D0756811

Frommer's®

Best RV and Tent Campgrounds in the U.S.A.

3rd Edition

Frommer's®
Best RV and Tent Campgrounds in the U.S.A.

3rd Edition

BICENTENNIAL
1807
WILEY
2007
BICENTENNIAL

Please note that prices fluctuate in the course of time, and travel information changes under the impact of many factors that influence the travel industry. We therefore suggest that you write or call ahead for confirmation when making your travel plans. Every effort has been made to ensure the accuracy of information throughout this book, and the contents of this publication are believed correct at the time of printing. Nevertheless, the publishers cannot accept responsibility for errors or omissions or for changes in details given in this guide or for the consequences of any reliance on the information provided by the same. Assessments of attractions and so forth are based upon the author's own experience, and therefore, descriptions given in this guide necessarily contain an element of subjective opinion, which may not reflect the publisher's opinion or dictate a reader's own experience on another occasion. Readers are invited to write the publisher with ideas, comments, and suggestions for future editions.

Published by:

John Wiley & Sons, Inc.
111 River Street
Hoboken, NJ 07030-5774

Copyright © 2007 by Robert W. Sehlinger. All rights reserved. No part of this publication may be reproduced, stored in a retrieval system or transmitted in any form or by any means, electronic, mechanical, photocopying, recording, scanning or otherwise, except as permitted under Sections 107 or 108 of the 1976 United States Copyright Act, without either the prior written permission of the Publisher, or authorization through payment of the appropriate per-copy fee to the Copyright Clearance Center, 222 Rosewood Drive, Danvers, MA 01923, (978) 750-8400, fax (978) 750-4744, or on the Web at www.copyright.com. You can contact the Publisher directly for permission by e-mail at permreq@ wiley.com or on the Web at www.wiley.com/about/permission.

Wiley, the Wiley logo and Unofficial Guide are registered trademarks of John Wiley & Sons, Inc. in the United States and other countries and may not be used without written permission. Used under license. All other trademarks are the property of their respective owners. John Wiley & Sons, Inc. is not associated with any product or vendor mentioned in this book.

Produced by Menasha Ridge Press
Cover design by Michael J. Freeland
Interior design by Michele Laseau

For information on our other products and services or to obtain technical support, please contact our Customer Care Department within the U.S. at (800) 762-2974, outside the U.S. at (317) 572-3993 or fax (317) 572-4002.

John Wiley & Sons, Inc. also publishes its books in a variety of electronic formats. Some content that appears in print may not be available in electronic formats.

ISBN 978-0-470-06929-5

Manufactured in the United States of America
5 4 3 2 1

Contents

Supplemental Directory of Campgrounds   929

Index   1056

List of Maps

Introduction

Frommer's Guide

The material in this guide has not been edited or in any way reviewed by the campgrounds profiled. In this guide we represent and serve you, the consumer. By way of contrast with other campground directories, no ads were sold to campgrounds, and no campground paid to be included. Through our independence, we're able to offer you the sort of objective information necessary to select a campground efficiently and with confidence.

Why Another Guide to Campgrounds?

We developed *Frommer's Best RV and Tent Campgrounds in the United States* because we recognized that campers are as discriminating about their choice of campgrounds as most travelers are about their choice of hotels. As a camper, you don't want to stay in any campground along your route. Rather, you prefer to camp only in the best. A comprehensive directory with limited information on each campground listed does little to help you narrow your choices. What you need is a reference that tells you straight out which campgrounds are the best, and that supplies detailed information, collected by independent inspectors, that differentiates those campgrounds from all of the also-rans. This is exactly what *Frommer's Best RV and Tent Campgrounds* delivers.

The Choice Is All Yours

Life is short, and life is about choices. You can stay in a gravel lot, elbow to elbow with other campers, with tractor-trailers roaring by just beyond the fence; or with this guide, you can spend the night in a roomy, shaded site, overlooking a sparkling blue lake. The choice is yours.

The authors of this guide have combed the country inspecting and comparing hundreds of campgrounds. Their objective was to create a hit parade of the very best, so that no matter where you travel, you'll never have to spend another night in a dumpy, gravel lot.

The best campgrounds in each state are described in detail in individual profiles so you'll know exactly what to expect. In addition to the fully profiled campgrounds, we provide a Supplemental Directory of Campgrounds that lists over five thousand additional properties that are quite adequate, but that didn't make the cut for the top 2,300 in the guide. Thus, no matter where you are, you'll have plenty of campgrounds to choose from. None of the campgrounds appearing in this guide, whether fully profiled or in the supplemental list, paid to be included. Rather, each earned its place by offering a superior product. Period.

Letters, Comments, and Questions from Readers

Many who use our guides write to us with questions, comments, and reports of their camping experiences. We appreciate all such input, both positive and critical. Readers' comments are frequently incorporated into revised editions of the Frommer's Guides and have contributed immeasurably to their improvement. Please write to:

Frommer's Best RV and Tent Campgrounds
P.O. Box 43673
Birmingham, AL 35243

For letters sent through the mail, please put your return address on both your letter and envelope; the two sometimes become separated. Also include your phone number and e-mail address if you are available for a possible interview.

U.S.A. Overview

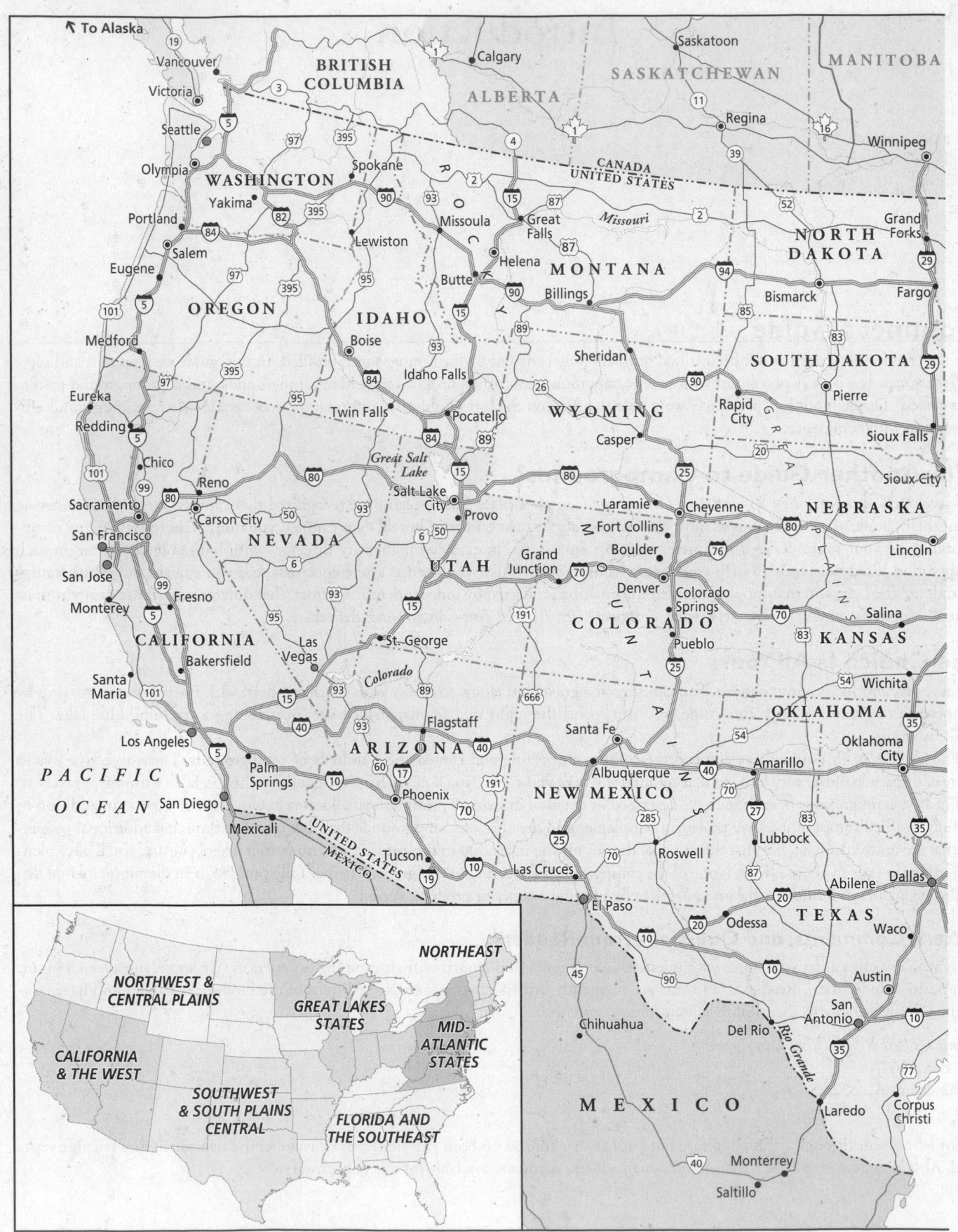

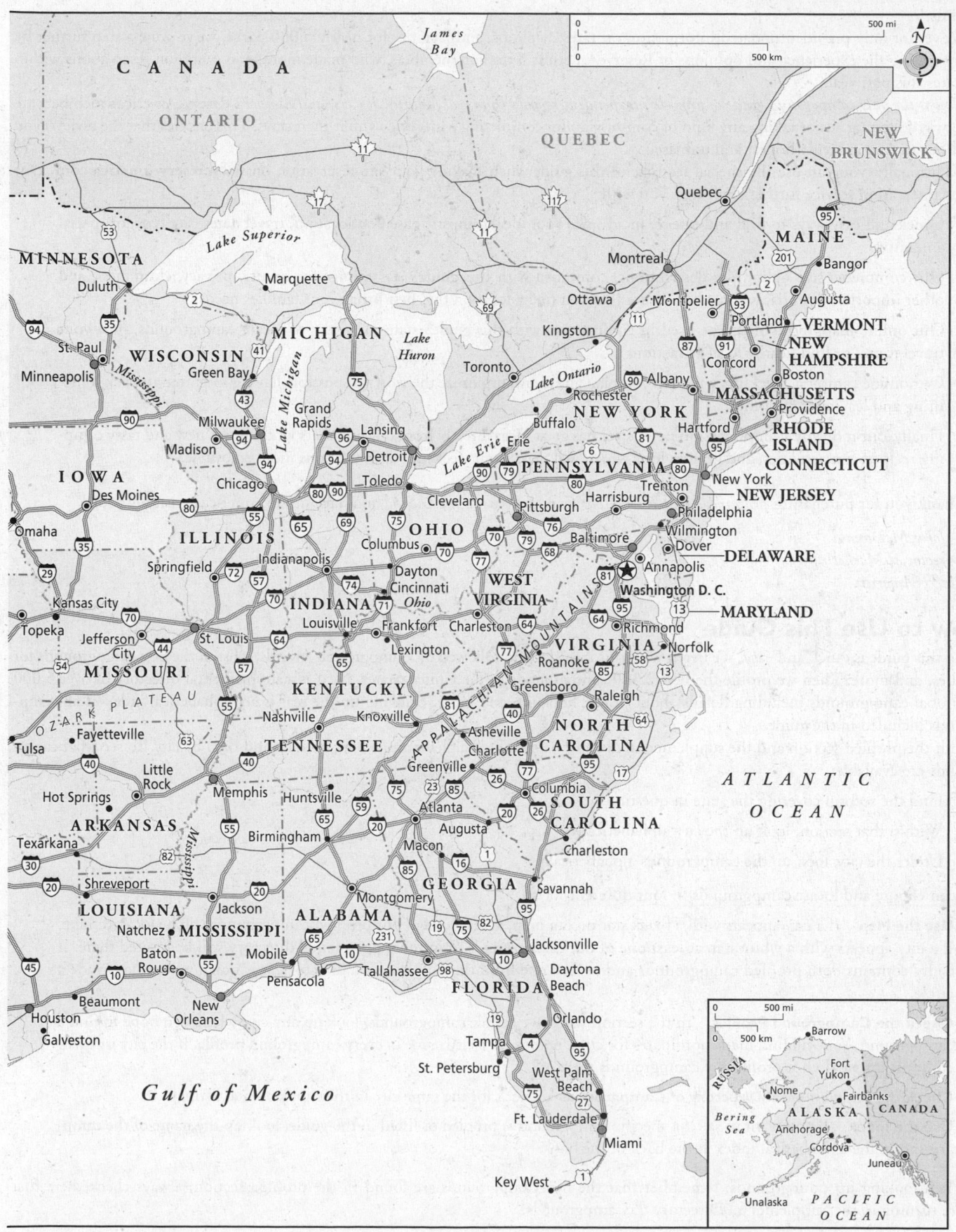

Welcome to the Official Guide of ReserveAmerica.com.

We've partnered with Frommer's to provide you the most comprehensive and complete guide to America's beautiful RV and tent campgrounds.

We've not only provided updated information on rates, hookups, and facilities for nearly 5,000 parks, we've gone a step further by incorporating the experience and opinions of ReserveAmerica's 5 million members, who made more than 4 million reservations within 48 states this past year.

This is the only campground guide to provide independent reviews from real families, RV'ers, and campers. ReserveAmerica's members are in no way soliciting ads or taking any kind of commission for completing park reviews after their stays. This ensures that the reviews you are about to read are truly honest and unbiased.

Additionally, you can use the special features of this guide when making your site reservation on **www.reserveamerica.com.** Our online reservation service further empowers you with:

- Quick and easy ways to find and reserve in advance your ideal campsite based on location, travel dates, site type, or special amenities.

- Our comprehensive online site descriptions, combined with this guide's star ratings for beauty, privacy, cleanliness, and other important criteria, will further ensure that you find a location that best meets your families needs.

- Our online mapping tool can be used in conjunction with this guide's state-road atlas to locate campgrounds, plan your travel route, or find nearby local attractions.

- Our online camping checklists will help you plan ahead and minimize the worry of possibly having forgotten to pack something and leaving it at home.

- Finally, our monthly Camping Club newsletter has great ideas directly from our members who submit new and tasty camping recipes, fun activities, and gear reviews which will make your weekends and vacations more enjoyable.

Thank you for purchasing *Frommer's Best RV & Tent Campgrounds in the U.S.A.,* and have fun in America's great outdoors!

—John McDonald
Director of Marketing
ReserveAmerica

How to Use This Guide

Using this guide is quick and easy. We begin with this introduction followed by Campground Awards, a list of the best campgrounds for families, and more. Then we profile the best 2,300 campgrounds in the United States. Next is a supplemental directory of over 5,000 additional campgrounds including details about prices, hookups, and more. Bringing up the rear is an alphabetical index of all campgrounds included in the guide.

Both the profiled section and the supplemental directory are ordered alphabetically, first by state and then by city. To see what campgrounds are available:

- Find the section covering the state in question.
- Within that section, look up the city alphabetically.
- Under the city, look up the campgrounds alphabetically.

You can choose and locate campgrounds in four different ways.

1. **Use the Map** If a city appears with a black star on our map, at least one of our profiled campgrounds will be located there. If a city appears with a white star, at least one of our campgrounds from the supplemental directory will be located there. If a city contains both profiled campgrounds and at least one from the supplemental directory, it is noted with a star inside a circle.

2. **Check the Campground Profiles** In the section where we profile campgrounds, look up any city where you hope to find a campground. You will find map coordinates for cities next to each city name in every campground profile. If the city isn't listed, it means we do not profile any campgrounds there.

3. **Check the Supplemental Directory of Campgrounds** Check for the same city in the supplemental listings.

4. **Use the Index** If you want to see if a specific campground is profiled or listed in the guide, look up the name of the campground in the alphabetical index at the back of the book.

When looking up campgrounds, remember that the best campgrounds are found in the profiled section; always check there first before turning to the Supplemental Directory of Campgrounds.

Understanding the Profiles

Each profile has eight important sections:

City Name and Map Coordinate   Use this information to find quickly a city on the corresponding state map.

Campground Name, Address, and Contact Information   In addition to the street address, we also provide phone numbers and Web site addresses.

Ratings   Using the familiar one- to five-star rating with five stars being best, we offer one overall rating for RV campers and a second overall rating for tent campers. The overall rating for each type of camper is based on a rough weighted average of the following eight individually rated categories:

Category	Weight
Beauty	15%
Site Privacy	10%
Site Spaciousness	10%
Quiet	15%
Security	13%
Cleanliness/upkeep	13%
Insect Control	10%
Facilities	14%

Beauty   This rates the natural setting of the campground in terms of its visual appeal. The highest ratings are reserved for campgrounds where the beauty of the campground can be enjoyed and appreciated both at individual campsites and at the campground's public areas. Views, vistas, landscaping, and foliage are likewise taken into consideration.

Site Privacy   This category rates the extent to which the campsites are set apart and/or in some way buffered (usually by trees and shrubs) from adjacent or nearby campsites. The farther campsites are from one another the better. This rating also reflects how busy the access road to the campsites is in terms of traffic. Campgrounds that arrange their sites on a number of cul-de-sacs, for example, will offer quieter sites than a campground where the sites are situated off of a busy loop or along a heavily traveled access road.

Site Spaciousness   This rates the size of the campsite. Generally, the larger the better.

Quiet   This rating indicates the relative quietness of the campground. There are three key considerations. The first is where the campground is located. Campgrounds situated along busy highways or in cities or towns are usually noisier, for example, than rural or wilderness campgrounds removed from major thoroughfares. The second consideration relates to how noise is managed at the campground. Does the campground forbid playing of radios or enforce a "quiet time" after a certain hour? Is there someone on site at night to respond to complaints about other campers being loud or unruly at a late hour? Finally, the rating considers the extent to which trees, shrubs, and the natural topography serve to muffle noise within the campground.

Security   This rating reflects the extent (if any) to which management monitors the campground during the day and night. Physical security is also included in this rating: Is the campground fenced? Is the campground gated? If so, is the gate manned? Generally, a campground located in a city or along a busy road is more exposed to thieves or vandals than a more remote campground, and should more actively supervise access.

Cleanliness   This rates the cleanliness, serviceability, and state of repair of the campground, including grounds, sites, and facilities.

Insect Control   This rating addresses questions regarding insect and pest control. Does management spray or take other steps to control the presence of mosquitoes and other insect pests? Does the campground drain efficiently following a rain? Are garbage and sewage properly collected and disposed of?

Facilities   This rates the overall variety and quality of facilities to include bath house/toilets, swimming pool, retail shops, docks, pavilions, playgrounds, etc. If the quality of respective facilities vary considerably within a given campground, inconsistencies are explained in the prose description of the campground.

Campground Description   This is an informative, consumer-oriented description of the campground. It includes what makes the campground special or unique and what differentiates it from other area campgrounds. The description may additionally include the following:

- The general layout of the campground.
- Where the campground is located relative to an easily referenced city or highway.
- The general setting (wilderness, rural, or urban).

- Description of the campsites including most and least desirable sites.
- Prevailing weather considerations and best time to visit.
- Mention of any unusual, exceptional, or deficient facilities.
- Security considerations, if any (gates that are locked at night, accessibility of campground to noncampers, etc.).

Basics   Key information about the campground including:

- *Operated By* Who owns and/or operates the campground.
- *Open* Dates or seasons the campground is open.
- *Site Assignment* How sites are most commonly obtained (first come, first served; reservations accepted; reservations only; assigned on check-in, etc. Deposit and refund policy.
- *Registration* Where the camper registers on arrival. Information on how and where to register after normal business hours (late arrival).
- *Fee* Cost of a standard campsite for one night for RV sites and tent sites respectively. Forms of payment accepted. Uses the following abbreviations for credit cards: V = VISA, AE = American Express, MC = MasterCard, D = Discover, CB = Carte Blanche, and DC = Diner's Club International.
- *Parking* Usual entry will be "At campsite" or "On road," though some campgrounds have a central parking lot from which tent campers must carry their gear to their campsite.

Facilities   This is a brief data presentation that provides information on the availability of specific facilities and services.

- *Number of RV Sites* Any site where RVs are permitted.
- *Number of Tent-Only Sites* Sites set aside specifically for tent camping, including pop-up tent trailers.
- *Hookups* Possible hookups include electric, water, sewer, cable TV, phone, and Internet connection. Electrical hookups vary from campground to campground. Where electrical hookups are available, the amperage available is stated parenthetically, for example: "Hookups: Electric (20 amps), water."
- *Each Site* List of equipment such as grill, picnic table, lantern pole, fire pit, water faucet, electrical outlet, etc., provided at each campsite. Are these items or services available on site? Dump station, laundry, pay phone, rest rooms and showers, fuel, propane, RV service, general store, vending, playground, etc.
- *Internal Roads* Indicates the type of road (gravel, paved, dirt), and in what condition.
- *Market* Location and distance of closest supermarket or large grocery store.
- *Restaurant* Location and distance of closest restaurant.
- *Other* Boat ramp, dining pavilion, miniature golf, tennis court, lounge, etc.
- *Activities* Activities available at the campground or in the area.
- *Nearby Attractions* Can be natural or artificial.
- *Additional Information* The best sources to call for general information on area activities and attractions. Sources include local or area chambers of commerce, tourist bureaus, visitors and convention authorities, U.S. Forest Service, etc.

Restrictions   Any restrictions that apply, including:

- *Pets* Conditions under which pets are allowed or not.
- *Fires* Campground rules for fires and fire safety.
- *Alcoholic Beverages* Campground rules regarding the consumption of alcoholic beverages.
- *Vehicle Maximum Length* Length in feet of the maximum size vehicle the campground can accommodate.
- *Other* Any other rules or restrictions, to include minimum and maximum stays; age or group size restrictions; areas off-limits to vehicular traffic; security constraints such as locking the main gate during the night; etc.

How to Get There   Clear and specific directions, including mileage and landmarks, for finding the campground.

Supplemental Directory of Campgrounds

If you're looking for a campground within the territory covered in this guide and can't find a profiled campground that is close or convenient to your route, check the Supplemental Directory of Campgrounds. This directory of hundreds of additional campgrounds is organized alphabetically by state and city name. Each entry provides the campground's name, address, reservations phone, Web site, number of sites, average fee per night, and hookups available.

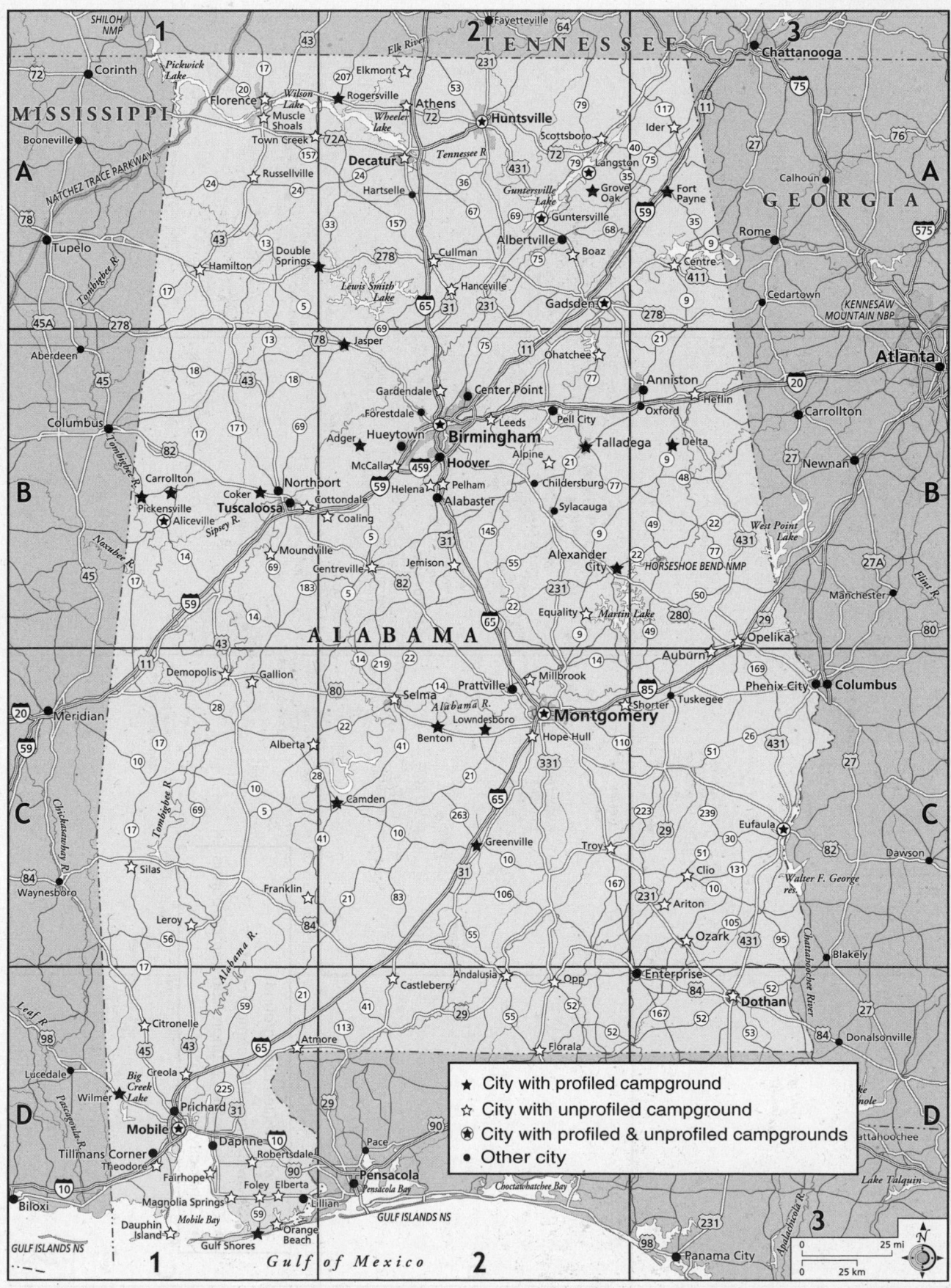

Legend:

★ City with profiled campground

☆ City with unprofiled campground

✪ City with profiled & unprofiled campgrounds

• Other city

Alaska

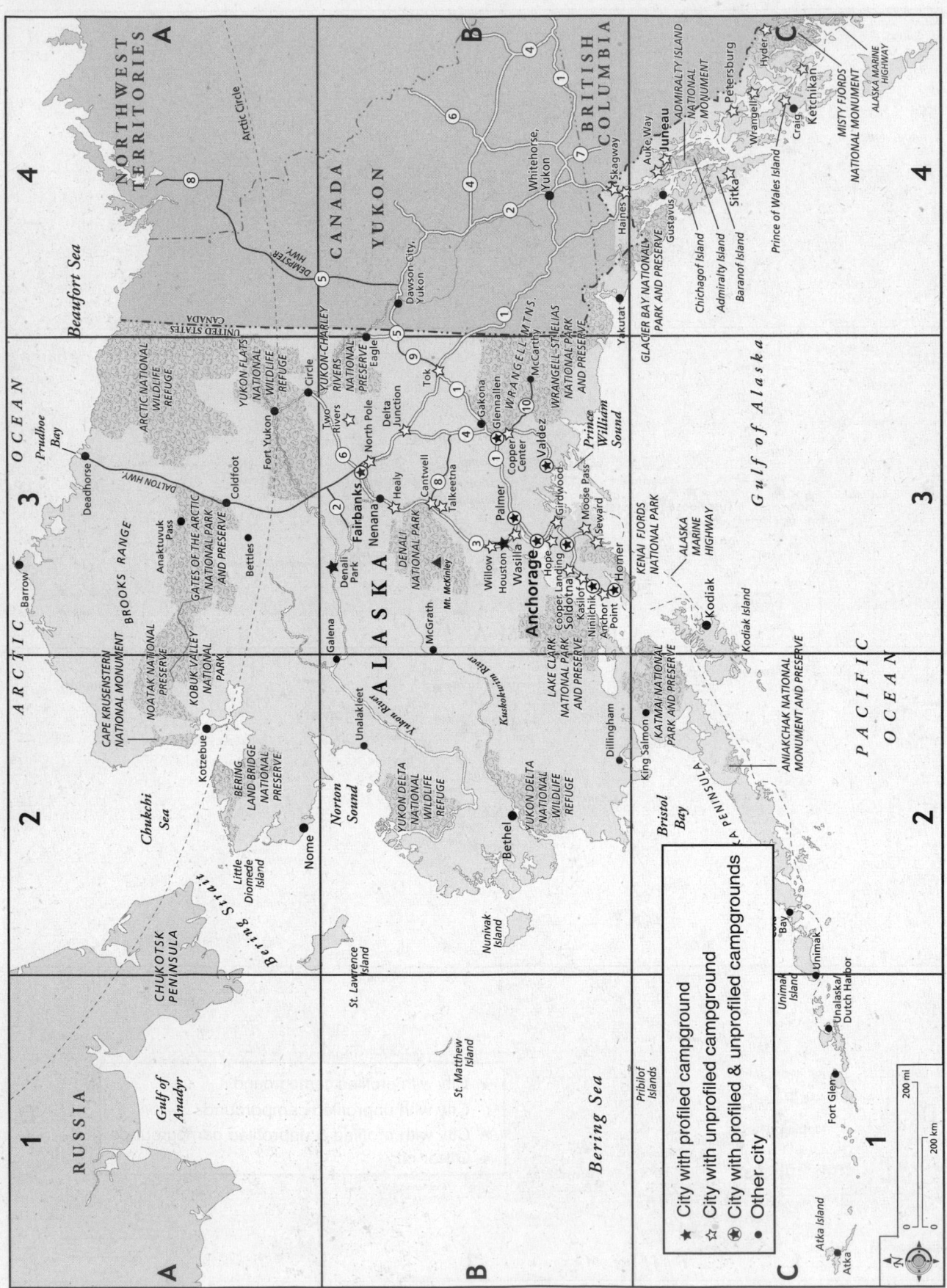

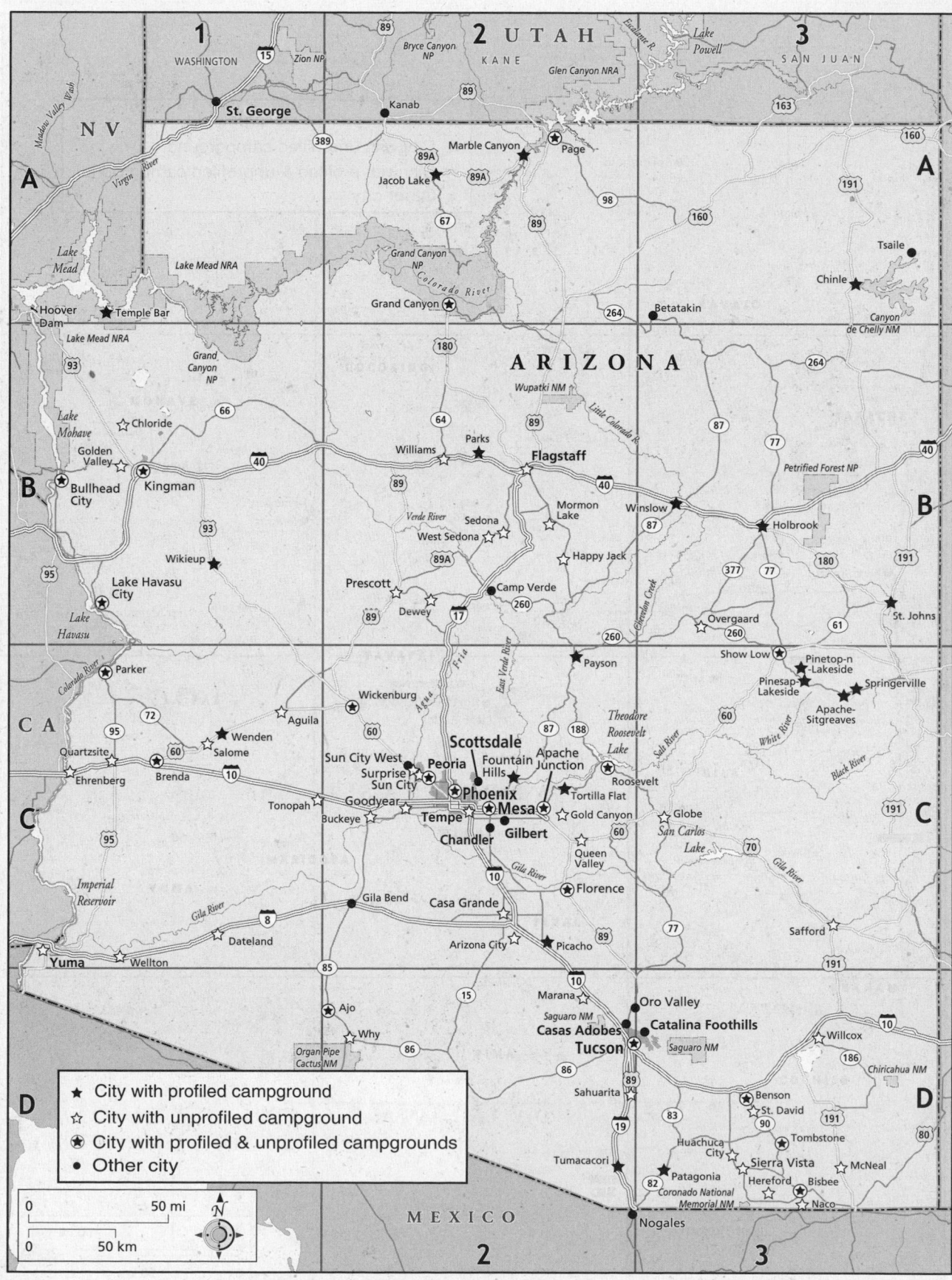

City with profiled campground

☆ **City with unprofiled campground**

⍟ **City with profiled & unprofiled campgrounds**

• **Other city**

Arkansas

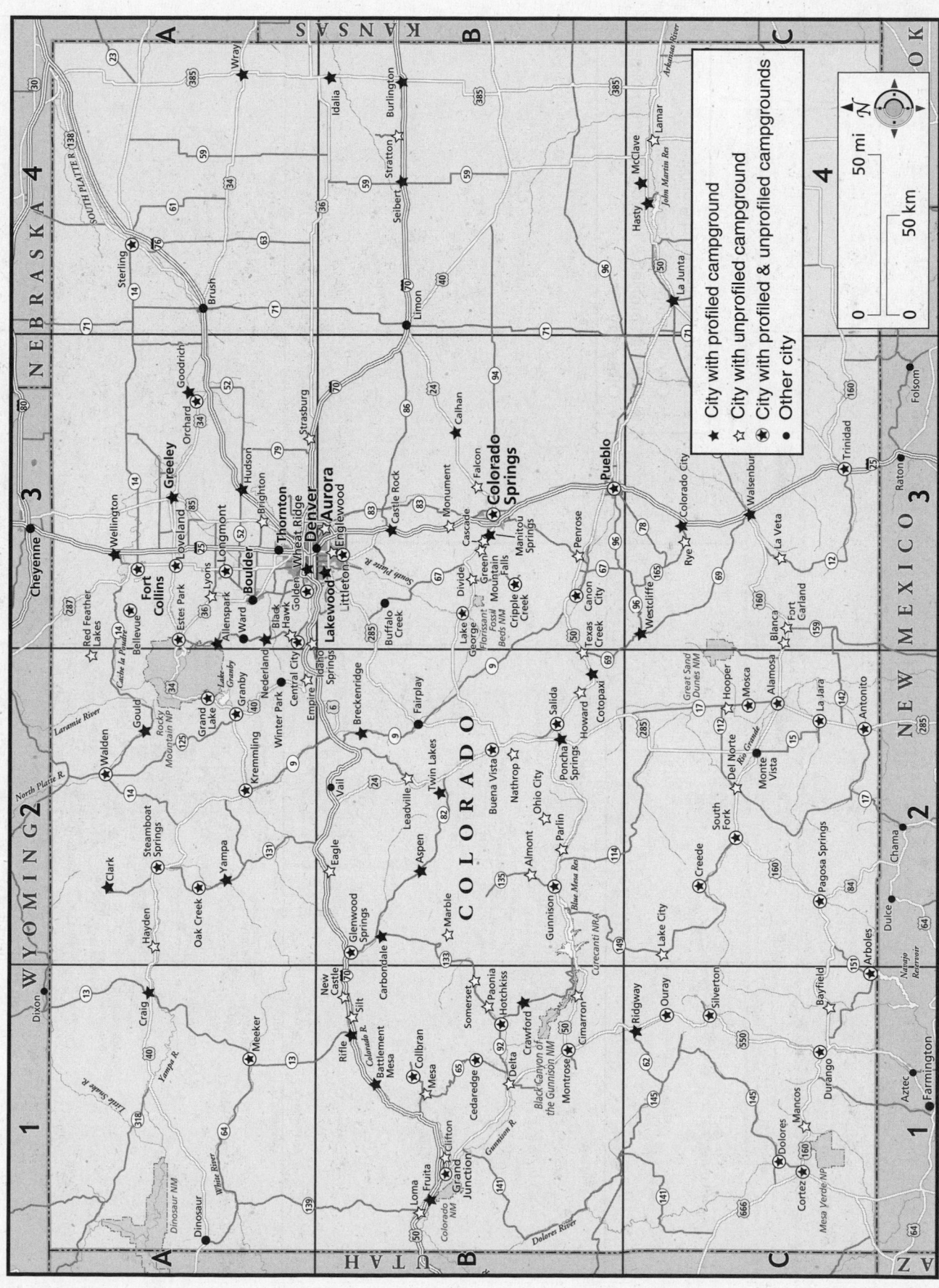

California North

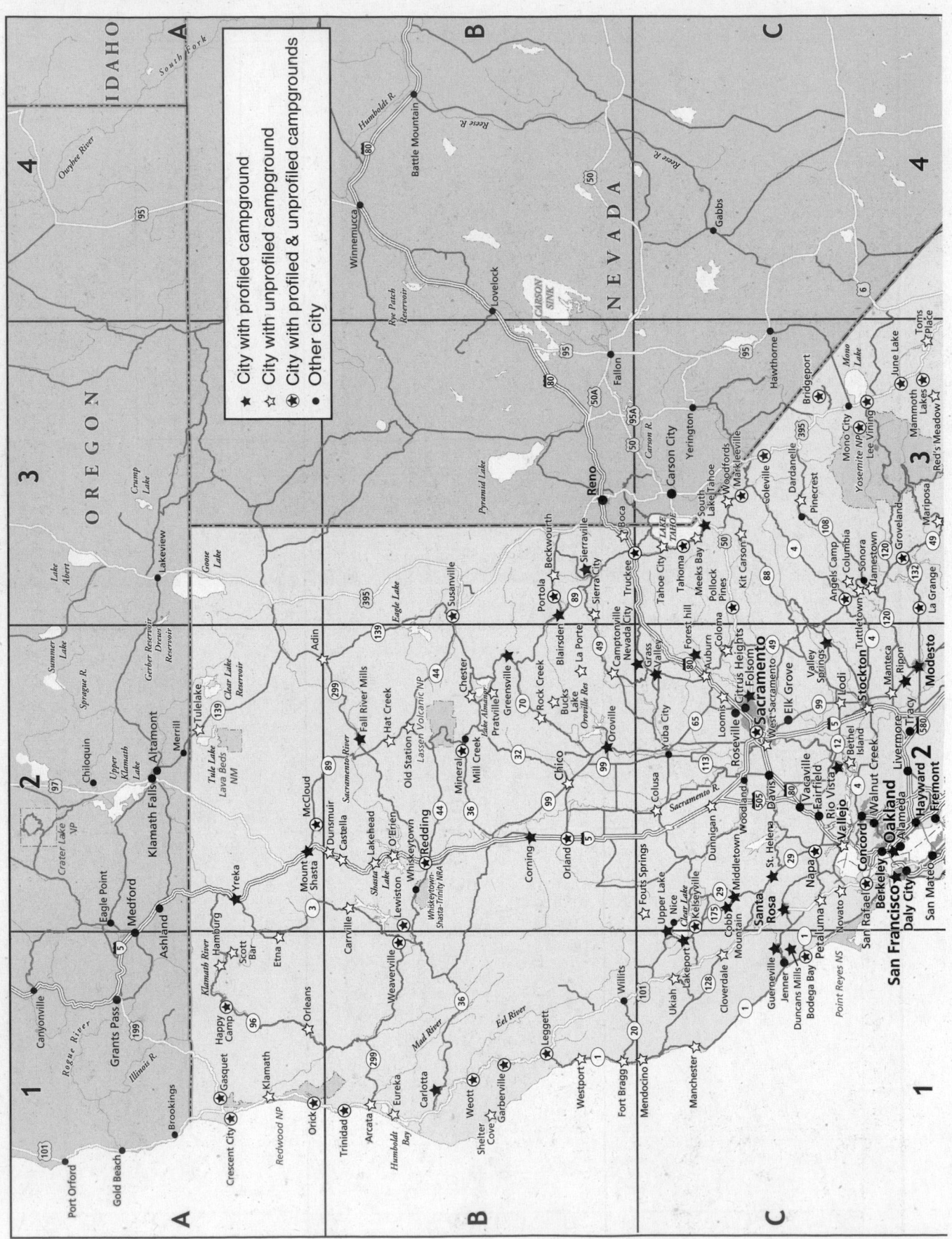

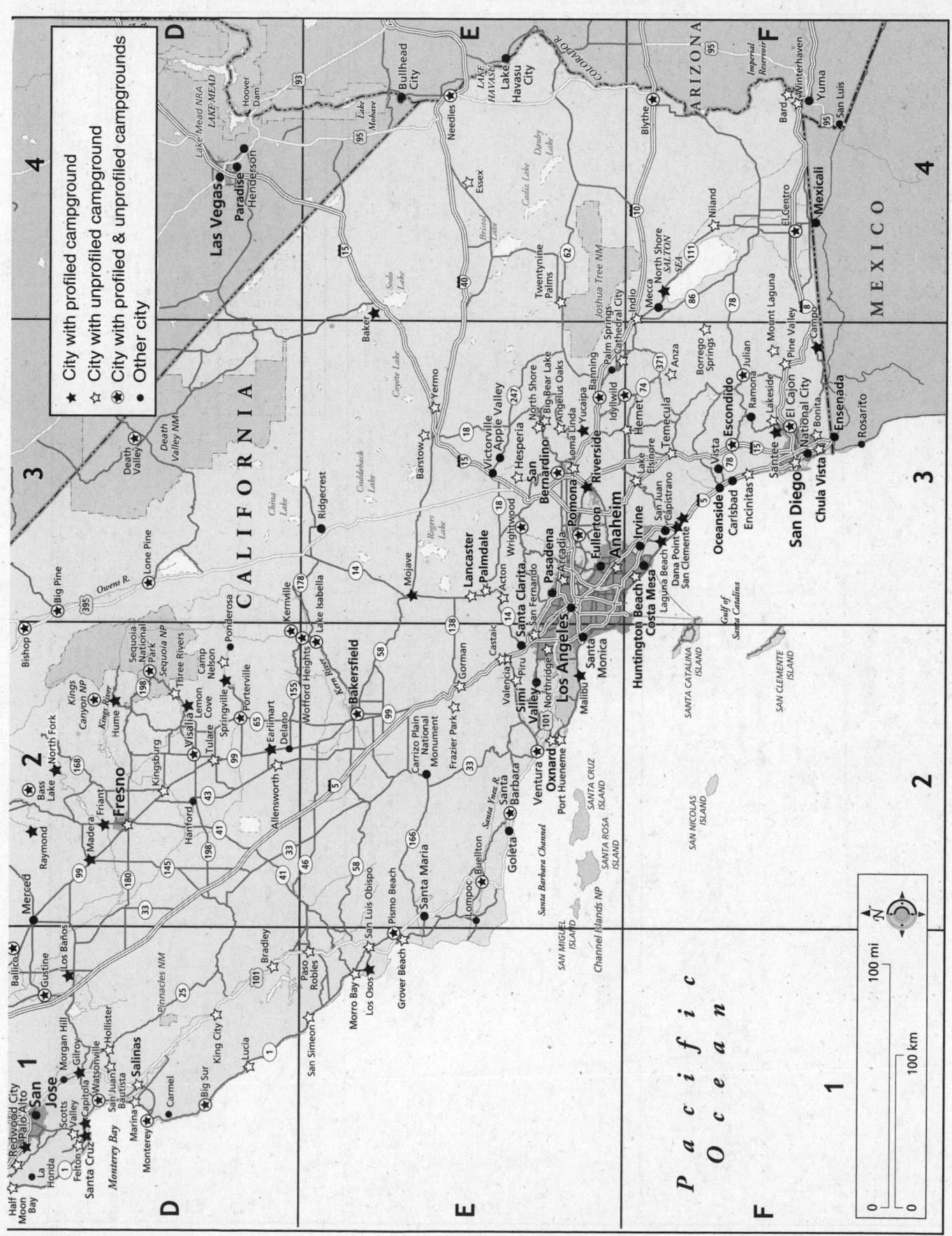

Connecticut

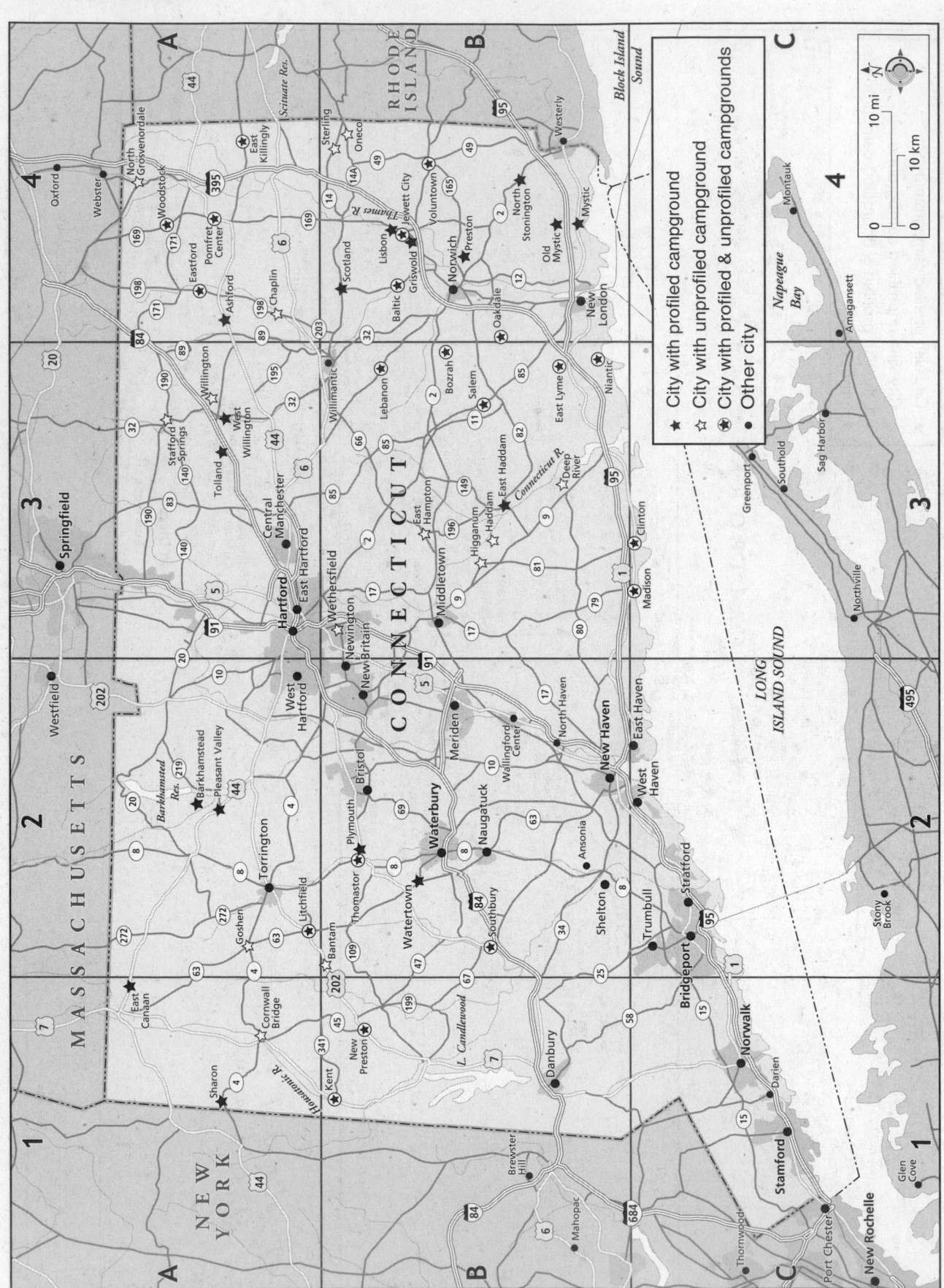

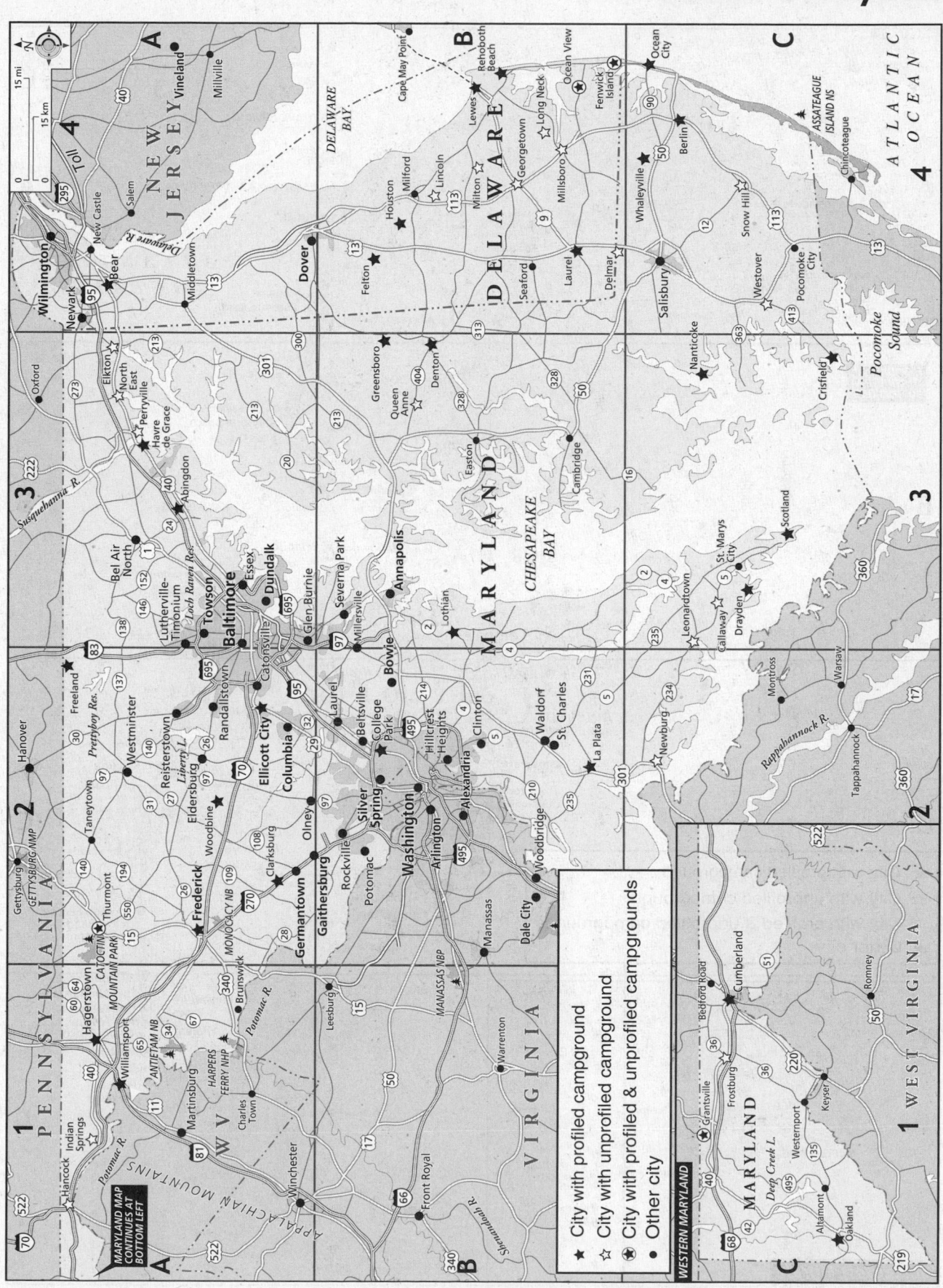

City with profiled campground
City with unprofiled campground
City with profiled & unprofiled campgrounds
Other city

WESTERN MARYLAND

Florida

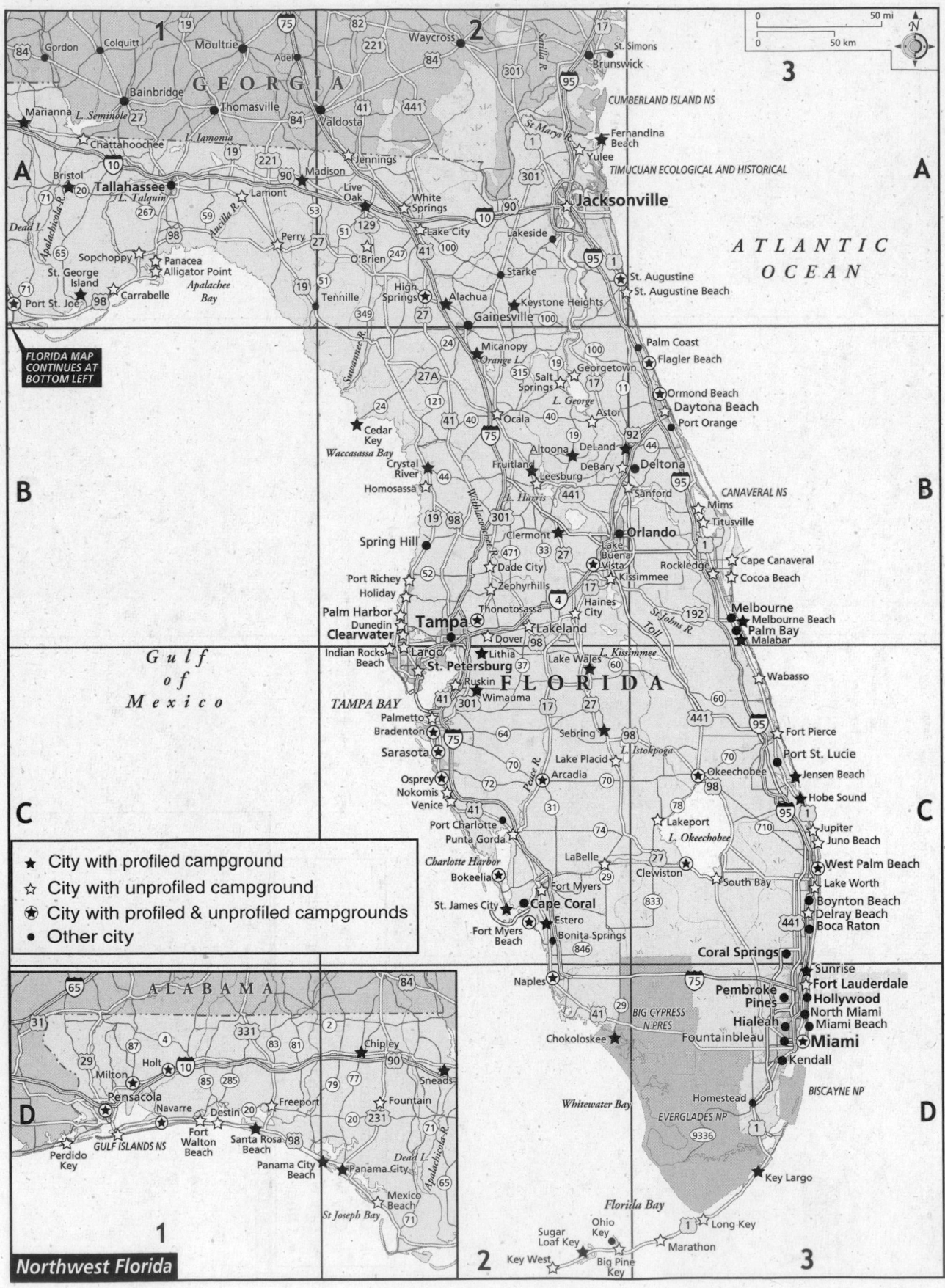

Legend:
- ★ City with profiled campground
- ☆ City with unprofiled campground
- ⊛ City with profiled & unprofiled campgrounds
- • Other city

Northwest Florida

Georgia

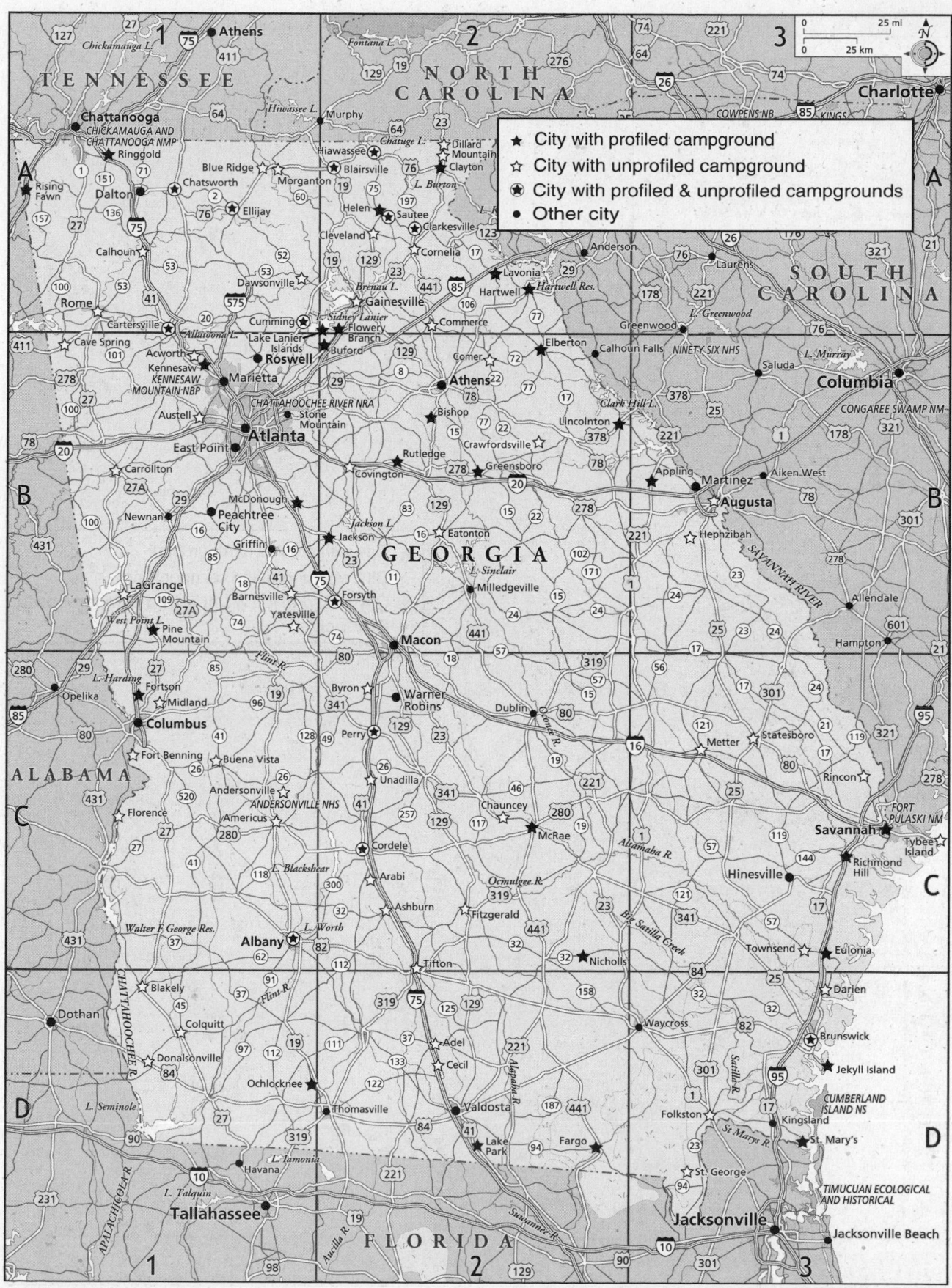

Idaho

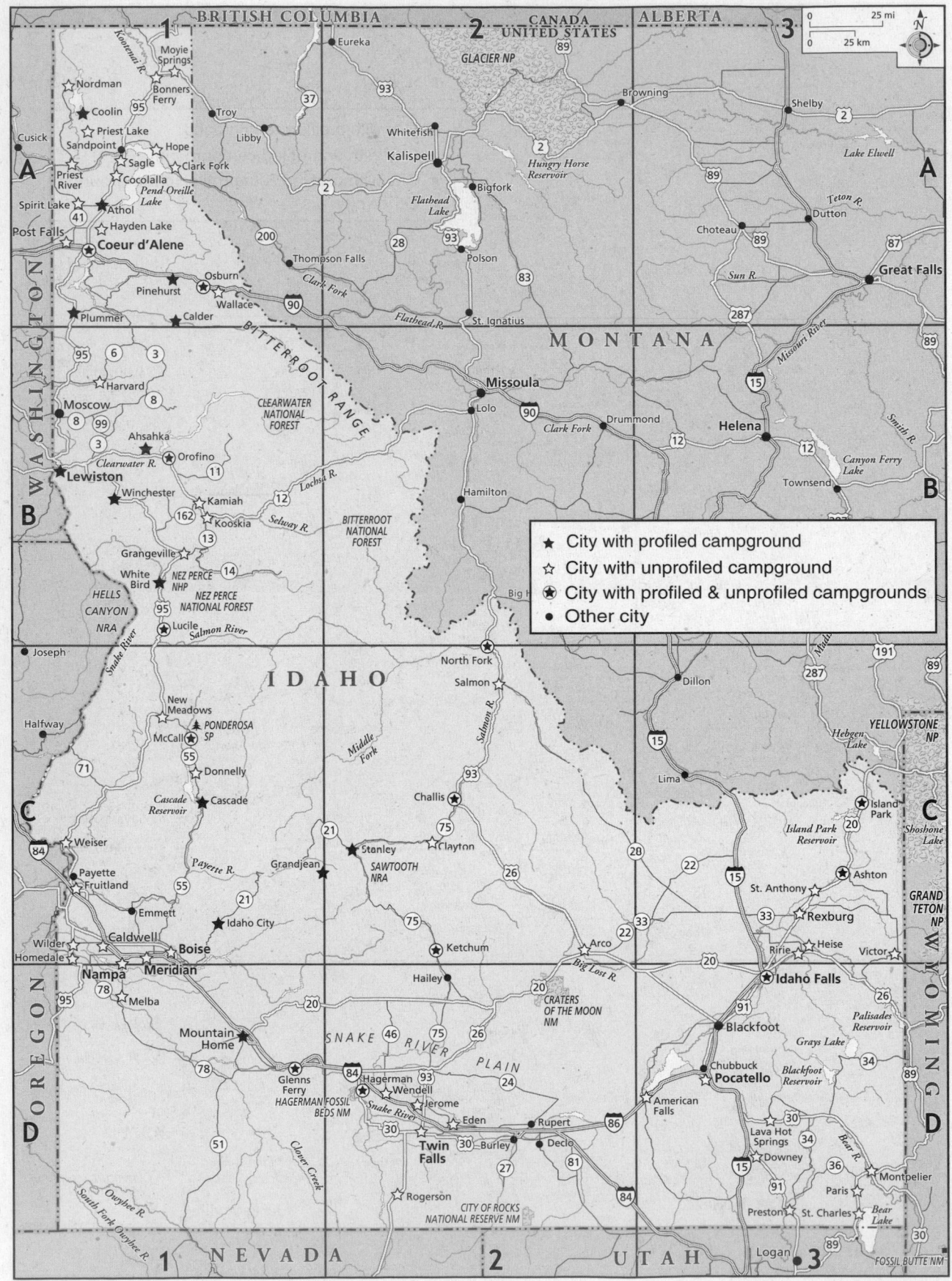

Legend:
- ★ City with profiled campground
- ☆ City with unprofiled campground
- ⊛ City with profiled & unprofiled campgrounds
- ● Other city

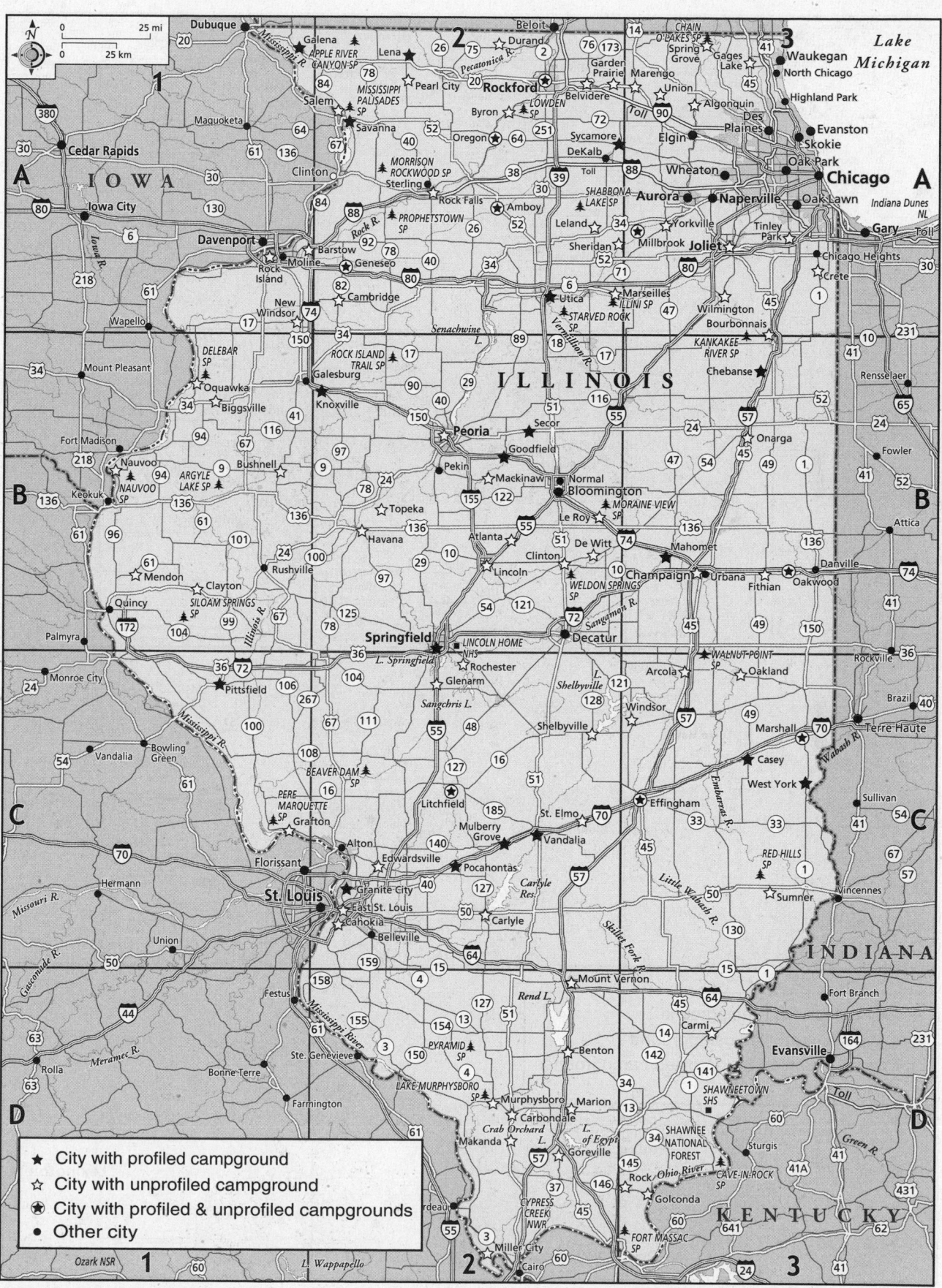

Illinois

City with profiled campground ★
City with unprofiled campground ☆
City with profiled & unprofiled campgrounds ✪
Other city •

Indiana

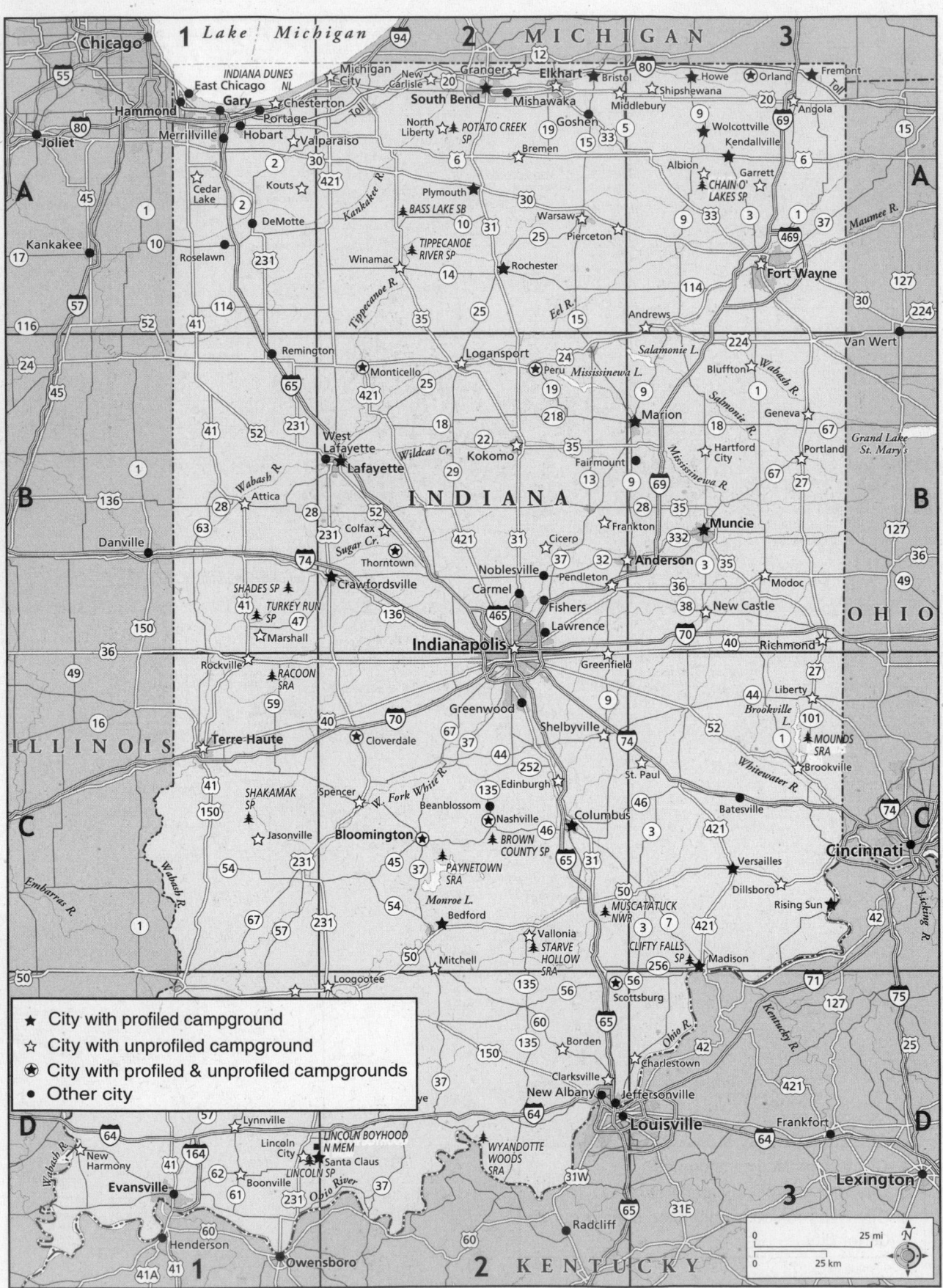

Legend:
- ★ City with profiled campground
- ☆ City with unprofiled campground
- ⊛ City with profiled & unprofiled campgrounds
- ● Other city

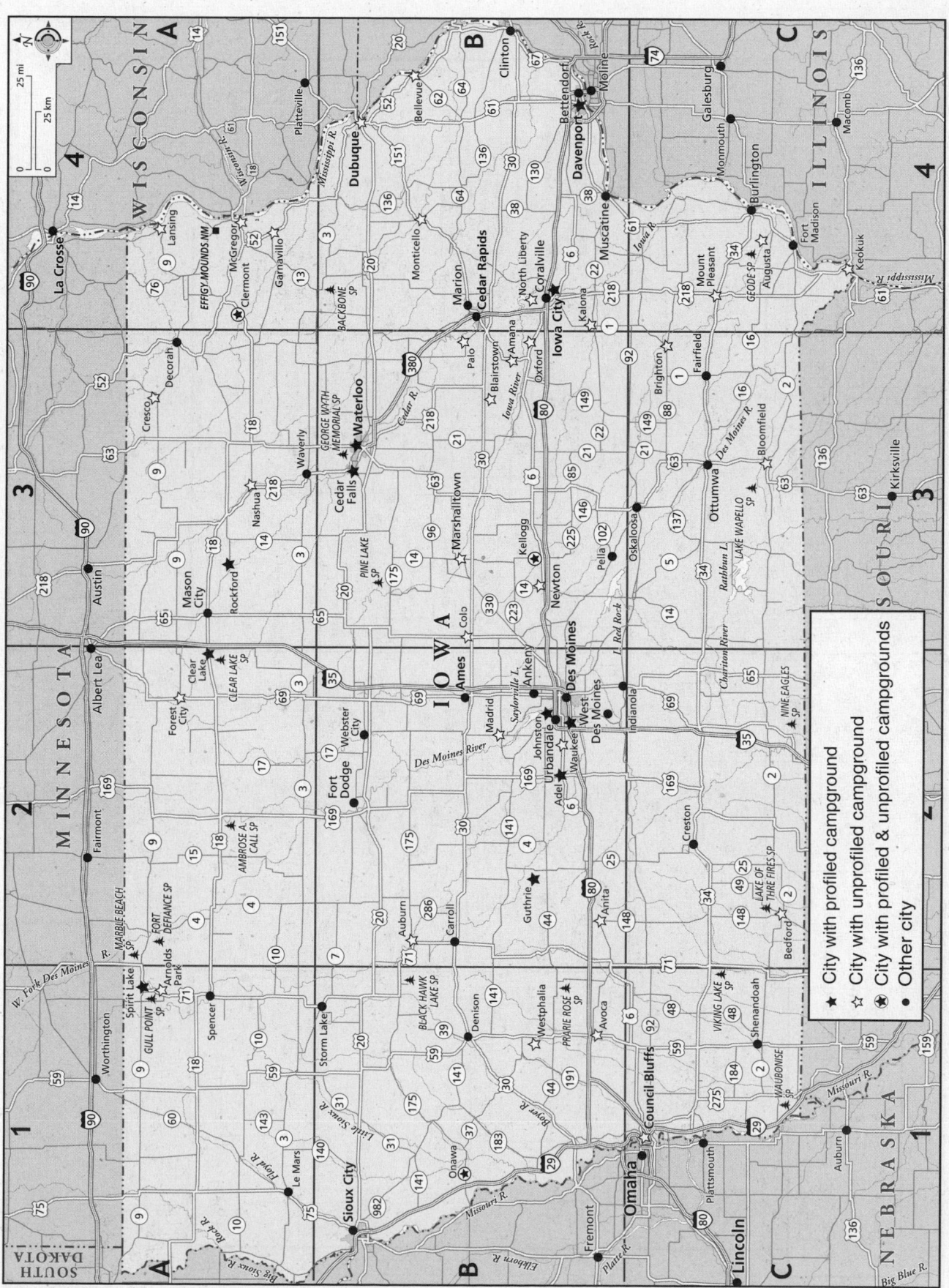

Kansas

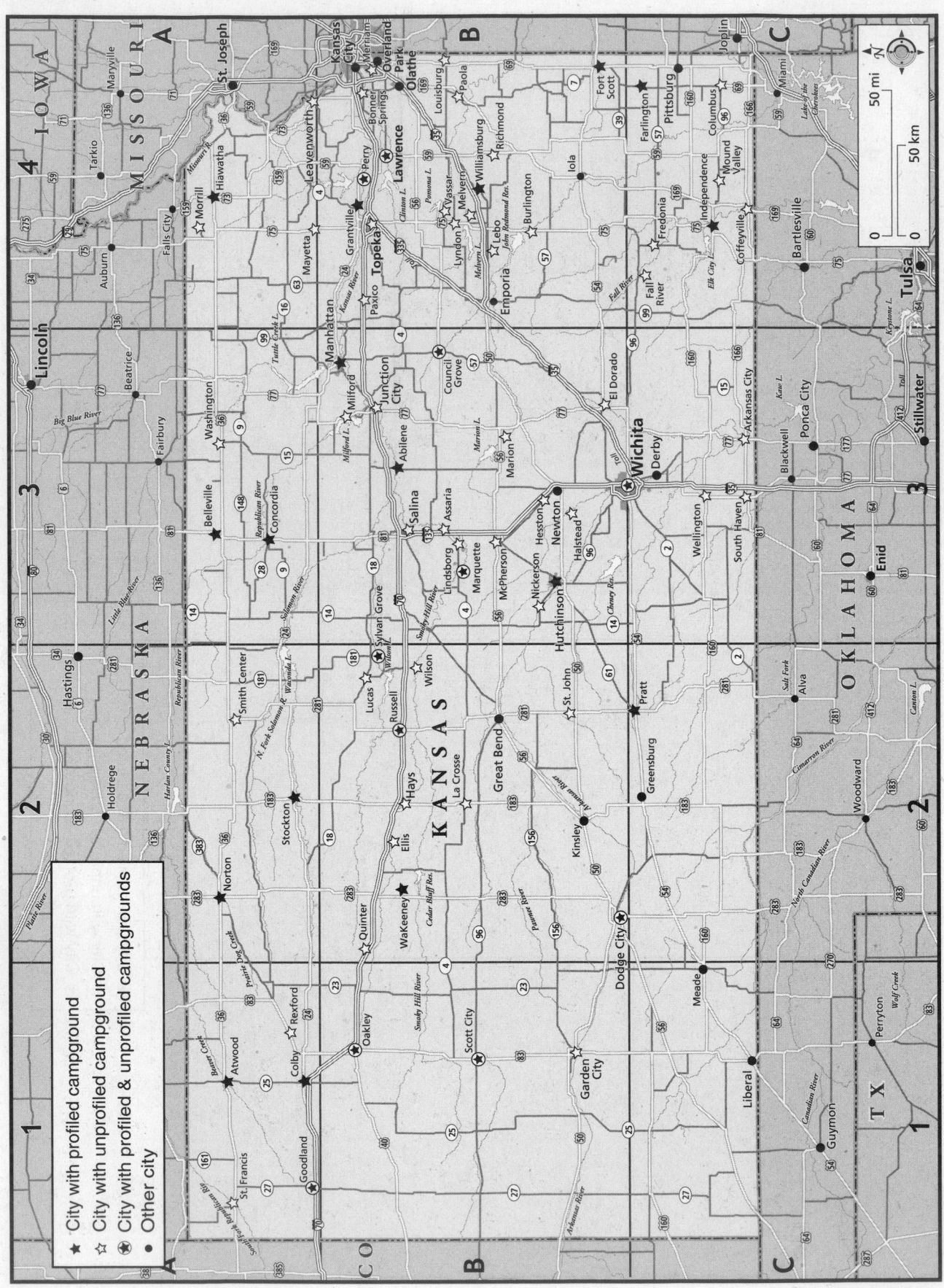

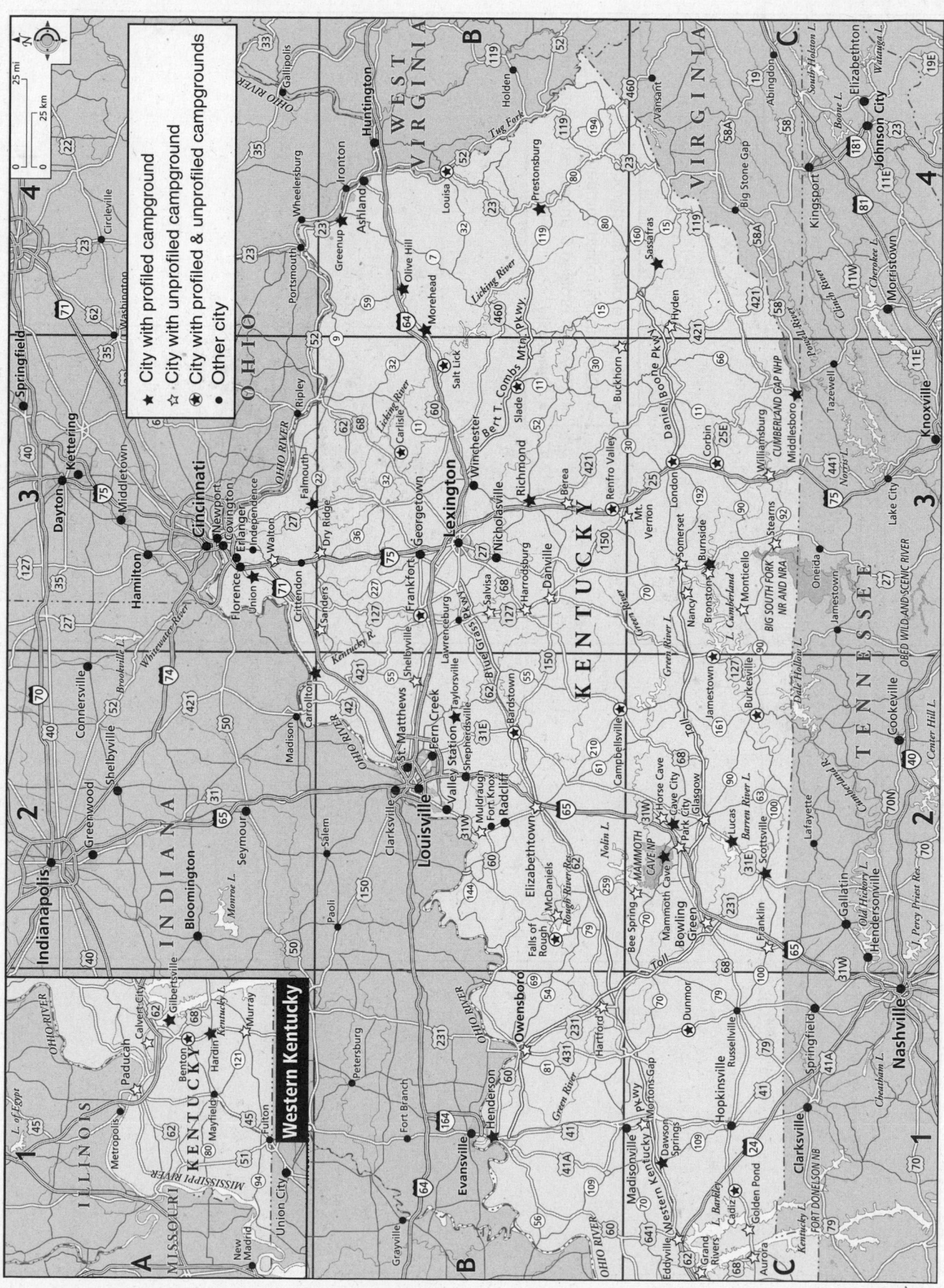

Louisiana

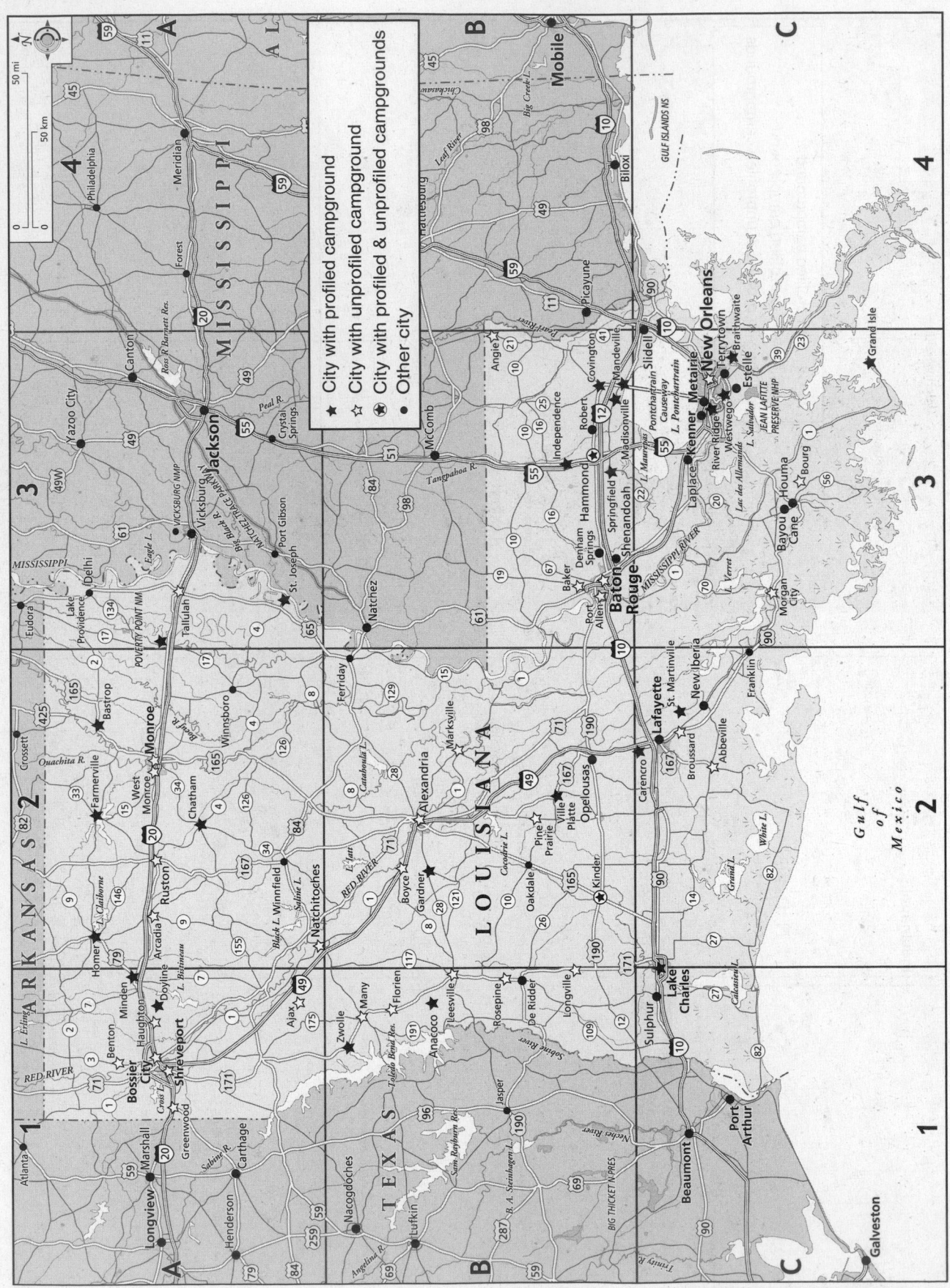

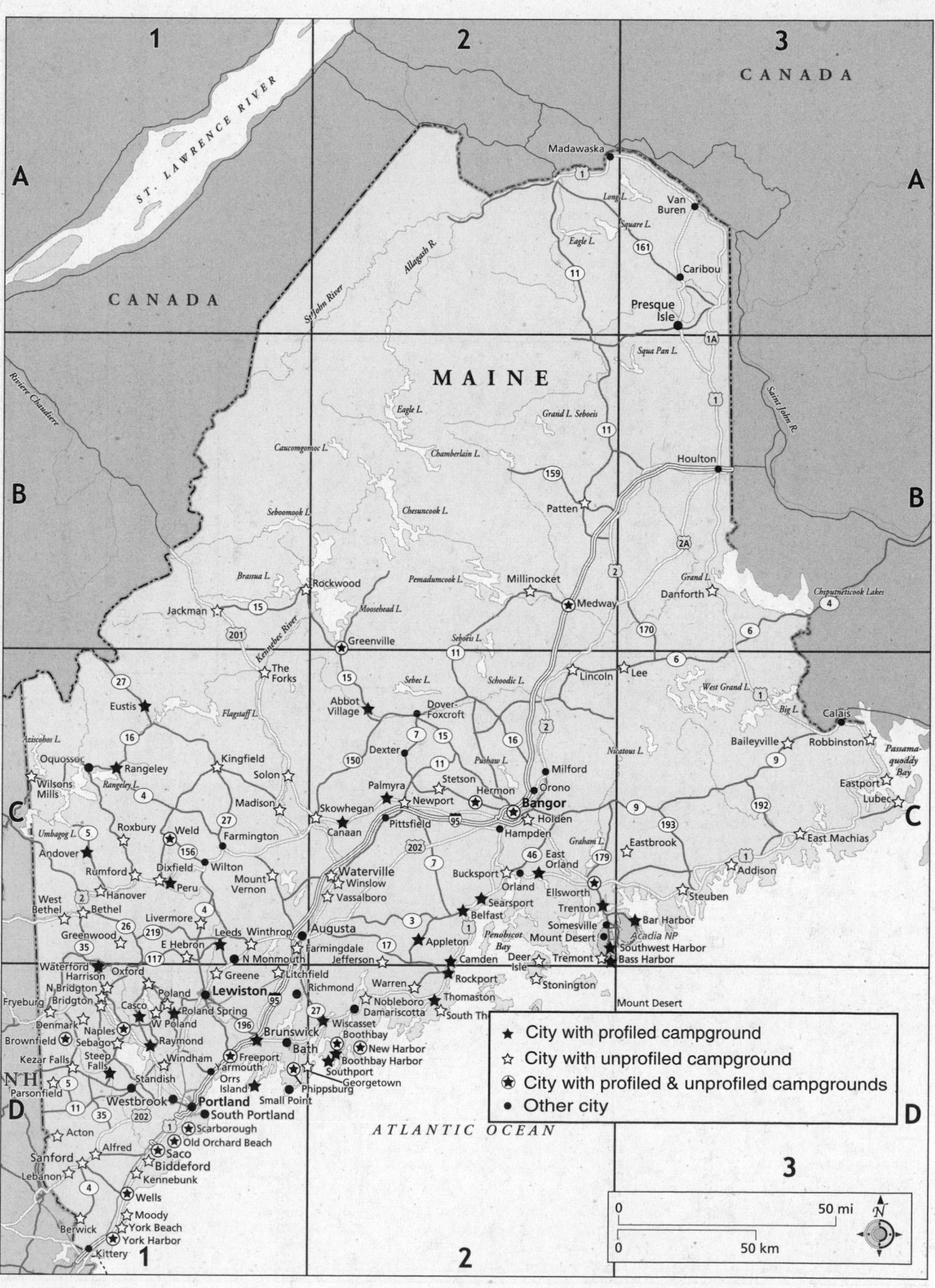

Maine

Legend:
- ★ City with profiled campground
- ☆ City with unprofiled campground
- ✪ City with profiled & unprofiled campgrounds
- • Other city

CANADA

ST. LAWRENCE RIVER

Rivière Chaudière

MAINE

St. John River

Allagash R.

Eagle L.

Caucomgomoc L.

Chamberlain L.

Seboomook L.

Chesuncook L.

Brassua L.

Pemadumcook L.

Moosehead L.

Rockwood ☆

Jackman ☆

201

15

Greenville ✪

The Forks ☆

27

Eustis ★

Flagstaff L.

16

Oquossoc •

Rangeley ★

Rangeley L.

Wilsons Mills ☆

Kingfield ☆

Solon ☆

4

Roxbury ☆

Weld ✪

156

Madison ☆

Umbagog L.

5

Andover ★

Rumford •

Dixfield ☆

Peru ★

Wilton ☆

Mount Vernon ☆

Farmington ✪

West Bethel ☆

Hanover •

Bethel ☆

Livermore ☆

2

26

219

Greenwood ☆

E Hebron ☆

Leeds ☆

Winthrop ☆

35

117

4

Abbot Village ★

Dover-Foxcroft ★

7

15

Dexter ★

11

150

Palmyra ★

Skowhegan ★

Newport ★

Canaan ★

Pittsfield ★

202

Waterville ✪

Winslow ☆

Vassalboro ☆

7

Augusta ★

Farmingdale ☆

17

3

Jefferson ☆

Appleton ☆

Stetson ☆

Hermon ★

Milford •

Orono ★

Bangor ✪

Holden ☆

Hampden ☆

1

46

Bucksport ★

Orland ★

East Orland ★

179

Searsport ★

Belfast ★

Camden ✪

Warren ☆

Thomaston ☆

Rockport ★

Rockland

South Th.

Noblaboro ☆

Damariscotta ☆

Deer Isle ☆

Stonington ☆

Ellsworth ✪

Trenton ★

Somesville ☆

Mount Desert ★

Acadia NP

Bar Harbor ★

Southwest Harbor ✪

Bass Harbor ★

Tremont ★

Mount Desert

Penobscot Bay

Graham L.

Eastbrook ☆

Steuben ☆

Addison ☆

East Machias ☆

Lubec ☆

Eastport ☆

Passamaquoddy Bay

Baileyville ☆

Robbinston ☆

Calais ✪

9

192

193

Nicatous L.

West Grand L.

Big L.

Lincoln ☆

Lee •

6

1

Lewiston

95

27

Poland ★

Poland Spring ★

W Poland ★

196

Brunswick ★

Bath ★

Wiscasset ☆

Boothbay ☆

Boothbay Harbor ★

New Harbor ★

Southport ☆

Georgetown ☆

Phippsburg ☆

Small Point ☆

Casco ★

Oxford ★

Harrison ★

N Bridgton ☆

Bridgton ☆

Fryeburg ☆

Naples ★

Sebago ★

Denmark ☆

Brownfield ☆

Kezar Falls ☆

Steep Falls ★

Raymond ☆

Windham ☆

Standish ☆

Yarmouth ☆

Freeport ★

Orrs Island ★

Greene ☆

Litchfield ☆

Richmond ☆

Waterford ★

N Monmouth ☆

Portland

South Portland

Westbrook ☆

202

1

Scarborough ✪

Old Orchard Beach ✪

Saco ✪

Biddeford

Kennebunk ☆

Wells ★

Moody ☆

York Beach ☆

York Harbor ★

Kittery ✪

NH

Parsonfield ☆

5

11

35

Acton ☆

Alfred ☆

Sanford ☆

Lebanon •

4

Berwick ★

ATLANTIC OCEAN

Madawaska ✪

Van Buren ★

Caribou ★

Presque Isle ★

161

1A

1

Long L.

Square L.

Eagle L.

Squa Pan L.

Grand L. Seboeis

11

159

Patten ☆

Houlton ●

Danforth ☆

Millinocket ★

Medway ★

Grand L.

Chiputneticook Lakes

4

170

2A

2

6

Seboeis L.

11

Schoodic L.

Sebec L.

Graham L.

0 ——— 50 mi

0 ——— 50 km

25

Massachusetts

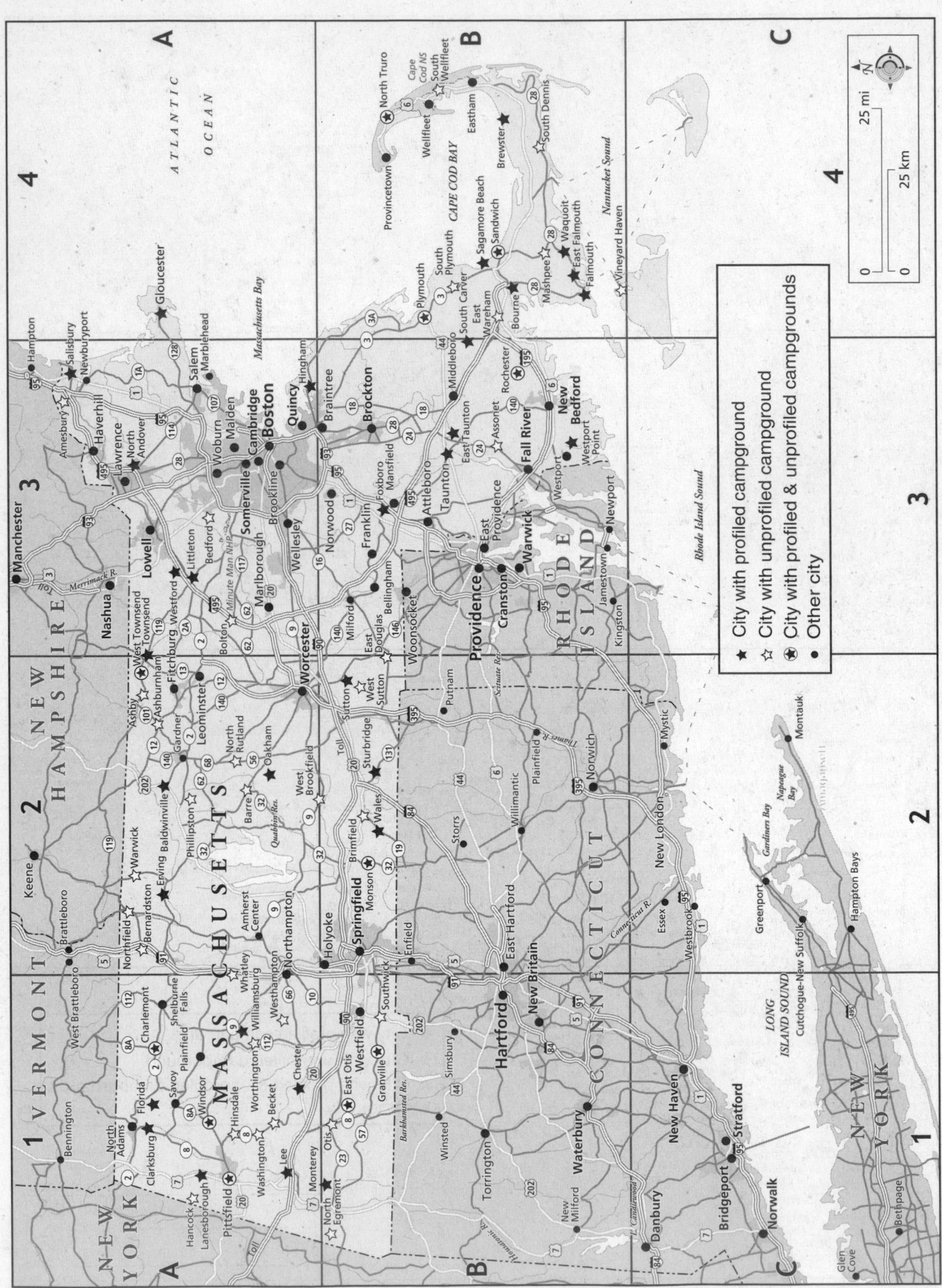

Michigan

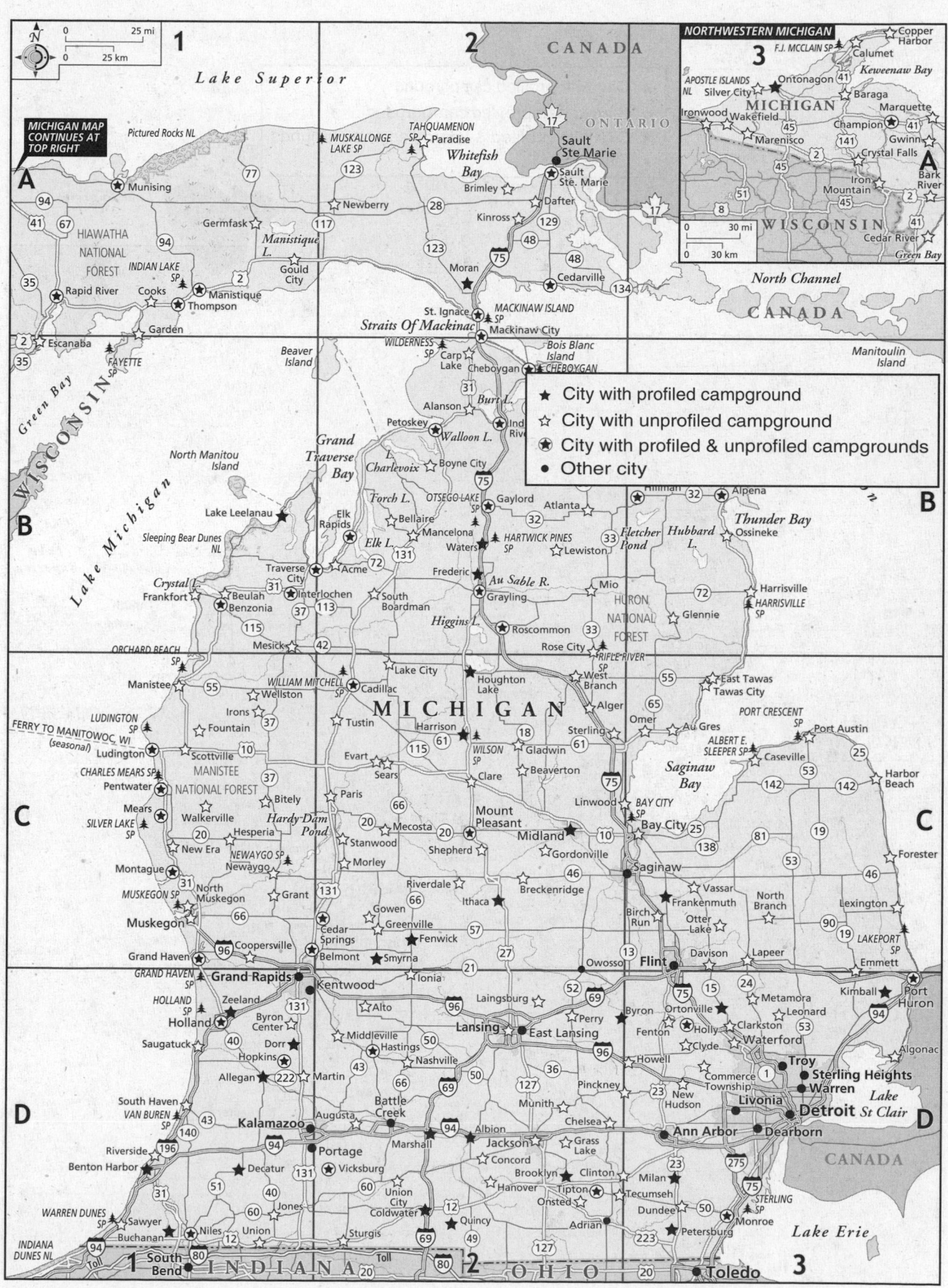

Legend:
- ★ City with profiled campground
- ☆ City with unprofiled campground
- ⍟ City with profiled & unprofiled campgrounds
- • Other city

NORTHWESTERN MICHIGAN (inset 3)

Copper Harbor, F.J. McCLAIN SP, Calumet, Keweenaw Bay, Apostle Islands NL, Silver City, Ontonagon, Baraga, Marquette, Ironwood, Wakefield, Champion, Gwinn, Marenisco, Crystal Falls, Iron Mountain, Bark River, Cedar River, Green Bay

WISCONSIN

Minnesota

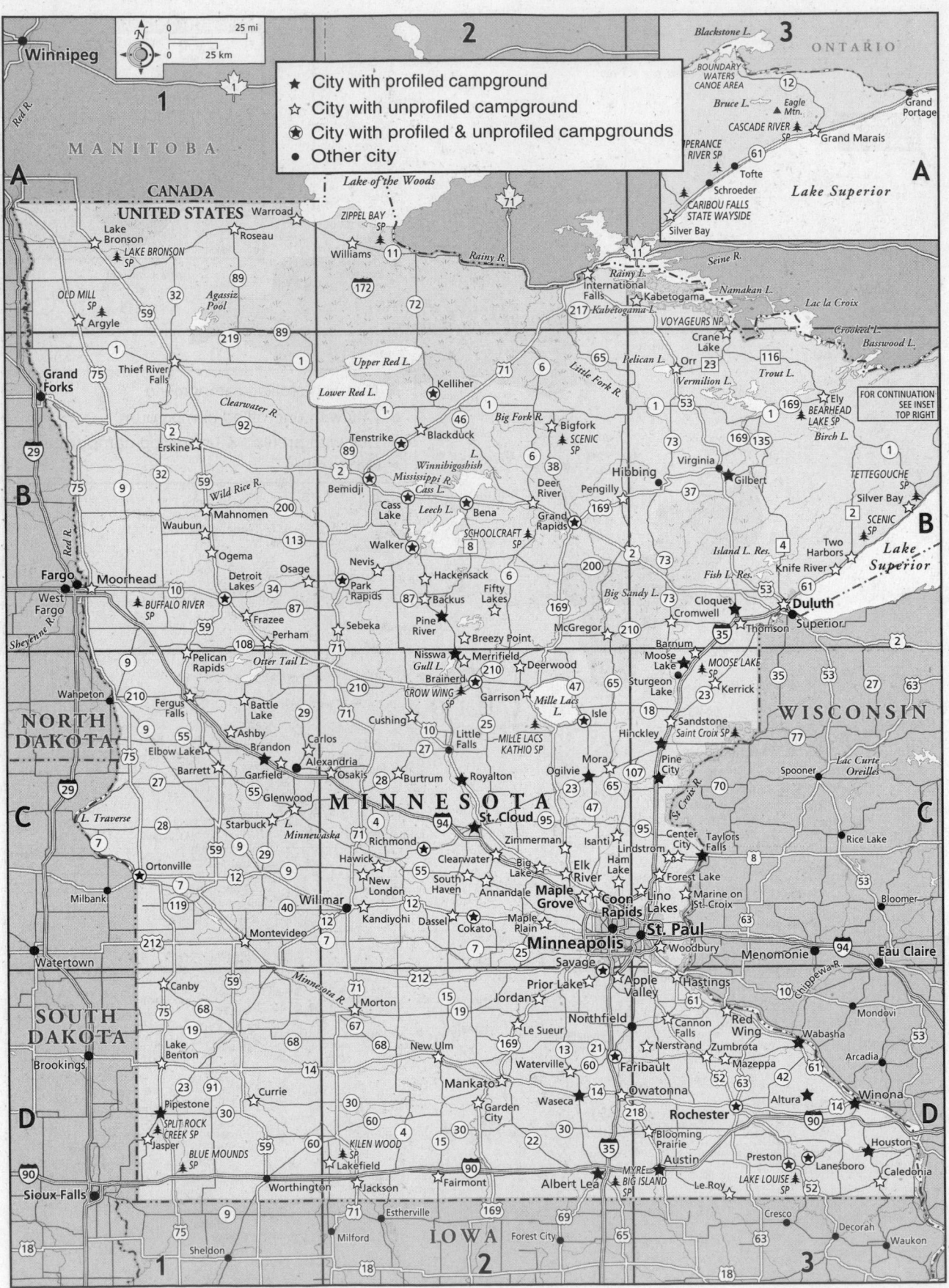

Legend:
- ★ City with profiled campground
- ☆ City with unprofiled campground
- ⊛ City with profiled & unprofiled campgrounds
- • Other city

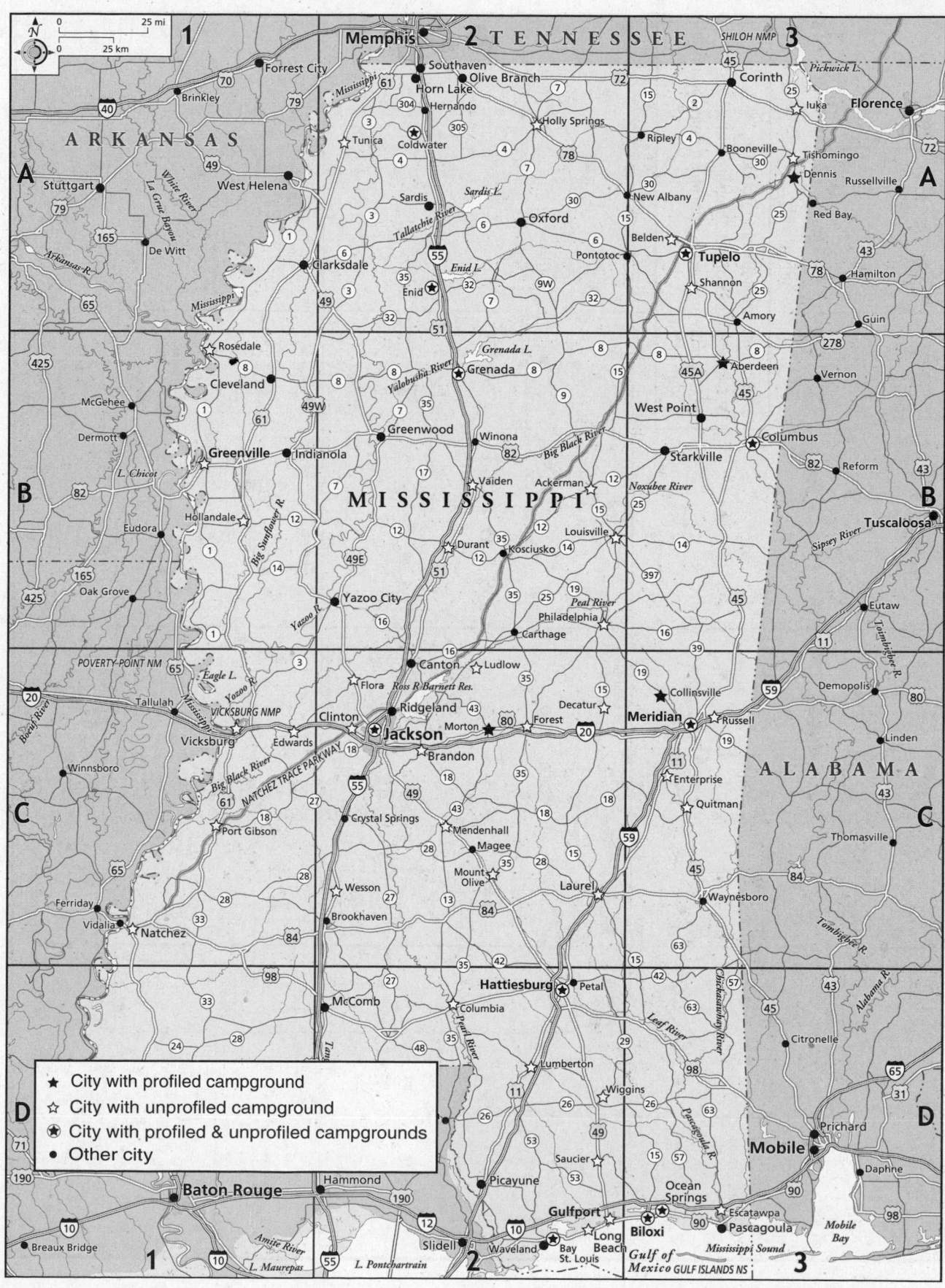

Missouri

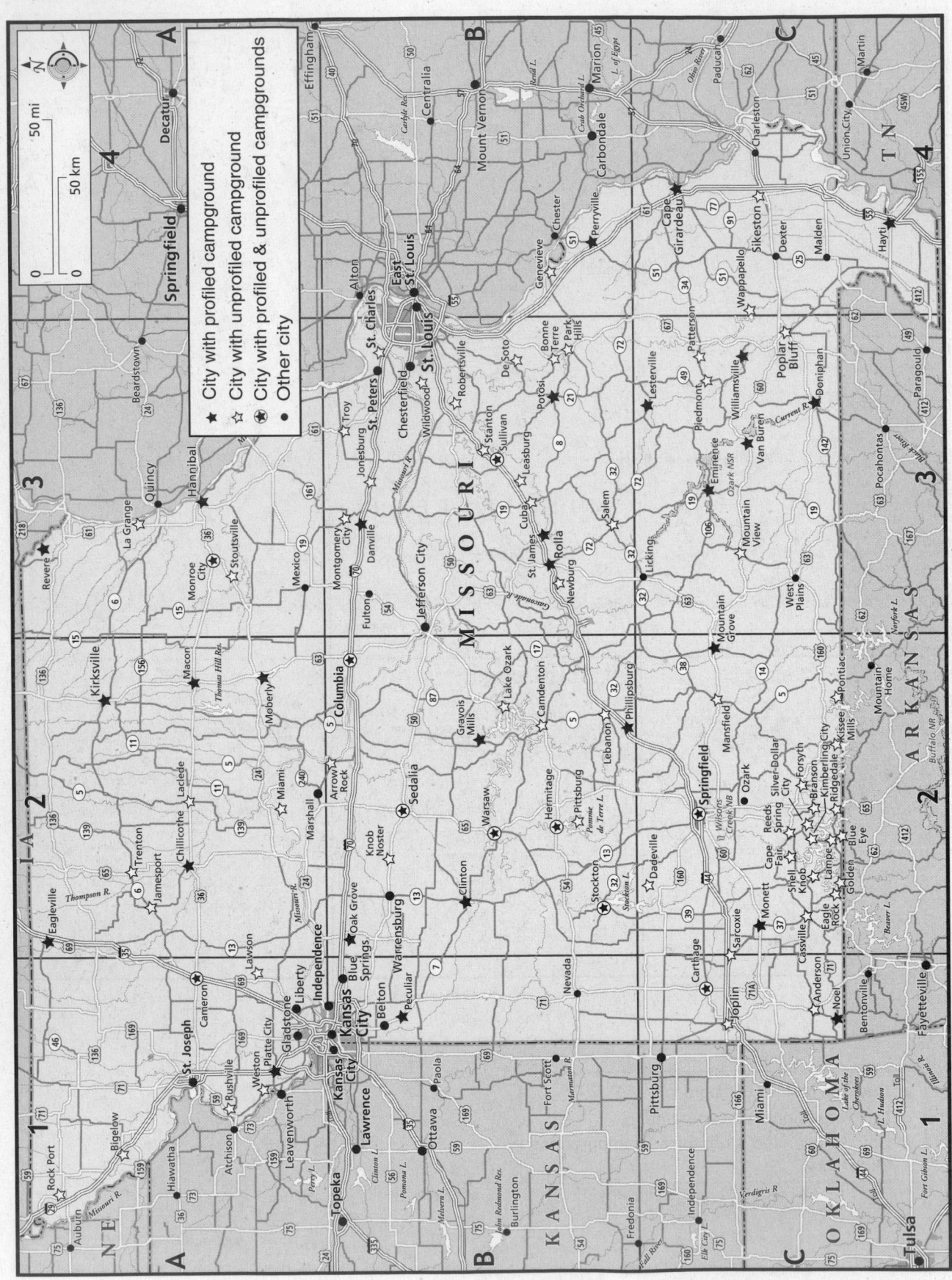

Legend:
- ★ City with profiled campground
- ☆ City with unprofiled campground
- ⊛ City with profiled & unprofiled campgrounds
- • Other city

50 mi
50 km

Montana

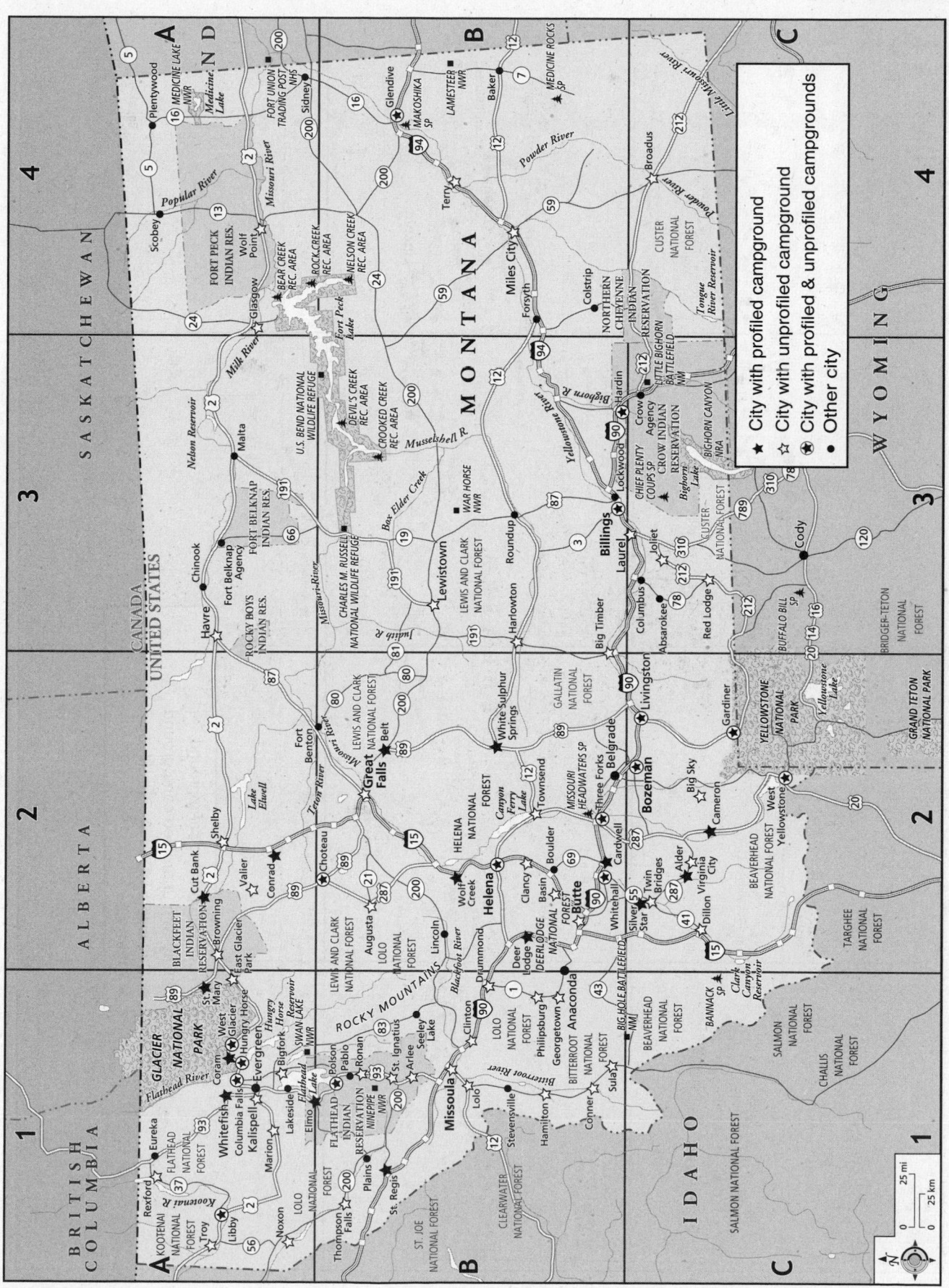

Nebraska

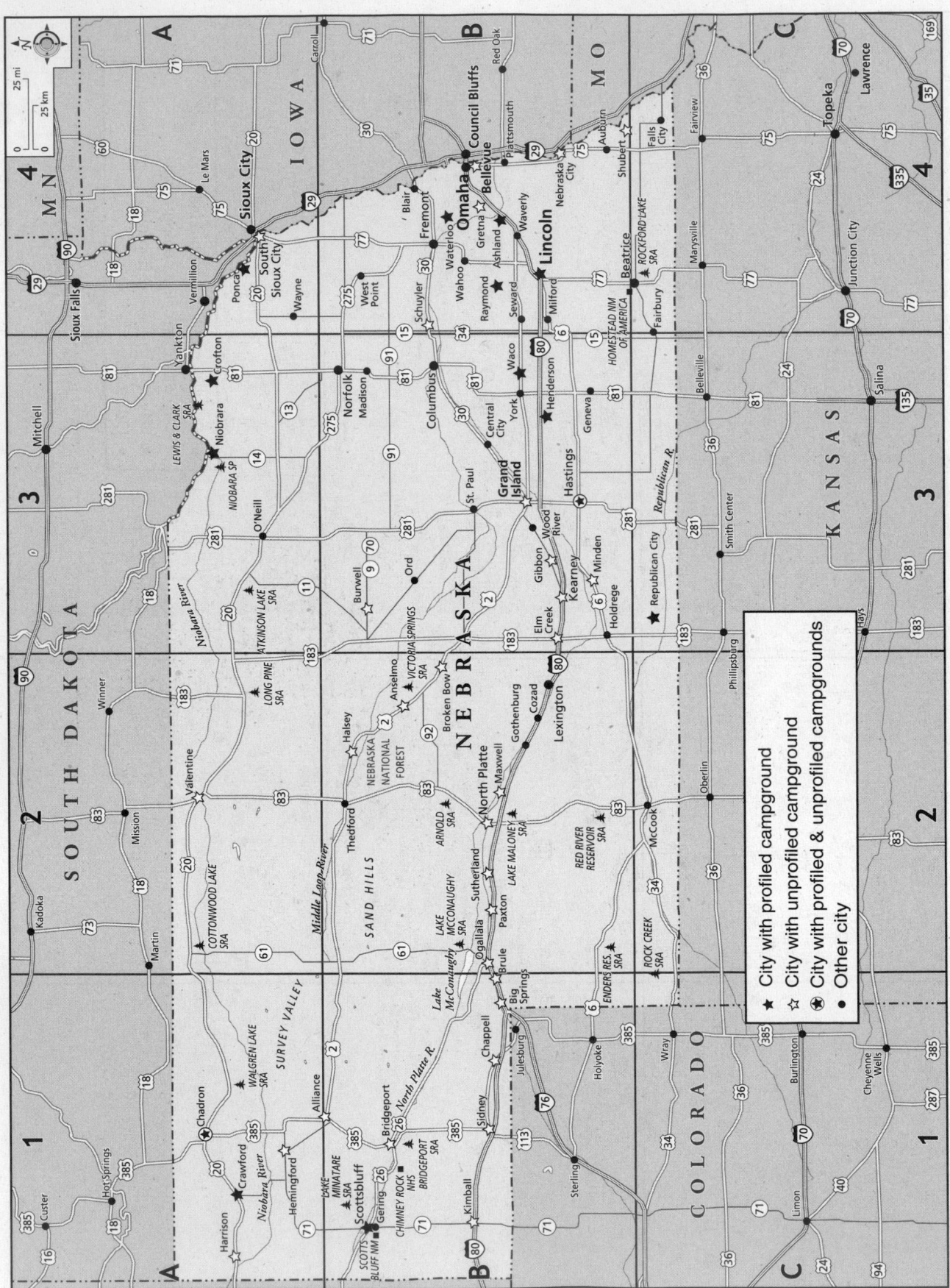

Nevada

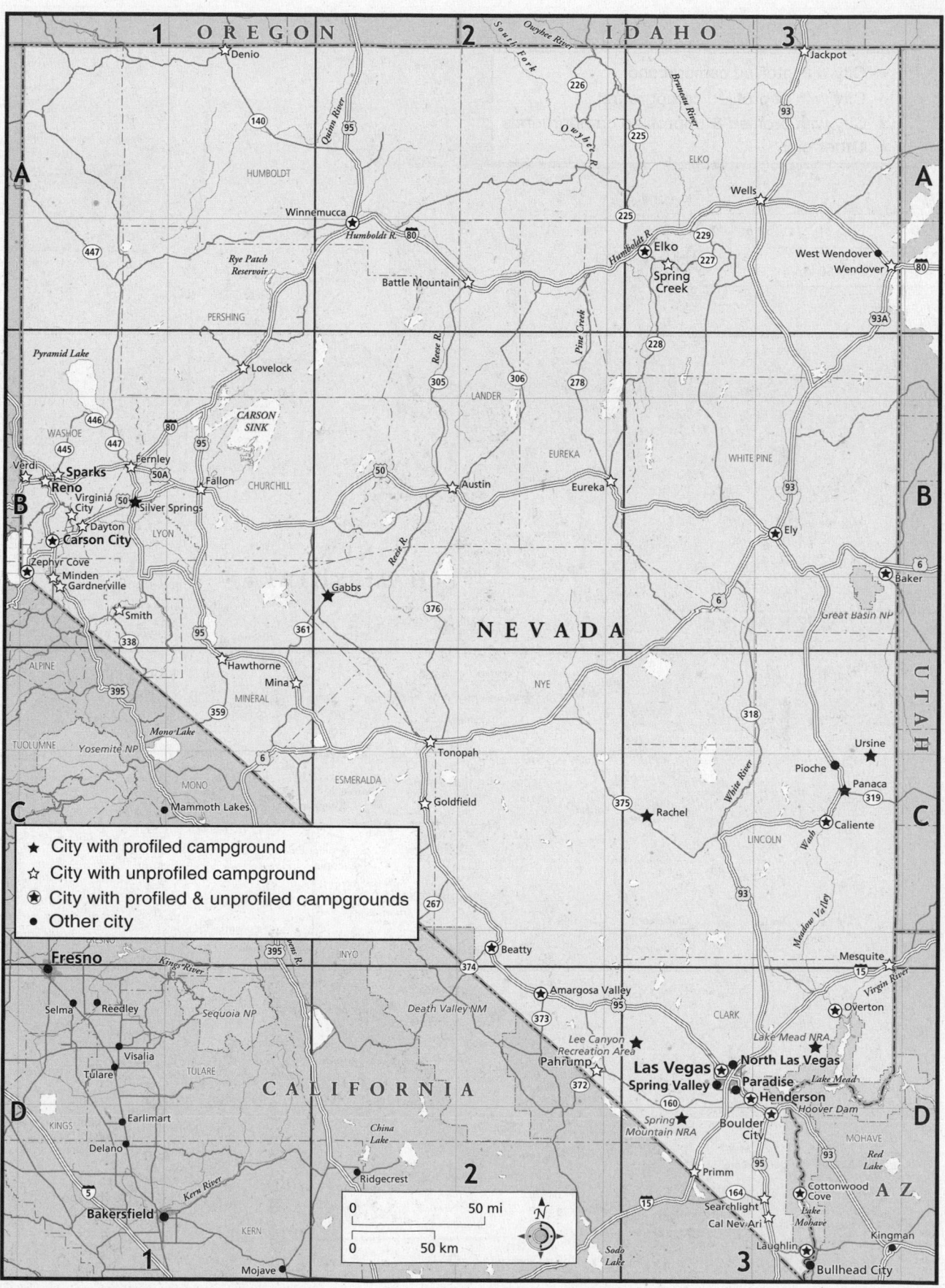

Legend:
- ★ City with profiled campground
- ☆ City with unprofiled campground
- ⍟ City with profiled & unprofiled campgrounds
- • Other city

Scale:
0 — 50 mi
0 — 50 km

New Hampshire

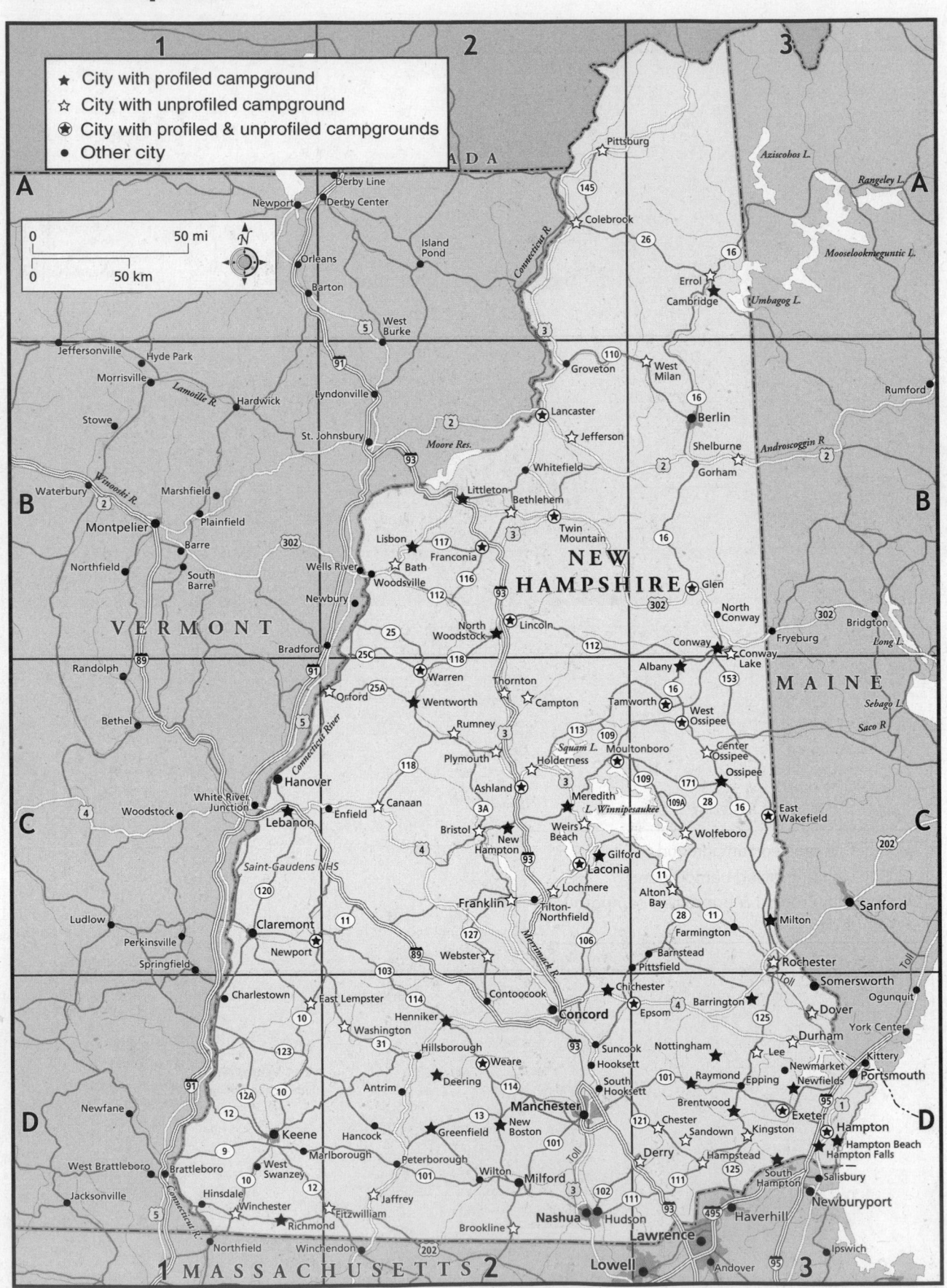

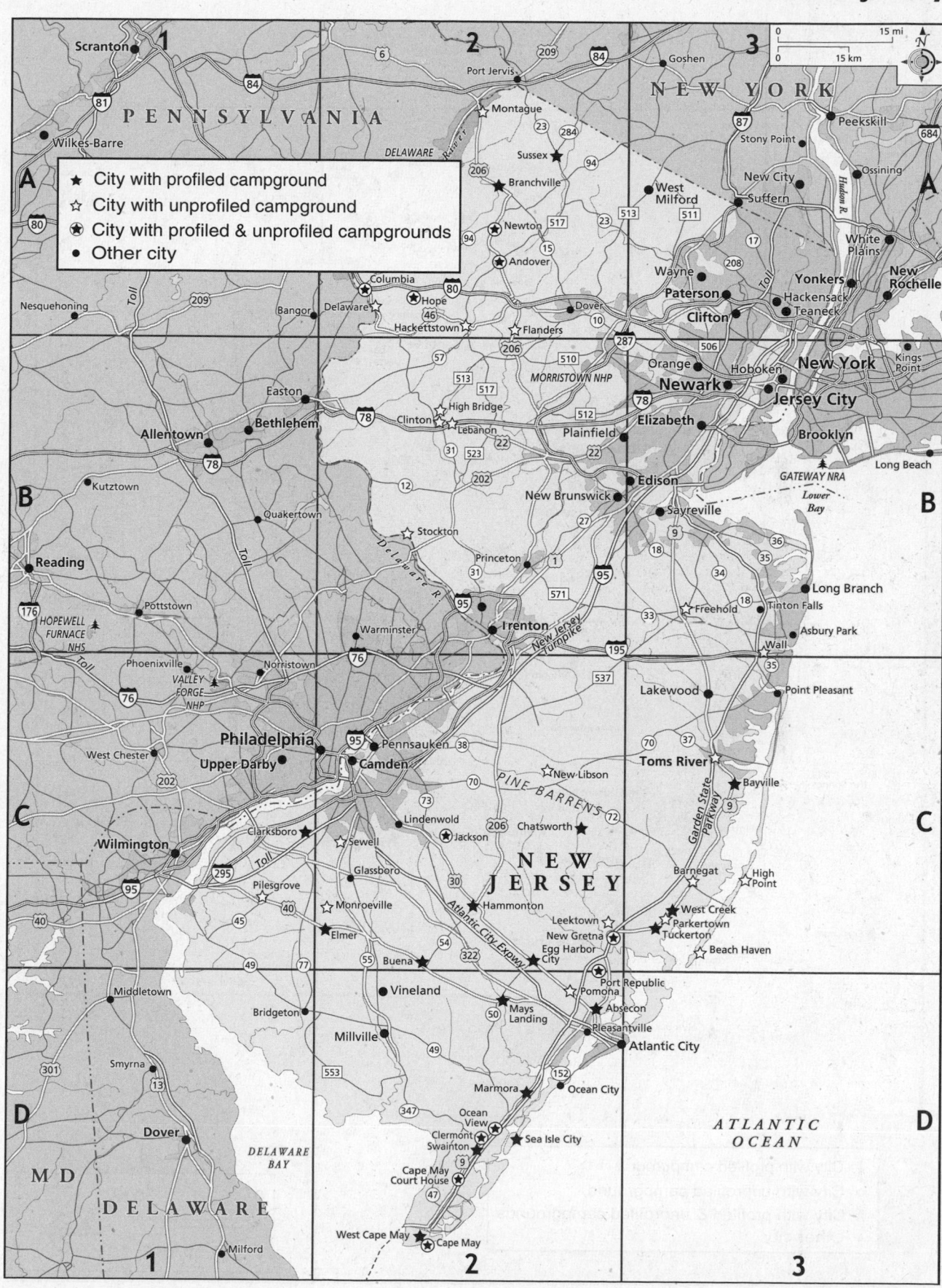

New Mexico

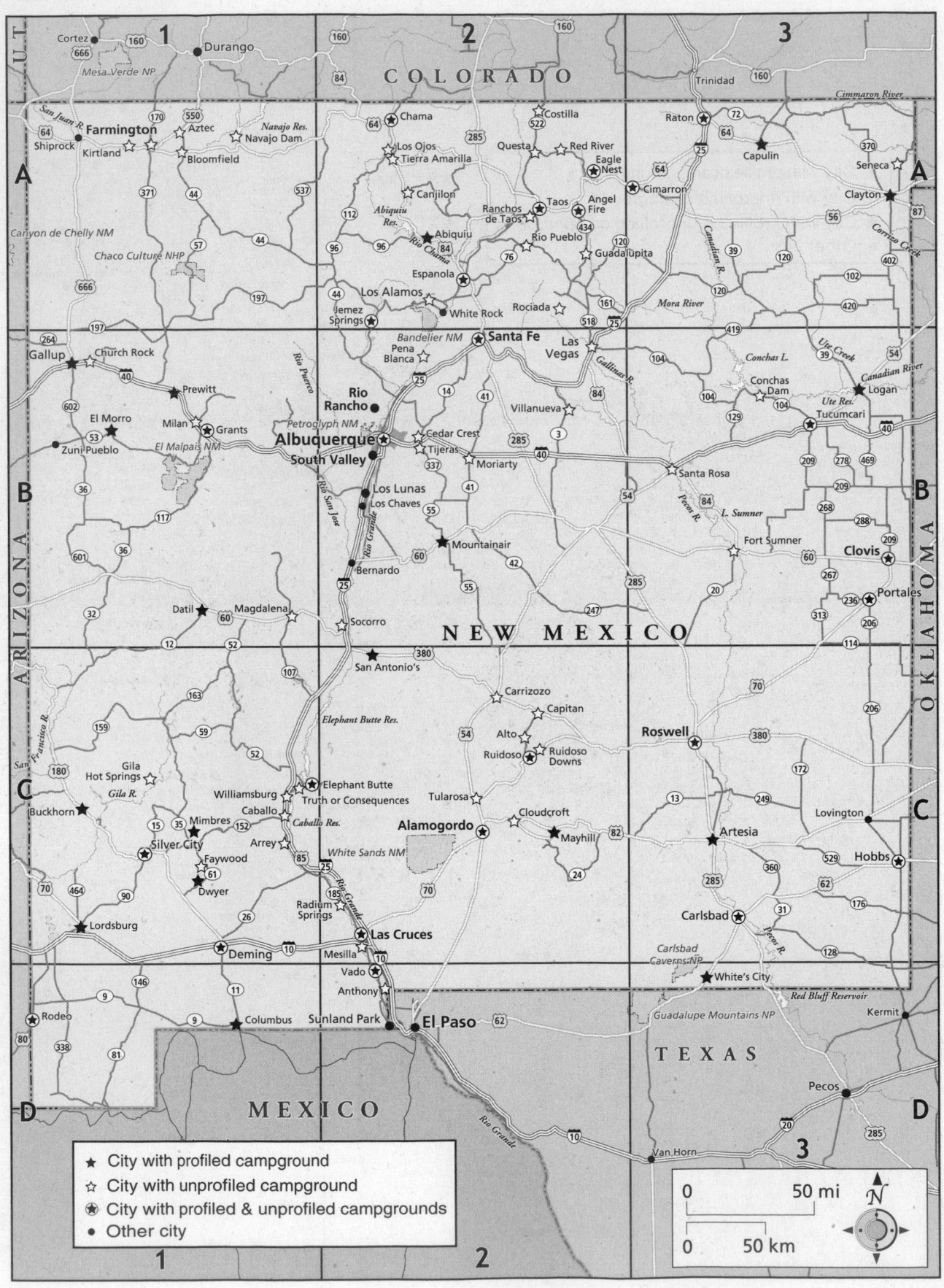

Legend:
- ★ City with profiled campground
- ☆ City with unprofiled campground
- ⊛ City with profiled & unprofiled campgrounds
- • Other city

0 50 mi

0 50 km

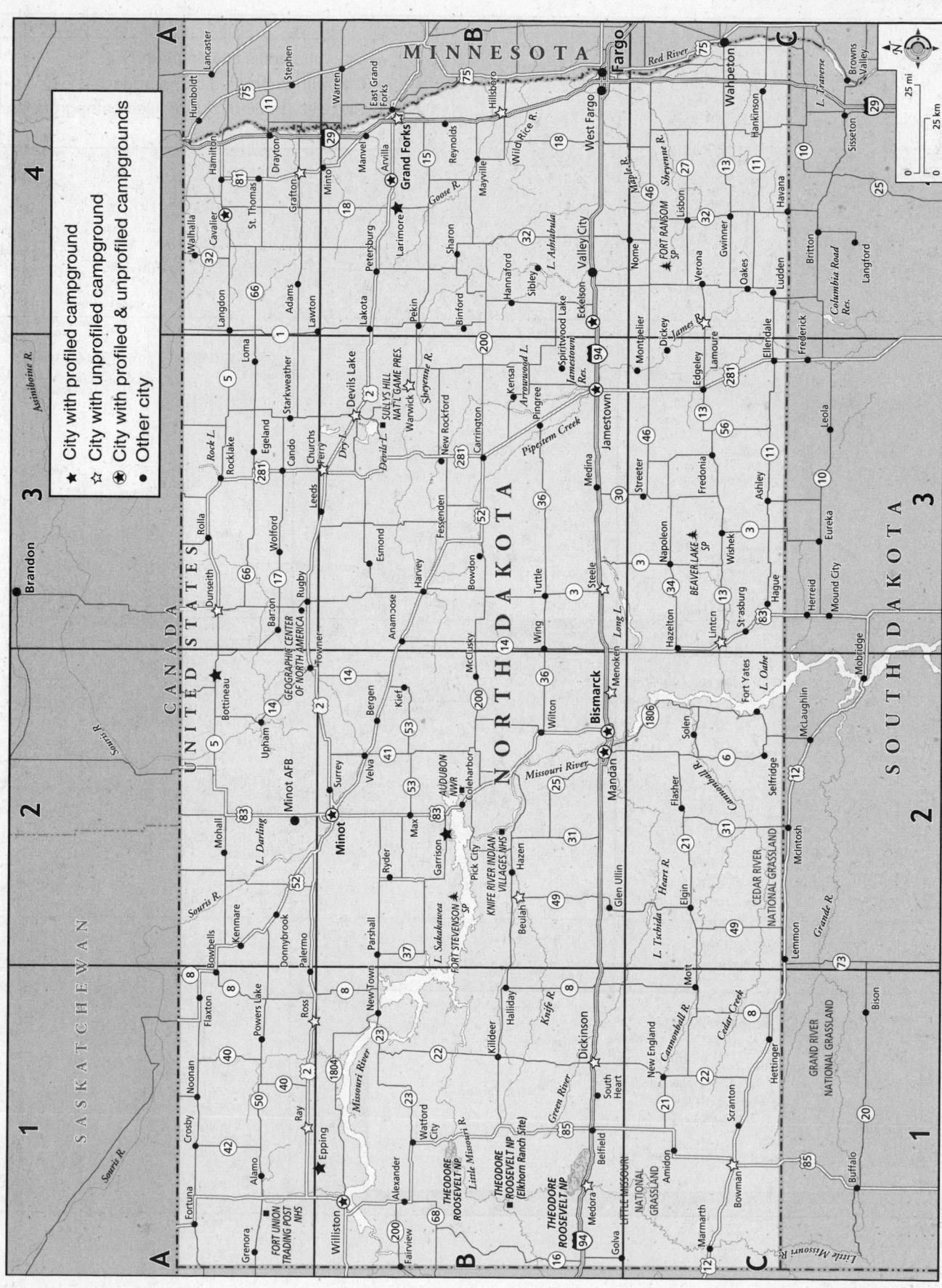

North Dakota

MINNESOTA

NORTH DAKOTA

SOUTH DAKOTA

SASKATCHEWAN

CANADA
UNITED STATES

Legend:
- ★ City with profiled campground
- ☆ City with unprofiled campground
- ✪ City with profiled & unprofiled campgrounds
- ● Other city

25 mi
25 km

New York West

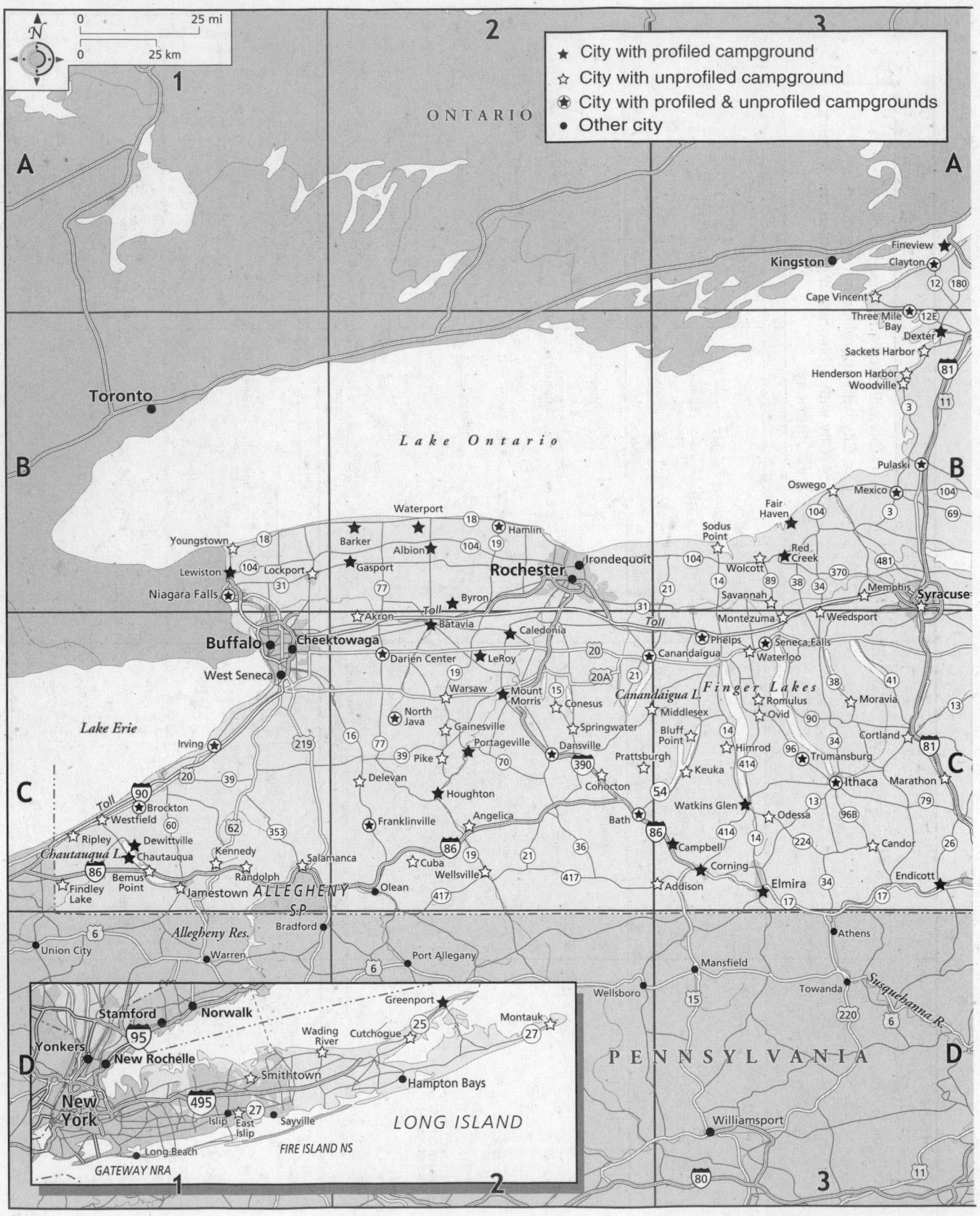

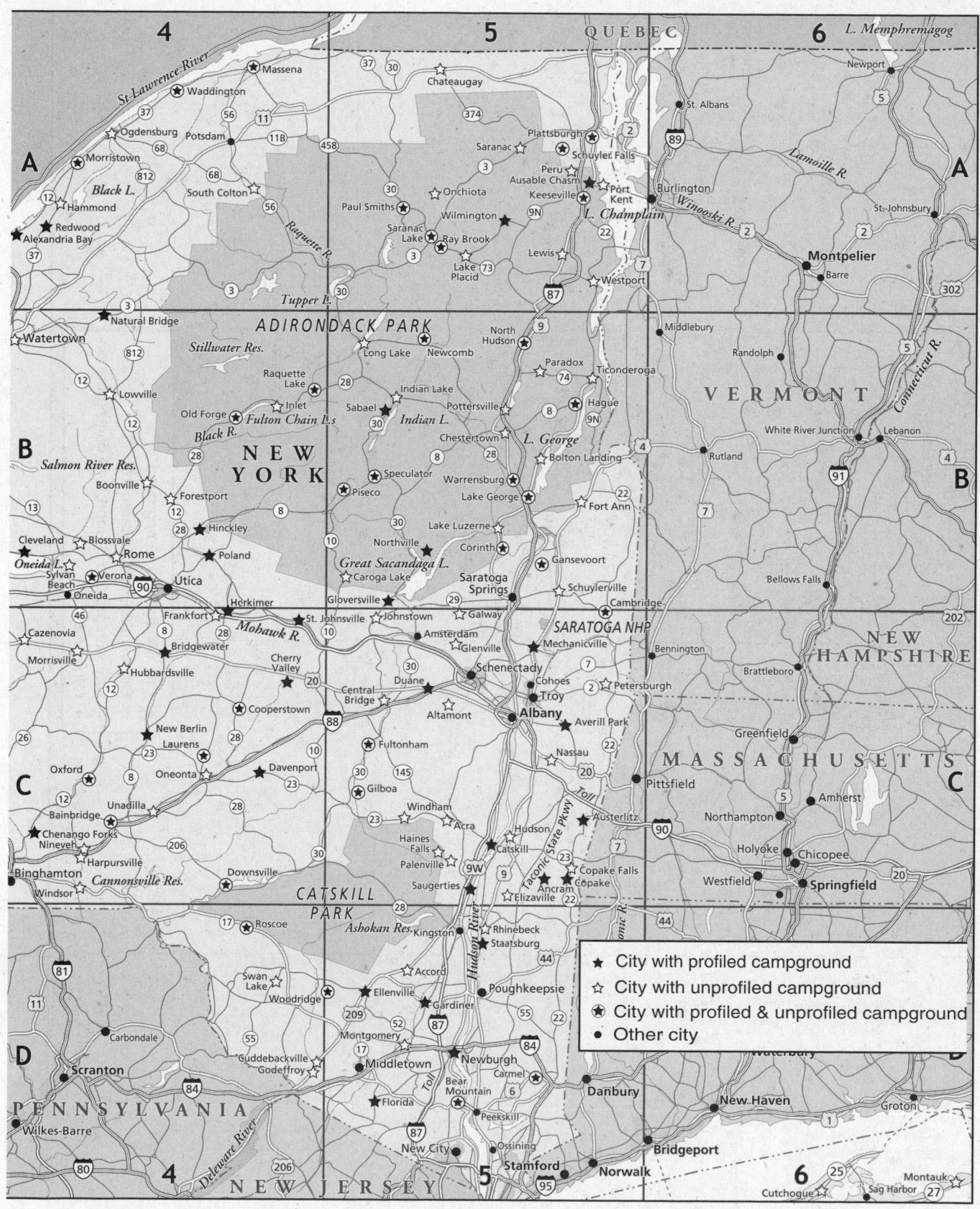

City with profiled campground

City with unprofiled campground

City with profiled & unprofiled campground

Other city

North Carolina West

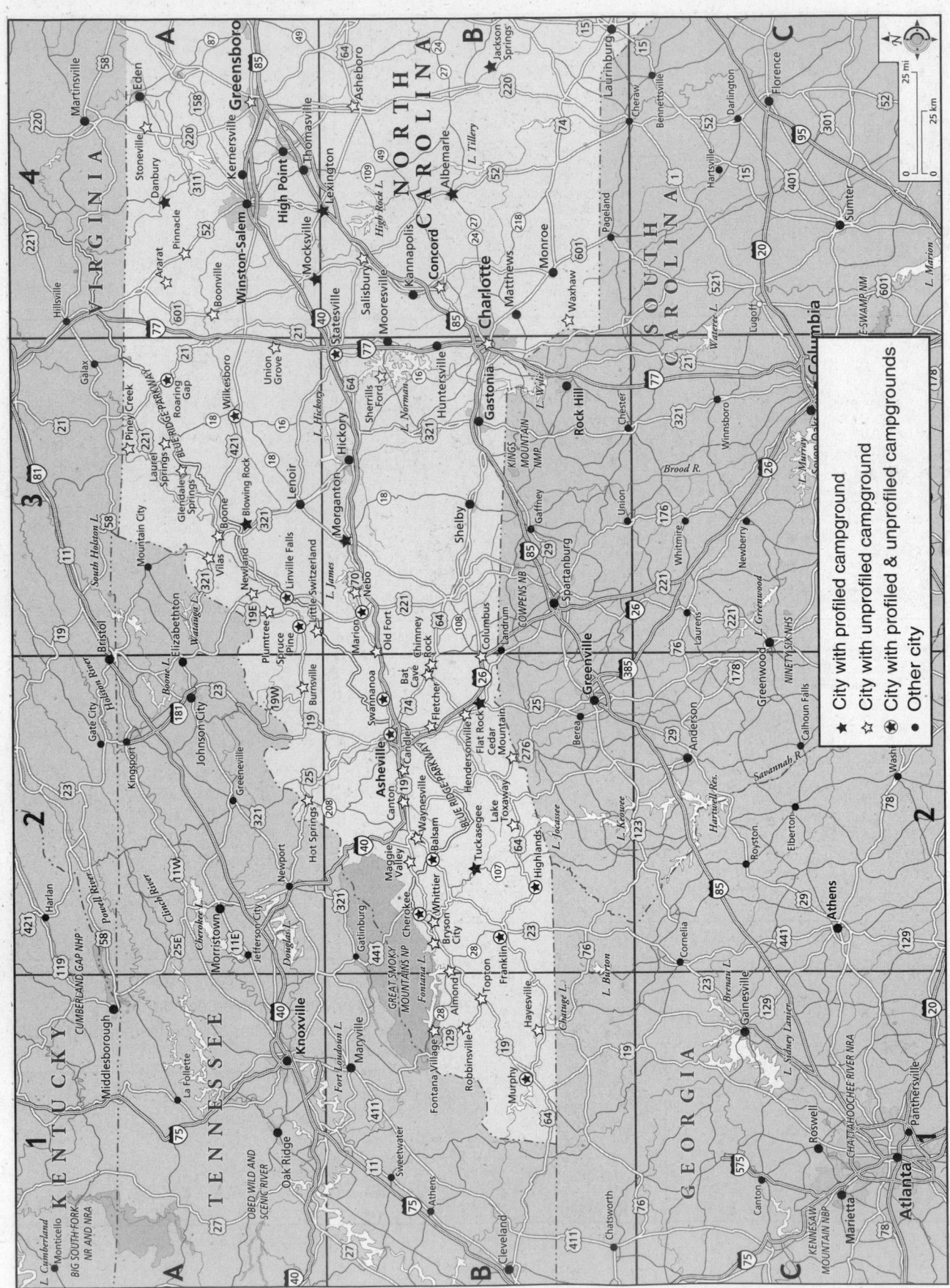

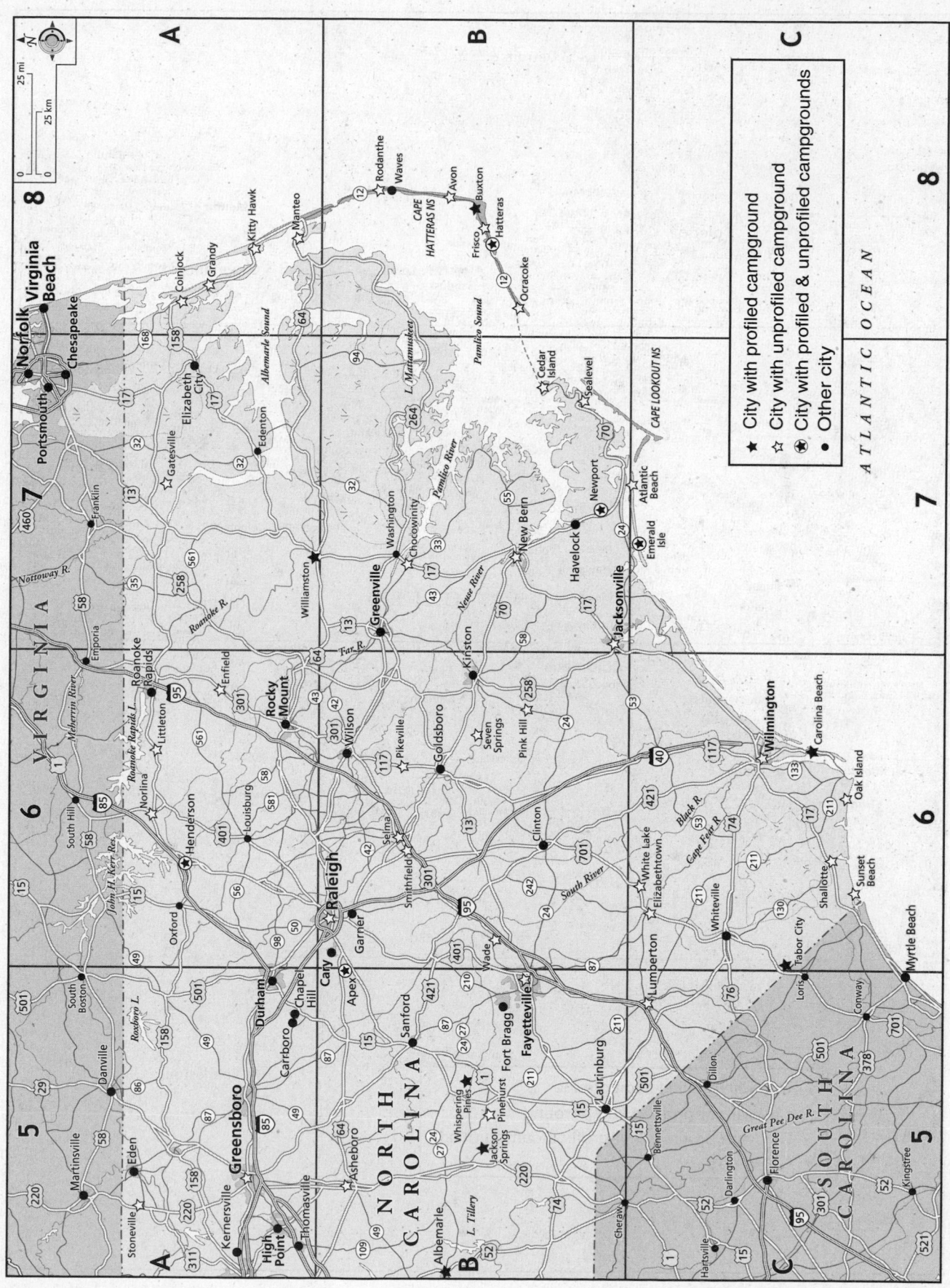

Ohio

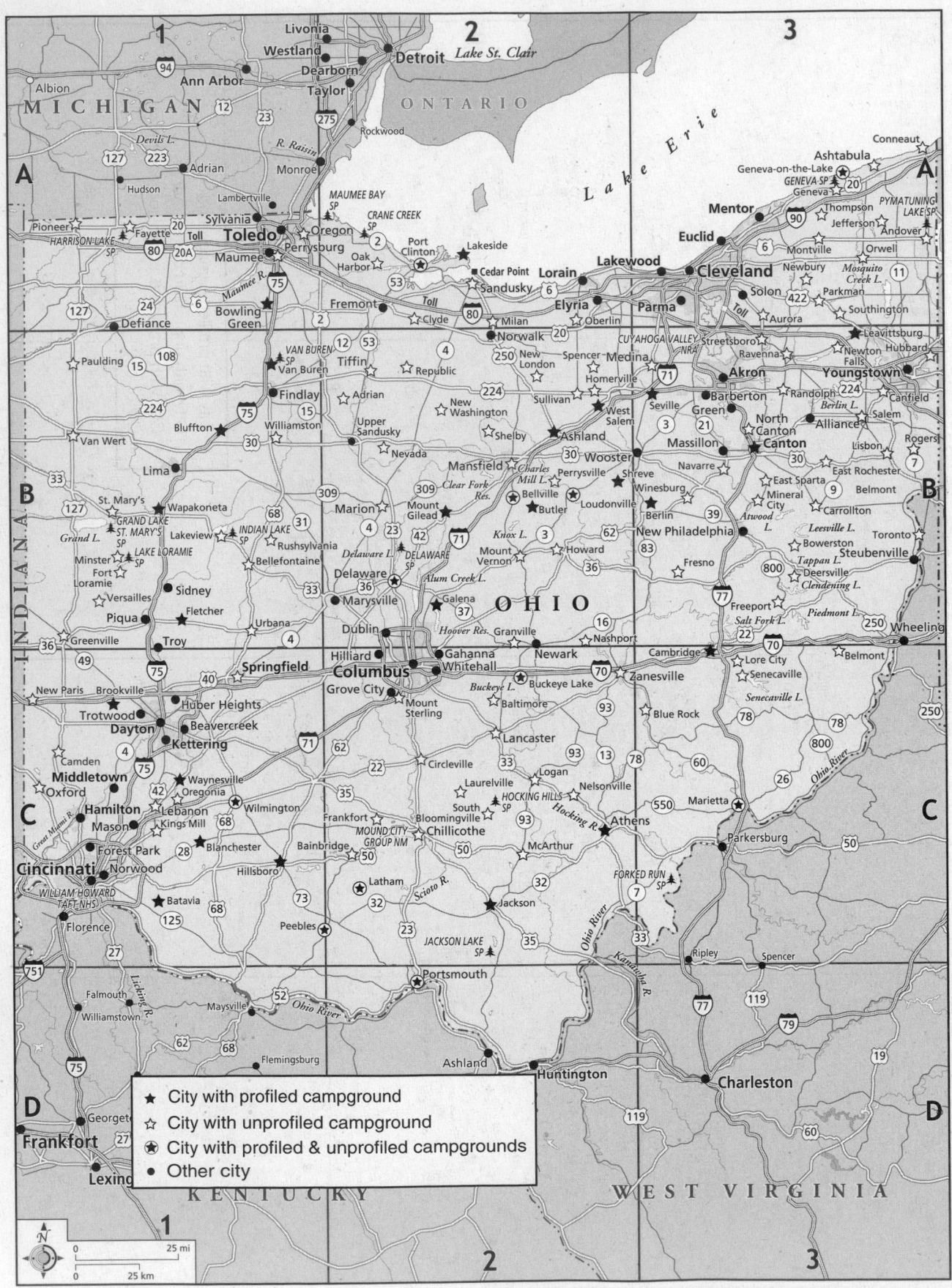

Legend:
- ★ City with profiled campground
- ☆ City with unprofiled campground
- ✪ City with profiled & unprofiled campgrounds
- • Other city

0 — 25 mi
0 — 25 km

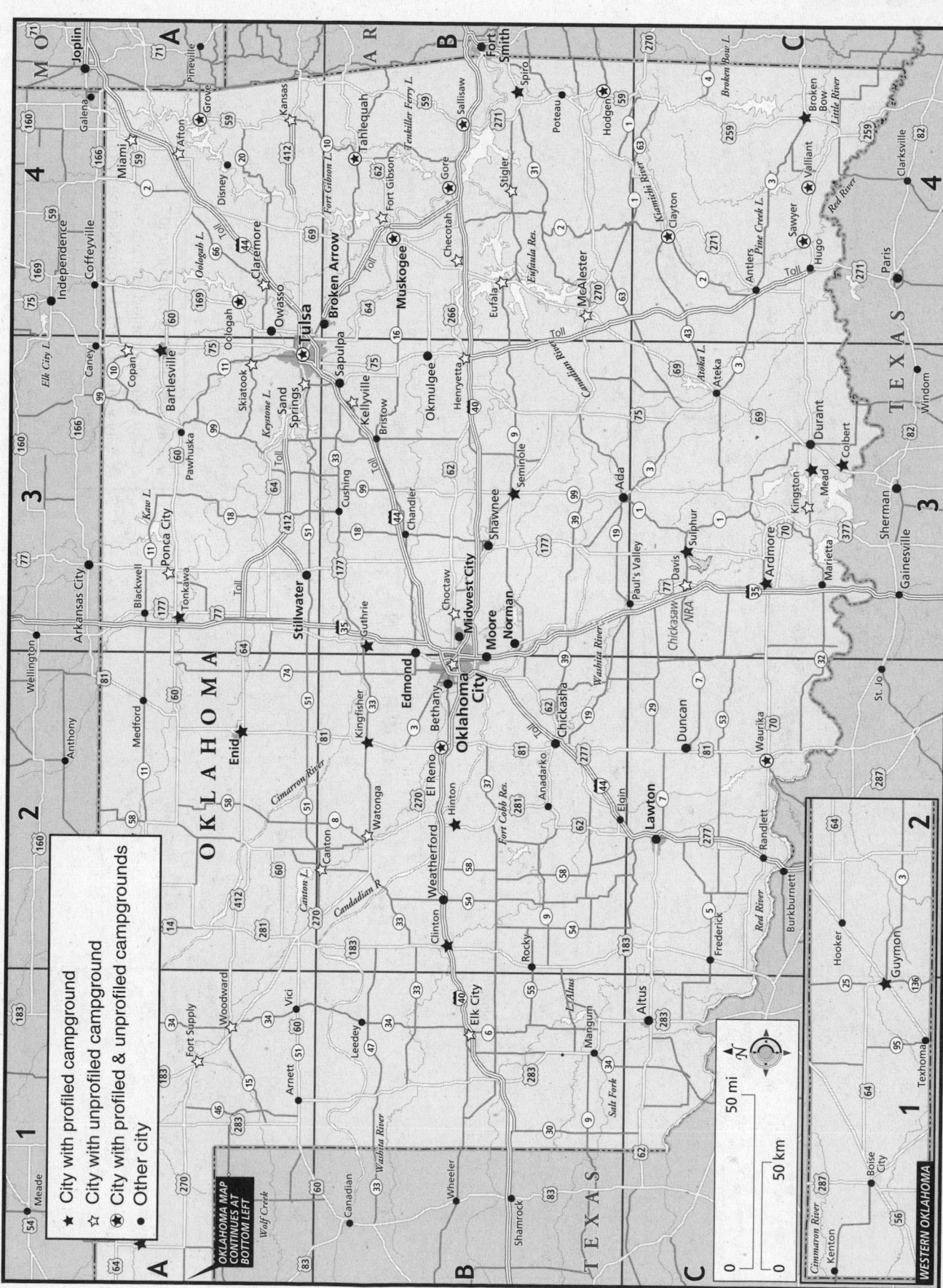

Oklahoma

Legend:
- ★ City with profiled campground
- ☆ City with unprofiled campground
- ⊛ City with profiled & unprofiled campgrounds
- • Other city

OKLAHOMA MAP CONTINUES AT BOTTOM LEFT

WESTERN OKLAHOMA

50 mi

50 km

43

Oregon

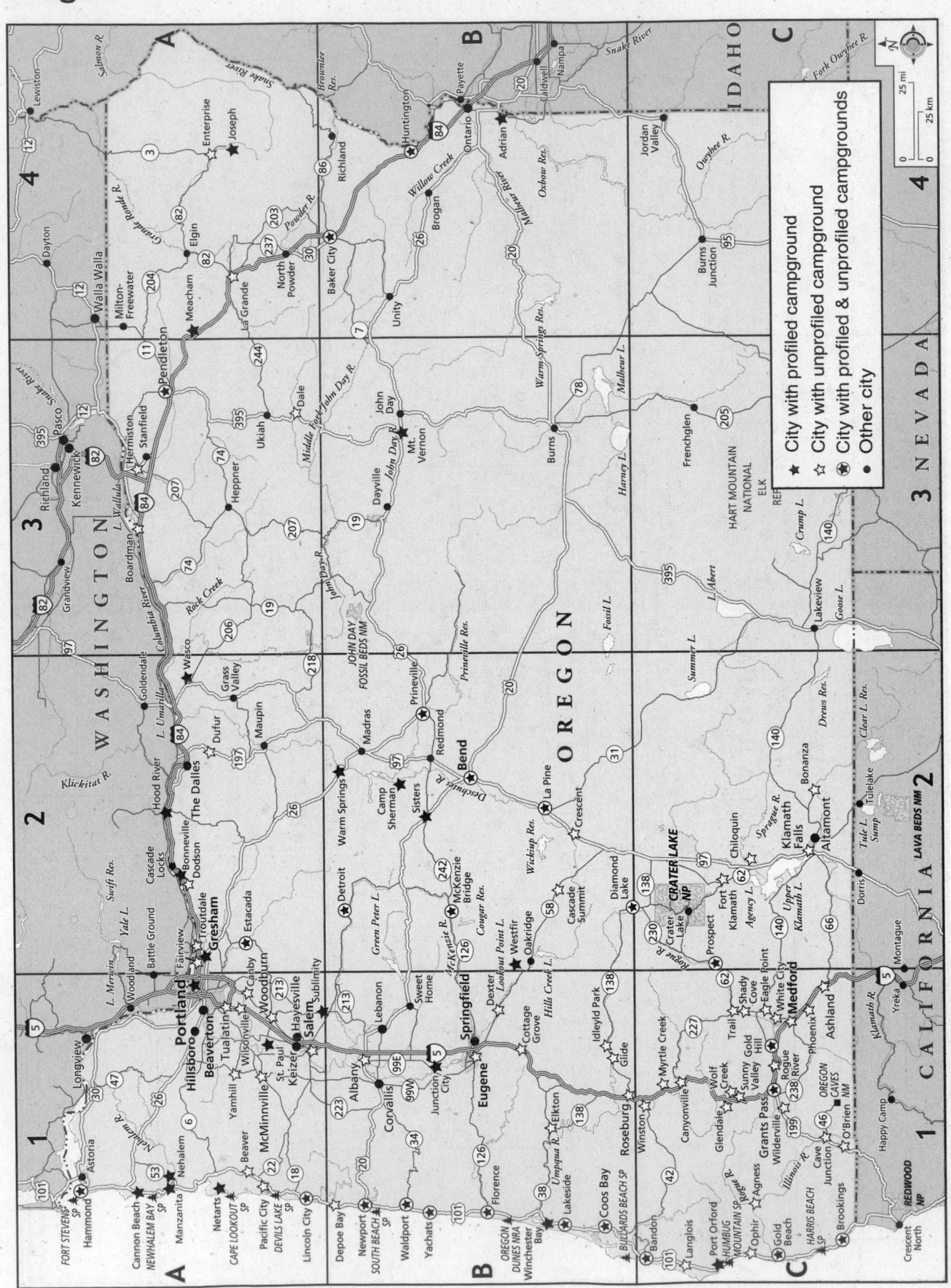

44

Rhode Island

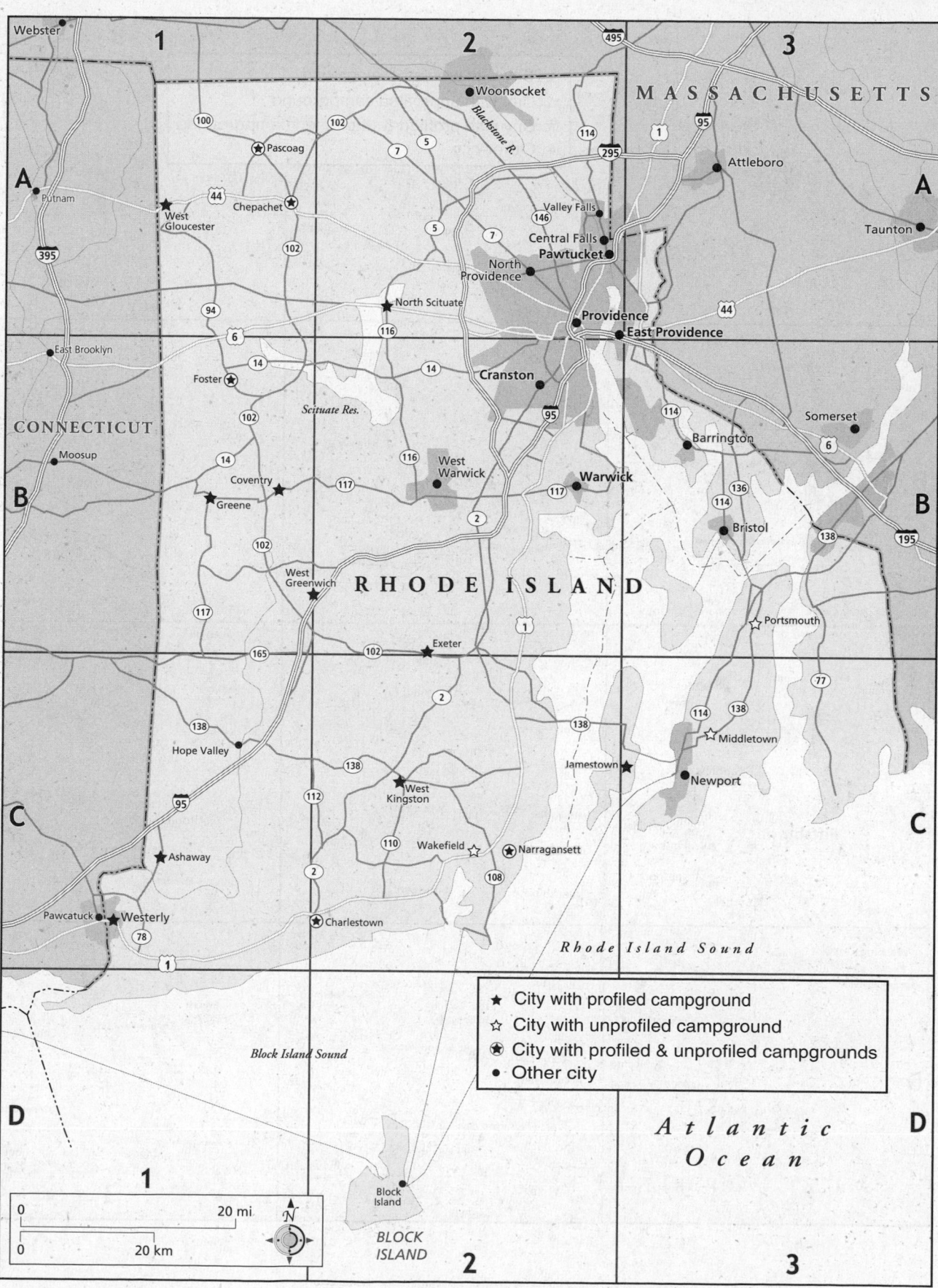

Webster

1

100

Pascoag

102

2

Woonsocket

495

MASSACHUSETTS

1

95

3

7

5

Blackstone R.

114

295

Attleboro

A

Putnam

44

Chepachet

West
Gloucester

5

7

146

Valley Falls

Central Falls

Pawtucket

North
Providence

44

Taunton

A

395

102

East Brooklyn

94

6

North Scituate

116

Providence

East Providence

14

14

Cranston

95

114

Somerset

CONNECTICUT

Foster

102

Scituate Res.

116

West
Warwick

Warwick

Barrington

6

B

Moosup

14

Coventry

Greene

117

117

2

RHODE ISLAND

117

114

136

114

Bristol

138

195

B

102

West
Greenwich

117

165

102

Exeter

1

2

Portsmouth

77

138

Jamestown

114

138

Middletown

C

138

Hope Valley

138

West
Kingston

138

Newport

C

112

Ashaway

95

110

Wakefield

Narragansett

2

108

Rhode Island Sound

Pawcatuck

Westerly

78

Charlestown

★ City with profiled campground
☆ City with unprofiled campground
✪ City with profiled & unprofiled campgrounds
● Other city

1

D

1

Block Island Sound

Atlantic
Ocean

D

1

0   20 mi.

N

0   20 km

Block
Island

BLOCK
ISLAND

2

3

45

Pennsylvania West

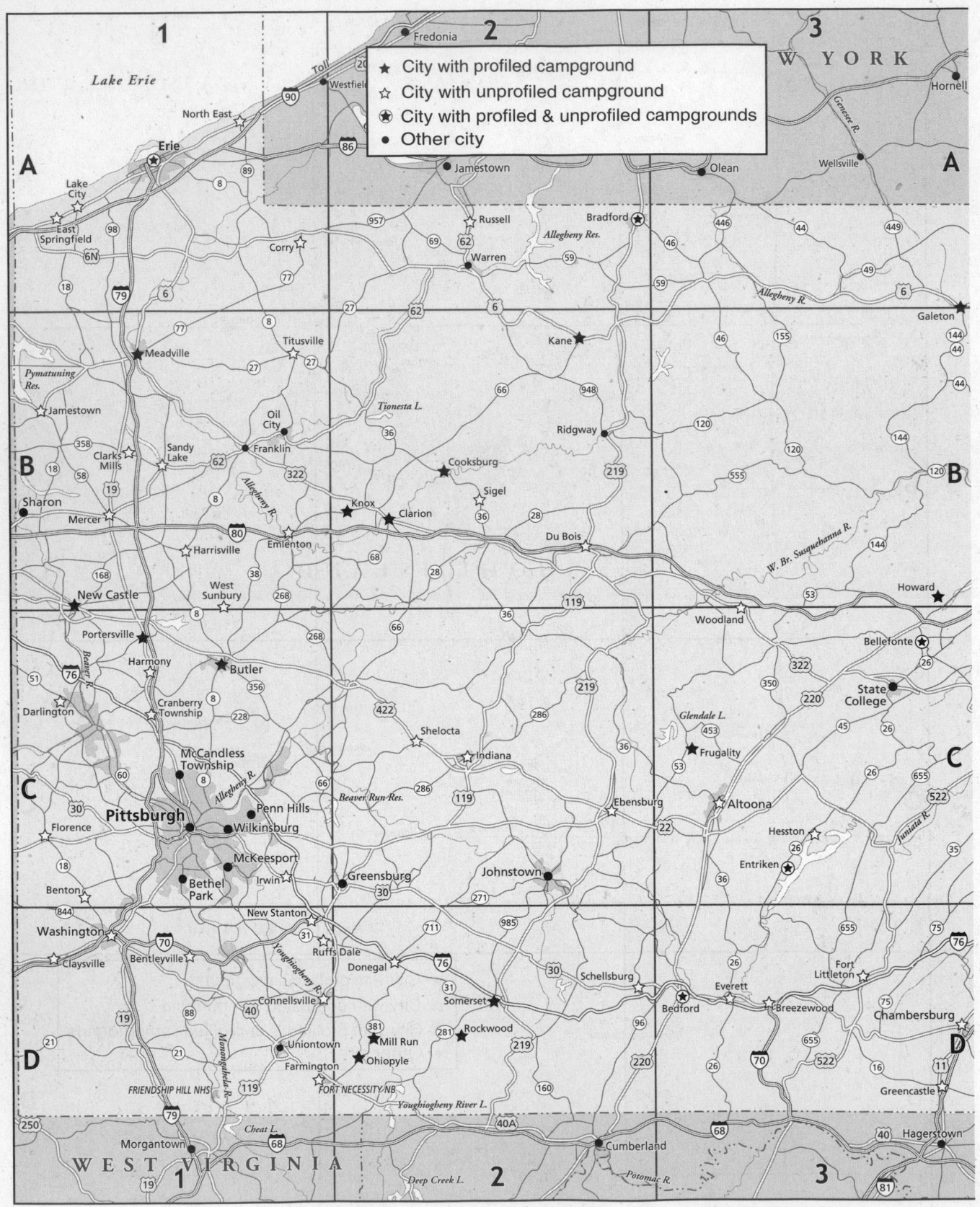

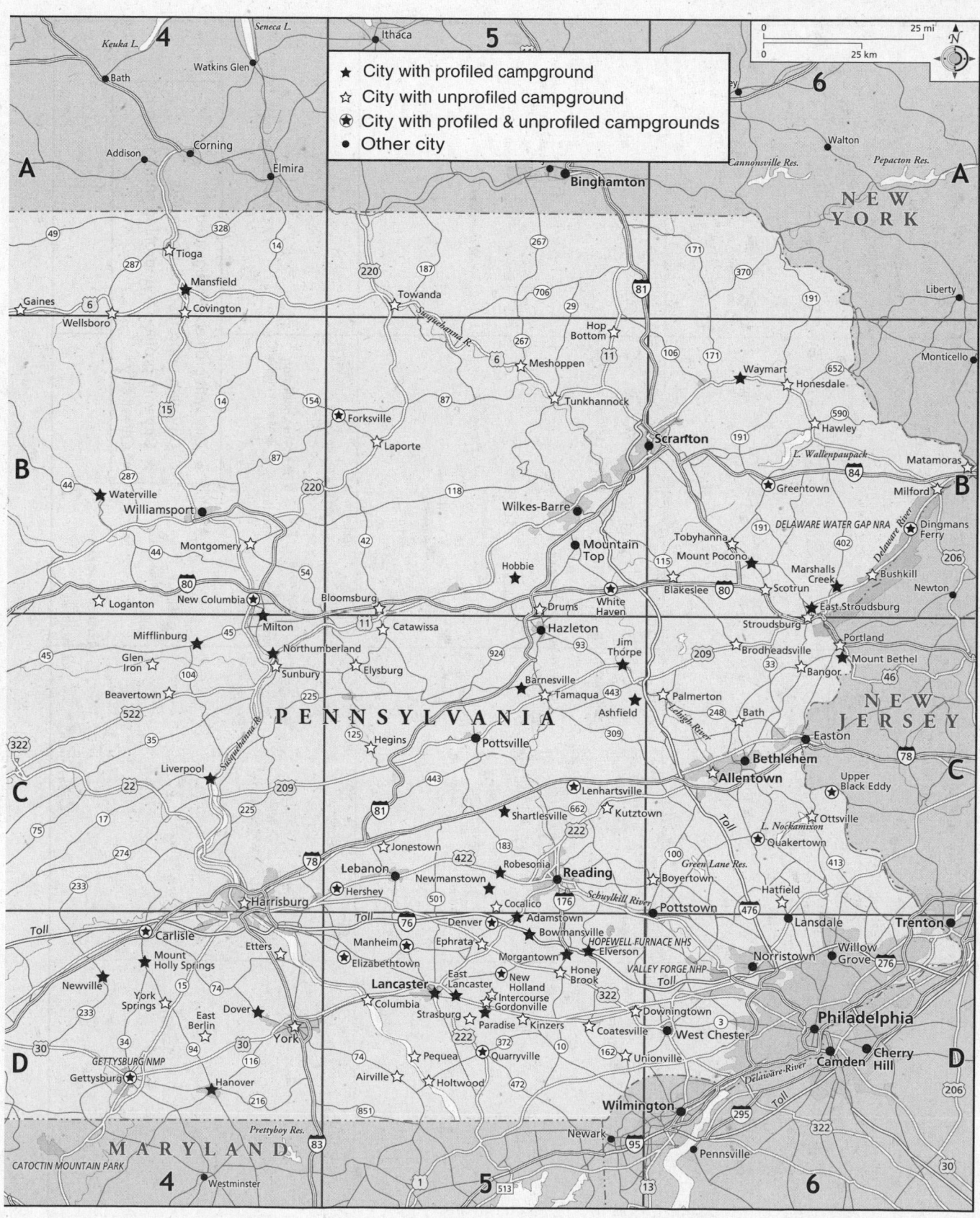

Pennsylvania East

South Carolina

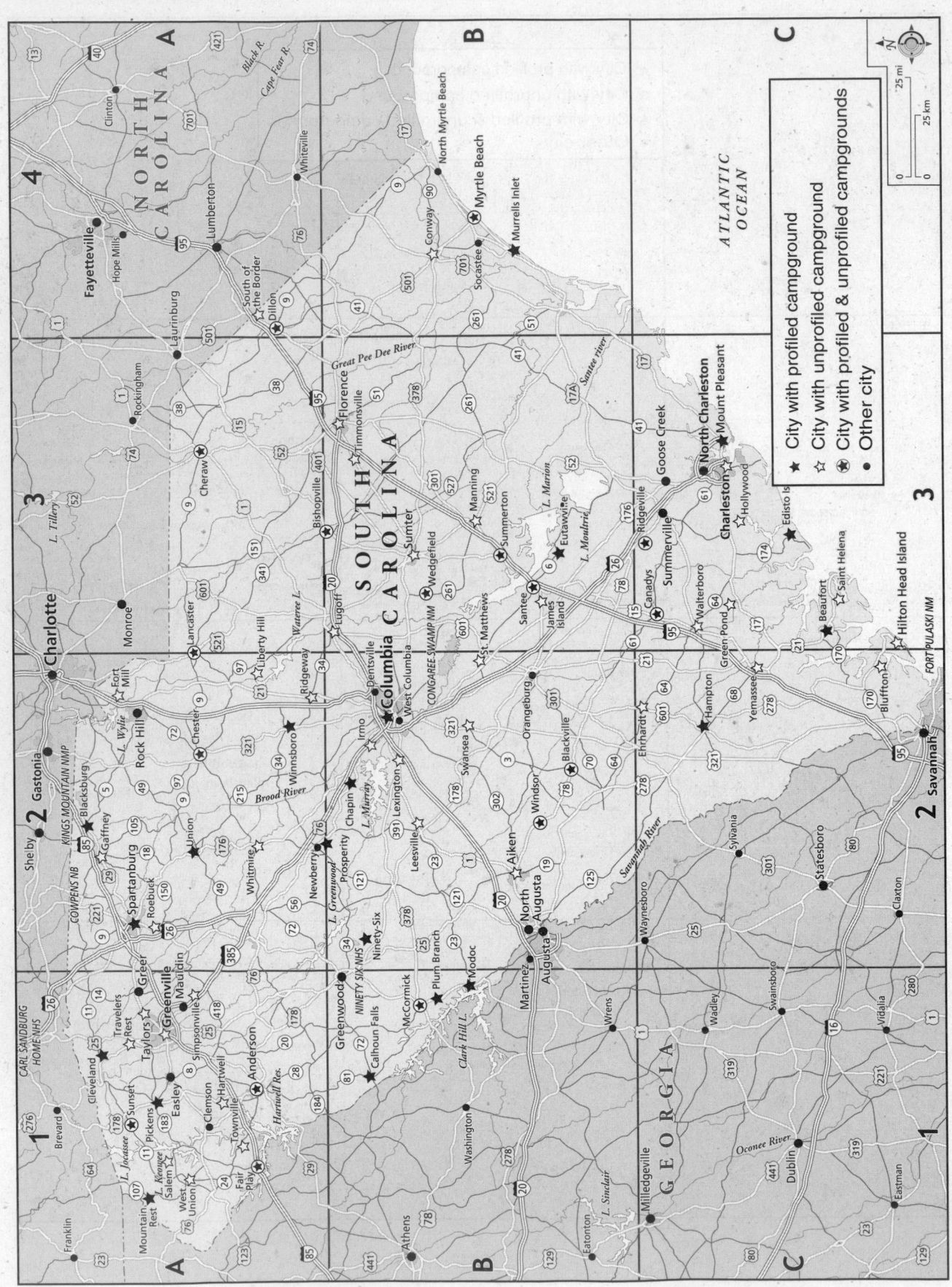

South Dakota

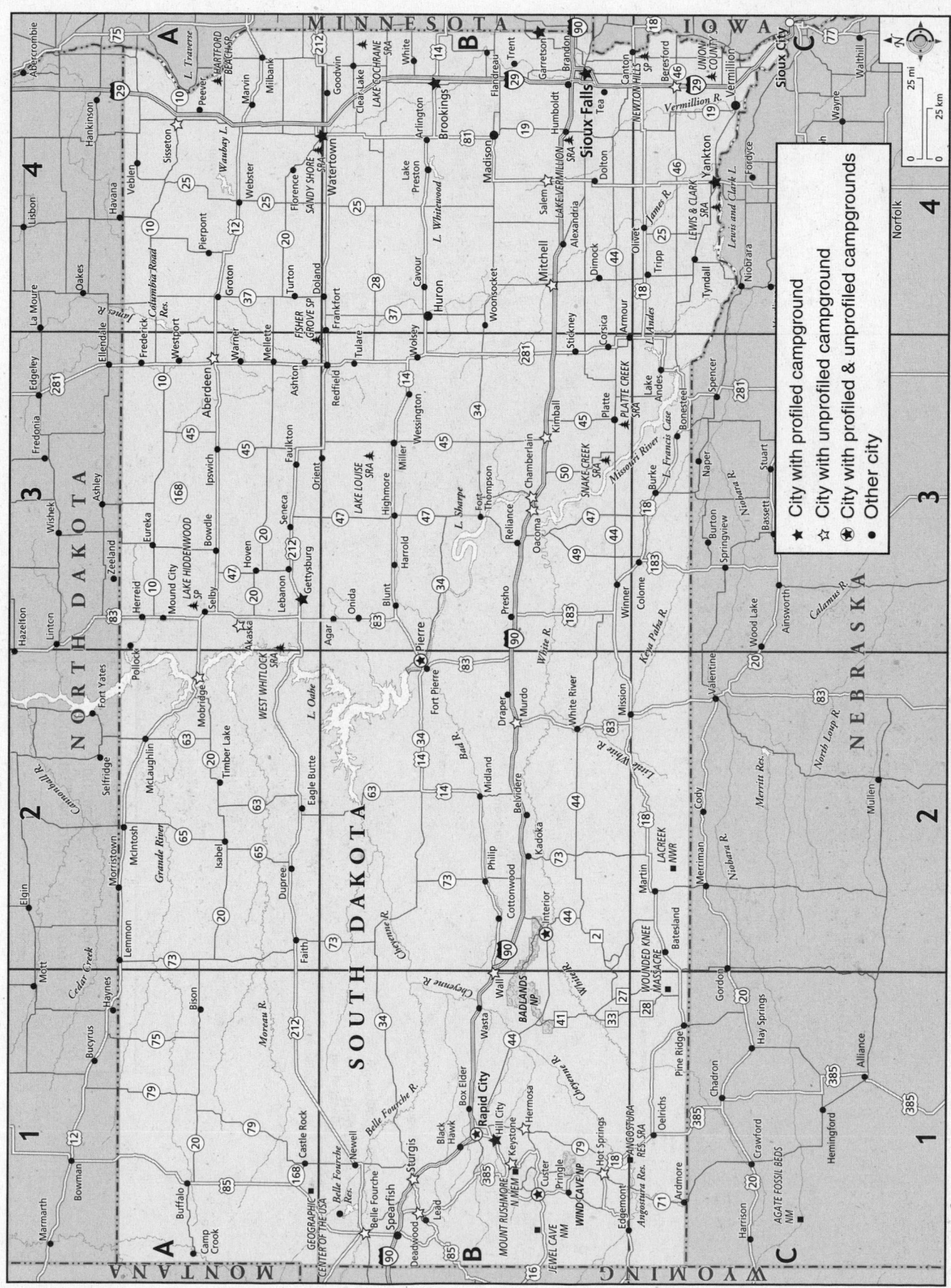

Tennessee West

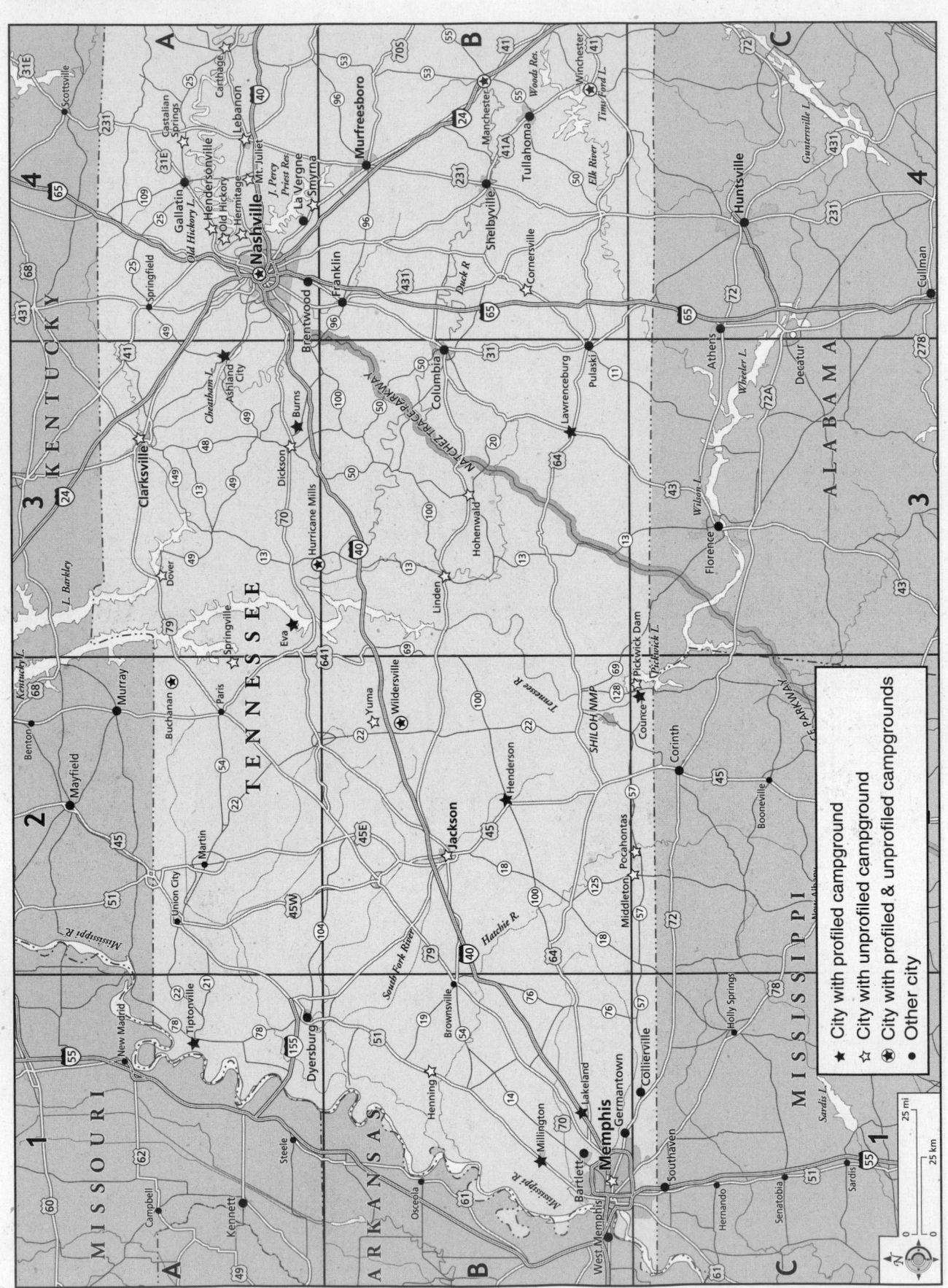

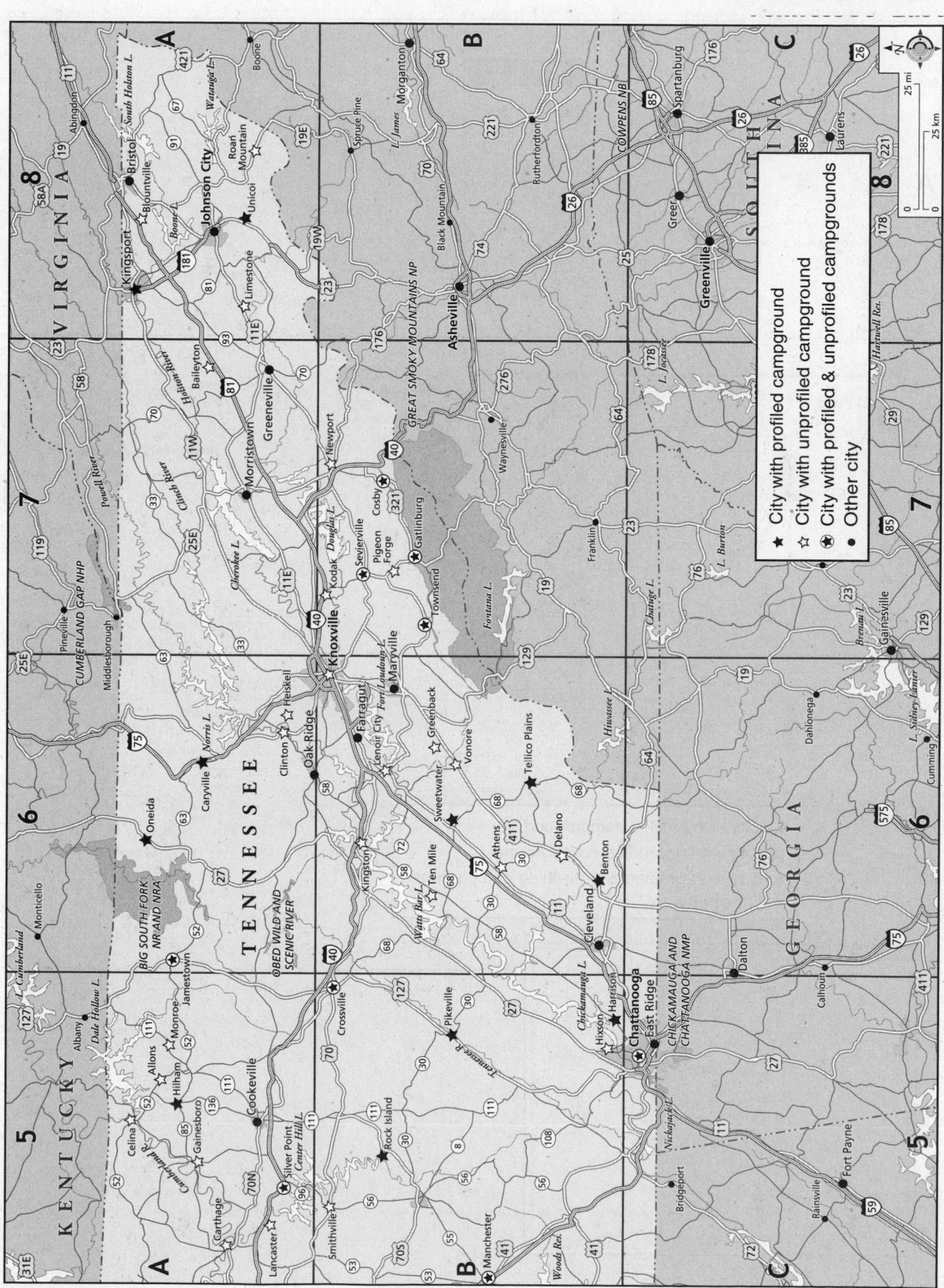

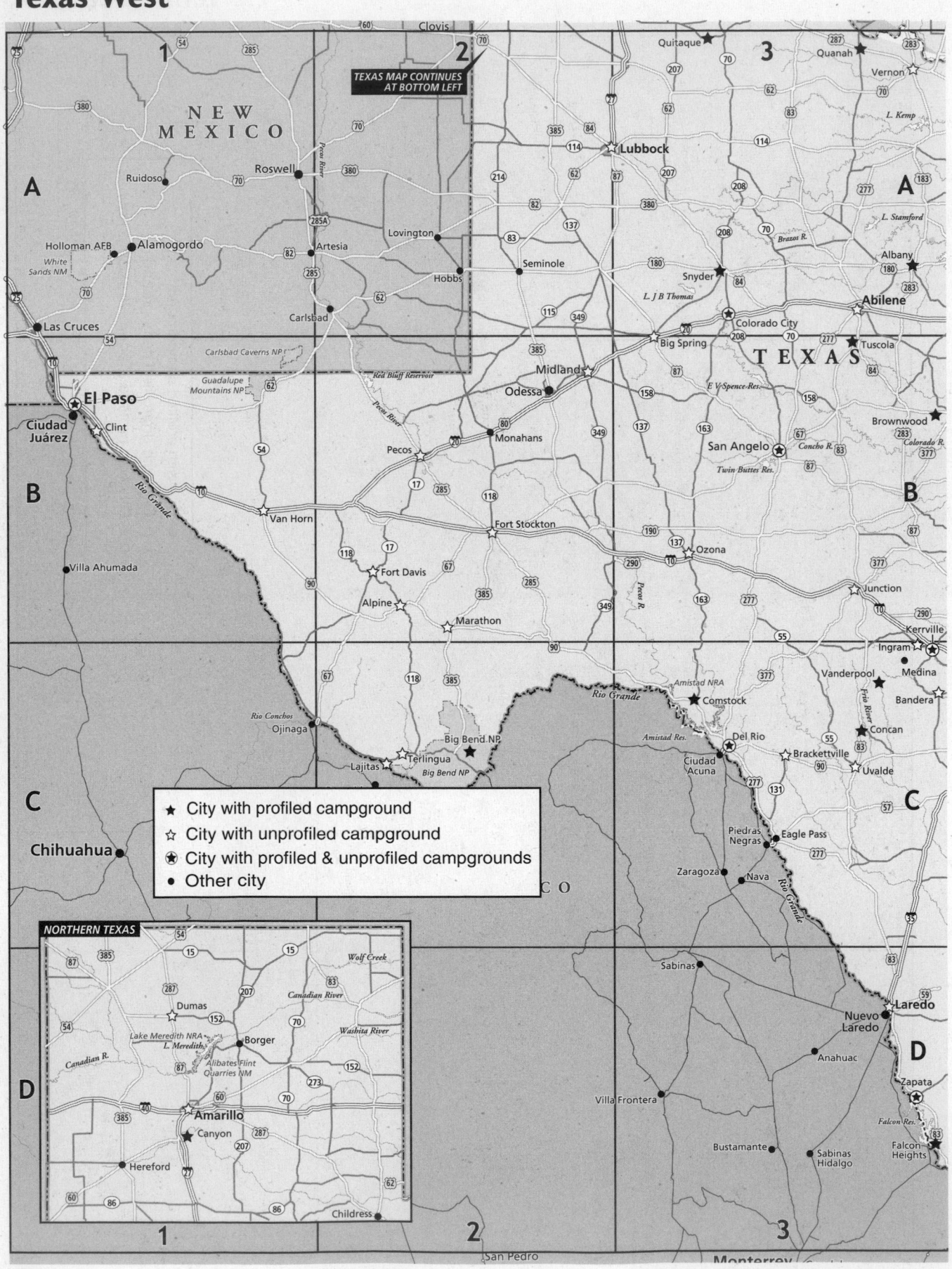

TEXAS MAP CONTINUES
AT BOTTOM LEFT

NEW
MEXICO

TEXAS

★ City with profiled campground
☆ City with unprofiled campground
✪ City with profiled & unprofiled campgrounds
• Other city

NORTHERN TEXAS

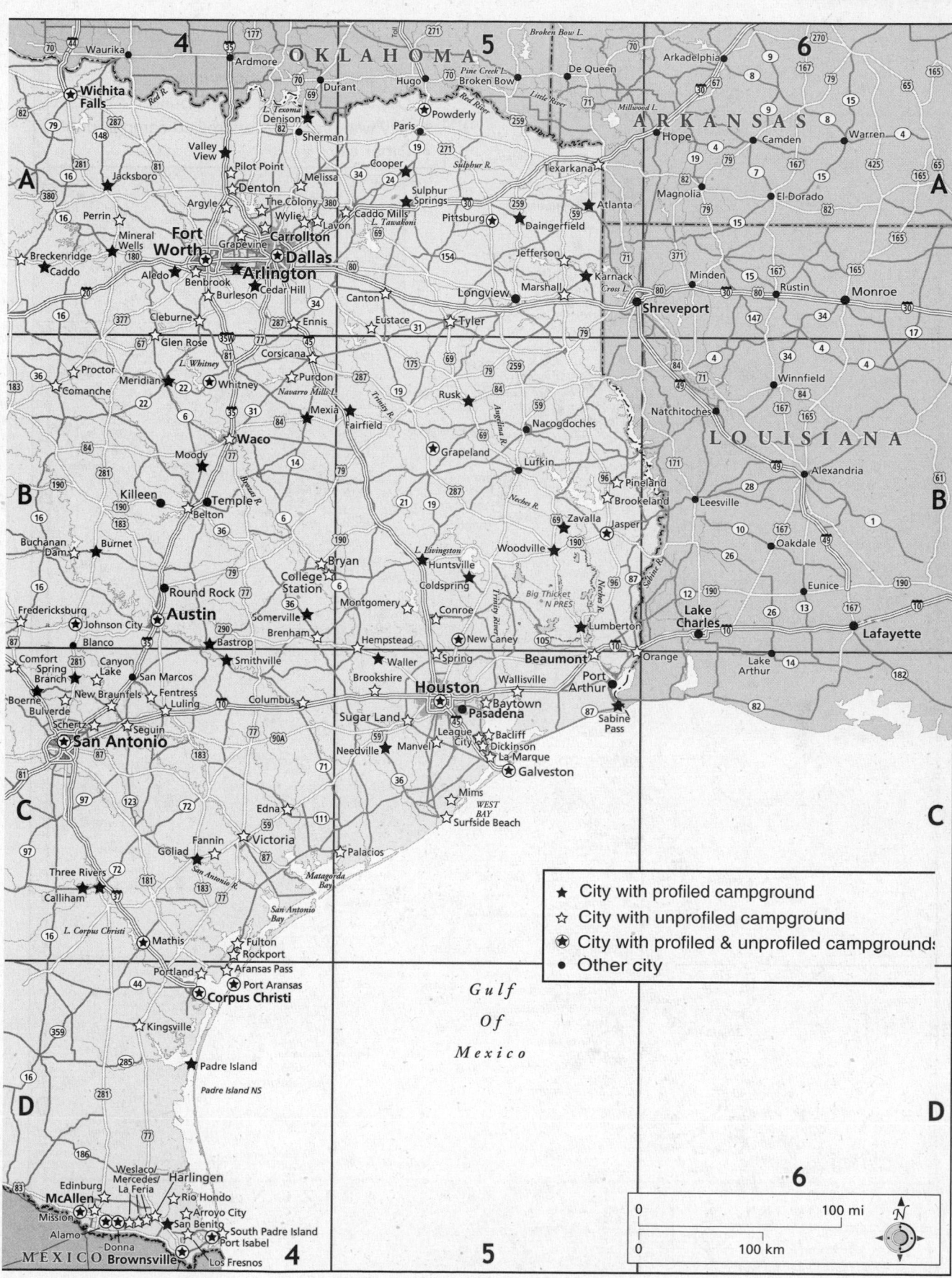

Legend:
- ★ City with profiled campground
- ☆ City with unprofiled campground
- ⍟ City with profiled & unprofiled campgrounds
- • Other city

Gulf Of Mexico

0 ——— 100 mi
0 ——— 100 km

Utah

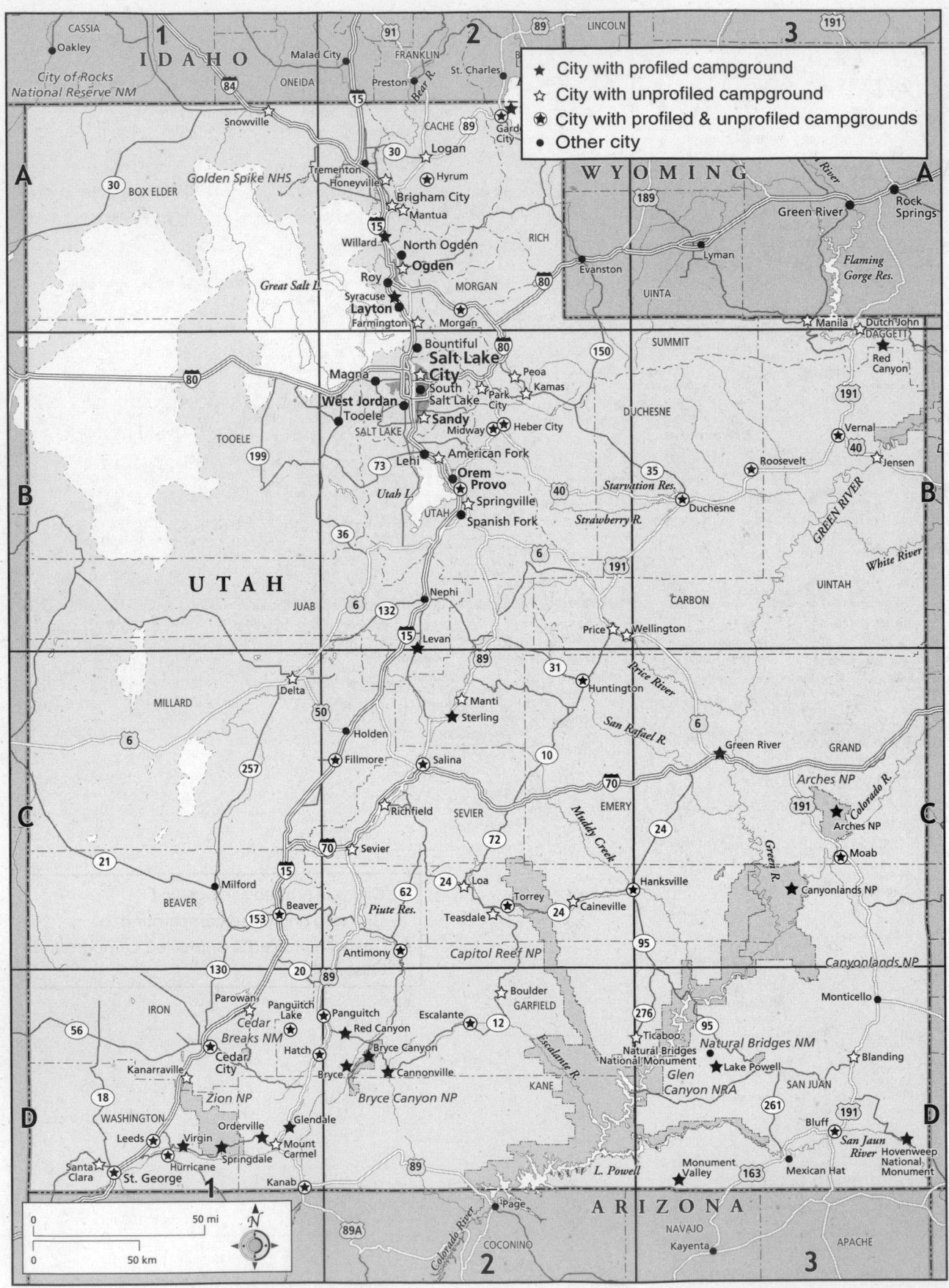

Legend:
- ★ City with profiled campground
- ☆ City with unprofiled campground
- ⊛ City with profiled & unprofiled campgrounds
- • Other city

Vermont

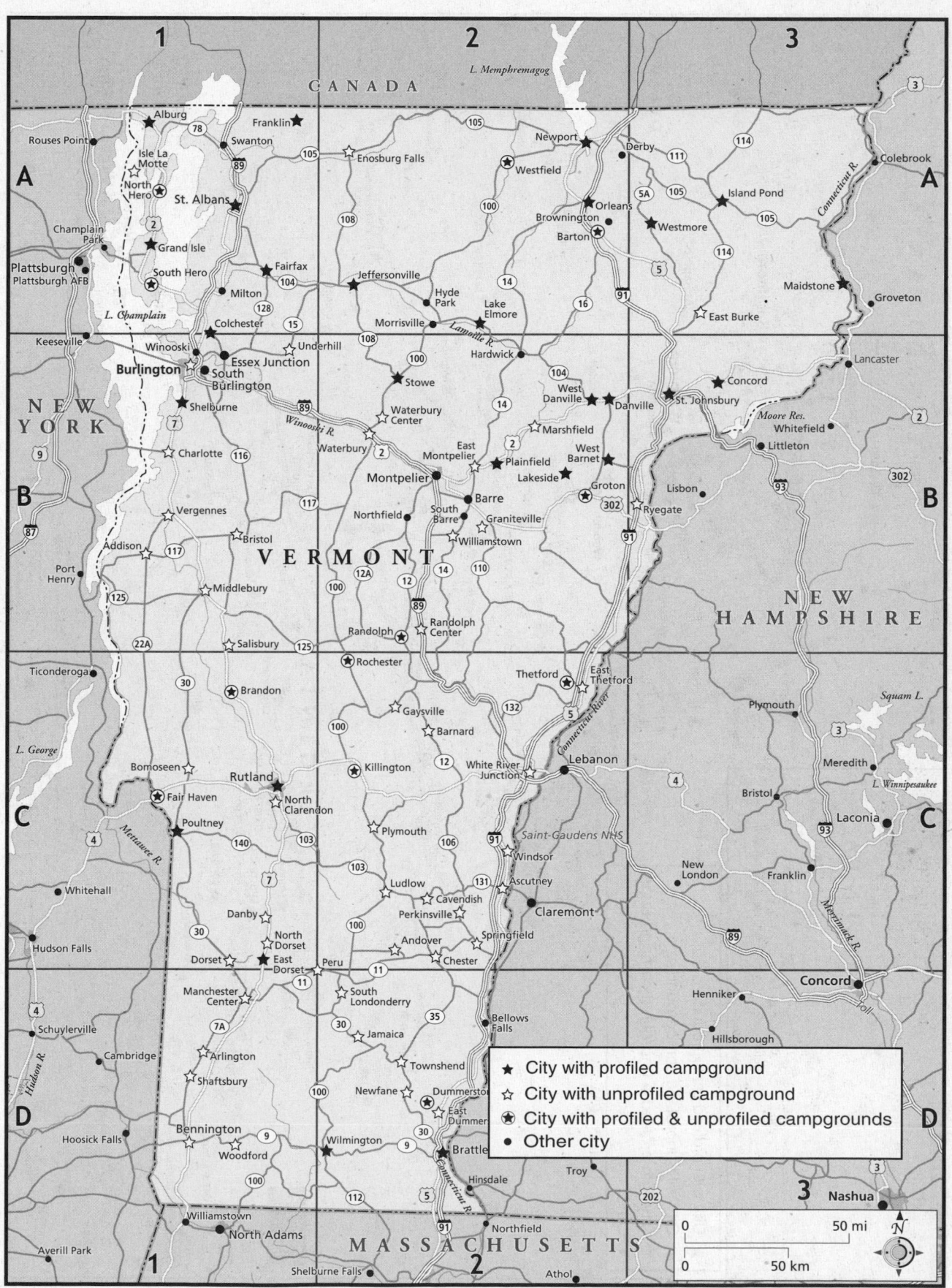

Legend:
- ★ City with profiled campground
- ☆ City with unprofiled campground
- ⊛ City with profiled & unprofiled campgrounds
- • Other city

0 ___ 50 mi

0 ___ 50 km

Virginia

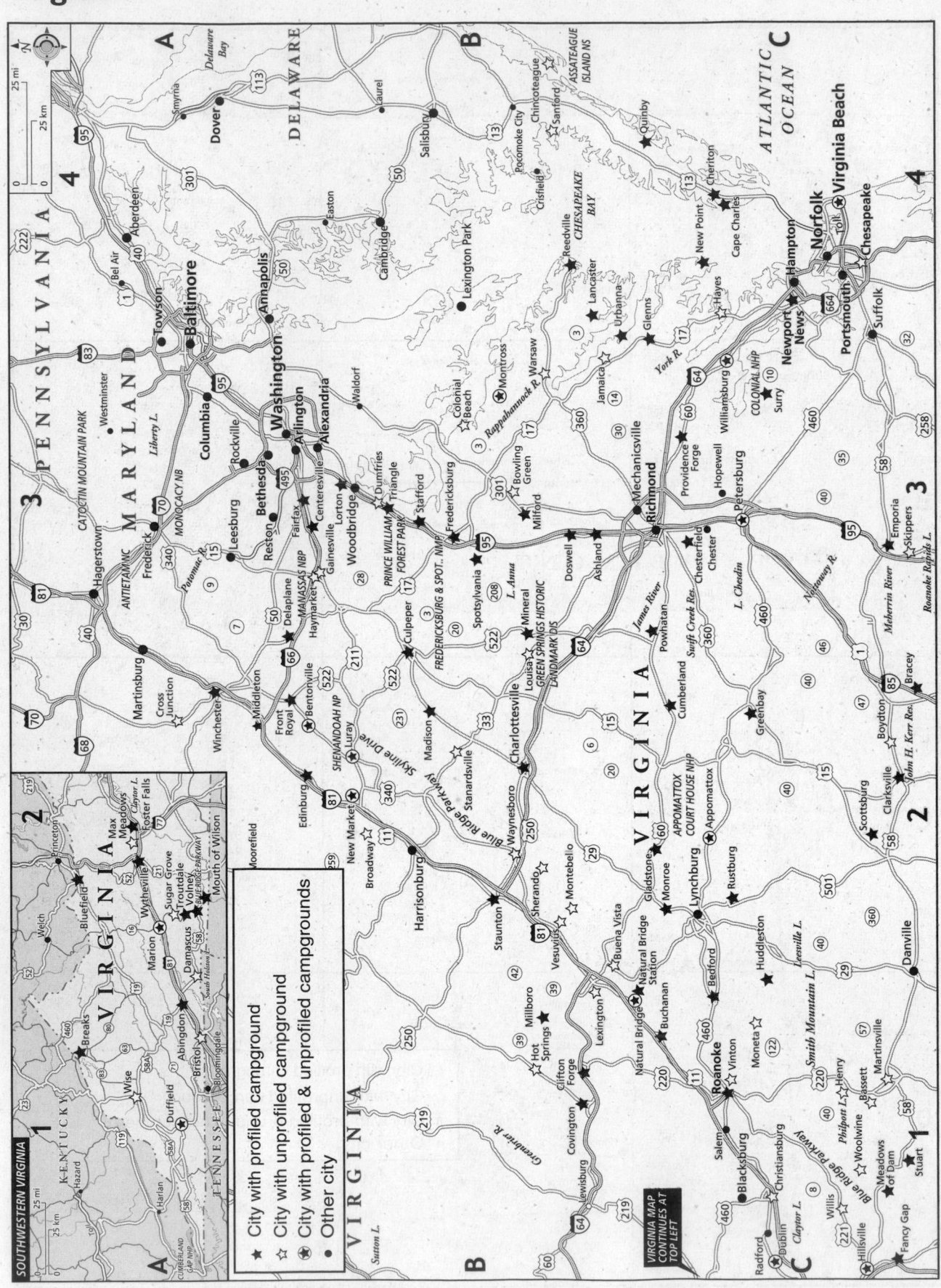

Legend:
- ★ City with profiled campground
- ☆ City with unprofiled campground
- ⊛ City with profiled & unprofiled campgrounds
- • Other city

SOUTHWESTERN VIRGINIA

VIRGINIA MAP CONTINUES AT TOP LEFT

Washington

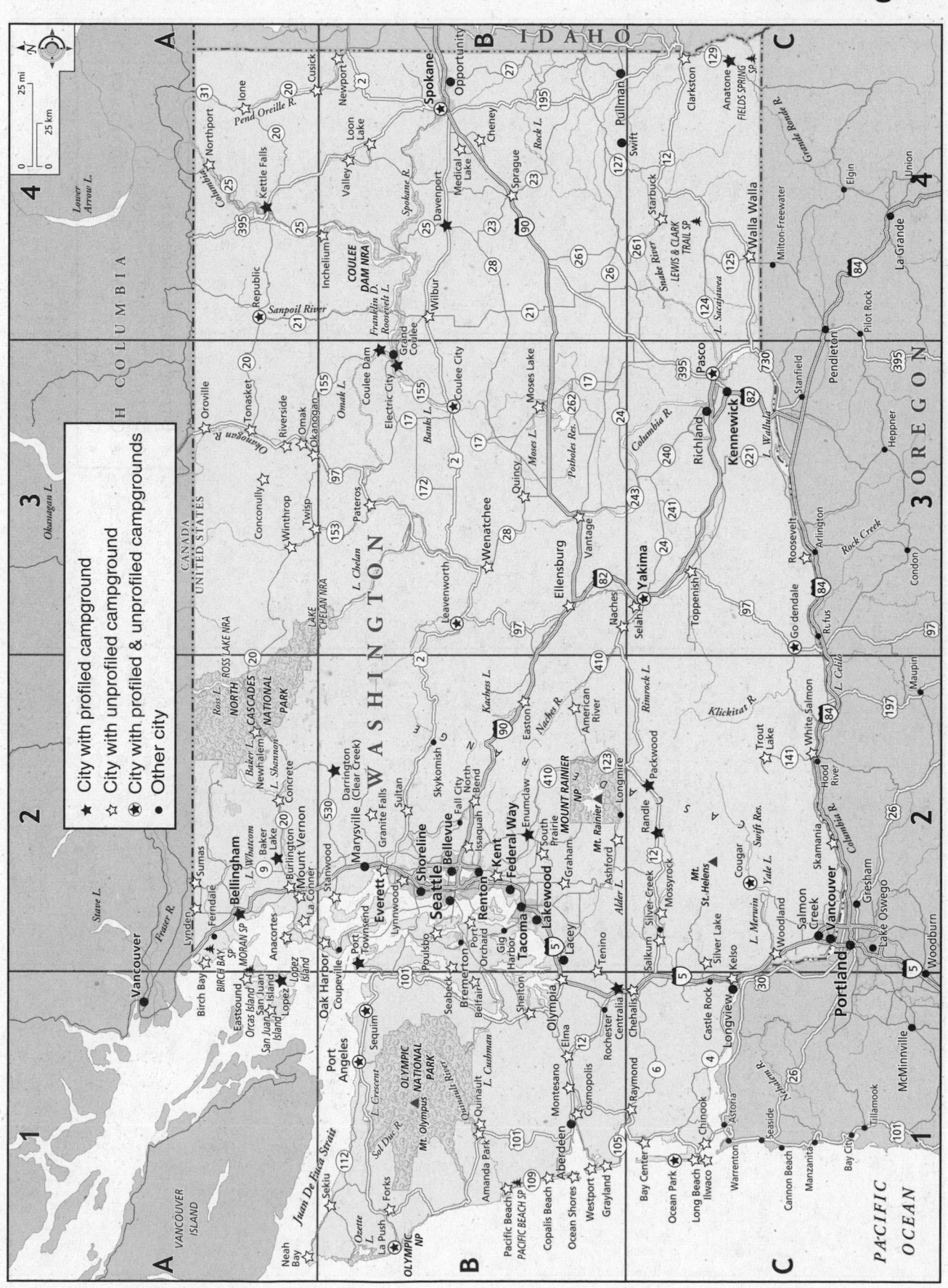

West Virginia

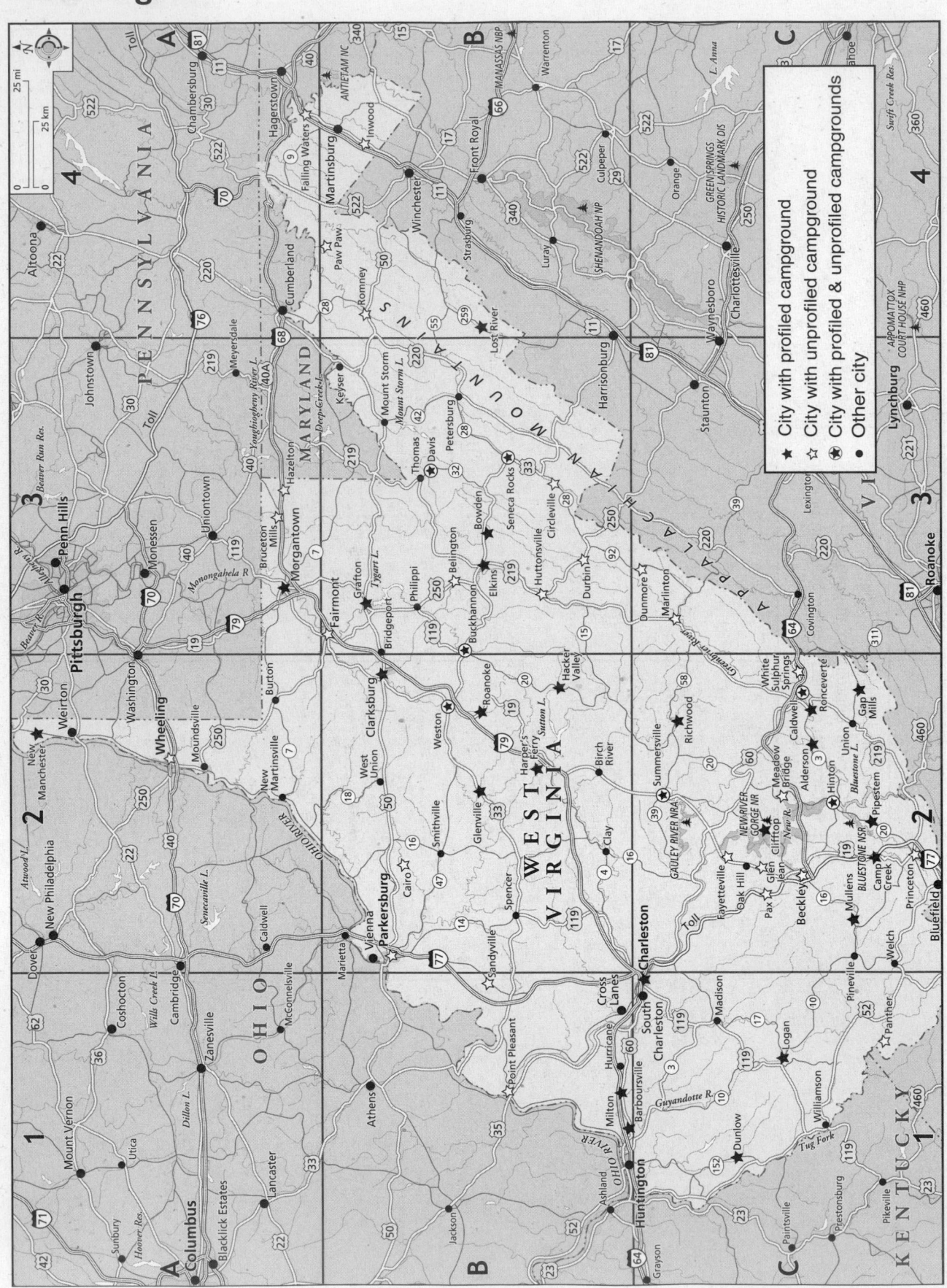

Wisconsin

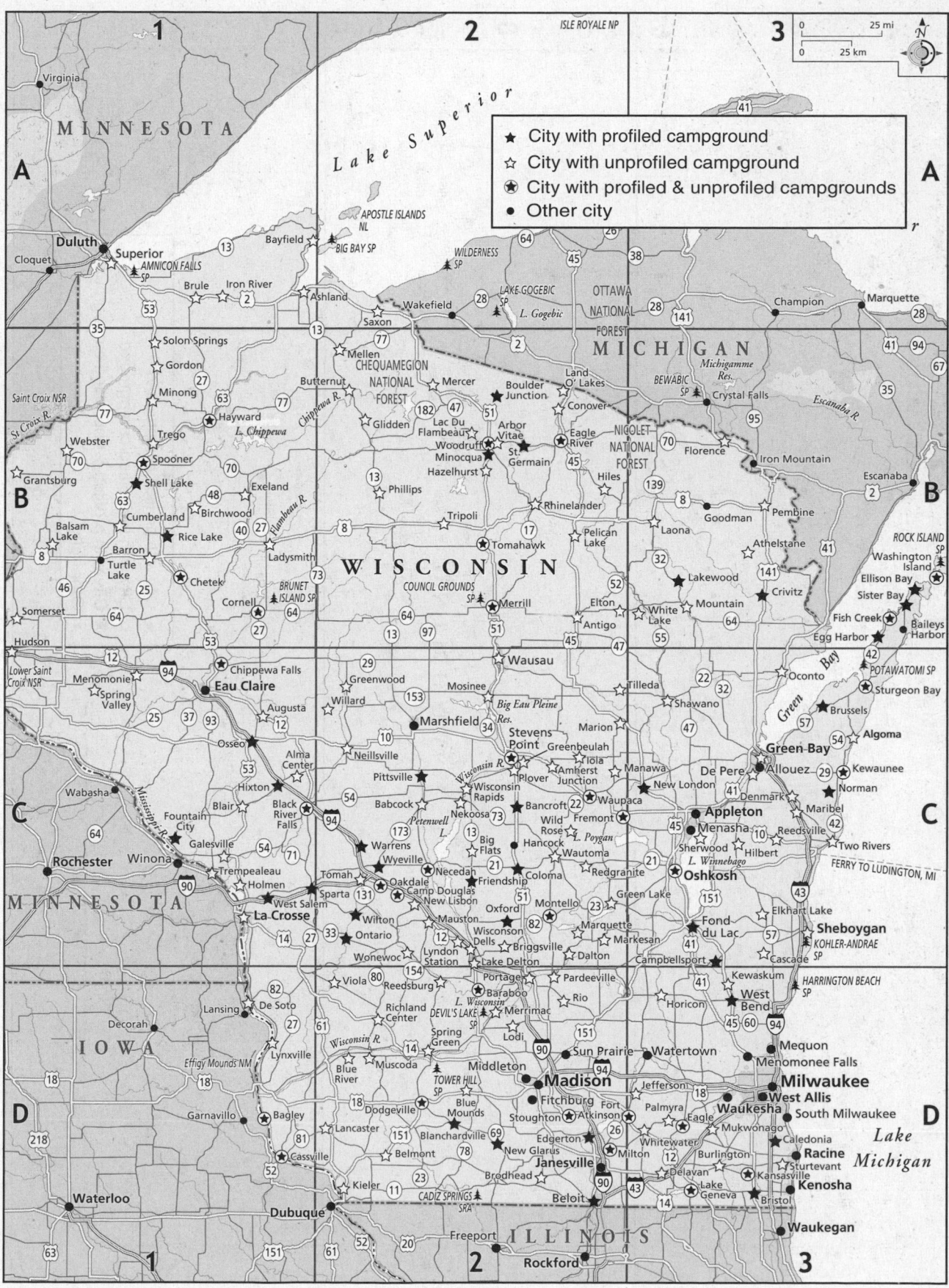

Legend:
- ★ City with profiled campground
- ☆ City with unprofiled campground
- ⬖ City with profiled & unprofiled campgrounds
- • Other city

MINNESOTA

Lake Superior

ISLE ROYALE NP

APOSTLE ISLANDS NL

BIG BAY SP

Virginia

Duluth
Cloquet
Superior
AMNICON FALLS SP
Bayfield
Brule
Iron River
Ashland
Wakefield
Saxon

WILDERNESS SP
LAKE-GOGEBIC
L. Gogebic
OTTAWA NATIONAL FOREST
MICHIGAN
Champion
Marquette

Michigamme Res.
BEWABIC SP
Crystal Falls
Iron Mountain
Escanaba R.
Escanaba

Solon Springs
Gordon
Minong
Hayward
Webster
Trego
Spooner
Grantsburg
Shell Lake
Balsam Lake
Cumberland
Birchwood
Rice Lake
Barron
Turtle Lake
Somerset
Chetek
Cornell

Mellen
CHEQUAMEGION NATIONAL FOREST
Butternut
Glidden
Lac Du Flambeau
Mercer
Boulder Junction
Land O' Lakes
Conover
Arbor Vitae
Eagle River
St. Germain
Woodruff
Minocqua
Hazelhurst
Phillips
Hiles
NICOLET NATIONAL FOREST
Florence
Rhinelander
Pelican Lake
Laona
Goodman
Pembine
Athelstane

WISCONSIN

Ladysmith
Exeland
Tomahawk
Tripoli
Antigo
Mountain
Crivitz
Lakewood
Elton
White Lake

BRUNET ISLAND SP
COUNCIL GROUNDS SP
Merrill

ROCK ISLAND SP
Washington Island
Ellison Bay
Sister Bay
Fish Creek
Baileys Harbor
Egg Harbor

MINNESOTA
Hudson
Menomonie
Spring Valley
Chippewa Falls
Eau Claire
Augusta
Osseo
Alma Center
Hixton
Blair
Black River Falls
Fountain City
Galesville
Wabasha
Rochester
Winona
Trempealeau
Holmen

Greenwood
Willard
Neillsville
Marshfield
Wausau
Mosinee
Big Eau Pleine Res.
Stevens Point
Greenwood
Tilleda
Shawano
Oconto
POTAWATOMI SP
Sturgeon Bay
Brussels
Algoma

Green Bay
De Pere
Allouez
Kewaunee
Denmark
Norman
Maribel
Two Rivers
Reedsville

Pittsville
Babcock
Wisconsin Rapids
Nekoosa
Wild Rose
Bancroft
Wautoma
Redgranite
Iola
Amherst Junction
Plover
Manawa
Waupaca
New London
Fremont
Appleton
Menasha
Sherwood
Hilbert
Oshkosh

Tomah
Oakdale
Camp Douglas
Sparta
New Lisbon
West Salem
La Crosse
Wilton
Ontario
Wonewoc
Necedah
Friendship
Coloma
Big Flats
Hancock
Montello
Marquette
Green Lake
Markesan
L. Winnebago
Fond du Lac
Elkhart Lake
Sheboygan
KOHLER-ANDRAE SP

Viola
Reedsburg
Portage
Baraboo
Pardeeville
Rio
Horicon
Kewaskum
West Bend
HARRINGTON BEACH SP

Lansing
De Soto
Decorah
IOWA
Garnavillo
Bagley
Cassville
Waterloo
Dubuque

Lynxville
Blue River
Muscoda
Richland Center
Spring Green
Blue Mounds
Dodgeville
Lancaster
Blanchardville
Belmont
Kieler

Viroqua
Wonewoc
Lyndon Station
Wisconsin Dells
Briggsville
Dalton
Lake Delton
Cascade
Campbellsport

DEVIL'S LAKE SP
Merrimac
Lodi
Spring Green
TOWER HILL SP
Middleton
Sun Prairie
Watertown
Mequon
Menomonee Falls
Milwaukee

Madison
Fitchburg
Fort Atkinson
Jefferson
Palmyra
West Allis
Waukesha
South Milwaukee

New Glarus
Edgerton
Janesville
Milton
Whitewater
Eagle
Mukwonago
Burlington
Delavan
Lake Geneva
Caledonia
Racine
Sturtevant
Kansasville
Kenosha
Bristol

Brodhead
Beloit
CADIZ SPRINGS SRA

ILLINOIS
Freeport
Rockford
Waukegan

Lake Michigan

Effigy Mounds NM

59

Wyoming

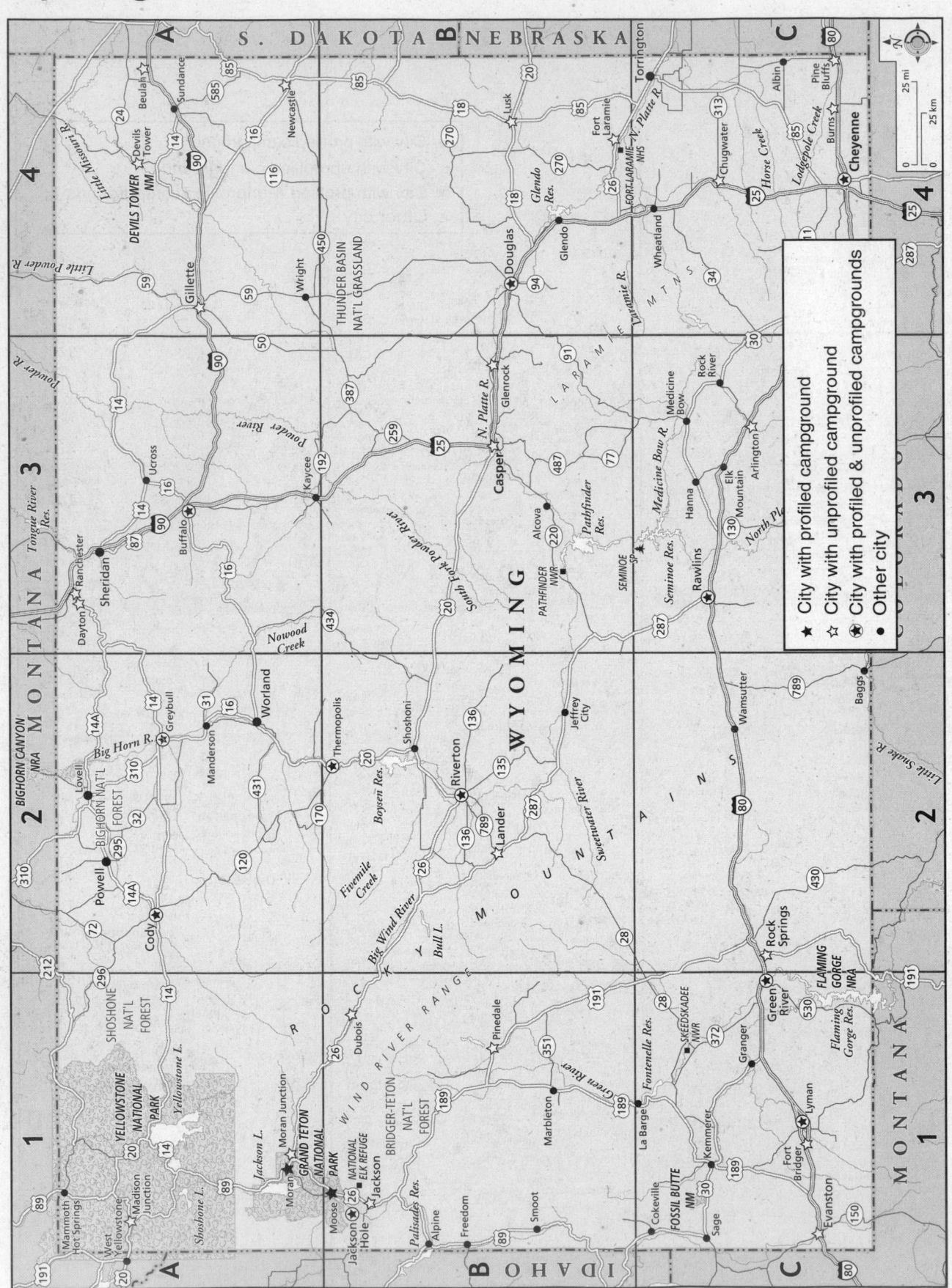

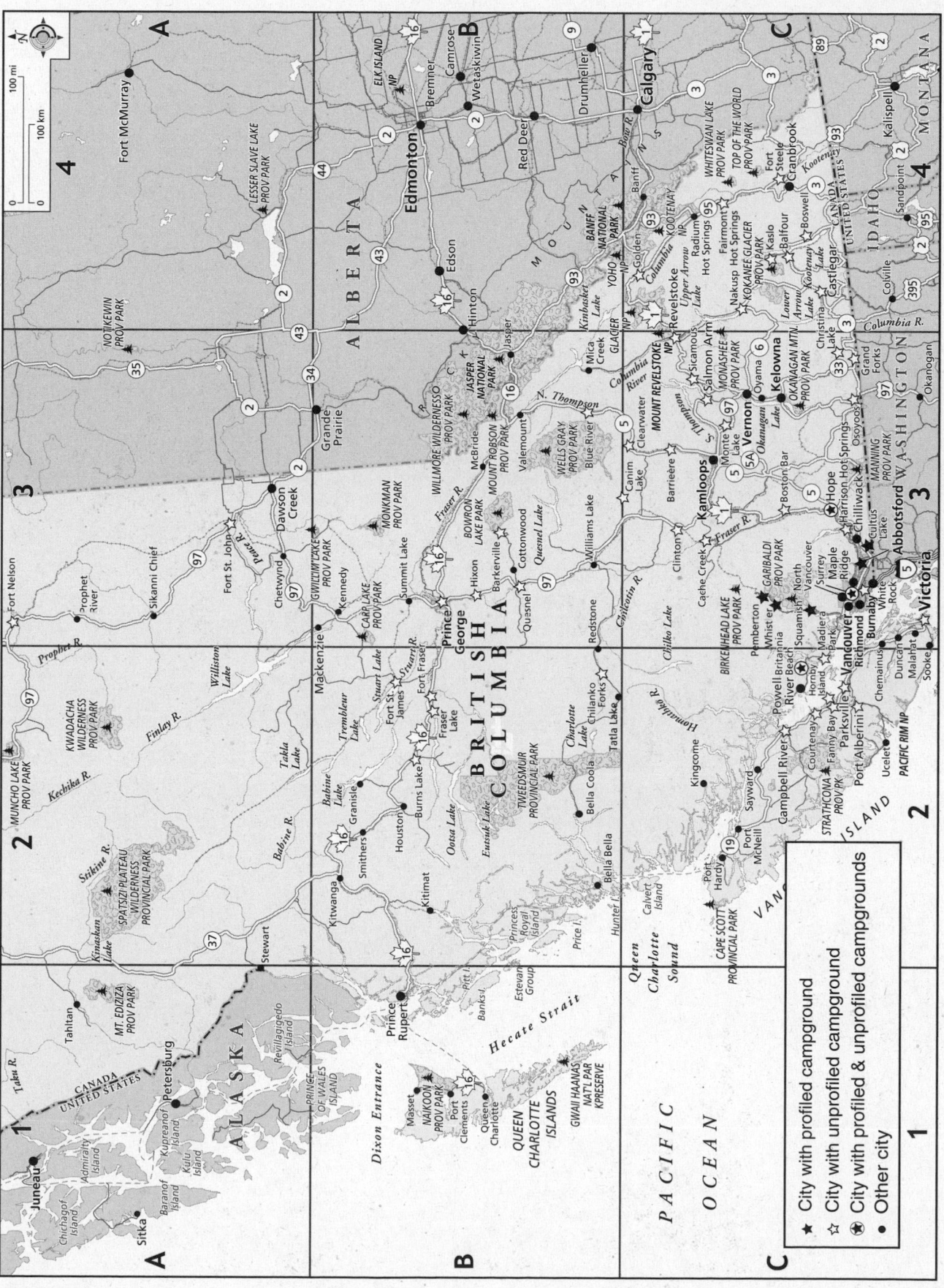

Legend

★ City with profiled campground
☆ City with unprofiled campground
✪ City with profiled & unprofiled campgrounds
● Other city

RESERVEAMERICA TOP 100 FAMILY CAMPGROUNDS

Alafia River State Park — Lithia, FL

Alexander Springs Recreation Area — Ocala National Forest — Altoona, FL

Angel Island State Park — Tiburon, CA

Austin Hawes Campground — American Legion State Forest — Pleasant Valley, SC

Big Bone Lick State Park — Union, KY

Black Rock State Park — Watertown, CT

Blue Licks Battlefield State Resort Park — Carlisle, KY

Bonny Lake State Park — Idalia, CO

Boston Harbor Islands State Park — Hingham, MA

Buckhorn State Park — Necedah, WI

Canning Creek Cove Park — Council Grove, KS

Carter Lake Campground — Oregon Dunes National Recreation Area — Lakeside, OR

Cedar Lake Recreation Area — Hodgen, OK

Charbonneau Campground — Burbank, WA

Chenango Valley State Park — Chenango Falls, NY

Chester State Park — Chester, SC

Chisos Basin Campground — Big Bend National Park, TX

Choke Canyon State Park — Calliham, TX

Clarence Fahnestock Memorial State Park — Carmel, NY

Claytor Lake State Park — Dublin, VA

Collier-Seminole State Park — Naples, FL

Cooper Lake State Park — Cooper, TX

Corinth Recreation Area — Double Springs, AL

Dale Hollow Lake State Resort Park — Burkesville, KY

Darien Lakes State Park — Darien Center, NY

Dent Acres Campground, Dworshak Dam & Reservoir — Ahsahka, Idaho

Devils Fork State Park — Salem, SC

Devils Garden Campground — Arches National Park — Moab, UT

DeWayne Hayes Campground — Columbus, MS

Douthat State Park — Millboro, VA

Fall Lake Campground — Superior National Forest — Ely, MN

Forked Lake Campground — Long Lake, NY

Fort Richardson State Park & Historic Site — Jacksboro, TX

Four Mile Creek State Park — Youngstown, NY

Frank Russell Campground — Monroe City, MO

Gamaliel Park — Norfork Lake — Gamaliel, AR

Granville State Forest — Granville, MA

Grayton Beach State Park — Santa Rosa Beach, FL

Green River State Park — Green River, UT

Greenbo Lake State Resort Park — Greenup, KY

Guadalupe River State Park — Spring Branch, TX

Hamilton Branch State Recreation Area — Plum Branch, SC

Hardin Ridge Recreation Area — Heltonville, IN

Highlands Hammock State Park — Sebring, FL

Hillsborough River State Park — Thonotosassa, FL

Hontoon Island State Park — Deland, FL

Housatonic Meadows State Park — Sharon, CT

Houston Mesa Family & Horse Camps — Tonto National Forest — Payson, AZ

Humboldt Redwoods State Park — Weott, CA

Hungry Mother State Park — Marion, VA

Joseph H. Stewart Campground — Joseph H. Stewart State Recreation Area — Trail, OR

Kodachrome Basin State Park — Cannonville, UT

Kring Point State Park — Redwood, NY

Lake Anna State Park — Spotsylvania, VA

Lake Hartwell State Recreation Area — Fair Play, SC

Lake Manatee State Park — Bradenton, FL

Lake Mineral Wells State Park & Trailway — Mineral Wells, TX

Lake Oroville State Recreation Area — Oroville, CA

Lake Powhatan Recreation Area — Asheville, NC

Lepage Park–Philippi Park Recreation Area — The Dalles, OR

Little Pond Campground — Andes, NY

Logger Campground — Tahoe National Forest — Truckee, CA

Meacham Lake Campground — Paul Smiths, NY

RESERVE AMERICA TOP 100 FAMILY CAMPGROUNDS (continued)

Millsite State Park — Huntington, UT

Natural Bridge State Resort Park — Slade, KY

Navajo State Park — Arboles, CO

New River Trail State Park — Foster Falls, VA

Oconee Point Campground — Seneca, SC

Oscar Scherer State Park — Osprey, FL

Plumas Eureka State Park — Blairsden, CA

Poinsett State Park — Wedgefield, SC

Prairie Flower Campground — Saylorville Lake, IA

Princess Campground — Giant Sequoia National Monument — Kings Canyon National Park, CA

Putnam Pond — Ticonderoga, NY

Ray Behrens Campground — Monroe City, MO

Rifle Falls/Rifle Gap/Harvey Gap State Park — Rifle, CO

Rio Grande Village Campground — Big Bend National Park, TX

Robert W. Craig Campground — Elk Garden, WV

Roche-A-Cri State Park — Friendship, WI

Rocky Neck State Park — Niantic, CT

Sacandaga Campground — Northville, NY

Salt Rock State Park — Baltic, CT

San Luis Reservoir State Recreation Area — Gustine, CA

Sand Hollow State Park — Hurricane, UT

Savoy Mountain State Forest — Florida, MA

Shawme-Crowell State Forest — Sandwich, MA

Signal Creek and Last Chance Campgrounds — Ward Lake Recreation Area — Tongass National Forest — Ketchikan, AK

Spring Cove Campground — Bass Lake Recreation Area — Sierra National Forest — Bass Lake, CA

St. Andrew State Park — Panama City, FL

Starvation State Park — Duchesne, UT

Stony Brook State Park — Dansville, NY

Torreya State Park — Tallahasse, FL

Trinidad State Park — Trinidad, CO

Twin Lake Campground — Hartwell, SC

Vega State Park — Collbran, CO

Waquoit Bay National Estuarine Research Reserve — Waquoit, MA

Watsadler Campground — Hartwell, GA

Wildwood State Park — Wading River, NY

Winhall Brook Camping Area — Jamaica, VT

Youghiogheny River Lake's Outflow Campground — Confluence, PA

ReserveAmerica Outdoor Awards

PARK BEACHES

Cape Florida State Park — Key Biscayne, FL

Edisto Beach State Park — Edisto Island, SC

False Cape State Park — Virginia Beach, VA

Green River Lake State Park — Campbellsville, KY

Henderson Beach State Park — Destin, FL

Huntington Beach State Park — Murrells Inlet, SC

Jackson Lake State Park — Orchard, CO

Myrtle Beach State Park — Myrtle Beach, SC

Oleta River State Park — North Miami, FL

Pope & Baldwin Beaches — Lake Tahoe, CA

Revere Beach — Revere, MA

Salisbury Beach State Reservation — Salisbury, MA

Shaw Beach — Jennings Randolph Lake — Elk Garden, West Virginia

South Cape Beach State Park — Mashpee, MA

Southwick Beach State Park — Woodville, NY

SCENIC VIEWS

Albion Basin Campground — Alta, UT

Caesars Head State Park — Cleveland, SC

Cape Florida State Park — Key Biscayne, FL

Columbus-Belmont State Park — Columbus, KY

Crown Point State Scenic Corridor — Corbett, OR

Cumberland Falls State Resort Park — Corbin, KY

Devils Lake State Park — Baraboo, WI

False Cape State Park — Virginia Beach, VA

Henderson Beach State Park — Destin, FL

Kingdom Come State Park — Cumberland, KY

Mt. Greylock State Recreation — Lanesborough, MA

Mt. Sugarloaf State Recreation — South Deerfield, MA

R.D. Bailey Lake (Visitor Center) — Justice, WV

Robert Treman State Park — Ithaca, NY

State Forest State Park — Walden, CO

TOURS/EVENTS

Arkansas Headwaters State Park — Salida, CO

Atalaya Festival — Huntington Beach State Park — Murrells Inlet, SC

Boston Harbor Islands — Hingham, MA

Douthat State Park — Millboro, VA

Great Brook Farm — Carlisle, MA

Grenada Lake — Grenada, MS

Hearst Castle — San Simeon, CA

Kenlake State Resort Park — Aurora, KY

Kentucky Dam Village State Resort Park — Gilbertsville, KY

Maudslay State Park — Newburyport, MA

KID-FRIENDLY PARKS

Beaver Brook Farm — Belmont/Waltham, MA

Carter Caves State Resort Park — Olive Hill, KY

Douthat State Park — Millboro, VA

Great Brook Farm — Carlisle, MA

James M. Robb — Colorado River State Park — Clifton, CO

Lake Ouachita, Vicksburg District — AR

Oleta River State Park — North Miami, FL

Santee State Park — Santee, SC

Sebago Cabin Camp — Bear Mountain, NY

Sesquicentennial State Park — Columbia, SC

PICNIC AREAS

Blue Hills State Recreation — Milton, MA

Canoe-Picnic Point State Park — Clayton, NY

Clarksburg State Forest — Clarksburg, MA

Cumberland Falls State Resort Park — Corbin, KY

Elrod Ferry Day Use Area — Hartwell, GA

Fish Dam Creek Park — W. Kerr Scott Lake — Wilkesboro, NC

Highway 7 Recreation Area — Arkadelphia, AR

Jones Gap State Park — Marietta, SC

Lake Warren State Park — Hampton, SC

Lathrop State Park — Walsenburg, CO

Oleta River State Park — North Miami, FL

Paris Mountain State Recreation Area — Greenville, SC

Pine Mountain State Resort Park — Pineville, KY

R.D. Bailey Lake — Justice, WV

Roche-A-Cri State Park — Friendship, WI

AMAZING SPOTS

Carter Caves State Resort Park — Olive Hill, KY

Hither Hills State Park — Montauck, NY

Iron Mountain Lodge and Marina — Arkadelphia, AR

John Pennekamp Coral Reef State Park — Key Largo, FL

Lake Ouachita, Vicksburg District — AR

Natural Bridge State Park — Slade, KY

Purgatory Chasm State Park — Sutton, MA

Table Rock State Park — Pickens, SC

Trinidad State Park — Trinidad, CO

Woods Bay State Park — Olanta, SC

UNIQUE CABINS

Allegany State Park — Salamanca, NY

Buckhorn State Park — Necedah, WI

Frog Meadow Guard Station — Giant Sequoia National Monument, CA

Interpreter's Cabin — Grayson Highlands State Park — Blue Ridge Mountains, VA

Lake Anna State Park — Spotsylvania, VA

Lake Barkley State Resort Park — Cadiz, KY

Mueller State Park — Divide, CO

Oconee State Park — Mountain Rest, SC

Topsail Hill Preserve State Park — Santa Rosa Beach, FL

Otter River State Forest — Baldwinville, MA

Pine Mountain State Resort Park — Pineville, KY

Santee State Park — Santee, SC

Savoy Mountain State Forest — Savoy, MA

Shawme-Crowell State Forest — Sandwich, MA

Silver River State Park — Ocala, FL

HIKING TRAILS

Appalachian Trail — MA

Cabin Creek Nature Trail-Grayson Highland State Park — Blue Ridge Mountains, VA

Caesars Head State Park — Cleveland, SC

Collier-Seminole State Park — Naples, FL

Cumberland Falls State Resort Park — Corbin, KY

Devils Lake State Park — Baraboo, WI

Douthat State Park — Millboro, VA

Edisto Beach State Park — Edisto Island, SC

Highlands Hammock State Park — Sebring, FL

Huntington Beach State Park — Murrells Inlet, SC

Joanna Trail — Monroe City, MO

Kings Mountain State Park — Blacksburg, SC

Lory State Park — Bellvue, CO

Middlesex Falls — Malden, MA

Mid-State Trail — Ayer, MA

Natural Bridge State Resort Park — Slade, KY

Oconee State Park — Mountain Rest, SC

Oscar Scherer State Park — Osprey, FL

Pine Mountain State Resort Park — Pineville, KY

Silver Falls State Park — Sublimity, OR

Silver River State Park — Ocala, FL

Table Rock State Park — Pickens, SC

Taughannock Falls State Park — Trumansburg, NY

Twin Pinnacles — Grayson Highlands State Park — Blue Ridge Mountains, VA

Wilson Creek Trail — Grayson Highlands State Park — Blue Ridge Mountains, VA

ROMANTIC SPOTS

Cape Florida State Park — Key Biscayne, FL

Golden Gate Canyon State Park — Golden, CO

Halibut Point State Park — Rockport, MA

Huntington Beach State Park — Murrells Inlet, SC

Kenlake State Resort Park — Aurora, KY

Moore State Park — Paxton, MA

Oleta River State Park — North Miami, FL

Pixley Falls State Park — Boonsville, NY

Tillicum Beach Campground — Waldport, OR

Wolf Creek Inn State Heritage Site — Wolf Creek, OR

CANOEING SPOTS

Black River State Park — Holt, FL

Blue Licks Battlefield State Resort Park — Carlisle, KY

Buckhorn State Park — Necedah, WI

Collier-Seminole State Park — Naples, FL

Connecticut River Greenway — Northampton, MA

Cumberland Falls State Resort Park — Corbin, KY

False Cape State Park — Virginia Beach, VA

Givhans Ferry State Park — Ridgeville, SC

Higley Flow State Park — Colton, NY

Hunting Island State Park — Hunting Island, SC

James River State Park — Gladstone, VA

Lake Ouachita — Royal, AR

Nickerson State Park — Brewster, MA

Pearl Lake State Park — Clark, CO

Salt Springs Recreation Area — Salt Springs, FL

EDUCATIONAL AND HISTORICAL FACILITIES

Blue Licks Battlefield State Resort Park — Carlisle, KY

Borderland State Park — Easton/Sharon, MA

Douthat State Park — Millboro, VA

John Martin Reservoir — Hasty, CO

Kam Wah Chung State Heritage Site — John Day, OR

Redcliff Plantation State Historic Site — Beech Island, SC

River's Bridge State Historic Site — Ehrhardt, SC

Robert Moses State Park — Massena, NY

Savanna Preserve State Park — Port St. Lucie, FL

Walden Pond State Reservation — Concord, MA

BIRD-WATCHING SPOTS

Caesars Head State Park — Cleveland, SC

Devils Lake State Park — Baraboo, WI

False Cape State Park — Virginia Beach, VA

J.A. Skinner State Park — Hadley, MA

John James Audubon State Park — Henderson, KY

Lake Erie State Park — Brocton, NY

Oscar Scherer State Park — Osprey, FL

Saylorville Lake — Johnston, IA

St. Vrain State Park — Longmont, CO

Wachusett Mountain State Reservation — Princeton, MA

BIKING TRAILS

Alpine Pedal Path — San Bernadino, CA

Ashuwilticook Rail Trail — Lanesborough, MA

Baker Creek State Park — McCormick, SC

Devils Lake State Park — Baraboo, WI

Douthat State Park — Millboro, VA

False Cape State Park — Virginia Beach, VA

General Butler State Resort Park — Carrollton, KY

Green River Lake State Park — Campbellsville, KY

Guyandotte Campground — R. D. Bailey Lake — Baileysville, WV

Highline Lake State Park — Loma, CO

Mills-Norrie State Park — Staatsburg, NY

Nashua River Rail — MA

Oleta River State Park — North Miami, FL

Paris Mountain State Park — Greenville, SC

Youghiogheny River Lake's Outflow Campground — Confluence, PA

FISHING SPOTS

Alafia State Park — Lithia, FL

Alfred A. Loeb State Park — Brooking, OR

Bowman Bridge Campground — Baldwin, MI

Claytor Lake State Park — Dublin, VA

Dreher Island State Recreation Area — Prosperity, SC

False Cape State Park — Virginia Beach, VA

Grass Point State Park — Clayton, NY

Greenbo Lake State Resort Park — Greenup, KY

Grenada Lake — Grenada, MS

Hickory Knob State Resort Park — McCormick, SC

Kenlake State Resort Park — Aurora, KY

Kentucky Dam Village State Resort Park — Gilbertsville, KY

Lake Manatee State Park — Bradenton, FL

Lake Ouachita, Vicksburg District — AR

Lake Warren State Park — Hampton, SC

Lake Wateree State Recreation Area — Winnsboro, SC

Leesylvania State Park — Woodbridge, VA

Lepage Park — Philippi Park Recreational Area — The Dalles, OR

Mark Twain Lake — Monroe City, MO

Norfork River-Quarry Park — Mountain Home, AR

North Branch Potomac River — Elk Garden, WV

North Sterling — Sterling, CO

Oleta River State Park — North Miami, FL

Pine Flat Lake — Piedra, CA

Scusset Beach State Reservation — Sandwich, MA

America's Ranger of the Year

Les Perry

SHAWME–CROWELL STATE FOREST — SANDWICH, MASSACHUSETTS

Les Perry has worked for the Massachusetts State Parks since 1966 and has worked at both ends of the state from Mt. Washington State Forest in the west to Shawme–Crowell State Forest in the east. Les is a graduate of Stockbridge School of Agriculture and University of Massachusetts Amherst and has earned two degrees in Park Management. He has managed Shawme–Crowell State Forest in a professional manner and has consistently made improvements to the facility and many life long friends among campers. Les developed The Friends of Shawme–Crowell State Forest Program which has grown consistently in both membership and popularity; last year the program generated $9,000 to support the construction of a new pavilion. Les was a driving force during the fund raising and pavilion construction.

TESTIMONIAL

We have been camping at this park for over 10 years now. Mr. Perry always greets us with a huge smile and a "Glad to see you back!" He truly loves his campground and the people that camp there. He goes out of his way to make sure everyone is safe and well informed of any potential hazards, such as coyotes. "Keep an eye on your dogs, we've got a pack of coyotes out back." One time, he drove up to all the sites to warn of potentially severe thunderstorms with possible tornados on the way. I remember him telling me to "tie down those little girls," meaning to get them into the truck before the weather hit. What a great guy! He was concerned about the safety of my children as well as all the campers in the park. What more could you ask in a park ranger? He loves his park and his people.

—Diane Brunelle

Alabama

Called the Cradle of the Confederacy, Alabama is steeped in Civil War history. Fascinating tours include Montgomery, the first capital of the Confederacy. During the Battle of Mobile Bay, Admiral Farragut exclaimed, "Damn the torpedoes! Full speed ahead!"

At the **USS *Alabama* Battleship Memorial Park** in Mobile, visitors can explore the park's namesake as well as over 20 other World War II ships, aircraft, and weapons. The recipient of nine battle stars in World War II, the "Mighty A" saw plenty of action as part of the Pacific Fleet—fighting in Leyte, the Gilbert Islands, and Okinawa. The *Alabama* is lovingly preserved and is open for tours all year. If you're traveling with a group, you can spend the night in the battleship's barracks. A World War II submarine, the **USS *Drum,*** is also open for tours. Exhibits in the park's Aircraft Pavilion include a B-52 bomber, and a Blackbird jet, in addition to several Medal of Honor–winning aircraft.

The Civil Rights movement thrust Alabama into the national media spotlight in the 1950s and 1960s. Defining events included the 1955 Montgomery bus boycott and the historic Selma-to-Montgomery march. You can gain a deeper understanding of the movement at the **Birmingham Civil Rights Institute.** Located across the street from the **Sixteenth Street Baptist Church,** site of the 1963 bombing that killed four little girls, the BCRI walks visitors through the many barriers that were overcome for the advancement of civil rights, with the aid of film, sound, and sculpture. An exhibit dedicated to human-rights activists around the world is equally as moving.

Natives call Alabama "the Beautiful," and we agree. Its northeast corner lies at the southernmost terminus of the **Appalachian Mountain** range. Quaint mountain towns, such as **Mentone,** offer rich fall foliage and excellent craft and antiques shopping. Check out the **Log Cabin Restaurant and Deli**—an intimate soup-and-sandwich shop that has the best root-beer float on **Lookout Mountain.** Mentone has plenty of campsites and cabins, but if the weather is nice, spaces are taken up fast—so take the time to call ahead. Mentone is also the getaway for several country music artists. In nearby **Fort Payne** ("The Sock Capitol of the World"), country music fans might want to check out the museum dedicated to hometown heroes Alabama.

Fort Payne's **Little River Canyon** is one of the deepest gorges east of the Mississippi. A national preserve, Little River Canyon is a sanctuary for a number of rare plants, such as the green pitcher and Kral's water plantain—an aquatic plant native to this region. Trails for hiking, horseback riding, and ATVs abound. Alabama also has four national forests, and numerous lakes throughout the state provide enthusiasts with plenty of hunting and fishing.

Campers who truly need to get away from it all can find solitude in the **Sipsey Wilderness.** A 25,000-acre spread in northeast Alabama's **Bankhead National Forest,** Sipsey is a popular spot for camping, hiking, hunting, and getting lost. With over 13 miles of trails, there is plenty of room to accommodate horseback riding, ATVs, and mountain bikes. Sipsey's climate has somewhat of a challenging for campers—temperature average between 50–75ºF with frequent rain—so be sure to pack accordingly.

Those looking for warmer climates will be inclined to head for the beach. Alabama's **Gulf Coast** region is home to moss-covered oak trees and white-sand beaches. **Orange Beach** is known for top-notch saltwater fishing. The **Alabama Coastal Birding Trail** dots historic **Mobile Bay** with spots for viewing both waders and shorebirds.

Golf is the feather in Alabama's outdoor cap. Anchoring the golf offerings are the eight facilities of the **Robert Trent Jones Golf Trail.** An ambitious project designed by the revered architect for which the course is named, the Robert Trent Jones Golf Trail is 378 holes of golf that will impress avid and novice players alike. Beautifully sculpted and reasonably priced, it's not a surprise that five of the eight courses are routinely listed as some of the best in the country.

NASCAR racing fans are familiar with the **Talladega Superspeedway,** home of the **Diehard 500** in April and the **Winston 500** in October. Combination tickets for year-round track tours and admission to the **International Motorsports Hall of Fame** are available. RVers should take note that race time in Talladega is tailgate heaven.

Campground Profiles

ADGER
Burchfield Branch Park
MAP, B-2

reserve america

15036 Bankhead Rd., 35006. T: (205) 553-9373 or (205) 497-9828; www.reserveamerica.com.

🚐 ★★★★   ⛺ ★★★★

Beauty: ★★★★
Spaciousness: ★★★★
Security: ★★★★
Insect Control: ★★★

Site Privacy: ★★★
Quiet: ★★★★
Cleanliness: ★★★★
Facilities: ★★★

Every site is situated on the water and features paved back-in parking. Sites are larger than average and nicely spaced, making them quiet. There are a few shade trees, but not enough greenery to provide privacy between sites. At press time, we could not tell which sites would be the nicest.

BASICS

Operated By: U.S. Army Corps of Engineers. **Open:** All year. **Site Assignment:** First come, first served; reservations accepted through National Recreation Reservation Service (NRRS) at (877) 444-6777 or www.recreation.gov; reservations can be made up to 240 days in advance, full payment required upon making reservation; credit card preferred (V, MC, D, AE), or pay by money order if at least 21 days in advance of arrival; $10 fee for cancellation or change of site or dates; cancellation w/in 3 days of arrival charged first night, no-show charged $20 plus first night. **Registration:** At gatehouse. **Fee:** $12. **Parking:** At site, limit 2 vehicles per site.

FACILITIES

Number of Tent-only Sites: 2. **Number of Multipurpose Sites:** 35. **Hookups:** Electric (50 amps), water. **Each Site:** Picnic table, grill, fire ring, lantern post, some decks. **Dump Station:** Yes. **Laundry:** Yes. **Pay Phone:** Yes. **Restrooms and Showers:** Yes. **Fuel:** No. **Propane:** No. **Internal Roads:** Paved. **RV Service:** 40 mi. west in Tuscaloosa. **Market:** Country store 4 mi.; Grocery 25 mi. east in Hueytown. **Restaurant:** 10 mi. north in Oak Grove. **General Store:** W/in 5 mi. **Vending:** Beverages. **Swimming:** Beach. **Playground:** 2. **Other:** Boat ramp, swimming beach, picnic shelter. **Activities:** Fishing, boating, hiking, biking in area, migratory eagle viewing Oct.–Feb., jet skiing, water skiing. **Nearby Attractions:** VisionLand, Mercedes-Benz Visitor Center, Birmingham & Tuscaloosa attractions. **Additional Information:** Tuscaloosa CVB, (800) 538-8696; Greater Birmingham CVB, (800) 458-8085; Holt Resource Office, (205) 553-9373.

RESTRICTIONS

Pets: On leash only. **Fires:** In grills, fire rings only. **Alcoholic Beverages:** Not allowed. **Vehicle Maximum Length:** No limit. **Other:** 14-day stay limit.

TO GET THERE

From I-59, take the Brookwood exit onto CR 59 and go north approximately 5 mi. to AL 216. Turn right and drive east for 2.5 mi. Then turn left back onto CR 59 and go north 18 mi. Turn left onto Lock 17 Rd. and go north. After 2 mi. (at Lock 17 Grocery) the road veers to the left. Continue 2.5 mi. north to the campground entrance.

ALEXANDER CITY
Wind Creek State Park
MAP, B-2

reserve america

4325 AL128, 35010. www.reserveamerica.com.

🚐 ★★★★   ⛺ ★★★★

Beauty: ★★★★
Spaciousness: ★★★
Security: ★★★★★
Insect Control: ★★★

Site Privacy: ★★
Quiet: ★★★
Cleanliness: ★★★★
Facilities: ★★★★

On the shores of 40,000-acre Lake Martin in east central Alabama, Wind Creek State Park is an excellent choice for families. Children will enjoy the large playground and variety of natural and recreational programs. Campers with lakefront sites are allowed to swim and dock boats right at the sites. Anglers will find catfish, crappie, and bluegill as well as largemouth, salt-water striped, white, and hybrid bass. Wind Creek State Park is not the top choice for peace and quiet as it is full of children and boats. The park should be assiduously avoided on holiday weekends. Security is outstanding at this gated and extremely remote park. The campground at Wind Creek State Park is laid out in 5 main sections including a primitive overflow area. The large, flat, grid-like Section B is nicely shaded by a stand of loblolly and longleaf pine. Section C includes sites on an open peninsula with unobscured views of Lake Martin. Sites C190, C191 and C192 are the prettiest in spite of their complete lack of privacy. Other attractive lakefront sites are found in Section D. Section E contains a few sites with lake views and a modicum of privacy (try E32, E33, E34, E36, E38, or E30). All the sites at Wind Creek State Park are small compared to other Alabama state parks. While some sites are extremely shady, the open sites tend to have better views of the lake. The back-in, paved parking spaces are in various states of repair and disrepair and may be peppered with pine straw, gravel, or grass. However, the bathhouses here are in excellent condition—large and clean with no frills.

BASICS

Operated By: Alabama State Parks. **Open:** All year. **Site Assignment:** First come, first served; Alabama State Park reservations system. **Registration:** At main entrance, open 24 hours in-season; night registration available in winter. **Fee:** RV camping, $17.44; tent, $15.26; $4 additional for sewer or waterfront sites. Fee includes 4 people; $2 per extra person; limit 8 people per site. **Parking:** Limit 2 cars per site, overflow parking available.

FACILITIES

Number of Multipurpose Sites: 642. **Hookups:** Electric (30 amps), water, 235 sites w/ sewer. **Each**

Site: Picnic table, grill. **Dump Station:** Yes. **Laundry:** Yes. **Pay Phone:** Yes. **Restrooms and Showers:** Yes. **Fuel:** No. **Propane:** No. **Internal Roads:** Paved. **RV Service:** 8 mi. northeast in Alexander City. **Market:** 8 mi. northeast in Alexander City. **Restaurant:** 8 mi. northeast in Alexander City. **General Store:** Camp store. **Vending:** Yes. **Swimming:** Beach. **Playground:** Yes. **Other:** Marina, boat launches, 210-ft. fishing pier, picnic pavilions. **Activities:** Hiking trails, fishing, lake swimming, boating (limited boat rentals), organized summer activities, volleyball, horseshoes. **Nearby Attractions:** Lake Martin, Horseshoe Bend Military Park, Charles E. Bailey Sportsplex. **Additional Information:** Alexander City Chamber of Commerce, (256) 234-3461.

RESTRICTIONS

Pets: On leash only. **Fires:** Allowed. **Alcoholic Beverages:** At site only. **Vehicle Maximum Length:** 50 ft. **Other:** 2-week stay limit on the same site. Some permanent sites available.

TO GET THERE

From Montgomery, take US 231 north for 9 mi. At Wetumpka, turn right onto AL 170 and go east for 10 mi. At Eclectic follow signs to AL 63 north. Follow AL 63 for 18 mi. until you see park signs. Turn right onto AL 128 and travel east 5 mi. to the park. From Birmingham, take US 280 east to Alexander City. Turn right onto AL 63 and go south for 7 mi. Turn left onto AL 128 and go east 5 mi.

ALICEVILLE
Cochrane
MAP, B-1

reserve america

707 Tenntom Park Rd., 35442. T: (662) 327-2142; www.reserveamerica.com.

🚐 ★★★★   ⛺ ★★★★

Beauty: ★★
Spaciousness: ★★★
Security: ★★★
Insect Control: ★★★

Site Privacy: ★★★
Quiet: ★★★
Cleanliness: ★★★★
Facilities: ★★★

Cochrane Campground is located on the Tennessee-Tombigbee Waterway. The Tenn-Tom Waterway is an outdoor-enthusiasts paradise. From picnicking to fishing to camping, the Tenn-Tom has it all. The Tombigbee River was originally navigable by early shallow-draft steamboats from Mobile Bay to Cotton Gin Port, Mississippi. From Chattanooga, Tennessee, it is only 100 river miles down the Tennessee River to Pickwick Lake in northern Alabama. But to ship goods from there to an ocean port, such as New Orleans, it would have been another 1,800 miles via the Tennessee, Ohio, and Mississippi Rivers. As part of the Rivers and Harbors Act of 1946, the U.S. Congress authorized the U.S. Army Corps of Engineers to plan for a canal between the Tennessee and the Tombigbee Rivers. Such a water connection could cut the distance between the developing industries of the mid-South and the ocean ports on the

Gulf of Mexico by over 800 miles. By 1951 construction of the Federal Interstate Highway system had begun. As a result, Congress felt a canal was unneeded and withdrew its authorization. Between 1956 and 1960, local Congressmen realized the need to invigorate the regional economy. They funded a new study to analyze benefits and cost for such a canal. In 1958 Alabama and Mississippi established the Tennessee-Tombigbee Waterway Development Authority to provide local initiative. The economic report these agencies wrote in 1961 was favorable. Based on that report, Congress accepted the older U.S. Army Corps of Engineers plans, but not until 1971 were funds appropriated for the waterway. The first spade of earth for the new Tennessee-Tombigbee Waterway was officially turned by President Nixon in May of 1971.

BASICS

Operated By: U.S. Army Corps of Engineers. **Open:** All year. **Site Assignment:** Reservations must be made at least 4 days in advance. **Registration:** At office. **Fee:** Single, $12–$14. **Parking:** At site.

FACILITIES

Number of Multipurpose Sites: 92. **Hookups:** Yes. **Dump Station:** Yes. **Laundry:** Yes. **Pay Phone:** Yes. **Restrooms and Showers:** Yes. **Fuel:** No. **Propane:** No. **Internal Roads:** Paved & gravel. **RV Service:** No. **Market:** No. **Restaurant:** No. **General Store:** No. **Vending:** No. **Swimming:** No. **Playground:** Yes. **Activities:** Fishing.

RESTRICTIONS

Pets: Pets must be restrained or on a leash at all times while in developed recreation areas. **Fires:** In fire rings, stoves, grills, or fireplaces provided for that purpose. **Alcoholic Beverages:** Not allowed. **Vehicle Maximum Length:** Call ahead.

TO GET THERE

From Aliceville, AL, take Hwy. 17 south 10 mi. Approximately 2 mi. past the Huyck Bridge, turn right at the sign for the Cochrane Recreation Area. Follow the paved road approximately 2 mi. The campground is located to the left.

BENTON   MAP, C-2
Prairie Creek Campground, Woodruff Lake

reserve america

8493 US 80 West, 36040. T: (479) 925-3957; www.reserveamerica.com.

🚐 ★★★★   ▲ ★★★★

Beauty: ★★★★	Site Privacy: ★★★★
Spaciousness: ★★★★	Quiet: ★★★★
Security: ★★★★	Cleanliness: ★★★★
Insect Control: ★★★	Facilities: ★★★

Prairie Creek is typical of the top quality campgrounds managed by the Army Corps of Engineers. Sites are extremely spacious and most have uncluttered views of the Alabama River. Spanish moss-laden oak trees provide shade and privacy. Two of the three camping areas, Beaver Point and Eagles Roost, are newer and feature paved back-in parking. The older Whitetail Bluff camping area contains pull-throughs but is now used for overflow camping. At Beaver Point, sites 56–62 are reserved for tent campers. RV campers will not be disappointed with any of the waterfront sites, 27–51. Since so many sites are excellent, choose your site based on proximity to facilities. The campgrounds located on the Alabama River Lake system are all extremely remote. Prairie Creek makes a great summer destination as it only fills to capacity on the busiest holiday weekends. Gates lock at night, making the park extremely safe. Prairie Creek is located 6 miles from Holy Ground Battlefield Park, site of 1813–1814 clashes between the Creek Indians and the U.S. Army, led by General Andrew Jackson. Today, Holy Ground Battlefield Park is a day-use-only recreation area with swimming beach, boat launch, playground, bathhouse, picnic shelters, multi-purpose court, hiking trails, and observation deck. Day-use fees are waived for Prairie Creek campground guests.

BASICS

Operated By: U.S. Army Corps of Engineers. **Open:** All year. **Site Assignment:** First come, first served; 60% of sites are available for reservations, accepted through National Recreation Reservation Service (NRRS) at (877) 444-6777 or www.recreation.gov; reservations can be made up to 240 days in advance, full payment required upon making reservation; credit card preferred (V, MC, D, AE), or pay by money order if at least 21 days in advance of arrival; $10 fee for cancellation or change of site or dates; cancellation w/in 3 days of arrival charged first night, no-show charged $20 plus first night. **Registration:** At gatehouse or night-access lane. **Fee:** Waterfront multipurpose, $16–$19; other multipurpose, $12; tent, $10. **Parking:** At sites, overflow parking available.

FACILITIES

Number of Tent-only Sites: 7. **Number of Multipurpose Sites:** 55. **Hookups:** Electric (50 amps), water. **Each Site:** Picnic table, grill, fire rings, tent pad at tent sites. **Dump Station:** Yes. **Laundry:** Yes. **Pay Phone:** Yes. **Restrooms and Showers:** Yes. **Fuel:** No. **Propane:** No. **Internal Roads:** Paved. **RV Service:** 20 mi. west in Selma. **Market:** 20 mi. west in Selma. **Restaurant:** 10 mi. southeast in Lowndesboro. **General Store:** 20 mi. west in Selma. **Vending:** No. **Swimming:** Yes. **Playground:** Yes. **Other:** Courtesy docks, boat ramp, fish-cleaning area, picnic shelters, sports court, scenic overlooks. **Activities:** Boating, waterskiing, hiking, hunting. **Nearby Attractions:** Brown Chapel A.M.E. Church & King Monument, Cahawba, National Voting Rights Museum & Institute, Old Depot Museum, Old Live Oak Cemetery Tour, Smitherman Historic Building. **Additional Information:** Selma/Dallas County Chamber of Commerce, (334) 875-7241.

RESTRICTIONS

Pets: On leash only. **Fires:** Fire ring only. **Alcoholic Beverages:** Allowed. **Vehicle Maximum Length:** 50 ft. **Other:** Limit 3 vehicles per site.

TO GET THERE

Turn east at the intersection of 2nd and Locust in Rogers. Travel east on Hwy. 12 for 4 mi. then turn left on North Park Rd. This road leads to Prairie Creek Rd.

BIRMINGHAM   MAP, B-2
Birmingham South Campground

222 Hwy. 33, 35124. T: (205) 664-8832 or (800) 772-8832.

🚐 ★★★★   ▲ ★★

Beauty: ★★★	Site Privacy: ★★
Spaciousness: ★★★	Quiet: ★★★
Security: ★★★	Cleanliness: ★★★
Insect Control: ★★★★	Facilities: ★★★★

Though not as attractive as nearby Oak Mountain State Park, KOA Birmingham South is tidy and offers comfortably spaced sites. Campers sometimes prefer the aesthetically bland sites at KOA to the state park because sites are level and hookups include cable television. The KOA may also be quieter, as many of the campers here are retirees. Back-in sites numbered B-8–B-30 are the shadiest, prettiest, and the most popular. If you prefer an open pull-through site, choose from sites numbered 1–36. All roads and RV parking spots are paved.

BASICS

Operated By: AIG Baker. **Open:** All year. **Site Assignment:** First come, first served; reservations accepted. **Registration:** At camp office. **Fee:** Water/electric, $32; tent, $25. Fee includes 2 people; extra charge for sewer, a/c, electric heat or 50 amp hookup. **Parking:** 2 vehicles per site, plus overflow lot.

FACILITIES

Number of RV-only Sites: 116. **Number of Tent-only Sites:** 6. **Hookups:** Electric (30, 50 amps), water, sewer, cable TV. **Each Site:** Picnic table, paved area, grill on request. **Dump Station:** Yes. **Laundry:** Yes. **Pay Phone:** Yes. **Restrooms and Showers:** Yes. **Fuel:** No. **Propane:** Yes. **Internal Roads:** Some gravel, majority paved. **RV Service:** 15 mi. **Market:** Located in campground. **Restaurant:** 0.5 mi. in Pelham. **General Store:** Camp store, Wal-Mart 2 mi. south in Pelham. **Vending:** Beverages. **Swimming:** Heated pool/hot tub. **Playground:** Yes. **Other:** Gift shop, hot tub, covered pavilion, rental cabins. **Activities:** Game room, horseshoes, basketball, clubhouse w/ television, planned activities. **Nearby Attractions:** Oak Mountain State Park (golf, fishing, horseback riding, boating, hiking), Birmingham Zoo & Botanical Gardens, Galleria Mall. **Additional Information:** Birmingham CVB, (800) 458-8085; Hoover Chamber of Commerce, (205) 988-5672.

RESTRICTIONS

Pets: On leash only. **Fires:** At tent sites only. **Alcoholic Beverages:** At site only. **Vehicle Maximum Length:** 50 ft.

TO GET THERE

From I-65, take Exit 242, then Hwy. 52 west, then right on Hwy. 33; campground 1 block on the right.

CAMDEN
MAP, C-2
Roland Cooper State Park

285 Deer Run Dr., 36726. T: (334) 682-4838; www.alapark.com.

🚐 ★★★   ▲ ★★★

Beauty: ★★★   Site Privacy: ★★★
Spaciousness: ★★★   Quiet: ★★★
Security: ★★★   Cleanliness: ★★★
Insect Control: ★★   Facilities: ★★★★

Golf and fishing are the primary draws at Roland Cooper State Park. Created by a dam on the Alabama River, 22,000-acre Dannelly Reservoir is home to numerous fish species, as well as beaver, waterfowl, and American alligator. The nine-hole golf course is a bargain; greens fees are only $9 for 9 holes and $13 for 18 holes. Here, the woodlands are dominated by pine. The majority of the campsites enjoy the shade of a mature stand of loblolly pine. A bit of privacy is provided by the trees, but none of the sites are entirely secluded. Most of the sites are situated on one loop and feature paved, back-in parking. Sites 22, 24, and 28 are pull-through sites, with views of the reservoir and gravel parking. In the primitive tent-camping area, site 10 has a nice view of the water. Site size is comfortable but not exceptional. Roland Cooper's rural location and gates that lock at night make it fairly secure. Avoid this park in July and August when summer heat crescendos. Also avoid Memorial Day, 4th of July, and Labor Day, when crowds are at a maximum.

BASICS

Operated By: Alabama State Parks. **Open:** All year. **Site Assignment:** Reservations accepted; cancellation w/ 72-hour notice; sites are first come, first served. **Registration:** At entrance office. **Fee:** Improved, $16.64; primitive, $8.32. **Parking:** Limit 3 vehicles per site, overflow parking available.

FACILITIES

Number of Tent-only Sites: 10. **Number of Multipurpose Sites:** 47. **Hookups:** Electric (30 amps), water, sewer. **Each Site:** Picnic table, grill, fire ring. **Dump Station:** Yes. **Laundry:** Yes. **Pay Phone:** Yes. **Restrooms and Showers:** Yes. **Fuel:** No. **Propane:** No. **Internal Roads:** Paved. **RV Service:** 75 mi. northeast in Montgomery. **Market:** Camp store. **Restaurant:** 5 mi. south in Camden. **General Store:** 5 mi. south in Camden. **Vending:** No. **Swimming:** No. **Playground:** Yes. **Other:** Clubhouse, picnic pavilion, 9-hole golf course, driving range, boat ramps, fish-cleaning area. **Activities:** Golf, fishing, boating, swimming, walking trails. **Nearby Attractions:** Bridgeport Beach, Dale Masonic Lodge, Wilcox Female Institute. **Additional Information:** Wilcox Development Council (334) 682-4929.

RESTRICTIONS

Pets: On leash only. **Fires:** Fire rings, grills only. **Alcoholic Beverages:** At site only. **Vehicle Maximum Length:** No limit.

TO GET THERE

From I-65, take Exit 128. Drive west on AL 10 for 40 mi. At Camden, turn right onto AL 41 and drive north for 4 mi. The park is on the left.

CARROLLTON
MAP, B-1
Pickensville Campground

reserve america

61 Camping Rd., 35447. T: (205) 373-6328; www.reserveamerica.com.

🚐 ★★★★   ▲ ★★★★

Beauty: ★★★   Site Privacy: ★★★
Spaciousness: ★★★   Quiet: ★★★
Security: ★★★   Cleanliness: ★★★★
Insect Control: ★★★   Facilities: ★★★

Pickensville Campground is on the Tennessee-Tombigbee Waterway. The Tenn-Tom Waterway is an outdoor-enthusiasts paradise. From picnicking to fishing to camping, the Tenn-Tom has it all. The Tombigbee River was originally navigable by early shallow-draft steamboats from Mobile Bay to Cotton Gin Port, Mississippi. From Chattanooga, Tennessee, it is only 100 river miles down the Tennessee River to Pickwick Lake in northern Alabama. But to ship goods from there to an ocean port, such as New Orleans, it would have been another 1,800 miles via the Tennessee, Ohio, and Mississippi Rivers. As part of the Rivers and Harbors Act of 1946, the U.S. Congress authorized the U.S. Army Corps of Engineers to plan for a canal between the Tennessee and the Tombigbee Rivers. Such a water connection could cut the distance between the developing industries of the mid-South and the ocean ports on the Gulf of Mexico by over 800 miles. By 1951 construction of the Federal Interstate Highway system had begun. As a result, Congress felt a canal was unneeded and withdrew its authorization. Between 1956 and 1960, local Congressmen realized the need to invigorate the regional economy. They funded a new study to analyze benefits and cost for such a canal. In 1958 Alabama and Mississippi established the Tennessee-Tombigbee Waterway Development Authority to provide local initiative. The economic report these agencies wrote in 1961 was favorable. Based on that report, Congress accepted the older U.S. Army Corps of Engineers plans, but not until 1971 were funds appropriated for the waterway. The first spade of earth for the new Tennessee-Tombigbee Waterway was officially turned by President Nixon in May of 1971.

BASICS

Operated By: U.S. Army Corps of Engineers. **Open:** All year. **Site Assignment:** Reservations must be made at least 4 days in advance. **Registration:** At office. **Fee:** Single, $16–$20. **Parking:** At site.

FACILITIES

Number of Multipurpose Sites: 424. **Hookups:** Yes. **Dump Station:** Yes. **Laundry:** Yes. **Pay Phone:** Yes. **Restrooms and Showers:** Yes. **Fuel:** No. **Propane:** No. **Internal Roads:** Paved. **RV Service:** No. **Market:** No. **Restaurant:** No. **General Store:** No. **Vending:** No. **Swimming:** No. **Playground:** Yes. **Activities:** Picnicking, fishing.

RESTRICTIONS

Pets: Pets must be restrained or on a leash at all times while in developed recreation areas. **Fires:** In fire rings, stoves, grills, or fireplaces provided for that purpose. **Alcoholic Beverages:** Not allowed. **Vehicle Maximum Length:** Call ahead.

TO GET THERE

From Tuscaloosa, take US 82 west to the junction with US 86. Turn left onto US 86 west to Pickensville. The entrance road to the campground is 2.5 mi. past the yellow caution light.

COKER
MAP, B-1
Lake Lurleen State Park

13226 Lake Lurleen Rd., 35452. T: (205) 339-1558; www.alapark.com.

🚐 ★★★★   ▲ ★★★★

Beauty: ★★★★   Site Privacy: ★★★
Spaciousness: ★★★★ Quiet: ★★★
Security: ★★★★   Cleanliness: ★★★
Insect Control: ★★   Facilities: ★★★

Named after Alabama's only woman governor, Lurleen Burns Wallace, this lake is popular with anglers. The 250-acre lake is stocked with bream, catfish, crappie, and largemouth and striped bass. Rather not fish? Swim, hike, or canoe. Located 12 miles northwest of Tuscaloosa, this park stays busy all summer, so we recommend weekday, spring, or fall visits. Four camping areas (A–D) offer nice sized sites. Most have paved back-in parking. A few sites have gravel parking. Section B is devoted to RV campers and contains 8 pull-through sites. Sites B33–B39 (odd numbers) feature wooden decks overlooking Lake Lurleen. In Section A, lakefront sites A2–A14 (even numbers) offer lovely views. While most sites have some shady trees, sites A15 and A16 are exceptionally shady and secluded. In spite of Lake Lurleen's proximity to Tuscaloosa, it feels remote. Gates lock at night, making the park extremely secure.

BASICS

Operated By: Alabama State Parks. **Open:** All year. **Site Assignment:** Reservations accepted w/ 1-night deposit; sites are first come, first served; 72-hour cancellation policy, except for football weekend. **Registration:** At entrance station. **Fee:** $16–$20. **Parking:** 2 vehicles per site.

FACILITIES

Number of Multipurpose Sites: 91. **Hookups:** Electric (30, 50 amps), water, 35 sites w/ sewer. **Each Site:** Picnic table, grill. **Dump Station:** Yes. **Laundry:** No. **Pay Phone:** Yes. **Restrooms and Showers:** Yes. **Fuel:** No. **Propane:** No. **Internal Roads:** Paved. **RV Service:** 15 mi. south in Tuscaloosa. **Market:** 7 mi. east in Northport. **Restaurant:** 7 mi. east in Northport. **General Store:** Yes. **Vending:** Yes. **Swimming:** Lake. **Playground:** Yes. **Other:** Boat ramps, fishing pier, marina, boat rentals, amphitheater, picnic area, group picnic shelters, swimming beach, beach snack stand, nature center, sports field. **Activities:** Fishing, boating, hiking, swimming. **Nearby Attractions:** Paul "Bear" Bryant Museum, Alabama Museum of Natural History, Moundville Indian Archeological Park, Mercedes-Benz Visitor Center, Denny Chimes, Gorgas House, Children's Hands-On

Museum, Kentucky Art Center, University of Alabama Arboretum. **Additional Information:** West Alabama Chamber of Commerce (205) 758-7588; Tuscaloosa CVB (800) 538-8696.

RESTRICTIONS

Pets: On leash only. **Fires:** Fire pit only. **Alcoholic Beverages:** Site only, not allowed at beach. **Vehicle Maximum Length:** No limit. **Other:** No ATVs or horses allowed.

TO GET THERE

From I-20/59 take Exit 71B, continue on I-35 D approximately 5 mi. to the intersection of US 82, turn left (west) on US 82 and continue 5 mi. to Tuscaloosa CR 21, turn right on it. Turn right at park sign.

DELTA
Cheaha State Park
MAP, B-3

2141 Bunker Loop, 36258. T: (256) 488-5111 or (800) 610-5801; www.cheahastpark.com.

🚐 ★★★★   ▲ ★★★★

Beauty: ★★★★	Site Privacy: ★★★
Spaciousness: ★★★★	Quiet: ★★★
Security: ★★★	Cleanliness: ★★★
Insect Control: ★★★★	Facilities: ★★★★

With an elevation of 2407 feet, Mt. Cheaha is the highest point in the state of Alabama. Park guests can enjoy the gorgeous mountain view from atop the observation tower. The campgrounds are also very attractive, with very spacious sites and a variety of shady hardwood trees. Site privacy varies, with dense foliage buffering some sites from their neighbors. There are two campgrounds at Cheaha, Number 1, or "Upper," and Number 2, or "Lower." Campground Number 1 features mostly back-in parking, but there are a few spacious pull-throughs. Parking spots are an amalgamation of dirt and gravel. In campground Number 1, sites 4 and 5 are extremely private and wooded. Large pull-throughs include 30, 31, 34, 35, and 36. Of these, 34 is the shadiest. In campground Number 2, sites 56 and 57 have a gorgeous view. Most sites in Number 2 are pull-throughs. The popularity of Cheaha's campgrounds can sometimes detract from their beauty. The campgrounds are fairly well maintained, but the potties and trash bins sometimes need more attention than they get. Security is fair at this rural state park. We got the idea that gates may or may not close at night. This Appalachian park stays cooler than most of Alabama during the summer. Nonetheless, we recommend avoiding Cheaha on summer weekends when the park's beauty and myriad activities attract the masses.

BASICS

Operated By: Alabama State Parks. **Open:** All year. **Site Assignment:** First come, first served; reservations accepted w/ 1-night fee in advance; no refunds allowed although date of stay can be changed. **Registration:** At country store. **Fee:** Improved, $16; semi-primitive, $12; primitive, $10. Discount (15%) for disabled & seniors (62 & over). **Parking:** Site, limit 2 vehicles per site.

FACILITIES

Number of Multipurpose Sites: 73. **Hookups:** Electric (30 amps), water, sewer. **Each Site:** Picnic table, grill. **Dump Station:** No. **Laundry:** Yes. **Pay Phone:** Yes. **Restrooms and Showers:** Yes. **Fuel:** Yes. **Propane:** No. **Internal Roads:** Paved. **RV Service:** 25 mi. east in Oxford. **Market:** 25 mi. east in Oxford. **Restaurant:** In park. **General Store:** Wal-Mart 25 mi. east in Oxford. **Vending:** Beverages. **Swimming:** Yes. **Playground:** Yes. **Other:** Observation tower, CCC Museum, picnic & play area, sandy swimming beach. **Activities:** Fishing, pedal-boat rental, hiking, mountain biking. **Nearby Attractions:** Anniston Museum of Natural History, Birmingham & Gadsden attractions.

RESTRICTIONS

Pets: On leash only. **Fires:** Allowed. **Alcoholic Beverages:** At site only. **Vehicle Maximum Length:** 40 ft. **Other:** 14-day stay limit.

TO GET THERE

From I-20 take Exit 191. Go south on US 431 for 5 mi. Turn right onto AL 281 and go south. This runs into the park.

DOUBLE SPRINGS
Corinth Recreation Area
MAP, A-1

reserve america

2540 CR 57, 35553. T: (205) 489-5111 or (205) 489-2527; www.reserveamerica.com.

🚐 ★★★★   ▲ ★★★★

Beauty: ★★★★	Site Privacy: ★★★
Spaciousness: ★★★★	Quiet: ★★★★
Security: ★★★★★	Cleanliness: ★★★★
Insect Control: ★★★★★	Facilities: ★★★

Located 28 miles from the hiking and equestrian trails at Sipsey Wilderness Area, Corinth Recreation Area offers 52 campsites with full hookups. Sites are attractive, spacious, and heavily wooded. Dense brush between sites provides privacy. The campground is laid out in two main loops plus a group camp loop. The Yellow Hammer loop is much prettier than the Firefly loop. All parking is paved. While most of the parking is back-in style, there are five huge pull-through sites. Pull-through sites 17 and 19 are lovely and very private. Although the bathhouses in Bankhead National Forest are small, they are some of the tidiest in the state. Security is excellent at Corinth; the campground is extremely remote and gated at all times. Day-use facilities at Corinth are minimal, so the atmosphere is usually incredibly laid back. This tranquil campground rarely fills up, so it's a good bet for a summer weekend (if you can stand the heat).

BASICS

Operated By: U.S. Forest Service. **Open:** Mar. 17–Nov. 1. **Site Assignment:** First come, first served; some loops reservable through National Recreation Reservation System (877) 444-6777; reservations must be made 4 days in advance. **Registration:** At gatehouse. **Fee:** RV, $22–$30; tent, $10. Fee includes 1 vehicle per site, $3 per extra vehicle. **Parking:** At site; wheels must be on pavement.

FACILITIES

Number of Tent-only Sites: 8. **Number of Multipurpose Sites:** 50. **Hookups:** Electric (50 amps), water, sewer. **Each Site:** Picnic table, fire ring, grill, lantern post, tent pad. **Dump Station:** Yes, $5 per vehicle. **Laundry:** No. **Pay Phone:** Yes. **Restrooms and Showers:** Yes. **Fuel:** No. **Propane:** No. **Internal Roads:** Paved. **RV Service:** 35 mi. east in Cullman. **Market:** 5 mi. northwest in Double Springs. **Restaurant:** 5 mi. northwest in Double Springs. **General Store:** 5 mi. northwest in Double Springs. **Vending:** No. **Swimming:** No. **Playground:** No. **Other:** Boat launch, swimming beach, paddle-boat rental, group picnic shelter. **Activities:** Fishing, swimming, hiking. **Nearby Attractions:** William B. Bankhead National Forest, Looney's Entertainment & Riverboat, Ave Maria Grotto in Cullman. **Additional Information:** Cullman Area Chamber of Commerce, (800) 313-5114.

RESTRICTIONS

Pets: On leash only. **Fires:** Fire ring only. **Alcoholic Beverages:** Not allowed. **Vehicle Maximum Length:** 50 ft. **Other:** 14-day stay limit. Electrical plug on sites.

TO GET THERE

Drive east of Double Springs on US 278 for about 5 mi., turn south on CR 57 for about 3 mi. to Corinth Recreation Area.

EUFAULA
Lakepoint Resort State Park
MAP, C-3

P.O. Box 267, 36072. T: (334) 687-8011 or (800) 544-5253; www.alapark.com.

🚐 ★★★★   ▲ ★★★★

Beauty: ★★★★	Site Privacy: ★★
Spaciousness: ★★★	Quiet: ★★★
Security: ★★★★	Cleanliness: ★★★★
Insect Control: ★★★	Facilities: ★★★★★

Hide your carrots. Lakepoint Resort Sate Park campgrounds are full of bunny rabbits. The flat campground is situated along Lake Eufaula, home to beaver and American alligator. Four camping areas provide over 500 sites. Of these areas, the Clark Loop, with sites along the lake, is the most attractive. Clark has only water and electric hookups, and is the best choice for tent campers. Even-numbered sites 20–42 have the prettiest views. RV campers should head for the Deer Court area, which has full hookups, and both back-in and pull-through sites. All parking is paved and ground cover consists of grass and pine straw. Site size varies, but sites are generally comfortable. Most sites are nicely wooded with a variety of tree species, some adorned with Spanish moss. None are very secluded. With excellent resort amenities, Lakepoint Resort State Park is a good choice for active families and couples, making its remote location worth the drive. Gated at all times, campground security is excellent. This park becomes chaotic on holiday weekends and should also be avoided in July and Aug. when it's bound to be unbearably hot and humid.

BASICS

Operated By: Alabama State Parks Conservation Dept. **Open:** All year, except Thanksgiving & Christmas. **Site Assignment:** First come, first served; reservations accepted through Conservation Dept. or directly, 1-night deposit, 7-day cancellation notice; 3-night minimum on holidays. **Registration:** At camp store, night registration available. **Fee:** Full hookup, $19.80; water/electric, $14.30. **Parking:** 2 cars per site, overflow parking available.

FACILITIES

Number of Multipurpose Sites: 244. **Hookups:** Electric (30 amps), water, 80 sites w/ sewer. **Each Site:** Picnic table, grill. **Dump Station:** Yes. **Laundry:** Yes. **Pay Phone:** Yes. **Restrooms and Showers:** Yes. **Fuel:** Boat fuel. **Propane:** Yes. **Internal Roads:** Paved. **RV Service:** 40 mi. north in Columbus, GA. **Market:** 6 mi. south in Eufaula. **Restaurant:** In park. **General Store:** Camp store. **Vending:** Yes. **Swimming:** No. **Playground:** Yes. **Other:** Marina, boat launches, swimming beach, picnic area, sports field, information/nature center, RV storage, tennis courts, volleyball courts, basketball courts, lodge, 18-hole golf course, lounge, resort motel, video arcade. **Activities:** Fishing, pontoon-boat rental, hiking, tennis courts, lodge, 18-hole golf, game room for kids. **Nearby Attractions:** Downtown Eufaula, antebellum homes, walking & driving tours, antique shopping. **Additional Information:** Eufaula Chamber of Commerce, (334) 687-6664.

RESTRICTIONS

Pets: On leash only. **Fires:** Grill, fire rings only. **Alcoholic Beverages:** At site only. **Vehicle Maximum Length:** 60 ft.

TO GET THERE

Located 7 mi. north of Eufala off US 431 on the Alabama–Georgia line.

FORT PAYNE   MAP, A-3
DeSoto State Park

13883 Co. Rd. 89, 35967. T: (256) 845-5075 or (800) 760-4089; www.desotostatepark.com.

🚐 ★★★★★   ⛺ ★★★★★

Beauty: ★★★★★	Site Privacy: ★★★★
Spaciousness: ★★★★★	Quiet: ★★★
Security: ★★★★★	Cleanliness: ★★★★
Insect Control: ★★★	Facilities: ★★★★

Situated about half way between De Soto Falls and Little River Canyon, De Soto State Park has a rugged ambiance even though it's less than 10 miles northeast of Fort Payne. Sometimes referred to as "The Grand Canyon of the East," Little River Canyon has drops of up to 600 feet. Hardcore outdoors folk climb the canyon's sandstone bluffs and paddle the Little River's Class III–V whitewater. The campground at De Soto State Park is laid out in two loops, each with its own playground and restrooms. Sites are nicely spaced and the campground is heavily wooded with a variety of hardwoods and pines, making site size outstanding and site privacy excellent. RV parking spaces are gravel. Of the 78 campsites, 10 are pull-throughs. Since all of the sites are nice, choose your site based on proximity to (or distance from) playgrounds and restrooms. RV campers may want to procure one of the 20 sites with full hookups. Gorgeous sites make this one of the most popular campgrounds in the state, so visit in the spring to avoid the masses. If you don't mind the constant crowds, visit for fall "leaf-peeping" in September and October. Security at De Soto State Park is excellent; at night the gate must be opened with a "key card."

BASICS

Operated By: Alabama State Parks. **Open:** All year. **Site Assignment:** Reservations required, a deposit by credit card for the first night should be made well in advance. **Registration:** At country store. **Fee:** Full hookup, $20; water/electric/sewer, $18.50; water/electric, $16. $2.14 per extra person. **Parking:** At site, limit 2 cars per site.

FACILITIES

Number of RV-only Sites: 78. **Number of Tent-only Sites:** 50 acres open camping. **Hookups:** Water, 58 w/ electric (30 amps), 20 w/ electric (30 amps), sewer. **Each Site:** Picnic table, grill, fire ring. **Dump Station:** Yes. **Laundry:** Yes. **Pay Phone:** Yes. **Restrooms and Showers:** Yes. **Fuel:** No. **Propane:** Yes. **Internal Roads:** Paved. **RV Service:** 35 mi. west in Rainsville. **Market:** Convenience 3 mi., grocery 7 mi. southwest in Fort Payne. **Restaurant:** In park. **General Store:** Convenience 3 mi., Wal-Mart 10 mi. southwest in Fort Payne. **Vending:** Yes. **Swimming:** Yes. **Playground:** Yes. **Other:** Boat launch (7 mi.), nature trails, tennis courts, volleyball court, sports equipment, picnic & play area, lodge, country store. **Activities:** Whitewater paddling (class I–IV), rock climbing, hiking. **Nearby Attractions:** Little River Canyon National Preserve, Mentone crafts & antiques, Depot Museum, Cloudmont Ski & Golf Resort, various waterfalls. **Additional Information:** Fort Payne Chamber of Commerce, (256) 845-2741; Gadsden Chamber of Commerce, (256) 543-3472.

RESTRICTIONS

Pets: On leash only. **Fires:** Grills fire rings only. **Alcoholic Beverages:** Not allowed. **Vehicle Maximum Length:** 50 ft. **Other:** 14-day stay limit.

TO GET THERE

From I-59, take Fort Payne Exit 218 and drive northeast on AL 35. Drive 8 mi. to the top of Lookout Mountain. At the flashing caution light, turn left onto CR 89 and drive 5 mi. to the park entrance.

GADSDEN   MAP, A-2
Noccalula Falls Park and Campground

P.O. Box 267, 35904. T: (256) 543-7412; www.noccalulafalls.org.

🚐 ★★★★   ⛺ ★★★★

Beauty: ★★★★	Site Privacy: ★★
Spaciousness: ★★★	Quiet: ★★★
Security: ★★★★	Cleanliness: ★★★
Insect Control: ★★★★	Facilities: ★★★★★

This city-owned park will be a big hit with the young'uns. The historic Pioneer Homestead consists of over 50 structures which have been preserved by the city of Gadsden. Buildings such as the blacksmith shop and the loom house contain tools typically used by early Appalachian pioneers. Children will also dig the passenger train, animal park, and mini-golf. Adults will appreciate the urban location, with shopping and choice of restaurants found within 6 miles of the park. Everybody will enjoy the park's center piece, 90-foot Noccalula Falls. The campground is attractive, with plenty of back-in sites and a handful of pull-throughs. A few sites have gravel parking, but most are paved. Here, site size varies greatly, with most sites being comfortably sized. The majority enjoy the shade of tall pine trees. But with little foliage between sites, privacy is poor. The prettiest sites (A19–A38) overlook the large bluff that leads down to Black Creek. Security is good at Noccalula Falls. Gates remain open throughout the night, but rangers patrol the park 24 hours a day. Avoid Gadsden in the hotter summer months. Avoid this park completely on holidays. School groups are more likely to visit the Pioneer Village on weekdays in Apr. and May. Call ahead if you would like to avoid them.

BASICS

Operated By: City of Gadsden. **Open:** All year. **Site Assignment:** First come, first served. Reservations available; call campground for details. **Registration:** At camp office. **Fee:** Full hookup, $21; water/electric, $16; tent, $16. Seventh night free; 10% senior discount. **Parking:** At site.

FACILITIES

Number of RV-only Sites: 83. **Number of Tent-only Sites:** 47. **Hookups:** 14 RV w/ electric (30, 50 amps), water, sewer, & cable TV; 13 RV w/ electric (30, 50 amps), water, sewer; 56 RV w/ electric (30, 50 amps), water; 20 tent w/ electric (30, 50 amps), water. **Each Site:** Picnic table, grill. (Available at most sites. Not guaranteed.) **Dump Station:** Yes. **Laundry:** Yes. **Pay Phone:** Yes. **Restrooms and Showers:** Yes. **Fuel:** No. **Propane:** No. **Internal Roads:** Gravel. **RV Service:** 5 mi. east in Gadsden. **Market:** 1 mi. south in Gadsden. **Restaurant:** In park. **General Store:** Country store in park; Wal-Mart, K-Mart & Lowe's 10 mi. south in Gadsden. **Vending:** No. **Swimming:** Yes. **Playground:** Yes. **Other:** Botanical gardens, Noccalula Falls, Pioneer Village, animal park, passenger train, picnic pavilions, souvenir shop, concession stand, rec hall, information center. **Activities:** Hiking, carpet golf, swimming, nature & history study. **Nearby Attractions:** Inquire at campground.

RESTRICTIONS

Pets: On leash only. **Fires:** Allowed. **Alcoholic Beverages:** Not allowed. **Vehicle Maximum Length:** No limit. **Other:** 2 car max. per site.

TO GET THERE

From I-59 take Exit 188 onto AL 211 (Noccalula Rd.). Go south 3.5 mi. to the first light and turn right. The park entrance is ahead.

GREENVILLE   MAP, C-2
Sherling Lake

P.O. Box 158, 36037. T: (800) 810-5253; www.gocampingamerica.com/sherlinglake.

🚐 ★★★★★   ⛺ ★★★★

Beauty: ★★★★★   Site Privacy: ★★★★
Spaciousness: ★★★★   Quiet: ★★★★★
Security: ★★★★★   Cleanliness: ★★★★★
Insect Control: ★★★★   Facilities: ★★★★

The city of Greenville operates this impeccably manicured campground. The tidy landscaping includes native azaleas and dogwoods with intermittent shade provided by tall pines. The park encompasses two fishing lakes, stocked with catfish, bluegill, brim, bass, and crappie. For golfers, 27-hole Cambrian Ridge (part of the Robert Trent Jones Golf Trail) is adjacent to Sherling Lake. Nearly deserted in the spring and fall, this campground is an excellent choice for golfers. For families, the playground is one of the nicest we've seen. The majority of the campsites are situated near the "Top Lake." All sites have ample paved parking and there are plenty of large pull-through sites. Folks with large campers should consider 1, 14, 18, and 25–41. Although all sites at Sherling Lake are spacious, back-in sites often feel a bit more secluded. Though most every site enjoys some shade, none are completely secluded by greenery. Sherling Lake is only 3 miles from Greenville, providing easy access to shopping and restaurants. The park fills to capacity on holidays and during coastal hurricane evacuations. The rest of the time it's an oasis of tranquility. Gates lock at night making security excellent.

BASICS

Operated By: City of Greenville. **Open:** All year. **Site Assignment:** First come, first served; reservations accepted, no deposit required. **Registration:** At office, late-comers register next morning. **Fee:** Developed (up to 4 people), $21.95; primitive (per tent), $19.95. **Parking:** Limit 1 car per site, overflow parking available.

FACILITIES

Number of Multipurpose Sites: 41. **Hookups:** Electric (30, 50 amps), water, sewer. **Each Site:** Picnic table, shelter, fire ring, grill; primitive area includes some tables, fire rings & grills. **Dump Station:** Yes. **Laundry:** No. **Pay Phone:** Yes. **Restrooms and Showers:** Yes. **Fuel:** No. **Propane:** No. **Internal Roads:** Paved. **RV Service:** 3.5 mi. south in Greenville. **Market:** 3.5 mi. south in Greenville. **Restaurant:** 3.5 mi. south in Greenville. **General Store:** Snack shop. **Vending:** Yes. **Swimming:** No. **Playground:** Yes. **Other:** Boat launches, picnic pavilions, small meeting room. **Activities:** Fishing lakes, boat rentals, walking trail. **Nearby Attractions:** Adjacent to Cambrian Ridge Robert Trent Jones 18-hole golf course, Historic Greenville, Preesters Pecan Factory & Outlet. **Additional Information:** Greenville Chamber of Commerce, (334) 382-3251.

RESTRICTIONS

Pets: On leash only. **Fires:** Grill, fire rings only. **Alcoholic Beverages:** At site only. **Vehicle Maximum Length:** 45 ft.

TO GET THERE

From I-65, take Exit 130 and head northwest on AL 185 for 1.5 mi. At AL 263, turn left and continue another 1.5 mi. The park entrance is on the left.

GROVE OAK   MAP, A-2
Buck's Pocket State Park

393 CR 174, 35975. T: (256) 659-2000; www.dcnr.state.al.us/parks.

🚐 ★★★★   ⛺ ★★★★★

Beauty: ★★★★★   Site Privacy: ★★★
Spaciousness: ★★★   Quiet: ★★★★★
Security: ★★★★   Cleanliness: ★★★★
Insect Control: ★★★★   Facilities: ★★★★

2,000-acre Buck's Pocket State park is exceedingly beautiful and not heavily visited. Built around the 400-foot deep Buck's Pocket Canyon and featuring five moderately difficult hiking trails, the park is appreciated by day hikers. Anglers can access Lake Guntersville at Morgan Cove, 7 miles from the park. We were very impressed with the quiet campground that lies in the flat valley of the canyon. Completely shaded by a stand of hardwood trees, the campground features sights adjacent to lovely boulder-lined Little South Sauty Creek. Campsites are not huge, but this campground rarely fills to capacity so you'll have plenty of elbow room. While internal roads are paved, sites offer back-in gravel parking. If you are looking for solitude, head for secluded site Number 17. At 900 feet above sea level, this little "pocket" of the southern Appalachians stays cooler than most of Alabama during the hot summer months. Visit Buck's Pocket comfortably during spring, summer, or fall. The park is very remote with poor signage. It is equipped with gates, but as one local said, "there ain't no need to lock 'em!"

BASICS

Operated By: Alabama State Parks. **Open:** All year. **Site Assignment:** First come, first served; reservations accepted for holiday weekends. **Registration:** At park office. **Fee:** Full hookup, $15; water/electric, $14. Fee includes 8 people; $1 per extra person; senior discount. **Parking:** At sites.

FACILITIES

Number of Tent-only Sites: 8. **Number of Multipurpose Sites:** 36. **Hookups:** 6 w/ electric (50 amps), water, sewer; 36 w/ electric (50 amps), water. **Each Site:** Picnic table, grill, fire ring, tent pad at tent sites. **Dump Station:** Yes. **Laundry:** Yes. **Pay Phone:** Yes. **Restrooms and Showers:** Yes. **Fuel:** No. **Propane:** No. **Internal Roads:** Paved. **RV Service:** 12 mi. east in Rainsville. **Market:** Convenience store 3 mi. south, Grocery 10 mi. south in Geraldine. **Restaurant:** 10 mi. south in Geraldine. **General Store:** 10 mi. south in Geraldine. **Vending:** Yes. **Swimming:** Fishing pier. **Playground:** Yes. **Other:** Boat launch, observation overlook, picnic area. **Activities:** Hiking & walking trails, fishing, boating. **Nearby Attractions:** Cathedral Caverns, Huntsville Space Museum, Lake Guntersville State Park, TVA Guntersville Dam, Depot Museum. **Additional Information:** Guntersville Chamber of Commerce, (256) 582-3612.

RESTRICTIONS

Pets: On leash only. **Fires:** Fire rings, grills only. **Alcoholic Beverages:** Not allowed. **Vehicle Maximum Length:** No limit. **Other:** 14-day stay limit.

TO GET THERE

From I-59, take Exit 218 at Fort Payne. Go north on AL 35 for 7 mi. At Rainsville, turn left and drive south on AL 75 for 4 mi. At Fyffe, turn right on CR 50, and go 8 mi. Watch carefully for park signs. Turn right onto CR 19 and right again onto CR 556, then left onto CR 73. The park is on the right.

GULF SHORES   MAP, D-1
Gulf State Park

22050 Campground Rd., 36542. T: (251) 948-7275; www.alapark.com.

🚐 ★★★★   ⛺ ★★★★

Beauty: ★★★★   Site Privacy: ★★★
Spaciousness: ★★★   Quiet: ★★★
Security: ★★★★   Cleanliness: ★★★★
Insect Control: ★★   Facilities: ★★★★★

Unfortunately, the large campground at Gulf State Park offers no campsites within walking distance of the beach. However, the campground is very attractive and perennially popular with families; don't expect any solitude here during the summer months. Site size is acceptable but the bustling atmosphere makes the campground feel crowded. 185 sites offer back-in parking and 25 offer pull-through parking. Parking areas may be paved, gravel, or packed sand. Many of the sites are shady and a few offer views of small Middle Lake. Tent sites offer soft-sand tent pads. Of those with lake views, sites 17–39 are the most picturesque. Unless you really want a pull-through, avoid the noisy, highly trafficked sites along the main road. Located just a few miles from the tourist town of Gulf Shores, campers have easy access to excellent dining and other tourist attractions. Amenities within the park are also outstanding, including the state's largest fishing pier (825 feet), an 18-hole golf course, and 2.5 miles of white sand beach. The gates at Gulf Shores State Park campground are locked at night and the entrance is staffed all day, making security excellent.

BASICS

Operated By: Alabama State Parks. **Open:** All year. **Site Assignment:** First come, first served; roughly half of the sites are available for reservation w/ a 1-night, nonrefundable deposit, 2 nights on weekends, & 3 nights on holidays. **Registration:** At camp entrance. **Fee:** $23–$25. Discount (15%) for disabled, seniors. **Parking:** At site, limit 2 vehicles per site.

FACILITIES

Number of Multipurpose Sites: 468. **Hookups:** Electric (15, 30 amps), water, sewer. **Each Site:** Picnic table, grill. **Dump Station:** Yes. **Laundry:** Yes. **Pay Phone:** Yes. **Restrooms and Showers:** Yes, 11 bathhouses. **Fuel:** No. **Propane:** No. **Internal Roads:** Paved. **RV Service:** No. **Market:** 3 mi. in Gulf Shores. **Restaurant:** In park. **General Store:** Yes. **Vending:** Beverages. **Swimming:** Yes. **Playground:** Yes. **Other:** Tennis courts, fishing pier, golf course, game room, bicycle rental, beach pavilion, boat ramp, nature center, resort hotel & conference center, picnic area. **Activities:** Swimming, hiking, fishing, golf. **Nearby Attractions:** Alabama Gulf Coast Zoo, Gulf

Shores Beach, Dauphin Island Sea Lab, Adventure Island, Bellingrath Gardens & Home, Biophilia Nature Center & Native Nursery, Gulf Coast Museum of Science, Gulf Coast Amusement Park, Mobile Bay Ferry, Pirate Island Adventure Golf, USS *Alabama* Battleship Memorial Park, Wildland Expeditions, Waterville USA. **Additional Information:** Alabama Gulf Coast Visitor Information, (800) 745-7263.

RESTRICTIONS

Pets: On leash only. **Fires:** In grills, designated bonfire areas. **Alcoholic Beverages:** At site only. **Vehicle Maximum Length:** No limit.

TO GET THERE

At the intersection of AL 59 and AL 182 (Beach Rd.), turn left. Drive east on AL 182 for 3.5 mi. Pass Gulf State Park Resort Hotel and take the next left onto CR 2. Campground is on the right.

GUNTERSVILLE MAP, A-2
Lake Guntersville State Park

7966 Hwy. 227, 35976-9126. T: (256) 571-5455; www.alapark.com.

🚐 ★★★★ ⛺ ★★★

Beauty: ★★★★	Site Privacy: ★★
Spaciousness: ★★★	Quiet: ★★
Security: ★★★	Cleanliness: ★★★
Insect Control: ★★★★	Facilities: ★★★★★

Lake Guntersville Sate Park is really lovely, but the campgrounds are often way too crowded for our tastes. Set in a beautiful stand of tall pines, the huge campground (with over 300 sites) stays full for much of the summer. If you don't mind spending your vacation with an entire village of new friends and neighbors, you may enjoy this park. Here you will find paved back-in sites with very little privacy. Sites are small compared to other Alabama State parks. The campground is laid out in eight grid-like areas (A–F). Tent campers should head for Area A, especially sites 16 and 17. RV campers should try to land a lakeside site in Area D or G. Sites G9, G11, G12, G13, G24, and G36 are among the most attractive. Area E should be avoided as it abuts the picnic pavilion and experiences heavy traffic. Families wishing to camp right next to the playground should head for C51–C59. Lake Guntersville State Park offers plenty of amenities and activities, but their pride and joy are the American bald eagles who winter there. The campground is gated and guarded, but security isn't fantastic because of the number of folks on the campground. We recommend visiting Lake Guntersville in spring or fall to avoid the crowds.

BASICS

Operated By: Alabama State Parks. **Open:** All year. **Site Assignment:** First come, first served; about half of the sites can be reserved; 3-night minimum weekends & holidays; 1-night deposit. **Registration:** At camp store, no late registration—after 9 p.m., beach parking lot has electric hookups for night parking. **Fee:** Full hookup, $18; water/electric, $16; primitive, $10. **Parking:** At site.

FACILITIES

Number of Multipurpose Sites: 321. **Hookups:** Electric (30 amps), water, 144 sites w/ sewer. **Each

Site: Picnic table, grill, fire ring. **Dump Station:** Yes. **Laundry:** Yes. **Pay Phone:** Yes. **Restrooms and Showers:** Yes. **Fuel:** No. **Propane:** No. **Internal Roads:** Paved. **RV Service:** Inquire at campground. **Market:** 7.5 mi. southwest in Guntersville, Town Creek Filling Station 5 mi. north. **Restaurant:** In park. **General Store:** Camp store, Wal-Mart 15 mi. southwest in Guntersville. **Vending:** Yes. **Swimming:** Beach. **Playground:** Yes. **Other:** Beach, nature center, art gallery, 18-hole golf course, RV storage, activity building, three fishing piers, picnic pavilion, 31 mi. of hiking trails. **Activities:** Swimming, fishing, boating, hiking, tennis, basketball, volleyball, golf. **Nearby Attractions:** American bald eagles Convention Center, Cathedral Caverns, Buck's Pocket State Park, Guntersville Museum & Cultural Center. **Additional Information:** Guntersville Chamber of Commerce, (256) 582-3612.

RESTRICTIONS

Pets: On leash only. **Fires:** Fire ring only. **Alcoholic Beverages:** At site only. **Vehicle Maximum Length:** No limit. **Other:** 14-day stay limit Apr.–Oct.

TO GET THERE

From I-59, take the Gadsden exit and go north on US 431 for approximately 38 mi. At Guntersville, turn right onto AL 227 and go northeast for 7 mi. The park entrance is on the left.

GUNTERSVILLE/ MAP, A-2
LANGSTON
Little Mountain Marina Resort

1001 Murphy Hill Rd., 35755. T: (256) 582-8211; www.wakefieldenterprises.com.

🚐 ★★★★ ⛺ n/a

Beauty: ★★★	Site Privacy: ★★
Spaciousness: ★★★	Quiet: ★★
Security: ★★★★	Cleanliness: ★★★
Insect Control: ★★★★	Facilities: ★★★★★

Little Mountain Resort is noteworthy for its modern amenities rather than its natural beauty. Located on Guntersville Lake, the resort caters to active families and large groups. For fishing and boating enthusiasts, there's a boat launch, marina, fishing pier, and two covered piers containing a total of 86 boat slips. Land amenities include a 500-seat great hall as well as multiple swimming pools and other activities. The gigantic campground is a no-frills affair with midsized sites. There are no barriers to provide privacy between sites. Back-in gravel parking is the rule and no tent camping is allowed. The prettiest sites are numbers 110–119 and 110A–119A, which are adjacent to the lake and have power and water only. The nicest sites with full hookups and views of the lake are 18–20, 27–29, 36, 37, 120, and 121. Avoid sites in the 200s and 300s, which have unattractive views of the boat and RV storage areas. Some sites are completely open while others provide plenty of shade. In spite of Little Mountain's extremely remote location, you may feel like you've arrived in lower Manhattan once you're here. We recommend weekday visits in the summertime, or visits in spring or autumn. The guard house is staffed 24 hours a day, making security good.

BASICS

Operated By: Earl & Elke Hodges. **Open:** All year. **Site Assignment:** First come, first served; 2-night minimum for reservations (must have credit card); cancellation penalty is 1-night fee on holidays. **Registration:** At guard house (24 hours). **Fee:** $24; includes 4 people; $2 per extra person. **Parking:** Limit 2 vehicles per site.

FACILITIES

Hookups: electric (30, 50 amps), water, sewer. **Each Site:** Picnic table, concrete patio, grill (at full-hookup sites only). **Dump Station:** No. **Laundry:** Yes, coin operated. **Pay Phone:** Yes. **Restrooms and Showers:** Yes. **Fuel:** No. **Propane:** Exchange only. **Internal Roads:** Gravel. **RV Service:** Mechanic on call. **Market:** Yes. **Restaurant:** 6 mi. south in Guntersville. **General Store:** Country store 1 mi., Wal-Mart 15 mi. south in Guntersville. **Vending:** Yes. **Swimming:** Pool. **Playground:** Yes. **Other:** Marina, boat launch, 86-slip covered pier, fishing pier, indoor & outdoor pools, spa, sauna, game room, club house w/ great hall, exercise room, library, TV/card room, Florida room, dining room, chapel, activity pavilion. **Activities:** Tennis, shuffleboard, basketball, horseshoes, mini-golf, fishing, boating, swimming, canoeing, volleyball, tennis, badminton. **Nearby Attractions:** Cathedral Caverns, Huntsville Space Museum, Lake Guntersville State Park, TVA Guntersville Dam, Depot Museum. **Additional Information:** Guntersville Chamber of Commerce, (256) 582-3612.

RESTRICTIONS

Pets: On leash only. **Fires:** Grill only. **Alcoholic Beverages:** At site only. **Vehicle Maximum Length:** 45 ft.

TO GET THERE

Take AL 79 or I-59 then US 431 to Guntersville. From Guntersville take AL 227 South to Five Points Store, turn left at Five Points Store. Go 0.5 mi. to resort.

HUNTSVILLE MAP, A-2
Monte Sano State Park

5105 Nolen Ave., 35801. T: (256) 534-3757; www.alapark.com.

🚐 ★★★★ ⛺ ★★★★

Beauty: ★★★★	Site Privacy: ★★★★
Spaciousness: ★★★★	Quiet: ★★★★
Security: ★★★★	Cleanliness: ★★★★
Insect Control: ★★★★	Facilities: ★★★★

This flat campground on top of Monte Sano features lovely hardwoods with foliage between all campsites. In some instances, sites are very secluded by dense foliage. Site size is ample, and parking is mostly back-in. Four pull-throughs (numbers 14, 30, 62, and 82) are extremely large. Parking spaces are fine gravel. The prettiest sites are odd numbers 49–61 and only have water and electric hookups. Avoid sites 31–44, as they parallel a noisy road. The campground is laid out in two loops, each having its own bathhouse. With over 32 miles of trails, Monte Sano is a hiker's heaven. This suburban park lies just outside of Huntsville city limits and is popular with the locals. Monte Sano Mountain has an elevation of approximately 1,500 feet, and stays about five degrees Fahrenheit cooler than Huntsville proper, making the park a fine summer destination. The park gates lock at night, but its suburban location necessitates caution with your valuables.

BASICS

Operated By: Alabama State Parks. **Open:** All year. **Site Assignment:** First come, first served; no reservations taken except for groups. Individuals must request cottages. **Registration:** At camp store, night registration available until 9 p.m. **Fee:** Full hookup, $18.90; water/electric, $16.80; primitive, $10.50. **Parking:** At site, overflow parking available.

FACILITIES

Number of RV-only Sites: 9. **Number of Tent-only Sites:** 20. **Hookups:** Electric (30 amps), water, sewer. **Each Site:** Picnic table, fire ring, grill. **Dump Station:** Yes. **Laundry:** Yes. **Pay Phone:** Yes. **Restrooms and Showers:** Yes. **Fuel:** No. **Propane:** No. **Internal Roads:** Paved. **RV Service:** 8 mi. south in Huntsville. **Market:** 6 mi. south in Huntsville. **Restaurant:** 6 mi. south in Huntsville. **General Store:** Inquire at campground. **Vending:** Yes. **Swimming:** No. **Playground:** Yes. **Other:** Japanese Gardens, 32 mi. of hiking trials, planetarium, camp store, amphitheater, cottage rentals. **Activities:** Hiking, walking, biking. **Nearby Attractions:** Huntsville: U.S. Space & Rocket Center, Huntsville Museum of Art, Twickenham Historic District, Alabama Constitution Village, Cathedral Caverns, Children's Museum, Alabama State Black Archives Research Center & Museum, Burritt Museum. **Additional Information:** Huntsville CVB, (800) SPACE-4-U.

RESTRICTIONS

Pets: On leash only; no pets in cottages. **Fires:** Fire ring only. **Alcoholic Beverages:** Not allowed. **Vehicle Maximum Length:** No limit. **Other:** 14-night stay-limit.

TO GET THERE

From I-65, take Exit 340 and go east on I-565 to Huntsville. From I-565 take Exit 17 and go east on Governor's Dr. Go through Huntsville and turn left onto Monte Sano Blvd. At the top of the mountain, turn right onto Nolen St. The park entrance is ahead.

JASPER — MAP, B-2
Clear Creek Recreation Area

reserve america

8079 Fall City Rd., 35501. T: (205) 384-4792 or (877) 444-6777; www.reserveamerica.com.

🚐 ★★★★★   ⛺ ★★★★★

Beauty: ★★★★★	Site Privacy: ★★★★★
Spaciousness: ★★★★★	Quiet: ★★★★★
Security: ★★★★★	Cleanliness: ★★★★★
Insect Control: ★★★★	Facilities: ★★★

In the heart of William B. Bankhead National Forest, Clear Creek offers incredibly spacious sites with majestic views of Lake Lewis Smith. The campground is incredibly remote and quiet, with a dense under story providing an additional noise barrier between campsites. Each site enjoys the cooling shade of mature trees. Parking is paved, and there are both back-in and pull-through spaces. Double sites are available for large families or small groups. Tent campers should head for picturesque lakefront sites 47, 49, and 51. For RV campers, we like a number of sites, including 5, 8, 17, 18, 51, 53, 55, 81, and 82. Site 53 is a pull-through with water view. Facilities here are nice, particularly the swimming beach. Bankhead National Forest and nearby Sipsey Wilderness (35 miles from campground) offer hiking galore. Security is excellent—the park is gated at all times. Visit in late spring, early summer, and fall. Avoid holiday weekends.

BASICS

Operated By: Cradle of Forestry in America Interpretive Assoc. **Open:** Mar. 17–Oct. 27. **Site Assignment:** First come, first served; reservations up to 3 days prior to arrival. **Registration:** At gatehouse Mon.–Thurs., 7 a.m.–6 p.m.; Fri. & Sat., 7 a.m.–10 p.m.; no late registration. **Fee:** $18.90–$29.40. Golden Age/Access discount. **Parking:** Limited space at sites, all wheels must be on pavement.

FACILITIES

Number of RV-only Sites: 102. **Hookups:** Electric (30 amps), water. **Each Site:** Picnic table, grill, fire ring, lantern post, tent pad. **Dump Station:** Yes, $5 per vehicle. **Laundry:** No. **Pay Phone:** Yes. **Restrooms and Showers:** Yes. **Fuel:** No. **Propane:** No. **Internal Roads:** Paved. **RV Service:** 15 mi. in Jasper. **Market:** 15 mi. in Jasper. **Restaurant:** 5 mi. west. **General Store:** 5 mi. south. **Vending:** No. **Swimming:** Yes. **Playground:** Yes. **Other:** Boat launch. **Activities:** Lake beach, basketball, hiking, mountain biking, fishing, Interpretive programs, wildlife education. **Nearby Attractions:** Arrowhead & Twin Lakes golf, Walker County Lake, Rickwood Caverns State Park, William B. Bankhead National Forest, Smith Lake. **Additional Information:** Walker County Chamber of Commerce, (888) 384-4571.

RESTRICTIONS

Pets: On leash only. **Fires:** Fire ring only. **Alcoholic Beverages:** Not allowed. **Vehicle Maximum Length:** Varies up to 50 ft. **Other:** 14-day stay limit.

TO GET THERE

From I-65, take US 78 west 41 mi. to Jasper, then Hwy. 195 north 8 mi. Turn right on CR 27, which dead ends in 5 mi. at the park entrance.

LOWNDESBORO — MAP, C-2
Prairie Creek

reserve america

582 Prairie Creek Rd., 36752. T: (334) 418-4919; www.reserveamerica.com.

🚐 ★★★★   ⛺ ★★★★

Beauty: ★★★	Site Privacy: ★★★
Spaciousness: ★★★	Quiet: ★★★
Security: ★★★	Cleanliness: ★★★★
Insect Control: ★★★	Facilities: ★★★

Camp year-round at Prairie Creek Campground beneath the majestic moss-draped oaks on the banks of the beautiful Alabama River. For anglers and hunters, the campground offers a wonderful opportunity to relax between trips. The Lowndes Wildlife Management area is located near the campground. The Alabama River, in the U.S. state of Alabama, is formed by the Tallapoosa and Coosa rivers, which unite about 6 miles above Montgomery. It flows west as far as Selma, then southwest until, about 45 miles from Mobile, it unites with the Tombigbee to form the Mobile and Tensaw rivers, which discharge into Mobile Bay. The course of the Alabama is tortuous. Its width varies from 200 to 300 yards, and its depth from 3 to 7 feet. Its length as measured by the United States Geological Survey is 312 miles, and by steamboat measurement, 420 miles. The river crosses the richest agricultural and timber districts of the state, and railways connect it with the mineral regions of north-central Alabama. The principal tributary of the Alabama is the Cahaba River about 200 miles long, which enters it about 10 miles below Selma. Of the rivers which form the Alabama, the Coosa crosses the mineral region of Alabama, and is navigable for light-draft boats from Rome, Georgia (where it is formed by the junction of the Oostanaula and Etowah rivers) to about 117 miles above Wetumpka (about 102 miles below Rome and 26 miles below Greensport), and from Wetumpka to its junction with the Tallapoosa; the channel of the river has been considerably improved by the federal government. The navigation of the Tallapoosa River, which has its source in Paulding County, Georgia, and is about 250 miles long, is prevented by shoals and a 60-foot fall at Tallassee, a few miles north of its junction with the Coosa. The Alabama is navigable throughout the year. The river played an important role in the growth of the economy in the region during the 19th century as a source of transportation of goods. The river is still used for transportation of farming produce; however, it is not as important as it was due to the presence of roads and railways.

BASICS

Operated By: U.S. Army Corps of Engineers. **Open:** All year. **Site Assignment:** Reservations must be made at least 2 days in advance. **Registration:** At office. **Fee:** Single, $12–$16. **Parking:** At site.

FACILITIES

Number of Multipurpose Sites: 440. **Hookups:** Yes. **Dump Station:** Yes. **Laundry:** Yes. **Pay Phone:** Yes. **Restrooms and Showers:** Yes. **Fuel:** No. **Propane:** No. **Internal Roads:** Paved. **RV Service:** No. **Market:** No. **Restaurant:** No. **General Store:** No. **Vending:** No. **Swimming:** Nearby. **Playground:** Yes. **Activities:** Basketball, biking, birdwatching, boating, canoeing, fishing, jet skiing, photography, sightseeing, water skiing, & wildlife viewing.

RESTRICTIONS

Pets: Pets must be restrained or on a leash at all times while in developed recreation areas. **Fires:** In fire rings, stoves, grills, or fireplaces provided for that purpose. **Alcoholic Beverages:** Not allowed. **Vehicle Maximum Length:** Call ahead.

TO GET THERE

From Montgomery, follow US 80 west, approximately 25 mi., turn right on CR 29, and follow the signs. From Selma, follow US 80 east for 25 mi., turn left on CR 23, and follow the signs.

MOBILE
Chickasabogue Park and Campground

MAP, D-1

reserve america

760 Aldock Rd., 36613. T: (251) 574-2267; www.reserveamerica.com.

🚐 ★★★★   ▲ ★★★★

Beauty: ★★★★	Site Privacy: ★★★★
Spaciousness: ★★★★	Quiet: ★★★★
Security: ★★★	Cleanliness: ★★★
Insect Control: ★★	Facilities: ★★★

Operated by the Mobile County Commission, Chickasabogue Park campground includes 47 incredibly spacious sites. Most of the sites are pull-throughs, with plenty of shade and privacy provided by magnolia and post and live oak complete with Spanish moss. These surprisingly lovely sites have gravel parking. Tent campers should head for sites 40–47. RV campers should try sites 1–13, which are commodious, private and attractive pull-throughs. The campground includes a group camp and three other areas. The washhouses are nothing to write home about. Bring your own Lysol. This suburban park offers plenty of outdoor activities including an 18-hole disc-golf course. Gates are not locked at night, but rangers patrol hourly, making security acceptable. The Mobile Bay should be avoided in July and August when heat and humidity can be unbearable.

BASICS

Operated By: Mobile County Commission. **Open:** All year. **Site Assignment:** First come, first served; reservations accepted w/ 1-night fee deposit by check or credit card. **Registration:** At camp store; w/ security guard after hours. **Fee:** Tent, $19; full hookup, $18; water/electric, $15. Fee includes 4 people. **Parking:** At site.

FACILITIES

Number of RV-only Sites: 47. **Number of Multipurpose Sites:** 21. **Hookups:** Electric (30, 50 amps), water, 24 sites w/ sewer. **Each Site:** Picnic table, fire ring, grill. **Dump Station:** Yes. **Laundry:** Yes. **Pay Phone:** Yes. **Restrooms and Showers:** Yes. **Fuel:** No. **Propane:** No. **Internal Roads:** Paved. **RV Service:** 5 mi. north in Saraland. **Market:** 5 mi. north in Saraland. **Restaurant:** 5 mi. north in Saraland. **General Store:** Camp store in park, Walmart 5 mi. north in Saraland. **Vending:** Yes. **Swimming:** Yes. **Playground:** Yes. **Other:** Canoe rentals, boat ramp, 18-hole disc-golf course, picnic area, sports field, nature center. **Activities:** Boating, hiking, biking. **Nearby Attractions:** USS *Alabama*, Dauphin Island Sea Lab, Mobile attractions. **Additional Information:** Mobile Convention & Visitors Corporation, (800) 5-MOBILE.

RESTRICTIONS

Pets: On leash only. **Fires:** In grills, fire rings only. **Alcoholic Beverages:** At site only. **Vehicle Maximum Length:** No limit. **Other:** 2-week stay limit in summertime.

TO GET THERE

From I-65 take Exit 13. If coming from the north, cross AL 158 (Industrial Rd.) and then turn left onto AL. 213 South (Shelton Beach Rd.). If coming from the south, turn left onto AL 158 (Industrial Rd.) and then left again onto AL 213 South. Go south on AL 213 for 2 mi. At the first flashing light turn left onto Whistler St. Take the second left onto Aldock Rd. Go 1 mi. to the park entrance.

MONTGOMERY
Gunter Hill

MAP, C-2

reserve america

561 Booth Rd., 36108. T: (334) 872-9554; www.reserveamerica.com.

🚐 ★★★★   ▲ ★★★★

Beauty: ★★★	Site Privacy: ★★★
Spaciousness: ★★★	Quiet: ★★★
Security: ★★★	Cleanliness: ★★★★
Insect Control: ★★★	Facilities: ★★

Gunter Hill Campground offers the peaceful scene of trees and nature overlooking the backwaters of the Alabama River. The fishing is excellent, providing challenges for the master angler as well as the occasional cane pole. The park also provides good bow-hunting opportunities for whitetail deer. The Alabama River, in the U.S. state of Alabama, is formed by the Tallapoosa and Coosa rivers, which unite about 6 miles above Montgomery. It flows west as far as Selma, then southwest until, about 45 miles from Mobile, it unites with the Tombigbee to form the Mobile and Tensaw rivers, which discharge into Mobile Bay. The course of the Alabama is tortuous. Its width varies from 200 to 300 yards, and its depth from 3 to 7 feet. Its length as measured by the United States Geological Survey is 312 miles, and by steamboat measurement, 420 miles. The river crosses the richest agricultural and timber districts of the state, and railways connect it with the mineral regions of north-central Alabama. The principal tributary of the Alabama is the Cahaba River about 200 miles long, which enters it about 10 miles below Selma. Of the rivers which form the Alabama, the Coosa crosses the mineral region of Alabama, and is navigable for light-draft boats from Rome, Georgia (where it is formed by the junction of the Oostanaula and Etowah rivers) to about 117 miles above Wetumpka (about 102 miles below Rome and 26 miles below Greensport), and from Wetumpka to its junction with the Tallapoosa; the channel of the river has been considerably improved by the federal government. The navigation of the Tallapoosa River, which has its source in Paulding County, Georgia, and is about 250 miles long, is prevented by shoals and a 60-foot fall at Tallassee, a few miles north of its junction with the Coosa. The Alabama is navigable throughout the year. The river played an important role in the growth of the economy in the region during the 19th century as a source of transportation of goods. The river is still used for transportation of farming produce; however, it is not as important as it was due to the presence of roads and railways.

BASICS

Operated By: U.S. Army Corps of Engineers. **Open:** All year. **Site Assignment:** Reservations must be made at least 2 days in advance. **Registration:** At office. **Fee:** Single, $16. **Parking:** At site.

FACILITIES

Number of Multipurpose Sites: 294. **Hookups:** Yes. **Dump Station:** Yes. **Laundry:** Yes. **Pay Phone:** Yes. **Restrooms and Showers:** Yes. **Fuel:** No. **Propane:** No. **Internal Roads:** Paved. **RV Service:** No. **Market:** No. **Restaurant:** No. **General Store:** Yes. **Vending:** No. **Swimming:** No. **Playground:** Yes. **Activities:** Fishing.

RESTRICTIONS

Pets: Pets must be restrained or on a leash at all times while in developed recreation areas. **Fires:** In fire rings, stoves, grills, or fireplaces provided for that purpose. **Alcoholic Beverages:** Not allowed. **Vehicle Maximum Length:** Call ahead. **Other:** No off-road driving; no ATVs allowed in park areas.

TO GET THERE

From I-65, take Exit 167 onto US 80 west for 9 mi. Turn right on CR 7. Follow signs into the campground.

PELHAM
Oak Mountain State Park

MAP, B-2

P.O. Box 278, 200 Terrace Dr., 35124. T: (205) 620-2520; www.alapark.com/parks.

🚐 ★★★★   ▲ ★★★★

Beauty: ★★★	Site Privacy: ★★★
Spaciousness: ★★★	Quiet: ★★★★
Security: ★★★	Cleanliness: ★★★
Insect Control: ★★★	Facilities: ★★★★★

While reasonably attractive, Oak Mountain State park doesn't boast the most gorgeous campground in the state. The camp sites are a little ghostly—we could tell that they used to be lovely. Sites are situated in two main areas, within which site shape, size and privacy vary immensely. Area A contains 71 sites, 24 of which have full hookups. Area A is prettier, shadier and more woodsy than B, which has 72 sites crammed into half the space of A. In fact, most of area B is downright unattractive, with the exception of tent sites B6, B8, B64, and B65. All RV parking is on untidy gravel and both areas have back-in and pull-through parking. Oak Mountain is exceptional for its proximity to Birmingham. It's a good place to stay while visiting Birmingham, and it's also the favored outdoor playground for the city's natives. This means that hiking, mountain biking, and other activities may not provide the solitude we would expect at other parks. Still, the park's broad offering of activities and its proximity to a number of restaurants and attractions make it a good choice for a visit. Security at Oak Mountain is fair. The back gate is never staffed, but both gates are locked at night. Avoid Oak Mountain State Park like the plague on holiday weekends and during the hotter summer months.

BASICS

Operated By: Alabama State Parks. **Open:** All year. **Site Assignment:** Reservations required for weekends & holidays, 2-night min. stay weekends, 3-night minimum holiday weekends (Memorial Day, Labor Day, & July 4th). **Registration:** At country store. **Fee:** Full hookup, $17; water/electric, $15; tent, $11; fee includes 3 people; $2.22 per extra person; senior discount (over 65). **Parking:** Limit 2 cars per site.

FACILITIES

Number of Tent-only Sites: 60. **Number of Multipurpose Sites:** 85. **Hookups:** Electric (30 amps), water, sewer. **Each Site:** Picnic table, grill, fire ring, lantern pole. **Dump Station:** Yes. **Laundry:** Yes. **Pay Phone:** Yes. **Restrooms and Showers:** Yes. **Fuel:** No. **Propane:** No. **Internal Roads:** Paved & gravel. **RV Service:** 2 mi. southwest. **Market:** 3 mi. southwest in Pelham. **Restaurant:** 3 mi. southwest in Pelham. **General Store:** Wal-Mart 6 mi. east in Inverness. **Vending:** Beverages. **Swimming:** Yes. **Playground:** Yes. **Other:** Boat ramp, lake beach, snack bar, petting zoo, information center, stables, marina, boat rental (no gasoline boats allowed on lake), tennis courts, BMX track, picnic area, Alabama Wildlife Rescue Center, 18-hole golf course, sports fields, picnic shelters. **Activities:** Horseback riding, hiking, mountain biking, fishing. **Nearby Attractions:** Vision Land, Birmingham Zoo & Botanical Gardens, Birmingham Museum of Art, Alabama Jazz Hall of Fame, Birmingham Civil Rights Institute, Sloss Furnaces, Galleria Shopping Mall. **Additional Information:** Birmingham CVB, (205) 458-8001; Hoover Chamber of Commerce, (205) 988-5672.

RESTRICTIONS

Pets: On leash only. **Fires:** Grill, fire rings only. **Alcoholic Beverages:** At site only. **Vehicle Maximum Length:** 56 ft. **Other:** 14-day stay limit.

TO GET THERE

From I-65, take Exit 246 and go west on US 119. Take an immediate left onto State Park Rd. Drive for 3.5 mi. to a 4-way stop. Turn left onto Findlay Dr. The main park gate is ahead. Go 5.5 mi. past the gate to Campground Rd. and turn left.

PICKENSVILLE   MAP, B-1
Aliceville Lake

reserve america

Pickensville Recreation Area, 61 Camping Rd., 35447. T: (205) 373-6328; www.reserveamerica.com.

🚐 ★★★★   ▲ ★★★★

Beauty: ★★★★   Site Privacy: ★★★★
Spaciousness: ★★★★   Quiet: ★★★★
Security: ★★★★★   Cleanliness: ★★★★
Insect Control: ★★   Facilities: ★★★

The necessity of a waterway connecting the Tennessee River to Mobile Bay was noted as far back as 1770, when the Marquis de Montcalm made a report to King Louis XV. Since before Alabama attained statehood, governors have asked Congress to fund such a project. Finally completed in 1985, the Tennessee-Tombigbee Waterway currently flows south from the Tennessee River. Aliceville Lake is now one of many recreation destinations along the Tenn-Tom. Straddling the Alabama–Mississippi border, the lake provides fishing, swimming, and other activities. The Pickensville campground consists of 176 sites laid out in three loops and two spurs. Though mostly flat, the campground is very attractive. Sites are shaded by a variety of tree species, and the water's edge is graced with lovely cypress trees. All roads and parking spaces are paved. Most of the sites offer back-in parking and a good deal of privacy. Eight pull-through sites are gigantic, but lacking in privacy. Riverside sites, numbered 105–138, have the nicest views of the water. Built next to a cypress-lined creek, sites 49–61 are also very pretty. Security at Pickensville Campground is outstanding, with 24-hour gate attendance. We recommend avoiding this area in July and August when insects, heat, and humidity can be oppressive.

BASICS

Operated By: U.S. Army Corps of Engineers. **Open:** All year. **Site Assignment:** First come, first served; reservations accepted through National Recreation Reservation Service (NRRS) at (877) 444-6777 or www.recreation.gov; reservations can be made up to 240 days in advance, full payment required upon making reservation; credit card preferred (V, MC, D, AE), or pay by money order if at least 21 days in advance of arrival; $10 fee for cancellation or change of site or dates; cancellation w/in 3 days of arrival charged 1-night, no-show charged $20 plus first night. **Registration:** At gatehouse. **Fee:** $18–$22. **Parking:** 2 vehicles per site, additional charge for more vehicles.

FACILITIES

Number of Multipurpose Sites: 176. **Hookups:** Electric (30, 50 amps), water, some sewer. **Each Site:** Picnic table, grill, fire ring, lantern post, concrete pads. **Dump Station:** Yes. **Laundry:** Yes. **Pay Phone:** Yes. **Restrooms and Showers:** Yes. **Fuel:** No. **Propane:** No. **Internal Roads:** Paved. **RV Service:** 25 mi. north in Columbus, MS. **Market:** 15 mi. southeast in Aliceville. **Restaurant:** 3 mi. east in Pickensville. **General Store:** 3 mi. east in Pickensville. **Vending:** Beverages. **Swimming:** Beach. **Playground:** Yes. **Other:** Boat launch, fish-cleaning station, picnic shelters, group campfire ring, game courts, swimming beach, wildlife viewing area. **Activities:** Fishing, tennis, volleyball, basketball, boating, walking trails. **Nearby Attractions:** Antebellum Visitors Center in Pickensville, U.S. Snagboat *Montgomery*, Aliceville Museum & Cultural Arts Center w/ German POW Camp, attractions in Columbus, MS. **Additional Information:** Aliceville Chamber of Commerce, (205) 373-2820.

RESTRICTIONS

Pets: On leash only, not allowed on beach. **Fires:** Fire rings, grills only. **Alcoholic Beverages:** Not allowed. **Vehicle Maximum Length:** No limit. **Other:** Title 36 policies apply, inquire at campground.

TO GET THERE

From Tuscaloosa, take US 82 west 20 mi. to AL 86. Go southwest 24 mi. to Pickensville. Continue 3 mi. west to the Recreation Area. From Columbus, MS take MS 69, which becomes AL 14, to Pickensville. Turn right onto AL 86, and go 3 mi. west to the Recreation Area. The entrance is on the right.

ROGERSVILLE   MAP, A-2
Joe Wheeler State Park

201 McLean Dr., 35652. T: (256) 247-5466 or (256) 247-5461; www.joewheelersstatepark.com.

🚐 ★★★★★   ▲ ★★★★★

Beauty: ★★★★★   Site Privacy: ★★★★
Spaciousness: ★★★★   Quiet: ★★★
Security: ★★★★★   Cleanliness: ★★★★
Insect Control: ★★★   Facilities: ★★★★★

Straddling Wheeler Lake, and connected by a bridge over Wheeler Dam, Joe Wheeler State Park is a favorite among anglers. A variety of fish species is found in the lake. Two boat launches serve Wheeler Lake, and a third provides access to adjoining Wilson Lake. A marina store augments the fishing experience with fuel and supplies. Joe Wheeler State Park provides a variety of activities on land as well as facilities for large groups. The campground is laid out in three loops with 116 improved sites, and one loop with primitive sites. Site size is ample but not outstanding. Parking is paved and most sites are back-in. The prettiest sites, 9, 10, 22, 24, and 26, have partial views of Lake Wheeler. The campground is surrounded by lovely thick woods, which provide shade at most sites but very little privacy between sites. The tent camping area consists of a nicely wooded loop of gravel road surrounded by trash cans and fire rings. Like many exceedingly attractive tent areas, there are no designated sites. This remote state park is gated and guarded, making security outstanding. Avoid late summer heat and humidity at Joe Wheeler State Park; plan a visit in spring, early summer, or fall.

BASICS

Operated By: Alabama State Parks. **Open:** All year. **Site Assignment:** First come, first served; reservations recommended Mar. 1–Oct. 31, 2-night minimum required & 3 nights on holidays. **Registration:** At campground office; security will register late-comers. **Fee:** Improved, $19.80; primitive, $11; V, MC, AE. **Parking:** At sites, limit 2 cars per site.

FACILITIES

Number of Multipurpose Sites: 116. **Hookups:** Electric (20, 30 amps), water, sewer. **Each Site:** Picnic table, grill. **Dump Station:** Yes. **Laundry:** Yes. **Pay Phone:** Yes. **Restrooms and Showers:** Yes. **Fuel:** Boat fuel. **Propane:** No. **Internal Roads:** Paved. **RV Service:** 15 mi. west toward Florence. **Market:** 4 mi. east in Rogersville. **Restaurant:** In park. **General Store:** Camp store. **Vending:** Yes. **Swimming:** Beach. **Playground:** Yes. **Other:** Marina, boat ramps, boat fuel, sandy beach, 18-hole golf course, group meeting room & lodge, resort lodge, picnic pavilions. **Activities:** Boating (rentals available), swimming, hiking trails, tennis, basketball, golf. **Nearby Attractions:** Athens, W.C. Handy Birthplace Museum & Library in Florence, Civil War Walking Trail, Cook's Natural Science Museum, Oakville Indian Park & Museum. **Additional Information:** Decatur/Morgan County CVB, (256) 350-2028.

RESTRICTIONS

Pets: On leash only. **Fires:** In grills, fire rings only. **Alcoholic Beverages:** Not allowed. **Vehicle Maximum Length:** 50 ft. **Other:** 2-week stay limit per site.

TO GET THERE

From I-65, take Hwy. 72 west for 22 mi. The Park entrance is on the left 2 mi. west of Rogersville. The campground is 3 mi. inside the park.

TALLADEGA   MAP, B-2, B-3
Logan Landing RV Resort and Campground

1036 Paul Bear Bryant Blvd., 35014. T: (256) 268-0045 or (888) 564-2671; www.loganlanding.com.

🚐 ★★★   ⛺ ★★★

Beauty: ★★★	Site Privacy: ★★★
Spaciousness: ★★★	Quiet: ★★★
Security: ★★★★	Cleanliness: ★★★
Insect Control: ★★★	Facilities: ★★★

Attractive and clean with friendly owners, Logan Landing is a good choice if you plan on spending a few days in the area. The campground offers boating and other activities and drive times are short to Logan Martin Lake, De Soto Caverns, and Talladega Superspeedway. Cheaha State Park can be reached in less than one hour. Because this is a popular recreation area, summer weekends are busy. By all means avoid the two biggest race weekends at Talladega Superspeedway—the Die Hard 500 in April and the Winston 500 in October. If you want to stay here on a race weekend, make advance reservations. Two camping areas are situated next to a small private lake. Section A contains no lakefront sites and may be preferred by tent campers because the sites are wooded. We prefer section B for RVs because sites are generally larger and more level. Even-numbered sites 58–80 have lake-views but little shade. As you move away from the lake in Section B, sites become shadier. Each of the midsized sites in section B has gravel parking and a cement patio. Section C is unattractive. The variety of tree species in the campground includes some dogwoods. Of the 145 campsites, only a few are pull-throughs. With its remote location in Alpine, Alabama, and gated entrance, this campground has very good security.

BASICS

Operated By: Gerald & Helen Rossman. **Open:** All year. **Site Assignment:** First come, first served;

reservations accepted for holiday weekends & recommended for Talladega Superspeedway race weekends. **Registration:** At office in camp store. **Fee:** Full hookup, $27.50; water/electric, $25.50; primitive, $20.50. **Parking:** At sites.

FACILITIES

Number of RV-only Sites: 140. **Number of Tent-only Sites:** 30. **Number of Multipurpose Sites:** 40. **Hookups:** Electric (30, 50 amps), water, some sewer. **Each Site:** Picnic table, grill (most sites), fire ring. **Dump Station:** Yes. **Laundry:** Yes. **Pay Phone:** Yes. **Restrooms and Showers:** Yes. **Fuel:** No. **Propane:** No. **Internal Roads:** Gravel. **RV Service:** 11 mi. north in Pell City. **Market:** 11 mi. north in Pell City. **Restaurant:** 3 mi. north. **General Store:** Yes. **Vending:** Inquire at campground. **Swimming:** Yes (no lifeguard). **Playground:** Yes. **Other:** Private lake, boat ramp, paddle boats, canoes, enclosed pavilion. **Activities:** Fishing, croquet, horseshoes, Lake Logan Martin swimming beach, live music, volleyball, planned activities on weekends. **Nearby Attractions:** Talladega Superspeedway (NASCAR), De Soto Caverns, Davey Allison Park, Kymulga Grist Mill & Covered Bridge, Cheaha State Park, Barber Motorcycle Speedway & Museum. **Additional Information:** Talladega Chamber of Commerce, (256) 362-9075.

RESTRICTIONS

Pets: On leash only. **Fires:** Fire ring, grill only. **Alcoholic Beverages:** At site only. **Vehicle Maximum Length:** 50 ft.

TO GET THERE

From I-20, take Exit 158 at Pell City. Go south on US 231 to Hwy. 34 and turn left. Go to Hwy. 207 and turn right (south). Take Hwy. 207 to Hwy. 54, turn right at Bama Grocery store. Follow signs for 2 mi. and turn right onto Paul Bear Bryant Rd. The campground is about 1 mi. ahead on the right.

WILMER   MAP, D-1
Escatawpa Hollow Campground

15551 Moffett Rd., 36587. T: (251) 649-4233.

🚐 ★★★★   ⛺ ★★★★

Beauty: ★★★★	Site Privacy: ★★★
Spaciousness: ★★★	Quiet: ★★★
Security: ★★★★	Cleanliness: ★★★
Insect Control: ★★★	Facilities: ★★★★

If your kids are the strong-swimming adventurous types, they will delight in the river and woods at

Escatawpa Hollow. In the vernacular of youth, "this place is cool!" Because of its popularity with gregarious families, this campground is anything but quiet on summer weekends. The picturesque private campground is situated on the bank of the Escatawpa River near the Alabama–Mississippi border. An exceptionally clean blackwater river, the Escatawpa here is lined with white-sand beach, creating a delightful swimming area. The bream, catfish, and bass in the river are purported to be the best-tasting in the state (if you can catch them). Paddlers enjoy the mellow flat-water of the Escatawpa. Boat rental and shuttle arrangements are available at the campground.

BASICS

Operated By: Larry & Janice Godfrey. **Open:** All year. **Site Assignment:** First come, first served; reservations accepted; deposit required on holidays; 2-day notice for refund. **Registration:** At office. **Fee:** $12–$22. **Parking:** 2 vehicles per site, overflow parking available.

FACILITIES

Hookups: Electric (20, 30 amps), water. **Each Site:** Picnic table, most sites have a grill. **Dump Station:** Yes. **Laundry:** No. **Pay Phone:** No. **Restrooms and Showers:** Yes. **Fuel:** No. **Propane:** No. **Internal Roads:** Most paved, some gravel & dirt. **RV Service:** 15 mi. southeast in Mobile. **Market:** 4 mi. east in Wilmer. **Restaurant:** 4 mi. east in Wilmer. **General Store:** Camp store, 1 mi. **Vending:** Yes. **Swimming:** Beach. **Playground:** No. **Other:** Canoe & tube rentals, canoe trips including shuttle service (reservations required), walking trails, rope swings. **Activities:** River swimming, canoeing, kayaking, fishing, golfing, swinging. **Nearby Attractions:** Bellingrath Gardens in Theodore, Robert Trent Jones Golf Trail, USS *Alabama*, Mobile attractions, HQH Western World Zoo. **Additional Information:** Mobile Convention & Visitors Corporation, (800) 5-MOBILE.

RESTRICTIONS

Pets: In RV sites only, on leash only. **Fires:** At tent sites only. **Alcoholic Beverages:** Not allowed. **Vehicle Maximum Length:** No limit. **Other:** Tent sites max. 1 week stay; read all warnings concerning river swimming.

TO GET THERE

From I-65, take Exit 5B at Moffett Rd. and US 98. Go 22 mi. west on US 98 to the 0-mile marker at the Mississippi state line. The park entrance is on the left.

Alaska

Alaska, seemingly the granddaddy of destinations for RVers and campers, lives up to its reputation as the last frontier in several ways. Glaciers, mountains, crystal-clear streams, and wildlife appear as otherworldy entities that make you reconsider your standard perceptions of an untamed wild. However, in this state you will also be entering another world of RV parks and campgrounds. After you cross the mountainous border, you notice that the quality of both state and private campgrounds changes dramatically. Here, many private RV parks look like they were constructed hastily, without consideration for aesthetics and privacy. Bulldozed lots that sandwich vehicles together are more standard than not. State campgrounds and facilities don't fare much better for RVers. Although generally more private, they tend to have bumpy roads, uneven campsites accommodating only the shortest of vehicles, few facilities, and no hookups.

Primitive though the campgrounds may be, they are nothing compared to the road system. Although most of the state's main roads are now paved (some just recently), what is considered a highway in Alaska is a backcountry road to the rest of the nation. Except for Anchorage and Fairbanks, even modern thoroughfares are mostly narrow, single lanes without shoulders, curb banks, or passing areas. Factor in the many unexpected curves, a stargazing trucker in front of you, slower speed limits, or the occasional moose blocking the way, and your travel time increases significantly. As a general rule, it would be very difficult to cover more than 300 miles in one day if you planned on making any pit stops. A three-week minimum stay is recommended to see Alaska, though travel agencies and tour guides say at least two months. Visitors are always surprised just how far it is from one civilized destination to another and how slow the pace can be. However, your trip will be worth every pothole, irregular campsite, and outhouse. Alaska is worth every square foot you drive.

If you're the adventuresome type and need a distraction from all the distractions, the 49th state has a few peculiarities for your fancy. If in Nome on the Seward Peninsula around Labor Day, make plans to attend the **Great American Bathtub Race.** If heading back east at the start of March, and you enjoy seeing frozen water get sculpted, Fairbanks holds the annual **World Ice Art Championships.** Arriving early could mean witnessing an ice harvest from O'Grady Pond. Still around Fairbanks in July? Might as well attend the city's **Golden Days** festival to witness the hairy chest, legs, and beard contest or the rubber duck race on the Chena River. To see the northernmost totem pole in the world, though, you'll have to head due north to **Barrow Point,** the northernmost inhabited locale in the United States.

The scenery in Alaska is unrivaled, and you will find yourself gasping and holding your breath countless times a day. Just when you begin to think you've captured the mountains from every possible angle, suddenly you turn a corner to see a heart-stopping scene that makes you feel like you're the first to glimpse these giant rocky wonders. The massive hanging and piedmont glaciers are visible right from the highway; the turquoise water of the lakes and streams, sprawling forests of spruce and birch, and seemingly endless fields of wildflowers all conspire to woo you.

In addition, if viewing wildlife is your goal, there is nowhere better than Alaska. Wake up very early to increase your chances of seeing moose by the roadside. Besides moose, there are caribou, Dall sheep, 300 varieties of migrating birds, whales, wolves, foxes, coyotes, and bears—just some of the animals you have a chance of glimpsing on your trip. If it's fish you came here for, then welcome, anglers, to the state where the fabled 98.5-pound king salmon and 395-pound halibut were caught. Fishing opportunities are as bountiful as mosquitoes are chummy in this state.

Campground Profiles

ANCHORAGE   MAP, B-3
Anchorage RV Park

reserve *america*

1200 North Muldoon Rd., 99506.
T: (800) 400-7275; www.reserveamerica.com.

🚐 ★★★★   ▲ n/a

Beauty: ★★★   Site Privacy: ★★★
Spaciousness: ★★★ Quiet: ★★★★
Security: ★★★   Cleanliness: ★★★★★
Insect Control: ★★ Facilities: ★★★★★

Anchorage RV Park, located 15 minutes east of downtown, takes camping in Alaska to an entirely new level. This immaculate and well-maintained campground spoils RV travelers for all other parks. With 195 full-hookup sites, one might think that campers feel overcrowded here; however, plenty of birch and spruce trees, coupled with manicured flower gardens, make it easy to forget that you are at the largest campground in the state's largest city. And besides, one can always seek reprieve in the cedar-lined lounge area, where a fireplace, television, games, books, and coffee make guests feel like they are back home in their living rooms. For travelers who don't want to waste time shopping, Anchorage RV Park has a general store and gift shop right on the premises. And for those who can't quite get used to the cooler temperatures of the state, Anchorage RV Park offers bathrooms with heated floors to keep those toes toasty. Both back-in and pull-through sites are available, although the latter are a bit more expensive. We preferred the most wooded sites, numbers 101 through 115, but keep in mind these are quite far from the restrooms and showers. Anchorage RV Park is located adjacent to Elmendorf Air Force Base, so if you hear a deep rumble, look up for F-16s flying daily maneuvers. Also keep your eyes peeled for the fox and moose that like this part of town.

BASICS

Operated By: CIRI Alaska Tourism. **Open:** May 15–Sept. 15 or later depending on the weather. **Site Assignment:** 24-hour advance notice of cancellation required. **Registration:** At office; 7 a.m.–10 p.m. If you arrive after hours, a map w/ site assignment will be posted on the door & payment can be settled by 8 a.m. the next morning. If you don't have a reservation, maps w/ highlighted available spaces. **Fee:** $41–$45; rates vary according to season. **Parking:** At site.

FACILITIES

Number of RV-only Sites: 195. **Hookups:** Electric (20, 30, 50 amps), water, sewer, cable TV, phone. **Each Site:** Picnic table, barbecue pavilion. **Dump Station:** Yes. **Laundry:** Yes, coin operated washers & dryers cost $1.50. Laundry soap & change dispensers are available. **Pay Phone:** Yes, several w/ a terrace & chairs. **Restrooms and Showers:** Yes. Facilities are clean, modern & heated. **Fuel:** Available 3 mi. down the road at Muldoon Texaco. **Propane:** Available at Muldoon Texaco. **Internal Roads:** Paved & gravel, pristine condition. **RV Service:** There are several service centers in Anchorage; some have mechanics that will come to you. Inquire in the office. **Market:** Grocery store w/in 1 mi. **Restaurant:** Several to choose from in Anchorage. Ask for suggestions at the front office. **General Store:** Yes. **Vending:** Soft drink, candy, & newspaper dispensers located by the restrooms. **Swimming:** No. **Playground:** No. **Other:** There is a covered picnic & grill area on the west side of the campground, cable connections. **Activities:** Trails & picnics. **Nearby Attractions:** The Native Heritage Center is just across the street, & downtown Anchorage is a 15-minute drive. There is also a paved bike trail & stop for the local bus service nearby. Information on activities & a variety of brochures can be found at the front office. **Additional Information:** www.anchrvpark.com.

RESTRICTIONS

Pets: Must be leashed. Waste bags are available throughout to clean up after pets. **Fires:** Not allowed. **Alcoholic Beverages:** Prohibited in communal areas. **Vehicle Maximum Length:** No limit. **Other:** A list of rules is distributed upon check-in.

TO GET THERE

Take the Glenn Hwy. to the Muldoon North Exit. Follow Muldoon north almost to the end of the road, where you will see the Elmendorf Air Force Base gates. Turn left just before these gates at the lighted Anchorage RV Park sign.

ANCHORAGE   MAP, B-3
Granite Creek Campground

reserve *america*

Alaska Recreational Management, Inc., 800 East Diamond Blvd., 99515. T: (907) 522-8368; www.reserveamerica.com.

🚐 ★★★★   ▲ ★★★★★

Beauty: ★★★★★ Site Privacy: ★★★★★
Spaciousness: ★★★★★ Quiet: ★★★★★
Security: ★★★   Cleanliness: ★★★★
Insect Control: ★★ Facilities: ★★

If you are looking for a truly Alaskan camping experience, Granite Creek campground, tucked into a trio of Chugach mountain peaks, will not disappoint you. This campground is only a half-mile off the Seward Hwy.; but it can still be considered "off the beaten track," since Anchorage locals tend to occupy the campground on weekends, and out-of-state visitors rarely find their way here. You'll have to come prepared with plenty of food and fuel (as well as mosquito spray from mid-June to mid-July) because you will not find convenience stores or other amenities for at least 25 miles in any direction. However, the nature-lover will be entertained merely by listening to the rushing waters of Granite Creek, taking in the stunning views of the Chugach mountains, or identifying the lush variety of wildflowers that fill in the gaps between spruce trees. All sites are back-in, spacious, and private. However, the loop layout is a bit tight for extra-long vehicles, and it is not recommended for RVs 30 feet or longer. You'll find the most impressive views at sites 8, 11, 12, and 16, although a bad site does not exist at Granite Creek campground. Chances of spotting moose are high here, particularly if you are an early riser. Ask the campsite manager where to look.

BASICS

Operated By: U.S. Forest Service. **Open:** All year; only managed/maintained from Memorial Day–Sept. 15. Sometimes snow prohibits opening until mid-June. **Site Assignment:** Reservations (must be made 5 days in advance) or first come, first served. **Registration:** Occupy a site & return to the entrance sign w/in 30 minutes, fill out a fee envelope & settle payment. Tear the stub off the envelope & make sure it is visible through your car or RV windshield. **Fee:** $10; Golden Age Passport, half price; 14-day limit per camper. **Parking:** At site.

FACILITIES

Number of RV-only Sites: 19. **Hookups:** 2 hand-operated water pumps for entire campground. **Each Site:** Picnic table, fire grate. **Dump Station:** No. **Laundry:** No. **Pay Phone:** No. **Restrooms and Showers:** 2 pit toilets cleaned & well maintained by a campground manager. **Fuel:** Girdwood, 27 mi. north, or Seward, 63 mi. south. **Propane:** No. **Internal Roads:** Gravel, sometimes impassible up until mid-June due to high snowfall in the area. **RV Service:** Girdwood, 27 mi. north, or Seward, 63 mi. south. **Market:** None in area. Go to Girdwood, 27 mi. north or Moose Pass, 34 mi. south. **Restaurant:** None in area. Go to Girdwood, 27 mi. north, Portage Lake Lodge near Portage Glacier, or Summit Lake Lodge 18 mi. south. **General Store:** None in area. Go to Girdwood, 27 mi. north, or Moose Pass, 34 mi. south. **Vending:** No. **Swimming:** No. **Playground:** No. **Other:** The Johnson Pass hiking trailhead can be found on the highway 0.5 mi. north; a great family hike. There is also an 8-mi. paved biking trail that begins there. **Activities:** Go fishing for Dolly Vardens in Granite Creek, or take a walk & look for the many moose that reside in the area; kayaking, rafting, paddling. **Nearby Attractions:** Portage Glacier & the access road to Whittier are only 30 minutes away & the gold mining town of Hope, although a 40-minute drive, would be worth an afternoon trip.

RESTRICTIONS

Pets: All pets should be leashed & under owner supervision. **Fires:** Fire grates only. **Alcoholic Beverages:** No restrictions. **Vehicle Maximum Length:** No limit (RVs over 30 ft. may have difficulties). **Other:** No more than 8 people per site. Firearms & fireworks are not allowed. Food that is not properly stored or left unattended subjects you to citation; 2 cars per group.

TO GET THERE

Take the Seward Hwy. to mi. 63.5 and look for the large blue-and-white sign for Granite Creek Campground w/ an arrow directing you to Granite Creek Rd. Follow the road approximately 0.5 mi., and you will find a large entrance sign and fee box.

ANCHORAGE MAP, B-3
Montana Creek Campground

816 Oceanview Dr., 99515.
T: (877) 475-2267;
www.montanacreekcampground.com.

🚐 ★★★★ ⛺ ★★★★

Beauty: ★★★★	Site Privacy: ★★★
Spaciousness: ★★★	Quiet: ★★★★
Security: ★★★	Cleanliness: ★★★★★
Insect Control: ★★	Facilities: ★★

If you've been traveling awhile and feel that all campgrounds look alike, Montana Creek will offer a refreshing change of pace. Attention to detail is what makes this campground stand out from the rest. Sheila Lankford, the owner and operator of the campground, tends her perennial gardens and campsite grounds personally, and vibrant displays of wildflowers and berries are sure to delight those with or without a green thumb. Sheila was born and raised on a homestead in this area, and she can offer guests great stories and solid traveling advice. Look for her with her dog, Cody. Montana Creek Campground has 18 back-in/pull-through sites with electric hookups available in a grassy area adjacent the creek. All-sized rigs can be easily accommodated here. These sites all have new fire pits and grills, as well as lanterns for the evening hours. For smaller RVs, more scenic, dry camping is available in the meandering campground loops tucked into birch and spruce woods. Campers will enjoy the private, heavily treed sites that have been uniquely named after regular guests. Our favorite spot was "Hilton's Hotel" located right next to the serene Montana Creek bed.

BASICS

Operated By: Owned & operated by Sheila Lankford; co-owned by Bill Nathis. **Open:** May–Oct.; exact days depend on snowmelt & weather conditions. **Site Assignment:** This campground is first come, first served only. Space is usually available, but it is recommended that you arrive by Fri. afternoon if you are planning to stay the weekend. **Registration:** A self-registration board & pay box are situated at the entrance of the campground. Find a site, then pay at box. **Fee:** Electric, $23; dry, $18; park & fish, $6 per day. **Parking:** At site.

FACILITIES

Hookups: 18 w/ electric (30, 50 amps); water is available near the store. **Each Site:** Picnic table, grill, lantern pole, fire pit, & some w/ electrical outlets. **Dump Station:** Available 3 mi. north at Tesoro Station or 5 mi. south at Mat-Su RV Park. **Laundry:** No. **Pay Phone:** Yes. **Restrooms and Showers:** No showers or flushable toilets. Only portables are available, but they are extremely well maintained & clean. **Fuel:** Available at Tesoro Station 3 mi. north or Ship Creek Lodge 8 mi. south. **Propane:** Available at Tesoro Station 3 mi. north or Mat-Su RV Park 5 mi. south. **Internal Roads:** Gravel, well maintained. **RV Service:** Talkeetna, 17 mi. **Market:** No. **Restaurant:** His & Hers Lounge & Restaurant located 3 mi. north. Also several restaurants to choose from in Talkeetna. The Store just north of the campground also has a small baker w/ soups & sandwiches. **General Store:** Yes. **Vending:** No. **Swimming:** No. **Playground:** No. **Other:** A paved walkway & pedestrian bridge allows guests views of Montana Creek & several access points to the creek offer excellent fishing opportunities for silvers, kings, pink (even-numbered years), grayling, & trout. A tackle shop on site offers fishing gea. **Activities:** Live music is available on the campground July 4th. Feature artists vary every year. The Talkeetna Bluegrass Festival takes place the first week of Aug. just 5 mi. north of the campground; fishing, hiking. **Nearby Attractions:** This campground is a hop, skip, & a jump from the endearing town of Talkeetna (the town which the show Northern Exposure was designed after). In addition, information is available at the campground on dog sledding, flight seeing, fishing.

RESTRICTIONS

Pets: Should be leashed at all times. **Fires:** In campground fire pits grills; forest fire conditions may trigger temporary fire restrictions. **Alcoholic Beverages:** No restrictions. **Vehicle Maximum Length:** No limit.

TO GET THERE

Take the Parks Hwy. to mi. 96.5 and look to the east. The large sign and a picnic table w/ a statue of two bear cubs sitting on it make this campground easy to find.

ANCHORAGE MAP, B-3
Williwaw Campground

reserve america

800 East Diamond Blvd., 99515. T: (877) 444-6777 or (907) 522-8368; www.reserveamerica.com.

🚐 ★★★★ ⛺ ★★★★★

Beauty: ★★★★★	Site Privacy: ★★★★★
Spaciousness: ★★★★★	Quiet: ★★★★
Security: ★★★	Cleanliness: ★★★★★
Insect Control: ★★	Facilities: ★★

Relatively new to the RV scene, this immaculate and newly paved campground is a stone's throw away from Portage and Whittier, as well as an ideal overnight stopover for travelers heading to Seward or Homer. Williwaw is a USFS campground, and therefore without hookups or other amenities—but waking up to the dynamic blue of the hanging Middle Glacier that is the campground backdrop is an experience sure to delight young and old alike. Campsites are spacious and private here and can easily accommodate the largest of RVs. With both pull-through and back-in spaces available, it is worth planning ahead and making reservations for a campsite with a view of the glacier. We recommend sites 2–6 or 34–36.

BASICS

Operated By: U.S. Forest Service. **Open:** May–Sept.; depending on weather. **Site Assignment:** By reservation (made at least 5 days in advance) or on a space-available basis. **Registration:** Occupy a site & return to the entrance sign w/in 30 minutes—fill out a fee envelope & settle payment. Tear the stub off the envelope & make sure it is visible through your RV windshield or on the front of your tent. **Fee:** $10. **Parking:** At site.

FACILITIES

Number of Multipurpose Sites: 60. **Hookups:** None. **Each Site:** Picnic table, fire pit. **Dump Station:** No. **Laundry:** No. **Pay Phone:** No, go to Portage Glacier Lodge 1.5 mi. down the road. **Restrooms and Showers:** Several pit toilets. No showers or wash facilities available. **Fuel:** None in area, fuel up in Anchorage or Girdwood before arriving. The next gas station will not be available until Seward. **Propane:** No. **Internal Roads:** Newly paved & in excellent condition. **RV Service:** No. **Market:** 10 mi. north in Girdwood. **Restaurant:** Several in Girdwood. **General Store:** The closest general store is in Girdwood, 10 mi. north. **Vending:** Soft drinks & candy machine at Portage Glacier Lodge. **Swimming:** No. **Playground:** No. **Other:** Check out the salmon-spawning viewing area adjacent the campground, or take the pleasant Williwaw Nature Trail to get a better look at the glacier. **Activities:** Bike trails, hiking, viewing the scenery. **Nearby Attractions:** Portage Lake & the Begich Boggs Visitor Center are just 1.5 mi. down the road. It is worth catching the movie Voices from the Ice at the visitor center (shown 20 minutes after every hour). Boat tours to the face of the glacier are also available. Portage road then continues to Whittier but there is a fee to drive through the tunnel. Many people catch glacier boat tours out of Whittier. **Additional Information:** www.recreation.gov.

RESTRICTIONS

Pets: All pets should be on leashed & under owner supervision. **Fires:** Fire grates only. **Alcoholic Beverages:** Inquire at campground. **Vehicle Maximum Length:** No limit.

TO GET THERE

Take the Seward Hwy. to mi. 78. Although your map may say Portage, the town was destroyed in the 1964 earthquake and only a few dilapidated remnants remain. Turn north on Portage Rd. and go 5 mi. to the Williwaw Campground sign (not to be confused w/ the Williwaw Viewing Area sign that you'll see 0.25 mi. before the campground). Turn right at the sign, and you will find the entrance board and campsite manager just down the road.

DENALI PARK MAP, B-3
Denali Grizzly Bear Cabins andCampground

Mile 231 Park Hwy., 99755.
T: (907) 683-2696 or (907) 374-8796;
www.denaligrizzlybear.com.

🚐 ★★★★ ⛺ ★★★★

Beauty: ★★★★	Site Privacy: ★★★
Spaciousness: ★★★	Quiet: ★★★★
Security: ★★★	Cleanliness: ★★★★★
Insect Control: ★★	Facilities: ★★★★

If you're looking to capture some of the hearty Alaskan spirit from the days of yore, Denali Grizzly Bear Campground will make you feel like you're back in the pioneer times. One of the highlights of this campground is chatting with the workers here. Most of them are part of the Reisland clan, descendents of the family that homesteaded this land decades ago. Siblings and cousins now run the campground in the summer, and they have gone to great lengths to preserve some of the flavor of yesteryear. Take a few moments to admire the unique Alaska paraphernalia that decorates the general store and office. Almost everything you see has a story behind it. With several thickly wooded back-in sites (and two pull-through sites) available, all-sized rigs can be accommodated, but longer vehicles may have some difficulty maneuvering if they wander beyond their designated area. This campground has many loops and turns, making campers feel like they're much farther away from the park highway than they really are. The rushing Nenana River that borders the campground, coupled with the snow-capped mountains in the background, completes the effect of being away from it all. Ask for a riverside site if possible.

BASICS

Operated By: Owned & operated by the Reislands. **Open:** May 15–Sept. 12; exact days depend on snowmelt & weather. **Site Assignment:** Reservations are recommended, particularly in June & July. A 1-night deposit is required to secure a campsite, & a 15% fee is charged for cancellations. No refunds are given w/in 48 hours of the reserved date. Walk-ins are also welcome, just check into the office before settling into a site. No charge if cancelled w/in 60 days of arrival. **Registration:** Payments should be made at the front office before you go to a site. Check-in 3–10 p.m. Late arrivals (after 10 p.m., before 8 a.m.) call ahead. A map will w/ site assignment will be waiting for you. **Fee:** $28–$32. **Parking:** At site for most spots. Some tent sites are walk-in only w/ designated parking in a separate area.

FACILITIES

Number of Multipurpose Sites: 45. **Hookups:** Electric (30 amps), water (most sites). **Each Site:** Picnic table & campfire circles. **Dump Station:** Yes, 2 on campground property. **Laundry:** Yes, tokens available for purchase at campground office. Laundry soap is sold in the general store. **Pay Phone:** Yes, 3. **Restrooms and Showers:** 3 buildings w/ flushable toilets & pay showers are available to park guests. Shower is coin operated; five minutes cost 75 cents. Facilities are clean & accessible. **Fuel:** A Tesoro station is located in Denali Village, 7 mi. north. **Propane:** Yes. **Internal Roads:** Dirt & gravel roads, curvy but well maintained. **RV Service:** No, 18 mi. in Healy. **Market:** Basic food items are available at the campground general store. **Restaurant:** Yes, across the street. **General Store:** A well-stocked general store is located adjacent the office & includes coffee & rolls, ice cream, snacks & groceries, ice, liquor, & Alaskan gifts. Hours are 8 a.m–10 p.m. **Vending:** No. **Swimming:** No. **Playground:** No. **Other:** There are 7 covered pavilions for picnics & barbecues. Cabins are available. **Activities:** Airplane rides & horseback riding (nearby), raft tours. **Nearby Attractions:** The Denali National Park entrance is located 6 mi. north of the RV Park. In addition, a wide array of local tours can be booked in the front office.

RESTRICTIONS

Pets: On leash; walked only in dog-walking area. Should not be left unattended. **Fires:** Restricted to pit areas only. **Alcoholic Beverages:** No restrictions. Liquor is sold in the campground general store. **Vehicle Maximum Length:** 45 ft. **Other:** A list of sensible campground rules is distributed to all campers.

TO GET THERE

Take the Parks Hwy. to mi. 231. When you near this mi., slow down—the large Denali Grizzly Bear Cabins & Campground sign on the west side of the road sneaks up on you suddenly.

GLENNALLEN — MAP, B-3
Mendeltna Creek Lodge

Mile 153 Glenn Hwy., 99588. T: (907) 822-3346.

🚐 ★★★   ⛺ ★★★

Beauty: ★★★	Site Privacy: ★★★
Spaciousness: ★★★	Quiet: ★★★
Security: ★★★	Cleanliness: ★★★
Insect Control: ★★	Facilities: ★★★

This campground, the halfway point between Tok and Anchorage, is not a destination in itself, but rather a place to lay over before journeying to your next checkpoint. However, the highway-weary traveler will find a surprisingly unique experience at Mendeltna Creek Lodge. Set in the gnarly black-spruce forest with the sinuous Mendeltna Creek flowing by, the campground has a bit of a rustic, wild feel to it. This campground has treed sites with plenty of back-ins and pull-throughs. The several loops and slightly bumpy road make some parts of the campground difficult for larger rigs, but ultimately all can be accommodated. The sites are not numbered and seem slightly scattered about. We preferred the creek-side sites, but they are the farthest away from the showers and restrooms. Overall, the campground is clean and on par with Alaska's other RV sites—it simply has a very "seasoned" feel to it.

BASICS

Operated By: Mabel & Russel Wimmer. **Open:** All year. **Site Assignment:** Reservations are recommended for holiday weekends & July 4th. Deposits are required during busy times. Otherwise, there is usually room for RVers who just show up. **Registration:** Stop In restaurant/office & pay before you park. If you arrive after hours, find a spot & settle payment in the morning. **Fee:** Full hookup, $20; dry, $10; tents, $6; cabins, $40–$50. Good Sam discount; cash, credit card, no checks. **Parking:** At site.

FACILITIES

Number of RV-only Sites: 60. **Number of Tent-only Sites:** Undesignated sites. **Hookups:** Electric (20 amps), water, sewer. **Each Site:** Picnic table & fire pits. **Dump Station:** Yes. **Laundry:** Yes, coin operated. **Pay Phone:** No, but calling cards may be used in the office. Phone cards available for purchase in the restaurant. **Restrooms and Showers:** Family-style bathrooms available in the restaurant & on the campground. Showers cost $1. **Fuel:** Yes, on site.

Propane: No. **Internal Roads:** Gravel, a bit bumpy. **RV Service:** Closest available is in Glenallen. **Market:** In Glenallen. **Restaurant:** A restaurant & bar are on site & are open from 6 a.m.–midnight. Hand-tossed pizzas; the cinnamon rolls come recommended. Sandwiches & simple meals are also available at relatively reasonable prices. **General Store:** Some basic items available for purchase in the restaurant. **Vending:** No. **Swimming:** No. **Playground:** No. **Other:** Cozy cabins are available for rent if you want a night out of your camper/tent. **Activities:** Fishing, hiking, outdoor museum. **Nearby Attractions:** The Drunken Forest museum is on site. This is a fenced in collection of unusually shaped wood pieces & artifacts that have been found in the local area.

RESTRICTIONS

Pets: Allowed on leash only, must be cleaned up after. **Fires:** Allowed. **Alcoholic Beverages:** No restrictions, alcohol available at the bar. **Vehicle Maximum Length:** No limit.

TO GET THERE

Take the Glenn Hwy. to mi. 153. You'll see the log lodge on the south side of the highway.

HOUSTON — MAP, B-3
Riverside Camper Park

Mile 57.7 Park Hwy., 99694. T: (907) 892-9020.

🚐 ★★★★   ⛺ ★★★

Beauty: ★★★	Site Privacy: ★★★
Spaciousness: ★★★	Quiet: ★★★
Security: ★★★	Cleanliness: ★★★★
Insect Control: ★★	Facilities: ★★★★

Riverside Camper Park is a clean, tranquil park that offers the perfect break before going to the big city of Anchorage just an hour's drive away. This loop-shaped campground is just off the Park Highway and is conveniently located within walking distance of a restaurant, post office, grocery store, and service station. It can also be commended for its clean bathrooms and home-style showers. For fishing fans, bank fishing on the Little Susitna River is available all summer, and boat charters can be arranged at the campground. There are plenty of spacious back-in and pull-through sites available. Spruce and birch line Riverside Camper Park, but no trees or flowers separate the grassy campsites. Request the spots farthest from the highway; sites 27 and 28 are next to the water.

BASICS

Operated By: Owned & operated by Kenny & Sheila Mortensen. **Open:** May–Sept., exact days depend on snowmelt & weather. **Site Assignment:** First come, first served or by reservation; sites held w/ credit card; 24-hour cancellation policy. **Registration:** Check in at the front office before settling on a site. Office hours are 9 a.m.–9 p.m. If you arrive after hours, instructions are on the front gate for check-in. **Fee:** Full hookup, $25. Good Sam & Military discount; V, MC, AE, D. **Parking:** At site.

FACILITIES

Number of RV-only Sites: 56. **Number of Tent-only Sites:** 2. **Hookups:** 60 full hookup sites. **Each**

Site: Picnic table, electrical outlet, water faucet. **Dump Station:** Yes. **Laundry:** Yes, $1.50 to wash & $1.50 to dry. An iron & ironing board are available free of charge. **Pay Phone:** Yes. **Restrooms and Showers:** Clean & modern bathroom facilities are available free of charge to all guests. **Fuel:** No. **Propane:** No. **Internal Roads:** Gravel, well maintained. **RV Service:** RV wash on site. **Market:** Grocery Store on site. **Restaurant:** Hamburgers are available at Miller's Place. For more variety, the Houston Lounge is located just down the road. **General Store:** Miller's Place stocks a variety of basic supplies. **Vending:** Vendable soft drinks, candy & news-papers at Riverside front office. Also, buy or trade used books here. **Swimming:** Lake. **Playground:** No. **Other:** There is a boat ramp & bank access to the Little Susitna River, & horseshoe pits on site. Post office available on grounds. **Activities:** The 3rd Sat. of Aug. is Houston's Annual Founder's Day. This is a community barbecue w/ games, activities, & the best fireworks display you've ever witnessed!. **Nearby Attractions:** This area of the state is famed for lake & river fishing. Houston is also renown for its fire-works stores.

RESTRICTIONS

Pets: Allowed on leash, must be cleaned up after. **Fires:** Restricted to pit areas only. **Alcoholic Beverages:** No restrictions. **Vehicle Maximum Length:** No limit. **Other:** Barcley, the office pooch, is not much of a watch dog, but he is fun to pet & play with!.

TO GET THERE

Take the Parks Hwy. to mi. 57.7. You cannot miss the tiny strip of convenience shops and the large, dark brown building w/ Riverside Camper Park displayed above the front door.

Arizona

Arizona blends a rich Native American past and present with a Wild West legacy of cowboys, cattle, and mining. Snowbirds annually flock to Arizona's deserts for the mild winter temperatures, golf, and Major League Baseball's spring training **Cactus League.** Hundreds of RV parks with every imaginable amenity come to life to accommodate the winter influx, and most book up well in advance of the annual RV migration.

The desert has its own distinctive brand of beauty. The hardiest of heat lovers will gladly brave summer temperatures soaring past 110°F in capital city Phoenix at **Organ Pipe Cactus National Monument** to take in the splendors of the **Sonoran Desert.** Many opt for the cooler months, from fall through the spring wildflower season. Though still in the 100s, Tucson summer temperatures are about 10°F cooler than those in Phoenix, and get even cooler if you visit the **Colossal Cave** and learn the legend behind the money supposedly hidden there. If that's not cool enough, the summer monsoons can be refreshing but generally bring flash floods. If you miss the monsoons, visit the world's tallest fountain in **Fountain Hills, Maricopa County,** and get downwind from a breeze to bask in the mist. By August, bird-watchers invade the **Upper San Pedro River Valley** southeast of Tucson, an area about 15°F cooler than Phoenix. History abounds in **Bisbee,** an old copper mining town with an RV park overlooking an open-pit mine. Few ghost towns rival Tombstone's ambiance, not to mention the world's largest rose bush, which blooms there every April. Water-formed **Kartchner Caverns,** where you can witness the largest natural column in the 48th state as well as the most minuscule of formations, satisfies an appetite for geological oddities.

Arizona is also a land of mountains, which means winter sports and summer campgrounds that are a refuge from the desert heat. Both deserts and mountains abound with lakes and reservoirs, and fishing and boating are a popular part of the cooling summer mix. Outside Flagstaff, you can venture to and climb Arizona's highest point, **Humphrey's Peak,** for a tremendous 360° view of the land. The **Colorado River** along Arizona's western border is a water playground with a collage of private RV parks, marinas, and state and county campgrounds between Parker and Lake Havasu, home of the old **London Bridge.** Nearby **Quartzsite** becomes a giant winter flea market and gem show, attracting over a million visitors who park their RVs on Bureau of Land Management land all over the desert. Equally as exciting but more intimate and obscure is the annual solar egg-frying contest every July 4 in **Oatman.** Anyone can enter, but your egg must be done within the 15-minute time limit. Don't forget to feed carrots to the wild burros that carouse freely around the town—over the years they have been fed and enjoyed one too many eggs, so they are on a more strict diet now.

The **Grand Canyon** to the north is an international attraction and gateway to the **Navajo Nation. Canyon de Chelly,** just east of the Hopi Indian mesas, is also on most international itineraries as a link to the past through the 1600-year-old-plus ruins, and through the Navajo who presently reside and farm here. There is no camping inside the **Painted Desert** or **Petrified Forest National Park,** but choices outside the parks, between Winslow and Holbrook, range from archaeological sites and power-plant cooling reservoirs to commercial campgrounds. While in the area and looking for something touristy to do, take a trip out to **Four Corners** and you might get invited to square dance in four states at the same time. South of the Petrified Forest is high-mountain country, with a number of forest, lake, and reservoir campgrounds, and even a White Mountain Apache casino RV park for those wanting some Nevada-style action.

Campground Profiles

AJO   MAP, D-2
Twin Peaks Campground

10 Organ Pipe Dr., 85321. T: (520) 387-6849; www.nps.gov/orpi.

🚐 ★★★   ⛺ ★★★★

Beauty: ★★★★★
Site Privacy: ★★★★★
Spaciousness: ★★★★★
Quiet: ★★★
Security: ★★★★
Cleanliness: ★★★★★
Insect Control: ★★★
Facilities: ★★

Designated an International Biosphere Reserve by the United Nations in 1976, Organ Pipe Cactus National Monument showcases Sonoran Desert plants (28 cactus species) and animals adapted to extremes like summer air temperatures of 118°F and ground temperatures of 175°F. The Monument's namesake organ pipe cactus copes in part by only opening its lavender-white flowers at night. Campers cope best by coming from October to April, when daytime temperatures are in the 60s and 70s. The campground stays open through the torrid summer, when the organ pipe and other cacti colorfully bloom and storms suddenly appear out of nowhere, triggering flash floods. Hardy tent campers can head to more primitive campgrounds, some in cooler mountains with juniper, oak, rosewood, agave, and jojoba. Lukeville has Mexican food, and plenty of hookups are available in Why and Ajo, 22 and 36 miles north, respectively.

BASICS

Operated By: National Park Service. **Open:** All year; closed Christmas day. **Site Assignment:** First come, first served. **Registration:** At visitor center (8 a.m.–5 p.m.). After 5 p.m. use self-register station. **Fee:** $10; Gold Access, $5; cash only; additional entry fee, $5; pass remains valid for 7 consecutive days. **Parking:** At site.

FACILITIES

Number of RV-only Sites: 208. **Hookups:** None. **Each Site:** Table, grill, cement pad. **Dump Station:** Yes. **Laundry:** No. **Pay Phone:** Yes. **Restrooms and Showers:** Restrooms but no showers. **Fuel:** No. **Propane:** No. **Internal Roads:** Paved. **RV Service:** No. **Market:** Lukeville, 5 mi. **Restaurant:** Lukeville, 5 mi. **General Store:** No. **Vending:** No. **Swimming:** No. **Playground:** No. **Other:** Amphitheater. **Activities:** Bird-watching, hiking, biking. **Nearby Attractions:** Mexico, Ajo, Tohono O'odham Indian Reservation. **Additional Information:** Ajo Chamber of Commerce, (520) 387-7742.

RESTRICTIONS

Pets: On leash under owner's control. Restricted from trails. **Fires:** Grill only. **Alcoholic Beverages:** Not allowed. **Vehicle Maximum Length:** 35 ft. **Other:** No wood gathering or removing anything natural from the park.

TO GET THERE

From Gila Bend, go 80 mi. south on AZ 85.

APACHE JUNCTION   MAP, C-2
Lost Dutchman State Park

6109 North Apache Tr., 85219. T: (480) 982-4485; www.pr.state.az.us.

🚐 ★★★★   ⛺ ★★★★★

Beauty: ★★★★★
Site Privacy: ★★★★★
Spaciousness: ★★★★★
Quiet: ★★★★★
Security: ★★★
Cleanliness: ★★★★
Insect Control: ★★★
Facilities: ★★

The big news at Lost Dutchman State Park is the addition of showers, though being without hookups this was never the sort of place people came for RV amenities. The major attractions here are the great views of the spire-like Praying Hand rock formation backed by the tall Flatiron formation, plus many nature trails for hiking and horseback riding. The area's intriguing eroded rock formations are fronted with saguaros, palo verde cholla, and other desert vegetation tall enough to screen the campsites and add privacy. The campground's 35 sites are divided into three small loops within a larger loop, so the natural environment predominates over camping neighbors. It is these natural environment qualities, not the presence or absence of standard amenities, that causes this campground to fill up fast. The group-camping area sometimes doubles as overflow.

BASICS

Operated By: Arizona State Parks. **Open:** All year. **Site Assignment:** First come, first served. **Registration:** At office or self-pay fee station. **Fee:** $12; V, MC. **Parking:** At site.

FACILITIES

Number of RV-only Sites: 70. **Hookups:** None. **Each Site:** Table, grill. **Dump Station:** Yes. **Laundry:** No. **Pay Phone:** Yes. **Restrooms and Showers:** Yes. **Fuel:** No. **Propane:** No. **Internal Roads:** Paved. **RV Service:** No. **Market:** Apache Junction, 5 mi. **Restaurant:** Apache Junction, 3 mi. **General Store:** No. **Vending:** Yes. **Swimming:** No. **Playground:** No. **Other:** Group pavilion, amphitheater, gift shop, native-plant trail near ranger station. **Activities:** Horseback riding, hiking. **Nearby Attractions:** Tortilla Flat, Phoenix; Boyce Thompson State Park; Superstition Mountains; Tonto National Forest; Apache Trail. **Additional Information:** Pinal County Visitor Center, (520) 868-9433.

RESTRICTIONS

Pets: On leash. **Fires:** Grill only; ground fires strictly prohibited; no wood gathering. **Alcoholic Beverages:** Allowed. **Vehicle Maximum Length:** No limit. **Other:** 15-day stay limit.

TO GET THERE

From junction of US 60 and AZ 88 go 6 mi. northeast on Hwy. 88.

APACHE JUNCTION   MAP, C-2
Mesa-Apache Junction KOA

1540 South Tomahawk Rd., 85220. T: (480) 982-4015 or (800) 562-3404; www.koa.com.

🚐 ★★★★   ⛺ ★★★

Beauty: ★★★
Site Privacy: ★★
Spaciousness: ★★★★
Quiet: ★★★★
Security: ★★★★
Cleanliness: ★★★★★
Insect Control: ★★★
Facilities: ★★★★

Without the age restriction of many of the mega-lots in the Apache Junction/Mesa area, this campground is a great family destination. The combination of decent-sized lots (50 by 25 feet on average), attractive landscaping, views of the Superstition Mountains, and full services makes this a campground worth your while to visit. Tent sites are well tucked away, but would be improved with grass instead of gravel. RV sites 116 and 177 sport a fine mature shade tree, making them the best for the money. Sites to avoid are 65, 113, 113A, 114, and 114A, as they have no trees to speak of and are located next to the rec room and an intersection in the campground road. Tent sites H–L are located next to shrubs along the border of the property, which adds to their charm. Tent sites E and F are situated closest to the playground, and worse, E has no trees whatsoever.

BASICS

Operated By: Mike & Rosemary Mortensen. **Open:** All year. **Site Assignment:** Assigned on registration. **Registration:** At office. (Late arrivals: select site from map of open sites, use drop slot in door.) **Fee:** $20–$30. **Parking:** At site.

FACILITIES

Number of RV-only Sites: 140. **Hookups:** Electric (30, 50 amps), water, sewer. **Each Site:** Picnic table, some shade trees, some trash receptacles. **Dump Station:** Yes. **Laundry:** Yes. **Pay Phone:** Yes. **Restrooms and Showers:** Yes. **Fuel:** No. **Propane:** Yes. **Internal Roads:** Hard-packed dirt, gravel, & pavement mix; in very drivable condition. **RV Service:** No. **Market:** On site. **Restaurant:** Next door. **General Store:** Yes. **Vending:** Yes. **Swimming:** Pool. **Playground:** Yes. **Other:** Rec building, "dog relief pen." **Activities:** River tubing, TV, some fitness equipment, ping pong, basketball, horseshoes, desert Jeep tours, horseback tours, helicopter tours, hot-air balloon rides, tennis, guided pack trips, hiking, golf. **Nearby Attractions:** Mesa Southwest Museum, Champlin Fighter Museum, Superstition Springs Center, Casa Grande Ruins, Roosevelt Dam, Tonto National Monument. **Additional Information:** Apache Junction Chamber of Commerce, (602) 982-3141.

RESTRICTIONS

Pets: On leash, clean up after. **Fires:** Allowed (only charcoal in grills). **Alcoholic Beverages:** At sites only. **Vehicle Maximum Length:** No limit. **Other:** No clotheslines, no generators, no FOR SALE signs.

TO GET THERE

From Hwy. 60, take Exit 197 onto Tomahawk Rd., turn north and drive for 1 mi. The entrance is on the left.

APACHE-SITGREAVES
MAP, C-3

Lakeside Campground—Apache-Sitgreaves National Forest

reserve america

P.O. Box 640, 85938. T: (928) 333-4301; www.reserveamerica.com.

🚐 ★★★★ 　　　 ⛺ ★★★★

Beauty: ★★★ 　　　 Site Privacy: ★★★
Spaciousness: ★★★ 　 Quiet: ★★★
Security: ★★★★ 　　 Cleanliness: ★★★★
Insect Control: ★★★★ 　Facilities: ★★

The elevation here is 6,700 ft. The campground is adjacent to NH 260 under Ponderosa pines. It is convenient for overnight stay. Not far from campground is the Porter Mountain Stable on Porter Mountain Rd. There, horses can be rented for guided trail rides. Firewood is available. Restrooms and sanitary dump station are provided. Popular activities include fishing, hiking, and sightseeing. Lakeside Campground is located within the Apache-Sitgreaves National Forest and has 34 lakes and reservoirs and more than 680 miles of rivers and streams—more than can be found in any other Southwestern national forest. The White Mountains contain the headwaters of several Arizona rivers including the Black, the Little Colorado, and the San Francisco. The Sitgreaves was named for Captain Lorenzo Sitgreaves, a government topographical engineer who conducted the first scientific expedition across Arizona in the early 1850s. In the Sitgreaves, the major attractions for visitors from the hot valleys of Phoenix or Tucson are the Mogollon Rim and the string of man-made lakes. From the Rim's 7,600-foot elevation, vista points provide inspiring views of the low country to the south and west.

BASICS

Operated By: U.S. Forest Service. **Open:** May 12–Oct. 27. **Site Assignment:** Reservations must be made at least 4 days in advance. **Registration:** At office. **Fee:** Single, $12–$14. **Parking:** At park.

FACILITIES

Number of Multipurpose Sites: 234. **Hookups:** None. **Each Site:** Call ahead. **Dump Station:** Yes. **Laundry:** No. **Pay Phone:** No. **Restrooms and Showers:** Yes. **Fuel:** Nearby. **Propane:** Nearby. **Internal Roads:** Paved. **RV Service:** No. **Market:** No. **Restaurant:** No. **General Store:** No. **Vending:** No. **Swimming:** No. **Playground:** No. **Activities:** Fishing, hiking, sightseeing.

RESTRICTIONS

Pets: Pets must be restrained or on a leash at all times while in developed recreation areas. **Fires:** In fire rings, stoves, grills, or fireplaces provided for that purpose. **Alcoholic Beverages:** Not allowed. **Vehicle Maximum Length:** Call ahead.

TO GET THERE

Located on AZ 260 in Lakeside, Arizona, across from the Lakeside Ranger Station office.

APACHE-SITGREAVES
MAP, C-3

Luna Lake Apache-Sitgreaves National Forest

reserve america

P.O. Box 640, 85938. T: (928) 333-4301; www.reserveamerica.com.

🚐 ★★★★ 　　　 ⛺ ★★★★

Beauty: ★★★ 　　　 Site Privacy: ★★★
Spaciousness: ★★★★ 　Quiet: ★★★
Security: ★★★★ 　　 Cleanliness: ★★★★
Insect Control: ★★★★ 　Facilities: ★★

Luna Lake is near a 75-acre lake, surrounded by a ponderosa pine forest, and near a large wetland for nesting waterfowl. With great rainbow, cutthroat, and brook trout, and close proximity to Alpine Arizona, Luna Lake is an excellent destination for weekend and vacationing anglers. Luna Lake is also known for ice fishing during winter freezes. Facilities include campgrounds, picnic tables, restrooms, and a boat launch. Luna Lake is located within the Apache-Sitgreaves National Forest and has 34 lakes and reservoirs and more than 680 miles of rivers and streams—more than can be found in any other southwestern national forest. The White Mountains contain the headwaters of several Arizona rivers including the Black, the Little Colorado, and the San Francisco. The Sitgreaves was named for Captain Lorenzo Sitgreaves, a government topographical engineer who conducted the first scientific expedition across Arizona in the early 1850s. In the Sitgreaves, the major attractions for visitors from the hot valleys of Phoenix or Tucson are the Mogollon Rim and the string of manmade lakes. From the Rim's 7,600-foot elevation, vista points provide inspiring views of the low country to the south and west.

BASICS

Operated By: U.S. Forest Service. **Open:** May 1–Nov. 13. **Site Assignment:** Reservations must be made at least 4 days in advance. **Registration:** At office. **Fee:** Single, $10; group, $50–$125. **Parking:** At park.

FACILITIES

Number of Multipurpose Sites: 122. **Hookups:** None. **Each Site:** Call ahead. **Dump Station:** No. **Laundry:** No. **Pay Phone:** No. **Restrooms and Showers:** Yes. **Fuel:** No. **Propane:** No. **Internal Roads:** Paved. **RV Service:** No. **Market:** No. **Restaurant:** No. **General Store:** Yes. **Vending:** No. **Swimming:** No. **Playground:** No. **Activities:** Interpretive programs, boating, fishing, wildlife viewing.

RESTRICTIONS

Pets: Pets must be restrained or on a leash at all times while in developed recreation areas. **Fires:** In fire rings, stoves, grills, or fireplaces provided for that purpose. **Alcoholic Beverages:** Not allowed. **Vehicle Maximum Length:** Call ahead.

TO GET THERE

Located 5 mi. east of Alpine, on Hwy. 180. Turn north of Hwy. 180 onto gravel road and proceed 2 mi. around the lake to the campground.

BENSON
MAP, D-3

Cochise Terrace RV Resort

1030 South Barrel Cactus Ridge, 85602. T: (520) 586-0600 or (800) 495-9005; www.cochise-terrace.com.

🚐 ★★★★ 　　　 ⛺ ★

Beauty: ★★★★ 　　　Site Privacy: ★★★★
Spaciousness: ★★★★ 　Quiet: ★★★★
Security: ★★★★ 　　　Cleanliness: ★★★★
Insect Control: ★★★★ 　Facilities: ★★★★

Far enough from the main highways so that the only external sound is the wind blowing, Cochise Terrace is like a little city with street lights. Streets have bird names like Raven Road and Quail Run, and an 80-foot-tall American flag near the front entrance office doubles as a navigation landmark. Barrel cactus, ocotillo, mesquite, and a dry wash are reminders that there is a desert surrounding this little oasis of paved streets. There are almost 100 annual residents of Cochise Terrace, and the 200-plus remaining RV sites are quite popular with snowbirds. So, if the largest 42-foot site is needed for a winter visit, call ahead and reserve it. As far as locations go, this is about as central a base for touring southeast Arizona as there is, being an easy drive to almost all the sights from Tucson and Tumacacori to Tombstone and Bisbee.

BASICS

Operated By: Art & Pat Bale. **Open:** All year. **Site Assignment:** First come, first served; winter reservations recommended. **Fee:** $19–$30. **Parking:** At site.

FACILITIES

Number of RV-only Sites: 223. **Hookups:** Electric (20, 30, 50 amps), water, sewer, cable TV, phone. **Each Site:** Table. **Dump Station:** Yes. **Laundry:** Yes. **Pay Phone:** Yes, winter only. **Restrooms and Showers:** Yes. **Fuel:** No. **Propane:** Yes. **Internal Roads:** Paved, excellent. **RV Service:** No. **Market:** Benson, 2 mi. **Restaurant:** Benson, 2 mi. **General Store:** No. **Vending:** Yes. **Swimming:** Pool. **Playground:** No. **Other:** Clubhouse, whirlpool, kitchen, barbecue, picnic area, basketball court, pet walk, mail service. **Activities:** Golf, horseshoes, square dancing. **Nearby Attractions:** Kartchner Caverns, Fort Huachuca, Tombstone, Bisbee, Dragoon Mountains, Cochise Stronghold, San Pedro Riparian National Conservation Area, Tucson, Arizona Desert Museum in Tucson. **Additional Information:** Benson Chamber of Commerce, (520) 586-2842, www.bensonchamberaz.com.

RESTRICTIONS

Pets: On leash, never left unattended. Max. 2 pets. **Fires:** No open fires. **Alcoholic Beverages:** Allowed on sites. **Vehicle Maximum Length:** 40 ft. **Other:** No firearms, no fireworks.

TO GET THERE

From I-10 Exit 302 go south on AZ 90 and west on S. Barrel Cactus Ridge.

BENSON   MAP, D-3
Kartchner Caverns State Park

Hwy. 90, P.O. Box 1849, 85602. T: (520) 586-4100
or (602) 542-4174; www.pr.state.az.us.

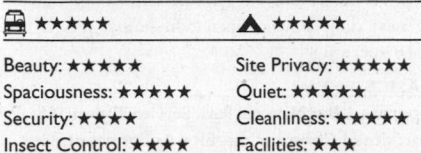

Beauty: ★★★★★   Site Privacy: ★★★★★
Spaciousness: ★★★★★   Quiet: ★★★★★
Security: ★★★★   Cleanliness: ★★★★★
Insect Control: ★★★★   Facilities: ★★★

The Caverns, which require separate admission tickets (phone (520) 586-CAVE) for cavern tour reservations), are limestone caves with pooling shelf-stones, spar crystals, cave pearls, dripping stalactites, stalagmites, coral pipes, columns, and drapery. Discovered 49 miles southeast of Tucson by two cave explorers in 1974, the caverns were kept secret until purchased as a state park in 1988. The Discovery Center has an explanatory video, plus a hummingbird garden. The campsites are very large, and include 16 50-amp pull-through sites. Thick mesquite barriers between sites provide privacy, and agave, ocotillo, and prickly pear make this campground one of the most beautiful in the desert. However, the attractive sites fill up early almost every day of the year. Since there are no campground reservations, be prepared to make this a day trip and find alternative campsites in Benson, Huachuca City, and other nearby areas.

BASICS

Operated By: Arizona State Parks. **Open:** All year; closed Christmas day. **Site Assignment:** First come, first served. **Registration:** Pay upon entrance (after-hours self-pay station). **Fee:** $22; V, MC, cash only (after hours). **Parking:** At site.

FACILITIES

Number of RV-only Sites: 64. **Hookups:** Electric (30, 50 amps), water. **Each Site:** Table. **Dump Station:** Yes. **Laundry:** No. **Pay Phone:** Yes. **Restrooms and Showers:** Yes. **Fuel:** No. **Propane:** No. **Internal Roads:** Paved, good. **RV Service:** No. **Market:** Benson, 10 mi. **Restaurant:** Benson, 10 mi. **General Store:** No. **Vending:** Yes. **Swimming:** No. **Playground:** No. **Other:** Some grills, Discovery Center. **Activities:** Cave tours, hiking, walking. **Nearby Attractions:** Ramsey Canyon Preserve, Patagonia Lake, Sonoita, Fort Huachuca, Tombstone. **Additional Information:** Sierra Vista Visitor Center, (800) 288-3861, www.visitsierravista.com; Sierra Vista Ranger District, (520) 378-0311.

RESTRICTIONS

Pets: On leash under owner's control. **Fires:** Allowed (gas stoves only, no wood or charcoal fires). **Alcoholic Beverages:** Allowed. **Vehicle Maximum Length:** 74 ft. **Other:** 14-day stay limit.

TO GET THERE

From I-10, 1 mi. west of Benson, take Exit 302 and go 9 mi. south on AZ 90.

BISBEE   MAP, D-3
Queen Mine RV Park

P.O. Box 488, 473 North Dart Rd., 85603.
T: (520) 432-5006.

🚐 ★★★★   ⛺ ★

Beauty: ★★★★   Site Privacy: ★★★★
Spaciousness: ★★★★   Quiet: ★★★★
Security: ★★★★   Cleanliness: ★★★★
Insect Control: ★★★★   Facilities: ★★★

Perched on a circular hilltop just opposite and above the Queen Mine Tour, with RVs circled around the perimeter like a wagon train, the Queen Mine RV Park looks out on orange, ochre, and gray hillside layers exposed by a deep pit copper mine known as the Lavender Pit. Some may call the pit mine a scar on the face of the Earth, but it has its beauty, particularly after a rain when the hillside colors become deeply saturated. For at least a brief moment it is possible to fantasize that a mighty river, rather than copper miners, carved out this three-quarter-mile wide, 950-foot-deep chasm filled with water at the bottom. In any event, it is just a block downhill from this clean, well-run, breezy hillside RV park to the start of Bisbee's historic old Main St. and all the shops, restaurants, hotels, galleries, theaters, and saloons.

BASICS

Operated By: Stan Dupuy. **Open:** All year. **Site Assignment:** First come, first served. **Registration:** At office. **Fee:** $23; cash, check. **Parking:** At site.

FACILITIES

Number of RV-only Sites: 25. **Hookups:** Electric (20, 30, 50 amps), water, sewer, cable TV. **Each Site:** Rock planter w/ small tree. **Dump Station:** Yes. **Laundry:** Yes. **Pay Phone:** Yes. **Restrooms and Showers:** Yes. **Fuel:** No. **Propane:** No. **Internal Roads:** Gravel, good. **RV Service:** No. **Market:** Bisbee, 2 mi. **Restaurant:** Bisbee, 2 blocks. **General Store:** No. **Vending:** No. **Swimming:** No. **Playground:** No. **Other:** Inquire at campground. **Activities:** Golf, bird-watching. **Nearby Attractions:** Mine tour, museums, Tombstone, San Pedro Riparian National Conservation Area. **Additional Information:** Bisbee Chamber of Commerce, (520) 432-5421, www.bisbeearizona.com.

RESTRICTIONS

Pets: On leash under owner's control. **Fires:** Allowed. **Alcoholic Beverages:** Allowed. **Vehicle Maximum Length:** No limit.

TO GET THERE

From AZ 80, take downtown Bisbee Exit and follow road to Queen Mine Tour.

BISBEE   MAP, D-3
Shady Dell RV Park

1 Douglas Rd., 85603. T: (520) 432-3567;
www.theshadydell.com.

🚐 ★★★★   ⛺ ★★

Beauty: ★★★★   Site Privacy: ★★★★
Spaciousness: ★★★★   Quiet: ★★★
Security: ★★★★   Cleanliness: ★★★★
Insect Control: ★★★★   Facilities: ★★★★

Located off a roundabout southeast of the Lavender Pit mine, Shady Dell got its start in 1927 when copper mining was going strong, and Bisbee was better known than Phoenix. Getting a campsite here is tough, and late afternoon arrivals are usually of out of luck, as most of the campground is rented out to year-round campers. Even more coveted than the camping sites are the furnished aluminum travel trailer rentals, an homage to American road travel that includes a 1949 Airstream, 1950 Spartanette, 1951 Royal Mansion, and 1954 Crown, all furnished in near original blonde woods and polished aluminum with vintage radios, black-and-white TVs, phonographs, and vinyl records of early rhythm and blues and big bands. Dot's Diner, a ten-stool 1957 art-deco Valentine model, makes Shady Dell a good early breakfast stop even if not camping.

BASICS

Operated By: Ed Smith & Rita Personette. **Open:** All year. **Site Assignment:** First come, first served. **Registration:** At office. **Fee:** $10–$15; cash, check. **Parking:** At site.

FACILITIES

Number of RV-only Sites: 10. **Number of Tent-only Sites:** 2. **Hookups:** Electric (30 amps), water, sewer, cable TV. **Each Site:** Grass, gravel. **Dump Station:** Yes. **Laundry:** Yes. **Pay Phone:** Yes. **Restrooms and Showers:** Yes. **Fuel:** Yes. **Propane:** Yes. **Internal Roads:** Gravel, good. **RV Service:** No. **Market:** Bisbee, 2 mi. **Restaurant:** Yes. **General Store:** No. **Vending:** No. **Swimming:** No. **Playground:** No. **Other:** Vintage travel trailer rentals. **Activities:** Golf, bird-watching, rock hunting. **Nearby Attractions:** Mine tour, museums, Tombstone, San Pedro Riparian National Conservation Area. **Additional Information:** Bisbee Chamber of Commerce, (520) 432-5421, www.bisbeearizona.com.

RESTRICTIONS

Pets: On leash. **Fires:** Allowed. **Alcoholic Beverages:** Allowed. **Vehicle Maximum Length:** 40 ft.

TO GET THERE

From AZ 80, 1.5 mi. southeast of Bisbee, follow the roundabout at the Chevron station to Douglas Rd.

BULLHEAD   MAP, D-3
Katherine Campground

601 Nevada Hwy., 2690 Katherine Spur Rd., 89005. T: (702) 293-8907; www.nps.gov/lame/index.html.

🚐 ★★★★   ⛺ ★★★★

Beauty: ★★★★   Site Privacy: ★★★★
Spaciousness: ★★★★   Quiet: ★★★★
Security: ★★★★   Cleanliness: ★★★★
Insect Control: ★★★   Facilities: ★★★★

About 5 miles north of Bullhead City and Laughlin's casinos, in the Lake Mead National Recreation Area, Katherine is divided into five smaller campgrounds with solar power, paved roads, and gravel sites separated by oleanders, eucalyptus, and palms. Though the National Park Service does not provide hookups, a private concessionaire (Lake Mojave Resort and Marina) offers sites with hookups ($18; register at motel), along with a trailer village, motel, marina, houseboat rentals, restaurant, and lounge. A favorite of Californians, on a recent three-day holiday weekend Katherine was overrun by 44,000 visitors. A warning to the wise: those who didn't snag a campsite on the Thursday prior to the holiday were backed up in a two-hour line of cars, only to be turned away. But when the crowds abate, Katherine offers enough true desert relaxation and water to make the rest of the world seem like memories from a distant planet.

BASICS

Operated By: National Park Service. **Open:** All year. **Site Assignment:** First come, first served; no reservations (except groups). **Registration:** At entrance kiosk. **Fee:** $10; Golden Age & Golden Access pass, $5; cash only. **Parking:** At site.

FACILITIES

Number of RV-only Sites: 173. **Hookups:** None (private Lake Mojave Resort & Marina concession offers sites w/ hookups). **Each Site:** Table, grill. **Dump Station:** Yes. **Laundry:** Yes. **Pay Phone:** Yes. **Restrooms and Showers:** Yes. **Fuel:** Yes. **Propane:** Yes. **Internal Roads:** Paved, in good condition. **RV Service:** Limited; better in Bullhead City or Laughlin. **Market:** Yes. **Restaurant:** Yes. **General Store:** Yes. **Vending:** Yes. **Swimming:** No. **Playground:** No. **Activities:** House-boat rentals, full marina, fishing. **Nearby Attractions:** Laughlin casinos & outlet shopping. **Additional Information:** Lake Mohave Resort, (520) 754-3245 or (800) 752-9669.

RESTRICTIONS

Pets: Must be kept on 6-ft. leash, not left alone. **Fires:** Allowed (in grills only). **Alcoholic Beverages:** In designated areas. **Vehicle Maximum Length:** 25 ft. **Other:** 30-day stay limit, NRA entry fee must also be paid.

TO GET THERE

From junction of Hwy. 95 and Hwy. 68, north of Bullhead City, go west 0.25 mi. on Hwy. 68, then north 3 mi. on Katherine Rd.

BULLHEAD CITY   MAP, B-1
Davis Camp

P.O. Box 2078, 2251 Hwy. 68, 86429.
T: (928) 754-4606, (928) 754-7250, or (877) 757-0915; www.daviscamp.com.

🚐 ★★★★	▲ ★★
Beauty: ★★★★	Site Privacy: ★★★
Spaciousness: ★★★	Quiet: ★★★
Security: ★★★★	Cleanliness: ★★★★
Insect Control: ★★★★	Facilities: ★★★★

On the northern outskirts of Bullhead City, along Hwy. 68, between Davis Dam and the Laughlin Bridge, there are three clusters of camping sites with palms and eucalyptus along the banks of the Colorado River. This former federal housing area for Davis Dam workers, now a regional county park, looks across the river a mile to Laughlin, Nevada's glimmering casinos, and is the area's best combination of outdoor activities and casino proximity. Hardy outdoor types can swim, boat, jet ski, fish for world record striped bass (59 lbs., 12 oz., caught just below Davis Dam), and walk to Laughlin for

---

food, gaming, and outlet shopping. Children have a safe, shallow swimming cove and spacious play areas with swings, slides, and basketball hoops. Dogs are commonplace, and the roar of the nearby highway and river traffic add to the noise. The most coveted sites, particularly for tents, are the 50 beachfront ramadas with tables and grills near the north beach fishing pier.

BASICS

Operated By: Mohave County Parks Dept. **Open:** All year; annual passes for local & nonresidents. **Site Assignment:** First come, first served; reservations required for group area. **Registration:** At entrance kiosk. **Fee:** $10–$19. **Parking:** At site.

FACILITIES

Number of RV-only Sites: 141. **Hookups:** Electric (up to 50 amps), water, sewer. **Each Site:** Wide pull-through. **Dump Station:** Yes. **Laundry:** Yes. **Pay Phone:** Yes. **Restrooms and Showers:** Yes. **Fuel:** No. **Propane:** Yes. **Internal Roads:** Paved, in good condition. **RV Service:** In Bullhead City & Laughlin. **Market:** In Bullhead City & Laughlin. **Restaurant:** Many in nearby Laughlin, Bullhead City. **General Store:** In Bullhead City & Laughlin. **Vending:** Yes. **Swimming:** Children's wading pool. **Playground:** Yes. **Other:** Boat ramp, dock. Storage, maintenance. **Activities:** River fishing, swimming, boating. **Nearby Attractions:** Laughlin casinos & outlet shopping; Colorado River Museum, Lake Mead National Recreation Area, Lake Mohave. **Additional Information:** Bullhead Area Chamber of Commerce, (520) 754-4121.

RESTRICTIONS

Pets: Must be under handler's control; leash laws strictly enforced; 2 dog limit; $1 each. **Fires:** Grill only. **Alcoholic Beverages:** Arizona law enforced by park rangers. **Vehicle Maximum Length:** 55 ft. **Other:** No loaded firearms, 14-day stay limit for beach sites.

TO GET THERE

At junction of Bullhead Pkwy. (Laughlin Casino Bridge) and Hwy. 68.

CHINLE   MAP, A-3
Cottonwood Campground

P.O. Box 588, 86503. T: (928) 674-5500 or (928) 674-5507; www.nps.gov/cach.

🚐 ★★★★	▲ ★★★★
Beauty: ★★★★	Site Privacy: ★★★★
Spaciousness: ★★★	Quiet: ★★★★
Security: ★★★★	Cleanliness: ★★★★
Insect Control: ★★★	Facilities: ★★★★

Ancient Puebloans occupied 83,000-acre Canyon de Chelly National Monument at least as long ago as 350 AD, and sites like the White House Ruins, Canyon del Muerto, and Spider Rock attract visitors from around the world. At least 20 Navajo families still seasonally graze their sheep and plant corn crops here, and four-wheel-drive and all-terrain vehicle guided tours into Canyon de Chelly are a tourist staple. Overlook views and the White House Ruins trail are free, as (amazingly enough) is the campground.

When Cottonwood's free sites are gone, private Spider Rock RV Park (P.O. Box 2509, Chinle, AZ 86503; (520) 674-8261; no hookups) 10 miles southeast on South Rim Drive is happy to have the business. But with tall cottonwood trees providing plenty of shade and the Thunderbird Lodge Cafeteria next door staying open odd hours, this is the place to camp.

BASICS

Operated By: National Park Service. **Open:** All year; closed Christmas day. **Site Assignment:** First come, first served; group (15 or more) site reservations (Apr. 1–Oct. 31). **Registration:** At visitor center. **Fee:** None. **Parking:** At site.

FACILITIES

Number of RV-only Sites: 96. **Hookups:** None. **Each Site:** Table, grill. **Dump Station:** Yes. **Laundry:** No. **Pay Phone:** Yes. **Restrooms and Showers:** No showers. **Fuel:** No. **Propane:** No. **Internal Roads:** Paved, good condition. **RV Service:** No. **Market:** Chinle, 1 mi. **Restaurant:** Thunderbird Lodge, adjacent. **General Store:** No. **Vending:** No. **Swimming:** No. **Playground:** No. **Other:** Museum, Visitor Center. **Activities:** Horseback riding, Canyon de Chelly guided tours, summer campfire programs & hogan talks, ranger-led hikes. **Nearby Attractions:** Hubbell Trading Post, Navajo National Monument, Kayenta Burger King Navajo Code Breakers exhibit. **Additional Information:** Canyon de Chelly National Monument, (928) 674-5500, www.nps.gov/cach.

RESTRICTIONS

Pets: On leash (do not feed stray dogs, which are being live trapped). **Fires:** Allowed (in grill, ground fires & wood collection prohibited). **Alcoholic Beverages:** Prohibited on Navajo reservation. **Vehicle Maximum Length:** 40 ft. **Other:** 7-day stay limit. Pets are not allowed on trails. Camping allowed only in specified campgrounds.

TO GET THERE

From junction of US 91 and Indian Hwy. 7 in Chinle, go 4 mi. east on Hwy. 7 and then 0.25 mi. south on South Rim Dr.

FLORENCE   MAP, C-2
Rancho Sonora Inn and RV Park

9160 North Hwy. 79, 85232.
T: (520) 868-8000 or (800) 205-6817; www.c2i2.com/~rancho/index.htm.

🚐 ★★★★★	▲ ★★★
Beauty: ★★★★	Site Privacy: ★★★★
Spaciousness: ★★★★★	Quiet: ★★★★★
Security: ★★★★	Cleanliness: ★★★★
Insect Control: ★★★★	Facilities: ★★★

An extremely attractive campground studded with saguaro cacti, Rancho Sonora fills with snowbirds every winter. Halfway between Tucson and Phoenix (60 miles), this extremely well-run family operation has an attractive pool area with relaxing desert views that attract visitors from as far away as Alaska. The surprising beauty found here makes it a welcome haven and escape for those visiting the neighboring state facility, as well as for those using Rancho Sonora as a tourism base to explore surrounding areas. Florence has a good Mexican restaurant and old street façades that show up in Hollywood movies and TV shows. Nearby Coolidge has major chain stores for stocking up on sundries. The extended host family is very welcoming, and does its best to help guests enjoy their stay to the maximum.

BASICS

Operated By: Linda Freeman (owner), Diane Ward (manager). **Open:** All year. **Site Assignment:** Reservations needed mid-Oct. to end of Mar. (45-day cancellation, or 1-month charge applicable to following year's space rental; $35 fee). **Registration:** At office. **Fee:** RV, $25; tent, $20; V, MC, AE. **Parking:** At site.

FACILITIES

Number of RV-only Sites: 62. **Number of Tent-only Sites:** 4. **Hookups:** Electric (20, 30, 50 amps), water, sewer, phone (modem). **Each Site:** Table, cement pad. **Dump Station:** Yes. **Laundry:** Yes. **Pay Phone:** No. **Restrooms and Showers:** Yes. **Fuel:** No. **Propane:** Yes. **Internal Roads:** Gravel, excellent. **RV Service:** No. **Market:** Florence, 5 mi. **Restaurant:** Florence, 5 mi. **General Store:** No. **Vending:** No. **Swimming:** Heated pool/spa. **Playground:** No. **Other:** Putting green, whirlpool, horseshoes, barbecue, kitchen, clubhouse, pet walk, fax service, Fri. night bonfire. **Activities:** Golf. **Nearby Attractions:** Casa Grande Ruins, McFarland Historical State Park, museums. **Additional Information:** Pinal County Visitor Center, (520) 868-9433.

RESTRICTIONS

Pets: On leash (not allowed in clubhouse). **Fires:** No (clubhouse fire pit only). **Alcoholic Beverages:** Drink all you want. **Vehicle Maximum Length:** 40 ft. width (optional). **Other:** Children must be supervised at all times.

TO GET THERE

Go 5 mi. south of Florence on AZ 79.

FOUNTAIN HILLS   MAP, C-2
McDowell Mountain
Regional Park

P.O. Box 18415, 15612 East Palisades Dr., 85269. T: (480) 506-2930 or (480) 471-0173; www.maricopa.gov/parks.

🚐 ★★★★	🏕 ★★★★
Beauty: ★★★★	Site Privacy: ★★★★
Spaciousness: ★★★★★	Quiet: ★★★★
Security: ★★★★	Cleanliness: ★★★★
Insect Control: ★★	Facilities: ★★★

One of the excellent Maricopa County Parks ringing the Phoenix area, McDowell Mountain attracts many groups, individuals using the Mayo Clinic in Fountain Hills, and mountain bikers coming to race on the competitive track. With over 100 picnic tables and grills, this is also a popular day-use park, featuring 50 miles of mountain biking and horseback riding trails traversing several ecosystems with six different rattlesnake species. Even though surrounded by the Superstition, McDowell, and Four Peaks Mountains, the park is conveniently located near urban areas. A Native American casino is nearby, downtown Phoenix is just 20 miles away, and Scottsdale is within 6 miles—for those wanting to shop and enjoy the urban amenities. The campsites at McDowell's E. I. Rowland Campground are very large and far apart. Barriers of tall desert plants like saguaro, ocotillo, and palo verde between the campsites make the privacy even more absolute.

BASICS

Operated By: Maricopa County Parks & Recreation. **Open:** All year. **Site Assignment:** First come, first served; group reservations. **Registration:** At self-pay fee station. **Fee:** $5–$18. **Parking:** At site.

FACILITIES

Number of RV-only Sites: 80. **Hookups:** Electric (20, 30 amps), water. **Each Site:** Table, grill, fire ring. **Dump Station:** Yes. **Laundry:** No. **Pay Phone:** Yes. **Restrooms and Showers:** Yes. **Fuel:** No. **Propane:** No. **Internal Roads:** Gravel, good. **RV Service:** No. **Market:** Fountain Hills, 5 mi. **Restaurant:** Fountain Hills, 5 mi. **General Store:** No. **Vending:** Yes. **Swimming:** No. **Playground:** Yes. **Other:** Competitive bike track. **Activities:** Horseback riding for horse owners, biking. **Nearby Attractions:** Phoenix, Scottsdale, Rio Verde. **Additional Information:** McDowell Park Assoc., (602) 837-3026; Fountain Hills Chamber of Commerce, (480) 837-1654, www.fhchamberofcommerce.org.

RESTRICTIONS

Pets: On 6-ft. leash. **Fires:** Allowed, Memorial Day–Labor Day only. **Alcoholic Beverages:** Allowed. **Vehicle Maximum Length:** No limit. **Other:** No glass bottles; 14-day stay limit.

TO GET THERE

From Fountain Hills go 4 mi. north on Fountain Hills Blvd. to N. McDowell Mountain Rd.

GRAND CANYON   MAP, A-2
Mather Campground

Grand Canyon National Park, South Rim, 86023. T: (928) 638-2631/6035.

🚐 ★★★★	🏕 ★★★★
Beauty: ★★★★	Site Privacy: ★★★
Spaciousness: ★★★★	Quiet: ★★
Security: ★★	Cleanliness: ★★★★
Insect Control: ★★	Facilities: ★★

One can imagine by looking at Mather Campground how the Anasazi slowly ground their way out of existence: a large number of people competing for limited resources. Campers are definitely advised to arrive early—the earlier, the better. Large numbers of people want to camp within the Grand Canyon's boundaries, and with hikers taking advantage of the maximum stay of seven nights, numerous campsites will already be taken when you arrive. By 4 p.m., it is a scramble to pick up any spot, which, naturally, leaves the slimmest picking for the late arrivals. Sites to avoid (if possible) are those closest to the restrooms, as the lights remain on all night and the doors slam with a thud that can raise the dead. In addition, try to avoid sites close to the busy roads (such as sites 53 and 54 on the Aspen Loop or 318 and 319 on the Pine Loop), with foot and car traffic that will annoy all but the soundest sleepers. Having said that, this is the Grand Canyon after all, and perhaps the greatest natural wonder of the world is only a few minutes' drive away. Further, the campground offers an extremely rugged and wild flavor. If you can abide the few annoyances inherent in a campground of this size, it is definitely worth the stay.

BASICS

Operated By: National Park Service. **Open:** All year. **Site Assignment:** Reservations recommended (Apr. 1–Nov. 30); first come, first served (Dec. 1–Mar. 31). **Registration:** At kiosk at entrance. **Fee:** $18. Golden Age/Access, half price; cash only. **Parking:** At site.

FACILITIES

Number of RV-only Sites: 312. **Hookups:** None. **Each Site:** Picnic table, grill. **Dump Station:** Yes. **Laundry:** Yes. **Pay Phone:** Yes. **Restrooms and Showers:** Yes. **Fuel:** 0.5 mi. in Market Plaza. **Propane:** No. **Internal Roads:** Paved. **RV Service:** No. **Market:** 0.5 mi. in Market Plaza. **Restaurant:** 0.5 mi. in Market Plaza. **General Store:** No. **Vending:** No. **Swimming:** No. **Playground:** No. **Other:** Inquire at campground. **Activities:** Hiking, helicopter, plane, & horseback rides through the Grand Canyon. **Nearby Attractions:** Grand Canyon National Park. **Additional Information:** North Rim park info: (520) 638-7864, South Rim park info: (520) 638-7888 or (520) 638-7770.

RESTRICTIONS

Pets: On leash, in campground only. **Fires:** Charcoal or wood in grills only. **Alcoholic Beverages:** At sites only. **Vehicle Maximum Length:** 50 ft. **Other:** 7-day stay limit; max. of 6 people or 1 family per site.

TO GET THERE

From the Grand Canyon South Entrance, take Hwy. 64 North for 2.6 mi., then turn left at the traffic light. Continue for 0.4 mi. and turn right onto Market Plaza Rd. Drive 0.9 mi., then turn right into the entrance at the sign for the campground.

HOLBROOK   MAP, B-3
Cholla Lake County Park

Navajo County Parks and Recreation Dept., 86025. T: (928) 524-4251 or (928) 288-3717; www.parksrec@navajo.az.us.

🚐 ★★★	🏕 ★★★
Beauty: ★★★★	Site Privacy: ★★★★
Spaciousness: ★★★★	Quiet: ★★★★
Security: ★★★★	Cleanliness: ★★★★
Insect Control: ★★★	Facilities: ★★

Situated around an artificial cattail-ringed lake whose waters cool and generate electricity at the four adjacent coal-burning Cholla Power Plant units, rustic Cholla Lake County Park provides travelers on I-40 between Flagstaff and Gallup, New Mexico, with a convenient overnight stop or a base for exploring the Petrified Forest, Painted Desert, Mogollon Rim, and nearby Hopi and Navajo Indian Reservations. The lake, one of the largest in northeastern Arizona, can be used for boating and water sports or fished for largemouth bass, sunfish, and catfish. For some campers, the power pylons, tall cement smokestacks, and piles of coal waiting to be pulverized will seem a visual blight. Others may enjoy the educational displays explaining how scrubbers remove sulfur dioxides and particulates.

BASICS

Operated By: Navajo County Parks & Recreation Dept. **Open:** All year. **Site Assignment:** First come, first served; reservations available by email. **Registration:** At self-pay fee station. **Fee:** $26. **Parking:** At site.

FACILITIES

Number of RV-only Sites: 25. **Hookups:** Electric (30 amps), water. **Each Site:** Table, grill. **Dump Station:** Yes. **Laundry:** No. **Pay Phone:** No. **Restrooms and Showers:** Yes. **Fuel:** No. **Propane:** No. **Internal Roads:** Gravel, good condition. **RV Service:** No. **Market:** Holbrook, 8 mi. **Restaurant:** Holbrook, 8 mi. **General Store:** No. **Vending:** Yes. **Swimming:** No. **Playground:** No. **Other:** Group pavilion, water ski course, jet ski landing, fishing dock, horseshoe pits, sand volleyball court. **Activities:** Fishing, boating, bird-watching. **Nearby Attractions:** Navajo Indian Reservation, Petrified Forest, Painted Desert, Homolovi Ruins, Mogollon Rim, White Mountains. **Additional Information:** Holbrook Chamber of Commerce, (800) 524-2459.

RESTRICTIONS

Pets: On leash, crated or caged (not allowed on swimming beach or in structures). **Fires:** Allowed (in grills only). **Alcoholic Beverages:** Allowed. **Vehicle Maximum Length:** 35 ft. **Other:** No glass bottles, boaters must observe no wake zone.

TO GET THERE

From Holbrook go 8 mi. west on I-40 to Exit 277 (Joseph City), then south onto park access road for 2 mi.

JACOB LAKE   MAP, A-2
Jacob Lake Campground

Jacob Lake Inn, Hwy. 89A and Hwy. 67, 86022. T: (928) 643-7298 or (928) 204-1698.

🚐 ★★★★	⛺ ★★★★
Beauty: ★★★★	Site Privacy: ★★★★★
Spaciousness: ★★★★★	Quiet: ★★★★★
Security: ★★★★	Cleanliness: ★★★★
Insect Control: ★★★	Facilities: ★★★★

It's camping at its best along five secluded loops in the pine forest at 7,900 feet, just an hour's drive (40 miles south via a slow, windy road) from the forested North Rim of the Grand Canyon. Widely dispersed pull-through sites provide plenty of forested privacy, yet Jacob Lake Campground is within one-quarter mile of a 24-hour gas station, general store, counter cafe, restaurant, ranger-staffed visitor center, and motel. However, water is scarce and available only by

the bucketful. In contrast to the North Rim Campground (see Appendix), which books up over a month in advance with reservations, the key to getting a spot here is a very early afternoon arrival, as Jacob Lake Campground fills up just after 4 p.m. most June, July, and August afternoons. Campers wanting hookups should head to nearby Kaibab Camper Village. For a more primitive experience at a smaller campground (23 sites; 30-foot maximum) run by the same concessionaire, head south on US 89A towards the North Rim another 23 miles to DeMotte Campground (see Appendix).

BASICS

Operated By: U.S. Forest Service/Resource Recreation Management (concessionaire). **Open:** May 15–Nov. 1; weather-dependent. **Site Assignment:** First come, first served; group site reservations. **Registration:** W/ campground hosts. **Fee:** $12; cash. **Parking:** Paved loop in front of site.

FACILITIES

Number of RV-only Sites: 54. **Hookups:** None. **Each Site:** Table, fire ring. **Dump Station:** No. **Laundry:** No. **Pay Phone:** No. **Restrooms and Showers:** No showers. **Fuel:** Gas station across the street. **Propane:** No. **Internal Roads:** Paved, bumpy in spots. **RV Service:** No. **Market:** 0.3 mi. south, near visitor center. **Restaurant:** 0.3 mi. south, near visitor center. **General Store:** No. **Vending:** No. **Swimming:** No. **Playground:** No. **Other:** Some wheelchair-accessible facilities. DeMotte Campground has smaller sites. **Activities:** Evening ranger programs, mule-deer watching, biking, hiking. **Nearby Attractions:** North Rim of Grand Canyon, Pipe Springs National Monument, Kanab, Lees Ferry. **Additional Information:** Kaibab Plateau Visitor Center, (928) 643-7298; North Kaibab Ranger District, (928) 643-7395.

RESTRICTIONS

Pets: On 6 ft leash under owner's control. **Fires:** Fire ring only. **Alcoholic Beverages:** At sites. **Vehicle Maximum Length:** 30 ft. & larger RVs. **Other:** 14-day stay limit; wheelchair accessible site; no fireworks.

TO GET THERE

From junction of US 89A and AZ 67, drive 0.3 mi. north on US 89A.

JACOB LAKE   MAP, A-2
Kaibab Camper Village

P.O. Box 3331, 86003. T: (928) 643-7804 (May 15–Oct. 15) or (800) 525-0924 (Oct. 15–May 15, outside AZ); www.canyoneers.com.

🚐 ★★★★	⛺ ★★★★
Beauty: ★★★★	Site Privacy: ★★★★
Spaciousness: ★★★★	Quiet: ★★★★
Security: ★★★★	Cleanliness: ★★★★
Insect Control: ★★★	Facilities: ★★★

Tall pines, grassy meadows with picnic tables, the closest hookups to the Grand Canyon's North Rim, and wide pull-through sites make Kaibab Camper Village a top choice for quiet relaxation and North Rim excursions. Management goes to great lengths

to keep the campground quiet, even banning electrical generators. Tent campers will appreciate the grassy sites separate from the RV loop. Although it feels isolated in a tall pine forest surrounded by horse pastures and mountain backdrops, the campground is only 1 mile (half via a dusty but extra-wide gravel road) from a 24-hour gas station anchoring the U.S. Forest Service's helpful Kaibab Plateau Visitor Center, a motel, an old-fashioned counter cafe, a sit-down restaurant decorated with Native American rugs, and a general store loaded with curios. All in all, it is hard to go wrong with this combination of wilderness and comforts.

BASICS

Operated By: Canyoneers (Flagstaff, AZ). **Open:** May 15–Oct. 15. **Site Assignment:** First come, first served; reservations accepted (nonrefundable prepayment of 1 night). **Registration:** At camp office. **Fee:** Hookup, $27; tent/dry, $13; cash, traveler's check, check w/ 2 valid IDs. **Parking:** At site.

FACILITIES

Number of RV-only Sites: 62. **Number of Tent-only Sites:** 34. **Hookups:** Electric (20, 30 amps), water, sewer. **Each Site:** Table, fire ring at most sites. **Dump Station:** Yes, for guests only. **Laundry:** Yes. **Pay Phone:** Yes. **Restrooms and Showers:** Yes, pay showers. **Fuel:** No. **Propane:** No. **Internal Roads:** Dirt & gravel. **RV Service:** No. **Market:** 1 mi., near visitor center. **Restaurant:** 1 mi., near visitor center. **General Store:** Yes, very small. **Vending:** No. **Swimming:** No. **Playground:** No. **Other:** Modem hookup at office; 30-ft.-wide pull-throughs; noon check-out. **Activities:** Inquire at campground. **Nearby Attractions:** Grand Canyon North Rim (40 mi.), Bryce (115 mi.). **Additional Information:** (928) 526-0924.

RESTRICTIONS

Pets: On 10 ft. leash & kept quiet at all times; designated dog walking area. **Fires:** Allowed (only in metal firepots, firewood sold). **Alcoholic Beverages:** Allowed. **Vehicle Maximum Length:** No limit. **Other:** Electrical generator use not allowed; no gathering of firewood; water is scarce, & cannot be used for washing people, pets, vehicles, or clothes.

TO GET THERE

From junction of US 89A and AZ 67, go 0.3 mi. south on Hwy. 67 and then 0.5 mi. west on gravel road.

KINGMAN   MAP, B-1
Kingman KOA

3820 North Roosevelt, 86401-3298. T: (928) 757-4397 or (800) 562-3991; www.koa.com.

🚐 ★★★	⛺ ★★★
Beauty: ★★★	Site Privacy: ★★★
Spaciousness: ★★★	Quiet: ★★★★
Security: ★★★★	Cleanliness: ★★★★★
Insect Control: ★★★★	Facilities: ★★★★

Kingman, a stop en route to the Grand Canyon from Las Vegas, had its heyday when local boy Andy Devine was playing Jingles in cowboy movies and Route 66 was still the place for getting your "kicks" when driving cross country from Chicago to Los Angeles. Downtown Kingman is just now coming out of a deep boarded-up funk, and the KOA is just about the only campground away from the noise of I-40 with a little space for campers to spread out, short of heading out of town into the Hualapai Mountains. The KOA is a little oasis with oleanders and trees between the campsites, a pleasant ambiance, free morning coffee, 50 TV channels, and newspaper machines. Tent campers have their own area, and a policy of not running generators ensures quiet.

BASICS

Operated By: KOA. **Open:** All year. **Site Assignment:** First come, first served; reservations accepted. **Registration:** At office. **Fee:** Kamping Kabin, $42–$52; RV, $30–$40, tent, $21–$24. **Parking:** At site.

FACILITIES

Number of RV-only Sites: 78. **Number of Tent-only Sites:** 12. **Hookups:** Electric (30, 50 amps), water, sewer, cable TV, phone (modem). **Each Site:** Table, grill. **Dump Station:** Yes. **Laundry:** Yes. **Pay Phone:** Yes. **Restrooms and Showers:** Yes. **Fuel:** No. **Propane:** Yes. **Internal Roads:** Paved, good. **RV Service:** No. **Market:** No. **Restaurant:** No. **General Store:** Yes. **Vending:** No. **Swimming:** Pool. **Playground:** Yes. **Other:** Rec hall w/ kitchen & TV, video game room, mini-golf, cabins. **Activities:** Golf. **Nearby Attractions:** Grand Canyon, Ghost Towns, museums. **Additional Information:** Kingman Chamber of Commerce, (928) 753-6253, Fax (928) 753-1049, www.kingmanchamber.org.

RESTRICTIONS

Pets: On leash & under owner's control; no pit-bulls or rottweilers. **Fires:** Allowed (only in approved grills). **Alcoholic Beverages:** Allowed. **Vehicle Maximum Length:** 70 ft. **Other:** No running of generators.

TO GET THERE

From I-40 Exits 51 and 53 take Stockton Hill Rd. or Andy Devine to intersection of Airway and Roosevelt.

LAKE HAVASU CITY   MAP, B-1
Islander RV Resort

751 Beachcomber Blvd., 86403. T: (928) 680-2000.

🚐 ★★★★	⛺ n/a
Beauty: ★★★★	Site Privacy: ★★★
Spaciousness: ★★★★	Quiet: ★★★★
Security: ★★★★★	Cleanliness: ★★★★★
Insect Control: ★★★★	Facilities: ★★★

On the shores of Lake Havasu, Islander boasts ample amenities, including two swimming pools, boat docks, fish-cleaning stations, and winter activities for snowbirds. Premium and waterfront sites have the best lake views, but inland sites have tall eucalyptus trees and some decent mountain views. Unlike Beachcomber Resort (see Appendix) down the road, which rents empty mobile home spots to RVs, Islander terminates the rental agreement of anyone showing signs of residency, like enrolling kids in local schools or taking a job in town. The typical 36-

foot wide space has a patio pad and enough space for parking a tow vehicle and boat. Those who like it quiet will appreciate that the park is far from noisy highways, though only a short jaunt from the London Bridge, whose 10,276 granite stones were reassembled in this planned desert city by developer Robert McCulloch.

BASICS

Operated By: Islander RV Resort. **Open:** All year. **Site Assignment:** Reservations do not guarantee specific sites. **Registration:** At office. **Fee:** Summer season (Apr. 1–Oct. 31), $49–$69; winter season (Nov. 1–Mar. 31), $39–$54. **Parking:** At site.

FACILITIES

Number of RV-only Sites: 500. **Hookups:** Electric (30, 50 amps), water, sewer. **Each Site:** Patio pad, table. **Dump Station:** No. **Laundry:** Yes. **Pay Phone:** Yes. **Restrooms and Showers:** Yes. **Fuel:** No. **Propane:** No. **Internal Roads:** Paved, excellent. **RV Service:** No. **Market:** Lake Havasu City, 1 mi. **Restaurant:** Lake Havasu City, 1 mi. **General Store:** Yes. **Vending:** Yes. **Swimming:** Lake, 2 Jacuzzis. **Playground:** Yes. **Other:** Rec hall, billiards, shuffleboard & horseshoe areas, boat docks & launch ramp, fish-cleaning station. **Activities:** Biking, swimming, fishing, boating, golf (nearby). Seasonal activities include dances, crafts, computer classes, & other special events as well as children's programs. **Nearby Attractions:** London Bridge, Havasu National Wildlife Refuge. **Additional Information:** Lake Havasu Tourism Bureau, (928) 453-3444, (800) 242-8278.

RESTRICTIONS

Pets: Allowed (subject to separate signed agreement; aggressive breeds like pit bulls not allowed). **Fires:** Not allowed. **Alcoholic Beverages:** Excessive use not allowed. **Vehicle Maximum Length:** 50 ft. **Other:** RVIA approved self-contained RVs; RVs must be 10 years of age or newer.

TO GET THERE

Get off AZ 95 at Mesquite Ave. and go east on Lake Havasu Blvd., south to McCullough Blvd., and west across the London Bridge.

LAKE HAVASU CITY   MAP, B-1
Lake Havasu State Park (Windsor Beach)

699 London Bridge Rd, 86403. T: (928) 855-2784; www.pr.state.az.us/parkhtml/havasu.html.

🚐 ★★★★	⛺ ★★★★★
Beauty: ★★★★	Site Privacy: ★★★★★
Spaciousness: ★★★★★	Quiet: ★★★★★
Security: ★★★★	Cleanliness: ★★★★
Insect Control: ★★★	Facilities: ★★

Formed when the Colorado River was dammed near Parker to end the area's annual spring floods and provide water for Arizona and southern California, 45-mile-long Lake Havasu's boating, fishing, and bird-watching recreational possibilities can be accessed at Lake Havasu State Park's Windsor Beach Campground. The large gravel campsites at Windsor Beach combine camping in the desert scrub with a

lakeside location. The palo verde, mesquite, and other desert plants are lush enough here to provide each campsite with a barrier of privacy. For those desiring even more of an escape, Lake Havasu State Park also has 55 campsites accessible only by boat. For those wanting to stay closer to urban amenities, Windsor Beach has the added advantage of being only 3 miles from the London Bridge and Lake Havasu City's restaurants, three microbreweries, movie theaters, nightclubs, and shops.

BASICS

Operated By: Arizona State Parks. **Open:** All year. **Site Assignment:** First come, first served. **Registration:** At entrance kiosk. **Fee:** $10–$22. **Parking:** At site.

FACILITIES

Number of RV-only Sites: 73. **Number of Tent-only Sites:** 55. **Hookups:** None. **Each Site:** Table, grill, fire ring. **Dump Station:** Yes. **Laundry:** No. **Pay Phone:** Yes. **Restrooms and Showers:** Yes. **Fuel:** No. **Propane:** No. **Internal Roads:** Paved, good. **RV Service:** No. **Market:** Lake Havasu City, 3 mi. **Restaurant:** Lake Havasu City, 2 mi. **General Store:** No. **Vending:** No. **Swimming:** Lake. **Playground:** No. **Other:** Botanical garden, group pavilion. **Activities:** Boating, fishing, water sports, bird-watching, golf. **Nearby Attractions:** London Bridge, Havasu National Wildlife Refuge. **Additional Information:** Lake Havasu Tourism Bureau, (928) 453-3444, (800) 242-8278.

RESTRICTIONS

Pets: On 6 ft leash; water & shade must be provided. **Fires:** Allowed (no fires when high winds). **Alcoholic Beverages:** Allowed (state liquor laws strictly enforced). No glass containers. **Vehicle Maximum Length:** No limit. **Other:** No glass containers on beaches or in day-use areas.

TO GET THERE

From the junction of London Bridge Rd. and AZ 95, go 2.5 mi. west on London Bridge Rd.

MARBLE CANYON   MAP, A-2
Lees Ferry Campground

Hwy. 89, 86036. T: (928) 355-2234; www.nps.gov/glca.

🚐 ★★★	⛺ ★★★★
Beauty: ★★★★	Site Privacy: ★★★★
Spaciousness: ★★★★	Quiet: ★★★★
Security: ★★★★	Cleanliness: ★★★★
Insect Control: ★★★	Facilities: ★★

The surrounding mountains have red, orange, chocolate brown, white, and green bands of sandstone that give the area its name, Marble Canyon. In the 1920s, this was an important area for crossing the Colorado River by ferry, as well as the site of Jerry Johnson's polygamous Mormon colony at Lonely Dell Ranch. Ferry service ended when the historic Navajo Bridge opened after a deadly accident in 1928. The boat launch near Lees Ferry Campground is still one of the best places to enter the Colorado River, where it flows smooth and green beneath both the old and new Navajo Bridges. The

National Park Service has an interpretative center at Navajo Bridge, near where the river splits into its upper and lower basins. Only a few camp sites have trees or manmade structures for shade. Noises echo at the campground, but when the neighbors are quiet this is a peaceful spot. Few places are better for river recreation, and it's away from the hubbub of Lake Powell and Page.

BASICS

Operated By: National Park Service. **Open:** All year. **Site Assignment:** First come, first served. **Registration:** At self-pay fee station at entrance. **Fee:** $10 (Golden Age/Access, $5; cash only). **Parking:** At site.

FACILITIES

Number of RV-only Sites: 25. **Number of Tent-only Sites:** 24. **Hookups:** None. **Each Site:** Table, fire grate. **Dump Station:** Yes. **Laundry:** No. **Pay Phone:** Yes. **Restrooms and Showers:** Restrooms but no showers. **Fuel:** No. **Propane:** No. **Internal Roads:** Paved, good condition. **RV Service:** No. **Market:** 4.5 mi. southwest at Marble Canyon Lodge. **Restaurant:** 4.5 mi. southwest at Marble Canyon Lodge. **General Store:** No. **Vending:** No. **Swimming:** No. **Playground:** No. **Other:** Boat launch ramp, fish-cleaning station (summers only). **Activities:** Colorado River fishing, canoeing, rafting. **Nearby Attractions:** Navajo Bridge, Lake Powell, Jacob Lake, Grand Canyon North Rim. **Additional Information:** National Park Service, Southern AZ Group, (602) 640-5250; Marble Canyon Lodge, (520) 355-2225; Glen Canyon National Recreation Area, (520) 608-6404.

RESTRICTIONS

Pets: On 6-ft. leash under owner's control. **Fires:** Fire receptacles only, no ground fires. **Alcoholic Beverages:** Allowed in moderation. **Vehicle Maximum Length:** 45 ft. **Other:** 14 consecutive days limit, 30 days per year max.; noon checkout.

TO GET THERE

From US 89A, go 5.7 mi. north at Marble Canyon.

MESA   MAP, C-2
Usery Mountain Recreation Area

3939 North Usery Pass Rd., 85207. T: (480) 984-0032; www.maricopa.gov/parks/usery.

🚐 ★★★★★   ▲ ★★★★★

Beauty: ★★★★★   Site Privacy: ★★★★★
Spaciousness: ★★★★★   Quiet: ★★★★★
Security: ★★★★★   Cleanliness: ★★★★
Insect Control: ★★★   Facilities: ★★★

Conveniently close to Mesa's urban amenities, Usery Mountain Recreation Area's Buckhorn Family Campground combines lower Sonoran Desert foreground scenery with the majestic backdrop of the Usery, Goldfield, McDowell, and Superstition mountains. Campsites at this excellent Maricopa County campground, named for King Usery, a cattle rancher who robbed stagecoaches to make ends meet, are very private thanks to intervening patches of mesquite, ocotillo, palo verde, cholla, and saguaro. During spring and fall, Mexican and Basque shep-

herds can be spotted with their dogs moving sheep across Usery Pass between the high country and the Salt River Valley, an area of ancient Native American village and canal ruins. Seven miles north is Saguaro Lake and Salt River tubing near Stewart Mountain Dam. Campers can also ride their horses or mountain bike park trails. During hot summer months, four covered sites are available ($110 a week in advance; 2-week limit).

BASICS

Operated By: Maricopa County Parks & Recreation Dept. **Open:** All year. **Site Assignment:** First come, first served; group reservations required. **Registration:** At host site near entrance. **Fee:** $18 Camping fee waives $5 entry fee. Additional fee for group camping; V, MC. **Parking:** At site.

FACILITIES

Number of RV-only Sites: 73. **Hookups:** Electric (30, 50 amps), water. **Each Site:** Table, grill. **Dump Station:** Yes. **Laundry:** No. **Pay Phone:** Yes. **Restrooms and Showers:** Yes. **Fuel:** No. **Propane:** No. **Internal Roads:** Paved, good. **RV Service:** No. **Market:** Mesa, 4 mi. north. **Restaurant:** Mesa, 4 mi. north. **General Store:** No. **Vending:** Yes. **Swimming:** No. **Playground:** Yes. **Other:** Horse staging area, archery range, gun range, model airplane field, flood lights for group area. **Activities:** Horseback riding, mountain biking, hiking. **Nearby Attractions:** Phoenix, colleges, museums, botanic gardens, river tubing. **Additional Information:** Mesa CVB, (602) 969-1307.

RESTRICTIONS

Pets: On leash under owner's control (horses OK). **Fires:** Grill only. **Alcoholic Beverages:** Allowed (glass bottles prohibited). **Vehicle Maximum Length:** No limit. **Other:** 2-week stay limit; no horses in picnic areas.

TO GET THERE

From Mesa go 7.5 mi. north on US 60 (Ellsworth/Usery Pass Rd.) to Usery Park Rd.

PAGE   MAP, A-2
Wahweap Campground

P.O. Box 1597, 86040. T: (928) 645-2433 or (800) 528-6154; www.visitlakepowell.com.

🚐 ★★★   ▲ ★★★★

Beauty: ★★★★   Site Privacy: ★★★★
Spaciousness: ★★★★   Quiet: ★★★★
Security: ★★★★   Cleanliness: ★★★★
Insect Control: ★★★   Facilities: ★★★★

Wahweap Campground is more spacious and private in feel than Wahweap RV Park, and the Lake Powell views are surpassed only by camping at Lone Rock Beach. However, RV campers may prefer downtown Page and the more amenity-laden Page–Lake Powell Campground (see Appendix) over Wahweap Campground when Wahweap RV Park's hookups are full. Indeed, the spacious campsites and small loops are tailored to tents and small trailers, with plenty of shade trees and desert scrub separating sites from each other along smallish loops. It is slightly over a mile to the showers ($2) and Wahweap Marina

amenities like pizza, a restaurant, groceries, and the Wahweap Lodge pool (open to campers). Overall, Wahweap Campground is a good tent and trailer choice, combining the feel of camping out with Lake Powell's nearby amenities.

BASICS

Operated By: Aramark. **Open:** Mar. 15–Oct. 31. **Site Assignment:** First come, first served w/ tents; reservations allowed for full hookups & groups. **Registration:** At office. **Fee:** $15–$27; V, MC, AE, D, DC. **Parking:** At site.

FACILITIES

Number of RV-only Sites: 112. **Hookups:** 90 w/ electric, water, sewer. **Each Site:** Table, grill. **Dump Station:** Yes. **Laundry:** Yes. **Pay Phone:** Yes. **Restrooms and Showers:** Yes. **Fuel:** No. **Propane:** No. **Internal Roads:** Paved, good condition. **RV Service:** No. **Market:** Limited groceries at office store; more at RV park. **Restaurant:** At Wahweap Marina. **General Store:** Yes. **Vending:** Yes. **Swimming:** Lodge pool, lake. **Playground:** No. **Other:** Fine dining at Wahweap Lodge. **Activities:** Boat tours & rentals; float trips on river. **Nearby Attractions:** Rainbow Bridge, Page, Glen Canyon Dam, Antelope Canyon, Lees Ferry, Escalante Staircase National Monument. **Additional Information:** Glen Canyon National Recreation Area, (928) 608-6404; Page–Lake Powell Chamber of Commerce, 644 North Navajo Dr., Dam Plaza, P.O. Box 727, Page, AZ 86040; (888) 261-7243, www.PageLakePowellChamber.org; info@pagelakepowellchamber.org.

RESTRICTIONS

Pets: On leash under owner's control (no barking). **Fires:** Grill only. **Alcoholic Beverages:** Allowed. **Vehicle Maximum Length:** 45 ft. **Other:** 14 consecutive days, 30 days per year camping limit; no loaded firearms, fireworks, or water balloon launchers.

TO GET THERE

Take US 198 north from Glen Canyon Dam for 4 mi., turn on Lake Shore Dr. and go to corner of Wahweap Blvd.

PAGE   MAP, A-2
Wahweap RV Park

Hwy. 89, 86040. T: (800) 528-6154 or (928) 645-2433; www.visitlakepowell.com.

🚐 ★★★★   ▲ n/a

Beauty: ★★★   Site Privacy: ★★★
Spaciousness: ★★★   Quiet: ★★★★
Security: ★★★★   Cleanliness: ★★★★
Insect Control: ★★★   Facilities: ★★★★

Wahweap RV Park offers plenty of boat parking for nearby Wahweap Marina. An attractive grassy area with trees separates the RV Park from the road, but once inside it is more like a huge parking lot full of boats and vehicles. If hookups and amenities are of more interest than boats and the lake, downtown Page and the Page–Lake Powell Campground (see Appendix) are an attractive alternative. For a more primitive beach-camping experience, head to Lone Rock Beach. The views are nothing to write home about, but the whole idea here seems to be get out on the water and play until dark. Despite the tightly packed nature of the RV park, it stays fairly quiet. Tables on cement and shade are among the nice touches. If boating on Lake Powell plus RV amenities equal a good time, then this is the best place to be.

BASICS

Operated By: Aramark. **Open:** All year. **Site Assignment:** First come, first served; reservations (1-night deposit). **Registration:** At office. **Fee:** $15–$27; V, MC, AE, D, DC. **Parking:** At site.

FACILITIES

Hookups: Electric (20, 30, 50 amps). **Each Site:** Table, grill. **Dump Station:** Yes. **Laundry:** Yes. **Pay Phone:** Yes. **Restrooms and Showers:** Yes. **Fuel:** Yes. **Propane:** Yes. **Internal Roads:** Gravel, good condition. **RV Service:** No. **Market:** Yes. **Restaurant:** At Wahweap Marina. **General Store:** Yes. **Vending:** Yes. **Swimming:** Lodge pool, lake. **Playground:** Yes. **Other:** Boat ramp & boat rentals. **Activities:** Fishing, boating, summer ranger programs, free use of lodge facilities. **Nearby Attractions:** Antelope Canyon, Glen Canyon Dam, Lees Ferry, Rainbow Bridge, Escalante Staircase National Monument. **Additional Information:** Glen Canyon National Recreation Area, (520) 608-6404; Page–Lake Powell Chamber of Commerce, 644 North Navajo Dr., Dam Plaza, P.O. Box 727, Page, AZ 86040; (888) 261-7243, www.pagelakepowell chamber.org; info@pagelakepowellchamber.org.

RESTRICTIONS

Pets: On leash under owner's control. **Fires:** Allowed. **Alcoholic Beverages:** Allowed. **Vehicle Maximum Length:** 45 ft. **Other:** No tents.

TO GET THERE

From Glen Canyon Dam go 4 mi. north on US 89, then take Lake Shore Dr. to 100 Stateline Dr.

PARKER · MAP, C-1
Buckskin Mountain State Park

5476 Hwy. 95, 85344. T: (928) 667-3231; www.azstateparks.com.

🚐 ★★★	🏕 ★★★
Beauty: ★★★★	Site Privacy: ★★★★
Spaciousness: ★★★★	Quiet: ★★★
Security: ★★★	Cleanliness: ★★★★
Insect Control: ★★★	Facilities: ★★

If relaxation and plenty of play space for the children are more important than partying, then Buckskin Mountain's paved sites separated by dirt and trees are a better choice than Fox's Pierpoint Landing and Tony's Road Runner. A group-use area with sheltered tables is 1 mile north at Buckskin Mountain State Park's River Island Unit, which has another 22 campsites and large grass play areas but no hookups on 420 acres with a boat ramp and a Colorado River swimming beach. Island Unit is closer to the highway and farther from the water, but is quieter when not overrun with weekend groups. During the cooler winter months, hiking the short steep trails into the surrounding mountains for spectacular overviews of the area is a worthwhile alternative to water play.

Some trails go by abandoned mines and have interpretative stops to get to better know the local ecosystems and vegetation.

BASICS

Operated By: Arizona State Parks. **Open:** All year. **Site Assignment:** First come, first served. **Registration:** At self-pay entrance fee station. **Fee:** $14–$22; cash, check, V, MC. **Parking:** At site.

FACILITIES

Number of RV-only Sites: 68. **Number of Tent-only Sites:** 21. **Hookups:** Electric (30 amps), water, sewer; 11 sites w/ full hookups. **Each Site:** Table, grill. **Dump Station:** Yes. **Laundry:** No. **Pay Phone:** Yes. **Restrooms and Showers:** Yes. **Fuel:** No; boat fuel offered during summers. **Propane:** No. **Internal Roads:** Paved, good. **RV Service:** No. **Market:** Buckskin Market, in park (seasonal). **Restaurant:** In park (seasonal). **General Store:** Yes (seasonal). **Vending:** Seasonal. **Swimming:** River. **Playground:** Yes. **Other:** Cactus garden, interpretative center, boutique, boat ramp, basketball court, volleyball, horseshoe pit. **Activities:** Boating, fishing, water sports, hiking. **Nearby Attractions:** Lake Havasu. **Additional Information:** Parker Chamber of Commerce, (928) 669-2174, www.riverinfo.com/parker.

RESTRICTIONS

Pets: On leash. **Fires:** Fire grill. **Alcoholic Beverages:** Allowed. **Vehicle Maximum Length:** No limit. **Other:** No loud noises; 14-day stay limit.

TO GET THERE

From Parker go 11 mi. north on AZ 95.

PARKER · MAP, C-1
Havasu Springs Resort

2581 Hwy. 95, 85344. T: (928) 667-3361; www.havasusprings.com.

🚐 ★★★★	🏕 n/a
Beauty: ★★★	Site Privacy: ★★★
Spaciousness: ★★★	Quiet: ★★★★
Security: ★★★★★	Cleanliness: ★★★★★
Insect Control: ★★★	Facilities: ★★★★★

A true destination resort with plenty of amenities, including an Olympic-sized pool, and enough winter activities to keep snowbirds happy, Havasu Springs Resort has over 250 boat slips, three motels, a restaurant with a bar and lounge, and everything from par 3 golf to houseboat and fishing-boat rentals. In contrast to the Colorado River and Havasu partying areas, even teenagers must be under tight adult reign here. Motorcycles are also banned, which helps keep the park quiet. Gate security is also relatively tight, and visitors must obtain passes. Though the cement pads here are good, it will be a few years before the trees are large enough to provide some shade to the RV sites. But if protection from noisy Harleys and rowdy party animals is part of the Colorado River recreation game plan, then reservations here may fit the bill.

BASICS

Operated By: Havasu Springs Resort, L.L.C., Bob Atkins. **Open:** All year. **Site Assignment:** First come, first served; reservations a necessity. **Regis-**

tration: At office. **Fee:** Full, $38; basic, $34; V, MC, AE, D. **Parking:** At site.

FACILITIES

Number of RV-only Sites: 150. **Hookups:** Electric (30, 50 amps), water, sewer, phone, cable TV. **Each Site:** Table, grill. **Dump Station:** No. **Laundry:** Yes. **Pay Phone:** Yes. **Restrooms and Showers:** Yes. **Fuel:** Yes (boat fuel also available). **Propane:** Yes. **Internal Roads:** Paved, good. **RV Service:** No. **Market:** On premises. **Restaurant:** On premises. **General Store:** Yes. **Vending:** Yes. **Swimming:** Pool. **Playground:** No. **Other:** Marina, houseboat & fishing boat rentals, fish-cleaning stations, lighted tennis courts, 9-hole golf course, 3 motels, sporting goods store, pool tables, video games. **Activities:** Boating, fishing, golf, tennis. No hunting. **Nearby Attractions:** Parker Dam, Lake Havasu. **Additional Information:** Parker Chamber of Commerce, (928) 669-2174, www.riverinfo.com/parker.

RESTRICTIONS

Pets: On leash at all times (subject to management discretion). **Fires:** Not allowed. **Alcoholic Beverages:** Allowed. **Vehicle Maximum Length:** 40 ft. **Other:** Only RVIA approved units w/ hard sides allowed; teenagers must be accompanied by parents; no motorcycles or go-carts; no hunting.

TO GET THERE

From Parker go 17 mi. north on AZ 95.

PARKER · MAP, C-1
LaPaz County Park

7350 Riverside Dr., 85344. T: (928) 667-2069; www.lapazcountypark.com.

🚐 ★★★★	🏕 ★★★★
Beauty: ★★★★	Site Privacy: ★★★★
Spaciousness: ★★★★	Quiet: ★★★★
Security: ★★★★	Cleanliness: ★★★★★
Insect Control: ★★★	Facilities: ★★★

Though lacking ice cream socials and some of the snowbird amenities of Branson's Resort next door, LaPaz offers lots of open space and green grass. Golfers can practice on the putting green and cross the street to use the driving range or play 18 holes, and there are a baseball field, tennis court, and plenty else to do besides boating, fishing, and swimming in the Colorado River. During the winter, tent campers have a prime dirt beachfront area along the river, and designated sites are kept open for RVs. But RV sites are open to tent camping during the summer months when the snowbird migration has reversed. Tents can also be placed under trees near the group area when it does not conflict with irrigation schedules. The 2-mile-long park has some big pines surrounding the inland RV sites, but beachfront RV sites 5–47 and 84–113 have the best river views.

BASICS

Operated By: LaPaz County Parks. **Open:** All year. **Site Assignment:** First come, first served. **Registration:** At self-pay entrance fee station. **Fee:** $16. **Parking:** At site.

FACILITIES

Number of RV-only Sites: 114. **Number of Multipurpose Sites:** 35. **Hookups:** Electric (20, 30, 50 amps), water, cable TV, phone. **Each Site:** Table, grill. **Dump Station:** Yes. **Laundry:** No. **Pay Phone:** Yes. **Restrooms and Showers:** Yes. **Fuel:** No. **Propane:** Yes (delivered). **Internal Roads:** Gravel, good. **RV Service:** No. **Market:** Parker, 8 mi. **Restaurant:** Parker, 2 mi. **General Store:** No. **Vending:** Seasonal. **Swimming:** River. **Playground:** Yes. **Other:** Boat ramps, putting green, tennis court, softball field, volleyball court, rec hall, horseshoe pits, some sites w/ sheltered tables. **Activities:** Boating, fishing, golf, horseshoes, volleyball, tennis. **Nearby Attractions:** Nellie E. Saloon, Blythe Intaglios (CA), Quartzsite, Lake Havasu. **Additional Information:** Parker Chamber of Commerce, (928) 669-2174, www.riverinfo.com/parker.

RESTRICTIONS

Pets: On leash at all times (barking dogs not tolerated; no dogs on beachfront walkways). **Fires:** Allowed. **Alcoholic Beverages:** Allowed. **Vehicle Maximum Length:** No limit. **Other:** No bands allowed; no firearms; no fireworks.

TO GET THERE

From Parker go 8 mi. north on US 95.

PARKER   MAP, C-1
Red Rock Resort

6400 Riverside Dr., 85344. T: (928) 667-3116; www.redrockresort.com.

🚐 ★★★   ▲ ★★★

Beauty: ★★★★   Site Privacy: ★★★
Spaciousness: ★★★   Quiet: ★★★★
Security: ★★★★   Cleanliness: ★★★★
Insect Control: ★★★   Facilities: ★★

Boating, fishing, and water sports are the chief attraction at Red Rock Resort, which is notable for its waterfront cabana campsites. The large pull-through sites (41–56) and sites 64–71 near the winter overflow and RV and trailer storage areas are farthest from the Colorado River. However, site 41, a large lawn corner pull-through is closer to the water and worth the small rental premium. The best sites are right on the Colorado River, and are open only to smaller vehicles and tent camping. These waterfront cabanas, which offer the opportunity to barbecue on the banks of the Colorado River and sit in the shade, are numbered 1–40 and are difficult to score, as they are often rented for four months solid during the peak winter season. Good boat facilities, including repair, salvage, and storage, as well as RV and trailer storage, also help make this small waterfront resort with its own bar and cafe a popular destination.

BASICS

Operated By: Red Rock Resort. **Open:** All year. **Site Assignment:** First come, first served; reservations advised for peak season, holidays, weekends. **Registration:** At front desk. **Fee:** $20–$25; V, MC. **Parking:** At site.

FACILITIES

Number of RV-only Sites: 90. **Hookups:** Electric (30, 50 amps), water, sewer, cable TV, phone. **Each**

Site: Table, grill. **Dump Station:** Yes. **Laundry:** Yes. **Pay Phone:** Yes. **Restrooms and Showers:** Yes. **Fuel:** No. **Propane:** Yes. **Internal Roads:** Paved, good. **RV Service:** No. **Market:** Parker, 9 mi. **Restaurant:** On premises. **General Store:** Yes. **Vending:** Yes. **Swimming:** River. **Playground:** No. **Other:** Boat ramp, RV & boat storage, boat repair, game room, cafe, bar. **Activities:** Fishing, boating, water sports. **Nearby Attractions:** Parker Dam, Lake Havasu. **Additional Information:** Parker Chamber of Commerce, (928) 669-2174, www.riverinfo.com/parker.

RESTRICTIONS

Pets: On leash. **Fires:** Allowed. **Alcoholic Beverages:** Allowed. **Vehicle Maximum Length:** No limit.

TO GET THERE

From Parker go 9 mi. north on AZ 95.

PARKS   MAP, B-2
Ponderosa Forest RV Park and RV Campground

P.O. Box 50640, 86018. T: (888) 635-0456 or (928) 635-0456.

🚐 ★★★   ▲ ★★★

Beauty: ★★   Site Privacy: ★★★★
Spaciousness: ★   Quiet: ★
Security: ★★   Cleanliness: ★★★
Insect Control: ★★★   Facilities: ★★★★

The pine trees make a pretty setting for this campground, with most sites set into the forest. (There is a treeless strip of gravel for seven larger rigs in the middle of the park that strikes one as slightly out of place.) A gorgeous ponderosa pine forest surrounds the park for at least ten acres, giving this campground both a rustic feel and the clean fresh air of a mountain forest. Accommodating both pull-throughs and back-ins, Ponderosa Forest gives the impression of being lost in the woods. Too bad the train tracks are so close—the engineers blow the train horn often! While the tent sites could stand a little more room, the overall experience is better than the campgrounds in Williams or Flagstaff. Whether your destination is the Grand Canyon or Flagstaff, this campground makes an adequate jumping-off point.

BASICS

Operated By: Private operator. **Open:** All year. **Site Assignment:** Upon registration. **Registration:** At office; late arrivals go to manager's office at back of park. **Fee:** RV, $26; tent, $19. **Parking:** At site.

FACILITIES

Number of RV-only Sites: 33. **Number of Tent-only Sites:** 16. **Hookups:** Electric (30, 50 amps), water, sewer. **Each Site:** Picnic table, fire ring, trash can, most have several trees. **Dump Station:** Yes. **Laundry:** Yes. **Pay Phone:** Yes. **Restrooms and Showers:** Yes. **Fuel:** No. Firewood for sale. **Propane:** Yes. **Internal Roads:** Packed dirt & gravel, mostly good condition. **RV Service:** No. **Market:** 0.5 mi. to parks. **Restaurant:** 0.5 mi. **General Store:** Yes, nearby. **Vending:** Yes. **Swimming:**

No. **Playground:** No. **Other:** Gift shop on premises; post office, fax, copies, hair salon. **Activities:** Hiking, fishing, hunting. **Nearby Attractions:** Kendrik Peak, historic Rte. 66, Lava River Cave, local hikes. **Additional Information:** Williams–Grand Canyon Chamber of Commerce, (928) 635-4061.

RESTRICTIONS

Pets: On leash; some dog-breed restrictions; do not leave unattended; no barking. **Fires:** Fire ring only; firewood for sale. **Alcoholic Beverages:** Allowed. **Vehicle Maximum Length:** No limit. **Other:** Motorcycles & ATVs in/out use only; no generators; no clotheslines; no wood gathering.

TO GET THERE

From Hwy. 40, take Exit 178, turn north, then take immediate left and follow the road behind the shops.

PATAGONIA   MAP, D-3
Patagonia Lake State Park

400 Patagonia Lake Rd., 85624. T: (520) 287-6965; www.pr.state.az.us.

🚐 ★★★★   ▲ ★★★★

Beauty: ★★★★   Site Privacy: ★★★★
Spaciousness: ★★★★   Quiet: ★★★★
Security: ★★★★   Cleanliness: ★★★★
Insect Control: ★★★   Facilities: ★★★★

Situated between Patagonia and Nogales on the Mexican border, Patagonia Lake is reached from AZ 82 via a curving paved road through housing developments and a hillside forest of mesquite and ocotillo. The campground is nestled in low rolling foothills amongst shady mesquite trees, yucca, and cacti. The best campsites for views of the 265-acre manmade lake are numbered 1–37, and are also nearest the swimming beach. Boaters may wish to opt for the other loops, nearer the launch ramps. There are a dozen tent-only areas scattered around the lake, but they are only accessible by boat. Besides being stocked with trout every three weeks between November and late February, the lake offers fishing for crappie, bluegill, bass, and catfish and birding tours. Almost every Friday the campground fills early for the weekend, and peak-season park closures are common.

BASICS

Operated By: Arizona State Parks. **Open:** All year. **Site Assignment:** First come, first served. **Registration:** At self-pay fee station. **Fee:** Full hookup, $19–$25; basic, $12–$15. **Parking:** At site (except for tent areas only accessible by boat).

FACILITIES

Number of RV-only Sites: 106. **Number of Tent-only Sites:** 12. **Hookups:** Electric (20, 30 amps), water. **Each Site:** Table, grill. **Dump Station:** Yes. **Laundry:** No. **Pay Phone:** Yes. **Restrooms and Showers:** Yes. **Fuel:** Yes. **Propane:** No. **Internal Roads:** Paved, good. **RV Service:** No. **Market:** Patagonia, 12 mi. **Restaurant:** Patagonia, 12 mi. **General Store:** Yes. **Vending:** Yes. **Swimming:** Lake. **Playground:** No. **Other:** Marina, boat rentals, disabled-access fishing dock, picnic area. **Activities:** Boating, fishing, bird-watching. **Nearby Attractions:**

Tubac Presidio, Tumacacori National Monument, Patagonia-Sonoita Creek Preserve. **Additional Information:** Mariposa Books/Patagonia Visitors Center, (520) 394-9186; Nogales Santa Cruz County Chamber of Commerce, (520) 287-3685.

RESTRICTIONS

Pets: On 6-ft. leash under owner's control. **Fires:** Grill provided; no wood gathering. **Alcoholic Beverages:** Allowed. **Vehicle Maximum Length:** 30 ft. **Other:** 2 weeks per month stay limit; 12 people & 2 vehicles per site; jet skis allowed on weekends May 1–Oct.1 , but unrestricted in fall & winter; no live fish bait; park gate closed 10 p.m.–4 a.m.

TO GET THERE

From AZ 82, go 4 mi. north on park access road.

PAYSON   MAP, B-2, C-2
Houston Mesa-Tonto National Forest

2100 N. Houston Mesa Rd, 85541.
T: (928) 468-7135; www.reserveamerica.com.

🚐 ★★★	🏕 ★★★
Beauty: ★★★	Site Privacy: ★★★
Spaciousness: ★★★	Quiet: ★★★
Security: ★★★★	Cleanliness: ★★★★
Insect Control: ★★★★	Facilities: ★★

Houston Mesa is located within the Tonto National Forest, Arizona. It embraces almost 3 million acres of rugged and spectacularly beautiful country, ranging from Saguaro cactus–studded desert to pine-forested mountains beneath the Mogollon Rim. This variety in vegetation and range in altitude (from 1,300 to 7,900 feet) offers outstanding recreational opportunities throughout the year, whether it's lake beaches or cool pine forest. The campground is located 1 mile north of Payson, Arizona. Restrooms and showers are provided. There is a 14-day stay limit within any 30-day period. Interpretive trails are nearby. These are single-family camping units only. No hookups available. Horse-camping facilities available across the road from the family campground. Must have horses or mules to camp at the horse facility (Mule Deer Loop).

BASICS

Operated By: U.S. Forest Service. **Open:** Apr. 15–Sept. 21. **Site Assignment:** Reservations must be made at least 4 days in advance. **Registration:** At office. **Fee:** Single, $12–$16. **Parking:** At park.

FACILITIES

Number of Multipurpose Sites: 235. **Hookups:** None. **Each Site:** Call ahead. **Dump Station:** Yes. **Laundry:** No. **Pay Phone:** No. **Restrooms and Showers:** Yes. **Fuel:** No. **Propane:** No. **Internal Roads:** Paved. **RV Service:** No. **Market:** No. **Restaurant:** No. **General Store:** No. **Vending:** No. **Swimming:** No. **Playground:** No. **Activities:** Horseback riding.

RESTRICTIONS

Pets: Pets must be restrained or on a leash at all times while in developed recreation areas. **Fires:** In

fire rings, stoves, grills, or fireplaces provided for that purpose. **Alcoholic Beverages:** Not allowed. **Vehicle Maximum Length:** Call ahead.

TO GET THERE

From Payson, AZ, go north for 1 mi. to the junction of Hwy. 87 (Beeline Hwy.) and FS 199 (Houston Mesa Rd.). Turn east onto FS 199 for 0.1 mi.; campground is on the north side of the Houston Mesa Rd.

PAYSON   MAP, C-2
Ox Bow Estates RV Park

HC 6 Box 1050 D, 85541. T: (800) 520-5239.

🚐 ★★★★	🏕 ★★
Beauty: ★★★	Site Privacy: ★★★
Spaciousness: ★★★★	Quiet: ★★★★
Security: ★★★	Cleanliness: ★★★★★
Insect Control: ★★★★	Facilities: ★★★

With its log cabin–style office and wooded lots and stream, this campground has a very woodsy atmosphere. And well it should, since it abuts Tonto National Forest on one side. (From an aerial photo in the office, you can see just how lost in the woods this campground really is.) The rest of the surrounding area is quiet residential property. Sites are laid out in a grid, with one section divided from the rest by a small creek. Most sites are shaded, including the tent sites, and average a spacious 40 by 50 feet. The campground is peaceful, laid-back, and quiet. Besides Tonto National Forest, which you can be lost in within five minutes of leaving the park, the other local attractions are a quick drive away, making this campground a relaxing yet convenient stop. Proprietors Fred and Mimi are friendly, helpful, and full of information about the region.

BASICS

Operated By: Fred & Mimi Hendrix. **Open:** All year. **Site Assignment:** Upon registration. **Registration:** At office; if no one is available, use courtesy phone & call number listed; late arrivals: pick a spot & use drop slot in door. **Fee:** $24. **Parking:** At site.

FACILITIES

Number of Multipurpose Sites: 46. **Hookups:** Electric (30, 50 amps), water, sewer, TV. **Each Site:** Picnic table, fire pit, charcoal grill, tree. **Dump Station:** Yes. **Laundry:** Yes. **Pay Phone:** Yes. **Restrooms and Showers:** Yes. **Fuel:** No. **Propane:** Yes. **Internal Roads:** Gravel, in very good condition. **RV Service:** No. **Market:** 2 mi. to casino. **Restaurant:** 2 mi. to casino. **General Store:** Yes. **Vending:** Yes. **Swimming:** No. **Playground:** No. **Other:** Creek. Normally dry during monsoon season only. **Activities:** Hiking, biking, fishing, summer potlucks. **Nearby Attractions:** Tonto National Forest, Tonto National Bridge Park, Tonto Cliff Dwellings, Mogollon Rim. **Additional Information:** Payson Chamber of Commerce, (928) 474-4515.

RESTRICTIONS

Pets: On leash. **Fires:** In pit or grill. **Alcoholic Beverages:** Not in buildings. **Vehicle Maximum Length:** 45 ft. **Other:** No clotheslines.

TO GET THERE

From the intersection of Hwy. 260 and Hwy. 87 in Payson, go south on 87 (towards Rye) for 4.2 mi., then turn right at the sign for the campground (there is no street sign). Drive 0.8 mi. through a residential area and turn into the entrance on the right.

PEORIA   MAP, C-2
Lake Pleasant Regional Park

41835 North Castle Hot Springs Rd., 85382.
T: (928) 501-1710; www.maricopa.gov/parks/
lake_pleasant/camping.aspx.

🚐 ★★★★	🏕 ★★★★
Beauty: ★★★★	Site Privacy: ★★★★
Spaciousness: ★★★★	Quiet: ★★★★
Security: ★★★★★	Cleanliness: ★★★★
Insect Control: ★★★	Facilities: ★★★

One of six excellent Phoenix area county parks, Lake Pleasant Regional Park contains both the Desert Tortoise and Roadrunner Campgrounds. Roadrunner's hillside sites 7–24 fill up first because of their excellent views. Desert Tortoise's tent-only and improved pull-through sites along Den and Bajada Loop Roads have coveted lake views that are also snapped up fast. On long holiday weekends it seems like all Phoenix is headed here with boats. Since there are no reservations, an early Thursday arrival is advised to ensure snagging a holiday-weekend campsite. Most sites easily accommodate vehicles in the mid-30 to mid-45-foot range, though the sites tend to be narrow (e.g. the 80-foot-long site is only 13-feet wide). The native desert hillside saguaro, ocotillo, and brittlebush landscape blooms with yellow, purple, and blue wildflowers after April showers. Park animals include bald eagles, wild burros, javelina, and desert tortoises.

BASICS

Operated By: Maricopa County Parks & Recreation Dept. **Open:** All year. **Site Assignment:** First come, first served. **Registration:** At entrance kiosk (or w/ camp host). **Fee:** $5–$18. **Parking:** At site.

FACILITIES

Number of RV-only Sites: 66. **Number of Tent-only Sites:** 10. **Hookups:** Electric (20, 30, 50 amps), water. **Each Site:** Sheltered table, grill. **Dump Station:** Yes. **Laundry:** No. **Pay Phone:** Yes. **Restrooms and Showers:** Yes. **Fuel:** No. **Propane:** No. **Internal Roads:** Paved, good. **RV Service:** No. **Market:** Peoria, 8 mi. **Restaurant:** Peoria, 8 mi. **General Store:** No. **Vending:** Yes. **Swimming:** Lake. **Playground:** Yes. **Other:** Boat ramp, dam visitor center. **Activities:** Boating, fishing, shooting range, golf. **Nearby Attractions:** Factory shops, museums, Cave Creek, Carefree. **Additional Information:** Carefree–Cave Creek Chamber of Commerce, (480) 488-3381.

RESTRICTIONS

Pets: On leash under owner's control. **Fires:** Grill only; no ground fires. **Alcoholic Beverages:** Allowed. **Vehicle Maximum Length:** 80 ft. **Other:** No wood gathering.

TO GET THERE

From I-17 north of Phoenix take Exit 223, go west on AZ 74 (Carefree Hwy.).

PHOENIX
Tortilla-Coronado National Forest

MAP, C-2

reserve america

2324 E. Mcdowell Rd., 85006. T: (602) 225-5200; www.reserveamerica.com.

🚐 ★★★★   ▲ ★★★★

Beauty: ★★★   Site Privacy: ★★★
Spaciousness: ★★★   Quiet: ★★★
Security: ★★★★   Cleanliness: ★★★★
Insect Control: ★★★★ Facilities: ★★★

Tortilla campground is located directly across the historic Apache Trail from Tortilla Flat, Arizona, and is located in the Coronado National Forest covering 1,780,000 acres of southeastern Arizona and southwestern New Mexico. Elevations range from 3000 feet to 10,720 feet in twelve widely scattered mountain ranges, or sky islands, that rise dramatically from the desert floor, supporting plant communities as biologically diverse as those encountered on a trip from Mexico to Canada. Views are spectacular from these mountains, and visitors may experience all four seasons during a single day's journey, wandering through the desert among giant saguaro cactus and colorful wildflowers in the morning, enjoying lunch beside a mountain stream, and playing in the snow later in the afternoon. The sky islands of the Coronado National Forest are unique and surprising, offering year-round recreation opportunities. Recreation activities that can be enjoyed on the Coronado are nearly as diverse as the people who come to visit. The most popular ones, however, are hiking, camping, birding, horseback riding, picnicking, sightseeing, and visiting historic areas. Fishing and boating are also available, but limited in this arid land, while opportunities for the fast-growing sport of mountain biking are growing. Winter sports are possible in the higher elevations; Mt. Lemmon Ski Valley is the most southern ski area in the United States.

BASICS
Operated By: U.S. Forest Service. **Open:** Oct. 1– Apr. 29. **Site Assignment:** Reservations must be made at least 4 days in advance. **Registration:** At office. **Fee:** Single, $12. **Parking:** Limited.

FACILITIES
Number of Multipurpose Sites: 30. **Hookups:** Yes. **Each Site:** Picnic table, grill. **Dump Station:** Yes. **Laundry:** No. **Pay Phone:** No. **Restrooms and Showers:** Yes. **Fuel:** No. **Propane:** No. **Internal Roads:** Paved. **RV Service:** No. **Market:** No. **Restaurant:** Yes. **General Store:** Yes. **Vending:** No. **Swimming:** No. **Playground:** No. **Activities:** Boating, fishing & picnicking.

RESTRICTIONS
Pets: Pets must be restrained or on a leash at all times while in developed recreation areas. **Fires:** In fire rings, stoves, grills, or fireplaces provided for that purpose. **Alcoholic Beverages:** Not allowed. **Vehicle Maximum Length:** Call ahead. **Other:** No

ATVs or ORVs in campground; no livestock in campground.

TO GET THERE
From Apache Junction, Arizona, take AZ 88 (Apache Trail) northeast for 18 mi. to Tortilla Flat. Tortilla Campground is directly across AZ 88 from Tortilla Flat.

PHOENIX
Welcome Home RV Park

MAP, C-2

2501 Missouri Ave., 85017. T: (602) 249-9852 or (602) 249-9854.

🚐 ★★★   ▲ n/a

Beauty: ★★★   Site Privacy: ★★★★
Spaciousness: ★★★★   Quiet: ★★★★
Security: ★★★   Cleanliness: ★★★★★
Insect Control: ★★★★ Facilities: ★★

Certainly one of the closest campgrounds to downtown Phoenix, this park accepts only RVs, but has a few remaining mobile homes. The grounds are laid out on a loop, with well-shaded, comfortable lots on either side. Lots are 30 feet wide, making them spacious enough for evening outdoor activities. Although situated right next to the highway, there is very little traffic noise spillover. Located on a quiet residential street, the park presents a great little urban getaway without an overly urban feel. Downtown Phoenix is a 20-minute drive away, while the quick access to I-17 provides a convenient way to depart for farther destinations.

BASICS
Operated By: Ed Little. **Open:** All year. **Site Assignment:** Upon registration; no reservations. **Registration:** At office; if closed, go to house next door. **Fee:** $21–$24; cash, no credit cards. **Parking:** At site.

FACILITIES
Number of RV-only Sites: 52. **Hookups:** Electric (30, 50 amps), water, sewer. **Each Site:** Trees & grass, some flowering bushes. **Dump Station:** No (sewer available at all sites). **Laundry:** Yes. **Pay Phone:** No (1 block). **Restrooms and Showers:** No shower. **Fuel:** No (1 block). **Propane:** No. **Internal Roads:** Paved. **RV Service:** No. **Market:** 1 mi. **Restaurant:** 2 mi. **General Store:** No (1 block). **Vending:** No. **Swimming:** Yes. **Playground:** No. **Activities:** Shuffleboard, clubhouse, Christmas dinner. **Nearby Attractions:** Mesa Southwest Museum, Champlin Fighter Museum, Superstition Springs Center, Casa Grande Ruins, Roosevelt Dam, Tonto National Monument. **Additional Information:** Phoenix Visitors Center, (602) 254-6500.

RESTRICTIONS
Pets: On leash, clean up after. **Fires:** Allowed (only charcoal in grills). **Alcoholic Beverages:** At sites only. **Vehicle Maximum Length:** No limit. **Other:** 30 ft. min. length, must be 1991 or newer RV.

TO GET THERE
From the junction of I-17 and Bethany Rd. (Exit 204), merge into the far right-hand lane heading south. Follow the frontage road 0.5 mi. to the entrance on the right.

PICACHO
Picacho Campground

MAP, C-2

I-10, Picacho Exit, 85241. T: (520) 466-7401 or (888) 562-7453; www.picachocampground.com.

🚐 ★★★★   ▲ ★★★★

Beauty: ★★★★   Site Privacy: ★★★
Spaciousness: ★★★★   Quiet: ★★★
Security: ★★★★   Cleanliness: ★★★★
Insect Control: ★★★★ Facilities: ★★★★

Just off I-10, 75 miles south of Phoenix and 42 miles north of Tucson, Picacho Campground is popular with horse owners because it provides corrals ($10). Children are also welcome here, though parents must keep them in sight and under control at all times, particularly around the pool. Visitors here are mostly snowbirds and overnighters. Many put out their TV antennas to pull in Phoenix and Tucson stations, which means two NBC and two CBS channels, one each from PBS and ABC, and two independents. An attractive oleander perimeter mutes much of the highway truck noise, though not all of it. Cacti, eucalyptus, and an abundance of other trees shade these extra long and extra wide sites, which easily accommodate sliders. The store and office stay open from 8 a.m. to 8 p.m., adding convenience at this well-run family operation.

BASICS
Operated By: Jerry & Frankie Cross. **Open:** All year. **Site Assignment:** First come, first served; winter reservations advised. **Registration:** At office. **Fee:** RV, $22–$24 (winter rates); tent, $17; corrals, $5 per horse. Seasonal rates ($15 summer rate); V, MC, D. **Parking:** At site.

FACILITIES
Number of RV-only Sites: 70. **Number of Tent-only Sites:** 8. **Hookups:** Electric (30, 50 amps), water, sewer. **Each Site:** Table. **Dump Station:** Yes. **Laundry:** Yes. **Pay Phone:** Yes. **Restrooms and Showers:** Yes. **Fuel:** Yes. **Propane:** Yes. **Internal Roads:** Gravel, good. **RV Service:** No. **Market:** Eloy, 4 mi. **Restaurant:** 4 mi. **General Store:** Yes. **Vending:** Yes. **Swimming:** Pool. **Playground:** Yes. **Other:** Hot tub, shuffleboard, dog walk, cabin, corrals. **Activities:** Hiking, outlet malls, & golf nearby. **Nearby Attractions:** Picacho Peak State Park, Casa Grande Ruins, Sasco ghost town, Desert Museum. **Additional Information:** Eloy Chamber of Commerce (520) 466-3411.

RESTRICTIONS
Pets: On leash under owner's control (horses welcome). **Fires:** Fire pits in tent picnic areas only. **Alcoholic Beverages:** Allowed. **Vehicle Maximum Length:** No limit. **Other:** No vehicle washing or repairs.

TO GET THERE
From I-10 Picacho Exit (211A from Phoenix; 212 from Tucson), go 0.5–1 mi. on Frontage Rd.

PICACHO MAP, C-2
Picacho Peak RV Resort

17065 East Peak Ln., 85241. T: (520) 466-7841.

🚐 ★★★★ ⛺ n/a

Beauty: ★★★	Site Privacy: ★★★
Spaciousness: ★★★★	Quiet: ★★★
Security: ★★★★	Cleanliness: ★★★★★
Insect Control: ★★★★	Facilities: ★★★★★

Often confused with Picacho Campground 7 miles to the north, Picacho Peak RV Resort exudes a very different atmosphere. Though the sites are attractively landscaped with medium-sized ocotillo, cacti, and trees, Picacho Peak RV Resort feels like an upscale RV parking annex for the mobile home park sharing the rear of the property. The benefit of mixing mobile homes and RVs is sharing the clean, well-maintained mobile-home amenities. The RVs are closer to the interstate highway than the mobile homes, and the sandstone-colored perimeter wall and trees do not keep out all the truck noises and nightly train sounds. Also, there is not a convenience store here with the long hours found at Picacho Campground. However, the Resort is affiliated with Adventure Outdoor Resorts, Coast to Coast Network, and Resort Parks International, and members of those groups are promised good deals here.

BASICS

Operated By: Picacho Peak Resort. **Open:** All year. **Site Assignment:** First come, first served; winter reservations advised. **Registration:** At office (hosts will come by site to collect money after hours). **Fee:** $25. **Parking:** At site.

FACILITIES

Number of RV-only Sites: 159. **Hookups:** Electric (30, 50 amps), water, sewer, phone (modem). **Each Site:** Table. **Dump Station:** Yes. **Laundry:** Yes. **Pay Phone:** Yes. **Restrooms and Showers:** Yes. **Fuel:** No, across street. **Propane:** Yes. **Internal Roads:** Paved, excellent. **RV Service:** No. **Market:** Picacho Peak, 1 mi. **Restaurant:** Picacho Peak, 1 mi. **General Store:** No. **Vending:** Yes. **Swimming:** Pool. **Playground:** No. **Other:** Rec room, whirlpool, shuffleboard & volleyball courts, horseshoes, planned activities. **Activities:** Golf. No horseback riding. **Nearby Attractions:** Picacho Peak State Park, Casa Grande Ruins. **Additional Information:** Picacho State Park, (520) 466-3183.

RESTRICTIONS

Pets: On leash under owner's control. **Fires:** Not allowed. **Alcoholic Beverages:** Allowed. **Vehicle Maximum Length:** No limit.

TO GET THERE

From I-10, get off at Exit 219 and go south 0.5 mi. on Frontage Rd.

PICACHO MAP, C-2
Picacho Peak State Park

Picacho Peak Rd, 85241. T: (520) 466-3183; www.azstateparks.com/parks/parkhtml/picacho.html.

🚐 ★★★★ ⛺ ★★★★★

Beauty: ★★★★★	Site Privacy: ★★★★★
Spaciousness: ★★★★★	Quiet: ★★★★
Security: ★★★★	Cleanliness: ★★★★
Insect Control: ★★	Facilities: ★★

Picacho Peak, an ancient Hohokam Indian site, is a colorful mixture of 22-million-year-old lava flows and sedimentary rock strata, rich in saguaro, cacti, grasses, and cottontail rabbits. Though it doesn't have the swimming pools and amenities of the nearby private campgrounds, Picacho Peak State Park is the best place to experience the raw nature of this historic area. The three loops are far enough back from the interstate highway that noise is not a problem. The 14-site hookup loop closest to the peak and park entrance is literally just a paved parking lot, albeit with a spectacular view and natural surroundings. Indeed, those who end up here as Catalina State Park overflow casualties are pleasantly surprised by the historic peak that served as a landmark for Father Kino, the Butterfield Overland Stage, and the Forty-Niners headed to the California gold fields.

BASICS

Operated By: Arizona State Parks. **Open:** All year. **Site Assignment:** First come, first served; group area requires reservations. **Registration:** At contact station or self-pay station. **Fee:** $12–$22; cash, check, V, MC, no debit cards. **Parking:** At site.

FACILITIES

Number of Tent-only Sites: Undesignated sites. **Number of Multipurpose Sites:** 85. **Hookups:** Electric (20, 30, 50 amps), water. **Each Site:** Table, grill. **Dump Station:** Yes. **Laundry:** No. **Pay Phone:** No. **Restrooms and Showers:** Yes. **Fuel:** No. **Propane:** No. **Internal Roads:** Paved, good. **RV Service:** No. **Market:** Picacho Peak, 1 mi. **Restaurant:** Picacho Peak, 1 mi. **General Store:** No. **Vending:** No. **Swimming:** No. **Playground:** Yes. **Other:** Small visitor center w/ gift shop, some sheltered tables. **Activities:** Horseback riding, hiking, bird & wildlife watching. No golf. **Nearby Attractions:** Casa Grande Ruins, Catalina State Park, Saguaro National Park West. **Additional Information:** Picacho State Park, (520) 466-3183 (602) 542-4174.

RESTRICTIONS

Pets: On leash under owner's control. **Fires:** Allowed (except summer, when fire danger). **Alcoholic Beverages:** Allowed. **Vehicle Maximum Length:** No limit. **Other:** No fireworks.

TO GET THERE

From I-10, take Exit 219, Picacho Peak Rd.

PINETOP–LAKESIDE MAP, C-3
Hawley Lake Resort

P.O. Box 448, 85930. T: (928) 335-7511.

🚐 ★★★★ ⛺ n/a

Beauty: ★★★★★	Site Privacy: ★★★★
Spaciousness: ★★★★★	Quiet: ★★★★★
Security: ★★★★★	Cleanliness: ★★★★★
Insect Control: ★★★	Facilities: ★★★★

Created in the 1950s by impounding Trout Creek, 300-acre Hawley Lake offers rustic waterfront camping on the lands of the White Mountain Apache. Tall ponderosa pine trees, boulder-strewn meadows, small waterfalls, roadside fishing (requires daily White Mountain Apache permit), and good lake views from many hillside campsites are among the attractions. Rainbow trout thrive in the lake, though Apache, brown, cutthroat, and brook trout are also caught summer and winter (ice fishing). Many prefer fall fishing when the browns come up in the shallows. Wild turkey, deer, elk, and black bear make for good wildlife viewing and attract hunters. Be prepared for cold weather here, as at 8,200 feet elevation, summer temperatures can drop below freezing at night. The last 2 miles into the lake are on a gravel road, and big vehicles should call ahead to make sure they can be accommodated.

BASICS

Operated By: White Mountain Apache Tribe. **Open:** All year. **Site Assignment:** First come, first served; reservations up to 1 year in advance. **Registration:** At office in store. **Fee:** Hookup, $25; regular, $8; V, MC, debit. **Parking:** At site.

FACILITIES

Number of RV-only Sites: 100. **Hookups:** Electric (30 amps), water, sewer. **Each Site:** Table, grill. **Dump Station:** Yes. **Laundry:** Yes. **Pay Phone:** Yes. **Restrooms and Showers:** Yes. **Fuel:** Yes. **Propane:** Yes. **Internal Roads:** Gravel, good (chains or 4x4 required in winter). **RV Service:** No. **Market:** Pinetop-Lakeside, 24 mi. **Restaurant:** Café on premises. **General Store:** Yes (summer only). **Vending:** No. **Swimming:** No. **Playground:** No. **Other:** Marina, boat rentals, lodge, cabins, summer home rentals. **Activities:** Boating, fishing, hunting, horseback riding, biking, backpacking, archery. **Nearby Attractions:** Lakes, forest, casino. **Additional Information:** White Mountain Apache Tribe Office of Tourism, (520) 338-1230, www.wmat.nsn.us.

RESTRICTIONS

Pets: On leash under owner's control. **Fires:** Allowed. **Alcoholic Beverages:** Allowed (drunk-driving laws strictly enforced). **Vehicle Maximum Length:** No stated limit (but check w/ tribe before bringing in big vehicles). **Other:** No tents, fireworks, ATVs, cattle rustling, or fence cutting.

TO GET THERE

From Pinetop-Lakeside, go 16 mi. southeast on AZ 260 and 8 mi. south on AZ 473.

PINETOP–LAKESIDE MAP, C-3
Hon-Dah RV Park

777 Hwy. 260, 85935. T: (928) 369-7400; www.hon-dah.com.

🚐 ★★★★ ⛺ n/a

Beauty: ★★★★	Site Privacy: ★★★
Spaciousness: ★★★★	Quiet: ★★★
Security: ★★★★★	Cleanliness: ★★★★★
Insect Control: ★★★★	Facilities: ★★★★

A popular destination requiring advance reservations, Hon-Dah RV Park is across the street from Hon-Dah Casino's 500 slot machines and offers ample amenities to those visiting the area for boating, fishing, or winter skiing at nearby (20 miles) Sunrise Park Resort. The RV Park is in a wetlands

area bisected by Corduroy Creek. There are 140 RV campsites south of the creek, and 58 reached by crossing a bridge and going uphill to the north side of the creek. Though the RV Park is near enough the highway to hear the hum of passing traffic, tall pines and gravel roads make the campground feel rustic, almost like camping in the wilderness. For those who want their forests and lake country with gambling and nighttime entertainment, this is a friendly place to put down after a day of fishing or boating.

BASICS

Operated By: White Mountain Apache Tribe. **Open:** All year. **Site Assignment:** First come, first served; reservations necessary. **Registration:** At office. **Fee:** $23; V, MC. **Parking:** At site.

FACILITIES

Number of RV-only Sites: 258. **Hookups:** Electric (20, 30, 50 amps), water, sewer, satellite TV, phone. **Each Site:** Table, grill. **Dump Station:** Yes. **Laundry:** Yes. **Pay Phone:** Yes. **Restrooms and Showers:** Yes. **Fuel:** Yes. **Propane:** Yes. **Internal Roads:** Gravel, well maintained. **RV Service:** No. **Market:** Pinetop-Lakeside, 5 mi. **Restaurant:** Casino, across street. **General Store:** Yes. **Vending:** Yes. **Swimming:** No. **Playground:** Yes. **Other:** Rec hall, casino, conference center, wheelchair-accessible facilities. **Activities:** Shuffleboard, horseshoes, gambling, fishing, hunting, boating, winter sports. **Nearby Attractions:** Lakes, forests. **Additional Information:** White Mountain Apache Tribe Office of Tourism, (520) 338-1230, www.wmat.nsn.us; Sunrise Park Resort, (520) 735-7600, www.sunriseskipark.com.

RESTRICTIONS

Pets: On leash (requires prior approval; loud barking not tolerated). **Fires:** Allowed. **Alcoholic Beverages:** At site only. **Vehicle Maximum Length:** No limit. **Other:** Pets must be walked along fence outside park perimeter; no smoking in buildings; pedestrians should carry flashlight at night; units over 10 years old must pass visual inspection (refund if turned away).

TO GET THERE

From Pinetop-Lakeside go 5 mi. east on AZ 260 to junction w/ AZ 73.

ROOSEVELT   MAP, C-2, C-3
Cholla Recreation Site

Tonto Basin Ranger District, HC02 Box 4800, 85545. T: (928) 467-3200; www.fs.fed.us/r3/tonto.

🚐 ★★★	🛖 ★★★★★
Beauty: ★★★★★	Site Privacy: ★★★★★
Spaciousness: ★★★★★	Quiet: ★★★★★
Security: ★★★★	Cleanliness: ★★★★★
Insect Control: ★★★	Facilities: ★★

The largest completely solar-powered campground in the United States, Cholla Campground and Boating Site is located on the shores of central Arizona's largest lake, Theodore Roosevelt Lake. Blue shelters make the campground look like a blue-roofed village with solar panels amidst the tall saguaro, mesquite, and palo verde providing the campsites a privacy barrier. The 13 tent-only sites farthest from the boat ramp on the steep slopes at the end of Christmas Cholla Loop and the five tent-only sites at Cane Cholla Loop on the slopes closer to the campground entrance have the best waterfront views. The gravel and sand campsites are flat, and many double sites are available for those with multiple vehicles and big boats. For those wanting a more primitive experience, head to Indian Point on the northeast side of the lake or checkout the sometimes crowded beach camping nearby at Bachelor Cove or Cholla Cove.

BASICS

Operated By: U.S. Forest Service. **Open:** All year. **Site Assignment:** First come, first served. **Registration:** At kiosk or self-pay station. **Fee:** $10–$15 (highest for double sites); Golden Age, half price; V, MC. **Parking:** At site; separate walk-in tent site parking near restrooms.

FACILITIES

Number of RV-only Sites: 188. **Number of Tent-only Sites:** 18. **Hookups:** None. **Each Site:** Sheltered table, grill, fire pit (most sites). **Dump Station:** No. **Laundry:** No. **Pay Phone:** Yes. **Restrooms and Showers:** Yes. **Fuel:** No. **Propane:** No. **Internal Roads:** Paved, good. **RV Service:** No. **Market:** Globe, 36 mi. **Restaurant:** Roosevelt, 5 mi. **General Store:** No. **Vending:** No. **Swimming:** Lake. **Playground:** Yes. **Other:** Boat ramp, campfire circle, fish-cleaning station, picnic tables, barrier-free wheelchair accessibility. **Activities:** Boating, fishing, waterskiing. **Nearby Attractions:** Tonto National Monument, Roosevelt Dam, Globe, Payson.

RESTRICTIONS

Pets: On leash under owner's control. **Fires:** Not allowed. **Alcoholic Beverages:** Allowed. **Vehicle Maximum Length:** No limit. **Other:** No ATVs or firearms. Generators must be off at 10 pm.

TO GET THERE

From Globe take AZ 88/188 west for 36 mi.

ROOSEVELT   MAP, C-2, C-3
Windy Hill Recreation Site

HC 02 Box 4800, 85545. T: (928) 467-3200; www.fs.fed.us/r3/tonto.

🚐 ★★★	🛖 ★★★★
Beauty: ★★★★	Site Privacy: ★★★★
Spaciousness: ★★★★	Quiet: ★★★
Security: ★★★★	Cleanliness: ★★★★
Insect Control: ★★★★	Facilities: ★★

Often packed full with local boaters on summer weekends, Windy Hill feels isolated because it is 2 miles from the main highway and the campsites are widely dispersed among ten loops. Each loop has its own trailheads and is named after a different animal that might be seen in the area, such as javelina, desert bighorn, gray fox, and coati. However, it is the rattlesnake (which does not have a loop named after it) which has to be watched out for here and in most other Arizona campgrounds. Double sites are big enough for a small beach party, packing in up to four cars, two boats, and 20 people. The level ground is good for tenting, and abundant desert plants like palo verde, ocotillo, and mesquite between the campsites add to the feeling of isolation and privacy.

BASICS

Operated By: U.S. Forest Service. **Open:** All year. **Site Assignment:** First come, first served; group reservations. **Registration:** At self-pay fee stations. **Fee:** $10–$15; V, MC, no checks. **Parking:** At site.

FACILITIES

Number of RV-only Sites: 320. **Number of Tent-only Sites:** 27. **Hookups:** None. **Each Site:** Sheltered table, grill (most sites). **Dump Station:** Yes (5 mi. east). **Laundry:** No. **Pay Phone:** Yes. **Restrooms and Showers:** Yes. **Fuel:** No. **Propane:** No. **Internal Roads:** Gravel, good. **RV Service:** No. **Market:** Globe, 27 mi. **Restaurant:** Roosevelt, 6 mi. **General Store:** No. **Vending:** No. **Swimming:** Lake. **Playground:** Yes. **Other:** Amphitheater, fish-cleaning station, high- & low-water boat ramps, day-use picnic sites, wheelchair-accessible sites. **Activities:** Boating, fishing. **Nearby Attractions:** Tonto National Monument, Roosevelt Dam, Globe. **Additional Information:** Salt River Project (for water level information), (602) 236-3929, www.srpnet.com; Roosevelt Lake Marina, (520) 467-2245.

RESTRICTIONS

Pets: On leash. **Fires:** Allowed (fires prohibited when high winds). **Alcoholic Beverages:** Allowed. **Vehicle Maximum Length:** No limit. **Other:** No glass containers; no ATVs.

TO GET THERE

From Globe take AZ 88/188 west for 25 mi., then go east for 2 mi. on Frontage Rd. 82 at Windy Hill Recreation Site entrance sign.

SALOME   MAP, C-1
Black Rock RV Village

reserve america

46751 East Hwy. 60, 85348. T: (928) 927-4206; www.reserveamerica.com.

🚐 ★★★★	🛖 n/a
Beauty: ★★★★	Site Privacy: ★★★
Spaciousness: ★★★★	Quiet: ★★★★
Security: ★★★★	Cleanliness: ★★★★★
Insect Control: ★★★★	Facilities: ★★★★★

A small, friendly village with a great little bakery guaranteed to defeat efforts to keep off the pounds, Black Rock is a welcome refuge from the January and February crowds jamming nearby Quartzsite. A few trees and cacti line gravel streets with names like Which Way, What Street, Wash Way, Fun Gully, and Easy Street. Desert amenities abound for snowbirds, and people here enjoy walking alongside the road. Winter activities include Sunday afternoon ice-cream socials, bean-bag baseball, line dancing, cribbage, crafts, painting classes, exercise programs, bingo, darts, pinochle, and jam sessions. The rec hall attracts entertainers like Terry Raff, the singing mountain man. The area to the north is BLM land with ATV and hiking trails, as well as 18 holes of golf and a remote-control airfield for flying model planes. For some this is enough to rent a post-office box and take up residence.

BASICS

Operated By: Black Rock RV Village. **Open:** All year. **Site Assignment:** First come, first served. **Registration:** At front office. **Fee:** $19.50–$25. **Parking:** At site.

FACILITIES

Number of RV-only Sites: 403. **Hookups:** Electric (30, 50 amps), water, sewer, phone (modem), satellite TV. **Each Site:** None. **Dump Station:** Yes. **Laundry:** Yes. **Pay Phone:** Yes. **Restrooms and Showers:** Yes. **Fuel:** No. **Propane:** Yes. **Internal Roads:** Gravel, good. **RV Service:** No. **Market:** Brenda, 0.5 mi. **Restaurant:** Yes. **General Store:** Yes. **Vending:** Yes. **Swimming:** No. **Playground:** No. **Other:** Soft water car/RV wash, barber, beauty shop, post office, motel, 9-hole golf, R/C model flying field, rec hall, reverse-osmosis water, oil-change area. **Activities:** Golf, horseshoes. **Nearby Attractions:** Colorado River. **Additional Information:** McMullen Valley Chamber of Commerce, (928) 859-3846, www.azoutback.com.

RESTRICTIONS

Pets: On leash. **Fires:** Allowed. **Alcoholic Beverages:** Allowed. **Vehicle Maximum Length:** 100 ft. **Other:** No subletting sites.

TO GET THERE

From Quartzsite go 11 mi. east on I-10 and take Exit 31 to US 60; stay on US 60 heading east for 4 mi.

SEDONA
Manzanita   MAP, B-2

reserve america

2323 East Greenlaw Ln., 86004. T: (928) 527-3600 or (928) 282-4119; www.reserveamerica.com.

🚐 ★★   ▲ ★★★★

Beauty: ★★★★★	Site Privacy: ★
Spaciousness: ★★★	Quiet: ★★★★★
Security: ★	Cleanliness: ★★★★
Insect Control: ★	Facilities: ★

Charming, gorgeous, breathtaking, revitalizing—pick any superlative, they all fit. But so does "filled quickly." This campsite is a favorite in the well-traveled Oak Creek Canyon—and for good reason. Striking red rock bursts out of the forested hills above the creek, while rocky crags jut overhead. The entire canyon is beautiful and, as one local resident put it, "plum fulla history." The campsites mostly string out along the creek, and these sites (along with 10 and 19 on the ends) are the most highly prized. The sites to avoid are 6 and 7 situated by the outhouse and up against the road. Admittedly, this campsite is not for everyone; in fact, no trailers or RVs are allowed due to the small size of the campground. (Those who can't "fit" here can press on down Hwy. 89A to the lovely Rio Verde in Cottonwood.) However, campers looking for a great base for outdoor activities or a really romantic nook should definitely try their luck at scoring one of these spots.

BASICS

Operated By: Coconano National Forest. **Open:** All year. **Site Assignment:** First come, first served. **Registration:** Pick a site, register w/ camp host. **Fee:** $18. **Parking:** At sites. Second vehicle, $7.

FACILITIES

Number of Tent-only Sites: 18. **Hookups:** None. **Each Site:** Picnic table, concrete fire pit. **Dump Station:** No. **Laundry:** No. **Pay Phone:** No. **Restrooms and Showers:** Pit toilets, no showers. **Fuel:** No. **Propane:** No. **Internal Roads:** Paved. **RV Service:** No. **Market:** No. **Restaurant:** No. **General Store:** No. **Vending:** No. **Swimming:** Creek. **Playground:** No. **Other:** Well water, murmur of Oak Creek. **Activities:** Hiking, fishing, swimming, mountain biking. **Nearby Attractions:** Oak Creek Canyon.

RESTRICTIONS

Pets: On leash. **Fires:** In pit or grill only. **Alcoholic Beverages:** At sites only. **Vehicle Maximum Length:** Trailers & RVs Not allowed. **Other:** 7-day stay limit. No trailers.

TO GET THERE

5 mi. north of "Midgely Bridgely" at the northernmost edge of town on Hwy. 89A.

SHOW LOW
Fool Hollow Lake   MAP, C-3
Recreation Area

1500 North Fool Hollow Lake Rd., 85901. T: (928) 537-3680; www.pr.state.az.us.

🚐 ★★★★★   ▲ ★★★★★

Beauty: ★★★★	Site Privacy: ★★★★
Spaciousness: ★★★★	Quiet: ★★★★★
Security: ★★★★★	Cleanliness: ★★★★★
Insect Control: ★★★	Facilities: ★★★

Established in 1991 as a partnership between the city of Show Low, the U.S. Forest Service, Arizona State Parks, and Arizona Game and Fish, Fool Hollow provides RV campers with large cement pads and hookups in four separate loops (Red Head, Mallard, Ruddy Duck, and Cinnamon Teal). Tent campers have good lake views from their three separate loops (Northern Harrier, Osprey, Bald Eagle). Pines, tall junipers, volcanic boulders, and jack rabbits contribute to the rustic feel. Show Low Creek feeds Fool Hollow Lake, which is stocked with rainbow trout by Arizona Game and Fish. There is also a good chance of catching brown trout, largemouth and smallmouth bass, black crappie, and green sunfish. Away from the water are 103 miles of hiking trails within 15 miles and golf links in the rapidly suburbanizing surrounding area.

BASICS

Operated By: Arizona State Parks. **Open:** All year. **Site Assignment:** First come, first served. **Registration:** At self-pay station, 8 a.m.–5 p.m. **Fee:** $12–$25. **Parking:** At site.

FACILITIES

Number of RV-only Sites: 92. **Number of Tent-only Sites:** 31. **Hookups:** Electric (30, 50 amps), water. **Each Site:** Table, grill. **Dump Station:** Yes.

Laundry: No. **Pay Phone:** Yes. **Restrooms and Showers:** Yes. **Fuel:** No. Nearest in Show Low, 4 mi. **Propane:** No. **Internal Roads:** Paved, excellent. **RV Service:** No. **Market:** Show Low, 4 mi. **Restaurant:** Show Low, 4 mi. **General Store:** No. **Vending:** No. **Swimming:** No. **Playground:** Yes. **Other:** Boat ramps, fish-cleaning station, fishing docks, covered picnic tables w/ grills, wildlife island. **Activities:** Boating, fishing, golf. **Nearby Attractions:** Lakes, forests, Mogollon Rim, Petrified Forest, Show Low. **Additional Information:** Show Low Chamber of Commerce, (928) 527-3680.

RESTRICTIONS

Pets: On leash (not allowed on beaches or in buildings). **Fires:** Grill only; firewood sold. **Alcoholic Beverages:** Allowed. **Vehicle Maximum Length:** No limit. **Other:** Entrance gate closed 10 p.m.–5 a.m.; no fireworks; food must be secured from bears; 10 horsepower limit on boat motors.

TO GET THERE

From junction of US 60 and AZ 260, go 2 mi. west on Hwy. 260 and 1.5 mi. east on Old Linden Rd. to Fool Hollow Rd.

SHOW LOW   MAP, C-3
Show Low Lake County Park

Navajo County Parks and Recreation Dept., 86025. T: (928) 537-4126; www.parksrec@navajo.az.us.

🚐 ★★★   ▲ ★★★★

Beauty: ★★★★	Site Privacy: ★★★★
Spaciousness: ★★★★★	Quiet: ★★★★
Security: ★★★★	Cleanliness: ★★★★★
Insect Control: ★★★	Facilities: ★★★★

Show Low Lake was formed when the Phelps Dodge Corporation built Show Low Dam as part of a water exchange agreement with the Salt River Project to supply water to its mining and metallurgical operations elsewhere in the state. Indeed, the park land is leased from Phelps Dodge. Navajo County recently issued a private vendor a special permit to run the park and take campsite reservations. At 7,000 feet elevation in the White Mountains, the area makes a relatively cool summer retreat for Phoenix and the hot desert valleys. Show Low Lake is also a popular fishing spot for trout, walleyes, bluegills, largemouth bass, and catfish. The large crushed brown volcanic gravel campsites are shaded by very tall pine trees. For electric hookups request sites 25, 26, 28, 31, 32, 33, or 35. When the need for manmade necessities strikes, the local Wal-Mart is only a mile away.

BASICS

Operated By: Recreation Resource Management of America. **Open:** All year. **Site Assignment:** First come, first served; reservations available. **Registration:** At store; use adjacent host trailer when store is closed. **Fee:** $12–$18. **Parking:** At site.

FACILITIES

Number of RV-only Sites: 73. **Hookups:** Electric (30 amps). **Each Site:** Table, fire pit. **Dump Station:** Yes. **Laundry:** No. **Pay Phone:** Yes. **Restrooms and Showers:** Yes. **Fuel:** No. Walmart, 1mi. **Propane:** No. **Internal Roads:** Gravel, good. **RV Service:** No. **Market:** Show Low, 1 mi. **Restaurant:** Show Low, 1 mi. **General Store:** Yes. **Vending:** Yes. **Swimming:** Lake. **Playground:** Yes. **Other:** Boat ramp, boat rental, visitor center. **Activities:** Boating, fishing. **Nearby Attractions:** Lakes, forests, Mogollon Rim, Petrified Forest. **Additional Information:** Show Low Chamber of Commerce, (520) 537-2326.

RESTRICTIONS

Pets: On leash. **Fires:** Allowed (firewood sold). **Alcoholic Beverages:** Allowed. **Vehicle Maximum Length:** No limit. **Other:** Boats limited to a 10 horsepower motor; no firearms or woodcutting; secure food from bears.

TO GET THERE

From Show Low go 6 mi. south on AZ 260.

SPRINGERVILLE   MAP, C-3
Winn—Apache Sitgreaves National Forest

reserve america

P.O. Box 640, 85938. T: (928) 333-4301; www.reserveamerica.com.

🚐 ★★★★   ⛺ ★★★★

Beauty: ★★★★	Site Privacy: ★★★
Spaciousness: ★★★★	Quiet: ★★★
Security: ★★★★	Cleanliness: ★★★★
Insect Control: ★★★★	Facilities: ★★

This campground is located in a heavily forested pine and aspen area at an elevation of 8,500 feet near Lee Valley and Big Lake in the Apache Sitgreaves National Forest. The Apache and the Sitgreaves National Forests were administratively combined in 1974 and are now managed as one unit from the Forest Supervisor's office in Springerville. The 2-million-acre forest encompasses magnificent mountain country in east-central Arizona along the Mogollon Rim and the White Mountains. What makes this forest so special? It's the water—lots of it—draining the high mountains and forming numerous lakes and streams. It's an angler's paradise in the arid Southwest. The Apache-Sitgreaves has 34 lakes and reservoirs and more than 680 miles of rivers and streams—more than can be found in any other Southwestern national forest. The White Mountains contain the headwaters of several Arizona rivers including the Black, the Little Colorado, and the San Francisco. The Sitgreaves was named for Captain Lorenzo Sitgreaves, a government topographical engineer who conducted the first scientific expedition across Arizona in the early 1850s. In the Sitgreaves, the major attractions for visitors from the hot valleys of Phoenix or Tucson are the Mogollon Rim and the string of artificial lakes. From the Rim's 7,600-foot elevation, vista points provide inspiring views of the low country to the south and west.

BASICS

Operated By: U.S. Forest Service. **Open:** May 1–Nov. 13. **Site Assignment:** First come, first served only; no reservations. **Registration:** At office. **Fee:** Single, $12–$14; group, $125. **Parking:** At park.

FACILITIES

Number of Multipurpose Sites: 156. **Hookups:** None. **Each Site:** Call ahead. **Dump Station:** No. **Laundry:** No. **Pay Phone:** No. **Restrooms and Showers:** Yes. **Fuel:** No. **Propane:** No. **Internal Roads:** Paved. **RV Service:** No. **Market:** No. **Restaurant:** No. **General Store:** No. **Vending:** No. **Swimming:** No. **Playground:** No. **Activities:** Fishing, hiking.

RESTRICTIONS

Vehicle Maximum Length: Call ahead.

TO GET THERE

From Show Low, take Hwy. 260 southeast 34.5 mi. Take Hwy. 273 south for 10.5 mi., campground is on the left.

ST. JOHNS   MAP, B-3
Lyman Lake State Park

P.O. Box 1428, 85936. T: (520) 337-4441; www.pr.state.az.us.

🚐 ★★★★   ⛺ ★★★★

Beauty: ★★★★	Site Privacy: ★★★★
Spaciousness: ★★★★	Quiet: ★★★★★
Security: ★★★★	Cleanliness: ★★★★★
Insect Control: ★★★★	Facilities: ★★★★

A favorite of local windsurfers and water-skiers because of the lake's smooth surface, boaters like 6,000-foot-elevation Lyman Lake because it doesn't have boat-size and motor-horsepower restrictions (though there is a no-wake area near the fishing dock). There is a self-guided petroglyph trail on Peninsula Point, as well as a ranger-guided weekend boat trip to another petroglyph trail on the opposite side of the lake. Rangers also lead a summer tour to 14th-century Rattlesnake Pueblo for those curious about the ancient Mogollon and Pueblo cultures formerly inhabiting this high-plains area. RV campers have 38 electrical and water hookup sites attractively separated by grass and aspen and juniper trees. Tent campers can opt out of the designated sites altogether for more of a wilderness experience and camp along the shoreline beaches of this 1,500-acre reservoir.

BASICS

Operated By: Arizona State Parks. **Open:** All year. **Site Assignment:** First come, first served; group reservations. **Registration:** At office. **Fee:** $12–$22. **Parking:** At site.

FACILITIES

Number of RV-only Sites: 61. **Number of Tent-only Sites:** Undesignated sites. **Hookups:** Electric (30 amps), water. **Each Site:** Table, fire pit. **Dump Station:** Yes. **Laundry:** No. **Pay Phone:** Yes. **Restrooms and Showers:** Yes. **Fuel:** No. **Propane:** No. **Internal Roads:** Paved, good. **RV Service:** No. **Market:** St. Johns, 10 mi. **Restaurant:** No. **General Store:** Yes. **Vending:** Yes. **Swimming:** Lake. **Playground:** No. **Other:** Boat ramp, fish-cleaning station, sheltered picnic tables, tournament-grade water-ski slalom course, petroglyph trails, yurts available for rent. **Activities:** Fishing, boating, water sports, volleyball, horseshoes. **Nearby Attractions:** Sunrise Ski Area, White Mountains, Petrified Forest,

Navajo Reservation, Indian ruins. **Additional Information:** St. Johns Regional Chamber of Commerce, (928) 337-4441.

RESTRICTIONS

Pets: On leash. **Fires:** Not allowed. **Alcoholic Beverages:** Allowed (provided quiet hours observed). **Vehicle Maximum Length:** No limit. **Other:** No harassing or removing birds.

TO GET THERE

From St. Johns go 11 mi. south on the combined US 191/180.

TEMPLE BAR   MAP, A-1
Temple Bar Resort

601 Nevada Hwy., 89005. T: (702) 293-8906; www.nps.gov/lame.

🚐 ★★★   ⛺ ★★★★

Beauty: ★★★★	Site Privacy: ★★★★
Spaciousness: ★★★★	Quiet: ★★★★
Security: ★★★★	Cleanliness: ★★★★★
Insect Control: ★★★	Facilities: ★★★

On the Arizona side of Lake Mead, across yucca-studded desert that yields to creosote bush interspersed with brown and black chunks of lava and white hills, Temple Bar is one of the most remote designated campgrounds on Lake Mead. The Temple, a huge monolithic chunk of sandstone that glows brilliant orange at sunset, was an early landmark for Mormon settlers and the site of placer mining operations in the 1800s. The campground is a tightly packed cluster of sites beautifully landscaped with palms, oleander, and eucalyptus that provide privacy. Gravel pads make for good tent camping, and lake and mountain views are common. The campground's remoteness and isolation are part of its beauty, and like the rest of Lake Mead, the activities center around the water. There are 64 boat slips.

BASICS

Operated By: National Park Service. **Open:** All year. **Site Assignment:** First come, first served. **Registration:** At self-pay entrance fee station. **Fee:** $18. **Parking:** At site.

FACILITIES

Number of RV-only Sites: 166. **Hookups:** None. **Each Site:** Table, grill. **Dump Station:** Yes. **Laundry:** Yes. **Pay Phone:** Yes. **Restrooms and Showers:** Yes. **Fuel:** Yes. **Propane:** Yes. **Internal Roads:** Paved, good. **RV Service:** No. **Market:** Boulder City, 60 mi. **Restaurant:** At Temple Bar Resort. **General Store:** Yes. **Vending:** Yes. **Swimming:** Lake (at own risk). **Playground:** No. **Other:** Wheelchair-accessible sites, boat ramp, row-boat rentals, motel, landing strip. **Activities:** Boating, fishing. **Nearby Attractions:** Lake Mead, Hoover Dam, Las Vegas. **Additional Information:** Temple Bar Resort (Seven Crowns), (800) 752-9669, (520) 767-3211.

RESTRICTIONS

Pets: On leash under owner's control. **Fires:** Allowed. **Alcoholic Beverages:** Allowed. **Vehicle Maximum Length:** No limit. **Other:** 30-night stay limit.

TO GET THERE

From Hoover Dam go 19 mi. southeast on US 93 and turn northeast on Temple Bar Rd. for 28 mi.

TOMBSTONE
Wells Fargo RV Park
MAP, D-3

P.O. Box 1076, 85638. T: (520) 457-3966 or (800) 269-8266; www.wellsfargorv.com.

🚐 ★★★   ⛺ ★★★

Beauty: ★★★   Site Privacy: ★★★★
Spaciousness: ★★★   Quiet: ★★★★
Security: ★★★   Cleanliness: ★★★★
Insect Control: ★★★★   Facilities: ★★★★

Though at the edge of Tombstone's historic boardwalk, Wells Fargo RV Park becomes almost as quiet as a tomb at night, as this once brawling, saloon- and brothel-filled frontier mining town now shuts down at sundown. Some claim to hear ghosts at night, but usually the only commotion at this tree-lined campground is dogs in a howling frenzy as deer and javelina strolling through like they own the place. Wells Fargo's year-round residents are mostly a friendly group, and many work at local establishments like Big Nose Kate's Saloon. Next door is what locals call the best breakfast place in town, the O.K. Cafe, which also charbroils emu, ostrich, and buffalo burgers. It's "just a biscuit sling from the OK Corral," where Doc Holliday joined Wyatt and the Earp brothers for the famous shootout with the Clanton and McLaury families.

BASICS
Operated By: Joe & Buff Huntsman. **Open:** All year. **Site Assignment:** First come, first served; reservations advised Dec. 26–Memorial Day. **Registration:** At office. **Fee:** $29. **Parking:** At site.

FACILITIES
Number of RV-only Sites: 71. **Hookups:** Electric (20, 30 amps), water, sewer, cable TV. **Each Site:** Table, cement pad. **Dump Station:** No. **Laundry:** Yes. **Pay Phone:** Yes. **Restrooms and Showers:** Yes. **Fuel:** No. **Propane:** No. **Internal Roads:** Gravel, good. **RV Service:** No. **Market:** Bisbee, 19 mi. **Restaurant:** Tombstone, next door. **General Store:** No. **Vending:** No. **Swimming:** No. **Playground:** No. **Activities:** 2 p.m. daily OK Corral shootout. **Nearby Attractions:** OK Corral, Tombstone Courthouse State Park, Bird Cage Theatre, Bisbee. **Additional Information:** Tombstone Chamber of Commerce, (520) 457-9317 or (888) 457-3929, www.tombstone.org.

RESTRICTIONS
Pets: On leash under owner's control. **Fires:** Not allowed, depends on season & conditions. **Alcoholic Beverages:** Allowed. **Vehicle Maximum Length:** 30 ft.

TO GET THERE
From junction of US 80 and AZ 82, go 3 mi. south on US 80.

TUBAC
De Anza Trails RV Resort
MAP, D-2

P.O. Box 1927, 85646. T: (520) 398-8628 or (866) 332-6022; www.deanzatrailsrvresort.com.

🚐 ★★★   ⛺ n/a

Beauty: ★★★   Site Privacy: ★★★
Spaciousness: ★★★   Quiet: ★★★★
Security: ★★★   Cleanliness: ★★★★
Insect Control: ★★★★   Facilities: ★★★★

A collection of mundane RV parking spaces packaged with an impressive array of amenities, including an indoor pool and weight room, De Anza Trails offers 50 amp electric power, unlike Mountain View next door. However, De Anza falls short in parking convenience, as its spaces are all back-ins and require a security guard to supervise placement, in contrast to Mountain View's pull-through sites. Higher prices than the RV park next door have not helped, and on a recent summer day (admittedly the slow season this far south), De Anza had one customer while the funkier Mountain View was packed with RVs. Tents are prohibited, as are noisy trucks, cars, and motorcycles. Noise from trucks traversing the adjacent highway linking Tucson and Mexico might bother some people, but inside the clubhouse, library, and other facilities it should not be a problem.

BASICS
Operated By: De Anza Trails. **Open:** All year. **Site Assignment:** First come, first served; reservations accepted (payment in full; 30-day notice for 90% refund, otherwise "no refunds! no exceptions!"). **Registration:** At self-pay entrance fee station. **Fee:** $25; V, MC. **Parking:** At site.

FACILITIES
Number of RV-only Sites: 82. **Hookups:** Electric (20, 30, 50 amps), water, sewer, cable TV, phone. **Each Site:** Pole lights. **Dump Station:** Yes. **Laundry:** Yes. **Pay Phone:** Yes. **Restrooms and Showers:** Yes. **Fuel:** No. **Propane:** No. **Internal Roads:** Paved, excellent. **RV Service:** No. **Market:** Green Valley, 15 mi. **Restaurant:** Tumacacori, seasonal coffee shop on premises. **General Store:** Yes. **Vending:** Yes. **Swimming:** Indoor pool. **Playground:** No. **Other:** Pet walk, Jacuzzi, rec center, library, exercise/weight room, modem access. **Activities:** Cards, billiards, golf, boating, fishing. **Nearby Attractions:** Missions, Tubac Presidio, Madera Canyon, Buenos Aires Wildlife Refuge, museums, copper mine tour. **Additional Information:** Green Valley Chamber of Commerce, (520) 625-7575, (800) 858-5872, sraney@concentric.net.

RESTRICTIONS
Pets: On leash under owner's control. **Fires:** Allowed (limited). **Alcoholic Beverages:** Allowed. **Vehicle Maximum Length:** 50 ft. **Other:** 1 RV & vehicle per site; no street parking; shirts & shoes required in clubhouse; swim attire permitted in swim area only; 11 a.m. checkout.

TO GET THERE
From I-19 south of Green Valley, take Exit 48 (Arivaca Junction) and go south 2 mi. on Frontage Rd.

TUCSON
Catalina State Park
MAP, D-2

Oracle Rd., P.O. Box 36986, 85740. T: (520) 628-5798; www.pr.state.az.us.

🚐 ★★★★   ⛺ ★★★★★

Beauty: ★★★★   Site Privacy: ★★★★
Spaciousness: ★★★★★   Quiet: ★★★★
Security: ★★★★   Cleanliness: ★★★★
Insect Control: ★★★   Facilities: ★★

Big patches of mesquite ensure privacy at Catalina State Park, where the smallest campsite length is 55 feet and half the sites have hookups. Ten years ago this Santa Catalina Mountains desert foothill cattle ranching area was considered remote. Now Tangerine Rd. between I-10 and the park and the whole Oro Valley is filling up with subdivisions for retirees and aerospace engineers commuting to Tucson. Park roads run through a floodplain with flat ridges that provided the ancient Hohokams a home with water. When Sutherland Wash, the key floodplain drainage, becomes impossible to cross, access to hiking trails and Romero Ruins is blocked, though the campground is still reachable. From January through April, Tucson's peak season, morning arrivals snag all the campsites by noon. Afternoon arrivals (overflow) are typically sent to either Gilbert Ray Campground or Picacho Peak State Park.

BASICS
Operated By: Arizona State Parks. **Open:** All year. **Site Assignment:** First come, first served; group reservations required. **Registration:** At self-pay station. **Fee:** $12–$22. **Parking:** At site.

FACILITIES
Hookups: Electric (20, 30, 50 amps), water. **Each Site:** Table, grill. **Dump Station:** Yes. **Laundry:** No. **Pay Phone:** Yes. **Restrooms and Showers:** Yes. **Fuel:** No. **Propane:** No. **Internal Roads:** Paved, good condition. **RV Service:** Yes. **Market:** Oro Valley, 2 mi. **Restaurant:** Oro Valley, 2 mi. **General Store:** No. **Vending:** Yes. **Swimming:** No. **Playground:** No. **Other:** Romero Ruin Hohokam Indian archaeological site. Mountain biking & hiking. **Activities:** Horseback riding, bird-watching, mountain biking, hiking, golf. **Nearby Attractions:** Santa Catalina Mountains, Coronado National Forest, Biosphere 2, observatory, museums. **Additional Information:** Santa Catalina Ranger District, (520) 749-8700.

RESTRICTIONS
Pets: On leash under owner's control. **Fires:** Allowed (charcoal only; no wood fires, except 1 campfire pit in group area). **Alcoholic Beverages:** Allowed. **Vehicle Maximum Length:** 136 ft. **Other:** 14-day stay limit.

TO GET THERE
Go 9 mi. north of Tucson on AZ 77 (Oracle Rd.) to mile marker 81.

TUCSON   MAP, D-2
Crazy Horse Campground and RV Park

6660 South Craycroft Rd., 85706. T: (520) 574-0157 or (800) 279-6279; www.crazyhorserv.com.

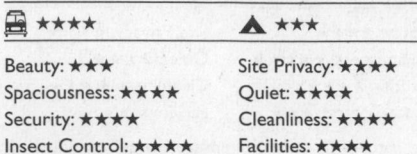 ★★★★   ▲ ★★★

Beauty: ★★★   Site Privacy: ★★★★
Spaciousness: ★★★★   Quiet: ★★★★
Security: ★★★★   Cleanliness: ★★★★
Insect Control: ★★★★   Facilities: ★★★★

Far enough back from I-10 to be quiet and near enough a truck stop to have a gas station, mini-mart, and restaurant next door, Crazy Horse is especially attractive to families with children. Thomas Jay Littletown Park, a quiet Pima County–run park two blocks north, is popular with kids and an easy walk from Crazy Horse. Most sites are pull-through, mostly 24-feet wide and accommodating vehicles up to 45 feet in length (one site accommodates a 60-foot vehicle). The attractive oleander, mesquite, and agave landscaping is concentrated around the front of the campground. For more amenities and the feel of a small luxury city, the adult-oriented Voyager RV Resort a few miles down the road is a good alternative. Cochise Terrace in Benson should also be considered if the objective is establishing a base camp near Tucson for exploring places like Tombstone and Bisbee.

BASICS
Operated By: Frank & Billie Anne Weingart. **Open:** All year. **Site Assignment:** First come, first served; reservations accepted seasonally (nonrefundable fee for confirmation by mail). **Registration:** At office. **Fee:** $25.50. **Parking:** At site.

FACILITIES
Number of RV-only Sites: 154. **Hookups:** Electric (20, 30, 50 amps), water, sewer, cable TV; phone available on request at most sites. **Each Site:** Table, most sites. **Dump Station:** Yes. **Laundry:** Yes. **Pay Phone:** Yes. **Restrooms and Showers:** Yes. **Fuel:** No. **Propane:** Yes. **Internal Roads:** Paved, good (Main road only). **RV Service:** No. **Market:** No. **Restaurant:** No. **General Store:** No. **Vending:** Soft drinks. **Swimming:** Pool. **Playground:** No, but w/in walking distance. **Other:** Dog walk, rec hall. **Activities:** Golf, horseback riding. **Nearby Attractions:** Pima Air & Space Museum, Saguaro National Park East, Colossal Cave, Kartchner Caverns, museums, Tucson. **Additional Information:** Tucson CVB, (800) 638-8350, www.visitTucson.org.

RESTRICTIONS
Pets: On leash under owner's control. **Fires:** Only in grills. **Alcoholic Beverages:** Not allowed. **Vehicle Maximum Length:** 60 ft.

TO GET THERE
Take Exit 268 from I-10 and go north on S. Craycroft Rd.

TUCSON   MAP, D-2
Gilbert Ray Campground

1204 West Silverlake Rd., 85713.
T: (520) 740-5830 or (520) 883-4200.

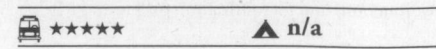 ★★★★   ▲ ★★★★

Beauty: ★★★★   Site Privacy: ★★★★
Spaciousness: ★★★★★   Quiet: ★★★★
Security: ★★★   Cleanliness: ★★★★
Insect Control: ★★★   Facilities: ★

A favorite of many for its low cost and location west of Tucson near Saguaro National Park West and the Desert Museum, Gilbert Ray's river-gravel sites are a particularly convenient stopping place when driving from Ajo or Organ Pipe Cactus National Monument through the Tohono O'odham Indian Reservation en route to Tucson on Arizona Hwy. 86 (Ajo Hwy.). This large, looping Pima County campground in Tucson Mountain Park is as close as camping gets to Saguaro National Park West without backpacking. Though there are hookups, the campground has few other amenities besides newspaper machines and a large recycling area. Campers here are mostly self-sufficient types whose idea of amenities is an undeveloped landscape with saguaro-studded mountains. Kinney, Gates Pass, and McCain Loop roads have roller coaster–like ups and downs near Gilbert Ray, and numerous roadside pullouts double as trailheads for traversing saguaro-rich Tucson Mountain Park.

BASICS
Operated By: Pima County Parks & Recreation. **Open:** All year. **Site Assignment:** First come, first served. **Registration:** At self-pay station. **Fee:** RV, $20; tent, $10; cash, check. **Parking:** At site.

FACILITIES
Number of RV-only Sites: 130. **Number of Tent-only Sites:** 5. **Hookups:** Electric (30 amps), water, sewer. **Each Site:** Table, grill. **Dump Station:** Yes. **Laundry:** No. **Pay Phone:** No. **Restrooms and Showers:** No showers. **Fuel:** No. **Propane:** No. **Internal Roads:** Paved, excellent. **RV Service:** No. **Market:** Tucson Estates, 5 mi. **Restaurant:** Tucson Estates, 5 mi. **General Store:** No. **Vending:** No. **Swimming:** No. **Playground:** No. **Other:** Some sheltered tables, recycling station. **Activities:** Rifle range, archery, horseback riding, biking. **Nearby Attractions:** Old Tucson Studios, Arizona-Sonora Desert Museum, Saguaro National Park West. **Additional Information:** Friends of Saguaro National Park, (520) 622-1080, www.friendsofsaguaro.org.

RESTRICTIONS
Pets: On leash under owner's control. **Fires:** Charcoal only in grills only; no wood fires. **Alcoholic Beverages:** Allowed. **Vehicle Maximum Length:** 30 ft. **Other:** 7-day stay limit; $160 automatic noncompliance citation if site not paid for w/in 15 min. of occupancy.

TO GET THERE
From intersection of W. Gates Pass and Kinney roads, go northwest to McCain Loop Rd.

TUCSON   MAP, D-2
Voyager RV Resort

8701 South Kolb Rd., 85706. T: (520) 574-5000 or (800) 424-9191; www.voyagerrv.com.

★★★★★   ▲ n/a

Beauty: ★★★   Site Privacy: ★★★
Spaciousness: ★★★★★   Quiet: ★★★★
Security: ★★★★★   Cleanliness: ★★★★★
Insect Control: ★★★★★   Facilities: ★★★★★

Tucson's largest RV resort opened in 1984 with 37,000 square feet of enclosed recreational space, including special crafts rooms for stained glass, lapidary, ceramics, and silver. With its own bank branch, restaurant, travel desk, store, and other facilities, Voyager has the feel of a small self-contained city. Streets are numbered 1st through 18th, and then skip by tens from 20th through 50th for the pull-through area surrounding the recreational facilities. Though daily RV rentals are welcome, the orientation is adult, like many southern Arizona RV parks catering to snowbird retirees. Except during summer, when kids are welcome, families with children will do better at the more child- and family-oriented Crazy Horse Campground. Since the fees are higher here, commensurate with the myriad of recreation options, Voyager is best thought of as a destination resort. But Voyager also works well as a luxury tourism base for exploring Tucson and southeastern Arizona.

BASICS
Operated By: Ike & Blanche Issacson. **Open:** All year. **Site Assignment:** First come, first served. **Registration:** At self-pay entrance fee station. **Fee:** $26.50–$41.50. **Parking:** At site.

FACILITIES
Number of RV-only Sites: 1,576. **Hookups:** Electric (20, 30, 50 amps), water, sewer, cable TV, phone. **Each Site:** Paved, table. **Dump Station:** Yes. **Laundry:** Yes. **Pay Phone:** Yes. **Restrooms and Showers:** Yes. **Fuel:** Yes. **Propane:** Yes. **Internal Roads:** Paved, excellent. **RV Service:** Yes. **Market:** Yes. **Restaurant:** Yes. **General Store:** Yes. **Vending:** Yes. **Swimming:** Pool. **Playground:** No. **Other:** Bocce, tennis, basketball & volleyball courts, mini-golf & 9-hole courses, exercise, poker, computer, & crafts rooms, ballroom, library, beautician, whirlpool, pet walk, pet grooming. **Activities:** Golf, shuffleboard, billiards. **Nearby Attractions:** Pima Air & Space Museum, Saguaro National Park East, Colossal Cave, Kartchner Caverns, museums. **Additional Information:** Tucson CVB, (800) 638-8350, www.visittucson.org.

RESTRICTIONS
Pets: Not allowed. **Fires:** Allowed. **Alcoholic Beverages:** At sites only. **Vehicle Maximum Length:** No limit. **Other:** Children welcome May 1–day after Labor Day.

TO GET THERE
From I-10 Exit 270 go 0.5 mi. south on Kolb Rd.

TUMACACORI   MAP, D-2
Mountain View RV Ranch

HCR 65 Box 380, 85640. T: (520) 398-9401; www.mtviewrvranch.com.

★★★   ▲ ★★

Beauty: ★★★★   Site Privacy: ★★★
Spaciousness: ★★★★   Quiet: ★★★
Security: ★★★   Cleanliness: ★★★
Insect Control: ★★   Facilities: ★★★★

Along the highway linking Tucson with Nogales, Mexico, a brick wall separates Mountain View RV Ranch from the newer De Anza Trails RV Resort next door. A loyal coterie of supporters keeps Mountain View humming year-round, even during the summer slow season when many other nearby RV parks look like deserted ghost towns. The virtually unlimited vehicle length and 49 40-ft.-wide pull-through spaces accommodating slide-outs is one reason for Mountain View's popularity. Tent campers can choose their spot anywhere along a grass strip extending from the small rear mobile home park to near the front of the park for pool, laundry, and snack-bar convenience. Sunday mornings the snack bar serves up free coffee with breakfast, and home-made soups and sandwiches top off the lunch menu. The action here includes Monday night football on a big screen TV, pot lucks, card games, Friday night bingo, and darts.

BASICS

Operated By: Esther Geisman. **Open:** All year. **Site Assignment:** First come, first served; winter reservations advised. **Registration:** At office. **Fee:** RV, $17–$21; tent, $16; V, MC, AE, D. **Parking:** At site.

FACILITIES

Number of RV-only Sites: 72. **Number of Tent-only Sites:** Undesignated sites. **Hookups:** Electric (20, 30 amps), water, sewer, cable TV, phone. **Each Site:** Table. **Dump Station:** Yes. **Laundry:** Yes. **Pay Phone:** Yes. **Restrooms and Showers:** Yes. **Fuel:** No. **Propane:** Yes. **Internal Roads:** Gravel, good condition. **RV Service:** No. **Market:** Green Valley, 15 mi. **Restaurant:** No. **General Store:** Yes. **Vending:** Soft drinks. **Swimming:** Yes. **Playground:** No. **Other:** Dog walk, rental cabins. **Activities:** Shuffleboard, golf, boating, fishing. **Nearby Attractions:** Tubac State Park, Presidio State Park, Tumacacori National Monument, Madera Canyon, Buenos Aires Wildlife Refuge, Native American casinos, museums, copper mine tour, 30 miles from Mexico. **Additional Information:** Green Valley Chamber of Commerce, (520) 625-7575, (800) 858-5872, sraney@concentric.net.

RESTRICTIONS

Pets: On leash. **Fires:** In designated area only. Only during summer. **Alcoholic Beverages:** Allowed. **Vehicle Maximum Length:** No limit.

TO GET THERE

From I-19 south of Green Valley, take Amado Exit 48 south or 42 north.

WENDEN MAP, C-1
Alamo Lake State Park

P.O. Box 38, 85357. T: (928) 669-2088; www.pr.state.az.us.

🚐 ★★★★	🏕 ★★★★
Beauty: ★★★★	Site Privacy: ★★★
Spaciousness: ★★★	Quiet: ★★★★
Security: ★★★★	Cleanliness: ★★★★
Insect Control: ★★★	Facilities: ★★★★

Nestled amongst saguaros and ocotillos where wild burros roam and golden and bald eagles soar above the Bill Williams River Valley, bass-filled Alamo Lake has a collection of eight developed and primitive camping areas on widely separated loops. The section of camping area A nearest the general store, sheltered picnic tables, and ranger station has 19 coveted sites with electric and water hookups. Camping areas A and B have sites with paved pads topped with a pebble layer, and are popular for both RVs and tents. Camping area C off Cholla Rd. also has hookups, though those willing to trade hookups for maximum privacy and beauty should continue down Cholla Rd. towards the lakeshore and camping areas D and E. Though farthest from the showers, store, and other amenities, camping area E, which has portable restrooms and picnic tables because it is sometimes underwater, is best situated to enjoy beautiful lake views.

BASICS

Operated By: Arizona State Parks. **Open:** All year. **Site Assignment:** First come, first served. **Registration:** At self-pay entrance fee station. **Fee:** $10–$19; cash, check. **Parking:** At site.

FACILITIES

Number of RV-only Sites: 250. **Hookups:** Electric (30 amps), water. **Each Site:** Table, grill, fire ring. **Dump Station:** Yes. **Laundry:** Yes. **Pay Phone:** Yes. **Restrooms and Showers:** Yes. **Fuel:** Yes. **Propane:** No. **Internal Roads:** Paved or pebbly, good condition. **RV Service:** No. **Market:** No. **Restaurant:** No. **General Store:** Yes. **Vending:** Soft drinks. **Swimming:** Lake. **Playground:** Yes. **Other:** Boat ramps, fish-cleaning & battery recharge station. **Activities:** Mountain biking, fishing, boating. **Nearby Attractions:** Desert. **Additional Information:** Alamo Lake Store (boat rental), (520) 925-0133.

RESTRICTIONS

Pets: On leash. **Fires:** Fire ring only. **Alcoholic Beverages:** Allowed. **Vehicle Maximum Length:** No limit. **Other:** ORVs must be street legal to operate in park.

TO GET THERE

From US 60 in Wenden, go 38 mi. north on Alamo Dam Access Rd.

WENDEN MAP, C-1
Morenga Palms RV Park

P.O. Box 68, 85357. T: (928) 859-3722.

🚐 ★★★★	🏕 ★★
Beauty: ★★★★	Site Privacy: ★★★
Spaciousness: ★★★★	Quiet: ★★★★★
Security: ★★★★	Cleanliness: ★★★★★
Insect Control: ★★★	Facilities: ★★

During the five-month winter season, this small RV park is filled by regulars from around the country and Canada, some of whom have been coming here for over a decade to form part of a small community that gathers for cocktails while watching the sunset from the clubhouse porch before evening games commence. During the hot summer, when there is space for tent campers to plug into the electric hookups left behind by migrating snowbirds, the surrounding fields are growing cotton, cantaloupes, watermelons, and a variety of fruit and vegetables for the Del Monte cannery. Parker and the Colorado River recreation is 64 miles to the north, but Alamo Lake State Park is within about 30 miles. Wickenburg's bowling alley and many restaurants are 46 miles to the west. All in all, a small isolated gem of a stopping place for those venturing into the Arizona outback.

BASICS

Operated By: Dorothy & Bruce O'Hara. **Open:** Closed during summer. **Site Assignment:** Winter reservations advised. **Registration:** At office. **Fee:** $18; plus tax. **Parking:** At site.

FACILITIES

Number of RV-only Sites: 52. **Hookups:** Electric (30 amps), water, sewer, phone. **Each Site:** Table, bench, fire ring (only at designated areas). **Dump Station:** No. **Laundry:** Yes. **Pay Phone:** No. **Restrooms and Showers:** Yes. **Fuel:** No. **Propane:** No. **Internal Roads:** Gravel, good. **RV Service:** No. **Market:** No. **Restaurant:** No. **General Store:** Yes. **Vending:** No. **Swimming:** No. **Playground:** No. **Other:** Clubhouse, exercise room, picnic area w/ fire ring. **Activities:** Lake is 40 miles away. **Nearby Attractions:** Alamo Lake State Park, Quartzsite. **Additional Information:** McMullen Valley Chamber of Commerce, (520) 859-3846.

RESTRICTIONS

Pets: On leash under owner's control. (Small dogs only.) **Fires:** In designated areas only. **Alcoholic Beverages:** Not allowed. **Vehicle Maximum Length:** No limit. **Other:** Need own satellite dish for TV.

TO GET THERE

From Wenden go 3 mi. east on US 60.

WICKENBURG MAP, B-1
Burro Creek Recreation Site

2475 Beverly Ave., 86401. T: (928) 692-4400.

🚐 ★★★★	🏕 ★★★★
Beauty: ★★★★	Site Privacy: ★★★★
Spaciousness: ★★★★	Quiet: ★★★★
Security: ★★★★	Cleanliness: ★★★★
Insect Control: ★★★	Facilities: ★★

Nine miles north of the town of Nothing and near old copper mining towns like Bagdad, Burro Creek Recreation Site is seemingly in the middle of nowhere, though it is just off US 93, the main artery linking Phoenix and Las Vegas, Nevada. Many regulars come back here every year because it is such a good place to just sit and relax, with little else to do besides hiking along the tree-lined creek and looking for the blue and purple agates and Apache tears that endear the area to rock hounds. Day use of the park is free, including the solar-lighted restrooms and the ample picnic area surrounded by saguaros and mesquite. The small cactus garden is a good introduction to desert botany and nesting desert pack rats. Fishing in the year-round water pools is taboo, as the Sonoran suckers and roundtail chub are endangered. Bird-watchers can spot great blue herons and bald eagles.

BASICS

Operated By: Bureau of Land Management. **Open:** All year. **Site Assignment:** First come, first served; group site reservations. **Registration:** At self-pay station. **Fee:** $10; cash, check. **Parking:** At site.

FACILITIES

Number of RV-only Sites: 30. **Hookups:** None. **Each Site:** Table, fire ring. **Dump Station:** Yes. **Laundry:** No. **Pay Phone:** No. **Restrooms and Showers:** No showers. **Fuel:** No. **Propane:** No. **Internal Roads:** Gravel, good. **RV Service:** No. **Market:** Wickenburg, 60 mi. **Restaurant:** Wickenburg, 60 mi. **General Store:** No. **Vending:** No. **Swimming:** No. **Playground:** No. **Other:** Some sheltered tables; 1 wheelchair-accessible site; cactus botanical garden. **Activities:** Rock collecting, bird-watching. **Nearby Attractions:** Hualapai Indian Reservation, Alamo Lake State Park. **Additional Information:** BLM Kingman Field Office, (928) 692-4400.

RESTRICTIONS

Pets: On leash under owner's control. **Fires:** Allowed. **Alcoholic Beverages:** Allowed. **Vehicle Maximum Length:** No limit.

TO GET THERE

From Kingman go 17 mi. east on I-40, then 53 mi. south on US 93 to signed turnoff 1 mi. south of Burro Creek Bridge and follow gravel road 1.5 mi. to campground.

WINSLOW
Homolovi Ruins State Park
MAP, B-3

HCR 63 Box 5, 86047. T: (520) 289-4106; www.pr.state.az.us.

🚐 ★★★★   ▲ ★★★

Beauty: ★★★★	Site Privacy: ★★★★
Spaciousness: ★★★★	Quiet: ★★★★
Security: ★★★★	Cleanliness: ★★★★★
Insect Control: ★★★	Facilities: ★★★

Mostly used as an overnight stop by travelers on I-40, Homolovi Ruins is farther from the highway and not near a power plant or lake like the nearby and more rustic Cholla Lake County Park. The paved sites have small trees provide some shade. Raised dirt pads make for comfortable tenting, though it is advisable to shake your boots for scorpions before putting them on in the morning. The name Homolovi means little hills in the Hopi language, and the area was a sacred gathering place of the clans and is still visited as a sacred place by the Hopi. The park opened in 1993, but archaeological excavations date to 1896. The over 1,000-room pueblo is the most accessible site in this park, which has good wildlife viewing areas along the Little Colorado River.

BASICS

Operated By: Arizona State Parks. **Open:** All year. **Site Assignment:** First come, first served. **Registration:** At entrance kiosk (use self-pay slot when closed). **Fee:** $10–$15; cash, check. **Parking:** At site.

FACILITIES

Number of RV-only Sites: 53. **Hookups:** Electric (30 amps), water. **Each Site:** Table, grill. **Dump Station:** Yes. **Laundry:** No. **Pay Phone:** Yes. **Restrooms and Showers:** Yes (showers May–Oct. only). **Fuel:** No. **Propane:** No. **Internal Roads:** Paved, excellent. **RV Service:** No. **Market:** Winslow, 3 mi. **Restaurant:** Winslow, 3 mi. **General Store:** No. **Vending:** Yes. **Swimming:** No. **Playground:** No. **Other:** Visitor center, museum, covered picnic tables, wildlife viewing turnouts, archaeological sites. **Activities:** Archaeological dig tours (June, July). **Nearby Attractions:** Little Painted Desert, Second Mesa, Mogollon Rim, Meteor Crater, Walnut Canyon, Flagstaff, Petrified Forest. **Additional Information:** Winslow Chamber of Commerce Visitor Center, (928) 289-2434, www.winslowarizona.org.

RESTRICTIONS

Pets: On leash (not allowed in buildings). **Fires:** In designated areas only. **Alcoholic Beverages:** Allowed. **Vehicle Maximum Length:** No limit. **Other:** Gates closed from 7 p.m.–6 a.m.

TO GET THERE

From Winslow go east 2 mi. on I-40 to Exit 257 and then north 1.5 mi. on AZ 87.

Arkansas

Rice paddies. Catfish fillets. Only country-and-western radio stations. A polite "sir" or "madam" in every sentence. Life in Arkansas draws on the Deep South in ways outsiders may consider out of sync with modern America. With county bans on alcohol sales reminiscent of Prohibition, one native went so far as to call the state "backward," but that depends on your perception. Residents possess an intimate knowledge and palpable love of the land they inhabit, and visitors are welcomed warmly in the best tradition of Southern hospitality.

Arkansas calls itself "the Natural State," and the moniker is reinforced by its inhabitants—even businesspeople take weekend hunting trips. Nearly everyone you meet has a fishing pole, knows where to catch a trophy bass (or maybe just dinner), or has photos from the last fishing trip. Perhaps the best way to get to know this state is to camp at some of the many state parks—they give you a feel for the breadth of the state's natural diversity and the depth of its history. Arkansas is also home to the country's one and only diamond mine. Rockhounds and fortune-seekers alike will want to visit **Crater of Diamonds State Park** near Murfreesboro, where visitors can keep whatever gems they uncover. Diamonds found in the park have all varied in size and color. One of the biggest finds was by one of the park's own employees, who found a whopping 16-carat diamond (about the size of a wild pecan) after a rainstorm.

Aside from the hunting, fishing, boating, and hot springs, even just driving through Arkansas is a pleasure. This is such a verdant state you can't help but revel in its greenery. **Bull Shoals** and the **Ouachita Mountains** are as representative of Arkansas as Little Rock and Texarkana. Lush vegetation wraps around small roads like clothing. Wildlife abounds, including armadillos and even alligators. Go for a drive through the **Ozark National Forest** or along the **Mississippi River,** and you'll never think of Arkansas the same way again. I-540, which passes through Fayetteville, is 38 miles of billboard-free driving—making for an obstruction-free view of the **Ozark Mountains.** Another inspiring view is **Byway 71,** which runs from Alma to Fayetteville. On this particularly dizzying drive, the amount of breathtaking sights is equaled only by many twists and dipping curves—sort of like a roller-coaster ride through the Ozarks. Need a tour guide? If you're around Fayetteville in late September or early October, you might be able to get a few folks from the **Bikes and Blues and Barbecue Motorcycle Roll and Music Festival** to give you guided tour. With all that music (everything from rock and country to blues and jazz), food, and great weather (highs averaging in the mid-70s) you might be tempted to stay in Fayetteville for the weekend.

In fact, it seems to be the natural state of being for most Arkansas natives to gather in large numbers and celebrate all things Arkansas. Some festivals of note include the **Arkansas Scottish Festival** (complete with bagpipe music and Highland dancing), the **Hot Springs Documentary Film Festival and Institute, Hot Springs Music Festival, Mount Ida's Good Ole Days** (originally called Charlie Weaver Day), the **Pink Tomato Festival, Riverfront Blues Festival, Purple Hull Pea Festival, Hope Watermelon Fest, Johnson County Arkansas Peach Festival, Greek Food Festival** (in Little Rock), **Mount Magazine International Butterfly Festival, Shakespeare Festival of Arkansas, White Water River Carnival, Turkey Trot Festival,** and (perhaps the most curiously titled festival of the lot) **Toad Suck Daze.**

The question to ask yourself isn't "Why should I go to Arkansas?" but "Why haven't I gone there before?"

Campground Profiles

ARKADELPHIA   MAP, C-2
Arkadelphia Campground and RV Park

221 Frost Rd., 71923-9610. T: (870) 246-4922; www.arkadelphiacampground.com.

🚐 ★★★★   ▲ ★★★

Beauty: ★★★★	Site Privacy: ★★★
Spaciousness: ★★★	Quiet: ★★★
Security: ★★★★	Cleanliness: ★★★★
Insect Control: ★★★★	Facilities: ★★★★

Most of the sites in this campground are well shaded, which is good news to summer campers in this part of the state. Laid out in an arc with internal sites, the main camping area has 12 sites around the perimeter that can be used for tents or for small RVs. Site 1 is very close to the road that leads to the northern camping area, and all other sites (except 7 and 8) require either pitching a tent on a serious slope or right on the internal road. RVers may find this normal, but tenters will not like the space. Sites 7 and 8 are the exceptions, with larger spaces and nice trees. Site 24 is an enormous (100-feet-long) pull-through, while the sites next to it (20–23) are half the size and only pull-throughs if the adjacent site is unoccupied. These sites are all next to the forest, under a canopy of trees. Nice 50-foot back-ins that are likewise shaded include 50, 52, 59, and 62. These sites are in the north area of the campground, off the main camping area. Pull-throughs include 51, 55, 58, 60, and 62, which can accommodate a rig of any size. Less pleasant are sites 30 and 31, which are very open, and site 27, which is close to the entrance, Frost Rd., and the propane-vending area. The laundry room is clean and spacious, and has a television to help while away the time while your clothes are being cleaned. The restroom is very clean. Overall, this is a nice campground, although RVers will enjoy it a little more than tenters.

BASICS

Operated By: The Cristoffersons. **Open:** All year. **Site Assignment:** Upon registration; credit card required for reservations; need 2–3 day notice during holidays; cancellation by 4 p.m. the day before arrival. **Registration:** At office. (Late arrivals use drop box.) **Fee:** RV full, $20; water/electric, $18; tent, $14. **Parking:** At site.

FACILITIES

Number of RV-only Sites: 44. **Number of Tent-only Sites:** 12. **Hookups:** Electric (30, 50 amps), water, sewer, cable TV. **Each Site:** Picnic table. **Dump Station:** Yes. **Laundry:** Yes. **Pay Phone:** Yes. **Restrooms and Showers:** Yes. **Fuel:** No. Sell kerosene. **Propane:** Yes. **Internal Roads:** Gravel. **RV Service:** No. RV service on-call nearby. **Market:** 7 mi. (Exit 73). **Restaurant:** 1 mi. **General Store:** Yes. **Vending:** Yes. **Swimming:** Outdoor pool. **Playground:** Yes. **Other:** Pet walk area, cabins, fishing pond, cottage (w/kitchen). Can tether horses. **Activities:** Fishing, horseshoes, tetherball, hopscotch, hiking, biking. **Nearby Attractions:** Lake DeGray, Lake Hamilton, Lake Catherine, Lake Ouachita, Hot Springs, Crater of Diamonds. **Additional Information:** Arkadelphia Area Chamber of Commerce (870) 246-5542.

RESTRICTIONS

Pets: On leash, cleaned up after. **Fires:** In grills; subject to seasonal bans. **Alcoholic Beverages:** At sites, not by pool, subject to dry county regulations. **Vehicle Maximum Length:** No limit.

TO GET THERE

From I-30, take Exit 78 and turn north onto Hwy. 7. Go 0.25 mi. and turn right onto Frost Rd. Go 1.5 mi. and turn left at the sign into the entrance.

ARKADELPHIA   MAP, C-1, C-2
Arlie Moore

729 Channel Rd., 71923-9364. T: (870) 246-5501; www.reserveamerica.com.

🚐 ★★★   ▲ ★★★★

Beauty: ★★★	Site Privacy: ★★★
Spaciousness: ★★★	Quiet: ★★★
Security: ★★★	Cleanliness: ★★★★
Insect Control: ★★★	Facilities: ★★★

At the foothills of the Ouachita Mountains on DeGray Lake, Arlie Moore is a favorite due to its location about midway of the lake and easy access from State Highway 7. The Arlie Moore Interpretive Trail was constructed in August of 1984. After many years of use, combined with the lack of attention due to personnel and budget restrictions, the trail required extensive renovation. Therefore, the DeGray Lake Field Office submitted a trail-renovation grant proposal in the Alcoa Foundation Grant Program. The grant proposal was selected and the DeGray Lake Field Office was awarded grants totaling $8,000. DeGray Lake encompasses 31,800 land and water acres with 13,500 water acres and 207 miles of shoreline. DeGray Lake is stocked with a variety of game fish and is a world-class hybrid striped bass fishery. Arlie Moore offers 87 Class A campsites with electrical hookups. Other amenities include a reservable picnic shelter, flush toilets, heated showers, water, two boat ramps, swimming beach, trailer dump station, playground, picnic sites, nature trail, amphitheater, and registration booth.

BASICS

Operated By: U.S. Army Corps of Engineers. **Open:** All year. **Site Assignment:** Reservations must be made at least 3 days in advance. **Registration:** At office. **Fee:** Single, $10–$16. **Parking:** At site.

FACILITIES

Number of Multipurpose Sites: 173. **Hookups:** Yes. **Dump Station:** Yes. **Laundry:** No. **Pay Phone:** No. **Restrooms and Showers:** Yes. **Fuel:** No. **Propane:** No. **Internal Roads:** Paved. **RV Service:** No. **Market:** No. **Restaurant:** No. **General Store:** No. **Vending:** No. **Swimming:** Yes. **Playground:** Yes. **Activities:** Amphitheater, picnicking, fishing.

RESTRICTIONS

Pets: Pets must be restrained or on a leash at all times while in developed recreation areas. **Fires:** In fire rings, stoves, grills, or fireplaces provided for that purpose. **Alcoholic Beverages:** Not allowed. **Vehicle Maximum Length:** Call ahead.

TO GET THERE

From I-30 take Exit 78. Take AR 7 north for 9 mi. Turn left onto Arlie Moore Rd., go 2 mi. to campground. From Hot Springs take AR 7 south to 2 mi. south of Bismarck. Turn right onto Arlie Moore Rd. and go 2 mi. to campground.

ARKADELPHIA   MAP, C-1, C-2
Caddo Drive

729 Channel Rd., 71923-9364. T: (870) 246-5501; www.reserveamerica.com.

🚐 ★★★   ▲ ★★★★

Beauty: ★★★	Site Privacy: ★★
Spaciousness: ★★	Quiet: ★★
Security: ★★	Cleanliness: ★★★★
Insect Control: ★★★	Facilities: ★★

The breathtaking view over a rock bluff at the west end of the lake is this site's most popular feature, as well as the lakes. At the foothill of the Ouachita Mountains on DeGray Lake, Caddo Drive is located on a tree covered ridge ending abruptly on a bluff that offers one of the more panoramic views of DeGray Lake. DeGray Lake encompasses 31,800 land and water acres with 13,500 water acres and 207 miles of shoreline. Caddo Drive offers 72 Class A campsites with electrical hookups. DeGray Lake, a 13,800-acre fishing paradise stocked with a variety of game fish and is a world-class hybrid striped bass fishery. This sparkling lake on the Caddo River offers Arkansas's finest fishing for hybrid striped bass and great angling for bass, crappie, bream, and catfish. In warm months, water-skiing, sailing, snorkeling, kayaking, and pleasure boating are popular lake activities. The lake's clear waters are also ideal for scuba diving or swimming.

BASICS

Operated By: U.S. Army Corps of Engineers. **Open:** All year. **Site Assignment:** Reservations must be made at least 3 days in advance. **Registration:** At office. **Fee:** Single, $6–$10. **Parking:** At site.

FACILITIES

Number of Multipurpose Sites: 147. **Hookups:** Yes. **Dump Station:** Yes. **Laundry:** No. **Pay Phone:** No. **Restrooms and Showers:** Yes. **Fuel:** No. **Propane:** No. **Internal Roads:** Paved. **RV Service:** No. **Market:** No. **Restaurant:** No. **General Store:** No. **Vending:** No. **Swimming:** Yes. **Playground:** No. **Other:** Caddo Drive is located in close proximity to DeGray Lake Resort State Park, which offers an 18-hole golf course, tennis course, restaurant & lodge, boat rentals, full-service marina, laundry facilities, & an equestrian trail.

RESTRICTIONS

Pets: Pets must be restrained or on a leash at all times while in developed recreation areas. **Fires:** In fire rings, stoves, grills, or fireplaces provided for that purpose. **Alcoholic Beverages:** Not allowed. **Vehicle Maximum Length:** Call ahead.

TO GET THERE

From I-30 take Exit 78. Take AR 7 north for 6 mi. Turn left onto Edgewood Rd. and go 3 mi. to Caddo Dr.

ARKADELPHIA   MAP, C-1,C-2
Iron Mountain

729 Channel Rd., 71923-9364. T: (870) 246-5501; www.reserveamerica.com.

🚐 ★★★★   ▲ ★★★

Beauty: ★★★	Site Privacy: ★★
Spaciousness: ★★	Quiet: ★★★
Security: ★★★	Cleanliness: ★★★★
Insect Control: ★★★	Facilities: ★★★★

At the foothills of the Ouachita Mountains on DeGray Lake, Iron Mountain lives up to its name because the terrain is mountainous by comparison to other developed areas at DeGray Lake. DeGray Lake encompasses 31,800 land and water acres with 13,500 water acres and 207 miles of shoreline. The history of the DeGray area dates back to 700 AD when the area was inhabited by the Caddo Indians. Hernando DeSoto then came and explored this area in 1541, After coming across Hot Springs. The Caddo Indians way of life was changed forever when coming in contact with the Spanish explorers, the Indians were introduced to the horse. Now the Indians had an advantage when hunting or going into war. In the 1700s French fur trappers brought trade to the area with their extensive trapping methods. DeGray Lake was in fact named after a French fur trader, DeGraff, who settled this region. Several artifacts have been found near the dam site, and many have been brought to a local university, Henderson State University. DeGray Lake is stocked with a variety of game fish and is a world-class hybrid striped bass fishery. Iron Mountain is the closest camping area mileage wise from Interstate 30. Iron Mountain offers 69 Class A campsites with electrical hookups. Other amenities include flush toilets, heated showers, water, boat ramp, trailer dump station, picnic sites, playground, registration booth, and full-service marina.

BASICS

Operated By: U.S. Army Corps of Engineers. **Open:** All year. **Site Assignment:** Reservations must be made at least 3 days in advance. **Registration:** At office. **Fee:** Single, $10–$16. **Parking:** At site.

FACILITIES

Number of Multipurpose Sites: 134. **Hookups:** Yes. **Dump Station:** Yes. **Laundry:** No. **Pay Phone:** No. **Restrooms and Showers:** Yes. **Fuel:**

No. **Propane:** No. **Internal Roads:** Paved. **RV Service:** No. **Market:** No. **Restaurant:** No. **General Store:** No. **Vending:** No. **Swimming:** No. **Playground:** Yes.

RESTRICTIONS

Pets: Pets must be restrained or on a leash at all times while in developed recreation areas. **Fires:** In fire rings, stoves, grills, or fireplaces provided for that purpose. **Alcoholic Beverages:** Not allowed. **Vehicle Maximum Length:** Call ahead.

TO GET THERE

From I-30 take Exit 78. Take AR 7 north 2.5 mi. Turn left onto Skyline Dr. Take Skyline Dr. 2.5 mi. Turn right on Iron Mountain Rd. and proceed to Iron Mountain. From Hot Springs take AR 7 south to Skyline Dr. Turn right onto Skyline Dr. for 2.5 mi. Turn right onto Iron Mountain Rd. and proceed to Iron Mountain.

ARKADELPHIA   MAP, C-1,C-2
Shouse Ford

729 Channel Rd. , 71923-9364. T: (870) 246-5501; www.reserveamerica.com.

🚐 ★★★★   ▲ ★★★★

Beauty: ★★★	Site Privacy: ★★★
Spaciousness: ★★★	Quiet: ★★
Security: ★★	Cleanliness: ★★★★
Insect Control: ★★★	Facilities: ★★★★

At the foothills of the Ouachita Mountains on DeGray Lake, Shouse Ford is a favorite due to the gentle terrain and a number of shoreline campsites. DeGray Lake encompasses 31,800 land and water acres, 13,500 water acres, and 207 miles of shoreline. The history of the DeGray area dates back to 700 AD when the area was inhabited by the Caddo Indians. Hernando DeSoto then came and explored this area in 1541, After coming across Hot Springs. The Caddo Indians way of life was changed forever when coming in contact with the Spanish explorers, the Indians were introduced to the horse. Now the Indians had an advantage when hunting or going into war. In the 1700s French fur trappers brought trade to the area with their extensive trapping methods. DeGray Lake was in fact named after a French fur trader, DeGraff, who settled this region. Several artifacts have been found near the dam site, and many have been brought to a local university, Henderson State University. DeGray Lake is stocked with a variety of game fish and is a world-class hybrid striped bass fishery. Shouse Ford offers 100 Class A campsites with electrical hookups. Other amenities include flush toilets, heated showers, water, boat ramp, trailer dump station, picnic sites, two swimming beaches, and a registration booth.

BASICS

Operated By: U.S. Army Corps of Engineers. **Open:** All year. **Site Assignment:** Reservations must be made at least 3 days in advance. **Registration:** At office. **Fee:** Single, $10–$16. **Parking:** At site.

FACILITIES

Number of Multipurpose Sites: 212. **Hookups:** Yes. **Dump Station:** Yes. **Laundry:** No. **Pay Phone:** No. **Restrooms and Showers:** Yes. **Fuel:** No. **Propane:** No. **Internal Roads:** Paved. **RV Service:** No. **Market:** No. **Restaurant:** No. **General Store:** No. **Vending:** No. **Swimming:** Yes. **Playground:** Yes. **Activities:** Fishing.

RESTRICTIONS

Pets: Pets must be restrained or on a leash at all times while in developed recreation areas. **Fires:** In fire rings, stoves, grills, or fireplaces provided for that purpose. **Alcoholic Beverages:** Not allowed. **Vehicle Maximum Length:** Call ahead.

TO GET THERE

From I-30 take Exit 78. Take AR 7 north to Bismarck. Turn left on AR 84 and go 9 mi. west to Point Cedar. Turn left onto Shouse Ford Rd. and go 4 mi. to Shouse Ford. From Hot Springs, take AR 7 south to Bismarck. Turn right on AR 84 and go 9 mi. west to Point Cedar. Turn left onto Shouse Ford Rd. and go 4 mi. to Shouse Ford.

CALICO ROCK   MAP, B-2
Cedar Ridge

P.O. Box 236, 72519. T: (870) 297-4282.

🚐 ★★★★★   ▲ ★★★★★

Beauty: ★★★★★	Site Privacy: ★★★★★
Spaciousness: ★★★★	Quiet: ★★★★★
Security: ★★★★★	Cleanliness: ★★★★
Insect Control: ★★★★	Facilities: ★★

This campground is wild, undeveloped, natural, and quiet. It is subtly but attractively landscaped with rock, cacti, and juniper. Sites 1–3 are 42-foot back-ins that back up to the (rather quiet) road. Site 4 is an unshaded site that also abuts the road, but backs to thick vegetation. Sites 5–7 are pull-throughs that average 55 feet in length; 5 and 7 are shaded, 6 is not. Two unnumbered sites in the northeast corner are in an open field, and can accommodate a rig of any size, as can a third site slightly below these two. (This third site, being sheltered somewhat by a juniper, is more welcoming than the two open sites next to it.) The largest sites are 9–11, which average 70 feet in length. The restroom and shower are contained in a single unit, which is modern and decently clean. There is an absolutely wonderful scenic view of the river down a gravel road at the southernmost edge of the campground, which campers should make a point of seeing. In fact, the campground itself is an extremely attractive natural setting that will please campers of all kinds—definitely a destination campground to return to.

BASICS

Operated By: Gene & Reva Lockie. **Open:** Mar. 1–Oct. 30. **Site Assignment:** First come, first served; verbal reservations OK. **Registration:** At office. (Late arrivals sign register; "Gene will see you later.") **Fee:** RV full, $12; water/electric, $10; tent, $7. **Parking:** At site.

FACILITIES

Number of RV-only Sites: 17. **Number of Tent-only Sites:** 3. **Hookups:** Electric (20, 30 amps), water, sewer. **Each Site:** Picnic table, grill. **Dump**

Station: Yes. Laundry: No. Pay Phone: No. Restrooms and Showers: Yes. Fuel: No. Propane: No. Internal Roads: Gravel. RV Service: No. Market: 3 mi. into town. Restaurant: 1 mi. into town. General Store: No. Vending: No. Swimming: No. Playground: Yes. Other: Firewood. Activities: Fishing, hunting. Nearby Attractions: Blanchard Springs Caverns, White River. Additional Information: Mountain Home, Chamber of Commerce, (870) 425-5111.

RESTRICTIONS

Pets: On leash, cleaned up after. Fires: Grill only. Alcoholic Beverages: At sites. Vehicle Maximum Length: No limit.

TO GET THERE

From the junction of Hwy. 56 and Hwy. 5, go 1 block south on Hwy. 5 (Main St.) to Calico St. Turn right and go 0.7 mi. Turn left at the sign into the campground.

CLINTON   MAP, B-2
Whispering Pines RV Park

8575 Hwy. 65 North, 72031. T: (888) 745-4291 or (501) 745-4291.

🚐 ★★★★   ⛺ ★★★★

Beauty: ★★★★
Spaciousness: ★★★★★
Security: ★★★★
Insect Control: ★★★★
Site Privacy: ★★★★★
Quiet: ★★★★
Cleanliness: ★★★★
Facilities: ★★★

Located in a residential area, this property is a quiet, campground, with a large forested area at the back. Sites are extremely large (85 by 50 feet), with a mixture of pull-throughs and back-ins. Sites 1–14 are divided up into three rows, with 1–5 off to the west of the others. Site 11 is a particularly nice pull-through located next to the pavilion. Sites 15–24 are back-ins along the eastern edge of the property. These sites back up to a strip of trees, beyond which lies the highway. (This proximity to the road and the requirement that drivers back in make these sites a little less desirable.) Tenting is possible in a huge open field to the west, beyond which lie acres of forest. (The owner tells of a bear that has been seen in these woods, so hiding food and toiletries in your vehicle couldn't hurt.) Two other sites are located in front of the office, right off the highway, but you'd have to be crazy to camp there: they are literally a dozen steps from the road. The laundry facility is exceptionally clean and cozy, as are the restrooms. The showers, while clean, are beginning to show their age and could use an overhaul. This is a cute campground with fruit trees, pines, and country kitsch decorating the grounds. RVers and tenters alike will be comfortable staying here.

BASICS

Operated By: Vilene Borgman & Donna Adkins. Open: Mar.–Nov. Site Assignment: Flexible, depending on availability; verbal reservations OK. Registration: At office. (Late arrivals pay in morning). Fee: RV full, $17; tent, $10; check, no credit cards. Parking: At site.

FACILITIES

Number of RV-only Sites: 35. Number of Tent-only Sites: Undesignated sites. Hookups: Electric (20, 30, 50 amps), water, sewer. Each Site: Picnic table, grill. Dump Station: No (sewer hookup at all sites). Laundry: Yes. Pay Phone: Yes. Restrooms and Showers: Yes. Fuel: No. Propane: No. Internal Roads: Gravel. RV Service: No. Market: 7.5 mi. south. Restaurant: 0.5 mi. north. General Store: Yes. Vending: No. Swimming: No. Playground: No. Other: Pavilion, dog run, rec room. Activities: Boating, swimming, fishing, darts, horseshoes. Nearby Attractions: Branson, Greers Ferry Lake. Additional Information: Clinton Chamber of Commerce, (501) 745-6500.

RESTRICTIONS

Pets: On leash, cleaned up after. Fires: Grill only. Alcoholic Beverages: At sites. Vehicle Maximum Length: No limit.

TO GET THERE

From the junction of Hwy. 16 and Hwy. 65, turn north onto Hwy. 65 (toward Marshall), and go 7.3 mi. Turn left into the campground at the sign.

CROSSETT   MAP, D-2
Crossett Harbor RV Park

5997 Hwy. 82 W, 71635. T: (870) 364-6136.

🚐 ★★★★   ⛺ ★★★★

Beauty: ★★★★
Spaciousness: ★★★★
Security: ★★★★
Insect Control: ★★★
Site Privacy: ★★★★
Quiet: ★★★★
Cleanliness: ★★
Facilities: ★★★

This campground is divided into a south loop and an east loop. The south loop is further divided into an inner and outer loop. The most desirable sites are in general on the outer loop 9, especially even (102–106, 109), and odd (113–117), as they have more space and back up to forest, not other campsites. Site 85 is set back away from the other sites, and therefore has more privacy. Site 67 (and 69, to a lesser extent) is adjacent to a pond. Sites 86–91 are doubles. Some sites (especially 86, 87, 95, 97, and 98) seem prone to flooding after a rain. Sites on the outside of the east loop back to seemingly endless forest, and the loop feels more "lost" (in a good way) because of this. Sites 1–3 are smack dab on the intersection of two roads, and certainly must receive more passing traffic due to their location. Sites 31, 33, 35, 48, and 50 seem prone to flooding. The restrooms in both areas look well used, and the floors are in a desperate need of a paint job. Despite the bizarre junk found in a few sites, the east loop seems the nicer of the two areas, and campers will certainly enjoy a stay here.

BASICS

Operated By: City of Crossett. Open: All year. Site Assignment: First come, first served; no reservations. Registration: At manager's trailer. Fee: $12; seniors, $9; no credit cards. Parking: At site.

FACILITIES

Number of RV-only Sites: 119. Hookups: Electric (30, 50 amps), water. Each Site: Picnic table, grill, fire ring, 50-ft. camping pad, 18x12 tent pad, lantern pole. Dump Station: Yes. Laundry: No. Pay Phone: Yes. Restrooms and Showers: Yes. Fuel: No. Propane: No. Internal Roads: Paved. RV Service: No. Market: 9 mi. east. Restaurant: 8.5 mi. east. General Store: Yes. Vending: Soft drinks. Swimming: No. Playground: Yes. Other: Boat ramp, picnic shelter. Activities: Hiking, boating, fishing. Nearby Attractions: Felsenthal Wildlife Refuge. Additional Information: Crossett Area Chamber of Commerce, (870) 364-6591, (870) 364-8648.

RESTRICTIONS

Pets: On leash, cleaned up after. Fires: In grills; subject to bans. Alcoholic Beverages: Not allowed. Vehicle Maximum Length: No limit.

TO GET THERE

From the junction of Hwy. 133 and Hwy. 82 in town, turn west onto Hwy. 82 and go 8.1 mi. Turn left at the sign into the entrance.

DIERKS   MAP, C-1
Jefferson Ridge

reserve america

952 Lake Rd P.O. Box 8, 71833. T: (870) 286-3214; www.reserveamerica.com.

🚐 ★★★★   ⛺ ★★★★

Beauty: ★★★
Spaciousness: ★★★
Security: ★★★★★
Insect Control: ★★★
Site Privacy: ★★★
Quiet: ★★★★★
Cleanliness: ★★★★
Facilities: ★★★★

Jefferson Ridge Campground is located on Dierks Lake in southwest Arkansas. Rugged ridges bordering the lake allow for a scenic view, while year-round camping, fishing, hunting, and water recreation provide visitors with hours of enjoyment. The purpose of Dierks Lake is flood control on the Saline River, recreation, water supply, and fish and wildlife conservation. As a part of the Little River Basin System the lake offers a high degree of flood protection to many acres of land both in the Little River Basin and the flood plain along the Red River. Recreation on the lake is very popular. The 1,360-acre lake provides and enjoyable experience for the boating enthusiast. Dierks Lake is known for its wonderful bass and crappie fishing. It is also a great place for swimming and skiing. Fishing provides many hours of enjoyment for the visitors at Dierks Lake. The species most actively sought are: smallmouth bass, largemouth bass, spotted bass, crappie, channel catfish, flathead catfish, and the various species of sunfish. Most of the species found in the lake are also found in the downstream area. Picnicking areas are available at many of the sites on Dierks Lake. There are four reservable picnic areas, which are great for family reunions or holidays. The picnic shelters are lighted and equipped with barbecue grills and electricity. These shelters are located at Jefferson Ridge, Horseshoe Bend, and Dierks Overlook. Jefferson Ridge Campground offers 84 sites with electric and water hookups. This extremely popular park has numerous sites located on the water's edge. Additional amenities include hot showers, a dump station, a playground, a swimming beach, and a picnic shelter.

BASICS

Operated By: U.S. Army Corps of Engineers. **Open:** Mar. 1–Oct. 31. **Site Assignment:** Reservations must be made at least 3 days in advance. **Registration:** At office. **Parking:** At site.

FACILITIES

Number of RV-only Sites: 130. **Hookups:** Yes. **Dump Station:** Yes. **Laundry:** No. **Pay Phone:** No. **Restrooms and Showers:** Yes. **Fuel:** No. **Propane:** No. **Internal Roads:** Paved. **RV Service:** No. **Market:** No. **Restaurant:** No. **General Store:** No. **Vending:** No. **Swimming:** Yes. **Playground:** Yes. **Activities:** Fishing, hunting, water recreation.

RESTRICTIONS

Pets: Pets must be restrained or on a leash at all times while in developed recreation areas. **Fires:** In fire rings, stoves, grills, or fireplaces provided for that purpose. **Alcoholic Beverages:** Not allowed. **Vehicle Maximum Length:** Call ahead.

TO GET THERE

From Dierks, AR, travel 5 mi. west on US 70, then 5 mi. north on Green Chapel Rd. Follow signs into campground.

EDGEMONT   MAP, B-2
Blue Clouds RV and Cabin Resort

10645 Edgemont Rd., 72044. T: (501) 723-4999; www.greersferry.com/members/blueclouds/index.htm.

🚐 ★★★★   ▲ ★★★★

Beauty: ★★★★★   Site Privacy: ★★★★
Spaciousness: ★★★★   Quiet: ★★★★
Security: ★★★★   Cleanliness: ★★★★
Insect Control: ★★★★   Facilities: ★★★

This campground is built at the bottom of a hill, upon which are the office and the cafe. As a result there is a very nice forested view from many of the sites, which are all naturally landscaped. (While this has some appeal, the dirt road may be tricky for some rigs. Sites 1 and 9 are 90-foot pull-throughs, and 14 is a 120-foot pull-through, making it the longest site in the campground. Sites 2–6 are 40-foot back-ins, and 17–25 are 60-foot back-ins. Sites 40–48 back to woods on the south side, making them very attractive sites. All of the sites in this campground, however, are forested and therefore well shaded. This is a very nice, natural campground for those who enjoy a woodsy feel without being 25 miles from the nearest conveniences. RVers and tenters alike will enjoy a stay here, although the forested setting and dirt road may make for challenging driving for long rigs—especially those with tows.

BASICS

Operated By: Janice. **Open:** All year. **Site Assignment:** Upon registration; credit card required or telephone number for reservation; 24-hour cancellation policy. **Registration:** At office, 9 a.m.–6 p.m. (Late arrivals select site & pay in the morning.) **Fee:** RV, $16–$24; V, MC, D, check. **Parking:** At site.

FACILITIES

Number of Multipurpose Sites: 50. **Hookups:** Electric (30, 50 amps), water, sewer. **Dump Station:** No. **Laundry:** Yes. **Pay Phone:** Courtesy phone w/ Internet access. **Restrooms and Showers:** Yes. **Fuel:** 2 mi. **Propane:** Yes. **Internal Roads:** Gravel. **RV Service:** 22 mi. at Heber Springs. **Market:** 3 mi. east. **Restaurant:** 3 mi. east. **General Store:** No. **Vending:** Yes. **Swimming:** Lake. **Playground:** Yes. **Other:** Cabins. **Activities:** Fishing, boating, swimming, golfing, folk music. **Nearby Attractions:** Greers Ferry Lake, Ozark Mt. Folk Museum. **Additional Information:** Greers Ferry Chamber of Commerce, (501) 362-2444.

RESTRICTIONS

Pets: On leash, cleaned up after. **Fires:** Grill only. **Alcoholic Beverages:** At sites. **Vehicle Maximum Length:** No limit.

TO GET THERE

From the westernmost town name sign on Hwy. 16, go west on Hwy. 16 for 0.4 mi. Turn left at the sign into the entrance.

EUREKA SPRINGS   MAP, B-1
Eureka Springs KOA

15020 Hwy. 187 South, 72632. T: (479) 253-8036; www.eureka-net.com/koa.

🚐 ★★★★   ▲ ★★★★★

Beauty: ★★★★★   Site Privacy: ★★★
Spaciousness: ★★★   Quiet: ★★★
Security: ★★★★   Cleanliness: ★★★★★
Insect Control: ★★★★   Facilities: ★★★★★

There are loads of neat ornaments, plants, logs, rocks, and garden spots in this campground, giving it a somewhat artsy wilderness feel. All of the sites in this campground are forested, undeveloped gravel sites. Sites 1–19 ranging from 30 to 45-feet long on either side of an internal road. Of these, 1–12 back to a hedge, beyond which lies the highway. Sites 11 and 12 are fenced off, giving them added privacy. Site 32 is an exceptionally large (120 feet) pull-through, and 58–69 are only slightly shorter at 115 feet. Sites 41–44 are 60-foot back-ins by the Garden of Meditation, but are slightly sloped. Better sites by the garden are 49–51, which are also 60-foot back-ins, but more level. Tents sites are to the north, away from the RV sites. An exceptional feature of these tent pads is that they contain sawdust instead of crushed gravel, giving tenters a much more comfy bed to sleep on. These dirt sites are located under a canopy of trees, ensuring that all sites are shaded. Many of these sites are along the highway, which is normally quite quiet, but does, of course, carry the occasional vehicle. Sites M and N are the most remote, and R and S are also quite secluded. The restrooms and showers are all very clean and spacious. Showers are all tile, which makes them seem as comfy as home. One really neat detail is the wooden number plates at each site, which each have a unique hand-carved cartoon. The Garden of Meditation, also a unique detail, comprises stone, twisted wood, plants, and sculptures, and is an extremely peaceful place to rest for a moment.

BASICS

Operated By: Ken Shonka. **Open:** Apr. 1–Oct. 31. **Site Assignment:** Upon registration; credit card required for reservation; 48-hour cancellation policy, 72-hour cancellation policy for cabins only. **Registration:** At office. (Late arrivals select site & pay in the morning.) **Fee:** RV, $25–$35; tent, $18–$22. **Parking:** At site.

FACILITIES

Number of RV-only Sites: 65. **Number of Tent-only Sites:** 24. **Hookups:** Electric (30, 50 amps), water, sewer. **Each Site:** Picnic table, fire pit. **Dump Station:** Yes. **Laundry:** Yes. **Pay Phone:** Yes. **Restrooms and Showers:** Yes. **Fuel:** No. **Propane:** Yes. **Internal Roads:** Paved. **RV Service:** No. **Market:** 5 mi. to Eureka Springs. **Restaurant:** 0.75 mi. toward Eureka. **General Store:** Yes. **Vending:** Yes. **Swimming:** Pool. **Playground:** Yes. **Other:** Mini-golf, game room, data port, picnic pavilion, Garden of Meditation. **Activities:** Fishing, boating, swimming. **Nearby Attractions:** White River, Beaver Lake, passion play, hoedowns, downtown (on National Registry of Historic Places), Onyx Cave Park. **Additional Information:** Eureka Springs Chamber of Commerce, (800) 638-7352 or (501) 253-8737.

RESTRICTIONS

Pets: On leash, cleaned up after. **Fires:** Grill only. **Alcoholic Beverages:** At sites. **Vehicle Maximum Length:** No limit. **Other:** Consult handout when registering.

TO GET THERE

From the junction of Hwy. 62 and Hwy. 187, turn south onto Hwy. 187 and go 1.1 mi. Turn left at the signed entrance.

HARDY   MAP, B-2
Hardy Camper Park

South Springs St., 72542. T: (870) 856-2356.

🚐 ★★★★   ▲ ★★★

Beauty: ★★★   Site Privacy: ★★★★★
Spaciousness: ★★★★★   Quiet: ★★★★
Security: ★★★★★   Cleanliness: ★★★
Insect Control: ★★★★   Facilities: ★★

While the north and east sides of this campground face an industrial complex, the south has gorgeous rock cliffs over the river, and the west faces lush vegetation. Just 2 blocks from Main Street, this campground is convenient for visiting Old Hardy Town on foot, and has a comfortable, city parklike feel. RV sites are mostly open-ended, and can take a vehicle of any size. River sites (42-foot back-ins) have truly wonderful views, and are worth the slightly higher price. While you can't go wrong with any of these sites, 20–23 are definitely the best of the bunch: they are well shaded and farthest from the entrance. Sites 10 and 11 are also well shaded, and close to the bath house, while shaded sites 1–5 are closest to the entrance/exit. For a cheaper site (not on the river) or a pull-through, 58–63 are better than average. They are well shaded, full-length (120-feet) pull-throughs. (The other pull-throughs have two sites in an area the same size.) The tenting area is a nice, unmarked grassy area behind the office. There is some shade, but no protection in the event of rain. A surprise arrives with every train—loud whistles and rumblings. While infrequent, this may be enough to put off some campers, which is a shame given the camp's enjoyable environment.

BASICS

Operated By: City of Hardy. **Open:** All year. **Site Assignment:** Flexible, depending on availability; reservations require deposit if made more than 3 weeks in advance; cancellation requires 24-hour notice. **Registration:** At office. (Late arrivals either use drop box or pay in the morning.) **Fee:** Riverside, $17.50; other, $15.30; tent, $4 per person. **Parking:** At site.

FACILITIES

Number of RV-only Sites: 76. **Number of Tent-only Sites:** Undesignated sites. **Hookups:** Electric (15, 30, 50 amps), water. **Each Site:** Picnic table. **Dump Station:** Yes. **Laundry:** Yes. **Pay Phone:** Yes. **Restrooms and Showers:** Yes. Renovated winter 2003. **Fuel:** No. **Propane:** No. **Internal Roads:** Gravel/dirt. **RV Service:** No. **Market:** 1 block (on Main). **Restaurant:** 1 block (on Main). **General Store:** No. **Vending:** Yes. **Swimming:** River. **Playground:** Under construction at press time. **Other:** Boat dock, half-mile walking trail, beach, spring river, biking. **Activities:** Swimming, canoeing, fishing. **Nearby Attractions:** Veterans Military Museum, Old Hardy Town, antique stores, museums. **Additional Information:** Spring River Area Chamber of Commerce, (870) 856-3210.

RESTRICTIONS

Pets: Dangerous pets on leash. **Fires:** In grills; subject to bans; campfires allowed. **Alcoholic Beverages:** Dry county regulations. **Vehicle Maximum Length:** No limit.

TO GET THERE

From the junction of Hwy. 62/412 and Hwy. 63, go 0.25 mi. on Hwy. 62/412 (Main St.) to Spring St. Turn south onto Spring St. (at a building with a large mural). Go 0.2 mi. (just south of the train depot) and turn right at the sign into the campground.

HARRISON MAP, B-1
Parkers RV Park

3629 Hwy. 65 North, 72601. T: (888) 590-2267 or (870) 743-2267; www.parkersrvinc.com.

🚐 ★★★★	🏕 ★★★
Beauty: ★★★★	Site Privacy: ★★★★
Spaciousness: ★★★★★	Quiet: ★★★
Security: ★★★★	Cleanliness: ★★★★★
Insect Control: ★★★★	Facilities: ★★★

This campground has very cute landscaping (including shrubs and a bridge), and very tidy gravel and grass sites. sites 1–3 are 75 by 44–foot pull-throughs on the north side of the park, near the highway. These are some of the largest sites. (Site 4, for example, is only 52 feet long.) The only sites that are larger are 10 (a 90-foot pull-through) and 24, which can be a 105-foot pull-through if site 23 is unoccupied. A strip in the middle of the park contains sites

12–17, which are 66 by 44–foot back-ins. On the north side of the "island" in the middle, sites 18–22 are slightly smaller (60-feet) back-ins. For more shade, try sites 25–39, which back to woods on the south side of the campground. There is a covered pavilion between sites 29 and 30, which increases traffic near these two sites. Tenting is restricted to small parties of responsible adults. Tenting groups are discouraged. The restroom facility is one of the nicest you'll find. It is modern, very clean, and extremely comfortable. This park is a very nice stop for RVers, but tenters with children or groups of more than two or three should look elsewhere.

BASICS

Operated By: Gregg Parker. **Open:** All year. **Site Assignment:** Upon registration; credit card required for reservation; 24-hour cancellation policy. **Registration:** At office. (Late arrivals park. Someone will be out to see you.) **Fee:** $17.95–$20.95: V, MC, AE, D, check. **Parking:** At site.

FACILITIES

Number of RV-only Sites: 42. **Hookups:** Electric (50 amps), water, sewer, cable TV, high-speed wireless internet service access. **Each Site:** Picnic table. **Dump Station:** Yes. **Laundry:** Yes. **Pay Phone:** Yes. **Restrooms and Showers:** Yes. **Fuel:** No. **Propane:** Yes. **Internal Roads:** Gravel. **RV Service:** Yes, full-service RV repair shop. **Market:** 1 mi. south. **Restaurant:** 1 mi. south. **General Store:** Yes, limited. **Vending:** Yes. **Swimming:** No. **Playground:** No. **Other:** RV supplies, rec room, pool table, foosball, data port, pavilion. **Activities:** Fishing, boating, swimming. **Nearby Attractions:** Buffalo River National Park, Hot Springs National Park. **Additional Information:** Harrison Chamber of Commerce, (870) 741-2659.

RESTRICTIONS

Pets: On leash, cleaned up after. **Fires:** Grill only. **Alcoholic Beverages:** At sites. **Vehicle Maximum Length:** No limit. **Other:** No fireworks.

TO GET THERE

From the junction of Hwy. 65 and Hwy. 62/412, turn right (south) onto Hwy. 65 and go 1.3 mi. Turn right at the sign into the entrance.

HEBER SPRINGS MAP, B-2
Choctaw

700 Heber Springs Rd. North, 72543-9022. T: (501) 362-2416; www.reserveamerica.com.

🚐 ★★★★	🏕 ★★★★
Beauty: ★★★	Site Privacy: ★★
Spaciousness: ★★	Quiet: ★★★★
Security: ★★★★	Cleanliness: ★★★★
Insect Control: ★★★	Facilities: ★★

Choctaw Campground is located on Greers Ferry Lake in north central Arkansas. The environment provides the ideal location for camping, fishing, boating, hiking, and a day of family excitement. The Choctaw Campground has 146 sites, 78 electric/68

nonelectric. Additional amenities include hot showers, dump station, reservable picnic shelter, boat launch, playground, swimming area, public marina, and public telephones. Greers Ferry Lake is the artificial reservoir formed by Greers Ferry Dam, a United States Army Corps of Engineers dam in North Central Arkansas. It is located about 60 miles north of Little Rock. Construction of the dam began in March 1959 and was completed in December 1962. The lake serves the Heber Springs area flood control, and is a site for recreation and power generation. When construction began on the dam in 1956, hundreds of workers showed up, looking for a job. Workers then rented empty houses next to the construction site, and workers were even making their own houses next to the soon-to-be lake. Once all the workers arrived, people and business owners saw an opportunity to this construction and built motels, shops, and stores next to the construction site, so workers would have a place to shop, and relax. Farmers also felt the benefit of the construction. The work on the lake created demand for livestock and agriculture. Once the lake was completed, it was dedicated on October 3, 1963, by John F. Kennedy. The trip was his last major public appearance before his fateful trip to Dallas on November 22, 1963, where he was assassinated. In his remarks in Heber Springs, Kennedy explained that the Greers Ferry project and others like it were investments in Arkansas and the nation's future. He was right—after the lake filled tourism boomed, businesses opened back up, and Greers Ferry Lake became one of Arkansas's leading destinations. Today, many resort communities dot the shores of Greers Ferry Lake. The reservoir consists of two lakes connected by a water-filled gorge called the Narrows. The area of the two lakes and the Narrows totals about 40,500 acres with a combined shoreline of just over 340 miles. Carl Garner, former Greers Ferry Lake Resident Engineer since 1959, started the Carl Garner Federal Lands Cleanup Day in 1985.

BASICS

Operated By: U.S. Army Corps of Engineers. **Open:** Apr. 1–Nov. 1. **Site Assignment:** Reservations must be made at least 2 days in advance. **Registration:** At office. **Fee:** Single, $10–$18; group, $65. **Parking:** At site.

FACILITIES

Number of Multipurpose Sites: 414. **Hookups:** Yes. **Dump Station:** Yes. **Laundry:** No. **Pay Phone:** Yes. **Restrooms and Showers:** Yes. **Fuel:** No. **Propane:** No. **Internal Roads:** Paved. **RV Service:** No. **Market:** No. **Restaurant:** No. **General Store:** No. **Vending:** No. **Swimming:** Yes. **Playground:** Yes. **Activities:** Fishing, boating, hiking.

RESTRICTIONS

Pets: Pets must be restrained or on a leash at all times while in developed recreation areas. **Fires:** In fire rings, stoves, grills, or fireplaces provided for that purpose. **Alcoholic Beverages:** Not allowed. **Vehicle Maximum Length:** Call ahead.

TO GET THERE

From Clinton, AR, take US 65 5 mi. south to AR 330 then 3.5 mi. east. Follow signs into campground.

HEBER SPRINGS   MAP, B-2
Devils Fork

reserve america

700 Heber Springs Rd. North, 72543-9022.
T: (501) 362-2416; www.reserveamerica.com.

🚐 ★★★★   ⛺ ★★★★

Beauty: ★★★	Site Privacy: ★★★
Spaciousness: ★★★	Quiet: ★★★★★
Security: ★★★★★	Cleanliness: ★★★★
Insect Control: ★★★	Facilities: ★★★★

Devils Fork Campground is located on Greers Ferry Lake in north central Arkansas. The environment provides the ideal location for camping, fishing, boating, hiking, and a day of family excitement. Devils Fork Campground has 55 electric sites. Additional amenities include hot showers, dump station, reservable picnic shelter, boat launch, playground, swimming area, and public telephones. Greers Ferry Lake is the artificial reservoir formed by Greers Ferry Dam, a United States Army Corps of Engineers dam in North Central Arkansas. It is located about 60 miles north of Little Rock. Construction of the dam began in March 1959 and was completed in December 1962. The lake serves the Heber Springs area flood control, and is a site for recreation and power generation. When construction began on the dam in 1956, hundreds of workers showed up, looking for a job. Workers then rented empty houses next to the construction site, and workers were even making their own houses next to the soon-to-be lake. Once all the workers arrived, people and business owners saw an opportunity to this construction and built motels, shops, and stores next to the construction site so workers would have a place to shop and relax. Farmers also felt the benefit of the construction. The work on the lake created demand for livestock and agriculture. Once the lake was completed, it was dedicated on October 3, 1963, by John F. Kennedy. The trip was his last major public appearance before his fateful trip to Dallas on November 22, 1963, where he was assassinated. In his remarks in Heber Springs, Kennedy explained that the Greers Ferry project and others like it were investments in Arkansas and the nation's future. He was right—after the lake filled tourism boomed, businesses opened back up, and Greers Ferry Lake became one of Arkansas's leading destinations. Today, many resort communities dot the shores of Greers Ferry Lake. The reservoir consists of two lakes connected by a water-filled gorge called the Narrows. The area of the two lakes and the Narrows totals about 40,500 acres with a combined shoreline of just over 340 miles. Carl Garner, former Greers Ferry Lake Resident Engineer since 1959, started the Carl Garner Federal Lands Cleanup Day in 1985.

BASICS

Operated By: U.S. Army Corps of Engineers. **Open:** Apr. 1–Nov. 1. **Site Assignment:** Reservations must be made at least 4 days in advance. **Registration:** At office. **Fee:** Single, $10–$15. **Parking:** At site.

FACILITIES

Number of Multipurpose Sites: 132. **Hookups:** Yes. **Dump Station:** Yes. **Laundry:** No. **Pay Phone:** Yes. **Restrooms and Showers:** Yes. **Fuel:** No. **Propane:** No. **Internal Roads:** Paved. **RV Service:** No. **Market:** No. **Restaurant:** No. **General Store:** No. **Vending:** No. **Swimming:** Yes. **Playground:** Yes. **Activities:** Fishing, boating, hiking.

RESTRICTIONS

Pets: Pets must be restrained or on a leash at all times while in developed recreation areas. **Fires:** In fire rings, stoves, grills, or fireplaces provided for that purpose. **Alcoholic Beverages:** Not allowed. **Vehicle Maximum Length:** Call ahead.

TO GET THERE

From Greers Ferry, AR, take SR 16.25 mi. north and follow signs into the campground.

HEBER SPRINGS   MAP, B-2
Narrows

reserve america

700 Heber Springs Rd. North , 72543-9022.
T: (501) 362-2416; www.reserveamerica.com.

🚐 ★★★   ⛺ ★★★★

Beauty: ★★★	Site Privacy: ★★★
Spaciousness: ★★★	Quiet: ★★★★★
Security: ★★★★★	Cleanliness: ★★★★
Insect Control: ★★★	Facilities: ★★★★

Narrows Campground is located on Greers Ferry Lake in north central Arkansas. The environment provides the ideal location for camping, fishing, boating, hiking, and a day of family excitement. The Narrows Campground offers 60 sites, all with electric hookups. Additional amenities include hot showers, a dump station, picnic shelters, public phones, and a boat ramp. Greers Ferry Lake is the artificial reservoir formed by Greers Ferry Dam, a United States Army Corps of Engineers dam in North Central Arkansas. It is located about 60 miles north of Little Rock. Construction of the dam began in March 1959 and was completed in December 1962. The lake serves the Heber Springs area flood control, and is a site for recreation and power generation. When construction began on the dam in 1956, hundreds of workers showed up, looking for a job. Workers then rented empty houses next to the construction site, and workers were even making their own houses next to the soon-to-be lake. Once all the workers arrived, people and business owners saw an opportunity to this construction and built motels, shops, and stores next to the construction site so workers would have a place to shop and relax. Farmers also felt the benefit of the construction. The work on the lake created demand for livestock and agriculture. Once the lake was completed, it was dedicated on October 3, 1963, by John F. Kennedy. The trip was his last major public appearance before his fateful trip to Dallas on November 22, 1963, where he was assassinated. In his remarks in Heber Springs, Kennedy explained that the Greers Ferry project and others like it were investments in Arkansas and the nation's future. He was right—after the lake filled tourism boomed, businesses opened back up, and Greers Ferry Lake became one of Arkansas's leading destinations. Today, many resort communities dot the shores of Greers Ferry Lake. The reservoir consists of two lakes connected by a water-filled gorge called the Narrows. The area of the two lakes and the Narrows totals about 40,500 acres with a combined shoreline of just over 340 miles. Carl Garner, former Greers Ferry Lake Resident Engineer since 1959, started the Carl Garner Federal Lands Cleanup Day in 1985.

BASICS

Operated By: U.S. Army Corps of Engineers. **Open:** All year. **Site Assignment:** Reservations must be made at least 4 days in advance. **Registration:** At office. **Fee:** Single, $15–18. **Parking:** At site.

FACILITIES

Number of Multipurpose Sites: 212. **Hookups:** Yes. **Dump Station:** Yes. **Laundry:** No. **Pay Phone:** Yes. **Restrooms and Showers:** Yes. **Fuel:** No. **Propane:** No. **Internal Roads:** Paved. **RV Service:** No. **Market:** No. **Restaurant:** No. **General Store:** No. **Vending:** No. **Swimming:** No. **Playground:** No. **Activities:** Fishing, boating, hiking.

RESTRICTIONS

Pets: Pets must be restrained or on a leash at all times while in developed recreation areas. **Fires:** In fire rings, stoves, grills, or fireplaces provided for that purpose. **Alcoholic Beverages:** Not allowed. **Vehicle Maximum Length:** Call ahead.

TO GET THERE

From Greers Ferry, AR, take SR 16 southwest for 2.5 mi. Follow signs into the campground.

HEBER SPRINGS   MAP, B-2
Sugar Loaf

reserve america

700 Heber Springs Rd. N, 72543-9022.
T: (501) 362-2416; www.reserveamerica.com.

🚐 ★★★★   ⛺ ★★★★

Beauty: ★★★★★	Site Privacy: ★★★
Spaciousness: ★★★	Quiet: ★★★★
Security: ★★★★	Cleanliness: ★★★★
Insect Control: ★★★	Facilities: ★

Sugar Loaf Campground is located on Greers Ferry Lake in north central Arkansas. The environment provides the ideal location for camping, fishing, boating, hiking, and a day of family excitement. Sugar Loaf Mountain Island National Nature Trail is located at the lake adjacent to this park. Access is by boat, and the 1.5-mile hike takes you 540 feet above the lake to 1,001 feet above sea level. Panoramic views of the surrounding lake and countryside make the moderately difficult two-hour hike worthwhile. The Sugar Loaf Campground offers 95 sites, 56 with electric hookups, and 39 without electricity. Additional amenities include hot showers, a dump station, a picnic shelter, public phones, and a boat ramp. Greers Ferry Lake is the artificial reservoir formed by Greers Ferry Dam, a U.S. Army Corps of Engineers dam in North Central Arkansas. It is located about 60 miles north of Little Rock. Construction of the dam began in March 1959 and was completed in December 1962. The lake serves the Heber Springs area flood control, and is a site for recreation and power generation. When construction began on the dam in 1956, hundreds of workers showed up, looking for a job. Workers then rented empty houses next to the construction site, and workers were even making their own houses next to the soon-to-be lake. Once all the workers arrived, people and business owners saw an opportunity to this construction and built motels, shops, and stores next to the construction site so workers would have a place to shop and relax. Farmers also felt the benefit of the construction. The work on the lake created demand for livestock and agriculture. Once the lake was completed, it was dedicated on October 3, 1963, by John F. Kennedy. The trip was his last major public appearance before his fateful trip to Dallas on November 22, 1963, where he was assassinated. In his remarks in Heber Springs, Kennedy explained that the Greers Ferry project and others like it were investments in Arkansas and the nation's future. He was right—after the lake filled tourism boomed, businesses opened back up, and Greers Ferry Lake became one of Arkansas's leading destinations. Today, many resort communities dot the shores of Greers Ferry Lake. The reservoir consists of two lakes connected by a water-filled gorge called the Narrows. The area of the two lakes and the Narrows totals about 40,500 acres with a combined shoreline of just over 340 miles. Carl Garner, former Greers Ferry Lake Resident Engineer since 1959, started the Carl Garner Federal Lands Cleanup Day in 1985.

BASICS

Operated By: U.S. Army Corps of Engineers. **Open:** Apr. 1–Nov. 1. **Site Assignment:** Reservations must be made at least 4 days in advance. **Registration:** At office. **Fee:** Single, $12–$17. **Parking:** At site.

FACILITIES

Number of Multipurpose Sites: 208. **Hookups:** Yes. **Dump Station:** Yes. **Laundry:** No. **Pay Phone:** Yes. **Restrooms and Showers:** Yes. **Fuel:** No. **Propane:** No. **Internal Roads:** Paved. **RV Service:** No. **Market:** No. **Restaurant:** No. **General Store:** No. **Vending:** No. **Swimming:** Yes. **Playground:** Yes. **Activities:** Fishing, boating, hiking.

RESTRICTIONS

Pets: Pets must be restrained or on a leash at all times while in developed recreation areas. **Fires:** In fire rings, stoves, grills, or fireplaces provided for that purpose. **Alcoholic Beverages:** Not allowed. **Vehicle Maximum Length:** Call ahead.

TO GET THERE

From Alma, NE: on Hwy. 183 turn east on South St. and travel 2.5 mi. Park entrance on south side of the road.

HOPE   MAP, C-1
Fair Park RV Park

Park Dr., Off Hwy. 174, 71802-0596.
T: (870) 777-7500.

🚐 ★★★   ⛺ ★★★

Beauty: ★★★	Site Privacy: ★★★★
Spaciousness: ★★★★	Quiet: ★★★★
Security: ★★★★★	Cleanliness: ★★★
Insect Control: ★★★	Facilities: ★★★★★

This campground is in a large city park, and there are hundreds of RV sites available, divided up into sections. Section A is open and grassy, to the north of the ball field and the coliseum, with open-ended pull-through sites. There are a few trees, but most sites are not shaded. A2 is between the barns and the coliseum, and consists of open, grassy sites. Section B is to the south of A, and is likewise an open grassy field with no real shade. C is similar, but consists of open-ended back-ins around the baseball field. Section D backs to the woods on the perimeter of the park. Sites to the southeast are better shaded, and are some of the better sites in the park for this reason. Sections E and F are on either side of the office, closest to the restrooms. This is where tenters are encouraged to stay. There is a decent grass covering, and a tree at the far end of the fence to the north of the office complex. The most outstanding area of the park, however, is Section G. This area is shaded, has full hookups, and backs to the woods. sites are open-ended pull-throughs, which means that any rig could fit in pretty much any site. RVers are advised to check out Section G, and tenters can pitch tents in a number of pleasant spots at no cost.

BASICS

Operated By: Paul G Henley. **Open:** All year. **Site Assignment:** First come, first served; no reservations. **Registration:** At office. (Late arrivals use drop box.) **Fee:** RV, $10; tent, $5; check, no credit cards. **Parking:** At site.

FACILITIES

Number of RV-only Sites: 400. **Number of Tent-only Sites:** Undesignated sites. **Hookups:** Electric (20 amps), water, sewer. **Dump Station:** Yes. **Laundry:** Yes. **Pay Phone:** Yes. **Restrooms and Showers:** Yes. **Fuel:** No. **Propane:** No (6 blocks). **Internal Roads:** Paved. **RV Service:** No. **Market:** 6 blocks west. **Restaurant:** Less than 1 mi. west. **General Store:** No. **Vending:** Yes. **Swimming:** Pool. **Playground:** Yes. **Other:** Arena, coliseum, wrestling matches, rodeo. All are pull-through sites. **Activities:** Basketball, swimming, baseball/softball, tennis. **Nearby Attractions:** Watermelon festival. **Additional Information:** Hope Hempstead County Chamber of Commerce, (800) 777-3640.

RESTRICTIONS

Pets: On leash, cleaned up after. **Fires:** Grill only. **Alcoholic Beverages:** Not allowed. **Vehicle Maximum Length:** No limit.

TO GET THERE

From I-30, take Exit 30 and go 1.35 mi. south on Hwy. 4. Turn right onto Hwy. 67 and go 0.25 mi. west. Turn left onto Hwy. 174 and go 0.3 mi. south. Turn right onto Park Dr. and go 0.5 mi. through the park to the T intersection. Turn right and go 0.5 block to the office (green building) on the left.

HOT SPRINGS   MAP, C-2
Young's Lakeshore RV Resort

1601 Lakeshore Dr., 71913. T: (501) 767-7946 or (800) 470-7875; www.hsnp.com/youngsrv.

🚐 ★★★★   ⛺ n/a

Beauty: ★★★★	Site Privacy: ★★★
Spaciousness: ★★★	Quiet: ★★★
Security: ★★★★★	Cleanliness: ★★★★
Insect Control: ★★★★	Facilities: ★★★

A campground whose motto is "In the city, on the lake," this RV park has nearly lakeside sites toward the back (37 is the closest). Most back-ins around the perimeter are open-ended, with no maximum vehicle size. These sites back to a row of trees that provide some shade, but sites elsewhere in the park are open to the sun. Sites 1–6 are 42-feet back-ins in a strip on the north side of the park. Of these, 6 is the nicest, as it is closest to the trees and farthest from the entrance. Sites 7–20 are in two rows along the entrance road. These are 60-foot pull-throughs with grassy strips. Site 24 is next to both the propane and the entrance, making it less desirable. The lower numbered sites (1, 12, 13) are closer to the entrance, while the higher numbers (6, 7, 20) are farther away. The laundry is slightly unkempt but clean and well lit. The restrooms are small with an open toilet, so guests may only want to use them one at a time (which is slightly inconvenient). Children must be accompanied and kept under supervision at all times, so families may want to reconsider this as a destination. Other campers who do not wish to camp with children will be happiest here.

BASICS

Operated By: Jimmy & Ev Young. **Open:** All year. **Site Assignment:** Upon registration; verbal reservations OK. **Registration:** At office. (Late arrivals use mailbox next to the door.) **Fee:** $25. **Parking:** At site.

FACILITIES

Number of RV-only Sites: 44. **Hookups:** Electric (30, 50 amps), water, sewer, cable TV. **Each Site:** Picnic table. **Dump Station:** Yes. **Laundry:** Yes. **Pay Phone:** Yes. **Restrooms and Showers:** Yes. **Fuel:** No. **Propane:** Yes. **Internal Roads:** Gravel. **RV Service:** No. **Market:** 1.5 mi. east on Highway 7. **Restaurant:** 1.5 mi. west or east. **General Store:** No. **Vending:** Yes. **Swimming:** No. **Playground:** No. **Other:** Data port, boat ramp, lake beach, rec room, picnic area by lake. **Activities:** Fishing, boating, hot-spring baths, canoeing, hiking, pavilion w/ barbecue pit, kitchen. **Nearby Attractions:** Hot Springs National Park, Josephine Tussaud Wax Museum, Arkansas Alligator Farm & Petting Zoo, Race Track, Golf. **Additional Information:** Hot Springs CVB: (800) 772-2489, (501) 321-2277.

RESTRICTIONS

Pets: On leash, cleaned up after. **Fires:** Not allowed. **Alcoholic Beverages:** At sites. **Vehicle Maximum Length:** No limit. **Other:** Adults preferred (children must be accompanied at all times).

TO GET THERE

From Hwy. 270 (south of town), take Exit 3 and go west onto McLeod St. Go 0.25 mi. straight into the entrance of the park.

JERSEY   MAP, D-2
Moro Bay State Park

6071 Hwy. 600, 71651. T: (870) 463-8555; www.arkansasstateparks.com.

🚐 ★★★★   ⛺ ★★★

Beauty: ★★★★   Site Privacy: ★★★★★
Spaciousness: ★★★★★   Quiet: ★★★★★
Security: ★★★★   Cleanliness: ★★★
Insect Control: ★★★   Facilities: ★★★

Sites 1–9 are built along the edge of a hill, and some of the space is unusable due to the extreme slope. However, there is a large fenced-in area that contains the picnic table and a large concrete slab for camping. Sites are 42-feet-long back-ins, with two pull-throughs (4 and 9), of 42 feet and 75 feet in length, respectively. Site 1 backs to a large open field, and can allow for recreation right off the site. The restroom is across from site 8, and noise from a large fan in the men's room may be bothersome at this site. The restrooms are relatively clean and modern, but upon our visit the shower needed a good cleaning. Site 10 is located at the crossroads of two internal roads, and may receive more traffic because of this fact. The rest of the sites are along this other road, and are all 42-foot back-ins. Of the sites on this strip, 16 and 17 have a more secluded location at the end of the roundabout. The other sites are pretty much indistinguishable. Tenters will enjoy the wooded sites, but may wish for grassy ground cover instead of a more developed site. Campers of any stripe will enjoy this campground—however, especially those with boats.

BASICS

Operated By: Arkansas State Parks. **Open:** All year. **Site Assignment:** First come, first served; reservations require cash, credit card, or postal money order deposit; in case of cancellation (cancel w/in 14 days of reservation), 1-night fee is not refunded. **Registration:** At office, Sun.–Thurs., 8 a.m.–5 p.m.; Fri. & Sat., 8 a.m.–8 p.m. (Late arrivals occupy an available site & register at 8 a.m. the next morning.) **Fee:** $9–$20.50. **Parking:** At site.

FACILITIES

Number of Multipurpose Sites: 20. **Hookups:** Electric (20, 30 amps), water. **Each Site:** Picnic table, grill, fire pit. **Dump Station:** Yes. **Laundry:** No. **Pay Phone:** Yes. **Restrooms and Showers:** Yes / bathhouse. **Fuel:** No, gas station/country store 5 mi. **Propane:** No. **Internal Roads:** Paved. **RV Service:** No. **Market:** 15 mi. to Strong or Hermitage. **Restaurant:** 15 mi. to Strong, Hermitage, or Union. **General Store:** Yes. **Vending:** Yes. **Swimming:** Bay, lake, river. **Playground:** Yes. **Other:** Picnic area, fishing licenses. **Activities:** Boating, fishing, basketball, soccer, volleyball, horseshoes, badminton. **Nearby Attractions:** Ouachita River, South Arkansas Arboretum. **Additional Information:** El Dorado Chamber of Commerce, (870) 863-6113.

RESTRICTIONS

Pets: On leash, cleaned up after. **Fires:** Grill only. **Alcoholic Beverages:** At sites. **Vehicle Maximum Length:** No limit.

TO GET THERE

From the junction of Hwy. 167 and Hwy. 15, go 20 mi. northeast on Hwy. 15. Turn left at the sign and continue to the park entrance.

JONESBORO   MAP, B-3
Craighead Forest Park

P.O. Box 1845, 72403. T: (870) 933-4604 or (870) 933-1645.

🚐 ★★★★   ⛺ ★★★★

Beauty: ★★★★   Site Privacy: ★★★★
Spaciousness: ★★★★   Quiet: ★★★★★
Security: ★★★★★   Cleanliness: ★★★
Insect Control: ★★★   Facilities: ★★★

Situated in the easternmost edge of the park, this small campground has forested sites on either side of a single road. All sites back to the forest. Sites on the northwest side slope down toward the lake, while those on the southeast side back to flat land, making these sites a little longer than the 50-foot paved parking spaces. All campsites are extremely well spaced: there is loads of room between you and your neighbor and plenty of space for extra vehicles. Sites 12–15 are closest to the fishing dock (but there is no swimming access). Sites 14 and 15 are the nicest, as they are adjacent to a grassy field that can be used for recreation and has picnic tables. The restrooms are a little unkempt, but not any more than those who often camp in public forests might come to expect. This is a small and comfortable campground, well away from even the recreation areas within the park, offering a night of tranquility.

BASICS

Operated By: City of Jonesboro. **Open:** All year. **Site Assignment:** First come, first served; no reservations, no refunds. **Registration:** W/ campsite attendant (across from site 8). **Fee:** Water/electric, $15; tent, $7.50; check, no credits cards. **Parking:** At site.

FACILITIES

Number of RV-only Sites: 26. **Hookups:** Electric (30 amps), water. **Each Site:** Picnic table, grill, trash. **Dump Station:** Yes. **Laundry:** No. **Pay Phone:** Yes. **Restrooms and Showers:** Yes. **Fuel:** No. **Propane:** No. **Internal Roads:** Paved. **RV Service:** No. **Market:** 4 mi. to Hwy. 63. **Restaurant:** 4 mi. to Hwy. 63. **General Store:** No. **Vending:** Yes. **Swimming:** Lake. **Playground:** Yes. **Other:** Picnic pavilions, ball fields, basketball court, paddle-boat rentals, ATV trails. **Activities:** Boating, swimming, fishing, hiking. **Nearby Attractions:** Craighead Forest Lake, Arkansas State University Museum. **Additional Information:** Chamber of Commerce, (870) 932-6691.

RESTRICTIONS

Pets: On leash, cleaned up after. **Fires:** Grill only. **Alcoholic Beverages:** Not allowed. **Vehicle Maximum Length:** 50 ft. **Other:** No ATVs in campground, no fireworks.

TO GET THERE

From the junction of Hwy. 63 and Hwy. 1B, turn south onto Hwy. 1B and take the first right onto the service road (Parker Rd.). Follow this road 0.9 mi., then turn left onto Hwy. 141 (Culberhouse St.), and go 1.9 mi. Turn left onto Forest Park Dr. and go 1.25 mi. to the east end of Forest Park Loop, past pavilion 1, to the campground.

LAKE VILLAGE   MAP, D-2
Pecan Grove RV Park

3768 Hwy. 82 and 65 South, 71653. T: (877) RV-4-FUNN or (870) 265-3005; www.pecangrove.net.

🚐 ★★★★   ⛺ ★★★★

Beauty: ★★★★   Site Privacy: ★★★★★
Spaciousness: ★★★★★   Quiet: ★★★
Security: ★★★★★   Cleanliness: ★★★
Insect Control: ★★★★   Facilities: ★★★★

An old pecan orchard, this campground has a small-farm feel to it. There is very cute landscaping around the grounds (flowers around trees and light poles), and remnants of the farm it once was (barn, farmhouse). Towering pecan trees grow at almost every site. There is also, however, an air of oldness that could be swept away: cobwebs in the corners, dirt from many hands opening doors, etc. The laundry is small, and while the restrooms are clean, the building itself looks old. Furthermore, the cement walls are speckled with reddish paint. But don't let that scare you. The campground is very nice, and nearly every site is an excellent choice. Numbered sites in the first five rows are reserved for overnighters—the rest are for monthly renters. All sites are 80-foot pull-throughs on grassy patches. Sites at the far end of the highway (10, 27, and 35 especially) are the best, as they receive less traffic noise and not much passing traffic. (18, also an end site, is directly across from the bathhouse.) Those at the highway end are a little noisier (9, 17, 26, 34, 42). The tent area is to the northwest of the bathhouse. There is an excellent grass cover. Several large trees lend shade, but may be too high to provide much protection from rain. While the campground needs a nice spring cleaning and a little less traffic noise to earn a full rating, it is very nice, and a destination that many campers will be sure to return to.

BASICS

Operated By: Bill & Dee Bunker. **Open:** All year. **Site Assignment:** Flexible, depending on availability; verbal reservations OK. **Registration:** At office. (Late arrivals use drop box.) **Fee:** RV full, $16.67; tent, $12.50; $1 extra for cable or 50 amps. **Parking:** At site.

FACILITIES

Number of RV-only Sites: 116. **Number of Tent-only Sites:** 4. **Hookups:** Electric (30, 50 amps), water, sewer, cable TV. **Each Site:** Picnic table. **Dump Station:** No (sewer at all sites). **Laundry:** Yes. **Pay Phone:** Yes. **Restrooms and Showers:** Yes. **Fuel:** Next door. **Propane:** 1 mi. **Internal Roads:** Gravel. **RV Service:** On-call. **Market:** 1.5 mi. north. **Restaurant:** 1 mi. north. **General Store:** Yes. **Vending:** Yes.

Swimming: Lake. **Playground:** Yes. **Other:** Cabins, rec hall, Lake Chicot, boat ramp, pavilion, data port, dock, fish-cleaning area. **Activities:** Fishing, swimming, boating, volleyball, horseshoes. **Nearby Attractions:** Lake Chicot, Mississippi River. **Additional Information:** Chamber of Commerce, (870) 265-5997.

RESTRICTIONS

Pets: On leash, cleaned up after. **Fires:** Fire ring only. **Alcoholic Beverages:** At sites. **Vehicle Maximum Length:** No limit. **Other:** OHV's must be street legal to operate in park.

TO GET THERE

From the junction of Hwy. 65 S, 82 E, and 278 E, go 2.8 mi. on Hwy. 65/82. Turn right at the sign into the entrance. The office is the white house on the left.

LITTLE ROCK   MAP, C-2
Little Rock North KOA

7820 Crystal Hill Rd., 72118. T: (800) KOA-4598 or (501) 758-4598; www.koa.com.

🚐 ★★★★	▲ ★★★★
Beauty: ★★★★	Site Privacy: ★★★
Spaciousness: ★★★	Quiet: ★★
Security: ★★★★	Cleanliness: ★★★★
Insect Control: ★★★★	Facilities: ★★★★★

Campers in large rigs will be happy with the numerous pull-throughs in this campground, which include all sites except those around the perimeter. Rows G19–24 and R8–14 are closest to the road, and include 40-foot back-ins. (G sites 15–24 are all in a forested corner of the campground, with gravel sites.) Sites R1–7 are well shaded 56-foot pull-throughs, while G11–14 are even longer (75 feet). Row B has 75-foot pull-throughs, of which 1–3 face a residence. B15–20 is along the northwest side of the grounds, and has 40-foot grassy back-ins. (19 is located directly next to the dog walk area.) Row Y, along the northern perimeter, has the least developed sites, but the many pine trees in this area give it a nice, natural feel. Sites Y1–13 are 75 pull-throughs amidst the trees, while Y14–28 back into the forest. Tent site T1 is off in the woods above RV site G24, and T2–3 are even more remote, in the northeast corner. All sites have a finely crushed gravel bed for a tent and plenty of trees. The restroom is very clean, and campers will be delighted to know that it has air-conditioning. The toilet stalls are a little narrow, but everything is clean as a whistle. This is a fine campground to make your home base while exploring the Little Rock area. It has a nice woodsy feel and is close enough to the attractions to allow for plenty of day trips.

BASICS

Operated By: The Clay Family. **Open:** All year. **Site Assignment:** Upon registration; reservations require credit card; 24-hour cancellation policy. **Registration:** At office. (Late arrivals use drop box.) **Fee:** RV, $30–$38; V, MC, AE, D, check. **Parking:** At site.

FACILITIES

Number of RV-only Sites: 100. **Number of Tent-only Sites:** 10. **Hookups:** Electric (20, 30, 50 amps), water, sewer, cable TV. **Each Site:** Picnic table, grill. **Dump Station:** Yes. **Laundry:** Yes. **Pay Phone:** Yes. **Restrooms and Showers:** Yes. **Fuel:** No. **Propane:** Yes. **Internal Roads:** Paved. **RV Service:** No. **Market:** 4 mi. west. **Restaurant:** Across the street. **General Store:** Yes. **Vending:** Yes. **Swimming:** Pool. **Playground:** Yes. **Other:** Data port, sauna, hot tub, exercise equipment, snack bar, pool table, dog walk, old-fashioned soda fountain, ice-cream parlor, computer center. **Activities:** Basketball, volleyball, horseshoes, swimming, golf, shopping, antiquing, fishing, tennis. **Nearby Attractions:** Burns Park, Wild River Country, Little Rock, Aerospace Education Center, State Capitol, Pinnacle Mountain State Park, Civil War Cemetery, flea markets. **Additional Information:** North Little Rock Advertising & Promotion Commission, (800) 643-4690, (501) 758-1424.

RESTRICTIONS

Pets: On leash, cleaned up after; do not leave unattended. **Fires:** Grill only. **Alcoholic Beverages:** At sites. **Vehicle Maximum Length:** 95 ft. **Other:** Need own satellite dish for TV.

TO GET THERE

If coming north from Little Rock on I-30, take I-40 West. From I-40, take Exit 148. Turn west onto Crystal Hill Rd. and go 1.2 mi. Turn right at the sign into the entrance.

MARION   MAP, B-3
America's Best Campground

7037 I-55, 72364. T: (888) 857-4890 or (870) 739-4801; www.camp_memphis.com.

🚐 ★★★★	▲ ★★★★
Beauty: ★★★★	Site Privacy: ★★★★
Spaciousness: ★★★	Quiet: ★★★
Security: ★★★★	Cleanliness: ★★★★★
Insect Control: ★★★	Facilities: ★★★★★

West of the highway, with a cornfield to the north and an agricultural field to the south, this campground has attractive landscaping (using bushes at the ends of rows) and towering shade trees. Nearly all sites in the park are very well shaded, with a grass floor. Sites 1, 2, 4, and 9 are enormous (100-feet) pull-throughs, while 3 and 5–8 are 75-foot back-ins. End sites 16, 24, 32, 40, 48, and H have enormous leftover space at the ends of the rows. Sites 50–54 are 60-foot back-ins in a strip across from the office. Adjacent to these sites are sites 55–62, arranged in a semicircle in the grass. These are undeveloped sites in a wooded area, with a very natural, almost wild, feel. (These sites can accommodate any size of rig, and can be pull-throughs if the adjacent area is clear.) Sites A–H face a residential area, and A and B are the least best sites in the campground, lacking shade trees. However, there is nary a truly bad site in the park. The restrooms and showers are immaculate, well lit, and tastefully decorated. The laundry is contained in its own cute little cabin and is open 24 hours. Located 15 miles to most attractions, and 22

miles to Graceland, this park boasts very friendly management and is worth the drive out, especially given the state of other local campgrounds.

BASICS

Operated By: Jim & Sue Alkire. **Open:** All year. **Site Assignment:** Upon registration; reservations require credit card or cell-phone number & are recommended; 24-hour cancellation policy. **Registration:** At office. (Late arrivals use drop box.) **Fee:** RV (full), $28; water/electric, $24; tent, $18. Winter: RV, $26; tent, $16. **Parking:** At site, w/ plenty of visitor parking.

FACILITIES

Number of Multipurpose Sites: 102. **Hookups:** Electric (30, 50 amps), water, sewer. **Each Site:** Picnic table, grill. **Dump Station:** Yes. **Laundry:** Yes. **Pay Phone:** Yes. **Restrooms and Showers:** Yes. **Fuel:** No. **Propane:** Yes. **Internal Roads:** Gravel. **RV Service:** No. **Market:** 4 mi. south (Exit 10). **Restaurant:** 4 mi. south (Exit 10). **General Store:** Yes. **Vending:** No. **Swimming:** Outdoor pool. **Playground:** Yes. **Other:** Data port, rec room, pet-walk area, horseshoes. **Activities:** Swimming, visiting museums, city tours, shopping. **Nearby Attractions:** Graceland, Sun Studio, Beale St., Pink Palace Museum, Rock 'n' Soul Museum, IMAX Theater. **Additional Information:** Arkansas Visitor information Desk, (901) 543-5333.

RESTRICTIONS

Pets: On leash, cleaned up after. **Fires:** Grill only. **Alcoholic Beverages:** At sites, no bottles. **Vehicle Maximum Length:** No limit. **Other:** No semis, operators prefer no large animals that must be kept outside of RVs.

TO GET THERE

From I-55, take Exit 14. Take the first right (following the sign for Memphis). Follow the road around and take the right turn so that you are driving parallel to the interstate on the west service road. Go 0.2 mi. and turn right at the sign into the campground.

MENA   MAP, C-1
Shadow Mountain

3708 Hwy. 71 South, 71953. T: (479) 394-6099.

🚐 ★★★★★	▲ ★★★★★
Beauty: ★★★★	Site Privacy: ★★★★
Spaciousness: ★★★★	Quiet: ★★★★
Security: ★★★★★	Cleanliness: ★★★★★
Insect Control: ★★★★	Facilities: ★★★★

Touted by the proprietor as the "only full-service campground within 50 miles," this campground has full hookups, a pool, and modern facilities in a forested, rural setting. Sites in this campground are not overly developed, adding to the natural charm of the grounds. All RV sites are 65-foot pull-throughs. Sites at the ends of the rows on the east side (2, 7, 13, 14, 28) are generally the best, as they face the forest and are slightly away from the other sites in the rows. Sites 41–51 are right off the highway, making them less desirable than other sites. Unnumbered tent sites are situated down the slope of the RV park and to the south, toward the highway. Sites are grassy with ample tree coverage, but due to some amount of passing traffic noise is inevitable. The restrooms are very clean and fairly modern. Showers are very spacious. The laundry room is spacious and contains enough machines for a campground of this size. This is a nice little getaway with an off-the-beaten-path feel but the convenience of a highway location.

BASICS

Operated By: Jerry & Anita Buffington. **Open:** All year. **Site Assignment:** Upon registration; reservations require credit card. **Registration:** At office. (Late arrivals use drop box.) **Fee:** RV full hookup (50 amp), $21; partial hookup (30 amp), $18; tent (water/electric), $13. **Parking:** At site.

FACILITIES

Number of RV-only Sites: 64. **Number of Tent-only Sites:** Undesignated sites. **Hookups:** Electric (20, 30, 50 amps), water, sewer. **Each Site:** Picnic table. **Dump Station:** Yes. **Laundry:** Yes. **Pay Phone:** Yes. **Restrooms and Showers:** Yes. **Fuel:** No. **Propane:** No. **Internal Roads:** Paved. **RV Service:** No. **Market:** 5 mi. to Mena. **Restaurant:** 5 mi. to Mena. **General Store:** Yes. **Vending:** Yes. **Swimming:** Pool. **Playground:** Yes. **Other:** Lake, antique soda fountain, firewood. **Activities:** Basketball, swimming. **Nearby Attractions:** Talimena Scenic Drive, Ouachita National Forest, Janssen Park, Queen Wilhelmina State Park. **Additional Information:** Mean–Polk County Chamber of Commerce, (501) 394-2912.

RESTRICTIONS

Pets: On leash, cleaned up after. **Fires:** In rings. **Alcoholic Beverages:** At sites; subject to dry county regulations. **Vehicle Maximum Length:** No limit.

TO GET THERE

From the junction of Hwy. 8 and Hwy. 59/71, in Mena, go 4.5 mi. south on Hwy. 59/71. Turn right at the sign into the entrance. The office is on the left; park to the right.

MORRILTON   MAP, B-2
Petit Jean State Park

1285 Petit Jean Mountain Rd., 72110.
T: (501) 727-5441; www.petitjeanstatepark.com.

🚐 ★★★★   ⛺ ★★★★★

Beauty: ★★★★★	Site Privacy: ★★★★★
Spaciousness: ★★★★★	Quiet: ★★★★★
Security: ★★★★★	Cleanliness: ★★★★
Insect Control: ★★★★	Facilities: ★★★★

Sites in this state park, Arkansas's first, are divided into four areas, A–D. Area A is east of the Visitors Center, and contains sites 1–35, all 80-foot pull-throughs (except 32, which is 105 feet). Many of these sites are along (or near) the lake, and therefore are preferred or premium sites, costing more than the others. Premium sites closest to the lake are 19, 26, and 27. Preferred sites near the lake are 8, 9, 29, and 30. The end sites 1 and 35 are closest to the entrance, and may not be as desirable. Area B contains the reservable sites. Of these, 44–48 are the nicest, as they back to thick woods and are quieter than other sites.

Sites 36–42 back to a road and suffer from more noise as a result. Area C contains 45–50-foot back-ins. Sites 74–76, 89, and 91 back to thick woods, making them quite nice. Site 71 is across from the bathhouse, making access quite convenient. Site 77 is right by the entrance. Area D is for overflow camping. The restrooms and showers in all of these areas are clean and spacious. This is a wonderful park with loads to do. It makes a great destination for families and anyone in a tent. RVers will enjoy their stay but do not have the benefit of full hookups.

BASICS

Operated By: Arkansas State Parks. **Open:** All year. **Site Assignment:** Upon registration during the day; first come, first served at night; reservations require deposit of 1-night stay, made 5 days in advance; cancellation requires 5-day notice; 1-night deposit nonrefundable; reservations can be made for 60% of the campsites. **Registration:** At visitor center. (Late arrivals select site & pay in the morning.) **Fee:** $12–$28. **Parking:** At site.

FACILITIES

Number of Multipurpose Sites: 127. **Hookups:** Electric (20, 30 amps), water. **Each Site:** Picnic table, grill, lantern pole. **Dump Station:** Yes. **Laundry:** No. **Pay Phone:** Yes. **Restrooms and Showers:** Yes. **Fuel:** No. Oppelo 14 mi. **Propane:** No. **Internal Roads:** Paved. **RV Service:** No. **Market:** 20 mi. to Morrilton. **Restaurant:** On site; 20 mi. to Morrilton. **General Store:** Yes. **Vending:** Yes. **Swimming:** Pool (Memorial Day–Labor Day). **Playground:** Yes. **Other:** Tennis courts, picnic pavilion, snack bar, boat rentals, amphitheater, Mather Lodge Restaurant, horse facilities. **Activities:** Fishing, boating, swimming, horseback riding, hiking, tennis. **Nearby Attractions:** Waterfall, Museum of Automobiles. **Additional Information:** Morrilton Chamber of Commerce, (501) 354-2393.

RESTRICTIONS

Pets: On leash, cleaned up after. **Fires:** Grill only. **Alcoholic Beverages:** At sites. **Vehicle Maximum Length:** No limit.

TO GET THERE

From the junction of Hwy. 9 and Hwy. 154, turn west onto Hwy. 154 and go 11.3 mi. to the park.

MOUNTAIN HOME   B-2
Oakland/Ozark Isle Park

reserve america

324 W. 7th St., 72653. T: (870) 431-5744;
www.reserveamerica.com.

🚐 ★★★★   ⛺ ★★★★

Beauty: ★★★★	Site Privacy: ★★
Spaciousness: ★★	Quiet: ★★★
Security: ★★★	Cleanliness: ★★★★
Insect Control: ★★★	Facilities: ★★★

Oakland/Ozark Isle is located on Bull Shoals Lake in north central Arkansas. The lake is known for its exceptional water quality and outstanding fisheries. The wooded shoreline and undeveloped nature of the

lake offers visitors a remote experience, with modern services. Bull Shoals Lake is a water-sports paradise. Almost 1,000 miles of pristine shoreline are open to visitors who come to fish, scuba dive, houseboat, water ski, wake board, camp, and relax. Bull Shoals Lake water is very clean and clear. Swimming is enjoyable from mid-May until late September. Fishing on Bull Shoals Lake is excellent all year, with peak action in March, April, and May. Marinas on Bull Shoals Lake have boats and motors for rent, supplies for sale, and guides for hire. The Corps of Engineers provides launching areas and ramps for those who bring their own boats. Water sports such as swimming and skiing are popular on Bull Shoals Lake, as is cruising the hundreds of miles of lake arms and coves by motorboat or sailboat. Scuba divers come to Bull Shoals from many states to enjoy their sport in the clear, blue water. Spearfishing is enjoyed year-round. The campground features flush toilets, warm showers, developed swimming area, boat launching ramps, group picnic shelter, and playgrounds.

BASICS

Operated By: U.S. Army Corps of Engineers. **Open:** Apr. 1–Oct. 31. **Site Assignment:** Reservations must be made at least 3 days in advance. **Registration:** At office. **Fee:** Single, $16; group, $40. **Parking:** At site.

FACILITIES

Number of Multipurpose Sites: 188. **Hookups:** Yes. **Dump Station:** Yes. **Laundry:** No. **Pay Phone:** Yes. **Restrooms and Showers:** Yes. **Fuel:** No. **Propane:** No. **Internal Roads:** Paved. **RV Service:** No. **Market:** No. **Restaurant:** No. **General Store:** No. **Vending:** No. **Swimming:** Yes. **Playground:** Yes. **Activities:** Fishing, boating.

RESTRICTIONS

Pets: Pets must be restrained or on a leash at all times while in developed recreation areas. **Fires:** In fire rings, stoves, grills, or fireplaces provided for that purpose. **Alcoholic Beverages:** Not allowed. **Vehicle Maximum Length:** Call ahead. **Other:** No ATVs allowed.

TO GET THERE

From Mountain Home, AR, take SR 5 north 14 mi. to SR 202, then go 10 mi. west on SR 202 to Oakland/Ozark Isle Park. Follow signs into the campground.

MURFREESBORO   MAP, C-1
Kirby Landing

reserve america

155 Dynamite Hill Rd, 71958-9720.
T: (870) 285-2151; www.reserveamerica.com.

🚐 ★★★★   ⛺ ★★★★

Beauty: ★★★	Site Privacy: ★★★
Spaciousness: ★★★	Quiet: ★★★
Security: ★★★	Cleanliness: ★★★★
Insect Control: ★★★	Facilities: ★★★

Kirby Landing Campground is located on Lake Greeson. The lake is approximately 12 miles long with

7,260 surface acres of water for fishing, skiing, boating, and other water sports. The lake is created by Narrows Dam, named after the area in which it is located, "The Narrows." Lake Greeson is named after developer Martin White Greeson. The lake also contains Daisy State Park. Lake Greeson has been recognized for its rich variety of fish, which include: largemouth, spotted, and white bass, and flathead and channel catfish. The area below Narrows Dam has a mighty supply of rainbow trout. Other game species exist around Lake Greeson beside fish. Rabbits, squirrels, bobwhite quail, and whitetail deer can also be found here. The 35,000 acre Lake Greeson Public Hunting Area, west of the lake, provides good hunting areas for hunters. Lake Greeson provides 45 miles of walking, nature, and cycling trails for public use. At the Parker Creek Recreational Area there is a nature trail that lets you experience the nature and beauty around an old cinnabar mine. The cinnabar mine was popular during the 1930s and 40s before the lake was made in 1950. The Bear Creek Cycle Trail allows riders to experience 31 miles of breathtaking beauty around the lake. The trail takes riders across pine-covered forest and rolling hills. Lake Greeson is next to the small town of Murfreesboro, which is next to the Crater of Diamonds State Park. The area around Murfreesboro is full of recreational areas. Martin White Greeson, who was born on November 7, 1868, was the main developer of Lake Greeson. Lake Greeson was made to prevent flooding of the Little Missouri River. Construction of the lake began in April 1947, but the first bucket of concrete wasn't poured until June 1948. The lake was then finished in 1950 and dedicated in 1951. Now after more than 50 years of serving the local area with recreation, flood control, power, water, and beauty, this 12-mile-long lake surely exceeds the dreams of its creator, Martin White Greeson. Bald eagles are an attraction for visitors each winter. The campground has a short nature trail for naturalists and birders to enjoy. The campground offers 87 campsites with electric hookups. Other amenities include a dump station, hot showers, a boat ramp, a playground, and a swim beach.

BASICS

Operated By: U.S. Army Corps of Engineers. **Open:** All year. **Site Assignment:** Reservations must be made at least 3 days in advance. **Registration:** At office. **Fee:** Single, $13–$16. **Parking:** At site.

FACILITIES

Number of Multipurpose Sites: 40. **Hookups:** Yes. **Dump Station:** Yes. **Laundry:** No. **Pay Phone:** No. **Restrooms and Showers:** Yes. **Fuel:** No. **Propane:** No. **Internal Roads:** Gravel. **RV Service:** No. **Market:** No. **Restaurant:** No. **General Store:** No. **Vending:** No. **Swimming:** Yes. **Playground:** Yes. **Other:** No sewer site hookups at this campground. **Activities:** Fishing, skiing, boating.

RESTRICTIONS

Pets: Pets must be restrained or on a leash at all times while in developed recreation areas. **Fires:** In fire rings, stoves, grills, or fireplaces provided for that purpose. **Alcoholic Beverages:** Not allowed. **Vehicle Maximum Length:** Call ahead. **Other:** ORVs are prohibited unless loaded on a trailer or in a vehicle.

TO GET THERE

From Texarkana: go east on I-30 for 46 mi. to Prescott, north on AR 19 for 3 mi. to Murfreesboro, and north on AR 27 for 15 mi. to Kirby. Go west on US 70 for 3 mi. to Kirby Landing access road, then south to Kirby Landing. From Hot Springs: go west on US 70 to Kirby Landing Access Rd., then south on access road to the campground.

MURFREESBORO   MAP, C-1
Miner's Camping and Rock Shop

2235 Hwy. 301 South, 71958. T: (870) 285-2722.

🚐 ★★★★	⛺ ★★★★
Beauty: ★★★★	Site Privacy: ★★★
Spaciousness: ★★★	Quiet: ★★★
Security: ★★★★	Cleanliness: ★★★
Insect Control: ★★★	Facilities: ★★★

This campground is divided into two sections on either side of the highway, the north and south sections. In the north section, sites are arranged on the outside of an internal loop. All sites are back-ins: 5–11 back to the forest, 12–17 to a dirt road. Sites are open-ended, meaning that a rig of any size can fit in most sites. Site 17 is somewhat less desirable due to its proximity to the highway. The main restrooms are in this section, and are small, modern, and cozy. The shower is extremely spacious, but shares one drawback with the restroom—a cement floor. Sites on the south side of the park all back to the woods. Sites H–K are the best sites, as they are farthest from the highway. Site A is closest to the highway, and therefore less desirable. There are two nonflush toilets here, which are as clean as can be expected. (Take the time to cross the highway and use the full restroom!) Tenting is allowed in an open field on the south side, to the east of the RV sites. There is a good grass cover, but no trees for shade or protection from the elements. Rock hounds—and others—will enjoy this campground just south of Murfreesboro and a couple hundred feet from the Crater of Diamonds State Park. The services are decent, and the campground is cute and woodsy.

BASICS

Operated By: J. Goodin. **Open:** All year. **Site Assignment:** Upon registration. Verbal reservations OK; call to cancel. **Registration:** At gift shop. (Late arrivals select & settle in the morning.) **Fee:** RV (full), $15. **Parking:** At site.

FACILITIES

Number of Multipurpose Sites: 33. **Hookups:** Electric (30, 50 amps), water, sewer. **Each Site:** Picnic table, trash can. **Dump Station:** Yes. **Laundry:** No. **Pay Phone:** No. **Restrooms and Showers:** Yes. **Fuel:** No. **Propane:** No. **Internal Roads:** Gravel. **RV Service:** No. **Market:** 2 mi. north. **Restaurant:** 2 mi. north. **General Store:** No, 2 mi. north. **Vending:** No. **Swimming:** No. **Playground:** Yes. **Other:** Gift shop, 3 cabins, firewood, fishing pond, pavilion. **Activities:** Hiking, rock collecting. **Nearby Attractions:** Crater of Diamonds State Park, Ka-Do-Ha Indian Village, Hot Springs, Quartz Mines, Washington State Park. **Additional Information:** Murfreesboro Chamber of Commerce, (870) 425-5111.

RESTRICTIONS

Pets: On leash, cleaned up after. **Fires:** In pits. **Alcoholic Beverages:** Subject to dry county regulations. **Vehicle Maximum Length:** No limit. **Other:** No washing of vehicles.

TO GET THERE

From the junction of Hwy. 26/27 and Hwy. 301, go 2.3 mi. east on Hwy. 301. Turn left at the sign into the entrance.

MURFREESBORO   MAP, C-1
Self Creek

reserve america

155 Dynamite Hill Rd, 71958. T: (870) 285-2151; www.reserveamerica.com.

🚐 ★★★★	⛺ ★★★★
Beauty: ★★★	Site Privacy: ★★
Spaciousness: ★★	Quiet: ★★★
Security: ★★★	Cleanliness: ★★★★
Insect Control: ★★★	Facilities: ★

Self Creek/Jim Wylie Campground is located on Lake Greeson. The lake is approximately 12 miles long with 7,260 surface acres of water for fishing, skiing, boating, and other water sports. The lake is created by Narrows Dam, named after the area in which it is located, "The Narrows." Lake Greeson is named after developer Martin White Greeson. The lake also contains Daisy State Park. Lake Greeson has been recognized by its rich variety of fish, which include: largemouth, spotted, and white bass, and flathead and channel catfish. The area below Narrows Dam has a mighty supply of rainbow trout. Other game species exist around Lake Greeson beside fish. Rabbits, squirrels, bobwhite quail, whitetail deer can also be found here. The 35,000 acre Lake Greeson Public Hunting Area is west of the lake and provides good hunting areas. Lake Greeson provides 45 miles of walking, nature, and cycling trails for public use. At the Parker Creek Recreational Area there is a nature trail that lets you experience the nature and beauty around an old cinnabar mine. The cinnabar mine was a popular mine during the 1930s and 40s before the lake was made in 1950. The Bear Creek Cycle Trail allows riders to experience 31 miles of breathtaking beauty around the lake. The trail takes riders across pine-covered forest and rolling hills. Lake Greeson is next to the small town of Murfreesboro, which is next to the Crater of Diamonds State Park. The area around Murfreesboro is full of recreational areas. Martin White Greeson, who was born on November 7, 1868, was the main developer of Lake Greeson. Lake Greeson was basically made to prevent flooding of the Little Missouri River. Construction of the lake began in April 1947, but the first bucket of concrete wasn't pored until June 1948. The lake was then finished in 1950 and dedicated in 1951. Now after more than 50 years of serving the local area with recreation, flood control, power, water, and beauty, this 12-mile long lake surely exceeds the dreams of the creator. Bald eagles are an attraction for visitors each winter. The campground offers 72 campsites, 41 with electric hookups. Other amenities include a dump station, hot showers, a boat ramp, and a swim beach.

BASICS

Operated By: U.S. Army Corps of Engineers. **Open:** All year. **Site Assignment:** Reservations must be made at least 3 days in advance. **Registration:** At office. **Fee:** Single, $10–$15. **Parking:** At site.

FACILITIES

Number of Multipurpose Sites: 169. **Hookups:** Yes. **Dump Station:** Yes. **Laundry:** No. **Pay Phone:** No. **Restrooms and Showers:** Yes. **Fuel:** No. **Propane:** No. **Internal Roads:** Paved. **RV Service:** No. **Market:** No. **Restaurant:** No. **General Store:** No. **Vending:** No. **Swimming:** Yes. **Playground:** No. **Other:** Outside the reservation season ORVs are prohibited in recreational areas, unless loaded on a trailer or in a vehicle. **Activities:** Fishing, skiing, boating, & other water sports.

RESTRICTIONS

Pets: Pets must be restrained or on a leash at all times while in developed recreation areas. **Fires:** In fire rings, stoves, grills, or fireplaces provided for that purpose. **Alcoholic Beverages:** Not allowed. **Vehicle Maximum Length:** Call ahead.

TO GET THERE

From Texarkana, take I-30 east (46 mi.) to Prescott, then AR 19 north to Murfreesboro (30 mi.), then AR 27 north (15 mi.) to Kirby. Go west on US 70 (6 mi.) to Self Creek/Jim Wylie Campground.

NEWPORT   MAP, B-3
Jacksonport State Park

205 Ave. St., 72112. T: (870) 523-2143; www.arkansasstateparks.com/stay/camping.

🚐 ★★★★	🏕 ★★★★★
Beauty: ★★★★★	Site Privacy: ★★★★★
Spaciousness: ★★★★★	Quiet: ★★★★★
Security: ★★★★★	Cleanliness: ★★★★★
Insect Control: ★★★★	Facilities: ★★★

This park is located in a wilderness setting about 5 miles out of town. There are a boat ramp, swimming beach, picnic area, and museum that explains the history of the area. All of the sites in this park are grassy 50-foot back-ins on either side of a looped road. Sites are extremely spacious, and most contain several shade trees. (All sites but 1, 10, and 11 are well shaded.) Site 1 has a parking pad for an extra vehicle. Even numbered sites 4–10 and 9, 13, and 16 back to the river, while 2, 5, 7, 11, 12, 15, and 19 back to a large, open recreation field on the interior of the looped drive. Site 7 and 9 are closest to the restrooms. The restrooms and showers are very clean, modern, and quite comfortable.

BASICS

Operated By: Arkansas Dept. of Parks & Tourism. **Open:** All year. **Site Assignment:** Reservations can be made or first come, first served; first night's reservation must be paid 5 days in advance of arrival date; no refunds. **Registration:** At visitor center or self-pay station. (Late arrivals use self-pay station.) **Fee:** $9–$18.50; V, MC, AE, D, check. **Parking:** At site.

FACILITIES

Number of RV-only Sites: 20. **Hookups:** Electric (20, 30, 50 amps), water. **Each Site:** Picnic table, grill, fire pit, lantern pole. **Dump Station:** Yes. **Laundry:** No. **Pay Phone:** Yes. **Restrooms and Showers:** Yes. **Fuel:** No. **Propane:** No. **Internal Roads:** Paved. **RV Service:** No. **Market:** 3 mi. to Newport. **Restaurant:** 3 mi. to Newport. **General Store:** Yes. **Vending:** Yes. **Swimming:** River. **Playground:** Yes. **Other:** Hunting & fishing licenses, picnic area, gift shop, boat ramp, nature trail. **Activities:** Fishing, swimming, boating, interpretive programs. **Nearby Attractions:** White River, Old Jacksonport Courthouse Museum, Paddleboat Museum. **Additional Information:** Newport Area Chamber of Commerce, (870) 523-3618.

RESTRICTIONS

Pets: On leash, cleaned up after. **Fires:** Grill or pits. **Alcoholic Beverages:** At sites. **Vehicle Maximum Length:** No limit. **Other:** No metal detectors, no glass near river, no gray-water discharge at site.

TO GET THERE

From the junction of Hwy. 367 and Hwy. 69, go 2.9 mi. north. Turn left onto Hwy. 69 Spur (south), and go 0.8 mi. Take a tricky left turn at the sign into the campground entrance.

PARAGOULD   MAP, B-3
Crowley's Ridge State Park

2092 Hwy. 168 North, 72450. T: (800) 264-2405 or (870) 573-6751; www.arkansasstateparks.com.

🚐 ★★★★	🏕 ★★★★★
Beauty: ★★★★	Site Privacy: ★★★★
Spaciousness: ★★★★★	Quiet: ★★★★★
Security: ★★★★	Cleanliness: ★★★
Insect Control: ★★★	Facilities: ★★★

Campsites in the park are situated along a single internal road. Sites on the north side have a steep slope at the rear, while those on the south side have a more gradual slope. (All parking strips are level.) Tent sites (19–26) are mostly 30 feet off the main road, although sites 22–24 are set farther back. These are extremely spacious (45-foot-wide) dirt campsites set, as all campsites in the park are, back in the forest. Of the RV sites (so designated solely by their electric hookups), 1 is a gigantic (120-foot) pull-through, while the others are mostly 45–50-foot back-ins. (Site 7 is an exception, being only 30 feet long and set very close to the road.) Site 9 offers the most privacy, being set well back from the road; while 8 has much less privacy due to its proximity to a hiking trailhead. The restrooms and showers are astonishingly clean, modern, and spacious (but lack air-conditioning). This is an intimate state park with extraordinarily clean facilities that both tenters and RVers will definitely enjoy.

BASICS

Operated By: Arkansas Dept. of Parks & Tourism. **Open:** All year. **Site Assignment:** First come, first served; reservations require 1-night deposit made 5 days in advance; cancellation requires 5-day notice; 1-night deposit nonrefundable; only 5 sites are reservable. **Registration:** At visitor center. (Late arrivals select site & register next morning after 8 a.m.) **Fee:** $9–$15.50; V, MC, AE, D, check. **Parking:** At site.

FACILITIES

Number of RV-only Sites: 18. **Number of Tent-only Sites:** 8. **Hookups:** Electric (30 amps), water, sewer. **Each Site:** Picnic table, grill, lantern pole. **Dump Station:** Yes. **Laundry:** No. **Pay Phone:** Yes. **Restrooms and Showers:** Yes. **Fuel:** No. **Propane:** No. **Internal Roads:** Paved. **RV Service:** No. **Market:** 9 mi. to Paragould. **Restaurant:** 9 mi. to Paragould. **General Store:** No. **Vending:** Yes. **Swimming:** Lake. **Playground:** Yes. **Other:** Gift shop. **Activities:** Boating, canoeing, hiking, swimming, paddle boating. **Nearby Attractions:** Lake Ponder, Walcott Lake. **Additional Information:** Paragould-Greene County Chamber of Commerce, (870) 236-7684.

RESTRICTIONS

Pets: On leash, cleaned up after. **Fires:** In pits. **Alcoholic Beverages:** At sites (preferably in nondescript containers). **Vehicle Maximum Length:** No limit.

TO GET THERE

From the junction of Hwy. 49 and Hwy. 412, go 9 mi. west on Hwy. 412. Turn left onto Hwy. 168 and go 2 mi. Turn left at the sign into campground.

PINE BLUFF   MAP, C-2
Saracen Trace RV Park

P.O. Box 7676, 71611. T: (870) 536-0920 or (870) 534-0711.

🚐 ★★★★	🏕 n/a
Beauty: ★★★★	Site Privacy: ★★★★
Spaciousness: ★★★★	Quiet: ★★★★★
Security: ★★★★	Cleanliness: ★★★★
Insect Control: ★★	Facilities: ★★★

Located within a large city park, this campground has open, grassy sites situated along a looped internal road. All sites are 60-foot back-ins, and most (if not all) are very well shaded. Sites on the eastern side of the campground (7–17) back to the lake, and seem to be sought after for this reason. Sites 21–24 back to a golf course adjacent to the campground. Site 43 is desirable for the large amount of open space (large enough for another RV site) adjacent to it. Sites 29 and 30, on the other hand, are less desirable, as they are very close to the entrance and receive more passing traffic than other sites. There is a disabled-access fishing pier between sites 12 and 13, which may also account for increased traffic past these two sites. This campground is on the whole a very pleasant, extremely quiet campground. Sites are grassy and shaded, and campers seeking a relaxing atmosphere should find them extremely comfortable.

BASICS

Operated By: Pine Bluff Parks Commission. **Open:** All year. **Site Assignment:** First come, first served; no reservations. **Registration:** At registration kiosk. **Fee:** $12. **Parking:** At site.

FACILITIES

Number of RV-only Sites: 52. **Hookups:** Electric (20, 30 amps), water. **Each Site:** Picnic table, grill, trees. **Dump Station:** Yes. **Laundry:** Yes. **Pay Phone:** Yes. **Restrooms and Showers:** No. **Fuel:** 3 mi. **Propane:** 3 mi. **Internal Roads:** Paved. **RV Service:** No. **Market:** 6 mi. to town. **Restaurant:** 6 mi. to town. **General Store:** No. **Vending:** Yes. **Swimming:** Lake (at boat dock). **Playground:** Yes. **Activities:** Swimming, fishing, baseball, soccer, horseshoes, hiking, golf. **Nearby Attractions:** Lake Langhofer, The Band Museum, Southeast Arkansas Arts & Science Center, Nature Center, railroad museum. **Additional Information:** Greater Pine Bluff Area Chamber of Commerce, (870) 535-0110.

RESTRICTIONS

Pets: On leash, cleaned up after. **Fires:** Grill only. **Alcoholic Beverages:** At sites. **Vehicle Maximum Length:** No limit.

TO GET THERE

From the junction of Hwy. 79B and Hwy. 65B, go 1.2 mi. east on Hwy. 65B. Turn left at the light onto Convention Center Drive and follow this road into the park. The campground is at the extreme north end of the park.

PINE BLUFF — MAP, C-2
Tar Camp

P.O. Box 7835, 71611-7835. T: (501) 397-5101; www.reserveamerica.com.

🚐 ★★★★   ⛺ ★★★★

Beauty: ★★★	Site Privacy: ★★
Spaciousness: ★★	Quiet: ★★★★
Security: ★★★★	Cleanliness: ★★★★
Insect Control: ★★★	Facilities: ★★★★

Tar Camp Campground is located on the Arkansas River by Pool 5 Lock and Dam. The area provides something for everyone whether it's camping, fishing, boating, or just relaxing in the sun. The Arkansas River is a major tributary of the Mississippi River. The Arkansas generally flows to the east and southeast, and traverses the states of Colorado, Kansas, Oklahoma, and Arkansas. At 1,450 miles it is the fourth longest river in the United States. Its origin is in the Colorado Rockies in Lake County near Leadville, and its outlet is at the historic site of Napoleon, Arkansas. It is the second largest tributary in the Mississippi–Missouri system, with a drainage basin of nearly 195,000 square miles. The Arkansas has three distinct characters in its long path through central North America. At its headwaters the Arkansas runs as a steep mountain torrent through the Rockies, dropping 4,600 feet in 120 miles. At Cañon City, Colorado, it leaves the mountains and enters Royal Gorge. This section sees extensive whitewater rafting in the spring and summer. For most of its length through the rest of Colorado and Kansas, it is a typical Great Plains riverway, with wide shallow banks, subject to seasonal flooding. Tributaries include the Cimarron River flowing from

NE New Mexico and the Salt Fork Arkansas River. The Tar Camp Campground offers 58 sites, 38 with electric and water hookups. Additional amenities include hot showers, a dump station, a boat launch, a playground, and public telephones. Click on the map to select a camping area within the campground or view a list of camping areas. To view definitions of the map icons see our legend page.

BASICS

Operated By: U.S. Army Corps of Engineers. **Open:** All year. **Site Assignment:** Reservations must be made at least 3 days in advance. **Registration:** At office. **Fee:** Single, $17. **Parking:** At site.

FACILITIES

Number of Multipurpose Sites: 115. **Hookups:** Yes. **Dump Station:** Yes. **Laundry:** No. **Pay Phone:** Yes. **Restrooms and Showers:** Yes. **Fuel:** No. **Propane:** No. **Internal Roads:** Paved. **RV Service:** No. **Market:** No. **Restaurant:** No. **General Store:** No. **Vending:** No. **Swimming:** No. **Playground:** Yes. **Activities:** Fishing, boating.

RESTRICTIONS

Pets: Pets must be restrained or on a leash at all times while in developed recreation areas. **Fires:** In fire rings, stoves, grills, or fireplaces provided for that purpose. **Alcoholic Beverages:** Not allowed. **Vehicle Maximum Length:** Call ahead.

TO GET THERE

From Redfield, AR, at the intersection of US 65 and SR 46, go east on SR 46, then to SR 365, then north 1 block, then 4 mi. east to Tar Camp Park. Follow signs into the campground.

POCAHONTAS — MAP, B-3
Old Davidsonville State Park

7953 Hwy. 166 South, 72455. T: (870) 892-4708 or (870) 892-7650; www.arkansasstateparks.com.

🚐 ★★★★   ⛺ ★★★★

Beauty: ★★★★	Site Privacy: ★★★★
Spaciousness: ★★★★★	Quiet: ★★★★★
Security: ★★★★	Cleanliness: ★★★★
Insect Control: ★★★★	Facilities: ★★★

RV sites in this park are located on either side of a single, internal, looped road. Tent sites are walk-ins from a common parking area in the southeast corner. All campsites are spacious, forested spaces with a (mostly) dirt floor. Of the RV sites, 4, 8, 16, and 20 are 120-foot pull-throughs, while the rest of the sites run from 45 feet (1) or 75 feet (3) in length. Sites 10 and 11 are a double, suitable for a group camping. Sites 18, 19, and 24 are slightly less desirable sites: 18 is set right on the road, with little privacy; 19 is extremely close to several tent sites; and 24 is located right on the path that leads to the bath house, ensuring loads of passing foot traffic. All other sites are very nice, and even these three are only slightly worse-off. The tenting area consists of a very spacious walk-in area behind site 19. One (unnumbered) site in the northeast corner of this area is situated well away from the others, and therefore offers more privacy. The restrooms and showers are extremely clean, modern, and spacious. The camp-

ground is very comfortable for both tenters and RVers, and offers a glimpse into frontier life in Arkansas from the early 1800s.

BASICS

Operated By: Arkansas Dept. of Parks & Tourism. **Open:** All year; limited service Dec.–Feb. **Site Assignment:** First come, first served; reservations require 1-night deposit made 5 days in advance; cancellation requires 5-day notice; 1-night deposit non-refundable. **Registration:** At visitor center, 8 a.m.–5 p.m. (Late arrivals select site & register next morning after 8 a.m.) **Fee:** $9–$18.50; V, MC, AE, D, check. **Parking:** At site.

FACILITIES

Number of RV-only Sites: 24. **Number of Tent-only Sites:** 15. **Hookups:** Electric (20 amps), water. **Each Site:** Picnic table, grill, fire pit, trees. **Dump Station:** Yes. **Laundry:** No. **Pay Phone:** Yes. **Restrooms and Showers:** Yes. **Fuel:** 10 mi. in Pocahontas. **Propane:** 10 mi. in Pocahontas. **Internal Roads:** Paved. **RV Service:** 45 min. to Jonesboro. **Market:** 10 mi. to Pocahontas. **Restaurant:** 10 mi. to Pocahontas. **General Store:** 1 mi. **Vending:** Yes. **Swimming:** No. **Playground:** Yes. **Other:** Pavilion, boat ramp, historical exhibits, canoe rentals, gift shop, campfire ring. **Activities:** Boating, hiking, fishing, volleyball. **Nearby Attractions:** Black River, Old Davidsonville. **Additional Information:** Randolph County Chamber of Commerce, (870) 892-3956.

RESTRICTIONS

Pets: On leash, cleaned up after. **Fires:** Grill only. **Alcoholic Beverages:** At sites (preferably in non-descript containers). **Vehicle Maximum Length:** No limit. **Other:** No fireworks, no firearms, no metal detectors, no excavating.

TO GET THERE

From the junction of Hwy. 62 and Hwy. 166, turn south onto Hwy. 166 and go 8.5 mi. (Be sure to follow Hwy. 166 as it turns to the left after 8 mi.) Follow the road straight into the park.

ROGERS — MAP, B-1
Rogers/Pea Ridge Garden RV and Campground

15170 Hwy. 62 East, 72732. T: (479) 451-8566; www.gardenrv.com.

🚐 ★★★★   ⛺ ★★★★

Beauty: ★★★★	Site Privacy: ★★★
Spaciousness: ★★★	Quiet: ★★★★★
Security: ★★★★	Cleanliness: ★★★★★
Insect Control: ★★★★	Facilities: ★★★★

Sites in this campground are mostly undeveloped, being grassy or, at most, gravel. However, this lends a natural feel to the entire campground that many campers will enjoy. Sites 1–15 are 75-foot pull-throughs, of which 1–8 are mostly without shade. (Sites 10–15 are forested.) Sites 22–26 are smaller (42–54-feet) back-ins, and a little crunched for space. 23 is a 60-foot pull-through at the tip of the island inside the looped road. Sites 44 and 45 are 75-foot back-ins that back to the forest, and are the most secluded sites in the park. The tent spaces,

32–40, are in fact one large open space fit for tents. This area has lots of trees but a rather thin grass cover. Tent sites 48 and 50, by the entrance, have crushed gravel pads and loads of shade. The laundry facility is small but very clean. The restrooms are likewise clean and very bright. This campground is a very comfortable stay for both RVers and tenters.

BASICS

Operated By: Leslie Thomas & Jack Maertens. **Open:** All year. **Site Assignment:** Upon registration; V or MC required for reservation, 24-hour cancellation policy. **Registration:** At office. (Late arrivals use drop box.) **Fee:** RV (full), $22; water/electric, $20; tent, $13.50; V, MC, check. **Parking:** At site.

FACILITIES

Number of RV-only Sites: 41. **Number of Tent-only Sites:** Undesignated sites. **Hookups:** Electric (20, 30, 50 amps), water, sewer. **Each Site:** Picnic table, grill (most sites). **Dump Station:** Yes. **Laundry:** Yes. **Pay Phone:** Yes. **Restrooms and Showers:** Yes. **Fuel:** No, 0.5 mi. **Propane:** No. **Internal Roads:** Gravel. **RV Service:** No, 0.5 mi. **Market:** 2 mi. on Hwy. 62. **Restaurant:** 0.5 mi. **General Store:** Yes. **Vending:** No. **Swimming:** Pool. **Playground:** Yes. **Other:** Game room, w/in 15 minutes of fishing areas, cabins, pet walk, swimming pool. **Activities:** Fishing, boating, swimming. **Nearby Attractions:** Pea Ridge Military Park, War Eagle Cavern, Beaver Lake. **Additional Information:** Rogers Chamber of Commerce, (501) 636-1240.

RESTRICTIONS

Pets: On leash, cleaned up after. **Fires:** Grill only. **Alcoholic Beverages:** At sites. **Vehicle Maximum Length:** No limit. **Other:** Extended-stay campers have a 3-dog limit.

TO GET THERE

From I-340 (Exit 82), exit onto Hwy. 62 and go 10.6 mi. Turn left at the sign into the entrance.

ROYAL   MAP, C-1
Joplin

reserve america™

1201 Blakely Dam Rd, 71968-9493.
T: (501) 767-2108; www.reserveamerica.com.

🚐 ★★★   ⛺ ★★★★

Beauty: ★★★★	Site Privacy: ★★★
Spaciousness: ★★★	Quiet: ★★★★★
Security: ★★★★★	Cleanliness: ★★★★
Insect Control: ★★★	Facilities: ★★★

Joplin Campground is located on Lake Ouachita in Arkansas. The lake at normal power pool extends approximately 30 miles and has a water surface of 40,000 acres. Come explore the scenic beauty of Lake Ouachita with its surrounding mountain ranges and beautiful array of seasonal colors. Have fun on the lake while exploring the many wonders of nature on one of the cleanest lakes in the country (according to the EPA). Nestled in the hills of the Ouachita National Forest, where no homes are

allowed, Lake Ouachita has over 1,000 miles of shoreline and over 200 islands where you can find your own private beach. One area of the lake features one of the largest crystal veins in the world. This lake is a scuba diver's heaven with crystal-clear water featuring rare jellyfish (nonstinging) and sponges found in only a very few of the cleanest freshwater lakes. World-class striped bass abound here as do most types of freshwater fish. Bald eagles are an attraction for the visitors during the winter. The campground consists of 64 sites, 62 with electric hookups. The campsites do not have water connections but a water faucet is located in each loop of sites for camper use. Other amenities include a dump station, fish cleaning station, hot showers, boat ramp, and a swim beach.

BASICS

Operated By: U.S. Army Corps of Engineers. **Open:** All year. **Site Assignment:** Reservations must be made at least 3 days in advance. **Registration:** At office. **Fee:** Single, $8–$14. **Parking:** At site.

FACILITIES

Number of Multipurpose Sites: 98. **Hookups:** Yes. **Dump Station:** Yes. **Laundry:** Yes. **Pay Phone:** No. **Restrooms and Showers:** Yes. **Fuel:** No. **Propane:** No. **Internal Roads:** Paved. **RV Service:** No. **Market:** No. **Restaurant:** No. **General Store:** No. **Vending:** No. **Swimming:** Yes. **Playground:** No. **Activities:** Skiing, scuba diving, boating, & other water activities.

RESTRICTIONS

Pets: Pets must be restrained or on a leash at all times while in developed recreation areas. **Fires:** In fire rings, stoves, grills, or fireplaces provided for that purpose. **Alcoholic Beverages:** Not allowed. **Vehicle Maximum Length:** Call ahead. **Other:** No ATVs allowed. No paved camping pads.

TO GET THERE

From Hot Springs, take US 270 west approx. 23.5 mi. to Mountain Harbor Rd. Turn right and follow access road 3 mi. north to the park.

SILOAM SPRINGS   MAP, B-1
Wilderness Hills RV Park and Campground

13776 Taylor Orchard Rd., 72734-8833.
T: (479) 524-4955.

🚐 ★★★★   ⛺ ★★★★

Beauty: ★★★★	Site Privacy: ★★★★★
Spaciousness: ★★★★★	Quiet: ★★★★★
Security: ★★★★	Cleanliness: ★★★★
Insect Control: ★★★★	Facilities: ★★

Located in a wilderness setting and surrounded by forest, this campground is shady and quiet. RV sites are huge pull-throughs (75–95-feet) laid out in two strips, and all are well shaded. Sites 1–10 are farthest from the office, but closest to the entrance. (Sites 1–5 are the farthest from everything—but not by much.) Sites 3 and 4, as well as 5 and 6, are angled into each other, which makes them slightly less private. The longest sites in the campground are 11–15,

which are an impressive 95 feet in length. Tenting space is located in the southeast corner. Like the RV sites, this area is well shaded, and it is closest to the undeveloped forest. While there is but thin grass cover, the dirt is soft and will easily take tent spikes. Tenters will especially enjoy the "lost" atmosphere of this park, although anyone in search of a quiet night in the woods will appreciate it.

BASICS

Operated By: Robert Hammersla. **Open:** All year. **Site Assignment:** Upon registration; verbal reservations OK; first come, first served. **Registration:** At office. (Late arrivals use drop box.) **Fee:** RV (full), $22; water/electric, $18; tent, $13; check, no credit cards. **Parking:** At site.

FACILITIES

Number of RV-only Sites: 25. **Number of Tent-only Sites:** 5. **Hookups:** Electric (30, 50 amps), water, sewer. **Each Site:** Picnic table, grill. **Dump Station:** No (sewer at all sites). **Laundry:** No. **Pay Phone:** Yes. **Restrooms and Showers:** Yes. **Fuel:** 2 mi. **Propane:** 2 mi. **Internal Roads:** Gravel. **RV Service:** No. **Market:** 2 mi. southwest to Siloam Springs. **Restaurant:** 2 mi. southwest to Siloam Springs. **General Store:** No. **Vending:** Yes. **Swimming:** No. **Playground:** No. **Other:** Data port, lake, stream, golf course, cabins, horseshoes. **Activities:** Fishing, golf, antique, flea markets, horseshoes. **Nearby Attractions:** Ozark National Forest, Beaver Lake. **Additional Information:** Chamber of Commerce, (501) 524-6466.

RESTRICTIONS

Pets: On leash, cleaned up after, quiet. **Fires:** Grill only. **Alcoholic Beverages:** At sites. **Vehicle Maximum Length:** No limit.

TO GET THERE

From the junction of Hwy. 595 and Hwy. 412 East in town (just west of the Arkansas state line), go east on Hwy. 412 for 1.5 mi. Turn left onto Mt. Olive St. and go 1.9 mi. Turn right onto Dawn Hill Rd. and go 1.85 mi. Turn left onto Taylor Orchard Rd. and go 1.3 mi. Turn right at the sign into the campground.

TICHNOR   MAP, C-2, C-3
Merrisach Lake

reserve america™

PFO 35 Wild Goose Lane , 72166.
T: (870) 548-2291; www.reserveamerica.com.

🚐 ★★★★   ⛺ ★★★★

Beauty: ★★★	Site Privacy: ★★★
Spaciousness: ★★★	Quiet: ★★★★
Security: ★★★★	Cleanliness: ★★★★
Insect Control: ★★★	Facilities: ★★★

The Merrisach Lake Campground is located near the Wilbur D. Mills Lock on the Arkansas Post Canal. The area provides an excellent opportunity for visitors to camp, fish, hike, and enjoy nature's wondrous beauty. Lock No. 2 is located on the artificial Arkansas Post Canal, which connects the Arkansas

River with the White River. Wilber D. Mills Dam is located on the main stem of the Arkansas River. Overnight camping is available in Merrisach Lake Park near Lock No. 2, Wilbur D. Mills Park downstream from the dam, and Pendleton Bend Park upstream from the dam. World-class bass and crappie fishing is found in Pool 2. The tailwaters of the dam and Joe Hardin Dam upstream provide excellent opportunities to catch catfish. In the Arkansas area visitors can experience history at the national memorial at Arkansas Post. Here, in 1686, Henri de Tonti established the first village west of the Mississippi River. In 1819 Arkansas Post became the capital of the Arkansas Territory and was so until the Civil War. Parks offer modern amenities such as boat-launching ramps, drinking water, camping areas, picnic sites and other facilities for the convenience of all.

BASICS

Operated By: U.S. Army Corps of Engineers. **Open:** All year. **Site Assignment:** Reservations must be made at least 3 days in advance. **Registration:** At office. **Fee:** Single, $9–$17; group, $30–$40. **Parking:** At site.

FACILITIES

Number of Multipurpose Sites: 179. **Hookups:** Yes. **Dump Station:** Yes. **Laundry:** No. **Pay Phone:** No. **Restrooms and Showers:** Yes. **Fuel:** Nearby. **Propane:** No. **Internal Roads:** Paved, gravel. **RV Service:** No. **Market:** No. **Restaurant:** Nearby. **General Store:** No. **Vending:** No. **Swimming:** No. **Playground:** Yes. **Activities:** Fishing, hunting, wildlife viewing.

RESTRICTIONS

Pets: Pets must be restrained or on a leash at all times while in developed recreation areas. **Fires:** In fire rings, stoves, grills, or fireplaces provided for that purpose. **Alcoholic Beverages:** Not allowed. **Vehicle Maximum Length:** Call ahead.

TO GET THERE

From DeWitt, take US 165 south for 8.1 mi. to AR 44. Follow AR 44 east for 5.3 mi. to Tichnor and travel Tichnor Blacktop Rd. 8.2 mi. south to Merrisach Lake Lane. Go 1 mi. west, following signs into the campground.

WIEDERKEHR   MAP, B-1
Wiederkehr Wine Cellars RV Park

3324 Swiss Family Dr., 72821. T: (800) 622-WINE or (479) 468-WINE.

🚐 ★★★	⛺ ★★★
Beauty: ★★★★	Site Privacy: ★★★
Spaciousness: ★★★	Quiet: ★★★★
Security: ★★★★	Cleanliness: ★★★★
Insect Control: ★★★★	Facilities: ★★

This campground is west of a restaurant, gift shop, and office complex, and north of Arkansas River Valley vineyards. The park itself is little more than a large open parking lot of a gravel, grass, and dirt. Sites 1–10 back up to woods, while 11–20 back up to a pretty agricultural setting. Site 1 is partly in long prairie-type grass, but is close to a shade tree. Sites 7

and 8 are shaded, as is 20. This latter site is probably in the nicest location, as it is farthest from the restaurant complex and next to a large tree. Sites 9–12 are closest to the visitor parking lot. While there is no real maximum length to the vehicles this park can accommodate during off-season, it is unrealistic to haul more than 50 feet during the September wine fest—the best time to come to this park (at least, if you don't mind crowds). Tents can cover the entire field to the west during the wine fest, making it difficult to find a spot. There are few trees anyway, so most tenters will be in the same boat—camping on a hill with no shower facility. Of course, the atmosphere of the festival can override other concerns, but tenters (and RVers without indoor showers) must remember that they will have to spend a day or so without showering. There is one modern unisex restroom that must surely be packed during the festival. This campground is a somewhat dull park without many facilities, although the atmosphere of the restaurant and the wine fest help make up for these shortcomings.

BASICS

Operated By: Gary Wiederkehr. **Open:** All year. **Site Assignment:** First come, first served (reservations only for wine fest). **Registration:** At office, shop, or restaurant. (Late arrivals select site & pay in the morning.) **Fee:** RV, $10 (water/electric); tent, $10; MC, AE, D, DC, CB, check. **Parking:** At site.

FACILITIES

Number of RV-only Sites: 20. **Number of Tent-only Sites:** Undesignated sites. **Hookups:** Electric (20, 30 amps), water. **Dump Station:** No. **Laundry:** No. **Pay Phone:** No. **Restrooms and Showers:** Restrooms; no shower. **Fuel:** No. **Propane:** No. **Internal Roads:** Gravel. **RV Service:** No. **Market:** 2 mi. to Altus. **Restaurant:** On site. **General Store:** No. **Vending:** No. **Swimming:** No. **Playground:** No. **Other:** Gift shop, vineyards. **Activities:** Picnics in vineyards, shopping, wine tasting. **Nearby Attractions:** Wineries, antique shops, museums, canoeing. **Additional Information:** Altus Chamber of Commerce, (479) 468-4684.

RESTRICTIONS

Pets: On leash, cleaned up after. **Fires:** Grill only; subject to seasonal bans. **Alcoholic Beverages:** At sites. **Vehicle Maximum Length:** No limit.

TO GET THERE

From I-40 (Exit 41), turn south onto Hwy. 186 and go 4.6 mi. Turn right at the sign into the entrance.

WYNNE   MAP, B-3
Village Creek State Park

201 CR 754, 72396. T: (870) 238-9406; www.arkansasstateparks.com.

🚐 ★★★★	⛺ ★★★★
Beauty: ★★★★	Site Privacy: ★★★★
Spaciousness: ★★★★	Quiet: ★★★★★
Security: ★★★★	Cleanliness: ★★★
Insect Control: ★★★	Facilities: ★★★★

This is a large campground divided up into three camping areas: South (1–41), West (42–73), and

North (74–104), in order from the entrance. All sites are forested and have a paved parking area for an RV or other vehicle. Most sites open to a grassy field that campers can use for recreation. The South Area consists of two loops in a figure 8, the more northerly of the two loops containing reservable sites. Sites 1 and 8 are set very close to the road, which makes them less desirable; while 7 is set back farther than most, making it rather more private. Sites 23 and 24 are on either side of a hiking trailhead, and may experience more foot traffic for this reason. Sites 25 and 26 together form a double. The West Area is close to Lake Dunn; sites 46–50 are the closest campsites to the swimming beach. Sites 53–57 back to the lake (with a strip of forest behind them), while 59 is close to the restroom. Sites 48 and 49 make a double, and 72 and 73 are very close to one another. 60–67 are located on a side street, making them slightly more private. Of these sites, 61 and 62 are the most remote. The North Area contains the most number of doubles, which will interest groups of campers. These include sites 75 and 76, 93 and 94, and 101 and 102. Site 74 is right at the entrance, but 85 and 86 are tucked away in a corner. This is a pleasant wilderness campground that will appeal to many campers for its quiet and natural setting.

BASICS

Operated By: Arkansas Dept. of Parks & Tourism. **Open:** All year. **Site Assignment:** First come, first served; reservations require 1-night deposit made 5 days in advance; cancellation requires 5-day notice; first night's deposit nonrefundable. **Registration:** At visitor center. (Late arrivals select site & register next morning after 8 a.m.) **Fee:** $9–$25.50; 8 person limit; V, MC, AE, D, check. **Parking:** At site.

FACILITIES

Number of RV-only Sites: 96. **Hookups:** Electric (20, 30, 50 amps), water. **Each Site:** Picnic table; fire pit; tent pad (only at 37 sites). **Dump Station:** Yes. **Laundry:** No. **Pay Phone:** Yes. **Restrooms and Showers:** Yes. **Fuel:** W/in 1 mi. **Propane:** W/in 1 mi. **Internal Roads:** Paved. **RV Service:** No. **Market:** 7 mi. to Wynne. **Restaurant:** 7 mi. to Wynne. **General Store:** Yes. **Vending:** Yes. **Swimming:** Lake. **Playground:** Yes. **Other:** Cabins, auditorium. **Activities:** Tennis, hiking, driving range, basketball, bicycles for rent. **Nearby Attractions:** Village Creek State Park, Parking Arch State Park. **Additional Information:** Chamber of Commerce, (870) 238-2601.

RESTRICTIONS

Pets: On leash, cleaned up after, not in cabins. **Fires:** Grill only. **Alcoholic Beverages:** At sites (preferably in nondescript containers). **Vehicle Maximum Length:** No limit.

TO GET THERE

From the junction of Hwy. 1 and Hwy. 64B/284, turn east onto Hwy. 64B/284, and go 1.9 mi., making sure to take the 2 turns w/in the first 0.7 mi. to stay on this highway. At the junction of Hwy. 64B and Hwy. 284, go 4.9 mi. south on Hwy. 284. Turn left at the sign into the park entrance.

YELLVILLE
Buffalo Point

MAP, B-2

2229 Hwy. 268 East, 72687. T: (870) 449-4311;
www.reserveamerica.com.

🚐 ★★★★   ⛺ ★★★★

Beauty: ★★★★	Site Privacy: ★★★
Spaciousness: ★★★★	Quiet: ★★★★
Security: ★★★★★	Cleanliness: ★★★★
Insect Control: ★★★	Facilities: ★★★★

Buffalo Point offers campsites with water and electricity and the only restaurant within the park. Two popular attractions within the Buffalo Point Area are the Indian Rockhouse Trail and the Rush Historic District. Rush was a zinc-mining community until the bottom fell out of the zinc market and the settlement became a ghost town. Buffalo Point is the former Buffalo River State Park, developed in the 1930s as project of the Civilian Conservation Corps (CCC). The area known as Buffalo Point was developed through cooperation among the National Park Service, the CCC, and the Arkansas State Parks Commission, and was established as Buffalo River State Park in 1938. All of the Civilian Conservation Corps structures are listed on the National Register of Historic Places. Several hiking trails ranging in length from 0.25 miles to 3.5 miles lead hikers to a scenic vista, caves, a waterfall, and other interesting features. Interpretive programs are given regularly in the summer. Schedules and trail guides are available at the fanger station. Doc Dillard built the original ferry (named Dillard's Ferry) with his sons Ira and Pate and W. Davenport in the early 1900s. The old ferry crossing is just a few yards downstream from the present bridge and was in operation until the bridge was completed in 1959. In December 1982 a flood covered the bridge. The river was about 65 feet above normal water level, making this the biggest flood in the river's recorded history.

BASICS

Operated By: National Park Service. **Open:** All year. **Site Assignment:** Reservations must be made 3 days in advance. **Registration:** At registration office. **Fee:** Single, $15–$20; group, $53. **Parking:** At site.

FACILITIES

Number of Multipurpose Sites: 236. **Hookups:** Yes. **Each Site:** Call ahead. **Dump Station:** Yes. **Laundry:** No. **Pay Phone:** Yes. **Restrooms and Showers:** Yes. **Fuel:** No. **Propane:** No. **Internal Roads:** Paved. **RV Service:** No. **Market:** No. **Restaurant:** Yes. **General Store:** No. **Vending:** No. **Swimming:** Yes. **Playground:** No. **Activities:** Amphitheater, biking, bird-watching, boating, campfire programs, fishing, hiking, kayaking, photography, sightseeing, wildlife viewing.

RESTRICTIONS

Pets: Pets are not allowed on trails. **Fires:** Allowed; Campfire Program. **Alcoholic Beverages:** Not allowed. **Vehicle Maximum Length:** Varies; call ahead. **Other:** Generators prohibited 8 p.m.–8 a.m. Draining wastewater onto the ground from vehicles or trailers is not allowed.

TO GET THERE

From Springfield, MO: Take Hwy. 65 South through Branson to Harrison. Stay on Hyw. 65 through Harrison. Turn left on Hwy. 62 and travel to Yellville. At Yellville turn right on Hwy. 14 East. Travel 17 mi. to Hwy. 268 East. Turn left on Hwy. 268 to Buffalo Point. From Little Rock, AR: Take Hwy. 65 North to Marshall; at Marshall turn right on Hwy. 27 North and go approx. 11 mi. to Harriet. Turn left on Hwy. 14 West and travel approx. 14 mi. to Hwy. 268 East. Turn right on Hwy. 268 to Buffalo Point.

California

California's motto, Eureka, means "I have found it!" That sentiment is just as applicable to campers today as it was when it was first adopted a century and a half ago by the forty niners of the Gold Rush era. Indeed, the camping prospects are richer by far than what remains of the Golden State's mineral resources. From its 840 miles of shoreline, millions of acres of federal land, and 264 state parks (with scores more on the county level), California's scenery is a glittering reflection of all that is rare and wonderful in the natural beauty of the United States. With the relatively mild climate, many campgrounds here remain open all year.

As one might expect in a state California's size, this is a land packed with extremes and superlatives: from **Mount Whitney,** the highest peak in the Lower 48 states, to **Badwater** in **Death Valley,** the lowest point in the Western Hemisphere. Its coast redwoods are the tallest trees in the world, and the bristlecone pines of the **Inyo National Forest** are the planet's oldest living organisms. To the south are sun-parched deserts awash in cacti and colorfully eroded landscapes that explode with wildflowers in the spring. Up north are the **Cascade Mountains,** iced with snow, scarred by lava, laced with trout streams, alpine lakes, and thousands of miles of hiking trails. In between are a few snow-crusted glaciers in the **Sierra Nevada Mountains,** one crashing waterfall after another, especially in **Yosemite Valley,** more national parks and monuments than any other state in the country, and a number of historical sites honoring Native American, Spanish, and Mexican explorers and African and Chinese pioneers, among others.

Beyond its silky-smooth beaches and tide pools, where passing whales and nesting seals can be observed, in addition to the superb fishing and boating in pristine lakes, rivers, and reservoirs, California's abundance of wildlife is icing on the camper's cake. Grizzly bears are long gone, but you will find Tule elk, Roosevelt elk, and fallow deer among the animals gracing the coastal preserves; bighorn sheep, kangaroo rats, and desert tortoises in the arid areas; and black bears, coyotes, and black-tail deer roaming throughout. One needn't be a sharp-eyed birder to enjoy the sight of condors, Canada geese, bald and golden eagles, acorn woodpeckers, hummingbirds, California quails, and herons of various types soaring above the oaks or winging across the marshlands.

Under the Clinton presidency, the Golden State gained the newly created **Mojave National Preserve** and two national monuments, **Carrizo Plain** and **Giant Sequoia.** The domains of **Pinnacles National Monument, Death Valley,** and **Joshua Tree National Parks** were substantially expanded. Hundreds of properties within California's national forests have been revamped and are now run by concessionaires intent on keeping them clean, secure, and profitable. Dispersed camping on lands administered by the U.S. Forest Service and Bureau of Land Management offers serious solitude-seekers and the budget-minded a less structured approach to camping.

The 31st state also is chockfull of fascinating destinations should you get an itch for the kitsch. Just outside San Francisco Airport in Burlingame, you can relive your childhood while at the **Museum of Pez Memorabilia.** Every October, the Santa Barbara County city of Carpinteria hosts its **Avocado Festival,** where it is highly probable that you will be encouraged by the locals to participate in helping create the world's largest bowl of guacamole. But if what you really desire is to be in the middle of things, we suggest a trek to Felicity, otherwise known as the **Center of the World**, and have your name not only inscribed on the **Wall for the Ages** but entered into the electronic archive.

Whatever your interests and however you like to camp, despite the confines of your itinerary, California has so much beauty and space that on pulling into a campground you may well feel inspired to imitate the Forty-Niners by exclaiming with exuberance, "Eureka!"

Campground Profiles

ANGELS CAMP   MAP, C-3
Glory Hole Recreation Area

reserve america

Glory Hole Rd., 95222. T: (209) 536-9094;
www.reserveamerica.com.

🚐 ★★★★   ⛺ ★★★★

Beauty: ★★★★	Site Privacy: ★★★
Spaciousness: ★★★	Quiet: ★★★★
Security: ★★★★	Cleanliness: ★★★★
Insect Control: ★★★	Facilities: ★★★★

Glory Hole Recreation Area is located at New Melones Lake. New Melones Lake, the fifth largest lake in California, is located on the Stanislaus River. The 12,500 surface acre lake is situated along the edge of the Mother Lode, the rich gold vein that prompted the 1849 California Gold Rush. New Melones Lake sits at an elevation of 1088 feet, with more than 100 miles of shoreline covered with trees and brushlands. The lake is administered by the Bureau of Reclamation, U.S. Department of the Interior. The dam and recreational facilities were constructed by the U.S. Army Corp of Engineers. There are two recreation areas at New Melones Lake with camping facilities. The Glory Hole Recreation Area contains 144 campsites for overnight use. The Tuttletown Recreation Area has 106 sites at present with another campground planned for future use. Fish to be found at New Melones include largemouth bass, rainbow and German brown trout, catfish, crappie, and bluegill are the most common. Fishing season is all year, and limits are set by the California Department of Fish and Game. The lake was constructed by the Corps of Engineers and transferred to the Bureau of Reclamation shortly after its completion in 1980. The responsibility to complete the cultural-resources programs was transferred to the Secretary of the Interior. The Washington office of the National Park Service's Interagency Archeological Services was assigned the task of completing the archeological mitigation. Reclamation was designated the lead federal agency for compliance with the National Historic Preservation Act, and was assigned to manage the historic properties, address the storage and management of the extensive collections, and develop an interpretative program.

BASICS
Operated By: U.S. Army Corps of Engineers. **Open:** All year. **Site Assignment:** Reservations must be made at least 2 days in advance. **Registration:** At office. **Fee:** Single, $12–$16. **Parking:** At site.

FACILITIES
Number of Multipurpose Sites: 504. **Hookups:** None. **Dump Station:** No. **Laundry:** No. **Pay Phone:** No. **Restrooms and Showers:** Yes. **Fuel:** No. **Propane:** No. **Internal Roads:** Paved. **RV Service:** No. **Market:** No. **Restaurant:** No. **General Store:** No. **Vending:** No. **Swimming:** No. **Playground:** Yes.

RESTRICTIONS
Pets: Pets must be restrained or on a leash at all times while in developed recreation areas. **Fires:** In fire rings, stoves, grills, or fireplaces provided for that purpose. **Alcoholic Beverages:** Not allowed. **Vehicle Maximum Length:** Total vehicle & equipment length must not exceed driveway length. No extra vehicles allowed. All vehicles must park on parking pads.

TO GET THERE
From Sacramento take Hwy. 99 south to Hwy. 12 at Lodi. Then take Hwy. 12 east to Hwy. 49 at San Andreas. Then take Hwy. 49 south approximately 15.2 mi. Turn right onto Glory Hole Rd. and follow the road 3 mi. to the campgrounds. From Central California take Hwy. 108 east from Modesto to Hwy. 49 at Sonora. Then take Hwy. 49 north approximately 17 mi. Turn left onto Glory Hole Rd. and follow the road 3 mi. to the campgrounds. Alternatively, take Hwy. 4 east from Stockton to Hwy. 49 at Angels Camp. Then take Hwy. 49 south approximately 3.3 mi. Turn right onto Glory Hole Rd. and follow the road 3 mi. to the campgrounds.

BAKER   MAP, E-4
Hole-in-the-Wall

Mojave National Preserve, Black Canyon Rd., 92311. T: (760) 928-2572 or (760) 252-6100; www.nps.gov/moja.

🚐 ★★★   ⛺ ★★★★

Beauty: ★★★★	Site Privacy: ★★★
Spaciousness: ★★★	Quiet: ★★★★
Security: ★★★	Cleanliness: ★★★★
Insect Control: ★★★★	Facilities: ★★★

If you chanced to visit this campground when the Mojave National Preserve was first created in 1994, there was a very good likelihood that you had the entire grounds to yourself. Times have changed as word has spread about the subtle beauty of this area, and now you will probably have neighbors. Unless, of course, you make the mistake of visiting this piece of desert in summer when it becomes a sweltering inferno without a single shade tree to be found in the camp's single loop. But at an elevation of 4,400 feet, Hole-in-the-Wall can be pretty comfortable in both autumn and spring, even if late afternoon winds often require the donning of jackets and hats for warmth. And while the yucca plants and pencil chollas don't provide much in the way of screening, sites, with both pull-through and back-in parking, are roomy, well spaced apart, and attractively positioned just below a rough looking canyon. The sunset view of the surrounding mountains is an added plus, as is the Rings Trail hike, with its trailhead half a mile to the south.

BASICS
Operated By: National Park Service. **Open:** All year. **Site Assignment:** First come, first served. **Registration:** At entrance kiosk. **Fee:** $12; cash, check. **Parking:** At site.

FACILITIES
Number of RV-only Sites: 35. **Number of Tent-only Sites:** 2. **Hookups:** None. **Each Site:** Picnic table, fire ring. **Dump Station:** Yes. **Laundry:** No. **Pay Phone:** Yes, at Hole-in-the Wall Visitor Center, 0.5 mi. south. **Restrooms and Showers:** Vaulted toilets, no showers. **Fuel:** No. **Propane:** No. **Internal Roads:** Dirt, in good condition. **RV Service:** No. **Market:** 60 mi. west in Baker. **Restaurant:** 60 mi. west in Baker. **General Store:** No, 28 mi. in Fenner. **Vending:** No. **Swimming:** No. **Playground:** No. **Other:** Some wheelchair-accessible sites, information center. **Activities:** Hiking, bicycling, horseback riding. **Nearby Attractions:** Mitchell Caverns, Kelso Dunes, Teutonia Peak. **Additional Information:** Mojave Desert Information Center, (760) 733-4040.

RESTRICTIONS
Pets: On 6-ft. leash. **Fires:** Fire ring only. **Alcoholic Beverages:** Allowed at site. **Vehicle Maximum Length:** No limit. **Other:** 14-day stay limit; no loaded firearms.

TO GET THERE
Exit I-40 at Essex Rd., drive 10 mi. north and turn right on Black Canyon Rd. Drive 10.3 mi. and turn left into campground. Or: Exit I-15 at Cima Rd. and drive south for 22 mi. Turn left on Cedar Canyon Rd. and after 6 mi. turn right on Black Canyon Rd. Proceed for 9.5 mi. to the campground on the right.

BALLICO   MAP, D-1
McConnell SRA

reserve america

8800 McConnell Rd., 95303. T: (209) 394-7755; www.reserveamerica.com.

🚐 ★★★   ⛺ ★★★★

Beauty: ★★★	Site Privacy: ★★★
Spaciousness: ★★★	Quiet: ★★★★
Security: ★★★★	Cleanliness: ★★★★
Insect Control: ★★★	Facilities: ★★

McConnell State Recreation Area is on the banks of the Merced River. Fishing is popular for catfish, black bass and perch. There are over 70 acres of picnic, camping, and play areas. Trees in the park attract migrant songbirds during migration and, in the winter, sparrows, thrushes, and woodpeckers. There are 21 sites for tents or RVs up to 24 feet long and two group sites for tents only. Piped water, fire grills, and picnic tables are provided. Flush toilets and hot showers are available. Supplies can be obtained in Delhi, 3 miles away. Leashed pets are permitted. Three sites are designated as accessible to the disabled. The campfire center has been redesigned and now includes an accessible path of travel and some spaces for wheelchair users. Group campsite B provides accessible tables and cooking facilities that are on a firm grass surface whose usability is best in dry weather. Parking includes two spaces designated accessible, and paths of travel to site and restroom are paved and accessible. The route to the restroom requires passing behind other vehicles in the small parking lot. For beach access, a beach wheelchair is available.

BASICS

Operated By: California State Parks. **Open:** All year. **Site Assignment:** Reservations can be made 7 months in advance. **Registration:** At office. **Fee:** Single, $13–$20; group, $32–$110. **Parking:** At site.

FACILITIES

Number of Multipurpose Sites: 21. **Hookups:** None. **Dump Station:** No. **Laundry:** No. **Pay Phone:** No. **Restrooms and Showers:** Yes. **Fuel:** No. **Propane:** No. **Internal Roads:** Paved. **RV Service:** No. **Market:** No. **Restaurant:** No. **General Store:** No. **Vending:** No. **Swimming:** Yes. **Playground:** No. **Activities:** Fishing, picnicking.

RESTRICTIONS

Pets: On 6-ft. leash in a tent or enclosed vehicle at night. Except for guide dogs, pets are not allowed in park buildings, on trails, or on most beaches. **Fires:** In designated fireplaces. **Alcoholic Beverages:** Not allowed. **Other:** Fees include entry for 1 vehicle & 1 legally towed vehicle or trailer, additional vehicles will be charged per night at the park.

TO GET THERE

The recreation area is 5 mi. southeast of Delhi on Hwy. 99, south of Turlock.

BASS LAKE — MAP, D-2
Lupine-Cedar Bluff

reserve america

C.R. 222, 93604. T: (559) 877-2218 or (877) 444-6777; www.reserveamerica.com.

🚐 ★★★★   ▲ ★★

Beauty: ★★★★	Site Privacy: ★★
Spaciousness: ★★	Quiet: ★★★
Security: ★★★	Cleanliness: ★★★
Insect Control: ★★	Facilities: ★★★

A question to ask before heading out to this campground is, how much time will you be spending at the site? Bass Lake, a pretty green mountain reservoir, is right across the street, an attractive venue for fishing, boating, and waterskiing. The surrounding national forest land and Yosemite National Park, 25 miles away, beckon to hikers. If you plan to put in most of your time soaking up the natural splendor of the environment, go ahead and book a spot at Lupine-Cedar Bluff. On second thought, make that a double. For while its hilltop setting, among an array of manzanita, oak, cedar, and pines, is superb, the exposed, grassy sites are disappointingly small and crammed right up against each other. In many cases the dimensions are so tight you won't be able to set up a tent and safely light a fire. The dozen walk-ins are a sop to tenters, as this is more of a camp for motor homes, with paved parking slips and the vast majority of its spots set aside as multiple units. There

are a handful of fine single sites, but the concession that runs this property—and dares to charge $18 a night—does not permit reservations by number, only by type (single, double, on up to quadruple).

BASICS

Operated By: California Land Management, concessionaire. **Open:** All year. **Site Assignment:** Reservations recommended w/ V, MC, D. **Registration:** At Forest Service office 2.7 mi. west of campground. **Fee:** Single site, $19; quadruple, up to $76; cash, check. **Parking:** At site or designated area for walk-ins.

FACILITIES

Number of RV-only Sites: 62. **Number of Tent-only Sites:** 12. **Hookups:** None. **Each Site:** Picnic table, fire grate. **Dump Station:** No, 2 mi. **Laundry:** No. **Pay Phone:** No. **Restrooms and Showers:** Flush toilets, no showers. **Fuel:** No. **Propane:** No. **Internal Roads:** Paved. **RV Service:** No. **Market:** 10 mi. west in Oakhurst. **Restaurant:** Several options on Bass Lake. **General Store:** No. **Vending:** No. **Swimming:** Bass Lake. **Playground:** No. **Other:** Some wheelchair-accessible facilities. **Activities:** Fishing, hiking, waterskiing, boating, eavesdropping on your neighbors. **Nearby Attractions:** Yosemite National Park; Fresno Flats Historical Site in Oakhurst; Yosemite Mountain Sugar Pine Railroad in Fish Camp, Nelder Grove of giant sequoias. **Additional Information:** Bass Lake Chamber of Commerce, (559) 642-3676.

RESTRICTIONS

Pets: On leash. **Fires:** Fire grates only. **Alcoholic Beverages:** Allowed. **Vehicle Maximum Length:** 40 ft. **Other:** 14-day stay limit.

TO GET THERE

From Oakhurst drive 3 mi. north on Hwy. 41. Turn right on CR 222 and continue for 7 mi., bearing right at 2 consecutive forks, to the campground on the right.

BIG PINE — MAP, D-3
Big Pine Creek

reserve america

Glacier Lodge Rd., 93513. T: (760) 873-2500 or (877) 444-6777; www.reserveamerica.com.

🚐 ★★★★   ▲ ★★★★

Beauty: ★★★★	Site Privacy: ★★★
Spaciousness: ★★	Quiet: ★★★
Security: ★★★	Cleanliness: ★★★
Insect Control: ★★★	Facilities: ★★

Of the several campgrounds along Glacier Lodge Rd., Big Pine Creek, at an elevation of 7,700 feet, is preferable for its green grassy look and close proximity to the rocky jaw-line of the overhanging mountains. It is a gorgeous, natural setting, shot-through with Sierra granite, a creek running by, and an abundance of Jeffrey pines complementing its flush of aspens. There is only one blemish to all this beauty, the presence of a handful of private cabins at the center of the property. As is typical of mountain camps,

many sites run toward the miniature, and seem to offer less privacy than you'd enjoy at a nudist colony. The exceptions, though, make this a winner, with the spots by the creek providing the best space and seclusion. The pick of the park are numbers 9, appealingly set in an old stone foundation, and 21–23, which are roomy and private. Showers, a snack bar, bait and tackle, and other basic supplies are available at the lodge.

BASICS

Operated By: American Land & Leisure, concessionaire. **Open:** May 12–Oct. 15, weather permitting. **Site Assignment:** First come, first served; reservations accepted w/ V, MC, D. **Registration:** At entrance kiosk. **Fee:** $13; cash, check. **Parking:** At site.

FACILITIES

Number of RV-only Sites: 25. **Number of Tent-only Sites:** 5. **Hookups:** None. **Each Site:** Picnic table, fire grate. **Dump Station:** No. **Laundry:** No. **Pay Phone:** No. **Restrooms and Showers:** Vault toilets, no showers. **Fuel:** No, available in Big Pine. **Propane:** No. **Internal Roads:** Paved, narrow & bumpy. **RV Service:** No. **Market:** 9.5 mi. east in Big Pine. **Restaurant:** 9.5 mi. east in Big Pine. **General Store:** Yes. **Vending:** No. **Swimming:** No. **Playground:** No. **Other:** Some wheelchair-accessible facilities. **Activities:** Hiking, fishing, horseback riding, photography. **Nearby Attractions:** Inyo National Forest; Ancient Bristlecone Pine Forest & Laws Railroad Museum & Historic Site in Bishop; Death Valley National Park; John Muir Wilderness. **Additional Information:** Bishop Area Chamber of Commerce & Visitors Bureau, (760) 873-8405.

RESTRICTIONS

Pets: On leash. **Fires:** Fire grates only. **Alcoholic Beverages:** Allowed. **Vehicle Maximum Length:** 35 ft. **Other:** 14-day stay limit.

TO GET THERE

From Big Pine on US 395 head west on Crocker St. (which becomes Glacier Lodge Rd.). Drive 9.5 mi. to the campground entrance on the left.

BIG PINE — MAP, D-3
Grandview

White Mountain Rd., 93514. T: (760) 873-2500; www.r5.fs.fed.us/inyo.

🚐 ★★★★   ▲ ★★★★★

Beauty: ★★★★	Site Privacy: ★★★★
Spaciousness: ★★★★★	Quiet: ★★★★★
Security: ★	Cleanliness: ★★★★
Insect Control: ★★★★	Facilities: ★

Your first question on arriving at this notably primitive place will probably be, "Where's the view?" Don't despair. While none of the remarkably spacious, well-separated sites offer vistas of anything much beyond the sage-covered meadow at the center of the large loop, walk a few minutes in almost any direction and you will find rewarding panoramas of the outlying valleys and mountain ranges. The best of this national forest land, though, lies 5 miles farther up the road, at the Ancient Bristlecone Pine

Forest, with trails leading past some of the oldest trees on the planet. (The relatively new visitor center there keeps irregular hours.) Pull-through parking slots are available at a number of sites, and most of the latter benefit at least partly from the shade cast by mature junipers, piñons, and other conifers. Weather can be scorching in late spring and early autumn, but at 8,600 feet of elevation, expect nights to be cool and quite breezy. There is no water available, and trash must be packed out.

BASICS

Operated By: Inyo National Forest, White Mountain Ranger District. **Open:** All year. **Site Assignment:** First come, first served. **Registration:** Not necessary. **Fee:** None. **Parking:** At site.

FACILITIES

Number of RV-only Sites: 26. **Hookups:** None. **Each Site:** Picnic table, fire grate. **Dump Station:** No. **Laundry:** No. **Pay Phone:** No. **Restrooms and Showers:** Vault toilets, no showers. **Fuel:** No. **Propane:** No. **Internal Roads:** Packed dirt, good condition. **RV Service:** No. **Market:** 13 mi. south in Big Pine. **Restaurant:** 13 mi. south in Big Pine. **General Store:** No. **Vending:** No. **Swimming:** No. **Playground:** No. **Activities:** Hiking, photography, stargazing. **Nearby Attractions:** Inyo National Forest; Ancient Bristlecone Pine Forest & Laws Railroad Museum & Historic Site in Bishop; Death Valley National Park. **Additional Information:** Bishop Area Chamber of Commerce & Visitors Bureau, (760) 873-8405.

RESTRICTIONS

Pets: On leash. **Fires:** Fire grates only. **Alcoholic Beverages:** Allowed. **Vehicle Maximum Length:** 40 ft. **Other:** 14-day stay limit.

TO GET THERE

From Big Pine on US 395 drive 13 mi. east on Hwy. 168. Turn left on White Mountain Rd. and continue 5.5 mi. to the campground entrance on the left.

BIG SUR · MAP, D-1
Pfeiffer Big Sur State Park

reserve america

Hwy. 1, 93920. T: (831) 667-2315 or (800) 444-7275; www.reserveamerica.com.

🚐 ★★★　　🏕 ★★★★

Beauty: ★★★★	Site Privacy: ★★
Spaciousness: ★★	Quiet: ★★★
Security: ★★★★	Cleanliness: ★★★
Insect Control: ★	Facilities: ★★★

The redwood trees of Pfeiffer Big Sur are neither the largest nor oldest along the California coast. In fact, there is a more impressive grove just 2 miles south, at the privately operated Ventana Campground. The trees are so numerous there and grow so close together that the property, with small sites priced around $40 a night, seems perpetually moist and dark. The trees at Pfeiffer, on the other hand, are big without blocking the sunlight. They comprise only

one part of three distinct habitats represented over the five dispersed loops, with an oak woodland and grassy meadows making up the balance. The Big Sur River parallels the campground, which consists of level sites of dirt and leaves. Those in the first two loops are a bit more spacious than elsewhere. There are some excellent hiking trails in this ever-popular park, with Buzzards Roost in particular delivering superb views of the surrounding hills. Poison oak is abundant around the campground and beggar squirrels can strip your table of food before you're even aware they've invaded.

BASICS

Operated By: California Dept. of Parks & Recreation. **Open:** All year. **Site Assignment:** Reservations recommended & can be made 7 months in advance for summer season; V, MC, D. **Registration:** At entrance booth. **Fee:** $16; cash, CA check. **Parking:** At site.

FACILITIES

Number of Multipurpose Sites: 214. **Hookups:** None. **Each Site:** Picnic table, fire grate, barbecue grill. **Dump Station:** Yes. **Laundry:** Yes, June–Labor Day. **Pay Phone:** Yes. **Restrooms and Showers:** Yes. **Fuel:** No. **Propane:** No. **Internal Roads:** Paved. **RV Service:** No. **Market:** 1 mi. north in Big Sur. **Restaurant:** In Big Sur Lodge, w/in the park. **General Store:** Yes. **Vending:** Yes. **Swimming:** No. **Playground:** No. **Other:** Some wheelchair-accessible facilities, Big Sur Lodge. Wood available at Big Sur Lodge. **Activities:** Hiking, beaching, winter whale-watching, redwoods exploring, photography. **Nearby Attractions:** Several state parks in the vicinity: Julia Pfeiffer Burns, Andrew Molera, Garrapata, Limekiln State Park in Lucia, Big Sur coastal vistas. **Additional Information:** Big Sur Chamber, (831) 667-2100.

RESTRICTIONS

Pets: On 6-ft. leash, not allowed on trails. **Fires:** Fire grates only. **Alcoholic Beverages:** Allowed at site. **Vehicle Maximum Length:** 32 ft. motor home, 27 ft. restriction on trailers. **Other:** 14-day stay limit (7-day limit in summers); no firearms; no wood gathering.

TO GET THERE

From the Big Sur Post Office on Hwy. 1, drive 1.5 mi. north and turn right into the campground.

BISHOP · MAP, D-2
East Fork

reserve america

Rock Creek Rd., 93514. T: (760) 873-2500 or (877) 444-6777; www.reserveamerica.com.

🚐 ★★★★　　🏕 ★★★

Beauty: ★★★★	Site Privacy: ★★★
Spaciousness: ★★	Quiet: ★★★
Security: ★★★	Cleanliness: ★★★
Insect Control: ★★★	Facilities: ★

East Fork is nestled in a rocky canyon with snow-capped Sierra peaks looming above, a thrilling set-

ting very near the gorgeous Rock Creek Lake. The creek itself gurgles through the property, which consists of a hodgepodge of sites, some shaded by lodgepole pines and junipers, others screened by aspen trees, and many exposed to the sun. While most are respectably scattered apart, sites are on the small side, with some so snug there's not enough room to set up anything but a bivvy tent. Still, we find this Inyo National Forest facility infinitely preferable to that at the lake, which is basically a campers corral in a parking lot. Creek-side site 86 is especially recessed and private, 108 is quite large, and 110–112 and 114 are very good runners-up. At 9,000 feet elevation, this high altitude camp can get hit by snow at almost any time of year, so plan your trip accordingly.

BASICS

Operated By: American Land & Leisure. **Open:** May 5–Oct. 14; weather permitting. **Site Assignment:** Reservations accepted w/ MC, V, D. **Registration:** At entrance kiosk. **Fee:** $13–$17; cash, check. **Parking:** At site.

FACILITIES

Number of RV-only Sites: 80. **Number of Tent-only Sites:** 53. **Hookups:** None. **Each Site:** Picnic table, fire grate, barbecue grill, food storage at some sites. **Dump Station:** No. **Laundry:** No. **Pay Phone:** No. **Restrooms and Showers:** Flush toilets, no showers. **Fuel:** No. **Propane:** No. **Internal Roads:** Paved. **RV Service:** No. **Market:** 21 mi. north in Mammoth Lakes. **Restaurant:** 3 mi. northeast in Toms Place. **General Store:** No. **Vending:** No. **Swimming:** No. **Playground:** No. **Activities:** Hiking, fishing, bicycling. **Nearby Attractions:** Devil's Postpile National Monument, outlet shopping in Mammoth Lakes, museums in Bishop, Ancient Bristlecone Pine Forest in the Inyo National Forest. **Additional Information:** Bishop Area Chamber of Commerce & Visitors Bureau, (760) 873-8405.

RESTRICTIONS

Pets: On leash. **Fires:** Fire grates only. **Alcoholic Beverages:** Allowed. **Vehicle Maximum Length:** 45 ft. **Other:** 14-day stay limit.

TO GET THERE

From Bishop head north on US 395 for 24 mi. Turn left (west) on Rock Creek Rd.; continue for 6 mi. and turn left to the campground access road.

BISHOP · MAP, C-3
Inyo National Forest

351 Pacu Lane, 93514. T: (760) 873-2400 or (760) 647-3044; www.fs.fed.us/r5/inyo.

🚐 ★★★★　　🏕 ★★★

Beauty: ★★★★★	Site Privacy: ★★
Spaciousness: ★★	Quiet: ★★
Security: ★★★★	Cleanliness: ★★★
Insect Control: ★	Facilities: ★

There is only one site here with a view of the camp's namesake Ellery Lake, lucky 13, a walk-in. Don't let that, or the overall lack of privacy and elbowroom, nettle you, though. This is an exquisite environment, surrounded by the jagged, snowy mountain peaks of Lee Vining Canyon, with a small creek gurgling by.

The ground is level, parking slips paved, and a smattering of lodgepole pines and low-lying willows vie with boulders and campers for ground space. You can fish for trout in the creek or, better still, the nearby lake. The campground, which is at an altitude of 9,500 feet, is also a fine base for day trips into Yosemite National Park's high country, its east entrance being a scant 3 miles away. Nearly half the sites are walk-ins for tenters, with access to them cutting directly through other sites, an unfortunate sacrifice in privacy. The better spots are 9–14, shielded from Hwy. 120 in a nook behind talus rock. A general store is 0.5 miles to the west.

BASICS

Operated By: Sierra Recreation, concessionaire. **Open:** June–Oct., weather permitting. **Site Assignment:** First come, first served. **Registration:** At entrance kiosk. **Fee:** $12; cash, check. **Parking:** At site.

FACILITIES

Number of RV-only Sites: 6. **Number of Tent-only Sites:** 6. **Hookups:** None. **Each Site:** Picnic table, fire grate. **Dump Station:** No. **Laundry:** No. **Pay Phone:** No. **Restrooms and Showers:** Vault toilets, no showers. **Fuel:** No. **Propane:** No. **Internal Roads:** Paved. **RV Service:** No. **Market:** 11 mi. east in Lee Vining. **Restaurant:** 11 mi. east in Lee Vining. **General Store:** No. **Vending:** No. **Swimming:** Yes. **Playground:** No. **Other:** Some wheelchair-accessible facilities. **Activities:** Fishing, hiking, photography, boating, swimming. **Nearby Attractions:** Yosemite National Park; Mono Lake Tufa State Reserve in Lee Vining; Bodie State Historic Park near Bridgeport. **Additional Information:** Lee Vining Chamber of Commerce, (760) 647-6629; Yosemite Area Traveler Information, (209) 723-3153.

RESTRICTIONS

Pets: On leash. **Fires:** Fire grates only. **Alcoholic Beverages:** Allowed. **Vehicle Maximum Length:** 30 ft. **Other:** 14-day stay limit.

TO GET THERE

Just south of Lee Vining on US 395, head west on Hwy. 120. Drive 10 mi. and turn left into the campground.

BLAIRSDEN — MAP, B-2, B-3
Grasshopper Flat— Plumas National Forest

reserve america

Mohawk Rd./ P.O. Box 7, 96103.
T: (530) 836-2575; www.reserveamerica.com.

🚐 ★★★★ ▲ ★★★★

Beauty: ★★★★   Site Privacy: ★★★
Spaciousness: ★★★   Quiet: ★★★
Security: ★★★★   Cleanliness: ★★★★
Insect Control: ★★★★   Facilities: ★★

Located in the northern Sierra Nevada, approximately 7 miles from the town of Portola, California, Grasshopper Flat Campground is within the Lake Davis Recreation Area. This campground is one of three located on Lake Davis. Overflow camping is available nearby. Popular activities include camping, fishing, and boating. Facilities provided include four boat ramps, three docks, an RV dump station (an eighth-mile from Grasshopper Flat Campground), numerous fishing access points, and a convenience store. Free fishing days are sponsored by the California Department of Fish and Game in June and September. Grasshopper Flat is located within Plumas National Forest and is versatile in its land features, uncrowded, and enhanced by a pleasant climate. Outdoor enthusiasts are attracted year-round to its many streams and lakes, beautiful deep canyons, rich mountain valleys, meadows, and lofty peaks.

BASICS

Operated By: U.S. Forest Service. **Open:** Apr. 28–Oct. 10. **Site Assignment:** Reservations must be made at least 4 days in advance. **Registration:** At office. **Fee:** Single, $16; group, $50. **Parking:** At park.

FACILITIES

Number of Multipurpose Sites: 62. **Hookups:** None. **Each Site:** Call ahead. **Dump Station:** Less than 1 mi. **Laundry:** No. **Pay Phone:** No. **Restrooms and Showers:** Yes. **Fuel:** No. **Propane:** No. **Internal Roads:** Paved. **RV Service:** No. **Market:** No. **Restaurant:** No. **General Store:** No. **Vending:** No. **Swimming:** Yes. **Playground:** No. **Activities:** Fishing, boating.

RESTRICTIONS

Pets: Pets must be restrained or on a leash at all times while in developed recreation areas. **Fires:** In fire rings, stoves, grills, or fireplaces provided for that purpose. **Alcoholic Beverages:** Not allowed. **Vehicle Maximum Length:** 32 ft.

TO GET THERE

From Reno, NV travel north on US 395 to Hwy. 70, turn west on Hwy. 70 and travel to Portola, CA. Turn north on West St., travel 6 mi. to Lake Davis. Cross dam and take first left; Grasshopper Flat is the second campground on left.

BLAIRSDEN — MAP, B-2, B-3
Grizzly—Plumas National Forest

reserve america

Mohawk Rd./ P.O. Box 7, 96103.
T: (530) 836-2575; www.reserveamerica.com.

🚐 ★★★★ ▲ ★★★★

Beauty: ★★★★   Site Privacy: ★★★
Spaciousness: ★★★   Quiet: ★★★
Security: ★★★★   Cleanliness: ★★★★
Insect Control: ★★★★   Facilities: ★★★

Grizzly Campground is located on the southeastern shore of Lake Davis at an elevation of 5,800 feet. This campground has 55 campsites with trailer space. Potable water and toilets are available, and there is a RV sanitation station in the area. Fishing, swimming, and boating are available on, or around, the lake. Grizzly Campground is situated in the Sierra Nevada, just south of the Cascade Range. The Plumas is versatile in its land features, uncrowded, and enhanced by a pleasant climate. Outdoor enthusiasts are attracted year-round to its many streams and lakes, beautiful deep canyons, rich mountain valleys, meadows, and lofty peaks.

BASICS

Operated By: U.S. Forest Service. **Open:** Apr. 29–Oct. 11. **Site Assignment:** Reservations must be made at least 4 days in advance. **Registration:** At office. **Fee:** Single, $16. **Parking:** At park.

FACILITIES

Number of Multipurpose Sites: 64. **Hookups:** None. **Each Site:** Call ahead. **Dump Station:** Yes. **Laundry:** No. **Pay Phone:** No. **Restrooms and Showers:** Yes. **Fuel:** No. **Propane:** No. **Internal Roads:** Paved. **RV Service:** No. **Market:** No. **Restaurant:** No. **General Store:** Yes. **Vending:** No. **Swimming:** Yes. **Playground:** No. **Activities:** Fishing, boating.

RESTRICTIONS

Pets: Pets must be restrained or on a leash at all times while in developed recreation areas. **Fires:** In fire rings, stoves, grills, or fireplaces provided for that purpose. **Alcoholic Beverages:** Not allowed. **Vehicle Maximum Length:** 32 ft. **Other:** No water-skiing.

TO GET THERE

From Reno, NV travel north on US 395 to Hwy. 70, turn west on Hwy. 70 and travel to Portola, CA. Turn north on West St., travel 6 mi. to Lake Davis. Cross dam and take first left; Grizzly will be the first campground on the left.

BLAIRSDEN — MAP, B-2, B-3
Plumas Eureka State Park

reserve america

310 Johnsonville Rd., 96103. T: (530) 836-2380; www.reserveamerica.com.

🚐 ★★★ ▲ ★★★★

Beauty: ★★★   Site Privacy: ★★★
Spaciousness: ★★   Quiet: ★★★★
Security: ★★★★   Cleanliness: ★★★★
Insect Control: ★★★   Facilities: ★★

If ever there was a park that held something for everyone, Sierra Plumas Eureka State Park is it! Established in 1959, "Plumas" (as it is commonly known by State Park folks and visitors alike) has been providing a bit of California's history, scenic beauty, and recreational opportunity to thousands of visitors for many years. The focal point of the park is the museum building. Originally constructed as a miners bunkhouse, it now serves as a visitor center. Outside and across the street from the museum stands the Mohawk Stamp Mill, Bushman five stamp mill, stable, mine office, and the blacksmith shop. All have been maintained in a "near-restored" condition. During the summer, tours of the buildings and blacksmithing demonstrations are conducted by park staff. Fishing opportunities at Plumas abound with two lakes, Madora and Eureka, plus Jamison Creek, which flows through the park. Some of the species to be caught include rainbow, brown and golden trout. You can also take part in supervised gold panning in Jamieson Creek. In the wintertime, the park is transformed into a winter paradise. Visitors can drive the well-cleared roads to enjoy the various cross-country ski loops, or continue on to Eureka Bowl, the birthplace of downhill ski racing. The Upper Jamison Creek campground offers an outstanding camping experience. Located at the foot of Eureka Mountain and divided by Jamison Creek, it is surrounded by a mixture of white fir, Jeffrey pine, and incense cedar. There are 67 well-spaced campsites, each with a table and fire pit. Hot showers are located within the campground. Those campers desiring a little more privacy might try one of the 14 walk-in sites. The maximum trailer length is 24 feet, motor homes 30 feet. A specially designed wheelchair-accessible campsite is also available.

BASICS

Operated By: California State Parks. **Open:** All year. **Site Assignment:** Reservations can be made 7 months in advance. **Registration:** At office. **Fee:** Call ahead. **Parking:** At site.

FACILITIES

Number of Multipurpose Sites: 62. **Hookups:** None. **Dump Station:** Yes. **Laundry:** Yes. **Pay Phone:** No. **Restrooms and Showers:** No. **Fuel:** No. **Propane:** No. **Internal Roads:** Paved. **RV Service:** No. **Market:** No. **Restaurant:** No. **General Store:** No. **Vending:** No. **Swimming:** No. **Playground:** No. **Activities:** Fishing, nature trails, picnicking.

RESTRICTIONS

Pets: On 6-ft. leash in a tent or enclosed vehicle at night. Except for guide dogs, pets are not allowed in park buildings, on trails, or on most beaches. **Fires:** In designated fireplaces. **Alcoholic Beverages:** Not allowed. **Other:** Bears can break into cars if they smell anything of interest. A car may not be sufficient to protect your food & belongings, even if the car is locked up. Camp at your own risk!.

TO GET THERE

In the northern Sierra Nevada, in Plumas County. 53 mi. northwest of Truckee via CA 89, and west of Gray Eagle. (1 hour north of Truckee, via CA 89; turn onto CR A-14 from CA 89 and go 5 mi.).

BLAIRSDEN   MAP, B-2
Upper Jamison Creek Campground

Plumas-Eureka State Park, 310 Johnsville Rd., 96103. T: (530) 836-2380; www.cal-parks.ca.gov.

🚐 ★★★★	🏕 ★★★★
Beauty: ★★★★	Site Privacy: ★★★
Spaciousness: ★★★	Quiet: ★★★★
Security: ★★★	Cleanliness: ★★★
Insect Control: ★★	Facilities: ★★★

"Stunning," "drop-dead gorgeous," and "breath-taking" all describe the spectacular beauty of this high altitude campground that is encircled by a series of jagged, snow-patched Sierra Nevada peaks. The rugged landscape is enhanced by its position next to Jamison Creek and the great variety of conifers, as well as willows, alders, and cottonwoods, that provide shade. Flourishing though the forest is, a fair degree of sunlight manages to warm the property.

Most sites are roomy and set pretty well apart along a small series of loops. Eureka Peak was once known as Gold Mountain, a testimony to the extensive mining activity that went on in the Jamison area from the Gold Rush days through the end of the first world war. A mining-history museum within the park preserves buildings and equipment from that era. Once a month, in summer, docents in period dress attempt to recreate a sense of what camp life was like in the 19th century.

BASICS

Operated By: California Dept. of Parks & Recreation. **Open:** May 15–Oct. 15, weather permitting. **Site Assignment:** First come, first served; no reservations. **Registration:** At park office. **Fee:** $15; cash or CA check. **Parking:** At site.

FACILITIES

Number of RV-only Sites: 55. **Number of Tent-only Sites:** 12. **Hookups:** None. **Each Site:** Picnic table, fire grate, bear-proof box. **Dump Station:** Yes. **Laundry:** No. **Pay Phone:** No, museum 1 mi. away. **Restrooms and Showers:** Yes. **Fuel:** No. **Propane:** No. **Internal Roads:** Paved. **RV Service:** No. **Market:** 6 mi. east in Graegle. **Restaurant:** Yes, in Johnsville. **General Store:** No. **Vending:** No. **Swimming:** Lake. **Playground:** No. **Other:** Some wheelchair-accessible facilities, visitor center & museum. **Activities:** Hiking, bicycling, fishing, swimming, summer tours. **Nearby Attractions:** Portola Railroad Museum; Lakes Basin Recreation Area in Graegle; Plumas County Museum in Quincy; Plumas National Forest. **Additional Information:** Plumas County Visitors Bureau, (530) 283-6345 or (800) 326-2247.

RESTRICTIONS

Pets: On 6-ft. leash. **Fires:** Fire grates only. **Alcoholic Beverages:** Allowed at site. **Vehicle Maximum Length:** 30 ft. (varies). **Other:** 14-day stay limit; no firearms; no wood gathering.

TO GET THERE

From Portola drive 10 mi. west on Hwy. 70. 1 mi. beyond Blairsden after the junction w/ Hwy. 89, turn left towards Johnsville and continue for 0.6 mi. At the stop sign turn right on the Graegle-Johnsville Rd./A14. The park entrance is 4.5 mi. ahead.

BLYTHE   MAP, F-4
Mayflower Park

4980 Colorado River Rd., 92225. T: (760) 922-4665; www.riversidecountyparks.org/parks/mayflower.htm.

🚐 ★★★★	🏕 ★★★
Beauty: ★★★	Site Privacy: ★★
Spaciousness: ★★	Quiet: ★★★
Security: ★★★★	Cleanliness: ★★★★
Insect Control: ★★★	Facilities: ★★★★

In the dusty desert landscape common to this part of the state, Mayflower is a welcome oasis and, situated just 7 miles north of I-10, a convenient one to pilgrims sailing along the highway. Well manicured, grassy sites are partially shaded by mesquite trees, eucalyptus, and cottonwoods, with the tent area—separated from two other RV loops—especially

appealing. The view of the Plomosa Mountains across the state line in Arizona is superb, but it is the border itself, marked here by the Colorado River (which flows just below the campground and is accessible via an in-camp boat ramp and swimming lagoon) that is the real attraction for most visitors. Peace-and-quiet seekers take note: boating on this stretch of river during summer months—weekends especially—is more popular than a high school prom queen, so be prepared to hear the constant whine of two-stroke engines being pushed to their limits. That activity largely fades away in the off-season, but winter brings hordes of a different sort of camper, snowbirds by the RV-load.

BASICS

Operated By: Riverside County. **Open:** All year. **Site Assignment:** First come, first served; reservations can be made for holidays. **Registration:** At entrance office. **Fee:** $15–$16; cash, CA check, V, MC. **Parking:** At site.

FACILITIES

Number of Tent-only Sites: 30. **Number of Multipurpose Sites:** 152. **Hookups:** Electric (30, 50 amps), water. **Each Site:** Picnic table, fire grate (tent sites only). **Dump Station:** Yes. **Laundry:** No. **Pay Phone:** Yes. **Restrooms and Showers:** Yes. **Fuel:** No. **Propane:** No. **Internal Roads:** Mostly paved. **RV Service:** No. **Market:** 7 mi. southwest in Blythe. **Restaurant:** 7 mi. southwest in Blythe. **General Store:** No. **Vending:** No. **Swimming:** Mud-wallow lagoon, Colorado River. **Playground:** No. **Other:** Some wheelchair-accessible facilities, boat ramp. **Activities:** Fishing, horseshoe pits, bowling lawn, shuffleboard, swimming, water activities. **Nearby Attractions:** Colorado River, Mojave National Preserve; Cibola & Imperial National Wildlife Refuges in Arizona. **Additional Information:** Riverside County, Regional Park & Open Space District, (909) 955-4397.

RESTRICTIONS

Pets: On leash, $2 fee. **Fires:** Fire grates only. **Alcoholic Beverages:** Allowed. **Vehicle Maximum Length:** No limit. **Other:** 14-day stay limit from Apr. 1–Sept. 30; no ORVs; no generators; no loaded firearms.

TO GET THERE

From I-10/US 95 drive 3.7 mi. north on Inlake Blvd. Turn right on 6th Ave. and drive 3.2 mi. into the campground.

BODEGA BAY   MAP, C-1
Bodega Dunes Campground

Sonoma Coast State Beach, Hwy. 1, 94923. T: (707) 875-3483 or (800) 444-7275; www.parks.ca.gov.

🚐 ★★★★	🏕 ★★★★
Beauty: ★★★★	Site Privacy: ★★★★
Spaciousness: ★★★	Quiet: ★★★★
Security: ★★★	Cleanliness: ★★★
Insect Control: ★★★	Facilities: ★★

This good-looking, spacious campground is right off of Hwy. 1, just a short trail's walk from the ocean. Three separate loops undulate across sandy dunes in a semi-forested environment colored by ferns, dune grass, Monterey pines, and eucalyptus. Sites of grass and sand are decently roomy and planted well apart, with a number of pull-through parking slips on hand. Of the latter, numbers 3 and 4 are very private and shaded by conifers. Similarly isolated are 24, 32, 36, 69, 86, and 88, and their nestled-in-the-dunes position is a welcome buffer against road noise and brisk coastal breezes. The steady drone of a distant foghorn is less a disturbing influence than a contributor to the pleasant seaside atmosphere. In spite of its beauty, this facility is often wonderfully underpopulated. With whales routinely passing in winter months and a seal rookery located by the egress of the Russian River, you will want to pack binoculars.

BASICS

Operated By: California Dept. of Parks & Recreation. **Open:** All year. **Site Assignment:** Reservations accepted w/ V, MC, D; recommended 7 months in advance. **Registration:** At entrance booth. **Fee:** $16; extra vehicle, $4; senior rates available; cash, CA check. **Parking:** At site.

FACILITIES

Number of Multipurpose Sites: 98. **Hookups:** None. **Each Site:** Picnic table, fire grate, food storage box. **Dump Station:** Yes. **Laundry:** No. **Pay Phone:** Yes. **Restrooms and Showers:** Yes. **Fuel:** No. **Propane:** No. **Internal Roads:** Paved. **RV Service:** No. **Market:** 2 mi. south in Bodega Bay. **Restaurant:** 2 mi. south in Bodega Bay. **General Store:** No. **Vending:** No. **Swimming:** No. **Playground:** No. **Other:** Some wheelchair-accessible facilities. En route camping for hikers & bikers ($2 night). **Activities:** Fishing, sunning, surfing, tide pooling, beachcombing, horseback riding, bicycling, winter whale-watching at Bodega Head. **Nearby Attractions:** Santa Rosa museums & Luther Burbank Home & Memorial Gardens; Fort Ross, Kruse Rhododendron State Reserve, & Salt Point State Park in Jenner. **Additional Information:** Bodega Bay Area Chamber of Commerce, (707) 875-3422.

RESTRICTIONS

Pets: On 6-ft. leash. **Fires:** Fire grates only. **Alcoholic Beverages:** Allowed at site. **Vehicle Maximum Length:** 31 ft. **Other:** 10-day stay limit from Apr. 1–Nov. 30; no firearms; no wood gathering.

TO GET THERE

From Bodega Bay drive 2 mi. north on Hwy. 1. Turn left into the park.

BORREGO SPRINGS   MAP, F-3
Borrego Palm Canyon Campground

Anza-Borrego Desert State Park, 200 Palm Canyon Dr., 92004. T: (760) 767-5341 or (800) 242-0044; www.cal-parks.ca.gov.

🚐 ★★★	⛺ ★★★
Beauty: ★★★	Site Privacy: ★★★
Spaciousness: ★★★	Quiet: ★★★
Security: ★★★	Cleanliness: ★★★
Insect Control: ★★★★	Facilities: ★★★

This campground is situated in the mouth of the expansive Borrego Palm Canyon near the heart of

---

Anza-Borrego Desert State Park. This central location ensures a level of use and popularity well beyond most of the many other camps in this, the largest state park in the lower 48 states. A good range of facilities adds to its appeal, with drinking water, showers, full hookups, and even a few partially enclosed stone shelters (complete with fireplaces) available. Though shade is scarce, ramadas over tables provide some relief from a sun that is scorching much of the year. Tent pads are of a coarse gravel, but the overall landscape is hardly lunar, with fan palms lining one stretch of the camp road and ironwood, ocotillo, staghorn cholla, and creosote bushes sprinkled throughout. Large sites are well spread apart, with a good number equipped with pull-through parking slots.

BASICS

Operated By: California Dept. of Parks & Recreation. **Open:** All year. **Site Assignment:** Reservations accepted w/ V, MC. **Registration:** At entrance booth. **Fee:** $29; cash, CA check, V, MC. **Parking:** At site.

FACILITIES

Number of RV-only Sites: 132. **Hookups:** Electric (30 amps), water, sewer, cable TV, phone. **Each Site:** Picnic table, fire grate, ramada (tent loop only). **Dump Station:** Yes. **Laundry:** Yes. **Pay Phone:** Yes. **Restrooms and Showers:** Yes. **Fuel:** No. **Propane:** No. **Internal Roads:** Paved. **RV Service:** No. **Market:** 2 mi. east in Borrego Springs. **Restaurant:** Yes. **General Store:** No. **Vending:** No. **Swimming:** No. **Playground:** No. **Other:** Some wheelchair-accessible facilities. **Activities:** Hiking, bicycling, seasonal nature programs, bird-watching, wildflower photography. **Nearby Attractions:** Anza-Borrego Desert State Park. **Additional Information:** Borrego Springs Chamber of Commerce, (760) 767-5976.

RESTRICTIONS

Pets: On 6-ft. leash. **Fires:** Fire grates only. **Alcoholic Beverages:** Allowed at site. **Vehicle Maximum Length:** 35 ft. **Other:** 14-day stay limit; no firearms; no wood gathering.

TO GET THERE

From Borrego Springs drive 1 mi. west on CR S22. At the bend in the road continue straight on Palm Canyon Dr. for 0.2 mi. The campground access road is 1 mi. ahead on the right.

BORREGO SPRINGS   MAP, F-3
Culp Valley Primitive Camp

200 Palm Canyon Dr., 92004. T: (760) 767-5311; www.reserveamerica.com.

🚐 ★★★★	⛺ ★★★★
Beauty: ★★★★	Site Privacy: ★★★★
Spaciousness: ★★★★	Quiet: ★★★★
Security: ★	Cleanliness: ★★★★
Insect Control: ★★★★	Facilities: ★

To those who appreciate the low-key beauty of the desert and enjoy roughing it, Culp Valley, 9 miles

---

west of Borrego Springs, is a hidden gem. Large granite boulders litter a chaparral landscape punctuated by buckwheat, cat's claw, staghorn cholla, and dwarf oak. Most sites are extraordinarily spacious, and several are shielded from view by high hedges of sugar bush, which makes for a more peaceful experience than what is possible in the more popular—and populated—developed campgrounds elsewhere in Anza-Borrego. The trade-off is that creature comforts are limited to surprisingly clean vaulted toilets; no water is available and you will have to pack out your trash. A greater nuisance though is the biting wind that tends to whistle through camp from late fall through early spring. That and an altitude of 3,400 feet will make you glad you packed a heavy sweater, should you visit in the off-season. If you come in summer, well, you'll very likely find yourself alone in the whole blazing park.

BASICS

Operated By: California Dept. of Parks & Recreation. **Open:** All year. **Site Assignment:** First come, first served. **Registration:** At entrance kiosk. **Fee:** $12–$29. **Parking:** At site.

FACILITIES

Number of RV-only Sites: 15. **Hookups:** None. **Dump Station:** No. **Laundry:** No. **Pay Phone:** No. **Restrooms and Showers:** Vault toilets, no showers. **Fuel:** No. **Propane:** No. **Internal Roads:** Hard sand, some rock, some washboard, negotiable. **RV Service:** No. **Market:** 9 mi. west in Borrego Springs. **Restaurant:** 9 mi. west in Borrego Springs. **General Store:** Yes. **Vending:** No. **Swimming:** No. **Playground:** No. **Activities:** Hiking, photography, stargazing, rock scrambling, bird-watching. **Nearby Attractions:** Anza-Borrego Desert State Park, historic Julian, scenic views. **Additional Information:** Borrego Springs Chamber of Commerce, (760) 767-5976.

RESTRICTIONS

Pets: On 6-ft. leash. **Fires:** Not allowed. **Alcoholic Beverages:** Allowed. **Vehicle Maximum Length:** 30 ft. **Other:** 14-day stay limit; no shooting.

TO GET THERE

From Borrego Springs drive 9 mi. east on CR S22. Check for a sign between mile markerss 9 and 10 on the right (north) side of the road.

BRIDGEPORT   MAP, C-3
Honeymoon Flat

reserve america

Twin Lakes Rd., 93517. T: (760) 932-7070 or (877) 444-6777; www.reserveamerica.com.

🚐 ★★★★	⛺ ★★★★
Beauty: ★★★★	Site Privacy: ★★★
Spaciousness: ★★★	Quiet: ★★★
Security: ★★★	Cleanliness: ★★★★
Insect Control: ★★	Facilities: ★

A campground sporting the name Honeymoon Flat had better be the sort of cozily romantic place you'd want to take your sweetheart. Well, go right ahead, as this idyllic spot lives up to that promise, and then some. Twin Lakes Rd. divides it into two sections, with both hugging Robinson Creek. Many of the grassy sites along the camp's series of sandy loops abut the water, allowing you to fish for trout from tent-side, or simply dangle your toes in the rippling water. Though sites are a shade small, privacy is well above average, with screening provided by a mix of pines and, especially, the luminescent leaves of quaking aspen. Most of the sites are back-ins, however, 7 pull-throughs are available. Site 3, very recessed and with water flowing by on three sides, might well be the envy of Diana. Number 5 is similarly romantic. Bear sitings in the park are common and generally cause little fuss. There are half a dozen other campgrounds in the neighborhood, but this is the only one that hasn't been smothered by an excess of asphalt. When you are at 7,000 feet, surrounded by the High Sierra, a campground shouldn't look like a parking lot. Due to the altitude, the road leading to the campground is extremely winding and not recommended for large RVs.

BASICS

Operated By: American Land & Leisure, concessionaire. **Open:** Late-Apr.–Oct.; weather permitting. **Site Assignment:** Reservations accepted w/V, MC, D. **Registration:** At entrance bulletin board. **Fee:** $11; cash, check. **Parking:** At site.

FACILITIES

Number of RV-only Sites: 31. **Number of Tent-only Sites:** 4. **Hookups:** None. **Each Site:** Picnic table, fire grate. **Dump Station:** No. **Laundry:** No, 2 mi. **Pay Phone:** No, 2 mi. **Restrooms and Showers:** Vault toilets, no showers. **Fuel:** No. **Propane:** No. **Internal Roads:** Sandy & somewhat bumpy. **RV Service:** No. **Market:** 2 mi. **Restaurant:** 2 mi. **General Store:** No. **Vending:** No. **Swimming:** No. **Playground:** No. **Other:** Bear sitings are common in the park. **Activities:** Hiking, fishing, whispering sweet nothings into your sweetheart's ear. **Nearby Attractions:** Bodie State Historic Park near Bridgeport; Lower Twin Lake, Mono Lake Tufa State Reserve in Lee Vining. **Additional Information:** Ranger Station (760) 932-7070.

RESTRICTIONS

Pets: On leash. **Fires:** Fire grates only. **Alcoholic Beverages:** Allowed. **Vehicle Maximum Length:** 45 ft. **Other:** 14-day stay limit, 6 people per site. The road leading to the campground is small & winding so large RVs may wish to opt for another park.

TO GET THERE

From US 395 on Bridgeport's west side, turn south onto Twin Lakes Rd. Drive 8.2 mi. to the campground entrance on both sides of the road.

BRIDGEPORT   MAP, C-3
Robinson Creek Campground— Humboldt-Toiyabe National Forest

HCR 1 Box 1000, 93517. T: (760) 932-7070; www.reserveamerica.com.

🚐 ★★★★   ⛺ ★★★★

Beauty: ★★★★	Site Privacy: ★★★
Spaciousness: ★★★	Quiet: ★★★
Security: ★★★★	Cleanliness: ★★★★
Insect Control: ★★★★	Facilities: ★

Robinson Creek Campground is located in the mountains with large Jeffrey pine trees and sagebrush. Robinson Creek runs by this campground, and nearby are the Lower and Upper Twin Lakes and Hoover Wilderness. Opening and closing dates depend on the weather condition. Bears are in the area. There is good fishing in Robinson Creek and Upper and Lower Twin Lakes and good hiking and hunting opportunities in the area. Interpretive programs are conducted July 4 through Labor Day. Robinson Creek is split into two separate campgrounds. Robinson Creek North has sites 26–54, Robinson Creek South has sites 1–25. Robinson Creek Campground is located within the Humboldt-Toiyabe National Forest along the far eastern edge of California. The name Humboldt comes from the explorer John C. Frémont. He named the East Humboldt Mountain Range and the Humboldt River after German naturalist Baron Alexander von Humboldt. Toiyabe is an ancient Shoshone word meaning mountain. The Humboldt-Toiyabe, or H-T, is the largest national forest in the lower 48 states. To manage the expansive acreage on the H-T, there are ten ranger districts throughout the state of Nevada and Northern California.

BASICS

Operated By: U.S. Forest Service. **Open:** Apr. 25–Oct. 31. **Site Assignment:** Reservations must be made at least 4 days in advance. **Registration:** At office. **Fee:** Single, $15. **Parking:** At park.

FACILITIES

Number of Multipurpose Sites: 106. **Hookups:** None. **Each Site:** Fire ring. **Dump Station:** No. **Laundry:** No. **Pay Phone:** No. **Restrooms and Showers:** Yes. **Fuel:** No. **Propane:** No. **Internal Roads:** Paved. **RV Service:** No. **Market:** No. **Restaurant:** No. **General Store:** No. **Vending:** No. **Swimming:** No. **Playground:** No. **Other:** Proper safe food storage is recommended. No refunds are given for bad weather. **Activities:** Fishing, hiking.

RESTRICTIONS

Pets: Pets must be restrained or on a leash at all times while in developed recreation areas. **Fires:** In fire rings, stoves, grills, or fireplaces provided for that purpose. **Alcoholic Beverages:** Not allowed. **Vehicle Maximum Length:** 35 ft.

TO GET THERE

US 395 runs through Bridgeport. Turn south on Twin Lakes Rd. at the MoMart Gas Station. Travel on the Twin Lakes Rd. for about 9.3 mi., turn left at Robinson Creek Campground.

CALISTOGA   MAP, C-2
Bothe-Napa Valley State Park

reserve america

3801 St. Helena Hwy. (Hwy. 29), 94515. T: (707) 942-4575 or (800) 444-7275; www.reserveamerica.com.

🚐 ★★★   ⛺ ★★★★

Beauty: ★★★★	Site Privacy: ★★★★
Spaciousness: ★★★	Quiet: ★★★
Security: ★★★	Cleanliness: ★★★
Insect Control: ★	Facilities: ★★

The Wappo Indians used to call this part of the valley home until being displaced by white settlers in the middle of the 19th century. In honor of its first inhabitants the park maintains a small "Native American garden" of herbs and vegetables the Wappos are believed to have cultivated. Indigenous plants are featured in a more natural setting around the campground, its lollipop loop being abundantly furnished with a variety of conifers and oaks, toyon, bay, madrone, manzanita, and poison oak. Most campers gravitate to the top of the cul-de-sac near the latrines. The more private sites, though, are 1–9 at the front end of the drive, and their gravel parking slips are long enough to accommodate almost any size RV. One of the better trails in Bothe-Napa leads to volcanic-ash cliffs atop Upper Ritchey Canyon. And for unusual amenities in a state park, how about the swimming pool, open from Memorial Day through Labor Day? That sure beats wading in the stream that trickles by one side of camp, spawning hordes of mosquitoes in the spring.

BASICS

Operated By: California Dept. of Parks & Recreation. **Open:** All year. **Site Assignment:** Reservations accepted w/V, MC, D; first come, first served sites available. **Registration:** At kiosk opposite site 11. **Fee:** $15 - $25; cash, CA check. **Parking:** At site. $4 per extra vehicle.

FACILITIES

Number of RV-only Sites: 40. **Number of Tent-only Sites:** 9. **Hookups:** None. **Each Site:** Picnic table, fire grate, food storage box. **Dump Station:** Yes. **Laundry:** No. **Pay Phone:** Yes. **Restrooms and Showers:** Yes. **Fuel:** No. **Propane:** No. **Internal Roads:** Paved. **RV Service:** No. **Market:** 3 mi. north in Calistoga. **Restaurant:** 3 mi. north in Calistoga. **General Store:** No. **Vending:** No. **Swimming:** Pool (seasonal). **Playground:** No. **Other:** Some wheelchair-accessible facilities, visitor center. **Activities:** Hiking, bicycling, horseback riding, birding, interpretive programs, horseshoe pit, Ritchey Canyon, picnicking, swimming. **Nearby Attractions:** Luther Burbank Home & Gardens, Annadel State Park & museums in Santa Rosa; winery tours; Native American Garden. **Additional Information:** Santa Rosa CVB, (800) 404-rose.

RESTRICTIONS

Pets: On 6-ft. leash. **Fires:** Fire grates only. **Alcoholic Beverages:** Allowed at site. **Vehicle Maximum**

Length: 31 ft. **Other:** 14-day stay limit; no firearms; no wood gathering.

TO GET THERE

From St. Helena follow Hwy. 29 north for 4.5 mi. The well-marked park entrance is on the left, beyond Bale Grist Mill State Park.

CAMPO   MAP, F-3, F-4
Lake Morena County Park, South Shore Campground

2550 Lake Morena Dr., 91906. T: (877) 565-3600; www.co.san-diego.ca.us/parks.

🚐 ★★★★   ⛺ ★★★

Beauty: ★★★★   Site Privacy: ★★★
Spaciousness: ★★★   Quiet: ★★★★
Security: ★★★   Cleanliness: ★★★
Insect Control: ★★   Facilities: ★★★

Lake Morena Reservoir is home to some of the better bass and trout fishing in the area, with the record for the former weighing in at a whopping 19 pounds, 3 ounces. But even when the water has been drawn down to the size of a pond, typically by late July or early August, there is still plenty to do here, from biking and hiking the nature trails to hooking up to the Pacific Crest Trail, which cuts through the park. Granite-spiked hills surround the domain, with the campground's grassy, fairly tightly concentrated sites well shaded by thick-limbed live oaks, incense cedars, and Jeffrey and Coulter pines. Best for spaciousness and lake view—at least when water levels are high—are sites 81 and 85, with 6–14 good fall-back options. And though restrooms are a bit shabby looking, they are kept reasonably clean. Dogs are supposed to be kept on leashes, but enforcement is lax. Tent campers looking for more space and privacy may want to stake out a spot at the North Shore primitive area.

BASICS

Operated By: County of San Diego, Dept. of Parks & Recreation. **Open:** All year. **Site Assignment:** Reservations accepted w/ V, MC, D; $3 reservation fee. **Registration:** At entrance booth or ranger office. **Fee:** $12–$16; cabins, $25; cash, V, MC, D. **Parking:** At site. $2 per extra vehicle.

FACILITIES

Number of RV-only Sites: 86. **Hookups:** Electric (20, 30 amps), water. **Each Site:** Picnic table, fire grate. **Dump Station:** Yes. **Laundry:** No. **Pay Phone:** Yes. **Restrooms and Showers:** Yes. **Fuel:** No. **Propane:** No. **Internal Roads:** Mostly paved. **RV Service:** No. **Market:** 1 mi. south in Lake Morena Village. **Restaurant:** 1 mi. south in Lake Morena Village. **General Store:** No. **Vending:** Yes. **Swimming:** No. **Playground:** No. **Other:** Some wheelchair-accessible facilities, boat launch. **Activities:** Fishing, bicycling, hiking, campfire programs, boat rentals. **Nearby Attractions:** Coral Canyon OHV Area, Pacific Crest Trail, only 8 mi. from the Mexican border, historic Campo. **Additional Information:** County of San Diego, Dept. of Parks & Recreation, (858) 694-3049.

RESTRICTIONS

Pets: On 6-ft. leash. Not allowed on trails. $1 per pet. **Fires:** Fire grates only. **Alcoholic Beverages:**

Allowed at site, not exceeding 40 proof. **Vehicle Maximum Length:** 60 ft. **Other:** 14-day stay limit; no firearms; no wood gathering.

TO GET THERE

From San Diego head east on I-8 for 54 mi. Exit on Buckman Springs Rd. and continue south for 5.5 mi. Turn right on Oak Dr. and proceed for 1.5 mi. Turn right again on Lake Morena Dr. The park is 0.5 mi. ahead.

CAPITOLA   MAP, D-1
New Brighton State Beach

reserve america

1500 Park Ave., Off Hwy. 1, 95010.
T: (831) 464-6330 or (800) 444-7275; www.reserveamerica.com.

🚐 ★★★★   ⛺ ★★★★

Beauty: ★★★★   Site Privacy: ★★★
Spaciousness: ★★★★   Quiet: ★★★
Security: ★★★   Cleanliness: ★★★★
Insect Control: ★★   Facilities: ★★

Tired of sweeping buckets of sand out of your tent or RV after every trip to the beach? Then you owe it to yourself to check out this splendid campground, located just 5 miles east of Santa Cruz off of Hwy. 1. The bluff-top real estate is lush and grassy, graced with a comforting balance of shade and sun that filters through a high canopy of pines and eucalyptus trees. Many of the refreshingly spacious spots enjoy great vistas of the crashing surf. And of those that do not, a hefty share have the edge in privacy, being buffered by dense hedges of coastal chaparral. Sites 25 and 94 are the most isolated, while 36 is the best screened of the view options. And if sand in your shelter isn't a problem, you can always bring a bucketful back from the idyllic beach, reachable via a short trail next to site 50. Poison oak thrives around the edges of this park.

BASICS

Operated By: California Dept. of Parks & Recreation. **Open:** All year. **Site Assignment:** Reservations recommended; V, MC, D. **Registration:** At entrance booth. **Fee:** $12; day-use fee, $3–$26 (depending on number of people); cash, CA check. **Parking:** At site.

FACILITIES

Number of RV-only Sites: 112. **Hookups:** None. **Each Site:** Picnic table, fire grate, food-storage box. **Dump Station:** Yes. **Laundry:** No. **Pay Phone:** Yes. **Restrooms and Showers:** Yes. **Fuel:** No. **Propane:** No. **Internal Roads:** Paved. **RV Service:** No. **Market:** 5 mi. west in Santa Cruz. **Restaurant:** 5 mi. west in Santa Cruz. **General Store:** No. **Vending:** No. **Swimming:** Pacific Ocean. **Playground:** No. **Other:** Some wheelchair-accessible facilities. **Activities:** Surf fishing, sunning, hiking, ranger-led programs in summer. **Nearby Attractions:** Santa Cruz Beach Boardwalk, mission, museums, Seymour Marine Discovery Center, Arboretum & Natural Bridges State Beach; Roaring Camp Railroads in Felton. **Additional Information:** Capitola Chamber of

Commerce, (831) 475-6522; Santa Cruz County Conference & Visitors Council, (831) 425-1234 or (800) 833-3494.

RESTRICTIONS

Pets: On 6-ft. leash. **Fires:** Fire grates only. **Alcoholic Beverages:** Allowed at site. **Vehicle Maximum Length:** 36 ft. **Other:** 7-day stay limit from Apr. 1–Oct. 31; no firearms; no wood gathering.

TO GET THERE

From Santa Cruz drive 5 mi. south on Hwy. 1 and take the New Brighton Beach Exit. Drive 1 block west to the stop sign. Turn left on McGregor Dr. After 0.2 mi. turn right into the park.

CARLOTTA   MAP, B-1
Grizzly Creek Redwoods State Park

reserve america

16949 Hwy. 36, 95528. T: (707) 777-3683; www.reserveamerica.com.

🚐 ★★★   ⛺ ★★★★

Beauty: ★★★   Site Privacy: ★★★
Spaciousness: ★★★   Quiet: ★★★★★
Security: ★★★★★   Cleanliness: ★★★★
Insect Control: ★★★   Facilities: ★★

The redwoods in the Grizzly Creek area were what inspired Owen R. Cheatham, founder of Georgia-Pacific Corporation, to preserve this site in perpetuity. The facilities include 30 campsites, access to canoeing and kayaking, fishing, and swimming in Van Duzen River, group camp and/or picnic area, 4.5 miles of hiking trails, a horseshoe pit, environmental camp, and visitor center with exhibits and bookstore. The campground is open year-round and can accommodate tents and up to 24-foot trailers and 30-foot motor homes. There are no hookups. Although Grizzly Creek Redwoods State Park covers only a few acres large enough to provide a sense of seclusion, and it receives so few visitors that on a weekday it is possible to be the only person in one of it groves of coast redwoods. The Cheatham Grove is an exceptional stand of coastal redwoods. The park is a quiet place to camp, hike, fish, swim, and picnic. The Van Duzen River flows beside the campground.

BASICS

Operated By: California State Parks. **Open:** All year. **Site Assignment:** Reservations can be made 7 months in advance. **Registration:** At office. **Fee:** Single, $15–$20. **Parking:** At site.

FACILITIES

Number of Multipurpose Sites: 28. **Hookups:** None. **Dump Station:** No. **Laundry:** No. **Pay Phone:** No. **Restrooms and Showers:** Yes. **Fuel:** No. **Propane:** No. **Internal Roads:** Paved. **RV Service:** No. **Market:** No. **Restaurant:** No. **General Store:** No. **Vending:** No. **Swimming:** Yes. **Playground:** No. **Activities:** Fishing, hiking, picnicking, nature trails.

RESTRICTIONS

Pets: On 6-ft. leash in a tent or enclosed vehicle at night. Except for guide dogs, pets are not allowed in park buildings, on trails, or on most beaches. **Fires:** In designated fireplaces. **Alcoholic Beverages:** Not allowed. **Other:** Fees include entry for 1 vehicle & 1 legally towed vehicle or trailer, additional vehicles will be charged per night at the park.

TO GET THERE

Grizzly Creek Redwoods State Park is 20 mi. southeast of Eureka on Hwy. 101, then 17 mi. east on Hwy. 36.

CARLSBAD   MAP, F-3
South Carlsbad State Beach

reserve america

7201 Carlsbad Blvd., 92008. T: (760) 438-3143 or (800) 444-7275; www.reserveamerica.com.

🚐 ★★★★   ⛺ ★★

Beauty: ★★★	Site Privacy: ★★
Spaciousness: ★★★	Quiet: ★
Security: ★★★	Cleanliness: ★★
Insect Control: ★★	Facilities: ★★★★

There is much to like about South Carlsbad State Beach, such as the pretty beach and its convenient location just off I-5, 25 miles north of San Diego. Sites are positioned side-by-side high above the sea on a sandy bluff, and are both spacious and buffered with thick hedges that provide a certain degree of privacy. The straight-in linear layout of the camp road endows half the property with fine views of the Pacific Ocean. Of course, the narrowness of the bluff means that you are likely to have neighbors on three of your spot's four sides when the camp is busy, which is most of the year, given its near-constant use by hordes of college-age campers. At those times the flow of traffic can seem never-ending, a problem compounded by the busy external road that parallels the park's entire length. True, that constant hum of vehicles helps drown out the boisterousness of other campers and the squealing whistles of Amtrak trains that tend to pass the property on an hourly basis, but that may be of small consolation to light sleepers. At least the ocean-side sites benefit from the sonorous sound of the surf. Overall, South Carlsbad is quieter than San Elijo State Beach to the south, where the deafening roar of railroad and highway vehicles seem to be bearing down on one's tent. San Elijo does, however, offer some sites with hookups.

BASICS

Operated By: California Dept. of Parks & Recreation. **Open:** All year. **Site Assignment:** Reservations recommended; V, MC, D. **Registration:** At entrance booth. **Fee:** $16; cash, CA check, V, MC, D. **Parking:** At site.

FACILITIES

Number of RV-only Sites: 222. **Hookups:** None. **Each Site:** Picnic table, fire ring. **Dump Station:** Yes. **Laundry:** Yes. **Pay Phone:** Yes. **Restrooms and Showers:** Yes. **Fuel:** No. **Propane:** Yes. **Internal Roads:** Paved. **RV Service:** No. **Market:** 4 mi. north in Carlsbad. **Restaurant:** 4 mi. north in Carlsbad. **General Store:** Yes. **Vending:** Yes. **Swimming:** Pacific Ocean. **Playground:** No. **Other:**

Some wheelchair-accessible facilities. **Activities:** Sunning, surfing, rock & shell hounding, surfboard rentals, fishing. **Nearby Attractions:** Coastal air tours, outlet shopping, Museum of Making Music, Legoland. **Additional Information:** Carlsbad CVB, (760) 434-6093; San Diego CVB, (619) 232-3101.

RESTRICTIONS

Pets: On leash no longer than 6 ft.; not allowed on the beach. **Fires:** Fire ring only. **Alcoholic Beverages:** Allowed at site. **Vehicle Maximum Length:** 35 ft. **Other:** 14-day stay limit; no firearms.

TO GET THERE

From Carlsbad drive 4.5 mi. south on Hwy. 101. Bear to the right into the campground, which is easy to overshoot since signs are lacking.

CARPINTERIA   MAP, E-2
Carpinteria State Beach

reserve america

5361 6th St., 93013. T: (805) 968-1033 or (800) 444-7275; www.reserveamerica.com.

🚐 ★★★   ⛺ ★★

Beauty: ★★★	Site Privacy: ★★
Spaciousness: ★★	Quiet: ★★
Security: ★★★	Cleanliness: ★★★
Insect Control: ★★★	Facilities: ★★★

The bad news about this state-run property is that many sites border the park road and some industrial buildings, and if you happen to occupy one of those near the railroad tracks you may confuse a passing freight train with an earthquake. The good news? Never mind the distant off-shore oil platforms, a fair number of sites enjoy stunning views of the ocean, and the crashing surf nearby will drown out most of the noise emanating from your neighbors. The campground, which features an attractive balance of palm trees, eucalyptus, conifers, and sycamores, is broken into four separate sections, with Santa Cruz, Santa Rosa, and San Miguel providing beach access, while the shady Anacapa is situated away from the water. Not so coincidentally, the latter is the quietest, least crowded area in which to camp, while the former three loops feature sandy sites that are packed together like sardines in a can. The beach at Carpinteria, which is just 1 mile from Hwy. 101, 12 miles south of Santa Barbara, is also open to day use and picnicking, and a large grassy meadow near it is excellent for kites and Frisbee.

BASICS

Operated By: California Dept. of Parks & Recreation. **Open:** All year. **Site Assignment:** Reservations highly recommended (especially in summer); V, MC, D. **Registration:** At entrance booth. **Fee:** $16–$26; cash, CA check, V, MC, D. **Parking:** At site. Gated lot available for additional parking.

FACILITIES

Number of RV-only Sites: 261. **Hookups:** Electric (30 amps), water, sewer at most sites; 120 sites w/ hookups. **Each Site:** Picnic table, fire grate. **Dump Station:** Yes. **Laundry:** No. **Pay Phone:** Yes. **Restrooms and Showers:** Yes. **Fuel:** No.

Propane: No. **Internal Roads:** Paved. **RV Service:** No. **Market:** 1 mi. north in Carpinteria. **Restaurant:** 1 mi. north in Carpinteria. **General Store:** No. **Vending:** No. **Swimming:** Pacific Ocean. **Playground:** No. **Other:** Some wheelchair-accessible facilities. **Activities:** Surfing, tide pool exploring, seal watching, volleyball. **Nearby Attractions:** Mission San Buenaventura, historic Ventura, Mission Santa Barbara, Santa Barbara & its museums, historic buildings, zoo, Stearns Wharf, botanic garden, historic Ventura. **Additional Information:** Santa Barbara Region Chamber of Commerce, (805) 965-3023.

RESTRICTIONS

Pets: On 6-ft. leash. **Fires:** Fire grates only, not on the beach. **Alcoholic Beverages:** Allowed at site. **Vehicle Maximum Length:** 35 ft. (in non-hookup areas). **Other:** 7-day stay limit from June 1–Oct. 15; no firearms; no wood gathering.

TO GET THERE

From Santa Barbara drive 12 mi. southeast on US 101 and exit on Casitas Pass. Follow Casitas Pass Rd. to the right for 0.2 mi., then turn right on Carpinteria Ave. After 1 block turn left onto Palm Ave. Continue for 0.4 mi. straight into the campground.

CASTELLA   MAP, B-2
Castle Crags State Park

reserve america

Castle Creek Rd., 96017-0080. T: (530) 235-2684 or (800) 444-7275; www.reserveamerica.com.

🚐 ★★★   ⛺ ★★★

Beauty: ★★★★	Site Privacy: ★★
Spaciousness: ★★	Quiet: ★★
Security: ★★★	Cleanliness: ★★★
Insect Control: ★★★	Facilities: ★★

The stark, saw-toothed spires that give this small park its name rise some 4,000 feet from the Sacramento River to the tips of their granite peaks. If the challenging, highly strenuous hike up there from the campground doesn't take your breath away, the spectacular views will. The park straddles I-5, with the larger part of it, including the crags, lying west of the highway. To the east, just beyond the railroad tracks and right alongside the river, are 12 grassy sites that are ideal for anglers. The main campground, though, is across the road, higher up toward the summit. Its three ascending loops snake through an attractively wooded hillside of oaks, cedars, and pines, with mediocre screening between closely set, shallow sites. The most private is 11, though its rear faces a chain-link fence. Similarly recessed are 14 and 15, and both 26 and 37 have pull-through parking. The stone masonry of the fire pits dates from when the Civilian Conservation Corps was active here in the early 20th century. The continuous roar of traffic emanating from the interstate is a jarring note to an otherwise splendid setting.

BASICS

Operated By: California Dept. of Parks & Recreation. **Open:** All year. **Site Assignment:** Reservations accepted w/ V, MC, D. **Registration:** At entrance booth. **Fee:** $14–$20 w/ senior discount; cash, CA check. **Parking:** At site.

FACILITIES

Number of RV-only Sites: 11. **Number of Tent-only Sites:** 52. **Hookups:** None. **Each Site:** Picnic table, fire grate, food storage box. **Dump Station:** No. **Laundry:** No. **Pay Phone:** No. **Restrooms and Showers:** Yes. **Fuel:** No. **Propane:** No. **Internal Roads:** Paved. **RV Service:** No. **Market:** 7 mi. north in Dunsmuir. **Restaurant:** 7 mi. north in Dunsmuir. **General Store:** Yes. **Vending:** No. **Swimming:** Sacramento River. **Playground:** No. **Activities:** Hiking, fishing, canoeing, rafting, bicycling nearby. **Nearby Attractions:** Lake Siskiyou; Mount Shasta Ski Park, Mount Shasta Hatchery & Sisson Museum; downtown Dunsmuir. **Additional Information:** Mount Shasta Chamber of Commerce & Visitors Bureau, (530) 926-4865 or (800) 926-4865; Dunsmuir Chamber of Commerce, (530) 235-2177.

RESTRICTIONS

Pets: On 6-ft. leash. **Fires:** Fire grates only. **Alcoholic Beverages:** Allowed at site. **Vehicle Maximum Length:** 27 ft. **Other:** 14-day stay limit from May 1–Sept. 30, 30-day limit the rest of the year; no firearms; no wood gathering.

TO GET THERE

From Dunsmuir on I-5 drive 6.5 mi. south to the Castella Exit. Turn right (west) and continue for 0.3 mi. Turn right into the well-signed park. The campground is 0.7 mi. beyond the entrance station.

CHINO   MAP, E-3
Prado Regional Park

16700 Euclid Ave., 91710. T: (909) 597-4260; www.co.san-bernardino.ca.us/parks/prado.htm.

🚐 ★★★★   ⛺ ★★★

Beauty: ★★★★	Site Privacy: ★★★
Spaciousness: ★★★★	Quiet: ★★★★
Security: ★★★★	Cleanliness: ★★★
Insect Control: ★★	Facilities: ★★★★

This attractive park is just 35 miles east of downtown Los Angeles, and yet to look at its verdant grounds you might think you were in the middle of farm country. That impression is accentuated by the presence of a neighboring ranch that pens cattle up near one of Prado's two loops. The pitiful sight of so many beasts herded together in a small parcel of muddy, denuded soil is outdone only by the powerful reek of ammonia emanating from their direction, a one-two sensory punch that could convert the most committed of meat eaters to vegetarianism. You won't have much to beef about though if you bring your fishing rod to Prado, as the lake is well stocked w/ trout in winter and catfish in summer. Grassy sites are exposed but roomy, set under young sycamores, eucalyptus, and pines. Aim for any of 7–75, as they are not only among the shadier, but also out of view of the bovine stalag. Of the great number of amenities here, one of the more unusual is an area set aside on the lake for radio-controlled model boats.

BASICS

Operated By: San Bernardino County, Regional Parks Dept. **Open:** All year. **Site Assignment:**

Reservations accepted w/ V, MC, D; walk-ins welcome. **Registration:** At entrance booth. **Fee:** $20; cash, check, V, MC, D. **Parking:** At site.

FACILITIES

Number of RV-only Sites: 75. **Number of Tent-only Sites:** 25. **Hookups:** Electric (50 amps), water, sewer. **Each Site:** Picnic table, fire ring. **Dump Station:** Yes. **Laundry:** Yes. **Pay Phone:** Yes. **Restrooms and Showers:** Yes. **Fuel:** No. **Propane:** No. **Internal Roads:** Paved. **RV Service:** No. **Market:** 8 mi. south in Corona. **Restaurant:** 8 mi. south in Corona. **General Store:** No. **Vending:** No. **Swimming:** No. **Playground:** Yes. **Other:** Some wheelchair-accessible facilities, boat ramp. **Activities:** Fishing, horseback riding rentals, soccer field, boat rentals, golf. **Nearby Attractions:** Disneyland, Six Flags Magic Mountain, Riverside & its museums, gardens, & historic buildings. **Additional Information:** San Bernardino County, Regional Parks Dept., (909) 38-PARKS.

RESTRICTIONS

Pets: On leash no longer than 6 ft., $1 fee per dog. **Fires:** Fire ring only. **Alcoholic Beverages:** Allowed at site. **Vehicle Maximum Length:** 60 ft. **Other:** 14-day stay limit; no loaded firearms; no wood gathering.

TO GET THERE

In Pomona exit Hwy. 60 on Euclid Ave./Hwy. 83 and head south for 0.6 mi. Turn left at the sign for the regional park.

CLAYTON   MAP, C-2
Mount Diablo State Park

reserve america

96 Mitchell Canyon Rd., 94517. T: (925) 837-2525 or (925) 838-9225; www.reserveamerica.com.

🚐 ★★   ⛺ ★★★★

Beauty: ★★★★	Site Privacy: ★★★
Spaciousness: ★★	Quiet: ★★★★
Security: ★★★	Cleanliness: ★★★
Insect Control: ★★★	Facilities: ★★

The rolling grass-covered hills that make up this highly scenic park are dappled with live oak, gray pines, and juniper. If the extraordinary valley views don't take your breath away, you had better check your pulse! Or come back in spring, when an explosion of wildflowers should stimulate even the most colorblind of campers. There are three campgrounds here set at different altitudes, with the no-reservations Junction the least appealing. We prefer the Juniper loop (3,000 feet elevation) because, in a park where sites run toward petite, its are the larger and better screened. Additionally, many are blessed with outstanding westward vistas. Prime among many fine choices is number 20, detached from its neighbors and nursed by a superannuated, overhanging tree. In summer months when the heat intensifies, the cool, shady Live Oak loop (1,450 feet elevation) is the sounder choice. As the risk of wildfires escalates in summer, the park may close.

Plan to call ahead, therefore, from June through September.

BASICS

Operated By: California Dept. of Parks & Recreation. **Open:** All year; but may close in summer w/ extreme fire danger—call ahead. **Site Assignment:** Reservations recommended; V, MC, D. **Registration:** At entrance kiosk. **Fee:** $12–$15; cash, CA check. Call camp for senior discount. **Parking:** At site.

FACILITIES

Number of Multipurpose Sites: 64. **Hookups:** None. **Each Site:** Picnic table, fire grate, food storage box in some sites. **Dump Station:** No. **Laundry:** No. **Pay Phone:** Yes. **Restrooms and Showers:** Yes. **Fuel:** No. **Propane:** No. **Internal Roads:** Paved & windy. **RV Service:** No. **Market:** 10 mi. south in Livermore. **Restaurant:** 10 mi. south in Livermore. **General Store:** No. **Vending:** No. **Swimming:** No. **Playground:** No. **Other:** Some wheelchair-accessible facilities, visitor center, observation deck, Summit Museum. **Activities:** Hiking, horseback riding, star gazing, mountain biking, rock climbing. **Nearby Attractions:** Berkeley Botanical Garden & museums; Dunsmuir House & Gardens Historic Estate, Chabot Space & Science Center, Jack London Square, museums, zoo, & more in Oakland. **Additional Information:** Walnut Creek Chamber of Commerce, (925) 934-2007.

RESTRICTIONS

Pets: On 6-ft. leash. Not allowed on trails. **Fires:** Fire grates only; restrictions are in effect when wildfire risk is extreme. **Alcoholic Beverages:** Not allowed. **Vehicle Maximum Length:** 20 ft. **Other:** 30-day stay limit; no firearms; no wood gathering.

TO GET THERE

From I-680 at Walnut Creek take the North Main St. Exit. Head east (toward downtown) to Ygnacio Valley Rd. Follow that for 2.1 mi. to the traffic light and turn right on Walnut Ave., which turns into North Gate Rd. Proceed to park entrance booth; Junction campground is 6.7 mi. beyond that.

COBB MOUNTAIN   MAP, C-2
Yogi Bear's Jellystone Park Camp-Resort

reserve america

14117 Bottle Rock Rd., 95426. T: (707) 928-4322 or (866) 928-4322; www.jellystonecobbmtn.com.

🚐 ★★★★   ⛺ ★★★★

Beauty: ★★★★	Site Privacy: ★★★
Spaciousness: ★★★	Quiet: ★★★
Security: ★★★★	Cleanliness: ★★★★
Insect Control: ★★★★	Facilities: ★★★★

Whether you are an RV park enthusiast, enjoy the comfort of a cabin in the woods, or just like to tent camp and sleep in the great outdoors, Jellystone Park's accommodations, amenities, and activities are top-notch. Amenities and activities include swimming, mini-golf, hay rides, tennis, volleyball, fishing, hiking, and appearances from Yogi Bear and friends,

BASICS

Operated By: Brian Barnhardt. **Open:** All year. **Site Assignment:** Reservations recommended. **Registration:** At office. **Fee:** RV, $30–$40; tent, $25; cabin, $55–$65.

FACILITIES

Number of RV-only Sites: 107. **Hookups:** Yes. **Each Site:** Picnic table, fire ring. **Dump Station:** Yes. **Laundry:** Yes. **Pay Phone:** Yes. **Restrooms and Showers:** Yes. **Fuel:** No. **Propane:** No. **Internal Roads:** Gravel. **General Store:** Camp store. **Vending:** Yes. **Swimming:** Yes. **Playground:** Yes. **Other:** Trout creek, gem mining, snack bar, pedal carts.

RESTRICTIONS

Pets: On leash attended only. **Fires:** Allowed. **Vehicle Maximum Length:** 40 ft. rigs easily accommodated.

TO GET THERE

From Bay Area, Points South Hwy. 29 N to Middletown Hwy, 175 N to Cobb Mountain., 8.5 mi. left on Bottle Rock Rd for 3 mi., left into campground.

COLEVILLE
Sonora Bridge
MAP, C-3

Hwy. 108, 96107.
T: (760) 932-7070;
www.r5.fs.fed.us/htnf/soncamp.htm.

🚐 ★★★★   ▲ ★★★★

Beauty: ★★★★	Site Privacy: ★★★
Spaciousness: ★★★	Quiet: ★★★★
Security: ★★★	Cleanliness: ★★★★
Insect Control: ★★★★	Facilities: ★

There is a rough-surfaced russet knob of granite on one flank of this expansive camp, a steep rocky slope on another, and all around are fabulous views of the mountains. Thick-trunked Jeffrey pines are the dominant trees in these parts, though the campground is also accented by juniper and such chaparral as salt bush and sage. Unlike Leavitt Meadows, just up the road, there's no river flowing by this turf, but sites here are clearly superior, and many offer pull-through parking. Most are roomier and largely more private, owing partly to a thick undergrowth of mountain mahogany, and partly to their wider distribution along a series of four loops. Additionally, the breathtaking views of the Sierra simply cannot be beat. Unless, that is, you strap a pack to your back and hoof it higher into the mountains, or head out to the Walker River to fish for rainbow trout. Elevation at Sonora Bridge, which is 20 miles west of Bridgeport, is 6,800 feet; icy winds whistle through camp early and late in the year, so bring along some warm clothing.

BASICS

Operated By: American Land & Leisure, concessionaire. **Open:** Mid-May–mid-Oct.; weather permitting. **Site Assignment:** First come, first served. **Registration:** At entrance kiosk. **Fee:** $10; cash, check. **Parking:** At site.

FACILITIES

Number of RV-only Sites: 23. **Hookups:** None. **Each Site:** Picnic table, fire grate. **Dump Station:** No. **Laundry:** No. **Pay Phone:** No. **Restrooms and Showers:** Vault toilets, no showers. **Fuel:** No. **Propane:** No. **Internal Roads:** Dirt but smooth. **RV Service:** No. **Market:** 19 mi. east in Bridgeport. **Restaurant:** 19 mi. east in Bridgeport. **General Store:** No. **Vending:** No. **Swimming:** No. **Playground:** No. **Activities:** Hiking, fishing, stargazing. **Nearby Attractions:** Bodie State Historic Park near Bridgeport; Sonora Pass. **Additional Information:** Eastern Sierra Interagency Visitor Center, (760) 876-6222; Bridgeport Chamber of Commerce, (760) 932-7500.

RESTRICTIONS

Pets: On leash. **Fires:** Fire grates only. **Alcoholic Beverages:** Allowed. **Vehicle Maximum Length:** 35 ft. **Other:** 14-day stay limit.

TO GET THERE

From Bridgeport drive 17 mi. north on US 395. Turn left (west) onto Hwy. 108 and drive 1.5 mi. to the campground entrance on the left.

CORNING
Woodson Bridge State Recreation Area
MAP, B-2

25340 South Ave., 96021-0616.
T: (530) 839-2112 or (800) 444-7275;
www.reserveamerica.com.

🚐 ★★★★   ▲ ★★★★

Beauty: ★★★★	Site Privacy: ★★★
Spaciousness: ★★★	Quiet: ★★★
Security: ★★★★	Cleanliness: ★★★★
Insect Control: ★	Facilities: ★★

The marked increase in visitation to this sweet gem of a park proves the secret is out. No wonder, with its grounds, which overlap the Sacramento River, so fertile and grassy, and its recessed, scattered campsites framed by massive, aged valley oaks. Unbelievably, this sylvan glade is not concealed in some forested outback, but instead is located a scant 6 miles east of Corning and I-5, 3 miles west of Hwy. 99 and Vina. If fishing is your game, prepare to mark your date book: king salmon runs are optimum from October through May, the peak for shad is in July and August, striped bass in early fall, steelhead in October and November, and catfish may be caught just about any time of year. If that is not enough to lure you to this appealing recreation area, perhaps its extraordinary birding will, with yellow-billed cuckoos, hummingbirds, pheasants, hawks, falcons, and many other species commonly seen. So are swarms of mosquitoes, from spring through mid-summer—plan to bring repellent. Older guidebooks list Woodson Bridge as having a dump station

but fallen trees now make that inaccessible. There are no plans yet to restore it.

BASICS

Operated By: California Dept. of Parks & Recreation. **Open:** All year. **Site Assignment:** Reservations accepted w/ V, MC, D. **Registration:** At entrance booth. **Fee:** $12 from May 15–Sept. 15, $9 the rest of the year; cash, CA check. **Parking:** At site.

FACILITIES

Number of RV-only Sites: 37. **Hookups:** None. **Each Site:** Picnic table, fire grate. **Dump Station:** No, inaccessible because of fallen trees. **Laundry:** Yes. **Pay Phone:** Yes. **Restrooms and Showers:** Yes. **Fuel:** No. **Propane:** No. **Internal Roads:** Paved. **RV Service:** No. **Market:** 6 mi. west in Corning. **Restaurant:** 6 mi. west in Corning. **General Store:** No. **Vending:** No. **Swimming:** Sacramento River. **Playground:** No. **Other:** Some wheelchair-accessible facilities. **Activities:** Fishing, hiking, birding, boating. **Nearby Attractions:** Tejama County Park in Corning; Chico museums & Bidwell Mansion State Historic Park; outlet shopping in Anderson; William B. Ide Adobe State Historic Park near Red Bluff. **Additional Information:** Corning District Chamber of Commerce, (530) 824-5550; Chico Chamber of Commerce & Visitor Bureau, (530) 891-5556 or (800) 852-8570.

RESTRICTIONS

Pets: On 6-ft. leash. **Fires:** Fire grates only. **Alcoholic Beverages:** Allowed at site. **Vehicle Maximum Length:** 31 ft. **Other:** 14-day stay limit from June through Sept., 30-day stay limit from Oct. through May; no firearms; no wood gathering.

TO GET THERE

In Corning on I-5 take the South Ave. Exit. Head east for 6.3 mi. and turn left into the campground.

CRESCENT CITY
Del Norte Coast Redwoods State Park
MAP, A-1

1375 Elk Valley Rd., 95531. T: (707) 464-6101;
www.reserveamerica.com.

🚐 ★★★★   ▲ ★★★★

Beauty: ★★★★	Site Privacy: ★★★★
Spaciousness: ★★★★	Quiet: ★★★
Security: ★★★	Cleanliness: ★★★★
Insect Control: ★★★	Facilities: ★★

Del Norte Coast Redwoods State Park was established in 1929 and comprises 6,400-acres with approximately 50 percent old-growth coast redwood and 8 miles of wild coastline. The park is a World Heritage Site and Biosphere Preserve. The mixed understory includes tanoak, madrone, red alder, big-leaf maple, and California bay. Ground cover is dense with a wide range of species. The campground development is located in an area that was logged in the 1920s. Wildlife is present in all areas. Salmon and steelhead spawn in Mill Creek. Bobcat, coyote, bear, deer, squirrels, and chipmunks are most frequently seen. Varied thrushes, Steller's jays, hawks, great blue herons, and dippers are common birds. The topography is fairly steep, with elevations from sea level to 1,277 feet. Approximately one-half mile of sandy beach is known as Wilson Beach or False Klamath Cove. This beach is unsafe for swimming due to steep beach slope, rocky conditions, and frequent rough seas and cold water, but does provide excellent tidepool opportunities at low tide. The park has 10 miles of hiking trails, beach and water access, and camping opportunities. Mill Creek Campground offers 145 campsites that can accommodate motor homes up to 31 feet and trailers to 27 feet. Some walk-in sites are available for tent campers. The campground is open year-round.

BASICS

Operated By: California State Parks. **Open:** May 1–Sept. 30. **Site Assignment:** Reservations from May 1–Sept. 5. **Registration:** At office. **Fee:** Single, $15–$20. **Parking:** At site.

FACILITIES

Number of Multipurpose Sites: 275. **Hookups:** None. **Dump Station:** Yes. **Laundry:** No. **Pay Phone:** More than 5 mi. **Restrooms and Showers:** Yes. **Fuel:** No. **Propane:** No. **Internal Roads:** Paved. **RV Service:** No. **Market:** No. **Restaurant:** No. **General Store:** No. **Vending:** No. **Swimming:** No. **Playground:** No. **Other:** Fees include entry for 1 vehicle & 1 legally towed vehicle or trailer, additional vehicles will be charged per night at the park. **Activities:** Hiking, nature trails, wildlife viewing.

RESTRICTIONS

Pets: On 6-ft. leash in a tent or enclosed vehicle at night. Except for guide dogs, pets are not allowed in park buildings, on trails, or on most beaches. **Fires:** In designated fireplaces. **Alcoholic Beverages:** Not allowed. **Other:** Fees include entry for 1 vehicle & 1 legally towed vehicle or trailer, additional vehicles will be charged per night at the park.

TO GET THERE

Park is 7 mi. south of Crescent City; turn east on the campground road. The campground entrance is 1.5 mi. east of the highway; campground is still 1 mi. after entrance. Park sign says in capital letters "MILL CREEK CAMPGROUND" and in small letters "DEL NORTE COAST REDWOODS STATE PARK."

CRESCENT CITY   MAP, A-1
Jedediah Smith Redwoods State Park

1375 Elk Valley Rd., 95531. T: (707) 464-6101/5112 or (800) 444-7275; www.reserveamerica.com.

🚐 ★★★★   ⛺ ★★★★

Beauty: ★★★★   Site Privacy: ★★★
Spaciousness: ★★★★   Quiet: ★★★
Security: ★★★   Cleanliness: ★★★★
Insect Control: ★★★   Facilities: ★★★

Heading south from Oregon along Hwy. 199, Jedediah Smith Redwoods State Park is the northernmost of several redwoods-focused state parks in California. Named for the first white man known to cross the Coast Range, "Jed Smith" is a striking introduction to Sequoia sempervirens. These giant redwood trees are the tallest living things in the world, with several old-growth groves towering over the 10,000-acre preserve. The campground is less than 10 miles northeast of Crescent City, set beside the emerald-green Smith River. Tan oaks, maples, and rhododendrons thrive among the red-barked atavars, with moss and lace lichen contributing to the cool, shady, rainforest atmosphere. The roomy and well-screened sites are spread decently apart over a series of loops, the most private being 68 (with a river view), 70 (a spacious end spot), and 77. Site 60 has pull-through parking. Years ago local Native Americans gathered the green, stringy lichen that hangs from the trees and dried it to use as soft bedding material. It—and all other vegetation within the park—is now protected by the state.

BASICS

Operated By: California Dept. of Parks & Recreation. **Open:** All year. **Site Assignment:** Reservations recommended; V, MC, D. **Registration:** At entrance booth. **Fee:** $15–$20; cash, CA check. **Parking:** At site.

FACILITIES

Number of RV-only Sites: 106. **Number of Tent-only Sites:** 5. **Hookups:** None. **Each Site:** Picnic table, fire grate, food storage box. **Dump Station:** Yes. **Laundry:** No. **Pay Phone:** Yes. **Restrooms and Showers:** Yes. **Fuel:** No. **Propane:** No. **Internal Roads:** Paved. **RV Service:** No. **Market:** 9 mi. west in Crescent City. **Restaurant:** 9 mi. west in Crescent City. **General Store:** No. **Vending:** No. **Swimming:** No. **Playground:** No. **Other:** Some wheelchair-accessible facilities. **Activities:** Hiking, fishing, bicycling, horseback riding, canoeing, rafting. **Nearby Attractions:** Redwood National & State Parks; Battery Point Lighthouse, Ocean World & Del Norte County Historical Museum in Crescent City. **Additional Information:** Crescent City–Del Norte County Chamber of Commerce, (707) 464-3174 or (800) 343-8300.

RESTRICTIONS

Pets: On 6-ft. leash. **Fires:** Fire grates only. **Alcoholic Beverages:** Allowed at site. **Vehicle Maximum Length:** 36 ft. **Other:** 14-day stay limit from May 1–Sept. 30; no firearms; no wood gathering.

TO GET THERE

From Crescent City drive 3.5 mi. north on US 101. Exit on US 199 and head east towards Grants Pass, OR. Continue for 5 mi. to the park entrance on the right.

CRESCENT CITY   MAP, A-1
Mill Creek Campground

Del Norte Coast Redwoods State Park, 1375 Elk Valley Rd., 95531. T: (707) 464-9533 or (800) 444-7275; www.cal-parks.ca.gov.

🚐 ★★★★   ⛺ ★★★★

Beauty: ★★★★   Site Privacy: ★★★★
Spaciousness: ★★★   Quiet: ★★★
Security: ★★★   Cleanliness: ★★★★
Insect Control: ★★★   Facilities: ★★

This campground is set in the heart of Mill Creek Canyon among a concentration of red alders and second-growth redwoods. It is a moist, antediluvian environment, with winter rainfall, which averages 100 inches, contributing to a fertile, mossy, jungle-like luminescence. Rhododendrons, azaleas, maples, and ferns thrive here, along with pale yellow slugs as thick as a thumb and a good deal longer. A sextet of loops features level grass and dirt sites that are small-ish and rather crowded together, but fairly well screened by the flourishing foliage and equipped with capacious car slips. One of the larger spots is 38, by the creek, and of the many walk-up units, 4, 5, and 6 offer the best privacy. A pristine stretch of beach is accessible via the challenging Damnation Creek Trail, an old Native American path that loses 1,000 feet as it descends through a grove of old-growth redwoods. Mill Creek is closed to fishing from October through April to protect spawning salmon.

BASICS

Operated By: California Dept. of Parks & Recreation. **Open:** Apr.–Oct. **Site Assignment:** Reservations accepted w/ V, MC, D. **Registration:** At entrance booth. **Fee:** $15; cash, CA check. **Parking:** At site.

FACILITIES

Number of RV-only Sites: 145. **Hookups:** None. **Each Site:** Picnic table, fire grate, food storage box. **Dump Station:** Yes. **Laundry:** No. **Pay Phone:** No. **Restrooms and Showers:** Yes. **Fuel:** No. **Propane:** No. **Internal Roads:** Paved, w/ bumps & potholes. **RV Service:** No. **Market:** 6 mi. north in Crescent City. **Restaurant:** 6 mi. north in Crescent City. **General Store:** No. **Vending:** No. **Swimming:** Smith River. **Playground:** No. **Other:** Some wheelchair-accessible facilities. **Activities:** Hiking, bicycling, fishing. **Nearby Attractions:** Redwood National & State Parks; Battery Point Lighthouse, Ocean World & Del Norte County Historical Museum in Crescent City. **Additional Information:** Crescent City–Del Norte County Chamber of Commerce, (707) 464-3174 or (800) 343-8300.

RESTRICTIONS

Pets: On 6-ft. leash. **Fires:** Fire grates only. **Alcoholic Beverages:** Allowed at site. **Vehicle Maximum Length:** 31 ft. **Other:** 14-day stay limit from May 1–Sept. 30; no firearms; no wood gathering; no mushroom-plucking.

TO GET THERE

From Crescent City head 6 mi. south on US 101 to the marked access road for the State Park. Turn left; the park entrance is 1.5 mi. ahead.

DANA POINT MAP, F-3
Doheny State Beach

reserve america

25300 Dana Point Harbor Dr., 92629.
T: (949) 496-6172 or (800) 444-7275;
www.reserveamerica.com.

🚐 ★★★★   ⛺ ★★★

Beauty: ★★★★   Site Privacy: ★★★
Spaciousness: ★★   Quiet: ★★
Security: ★★★   Cleanliness: ★★★★
Insect Control: ★   Facilities: ★★

This state park provides sun and surf lovers access to more than a mile of beautiful beach, with the good news for campers being that a healthy number of sites are set right on the sand. Stroll from your tent to the shore in one fluid motion, or bask in a sunset radiating over the water from the comfort of your picnic table. If it is high tide, this must be "surfin' USA!" And if the water is low, grab your children and go check out the tide pools. All of these somewhat tightly packed sites benefit from the fresh breeze of the salty sea, but the ones to the rear of camp are annoyingly close to railroad tracks, and also have the dubious distinction of facing a large housing development across the interstate. Best by far are those on the beach, such as 38–43, and odd numbers from 45–59. Though swimming is ideal from late June through early autumn, solitude-seekers will enjoy camping here in winter, when daytime temperatures are still comfortable.

BASICS

Operated By: California Dept. of Parks & Recreation. **Open:** All year. **Site Assignment:** Reservations recommended w/ V, MC, D. **Registration:** At entrance booth. **Fee:** $16–$25; cash, CA check. **Parking:** At site. $5 per day.

FACILITIES

Number of RV-only Sites: 122. **Hookups:** None. **Each Site:** Picnic table, fire grate, paved parking pad. **Dump Station:** Yes, $5 fee. **Laundry:** No. **Pay Phone:** Yes. **Restrooms and Showers:** Yes, coin-operated hot showers. **Fuel:** No. **Propane:** No. **Internal Roads:** Paved. **RV Service:** No. **Market:** 1 mi. east in Dana Point. **Restaurant:** 1 mi. east in Dana Point. **General Store:** No. **Vending:** No. **Swimming:** Pacific Ocean. **Playground:** No. **Other:** Some wheelchair-accessible facilities. **Activities:** Surfing, swimming, fishing, people-watching, tide pool exploring, volleyball, whale-watching. **Nearby Attractions:** San Clemente, Dana Point, Mission San Juan Capistrano. **Additional Information:** Dana Point Chamber of Commerce, Tourism & Visitors Center, (949) 496-1555.

RESTRICTIONS

Pets: On 6-ft. leash. **Fires:** Fire grates only. **Alcoholic Beverages:** Not allowed. **Vehicle Maximum Length:** 35 ft. **Other:** 7-day stay limit from June 1–Sept. 30, 14-day stay limit for the rest of the year; no firearms; no wood gathering.

TO GET THERE

From San Juan Capistrano head 3 mi. south on I-5 to the Beach Cities/Pacific Coast Hwy. Exit. Turn left onto Dana Point Harbor Dr., then left again onto Park Lantern into the park.

DEATH VALLEY MAP, D-3
Furnace Creek

Death Valley National Park, Hwy. 190, 92328.
T: (760) 786-3200 or (800) 365-2267;
www.nps.gov/deva.

🚐 ★★★★   ⛺ ★★★

Beauty: ★★★★   Site Privacy: ★★
Spaciousness: ★★   Quiet: ★★★
Security: ★★★★   Cleanliness: ★★★
Insect Control: ★★★★   Facilities: ★★

Visit this campground between May and September and you'll have a good idea of what Hades is all about; you are also likely to have most of the domain to yourself. Certainly the "furnace" half of its name seems apt, with an oppressive blanket of heat clinging to the dry terrain in much the manner that bark hugs the trunk of a tree. As to the "creek," just be thankful for water spigots. Level sites of hard clay are closely grouped around a series of loops, with a bit of shade provided by mesquite, creosote bushes, and tamarisk trees. The blistering heat seems magnified by the camp's position at 196 feet below sea level, but we prefer it to Stovepipe Wells, which is little more than a pebbly parking lot without a twig of shade. The park visitor center is next to the campground, and a number of excellent hikes and drives are in the vicinity. Laundry machines, showers, swimming pool, general store, and gasoline are available at Furnace Creek Ranch.

BASICS

Operated By: National Park Service. **Open:** All year. **Site Assignment:** Reservations recommended, accepted Oct. 15–Apr. 15; V, MC, D. **Registration:** At entrance booth. **Fee:** $10–$16; cash, check (plus park entrance fee). **Parking:** At site.

FACILITIES

Number of RV-only Sites: 101. **Number of Tent-only Sites:** 35. **Hookups:** None. **Each Site:** Picnic table, fire grate, barbecue grill. **Dump Station:** Yes. **Laundry:** No. **Pay Phone:** Yes. **Restrooms and Showers:** Flush toilets, no showers. **Fuel:** No. **Propane:** No. **Internal Roads:** Paved. **RV Service:** No. **Market:** 47 mi. north in Beatty. **Restaurant:** At Furnace Creek Ranch. **General Store:** No. **Vending:** No. **Swimming:** No. **Playground:** No. **Other:** Some wheelchair-accessible facilities, visitor center, museum. **Activities:** Hiking, driving tours, ranger-led activities, photography, frying eggs on the sidewalk. **Nearby Attractions:** Badwater, Scotty's Castle, Dantes View, Stovepipe Wells Village, mountains, mines, & more in Death Valley National Park. **Additional Information:** Death Valley Chamber of Commerce, (760) 852-4524.

RESTRICTIONS

Pets: On 6-ft. leash; not allowed on trails or off of roads. **Fires:** Fire grates only. **Alcoholic Beverages:** Allowed at site. **Vehicle Maximum Length:** 50 ft. **Other:** 14-day stay limit; no loaded firearms; no wood gathering.

TO GET THERE

From the Furnace Creek Visitor Center drive 0.5 mi. north on Hwy. 190 to the campground entrance on the left.

DEATH VALLEY MAP, D-3
Mesquite Spring

Death Valley National Park, Grapevine Rd., 92328.
T: (760) 786-3200; www.nps.gov/deva.

🚐 ★★★   ⛺ ★★★

Beauty: ★★★★   Site Privacy: ★★★
Spaciousness: ★★★   Quiet: ★★★
Security: ★★★★   Cleanliness: ★★★
Insect Control: ★★★★   Facilities: ★★

The vast tract of land that is Death Valley National Park is far more than a barren, stagnant desert. Give it a chance and your appreciation for the parched beauty of the scenery will likely grow as you explore the park: from the volcanic craters in the north to the salt water basins to its south, from its shifting sand dunes to the multicolored mountains that range like twin spines up its entire length. You'll be in good position at Mesquite Spring to check out Ubehebe Crater and Scotty's Castle, a lavish 1920s vacation home built in Spanish-mission style. This campground is more exposed than Furnace Creek, but it benefits, after the sun goes down, from being 2,000 feet higher. It is set against a mud-colored canyon wall and a dry creek, with two low mountain ridges paralleling its double loop. Dusty, pebbly sites are on the spacious side, and they are grouped farther apart than at Furnace Creek, allowing for a greater degree of privacy. A couple of cottonwoods mark the spring. The nearest pay phone is at the Grapevine Ranger Station, 2.5 miles north; fuel is available at Scotty's Castle; a general store is in Stovepipe Wells, 41 miles south.

BASICS

Operated By: National Park Service. **Open:** All year. **Site Assignment:** First come, first served. **Registration:** At entrance kiosk. **Fee:** $10; cash, check (plus park entrance fee). **Parking:** At site.

FACILITIES

Number of RV-only Sites: 30. **Hookups:** None. **Each Site:** Picnic table, fire grate. **Dump Station:** Yes. **Laundry:** No. **Pay Phone:** No. **Restrooms and Showers:** Flush toilets, no showers. **Fuel:** No. **Propane:** No. **Internal Roads:** Paved. **RV Service:** No. **Market:** 53 mi. east in Beatty. **Restaurant:** 41 mi. south in Stovepipe Wells. **General Store:** No. **Vending:** No. **Swimming:** No. **Playground:** No. **Other:** Some wheelchair-accessible facilities. **Activities:** Hiking, driving tours, stargazing, photography. **Nearby Attractions:** Badwater, Scotty's Castle, Dantes View, Stovepipe Wells Village, mountains, mines, & more in Death Valley National Park. **Additional Information:** Death Valley Chamber of Commerce, (760) 852-4524.

RESTRICTIONS

Pets: On leash no longer than 6 ft., not allowed on trails or off of roads. **Fires:** Fire grates only.

Alcoholic Beverages: Allowed at site. **Vehicle Maximum Length:** 50 ft. **Other:** 30-day stay limit; no loaded firearms; no wood gathering.

TO GET THERE

From Furnace Creek head north on Hwy. 190 and drive 19 mi. to Sand Dune Junction. Turn right, toward Scotty's Castle, and continue for 32 mi. Turn left onto the campground access road. Proceed for another 2 mi. into the campground.

DEATH VALLEY   MAP, D-3
Wildrose

Hwy. 190. P.O. box 579, Wildrose Canyon Rd., 92328. T: (760) 786-3200; www.nps.gov/deva.

🚐 ★★★★   ⛺ ★★★★

Beauty: ★★★★   Site Privacy: ★★★
Spaciousness: ★★★★   Quiet: ★★★★
Security: ★★   Cleanliness: ★★★★
Insect Control: ★★★★ Facilities: ★

The wonderful, oleander-shaded picnic area in the dramatically eroded Wildrose Canyon is misleading. You will find nothing so pleasant in the way of plantings at the similarly named campground. Still, there is a Spartan beauty to this arid, primitive camp. Very Spartan. It is located in a side gully of the canyon, with rumpled hills on either side. There are no shade trees to shelter the dusty, pebbly ground, only such scrub as creosote and salt bush. The same, of course, might also be said of most of Death Valley's other campgrounds; at least Wildrose has potable water. Because the campground, which is 30 miles south of Stovepipe Wells Village, is at 4,100 feet of elevation, evenings are blessedly cooler here than elsewhere in the park. Comparable spots are roomy but exposed, and dispersed in two sections (the upper one being reserved for tents). Even when Furnace Creek and Stovepipe Wells are brimming with campers, you are likely to find plenty of space and tranquility at this remote place. Use it as a base for exploring such Death Valley attractions as the beehive-shaped charcoal kilns, Skidoo, a ghost town, and the Eureka mine.

BASICS

Operated By: National Park Service. **Open:** All year. **Site Assignment:** First come, first served. **Registration:** Not necessary. **Fee:** None (pay park entrance fee). **Parking:** At site.

FACILITIES

Number of RV-only Sites: 11. **Number of Tent-only Sites:** 11. **Hookups:** None. **Each Site:** Picnic table, fire grate &/or barbecue grill. **Dump Station:** No. **Laundry:** No. **Pay Phone:** No. **Restrooms and Showers:** Vault toilets, no showers. **Fuel:** No. **Propane:** No. **Internal Roads:** Gravel, good condition. **RV Service:** No. **Market:** 65 mi. south in Ridgecrest. **Restaurant:** 30 mi. north in Stovepipe Wells. **General Store:** No. **Vending:** No. **Swimming:** No. **Playground:** No. **Activities:** Hiking, solitudinous meditation, stargazing. **Nearby Attractions:** Ballarat Ghost Town; Trona Pinnacles. **Additional Information:** Death Valley Chamber of Commerce, (760) 852-4524.

RESTRICTIONS

Pets: On leash no longer than 6 ft., not allowed on trails. **Fires:** Fire grates only. **Alcoholic Beverages:** Allowed at site. **Vehicle Maximum Length:** 25 ft. **Other:** 30-day stay limit; no loaded firearms; no wood gathering.

TO GET THERE

From Ridgecrest drive 13 mi. east on Hwy. 178. Turn left on Trona Rd. and continue for 42 mi. to Wildrose Canyon Rd. Turn right and proceed for 9 mi. Bear right at the fork in the road; the campground is 0.25 mi. ahead on the left.

DUNCANS MILLS   MAP, C-1
Casini Ranch Family Campground

P.O. Box 22, 95430. T: (707) 865-2255 or (800) 451-8400; www.casiniranch.com.

🚐 ★★★★★   ⛺ ★★★★

Beauty: ★★★★   Site Privacy: ★★★★
Spaciousness: ★★★★   Quiet: ★★★★
Security: ★★★★   Cleanliness: ★★★
Insect Control: ★★★   Facilities: ★★★★

Not too many years ago this family-operated campground was a dairy farm, and many of the rustic buildings from that era remain, along with miscellaneous farm implements that have been decoratively strewn about the property. It is hard to imagine, though, that the scene was any prettier when cows lowed through the grassy meadows and varied woodland than it is today, even when brimming with campers. The level property sits in an oxbow bend of the Russian River, a perfect position that blesses it not only with a number of water-view sites but also a greater amount of serenity than the bucolic camp's roadside counterparts. True, the full-hookup area next to a row of pollarded trees at Casini's core is typically congested. If you don't require pull-through parking and can get by without a sewer connection, such pleasantly secluded spots as 88–90, 92–94, and 96–98 are infinitely more appealing. Similarly, 36–40 are the pick of the primitive options, where grassy sites are so spacious and well buttressed by vegetation as to satisfy even the most finicky of tent campers.

BASICS

Operated By: Casini family. **Open:** All year. **Site Assignment:** Reservations accepted w/ V, MC, D, AE or advance check payments. **Registration:** At entrance booth or office. Register at store during the off season. **Fee:** $26–$34; 9% local tax; cash, V, MC, AE, D. **Parking:** At site.

FACILITIES

Number of RV-only Sites: 225. **Hookups:** Electric (30 amps), water, sewer, cable TV. **Each Site:** Picnic table, fire grate. **Dump Station:** Yes. **Laundry:** Yes. **Pay Phone:** Yes. **Restrooms and Showers:** Yes. **Fuel:** No. **Propane:** Yes. **Internal Roads:** Packed gravel & dirt, good condition. **RV Service:** No. **Market:** 0.75 mi. in Duncans Mills. **Restaurant:** 0.75 mi. in Duncans Mills. **General Store:** Yes. **Vending:** Yes. **Swimming:** Russian River. **Playground:** Yes. **Other:** Some wheelchair-accessible facilities, rec hall, boat ramp. **Activities:** Fishing, kayak & canoe rentals. **Nearby Attractions:** Fort

Ross State Historic Park, Kruse Rhododendron State Reserve & Salt Point State Park in Jenner; Austin Creek State Recreation Area & Armstrong Redwoods State Reserve in Guerneville; winery tours. **Additional Information:** Russian River Chamber of Commerce & Visitors Center, (707) 869-9212 or (877) 644-9001.

RESTRICTIONS

Pets: On leash. **Fires:** Fire grates only. **Alcoholic Beverages:** Allowed. **Vehicle Maximum Length:** No limit. **Other:** 30-day stay limit; no firearms; no wood gathering.

TO GET THERE

From Guerneville head west on Hwy. 116 and drive 8.4 mi. to Duncans Mills. Turn left on Moscow Rd. and continue for 0.75 mi. to the well-signed campground entrance.

EARLIMART   MAP, D-2
Colonel Allensworth State Historic Park

reserve america

Star Rte. 1, Box 148, 93219. T: (661) 849-3433; www.reserveamerica.com.

🚐 ★★★★   ⛺ ★★★★

Beauty: ★★★★   Site Privacy: ★★
Spaciousness: ★★   Quiet: ★★★★★
Security: ★★★★★   Cleanliness: ★★★★
Insect Control: ★★★   Facilities: ★★

Colonel Allensworth State Historic Park is the only California town to be founded, financed, and governed by African Americans. The small farming community was founded in 1908 by Colonel Allen Allensworth and a group dedicated to improving the economic and social status of African Americans. Uncontrollable circumstances, including a drop in the area's water table, resulted in the town's demise. With continuing restoration and special events the town is coming back to life as a State Historic Park. The parks visitor center features a film about the site. A yearly rededication ceremony reaffirms the vision of the pioneers. Fifteen campsites, open all year, will accommodate RVs or tents. Each site includes a picnic table and a camp stove; flush toilets are nearby. Facilities for disabled people are available. Turf, trees, and shade ramadas are other features. A nearby picnic area is shaded by 75 large trees, planted by the California Conservation Corps.

BASICS

Operated By: California State Parks. **Open:** All year. **Site Assignment:** Reservations available year-round. **Registration:** At office. **Fee:** Single, $10. **Parking:** At site.

FACILITIES

Number of Multipurpose Sites: 15. **Hookups:** None. **Dump Station:** Yes. **Laundry:** No. **Pay Phone:** No. **Restrooms and Showers:** Yes. **Fuel:** No. **Propane:** No. **Internal Roads:** Paved. **RV Service:** No. **Market:** No. **Restaurant:** No. **General Store:** No. **Vending:** No. **Swimming:** No.

Playground: No. **Activities:** Picnicking.

RESTRICTIONS

Pets: On 6-ft. leash in a tent or enclosed vehicle at night. Except for guide dogs, pets are not allowed in park buildings, on trails, or on most beaches. **Fires:** In designated fireplaces. **Alcoholic Beverages:** Not allowed. **Vehicle Maximum Length:** No longer than 35 ft. **Other:** Fees include entry for 1 vehicle & 1 legally towed vehicle or trailer, additional vehicles will be charged per night at the park.

TO GET THERE

The park is north of Bakersfield; 20 mi. north of Wasco on Hwy. 43; 7 mi. west of Earlimart on CR J22.

EL CENTRO   MAP, F-4
Rio Bend RV and Golf Resort

1589 Drew Rd., 92243. T: (800) 545-6481; www.riobendrvgolfresort.com.

🚐 ★★★★   ▲ ★

Beauty: ★★	Site Privacy: ★★
Spaciousness: ★★	Quiet: ★★★
Security: ★★★	Cleanliness: ★★★★
Insect Control: ★	Facilities: ★★★★

In many ways Rio Bend is a community unto itself. RVs are parked side by side along dirt lanes attractively lined with palms, eucalyptus, and citrus trees; the central plaza is colorfully accented with flowering oleanders, a couple of Conestoga wagons, and some bales of hay; there are even a post office, swimming pool, nine-hole golf course, and two stocked fishing ponds on the premises. No wonder then that the resort is also well stocked each winter with snowbirds looking to ride out the cooler months at 50 feet below sea level. True, shade trees are scarce in the short-term camping area, and tents, relegated to the thick grass outside the office, are given short shrift. But with so many amenities, these small hardships are a little easier to wink at.

BASICS

Operated By: Bill & Wanda Camp, managers. **Open:** All year. **Site Assignment:** Reservations accepted w/ V, MC. First come, first served. **Registration:** At office at the end of the driveway. **Fee:** $38; cash, V, MC. **Parking:** At site.

FACILITIES

Number of RV-only Sites: 500. **Hookups:** Electric (50 amps), water, cable TV, Internet available on request. **Each Site:** Full hookups. **Dump Station:** Yes. **Laundry:** Yes. **Pay Phone:** Yes. **Restrooms and Showers:** Yes. **Fuel:** No. **Propane:** No. **Internal Roads:** Paved & packed dirt. **RV Service:** No. **Market:** 8.5 mi. east in El Centro. **Restaurant:** 8.5 mi. east in El Centro. Only open in the winter. **General Store:** Yes. **Vending:** No. **Swimming:** Heated pool. **Playground:** No. **Other:** Some wheelchair-accessible facilities, post office, 2 fishing ponds. **Activities:** 9-hole golf course, pool, spa, fishing, shuffleboard, horseshoe pit. **Nearby Attractions:** Shopping in Mexicali across the Mexican border, Anza-Borrego Desert State Park, Salton Sea National Wildlife Refuge, Sand Dunes (east of El Centro). **Additional Informa-**

tion: El Centro Chamber of Commerce & Visitors Bureau, (760) 352-3681.

RESTRICTIONS

Pets: On leash; keep pets in the pet area. **Fires:** Not allowed. **Alcoholic Beverages:** Allowed. **Vehicle Maximum Length:** 40 ft. **Other:** No stay limit.

TO GET THERE

From El Centro head west on I-8 for 8 mi. Take the Drew Rd. Exit and turn left (south). Drive 0.5 mi. to the resort on the right.

ESCONDIDO   MAP, F-3
Dixon Lake Recreation Area

1700 North La Honda Dr., 92027.
T: (760) 839-4680; www.dixonlake.com.

🚐 ★★★   ▲ ★★★★

Beauty: ★★★★	Site Privacy: ★★★★
Spaciousness: ★★★	Quiet: ★★★★
Security: ★★★	Cleanliness: ★★★
Insect Control: ★★	Facilities: ★★★

Dixon Lake is almost too good to be true: the camp's hilltop location lies at just over 1,000 feet elevation, with a dramatic panorama of greater Escondido on one side and the small lake on the other. This latter is actually a stocked reservoir with great fishing for trout in the fall and catfish and bass year-round. Like the fish you'll throw back, some sites may be a tad small, but they are spaced fairly well apart amid a field of granite boulders that just beg to be scrambled over, and amply shaded by an appealing potpourri of trees, including the ubiquitous eucalyptus, live oak, a variety of pines, toyon, and ceanothus, as well as a healthy accent of agave. Aside from the handful of spots near the park road, it is hard to go wrong, with numbers 8, 11, 12, and 37 particularly private and 26 and 29 yielding great city views. And when you tire of boating, fishing, and hiking, the San Diego Wild Animal Park is just a 15 minutes' drive away.

BASICS

Operated By: City of Escondido. **Open:** All year. **Site Assignment:** First come, first served; reservations accepted w/ V, MC; $5 reservation fee. **Registration:** At ranger office. **Fee:** $16–$24; cash, V, MC. **Parking:** At site.

FACILITIES

Number of Multipurpose Sites: 46. **Hookups:** Electric (20, 30 amps), water, sewer. **Each Site:** Picnic table, fire grate, trash bin. **Dump Station:** Yes. **Laundry:** No. **Pay Phone:** Yes. **Restrooms and Showers:** Yes. **Fuel:** No. **Propane:** No. **Internal Roads:** Paved. **RV Service:** No. **Market:** 3 mi. south in Escondido. **Restaurant:** 3 mi. south in Escondido. **General Store:** Yes. **Vending:** No. **Swimming:** No. **Playground:** Yes. **Other:** Some wheelchair-accessible facilities, snack bar, boat launch. **Activities:** Fishing, bicycling, hiking, horseshoe pit, boat rentals. **Nearby Attractions:** Heritage Walk & Museum, San Pascal Battlefield State Historic Park, Deer Park Auto Museum, San Diego Wild Animal Park. **Additional Information:** Escondido Chamber of Commerce, (760) 745-2125.

RESTRICTIONS

Pets: Not allowed. **Fires:** Not allowed. **Alcoholic Beverages:** Allowed at campground only. **Vehicle Maximum Length:** 50 ft. **Other:** 14-day stay limit; no firearms.

TO GET THERE

From I-15 in Escondido take the El Norte Pkwy. Exit and drive 3.3 mi. north. Turn left on La Honda Dr. and continue 1.2 mi. straight into the rec area.

ESCONDIDO   MAP, F-3
Palomar Mountain State Park

reserve america

P.O. Box 175, 92060. T: (760) 742-3462; www.reserveamerica.com.

🚐 ★★★   ▲ ★★★★

Beauty: ★★★★	Site Privacy: ★★★
Spaciousness: ★★★	Quiet: ★★★
Security: ★★★	Cleanliness: ★★★
Insect Control: ★★★★	Facilities: ★★

Palomar Mountain State Park is located very near the observatory that houses one of America's largest ground-based telescopes, a testimony to the clarity of the night sky in these parts. That facility is off-limits to the public, but barring an overcast sky you should be able to see plenty of stars from the privacy of your campsite. Most are spacious and hug the contours of the hilly mountainside, which compensates for an overall lack of screening. Which is not to suggest that the terraced loops meander over a denuded knob (though there is a fair share of gray granite and mossy rocks scattered about the domain). On the contrary, this charming campground is well forested with cedars, live oak, Douglas firs, and Coulter pines. The restrooms and a couple of sites are wheelchair accessible, but most of the rest involve negotiating a few stone stairs, solid relics from when the Civilian Conservation Corps was working in the area in the early 20th century. The best seasons to camp here are spring and fall, though at an elevation of 4,700 feet the risk of snowfall exists from November through early April. Plan accordingly.

BASICS

Operated By: California Dept. of Parks & Recreation. **Open:** All year. **Site Assignment:** Reservations accepted w/ V, MC, D. **Registration:** At entrance kiosk. **Fee:** $12; cash, CA check. **Parking:** At site.

FACILITIES

Number of RV-only Sites: 12. **Number of Tent-only Sites:** 19. **Hookups:** None. **Each Site:** Picnic table, fire grate, barbecue grill, food storage box. **Dump Station:** No. **Laundry:** No. **Pay Phone:** Yes. **Restrooms and Showers:** Yes. **Fuel:** No. **Propane:** No. **Internal Roads:** Paved. **RV Service:** No. **Market:** 47 mi. northwest in Temecula. **Restaurant:** 47 mi. northwest in Temecula. **General Store:** No. **Vending:** No. **Swimming:** No. **Playground:** No. **Other:** Some wheelchair-accessible facilities. **Activities:** Hiking, fishing, ranger-led activities in summer. **Nearby Attractions:** Palomar Mountain

Observatory, San Diego Wild Animal Park, Mission San Antonio de Pala. **Additional Information:** Escondido Chamber of Commerce, (760) 745-2125.

RESTRICTIONS

Pets: On 6-ft. leash. **Fires:** Fire grates only. **Alcoholic Beverages:** Allowed at site. **Vehicle Maximum Length:** 27 ft. **Other:** 7-day stay limit; no firearms; no wood gathering.

TO GET THERE

From Escondido on I-15 drive 15 mi. north. Turn east on Hwy. 76 and continue for 21 mi. Turn left on CR S6 direction Palomar Mountain. Follow S6/South Grade Rd. for 7 mi., then turn left on East Grade/State Park Rd. The park entrance is 3.5 mi. ahead.

FALL RIVER MILLS MAP, B-2
Hat Creek—Lassen National Forest

reserve america

43225 E. Hwy. 299/ P.O. Box 220, 96028.
T: (530) 336-5521; www.reserveamerica.com.

🚐 ★★★★ ⛺ ★★★★

Beauty: ★★★	Site Privacy: ★★★
Spaciousness: ★★★	Quiet: ★★★
Security: ★★★★	Cleanliness: ★★★★
Insect Control: ★★★★	Facilities: ★

Located 1 mile west of the town of Old Station. Facilities provided include lighted restrooms with flush toilets and wash basins, picnic tables, fire rings, running water, and accessible fishing pier. Campground situated in a mixed coniferous forest, adjacent to Hat Creek. Elevation is 4,390 feet. Hat Creek is located within the Lassen National Forest, which is a total of 1.2 million acres or 1,875 square miles. It lies within seven counties; Lassen, Shasta, Tehama, Butte, Plumas, Siskiyou, and Modoc. The Forest lies at the heart of one of the most fascinating areas of California, called the Crossroads. Here the granite of the Sierra Nevada, the lava of the Cascades and the Modoc Plateau, and the sagebrush of the Great Basin meet and blend. It is an area of great variety, greeting visitors and residents alike with a wide array of recreational opportunities and adventures. Fishing, hunting, camping, hiking, bicycling, boating, snowmobiling, cross-country skiing, and just exploring and learning about nature are among the many popular pastimes. Within the Lassen National Forest you can explore a lava tube or the land of Ishi, the last survivor of the Yahi Yana Native American tribe; watch pronghorn glide across sage flats or an osprey snatch fish from lake waters; drive four-wheel trails into high granite country appointed with sapphire lakes or discover spring wildflowers on foot. The Lassen National Forest is managed for all of these and more—timber for homes, forage for livestock, water, minerals, and many other resources the land offers. It is a challenging mission aimed at providing the greatest good for the most people over the long run.

BASICS

Operated By: U.S. Forest Service. **Open:** All year. **Site Assignment:** Reservations must be made at least 4 days in advance. **Registration:** At office. **Fee:** Single, $16; group, $85. **Parking:** At park.

FACILITIES

Number of Multipurpose Sites: 42. **Hookups:** None. **Each Site:** Call ahead. **Dump Station:** 1 mi. east. **Laundry:** No. **Pay Phone:** No. **Restrooms and Showers:** Yes. **Fuel:** No. **Propane:** No. **Internal Roads:** Paved. **RV Service:** No. **Market:** No. **Restaurant:** No. **General Store:** No. **Vending:** No. **Swimming:** No. **Playground:** No. **Other:** No ATVs or ORVs may be operated w/in campground. **Activities:** Hiking, picnicking, sightseeing, caving, hunting, & fishing.

RESTRICTIONS

Pets: Pets must be restrained or on a leash at all times while in developed recreation areas. **Fires:** In fire rings, stoves, grills, or fireplaces provided for that purpose. **Alcoholic Beverages:** Not allowed. **Vehicle Maximum Length:** Call ahead.

TO GET THERE

From Hwy. 44 and Hwy. 89 junction, go through Old Station and 1 mi. west to Hat Creek Campground.

FELTON MAP, D-1
Henry Cowell Redwoods State Park

reserve america

101 North Big Trees Park Rd., 95018.
T: (831) 438-2396 or (831) 335-4598;
www.reserveamerica.com.

🚐 ★★★ ⛺ ★★★

Beauty: ★★★★	Site Privacy: ★★★
Spaciousness: ★★★	Quiet: ★★
Security: ★★	Cleanliness: ★★★
Insect Control: ★★★	Facilities: ★★

The first thing you may notice on pulling into the pair of double loops that comprise this campground is that despite the park's name there are precious few burly looking redwoods in evidence. The natural forested atmosphere derives from an abundance of knobcone pines, madrone trees, and moss-covered oaks. The Cowell grove of redwoods is a 40-minute hike (or 5-minute drive) away. Such minor misrepresentations aside, this is a fine park with roomy leaf- and dirt-based sites ranging from sun-dappled to shady, from exposed to well shielded. Unfortunately, noise carries here and can be a big problem on weekends, when Bay Area residents descend in droves. The presence of a summer-time host augments an otherwise lax enforcement of quiet time. Trash tossed into fire grates is another nuisance. Be alert to poison oak, and if you plan to visit in the spring pack along insect repellent.

BASICS

Operated By: California Dept. of Parks & Recreation. **Open:** Feb. 15–Nov. 30. **Site Assignment:** Reservations accepted 48 hours in advance w/ V, MC.

Registration: At entrance booth. **Fee:** $25; cash, CA check. **Parking:** 1 vehicle per reservation at site. $5 for additional vehicle.

FACILITIES

Number of RV-only Sites: 112. **Hookups:** None. **Each Site:** Picnic table, fire grate, food storage box. **Dump Station:** No. **Laundry:** No. **Pay Phone:** Yes. **Restrooms and Showers:** Yes. **Fuel:** No. **Propane:** No. **Internal Roads:** Paved. **RV Service:** No. **Market:** 2 mi. west in Felton. **Restaurant:** 2 mi. west in Felton. **General Store:** No. **Vending:** Yes. **Swimming:** River. **Playground:** No. **Other:** Some wheelchair-accessible facilities. **Activities:** Hiking, bicycling, horseback riding, horseshoe pit. **Nearby Attractions:** Santa Cruz Beach Boardwalk, mission, museums, Seymour Marine Discovery Center, Arboretum & Natural Bridges State Beach; Roaring Camp Railroads in Felton, Redwood Trees. **Additional Information:** Santa Cruz County Conference & Visitors Council, (831) 425-1234 or (800) 833-3494.

RESTRICTIONS

Pets: On 6-ft. leash. **Fires:** Fire grates only, attended at all times. **Alcoholic Beverages:** Allowed only in picnic areas. **Vehicle Maximum Length:** 35 ft. **Other:** 7-day stay limit from Apr. 1–Oct. 31; 30-day limit rest of year, no firearms; no wood gathering, no unattended fires.

TO GET THERE

From Santa Cruz on Hwy. 1 take Hwy. 9 north. Drive 6.5 mi. to the stop light; bear right on Graham Hill Rd. The campground is 2.7 mi. ahead on the right.

FOLSOM MAP, C-2
Beal's Point Campground

Folsom Lake State Recreation Area, 7806 Folsom-Auburn Rd., 95630-1797. T: (916) 988-0205 or (800) 444-7275; www.parks.ca.gov.

🚐 ★★★★ ⛺ ★★★★

Beauty: ★★★★	Site Privacy: ★★★
Spaciousness: ★★★★	Quiet: ★★★
Security: ★★★★	Cleanliness: ★★★
Insect Control: ★★★	Facilities: ★★★

Beal's Point is just 20 miles from Sacramento, a convenient proximity that explains why camping reservations are essential between May and mid-September. Once you get over the shock of so many people—and the absence of lake vistas from the campground—you'll be in for a treat. That's because this is a splendid woodland habitat that offers a little bit of something for everyone. At the top of that list are grassy campsites that are roomy, recessed, and shaded by conifers, blue and live oaks, and buttonwood trees. The many walk-ins make tenting here especially pleasant, though RVers do well with any of 16–38, which are level and shady. The lake features 75 miles of shoreline when it is full, and there are hiking, riding, and biking trails in the surrounding foothills. The marina offers both wet and dry slips (the latter when the water drops below 435 feet), as well as a snack bar, marine supplies, and fuel.

BASICS

Operated By: California Dept. of Parks & Recreation. **Open:** All year. **Site Assignment:** Reservations recommended; V, MC, D; off season is first come, first served. **Registration:** At entrance booth. **Fee:** $15–$20; cash, CA check. **Parking:** At site.

FACILITIES

Number of RV-only Sites: 31. **Number of Tent-only Sites:** 18. **Hookups:** None. **Each Site:** Picnic table, fire grate. **Dump Station:** Yes. **Laundry:** No. **Pay Phone:** Yes. **Restrooms and Showers:** Yes. **Fuel:** No. **Propane:** No. **Internal Roads:** Paved. **RV Service:** No. **Market:** 3 mi. south in Folsom. **Restaurant:** 3 mi. south in Folsom. **General Store:** No. **Vending:** No. **Swimming:** Folsom Lake. **Playground:** No. **Other:** Some wheelchair-accessible facilities, 4-lane boat ramp, marina, beach, snack bar in summer. **Activities:** Fishing, boat rentals, horseback riding, hiking, bicycling. **Nearby Attractions:** Folsom City Zoo, Dam, Powerhouse, museums, historic downtown, & outlet shopping; Sacramento Zoo, museums, Esquire Imax Theatre, & state parks. **Additional Information:** Folsom Chamber of Commerce & Visitors Center, (916) 985-2698; Sacramento CVB, (916) 264-7777 or (800) 292-2334.

RESTRICTIONS

Pets: On 6-ft. leash. **Fires:** Fire grates only. **Alcoholic Beverages:** Allowed at site. **Vehicle Maximum Length:** 31 ft. **Other:** 7-day stay limit from May 18 to Sept. 30, 30-day stay limit for the rest of the year; no firearms; no wood gathering.

TO GET THERE

From Sacramento drive 15 mi. east on US 50 and take Folsom Blvd. Exit. Head north on Folsom Blvd. (which becomes Folsom–Auburn Rd.). After 6.3 mi. turn right into the park.

FOLSOM
Folsom Lake SRA
MAP, C-2

7806 Folsom-Auburn Rd., 95630-1797.
T: (916) 988-0205; www.reserveamerica.com.

🚐 ★★★   ⛺ ★★★★

Beauty: ★★★	Site Privacy: ★★★
Spaciousness: ★★★	Quiet: ★★★
Security: ★★★	Cleanliness: ★★★★
Insect Control: ★★★	Facilities: ★

Folsom Lake offers an area of 40-foot sites available for reservations year-round. Located at the base of the Sierra foothills, the 18,000-acre lake and recreation area offers opportunities for hiking, biking, running, camping, picnicking, horseback riding, water-skiing, and boating. Fishing offers trout, catfish, bigmouth and smallmouth bass, and perch. Visitors can also see the Folsom Powerhouse (once called "the greatest operative electrical plant on the American continent"), which from 1885 to 1952 produced electricity for Sacramento residents. For cyclists, there is a 32-mile-long bicycle path that connects Folsom Lake with many Sacramento County parks before reaching Old Sacramento. The bike path is considered to be one of the finest of its kind in the nation. The park also includes Lake Natoma, downstream from Folsom Lake, which is popular for crew races, sailing, kayaking, and other aquatic sports. Reservations for camping in the busy season (April through September) should be made in advance. There is a group picnic site at Granite Bay on Folsom Lake; reservations are handled through the District office and can be made up to 90 days in advance.

BASICS

Operated By: California Dept. of Parks & Recreation. **Open:** All year. **Site Assignment:** Reservations can be made 7 months in advance; reservations from May 21–Sept. 3. **Registration:** At office. **Fee:** Single, $15–$20; group, $34–$111. **Parking:** At site.

FACILITIES

Number of Multipurpose Sites: 157. **Hookups:** None. **Dump Station:** No. **Laundry:** No. **Pay Phone:** No. **Restrooms and Showers:** No. **Fuel:** No. **Propane:** No. **Internal Roads:** Paved. **RV Service:** No. **Market:** No. **Restaurant:** No. **General Store:** No. **Vending:** No. **Swimming:** No. **Playground:** No. **Other:** Fees include entry for 1 vehicle & 1 legally towed vehicle or trailer; additional vehicles will be charged per night at the park. Max. of 2 vehicles parked at the campsite. **Activities:** Hiking, biking, running, camping, picnicking, horseback riding, water-skiing, & boating.

RESTRICTIONS

Pets: On 6-ft. leash in a tent or enclosed vehicle at night. Except for guide dogs, pets are not allowed in park buildings, on trails, or on most beaches. **Fires:** In designated fireplaces. **Alcoholic Beverages:** Not allowed. **Vehicle Maximum Length:** 40 ft.

TO GET THERE

The park, located near the town of Folsom, can be reached via either Hwy. 50 or I-80.

FORESTHILL
French Meadows— Tahoe National Forest
MAP, C-2

reserve america

22830 Foresthill Rd., 95631. T: (530) 367-2224; www.reserveamerica.com.

🚐 ★★★★   ⛺ ★★★★

Beauty: ★★★★	Site Privacy: ★★★
Spaciousness: ★★★★	Quiet: ★★★
Security: ★★★★	Cleanliness: ★★★★
Insect Control: ★★★★	Facilities: ★★

The campground, on the northeastern shore of French Meadows Reservoir, has two sections—one for reservations and the other first come, first served. A pleasant mixture of conifer trees provides ample shade to most camp sites. While both sections have camp sites with views of the reservoir, the first-come, first-serve section has better views and easier water access. It is also possible to moor boats at some camp sites. It can be a long drive to this attractive campground but worth the effort. Consider a day trip to Big Trees Interpretive Trail. Summer days are warm to hot, evenings are cool. This is a remote, forested basin that is peaceful and lovely because of its location. However, the reservoir is usually drawn down to low-water levels by late summer. Elevation is 5,263 feet with a season of late June through October. The lake also makes a good base camp for day-hiking into the Granite Chief Wilderness from the west side. French Meadows is located within the Tahoe National Forest, which is located northeast of Sacramento and is bordered on the east by Nevada. It consists of 832,511 acres. In the middle of California's central Sierra Nevada Mountains is the Tahoe National Forest. Although the word "Tahoe" is thought to be derived from the Washoe Indian phrase for "big water," there is a lot more to this forest than a magnificent body of water. (Actually, Lake Tahoe isn't inside the Forest's boundaries; a fact that can confuse visitors.) Visitors to Tahoe National Forest find fishing and canoeing available in ice cold, crystal-clear, high-mountain lakes tucked in among geological features of towering granite ridges and glacially serrated rock outcroppings. There are trails along sparkling rivers that crisscross the forest and meander through wildflower-dotted meadows. In addition, swimming beaches, challenging trails, camp locations of every description, and many recreation opportunities are available in the Tahoe National Forest.

BASICS

Operated By: U.S. Forest Service. **Open:** May 18–Sept. 30. **Site Assignment:** Reservations must be made at least 4 days in advance. **Registration:** At office. **Fee:** Single, $16. **Parking:** At park.

FACILITIES

Number of Multipurpose Sites: 120. **Hookups:** None. **Each Site:** Call ahead. **Dump Station:** No. **Laundry:** No. **Pay Phone:** No. **Restrooms and Showers:** Yes. **Fuel:** No. **Propane:** No. **Internal Roads:** Paved. **RV Service:** No. **Market:** No. **Restaurant:** No. **General Store:** No. **Vending:** No. **Swimming:** Yes. **Playground:** No. **Activities:** Biking, hiking.

RESTRICTIONS

Pets: Pets must be restrained or on a leash at all times while in developed recreation areas. **Fires:** In fire rings, stoves, grills, or fireplaces provided for that purpose. **Alcoholic Beverages:** Not allowed. **Vehicle Maximum Length:** 35 ft. **Other:** No refunds are given for bad weather. The area is a State Game Refuge, so no firearms.

TO GET THERE

Take I-80 to Foresthill Rd. just north of Auburn and travel 17 mi. east to Foresthill. Turn right on Mosquito Ridge Rd. and travel 34 mi. east to the French Meadow Reservoir; the French Meadows Campground is on the south shore.

FRESNO
Pine Flat Lake Recreation Area
MAP, D-2

Pine Flat Rd., 93649-0117. T: (559) 488-3004 or (559) 787-2589.

🚐 ★★★★   ⛺ ★★★

Beauty: ★★★	Site Privacy: ★★
Spaciousness: ★★★	Quiet: ★★★★
Security: ★★★★	Cleanliness: ★★
Insect Control: ★★★	Facilities: ★★

One of the more pleasant aspects of this county park is that it does not get overrun by hordes of campers, unlike other lakeside camps in the area. Boaters are not in dry-dock country, though; there is good fishing in the Kings River, which flows from the Pine Flat Dam past one side of camp, and boat-ramp access to the reservoir is nearby. The level, grassy turf is attractively punctuated here and there by a great range of such shade trees as oak, sycamore, and black walnut, and encompassed by undulating hills of golden grass and traces of granite. There is a uniformity to the double-loop layout, with open sites so comparable that one is as good as another. This is an invaluable oasis during the summer, which runs in these parts from May through September. The grounds are raked and well maintained, though some restrooms lack taps and have a neglected air to them. There is a general store and fuel station in Piedra, 3 miles to the west.

BASICS
Operated By: Fresno County Parks Dept. **Open:** All year. **Site Assignment:** First come, first served. **Registration:** At entrance booth. **Fee:** $16; cash, CA check. **Parking:** At site.

FACILITIES
Number of RV-only Sites: 55. **Hookups:** None. **Each Site:** Picnic table, barbecue grill. **Dump Station:** Yes. **Laundry:** No. **Pay Phone:** Yes. **Restrooms and Showers:** Flush toilets, no showers. **Fuel:** No. **Propane:** No. **Internal Roads:** Paved. **RV Service:** No. **Market:** 20 mi. southwest in Sanger. **Restaurant:** 20 mi. southwest in Sanger. **General Store:** No. **Vending:** No. **Swimming:** Kings River. **Playground:** No. **Other:** Some wheelchair-accessible facilities. **Activities:** Fishing, hiking. **Nearby Attractions:** Museums, Forestiere Underground Gardens, Chaffee Zoological Gardens, Rotary Storyland & Playland in Fresno; Sanger Depot Museum. **Additional Information:** Sanger District Chamber of Commerce, (559) 875-4575; Fresno City & County CVB, (800) 788-0836.

RESTRICTIONS
Pets: On 6-ft. leash. **Fires:** Fire grills only. **Alcoholic Beverages:** Allowed. **Vehicle Maximum Length:** No limit. **Other:** 14-day stay limit.

TO GET THERE
From Fresno drive 15 mi. east on Hwy. 180/Kings Canyon Rd. to Centerville. Bear left on Trimmer Springs Rd. Continue for 10 mi., past the small town of Piedra, then turn right on Pine Flat Rd. Proceed for 2.5 mi., over the bridge, to the campground entrance on the right.

FRIANT
Millerton Lake State Recreation Area
MAP, D-2

reserve america

5290 Millerton Rd., 93626. T: (559) 822-2332 or (800) 444-7275; www.reserveamerica.com.

🚐 ★★★★   ⛺ ★★★★

Beauty: ★★★★	Site Privacy: ★★★★
Spaciousness: ★★★	Quiet: ★★★
Security: ★★★	Cleanliness: ★★★
Insect Control: ★★	Facilities: ★★★

State officials estimate that on holiday weekends as many as 25,000 people descend on Millerton Lake, an indication of its popularity, as well as when to avoid visiting. Beyond the charming setting, amid a series of wrinkly, dimpled hills, with long, golden grass and monzo-granite gleaming in the sun, the attraction is obvious, given the scorching temperatures here during summer months. But while the lake is the main show, the campground is no ugly stepchild. Its level sites of grass and dirt are very well scattered over an extended series of loops, endowing many with privacy and prime vantages of the water. Several kinds of oak grace the domain, as well as sycamores, willows, eucalyptus, and various conifers, providing a balance of shade and filtered sun. The best of many fine sites is 59, on a point of land jutting out into the lake; 6–8 are on the small side but secluded. There are also 25 boat-in spots, and a marina with a snack bar and vending machines. Be sure to visit the Millerton Courthouse, circa 1867, preserved within the park.

BASICS
Operated By: California Dept. of Parks & Recreation. **Open:** All year. **Site Assignment:** Reservations accepted w/ V, MC, D; first come, first served. **Registration:** At entrance booth. **Fee:** $15–$34; cash, CA check; seasonal prices. **Parking:** At site.

FACILITIES
Number of RV-only Sites: 138. **Hookups:** Electric (20, 30, 50 amps), water, sewer. **Each Site:** Picnic table, fire grate, some sites have food storage box &/or ramada. **Dump Station:** Yes. **Laundry:** No. **Pay Phone:** Yes. **Restrooms and Showers:** Yes. **Fuel:** No. **Propane:** No. **Internal Roads:** Paved. **RV Service:** No. **Market:** 23 mi. west in Madera. **Restaurant:** 23 mi. west in Madera. **General Store:** No. **Vending:** No. **Swimming:** Millerton Lake. **Playground:** No. **Other:** Some wheelchair-accessible facilities, marina, boat launch, beach when water level drops. **Activities:** Fishing, boat rentals, horseback riding, hiking, waterskiing, windsurfing. **Nearby Attractions:** Museums, Forestiere Underground Gardens, Chaffee Zoological Gardens, Rotary Storyland & Playland in Fresno; Madera County Historical Museum & Quady Winery, Indian Gambling Casino. **Additional Information:** Fresno City & County CVB, (800) 788-0836; Madera Chamber of Commerce, (559) 673-3563.

RESTRICTIONS
Pets: On 6-ft. leash. **Fires:** Fire grates only. **Alcoholic Beverages:** Allowed at site; no alcohol on the shoreline. **Vehicle Maximum Length:** 36 ft. **Other:** 14-day stay limit from May 1–Sept. 15, 30 for the rest of the year; no firearms; no wood gathering; no glass bottles allowed.

TO GET THERE
From Madera drive 16 mi. east on Hwy. 145. Proceed through the intersection w/ Hwy. 41 (where Hwy. 145 becomes Millerton Rd.). Continue 3.5 mi., then bear left. After 1.3 mi. turn right. The campground is 2.2 mi. ahead.

GARBERVILLE
Benbow Lake State Recreation Area
MAP, B-1

reserve america

1600 US 101, 95542. T: (707) 923-3238; www.reserveamerica.com.

🚐 ★★★★   ⛺ ★★★★

Beauty: ★★★	Site Privacy: ★★
Spaciousness: ★★	Quiet: ★★★
Security: ★★★	Cleanliness: ★★★★
Insect Control: ★★★	Facilities: ★★★★

A popular destination, Benbow Lake State Recreation Area was first established in 1958. Prior to that, the area was used by settlers, ranchers, and loggers until 1922, when the Benbow family purchased much of the land in the valley. Some of the land was subdivided and sold for home sites. The Benbow Hotel, as it was originally named, was built in 1925 and opened for business in 1926. To provide power for the new development in the valley, a concrete dam was constructed across the south fork of the Eel River in 1928. The dam not only provided power but also created Benbow Lake. The Benbow family, interested in preserving the natural scene around the hotel and along the river, made efforts to place the land under state protection. In 1956, funds were approved for the Benbow Project, and the first 207 acres were purchased in 1958. Today the park consists of about 1,200 acres with 75 campsites and a large day-use picnic area. The campground is open year-round and reservations can be made from Memorial Day weekend to Labor Day weekend. Hiking, swimming, picnicking, and camping are popular summertime activities, while salmon and steelhead fishing are popular in the winter. There are no hookups in the campgrounds.

BASICS
Operated By: California Dept. of Parks & Recreation. **Open:** All year. **Site Assignment:** Reservations can be made 11 months in advance. **Registration:** At office. **Fee:** Single, $15–$28. **Parking:** At site.

FACILITIES
Number of Multipurpose Sites: 77. **Hookups:** Yes. **Each Site:** Fire ring. **Dump Station:** Yes. **Laundry:** No. **Pay Phone:** No. **Restrooms and**

Showers: Yes. **Fuel:** No. **Propane:** No. **Internal Roads:** Paved. **RV Service:** No. **Market:** No. **Restaurant:** No. **General Store:** No. **Vending:** No. **Swimming:** Yes. **Playground:** No. **Other:** No motorized boats are allowed on the lake. **Activities:** Boating, fishing, hiking, picnicking.

RESTRICTIONS

Pets: On 6-ft. leash in a tent or enclosed vehicle at night. Except for guide dogs, pets are not allowed in park buildings, on trails, or on most beaches. **Fires:** In designated fireplaces. **Alcoholic Beverages:** Not allowed.

TO GET THERE

Park is 2 mi. south of Garberville on Hwy. 101.

GARBERVILLE   MAP, B-1
Richardson Grove State Park

reserve america

1600 Hwy. 101 #8, 95542. T: (707) 247-3318; www.reserveamerica.com.

🚐 ★★★   ▲ ★★★★

Beauty: ★★★★	Site Privacy: ★★★★
Spaciousness: ★★★★	Quiet: ★★★★
Security: ★★★★	Cleanliness: ★★★★
Insect Control: ★★★	Facilities: ★★★★

Established in 1922 and named after Friend W. Richardson, the 25th governor of California, the park is bisected by Hwy. 101 and the south fork of the Eel River. Camping, hiking, swimming, and just relaxing are popular activities throughout much of the year. Fishing for salmon and steelhead is available during the winter. Richardson Grove State Park is a good place to find significant old growth redwood forest. The ninth tallest coast redwood, a fallen tree ring study conducted in 1933, and a walk-through tree are just a few of the sights available here. The park offers a variety of summer nature programs during the summer including evening campfire programs, Junior Rangers, and guided nature walks. A visitor center and nature store are located in the historic 1930s Richardson Grove lodge and are also open in the summer. The park has family campgrounds and a group camp totaling 159 campsites. Campsites can accommodate tents, up to 24-foot trailers, and 30-foot motor homes. There are no hookups.

BASICS

Operated By: California Dept. of Parks & Recreation. **Open:** All year. **Site Assignment:** Reservations can be made 7 months in advance; reservations from July 1–Sept. 5. **Registration:** At office. **Fee:** Single, $15–$20; group, $54–$90. **Parking:** At site.

FACILITIES

Number of Multipurpose Sites: 171. **Hookups:** None. **Dump Station:** 5 mi. **Laundry:** No. **Pay Phone:** No. **Restrooms and Showers:** Yes. **Fuel:** No. **Propane:** No. **Internal Roads:** Paved. **RV Service:** No. **Market:** No. **Restaurant:** No. **General Store:** Yes. **Vending:** No. **Swimming:** Yes. **Playground:** No. **Other:** Fees include entry for 1 vehi-

cle & 1 legally towed vehicle or trailer, additional vehicles will be charged per night at the park. **Activities:** Picnicking, fishing, hiking, nature trails.

RESTRICTIONS

Pets: On 6-ft. leash in a tent or enclosed vehicle at night. Except for guide dogs, pets are not allowed in park buildings, on trails, or on most beaches. **Fires:** In designated fireplaces. **Alcoholic Beverages:** Not allowed. **Vehicle Maximum Length:** 18 ft. max.

TO GET THERE

Richardson Grove SP is located 7 mi. south of Garberville on Hwy. 101.

GASQUET   MAP, A-1
Panther Flat Campground

reserve america

P.O. Box 228, 95543. T: (707) 457-3131; www.reserveamerica.com.

🚐 ★★★★   ▲ ★★★★

Beauty: ★★★★	Site Privacy: ★★★
Spaciousness: ★★★★	Quiet: ★★★
Security: ★★★	Cleanliness: ★★★★
Insect Control: ★★★	Facilities: ★★

This tidy, well-maintained campground is perched just above the Middle Fork of the Smith River, about 20 miles northeast of Crescent City along Hwy. 199. Though a rather average facility, it is a worthy alternative to Jedediah Smith Redwood State Park, just down the road, if the latter is full, or if the wild, moldering atmosphere of a moss-encrusted old-growth forest leaves you shivering. Its central location within the Smith River National Recreation Area also makes Panther Flat a suitable base camp for day hikes and fishing the several rivers in the locale. There are only a few redwoods here, of the spindly second-growth variety, and they are overshadowed by tan oaks and madrones. Level gravel sites, well groomed, and equipped with large back-in parking slips, are moderately spacious and evenly distributed around a small grassy meadow at the heart of the elongated double-oval camp lane. The nearest telephone is in Gasquet, 3 miles west.

BASICS

Operated By: Six Rivers National Forest, Smith River National Recreation Area. **Open:** All year. **Site Assignment:** Reservations accepted w/ V, MC. **Registration:** At entrance kiosk. **Fee:** $15; double site, $30; cash, check. **Parking:** At site.

FACILITIES

Number of RV-only Sites: 39. **Hookups:** None. **Each Site:** Picnic table, fire grate. **Dump Station:** No. **Laundry:** No. **Pay Phone:** No. **Restrooms and Showers:** Yes. **Fuel:** No. **Propane:** No. **Internal Roads:** Paved. **RV Service:** No. **Market:** 2 mi. south in Gasquet. **Restaurant:** 2 mi. south in Gasquet. **General Store:** No. **Vending:** No. **Swimming:** Smith River. **Playground:** No. **Other:** Some wheelchair-accessible facilities. **Activities:** Fishing, hiking, kayaking. **Nearby Attractions:** Redwood National & State Parks; Battery Point Lighthouse,

Ocean World, & Del Norte County Historical Museum in Crescent City; Rowdy Creek Fish Hatchery in Smith River. **Additional Information:** Crescent City–Del Norte County Chamber of Commerce, (707) 464-3174 or (800) 343-8300.

RESTRICTIONS

Pets: On leash. **Fires:** Fire grates only. **Alcoholic Beverages:** Allowed. **Vehicle Maximum Length:** 40 ft. **Other:** 14-day stay limit.

TO GET THERE

From Crescent City drive 3.5 mi. north on US 101. Exit on US 199 and head east toward Grants Pass, OR. Continue for 17 mi. to the well-marked campground entrance on the left.

GREENVILLE   MAP, B-2
Lake Almanor Campground

15778 Hwy. 89, 95923. T: (916) 386-5164; www.r5.fs.fed.us/lassen.

🚐 ★★★★   ▲ ★★★★

Beauty: ★★★★	Site Privacy: ★★★
Spaciousness: ★★★	Quiet: ★★★
Security: ★★★	Cleanliness: ★★★★
Insect Control: ★★★	Facilities: ★★

Of the many level, rather spacious sites here, there is a healthy balance between those that are open and exposed and others that are flanked by incense cedars, manzanita, Douglas firs, and ponderosa pines. Shade or sun, boating and fishing versus hiking or swimming, one thing that everybody can agree on is that the sightlines are magnificent from camp to glimmering Lake Almanor and the rumpled mountains looming above. Access to the lake is easy, too, with only a gentle tilt to the ground near the water—instead of the steep embankments of many other reservoir lakes—and loops that hug the meandering contours of the shore. Arguably, the very finest site is 40, isolated on a finger of land projecting into the lake; its neighbor, 41, is a very good runner-up. Similarly situated is 50, a double site that's ideal for large groups or oversize RVs. Tent campers should angle for 12, a cedar-shaded walk-in near the shore. A "camp library" of paperbacks is located in a cabinet across from the "supervisor," an on-site employee of American Land & Leisure, which operates the property for Pacific Gas & Electric.

BASICS

Operated By: American Land & Leisure, concessionaire. **Open:** May 15–Oct. 1. **Site Assignment:** First come, first served. **Registration:** At entrance kiosk. **Fee:** $15; cash, check. **Parking:** At site.

FACILITIES

Number of RV-only Sites: 125. **Number of Tent-only Sites:** 6. **Hookups:** None. **Each Site:** Picnic table, fire grate, food storage box. **Dump Station:** Yes. **Laundry:** No. **Pay Phone:** Yes. **Restrooms and Showers:** Vault toilets, no showers. **Fuel:** No. **Propane:** No. **Internal Roads:** Paved. **RV Service:** No. **Market:** 12 mi. south in Greenville. **Restaurant:** 12 mi. south in Greenville. **General Store:** No. **Vending:** No. **Swimming:** Lake Almanor. **Playground:** No. **Other:** Some wheelchair-accessible facilities, boat ramp. **Activities:** Fishing, boating, waterskiing, hiking, birding. **Nearby Attractions:** Westwood Museum, Paul Bunyan & Babe the Blue Ox statues; Lassen National Scenic Byway (Hwys. 89-44-36); Lassen Volcanic National Park. **Additional Information:** Chester–Lake Almanor Chamber of Commerce, (530) 258-2426 or (800) 350-4838.

RESTRICTIONS

Pets: On leash, $1 fee. **Fires:** Fire grates only. **Alcoholic Beverages:** Allowed. **Vehicle Maximum Length:** 34 ft. **Other:** 14-day stay limit.

TO GET THERE

From Greenville drive 12 mi. north on Hwy. 89. The campground entrance is on the right.

GROVELAND   MAP, C-3
Moccasin Point

Jacksonville Rd., 95347. T: (209) 852-2396 or (209) 989-2206 (marina); www.donpedrolake.com.

🚐 ★★★★   ▲ ★★★

Beauty: ★★★★	Site Privacy: ★★★
Spaciousness: ★★★	Quiet: ★★★
Security: ★★★★	Cleanliness: ★★★
Insect Control: ★★★	Facilities: ★★★★

Given a choice between camping at Moccasin Point or Fleming Meadows, just down the road, the first wins hands down. For one thing, sites at Moccasin are not wedged together quite as tightly, and they benefit from a greater concentration of such shade and privacy providers as oaks, various conifers, and manzanita. Another point in its favor is the picturesque landscape, which ranges from chaparral-covered Sierra foothills to rolling fields of wildflower-dotted golden grass. The layout consists of a figure-8 loop and a triple circuit, both of which descend toward the jade-green water over a series of tiers. The most private sites are B 6, 10, 17, C 7, 8, 15, and 16. One drawback of this fine campground is the dearth of lake views. Oddly, the best water access is available via its primitive D and E overflow loops, the latter being graced with its own lagoon. Site distribution is more concentrated there, but shade is abundant.

BASICS

Operated By: Don Pedro Recreation Agency. **Open:** All year. **Site Assignment:** Reservations accepted w/ V, MC or check. **Registration:** At entrance booth. **Fee:** $12–$25; cash, V, MC. **Parking:** At site.

FACILITIES

Number of Multipurpose Sites: 96. **Hookups:** Electric (20, 30 amps), water, sewer. **Each Site:** Picnic table, barbecue grill, food storage box. **Dump Station:** Yes. **Laundry:** No. **Pay Phone:** Yes. **Restrooms and Showers:** Yes. **Fuel:** No. **Propane:** Yes. **Internal Roads:** Paved. **RV Service:** No. **Market:** 8 mi. east in Groveland. **Restaurant:** 8 mi. east in Groveland. **General Store:** Yes. **Vending:** Yes. **Swimming:** Don Pedro Lake. **Playground:** No. **Other:** Some wheelchair-accessible facilities, boat ramp, marina. **Activities:** Fishing, waterskiing, motorboat & houseboat rentals, sailing. **Nearby Attractions:** Northern Mariposa County History Center in

Coulterville; Tuolumne County Museum & History Center in Sonora; Yosemite National Park. **Additional Information:** Coulterville Visitors Center, (209) 878-3074; Tuolumne County Visitors Bureau, (209) 533-4420 or (800) 446-1333.

RESTRICTIONS

Pets: Not allowed. **Fires:** Ground fires not allowed. **Alcoholic Beverages:** Allowed. **Vehicle Maximum Length:** No limit. **Other:** 14-day stay limit; no fireworks.

TO GET THERE

From Groveland on Hwy. 120 head 7 mi. west to the junction w/ Hwy. 49. Turn right (north) on Hwy. 49 and continue for 2 mi. Turn right on Jacksonville Rd., followed by another right into the campground.

GUERNEVILLE   MAP, C-1
Bullfrog Pond Campground

Austin Creek State Recreation Area, 17000 Armstrong Woods Rd., 95446-9587. T: (707) 869-2015; www.cal-parks.ca.gov.

🚐 ★★★   ▲ ★★★★

Beauty: ★★★★	Site Privacy: ★★★
Spaciousness: ★★★	Quiet: ★★★★
Security: ★★★	Cleanliness: ★★★★
Insect Control: ★★	Facilities: ★★

Shortly after the end of World War II, renowned ceramist Marguerite Wildenhain of the Bauhaus school came to settle in this area. She found inspiration in the sublime beauty of her surroundings, a feeling that countless campers have shared since then. If you are able to get your vehicle up the steep, narrow, meandering access road—and that's a big if—you will find stunning mountain views and an enchanting forested atmosphere. Feral pigs, wild turkeys, bobcats, and the elusive spotted owl make their homes in these redwood- and tan oak-covered hills. You are more likely, though, to see frogs by the pond, where the camp lane ends. Fern-freckled sites are distributed fairly well apart and though they are a tad small and some are planted on slanting ground, such minor discomforts seem an acceptable tradeoff for camping in so attractive a place. The park closes when the fire risk is extreme, so be sure to call ahead in summer.

BASICS

Operated By: California Dept. of Parks & Recreation. **Open:** All year; weather & fire danger permitting. **Site Assignment:** First come, first served. **Registration:** At kiosk, 3.2 mi. beyond entrance booth. **Fee:** $15 for 1 vehicle w/ up to 8 people, $6 extra vehicle; cash, CA check. **Parking:** At site.

FACILITIES

Number of Tent-only Sites: 23. **Hookups:** None. **Each Site:** Picnic table, fire grate, food storage box. **Dump Station:** No. **Laundry:** No. **Pay Phone:** Yes. **Restrooms and Showers:** Flush toilets, no showers. **Fuel:** No. **Propane:** No. **Internal Roads:** Paved, narrow & bumpy. **RV Service:** No. **Market:** 5.5 mi. south in Guerneville. **Restaurant:** 5.5 mi. south in Guerneville. **General Store:** No. **Vending:**

No. **Swimming:** No. **Playground:** No. **Other:** Some wheelchair-accessible facilities. Three backcountry campsites are available. **Activities:** Hiking, fishing, horseback riding, birding. **Nearby Attractions:** Healdsburg Museum & Sonoma County Wine Library; Fort Ross State Historic Park, Kruse Rhododendron State Reserve & Salt Point State Park in Jenner; Brooks Canoes; winery tours. **Additional Information:** Healdsburg Chamber of Commerce & Visitors Center, (707) 823-3032 or (877) 828-4748; Russian River Chamber of Commerce & Visitors Center, (707) 869-9212 or (877) 644-9001.

RESTRICTIONS

Pets: On 6-ft. leash; not allowed on trails. **Fires:** Fire grates only; not allowed when fire danger is extreme. **Alcoholic Beverages:** Allowed at site. **Vehicle Maximum Length:** 20 ft. (no trailers allowed). **Other:** 14-day stay limit; no firearms; no wood gathering.

TO GET THERE

From downtown Guerneville on Hwy. 116, turn north on Armstrong Woods Rd. The park entrance is 2.3 mi. ahead; the campground entrance is 3.2 mi. beyond that.

GUSTINE   MAP, D-1
San Luis Creek Campground

reserve america

San Luis Reservoir State Recreation Area, 31426 Gonzaga Rd., 95322. T: (209) 826-1197 or (800) 346-2711; www.reserveamerica.com.

🚐 ★★★★   ▲ ★★★

Beauty: ★★★★	Site Privacy: ★★
Spaciousness: ★★★	Quiet: ★★★★
Security: ★★★★	Cleanliness: ★★★★
Insect Control: ★★★	Facilities: ★★★

San Luis Reservoir lies in the heart of California's central valley, just off of I-5, about 40 miles south of Modesto. Summer starts early in these parts, with the sun scorching the neighboring hills brown by April. Water sports are therefore the logical activity of choice and fortunately there is usually enough water in the reservoir to satisfy boaters and swimmers throughout the hot season. Of the three campgrounds in the park, only San Luis Creek on the O'Neill Forebay has hookups. It is a grassy, peaceful camp with many of its fairly exposed, roomy sites set close to the shore. Adding a splash of color to the setting are eucalyptus trees, pines, and sycamores. The latter are still too small to cast much shade but they are just large enough to attract larks and other songbirds. The only off-key note is the presence of power lines looming above a few of the sites. Showers are available across the street at Basalt Campground.

BASICS

Operated By: California Dept. of Parks & Recreation. **Open:** All year. **Site Assignment:** Reservations accepted w/ V, MC, D. **Registration:** At entrance booth. **Fee:** $15–$20; cash, CA check. **Parking:** At site.

FACILITIES

Number of Multipurpose Sites: 132. **Hookups:** Electric (30 amps), water. **Each Site:** Picnic table, fire grate. **Dump Station:** Yes. **Laundry:** No. **Pay Phone:** Yes. **Restrooms and Showers:** Pit toilets, no showers. **Fuel:** No. **Propane:** No. **Internal Roads:** Paved. **RV Service:** No. **Market:** 15 mi. east in Los Baños. **Restaurant:** 15 mi. east in Los Baños. **General Store:** No. **Vending:** No. **Swimming:** Reservoir. **Playground:** No. **Other:** Some wheelchair-accessible facilities. **Activities:** Fishing, boating, birding, hiking, picnicking. **Nearby Attractions:** Modesto museums; Mission San Juan Bautista; Los Baños Great Valley Grasslands State Park & Wildlife Area. **Additional Information:** Santa Nella Chamber of Commerce, (209) 826-8282; Los Baños Chamber of Commerce, (209) 826-2495.

RESTRICTIONS

Pets: On 6-ft. leash. $1 fee. **Fires:** Fire grates only. **Alcoholic Beverages:** Allowed at site. **Vehicle Maximum Length:** 30 ft. **Other:** 14-day stay limit from May 1–Sept. 30; no firearms; no wood gathering.

TO GET THERE

From Gilroy on US 101 follow Hwy. 152 east for 36 mi. Turn left into the park. The campground entrance is 1 mi. ahead to the left.

HAPPY CAMP   MAP, A-1, A-2
Sarah Totten

reserve america

63822 Hwy. 96, 96039. T: (530) 493-2243; www.reserveamerica.com.

🚐 ★★★   ⛺ ★★★★

Beauty: ★★★★	Site Privacy: ★★★★
Spaciousness: ★★★★	Quiet: ★★★
Security: ★	Cleanliness: ★★★
Insect Control: ★★★	Facilities: ★★

A popular rafting stretch of the Klamath River flows right by this pretty little campground, with easy put-in access to the water. Like Fort Goff to the west, this is a roadside facility, with a key difference being that Sarah Totten is recessed from Hwy. 96 and thus approaching autos do not seem to be bearing down on one's tent. In fact, road noise in most sites is pretty effectively muffled by the melodious churning of the Klamath. Of the two neighboring loops, the left-hand one contains five walk-in sites, with the oak-shaded number 3 the most spacious. Oak, pines, and horsetail grass also thrive in the second circuit, where peculiar mounds of river stones near the entrance are relics from the Gold Rush era, circa 1850, when extensive mining of the river occurred. Sites 6 and 7, with paved back-in parking, are tailor-made for RVs. The most private spot is 9, hidden behind an overgrown thicket of vines and weeds; it also has a water view. This is a splendid property, 40 miles east of Happy Camp, albeit somewhat neglected and overgrown.

BASICS

Operated By: Klamath National Forest. **Open:** May 15–Oct. 15. **Site Assignment:** First come, first served; reservations required for group site. **Regis-**

---

tration: At entrance kiosk. **Fee:** $30; cash, check; no fee when in winter when spigots are capped. **Parking:** At site.

FACILITIES

Number of RV-only Sites: 5. **Number of Tent-only Sites:** 12. **Hookups:** None. **Each Site:** Picnic table, barbecue grill, fire ring. **Dump Station:** No. **Laundry:** No. **Pay Phone:** No, emergency phone only. **Restrooms and Showers:** Vault toilets, no showers. **Fuel:** No. **Propane:** No. **Internal Roads:** Mostly paved, also dirt & rocks. **RV Service:** No. **Market:** 10 mi. east in Seiad Valley. **Restaurant:** 10 mi. east in Seiad Valley. **General Store:** No. **Vending:** No. **Swimming:** Klamath River. **Playground:** No. **Other:** Limited wheelchair-accessible facilities. **Activities:** Fishing, hiking, rafting, kayaking, birding. **Nearby Attractions:** Klamath National Forest; Yreka National Historic District, Western Railroad, Siskiyou County Courthouse & Museum in Yreka. **Additional Information:** Siskiyou County Visitors Bureau, (530) 926-3850; Yreka Chamber of Commerce, (530) 842-1649.

RESTRICTIONS

Pets: On 6-ft. leash. **Fires:** Fire ring only. **Alcoholic Beverages:** Allowed. **Vehicle Maximum Length:** 22 ft. **Other:** 14-day stay limit.

TO GET THERE

From Happy Camp drive 30 mi. east on Hwy. 96. The campground entrance is on the left side of the road.

HAPPY CAMP   MAP, A-2
Tree of Heaven

reserve america

P.O. Box 377, 96039. T: (530) 493-2243; www.reserveamerica.com.

🚐 ★★★★   ⛺ ★★★

Beauty: ★★★★	Site Privacy: ★★
Spaciousness: ★★★	Quiet: ★★★
Security: ★★	Cleanliness: ★★★
Insect Control: ★★★	Facilities: ★★

Tree of heaven is the common name for *Ailanthus altissima,* a nonnative tree that grows in this small campground, which lies just 8 miles west of I-5. The forest service has thoughtfully installed a sign informing visitors that *Ailanthus altissima* were "planted by early settlers for soil conservation and resistance to air pollution." That they were a fast-growing source of shade is a more likely reason miners settled on them, something campers can be glad of, too. Pines, junipers, and maples round out the shady mix of trees here, with grassy, level sites evenly spaced out along a single loop. The grounds and limited facilities show none of the neglect so ubiquitous to Forest Service campgrounds elsewhere. On the contrary, scrupulous manicuring may leave some campers feeling that the "wilderness" has been snipped right out of the domain. The frothy waters of the Klamath River, which is popular for its rafting opportunities, churn right alongside the property. A fish-cleaning station is located next to the river.

BASICS

Operated By: Klamath National Forest, Scott River Ranger District. **Open:** All year; no water in winter. **Site Assignment:** Reservations accepted w/ V, MC; make reservations at least 2 weeks in advance. **Registration:** At central kiosk. **Fee:** $10; cash, check. **Parking:** At site.

FACILITIES

Number of RV-only Sites: 19. **Hookups:** None. **Each Site:** Picnic table, fire grate, barbecue grill. **Dump Station:** No. **Laundry:** No. **Pay Phone:** No. **Restrooms and Showers:** Vault toilets, no showers. **Fuel:** No. **Propane:** No. **Internal Roads:** Paved. **RV Service:** No. **Market:** 12 mi. east in Yreka. **Restaurant:** 12 mi. east in Yreka. **General Store:** No. **Vending:** No. **Swimming:** Klamath River. **Playground:** No. **Other:** Some wheelchair-accessible facilities, small boat ramp. **Activities:** Fishing, hiking, rafting, kayaking, canoeing. **Nearby Attractions:** Klamath National Forest; Yreka National Historic District, Western Railroad, Siskiyou County Courthouse & Museum in Yreka. **Additional Information:** Siskiyou County Visitors Bureau, (530) 926-3850; Yreka Chamber of Commerce, (530) 842-1649.

RESTRICTIONS

Pets: On leash. **Fires:** Fire grates only. **Alcoholic Beverages:** Allowed. **Vehicle Maximum Length:** 34 ft. **Other:** 14-day stay limit.

TO GET THERE

From Yreka drive 8 mi. north on Hwy. 263. Turn left (west) on Hwy. 96 and continue for 4 mi. to the campground entrance on the left.

IDYLLWILD   MAP, E-3, F-3
Mt. San Jacinto State Park

reserve america

25905 Hwy. 243, 92549. T: (951) 659-2607; www.reserveamerica.com.

🚐 ★★★   ⛺ ★★★★

Beauty: ★★★★	Site Privacy: ★★★★
Spaciousness: ★★★★	Quiet: ★★★
Security: ★★★	Cleanliness: ★★★★
Insect Control: ★★★	Facilities: ★★

The deeply weathered summit of Mount San Jacinto stands 10,804 feet above sea level, the highest point in the San Jacinto Range and second highest in Southern California. The mountain's magnificent granite peaks, subalpine forests, and fern-bordered mountain meadows offer a unique opportunity to explore and enjoy a scenic, high-country wilderness area. The park, accessible by hiking or via the Palm Springs Aerial Tramway, has primitive camping, picnic areas, and 54 miles of hiking trails. You can take guided mule rides through the wilderness during snow-free months. The Nordic Ski Center rents cross-country ski equipment. You must get a free permit before coming for day or overnight wilderness hiking. The park also offers two drive-in campgrounds near the town of Idyllwild. The Aerial Tram starts in Chino Canyon near Palm Springs and takes passengers from Valley Station at 2,643 feet elevation to Mountain Station on the edge of the Wilderness, elevation 8,516 feet. The Pacific Crest Trail is the jewel in the crown of America's scenic trails, spanning 2,650 miles from Mexico to Canada through three western states. The trail passes through five California State Parks including Mount San Jacinto.

BASICS

Operated By: California Dept. of Parks & Recreation. **Open:** All year. **Site Assignment:** Reservations can be made 7 months in advance. **Registration:** At office. **Fee:** Single, $11–$20. **Parking:** At site.

FACILITIES

Number of Multipurpose Sites: 82. **Hookups:** None. **Dump Station:** No. **Laundry:** Yes. **Pay Phone:** No. **Restrooms and Showers:** Yes. **Fuel:** No. **Propane:** No. **Internal Roads:** Paved. **RV Service:** No. **Market:** No. **Restaurant:** No. **General Store:** No. **Vending:** No. **Swimming:** No. **Playground:** No. **Other:** Fees include entry for 1 vehicle & 1 legally towed vehicle or trailer, additional vehicles will be charged per night at the park. Stone Creek & Idyllwild are separate campgrounds 6 mi. apart. **Activities:** Fishing, hiking, nature trails, picnicking.

RESTRICTIONS

Pets: On 6-ft. leash in a tent or enclosed vehicle at night. Except for guide dogs, pets are not allowed in park buildings, on trails, or on most beaches. **Fires:** In designated fireplaces. **Alcoholic Beverages:** Not allowed.

TO GET THERE

The park is accessible via Hwy. 243 from Idyllwild.

IDYLLWILD   MAP, E-3
Stone Creek Campground

Mount San Jacinto State Park, 25905 Hwy. 243, 92549. T: (909) 659-2607 or (800) 444-7275; www.sanjac.statepark.org.

🚐 ★★★★   ▲ ★★★

Beauty: ★★★★	Site Privacy: ★★★
Spaciousness: ★★★	Quiet: ★★★
Security: ★★★	Cleanliness: ★★★★
Insect Control: ★	Facilities: ★★

The scenic mountain drive along Hwy. 243 to Stone Creek is a good warm-up for your arrival at this gorgeous highland park. Set in a hilly, boulder-strewn forest of oak, incense cedar, manzanita, and ponderosa pine, the camp lies at 5,900 feet of elevation, so plan for cool evenings throughout the year. Regrettably, the somewhat wild, natural look of the place is balanced by sites that tend to be grouped a bit close together, with several lacking level tenting space. Best choices for RVers from the series of loops are sites 45, with a large pull-through slot, and 50, for privacy. Site 26 is the most secluded among the tent options. Birders will enjoy the lively community of acorn woodpeckers nesting in the vicinity and hikers should aim their boots in the direction of trails that lead into the neighboring San Jacinto Wilderness.

BASICS

Operated By: California Dept. of Parks & Recreation. **Open:** All year. **Site Assignment:** First come, first served; reservations accepted w/ V, MC, D. **Registration:** At entrance kiosk. **Fee:** $10–$12 (Sept. 15–May 14, $7); cash, CA check. **Parking:** At site.

FACILITIES

Number of RV-only Sites: 23. **Number of Tent-only Sites:** 27. **Hookups:** Electric, water, sewer; ranges from no hookup–full hookup. **Each Site:** Picnic table, fire grate, food storage box. **Dump Station:** No. **Laundry:** No. **Pay Phone:** No. **Restrooms and Showers:** Vault toilets, no showers. Idyllwild has flush toilets & showers. **Fuel:** No. **Propane:** No. **Internal Roads:** Paved. **RV Service:** No. **Market:** Idyllwild w/in walking distance. **Restaurant:** Idyllwild w/in walking distance. **General Store:** Idyllwild. **Vending:** No. **Swimming:** No. **Playground:** No. **Other:** Some wheelchair-accessible facilities. Movie theater in Idyllwild. **Activities:** Hiking, birding, nature programs in summer, Movie theater in Idyllwild. **Nearby Attractions:** Palm Springs Aerial Tramway, Palm Springs Desert Museum, Oasis Water Park in Palm Springs, Gilman Historic Ranch & Wagon Museum in Banning, County Nature Center. **Additional Information:** Idyllwild Chamber of Commerce, (909) 659-3259.

RESTRICTIONS

Pets: On 6-ft. leash. **Fires:** Fire grates only. **Alcoholic Beverages:** Allowed at site. **Vehicle Maximum Length:** 24 ft. **Other:** 15-day stay limit; no firearms; no wood gathering.

TO GET THERE

From I-10 in Banning exit south on Hwy. 243. Drive 20 mi. and turn left at the campground sign.

JULIAN   MAP, F-3
Paso Picacho Campground

Cuyamaca Rancho State Park, 12551 Hwy. 79, 91916. T: (760) 765-3020; www.cuyamaca.statepark.org.

🚐 ★★★   ▲ ★★★★

Beauty: ★★★★	Site Privacy: ★★★
Spaciousness: ★★★	Quiet: ★★★
Security: ★★★★	Cleanliness: ★★★
Insect Control: ★★★	Facilities: ★★

Paso Picacho is open year-round; if you come in winter, plan to dress warmly and don't be surprised if there is snow on the ground. That's because at an elevation of nearly 5,000 feet, this is one of the higher camps in southern California and thus one of the more pleasant—and hugely popular—in summer. Of course its rough-hewn mountainous setting has something to do with that appeal, with roomy sites shaded by oak, manzanita, and pines, and dispersed through a series of loops that snake across the hilly contours of the park. As with many mountain camps, finding a level site can be a challenge: best in that department (as well as for privacy and space) are numbers 3–12. Rangers report that area mountain lions have become bold, with a number of sightings and a few attacks in the last several years.

BASICS

Operated By: California Dept. of Parks & Recreation. **Open:** All year. **Site Assignment:** First come, first served; reservations recommended; V, MC, AE. **Registration:** At entrance booth. **Fee:** $15; cash, CA check. **Parking:** At site.

FACILITIES

Number of RV-only Sites: 85. **Hookups:** None. **Each Site:** Picnic table, fire grate. **Dump Station:** Yes. **Laundry:** No. **Pay Phone:** Yes. **Restrooms and Showers:** Yes. **Fuel:** No. **Propane:** No. **Internal Roads:** Paved. **RV Service:** No. **Market:** 11 mi. north in Julian. **Restaurant:** 11 mi. north in Julian. **General Store:** No. **Vending:** No. **Swimming:** No. **Playground:** No. **Other:** Some wheelchair-accessible facilities. **Activities:** Hiking, horseback riding, boating & fishing in Lake Cuyamaca less than 2 mi. away, ranger-led activities in summer. **Nearby Attractions:** San Diego Wild Animal Park in Escondido, historic Julian. **Additional Information:** Julian Chamber of Commerce, (760) 765-1857.

RESTRICTIONS

Pets: On 6-ft. leash, not allowed on trails. **Fires:** Fire grates only. **Alcoholic Beverages:** Allowed at site. **Vehicle Maximum Length:** 27 ft. **Other:** 30-day stay limit; no firearms; no wood gathering.

TO GET THERE

From San Diego head east on I-8 for 43 mi. Exit on Hwy. 79 north and drive 12.2 mi. The campground entrance is on the left.

JULIAN   MAP, F-3
William Heise County Park

4945 Heise Park Rd., 92036. T: (760) 765-0650 (the ranger) or (888) 565-3600; www.sdparks.org.

🚐 ★★★   ▲ ★★★

Beauty: ★★★★	Site Privacy: ★★★
Spaciousness: ★★★	Quiet: ★★★
Security: ★★★	Cleanliness: ★★★
Insect Control: ★	Facilities: ★★★

This agreeable campground mixes grassy meadows with a forest environment and comes up with a series of loops laid out in a terracing of such shade trees as live oaks, Coulter pines, and incense cedars. The largely comparable sites have coarse sand and dirt for tent pads, with 73 and 84 giving tenters the most space and 36 optimum for RVers. You're likely to hear acorn woodpeckers clowning around up in the leafy canopy, and last time we camped here a number of wild turkeys gobbled through our site. There are 7 miles of hiking trails in the park, with the scenic overlook on Desert View Trail especially rewarding. Looking for more? How about heated restrooms, a nicely civilized touch of comfort. The park is just 6 miles from the scenic mountain town of Julian, making it a great base when the latter holds its Apple Days festival throughout October.

BASICS

Operated By: County of San Diego, Dept. of Parks & Recreation. **Open:** All year. **Site Assignment:** First come, first served; reservations accepted w/ V, MC, D. **Registration:** At entrance booth & park office. **Fee:** $12–$16; cash, V, MC, D. **Parking:** At site.

FACILITIES

Number of Tent-only Sites: 41. **Number of Multipurpose Sites:** 40. **Hookups:** None. **Each Site:** Picnic table, fire ring, some w/ a barbecue grill. **Dump Station:** Yes. **Laundry:** No. **Pay Phone:** Yes. **Restrooms and Showers:** Yes. **Fuel:** No. **Propane:** No. **Internal Roads:** Gravel, some paved. **RV Service:** No. **Market:** 5.5 mi. north in Julian. **Restaurant:** 5.5 mi. north in Julian. **General Store:** No. **Vending:** No. **Swimming:** No. **Playground:** Yes. **Other:** Some wheelchair-accessible facilities. **Activities:** Hiking, bicycling, horseback riding (must provide your own horse), horseshoe pit. **Nearby Attractions:** Anza-Borrego Desert State Park, historic Julian, Lake Cuyamaca. **Additional Information:** Julian Chamber of Commerce, (760) 765-1857.

RESTRICTIONS

Pets: On 6-ft. leash; $1 fee. **Fires:** Fire ring only. **Alcoholic Beverages:** Allowed at site, not exceeding 40 proof. **Vehicle Maximum Length:** 40 ft. **Other:** 14-day stay limit; no firearms.

TO GET THERE

From Julian head west on Hwy. 78 for 1 mi. Turn left on Pine Hills Rd. and drive 2.3 mi. Turn left again on Frisius Rd. and continue for 2.2 mi. to the park.

KELSEYVILLE
Clear Lake State Park
MAP, C-1, C-2

reserve america

5300 Soda Bay Rd., 95451. T: (707) 279-4293 or (800) 444-7275; www.reserveamerica.com.

🚐 ★★★★	⛺ ★★★★
Beauty: ★★★★	Site Privacy: ★★★
Spaciousness: ★★★	Quiet: ★★★
Security: ★★★★	Cleanliness: ★★★
Insect Control: ★★	Facilities: ★★★

Clear Lake is one of the largest freshwater lakes in California. The angling in its shimmering blue-green waters is so good, particularly for bass, bluegill, and catfish, that you just might forget for a moment the other liquids for which this wine-producing region is renowned. There is an appealingly wild, untamed air to the forested hills around the lake, and the park takes full advantage of that by dispersing its campground into four zones, ranging from lake and creek-side on up into the higher woodland. The prime water sites are 58–60 in the Kelsey Creek loop, where plant life is highlighted by manzanita, willow, cottonwood, and black walnut. The opposite side of that loop overlooks a creek (very buggy in spring) and numbers 29, 31, 32, 38, 39, 41, 42, 44, and 45 are gratifyingly spacious and private. Pines, oak, and sycamore are the dominant tree species at the two Bayview circuits up the road, with 110–112, shady and overlooking the lake, ideal for small RVs. Cole Creek, close and parallel to the access road near the park entrance, is the least attractive of the camping areas.

BASICS

Operated By: California Dept. of Parks & Recreation. **Open:** All year. **Site Assignment:** Reservations accepted May 15–Sept. 15 w/ V, MC, D; first come, first served sites available. **Registration:** At entrance booth. **Fee:** $12 off season, $15 May 15–Sept. 15; cash, CA check. Premium sites $4 extra. **Parking:** At site.

FACILITIES

Number of RV-only Sites: 145. **Number of Tent-only Sites:** 2. **Hookups:** None. **Each Site:** Picnic table, fire grate. **Dump Station:** Yes. **Laundry:** No. **Pay Phone:** Yes. **Restrooms and Showers:** Yes. **Fuel:** No. **Propane:** No. **Internal Roads:** Paved. **RV Service:** No. **Market:** 4 mi. south in Kelseyville. **Restaurant:** 4 mi. south in Kelseyville. **General Store:** No. **Vending:** No. **Swimming:** Clear Lake. **Playground:** No. **Other:** Some wheelchair-accessible facilities, boat ramp, visitor center, fire wood available. **Activities:** Fishing, hiking, waterskiing, birding, kayak rentals. **Nearby Attractions:** Lakeport County Museum in Lakeport; Clear Lake Queen, Outrageous Waters Water Park & Fun Center & Anderson Marsh State Historic Park in Clearlake. **Additional Information:** Lakeport Chamber of Commerce, (707) 263-5092; Clearlake Chamber of Commerce, (707) 994-3600.

RESTRICTIONS

Pets: On 6-ft. leash. **Fires:** Fire grates only. **Alcoholic Beverages:** Allowed at site. **Vehicle Maximum Length:** 35 ft. **Other:** 14-day stay limit from Apr. 1–Oct. 30 annually; no firearms; no wood gathering.

TO GET THERE

From Lakeport head 8 mi. south on Hwy. 29 to Kelseyville. Turn left on Merritt Rd. which leads into Gaddy Ln. Drive 3.5 mi., then turn right on Soda Bay and continue for 1 mi. to the park entrance on the left.

KERNVILLE
Fairview
MAP, D-3

reserve america

P.O. Box 1640, 93238. T: (760) 376-3781; www.reserveamerica.com.

🚐 ★★★★	⛺ ★★★
Beauty: ★★★★	Site Privacy: ★★★
Spaciousness: ★★	Quiet: ★★★
Security: ★★★	Cleanliness: ★★★
Insect Control: ★★★	Facilities: ★★

The turbulent Kern River is a rafters delight, and Fairview puts campers where the action is, right alongside that purling cascade of water. The saw-toothed Sierra range circles this rocky, mountainous setting, which is at an altitude of 3,500 feet. Very small, level sites, with equally tight parking slips, are crowded together over rocky, sandy ground. The host's spot has the best shade; elsewhere over the three loops it is sparsely provided by a few pines and cottonwoods, with Mormon tea and other chaparral making up the ground cover. Spring, when snow-

melt adds to the Kern's power, is the best time to visit, but bear in mind that the concession operating this national forest property charges the same fee whether you picnic, day-use, or camp. There are many maverick camps along the Kern that budget-minded campers may want to investigate. Many are sizable enough to handle small RVs, and if they don't have facilities, at least they offer more seclusion and fairer river access than this and the many other developed camps in the area.

BASICS

Operated By: California Land Management, concessionaire. **Open:** Apr. 1–Oct. 31. **Site Assignment:** First come, first served; reservations recommended; V, MC, D. **Registration:** W/ campground host. **Fee:** $15; double site, $30; cash, check; add $2 per night for holiday weekends. **Parking:** At site.

FACILITIES

Number of RV-only Sites: 55. **Hookups:** None. **Each Site:** Picnic table, fire grate. **Dump Station:** No. **Laundry:** No. **Pay Phone:** No. **Restrooms and Showers:** Vault toilets, no showers. **Fuel:** No. **Propane:** No. **Internal Roads:** Paved & meandering. **RV Service:** No. **Market:** 17 mi. south in Kernville. **Restaurant:** 17 mi. south in Kernville. **General Store:** Yes. **Vending:** No. **Swimming:** No. **Playground:** No. **Other:** Some wheelchair-accessible facilities. **Activities:** Rafting, fishing, hiking, bicycling. **Nearby Attractions:** Sequoia National Forest; Isabella Lake; California Hot Springs; Porterville Historical Museum. **Additional Information:** Porterville Chamber of Commerce, (559) 784-7503.

RESTRICTIONS

Pets: On 6-ft. leash. **Fires:** Fire grates only, in designated areas. **Alcoholic Beverages:** Allowed. **Vehicle Maximum Length:** 40 ft. **Other:** 14-day stay limit. 10 p.m.–6 a.m. quiet time.

TO GET THERE

From Kernville drive 17 mi. north on Sierra Way. The campground entrance is on the left.

KERNVILLE
Hume Lake
MAP, D-2

reserve america

P.O. Box 1640, 93238. T: (559) 335-2232; www.reserveamerica.com.

🚐 ★★★	⛺ ★★★
Beauty: ★★★★	Site Privacy: ★★★
Spaciousness: ★★★	Quiet: ★★★
Security: ★★★★	Cleanliness: ★★★
Insect Control: ★★	Facilities: ★★

Hume Lake lies just below this good-looking woodland campground. Fishing and boating are popular pastimes here, so much so that you'll need reservations on summer weekends. It is well situated as a base camp for exploring the Giant Sequoia National Monument, of which it is a part, and launching into the neighboring Kings Canyon National Park. Manzanita, Jeffrey and ponderosa pines, oak, and cedar thrive across this hilly domain, where dirt- and pine needle–surfaced sites are spread decently apart over a convoluted series of six loops. That's the good news. The bad news is that few spots are blessed with lake vistas, and those that are, such as 63 and 64, are not specifically reservable. The concession that manages Hume Lake for the national forest service restricts reservations to "type," not site number. Thus, car campers with a tent might reserve a "type one" spot, while a motor home would require a "type two" or "type three," at a higher fee. Unfortunately, many in the first category have parking slips that are so tight you may wish you rolled in on two wheels instead of four. Gasoline and a general store are available at the Christian camp in Hume, 2 miles south.

BASICS

Operated By: California Land Management, concessionaire. **Open:** May–Sept., weather permitting. **Site Assignment:** Reservations accepted w/ V, MC, D. **Registration:** At entrance booth. **Fee:** $17, cash, check; $34 for a double site; add $2 per night for holiday weekends. **Parking:** At site.

FACILITIES

Number of RV-only Sites: 74. **Hookups:** None. **Each Site:** Picnic table, fire grate, some sites have bear proof box. **Dump Station:** No. **Laundry:** No. **Pay Phone:** No. **Restrooms and Showers:** Flush toilets, no showers. **Fuel:** No. **Propane:** No. **Internal Roads:** Paved. **RV Service:** No. **Market:** 41 mi. west in Sanger. **Restaurant:** 10 mi. southwest in Grant Grove Village. **General Store:** Yes. **Vending:** No. **Swimming:** Hume Lake. **Playground:** No. **Other:** Boat ramp. **Activities:** Fishing, boat rentals, hiking, kayaking, swimming, canoeing, horseback riding. **Nearby Attractions:** Giant Sequoia National Monument; Kings Canyon & Sequoia National Parks; Reedley Opera House, Museum & Mennonite Quilting Center. **Additional Information:** Fresno City & County CVB, (800) 788-0836; Reedley District Chamber of Commerce & Visitors Bureau, (559) 638-3548.

RESTRICTIONS

Pets: On leash. **Fires:** Fire grates only. **Alcoholic Beverages:** Allowed. **Vehicle Maximum Length:** 30 ft. **Other:** 14-day stay limit.

TO GET THERE

From Grant Grove on Hwy. 180 in Kings Canyon National Park drive 6.2 mi. north, toward Cedar Grove. At the sign for Hume Lake make a right onto Hume Rd. and continue for 3.2 mi. to the Hume Lake campground turnoff. Make a left and proceed for 0.4 mi. to the campground straight ahead.

LA GRANGE   MAP, C-3
Fleming Meadows

Bonds Flat Rd. 31, 95329. T: (209) 852-2396; www.donpedrolake.com.

🚐 ★★★★	⛺ ★★★
Beauty: ★★★★	Site Privacy: ★★
Spaciousness: ★★★	Quiet: ★★★
Security: ★★★★	Cleanliness: ★★★
Insect Control: ★★★	Facilities: ★★★★

In an area where summers are long and hot, Don Pedro Lake, 35 miles east of Modesto, is a marvelous sight. The rolling hills around its multi-pronged arms are speckled green with oaks and awash in golden grass. The reservoir features 160 miles of shoreline, endowing Fleming Meadows campground with no end of water vistas. There is a trade-off for those splendid views; many of the dirt-surfaced sites lack privacy and space. Of the four loops, sites in the A group are better shaded and seem a little more spacious. The optimum are A 24 and 25, which overlook the lake and are framed by a large oak; A 34, a comfortable unit with pull-through parking; and A 58, 59, 61, 62, and 64. Boaters may also indulge in primitive camping along the opposite shoreline. Not that a boat is necessary to enjoy this huge recreation area. Facilities include a sandy swimming lagoon that is six-feet deep and two acres across, a softball field, horseshoe pits, volleyball, and no end of fishing opportunities. Boat service, fuel, a snack bar, and store are available at the marina.

BASICS

Operated By: Don Pedro Recreation Agency. **Open:** All year. **Site Assignment:** Reservations accepted w/ V, MC, or check. **Registration:** At entrance booth. **Fee:** $12–$25; cash, V, MC. **Parking:** At site or designated area for walk-ins.

FACILITIES

Number of RV-only Sites: 231. **Number of Tent-only Sites:** 36. **Hookups:** Electric (20, 30 amps), water, sewer. **Each Site:** Picnic table, fire grate, food storage box, some sites have a ramada. **Dump Station:** Yes. **Laundry:** No. **Pay Phone:** Yes. **Restrooms and Showers:** Yes. **Fuel:** No, at Marina. **Propane:** At Marina. **Internal Roads:** Paved. **RV Service:** No. **Market:** 8.5 mi south in La Grange. **Restaurant:** 8.5 mi. south in La Grange. **General Store:** Yes. **Vending:** Yes. **Swimming:** Lagoon. **Playground:** No. **Other:** Some wheelchair-accessible facilities, boat ramp, marina, beach. **Activities:** Fishing, waterskiing, motorboat & houseboat rentals, sailing, horseshoe pit, volleyball, softball. **Nearby Attractions:** Northern Mariposa County History Center in Coulterville; Turlock Lake State Recreation Area; Yosemite National Park. **Additional Information:** Tuolumne County Visitors Bureau, (209) 533-4420 or (800) 446-1333.

RESTRICTIONS

Pets: Not allowed. **Fires:** Fire grates only. **Alcoholic Beverages:** Allowed. **Vehicle Maximum Length:** No limit. **Other:** 14-day stay limit; no fireworks.

TO GET THERE

From La Grange on Hwy. 132 drive 5 mi. north on La Grange Rd./J59. Turn right on Bonds Flat Rd. and proceed for another 3.3 mi. to the park entrance on the left.

LA GRANGE   MAP, C-3
Turlock Lake State Recreation Area

reserve america

22600 Lake Rd., 95329. T: (209) 874-2056; www.reserveamerica.com.

🚐 ★★★★	⛺ ★★★★
Beauty: ★★★	Site Privacy: ★★
Spaciousness: ★★	Quiet: ★★★★★
Security: ★★★★★	Cleanliness: ★★★★
Insect Control: ★★★	Facilities: ★★

Nestled in the rolling foothills of eastern Stanislaus County, Turlock Lake State Recreation Area is an ideal place for day- or week-long outings. Open all year and featuring camping, picnicking, fishing, swimming, boating, water skiing, and clean country air, the area offers visitors an opportunity to see the wonderful variety of native plant life that once flourished alongside the rivers of the San Joaquin Valley. Bounded on the north by the Tuolumne River and on the south by Turlock Lake, the recreation area provides an ideal setting for water-oriented outdoor activities. The recreation area features the lake with its 26 miles of shoreline and the foothill country leased from the Turlock Irrigation District in 1950. Picnicking, day use, and boat-launch ramps are offered at the lake. Overnight visitors are welcome at the 66 site campground located on the shady south bank of the Tuolumne River about 1 mile from the lake. From several lookout points, visitors can view the surrounding savannas and some of the cattle ranches and orchards nearby. And from Lake Road, which separates the campground from the day-use area, an excellent perspective is shown of the campground, the river and sloughs, and miles of dredger tailing piles—the by-product of a half century of gold mining.

BASICS

Operated By: California Dept. of Parks & Recreation. **Open:** All year. **Site Assignment:** Reservations can be made 7 months in advance. **Registration:** At office. **Fee:** Single, $13–$20. **Parking:** At site.

FACILITIES

Number of Multipurpose Sites: 59. **Hookups:** None. **Dump Station:** No. **Laundry:** No. **Pay Phone:** No. **Restrooms and Showers:** Yes. **Fuel:** No. **Propane:** No. **Internal Roads:** Paved. **RV Service:** No. **Market:** No. **Restaurant:** No. **General Store:** No. **Vending:** No. **Swimming:** Yes. **Playground:** No. **Other:** Fees include entry for 1 vehicle & 1 legally towed vehicle or trailer, additional vehicles will be charged per night at the park. **Activities:** boating, fishing, hiking, picnicking.

RESTRICTIONS

Pets: On 6-ft. leash in a tent or enclosed vehicle at night. Except for guide dogs, pets are not allowed in park buildings, on trails, or on most beaches. **Fires:** In designated fireplaces. **Alcoholic Beverages:** Not allowed.

TO GET THERE

Park is located about 25 mi. east of Modesto on the south side of the Tuolumne River. From Modesto take Hwy. 132 east 14 mi. to Waterford; in Waterford turn right on Hickman Rd. (CR J-9) and drive 1 mi. to Lake Rd. Turn left on Lake Rd. and drive 10 mi. to Turlock Lake State Recreation Area.

LA HONDA · · · · · · · · · · MAP, D-1
Portola Redwoods State Park

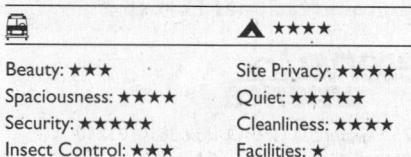

9000 Portola State Park Rd. #F, 94020.
T: (650) 948-9098 or (800) 444-7275;
www.reserveamerica.com.

🚐 ★★★   ⛺ ★★★★

Beauty: ★★★★	Site Privacy: ★★★
Spaciousness: ★★★	Quiet: ★★★★
Security: ★★	Cleanliness: ★★★
Insect Control: ★★★	Facilities: ★★

As you make your way along the access road to Portola Redwoods State Park, you'll enjoy some breathtaking valley views. Some may feel that is small reward for the clutch-grinding, white-knuckle drive from one hairpin curve to another. But on finally arriving at the park, you may have the entire campground to yourself, especially if visiting midweek or out of season. The two small loops are deftly arranged across a hilly canyon to maximize the usable space. That is a good thing, as aside from the fallen giants that border some of the fern-dappled sites, screening is minimal. Still, this is a handsomely forested camp, with ancient moss-covered sentinels surrounded by their smaller, second-growth descendants, as well as oaks and azaleas. Site 28 overlooks a creek and is, with neighboring 29, among the better ones for privacy. Numbers 37 and 39 are attractive, too, though on the small side. Pull-through sites are available but drivers of long rigs should think twice about trying to navigate the goat-path of a road up to Portola. Also remember to fill up your gas tank before entering the mountains.

BASICS

Operated By: California Dept. of Parks & Recreation. **Open:** Mar.–Nov. **Site Assignment:** Reservations accepted w/ V, MC, D. **Registration:** At entrance booth or visitor center. **Fee:** $25; cash, CA check (ID required); extra vehicle, $5. **Parking:** At site.

FACILITIES

Number of RV-only Sites: 9. **Number of Tent-only Sites:** 42. **Hookups:** None. **Each Site:** Picnic table, fire ring. **Dump Station:** No. **Laundry:** No. **Pay Phone:** Yes. **Restrooms and Showers:** Yes. **Fuel:** No. **Propane:** No. **Internal Roads:** Paved. **RV Service:** No. **Market:** 25 mi. east in Palo Alto. **Restaurant:** 25 mi. east in Palo Alto. **General Store:** No. **Vending:** No. **Swimming:** No. **Playground:** No. **Activities:** Hiking, ranger-led activities in summer, exploring redwood forests. **Nearby Attractions:** Palo Alto museums; state beaches along the coast; Mission Santa Clara de Asis & vari-

ous museums in Santa Clara; San Jose museums, architecture & zoo. **Additional Information:** Palo Alto Chamber of Commerce, (650) 324-3121; Santa Clara CVB, (408) 224-9660 or (800) 272-6822; San Jose CVB, (888) san-jose.

RESTRICTIONS

Pets: On 6-ft. leash; not allowed on trails or in creeks. **Fires:** Fire ring only. **Alcoholic Beverages:** Allowed at site. **Vehicle Maximum Length:** 24 ft. **Other:** 15-day stay limit from Apr. 1–Oct. 31; no loaded firearms; no wood gathering; no bicycling; no horseback riding; no fishing. Food must be stored in vehicles.

TO GET THERE

From Palo Alto drive south on I-280 and take the Page Mill Rd. Exit. Turn right (south) and drive 8.8 mi., straight through the stop sign, to Alpine Rd. Follow this road for 3.5 mi., then turn left on Portola State Park Rd. The park entrance is 3.1 mi. ahead.

LAGUNA BEACH · · · · · · · · MAP, F-3
Crystal Cove State Park

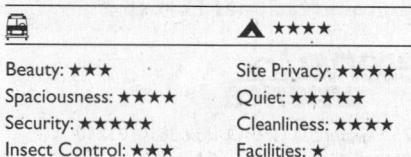

8471 PCH, 92651. T: (949) 494-3539;
www.reserveamerica.com.

🚐   ⛺ ★★★★

Beauty: ★★★	Site Privacy: ★★★★
Spaciousness: ★★★★	Quiet: ★★★★★
Security: ★★★★★	Cleanliness: ★★★★
Insect Control: ★★★	Facilities: ★

Crystal Cove State Park has 3.5 miles of beach and 2,000 acres of undeveloped woodland, which are popular for hiking and horseback riding. The offshore waters are designated as an underwater park. Crystal Cove is used by mountain bikers inland and scuba and skin divers underwater. The beach is popular with swimmers and surfers. Visitors can explore tidepools and sandy coves. Crystal Cove offers sand and surf, rocky reefs, ridges and canyon, plus recreational opportunities that appeal to everyone. State-park rangers conduct nature hikes in the winter. Camping at the park is not beach camping. After you park your car in El Moro lot, to reach the campground you must hike inland about 3 miles, mostly uphill. The trail is strenuous at times and is in the opposite direction from the beach. Some people report that it takes two hours to reach the campground, one way, while others report six hours. You must pack everything in, including water.

BASICS

Operated By: California Dept. of Parks & Recreation. **Open:** All year. **Site Assignment:** Reservations can be made 7 months in advance. **Registration:** At office. **Fee:** Dorm room–cottage, $30–$295. **Parking:** At park office.

FACILITIES

Number of Tent-only Sites: 32. **Hookups:** None. **Each Site:** Picnic table. **Dump Station:** No. **Laundry:** No. **Pay Phone:** No. **Restrooms and Show-**

ers: Yes. **Fuel:** No. **Propane:** No. **Internal Roads:** Paved. **RV Service:** No. **Market:** No. **Restaurant:** No. **General Store:** No. **Vending:** No. **Swimming:** No. **Playground:** No. **Activities:** Hiking.

RESTRICTIONS

Pets: No pets allowed. **Fires:** Restricted to backpack stoves. **Alcoholic Beverages:** Not allowed. **Other:** No drinking water available, must pack it in. No trash cans available—pack it in, pack it out. Fees include entry for 1 vehicle & 1 legally towed vehicle or trailer, additional vehicles will be charged per night at the park. All sites are a 3 mi. hike from the beach.

TO GET THERE

The park is located off Pacific Coast Hwy. between Corona del Mar and Laguna Beach.

LAGUNITAS · · · · · · · · MAP, C-1, C-2
Samuel P. Taylor State Park

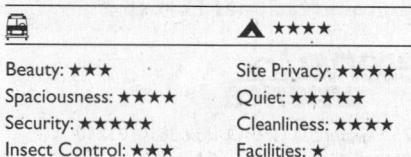

Sir Francis Drake Blvd., 94938. T: (415) 488-9897 or (800) 444-7275; www.reserveamerica.com.

🚐 ★★★   ⛺ ★★★

Beauty: ★★★★	Site Privacy: ★★★
Spaciousness: ★★★	Quiet: ★★★
Security: ★★★	Cleanliness: ★★★★
Insect Control: ★★	Facilities: ★★

In 1854 Samuel Taylor stumbled into a redwood grove here and was so enchanted by the sight that he promptly purchased 100 acres of land and set up a paper mill. Present-day visitors to this dark, densely forested park may wish that he had exercised less discretion in his timber harvesting to allow more sunshine to penetrate. No matter, it remains an appealing woodland of intermingled second-growth redwoods, tan oaks, madrones, bays, and Douglas firs. The compact campground is tightly woven through two loops, with small dirt-surfaced sites rather crowded together. Although the preserve is open to RVs and even has six pull-through spots, narrow cornering and limited parking space make it more practical for tenting. Yet even the nylon-roof set may find most sites a bit shy of elbow room. Of the two circuits, there is slightly more space and privacy in Orchard Hill (numbers 25–60). If you plan on coming between May and October, you will need to reserve far ahead.

BASICS

Operated By: California Dept. of Parks & Recreation. **Open:** All year. **Site Assignment:** Reservations accepted all year w/ V, MC, D; first come, first served sites available. **Registration:** At entrance booth. **Fee:** $15–$25; cash, CA check. **Parking:** At site or adjacent to site.

FACILITIES

Number of Tent-only Sites: 24. **Number of Multipurpose Sites:** 36. **Hookups:** None. **Each Site:** Picnic table, fire grates, food storage box. **Dump Station:** No. **Laundry:** No. **Pay Phone:** Yes. **Restrooms and Showers:** Yes. **Fuel:** No. **Propane:** No. **Internal Roads:** Paved, narrow,

& windy. **RV Service:** No. **Market:** 2 mi. southeast in Lagunitas. **Restaurant:** 2 mi. southeast in Lagunitas. **General Store:** No. **Vending:** No. **Swimming:** No. **Playground:** No. **Other:** Some wheelchair-accessible facilities. **Activities:** Hiking, mountain biking, horseback riding. **Nearby Attractions:** Mission San Rafael Archangel, Marin County Frank Lloyd Wright Civic Center & China Camp State Park in San Rafael; Muir Woods National Monument & Mount Tamalpais State Park in Mill Valley. **Additional Information:** San Rafael Chamber of Commerce, (415) 454-4163; Mill Valley Chamber of Commerce, (415) 388-9700.

RESTRICTIONS

Pets: On leash no longer than 6 ft., not allowed on trails. **Fires:** Fire grates only. **Alcoholic Beverages:** Allowed at site. **Vehicle Maximum Length:** 24 ft. **Other:** 7-day stay limit from Apr. 1–Oct. 31; no firearms; no wood gathering.

TO GET THERE

From San Rafael take Hwy. 101 south to the Sir Francis Drake Blvd. Exit. Head west for 17 mi. The park entrance is on the left.

LAKE ISABELLA   MAP, D-2, E-2
Boulder Gulch—Sequoia National Forest

4875 Ponderosa Dr./P.O. Box 3810, 93240.
T: (760) 379-5646; www.reserveamerica.com.

🚐 ★★★★   ⛺ ★★★★

Beauty: ★★★★	Site Privacy: ★★★
Spaciousness: ★★★	Quiet: ★★★
Security: ★★★★	Cleanliness: ★★★★
Insect Control: ★★★★	Facilities: ★★★

Boulder Gulch Campground is located around Lake Isabella, one of the largest reservoirs in southern California, with over 11,000 surface acres. The campground is a series of overlapping loops on the shores of Lake Isabella. A few cottonwoods and gray pine provide some shade. The camp sites are mostly in the open, with sagebrush and boulders. There are a variety of recreational opportunities within the campground or nearby, ranging from fishing, boating, or picknicking. The lake offers terrific freshwater recreation experiences and is in close proximity to Los Angeles and Bakersfield. Elevation ranges from 2,500 to 2,600 feet and fishing on the lake is open year-round. All developed campgrounds and group camping areas operate under a concessionaire program with California Land Management (CLM). Boulder Gulch is located in the Sequoia National Forest; the forest and Giant Sequoia National Monument are named for the giant sequoia, the world's largest tree. The landscape is as spectacular as the 38 groves of giant sequoia. Majestic granite monoliths, glacier-torn canyons, roaring whitewater, and lush meadows await your discovery at the southern end of the Sierra Nevada.

BASICS

Operated By: U.S. Forest Service. **Open:** May 15–Sept. 14. **Site Assignment:** Reservations must be made at least 1 day in advance. **Registration:** At office. **Fee:** Single, $17. **Parking:** At park.

FACILITIES

Number of Multipurpose Sites: 12. **Hookups:** None. **Each Site:** Fire ring. **Dump Station:** Less than 2 mi. **Laundry:** No. **Pay Phone:** No. **Restrooms and Showers:** Yes. **Fuel:** Less than 2 mi. **Propane:** No. **Internal Roads:** Paved. **RV Service:** No. **Market:** Less than 2 mi. **Restaurant:** Less than 2 mi. **General Store:** Less than 2 mi. **Vending:** No. **Swimming:** No. **Playground:** Yes. **Activities:** Biking, bird-watching, hiking, photography, wildlife viewing.

RESTRICTIONS

Pets: Pets must be restrained or on a leash at all times while in developed recreation areas. **Fires:** In fire rings, stoves, grills, or fireplaces provided for that purpose. **Alcoholic Beverages:** Not allowed. **Vehicle Maximum Length:** 45 ft. **Other:** No battery charging in the restrooms. Hair dryers are not allowed in the shower building. No livestock allowed in the campground.

TO GET THERE

From the town of Lake Isabella, go 4 mi. north on CA 155.

LAKE ISABELLA   MAP, D-2, E-2
Camp 9 Campground—Sequoia National Forest

4875 Ponderosa Dr./P.O. Box 3810, 93240.
T: (760) 379-5646; www.reserveamerica.com.

🚐 ★★★★   ⛺ ★★★★

Beauty: ★★★★	Site Privacy: ★★★
Spaciousness: ★★★★	Quiet: ★★★
Security: ★★★★	Cleanliness: ★★★★
Insect Control: ★★★★	Facilities: ★★★

You will find a 2,600-foot elevation at Camp 9 Campground including 109 campsites and 12 group areas, which accommodate between 24–50 people, on Lake Isabella in Sequoia National Forest. The Sequoia National Forest and Giant Sequoia National Monument are named for the giant sequoia, one of the world's largest trees. The landscape is as spectacular as its 38 groves of giant sequoia. Majestic granite monoliths, glacier-torn canyons, roaring whitewater, and lush meadows await your discovery at the southern end of the Sierra Nevada Mountain Range. The Sequoia is one of 19 national forests in California.

BASICS

Operated By: U.S. Forest Service. **Open:** All year. **Site Assignment:** Reservations must be made at least 3 days in advance. **Registration:** At office. **Fee:** Single, $10; other, $40–$110. **Parking:** At park.

FACILITIES

Number of Multipurpose Sites: 282. **Hookups:** None. **Each Site:** Call ahead. **Dump Station:** Yes. **Laundry:** 4 mi. **Pay Phone:** No. **Restrooms and Showers:** Yes. **Fuel:** No. **Propane:** No. **Internal Roads:** Paved. **RV Service:** No. **Market:** 4 mi.

Restaurant: 4 mi. **General Store:** 4 mi. **Vending:** No. **Swimming:** Yes. **Playground:** No. **Activities:** Biking, bird-watching, boating, fishing, jet skiing, photography, volleyball.

RESTRICTIONS

Pets: Pets must be restrained or on a leash at all times while in developed recreation areas. **Fires:** In fire rings, stoves, grills, or fireplaces provided for that purpose. **Alcoholic Beverages:** Not allowed. **Other:** No ATVs or ORVs in the campground. No loud music or yelling & screaming. Cars are not allowed to be used as a stereo system.

TO GET THERE

From Kernville, go south on Sierra Way/CR 521, then turn west on access road to the lake.

LAKE ISABELLA   MAP, D-2, E-2
Tillie Creek Campground—Sequoia National Forest

4875 Ponderosa Dr./P.O. Box 3810, 93240.
T: (760) 379-5646; www.reserveamerica.com.

🚐 ★★★★   ⛺ ★★★★

Beauty: ★★★★	Site Privacy: ★★★
Spaciousness: ★★★	Quiet: ★★★
Security: ★★★★	Cleanliness: ★★★★
Insect Control: ★★★★	Facilities: ★★★★

Tillie Creek Campground is located in the Sequoia National Forest. Giant Sequoia National Monument is named for the giant sequoia, one of the world's largest trees. The landscape is as spectacular as the 38 groves of giant sequoia. Majestic granite monoliths, glacier-torn canyons, roaring whitewater, and lush meadows await your discovery at the southern end of the Sierra Nevada. The Sequoia is one of 19 national forests in California. The Sequoia National Forest offers a huge range of outdoor recreation activities. The trails offer hiking, backpacking, horseback riding, and mountain biking. The many developed campgrounds or dispersed areas provide the full range of camping experiences. The rivers, lakes, and reservoirs offer boating, fishing, water-skiing, swimming, whitewater rafting, and kayaking. In the winter, the high elevations provide downhill skiing and snowboarding, cross-country skiing, snowshoeing, and snowmobiling.

BASICS

Operated By: U.S. Forest Service. **Open:** All year. **Site Assignment:** Reservations must be made at least 1 day in advance. **Registration:** At office. **Fee:** Single, $15. **Parking:** At park.

FACILITIES

Number of Multipurpose Sites: 324. **Hookups:** None. **Each Site:** Fire ring, picnic table. **Dump Station:** Yes. **Laundry:** No. **Pay Phone:** No. **Restrooms and Showers:** Yes. **Fuel:** Less than 1 mi. **Propane:** Less than 1 mi. **Internal Roads:** Paved. **RV Service:** No. **Market:** Less than 1 mi. **Restaurant:** Less than 1 mi. **General Store:** Less than 1 mi. **Vending:** No. **Swimming:** No. **Playground:** Yes.

RESTRICTIONS

Pets: Pets must be restrained or on a leash at all times while in developed recreation areas. **Fires:** In fire rings, stoves, grills, or fireplaces provided for that purpose. **Alcoholic Beverages:** Not allowed. **Vehicle Maximum Length:** 30 ft. **Other:** No livestock. All equipment must fit on the site pad.

TO GET THERE

From Bakersfield take Hwy. 178 east to the town of Lake Isabella. From Lake Isabella take Hwy. 155 north, traveling 6 mi. to the entry station of Tillie Creek Campground.

LAKEHEAD   MAP, B-2
Antlers RV Park and Campground

20682 Antler Rd., 96051. T: (530) 238-2322 or (800) 642-6849; www.antlersrv.com.

🚐 ★★★★★   ⛺ ★★★★

Beauty: ★★★★   Site Privacy: ★★★★
Spaciousness: ★★★★   Quiet: ★★★
Security: ★★★   Cleanliness: ★★★★
Insect Control: ★★★   Facilities: ★★★★

During a recent winter, snow and rain combined with gale-force winds to topple dozens of trees in Antlers RV Park. A lesser property would have been left scarred for years to come by such decimation. Not Antlers. The trunks and limbs were carved up and hauled away, and the campground continues to be a standout beauty. Its lovely perch above the iridescent Shasta Lake offers campers a balance of sun and shade among an abundance of such trees as oak, pine, cedar, and manzanita. Most sites are level, grassy, and surprisingly spacious for an RV-oriented campground. Even those with full hookups have plenty of elbow-room, with 108 one of the best in that class. In the ever-popular lake-view area, A 38 and A 39, decked with ramadas as well as shade trees, are the prime slots. Tent campers, too, will find more than enough space to spread their tents, with the forested loops, where mossy boulders accentuate the natural look, providing the most privacy. Although Antlers is a mere 2 miles from I-5, surprisingly little road noise reaches it.

BASICS

Operated By: Antlers RV Park & Campground. **Open:** All year. **Site Assignment:** Reservations accepted w/ V, MC, D. **Registration:** At office. **Fee:** RV, $20–$31.50; tent: $14–$20.50; cash, V, MC, D. **Parking:** At site.

FACILITIES

Number of RV-only Sites: 70. **Number of Tent-only Sites:** 37. **Hookups:** Electric (30, 50 amps), water, sewer, internet. **Each Site:** Picnic table, fire grate, food storage box. **Dump Station:** No. **Laundry:** Yes. **Pay Phone:** Yes. **Restrooms and Showers:** Yes. **Fuel:** No. **Propane:** No. **Internal Roads:** Paved & gravel. **RV Service:** No. Mobile mechanic. **Market:** 2 mi. north in Lakehead. **Restaurant:** 1 mi. south. **General Store:** Yes, open from Memorial Day to Labor Day, w/ snack bar. **Vending:** No. **Swimming:** Pool. **Playground:** Yes. **Other:** Some wheelchair-accessible facilities, marina, game room, video rentals. **Activities:** Fishing, boat rentals, water-

skiing, hiking, horseshoe pit, ping pong, volleyball, basketball. **Nearby Attractions:** Carter House Natural Science Museum, Turtle Bay Museums & Arboretum, Waterworks Park in Redding; Shasta Lake, Caverns & Dam; Shasta State Historic Park; Whiskeytown National Recreation Area. **Additional Information:** Redding CVB, (530) 225-4100.

RESTRICTIONS

Pets: On leash, $3 fee. **Fires:** Fire grates only. **Alcoholic Beverages:** Allowed. **Vehicle Maximum Length:** 40 ft. **Other:** 30-day stay limit; no wood gathering.

TO GET THERE

From Redding drive 26 mi. north on I-5 and exit at Lakeshore/Antlers Rd. Turn right and drive 1 block, then turn right again on Antlers Rd. Continue for 1.5 mi. to the campground entrance straight ahead.

LAKESIDE   MAP, F-3
Lake Jennings County Park

10108 Bass Rd., 92040. T: (858) 694-3049 or (858) 565-3600; www.co.san-diego.ca.us/parks.

🚐 ★★★★   ⛺ ★★★

Beauty: ★★★★   Site Privacy: ★★★★
Spaciousness: ★★★   Quiet: ★★★
Security: ★★★★   Cleanliness: ★★★
Insect Control: ★★★   Facilities: ★★★

People familiar with Lake Jennings from previous years may be excused if they fail to recognize it in its current state. The most obvious change is the spruced up landscaping, with geraniums and other annuals lending a welcome splash of color to a ridge-top setting marked by holly, acacia, prickly pear cacti, eucalyptus, pepper trees, and a variety of conifers. That's not all, as structural renovations have encompassed the restrooms and showers, as well as upgraded electrical hookups. Unaffected by these alterations, alas, are the gravel sites themselves, which are shoe-horned close together, several resting on ground so tilted that hammocks might seem preferable to tents. Thankfully, abundant vegetation yields some privacy and many units along the park's spiraling loop road enjoy excellent vistas. Numbers 20, 22, 24, 43, and 45 are among the standout tenting options, with 89–91 tops for RVs. The lake is stocked with trout in the winter and catfish summertime, but boating is only allowed on weekends.

BASICS

Operated By: County of San Diego, Dept. of Parks & Recreation. **Open:** All year. **Site Assignment:** Reservations accepted w/ V, MC, D. **Registration:** At entrance booth. **Fee:** $12–$18; cash, V, MC, D. **Parking:** At site.

FACILITIES

Number of RV-only Sites: 94. **Number of Tent-only Sites:** 6. **Hookups:** Electric (20, 30 amps), water, sewer. **Each Site:** Picnic table, fire grate, barbecue grill. **Dump Station:** Yes. **Laundry:** No. **Pay Phone:** Yes. **Restrooms and Showers:** Yes. **Fuel:** No. **Propane:** No. **Internal Roads:** Paved. **RV Service:** No. **Market:** 2 mi west in Lakeside. **Restaurant:** 2 mi. west in Lakeside. **General Store:** No.

Vending: Yes. **Swimming:** No. **Playground:** Yes. **Other:** Some wheelchair-accessible facilities. **Activities:** Fishing, hiking, horseshoe pit. **Nearby Attractions:** San Diego & its waterfront, museums, zoo, historic district. **Additional Information:** Lakeside Chamber of Commerce, (619) 561-1031; City of El Cajon, (619) 441-1776.

RESTRICTIONS

Pets: On 6-ft. leash; $1 fee. **Fires:** Fire grates only. **Alcoholic Beverages:** Allowed at site, not exceeding 40 proof. **Vehicle Maximum Length:** 35 ft. **Other:** 14-day stay limit; no firearms.

TO GET THERE

From I-8 in El Cajon take Hwy. 67 north and drive 4.5 mi. Turn right onto Maple View St. and drive 2.2 mi. The road changes into Lake Jennings Park Rd. The campground entrance is on the left.

LEE VINING   MAP, C-3
Lundy Canyon Campground

Lundy Lake Rd., 93541. T: (760) 932-5440; www.dogfriendly.com.

🚐 ★★★★   ⛺ ★★★★

Beauty: ★★★★   Site Privacy: ★★★★
Spaciousness: ★★★★   Quiet: ★★
Security: ★★   Cleanliness: ★★
Insect Control: ★★★   Facilities: ★

Lundy Canyon, a county park, is one of the better bargains around, especially with the explosion of price hikes at the concession-run national forest options. There is a subtle, understated beauty to this scruffy glen, where Lundy Creek discreetly trickles through and Sierra Nevadas tower above. Level, largely grassy sites, which range in size from shoe-box to palatial, are spread out over several access points along Lundy Lake Rd. Skip the first 15 or so, as many later choices are endowed with superior privacy and a more generous amount of space. Excellent screening between spots is derived from thickets of aspen, as well as juniper and high-desert chaparral. This diamond-in-the-rough, at 7,800 feet elevation, lacks potable water. A boat ramp, boat rentals, and groceries are available at Lundy Lake Resort, just up the road.

BASICS

Operated By: Mono County Public Works Dept. **Open:** May–Oct.; weather permitting. **Site Assignment:** First come, first served. **Registration:** At entrance kiosk, pay at site 37. **Fee:** $8; cash, CA check. **Parking:** At site.

FACILITIES

Number of RV-only Sites: 54. **Hookups:** None. **Each Site:** Picnic table, fire grate. **Dump Station:** No. **Laundry:** No. **Pay Phone:** No. **Restrooms and Showers:** Pit & vault toilets, no showers. **Fuel:** No. **Propane:** No. **Internal Roads:** Gravel & dirt, decent condition. **RV Service:** No. **Market:** 10 mi. southeast in Lee Vining. **Restaurant:** 10 mi. southeast in Lee Vining. **General Store:** No. **Vending:** No. **Swimming:** No. **Playground:** No. **Other:** Some wheelchair-accessible facilities. **Activities:** Fishing, hiking, boating. **Nearby Attractions:**

Yosemite, Mono Lake Tufa State Reserve in Lee Vining; Lundy Lake; Bodie State Historic Park near Bridgeport. **Additional Information:** Mono County Tourism Commission, (760) 924-3699; Lee Vining Chamber of Commerce, (760) 647-6629.

RESTRICTIONS

Pets: On 10 ft. leash. **Fires:** Fire grates only. **Alcoholic Beverages:** Allowed at site. **Vehicle Maximum Length:** 24 ft. **Other:** No stay limit.

TO GET THERE

From Lee Vining drive 7 mi. north on US 395. Turn left on Lundy Lake Rd. and continue for 2.5 mi. to the campground entrance on the left. Lundy Lake Rd. offers several access points.

LEGGETT   MAP, B-1
Standish-Hickey State Recreation Area

reserve america

69350 Hwy. 101, #2, 95585. T: (707) 925-6482; www.reserveamerica.com.

🚐 ★★★★   ⛺ ★★★★

Beauty: ★★★   Site Privacy: ★★★
Spaciousness: ★★★   Quiet: ★★★★★
Security: ★★★★★   Cleanliness: ★★★★
Insect Control: ★★★   Facilities: ★★

Standish-Hickey began as a 40-acre campground acquired by the Save-the-Redwoods League in 1922. It was named to honor Edward Ritter Hickey, a local lumberman who died of influenza while caring for the victims of the epidemic of 1918. In the late 1950s, the Standish family donated over 500 acres, and additional acquisitions through the years have brought the park's total acreage to 1,012. Much of the land, clear-cut and then burned over in a disastrous fire in the mid-1940s, is just now regaining its former beauty. At the "gateway to the tall trees country," the area offers camping, picnicking, hiking, fishing, and swimming on the South Fork of the Eel River, which winds through the park for almost 2 miles. One of the few virgin redwood stands remaining in this area can be seen on the Grove Trail. The park's three campgrounds contain a total of 162 family campsites. Campsites can accommodate equipment ranging from tents to 24-foot trailers and 27-foot motor homes. Camping is available year-round.

BASICS

Operated By: California Dept. of Parks & Recreation. **Open:** All year. **Site Assignment:** Reservations can be made 7 months in advance. Hickey & Rock Creek, May 25–Sept. 5; Redwood Campground, July 17–Sept. 5. **Registration:** At office. **Fee:** Single, $15–$20. **Parking:** At site.

FACILITIES

Number of Multipurpose Sites: 161. **Hookups:** None. **Dump Station:** No. **Laundry:** No. **Pay Phone:** No. **Restrooms and Showers:** Yes. **Fuel:** No. **Propane:** No. **Internal Roads:** Paved. **RV Service:** No. **Market:** No. **Restaurant:** No. **General**

Store: No. **Vending:** No. **Swimming:** Yes. **Playground:** No. **Activities:** Hiking, nature trails, picnicking.

RESTRICTIONS

Pets: On 6-ft. leash in a tent or enclosed vehicle at night. Except for guide dogs, pets are not allowed in park buildings, on trails, or on most beaches. **Fires:** In designated fireplaces. **Alcoholic Beverages:** Not allowed.

TO GET THERE

1.5 mi. north of Leggett on Hwy. 101.

LEMON COVE   MAP, D-2
Horse Creek Campground

reserve america

P.O. Box 44270, Hwy. 198, 93244.
T: (559) 597-2301 or (877) 444-6777;
www.reserveamerica.com.

🚐 ★★★★   ⛺ ★★★

Beauty: ★★★★   Site Privacy: ★★
Spaciousness: ★★★   Quiet: ★★★
Security: ★★★★   Cleanliness: ★★★
Insect Control: ★★   Facilities: ★★★

Lake Kaweah is a refreshing body of water that provides welcome relief in a part of the state where summer starts early and runs late. Its level was so high one recent spring that several of Horse Creek's sites were underwater. Nonetheless it remains a popular weekend retreat for area families, and for good reason: you can soak yourself in Kaweah's cool waters while the campgrounds in Sequoia and Kings Canyon national parks are still under snow. Nestled in the Sierra foothills at an elevation of 694 feet, Horse Creek's environment is framed by the boulder-streaked, grassy ridges that hover over it. Nearer at hand, sites are plentifully shaded by oak, sycamore, buckeye, and cottonwood trees. An elongated loop, with three spur circuits, puts a great number of grass and dirt sites right at the edge of the lake. Privacy-seekers, though, should look toward higher ground, where numbers 4 and 5 are roomy, set back from the camp lane and enjoy a premium vantage of the water. The marina at Lemon Hill has propane and basic supplies.

BASICS

Operated By: U.S. Army Corps of Engineers. **Open:** All year. **Site Assignment:** Reservations recommended; V, MC, D, AE; first come, first served sites available. **Registration:** At entrance booth. **Fee:** $16; cash, check. **Parking:** At site. Only 2 vehicles permitted per site.

FACILITIES

Number of RV-only Sites: 80. **Hookups:** None. **Each Site:** Picnic table, fire grate, lantern pole. **Dump Station:** Yes, but not on site. **Laundry:** No. **Pay Phone:** Yes. **Restrooms and Showers:** Yes. **Fuel:** No. **Propane:** No. **Internal Roads:** Paved & occasionally flooded. **RV Service:** No. **Market:** 8 mi. east in Three Rivers. **Restaurant:** 8 mi. east in Three Rivers. **General Store:** No. **Vending:** No. **Swimming:** Lake Kaweah. **Playground:** Yes. **Other:** Some wheelchair-accessible facilities, boat

ramp not at the campground. **Activities:** Fishing, boat rentals, waterskiing, hiking, whitewater rafting on the Kaweah River, bailing out your tent. **Nearby Attractions:** Sequoia & Kings Canyon national parks; Tulare County Museum in Visalia; Kaweah Oaks Preserve in Exeter. **Additional Information:** Visalia Chamber of Commerce & Visitors Bureau, (559) 734-5876; Three Rivers–Lemoncove Business Assoc., (550) 561-0410.

RESTRICTIONS

Pets: On leash. **Fires:** Fire grates only. **Alcoholic Beverages:** Allowed. **Vehicle Maximum Length:** 45 ft. **Other:** 14-day stay limit; only 2 vehicles per site; 8 people per site; quiet hours after 10 p.m.

TO GET THERE

From Visalia drive 24 mi. east on Hwy. 198 to Lake Kaweah's south shore. The well-signed campground entrance is on the left.

LIVERMORE   MAP, C-2
Del Valle Regional Park

7000 Del Valle Rd., 94550. T: (510) 636-1684 or (510) 562-2267; www.ebparks.org.

🚐 ★★★★   ⛺ ★★★★

Beauty: ★★★★   Site Privacy: ★★★
Spaciousness: ★★★   Quiet: ★★★
Security: ★★★★   Cleanliness: ★★
Insect Control: ★★★   Facilities: ★★★

Del Valle Regional Park is a quiet, unassuming place that just happens to be one of the more beautiful of the many parklands in the Bay Area. A part of the Diablo Range, this rugged canyon setting consists of grassy hills, meadows punctuated by thick concentrations of oak, eucalyptus, knobcone pine, and sycamore, and at its heart a narrow reservoir that stretches 5 miles from end to end. Windsurfers and sailing enthusiasts take to the water like a child to chocolate, with motorboats restricted to a maximum speed of 10 miles per hour. Fishing conditions are only average, despite regular plantings of rainbow trout. There are no views of the lake from the campground, but roomy, grass-covered sites are spaced well apart over a double loop, helping to compensate for that handicap. Birders will find pleasure in the many species that make this territory their home, including several wild turkeys and a pair of peacocks.

BASICS

Operated By: East Bay Regional Park District. **Open:** All year. **Site Assignment:** Reservations accepted w/ V, MC, fee is $7. First come, first served. **Registration:** At entrance booth. **Fee:** $18; cash, V, MC. **Parking:** At site.

FACILITIES

Number of RV-only Sites: 150. **Hookups:** Water, sewer. **Each Site:** Picnic table, fire grate. **Dump Station:** Yes. **Laundry:** No. **Pay Phone:** Yes. **Restrooms and Showers:** Yes. **Fuel:** No. **Propane:** No. **Internal Roads:** Paved. **RV Service:** No. **Market:** 9.5 mi. north in Livermore. **Restaurant:** 9.5 mi. north in Livermore. **General Store:** Yes, in summer. **Vending:** No. **Swimming:** Designated areas of Lake Del Valle. **Playground:** No. **Other:** Some wheelchair-accessible facilities, marina, boat launch. **Activities:** Hiking, fishing, bicycling, windsurfing, sailing, nature programs. **Nearby Attractions:** Mission San Jose & Ardenwood Historic Farm in Fremont; winery tours; Waterslide Park in Pleasington. **Additional Information:** Livermore Chamber of Commerce, (925) 447-1606.

RESTRICTIONS

Pets: On leash, $1 fee per night. **Fires:** Fire grates only. **Alcoholic Beverages:** Beer & wine only. Allowed at site & picnic areas. **Vehicle Maximum Length:** 35 ft. **Other:** 14-day stay limit; no firearms. Gates lock at 10 p.m. every night. Quiet hours from 10 p.m.–8 a.m.

TO GET THERE

From Livermore and Hwy. 84 head south on South Livermore Ave., which changes into Tesla Rd. After 2.4 mi. turn right on Mines Rd. Continue for 3.6 mi. and bear right on Del Valle Park Rd. The park entrance is 3.2 mi. ahead.

LONE PINE   MAP, D-3
Whitney Portal

P.O. Box 8, 93545. T: (760) 876-6200 (ranger station) or (877) 444-6777; www.fs.fed.us/r5/inyo.

🚐 ★★★★   ⛺ ★★★★

Beauty: ★★★★★	Site Privacy: ★★★
Spaciousness: ★★★	Quiet: ★★★
Security: ★★★	Cleanliness: ★★★
Insect Control: ★★★	Facilities: ★★

Even if you don't plan to hike Mt. Whitney, which, at 14,495 feet, is the highest peak in the lower 48 states, this campground is a worthwhile, breathtaking retreat. From its rocky, pine-shrouded sites, up to the aspen-fringed trailhead, from the many streams noisily cascading down the mountain to the saw-toothed, jaw-like peaks that hover menacingly above, this is one spectacular, picture-perfect scene. As you lounge by your tent at 8,000 feet elevation, low-floating clouds seem close enough to reach out and grab. Boulders provide respectable privacy between closely grouped sites, and shade is derived from Jeffrey and ponderosa pines, as well as mountain mahogany. The most secluded sites are 8 and 9, flanked by large slabs of granite. Avoid the spots just below Whitney Portal Rd., which pick up more traffic noise than the others, and try to visit on a weekday, when there are fewer mountain climbers in camp. The trailhead picnic area is an Arcadian delight.

BASICS

Operated By: Campground concessionaire. **Open:** Mid-May–mid-Oct.; weather permitting. **Site Assignment:** Reservations accepted w/ V, MC, D. **Registration:** At entrance. **Fee:** $14; cash, check. **Parking:** At site.

FACILITIES

Number of RV-only Sites: 44. **Hookups:** None. **Each Site:** Picnic table, fire grate or barbecue grill, sites have bear proof box. **Dump Station:** No. **Laundry:** No. **Pay Phone:** No. **Restrooms and Showers:** Chemical toilets, no showers. **Fuel:** No. **Propane:** No. **Internal Roads:** Paved, winding. **RV Service:** No. **Market:** 12 mi. east in Lone Pine.

Restaurant: Yes. **General Store:** Yes. **Vending:** No. **Swimming:** No. **Playground:** No. **Other:** Some wheelchair-accessible facilities. Water is available, but must be purified before consuming. **Activities:** Hiking, fishing, photography, picnicking, backpacking, rock climbing. **Nearby Attractions:** Manzanar National Historic Site & Eastern California Museum in Independence; Diaz Lake Recreation Area in Lone Pine; Mount Whitney. **Additional Information:** Lone Pine Chamber of Commerce, (760) 876-4444; Independence Chamber of Commerce, (760) 878-0084.

RESTRICTIONS

Pets: On 6-ft. leash. **Fires:** Fire grates only. **Alcoholic Beverages:** Allowed. **Vehicle Maximum Length:** 32 ft. **Other:** 7-day stay limit.

TO GET THERE

From Lone Pine on US 395 drive 12 mi. west on Whitney Portal Rd. to the campground on the left.

MALIBU   MAP, E-2
Leo Carillo State Park

reserve america

Pacific Coast Hwy., 90265. T: (805) 488-5223 or (800) 444-7275; www.reserveamerica.com.

🚐 ★★★★   ⛺ ★★★★

Beauty: ★★★★	Site Privacy: ★★★
Spaciousness: ★★★★	Quiet: ★★★
Security: ★★★★	Cleanliness: ★★★
Insect Control: ★★	Facilities: ★★★

The campground at Leo Carillo State Park is located directly across the Pacific Coast Hwy. from a wide sandy beach. While this detached position may at first appear to be a drawback, it is in fact the best of two worlds, with easy access to the ocean via a walkway under the road and a campground free of coastal winds due to its dramatic nest by the base of the steep Santa Monica Mountains. Gnarly sycamore trees overhang grassy sites along a double loop, with most being fairly spacious and decently screened by such trees as bay, willow, and black walnut. The largest and most private sites, 54, 57, 59, 61, 63, and 66, are on the west side of camp along the creek. On weekends, restrooms can be in an atrocious state, but overall the campground is surprisingly clean, given the high traffic it receives from large family groups. Reservations are highly recommended from Easter through mid-September. Rangers routinely patrol the grounds.

BASICS

Operated By: California Dept. of Parks & Recreation. **Open:** All year. **Site Assignment:** Reservations recommended; V, MC, D; some first come, first served sites. **Registration:** At entrance booth. **Fee:** $15–$25; cash, CA check. **Parking:** At site.

FACILITIES

Number of RV-only Sites: 139. **Number of Tent-only Sites:** 1. **Hookups:** None. **Each Site:** Picnic table, fire ring. **Dump Station:** Yes. **Laundry:** No. **Pay Phone:** Yes. **Restrooms and Showers:** Yes. **Fuel:** No. **Propane:** No. **Internal Roads:** Paved.

RV Service: No. **Market:** 5.5 mi. east in Malibu. **Restaurant:** 5.5 mi. east in Malibu. **General Store:** No. **Vending:** No. **Swimming:** Pacific Ocean. **Playground:** No. **Other:** Some wheelchair-accessible facilities. **Activities:** Surfing, fishing, beachcombing, tide pools, cave & reef exploring, nature walks, wind surfing, hiking. **Nearby Attractions:** Hollywood's theme parks, J. P. Getty Museum, La Brea Tar Pits, Will Rogers State Historic Park, Disneyland, historic Ventura. **Additional Information:** Santa Monica Mountains District, (810) 706-1310.

RESTRICTIONS

Pets: On 6-ft. leash. **Fires:** Fire ring only. **Alcoholic Beverages:** Allowed at site. **Vehicle Maximum Length:** 36 ft. **Other:** 7-day stay limit in summer, 14-day stay limit for the rest of the year; no firearms; no wood gathering.

TO GET THERE

At the intersection of Trancas Canyon and Broad Beach in Malibu, drive 5.5 mi. west on the Pacific Coast Hwy. (Hwy. 1). The park entrance is on the right (north) side of the road.

MALIBU   MAP, E-2
Malibu Beach RV Park

reserve america

25801 Pacific Coast Hwy., 90265. T: (800) 622-6052 or (310) 456-6052; www.reserveamerica.com.

🚐 ★★★★   ⛺ ★★★

Beauty: ★★★★	Site Privacy: ★★
Spaciousness: ★★	Quiet: ★★★
Security: ★★★	Cleanliness: ★★★★
Insect Control: ★★★	Facilities: ★★★★★

On the surface Malibu Beach looks like just another run-of-the-mill RV facility. Caravans are wedged one next to another, with a tenting area attached to the end of the serpentine camp lane seemingly as an afterthought. Probe a bit, though, and you will find this a superior property, just 6 miles west of Malibu on the Pacific Coast Hwy. on the inland side of the road. Shrewd terracing stretches sites up a bluff, thus maximizing vistas of the ocean. Yes, site privacy is nearly nil, but with that ocean panorama and the beautiful sunsets, who cares! Eucalyptus, palms, pines, and sycamores decorate the landscape and while they do little to provide shade, at least they don't obstruct the view. Though they will probably be taken already, try to get any of numbers 6–33 or V1–V13. Even the dirt walk-in tenting area atop the bluff is attractive, with small sycamores providing shade. Double-wide sites and pull-throughs are available, as well as a hot tub, game room, and Internet connection.

BASICS

Operated By: Malibu Beach RV Park. **Open:** All year. **Site Assignment:** Reservations recommended; V, MC, D, AE, DC; walk-ins accepted. **Registration:** At entrance office. **Fee:** RV summer (May 1–Sept. 30), $33–$53; RV winter (Oct. 1–Apr. 30), $26–$45; tent summer, $21–24; tent winter, $16–$18. **Parking:** At site.

FACILITIES

Number of RV-only Sites: 150. **Number of Tent-only Sites:** 50. **Hookups:** Electric (30, 50 amps), water, sewer, cable TV, Internet (in a community room). **Each Site:** Picnic table, barbecue grill. **Dump Station:** Yes. **Laundry:** Yes. **Pay Phone:** Yes. **Restrooms and Showers:** Yes. **Fuel:** Yes. **Propane:** Yes. **Internal Roads:** Paved. **RV Service:** No. **Market:** 3 mi. east in Malibu. **Restaurant:** 3 mi. east in Malibu. **General Store:** Yes. **Vending:** Yes. **Swimming:** Pacific Ocean, adult spa. **Playground:** Yes. **Other:** Some wheelchair-accessible facilities, game room. **Activities:** Surfing, fishing, hiking, dolphin & whale-watching. **Nearby Attractions:** Hollywood's theme parks, J. P. Getty Museum, La Brea Tar Pits, Will Rogers State Historic Park, Venice Beach Boardwalk, Santa Monica Pier & museums, Universal Studios. **Additional Information:** Malibu Chamber of Commerce, (310) 456-9025.

RESTRICTIONS

Pets: Well-behaved pets in RV sites only. Some breeds not allowed including: rottweilers, pit bulls, German shepherds, Doberman pinschers, akitas, alapaha Blue Blood bulldogs, American bulldogs, Staffordshire terriers, chows. **Fires:** No wood fires allowed. **Alcoholic Beverages:** Allowed. **Vehicle Maximum Length:** 45 ft. **Other:** 7-month stay limit.

TO GET THERE

From the Pacific Coast Hwy. in Malibu turn inland just 3 mi. west of Coral Canyon Rd. The campground is well signed.

MALIBU   MAP, E-2
Malibu Creek State Park

reserve america

1925 Las Virgenes Rd., 91302. T: (818) 880-0367 or (800) 444-7275; www.reserveamerica.com.

🚐 ★★★   ⛺ ★★★★

Beauty: ★★★★	Site Privacy: ★★★
Spaciousness: ★★★	Quiet: ★★★
Security: ★★★★	Cleanliness: ★★★
Insect Control: ★★★	Facilities: ★★

If you managed to get a site here without a reservation it may be time to buy a lottery ticket, that's how good your luck is. "Popular" doesn't begin to describe this park, which lies just 6 miles north of Malibu, on the sloping side of a grassy hill in the shadow of the Santa Monica Mountains. Though a forest of live oak borders the camp, there is little shade to be found within its single loop. A recent round of plantings holds the promise of many shade trees to come. And while the tilt of the terrain and small parking slips make RV camping a challenge, most sites are large enough for tenters to scratch out a satisfactory patch of turf. Heavy visitation means that restrooms tend toward the messy, especially on weekends. Overall, though, this is a remarkably well-maintained place. There are some Hollywood sets in the park, leftover from when it was owned by Universal Studios, but most people come for the great

---

hiking, mountain biking, and horseback riding. Try to get here in spring, while the long flowing grass is still green and wildflowers are in bloom.

BASICS

Operated By: California Dept. of Parks & Recreation. **Open:** All year. **Site Assignment:** Reservations highly recommended; V, MC, D. **Registration:** At entrance booth. **Fee:** $15–$25; cash, CA check. **Parking:** At site.

FACILITIES

Number of RV-only Sites: 63. **Hookups:** None. **Each Site:** Picnic table, fire grate. **Dump Station:** Yes. **Laundry:** No. **Pay Phone:** Yes. **Restrooms and Showers:** Yes. **Fuel:** No. **Propane:** No. **Internal Roads:** Paved. **RV Service:** No. **Market:** 6 mi. south in Malibu. **Restaurant:** 6 mi. south in Malibu. **General Store:** No. **Vending:** No. **Swimming:** No. **Playground:** No. **Other:** Some wheelchair-accessible facilities. **Activities:** Hiking, mountain biking, horseback riding, birding, fishing. **Nearby Attractions:** Santa Monica Pier & museums, Venice Beach Boardwalk, Hollywood's theme parks, La Brea Tar Pits. **Additional Information:** Malibu Chamber of Commerce, (310) 456-9025.

RESTRICTIONS

Pets: On 6-ft. leash. **Fires:** Fire grates only, not allowed after the grass turns brown late spring/early summer. **Alcoholic Beverages:** Allowed at site. **Vehicle Maximum Length:** 30 ft. **Other:** 7-day stay limit June 1–Sept. 30, 14-day stay limit Oct. 1–May 31; no firearms; no wood gathering.

TO GET THERE

From the Pacific Coast Hwy. in Malibu head north on CR N1/Malibu Canyon Rd. Drive 6 mi. to the campground entrance on the left.

MAMMOTH LAKES   MAP, C-3
Glass Creek

Glass Creek Rd. off of I-395, 93546.
T: (760) 647-3044; www.fs.fed.us/r5/inyo.

🚐 ★★★★   ⛺ ★★★★

Beauty: ★★★	Site Privacy: ★★★
Spaciousness: ★★★★	Quiet: ★★★
Security: ★	Cleanliness: ★★★
Insect Control: ★★★★	Facilities: ★

It may be true that there is no such thing as a free lunch, but fortunately for budget-minded campers there are still a few no-fee campgrounds left. Glass Creek is one of those, a primitive national forest camp with no potable water, no trash pickup, and rickety-looking vaulted toilets. It is also a quietly attractive piece of land that straddles its namesake creek (where the fishing for trout is pretty good), with generously large, dispersed sites on either side of the smooth, dirt access road. The slightly rolling terrain is partly shaded by very mature Jeffrey and ponderosa pines, and aspens that grow alongside the creek. Its great location, just 12 miles north of Mammoth Lakes, makes Glass Creek a popular base camp for the RV set. While ranger patrols are few and far between, the presence of vacation homes at the perimeter of the property is a reassuring sign of civilization.

BASICS

Operated By: Inyo National Forest, Mono Lake Ranger District. **Open:** Apr. 25–Nov. 1; weather permitting. **Site Assignment:** First come, first served. **Registration:** Not necessary. **Fee:** None. **Parking:** At site.

FACILITIES

Number of RV-only Sites: 50. **Hookups:** None. **Each Site:** Picnic table, fire grate or pit. **Dump Station:** Yes. **Laundry:** No. **Pay Phone:** No. **Restrooms and Showers:** Vault toilets, no showers. **Fuel:** No. **Propane:** No. **Internal Roads:** Dirt, sand, & rocks, but negotiable. **RV Service:** No. **Market:** 12 mi. south in Mammoth Lakes. **Restaurant:** 12 mi. south in Mammoth Lakes. **General Store:** No. **Vending:** No. **Swimming:** No. **Playground:** No. **Activities:** Fishing, hiking, photography, backpacking. **Nearby Attractions:** Mono Lake Tufa State Reserve in Lee Vining; Devils Postpile National Monument, Mammoth Mountain Bike Park, Mammoth Museum & outlet shopping in Mammoth Lakes, Yosemite. **Additional Information:** Mono County Tourism Commission, (760) 924-3699; Mammoth Lakes Visitors Bureau, (888) GO-MAMMOTH.

RESTRICTIONS

Pets: On leash. **Fires:** Fire grates or pits only. **Alcoholic Beverages:** Allowed. **Vehicle Maximum Length:** 40 ft. **Other:** 21-42 day stay limit.

TO GET THERE

From Mammoth Junction drive 10 mi. north on US 395, past the Caltrans Crestview Maintenance Station. Make a U-turn and head 0.5 mi. south on US 395. Turn right on Glass Creek Rd., a Forest Service road, and continue for 0.3 mi. to the campground access road on the right.

MAMMOTH LAKES   MAP, C-3
Pine Cliff Resort

P.O. Box 2, 93546. T: (760) 934-2447;
www.pinecliff.net.

🚐 ★★★★   ⛺ ★★★

Beauty: ★★★★	Site Privacy: ★★
Spaciousness: ★★	Quiet: ★★★★
Security: ★★★★	Cleanliness: ★★★★
Insect Control: ★★★	Facilities: ★★★★

June Lake is a lovely body of water, encircled by wavy, golden grasslands, with the choppy, rocky eastern Sierra range looming above. Pine Cliff Resort capitalizes on this rugged setting by positioning many of its sandy, mostly level sites among large gray boulders, while others rub up against high desert chaparral. Jeffrey pines thrive throughout the tilting, mountainous domain, providing shade and highlighting its natural beauty. Despite the trees, there is little screening here, and sites, which are on the small side, are too often crowded together. For the most privacy, try to reserve such perimeter slots as 133, 135, and 136; or any of 66–72, for their dramatic location amid a rift of Sierra uplift. Management deserves credit for the competitive pricing of its fuel and basic supplies, though for "people skills," campers give it mixed reviews. Pine Cliff Resort lies at 7,600 feet altitude, less than 15 miles south of Lee

Vining. The sandy access road to the beach and boat ramp is very bumpy.

BASICS

Operated By: Pine Cliff Resort. **Open:** Apr.–Nov. **Site Assignment:** First come, first served; reservations recommended; checks only. **Registration:** At entrance booth. **Fee:** Call ahead or see Web site for pricing details. **Parking:** At site.

FACILITIES

Number of RV-only Sites: 190. **Number of Tent-only Sites:** 60. **Hookups:** Electric (20, 30 amps), water, sewer. **Each Site:** Half-size picnic table, fire ring. **Dump Station:** No. **Laundry:** Yes. **Pay Phone:** Yes. **Restrooms and Showers:** Yes. **Fuel:** Yes. **Propane:** Yes. **Internal Roads:** Gravel. **RV Service:** No. **Market:** 13 mi. north in Lee Vining. **Restaurant:** 13 mi. north in Lee Vining. **General Store:** Yes. **Vending:** No. **Swimming:** June Lake. **Playground:** Yes. **Other:** Some wheelchair-accessible facilities, boat launch, beach, ATM machine & gift shop. **Activities:** Fishing, hiking, volleyball, basketball, horseshoe pit. **Nearby Attractions:** Mono Lake Tufa State Reserve in Lee Vining; Devils Postpile National Monument, Mammoth Mountain Bike Park, Mammoth Museum & outlet shopping in Mammoth Lakes. **Additional Information:** Mono County Tourism Commission, (760) 924-3699; Mammoth Lakes Visitors Bureau, (888) GO-MAMMOTH.

RESTRICTIONS

Pets: On leash; 2 max. per site. **Fires:** Fire grates only & out by 10:30 p.m. **Alcoholic Beverages:** Allowed. **Vehicle Maximum Length:** 40 ft. **Other:** Quiet time is 10:30 pm-7 a.m.; no motorcycles or ATVs.

TO GET THERE

From Lee Vining drive 11 mi. south on US 395, ignoring the 1st turnoff for Hwy. 158 north. Turn right on the 2nd turnoff, Hwy. 158 south, for the June Lake Loop. Drive 1 mi. to North Shore Dr. and turn right. Continue for 0.6 mi., then turn left on Pine Cliff Rd. The well-signed campground entrance is 0.4 mi. ahead on the right.

MAMMOTH LAKES   MAP, C-3
Twin Lakes

2500 Main St., 93546. T: (760) 924-5500; www.reserveamerica.com.

🚐 ★★★★	🏕 ★★★★
Beauty: ★★★★★	Site Privacy: ★★
Spaciousness: ★★★	Quiet: ★★★
Security: ★★★	Cleanliness: ★★★
Insect Control: ★★	Facilities: ★★★

To describe this camp as dramatic and pretty, peaceful and exhilarating, is to fall frustratingly short of its true splendor. The pair of lakes that inspired its name rest smack in the middle of a high Sierra canyon, jagged granite spires soaring well above the tops of the highest lodgepole pines. In spring, snow melt courses into Twin Falls, making for a spectacular cascade, visible from the campground. The very best site, with a prime panorama of the lakes, has been taken by the host. But there are many other agreeable options among the three zones that make up this park-like setting. Forget about the area by the entrance; those sites are too exposed to passing traffic. Better by far are the spots just across the bridge that divides the two lakes: 23, 25, 26, and 28 are small but enjoy their own private lakefront; 31, 33, 36, and 39, at the base of a steep hill, are fairly roomy, and detached from their neighbors; 62 and 70 are tucked into a thicket and blessed with a stunning view of the craggy canyon. The upper loop, in a more mountainous setting away from the lakes, is the roomiest; even the interior sites seem well separated. Given the elevation of 8,600 feet, you'll want to pack, along with a fishing rod, some heavy-weight fleece as a precaution against windy evenings.

BASICS

Operated By: Rocky Mountain Recreation Company, concessionaire. **Open:** May–Oct., weather permitting. **Site Assignment:** First come, first served. **Registration:** At entrance kiosk. **Fee:** $16; cash, check. **Parking:** At site.

FACILITIES

Number of RV-only Sites: 95. **Hookups:** None. **Each Site:** Picnic table, fire grate, barbecue grill. **Dump Station:** Yes. **Laundry:** No. **Pay Phone:** Yes. **Restrooms and Showers:** Yes. **Fuel:** No. **Propane:** No. **Internal Roads:** Paved. **RV Service:** No. **Market:** 4 mi. northeast in Mammoth Lakes. **Restaurant:** 4 mi. northeast in Mammoth Lakes. **General Store:** Yes. **Vending:** No. **Swimming:** Yes. **Playground:** No. **Other:** Some wheelchair-accessible facilities, boat launch. **Activities:** Fishing, horseback riding, hiking, boat rentals, paddling, water skiing. **Nearby Attractions:** Mono Lake Tufa State Reserve in Lee Vining; Devils Postpile National Monument, Mammoth Mountain Bike Park, Mammoth Museum & outlet shopping in Mammoth Lakes. **Additional Information:** Mono County Tourism Commission, (760) 924-3699; Mammoth Lakes Visitors Bureau, (888) GO-MAMMOTH.

RESTRICTIONS

Pets: On leash. **Fires:** Fire grates only. **Alcoholic Beverages:** Allowed. **Vehicle Maximum Length:** 46 ft. **Other:** 7-day stay limit.

TO GET THERE

From Mammoth Junction on US 395 head west on Hwy. 203, leading into Mammoth Lakes' Main St., and continue 4 mi. to where Main St. becomes Lake Mary Rd. Proceed straight ahead for 2.3 mi., then turn right onto Twin Lakes Loop Rd. The campground is 0.5 mi. ahead.

MARKLEEVILLE   MAP, C-3
Grover Hot Springs State Park

3415 Hot Springs Rd., 96120. T: (530) 694-2248 or (800) 444-7275; www.reserveamerica.com.

🚐 ★★★★	🏕 ★★★★
Beauty: ★★★★★	Site Privacy: ★★★
Spaciousness: ★★★★	Quiet: ★★★★
Security: ★★★	Cleanliness: ★★★
Insect Control: ★★★	Facilities: ★★

The mineral springs of Grover Hot Springs remain a constant 102° year-round, making its hot and cool pools a major therapeutic attraction. There is more to this state park, though, than the chance to bathe oneself in simmering water. Like miles of hiking and riding trails, as well as cross-country skiing in winter. First and foremost, though, is its strikingly beautiful campground, set at 5,900 feet of altitude, with a series of corrugated Sierra peaks contributing an Arcadian quality to its forested, creek-side location. The undefiled, natural look of this gorgeous preserve is furthered by its undulating terrain being salted with granite boulders, juniper, incense cedar and Jeffrey and lodgepole pines. Sites, covered with grass and pine needles, are generally shady, generously large, and fairly well separated, though several lie on uneven turf. The most private are 11, tucked behind boulders, and 22, by a row of Jeffrey pines and a grassy meadow; 58, 66–68, and 73–75 are also worth shooting for. The pools close for maintenance the last two weeks of September, and shut down during thunderstorms, which occur regularly throughout July and August.

BASICS

Operated By: California Dept. of Parks & Recreation. **Open:** All year. **Site Assignment:** Reservations recommended; V, MC, D; first come, first served. **Registration:** At entrance booth. **Fee:** $15–$25; cash, CA check. For seniors 62 & older, $13. **Parking:** At site.

FACILITIES

Number of RV-only Sites: 76. **Hookups:** None. **Each Site:** Picnic table, fire grate, bear-proof box. **Dump Station:** No. **Laundry:** No. **Pay Phone:** Yes. **Restrooms and Showers:** Yes. **Fuel:** No. **Propane:** No. **Internal Roads:** Paved. **RV Service:** No. **Market:** 3.6 mi. east in Markleeville. **Restaurant:** 3.6 mi. east in Markleeville. **General Store:** No. **Vending:** No. **Swimming:** Hot springs pool. **Playground:** No. **Other:** Some wheelchair-accessible facilities. **Activities:** Hiking, fishing, bicycling, swimming. **Nearby Attractions:** Alpine County Museum in Markleeville; Lake Tahoe & Lake Tahoe Historical Museum in South Lake Tahoe. **Additional Information:** Alpine County Chamber of Commerce, (530) 694-2475.

RESTRICTIONS

Pets: On 6-ft. leash. **Fires:** Fire grates only. **Alcoholic Beverages:** Allowed at site. **Vehicle Maximum Length:** 24 ft. **Other:** 14-day stay limit from May 15 to the first week in Sept., 30-day stay limit for the rest of the year; no firearms; no wood gathering, park on pavement.

TO GET THERE

From Markleeville on Hwy. 89 turn west on Hot Springs Rd. and drive 3.6 mi. The well-signed state park entrance is on the right.

MARKLEEVILLE
Indian Creek
MAP, C-3

Airport Rd., 96120. T: (775) 885-6000;
www.nv.blm.gov/carson/information.html.

🚐 ★★★★   ⛺ ★★★★

Beauty: ★★★★   Site Privacy: ★★★
Spaciousness: ★★★   Quiet: ★★★★
Security: ★★★   Cleanliness: ★★★★
Insect Control: ★★★   Facilities: ★★

Indian Creek is easily reached along a well-signed, smoothly paved roadway, a rare double-treat for a Bureau of Land Management property. Then, when you pull into camp—the trifecta!—as this is as sweet as it gets for BLM land. It's a beautiful lakeside campground, backed up against the Sierra range, with its two loops enhanced by mature stands of piñon, ponderosa, and Jeffrey pines, as well as a few boulders and such high-desert shrubs as salt bush and brittle bush. The first loop, which features walk-in sites for tents, offers the better vantage over Indian Creek Reservoir, where white pelicans were noisily cavorting our last time through. Birding is no less rewarding at the second circuit, which faces the lake on one side and a grassy marsh on another. The optimum sites there are 44, 48, and 49. The ground slopes gently toward the water, but most units are level, distributed well apart and surprisingly clean; even the sandy tent pads are raked by a conscientious host. Situated on the west side of the reservoir, Indian Creek is pleasantly illuminated by morning light, when it is almost too pretty for words.

BASICS
Operated By: Bureau of Land Management, Carson City Field Office. **Open:** Mid-Apr.–mid-Oct. **Site Assignment:** First come, first served; reservations only for group sites. **Registration:** Separate fee collection tubes. **Fee:** RV, $20–$32; tent, $14–$20; cash, check; fee per additional person, $5. **Parking:** At site or in parking lot for walk-ins.

FACILITIES
Number of RV-only Sites: 19. **Number of Tent-only Sites:** 10. **Hookups:** None. **Each Site:** Picnic table, makeshift fire ring, barbecue grill, bear-proof box. **Dump Station:** Yes, $5 fee. **Laundry:** No. **Pay Phone:** No. **Restrooms and Showers:** Yes. **Fuel:** No. **Propane:** No. **Internal Roads:** Paved. **RV Service:** No. **Market:** 6.5 mi. south in Markleeville. **Restaurant:** 6.5 mi. south in Markleeville. **General Store:** No. **Vending:** No. **Swimming:** Lake. **Playground:** No. **Other:** Boat ramp. **Activities:** Fishing, hiking, birding, horseback riding, sailing, mountain biking, swimming. **Nearby Attractions:** Alpine County Museum in Markleeville; Lake Tahoe & Lake Tahoe Historical Museum in South Lake Tahoe. **Additional Information:** Alpine County Chamber of Commerce, (530) 694-2475. Markleeville Chamber of Commerce, (530) 694-2475.

RESTRICTIONS
Pets: On leash. **Fires:** Fire ring only. **Alcoholic Beverages:** Allowed. **Vehicle Maximum Length:** 30 ft. **Other:** 14-day stay limit.

TO GET THERE
From Markleeville drive 2.5 mi. north on Hwy. 89. Turn right onto Airport Rd. and continue for 4 mi., then make a left into the campground.

MCCLOUD
Fowlers Campground
MAP, A-2

F.R. 39N28, 96057. T: (530) 964-2184;
www.fs.fed.us/r5/shastatrinity.

🚐 ★★★   ⛺ ★★★★

Beauty: ★★★★   Site Privacy: ★★★
Spaciousness: ★★★   Quiet: ★★★★
Security: ★★★   Cleanliness: ★★★
Insect Control: ★★★   Facilities: ★★

You are barreling along on Hwy. 89 bound toward McCloud, with a fishing rod in the back of your vehicle and a kayak strapped to its roof. Where do you pull over for some R&R? Fowlers Campground is one of the better options in the area. The McCloud River flows right behind this clean, well-maintained national forest–operated property. Brown trout inhabit the river and rainbow trout are regularly stocked from this point clear down to Lake McCloud. A small put-in for kayaks and canoes is just past the photogenic series of cascades by the day-use picnic area, 0.5 miles beyond camp along the dirt road. The campground's double loop threads by level sites that are situated reasonably well apart and decently shielded by a densely forested mix of incense cedar, manzanita, and various conifers. The tree-to-tree carpet of pine needles is speckled with pumice rocks, which enhances the natural beauty of this wheelchair-accessible camp.

BASICS
Operated By: Shasta-Trinity National Forest, McCloud Ranger District. **Open:** May 1–Oct. 31; weather permitting. **Site Assignment:** First come, first served. **Registration:** At entrance kiosk. **Fee:** $12; cash, check. **Parking:** At site.

FACILITIES
Number of RV-only Sites: 38. **Hookups:** None. **Each Site:** Picnic table, fire grate. **Dump Station:** No. **Laundry:** No. **Pay Phone:** No. **Restrooms and Showers:** Vault toilets, no showers. **Fuel:** No. **Propane:** No. **Internal Roads:** Paved, narrow. **RV Service:** No. **Market:** 6 mi. west in McCloud. **Restaurant:** 6 mi. west in McCloud. **General Store:** No. **Vending:** No. **Swimming:** Base of Middle & Lower Falls. **Playground:** No. **Other:** Some wheelchair-accessible facilities, small boat launch, cattle camp, overflow campground 11 mi. east w/ 27 sites, $12 fee. **Activities:** Fishing, hiking, kayaking. **Nearby Attractions:** McCloud River Falls & Shasta Sunset Dinner Train; Mount Shasta Ski Park, Mount Shasta Fish Hatchery, & Sisson Museum in Mount Shasta; Lake Siskiyou, old dDowntown McCloud. **Additional Information:** Mount Shasta Chamber of Commerce & Visitors Bureau, (530) 926-4865 or (800) 926-4865; McCloud Chamber of Commerce, (530) 964-3113.

RESTRICTIONS
Pets: On leash; not allowed in wilderness areas. **Fires:** Fire grates only. **Alcoholic Beverages:**

Allowed. **Vehicle Maximum Length:** 30 ft. **Other:** 14-day stay limit; no fireworks.

TO GET THERE
From Mount Shasta drive 2 mi. south on I-5. Head east on Hwy. 89 and drive 16 mi., past the town of McCloud, and turn right at the campground sign. Continue for 0.6 mi. and bear left at the fork. The campground is straight ahead.

MECCA
Headquarters Campground
MAP, F-4

Salton Sea State Recreation Area,
100–225 State Park Rd., 92254. T: (760) 393-3052;
www.saltonsea.statepark.org.

🚐 ★★★   ⛺ ★★★

Beauty: ★★★   Site Privacy: ★★★
Spaciousness: ★★★   Quiet: ★★★
Security: ★★★   Cleanliness: ★★★
Insect Control: ★★   Facilities: ★★★

The attraction here is the Salton Sea, a vast lake that lies 227 feet below sea level and is 25 percent saltier than the Pacific Ocean. The palm-fringed body of water is a Mecca of sorts to boaters and anglers, as well as birders drawn by hopes of sighting some of the great range of migratory fowl that wing through between late fall and early spring. The mildest weather is from January through March, a time that coincides with free ranger-led kayak tours of the lake (call ahead to make reservations). Of the state-run campgrounds in the area, Mecca Beach gives tenters the best beach access, but only has six spots with hookups. Headquarters, on the other hand, has the better fishing. It consists of two loops; one with 15 full-hookup sites facing the water across a paved, level parking area, the other with more space and privacy among desert ironwood trees, brittle bush, and desert scrub. A visitor center, located between the loops, has a short film strip on the lake and some interesting exhibits. This would be a delightfully peaceful bivouac if not for the occasional rattling of trains along the tracks by the park road. When the winds blow from the west side of the lake, that sweet briny air that is so reminiscent of the seaside can change in the twitch of a nose to such a strong stench of sulphur you may think you're camping next to a match factory.

BASICS
Operated By: California Dept. of Parks & Recreation. **Open:** All year. **Site Assignment:** First come, first served; reservations accepted w/ V, MC, D. **Registration:** At entrance booth. **Fee:** Call for pricing details. **Parking:** At site.

FACILITIES
Number of RV-only Sites: 50. **Hookups:** Electric (30 amps), water. **Each Site:** Picnic table, barbecue grill, some w/ a ramada. **Dump Station:** Yes. **Laundry:** No. **Pay Phone:** Yes. **Restrooms and Showers:** Yes. **Fuel:** No. **Propane:** No. **Internal Roads:** Paved. **RV Service:** No. **Market:** 11 mi. north in Mecca. **Restaurant:** 11 mi. north in Mecca. **General Store:** No. **Vending:** No. **Swimming:** Salton Sea. **Playground:** Yes. **Other:** Some wheelchair-accessible facilities. **Activities:** Fishing, boating, hiking, birding, horseshoe pit. **Nearby Attractions:** Joshua Tree

National Park, San Andreas Trail, Wister Mud Pots. **Additional Information:** Coachella Chamber of Commerce, (760) 398-8089.

RESTRICTIONS

Pets: On 6-ft. leash. **Fires:** No ground fires. **Alcoholic Beverages:** Allowed at site. **Vehicle Maximum Length:** 32 ft. **Other:** 30-day stay limit; no firearms; no wood gathering.

TO GET THERE

Take Hwy. 111 south from Mecca, drive 12 mi., and turn right into the state recreation area.

MINERAL   MAP, B-2
Butte Lake

reserve america

Lassen Volcanic National Park, P.O. Box 100, 96063. T: (530) 595-4444; www.reserveamerica.com.

🚐 ★★★★   ▲ ★★★★

Beauty: ★★★★   Site Privacy: ★★★
Spaciousness: ★★★   Quiet: ★★★
Security: ★★★★   Cleanliness: ★★★
Insect Control: ★★★   Facilities: ★

The remote location of Butte Lake campground provides a tranquil respite from the crowds of sightseers thronging to Manzanita Lake, Summit Lakes, and such main attractions of Lassen Volcanic National Park as Bumpass Hell and the Sulfur Works. While only one site, B-1, actually enjoys a view of the stunning Butte Lake, the campground's proximity to the water, to a cinder peak, and to several fine hikes, makes it a winner. Roomy sites, evenly positioned across a slightly undulating hillside, are partially shaded by lodgepole pines and a smattering of ponderosas. As is typical in national park venues, few of them offer much privacy. Of the A and B circuits, the second area has the larger sites and more pull-through parking: best bets, in addition to B-1, are B-3, which overlooks the lava flow field, and the partly screened B-55. A pay phone, gasoline, and a general store are available at Old Station, 17 miles west on Hwy. 44. Butte Creek, a national forest camp on the dirt and gravel access road to Butte Lake, is a passable alternative when the latter is full or closed.

BASICS

Operated By: National Park Service. **Open:** June 2–Sept. 18, weather permitting. **Site Assignment:** First come, first served. **Registration:** At entrance kiosk. **Fee:** $14; cash, check; plus park entrance fee, $10. **Parking:** At site.

FACILITIES

Number of Multipurpose Sites: 98. **Hookups:** None. **Each Site:** Picnic table, fire grate, bear-proof box. **Dump Station:** No. **Laundry:** No. **Pay Phone:** No. **Restrooms and Showers:** Flush toilets, no showers. **Fuel:** No. **Propane:** No. **Internal Roads:** Gravel, good condition. **RV Service:** No. **Market:** 48 mi. east in Susanville. **Restaurant:** 48 mi. east in Susanville. **General Store:** No. **Vending:** No. **Swimming:** Butte Lake. **Playground:** No. **Other:** Some wheelchair-accessible facilities, boat

launch. **Activities:** Hiking, fishing, boating (no motors), birding. **Nearby Attractions:** Hat Creek Recreation Area in Old Station; Lassen Historical Museum & Railroad Depot in Susanville. **Additional Information:** Burney Chamber of Commerce, (530) 335-2111.

RESTRICTIONS

Pets: On 6-ft. leash; not allowed on trails. **Fires:** Fire grates only. **Alcoholic Beverages:** Allowed at site. **Vehicle Maximum Length:** 35 ft. **Other:** 14-day stay limit; no loaded firearms.

TO GET THERE

From Old Station at the junction of Hwys. 44 and 89, drive 11 mi. east on Hwy. 44. Turn right (south) on Butte Lake Rd. and follow this dirt road 6.5 mi. to the campground entrance on the right.

MINERAL   MAP, B-2
Manzanita Lake

reserve america

Lassen Volcanic National Park, P.O. Box 100, 96063. T: (530) 595-4444; www.reserveamerica.com.

🚐 ★★★   ▲ ★★★

Beauty: ★★★★   Site Privacy: ★★★
Spaciousness: ★★★   Quiet: ★★
Security: ★★★   Cleanliness: ★★★
Insect Control: ★★★   Facilities: ★★★

Lassen Volcanic National Park was established as a monument in 1907, and upgraded to national park status nine years later. An astoundingly beautiful chunk of the Cascade Mountain range, the park has hundreds of miles of hiking trails, several geothermal attractions, an abundance of wildlife, and a handful of excellent campgrounds. Of those, Manzanita Lake is one of the best, with its namesake body of glimmering water abutting it and snow-capped Mt. Lassen hovering above. Just 5 miles from Lassen's north entrance, the camp enjoys an illusion of privacy that stems in part from its thick concentration of various conifers, as well as from the pull-through and back-in sites being well dispersed through a series of many loops. The shade provided by those evergreens keeps things cool and on the dark side, but tenters will find comfort in the spongy layer of pine needles that has accumulated on the forest floor. Best time to visit is September to mid-October, when the park sees fewer visitors. Just remember, at an altitude of 5,890 feet, Manzanita Lake can be chilly most anytime of year: extra layers of clothing and rain gear are advised. And use the bear-proof boxes to protect your vehicle from a furry intruder. Many sites are wheelchair accessible.

BASICS

Operated By: National Park Service. **Open:** May 19–Sept. 18; w/ water; no water w/ snow closing. **Site Assignment:** First come, first served; reservations must be made at least 4 days in advance. **Registration:** Self-registration at entrance kiosk. **Fee:** $16 (summer); plus park entrance fee; cash, check. **Parking:** At site.

FACILITIES

Number of Multipurpose Sites: 179. **Hookups:** None. **Each Site:** Picnic table, fire ring, barbecue grill, bear-proof box. **Dump Station:** Yes, fee charged. **Laundry:** Yes. **Pay Phone:** Yes. **Restrooms and Showers:** Yes. **Fuel:** No. **Propane:** Yes. **Internal Roads:** Paved. **RV Service:** No. **Market:** 50 mi. west in Redding. **Restaurant:** 19 mi. west in Shingletown. **General Store:** Yes. **Vending:** Yes. **Swimming:** Manzanita Lake. **Playground:** No. **Other:** Some wheelchair-accessible facilities, boat launch, Loomis Museum. **Activities:** Hiking, fishing, boating (no motors), bike rentals, ranger-led programs. **Nearby Attractions:** Westwood Museum, Paul Bunyan & Babe the Blue Ox statues; Lassen National Scenic Byway (Hwys. 89-44-36); Lake Almanor; Hat Creek Recreation Area in Old Station. **Additional Information:** Burney Chamber of Commerce, (530) 335-2111.

RESTRICTIONS

Pets: On 6-ft. leash; not allowed on trails. **Fires:** Fire ring only. **Alcoholic Beverages:** Allowed at site. **Vehicle Maximum Length:** 35 ft. **Other:** 14-day stay limit; no firearms; no fireworks.

TO GET THERE

From Redding drive 48 mi. east on Hwy. 44 to the junction w/ Hwy. 89. Drive 1 mi. south on Hwy. 89 (which becomes Lassen Park Rd. once you pass the park entrance station). Turn right onto the campground access road and continue for 0.5 mi. to the campground.

MODESTO   MAP, C-2
Modesto Reservoir Regional Park

Reservoir Rd. 18143, 95386. T: (209) 874-9540; www.co.stanislaus.ca.us.

🚐 ★★★★   ▲ ★★

Beauty: ★★★★   Site Privacy: ★★
Spaciousness: ★★   Quiet: ★★★
Security: ★★★   Cleanliness: ★★★
Insect Control: ★★   Facilities: ★★★★

Summer seems to last for six or seven months in this steamy stretch of California's Central Valley. That's a major reason why Modesto Reservoir is so popular for much of the year; its cool, shimmering water brings relief from temperatures that frequently top 100°F. Even on busy weekends, you are apt to find spots available in the sparsely shaded, full-hookup parking meadow. Far better are the smaller slots that are lined up one against another following the amoeba-like contours of the reservoir's wandering shoreline. What those lack in privacy they more than gain in shade from eucalyptus, plane trees, pines, and junipers. Their tent-side access to the lake is an added bonus. The many small islands that dot the surface of the water not only bless it with pleasing aesthetics, but also serve as safe havens for a variety of bird life, including pelicans, Canada geese, great blue herons, bald eagles, redtailed hawks, pheasants, and burrowing owls. An undeveloped section on the opposite side of the lake allows for more privacy, but lacks tables, fire rings, and potable water.

BASICS

Operated By: Stanislaus County Parks Dept. **Open:** All year. **Site Assignment:** First come, first served. **Registration:** At entrance kiosk. **Fee:** $12–$16; cash, CA check, V, MC; $2 per night extra for 3-day holiday weekends. **Parking:** At site.

FACILITIES

Number of RV-only Sites: 186. **Number of Tent-only Sites:** Undesignated sites. **Hookups:** Electric (20, 30 amps), water, sewer. **Each Site:** Picnic table, fire grate, barbecue grill. **Dump Station:** Yes. **Laundry:** No. **Pay Phone:** Yes. **Restrooms and Showers:** Yes. **Fuel:** No. **Propane:** No. **Internal Roads:** Paved. **RV Service:** No. **Market:** 7 mi. west in Waterford. **Restaurant:** 7 mi. west in Waterford. **General Store:** Yes. **Vending:** No. **Swimming:** Modesto Reservoir. **Playground:** No. **Other:** Some wheelchair-accessible facilities, boat ramp, marina, beach, archery range. **Activities:** Fishing, boat rentals, waterskiing,. **Nearby Attractions:** McHenry Mansion & museums in Modesto; Turlock Lake State Recreation Area in La Grange. **Additional Information:** Modesto CVB, (209) 571-6480 or (800) 266-4282.

RESTRICTIONS

Pets: Not allowed. **Fires:** Fire grates only. **Alcoholic Beverages:** Allowed at site. **Vehicle Maximum Length:** No limit. **Other:** 14-day stay limit; MBTE-free fuel only; no fuel containers; no firearms; no wood gathering.

TO GET THERE

From Modesto drive 13 mi. east on Hwy. 132/ Yosemite Blvd. Turn left on Reservoir Rd. and continue 0.5 mi. to the park entrance.

MOJAVE   MAP, E-3
Ricardo Campground

Red Rock Canyon State Park, Hwy. 14 at Abbott Dr., 93519. T: (661) 942-0662; www.parks.ca.gov.

🚐 ★★★★   ⛺ ★★★★

Beauty: ★★★★★	Site Privacy: ★★★
Spaciousness: ★★★★	Quiet: ★★★
Security: ★★★	Cleanliness: ★★★★
Insect Control: ★★★★	Facilities: ★

White House Cliffs is a fabulous fairyland canyon of melting sandstone and fluted folds, where cliff swallows nest and great-horned owls occasionally perch during their nocturnal vigils. This feast for the eyes, a part of the El Paso Mountain range, serves as host to Ricardo Campground, right at its base, and has been a featured backdrop in more than 130 movies. Coarse sand-surfaced sites are backed up against the eroded nooks and alcoves of the canyon, gaining, in addition to a touch of privacy from their neighbors, a solid shield from the afternoon sun. From this primitive setting one can look across the valley floor, an arid landscape that is enlivened by creosote bushes, Joshua trees, and rabbit brush, to the headlights of distant autos humming along on Hwy. 14, while still enjoying a brilliantly starry sky. Indeed, the stargazing here is so exceptional that star charts have been posted by the latrines and kiosk. A visitor center and the remains of an 1890s mining operation are in the vicinity. The nearest pay phone is 14 miles south by the Cantil post office.

BASICS

Operated By: California Dept. of Parks & Recreation. **Open:** All year. **Site Assignment:** First come, first served. **Registration:** At entrance booth. **Fee:** $9; cash, CA check. **Parking:** At site.

FACILITIES

Number of Multipurpose Sites: 50. **Hookups:** None. **Each Site:** Picnic table, fire grate. **Dump Station:** Yes. **Laundry:** No. **Pay Phone:** No. **Restrooms and Showers:** Pit toilets, no showers. **Fuel:** No. **Propane:** No. **Internal Roads:** Gravel, good condition. **RV Service:** No. **Market:** 35 mi. northeast in Ridgecrest. **Restaurant:** 25 mi. southwest in Mojave. **General Store:** No. **Vending:** No. **Swimming:** No. **Playground:** No. **Other:** Some wheelchair-accessible facilities, visitor center. **Activities:** Hiking, driving tour, photography, birding, stargazing, ranger-led activities. **Nearby Attractions:** Trona Pinnacles; Fossil Falls; Last Chance Canyon & Maturango Museum in Ridgecrest; Desert Tortoise Natural Area in California City. **Additional Information:** Mojave Chamber of Commerce, (661) 824-2481; Ridgecrest Area CVB, (760) 375-8202 or (800) 847-4830.

RESTRICTIONS

Pets: On 6-ft. leash. **Fires:** Fire grates only. **Alcoholic Beverages:** Allowed at site. **Vehicle Maximum Length:** 30 ft. **Other:** 14-day stay limit; no firearms.

TO GET THERE

From Mojave on Hwy. 14 drive 24 mi. northeast to the park entrance on the left. The campground is 1 mi. ahead.

MONTEREY   MAP, D-1
Fremont Peak State Park

reserve america

221 Garden Rd., 93940. T: (831) 623-4255; www.reserveamerica.com.

🚐 ★★★   ⛺ ★★★★

Beauty: ★★★	Site Privacy: ★★★
Spaciousness: ★★★	Quiet: ★★★
Security: ★★★	Cleanliness: ★★★★
Insect Control: ★★★	Facilities: ★★★★

Fremont Peak State Park (elevation 3,169 feet) features expansive views of Monterey Bay, and hiking trails in the grasslands of the Gavilan Range. Other views include the San Benito Valley, Salinas Valley, and the Santa Lucia Mountains east of Big Sur. Pine and oak woodlands in the park are home to many birds and mammals. Fremont Peak has ten primitive family campsites and 40 picnic sites, each with table and stove; pit toilets and water are nearby. During the summer, campers enjoy informal campfire programs and nature hikes. There are also 6 group camps, which will accommodate 50 people which can be reserved. The group picnic area is on a first come, first serve basis. The park also features an astronomical observatory with a 30-inch telescope, which is open for public programs on selected evenings. As a courtesy, it is suggested that headlights be dimmed when entering observing areas after sundown. If you are not familiar with the area, it is best to arrive before dark.

BASICS

Operated By: California Dept. of Parks & Recreation. **Open:** All year. **Site Assignment:** Reservations can be made 7 months in advance; family & group site reservations Mar. 1–Nov. 30. **Registration:** At office. **Fee:** Single, $11–$15; group, $50–$75. **Parking:** At site.

FACILITIES

Number of Multipurpose Sites: 29. **Hookups:** None. **Dump Station:** No. **Laundry:** No. **Pay Phone:** No. **Restrooms and Showers:** Outhouse. **Fuel:** No. **Propane:** No. **Internal Roads:** Gravel. **RV Service:** No. **Market:** No. **Restaurant:** No. **General Store:** No. **Vending:** No. **Swimming:** No. **Playground:** No. **Other:** Fees include entry for 1 vehicle & 1 legally towed vehicle or trailer, additional vehicles will be charged per night at the park. **Activities:** Hiking, nature trails, stargazing.

RESTRICTIONS

Pets: On 6-ft. leash in a tent or enclosed vehicle at night. Except for guide dogs, pets are not allowed in park buildings or on trails. **Fires:** In designated fireplaces. **Alcoholic Beverages:** Not allowed.

TO GET THERE

From San Juan Bautista and Hwy. 156, take San Juan Canyon Rd. south for 11 mi.; follow the signs to the park entrance station.

MORRO BAY   MAP, E-1
LOS OSOS
Montaña de Oro State Park

reserve america

3550 Pecho Valley Rd., 93402. T: (805) 528-0512; www.reserveamerica.com.

🚐 ★★★   ⛺ ★★★★

Beauty: ★★★★	Site Privacy: ★★
Spaciousness: ★★★	Quiet: ★★★★
Security: ★★★	Cleanliness: ★★★★
Insect Control: ★★★	Facilities: ★

In many respects this is a very ordinary campground, with adequate elbow room in the grass and dirt sites but little privacy. Facilities are minimal, and even the camp's immediate setting, with a few bishop pines punctuating the green confines of the narrow canyon, is just a notch or two above average in pulchritude. Give the park a chance, though—all 8,000 acres of it—and what you will find is a spectacular coastal wilderness that rivals the Big Sur area in its unspoiled beauty. The drive into Montaña de Oro threads past dense groves of aromatic eucalyptus, with eye-popping views of the dune-draped shore and Morro Rock out in the bay. Tall stands of cottonwood, oak, maple, willow, and box elder thrive. Add to that miles of pristine beaches, highland bluffs and miscellaneous meadows, and you have a nature-lovers nirvana. For sun bathers there is Spooner's Cove, a romantic patch of sand and tide pools, just below the campground off the road. The vast array of wildflowers scattered over the hills in late spring is a heaven-scent sight.

BASICS

Operated By: California Dept. of Parks & Recreation. **Open:** All year. **Site Assignment:** Reservations accepted w/ V, MC, D; reservations recommended Memorial Day–Labor Day; first come, first served. **Registration:** At entrance kiosk. **Fee:** $11–$15; cash, CA check. **Parking:** At site.

FACILITIES

Number of Tent-only Sites: 4. **Number of Multipurpose Sites:** 50. **Hookups:** None. **Each Site:** Picnic table, fire grate, food storage box. **Dump Station:** No. **Laundry:** No. **Pay Phone:** Yes. **Restrooms and Showers:** Vault toilets, no showers. **Fuel:** No. **Propane:** No. **Internal Roads:** Paved. **RV Service:** No. **Market:** 5 mi. northeast in Los Osos. **Restaurant:** 5 mi. northeast in Los Osos. **General Store:** No. **Vending:** No. **Swimming:** Pacific Ocean. **Playground:** No. **Activities:** Hiking, birding, bicycling, horseback riding, tide pooling, fishing, nature programs. **Nearby Attractions:** Mission San Luis Obispo; Morro Bay State Beach & Museum of Natural History. **Additional Information:** Los Osos/Baywood Park Chamber of Commerce, (805) 528-4884.

RESTRICTIONS

Pets: On 6-ft. leash, not allowed on trails or beaches. **Fires:** Fire grates only, except on primitive sites. **Alcoholic Beverages:** Allowed at site. **Vehicle Maximum Length:** 27 ft. **Other:** 10-day stay limit; no firearms; no wood gathering. No pets or fires in primitive camping area.

TO GET THERE

From San Luis Obispo head 3 mi. south on US 101 and exit at Los Osos Valley Rd. Drive 11.7 mi. west, then bear left on Pecho Valley Rd. The park entrance is 1 mi. ahead and the campground is to the left after that.

MOUNT SHASTA   MAP, A-2
KOA Mount Shasta

900 North Mount Shasta Blvd., 96067. T: (530) 926-4029 or (800) 562-3617; www.koa.com.

🚐 ★★★★		⛺ ★★
Beauty: ★★★		Site Privacy: ★★
Spaciousness: ★★		Quiet: ★★★
Security: ★★★★		Cleanliness: ★★★★
Insect Control: ★★★		Facilities: ★★★★★

Admit it, you've always wondered what it was like to camp at a KOA. Well, stop your wondering and get your butane-burner over to this campground. As you might expect, the facilities are top-notch, ranging from a small pool (summer season) and cabin rentals to a game room, volleyball, basketball, and even a horse corral. With snow-capped Mt. Shasta towering over the downtown property, you can imagine that you are roughing it while flipping burgers by the barbecue grill. Sites are crowded into two environments, open meadow and sparsely forested. The latter is composed mostly of pines, with support from cottonwoods, cedars, maples, and manzanita. The resulting shade and screening make that area preferable, especially for tent campers, but the narrow, meandering lanes are not recommended for big rigs. The meadow, on the other hand, while exposed to both sun and neighbors, has the virtue of pull-through parking.

BASICS

Operated By: KOA. **Open:** All year. **Site Assignment:** Reservations accepted w/ V, MC, D. **Registration:** At entrance office. **Fee:** Call or see Web site for pricing details. **Parking:** At site.

FACILITIES

Number of RV-only Sites: 50. **Number of Tent-only Sites:** 51. **Hookups:** Electric (30, 50 amps), water, sewer. **Each Site:** Half-size picnic table, some sites have a barbecue grill. **Dump Station:** Yes. **Laundry:** Yes. **Pay Phone:** Yes. **Restrooms and Showers:** Yes. **Fuel:** No. **Propane:** Yes. **Internal Roads:** Paved & forest floor. **RV Service:** Yes, mobile. **Market:** 1 mi. south in Mount Shasta. **Restaurant:** All throughout Mount Shasta. **General Store:** Yes. **Vending:** Yes. **Swimming:** Small pool, seasonal (May. 27–Sept. 15). **Playground:** Yes. **Other:** Some wheelchair-accessible facilities, game room, movie rentals. **Activities:** Horseshoe pit, volleyball, basketball, shuffleboard, nearby hiking, rafting, & fishing. **Nearby Attractions:** Lake Siskiyou; Mount Shasta Ski Park, Mount Shasta Hatchery & Sisson Museum; downtown Dunsmuir; Castle Crags State Park in Castella. **Additional Information:** Mount Shasta Chamber of Commerce & Visitors Bureau, (530) 926-4865 or (800) 926-4865; Dunsmuir Chamber of Commerce, (530) 235-2177.

RESTRICTIONS

Pets: On leash. No pit bulls, Dobermans, or rottweilers. **Fires:** At site & contained. **Alcoholic Beverages:** Allowed. **Vehicle Maximum Length:** 80 ft. **Other:** No fireworks.

TO GET THERE

On I-5 take the central Mount Shasta Exit and drive 0.5 mi. into town on West Lake St. At the stoplight turn left on North Mount Shasta Blvd. and proceed for 0.6 mi. Turn right on East Hinkley Blvd. and drive 1 block to the campground entrance on the left.

MOUNTAIN CENTER   MAP, E-3
Lake Hemet

56570 Hwy. 74, #4, 92561. T: (909) 659-2680.

🚐 ★★★★		⛺ ★★★
Beauty: ★★★		Site Privacy: ★★
Spaciousness: ★★		Quiet: ★★★★
Security: ★★★★★		Cleanliness: ★★★
Insect Control: ★★		Facilities: ★★★★

To paraphrase Dickens, Lake Hemet offers the best of campgrounds and the worst of campgrounds. It has a fine sandy beach but doesn't allow swimming in its namesake lake (wading is allowed in Hurkey Creek by the playground). The rugged, natural atmosphere radiating from the surrounding San Jacinto and Thomas mountain ranges is partly diminished by the cluttered cluster of the long-term residences. Several stands of mature ponderosa pines are scattered around the property, but sites of dirt, sand, and a smattering of grass are largely exposed to the sun. And unless you like plenty of company, forget about a waterside location, especially among the RV hookups; the outlying areas without electricity are your best bet for space and seclusion. Security is one feature this facility is unequivocal about, with an entrance gate, regular patrols, and a county sheriff's office on the edge of the grounds.

BASICS

Operated By: Lake Hemet Municipal Water District. **Open:** All year. **Site Assignment:** First come, first served. **Registration:** At entrance office. **Fee:** $17; V, MC, cash. **Parking:** At site.

FACILITIES

Number of RV-only Sites: 367. **Number of Tent-only Sites:** Undesignated sites. **Hookups:** Electric (20, 30 amps), water, sewer. **Each Site:** Picnic table, fire ring, some w/ a barbecue grill. **Dump Station:** Yes. **Laundry:** Yes. **Pay Phone:** Yes. **Restrooms and Showers:** Yes. **Fuel:** No, Idyllwild. **Propane:** Yes. **Internal Roads:** Mostly paved, some dirt roads. **RV Service:** No. **Market:** 9 mi. north in Idyllwild. **Restaurant:** 9 mi. north in Idyllwild. **General Store:** Yes. **Vending:** No. **Swimming:** No. **Playground:** Yes. **Other:** Wheelchair-accessible facilities, boat launch. **Activities:** Fishing, hiking, volleyball, basketball, horseshoe pit, boat rentals. **Nearby Attractions:** Pacific Crest Trail, Gilman Historic Ranch & Wagon Museum in Banning, San Jacinto Valley Museum. **Additional Information:** Banning Chamber of Commerce, (909) 849-4695.

RESTRICTIONS

Pets: On leash no longer than 15 ft., $1 fee. **Fires:** Fire ring only. **Alcoholic Beverages:** Allowed. **Vehicle Maximum Length:** 40 ft. **Other:** 14-day stay limit for tents, no shooting.

TO GET THERE

From Banning, head south on Hwy. 243 and drive 31 mi. Turn left on Hwy. 74 and continue for 5 mi. to the campground on the right.

NAPA   MAP, C-2
Putah Creek Resort

7600 Knoxville Rd., 94558.
T: (707) 966-0794 or (707) 966-0770;
www.napavalleyonline.com/directory/wsparks.html.

🚐 ★★★★		⛺ ★★
Beauty: ★★★		Site Privacy: ★★
Spaciousness: ★★		Quiet: ★★★
Security: ★★★★		Cleanliness: ★★★
Insect Control: ★★★		Facilities: ★★★★★

Like every story, there are two sides to Putah Creek Resort. As in lakeside and creek side. The main compound overlooks lovely Lake Berryessa, a glimmering body of water that was created by the Bureau of Land Reclamation back in the 1950s. Yuccas and palms, knobcone pines and oaks, oleanders and pollarded hibiscus lend an appealing dash of beauty to a camp so developed it even has motel rooms and a restaurant-bar. Partial hookups are available near the boat launch, painfully close to the bar's open-air patio and within easy earshot of the motorboats and jet skis that often zip by. Across the road is the creek camp, in a greener, more serene setting. It is also endowed with a boat launch, and though many sites are too close to each other for camping comfort, a healthy majority overlook the water. Of the latter, 21–28 offer RVers a fine lateral view of the creek, while 3–8 put tent campers at the shore's edge. One negative to the creek area is that upkeep of restrooms is sometimes neglected. Both zones are fenced and protected by gatehouse entrance booths.

BASICS

Operated By: Putah Creek Resort. **Open:** All year. **Site Assignment:** Reservations accepted w/ V, MC. **Registration:** At entrance gate or in store. **Fee:** $21–$26; cash, V, MC. **Parking:** At site.

FACILITIES

Number of RV-only Sites: 55. **Number of Tent-only Sites:** 120. **Hookups:** Electric (30, 50 amps), water, sewer; 35 full hookup, 20 partial hookup. **Each Site:** Picnic table, barbecue grill. **Dump Station:** Yes. **Laundry:** Yes. **Pay Phone:** Yes. **Restrooms and Showers:** Yes. **Fuel:** Yes. **Propane:** Yes. **Internal Roads:** Paved. **RV Service:** No. **Market:** 27 mi. east in St. Helena. **Restaurant:** Yes. **General Store:** Yes, also deli & snack bar. **Vending:** Yes. **Swimming:** Lake Berryessa. **Playground:** No. **Other:** Boat ramp, motel, restaurant, lounge. **Activities:** Fishing, Jet-ski rental. **Nearby Attractions:** Bale Gristmill State Historic Park & Bothe–Napa Valley State Park in St. Helena; winery tours. **Additional Information:** Winters District Chamber of Commerce, (530) 795-2329; Napa-Sonoma Wine Country Visitor Center, (707) 624-0686 or (800) 723-0575.

RESTRICTIONS

Pets: On leash, $2. **Fires:** Not allowed. **Alcoholic Beverages:** Allowed. **Vehicle Maximum Length:** 40 ft. **Other:** 14-day stay limit from May 15–Oct. 15, 3-month stay limit in winter.

TO GET THERE

From Napa head 16 mi. north on Hwy. 121/Monticello Rd. Turn left on Hwy. 128 and drive 5 mi. Turn right on Berryessa Knoxville Rd. and continue for 13 mi. The resort entrance is on the right, just after the Pope Canyon Rd. turnoff.

NEEDLES   MAP, E-4
Needles Marina Park

100 Marina Dr., 92363. T: (760) 326-2197; www.needlesmarinapark.com.

🚐 ★★★★   ⛺ ★★

Beauty: ★★★	Site Privacy: ★★
Spaciousness: ★★	Quiet: ★★
Security: ★★★	Cleanliness: ★★★★
Insect Control: ★★★	Facilities: ★★★★

Of the many campgrounds located along the Colorado River, few are quite as visually appealing as Needles Marina Park, where palm trees blend seamlessly with eucalyptus, mulberry with mesquite, and flowering oleanders lend a splash of color to the desert scene. Add to that a swimming pool and lagoon, a small sandy beach by the river, a boat ramp and marina, a hot tub, and cabin rentals and you've got the recipe for one fine vacation spot. All of which is not exactly a well-kept secret, as is easily observed in winter when the campground seems crowded. Even though loops are dispersed in clusters and many sites feature pull-through parking, space is definitely on the small side, and the hard-packed pebbly dirt is inhospitable to comfortable tenting. Sites 162–166, overlooking the lagoon, are the best screened for privacy.

BASICS

Operated By: Needles Marina Park. **Open:** All year. **Site Assignment:** Reservations accepted w/ V, MC. **Registration:** At office in store. **Fee:** $30–$32; cash, V, MC. **Parking:** At sites.

FACILITIES

Number of RV-only Sites: 83. **Number of Tent-only Sites:** 75. **Hookups:** Electric (30, 50 amps), water, sewer. **Each Site:** Picnic table, barbecue grill. **Dump Station:** Yes. **Laundry:** Yes. **Pay Phone:** Yes. **Restrooms and Showers:** Yes. **Fuel:** No, boat fuel is available. **Propane:** No. **Internal Roads:** Paved. **RV Service:** No. **Market:** 1 mi. south in Needles. **Restaurant:** 1 mi. south in Needles. **General Store:** Yes. **Vending:** Yes. **Swimming:** Pool, lagoon. **Playground:** Yes. **Other:** Boat ramp & boat slips, marina, spa. **Activities:** Fishing, waterskiing, Needles Municipal Golf Course. **Nearby Attractions:** London Bridge, Mitchell Caverns, Lake Havasu, Providence Mountains State Recreation Area. **Additional Information:** Needles Area Chamber of Commerce, (760) 326-2050.

RESTRICTIONS

Pets: On leash. $2.50 per day, per pet. **Fires:** In barbecue grills only. **Alcoholic Beverages:** Allowed. **Vehicle Maximum Length:** No limit. **Other:** No washing of vehicles; no motorcycle riding; no ATVs.

TO GET THERE

From Needles drive 0.8 mi. north on Needles Hwy. Bear right as it turns into River Rd. Take a left on Marina Dr. and continue 0.1 mi. to the park entrance on the left side.

NEVADA CITY   MAP, B-2, C-2
Malakoff Diggins State Park

23579 North Bloomfield Rd., 95959.
T: (530) 265-2740; www.reserveamerica.com.

🚐 ★★★★   ⛺ ★★★★

Beauty: ★★★	Site Privacy: ★★
Spaciousness: ★★	Quiet: ★★★★
Security: ★★★★	Cleanliness: ★★★★
Insect Control: ★★★	Facilities: ★★

Malakoff Diggins State Historic Park, a forested 3,000 acre park, is the site of California's largest hydraulic gold mine. As you enter the park, you can see the devastation caused by this form of mining. The miners used huge nozzles, which look like cannons, to wash away entire hillsides, looking for gold. Legal battles between mine owners and downstream farmers ended this method. The park also contains a 7,847 foot bedrock tunnel that serves as a drain. You can pan for gold for free. You can sign out a pan without charge, take a how-to sheet, and pan for gold by yourself in a designated area of Humbug Creek. Town-site tours and evening campfire programs are scheduled during the summer. The park contains the old gold-mining town of North Bloomfield, with several preserved buildings, including Park Museum, the park's visitor's center. You can enjoy a picnic area, and a campground with 30 spaces. There are also three rustic cabins that hold 4 campers each. You can also swim and fish at Blair Pond, within the park. The park is set in the beautiful forest of the Sierra. The park offers unique hiking and outdoor opportunities with a blend of a unique history and scenery.

BASICS

Operated By: California Dept. of Parks & Recreation. **Open:** All year. **Site Assignment:** Reservations can be made 7 months in advance; Mar. 31–Sept. 16. **Registration:** At office. **Fee:** Single, $11–$15; group, $67–$111. **Parking:** At site.

FACILITIES

Number of Multipurpose Sites: 34. **Hookups:** None. **Dump Station:** No. **Laundry:** No. **Pay Phone:** No. **Restrooms and Showers:** Yes. **Fuel:** No. **Propane:** No. **Internal Roads:** Paved. **RV Service:** No. **Market:** No. **Restaurant:** No. **General Store:** No. **Vending:** No. **Swimming:** Yes. **Playground:** No. **Activities:** Fishing, hiking, nature trails, picnicking.

RESTRICTIONS

Pets: On 6-ft. leash in a tent or enclosed vehicle at night. Except for guide dogs, pets are not allowed in park buildings, on trails, or on most beaches. **Fires:** In designated fireplaces. **Alcoholic Beverages:** Not allowed. **Other:** Fees include entry for 1 vehicle & 1 legally towed vehicle or trailer, additional vehicles will be charged per night at the park. Bears can break into cars if they smell anything of interest. A car may not be sufficient to protect your food & belongings, even if the car is locked up. Camp at your own risk.

TO GET THERE

The park is located 16 mi. northeast of Nevada City on North Bloomfield Rd.

NORTH FORK   MAP, D-2
Spring Cove—Sierra National Forest

57003 Rd 225, 93643. T: (209) 966-3638; www.reserveamerica.com.

🚐 ★★★★   ⛺ ★★★★

Beauty: ★★★★ Site Privacy: ★★★
Spaciousness: ★★★ Quiet: ★★★
Security: ★★★★ Cleanliness: ★★★★
Insect Control: ★★★★ Facilities: ★★★★

Spring Cove Campground is located in a mountainous environment with lakes, streams, and trees. Restrooms are provided, and firewood is available for sale at the site. Pay showers, laundry, gas, telephones, and a marina are available at nearby Millers Landing Resort. Popular activities include water-skiing, fishing, hiking, a local Native American museum in North Fork, and a local history museum in Oakhurst. Yosemite Valley is a short drive away. Spring Cove Campground, located within the Sierra National Forest located on the western slope of the central Sierra Nevada, is known for its spectacular mountain scenery and abundant natural resources. The Sierra National Forest encompasses more than 1.3 million acres between 900 and 13,986 feet in elevation. The terrain includes rolling, oak-covered foothills, heavily forested middle-elevation slopes, and the starkly beautiful alpine landscape of the High Sierra. Abundant fish and wildlife, varied mountain flora and fauna, and numerous recreational opportunities make the Sierra National Forest an outdoor lovers paradise. Placed under federal protection and management in 1893, when the area was designated the Sierra Forest Reserve, these lands have met public needs for wood, water, and outdoor recreation for more than a century. Today, the Forest's many rugged wilderness areas makes it one of the most popular national forests in the United States.

BASICS

Operated By: U.S. Forest Service. **Open:** May 4–Sept. 3. **Site Assignment:** Reservations must be made at least 1 day in advance. **Registration:** At office. **Fee:** Single, $14; double, $30; group, $50–$100. **Parking:** At site.

FACILITIES

Number of Multipurpose Sites: 252. **Hookups:** None. **Each Site:** Call ahead. **Dump Station:** No. **Laundry:** Yes. **Pay Phone:** Yes. **Restrooms and Showers:** Yes. **Fuel:** No. **Propane:** No. **Internal Roads:** Gravel. **RV Service:** No. **Market:** No. **Restaurant:** No. **General Store:** No. **Vending:** No. **Swimming:** Yes. **Playground:** No. **Activities:** Water-skiing, fishing, hiking.

RESTRICTIONS

Pets: Pets must be restrained or on a leash at all times while in developed recreation areas. **Fires:** In fire rings, stoves, grills, or fireplaces provided for that purpose. **Alcoholic Beverages:** Not allowed. **Vehicle Maximum Length:** Call ahead. **Other:** No ATVs or ORVs allowed. All equipment must fit on the site pad. No firearms or fireworks.

TO GET THERE

Located about 20 mi. south of Yosemite National Park. From Hwy. 41, take Bass Lake turn-off (Road 222). Head southeast about 3.5 mi. to the Bass Lake Campground registration office for check-in (keep to right). The campground is southeast another 4 mi.

NORTH SHORE MAP, F-4
Salton Sea State Recreation Area

reserve america

100-225 State Park Rd., 92254.
T: (760) 393-3052; www.reserveamerica.com.

🚐 ★★★ ⛺ ★★★★

Beauty: ★★★ Site Privacy: ★★
Spaciousness: ★★ Quiet: ★★★★
Security: ★★★★ Cleanliness: ★★★★
Insect Control: ★★★ Facilities: ★★★★

One of the world's largest inland seas, Salton Sea was created by accident in 1905 when increased flooding on the Colorado River allowed water to crash through canal barriers; for the next 18 months the entire flow of the Colorado River rushed downhill into the Salton Trough. By the time engineers were finally able to stop the breaching water in 1907, the Salton Sea had been born—45 miles long and 20 miles wide—equaling 110 miles of shoreline. This 360-square-mile basin is a popular site for boaters, water-skiers, and anglers. Catches include ocean corvina, gulf croaker, tilapia, and sargo. Swimmers, birdwatchers, kayakers, and other visitors can enjoy the site's many recreational opportunities. Because of the sea's low altitude (228 feet below sea level), atmospheric pressure improves speed and ski-boat engine performance. The park has five campgrounds with a total of 1,600 campsites. The popular full-hookup sites at the Headquarters Camp should be reserved in advance. The pleasant developed campsites are the most frequently used, and are well suited for RV or tent camping. Developed sites can be found by Varner Harbor and at Mecca Beach Campgrounds. Three beach campgrounds—Corvina, Salt Creek, and Bombay Beach—provide a more primitive camping experience along the lake's shoreline.

BASICS

Operated By: California Dept. of Parks & Recreation. **Open:** All year. **Site Assignment:** Reservations can be made 7 months in advance; open for reservations Oct. 1–May 31. **Registration:** At office. **Fee:** Single, $12–$23. **Parking:** At site.

FACILITIES

Number of Multipurpose Sites: 59. **Hookups:** Yes. **Dump Station:** Yes. **Laundry:** No. **Pay Phone:** No. **Restrooms and Showers:** Yes. **Fuel:** No. **Propane:** No. **Internal Roads:** Paved. **RV Service:** No. **Market:** No. **Restaurant:** No. **General Store:** No. **Vending:** No. **Swimming:** Yes. **Playground:** No. **Activities:** Boating, fishing, hiking, nature trails, picnicking.

RESTRICTIONS

Pets: On 6-ft. leash in a tent or enclosed vehicle at night. Except for guide dogs, pets are not allowed in park buildings, on trails, or on most beaches. **Fires:** In designated fireplaces. **Alcoholic Beverages:** Not allowed. **Other:** Fees include entry for 1 vehicle & 1 legally towed vehicle or trailer, additional vehicles will be charged per night at the park.

TO GET THERE

Park is located 155 mi. southeast of Los Angeles on Hwy. 10. The park's visitor center is 25 mi. southeast of Indio, via Hwy. 111. The nearest city is North Shore.

OAKLAND MAP, C-2
Anthony Chabot Regional Park

9999 Redwood Rd., 94619. T: (510) 562-2267; www.ebparks.org.

🚐 ★★★★ ⛺ ★★★

Beauty: ★★★★ Site Privacy: ★★
Spaciousness: ★★★ Quiet: ★★★★
Security: ★★★ Cleanliness: ★★★
Insect Control: ★★ Facilities: ★★★

This wooded, pastoral setting is an oasis of calm and beauty only a few minutes drive from the urban bustle of Oakland and Berkeley. Five small loops are spread over a hilltop that is abundantly populated with fragrant eucalyptus trees—though contrary to what may be implied by the name of the access lane, Redwood Rd.—and a few sycamores. Some of the slim, exposed sites enjoy vistas of Lake Chabot, while others overlook a fertile pasture where goats often graze. Best of the latter are 10–12 in the hookup area. The most private of the drive-to sites is number 69, but ardent tenters should consider the even more secluded walk-ins in the direction of the water. In addition to several hiking trails there is a 12–14-mile bicycling loop that is very popular with the fat tire set. The lake, which covers 315 acres, is stocked with fish on a regular basis. Security is good, with ranger patrols and a gate that is locked nightly at 10 p.m.

BASICS

Operated By: East Bay Regional Park District. **Open:** All year. **Site Assignment:** Reservations recommended; must be made at least 12 weeks in advance. V, MC. **Registration:** At entrance booth. **Fee:** $18–$22; cash, V, MC. **Parking:** At site. Parking fee.

FACILITIES

Number of RV-only Sites: 63. **Number of Tent-only Sites:** 12. **Hookups:** Electric (30 amps), water, sewer. **Each Site:** Picnic table, fire grate. **Dump Station:** Yes. **Laundry:** No. **Pay Phone:** Yes. **Restrooms and Showers:** Yes. **Fuel:** No. **Propane:** No. **Internal Roads:** Paved. **RV Service:** No. **Market:** 8 mi. east in Castro Valley. **Restaurant:** 8 mi. east in Castro Valley. **General Store:** No. **Vending:** No. **Swimming:** No. **Playground:** No. **Other:** Some wheelchair-accessible facilities, boat launch, marina, shooting range (nearby). **Activities:** Hiking, fishing, bicycling, kayaking, canoeing. **Nearby Attractions:** Berkeley Botanical Garden & museums; Oakland museums, zoo, Dunsmuir House & Gardens Historic Estate, Chabot Space & Science Center, Jack London Square & more. **Additional Information:** Oakland CVB, (510) 839-5924.

RESTRICTIONS

Pets: On 6-ft. leash; $1 fee. **Fires:** Fire grates only. **Alcoholic Beverages:** Allowed at site, beer & wine only. **Vehicle Maximum Length:** 40 ft. **Other:**

15-day stay limit; no loaded firearms; no wood gathering. Gates lock at 10 p.m.

TO GET THERE

From Oakland on I-580 drive 5.5 mi. east. Exit on Hwy. 13 north and after 1 mi. turn right onto Redwood Rd. Continue for 7.8 mi. to the park entrance on the right. The campground is 2 mi. ahead.

OCEANO   MAP, E-2
Pismo State Beach

555 Pier Ave., 93445. T: (805) 489-2684 or (800) 444-7275; www.parks.ca.gov.

🚐 ★★★   ⛺ ★★★★

Beauty: ★★★★   Site Privacy: ★★★
Spaciousness: ★★★   Quiet: ★★★
Security: ★★★   Cleanliness: ★★★
Insect Control: ★★   Facilities: ★★

Sand and surf, in a nutshell, are two attributes that make this a central-coast standout, one of the prettier stretches of beach in the area. Add to that the wintertime presence of tens of thousands of monarch butterflies, drawn to the park by its towering eucalyptus trees, and it's clear why swarms of tourists descend on the camp like ants to a picnic throughout the summer and most weekends the rest of the year. Located just off of Hwy. 1, 1 mile south of town, North Beach is separated from the water by a high series of dunes. These obstruct views of the ocean, but also buffer the campground from its blustery breezes. Grassy sites are level and of average size, with Monterey pines and flowering bottle brush enhancing the modest screening provided by the fragrant eucalyptus. Unlike Oceano, 2 miles to the south, North Beach does not allow day use, meaning that campers enjoy their piece of shore without the added crush of day-trippers. This is also the prettier of the two camps, but its lack of hookups means that if you need electricity Oceano is the place to be.

BASICS

Operated By: California Dept. of Parks & Recreation. **Open:** All year. **Site Assignment:** Reservations accepted w/V, MC, D. **Registration:** At entrance booth. **Fee:** $13–$22; cash, CA check. **Parking:** At site.

FACILITIES

Number of RV-only Sites: 103. **Hookups:** Yes. **Each Site:** Picnic table, fire grate, food storage box. **Dump Station:** Yes. **Laundry:** No. **Pay Phone:** Yes. **Restrooms and Showers:** Yes. **Fuel:** No. **Propane:** No. **Internal Roads:** Paved. **RV Service:** No. **Market:** 1 mi. north in Pismo Beach. **Restaurant:** 1 mi. north in Pismo Beach. **General Store:** No. **Vending:** Yes. **Swimming:** Pacific Ocean. **Playground:** No. **Other:** Some wheelchair-accessible facilities, visitor's center. **Activities:** Fishing, surfing, clamming, horseback riding, hiking. **Nearby Attractions:** Wineries; San Luis Obispo mission & museums; Oceano Dunes State Vehicular Recreation Area. **Additional Information:** Pismo Beach Chamber of Commerce, (805) 773-4382; San Luis Obispo County Visitors & Conference Bureau, (800) 634-1414 or (805) 541-8000.

RESTRICTIONS

Pets: On 6-ft. leash. **Fires:** Fire grates only. **Alcoholic Beverages:** Allowed at site. **Vehicle Maximum Length:** 36 ft. **Other:** 7-day stay limit from Apr. 1–Oct. 29; no firearms; no wood gathering.

TO GET THERE

In Pismo Beach on US 101 take the Pismo Beach State Park Exit. Drive 2.8 mi. west (toward the ocean) on East Grand Ave. and turn right on Hwy. 1. After 0.8 mi. turn left into the campground.

ORICK   MAP, A-1
Elk Prairie Campground

Prairie Creek Redwoods State Park, Newton B. Drury Scenic Pkwy., 95555. T: (707) 464-6101/5301 or (877) 444-7275; www.cal-parks.ca.gov.

🚐 ★★★★   ⛺ ★★★★

Beauty: ★★★★   Site Privacy: ★★★★
Spaciousness: ★★★★   Quiet: ★★★★
Security: ★★★   Cleanliness: ★★★★
Insect Control: ★★★   Facilities: ★★

Tall as they are, it is easy to overlook the redwood trees when you visit this delightful park. That is largely due to the presence of a good-sized herd of photogenic Roosevelt elk, which can usually be observed grazing in the open grassland near the park's entrance along US 101, as well as down by the shore close to the primitive Gold Bluff Beach campground. The latter is in a beautiful location, between the ocean and 100-foot-high bluffs, but to reach it you will have to navigate 6 miles along a dirt minefield of potholes, a stress test for your nerves as well as your vehicle's axles. Prairie Creek's other campground, Elk Prairie, is inland from the bluffs and far easier to reach. Its single meadow loop—favored by RVs—is prime elk-viewing territory, and its wooded double loop allows for shade, space, and privacy. Curiously, there are few redwoods present, but an abundance of other conifers as well as maples and moss-encrusted alders contribute to a lush, rain forest atmosphere. The largest, most private sites are those nearest to the creek, where the gently gurgling water will serenade you to sleep at night.

BASICS

Operated By: California Dept. of Parks & Recreation. **Open:** All year. **Site Assignment:** Reservations recommended; V, MC, D. **Registration:** At entrance kiosk. **Fee:** Memorial Day–Labor Day, $15; off-season, $12; cash, CA check. **Parking:** At site.

FACILITIES

Number of RV-only Sites: 75. **Hookups:** None. **Each Site:** Picnic table, fire grate, food storage box. **Dump Station:** Yes. **Laundry:** No. **Pay Phone:** Yes. **Restrooms and Showers:** Yes. **Fuel:** No. **Propane:** No. **Internal Roads:** Paved, narrow, & winding. **RV Service:** No. **Market:** 4 mi. south in Orick. **Restaurant:** 4 mi. south in Orick. **General Store:** No. **Vending:** No. **Swimming:** No. **Playground:** No. **Other:** Some wheelchair-accessible facilities, visitor center. **Activities:** Hiking, bicycling, wildlife viewing, photography, beachcombing. **Nearby**

Attractions: Humboldt Lagoons State Park & Redwood National & State Parks in Orick; Trees of Mystery in Klamath. **Additional Information:** Orick Chamber of Commerce, (707) 488-2885; Klamath Chamber of Commerce, (707) 482-7165.

RESTRICTIONS

Pets: On 6-ft. leash. **Fires:** Fire grates only. **Alcoholic Beverages:** Allowed at site. **Vehicle Maximum Length:** 27 ft. **Other:** 14-day stay limit from May 1–Sept. 30; no firearms; no wood gathering; no mushroom-plucking.

TO GET THERE

From Crescent City drive 37 mi. south on US 101. Exit and turn right on the Newton B. Drury Scenic Pkwy. Continue for 1.2 mi. to the park entrance on the left.

ORICK   MAP, A-1
Prairie Creek Redwoods State Park

127011 Newton B. Drury Parkway, 95555. T: (707) 464-6101; www.reserveamerica.com.

🚐 ★★★   ⛺ ★★★★

Beauty: ★★★   Site Privacy: ★★★
Spaciousness: ★★   Quiet: ★★★★★
Security: ★★★★★   Cleanliness: ★★★★
Insect Control: ★★★   Facilities: ★★

Set aside in the early 1920s by the forethought of the people of California and the generosity of the Save-the-Redwoods League, Prairie Creek is a 14,000-acre sanctuary of old-growth coast redwood. Designated as a World Heritage Site and Man in the Biosphere Preserve, the park has over 280 Save-the-Redwoods League memorial groves. There are over 70 miles of hiking trails through lush forests and along wild and scenic beaches. As the park is a preserve of uncut forest, all trails lead you through the world's tallest trees. There are all-day hikes and short leisurely strolls. The terrain is relatively mild with only 800 feet of elevation gain throughout the park. The park has two developed campgrounds. The Elk Prairie has 75 campsites that can accommodate up to 24-foot trailers and 27-foot motor homes. The Gold Bluffs Beach campground has 25 campsites. Both campgrounds offer fire rings, tables, and bear-proof food lockers with water nearby. There are restrooms with flush toilets and hot showers. Both campgrounds are open all year. The Gold Bluff Beach camp is on first-come, first-serve basis. The Elk Prairie camp can be reserved during the summer. The park also has two backcountry camps and an environmental camp. Backcountry campers must register and park at the visitor center and must camp in the designated campsites at Ossagon Trail camp and Miner's Ridge camp. Both camps are open all year. Prairie Creek offers hiking, nature study, wildlife viewing, beach combing, fishing, picnicking, a visitor center with exhibits, and a nature store.

BASICS

Operated By: California Dept. of Parks & Recreation. **Open:** All year. **Site Assignment:** Reservations can be made 7 months in advance; May 1–Sept. 30. **Registration:** At office. **Fee:** Single, $15–$20. **Parking:** At site.

FACILITIES

Number of Multipurpose Sites: 142. **Hookups:** None. **Dump Station:** Yes. **Laundry:** No. **Pay Phone:** No. **Restrooms and Showers:** Yes. **Fuel:** No. **Propane:** No. **Internal Roads:** Paved. **RV Service:** No. **Market:** No. **Restaurant:** No. **General Store:** No. **Vending:** No. **Swimming:** No. **Playground:** No. **Activities:** Biking, hiking, interpretive programs, nature trails.

RESTRICTIONS

Pets: On 6-ft. leash in a tent or enclosed vehicle at night. Except for guide dogs, pets are not allowed in park buildings, on trails, or on most beaches. **Fires:** In designated fireplaces. **Alcoholic Beverages:** Not allowed. **Other:** Bears are common! Keep food locked up! Use bear boxes! Fees include entry for 1 vehicle & 1 legally towed vehicle or trailer, additional vehicles will be charged per night at the park.

TO GET THERE

Take the Newton B. Drury Scenic Pkwy. exit off of Hwy. 101. The visitor center and Elk Prairie Campground are located at the southern end of the Pkwy. Gold Bluffs Beach Campground and Fern Canyon are accessed by Davison Rd., which is located 3 mi. north of Orick off of Hwy. 101, 50 mi. from Eureka and Crescent City.

ORLAND   MAP, B-2
Buckhorn

reserve america

19225 Newville Rd., 95963-8901. T: (530) 865-4781 or (877) 444-6777; www.reserveamerica.com.

🚐 ★★★★   ▲ ★★★★

Beauty: ★★★★   Site Privacy: ★★
Spaciousness: ★★★   Quiet: ★★★
Security: ★★★★   Cleanliness: ★★★
Insect Control: ★★★   Facilities: ★★★★

Black Butte Lake may seem like a mirage at first glance, its blue-green surface shimmering in the middle of sun-baked brown hills, with black-mauve volcanic rocks crowning the scene. Go ahead and pinch yourself, it's really there. It is also, as one of the largest lakes in the region, a hugely popular summertime recreation area that attracts anyone with a boat from miles around. Buckhorn is one of two campgrounds on this U.S. Army Corps of Engineers domain, 12 miles west of Orland and I-5. Several loops cling to the undulating contours of the hillside abutting the lake, which results in a high percentage of lake-view sites. A sprinkling of oaks sheds adequate shade, and screening and space are average. While all types of watercrafts are permitted, the stiff breezes that often sweep across the lake make sailing especially rewarding. Black Butte Lake is one of the better locations for crappie fishing in northern California.

BASICS

Operated By: U.S. Army Corps of Engineers. **Open:** All year. **Site Assignment:** Reservations accepted w/ V, MC, D; first-come, first-serve sites available. **Registration:** At entrance booth. **Fee:** $15 from Apr. 1–Oct. 31; $10 the rest of the year; cash, check. **Parking:** At site.

FACILITIES

Number of RV-only Sites: 60. **Number of Tent-only Sites:** 5. **Hookups:** None. **Each Site:** Picnic table, fire grate, barbecue grill. **Dump Station:** Yes. **Laundry:** No. **Pay Phone:** Yes. **Restrooms and Showers:** Yes. **Fuel:** No. **Propane:** Yes. **Internal Roads:** Paved. **RV Service:** No. **Market:** 12 mi. east in Orland. **Restaurant:** 12 mi. east in Orland. **General Store:** Yes, at marina. **Vending:** No. **Swimming:** Black Butte Lake. **Playground:** Yes. **Other:** Some wheelchair-accessible facilities, boat launch, marina. **Activities:** Fishing, hiking, sailing, windsurfing. **Nearby Attractions:** Tejama County Park in Corning; Chico museums & Bidwell Mansion State Historic Park; outlet shopping in Anderson; William B. Ide Adobe State Historic Park near Red Bluff. **Additional Information:** Corning District Chamber of Commerce, (530) 824-5550; Chico Chamber of Commerce & Visitor Bureau, (530) 891-5556 or (800) 852-8570.

RESTRICTIONS

Pets: On leash. **Fires:** Fire grates only. **Alcoholic Beverages:** Allowed. **Vehicle Maximum Length:** 35 ft. (varies depending on site). **Other:** 14-day stay limit.

TO GET THERE

In Orland on I-5 take the Black Butte Lake Exit. Head west on Rd. 200/Newville Rd. for 12 mi. Turn left on Buckhorn Rd. and continue straight to the campground.

OROVILLE   MAP, B-2
Bidwell Canyon Campground

Lake Oroville State Recreation Area, Arroyo Dr., 95966. T: (530) 538-2219 or (530) 538-2200; www.parks.ca.gov.

🚐 ★★★★   ▲ ★★

Beauty: ★★★   Site Privacy: ★★
Spaciousness: ★★   Quiet: ★★★
Security: ★★★   Cleanliness: ★★★
Insect Control: ★★★ Facilities: ★★★★

When Lake Oroville is full it is a beautiful sight. Unfortunately, its level depends both on winter snow melt and how much it has been drawn down during the summer. Management tries to keep the water near capacity at least through the Fourth of July holiday, when the recreation area overflows with campers, but Mother Nature does not always cooperate. Not that campsites are affected either way, since few are endowed with water views. Of the two double circuits, Loop I (numbers 1–39) is the grassier, with limited space between pine- and live oak–shaded sites. The crowding is no better in Loop II (40–75), where the live oaks are complemented by madrone and manzanita. Two of the better sites for privacy are 31 and 44, but overall the constricted layout of this facil-

ity makes it more suitable for RV campers than tenters. The exceptions are the remote boat-in sites, assuming there is water available to provide access.

BASICS

Operated By: California Dept. of Parks & Recreation. **Open:** All year. **Site Assignment:** Reservations accepted w/ V, MC, D; limited first come, first served sites. **Registration:** At entrance booth. **Fee:** $13–$24; cash, CA check. **Parking:** At site.

FACILITIES

Number of RV-only Sites: 74. **Hookups:** Electric (20, 30 amps), water, sewer. **Each Site:** Picnic table, fire grate. **Dump Station:** Yes. **Laundry:** No. **Pay Phone:** No. **Restrooms and Showers:** Yes. **Fuel:** No. **Propane:** No. **Internal Roads:** Paved. **RV Service:** No. **Market:** 10 mi. west in Oroville. **Restaurant:** 10 mi. west in Oroville. **General Store:** Yes, w/ snack bar at the end of Kellyridge Rd. **Vending:** No. **Swimming:** Lake Oroville. **Playground:** No. **Other:** Some wheelchair-accessible facilities, 7-lane boat ramp, marina. **Activities:** Fishing, waterskiing, hiking, windsurfing, horseback riding, boat rentals. **Nearby Attractions:** Oroville Dam, Chinese Temple & Garden, Pioneer Museum, Freeman Bicycle Trail; Gold Nugget Museum in Paradise. **Additional Information:** Oroville Area Chamber of Commerce, (530) 538-2542 or (800) 655-GOLD.

RESTRICTIONS

Pets: On 6-ft. leash. **Fires:** Fire grates only. **Alcoholic Beverages:** Allowed at site. **Vehicle Maximum Length:** 40 ft. **Other:** 30-day stay limit; no firearms; no wood gathering.

TO GET THERE

From Oroville drive 7 mi. east on Hwy. 162. Turn left on Kelly Ridge Rd. and continue for 1.6 mi. to Arroyo Dr. Turn right and proceed to the park entrance 0.5 mi. ahead.

OROVILLE   MAP, B-2
Lake Oroville State
Recreation Area

reserve america

400 Glen Dr., 95966-9222. T: (530) 538-2200; www.reserveamerica.com.

🚐 ★★★★   ▲ ★★★★

Beauty: ★★★★   Site Privacy: ★★★★
Spaciousness: ★★★★   Quiet: ★★★★
Security: ★★★★   Cleanliness: ★★★★
Insect Control: ★★★   Facilities: ★★★★

This artificial lake was formed by the tallest earth-filled dam (770 feet above the stream bed of the Feather River) in the country. Encompassing approximately 28,450 acres near the City of Oroville, the park features family and group camping, boating, an extensive system of horse, bicycle, and hiking trails and a state-of-the-art horse camp. The park features "floating campsites," moored in a cove. Lake Oroville Visitor Center has a museum, exhibits, videos, and a store. The view from the 47-foot tower, with two high-powered telescopes, is a spectacular panoramic view of the lake, Sierra Nevadas, valley, foothills, and the Sutter Buttes mountain range. The area includes the Feather River Fish Hatchery, built by the Department of Water Resources to replace lost spawning areas for salmon and steelhead. Displays of the State Water Project and the area's natural and cultural history are featured at the visitor's center. The lake offers a wide variety of outdoor activities including camping, picnicking, horseback riding, hiking, sail and powerboating, waterskiing, fishing, swimming, boat-in camping, floating campsites, and horse camping.

BASICS

Operated By: California Dept. of Parks & Recreation. **Open:** All year. **Site Assignment:** Reservations can be made 7 months in advance. **Registration:** At office. **Fee:** Single, $13–$30; group, $36–$60. **Parking:** At site.

FACILITIES

Number of Multipurpose Sites: 287. **Hookups:** None. **Dump Station:** Yes. **Laundry:** Yes. **Pay Phone:** No. **Restrooms and Showers:** Yes. **Fuel:** No. **Propane:** No. **Internal Roads:** Paved. **RV Service:** No. **Market:** No. **Restaurant:** No. **General Store:** Yes. **Vending:** No. **Swimming:** Yes. **Playground:** No. **Activities:** Boating, fishing, hiking, picnicking, nature trails, horseback riding.

RESTRICTIONS

Pets: Pets are prohibited on the floating campsites. **Fires:** In designated fireplaces. **Alcoholic Beverages:** Not allowed. **Other:** Fees include entry for 1 vehicle & 1 legally towed vehicle or trailer, additional vehicles will be charged per night at the park.

TO GET THERE

68 mi. north of Sacramento on Hwy. 70 to Hwy. 162; 8 mi. east on Hwy. 162 to Kelly Ridge Rd, left on Kelly Ridge Rd to Arroyo Drive.

PACIFICA MAP, C-1, C-2
San Francisco RV Resort

reserve america

700 Palmetto Ave., 94044. T: (800) 822-1250 or (650) 355-7093; www.reserveamerica.com.

🚐 ★★★★   ⛺ n/a

Beauty: ★★★	Site Privacy: ★
Spaciousness: ★	Quiet: ★★
Security: ★★★★	Cleanliness: ★★★★
Insect Control: ★★★★	Facilities: ★★★★★

Pacific Park RV Resort is conveniently located just 10 miles south of San Francisco, just off of Hwy. 1 in Pacifica. It is loaded with amenities, from cable television and Internet connections to a small swimming pool and Jacuzzi, from a horseshoe pit to a video-game room. The Pacific Ocean abuts the lot, filling the air with a pleasant brininess, and a very short trail leads down to the sandy beach. The view across the busy road is not bad either, highlighted by a wavy series of grass-covered hills. The bad news is the parking slots are wedged one against another, and there are no shade trees, no privacy, and no tents allowed. The best bet is to set up as far to the western

---

edge of the grounds as possible, where an unobstructed view of the sun setting into the water is a killer, and the crashing surf is almost loud enough to drown out the noise of incessant air and auto traffic. A shuttle service is available to ferry campers to downtown San Francisco.

BASICS

Operated By: San Francisco RV Resort; Charley Winter, manager. **Open:** All year. **Site Assignment:** Reservations recommended; V, MC. **Registration:** At entrance office. **Fee:** $38–$69 plus 10% local tax; cash, V, MC. **Parking:** At site.

FACILITIES

Number of RV-only Sites: 182. **Hookups:** Electric (30, 50 amps), water, sewer, cable TV, Internet. **Each Site:** Communal picnic table. **Dump Station:** Yes. **Laundry:** Yes. **Pay Phone:** Yes. **Restrooms and Showers:** Yes. **Fuel:** No. **Propane:** Yes. **Internal Roads:** Paved. **RV Service:** No. **Market:** 0.25 mi. in Pacifica. **Restaurant:** 0.25 mi. in Pacifica. **General Store:** Yes. **Vending:** Yes. **Swimming:** Small heated pool. **Playground:** Yes. **Other:** Some wheelchair-accessible facilities, spa, game room. **Activities:** Sunning, surfing, beachcombing, horseshoe pit, touring San Francisco. **Nearby Attractions:** Museums, Ghirardelli Square, Fisherman's Wharf, zoo, aquarium, Golden Gate Park, & much more in San Francisco; Montara & Gray Whale Cove State Beaches. **Additional Information:** San Francisco CVB, (415) 391-2000.

RESTRICTIONS

Pets: On leash, must be under 20 pounds. **Fires:** Not allowed. **Alcoholic Beverages:** Allowed. **Vehicle Maximum Length:** 60 ft. **Other:** No stay limit; no generators.

TO GET THERE

From San Francisco drive 8 mi. south on Hwy. 1 to Pacifica. Exit on Manor Dr. and continue straight through the stop sign. Manor Dr. becomes Palmetto Ave. The resort entrance is 0.5 mi. ahead on the right.

PERRIS MAP, E-3
Luiseño Campground

Lake Perris State Recreation Area, 17801 Lake Perris Dr., 92571. T: (909) 940-5603 or (800) 444-7275; www.parks.ca.gov.

🚐 ★★★★   ⛺ ★★★★

Beauty: ★★★★	Site Privacy: ★★★★
Spaciousness: ★★★★	Quiet: ★★★
Security: ★★★★	Cleanliness: ★★★
Insect Control: ★★	Facilities: ★★★★

If time weighs heavily on your hands during your stay at Lake Perris you will only have yourself to blame. That's because this recreation area has a little bit of something for everyone, from fishing and boating (rentals available at the marina), hiking, biking, and horseback riding trails, and an Native American museum (open Wednesdays and weekends), to a pair of swimming beaches and a waterslide (summer season only). It is a pretty park, too, with lush grassy turf sloping gently toward the water and rocky hills coloring the horizon. Sites are open but spacious, many shaded by conifers, eucalyptus,

---

and pepper trees. That shade is essential, as summer temperatures typically hit 110 degrees, scorching the grass brown and sending everyone with a swimsuit into the water. The weather is milder in the spring, when a fabulous explosion of wildflowers makes this place a must-see. Boating to Alessandro Island for a romantic picnic is considered by many to be a Lake Perris rite-of-passage.

BASICS

Operated By: California Dept. of Parks & Recreation. **Open:** All year. **Site Assignment:** Reservations accepted w/ V, MC, D. **Registration:** At office. **Fee:** $23–$34; cash, CA check. **Parking:** At site.

FACILITIES

Number of RV-only Sites: 254. **Number of Tent-only Sites:** 177. **Hookups:** Electric (30, 50 amps), water. **Each Site:** Picnic table, fire ring. **Dump Station:** Yes. **Laundry:** No. **Pay Phone:** Yes. **Restrooms and Showers:** Yes. **Fuel:** No. **Propane:** No. **Internal Roads:** Paved. **RV Service:** No. **Market:** 5 mi. south in Perris. **Restaurant:** 5 mi. south in Perris. **General Store:** Yes. **Vending:** No. **Swimming:** Lake Perris, swim beach. **Playground:** Yes. **Other:** Some wheelchair-accessible facilities, boat ramp, coffee shop. **Activities:** Fishing, bicycling, hiking, horseback riding, horseshoe pit, wind surfing, boat rentals, golf. **Nearby Attractions:** Perris Valley Historical Museum & Orange Empire Railway Museum; Riverside & its museums, gardens & historic buildings. **Additional Information:** Perris Valley Chamber of Commerce, (909) 657-3555.

RESTRICTIONS

Pets: On 6-ft. leash. **Fires:** Fire grates only. **Alcoholic Beverages:** Allowed at site but not in day-use areas. **Vehicle Maximum Length:** 31 ft. **Other:** 14-day stay limit from June 1–Sept. 30, 30-day stay limit for the rest of the year; no firearms; no wood gathering.

TO GET THERE

From Riverside follow I-215/Hwy. 60 east. When the two roads split remain on Hwy. 60 for another 4.6 mi. Exit on Moreno Beach Dr. and continue south for 3.5 mi. Turn left on Via del Lago. The park entrance is just 1 mi. ahead.

PESCADERO MAP, D-1
Butano State Park

reserve america

1500 Cloverdale Rd., 94060. T: (650) 879-2040 or (800) 444-7275; www.reserveamerica.com.

🚐 ★★★   ⛺ ★★★★

Beauty: ★★★★	Site Privacy: ★★★★
Spaciousness: ★★★★	Quiet: ★★★
Security: ★★★★	Cleanliness: ★★★★
Insect Control: ★★★	Facilities: ★★

You've heard the expression "good things come in small packages"? That is certainly true of this beautiful park, another in the fine constellation of coast redwood preserves that are located north of Santa Cruz and east of San Jose. The drive to Butano is easier than the others, along a marginally wider road without quite as many mountainous turns. Sites, too, are roomier and scattered farther apart than those at Portola Redwoods State Park a few miles away. Direct sunlight onto the double loop is largely blocked by the magnificent stands of *Sequoia sempervirens,* which are so dominant that only a few tan oaks have been able to lay down roots. Tenters will enjoy the privacy of the many recessed walk-in sites, and of the drive-to options, 6 is level and very roomy, and 9, tucked behind a fallen giant, is quite private. We encountered quails, rabbits, and a doe and its tiny fawn on our last visit; they were attracted to the grounds by a small creek that runs through camp.

BASICS

Operated By: California Dept. of Parks & Recreation. **Open:** All year. **Site Assignment:** Reservations accepted w/ V, MC, D. **Registration:** At entrance booth. **Fee:** $20–$25; cash, CA check. 8 people occupancy; additional vehicles, $4. **Parking:** At site; some walk-in sites.

FACILITIES

Number of RV-only Sites: 21. **Number of Tent-only Sites:** 17. **Hookups:** None. **Each Site:** Picnic table, fire grate, food storage box. **Dump Station:** No. **Laundry:** No. **Pay Phone:** Yes. **Restrooms and Showers:** Flush & pit toilets, no showers. **Fuel:** No. **Propane:** No. **Internal Roads:** Paved. **RV Service:** No. **Market:** 24 mi. north in Half Moon Bay. **Restaurant:** 24 mi. north in Half Moon Bay. **General Store:** No. **Vending:** No. **Swimming:** No. **Playground:** No. **Other:** Some wheelchair-accessible facilities, visitor center. **Activities:** Hiking, birding, exploring redwood forests, backpacking. **Nearby Attractions:** Pigeon Point Lighthouse & downtown Half Moon Bay; Montara & Gray Whale Cove State Beaches; several redwood forests. **Additional Information:** Half Moon Bay Coastside Chamber of Commerce & Visitors Bureau, (650) 726-8380.

RESTRICTIONS

Pets: On 6-ft. leash. **Fires:** Fire grates only. **Alcoholic Beverages:** Allowed at site. **Vehicle Maximum Length:** 27 ft. **Other:** 14-day stay limit; no firearms; no wood gathering.

TO GET THERE

From the junction of Hwy. 1 and Hwy. 92 in Half Moon Bay, drive 17 mi. south on Hwy. 1. Turn left on Pescadero Rd., drive 3 mi. and turn right on Cloverdale Rd. The park entrance is 5.5 mi. ahead on the left.

PINECREST
Pinecrest
MAP, C-3

reserve america

Pinecrest Lake Rd., 95364. T: (209) 965-3116 or (877) 444-6777; www.reserveamerica.com.

🚐 ★★★★	🛖 ★★★
Beauty: ★★★★	Site Privacy: ★★★
Spaciousness: ★★★	Quiet: ★★
Security: ★★	Cleanliness: ★★
Insect Control: ★★★	Facilities: ★★★

There is more than merely the aura of a resort town to Pinecrest, it actually delivers the goods. Activities range from hiking and bicycling to fishing, swimming, and boating; amenities include an expansive picnic area near the water, a marina, and, across the street, a post office, restaurant, and general store stocked with everything from fresh produce to liquor to hardware. The huge campground, which is 30 miles east of Sonora, is handsomely framed by its high-altitude (5,600 feet) Sierra Nevada locale, rubbing up against the clear blue Pinecrest Lake, with pine- and granite-studded hills all around. Even Shangri-la had its downside, however, and Pinecrest is no different. Sites of grass and pine needles pinch a bit as space is at a premium over the camp's multiple series of loops. That constricted feeling is accentuated by the presence of private vacation cabins off to one side of the property, which also detract from the rustic atmosphere. Nonetheless, privacy is not bad, as thick groves of cedars, ponderosa, and lodgepole pines, as well as a widespread debris field of glacial erratics, contribute a degree of screening.

BASICS

Operated By: Dodge Ridge Corp, concessionaire. **Open:** Apr. 17–Oct. 11, weather permitting. **Site Assignment:** Reservations required May 15–Sept. 5; required at least 2 days in advance; V, MC, D, AE. **Registration:** At entrance booth. **Fee:** $19; cash, check. **Parking:** At site, 2 vehicles per site.

FACILITIES

Number of RV-only Sites: 200. **Hookups:** None. **Each Site:** Picnic table, fire ring w/grate. **Dump Station:** No, Pinecrest RV dump 0.5 mi. **Laundry:** No. **Pay Phone:** Yes. **Restrooms and Showers:** Yes, fee. **Fuel:** No. **Propane:** No. **Internal Roads:** Paved. **RV Service:** No. **Market:** Across the street is a large, well-stocked general store. **Restaurant:** Across the street. **General Store:** Yes. **Vending:** No. **Swimming:** Pinecrest Lake. **Playground:** No. **Other:** Limited wheelchair-accessible facilities, boat ramp, marina. **Activities:** Hiking, fishing, boat rentals, bicycling. **Nearby Attractions:** Tuolumne County Museum & History Center in Sonora; Yosemite National Park; Ahwahnee Whitewater Rafting in Columbia. **Additional Information:** Yosemite Area Traveler Information, (209) 723-3153; Tuolumne County Visitors Bureau, (209) 533-4420 or (800) 446-1333.

RESTRICTIONS

Pets: On leash. **Fires:** Fire ring only. **Alcoholic Beverages:** Allowed. **Vehicle Maximum Length:** 40 ft. **Other:** 14-day stay limit.

TO GET THERE

From Sonora drive 30 mi. east on Hwy. 108. Turn right at the sign for Pinecrest Lake and continue for 0.7 mi. to the campground entrance on the right.

POLLOCK PINES
Ice House Resort
MAP, C-3

reserve america

9000 Ice House Rd., 95726. T: (530) 644-2348 or (877) 444-6777; www.reserveamerica.com.

🚐 ★★★★	🛖 ★★★★
Beauty: ★★★★	Site Privacy: ★★★
Spaciousness: ★★★	Quiet: ★★★★
Security: ★★★	Cleanliness: ★★★
Insect Control: ★★★	Facilities: ★★

The concession that operates Ice House delivers primitive camping conditions for its nightly fee of $15, which seems appalling at first blush. Don't let price-gouging deter you, though, from coming to this beautiful, rough-cut campground. Its wild, unspoiled appearance is an idiosyncratic reminder of the relative youth and vitality of the Sierra Nevada range, and a bit reminiscent of Grover Hot Springs State Park, at Markleeville. Ice House reflects two sorts of environments, from the reservoir below its two undulating loops to the lofty, snow-dusted mountain peaks high above. Sites of dirt and pine needles are grouped closely together, but are well buffered by an abundance of enormous boulders and concentrations of ponderosa and Jeffrey pines, incense cedar, and manzanita. The latter appears in especially thick concentrations in the second circuit, which also holds more of the quirkily engaging sites. With an elevation of 5,436 feet, roads in this area can be snow-covered from late October until mid-May.

BASICS

Operated By: American Land & Leisure, concessionaire. **Open:** Mid-May–mid-Oct.; weather permitting. **Site Assignment:** Reservations accepted w/ V, MC, D. **Registration:** At entrance kiosk. **Fee:** $15; double site, $30; cash, check. **Parking:** At site.

FACILITIES

Number of RV-only Sites: 66. **Number of Tent-only Sites:** 17. **Hookups:** None. **Each Site:** Picnic table, fire grate, barbecue grill. **Dump Station:** Yes. **Laundry:** No. **Pay Phone:** No. **Restrooms and Showers:** Vault toilets, no showers. **Fuel:** No. **Propane:** No. **Internal Roads:** Paved but bumpy, winding, & narrow. **RV Service:** No. **Market:** 21 mi. southwest in Pollock Pines. **Restaurant:** 21 mi. southwest in Pollock Pines. **General Store:** No. **Vending:** No. **Swimming:** Ice House Reservoir. **Playground:** No. **Other:** Some wheelchair-accessible facilities, boat ramp. **Activities:** Fishing, hiking, boating, bicycling, boulder scrambling. **Nearby Attractions:** Fountain-Tallman Museum in Placerville; El Dorado National Forest in Camino; Sly Park Recreation Area in Pollock Pines. **Additional Information:** El Dorado County Visitors Authority, (530) 642-8029 or (887) 588-4FUN; Pollock Pines–Camino Chamber of Commerce, (530) 644-3970 or (530) 644-2498.

RESTRICTIONS

Pets: On leash. **Fires:** Fire grates only. **Alcoholic Beverages:** Allowed. **Vehicle Maximum Length:** 22 ft. **Other:** 14-day stay limit.

TO GET THERE

From Placerville drive 20 mi. east on US 50. Turn left (north) on Ice House Rd. and continue for 11 mi. to FR 32. Turn right toward Ice House Reservoir, and proceed for 1.2 mi. to the campground entrance.

PONDEROSA
Peppermint
MAP, D-2, D-3

F.R. 21S07A, 93208. T: (559) 539-2607 or
(877) 444-6777; www.r5.fs.fed.us/sequoia.

🚐 ★★★★ 　 ⛺ ★★★★

Beauty: ★★★★	Site Privacy: ★★★★
Spaciousness: ★★★★	Quiet: ★★★
Security: ★	Cleanliness: ★★
Insect Control: ★★★	Facilities: ★

The last time we stopped by this primitive camp we were surprised to find half a dozen motor homes in residence. Not that the dirt access road off of Western Divide Hwy. is bad—it isn't (though the internal lane verges on abominable in places). It's just that for ages Peppermint has been a refuge for budget-minded tenters. Word of its rustic appeal must have spread. There are about a dozen tables scattered around this rocky, forested mountain knoll, mostly downhill by Peppermint Creek. There is also a dilapidated outhouse, of a similar vintage to the one at Quaking Aspen, just up the road. If you want more in creature comforts, you best bring 'em with you or go elsewhere. Undesignated sites are well hidden among lodgepole, ponderosa, and Jeffrey pines, alders and aspens, cedars and dirt. Those with tables are snapped up first, but there are many more across the hill with simply a crude ring of stones as an amenity. Bring your own drinking water, pack out trash, and, since you'll be camping at an altitude of 7,100 feet, dress warmly. Telephone, gasoline, propane, and a general store are available 1.5 miles north at Ponderosa Lodge.

BASICS
Operated By: Sequoia National Forest, Tule River Ranger District. **Open:** May–Oct.; weather permitting. **Site Assignment:** First come, first served. **Registration:** Not necessary. **Fee:** None. **Parking:** No restriction.

FACILITIES
Number of Multipurpose Sites: Undesignated, dispersed camping. **Hookups:** None. **Each Site:** 12 scattered picnic tables, many makeshift fire rings. **Dump Station:** No. **Laundry:** No. **Pay Phone:** No. **Restrooms and Showers:** Vault toilets, no showers. **Fuel:** No. **Propane:** No. **Internal Roads:** Rocky forest floor. **RV Service:** No. **Market:** 45 mi. west in Porterville. **Restaurant:** 3 mi. in Ponderosa. **General Store:** 3 mi. in Ponderosa. **Vending:** No. **Swimming:** No. **Playground:** No. **Activities:** Hiking, fishing, whittling. **Nearby Attractions:** Sequoia National Forest; Porterville Historical Museum & Zauld House & Gardens; California Hot Springs. **Additional Information:** Springville Chamber of Commerce, (559) 539-2312; Porterville Chamber of Commerce, (559) 784-7503.

RESTRICTIONS
Pets: On leash. **Fires:** By permit, issued at the Tule River Ranger District in Springville; use fire ring. **Alcoholic Beverages:** Allowed. **Vehicle Maximum Length:** 22 ft. **Other:** 14-day stay limit.

TO GET THERE
From Porterville drive 44 mi. east on Hwy. 190 (which becomes the Western Divide Hwy.). Turn left on FS 21S07B and after 0.5 mi. turn left again on FS 21S07A. The campground lies straight ahead.

PORTERVILLE
Tule Recreation Area
MAP, D-2

reserve america

P.O. Box 1072, 93258-1072. T: (559) 784-0215 or (877) 444-6777; www.reserveamerica.com.

🚐 ★★★★ 　 ⛺ ★★★

Beauty: ★★★	Site Privacy: ★★
Spaciousness: ★★★★	Quiet: ★★★
Security: ★★★★	Cleanliness: ★★★
Insect Control: ★★★	Facilities: ★★★

Sun-scorched buttes rise above the multi-pronged lake that serves as a focal point to this recreation area. How people cooled off here before the U.S. Army Corps of Engineers created Lake Success in 1961 is anybody's guess. With plenty of iced-down beer, perhaps, and that might still be considered an essential ingredient to any summertime visit. There is a scattered presence of such trees as oak, eucalyptus, buttonwood, oleander, juniper, and various conifers throughout the double-looped campground, but shade remains scarcer than candy in a dentist's office. In a facility that appears to put function ahead of aesthetics, ramadas would be a welcome addition to the sites. But the extra exposure to the blazing sun is just one more excuse to jump in the water. Not convinced? Then try to land 26, 29, 30, or 41, some of the few, the proud, the shaded. Located just off Hwy. 190 9 miles east of Porterville, the campground is subject to traffic noise. Unfortunately, an above average amount of bottles, 'butts, and plastic pollute the grounds.

BASICS
Operated By: U.S. Army Corps of Engineers. **Open:** All year. **Site Assignment:** Reservations recommended; V, MC, D; 17 first-come, first-serve sites. **Registration:** At office at the end of the driveway. **Fee:** $16–$21; cash, check. **Parking:** At site; 2 vehicle limit per site.

FACILITIES
Number of RV-only Sites: 104. **Hookups:** Electric (30, 50 amps), water. **Each Site:** Picnic table, fire grate, barbecue grill, lantern pole. **Dump Station:** Yes. **Laundry:** No. **Pay Phone:** Yes. **Restrooms and Showers:** Yes. **Fuel:** No. **Propane:** No. **Internal Roads:** Paved. **RV Service:** No. **Market:** 9 mi. west in Porterville. **Restaurant:** 9 mi. west in Porterville. **General Store:** Yes. **Vending:** Yes. **Swimming:** At your own risk. **Playground:** Yes. **Other:** Some wheelchair-accessible facilities, 2 boat ramps, marina. **Activities:** Fishing, boat rentals, sailing, waterskiing, hiking, horseback riding (not allowed in the campground area). **Nearby Attractions:** Porterville Historical Museum & Zauld House & Gardens; Kaweah Oaks Preserve in Exeter; California Hot Springs. **Additional Information:** Porterville Chamber of Commerce, (559) 784-7503.

RESTRICTIONS
Pets: On leash no longer than 6 ft. **Fires:** Fire grates only. **Alcoholic Beverages:** Allowed. **Vehicle Maximum Length:** 30 ft. **Other:** 14-day stay limit w/in a 30-day period.

TO GET THERE
From Porterville drive 9 mi. east on Hwy. 190 to Lake Success. The campground entrance is on the left.

PORTOLA
Grasshopper Flat
MAP, B-3

reserve america

Grizzly Rd., 96129. T: (530) 832-1076; www.reserveamerica.com.

🚐 ★★★★ 　 ⛺ ★★★★

Beauty: ★★★★	Site Privacy: ★★★
Spaciousness: ★★★	Quiet: ★★★
Security: ★★★	Cleanliness: ★★★★
Insect Control: ★★★	Facilities: ★★

If you are not towing a boat to this delightful lakeside facility, you will probably be in the minority. A simple fishing rod will do, though pole-less nature lovers should find the natural beauty of the setting gratifying enough. No sites verge on Lake Davis, but many of them offer excellent pine-filtered vistas of the water and short trails make access to the shore as easy as putting a night crawler on a hook. The tidy campground's three loops wind through medium-size Jeffrey and ponderosa pines. As a result, this facility, at 5,785 feet of altitude, is carpeted with pine needles and cones. There is a respectable amount of space between most sites, and the presence of both double units and pull-through parking simplifies the maneuvering of larger vehicles and trailers. A dump station is located on the opposite side of the street, 0.2 miles south of camp, and the Grizzly store, 2 miles south across the dam, has basic supplies and pay showers.

BASICS
Operated By: U.S.T. Wilderness Management Corp, concessionaire. **Open:** Apr. 28–Oct. 10. **Site Assignment:** Reservations accepted w/ V, MC, D for a limited number of sites. **Registration:** At entrance kiosk. **Fee:** $16; cash, check. **Parking:** At site.

FACILITIES
Number of Multipurpose Sites: 70. **Hookups:** None. **Each Site:** Picnic table, fire grate. **Dump Station:** Yes. **Laundry:** No. **Pay Phone:** Yes. **Restrooms and Showers:** Yes. **Fuel:** No. **Propane:** No. **Internal Roads:** Paved. **RV Service:** No. **Market:** 8 mi. south in Portola. **Restaurant:** 8 mi. south in Portola. **General Store:** No. **Vending:** No. **Swimming:** Frenchman Lake. **Playground:** No. **Other:** Boat launch 1 mi. north. **Activities:** Fishing, boating, hiking. **Nearby Attractions:** Portola Railroad Museum; Lakes Basin Recreation Area & Plumas-Eureka State Park in Graegle; Plumas County Museum in Quincy; Plumas National Forest. **Additional Information:** Plumas County Visitors Bureau, (530) 283-6345 or (800) 326-2247.

RESTRICTIONS

Pets: On leash. **Fires:** Fire grates only. **Alcoholic Beverages:** Allowed. **Vehicle Maximum Length:** 32 ft. **Other:** 14-day stay limit.

TO GET THERE

From downtown Portola head north on West St. and follow the sign for Lake Davis Recreation Area. West St. becomes Lake Davis Rd. Drive 7.7 mi. to the stop sign across the dam and turn left onto Beckwourth-Taylorsville Rd. The campground is 0.5 mi. ahead on the left.

PORTOLA — MAP, B-3
Spring Creek

Frenchman Lake Rd., 96105. T: (530) 836-2575 or (877) 444-6777; www.reserveamerica.com.

🚐 ★★★★　　🏕 ★★★★

Beauty: ★★★★	Site Privacy: ★★★
Spaciousness: ★★★★	Quiet: ★★★
Security: ★★★	Cleanliness: ★★★★
Insect Control: ★★★	Facilities: ★★

Spring Creek is a splendid oasis of pines and saltbush, and a smattering of aspen, standing in contrast to the refreshing blue-green waters of Frenchman Lake, just below the campground. This arid, mountain-fringed, high-desert domain sits on a hillside that is handsomely studded with volcanic rocks and tufa outcroppings. There is little screening between the level, pine-needle–carpeted sites, but they are decently spaced apart, with many—even those on the upper tier of the double loop—enjoying great pine-filtered views of the lake. While sites on average are rather spacious, the central positioning of fire rings and tables may pose problems for campers with large tents. Despite the rock-rimmed shore, access to the lake for boating and fishing is as easy as capsizing a canoe, with a boat ramp located at Frenchman Campground, just up the road. Of the reservable spots, the best for space, privacy, and water view are 30, 32, and 35. The concession that operates this Plumas National Forest facility offers double-size sites for twice the price of singles, and small bundles of firewood for $6, indications that inflation is making a comeback.

BASICS

Operated By: U.S.T. Wilderness Management Corp, concessionaire. **Open:** Apr. 29–Oct. 11; weather permitting. **Site Assignment:** Reservations accepted w/ V, MC, D. **Registration:** At entrance kiosk. **Fee:** $16; double site, $32; cash, check. **Parking:** At site.

FACILITIES

Number of RV-only Sites: 35. **Hookups:** None. **Each Site:** Picnic table, fire grate. **Dump Station:** No. **Laundry:** No. **Pay Phone:** No. **Restrooms and Showers:** Vault toilets, no showers. **Fuel:** No. **Propane:** No. **Internal Roads:** Paved. **RV Service:** No. **Market:** 10 mi. south in Chilcoot. **Restaurant:** 10 mi. south in Chilcoot. **General Store:** No. **Vending:** No. **Swimming:** Lake Davis. **Playground:** No. **Other:** Some wheelchair-accessible facilities. **Activi-**

ties: Fishing, boating, birding, hiking. **Nearby Attractions:** Frenchman Lake; Portola Railroad Museum; Lakes Basin Recreation Area in Graeagle; Plumas National Forest; Plumas-Eureka State Park near Graeagle. **Additional Information:** Plumas County Visitors Bureau, (530) 283-6345 or (800) 326-2247.

RESTRICTIONS

Pets: On leash. **Fires:** Fire grates only. **Alcoholic Beverages:** Allowed. **Vehicle Maximum Length:** 55 ft. **Other:** 14-day stay limit; no wood gathering.

TO GET THERE

From Portola on Hwy. 70 drive 17 mi. to Chilcoot and turn left on Frenchman Lake Rd. Continue for 8.6 mi., bear right and cross the dam. Proceed for 1.2 mi. and turn left into the campground.

QUAKING ASPEN — MAP, D-2
Quaking Aspen

Western Divide Hwy., 93208. T: (559) 539-3004 or (877) 444-6777; www.reserveamerica.com.

🚐 ★★★　　🏕 ★★★

Beauty: ★★★★	Site Privacy: ★★★
Spaciousness: ★★★	Quiet: ★★★★
Security: ★★★	Cleanliness: ★★★
Insect Control: ★★★	Facilities: ★

In most respects Quaking Aspen is a very average, unextraordinary campground. Yet its position, at 7,000 feet elevation in the heart of Giant Sequoia National Monument's southern unit, makes it an ideal base for day hikes into the area's sequoia groves. There is a grassy meadow on one side of this pretty, peaceful, hillside camp, and Freeman Creek flows nearby. Fair-sized sites of dirt and pine needles are set reasonably far apart around the double loop, and shaded by an abundance of lodgepole pines—but curiously few aspens. Units 12, 19, 21, and 29 are among the more recessed and shady, and 23 and 24 the more private ones in the meadow area. Tenters may want to consider Belknap (no trailers or RVs allowed), 9 miles west on Hwy. 190, where they can make camp under the protective aura of sequoia trees. Telephone, gasoline, propane, and a general store are available 2 miles south at Ponderosa Lodge.

BASICS

Operated By: California Land Management, concessionaire. **Open:** Mid-Apr.–mid-Nov.; weather permitting. **Site Assignment:** Reservations accepted w/ V, MC, D. **Registration:** At entrance kiosk. **Fee:** $14; cash, check. **Parking:** At site or in designated area.

FACILITIES

Number of RV-only Sites: 32. **Hookups:** None. **Each Site:** Picnic table, fire grate. **Dump Station:** No. **Laundry:** No. **Pay Phone:** No. **Restrooms and Showers:** Vault toilets, no showers. **Fuel:** No. **Propane:** No. **Internal Roads:** Paved. **RV Service:** No. **Market:** 40 mi. west in Porterville. **Restaurant:** 25 mi. west in Springville. **General Store:** No. **Vending:** No. **Swimming:** No. **Playground:** No.

Other: Some wheelchair-accessible facilities. **Activities:** Hiking, fishing, horseback riding. **Nearby Attractions:** Sequoia National Forest; Porterville Historical Museum & Zauld House & Gardens; California Hot Springs. **Additional Information:** Springville Chamber of Commerce, (559) 539-2312; Porterville Chamber of Commerce, (559) 784-7503.

RESTRICTIONS

Pets: On leash. **Fires:** Fire grates only. **Alcoholic Beverages:** Allowed. **Vehicle Maximum Length:** 24 ft. **Other:** 14-day stay limit.

TO GET THERE

From Porterville drive 40 mi. east on Hwy. 190 (which becomes the Western Divide Hwy.). The campground entrance is on the right.

RAMONA — MAP, F-3
Dos Picos Regional Park

17953 Dos Picos Park Rd., 92065. T: (858) 565-3600 or (877) 565-3600; www.sdparks.org.

🚐 ★★★★　　🏕 ★★★

Beauty: ★★★★	Site Privacy: ★★
Spaciousness: ★★★	Quiet: ★★★
Security: ★★	Cleanliness: ★★
Insect Control: ★	Facilities: ★★★

In the "location is everything" department, Dos Picos comes up a winner. It lies in a hillside riparian forest just a half-hour drive from downtown San Diego, and a little less than that from the San Diego Wild Animal Park in Escondido. The dirt- and grass-surfaced sites, spread out over several loops, are amply shaded by eucalyptus and live oak, with several enormous 300-year-olds among the latter. Of the many amenities here, highlights include a jogging track, soccer field, hiking trails, and a kids-only fishing pond. The park loses points, though, for such noise problems as many low-flying aircraft and neighborhood dogs barking throughout the night. Drivers of long RVs should plan to reserve site 56, one of the few with pull-through parking, while 9 and 12 are the more private, roomier tent options.

BASICS

Operated By: County of San Diego, Dept. of Parks & Recreation. **Open:** All year. **Site Assignment:** Reservations accepted w/ V, MC. **Registration:** At entrance booth. **Fee:** $12–$16; cash, V, MC. **Parking:** At site.

FACILITIES

Number of RV-only Sites: 62. **Hookups:** Electric (20 amps), water. **Each Site:** Picnic table, fire grate, barbecue grill. **Dump Station:** Yes. **Laundry:** No. **Pay Phone:** Yes. **Restrooms and Showers:** Yes. **Fuel:** No. **Propane:** No. **Internal Roads:** Paved. **RV Service:** No. **Market:** 5.5 mi. northeast in Ramona. **Restaurant:** 5.5 mi. northeast in Ramona. **General Store:** No. **Vending:** Yes. **Swimming:** No. **Playground:** Yes. **Other:** Limited wheelchair-accessible facilities. **Activities:** Hiking, children's fishing, horseshoe pit, jogging track, soccer field. **Nearby Attractions:** San Diego Wild Animal Park, San Pasqual Battlefield. **Additional Information:** Ramona Chamber of Commerce, (760) 789-1311.

RESTRICTIONS

Pets: On leash, not permitted on hiking trails. **Fires:** Fire grates only. **Alcoholic Beverages:** Allowed at site, not exceeding 40 proof. **Vehicle Maximum Length:** 35 ft. **Other:** 14-day stay limit; no firearms.

TO GET THERE

In Escondido drive 20 mi. east on Hwy. 78 to Ramona. Turn south on Hwy. 67 and drive 3.5 mi., then turn left on Mussey Grade Rd. and drive 1.1 mi. Turn right on Dos Picos Park Rd. The entrance is less than 1 mi. ahead.

RAYMOND MAP, D-2
Codorniz

reserve america

P.O. Box 67, 93653-0067. T: (559) 689-3255; www.reserveamerica.com.

🚐 ★★★★ ⛺ ★★★★

Beauty: ★★★	Site Privacy: ★★★
Spaciousness: ★★★	Quiet: ★★★★
Security: ★★★★	Cleanliness: ★★★★
Insect Control: ★★★	Facilities: ★★★

Codorniz Campground is located at Eastman Lake in the Sierra Nevada foothills about an hour drive north of Fresno. Eastman Lake is nestled in the Sierra Nevada foothills surrounded by grasslands and blue oaks. At maximum capacity, the lake has 1,780 surface acres and holds 150,000-acre feet of water. The lake was created by the construction of Buchanan Dam on the Chowchilla River. The dam is an earth- and rock-fill structure 205 feet high and 1,800 feet in length. At 600 feet elevation, summers are warm and the winters mild, allowing for year-round recreation. Built by the U.S. Army Corps of Engineers for flood control, irrigation, and recreation, the lake is a popular destination for visitors of all ages. Tall grasses and scattered oak trees cover the rolling hills surrounding the lake. Wildlife is abundant. Local residents include bobcats, golden eagles, mountain lions, hawks, wood ducks, deer, snakes, and bald eagles. The Codorniz Campground has 65 sites and is open all year. Three group camping areas in the Codorniz Recreation Area are available by reservation. Equestrian groups and non-profit organizations may also reserve the group equestrian area. The lake attracts a great number of boaters, water-skiers, sailors, pleasure boaters, and anglers. Launch ramps are located in the Chowchilla and Codorniz recreation areas. Eastman Lake has been designated as California's first Trophy Bass Fishery by the California Department of Fish and Game. Whether you are a beginner or an old pro, the lake offers a challenging fishing opportunity.

BASICS

Operated By: U.S. Army Corps of Engineers. **Open:** Apr. 20–Sept. 15. **Site Assignment:** Reservations must be made at least 3 days in advance. **Registration:** At office. **Fee:** $14–$22; group, $25–$75. **Parking:** At site.

FACILITIES

Number of Multipurpose Sites: 219. **Hookups:** Yes. **Dump Station:** Yes. **Laundry:** No. **Pay**

Phone: Yes. **Restrooms and Showers:** Yes. **Fuel:** No. **Propane:** No. **Internal Roads:** Paved. **RV Service:** No. **Market:** No. **Restaurant:** No. **General Store:** No. **Vending:** No. **Swimming:** Yes. **Playground:** Yes. **Activities:** Fishing, sightseeing, scuba diving, & picnicking.

RESTRICTIONS

Pets: Pets must be restrained or on a leash at all times while in developed recreation areas. **Fires:** In fire rings, stoves, grills, or fireplaces provided for that purpose. **Alcoholic Beverages:** Not allowed. **Vehicle Maximum Length:** Call ahead.

TO GET THERE

Codorniz is 30 mi. northeast of Madera, 25 mi. east of Chowchilla, and 50 mi. north of Fresno. From Hwy. 99, travel east on Ave. 26 then north on Rd 29. Follow signs into the campground.

REDDING MAP, B-2
Cooper Gulch

Trinity Dam Blvd., ,. T: (530) 226-2500; www.fs.fed.us/r5/shastatrinity.

🚐 ★★★★ ⛺ ★★★

Beauty: ★★★★	Site Privacy: ★★
Spaciousness: ★★	Quiet: ★★★
Security: ★★★★	Cleanliness: ★★★★
Insect Control: ★★★	Facilities: ★

The first thing you may notice about Cooper Gulch is the high-tension wires that run directly over the campground. That impression won't linger. Not when you see how close the five level sites are to the edge of Lewiston Lake. That they are also close to each other and lack privacy is not really a problem, either, since almost everybody devotes their attention to the rippling water just a few steps away. Bring your hammock and anchor it to a couple of the pines and incense cedars that shade this charming spot. And don't forget your canoe or kayak, which can be launched from the small dirt ramp right in camp. It is hard to go wrong with any of these medium-small, pine needle–carpeted sites, but 4 is closest to the lake and 5, sheltered by oaks, is the most private. Amazingly, a host occupies one of the five coveted slots in summer.

BASICS

Operated By: Hodge Management, concessionaire. **Open:** Apr.–Oct. **Site Assignment:** First come, first served. **Registration:** At entrance kiosk. **Fee:** $14; cash, check. **Parking:** At site.

FACILITIES

Number of RV-only Sites: 5. **Hookups:** None. **Each Site:** Picnic table, fire grate. **Dump Station:** No. **Laundry:** No. **Pay Phone:** No. **Restrooms and Showers:** Vault toilets, no showers. **Fuel:** No. **Propane:** No. **Internal Roads:** Paved. **RV Service:** No. **Market:** 4 mi. south in Lewiston. **Restaurant:** 4 mi. south in Lewiston. **General Store:** No. **Vending:** No. **Swimming:** No. **Playground:** No. **Other:** Some wheelchair-accessible facilities, small boat launch. **Activities:** Fishing, boating, hiking, birding. **Nearby Attractions:** Weaverville museums, National Historic District & Joss House State Historic Park; Historic Trinity River Bridge in Lewiston,

Trinity Alps Wilderness. **Additional Information:** Weaverville Chamber of Commerce, (530) 623-3840; Trinity County Chamber of Commerce, (530) 623-6101 or (800) 487-4648.

RESTRICTIONS

Pets: On 6-ft. leash. **Fires:** Fire grates only. **Alcoholic Beverages:** Allowed. **Vehicle Maximum Length:** 16 ft. **Other:** 14-day stay limit.

TO GET THERE

From Redding drive 26 mi. west on Hwy. 299 to Trinity Dam Blvd./Lewiston Exit. Turn right and continue for 8.6 mi. to the campground entrance on the right.

REDDING MAP, B-2
Nelson Point

reserve america

14538 Wonderland Blvd., 96051. T: (530) 275-1587 or (877) 444-6777; www.reserveamerica.com.

🚐 ★★★ ⛺ ★★★★

Beauty: ★★★★	Site Privacy: ★★★★
Spaciousness: ★★	Quiet: ★★
Security: ★	Cleanliness: ★★
Insect Control: ★	Facilities: ★

Nelson Point is a cozy property that rests on a grassy hill just above one rippling arm of Shasta Lake, a little more than 20 miles north of Redding. It is a convenient hop just off I-5, and that is also its major drawback: you may wake up in the middle of the night to the sound of traffic and think for a moment you're in a highway rest area. Oaks and pines hover over the dirt-surfaced sites, which are also spaced well apart along the meandering camp lane. While most spots enjoy water views, number 5, a walk-in of some 20 steps, is tops in spaciousness and occupies a small promontory that is blessed with a 180-degree panorama of the lake. More private is 7, though it lies close to the road, and 6, too, is tucked away from its neighbors. The appalling amount of broken glass, food debris, bottle caps, and even bullet shells littering the ground indicates that the concessionaire operating this diamond-in-the-rough for the Forest Service must do more to maintain the property than simply emptying the cash box. An elevation of just 1,000 feet makes for very comfortable evenings early and late in the year.

BASICS

Operated By: Shasta Recreation Company, concessionaire. **Open:** Apr. 1–Sept. 30. **Site Assignment:** Reservations accepted w/ V, MC, D for groups & limited number of sites; otherwise first come, first served. **Registration:** At entrance kiosk. **Fee:** $8; cash, check. **Parking:** At site.

FACILITIES

Number of Multipurpose Sites: 8. **Hookups:** None. **Each Site:** Picnic table, fire grate, some sites have stone fire ring. **Dump Station:** No. **Laundry:** No. **Pay Phone:** No. **Restrooms and Showers:** Vault toilets, no showers. **Fuel:** No. **Propane:** No. **Internal Roads:** Paved. **RV Service:** No. **Market:**

4 mi. north in Lakehead. **Restaurant:** 14 mi. south in Shasta Lake. **General Store:** No. **Vending:** No. **Swimming:** Shasta Lake inlet. **Playground:** No. **Activities:** Fishing, boating, waterskiing. **Nearby Attractions:** Turtle Bay Museums & Arboretum, Waterworks Park in Redding; Shasta Lake, Caverns, & Dam; Shasta State Historic Park; Whiskeytown National Recreation Area. **Additional Information:** Redding CVB, (530) 225-4100.

RESTRICTIONS

Pets: On 6-ft. leash. **Fires:** Fire grates only. **Alcoholic Beverages:** Allowed. **Vehicle Maximum Length:** 16 ft. **Other:** 14-day stay limit.

TO GET THERE

From Redding drive 22 mi. north on I-5 and exit at Salt Creek Rd./Gilman Rd. Turn left and drive 1 block, then veer right onto Salt Creek Rd. After 0.3 mi. turn left onto Conflict Point Rd. (opposite the highway underpass). The campground is 0.3 mi. ahead on the left.

RIDGECREST
Fossil Falls
MAP, E-3

300 Richmond Rd., 93555. T: (760) 384-5400; www.ca.blm.gov/caso/index.html.

🚐 ★★★★   ⛺ ★★★★

Beauty: ★★★★	Site Privacy: ★★★★
Spaciousness: ★★★★	Quiet: ★★★
Security: ★	Cleanliness: ★★★★
Insect Control: ★★★★	Facilities: ★

Heading north toward Lone Pine along US 395, there is a sign pointing the way to Fossil Falls, a geological site and campground. The falls in question are not fossilized, but rather a fantastic flow of hardened basaltic lava, spewed out of the eastern Coso Mountain range during a massive eruption 440,000 years ago. This little-known campground lies in a volcanic debris field in the arid Rose Valley, between the green-dappled Sierra Nevada to the west, China Lake naval base to the east, and a red cinder peak to the north. The sublime beauty of this desolate place is not universally appreciated, especially as the grounds are exposed to an unyielding sun and periodic high winds. There are no shade trees here, just low-lying desert scrub across the mildly undulating terrain. Level cinder-based sites, spread well apart over three loops, are among the largest we've come across, and they take advantage of volcanic tufts, spires, and mounds as privacy screening. Though this Bureau of Land Management facility lacks potable water and trash pick-up, the absence of ramadas is the most sorely felt omission. Gasoline and a pay phone are available 3 miles south at Little Lake.

BASICS

Operated By: Bureau of Land Management, Ridgecrest Field Office. **Open:** All year. **Site Assignment:** First come, first served. **Registration:** At entrance kiosk. **Fee:** $6; cash, check. **Parking:** At site.

FACILITIES

Number of RV-only Sites: 5. **Number of Tent-only Sites:** 6. **Hookups:** None. **Each Site:** Picnic table, fire grate. **Dump Station:** No. **Laundry:** No.

Pay Phone: No. **Restrooms and Showers:** Vault toilets, no showers. **Fuel:** W/in a few mi. **Propane:** No. **Internal Roads:** Cinder gravel, wide, & bumpy. **RV Service:** No. **Market:** 31 mi. south in Ridgecrest. **Restaurant:** 21 mi. south in Inyokern. **General Store:** No. **Vending:** No. **Swimming:** No. **Playground:** No. **Other:** Limited wheelchair-accessible facilities, Fossil Falls geological site. **Activities:** Hiking, birding, stargazing, rock scrambling, philosophical ruminating. **Nearby Attractions:** Trona Pinnacles; Last Chance Canyon & Maturango Museum/Death Valley Tourist Center in Ridgecrest; Death Valley National Park; Mount Whitney view; Lone Pine town. **Additional Information:** Ridgecrest Area CVB, (760) 375-8202 or (800) 847-4830.

RESTRICTIONS

Pets: On leash. **Fires:** Fire grates only. **Alcoholic Beverages:** Allowed. **Vehicle Maximum Length:** 30 ft. **Other:** 14-day stay limit.

TO GET THERE

From Ridgecrest drive 14 mi. west on Hwy. 178. Turn right on Hwy. 14/US 395. Continue 15 mi. and turn right at the sign for Fossil Falls. Proceed for 0.5 mi. and turn right again. The campground is 0.5 mi. ahead on the left.

RIO VISTA
Brannan Island State Recreation Area
MAP, C-2

reserve america

17645 CA 160, 94571. T: (916) 777-6671; www.reserveamerica.com.

🚐 ★★★★   ⛺ ★★★★

Beauty: ★★★	Site Privacy: ★★
Spaciousness: ★★	Quiet: ★★★★
Security: ★★★★	Cleanliness: ★★★★
Insect Control: ★★★	Facilities: ★★★

Brannan Island SRA is a maze of waterways through the Sacramento–San Joaquin Delta. This park northeast of San Francisco Bay has countless islands and marshes with many wildlife habitats and many opportunities for recreation, including boating, windsurfing, and swimming. The area offers great fishing, including striped bass, sturgeon, catfish, bluegill, perch, and bullhead. To the southeast and accessed by the San Joaquin River, Frank's Tract, a protected wetland marsh, is home to beaver, muskrat, river otter, mink, and 76 species of birds. Brannan Island Park, about 336 acres in size, has a six-lane launch ramp, over 140 campsites, and areas for picnicking and swimming. Day-use areas include the Windy Cove windsurfing access, the group picnic area located at the Ramadas, and Seven Mile Slough picnic area. Seven Mile Slough's swim beach has lifeguards from Memorial Day through Labor Day. Ample parking is close to the beach. The Ramadas have shaded picnic structures with large barbecues, picnic tables, water, and trash receptacles. A large open grassy area is adjacent to the site for games. The closest restroom to the Ramadas is located north of the swim beach along Seven Mile Slough.

BASICS

Operated By: California Dept. of Parks & Recreation. **Open:** All year. **Site Assignment:** Reservations can be made 7 months in advance. **Registration:** At office. **Fee:** Single, $15–$20; group, $40–$66. **Parking:** At site.

FACILITIES

Number of Multipurpose Sites: 103. **Hookups:** None. **Each Site:** Fire ring. **Dump Station:** Yes. **Laundry:** No. **Pay Phone:** No. **Restrooms and Showers:** Yes. **Fuel:** No. **Propane:** No. **Internal Roads:** Paved. **RV Service:** No. **Market:** No. **Restaurant:** No. **General Store:** No. **Vending:** No. **Swimming:** Yes. **Playground:** No. **Activities:** Boating, fishing, hiking, picnicking.

RESTRICTIONS

Pets: On 6-ft. leash in a tent or enclosed vehicle at night. Except for guide dogs, pets are not allowed in park buildings, on trails, or on most beaches. **Fires:** In designated fireplaces. **Alcoholic Beverages:** Not allowed.

TO GET THERE

The park is on Hwy. 160, 3 mi. south of Rio Vista.

RIPON
Caswell Memorial State Park
MAP, C-2

reserve america

28000 South Austin Rd., 95366-9527.
T: (209) 599-3810; www.reserveamerica.com.

🚐   ⛺ ★★★★

Beauty: ★★★★★	Site Privacy: ★★★
Spaciousness: ★★	Quiet: ★★★★★
Security: ★★★★★	Cleanliness: ★★★★
Insect Control: ★★★	Facilities: ★★

Caswell Memorial State Park is a small, wild refuge in the midst of Central Valley of California. This unique park protects one of the last remaining riparian oak woodlands that once flourished throughout the valley. The Native Americans who lived along this river and collected acorns among these ancient groves were Yokuts. In the early 1800s, Spanish explorers traversed this area, and fur trappers found the river bountiful. The 258-acre park was started with a donation of 134 acres by the descendants of Thomas Caswell, a landowner in the area. It grew to its current size through additional donations and state purchases, and Caswell Memorial State Park was open to the public in 1958. The Stanislaus River meanders through the park, with beaches and swimming areas near the parks day-use and campground facilities. The seemingly endless natural trails allow a glimpse of what the riparian ecosystem of the valley would have looked like in pristine times. A majestic oak forest is surrounded by many other lush plant species, some of which are rarely found anywhere else in the area. The park offers a rich variety of wildlife viewing. While many of the wildlife species here are nocturnal and rarely seen, bird-watching is a favorite among nature lovers. Red-shouldered and red-tailed hawks are often seen, along with dozens of other winged artists. In a pleasant wooded area beside the river there are 64 family campsites. Drinking water taps and restrooms with hot showers are nearby. Hookups are not available. The group campground will accommodate tent camping for 50 people.

BASICS

Operated By: California Dept. of Parks & Recreation. **Open:** All year. **Site Assignment:** Reservations can be made 7 months in advance. **Registration:** At office. **Fee:** Single, $13–$20; group, $67–$110. **Parking:** At site.

FACILITIES

Number of Multipurpose Sites: 59. **Hookups:** None. **Each Site:** Fire ring. **Dump Station:** No. **Laundry:** No. **Pay Phone:** No. **Restrooms and Showers:** Yes. **Fuel:** No. **Propane:** No. **Internal Roads:** Paved. **RV Service:** No. **Market:** No. **Restaurant:** No. **General Store:** No. **Vending:** No. **Swimming:** Yes. **Playground:** No. **Activities:** Fishing, hiking, picnicking.

RESTRICTIONS

Pets: On 6-ft. leash in a tent or enclosed vehicle at night. Except for guide dogs, pets are not allowed in park buildings, on trails, or on most beaches. **Fires:** In designated fireplaces. **Alcoholic Beverages:** Not allowed.

TO GET THERE

In Ripon, take the Austin Rd. exit off of SR 99. Travel south on Austin Rd. for approximately 6 mi. Austin Rd. leads directly into the park.

SAN CLEMENTE   MAP, F-3
San Clemente State Beach

reserve america

3030 Avenida del Presidente, 92672. T: (949) 492-3156 or (800) 444-7275; www.reserveamerica.com.

🚐 ★★★★   ⛺ ★★★

Beauty: ★★★	Site Privacy: ★★★
Spaciousness: ★★★	Quiet: ★★
Security: ★★★★	Cleanliness: ★★★★
Insect Control: ★★★★	Facilities: ★★★

San Clemente seems to be in a constant state of renewal. Your best bet is to steer toward the two loops that lack hookups; marginally more spacious and with a bit of screening, sites there are also positioned on grass instead of the dirt surface of the RV lot. Especially roomy are 83 and 85, both of which overlook the beach and cliffs. Monterey pines, eucalyptus, and flowering ceanothus are scattered throughout the park, lending an attractive look to the domain. Less appealing is the occasional use of prison labor for landscaping.

BASICS

Operated By: California Dept. of Parks & Recreation. **Open:** All year. **Site Assignment:** Reservations recommended; V, MC, D; first come first served. **Registration:** At entrance booth. **Fee:** $16–$34; cash, CA check. **Parking:** At site. $5 per vehicle.

FACILITIES

Number of RV-only Sites: 160. **Hookups:** Electric (30 amps), water, sewer. **Each Site:** Picnic table, fire ring; non-hookup sites have ramada, barbecue grill, spigot. **Dump Station:** Yes. **Laundry:** No. **Pay Phone:** Yes. **Restrooms and Showers:** Yes, coin operated showers. **Fuel:** No, for boats only. **Propane:** No. **Internal Roads:** Paved. **RV Service:** No. **Market:** 2 mi. north in San Clemente. **Restaurant:** 2 mi. north in San Clemente. **General Store:** Yes, the marina & beach store. **Vending:** No. **Swimming:** Pacific Ocean (less than 0.5 mi.). **Playground:** No. **Other:** Some wheelchair-accessible facilities, boat launch, marina. **Activities:** Surfing, swimming, bicycling, 2 mi. of hiking trails, boat rentals. **Nearby Attractions:** Pacific Crest Trail. **Additional Information:** San Clemente Chamber of Commerce, (949) 492-1131.

RESTRICTIONS

Pets: On 6-ft. leash. Must have current shots, visible tags, or paperwork. **Fires:** Fire grates only; no fires in the boating areas or Miller Canyon. **Alcoholic Beverages:** Allowed at site. **Vehicle Maximum Length:** 34 ft. **Other:** 7-day stay limit; no firearms; no wood gathering.

TO GET THERE

In San Clemente exit I-5 on Avenida Calafia and proceed for 0.2 mi. Turn left (west) into the park.

SAN CLEMENTE   MAP, F-3
San Mateo Campground

San Onofre State Beach, 3030 Avenida Del Presidente, 92672. T: (949) 361-2531; www.cal-parks.ca.gov or www.caescapes.com.

🚐 ★★★★   ⛺ ★★★

Beauty: ★★★	Site Privacy: ★★★
Spaciousness: ★★★	Quiet: ★★★
Security: ★★★	Cleanliness: ★★★
Insect Control: ★★★	Facilities: ★★★

San Onofre State Beach is composed of two campgrounds, the Bluff Area by the beach and San Mateo, 1 mile inland off of I-5. Forget about privacy at the Bluff Area, where sites are lined up one after another on a tiny stretch of turf alongside the parking area. Tranquility is another lost cause: trains hurtle along tracks just 100 feet from camp, basically paralleling its linear layout, and a few yards beyond an interstate highway reverberates to the continuous roar of traffic. Then there is the multitude of college-age campers that descends on the park from mid-spring through early September, filling it with the off-key melodies of their raucous partying and straining facilities beyond the capacity of the maintenance staff. Sites at San Mateo, by contrast, while not large, are at least scattered over three loops and enjoy decent privacy. The atmosphere is calmer—dare we say more sedate?—and setting more lush, though fine views of the coastal hills are somewhat offset by opposing vistas of power lines and produce fields. Both camps suffer from occasional helicopter overflights from neighboring Camp Pendleton. The best time to visit is from early spring through mid-

summer, while the grass in the sites is still soft and green. Your San Mateo receipt covers the day-use fee at the Bluff Area beach.

BASICS

Operated By: California Dept. of Parks & Recreation. **Open:** All year. **Site Assignment:** Reservations recommended; V, MC, D. **Registration:** At entrance booth. **Fee:** Off-season rates (Dec. 1–Feb. 28): $13–$19. Peak rates (Mar. 1–Nov. 30): $16–$22. $5 fee for additional vehicle. Cash or CA check, good for day use at San Onofre State Beach Bluffs Area. **Parking:** At site. Extra car is $5 per night.

FACILITIES

Number of RV-only Sites: 67. **Number of Multipurpose Sites:** 90. **Hookups:** Electric (30 amps), water. **Each Site:** Picnic table, fire grate. **Dump Station:** Yes. **Laundry:** No. **Pay Phone:** Yes. **Restrooms and Showers:** Yes, showers are coin operated. **Fuel:** No, in San Clemente. 2 mi. north. **Propane:** No. **Internal Roads:** Paved. **RV Service:** No, in San Clemente. 2 mi. north. **Market:** No, in San Clemente. 2 mi. north. **Restaurant:** No, in San Clemente. 2 mi. north. **General Store:** No. **Vending:** No. **Swimming:** Pacific Ocean (1.1 mi.). **Playground:** No. **Other:** Some wheelchair-accessible facilities. **Activities:** Surfing, bicycling, nature trails, skate boarding, helicopter spotting. **Nearby Attractions:** San Clemente, Dana Point, Mission San Juan Capistrano. **Additional Information:** San Clemente Chamber of Commerce, (949) 492-1131.

RESTRICTIONS

Pets: On 6-ft. leash. **Fires:** Fire grates only. **Alcoholic Beverages:** Allowed at site. **Vehicle Maximum Length:** 36 ft. at sites w/ no hookups; 32 ft. max. at hookup sites. **Other:** 14-day stay limit from Memorial Day through Labor Day.

TO GET THERE

From I-5 in San Clemente take the Cristianitos Rd. Exit and proceed inland for 1 mi. Turn right into the campground, which lacks adequate signposting.

SAN DIMAS   MAP, E-3
East Shore RV Park

1440 Camperview Rd., 91773. T: (909) 599-8355; www.eastshorervpark.com.

🚐 ★★★★   ⛺ ★★

Beauty: ★★	Site Privacy: ★★
Spaciousness: ★★★	Quiet: ★★★
Security: ★★★★	Cleanliness: ★★★
Insect Control: ★★★	Facilities: ★★★★★

When you arrive at East Shore RV Park you will be handed map of the property, which is a good thing, as without it you can forget about navigating your way through its maze of loops. Located just 30 miles east of downtown Los Angeles, above the shores of Puddingstone Lake and within Frank Bonelli Regional Park, not only is this place attractively landscaped, with undulating meadows accented by such trees as alder, eucalyptus, sycamore, magnolia, and a range of conifers, but it also is well endowed with a whole host of facilities. You want boating or fishing? You've got it. Looking to play some golf? No problem. Need to hook up to the Internet? That's a "can-do," too. And security is tighter than a martinet's collar, with both an entrance-booth checkpoint and regular ranger patrols. That sites tend to be wedged rather snugly together only really impacts tenters. And for them East Shore has set aside a wilderness-area meadow, a dubious amenity with undesignated sites on ground so curvaceous as to be unusable by RVs. Two small knocks on this outfit are the occasional buzz of airplanes using the neighboring county airport and restrooms that should be equipped with real mirrors instead of the shatterproof stainless steel more commonly seen in cut-rate national-forest properties.

BASICS

Operated By: East Shore RV Park, Phyllis Cook. **Open:** All year. **Site Assignment:** Reservations accepted w/ MC, V, D. **Registration:** At office. **Fee:** $32–$34. **Parking:** At site.

FACILITIES

Number of RV-only Sites: 519. **Number of Tent-only Sites:** 14. **Hookups:** Electric (20, 30, 50 amps), water, sewer, cable TV. **Each Site:** Picnic table, fire grate (not at every site). **Dump Station:** Yes, $5 fee. **Laundry:** Yes. **Pay Phone:** Yes. **Restrooms and Showers:** Yes. **Fuel:** No. **Propane:** Yes. **Internal Roads:** Paved. **RV Service:** No. **Market:** Yes. **Restaurant:** 3 mi. north in San Dimas. **General Store:** Yes. **Vending:** Yes. **Swimming:** 2 pools. **Playground:** Yes. **Other:** Some wheelchair-accessible facilities. **Activities:** Fishing, boating, waterskiing, hiking, bicycling, volleyball, horseshoe pit, horseback riding rentals, golf. **Nearby Attractions:** Disneyland, Six Flags Magic Mountain, Riverside & its museums, gardens, & historic buildings. **Additional Information:** Pomona Chamber of Commerce, (909) 622-1256.

RESTRICTIONS

Pets: On leash, $2 fee per night for dogs. **Fires:** Fire grates only; 20 inches off the ground in other areas. **Alcoholic Beverages:** Allowed. **Vehicle Maximum Length:** 45 ft. **Other:** 7-day stay limit for tents, 28-day stay limit for RVs.

TO GET THERE

From I-10 at Pomona, take Exit 44A/Fairplex Dr. Proceed north for 0.7 mi. and turn left on Via Verde. After 0.5 mi., at the stop sign, turn right on Campers View. The park is straight ahead.

SAN FRANCISCO   MAP, C-1, C-2
Candlestick RV Park

650 Gilman Ave., 94124. T: (415) 822-2299 or (800) 888-CAMP; www.sanfranciscorvpark.com.

🚐 ★★★★	🏕 ★
Beauty: ★★★	Site Privacy: ★
Spaciousness: ★	Quiet: ★★
Security: ★★★★	Cleanliness: ★★★★
Insect Control: ★★★★	Facilities: ★★★★

Short of setting up camp in Golden Gate Park, it is hard to imagine bivouacking much closer to San Francisco than in Candlestick RV Park. This facility is located directly across the street from 3Com Stadium, nee Candlestick Park, just 5 miles south of downtown. While its parking-lot layout and the chain-link security fence that encompasses the compound are not very appealing, management has done an admirable job of sowing a variety of exotic plants and trees around the perimeter. As usual for this sort of property, parking slots seem crowded together on the asphalt with no screening and negligible shade. A narrow strip of grass has been set aside for tenters but it seems to get more traffic from dogs, despite a rule that mandates dog-walking outside the fence. The washrooms, on the other hand, tend to be immaculate. Just down the street is Candlestick Point State Recreation Area, with a bike trail, picnic area, and bay access via a boat ramp. Also nearby, alas, is the airport, with loud flyovers common enough to make you wish your RV had double-pane glass. A shuttle service is available to ferry campers to downtown San Francisco.

BASICS

Operated By: Candlestick RV Park. **Open:** All year. **Site Assignment:** Reservations recommended; V, MC, AE. **Registration:** At entrance office. **Fee:** $46–$49; cash, V, MC, AE. **Parking:** At site.

FACILITIES

Number of RV-only Sites: 118. **Number of Tent-only Sites:** 47. **Hookups:** Electric (30, 50 amps), water, sewer, Internet in the office. **Each Site:** Picnic table in some sites. **Dump Station:** No. **Laundry:** Yes. **Pay Phone:** Yes. **Restrooms and Showers:** Yes. **Fuel:** Less than 1 mi. **Propane:** Yes. **Internal Roads:** Paved. **RV Service:** Inquire in office. **Market:** 4 mi. south in San Francisco. **Restaurant:** 1 mi. south in San Francisco. **General Store:** Yes. **Vending:** Yes. **Swimming:** No. **Playground:** No. **Other:** Some wheelchair-accessible facilities, game room, free video tapes. **Activities:** Touring San Francisco, hiking the San Francisco Bay shoreline, surfing. **Nearby Attractions:** Candlestick Point State Recreation Area; museums, Ghirardelli Square, Fisherman's Wharf, zoo, aquarium, Golden Gate Park, & much more in San Francisco. **Additional Information:** San Francisco CVB, (415) 391-2000.

RESTRICTIONS

Pets: On leash. **Fires:** Grill only. **Alcoholic Beverages:** Allowed. **Vehicle Maximum Length:** 45 ft. **Other:** 29-day stay limit; no generators.

TO GET THERE

From San Francisco drive south on US 101 to the 3Com Stadium Exit. Drive around the stadium, about 1 mi., to gate 4. The park entrance is directly opposite to that, on the right.

SANTA BARBARA   MAP, E-2
Cachuma Lake Recreation Area

Hwy. 154, 93105. T: (805) 686-5054; www.cachuma.com.

🚐 ★★★★	🏕 ★★★
Beauty: ★★★★	Site Privacy: ★★★
Spaciousness: ★★★	Quiet: ★★★
Security: ★★★★	Cleanliness: ★★★★
Insect Control: ★★	Facilities: ★★★★★

Confusion is an understandable state of mind for first-time visitors to Cachuma Lake. This is a huge campground, with more than 500 mostly level, grassy sites dispersed through an intricate maze of loops. Though the recreation area is less than 20 miles from Santa Barbara, the large shimmering body of water is surrounded by the relatively undeveloped Santa Ynez and San Rafael Mountains. There will be no roughing it here, though, because Cachuma has just about every possible amenity necessary to comfortable camping (and a good deal that probably aren't), including a snack bar and on-site gas station, and rentals of various size boats, bikes, golf clubs, and even yurts. The large domain is semiforested with mature sycamores, oaks, manzanita, and holly, and if most sites lack privacy, at least a good percentage overlook the water. At an elevation of only 800 feet, weather at this park is pleasant throughout the year. Be sure to check out the excellent nature center (open weekends) for its Native American exhibits and to make reservations for naturalist-led wildlife cruises.

BASICS

Operated By: Santa Barbara County Parks. **Open:** All year. **Site Assignment:** Reservations accepted for group camping only w/ V, MC, D. **Registration:** At entrance booth. **Fee:** $18–$25; cash, CA check. AAA, FMCA, Good Sam, & senior discounts available. **Parking:** At site, 2-car limit.

FACILITIES

Number of RV-only Sites: 154. **Number of Multipurpose Sites:** 339. **Hookups:** Electric (20, 30 amps), water, sewer. **Each Site:** Picnic table, fire ring (not in full-hookup sites). **Dump Station:** Yes. **Laundry:** Yes. **Pay Phone:** Yes. **Restrooms and Showers:** Yes. **Fuel:** Yes. **Propane:** Yes. **Internal Roads:** Paved. **RV Service:** No. **Market:** 10 mi. west in Santa Ynez. **Restaurant:** In campground or 10 mi. west in Santa Ynez. **General Store:** Yes. **Vending:** No. **Swimming:** Pool ($1 per hour). **Playground:** Yes. **Other:** Some wheelchair-accessible facilities, marina, boat launch, family fun center, nature center. **Activities:** Fishing, hiking, horseshoe pit, boat & bicycle rentals, mini-golf, volleyball, horseback riding, wildlife cruises. **Nearby Attractions:** Solvang & its mission & museums; Chumash Painted Cave State Historic Park; Santa Barbara & its mission, museums, historic buildings, zoo, Stearns Wharf, & botanic garden. **Additional Information:** Santa Barbara Region Chamber of Commerce, (805) 965-3023.

RESTRICTIONS

Pets: On 6-ft. leash; proof of rabies vaccination required; $3 fee; not w/in 50 ft. of shoreline not in boats. **Fires:** Fire ring only. **Alcoholic Beverages:** Allowed at site. **Vehicle Maximum Length:** No limit. **Other:** 14-day stay limit from Apr. 1–Sept. 14, 90-day limit the rest of the year.

TO GET THERE

In Santa Barbara exit US 101 on Hwy. 154 and drive 18 mi. north to the park entrance on the right.

SANTA BARBARA   MAP, E-2
El Capitan State Beach

reserve america

10 Refugio Beach Rd., 93117. T: (805) 968-1033 or (800) 444-7275; www.reserveamerica.com.

🚐 ★★★★   ▲ ★★★★

Beauty: ★★★★   Site Privacy: ★★★
Spaciousness: ★★★   Quiet: ★★★
Security: ★★★   Cleanliness: ★★★★
Insect Control: ★★★   Facilities: ★★★

El Capitan is not your typical beach campground. Though its four loops are set amidst a series of coastal bluffs, there is more of grass and dirt than sand in the surprisingly roomy, agreeably private sites. And aside from the time you spend on the beach, you won't need a parasol: much of the domain, which is just off Hwy. 101, 17 miles northwest of Santa Barbara, lies within a lush forest of live oak, with a few eucalyptus, sycamores, and pines tossed in for good measure. Tent campers looking for a water view should try for sites 75, 76, 78, and 80 in the third loop; RVers desiring the same will do well with 110, 111, 114, and 116 in the fourth and highest loop. The first circuit (sites 1–31), on the other hand, is one to avoid, lying nearest the railroad tracks and with no view of the ocean. This is one of the prettier beach campgrounds we've seen, with the terrain particularly green and delightful in spring.

BASICS

Operated By: California Dept. of Parks & Recreation. **Open:** All year. **Site Assignment:** First come, first served; reservations recommended; V, MC, D. **Registration:** At entrance booth. **Fee:** $16–$25; additional vehicles, $4; cash, CA check. **Parking:** At site. 3 vehicle max. $4 per additional vehicle.

FACILITIES

Number of RV-only Sites: 142. **Hookups:** None. **Each Site:** Picnic table, barbecue pit w/ grill. **Dump Station:** Yes. **Laundry:** No. **Pay Phone:** Yes. **Restrooms and Showers:** Yes, fee for showers. **Fuel:** No. **Propane:** No. **Internal Roads:** Paved. **RV Service:** No. Market: 13 mi. east in Goleta. **Restaurant:** 13 mi. east in Goleta. **General Store:** Yes, seasonal (Memorial Day thru Labor Day). **Vending:** Yes. **Swimming:** Pacific Ocean. **Playground:** No. **Other:** Some wheelchair-accessible facilities. **Activities:** Fishing, hiking, bicycling, boogie-board rentals. **Nearby Attractions:** Santa Barbara & its museums, historic buildings, zoo, Stearns Wharf, botanic garden, Mission Santa Barbara, Goleta South Coast Railroad Museum. **Additional Information:** Goleta Valley Chamber of Commerce, (805) 967-4618.

RESTRICTIONS

Pets: On 6-ft. leash under owner's supervision. Not allowed on beach. **Fires:** Fire ring only. **Alcoholic Beverages:** Allowed at site. **Vehicle Maximum Length:** 30 ft. **Other:** 7-day stay limit from June 1– Sept. 30; no firearms; no wood gathering.

TO GET THERE

From Santa Barbara drive 17 mi. west on US 101 and exit on El Capitan State Beach. Turn left (west) and proceed for 0.3 mi., under the railroad trestle, straight into the campground.

SANTA BARBARA   MAP, E-2
Gaviota State Park

reserve america

Hwy. 101, 93117. T: (805) 968-1033; www.reserveamerica.com.

🚐 ★★★   ▲ ★★★

Beauty: ★★★★   Site Privacy: ★★
Spaciousness: ★★   Quiet: ★★
Security: ★★★   Cleanliness: ★★★
Insect Control: ★★★   Facilities: ★★

Aside from the mature eucalyptus trees at the edge of the dusty campground, the few saplings here have only recently been planted; it will be years before they mature into shade trees—if they survive. Yet this park, which lies just off Hwy. 101, 30 miles northwest of Santa Barbara, is thrillingly set between a steep series of scenic bluffs and an unspoiled beach. To reach the shore you must walk beneath a century-old railroad trestle (more of a curiosity than noise nuisance) elevated some 75 feet off the ground. The pier by the water is fine for fishing and is equipped with a hoist for launching boats. A hot spring is located in the hills above Gaviota. The strong coastal breezes funneling through camp most afternoons and evenings make the packing of a jacket or sweater advisable.

BASICS

Operated By: California Dept. of Parks & Recreation. **Open:** All year. **Site Assignment:** First come, first served. **Registration:** At entrance booth. **Fee:** $8–$13; cash, CA check. **Parking:** At site.

FACILITIES

Number of RV-only Sites: 52. **Hookups:** None. **Each Site:** Picnic table, fire grate. **Dump Station:** No. **Laundry:** No. **Pay Phone:** Yes. **Restrooms and Showers:** Yes. **Fuel:** No. **Propane:** No. **Internal Roads:** Paved. **RV Service:** No. **Market:** 11 mi. north in Buëllton. **Restaurant:** 11 mi. north in Buëllton. **General Store:** Yes (summer only). **Vending:** No. **Swimming:** Pacific Ocean. **Playground:** No. **Other:** Some wheelchair-accessible facilities. **Activities:** Fishing, hiking, surfing, horseback riding. **Nearby Attractions:** Mission Santa Inés & museums in Solvang, La Purísima Mission State Historic Park in Lompoc, Santa Barbara & its museums, historic buildings, zoo, Stearns Wharf, botanic garden. **Additional Information:** Goleta Valley Chamber of Commerce, (805) 967-4618.

RESTRICTIONS

Pets: On 6-ft. leash. **Fires:** Fire grates only. **Alcoholic Beverages:** Allowed at site. **Vehicle Maximum Length:** 27 ft. **Other:** 14-day stay limit; no firearms; no wood gathering.

TO GET THERE

From Santa Barbara drive 30 mi. west on US 101 and take the Gaviota State Beach Exit to the left. Continue straight for 5 mi. to the park entrance.

SANTA CRUZ   MAP, D-1
Big Basin Redwoods State Park

reserve america

21600 Big Basin Way, 95006. T: (831) 338-8860 or (800) 444-7275; www.reserveamerica.com.

🚐 ★★★★   ▲ ★★★★

Beauty: ★★★★★   Site Privacy: ★★★
Spaciousness: ★★★   Quiet: ★★
Security: ★★★   Cleanliness: ★★★★
Insect Control: ★★★   Facilities: ★★★

Unlike the nearby Henry Cowell Redwoods State Park, Big Basin puts campers right in the center of a dramatic redwood forest. A fair amount of sunlight filters through the dense cluster of giants—which dwarf the tan oaks and hemlocks among them—and an abundance of mossy rocks and fallen trees decorate the thick blanket of redwood needles layered on the ground. Average-size sites offer minimal privacy but their distribution over four separate campgrounds helps to reduce incidental noise. Big Basin was established in 1902 as California's first state park. Of its more than 80 miles of trails, the Berry Creek Falls hike (11 miles round trip), which threads past a superb series of redwoods to a pretty waterfall, should be atop your to-do list. Although just 24 miles northwest of Santa Cruz, the road into the park, Hwy. 236, is very slow and winding. Tent cabins are in separate loop and are reserved by a concessionaire at (831) 338-4745

BASICS

Operated By: California Dept. of Parks & Recreation. **Open:** All year; most campgrounds closed in winter (except Huckleberry). **Site Assignment:** Reservations recommended during summer; V, MC, D. **Registration:** At park headquarters. **Fee:** $20–$25; additional vehicle, $5; cash, CA check. **Parking:** At site. $5 fee for any additional vehicles.

FACILITIES

Number of RV-only Sites: 31. **Number of Tent-only Sites:** 68. **Number of Multipurpose Sites:** 38. **Hookups:** None. **Each Site:** Picnic table, fire grate, food storage box. **Dump Station:** Yes. **Laundry:** Yes, only in the tent cabin loop which is a separate concessionaire. **Pay Phone:** Yes. **Restrooms and Showers:** Yes. **Fuel:** No. **Propane:** Yes. **Internal Roads:** Paved, some potholes. **RV Service:** No. **Market:** 9.5 mi. southeast in Boulder Creek. **Restaurant:** 9.5 mi. southeast in Boulder Creek. **General Store:** Yes. **Vending:** No. **Swimming:** No. **Playground:** No. **Other:** Some wheelchair-accessible facilities. **Activities:** Hiking, photography, exploring redwood forests. **Nearby Attractions:** Mission Santa Clara de Asis & various museums in Santa Clara; Hakone Japanese Gardens & Saso Herb Gardens in Saratoga; state beaches along the coast. **Additional Information:** Santa Clara CVB,

(408) 224-9660 or (800) 272-6822; Saratoga Chamber of Commerce, (408) 867-0753.

RESTRICTIONS

Pets: On 6-ft. leash. Not allowed on trails. **Fires:** Fire grates only. **Alcoholic Beverages:** Allowed at site. **Vehicle Maximum Length:** 27 ft. **Other:** 30-day stay limit; no firearms; no wood gathering.

TO GET THERE

From Santa Cruz drive 13.3 mi. north on Hwy. 9 to Boulder Creek. Turn left (west) on Hwy. 236 and continue for 8 mi. to the park entrance. The park headquarters are 1 mi. down the road.

SANTA ROSA   MAP, C-2
Spring Lake Regional Park

391 Violetti Dr., 95403. T: (707) 539-8092 or (707) 565-2267; www.sonoma-county.org/parks.

🚐 ★★★   ▲ ★★★

Beauty: ★★★★	Site Privacy: ★★★
Spaciousness: ★★★	Quiet: ★★★
Security: ★★★	Cleanliness: ★★★
Insect Control: ★★★	Facilities: ★★★

Spring Lake is a small body of water encircled by rolling hills of mature oaks, pines, and bay trees. It is a calm retreat just a few minutes from the heart of suburban Santa Rosa. As such, it is hardly a well-kept secret, and you are liable to have company here at almost any time of year. No problem, the grass-covered sites are large enough for you to comfortably spread out your gear, and decently spaced apart around a tree-dotted meadow. Lichen-speckled rocks are scattered across the turf, adding to the natural feel of this agreeable camp. Some sites are impacted by a gentle slope toward the water, and none are graced with a view of the lake. Still, there is a good amount of fine slots, with 28 and 30, at the loop's periphery, ideal for RVers desiring privacy. Sites 5, 26, and 27 are equipped with pull-through parking. Tent campers who don't mind being some distance from their cars should grab 12 or 14, which are secluded and give access to the lake. Note that from October 1 through April the campground is only open on weekends and holidays.

BASICS

Operated By: County of Sonoma, Regional Parks Dept. **Open:** May 1–Sept. 30; weekends & holidays only from Oct. 1–Apr. 30; group sites open year-round. **Site Assignment:** Reservations recommended especially during summer. (V, MC). **Registration:** At entrance office. **Fee:** $16, cash or CA check. $5 fee for each additional vehicle. **Parking:** At site. $5 fee for each additional vehicle.

FACILITIES

Number of RV-only Sites: 27. **Number of Tent-only Sites:** 4. **Hookups:** None. **Each Site:** Picnic table, fire grate, food storage box. **Dump Station:** Yes. **Laundry:** No. **Pay Phone:** Yes. **Restrooms and Showers:** Yes. **Fuel:** No. **Propane:** No. **Internal Roads:** Paved. **RV Service:** No. **Market:** 2 mi. west in Santa Rosa. **Restaurant:** 2 mi. west in Santa Rosa. **General Store:** No, snack stand 0.5 mi. from campground. **Vending:** No. **Swimming:** Swimming lagoon (Memorial Day–Labor Day). **Playground:** No.

Other: Some wheelchair-accessible facilities, boat ramp, fishing pier, visitor center, snack stand nearby. **Activities:** Hiking, bicycling, horseback riding, windsurfing. **Nearby Attractions:** Annadel State Park, Santa Rosa museums & Luther Burbank Home & Gardens; San Francisco Solano Mission & winery tours in Sonoma, Santa Rosa City Park. **Additional Information:** Santa Rosa CVB, (800) 404-ROSE; Sonoma County Tourism Program, (800) 5-SONOMA or (707) 565-5383.

RESTRICTIONS

Pets: On 6-ft. leash; rabies certificate required; $1 fee. **Fires:** Fire grates only. **Alcoholic Beverages:** Allowed at site. **Vehicle Maximum Length:** 40 ft. (some 70 ft. available. Call for details). **Other:** 10-day stay limit; no firearms; no wood gathering.

TO GET THERE

From Santa Rosa on US 101 take Hwy. 12 east. After 1.25 mi. exit onto Hoen Frontage Rd. which turns into Hoen Ave. After 1.5 mi. turn left on Newanga Ave., which veers sharply to the right. The park entrance is 0.6 mi. ahead.

SANTEE   MAP, F-3
Santee Lakes Regional Park and Campground

9310 Fanita Parkway, 92071. T: (619) 596-3141; www.santeelakes.com/campinghome.htm.

🚐 ★★★★   ▲ ★★

Beauty: ★★★★★	Site Privacy: ★★★
Spaciousness: ★★★★★	Quiet: ★★★
Security: ★★★★★	Cleanliness: ★★★★
Insect Control: ★★	Facilities: ★★★★★

For comfort in camping, Santee Lakes merits an enthusiastic "thumbs up." From tight security to remarkably clean restrooms, from a heated pool to modem hookup in the office, RV camping does not get much better than this. California sycamores, eucalyptus, and palm trees hover over the lush, grassy grounds, which also encompass a series of seven lakes—ponds, really. One of those is dotted with tiny islands and has been set aside for canoeing and pedal boats. Two others are stocked with fish, and the great number of waterfront sites means that anglers can camp where the action is. Still, despite respectable screening and level terrain, tent-camping purists are likely to find the slots a bit too close together. Their best option—short of decamping altogether—is the remote and barren-looking Cottonwood loop (only open weekends), where an absence of such amenities as shade, screening, and barbecue grills guarantees a high level of solitude. An added plus for this park is its close proximity to a San Diego trolley stop.

BASICS

Operated By: Padre Dam Municipal Water District. **Open:** All year. **Site Assignment:** Reservations accepted w/ V, MC, D. **Registration:** At entrance booth. **Fee:** $26–$42; cash, V, MC, D. **Parking:** At site.

FACILITIES

Number of RV-only Sites: 224. **Hookups:** Electric (20, 30, 50 amps), water, sewer, internet. **Each Site:**

Picnic table, barbecue grill. **Dump Station:** Yes. **Laundry:** Yes. **Pay Phone:** Yes. **Restrooms and Showers:** Yes. **Fuel:** No. **Propane:** Yes. **Internal Roads:** Paved. **RV Service:** No. **Market:** 3 mi. east in Santee. **Restaurant:** 3 mi. east in Santee. **General Store:** Yes. **Vending:** Yes. **Swimming:** Heated pool. **Playground:** Yes. **Other:** Some wheelchair-accessible facilities. **Activities:** Fishing, bicycling, horseshoe pit, volleyball, canoe & pedal boat rentals. **Nearby Attractions:** San Diego & its waterfront, museums, zoo, historic district. **Additional Information:** San Diego CVB, (619) 232-3101.

RESTRICTIONS

Pets: On leash; not allowed in day-use area; $1 fee. **Fires:** Not allowed. **Alcoholic Beverages:** Allowed. **Vehicle Maximum Length:** 45 ft. **Other:** 14-day stay limit.

TO GET THERE

From Hwy. 67 in Santee exit at Woodside/Santee. Woodside changes into Mission Gorge. Drive 2 mi. on Mission Gorge, turn right onto Carlton Hills Blvd., and after 0.5 mi. turn left onto Carlton Oaks. The campground is 0.4 mi. ahead on the right.

SEQUOIA NATIONAL PARK   MAP, D-2
Potwisha

Sequoia National Park, Generals Hwy., 93262. T: (559) 565-3341; www.americanparknetwork.com.

🚐 ★★★★   ▲ ★★★

Beauty: ★★★★	Site Privacy: ★★★
Spaciousness: ★★★	Quiet: ★★★
Security: ★★★	Cleanliness: ★★★★
Insect Control: ★★	Facilities: ★★

Potwisha is named for the Native Americans who once roamed these parts. It is 4 miles north of Sequoia National Park's south entrance station, 12 miles from the Giant Forest grove of impossibly large sequoia trees. Situated at 2,100 feet elevation, Potwisha enjoys an understated beauty, especially in spring when buttercups and other wildflowers decorate its tall green grass, the buckeye trees are ablaze with white blossoms, and the steeply sloping hills are ripe with flowering yucca. There is an authentically natural flavor to this campground, in contrast to the mega-sized lodgepole, a camper-corral in the heart of the park. Several sites are equipped with pull-through parking, and those along the lower loop, nearer the river, are the more private. Number 18 is all by itself next to a large boulder; 21, 22, and 24, above the river, are roomy and shaded by oaks. Regular bear sightings make using the metal storage lockers a necessity. A highly scenic trail along the Marble Fork leads out of camp by site 17. The road from Potwisha to the Giant Forest and Lodgepole, an uphill, serpentine, white-knuckle drive, ascends 4,500 feet and is not recommended for vehicles over 22 feet in length.

BASICS

Operated By: National Park Service. **Open:** All year. **Site Assignment:** First come, first served. **Registration:** At entrance kiosk. **Fee:** $14, cash, check. $5 park entrance fee. $20 annual parking pass fee. **Parking:** At site. $20 fee for annual parking pass.

FACILITIES

Number of Multipurpose Sites: 43. Hookups: None. **Each Site:** Picnic table, fire grate, bear proof box. **Dump Station:** Yes. **Laundry:** No. **Pay Phone:** Yes. **Restrooms and Showers:** Flush toilets, no showers. **Fuel:** No. **Propane:** No. **Internal Roads:** Paved. **RV Service:** No. **Market:** 10 mi. southwest in Three Rivers. **Restaurant:** 10 mi. southwest in Three Rivers. **General Store:** No. **Vending:** No. **Swimming:** No. **Playground:** No. **Other:** Some wheelchair-accessible facilities. **Activities:** Hiking, wildlife viewing, whitewater rafting on Kaweah River. **Nearby Attractions:** Kings Canyon National Park; Tulare County Museum in Visalia; Kaweah Oaks Preserve in Exeter; Kaweah Lake. **Additional Information:** Visalia Chamber of Commerce & Visitors Bureau, (559) 734-5876; Three Rivers–Lemoncove Business Assoc., (550) 561-0410.

RESTRICTIONS

Pets: On 6-ft. leash; not allowed on trails. **Fires:** Fire grates only. **Alcoholic Beverages:** Allowed at site. **Vehicle Maximum Length:** 32 ft. **Other:** 14-day stay limit; no loaded firearms; no food in vehicles.

TO GET THERE

From Visalia drive 37 mi. east on Hwy. 198 to the park's Ash Mountain entrance station. Continue 4 mi. north on Generals Hwy. The well-signed campground entrance is on the left.

SIERRAVILLE   MAP, B-3
Cottonwood—Tahoe National Forest

reserve america

Hwy. 89 North/ P.O. Box 95, 96126.
T: (530) 994-3401; www.reserveamerica.com.

🚐 ★★★★   ⛺ ★★★★

Beauty: ★★★★   Site Privacy: ★★★
Spaciousness: ★★★   Quiet: ★★★
Security: ★★★★   Cleanliness: ★★★★
Insect Control: ★★★★   Facilities: ★★

Located in the northern Sierra Nevada mountains, approximately 10 miles from the town of Chilcoot, Cottonwood Springs Campground is situated within the Frenchman Lake Recreation Area in Tahoe National Forest. Loops A and C contain single-family sites and Loops B and D are group sites. Cottonwood Springs Loop B has accessible campsites, table, and restrooms. The views include mountains, valleys, open space, and Frenchman Lake. Although the word "tahoe" is thought to be derived from the Washoe Indian phrase for big water, there is a lot more to this forest than a magnificent body of water. (Actually, Lake Tahoe isn't inside the forest's boundaries; a fact that can confuse visitors.) Visitors to Tahoe National Forest find fishing and canoeing available in ice cold, crystal-clear high mountain lakes tucked in among geological features of tower-

ing granite ridges and glacially serrated rock outcroppings. There are trails along sparkling rivers that crisscross the forest and meander through wildflower-dotted meadows. In addition, swimming beaches, challenging trails, camp locations of every description, and many recreational opportunities are available in Tahoe National Forest.

BASICS

Operated By: U.S. Forest Service. **Open:** Apr. 27–Sept. 4. **Site Assignment:** Reservations must be made at least 4 days in advance. **Registration:** At office. **Fee:** Single, $16; group, $50–$90. **Parking:** At park.

FACILITIES

Number of Multipurpose Sites: 192. Hookups: None. **Each Site:** Call ahead. **Dump Station:** Yes. **Laundry:** No. **Pay Phone:** No. **Restrooms and Showers:** Yes. **Fuel:** No. **Propane:** No. **Internal Roads:** Paved. **RV Service:** No. **Market:** No. **Restaurant:** No. **General Store:** 5 mi. **Vending:** No. **Swimming:** No. **Playground:** No. **Other:** A short interpretive loop trail is available. **Activities:** Hiking, fishing, boating, water skiing. **Nearby Attractions:** Sierra Valley Hot Springs.

RESTRICTIONS

Pets: Pets must be restrained or on a leash at all times while in developed recreation areas. **Fires:** In fire rings, stoves, grills, or fireplaces provided for that purpose. **Alcoholic Beverages:** Not allowed.

TO GET THERE

From Reno, NV, travel north on Hwy. 395 to Hwy. 70, turn west on Hwy. 70 and travel 5 mi. to Chilcoot, CA. Turn north on Hwy. 284, travel 8 mi. to the Frenchman Lake Reservoir, turn left (do not cross dam) and travel 2.5 mi.

SONORA   MAP, C-3
Boulder Flat

Stanislaus National Forest, Hwy. 108, 95364.
T: (209) 965-3434; www.fs.fed.us/r5/stanislaus.

🚐 ★★★★   ⛺ ★★★

Beauty: ★★★★   Site Privacy: ★★★
Spaciousness: ★★★   Quiet: ★★★
Security: ★★★   Cleanliness: ★★
Insect Control: ★★★★   Facilities: ★★

Of the great number of Stanislaus National Forest campgrounds along Hwy. 108, Boulder Flat is perhaps the most appropriately named, given its granite-strewn appearance. It is also arguably one of the prettier facilities, reflecting something of a wild, high Sierra Nevada ambiance. A spiny alpine ridge flanks one side of camp, the Stanislaus River purls by another, while a series of pointy peaks hover over the scene. Grass and dirt sites, punctuated by several stands of enormous red-bark cedars, are larger and more dispersed than at nearby Brighton Flat, and less barren-looking and exposed than those at Eureka Valley (though the latter also features an impressive array of boulders, and has the river sluicing past on two sides). It is true that Boulder Flat picks up auto noise from the Sonora Pass, but the same might be said of all the other campgrounds along this stretch

of road. The town of Sonora is 50 miles west, and Dardanelle, where you will find a telephone and general store, 2 miles east.

BASICS

Operated By: Dodge Ridge Corp, concessionaire. **Open:** May–Oct.; weather permitting. **Site Assignment:** First come, first served. **Registration:** At entrance kiosk. **Fee:** Single, $15; double, $17; cash, check. **Parking:** At site.

FACILITIES

Number of RV-only Sites: 20. Hookups: None. **Each Site:** Picnic table, fire grate. **Dump Station:** No. **Laundry:** No. **Pay Phone:** No. **Restrooms and Showers:** Vault toilets, no showers. **Fuel:** No. **Propane:** No. **Internal Roads:** Paved. **RV Service:** No. **Market:** 36 mi. southwest in Twain Harte or a small one at Dardanelle. **Restaurant:** 36 mi. southwest in Twain Harte. **General Store:** No. **Vending:** No. **Swimming:** No. **Playground:** No. **Activities:** Fishing, hiking, horseback riding nearby. **Nearby Attractions:** Tuolumne County Museum & History Center in Sonora; Pinecrest Lake; Sonora Pass. **Additional Information:** Tuolumne County Visitors Bureau, (209) 533-4420 or (800) 446-1333.

RESTRICTIONS

Pets: On 6-ft. leash. **Fires:** Fire grates only. **Alcoholic Beverages:** Allowed. **Vehicle Maximum Length:** 22 ft. **Other:** 14-day stay limit.

TO GET THERE

From Sonora drive 49 mi. east on Hwy. 108. The campground entrance is on the left, just beyond Clark Fork Rd.

SOUTH LAKE TAHOE   MAP, C-3
D. L. Bliss State Park

reserve america

West Shore Lake Tahoe, Hwy. 89, 96142.
T: (530) 525-7277 or (530) 525-9529; www.reserveamerica.com.

🚐 ★★★   ⛺ ★★★

Beauty: ★★★★   Site Privacy: ★★
Spaciousness: ★★★   Quiet: ★★★
Security: ★★★   Cleanliness: ★★★
Insect Control: ★★★   Facilities: ★★

D. L. Bliss was a pioneering lumberman, banker, and railroad owner whose family donated 744 acres of land to the state park system in 1929. More than 70 years later, the campground retains an appealingly rustic look. That it lacks the "Hooverville" feel of so many other facilities its size may be chalked up to its pleasingly chaotic Sierra Nevada setting. Huge granite boulders vie for space with incense cedars and lodgepole and Jeffrey pines across a steep hillside that ends at a sandy beach and picnic area on the shore of Lake Tahoe. Roomy sites are tightly clustered over a series of loops, but they don't seem crowded, due to a degree of buffering provided by the boulders. For the most space and best views of the indigo water, try for the loop with sites 141–168, which also has a number of pull-through parking slots. Make time for hiking the Rubicon trail (4.5 miles, one way), which offers stellar views of the lake and a chance to see osprey nesting in the tall trees. It ends at Vikingsholm Mansion (worth a visit), at scenic Emerald Bay. The shorter Balancing Rock nature trail (0.5 miles long) winds through the forest to a precariously positioned granite boulder.

BASICS

Operated By: California Dept. of Parks & Recreation. **Open:** Late May–mid-Sept.; weather permitting. **Site Assignment:** Reservations recommended; V, MC, D. **Registration:** At entrance booth. **Fee:** $15–$35; cash, CA check. **Parking:** At site.

FACILITIES

Number of RV-only Sites: 168. **Hookups:** None. **Each Site:** Picnic table, fire grate, bear-proof box, some sites have barbecue grill. **Dump Station:** Yes. **Laundry:** No. **Pay Phone:** Yes. **Restrooms and Showers:** Yes. **Fuel:** No. **Propane:** No. **Internal Roads:** Paved. **RV Service:** No. **Market:** 11 mi. south in South Lake Tahoe. **Restaurant:** 11 mi. south in South Lake Tahoe. **General Store:** No. **Vending:** No. **Swimming:** Lake Tahoe. **Playground:** No. **Other:** Beach. **Activities:** Hiking, fishing, birding. **Nearby Attractions:** Emerald Bay State Park & Vikingsholm Mansion in Tahoma; Lake Tahoe Historical Museum in South Lake Tahoe. **Additional Information:** South Lake Tahoe Chamber of Commerce, (530) 541-5255.

RESTRICTIONS

Pets: On 6-ft. leash. **Fires:** Fire grates only. **Alcoholic Beverages:** Allowed at site. **Vehicle Maximum Length:** 18 ft. **Other:** 14-day stay limit; no firearms; no wood gathering.

TO GET THERE

From South Lake Tahoe, at the junction of US 50 and Hwy. 89, follow Hwy. 89 north for 11.4 mi. to the entrance of the state park on the right. After making that turn, the campground is straight ahead.

---

small bridge, where aged, spidery-limbed oaks bestow the gift of shade. Additional shelter and screening are provided by ponderosa pines, madrone, manzanita, and cedar. Sites 20, 21, and 28, tucked behind boulders, are the most private. This national forest campground is in the southern unit of the Giant Sequoia National Monument, making it a great base for exploring trails in the area. The host's residence is adjacent to the property.

BASICS

Operated By: California Land Management, concessionaire. **Open:** All year; weather permitting. **Site Assignment:** Reservations accepted w/ V, MC, D. **Registration:** At entrance kiosk. **Fee:** $15; double, $28; cash, check. **Parking:** At site.

FACILITIES

Number of RV-only Sites: 36. **Hookups:** None. **Each Site:** Picnic table, fire grate, barbecue grill. **Dump Station:** No. **Laundry:** No. **Pay Phone:** No. **Restrooms and Showers:** Vault toilets, no showers. **Fuel:** No. **Propane:** No. **Internal Roads:** Paved. **RV Service:** 10 mi. west in Springville. **Market:** 28 mi. west in Porterville. **Restaurant:** 10 mi. west in Springville. **General Store:** 10 mi. west in Springville. **Vending:** No. **Swimming:** No. **Playground:** No. **Activities:** Hiking, fishing. **Nearby Attractions:** Sequoia National Forest; Porterville Historical Museum & Zauld House & Gardens; California Hot Springs. **Additional Information:** Springville Chamber of Commerce, (559) 539-2312; Porterville Chamber of Commerce, (559) 784-7503.

RESTRICTIONS

Pets: On leash. **Fires:** Fire grates only. **Alcoholic Beverages:** Allowed. **Vehicle Maximum Length:** 24 ft. **Other:** 14-day stay limit.

TO GET THERE

From Porterville drive 24 mi. east on Hwy. 190 to Camp Wishon Rd. Turn left and proceed 4 mi. to the campground entrance on the right.

---

melodic cascade. Pine trees and grassy meadows contribute to a peaceful atmosphere that is marred only occasionally by the buzzing of a passing military jet. Biting flies can be a nuisance from mid-spring through early summer, so bring repellent. Susanville lies less than 20 miles to the east.

BASICS

Operated By: CSU Chico Research Foundation, concessionaire, & Lassen National Forest, Eagle Lake Ranger District. **Open:** May–Oct.; weather permitting. **Site Assignment:** First come, first served. **Registration:** At entrance kiosk. **Fee:** $8; cash, check. **Parking:** At site.

FACILITIES

Number of RV-only Sites: 5. **Hookups:** None. **Each Site:** Picnic table, fire grate. **Dump Station:** No. **Laundry:** No. **Pay Phone:** No. **Restrooms and Showers:** Vault toilets, no showers. **Fuel:** No. **Propane:** No. **Internal Roads:** Packed dirt & volcanic cinder, decent condition. **RV Service:** No. **Market:** 16 mi. east in Susanville. **Restaurant:** 16 mi. east in Susanville. **General Store:** No. **Vending:** No. **Swimming:** No. **Playground:** No. **Activities:** Hiking, bicycling, horseback riding, birding. **Nearby Attractions:** Lassen National Scenic Byway (Highways 89/44/36); Lassen Volcanic National Park; Bizz Johnson National Recreation Trail & Lassen Historical Museum in Susanville; Lake Almanor. **Additional Information:** Lassen County Chamber of Commerce, (530) 257-4323.

RESTRICTIONS

Pets: On leash. **Fires:** Fire grates only. **Alcoholic Beverages:** Allowed. **Vehicle Maximum Length:** 30 ft. **Other:** 14-day stay limit.

TO GET THERE

From Susanville drive 6 mi. west on Hwy. 36. Turn right on Hwy. 44 and continue for 7.1 mi. Turn left on FR 30N03/Goumaz Rd. The campground is 3.4 mi. ahead on the right.

SPRINGVILLE — Wishon | MAP, D-2

reserve america

Camp Wishon Rd./C.R. 208, 93265.
T: (559) 539-3004; www.reserveamerica.com.

🚐 ★★★	🏕 ★★★★
Beauty: ★★★★	Site Privacy: ★★★
Spaciousness: ★★★	Quiet: ★★★★
Security: ★★★★	Cleanliness: ★★★
Insect Control: ★★	Facilities: ★★

Wishon, at 4,000 feet elevation, is not for the tidy at heart. It's a sprawling campground that overlaps a congested tangle of trees and rocks. The boulder-larded landscape adds convincingly to the mountainous feel here, and to the difficulty in walking through the domain after dark. The unspoiled allure of this primitive, peaceful setting is accentuated by craggy Sierra ridges that seem to brush the sky overhead. Middle Fork of the North Tule River cuts the camp in half, with the more appealing sites across the

---

SUSANVILLE — Goumaz | MAP, B-3

F.R. 30N03, 96130. T: (530) 257-4188;
www.r5.fs.fed.us/lassen.

🚐 ★★★★	🏕 ★★★★
Beauty: ★★★★	Site Privacy: ★★★
Spaciousness: ★★★	Quiet: ★★★★
Security: ★	Cleanliness: ★★★
Insect Control: ★	Facilities: ★

Aside from a vaulted toilet which is shared with hikers doing the Bizz Johnson "rails to trails" path that runs by the camp, this place has nada for facilities. If you can do without the other comforts, though, you'll have it made in the glade. Goumaz, at 5,200 feet elevation, is a thinly forested, delightfully pretty, alpine campground in a level, sunny spot right alongside the Susan River. There is plenty of elbow room between the five sites, and four of those abut the water. Thus, it is hard to go wrong with any of these units, though number 2 enjoys a commanding view of a bend in the river; and 4, which has pull-through parking (as does 1), is just 15 feet from a

---

SUSANVILLE — Merrill | MAP, B-3

reserve america

477-050 Eagle Lake Rd., 96130. T: (530) 257-4188
or (877) 444-6777; www.reserveamerica.com.

🚐 ★★★★	🏕 ★★★★
Beauty: ★★★★	Site Privacy: ★★★
Spaciousness: ★★★	Quiet: ★★★
Security: ★★★★	Cleanliness: ★★★
Insect Control: ★★★	Facilities: ★★

The deep blue Eagle Lake is California's second largest natural body of water, a magnificent mountain lake that is ringed by ponderosa, Jeffrey, and white pines, with low peaks nuzzling the horizon. The beauty of the scene more than compensates for the shocking impression made by the clear-cutting of national-forest land along the drive to Eagle Summit, a process that appears to be turning large patches of forest into mountain heath. Sites at Merrill are evenly distributed over six loops and are either grassy or covered in pine needles, and partially shaded by pines. Many of those lie just 100 feet from the water, with 164 and 180 the most isolated. Also worth reserving are 167, 169, 171, 172, 174, 176, and 178. Security is above average for a national-forest camp, with two separate hosts patrolling the domain. Also vigilant in summer are omnipresent game wardens, something to remember if you intend to fish. Showers, pay phones, fuel, groceries, and laundry machines are available at the marina, 3 miles away.

BASICS

Operated By: CSU Chico Research Foundation, concessionaire, & Lassen National Forest, Eagle Lake Ranger District. **Open:** May 9.–Dec. 31; weather permitting. **Site Assignment:** Reservations accepted w/ V, MC, D for Aspen & Pine loops. **Registration:** At entrance kiosk. **Fee:** $19–$33; cash, check. **Parking:** At site.

FACILITIES

Number of Multipurpose Sites: 180. **Hookups:** None, but planned. **Each Site:** Picnic table, fire grate. **Dump Station:** Yes. **Laundry:** No. **Pay Phone:** No. **Restrooms and Showers:** Flush toilets, no showers. **Fuel:** No. **Propane:** No. **Internal Roads:** Paved. **RV Service:** No. **Market:** 14 mi. north in Spaulding. **Restaurant:** 14 mi. north in Spaulding. **General Store:** No. **Vending:** No. **Swimming:** Eagle Lake. **Playground:** No. **Other:** Some wheelchair-accessible facilities, boat ramp, marina. **Activities:** Fishing, waterskiing, canoeing, bicycling. **Nearby Attractions:** Bizz Johnson National Recreation Trail; Railroad Depot & Lassen Historical Museum in Susanville; Lassen Volcanic National Park. **Additional Information:** Lassen County Chamber of Commerce, (530) 257-4323.

RESTRICTIONS

Pets: On leash. **Fires:** Fire grates only. **Alcoholic Beverages:** Allowed. **Vehicle Maximum Length:** 45 ft. **Other:** 14-day stay limit except in 1 loop w/ a 30-day stay limit.

TO GET THERE

From Susanville drive 4 mi. west on Hwy. 36. Turn right on Eagle Lake Rd./CR A1 and continue for 13.7 mi. to Gallatin Rd. Take a right and proceed for 1 mi. to the campground entrance on the right. The marina is 1 mi. ahead.

TAHOMA   MAP, C-3
General Creek Campground

Sugar Pine Point State Park, West Shore Lake Tahoe/Hwy. 89, 96142. T: (530) 525-7982 or (800) 444-7275; www.parks.ca.gov.

🚐 ★★★   ⛺ ★★★

Beauty: ★★★★	Site Privacy: ★★★
Spaciousness: ★★★	Quiet: ★★★
Security: ★★★	Cleanliness: ★★★
Insect Control: ★★★	Facilities: ★★★

So close to Lake Tahoe, and yet so far. That, in a phrase, sums up one of the more frustrating aspects of this otherwise fine state park. General Creek Campground, at an altitude of 6,250 feet, consists of several loops that wind through a level pine forest that is uphill and across the street from the lake, but offers no

views of the water. There is decent screening between sites, which is fortunate, given how closely they are clustered. The circuit with units 126–175 features the most dispersed spots, while that containing 76–125 runs a close second. This is the only state park in the area to stay open all year, a boon to cross-country skiers and hardy, hot-blooded campers. Spring, though, is one of the better times to come, before the roads are clogged by tourists, and while the manzanita are in bloom. The Hellman-Ehrman Mansion, an opulent, pine-paneled summer home built a century ago, is open for tours from July through Labor Day.

BASICS

Operated By: California Dept. of Parks & Recreation. **Open:** All year. **Site Assignment:** Reservations recommended; V, MC, D. **Registration:** At entrance booth. **Fee:** $15–$25; cash, CA check. **Parking:** At site.

FACILITIES

Number of Multipurpose Sites: 175. **Hookups:** None. **Each Site:** Picnic table, fire ring, bear-proof box, most sites have barbecue grill. **Dump Station:** Yes. **Laundry:** No. **Pay Phone:** Yes. **Restrooms and Showers:** Yes, showers closed in winter. **Fuel:** No. **Propane:** No. **Internal Roads:** Paved. **RV Service:** No. **Market:** 1 mi. north in Tahoma. **Restaurant:** 1 mi. north in Tahoma. **General Store:** No. **Vending:** No. **Swimming:** Lake Tahoe. **Playground:** No. **Other:** Lighthouse, beach, nature center, Hellman-Ehrman Mansion. **Activities:** Hiking, fishing, birding, cross-country skiing. **Nearby Attractions:** Gatekeeper's Museum/Marion Steinbach Indian Basket Museum & Watson Cabin Museum in Tahoe City; Emerald Bay State Park & Vikingsholm Mansion in Tahoma. **Additional Information:** South Lake Tahoe Chamber of Commerce, (530) 541-5255.

RESTRICTIONS

Pets: On 6-ft. leash. **Fires:** Fire ring only. **Alcoholic Beverages:** Allowed at site. **Vehicle Maximum Length:** RVs, 32 ft.; trailers, 26 ft. **Other:** 14-day stay limit from June 15 to Sept. 30, 30-day stay limit for the rest of the year; no firearms; no wood gathering.

TO GET THERE

From Tahoe City drive 9.7 mi. south on Hwy. 89, past Tahoma. The campground entrance is on the right.

TAHOMA   MAP, C-3
Meeks Bay

7941 Emerald Bay Rd., Hwy. 89, 94612. T: (530) 525-6946 or (877) 326-3357; www.reserveamerica.com.

🚐 ★★★   ⛺ ★★

Beauty: ★★★★	Site Privacy: ★★
Spaciousness: ★★★	Quiet: ★★
Security: ★★★	Cleanliness: ★★★
Insect Control: ★★★	Facilities: ★★

If your idea of a restful vacation spot is a quiet place to pitch your tent or park your camper, don't even

think about stopping at Meeks Bay. Just 11 miles south of Tahoe City, this national-forest camp is hunkered up against a bend in Hwy. 89 as it follows the contours of Lake Tahoe, subjecting it to the roar of an ongoing stream of traffic. If, on the other hand, beach time is what makes you tick, drive on in and sink your toes into the soft, sandy stretch of shore here at the heart of the scenically gorgeous Meeks Bay. Soak up the rays and enjoy the hazy view of Nevada and its mountains across the lake. Or get out on the water via the boat ramp at the resort next door. As for the attractive campground, at 6,300 feet elevation, its level, sandy, and grassy sites are dispersed around a convoluted series of loops. Though they are rather exposed, many are shaded by mature Jeffrey pines, with smaller conifers, some manzanita, and young incense cedars adding to the beauty of the scene. The Meeks Bay trailhead leads into the Desolation Wilderness, across the road.

BASICS

Operated By: Concessionaire. **Open:** Mid-May–Oct. 31. **Site Assignment:** Reservations recommended; V, MC, D. **Registration:** At general store. **Fee:** RV w/hookup, $30; RV no hookup, $25; tent, $20. **Parking:** At site.

FACILITIES

Number of RV-only Sites: 38. **Hookups:** Electric, water, sewer. **Each Site:** Picnic table, fire ring, barbecue grill. **Dump Station:** Yes. **Laundry:** No. **Pay Phone:** Yes. **Restrooms and Showers:** Yes. **Fuel:** No. **Propane:** No. **Internal Roads:** Paved. **RV Service:** No. **Market:** 4 mi. north in Homewood. **Restaurant:** 2 mi. north in Tahoma. **General Store:** Yes. **Vending:** No. **Swimming:** Lake Tahoe. **Playground:** No. **Other:** Beach. **Activities:** Fishing, boating, volleyball, hiking. **Nearby Attractions:** Gatekeeper's Museum/Marion Steinbach Indian Basket Museum & Watson Cabin Museum in Tahoe City; Emerald Bay State Park & Vikingsholm Mansion in Tahoma, shopping, restaurants. **Additional Information:** South Lake Tahoe Chamber of Commerce, (530) 541-5255.

RESTRICTIONS

Pets: Not allowed. **Fires:** Fire ring only. **Alcoholic Beverages:** Allowed at site. **Vehicle Maximum Length:** 60 ft. **Other:** 14-day stay limit.

TO GET THERE

From Tahoe City drive 11.2 mi. south on Hwy. 89. The campground entrance is on the left, right after Meeks Bay RV Resort and Marina.

TAHOMA   MAP, C-3
Sugar Pine Point State Park

reserve america

7360 West Lake Blvd., 96142. T: (530) 525-7982; www.reserveamerica.com.

🚐 ★★★★   ⛺ ★★★★

Beauty: ★★★	Site Privacy: ★★
Spaciousness: ★★	Quiet: ★★★
Security: ★★	Cleanliness: ★★★★
Insect Control: ★★★	Facilities: ★★★

Sugar Pine Point State Park contains one of the finest remaining natural areas on Lake Tahoe. With nearly 2 miles of lake frontage, the park has dense forests of pine, fir, aspen, and cedar. Deep-line anglers fish the lake's 300-foot-deep underwater ledges for trout and salmon. Another attraction is the museum in the Hellman-Ehrman Mansion (also known as Pine Lodge), a summer home built in 1903 in a grove of pine and cedar. From the turn of the 20th century until 1965, the lands of what is now Ed Z'berg–Sugar Pine Point State Park were owned by financier Isaiah W. Hellman, and later by his daughter Florence Hellman. Today their house is maintained as a house museum and as an example of the opulent tradition in Tahoe summer homes. During winter, the park features cross-country skiing. There are 175 campsites in the campground. Each site has a table and stove. Restrooms with sinks and flush toilets are located nearby. Shower facilities and a sanitary dump station are also available during the summer. Family campsites can accommodate a maximum of eight people and three vehicles. Ten group campsites can each accommodate up to 40 people and 10 vehicles. The campsites are suitable for tents, trailers up to 40 feet, and motor homes up to 30 feet.

BASICS

Operated By: California Dept. of Parks & Recreation. **Open:** All year. **Site Assignment:** Reservations can be made 7 months in advance; reserve Front & Middle Family Loops & group sites May 26–Sept. 23; reserve Back Family Loop May 26–Sept. 16. **Registration:** At office. **Fee:** Single, $15–$25; group, $67–$111. **Parking:** At site.

FACILITIES

Number of Multipurpose Sites: 123. **Hookups:** None. **Dump Station:** Yes. **Laundry:** No. **Pay Phone:** No. **Restrooms and Showers:** Yes. **Fuel:** No. **Propane:** No. **Internal Roads:** Paved. **RV Service:** No. **Market:** No. **Restaurant:** No. **General Store:** No. **Vending:** No. **Swimming:** Yes. **Playground:** No. **Other:** This park is above 6,200-ft elevation. Campsite availability is subject to unpredictable & adverse weather conditions including snow closures, which may result in cancelled reservations. Campers are strongly advised to bring appropriate clothing. **Activities:** Boating, fishing, hiking, nature trails, picnicking.

RESTRICTIONS

Pets: On 6-ft. leash in a tent or enclosed vehicle at night. Except for guide dogs, pets are not allowed in park buildings, on trails, or on most beaches. **Fires:** In designated fireplaces. **Alcoholic Beverages:** Not allowed.

TO GET THERE

The park is located 10 mi. south of Tahoe City on Hwy. 89.

THREE RIVERS
Azalea
MAP, D-2

47050 Generals, 93271-9700. T: (559) 565-3341; www.nps.gov/seki.

🚐 ★★★★   ⛺ ★★★

Beauty: ★★★★   Site Privacy: ★★
Spaciousness: ★★★   Quiet: ★★★
Security: ★★★   Cleanliness: ★★★
Insect Control: ★★★   Facilities: ★★

One of the more appealing aspects of this campground is its central location, within easy walking distance of the General Grant Grove of massive dequoia trees and the Grant Grove Visitor Center. The first thing you may notice, though, on driving in is that many sites are considerably less than mediocre—tiny, unshaded, and exposed, as if carved out of the evergreen needle–packed ground as an afterthought. Indeed, for a rugged, hilly setting that is rich in sequoia, cedar, manzanita, madrone, and various pines, the overall absence of privacy throughout the many loops is hugely disappointing. Still, spacing between sites is not that bad, and if you persevere you'll notice a few that take advantage of protruding boulders for a little extra cover, with 89 and 113 in this better category. There are also several tent-only spots, though many are grouped closely together. If you have the time, be sure to drive the awe-inspiring Kings Canyon Scenic Byway (closed in winter). Sentinel, near the road's end, is a beautiful, wooded campground laid out around a small meadow.

BASICS

Operated By: National Park Service. **Open:** All year. **Site Assignment:** First come, first served. **Registration:** At entrance kiosk. **Fee:** $18; plus park entrance fee; cash, check. **Parking:** At site.

FACILITIES

Number of RV-only Sites: 57. **Number of Tent-only Sites:** 56. **Hookups:** None. **Each Site:** Picnic table, fire grate, some sites have bear-proof box. **Dump Station:** No. **Laundry:** No. **Pay Phone:** Yes. **Restrooms and Showers:** Yes. **Fuel:** No. **Propane:** No. **Internal Roads:** Paved. **RV Service:** No. **Market:** 31 mi. west in Sanger. **Restaurant:** In Grant Grove Village. **General Store:** Yes. **Vending:** Yes. **Swimming:** No. **Playground:** No. **Other:** Some wheelchair-accessible facilities. **Activities:** Hiking, horseback riding, ranger-led activities. **Nearby Attractions:** Giant Sequoia National Monument; Sequoia National Park; Reedley Opera House, Museum & Mennonite Quilting Center. **Additional Information:** Fresno City & County CVB, (800) 788-0836; Reedley District Chamber of Commerce & Visitors Bureau, (559) 638-3548.

RESTRICTIONS

Pets: On 6-ft. leash; not allowed on trails. **Fires:** Fire grates only. **Alcoholic Beverages:** Allowed at site. **Vehicle Maximum Length:** 32 ft. **Other:** 14-day stay limit; no firearms; no food in vehicles (bear habitat).

TO GET THERE

From Grant Grove Village drive 0.2 mi. north on Hwy. 180. Turn left at the sign for Azalea and a quick left again into the campground.

TRINIDAD
Patrick's Point State Park
MAP, B-1

reserve america

4150 Patrick's Point Dr., 95570. T: (707) 677-3570; www.reserveamerica.com.

🚐 ★★★★   ⛺ ★★★★★

Beauty: ★★★★   Site Privacy: ★★★★★
Spaciousness: ★★★★   Quiet: ★★★★
Security: ★★★   Cleanliness: ★★★
Insect Control: ★★★   Facilities: ★★

Visitors to this breathtakingly beautiful state park are in for a special treat. We're not referring to Sumeg, its reconstructed Yurok Indian village. Nor to the thriving tide pools and pretty beach. Beyond the chance of seeing passing whales from towering, pine-shrouded bluffs, Patrick's Point has an ace up its figurative sleeve: its campground is one of the finest in the entire state-park system. There is a wild, untamed atmosphere to the domain, with the rock-studded undergrowth thick with ferns and moss. Three detached loop areas feature sites that are uncommonly spacious and well screened, a generous allowance of space that grants campers a refreshing dignity of privacy. Those in the shady Abalone circuit (from 16–85) are the roomiest, while Agate's (86–97) enjoy more sun exposure and have stunning views of the surf. The RV section, admittedly, is typically tight, but its ocean vistas are a balancing amelioration. Cabin and yurt rentals are also available.

BASICS

Operated By: California Dept. of Parks & Recreation. **Open:** All year. **Site Assignment:** First come, first served. **Registration:** At entrance booth. **Fee:** $15; cash, CA check. **Parking:** At site.

FACILITIES

Number of RV-only Sites: 124. **Hookups:** None. **Each Site:** Picnic table, fire grate, food storage box. **Dump Station:** No. **Laundry:** No. **Pay Phone:** Yes. **Restrooms and Showers:** Yes. **Fuel:** No. **Propane:** No. **Internal Roads:** Paved. **RV Service:** No. **Market:** 6.5 mi. south in Trinidad. **Restaurant:** 6.5 mi. south in Trinidad. **General Store:** No. **Vending:** No. **Swimming:** No. **Playground:** No. **Other:** Some wheelchair-accessible facilities, gift shop in the visitor center. **Activities:** Hiking, fishing, whale-watching, tide pooling. **Nearby Attractions:** Trinidad State Beach, museums, Memorial Lighthouse & aquarium in Trinidad; Sumeg Village; Fort Humboldt State Historic Park, Humboldt Bay Harbor Cruise & Maritime Museum, Romano Gabriel Wooden Sculpture Garden, Carson Mansion, Main St., zoo, & more in Eureka. **Additional Information:** Trinidad Chamber of Commerce, (707) 677-1610; Greater Eureka Chamber of Commerce, (707) 442-3738.

RESTRICTIONS

Pets: On 6-ft. leash. **Fires:** Fire grates only. **Alcoholic Beverages:** Allowed at site. **Vehicle Maximum Length:** 31 ft. **Other:** 14-day stay limit from May 1–Sept. 30; no firearms; no wood gathering.

TO GET THERE

From Eureka drive 28 mi. north on US 101 and take the Patrick's Point State Park exit. Drive 0.4 mi. west on Patrick's Point Dr. to the park entrance on the right.

TRUCKEE   MAP, B-3
Logger

reserve america

Stampede Valley Rd., 96161. T: (530) 587-9281 or (530) 544-0426; www.reserveamerica.com.

🚐 ★★★★	⛺ ★★★
Beauty: ★★★★	Site Privacy: ★★
Spaciousness: ★★★	Quiet: ★★★
Security: ★★★	Cleanliness: ★★★
Insect Control: ★★★	Facilities: ★★

Campers who make a practice of shying away from oversize properties with numerous loops may want to make an exception for Logger, which is so vast it has west and east entrances. In spite of its inauspicious name, there is an abundance of ponderosa pines across its hillside perch, above the south shore of the deep blue Stampede Reservoir. Sage-colored salt bush and other low-lying shrubs don't add much to the minimal screening between dirt- and pine needle–surfaced sites, but in general space and shade are above average for such a crowded campground. One of the more private sites is 22, and 39 is well shaded, with a water view; two of the larger pull-through slots are 32, also with a lake view, and 37. Other fine options include 25, 79, 83, and 84. Logger, which is less than 20 miles from Truckee, is at an elevation of 5,949 feet, making a coat or sweater essential apparel, even in summer. Stampede Reservoir is a popular fishing spot for Kokanee salmon, so don't forget your rod. Seasonal drawdowns, however, can leave the lake disappointingly low by late summer.

BASICS

Operated By: California Land Management, concessionaire. **Open:** May 15–Sept. 30; weather permitting. **Site Assignment:** Reservations accepted w/ V, MC, D. **Registration:** At entrance booth. **Fee:** $16; cash, check. **Parking:** At site.

FACILITIES

Number of RV-only Sites: 252. **Hookups:** None. **Each Site:** Picnic table, fire grate, barbecue grill. **Dump Station:** Yes. **Laundry:** No. **Pay Phone:** No. **Restrooms and Showers:** Vault toilets, no showers. **Fuel:** No. **Propane:** No. **Internal Roads:** Paved. **RV Service:** No. **Market:** 11 mi. south in Boca. **Restaurant:** 18 mi. south in Truckee. **General Store:** No. **Vending:** No. **Swimming:** Stampede Reservoir. **Playground:** No. **Other:** Some wheelchair-accessible facilities, boat ramp. **Activities:** Fishing, boating, waterskiing, hiking, meeting your neighbors. **Nearby Attractions:** Boreal Mountain Ski Resort, Donner Memorial State Park, Western Skisport Museum, & historic downtown in Truckee; Lake Tahoe. **Additional Information:** Truckee Donner Chamber of Commerce & Visitors Center, (530) 587-2757.

RESTRICTIONS

Pets: On leash. **Fires:** Fire grates only. **Alcoholic Beverages:** Allowed. **Vehicle Maximum Length:** 32 ft. **Other:** 14-day stay limit.

TO GET THERE

From Truckee drive 7 mi. east on I-80. Take the Boca/Stampede-Hirschdale Rd. Exit and proceed north for 8.7 mi., past the Boca Reservoir. Turn left onto CR S261 and drive 2 mi. to the campground entrance on the right.

TRUCKEE   MAP, C-2
Schoolhouse

P.O. Box 9147, 95922. T: (530) 288-3231 or (530) 692-3200 (marina); www.r5.fs.fed.us/tahoe.

🚐 ★★★★	⛺ ★★★
Beauty: ★★★★	Site Privacy: ★★★
Spaciousness: ★★★	Quiet: ★★★★
Security: ★★★	Cleanliness: ★★★
Insect Control: ★★★	Facilities: ★★

Dark Day Campground, a tent-only, walk-in facility just up the road from Schoolhouse, is blessed from its bluff-top aerie with a heavenly vista of Bullards Bar Reservoir. Sites at Schoolhouse, on the other hand, enjoy no water views. Even so, it is a peaceful, engaging camp, located above the lake on a hill that is thick with conifers, madrone, toyon, and dogwood. The triple loop winds its way across an undulating terrain, where roomy sites are granted a fair degree of privacy. There is plenty of pull-through parking available, and many of the back-ins are large enough for vehicles hauling boats. The most secluded spots are 24, 37, and 40, while 26, a pull-through, is very deep. From mid-October through early spring only sites 1–14 are kept open and no potable water is available. Bullards Bar Dam, constructed in 1969, is California's largest and ranks fourth in size in the United States.

BASICS

Operated By: Tahoe National Forest, North Yuba/Downieville Ranger District & Yuba City Water Agency. **Open:** All year. **Site Assignment:** Reservations accepted w/ V, MC; recommended during the winter. **Registration:** At Emerald Cove Marina at the dam; permit required. **Fee:** $17 (Apr. 15–Oct); cash, check, V, MC; no fee in winter when water spigots are capped. **Parking:** At site.

FACILITIES

Number of RV-only Sites: 56. **Hookups:** None. **Each Site:** Picnic table, fire grate. **Dump Station:** No. **Laundry:** No. **Pay Phone:** Yes. **Restrooms and Showers:** Flush & vault toilets, no showers. **Fuel:** No. **Propane:** No. **Internal Roads:** Paved, some potholes. **RV Service:** No. **Market:** 26 mi. east in Downieville. **Restaurant:** 26 mi. east in Downieville. **General Store:** Yes, at marina. **Vending:** No. **Swimming:** Bullards Bar Reservoir. **Playground:** No. **Other:** Boat ramp, marina. **Activities:** Fishing, hiking, horseback riding, mountain biking, boating. **Nearby Attractions:** Empire Mine State Historic Park in Grass Valley; Malakoff Diggins State Historic Park in Nevada City; Downieville Foundry/Museum, Gallows & County Museum. **Addi-**

tional Information: Grass Valley–Nevada County Chamber of Commerce, (530) 273-4667; Sierra County Chamber of Commerce, (530) 862-0308 or (800) 200-4949.

RESTRICTIONS

Pets: On leash. **Fires:** Fire grates only. **Alcoholic Beverages:** Allowed. **Vehicle Maximum Length:** 35 ft. **Other:** 14-day stay limit.

TO GET THERE

Exit Hwy. 70 at Marysville and drive 12 mi. east on Hwy. 20. Turn left on Marysville Rd./E21, at the sign for Bullards Bar Reservoir, and continue for 11 mi. Head right on Old Marysville Rd. and drive 17 mi., across the dam, to the campground on the left.

TULELAKE   MAP, A-2
Indian Well

Lava Beds National Monument, Lava Beds National Monument Rd., 96134.
T: (530) 667-8100; www.nps.gov/labe.

🚐 ★★★	⛺ ★★★
Beauty: ★★★★	Site Privacy: ★★★
Spaciousness: ★★★	Quiet: ★★★
Security: ★★★	Cleanliness: ★★★★
Insect Control: ★★★★	Facilities: ★★

At just over 46,000 acres, Lava Beds National Monument may not seem a very large preserve. It manages, though, to pack a great deal within the confines of its boundaries. Located 55 miles south of Klamath Falls, Oregon, this high desert terrain has been dramatically painted by lava runoff from the Medicine Lake volcano, and a large swath of its rugged, rocky tufa–terrain saw the final curtain drawn on the Modoc war. Most dramatically, there are over 380 lava tube caves in the park, with two dozen developed for easy—and often thrilling—exploration. Most of those are a short drive from the campground, which is divided into a pair of loops. Cinder and spatter cones mark the approach to camp, and such desert scrub as sage brush, rabbit brush, bitter brush, and mountain mahogany contribute a hint of green to the bituminous landscape. Aged, gnarly junipers scattered over the undulating lava meadow shed shade on a few fortunate sites, such as the roomy, recessed B 25 and both A 5 and A 6, the latter two also being graced with expansive valley views. At 4,770 feet of elevation, nights at Indian Well can be quite windy and cold from late Oct. through early Apr. Keep an eye out for kangaroo rats after dark.

BASICS

Operated By: National Park Service. **Open:** All year. **Site Assignment:** First come, first served. **Registration:** Self-registration. **Fee:** $10; cash, check. **Parking:** At site.

FACILITIES

Number of Tent-only Sites: 43. **Hookups:** None. **Each Site:** Picnic table, fire ring, barbecue grill. **Dump Station:** No. **Laundry:** No. **Pay Phone:** Yes, calling cards only. **Restrooms and Showers:** Flush toilets, vault toilets, no showers. **Fuel:** No. **Propane:** No. **Internal Roads:** Paved. **RV Service:** No. **Market:** 14 mi. south in Tionesta (basic supplies). **Restaurant:** 30 mi. north in

Tulelake. **General Store:** No. **Vending:** Yes. **Swimming:** No. **Playground:** No. **Other:** Some wheelchair-accessible facilities, visitor center. **Activities:** Hiking, lava-tube caving, birding, ranger programs (summer only). **Nearby Attractions:** Tule Lake & Klamath national wildlife refuges; Medicine Lake Recreation Area; Petroglyph Section at the northeast entrance of Lava Beds National Monument. **Additional Information:** Tulelake Chamber of Commerce, (530) 667-5312.

RESTRICTIONS

Pets: On 6-ft. leash; not allowed on trails. **Fires:** Fire ring only. **Alcoholic Beverages:** Allowed at site. **Vehicle Maximum Length:** No limit. **Other:** 14-day stay limit; no loaded firearms; wood gathering only in designated area. Very limited space available for RVs.

TO GET THERE

From Tulelake drive 26 mi. south on Hwy. 139. Turn right (west) on Tionesta Rd. and continue for 2.7 mi. Turn right again on Lava Beds National Monument Rd. and proceed for 14 mi. The campground entrance is to the right, directly across the visitor center.

UKIAH
Ky-en
MAP, C-1

reserve america

1160 Lake Mendocino Dr., 95482-9404.
T: (707) 462-7581 or (877) 444-6777;
www.reserveamerica.com.

🚐 ★★★	🏕 ★★★
Beauty: ★★★★	Site Privacy: ★★★
Spaciousness: ★★	Quiet: ★★★
Security: ★★★★	Cleanliness: ★★
Insect Control: ★★★	Facilities: ★★★

You do not need to have a fishing rod or boat to enjoy Lake Mendocino, but it will certainly add to your pleasure. This green gleaming body of water receives quite a lot of use, with most of that falling between Memorial Day and Labor Day. Ky-en (also rendered Kyen) is typical of the three campgrounds here (a fourth, Miti, is a boat-in camp), nestled against a sloping hillside between Hwy. 20 and the lake. The most popular sites abut the shore, with 75, 82, and 103 the most private. The screening and shade are far better, though, up the hill where the loops snake through such varied vegetation as juniper, pine, oak, toyon, manzanita, and flowering ceanothus. Best of that section are 18 and 22 (both with pull-through parking), and 15, 16, 26, and 42. Security is good, with regular ranger patrols and entrance gates that are locked between 10:30 p.m. and 7:30 a.m.

BASICS

Operated By: U.S. Army Corps of Engineers. **Open:** All year. **Site Assignment:** Reservations accepted w/ V, MC, D, AE. **Registration:** At entrance booth. **Fee:** $20–$22; cash, check. **Parking:** At site.

FACILITIES

Number of RV-only Sites: 103. **Hookups:** None. **Each Site:** Picnic table, fire grate, lantern holder. **Dump Station:** Yes. **Laundry:** No. **Pay Phone:** Yes. **Restrooms and Showers:** Yes. **Fuel:** No. **Propane:** No. **Internal Roads:** Paved & narrow. **RV Service:** No. **Market:** 1 mi. east in Calpella. **Restaurant:** 1 mi. east in Calpella. **General Store:** Yes, in summer. **Vending:** No. **Swimming:** Lake Mendocino. **Playground:** Yes. **Other:** Some wheelchair-accessible facilities, 6-lane boat ramp, visitor center. **Activities:** Fishing, waterskiing, sailing, boat rentals, hiking, disc golf. **Nearby Attractions:** Ukiah museums & Cow Mountain Recreation Area; Mendocino County Museum & Roots of Motive Power/Antique Steam Logging Equipment in Willits; Skunk Train from Willits to Fort Bragg. **Additional Information:** Greater Ukiah Chamber of Commerce, (707) 462-4705.

RESTRICTIONS

Pets: On 6-ft. leash. **Fires:** Fire grates only. **Alcoholic Beverages:** Allowed. **Vehicle Maximum Length:** 35 ft. **Other:** 14-day stay limit.

TO GET THERE

Drive 6 mi. north of Ukiah on US 101. Turn east on Hwy. 20 and after 2.3 mi. turn right on Marina Drive Rd. The campground is 0.3 mi. ahead.

UPPER LAKE
Pogie Point
MAP, C-2

Hull Mountain Rd., 95469. T: (916) 386-5164;
www.r5.fs.fed.us/mendocino.

🚐 ★★★	🏕 ★★★
Beauty: ★★★★	Site Privacy: ★★★
Spaciousness: ★★	Quiet: ★★★
Security: ★★★	Cleanliness: ★★★
Insect Control: ★★	Facilities: ★★

Forget the jokes about "doughboy" campers and "poppin' fresh" fish: Lake Pillsbury is one pretty haven for boating, fishing, hiking, or just lazing around. There are four campgrounds in this region of the Mendocino National Forest, with Oak Flat, 2 miles up the road, offering better lake access than Pogie Point. The former, though, is a primitive facility and there is some truth to the waggish suggestion that this status owes more to the people it attracts than its limited amenities. Pogie Point is marginally better in the creature comforts department (though its latrines could use more regular maintenance), but leagues ahead in aesthetics. It rests above a tiny cove that is ideal for launching canoes and kayaks. The grounds are thinly forested with tan oak, moss-covered pines, madrone, and oversize manzanita. Sites along its double loop range from uncomfortably small and exposed to reasonably roomy and recessed. Elk, black-tailed deer, and wild turkey frequent these parts.

BASICS

Operated By: Pacific Gas & Electric. **Open:** All year; weather permitting. **Site Assignment:** First come, first served. **Registration:** At entrance kiosk. **Fee:** Call for pricing details. **Parking:** At site.

FACILITIES

Number of RV-only Sites: 45. **Hookups:** None. **Each Site:** Picnic table, fire grate. **Dump Station:** No. **Laundry:** No. **Pay Phone:** No. **Restrooms and Showers:** Vault toilets, no showers. **Fuel:** No. **Propane:** No. **Internal Roads:** Paved. **RV Service:** No. **Market:** 19 mi. west in Potter Valley. **Restaurant:** 19 mi. west in Potter Valley. **General Store:** No. **Vending:** No. **Swimming:** Lake Pillsbury. **Playground:** No. **Other:** Some wheelchair-accessible facilities, small boat launch. **Activities:** Fishing, hiking, horseback riding, mountain biking, windsurfing, boating. **Nearby Attractions:** Lakeport County Museum & Clear Lake in Lakeport. **Additional Information:** Lake County Marketing Program/Visitor Information Center, (707) 263-9544 or (800) 525-3743; Mendocino National Forest, Upper Lake Ranger District, (707) 275-2361.

RESTRICTIONS

Pets: On leash, $1 fee. **Fires:** Fire grates only. **Alcoholic Beverages:** Allowed. **Vehicle Maximum Length:** 40 ft. **Other:** 14-day stay limit.

TO GET THERE

From Hwy. 20 in Upper Lake head north on Mendenhall Ave., which becomes Elk Mountain Rd./FS M1. After 17 mi. the scenic road turns to graded dirt, then pavement again after another 9 mi. From that point, the campground access is 5.5 mi. ahead on the right.

VALLEY SPRINGS
Acorn Camp
MAP, C-2

reserve america

New Hogan Lake, 2713 Hogan Dam Rd., 95255-9501. T: (209) 772-1343 or (877) 444-6777; www.reserveamerica.com.

🚐 ★★★★	🏕 ★★★
Beauty: ★★★★	Site Privacy: ★★
Spaciousness: ★★★	Quiet: ★★
Security: ★★★★	Cleanliness: ★★
Insect Control: ★★★	Facilities: ★★★★

The U.S. Army Corps of Engineers created this reservoir in 1964 and continues to manage it. Which is not to suggest that you'll be rousted out of your sleeping bag by reveille at 0500 hours. It's more likely that the roar of motorboats will get you up, as this is a popular—though seldom full—boating and fishing spot. The only overt reminders that this is army land is the presence of uniformed volunteers at the entrance booths. In a sense that's a shame, since the oak-fringed, grassy meadows of the three camp loops, which slope water-ward, could tolerate more thorough litter control. On weekend nights, too, excessive noise, including barking, wandering dogs, can be severe enough to make you want to call in the MPs. Yet sites are well dispersed, if somewhat open, and many are shaded by toyon, pines, and oaks. There are also 30 boat-in spots available (first come, first served) from May through September. Oak Knoll, the primitive overflow area, costs $6 less per night and offers a few decently private, lake view sites.

BASICS

Operated By: U.S. Army Corps of Engineers.
Open: All year. **Site Assignment:** Reservations for 90% of the sites accepted w/ V, MC, D. **Registration:** At entrance booth. **Fee:** $12; cash, check. **Parking:** At site.

FACILITIES

Number of RV-only Sites: 127. **Hookups:** None. **Each Site:** Picnic table, fire grate, lantern pole. **Dump Station:** Yes. **Laundry:** No. **Pay Phone:** Yes. **Restrooms and Showers:** Yes. **Fuel:** No. **Propane:** No. **Internal Roads:** Paved. **RV Service:** No. **Market:** 3 mi. northwest in Valley Springs. **Restaurant:** 3 mi. northwest in Valley Springs. **General Store:** No. **Vending:** No. **Swimming:** New Hogan Lake. **Playground:** No. **Other:** Some wheelchair-accessible facilities, boat ramp, marina. **Activities:** Fishing, hiking, birding, horseback riding, mountain biking, cussing out your noisy neighbors. **Nearby Attractions:** Calaveras County Historical Society & Museum Complex in San Andreas; Amador County Museum in Jackson; planetarium & museums in Stockton. **Additional Information:** Calaveras County Visitors Bureau, (209) 736-0049.

RESTRICTIONS

Pets: On leash. **Fires:** Fire grates only. **Alcoholic Beverages:** Allowed. **Vehicle Maximum Length:** No limit. **Other:** 14-day stay limit.

TO GET THERE

From Stockton on Hwy. 99 drive 30 mi. east to Hogan Dam Rd. Turn right and continue for 1 mi. to the well-signed campground access road on the left. The campground entrance is 0.8 mi. from there.

VENTURA   MAP, E-2
Emma Wood SB

900 West Main St., 93001. T: (805) 968-1033; www.reserveamerica.com.

🚐 ★★★★	🏕
Beauty: ★★★	Site Privacy: ★★★
Spaciousness: ★★★	Quiet: ★★★
Security: ★★★	Cleanliness: ★★★★
Insect Control: ★★★	Facilities: ★★

Moderate ocean temperature at Emma Wood State Beach makes the area a great place for swimming, surfing and fishing. Catches include perch, bass, cabezon, and corbina. The Ventura River estuary is at the mouth of the Ventura River, at the southeast end of the park. This freshwater marsh at the southwest end of the beach attracts raccoons, songbirds, and red-tailed hawks. The beach also features the crumbling ruins of a World War II coastal artillery site. There is a grassy area for groups and a campground for hikers and bikers. The beach offers a view of Anacapa Island—and occasional dolphins. In the South End there are four developed group camps, one undeveloped group camp, and one hike-and-bike camp. In the North End, there are primitive family sites (no restrooms or showers). Please contact the park directly for detailed camping availability.

BASICS

Operated By: California Dept. of Parks & Recreation. **Open:** All year. **Site Assignment:** Reservations can be made 7 months in advance from May 14–Sept. 3; family sites are first come, first served when not reserved; group sites reservable year-round. **Registration:** At office. **Fee:** Group, $40–$186. **Parking:** At site.

FACILITIES

Number of Multipurpose Sites: 91. **Hookups:** None. **Dump Station:** No. **Laundry:** No. **Pay Phone:** No. **Restrooms and Showers:** Yes. **Fuel:** No. **Propane:** No. **Internal Roads:** Paved. **RV Service:** No. **Market:** No. **Restaurant:** No. **General Store:** No. **Vending:** No. **Swimming:** Yes. **Playground:** No. **Activities:** Hiking, fishing, nature trails, picnicking, wildlife viewing.

RESTRICTIONS

Pets: Dogs must be kept on a leash at all times. Dogs are not permitted on the beach. **Fires:** In designated fireplaces. **Alcoholic Beverages:** Not allowed. **Other:** Family sites accommodate self-contained vehicles only. There is no running water & there is no electricity available to campers. No tent camping. Fees include entry for 1 vehicle & 1 legally towed vehicle or trailer, additional vehicles will be charged per night at the park.

TO GET THERE

Emma Wood State Beach (family campground) is 2 mi. west of Ventura via Hwy. 101. The group camp's entrance is at the west end of Main St. in Ventura.

WATSONVILLE   MAP, D-1
Mount Madonna County Park

7850 Pole Line Rd., 95076. T: (408) 842-2341; www.parkhere.org/prkpages/madonna.htm.

🚐 ★★★★	🏕 ★★★★
Beauty: ★★★★	Site Privacy: ★★★
Spaciousness: ★★★	Quiet: ★★★★
Security: ★★★	Cleanliness: ★★★
Insect Control: ★★★	Facilities: ★★★

Redwood trees are what this park is all about, with some groves so dense you may find yourself wondering whether the sun has gone into eclipse. Madrone trees and tan oaks round out a very natural, attractive hilltop forest habitat that is laced with 20 miles of hiking trails. Sites of matted leaves and grass are above average in size and distributed over four separate loops, with those in Tan Oak both more private and open to diffused sunlight. There is also a generous amount of gravel-surfaced pull-through parking slips available throughout the campground. The Civilian Conservation Corps was based here in the early 1930s; fieldstone fire pits in some sites are solid reminders of their efforts. Around the same time, William Hearst donated a pair of white fallow deer to the park. Their descendants are still present, housed in a pen near the visitor center. Black-tailed deer, coyotes, foxes, and bobcats also call this part of the Santa Cruz Mountains home.

BASICS

Operated By: County of Santa Clara, Parks & Recreation Dept. **Open:** All year. **Site Assignment:** First come, first served; reservations accepted. **Registration:** At entrance booth. **Fee:** $15–$25; cash, CA check, V, MC. **Parking:** At site.

FACILITIES

Number of RV-only Sites: 118. **Hookups:** Electric (20, 30 amps), water. **Each Site:** Picnic table, fire grate, food storage box. **Dump Station:** Yes. **Laundry:** No. **Pay Phone:** Yes. **Restrooms and Showers:** Yes. **Fuel:** No. **Propane:** No. **Internal Roads:** Paved. **RV Service:** No. **Market:** 8 mi. west in Watsonville. **Restaurant:** 8 mi. west in Watsonville. **General Store:** No. **Vending:** No. **Swimming:** No. **Playground:** No. **Other:** Some wheelchair-accessible facilities, visitor center. **Activities:** Hiking, horseback riding, picnics. **Nearby Attractions:** Mission San Juan Bautista; John Steinbeck House & Library in Salinas; outlet shopping in Gilroy; Monterey peninsula. **Additional Information:** Mount Madonna county Park, (408) 842-2341.

RESTRICTIONS

Pets: On 6-ft. leash, 2 pet limit. **Fires:** Fire grates only. **Alcoholic Beverages:** Allowed at site & picnic area. **Vehicle Maximum Length:** 35 ft. **Other:** 14-day stay limit; no firearms; no wood gathering.

TO GET THERE

From Gilroy on US 101 take the Hwy. 152 Exit and drive west for 10.5 mi. Turn right on Pole Line Rd., which leads to the park.

WATSONVILLE   MAP, D-1
Sunset State Beach

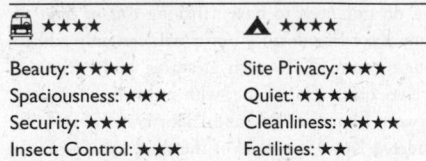

201 Sunset Beach Rd., 95076. T: (831) 763-7063 or (800) 444-7275; www.reserveamerica.com.

🚐 ★★★★	🏕 ★★★★
Beauty: ★★★★	Site Privacy: ★★★
Spaciousness: ★★★	Quiet: ★★★★
Security: ★★★	Cleanliness: ★★★★
Insect Control: ★★★	Facilities: ★★

Too often beach-side campgrounds are a compromise in comfort, especially in the southern part of the state. Sites are compact, they are laid out in a parking lot, there's no view of the water, trains thunder by at regular intervals. Sunset State Beach, located just 15 miles south of Santa Cruz, avoids most of those pitfalls, presenting campers with a stellar setting in the process. Plenty of shade is provided by the Monterey pines and eucalyptus trees that thrive throughout the property's three loops, yet sun-worshippers will appreciate that there is also an abundance of open space. Level sites are grassy, surprisingly roomy, and buffered from ocean breezes by a series of high sand dunes. Arguably, the most appealing loop is South Camp, with 26 particularly private and 25 offering a decent ocean view. The sandy beach is stunningly gorgeous, though slightly marred by the presence of a cookie-cutter housing development at its south end. Surf fishing here is reportedly very good. If you value tranquility don't even think about arriving on weekends from Easter through Labor Day.

BASICS

Operated By: California Dept. of Parks & Recreation. **Open:** All year. **Site Assignment:** Reservations recommended; V, MC, D. **Registration:** At entrance booth. **Fee:** $20–$25; cash, CA check. **Parking:** At site.

FACILITIES

Number of RV-only Sites: 90. **Hookups:** None. **Each Site:** Picnic table, fire grate, food storage box. **Dump Station:** No. **Laundry:** No. **Pay Phone:** Yes. **Restrooms and Showers:** Yes. **Fuel:** No. **Propane:** No. **Internal Roads:** Paved. **RV Service:** No. **Market:** 3 mi. northeast in Watsonville. **Restaurant:** 3 mi. northeast in Watsonville. **General Store:** No. **Vending:** No. **Swimming:** Pacific Ocean. **Playground:** No. **Other:** Some wheelchair-accessible facilities. **Activities:** Fishing, surfing, beachcombing, hiking, hang gliding. **Nearby Attractions:** Mission San Juan Bautista; John Steinbeck House & Library in Salinas; outlet shopping in Gilroy; Monterey peninsula. **Additional Information:** Castroville Chamber of Commerce, (831) 633-6545.

RESTRICTIONS

Pets: On 6-ft. leash. Not allowed on beach. **Fires:** Fire grates only. **Alcoholic Beverages:** Allowed at site, not on the beach. **Vehicle Maximum Length:** 31 ft. **Other:** 7-day stay limit from Apr. 1–Oct. 31; no wood gathering.

TO GET THERE

From Hwy. 1 near Watsonville take the Riverside Dr. Exit and head toward the ocean. Turn right after 1 block onto Lee Rd., then a quick left onto West Beach St. Proceed for 1.5 mi. to San Andreas Rd., where you should hang a right. In 2.1 mi. steer left onto Sunset Beach Rd. and follow it into the park.

WEAVERVILLE MAP, B-1
Tannery Gulch

reserve america

Hwy. 3, 96093. T: (530) 623-2121 or (877) 444-6777; www.reserveamerica.com.

🚐 ★★★★   ⛺ ★★★

Beauty: ★★★★	Site Privacy: ★★
Spaciousness: ★★★	Quiet: ★★★★
Security: ★★★	Cleanliness: ★★★★
Insect Control: ★★★	Facilities: ★★

Gold was discovered in the Trinity River in 1848. The rush that followed left its mark on this entire region, from hillsides washed away with hydraulic pumps to the colorful names attached to various locales. Tannery Gulch is an example of the second, and fortunately in its beautiful pine-forested perch above the jade-green Trinity Lake there is little evidence of the first. A few oaks and dogwoods are sprinkled among the tall conifers, and while the forest is fairly dense, a good deal of sunlight radiates through the canopy. As in any hilly area, some sites lack level ground. Most, though, are fine, being above average in spaciousness and distributed reasonably far apart over the property's five loops. Among the better choices for space and their partial views of the lake are 33, 34, 35, 40, 41, and 42. Most people come here for the water sports, but hikers (and horse riding enthusiasts) won't have to sit idly by watching the moss grow: there are many outstanding trails immediately to the north in the Trinity Alps Wilderness. Weaverville is 12 miles south along Hwy. 3.

BASICS

Operated By: Hodge Management, concessionaire. **Open:** May 1–Sept. 31. **Site Assignment:** Reservations accepted w/ V, MC, D for most sites; first come, first served for sites 50–62. **Registration:** At entrance kiosk. **Fee:** $15–$20; cash, check; additional vehicles, $5. **Parking:** At site. Additional vehicles $5.

FACILITIES

Number of RV-only Sites: 82. **Hookups:** None. **Each Site:** Picnic table, fire grate. **Dump Station:** No. **Laundry:** No. **Pay Phone:** No. **Restrooms and Showers:** Flush & vault toilets, no showers. **Fuel:** No. **Propane:** No. **Internal Roads:** Paved. **RV Service:** No. **Market:** 13 mi. south in Weaverville. **Restaurant:** 13 mi. south in Weaverville. **General Store:** Yes. **Vending:** No. **Swimming:** Trinity Lake. **Playground:** No. **Other:** No wheelchair-accessible facilities, seasonal boat ramp for campground use only. **Activities:** Fishing, hiking, boating, waterskiing. **Nearby Attractions:** Weaverville museums, National Historic District, & Joss House State Historic Park; Historic Trinity River Bridge in Lewiston. **Additional Information:** Weaverville Chamber of Commerce, (530) 623-3840; Trinity County Chamber of Commerce, (530) 623-6101 or (800) 487-4648.

RESTRICTIONS

Pets: On leash. **Fires:** Fire grates only. **Alcoholic Beverages:** Allowed. **Vehicle Maximum Length:** 40 ft. **Other:** 14-day stay limit.

TO GET THERE

Exit Hwy. 299 in Weaverville onto Hwy. 3, northward direction. After 12 mi. turn right on CR 172. The campground entrance is 1.25 mi. ahead.

WEOTT MAP, B-1
Humboldt Redwoods State Park

reserve america

P.O. Box 100, 95571. T: (707) 946-2409; www.reserveamerica.com.

🚐 ★★★   ⛺ ★★★★

Beauty: ★★★★	Site Privacy: ★★★
Spaciousness: ★★★	Quiet: ★★★★★
Security: ★★★★★	Cleanliness: ★★★★
Insect Control: ★★★	Facilities: ★★★

Humboldt Redwoods State Park encompasses over 52,000 acres, including 17,000 acres of old-growth coast redwoods. Created in 1921 with a small memorial grove, the park has grown to include a diverse ecosystem including the entire Bull Creek watershed and the Rockefeller Forest, the largest remaining old-growth redwood forest in the world. As well the park features the 32-mile Avenue of the Giants scenic highway, the very popular Founders Grove Nature Trail, and the delightful and unique Humboldt Redwoods Visitor Center. A wide variety of activities and facilities are available. There are over 250 family campsites in three different campgrounds, plus environmental camps, group camps, trail camps, and horse camps. Over 100 miles of trail await exploration by hikers, bikers, and equestrians. The South Fork Eel River provides fishing, boating, and swimming opportunities, and there are many day-use areas for picnicking, family activities, or just enjoying the pristine environment.

BASICS

Operated By: California Dept. of Parks & Recreation. **Open:** All year. **Site Assignment:** Reservations can be made 7 months in advance. **Registration:** At office. **Fee:** Single, $15–$20; group, $54–$100. **Parking:** At designated parking spur.

FACILITIES

Number of Multipurpose Sites: 253. **Hookups:** None. **Dump Station:** No. **Laundry:** No. **Pay Phone:** No. **Restrooms and Showers:** Yes. **Fuel:** No. **Propane:** No. **Internal Roads:** Paved. **RV Service:** No. **Market:** No. **Restaurant:** No. **General Store:** Yes. **Vending:** No. **Swimming:** Yes. **Playground:** No. **Activities:** Fishing, picnicking, hiking, nature trails, horseback riding.

RESTRICTIONS

Pets: Pets are welcome at the park. However, they must be on leash at all times & are never allowed on trails or in undeveloped areas. **Fires:** In designated fireplaces. **Alcoholic Beverages:** Not allowed. **Other:** Fees are for 1 vehicle & 1 legally towed vehicle. Additional vehicles will be charged a fee at the park.

TO GET THERE

45 mi. south of Eureka (along the Ave. of the Giants) and 20 mi. north of Garberville.

WINCHESTER MAP, F-3
Lake Skinner Recreation Area

37701 Warren Rd., 92596. T: (951) 926-1541 or (800) 234-7275; www.riversidecountyparks.org.

🚐 ★★★★   ⛺ ★★

Beauty: ★★★	Site Privacy: ★★
Spaciousness: ★★★	Quiet: ★★★★
Security: ★★★★	Cleanliness: ★★
Insect Control: ★★★	Facilities: ★★★★★

Forget the hiking and equestrian trails at Lake Skinner and its proximity to nearly a dozen wineries. There is really only one reason to visit this huge campground, and that reason is spelled f-i-s-h-i-n-g. The lake is stocked weekly from November through May, making it one of the better fishing spots in southern California for trout, bass, bluegill, catfish, and crappie. Serious anglers will appreciate the lake-wide speed limit of 10 miles per hour and may want to plan their trips around the derbies held for catfish in August and trout in November, when cash prizes are awarded. Keep in mind, though, that boats must be at least ten feet long, and canoes and kayaks are not permitted on the water. Of the campground itself, there are three large loops spread over grassy meadows, with few of the average-looking sites endowed with a lake view. Shade, too, is scarce, despite the scattered presence of sycamores and pepper trees. B and C loops offer sites that appear marginally less crowded together than those in loop A.

BASICS

Operated By: Riverside County Regional Park. **Open:** All year. **Site Assignment:** Reservations accepted w/ V, MC, D. **Registration:** At entrance booth. **Fee:** $15–$18; cash, CA check. **Parking:** At site.

FACILITIES

Number of Multipurpose Sites: 300. **Hookups:** Electric (30, 50 amps), water, sewer. **Each Site:** Picnic table, fire grate. **Dump Station:** Yes. **Laundry:** Yes. **Pay Phone:** Yes. **Restrooms and Showers:** Yes. **Fuel:** Yes, for boats. **Propane:** Yes. **Internal Roads:** Paved. **RV Service:** No. **Market:** 8 mi. southwest in Temecula. **Restaurant:** 8 mi. southwest in Temecula. **General Store:** Yes. **Vending:** Yes. **Swimming:** Pool (seasonal). **Playground:** No. **Other:** Some wheelchair-accessible facilities, 2 boat ramps. **Activities:** Fishing, hiking, horseback riding, horseshoe pit, volleyball, boat rentals. **Nearby Attractions:** Numerous wineries, Palomar Mountain Observatory. **Additional Information:** Temecula Valley Chamber of Commerce (909) 676-5090.

RESTRICTIONS

Pets: On 6-ft. leash; $2. **Fires:** Fire grates only. **Alcoholic Beverages:** Allowed at site. **Vehicle Maximum Length:** 45 ft. **Other:** 30-day stay limit; no firearms.

TO GET THERE

From I-15 in Temecula take Rancho California Rd. Exit and head east for 9.5 mi. Turn right on Warren Rd. Campground entrance is straight ahead.

WOFFORD HEIGHTS   MAP, E-2
Tillie Creek

reserve america

Hwy. 155, 93285. T: (760) 376-1815 or (877) 444-6777; www.reserveamerica.com.

🚐 ★★★★	🏕 ★★★
Beauty: ★★★★	Site Privacy: ★★★
Spaciousness: ★★	Quiet: ★★★
Security: ★★★	Cleanliness: ★★★
Insect Control: ★★★	Facilities: ★★★

Isabella Lake is a Mecca of sorts for windsurfing, waterskiing, and year-round fishing. Cottonwoods skirt its meandering shoreline, whereas oak trees and pines populate the higher ground, especially around Tillie Creek, on the lake's western rim. The rocky locale, in the foothills of the Sierra Nevadas, is attrac-

tively wild, in a sun-baked area of wavy brown hills. There is plenty of shade throughout most of the multiple loops, with the exception of sites nearest the water, which are uncomfortably exposed. Across the domain, units are so shallow and small that tent campers will find it challenging to use the fire ring without singing their nylon. There are some larger-size spots available in the type three and four categories, but none may be reserved by specific number. Thus, you have no guarantee of getting a shady site, or even a lake view. A distressing amount of broken glass litters an otherwise tidy camp. Basic supplies and laundry machines are available in Wofford Heights.

BASICS

Operated By: California Land Management, concessionaire. **Open:** All year. **Site Assignment:** First come, first served; reservations accepted w/ V, MC, D. **Registration:** W/ campground host. **Fee:** $17; cash, check. **Parking:** At site.

FACILITIES

Number of RV-only Sites: 155. **Hookups:** None. **Each Site:** Picnic table, fire grate, barbecue grill. **Dump Station:** Yes. **Laundry:** No. **Pay Phone:** Yes. **Restrooms and Showers:** Yes. **Fuel:** No. **Propane:** No. **Internal Roads:** Paved. **RV Service:** No. **Market:** 6.5 mi. south in Lake Isabella. **Restaurant:** 6.5 mi. south in Lake Isabella. **General Store:** Yes. **Vending:** No. **Swimming:** Lake Isabella. **Playground:** Yes. **Other:** Some wheelchair-accessible facilities. **Activities:** Fishing, hiking, boating, waterskiing. **Nearby Attractions:** Sequoia National Forest; California Hot Springs; Greenhorn Mountain Park in Alta Sierra. **Additional Information:** Kern County Board of Trade, (661) 861-2367 or (800) 500-KERN.

RESTRICTIONS

Pets: On leash. **Fires:** Fire grates only. **Alcoholic Beverages:** Allowed. **Vehicle Maximum Length:** 45 ft. **Other:** 14-day stay limit.

TO GET THERE

From Wofford Heights drive 1 mi. south on Hwy. 155. Turn left at the campground sign; the entrance is just ahead.

WRIGHTWOOD   MAP, E-3
Table Mountain—
Angeles National Forest

reserve america

22223 Big Pines Hwy., 92397. T: (661) 296-9710; www.reserveamerica.com.

🚐 ★★★★	🏕 ★★★★
Beauty: ★★★	Site Privacy: ★★★★
Spaciousness: ★★★★	Quiet: ★★★
Security: ★★★★	Cleanliness: ★★★★
Insect Control: ★★★★	Facilities: ★

The campground has eight loops and a spur (Knoll)—Zuni, Apache, Cherokee, Mohave, Pima, Osage Way, Broken Blade, and Twisted Arrow. It meanders around the mountaintop through a stand of large, mature ponderosa pine. Many of the camp sites have magnificent views of the surrounding

mountains or the Mojave Desert. Some sites have bear-proof food containers. Big, spacious, widely separated campsites provide ample privacy. The Knoll (sites 12–15) are on a dead-end with no turn-around; only tents are recommended. Pima, Osage Way, and Mohave Rim loops have the campground's shortest parking aprons and tight, winding interior roads. The lodge at adjacent Ski Sunrise offers a cook's night out, public phone, 27-hole disc golf, and occasional entertainment. Table Mountain is located within the Angeles National Forest and was established by executive order in December 1892. It covers over 650,000 acres and is the backyard playground to the huge metropolitan area of Los Angeles. The land within the forest is as diverse in appearance and terrain as it is in the opportunities it provides for enjoyment. Elevations range from 1,200 to 10,064 feet. Much of the forest is covered with dense chaparral which changes to pine- and fir-covered slopes as you reach the majestic peaks of the higher elevations.

BASICS

Operated By: U.S. Forest Service. **Open:** Apr. 21–Nov. 13. **Site Assignment:** Reservations must be made at least 4 days in advance. **Registration:** At office. **Fee:** Single, $15; double, $30; quadruple, $60; group, $185. **Parking:** At park.

FACILITIES

Number of Multipurpose Sites: 148. **Hookups:** None. **Each Site:** Call ahead. **Dump Station:** No. **Laundry:** No. **Pay Phone:** No. **Restrooms and Showers:** Yes. **Fuel:** No. **Propane:** No. **Internal Roads:** Paved. **RV Service:** No. **Market:** No. **Restaurant:** No. **General Store:** No. **Vending:** No. **Swimming:** No. **Playground:** No. **Activities:** Amphitheater, hiking, sightseeing, picnicking.

RESTRICTIONS

Pets: Pets must be restrained or on a leash at all times while in developed recreation areas. **Fires:** In fire rings, stoves, grills, or fireplaces provided for that purpose. **Alcoholic Beverages:** Not allowed. **Vehicle Maximum Length:** Call ahead. **Other:** No refunds are given for bad weather. Food must be kept in approved containers.

TO GET THERE

The campground is located 5 mi. from Wrightwood, and approximately 1 mi. form the Forest Service Big Pines Station.

YOSEMITE   MAP, C-3
NATIONAL PARK
North Pines

Yosemite Valley, Southside Dr., 95389. T: (209) 372-8502 or (800) 436-7275; www.nps.gov/yose.

🚐 ★★★★	🏕 ★★★
Beauty: ★★★★	Site Privacy: ★★
Spaciousness: ★★★	Quiet: ★★
Security: ★★★★	Cleanliness: ★★★
Insect Control: ★★	Facilities: ★★★

Given a choice, it is best to see Yosemite Valley in late spring, when its many waterfalls are at their peak and the dogwoods are in bloom. You'll be joining thousands of others then, so make your campground reservations well in advance. There are three campgrounds situated near each other, and which you end up at may come down to the one with available space. If possible, aim for North Pines, which is superior for its views of the granite environs and its thrilling position at the confluence of the Merced River and Tenaya Creek. Like the neighboring camps, this is a family-friendly atmosphere that makes a great launching point for a number of excellent hikes. Level sites are, alas, packed rather closely together, and the many stands of lodgepole pine and oak provide only minimal screening. Best for privacy and access to the river are 136, 502, 503, 504, and 506. Do pay attention to the bear warnings, use the metal food lockers, and keep a whistle—or other noise maker—handy after dark. The nearest gas station is at Crane Flat, just outside the valley.

BASICS

Operated By: National Park Service. **Open:** Mar.–Sept.; weather permitting. **Site Assignment:** Reservations required; V, MC. **Registration:** At reservation office. **Fee:** $20; plus park entrance fee; cash, check, V, MC. **Parking:** At site.

FACILITIES

Number of RV-only Sites: 85. **Hookups:** None. **Each Site:** Picnic table, fire ring, barbecue grill, bear-proof box. **Dump Station:** Yes. **Laundry:** Yes. **Pay Phone:** Yes. **Restrooms and Showers:** Yes. **Fuel:** No. **Propane:** No. **Internal Roads:** Paved. **RV Service:** No. **Market:** In Yosemite Valley. **Restaurant:** In Yosemite Valley. **General Store:** Yes. **Vending:** No. **Swimming:** Ahwahnee Lodge & Curry Village. **Playground:** No. **Other:** Visitor center, several stores, post office. **Activities:** Hiking, fishing, horse & bicycle rentals, rafting, ranger-led activities, bear-spotting. **Nearby Attractions:** El Capitan, waterfalls, LeConte Memorial Lodge, sightseeing tours, museum & gallery in Yosemite Valley. **Additional Information:** Yosemite Public Information Office, (209) 372-0200.

RESTRICTIONS

Pets: On 6-ft. leash; not allowed on trails. **Fires:** Fire ring only, May 1–Oct. 15, 5–10 p.m. only. **Alcoholic Beverages:** Allowed at site. **Vehicle Maximum Length:** 45 ft. **Other:** 14-day stay limit; no firearms; no fireworks; no metal detectors; no food in vehicles (bear habitat); no wood gathering.

TO GET THERE

On entering the park from the west via Hwy. 120, follow the signs first to Yosemite Valley, then to Curry Village. Proceed straight ahead, past Lower and Upper Pines, drive over Clarks Bridge and turn left into the campground.

YOSEMITE NATIONAL PARK
Tuolumne Meadows
MAP. C-3

Tioga Rd./Hwy. 120, 95389. T: (209) 372-8502 or (800) 436-7275; www.nps.gov/yose.

★★★★   ★★★★

Beauty: ★★★★   Site Privacy: ★★
Spaciousness: ★★★   Quiet: ★★
Security: ★★★★   Cleanliness: ★★★★
Insect Control: ★   Facilities: ★★★

Summer doesn't last long in Yosemite National Park's high country, which translates to a short season for Tuolumne Meadows Campground, elevation 8,600 feet. Perhaps it's that scarcity of available time that lends an extra frisson to the delights of being in this glacier-wracked wilderness camp, which is only 20 miles west of Lee Vining. It is surprisingly attractive, given its enormous dimensions. Young lodgepole pines rise up off ubiquitous slanting slabs of granite and poke past giant boulders, while the fresh, clear Tuolumne River twists and bends, churning noisily by the campground. In late spring, and after heavy rainfalls, the river brims to the very edge of sites, verging on overflowing the campground. Of this camp's two sections, the A loops run closer to the river and offers vistas of Lembert Dome. Best for views, river access or privacy are A 50, 51, 52, 55, 63, 65, 66, 67, 71, 74, and 89. Sites in the B area are in a more forested setting, recessed from the road and a touch roomier. We find the $18 fee outrageous, given the austere facilities, but if you don't take the site, some one else will. The Tioga Rd. closes in winter, depending on snowfall; call ahead if traveling in late fall or early spring.

BASICS

Operated By: National Park Service. **Open:** May–Oct.; weather permitting. **Site Assignment:** Half by advance reservations, half by same-day reservations; V, MC. **Registration:** At entrance kiosk. **Fee:** $20; plus park entrance fee; cash, check, V, MC. **Parking:** At site.

FACILITIES

Number of RV-only Sites: 304. **Number of Tent-only Sites:** 25. **Hookups:** None. **Each Site:** Picnic table, fire pit, barbecue grill, bear-proof box (grill & bear box at some sites). **Dump Station:** Yes. **Laundry:** No. **Pay Phone:** Yes. **Restrooms and Showers:** Yes. **Fuel:** Yes. **Propane:** Yes. **Internal Roads:** Partly paved, partly dirt, but decent. **RV Service:** No. **Market:** 20 mi. east in Lee Vining. **Restaurant:** In Tuolumne Meadows. **General Store:** Yes. **Vending:** No. **Swimming:** No. **Playground:** No. **Other:** Visitor center, bookstore, sport shop, post office. **Activities:** Hiking, fishing, horse rentals, mountaineering classes, ranger-led activities, backpacking. **Nearby Attractions:** Mono Lake Tufa State Reserve in Lee Vining; Bodie State Historic Park near Bridgeport. **Additional Information:** Yosemite Public Information Office, (209) 372-0200.

RESTRICTIONS

Pets: On 6-ft. leash; not allowed on trails. **Fires:** Fire ring only. **Alcoholic Beverages:** Allowed at site. **Vehicle Maximum Length:** 35 ft. **Other:** 14-day stay limit; no firearms; no fireworks; no food in vehicles (bear habitat).

TO GET THERE

Just south of Lee Vining on US 395 head west on Hwy. 120. Drive 20 mi., past the Yosemite National Park entrance, to the campground on the left.

YOSEMITE NATIONAL PARK
Wawona
MAP. C-3

Wawona Rd./Hwy. 41, 95389. T: (209) 372-0265 or (800) 436-7275; www.nps.gov/yose.

★★★★   ★★★

Beauty: ★★★★   Site Privacy: ★★
Spaciousness: ★★★   Quiet: ★★★
Security: ★★★★   Cleanliness: ★★★
Insect Control: ★★   Facilities: ★★★

Sitting in a camp chair, gazing over the South Fork Merced River as the afternoon sun radiates through the oaks, cedars, and cinnamon-barked ponderosa pines onto the enormous boulders protruding from the hilly domain, you may well feel a part of Eden. Go ahead and look for snakes, though bears are more likely nighttime visitors. Wawona, 21 miles north of Oakhurst, near Yosemite's southern entrance, is one of the National Park's prettier, more sedate campgrounds. It is also one of the more spacious, as its series of loops are elongated alongside the Merced, rather than being concentrated one against another. As a result of that thoughtful layout, dirt- and grass-covered sites seem less jammed together, and a high number are favored with waterfront locations. Highly recommended are 34 and 37, and to a lesser extent, 51–53; while tent campers should consider such prime river sites as walk-ins 1–4. Away from the water, 42 and 44 are among the more private. The nearby Mariposa Grove trail leads into a forest of numerous spectacular sequoia trees, as well as many other impressive conifers.

BASICS

Operated By: National Park Service. **Open:** Oct.–Apr. **Site Assignment:** Reservations required May–Oct.; V, MC; first come, first served Nov.–Apr. **Registration:** At entrance kiosk. **Fee:** $20; plus park entrance fee; cash, check, V, MC. **Parking:** At site.

FACILITIES

Number of RV-only Sites: 89. **Number of Tent-only Sites:** 11. **Hookups:** None. **Each Site:** Picnic table, fire pit, bear-proof box (some sites). **Dump Station:** Yes. **Laundry:** No. **Pay Phone:** No. **Restrooms and Showers:** Flush toilets, no showers. **Fuel:** No. **Propane:** No. **Internal Roads:** Paved, many potholes. **RV Service:** No. **Market:** 20 mi. east in Lee Vining. **Restaurant:** 20 mi. east in Lee Vining. **General Store:** Yes. **Vending:** No. **Swimming:** South Fork Merced River. **Playground:** No. **Other:** Some wheelchair-accessible facilities, hotel, golf course, bookstore. **Activities:** Hiking, fishing, ranger-led walks, campfire programs, horseback riding, swimming. **Nearby Attractions:** Mariposa Grove of giant sequoia; Yosemite Mountain Sugarpine Railroad in Fish Camp; Yosemite Valley & its attractions, Yosemite waterfalls. **Additional Information:** Yosemite Sierra Visitors Bureau, (559) 683-5697.

RESTRICTIONS

Pets: On 6-ft. leash; not allowed on trails. **Fires:** Fire pit only. **Alcoholic Beverages:** Allowed at site. **Vehicle Maximum Length:** 40 ft. **Other:** 7-day stay limit; no firearms; no fireworks; no food in vehicles (bear habitat).

Reserve your campsite online at www.ReserveAmerica.com

To Get There

From Oakhurst drive 15 mi. north on Hwy. 41 to the Yosemite National Park entrance station. Continue for 6 mi. to the campground on the left.

YUCAIPA   MAP, E-3
Yucaipa Regional Park

33900 Oak Glen Rd., 92399. T: (909) 790-3127; www.co.san-bernardino.ca.us/parks.

🚐 ★★★★	▲ ★★★★
Beauty: ★★★★	Site Privacy: ★★
Spaciousness: ★★★★	Quiet: ★★★
Security: ★★★★★	Cleanliness: ★★★★
Insect Control: ★★	Facilities: ★★★

There is quite a lot to like about Yucaipa Regional Park, from its easy-to-find suburban location just 5 miles off of I-10, to the lushly manicured grounds that include three ponds stocked with trout and catfish and a one acre swimming lagoon. Add to this a sandy beach and a pair of 350-foot waterslides, pull-through parking large enough to handle most of the larger RVs, and a separate area for tents complete with soft, sandy pads, and you have the makings for good family fun. Security is tight, with a gate that typically closes at dusk, and there are hosts in residence throughout the year. Critics may carp that the handsome mix of trees does not do much to shade sites, but at least they don't obscure the fine view of the San Bernardino Mountains.

BASICS

Operated By: San Bernardino County Regional Parks Dept. **Open:** Memorial Day–Labor Day. **Site Assignment:** Reservations accepted up to 1 year in advance w/ V, MC, D. **Registration:** At entrance booth. **Fee:** $18–$27; cash, check, V, MC, D. **Parking:** At site.

FACILITIES

Number of RV-only Sites: 26. **Number of Tent-only Sites:** 9. **Hookups:** Electric (50 amps), water. **Each Site:** Picnic table, barbecue grill. **Dump Station:** Yes. **Laundry:** No. **Pay Phone:** Yes. **Restrooms and Showers:** Yes. **Fuel:** No. **Propane:** No. **Internal Roads:** Paved. **RV Service:** No. **Market:** 0.5 mi. south. **Restaurant:** 0.5 mi. south. **General Store:** Yes. **Vending:** Yes. **Swimming:** Swim lagoon w/ waterslide (seasonal). **Playground:** Yes. **Other:** Wheelchair-accessible facilities, snack bar. **Activities:** Fishing, horseshoe pit, pedal boat rentals (Memorial–Labor Day). **Nearby Attractions:** Asistencia Misión de San Gabriel, Historical Glass Museum, both in Redlands. Oak Glen Apple Orchards, San Gorgonio Wilderness Area. **Additional Information:** San Bernardino County Regional Parks, (909) 38-PARKS.

RESTRICTIONS

Pets: On 6-ft. leash. **Fires:** Allowed (In grills only). **Alcoholic Beverages:** Allowed at site. **Vehicle Maximum Length:** No limit. **Other:** 14-day stay limit; no firearms.

To Get There

From San Bernardino follow I-10 east for 15 mi. to the Yucaipa Exit. Drive 2.8 mi. east on Yucaipa Blvd., exit on Oak Glen Rd. and proceed for 4 mi. to the campground on the left.

Colorado

Colorado boasts the somewhat arguable claim that it has some of the best camping in the whole world. As far as mountains, rivers, forests, lakes, cliffs, wildlife, fishing, hiking, and canoeing go, Colorado has it all. Ranging from forested mountains to almost desert plains, the geography and climate vary wildly by region and month. Some would even say by the minute, as it can be 80° and gorgeous in Denver with blizzard conditions in the mountains less than two hours away. For this reason, campers in the mountains should plan to bring much warmer clothing than would be necessary for the lower lands and cities. Normally, the weather in the mountains changes quickly—even summer nights can be downright cold.

Interstate 25 slices the 38th state neatly into two vastly differing regions: the almost featureless grasslands of the east, and the mountainous west, where the lion's share of exciting camping opportunities exist. **Bonny State Park** is a great starting point and an excellent welcome to visitors in search of outdoor recreation on entering Colorado from Kansas. To the west, **Dinosaur National Monument,** with possibly the highest concentration in the world of fossilized dinosaur remains from the Jurassic period, and the **Grand Mesa** area likewise show the state at its best. In fact, entering Colorado on nearly any road from the surrounding states quickly puts you in prime camping territory. Once you've made it to the center, opportunities for outdoor recreation abound. If you count rocking as an activity, Freemont County boasts the **World's Largest Rocking Chair**—21 feet tall, 14 feet wide, 9,100 pounds—in the city of Penrose.

With large tracts of national forest, plenty of state parks, and numerous private campgrounds, the mountains of Colorado provide endless possibilities for those who like to stretch their legs and breathe clean mountain air. Speaking of clean, if you manage to make it up to the northern county of Weld, go out of your way to track down and launder some time at the **Antique Washing Machine Museum** in Eaton, where more than 800 of the devices have been rebuilt to working order. But let's not forget skiing. In some people's dictionaries, the entry for snow skiing says "see Colorado." **Vail, Aspen, Breckenridge** (where the **International Snow Sculpture** competition is held every January), **Steamboat Springs**—these are ski towns with nearly mythical status. All of these areas accommodate campers, whether they come in the largest RVs available or hike in with little more than a tent. Every level of amenity is available, from the most basic primitive campgrounds with no running water to full-service resorts with hot tubs, Internet connections, and ice-cream socials.

In-state attractions are nearly too numerous to mention, but if you're into getting a different experience out of Colorado, why not check out El Paso County's **Great Fruitcake Toss,** held every year the first week of January in Manitou Springs. Contestants get to let out their pent-up frustrations with the colorful holiday icon. Other attractions on the list are **Mesa Verde National Park, Rocky Mountain National Park,** the **Great Sand Dunes National Monument, Telluride,** the **Durango and Silverton Narrow Gauge Railroad, Royal Gorge, Garden of the Gods, Denver** (which harbors the obscure but popular homage to taxidermy, the **Buckhorn Exchange**), **Boulder, Leadville, Cache La Poudre** wilderness, and **Central City,** which all deserve a mention as well as a visit. If you're desperately hard up for a smile, there's always the option of playing a game or two of Twister at **Four Corners** or heading to **Fruita,** if you're in Mesa County in May, for the annual festival dedicated to **Mike the Headless Chicken.** Any way you approach it, Colorado is a camping enthusiast's state and boasts enough opportunities to keep even the most fickle outdoors person from getting bored.

ALAMOSA MAP, C-2
Alamosa KOA

6900 Juniper Ln., 81101. T: (800) 562-9157 or
(719) 589-9757; www.koakampgrounds.com.

🚐 ★★★★   ⛺ ★★★

Beauty: ★★★★   Site Privacy: ★★★
Spaciousness: ★★★   Quiet: ★★★★
Security: ★★★★   Cleanliness: ★★★★
Insect Control: ★★★★   Facilities: ★★★★

This campground, offering spectacular views of
mountains to the east, has pull-through sites that
average 60 by 22 feet in size—large enough to camp
comfortably in almost any vehicle. End sites 16, 24,
32, and 42 have superb views, making them more
attractive. Sites 41 and 42 are even longer (80-foot)
pull-throughs, also with excellent views, although 42
shares space with a light standard. The last row of RV
sites on Rd. 6 (sites 33–42) are arguably the nicest, as
they are away from the office and closest to the grassy
tent sites. (Of course, this row is also farthest from
the restrooms, so some campers may prefer not to
take a site.) Tent sites on the north side of the campground have nice grass and great views but no shade.
(Tent sites at the northwest side have more trees and
are therefore a better bet for tenters.) The restroom
and shower facilities are clean and spacious, although
the showers have a cement floor, which is slightly less
comfortable and clean-looking than tile. The laundry is clean, with loads of room.

BASICS

Operated By: Private operator. **Open:** All year.
Site Assignment: Upon registration; credit card
required for reservation; 24-hour cancellation policy,
$5 fee. **Registration:** At office. (Late arrivals use
drop box.) **Fee:** RV (full), $25; water/electric, $22;
tent, $19. **Parking:** At site.

FACILITIES

Number of RV-only Sites: 42. **Number of Tent-
only Sites:** 15. **Hookups:** Electric (50 amps), water,
sewer. **Each Site:** Picnic table, grill. **Dump Station:**
Yes. **Laundry:** Yes. **Pay Phone:** Yes. **Restrooms
and Showers:** Yes. **Fuel:** No. **Propane:** No. **Internal Roads:** Gravel. **RV Service:** No. **Market:** 5 mi.
west. **Restaurant:** 1 mi. west. **General Store:** Yes.
Vending: No. **Swimming:** No. **Playground:** Yes.
Other: Pool table, video games, cabins, dog-walk
area. **Activities:** Hiking, viewing wildlife, volleyball,
horseshoes. **Nearby Attractions:** Great Sand
Dunes, Alamosa National Wildlife Refuge, San Luis
Valley Alligator Farm. **Additional Information:**
Alamosa County Chamber of Commerce,
(800) 258-7597 or (719) 589-3681.

RESTRICTIONS

Pets: 1 per camper; on leash, cleaned up after. **Fires:**
In community fire pit. **Alcoholic Beverages:** At
sites. **Vehicle Maximum Length:** 40 ft.

TO GET THERE

From the junction of Hwy. 17 and Hwy. 160, go
3.2 mi. east on Hwy. 160. Turn north onto Juniper
Ln., then take the first right into the campground.
The office is on the left.

ALLENSPARK MAP, A-3
Olive Ridge Campground

Hwy. 7, 80301. T: (303) 444-6600 or
(877) 444-6777; www.reserveamerica.com.

🚐 ★★★★   ⛺ ★★★★

Beauty: ★★★★★   Site Privacy: ★★★★
Spaciousness: ★★★★   Quiet: ★★★★
Security: ★★★★   Cleanliness: ★★★★
Insect Control: ★★★★   Facilities: ★

Almost in the shadow of Long's Peak, this campground has very natural campsites scattered in a
ponderosa pine forest. Sites average 40 feet, and all
but 50 are back-ins. (Site 50 is a 45-foot "parallel-
parking" site similar to a pull-through.) Sites 26 and
40 are oversized sites, roughly twice as large as a regular site. Sites 10, 42, 45, and 46 are reserved for
campground hosts and administration. There is a
hiking trail that starts by site 35, perhaps increasing
foot traffic past this site. Water pumps are located
near sites 2, 8, 16, 20, 30, 34, 36, and 49. Several
sites have huge boulders that may either be seen as an
encroachment on site space or as a source of shade
and beauty. This is a slice of nature developed with a
minimal impact, allowing campers to experience the
beauty of nature. Facilities are limited to pit toilets,
but the photos on the walls are an attempt to make
the campground as comfortable as possible, considering its basic facilities. Tenters in particular may prefer this campground, but there is no reason why
RVers willing to forego hookups for a night shouldn't
enjoy it equally well.

BASICS

Operated By: Thousand Trails Management. **Open:**
May–Oct.; dates may vary. **Site Assignment:** First
come, first served; credit card required for reservation; 3-day cancellation policy, less $10; refunds must
be requested w/in 30 days. Group rates available.
Registration: At pay kiosk. (Camp host will verify
that campers have paid.) **Fee:** $14 ($8.65 for reservations); oversized site, $17; check, no credit cards.
Parking: At site.

FACILITIES

Number of RV-only Sites: 56. **Hookups:** None.
Each Site: Picnic table, grill, fire pit. **Dump Sta-
tion:** No. **Laundry:** No. **Pay Phone:** No.
Restrooms and Showers: Restrooms; no shower.
Fuel: No. **Propane:** No. **Internal Roads:** Paved.
RV Service: No. **Market:** 12 mi. to Estes Park.
Restaurant: 2 mi. to Allenspark. **General Store:**
No. **Vending:** No. **Swimming:** No. **Playground:**
Yes. **Other:** Amphitheater, 1 free picnic site. **Activi-
ties:** Fishing, hiking, mountain climbing, cross-country
skiing. **Nearby Attractions:** Rocky Mountain
National Park, Blackhawk, Central City Casinos.
Additional Information: Thousand Trails Manage-
ment, (303) 258-3610.

RESTRICTIONS

Pets: On leash, cleaned up after. **Fires:** Fire pit only.
Alcoholic Beverages: At sites. **Vehicle Maximum
Length:** 40 ft. **Other:** 8 people allowed per site.

TO GET THERE

From the junction of Hwy. 72 and Hwy. 7, turn
north onto Hwy. 7 and go 5.6 mi. Turn left at the
sign into the entrance, then take the immediate left
to go to the fee station.

ARBOLES MAP, C-1, C-2
Navajo State Park

Box 1697, 81121. T: (970) 883-2208;
www.reserveamerica.com.

🚐 ★★★★   ⛺ ★★★★

Beauty: ★★★★   Site Privacy: ★★★
Spaciousness: ★★★   Quiet: ★★★★★
Security: ★★★★★   Cleanliness: ★★★★
Insect Control: ★★★   Facilities: ★★★★

Many visitors describe their first view of Navajo
Lake, Colorado's answer to Lake Powell, as "unbe-
lievable." This huge (15,000 surface acres and 150
miles of shoreline) reservoir extends for 21 miles
south into New Mexico. Fish for record-size German
brown trout, northern pike, or catfish in open waters
without crowds. Camp on your boat or enjoy beautiful lakeside camping with lots of trees. Gather your
family and friends and enjoy Navajo Lake from the
comfort of a houseboat. Explore three major rivers
and sail or waterski on open waters. Take advantage
of the opportunity to see wildlife such as foxes, deer,
grouse and turkeys in the midst of one of Colorado's
most historic and scenic areas. The Lake usually
doesn't freeze in the wintertime, and therefore park
visitors are able to enjoy boating and open-water
fishing year-round. Other winter activities include
cross-country skiing and wildlife viewing (including
an opportunity to view bald eagles). Navajo offers
campsites and three beautiful full-service cabins. The
park's campground is open year-round with limited
facilities in the winter.

BASICS

Operated By: Colorado State Parks. **Open:** All
year. **Site Assignment:** Reservations can be made 6
months in advance. **Registration:** At office. **Fee:**
Single, $7–$20; yurt, $60; cabin, $80–$160. **Parking:**
At park.

FACILITIES

Number of Multipurpose Sites: 122. **Hookups:**
Yes. **Each Site:** Fire ring. **Dump Station:** Yes.
Laundry: Yes. **Pay Phone:** Yes. **Restrooms and
Showers:** Yes. **Fuel:** No. **Propane:** No. **Internal
Roads:** Paved. **RV Service:** No. **Market:** No.
Restaurant: No. **General Store:** Yes. **Vending:**
No. **Swimming:** Yes. **Playground:** No. **Activities:**
Biking, bird-watching, boating, fishing, hiking, horse-
back riding, horseshoe pits, hunting, jet skiing, pho-
tography, picnicking, sailing, sailboarding, waterskiing,
wildlife viewing.

RESTRICTIONS

Pets: Pets must be on a leash no longer than 6 ft. in
length. **Fires:** In designated fireplaces. **Other:** Quiet
hours will be enforced 10 p.m.–6 a.m. All generators,

loud radios, or other loud noises that may disturb the peace are prohibited during these hours.

To Get There

Take US 160 west out of Pagosa Springs 17 mi. Turn southwest on CO 151, go 18 mi. to the town of Arboles. Go 2 mi. south on CR 982.

ARBOLES   MAP, C-2
Pinon Park Campground and RV Resort

19 Lazy Ln., 81121. T: (970) 883-3636; www.navajolake.com.

🚐 ★★★★   ⛺ ★★★★

Beauty: ★★★★	Site Privacy: ★★★★
Spaciousness: ★★★	Quiet: ★★★★
Security: ★★★★	Cleanliness: ★★★★★
Insect Control: ★★★	Facilities: ★★★★

The facilities are in good shape here. The restrooms are clean, spacious, and extremely comfortable, as is the laundry facility. Anyone who frets over questionable restrooms may want to stay an extra few days to luxuriate in the clean and comfortable facilities. The park itself is in a wilderness setting, not too far (0.5 miles) from Navajo State Park, which offers lake recreation. Both back-ins and pull-throughs are grassy but open. Sites 14–26 offer no shade at all, making them slightly less attractive. (There is not a lot of shade to begin with.) Tenters, on the other hand, will delight in the trees offered for the tenting area. All tent sites have water and a grill, and the sites are a mix of grass and dirt. Campers of either stripe (RV or tent) will be happy to stay in this park, which offers great views of the reservoir to the east. The RV experience would, however, be improved with the addition of more shade trees.

Basics

Operated By: Nannette Colaizzy. **Open:** Apr.–Nov. **Site Assignment:** Upon registration; flexible, depending on site availability; credit card required for reservation; $5 fee w/ 14-day notice & 50% of deposit w/ less than 14-day notice. **Registration:** At office. (Late arrivals use drop box.) **Fee:** RV (full hookup), $18; water/electric, $15; tent, $12; V, MC, D. **Parking:** At site, except for tent areas.

Facilities

Number of RV-only Sites: 35. **Number of Tent-only Sites:** 30. **Hookups:** Electric (30, 50 amps), water, sewer. **Each Site:** Picnic table, grill. **Dump Station:** Yes. **Laundry:** Yes. **Pay Phone:** Yes. **Restrooms and Showers:** Yes. **Fuel:** No. **Propane:** No. **Internal Roads:** Gravel. **RV Service:** No. **Market:** 0.25 mi. to Arboles. **Restaurant:** 0.25 mi. to Arboles. **General Store:** Yes. **Vending:** No. **Swimming:** Lake. **Playground:** No; park is next door. **Other:** RV rentals, pavilion, dog-walk area, storage. **Activities:** 6 organized parties in summer, horseshoes. **Nearby Attractions:** Durango Silverton Railroad, Chimney Rock Archaeological Site, San Juan National Forest, Vallecito Reservoir, Florida River, Mesa Verde National Park. **Additional Information:** Durango Chamber of Commerce, (800) 525-8855.

RESTRICTIONS

Pets: On leash, cleaned up after. **Fires:** Community fire pit only. **Alcoholic Beverages:** At sites. **Vehicle Maximum Length:** 40 ft. **Other:** No tent camping allowed in RV areas.

To Get There

From Hwy. 151 in town, go 0.2 mi. north of Navajo State Park—look for the sign on the east side. Turn east into the driveway, then, at the T intersection, take the 2nd left into the campground. The office is the brown building ahead and to the right.

ASPEN   MAP, B-2
Aspen-Basalt Campground

20640 Hwy. 82, 81621. T: (800) KMP-ASPEN or (970) 927-3405.

🚐 ★★★★   ⛺ n/a

Beauty: ★★★★	Site Privacy: ★★★★
Spaciousness: ★★★★	Quiet: ★★★
Security: ★★★★	Cleanliness: ★★★★★
Insect Control: ★★★★	Facilities: ★★★★★

With red hills to the southwest; forested hills to the east, south, and west; and loads of trees in and around the park, this campground is a comfortable location for an overnight or extended stay. Each site has at least one shade tree and a section of fence for increased privacy. Sites 1–6 are small (30-foot) back-ins and have no hookups. Sites 54–61, right next to these sites, are even smaller (25 feet in length), but have larger fences and are located in a beautiful, shaded corner. These are by far the most attractive sites, but very small. Sites 8–27 and 37–53 are 60-foot pull-throughs laid out in two rows. There are mobile homes located to the east of the row containing sites 8–27. Sites 28–36 to the south and 64–90 to the north (by the entrance) are reserved for monthly guests. These are 45-foot back-ins that back to trees and the road (in both areas). The restrooms and showers are very clean, and the laundry is big and clean. This is an extremely pleasant destination located in a wonderful area.

Basics

Operated By: Rich & Bonnie Nichols. **Open:** All year. **Site Assignment:** Upon registration; credit card required for reservation; 24-hour cancellation policy. **Registration:** At office. (Late arrivals use drop box.) **Fee:** $33–$36; check, V, MC. **Parking:** At site.

Facilities

Number of RV-only Sites: 75. **Hookups:** Electric (20, 30, 50 amps), water, sewer, cable TV, wireless Internet. **Each Site:** Picnic table. **Dump Station:** Yes. **Laundry:** Yes. **Pay Phone:** Yes. **Restrooms and Showers:** Yes. **Fuel:** No. **Propane:** Yes. **Internal Roads:** Gravel. **RV Service:** On-call. **Market:** 1 mi. north. **Restaurant:** 1 mi. north. **General Store:** Yes. **Vending:** Yes. **Swimming:** Pool, hot tub. **Playground:** Yes. **Other:** Data port, game room. **Activities:** Movies, skiing, ATV riding, fishing, golfing, hunting, mountain biking, rafting, horseback riding, swimming, hiking. **Nearby Attractions:** Roaring Fork River, Aspen, golf courses. **Additional Infor-**

mation: Aspen Chamber of Commerce, (970) 925-1940. www.coloradodirectory.com.

RESTRICTIONS

Pets: On leash, cleaned up after; no more than 2 pets. **Fires:** Grill only. **Alcoholic Beverages:** At sites. **Vehicle Maximum Length:** No limit. **Other:** No smoking in buildings.

To Get There

From the junction of Hwy. 133 and Hwy. 82, turn southeast onto Hwy. 82 and go 8.8 mi. Turn right, then take the immediate left and go straight into the campground.

BATTLEMENT MESA   MAP, B-1
Battlement Mesa RV Park

95 Eldora Dr., 81635. T: (888) 828-0681 or (970) 285-7023; www.battlementmesa.com/rvs.html

🚐 ★★★★   ⛺ ★★

Beauty: ★★★★	Site Privacy: ★★★
Spaciousness: ★★★	Quiet: ★★★★★
Security: ★★★★	Cleanliness: ★★★★★
Insect Control: ★★★★	Facilities: ★★★

This campground offers wondrous views of Battlement Mesa and other volcano-like peaks from any site. The location is very rural, and sites are level, grassy, and large. Super-long (70-foot) forked pull-throughs share a common entrance but angle so that privacy is maximized given the site arrangement. Site 106 is next to a residence, and 139 and 144 are adjacent to electrical hardware, making these the least desirable sites. Sites 133 and 145 have superior grass, bushes, and views, making these two highly desirable. Other coveted sites include odd numbers 101–109, which back to a dried river bed and forested hills and therefore receive less traffic and noise. The restrooms and showers are very clean and modern; this is a pleasant RV experience. However, tenters are at the mercy of the high winds and the occasional rainstorm, as there is absolutely no coverage to protect a tent. RVers should definitely check out this park, but tenters should consider moving on to Rifle, if possible.

Basics

Operated By: Helena Johnson. **Open:** All year. **Site Assignment:** Upon registration; verbal reservations OK. **Registration:** At office. (Late arrivals go to 86 Parachute Way.) **Fee:** RV, $22.86; check, V, MC, AE, D, CB, DC. Good Sam discounts available. **Parking:** At site. 2 vehicles allowed per site.

Facilities

Number of RV-only Sites: 118. **Hookups:** Electric (30, 50 amps), water, sewer, cable TV. **Dump Station:** Yes. **Laundry:** Yes. **Pay Phone:** Yes. **Restrooms and Showers:** Yes. **Fuel:** No. **Propane:** Yes. **Internal Roads:** Paved. **RV Service:** No. **Market:** 2.5 mi. into Battlement Mesa. **Restaurant:** 2.5 mi. into Battlement Mesa. **General Store:** No. **Vending:** No. **Swimming:** Yes (3 mi.). **Playground:** No. **Other:** Data port, dog walk, rec center (2.5 mi. away; free w/ park receipt). **Activities:** Skiing, fishing, swimming, golf, biking, horseshoes, tennis (nearby). **Nearby Attractions:** Aspen, Powderhorn, Vail, Grand Mesa, natural hot springs. **Additional Information:** Rifle Visitor Information Center, (970) 625-2085.

RESTRICTIONS

Pets: On 6-ft. leash, cleaned up after. No pets over 50 lbs. **Fires:** Charcoal in grills; no open or wood fires. **Alcoholic Beverages:** At sites. **Vehicle Maximum Length:** No limit. **Other:** Call if late, no motorcycles or ATVs. No open fires or wood fires. 2-vehicle max.

TO GET THERE

From I-70, take Exit 75, turn south, and go 0.75 mi. Turn right onto West Battlement Pkwy., drive 1.5 mi., then turn right onto Stone Quarry Rd. Drive 2 mi., then turn right onto Thunderberg Trail. Take the 2nd left and keep straight to get to the office.

BELLEVUE   MAP, A-3
Dowdy Lake Campground

Red Feather Lakes, 80512. T: (877) 444-6777; www.reserveamerica.com.

🚐 ★★   ⛺ ★★★★

Beauty: ★★★★★		Site Privacy: ★★★
Spaciousness: ★★★		Quiet: ★★★★
Security: ★★★★		Cleanliness: ★★★★
Insect Control: ★★★		Facilities: ★

This National Forest campground is divided up into Loops A–E, each containing a varying number of campsites. The average size of a site is 24 by 18 feet, which, of course, limits the number of RVs that can camp here. As there are no RV hookups, the campground is more geared toward tenters. However, RVers who don't mind roughing it for a night or two will also enjoy the natural beauty and the quiet this campground has to offer. Sites 1–3 in Loop A are spacious and quite close to the lake (3 is closest) and some neat rock formations. These are quite possibly the best sites in the campground, as they boast terrific views of the lake, are close to the camp hosts, and aren't bothered by too much passing traffic. Sites right on the water include 27, 28, 30–32, 35, and 37. Sites 33 and 34 are very close together, and they may be best for a group that is camping together. Group sites that require a double fee include 44–46, 50, 53, and 54. These are aimed at groups of 10 people or more. Sites 52 and 57 are outside the woods that most of the other sites are located in. The restrooms are pit toilets, and, unfortunately, there are no showers. Some RVers may hesitate to camp in a park without hookups, but those hardy enough to do so will join adventurous tenters in an excellent wilderness of woods, grass, wildflowers, rock outcroppings, and gorgeous lake views.

BASICS

Operated By: Thousand Trails. **Open:** May 15–Sept. **Site Assignment:** First come, first served; reservations can be made 5–240 days in advance; credit card required for reservation; 24-hour cancellation policy. **Registration:** At self-pay station. **Fee:** $13–$26; check, no credits cards. **Parking:** At site, Loop C parking lot.

FACILITIES

Number of RV-only Sites: 52. **Number of Tent-only Sites:** 10. **Hookups:** None. **Each Site:** Picnic table, fire grate, flat tent space. **Dump Station:** No. **Laundry:** No. **Pay Phone:** No. **Restrooms and Showers:** Toilets; no shower. **Fuel:** No. **Propane:** No. **Internal Roads:** Dirt. **RV Service:** No. **Market:** 35 mi. west to Wellington. **Restaurant:** 3 mi. west. **General Store:** No. **Vending:** No. **Swimming:** No. **Playground:** No. **Other:** Boat ramp, no-fee day use. **Activities:** Fishing, boating, hiking, cycling, mountain biking. **Nearby Attractions:** Dowdy Lake, North Park, Red Feather Village. **Additional Information:** Red Feather Lakes Tourist Council, (800) 462-5870.

RESTRICTIONS

Pets: On leash, cleaned up after. **Fires:** Fire pit only. **Alcoholic Beverages:** At sites. **Vehicle Maximum Length:** 40 ft. **Other:** Boating w/ no wakes, no swimming, do not fill water reserves, no ATVs.

TO GET THERE

From the junction of Prairie Divide Rd. and Red Feather Lakes Rd. (74 East), go 1 mi. east on 74 East. Turn north onto Dowdy Lake Rd. and go 1 mi. (keep right on Dowdy Rd.) to pay station.

BELLEVUE   MAP, A-3
Glen Echo Resort

31503 Poudre Canyon Dr./Hwy. 14, 80512. T: (800) 348-2208 or (970) 881-2208.

🚐 ★★★★   ⛺ ★★★

Beauty: ★★★★		Site Privacy: ★★★
Spaciousness: ★★		Quiet: ★★★★★
Security: ★★★★		Cleanliness: ★★★★★
Insect Control: ★★★		Facilities: ★★★

Situated on scenic Hwy. 14, this campground delivers on the beauty promised by the scenic drive to get there. Hills surround the campground on all four sides, and a river runs behind the cabins. The air is fresh, birds sing constantly, and there is green everywhere you look. Even the wood and stone buildings blend in well with the natural surroundings. Now, for the sites themselves. The best sites by far are those in the south portion of the park, which is divided by a retaining wall running east–west down the middle. Unfortunately, nearly half of the sites in the park (including, you guessed it, the choicest south sites) are occupied by long-term residents. There are still some very nice sites available (pull-throughs 64–68 are 80 feet long and have good tree coverage), but chances are good that you will end up on the north side, in a back-in facing to the highway. Not that that's a bad place to be. Sites are level, grassy, and for the most part, shaded by numerous trees. (Sites 14–21, one row in from the highway, have no shade to speak of and are therefore less desirable.) The restroom and shower facilities (both in the main living and laundry complex and the secondary building to the south) are immaculate. The laundry is likewise clean and comfortable, with a sofa and bookshelf stocked with loaners. Note that the "playground" consists of one merry-go-round, but since most of the residents are retirees, there probably isn't call for

much more than that. There is a fine group picnic shelter that even has electric outlets. Living up to the name of the town, this campground is "rustic," and makes a scenic as well as comfortable destination. Make a special trip to come out!

BASICS

Operated By: Lloyd & Gaile Rowe. **Open:** All year. **Site Assignment:** First come, first served. **Registration:** At store until 7 p.m. (Late arrivals not allowed.) **Fee:** RV, $32; tent, $20; V, MC; 10% off during winter. **Parking:** At site.

FACILITIES

Number of RV-only Sites: 87. **Number of Tent-only Sites:** 9. **Hookups:** Electric (30, 50 amps), water, sewer. **Each Site:** Picnic table, trees. **Dump Station:** No (sewer at all sites). **Laundry:** Yes. **Pay Phone:** Yes. **Restrooms and Showers:** Yes. **Fuel:** Yes, including diesel. **Propane:** Yes. **Internal Roads:** Dirt, in good condition. **RV Service:** No. **Market:** Limited on-site (full, 40 mi. east to La Porte). **Restaurant:** Yes. **General Store:** Yes. **Vending:** No. **Swimming:** No. **Playground:** Yes. **Other:** 12 cabins, 2 duplex cabins, group picnic shelter. **Activities:** Special dinner on Mother's Day, hiking, driving. **Nearby Attractions:** Roosevelt National Forest, Cache La Poudre Scenic Byway. **Additional Information:** North Park Chamber of Commerce, (970) 723-4600.

RESTRICTIONS

Pets: On leash. **Fires:** Grill only. **Alcoholic Beverages:** No alcohol permitted. **Vehicle Maximum Length:** 36 ft.

TO GET THERE

On Hwy. 14, just west of the Rustic town name sign and mile marker 91.

BRECKENRIDGE   MAP, B-2
Tiger Run RV Resort

85 Tiger Run Rd., 80424. T: (970) 453-9690; www.tigerrunresort.com.

🚐 ★★★★★   ⛺ n/a

Beauty: ★★★★★		Site Privacy: ★★★★★
Spaciousness: ★★★★★		Quiet: ★★★★★
Security: ★★★★★		Cleanliness: ★★★★★
Insect Control: ★★★★★		Facilities: ★★★★★

The manager here calls this resort "its own little town," and this is not an exaggeration. With roughly 400 sites (70% of which are available to overnighters), tennis courts, indoor swimming pools, a recreation building with TV rooms and pool tables, laundry facilities, double-wide parking spaces, and chalet-style cabins on nearly each RV site, as well as incredible landscaping (lawns, trees, and brick walks), this resort feels more like a quiet suburban neighborhood than an overnight RV park. RVers who wish to use this resort as a travel park (as opposed to buying property) should speak to the manager about which sites are available, as some are privately owned or up for sale. Sites 122–129 and 147–151 are closest to the lake, while 1–7, 129–147, 204–243, and 345–367 are riverside sites. For those who like proximity to the facilities, sites 16–39 and 275–291 are closest to the recreation building. This is a top-notch RV park that deserves the title "resort."

BASICS

Operated By: The Whitt family. **Open:** All year. **Site Assignment:** Upon registration; credit card required for reservation; 48-hour cancellation policy. **Registration:** At office 24 hours (Dial *9). **Fee:** RV, $29–$54; check, V, MC, AE, D, DC, CB; 10% cash discount. **Parking:** At site.

FACILITIES

Number of RV-only Sites: 400. **Hookups:** Electric (30, 50 amps), water, sewer, cable TV. **Each Site:** Picnic table, full-service cabin. **Dump Station:** No (sewer at all sites). **Laundry:** Yes. **Pay Phone:** Yes. **Restrooms and Showers:** Yes. **Fuel:** No. **Propane:** Yes. **Internal Roads:** Paved. **RV Service:** No. **Market:** 3.5 mi. to Breckenridge. **Restaurant:** 3.5 mi. to Breckenridge. **General Store:** Yes. **Vending:** Yes. **Swimming:** Pool, hot tub. **Playground:** Yes. **Other:** Cabins, data port, TV room, pool table, free bus service, lake. **Activities:** Rafting, fishing, Ping-Pong, biking, Wed. night free wine & cheese, Fri. night smores, live entertainment on weekends, tennis, rock climbing, GPS orienteering, teambuilding activities. **Nearby Attractions:** 14,000-ft.-plus mountains, Summit County. **Additional Information:** Breckenridge Resort Chamber, (970) 453-5579.

RESTRICTIONS

Pets: On leash, cleaned up after. **Fires:** Grill only. **Alcoholic Beverages:** At sites. **Vehicle Maximum Length:** No limit. **Other:** No pop-ups or tents.

TO GET THERE

From I-70 Exit 203, turn south onto Hwy. 9 and go 6.3 mi. Turn left at the sign onto the entrance (past mile marker 91) and turn left into the office complex.

BRUSH MAP, A-4
Memorial Park

Mayor of Brush, P.O. Box 363, 80723.
T: (970) 842-5001; www.brushcolo.com.

🚐 ★★★ ⛺ ★★★

Beauty: ★★★   Site Privacy: ★★★★
Spaciousness: ★★★★   Quiet: ★★★
Security: ★★★   Cleanliness: ★★★
Insect Control: ★★★★ Facilities: ★★★

A city park set in an urban environment with industrial and commercial lots around the perimeter, this park tries its best to present a comfortable stay to Brush visitors. Grassy areas and a cute schoolhouse definitely add to the attractiveness of the park, and visitors here should feel rather comfortable (especially knowing that their first night is free!). The sites are somewhat undistinguished and can number more than the electrical boxes that dot the parking area, depending on how people park. There are rows of seemingly just 3–6 sites each, but the city employees who tend to the RV park insist that there are 50 possible sites. The south side of the park is conducive to pull-alongside, while the north is better suited to back-ins. The south side is slightly more industrial and therefore less visibly attractive.

All sites are located on the gravel interior road and do not have a picnic area in their immediate vicinity. Tenters can camp on the lush grass or the crushed gravel tent pads located at the entrance to the RV park. The facilities are city-park clean, and the shower is enormous. They are all open, lacking curtains or dividers of any kind. Overall, this is a rather comfortable city park.

BASICS

Operated By: City of Brush. **Open:** All year. **Site Assignment:** First come, first served; no reservations. **Registration:** At pay station. **Fee:** First night free; each night thereafter, $10; check. **Parking:** At site.

FACILITIES

Number of Tent-only Sites: Undesignated sites. **Hookups:** Electric (20, 30, 50 amps). **Each Site:** Picnic table, grill (tent pads at tent sites). **Dump Station:** Yes. **Laundry:** Yes, in town. **Pay Phone:** Yes. **Restrooms and Showers:** Yes. **Fuel:** No. **Propane:** No. **Internal Roads:** Gravel. **RV Service:** No. **Market:** 0.5 mi. northwest. **Restaurant:** 0.5 mi. north. **General Store:** No. **Vending:** No. **Swimming:** Pool. **Playground:** Yes. **Other:** Covered picnic area, schoolhouse museum. **Activities:** Basketball, volleyball, baseball, swimming. **Nearby Attractions:** Brush Rodeo (July 1–4), buildings on National Historic Registry, Doty Pond. **Additional Information:** Brush Chamber of Commerce, (970) 842-2666.

RESTRICTIONS

Pets: On leash, cleaned up after; only small animals, large animals boarded. **Fires:** Grill only. **Alcoholic Beverages:** Beer only. **Vehicle Maximum Length:** No limit.

TO GET THERE

From I-76 (Exit 90A), turn south onto Hwy. 1 and go 0.75 mi. Turn right onto Hwy. 34, then take the first left onto Clayton. Go 0.4 mi. Turn right at the sign into the entrance.

BUENA VISTA MAP, B-2
Arkansas River Rim Campground and RV Park

33198 Hwy. 24 North, 81211. T: (719) 395-8883; www.coloradodirectory.com/arkansasriverrimcamp.

🚐 ★★★★ ⛺ ★★★★★

Beauty: ★★★★★   Site Privacy: ★★★★
Spaciousness: ★★★★   Quiet: ★★★★
Security: ★★★★   Cleanliness: ★★★★
Insect Control: ★★★★ Facilities: ★★★★

Located in a beautiful valley next to the Arkansas River, this campground offers comfortable sites with beautiful mountain views to the northeast. Sites 1–15 are 75-foot pull-throughs, and 16–24 are 40-foot back-ins located in the north part of the campground. Behind these sites are woods, and beyond those, distant mountains. Sites 25–31 are smaller back-ins (30-foot), while 28–32 are slightly larger (40-foot). Sites 30–32 back to a residence. Sites 33–36 are 60-foot pull-throughs, and 37 and 38, in

the same row, are 42-foot pull-throughs. All sites are mostly open, although there is some shade throughout the park. Tent sites are located at the top of the embankment above the Arkansas River. These sites are wooded and very attractive in their natural state. The restrooms and showers are located in a mobile home. The facilities aren't elaborate but are comfortably clean. This is a very attractive campground in a stunning part of the state—a worthwhile stop in a highly recommended area.

BASICS

Operated By: Dale & Debbie Jantz. **Open:** All year. **Site Assignment:** Flexible, depending on site availability; reservations highly recommended in summer; credit card required for reservation; call to cancel. **Registration:** At office. (Late arrivals select site & pay in the morning.) **Fee:** RV (full), $27; tent, $20; check, V, MC, D. **Parking:** At site.

FACILITIES

Number of RV-only Sites: 36. **Number of Tent-only Sites:** 7. **Hookups:** Electric (30, 50 amps), water, sewer. **Each Site:** Picnic table. **Dump Station:** Yes. **Laundry:** Yes. **Pay Phone:** No. **Restrooms and Showers:** Yes. **Fuel:** No. **Propane:** No. **Internal Roads:** Gravel. **RV Service:** No. **Market:** 4.5 mi. south. **Restaurant:** 4 mi. south. **General Store:** Yes. **Vending:** No. **Swimming:** No. **Playground:** No. **Other:** Ice, fishing licenses, cabins available. **Activities:** Fishing, gold panning, hiking, mountain climbing. **Nearby Attractions:** Classic auto show (July), ghost towns. **Additional Information:** Buena Vista Chamber of Commerce, (719) 395-6612.

RESTRICTIONS

Pets: On leash, cleaned up after; small pets only. 2-pet limit. **Fires:** Grill only. **Alcoholic Beverages:** At sites. **Vehicle Maximum Length:** 70 ft. (some sites). **Other:** Children & groups discouraged.

TO GET THERE

From the junction of Hwy. 285 and Hwy. 24, turn north onto Hwy. 24 and go 7 mi. Turn right at the sign into the entrance. The office is to the right.

BUFFALO CREEK MAP, B-3
Kelsey Campground

Woodland Park, P.O. Box 636, 80866.
T: (800) 416-6992 or (877) 444-6777; www.reserveamerica.com.

🚐 ★★★ ⛺ ★★★★

Beauty: ★★★★★   Site Privacy: ★★★★
Spaciousness: ★★★★   Quiet: ★★★★
Security: ★★★★   Cleanliness: ★★★★
Insect Control: ★★★★ Facilities: ★

Of the many campgrounds in the area, this is perhaps the best for RVers, as the sites are paved. Having said that, of course, there are no hookups, and some of the sites are quite severely sloped. A refined statement might read: this is the area's best campground for adventurous RVers in small rigs. Some of the sites (of which all are back-ins) are truly small: 1 is the smallest at 35 feet, 5 is 40 feet, and most of the rest range from 51 to 60 feet. Site 13 is by far the largest at 66 feet. Sites 8 and 9 are quite a bit less shaded than the rest of the sites. Sites 10, 11, and 13 are also somewhat unshaded and are quite noticeably sloped. The best bets for RVers are 13 (for its size), 12 (level and close to the restroom), or one of the smaller sites 1–5. Tenters need not worry as much about the slope, as there is plenty of level ground to pitch a tent. In fact, this campground is practically a tenter's paradise, and the scenery is absolutely unbeatable. More adventurous RVers can also enjoy a foray into the wild at this campground.

BASICS

Operated By: U.S. Forest Service. **Open:** May 24–Sept. 1 or later. **Site Assignment:** First come, first served; credit card required for reservation; reservations can be made 4–240 days in advance. $8.65 reservation fee, $10 cancellation fee; cancellations w/in 3 days pay first night, no-shows pay $20 fee. (2-night minimum stay on weekends, 3 nights on holidays.) **Registration:** At pay station. **Fee:** $13; check. **Parking:** At site.

FACILITIES

Number of RV-only Sites: 17. **Hookups:** None. **Each Site:** Picnic table, grill. **Dump Station:** No. **Laundry:** No. **Pay Phone:** No. **Restrooms and Showers:** Pit toilets; no shower. **Fuel:** No. **Propane:** No. **Internal Roads:** Gravel. **RV Service:** No. **Market:** 18 mi. to Conifer. **Restaurant:** 9 mi. to Pine. **General Store:** No. **Vending:** No. **Swimming:** No. **Playground:** No. **Activities:** Hiking, mountain biking, fishing. **Nearby Attractions:** Arapaho National Forest. **Additional Information:** South Platte Peak Ranger District, (303) 275-5610.

RESTRICTIONS

Pets: On leash, cleaned up after. **Fires:** Grill only. **Alcoholic Beverages:** Not allowed. **Vehicle Maximum Length:** 20 ft.–99 ft. **Other:** $4 per day park pass; $5 dollar 2nd vehicle fee (2-night min. on weekends, 3 nights on holidays).

TO GET THERE

From the junction of Hwy. 285 and Hwy. 126, turn southeast onto Hwy. 126 and go 19.9 mi. (7.2 mi. from National Forest Service Buffalo Creek Work Center). Turn right at the sign into the entrance.

CALHAN   MAP, B-3
Cadillac Jack's Campground

1001 5th St., 80808. T: (719) 347-2000.

🚐 ★★★		🏕 ★★★
Beauty: ★★★		Site Privacy: ★★★
Spaciousness: ★★★		Quiet: ★★★
Security: ★★★★		Cleanliness: ★★★★
Insect Control: ★★★★		Facilities: ★★

Like most of eastern Colorado, this campground is largely barren and unshaded. It is, however, a comfortable place to camp that offers several pull-throughs (1–6) able to accommodate a rig of any size, including a tow. Sites 7–16 (mostly unnumbered) are 30-foot back-ins that back to a row of large shrubs. These are the most shaded sites in the campground, but quite small. Larger sites (but not as large as 1–6) are laid out in a row along the northern edge of the campground. These sites are 33-foot (17–25) and 42-foot (26–37) pull-throughs that offer full hookups. Sites 15 and 16 should be avoided is possible, as they are quite close to the highway that passes by the campground. The tent area is an open grassy space near the storage units in the southern part of the campground. Tenters will not enjoy this campground as much as self-contained RVs with shower and toilet, as there are no facilities for campers to use.

BASICS

Operated By: Tom Covington. **Open:** Mar.–Nov. 1. **Site Assignment:** First come, first served; reservations available. **Registration:** At campground. **Fee:** RV (full), $22; water/electric, $20; tent, $10; check. **Parking:** At site, extra parking for tows.

FACILITIES

Number of RV-only Sites: 42. **Number of Tent-only Sites:** 5. **Hookups:** Electric (30, 50 amps), water, sewer. **Dump Station:** No. **Laundry:** 1 block. **Pay Phone:** Adjacent to campground. **Restrooms and Showers:** No. **Fuel:** Next door. **Propane:** Across street. **Internal Roads:** Gravel. **RV Service:** No. **Market:** 20 mi. west. **Restaurant:** Yes. **General Store:** Yes. **Vending:** No. **Swimming:** No. **Playground:** No. **Other:** Covered pavilion, antique store, barber shop, bowling alley. **Activities:** Bowling, antique shopping. **Nearby Attractions:** Paint Mines, El Paso County Fair (late July), Colorado Springs. **Additional Information:** Colorado Springs Chamber of Commerce, (719) 635-1551.

RESTRICTIONS

Pets: On leash, cleaned up after. **Fires:** Grill only. **Alcoholic Beverages:** At sites. **Vehicle Maximum Length:** No limit.

TO GET THERE

From Hwy. 24, 0.75 mi. west of the town center on the north side of the street. (Look for the antique shop.)

CANON CITY   MAP, B-3
Yogi Bear's Jellystone
Park Royal Gorge

reserve america

43595 Hwy. 50, 81212. T: (719) 275-2128 or (800) 341-4471; www.royalgorgejellystone.com.

🚐 ★★★★		🏕 ★★★★
Beauty: ★★★★		Site Privacy: ★★
Spaciousness: ★★		Quiet: ★★
Security: ★★★★		Cleanliness: ★★★
Insect Control: ★★★		Facilities: ★★★★

Whether you are an RV-park enthusiast, enjoy the comfort of a cabin in the woods, or just like to tent camp and sleep in the great outdoors, Jellystone Park's accommodations, amenities, and activities are waiting for you and your family to enjoy a quality camping experience. Activities available include swimming, mini-golf, hay rides, tennis, volleyball, fishing, hiking, and appearances from Yogi Bear™ and friends.

BASICS

Operated By: Danny & Gwen DeGeorge. **Open:** Mar. 1–Oct. 1. **Site Assignment:** Reservations recommended. **Fee:** RV, $28–$37; tent, $17–$19; cabin, $50–$118.

FACILITIES

Number of RV-only Sites: 77. **Number of Tent-only Sites:** 28. **Hookups:** Yes. **Dump Station:** Yes. **Laundry:** Yes. **Pay Phone:** Yes. **Restrooms and Showers:** Yes. **Fuel:** No. **Propane:** Yes. **Internal Roads:** Gravel. **General Store:** Camp store. **Vending:** Yes. **Swimming:** Yes. **Playground:** Yes. **Activities:** Sand volleyball, hot tub, horseshoes, hayrides, pedal carts. **Nearby Attractions:** Bike & hiking trails, casinos, Pikes Peak, ATV tours.

RESTRICTIONS

Pets: On leash, attended only. **Vehicle Maximum Length:** 80 ft.

TO GET THERE

Located 9 mi. west of Canon City, on US 50, 1 mi. west of the Royal Gorge turnoff.

CARBONDALE   MAP, B-1, B-2
BRB Crystal River Resort

7202 Hwy. 133, 81623. T: (800) 963-2341 or (970) 963-2341; www.cabinscolorado.com.

🚐 ★★★★		🏕 ★★★★
Beauty: ★★★★		Site Privacy: ★★★★
Spaciousness: ★★★		Quiet: ★★★★
Security: ★★★★		Cleanliness: ★★★★
Insect Control: ★★★		Facilities: ★★

This campground bills itself as the "ultimate resort," which isn't far from the truth. It is surrounded on three sides by towering hills and a mountain and offers a relaxing rustic experience and wonderful views from any site. Sites K–O and 24–31, on the river's edge, are smaller (21-foot) back-ins for pop-ups. Site 25 looks a little cramped, but 26 and N have nice trees and grass. Sites A and B have tall trees, nice grass, and easy access. Tent sites are inside a loop, with excellent trees and wild grass (7–9, right off the highway, are less desirable). Sites E-J and V (all back-ins; there are no pull-throughs in the park) are a little too open and lacking in shade, are situated by the highway, and have more gravel than grass. The restroom and shower facility is a wooden structure that is rustic but cozy—probably chilly on a cold fall day but great in summer. A sign warns campers to keep the doors closed "due to bears." There is rather intimate space between the showers, but on the whole, the facility—as well as the park itself—is quite comfortable.

BASICS

Operated By: Omar Sultan. **Open:** Memorial Day–Oct. 31. **Site Assignment:** Flexible, depending on availability; credit card or check required for reservation; 24-hour cancellation policy. **Registration:** At office. (Late arrivals select site & pay in the morning.) **Fee:** RV on river, $29; tent on river, $19; tent off river, $17; V, MC, D. **Parking:** At site.

FACILITIES

Number of RV-only Sites: 24. **Number of Tent-only Sites:** 24. **Hookups:** Electric (30 amps), water. **Each Site:** Picnic table (most sites). **Dump Station:** Yes. **Laundry:** No. **Pay Phone:** Yes. **Restrooms and Showers:** Yes. **Fuel:** No. **Propane:** No. **Internal Roads:** Gravel. **RV Service:** No. **Market:** 5 mi. in Carbondale. **Restaurant:** 5 mi. in Carbondale. **General Store:** Yes. **Vending:** No. **Swimming:** Pool. **Playground:** Yes. **Other:** River, cabins. **Activities:** Volleyball, basketball, horseshoes, fishing, swimming. Rafting & castle tours are nearby. **Nearby Attractions:** McClure Pass, Hanging Lake, Aspen, Redstone Mansions. **Additional Information:** Glenwood Springs Chamber Resort Assoc., (970) 945-6589.

RESTRICTIONS

Pets: On leash, cleaned up after; small pets only. **Fires:** Varies; call campground for details. **Alcoholic Beverages:** At sites. **Vehicle Maximum Length:** 40 ft.

TO GET THERE

From the junction of Hwy. 82 and Hwy. 133, go 7 mi. south on Hwy. 133. The entrance is on the left, and the office to the right.

CARBONDALE   MAP, B-3
Castle Rock Campground

7202 Hwy. 133, 80109. T: (800) 562-3102 or (303) 681-3169; www.castlerockcampground.com.

🚐 ★★★★   ⛺ ★★★★

Beauty: ★★★★	Site Privacy: ★★★★★
Spaciousness: ★★★★★	Quiet: ★★★★
Security: ★★★★★	Cleanliness: ★★★★★
Insect Control: ★★★★	Facilities: ★★★★

A large campground with sites scattered over the side of a hill, this KOA offers extremely private sites separated from each other by large swaths of vegetation. Sites 1 and 2 are 75-foot pull-throughs right by the entrance. Sites 12, 14, 15, 17, and 19 are "pull-alongsides" that can accommodate 70-foot RVs. Site 72 is an extra-long (100-foot) pull-through. Back-in sites in this area average 54 by 24 feet. Even sites 74–78 and 127 and 129 command a view to the northeast from the top of the hill, making these quite attractive sites. Sites 85–89 are unshaded pull-throughs in the eastern section of the campground. Sites 174 and 175 have views of the volcano cones to the east. Sites 160–169 have approximately 45 feet of usable space (the rest has too much slope). Even 140–148 have views to the east but are completely unshaded and are closest to the railroad tracks. Tent sites are mostly open and unshaded. These include walk-in sites T9–11 and sites T3–8, which are located on the side of the hill. This is quite an attractive campground with lots of vegetation. It is a very nice destination for both tenters and RVers.

BASICS

Operated By: Private operator. **Open:** May 15–Oct. 15; call campground for details. **Site Assignment:** Upon registration.; credit card required for reservation; 24-hour cancellation policy. **Registration:** At office. (Late arrivals use drop box.) **Fee:** $24.50–$37.50; check, V, MC, D. **Parking:** At site.

FACILITIES

Number of RV-only Sites: 179. **Number of Tent-only Sites:** 24. **Hookups:** Electric (30, 50 amps), water, sewer. **Each Site:** Picnic table, grill. **Dump Station:** Yes. **Laundry:** Yes. **Pay Phone:** Yes. **Restrooms and Showers:** Yes. **Fuel:** No. **Propane:** Yes. **Internal Roads:** Dirt. **RV Service:** No. **Market:** 8 mi. north. **Restaurant:** 8 mi. north. **General Store:** Yes. **Vending:** Yes. **Swimming:** Pool. **Playground:** Yes. **Other:** Snack bar, cabins, movie caboose, video games, dog walk. **Activities:** Shopping, swimming. **Nearby Attractions:** Castlewood Canyon State Park, outlet stores, Denver, Colorado Springs, Roxborough State Park. **Additional Information:** Castle Rock Chamber of Commerce, (303) 688-4597.

RESTRICTIONS

Pets: On leash, cleaned up after. **Fires:** Grill only. **Alcoholic Beverages:** At sites. **Vehicle Maximum Length:** No limit. **Other:** No ATVs or motorcycles.

TO GET THERE

From I-25 (Exit 174), turn west onto Tomah Rd. and go across the railroad tacks. Take the first left into the campground parking lot.

CEDAREDGE   MAP, B-1
Aspen Trails Campground and Resort

1997 Hwy. 65, 81413. T: (888) 856-1101 or (970) 856-6321.

🚐 ★★★★★   ⛺ ★★★★★

Beauty: ★★★★	Site Privacy: ★★★★
Spaciousness: ★★★★	Quiet: ★★★★★
Security: ★★★★	Cleanliness: ★★★★
Insect Control: ★★★★	Facilities: ★★★★★

This campground is beautifully landscaped with grass, trees lining the perimeter and dotting the park, and rocks demarking RV sites. (Sites 1–12 are clearly marked, but 13–22 as yet do not have numbers.) All pull-throughs are 72 by 28 feet. The RV site possibly numbered 13 (at any rate, the site southeast of 1) is closest to the road, although a fence does add some extra security. While there is no shade in the RV park, angling your vehicle can reduce direct sunlight dramatically—especially in conjunction with the use of an awning. The large tenting area to the west of the RV sites is wild and good: with lots of grass and tons of trees. Children should be careful of large rocks in the grass around the playground area near the tenting sites. The restrooms have finely finished wood interiors with a Western theme. Showers share a partition and a drain, and the toilet stall doors are only five feet high—but otherwise, the facilities are quite comfortable. Located on a scenic byway, this campground is worth the drive up.

BASICS

Operated By: Dolly, Pat, & Tony Mercep. **Open:** Memorial Day–Nov 15. **Site Assignment:** Flexible depending on availability; credit card required for reservation; 7-day cancellation policy, less 1 night's fee. **Registration:** At office. **Fee:** RV, $22–$24; tent, $15; check, V, MC, AE, D. **Parking:** At site.

FACILITIES

Number of RV-only Sites: 30. **Number of Tent-only Sites:** 20. **Hookups:** Electric (30, 50 amps), water, sewer. **Each Site:** Picnic table, grill. **Dump Station:** Yes. **Laundry:** No. **Pay Phone:** No. **Restrooms and Showers:** Yes. **Fuel:** No. **Propane:** Yes. **Internal Roads:** Dirt/gravel. **RV Service:** No. **Market:** 2 mi. to Cedaredge. **Restaurant:** Yes. **General Store:** No. **Vending:** No. **Swimming:** No. **Playground:** No. **Other:** Ice cream & soda fountain, deli, cabins, pavilion, pet exercise area, groups welcome. **Activities:** Skiing, biking, hiking, fishing. **Nearby Attractions:** Grand Mesa, motorcycle rally (early Aug.). **Additional Information:** Delta Area Chamber of Commerce, (970) 874-8616.

RESTRICTIONS

Pets: On leash, cleaned up after; not allowed to chase deer. **Fires:** Depends on seasonal bans. **Alcoholic Beverages:** At sites. **Vehicle Maximum Length:** No limit.

TO GET THERE

From the Cedaredge town name signpost, go 2 mi. north. Turn west at the signs into the entrance.

CENTRAL CITY   MAP, A-2
Gambler's Edge RV Park

605 Lake Gulch Rd., 80427. T: (877) 660-3465 or (303) 582-9345; www.gamblersedgervpark.com.

🚐 ★★★★★   ⛺ n/a

Beauty: ★★★★★	Site Privacy: ★★★★
Spaciousness: ★★★★	Quiet: ★★★★★
Security: ★★★★★	Cleanliness: ★★★★★
Insect Control: ★★★★	Facilities: ★★★★

This campground is a very nice destination. Sites are uniform gravel back-ins 55 by 30 feet with exceptional landscaping. In addition to an attractive interior, this park benefits from stunning views to the east and northwest. Sites 1–10 back to a stone retaining wall and a beautiful view of Central City and the hills beyond. Sites 11–25 are laid out in two rows on the "island" inside the road that loops around the park. These are nice, but don't offer the views that most other sites enjoy. Sites 33–42 back to an open view to the east and are among the best sites in the park. While there are 80 sites planned for this park, work is still being done on about half. However, from the looks of the existing sites and facilities, this park promises to be a top-notch resort well worth a return trip.

BASICS

Operated By: Barb & Bob. **Open:** All year. **Site Assignment:** First come, first served; reservations recommended & preferred; credit card required for reservation; 24-hour cancellation policy. **Registration:** At office. (Late arrivals come to office or use drop box.) **Fee:** RV, $32.97–$39.56; check, V, MC, D. **Parking:** At site, next to huge parking lot.

FACILITIES

Number of Multipurpose Sites: 67. **Hookups:** Electric (30, 50 amps), water, sewer, phone, data port. **Dump Station:** Yes. **Laundry:** Yes. **Pay Phone:** Yes. **Restrooms and Showers:** Yes. **Fuel:** No. **Propane:** Yes. **Internal Roads:** Gravel. **RV Service:** No. **Market:** 8 mi. to Idaho Springs. **Restaurant:** 1 mi. to

Central City. **General Store:** Yes. **Vending:** No. **Swimming:** No (hot tub). **Playground:** No. **Other:** Clubhouse. **Activities:** Rafting, hiking, mountain biking, skiing, fishing. **Nearby Attractions:** Ghost towns, Coors Brewery, aquarium, zoo. **Additional Information:** Gilpin County Chamber of Commerce, (303) 582-5077.

RESTRICTIONS

Pets: On leash, cleaned up after. **Fires:** Grill only. **Alcoholic Beverages:** At sites. **Vehicle Maximum Length:** No limit. **Other:** 1 vehicle only.

TO GET THERE

From I-70 (Exit 244), turn east onto Hwy. 6 and go 2.85 mi. Turn north onto Hwy. 119 and go 7.3 mi. Turn left onto Gregory St. and go 1 mi. Turn left onto Spring St. (turns into Hooper) and go 2 mi. Turn right onto Lake Gulch Rd. and go 0.15 mi. Turn left at the sign into the entrance.

CLARK   MAP, A-2
Pearl Lake State Park

Box 750, 80428. T: (970) 879-3922; www.reserveamerica.com.

🚐 ★★★★	⛺ ★★★★
Beauty: ★★★★★	Site Privacy: ★★★
Spaciousness: ★★★★	Quiet: ★★★★★
Security: ★★★★	Cleanliness: ★★★★
Insect Control: ★★★	Facilities: ★

Pearl Lake State Park is by far one of the most beautiful parks in the Colorado State Park system. Nestled in the mountains north of Steamboat Springs and west of the Continental Divide, Pearl Lake offers peace and quiet in a lush forest setting. Surrounded by towering pines, visitors camp along the lake and up a gentle hill which is deep in the cozy woods. It features a 167-surface-acre lake, and draws most of its visitors for trout fishing. Excellent fly- and lure-fishing is available at the park where native cutthroat trout flash their dramatic red throats when pulled from the water. Interpretive programs through Steamboat Lake State Park are available during the summer months. The road into the park is not maintained during the winter months but ice fishing, cross-country skiing, snowshoeing, and snowmobiling are permitted in the park. The 40 campsites and two yurts are shaded by dense stands of spruce, fir and lodgepole pines. Large motor homes cannot be accommodated here, but smaller camping vehicles can enjoy sites with a table, grill, and vault toilets. South of the campground is a boat ramp and a fishing trail that leads around the lake.

BASICS

Operated By: Colorado State Parks. **Open:** May 1–Sept. 4. **Site Assignment:** Reservations can be made 6 months in advance. **Registration:** At office. **Fee:** Single, $7–$20; yurt, $60; cabin, $80–$160. **Parking:** At park.

FACILITIES

Number of Multipurpose Sites: 38. **Hookups:** None. **Each Site:** Fire ring. **Dump Station:** No.

Laundry: No. **Pay Phone:** No. **Restrooms and Showers:** Yes. **Fuel:** No. **Propane:** No. **Internal Roads:** Paved. **RV Service:** No. **Market:** No. **Restaurant:** No. **General Store:** No. **Vending:** No. **Swimming:** No. **Playground:** No. **Activities:** Bird watching, boating, cross-country skiing, fishing, hiking, hunting, ice fishing, interpretive programs, photography, picnicking, snowshoeing, wildlife viewing.

RESTRICTIONS

Pets: Pets must be on a leash no longer than 6 ft. in length. **Fires:** In designated fireplaces. **Other:** Quiet hours will be enforced 10 p.m.–6 a.m. All generators, loud radios, or other loud noises that may disturb the peace are prohibited during these hours.

TO GET THERE

From Steamboat Springs go west 2 mi. on Hwy. 40 to CR 129. Turn north and go 23 mi. to Pearl Lake Rd. Go east 2 mi. to park entrance.

CLARK   MAP, A-2
Steamboat Lake State Park

P.O. Box 750, 80428. T: (800) 678-CAMP or (970) 879-7019; www.reserveamerica.com.

🚐 ★★★★	⛺ ★★★★★
Beauty: ★★★★	Site Privacy: ★★★★
Spaciousness: ★★★★	Quiet: ★★★★★
Security: ★★★★	Cleanliness: ★★★★
Insect Control: ★★★★	Facilities: ★★★

This campground has forested campsites that include 60-foot back-ins and some 90-foot pull-throughs (pull-throughs include 116, 118, 120, 121, 123, and 127). Sites with electric hookups are limited to 116–165. All sites are laid out in loops, with the Baker Loop being slightly closer to the boat ramps and the swimming beach. Sites 131, 146, and 160 are all located at the end of roundabouts, and they are therefore more secluded than most others. Bridge Island is a separate section of the campground connected by the interior road. It contains sites 166–200, of which about half (181–200) are walk-in tent sites. The restrooms and showers are large, clean, and comfortable. The showers cost 50 cents for three minutes. There are change machines in the restrooms.

BASICS

Operated By: Colorado State Parks. **Open:** All year; weather permitting. **Site Assignment:** First come, first served; credit card required for reservation; 3-day cancellation policy. **Registration:** At pay station. **Fee:** $7–$20; check, no credits cards. **Parking:** At site.

FACILITIES

Number of RV-only Sites: 50. **Number of Tent-only Sites:** 148. **Hookups:** Electric (20, 30, 50 amps). **Each Site:** Picnic table, grill, fire pit, tent pad. **Dump Station:** Yes (at Dutch Hill). **Laundry:** Yes (at Dutch Hill). **Pay Phone:** Yes (at Visitor Center). **Restrooms and Showers:** Yes (at Dutch Hill). **Fuel:** No. **Propane:** No. **Internal Roads:** Gravel. **RV Service:** No. **Market:** 26 mi. south. **Restaurant:** 26 mi. south. **General Store:** Marina. **Vending:** Yes. **Swim-**

ming: Lake. **Playground:** No. **Other:** Boat ramp, firewood, amphitheater, cabins, boat rentals, indoor picnic area. **Activities:** Fishing, boating, swimming, hiking. **Nearby Attractions:** Steamboat Springs. **Additional Information:** Steamboat Springs Chamber Resort Assoc., (970) 879-0880.

RESTRICTIONS

Pets: On leash, cleaned up after. **Fires:** Grill only. **Alcoholic Beverages:** At sites. **Vehicle Maximum Length:** No limit. **Other:** $4 per vehicle for day-use fee.

TO GET THERE

From the junction of Hwy. 40 and CR 129, turn north onto CR 129 and go 25 mi. to visitor center. Continue 0.9 mi. to first campground on the left.

CLIFTON   MAP, B-1
RV Ranch at Grand Junction

3238 East I-70 Business Loop, 81520. T: (800) 793-0041 or (970) 434-6644; www.rvranches.com.

🚐 ★★★★★	⛺ ★★
Beauty: ★★★★	Site Privacy: ★★
Spaciousness: ★★★	Quiet: ★★★★
Security: ★★★★	Cleanliness: ★★★★★
Insect Control: ★★★★	Facilities: ★★★★★

This perfectly manicured, wonderfully clean park has loads of trees offering shade, nice landscaping, and long (75-foot) pull-throughs. The one downside is that sites are slightly narrow: the RVs with slide-outs on some of the 30-foot-wide spaces were practically touching on my visit. Besides this, however, it is hard to find a less-than-wonderful site in this park (although, 53 seems slightly chintzed on space and doesn't have a tree, and 54 is a little close to the basketball court). Pull-throughs 44–52 and back-ins 23–35 are personal favorites due to their semi-isolated feeling and good trees. The restrooms are immaculate and beautiful, with nice tiling and decorations. Showers have inner and outer doors for added privacy and are spacious enough for anyone. A sign in the restrooms asks guests to report any problems to management, and you can tell that these folks are on top of things. Tenters, unfortunately, don't fare quite as well, and the concrete slabs that pass for tent sites (ouch!) might as well be converted to RV sites for all they're worth. Tent campers should skip this park. However, anyone with an RV who is passing through Colorado should make a point to check out this park—it is what an RV park is supposed to be!

BASICS

Operated By: RV Resorts Co. **Open:** All year. **Site Assignment:** Upon registration; credit card required for reservation; 24-hour cancellation policy. **Registration:** At office. (Late arrivals use drop box.) **Fee:** RV, $26–$33; tent, $28; V, MC, AE, D. **Parking:** At site.

FACILITIES

Number of RV-only Sites: 139. **Hookups:** Electric (20, 30, 50 amps), water, sewer. **Each Site:** Picnic table, grill. **Dump Station:** Yes. **Laundry:** Yes. **Pay Phone:** Yes. **Restrooms and Showers:** Yes. **Fuel:** No. **Propane:** Yes. **Internal Roads:** Perfect, paved. **RV Service:** Can call. **Market:** 0.5 mi. east.

Restaurant: 0.5 mi. east (café on-site). **General Store:** Yes. **Vending:** Yes. **Swimming:** Pool. **Playground:** Yes. **Other:** Dog walk area, TV room, e-mail booth, exercise room, kitchen, nightly movies in summer, RV supplies. **Activities:** Hiking, wine-tasting, swimming, volleyball, horseshoes, pancake breakfasts, ice-cream socials, fishing, golf, crafts. **Nearby Attractions:** Colorado National Monument, Dinosaur National Monument, Dinosaur Trail, Grand Mesa, wineries. **Additional Information:** Grand Junction CVB, (800) 962-2547 or (970) 244-1480.

RESTRICTIONS

Pets: On leash, cleaned up after. **Fires:** Fire pit only. **Alcoholic Beverages:** At sites. **Vehicle Maximum Length:** No limit. **Other:** No generators, no kennels, no clotheslines, no vehicle washing.

TO GET THERE

From I-70, take Exit 30 onto the I-70 Business Loop. Go 0.75 mi. southwest, then turn right at the light onto F Rd. and take the first (sharp) right turn behind the Park-Ride. Drive 0.1 mi. and take the first left into the entrance.

COLLBRAN   MAP, B-1
Vega State Recreation Area

reserve america

Box 186, 81624. T: (970) 487-3407; www.reserveamerica.com.

🚐 ★★★★	⛺ ★★★★
Beauty: ★★★	Site Privacy: ★★★
Spaciousness: ★★★	Quiet: ★★★★★
Security: ★★★★★	Cleanliness: ★★★★
Insect Control: ★★★	Facilities: ★★★★

Vega Lake is a beautiful high-mountain lake that sits in a glorious alpine meadow on the west edge of Grand Mesa National Forest. Vega State Park lies 55 miles east of Grand Junction on the northern edge of the Grand Mesa National Forest. The focus of recreation activity in the park is a 900-surface-acre reservoir. Vega State Park provides visitors with several camping options. Early Settlers Campground offers 33 pull-through and back-in sites, with electric and water hookups, flush toilets, and coin-operated showers. Aspen Grove Campground has 27 pull-through and back-in sites with centrally located water pumps and vault toilets. Oak Point Campground provides 39 pull-through and back-in sites with centrally located water pumps and vault toilets. For a more unique experience, Pioneer Campground offers 10 walk-in tent sites and 5 rustic cabins with centrally located water pumps and vault toilets. Most users of Vega Lake come for boating, fishing, and camping. Picnicking, waterskiing, jet skiing, sailing, and hiking are also available for visitors. The extensive trail systems of the Grand Mesa National Forest are located close to the park boundaries.

BASICS

Operated By: Colorado State Parks. **Open:** All year. **Site Assignment:** Reservations can be made 6 months in advance. **Registration:** At office. **Fee:**

Single, $7–$20; yurt, $60; cabin, $80–$160. **Parking:** At park.

FACILITIES

Number of Multipurpose Sites: 116. **Hookups:** Yes. **Each Site:** Fire ring. **Dump Station:** Yes. **Laundry:** No. **Pay Phone:** Yes. **Restrooms and Showers:** Yes. **Fuel:** No. **Propane:** No. **Internal Roads:** Paved. **RV Service:** No. **Market:** No. **Restaurant:** No. **General Store:** No. **Vending:** No. **Swimming:** No. **Playground:** Yes. **Activities:** Biking, bird-watching, boating, cross-country skiing, fishing, hiking, hunting, ice fishing, interpretive programs, jet skiing, photography, picnicking, sailing, sailboarding, snowmobiling, waterskiing, wildlife viewing.

RESTRICTIONS

Pets: Pets must be on a leash no longer than 6 ft. in length. **Fires:** Permitted in designated fireplaces. **Other:** Quiet hours will be enforced 10 p.m.–6 a.m. All generators, loud radios, or other loud noises that may disturb the peace are prohibited during these hours.

TO GET THERE

From I-70 go south on Hwy. 65 then east on Hwy. 330 through Collbran. Continue 12 mi. to the park entrance 55 mi. from Grand Junction.

COLORADO CITY   MAP, C-3
Pueblo South/Colorado City KOA

9040 I-25 South, 81004. T: (800) 562-8646 or (719) 676-3376; www.koakampground.com.

🚐 ★★★★★	⛺ ★★★★★
Beauty: ★★★★	Site Privacy: ★★★★
Spaciousness: ★★★★	Quiet: ★★★
Security: ★★★★★	Cleanliness: ★★★★
Insect Control: ★★★★	Facilities: ★★★★

This desert campground uses attractive indigenous plants and rocks in its landscaping, including at least one huge flowering cactus. RV sites are laid out in three rows, with tent sites occupying another distinct row. Row A, along the north side of the campground, has 60-foot back-ins that are mostly quite shady. (Sites 13 and 14 do not have shade trees.) Site A2 is next to the hot tub, which is convenient, but may attract more foot traffic. Site A9 has an extra large grassy site (27 feet wide), which makes it more desirable. Site A14, on the other hand, has "views" of a gas station and residences and backs to a mobile home, making it the least desirable site in the campground. Row B has grassy pull-throughs 60 by 18 feet. Sites B7–10 are especially shaded. Site B1 has a giant overhanging tree and is closest to the restrooms. Sites in Row C have views of an open field to the east, which is more attractive than, for example, A14's view. These sites are all grassy, and C7–10 are especially shaded. Site C16 has an electric pole and wires that encroach on its space. Tent sites are located along the south side of the campground. These sites have beautiful grass and loads of trees. There are also some very nice views of hills to the southwest. (Unfortunately, there is RV storage to the southeast.) Each of these spacious sites is separated by shrubs.

The restrooms are very nicely decorated but had soap residue on the shower floors. Otherwise, the restrooms were spotless. This is a very attractive campground that will appeal to most RV campers and has excellent facilities for tenters.

BASICS

Operated By: Tim & Elena Johnson. **Open:** All year. **Site Assignment:** Upon registration; reservations recommended (credit card required); 24-hour cancellation policy. **Registration:** At office. (Late arrivals use drop box.) **Fee:** RV (full), $34; tent, $17; check, V, MC, D. **Parking:** At site.

FACILITIES

Number of RV-only Sites: 71. **Number of Tent-only Sites:** 14. **Hookups:** Electric (30, 50 amps), water, sewer. **Each Site:** Picnic table. **Dump Station:** Yes. **Laundry:** Yes. **Pay Phone:** Yes. **Restrooms and Showers:** Yes. **Fuel:** No. **Propane:** Yes. **Internal Roads:** Gravel w/ paved entrance. **RV Service:** No. **Market:** 2 mi. west. **Restaurant:** 0.25 mi. west. **General Store:** Yes. **Vending:** Yes. **Swimming:** Heated pool. **Playground:** Yes. **Other:** Mini-golf, pavilion, pet walk, cabins. **Activities:** Basketball, fishing (nearby), off-road riding, swimming, volleyball, golf (nearby). **Nearby Attractions:** Hollydot Golf Course, Bishop's Castle, Lake Beckweth, Lake Isabel, Pueblo Riverwalk, Pueblo Museum, Colorado State Fair, Art & Conference Center. **Additional Information:** Visitor Information Center, (719) 543-1742.

RESTRICTIONS

Pets: On leash, cleaned up after. **Fires:** Fire pit only. **Alcoholic Beverages:** At sites. **Vehicle Maximum Length:** 55 ft.

TO GET THERE

From I-25 (Exit 74): From the south side of the exit, take the first right after the highway and go 0.25 mi. Turn left at the sign into the entrance.

COLORADO SPRINGS   MAP, B-3
Garden of the Gods Campground

3704 West Colorado Ave., 80904. T: (800) 248-9451 or (719) 475-9450; www.coloradocampgrounds.com.

🚐 ★★★★	⛺ ★★★★
Beauty: ★★★★	Site Privacy: ★★★
Spaciousness: ★★★	Quiet: ★★★
Security: ★★★★	Cleanliness: ★★★★
Insect Control: ★★★★	Facilities: ★★★★

This is a vast campground that offers a large selection of back-ins and pull-throughs, with some creek side spaces. Most sites are very well shaded (the M, N, and O sites being one notable exception). Back-in sites range from 30 feet (A, B, and P sections), to 45 feet (D, E, K, and S sections), to 60 feet (C section) long. Pull-throughs are located in the F, G, M, N, and O sections. F and G sites are extra-long, 80-feet, sites used as end-to-end doubles, making each site roughly 40 feet. Longer single sites are located in sections M, N, and O, which are 60 feet in length. Creek side sites (indicated on the campground map by "CS") are located in the southwest corner. The tenting area is found on the west side of the campground, but there are also creek side tenting sites, marked on the map as "CRT." These are nice, shaded sites with some grass cover. Although they are closer to the road that passes by the campground, tenters may prefer these sites for their natural feel and the sound of the creek at night. The pool, the laundry, the restrooms, and all other facilities are well-maintained, clean, and comfortable. This is a great campground to stay at while visiting the Garden of the Gods or any of the other numerous attractions in the area.

BASICS

Operated By: Chuck Murphy. **Open:** All year. **Site Assignment:** Upon registration; credit card required for reservation (groups welcome); specific sites not guaranteed, 24-hour cancellation policy, less $5 fee. **Registration:** At office. (Late arrivals use drop box.) **Fee:** Summer, $28–$40; winter, $26–$30; V, MC, D. **Parking:** At site.

FACILITIES

Number of RV-only Sites: 300. **Number of Tent-only Sites:** 30. **Number of Multipurpose Sites:** 325. **Hookups:** Electric (30, 50 amps), water, sewer, phone. **Each Site:** Picnic table, grill. **Dump Station:** Yes. **Laundry:** Yes. **Pay Phone:** Yes. **Restrooms and Showers:** Yes. **Fuel:** No. **Propane:** No. **Internal Roads:** Paved. **RV Service:** No. **Market:** 0.5 mi. east. **Restaurant:** 1 block east. **General Store:** Yes. **Vending:** Yes. **Swimming:** Pool. **Playground:** Yes. **Other:** Clubhouse, jukebox, gift shop, coffee & donuts, pancake breakfasts, watermelon feasts, ice-cream socials, fajitas, bus stop in front, firewood, Internet access, cabins. **Activities:** Bus tours, basketball, socials, sunbathing, food socials. **Nearby Attractions:** Garden of the Gods, Florissant Fossil Beds National Monument, Cripple Creek & Victor Narrow Gauge Railroad, Air Force Base Visitor Center, Mining Museum. **Additional Information:** Colorado Springs Chamber of Commerce, (719) 635-1551.

RESTRICTIONS

Pets: On leash, cleaned up after. **Fires:** Grill, dependent on current fire bans. **Alcoholic Beverages:** At sites. **Vehicle Maximum Length:** 70 ft. **Other:** No schoolbuses, no washing or repairing vehicles.

TO GET THERE

From I-25 (Exit 141), turn west onto Hwy. 24 and go 2.6 mi. Turn north onto 31st St. and go 1 block. Turn left onto Colorado Ave. and go 0.8 mi. Turn right at the sign into the entrance.

CORTEZ   MAP, C-1
Cortez/Mesa Verde KOA

27432 East Hwy. 160, 81321. T: (800) 562-3901 or (970) 565-9301; www.koakampground.com.

🚐 ★★★★   ⛺ ★★★★

Beauty: ★★★★	Site Privacy: ★★★★
Spaciousness: ★★★★	Quiet: ★★★
Security: ★★★★	Cleanliness: ★★★★★
Insect Control: ★★★★	Facilities: ★★★★★

This beautiful campground is surrounded on three sides by mountains and has an excellent view of Sleeping Ute Mountain to the north. To the south are scrub-covered hills, and over everything looms big,

open sky. RV sites are almost exclusively 70-foot pull-throughs, with a handful of 45-foot back-ins mostly used by long-term guests. Tent sites have both water and electric hookups. The tenting area is grassy, shaded, and very comfortable. The restrooms and showers are spacious, comfortable, and absolutely spotless. The laundry room is bright and roomy, and all other facilities (pool, game room) are clean and tidy. This campground is centrally located for trips to Mesa Verde, Four Corners, and even farther reaches such as Canyonlands or Monument Valley. Campers in tents or RVs will be pleased by this campground, which is worth making a destination on their itinerary.

BASICS

Operated By: Shawn & Bernie Bender. **Open:** Apr. 1–Oct. 15. **Site Assignment:** Upon registration. **Registration:** At office. (Late arrivals use drop box.) **Fee:** RV (full), $29; water/electric, $27; primitive tent, $21; deluxe, $35; Indian tepees, $30; V, MC, D. **Parking:** At site.

FACILITIES

Number of RV-only Sites: 78. **Number of Tent-only Sites:** 26. **Hookups:** Electric (30, 50 amps), water, sewer. **Each Site:** Picnic table, grill. **Dump Station:** Yes. **Laundry:** Yes. **Pay Phone:** Yes. **Restrooms and Showers:** Yes. **Fuel:** No. **Propane:** No. **Internal Roads:** Gravel. **RV Service:** No. **Market:** 1 mi. west. **Restaurant:** 0.25 mi. west. **General Store:** Yes. **Vending:** No. **Swimming:** Pool. **Playground:** Yes. **Other:** Data port, hot tub/sauna, firewood, game room, cabins, pet walk, tepees. **Activities:** Fishing, boating, swimming, golf, horseback riding, visiting ruins, volleyball, basketball. **Nearby Attractions:** Mesa Verde, Four Corners, Lake McPhee, Monument Valley, Canyonlands, Hovenweep National Monument. **Additional Information:** Cortez Area Chamber of Commerce, (800) 346-6526 or (970) 565-3414.

RESTRICTIONS

Pets: On leash, cleaned up after. **Fires:** Fire pit only. **Alcoholic Beverages:** At sites. **Vehicle Maximum Length:** No limit. **Other:** Seasonal restrictions; inquire at campground.

TO GET THERE

From the junction of Hwy. 145 and Hwy. 160, turn east onto Hwy. 160 and go 0.4 mi. Turn right at the sign into the entrance.

COTOPAXI   MAP, B-2
Arkansas River KOA

21435 US 50, 81223. T: (800) 562-2686 or (719) 275-9308; www.koakampground.com.

🚐 ★★★★   ⛺ ★★★★

Beauty: ★★★★	Site Privacy: ★★★
Spaciousness: ★★★★	Quiet: ★★★
Security: ★★★★	Cleanliness: ★★★★
Insect Control: ★★★★	Facilities: ★★★★

This riverside campground has three strips of pull-throughs (1–13, 14–29, and 30–49) between the highway and the river. These pull-through sites range from 60 feet to 80 feet in length. Sites with nice shade trees include 14, and 17–23. These sites also have beautiful vistas of the rocky hills across the river

to the west. End site 30 is a slightly shorter (50-foot) pull-through, but has extra space around it. This site might be a tough spot to park in for a larger rig, due to its proximity to a cabin. Tent sites are back-ins, 35 by 18 feet, along the riverfront. These sandy sites (51–80) have trees and vegetation, and they face the river and the woods on the far shore. These are excellent sites that tenters will be happy to occupy for a stay of any length. The restrooms are clean, though slightly run-down, and appear to have been decorated in the 1970s. (There are additional porta-potties along the river for tenters' use.) Likewise, the laundry is dark and a little musty, but spacious and relatively clean. This is a pleasant campground in a beautiful setting that will appeal slightly more to tenters, but is still an excellent stay for RVers.

BASICS

Operated By: Jim & Amy Burnham. **Open:** Apr. 15–Oct. 30. **Site Assignment:** Flexible, depending on site availability; credit card required for reservation; cancellation by 4 p.m. same day. **Registration:** At office. (Late arrivals go to night registration at building to left of entrance.) **Fee:** RV, $25–$45; tent, $22–$26; V, MC, D. **Parking:** At site.

FACILITIES

Number of RV-only Sites: 49. **Number of Tent-only Sites:** 30. **Hookups:** Electric (30, 50 amps), water, sewer. **Each Site:** Picnic table, fire pit. **Dump Station:** Yes. **Laundry:** Yes. **Pay Phone:** Yes. **Restrooms and Showers:** Yes. **Fuel:** No. **Propane:** Yes. **Internal Roads:** Gravel. **RV Service:** No. **Market:** 25 mi. to Salida or Canon City. **Restaurant:** 25 mi. to Salida or Canon City. **General Store:** Yes. **Vending:** Soft drinks. **Swimming:** Pool. **Playground:** Yes. **Other:** Pool table. **Activities:** Basketball, fishing, rafting, horseshoes, nightly hay ride, nightly kids movies, mini-golf, tetherball, shuffleboard. **Nearby Attractions:** Royal Gorge, Buckskin Joe's Frontierland & Railway, Royal Gorge Railroads. **Additional Information:** Canon City Chamber of Commerce, (719) 275-2331.

RESTRICTIONS

Pets: On leash, cleaned up after, $5 per pet, in designated campground areas. **Fires:** Fire pit only. **Alcoholic Beverages:** At sites. **Vehicle Maximum Length:** 75 ft. **Other:** Protect trees; do not tie anything to trees.

TO GET THERE

From the easternmost town name sign, go 1.3 mi. east on Hwy. 50 (just south of mile marker 247). Turn left at the sign into the entrance. The office is on the right; night registration is to the left.

CRAIG   MAP, A-1
Craig KOA Kampground

2800 East US 40, 81625. T: (970) 824-5105; www.koakampground.com.

🚐 ★★★   ⛺ ★★

Beauty: ★★★	Site Privacy: ★★★
Spaciousness: ★★★	Quiet: ★★★
Security: ★★★★	Cleanliness: ★★★★★
Insect Control: ★★★★	Facilities: ★★★★★

Just at the east end of town, and 2 miles from downtown Craig, this campground has grassy fields and plenty of trees to the south and west. Its super-long (90-foot) double pull-throughs (sites 28–44) can be used by one long rig if the campground is not too full. Sites are level and grassy, averaging 27 feet wide. Sites 6–10 are wide open in the middle of the interior road with only two decent trees, thus they are the least desirable sites. Tent sites are located along the south fence, which presents one significant drawback: trains roll right past the park boundary by the fence. The restroom and shower facilities are spotless and well lit. The laundry is spacious and clean, with a pleasant waiting area. Overall, the park is a decent place to stay, but tenters might have better luck elsewhere.

BASICS

Operated By: Rocky Mountain. **RV Park. Open:** All year; monthly tenants only Dec. 1–Apr. 15. **Site Assignment:** Reservations recommended Apr. 1–Nov. 30; first come, first served Dec. 1–Mar. 31. **Registration:** At store. (Late arrivals use drop box.) **Fee:** RV, $31–$41; tent, $23–$33; V, MC, AE, D. **Parking:** At site only.

FACILITIES

Number of RV-only Sites: 83. **Number of Tent-only Sites:** 20. **Hookups:** Electric (30, 50 amps), water, sewer. **Each Site:** Picnic table, tree. **Dump Station:** Yes. **Laundry:** Yes. **Pay Phone:** Yes. **Restrooms and Showers:** Yes. **Fuel:** No. **Propane:** Yes. **Internal Roads:** Gravel. **RV Service:** No. **Market:** 2 mi. west. **Restaurant:** 2 mi. west. **General Store:** Yes. **Vending:** Yes. **Swimming:** Pool. **Playground:** Yes. **Other:** 4 cabins, RV parts, data port, pet walk area, hot tub, rec room, soccer field. **Activities:** Soccer, swimming, horseshoes, hiking. **Nearby Attractions:** Sandrocks Nature Trail & Petroglyphs, Museum of Northwest Colorado, Dinosaur National Monument. **Additional Information:** Craig Chamber of Commerce, (970) 824-5689.

RESTRICTIONS

Pets: On leash, cleaned up after. **Fires:** Fire pits; subject to seasonal bans. **Alcoholic Beverages:** At sites only. **Vehicle Maximum Length:** No limit.

TO GET THERE

On Hwy. 40, go 0.5 mi. west of the easternmost Craig town name signpost. Turn south into the entrance. The office is straight ahead.

CRAWFORD   MAP, B-1
Crawford State Park

Box 147, 81415. T: (970) 921-5721; www.reserveamerica.com.

🚐 ★★★★	🏕 ★★★★
Beauty: ★★★★	Site Privacy: ★★★
Spaciousness: ★★★	Quiet: ★★★★★
Security: ★★★★★	Cleanliness: ★★★★
Insect Control: ★★★	Facilities: ★★★★

The focal attraction of Crawford State Park is the 397-surface-acre lake. Facilities line the lake on the northern, eastern, and western shores. The northern shore provides access to a day-use area with several picnic sites and a beach. Goodwin Cove day-use area lies on the western shore of the lake and includes shore-fishing access, picnic tables, pit toilets, and the Indian Fire Nature Trail. The eastern shore of Crawford Lake supports the overnight-use areas of the park. These areas include 53 modern campsites with electrical hookups, parking pads, showers, flush toilets, picnic tables, water hydrants, and grills. A boat ramp, swimming area, and dump station are also located on the eastern shore of Crawford Reservoir. Fishing is the main reason people visit Crawford State Park. The lake is stocked with perch, bass, catfish and trout. Boating, swimming, waterskiing, jet skiing, sailing, hiking, camping, and picnicking can also be enjoyed by visitors to this state park. Hunters use the camping facilities of the park as a base for big game hunting during the autumn months. Ice fishing, ice skating, snowmobiling, and cross-country skiing may be enjoyed by visitors in the winter months.

BASICS

Operated By: Colorado State Parks. **Open:** All year. **Site Assignment:** Reservations can be made 6 months in advance. **Registration:** At office. **Fee:** Single, $7–$20; yurt, $60; cabin, $80–$160. **Parking:** At park.

FACILITIES

Number of Multipurpose Sites: 66. **Hookups:** Yes. **Each Site:** Fire ring. **Dump Station:** Yes. **Laundry:** No. **Pay Phone:** Yes. **Restrooms and Showers:** Yes. **Fuel:** No. **Propane:** No. **Internal Roads:** Paved. **RV Service:** No. **Market:** No. **Restaurant:** No. **General Store:** No. **Vending:** No. **Swimming:** Yes. **Playground:** Yes. **Activities:** Beach, biking, bird-watching, boating, cross-country skiing, fishing, hiking, hunting, ice fishing, jet skiing, photography, picnicking, sailing, sailboarding, snowshoeing, sledding, waterskiing, wildlife viewing.

RESTRICTIONS

Pets: Pets must be on a leash no longer than 6 ft. in length. **Fires:** Permitted in designated fireplaces. **Other:** Quiet hours will be enforced 10 p.m.–6 a.m.; all generators, loud radios or other loud noises that may disturb the peace are prohibited during these hours.

TO GET THERE

From Delta, take CO 92 east to Hotchkiss. Stay right on 92 where it intersects Colorado Highway 133 and drive 10 miles to Crawford. The park is 1 mile south of town.

CRAWFORD   MAP, B-1
Paonia State Park

P.O. Box 147, 81415. T: (800) 678-2267 or (970) 921-5721; www.reserveamerica.com.

🚐 ★★★	🏕 ★★★★
Beauty: ★★★★★	Site Privacy: ★★★★
Spaciousness: ★★★★	Quiet: ★★★★
Security: ★★★★	Cleanliness: ★★★★
Insect Control: ★★★★	Facilities: ★

Of the two campgrounds in this state park, Hawsapple Campground is the closest to the reservoir boat and swimming access areas. Sites 1–3 are scrunched together at the end of the roundabout, near a pit toilet. These are 27 feet long but have ample parking space, as they are 25 feet wide. Site 0 is a "pull-alongside" that can accommodate RVs 42–45 feet. If you turn left at the entrance, you continue on to sites 4–7. Of these, 4–6 are large pull-throughs, measuring 84–90 feet each. Site 7 is a 54-foot shaded back-in. The reservoir access area is a mile farther up this road. Spruce Campground is located just off Hwy. 133, and contains sites 8–15. Sites 8–12 are located together by the entrance, and sites 8 and 10 seem to be sharing parking spaces as do 11 and 12. Site 13 is a smallish back-in (36 feet long), but extremely well shaded. Site 15 is a 60-foot "pull-alongside" with an open picnic area down by the edge of the river. The two campgrounds in this state park offer a variety of recreational opportunities related to the reservoir, and campers of all stripes will enjoy an adventurous stay here.

BASICS

Operated By: Colorado State Parks. **Open:** Year-round; weather permitting. Call park for details. **Site Assignment:** First come, first served; credit card or check required for reservation; 24-hour cancellation policy. **Registration:** At pay station. **Fee:** $7 plus $5 day-use fee; check. **Parking:** At site.

FACILITIES

Number of Multipurpose Sites: 15. **Hookups:** None. **Each Site:** Picnic table, grill. **Dump Station:** No. **Laundry:** No. **Pay Phone:** No. **Restrooms and Showers:** Pit toilets; no shower. **Fuel:** No. **Propane:** No. **Internal Roads:** Gravel. **RV Service:** No. **Market:** 16 mi. to Paonia. **Restaurant:** At bottom of reservoir. **General Store:** No. **Vending:** No. **Swimming:** Reservoir. **Playground:** No. **Other:** Boat ramp, picnic area. **Activities:** Fishing, boating, swimming, hiking, waterskiing. **Nearby Attractions:** Gunnison National Forest. **Additional Information:** Gunnison National Forest, (970) 921-5721.

RESTRICTIONS

Pets: On 6-ft. leash, cleaned up after. **Fires:** Grill only; check w/ park for current fire restrictions. **Alcoholic Beverages:** Beer only. **Vehicle Maximum Length:** No limit. **Other:** No drinking water is available.

TO GET THERE

From the junction of Hwy. 133 and CR2 (at the sign for Paonia State Park), turn left and cross the bridge. (A 2nd campground is 0.1 mi. south on Hwy. 133, on the left.) Take the first right and go 0.5 mi. Turn right into the campground.

CREEDE   MAP, C-2
Mountain Views at River's Edge RV Resort

539 Airport Rd., 81130. T: (719) 658-2710; www.reserveamerica.com.

🚐 ★★★★★   ▲ n/a

Beauty: ★★★	Site Privacy: ★★★★★
Spaciousness: ★★★★★	Quiet: ★★★★★
Security: ★★★★	Cleanliness: ★★★★★
Insect Control: ★★★★	Facilities: ★★★★★

This beautiful park is surrounded on all four sides by mountains and features modern facilities. The laundry is spacious, clean, well-lit, and has lots of machines. The restrooms are modern and immaculate. There is truly a space for any rig of any size in this park: back-ins are 60-feet long, while pull-throughs are a lengthy 70 feet; both types are 40-feet wide, with a designated space for extra vehicles to the side of the main parking area. The best sites in this park (which is a difficult thing to judge!) are probably 107–110 on the north side, as they face nice pasture land, hills, and an attractive wooden fence, they are as long as anyone would need, and they are close to the restrooms without being right next to them. Although shade trees—and perhaps a paved road—would improve this park, the location is so nice, the spaces so big, and the facilities so clean that it deserves top honors. This is a top-notch resort; make sure to get reservations, or you may not get in.

BASICS

Operated By: Roland & Helen Zimmerman. **Open:** May–Oct. 1. **Site Assignment:** Upon registration; reservations require deposit; $20 cancellation fee. **Registration:** At office. (Late arrivals use map on bulletin board to find available site; pay in the morning.) **Fee:** $23; no credit cards. **Parking:** At site.

FACILITIES

Number of RV-only Sites: 100. **Hookups:** Electric (30, 50 amps), water, sewer. **Each Site:** Picnic table, sectioned-off picnic area. **Dump Station:** No (sewer at all sites). **Laundry:** Yes. **Pay Phone:** Yes. **Restrooms and Showers:** Yes. **Fuel:** No. **Propane:** Yes. **Internal Roads:** Gravel. **RV Service:** No. **Market:** 1.4 mi. west. **Restaurant:** 1.2 mi. west. **General Store:** Small store. **Vending:** No. **Swimming:** No. **Playground:** No. **Other:** Enclosed phone, group picnic/barbecue area, extremely large rec room, pool table, sofa, TV. **Activities:** Potlucks, themed dinners. **Nearby Attractions:** Creede Repertory Theater, Creede Underground Mining Museum, The Great Sand Dunes. **Additional Information:** Creede-Mineral Chamber of Commerce, (800) 327-2102 or (719) 658-2374.

RESTRICTIONS

Pets: On leash, cleaned up after, no barking. **Fires:** Restrictions, inquire at campground. **Alcoholic Beverages:** Not allowed in public gathering areas. **Vehicle Maximum Length:** No limit.

TO GET THERE

From the south edge of Creede, take Hwy. 149 0.75 mi. southwest. Turn south onto Airport Rd. (unmarked—look for blue trailer sign). Drive 0.5 mi. and take the first left into the gravel driveway. Continue straight ahead to get to the office.

CRIPPLE CREEK   MAP, B-3
Lost Burro Campground and Lodging

4023 Teller Rd. #1, 80813. T: (719) 689-2345; www.lostburro.com.

🚐 ★★★★★   ▲ ★★★★

Beauty: ★★★★★	Site Privacy: ★★★★★
Spaciousness: ★★★★★	Quiet: ★★★★★
Security: ★★★★	Cleanliness: ★★★★★
Insect Control: ★★★★	Facilities: ★★★

Get lost in the pines! If you'd like to, you certainly can at the Lost Burro. Located in a small valley with wooded and rocky hills on all four sides, imposing cliffs to the north, and dense forest to the south, this campground feels truly "lost." Campsites are located in tiers up the hillside and down near the stream. Sites are well spaced, and include some enormous pull-throughs (16 measures 100 feet), as well as long (60-foot) back-ins (8, 12, 13, 14, 15). RV site 11 is a long pull-through like the others, but only about 48 feet are level—the rest drop off quite quickly. Tent sites (by the stream) are mostly open, although sites 15 and 16 (up in the forest away from the stream) are wooded and separated from the rest, making them the best tent sites. The campground is wild and not overly built-up: sites are not much more than bull-dozed strips in the woods, making them quite natural and beautiful. For some, the primitive sites, along with the lack of full hookups at every site, may represent too much of a step away from civilization. However, those savvy enough to realize that water spouts and a dump station make full hookups unnecessary will love this campground. Make sure you have reservations—once others "discover" the Lost Burro, it may be harder to get lost than you'd like.

BASICS

Operated By: Kent Goza & Mary Eddleman. **Open:** All year. **Site Assignment:** Upon registration; credit card or check required for reservation; 24-hour cancellation policy. **Registration:** At office. (Late arrivals select site & pay in the morning.) **Fee:** RV, $25; tent, $14; check, V, MC, D. **Parking:** At site.

FACILITIES

Number of Multipurpose Sites: 27. **Hookups:** Electric (30, 50 amps). **Each Site:** Picnic table, fire pit. **Dump Station:** Yes. **Laundry:** No. **Pay Phone:** Yes. **Restrooms and Showers:** Yes. **Fuel:** No. **Propane:** No. **Internal Roads:** Dirt. **RV Service:** No. **Market:** 20 mi. to Woodland/Divide. **Restaurant:** 4 mi. to Cripple Creek. **General Store:** Yes. **Vending:** Yes. **Swimming:** No. **Playground:** No. **Other:** Stream, burgers. **Activities:** Hiking. **Nearby Attractions:** Casinos, Cripple Creek, Royal Gorge, Florissant Fossil Beds National Monument, Pike's Peak, Cripple Creek & Victor Narrow Gauge Railroad, 30-ft. waterfall in back of campground. **Addi-**

tional Information: Cripple Creek Chamber of Commerce, (719) 689-2169.

RESTRICTIONS

Pets: On leash, cleaned up after. **Fires:** Fire pit only. **Alcoholic Beverages:** At sites. **Vehicle Maximum Length:** No limit. **Other:** Quiet at 9 p.m., no ATVs or motorcycles, no wood cutting or gathering.

TO GET THERE

From the northwestern sign for the town of Cripple Creek on Carr Ave. (CR Teller 1), go 3.2 mi. north. Turn left at the signs into the entrance. (Those coming from Canon City on CR Teller 1 will find the campground on their right, just at the Open Air Chapel dome.) Follow the dirt drive down to the office on the right.

DELTA   MAP, B-1
Riverwood Inn

677 Hwy. 50 Delta, 81416. T: (970) 874-5787.

🚐 ★★★   ▲ ★★★

Beauty: ★★★	Site Privacy: ★★★★
Spaciousness: ★★★	Quiet: ★★★
Security: ★★★	Cleanliness: ★★★
Insect Control: ★★★	Facilities: ★★★

This park, on the Gunnison River, has large back-ins (56–70-foot) and absolutely enormous pull-throughs (90–100-foot). Furthermore, there are loads of trees throughout the park, making shade a given for any site. Arguably, the best sites are 5–7 in the northeast corner near the tenting area, with fine towering trees at the back, nice grass, and enough distance from the mobile homes to the west (behind 8–13) to allow increased privacy. The least desirable sites are 14 and 15, right along Hwy. 50 (with no fence at the perimeter), and sites 16 and 17, which back to the park entrance (again without a fence). The laundry facility is a little small (1 of each machine) and dingy. The tent sites are located on an "island" to the northeast of the RV sites. These are unmarked, virtually unlimited, and unkempt. While the wild grass and other vegetation, including lots of trees, is appealing to tenters, there was old wood and some cast-away furniture littering the area during our inspection. Additionally, the only restroom on the "island" is a porta-potty. Disregarding this slight slap in the face to tenters, the actual tenting area is quite nice. Campers of all stripes will find it a reasonable stop, as it is easily accessed from Hwy. 50 or 92, and is quite close to town.

BASICS

Operated By: Loren & Merced Pogue. **Open:** All year. **Site Assignment:** Upon registration; credit card required for reservation; 24-hour cancellation policy. **Registration:** At office. (Late arrivals select site & pay in the morning.) **Fee:** RV, $21–$30; tent, $12; check, V, MC, D, DC, CB. **Parking:** At site.

FACILITIES

Number of RV-only Sites: 29. **Number of Tent-only Sites:** 50. **Hookups:** Electric (30, 50 amps), water, sewer. **Each Site:** Picnic table, grill; most have several trees & shrubs. **Dump Station:** No (sewer at all sites). **Laundry:** Yes. **Pay Phone:** Yes.

Restrooms and Showers: Yes. **Fuel:** No. **Propane:** Yes. **Internal Roads:** Gravel. **RV Service:** No. **Market:** 0.5 mi. **Restaurant:** On site. **General Store:** No. **Vending:** No. **Swimming:** No. **Playground:** No. **Other:** River, 11-room hotel. **Activities:** Fishing, hiking, biking. **Nearby Attractions:** Grand Mesa, Fort Uncompahgre, Delta County Museum. **Additional Information:** Delta Area Chamber of Commerce, (970) 874-8616.

RESTRICTIONS

Pets: On leash, cleaned up after. **Fires:** Fire pit only. **Alcoholic Beverages:** At sites. **Vehicle Maximum Length:** No limit.

TO GET THERE

From the junction of Hwy. 92 and Hwy. 50, turn north onto Hwy. 50, go 0.5 mi., and turn right into the entrance.

DOLORES — MAP, C-1
Mancos

Box 1047, 81323. T: (970) 533-7065; www.reserveamerica.com.

🚐 ★★★★   ⛺ ★★★★

Beauty: ★★★	Site Privacy: ★★★
Spaciousness: ★★★	Quiet: ★★★★★
Security: ★★★★★	Cleanliness: ★★★★
Insect Control: ★★★	Facilities: ★★

Mancos State Park encompasses 338 acres surrounding Jackson Gulch Dam and Reservoir. The reservoir is the recreation focus of the park. It is composed of 216 surface acres. Because it lies at 7,800 feet. Mancos Lake is considered an alpine lake. Facilities at the park include two campgrounds. On the southern shore you'll find a 24-site campground with tables, grills, vault toilets, and water hydrants. Volleyball and horseshoe facilities are located in this area and open to visitors. A dump station is at the entrance to this site. A group picnicground, boat ramp, and ranger station are also located in this area. The other campground lies on the northern shore of the lake. It is considered a primitive site, because there is no drinking water available. Each site includes a grill, table, and access to vault toilets. Two picnic areas are along the northern shore of the lake. This is also where hikers can gain access to the Chicken Creek Trail, which leads into the San Juan National Forest. The area is rich in western history, especially that of the ancestral Puebloans whose ruins are preserved and displayed at the nearby Anasazi Heritage Center, a museum in Dolores, approximately 20 miles northwest of Mancos. The Durango–Silverton Narrow Gauge railroad in nearby Durango—27 miles east of Mancos—offers visitors a scenic trip through remote wilderness areas of the San Juan National Forest.

BASICS

Operated By: Colorado State Parks. **Open:** All year. **Site Assignment:** Reservations can be made 6 months in advance. **Registration:** At office. **Fee:** Single, $7–$20; yurt, $60; cabin, $80–$160. **Parking:** At park.

FACILITIES

Number of Multipurpose Sites: 34. **Hookups:** None. **Each Site:** Fire ring. **Dump Station:** Yes. **Laundry:** No. **Pay Phone:** No. **Restrooms and Showers:** Yes. **Fuel:** No. **Propane:** No. **Internal Roads:** Paved. **RV Service:** No. **Market:** No. **Restaurant:** No. **General Store:** No. **Vending:** No. **Swimming:** No. **Playground:** No. **Activities:** Amphitheater, biking, bird-watching, boating, fishing, hiking, horseback riding, horseshoe pits, ice fishing, photography, picnicking, snowshoeing, volleyball, wildlife viewing.

RESTRICTIONS

Pets: Pets must be on a leash no longer than 6 ft. in length. **Fires:** Permitted in designated fireplaces. **Other:** Quiet hours will be enforced 10 p.m.–6 a.m. All generators, loud radios, or other loud noises that may disturb the peace are prohibited during these hours.

TO GET THERE

From Durango take Hwy. 160 west 27 mi. to the town of Mancos. Go north on Hwy. 184 0.5 mi. and turn east onto CR 42 (FS 561). Go 5 mi. and take Rd. N to the park entrance.

DURANGO — MAP, C-1
Durango East KOA

30090 US 160, 81301. T: (800) KOA-0793 or (970) 247-0783; www.koakampground.com.

🚐 ★★★★   ⛺ ★★★★

Beauty: ★★★★	Site Privacy: ★★★★
Spaciousness: ★★★★	Quiet: ★★★★
Security: ★★★★	Cleanliness: ★★★★★
Insect Control: ★★★★	Facilities: ★★★★★

This campground, on the northeast side of town, has mostly back-ins, but of such large proportions (40–60 feet) that campers should not be put off by the prospect of not finding a pull-through. Indeed, the pull-throughs on the east side of the campground are less desirable than most back-ins due to the absence of any shade trees, and their "views" of nearby houses. Site 43 is a gigantic pull-through that will accommodate any rig, while 66 is a pull-through with a great view. Most sites have a row of trees and shrubs between them for an added sense of privacy. With the exception of the more-open sites to the east, many spots have a lost-in-the-woods feel. The least desirable sites (1 and 2), however, are quite open and close to the propane storage, a separate storage unit, and the registration office; hopefully they are only used as overflow sites. This campground's ruggedness will appeal especially to tenters, who have lots of protection in a wilderness atmosphere. The restrooms are clean, modern, and spacious, as is the laundry. This is a great campground in a wonderful location and will suit both tenters and RVers.

BASICS

Operated By: Jay & Carol Coates. **Open:** May 1–Oct. 15. **Site Assignment:** Upon registration; reservations require deposit; 24-hour cancellation policy. **Registration:** At office. (Late arrivals use

drop box.) **Fee:** RV (full), $29; water/electric, $27; tent, $22; check, V, MC. **Parking:** At site.

FACILITIES

Number of RV-only Sites: 60. **Number of Tent-only Sites:** 24. **Hookups:** Electric (30, 50 amps), water, sewer, cable TV. **Each Site:** Picnic table, grill, trees. **Dump Station:** Yes. **Laundry:** Yes. **Pay Phone:** Yes. **Restrooms and Showers:** Yes. **Fuel:** No. **Propane:** Yes. **Internal Roads:** Gravel. **RV Service:** No. **Market:** 4 mi. southwest. **Restaurant:** 5 mi. southwest. **General Store:** Yes. **Vending:** Yes. **Swimming:** Pool. **Playground:** Yes. **Other:** Cabins, cottage, game room, TV lounge, group site, data port, pool table, river. **Activities:** Mini-golf, volleyball, fishing, ice-cream socials, pancake breakfast, nightly movie. **Nearby Attractions:** Durango/Silverton Railroad, Mesa Verde. **Additional Information:** Durango Chamber of Commerce, (800) 525-8855.

RESTRICTIONS

Pets: On leash, cleaned up after; do not leave unattended. **Fires:** Subject to seasonal bans. **Alcoholic Beverages:** At sites. **Vehicle Maximum Length:** No limit.

TO GET THERE

From the northwest junction of Hwy. 550 and Hwy. 160/550 (at the western edge of town), go 2.7 mi. northeast on Hwy. 550. Turn right at the sign into the entrance. The office is straight ahead.

ESTES PARK — MAP, A-3
Estes Park KOA

2051 Big Thompson Ave., 80517. T: (800) KOA-1887 or (970) 586-2888; www.koakampground.com.

🚐 ★★★★   ⛺ ★★★

Beauty: ★★★★★	Site Privacy: ★★★
Spaciousness: ★★★	Quiet: ★★★★
Security: ★★★★	Cleanliness: ★★★★★
Insect Control: ★★★★★	Facilities: ★★★★★

The fourth KOA campground ever built, this tiered campground is admittedly not for big rigs. Sites are somewhat cramped by today's standards (although the odd, large fifth wheel can still be found, tucked in sideways), and space between sites is negligible. And yet the campground is still worth a visit—after all, you can't beat the gorgeous mountain views from all sides or the cooler weather in summer, and even the natural landscaping is very attractive. Sites 1–7 in the southwest corner along the highway are rather small back-ins (30 by 22 feet). Sites 8–29 are larger (40-foot) back-ins, as are 37–48 (40–42-feet). Sites 30–36 and 49–54 are longer (40–45-feet) "parallel parking" sites that resemble pull-throughs and may be more convenient than a straight back-in. There are stairs between the tiered levels at sites 24, 26, and 44, increasing the likelihood of foot traffic past these sites. Tent sites are located in the southeast corner (accessed on the road by cabins 9 and 12). Each tent site has at least one (two maximum) sides fenced in by a solid fence, with a wooden barricade on one other side, lending more privacy to these sites. There is one gravel pad and one Astroturf pad per tent site. At 21 by 33 feet, the sites are medium-sized, but they are packed in one atop the other with little space between them. Despite the confined spaces, this is a beautiful campground and well worth a visit.

BASICS

Operated By: Jim & Ruth Turner. **Open:** May 1–Oct. 19. **Site Assignment:** Upon registration; credit card required for reservation; 24-hour cancellation policy. **Registration:** At office. (Late arrivals use drop box.) **Fee:** RV, $32–$42; tent, $21–$28; V, MC. **Parking:** At site.

FACILITIES

Number of RV-only Sites: 46. **Number of Tent-only Sites:** 19. **Hookups:** Electric (30 amps), water, sewer, cable TV. **Each Site:** Picnic table on wooden platform, grill. **Dump Station:** Yes. **Laundry:** Yes. **Pay Phone:** Yes. **Restrooms and Showers:** Yes. **Fuel:** No. **Propane:** Yes. **Internal Roads:** Dirt. **RV Service:** No. **Market:** 1.5 mi. west. **Restaurant:** 1.5 mi. west. **General Store:** Yes. **Vending:** No. **Swimming:** No. **Playground:** Yes. **Other:** 20 cabins, 7 cottages, gift shop, lounge, game room, across from lake. **Activities:** Fishing, boating, swimming, hiking, skiing, mountain climbing. **Nearby Attractions:** Rocky Mountain National Park, elk bugling, aspens turning. **Additional Information:** Estes Park Chamber of Commerce, (800) 443-7837 or (970) 586-4431.

RESTRICTIONS

Pets: On leash, cleaned up after. **Fires:** Fire pit only. **Alcoholic Beverages:** At sites. **Vehicle Maximum Length:** 36 ft.

TO GET THERE

From the junction of Hwy. 36 and Hwy. 34, turn east onto Hwy. 34 and go 1.8 mi. Turn left at the sign into the entrance.

ESTES PARK — MAP, A-3
Yogi Bear's Jellystone Park of Estes

reserve america

5495 US 36, 80517. T: (970) 586-4230 or (800) 722-2928; www.jellystoneofestes.com.

🚐 ★★★★   ⛺ ★★★★

Beauty: ★★★★   Site Privacy: ★★★★
Spaciousness: ★★★★   Quiet: ★★★★
Security: ★★★★   Cleanliness: ★★★★
Insect Control: ★★★★   Facilities: ★★★★

The Yogi Bear's Jellystone Park™ Camp-Resort is great fun whether you are an RV-park enthusiast, enjoy the comfort of a cabin in the woods, or just like to tent camp and sleep in the great outdoors, Jellystone Park's accommodations, amenities, and activities help provide a quality camping experience. Activities include swimming, mini-golf, hay rides, tennis, volleyball, fishing, hiking, and appearances from Yogi Bear™.

BASICS

Operated By: Kathy & Tony Palmeri. **Open:** May–Oct. **Site Assignment:** Reservations recommended. **Registration:** At ranger station. **Fee:** RV, $43; water/electric, $36; tent, $27; for 2 people; additional fee per person (over 3 years old), $3.50; max. of 6 people per site. **Parking:** Limit 1 car per site.

FACILITIES

Number of RV-only Sites: 30. **Number of Tent-only Sites:** 16. **Number of Multipurpose Sites:** 61. **Hookups:** Water, electric, sewer. **Each Site:** Picnic table, fire pit. **Dump Station:** Yes. **Laundry:** Yes. **Pay Phone:** Yes. **Restrooms and Showers:** Yes. **Fuel:** No. **Propane:** Yes. **Internal Roads:** Yes. **RV Service:** 5 mi. **Market:** 5mi. **Restaurant:** 5 mi. in Estes Park. **General Store:** Camp store. **Vending:** Yes. **Swimming:** Yes. **Playground:** Yes. **Activities:** Organized activities, theme weekends, mini-golf, hiking trails, horseshoes, basketball court. **Nearby Attractions:** Rocky Mountain National Park, downtown Estes park.

RESTRICTIONS

Vehicle Maximum Length: 40 ft.

TO GET THERE

From Denver take I-25 north to Exit 243 (Hwy. 66). Go west to Lyons where you will merge with Hwy. 36 to Estes Park. Look for Jellystone on the right side of the road just 15 mi. past Lyons.

FORT COLLINS — MAP, A-3
Horsetooth Reservoir

1800 South CR 31, 80537. T: (970) 679-4570 or (970) 679-4554; www.abouthorsetooth.com; www.co.larimer.co.us/parks.

🚐 ★★★★   ⛺ ★★★★★

Beauty: ★★★★★   Site Privacy: ★★★★★
Spaciousness: ★★★★★   Quiet: ★★★★
Security: ★★★★   Cleanliness: ★★★★
Insect Control: ★★★★   Facilities: ★★

Beautiful views of rocks, hills, and trees surround this park to the northeast and northwest. In addition to its beauty, the lake offers many recreational opportunities, including swimming, boating, and scuba diving. There are lots of trees throughout the park, and most sites are at least partially shaded. Site 1 is close to the entrance and the restrooms. Site 8 is a 90-foot pull-through, and 14 and 15 are even longer (105-foot) pull-throughs. Sites 21, 26, 27, 29, and 30 are among the handful of back-ins in the park. Sites 32–42 are on a separate loop to the southeast of the main campground area. Site 37 has a water pump. Tent sites are walk-ins, with a central parking area for all sites. (There are a large number of tenting sites around the reservoir.) This campground is a decent stop for outdoor enthusiasts, and although it does not offer full services, many campers will enjoy a stay here.

BASICS

Operated By: Larimer County. **Open:** All year. **Site Assignment:** First come, first served; no reservations. **Registration:** Ranger or camp host will collect fees. **Fee:** Electric, $10; tent, $7; check. **Parking:** At site.

FACILITIES

Number of Multipurpose Sites: 42. **Hookups:** Electric (20, 30, 50 amps). **Each Site:** Picnic table,

grill, tent pad. **Dump Station:** Yes. **Laundry:** No. **Pay Phone:** No. **Restrooms and Showers:** Pit toilets; no shower. **Fuel:** No. **Propane:** No. **Internal Roads:** Gravel. **RV Service:** No. **Market:** 6.5 mi. east. **Restaurant:** 6.5 mi. east. **General Store:** Yes. **Vending:** No. **Swimming:** Reservoir. **Playground:** No. **Other:** Boat ramp, covered picnic area. **Activities:** Fishing, boating, swimming, hiking, rock climbing, scuba diving, horseback riding, waterskiing. **Nearby Attractions:** Lory State Park, Horsetooth Mountain Park. **Additional Information:** Larimer City Parks & Open Lands Dept., (970) 679-4570.

RESTRICTIONS

Pets: On leash, cleaned up after. **Fires:** Grill only; no open fires or fireworks. **Alcoholic Beverages:** Beer only; no alcohol above 3.2%. **Vehicle Maximum Length:** No limit. **Other:** Counter-clockwise boating only; $6 day pass for all vehicles; no fireworks; 14-day stay limit w/in 30-day period.

TO GET THERE

From I-25 (Exit 265), turn west onto Harmony Rd. and go 10.8 mi. Turn right at the sign into the entrance.

FRUITA — MAP, B-1
James M. Robb-Colorado River State Park

reserve america

595 Hwy. 340, 81521. T: (970) 858-9188; www.reserveamerica.com.

🚐 ★★★★   ⛺ ★★★★

Beauty: ★★★   Site Privacy: ★★★
Spaciousness: ★★★   Quiet: ★★★★★
Security: ★★★   Cleanliness: ★★★★
Insect Control: ★★★   Facilities: ★★★★

The Island Acres area of this state park is the most eastern. It boasts four lakes. Lakes numbered 1, 3, and 4 are open to fishing and boating; and Lake 2 is reserved for swimming. (Only nonmotorized and electric-trolling motorized boats are permitted.) There are three picnic areas amid the lakes, which provide 50 picnic sites, and one campground with 60 sites that lies north of Lake 4. A group picnic ground and dump station are also available at this site. Traveling west from Island Acres visitors will come to the Corn Lake section of Colorado River State Park. This is a day-use area that encompasses 20 acres and 15 surface acres of water. Corn Lake affords picnicking, fishing, and hiking opportunities and includes a pier that is wheelchair accessible. The lake is stocked with bass, trout, bluegill, catfish, and crappie. A one and a half mile trail leads west and accesses the Colorado River Wildlife Area. On D Road a short distance west of Corn Lake lies the Colorado River Wildlife Area. The area is a haven for bird-watchers who will see blue heron, hawks, owls, eagles, and geese. Fishing is good on the river, and a large parking lot provides access for plenty of visitors. Restrooms, picnic sites, and interpretive kiosks are facilities included in this part of the park. Connected Lakes is the westernmost section of the park. A boat ramp in this area provides access to the river, and nonmotorized boating is permitted on the lakes. The facilities include paved trails, gravel walkways, interpretive panels, concrete fishing piers, and picnic sites.

BASICS

Operated By: Colorado State Parks. **Open:** All year. **Site Assignment:** Reservations can be made 6 months in advance. **Registration:** At office. **Fee:** Single, $7–$20; yurt, $60; cabin, $80–$160. **Parking:** At park.

FACILITIES

Number of Multipurpose Sites: 57. **Hookups:** Yes. **Each Site:** Fire ring. **Dump Station:** Yes. **Laundry:** Yes. **Pay Phone:** Yes. **Restrooms and Showers:** Yes. **Fuel:** No. **Propane:** No. **Internal Roads:** Paved. **RV Service:** No. **Market:** No. **Restaurant:** No. **General Store:** No. **Vending:** Yes. **Swimming:** Yes. **Playground:** Yes. **Activities:** Beach, biking, birdwatching, boating, fishing, hiking, photography, picnicking, sailing, sailboarding, wildlife viewing.

RESTRICTIONS

Pets: Pets must be on a leash no longer than 6 ft. in length. **Fires:** Permitted in designated fireplaces. **Other:** Quiet hours will be enforced 10 p.m.–6 a.m. All generators, loud radios, or other loud noises that may disturb the peace are prohibited during these hours.

TO GET THERE

Take I-70 to Exit 19, go south on CO 340 approximately 0.4 mi. to the park entrance.

GLENWOOD SPRINGS   MAP, B-2
Ami's Acres

P.O. Box 1239, 81602. T: (970) 945-5340; www.coloradodirectory.com/amisacrescg.

🚐 ★★★★   ⛺ ★★★★

Beauty: ★★★★		Site Privacy: ★★★	
Spaciousness: ★★		Quiet: ★★	
Security: ★★★★		Cleanliness: ★★★★★	
Insect Control: ★★★★		Facilities: ★★★	

This terraced RV park on the slope of a hill facing gorgeous rock cliffs across the highway has long (90-foot) but narrow (15-foot) pull-throughs. Sites 51–56 are smaller back-ins for pop-ups, but back to a beautiful grassy hill and are quite attractive. Tent sites are located up the slope from the RV sites, some distance from park traffic. These are nice, natural sites with plenty of tree coverage and soft dirt floors. The restroom and shower facilities are quite clean and modern, although the building they are housed in looks a little run-down. The laundry is small but clean. The landscaping is rather attractive, with plenty of trees and shrubs enhancing the natural setting. Another nice touch are the picnic tables, which are painted a variety of colors. One downside is that the park is plagued by both train and traffic noise. However, if you can get past the minor inconvenience, this park is a nice stay.

BASICS

Operated By: John & Roxanne Christner. **Open:** Mar. 15–Nov. 15. **Site Assignment:** Upon registra-

tion; credit card required for reservation; 48-hour cancellation policy. **Registration:** At office. (Late arrivals use drop box.) **Fee:** $20–$28; V, MC. **Parking:** At site.

FACILITIES

Number of RV-only Sites: 53. **Number of Tent-only Sites:** 14. **Hookups:** Electric (30, 50 amps), water, sewer, phone (upon request). **Each Site:** Picnic table, tree. **Dump Station:** No (sewer at all sites). **Laundry:** Yes. **Pay Phone:** Yes. **Restrooms and Showers:** Yes. **Fuel:** No. **Propane:** No. **Internal Roads:** Gravel. **RV Service:** No. **Market:** 1 mi. east. **Restaurant:** 1 mi. east. **General Store:** No. **Vending:** No. **Swimming:** No. **Playground:** Yes. **Other:** Easy access from I-70. **Activities:** Rafting, hiking, biking, hunting, fishing, golf. **Nearby Attractions:** Glenwood Hot Springs Pool, Hanging Lake, Frontier Historical Museum, Yampa Spa & Vapour Cave. **Additional Information:** Glenwood Springs Chamber Resort Assoc., (970) 945-6589.

RESTRICTIONS

Pets: On leash, cleaned up after; no pets in tent sites. **Fires:** No wood fires. **Alcoholic Beverages:** At sites. **Vehicle Maximum Length:** No limit. **Other:** No ATVs or motorcycles.

TO GET THERE

From I-70, take Exit 114, go 1 mi. west on the frontage road to the north of the highway. The entrance is on the right.

GOLDEN   MAP, A-3
Chief Hosa Campground

27661 Genesee Dr., 80401. T: (303) 526-1324; www.chiefhosa.com.

🚐 ★★★   ⛺ ★★★★

Beauty: ★★★★		Site Privacy: ★★★★	
Spaciousness: ★★★★		Quiet: ★★★★	
Security: ★★★★		Cleanliness: ★★★★	
Insect Control: ★★★★		Facilities: ★★	

This is a giant campground that occupies both sides of the highway. (The western side of the campground closes on September 1.) All of the sites in this campground are back-ins, averaging 40 feet in length. Sites 1–13 are 40-foot sites in a row along the northeast side. Sites 14–19 are located in the southeast, and 20–42 are in the central "island" of the park. Sites 43–48 are clustered around the bathhouse. There are numerous tent sites in this campground. The heavily forested sites are rough and natural. The road leading up to the hill on which sites 26–40 are located is very poorly maintained and difficult to negotiate. Other tent sites are scattered around the park and not quite as challenging to get to. The restrooms and showers are located in a mobile home parked in the southwest corner. The facilities are quite clean, the showers are slightly less so than the restrooms. This is an enjoyable place to take the family for a camping outing or just to get away for a weekend alone.

BASICS

Operated By: City & County of Denver. **Open:** All year; limited services Labor Day–Memorial Day. **Site Assignment:** Upon registration; credit card

required for reservation; 24-hour cancellation policy. **Registration:** At office or use drop box. **Fee:** RV (water/electric), $26; tent, $22; V, MC, AE, D. **Parking:** At site.

FACILITIES

Number of RV-only Sites: 35. **Number of Tent-only Sites:** 26. **Hookups:** Electric (30, 50 amps), water. **Each Site:** Picnic table. **Dump Station:** Yes. **Laundry:** No. **Pay Phone:** Yes. **Restrooms and Showers:** Yes. **Fuel:** No. **Propane:** No. **Internal Roads:** Gravel. **RV Service:** No. **Market:** 1 mi. **Restaurant:** 1 mi. east or west. **General Store:** No. **Vending:** No. **Swimming:** No. **Playground:** Yes. **Other:** Communal fire pit, dog walk. **Activities:** Volleyball, basketball, horseshoes, hiking. **Nearby Attractions:** Buffalo Bill's Grave, Buffalo Herd Overlook. **Additional Information:** Golden Chamber of Commerce, (303) 279-3113.

RESTRICTIONS

Pets: On leash, cleaned up after; no vicious dogs. **Fires:** Grill only. **Alcoholic Beverages:** At sites. **Vehicle Maximum Length:** No limit.

TO GET THERE

From I-70 (Exit 253), on the southeast side of the highway, go straight on Genesee Rd. to campground entrance on right.

GOLDEN   MAP, A-3
Golden Gate State Park

reserve america

92 Crawford Gulch Rd., 80403. T: (303) 582-3707; www.reserveamerica.com.

🚐 ★★★★   ⛺ ★★★★

Beauty: ★★★		Site Privacy: ★★★	
Spaciousness: ★★★		Quiet: ★★★★★	
Security: ★★★★★		Cleanliness: ★★★★	
Insect Control: ★★★		Facilities: ★★★★	

Only 30 miles away from Denver, 12,000 acres of Golden Gate Canyon State Park awaits you with hiking, picnicking, and camping among dense forest, rocky peaks and aspen-filled meadows. The mountain splendor of Golden Gate Canyon's wildflower meadows, glorious autumn colors, and the spectacular view from the famous Panorama Point of over 100 miles of the Continental Divide make the park ideal for sightseers and photographers. Miles upon miles of mountain trails for hiking, biking, and horseback riding and 155 campsites make Golden Gate Canyon accessible to everyone. Golden Gate Canyon is a great place for young anglers and fall-color viewing. The park has also hosted countless weddings and other special celebrations at Panorama Point. There are five cabins and two yurts located at Reverend's Ridge Campground. There are tent and electric campsites at Reverend's Ridge Campground available on the reservation system during the summer. Tent sites at Aspen Meadow Campground can also be reserved during the summer. There are flush toilets and sinks available at Reverend's Ridge. However, the dump station, showers, and laundry facilities will be closed during the winter months. Golden

Gate Canyon State Park offers 35 miles of trails for winter hiking and snowshoeing. There are stocked ponds for ice fishing and spectacular views of the Continental Divide from Panorama Point.

BASICS

Operated By: Colorado State Parks. **Open:** All year. **Site Assignment:** Reservations can be made 6 months in advance. **Registration:** At office. **Fee:** Single, $7–$20; yurt, $60; cabin, $80–$160. **Parking:** At park.

FACILITIES

Number of Multipurpose Sites: 139. **Hookups:** Yes. **Each Site:** Fire ring. **Dump Station:** Yes. **Laundry:** Yes. **Pay Phone:** Yes. **Restrooms and Showers:** Yes. **Fuel:** No. **Propane:** No. **Internal Roads:** Paved. **RV Service:** No. **Market:** No. **Restaurant:** No. **General Store:** No. **Vending:** No. **Swimming:** No. **Playground:** No. **Activities:** Biking, bird-watching, fishing, hiking, hunting, ice fishing, photography, picnicking, skating, showshoeing, wildlife viewing.

RESTRICTIONS

Pets: Pets must be on a leash no longer than 6 feet in length. **Fires:** Permitted in designated fireplaces. **Other:** Quiet hours will be enforced 10 p.m.–6 a.m. All generators, loud radios, or other loud noises that may disturb the peace are prohibited during these hours.

TO GET THERE

From Colorado Springs, take Hwy. 24 west 38 mi. through Lake George. West of Lake George, turn left (south) on CR 90 and follow it 4 mi. From that point, continue south on CR 92 6 mi. to the park.

GRANBY   MAP, A-2
Stillwater Campground

reserve america

8590 US 34, 80446. T: (877) 444-6777 or (970) 887-4100; www.reserveamerica.com.

🚐 ★★★★   ⛺ ★★★★

Beauty: ★★★★	Site Privacy: ★★★★
Spaciousness: ★★★	Quiet: ★★★★
Security: ★★★★	Cleanliness: ★★★★
Insect Control: ★★★★	Facilities: ★★★

Overlooking Lake Granby, this campground has a myriad of sites offering a combination of camping possibilities: great views, electrical hookups, facilities. One combination that does not seem possible, however, is an electric site with a superb view, as all of the electric sites are on the north side of the hill, and the lake is farther south. However, most sites are at least partially forested, and all seem very comfortable. Sites 1–4 accommodate tents only, as there is separate parking away from these sites. Electric sites include 12–14, 16–18, 20–23, and about half of the sites numbered in the 30s, 40s, and 50s. These sites range from 25-foot back-ins (12) to 42-foot back-ins (14). The only electric sites that have somewhat of a view are 12 and 23. Sites 61–92 offer spectacular views of the lake and the marina but are entirely unshaded. Moreover, a number of these sites (76–83)

do not permit tent camping. Loop C offers some great views—especially among the higher numbers—but is mostly unshaded. Tent sites include 24–28 and 32–35, which are walk-in sites overlooking the lake. The restroom is small and the showers made of crude cement, but they are otherwise modern and comfortable. This is a large and attractive campground that will appeal mostly to those interested in water recreation.

BASICS

Operated By: Thousand Trails Management Services Inc. **Open:** Memorial Day–early Sept. **Site Assignment:** First come, first served; credit card required for reservation; 3-day cancellation policy, less $10. **Registration:** W/ campground host. **Fee:** Water/electric, $22; premium, $20; no hookup, $17; double, $33; check. **Parking:** At site.

FACILITIES

Number of RV-only Sites: 20. **Number of Tent-only Sites:** 128. **Hookups:** Electric (10, 20, 30, 50 amps), water. **Each Site:** Picnic table, fire pit. **Dump Station:** Yes. **Laundry:** No. **Pay Phone:** Yes. **Restrooms and Showers:** Yes. **Fuel:** No. **Propane:** No. **Internal Roads:** Gravel. **RV Service:** No. **Market:** 9 mi. south. **Restaurant:** 9 mi. south. **General Store:** No. **Vending:** No. **Swimming:** Lake. **Playground:** No. **Other:** Boat ramp, amphitheater. **Activities:** Fishing, boating, swimming, hiking, skiing, wildlife viewing. **Nearby Attractions:** Lake Granby. **Additional Information:** Forestry Office, (970) 887-4100.

RESTRICTIONS

Pets: On leash, cleaned up after. **Fires:** Grill only. **Alcoholic Beverages:** At sites. **Vehicle Maximum Length:** No limit. **Other:** Max. 5 people per site.

TO GET THERE

From the junction of Hwy. 40 and Hwy. 34, turn north onto Hwy. 34 and go 8.5 mi. Turn right at the sign into the entrance.

GRAND LAKE   MAP, A-2
Elk Creek Campground

reserve america

143 CR 48 (Golf Course Rd.), P.O. Box 689, 80447. T: (800) ELK-CREEK or (970) 627-8502; www.reserveamerica.com.

🚐 ★★★★   ⛺ ★★★★

Beauty: ★★★★	Site Privacy: ★★★★
Spaciousness: ★★★★	Quiet: ★★★★
Security: ★★★★	Cleanliness: ★★★★★
Insect Control: ★★★★	Facilities: ★★★★★

Located in a very rural area just outside of town, this campground has campsites laid out in a loop that extends almost into the forest. As a result, most sites are well shaded. (Sites 1–3 and 27–33 are on the edge of a clearing and are therefore less shaded.) All sites are back-ins, averaging 45 feet in length, with little variation. Sites 20 and even numbers 34–40 are located at the foot of a forested hill, which makes these sites somewhat more attractive. Site 42 is by far

the most secluded site, set well into the forest at the far end of the internal road loop. Tent sites are located across the Elk River opposite the playground. The management is planning to build more cabins, however, and these sites may no longer be available. The rec room is extremely cozy and contains comfortable sofas as well as cable TV. The restrooms are spic-and-span. The showers are individual unisex units just outside the restrooms. While clean, they are extremely narrow, a little dark, and almost intimidating. Otherwise, this campground is a wonderful destination for any camper, alone or with a family.

BASICS

Operated By: Chris & Kathy Janosko. **Open:** All year. **Site Assignment:** Upon registration; reservations recommended; credit card required for reservation; cancellation required by noon the day before a scheduled stay. **Registration:** At office. (Late arrivals select site & pay in the morning.) **Fee:** RV, $30–$33; tent, $22; check, V, MC, D, AE. Subject to change. Call campground for current rates. **Parking:** At site.

FACILITIES

Number of RV-only Sites: 50. **Number of Tent-only Sites:** 11. **Hookups:** Electric (30, 50 amps), water, sewer. **Each Site:** Picnic table, grill, fire pit. **Dump Station:** Yes. **Laundry:** Yes. **Pay Phone:** Yes. **Restrooms and Showers:** Yes. **Fuel:** No. **Propane:** Yes. **Internal Roads:** Gravel. **RV Service:** No. **Market:** 0.5 mi. toward Grand Lake. **Restaurant:** 0.75 mi. toward Grand Lake. **General Store:** Yes. **Vending:** No. **Swimming:** Nearby. **Playground:** Yes. **Other:** 14 cabins, game room, rec room (w/ cable TV & pool table), data port, RV supplies, fishing pond. **Activities:** Fishing, boating, swimming, hiking, golfing, horseback riding, hunting, snowmobiling, tennis, horseshoes, volleyball. **Nearby Attractions:** Rocky Mountain National Park. **Additional Information:** Grand Lake Chamber of Commerce, (970) 627-3402.

RESTRICTIONS

Pets: On leash, cleaned up after. No pets or food in game room or rec room. **Fires:** Grill only. **Alcoholic Beverages:** At sites. **Vehicle Maximum Length:** No limit.

TO GET THERE

From the junction of Hwy. 278 and Hwy. 34, turn north onto Hwy. 34 and go 0.25 mi. Turn west onto CR 48 (Golf Course Rd.) and go 0.2 mi. Turn right at the sign into the entrance.

GREELEY   MAP, A-3
Greeley Campground and RV Park

501 East 27 St., 80631. T: (970) 353-6476; www.greeleyrvpark.com.

🚐 ★★★★   ⛺ ★★★

Beauty: ★★★★	Site Privacy: ★★★★
Spaciousness: ★★★★	Quiet: ★★★
Security: ★★★★	Cleanliness: ★★★★
Insect Control: ★★★★	Facilities: ★★★

Made up of uniform 65-foot pull-throughs, this campground offers many shaded sites and a comfortable environment. The western side of the campground is more shaded than the east. Many sites have a cement pad for picnicking, although some (especially toward the southwest) do not. Sites 2–12 along the north side face a row of vegetation, offering a very pleasant view. This row, and perhaps the row immediately to the south (60–71), is the nicest area in the park due to the large amount of shade and the view. There is a storage unit by sites 2 and 71 that makes these sites less desirable. Site 15, on the other hand, has exceptionally attractive landscaping (including flowers and a section of fence) that makes it the prettiest site in the park. The row containing sites 39–52 is closest to the highway and therefore a less desirable place to camp. The tenting area is located to the east of the office and consists of a large grassy area with two huge shade trees. This area is even closer to the highway than the closest row of RV sites. The restrooms and showers are aging slightly, but are very clean. This campground provides a pretty location for campers who wish to explore the Greeley area, and is very convenient for longer rigs.

BASICS

Operated By: Marlin & Shirley Ness. **Open:** All year. **Site Assignment:** Upon registration; credit card required for reservation; 24-hour cancellation policy. **Registration:** At office. (Late arrivals use drop box.) **Fee:** RV (full, 30 amp), $23.50; (full, 50 amp), $23.50; tent, $13; check, V, MC. **Parking:** At site, plenty of extra parking.

FACILITIES

Number of RV-only Sites: 95. **Number of Tent-only Sites:** 10. **Hookups:** Electric (30, 50 amps), water, sewer. **Each Site:** Picnic table. **Dump Station:** No (sewer at all sites). **Laundry:** Yes. **Pay Phone:** Yes. **Restrooms and Showers:** Yes. **Fuel:** No. **Propane:** Yes. **Internal Roads:** Paved. **RV Service:** No. **Market:** 1 mi. west. **Restaurant:** 1 mi. west. **General Store:** Yes. **Vending:** Yes. **Swimming:** No. **Playground:** No. **Other:** RV parts, data port, woodworking shop, dog walk area, cabins. **Activities:** Hiking, woodworking. **Nearby Attractions:** Pawnee Grasslands, Centennial Village, Greeley Independence Stampede (July 4th). **Additional Information:** Greeley/Weld Chamber of Commerce, (970) 352-3566.

RESTRICTIONS

Pets: On leash, cleaned up after, small pets only. **Fires:** Grill only. **Alcoholic Beverages:** At sites. **Vehicle Maximum Length:** No limit. **Other:** Adult-oriented.

TO GET THERE

From the junction of Hwy. 85 and Hwy. 34 (Fort Morgan Exit), turn east onto Hwy. 34 and go 0.6 mi. Turn north at the blue trailer sign onto an unmarked road. Turn right at the sign into the entrance.

GUNNISON
Elk Creek Campground
MAP, B-2

reserve america

102 Elk Creek, 81230. T: (970) 641-2337; www.reserveamerica.com.

🚐 ★★★★   🔺 ★★★★

Beauty: ★★★★   Site Privacy: ★★★
Spaciousness: ★★★★   Quiet: ★★★
Security: ★★★★★   Cleanliness: ★★★★
Insect Control: ★★★   Facilities: ★★★★

Curecanti National Recreation Area is situated between Montrose and Gunnison, Colorado. Elk Creek Campground is located on the north shore of Blue Mesa Lake, just off Hwy. 50 approximately 16 miles west of Gunnison. Altitude is 7,800 feet. Blue Mesa Reservoir is Colorado's largest body of water and is the largest Kokanee Salmon fishery in the United States. Morrow Point Reservoir is the beginning of the Black Canyon of the Gunnison and below. Crystal Reservoir is the site of the Gunnison Diversion Tunnel, a National Historic Civil Engineering Landmark. Recently discovered dinosaur fossils, a 5,000-acre archeological district, a narrow gauge train, and traces of 6,000-year-old dwellings further enhance the offerings of Curecanti. The campground is located within a prairie dog colony. Three reservoirs, named for corresponding dams on the Gunnison River, form the heart of Curecanti National Recreation Area. Panoramic mesas, fork-like reservoirs, and deep, steep, and narrow canyons abound.

BASICS

Operated By: National Park Service. **Open:** All year. **Site Assignment:** Reservations must be made at least 3 days in advance; reservable season is May 20–Sept. 9. **Registration:** At registration office. **Fee:** Single, $12–$18. **Parking:** At park.

FACILITIES

Number of Multipurpose Sites: 248. **Hookups:** Yes. **Each Site:** Call ahead. **Dump Station:** Yes. **Laundry:** No. **Pay Phone:** Yes. **Restrooms and Showers:** Yes. **Fuel:** No. **Propane:** No. **Internal Roads:** Paved. **RV Service:** No. **Market:** No. **Restaurant:** Yes. **General Store:** No. **Vending:** No. **Swimming:** Yes. **Playground:** No. **Other:** All boats require a boat permit. **Activities:** Amphitheater, biking, bird-watching, boating, campfire programs, canoeing, fishing, hiking, hunting, jet skiing, kayaking, photography, scuba diving, sightseeing, snowshoeing, waterskiing, wildlife viewing, wind surfing.

RESTRICTIONS

Pets: Pets must be on a leash at all times. **Fires:** Allowed; campfire program. **Alcoholic Beverages:** Not allowed. **Vehicle Maximum Length:** Varies; call ahead.

TO GET THERE

Elk Creek is located off of US 50 between Gunnison and Montrose, along Blue Mesa reservoir.

GUNNISON
Gunnison KOA
MAP, B-2

105 CR 50, 81230. T: (800) 562-1248 or (970) 641-1358; www.koakampground.com.

🚐 ★★★★   🔺 ★★★

Beauty: ★★★★   Site Privacy: ★★★★
Spaciousness: ★★★   Quiet: ★★★★
Security: ★★★★   Cleanliness: ★★★★★
Insect Control: ★★★★   Facilities: ★★★★★

This campground on the southwest side of town features level, grassy sites laid out on two loops. The rural location and the attractive decor make for a pleasant camping experience. There is a farm to the southwest, and cars are greeted by curious geese upon entry. The interior spaces of the loops are large enough that vehicles of any size can park on the sites (which average 75 feet long). Except for the lack of shade, most sites are extremely nice. RV sites E-H are very close to the playground, which some campers may wish to avoid. Tent areas are grassy, with some large trees to the northeast. While the RV experience would be improved with more trees, this campground is pleasant enough to warrant a return visit. Tenters will likewise be pleased.

BASICS

Operated By: Dave & Susie Taylor. **Open:** May 1–Oct. 15. **Site Assignment:** Upon registration; credit card required for reservation; 24-hour cancellation policy. **Registration:** At office. (Late arrivals use drop box.) **Fee:** RV, $27–$35; tent, $20; V, MC, AE, D. **Parking:** At site.

FACILITIES

Number of RV-only Sites: 126. **Hookups:** Electric (30, 50 amps), water, sewer. **Each Site:** Picnic table, grill. **Dump Station:** Yes. **Laundry:** Yes. **Pay Phone:** Yes. **Restrooms and Showers:** Yes. **Fuel:** No. **Propane:** Yes. **Internal Roads:** Gravel. **RV Service:** Can call. **Market:** 1.5 mi. **Restaurant:** 1 mi. **General Store:** Yes. **Vending:** No. **Swimming:** No. **Playground:** Yes. **Other:** Trout pond, covered picnic area, pet walk area, cabins. **Activities:** Fishing, golf, hunting, ATV riding. **Nearby Attractions:** Aspen trees at Kebler Pass, Curecanti National Recreation Area. **Additional Information:** Gunnison Chamber of Commerce, (800) 274-7580 or (970) 641-1501.

RESTRICTIONS

Pets: On leash, cleaned up after. **Fires:** Fire pit only. **Alcoholic Beverages:** At sites. **Vehicle Maximum Length:** No limit. **Other:** No clotheslines, no vehicle washing/maintenance.

TO GET THERE

From the junction of Hwy. 135 and US 50, go 1.6 mi. west on Hwy. 50. Turn south onto CR 38 (just east of the bridge across the street). Go 0.5 mi., then turn right after the sign. Take the first right into the entrance. The office is on the right.

GUNNISON MAP, B-2
Lake Fork Campground

reserve america

102 Elk Creek, 81230. T: (970) 641-2337;
www.reserveamerica.com.

🚐 ★★★★   ⛺ ★★★★

Beauty: ★★★★	Site Privacy: ★★★
Spaciousness: ★★★★	Quiet: ★★★
Security: ★★★★★	Cleanliness: ★★★★
Insect Control: ★★★	Facilities: ★★★★

Lake Fork Campground is located just off Highway 50 near Blue Mesa Dam, approximately 37 miles east of Montrose and 28 miles west of Gunnison. This a semi-arid shrub land with vast expanses of sagebrush. A part of the Curecanti National Recreation Area where there are three reservoirs, named for corresponding dams on the Gunnison River, forms the heart of Curecanti National Recreation Area. Panoramic mesas, fjord-like reservoirs, and deep, steep, and narrow canyons abound. Blue Mesa Reservoir is Colorado's largest body of water and is the largest Kokanee Salmon fishery in the United States. Morrow Point Reservoir is the beginning of the Black Canyon of the Gunnison and below. Crystal Reservoir is the site of the Gunnison Diversion Tunnel, a National Historic Civil Engineering Landmark. Recently discovered dinosaur fossils, a 5,000-acre archeological district, a narrow gauge train, and traces of 6,000-year-old dwellings further enhance the offerings of Curecanti.

BASICS
Operated By: National Park Service. **Open:** May 1–Sept. 13. **Site Assignment:** Reservations must be made 3 days in advance; reservable season May 20–Sept 9. **Registration:** At registration office. **Fee:** Single, $10. **Parking:** At park.

FACILITIES
Number of Multipurpose Sites: 218. **Hookups:** None. **Each Site:** Call ahead. **Dump Station:** Yes. **Laundry:** No. **Pay Phone:** Yes. **Restrooms and Showers:** Yes. **Fuel:** No. **Propane:** No. **Internal Roads:** Paved. **RV Service:** No. **Market:** No. **Restaurant:** No. **General Store:** No. **Vending:** No. **Swimming:** Yes. **Playground:** No. **Activities:** Biking, bird-watching, boating, campfire programs, canoeing, fishing, hiking, hunting, jet skiing, kayaking, photography, scuba diving, sightseeing, snowshoeing, waterskiing, wildlife viewing, windsurfing.

RESTRICTIONS
Pets: Pets must be on a leash at all times. **Fires:** Allowed; campfire program. **Alcoholic Beverages:** Not allowed. **Vehicle Maximum Length:** Varies; call ahead. **Other:** Cell phone coverage is limited, if at all. All boats require a Curecanti NRA boat permit. Registered sites must be occupied, meaning the site has to be used or slept w/in a 12-hr. period or it can forfeited.

TO GET THERE
Lake Fork campground is located off of Hwy. 50 between Gunnison and Montrose, along Blue Mesa reservoir.

HASTY MAP, C-4
John Martin Reservoir

reserve america

30703 CO. Rd. 24, 81044. T: (719) 829-1801;
www.reserveamerica.com.

🚐 ★★★★   ⛺ ★★★★

Beauty: ★★★★	Site Privacy: ★★★
Spaciousness: ★★★	Quiet: ★★★★★
Security: ★★★★★	Cleanliness: ★★★★
Insect Control: ★★★	Facilities: ★★★★

Welcome to John Martin Reservoir State Park, an oasis on the plains of southeastern Colorado. Located in the Lower Arkansas River Valley, visitors come to John Martin to take advantage of modern campgrounds, great fishing, uncrowded boating waters, and diverse wildlife-viewing opportunities, and to see historical sites. The park has a total of 213 campsites, which can accommodate recreational vehicles, trailers, and tents. The Lake Hasty Campground, located below the dam provides plentiful shade with large trees. Camping is available year-round in Lake Hasty. The Point Campground, located on the north shore, sits on a ridge overlooking the reservoir. John Martin is a large reservoir that accommodates all forms of water recreation including waterskiing, jet skiing, sailing, windsurfing, and swimming. Anglers catch walleye, saugeye, bass, wiper, crappie, perch, and catfish. John Martin supports a diverse community of wildlife. Resident and migratory birds abound here, making the park a bird-watchers' paradise. Every year from mid-April to late August visitors share the sand and gravel shores of the reservoir with the threatened piping plover and endangered interior least tern. John Martin Reservoir is among the few suitable nesting areas for these birds in Colorado. During the winter months, bald eagles can be seen throughout the area.

BASICS
Operated By: Colorado State Parks. **Open:** All year. **Site Assignment:** Reservations can be made 6 months in advance. **Registration:** At office. **Fee:** Single, $7–$20; yurt, $60; cabin, $80–$160. **Parking:** At park.

FACILITIES
Number of Multipurpose Sites: 213. **Hookups:** Yes. **Each Site:** Fire ring. **Dump Station:** Yes. **Laundry:** Yes. **Pay Phone:** Yes. **Restrooms and Showers:** Yes. **Fuel:** No. **Propane:** No. **Internal Roads:** Paved. **RV Service:** No. **Market:** No. **Restaurant:** No. **General Store:** No. **Vending:** Yes. **Swimming:** Yes. **Playground:** Yes. **Activities:** Beach, bird-watching, boating, fishing, hiking, interpretive programs, jet skiing, photography, picnicking, sailing, sailboarding, waterskiing, wildlife viewing.

RESTRICTIONS
Pets: Pets must be on a leash no longer than 6 f.t in length. **Fires:** Permitted in designated fireplaces. **Other:** Quiet hours will be enforced 10 p.m.–6 a.m. All generators, loud radios, or other loud noises that may disturb the peace are prohibited during these hours.

TO GET THERE
Hwy. 50 to Hasty. Go south from Hasty on Road 24 and travel 2 mi. The park visitor center will be on your right. Please check in before going to your campsite.

HOTCHKISS MAP, B-1
Mountain Valley Meadows RV Park

1083 Hwy. 133, P.O. Box 893, 81419.
T: (800) 782-4037 or (970) 872-2351;
www.mountainvalleymeadows.com.

🚐 ★★★   ⛺ ★★

Beauty: ★★★	Site Privacy: ★★★
Spaciousness: ★★★★	Quiet: ★★★★
Security: ★★★★	Cleanliness: ★★★
Insect Control: ★★★★	Facilities: ★★

This campground offers 54-foot grassy back-ins in a loop, with a 40-foot space at each site for an extra vehicle. Sites 15–17 at the end of the loop border woods to the west and a fence to the rear. They feel slightly apart from the other site, and have an incomparable view of the mountains to the east (as do 28–30). Sites 21 and 24 are at the corner of two internal roads and so may receive more traffic due to this location. Long-term residents occupy several of the RV sites. Tent sites are to the southeast of the RV sites in a strip, on either side of the internal road. While these sites have gorgeous grass, there is no shade to protect from the sun or rain. Site T2 is less desirable due to a dumpster that encroaches on it. The restrooms have composting, nonflush toilets. and curtained-off showers that are extremely clean. This is a worthwhile campground for both tenters and RVers, although RVers may find it slightly more comfortable.

BASICS
Operated By: Private operator. **Open:** All year. **Site Assignment:** First come, first served. **Registration:** At office. (Late arrivals use drop box.) **Fee:** RV (full), $18.90; water/electric, $15.75; tent, $10.50; V, MC, D. **Parking:** At site.

FACILITIES
Number of RV-only Sites: 30. **Number of Tent-only Sites:** 5. **Hookups:** Electric (30, 50 amps), water, sewer. **Each Site:** Picnic table, fire ring. **Dump Station:** Yes. **Laundry:** Yes. **Pay Phone:** Yes. **Restrooms and Showers:** Yes. **Fuel:** No. **Propane:** No. **Internal Roads:** Gravel/dirt. **RV Service:** No. **Market:** No. **Restaurant:** No. **General Store:** No. **Vending:** No. **Swimming:** No. **Playground:** Yes. **Other:** Wellwater. **Activities:** Hiking, fishing, hunting, boating, swimming. **Nearby Attractions:** Gunnison National Forest, Crawford State Park, Gunnison Gorge National Conservation Area. **Additional Information:** Delta Chamber of Commerce, (970) 874-8616.

RESTRICTIONS
Pets: On leash, cleaned up after. **Fires:** Fire pit only. **Alcoholic Beverages:** At sites. **Vehicle Maximum Length:** No limit.

TO GET THERE
From the junction of Hwy. 92 and Hwy. 133, turn east onto Hwy. 133 and go 1 mi. Turn left at the

sign into the entrance. The office is the first building on the left.

HUDSON   MAP, A-3
Pepper Pod Campground

P.O. Box 445, 80642. T: (303) 536-4763 or (303) 536-9554; www.pepperpodcamp.com.

🚐 ★★★★   ⛺ ★★★

Beauty: ★★	Site Privacy: ★★★★
Spaciousness: ★★★★	Quiet: ★★
Security: ★★★★	Cleanliness: ★★★★
Insect Control: ★★★★	Facilities: ★★★★

Laid out as a square with rows on the inside and sites ringing the perimeter, this campground is adjacent to some industrial and commercial areas, and it has a definite urban feel. There is a railroad that passes to the east of the campground. Sites to the northwest (especially 19 and 29) have the most industrial views and are less attractive as a result. Sites 2–10 are 30-foot back-ins on thick grass that is even better than the grass in the tenting area. Site 2 is directly next to the trash dumpster and the RV dump and is the least desirable site. The row containing 32–39 is perhaps the nicest section, as it is farthest from the highway and the residences around the park. Sites 42 and 52 are adjacent to the manager's residence, and sites 52–59 border an external residential area. The tenting area occupies the entire western side of the campground. There is sparse vegetation covering the ground and little shade except in the northwest corner. The camper kitchen did not have running water at the time of this review. This is an acceptable overnight campground, but neither the area nor the campground itself present any reason to make a special trip out.

BASICS

Operated By: Neal Pontius. **Open:** All year. **Site Assignment:** Upon registration; credit card required for reservation; 24-hour cancellation policy. **Registration:** At office. (Late arrivals use drop box.) **Fee:** RV, $26.75–$29; tent, $20; check, V, MC, D. **Parking:** At site.

FACILITIES

Number of RV-only Sites: 65. **Number of Tent-only Sites:** 10. **Hookups:** Electric (20, 30, 50 amps), water, sewer. **Each Site:** Picnic table, grill. **Dump Station:** Yes. **Laundry:** Yes. **Pay Phone:** Yes. **Restrooms and Showers:** Yes. **Fuel:** No. **Propane:** Yes. **Internal Roads:** Gravel. **RV Service:** Yes. **Market:** 18 mi. to Brighton. **Restaurant:** 1 block. **General Store:** Yes. **Vending:** No. **Swimming:** Pool. **Playground:** Yes. **Other:** 2 cabins, game room, pet walk, data port, community building. **Activities:** Swimming, meetings, volleyball, touring Denver. **Nearby Attractions:** Denver. **Additional Information:** Fort Lupton Chamber of Commerce, (303) 857-4474.

RESTRICTIONS

Pets: On leash, cleaned up after. **Fires:** Grill only. **Alcoholic Beverages:** At sites. **Vehicle Maximum Length:** 50 ft.

TO GET THERE

From I-76 (Exit 31), turn east onto Hwy. 52 and go 0.1 mi., then turn right and go 0.2 mi. Turn left at the sign into the entrance. The office is on the right.

IDALIA   MAP, B-4
Bonny Lake State Park Campground

reserve america

30010 CR 3, 80735. T: (800) 678-CAMP or (970) 354-7306; www.reserveamerica.com.

🚐 ★★★★   ⛺ ★★★★

Beauty: ★★★★★	Site Privacy: ★★★★
Spaciousness: ★★★★	Quiet: ★★★★★
Security: ★★★	Cleanliness: ★★★★★
Insect Control: ★★★	Facilities: ★★★★

The best time to go to this campground, strung along the perimeter of Lake Bonny, is in later spring or summer, when full facilities are provided and it's warm enough to tempt you into the water. Variety is the name of the game here: laid out in a series of loops, the campground offers sites both lakeside and farther up the banks in the forest. (All sites are within a quarter mile of the lake.) There are both pull-throughs (average length 50 feet) and back-ins (average length 35 feet), all of which are grassy and mostly level. Tents or RVs can occupy any sites, although you may see primitive sites (without hookups) referred to as "tent sites." This forested campground has a secluded, wilderness feel to it and is a fun destination for families who enjoy lake recreation. Campers should remember to bring along enough provisions for their stay because the campground is a fair hike (25 miles) from the nearest full services. The marina inside the campground can, however, provide limited groceries, propane, and gasoline in proper containers.

BASICS

Operated By: Colorado State Parks. **Open:** All year; limited services, Oct.–mid-Apr. **Site Assignment:** First come, first served; reservations recommended in summer; credit card required; cancellation fees are $12 w/ 14-day notice & $7 plus 1 night w/ less than 14-day notice. **Registration:** At visitor station or at booth. **Fee:** Electric, $16–$18; primitive, $7; plus $5 day pass (cash only for pay station). **Parking:** At site, some parking in lots.

FACILITIES

Number of RV-only Sites: 100. **Number of Tent-only Sites:** 90. **Hookups:** Electric (30, 50 amps). **Each Site:** Picnic table, grill. **Dump Station:** Yes. **Laundry:** Yes. **Pay Phone:** Yes. **Restrooms and Showers:** Yes. **Fuel:** Yes (marina). **Propane:** Yes (marina). **Internal Roads:** Mostly dirt, some paved. **RV Service:** No. **Market:** 25 mi. to Burlington. **Restaurant:** 25 mi. to Burlington. **General Store:** Marina. **Vending:** No. **Swimming:** Yes. **Playground:** No. **Other:** Boat ramp, amphitheater. **Activities:** Swimming, boating, fishing, ranger presentations. **Nearby Attractions:** Bonny Lake, wildlife viewing areas. **Additional Information:** Burlington Chamber of Commerce, (719) 346-8070.

RESTRICTIONS

Pets: On 6-ft. leash, cleaned up after. **Fires:** Fire pit only. **Alcoholic Beverages:** No glass bottles, 3.2 alcohol only. **Vehicle Maximum Length:** No limit. **Other:** Vehicle pass required.

TO GET THERE

From I-70, take Exit 437, then turn north onto Hwy. 385 and go 22 mi. Turn right at the sign (0.7 mi. after mile marker 209) onto CR 2, and follow the road 3.7 mi. to the park entrance. (You can also take CR 3, 1 mi. farther north on Hwy. 385, to go directly to the north side of the lake.)

KREMMLING   MAP, A-2
Red Mountain RV Park

2201 Central Ave, 80459. T: (970) 724-9593 or (877) 375-9593; www.redmtnrvpark.com.

🚐 ★★★   ⛺ ★★★

Beauty: ★★★	Site Privacy: ★★★
Spaciousness: ★★★	Quiet: ★★★★
Security: ★★★★	Cleanliness: ★★★★★
Insect Control: ★★★★	Facilities: ★★★★

The presence or absence of trees in this park will make or break your stay—at least in summer. Sites 1–10 are shaded 54-foot gravel pull-throughs laid out horizontally to the highway. The dump station is right at site 10, making this site less desirable. The rest of the sites, however, are entirely unshaded. In effect, this park consists of hookups set around a large, open gravel space. To the north are long-term residents and RV storage. There is a baseball field to the east and a large antenna to the west. The sites that have grass (mostly to the north) are in large part overgrown. The tent area is a cordoned-off section of thick grass that has two covered picnic tables. This area is nice but only large enough to comfortably fit about six tents. The restrooms and showers are very clean and roomy enough. They are often used by hunters who only pass through for a shower. For campers who wish to explore the area, this park is a pleasant stay.

BASICS

Operated By: Jeff & Sara Miller. **Open:** All year. **Site Assignment:** Flexible, depending on site availability; credit card required for reservation; 24-hour cancellation policy. **Registration:** At office. (Late arrivals select site & pay in the morning.) **Fee:** RV (full), $23; tent, $8–$15; check, V, MC, & D. **Parking:** At site.

FACILITIES

Number of RV-only Sites: 45. **Number of Tent-only Sites:** Undesignated sites. **Hookups:** Electric (30, 50 amps), water, sewer. **Each Site:** Picnic table. **Dump Station:** Yes. **Laundry:** Yes. **Pay Phone:** Yes. **Restrooms and Showers:** Yes. **Fuel:** No. **Propane:** Yes. **Internal Roads:** Gravel. **RV Service:** No. **Market:** 1 mi. west. **Restaurant:** 1 mi. west. **General Store:** No. **Vending:** No. **Swimming:** No. **Playground:** Yes. **Other:** Data port, lounge, RV storage. **Activities:** Hunting, fishing, hiking. **Nearby Attractions:** Rocky Mountain National Park, Steamboat Springs. **Additional Information:** Kremmling Area Chamber of Commerce, (970) 724-3472.

RESTRICTIONS

RESTRICTIONS

Pets: On leash, cleaned up after. **Fires:** Grill only. **Alcoholic Beverages:** At sites. **Vehicle Maximum Length:** No limit.

TO GET THERE

From the junction of Hwy. 9 and Hwy. 40, turn east onto Hwy. 40 and go 1 mi. Turn north onto CR 22 and go 1 block. Turn right at the sign into the entrance.

LA JARA   MAP, C-2
Mogote–Rio Grande National Forest

Conejos Peak Rd 15571 Cr T-5, 81140. T: (719) 852-5941; www.reserveamerica.com.

🚐 ★★★★   ⛺ ★★★★

Beauty: ★★★★	Site Privacy: ★★★
Spaciousness: ★★★★	Quiet: ★★★
Security: ★★★★	Cleanliness: ★★★★
Insect Control: ★★★★	Facilities: ★

The lower level of this campground is near or along the Conejos River. Elevation is 8,300 feet. Mogote Campground is located in the Rio Grande National Forest which is 1.86 million acres and remains one of the true undiscovered jewels of Colorado. The Continental Divide runs for 236 miles along most of the western border of the forest. The forest presents myriad ecosystems from 7,600-foot alpine desert to over 14,300 feet in the majestic Sangre de Cristo Wilderness on the eastern side. The forest embraces the San Luis Valley, the largest agricultural alpine valley in the world and includes all or parts of four wilderness areas (South San Juan, Weminuche, La Garita, and Sangre de Cristo). The forest also is the headwaters of the Rio Grande River and has the moonscape wonder of the Wheeler Geologic Area, established by Theodore Roosevelt in 1911. The Anasazi were visitors here, and many of their sites remain. Denver is four hours north and Albuquerque is four hours south.

BASICS

Operated By: U.S. Forest Service. **Open:** May 19–Sept. 4. **Site Assignment:** Reservations must be made at least 4 days in advance. **Registration:** At office. **Fee:** Single, $14; group, $85–$95. **Parking:** At park.

FACILITIES

Number of Multipurpose Sites: 128. **Hookups:** None. **Each Site:** Call ahead. **Dump Station:** No. **Laundry:** No. **Pay Phone:** No. **Restrooms and Showers:** Yes. **Fuel:** No. **Propane:** No. **Internal Roads:** Paved. **RV Service:** No. **Market:** No. **Restaurant:** No. **General Store:** No. **Vending:** No. **Swimming:** No. **Playground:** No.

RESTRICTIONS

Pets: Pets must be restrained or on a leash at all times while in developed recreation areas. **Fires:** In fire rings, stoves, grills, or fireplaces provided for that purpose. **Alcoholic Beverages:** Not allowed. **Vehicle Maximum Length:** Call ahead. **Other:** No

ATVs or ORVs allowed in the campground. No refunds are given for bad weather. No horses/pack animals allowed.

TO GET THERE

From Antonio, go west on Hwy. 17 approximately 15 mi. to campground access road. Turn right, and travel 0.25 mi. to the Upper Loop Rd.

LA JUNTA   MAP, C-4
La Junta KOA

26680 West Hwy. 50, 81050. T: (800) 562-9501 or (719) 384-9580; www.lajuntakoa.com or www.koakampground.com.

🚐 ★★★★   ⛺ ★★★

Beauty: ★★	Site Privacy: ★★★
Spaciousness: ★★★★	Quiet: ★★★
Security: ★★★★	Cleanliness: ★★★★
Insect Control: ★★★★	Facilities: ★★★★

Pull-throughs in this campground range from 30 feet to 60 feet in length, and all are very level, grassy, and open. End sites 31, 41, and 49 are at the small end of this scale, making them slightly less desirable. The best RV site is 25, as it contains large shade trees on both sides. This is an important consideration, as most sites (and most campgrounds in the area) have very little shade. Site 49 comes in second thanks to a single towering shade tree. Tenters have it a little nicer with regards to shade. The strip of tent sites at the north end of the campground (just off the highway, unfortunately) and to the west of the pool have a line of overarching trees that protect tenters from the sun's rays. The earth is quite hard here, however, and the sites receive a fair amount of traffic noise. The group tenting area at the extreme south end of the campground does not have shade trees like the strip at the north end and is therefore not quite as nice. The restroom facility is a little small but quite clean. The shower curtains and floors look dated, but the facility is otherwise comfortable. The laundry room is clean and roomy, and is open 24 hours. RVers will enjoy this campground, but tenters may want to push on.

BASICS

Operated By: Gene & Michelle Rowland. **Open:** All year. **Site Assignment:** Upon registration; credit card required for reservation; 24-hour cancellation policy. **Registration:** At office. (Late arrivals), **Fee:** $24.50–$27.50; V, MC, D. **Parking:** At site.

FACILITIES

Number of RV-only Sites: 39. **Number of Tent-only Sites:** 3. **Hookups:** Electric (30, 50 amps), water, sewer, cable TV. **Each Site:** Picnic table, tree, or shrub. **Dump Station:** Yes. **Laundry:** Yes. **Pay Phone:** Yes. **Restrooms and Showers:** Yes. **Fuel:** No. **Propane:** Yes. **Internal Roads:** Gravel. **RV Service:** No. **Market:** 0.2 mi. west (limited on site). **Restaurant:** 0.2 mi. west. **General Store:** Yes. **Vending:** No. **Swimming:** Pool. **Playground:** Yes. **Other:** Meeting room, dog walk area, pool table, covered patio, data port, cabins. **Activities:** Fishing (nearby), golf (nearby), boating, horseshoes, video games. **Nearby Attractions:** Bent's Fort, Dinosaur Track Site, Koshare Indian Museum. **Additional**

Information: La Junta Chamber of Commerce, (719) 384-7411.

RESTRICTIONS

Pets: On leash, cleaned up after, max. of 2 (small) dogs. **Fires:** Grill only. **Alcoholic Beverages:** At sites. **Vehicle Maximum Length:** 65 ft.

TO GET THERE

From the junction of Hwy. 10 and Hwy. 50, go 1.5 mi. west on Hwy. 50. Turn left at the sign into the entrance. Keep straight to enter the campground. The office is on the left.

LAKE GEORGE   MAP, B-3
Eleven Mile State Park

4230 CR 92, 80827-9202. T: (719) 748-3402; www.reserveamerica.com.

🚐 ★★★★   ⛺ ★★★

Beauty: ★★★★	Site Privacy: ★★★
Spaciousness: ★★★	Quiet: ★★★★★
Security: ★★★★★	Cleanliness: ★★★★
Insect Control: ★★★	Facilities: ★★★★

This site is located at an elevation of 8,600 feet in the southeastern corner of South Park, a large, natural mountain park in central Colorado. The focus of the park is 3,400-acre Eleven Mile Reservoir, one of the largest reservoirs in Colorado. The nearby Front Range and interesting rock formations provide spectacular scenery. Eleven Mile Reservoir is known for its excellent fishing. Rainbow, brown and cutthroat trout, kokanee salmon, northern pike, and carp are all found within the waters of Eleven Mile. Power-boating, sailing, and windsurfing are also very popular during the summer and fall months. Two boat ramps are available on the shores of the reservoir. A multitude of camping and picnicking sites are available around the lake. The park is open year-round, offering spectacular Rocky Mountain sunsets and plenty of room to breathe. Visitors may choose from a variety of campsites at Eleven Mile State Park's 350-site facility. Showers and laundry facilities are located at the park office.

BASICS

Operated By: Colorado State Parks. **Open:** All year. **Site Assignment:** Reservations can be made 6 months in advance. **Registration:** At office. **Fee:** Single, $7–$20; yurt, $60; cabin, $80–$160. **Parking:** At park.

FACILITIES

Number of Multipurpose Sites: 349. **Hookups:** Yes. **Each Site:** Fire ring. **Dump Station:** Yes. **Laundry:** Yes. **Pay Phone:** Yes. **Restrooms and Showers:** Yes. **Fuel:** No. **Propane:** No. **Internal Roads:** Paved. **RV Service:** No. **Market:** No. **Restaurant:** No. **General Store:** Yes. **Vending:** No. **Swimming:** Yes. **Playground:** Yes. **Activities:** Amphitheater, biking, bird-watching, boating, cross-country skiing, fishing, hiking, hunting, ice fishing, photography, picnicking, sailing, sailboarding, show-shoeing, wildlife viewing.

RESTRICTIONS

Pets: Pets must be on a leash no longer than 6 ft. in length. **Fires:** Permitted in designated fireplaces. **Other:** Quiet hours will be enforced 10 p.m.–6 a.m. All generators, loud radios, or other loud noises that may disturb the peace are prohibited during these hours.

TO GET THERE

From Colorado Springs, take Hwy. 24 west 38 mi. through Lake George. West of Lake George, turn left (south) on CR 90 and follow it 4 mi. From that point, continue south on CR 92 6 mi. to the park.

LONGMONT   MAP, A-3
Barbour Ponds State Park–St. Vrain State Park

4995 Weld CR 24 1/2, 80504. T: (303) 678-9402; www.parks.state.co.us.

🚐 ★★★   🏕 ★★★

Beauty: ★★★   Site Privacy: ★★★★
Spaciousness: ★★★★   Quiet: ★★★
Security: ★★★★   Cleanliness: ★★★
Insect Control: ★★★★   Facilities: ★★★

Divided into the North, West, and East campgrounds, this park offers rather undeveloped sites with both back-ins and pull-throughs. The North Campground is located quite close to I-25 and cannot be recommended due to the amount of traffic noise it receives. Sites in this campground include 40-foot (57–60) to 66-foot back-ins (48–50, 52–54), and 70-foot pull-throughs (46, 47, 51). Many of these sites are well-shaded. West Campground has 45–54-foot back-ins that lie closest to the water. Some of these sites are right on the banks of the ponds. Farthest west, the unattractive view of mines to the south opens up. The views to the north, however, are much nicer. East Campground has several tent sites in a stand of trees right at the entrance (site 28). Other sites are 45-foot back-ins, and many of these are unshaded. Facilities are limited to pit toilets (no showers). This is a pleasant but rather small state park that attracts mostly fishermen and does not offer much in terms of facilities or activities.

BASICS

Operated By: Colorado State Parks. **Open:** All year. **Site Assignment:** First come, first served (winter only); reservations available Memorial Day–Labor Day; credit card required for reservation; 3-day cancellation policy. **Registration:** At pay kiosk. **Fee:** $12; check, no credits cards. **Parking:** At site, lots of extra parking.

FACILITIES

Number of RV-only Sites: 59. **Number of Tent-only Sites:** 1. **Hookups:** None. **Each Site:** Picnic table, grill, fire pit, tent pad. **Dump Station:** No. **Laundry:** No. **Pay Phone:** No. **Restrooms and Showers:** Restrooms; no shower. **Fuel:** No. **Propane:** No. **Internal Roads:** Dirt & gravel. **RV Service:** No. **Market:** Less than 10 mi. to 17th & Pace Sts. **Restaurant:** 3 mi. to I-25. **General Store:** No. **Vending:** No. **Swimming:** No. **Playground:** Yes. **Other:** Firewood, nature trails, wildlife, views of

Rocky Mountains, covered picnic areas, volleyball court, horseshoe pit. **Activities:** Nonmotorized boating, fishing. **Nearby Attractions:** Denver, Boulder, Rocky Mountain National Park, Ft. Collins. **Additional Information:** Boulder CVB, (303) 442-2911.

RESTRICTIONS

Pets: On 6-ft. leash, cleaned up after. **Fires:** Fire pit only. **Alcoholic Beverages:** At sites; 3.2% or less. **Vehicle Maximum Length:** No limit. **Other:** $5 entrance fee, no swimming, no bills larger than $20, preferably.

TO GET THERE

From the junction of I-25 (Exit 240), turn west onto Hwy. 179 and go 1.1 mi. Turn right onto Rd. 7 and go 1.3 mi. to the entrance.

LOVELAND   MAP, A-3
Boyd Lake State Recreation Area

reserve america

3720 N. County Rd., 80538. T: (970) 669-1739; www.reserveamerica.com.

🚐 ★★★★   🏕 ★★★★

Beauty: ★★★★   Site Privacy: ★★★
Spaciousness: ★★★   Quiet: ★★★★★
Security: ★★★   Cleanliness: ★★★★
Insect Control: ★★★   Facilities: ★★★★

The pelicans display their full wingspan as they glide gracefully to a landing on the clear surface of the lake. The sun reflects across the gentle ripples made in their wake. In the distance, a sailboat flies on the breeze, fishermen cast for that trophy catch and families play and picnic on a sandy beach. This is Boyd Lake State Park. The most modern water sports facility in northern Colorado, Boyd Lake State Park boasts over 1,700 surface acres of water for boating, fishing, sailing, and more. Hunting for waterfowl is allowed in season. A sandy beach and seasonally warm water make Boyd Lake a favorite for windsurfing, canoeing, waterskiing, and swimming. With 148 sites for camping, and other facilities, including picnic areas, a playground and a trail system, this family-oriented park is the perfect place for visitors of all ages.

BASICS

Operated By: Colorado State Parks. **Open:** Apr. 1–Sept. 30. **Site Assignment:** Reservations can be made 6 months in advance. **Registration:** At office. **Fee:** Single, $7–$20; yurt, $60; cabin, $80–$160. **Parking:** At park.

FACILITIES

Number of Multipurpose Sites: 148. **Hookups:** Yes. **Each Site:** Fire ring. **Dump Station:** Yes. **Laundry:** Yes. **Pay Phone:** Yes. **Restrooms and Showers:** Yes. **Fuel:** No. **Propane:** No. **Internal Roads:** Paved. **RV Service:** No. **Market:** No. **Restaurant:** No. **General Store:** Yes. **Vending:** No. **Swimming:** Yes. **Playground:** Yes. **Activities:** Beach, biking, bird-watching, boating, fishing, hiking, hunting, ice fishing, jet skiing, photography, picnicking, sailing, sailboarding, waterskiing, wildlife viewing.

RESTRICTIONS

Fires: Permitted in designated fireplaces. **Other:** Quiet hours will be enforced 10 p.m.–6 a.m. All generators, loud radios or other loud noises that may disturb the peace are prohibited during these hours.

TO GET THERE

One mi. east of Loveland. Take Hwy. 34 west of I-25; turn north on Madison Ave. and follow the signs.

LOVELAND   MAP, A-3
Carter Valley Campground

1326 North Carter Lake Rd., 80537. T: (970) 663-3131.

🚐 ★★★★   🏕 ★★★

Beauty: ★★★★   Site Privacy: ★★★
Spaciousness: ★★★   Quiet: ★★★★
Security: ★★★★   Cleanliness: ★★★★★
Insect Control: ★★★★   Facilities: ★★★

Sites in this campground are laid out in rows on three tiers up a hillside. The campground is surrounded by farms, and there are forests and mountains to the northwest. Sites around the office are open-ended back-ins that can accommodate a vehicle of about 40 feet. Sites 15–25 on the second tier are 40-foot angled back-ins with parking in front of the sites. Sites 53–62 measure 25 by 35 feet and are laid out by the highway. These sites are somewhat cramped and (although well shaded) rather undesirable. The top tier, adjacent to a large grassy hill, contains long-term residents. This is probably the nicest section of the park. Sites 37–40 are located along the south edge, perpendicular to the rows on the three tiers. There is RV storage to the west of site 37, making this area less attractive. Tent sites are located on the second tier, above the office. These are grassy but unshaded sites. This campground is in an attractive area and close to a number of recreation opportunities. It is a pleasant stay for RVers or tenters.

BASICS

Operated By: Tammy Johnson. **Open:** All year. **Site Assignment:** Upon registration; verbal reservations OK. **Registration:** At office. (Late arrivals ring bell.) **Fee:** RV (full), $20; water/electric, $18; tent, $10; check, V, MC, D. **Parking:** At site.

FACILITIES

Number of RV-only Sites: 58. **Number of Tent-only Sites:** 6. **Hookups:** Electric (30, 50 amps), water, sewer. **Each Site:** Picnic table. **Dump Station:** Yes. **Laundry:** Yes. **Pay Phone:** Yes. **Restrooms and Showers:** Yes. **Fuel:** No. **Propane:** No. **Internal Roads:** Gravel. **RV Service:** No. **Market:** 4 mi. east. **Restaurant:** 2.5 mi. east. **General Store:** Yes. **Vending:** Yes. **Swimming:** None. **Playground:** Yes. **Other:** Potlucks every 2 weeks, rec room w/ pool table & TV. **Activities:** Skiing, hiking, rock climbing, fishing, boating, swimming, bicycling, mountain climbing. **Nearby Attractions:** Golf courses, Rocky Mountain National Park, flea markets, antique malls. **Additional Information:** Loveland Visitor Center, (970) 667-5728.

RESTRICTIONS

Pets: On leash, cleaned up after. **Fires:** Grill only.

Alcoholic Beverages: At sites. **Vehicle Maximum Length:** 42 ft.

TO GET THERE

From the junction of Hwy. 287 and Hwy. 34, turn west onto Hwy. 34 and go 7.25 mi. Turn left onto Carter Lake Rd. and go 0.45 mi. Turn left at the sign into the entrance.

MOGOTE   MAP, C-2
Mogote Meadow Cottages and RV Park

34127 Hwy. 17, 81120. T: (719) 376-5774; www.mogotemeadow.com.

🚐 ★★★★   ▲ ★★★★

Beauty: ★★★★	Site Privacy: ★★★★
Spaciousness: ★★★★	Quiet: ★★★★
Security: ★★★★	Cleanliness: ★★★★★
Insect Control: ★★★	Facilities: ★★★

This park consists of a large field that can take any size rig (except for sites 8–16, which are restricted to 55 feet in length). 40-foot-wide sites are in a rural location with trees on all sides. (Some houses to the north belie the proximity to human habitation, but do not damage the scenery.) End site 27 is set slightly apart from the others and has a large open space to the west. Sites 1–7 are situated along the entrance and therefore receive more traffic than other sites. The laundry facility is slightly cramped and hot (it shares the building with a furnace and has no windows). The men's and women's restrooms are separated—the men's being out in the middle of the park, the women's in the same building as the laundry facility. These facilities are quite clean and comfortable. This is a fine campground in a great location.

BASICS

Operated By: Mark & Sharon Melvin. **Open:** May 1–Oct. 20. **Site Assignment:** Flexible, depending on availability; reservations available. **Registration:** At office. (Late arrivals select site & pay in the morning.) **Fee:** $18 plus tax; check, no credit cards. **Parking:** At site.

FACILITIES

Number of RV-only Sites: 45. **Hookups:** Electric (30, 50 amps), water, sewer. **Each Site:** Most have cement slab & large cottonwood. **Dump Station:** No (sewer at all sites). **Laundry:** Yes. **Pay Phone:** Yes. **Restrooms and Showers:** Yes. **Fuel:** No. **Propane:** Yes. **Internal Roads:** Gravel. **RV Service:** No. **Market:** 5 mi. to Antonito. **Restaurant:** 5 mi. to Antonito. **General Store:** No. **Vending:** Soft drinks. **Swimming:** No. **Playground:** Yes. **Other:** Cabins, meeting hall. **Activities:** Fishing, volleyball, horseshoes, potluck dinner (Wed. nights), pancake breakfast (Sun. mornings). **Nearby Attractions:** Scenic byway, Cumbres & Toltect Scenic Railroad, Colorado Alligator Park, Jack Demsey Museum. **Additional Information:** Antonito Tourist Information Center & Chamber of Commerce, (719) 376-5441.

RESTRICTIONS

Pets: On leash, cleaned up after. **Fires:** No fires at sites. **Alcoholic Beverages:** At sites. **Vehicle Maximum Length:** No limit.

TO GET THERE

From the junction of Hwy. 285 and Hwy. 17, go 4.8 mi. southwest on Hwy. 17. Turn right at the sign into the entrance. The office is immediately on the left.

MANITOU SPRINGS   MAP, B-3
Pike's Peak RV Park and Campground

320 Manitou Dr., 80829. T: (719) 685-9459 or (719) 685-1871.

🚐 ★★★★   ▲ ★★★

Beauty: ★★★★	Site Privacy: ★★★
Spaciousness: ★★	Quiet: ★★★
Security: ★★★★	Cleanliness: ★★★★
Insect Control: ★★★★	Facilities: ★★★

Laid out in a giant loop that rings the entire campground, RV sites are a tight 19 feet wide and a maximum of 40 feet long. Sites 1–19 back to woods along the northern edge of the campground. Besides 24–27, which are quite near the basketball court and may find games there disruptive, these are among the best sites due to the natural scenery. Sites 26–47 back to the creek, which would make these the nicest sites, except the highway lies just beyond, bringing traffic noise. Sites 48–58 are in the middle of the park. Sites 58 and 59 are close to a private residence, but definitely the most spacious sites. Tent sites are on a crushed gravel drive. Sites 70 and 71 are wide open to the sun, but 72–74 are very well shaded. All of these sites are just off the highway.

BASICS

Operated By: Allen & Jackie Branine. **Open:** Apr. 1–Oct. 31. **Site Assignment:** Upon registration; credit card required for reservation; 24-hour cancellation policy. **Registration:** At office. (Late arrivals select site & pay in the morning.) **Fee:** RV (full), $26; water/electric, $26; tent, $20; check, V, MC. **Parking:** At site.

FACILITIES

Number of RV-only Sites: 60. **Number of Tent-only Sites:** 6. **Hookups:** Electric (30, 50 amps), water, sewer. **Each Site:** Picnic table. **Dump Station:** No. **Laundry:** Yes. **Pay Phone:** Yes. **Restrooms and Showers:** Yes. **Fuel:** No. **Propane:** No. **Internal Roads:** Gravel. **RV Service:** On-call. **Market:** Less than 0.25 mi. **Restaurant:** Across the street. **General Store:** Yes. **Vending:** Yes. **Swimming:** Pool. **Playground:** No. **Other:** Data port, next door to city park & pool, central location, fishing in creek. **Activities:** Swimming, fishing, sightseeing, mountain climbing, hiking, tours. **Nearby Attractions:** Garden of the Gods, Pike's Peak. **Additional Information:** Manitou Springs Chamber of Commerce, (719) 685-5089.

RESTRICTIONS

Pets: On leash, cleaned up after. **Fires:** Grill only. **Alcoholic Beverages:** At sites. **Vehicle Maximum Length:** 40 ft.

TO GET THERE

From the junction of Hwy. 24 and Hwy. Business 24 (Manitou Ave.), turn west onto Manitou Ave. and go 0.25 mi. Turn right at the sign into the entrance.

MCCLAVE   MAP, C-4
Hud's Campground

29995 Hwy. 50, 81057. T: (719) 829-4344.

🚐 ★★★   ▲ ★★★

Beauty: ★★★	Site Privacy: ★★★★
Spaciousness: ★★★★	Quiet: ★★★
Security: ★★★★	Cleanliness: ★★★
Insect Control: ★★★★	Facilities: ★★★★

This rural campground consists of a large open field. There is a mobile home to the west of the park, which is slightly unattractive, and the highway is just off the east edge. A big plus in this campground is that sites are defined by width, but not by length. Therefore, pull-throughs measure 30 by 60 feet or longer. Rigs of any size can easily park here. Sites are open, grassy spaces situated in rows. The campground contains only sparse bushes, and, as a result, not much shade. The best sites, at the northern edge of the campground, are slightly larger but situated right on the internal road. Tenting sites, to the south of the pool, are also quite open, but the grass is rather thick, making for a decent ground covering. The shower and restroom facility is a large concrete building, reminiscent of a public-swimming pool changing room. The floor needed painting during our inspection, and the showers, while certainly adequate, were due for a good scrubbing.

BASICS

Operated By: Bob & Patty Boyer. **Open:** All year; limited facilities in winter. **Site Assignment:** First come, first served; verbal reservations OK. **Registration:** At store. (Late arrivals select site & pay in the morning.) **Fee:** RV, $16; tent, $12. **Parking:** At site.

FACILITIES

Number of RV-only Sites: 20. **Number of Tent-only Sites:** 5. **Hookups:** Electric (30 amps), water, sewer. **Each Site:** Some picnic tables. **Dump Station:** Yes. **Laundry:** Yes. **Pay Phone:** Yes. **Restrooms and Showers:** Yes. **Fuel:** Nearby. **Propane:** Nearby. **Internal Roads:** Gravel. **RV Service:** No. **Market:** 15 mi. into Lamar. **Restaurant:** 15 mi. into Lamar. **General Store:** Yes. **Vending:** No. **Swimming:** Pool. **Playground:** Yes. **Other:** RV parts, horseshoes, lake (7 mi. away). **Activities:** Swimming, fishing (nearby). **Nearby Attractions:** John Martin Lake, Benson Fort. **Additional Information:** Lamar Chamber of Commerce, (719) 336-4379.

RESTRICTIONS

Pets: On leash, cleaned up after. **Fires:** Fire pit only. **Alcoholic Beverages:** At sites. **Vehicle Maximum Length:** No limit. **Other:** No BB guns.

TO GET THERE

At the junction of Hwy. 50 and Hwy. 196, on the southwest side.

MEEKER   MAP, A-1
Stagecoach Campground

39084 Hwy. 13, 81641. T: (970) 878-4334.

🚐 ★★★★   ▲ ★★★

Beauty: ★★★★   Site Privacy: ★★★★
Spaciousness: ★★★★★   Quiet: ★★★★
Security: ★★★★   Cleanliness: ★★★
Insect Control: ★★★   Facilities: ★★

This is a beautiful campground with lush grass and giant cottonwoods surrounded by natural scenery on all sides: grassy hills to the south and west, a rocky hill to the north, and wetlands to the east. Sites 30–34 are long enough (120 feet) to be used as doubles, but, surprisingly, are not. Sites are a generous 45 feet wide, grassy, and forested. Sites 11–18C may require some maneuvering to park in but are still excellent places to camp. RV sites 1–10 are shorter (36-foot) back-ins, much more cramped than the humongous pull-throughs. Tent sites are on a strip of thick grass to the west of the RV sites, but there is only one fire pit, under a cottonwood by the river. Whoever can grab that one spot has quite possibly the best tenting space for 20 miles around! The laundry is small, and the restrooms are small and darkish, with sealant flaking off the cement floors. Showers are spacious, but one light didn't work when inspected. These facilities are rough but not uncomfortable. Don't let the less-than-perfect toilet facilities put you off: this is a park to return to again and again!

BASICS

Operated By: Gerry Meislohn. **Open:** May 15–Nov. 1. **Site Assignment:** Flexible, depending on availability; verbal reservations OK. **Registration:** At office. (Late arrivals knock on door or use drop box.) **Fee:** RV (full), $20; water/electric, $18; tent, $15; V, MC. **Parking:** At site.

FACILITIES

Number of RV-only Sites: 41. **Number of Tent-only Sites:** Undesignated sites. **Hookups:** Electric (20, 30, 50 amps), water, sewer. **Each Site:** Picnic table, fire ring. **Dump Station:** Yes. **Laundry:** Yes. **Pay Phone:** Yes. **Restrooms and Showers:** Yes. **Fuel:** No. **Propane:** No. **Internal Roads:** Gravel. **RV Service:** No. **Market:** 2 mi. into town. **Restaurant:** 2 mi. into town. **General Store:** No. **Vending:** No. **Swimming:** No. **Playground:** No. **Other:** River, meat-hanging area for hunters, cottonwoods, wildlife. **Activities:** Fishing, hunting, skiing, backpacking, snowmobiling. **Nearby Attractions:** White River Museum, White River National Forest, Meeker Classic Sheepdog Trials (Sept.). **Additional Information:** Meeker Chamber of Commerce, (970) 878-5510.

RESTRICTIONS

Pets: On leash, cleaned up after. **Fires:** Fire rings/pits. **Alcoholic Beverages:** At sites. **Vehicle Maximum Length:** No limit.

TO GET THERE

On the south side at the junction of Hwy. 13 and Hwy. 64 (2 mi. out of town). The office is on the left of the driveway.

MONTROSE   MAP, B-1
Montrose RV Resort

200 North Cedar Ave., 81401. T: (888) 249-9554 or (970) 249-9177.

🚐 ★★★★   ▲ ★★★

Beauty: ★★★   Site Privacy: ★★★★
Spaciousness: ★★★★   Quiet: ★★★★★
Security: ★★★★   Cleanliness: ★★★★★
Insect Control: ★★★★   Facilities: ★★★★★

All sites are level and grassy here, and the landscaping makes this an attractive park. (Storage units to the south detract a little from the beauty.) Sites 1–7 are 36-foot back-ins; although 4 does not have a shade tree, making it less desirable. Sites 8–13 and 18–23 are 56-foot pull-throughs with a shared covered picnic area separated by a wooden divider. 24–31 are slightly larger (66 by 24 feet). Tent sites are in a fenced-off area to the north of the RV sites and west of the cabins. Beyond this, there is an open grassy field with trees at the far end and views of distant hills to the north and west. (Site 43 has the only shade tree among the tent sites.) The restrooms and showers are spotless, modern, and spacious. There is a bench running along one side for towels and toiletries as well as a clothes rack. Note that the door locks are a little complicated. The laundry is spacious and clean. All in all, this is quite a nice park—especially for RVers.

BASICS

Operated By: Ray & Angeline Wells. **Open:** All year. **Site Assignment:** Flexible, depending on availability; credit card required for reservation; 24-hour cancellation policy. **Registration:** At office. (Late arrivals use drop box.) **Fee:** RV, $19.95–$27.50; tent, $19.95; V, MC, AE, D. **Parking:** At site.

FACILITIES

Number of RV-only Sites: 26. **Number of Tent-only Sites:** 17. **Hookups:** Electric (30, 50 amps), water, sewer. **Each Site:** Picnic table, grill. **Dump Station:** Yes. **Laundry:** Yes. **Pay Phone:** Yes. **Restrooms and Showers:** Yes. **Fuel:** No. **Propane:** Yes. **Internal Roads:** Nice gravel. **RV Service:** No. **Market:** 1 mi. into town. **Restaurant:** 1 mi. into town. **General Store:** Yes. **Vending:** No. **Swimming:** Pool. **Playground:** Yes. **Other:** Dog-walk area, nightly movies on large screen TV, covered pavilion, cabins. **Activities:** Basketball, movies, swimming, hunting, hiking, biking, rafting, boating. **Nearby Attractions:** Montrose County Historical Museum, Ute Indian Museum & Ouray Memorial Park. **Additional Information:** Montrose Chamber of Commerce, (800) 923-5515 or (970) 249-5000.

RESTRICTIONS

Pets: On leash, cleaned up after. **Fires:** Grill only. **Alcoholic Beverages:** At sites. **Vehicle Maximum Length:** No limit.

TO GET THERE

From the junction of Hwy. 50 and Hwy. 550, go 0:8 mi. east on Hwy. 50 (Main St. in town), then 0.2 mi. north on Cedar Ave. Turn right at the sign into the entrance.

MONTROSE   MAP, B-1
South Rim Campground

reserve america

Black Canyon National Park, 81230.
T: (970) 641-2337; www.reserveamerica.com.

🚐 ★★★★   ▲ ★★★★

Beauty: ★★★★   Site Privacy: ★★★
Spaciousness: ★★★★   Quiet: ★★★★
Security: ★★★★★   Cleanliness: ★★★★
Insect Control: ★★★   Facilities: ★★★

South Rim Campground is located in Black Canyon National Park. The Black Canyon of the Gunnison's unique and spectacular landscape was formed slowly by the action of water and rock scouring down through hard Proterozoic crystalline rock. No other canyon in North America combines the narrow opening, sheer walls, and startling depths offered by the Black Canyon of the Gunnison. The canyon has been a mighty barrier to humans. Only its rims, never the gorge, show evidence of human occupation—not even by Ute Indians living in the area since written history began. Though the 6-mile drive that leads to the south rim of Black Canyon is unassuming, one quick glimpse over the edge of this magnificent, precipitous gorge will give anyone a tremendous appreciation for why the area was set aside as a national monument. Black Canyon, one of the most astounding canyons in the world, is as narrow as 1,100 feet across in places, yet its walls plummet 2,900 feet down to the Gunnison River far below. Established in 1933 by President Hoover, the Black Canyon of the Gunnison National Park protects the most spectacular 12 miles of the canyon. The Gunnison River began carving through the Precambrian stone millions of years ago, slowly etching out its path through the layers of rock and volcanic debris. Geologists marvel at this incredible display of natural history—the dark colored schists date back at least 1.7 billion years.

BASICS

Operated By: National Park Service. **Open:** All year. **Site Assignment:** Reservations must be made at least 3 days in advance; reservable season May 20–Sept. 9. **Registration:** At registration office. **Fee:** Single, $12–$18. **Parking:** At park.

FACILITIES

Number of Multipurpose Sites: 198. **Hookups:** Yes. **Each Site:** Call ahead. **Dump Station:** Yes. **Laundry:** No. **Pay Phone:** Near park. **Restrooms and Showers:** Yes. **Fuel:** No. **Propane:** No. **Internal Roads:** Paved. **RV Service:** No. **Market:** No. **Restaurant:** No. **General Store:** No. **Vending:** No. **Swimming:** No. **Playground:** No. **Activities:** Amphitheater, bird-watching, campfire programs, climbing, photography, showshoeing, wildlife viewing.

RESTRICTIONS

Pets: Pets must be on a leash at all times. **Fires:** Allowed; campfire program. **Alcoholic Beverages:** Not allowed. **Vehicle Maximum Length:** Varies; call ahead. **Other:** Bears frequent! All food must be kept in approved containers; no generator use; 2 primary recreation units per pad.

TO GET THERE

The park is located approximately 250 mi. south-west of Denver. South Rim: 15 mi. east of Montrose, via US 50 and CO 347. Campground in Oak-brush forest.

MORRISON — MAP, B-3
Bear Creek Lake Park

15600 West Morrison Rd., 80465.
T: (303) 697-6159.

🚐 ★★★★　　🏕 ★★★★

Beauty: ★★★★	Site Privacy: ★★★★
Spaciousness: ★★★★	Quiet: ★★★★
Security: ★★★★	Cleanliness: ★★★★
Insect Control: ★★★	Facilities: ★★★★

Almost appearing out of place, this campground is in a desert-like field with few trees and low, sparse vegetation. Sites are mostly dirt, with some vegetation. The campground is at the far southeast end of the park. The electric sites (more suitable for RVs) are on a hill overlooking the primitive sites. Sites are laid out in rows of roughly five units. Sites 13–16 are closest to the railroad that passes by the park and are therefore less desirable. Of the primitive sites, 45–49 are extremely long (100–105-foot) pull-throughs. Others are quite long (65–70-foot) back-ins. Sites 65–70 are located just off the internal road, making them more susceptible to passing vehicular traffic. Walk-in tent sites are found to the northeast of the RV sites. These are surrounded by both fences and trees. This is a nice, wild campground located surprisingly close to the highway to Denver. It is a welcome relief from the busy city, which most campers should enjoy.

BASICS

Operated By: Lakewood Community Resources. **Open:** Apr. 1–Oct. 31. **Site Assignment:** First come, first served; no reservations. **Registration:** At pay station. **Fee:** Electric, $18; primitive, $14; check. **Parking:** At site. $4 per vehicle per day.

FACILITIES

Number of Multipurpose Sites: 52. **Hookups:** Electric (20, 30 amps). **Each Site:** Picnic table, fire pit. **Dump Station:** No. **Laundry:** No. **Pay Phone:** Yes. **Restrooms and Showers:** Yes. **Fuel:** No. **Propane:** No. **Internal Roads:** Paved/gravel. **RV Service:** No. **Market:** 3 mi. east. **Restaurant:** 0.5 mi. into Morrison. **General Store:** Concession stand at marina. **Vending:** No. **Swimming:** Lake. **Playground:** Yes. **Other:** Amphitheater, swim beach, picnic areas, horse rentals, archery range, boat rentals, boat ramp, yurt, concession stand. **Activities:** Fishing, boating, swimming, hiking, volleyball. **Nearby Attractions:** Denver. **Additional Information:** Denver Chamber of Commerce, (303) 458-0220.

RESTRICTIONS

Pets: On 6-ft. leash, cleaned up after. **Fires:** Grill only. **Alcoholic Beverages:** Beer only. **Vehicle Maximum Length:** No limit. **Other:** $4/vehicle/day. $3 for seniors 62 & over. No glass.

TO GET THERE

From the junction of Hwy. 470 (Bear Creek Lake Exit), turn east onto Hwy. 8. Go 1 mi. Turn right at the sign into the entrance.

MOSCA — MAP, C-2
San Luis Lakes State Park

reserve america

P.O. Box 150, 81146. T: (719) 738-2376; www.reserveamerica.com.

🚐 ★★★★　　🏕 ★★★★

Beauty: ★★★★	Site Privacy: ★★★★
Spaciousness: ★★★	Quiet: ★★★★★
Security: ★★★★★	Cleanliness: ★★★★
Insect Control: ★★★	Facilities: ★★★★

In the shadow of the Great Sand Dunes National Monument is peaceful San Luis Lakes State Park and San Luis Lakes Wildlife Area. Nestled among low sand dunes in this unique desert are wildlife-laden wetlands and approximately 9 miles of easy, level hiking and biking trails. The combination of wetlands, lakes and dry valley floor environments provides a fantastic wildlife-viewing and recreation area. Migratory waterfowl and other birds are frequent visitors to these tranquil waters. Coyotes, kangaroo rats, and rabbits are common sight in the surrounding dunes. Elk, songbirds, raptors, reptiles, and amphibians all find refuge in this unlikely riparian oasis hidden in the low dunes of the San Luis Valley. The park features fishing, windsurfing, boating, waterskiing, picnicking, and photographic and amateur archaeology opportunities. San Luis Lakes State Park features a modern campground with showers and electricity. The campsites have a view of the lake and can accommodate motor homes, trailers, and tents. The park is located just 15 minutes west of the Great Sand Dunes on the Los Caminos Antiguos Scenic and Historic Byway.

BASICS

Operated By: Colorado State Parks. **Open:** May 26–Sept. 4. **Site Assignment:** Reservations can be made 6 months in advance. **Registration:** At office. **Fee:** Single, $7–$20; yurt, $60; cabin, $80–$160. **Parking:** At park.

FACILITIES

Number of Multipurpose Sites: 51. **Hookups:** Yes. **Each Site:** Fire ring. **Dump Station:** Yes. **Laundry:** Yes. **Pay Phone:** No. **Restrooms and Showers:** Yes. **Fuel:** No. **Propane:** No. **Internal Roads:** Paved. **RV Service:** No. **Market:** No. **Restaurant:** No. **General Store:** No. **Vending:** No. **Swimming:** No. **Playground:** No. **Activities:** Bird watching, boating, fishing, hiking, hunting, ice fishing, jet skiing, picnicking, photography, sailing, sailboarding, waterskiing, wildlife viewing.

RESTRICTIONS

Pets: Pets must be on a leash no longer than 6 ft. in length. **Fires:** Permitted in designated fireplaces. **Other:** Quiet hours will be enforced 10 p.m.–6 a.m. All generators, loud radios, or other loud noises that may disturb the peace are prohibited during these hours.

TO GET THERE

Take Hwy. 160 west from Walsenburg 60 mi. Travel north 13.5 mi. on Hwy. 150. Go left on Six Mile Lane 8 mi., then north 0.125 mi. to park entrance.

NEDERLAND — MAP, A-2
Kelly-Dahl Campground

reserve america

Hwy. 119/72, 80301. T: (877) 444-6777 or (303) 541-2500; www.reserveamerica.com.

🚐 ★★★★　　🏕 ★★★★

Beauty: ★★★★	Site Privacy: ★★★★
Spaciousness: ★★★★	Quiet: ★★★★
Security: ★★★★	Cleanliness: ★★★
Insect Control: ★★★★	Facilities: ★

The campgrounds in this area of the Roosevelt National Forest unfortunately do not include hookups. RVers wishing to camp here therefore have to make a bit of a sacrifice. However, this sacrifice may well be worth it, as the forest and the surrounding area is beautiful and wonderfully peaceful. This campground is laid out in three loops, with site driveways ranging from 20 feet (site 39) to 45 feet (site 30) in length. Average length is between 35 feet and 40 feet. Site 11 is a 72-foot quasi pull-through (that actually requires parallel parking). The rest of the sites are straightforward back-ins. Sites 16, 18, and 20 have a hill that provides a view when climbed. Both the Aspen Loop and the Pine Loop are quite forested. The Fir Loop is more open. Reservable sites are located in the Fir and Pine Loops. Site 30 (in the Pine Loop) is located extremely close to the playground, which may make it less desirable to some campers. The toilets are typical pit toilets, with no running water or showers. This campground offers the chance to get close to nature, which, of course, entails giving up some modern conveniences.

BASICS

Operated By: Thousand Trails Management. **Open:** May–Oct.; dates may vary. **Site Assignment:** First come, first served; credit card required for reservation; 3-day cancellation policy, less $10 fee. **Registration:** At pay kiosk. (Camp host will verify that campers have paid.) **Fee:** $14; check, no credit cards. **Parking:** At site.

FACILITIES

Number of Multipurpose Sites: 46. **Hookups:** None. **Each Site:** Picnic table, grill, fire pit. **Dump Station:** No. **Laundry:** No. **Pay Phone:** No (in Rollingsville). **Restrooms and Showers:** Restrooms; no shower (showers in downtown Nederland mall). **Fuel:** No. **Propane:** No. **Internal Roads:** Gravel/dirt. **RV Service:** No. **Market:** 3.5 mi. to Nederland. **Restaurant:** 3.5 mi. to Nederland. **General Store:** No. **Vending:** No. **Swimming:** No. **Playground:** Yes. **Other:** Firewood for sale. **Activities:** Hiking, gambling, horseback riding, mountain biking. **Nearby Attractions:** Rocky Mountain National Park, Blackhawk, Central City. **Additional Information:** Thousand Trails Management, (303) 258-3610.

RESTRICTIONS

Pets: On leash, cleaned up after. **Fires:** Fire pit only. **Alcoholic Beverages:** At sites. **Vehicle Maximum Length:** 40 ft.

TO GET THERE

From the junction of Hwy. 72 and Hwy. 119, turn south onto Hwy. 119/72 and go 3 mi. Turn left at the sign into the entrance and follow the dirt road to the pay kiosk.

OAK CREEK   MAP, A-2
Stagecoach

reserve america

P.O. Box 98, 80467. T: (970) 736-2436; www.reserveamerica.com.

🚐 ★★★★   ⛺ ★★★★

Beauty: ★★★   Site Privacy: ★★★
Spaciousness: ★★★   Quiet: ★★★★★
Security: ★★★★★   Cleanliness: ★★★★
Insect Control: ★★★   Facilities: ★★★★

Located in the verdant Yampa Valley south of Steamboat Springs, Stagecoach State Park offers visitors a wonderful area to enjoy Colorado's outdoors. The park is centered around a 780-acre reservoir with full-service marina. Learn the fascinating history of mining and logging near Stagecoach while you enjoy an unlimited array of activities, including fabulous boating and fishing in the summer and cross-country skiing and ice fishing in the winter. Fishing for rainbow, brook, brown, and Snake River cutthroat trout challenges anglers. Northern Pike and Kokanee salmon are also present in the lake. The Elk Run Trail (along the south shore) and the Wetlands Trail (located at the inlet) provide great opportunities for nature observation and recreation. The park has 4 campgrounds with 100 campsites spread among the lush and fragrant sagebrush of the Yampa Valley accommodating trailers, motor homes, pick-up campers, and tents. During the winter, a few electric campsites are available on a first-come, first-served basis.

BASICS

Operated By: Colorado State Parks. **Open:** All year. **Site Assignment:** Reservations can be made 6 months in advance. **Registration:** At office. **Fee:** Single, $7–$20; yurt, $60; cabin, $80–$160. **Parking:** At park.

FACILITIES

Number of Multipurpose Sites: 92. **Hookups:** Yes. **Each Site:** Fire ring. **Dump Station:** Yes. **Laundry:** No. **Pay Phone:** Yes. **Restrooms and Showers:** Yes. **Fuel:** No. **Propane:** No. **Internal Roads:** Paved. **RV Service:** No. **Market:** No. **Restaurant:** No. **General Store:** Yes. **Vending:** No. **Swimming:** Yes. **Playground:** No. **Activities:** Beach, biking, birdwatching, boating, cross-country skiing, fishing, hiking, hunting, ice fishing, interpretive programs, jet skiing, picnicking, photography, sailing, sailboarding, showshoeing, snowmobiling, waterskiing, wildlife viewing.

RESTRICTIONS

Pets: Pets must be on a leash no longer than 6 ft. in length. **Fires:** Permitted in designated fireplaces. **Other:** Quiet hours will be enforced 10 p.m.–6 a.m. All generators, loud radios, or other loud noises that may disturb the peace are prohibited during these hours.

TO GET THERE

From I-70 go north 44 mi. on Hwy. 9 to Hwy. 134, then go west 27 mi. to Hwy. 131. Proceed north 17 mi. to CR 14, and follow the signs.

ORCHARD   MAP, A-3
Jackson Lake State Park
Cove Campground

reserve america

26363 CR 3, 80649. T: (877) 444-6777 or (970) 645-2551; www.reserveamerica.com.

🚐 ★★★   ⛺ ★★★★

Beauty: ★★★★   Site Privacy: ★★★
Spaciousness: ★★★★   Quiet: ★★★★
Security: ★★★★   Cleanliness: ★★★★
Insect Control: ★★★★   Facilities: ★★★

Seemingly its own little world, this state park offers water-oriented recreation in a wilderness setting. The sparse grass and low vegetation gives it a typical southwestern feel, and it is beautiful in its own way. There are several campgrounds with several hundred sites; those reviewed here are the Cove and Pelican Campgrounds, containing roughly 20 sites combined. Sites 1–4 in Cove Campground are unshaded 40-foot back-ins that do not provide much in the way of privacy. Sites 5 and 6 are 63-foot pull-throughs located near the amphitheater. Site 5 has much better shade than 1–4 or 6. There is an unnumbered, 60-foot "pull-alongside" near the swimming beach, and several possible campsites along the parking lot for the swim beach. (If the parking lot is full, there is no parking for these sites.) Sites 7–10 and 13–14 are 40-foot back-ins that back to woods. These sites have the best shade in the park. (Sites 15 and 16 are also well shaded.) Sites 11 and 12 are much more open 45-foot back-ins. In the Pelican Campground, sites 5–10 are 60-foot pull-throughs that overlook the beach. There are also some tenting sites that are even closer to the edge of the beach. These are undoubtedly among the best tenting sites. The low shade trees and sandy cover make tent camping quite comfortable. This is a fun park for the entire family, whether in tents or an RV.

BASICS

Operated By: Colorado State Parks. **Open:** All year. **Site Assignment:** First come, first served; credit card required for reservation; 3-day cancellation policy, less $10. **Registration:** At pay station. **Fee:** $7–$30; check. **Parking:** At site.

FACILITIES

Number of RV-only Sites: 260. **Hookups:** Electric (20, 30, 50 amps). **Each Site:** Picnic table, grill, fire pit. **Dump Station:** Yes. **Laundry:** Yes, seasonally. **Pay Phone:** Yes. **Restrooms and Showers:** Yes. **Fuel:** No. **Propane:** Yes, summers only. **Internal Roads:** Paved/dirt. **RV Service:** No. **Market:** 18 mi. south in Wiggins. **Restaurant:** 18 mi. south in Wiggins. **General Store:** Marina, seasonally. **Vending:** Soft drinks. **Swimming:** Lake. **Playground:** No. **Other:** Boat ramp, amphitheater, hunting blinds, nature trails. **Activities:** Fishing, boating, swimming,

hiking, ice skating, interpretive programs, hunting. **Nearby Attractions:** Pawnee National Grasslands. **Additional Information:** Fort Morgan Chamber of Commerce, (970) 867-6702.

RESTRICTIONS

Pets: On 6-ft. leash, cleaned up after. **Fires:** Grill only. **Alcoholic Beverages:** 3.2% beer only. **Vehicle Maximum Length:** Varies. **Other:** $4-per-day park pass; no cutting of firewood.

TO GET THERE

From the junction of I-76 and Hwy. 39, turn north onto Hwy. 39 and go 7.65 mi. Turn west onto CR Y5 and go 2.4 mi. Turn right to go to the south end or continue straight to the north end and the office.

OURAY   MAP, C-1
4J+1+1 Trailer Park

P.O. Box F, 81427. T: (970) 325-4418.

🚐 ★★★★   ⛺ ★★★★

Beauty: ★★★★   Site Privacy: ★★★★
Spaciousness: ★★★★   Quiet: ★★★★
Security: ★★★★   Cleanliness: ★★★★
Insect Control: ★★★★   Facilities: ★★★★

Located in an outstandingly beautiful part of Colorado, this campground offers spectacular scenes from any site. This rural park has level gravel sites close to the river as well as farther back. "R" sites are back-ins by the river. 1–6 are quite small (24 feet long), but 7–13 get progressively longer: 27 feet to 45 feet. The pull-throughs in the middle of the park (14–19) are 55–60 feet long and contain shade trees, making them the best pull-through sites. Tent sites are along the western edge of the park right at the base of the mountain. (Don't worry about rock fall, though, as the mountainside is all trees.) The least appealing spot is 15, which is located next to a concrete slab as well as a telephone pole and dumpster. The rest of the tent sites are quite nice, however, and 6–10 are all the nicer for the overhanging trees they contain. Tent sites 1–4 have attractive wooden fencing for added privacy, and it appears as though all tent sites will soon have this added feature. The restrooms are clean but rather cramped—so much so, in fact, that only 1 of 4 stalls has a door, and only 1 of 3 showers has a curtain—which may make for an awkward bathroom experience. The playground is located across a road, and, while it is fenced in, it would be wise to keep an eye on children playing there. The RV experience here would be improved with more trees, and tenters would enjoy more grass, but either experience is quite satisfactory in this campground.

BASICS

Operated By: Jack & Jackie Clark & family. **Open:** May 15–Oct. 15; fully self-contained units may come before & after these dates. **Site Assignment:** Flexible, depending on availability; credit card required for reservation; 24-hour cancellation policy, 72-hour for Fourth of July. **Registration:** At office. (Late arrivals park & register in the morning.) **Fee:** RV (full), $20–$26; tent, $20; V, MC. **Parking:** At site.

FACILITIES

Number of RV-only Sites: 57. **Number of Tent-only Sites:** 10. **Hookups:** Electric (30, 50 amps),

water, sewer. **Each Site:** Picnic table, grill. **Dump Station:** Yes. **Laundry:** Yes. **Pay Phone:** Yes. **Restrooms and Showers:** Yes. **Fuel:** No. **Propane:** No. **Internal Roads:** Paved. **RV Service:** No. **Market:** 3 blocks. **Restaurant:** 1 block. **General Store:** No. **Vending:** Soft drinks. **Swimming:** Yes. **Playground:** Yes. **Other:** River; conveniently located near downtown & hot springs. **Activities:** Jeep tours, hiking, mountain biking, skiing (Telluride). **Nearby Attractions:** Hot springs, historic district. **Additional Information:** Ouray Chamber Resort Assoc., (800) 228-1876 or (970) 325-4746.

RESTRICTIONS

Pets: On leash, cleaned up after. **Fires:** Fire pit only. **Alcoholic Beverages:** At sites. **Vehicle Maximum Length:** No limit.

TO GET THERE

From Hwy. 550 in town, turn west onto 7th Ave. Drive 2 blocks to the end (just past the river), then turn right at the end of 7th Ave. onto Oak St. Take the first right into the entrance. The office is on the left.

PAGOSA SPRINGS   MAP, C-2
Cool Pines RV Park

1501 West Hwy. 160, 81147. T: (970) 264-9130 or (877) 250-4811.

🚐 ★★★★   ▲ ★★★

Beauty: ★★★★	Site Privacy: ★★★★
Spaciousness: ★★★	Quiet: ★★★★
Security: ★★★★	Cleanliness: ★★★★★
Insect Control: ★★★	Facilities: ★★★★

This attractive park is surrounded by "cool pines" and offers some mountain views from within. Terraced sites are situated on a loop with a grassy patch between each site. Pull-throughs are 60-feet long, while back-ins are only slightly smaller (50–55-feet long). There is one unmarked RV site directly by the office, which may get more traffic but also has a better view of the mountains. Tent sites are unmarked on a grassy patch behind the shops to the north, which could comfortably fit about five tents. (There are only three trees to provide coverage, however, and one fire ring.) The restrooms are individual units, which can be locked when in use. They are all very clean and spacious. The rec room, which houses the restrooms, is likewise very clean and comfortable. RVers should definitely make a point to come to Cool Pines. Tenters will also be comfortable, but would benefit from more coverage and more fire rings or pits, and some tables. This is a peaceful, wilderness location convenient both to the highway and to town.

BASICS

Operated By: The Robinsons. **Open:** Mid-Apr.–mid-Nov. **Site Assignment:** Flexible, depending on availability; credit card required for reservation; 3-day cancellation policy. **Registration:** At office. (Late arrivals come to office.) **Fee:** RV, $24; tent, $16; V, MC. **Parking:** At site.

FACILITIES

Number of RV-only Sites: 23. **Number of Tent-only Sites:** Undesignated sites. **Hookups:** Electric (30, 50 amps), water, sewer, cable TV. **Each Site:** Pic-

---

nic table, several trees at most sites. **Dump Station:** Yes. **Laundry:** Yes. **Pay Phone:** Yes. **Restrooms and Showers:** Yes. **Fuel:** No. **Propane:** No. **Internal Roads:** Paved/gravel. **RV Service:** No. **Market:** 1 mi. **Restaurant:** 1 mi. **General Store:** No. **Vending:** No. **Swimming:** No (hot tub). **Playground:** Yes. **Other:** Wheelchair accessible. **Activities:** Hiking, mountain biking, river rafting, fishing. **Nearby Attractions:** Chimney Rock, Red Rider Museum. **Additional Information:** Pagosa Springs Area Chamber of Commerce, (800) 252-2204 or (970) 264-2360.

RESTRICTIONS

Pets: On leash, cleaned up after. **Fires:** Grill only. **Alcoholic Beverages:** At sites. **Vehicle Maximum Length:** 42 ft.

TO GET THERE

From the junction of Hwy. 84 and Hwy. 160, go 2.5 mi. west on Hwy. 160. Turn right at the sign, and drive down behind the store fronts to get to the RV park.

PONCHA SPRINGS   MAP, B-2
Monarch Spur RV Park and Campground

18989 West Hwy. 50, P.O. Box 457, 81242. T: (888) 814-3001 or (719) 530-0341; www.monarchspurrvpark.com.

🚐 ★★★★   ▲ ★★★★

Beauty: ★★★★	Site Privacy: ★★★★
Spaciousness: ★★★★	Quiet: ★★★★
Security: ★★★★	Cleanliness: ★★★
Insect Control: ★★★★	Facilities: ★★★

Billing itself as a "big rig park," this campground makes good on its promise with decent 60-foot sites. This park uses its natural setting to its best advantage, employing rows of large rocks to designate site boundaries, and setting tent sites (and some RV sites) in the thick forest and on the grassy hills that encompass the park. RV sites are arranged in two rows of sites 60 by 30 feet. All pull-throughs are level with a grass and gravel mix. Unmarked tent sites are scattered along the river on grassy patches. These are fairly wild sites with good grass, lots of trees, and the constant sound of the river (which helps drown out traffic noise). There are many sites in the forest, which are slightly more isolated and definitely more shaded. The laundry room is clean and spacious, as are the restrooms. The showers are, however, slightly dingy. Tucked away on Hwy. 50, this campground can be a little difficult to locate. However, if you call, the staff will help you locate the park and even come out to get you.

BASICS

Operated By: Jerry Gunkel. **Open:** All year. **Site Assignment:** Flexible, depending on availability; credit card required for reservation; 48-hour cancellation policy, less $5 fee. **Registration:** At office. (Late arrivals select site & pay in the morning.) **Fee:** RV, $30; tent, $23; more than 4 adults, added fee; children, no extra charge. **Parking:** At site.

FACILITIES

Number of RV-only Sites: 29. **Number of Tent-only Sites:** 12. **Hookups:** Electric (20, 30, 50 amps),

---

water, sewer. **Each Site:** Picnic table, grass strip. **Dump Station:** No (sewer at all sites). **Laundry:** Yes. **Pay Phone:** Yes. **Restrooms and Showers:** Yes. **Fuel:** No. **Propane:** Yes. **Internal Roads:** Gravel/dirt. **RV Service:** No. **Market:** 10 mi. to Salida. **Restaurant:** 7 mi. to Poncha Springs. **General Store:** Yes. **Vending:** Yes. **Swimming:** No. **Playground:** No. **Other:** ATV rentals, picnic deck, video & VCR rentals, souvenir shop, firewood for sale. **Activities:** Hiking, ATV trails, horseshoes, swimming, hunting, gold panning. **Nearby Attractions:** San Isabel National Forest, San Juan National Forest. **Additional Information:** Heart of the Rockies Chamber of Commerce, (877) 772-5432 or (719) 539-2068.

RESTRICTIONS

Pets: On leash, cleaned up after. **Fires:** Fire pits; subject to seasonal bans. **Alcoholic Beverages:** At sites. **Vehicle Maximum Length:** 60 ft. **Other:** Read policy sheet; quiet time 10 p.m.–7a.m.; must have a sewer adapter to dump in park's septic.

TO GET THERE

From the junction of Hwy. 285 and Hwy. 50 in Salida, go 8.2 mi. west on Hwy. 50. Turn south at the sign onto a dirt road and follow it to the office.

PUEBLO   MAP, B-3
Lake Pueblo State Park

reserve america

640 Pueblo Reservoir Rd., 81005. T: (719) 561-9320; www.reserveamerica.com.

🚐 ★★★★   ▲ ★★★★

Beauty: ★★★★	Site Privacy: ★★★
Spaciousness: ★★★	Quiet: ★★★★★
Security: ★★★★	Cleanliness: ★★★★
Insect Control: ★★★	Facilities: ★★★★

Opened to the public in 1975, Lake Pueblo State Park quickly became one of the prime recreation destinations in Colorado. Known widely by sun-lovers and water-sports enthusiasts for its 4,646-surface-acre reservoir, the park also offers 400 campsites spread throughout its 9,600-acre park. Whether you want to boat, waterski, sail, swim, fish, camp, hike, or just relax, Lake Pueblo has something to offer for everyone. The park offers two full-service marinas, two boat ramps for easy boating access, prime fishing waters, plenty of camping with or without electrical hookups, a swim beach with a five-story waterslide, a visitor's center with fun displays and gift shop, as well as hundreds of picnic tables. Set against a background of the Greenhorn and Sangre de Cristo mountain ranges to the south and west and the magnificent Pikes Peak to the north, Lake Pueblo is an area of great contrasts. The miles of hiking and biking trails make it easy to discover the beauty of the shady Arkansas River below the dam or the splendor of hundred-year-old piñon juniper trees that overlook the 11-mile-long reservoir. Add the year-round mild and sunny weather of Pueblo, and it is no wonder that Lake Pueblo is a favorite vacation destination for so many people every year.

BASICS

Operated By: Colorado State Parks. **Open:** All year. **Site Assignment:** Reservations up to 6 months in advance. **Registration:** At office. **Fee:** Single, $7–$20; yurt, $60; cabin, $80–$160. **Parking:** At park.

FACILITIES

Number of Multipurpose Sites: 383. **Hookups:** Yes. **Each Site:** Fire ring. **Dump Station:** Yes. **Laundry:** Yes. **Pay Phone:** Yes. **Restrooms and Showers:** Yes. **Fuel:** No. **Propane:** No. **Internal Roads:** Paved. **RV Service:** No. **Market:** No. **Restaurant:** No. **General Store:** Yes. **Vending:** Yes. **Swimming:** Yes. **Playground:** Yes. **Activities:** Beach, biking, bird-watching, boating, fishing, hiking, hunting, interpretive programs, jet skiing, model airplane flying, photography, picnicking, sailing, sailboarding, waterskiing, wildlife viewing.

RESTRICTIONS

Pets: Pets must be on a leash no longer than 6 ft. in length. **Fires:** Permitted in designated fireplaces. **Other:** No airborne fireworks or any that explode or consist of any incendiary device or can result in secondary burns will be permitted. Quiet hours will be enforced 10 p.m.–6 a.m. All generators, loud radios, or other loud noises that may disturb the peace are prohibited during these hours.

TO GET THERE

Take I-25 to Pueblo, then Hwy. 50 west 4 mi. Turn south on Pueblo Blvd. and go 4 mi. to Thatcher Ave. Turn west and go 6 mi. to park entrance. Alternate route: best for North Plains Campground and Juniper Breaks Campground. Travel west on Hwy. 50 to McCulloch Blvd. then south and west on McCulloch to Nichols Rd. Then south to the north entrance.

PUEBLO
Pueblo KOA   MAP, B-3

4131 I-25 North, 81008. T: (800) 562-7453 or (719) 542-2273; www.koakampground.com.

🚐 ★★★★   ⛺ ★★★

Beauty: ★★★★	Site Privacy: ★★★
Spaciousness: ★★★★	Quiet: ★★★
Security: ★★★★★	Cleanliness: ★★★★★
Insect Control: ★★★★	Facilities: ★★★★

This campground in a desert setting has scattered rows of sites, each designated by a letter. Row A has pull-throughs measuring 60 by 18 feet that are separated from each other by a row of bushes. Sites A5 and A6 share a large shade tree. Toward the south are rows N and P. Row N has pull-throughs of 45 by 30 feet and is separated from row P by a hedge. All sites are well-shaded. Row P, at the southern edge of the campground, has 40-foot back-ins. Sites P1 and P2 are separated from each other by a wooden fence, which offers these sites more privacy than practically any others. They back to the hedge and open to the pool and a dirt road. There is a private residence next to P6. On the other side of P6 is a hedge that separates it from P5, making this latter site very private. In the middle and on the northern side of the campground, Rows B, C, D, and E have unshaded pull-throughs that average 60 feet in length. (Row C has

some slightly shorter pull-throughs, 42–57 feet long.) Rows F, G, and H are primitive sites good for tenting and possibly a pop-up. These sites are nicer, in fact, than the designated tent area between rows C and D, which has completely open sites on sparse grass set among a number of RV sites. The restrooms are pristine; the showers are a little worn but still acceptable. This is a beautiful campground for those who appreciate the austere beauty of the desert.

BASICS

Operated By: Michael & Carolyn Stowe. **Open:** All year. **Site Assignment:** Upon registration; credit card required for reservation; 24-hour cancellation policy. **Registration:** At office. (Late arrivals use drop box.) **Fee:** RV (full), $28; water/electric, $25; tent, $18; Colorado check, V, MC, AE, D. **Parking:** At site.

FACILITIES

Number of RV-only Sites: 60. **Number of Tent-only Sites:** 25. **Hookups:** Electric (50 amps), water, sewer. **Each Site:** Picnic table. **Dump Station:** Yes. **Laundry:** Yes. **Pay Phone:** Yes. **Restrooms and Showers:** Yes. **Fuel:** No. **Propane:** Yes. **Internal Roads:** Gravel. **RV Service:** No. **Market:** 8 mi. south to Hwy. 50. **Restaurant:** 2 mi. north. **General Store:** Yes. **Vending:** Yes. **Swimming:** Pool. **Playground:** Yes. **Other:** Rec room (pool table, video games), data port, dog walk, nature trail. **Activities:** Swimming, hiking, mountain climbing, boating. **Nearby Attractions:** Lake Pueblo State Park, Royal Gorge Bridge, Pikes Peak, Seven Falls, Cave of the Winds, Garden of the Gods, Manitou Cliff Dwellings. **Additional Information:** Visitor Information Center, (719) 543-1742.

RESTRICTIONS

Pets: On leash, cleaned up after; or must stay inside at night. **Fires:** Grill only. **Alcoholic Beverages:** At sites. **Vehicle Maximum Length:** No limit.

TO GET THERE

From I-25 (Exit 108): on the west side of the highway, take the first right and go 0.6 mi. straight into the campground. (From northbound I-25, there is a single lane underpass 13 ft. 6 in. high to negotiate. The owner assures there has never been a rig that can't pass through.)

RIDGWAY
Ridgway State Park   MAP, C-1

reserve america

28555 Hwy. 550, 81432. T: (800) 678-2267 or (970) 626-5822; www.reserveamerica.com.

🚐 ★★★★   ⛺ ★★★★

Beauty: ★★★★	Site Privacy: ★★★★
Spaciousness: ★★★	Quiet: ★★★★★
Security: ★★★★	Cleanliness: ★★★★
Insect Control: ★★★	Facilities: ★★

This state park includes three separate campgrounds (Elk Ridge, Dakota Terraces, and Pa-Co-Chu-Puk), each offering a slightly different experience. All campgrounds are organized in loops, offering 25-foot

back-ins for pop-ups to 65-foot pull-throughs for longer RVs. The first campground on the way in from the entrance and the visitor center, Dakota Terraces is also closest to the swimming beach at the reservoir (especially sites 56–79 in Loop C). Elevated wooden tent decks are offered at sites 10 and 50, while shade shelters can be found at 4, 6, 8–10, 79, and others (indicated on the state park map). This campground has many trees, and is the best bet for those who want to take advantage of the reservoir. Elk Ridge Campground is located on top of a hill overlooking the reservoir. It is thus a little farther from the water than Dakota Terraces, as well as more open. The most remote, and thus most private, sites are odd numbers 139–149 in Loop E, as well as 184–187. Wooden tent decks are provided at sites 99–103 (and others), while improved tent sites include 80, 83, 87, 123, 124, 165, 170, and others. Most difficult to pronounce, Pa-Co-Chu-Pak (also known as "Cow Creek") offers full hookups (sites 200–280) and walk-in tent sites (281–295). This campground is the most remote, and possibly the best for tenters—as long as they don't mind parking first and trekking in with their stuff. This campground offers two fishing ponds and almost exclusively pull-throughs. The most private sites include 200–208 in Loop F and 251, 254, and 257 in Loop G. This is a rare example of a state park offering full hookups, and those campers who enjoy getting out into the wild a little should definitely take advantage of these campgrounds.

BASICS

Operated By: Colorado State Parks. **Open:** All year; closed during bad weather; limited facilities in winter. **Site Assignment:** First come, first served; reservations can be made 3–90 days in advance; credit card required for reservation. **Registration:** At self-pay kiosk. **Fee:** $7–$20; park pass, $5; check, no credit cards. **Parking:** At site.

FACILITIES

Number of RV-only Sites: 295. **Number of Tent-only Sites:** 15. **Hookups:** Electric (50 amps), water, sewer; hookup availability varies by campground. **Each Site:** Picnic table, grill. **Dump Station:** Yes. **Laundry:** Yes. **Pay Phone:** Yes. **Restrooms and Showers:** Yes. **Fuel:** No. **Propane:** No. **Internal Roads:** Paved. **RV Service:** No. **Market:** 6 mi. in Ridgway. **Restaurant:** 6 mi. in Ridgway. **General Store:** Yes. **Vending:** Yes. **Swimming:** Lake. **Playground:** Yes. **Other:** Marina, beach house, some wheelchair accessible facilities. **Activities:** Hiking, swimming, biking, hunting, fishing, boating, scuba diving, water-skiing, windsurfing. **Nearby Attractions:** Ridgway Reservoir. **Additional Information:** Ridgway Visitor Center, (970) 626-5868.

RESTRICTIONS

Pets: On 6-ft. leash, cleaned up after. **Fires:** Fire pits/grills, check w/ park for current fire restrictions. **Alcoholic Beverages:** Beer only. **Vehicle Maximum Length:** 65 ft. **Other:** No gathering firewood; no fireworks; 28-day stay limit.

TO GET THERE

From the junction of Hwy. 62 and Hwy. 550, go 4.6 mi. north on Hwy. 550. Turn northwest at "Dutch Charlie" sign into the entrance. Go 0.4 mi. to the pay station or to the park HQ.

RIFLE   MAP, B-1
Rifle Falls/Rifle Gap State Park

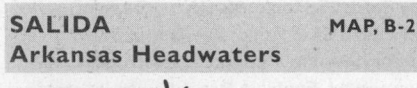

5775 Hwy. 325, 81650. T: (800) 678-2267 or
(970) 625-1607; www.reserveamerica.com.

🚐 ★★★★   ⛺ ★★★★

Beauty: ★★★★★	Site Privacy: ★★★★
Spaciousness: ★★★★	Quiet: ★★★★★
Security: ★★★	Cleanliness: ★★★★★
Insect Control: ★★★	Facilities: ★★★★

The Rifle Falls/Rifle Gap State Park Camping area consists of five small campgrounds—four in Rifle Gap, one in Rifle Falls—each of which is described below. The Cottonwood Campground in Rifle Gap has absolutely huge pull-throughs that can accommodate a rig of any size. These sites, which average 100 by 100 feet, are scattered around the lake edge—some right up to the water, which would allow for an easy morning dip or an afternoon cast. This is the first campground one would approach from the main entrance, and well worth occupying for the night. Next in line is Cedar Campground, which contains mostly back-ins (average 48 feet in length), and one single pull-through. Also close to the water, this campground is better for smaller RVs, such as pop-ups or vans. Sage Campground, as the name implies, is "dry"—that is, has no direct water access. There are, however, 100-foot pull-throughs in a loop along the road, each with a large covered picnic area—ideal for landlubbers who only want to dip once or twice in the lake. Pinion Campground is perhaps the prettiest, crowded as it is with pinions and juniper. Like Cedar Campground, sites are smaller and best suited for small vehicles or tents. (Tenters won't be thrilled by the gravel bed in each site, however.) Rifle Falls Campground, which offers easy access to the falls and caves that accompany them, has back-ins and pull-throughs that range in length from 28 feet to 120 feet. Tent sites are walk-ins to the south of the RV sites. The more remote sites, while offering better privacy, also require lugging equipment several hundred feet. Campers in tents or RVs will enjoy the beautiful sites—and sights—of Rifle Falls and should definitely consider making a stop here.

BASICS

Operated By: Colorado State Parks. **Open:** All year. **Site Assignment:** First come, first served. **Registration:** At pay kiosk. **Fee:** $7–$20, park pass, $5; check. **Parking:** At site.

FACILITIES

Number of RV-only Sites: 13. **Number of Tent-only Sites:** 56. **Hookups:** Electric (30, 50 amps). **Each Site:** Picnic table, grill. **Dump Station:** Yes. **Laundry:** No. **Pay Phone:** No (at golf course). **Restrooms and Showers:** Pit toilets; no shower. **Fuel:** No. **Propane:** No. **Internal Roads:** Gravel. **RV Service:** No. **Market:** 10 mi. to Rifle. **Restaurant:** 10 mi. to Rifle. **General Store:** No. **Vending:** No. **Swimming:** Lake. **Playground:** No. **Other:** Creek, lake, falls. **Activities:** Boating, swimming, fishing, waterskiing, scuba diving, ice-skating, golf, caving,

hiking, windsurfing. **Nearby Attractions:** Rifle Falls, Rifle Gap Reservoir. **Additional Information:** Rifle Visitor Information Center/Chamber of Commerce, (970) 625-2085.

RESTRICTIONS

Pets: On 6-ft. leash, cleaned up after. No pets in hatchery. **Fires:** Fire pit only; check w/ park for current fire restrictions. **Alcoholic Beverages:** Beer only. **Vehicle Maximum Length:** No limit. **Other:** No removing of plants or artifacts; cell phones may not work. No gathering firewood.

TO GET THERE

From the junction of Hwy. 13 and Hwy. 325, go 6 mi. northeast on Hwy. 325. At the fork, stay on the paved road to reach the campground. (You can take the dirt road to the park office.) Turn left at the sign into the Rifle Gap Reservation, or continue another 4 mi. to get to Rifle Falls.

SALIDA   MAP, B-2
Arkansas Headwaters

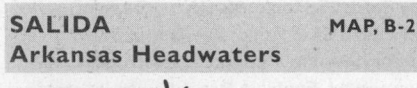

307 W. Sackett Ave, 81201. T: (719) 539-7289; www.reserveamerica.com.

🚐 ★★★★   ⛺ ★★★★

Beauty: ★★★★★	Site Privacy: ★★★
Spaciousness: ★★★	Quiet: ★★★★★
Security: ★★★★★	Cleanliness: ★★★★
Insect Control: ★★★	Facilities: ★

Arkansas Headwaters is one of the nation's most unusual recreation areas. The region stretches 148 miles along one of the West's premier recreation rivers, the Arkansas. From its northern boundary below the fabled mining town of Leadville to the bass-filled waters of Pueblo Reservoir, the area is a recreation paradise. Here, massive 14,000-foot mountains contrast wide valleys, and steep gorges provide a path for the rapid waters of the Arkansas River. In such a diverse terrain, you'll find a wide range of recreational opportunities. Most popular are the whitewater activities such as rafting or kayaking; however, fishing, wildlife watching, hiking, mountain climbing, and camping are also available. Hecla Junction provides great fishing for brown trout, and wildlife watching is ideal at any of the Five Points Watchable Wildlife Areas in Bighorn Sheep Canyon, aptly named for the thriving population and frequent sightings of bighorn sheep. The cities and towns along the river—Leadville, Buena Vista, Poncha Springs, Salida, Cañon City, Florence, and Pueblo—offer fine dining, lodging, and plenty of Western hospitality.

BASICS

Operated By: Colorado State Parks. **Open:** Apr. 1–Sept. 30. **Site Assignment:** Reservations can be made 6 months in advance. **Registration:** At office. **Fee:** Single, $10–$13. **Parking:** At site.

FACILITIES

Number of Multipurpose Sites: 101. **Hookups:** None. **Each Site:** Fire ring. **Dump Station:** No. **Laundry:** No. **Pay Phone:** No. **Restrooms and**

Showers: Yes. **Fuel:** No. **Propane:** No. **Internal Roads:** Paved. **RV Service:** No. **Market:** No. **Restaurant:** No. **General Store:** No. **Vending:** No. **Swimming:** No. **Playground:** No. **Activities:** Biking, bird-watching, fishing, hiking, horseback riding, interpretive programs, photography, picnicking, wildlife viewing.

RESTRICTIONS

Pets: Pets must be on a leash no longer than 6 ft. in length. **Fires:** Permitted in designated fireplaces. **Other:** Quiet hours will be enforced 10 p.m.–6 a.m. All generators, loud radios, or other loud noises that may disturb the peace are prohibited during these hours.

TO GET THERE

The campground is 8 mi. east of Salida and accessed off US 50 at mile marker 231 between the towns of Swissvale and Howard. It is located on the north side of the highway in a very curvy section. (See Web site for more details.)

SALIDA   MAP, B-2
Four Seasons RV Park

4305 East US 50, 81201. T: (888) 444-3626 or (719) 539-3084.

🚐 ★★★★★   ⛺ n/a

Beauty: ★★★★	Site Privacy: ★★★★★
Spaciousness: ★★★★★	Quiet: ★★★★
Security: ★★★★	Cleanliness: ★★★★★
Insect Control: ★★★★	Facilities: ★★★★★

This two-tiered campground offers sites just off the highway as well as sites down by the river. All of the long back-ins in the B row are gorgeous, and most river sites are equally nice. (R15 has exceptionally great shade.) The D row, one in from the river, is also quite pleasant, with lush grass, two pull-throughs (in addition to the lengthy back-ins), and fencing between sites. Most sites in the park have one side to either the river or to an embankment, adding privacy and security, and a shade tree of considerable size. The exceptions to this are 11–13 by the river, which lack grass as well as shade and are undoubtedly the least desirable sites. The restrooms are immaculate and spacious, as is the laundry. There is also a community room with microwave, fridge, books, and nine tables. Although big rigs will have to unhook, you really can't go wrong with any site in the D or R rows. Ask for a site on the lower tier by the river, and you will be pleased with virtually any site you get.

BASICS

Operated By: Paul & Candy Draper. **Open:** May–Oct. 1. **Site Assignment:** Upon registration; credit card required for reservation. 72-hour to 1-week cancellation policy, depending on length of stay. **Registration:** At office. (Late arrivals use drop box.) **Fee:** $32.40–$36.15; V, MC, D. **Parking:** At site.

FACILITIES

Number of RV-only Sites: 67. **Hookups:** Electric (30, 50 amps), water, sewer. **Each Site:** Picnic table. **Dump Station:** No (sewer at all sites). **Laundry:** Yes. **Pay Phone:** Yes. **Restrooms and Showers:** Yes. **Fuel:** No. **Propane:** Yes. **Internal Roads:**

Gravel. **RV Service:** No. **Market:** 2 mi. west to Salida. **Restaurant:** 2 mi. west to Salida. **General Store:** No. **Vending:** No. **Swimming:** No. **Playground:** No. **Other:** Meeting room, storage. **Activities:** Rafting, horseshoes, shuffleboard, fishing, Jeep tours, hiking, mountain biking, skiing, golf, hunting, rock hounding. **Nearby Attractions:** Hot springs pools, ghost towns, kayaking competition. **Additional Information:** Heart of the Rockies Chamber of Commerce, (877) 772-5432 or (719) 539-2068.

RESTRICTIONS

Pets: On leash, cleaned up after. **Fires:** No open fires. **Alcoholic Beverages:** At sites. **Vehicle Maximum Length:** No limit.

TO GET THERE

From the junction of Hwy. 291 and Hwy. 50, go 1.4 mi. east on Hwy. 50. Turn north at the sign into the entrance. The office is on the right.

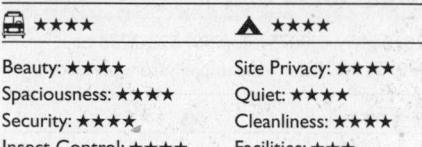

SEIBERT   MAP, B-4
Shadey Grove Campground

306 Colorado Ave., P.O. Box 178, 80834.
T: (970) 664-2218.

🚐 ★★★★   ⛺ ★★★★

Beauty: ★★★★	Site Privacy: ★★★★
Spaciousness: ★★★★	Quiet: ★★★★
Security: ★★★★	Cleanliness: ★★★★
Insect Control: ★★★★	Facilities: ★★★

This campground is split up into three separate areas. The two main camping areas are on either side of the office. On the north side, there are 11 50-foot pull-throughs with cable TV hookups. These sites are mainly open, with some trees. The second main area is on the south side of the office. There are 11 60-foot pull-throughs in this area (without cable). This area is more heavily forested, and almost every site is shaded. The third area, for overflow, consists of an open grassy field with six 70-foot back-ins. These sites are completely unshaded and do not offer any facilities (other than electric hookups). The town and surrounding area is full of historical attractions but offers little else in the realm of entertainment.

BASICS

Operated By: Jim & Lisa Ensz. **Open:** All year. **Site Assignment:** Upon registration; reservations accepted. **Registration:** At office, which is open until 1 a.m. for late arrivals. **Fee:** RV (full), $20; tent, $15; check, no credits cards. Honors most discounts. **Parking:** At site.

FACILITIES

Number of RV-only Sites: 30. **Number of Tent-only Sites:** 10. **Hookups:** Electric (20, 30, 50 amps), water, sewer, cable TV. **Each Site:** Most have picnic tables. **Dump Station:** Yes. **Laundry:** Yes. **Pay Phone:** Yes. **Restrooms and Showers:** Yes, free showers. **Fuel:** No. **Propane:** No. **Internal Roads:** Gravel. **RV Service:** No. **Market:** Less than 0.25 mi. north. **Restaurant:** Less than 1 mi. south. **General Store:** 2 blocks. **Vending:** No. **Swimming:** Pool, hot tub. **Playground:** No. **Other:** Full grocery, bank, post office only 2 blocks away, cabin rentals & modem hookup available. **Activities:** Boating, swim-

ming, hiking, biking (extra bikes, no charge). **Nearby Attractions:** Bonny State Park, Old Town Burlington, historical sites, fishing. **Additional Information:** Burlington Chamber of Commerce, (719) 346-8070.

RESTRICTIONS

Pets: On leash, cleaned up after. **Fires:** Grill only. **Alcoholic Beverages:** At sites. **Vehicle Maximum Length:** Big rigs welcome. **Other:** No extra charge for premium sites.

TO GET THERE

From I-70 (Exit 405), turn north onto Hwy. 59 and go 0.2 mi. Turn right onto 4th St. and go 0.2 mi. Turn right onto Colorado and go 1 block to the office on the right.

SILVERTON   MAP, C-1
Silver Summit

640 Mineral St., P.O. Box 656, 81433.
T: (800) 352-1637 or (970) 387-0240;
www.silversummitrvpark.com.

🚐 ★★★★   ⛺ ★★★

Beauty: ★★★★	Site Privacy: ★★★
Spaciousness: ★★★	Quiet: ★★★★★
Security: ★★★★	Cleanliness: ★★★★★
Insect Control: ★★★★	Facilities: ★★★★

At the southern edge of town, this campground is surrounded on all four sides by mountains (including Kendell Mountain to the east). There are beautiful vistas from anywhere inside this campground, making it a wonderful place to stop and relax. While there are no shade trees around the park, summers do not get overly hot and the park remains quite comfortable. End site 23 is an open pull-through that could accommodate a rig of any size. All other sites (pull-throughs and back-ins) range from 50 feet to 55 feet. Tents are allowed on any of the RV spaces, which are all level, grassy, and open, making them a fine place to set up a tent. The restrooms are fantastically clean, and there is plenty of space in the showers. The laundry room is also quite clean and spacious. This is a very pretty campground with unbeatable vistas that both tenters and RVers will enjoy.

BASICS

Operated By: Denny & Sigrun Martin. **Open:** May 15–Oct. 15. **Site Assignment:** Upon registration; credit card required for reservation; 48-hour cancellation policy; reservations required in peak season (July & Aug.). **Registration:** At office. (Late arrivals select site & pay in the morning.) **Fee:** RV, $28; tent, $17; V, MC, AE, D. **Parking:** At site. Perimeter parking available.

FACILITIES

Number of RV-only Sites: 39. **Hookups:** Electric (30, 50 amps), water, sewer, cable TV. **Each Site:** Picnic table. **Dump Station:** Yes. **Laundry:** Yes. **Pay Phone:** Yes. **Restrooms and Showers:** Yes. **Fuel:** In Silverton. **Propane:** In Silverton. **Internal Roads:** Gravel. **RV Service:** No. **Market:** 1 block. **Restaurant:** 6 blocks. **General Store:** Yes. **Vending:** No. **Swimming:** No (hot tub). **Playground:** No. **Other:** Jeep rentals; 1 wheelchair-accessible site. **Activities:** Jeeping, hiking, fishing, horseback riding,

guided tours, gold-mining tours. **Nearby Attractions:** Ghost towns, railroad, scenic byway, national historic district, wildflowers, native crafts, museum. **Additional Information:** Silverton Chamber of Commerce, (800) 752-4494 or (970) 387-5654.

RESTRICTIONS

Pets: On leash, cleaned up after. **Fires:** Not allowed. **Alcoholic Beverages:** At sites. **Vehicle Maximum Length:** 45 ft.

TO GET THERE

From the junction of Hwy. 550 and Hwy. 110, go 0.2 mi. north on Hwy. 110. Turn east onto East 7th St. Turn right onto Mineral St. The office is on the left.

SOUTH FORK   MAP, C-2
Grandview Cabins and RV

P.O. Box 189, 81154. T: (719) 873-5541;
www.grandview.com.

🚐 ★★★★   ⛺ n/a

Beauty: ★★★	Site Privacy: ★★★
Spaciousness: ★★★	Quiet: ★★★★
Security: ★★★★	Cleanliness: ★★★★
Insect Control: ★★★	Facilities: ★★★★

This campground has quite attractive sites in the southern part, but more open and unshaded sites to the north. There are level grassy pull-throughs as well as back-ins, which average 35 by 25 feet. Back-ins in the southwest (16–24) back to a wall of trees that makes these sites quite attractive. Sites 25–34 are larger (40 by 27 feet) but do not have as many trees. Sites 51–54 are very nice back-ins with shade trees and attractive landscaping that back to a fence. Site 48, next to the cabins, is also quite a good spot, with several trees in the corner. The laundry, which shares a room with a furnace and water tanks, is a little hot and cramped and in need of a paint job, but has quite a few machines. The restrooms are housed individually and are very clean and comfortable.

BASICS

Operated By: Gary & Maria Hodges. **Open:** All year. **Site Assignment:** Upon registration; credit card required for reservation; 30-day cancellation policy. **Registration:** At office. **Fee:** $22; V, MC, D. **Parking:** At site.

FACILITIES

Number of RV-only Sites: 92. **Hookups:** Electric (30 amps), water, sewer, cable TV. **Each Site:** Picnic table. **Dump Station:** No. **Laundry:** Yes. **Pay Phone:** Modem available. **Restrooms and Showers:** Yes. **Fuel:** 0.5 mi. in Southfork. **Propane:** No. **Internal Roads:** Gravel. **RV Service:** 0.5 mi. in South Fork. **Market:** 0.5 mi. in South Fork. **Restaurant:** 0.5 mi. in South Fork. **General Store:** No. **Vending:** No. **Swimming:** No (seasonal hot tub—winter only). **Playground:** No. **Other:** Fish-cleaning station, cabins, meeting room, RV storage, kitchenette, rec room. **Activities:** Hunting, fishing, Jeep tours, evening camp fires, skiing, snowmobiling, rafting, hiking, local country & western dancing, potlucks, ice-cream socials. Campground is 5 minutes from river. **Nearby Attractions:** Great Sand Dunes, Creede, Silver Thread Scenic Byway, Mesa

Verde, Rio Grande River, Durango–Silverton RR, Royal Gorge Bridge, country & western dancing. **Additional Information:** South Fork Visitor Center, (719) 873-5412.

RESTRICTIONS

Pets: Only in north RV sites; on leash, cleaned up after. **Fires:** Fire pit only. **Alcoholic Beverages:** At sites. **Vehicle Maximum Length:** No limit. **Other:** 5 miles per hour through the park.

TO GET THERE

From the junction of Hwy. 148 and Hwy. 160, go 0.6 mi. northwest on Hwy. 149. Turn left at the sign onto a dirt road. Keep straight and follow the signs to the office.

STEAMBOAT SPRINGS   MAP, A-2
Steamboat Campground

3603 Lincoln Ave., 80487.
T: (888) 451-2243 or (970) 879-0273;
www.steamboatcampground.com.

🚐 ★★★★   ⛺ ★★★★

Beauty: ★★★★		Site Privacy: ★★★
Spaciousness: ★★★		Quiet: ★★★
Security: ★★★★		Cleanliness: ★★★★
Insect Control: ★★★★		Facilities: ★★★★★

At the very western tip of town, this campground is split in half by the Yampa River: RVs on the north side, tents on the south. There are stunning mountain views from practically anywhere in the campground. However, Hwy. 40 is just a stone's throw away, and noise can be heard as far away as in the tent sites. The grounds are clean, with immaculately manicured, lush grass. The restroom facilities are clean and modern, as is the laundry, although the latter is a little cramped. Some of the best sites (36–39, 41, 42) are back-ins that may exclude some larger rigs, but they sport nice trees along the southwest fence. Another drawback to this area is the mobile homes parked along this strip—some of which look quite run-down. Other RV sites are laid out in a grid, with decent-sized pull-throughs among them (73 by 28 feet). (Back-in spaces run 42 feet in length and a comparable width.) The RV section of the park is mostly open, and all sites are level and grassy. The tent area is a whole different ballgame, left nicely wild with loads of trees and grass. Some tent sites (99A–106) are right on the river's edge, while the rest have a more forested feel. In all, this park offers a very nice stay in a location that can't be beat.

BASICS

Operated By: The Sabia family. **Open:** All year. **Site Assignment:** Upon registration. **Registration:** At office. (Late arrivals use drop box.) **Fee:** RV, $20–$40; tent, $17–$24; V, MC, D; 10% discount for AAA & AARP. **Parking:** At site.

FACILITIES

Number of RV-only Sites: 98. **Number of Tent-only Sites:** 36. **Hookups:** Electric (30, 50 amps), water, sewer, cable TV (fee required). **Each Site:** Picnic table, grill. **Dump Station:** Yes. **Laundry:** Yes. **Pay Phone:** Yes. **Restrooms and Showers:** Yes. **Fuel:** No. **Propane:** Yes. **Internal Roads:** Paved, gravel to tent area. **RV Service:** No. **Market:** 2 mi. into town.

Restaurant: 2 mi. into town. **General Store:** Yes. **Vending:** Yes. **Swimming:** Pool. **Playground:** Yes. **Other:** TV room w/ pool table, RV parts, mini-golf, free local bus service, cabins, river, data port, hot tub, breakfast patio, snack bar, pet walk area. **Activities:** Volleyball, horseshoes, fishing, hiking, skiing. **Nearby Attractions:** Steamboat Springs ski area, Routt National Forest, Fish Creek Falls, Haymaker Golf Course, Flat Tops Wilderness Area, Tread of Pioneers Museum. **Additional Information:** Steamboat Springs Chamber Resort Assoc., (970) 879-0880.

RESTRICTIONS

Pets: On leash, cleaned up after; use pet-walk area. **Fires:** Fire ring only. **Alcoholic Beverages:** At sites. **Vehicle Maximum Length:** No limit. **Other:** In winter, only open to monthly rentals.

TO GET THERE

0.1 mi. from the western town name signpost on Hwy. 40. Entrance is on the south side.

STERLING   MAP, A-4
North Sterling State Park

reserve america

24005 CR 330, 80751. T: (970) 522-3657;
www.reserveamerica.com.

🚐 ★★★★   ⛺ ★★★★

Beauty: ★★★		Site Privacy: ★★★
Spaciousness: ★★★		Quiet: ★★★★★
Security: ★★★		Cleanliness: ★★★★
Insect Control: ★★★		Facilities: ★★★★

Majestic bluffs and expansive views of the high plains greet visitors to one of Colorado's newest state parks, North Sterling State Park. The focal point of North Sterling State Park is Sterling Reservoir. This man-made body of water is fed by the South Platte River and is one of the deepest reservoirs in Colorado. (Its depths reach over 50 feet.) This boater's paradise offers 3,000 acres of pristine waters, providing an interesting array of coves and fingers to explore. Modern facilities are located nearby and support a wide variety of recreational activities available at North Sterling State Park. Three boat ramps line the eastern shore, one of which is made specifically for low water. Campgrounds at North Sterling State Park can accommodate recreational vehicles, trailers, or tents, and there is a total of 141 sites with more being developed. Recreation in North Sterling State Park is focused upon water. Boating and fishing are the most popular activities. Swimming, waterskiing, jet skiing, and sailing may be enjoyed by many visitors. Picnicking, camping, bird-watching, and hunting are also very popular within the park.

BASICS

Operated By: Colorado State Parks. **Open:** All year. **Site Assignment:** Reservations can be made 6 months in advance. **Registration:** At office. **Fee:** Single, $7–$20; yurt, $60; cabin, $80–$160. **Parking:** At park.

FACILITIES

Number of Multipurpose Sites: 141. **Hookups:** Yes. **Each Site:** Fire ring. **Dump Station:** Yes.

Laundry: Yes. **Pay Phone:** No. **Restrooms and Showers:** Yes. **Fuel:** No. **Propane:** No. **Internal Roads:** Paved. **RV Service:** No. **Market:** No. **Restaurant:** No. **General Store:** Yes. **Vending:** No. **Swimming:** Yes. **Playground:** Yes. **Activities:** Biking, bird-watching, boating, fishing, hiking, hunting, ice fishing, interpretive programs, jet skiing, photography, picnicking, sailing, sailboarding, skating, waterskiing, wildlife viewing.

RESTRICTIONS

Pets: Pets must be on a leash no longer than 6 ft. in length. **Fires:** Permitted in designated fireplaces. **Other:** Quiet hours will be enforced 10 p.m.–6 a.m. All generators, loud radios, or other loud noises are prohibited during these hours.

TO GET THERE

I-76 to Sterling Exit 125, west on Chestnut St. (US 6). Continue west on Platte St., turn right on N. 3rd Ave., go 4 blocks. Turn left on Broadway and go west 4 blocks. Turn right on N. 7th Ave., go north 12 mi., turn west on CR 46, follow the signs to the reservoir.

STERLING   MAP, A-4
Yogi Bear's Jellystone
Camp Resort

22018 Hwy. 6, 80751. T: (970) 522-2233 or
(970) 522-6701; www.campjellystonepark.com.

🚐 ★★★★   ⛺ ★★★★

Beauty: ★★★		Site Privacy: ★★★
Spaciousness: ★★★		Quiet: ★★★★
Security: ★★★★★		Cleanliness: ★★★★
Insect Control: ★★★★		Facilities: ★★★★

This family-oriented campground offers lots of activities within the park itself, with facilities from a swimming pool to volleyball nets to meeting rooms. There are two separate RV areas, offering very different experiences. Sites E1–E14 are laid out in two wings along a central row, and are entirely unshaded. These are, of course, electric sites only, and lack of other hookups and shade trees makes them less desirable than sites in the main camping area. The main camping area contains both RV sites (laid out in a large loop) and tenting sites (occupying the middle of the loop). These 47 RV sites are uniformly forested, and all of them are pull-throughs. Sites average 75 feet in length—easily large enough for any vehicle, even with a tow. About half of these sites are large enough for double slide-outs, but all sites are certainly roomy enough for pleasant family camping. Sites with the highest numbers (40–47) are closest to the pool and the office, while those in the 20s and 30s are farthest away from the action. The tenting area is likewise well shaded, and very comfortable. The restrooms and showers are exceptionally clean and comfortable. This is a family-oriented campground that offers enough in the way of recreation opportunities to be a destination in itself.

BASICS

Operated By: "Ranger" Bill. **Open:** All year. **Site Assignment:** Upon registration. **Registration:** At office. (Late arrivals use drop box.) **Fee:** RV (full), $28.50; water/electric, $26.50; tent, $20; check, V, MC. **Parking:** At site.

FACILITIES

Number of RV-only Sites: 61. **Number of Tent-only Sites:** 25. **Hookups:** Electric (20, 30 amps), water, sewer. **Each Site:** Picnic table, most have grills. **Dump Station:** Yes. **Laundry:** Yes. **Pay Phone:** Yes. **Restrooms and Showers:** Yes. **Fuel:** No. **Propane:** Yes. **Internal Roads:** Gravel. **RV Service:** No. **Market:** 5 mi. to Sterling. **Restaurant:** 0.25 mi. on Hwy. 6. **General Store:** Yes. **Vending:** Yes. **Swimming:** Outdoor Pool. **Playground:** Yes. **Other:** Mini-golf, game room, meeting room, pet walk. **Activities:** Volleyball, swimming, planned activities, horseshoes, basketball, fishing, boating. **Nearby Attractions:** North Sterling State Park, North Sterling Reservoir. **Additional Information:** Logan County Chamber of Commerce, (800) 544-8609 or (970) 522-5070.

RESTRICTIONS

Pets: On leash, cleaned up after. **Fires:** Grill only. **Alcoholic Beverages:** At sites. **Vehicle Maximum Length:** No limit.

TO GET THERE

From I-76 take Exit 125, turn east onto Hwy. 6 and go 0.5 mi. Turn right at the sign into the entrance.

TRINIDAD   MAP, C-3
Trinidad Lake State Park

reserve america

32610 Hwy. 12, 81082. T: (719) 846-6951; www.reserveamerica.com.

🚐 ★★★★   ⛺ ★★★★

Beauty: ★★★★	Site Privacy: ★★★
Spaciousness: ★★★	Quiet: ★★★★★
Security: ★★★	Cleanliness: ★★★★
Insect Control: ★★★	Facilities: ★★★★

Trinidad Lake State Park lies in the foothills of the Sangre de Cristo Mountains of southeastern Colorado. The lake is a few miles west of Interstate 25. The biggest attraction to this state park is 700-surface-acre Trinidad Lake. The entire park encompasses 2,300 acres. The facilities at Trinidad Lake include a campground with 62 modern sites. Each site has a table, grill, access to water, toilets, laundry facilities, and showers. Electrical hookups are available at 49 sites in the campground. The eastern entrance to the park from CO 12 provides access to the boat ramp. Most visitors to Trinidad Lake State Park come to participate in water sports. Boating, waterskiing, sailboarding, and jet skiing are permitted on Trinidad Lake. Fishing is popular and the lake is stocked with rainbow and brook trout, largemouth bass, channel catfish, walleye, crappie, bluegill, and wipers. Several maintained trails within the park provide terrain for hikers, walkers, and mountain bikers. Interpretive programs are provided throughout the summer months. During the winter, visitors can enjoy ice fishing and cross-country skiing.

BASICS

Operated By: Colorado State Parks. **Open:** All year. **Site Assignment:** Reservations can be made 6 months in advance. **Registration:** At office. **Fee:** Single, $7–$20; yurt, $60; cabin, $80–$160. **Parking:** At park.

FACILITIES

Number of Multipurpose Sites: 62. **Hookups:** Yes. **Each Site:** Fire ring. **Dump Station:** Yes. **Laundry:** Yes. **Pay Phone:** Yes. **Restrooms and Showers:** Yes. **Fuel:** No. **Propane:** No. **Internal Roads:** Paved. **RV Service:** No. **Market:** No. **Restaurant:** No. **General Store:** No. **Vending:** No. **Swimming:** No. **Playground:** Yes. **Activities:** Amphitheater, biking, bird-watching, boating, fishing, hiking, horseback riding, hunting, ice fishing, interpretive programs, jet skiing, photography, picnicking, sailing, sailboarding, waterskiing, wildlife viewing.

RESTRICTIONS

Pets: Pets must be on a leash no longer than 6 ft. in length. **Fires:** Permitted in designated fireplaces. **Other:** Quiet hours will be enforced 10 p.m.–6 a.m. All generators, loud radios, or other loud noises that may disturb the peace are prohibited during these hours.

TO GET THERE

3 mi. west of Trinidad on Hwy. 12. Follow signs to park.

TWIN LAKES   MAP, B-2
Parry Peak Campground

2015 North Poplar, 80461. T: (719) 486-0749.

🚐 ★★★★   ⛺ ★★★★

Beauty: ★★★★★	Site Privacy: ★★★★
Spaciousness: ★★★★	Quiet: ★★★★
Security: ★★★★	Cleanliness: ★★★★
Insect Control: ★★★★	Facilities: ★

At the foot of a large mountain and by a river, this campground offers a very natural escape from the world. Unfortunately, that world drives past quite close to the campground, and no site is immune to passing traffic noise. Sites 1, 3–5, 7, and 9 back to the highway and receive the worst traffic noise. Most of the sites are 50–54-foot back-ins, although there are large pull-throughs, including 6 (78-foot) and 8 (70-foot), as well as an oversized back-in (site 26 measures 30 by 36 feet) and at least one smaller site (5 is a 30-foot back-in). While most sites in this forested campground are well shaded, 12 is an exception, and many campers may wish to avoid this site for that reason. Sites 16–26, located across a small bridge from the main campground area, also offer tent pads at each site. Some of these sites (17–21 especially) are among the quietest, as they are farthest from the highway. Although there are no hookups in this campground, drinking water is found at several sites, including 10 and between 17 and 18. Besides the RV sites and the sites with tent pads, tenters can also choose from several extremely attractive walk-in sites. These are just off the road (no fear of dragging your gear for hundreds of yards), and three are located just off the river. While lacking hookups, this campground offers a great escape for those willing to give up luxury for a night or two.

BASICS

Operated By: National Forest Service. **Open:** Memorial Day–after Labor Day. **Site Assignment:** First come, first served. **Registration:** At pay station. **Fee:** $13; check. **Parking:** At site.

FACILITIES

Number of RV-only Sites: 26. **Number of Tent-only Sites:** 4. **Hookups:** None. **Each Site:** Picnic table, grill. **Dump Station:** No. **Laundry:** No. **Pay Phone:** No. **Restrooms and Showers:** Pit toilets; no shower. **Fuel:** No. **Propane:** No. **Internal Roads:** Gravel. **RV Service:** No. **Market:** 22 mi. to Leadville. **Restaurant:** 2.8 mi. to Twin Lakes. **General Store:** No. **Vending:** No. **Swimming:** Lake. **Playground:** No. **Other:** Firewood. **Activities:** Fishing, boating, swimming, hiking. **Nearby Attractions:** Leadville, Rocky Mountains, San Isabel National Forest. **Additional Information:** Leadville Chamber of Commerce, (719) 486-3900.

RESTRICTIONS

Pets: On leash, cleaned up after. **Fires:** Grill only. **Alcoholic Beverages:** At sites. **Vehicle Maximum Length:** 32 ft. **Other:** $3 day-use fee.

TO GET THERE

From the junction of Hwy. 24 and Hwy. 82, turn west onto Hwy. 82 and go 9 mi. Turn left at the sign into the entrance.

WALDEN   MAP, A-2
North Park/Gould KOA

53337 Hwy. 14, 80480. T: (800) 562-3596 or (970) 723-4310; www.koakampground.com.

🚐 ★★★★★   ⛺ ★★★★★

Beauty: ★★★★★	Site Privacy: ★★★★★
Spaciousness: ★★★★	Quiet: ★★★★★
Security: ★★★★	Cleanliness: ★★★★★
Insect Control: ★★★★	Facilities: ★★★★★

Ahhh. This is what camping is all about! Smack-dab in the middle of the forest in North Park, this campground is wooded, quiet, and clean. Now, campers should keep in mind the fact that North Park is 8,900 feet above sea level, and nights get pretty chilly here—even well into spring, when there can still be snow on the ground. Bring your long johns (especially tent campers) for cold nights and possible use during the day. Tenters should count on bringing more "winter woolies" and bed layers when camping at lower elevations. That said, this is a gorgeous campground that RVers and tenters alike will love. Back-in sites are quite long (50-foot), while pull-throughs are an incredible 90 feet—there's something for every rig here! Sites could be wider (they are just 22 feet), but should suffice for all but the widest RVs with slide-outs. Sites are well-spaced and private, located along a single giant loop. The only site that may present any inconvenience is 30, which is located on the tip of the inner "island" of the loop and may thus get a little more passing traffic than the others. All other sites are a camper's delight. The playground includes a neat wooden fort, and all of the facilities are spotless. There are a number of state, national, and private campgrounds in the area, but this campground is unequalled in services. If you are considering a trip to this region, by all means, plan to stop for a night at this KOA.

BASICS

Operated By: The Vlasmans. **Open:** May 26–Nov 15. **Site Assignment:** Upon registration. **Registration:** At office. (Late arrivals use drop box.) **Fee:** RV, $27–$40; water/electric, $22; tent, $25–$30. **Parking:** At site.

FACILITIES

Number of RV-only Sites: 30. **Number of Tent-only Sites:** 7. **Hookups:** Electric (30 amps), water, sewer. **Each Site:** Picnic table. **Dump Station:** Yes. **Laundry:** Yes. **Pay Phone:** Yes. **Restrooms and Showers:** Yes. **Fuel:** Yes. **Propane:** Yes. **Internal Roads:** Gravel. **RV Service:** No. **Market:** 3 mi. to Gould. **Restaurant:** 3 mi. to Gould. **General Store:** Yes. **Vending:** No. **Swimming:** No. **Playground:** Yes. **Other:** Game room. **Activities:** Fishing, hiking, mountain biking, hunting, horseshoes, basketball. **Nearby Attractions:** North Park, North Sandhills Recreation Area, Arapahoe National Wildlife Refuge. **Additional Information:** North Park Tourism Information Center, (970) 723-4344.

RESTRICTIONS

Pets: On leash, cleaned up after. **Fires:** Fire pit only. **Alcoholic Beverages:** At sites. **Vehicle Maximum Length:** No limit.

TO GET THERE

From the westernmost Gould town name signpost, drive 2.7 mi. west on Hwy. 14. Turn north at the sign into the campground entrance. The office is straight ahead.

WALDEN   MAP, A-2
Roundup Motel

365 Main St., 80480. T: (970) 723-4680 or (866) 689-2866.

🚐 ★★★   ⛺ n/a

Beauty: ★★★	Site Privacy: ★★★
Spaciousness: ★★★	Quiet: ★★★★
Security: ★★★★	Cleanliness: ★★★★
Insect Control: ★★★★	Facilities: ★★★

Recently opened as an RV park, the Roundup Motel has only a few spaces available, but these are the only full hookups within several miles of town. (There are two other pull-through sites with full hookups at the North Park Motel, also on Main.) The "park" consists of five back-ins, 25 feet wide and virtually as long as you want. On the opposite side of the fence that runs around the park are mobile homes, and the surrounding area has a distinct small-town feel. The sites are a mix of gravel and grass. The middle sites are slightly more desirable, as they do not abut a residence. The advantage of this park over the National Forest campgrounds in the surrounding area is twofold: full hookups and proximity to town. Everything in town is within walking distance of this park. Tenters can pitch a tent in the town park or continue on to one of the fational forest parks. This RV park is extremely small but convenient.

BASICS

Operated By: Mark & Bobbie Scott. **Open:** All year. **Site Assignment:** First come, first served; credit card required for reservation; 24-hour cancel-lation policy. **Registration:** At office. (Late arrivals ring manager's number on phone.) **Fee:** RV, $20; check, V, MC, D, AE. Long-term rates available. **Parking:** At site.

FACILITIES

Number of RV-only Sites: 5. **Hookups:** Electric (20, 30 amps), water, sewer, cable TV. **Dump Station:** No (sewer at all sites). **Laundry:** No (in town). **Pay Phone:** Yes. **Restrooms and Showers:** No. **Fuel:** In town. **Propane:** No. In town. **Internal Roads:** Gravel. **RV Service:** No. **Market:** Less than 1 mi. north. **Restaurant:** 1 block south. **General Store:** In town. **Vending:** No. **Swimming:** No (indoor pool 3 blocks). **Playground:** No. Town park 2 blocks. **Other:** Motel rooms. **Activities:** Fishing, boating, swimming, hiking, cross-country skiing, hunting. **Nearby Attractions:** Steamboat Springs, Laramie, wildlife, natural sand dunes, Big Creek Lakes, North Platte River, Routt National Forest. **Additional Information:** North Park Chamber of Commerce, (970) 723-4600.

RESTRICTIONS

Pets: On leash, cleaned up after. **Fires:** Grill only. **Alcoholic Beverages:** At sites. **Vehicle Maximum Length:** No limit.

TO GET THERE

From the junction of Hwy. 14 and Hwy. 125, turn right at the sign into the entrance.

WALDEN   MAP, A-2
State Forest State Park

reserve america

56750 Hwy. 14, 80480. T: (970) 723-8366; www.reserveamerica.com.

🚐 ★★★★   ⛺ ★★★★

Beauty: ★★★	Site Privacy: ★★★
Spaciousness: ★★★	Quiet: ★★★★★
Security: ★★★★★	Cleanliness: ★★★★
Insect Control: ★★★	Facilities: ★★★

The ultimate in rugged Colorado wilderness, the Colorado State Forest offers visitors 71,000 acres of unaltered forest, jagged peaks, and alpine lakes, a true backcountry hiking, camping or hunting experience. If you want to get away from the crowds and enjoy the unspoiled natural landscape Colorado is famous for, the Colorado State Forest is for you. The state forest lies on the eastern slope of the Medicine Bow Mountains and the northern tip of the Never Summer Mountains in North Park. Elevations in the forest begin at about 8,500 feet and reach 12,644 feet. An extensive trail system (110 miles) in the southern part of the forest supports hiking, biking, and horseback riding. The Never Summer Nordic Yurt System includes six yurts and one hut, open for winter and summer use. This region supports a variety of hiking, mountain biking, horseback riding, fishing, and mountaineering opportunities. During the winter months cross-country and backcountry skiers can enjoy the pristine beauty of the state forest. Mountain bikers and hikers in the summer and cross-country skiers and snowshoers in the winter make use of the Never Summer Yurt System.

BASICS

Operated By: Colorado State Parks. **Open:** All year. **Site Assignment:** Reservations can be made 6 months in advance. **Registration:** At office. **Fee:** Single, $7–$20; yurt, $60; cabin, $80–$160. **Parking:** At park.

FACILITIES

Number of Multipurpose Sites: 164. **Hookups:** Yes. **Each Site:** Fire ring. **Dump Station:** Yes. **Laundry:** No. **Pay Phone:** No. **Restrooms and Showers:** Yes. **Fuel:** No. **Propane:** No. **Internal Roads:** Paved. **RV Service:** No. **Market:** No. **Restaurant:** No. **General Store:** No. **Vending:** No. **Swimming:** No. **Playground:** No. **Activities:** Amphitheater, biking, bird-watching, boating, cross-country skiing, fishing, hiking, horseback riding, hunting, ice fishing, interpretive programs, photography, picnicking, snowshoeing, snowmobiling, wildlife viewing.

RESTRICTIONS

Pets: Pets must be on a leash no longer than 6 ft. in length. **Fires:** Permitted in designated fireplaces. **Other:** Quiet hours will be enforced 10 p.m.–6 a.m. All generators, loud radios, or other loud noises that may disturb the peace are prohibited during these hours.

TO GET THERE

75 mi. west of Ft. Collins on Hwy. 14, over Cameron Pass or 150 mi. north of Denver on Hwy. 40 over Berthoud Pass.

WALSENBURG   MAP, C-3
Lathrop State Park

reserve america

70 CR 502, 81089. T: (719) 738-2376; www.reserveamerica.com.

🚐 ★★★★   ⛺ ★★★★

Beauty: ★★★	Site Privacy: ★★★
Spaciousness: ★★★	Quiet: ★★★★★
Security: ★★★	Cleanliness: ★★★★
Insect Control: ★★★	Facilities: ★★★★

Lying on a high plains grassland, dotted with piñon and juniper, which is typical of southeastern Colorado, is Lathrop State Park. To the west, the beautiful Sangre de Cristo range; to the south, the towering Spanish Peaks 13,610 and 12,669 feet in elevation. Early Native Americans named the peaks Huajatollas (We-ha-toy-as), which means "Breasts of the World." They believed that rain clouds, the source of all life, originated there. Lathrop State Park's gentle climate, clear air, beautiful campsites, excellent fishing, waterskiing and great views of the nearby mountain ranges lure Colorado travelers and other visitors to the state for regular visits to this remarkable area. The state's first state park, Lathrop State Park is 1,594 acres of recreational enjoyment. The park has two lakes, Martin Lake and Horseshoe Lake, which, with a combined acreage of 320 acres, offer a variety of boating and angling opportunities.

A nine-hole golf course at the park is also popular. Stop by the Lathrop Visitors Center for a look at artists' murals showcasing the area's rich history and heritage, and access information about the surrounding area. The park's campsites accommodating motor homes, trailers, and tents.

BASICS

Operated By: Colorado State Parks. **Open:** All year. **Site Assignment:** Reservations can be made 6 months in advance. **Registration:** At office. **Fee:** Single, $7–$20; yurt, $60; cabin, $80–$160. **Parking:** At park.

FACILITIES

Number of Multipurpose Sites: 103. **Hookups:** Yes. **Each Site:** Fire ring. **Dump Station:** Yes. **Laundry:** Yes. **Pay Phone:** No. **Restrooms and Showers:** Yes. **Fuel:** No. **Propane:** No. **Internal Roads:** Paved. **RV Service:** No. **Market:** No. **Restaurant:** No. **General Store:** No. **Vending:** No. **Swimming:** Yes. **Playground:** Yes. **Activities:** Amphitheater, beach, biking, bird-watching, boating, fishing, hiking, hunting, interpretive programs, jet skiing, photography, picnicking, sailing, sailboarding, showshoeing, waterskiing, wildlife viewing.

RESTRICTIONS

Pets: Pets must be on a leash no longer than 6 ft. in length. **Fires:** Permitted in designated fireplaces. **Other:** Quiet hours will be enforced 10 p.m.–6 a.m. All generators, loud radios, or other loud noises that may disturb the peace are prohibited during these hours.

TO GET THERE

3 mi. west of Walsenburg on Hwy. 160, on the north side of the road.

WARD   MAP, A-3
Camp Dick

reserve america

Hwy. 72, 80301. T: (877) 444-6777 or (303) 444-6600; www.reserveamerica.com.

🚐 ★★★	⛺ ★★★★★
Beauty: ★★★★★	Site Privacy: ★★★★
Spaciousness: ★★★★	Quiet: ★★★★★
Security: ★★★★	Cleanliness: ★★★
Insect Control: ★★★★	Facilities: ★

Nature lovers will enjoy this campground, but those who rely on campground facilities may have mixed feelings. The beauty of this location is undeniable: the entire campground is surrounded by forested hills and most of the sites are at least partially forested. On the downside, of course, is the lack of RV hookups and narrow road in—hopefully, two giant 5th wheels will never meet on this road. Most of the sites are 40-foot back-ins, but there are exceptions to this. Site 16 is a large (75-foot) pull-through, and sites 7 and 21 are oversized sites—large enough for two vehicles and much wider than ordinary sites. Sites to the north (10, 12, and 13–16) back to a lovely stream, making these more desirable. Sites 26 and 28, on the other hand, are totally unshaded,

making them less desirable. Site 35 offers more privacy, located as it is at the end of a roundabout. Sites 30–38 offer somewhat more seclusion, as they are located on a separate road from the other sites. The facilities include pit toilets but no showers or running water. Hardier campers will enjoy the chance to be close to nature, but those who prefer to be pampered will want to look elsewhere.

BASICS

Operated By: Thousand Trails Management. **Open:** May–Oct.; dates may vary. **Site Assignment:** First come, first served; credit card required for reservation; 3-day cancellation policy, less $10; call at least 5 days in advance for reservation. **Registration:** At pay kiosk. (Camp host will verify that campers have paid.) **Fee:** $14–$17; check, no credit cards. **Parking:** At site.

FACILITIES

Number of RV-only Sites: 41. **Hookups:** None. **Each Site:** Picnic tables, fire rings, grills. **Dump Station:** No. **Laundry:** No. **Pay Phone:** No. **Restrooms and Showers:** Vault Toilets. No showers. **Fuel:** No. **Propane:** No. **Internal Roads:** Paved. **RV Service:** No. **Market:** 12 mi. (in Nederland). **Restaurant:** 5 mi. north (in town). **General Store:** No. **Vending:** No. **Swimming:** No. **Playground:** No. **Other:** Dump water & trash services. **Activities:** Fishing, hiking, mountain climbing, crosscountry skiing, gambling, off-roading w/ 4x4, mountain biking. **Nearby Attractions:** Rocky Mountain National Park, Blackhawk, Central City. **Additional Information:** Thousand Trails Management, (303) 258-3610.

RESTRICTIONS

Pets: On leash, cleaned up after. **Fires:** Fire pit only. **Alcoholic Beverages:** At sites. **Vehicle Maximum Length:** 55 ft. **Other:** 8 people per regular site & 12 people per oversized site.

TO GET THERE

From the junction of Hwy. 7 and Hwy. 72, turn south onto Hwy. 72 and go 4.1 mi. Turn right at the sign into the entrance. Pass through Peaceful Valley Campground to get to Camp Dick.

WELLINGTON   MAP, A-3
Fort Collins/Wellington KOA

4821 East Co. Rd. 70, 80549. T: (800) KOA-8142 or (970) 568-7486; www.koakampground.com.

🚐 ★★★★	⛺ ★★★★
Beauty: ★★★★	Site Privacy: ★★★★
Spaciousness: ★★★★	Quiet: ★★★★
Security: ★★★★	Cleanliness: ★★★★★
Insect Control: ★★★★	Facilities: ★★★★★

With the exception of a small row of back-ins for long-term guests, this campground offers all pull-throughs. Sites average 70 feet (60 feet in Row Cougar). The sites consist of gravel and sparse grass and have only limited amounts of shade from small trees. The views to the west are best enjoyed from sites A12, B14, C10, and D10. These end sites are also the farthest from the entrance (especially in rows Antelope, Buffalo, and Cougar) and the office. The

50-amp sites are in the southeast corner of the RV sites (A 1–5 and B 1–5). There are 19 tent sites on a semi-circle to the southeast. These sites are also sparsely shaded at best. The restrooms and showers are very clean and spacious. There are four individual units inside the office complex that are open during business hours. These are equally spotless. This campground is a pleasant place to stay, whether visiting the Ft. Collins area or continuing on to the Poudre valley.

BASICS

Operated By: Guenter Kippschull, Helmut Roy. **Open:** All year. **Site Assignment:** Credit card required for reservation; 48-hour cancellation policy, less $5. **Registration:** At office. (Late arrivals use drop box.) **Fee:** RV (full), $30; water/electric, $28.50; tent, $24; check, V, MC, AE. Discounts available, call office for more info. **Parking:** At site.

FACILITIES

Number of RV-only Sites: 75. **Number of Tent-only Sites:** 19. **Hookups:** Electric (30, 50 amps), water, sewer. **Each Site:** Picnic table. **Dump Station:** Yes. **Laundry:** Yes. **Pay Phone:** Yes. **Restrooms and Showers:** Yes. **Fuel:** No. **Propane:** Yes. **Internal Roads:** Gravel. **RV Service:** No. **Market:** 12 mi. south to Fort Collins. **Restaurant:** 12 mi. south to Fort Collins. **General Store:** Yes. **Vending:** No. **Swimming:** Pool. **Playground:** Yes. **Other:** Pavilion, rec room (w/ TV), dog walk, storage, patio, bicycle rentals. **Activities:** Rafting, fishing, swimming. **Nearby Attractions:** Cache La Poudre, Fort Collins, Budweiser Brewery, Cheyenne Days Rodeo (July). **Additional Information:** Fort Collins CVB, (970) 491-3388.

RESTRICTIONS

Pets: On leash, cleaned up after; monthly guests must pay deposit. **Fires:** Grill only. **Alcoholic Beverages:** At sites. **Vehicle Maximum Length:** No limit. **Other:** No speeding (5-mph limit).

TO GET THERE

From I-25 (Exit 281), turn east onto CR 70 and go 0.3 mi. Turn into 2nd driveway (to the east) and continue to the office.

WESTCLIFFE   MAP, C-3
Grape Creek RV Park

56491 Hwy. 69, 81252. T: (719) 783-2588; www.coloradovacations.com/camp/grape.

🚐 ★★★★★	⛺ ★★★
Beauty: ★★★★	Site Privacy: ★★★★
Spaciousness: ★★★★	Quiet: ★★★★★
Security: ★★★★	Cleanliness: ★★★★★
Insect Control: ★★★★	Facilities: ★★★★

A destination for peace, quiet, and, in the words of Mr. Latham, "some of the most beautiful sunsets you've ever seen," this campground has beautiful sites with lush grass and gorgeous views of snow-capped peaks to the west. Pretty much all sites are wonderful, although 25–32 are closest to the offices and may get a little more passing traffic than other sites. Sites 1–12 and end site 24 have the best views of the mountains and the valley and are therefore more desirable. All RV sites are grassy pull-throughs averaging 50 by 30 feet. The restrooms and showers are immaculate, spacious, and modern, as is the laundry room. Tenting is possible to the west of the RV sites or below the park by the river. Either location has beautiful grass but no cover. In fact, pretty much the only conceivable complaint anyone could have here is the lack of shade. But why complain when you're in such a beautiful site? Sit back, relax, and enjoy the quiet and scenery!

BASICS

Operated By: Zane & Diana Latham. **Open:** May 10–Sept. 30. **Site Assignment:** Upon registration; credit card required for reservation; 30-day cancellation policy. **Registration:** At office. (Late arrivals come to office.) **Fee:** RV (full), $25; water/electric, $21; tent, $15. **Parking:** At site.

FACILITIES

Number of RV-only Sites: 34. **Number of Tent-only Sites:** 10. **Hookups:** Electric (30, 50 amps), water, sewer. **Each Site:** Bushes between sites, space for extra vehicle. **Dump Station:** Yes. **Laundry:** Yes. **Pay Phone:** Yes. **Restrooms and Showers:** Yes. **Fuel:** No. **Propane:** No. **Internal Roads:** Gravel. **RV Service:** No. **Market:** 2 mi. to Westcliffe. **Restaurant:** 2 mi. to Westcliffe. **General Store:** No. **Vending:** No. **Swimming:** No. **Playground:** No. **Other:** Cabins. **Activities:** Fishing, mountain climbing, mountain biking, hunting. **Nearby Attractions:** Bishop Castle, Kit Carson Mountain, Carson Mountain, Crestone Peak, Crestone Needle, Humboldt Peak, Grape Creek. **Additional Information:** Custer County Chamber, (719) 783-9163.

RESTRICTIONS

Pets: On leash, cleaned up after. **Fires:** In rings (not at sites). **Alcoholic Beverages:** At sites. **Vehicle Maximum Length:** 45 ft.

TO GET THERE

From the junction of Hwy. 96 and Hwy. 69, go 2 mi. south on Hwy. 69. Turn right at the sign onto a dirt lane and follow it into the campground.

WHEAT RIDGE   MAP, A-3
Prospect RV Park

11600 West 44th Ave., 80033. T: (800) 344-5702 or (303) 424-4414; www.prospectrv.com.

🚐 ★★★★   ▲ n/a

Beauty: ★★★★	Site Privacy: ★★★
Spaciousness: ★★★	Quiet: ★★★★
Security: ★★★★★	Cleanliness: ★★★★★
Insect Control: ★★★★	Facilities: ★★★★

Although this campground is located in an urban residential area, it abuts a park and a lake, so it feels much more like a hideaway. The red barn and horses in the southwest corner only add to this feeling. Sites consist of shaded gravel spaces a uniform 24 feet wide. Pull-throughs average 50 feet in length, and back-ins average 35 feet. Sites 5–10 have a very nice view of the neighboring lake. Sites 21–35 and 42–47 are quite attractive back-ins that back to a hedge that runs along the perimeter of the manager's residence.

Sites 49–71 are laid out in three rows. These pull-throughs are somewhat smaller than the others in the park (30–42 feet). Sites 41 and 55 have the nicest views of the farmland to the southwest, but 64 has the least desirable view (a storage shed). The restrooms are bright, modern, and absolutely immaculate. This campground offers urban convenience, but the surprise it holds up its sleeve is the quiet, pretty retreat it creates in the middle of the city.

BASICS

Operated By: Nancy Laird. **Open:** All year. **Site Assignment:** Upon registration; credit card required for reservation; call to cancel. **Registration:** At office. (Late arrivals select site & pay in the morning.) **Fee:** $27–$29; check, V, MC. **Parking:** At site.

FACILITIES

Number of RV-only Sites: 70. **Hookups:** Electric (30, 50 amps), water, sewer. **Each Site:** Picnic table on concrete slab. **Dump Station:** Yes. **Laundry:** Yes. **Pay Phone:** Yes. **Restrooms and Showers:** Yes. **Fuel:** No. **Propane:** No. **Internal Roads:** Gravel. **RV Service:** On-call. **Market:** 6 blocks west. **Restaurant:** 3 blocks west. **General Store:** No. **Vending:** Yes. **Swimming:** No. **Playground:** Yes (next door). **Other:** Pet walk, data port. **Activities:** Fishing, biking, hiking. **Nearby Attractions:** Prospect Park, Prospect Lake. **Additional Information:** Denver Chamber of Commerce, (303) 458-0220.

RESTRICTIONS

Pets: On leash, cleaned up after, some problem breeds not allowed. **Fires:** Grill only. **Alcoholic Beverages:** At sites. **Vehicle Maximum Length:** No limit.

TO GET THERE

From the junction of I-25 and I-70, take Exit 214A and turn west onto I-70. Go 8.1 mi. to Exit 266, then turn south onto Ward Rd. and go 1 block south. Turn east onto 44th Ave. and go 0.6 mi. (past the RV service center). Turn right at the sign into the entrance. The office is on the right.

WRAY   MAP, A-4
Hitchin' Post RV Park

34172 Hwy. 385, 80758. T: (970) 332-3128; www.plains.net/hitchinpost.

🚐 ★★★★   ▲ ★★★★

Beauty: ★★★	Site Privacy: ★★★★
Spaciousness: ★★★★	Quiet: ★★★★
Security: ★★★★	Cleanliness: ★★★★
Insect Control: ★★★★	Facilities: ★★★

This campground consists solely of two rows of pull-throughs. These unshaded gravel sites can accommodate RVs of any size. There is a third row of back-ins/tent sites to the south of the RV sites. These back-ins (which can also be used by tents), are located on a lush grassy field. Sites are 40 feet in length. While the sites themselves do not offer any facilities, the campground has attractive landscaping that uses flowers, trees, and white fencing. The restrooms are perfectly clean, and the showers only slightly less so. This is a pleasant campground that

will appeal equally well to tenters and to RVers.

BASICS

Operated By: Noble & Virgene Burns. **Open:** All year. **Site Assignment:** Upon registration; verbal reservations OK. **Registration:** At office. (Late arrivals select site & pay in the morning.) **Fee:** $25; check, no credits cards. **Parking:** At site.

FACILITIES

Number of RV-only Sites: 20. **Number of Tent-only Sites:** Undesignated sites. **Hookups:** Electric (20, 30, 50 amps), water, sewer. **Each Site:** Covered picnic tables. **Dump Station:** Yes. **Laundry:** Yes. **Pay Phone:** Yes. **Restrooms and Showers:** Yes. **Fuel:** No. **Propane:** Yes. **Internal Roads:** Gravel. **RV Service:** No. **Market:** 1 mi. north. **Restaurant:** 1 mi. north. **General Store:** No. **Vending:** No. **Swimming:** No. **Playground:** No. **Other:** Dog pen. **Activities:** Fishing, boating, swimming, horseback riding. **Nearby Attractions:** Bonny State Park, golf, museums, movie theater, city parks, playgrounds. **Additional Information:** Chamber of Commerce, (970) 332-4609.

RESTRICTIONS

Pets: On leash, cleaned up after. **Fires:** Grill only. **Alcoholic Beverages:** At sites. **Vehicle Maximum Length:** No limit. **Other:** See rule sheet upon arrival.

TO GET THERE

From the junction of Hwy. 34 and Hwy. 385, turn south onto Hwy. 385 and go 1.1 mi. Turn left at the sign into the entrance, then right toward the office.

YAMPA   MAP, A-2
Stillwater Campground

300 Roselawn Ave., 80483. T: (970) 879-1870.

🚐 ★★★★   ▲ ★★★★

Beauty: ★★★★★	Site Privacy: ★★★★★
Spaciousness: ★★★★★	Quiet: ★★★★★
Security: ★★★★	Cleanliness: ★★★
Insect Control: ★★★★	Facilities: ★

The long but beautiful drive in to this campground is worth the effort once you are there, as this campground offers spectacular views of lakes and the mountains that rise above them. The recreational opportunities for outdoor enthusiasts are also limitless. The campground itself is very small (7 sites), but there are a number of campsites along the road in. Some of these (including 28, just across from the campground, and 33, a pull-through overlooking Bear Lake) are at the tops of hills, allowing a view overlooking the entire area. Site 1 in the campground is right by the entrance and may be less desirable for this location. Sites 2–4 are 45–50-foot back-ins; of these, 3 has the best views to the southeast. Site 5 is an 80-foot back-in, and 6 and 7 are 75-foot pull-throughs. All of these sites are at least partially forested and some (2 and 4) are completely lost in the trees. Come to this campground in September, when the aspens are turning. You will see a startle of yellow aspens among the stately deep-green ponderosa pines. This campground offers wonderful scenic and recreational opportunities but next to nothing in the way of facilities. As such, it may appeal most to tenters and RVers with a sense of adventure.

BASICS

Operated By: U.S. Forest Service. **Open:** All year. **Site Assignment:** First come, first served; no reservations. **Registration:** At pay station. **Fee:** Site in campground, $10; developed campsites along road, $3; check. **Parking:** At site.

FACILITIES

Number of RV-only Sites: 29. **Hookups:** Electric. **Each Site:** Picnic table, fire pit. **Dump Station:** Yes. **Laundry:** No. **Pay Phone:** No. **Restrooms and** **Showers:** Yes. **Fuel:** No. **Propane:** No. **Internal Roads:** Dirt. **RV Service:** No. **Market:** 16 mi. northeast. **Restaurant:** 16 mi. northeast. **General Store:** No. **Vending:** No. **Swimming:** Reservoir. **Playground:** No. **Activities:** Fishing, boating, swimming, hiking, hunting, horseback riding. **Nearby Attractions:** Stillwater Reservoir, Yamcolo Reservoir, Bear Lake, Devil's Causeway, Stagecoach State Park. **Additional Information:** Yampa Ranger District, (970) 638-4516.

RESTRICTIONS

Pets: On leash, cleaned up after. **Fires:** Grill only. **Alcoholic Beverages:** At sites. **Vehicle Maxi-** mum Length: No limit. **Other:** $3 per vehicle day-use pass, no cutting firewood.

TO GET THERE

From the junction of Hwy. 131 and Moffat Ave. (by gas station complex at southeastern edge of town), turn southwest onto Moffat Ave. and go 0.4 mi. to Main St. Cross over Main and continue on CR 7 (which becomes unpaved FR 900) 13.3 mi. to Bear Lake Campground. The campground is on the left.

Connecticut

A comparitively tiny state with a surprising variety of terrain, including wetlands, woods, and beach, Connecticut offers an impressive array of options for whatever type of camping you may be seeking. Though even the most remote parts of the state aren't far from civilization (or for that matter a shopping complex), campgrounds range from isolated to middle-of-town. There's almost no type of camping that you can't find here, and if you're looking for variety, you could easily spend one day at a rural site, another near the ocean, and the next by a small mountain.

For those anxious to head off into the relative obscurity of the wild, the Constitution State maintains more than 100 state parks and forests, 13 of which offer camping facilities, not to mention some great hiking and trail riding. In the western portion of the state, your options are **American Legion State Forest, Macedonia Brook, Lake Waramaug, Housatonic Meadows, Kettletown,** and **Black Rock State Parks.** To the east lie the **Natchaug** and **Pachaug State Forests, Mashamoquet Brook, Salt Rock, Devil's Hopyard,** and **Hopeville Pond State Parks.** Along the coast are the **Hammonasset** and **Rocky Neck State Parks.**

Outdoor enthusiasts may be overwhelmed by the vast array. Connecticut has 250 miles of coastline and countless boat launches, which is conducive to fishing if you don't mind catching cod, flounder, shark, tuna, or striped bass. While at the ocean you may want to take one of the many guided lighthouse tours. There are numerous ski slopes, too. Visiting skiers and snowboarders alike are encouraged to try out the likes of **Mount Southington, Mohawk Mountain, Powder Ridge,** or **Ski Sundown,** to name a few. Because it only takes at most three hours to drive across Connecticut, you're never that far from anything. The big attractions for most folks are the **Foxwoods** and **Mohegan Sun** casinos. These gigantic, Native American–run facilities are easily accessible from nearly anywhere in the state and are close to numerous campgrounds. For fans of NASCAR, Stafford Springs is home to **Stafford Motor Speedway,** in case you're fiending for some speed. While you're on the road and have three days to spare, a fun and informative time is guaranteed on the **Connecticut Wine Trail,** which snakes through the state and lets you sample some of the region's finest grapes.

A big tourist attraction in Connecticut is the town of Mystic, with its aquarium, seaport, and numerous quaint attractions. There are also an uncountable number of villages with lively downtowns full of little shops, restaurants, and attractions. Visitors to Stamford in March might be interested in partaking in the **American Crossword Puzzle Tournament.** Hungry travelers through Norwalk desiring a little distraction from reality may want to stop off at **Stew Leonard's,** the world's largest dairy store, to be serenaded by animatronic milk cartons, vegetables, and a cow. Despite this anomaly, much of the state is traditional New England, where the center of town is still the center of activity. For an excellent guide and itinerary planner customized to help you experience all the fifth state is made of, visit www.tourism.state.ct.us.

In addition to the varying topography in conjunction with the state's campgrounds, its cities and towns tend to vary quite a bit within a small distance. Take the capital, Hartford, as an example—a city with most of the amenities of its bigger counterparts that's also a five-minute ride from open space. If you go in different directions you get a wide choice of towns that conveniently cater to different needs. Some offer gourmet dining and theater, whereas others have great pizza joints, movie theaters, and bowling alleys.

For campers, the main appeal of Connecticut has to be its accessibility—it's easy to do anything from anywhere in this state, with enough to keep you busy for a while. In general, if you're looking for rustic and respite, you'll not want to dip too far into the southern parts of the state, and there might be fewer amenities outside your campground to the west. But with the small size and many highways, you're never more than a half-hour ride from any facet of culture in Connecticut's well-polished spectrum.

Campground Profiles

ASHFORD MAP, A-4
Brialee RV and Tent Park

174 Laurel Lane, P.O. Box 125, 06278-0125.
T: (860) 429-8359 or (800) 303-CAMP;
www.brialee.net.

🚐 ★★★★　　🏕 ★★★★

Beauty: ★★★★　　Site Privacy: ★★★★
Spaciousness: ★★★　　Quiet: ★★★
Security: ★★★★　　Cleanliness: ★★★★
Insect Control: ★★★　　Facilities: ★★★★

Three ponds, a sandy beach, a heated pool, and non-stop activities make this a popular family vacation destination. The campground, nestled in Connecticut's northeast quiet corner, is close to the Natchaug State Forest, which offers wilderness trails and wildlife viewing. But most campers stick around the campground to enjoy the on-site amenities. There are three walking trails within the park, including a pleasant boardwalk that meanders through marshes and woodlands. No fishing license is required to drop a line in the stocked, catch-and-release trout and bass ponds. Live entertainment and dances are common throughout the season and two full-time on-site recreation directors have developed a host of fun activities for the entire family. RV campers take up most of the sites (there are a number of seasonal renters, too), but tenters can find a handful of woodsy, quiet sites (try 128A and 128C). All sites are of a good size, with an average width of about 40–45 feet.

BASICS

Operated By: Brian, Addie, & Ed Specyalski. **Open:** Apr. 1–Oct. 31. **Site Assignment:** Reservations suggested; 1-night deposit; 7-day cancellation policy minus 10%; V, MC. **Registration:** At office. **Fee:** Waterfront, $48; water/electric, $43; no hookup, $39; cable: $47; sewer: $51. **Parking:** At site.

FACILITIES

Number of RV-only Sites: 10. **Number of Tent-only Sites:** 20. **Number of Multipurpose Sites:** 165. **Hookups:** Electric (20, 30, 50 amps), water, sewer, cable TV, Internet. **Each Site:** Picnic table, fire ring. **Dump Station:** Yes. **Laundry:** Yes. **Pay Phone:** Yes. **Restrooms and Showers:** Yes. **Fuel:** No. **Propane:** Yes. **Internal Roads:** Gravel (good). **RV Service:** No. **Market:** Ashford, 4 mi. **Restaurant:** Snack bar on site. **General Store:** Yes. **Vending:** Yes, & ATM. **Swimming:** Pool, pond. **Playground:** Yes. **Other:** Ponds, beach, boat rentals, stocked fishing, pavilion, rec hall, arcade, safari field, sports fields, trails, trailer rentals, planned activities. **Activities:** Swimming, boating, fishing, hiking, basketball, volleyball, softball, horseshoes, game room w/ pool, Ping-Pong, shuffleboard. **Nearby Attractions:** Farms, antiques shops, swimming, boating, fishing, biking, hiking, Woodstock. **Additional Information:** Town of Woodstock, 415 Hwy. 169, Woodstock, CT 06281, (860) 928-6595, www.townofwoodstock.com. Northeast Connecticut Visitors District, 13 Canterbury Rd., Suite 3, P.O. Box 145, Brooklyn, CT 06234-0145, (860) 779-6383, www.ctquietcorner.org.

RESTRICTIONS

Pets: On leash only (5 feet max.). All vaccination papers required, 2-pet limit per site. **Fires:** Fire pits, grills only. **Alcoholic Beverages:** At site. **Vehicle Maximum Length:** 45 ft.

TO GET THERE

From Hwy. 84 East Exit 62, follow Hwy. 74 east 8 mi. to Hwy. 44. Turn left on Hwy. 44. Go east 1 mi. to Hwy. 89 North. Take first left onto Perry Hill Rd., then second right onto Laurel Lane to campground.

BALTIC MAP, B-4
Salt Rock Campground

reserve america

173 Scotland Rd. (Hwy. 97), 06330.
T: (860) 822-0884; www.reserveamerica.com.

🚐 ★★★★　　🏕 ★★★★

Beauty: ★★★　　Site Privacy: ★★★
Spaciousness: ★★★　　Quiet: ★★★★
Security: ★★★★　　Cleanliness: ★★★★
Insect Control: ★★★　　Facilities: ★★★★

Salt Rock State Campground covers 120 wooded acres in a rural setting that was once farmland. Located in eastern Connecticut, the park is near many tourist destinations including Mystic and New London attractions. Salt Rock is a unique campground for the State Parks Division as it is the only state campground that provides the opportunity for long-term camping. Salt Rock State Campground has 60 campground sites open for tent and recreational vehicle (RV) camping with utilities to some sites. There are also two in-ground swimming pools for patrons to enjoy. A visit to Baltic Historic District rejuvenates the soul, and Natchaug River has a great whitewater-paddling spot nearby. Everybody loves Occum Playground and going for a hike along the Narragansett Trail will let you absorb the natural beauty of this area. A trip to Quinebaug and Shetucket Rivers Valley National Heritage Corridor is worthwhile, and paddling on Salmon River is so much fun. A round of golf at nearby River Ridge Golf Course is a great way to kill some time, and if you like skiing you're in luck: Yawgoo Valley is quite near. Whitewater paddling is great on Quinebaug River; going for a hike on the Nipmuck Trail is always a great adventure, and Blackstone River Valley National Heritage Corridor is a wonderful national park.

BASICS

Operated By: Connecticut Dept. Environmental Protection. **Open:** May 18–Oct. 8. **Site Assignment:** Reservations must be made at least 2 days in advance. **Registration:** At office. **Fee:** Single, $25–$28. **Parking:** At site.

FACILITIES

Number of Multipurpose Sites: 72. **Hookups:** Yes. **Dump Station:** Yes. **Laundry:** W/in 10 mi. **Pay**

Phone: Yes. **Restrooms and Showers:** Yes. **Fuel:** No. **Propane:** No. **Internal Roads:** Paved. **RV Service:** No. **Market:** W/in 10 mi. **Restaurant:** No. **General Store:** W/in 10 mi. **Vending:** No. **Swimming:** No. **Playground:** No. **Activities:** Canoeing, fishing, hiking, horseshoe pits, kayaking, softball, tubing, volleyball.

RESTRICTIONS

Pets: No pets allowed in campground. **Fires:** Permitted in designated fireplaces. **Alcoholic Beverages:** Alcohol not allowed. **Vehicle Maximum Length:** Trailers & RVs exceeding 35 ft. in length are not permitted.

TO GET THERE

From I-395 (Exit 83): At the end of exit ramp take left onto Hwy. 97 north. Continue approximately 5 mi. Campground entrance is located on left-hand side on Hwy. 97 in Baltic.

BARKHAMSTED MAP, A-2
White Pines Campsites

232 Old North Rd., 06063. T: (860) 379-0124 or (800) 622-6614 (reservations); www.whitepinescamp.com.

🚐 ★★★　　🏕 ★★★

Beauty: ★★　　Site Privacy: ★★
Spaciousness: ★★★　　Quiet: ★★★
Security: ★★★★　　Cleanliness: ★★★
Insect Control: ★★★　　Facilities: ★★★

This pleasantly woodsy campground offers a blend of outdoor fun and planned activities, with nearly all the conveniences of home: cable TV hookups, the Happy Camper Café, and a modem, so you can check that e-mail if you must. Sites are set in two loops, with some alongside a pond and stream. Some sites are grass, some are gravel, and most offer a fair amount of shade. They also have a grassy field for bigger rigs, and for campers who like nothing better than to bask in the sun alongside their RV. There are even a few "wilderness" tent sites hidden among the pines. White Pines offers plenty to do, from pedal-boating on the pond to casting a line or scaring up some teammates for volleyball in a sand pit. It occupies a pleasant niche between resort and rustic camping experience.

BASICS

Operated By: Private operator. **Open:** Apr. 14–Oct. 15; peak season, May 26–Sept. 4. **Site Assignment:** Reserve online or by phone; deposit of 50% due at time of reservation; refunds offered for 7-day cancellations, minus $10; late cancellations or no-shows forfeit deposits; 3-night minimum on holidays; on holiday weekends, 100% deposit is due w/ reservation. **Registration:** At office. **Fee:** Water/electric/cable, $42; no hookup, $32; holiday weekend rates vary; special club rates may apply. **Parking:** At site, no mopeds or ATVs.

FACILITIES

Number of RV-only Sites: 9. **Number of Tent-only Sites:** 9. **Number of Multipurpose Sites:** 200. **Hookups:** Electric, water, modem, cable. **Each**

Site: Picnic table, fire ring. **Dump Station:** Yes. **Laundry:** Laundromat nearby. **Pay Phone:** Yes. **Restrooms and Showers:** Yes. **Fuel:** No. **Propane:** Yes. **Internal Roads:** Gravel, fair condition. **RV Service:** No. **Market:** 5 mi. in town. **Restaurant:** On-site café. **General Store:** Yes. **Vending:** Yes. **Swimming:** Pool. **Playground:** Yes. **Other:** Rec hall, pavilion, sports field. **Activities:** Pedal-boat rentals, pond fishing, badminton, volleyball, swimming, basketball, horseshoe pits. **Nearby Attractions:** Lakes, indoor sports dome. **Additional Information:** Litchfield Hills Visitors Bureau; (860) 567-4507; www.litchfieldhills.com.

RESTRICTIONS

Pets: On leash only; must be quiet cleaned up after. Proof of current rabies vaccination required. No rottweilers, pit bulls, chows, guard dogs, or other aggressive dogs permitted. **Fires:** In fire rings only. **Alcoholic Beverages:** At site. **Vehicle Maximum Length:** 40 ft.

TO GET THERE

Located 2 mi. north of Winsted Center; east of Hwy. 3, south of Hwy. 20, and north of Hwy. 44. From Winsted Center, continue north on Hwy. 8, go right onto Wallens St. and left onto Wallens Hill Rd. Go straight onto Wallens Hill 3 mi., right onto Old North Rd.

BOZRAH — MAP, B-3
Acorn Acres

135 Lake Rd., 06334. T: (860) 859-1020; www.acornacrescampsites.com.

🚐 ★★★★ ⛺ ★★★★

Beauty: ★★★★	Site Privacy: ★★★★
Spaciousness: ★★★★	Quiet: ★★★
Security: ★★★★★	Cleanliness: ★★★★
Insect Control: ★★★	Facilities: ★★★★

You'll find plenty of room to roam and large sites at this rolling, wooded campground tucked into the side of a hill. Sites are terraced, and the property weaves up and down and around more than 200 acres in the hills of southeastern Connecticut. There are outdoor pursuits for nature lovers, like fishing in the stocked trout stream, swimming in the two-acre private pond, or hiking the miles of old Mohegan hunting grounds. But many campers, especially families, take part in the planned activities, like diving and tennis lessons, free swimming lessons in the Olympic-sized pool, arts and crafts, and sports tournaments. The campground has been family-owned for more than 35 years and draws a solid base of returning campers. Sites are spacious, wooded or open, and the on-site cabins for rent, tucked in the woods for added privacy, are a nice option.

BASICS

Operated By: Sis O'Neil. **Open:** May–Columbus Day. **Site Assignment:** Reservations suggested; 1-night deposit; 7-day cancellation policy; V, MC. **Registration:** At office. **Fee:** Water/electric/sewer/cable, $50; water/electric, $45; no hookup, $40. **Parking:** At site.

FACILITIES

Number of RV-only Sites: 500. **Hookups:** Electric (20, 30, 50 amps), water, sewer, cable TV. **Each Site:**

Picnic table, fire ring. **Dump Station:** Yes. **Laundry:** Yes. **Pay Phone:** Yes. **Restrooms and Showers:** Yes. **Fuel:** No. **Propane:** Yes. **Internal Roads:** Paved, gravel (good). **RV Service:** No. **Market:** Bozrah, 0.5 mi. **Restaurant:** Bozrah, 0.5 mi. **General Store:** Yes. **Vending:** Yes. **Swimming:** Olympic swimming pool, hot tub, pond. **Playground:** Yes. **Other:** Mini-golf, rec hall, tennis courts, river frontage, beach, sports fields, cabin rentals, fishing pond, hiking trails, snack bar, lounge. **Activities:** Swimming, fishing, boating, tennis, softball, shuffleboard, volleyball, horseshoes, basketball, badminton, hiking, planned activities like arts & crafts, hay rides, live music. **Nearby Attractions:** Swimming, boating, fishing, hiking, biking, Norwich, Mystic, Foxwoods & Mohegan Sun casinos, golf, horseback riding. **Additional Information:** Mystic Chamber of Commerce, 14 Holmes St., P.O. Box 143, Mystic, CT 06355, (860) 572-9578; Foxwoods Resort Casino, Hwy. 2 P.O. Box 3777, Mashantucket, CT 06338, www.foxwoods.com.

RESTRICTIONS

Pets: On leash only, vaccination papers required, 2 per site. **Fires:** Fire pits, grills only. **Alcoholic Beverages:** At site. **Vehicle Maximum Length:** 40 ft.

TO GET THERE

From Norwich, take Hwy. 82 West 6 mi., then Hwy. 163 North 1 mi. Take left on Lake Rd. 1 mi. to campground.

BOZRAH — MAP, B-3
Odetah Campground

38 Bozrah St. Extension, P.O. Box 151, 06334. T: (860) 889-4144 or (800) 448-1193; www.odetah.com.

🚐 ★★★★★ ⛺ ★★★★★

Beauty: ★★★★★	Site Privacy: ★★★★
Spaciousness: ★★★★	Quiet: ★★★
Security: ★★★	Cleanliness: ★★★★
Insect Control: ★★★	Facilities: ★★★★★

This attractive and amenities-laden campground is one of Connecticut's finest. The campground sits on the shores of a crystal-clear, 32-acre lake with pretty views and a private sandy beach. It offers lakeside activities, like swimming and boating (boat rentals are available at the campground), and fishing. Off the lake, there's an 18-hole mini-golf course, large swimming pool, sports fields, and a slew of planned activities scheduled throughout the season. Everything you'll want is here; if not, the campground is just off the highway and close to some of southeast Connecticut's popular attractions, including Norwich Navigators baseball, Foxwoods and Mohegan Sun casinos, and Mystic. Sites are quite roomy, with choice of open or shaded areas. There are also several with lake frontage or lake views. The 12 rental cabins tucked up in the woods and the 3 yurts near the pool are fun and easy options for vacationing families.

BASICS

Operated By: Linda & Nathan Adelman. **Open:** May–Oct. **Site Assignment:** Reservations highly recommended; can be made by phone or in person starting Apr. 1 at 8 a.m. **Registration:** At office. **Fee:** Full hookup, $40; water/electric, $35; no hookup, $30. **Parking:** At site.

FACILITIES

Number of RV-only Sites: 28. **Number of Tent-only Sites:** 33. **Number of Multipurpose Sites:** 231. **Hookups:** Electric (20, 30, 50 amps), water, sewer. **Each Site:** Picnic table, fire ring. **Dump Station:** Yes. **Laundry:** Yes. **Pay Phone:** Yes. **Restrooms and Showers:** Yes. **Fuel:** No. **Propane:** Yes. **Internal Roads:** Half paved, half gravel. **RV Service:** No. **Market:** Bozrah, 0.5 mi. **Restaurant:** Snack shop on site. **General Store:** Yes. **Vending:** Yes, soft drinks. **Swimming:** Pool, lake. **Playground:** Yes. **Other:** Lake frontage, beach, boat rentals, tennis courts, social hall, game room pavilion, safari area, sports fields, mini-golf, trails, cabin & yurt rentals, outdoor fitness facility. **Activities:** Swimming, boating, fishing, hiking, mini-golf, tennis, bocce, horseshoes, basketball, volleyball, planned activities like arts & crafts, hay rides, contests, movies. **Nearby Attractions:** Swimming, boating, hiking, biking, fishing, Norwich, Mystic, Foxwoods & Mohegan Sun casinos. **Additional Information:** Mystic Chamber of Commerce, 14 Holmes St., P.O. Box 143, Mystic, CT 06355, (860) 572-9578. Foxwoods Resort Casino, Hwy. 2 P.O. Box 3777, Mashantucket, CT 06338, www.foxwoods.com.

RESTRICTIONS

Pets: On leash only. **Fires:** Fire pits, grills only. **Alcoholic Beverages:** At site.

TO GET THERE

From I-395 Exit 81 west, go 2 mi. west on Hwy. 2 to Exit 23, turn left. Go straight through stop sign, campground is 1,000 ft. on the right.

CHAPLIN — MAP, A-4
Nickerson Park Campground

1036 Phoenixville Rd., 06235. T: (860) 455-0007; www.nickersonpark.com.

🚐 ★★★ ⛺ ★★★★

Beauty: ★★★	Site Privacy: ★★★
Spaciousness: ★★★	Quiet: ★★★★
Security: ★★★	Cleanliness: ★★★★
Insect Control: ★★★	Facilities: ★★★

This is an outdoor lover's haven. Anglers and hunters (in season) flock to this campground, nestled on the banks of the Natchaug River. The state-stocked river is known for its fine trout fishing, and you'll have direct access to some of the best fishing holes on the river, right from your campsite. Half of the sites (50) have river frontage. Sites R30 and R38 are favorites for their woodsy, riverfront locations. If you can snag site W7, go for it. This one is roomy, on the river, circled with trees for added privacy, and next to the River Trail. The large lodge/rec hall, with its stone fireplace, is a popular place to hang out. Across the river sits the dense 12,000-acre Natchaug State Forest, with miles of hiking and biking trails and abundant wildlife. In winter, bring your skis and snowshoes; the campground is open year-round.

BASICS

Operated By: Chris & Diane Nickerson. **Open:** All year. **Site Assignment:** Reservations suggested; 1-night deposit; 2-night minimum stay on weekends, 3-night minimum on holidays; 14-day cancellation policy; cancellations made 7–14 days before scheduled arrival receive credit; no refunds or credit for cancellations made less than 7 days prior to arrival; V, MC. **Registration:** At office. **Fee:** Full hookup, $27.50; water/electric, $25. **Parking:** At site.

FACILITIES

Number of RV-only Sites: 25. **Number of Tent-only Sites:** 25. **Number of Multipurpose Sites:** 50. **Hookups:** Electric (20, 30 amps), water, sewer, cable TV, some sites w/ Internet. **Each Site:** Picnic table, fire ring. **Dump Station:** Yes. **Laundry:** Yes. **Pay Phone:** Yes. **Restrooms and Showers:** Yes. **Fuel:** No. **Propane:** Yes. **Internal Roads:** Gravel, dirt (good). **RV Service:** No. **Market:** North Windham, 5 mi. **Restaurant:** North Windham, 5 mi. **General Store:** Yes, but limited. **Vending:** Yes. **Swimming:** River. **Playground:** Yes. **Other:** River frontage, rec hall, pavilion, game room, 14,000 acres of wilderness w/ hiking trails. **Activities:** Swimming, boating, fishing, hiking, hunting, cross-country skiing, basketball. **Nearby Attractions:** Farms, boating, fishing, hiking, swimming, biking, Natchaug State Forest. **Additional Information:** Northeast Connecticut Visitors District, 13 Canterbury Rd., Suite 3, P.O. Box 145, Brooklyn, CT 06234-0145, (860) 779-6383; www.ctquietcorner.org.

RESTRICTIONS

Pets: On leash only (no rottweilers or pit bulls). **Fires:** Fire pits, grills only. **Alcoholic Beverages:** At site.

TO GET THERE

From Willimantic, take Hwy. 6 East to Hwy. 198. Follow Hwy. 198 North 4.5 mi. to campground.

EAST CANAAN   MAP, A-1
Lone Oak Campsites

360 Norfolk Rd., P.O. Box 640, 06024. T: (860) 824-7051 or (800) 422-2267; www.loneoakcampsites.com.

🚐 ★★★★   ⛺ ★★★

Beauty: ★★★   Site Privacy: ★★
Spaciousness: ★★★   Quiet: ★★
Security: ★★★   Cleanliness: ★★★
Insect Control: ★★   Facilities: ★★★★

Set in the Berkshire foothills at the base of Canaan Mountain, this lively, resort-ish campground is continually busy. Check out the corn roast, Christmas in August, the magic show, or the ever-popular softball game versus White Pines Campground. With all of this activity—plus a hot tub, a sauna, even a lounge for grown-ups—you won't get bored here! This may not be the most unspoiled natural setting you'll ever find, but it's not bad in terms of outdoor beauty. The campground is set on the Blackberry River, with some sites protected by trees and others open to the rolling, grassy fields. The river and pond provide an opportunity to cast a line and watch the world go by. Family campers looking for a real vacation experience in the Litchfield Hills will have a blast here.

BASICS

Operated By: Private operator. **Open:** Mid-Apr.–mid-Oct. **Site Assignment:** Reservations taken year-round; 50% deposit required; refunds for cancellations made 7 days or more prior to stay, minus

---

$10; no refunds for cancellations of 6 days or less prior to arrival date; 3-night minimum on holidays. **Registration:** At office. **Fee:** Water/electric/cable/sewer, $46; water/electric/cable, $43; no hookup: $38. **Parking:** At site.

FACILITIES

Number of Tent-only Sites: 390. **Number of Multipurpose Sites:** 110. **Hookups:** Electric, water, sewer, cable, free Wi-Fi. **Each Site:** Picnic table, fire ring. **Dump Station:** Yes. **Laundry:** Yes. **Pay Phone:** Yes. **Restrooms and Showers:** Yes, coin operated. **Fuel:** No. **Propane:** Yes. **Internal Roads:** Gravel & paved. **RV Service:** Yes. **Market:** In town, about 3 mi. **Restaurant:** Deli on site. **General Store:** Yes. **Vending:** No. **Swimming:** 2 pools (heated). **Playground:** Yes. **Other:** Hot tub, sauna, arcade, nightclub (adult lounge), live entertainment, children's activities. **Activities:** Fishing (river, pond, stream), children's club, basketball, volleyball, planned activities. **Nearby Attractions:** Appalachian Trail, Norman Rockwell Museum, Lime Rock Race Park, Tanglewood Music Festival, golf, hiking. **Additional Information:** Litchfield Hills Visitors Bureau; (860) 567-4506; www.litchfieldhills.com.

RESTRICTIONS

Pets: On leash only; must be quiet, cleaned up after. Proof of current rabies vaccination required. Allowed in designated areas only (not allowed in rental properties). **Fires:** In fire rings only. **Alcoholic Beverages:** At site.

TO GET THERE

From junction of US 7 and US 44, go 3.5 mi. east on US 44. Campground entrance is on the right.

EAST HADDAM   MAP, B-3
Devil's Hopyard

reserve america

366 Hopyard Rd., 06423. T: (860) 526-2336; www.reserveamerica.com.

🚐 ★★★★   ⛺ ★★★★

Beauty: ★★★★   Site Privacy: ★★★
Spaciousness: ★★★   Quiet: ★★
Security: ★★★   Cleanliness: ★★★★
Insect Control: ★★★   Facilities: ★★★

Devil's Hopyard consists of 940 acres and is located in East Haddam, Connecticut. The primary focal point of the park is the Chapman Falls whose water tumbles more than 60 feet over the rocky escarpment. The water from the splash pool at the base of the falls, continuing as the Eight Mile River, flows through the hemlock-canopied picnic area, providing a tranquil setting for a family outing. No less than half a dozen myths surround the name of the park. The numerous potholes at the base of the falls are the basis for one tale that suggests these formations were the result of the devil hopping from ledge to ledge in order not to get wet. The cylindrical holes were "burned" into the rock by the "hot hoofs." Activities and facilities at the park include picnicking, camping, stream fishing, hiking, mountain biking, picnic shelter, outhouses, gravel parking, and

---

drinking water. The campground contains 22 campsites in an open field setting.

BASICS

Operated By: Connecticut Dept. Environmental Protection. **Open:** Apr. 13–May 29. **Site Assignment:** Reservations must be made at least 2 days in advance. **Registration:** At office. **Fee:** $15 per day. **Parking:** At site.

FACILITIES

Number of Multipurpose Sites: 22. **Hookups:** None. **Dump Station:** Yes. **Laundry:** W/in 10 mi. **Pay Phone:** Yes. **Restrooms and Showers:** Yes. **Fuel:** No. **Propane:** No. **Internal Roads:** Paved. **RV Service:** No. **Market:** No. **Restaurant:** No. **General Store:** W/in 10 mi. **Vending:** No. **Swimming:** No. **Playground:** No. **Activities:** Biking, bird-watching, fishing, hiking, horseshoe pits, nature center, photography, wildlife viewing.

RESTRICTIONS

Pets: No pets allowed in campground. **Fires:** Permitted in designated fireplaces. **Alcoholic Beverages:** Beer in containers larger than 1 liter is not allowed. State law limits the possession of alcoholic beverages to individuals 21 years or older. **Vehicle Maximum Length:** Trailers & RVs exceeding 35 ft. in length are not permitted.

TO GET THERE

From CT 9, take Exit 7. Left at end of ramp onto CT 154 north. Right at first traffic light and follow the signs. From I-395, Exit 80 west. Right onto CT 82 west. Right onto Hopyard Rd. and follow signs.

EAST LYME   MAP, B-3
Aces High RV Park

301 Chesterfield Rd., Hwy. 161, 06333. T: (860) 739-8858 or (877) PUL-THRU; www.aceshighrvpark.com.

🚐 ★★★★★   ⛺ n/a

Beauty: ★★★★   Site Privacy: ★★★
Spaciousness: ★★★★   Quiet: ★★★★
Security: ★★★★★   Cleanliness: ★★★★★
Insect Control: ★★★   Facilities: ★★★★★

This ultra-clean, modern RV-only park (no tents allowed) is most popular with adult campers who use it as a base for exploring southeast Connecticut or for spending days relaxing around the campground. The nearby Foxwoods and Mohegan Sun casinos, Mystic, and coastal beaches are popular day trips. Open, rolling fields, three ponds, and surrounding woods combine to make this an attractive setting. On site there's a stocked trout-fishing pond and a larger pond for swimming. Planned activities are offered most weekends. Nature trails roam through woodlands and along pretty streams and ponds. Campsites are large (average width is about 45 feet), and most are in the open. The park has been named Best Small Park in the Country by the National Association of RV Parks and Campgrounds.

BASICS

Operated By: Quinn family. **Open:** All year. **Site Assignment:** Reservations for stays less than 1 week are not accepted before Apr. 1; deposits on credit cards or checks. **Registration:** At office. **Fee:** $45–$48. **Parking:** At site.

FACILITIES

Number of Multipurpose Sites: 90. **Hookups:** Electric (20, 30, 50 amps), water, sewer, cable TV. **Each Site:** Picnic table, fire ring. **Dump Station:** Yes. **Laundry:** Yes. **Pay Phone:** Yes. **Restrooms and Showers:** Yes, coin operated. **Fuel:** No. **Propane:** Yes. **Internal Roads:** Gravel (good). **RV Service:** No. **Market:** Oakdale, 5 mi. **Restaurant:** East Lyme, 3 mi. **General Store:** Yes. **Vending:** No. **Swimming:** Pond, beach. **Playground:** Yes. **Other:** Rec room, beach, fishing pond, boat rentals, nature trails, sports fields, game room. **Activities:** Swimming, fishing, hiking, boating, volleyball, horseshoes, shuffleboard. **Nearby Attractions:** Foxwoods & Mohegan Sun casinos, Mystic, saltwater beaches. **Additional Information:** Mystic Shoreline Visitor's Information Center, Olde Mistick Village, Bldg. 1D, Mystic, CT 06355; (860) 536-1641; www.visitconnecticut.com/visitorscenter.

RESTRICTIONS

Pets: On leash only. **Fires:** Fire pits, grills only. **Alcoholic Beverages:** At site.

TO GET THERE

From I-95 Exit 74, follow Hwy. 161 north 3 mi. Campground is on the right.

EAST LYME — MAP, B-3
Island Campground and Cottages

20 Islanda Ct., P.O. Box 2, 06333.
T: (860) 739-8316.

🚐 ★★★   ⛺ ★★★★

Beauty: ★★★★★	Site Privacy: ★★★★
Spaciousness: ★★★	Quiet: ★★★★★
Security: ★★★★	Cleanliness: ★★★★
Insect Control: ★★★	Facilities: ★★

"There's nothing here," the owners tell us. "Just our cottages, and a few campsites, and a really pretty beach." And that's exactly why folks fill this tiny campground, which is set in the middle of Lake Pattagansett. This is a little, old-fashioned place with nothing but water, woods, and relaxation. Cast a fishing line; dangle your feet in the clear, warm lake waters; take a nap at the beach; and let the world go by. Most of the sites are tucked under trees overlooking the lake. All have water and electric, and most can accommodate large RVs.

BASICS

Operated By: Steve Harney. **Open:** May–Oct. **Site Assignment:** Reservations accepted; no deposit required; no credit cards. **Registration:** At office. **Fee:** $40–$50. **Parking:** At site.

FACILITIES

Number of Multipurpose Sites: 35. **Hookups:** Electric (20, 30 amps), water, cable. **Each Site:** Picnic table, fire ring. **Dump Station:** Yes. **Laundry:** No, Laundromat nearby. **Pay Phone:** No. **Restrooms and Showers:** Yes. **Fuel:** No. **Propane:** No. **Internal Roads:** Gravel (good). **RV Service:** No. **Market:** East Lyme, 1 mi. **Restaurant:** East Lyme, 1 mi. **General Store:** No. **Vending:** No. **Swimming:**

Lake. **Playground:** Yes. **Other:** Private beach, cottage rentals, rec room (pool table, darts) horseshoes. **Activities:** Swimming, fishing. **Nearby Attractions:** Foxwoods & Mohegan Sun casinos, Mystic, seaport. **Additional Information:** Mystic Shoreline Visitor's Information Center, Olde Mistick Village, Bldg. 1D, Mystic, CT 06355; (860) 536-1641; www.visitconnecticut.com/visitorscenter.

RESTRICTIONS

Pets: On leash only. **Fires:** Fire pits, grills only. **Alcoholic Beverages:** At site. **Vehicle Maximum Length:** Call for availability.

TO GET THERE

From I-95 Exit 74, take Hwy. 161 to Hwy. 1. Turn left and go 1 mi. to Islanda Court Rd.; turn right to campground.

GRISWOLD — MAP, B-4
Countryside RV Park

75 Cook Hill Rd., 06351.
T: (860) 376-0029 or (866) 247-8316;
www.countrysidecampground.com.

🚐 ★★★★   ⛺ ★★★

Beauty: ★★★	Site Privacy: ★★★★
Spaciousness: ★★★★	Quiet: ★★★★
Security: ★★★	Cleanliness: ★★★★
Insect Control: ★★★	Facilities: ★★★

"The strength of our nation is in the family." That's the motto of this campground, and it illustrates the family-friendly, close-knit atmosphere of the rural property. The campground has been in the Mackin family for more than two decades, and they've built up a loyal clientele. About half the sites are seasonals; the rest are taken by traveling families and transient campers touring Connecticut sites. This is a quiet, relaxed campground with lots of open space. There are two small ponds: one for fishing (it's also a favorite hangout for migrating Canada geese), the other for swimming. All the sites are especially large; 43 sits by itself with extra space. If you like the woods, ask about sites 37, 38, and 44 (among others). Sites 7 and 8 are pretty, too, with views through the woods of the pond.

BASICS

Operated By: Linda & James Mackin. **Open:** May 1–Oct. 9. **Site Assignment:** Reservations suggested; $40 deposit, 14-day cancellation policy; V, MC. **Registration:** At office. **Fee:** $40. **Parking:** At site.

FACILITIES

Number of Tent-only Sites: 89. **Number of Multipurpose Sites:** 25. **Hookups:** Electric (50 amps), water, sewer. **Each Site:** Picnic table, fire ring. **Dump Station:** Yes. **Laundry:** No. **Pay Phone:** Yes. **Restrooms and Showers:** Yes. **Fuel:** No. **Propane:** Yes. **Internal Roads:** Gravel (good). **RV Service:** No. **Market:** Voluntown, 4 mi. **Restaurant:** Voluntown, 4 mi. **General Store:** No. **Vending:** Yes. **Swimming:** Pond. **Playground:** Yes. **Other:** 1 swimming pond, 1 fishing pond, game room. **Activities:** Swimming, fishing, shuffleboard, horseshoes, volleyball. **Nearby Attractions:** Fishing, hiking, Mystic, Foxwoods. **Additional Information:** Mystic Chamber of Commerce, 14 Holmes St., P.O.

Box 143, Mystic, CT 06355, (860) 572-9578; Milford Chamber of Commerce, 5 Broad St., Milford, CT 06460, (203) 878-0681; www.milfordct.com.

RESTRICTIONS

Pets: On leash only. **Fires:** Fire pits, grills only. **Alcoholic Beverages:** At site.

TO GET THERE

From I-395 Exit 85, go 4 mi. east on Hwy. 138 to Hwy. 201 South. Go 1 mi. to Cook Hill Rd.; campground is 0.5 mi. on right.

JEWETT CITY — MAP, B-4
Hopeville Pond State Park

reserve america ☼

193 Roode Rd., 06351. T: (860) 376-2920;
www.reserveamerica.com.

🚐 ★★★★   ⛺ ★★★

Beauty: ★★★	Site Privacy: ★★★
Spaciousness: ★★★	Quiet: ★★★
Security: ★★★	Cleanliness: ★★★★
Insect Control: ★★★	Facilities: ★★★★

Visitors can fish, swim, or camp on the serene shores of Hopeville Pond. The site, which once boasted several successful mill operations, offers a fine mix of quality recreation and local history. The Pachaug River was a major fishing ground for the Mohegan tribe of Native Americans. Until blocked up by a dam, constructed in 1828 at Greenville, shad passed up the Quinebaug River in great numbers. Between 1711 and 1908, various mills were operated on the site; in 1711, a sawmill and cornmill were erected; in 1818 a woolen mill went up; later all of these were purchased by John Slater, and a satinet mill was added. He named the area Hope Mill, from which the name Hopeville was derived. Between 1881 and 1908, several fires destroyed the mills and most of the buildings in the area. The site's suitability for recreational activities was recognized in the 1930s when the federal government purchased considerable acreage in eastern Connecticut. These lands were managed by the Civilian Conservation Corps with evidence of much of the work done by the CCC still visible in the pine plantations, forest roads, and fire-control ponds. Hopeville Pond Campground offers 81 sites in a wooded setting that includes a dumping station, drinking water, and showers. Activities and services in the park include picnicking, freshwater fishing, swimming, boating, field sports, nature trail, hiking, clivus composters, mountain biking, concessions, paved parking, change houses, drinking water, and boat-launch ramp.

BASICS

Operated By: Connecticut Dept. Environmental Protection. **Open:** Apr. 20–Sept. 30. **Site Assignment:** Reservations must be made at least 2 days in advance. **Registration:** At office. **Fee:** Single, $13. **Parking:** At site.

FACILITIES

Number of Multipurpose Sites: 81. **Hookups:** None. **Dump Station:** Yes. **Laundry:** Yes. **Pay Phone:** Yes. **Restrooms and Showers:** Yes. **Fuel:**

No. **Propane:** No. **Internal Roads:** Paved. **RV Service:** No. **Market:** Yes. **Restaurant:** Yes. **General Store:** Yes. **Vending:** Yes. **Swimming:** Yes. **Playground:** No. **Activities:** Baseball, berry picking, biking, bird-watching, boating, canoeing, fishing, hiking, horseback riding, hunting, kayaking, scuba diving, softball, volleyball, wildlife viewing.

RESTRICTIONS

Pets: No pets allowed in campground. **Fires:** Permitted in designated fireplaces. **Alcoholic Beverages:** Beer in containers larger than 1 liter is not allowed. State law limits the possession of alcoholic beverages to individuals 21 years or older. **Vehicle Maximum Length:** Trailers & RVs exceeding 35 ft. in length are not permitted.

TO GET THERE

I-395 to Exit 86 to CT 201 east. At second stop sign take right and continue to follow CT 201. Campground is located approximately 1 mi. on the right.

KENT   MAP, B-1
Macedonia Brook State Park

159 Macedonia Brook Rd., 06757.
T: (860) 927-4100 or (877) 668-2267;
www.reserveamerica.com.

🚐 ★★★	▲ ★★★
Beauty: ★★★★	Site Privacy: ★★★★
Spaciousness: ★★★	Quiet: ★★★
Security: ★★★	Cleanliness: ★★★
Insect Control: ★★	Facilities: ★★★

If you don't mind roughing it and you love to hike, this huge state park is an excellent option for tent campers, or those in smaller or self-contained rigs. Sites are set in the woodlands, in the meadows, and at brookside here, where you'll feel surrounded by wilderness, even though the upscale pleasures of Litchfield County are a short drive away. Among the features here are two peaks, each nearly 1,400 feet in elevation. Climb a summit and enjoy wonderful views of the Catskills and Taconic ranges of New York State. If you like fishing, Macedonia Brook will surely tempt you. The brook, in fact, winds through the camping area, with several sites near the water. Site 27T (for tenting) is a pretty brookside spot. A couple of days of this, and you really won't mourn the lack of hot showers here (although you probably will once you're back in the car).

BASICS

Operated By: Connecticut Dept. of Environmental Protection, State Parks Division. **Open:** Apr. 14–Oct. 1. **Site Assignment:** Reserve by phone; 2-night minimum. **Registration:** At office. **Fee:** $11; reservation fee, $9; walk-in fee, $3. **Parking:** At site.

FACILITIES

Number of Multipurpose Sites: 51. **Hookups:** None. **Each Site:** Picnic table, fire ring. **Dump Station:** Yes. **Laundry:** No. **Pay Phone:** Yes. **Restrooms and Showers:** Yes, pit toilets/no showers. **Fuel:** No. **Propane:** No. **Internal Roads:**

Gravel (fair). **RV Service:** No. **Market:** In town. **Restaurant:** In town. **General Store:** No. **Vending:** No. **Swimming:** No. **Playground:** No. **Other:** Hiking trails, sports fields. **Activities:** Stream fishing, hiking, picnicking. **Nearby Attractions:** Appalachian Trail, White Memorial Conservation Center nature museum, antiquing. **Additional Information:** Litchfield Hills Visitors Bureau; (860) 567-4506; www.litchfieldhills.com.

RESTRICTIONS

Pets: Not allowed in campground, but permitted in picnic area on a leash. **Fires:** In fire rings only. **Alcoholic Beverages:** Not allowed. **Vehicle Maximum Length:** 35 ft. **Other:** 14-day stay limit.

TO GET THERE

From junction of US 7 and Hwy. 341, go 1.5 mi. northwest on Hwy. 341, then 2 mi. north on Macedonia Brook Rd.

LEBANON   MAP, B-3
Water's Edge Family Campground

271 Leonard Bridge Rd., 06249. T: (860) 642-7470 or (800) 828-6478 reservations; www.watersedgecampground.com.

🚐 ★★★★★	▲ ★★★★
Beauty: ★★★★	Site Privacy: ★★★★
Spaciousness: ★★★★	Quiet: ★★★★
Security: ★★★★★	Cleanliness: ★★★★
Insect Control: ★★★	Facilities: ★★★★★

This very pretty, well-maintained, and manicured campground surrounds a private, 10-acre lake. The clear, spring-fed waters are perfect for swimming, fishing (large bass between six and seven pounds have been caught from the lake), and boating (non-motorized). The campground offers paddleboat and rowboat rentals and a large sandy beach area, the perfect spot for hanging out on hot summer days. A roster of planned activities is offered throughout the season, popular with kids and adults alike. Sites are spacious and many are scattered around the edge of the pond. If you like to be in the woods, a little away from the action, consider sites 1–23, which are nicely spaced out and private.

BASICS

Operated By: Julie & Bob Korten. **Open:** Apr. 15–Oct. 15. **Site Assignment:** Reservations suggested; 2-night deposit; 2-week cancellation policy minus $5. V, MC, D, AE. **Registration:** At office. **Fee:** $32–$37. **Parking:** At site.

FACILITIES

Number of Multipurpose Sites: 180. **Hookups:** Electric (20, 30 amps), water, cable TV. **Each Site:** Picnic table, fire ring. **Dump Station:** Yes. **Laundry:** Yes. **Pay Phone:** Yes. **Restrooms and Showers:** Yes. **Fuel:** No. **Propane:** Yes. **Internal Roads:** Gravel (good). **RV Service:** No. **Market:** Willimantic & Norwich, 6 mi. **Restaurant:** New London, 5 mi. **General Store:** Yes. **Vending:** Yes. **Swimming:** Lake, pool. **Playground:** 2. **Other:** Lake frontage, beach, boat rentals, docks, arcade, sports fields, pavilion, cabin rentals. **Activities:** Swimming, boating,

fishing, basketball, horseshoes, planned activities, like arts & crafts, potluck dinners, contests, live entertainment, & dancing. **Nearby Attractions:** Swimming, boating, fishing, biking, hiking, Mystic, Foxwoods & Mohegan Sun casinos. **Additional Information:** Mystic Chamber of Commerce, 14 Holmes St., P.O. Box 143, Mystic, CT 06355, (860) 572-9578; Foxwoods Resort Casino, Hwy. 2 P.O. Box 3777, Mashantucket, CT 06338, www.foxwoods.com.

RESTRICTIONS

Pets: On leash only. Max. 2 pets per site. **Fires:** Fire pits, grills only. **Alcoholic Beverages:** At site.

TO GET THERE

From Hwy. 2 Exit 13, take Hwy. 66 East to Hwy. 85 South 1.5 mi. Turn left on Hwy. 207 to Leonard Bridge Rd.; campground is 0.5 mi. on the left.

LISBON   MAP, B-4
Ross Hill Park

170 Ross Hill Rd., 06351. T: (860) 376-9606 or (800) 308-1089; www.rosshillpark.com.

🚐 ★★★	▲ ★★★★
Beauty: ★★★	Site Privacy: ★★★
Spaciousness: ★★★	Quiet: ★★★
Security: ★★★★★	Cleanliness: ★★★★
Insect Control: ★★★	Facilities: ★★★★

This 50-acre campground in southeast Connecticut offers a nice blend of activities and amenities mixed with natural scenery and outdoor pursuits. You'll find pool tables and a snack bar but also a sandy beach circling a pretty swimming pond and frontage along the rippling waters of the Quinebaug River. The campground commands more than a half acre of prime river frontage, at the point where the river expands to create Aspinook Pond. There are pretty vistas off the ledges and rocks along the river, plus some great canoeing and kayaking. Boat rentals are available at the campground. A walk to Observation Rock overlooking Aspinook Pond is a must-do for campers. You'll have a choice of sites: both shaded and open are available. There are also several nice riverfront sites. Sites 90, 91A, 91B, and 91C sit out on a small promontory overlooking the river and are especially nice. But no matter where you stake your home away from home, you'll have plenty of elbow room here.

BASICS

Operated By: Gregory Pappas. **Open:** Apr.–Oct. **Site Assignment:** Reservations by phone; 50% deposit required w/ reservation. **Registration:** At office. **Fee:** Full hookup, $38; water/electric, $35; no hookup, $35; for 2 people; each additional person per night, $2. **Parking:** At site.

FACILITIES

Number of RV-only Sites: 12. **Number of Tent-only Sites:** 20. **Number of Multipurpose Sites:** 98. **Hookups:** Electric (30, 50 amps), water, sewer, cable TV. **Each Site:** Picnic table, fire ring. **Dump Station:** Yes. **Laundry:** Yes. **Pay Phone:** Yes. **Restrooms and Showers:** Yes. **Fuel:** No. **Propane:** Yes. **Internal Roads:** Gravel, dirt (fair). **RV Service:** No. **Market:** Yes. **Restaurant:** Snack bar on site. **General Store:** Yes. **Vending:** Yes.

Swimming: Pond w/ beach. **Playground:** Yes. **Other:** Safari field, cabin rentals, private pond, river frontage, rec hall, nature trails, boat rentals (canoes & kayaks). **Activities:** Swimming, fishing, hiking, boating, basketball, horseshoes, volleyball, baseball, planned activities like dances, arts & crafts, hay rides, contests, ceramics, scrapbooking. **Nearby Attractions:** Antiques shops, farms, hiking, biking, boating, fishing, Norwich, Foxwoods & Mohegan Sun casinos, Stonington, Mystic. **Additional Information:** Mystic Chamber of Commerce, 14 Holmes St., P.O. Box 143, Mystic, CT 06355, (860) 572-9578; Milford Chamber of Commerce, 5 Broad St., Milford, CT 06460, (203) 878-0681; www.milfordct.com.

RESTRICTIONS

Pets: On leash only. Valid rabies certification must be presented at check-in. Max. 2 pets per site. **Fires:** Fire pits, grills only. **Alcoholic Beverages:** At site.

TO GET THERE

From I-395 Exit 84, take Hwy. 12 north 0.5 mi. to Hwy. 138. Take a right on Hwy. 138, 0.5 mi. to Ross Hill Rd.; right 1 mi. to the campground.

LITCHFIELD   MAP, A-2
Hemlock Hill Camp Resort

P.O. Box 475, Hemlock Hill Rd., 06759. T: (860) 567-CAMP; www.hemlockhillcamp.com.

🚐 ★★★   ⛺ ★★★

Beauty: ★★★   Site Privacy: ★★★★
Spaciousness: ★★★   Quiet: ★★★★
Security: ★★★   Cleanliness: ★★★
Insect Control: ★★★   Facilities: ★★★

Located in the picture-postcard-pretty town of Litchfield in the northwest corner of Connecticut, this hilly campground is shaded with hemlock trees. It's a peaceful, rural setting, complete with a pond, meandering brook, and footbridge. Campsites are set in clusters around the pools, playground, and public areas. The choicest sites surround the pond (20–24A are nice), with tenters tucked in at the rear of the property, farthest back from the road. The pond is fishable and canoeable. They've also got a hot tub, perfect for soothing the muscles after a long trip or a long hike on the Appalachian Trail (nearby). Adding to the fun: a host of neighborly get-togethers, like potluck suppers. There are ownership sites at this park, so there's a fairly chummy group of regulars. It's not a super-fancy place, but it's friendly and low-key.

BASICS

Operated By: Private operator. **Open:** Apr. 28–Oct. 15. **Site Assignment:** Phone reservations accepted; 1-night deposit required; 50% deposit for stays of 3 days or more; $10 fee on all cancellations; 3-night minimum stay on holidays; 2-night minimum on weekends. **Registration:** At office. **Fee:** $33–$45. **Parking:** At site.

FACILITIES

Number of Multipurpose Sites: 140. **Hookups:** Electric (20, 30 amps), water. **Each Site:** Picnic table, fire ring. **Dump Station:** Yes. **Laundry:** Yes. **Pay Phone:** No. **Restrooms and Showers:** Yes, coin operated. **Fuel:** No. **Propane:** Yes. **Internal Roads:** Gravel (fair). **RV Service:** No. **Market:** 3.5 mi.

Restaurant: Litchfield, 3.5 mi. **General Store:** Yes. **Vending:** Yes. **Swimming:** 2 pools. **Playground:** Yes. **Other:** Rec room/pavilion, hot tub, sports field, arcade. **Activities:** Fishing (pond), hiking trails, basketball, volleyball, badminton, horseshoes, planned activities. **Nearby Attractions:** Appalachian Trail, White Memorial Conservation Center nature museum, antiquing. **Additional Information:** Litchfield Hills Visitors Bureau; (860) 567-4506; www.litchfieldhills.com.

RESTRICTIONS

Pets: On leash only; must be quiet, cleaned up after. Must not be left unattended. Vaccination papers required upon arrival. **Fires:** In fire rings only. **Alcoholic Beverages:** At site. **Vehicle Maximum Length:** 38 ft.

TO GET THERE

From junction of Hwy. 63 and US 202, go 0.75 mi. west on US 202, then 3 mi. north on Milton Rd. Then, head 1.25 mi. north on Maple, then 0.5 mi. east on Hemlock Hill Rd. Campground entrance is on the left.

LITCHFIELD   MAP, A-2
White Memorial Family Campground

P.O. Box 368, 80 Whitehall Rd., 06759. T: (860) 567-0857; www.whitememorialcc.org.

🚐 n/a   ⛺ ★★★★

Beauty: ★★★★   Site Privacy: ★★★
Spaciousness: ★★★   Quiet: ★★★
Security: ★★★★   Cleanliness: ★★★★
Insect Control: ★★★   Facilities: ★★★

Two family campgrounds (and one group camping area) here are part of a 4,000-acre wildlife refuge and environmental education center. The property includes a very good nature museum and more than 35 miles of multiuse trails plus an interpretive nature trail and a boardwalk—great for observing the rich bird life in the wetlands here. It's a pristine haven of fields, water, and woodlands. The two campgrounds here offer really different experiences: Windmill Hill is set in the woods and Point Folly's 47 sites are set on a peninsula in Bantam Lake. This spot is every bit as lovely as it sounds. Point Folly has a slightly longer season. If you don't luck into a camping spot, come back in the winter with your cross-country skis or snowshoes; this place is famous for its terrific Nordic ski trails.

BASICS

Operated By: White Memorial Foundation. **Open:** Early May–Columbus Day; fully operational Memorial Day–Labor Day. **Site Assignment:** Reservations recommended, but not accepted by phone (only by mail or in person; call for details); 14-day stay limit. **Registration:** At office. **Fee:** $12–$14.25 (Pt. Folly); $8.50 (Windmill Hill). **Parking:** At site.

FACILITIES

Number of Multipurpose Sites: 45. **Hookups:** None. **Each Site:** Picnic table, fire ring. **Dump Station:** Yes. **Laundry:** No. **Pay Phone:** Yes. **Restrooms and Showers:** Pit toilets, no showers.

Fuel: No. **Propane:** No. **Internal Roads:** Paved, gravel. **RV Service:** No. **Market:** In town, 3 mi. east. **Restaurant:** In town, 3 mi. east. **General Store:** Yes. **Vending:** No. **Swimming:** Lake. **Playground:** No. **Other:** Boat ramp. **Activities:** Lake swimming, boating, canoeing, lake fishing, hiking trails. **Nearby Attractions:** White Memorial Conservation Center nature museum, Topsmead State Park, antiquing, Appalachian Trail. **Additional Information:** Litchfield Hills Visitors Bureau; (860) 567-4506; www.litchfieldhills.com.

RESTRICTIONS

Pets: On leash only; must be quiet, cleaned up after. Must not be left unattended. **Fires:** In fire rings only. **Alcoholic Beverages:** Allowed. **Vehicle Maximum Length:** 28 ft.

TO GET THERE

Located off US 202 between Litchfield and Bantam, approximately 2 mi. west of Litchfield on Whitehall Rd.

MADISON   MAP, C-3
Hammonasset Beach State Park

reserve america

P.O. Box 271, 06443. T: (203) 245-1817 (summer) or (203) 245-2785 (winter); www.reserveamerica.com.

🚐 ★★★★   ⛺ ★★★★

Beauty: ★★★★★   Site Privacy: ★★★
Spaciousness: ★★★★   Quiet: ★★★
Security: ★★★   Cleanliness: ★★★
Insect Control: ★★★   Facilities: ★★★

More than a million people visit this huge oceanfront state park each year, making it one of Connecticut's most popular. It's no surprise: the park boasts more than 2 miles of ocean shoreline, with more than 900 surrounding acres. The beach is the big draw and can get super-crowded on summer weekends. Saltwater fishing (there's a carry-in boat launch) and birdwatching (look for herons, egrets, and hawks) are also popular. Both kids and adults enjoy the nature walks and programs offered at the Meigs Point Nature Center. Grassy sites are in the open, located away from the beach area. There's a walking/biking path from the campground to the beach.

BASICS

Operated By: State of Connecticut. **Open:** May–mid-Oct. **Site Assignment:** First-come, first-serve sites available; reservations may be made for campsites reserved Memorial Day–Labor Day; reservations must be made at least 2 days in advance & can be made as much as 11 months in advance. **Registration:** At office. **Fee:** $15; reservation fee, $9. **Parking:** At site.

FACILITIES

Number of Multipurpose Sites: 552. **Each Site:** Picnic table. **Dump Station:** Yes. **Laundry:** No. **Pay Phone:** Yes. **Restrooms and Showers:** Yes. **Fuel:** No. **Propane:** No. **Internal Roads:** Paved. **RV Service:** No. **Market:** Madison, 2 mi. **Restaurant:** Madison, 2 mi. **General Store:** Yes. **Vending:** Yes.

Swimming: Ocean beach. **Playground:** Yes. **Other:** Nature center, carry-in boat launch, picnic areas, pavilion, beach, boardwalk, nature trails, bathhouse. **Activities:** Swimming, fishing, boating, hiking, planned activities at the nature center. **Nearby Attractions:** Long Island Sound beaches, New Haven. **Additional Information:** The Greater New Haven CVB, 59 Elm St., New Haven, CT 06510, (203) 777-8550 or (800) 332-STAY, www.newhavencvb.org; Madison Town Visitor Information Center, 12 School St., Madison, CT 06443, (203) 245-5659.

RESTRICTIONS

Pets: Not allowed. **Fires:** Bring your own containers/grills or use community fireplaces. **Alcoholic Beverages:** Permitted. No boisterous behavior or profane language. If guests get out of control, they will be asked to leave.

TO GET THERE

From I-95 Exit 62, take a right off the exit and go approximately 1 mi. Go straight through the traffic light, crossing Hwy. 1 (Boston Post Rd.) into the park.

NEW PRESTON   MAP, B-1
Lake Waramaug State Park

reserve america

30 Lake Waramaug Rd., 06777. T: (860) 868-0220; www.reserveamerica.com.

🚐 ★★★   ⛺ ★★★★

Beauty: ★★★★	Site Privacy: ★★★
Spaciousness: ★★★	Quiet: ★★★
Security: ★★★	Cleanliness: ★★★
Insect Control: ★★	Facilities: ★★★

Lake Waramaug, tucked between two peaks (Mt. Bushnell and Above All Mountain) is one of Connecticut's most treasured beauty spots. It's a dazzling setting especially in autumn, when fiery trees are reflected in the mirror-like surface of the lake. Come in September and you'll get a taste of it, plus the summer crowds have gone home. Campsites are both wooded and open, with those lining the lake naturally the most desirable. (Site 9 is a favorite.) Keep in mind, though, that those spots closest to the lake are also the farthest from the restrooms! They offer ranger-led nature programs here and, happily, rent canoes and pedal boats for exploring the lake–an absolute must-do here. If that's not enough exercise for you, simply hike one of those peaks or have a go at the Connecticut portion of the Appalachian Trail (tougher than you'd think, in places).

BASICS

Operated By: Connecticut Dept. of Environmental Protection, State Parks Division. **Open:** Memorial Day weekend–Sept. 30. **Site Assignment:** Reservations recommended. **Registration:** At office. **Fee:** $13; reservation fee, $9; no credit cards; cash or checks only. **Parking:** At site.

FACILITIES

Number of Multipurpose Sites: 77. **Hookups:** None. **Each Site:** Picnic table, fire ring. **Dump Station:** Yes. **Laundry:** No. **Pay Phone:** Yes.

Restrooms and Showers: Yes. **Fuel:** No. **Propane:** No. **Internal Roads:** Paved, gravel. **RV Service:** No. **Market:** 5 mi. west. **Restaurant:** 5 mi. west. **General Store:** No; however, there is a concession stand. **Vending:** No. **Swimming:** Lake. **Playground:** No. **Other:** Pavilion, sports field. **Activities:** Fishing, lake swimming, boating, canoeing, hiking trails, nature programs. **Nearby Attractions:** Appalachian Trail, covered bridges, antiquing. **Additional Information:** Litchfield Hills Visitors Bureau; (860) 567-4506; www.litchfieldhills.com.

RESTRICTIONS

Pets: Not allowed. **Fires:** In fireplaces only. **Alcoholic Beverages:** W/ discretion. Beer in containers larger than 1 liter is not allowed. **Vehicle Maximum Length:** 35 ft.

TO GET THERE

From the junction of US 202 and Hwy. 45, go 1.5 mi. north on Hwy. 45 to Lake Waramaug, then follow signs around lake.

NIANTIC   MAP, B-3
Rocky Neck State Park

reserve america

244 West Main St. P.O. Box 676, 06357. T: (860) 739-5471; www.reserveamerica.com.

🚐 ★★★   ⛺ ★★★★

Beauty: ★★★★	Site Privacy: ★★★★
Spaciousness: ★★★★	Quiet: ★★★
Security: ★★★	Cleanliness: ★★★
Insect Control: ★★★	Facilities: ★★

This 700-acre oceanfront state park is a jewel, boasting woods, pristine marshlands, sand dunes, a rocky coastline, and sandy beach areas. Campers have access to prime oceanfront real estate—the smell of salty air and the feel of the cool ocean breezes—for ridiculously low state-park prices. Campsites are in the woods set in five major loops. There's a small nature center at the park, a web of hiking trails, and a lovely stone pavilion for group gatherings. Note that there are no on-site fire pits or grills, so you'll need to bring your own container or use the community fireplace at the campground. This is a great spot for bird-watching (look for great blue herons, osprey, and migrating shorebirds) and hanging out at the beach. The coastline views are great. Expect crowds at the day-use beach area on hot summer days, but campers have the advantage of rising early before the gangs arrive.

BASICS

Operated By: State of Connecticut. **Open:** Memorial Day–Sept. **Site Assignment:** First-come, first-serve sites available; reservations may be made for campsites reserved Memorial Day–Labor Day; reservations must be made at least 2 days in advance & can be made as much as 11 months in advance. **Registration:** At office. **Fee:** $15; processing fee for walk-ins, $3. **Parking:** At site.

FACILITIES

Number of Multipurpose Sites: 160. **Hookups:** No RV hookups. **Each Site:** Picnic table, fire ring.

Dump Station: Yes. **Laundry:** No. **Pay Phone:** Yes. **Restrooms and Showers:** Yes. **Fuel:** No. **Propane:** No. **Internal Roads:** Paved, gravel (good). **RV Service:** No. **Market:** Niantic, 3 mi. **Restaurant:** Niantic, 3 mi. **General Store:** No. **Vending:** No. **Swimming:** Ocean beach. **Playground:** No. **Other:** Pavilion, nature center, community fire pits, trails, oceanfront beach. **Activities:** Swimming, fishing, crabbing, hiking, biking, bird-watching. **Nearby Attractions:** Mystic, Norwich, Foxwoods & Mohegan Sun casinos, beaches. **Additional Information:** Mystic Shoreline Visitor's Information Center, Olde Mistick Village, Bldg. 1D, Mystic, CT 06355; (860) 536-1641; www.visitconnecticut.com/visitorscenter.

RESTRICTIONS

Pets: Allowed in picnic areas on the hiking trails, but not permitted in the campgrounds or on the beach. **Fires:** Fire pits, grills, community fire places. **Alcoholic Beverages:** Allowed if under 1 liter.

TO GET THERE

From I-91 Exit 22 to Hwy. 9 South or from I-95 East Exit 72.

NORTH STONINGTON   MAP, B-4
Highland Orchards Resort Park

Hwy. 49, P.O. Box 222, 06359. T: (800) 624-0829; www.highlandorchards.com.

🚐 ★★★★   ⛺ ★★★

Beauty: ★★★	Site Privacy: ★★★
Spaciousness: ★★★	Quiet: ★★★
Security: ★★★★★	Cleanliness: ★★★★★
Insect Control: ★★★	Facilities: ★★★★

Location, service, and convenience are the keys to this campground's success. Just off the highway in southeast Connecticut, the campground is minutes from Foxwoods and Mohegan Sun casinos, Mystic Seaport, and Connecticut and Rhode Island beaches. The large, 270-site property is dominated by RVs perched in rows in open fields. More than 250 years ago, this area was farmland, and the campground still has a rolling, open feel to it. Grassy sites are a bit cramped (average width is about 35 feet) and in the open, which only adds to the communal feel of the campground. The lounge, with a large fireplace, pavilion, and 10-acre event field are popular gathering spots. After a day of exploring area attractions, the two-pool complex is a welcome sight. There are a few planned activities on summer weekends, but most campers take advantage of the many festivals and events held in nearby towns throughout the summer.

BASICS

Operated By: Boissevain family. **Open:** Seasonal; call for winter availability. **Site Assignment:** Reservations suggested; 1-night deposit; 7-day cancellation policy minus $10; 3-day minimum stay on holidays, paid in advance; V, MC, D, AE; visitors must be registered, some fees & restrictions apply; 1 car per site, each site accommodates 2 adults & 2 children (age 16 & under). **Registration:** At office. **Fee:** Full hookup (50 amp), $55; full hookup (30 amp), $51; water/electric, $46; no hookup, $41; off-season rates are lower. **Parking:** At site.

FACILITIES

Number of Multipurpose Sites: 270. **Hookups:** Electric (30, 50 amps), water, sewer, cable TV, Wi-Fi. **Each Site:** Picnic table, fire ring. **Dump Station:** Yes. **Laundry:** Yes. **Pay Phone:** Yes. **Restrooms and Showers:** Yes. **Fuel:** No. **Propane:** Yes. **Internal Roads:** Paved, gravel (good). **RV Service:** Yes. **Market:** 5 mi. **Restaurant:** North Stonington, 5 mi. **General Store:** Yes. **Vending:** Yes. **Swimming:** Pool. **Playground:** Yes. **Other:** Lodge, pavilion, safari area, arcade, mini-golf, cabin & trailer rentals, fishing pond. **Activities:** Swimming, fishing, mini-golf, shuffleboard, horseshoes, volleyball, basketball. **Nearby Attractions:** Mystic, Foxwoods & Mohegan Sun casinos, beaches. **Additional Information:** Mystic Shoreline Visitor's Information Center, Olde Mistick Village, Bldg. 1D, Mystic, CT 06355; (860) 536-1641; www.visitconnecticut.com/visitorscenter.

RESTRICTIONS

Pets: On leash only; 1 pet per site. Each additional pet is charged a $4 fee. **Fires:** Fire pits, grills only. **Alcoholic Beverages:** At site. **Vehicle Maximum Length:** 45 ft.

TO GET THERE

From I-95 North Exit 92, go left on Hwy. 2, then right at Service Rd. to Hwy. 49. Take a left on Hwy. 49; the campground entrance is the first drive on the right.

OLD MYSTIC   MAP, B-4
Seaport Campground

Hwy. 184, P.O. Box 104, 06372. T: (860) 536-4044; www.seaportcampground.com.

🚐 ★★★★	🏕 ★★★
Beauty: ★★	Site Privacy: ★★★
Spaciousness: ★★★★	Quiet: ★★★
Security: ★★★★★	Cleanliness: ★★★★
Insect Control: ★★★	Facilities: ★★★★

Its close proximity to Mystic Seaport, one of southern New England's top attractions, is the big draw of this campground near the Connecticut shoreline. Cookie-cutter open sites are set in rows. But what they lack in personality they make up for in size. These sites are some of the largest we've seen in the area, averaging about 60 feet in width. Most campers use the property as a base for exploring local attractions, but there's plenty of recreation on site, too. Kids can dangle a line in the small fishing pond, splash around in the pool, or try a round of mini-golf. There's live entertainment on Saturday nights and a pavilion and large barbecue pit for group gatherings.

BASICS

Operated By: Joanna Oat & Robert Ranger. **Open:** Apr.–mid-Nov. **Site Assignment:** Reservations suggested; 1-night deposit; 14-day cancellation policy minus $10; 3-night minimum on holidays, paid in advance; V, MC. 30-night cancellation policy; fee for cancellations on holiday weekends. **Registration:** At office. **Fee:** Water/electric (30, 50 amp), $42; water/electric (20, 30 amp), $40; cable on all sites. **Parking:** At site (max. 2 cars per site).

FACILITIES

Number of Multipurpose Sites: 130. **Hookups:** Electric (20, 30, 50 amps), water, cable TV, Wi-Fi. **Each**

Site: Picnic table, fire ring. **Dump Station:** Yes, pump-out service is also available for a $4 fee. Dump station fee is included in base price. **Laundry:** Yes. **Pay Phone:** Yes. **Restrooms and Showers:** Yes. **Fuel:** No. **Propane:** Yes. **Internal Roads:** Gravel (good). **RV Service:** No. **Market:** Groton, 5 mi. **Restaurant:** Mystic, 0.5 mi. **General Store:** Yes. **Vending:** Yes. **Swimming:** Pool. **Playground:** Yes. **Other:** Fishing pond, mini-golf, pavilion, rec hall, group barbecue pit, arcade, sports fields, volleyball courts. **Activities:** Swimming, fishing, horseshoes, softball, mini-golf. **Nearby Attractions:** Mystic, Foxwoods & Mohegan Sun casinos, beaches. **Additional Information:** Mystic Shoreline Visitor's Information Center, Olde Mistick Village, Bldg. 1D, Mystic, CT 06355, (860) 536-1641; www.visitconnecticut.com/visitorscenter.

RESTRICTIONS

Pets: On leash only. 2 pets per site. First pet is free; second pet is $2/day. Vaccination papers required upon arrival. **Fires:** Fire pit, grills only. **Alcoholic Beverages:** At site.

TO GET THERE

From I-95 North Exit 89, take a left onto Allyn St., then a right onto Hwy. 184 (Goldstar Hwy.). The campground is 1 mi. on the left.

ONECO   MAP, B-4
River Bend Campground

reserve america

Hwy. 14A, P.O. Box 23, 06373. T: (860) 564-3440; www.riverbendcamp.com.

🚐 ★★★	🏕 ★★★
Beauty: ★★★	Site Privacy: ★★
Spaciousness: ★★	Quiet: ★★★
Security: ★★★	Cleanliness: ★★★
Insect Control: ★★★	Facilities: ★★★★

Kids, kids, and more kids. You better like 'em if you come to this family-friendly campground. All aboard! Here comes the mini-express train. Next up: archery lessons, gemstone panning, mini-golf, and then a dip in the pool. This activity-centered campground has some unique attractions, too, like the mounted wildlife exhibit (more than 40 animals) and the Lucky Strike Mine, where you can search for gems, fossils, and shells from around the world. There are sing-alongs with costumed characters, dances, tournaments, and more. The sites and the campground in general are crowded. To get away, rent a canoe or kayak and paddle Oneco Pond. If you head up the Moosup River, you can make a day of it.

BASICS

Operated By: Tony & Dolores Sinko. **Open:** Late Apr.–mid-Oct. **Site Assignment:** Reservations recommended; 1-night deposit; holiday weekends paid in advance; 10-day cancellation policy; V, MC; rates based on a family of 5 (2 adults & 3 children under 19 years old). **Registration:** At office. **Fee:** Full hookup, $42; water/electric, $39; no hookup, $30. **Parking:** At site.

FACILITIES

Number of Multipurpose Sites: 160. **Hookups:** Electric (30, 50 amps), water, sewer. **Each Site:** Picnic table, fire ring. **Dump Station:** Yes. **Laundry:** Yes.

Pay Phone: Yes. **Restrooms and Showers:** Yes. **Fuel:** No. **Propane:** Yes. **Internal Roads:** Gravel (good). **RV Service:** No. **Market:** Oneco, 1 mi. **Restaurant:** Oneco, 1 mi. **General Store:** Yes. **Vending:** Yes. **Swimming:** Pool. **Playground:** Yes. **Other:** Pond, boat rentals, dock, safari area, pavilion, mini-golf, natural wildlife museum, gemstone mining & panning, rec hall, cabin & trailer rentals. **Activities:** Swimming, boating, fishing, gemstone panning, archery, basketball, volleyball, tennis, horseshoes, planned activities like arts & crafts, contests, movies, hayrides, train rides. **Nearby Attractions:** Swimming, boating, hiking, biking, fishing, Mystic, Foxwoods. **Additional Information:** Mystic Chamber of Commerce, 14 Holmes St., P.O. Box 143, Mystic, CT 06355, (860) 572-9578; Milford Chamber of Commerce, 5 Broad St., Milford, CT 06460, (203) 878-0681, www.milfordct.com.

RESTRICTIONS

Pets: On leash only. Must present current vaccination records at check-in. Not allowed in rental units. **Fires:** Fire pits, grills, bonfire area. **Alcoholic Beverages:** At site. **Vehicle Maximum Length:** 36 ft.

TO GET THERE

From I-395 Exit 88, go east 5.5 mi. on Hwy. 14A to Oneco. Turn right at the River Bend sign just before the bridge.

PLEASANT VALLEY   MAP, A-2
American Legion State Forest (Hawes)

reserve america

West River Rd. (P.O. Box 1), 06063. T: (860) 379-0922; www.reserveamerica.com.

🚐 ★★★★	🏕 ★★★
Beauty: ★★★	Site Privacy: ★★★★
Spaciousness: ★★★★	Quiet: ★★★
Security: ★★★	Cleanliness: ★★★★
Insect Control: ★★★	Facilities: ★★★

American Legion State Forest covers roughly 900 acres in the town of Barkhamsted, on the west side of the West Branch of the Farmington River. The American Legion gave most of this forest to the state. The first deed was received in 1927 and the most recent acquisition was in 2004. The Civilian Conservation Corps established Camp White in the Forest in 1934, and the remnants are still visible in and around the present day Youth Group Camping Area. The C's made many improvements to the forest such as building the main access road in the Forest (Legion Road) and building firebreaks and trails. The Austin F. Hawes Memorial Campground provides 30 spacious and wooded campsites near the river. In 1994, this stretch of the West Branch of the Farmington River was designated by Congress as a Wild and Scenic River and is a center point for river-based activities. The forest is a mosaic of forest-tree species commonly found in northwest Connecticut. The slopes are steep, rugged, and rocky. In 1922 the entire area was burned over. It was reported that the residents of Pleasant Valley started to leave their homes as they expected the village would be lost to the fire. The forest is managed for saw timber, firewood, wildlife habitat, and recreational activities such as hiking, hunting, bird-watching, and camping.

BASICS

Operated By: Connecticut Dept. Environmental Protection. **Open:** Apr. 20–Oct. 8. **Site Assignment:** Reservations must be made at least 2 days in advance. **Registration:** At office. **Fee:** Single, $13. **Parking:** At site.

FACILITIES

Number of Multipurpose Sites: 30. **Hookups:** None. **Dump Station:** Yes. **Laundry:** No. **Pay Phone:** W/in 10 mi. **Restrooms and Showers:** Yes. **Fuel:** No. **Propane:** No. **Internal Roads:** Paved. **RV Service:** No. **Market:** W/in 10 mi. **Restaurant:** W/in 10 mi. **General Store:** W/in 10 mi. **Vending:** No. **Swimming:** Yes. **Playground:** No. **Activities:** Biking, bird-watching, canoeing, climbing, fishing, hunting, interpretive programs, kayaking, softball, tubing, wildlife viewing.

RESTRICTIONS

Pets: Pets are permitted at state forest campgrounds. Limited to one per site. Must be leashed. **Fires:** Permitted in designated fireplaces. **Alcoholic Beverages:** Beer in containers larger than 1 liter is not allowed. **Vehicle Maximum Length:** Trailers & RVs exceeding 35 ft. in length are not permitted.

TO GET THERE

From Hartford, take Hwy. 44 west to Hwy. 318 east in Barkhamsted. Take a left at the stop sign onto West River Rd. The campground is approximately 2 mi. on the right side.

POMFRET   MAP, A-4
Mashamoquet Brook State Park

reserve america

147 Wolf Den Dr., 06259. T: (860) 928-6121 or (877) 668-2267 (reservations); www.reserveamerica.com.

🚐 ★★★   ▲ ★★★★

Beauty: ★★★★	Site Privacy: ★★★★
Spaciousness: ★★★★	Quiet: ★★★
Security: ★★★	Cleanliness: ★★★★
Insect Control: ★★★	Facilities: ★★

This small, woodsy state-park campground, set along the Mashamoquet Brook, is best for campers who don't mind roughing it in exchange for peaceful surroundings. Mashamoquet is the Native American name for "stream of good fishing," and modern anglers can still take advantage of the fish-rich waters. There are decent swimming spots along the brook, too, and several nice picnic areas. Nature trails, accessible from the campground, criss-cross the 900 acres of forests and fields. Campsites are tucked into the woods for privacy, with lots of elbow room. Wolf Den state campground is next door and offers similar surroundings (but with flush toilets and hot showers).

BASICS

Operated By: State of Connecticut. **Open:** Mid-Apr.–mid-Oct. **Site Assignment:** First-come, first-serve sites available; reservations may be made for sites reserved Memorial Day–Labor Day; reservations must be made at least 2 days in advance & can be made as much as 11 months in advance. **Registration:** At office. **Fee:** $11; reservation fee, $9; walk-in processing fee, $3. **Parking:** At site.

FACILITIES

Number of Multipurpose Sites: 20. **Each Site:** Picnic table, fire ring. **Dump Station:** Yes. **Laundry:** No. **Pay Phone:** Yes. **Restrooms and Showers:** Flush toilets & showers. **Fuel:** No. **Propane:** No. **Internal Roads:** Gravel, dirt (good), some paved. **RV Service:** No. **Market:** 4.5 mi. in Dayville. **Restaurant:** 1.5 mi. **General Store:** No. **Vending:** No. **Swimming:** River, pond. **Playground:** No. **Other:** Nature trails, river frontage, open-sided stone lodge. **Activities:** Swimming, fishing, hiking. **Nearby Attractions:** Antiques shops, biking, fishing, boating, hiking, Woodstock. **Additional Information:** Town of Woodstock, 415 Hwy. 169, Woodstock, CT 06281; (860) 928-6595; www.townofwoodstock.com.

RESTRICTIONS

Pets: Not allowed. **Fires:** Fire pits, grills only. **Alcoholic Beverages:** Allowed, but only if kept under control. No boisterous behavior. **Vehicle Maximum Length:** 35 ft. **Other:** No glass.

TO GET THERE

From junction of Hwy. 44 and Hwy. 101, go west 1.5 mi. on Hwy. 44; campground is on the left.

POMFRET   MAP, A-4
Wolf Den Campground

147 Wolf Den Dr., 06259. T: (860) 928-6121; www.dep.state.ct.us/stateparks/parks/wolfden.htm.

🚐 ★★★   ▲ ★★★★

Beauty: ★★★★	Site Privacy: ★★★★
Spaciousness: ★★★★	Quiet: ★★★
Security: ★★★	Cleanliness: ★★★★
Insect Control: ★★★	Facilities: ★★

Despite the campground name, there are no wolves haunting the grounds, though there once were. (The ranger will be happy to share an interesting story on how the campground got its name.) You will find a loop of large private campgrounds, tucked into the woods. This campground is part of the Mashamoquet Brook State Park and features river frontage on the Mashamoquet Brook (with great fishing) and a network of hiking trails. Unlike the Mashamoquet campground next door, Wolf Den has flush toilets and hot showers. It's a nice option for campers who enjoy a natural, no-frills experience.

BASICS

Operated By: State of Connecticut. **Open:** Mid-Apr.–mid-Oct. **Site Assignment:** First-come, first-serve sites available; reservations may be made for campsites reserved Memorial Day–Labor Day; make reservations at least 2 days in advance & as much as 11 months in advance. **Registration:** At office. **Fee:** $11; reservation fee, $9; walk-in fee, $3. **Parking:** At site.

FACILITIES

Number of Multipurpose Sites: 35. **Each Site:** Picnic table, fire ring. **Dump Station:** Yes. **Laundry:** No. **Pay Phone:** Yes. **Restrooms and Showers:** Yes. **Fuel:** No. **Propane:** No. **Internal Roads:** Gravel, dirt (good); Some paved. **RV Service:** No. **Market:** 4.5 mi. in Dayville. **Restaurant:** 1.5 mi. **General Store:** No. **Vending:** No. **Swimming:** River, pond. **Playground:** No. **Other:** Nature trails. **Activities:** Swimming, fishing, hiking. **Nearby Attractions:** Antiques shops, biking, fishing, boating, hiking, Woodstock. **Additional Information:** Town of Woodstock, 415 Hwy. 169, Woodstock, CT 06281; (860) 928-6595; www.townofwoodstock.com.

RESTRICTIONS

Pets: Not allowed. **Fires:** Fire pits, grills only. **Alcoholic Beverages:** Allowed if kept under control. No boisterous behavior. **Vehicle Maximum Length:** 35 ft. **Other:** No glass.

TO GET THERE

From junction of Hwy. 44 and Hwy. 101, go west 1.5 mi. on Hwy. 44; campground is on the left.

POMFRET CENTER   MAP, A-4
Mashamoquet Brook State Park

reserve america

147 Wolf Den Dr., 06259. T: (860) 928-6121; www.reserveamerica.com.

🚐 ★★★★   ▲ ★★★★

Beauty: ★★★★	Site Privacy: ★★
Spaciousness: ★★★	Quiet: ★★★★
Security: ★★★★	Cleanliness: ★★★★
Insect Control: ★★★	Facilities: ★★★★

Mashamoquet Brook State Park consists of 1,000 acres and is located in Pomfret. The present park was formed by combining three parks: Mashamoquet Brook, Wolf Den, and Saptree Run. An interesting trail system provides access to the various areas and features of the park. The most famous of the park features is the Wolf Den into which, on a night in 1742, Israel Putnam crept and shot a wolf that for years had preyed upon local sheep and poultry. The same Israel Putnam was later to gain fame as a major general in the Continental Army during the Revolutionary War. Near the Den are the Table Rock and Indian Chair stone formations. Activities and services in the park include picnicking, fishing, swimming, field sports, drinking water, concession, picnic shelter and camping at two different areas. The Mashamoquet Brook Campground contains 19 wooded campsites with outhouses, drinking water and a nearby dumping station. The Wolf Den Field campground contains 35 mostly open campsites with flush toilets, showers, drinking water, and dumping station.

BASICS

Operated By: Connecticut Dept. Environmental Protection. **Open:** Apr. 20–Oct. 1. **Site Assignment:** Reservations must be made at least 2 days in advance. **Registration:** At office. **Fee:** Single, $11. **Parking:** At site.

FACILITIES

Number of Multipurpose Sites: 54. **Hookups:** None. **Dump Station:** Yes. **Laundry:** W/in 10 mi. **Pay Phone:** Yes. **Restrooms and Showers:** Yes. **Fuel:** No. **Propane:** No. **Internal Roads:** Paved. **RV Service:** No. **Market:** W/in 10 mi. **Restaurant:** W/in 10 mi. **General Store:** W/in 10 mi. **Vending:** No. **Swimming:** Yes. **Playground:** No. **Activities:** Picking, biking, bird-watching, fishing, hiking, photography, walking, wildlife viewing.

RESTRICTIONS

Pets: No pets allowed in campground. **Fires:** Permitted in designated fireplaces. **Alcoholic Beverages:** Beer in containers larger than 1 liter is not allowed. State law limits the possession of alcoholic beverages to individuals 21 years or older. **Vehicle Maximum Length:** Trailers & RVs exceeding 35 ft. in length are not permitted.

TO GET THERE

Travel west on Hwy. 101 through Dayville until it ends at Hwy. 44 in Pomfret. Continue straight ahead onto Hwy. 44 west approximately 1 mi. Mashamoquet Brook State Park is on the left.

PRESTON
Hidden Acres
MAP, B-4

47 River Rd., 06365. T: (860) 887-9633; www.hiddenacrescamp.com.

🚐 ★★★	⛺ ★★★★
Beauty: ★★★	Site Privacy: ★★★
Spaciousness: ★★★	Quiet: ★★★
Security: ★★★	Cleanliness: ★★★
Insect Control: ★★★	Facilities: ★★★★

"Sufferin' succotash, we're finally there!" announces the cute sign at the entrance. Three wooden, log cabin–style buildings housing the store, a TV room, and a crafts shop cluster around the entrance. A handwritten wooden sign tells us that there are worms for sale. A strutting peacock greets us when we step out of the car. We notice a pen full of roosters, goats, and sheep and a gaggle of kids petting them. Welcome to Hidden Acres, an old-fashioned, laid-back campground, reminiscent of days gone by. The campground is nestled on the Quinebaug River with a small beach area. Floating the river is a popular pastime, as are the many planned, kid-friendly activities. This cluttered campground can get quite busy and a bit noisy. Families, especially those who appreciate old-style camping, don't seem to mind. River sites are the most spacious and scenic. Sites 8–15 are best for tenters or small pop-up campers (there are no hookups on these sites), and sites 40–50 offer water and electric hookups and river views.

BASICS

Operated By: Migliaccio family. **Open:** May–Columbus Day. **Site Assignment:** Reservations accepted; 1-night deposit; 30-day notice required for refunds; 7-day notice required for credit. **Registration:** At main office. **Fee:** Full hookup, $35; water/electric, $36; no hookup, $28; extra fee for riverfront sites, $5. **Parking:** At site.

FACILITIES

Number of RV-only Sites: 15. **Number of Tent-only Sites:** 20. **Number of Multipurpose Sites:** 145. **Hookups:** Electric (15, 50 amps), water, sewer. **Each Site:** Picnic table, fire ring. **Dump Station:** Yes. **Laundry:** Yes. **Pay Phone:** Yes. **Restrooms and Showers:** Yes (coin-op). **Fuel:** No. **Propane:** Yes. **Internal Roads:** Gravel, dirt (good). **RV Service:** No. **Market:** Preston, 4 mi. **Restaurant:** Snack bar on site. **General Store:** Yes. **Vending:** Yes. **Swimming:** Pool, river, pond. **Playground:** Yes. **Other:** Rec hall, petting farm, river & pond frontage, movie house, sports fields, cabin & trailer rentals, safari area, crafts shop. **Activities:** Swimming, fishing, tubing, shuffleboard, horseshoes, softball, basketball, badminton, dancing, planned activities like hayrides, arts & crafts, contests. **Nearby Attractions:** Farms, swimming, hiking, biking, boating, fishing, Mystic, Norwich, Foxwoods & Mohegan Sun casinos. **Additional Information:** Mystic Chamber of Commerce, 14 Holmes St., P.O. Box 143, Mystic, CT 06355, (860) 572-9578; Foxwoods Resort Casino, Hwy. 2, P.O. Box 3777, Mashantucket, CT 06338, www.foxwoods.com.

RESTRICTIONS

Pets: On leash only. **Fires:** Fire pits, grills only. **Alcoholic Beverages:** At site. **Vehicle Maximum Length:** 35 ft.

TO GET THERE

From I-395 Exit 85, take Hwy. 164 1 mi. south to George Palmer Rd. Turn right on George Palmer Rd. and drive 3 mi. to the campground.

PRESTON
Strawberry Park Resort
Campground
MAP, B-4

42 Pierce Rd., 06365. T: (860) 886-1944 or (888) 794-7944; www.strawberrypark.net.

🚐 ★★★★★	⛺ ★★★★
Beauty: ★★★	Site Privacy: ★★★
Spaciousness: ★★★	Quiet: ★★★
Security: ★★★★★	Cleanliness: ★★★★★
Insect Control: ★★★	Facilities: ★★★★★

This top-notch, highly rated campground in southeast Connecticut is a true vacation destination with all the amenities and activities of a bustling resort. You name it and they have it at this action-packed, family-friendly campground that's been around for three decades—and it just keeps getting better. It will take you awhile to read through all the activities and events offered throughout the summer, much less participate in them! Some of the kid's activities include horseback riding, pony rides, arts and crafts, sports camps, contests, and story hours. There are also plenty of adult and teen activities, from dances to tournaments. Several times a year, the campground hosts major music festivals, with live bands, special dinners, and events. The three-pool complex is a hot spot, with a diving pool, a large (all ages) pool, and a special kiddy pool. There's also a spa and sauna reserved for adult

campers. Don't feel like cooking? Head to the on-site restaurant for breakfast, lunch, or dinner. Who said camping was roughing it? Not at this super-deluxe resort!

BASICS

Operated By: Buck Biber. **Open:** All year; limited facilities in winter. **Site Assignment:** Reservations are strongly suggested; reservations for spring & summer stay of 7 days or longer are accepted beginning Jan. for upcoming camping season; reservations for summer stays less than 7 nights can be made 2 months in advance; 2-night minimum (3 nights on holidays) & no Sat. arrivals or departures can be reserved; 1-night stays w/o reservations are welcome; weekend reservations must be paid in full; midweek stays (2–5 nights, not including a weekend) require $100 deposit; week or longer, $200; 7-day cancellation policy; cancellations made less than 30 days but at least 7 days receive a credit for future stay minus $20. **Registration:** At office. **Fee:** Weekday, $25; weekly (5 nights), $25 plus additional weekend fee depending on specific weekend & events. Additional weekend rates run from $34 (no hookups, early spring) to $222 (full hookups, July 4 holiday). **Parking:** At site.

FACILITIES

Number of Multipurpose Sites: 500. **Hookups:** Electric (20, 30, 50 amps), water, sewer, cable TV, Wi-Fi. **Each Site:** Picnic table, fire ring. **Dump Station:** Yes. Pump-out service & trash service. **Laundry:** Yes. **Pay Phone:** Yes. **Restrooms and Showers:** Yes. **Fuel:** No. **Propane:** Yes. **Internal Roads:** Gravel, paved (good). **RV Service:** Yes. **Market:** Preston City, 1 mi. **Restaurant:** On-site. **General Store:** Yes. **Vending:** Yes. **Swimming:** 3 pools. **Playground:** Yes. **Other:** Spa, sauna, game room, adult rec center, amphitheater, dance floors, sports fields, trailer rentals, entertainment, hot tub. **Activities:** Horseback riding, softball, basketball, horseshoes, volleyball, swimming, washer toss, soccer, shuffleboard, bocce, sports camps, planned events & activities like classes, contests, golf, music festivals. **Nearby Attractions:** Farms, swimming, hiking, biking, boating, fishing, Norwich, Mystic, Foxwoods & Mohegan Sun casinos. **Additional Information:** Mystic Chamber of Commerce, 14 Holmes St., P.O. Box 143, Mystic, CT 06355, (860) 572-9578; Foxwoods Resort Casino, Hwy. 2 P.O. Box 3777, Mashantucket, CT 06338, www.foxwoods.com.

RESTRICTIONS

Pets: Must remain at site. No walking or carrying pets around the campground. Certain breeds not allowed. Dog park is available to all guests. **Fires:** Fire pits, grills only. **Alcoholic Beverages:** At site. **Vehicle Maximum Length:** 50 ft. **Other:** No skateboards.

TO GET THERE

From I-395 Exit 85, take Hwy. 164 4 mi. south to Hwy. 165. Campground is 1 mi. east on Hwy. 165.

SHARON   MAP, A-1
Housatonic Meadows State Park

reserve **america**

US 7, 06757. T: (860) 927-3238 or (877) 668-2267 (reservations); www.reserveamerica.com.

🚐 ★★   ▲ ★★★

Beauty: ★★★	Site Privacy: ★★★★
Spaciousness: ★★★	Quiet: ★★★
Security: ★★★	Cleanliness: ★★★
Insect Control: ★★	Facilities: ★★★

Located in the scenic valley of the Housatonic River amid the rugged hills of northwestern Connecticut, this campground is a delicious slice of wilderness. The surrounding towns showcase covered bridges, white-steepled churches, and antiques. It's all about unspoiled nature. Fly-fishing enthusiasts have discovered this park, beckoned by the clear, cold water of the Housatonic. A 2-mile stretch of river (including the park's shoreline) is limited to fly fishing. Sites are set under tall trees on the riverbanks, and they couldn't be prettier. Some are grass; some are gravelly. Everybody wants a site right on the river, of course, and the spots that are near water, but also farthest from Route 7 traffic are 18–24. Sites 1–24 are considered the riverside area. We'd steer clear of 92–97 and 76–81 if you're tenting due to proximity to the roadway.

BASICS

Operated By: Connecticut Dept. of Environmental Protection, State Parks Division. **Open:** Mid-Apr.–Dec. **Site Assignment:** Reserve in advance; no reservations taken after Sept. 1 when campground is first come, first served. **Registration:** At office. **Fee:** $13; reservation fee, $9; processing fee for walk-ins, $3. **Parking:** At site.

FACILITIES

Hookups: None. **Each Site:** Picnic table, fire ring. **Dump Station:** Yes. **Laundry:** No. **Pay Phone:** Yes. **Restrooms and Showers:** Yes. **Fuel:** No. **Propane:** No. **Internal Roads:** Paved. **RV Service:** No. **Market:** 3 mi. north. **Restaurant:** 3 mi. north. **General Store:** No. **Vending:** No. **Swimming:** No. **Playground:** No. **Activities:** Fly fishing, canoeing, hiking trails. **Nearby Attractions:** Covered bridges, Appalachian Trail, Sharon Audubon Center. **Additional Information:** Litchfield Hills Visitors Bureau; (860) 567-4506; www.litchfieldhills.com.

RESTRICTIONS

Pets: Not allowed. **Fires:** In fire rings only. **Alcoholic Beverages:** Not allowed. **Vehicle Maximum Length:** 35 ft. **Other:** 14-day stay limit.

TO GET THERE

From junction of US 7 and Hwy. 4, go 2 mi. north on US 7. Campground is located on the right (east) side of US 7.

SOUTHBURY   MAP, B-2
Kettletown State Park

reserve **america**

1400 Georges Hill Rd., 06488. T: (203) 264-5169; www.reserveamerica.com.

🚐 ★★★★   ▲ ★★★★

Beauty: ★★★	Site Privacy: ★★★★
Spaciousness: ★★★★	Quiet: ★★★★
Security: ★★★★	Cleanliness: ★★★★
Insect Control: ★★★	Facilities: ★★★★

With opportunities for swimming, picnicking, fishing, and hiking, Kettletown State Park in Southbury ensures a wonderful afternoon or weekend for anyone who loves the outdoors. The main attraction here, however, is camping. Kettletown offers 68 camping sites in open and wooded settings, each equipped with a picnic table and fire pit. Day visitors can also enjoy the variety of recreational activities Kettletown offers. People can be found sunbathing on the shores of Lake Zoar or taking a dip in the cool water on a warm sunny day. No matter what time of day it is, fishermen can be seen baiting and casting their hooks. Hikers have numerous trails to choose from, each with breathtakingly scenic lake views. Picnic areas are also located throughout the hiking trails and around Lake Zoar. Legend has it that the name Kettletown refers to a great trade that took place in 1758 between early colonists and the Pootatuck tribe of Native Americans who inhabited the area currently occupied by Kettletown State Park. According to the Connecticut state parks and forests Web site, early settling colonists traded one brass kettle to the Native Americans for use of the land to fish and hunt on. Eventually, the settlers acquired all of the land after the Pootatucks either migrated north or died. Occasionally, an arrowhead of the Pootatucks can be found on the hiking trails or the woods located directly behind some of the campsites.

BASICS

Operated By: Connecticut Dept. Environmental Protection. **Open:** May 18–Sept. 30. **Site Assignment:** Reservations must be made at least 2 days in advance. **Registration:** At office. **Fee:** Single, $13. **Parking:** At site.

FACILITIES

Number of Multipurpose Sites: 68. **Hookups:** None. **Dump Station:** Yes. **Laundry:** W/in 10 mi. **Pay Phone:** Yes. **Restrooms and Showers:** Yes. **Fuel:** No. **Propane:** No. **Internal Roads:** Paved. **RV Service:** No. **Market:** W/in 10 mi. **Restaurant:** W/in 10 mi. **General Store:** No. **Vending:** No. **Swimming:** Yes. **Playground:** No. **Activities:** Beachcombing, biking, bird-watching, boating, hiking, photography, wildlife viewing.

RESTRICTIONS

Pets: No pets allowed in campground. **Fires:** Permitted in designated fireplaces. **Alcoholic Beverages:** Beer in containers larger than 1 liter is not allowed. State law limits the possession of alcoholic

beverages to individuals 21 years or older. **Vehicle Maximum Length:** Trailers & RVs exceeding 35 ft. in length are not permitted.

TO GET THERE

Exit 15 off I-84, south onto CT 67. Take a right at first traffic light onto Kettletown Rd. Continue approximately 3 mi. on Kettletown Rd. Take a right onto Georges Hill Rd. Park is located on left approximately 0.6 mi.

VOLUNTOWN   MAP, B-4
Circle C Campground

reserve **america**

21 Bailey Rd., 06384. T: (800) 424-4534; www.campcirclec.com.

🚐 ★★★   ▲ ★★★

Beauty: ★★★	Site Privacy: ★★★
Spaciousness: ★★★	Quiet: ★★★★
Security: ★★★★★	Cleanliness: ★★★★
Insect Control: ★★★	Facilities: ★★★

"It better be worth it," we mumbled to ourselves on the way to this campground. We drove the skinny, two-lane blacktop roads, winding through rolling farmlands and forests. In truth, the campground is only about 5 miles off Hwy. 49; it just seems farther as you travel the backcountry roads. This rural campground is a quiet oasis, nestled on the shores of 80-acre Bailey Pond. The pond is a great fishing and boating spot. Boat rentals are available through the campground office and there's a launch and dock for campers who tow their own watercraft (which many regular guests tend to do). Also on the property is a swimming pond and another small, kid-friendly fishing pond. There are some seasonals at the campground, but they're contained in a separate area. The sites are a bit cramped for our taste, and most offer little privacy. Tent sites are located in an open field overlooking Bailey's Pond.

BASICS

Operated By: John & Jeannette Richard. **Open:** Late Apr.–Columbus Day. **Site Assignment:** Reservations suggested; 1-night deposit; holiday weekends (3-night minimum) paid in full; 15-day cancellation policy minus $3; V, MC, D. **Registration:** At office. **Fee:** Water/electric, $31; no hookup, $27. **Parking:** At site.

FACILITIES

Number of RV-only Sites: 4. **Number of Multipurpose Sites:** 114. **Hookups:** Electric (30, 50 amps), water. **Each Site:** Picnic table, fire ring. **Dump Station:** Yes. **Laundry:** Yes. **Pay Phone:** Yes. **Restrooms and Showers:** Yes. **Fuel:** No. **Propane:** Yes. **Internal Roads:** Gravel (good). **RV Service:** No. **Market:** Voluntown, 10 mi. **Restaurant:** Voluntown, 6 mi. **General Store:** Yes. **Vending:** No. **Swimming:** Pond. **Playground:** Yes. **Other:** Mini-golf, ponds, arcade, rec hall, adult lounge. **Activities:** Swimming, fishing, boating, horseshoes, volleyball, basketball, planned activities like arts

& crafts, potluck dinners, dances, contests. **Nearby Attractions:** Biking, hiking, boating, fishing, Mystic, Foxwoods & Mohegan Sun casinos. **Additional Information:** Mystic Chamber of Commerce, 14 Holmes St., P.O. Box 143, Mystic, CT 06355, (860) 572-9578; Milford Chamber of Commerce, 5 Broad St., Milford, CT 06460, (203) 878-0681, www.milfordct.com.

RESTRICTIONS

Pets: On leash only; vaccination papers required. **Fires:** Fire pits, grills only. **Alcoholic Beverages:** At site.

TO GET THERE

Take I-395 Exit 85 to Hwy. 138 East. Go left on Hwy. 49 North 2.5 mi. to Brown Rd.; turn right and follow to end. Turn right on Gallup Homestead Rd. to end, then right on Bailey Pond Rd.

VOLUNTOWN   MAP, B-4
Nature's Campsites

96 Ekonk Hill Rd., 06384. T: (860) 376-4203; www.naturescampsites.com.

🚐 ★★★★★   ⛺ ★★★★★

Beauty: ★★★★   Site Privacy: ★★★★
Spaciousness: ★★★★★   Quiet: ★★★
Security: ★★★★★   Cleanliness: ★★★★
Insect Control: ★★★   Facilities: ★★★★

This campground is one of Connecticut's finest, offering a plethora of activities, facilities, space, natural beauty, and a friendly, rural atmosphere. The property rolls through pine woods and fields along the scenic Pachaug River and two pretty ponds. Anglers will appreciate the state-stocked Pachaug, known for its bass and trout fishing. There's also fishing on Beachdale Pond and an additional two fishing ponds for children to cast a line. Many campers spend a morning or afternoon paddling the river; canoe rentals are available at the campground. Near the front entrance of the campground is a two-pool complex and bathhouse area, a popular gathering spot. There are sports fields and playgrounds and lots of planned activities offered throughout the summer. Sites are super-large and private, with a choice of open or shaded spots. There are sites along the river (R31 and R32 are exceptionally nice), flanking the ponds, and in the woods. You really can't go wrong with any site; they're all lovely.

BASICS

Operated By: Lazourack family. **Open:** May–Oct. 15. **Site Assignment:** Reservations suggested; 1-night deposit; holidays (3-day minimum) paid in full; V, MC, D, AE. **Registration:** At office. **Fee:** Full hookup, $45; water/electric, $40; no hookup, $34. **Parking:** At site.

FACILITIES

Number of Multipurpose Sites: 150. **Hookups:** Electric (20, 30 amps), water, sewer; 2 50-amp sites available. **Each Site:** Picnic table, fire ring. **Dump Station:** Yes. **Laundry:** Yes. **Pay Phone:** No. **Restrooms and Showers:** Yes. **Fuel:** No. **Propane:** Yes. **Internal Roads:** Gravel (fair). **RV**

Service: No. **Market:** Voluntown, 1 mi. **Restaurant:** Voluntown, 1 mi. **General Store:** Yes. **Vending:** Yes. **Swimming:** 2 pools, river. **Playground:** Yes. **Other:** Arcade, river frontage, fishing ponds, pavilion, safari area, rec hall, canoe rentals, cabin rentals. **Activities:** Swimming, fishing, boating, bocce, horseshoes, shuffleboard, volleyball, basketball, paintball, planned activities: hayrides, dances, tournaments, potluck parties. **Nearby Attractions:** Fishing, hiking, Mystic, Foxwoods & Mohegan Sun casinos. **Additional Information:** Mystic Chamber of Commerce, 14 Holmes St., P.O. Box 143, Mystic, CT 06355, (860) 572-9578; Milford Chamber of Commerce, 5 Broad St., Milford, CT 06460, (203) 878-0681; www.milfordct.com.

RESTRICTIONS

Pets: On leash only. 1 pet per site. Vaccination papers required upon arrival. **Fires:** Fire pits, grills only. **Alcoholic Beverages:** At site.

TO GET THERE

From I-395 Exit 85, follow Hwy. 138 6 mi. to Voluntown, then left onto Hwy. 49 north 0.5 mi.

WATERTOWN   MAP, B-2
Black Rock State Park

Watertown Rd., US 6, 06759. T: (860) 283-8088; www.reserveamerica.com.

🚐 ★★★   ⛺ ★★★

Beauty: ★★★   Site Privacy: ★★★
Spaciousness: ★★★   Quiet: ★★★
Security: ★★★   Cleanliness: ★★★
Insect Control: ★★   Facilities: ★★★

The name Black Rock refers to the local granite deposits here, where the backdrop is the western highlands of Connecticut, laced with brooks and streams. Sites here, wooded and open, are set in six loops, clustered around Black Rock Pond and Branch Brook. The "T" lots, 37–43 are nice, as are 76–96, near the brook. Sites are a mixture of grass and gravel. This campground is a real mecca for hikers; the blue-blazed Mattatuck Trail connects the park with the woodlands of Mattatuck State Forest. Always spectacular, it's especially inviting in late September, when the surrounding hillsides are ablaze in vivid color.

BASICS

Operated By: Connecticut Dept. of Environmental Protection, State Parks Division. **Open:** Mid-Apr.–Sept. 30. **Site Assignment:** Reserve in advance; no reservations after Sept. 1, when campground is first come, first served. **Registration:** At office. **Fee:** $13; reservation fee, $9; no credit cards; cash or checks only. **Parking:** At site.

FACILITIES

Number of Multipurpose Sites: 96. **Hookups:** None. **Each Site:** Picnic table, fire ring. **Dump Station:** Yes. **Laundry:** No. **Pay Phone:** No. **Restrooms and Showers:** Yes. **Fuel:** No.

Propane: No. **Internal Roads:** Paved. **RV Service:** No. **Market:** 3 mi. south in Thomaston. **Restaurant:** Snack bar on site. **General Store:** Yes. **Vending:** No. **Swimming:** Pond. **Playground:** No. **Other:** Sports field. **Activities:** Pond swimming, stream fishing, hiking trails, nature programs. **Nearby Attractions:** Mattatuck Museum, Timexpo Museum, Naugatuck Railroad & Railroad Museum of New England. **Additional Information:** Waterbury Region CVB; (203) 597-9539 or (888) 588-7880; www.waterburyregion.com.

RESTRICTIONS

Pets: Not allowed. **Fires:** In fire rings only. **Alcoholic Beverages:** Not allowed. **Vehicle Maximum Length:** 35 ft. **Other:** 14-day stay limit.

TO GET THERE

Take Exit 38 off Hwy. 8 North. Turn left at end of ramp to first traffic light. Take left to US 6 West. Park entrance is 0.5 mi. on right of US 6.

WEST WILLINGTON   MAP, A-2
Moose Meadow

P.O. Box 38, 06279. T: (860) 429-7451; www.moosemeadow.com.

🚐 ★★★★   ⛺ ★★★★

Beauty: ★★★★   Site Privacy: ★★★★
Spaciousness: ★★★★   Quiet: ★★★
Security: ★★★   Cleanliness: ★★★★★
Insect Control: ★★★   Facilities: ★★★★★

Want to get away from it all but don't want to give up your creature comforts? This campground, just off the highway in northeast Connecticut, could be what you're looking for. On the way in, you'll pass fields with grazing cows. It's a pleasant entrance to this rural, 53-acre campground, which is surrounded by pine-covered hills. The campground has a relaxed, family-friendly appeal, with lots of repeat business. A full-time recreation director plans a roster of ongoing activities for children and adults. There's mini-golf and a tennis court, fishing ponds, and river frontage, as well as a large heated pool. Campsites are generously situated. If you want to be away from the action, check out the in-the-woods sites 105–113. Families tend to congregate along the row-by-row pool-area sites.

BASICS

Operated By: Hasapes family. **Open:** Mid-Apr.–mid-Oct. **Site Assignment:** Reservations accepted; 1-night deposit; 2-week cancellation policy; V, MC. **Registration:** At office. **Fee:** Full hookup, $41; water/electric, $35; no hookup, $28. **Parking:** At site.

FACILITIES

Number of Multipurpose Sites: 150. **Hookups:** Electric (20, 30 amps), water, sewer, cable TV. **Each Site:** Picnic table, fire ring. **Dump Station:** Yes. **Laundry:** Yes. **Pay Phone:** No. **Restrooms and Showers:** Yes. **Fuel:** No. **Propane:** Yes. **Internal Roads:** Gravel (good). **RV Service:** No. **Market:** Willington, 4 mi. **Restaurant:** Willington, 4 mi. **General Store:** Yes. **Vending:** Yes. **Swimming:** Pool.

Playground: Yes. **Other:** Fishing pond, river frontage, sports fields, mini-golf, pavilion, tennis court, safari field, cabin rentals, Internet access. **Activities:** Swimming, fishing, mini-golf, volleyball, shuffleboard, horseshoes, softball. **Nearby Attractions:** Farms, antiques shops, hiking, biking, boating, fishing, swimming, University of Connecticut, Woodstock. **Additional Information:** Town of Woodstock, 415 Hwy. 169, Woodstock, CT 06281, (860) 928-6595, www.townofwoodstock.com. Northeast Connecticut Visitors District, 13 Canterbury Rd., Suite 3, P.O. Box 145, Brooklyn, CT 06234-0145, (860) 779-6383, www.ctquietcorner.org.

RESTRICTIONS

Pets: On leash only. **Fires:** Fire pits, grills only. **Alcoholic Beverages:** At site. **Vehicle Maximum Length:** 50 ft.

TO GET THERE

From I-84 Exit 69, take Hwy. 74 4 mi. At the blinking yellow light, turn left onto Moosemeadow Rd.; campground is 1.5 mi. on the left.

WOODSTOCK MAP, A-4
Beaver Pines Campground

1728 Hwy. 198, 06281. T: (860) 974-0110; www.beaverpinescampground.com.

🚐 ★★★   ⛺ ★★★★

Beauty: ★★★	Site Privacy: ★★★★★
Spaciousness: ★★★★★	Quiet: ★★★★
Security: ★★★★★	Cleanliness: ★★★★★
Insect Control: ★★★	Facilities: ★★★

Tenters and nature lovers will appreciate the seclusion and natural setting at this woodsy campground near the Massachusetts border. Big RVs are welcome, and there are some amenities and comforts (like hot showers, laundry, and water and electric hookups) but the main draw is the great outdoors. The campground is surrounded by 7,500-acre Nipmuck State Forest with more than 25 miles of hiking and biking trails. Campers can walk to pretty Griggs Pond for a picnic, or bring their own canoe or kayak for paddling. Sites are extra-large, most surrounded by trees, offering a good amount of privacy. If you'd like even more seclusion, reserve one of the remote tent sites, tucked in the woods near Griggs Pond.

BASICS

Operated By: Duane & Kathy Frederick. **Open:** Late Apr.–mid-Oct. **Site Assignment:** Reservations accepted; 1-night deposit; holidays paid in full; 14-day cancellation policy w/ 10% fee; V, MC. **Registration:** At office. **Fee:** Water/electric, $34; no hookup, $27; cable TV, $2.50/day. **Parking:** At site, some walk-in tent sites.

FACILITIES

Number of RV-only Sites: 38. **Number of Tent-only Sites:** 12. **Hookups:** Electric (20, 30, 50 amps), water, sewer, cable TV, Wi-Fi on most sites. **Each Site:** Picnic table, fire ring. **Dump Station:** Yes. **Laundry:** Yes. **Pay Phone:** Yes. **Restrooms and Showers:** Yes. **Fuel:** No. **Propane:** Yes. **Internal Roads:** Gravel, dirt (good). **RV Service:** No. **Market:** Union, 6 mi. **Restaurant:** Union, 6 mi. **General Store:** Yes. **Vending:** No. **Swimming:** No. **Playground:** Yes. **Other:** Pond, game room, sports fields. **Activities:** Volleyball, horseshoes, fishing, boating. **Nearby Attractions:** Fishing, swimming, hiking, biking, antiques shops, Woodstock. **Additional Information:** Town of Woodstock, 415 Hwy. 169, Woodstock, CT 06281, (860) 928-6595; www.townofwoodstock.com.

RESTRICTIONS

Pets: On leash only, vaccination registration papers required upon arrival. Max. of 2 pets per site. Restrictions on certain breeds. **Fires:** Fire pits, grills only. **Alcoholic Beverages:** At site.

TO GET THERE

From I-84 Exit 73, go east 2 mi. on Hwy. 190 to Union. Turn right on Hwy. 171 2.2 mi., then left on Hwy. 197 2 mi. Turn left on Hwy. 198 North 1.5 mi.; campground is on the left.

WOODSTOCK MAP, A-4
Chamberlain Lake

1397 Hwy. 197, 06281. T: (860) 974-0567.

🚐 ★★★   ⛺ ★★★

Beauty: ★★★	Site Privacy: ★★★
Spaciousness: ★★★	Quiet: ★★★★
Security: ★★★★★	Cleanliness: ★★★★
Insect Control: ★★★	Facilities: ★★★

If you like lakeside camping, this is a pleasant, comfortable place in the northeast corner of the state near the Massachusetts border. The large beach and warm, clear waters of Lake Chamberlain are the campground's top assets. There's a boat launch (many campers, especially seasonal renters, bring their own watercraft), a white sandy beach, and canoe and boat rentals on site. Unfortunately, the lake is not visible from most sites. If you're a tenter or small pop-up camper, snag one of the few lakefront sites (sites 39–41 are right on the water). The rest of the campsites are small, about 30 feet in width, mostly shaded, set in rows along gravel roads. About half the sites are rented by the season and sport the usual lawn ornaments, flowerboxes, piles of gear, and built-on decks. There are planned activities on summer weekends.

BASICS

Operated By: David Trudeau. **Open:** May 1–Columbus Day. **Site Assignment:** Reservations suggested; 1-night deposit; holidays (3-night minimum) paid in full; V, MC. **Registration:** At office. **Fee:** Water/electric (50 amp), $36–$38; water/electric (20, 30 amp), $34–$36; no hookup, $32–$34. **Parking:** At site; 2 car max.

FACILITIES

Number of Tent-only Sites: 16. **Number of Multipurpose Sites:** 100. **Hookups:** Electric (20, 30, 50 amps), water. **Each Site:** Picnic table, fire ring. **Dump Station:** Yes. **Laundry:** Yes, coin operated. **Pay Phone:** Yes. **Restrooms and Showers:** Yes, coin operated. **Fuel:** No. **Propane:** Yes. **Internal Roads:** Gravel, dirt (good). **RV Service:** No. **Market:** Union, 5 mi. **Restaurant:** Union, 5 mi. **General Store:** Yes. **Vending:** No. **Swimming:** Lake. **Playground:** Yes. **Other:** Beach, boat rentals, game room, rec hall, sports fields, safari field. **Activities:** Swimming, boating, fishing, badminton, basketball, bocce, horseshoes, shuffleboard, volleyball, planned activities like ice-cream socials, fishing derbies, contests on major holidays. **Nearby Attractions:** Fishing, swimming, hiking, biking, antiques shops, Woodstock. **Additional Information:** Town of Woodstock, 415 Hwy. 169, Woodstock, CT 06281; (860) 928-6595; www.townofwoodstock.com.

RESTRICTIONS

Pets: On leash only. Valid rabies certification must be presented at check-in. Pets are prohibited from lake area sites, beach area, trailer rentals. $5 per pet (max. 2 pets) on holiday weekends. **Fires:** Fire pits, grills only. **Alcoholic Beverages:** At site. **Vehicle Maximum Length:** 55 ft.

TO GET THERE

From I-84 Exit 73, go east 2 mi. on Hwy. 190 to Union. Turn right on Hwy. 171 East 2.2 mi. then left on Hwy. 197 3.4 mi.; campground is on the left.

Delaware

From the rolling hills and sprawling meadows of Brandywine Valley to the picturesque beach towns dotting the Atlantic Coast, Delaware is a compact but diverse place. America's second-smallest state after Rhode Island, Delaware earns one of its nicknames, Small Wonder, not only because there's so much squeezed into its borders but also because it's rich with early-American history, natural splendor, and small-town charm.

The state capital of Dover was laid out by William Penn around a beautiful green. A contrasting landscape, Delaware features forested hills in the north, stretches of sand dunes in the south, and miles of marshland along the coast.

In northern Delaware, historic New Castle is a well-preserved colonial town and was the state's first capital; its cobblestone streets are still intact and resound with the echoes of horse hooves and carriage wheels clacking out a rhythm in time with the town's abundantly evident easy pace. The First State's largest city is Wilmington, settled in the Brandywine Valley by Swedes in the 17th century and regarded as the chemical capital of the world. Minutes from Wilmington's skyline are numerous lavish country estates, including the 300-acre Nemours Mansion and Gardens, once the home of Alfred I. DuPont. Options for outdoor jaunts in this region among Delaware's 14 state parks include the 1,000-acre day-use **Brandywine Creek State Park,** which offers nature trails, fishing holes, excellent photography subject matter, and a nature center with interpretive programs. **Fort Delaware State Park,** the purpose of which was to protect the cities of Wilmington and Philadelphia, captures and re-creates what life was like for Confederate prisoners in a Civil War prison camp. **White Clay Creek State Park** is a hiker and mountain biker paradise—its cliff overlooks and **Arc Corner Monument,** marking the state line between Delaware and Pennsylvania, serve as much-needed distractions from the proximal urban sprawl.

Set in the heart of Delaware, Dover is known for its tranquil beauty, capped off by its intact 18th-century cupola-topped state house. The **Delaware State Museums Complex** includes the Delaware **Archaeology Museum,** the **Johnson Victrola Museum,** and the **Museum of Small Town Life. Killens Pond State Park** and the **Delaware Agricultural Museum and Village** are also located in the Dover area.

The coastal edge of southern Delaware is renowned for its mammoth sandy beaches and seaside small-town jaunts. Hence it is the most popular destination in the Diamond State for beach bums from all walks of life. **Bethany Beach** and **Dewey Beach** are popular oceanside towns, complete with a wide array of nightlife entertainment as well as excellent opportunities for the kids or the kids at heart. **Rehoboth Beach** is one of the Atlantic Coast's busiest resort areas and sports a boardwalk with rides, games, or an excuse to nuzzle up to a funnel cake or three. As the beach season winds down, pick up your favorite instrument or just improvise and participate in summer's send-off during Rehoboth's annual jazz funeral parade. In November, cinema buffs looking for a respite from the usual silver-screen fodder offered up by Hollywood can get whisked away by a generous heaping of independent celluloid at the annual **Rehoboth Beach Film Festival.**

Away from the bustle of the resort area, **Delaware Seashore State Park** is a seven-mile strip of land separating Rehoboth and Indian River Bays from the Atlantic Ocean where the lifeguards are on duty from 9 a.m. to 5 p.m. Lewes, originally called Zwaanendael when it was the first Dutch settlement in Delaware, is a quaint town perched on Delaware Bay. Outdoor recreation is plentiful at **Cape Henlopen State Park.** Day-trippers can board the **Lewes–Cape May Ferry** and visit Cape May, New Jersey, the immaculately preserved town that boasts more Victorian homes than any community in the United States.

If you happen to be in the Lewes area around the first Saturday in November and you have an affinity for witnessing gourds fly through the sky, there is no excuse not to stop by and be completely awed by the annual **World Championship Punkin' Chunkin' Festival.** Basically, the contestants can use anything at their disposal to hurl the pumpkins—anything, that is, except for explosives. If you have a difficult time believing the current record is 4,434.28 feet, then perhaps you should make the time to see for yourself. Also located in Lewes is a fountain of youth, which unfortunately has dried up since being discovered by the original Dutch settlers.

If you can't resist a good flea market, Delaware hosts some of the most intriguing secondhand shopping in the country, located along an otherwise featureless Route 13. Along this stretch of highway you will bump into several quaint and curious small towns, like Laurel and Seaford, which happens to be the Nylon Capital of the World.

Campground Profiles

BEAR
Lums Pond State Park
MAP, A-4

1068 Howell School Rd., 19701. T: (877) 987-2757
or (302) 368-6989; www.destateparks.com.

🚐 ★★★ ▲ ★★★★

Beauty: ★★★★	Site Privacy: ★★★★
Spaciousness: ★★★★	Quiet: ★★★★
Security: ★★★★	Cleanliness: ★★★★
Insect Control: ★★★★	Facilities: ★★★★

Built around the largest freshwater pond in Delaware, Lums Pond State Park is located on the north side of the Chesapeake and Delaware Canal south of Newark and southwest of culture-rich Wilmington. Covering 200 acres, Lums Pond itself has a sandy swimming beach and a place where row-boats, sailboats, canoes, and pedal boats are rented. For campers who bring their own boats, a launching ramp and two piers allow easy access to the water. The campground is located off Hwy. 71 south of the widest section of the pond, not far from the boat ramp. Sites are spacious and wooded, and six have electric hookups. The shower facilities here are modern and clean. The swimming area, boat-rental station, sports complex, nature center, and park office are located on the opposite end of the pond. These sites are accessible through the main entrance off Howell School Rd.

BASICS
Operated By: State of Delaware. **Open:** Mar. 1–Nov. 30. **Site Assignment:** Reservations accepted; pay in advance to confirm site; $10 fee for cancelling reservation w/ 30-day notice; 1-night charge for cancelling reservation w/ less than 30-day notice; walk-ins accepted. **Registration:** At campground office. **Fee:** $20–$24; V, MC; $2 fee for each person. **Parking:** At site.

FACILITIES
Number of RV-only Sites: 68. **Hookups:** Electric (30, 50 amps). **Each Site:** Grill, picnic table, fire ring. **Dump Station:** Yes. **Laundry:** No. **Pay Phone:** Yes. **Restrooms and Showers:** Yes. **Fuel:** No. **Propane:** No. **Internal Roads:** Paved, in good condition. **RV Service:** No. **Market:** W/in 5 mi. **Restaurant:** W/in 5 mi. **General Store:** No. **Vending:** Soft drinks. **Swimming:** No. **Playground:** To the side of the park. **Other:** Yurt (tent) rentals, nature center, gift shop in park office. **Activities:** Disc golf, fishing, boating, boat rentals, tennis, badminton, sports field, hiking trails, volleyball, horseshoes. **Nearby Attractions:** Wilmington, Fort Delaware State Park, Brandywine Zoo & Park, Brandywine Springs Park, Delaware Art Museum, Fort Christina Monument, Delaware Museum of Natural History, Rockwood Museum, Nemours Mansion & Gardens, New Castle, Amstel House Museum, Old New Castle Court House, University of Delaware. **Additional Information:** Greater Wilmington CVB, (800) 489-6664.

RESTRICTIONS
Pets: On leash. **Fires:** At site. **Alcoholic Beverages:** No alcohol permitted. Strictly enforced. **Vehicle Maximum Length:** No limit. **Other:** 14-day stay limit during 21-day period Memorial Day–Labor Day.

TO GET THERE
From Glasgow, go 3 mi. south on Hwy. 896 and east on Howell School Rd. Turn left on Redline Rd./Hwy. 71 North.

FELTON
Killens Pond State Park
MAP, B-4

5025 Killens Pond Rd., 19943. T: (302) 284-4526 or (302) 284-3412 or (877) 987-2757; www.destateparks.com.

🚐 ★★★★ ▲ ★★★★

Beauty: ★★★★	Site Privacy: ★★★
Spaciousness: ★★★	Quiet: ★★★★
Security: ★★★★	Cleanliness: ★★★★
Insect Control: ★★★★	Facilities: ★★★★

Located in the heart of Kent County about 15 miles south of Dover, Killens Pond State Park is within a 1.5-hour drive from the northern and southern borders of Delaware, making the campground an ideal base to explore the state. The wooded sites for both RVs and tents are arranged around six loops, all a short walk from the southeastern end of Killens Pond. A secluded primitive tenting area is separated from the other sites. The park office and waterpark complex are located on the north side of the pond, a short drive from the campground. Killens Pond is stocked with largemouth bass, catfish, carp, perch, crappie, bluegill, and pickerel. Canoes, rowboats, surf bikes, kayaks, and pedal boats are available for rent during the summer. The waterpark has a concession stand and swim shop. An 18-hole disc golf course and a network of wooded hiking trails offer additional recreation.

BASICS
Operated By: State of Delaware. Debbie Smith, Supervisor. **Open:** All year. **Site Assignment:** Reservations accepted; pay in advance to confirm site; $10 fee for cancelling reservation w/ 30-day notice; 1-night charge for cancelling reservation w/ less than 30-day notice; walk-ins accepted. **Registration:** At campground office. **Fee:** $18–$24; V, MC. **Parking:** At site.

FACILITIES
Number of RV-only Sites: 59. **Number of Tent-only Sites:** 17. **Hookups:** Electric (20 amps), water. **Each Site:** Fire ring, picnic table. **Dump Station:** Yes. **Laundry:** No. **Pay Phone:** Yes. **Restrooms and Showers:** Yes. **Fuel:** No. **Propane:** No. **Internal Roads:** Paved & dirt, in fair condition. **RV Service:** No. **Market:** W/in 2 mi. **Restaurant:** W/in 2 mi. **General Store:** No. **Vending:** Yes. **Swimming:** Yes. **Playground:** Yes. **Other:** Cabin rentals, Killens Pond Water Park. **Activities:** Swimming, boating, canoeing, boat rentals, pond fishing, shuffleboard, sports field, volleyball, hiking trails, horseshoes, badminton, disc golf. **Nearby Attractions:** Delaware Archaeology Museum, Museum of Small Town Life, Johnson Victrola Museum, Delaware State Visitor Center, Dover Heritage Trail, John Dickinson Plantation, Old State House, Delaware State Fair. **Additional Information:** Kent County CVB, (800) 233-KENT, www.visitdover.com.

RESTRICTIONS
Pets: On leash. **Fires:** At site. **Alcoholic Beverages:** At site. **Vehicle Maximum Length:** 30 ft. **Other:** 14-day stay limit during 21-day period Memorial Day–Labor Day.

TO GET THERE
From Felton, go 1 mi. south on US 13 and 1.5 mi. east on Paradise Alley Rd. Follow signs to campground.

FENWICK ISLAND
Treasure Beach RV Park and Campground
MAP, B-4

37291 Lighthouse Rd., P.O. Box 150A, 19975. T: (302) 436-8001; www.treasurebeachrvpark.com.

🚐 ★★★★ ▲ ★★★★

Beauty: ★★★★	Site Privacy: ★★★
Spaciousness: ★★★	Quiet: ★★★★
Security: ★★★★	Cleanliness: ★★★★
Insect Control: ★★★★	Facilities: ★★★★

Watching the sun set over the Atlantic Ocean is a spectacular sight from Treasure Island RV Park and Campground, located along the ocean and Little Assawoman Bay 1 mile west of Fenwick Island at the southeastern tip of Delaware. Rehoboth Beach is a 20-minute drive to the north, and Ocean City (MD) is a 20-minute jaunt to the south. With 1,000 sites in a relatively small area, campers have little privacy, but the campground has many amenities, such as a crabbing pier, two swimming pools, and a recreation center. The campground is close to the Bayville Marina and the well-kept Bayville Shopping Center. Sailboats are rented here. For an added adventure, campers can drive to Lewes, less than 10 miles north of Rehoboth Beach and board the Lewes–Cape May (NJ) Ferry. The 16-mile, 70-minute journey ends at historic Cape May, where a tour of the town's historic Victorian district is a must for history enthusiasts.

BASICS
Operated By: Private operator. **Open:** May 1–Oct. 15. **Site Assignment:** Reservations accepted; 3-day minimum stay on weekends in July & Aug., & on holiday weekends; walk-ins accepted. **Registration:** At campground office. **Fee:** RV, $40–$50; tent, $25; each additional person, $2. **Parking:** At site.

FACILITIES
Number of RV-only Sites: 900. **Number of Tent-only Sites:** 100. **Hookups:** Electric (30, 50 amps), water, sewer, cable TV. **Each Site:** Fire ring, picnic table. **Dump Station:** Yes. **Laundry:** Yes. **Pay Phone:** Yes, at convenience store. **Restrooms and Showers:** Yes. **Fuel:** No. **Propane:** Yes. **Internal Roads:** Gravel & paved, in good condition. **RV Service:** No. **Market:** W/in 2 mi. **Restaurant:** W/in 2 mi. **General Store:** Yes. **Vending:** Yes. **Swimming:** Yes. **Playground:** Yes. **Other:** Little Assawoman Bay,

boat ramp, rec hall, game room. **Activities:** Saltwater fishing, boating, shuffleboard, planned activities, crabbing, basketball. **Nearby Attractions:** Fenwick Island Lighthouse, DiscoverSea Shipwreck Museum, Thunder Lagoon, Fenwick Island State Park, Bethany Beach, Rehoboth Beach, Ocean City (MD).
Additional Information: Bethany-Fenwick Area Chamber of Commerce, (800) 962-7873, www.bethany-fenwick.org.

RESTRICTIONS

Pets: On leash; not allowed at tent sites. Small pets only. **Fires:** In fireplace, extinguished by midnight & cleaned up. **Alcoholic Beverages:** At site only. **Vehicle Maximum Length:** 40 ft. **Other:** 2 cars & 1 RV per campsite.

TO GET THERE

From SR 1, go 2 mi. west on SR 54. Follow sign to campground.

LAUREL
Trap Pond State Park
MAP, B-4

Baldcypress Ln., 19956. T: (302) 875-5153 or (302) 875-2392; www.destateparks.com.

🚐 ★★★ ⛺ ★★★★

Beauty: ★★★★	Site Privacy: ★★★★
Spaciousness: ★★★★	Quiet: ★★★★
Security: ★★★★	Cleanliness: ★★★★
Insect Control: ★★★★	Facilities: ★★★

Trap Pond State Park retains the picturesque mystique of the freshwater wetlands of southwestern Delaware. In fact, Trap Pond contains the northernmost stand of bald cypress trees in the nation. Hiking trails surround the pond, and observant hikers may spot a great blue heron, hummingbird, warbler, bald eagle, or pileated woodpecker. Our favorite activity at Trap Pond is boating amid the bald cypress. Guided pontoon boat tours hosted by a park interpreter are conducted on weekends and holidays. One of the streams that flows into Trap Pond has been marked as a wilderness canoe trail, which leads farther into the swamp's interior. The campground is located at the northwest end of the pond, and sites are arranged in five loops beneath tall pines. Overall, 130 sites are equipped with water and electric hookups. Two primitive camping areas are also available for youth groups by reservation.

BASICS

Operated By: State of Delaware. **Open:** Apr. 1– Oct. 31. **Site Assignment:** Reservations accepted; pay in advance to confirm site; $10 fee for cancelling reservation w/ 30-day notice; 1-night charge for cancelling reservation w/ less than 30-day notice; walk-ins accepted. **Registration:** At the log-cabin store. **Fee:** $20–$55. **Parking:** At site. 1 car per site.

FACILITIES

Number of RV-only Sites: 130. **Number of Tent-only Sites:** 12. **Hookups:** Electric (20 amps), water. **Each Site:** Fire ring, picnic table. **Dump Station:** Yes. **Laundry:** Yes. **Pay Phone:** Yes. **Restrooms and Showers:** Yes. **Fuel:** No. **Propane:** No. **Internal Roads:** Dirt, in fair condition. **RV Service:** No. **Market:** W/in 5 mi. **Restaurant:** W/in 5 mi. **General Store:** Yes. **Vending:** Soft drinks. **Swimming:**

No. **Playground:** Yes. **Other:** Trap Pond, Bald Cypress Nature Center. **Activities:** Fishing, boating, canoeing, boat rentals, hiking trails, volleyball, horseshoes. **Nearby Attractions:** Barnes Woods Nature Preserve, Old Christ Church, Nutter D. Marvel Carriage Museum, Fenwick Island, Nanticoke River, Delaware Seashore State Park, Rehoboth Beach. **Additional Information:** Laurel Chamber, (302) 875-9319, www.laurelchamber.com.

RESTRICTIONS

Pets: On leash, under control. **Fires:** At site. **Alcoholic Beverages:** Allowed in moderation. **Vehicle Maximum Length:** 40 ft. **Other:** 14-day stay limit during 21-day period Memorial Day–Labor Day.

TO GET THERE

From US 13, go 4 mi. east on Hwy. 24 and 1 mi. south on CR 449. Follow signs to campground.

LEWES
Cape Henlopen State Park
MAP, B-4

42 Cape Henlopen Dr., 19958.
T: (302) 645-8983 or (302) 645-2103; www.destateparks.com/chsp/chsp.html.

🚐 ★★★ ⛺ ★★★★

Beauty: ★★★★★	Site Privacy: ★★★★
Spaciousness: ★★★★	Quiet: ★★★★★
Security: ★★★★	Cleanliness: ★★★★
Insect Control: ★★★★	Facilities: ★★★★

The beaches attract most visitors to Cape Henlopen State Park, located on the Atlantic Ocean at the mouth of Delaware Bay. Yet this park on Delaware's southeastern shore is not just about basking in the sun and swimming in the ocean. Gordon's Pond Wildlife Area has a unique saltwater impoundment. Along the coast, the Great Dune rises 80 feet above sea level. Farther inland, the famous "walking dunes" stretch across the pine forests. A broad salt marsh meanders along the park's western boundary. Fittingly, the campground is nestled amid pine-covered dunes and has 159 back-in sites, most of which have water hookups. For anglers, a quarter-mile-long pier offers access to Delaware Bay. The pier's bait and tackle shop also sells snacks and beverages. Two designated swimming beaches are monitored by lifeguards, and the northern swimming area has a modern bathhouse with showers, changing rooms, and a concession stand.

BASICS

Operated By: State of Delaware. **Open:** Mar. 1–Nov. 30. **Site Assignment:** Reservations accepted; pay in advance to confirm site; $10 fee for cancelling reservation w/ 30-day notice; 1-night charge for cancelling reservation w/ less than 30-day notice; walk-ins accepted. **Registration:** At campground office. **Fee:** $27–$29. **Parking:** At site.

FACILITIES

Number of RV-only Sites: 142. **Number of Tent-only Sites:** 17. **Hookups:** Water. **Each Site:** Grill, picnic table. **Dump Station:** Yes. **Laundry:** Yes. **Pay Phone:** Yes. **Restrooms and Showers:** Yes. **Fuel:** No. **Propane:** Yes, pier. **Internal Roads:** Paved, in good condition. **RV Service:** No. **Market:** W/in 4 mi. **Restaurant:** W/in 4 mi. **General Store:** No.

Vending: Yes. **Swimming:** Ocean. **Playground:** No. **Other:** Seaside Nature Center. **Activities:** Saltwater fishing & swimming, basketball, disc golf, tennis, hiking trails, sports field, rec hall. **Nearby Attractions:** Lewes–Cape May (NJ) Ferry, Beach Plum Island Nature Preserve, Lewes Historical Society Complex (including Cannon Ball House & Marine Museum, Thompson Country Store, Doctor's Office, log cabins & farmhouse), Zwaanendael Museum, Rehoboth Beach. **Additional Information:** Lewes Chamber of Commerce Visitors Bureau, (302) 645-8073, www.leweschamber.com.

RESTRICTIONS

Pets: On leash, must be attended. **Fires:** At site. **Alcoholic Beverages:** Allowed, no kegs. **Vehicle Maximum Length:** 35 ft. **Other:** 14-day stay limit during 21-day period Memorial Day–Labor Day.

TO GET THERE

From Hwy. 1, go 4 mi. northeast on US 9. Follow signs to the campground.

LEWES
Tall Pines
MAP, B-4

29551 Persimmon Rd., P.O. Box 221, 19958.
T: (302) 684-0300; www.tallpines-del.com.

🚐 ★★★★ ⛺ ★★★★

Beauty: ★★★★	Site Privacy: ★★★
Spaciousness: ★★★★	Quiet: ★★★★
Security: ★★★★	Cleanliness: ★★★★
Insect Control: ★★★★	Facilities: ★★★★

As the name suggests, Tall Pines is a camping resort snuggled beneath a forest of loblolly pines. Located in Lewes near Delaware's southeastern shore, the campground is only a few minutes from the Atlantic Ocean and the mouth of Delaware Bay, where campers can frolic on beaches and explore the rolling sand dunes at Cape Henlopen State Park. The bulk of the RV sites are situated in the center and north end of Tall Pines; only five of these are pull-throughs. Seasonal sites are concentrated from the center to the north, while transient sites are located from the center to the south. Though Tall Pines is shaded by pines and is well maintained, campers should know that the eastern side of the campground is bordered by railroad tracks. Tent sites are located on the southwestern end of the campground along the stream. A majority of the RV sites are rented out for an entire season. Only 23 sites are available with water and electric hookups for daily rental.

BASICS

Operated By: Private operator. **Open:** All year. **Site Assignment:** Reservations accepted; 2-night deposit required; 3 nights on holiday weekends; walk-ins accepted. **Registration:** At campground office. **Fee:** $33–$36; V, MC. **Parking:** At site.

FACILITIES

Number of RV-only Sites: 23. **Number of Tent-only Sites:** 26. **Hookups:** Electric (20, 30 amps), water; at daily sites, 26 tent sites w/ water only & 23 RV sites w/ electric, water. **Each Site:** Fire ring, picnic table. **Dump Station:** Yes. **Laundry:** Yes. **Pay Phone:** Yes. **Restrooms and Showers:** Yes. **Fuel:** No. **Propane:** Yes. **Internal Roads:** Paved, in fair condition. **RV Service:** No. **Market:** W/in 4 mi. **Restaurant:** W/in 4 mi. **General Store:** Yes. **Vending:** Yes. **Swimming:** Pool. **Playground:** Yes. **Other:** Pavilion. **Activities:** Basketball, rec hall, Olympic-size pool, game room, badminton, shuffleboard, volleyball, horseshoes. **Nearby Attractions:** Lewes–Cape May (NJ) Ferry; Cape Henlopen State Park, Lewes Historical Society Complex (including Cannon Ball House & Marine Museum, Thompson Country Store, Doctor's Office, log cabins & farmhouse), Zwaanendael Museum, Rehoboth Beach. **Additional Information:** Lewes Chamber of Commerce Visitors Bureau, (302) 645-8073, www.leweschamber.com.

RESTRICTIONS

Pets: On leash, at site; no pets permitted in recreation areas. **Fires:** At site. **Alcoholic Beverages:** At site. **Vehicle Maximum Length:** No limit. **Other:** Quiet hours 11 p.m.–9 a.m.; rates are based on a family of four people. Additional campers may stay at a rate of $2 per person per day.

TO GET THERE

From Hwy. 1, go 3 mi. southwest on US 9 and 0.75 mi. southwest on service road. Entrance is on the right.

OCEAN VIEW   MAP, B-4
Sandy Cove Campground

RD 1 Box 256, 19970. T: (302) 539-6245; www.sandycovede.com.

🚐 ★★★   ▲ ★★★

Beauty: ★★★	Site Privacy: ★★★
Spaciousness: ★★★	Quiet: ★★★
Security: ★★★★	Cleanliness: ★★★★
Insect Control: ★★★★	Facilities: ★★★

We like sunsets over the water, and the sunset from Sandy Cove Campground's location on Indian River Bay did not disappoint us. Sandy Cove is based in Ocean View, a few miles west of the Atlantic Ocean, where the waters of Indian River Bay flow. Sandy Cove is central to Rehoboth Beach (about 12 miles north) and Fenwick Island (about 8 miles south). Campers have their choice of open and wooded sites, all of which have water and electric hookups. Campers tend to favor the areas near the bay. Sandy Cove does not have a swimming pool, but it does have a private beach. The marina rents rowboats and canoes, and the campground has a crabbing pier that lures the youngsters, who also flock to the game room and playground. If you want to enjoy the ocean and the beach without the crowds that often gather at Ocean City and Rehoboth Beach, try Bethany Beach, which is just south of Ocean View.

BASICS

Operated By: Kevin Sagers. **Open:** Apr. 1–Nov. 1. **Site Assignment:** Reservations accepted; 3-night minimum June 15–Aug. 15); walk-ins accepted. **Registration:** At campground office. **Fee:** $15–$35. **Parking:** At site. No additional parking.

FACILITIES

Number of RV-only Sites: 180. **Hookups:** Electric (20, 30 amps), water. **Each Site:** Fire ring, picnic table. **Dump Station:** Yes. **Laundry:** No. **Pay**

Phone: Yes. **Restrooms and Showers:** Yes. **Fuel:** No. **Propane:** Yes. **Internal Roads:** Gravel, in good condition. **RV Service:** Yes. **Market:** W/in 2 mi. **Restaurant:** W/in 2 mi. **General Store:** Yes. **Vending:** Yes. **Swimming:** Bay (very shallow). **Playground:** Yes. **Other:** Boat ramp & dock. **Activities:** Boating, canoeing, boat rentals, saltwater fishing, volleyball, horseshoes. **Nearby Attractions:** Indian River Bay, Fenwick Island, DiscoverSea Shipwreck Museum, Fenwick Island Lighthouse, Bethany Beach, Fenwick Island State Park, Delaware Seashore State Park, Rehoboth Beach, Lewes–Cape May Ferry, Ocean City (MD). **Additional Information:** Bethany-Fenwick Area Chamber of Commerce, (800) 962-7873, www.bethany-fenwick.org.

RESTRICTIONS

Pets: On leash. **Fires:** At site. **Alcoholic Beverages:** At site. **Vehicle Maximum Length:** 40 ft. (min. 20 ft.). **Other:** Pets & fires may not be left unattended.

TO GET THERE

From Hwy. 1, go 2 mi. west on Hwy. 26, 2.5 mi. north on Central Ave., and 0.5 mi. west on CR 358. Entrance is on the left.

REHOBOTH BEACH   MAP, B-4
Big Oaks Family Campground

35567 Big Oak Lane, P.O. Box 53, 19971. T: (302) 645-6838; www.bigoakscamping.com.

🚐 ★★★★   ▲ ★★★★

Beauty: ★★★★	Site Privacy: ★★★★
Spaciousness: ★★★★	Quiet: ★★★★
Security: ★★★★	Cleanliness: ★★★★
Insect Control: ★★★★	Facilities: ★★★★

Located 3 miles north of Rehoboth Beach and 3 miles south of the Lewes–Cape May Ferry, Big Oaks Family Campground caters to campers interested in boardwalk amusements and beach frolicking. Big Oaks operates a free shuttle service to and from Rehoboth Beach. Campers can choose from level open and wooded back-in sites, 125 of which have full hookups. Yes, the wooded sites are snuggled under mighty oak trees. The campground has a swimming pool, as well as a clubhouse, game room, and snack bar. The restrooms and shower facilities at Big Oaks are well maintained. During the summer, Big Oaks stirs with special activities like dances, hayrides, art contests, and bingo games, as well as tournaments for basketball, horseshoes, shuffleboard, and billiards. For those without RVs or tents, Big Oaks has two-room cabins, RVs, and mobile homes for rent. Big Oaks also sells tickets to Atlantic City casinos, a short drive north of Lewes.

BASICS

Operated By: Private operator. **Open:** May 1–Oct. 1. **Site Assignment:** Reservations accepted; 2-night minimum July & Aug.; walk-ins accepted. **Registration:** At campground office. **Fee:** $36–$48; V, MC. **Parking:** At site.

FACILITIES

Number of RV-only Sites: 150. **Number of Tent-only Sites:** 25. **Hookups:** Electric (20, 30, 50 amps), water, cable TV, phone. **Each Site:** Fire ring, picnic

table. **Dump Station:** Yes. **Laundry:** Yes. **Pay Phone:** Yes. **Restrooms and Showers:** Yes. **Fuel:** No. **Propane:** No. **Internal Roads:** Gravel & paved, in good condition. **RV Service:** No. **Market:** W/in 1 mi. **Restaurant:** W/in 1 mi. **General Store:** Yes. **Vending:** Yes. **Swimming:** Pool. **Playground:** Yes. **Other:** RV rentals, beach shuttle. **Activities:** Basketball, game room, rec hall, shuffleboard, movies, planned activities on weekends, horseshoes. **Nearby Attractions:** Rehoboth Beach boardwalk attractions & beach, Cape Henlopen State Park, Delaware Seashore State Park, Lewes–Cape May (NJ) Ferry. **Additional Information:** Rehoboth Beach–Dewey Beach Chamber of Commerce, (800) 441-1329, www.beach-fun.com.

RESTRICTIONS

Pets: On leash; pets may not be left unattended. **Fires:** At site. **Alcoholic Beverages:** Not allowed. **Vehicle Maximum Length:** 40 ft. **Other:** 1 camping unit for site.

TO GET THERE

At Hwy. 1 and Hwy. 24, go 0.5 mi. east on CR 270. Entrance is on the left.

REHOBOTH BEACH   MAP, B-4
Delaware Seashore State Park

130 Coastal Hwy., 19971. T: (302) 227-2800 or (302) 539-7202; www.destateparks.com.

🚐 ★★★★   ▲ ★★★★

Beauty: ★★★★	Site Privacy: ★★★
Spaciousness: ★★★★	Quiet: ★★★★
Security: ★★★★	Cleanliness: ★★★★
Insect Control: ★★★★	Facilities: ★★★★

Bounded on the east by the Atlantic Ocean and on the west by Rehoboth Bay and Indian River Bay, the 2,799-acre Delaware Seashore State Park covers 6 miles of ocean and bay shoreline. Surf fishing is big here, and several charter boats offer deep-sea excursions. Also, fishing boats operate from the Indian River Marina, located on the bay side north of the inlet. A special access pier at the inlet allows people with disabilities to fish more easily. Umbrellas, chairs, and rafts can be rented on the beach. The park office and the Indian River Marina are located north of Indian River Inlet, while the campground is situated on the water south of the inlet. Of the 278 sites, 145 have full hookups and all are pull-through sites. Thompson Island Preserve, located on Rehoboth Bay northwest of the inlet, is a prime example of the salt-marsh habitat that once thrived around inland bays.

BASICS

Operated By: State of Delaware. **Open:** All year; fully operational mid-Mar.–mid-Nov. **Site Assignment:** Reservations accepted; pay in advance to confirm site; $10 fee for cancelling reservation w/ 30-day notice; 1-night charge for cancelling reservation w/ less than 30-day notice; walk-ins accepted. **Registration:** At campground office. **Fee:** $35; V, MC. **Parking:** At site.

FACILITIES

Number of RV-only Sites: 145. **Number of Tent-only Sites:** 133. **Hookups:** Electric (20, 50 amps).

Each Site: Picnic table. **Dump Station:** Yes. **Laundry:** Yes. **Pay Phone:** Yes. **Restrooms and Showers:** Yes. **Fuel:** No. **Propane:** No. **Internal Roads:** Paved & dirt, in good condition. **RV Service:** No. **Market:** W/in 3 mi. **Restaurant:** W/in 3 mi. **General Store:** No. **Vending:** Soft drinks. **Swimming:** Beaches. **Playground:** Yes. **Other:** Indian River Bay. **Activities:** Saltwater fishing, swimming, boating, hiking trails. **Nearby Attractions:** Rehoboth Beach boardwalk attractions & beach, Fenwick Island, Lewes–Cape May Ferry, Cape Henlopen State Park. **Additional Information:** Rehoboth Beach–Dewey Beach Chamber of Commerce, (800) 441-1329, www.beach-fun.com.

RESTRICTIONS

Pets: On leash. **Fires:** Not allowed. **Alcoholic Beverages:** No alcohol permitted. **Vehicle Maximum Length:** 40 ft. **Other:** 14-day stay limit during 21-day period Memorial Day–Labor Day.

TO GET THERE

From Rehoboth Beach, go 2 mi. south on Hwy. 1. Follow signs to campground.

REHOBOTH BEACH   MAP, B-4
Holly Lake Campsites

32087 Holly Lake Rd., P.O. Box 141, 19966. T: (302) 945-3410 or (800) 227-7170; www.hollylakecampsites.com.

🚐 ★★★	⛺ ★★★
Beauty: ★★★	Site Privacy: ★★★
Spaciousness: ★★★	Quiet: ★★★★
Security: ★★★★	Cleanliness: ★★★
Insect Control: ★★★★	Facilities: ★★★

A kidney-shaped 4,000-square-foot swimming pool, 2 miles of hiking trails through dense woodlands, a wildlife area with two observation platforms, and a petting zoo where barnyard animals roam are among the attractions that lure campers to Holly Lake Campsites, located outside of Rehoboth Beach. The campground also has Old Holly River, Deep Branch Creek, and Ivy Branch Creek within its boundaries. The camp store serves breakfast, lunch, and dinner and sells ice cream, camping supplies, snacks, beverages, and ice. With 600 pull-through sites, including 500 with full hookups, Holly Lake is a large campground with 11 bathhouses scattered about. Sites are arranged in four large areas. Many sites are nestled between Deep Branch Creek and Old Holly Lake. A

mass of sites is also located east of Deep Branch. Though the campground is adorned with lush woods around the bodies of water, and some sites are wooded with oak, maple or cedar, many sites have little privacy.

BASICS

Operated By: Private operator. **Open:** All year; fully operational May 1–Sept. 30. **Site Assignment:** Reservations accepted; 2-night minimum on weekends; 3-night minimum on holiday weekends; walk-ins accepted. **Registration:** At campground office. **Fee:** $40–$48; V, MC. **Parking:** At site.

FACILITIES

Number of RV-only Sites: 500. **Number of Tent-only Sites:** 100. **Hookups:** Electric (20, 30 amps), water. **Each Site:** Fire ring, picnic table. **Dump Station:** Yes. **Laundry:** Yes. **Pay Phone:** Yes. **Restrooms and Showers:** Yes. **Fuel:** Yes. **Propane:** Yes. **Internal Roads:** Dirt, in fair condition. **RV Service:** No. **Market:** W/in 6 mi. **Restaurant:** W/in 4 mi. **General Store:** Yes. **Vending:** Yes. **Swimming:** Pool. **Playground:** Yes. **Other:** Petting zoo. **Activities:** Hiking trails, game room, volleyball, horseshoes, rec hall, planned activities on weekends. **Nearby Attractions:** Rehoboth Beach boardwalk attractions & beach, Cape Henlopen State Park, Delaware Seashore State Park, Lewes–Cape May Ferry. **Additional Information:** Rehoboth Beach–Dewey Beach Chamber of Commerce, (800) 441-1329, www.beach-fun.com.

RESTRICTIONS

Pets: On leash, do not leave unattended. **Fires:** At site. **Alcoholic Beverages:** No alcohol permitted. **Vehicle Maximum Length:** 45 ft. **Other:** No motorcycles or mini-bikes; no outside refrigerators.

TO GET THERE

From Hwy. 1, go 6 mi. southwest on Hwy. 24. Entrance is on the right.

REHOBOTH BEACH   MAP, B-4
Sea Air Village

Hwy. 1 and Sea Air Ave., 19971. T: (302) 227-8118.

🚐 ★★★★	⛺ n/a
Beauty: ★★	Site Privacy: ★★
Spaciousness: ★★★	Quiet: ★★★
Security: ★★★★	Cleanliness: ★★★★
Insect Control: ★★★★	Facilities: ★★★★

Convenient to boardwalk attractions, outlet malls, and the eponymous beach in Rehoboth Beach, Sea Air Village is an RV and manufactured-home community and park where no tents are allowed. In fact, Sea Air Village only accepts full hookup units. The park has two swimming pools, a large playground, a softball diamond, and a volleyball court. There is also a rec room and a pavilion for special events. Sea Air Village is ideal for campers who want clean facilities while enjoying Rehoboth Beach's attractions, of which there are many. Funland, a family-operated amusement center along the boardwalk, has 18 rides, 12 midway games, and a video arcade. Even closer to Sea Air Village, in the Midway Shopping Center, is Midway Speedway and Water Park. Many Sea Air Village campers wander over to Rehoboth Outlets, where 140 stores line a 2-mile stretch of Hwy. 1.

BASICS

Operated By: Private operator. **Open:** Apr. 15–Nov. 15. **Site Assignment:** Reservations & walk-ins accepted. **Registration:** At community office. **Fee:** $55; V, MC. **Parking:** At site.

FACILITIES

Number of RV-only Sites: 157. **Hookups:** Electric (20, 30, 50 amps), cable TV, phone. **Each Site:** Fire ring, picnic table. **Dump Station:** No. **Laundry:** No. **Pay Phone:** No. **Restrooms and Showers:** Yes. **Fuel:** No. **Propane:** No. **Internal Roads:** Paved, in good condition. **RV Service:** No. **Market:** W/in 2 mi. **Restaurant:** W/in 2 mi. **General Store:** No. **Vending:** No. **Swimming:** Pool. **Playground:** No. **Other:** Pavilion. **Activities:** Badminton, pool. **Nearby Attractions:** Rehoboth Beach boardwalk attractions & beach, Cape Henlopen State Park, Delaware Seashore State Park, Lewes–Cape May Ferry. **Additional Information:** Rehoboth Beach–Dewey Beach Chamber of Commerce, (800) 441-1329, www.beach-fun.com.

RESTRICTIONS

Pets: On leash. **Fires:** Not allowed. **Alcoholic Beverages:** At site. **Vehicle Maximum Length:** Depends on the site. **Other:** No tents allowed.

TO GET THERE

From Hwy. 274, go 1.5 mi. south on Hwy. 1 and 2 blocks west on Sea Air Ave. Entrance is on the right.

Florida

RVers and campers alike in search of sun, sand, and surf will discover (if they didn't already know), that Florida tends to be number one on the itinerary of those away from home when it comes to relaxation and fun in all its forms. Because it's extremely rare that the temperature in the Sunshine State drops below 60º, visitors the world over make Florida a destination mandatory at some point during the year to fulfill their leisure quota.

Although it seceded from the Union during the Civil War and joined the Confederacy, the 27th state instantly became a hotly contested stretch of land for those seeking a piece of the Sunshine State. The U.S. government succeeded in removing from Florida all but about 300 members of the Seminole Tribe, who hid in the swamps from the invading army. It was because of this resiliency that the Seminole descendants call themselves the Unconquered People.

Except for mountain climbing, Florida is home to every possible form of recreation imaginable, from cave diving to curiosity seeking to alligator wrestling. Whether you are tanning in the panhandle or helping celebrate Key West's independence from the United States in the Conch Republic's annual festival in April, you may find it difficult to distinguish your locale in Florida based solely on the geography.

On the Gulf side, wind surfing, clamming, parasailing, kayaking, fishing, and beachcombing comprise the left and north coasts' sun-soaked activities. For those who are qualified and after something a little more extreme, the north-central region is home to some of the world's most incredible cave diving. Here and also all over the rest of the state, there are numerous opportunities to hike trails, spot exotic wildlife, and maybe take refuge from the heat under the canopies of the state parks.

Depending on the swell and tide, the Atlantic side boasts some of the most unique yet unpredictable surfing spots along the East Coast; when there are no waves to be ridden, an early evening of surf-fishing will relax you. Heading south along the water toward the Keys, the opportunities for scuba diving and snorkeling increase in proportion to the frequency of coral reefs.

Florida is famous for its swampland, as it complements the obvious other half of the state's vital tourism industry. **Everglades National Park,** the only subtropical preserve in North America and the world's only cohabitation of crocodiles and alligators, offers many interpretive programs, sloughing, and airboat rides for those who don't mind the muck.

Prepare as you would for venturing into any subtropical climate, especially in the summer and early fall, when the insects and humidity may seem to be conspiring against you. Tackling Florida during this time of year will definitely make for a less crowded adventure, but the elements will be out in full force. If you don't mind the crowds and bumper-to-bumper shuffle, late fall through late spring draws hundreds of thousands worldwide as they take advantage of the more manageable climate and social life.

If you're looking for something funky, something a bit out of the ordinary, but the nightclub scene isn't your speed, Florida is teeming with an assortment of fringe elements that do more than just contribute to that overwhelming feeling you get from experiencing Americana firsthand. **Coral Castle** in Homestead is probably one of most perplexing anomalies in the world. The physics that permit the swinging gate to move cannot be explained, so don't wrack your brain attempting to figure it out.

Every April, Pensacola holds its **Interstate Mullet Toss**—the fish, not the postironic hairstyle—where patrons at the **Flora-Bama Package & Lounge** hurl the balled-up bottomfeeder from the Florida side over the state line into Alabama in one of the bar's many events during the contest.

Along US 98 passing through Carrabelle, travelers who feel like reporting suspicious activity in the area can stop off at the world's smallest police station. Easy to miss, it is located in a phone booth—or actually, is the phone booth—along the route, so it's hard to say whether someone will be on duty.

You may think of Florida as the home of Mickey Mouse, roller coasters, and long, long lines. Or maybe the Sunshine State inspires dreams of endless surf and all-night parties on glittery South Beach. You'd be right, but you'd also be missing out on about 54,000 other unique square miles. Although much of Florida's 1,197 miles of coastline is obscured by high-rise condos, there is still a wealth of undiscovered beauty and charm behind the glamorous facade along the back roads and quiet coastal towns. Perhaps you've visited the Space Coast, the Treasure Coast, and the Gold Coast, but next time you come to Florida, take time to explore the Undiscovered Coast, the Forgotten Coast, the Nature Coast, the Emerald Coast, the First Coast, and the Interior.

Try a tour of US 19/98 along the Gulf Coast through Pasco County and head north to the Nature Coast, a beautiful old road through the countryside where signs warn of bear habitats and others point to such Florida staples as churches, guns, palm readers, boiled peanuts, fresh scallops, and oysters. We take Interstate 10 antiquing across the top to the First Coast and stop by **Amelia Island** for succulent copper shrimp. We canoe the rivers that course through the central part of the state, kayak the east and west shorelines, and scuba dive and snorkel the coral reef in the south. We enjoy an airboat ride into the depths of the **Everglades** and sample gator tail, frog legs, and swamp cabbage along with a little Indian fry bread. We amble around the 700 square miles of **Lake Okeechobee,** buying juicy mangoes and crisp okra from local farmers who've been here all their lives. When we're done with all that, we hit the beach. We like to dig for shark's teeth and tales of pirates, and we're always on the lookout for giant sea turtles, dolphins, and manatees.

Campers need to remember that summertime is swelter time in this fair state, when temperatures can soar into the 90s and higher. Afternoon rains help cool the air, but the heat can be brutal for those who aren't acclimated to it. Bugs are worse in summer, especially at night. Mosquitoes and no-see-ums, too small to see and tiny enough to pass through window screens, are the most annoying. Bug sprays and citronella candles will help, but there will be times when the only solution is to seek shelter. Some folks prefer Florida in the winter, when bugs and temperatures are more moderate; but expect to encounter more crowds then, too. No need to let a little nature scare you off—be prepared, and you can count on an adventure you'll never forget.

Campground Profiles

ALACHUA — MAP, A-2
Travelers Campground

17701 April Blvd., 32615. T: (386) 462-2505.

🚐 ★★★★★   ⛺ ★★

Beauty: ★★★	Site Privacy: ★★
Spaciousness: ★★	Quiet: ★★★★
Security: ★★★	Cleanliness: ★★★★
Insect Control: ★★★★	Facilities: ★★★★

Designed for travelers, as its name implies, this campground is super convenient to the highway, clean, and quick to get in and out of. Although some larger sites occupy a friendly hill graced with tall trees, most overnighters are placed in the back lot, six rows of seven drive-through sites. Privacy is not an option. The shower house is impeccably clean and hookups are updated. The perimeter of the campground houses the owners menagerie, which includes a single horse, donkeys, an emu, a pink pig, chickens and chicks, albino peacocks, goats, and an aviary with macaws and other exotic birds. A quiet rec hall hosts occasional dinners, and there is an Internet connection in the office.

BASICS
Operated By: Owners Harold & Linda. **Open:** All year. **Site Assignment:** First come, first served, except during football games; reservations can also be made. **Registration:** At office. **Fee:** 30 amp, $22; 50 amp, $25; tent, $16; cash, check only. **Parking:** Yes.

FACILITIES
Number of RV-only Sites: 100. **Number of Tent-only Sites:** 20. **Hookups:** Electric (20, 30, 50 amps), water, sewer, cable TV, modem in office. **Each Site:** Picnic table on request. **Dump Station:** Yes, at the sites. **Laundry:** Yes. **Pay Phone:** Yes. **Restrooms and Showers:** Yes. **Fuel:** No. **Propane:** Yes. **Internal Roads:** Lime-rock, all in good condition. **RV Service:** Referral. **Market:** 1.5 mi. east on US 441. **Restaurant:** 2 mi. east on US 441. **General Store:** Yes, small store in the office. **Vending:** No. **Swimming:** Yes. **Playground:** No. **Other:** Rec hall, horseshoes, shuffleboard, field for golf & ballgames. **Activities:** Monthly pot-luck dinner. **Nearby Attractions:** Freshwater springs offer tubing & canoeing; antique mall in Micanopy, University of Florida in Gainesville. **Additional Information:** Alachua County CVB, (352) 374-5260.

RESTRICTIONS
Pets: On leash only. **Fires:** Grill only. **Alcoholic Beverages:** Allowed, but not openly displayed. **Vehicle Maximum Length:** 80 ft.

TO GET THERE
I-75 Exit 78 at US 441 east 200 ft. to April Blvd. (on north side of road next to Waffle House), north 1 mi. to campground on right.

ALTOONA — MAP, C-2
Alexander Springs

reserve america™

Ocala National Forest, 49525 CR 445, 32702. T: (352) 669-3522; www.reserveamerica.com.

🚐 ★★★   ⛺ ★★★★★

Beauty: ★★★★★	Site Privacy: ★★★
Spaciousness: ★★★	Quiet: ★★★
Security: ★★★★★	Cleanliness: ★★★★★
Insect Control: ★★★	Facilities: ★★★★★

If you're in the mood to take a break from luxury camping for a dip into the wild side, the Ocala National Forest is a great place for the adventure. Rangers report finding bear droppings and paw prints on the beaches in the mornings, and say that a mama bear and her cubs have been known to reside nearby. Sightings are frequent along CR 445 leading to the Alexander Springs Recreation Area—you may want to cruise a bit more slowly than the 55-mph speed limit allows. Other creatures include alligators in the springs (yes, the place is crowded with swimmers), wild hogs, and deer. Osprey and American bald eagles can be seen above. Camping is confined to four loops, each site shielded by a rim of brush and trees offering a little privacy, but paths cross through the back of some sites to the bathhouses, so you might get to know your neighbors. The nights are so quiet, you'll probably get to hear the giggles of other scouts and campers even if you don't get to meet them—even generators must be silenced during the night. But if you get a little sweaty at night, you'll be instantly refreshed if you take a dip in the perpetually 70° water that replenishes itself at the rate of 70 million gallons a day.

BASICS
Operated By: Recreation Resource Management. **Open:** All year. **Site Assignment:** First come, first served. **Registration:** At park office. **Fee:** $17; MC,V for bills of $20 or more. **Parking:** Yes.

FACILITIES
Number of RV-only Sites: 67. **Hookups:** None. **Each Site:** Picnic table, grill, lantern pole. **Dump Station:** Yes. **Laundry:** No. **Pay Phone:** Yes. **Restrooms and Showers:** Yes. **Fuel:** No. **Propane:** No. **Internal Roads:** Paved, in good condition. **RV Service:** Referral. **Market:** 3 mi. south on Hwy. 445 to convenience market, 6 mi. north on Hwy. 445 to supermarket in Astor. **Restaurant:** 6 mi. north on Hwy. 445 to Astor. **General Store:** Yes. **Vending:** Soft drinks. **Swimming:** Freshwater-spring swimming area w/ beach. **Playground:** No. **Other:** Hiking & biking trails, canoe launch, pavilion. **Activities:** Hiking, biking, swimming, fishing, canoeing. **Nearby Attractions:** National forest surrounds recreation area. **Additional Information:** Ocala National Forest Visitors Center, (352) 669-7495.

RESTRICTIONS
Pets: On leash only, designated areas. **Fires:** Grill & fire rings. **Alcoholic Beverages:** Not allowed. **Vehicle Maximum Length:** 35 ft. Some larger lots. **Other:** Gate closes at 8 p.m.; quiet time 10 p.m.–6 a.m.

TO GET THERE
From US 441, 6 mi. north on Hwy. 19 to CR 445, 6 mi. north to entrance on left.

ARCADIA — MAP, C-2
Craig's RV Park, Inc.

7895 Cubitis Ave., 34266. T: (863) 494-1820 or (877) 750-5129; www.craigsrv.com.

🚐 ★★★★   ⛺ ★★★

Beauty: ★★★	Site Privacy: ★★★★
Spaciousness: ★★★★★	Quiet: ★★★★★
Security: ★★★★★	Cleanliness: ★★★★★
Insect Control: ★★★★★	Facilities: ★★★★★

Tucked into Florida's beautiful countryside, Arcadia is a rural town surrounded by a long-standing agricultural community. The scenic Peace River meanders through the cattle ranches, forests, and swamps without a trace of commercial interference for miles on end. The river is very popular for canoeists who pack a few days' worth of supplies and camp along its banks. The practice is allowed by the ranch owners, but you're at your own risk—the territory is rich with alligators and other wildlife. Craig's RV Park is conveniently situated, with river access just 3 miles away, and it provides a peaceful place for those seeking the country atmosphere but who still love country fun, such as the bluegrass festivals and informal music nights. Laid out like a suburban neighborhood, sites are tightly packed though spacious, with more trees on the north side of the park than on the south, and a few dozen pull-through sites as well. Camper's favorite sites include 19, 62–65. One great feature is the private bathrooms and showers, but campers must pay 25 cents for 6 minutes of water, thanks to some vandals who once left the taps running and drained the water supply. The camp is run very professionally and kept immaculate by its family owners.

BASICS

Operated By: Owners Vicky & Allen Wickey & Sara & Victor Craig. **Open:** All year. **Site Assignment:** Reservations accepted; $20 deposit required, 24-hour cancellation policy, less 10% fee. **Registration:** At office. **Fee:** $25; M, V, D. **Parking:** Yes.

FACILITIES

Number of RV-only Sites: 356. **Hookups:** Electric (20, 30, 50 amps), water, sewer. **Each Site:** Concrete pad. **Dump Station:** Yes. **Laundry:** Yes. **Pay Phone:** Yes. **Restrooms and Showers:** Yes. **Fuel:** No. **Propane:** Yes. **Internal Roads:** Paved, in good condition. **RV Service:** Referral. **Market:** 9 mi. south to Arcadia, convenience mart 2 mi. south. **Restaurant:** 9 mi. south to Arcadia. **General Store:** No. **Vending:** Yes. **Swimming:** Yes. **Playground:** Swing set only. **Other:** Shuffleboard, bocce court, horseshoes, game room w/ pool tables, golf driving range. **Activities:** Monthly events Nov.–Apr. includes bingo, live music, bluegrass festivals in Nov. & Mar., shuffleboard, bocce & horseshoe tournaments. **Nearby Attractions:** Peace River canoe ramp 3 mi. south, antique shops in Arcadia. **Additional Information:** DeSoto County Chamber of Commerce, (863) 494-4033.

RESTRICTIONS

Pets: On leash & in designated areas only, proof of insurance policy for dogs over 30 lbs. required. **Fires:** In grill or designated campfire areas only. **Alcoholic Beverages:** At sites only. **Vehicle Maximum Length:** 45 ft. (call ahead for availability).

TO GET THERE

I-75 Exit 29/Hwy. 17 north 32 mi. to campground.

ARCADIA   MAP, C-2
Peace River Campground

2998 NW Hwy. 70, 34266.
T: (863) 494-9693 or (800) 559-4011;
www.peacerivercampground.com.

🚐 ★★★★	🏕 ★★★★
Beauty: ★★★★	Site Privacy: ★★★
Spaciousness: ★★★★	Quiet: ★★★★
Security: ★★★★	Cleanliness: ★★★★
Insect Control: ★★	Facilities: ★★★★

This wonderfully rustic and wooded campground might let you forget you're in a campground at all—almost. The shady camp overlooks the Peace River, and the campground has become home to a fossil museum, thanks to the excavation of the bones of three mammoths from the riverbed. Sharks' teeth continue to be a popular find for those who like to wade in the scenic river waters and sift through the sands along the bottom and shorelines. The laid-back, peaceful campground hosts an interesting group each year—the Ruckus Society gathers here in the spring to train peaceful demonstrators in the techniques of getting attention without getting in trouble. Lots of wildlife live in the surrounding environs, including alligators, bobcats, deer, gray foxes; even the occasional panther passes through. There are a few pull-through sites among the trees, and although there is plenty of room and plenty of trees, there are not specific site buffers in many cases.

BASICS

Operated By: Owners George & Johnny Lempenau. **Open:** All year. **Site Assignment:** First come, first served; reservations accepted; $50 deposit plus 3-night minimum required for holidays. **Registration:** At office. **Fee:** $15–$43. **Parking:** Yes.

FACILITIES

Number of RV-only Sites: 182. **Hookups:** Electric (20, 30, 50 amps), water, sewer. **Each Site:** Picnic table. **Dump Station:** Yes. **Laundry:** Yes. **Pay Phone:** Yes. **Restrooms and Showers:** Yes. **Fuel:** No. **Propane:** Yes. **Internal Roads:** Crushed shell, in good condition. **RV Service:** Referral. **Market:** 4 mi. east to Arcadia. **Restaurant:** 4 mi. east to Arcadia. **General Store:** Yes. **Vending:** Yes. **Swimming:** Pool, river. **Playground:** Yes. **Other:** Boat ramp, video room w/ pool tables, shuffleboard, horseshoes, fishing pond, miniature animal farm, snowbird dance hall, computers. **Activities:** Canoeing, fishing, fossil hunting. **Nearby Attractions:** Peace River, antique shops in Arcadia. **Additional Information:** DeSoto County Chamber of Commerce, (863) 494-4033.

RESTRICTIONS

Pets: On leash only. **Fires:** Allowed, in designated areas. **Alcoholic Beverages:** Allowed. **Vehicle Maximum Length:** No limit.

TO GET THERE

I-75 Exit 29/Hwy. 17, 22 mi. east to Hwy. 70, north/left 4 mi. to campground.

BIG PINE KEY   MAP, D-2
Sunshine Key RV Park

38801 Overseas Hwy., 33043. T: (305) 872-2217;
www.rvonthego.com.

🚐 ★★★	🏕 ★★★
Beauty: ★★	Site Privacy: ★
Spaciousness: ★	Quiet: ★★
Security: ★★★★★	Cleanliness: ★★★★★
Insect Control: ★★★★	Facilities: ★★★★★

A great campground for RVers who love to boat and fish—this Encore property offers a boat dock as well as a few waterfront sites under the perpetual sunshine of the Florida Keys. Book early, especially for winter visits. Most of the sites are pull-throughs.

Gravel and white sand underfoot and scattered small trees and bushes give a stark appearance. There are virtually no buffers between sites: this location is here for recreation, not the wilderness experience, although registered campers can visit a bird sanctuary across the highway. Tennis and basketball courts at the campground add to the fun, and a poolside snack bar provides refreshment.

BASICS

Operated By: National Homes Community/Encore. **Open:** All year. **Site Assignment:** By request on site or by phone in advance; 1-night rental deposit by credit card, refundable up to 7 days prior. **Registration:** At office. **Fee:** $25; tent, $30–$64; MC, V, D, AE. **Parking:** Yes.

FACILITIES

Number of Multipurpose Sites: 400. **Hookups:** Electric (30, 50 amps), water, sewer, cable TV. **Each Site:** Table. **Dump Station:** Yes. **Laundry:** Yes. **Pay Phone:** Yes. **Restrooms and Showers:** Yes. **Fuel:** Yes. **Propane:** Yes. **Internal Roads:** Paved & gravel, in good condition. **RV Service:** Referral. **Market:** 8 mi. south to Big Pine Key. **Restaurant:** 8 mi. south to Big Pine Key (plus poolside café for breakfast & lunch). **General Store:** Yes. **Vending:** Yes. **Swimming:** Heated pool. **Playground:** Yes. **Other:** Game room, basketball, volleyball, horseshoes, tennis court, shuffleboard, boat marina. **Activities:** Boating, fishing, kayaking, scuba, snorkeling (rentals available), winter recreation program includes bingo, shows, & dinners. **Nearby Attractions:** Beach, Key West is 39 mi. away. **Additional Information:** Florida Keys & Key West Tourist Council, (800) 648-5510, www.fla-keys.com.

RESTRICTIONS

Pets: On leash only. **Fires:** In grill only (not provided); no open fires. **Alcoholic Beverages:** Allowed. **Vehicle Maximum Length:** No limit. **Other:** Max. 6 campers per site.

TO GET THERE

US 1 south from Miami 61 mi. to mile marker 39, campground on west (Gulfside).

BOKEELIA   MAP, C-2
Cayo Costa State Park

reserve america

Pineland Rd., 33922. T: (941) 964-0375;
www.reserveamerica.com.

🚐	🏕 ★★★★
Beauty: ★★★	Site Privacy: ★★★
Spaciousness: ★★★	Quiet: ★★★★
Security: ★★★	Cleanliness: ★★★★
Insect Control: ★★★	Facilities: ★★

Over 2,000 acres, 5 multiuse trails, and 7 miles of beach make this visit a memorable occasion. This park is accessible by boat or ferry only which is wonderful for those who make the effort of visiting. A favorite at this park besides the solitude is the cabin community. Cayo Costa ("key by the coast") State Park occupies most of an island, which lies in a chain of barrier islands that shelter Charlotte Harbor and

Pine Island Sound from the storms of the Gulf of Mexico. The natural features of the island are stunning. Miles of beaches, acres of pine forests, oak palm hammocks, mangrove swamps, and a spectacular display of birdlife welcome visitors to this subtropical dreamland. Recreational activities include picnicking, fishing, boating, primitive camping, rental cabins, and beach activities. Shelling is especially good during the winter months. As there is no lifeguard on duty guests swim at their own risk.

BASICS

Operated By: Florida State Parks. **Open:** All year. **Site Assignment:** Reservations can be made 11 months in advance. **Registration:** At office. **Fee:** Cabin, $27.52; tent, $16.51. **Parking:** At park.

FACILITIES

Number of Multipurpose Sites: 140. **Hookups:** None. **Dump Station:** No. **Laundry:** No. **Pay Phone:** No. **Restrooms and Showers:** Yes. **Fuel:** No. **Propane:** No. **Internal Roads:** Paved. **RV Service:** No. **Market:** No. **Restaurant:** No. **General Store:** No. **Vending:** No. **Swimming:** Yes. **Playground:** No. **Activities:** Amphitheaters, beach combing, biking, bird-watching, boating, canoeing, fishing, hiking, kayaking, nature programs, picnicking, snorkeling, star gazing.

RESTRICTIONS

Pets: Pets are permitted in designated day-use areas. **Fires:** Permitted in designated fireplaces. **Alcoholic Beverages:** Not allowed. **Other:** There is no electricity at the park. No stores or restaurants on island. Food should be brought in animal-proof containers. No generators allowed at this park. Park accessible by ferry.

TO GET THERE

Accessible only by passenger ferry or private boat. Reservations are required on the ferry service. Call Tropic Star of Pine Island at (239) 283-0015.

BRADENTON MAP, C-2
Lake Manatee State Park

reserve america

20007 State Rd. 64, 34212. T: (941) 741-3028; www.reserveamerica.com.

🚐 ★★★★	🏕 ★★★★
Beauty: ★★★★	Site Privacy: ★★★
Spaciousness: ★★★	Quiet: ★★★★
Security: ★★★★★	Cleanliness: ★★★★
Insect Control: ★★★	Facilities: ★★★★

Lake Manatee State Park is a 556-acre park extending 3 miles along the south shore of Lake Manatee. This 2,400-acre reservoir supplies the drinking water for Manatee and Sarasota counties. The rest of the park is primarily pine flatwoods and sand pine scrub with some depression marshes and hardwood forests. A boat ramp provides easy access to the lake; boat motors must be less than 20 horsepower. Canoeing and kayaking are also popular activities. The lake offers excellent freshwater fishing, and anglers can fish from their boats or from the park's fishing dock. Swimming is permitted in a designated area of Lake

Manatee; a facility with showers is located nearby. A large picnic area is nestled in a sand pine scrub area near the lake. Five miles of multiuse trails offer interior and lakeside hikes. Mountain bikes and equestrians welcome. A picnic pavilion may be reserved for a fee. Campers can enjoy full-facility camping, just a short walk from the lake. A wide variety of plants and animals can be observed at the park.

BASICS

Operated By: Florida State Parks. **Open:** All year. **Site Assignment:** Reservations can be made 11 months in advance. **Registration:** At office. **Fee:** Single, $18. **Parking:** At park.

FACILITIES

Number of Multipurpose Sites: 216. **Hookups:** Yes. **Dump Station:** Yes. **Laundry:** No. **Pay Phone:** Yes. **Restrooms and Showers:** Yes. **Fuel:** No. **Propane:** No. **Internal Roads:** Paved. **RV Service:** No. **Market:** 5 mi. **Restaurant:** Less than 20 mi. **General Store:** Less than 3 mi. **Vending:** No. **Swimming:** Yes. **Playground:** Yes. **Activities:** Biking, bird-watching, boating, canoeing, fishing, hiking, interpretive programs, kayaking, photography, picnicking, sailing, wildlife viewing.

RESTRICTIONS

Pets: Pets are permitted in designated day-use areas. **Fires:** Permitted in designated fireplaces. **Alcoholic Beverages:** Not allowed. **Vehicle Maximum Length:** 65 ft. **Other:** Boat motors are restricted to 20 horsepower or less. A Florida freshwater fishing license is required for persons 16 years of age & older.

TO GET THERE

Lake Manatee State Park is 9 mi. east of I-75 on FL 64 in Bradenton, Florida.

BRISTOL MAP, A-1
Torreya State Park

reserve america

HC 2 Box 70, 32321. T: (850) 643-2674; www.reserveamerica.com.

🚐 ★★★★	🏕 ★★★★
Beauty: ★★★★	Site Privacy: ★★★
Spaciousness: ★★★	Quiet: ★★★★
Security: ★★★★	Cleanliness: ★★★★
Insect Control: ★★★	Facilities: ★★★★

High bluffs overlooking the Apalachicola River make Torreya one of Florida's most scenic places. The park is named for an extremely rare species of Torreya tree that only grows on the bluffs along the Apalachicola River. This once-plentiful tree was nearly destroyed by disease in the early 1960s and may be doomed to extinction. Torreya is popular for camping, hiking, and picnicking as well as bird-watching. Over 100 species of birds have been spotted in the park. But animals were not the only inhabitants known to exist in the area over the centuries. Archaeologists have discovered a number of Native American sites here. During the first Seminole Indian War in 1818, General Andrew Jackson crossed the river here with his army. Forests of hardwood trees provide the finest

display of fall color found in Florida. The main campground offers full-facility campsites and a YURT (Year-round Universal Recreational Tent). Primitive campsites and a youth campground are also available. Ranger-guided tours of the Gregory House, a fully furnished plantation home built in 1849, are given by park staff throughout the year.

BASICS

Operated By: Florida State Parks. **Open:** All year. **Site Assignment:** Reservations can be made 11 months in advance. **Registration:** At office. **Fee:** Single $12–$30. **Parking:** At park.

FACILITIES

Number of Multipurpose Sites: 105. **Hookups:** Yes. **Dump Station:** No. **Laundry:** No. **Pay Phone:** No. **Restrooms and Showers:** Yes. **Fuel:** No. **Propane:** No. **Internal Roads:** Paved. **RV Service:** No. **Market:** No. **Restaurant:** No. **General Store:** Yes. **Vending:** Yes. **Swimming:** No. **Playground:** Yes. **Activities:** Bird watching, hiking, picnicking.

RESTRICTIONS

Pets: Pets are permitted in designated day-use areas. **Fires:** Permitted in designated fireplaces. **Alcoholic Beverages:** Not allowed. **Vehicle Maximum Length:** 30 ft. **Other:** The park gates close at sunset. If you plan to arrive late, please contact the park before 3 p.m. on the day of your arrival.

TO GET THERE

Off I-10, take Exit 24 (north) on CR 270A. Go to the stop sign and turn left (south), on CR 269 (start following the signs). Go to CR 270 and turn right (south). Go several miles to Phillips Rd. Turn right to dead end, then turn right (west) in CR 1641. Follow that to park. Hwy. 20 at Bristol, FL. Turn (north) about 7 mi. to CR 1641, turn left (west) and follow signs to park (about 7 mi.).

CEDAR KEY MAP, C-2
Sunset Isle RV Park

11850 SW SR 24, P.O. Box 150, 32625. T: (352) 543-5375 or (800) 810-1103; www.cedarkeyrv.com.

🚐 ★★★★	🏕 ★★★
Beauty: ★★★	Site Privacy: ★
Spaciousness: ★★	Quiet: ★★★
Security: ★★★★	Cleanliness: ★★★★★
Insect Control: ★★	Facilities: ★★★

This is the only RV park on the island. The campground offers tours of the island, as well as the many smaller islands that surround. There is a clubhouse and four docks. The campground has 8 pull-through sites, while the rest are back-ins. For the nature lover, there are palm and pine trees. Among some of the birds and animals on this island, there are eagles, herons, pelicans, and kingfishers. Kayaking among the smaller islands is enjoyable. They also offer arts and craft classes and downtown is only a short hike away.

BASICS

Operated By: The Wilson family. **Open:** All year. **Site Assignment:** Reservations accepted by phone w/ credit card; deposits also accepted by mail.

Registration: At office. **Fee:** Motel rooms, $75–$85; RV waterfront (full hookup), $42; RV interior (full hookup), $38; MC, V, local check. **Parking:** Yes.

FACILITIES

Number of RV-only Sites: 53. **Number of Tent-only Sites:** Undesignated sites. **Hookups:** Electric (30, 50 amps), water, sewer, cable TV, Internet hookup in clubhouse. **Each Site:** Picnic table, grills. **Dump Station:** Yes. **Laundry:** No. **Pay Phone:** In clubhouse. **Restrooms and Showers:** Yes. **Fuel:** No. **Propane:** Yes. **Internal Roads:** Gravel in good condition. **RV Service:** No. **Market:** 3 blocks south, 3 blocks east to downtown Cedar Key. **Restaurant:** 3 blocks south. **General Store:** In town. **Vending:** No. **Swimming:** No. **Playground:** Yes. **Other:** Clubhouse, 4 docks, cabins available. **Activities:** Fishing, crabbing, clamming, bird-watching, island tours, seminars & arts & craft classes. **Nearby Attractions:** State Museum & County Museum, Fanning Springs. **Additional Information:** Cedar Key Chamber of Commerce, (352) 543-5600, www.cedarkey.org.

RESTRICTIONS

Pets: On leash only; $2 per day pet fee. **Fires:** In central fire area. **Alcoholic Beverages:** Allowed on site. **Vehicle Maximum Length:** 45 ft. **Other:** Office hours are 9 a.m.–8 p.m.

TO GET THERE

From I-75 in Gainesville, take Exit Hwy. 24. Go 70 mi. west to Cedar Key (24 mi. west on Hwy. 24 past US 19/98). Turn right on 6th St. to G St. Go right to campground at 7th St.

CHIPLEY MAP, D-2 INSET
Falling Waters State Recreation Area

reserve america

1130 State Park Rd., 32428. T: (850) 638-6130 or (800) 326-3521; www.reserveamerica.com.

🚐 ★★★		▲ ★★★★★
Beauty: ★★★★★		Site Privacy: ★★★★
Spaciousness: ★★★★		Quiet: ★★★★★
Security: ★★★★★		Cleanliness: ★★★★★
Insect Control: ★★★★★		Facilities: ★★★★

Falling Waters State Recreation Area boasts an unusually high elevation for Florida—and that's a great advantage during mosquito season when larvae thrive in puddles and lakes. The campground itself is particularly high within the park, which adds to the interest of the area. Once a camper has made the slow climb to the top of the hill, campsites form a single small circle around central restrooms and a playground for kids. The quiet, wooded setting is peaceful and friendly. For the nature lover, there are long-leaf pines, palm trees, magnolia trees, and honeysuckle. Among the wildlife, most common are cardinals, blue jays, woodpeckers, foxes, and squirrels. Six of the sites are pull-through half circles and 16 are back-ins.

BASICS

Operated By: Florida Dept. of Environmental Protection, Division of Recreation & Parks. **Open:** All year. **Site Assignment:** First come, first served;

reservations w/ 1-night deposit; 24-hour cancellation policy. **Registration:** At office. **Fee:** $15; MC, V. **Parking:** Yes.

FACILITIES

Number of RV-only Sites: 24. **Hookups:** Electric (30 amps), water. **Each Site:** Picnic table, grill. **Dump Station:** Yes. **Laundry:** No. **Pay Phone:** Yes. **Restrooms and Showers:** Yes. **Fuel:** No. **Propane:** No. **Internal Roads:** Paved, in good condition. **RV Service:** Referral. **Market:** 3 mi. north on 77A to supermarket. **Restaurant:** 3 mi. north on 77A. **General Store:** No. **Vending:** Soft drinks. **Swimming:** Lake. **Playground:** Yes. **Other:** Lake, hiking trails, sinkholes, waterfall, amphitheater. **Activities:** Hiking, swimming, fishing. **Nearby Attractions:** Florida Caverns State Park. **Additional Information:** Washington County Chamber of Commerce, (850) 638-4157, www.washcomall.com.

RESTRICTIONS

Pets: On leash only, proof of vaccinations required. Tags will not be accepted. **Fires:** Grill only. **Alcoholic Beverages:** Not allowed. **Vehicle Maximum Length:** 45 ft. **Other:** No firearms, no fireworks, quiet time 11 p.m.

TO GET THERE

Exit I-10 or Hwy. 90 at Chipley, 3 mi. south of town on Hwy. 77A.

CHOKOLOSKEE MAP, D-2
Outdoor Resorts—Chokoloskee Island RV Resort and Marina

P.O. Box 39, 34138. T: (239) 695-2881; www.outdoor-resorts.com/chokmap.htm.

🚐 ★★★★★		▲ ★★★★
Beauty: ★★★		Site Privacy: ★★★
Spaciousness: ★★★		Quiet: ★★★
Security: ★★★★		Cleanliness: ★★★★★
Insect Control: ★★★		Facilities: ★★★★

This owner-occupied park offers rental units as well as sites for travelers. Sites are large, with concrete pads and grass, some on the waterfront. On the Turner River, which runs from the Everglades and out to the Gulf of Mexico after passing through the Ten Thousand Islands, the park offers a marina and boat, canoe, and kayak rentals as well as fishing gear. But with many other amenities, such as three swimming pools and tennis courts, there's plenty to do for those who aren't interested in fishing.

BASICS

Operated By: Manager Kenny Brown. **Open:** All year. **Site Assignment:** Reservations accepted w/ $25 deposit; 7-day cancellation policy. **Registration:** At office. **Fee:** $49. **Parking:** Yes.

FACILITIES

Number of RV-only Sites: 283. **Hookups:** Electric (30, 50 amps), water, sewer, cable TV, phone. **Each Site:** Table (most sites). **Dump Station:** Yes. **Laundry:** Yes. **Pay Phone:** No. **Restrooms and Showers:** Yes. **Fuel:** Yes. **Propane:** No. **Internal Roads:** Paved, in good condition. **RV Service:** Referral. **Market:** 2 mi. north in Everglades City. **Restaurant:** 2 mi. north in Everglades City. **Gen-**

eral Store: Yes. **Vending:** No. **Swimming:** 3 pools. **Playground:** No. **Other:** Tennis courts, shuffleboard, rec hall, weight room, marina, boat rentals, fishing guides, bait shop, 24-hour security. **Activities:** Winter activities include dinners, bingo, ice-cream socials, craft exhibits, etc. Fishing. **Nearby Attractions:** Ten Thousand Islands, Everglades National Park. **Additional Information:** Everglades Chamber of Commerce.

RESTRICTIONS

Pets: Allowed. **Fires:** Grill only. **Alcoholic Beverages:** Allowed, in moderation. **Vehicle Maximum Length:** 45 ft. plus. **Other:** No vans or tents.

TO GET THERE

US 41 from Miami (60 mi.) or Naples (40 mi.) to CR 29, south through Everglades City across 3-mi. causeway to Chokoloskee, to campground on left.

CLERMONT MAP, B-2
Lake Louisa State Park

reserve america

7305 US 27, 34714. T: (352) 394-3969; www.reserveamerica.com.

🚐 ★★★★		▲ ★★★★
Beauty: ★★★★		Site Privacy: ★★★
Spaciousness: ★★★		Quiet: ★★★★
Security: ★★★★		Cleanliness: ★★★★
Insect Control: ★★★		Facilities: ★★★

A short drive from Orlando, this park is noted for its six beautiful lakes, rolling hills, and scenic landscapes. Lake Louisa is the largest in a chain of 13 lakes connected by the Palatlakaha River, which is designated as an Outstanding Florida Waterway. Lake Louisa, Dixie Lake, and Hammond Lake, the park's most accessible lakes, provide access for fishing, canoeing, and kayaking. Anglers can fish in four of the park's six lakes, but gasoline-powered boats are not allowed; only boats powered by trolling motors or without motors are permitted. Swimmers regularly use the small, nonguarded beach on summer weekends. The park is relatively large, encompassing 4,372-acres of bald cypress, live oak, and saw palmettos. Birdwatching and picnicking are other recreations enjoyed. More than 15 miles of horse trails are available for equestrians. For hikers and backpackers, the park has over 20 miles of hiking trails with excellent opportunities for wildlife viewing. Dixie Lake has a fishing pier, canoe/kayak launch, and a picnic pavilion. The park also has a full-facility campground and primitive campsites. Cabins are also available.

BASICS

Operated By: Florida State Parks. **Open:** All year. **Site Assignment:** Reservations can be made 11 months in advance. **Registration:** At office. **Fee:** Single, $21; cabin, $110; 6 people. **Parking:** At park.

FACILITIES

Number of Multipurpose Sites: 179. **Hookups:** Yes. **Dump Station:** Yes. **Laundry:** No. **Pay Phone:** No. **Restrooms and Showers:** Yes. **Fuel:** No. **Propane:** No. **Internal Roads:** Paved. **RV Service:** No. **Market:** Less than 3 mi. **Restaurant:** No.

General Store: No. **Vending:** No. **Swimming:** No. **Playground:** No. **Activities:** Biking, boating, fishing, hiking, interpretive programs, photography.

RESTRICTIONS

Pets: Pets are permitted in designated day-use areas. **Fires:** Permitted in designated fireplaces. **Alcoholic Beverages:** Not allowed. **Other:** No skateboards or ORVs are allowed at this park. No swimming in Dixie or Hammond Lakes. Cabins require a 2-night min. on weekends, 3-night on holidays.

TO GET THERE

Campground is 7 mi. south of Hwy. 50 on US 27.

CLEWISTON   MAP, C-3
Big Cypress State Preserve

HC Box 54-A, 33440. T: (863) 983-1330 or (800) 437-4102; www.bigcypressrvresort.com.

🚐 ★★★   🏕 ★★★

Beauty: ★★★	Site Privacy: ★★★
Spaciousness: ★★★★	Quiet: ★★★★★
Security: ★★★★	Cleanliness: ★★★
Insect Control: ★★	Facilities: ★★★

If you're looking for wilderness in the Everglades, you've found it here in the Big Cypress National Preserve and the Big Cypress Seminole Indian Reservation. And if you think the glades are just a big swamp, you'll be pleasantly surprised to find that there is plenty of high ground, thickly forested with flora, including water oak trees, sabal palms, and shrubbery. The large park also has abundant hibiscus flowers and a pretty pond and garden area. Six of the 110 sites are pull-throughs.

BASICS

Operated By: Seminole Indian Reservation. **Open:** All year. **Site Assignment:** Reservations accepted; $50 credit card deposit; at least 30-day cancellation. **Registration:** At park office. **Fee:** Cabin, $65–$75; RV, $24; RV/tent, $19; tent, $17. **Parking:** Yes.

FACILITIES

Number of RV-only Sites: 110. **Number of Tent-only Sites:** 75. **Hookups:** Electric (30, 50 amps), water, sewer, phone. **Each Site:** Picnic table, grill. **Dump Station:** Yes. **Laundry:** Yes. **Pay Phone:** Yes. **Restrooms and Showers:** Yes. **Fuel:** Yes. **Propane:** Yes. **Internal Roads:** Paved & gravel, in good condition. **RV Service:** Referral. **Market:** 2 mi. southeast on CR 833. **Restaurant:** 3 mi. west on Safari Road. **General Store:** Yes. **Vending:** Yes. **Swimming:** Yes. **Playground:** Yes. **Other:** Rec hall, mini-golf, shuffleboard, basketball, horseshoes. **Activities:** Fishing, swimming, boating, safari airboat & swamp buggy rides. **Nearby Attractions:** Boat ramp, Lake Okeechobee, Billie Swamp Safari Wildlife Park, Seminole Indian park featuring airboat rides, eco-tours, restaurant w/ authentic Indian food; Ah-Tah-Thi-Ki Museum w/ exhibits depicting the history of the Seminole Indians in Florida. **Additional Information:** Big Cypress National Preserve, (941) 695-2000.

RESTRICTIONS

Pets: On leash only, max. 2 pets per rig. **Fires:** In grill or designated area only. **Alcoholic Beverages:** Not allowed. **Vehicle Maximum Length:** 36 ft. **Other:** No firearms or fireworks.

TO GET THERE

I-75 (Alligator Alley between Fort Lauderdale and Naples) Exit 14 at mile marker 49 onto Snake Rd., north 19 mi. to park.

CRYSTAL RIVER   MAP, C-2
Rock Crusher Canyon
RV and Music Park

reserve america

275 South Rock Crusher Rd., 34429. T: (352) 795-3870 or (352) 795-1313; www.rccrvpark.com or www.reserveamerica.com.

🚐 ★★★★★   🏕 ★★★

Beauty: ★★★★	Site Privacy: ★★★
Spaciousness: ★★★★★	Quiet: ★★★★★
Security: ★★★★★	Cleanliness: ★★★★★
Insect Control: ★★★	Facilities: ★★★

This hidden RV paradise of rolling hills with shaded, level, grassy sites is like an oasis on Florida's west-central coast. Once you've found it, though, you're not likely to forget it, especially if you're a music lover. The park offers regular concerts with famous vintage and country headliners like Glen Campbell, the Tommy Dorsey Orchestra, and The Ink Spots. The top-rated park features individual restrooms/showers, wide sites with plenty of bushes and trees providing privacy, and the unusual bonus of several elevations. The park also offers a fitness center, country store, pool, and clubhouse. It's easy to see how this park has received top ratings from industry experts.

BASICS

Operated By: Private operator. **Open:** All year. **Site Assignment:** Reservations accepted; 1-night deposit required except for special events, which require multinight stays & nonrefundable tickets. **Registration:** At park office. **Fee:** Daily fee, $17–$23 (w/ Good Sam rate); $35 (w/out Good Sam rate). **Parking:** Yes.

FACILITIES

Number of RV-only Sites: 398. **Hookups:** Electric (50 amps), water, sewer, cable TV, phone. **Each Site:** Picnic table. **Dump Station:** Yes. **Laundry:** Yes. **Pay Phone:** Yes. **Restrooms and Showers:** Yes. **Fuel:** No. **Propane:** Yes. **Internal Roads:** Paved, in good condition. **RV Service:** Referral. **Market:** 2.5 mi. west to Crystal River/Hwy. 19. **Restaurant:** 2.5 mi. west to Crystal River/Hwy. 19. **General Store:** Yes. **Vending:** Yes. **Swimming:** Yes. **Playground:** Yes. **Other:** Amphitheater, lakes, shuffleboard, horseshoes, fitness center, modem access available, paddleboats, golf, golf cart rental. **Activities:** Country music & bluegrass concerts & festivals, fishing. **Nearby Attractions:** Crystal River Springs, Homosassa Springs (home to manatees), Weeki Wachee Springs, mermaid amusement park. **Additional Information:** Nature Coast Tourism Development, Inc. & Welcome Center, (352) 564-9197, www.crystalriver-ecotours.com.

RESTRICTIONS

Pets: On leash only. **Fires:** Designated areas only. **Alcoholic Beverages:** Allowed. **Vehicle Maxi-**

mum **Length:** No limit. **Other:** Quiet hours 11 p.m.–7:30 a.m.

TO GET THERE

From Hwy. 19/Crystal River, turn east on Venable Rd. (by the Home Depot store), 2.3 mi. to Rock Crusher Rd., right/south to entrance on the left.

DELAND   MAP, B-2, B-3
Hontoon Island State Park

reserve america

2309 River Ridge Rd., 32720. T: (386) 736-5309; www.reserveamerica.com.

🚐   🏕 ★★★★

Beauty: ★★★★	Site Privacy: ★★
Spaciousness: ★★★	Quiet: ★★★★
Security: ★★★	Cleanliness: ★★★★
Insect Control: ★★★	Facilities: ★★★★

Long before Hontoon Island became a state park, the Timucuan tribe of Native Americans, who thrived off the region's shellfish, inhabited it. As a result of consuming the scrumptious food source for generations, shell middens were formed and are still visible today. It is a unique experience to visit this boat-access only island, and then hike to the top of a shell midden to perch on a park bench and enjoy the silence of nature. Soaring overhead is the wonderful birdlife. Eagles and osprey will catch your eye first. Located in central Florida, Hontoon Island State Park was purchased by the Florida State Parks System in 1967 and today remains a relatively undeveloped site enjoyed by nature and recreation enthusiasts. This park is a fun excursion that takes little effort to reach. All day a ferry transports small numbers of visitors back and forth from the mainland to the park. In addition, there are 40 boat slips on the island. Shore power and water hookup are available for overnight accommodations at the slips. No reservations are accepted for the slips. Fishing is a natural recreation at the park. Many anglers cast a line from shore and reel in largemouth bass, shellcrackers, catfish, and bluegill. Hiking a short distance from the ranger station to the 80-foot observation tower gives the visitor a bird's-eye view of the surrounding area and the park's accommodations. Picnic tables, grills, restrooms, biking roads, and trails are visible from the higher elevation. A campground, primitive cabin community, and canoe rental are available for a small fee.

BASICS

Operated By: Florida State Parks. **Open:** All year. **Site Assignment:** Reservations can be made 11 months in advance. **Registration:** At office. **Fee:** Single, $12; cabin, $25–$30; 4–6 people minimum. **Parking:** At park.

FACILITIES

Number of Multipurpose Sites: 58. **Hookups:** Yes. **Dump Station:** No. **Laundry:** No. **Pay Phone:** Yes. **Restrooms and Showers:** Yes. **Fuel:** No. **Propane:** No. **Internal Roads:** Paved. **RV Service:** No. **Market:** No. **Restaurant:** No. **General Store:** Yes. **Vending:** Yes. **Swimming:** No. **Playground:** Yes. **Activities:** Bank fishing, biking, bird-watching, boating canoeing, fishing, hiking, horse-shoes, kayaking, photography, picnicking, star gazing, volleyball, wildlife viewing.

RESTRICTIONS

Pets: Pets are permitted in designated day-use areas. **Fires:** Permitted in designated fireplaces. **Alcoholic Beverages:** Not allowed. **Other:** Hontoon Island is accessible by passenger-ferry service or private boat only. Ferry service runs 8 a.m.–1 hour before sunset Sun.–Thurs., & until 7 p.m. on Fri. & Sat. year-round.

TO GET THERE

Hontoon Island is located west of DeLand off of FL 44. Turn on CR 4110 (Old New York Ave.), left if you are traveling west on FL 44, right if you are traveling east on FL 44. Follow CR 4110 to CR 4125 (Hontoon Rd.) make a left, go to River Ridge Rd. (continuation of CR 4125) and make a left onto River Ridge Rd.

ESTERO
Koreshan State Historic Site
MAP, C-2

reserve america

P.O. Box 7, 33928. T: (239) 992-0311 or (800) 326-3521; www.reserveamerica.com.

★★★★ / ★★★★

Beauty: ★★★★★
Spaciousness: ★★★★
Security: ★★★★★
Insect Control: ★★★
Site Privacy: ★★★★
Quiet: ★★★★
Cleanliness: ★★★★★
Facilities: ★★★★★

This small, unassuming park with the somewhat daunting name (the 'e' in Koreshan is pronounced as a short vowel like 'ch') offers a fascinating glimpse into a tiny but powerful piece of history. The site is the pre-served settlement of a religious sect founded in 1894 by New York doctor Cyrus Teed, who called himself by the Biblical name Koresh. Teed believed in immor-tality, therefore the sect practiced celibacy. Teed died in 1908, but not before establishing the settlement of a few hundred followers, which included a group kitchen, machine shop, and cultural-arts hall, where several paintings are still displayed. One depicts Teed's vision of the world, an inverted Earth with Heaven in its center. The buildings and their well-preserved con-tents make it clear that the group was well educated, musical, and artistic. The gardens they created of bam-boo, monkey trees, pineapple, citrus, and mangoes still stand, although the last of the sect members expired in the early 1960s, leaving the settlement to the state for preservation. Campers will enjoy the long loops of very private sites surrounded by an abun-dance of trees, in close proximity to the Estero River, a prime site for canoeing (rentals available); swimming is prohibited, perhaps because of alligators.

BASICS

Operated By: Florida Dept. of Environmental Pro-tection, Division of Recreation & Parks. **Open:** All year. **Site Assignment:** Reservations highly recom-mended & accepted up to 11 months in advance; 1-night deposit; 24-hour cancellation policy. **Regis-tration:** At office. **Fee:** $22. **Parking:** Yes.

FACILITIES

Number of RV-only Sites: 48. **Number of Tent-only Sites:** 12. **Hookups:** Electric (20, 30 amps), water. **Each Site:** Picnic table, fire ring. **Dump Sta-tion:** Yes. **Laundry:** Yes. **Pay Phone:** Yes. **Restrooms and Showers:** Yes. **Fuel:** No. **Propane:** No. **Internal Roads:** Paved & crushed shell, in good condition. **RV Service:** Referral. **Mar-ket:** 0.25 mi. across US 41. **Restaurant:** 0.25 mi. across US 41. **General Store:** No. **Vending:** Yes. **Swimming:** No. **Playground:** Yes. **Other:** Beach (nearby), volleyball court, boat launch, historic settle-ment. 4 wheelchair-accessible sites. **Activities:** Fish-ing, canoeing (rentals available). **Nearby Attractions:** Corkscrew Swamp Sanctuary, an Audubon Society nature preserve; Everglades Won-der Gardens in Bonita Springs; Teco Arena; Dog Rac-ing Track in Bonita Springs; beach; Mound Key Archaeological State Park, an adjacent island; Edison Ford estate in Fort Myers. **Additional Informa-tion:** Lee Island Coast CVB, (800) 237-6444, www.leeislandcoast.com.

RESTRICTIONS

Pets: On leash only, proof of vaccinations required, not allowed in buildings or canoes. **Fires:** In grill or fire ring only. **Alcoholic Beverages:** Not allowed. **Vehicle Maximum Length:** 40 ft. **Other:** No firearms or fireworks. No vehicle washing.

TO GET THERE

I-75 Exit 19, Estero onto Corkscrew Rd., 2 mi. west to Koreshan State Historic Site just 0.3 mi. west of US 41.

FERNANDINA BEACH
Amelia Island, Fort Clinch State Park
MAP. A-2. A-3

2601 Atlantic Ave., 32034.
T: (904) 277-7274 or (800) 326-3521; www.floridastateparks.org/fortclinch.

★★★★ / ★★★★

Beauty: ★★★★★
Spaciousness: ★★★★
Security: ★★★★★
Insect Control: ★★★
Site Privacy: ★★★
Quiet: ★★★★
Cleanliness: ★★★★
Facilities: ★★★★★

How does watching the sunset from the riverfront or the beach sound? It's not unlikely that you might see dolphins jumping in the surf, and even possible you might catch sight of the elusive right whales that come to calve in the offshore waters. Train your binoculars on Cumberland Island across the channel and you just might see the wild horses that still live there, left over from the island's days of glory as home to Carnegies and Rockefellers. The camp-grounds at Fort Clinch State Park provide shore side benches to enjoy the view. Campsites are all back in, but fairly spacious, with a path through the woods behind sites at the river campground leading to the beach—watch out for huge wolf spiders that weave webs among the trees! Take time for a tour of historic Fort Clinch itself, built for the Civil War but never used in battle; the place is fully equipped as a living-history exhibit, with touchable replicas so kids—and adults—can really feel what military life in the late 1800s must have been like. While you're on the island, be sure to sample the delicious local copper shrimp that makes the region famous.

BASICS

Operated By: Florida Dept. of Environmental Pro-tection, Division of Recreation & Parks. **Open:** All year. **Site Assignment:** First come, first served, reservations w/ 1-day deposit; 24-hour cancellation policy. **Registration:** At ranger station. **Fee:** $20.67; MC,V, D. **Parking:** Yes.

FACILITIES

Number of RV-only Sites: 21. **Number of Tent-only Sites:** 6. **Hookups:** Electric (30 amps), water. **Each Site:** Picnic table, fire ring. **Dump Station:** Yes. **Laundry:** Yes. **Pay Phone:** No. **Restrooms and Showers:** Yes. **Fuel:** No. **Propane:** No. **Inter-nal Roads:** Paved in good condition. **RV Service:** Referral. **Market:** 1.4 mi. south from main gate on Atlantic Blvd. (A1A). **Restaurant:** 0.25 mi. south on Atlantic Blvd., continuing 1.5 mi. **General Store:** Yes, firewood & souvenirs. Gift Shop. **Vending:** Yes. **Swimming:** Ocean. **Playground:** Yes. **Other:** Civil War–era Fort Clinch, beach, pier, river, forest. **Activi-ties:** Tours of historic fort, Civil War reenacts (first weekend of each month), Civil War encamp-ment (first weekend in May), guided nature hikes (9 a.m. Sat.), kids fishing clinic (June), Memorial & Veter-ans Day observations. **Nearby Attractions:** His-toric town of Fernandina Beach. **Additional Information:** Amelia Island Tourist Development Council, (800) 2-AMELIA, www.ameliaisland.org.

RESTRICTIONS

Pets: On leash in designated areas only; proof of vaccinations required; no pets on beach, in buildings, or on boardwalks. **Fires:** Grill only. **Alcoholic Bev-erages:** Not allowed. **Vehicle Maximum Length:** 50 ft. **Other:** No firearms or fireworks; do not dam-age or disturb dunes, nature, or wildlife; digging pro-hibited; quiet time 11 p.m.–7 a.m.

TO GET THERE

Exit I-95 north of Jacksonville onto A1A, east 14 mi. to Fernandina Beach, right on Atlantic Ave. 3 mi. to park.

FLAGLER BEACH
Beverly Beach Camptown RV Resort
MAP, B-3

2816 North Oceanshore Blvd. (Hwy. A1A), 32136. T: (386) 439-3111 or (800) 255-2706; www.beverlybeachcamptown.com.

★★★★ / ★★★

Beauty: ★★★★
Spaciousness: ★
Security: ★★★★
Insect Control: ★★★★
Site Privacy: ★
Quiet: ★★
Cleanliness: ★★★★★
Facilities: ★★★★★

We're generally not impressed with campgrounds that look like parking lots, but this one's directly on the beach—campers pull right up to the seawall, so they can literally wake up and watch the sun rise over the ocean without leaving their beds. That's pretty hard to beat, even without trees and wall-to-wall neighbors. The campground also offers a few tent sites right on the beach. Beverly Beach Camptown has a well-stocked store, too, with everything from souvenirs to beer and wine, plus a small restaurant, in case you're tired of cooking. But the best bonus here—at least for those who like to travel with their pets—is that leashed dogs are allowed on the beach, an unusual treat for our furry friends.

BASICS

Operated By: Manager Karen Siefken. **Open:** All year. **Site Assignment:** Reservations accepted w/ credit card; recommended on holidays & during Daytona special events. **Registration:** At office. **Fee:** Oct.–Jan., $50–$55; Feb.–Apr., $65–$70; May–Sept., $55–$60; tent, $35. **Parking:** Yes.

FACILITIES

Number of RV-only Sites: 130. **Number of Tent-only Sites:** 5. **Hookups:** Electric (30, 50 amps), water, sewer, cable TV. **Each Site:** Picnic table. **Dump Station:** Yes. **Laundry:** Yes. **Pay Phone:** Yes. **Restrooms and Showers:** Yes. **Fuel:** No. **Propane:** No. **Internal Roads:** Paved, in good condition. **RV Service:** On site. **Market:** 4 mi. south on A1A. **Restaurant:** On site for breakfast & lunch or 4 mi. south on A1A. **General Store:** Yes. **Vending:** Yes. **Swimming:** Beach. **Playground:** No. **Other:** Beach, meeting room, & café. **Activities:** Swimming, fishing, boogie-board surfing. **Nearby Attractions:** Daytona Beach 20 mi. south. **Additional Information:** Flagler Beach Chamber of Commerce, (800) 298-0995 www.flaglercounty.com/fbcc.

RESTRICTIONS

Pets: On leash only, must be picked up after. **Fires:** On beach when weather permitting. **Alcoholic Beverages:** Allowed. **Vehicle Maximum Length:** 45 ft.

TO GET THERE

I-95 Exit 91, 3.5 mi. east on SR 100 to A1A, 3 mi. north to campground.

FLAGLER BEACH   MAP, B-3
Gamble Rogers Memorial State Recreation Area

reserve america

3100 South A1A, 32136. T: (386) 517-2086 or (800) 326-3521; www.reserveamerica.com.

🚐 ★★★★   ⛺ ★★★★

Beauty: ★★★★	Site Privacy: ★★
Spaciousness: ★★	Quiet: ★★★★
Security: ★★★★★	Cleanliness: ★★★★★
Insect Control: ★★★	Facilities: ★★★★

This park was named for troubadour Gamble Rogers, a Floridian who drowned off Flagler Beach while saving another man from drowning in the mid-1980s. The campground, on the beachside, or east of A1A, is a small, gated facility with closely packed sandy sites shielded from the ocean by a bushy barrier of sea oats. Boardwalk paths lead to the beach, but there is no ocean view for campers. Sites have slight bushy buffers, but no trees to break the

---

ocean breezes. The rest of the park is on the west side of A1A—a thin strip of native land bordered by the highway and the Intracoastal Waterway. The park office displays an interesting but sad collection of roadkill collected from the highway—a skunk, ruby-throated hummingbird, Luna moth, rattlesnake, and a dozen or so other snakes. All victims of progress, reminding visitors to drive carefully.

BASICS

Operated By: Florida Dept. of Environmental Protection, Division of Recreation & Parks. **Open:** All year. **Site Assignment:** Reservations recommended & accepted up to 11 months in advance. **Registration:** At park office (across Hwy. A1A from the beach campground). **Fee:** No electric, $18.53; electric, $20.67 (tax included). **Parking:** At site.

FACILITIES

Number of RV-only Sites: 24. **Number of Tent-only Sites:** 10. **Hookups:** Electric (30 amps), water. **Each Site:** Picnic table, ground grill. **Dump Station:** Yes. **Laundry:** No. **Pay Phone:** Yes. **Restrooms and Showers:** Yes. **Fuel:** No. **Propane:** No. **Internal Roads:** Sand roads in good condition. **RV Service:** Referral. **Market:** 3 mi. north on A1A. **Restaurant:** 3 mi. north on A1A. **General Store:** No. **Vending:** No. **Swimming:** Beach. **Playground:** No. **Other:** Sand box, boat ramp, nature trails. **Activities:** Swimming, fishing, boating, hiking. **Nearby Attractions:** None. **Additional Information:** Flagler Chamber of Commerce (386) 439-0995.

RESTRICTIONS

Pets: Leash only, not in buildings or on beach. Proof of vaccination required. **Fires:** Grill/fire ring only. **Alcoholic Beverages:** Not allowed. **Vehicle Maximum Length:** 46 ft. (call ahead to ensure availability). **Other:** No firearms, no fireworks.

TO GET THERE

Exit I-95 at SR 100, 6 mi. east to Hwy. A1A, 3 mi. south to park.

FRUITLAND   MAP, B-2
Lake Griffin State Park

reserve america

3089 US 441/27, 34731. T: (352) 360-6760; www.reserveamerica.com.

🚐 ★★★★   ⛺ ★★★★

Beauty: ★★★★★	Site Privacy: ★★★
Spaciousness: ★★★	Quiet: ★★★★
Security: ★★★★	Cleanliness: ★★★★
Insect Control: ★★★	Facilities: ★★★★

Located near the western shores of Lake Griffin, the park is a well-known destination for canoeing, boating, camping, and especially fishing. The park is just shy of 500 acres composed of swampland and hardwood upland. Between the park's upland and Lake Griffin is an expansive marsh that provides the setting for one of its most distinctive features—the floating islands. Floating in only a few feet of water, these islands are considered prime real estate by the wading birds. The park-entrance hallmark is a 100-year-old

---

live oak tree measuring over 150 feet tall and 10 feet in circumference. Visitors to the recreation area will find it located on the shores of a small lobe of Lake Griffin, a well-known bass fishery. Park amenities include a 40-site campground, boat launch, hiking trails, and large picnic area with reservable pavilion. The 460-plus-acre park was established in the 1960s providing access to Lake Griffin via a small canal. Boaters enjoy fishing along the canal and viewing the abundant wildlife en route to the lake. Campers will find interpretive programs, modern facilities, and a liberal stay policy (extended stays of up to 120 days in a six-month period are permitted). Lake Griffin State Park is best known for its springtime bass fishing. Canoeists and boaters use the launch for access into the canal, which pours into Lake Griffin. Picnickers will find plenty of individual tables.

BASICS

Operated By: Florida State Parks. **Open:** All year. **Site Assignment:** Reservations can be made 11 months in advance. **Registration:** At office. **Fee:** Single, $15. **Parking:** At park.

FACILITIES

Number of Multipurpose Sites: 132. **Hookups:** Yes. **Dump Station:** Yes. **Laundry:** Yes. **Pay Phone:** Yes. **Restrooms and Showers:** Yes. **Fuel:** No. **Propane:** No. **Internal Roads:** Paved. **RV Service:** No. **Market:** No. **Restaurant:** No. **General Store:** No. **Vending:** Yes. **Swimming:** No. **Playground:** Yes. **Activities:** Amphitheaters, bird-watching, canoeing, fishing, horseshoes, interpretive programs, picnicking, volleyball.

RESTRICTIONS

Pets: Pets are permitted in designated day-use areas. **Fires:** Permitted in designated fireplaces. **Alcoholic Beverages:** Not allowed. **Vehicle Maximum Length:** 40 ft. **Other:** Site 39 is considered a "pull-in" site due to the location of the utilities.

TO GET THERE

From I-75, take Exit 329 (Wildwood/Leesburg), following SR 44 east about 10 mi. to US 27 north. Do not make any right turns off of SR 44. Turn left onto US 27 and travel north about 5 mi. Park entrance is on the right about 1 mi. past Wal-mart. From Orlando, take the Florida Turnpike north to Exit 285 (Clermont/Leesburg), and follow US 27 north about 17 mi. Park entrance is on the right about 1 mi. past Wal-mart. From Ocala, take US 27 south about 28 mi. Park entrance is on the left about 1 mi. past Florida Hwy. Patrol Station.

HIGH SPRINGS   MAP, A-2
O'leno State Park

reserve america

410 SE O'leno Park Rd., 32643. T: (386) 454-1853; www.reserveamerica.com.

🚐 ★★★★   ⛺ ★★★★

Beauty: ★★★	Site Privacy: ★★★
Spaciousness: ★★★	Quiet: ★★★★
Security: ★★★	Cleanliness: ★★★★
Insect Control: ★★★	Facilities: ★★★★

Located along the banks of the scenic Santa Fe River, a tributary of the Suwannee River, the park features sinkholes, hardwood hammocks, river swamps, and sandhills. As the river courses through the park, it disappears underground and reemerges over 3 miles away in the River Rise State Preserve. Visitors can picnic at one of the pavilions or fish in the river for their dinner. Canoes and bicycles are available for rent. While hiking the nature trails, visitors can look for wildlife and enjoy the beauty of native plants. The shady, full-facility campgrounds provide 61 sites, the majority with electric hookup. The cabin community and youth group area are footsteps away from the main campground. The primitive camping area is located in the Reserve off River Rise Trail. It is located near Sweetwater Lake and is very popular with hikers. In addition, horse camping is provided just north of High Springs on Highway 27. This area includes a 20-stall barn, restrooms, pavilion, and tables. O'leno State Park is joined with River Rise State Preserve, separated only by Bellamy Road. The total area encompasses 6,000 acres, where miles of multiuse trails offer a variety of recreation. River swimming is a favorite recreation at O'leno. Canoeists and anglers enjoy the clean waters as well; however, fishing success is rather unpredictable. When the fish do bite, anglers pull in largemouth bass, bream, and catfish. A freshwater fishing license is required for individuals 16 years and older. The park does offer canoe rentals.

BASICS

Operated By: Florida State Parks. **Open:** All year. **Site Assignment:** Reservations can be made 11 months in advance. **Registration:** At office. **Fee:** Single, $15. **Parking:** At park.

FACILITIES

Number of Multipurpose Sites: 201. **Hookups:** Yes. **Dump Station:** Yes. **Laundry:** No. **Pay Phone:** No. **Restrooms and Showers:** Yes. **Fuel:** No. **Propane:** No. **Internal Roads:** Paved. **RV Service:** No. **Market:** Less than 10 mi. **Restaurant:** Less than 10 mi. **General Store:** Less than 10 mi. **Vending:** Yes. **Swimming:** Yes. **Playground:** Yes. **Activities:** Bank fishing, biking, bird-watching, canoeing, fishing, hiking, picnicking, wildlife viewing.

RESTRICTIONS

Pets: Pets are permitted in designated day-use areas. **Fires:** Permitted in designated fireplaces. **Alcoholic Beverages:** Not allowed. **Vehicle Maximum Length:** 76 ft. **Other:** Boating is currently not allowed. Please call (386) 454-1853 for further information.

TO GET THERE

O'leno State Park is located approximately 6 mi. north of High Springs, Florida on US 441.

HOBE SOUND   MAP, C-3
Jonathan Dickinson State Park

16450 SE Federal Hwy., 33455. T: (772) 546-2771; www.reserveamerica.com.

🚐 ★★★★   ⛺ ★★★★★

Beauty: ★★★★★	Site Privacy: ★★★★
Spaciousness: ★★★★	Quiet: ★★★★★
Security: ★★★★★	Cleanliness: ★★★★
Insect Control: ★★★	Facilities: ★★★★★

Frequently cited as one of the best camping opportunities in South Florida, Jonathan Dickinson State Park offers a range of ecosystems to study and enjoy, from the Loxahatchee River, Florida's first federally designated Wild and Scenic River (which protects the river from future development and restructuring), to the pine scrub, cypress swamp, and pine flatwoods laced with hiking, biking, and nature trails. Try to visit Trapper Nelson's place on the Loxahatchee—the restored home site of a Florida pioneer trapper who died in 1968 under mysterious circumstances. Boat tours are offered Wednesday–Sunday. The park offers two campgrounds for RVers plus primitive trail camping areas for backpackers. The Pine Grove campground near the park entrance just off US 1 is the largest and provides both small and large sites. Most offer bushy buffers and shade cover from the many tall pine trees throughout the campground. Groups may appreciate the conference building and campfire circle at Pine Grove. The river campground, named for its proximity to the Loxahatchee River that runs along the western border of the park, has fewer tall trees but more native bushy vegetation, which provides greater privacy at each site but little shade. There are no pull-through sites at either campground.

BASICS

Operated By: Florida Dept. of Environmental Protection, Division of Recreation & Parks. **Open:** All year. **Site Assignment:** First come, first served; reservations accepted; deposit required (call for amount). **Registration:** At ranger station. **Fee:** $14–$17; M, V, D, AE. **Parking:** Yes.

FACILITIES

Number of RV-only Sites: 135. **Hookups:** Electric (30 amps), water. **Each Site:** Picnic table, grill. **Dump Station:** Yes. **Laundry:** No. **Pay Phone:** Yes. **Restrooms and Showers:** Yes. **Fuel:** No. **Propane:** No. **Internal Roads:** Paved, in good condition. **RV Service:** Referral. **Market:** 3–5 mi. north or south on US 1. **Restaurant:** 3–5 mi. north or south on US 1. **General Store:** No. **Vending:** Yes. **Swimming:** Beach. **Playground:** Yes. **Other:** Boat dock, hiking trails, observation tower, paved & off-road bike trails, nature trails. **Activities:** Hiking, boating (rentals available include motorboats, canoes, & kayaks), fishing, biking, bird & nature study, boat tours. **Nearby Attractions:** Beaches. **Additional Information:** Hobe Sound Chamber of Commerce, (561) 546-4724.

RESTRICTIONS

Pets: On leash & in designated areas only, proof of rabies vaccination required. **Fires:** Grill only. **Alcoholic Beverages:** After hours only. **Vehicle Maximum Length:** 40 ft. **Other:** No firearms or fireworks.

TO GET THERE

Exit I-95 at SR 708 (Hobe Sound Exit), east to US 1, south to park.

HOLT   MAP, D-1 INSET
Blackwater River State Park

7720 Deaton Bridge Rd., 32564. T: (850) 983-5363 or (800) 326-3521; www.reserveamerica.com.

🚐 ★★★★   ⛺ ★★★★★

Beauty: ★★★★★	Site Privacy: ★★★★★
Spaciousness: ★★★★	Quiet: ★★★★★
Security: ★★★	Cleanliness: ★★★★★
Insect Control: ★★	Facilities: ★★★★

Amazingly remote, this campground entrance was unmanned when we arrived, with self-registration instructions, based on the honor system. Campers were advised to revisit the camp office between 5 and 7 p.m. to register and pay for the campsite. Sites around the two circles were all back-in or pull-in sites, but quite large, with generous buffers. Although peaceful and quiet, the campground was nearly full, and even more visitors were found at the river's edge—Blackwater River is said to be one of the cleanest, most pristine rivers in the world. Happy groups of canoeists, swimmers, kayakers, and tubing enthusiasts frolicked in the cold, fresh, dark water as it wound its way through the park, dotted with wide, white-sand shores. Bobcats and deer are said to be common in this section of state forest. This one is clearly a Florida treasure. Pack the cooler and plan to stay a few days to enjoy the wilderness.

BASICS

Operated By: Florida Dept. of Environmental Protection, Division of Recreation & Parks. **Open:** All year. **Site Assignment:** First come, first served; reservations accepted. **Registration:** At office. **Fee:** $8–10; M, V, D. **Parking:** Yes.

FACILITIES

Number of RV-only Sites: 30. **Hookups:** Electric, water. **Each Site:** Picnic table, fire ring, clothesline poles. **Dump Station:** Yes. **Laundry:** No. **Pay Phone:** Yes. **Restrooms and Showers:** Yes. **Fuel:** No. **Propane:** No. **Internal Roads:** Gravel. **RV Service:** No. **Market:** 2 mi. south on Deaton Bridge Rd. **Restaurant:** 3 mi. south to Hwy. 90. **General Store:** No. **Vending:** No. **Swimming:** Yes. **Playground:** Yes. **Other:** Picnic pavilions, hiking trails & boardwalks, river. **Activities:** Fishing, hiking, swimming, canoeing, & kayaking. **Nearby Attractions:** Blackwater Canoe Outpost—rents canoes & tubes. **Additional Information:** Main Street Milton, (850) 623-2339, www.srcchamber.com; Pensacola CVB, (800) 874-1234, www.visitpensacola.com.

RESTRICTIONS

Pets: On leash only, not allowed on beaches or in river. Also must have proof of vaccination. **Fires:** Grill only. **Alcoholic Beverages:** Not allowed. **Vehicle Maximum Length:** 35 ft. **Other:** No firearms or intoxicants.

TO GET THERE

Exit Hwy. 90 at Harold onto Deaton Bridge Rd., north 3 mi. to park.

JENSEN BEACH MAP, C-3
Nettles Island

9803 South Ocean Dr., 34957. T: (772) 229-1300; www.vnirealty.com.

🚐 ★★★★★   ⛺ n/a

Beauty: ★★	Site Privacy: ★
Spaciousness: ★	Quiet: ★★★
Security: ★★★★★	Cleanliness: ★★★★★
Insect Control: ★★★★★	Facilities: ★★★★★

Quite different from most of the RV parks we've visited, Nettles Island is very popular with retirees who want Florida's great lifestyle at a high value. Nettles Island is wall-to-wall, privately owned sites, some available as rentals, others available for travelers and snowbirds. It is a complete village unto itself, with streets and nicely landscaped grassy lawns on the perimeter sites. Nettles Island includes a recreational section of property across the road, directly on the beach, with pool and cabana club. Fisher's delight.

BASICS
Operated By: VNI Realty. **Open:** All year. **Site Assignment:** First come, first served; reservations necessary Jan.–Mar.; full payment due 30 days before arrival. **Registration:** At office. **Fee:** $39–54. $2 fee for electric hookup. **Parking:** Yes.

FACILITIES
Number of RV-only Sites: 1,578. **Hookups:** Electric (30, 50 amps), water, sewer, cable TV, phone. **Each Site:** Varies—some tables. **Dump Station:** No. **Laundry:** Yes. **Pay Phone:** Yes. **Restrooms and Showers:** Yes. **Fuel:** Yes. **Propane:** Yes. **Internal Roads:** Paved, in good condition. **RV Service:** Referral. **Market:** On site. **Restaurant:** On site. **General Store:** Yes. **Vending:** Soft drinks. **Swimming:** Yes. **Playground:** Yes. **Other:** Mini-golf, volleyball & tennis courts, Jacuzzi, sauna, gas station, bank, hair salon, shuffleboard, marina, clothing store. **Activities:** Fishing off sites, off bridges, in the ocean. **Nearby Attractions:** Ocean, Elliot Museum, Observation & Education Center. **Additional Information:** Jensen Beach Chamber of Commerce, (772) 334-3444, www.jensenchamber.com.

RESTRICTIONS
Pets: On leash only. **Fires:** In grill only (not provided). **Alcoholic Beverages:** Allowed. **Vehicle Maximum Length:** 45 ft. **Other:** No tents or pop-ups—full hookups only.

TO GET THERE
Exit I-95 66 at Fort Pierce (Orange Ave.), east to US 1, north 0.5 mi. to A1A, east across Indian River (Fort Pierce Bridge to Hutchinson Island) then continue south on A1A about 14 mi. to Nettles Island.

KEY LARGO MAP, D-3
John Pennekamp Coral Reef State Park

reserve america

P.O. Box 487, 33037. T: (305) 451-1202; www.reserveamerica.com.

🚐 ★★★★   ⛺ ★★★★

Beauty: ★★★★	Site Privacy: ★★
Spaciousness: ★★★	Quiet: ★★★★
Security: ★★★★★	Cleanliness: ★★★★★
Insect Control: ★★★	Facilities: ★★★★★

Boasting numerous awards as one of the best parks and campgrounds in the state, John Pennekamp Coral Reef State Park offers several unique treats thanks to its location in the Florida Keys, just minutes from Miami. The first undersea park in the nation, 178 square miles of this park extend into the Atlantic Ocean, including a portion of the only coral reef in the country. Park management takes advantage of the prime location to offer boat tours for snorkelers, scuba divers, and scenic viewers—glass-bottom boat rides are also offered daily. Equipment and instruction are available. All RV campsites are back-in only, and many are waterfront but don't afford a view because the camping area is surrounded by protected mangrove trees, revered around the world for their erosion protection and their root system (which can get a little smelly at times), which provide nutrients for the tiniest sea creatures forming the foundation of the food chain.

BASICS
Operated By: Florida Dept. of Environmental Protection, Division of Recreation & Parks. **Open:** All year. **Site Assignment:** Reservations recommended; accepted up to 11 months in advance; 1-night deposit; 24-hour cancellation policy. **Registration:** At park office. **Fee:** $19 standard rate. **Parking:** Yes.

FACILITIES
Number of RV-only Sites: 41. **Number of Tent-only Sites:** 6. **Hookups:** Electric (30, 50 amps), water. **Each Site:** Picnic table, grill. **Dump Station:** Yes. **Laundry:** Less than 3 mi. **Pay Phone:** Yes. **Restrooms and Showers:** Yes. **Fuel:** No. **Propane:** No. **Internal Roads:** Paved & gravel, in good condition. **RV Service:** Referral. **Market:** 1 mi. south or north of the campground entrance. **Restaurant:** 1 mi. north or south of the campground entrance. **General Store:** Yes. **Vending:** Yes. **Swimming:** Yes. **Playground:** Yes. **Other:** Coral reef, nature trails, canoe trails, scuba & snorkel-boat tours. **Activities:** Swimming, hiking, fishing, boating, scuba, snorkeling. **Nearby Attractions:** Florida Keys Wild Bird Center, Tavernier; Key West (100 mi. south). **Additional Information:** Key Largo Chamber of Commerce, (800) 822-1088, www.keylargo.org.

RESTRICTIONS
Pets: Not allowed. **Fires:** Grill only. **Alcoholic Beverages:** Used discreetly after park hours only. **Vehicle Maximum Length:** 40 ft. **Other:** No firearms or fireworks.

TO GET THERE
US 1 south from Miami to mile marker 102.5.

KEY LARGO MAP, D-3
Key Largo Kampground and Marina

101551 Overseas Hwy., 33037.
T: (305) 451-1431 or (800) 526-7688; www.memberstripod.com/klkamp.

🚐 ★★★★   ⛺ ★★

Beauty: ★★★	Site Privacy: ★★
Spaciousness: ★★★	Quiet: ★★★★
Security: ★★★★★	Cleanliness: ★★★★
Insect Control: ★★★	Facilities: ★★★★

This campground is occupied partly by those who own the sites; rentals are not uncommon but are made available on an individual basis through the office. Travelers can overnight in the tent area—a grassy, shaded park near the entrance. The atmosphere is made even more peaceful with coconut palm trees, mahogany, gumbo limbo, and mangroves lining the park, providing habitat to tiny crabs and raccoons. Manatees sometimes venture into the marina from the surrounding bone flats—shallow waterways dotted with protected mangrove islands. Owner's sites reveal an interesting crowd, with fragrant flower and tropical-fruit gardens, wind chimes, and colorful flags. The campground employs interpreters during the winter season to accommodate guests from German-, French-, and Spanish-speaking countries.

BASICS
Operated By: Key Largo Kampground, Inc. **Open:** All year. **Site Assignment:** Reservations requested; 1-night nonrefundable deposit. **Registration:** At office. **Fee:** RV, $46–$63; tent, $30–$33. **Parking:** Yes.

FACILITIES
Number of RV-only Sites: 171. **Number of Tent-only Sites:** 38. **Hookups:** Electric (20, 30, 50 amps), water, sewer, cable TV. **Each Site:** Some tables & grills. **Dump Station:** Yes. **Laundry:** Yes. **Pay Phone:** Yes. **Restrooms and Showers:** Yes. **Fuel:** No. **Propane:** No. **Internal Roads:** Paved, in good condition. **RV Service:** Referral. **Market:** 2 blocks south. **Restaurant:** 2 blocks south. **General Store:** Yes. **Vending:** Yes. **Swimming:** Yes. **Playground:** Yes. **Other:** Marina, boat dock, beach, volleyball, horseshoe & shuffleboard courts. **Activities:** Bingo, game nights, potluck dinners, barbecue nights. **Nearby Attractions:** Coral reef, scuba, snorkeling, deep-sea fishing. **Additional Information:** Key Largo Chamber of Commerce, (800) 822-1088, www.keylargo.org.

RESTRICTIONS
Pets: On leash only. **Fires:** Grill only. **Alcoholic Beverages:** At site only, no offensive behavior. **Vehicle Maximum Length:** 35 ft. **Other:** No firearms or fireworks.

TO GET THERE
US 1 south from Miami to Key Largo (first Key), left on Samson Rd. at mile marker 101.5, 2 blocks to campground.

KEYSTONE HEIGHTS   MAP, A-2
Gold Head Branch State Park

reserve america™

6239 FL 21, 32656. T: (352) 473-4701;
www.reserveamerica.com.

🚐 ★★★   ⛺ ★★★★

Beauty: ★★★★   Site Privacy: ★★★
Spaciousness: ★★★   Quiet: ★★★★
Security: ★★★   Cleanliness: ★★★★
Insect Control: ★★★   Facilities: ★★★★

Mike Roess Gold Head Branch State Park is located on rolling sandhills in an area known as the central ridge of Florida. A deep ravine with springs issuing from its side bisects the area and forms Gold Head Branch. Marshes, lakes, and scrub provide a habitat for a wide variety of wildlife. Gold Branch State Park rests on nearly 2,100 acres and includes several lakes including Little Lake Johnson and Big Lake Johnson, which offer fishing and boating. Others provide scenic wildlife viewing. A large picnic area with tables and grills overlooks Little Lake Johnson. A designated lakeshore swimming area is located adjacent to the picnic area and within easy walking distance from the cabins. No lifeguards are provided. Several nature trails of varying length from a short 10-minute walk to a several-hour hike are offered. These trails meander through the parks' diverse habitats of open sand hills, lush ravine system with its seepage springs, and flowing stream and lakes. The Florida Trail traverses the park for approximately 3 miles. A primitive campsite is available to distance hikers. It is located about midway in the park's trail segment located off a short spur just beyond the intersection with Ridge Nature Trail. You'll have the opportunity to see such wildlife as the Sherman's fox squirrel, southeastern kestrel, red-tailed hawks, bald eagles, various water and wading birds, foxes, and deer.

BASICS

Operated By: Florida State Parks. **Open:** All year. **Site Assignment:** Reservations can be made 11 months in advance. **Registration:** At office. **Fee:** Single, $16; cabin, $346–$567. **Parking:** At park.

FACILITIES

Number of Multipurpose Sites: 225. **Hookups:** Yes. **Dump Station:** Yes. **Laundry:** Less than 5 mi. **Pay Phone:** Yes. **Restrooms and Showers:** Yes. **Fuel:** No. **Propane:** No. **Internal Roads:** Paved. **RV Service:** No. **Market:** Less than 10 mi. **Restaurant:** Less than 10 mi. **General Store:** Less than 10 mi. **Vending:** Yes. **Swimming:** No. **Playground:** Yes. **Other:** Toiletries & dishwashing soap are not provided in the cabins; linens & basic cooking & eating utensils are provided in the cabins. **Activities:** Bank fishing, biking, bird-watching, canoeing, fishing, hiking, interpretive programs, nature programs, picnicking, star gazing, wildlife viewing.

RESTRICTIONS

Pets: Pets are permitted in designated day-use areas. **Fires:** Permitted in designated fireplaces. **Alcoholic Beverages:** Not allowed. **Vehicle Maximum Length:** 45 ft.

TO GET THERE
Park is located 6 mi. north of Keystone Heights on FL 21 midway between Gainesville and Jacksonville in northeast Florida.

LAKE BUENA VISTA   MAP, C-2
Disney's Fort Wilderness Resort and Campground

4510 North Fort Wilderness Trail, 32830.
T: (407) 824-2900; www.disneyworld.com.

🚐 ★★★★   ⛺ ★★★

Beauty: ★★★★   Site Privacy: ★★★
Spaciousness: ★★★★   Quiet: ★★★★
Security: ★★★★★   Cleanliness: ★★★★★
Insect Control: ★★★★★   Facilities: ★★★★★

There's something very different at Disney's Campground. Just as the Magic Kingdom is like no other country and its Main Street like no other town, Disney's Fort Wilderness is a far cry from any other campground we've seen in Florida. For example, you'll be hard-pressed to find a mosquito here, even though the little blood-sucking bugs are a veritable plague throughout most of the rest of the state and beyond. Just as in the Magic Kingdom, the campgrounds are perfectly landscaped and maintained, and plenty of trees and shrubs create a nice sense of seclusion from neighboring campsites. Fort Wilderness offers 20 loops of campsites, plus another 8 for cabins, all spread comfortably across the more than 700-acre campground. Entertainment is also true Disney style, with two video arcades, nightly musical shows around the campfire, two swimming pools, a beach, fitness walks, and bike, boat, and ski rentals available. Horseback trails, pony rides and hayrides, canoeing, and kayaking add to the fun. But perhaps the best thing about Fort Wilderness is its convenient location close to all of Disney's parks—and early daily admission and free transportation to them all is allowed for campers. Enjoy!

BASICS

Operated By: Walt Disney World. **Open:** All year. **Site Assignment:** Reservations accepted through www.disneyworld.com or (407) 934-7639; 1-night deposit; 72-hour cancellation policy. **Registration:** At park office. **Fee:** Tent, $39–$53; cabin, $239; M, V, D, AE, DC, CB. **Parking:** Yes.

FACILITIES

Number of RV-only Sites: 784. **Number of Tent-only Sites:** 83. **Hookups:** Electric (20, 30, 50 amps), water, sewer, cable TV. **Each Site:** Picnic table, grill. **Dump Station:** No. **Laundry:** Yes. **Pay Phone:** Yes. **Restrooms and Showers:** Yes. **Fuel:** No. **Propane:** Yes. **Internal Roads:** Paved, in good condition. **RV Service:** Referral. **Market:** Yes. **Restaurant:** Yes. **General Store:** Yes. **Vending:** Yes. **Swimming:** Yes. **Playground:** Yes. **Other:** Tennis, basketball, & volleyball courts, beach, bike paths, fitness trail, marina, shuffleboard, horseshoes, horse stables, petting farm. **Activities:** Fishing, musical campfire shows, boating, biking, horseback riding, sports. **Nearby Attractions:** Disneyworld Magic Kingdom & MGM, Epcot Center & Animal Kingdom theme parks. **Additional**

Information: Orlando Official Visitor Center, (407) 363-5872, www.orlandoinfo.com.

RESTRICTIONS

Pets: On leash only, proof of rabies, please mention pets when booking reservation. **Fires:** Grill only. **Alcoholic Beverages:** Allowed. **Vehicle Maximum Length:** No limit. **Other:** No fireworks, firearms must be stored at front desk.

TO GET THERE
Exit I-4 at and follow signs to the Magic Kingdom.

LAKE WALES   MAP, C-2
Lake Kissimmee State Park

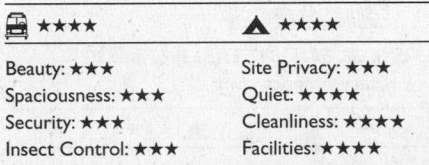

14248 Camp Mack Rd., 33898. T: (863) 696-1112;
www.reserveamerica.com.

🚐 ★★★★   ⛺ ★★★★

Beauty: ★★★   Site Privacy: ★★★
Spaciousness: ★★★   Quiet: ★★★★
Security: ★★★   Cleanliness: ★★★★
Insect Control: ★★★   Facilities: ★★★★

Rich in history, Lake Kissimmee was a prominent site during the Seminole War and the Civil War and served as an important early-American industrial site. Today, visitors can enjoy the 5,930-acre park through many recreational activities. A living history farm, open weekends and holidays, is a favorite for individuals of all ages. The park has always harbored a large number of plant and animal species and even today the park boasts 50 species of plants and animals that are either threatened or endangered. Nestled between three large lakes, one being Florida's third-largest lake, the park is a favorite recreation destination especially with anglers. Lake Kissimmee has been known for years as the host-site for many large fishing tournaments. In addition, nature lovers of all kinds flock to Lake Kissimmee State Park. Photographers, bird-watchers, hikers, and others find relaxing easy amid the pine flatwoods and floodplain prairies. Lake Kissimmee State Park is a quiet destination that offers a variety of recreations including mountain biking, horseback riding, hiking, boating, canoeing, picnicking, nature photography, bird-watching, camping, and more.

BASICS

Operated By: Florida State Parks. **Open:** All year. **Site Assignment:** Reservations can be made 11 months in advance. **Registration:** At office. **Fee:** Single, $12. **Parking:** At park.

FACILITIES

Number of Multipurpose Sites: 198. **Hookups:** Yes. **Dump Station:** Yes. **Laundry:** Yes. **Pay Phone:** No. **Restrooms and Showers:** Yes. **Fuel:** No. **Propane:** No. **Internal Roads:** Paved. **RV Service:** No. **Market:** Less than 1 mi. **Restaurant:** Less than 1 mi. **General Store:** Less than 0.5 mi. **Vending:** No. **Swimming:** No. **Playground:** No. **Other:** Wildlife has the right of way on all roads. **Activities:** Biking, bird-watching, hiking, horseback riding, interpretive programs, photography, picnicking, star gazing.

RESTRICTIONS

Pets: Pets are permitted in designated day-use areas. **Fires:** Permitted in designated fireplaces. **Alcoholic Beverages:** Not allowed. **Vehicle Maximum Length:** 40 ft.

TO GET THERE

From Florida Turnpike, take FL 60 west to Boyscout Rd. Turn right (north) onto Boyscout Rd. and go to Camp Mack Rd. Turn right onto Camp Mack Rd. and go 5.5 mi. to park main entrance. From US 27, take FL 60 east to Boyscout Rd. Turn left (north) onto Boyscout Rd. and go to Camp Mack Rd. Turn right onto Camp Mack Rd. and go 5.5 mi. to park entrance.

LITHIA
Alafia River State Park
MAP, C-2

reserve america

14325 S. CR 39, 33547. T: (813) 672-5320; www.reserveamerica.com.

🚐 ★★★★ 　　　　　 ⛺ ★★★★

Beauty: ★★★　　　　 Site Privacy: ★★★
Spaciousness: ★★★　 Quiet: ★★★★
Security: ★★★★　　　 Cleanliness: ★★★★
Insect Control: ★★★　 Facilities: ★★★★

Once the site of a phosphate mine, the reclaimed land has a unique topography that offers some of the most radical elevation changes in Florida, making Alafia's off-road bicycling trails the most challenging in the area. Helmets are required on the trails. Equestrians and hikers can explore 20 miles of trails that travel through mixed hardwood forests, pine flatwoods, and rolling hills. Bird-watchers and nature enthusiasts will delight in the abundance of wildlife along the trails. Scattered lakes and the south prong of the Alafia River provide opportunities for canoeing, kayaking, and fishing. Picnic pavilions, a playground, horseshoe pit, and volleyball court are available. For overnight stays, the park has a full-facility campground and equestrian-friendly campsites. Alafia River State Park's camping facilities include water, 50-amp electrical service, independent dump station, volleyball area, horseshoe pits, restroom facilities with showers, and ADA-accessible picnic shelters. Pets are welcome. Alafia River State Park offers numerous lakes for fishing. Bass, bluegill, and catfish are among the fish that you may catch. A fishing license is required for all freshwater fishing for people 16 and older.

BASICS

Operated By: Florida State Parks. **Open:** All year. **Site Assignment:** Reservations can be made 11 months in advance. **Registration:** At office. **Fee:** Single, $18. **Parking:** At park.

FACILITIES

Number of Multipurpose Sites: 68. **Hookups:** Yes. **Each Site:** Fire ring. **Dump Station:** Yes. **Laundry:** No. **Pay Phone:** Less than 0.5 mi. **Restrooms and Showers:** Yes. **Fuel:** No. **Propane:** No. **Internal Roads:** Paved. **RV Service:** No. **Market:** Less than 10 mi. **Restaurant:** Less than 10 mi. **General Store:** Less than 0.5 mi. **Vend-**ing: No. **Swimming:** No. **Playground:** Yes. **Activities:** Bank fishing, biking, bird-watching, boating, canoeing, fishing, hiking, horseback riding, interpretive programs, kayaking, photography, wildlife viewing.

RESTRICTIONS

Pets: Pets are permitted in designated day-use areas. **Fires:** Permitted in designated fireplaces. **Alcoholic Beverages:** Not allowed. **Other:** Firearms & fireworks not allowed.

TO GET THERE

Alafia River State Park is located in southeastern Hillsborough County, about 30 mi. southeast of Tampa. Access to the park is gained from CR 39, between CR 640 and CR 672.

LIVE OAK
Spirit of the Suwannee Music Park
MAP, A-1

3076 95th Dr., 32060. T: (386) 364-1683 or (800) 224-5656; www.musicliveshere.com.

🚐 ★★★★ 　　　　　 ⛺ ★★★★★

Beauty: ★★★★★　　 Site Privacy: ★★★
Spaciousness: ★★★★★ Quiet: ★★★★
Security: ★★★★★　　 Cleanliness: ★★★★
Insect Control: ★★★★　 Facilities: ★★★★★

Music is a mainstay of the local activities—bring your own and join in or come for the frequent concerts, which include nationally known musicians of a variety of genres, from bluegrass and country to Christian and rock. Campers can choose from full-hookup RV sites to rentable trailers called cabins to a treehouse overlooking the outdoor amphitheater. Seventy-five of the sites are pull-throughs.

BASICS

Operated By: The Cornett family. **Open:** All year. **Site Assignment:** Reservations accepted; payment in full, refundable up to 15 days in advance. **Registration:** At park office. **Fee:** RV, $20–$25; tent, $15; V, MC, D. **Parking:** Yes.

FACILITIES

Number of RV-only Sites: 1,000. **Number of Tent-only Sites:** Undesignated sites. **Hookups:** Electric (20, 30, 50 amps), water, sewer, cable TV. **Each Site:** Picnic table. **Dump Station:** Yes. **Laundry:** Yes. **Pay Phone:** Yes. **Restrooms and Showers:** Yes. **Fuel:** No. **Propane:** No. **Internal Roads:** Paved & gravel, in good condition. **RV Service:** Referral. **Market:** 4.5 mi. south on Hwy. 129 to I-10. **Restaurant:** 4.5 mi. north on Hwy. 129 to I-75. **General Store:** Yes. **Vending:** Yes. **Swimming:** Pool. **Playground:** Yes, 4. **Other:** Paddleboat & canoe rentals, amphitheater, restaurant, pickin' shed, horse stables, 15 mi. of trails, 3 stages, game field for up to 20,000 people. **Activities:** Playing and/or listening to music, canoeing, fishing, hiking, horseback riding. **Nearby Attractions:** Inquire at campground. **Additional Information:** Suwannee County Tourist Development Council, (386) 362-3071, www.suwanneechamber.com.

RESTRICTIONS

Pets: On leash only. **Fires:** Must be attended. **Alcoholic Beverages:** Allowed. **Vehicle Maximum Length:** No limit. **Other:** No firearms or ATVs.

TO GET THERE

4.5 mi. south of I-75 at Hwy. 129/Live Oak; 4.5 mi. north of I-10 at Hwy. 129/Live Oak.

LOXAHATCHEE
Lion Country Safari KOA
MAP, C-3

2000 Lion Country Safari Rd., 33470. T: (561) 793-9797 or (800) 562-9115; www.lioncountrysafari.com.

🚐 ★★★★★ 　　　　 ⛺ ★★★★

Beauty: ★★★　　　　 Site Privacy: ★★
Spaciousness: ★★★　 Quiet: ★★★
Security: ★★★★★　　 Cleanliness: ★★★★★
Insect Control: ★★★★　 Facilities: ★★★★★

Through the village of Royal Palm Beach and past the interesting city of Wellington, where many residents are aviators and share runways for driveways, finally you'll find a very unique attraction—Lion Country Safari, home to hundreds of African animals for more than 30 years. There are 58 back-in sites and most sites are not shielded from one another.

BASICS

Operated By: Managers. **Open:** All year. **Site Assignment:** Reservations accepted; 1-night deposit, 48-hour cancellation policy, less $4 fee. **Registration:** At park office. **Fee:** $32–$44; M, V, D, AE. **Parking:** Yes.

FACILITIES

Number of RV-only Sites: 214. **Number of Tent-only Sites:** 19. **Hookups:** Electric (30, 50 amps), water, sewer. **Each Site:** Picnic table, concrete pad. **Dump Station:** Yes. **Laundry:** Yes. **Pay Phone:** Yes. **Restrooms and Showers:** Yes. **Fuel:** No. **Propane:** Yes. **Internal Roads:** Paved, in good condition. **RV Service:** Referral. **Market:** Approx. 5.5 mi. east on Southern Blvd. **Restaurant:** Approx. 4 mi. east on Southern Blvd. **General Store:** Yes. **Vending:** Yes. **Swimming:** Yes. **Playground:** Yes. **Other:** Horseshoes, shuffleboard, volleyball, basketball & petanque (similar to bocce) courts. **Activities:** Swimming, horseshoes, shuffleboard, basketball, petanque, visiting the adjacent Lion Country Safari. **Nearby Attractions:** Lion Country Safari, a 500-acre wildlife preserve park where African animals such as rhinoceroses, elephants, lions, & tigers are among the more than 1,000 animals who roam free throughout the preserve. Visitors may observe the animals from the safety of enclosed vehicles as they drive through the preserve. An amusement park offers rides, mini-golf, paddleboats, petting zoo. **Additional Information:** Palm Beach County CVB, (800) 554-PALM, www.palmbeachfl.com.

RESTRICTIONS

Pets: On leash only; 2 per site. Kennels available for $5. **Fires:** In grill, charcoal only; no wood fires. **Alcoholic Beverages:** At site only. **Vehicle Maximum Length:** Big rigs welcome. **Other:** Quiet hours 10 p.m.–8 a.m., no bike riding after dusk, children must wear helmets when riding.

TO GET THERE

Exit I-95 at Southern Blvd., west 20 mi. to campground.

MADISON MAP, A-1, **A-2**
Yogi Bear's Jellystone Park Camp-Resort

1051 Old St. Augustine Rd., 32340.
T: (850) 973-8269; www.jellystoneflorida.com.

🚐 ★★★★★ ⛺ ★★★★

Beauty: ★★★ · Site Privacy: ★★★
Spaciousness: ★★★★ · Quiet: ★★★★
Security: ★★★★ · Cleanliness: ★★★★★
Insect Control: ★★★★ · Facilities: ★★★★★

Although this campground is conveniently situated right off the highway in north-central Florida, it's much more than a parking lot for overnight travelers. This campground offers plenty of opportunities for play—it is quickly becoming a destination in itself. It is the only Yogi Bear Jellystone campground in Florida, and Yogi himself often visits to cheer the children in a wide variety of activities, from mini-golf to a water slide. Regular tram rides take visitors to the back lot to see the frontier village, often the site of paint-ball showdowns. Some of the largest and most scenic sites are located on the lakeshore. Others are opposite a small pine forest, giving the campground a very spacious and comfortable feel with grass underfoot. Restrooms are private, individual shower/toilet rooms. 75 of the sites are pull-throughs, but most people want to stay awhile to relax and enjoy the activities. Kids are entertained throughout the days, and karaoke and even an "opry" hall features occasional performances for older travelers.

BASICS

Operated By: Jim & Latrelle Ragans. **Open:** All year. **Site Assignment:** Reservations accepted w/ credit card; $25 deposit; 48-hour cancellation policy. **Registration:** At park office. **Fee:** $27–$34. **Parking:** Yes.

FACILITIES

Number of RV-only Sites: 98. **Number of Tent-only Sites:** 8. **Hookups:** Electric (30, 50 amps), water, sewer, free local TV stations. **Each Site:** Picnic table, grill, fire ring, lantern. **Dump Station:** Yes. **Laundry:** Yes. **Pay Phone:** Yes. **Restrooms and Showers:** Yes. **Fuel:** No. **Propane:** No. **Internal Roads:** Gravel, in good condition. **RV Service:** Referral. **Market:** 4 mi. north on Hwy. 53. **Restaurant:** 2 mi. north on Hwy. 53. **General Store:** Yes. **Vending:** Yes. **Swimming:** Yes. **Playground:** Yes. **Other:** Lake, waterslide, frontier town, tram tours, mini-golf, rec hall, movie room. **Activities:** Holiday parties, volleyball tournaments (June), kids weekends (July), bingo, paintball, RV rally park. **Nearby Attractions:** Capital city, Tallahassee. **Additional Information:** Madison County Tourism Development Council, (850) 973-2788, www.madisonfl.org.

RESTRICTIONS

Pets: On leash only, in designated areas. **Fires:** In grill fire rings only. **Alcoholic Beverages:** At site only. **Vehicle Maximum Length:** No limit. **Other:** Don't feed the alligators.

TO GET THERE

Exit I-10 east of Tallahassee at Madison, Exit 37, take Hwy. 53 south to Ragans Lake Rd. (first road to right), turn right and follow 0.75 mi. to campground.

MALABAR MAP, B-3
Camelot RV Park

1600 US 1, 32950. T: (321) 724-5396; www.camelotrvpark.com.

🚐 ★★★★★ ⛺ n/a

Beauty: ★★★ · Site Privacy: ★★★
Spaciousness: ★★★ · Quiet: ★★★
Security: ★★★★★ · Cleanliness: ★★★★★
Insect Control: ★★★★★ · Facilities: ★★★★★

More like a small village than a typical RV park, this 15-acre complex seems a comfortable location for travelers with time to stay awhile in this quiet and peaceful section of Florida's central east coast. Owners help visitors get to know their neighbors by organizing frequent leisure events such as pitch-in dinners and dances. If the office happens to be closed when you arrive, you may self-select from among many large, grassy sites dotted with oak and palm trees, then register at your convenience. There are approximately 16 pull-through sites. The campground offers a nice view of the Intracoastal Waterway/Indian River across the road, where a private fishing dock is available for guests. Dolphins and manatees can often be spotted passing by in the river. Snowbirds will appreciate that this park offers RV storage, too.

BASICS

Operated By: Owners Bobby, Liz, & John Ritter. **Open:** All year. **Site Assignment:** Reservations accepted; deposit recommended. **Registration:** At office. **Fee:** $33–$36. **Parking:** Yes.

FACILITIES

Number of RV-only Sites: 130. **Hookups:** Electric (30, 50 amps), water, sewer, cable TV, phone, modem. **Each Site:** Picnic table & patio. **Dump Station:** Yes. **Laundry:** Yes. **Pay Phone:** Yes. **Restrooms and Showers:** Yes. **Fuel:** No. **Propane:** Yes. **Internal Roads:** Paved, in good condition. **RV Service:** Referral. **Market:** 2 mi. west. **Restaurant:** Walking distance north. **General Store:** No. **Vending:** Yes. **Swimming:** No. **Playground:** No. **Other:** Basketball, shuffleboard, & bocce courts, rec hall, fishing dock. **Activities:** Bingo, musical performances & dances, barbecue dinners, craft groups, fishing. **Nearby Attractions:** Intracoastal Waterway (Indian River), beach. **Additional Information:** Melbourne/Palm Bay Area Chamber of Commerce, (800) 771-9922, www.melpb-chamber.org.

RESTRICTIONS

Pets: On leash only. **Fires:** Grill only. **Alcoholic Beverages:** Allowed. **Vehicle Maximum Length:** Big rigs welcome. **Other:** Quiet time 10 p.m.–8 a.m.

TO GET THERE

I-95 Exit 70 east on Hwy. 514, 4.5 mi. to US 1, south 2 blocks to park.

MARIANNA MAP, A-1
Arrowhead Camping and RV Park

4820 US 90 East, 32446. T: (850) 482-5583 or (800) 643-9166; www.arrowheadcamp.com.

🚐 ★★★★ ⛺ ★★★

Beauty: ★★★ · Site Privacy: ★★
Spaciousness: ★★ · Quiet: ★★★★
Security: ★★★★★ · Cleanliness: ★★★★
Insect Control: ★★★★ · Facilities: ★★★★

This large, friendly campground offers a comfortable place to stay for those visiting the Marianna area not far from Tallahassee. Although it is on the main highway of the small town, the adjacent lake and plenty of tall trees give the camp a rural atmosphere. The half of the campground north of the pool and pavilion and running along the water's edge is more desirable, with curving roads and more-wooded sites, although even the less private sites are still pleasant, with grass underfoot and a few trees. There's plenty to do here, too, with boat rentals and fishing docks on Merritt's Mill Pond, a spring-fed lake that boasts the world-record red-eye fish (called a shell cracker in these parts) ever caught. Kids like the mini-golf and game room, and families appreciate the security of the gated entrance adjacent to the office.

BASICS

Operated By: Bill Reddoch. **Open:** All year. **Site Assignment:** Reservations accepted. **Registration:** At park office. **Fee:** $21; cable, $2 fee. **Parking:** Yes.

FACILITIES

Number of RV-only Sites: 262. **Number of Tent-only Sites:** 45. **Hookups:** Electric (20, 30 amps), water, sewer, cable TV. **Each Site:** Picnic table, trash can. **Dump Station:** Yes. **Laundry:** Yes. **Pay Phone:** Yes. **Restrooms and Showers:** Yes. **Fuel:** Yes. **Propane:** Yes. **Internal Roads:** Hard-packed dirt, in good condition. **RV Service:** Referral. **Market:** 0.5 mi. **Restaurant:** 0.5 mi. west on US 90. **General Store:** Yes. **Vending:** Yes. **Swimming:** Yes. **Playground:** Yes. **Other:** Lake, boat launch, fishing docks, rec pavilion, game room. **Activities:** Swimming, fishing, boating. **Nearby Attractions:** Florida Caverns State Park, Falling Waters State Park, 3 golf courses. **Additional Information:** Jackson County Tourist Development Council, (850) 482-8061.

RESTRICTIONS

Pets: On leash only. **Fires:** Fire ring only. **Alcoholic Beverages:** Allowed. **Vehicle Maximum Length:** No limit.

TO GET THERE

1.5 mi. from I-10 Exit 21 (Marianna), 1 mi. north on Hwy. 71 to US 90, 0.5 mi. west to campground.

MARIANNA   MAP, A-1
Florida Caverns State Park

reserve america

3345 Caverns Rd. (S.R. 166), 32446.
T: (850) 482-9598 or (800) 326-3521;
www.reserveamerica.com.

🚐 ★★★★★   ⛺ ★★★★★

Beauty: ★★★★★	Site Privacy: ★★★★
Spaciousness: ★★★★	Quiet: ★★★★★
Security: ★★★★★	Cleanliness: ★★★★★
Insect Control: ★★★★	Facilities: ★★★★★

Who knew there were caves in Florida? Sure enough when the land rises just a bit above sea level, caverns are revealed beneath the surface of the Earth. Left behind by the retreating sea millions of years ago, a dozen caves have been discovered in this state park (but only one is open for public exploration). The park also features a beautiful blue swimming hole. This is one of the nicest parks we've visited in Florida.

BASICS

Operated By: Florida Dept. of Environmental Protection, Division of Recreation & Parks. **Open:** All year. **Site Assignment:** Reservations accepted. **Registration:** At park office. **Fee:** Electric, $14; no electric, $12; MC, V. **Parking:** Yes.

FACILITIES

Number of RV-only Sites: 32. **Number of Tent-only Sites:** 3. **Hookups:** Electric (30 amps), water. **Each Site:** Picnic table, fire ring, clothes poles. **Dump Station:** Yes. **Laundry:** No. **Pay Phone:** Yes. **Restrooms and Showers:** Yes. **Fuel:** No. **Propane:** No. **Internal Roads:** Paved, in good condition & somewhat bumpy dirt roads. **RV Service:** No. **Market:** 3 mi. south on SR 166 to US 90, 2 mi. east to town. **Restaurant:** 3 mi. south on SR 166 to US 90, 2 mi. east to town. **General Store:** Yes. **Vending:** Yes. **Swimming:** Blue Hole spring-fed pond & beach. **Playground:** Yes. **Other:** Cave, visitors center features geologic & historic exhibits, golf course, boat launch. **Activities:** Guided cave tours, swimming, canoeing, hiking, fishing, golf. **Nearby Attractions:** Blue Springs Swimming Area, historic district, marina. **Additional Information:** Jackson County Chamber of Commerce, (850) 482-8061.

RESTRICTIONS

Pets: On leash only; must have proof of rabies vaccination. **Fires:** Fire ring only. **Alcoholic Beverages:** Allowed, in campground after dark. **Vehicle Maximum Length:** 34 ft. **Other:** No firearms, no fireworks. Check Web site for other restrictions.

TO GET THERE

On SR 166 (Caverns Rd), 3 mi. north of US 90.

MELBOURNE BEACH   MAP, B-3
Sebastian Inlet State Recreation Area

reserve america

9700 South A1A, 32951. T: (321) 984-4852;
www.reserveamerica.com.

🚐 ★★★★   ⛺ ★★★★

Beauty: ★★★★	Site Privacy: ★★
Spaciousness: ★★★	Quiet: ★★★★
Security: ★★★★★	Cleanliness: ★★★★★
Insect Control: ★★★★	Facilities: ★★★★★

Although there aren't a lot of trees to shade the campsites at Sebastian Inlet State Recreation Area, neither are there many obstructions to the view. This is one of the few campgrounds we found that allows campers overnight positions on the waterfront. In this case, sites 1–14 look across the road and directly over Sebastian Inlet, and sites 35–50 on the other side of the campground sit on a tidal lagoon, although the view may be somewhat obscured by brush and sea grape trees, a few strangler figs, sabal palm, and gumbo limbo trees. Wood storks and mockingbirds can be seen foraging along the shoreline and among the plants. This state park also offers an unusual bonus, the waterfront restaurant that serves lunch and breakfast. Finally, this beach is known as one of the best surfing areas in the world and hosts several international surfing competitions. Five of the sites are pull-throughs.

BASICS

Operated By: Florida Dept. of Environmental Protection, Division of Recreation & Parks. **Open:** All year. **Site Assignment:** First come, first served; reservations accepted up to 11 months in advance; 1-night deposit; 24-hour cancellation policy. **Registration:** At ranger's office or park entrance gate. **Fee:** $23. **Parking:** Yes.

FACILITIES

Number of RV-only Sites: 51. **Hookups:** Electric (30 amps), water. **Each Site:** Picnic table, fire ring. **Dump Station:** Yes. **Laundry:** Yes. **Pay Phone:** Yes. **Restrooms and Showers:** Yes. **Fuel:** No. **Propane:** No. **Internal Roads:** Paved, in good condition. **RV Service:** Referral. **Market:** About 6 mi. north on Hwy. A1A in Melbourne Beach. **Restaurant:** Park offers oceanside café serving breakfast & lunch, or 6 mi. north on A1A. **General Store:** Yes. **Vending:** Yes. **Swimming:** Indian River, ocean. **Playground:** Yes, small one. **Other:** Boat dock, ramp, & marina w/ boat, canoe, kayak, & pontoon rentals; Fishing museum & treasure museum. **Activities:** Fishing, boating, swimming, surfing. **Nearby Attractions:** Pelican Island National Wildlife Refuge, immediately south of Sebastian Inlet State Recreation Area on A1A. **Additional Information:** Melbourne/Palm Bay Area Chamber of Commerce, (800) 771-9922, www.melpb-chamber.org.

RESTRICTIONS

Pets: On leash only. **Fires:** In grill or fire ring only. **Alcoholic Beverages:** Not allowed. **Vehicle Maxi-** mum Length: No limit. **Other:** Quiet time 11 p.m.–8 a.m., no firearms or fireworks.

TO GET THERE

US 1 to Wabasso, CR 510 east 5 mi. through "Town of Orchid" to A1A, north 7 mi. to Sebastian State Recreation Area.

MIAMI   MAP, D-3
Miami Everglades Campground

20675 SW 162nd Ave., 33187. T: (305) 233-5300;
www.miamicamp.com.

🚐 ★★★★   ⛺ ★★★★

Beauty: ★★★★	Site Privacy: ★★★
Spaciousness: ★★	Quiet: ★★
Security: ★★★	Cleanliness: ★★★
Insect Control: ★★★	Facilities: ★★★★

Miami Everglades Campground is a gated camping community located in the countryside amid avocado and mango groves. It lies near the southernmost tip of Florida, 25 south of Miami and 10 miles east of the vast mangrove forests and watery sawgrass plains of the Everglades National Park. This area is perhaps the state's most diverse region. Numerous area attractions include Miami Metrozoo, Parrot Jungle, and Coral Castle. This is a great place to pitch your tent in a shady tropical setting or drive your RV into one of the many spacious pull-through sites.

BASICS

Operated By: Legacy RV Resorts. **Open:** All year. **Site Assignment:** First come, first served. **Registration:** At main entrance. **Fee:** RV summer, $39. **Parking:** Limit 2 cars.

FACILITIES

Number of RV-only Sites: 305. **Number of Tent-only Sites:** 26. **Hookups:** Electric (30, 50 amps), water, 253 sites w/sewer. **Each Site:** Picnic table. **Dump Station:** Yes. **Laundry:** Yes. **Pay Phone:** Yes. **Restrooms and Showers:** Yes. **Fuel:** No. **Propane:** Yes. **Internal Roads:** Paved, gravel. **RV Service:** 10 mi. southeast of park. **Market:** 1.5 mi. west of park. **Restaurant:** Gators Groveside Grill in campground. **General Store:** Camp store. **Vending:** Yes. **Swimming:** Pool. **Playground:** Yes. **Other:** Paved hiking, biking, walking trail. **Activities:** Shuffleboard, horseshoes, Internet, volleyball court, basketball, pool table, Ping-Pong. **Nearby Attractions:** Miami Zoo, Monkey Jungle, Everglades National Park, Coral Castle, Florida Keys, beaches. **Additional Information:** Homestead Chamber of Commerce, (305) 247-2332.

RESTRICTIONS

Fires: Fire ring. **Alcoholic Beverages:** Allowed. **Vehicle Maximum Length:** 45 ft. **Other:** Daily, monthly, 3-month & 6-month packages.

TO GET THERE

From the Florida Turnpike, take Exit 13 to Quail Roost Rd. Turn right (west) and travel 6 mi. to campground sign.

MICANOPY   MAP, C-2
Paynes Prairie Preserve

reserve america

100 Savannah Blvd., 32667-9702.
T: (352) 466-3397; www.reserveamerica.com.

🚐 ★★★★   ⛺ ★★★★

Beauty: ★★★   Site Privacy: ★★★
Spaciousness: ★★★   Quiet: ★★★★
Security: ★★★   Cleanliness: ★★★★
Insect Control: ★★★   Facilities: ★★★★

Paynes Prairie is biologically, geologically, and historically unique. This park encompasses 21,000 acres and became Florida's first state preserve in 1971 and is now designated as a National Natural Landmark. Noted artist and naturalist William Bartram called it the "great Alachua Savannah" when he wrote about his visit to the prairie in 1774. Artifacts from 10,000 years ago have been recovered on this site. The last known Native American tribe to inhabit the prairie was the Seminole Tribe. During the 1600s, this prairie was the site of the Spanish colonists' largest cattle ranch. Over 20 distinct biological communities provide a rich array of habitats for wildlife, including alligators, bison, wild horses, and over 270 species of birds. Exhibits and an audio-visual program at the visitor center explain the area's natural and cultural history. A 50-foot-high observation tower near the visitor center provides a panoramic view of the preserve. Eight trails provide opportunities for hiking, horseback riding, and bicycling. Ranger-led activities are offered on weekends, November through April. Fishing on Lake Wauberg is allowed, and a boat ramp provides access for canoes and boats with electric motors. Gasoline-powered boats are not allowed. Full-facility campsites are available for overnight visitors.

BASICS
Operated By: Florida State Parks. **Open:** All year. **Site Assignment:** Reservations can be made 11 months in advance. **Registration:** At office. **Fee:** Single, $15. **Parking:** At park.

FACILITIES
Number of Multipurpose Sites: 136. **Hookups:** Yes. **Each Site:** Picnic table, grill. **Dump Station:** Yes. **Laundry:** No. **Pay Phone:** Yes. **Restrooms and Showers:** Yes. **Fuel:** No. **Internal Roads:** Paved. **RV Service:** No. **Market:** Less than 10 mi. **Restaurant:** Less than 10 mi. **General Store:** Less than 1 mi. **Vending:** No. **Swimming:** No. **Playground:** Yes. **Activities:** Bank fishing, biking, boating, canoeing, fishing, hiking, interpretive programs, kayaking, photography, picnicking, sailing, star gazing, wildlife viewing.

RESTRICTIONS
Pets: Pets are permitted in designated day-use areas. **Fires:** Permitted in designated fireplaces. **Alcoholic Beverages:** Not allowed. **Other:** No collecting of firewood. Camping gear must be placed in designated areas only. No hanging or tying of anything on vegetation.

TO GET THERE
The main entrance to the park is located 10 mi. south of Gainesville, or 1 mi. north of Micanopy, on US 441. From I-75 take Exit 374 (Micanopy), take CR 234 east 1 mi. to US 441, proceed north on US 441 0.25 mi. to park entrance (Savannah Blvd.).

MICANOPY   MAP, C-2
Paynes Prairie State Preserve

reserve america

100 Savannah Blvd., 32667. T: (352) 466-3397 or (800) 326-3521; www.reserveamerica.com.

🚐 ★★★★   ⛺ ★★★★★

Beauty: ★★★★★   Site Privacy: ★★★★
Spaciousness: ★★★★   Quiet: ★★★★
Security: ★★★★★   Cleanliness: ★★★★★
Insect Control: ★★★   Facilities: ★★★★

This 21,000-acre wildlife preserve is quite unique, as it provides a safe home for free-roaming wild horses, herds of bison, and "cracker" cattle brought to the state by Spanish pioneers. Visitors are quite likely to encounter deer and perhaps even more unusual animals during a camp stay. An observation tower provides a panoramic view of the prairie—take binoculars so you'll be sure to capture images when you see the buffalo roam across the prairie. The two small campground loops of the Puc Puggy Campground (named for the prairie's founder, William Bartram) provide a quiet hideaway, with wooded terrain and sand and dirt underfoot. None of the sites are pull-through, but there is some vegetation separating each from the next. The camping area is a short hike from the lake.

BASICS
Operated By: Florida Dept. of Environmental Protection, Division of Recreation & Parks. **Open:** All year. **Site Assignment:** First come, first served; reservations recommended up to 11 months in advance by credit card; 24-hour cancellation policy. **Registration:** At park office. **Fee:** $15. **Parking:** Yes.

FACILITIES
Number of RV-only Sites: 35. **Number of Tent-only Sites:** 15. **Hookups:** Electric (20, 30, 50 amps), water. **Each Site:** Picnic table, grill. **Dump Station:** Yes. **Laundry:** No. **Pay Phone:** Yes. **Restrooms and Showers:** Yes. **Fuel:** No. **Propane:** No. **Internal Roads:** Paved, in good condition. **RV Service:** No. **Market:** US 441 south 1 mi. to small grocery store. **Restaurant:** U.S. 441 north 8 mi. to Gainesville. **General Store:** No. **Vending:** No. **Swimming:** No. **Playground:** Yes. **Other:** Wildlife preserve, hiking, biking, horse trails, observation tower, visitors center. **Activities:** Fishing, boating, hiking, horseback riding, educational programs, guided trail hikes. **Nearby Attractions:** Antique stores in historic Old Micanopy, historic home of Marjorie Kinnan Rawlings in nearby Cross Creek. **Additional Information:** Alachua County CVB, (352) 374-5260.

RESTRICTIONS
Pets: Not allowed. **Fires:** Grill, unless restrictions in effect. **Alcoholic Beverages:** Not allowed. **Vehicle Maximum Length:** No limit. **Other:** No firearms, no fireworks, no feeding wildlife, no collecting firewood, stay on established trails.

TO GET THERE
Take I-75 to Exit 75/Micanopy. Go 2 mi. east to US 441 north, then 1 mi. to park entrance on right.

MILTON   MAP, D-1
Milton/Gulf Pines KOA RV Park

8700 Gulf Pines Dr., 32583. T: (850) 623-0808; www.gulfpinesrv.com.

🚐 ★★★★   ⛺ ★★★★

Beauty: ★★★★   Site Privacy: ★★★
Spaciousness: ★★   Quiet: ★★
Security: ★★★   Cleanliness: ★★★
Insect Control: ★★★   Facilities: ★★★★

Milton/Gulf Pines KOA RV Park is located 20 minutes from Pensacola and Navarre Beach. Site amenities include a heated pool and mini-golf. There are also a beautiful tent area and cabins available for rent. Large pull-through sites accommodate the largest rigs with ease. This is a clean and modern park—a very nice destination.

BASICS
Operated By: Legacy RV Resorts. **Open:** All year. **Site Assignment:** Site assigned at time reservation made. **Registration:** At main entrance, open 12 hours daily; night self-check-in available. **Fee:** RV, $36; tent, $24; includes 2 people; each additional person, $3; storage (per day), $3. **Parking:** Limit 2 cars per site, overflow parking available.

FACILITIES
Number of RV-only Sites: 100. **Number of Tent-only Sites:** 32. **Hookups:** Water, electric (20, 30, 50 amps), sewer, cable, phone, Internet connection. **Each Site:** Picnic table. **Dump Station:** Yes. **Laundry:** 2 facilities. **Pay Phone:** Yes. **Restrooms and Showers:** Yes; 2 bathhouses. **Fuel:** No. **Propane:** Yes. **Internal Roads:** Paved, excellent condition. **RV Service:** No. **Market:** 5 mi. northwest in Milton. **Restaurant:** 0.1 mi. from campground. **General Store:** Camp store. **Vending:** Yes. **Swimming:** Pool & 18 mi. north of beach. **Playground:** Yes. **Other:** Picnic areas, mini-golf, game room, clubhouse, basketball, horseshoes. **Activities:** Hiking trails, bikes to rent, basketball, horseshoes, swimming pool, mini-golf, game room. **Nearby Attractions:** Canoeing & tubing at Blackwater River, 18 miles north of Navarre Beach, 20 miles east of Pensacola Naval Air Base.

RESTRICTIONS
Pets: On leash only. No aggressive dogs allowed. **Fires:** Allowed in tent area & community fire pit. **Alcoholic Beverages:** At site only. **Vehicle Maximum Length:** 100 ft. **Other:** 2-week stay limit in tent sites, some long-term RV sites available. Speed limit in park 10 mph, no modified golf carts or gas-powered ORVs allowed.

TO GET THERE

In Florida take Exit 31 off I-10. Campground is located north of I-10 on Hwy. 87.

NAPLES   MAP, D-2
Collier–Seminole State Park

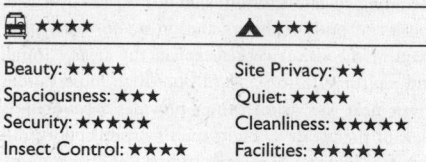

20200 East Tamiami Trail, 34114.
T: (239) 394-3397; www.reserveamerica.com.

🚐 ★★★★   ⛺ ★★★★

Beauty: ★★★★   Site Privacy: ★★★
Spaciousness: ★★★   Quiet: ★★★★
Security: ★★★   Cleanliness: ★★★★
Insect Control: ★★★   Facilities: ★★★★

Collier–Seminole State Park is a wonderful example of the former ecosystem found throughout southern Florida. Once inhabited by various Native American tribes and then preserved by entrepreneur Barron Collier, the park is a reflection of the past. This park is also the gateway to a well-known canoe route within the Ten Thousand Islands and Blackwater River. Nature enthusiasts will not be disappointed. From mammals to birdlife to one of the world's largest mangrove forests, the park highlights these unique features through its nature programs, guided boat tours, and observation tower. Collier–Seminole is home to a 4,760-acre wilderness preserve located in the mangrove swamp. A limited number of visitors are allowed to visit the preserve each day by canoe. It is a 13.5-mile canoe trip to the preserve which offers primitive camping for overnight stays. Tent and RV camping is available at Collier–Seminole State Park. Fishing, boating, and canoeing are popular activities at the park, where the Blackwater River flows, allowing access to the Ten Thousand Islands and the Gulf of Mexico. A 6.5-mile hiking trail winds through pine flatwoods and cypress swamp, allowing visitors to observe the great variety of vegetation and wildlife found in the park. A self-guided nature trail featuring a boardwalk system and observation platform overlooking the salt marsh is also available. Additional exhibits of plants and wildlife may be seen in the park's interpretive center.

BASICS

Operated By: Florida State Parks. **Open:** All year. **Site Assignment:** Reservations can be made 11 months in advance & are highly recommended Nov.–Mar. **Registration:** At office. **Fee:** Single, $18. **Parking:** At park.

FACILITIES

Number of Multipurpose Sites: 492. **Hookups:** Yes. **Each Site:** Grill, water, picnic table. **Dump Station:** Yes. **Laundry:** Yes. **Pay Phone:** Yes. **Restrooms and Showers:** Yes. **Fuel:** No. **Propane:** No. **Internal Roads:** Paved. **RV Service:** No. **Market:** No. **Restaurant:** No. **General Store:** Yes. **Vending:** No. **Swimming:** No. **Playground:** Yes. **Activities:** Amphitheaters, bank fishing, basketball, biking, bird-watching, boating, canoeing, fishing, golf, hiking, interpretive programs, kayaking, nature programs, picnicking, wildlife viewing.

RESTRICTIONS

Pets: Pets are permitted in designated day-use areas. **Fires:** Permitted in designated fireplaces. **Alcoholic Beverages:** Not allowed. **Vehicle Maximum Length:** 30 ft.

TO GET THERE

Going south from Tampa on I-75, take Exit 15 (SR 951 and SR 84) and turn right. Follow 951 to US 41. Turn left on US 41 and the Collier–Seminole State Park will be 8 mi. on the right just past CR 92. Going west from Fort Lauderdale, take Exit 14A (SR 29), go south to US 41 and turn right. Follow US 41 about 15 mi., and the Collier–Seminole State Park will be on your left.

OKEECHOBEE   MAP, C-3
Kissimmee Prairie Preserve State Park

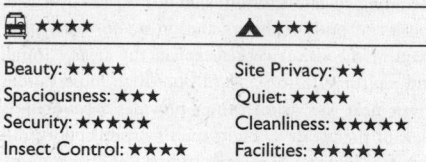

33104 NW 192nd Ave, 34972. T: (863) 462-5360; www.reserveamerica.com.

🚐 ★★★★   ⛺ ★★★★

Beauty: ★★★★   Site Privacy: ★★
Spaciousness: ★★   Quiet: ★★★★
Security: ★★★   Cleanliness: ★★★★
Insect Control: ★★★   Facilities: ★★★★

Located along the east bank of the Kissimmee River, the 46,000-acre preserve is one of the largest remaining stretches of Florida dry prairie, home to an array of endangered plants and animals. These species include the Florida grasshopper sparrow, snail kite, Florida sandhill crane, and crested caracara. The preserve offers a wilderness-type recreational experience with outstanding opportunities for wildlife viewing. Kissimmee Prairie Preserve State Park offers 20 beautiful, shady sites with electric, water, and dump station and 15 primitive sites for horseback campers. A spacious bathhouse with clean showers and laundry facilities is available in the family camping area, and horse paddocks are currently under construction at the horseback campground. Riding the trails in Kissimmee Prairie Preserve State Park on horseback is one of the best ways to see the real Florida. With more than 110 miles of two-trail roads, horseback riders are apt to see an abundance of wildlife. In early spring it's possible to hear the endangered Florida grasshopper sparrow singing in its dry prairie habitat. The trails take you through dry prairie, moist wetlands, and cool, shady hammocks. Bring your own horses and enjoy a day's ride or stay overnight in our beautiful horseback campground.

BASICS

Operated By: Florida State Parks. **Open:** All year. **Site Assignment:** Reservations can be made 11 months in advance. **Registration:** At office. **Fee:** Single, $12. **Parking:** At park.

FACILITIES

Number of Multipurpose Sites: 114. **Hookups:** Yes. **Dump Station:** Yes. **Laundry:** Yes. **Pay Phone:** No. **Restrooms and Showers:** Yes. **Fuel:**

No. **Propane:** No. **Internal Roads:** Paved. **RV Service:** No. **Market:** No. **Restaurant:** No. **General Store:** No. **Vending:** No. **Swimming:** No. **Playground:** No. **Activities:** Biking, bird-watching, hiking, horseback riding, photography, picnicking, stargazing.

RESTRICTIONS

Pets: Pets are prohibited in the campground. **Fires:** Permitted in designated fireplaces. **Alcoholic Beverages:** Not allowed. **Vehicle Maximum Length:** 40 ft. **Other:** On-site firewood collection is not allowed.

TO GET THERE

Kissimmee Prairie Preserve State Park is located approximately 25 mi. north of the city of Okeechobee. The Preserve is located 5 mi. north of the western terminus of Okeechobee CR 724. The road to the park is shell and is not paved. US 441 and Okeechobee CR 700A intersect CR 742. The campground is located 5 mi. inside the park entrance gate.

OKEECHOBEE   MAP, C-3
Zachary Taylor Camping Resort

2995 Hwy. 441 SE, 34974. T: (863) 763-3377 or (888) 282-6523; www.campfloridarv.com.

🚐 ★★★★   ⛺ ★★★

Beauty: ★★★★   Site Privacy: ★★
Spaciousness: ★★★   Quiet: ★★★★
Security: ★★★★★   Cleanliness: ★★★★★
Insect Control: ★★★★   Facilities: ★★★★★

This rural campground has been run by Chuck Freed for a quarter century. A haven for fisher people, the most scenic campsites abut Taylor creek, which flows into Lake Okeechobee, the state's largest lake, well known for its premium bass fishing. In times of drought the connection to the lake is blocked by a man-made dike. Nonetheless, proximity to the lake makes this campground a favorite for those who love to fish. Supplies are only a short distance away in the town of Okeechobee, too. Tall moss-draped cypress trees shade many sites and lean out over the river, narrow wooden docks lead out from the waterfront sites for boaters' access, and alligators, turtles, and herons share the river while gray squirrels scamper along the banks. Bird calls and the whistling of a nearby train provide a nighttime lullaby. Paved circular roads shared by about 100 permanent renters and 150 sites for travelers (each with concrete pads surrounded by grass and trees) wind through the camp. Cabins, a rec hall, and screened pool are provided as well as small separate toilet and shower stalls—be sure to ask for the key to the always-locked facilities reserved for overnight guests. Late arrivals can call ahead, and instructions will be posted at the entrance gate or an on-site security guard will greet and guide you after hours.

BASICS

Operated By: Owners Chuck & Fran Freed. **Open:** All year. **Site Assignment:** Reservations welcome; nonrefundable deposit required. **Registration:** At office. **Fee:** $35. **Parking:** Yes.

FACILITIES

Number of RV-only Sites: 250. **Hookups:** Electric (30 amps), water, sewer. **Each Site:** Picnic table, fire rings on waterfront sites. **Dump Station:** Yes. **Laundry:** Yes. **Pay Phone:** Yes. **Restrooms and Showers:** Yes ($2 key deposit). **Fuel:** No. **Propane:** No. **Internal Roads:** Paved, in good condition. **RV Service:** Referral. **Market:** 3 mi. north on US 441 in Okeechobee. **Restaurant:** 3 mi. north on US 441 in Okeechobee. **General Store:** Yes. **Vending:** Yes. **Swimming:** Yes. **Playground:** No. **Other:** Boat ramp, open grassy field for play. **Activities:** Fishing, boating (rental available), shuffleboard, horseshoes, group crafts in winter, holiday parties, fishing tournaments. **Nearby Attractions:** Lake Okeechobee, Brighton Indian gaming casino. **Additional Information:** Okeechobee County Tourist Development Council, (863) 763-3959 or (800) 871-4403.

RESTRICTIONS

Pets: On leash only. **Fires:** In grill or fire ring only. **Alcoholic Beverages:** Allowed. **Vehicle Maximum Length:** 40 ft. (call for availability). **Other:** 1 car per site, 1 family per site.

TO GET THERE

From US 441 south from Okeechobee 2 mi. to US 441 east 1 mi. to SE 30th Terrace, left (north) to campground entrance.

ORMOND BEACH — MAP, B-3
Tomoka State Park

2099 North Beach St., 32174. T: (386) 676-4050; www.reserveamerica.com.

Beauty: ★★★★ / Site Privacy: ★★★
Spaciousness: ★★★ / Quiet: ★★★★
Security: ★★★★ / Cleanliness: ★★★★
Insect Control: ★★★ / Facilities: ★★★★

Encompassing nearly 1,800 acres of land with 25 miles lying along the coast, Tomoka State Park is just minutes from one of America's most popular beaches, Daytona Beach. This forested park is perfect for picnicking and camping. The park actually rests on a peninsula bordered by the Halifax River, Tomoka River and the Tomoka Basin. Once inhabited by the Timucuan Indians, their burial grounds and shell middens are still visible today. Spanish explorers from the 1600s found the site a favorable vantage point. Today, these waters are popular for canoeing, boating, and fishing. The park protects a variety of wildlife habitats and endangered species, such as the West Indian manatee. Tomoka is a bird-watcher's paradise, with over 160 species sighted, especially during the spring and fall migrations. Visitors can stroll a one-half mile nature trail through a hardwood hammock that was once an indigo field for an 18th century British landowner. A museum houses artworks by artist Fred Dana Marsh, wildlife displays, Native American artifacts, and exhibits about Florida's history. A boat ramp gives boaters and canoeists access to the river. A park store and restaurant offers breakfast, lunch, snacks, camping supplies, and canoe rentals. For overnight stays, the park has full-facility campsites and youth camping.

BASICS

Operated By: Florida State Parks. **Open:** All year. **Site Assignment:** Reservations can be made 11 months in advance. **Registration:** At office. **Fee:** Single, $20. **Parking:** At park.

FACILITIES

Number of Multipurpose Sites: 353. **Hookups:** None. **Dump Station:** Yes. **Laundry:** No. **Pay Phone:** No. **Restrooms and Showers:** Yes. **Fuel:** No. **Propane:** No. **Internal Roads:** Paved. **RV Service:** No. **Market:** Less than 5 mi. **Restaurant:** No. **General Store:** No. **Vending:** Yes. **Swimming:** No. **Playground:** Yes. **Other:** The first week of Mar. is Bike Week & the third week of Oct. is Biketoberfest every year. Park becomes a paradise for motorcycle enthusiasts during this season. **Activities:** Bank fishing, biking, bird-watching, boating, canoeing, interpretive programs, kayaking, photography, picnicking.

RESTRICTIONS

Pets: Pets are permitted in designated day-use areas. **Fires:** Permitted in designated fireplaces. **Alcoholic Beverages:** Not allowed.

TO GET THERE

From I-95 take Exit 268 (SR 40) east approximately 6.5 mi. At the base of the bridge over the Intracoastal Waterway, turn left (north) on North Beach St. Proceed 3.5 mi. to main park entrance.

OSPREY — MAP, C-2
Oscar Scherer State Park

1843 S. Tamiami Trail, 34229. T: (941) 483-5956; www.reserveamerica.com.

Beauty: ★★★ / Site Privacy: ★★★
Spaciousness: ★★★ / Quiet: ★★★★
Security: ★★★ / Cleanliness: ★★★★
Insect Control: ★★★ / Facilities: ★★★★

A large acreage of scrubby flatwoods makes this park one of the best places to see Florida scrub-jays, a threatened species found only in Florida. The park protects scrubby and pine flatwoods that were once widespread throughout Sarasota County. Fifteen miles of trails through these beautiful natural areas provide opportunities for hiking, bicycling, and wildlife viewing. Canoeists and kayakers can paddle along South Creek, a blackwater stream that flows to the Gulf of Mexico. Canoe and kayak rentals are available, but motorized boats are not permitted in the park boundaries. Freshwater and saltwater fishing are available along the creek. Anglers can fish along the shores of Lake Osprey, which is also the park's swimming destination. Picnic areas along South Creek are equipped with grills; pavilions can be reserved for a fee. The park has full-facility campsites and a youth/group campground. The park nature center has exhibits and videos about the park's natural communities.

BASICS

Operated By: Florida State Parks. **Open:** All year. **Site Assignment:** Reservations can be made 11 months in advance. **Registration:** At office. **Fee:** Single, $22. **Parking:** At park.

FACILITIES

Number of Multipurpose Sites: 365. **Hookups:** Yes. **Dump Station:** Yes. **Laundry:** No. **Pay Phone:** Yes. **Restrooms and Showers:** Yes. **Fuel:** No. **Propane:** No. **Internal Roads:** Paved. **RV Service:** No. **Market:** Less than 3 mi. **Restaurant:** Less than 5 mi. **General Store:** Less than 1 mi. **Vending:** Yes. **Swimming:** Yes. **Playground:** Yes. **Activities:** Bank fishing, biking, bird-watching, fishing, hiking, interpretive programs, nature programs, photography, picnicking, wildlife viewing.

RESTRICTIONS

Pets: Pets are permitted in designated day-use areas. Campsites 1–35 & 68–98 are non-pet sites. Pets are not allowed on these sites. Pets are allowed on sites 36–67 & 99–104. **Fires:** Permitted in designated fireplaces. **Alcoholic Beverages:** Not allowed.

TO GET THERE

Oscar Scherer State Park is located on US 41, 2 mi. south of Osprey, FL. Traveling south from Tampa on I-75, take Exit 200 (old 36) to US 41. Traveling north from Ft. Myers on I-75, take Exit 195 (old 35A) to US 41.

PANAMA CITY — MAP, D-1 INSET
St. Andrews State Park

4607 State Park Lane, 32408. T: (850) 233-5140; www.reserveamerica.com.

Beauty: ★★★★ / Site Privacy: ★★★
Spaciousness: ★★★ / Quiet: ★★★★
Security: ★★★ / Cleanliness: ★★★★
Insect Control: ★★★ / Facilities: ★★★★

Well known for its sugar-white sands and emerald-green waters, this 1,260-acre former military reservation has over one-and-a-half miles of beaches on the Gulf of Mexico and Grand Lagoon. Water sports enthusiasts can enjoy swimming, snorkeling, scuba diving, kayaking, and canoeing. Two fishing piers, a jetty, and a boat ramp provide ample fishing opportunities for anglers. Two nature trails wind through a rich diversity of coastal plant communities—a splendid opportunity for bird-watching. Those wanting to relax can sunbathe on the beach or enjoy a leisurely lunch under the shade of a picnic pavilion. A concession offers snacks, souvenirs, and fishing amenities. Two campground loops are situated in the pinewoods near Grand Lagoon. There are 176 campsites with electricity, water, picnic tables, and grills. The sites will accommodate camping units ranging in size from tents to RVs up to 40 feet in length. Dump stations are located in the campground. There are also five bathhouses and one laundry facility.

BASICS

Operated By: Florida State Parks. **Open:** All year. **Site Assignment:** Reservations can be made 11 months in advance. **Registration:** At office. **Fee:** Single, $24. **Parking:** At park.

FACILITIES

Number of Multipurpose Sites: 467. **Hookups:** Yes. **Dump Station:** Yes. **Laundry:** Yes. **Pay Phone:** Yes. **Restrooms and Showers:** Yes. **Fuel:** No. **Propane:** No. **Internal Roads:** Paved. **RV Service:** No. **Market:** Less than 3 mi. **Restaurant:** Less than 0.5 mi. **General Store:** Less than 0.5 mi. **Vending:** Yes. **Swimming:** Yes. **Playground:** Yes. **Activities:** Amphitheaters, bank fishing, biking, bird-watching, boating, body surfing, fishing, hiking, interpretive programs, jet skiing, kayaking, photography, picnicking, sailing, snorkeling, surfing, wildlife viewing, windsurfing.

RESTRICTIONS

Pets: Pets are permitted in designated day-use areas. **Fires:** Permitted in designated fireplaces. **Alcoholic Beverages:** Not allowed. **Vehicle Maximum Length:** 40 ft. **Other:** No collecting of firewood.

TO GET THERE

4 mi. east of Panama City Beach off FL 392 (Thomas Dr.).

PANAMA CITY BEACH   MAP. D-1 INSET
Emerald Coast RV Beach Resort

1957 Allison Ave., 32407. T: (850) 235-0924 or (800) BEACH-RV; www.rvresort.com.

🚐 ★★★★★   ⛺ n/a

Beauty: ★★★	Site Privacy: ★★
Spaciousness: ★★★	Quiet: ★★★
Security: ★★★★★	Cleanliness: ★★★★★
Insect Control: ★★★★★	Facilities: ★★★★★

Given top designations by industry campground rating services, the Emerald Coast RV Beach Resort bills itself as "the highest-rated resort in North America." The resort has earned the compliment by creating a clean, well-manicured park with comfortable clubhouse and amenities—including big-screen TV—all kept in top condition. Premium cable channels are available on site as well. For those who find concrete roads, pads, and patios plus two trees too ascetic, a pair of stocked fishing lakes and recreational area abut the camper lots, providing a taste of nature. Colorful lilies and oleander bloom throughout the park, lending the tropical flair of Florida to the easy living provided at Emerald Coast. Even mosquitoes aren't too bad, thanks to an underground drainage system that eliminates bug-breeding grounds. Daily trash pickup at each site is another big plus that helps keep the park spotless and vermin-free. Some sites are pull-through, and "super sites" can accommodate the largest vehicles with triple slideouts.

BASICS

Operated By: Owners Mr. & Mrs. Hartka. **Open:** All year. **Site Assignment:** Reservations accepted by phone w/ 1-day deposit, $50 for week, or $100 for month; cancellations w/ 14-day notice, less $10 fee. **Registration:** At office. **Fee:** $43.95. **Parking:** Yes.

FACILITIES

Number of RV-only Sites: 164. **Number of Tent-only Sites:** No tents or pop-ups allowed. **Hookups:** Electric (30, 50 amps), water, sewer, cable TV, phone. **Each Site:** Table. **Dump Station:** Yes. **Laundry:** Yes. **Pay Phone:** Yes. **Restrooms and Showers:** Yes. **Fuel:** No. **Propane:** Yes. **Internal Roads:** Paved, in good condition. **RV Service:** Referral. **Market:** 0.75 mi. west on US 98 to supermarket. **Restaurant:** 0.75 mi. west on US 98. **General Store:** Yes. **Vending:** Yes. **Swimming:** Yes. **Playground:** Yes. **Other:** Rec room w/ computer & free e-mail, free coffee, putting green, shuffleboard, sand volleyball, fishing lake, bike rentals, horseshoes, sandbox. **Activities:** Free shuttle to the beach, family cookouts, breakfasts, bingo, card games, movies, organized outings to area restaurants & attractions. **Nearby Attractions:** Zoo next door, beach, pier, & boat charters, outlet shopping mall, 18-hole golf course, amusement park. **Additional Information:** Panama City Beach CVB, (800) PC-BEACH, www.800pcbeach.com.

RESTRICTIONS

Pets: Gentle breeds only, leash required. **Fires:** Grill only. **Alcoholic Beverages:** Allowed. **Vehicle Maximum Length:** No limit. **Other:** No tents or pop-ups.

TO GET THERE

Park is on Allison Ave. between US 98 and Alt. US 98, 1.5 mi. west of Hathaway Bridge (SR 231).

PENSACOLA   MAP, D-1 INSET
Big Lagoon State Park

reserve america

12301 Gulf Beach Hwy., 32507. T: (850) 492-1595; www.reserveamerica.com.

🚐 ★★★★   ⛺ ★★★★

Beauty: ★★★	Site Privacy: ★★★
Spaciousness: ★★★	Quiet: ★★★★
Security: ★★★	Cleanliness: ★★★★
Insect Control: ★★★	Facilities: ★★★★

This coastal park sits on the northern shoreline of its namesake, Big Lagoon, which separates the mainland from Perdido Key and the Gulf of Mexico. Natural communities, ranging from saltwater marshes to pine flatwoods, attract a wide variety of birds, especially during the spring and fall migrations. Beaches, shallow bays, nature trails, and open woodlands offer splendid opportunities for nature study. The park also beckons visitors with opportunities for camping, swimming, fishing, boating, canoeing, and hiking. Crabbing in the shallow waters of Big Lagoon is a popular activity as well. More than 75 campsites are located on a pine ridge in the center of the 698-acre park. Modern facilities and a dump station are on the premises. A variety of water sports attracts visitors to the park. Swimming and beach activities are enjoyed on the shore of Big Lagoon. A boat ramp with dock provides easy access to the lagoon and the Intracoastal Waterway. Fishing brings in redfish, bluefish, flounder, and sea trout seasonally. Crabbing and cast netting for mullet in the lagoon are also popular. The beaches, shallow bays, boardwalks, nature trails, and open woodlands offer ample opportunity for nature study. An observation tower at the East Beach area provides a panoramic view of Big Lagoon, the park, and Gulf Islands National Seashore across the Intracoastal Waterway. Numerous interpretive exhibits are located throughout the park.

BASICS

Operated By: Florida State Parks. **Open:** All year. **Site Assignment:** Reservations can be made 11 months in advance. **Registration:** At office. **Fee:** Single, $16. **Parking:** At park.

FACILITIES

Number of Multipurpose Sites: 140. **Hookups:** Yes. **Dump Station:** Yes. **Laundry:** Less than 0.4 mi. **Pay Phone:** Yes. **Restrooms and Showers:** Yes. **Fuel:** No. **Propane:** No. **Internal Roads:** Paved. **RV Service:** No. **Market:** Less than 0.25 mi. **Restaurant:** Less than 0.25 mi. **General Store:** Less than 0.25 mi. **Vending:** No. **Swimming:** Yes. **Playground:** Yes. **Other:** This park is located near the Intercoastal Waterway. There are 2 boardwalks that run the course of the park that connect to the beach, which is approximately a 15–20 minute walk; or roughly 0.25 mi. (from most of the campsites). **Activities:** Bank fishing, biking, boating, fishing, hiking, interpretive programs, nature programs, photography, picnicking, volleyball, waterskiing, wildlife viewing.

RESTRICTIONS

Pets: Pets are permitted in designated day-use areas. **Fires:** Permitted in designated fireplaces. **Alcoholic Beverages:** Not allowed. **Vehicle Maximum Length:** 30 ft.

TO GET THERE

Big Lagoon State Park is located approximately 10 mi. southwest of Pensacola. From I-10, take Exit 7 (Pensacola), and go south on Pineforest Rd. Take US 98 to CR 293, and go south on CR 293 to Big Lagoon State Park.

PENSACOLA   MAP, D-1 INSET
Pensacola/Perdido Bay/ Lillian KOA

33951 Spinnaker Dr., 36549. T: (251) 961-1717 or (800) 562-3471; www.koakampground.com.

🚐 ★★★★   ⛺ ★★★

Beauty: ★★★	Site Privacy: ★★
Spaciousness: ★★★★	Quiet: ★★★★
Security: ★★★★★	Cleanliness: ★★★★★
Insect Control: ★★★	Facilities: ★★★★★

We planned to end our day on Perdido Key outside Pensacola so we could spend the evening at the legendary rock/country pub and club, the Florabama on the state line. Alas, each campground we found on the island appeared to be nothing more than a beachside or near-beach parking lot, wall-to-wall with metal traveling vehicles. We kept on going, right across the Florida line into Alabama, where suddenly rolling green hills and a herd of frolicking deer in the twilight convinced us that we had found the best place around. We settled in at the KOA on Perdido Bay. With 80 pull-through sites and a dock that runs down to the bay, this campground looked like paradise.

BASICS

Operated By: Owner Denise Valentyne. **Open:** All year. **Site Assignment:** Reservations accepted; 1-night deposit; 24-hour cancellation policy. **Registration:** At park office. **Fee:** RV, $28–$35; tent, $22–$30; Kamping Kabins, $55–$85. **Parking:** Yes.

FACILITIES

Number of RV-only Sites: 100. **Number of Tent-only Sites:** 10. **Hookups:** Electric (30, 50 amps), water, sewer, cable TV. **Each Site:** Picnic table. **Dump Station:** Yes. **Laundry:** Yes. **Pay Phone:** Yes. **Restrooms and Showers:** Yes. **Fuel:** No. **Propane:** No. **Internal Roads:** Paved, in good condition. **RV Service:** Referral. **Market:** 4 mi. east. **Restaurant:** 3 mi. east or west. **General Store:** Yes. **Vending:** Yes. **Swimming:** Yes. **Playground:** Yes. **Other:** Basketball court, boat ramp & pier, rec room, shuffleboard, horseshoes, RV wash station. **Activities:** Sat. wagon rides & ice-cream socials. **Nearby Attractions:** Gulf Shores National Seashore. **Additional Information:** Pensacola CVB, (800) 874-1234, www.visitpensacola.com; Perdido Key Area Chamber of Commerce, (800) 328-0107, www.perdidochamber.com.

RESTRICTIONS

Pets: On leash only. **Fires:** In grills, designated areas only. **Alcoholic Beverages:** Allowed. **Vehicle Maximum Length:** No limit. **Other:** No fireworks, no generators, no clotheslines, quiet hours 10 p.m.–8 a.m.

TO GET THERE

From I-10 or Alt. 90 in Pensacola, go west to Hwy. 297 and south to Blue Angel Rd. Go south to Bauer Rd./US 98, then 3 mi. west across Perdido Bay into Alabama. The first left after bridge is Hwy. 99; go south to campground.

PORT ST. JOE MAP, A-1
St. Joseph Peninsula State Park

reserve america

8899 Cape San Blas Rd., 32456. T: (850) 227-1327; www.reserveamerica.com.

🚐 ★★★★ ⛺ ★★★★

Beauty: ★★★★	Site Privacy: ★★★
Spaciousness: ★★★	Quiet: ★★★★
Security: ★★★★★	Cleanliness: ★★★★
Insect Control: ★★★	Facilities: ★★★★

Native Americans once inhabited the peninsula and gathered shellfish for meals from the bay's shallow waters. Before the area was purchased for development as a state park, it was used as a U.S. Army training facility during World War II. With miles of white sugar sand, this park has one of the top rated beaches in the United States. Sunbathing, snorkeling, and swimming are popular activities along the

Gulf of Mexico and St. Joseph Bay. From offshore, canoeists and kayakers can take in a superb view of the high dunes and sand pine scrub. Outdoor enthusiasts can enjoy camping, fishing, hiking, and bicycling. As a coastal barrier peninsula, St. Joseph provides excellent opportunities for bird-watching; over 240 species have been sighted in the park. A boat ramp is located at Eagle Harbor on the bay side. Campers can stay in a full-facility campground, a short walk from the beach, or at primitive campsites in the wilderness preserve. Eight cabins on the bay side offer alternative overnight accommodations. Visitors to St. Joseph Peninsula enjoy fabulous scenery, beachcombing, snorkeling, sunbathing, camping, canoeing, boating, saltwater fishing, hiking, and bird-watching.

BASICS

Operated By: Florida State Parks. **Open:** All year. **Site Assignment:** Reservations can be made 11 months in advance. **Registration:** At office. **Fee:** Single, $20; cabin, $90; minimum 7. **Parking:** At park.

FACILITIES

Number of Multipurpose Sites: 425. **Hookups:** Yes. **Dump Station:** Yes. **Laundry:** No. **Pay Phone:** Yes. **Restrooms and Showers:** Yes. **Fuel:** No. **Propane:** No. **Internal Roads:** Paved. **RV Service:** No. **Market:** Greater than 20 mi. **Restaurant:** Less than 10 mi. **General Store:** Less than 10 mi. **Vending:** No. **Swimming:** Yes. **Playground:** Yes. **Activities:** Amphitheaters, beach combing, biking, bird-watching, boating, body surfing, fishing, hiking, photography, picnicking, sailing, snorkeling, stargazing, wildlife viewing, windsurfing.

RESTRICTIONS

Pets: Pets are permitted in designated day-use areas. **Fires:** Permitted in designated fireplaces. **Alcoholic Beverages:** Not allowed. **Vehicle Maximum Length:** 38 ft. **Other:** No more than 2 vehicles are allowed on a site. Please be set up by the 11 p.m. quiet hour.

TO GET THERE

St. Joseph Peninsula State Park is located between Port St. Joe and Apalachicola, off FL 30-E, off FL 30-A, off US 98 in the Florida Panhandle.

PORT ST. JOE MAP, A-1
Indian Pass Campground

2817 Indian Pass Rd., 32456. T: (850) 227-7203; www.indianpasscamp.com/campground.

🚐 ★★★ ⛺ ★★★★

Beauty: ★★★★	Site Privacy: ★★★
Spaciousness: ★★★	Quiet: ★★★★
Security: ★★★	Cleanliness: ★★★
Insect Control: ★★	Facilities: ★★★★

Bugs! A pod of dolphin has been seen playing in adjacent Indian Pass Sound, alligators live there and swim past the campground occasionally. A 12-foot shark has been sighted in recent years, swimming the off-shore waters. St. Vincent Island, visible from the campground, is a national wildlife refuge and home to a red wolf–breeding and reintroduction program as well as to 500–600-pound sambar deer, exotic ani-

mals from southeast Asia, introduced by the island's previous private owners in the early 1900s along with other nonnative game for hunters. The campground itself is beautiful and scenic, with honeysuckle-scented air, although just as rustic as you might guess for a fisherman's hideout.

BASICS

Operated By: Dead Fish, Inc. **Open:** All year. **Site Assignment:** First come, first served; reservations accepted, no deposit required. **Registration:** At office. **Fee:** Tent: Call ahead for details; RV, $38–$42; cabin, $85–$120. **Parking:** Yes.

FACILITIES

Number of RV-only Sites: 44. **Hookups:** Electric (30, 50 amps), water, cable TV, phone. **Each Site:** Picnic table. **Dump Station:** Yes. **Laundry:** Yes. **Pay Phone:** Yes. **Restrooms and Showers:** Yes. **Fuel:** Yes. **Propane:** No. **Internal Roads:** Gravel. **RV Service:** Referral. **Market:** 3.5 mi. west to Indian Pass. **Restaurant:** 3.5 mi. west to Indian Pass. **General Store:** Yes. **Vending:** Yes. **Swimming:** Pool, beach. **Playground:** No. **Other:** Boat ramp. **Activities:** Fishing, charters available. **Nearby Attractions:** National Wildlife Habitat. **Additional Information:** Apalachicola Bay Chamber of Commerce, (850) 653-9419, www.baynavigator.com.

RESTRICTIONS

Pets: Welcome, leashed if necessary. **Fires:** Fire ring only. **Alcoholic Beverages:** Allowed. **Vehicle Maximum Length:** 45 ft.

TO GET THERE

From Apalachicola, travel west on Hwy. 98 approximately 6 mi., follow left fork on C30. Go 9 mi. west (left) to C30B/Indian Pass Rd., then south (left) 3.5 mi. to the campground.

SANTA ROSA BEACH MAP, D-1 INSET
Grayton Beach State Recreation Area

reserve america

357 Main Park Rd., 32459. T: (850) 231-4210 or (800) 326-3521; www.reserveamerica.com.

🚐 ★★★★ ⛺ ★★★★★

Beauty: ★★★★★	Site Privacy: ★★★★
Spaciousness: ★★★	Quiet: ★★★★★
Security: ★★★★★	Cleanliness: ★★★★★
Insect Control: ★★★	Facilities: ★★★★★

Sandwiched between the tourist meccas of Seaside—an urban demonstration project touted as an ecologically sound pedestrian community but looking more like a lot of tightly packed tourist dwellings—and Sandestin, a resort hotel community that similarly packs in huge numbers of vacationers, Grayton Beach State Recreation Area offers a glimpse of the world's best beaches without being marred by rows of rooftops or other burdens of civilization. Here is a place where citizens can really appreciate the preservation of land via government park systems. The broad, white-sand beaches and turquoise waters clearly deserve the recurring annual recognitions they receive, and thousands upon thousands of people (and birds) flock to this haven of American beauty. Park rangers distribute a guide to area birds visitors might watch for, from grosbeaks to grebes, herons to hawks, with a cuckoo or two, loons, and starlings. Though small, Grayton Beach provides a perfect, quiet respite from the booming cities surrounding it, perhaps one of the last bastions of safety for passing birds and snowbirds alike.

BASICS

Operated By: Florida Dept. of Environmental Protection, Division of Recreation & Parks. **Open:** All year. **Site Assignment:** Reservations accepted up to 11 months in advance; 1-night deposit required. **Registration:** At office. **Fee:** Tent, $19; cabin, $110. **Parking:** Yes.

FACILITIES

Number of RV-only Sites: 37. **Hookups:** Electric, water. **Each Site:** Picnic table, fire ring, clothesline poles. **Dump Station:** Yes. **Laundry:** No. **Pay Phone:** Yes. **Restrooms and Showers:** Yes. **Fuel:** No. **Propane:** No. **Internal Roads:** Paved & shell, in good condition. **RV Service:** Referral. **Market:** 12 mi. west on Hwy. 98. **Restaurant:** 12 mi. west on Hwy. 98. **General Store:** No. **Vending:** Yes. **Swimming:** No. **Playground:** No. **Other:** One of the best beaches in the nation, hiking trails, boat ramp. **Activities:** Swimming, fishing, boating, hiking, birding. **Nearby Attractions:** Eglin Air Force Base. **Additional Information:** South Walton Tourist Development Council, (800) 822-6877, www.beachesofsouthwalton.com.

RESTRICTIONS

Pets: Not allowed in campground. **Fires:** Grill only. **Alcoholic Beverages:** Not allowed. **Vehicle Maximum Length:** No limit.

TO GET THERE

US 98 west from Panama City Beach to CR 30A—scenic coastal route—to park, just west of Seaside.

SANTA ROSA BEACH   MAP. D-1 INSET
Gregory E. Moore RV Resort

Top Sail Hill Preserve State Park, 7525 West Scenic Hwy. 30A, 32459. T: (850) 267-0299 or (877) BEACH-RV; www.floridastateparks.org.

🚐 ★★★★★   🏕 n/a

Beauty: ★★★	Site Privacy: ★★★★
Spaciousness: ★★★★	Quiet: ★★★★
Security: ★★★★★	Cleanliness: ★★★★★
Insect Control: ★★★★★	Facilities: ★★★★★

Proud recipient of top ratings from two RV-industry watchdogs, the Gregory E. Moore RV Resort at Topsail Hill Preserve State Park is the crown of camper habitats. Well-manicured and trimmed, the RV parking areas offer bushy buffers amid scattered tall pines lining concrete drives, pads, and patios. Twenty pull-through sites are available for the largest rigs around.

BASICS

Operated By: Florida Dept. of Environmental Protection, Division of Recreation & Parks. **Open:** All year. **Site Assignment:** First come, first served or by reservations w/ deposit; 24-hour cancellation policy. **Registration:** At office. **Fee:** $38. **Parking:** At site.

FACILITIES

Number of RV-only Sites: 156. **Hookups:** Electric (30, 50 amps), water, sewer, cable TV. **Each Site:** Picnic table, grills at pull-through sites. **Dump Station:** No. **Laundry:** Yes. **Pay Phone:** Yes. **Restrooms and Showers:** Yes. **Fuel:** No. **Propane:** No. **Internal Roads:** Paved. **RV Service:** Referral. **Market:** 2 mi. east on Hwy. 98. **Restaurant:** 0.25 mi. south on Hwy. 30A. **General Store:** Yes. **Vending:** Yes. **Swimming:** Pool, gulf. **Playground:** No. **Other:** 1,650-acre preserve w/ hiking trails & bike path, tennis courts, shuffleboard, basketball, 3 lakes, clubhouse w/ library. **Activities:** Fishing, biking, hiking. **Nearby Attractions:** 1 mi. walking trail to top-rated beach. **Additional Information:** South Walton Tourist Development Council, (800) 822-6877, www.beachesofsouthwalton.com.

RESTRICTIONS

Pets: On leash only, proof of vaccinations required. **Fires:** Grill only. **Alcoholic Beverages:** After hours only. **Vehicle Maximum Length:** No limit. **Other:** No tents (pop-ups okay), quiet hours 11 p.m.–7 a.m.

TO GET THERE

From US 98 and Hwy. 30A near Sandestin, south 0.25 mi. on 30A to park entrance.

SANTA ROSA BEACH   MAP. D-1 INSET
Topsail Hill Preserve State Park

reserve america

7525 W. Scenic Hwy. 30A, 32459.
T: (850) 267-0299; www.reserveamerica.com.

🚐 ★★★★   🏕 ▲

Beauty: ★★★	Site Privacy: ★★
Spaciousness: ★★	Quiet: ★★★★
Security: ★★★	Cleanliness: ★★★★
Insect Control: ★★★	Facilities: ★★★★

This 1,643-acre park offers a wide variety of natural resources. Swim, sun, beach comb for sea beans, and watch shorebirds along 3.2 miles of secluded, white sand beaches with majestic dunes over 25 feet tall as the emerald waters of the Gulf of Mexico lap at the shore. Three rare coastal dune lakes provide excellent freshwater fishing. Although boats are not allowed, fishing from the shoreline yields bass, bream, panfish, and catfish. Lakes, pristine beaches, old-growth long-leaf pines, sand pine scrub, and a variety of wetlands offer a bird-watching and hiking paradise. Visitors may bike, walk, or enjoy a quick ride to the beach on our timely tram service to swim, fish, sunbathe, or beach comb. The full-facility campground has the highest rating possible from *Trailer Life* and *Woodalls*, placing the resort in the top 1% of the

---

nation, and features a swimming pool, tennis courts, and shuffleboard courts. Furnished bungalows are available for weekly stays. A camp store offers a variety of camping items, as well as snacks and drinks.

BASICS

Operated By: Florida State Parks. **Open:** All year. **Site Assignment:** Reservations can be made 11 months in advance. **Registration:** At office. **Fee:** Single, $38; cabin (4 person), $690. **Parking:** At park.

FACILITIES

Number of Multipurpose Sites: 363. **Hookups:** None. **Dump Station:** No. **Laundry:** Yes. **Pay Phone:** Yes. **Restrooms and Showers:** Yes. **Fuel:** No. **Propane:** No. **Internal Roads:** Paved. **RV Service:** No. **Market:** Less than 10 mi. **Restaurant:** Less than 10 mi. **General Store:** Less than 1 mi. **Vending:** Yes. **Swimming:** Yes. **Playground:** No. **Activities:** Bank fishing, beach combing, biking, bird-watching, body surfing, fishing, hiking, interpretive programs, shuffle board, snorkeling, stargazing, surfing.

RESTRICTIONS

Pets: Pets are permitted in designated day-use areas. No pets in cabins. **Fires:** Permitted in designated fireplaces. **Alcoholic Beverages:** Not allowed. **Vehicle Maximum Length:** 55 ft. **Other:** No tent camping. Cabin rentals are weekly & monthly only. No smoking in cabins. Limit of 4 people.

TO GET THERE

The park is located on West CR 30A, 0.25 mi. from US 98. From Destin, FL, take US 98 to West CR 30A. Turn right (south) to entrance 0.25 mi. on the right. From Panama City, go 6 mi. past the US 331 intersection; turn left onto West CR 30A, 0.25 mi. on the right. From I-10, take Exit 85 (Defuniak Springs). Go south approximately 25 mi. to US 98; turn right heading west about 6 mi. and look for sign to turn left on West CR 30A. Entrance is 0.25 mi. on right.

SARASOTA   MAP. C-2
Myakka River State Park

reserve america

13207 SR 72, 34241. T: (941) 361-6511 or (800) 326-3521; www.reserveamerica.com.

🚐 ★★★   🏕 ★★★★

Beauty: ★★★★★	Site Privacy: ★★★
Spaciousness: ★★★	Quiet: ★★★★★
Security: ★★★★★	Cleanliness: ★★★★
Insect Control: ★★★	Facilities: ★★★★

Scenic and swampy, this alligator habitat is well known as home to a number of incredible birds, including bald eagles, great blue herons, great horned owls, sandhill cranes, wild turkeys, and ruby-throated hummingbirds, and as rest stop for passers-by, such as the roseate spoonbill, loons, Canadian geese, mallards, and peregrine falcons. Local volunteers even built a bridge that lifts observers seven flights of stairs into the treetops to gain perspective on life among their feathered friends. Other creatures include fox, bobcat, deer, wild hogs, and the occasional black bear. Campers can enjoy the campgrounds, which can get a bit swampy during rainy season, usually August and September, when the mosquitoes are out in full force. Many visitors bring their boats along to explore the lakes and the wild and scenic Myakka River, so named as part of a government preservation program that will protect it from scientific "engineering," a common practice designed to improve conditions but which ultimately is often discovered to bring negative results for tampering with nature. Myakka was one of Florida's first state parks, so it has been well preserved. Cabins here are very nice, built by the Civilian Conservation Corps in the 1930s and still sturdy—much larger and nicer than modern campground "cabins."

BASICS

Operated By: Florida Dept. of Environmental Protection, Division of Recreation & Parks. **Open:** All year. **Site Assignment:** Reservations accepted up to 11 months in advance, 1-night deposit. **Registration:** At office. **Fee:** Tent, $22; cabin, $60. **Parking:** At site.

FACILITIES

Number of RV-only Sites: 48. **Number of Tent-only Sites:** 28. **Hookups:** Electric (20, 30 amps), water. **Each Site:** Picnic table, grill or fire ring. **Dump Station:** Yes. **Laundry:** Yes. **Pay Phone:** Yes. **Restrooms and Showers:** Yes. **Fuel:** No. **Propane:** No. **Internal Roads:** Paved & gravel, in good condition. **RV Service:** Referral. **Market:** A little less than 10 mi. west to Sarasota. **Restaurant:** A little less than 10 mi. west to Sarasota. **General Store:** Yes. **Vending:** Yes. **Swimming:** No. **Playground:** Yes. **Other:** Canopy walkway for tree-top-level bird-watching, bird walk, boat ramp, tram & airboat rides, nature trails. **Activities:** Fishing, birding (a favorite Audubon Society bird habitat), hiking, horseback riding, biking. **Nearby Attractions:** Selby Botanical Gardens & Ringling Museum in Sarasota. **Additional Information:** Sarasota CVB, (800) 522-9799, www.sarasotafl.org.

RESTRICTIONS

Pets: Not allowed in camping areas because of alligators. **Fires:** Contained only, provided there is no burn ban. **Alcoholic Beverages:** Not allowed. **Vehicle Maximum Length:** 34 ft. **Other:** No firearms or fireworks.

TO GET THERE

From I-75 take Exit 37, SR 72. Go east 9 mi. to park on left.

This beautiful central Florida state park boasts a pristine hardwood hammock featuring tall pines and oak trees alongside cypress and native palms. Nature trails wind through samples of ancient hardwoods as well as swampy marshlands. A wide variety of native fauna has been found in the decades-old protected area, including the rare Florida panthers, black bears, river otters, raccoons, and foxes. Dual camping rings offer quiet sites under cover of the trees with easy access to shower and laundry facilities. Back-in only, dirt-ground sites are about 20 by 30 to 50 feet, with slight wooded buffer between each. A community campfire circle is available for evening activities. Although Florida summers are known for their heat, humidity, and mosquitoes, this forested atmosphere in the central state offers the promise of cooler, less humid nights than some. Park gates are locked at night, with security lock codes distributed to campers for access.

BASICS

Operated By: Florida Dept. of Environmental Protection. **Open:** All year. **Site Assignment:** Reservations up to 11 months in advance. **Registration:** At park ranger office. **Fee:** $18. **Parking:** Yes, 1 car per site. Fee charged for additional vehicles.

FACILITIES

Number of Multipurpose Sites: 138. **Hookups:** Electric, water. **Each Site:** Picnic tables, fire rings. **Dump Station:** Yes. **Laundry:** Yes. **Pay Phone:** Yes. **Restrooms and Showers:** Yes. **Fuel:** 4.5 mi. to town. **Propane:** No. **Internal Roads:** Paved & smooth dirt roads, good condition. **RV Service:** Referral. **Market:** 6 mi. south on US 27. **Restaurant:** Yes. **General Store:** 2 mi. from park. **Vending:** Yes. **Swimming:** No. **Playground:** Yes. **Other:** Horseshoes, shuffleboard, horse camping, firewood available. **Activities:** Horse trails (bring your own horse), nature trails, bike trails, guided ranger walks (winter) & tram tours. **Nearby Attractions:** Disney World, Prestigious annual auto race & year-round activities at nearby Sebring Raceway. **Additional Information:** Highlands County CVB, (863) 385-1316 or (800) 255-1711.

RESTRICTIONS

Pets: On leash only, must have proof of vaccination, not allowed on boardwalk. $2.18 per night. **Fires:** Fire ring only. **Alcoholic Beverages:** Not allowed. **Vehicle Maximum Length:** 45 ft. **Other:** No firearms, no fireworks, no intoxicants.

TO GET THERE

4 mi. west of Sebring on SR 634.

Where Florida meets the southwest corner of Georgia, the Chattahoochee and Flint rivers converge to form Lake Seminole, the setting for this peaceful park. The high hills and many ravines are similar to the Appalachian Mountain Range and have many of the same type plants. These consist primarily of hardwood hammocks and high pineland communities. Hiking through the 682 acres of forested hills, visitors might catch sight of fox squirrels, white-tailed deer, gray foxes, or many species of native and migratory birds. Anglers can launch from a boat ramp on the 37,000-acre lake to enjoy some of the best freshwater fishing in the state, or fish from a 100-foot pier in the camping area. Alligators and snapping turtles are commonly seen around the lake, which is well known to support large- and small-mouth bass, catfish, bluegill, speckled perch, and bream. A shady picnic area, with tables and grills, overlooks the lake. For large gatherings, a picnic pavilion that seats up to 60 people is available for rental. Overnight visitors can stay in a full-facility campground next to the lake or enjoy the comforts of a modern cabin.

BASICS

Operated By: Florida State Parks. **Open:** All year. **Site Assignment:** Reservations can be made 11 months in advance. **Registration:** At office. **Fee:** Single, $12; cabin, $55 (4-person min.). **Parking:** At park.

FACILITIES

Number of Multipurpose Sites: 105. **Hookups:** Yes. **Dump Station:** Yes. **Laundry:** No. **Pay Phone:** Yes. **Restrooms and Showers:** Yes. **Fuel:** No. **Propane:** No. **Internal Roads:** Paved. **RV Service:** No. **Market:** Less than 5 mi. **Restaurant:** Less than 5 mi. **General Store:** Less than 5 mi. **Vending:** No. **Swimming:** No. **Playground:** No. **Activities:** Amphitheaters, bank fishing, bird-watching, boating, canoeing, fishing, interpretive programs, jet skiing, kayaking, sailing.

RESTRICTIONS

Pets: Pets are permitted in designated day-use areas. **Fires:** Permitted in designated fireplaces. **Alcoholic Beverages:** Not allowed. **Vehicle Maximum Length:** 40 ft. **Other:** The park gates close at sunset. If you plan to arrive late, please contact the park prior to 5 p.m. on the day of your arrival.

TO GET THERE

2 mi. north of Sneads on River Rd.

SEBRING   MAP, C-2
Highlands Hammock State Park

reserve america

5931 Hammock Rd., 33872. T: (863) 386-6094 or (800) 326-3521; www.reserveamerica.com.

🚐 ★★★★	⛺ ★★★★★
Beauty: ★★★★★	Site Privacy: ★★★
Spaciousness: ★★★	Quiet: ★★★★
Security: ★★★★★	Cleanliness: ★★★★★
Insect Control: ★★★★	Facilities: ★★★★

SNEADS   MAP, D-2
Three Rivers State Park

reserve america

7908 Three Rivers Park Rd., 32460. T: (850) 482-9006; www.reserveamerica.com.

🚐 ★★★★	⛺ ★★★★
Beauty: ★★★	Site Privacy: ★★★
Spaciousness: ★★★	Quiet: ★★★★
Security: ★★★★	Cleanliness: ★★★★
Insect Control: ★★★	Facilities: ★★★★

ST. AUGUSTINE   MAP, A-3
Anastasia State Park

reserve america

1340A A1A South, 32080. T: (904) 461-2033 or (800) 326-3521; www.reserveamerica.com.

🚐 ★★★★	⛺ ★★★★★
Beauty: ★★★★★	Site Privacy: ★★★
Spaciousness: ★★	Quiet: ★★★
Security: ★★★★★	Cleanliness: ★★★★
Insect Control: ★★★	Facilities: ★★★★★

Crowded and very popular, this ocean-side park provides a beautiful example of Florida's coastal dunes undisturbed by development. Although all sites are back-in in the seven U-shaped camping areas, some are more crowded than others, and none are actually on the water. The Sea Bean circle seemed to offer the most privacy, and the Coquina circle, where we stayed, was most crowded. Nonetheless, the park was quiet by 11 p.m., and the dense trees and bush buffer provided a sense of seclusion. In addition to preserved and protected sand dunes and sea oats, endangered sea turtles are common to the shoreline here during nesting season, May to September. If you should happen to be lucky enough to spot a turtle laying eggs, or her hatchlings making their way from nest back to the ocean, be careful not to interfere with the process with sound or lights.

BASICS

Operated By: Florida Dept. of Environmental Protection, Division of Recreation & Parks. **Open:** All year. **Site Assignment:** First come, first served; reservations accepted up to 11 months in advance, 1-night deposit; 24-hour cancellation policy. **Registration:** At ranger station. **Fee:** $25.07. **Parking:** Yes.

FACILITIES

Number of RV-only Sites: 104. **Number of Tent-only Sites:** 35. **Hookups:** Electric, water. **Each Site:** Picnic table, fire ring. **Dump Station:** Yes. **Laundry:** Yes. **Pay Phone:** Yes. **Restrooms and Showers:** Yes. **Fuel:** No. **Propane:** No. **Internal Roads:** Paved, in good condition. **RV Service:** Referral. **Market:** 3 mi. south from park entrance. **Restaurant:** 1 mi. north or south from park entrance. **General Store:** Yes. **Vending:** Yes. **Swimming:** Beach. **Playground:** Yes. **Other:** Windsurfing, kayak & canoe rentals; beach, fishing pier, hiking trails. **Activities:** Summer evening programs at the campfire circle, surfing, kayaking, canoeing, sailing, swimming, fishing, hiking. **Nearby Attractions:** Historic Fort Castillo de San Marcos; Lighthouse Museum; historic St. Augustine, Florida's oldest city; farmer's market (south from park on A1A about 3 mi. at public fishing pier & information center), dog-friendly beach 3 mi. south of the city fishing pier. **Additional Information:** St. Augustine, Ponte Vedra & the Beaches CVB, (800) OLD-CITY, www.visitoldcity.com.

RESTRICTIONS

Pets: In designated areas (not on beach), on leash only, proof of vaccination. **Fires:** In grills, designated areas only. **Alcoholic Beverages:** Not during park hours. **Vehicle Maximum Length:** 35 ft. (call ahead for up to 40 ft.). **Other:** No driving on beach; do not damage or disturb dunes, nature, or wildlife.

TO GET THERE

Exit I-95 at Hwy. 207, north approximately 5 mi. to SR 312, east 3 mi. to Anastasia Island, left on A1A 1.5 mi. north to park on right.

ST. GEORGE ISLAND   MAP, A-1
St. George Island State Park

reserve america

1900 East Gulf Beach Dr., 32328.
T: (850) 927-2111 or (800) 326-3521;
www.reserveamerica.com.

🚐 ★★★★   ⛺ ★★★★

Beauty: ★★★★★	Site Privacy: ★★★★
Spaciousness: ★★★★	Quiet: ★★★★★
Security: ★★★★★	Cleanliness: ★★★★★
Insect Control: ★★★★	Facilities: ★★★★★

St. George Island Park is a beautifully preserved example of Florida's famous Emerald Coast beaches—the park has 9 miles of pristine beachfront, half accessible only by boat or foot. The rather stark park is largely made up of drifts of snow-white sands covered with small, wind-bent pines and sea oats, with pink and purple flower vines crawling across them. The smooth, soft slopes may call upon your instincts to climb, but you must resist the urge—this weather-shaped landscape is fragile, and the island depends on the dunes to protect against erosion. A number of interesting creatures make their home in the park and on the island. There were eight eagles nests when we visited, and we saw several eagles, standing proudly atop pine trees, light poles, and cellular towers, living comfortably amid civilization. Strangely, a coyote has been detected on the island, and there are alligators, nesting sea turtles, cardinals, pelicans, and osprey. Campers will appreciate the nicely wooded camping areas, with nice bushy buffers around the rather smallish sites. The full-facility campground offers 60 back-in sites, but no pull-throughs. A primitive camping area is available for tenters willing to hike 2.5 miles.

BASICS

Operated By: Florida Dept. of Environmental Protection, Division of Recreation & Parks. **Open:** All year. **Site Assignment:** Reservations accepted up to 11 months in advance; 1-night deposit; 24-hour cancellation policy. **Registration:** At park office. **Fee:** $19. **Parking:** Yes.

FACILITIES

Number of Tent-only Sites: Undesignated sites. **Number of Multipurpose Sites:** 60. **Hookups:** Electric, water. **Each Site:** Picnic table, fire ring. **Dump Station:** Yes. **Laundry:** No. **Pay Phone:** Yes. **Restrooms and Showers:** Yes. **Fuel:** No. **Propane:** No. **Internal Roads:** Paved & crushed shell, in good condition. **RV Service:** Referral. **Market:** Approx. 4 mi. west on Gulf Beach Dr. to St. George. **Restaurant:** Approx. 4 mi. west on Gulf Beach Dr. to St. George. **General Store:** No. **Vending:** Soft drinks. **Swimming:** Beach. **Playground:** Yes. **Other:** Boat ramp, nature trails. **Activities:** Swimming, fishing, hiking, kayaking, & boating. **Nearby Attractions:** Panama City (75 miles). **Additional Information:** Apalachicola Bay Chamber of Commerce, (850) 653-9419, www.baynavigator.com.

RESTRICTIONS

Pets: On leash only, not allowed on beaches, boardwalks, or dunes. **Fires:** Grill only. **Alcoholic Beverages:** Not during park hours. **Vehicle Maximum Length:** 40 ft. **Other:** No firearms or fireworks; no vehicles off roadways; do not walk over dunes or vegetation; do not feed wildlife; quiet hours starting at 11 p.m.

TO GET THERE

From US 98 at Eastpoint (just east of Apalachicola), cross Eastpoint Bridge/Hwy. 300 to St. George Island, then turn left on Gulf Beach Blvd. (still Hwy. 300) to park, about 5 mi.

ST. JAMES CITY   MAP, C-2
Fort Myers Pine Island KOA

5120 Stringfellow Rd, 33956. T: (239) 283-2415 or (800) KOA-8505; www.pineislandkoa.com.

🚐 ★★★★   ⛺ ★★

Beauty: ★★	Site Privacy: ★★
Spaciousness: ★★★★	Quiet: ★★★★
Security: ★★★★★	Cleanliness: ★★★★★
Insect Control: ★★	Facilities: ★★★★★

To say that this RV park is out of the way would be a great understatement—and that is exactly why so many campers love it. Pine Island is one of the last remaining rural outposts on Florida's southwest coast, offering a down-home feeling, farmers markets, and fishing villages. Although there are no pull-through sites, most are very large. The campground is on the waterfront, but views are completely obscured by mangrove trees. Most sites have a palm tree, and there is a nice expanse of green grass, but little shade. If you plan to visit in July, be sure to ask about MangoMania, an island festival that celebrates the many varieties of mangoes and avocados that grow on the island, and features live music and entertainment plus foods from area restaurants.

BASICS

Operated By: Manager John Streeter. **Open:** All year. **Site Assignment:** Reservations accepted; $20 deposit; 24-hour cancellation policy. **Registration:** At office. **Fee:** $27–$59. **Parking:** Yes.

FACILITIES

Number of RV-only Sites: 368. **Hookups:** Electric (30, 50 amps), water, sewer, cable TV; 50-amp hookups available w/ limited service. **Each Site:** Picnic table. **Dump Station:** Yes. **Laundry:** Yes. **Pay Phone:** No. **Restrooms and Showers:** Yes. **Fuel:** No. **Propane:** Yes. **Internal Roads:** Paved, in good condition. **RV Service:** Maintenance on-site & referral. **Market:** 5 mi. north or convenience mart 2 mi. south. **Restaurant:** 2–4 mi. south. **General Store:** Yes. **Vending:** Yes. **Swimming:** Heated pool, hot tub. **Playground:** Yes. **Other:** Clubhouse, exercise room, hot tub, tennis court, game room w/ computers & Internet access, library, big-screen TV. **Activities:** Shuttle to beach, cultural activities, flea market, museums, shopping, fishing, golfing. **Nearby Attractions:** Island is in the Gulf of Mexico. **Additional Information:** Greater Pine Island Chamber, (941) 283-0888, www.pineislandchamber.org.

RESTRICTIONS

Pets: On leash only, max. 2 pets. **Fires:** Grill only. **Alcoholic Beverages:** Allowed. **Vehicle Maximum Length:** 60 ft. **Other:** Quiet time 10 p.m., no swimming in lakes.

TO GET THERE

From I-75 take Exit 26 at Hwy. 78/Bayshore Rd. (becomes Pine Island Rd.). Head west 21 mi. to Stringfellow then go south 6 mi. to KOA.

SUNRISE — MAP, D-3
Markham Park

16001 West SR 84, 33326. T: (954) 389-2000; • www.broward.org/parks.

🚐 ★★★   ⛺ ★★★★

Beauty: ★★★   Site Privacy: ★★★
Spaciousness: ★★★   Quiet: ★★★★
Security: ★★★★   Cleanliness: ★★★★★
Insect Control: ★★★   Facilities: ★★★★★

Markham Park may be smaller than other nearby RV campgrounds like C. B. Smith Park, but its proximity to the Everglades gives this park an edge than can't be matched in the area. An abundance of alligators fill the waterways, canals, and lakes of the park, so keep dogs leashed and away from water. Other fauna include raccoons, foxes, and deer, and there have even been sightings of Florida's endangered panther on the outskirts of the park. Hike through the woods in the southwest corner of the park to a land bridge over the canal and to the dike, which provides a rare hilltop hike along the edge of the Everglades. It's a great place to enjoy the sunset—but don't stay too late, the walk back through darkened woodlands can be eerie! Ample trees give a wilderness feel that is largely missing in most of South Florida. Cul-de-sacs provided for camping create small, private enclaves for small groups.

BASICS

Operated By: Broward County. **Open:** All year. **Site Assignment:** First come, first served; weekends fill up fast so reservations suggested; deposit full amount or by agreement. **Registration:** At park office. **Fee:** $17–$23. **Parking:** Yes.

FACILITIES

Number of RV-only Sites: 88. **Number of Tent-only Sites:** 10. **Hookups:** Electric (20, 50 amps), water, sewer. **Each Site:** Grills or fire ring, picnic table. **Dump Station:** Yes. **Laundry:** No. **Pay Phone:** Yes. **Restrooms and Showers:** Yes. **Fuel:** No. **Propane:** No. **Internal Roads:** Paved, in good condition. **RV Service:** No. **Market:** Grocery & pharmacy across the street from entrance to the park. **Restaurant:** Snack bar at pool Feb.–Labor Day, restaurants across the street from the park entrance. **General Store:** No. **Vending:** Soft drinks. **Swimming:** Pool (seasonal). **Playground:** Yes. **Other:** Boat ramp. **Activities:** Bike rentals, bike & jogging paths, canoe, paddleboat & johnboat rentals, fishing permitted, model-airplane field, tennis, racquetball, &

target range. **Nearby Attractions:** Sawgrass Mills Mall (the world's largest outlet mall) is 5 mi. northwest, beaches are 15 mi. east in Fort Lauderdale & Hollywood. **Additional Information:** Greater Fort Lauderdale CVB, (800) 231-SUNNY, www.sunny.org.

RESTRICTIONS

Pets: On leash only, $1 fee. **Fires:** Ground fires in fire pits. **Alcoholic Beverages:** In designated areas only, no glass containers. **Vehicle Maximum Length:** No limit.

TO GET THERE

Take I-595 west from Fort Lauderdale about 15 mi. to Exit at SW 136th Ave. Continue west on SR 84 about 1 mi. to park entrance on right.

THONOTOSASSA — MAP, C-2
Hillsborough River State Park

reserve america™

15402 US 301 North, 33592. T: (813) 987-6771 or (800) 326-3521; www.reserveamerica.com.

🚐 ★★★★   ⛺ ★★★★★

Beauty: ★★★★★   Site Privacy: ★★★
Spaciousness: ★★★★   Quiet: ★★★★★
Security: ★★★★★   Cleanliness: ★★★
Insect Control: ★★★   Facilities: ★★★★

Designated a park in 1936, this 2,994-acre plot of land boasts oak, hickory, magnolia, and native sabal palm trees, with an undergrowth of palms that ensures you'll remember you're in Florida. Wild deer, bobcat, foxes, alligators, raccoons, gray squirrels, armadillos, and snakes take cover in the brush and along the scenic Hillsborough River, which runs through the park and features a unique set of rapids for canoeists and kayakers. A suspension bridge carries hikers across the river to hike a section of the Florida Trail. There are no pull-through sites.

BASICS

Operated By: Florida Dept. of Environmental Protection, Division of Recreation & Parks. **Open:** All year. **Site Assignment:** First come, first served; reservations (at least 2 days in advance) accepted by phone w/ credit card up to 11 months in advance, $10 cancellation fee. **Registration:** At park office. **Fee:** $20; MC,V; $2 per night for each pet. **Parking:** At site. 2 vehicle max. $3 for each additional vehicle.

FACILITIES

Number of Multipurpose Sites: 106. **Hookups:** Electric (30 amps), water. **Each Site:** Picnic table, fire ring, grill. **Dump Station:** Yes. **Laundry:** Yes. **Pay Phone:** Yes. **Restrooms and Showers:** Yes. **Fuel:** No. **Propane:** No. **Internal Roads:** Paved & crushed shell, in good condition. **RV Service:** No. 6 mi. to Zephyrhills. **Market:** Super Wal-mart in Zephyrhills. **Restaurant:** 6 mi. to Zephyrhills. **General Store:** Yes, concession outpost. **Vending:** Yes. **Swimming:** Yes. **Playground:** No. **Other:** Canoe launch, canoe rentals, hiking trails, bridges over river, historic Fort Foster. **Activities:** Hiking, canoeing, fishing, guided tours of fort on weekends, special events. **Nearby Attractions:** Busch Gardens,

Adventure Island Water Park, Museum of Science & Industry. **Additional Information:** Tampa Bay CVB, (800) 44-TAMPA, www.visittampabay.com.

RESTRICTIONS

Pets: On leash only in designated areas only, proof of rabies vaccination. $2 each pet per night. **Fires:** Grill or fire rings only. **Alcoholic Beverages:** Not allowed. **Vehicle Maximum Length:** No limit. **Other:** No firearms, no fireworks, no collecting of firewood or any other flora or fauna, no feeding of wildlife.

TO GET THERE

From I-75 take exit at Fowler Ave. Go east 5 mi. to US 301, then north 9 mi. to park on left.

WIMAUMA — MAP, C-2
Little Manatee River State Park

reserve america™

215 Lightfoot Rd., 33598. T: (813) 671-5005; www.reserveamerica.com.

🚐 ★★★★   ⛺ ★★★★

Beauty: ★★★   Site Privacy: ★★★
Spaciousness: ★★★   Quiet: ★★★★
Security: ★★★   Cleanliness: ★★★★
Insect Control: ★★★   Facilities: ★★★★

Little Manatee River is a peaceful suburban park featuring one of Florida's remaining sand-scrub habitats. Dense hardwood hammocks and 4.5 miles of riverfront also entice wildlife into establishing residence. Saw palmettos, blueberries, greenbrier, grapevine, and prickly pear cactus support the various species including the endangered Florida scrub jays, warblers, foxes, raccoons, armadillos, and bobcats. The Little Manatee River has been designated an Outstanding Florida Waterway, part of the Cockroach Bay Aquatic Preserve. Here, alligators and river otters nest and feed. Incidentally, you will not see river otters living in polluted waterways. Developed in 1974 as a recreation site for the suburban Tampa Bay area, the 2,000-acre park is divided into two sections. Visitors are invited to enjoy the day-use area and several of the overnight opportunities. The most obvious recreation at the park is centered on the banks of the river. Here, folks swim, picnic, and launch canoes. Beyond the day-use area, horse-trailer parking enables equestrians to ride on over 10 miles of trail and camp at an overnight horse campground. At the end of the park road, up to 30 individuals are invited to stay at the group site. The main campground has 34 full-service sites. For folks in search of a remote excursion, stop at the park office for details pertaining to the 6.5-mile loop trail. This trail and its trailhead are located north of the river through a locked gate.

BASICS

Operated By: Florida State Parks. **Open:** All year. **Site Assignment:** Reservations can be made 11 months in advance. **Registration:** At office. **Fee:** Single, $18. **Parking:** At park.

FACILITIES

Number of Multipurpose Sites: 120. **Hookups:** Yes. **Dump Station:** Yes. **Laundry:** Yes. **Pay Phone:** Yes. **Restrooms and Showers:** Yes. **Fuel:** No. **Propane:** No. **Internal Roads:** Paved. **RV Service:** No. **Market:** Less than 5 mi. **Restaurant:** Less than 5 mi. **General Store:** Less than 1 mi. **Vending:** No. **Swimming:** No. **Playground:** Yes. **Activities:** Bank fishing, biking, bird-watching, canoe-ing, fishing, hiking, horseback riding, interpretive programs, kayaking, nature programs, photography, picnicking, star gazing, wildlife viewing.

RESTRICTIONS

Pets: Pets are permitted in designated day-use areas. **Fires:** Permitted in designated fireplaces. **Alcoholic Beverages:** Not allowed. **Vehicle Maximum Length:** 68 ft. **Other:** Proof of negative Coggins test is required for each horse brought into the park.

TO GET THERE

Little Manatee River State Park is located on Lightfoot Rd., just off US 301, 6 mi. south of Sun City Center. Take the Sun City Center exit off I-75 (Exit 240A). Travel east 3 mi. to US 301. Turn right (south) onto US 301 and go about 5 mi. to Lightfoot Rd. Turn right onto Lightfoot Rd.; park entrance is less than 0.5 mi. on right.

Georgia

Georgia beckons visitors with her high Appalachian views; her rich history memorialized in stately mansions and great plantations; her primordial swamps, crawling with creatures and draped in moss; her golden coast graced with wide beaches and magical islands; and her great winding rivers feeding the land and imagination. Likely, after you journey through the state and experience this richness firsthand, the memory of your stay will be slow to fade. Oh, there's a Six Flags, too!

Begin your camping expedition in north Georgia's mountainous region. The days are cool, even when summer swelters to the south. In the fall, the north Georgia landscape is adorned with pumpkins, which contribute mightily to the area's remarkable fall canvas. Halloween travelers in search of the Great Pumpkin need look no farther than **Berry Patch Farms** in **Woodstock**. Pumpkin hunters are treated to warm apple cider while enjoying a scenic hayride into the farm's abundant pumpkin patch. Those on the hunt for indigenous culture should pay a visit to **Cherokee Indian Princess Trahlyta's** grave in **Dahlonega**. Legend has it that Trahlyta's tribe knew the location of a magic spring that would grant eternal youth. Abducted by a would-be suitor, Trahlyta lost her beauty and began to die. Her suitor buried her near her home and marked the grave with a few stones—thus creating a tradition among the grave's many visitors.

Kids, toy collectors, or travelers on the hunt for the arcane should pay a visit to **Babyland General Hospital** in Cleveland. Visitors not only witness the "birth" of a **Cabbage Patch Kid,** but (for a sizable fee) can "adopt" one as well. For travelers looking to keep it simple, north Georgia's thundering waterfalls, miles of hiking trails, and lazy floats down the **Chattahoochee River** are great ways to spend free time. Just around the corner, you might be surprised by **Helen,** a Bavarian town seemingly transplanted from the Alps to America's Deep South. Lots of fun shops and tourist spots abound, but (sadly) Helen's Fantasy Kingdom has fallen.

Move on to the **Atlanta** metro region. Although it may seem strange to choose a campsite near this bustling metropolis, the number of recreational opportunities in this area will surprise you. The Chattahoochee River meanders through Atlanta, where river-recreation opportunities await. Be sure to visit **Stone Mountain,** a monolith of granite displaying one of the world's largest relief sculptures. Venture on foot up the side of the mountain or take a skylift to the top to enjoy a breathtaking view. Below, visit the **Antebellum Plantation,** where you can wander through an 1800s mansion. Plenty of campsites are available. And there is the occasional laser light display or rock concert. After exploring, brush yourself off and visit some of Atlanta's cultural treasures, including the **Civil War Museum, High Museum of Art,** and the **Margaret Mitchell House,** where one of America's classic novels, *Gone with the Wind,* was written.

As you travel southward, you can't help but be mesmerized by the scenic expanse of 90 miles of Georgian coastline. Feel the warm salt air hug you as you venture to one of the state's many islands. Cumberland Island admits only 300 visitors each day to enjoy and explore its untamed wilderness, but camping is allowed. Enjoy the **Okefenokee National Wildlife Refuge** from a chartered boat or, if you dare, paddle through the blackwater swamp yourself in a canoe. The swamp is one of the oldest and most well-preserved freshwater areas in America. It's pretty big, too—extending 38 miles south, and 25 miles east to west—and lies up to 128 feet above sea level. Visit sweet **Savannah,** whose curious inhabitants and beautiful scenery were popularized by the book (and its film adaptation) *Midnight in the Garden of Good and Evil.* Since then, Savannah has become quite a tourist attraction. If you haven't read the book, don't worry—you can buy it just about anywhere in town. In addition to its regal Southern charms, you might want to check out the **Big Cow**—a 15-foot tall, 22-foot-long statue of . . . a cow. You'll soon learn that Savannah didn't need Hollywood's endorsement—she is a star of her own making.

Savannah makes a nice transition to Georgia's historic South, where campers can hike the trails of **Oconee National Forest** or fish on **Oconee Lake.** Canoeing and camping along the **Altamaha River,** lined by swamps and sandbars, provides campers and nature lovers a grand adventure. With so much to do, Georgia and her charm will likely entice you to make more visits.

Campground Profiles

ALBANY
The Parks at Chehaw

MAP, C-1

Philema Rd. (Hwy. 91N), 31701. T: (229) 430-5277; www.parksatchehaw.org.

★★★★ ▲ ★★★★

Beauty: ★★★★   Site Privacy: ★★
Spaciousness: ★★★★   Quiet: ★★★★
Security: ★★★★   Cleanliness: ★★★★
Insect Control: ★★★   Facilities: ★★★★★

Located just outside of Albany, this 800-acre park is a great destination for families. Fairly suburban in nature, the park has 52 RV sites that are moderately spaced but offer little privacy. Each site has water and electrical hookups and all back-in parking. The camping is not remarkable, but the activities nearby are. Within short walking distance is an amazing contemporary playground with slides, rungs, and other fun activities. Fishing, cycling, mountain biking, and hiking are all recreation possibilities, and those wishing to see cheetahs, beers, bison, or elk in the Georgia piney woods only need walk a short distance to the Wild Animal Park.

BASICS

Operated By: Glen Dobrogosz. **Open:** All year. **Site Assignment:** First come, first served. **Registration:** At ticket booth prior to set up. **Fee:** RV, $15; tent, $10. **Parking:** 2 vehicles per site.

FACILITIES

Number of Multipurpose Sites: 52. **Hookups:** Electric (30 amps), water. **Dump Station:** Yes. **Laundry:** Yes. **Pay Phone:** No. **Restrooms and Showers:** Yes. **Fuel:** 1 min. on Philema Rd. **Propane:** No. **Internal Roads:** Dirt. **RV Service:** No. **Market:** 5 min. on Philema Rd. **Restaurant:** Savanna Café. **General Store:** Gift shop. **Vending:** Yes. **Swimming:** No. **Playground:** Yes. **Other:** Covered picnic shelters can be reserved, fishing pond, lake. **Activities:** BMX riding, hiking, fishing, mountain biking, train rides, playground. **Nearby Attractions:** Public boat ramp (1 mi.), Wild Animal Park, Mt. Zion Albany Civil Rights Movement Museum, Albany Museum of Art. **Additional Information:** Albany Chamber of Commerce (229) 434-8715.

RESTRICTIONS

Pets: On leash only. **Fires:** Allowed. **Alcoholic Beverages:** Not allowed. **Vehicle Maximum Length:** No limit. **Other:** 14-day stay limit.

TO GET THERE

From Atlanta, take I-75S to Exit 32 (Hwy. 300). Go south on Hwy. 300, then turn right on Hwy. 32. Follow Hwy. 32 and turn left on Hwy. 91 (Philema Rd.); go 9 mi. to the park, which is on the right.

APPLING
Mistletoe State Park

MAP, B-3

3723 Mistletoe Rd., 30802.
T: (706) 541-0321 or (800) 864-7275;
www.gastateparks.org/info/mistletoe.

 ★★★★    ▲ ★★★★

Beauty: ★★★★★   Site Privacy: ★★★★
Spaciousness: ★★★★   Quiet: ★★★
Security: ★★★★★   Cleanliness: ★★★★
Insect Control: ★★★★   Facilities: ★★★

Located immediately northwest of Augusta, Mistletoe State Park is known as one of the best bass-fishing destinations in the United States. Camping is relegated to the northern part of the 1,900-acre park but comes with great views of the lake. Primitive camping is limited to four walk-in sites. For RVs, back-in sites dominate, but there are a few pull-throughs. Site size and privacy vary quite a bit; look around, and try to get sites 20 or 79—these are the cream of the crop. Volleyball and hiking are available, if you didn't come to fish. Two trails leave from the campground to connect with the rest of the park.

BASICS

Operated By: Georgia Dept. of Natural Resources. **Open:** All year. **Site Assignment:** Reservations or first come, first served. **Registration:** At camp office. **Fee:** $8–$20. **Parking:** Yes.

FACILITIES

Number of Multipurpose Sites: 92. **Hookups:** Electric (30 amps), water. **Each Site:** Grill, fire ring, picnic table, lantern pole. **Dump Station:** Yes. **Laundry:** Yes. **Pay Phone:** No. **Restrooms and Showers:** Yes. **Fuel:** No. **Propane:** No. **Internal Roads:** Gravel. **RV Service:** 15 mi. in Thompson. **Market:** In Thompson. **Restaurant:** In Thompson. **General Store:** Yes. **Vending:** Yes. **Swimming:** Lake. **Playground:** Yes. **Other:** 3 boat ramps. **Activities:** Volleyball, canoe rental, hiking, biking, fishing, swimming. **Nearby Attractions:** Augusta, Fun City, Golf Museum, Riverwalk.

RESTRICTIONS

Pets: On leash only. **Fires:** Allowed. **Alcoholic Beverages:** Not allowed. **Vehicle Maximum Length:** 50 ft. **Other:** 14-day tay limit.

TO GET THERE

From I-20, take Exit 175 (Hwy. 150). Go north 7.9 mi. to the park.

BISHOP
Pine Lake RV Campground

MAP, B-2

5540 High Shoals Rd., 30621. T: (706) 769-5486; www.members.aol.com/pinelakerv/index.html.

★★★★   ▲ ★★★

Beauty: ★★★★   Site Privacy: ★★★★
Spaciousness: ★★   Quiet: ★★★★
Security: ★★★   Cleanliness: ★★★★
Insect Control: ★★★   Facilities: ★★★

If you can get past the kitschy "Happy Campers are Our Business" slogan, this is a surprisingly nice, nature-oriented private campground. The pretty setting and the people (a mostly older crowd when we visited) together make this a pleasant place to be, picturesque and heavily wooded. It is a rural spot in north-central Georgia, with good security in part due to its remoteness. There are both back-in and pull-through sites, and although they are smallish, they have foliage between them for better privacy than is offered at a lot of commercial campgrounds. Also, despite the lovely hilly surroundings, the campsites themselves are flat, with gravel ground cover. We recommend sites 3, 15, and 16 in particular. The ponds here are stocked with catfish, bass, and bluegill, but they do have a bit of an algae problem. For its privacy, beauty, friendliness, and character, this campground is a delight.

BASICS

Operated By: Britt, Linda, & John Chandler. **Open:** All year. **Site Assignment:** Reservations preferred. **Registration:** At camp office. **Fee:** RV, $21–$23; tent, $17.50. **Parking:** At site.

FACILITIES

Number of RV-only Sites: 23. **Number of Tent-only Sites:** 7. **Hookups:** Electric (30, 50 amps), water, sewer. **Each Site:** Gravel site & picnic tables. **Dump Station:** No. **Laundry:** Yes. **Pay Phone:** Yes. **Restrooms and Showers:** Yes. **Fuel:** No. **Propane:** No. **Internal Roads:** Gravel. **RV Service:** In Athens. **Market:** In Athens or Watkinsville. **Restaurant:** In Athens or Watkinsville. **General Store:** Yes. **Vending:** Yes. **Swimming:** No. **Playground:** Yes. **Activities:** Bird-watching, nature trails, fishing. **Nearby Attractions:** State Botanical Gardens, antebellum homes, University of Georgia.

RESTRICTIONS

Pets: On leash only. **Fires:** Not allowed. **Alcoholic Beverages:** Not allowed. **Vehicle Maximum Length:** No limit; 30 ft. & over, please contact before arrival.

TO GET THERE

From I-20, go north on Hwy. 441-129 to Bishop. Turn west on Hwy. 186 and go 1.4 mi. to entrance.

BLAIRSVILLE
Vogel State Park

MAP, A-2

7485 Vogel State Park Rd., 30512. T: (706) 745-2628 or (800) 864-7275; www.gastateparks.org.

★★★★   ▲ ★★★★

Beauty: ★★★★★   Site Privacy: ★★★★
Spaciousness: ★★★★   Quiet: ★★★
Security: ★★★★   Cleanliness: ★★★★
Insect Control: ★★★★   Facilities: ★★★

Many of today's state parks wouldn't exist, at least not as we recognize them, if not for the work of the Civilian Conservation Corps—Vogel State Park is one such park. The CCC's handiwork is easily seen here, and a small museum honors their work. When the heat of the summer hits the rest of the state, Vogel is a great place to visit. The 85 sites have electric and water hookups (there are 18 walk-in sites without these amenities). The sites are all large, but some of them are practically on top of one another. This place is very woody, hence quite shady, but the ground cover is minimal, reducing privacy in some areas. Recommended sites are toward the back of the campground. In addition to hiking, visitors can take a boat out on beautiful Lake Trahlyta.

BASICS

Operated By: Georgia Dept. of Natural Resources. **Open:** All year. **Site Assignment:** Reservations or first come, first served. **Registration:** At visitor center. **Fee:** RV, $20–$22; tent, $12. **Parking:** Yes.

FACILITIES

Number of RV-only Sites: 84. **Number of Tent-only Sites:** 18. **Hookups:** Electric (30, 50 amps), water. **Each Site:** Grassy, gravel pads. **Dump Station:** Yes. **Laundry:** Yes. **Pay Phone:** Yes. **Restrooms and Showers:** Yes. **Fuel:** No. **Propane:** No. **Internal Roads:** Paved. **RV Service:** No. **Market:** In Blairsville. **Restaurant:** In Owltown or Hiawasee. **General Store:** Yes. **Vending:** Yes. **Swimming:** Beach. **Playground:** 2. **Activities:** Swimming, fishing, hiking, paddle boating, mini-golf. **Nearby Attractions:** CCC Museum, Appalachian Trail, Walasi-Yi Center, Dahlonega Gold Museum, numerous waterfalls.

RESTRICTIONS

Pets: On leash only. Not allowed in cabin areas. **Fires:** Fire ring only. **Alcoholic Beverages:** Restricted. **Vehicle Maximum Length:** 50 ft.

TO GET THERE

11 mi. south of Blairsville via US 19-129.

BRUNSWICK   MAP, D-3
Blythe Island Regional Park

6616 Blythe Island Hwy., 31525.
T: (800) 343-7855 or (912) 261-3805;
www.glynncounty.org

🚐 ★★★★   ▲ ★★★★

Beauty: ★★★★★	Site Privacy: ★★★★
Spaciousness: ★★★★★	Quiet: ★★★★★
Security: ★★★★	Cleanliness: ★★★★
Insect Control: ★★★	Facilities: ★★★

This campground is a great place to use as a base for touring the Jekyll Island area and nearby beaches. Pretty and well maintained, Blythe Island's sites are surprisingly large. Lovely shade trees and a variety of native scrub brush provide some privacy between sites. Sites 54, 56, 57, 60, 61, 63, 65, and 67 are the largest, most secluded, and most attractive in the campground. The small lake is stocked with fish for anglers, and a nice swimming beach serves one section. None of the sites are actually lakeside, though none are very far from the water; the closest sites to the swimming beach are 1–13. The wide variety of on-site activities include hiking and biking trails, boat and kayak rentals, tournament horseshoes, and a field-archery range. Campers can also make use of the nearby Blythe Island Marina to arrange for fishing or touring excursions or to dock their own boats.

BASICS

Operated By: Glynn County. **Open:** All year. **Site Assignment:** Reservations or first come, first served. **Registration:** At camp office. **Fee:** $25–$27. **Parking:** Yes.

FACILITIES

Number of RV-only Sites: 97. **Number of Tent-only Sites:** 26. **Hookups:** Electric (30, 50 amps),

water, sewer, cable TV. **Each Site:** Shell covering, picnic table, fire pit. **Dump Station:** Yes. **Laundry:** Yes. **Pay Phone:** Yes. **Restrooms and Showers:** Yes. **Fuel:** No. **Propane:** Yes. **Internal Roads:** Gravel. **RV Service:** In Brunswick. **Market:** In Brunswick or Dock Junction. **Restaurant:** In Fancy Bluff or Brunswick. **General Store:** No. **Vending:** Yes. **Swimming:** Yes. **Playground:** Yes. **Other:** Wi-Fi available. **Activities:** Swimming, fishing, boating, horseshoes, archery. **Nearby Attractions:** Saint Simons, Sea Island, Jekyll Island, Cumberland Island.

RESTRICTIONS

Pets: On leash only. **Fires:** Allowed. **Alcoholic Beverages:** Not allowed. **Vehicle Maximum Length:** 40 ft.

TO GET THERE

From I-95, take Exit 29 (US 17 S.). Go 1 mi. to GA 303 N. then 3 mi. to campground.

BUFORD   MAP, B-1
Shoal Creek

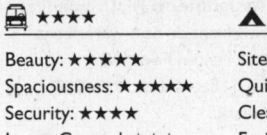

6300 Shadburn Ferry Rd., P.O. Box 567, 30518.
T: (877) 444-6777; www.reserveamerica.com.

🚐 ★★★★★   ▲ ★★★★★

Beauty: ★★★★★	Site Privacy: ★★★★★
Spaciousness: ★★★★★	Quiet: ★★★★★
Security: ★★★★★	Cleanliness: ★★★★★
Insect Control: ★★★	Facilities: ★★★

This pretty, well-run campground is one of the finest in Georgia. Set on the shores of Lake Lanier in a ritzy, suburban neighborhood and overseen by the US Army Corps of Engineers, Shoal Creek is a popular place that can get packed with campers. In addition, the lakeside setting means that boat noise is a fact of life for visitors; ask attendants for recommendations on quieter campsites. All sites here are quite large, with lovely shade trees above and screening foliage in between. Sites 55–57 are particularly shady and private; nearby, sites 36–39 and 51–54 are also particularly sizable and secluded, site 40 even more so. The half-loop that makes up sites 31–35 has breathtaking lake views. Lake Lanier features ten other campgrounds (see profiles for Lake Lanier Islands and Chestnut Ridge in Flowery Branch), 43 day-use parks, ten marinas, and nine state, county, and city parks.

BASICS

Operated By: U.S. Army Corps of Engineers. **Open:** Apr. 4–Sept. 28. **Site Assignment:** Reservations accepted. **Registration:** At entrance station. **Fee:** $16–$22, plus day-use fees. **Parking:** Limited.

FACILITIES

Number of Multipurpose Sites: 107. **Hookups:** Electric (30 amps), water. **Each Site:** Table, grill, lantern posts, fire pit. **Dump Station:** Yes. **Laundry:** Yes. **Pay Phone:** Yes. **Restrooms and Showers:** Yes. **Fuel:** No. **Propane:** No. **Internal Roads:** Paved. **RV Service:** No. **Market:** In Buford. **Restaurant:** In Buford. **General Store:** Less than

10 mi. **Vending:** Drinks. **Swimming:** Yes. **Playground:** Yes. **Other:** Swim area, boat ramp. **Activities:** Baseball, horseshoes. **Nearby Attractions:** Lake Lanier Island waterpark & golf course, concerts. **Additional Information:** Visitor center, (770) 945-9531.

RESTRICTIONS

Pets: On leash only. **Fires:** Fire ring only. **Alcoholic Beverages:** Not allowed. **Vehicle Maximum Length:** No limit. **Other:** 14-day stay limit.

TO GET THERE

From Atlanta, take I-85N to I-985. Take Exit 8 and turn left onto Hwy. 347. Turn left onto McEver Rd. then right on Shadburn Ferry Rd., which ends at the campground.

CARTERSVILLE   MAP, A-1
Allatoona Landing Campground

24 Allatoona Landing Rd., 30121.
T: (770) 974-6089 or (770) 974-6143;
www.westrec.com/allatoona.html.

🚐 ★★★   ▲ ★★★

Beauty: ★★★★	Site Privacy: ★★★
Spaciousness: ★★	Quiet: ★★★
Security: ★★★★	Cleanliness: ★★★★
Insect Control: ★★★★	Facilities: ★★★

This large campground is very popular, which means it's often crowded. Combine that with small- to mid-size campsites, and you lose a little when it comes to spaciousness and privacy. The owners of Allatoona Landing do run a tight ship, so the property is well-maintained and reasonably clean. Be aware that railroad tracks pass very near the campground, so some train noise is inevitable (especially for those sites nearest the campground office). Allatoona Lake offers plenty of options for water-sports enthusiasts, including elaborate boating facilities, and an extensive swimming beach. Sites 85, 86, 93, 95–101, and 103 are shaded and pretty, while 87 and 89–92 are the nicest waterfront sites. Sites 60–73 and 75, 77, 79, 81, 83, and 88 are closest to the swimming beach.

BASICS

Operated By: Private operator. **Open:** All year. **Site Assignment:** By reservation. **Registration:** At camp office. **Fee:** $20–$25. **Parking:** 2 vehicles per site.

FACILITIES

Number of RV-only Sites: 120. **Number of Tent-only Sites:** 20. **Hookups:** Electric (30, 50 amps), water, sewer. **Each Site:** Picnic table. Most have fire pit. **Dump Station:** Yes. **Laundry:** Yes. **Pay Phone:** Yes. **Restrooms and Showers:** Yes. **Fuel:** Yes. **Propane:** Yes. **Internal Roads:** Paved. **RV Service:** Yes. **Market:** In Bartow or Acworth. **Restaurant:** In Cartersville or Acworth. **General Store:** Yes. **Vending:** Yes. **Swimming:** Memorial Day–Labor Day. **Playground:** Yes. **Activities:** Fishing, boating, biking, kayaking, basketball. **Nearby Attractions:** Barnsly Gardens, Coopers Iron Works, Dellinger Park Complex, Etowah Arts Gallery, Etowah Indian Mounds, Lake Allatoona, Red Top State Park, Royal Oaks Golf Course. **Additional Information:**

Cartersville–Barton County Welcome Center, (770) 387-1357.

RESTRICTIONS

Pets: On leash, some restrictions. **Fires:** In designated areas only. **Alcoholic Beverages:** Allowed. **Vehicle Maximum Length:** 25 ft.

TO GET THERE

From I-75, take Exit 283. Go 2 mi. to campground entrance (in front of 2nd set of RR tracks).

CARTERSVILLE   MAP, A-1
Red Top Mountain State Park

50 Lodge Rd., 30121. T: (770) 975-0055 or (800) 864-7275; www.gastateparks.org.

🚐 ★★★★   ▲ ★★★★

Beauty: ★★★★   **Site Privacy:** ★★★
Spaciousness: ★★★   **Quiet:** ★★★★
Security: ★★★★★   **Cleanliness:** ★★★★
Insect Control: ★★★★   **Facilities:** ★★★

Red Top Mountain was once an important mining area for iron—the red-colored soil gives this away. Located a short distance from I-75 and near the town of Acworth, this park offers great camping opportunities on Allatoona Lake. Tent campers have a section all to themselves (sites 37–60), but water and power hookups are only available in the 63 other sites. Sites 1–12 are pull-throughs; the rest are back-ins. The area is nicely wooded, offering shade to small but picturesque sites. Every Saturday from May until early September, the park has a bluegrass and storytelling program. In addition to tennis, mini-golf, and boating, the park has 11.5 miles of trails to explore.

BASICS

Operated By: Georgia Dept. of Natural Resources. **Open:** All year. **Site Assignment:** Reservations or first come, first served. **Registration:** At visitor center or lodge. **Fee:** $16–$24. **Parking:** 2 vehicles per site.

FACILITIES

Number of RV-only Sites: 63. **Number of Tent-only Sites:** 29. **Hookups:** Electric (50 amps), water. **Each Site:** Wooded w/ tent pad, fire ring. **Dump Station:** Yes. **Laundry:** No. **Pay Phone:** No. **Restrooms and Showers:** Yes. **Fuel:** No. **Propane:** No. **Internal Roads:** Paved. **RV Service:** In Acworth. **Market:** In Acworth. **Restaurant:** Yes. **General Store:** No. **Vending:** Soft drinks. **Swimming:** Yes. **Playground:** Yes. **Other:** Gated park, boat rentals. **Activities:** Tennis, mini-golf, hiking, boating, swimming, fishing. **Nearby Attractions:** Etowah Indian Mounds State Historic Site, Kennesaw Mountain National Battlefield Park, Weinman Mineral Museum. **Additional Information:** Cartersville–Barton County Welcome Center, (770) 387-1357.

RESTRICTIONS

Pets: On leash only. **Fires:** Fire ring only. **Alcoholic Beverages:** At sites only. **Vehicle Maximum Length:** 40 ft. **Other:** No bicycles allowed on trails.

TO GET THERE

From Atlanta, go north on I-75 to Exit 285. Go right on Red Top Mountain Rd. across Lake Allatoona to the state park.

CLARKESVILLE   MAP, A-2
Moccasin Creek State Park

3655 Hwy. 197, P.O. Box 1634, 30523. T: (706) 947-3194 or (800) 864-7275.

🚐 ★★★★   ▲ ★★★★

Beauty: ★★★★   **Site Privacy:** ★★★★
Spaciousness: ★★★★   **Quiet:** ★★★★
Security: ★★★★   **Cleanliness:** ★★★★
Insect Control: ★★★★   **Facilities:** ★★★

High in the Blue Ridge Mountains and surrounded on three sides by the enormous Lake Burton, Moccasin Creek State Park offers a unique opportunity for campers with disabilities. The majority of the property is wheelchair-accessible, including a fishing pier reserved exclusively for handicapped visitors, seniors, and children. Despite its mountainous location, the campground is relatively flat. This makes it easy to maneuver around in large RVs, bicycles, and wheelchairs. Canoeing on the lake is a treat, though the high elevation and terrain mean that sudden winds can blow up (some strong enough to tip canoes over in the lake's center). Several trails wind through the mountains around the lake, including an easy walk to Hemlock Falls and a more rugged trek to Moccasin Creek Falls. The fall colors are especially beautiful here, making it very difficult to score a vacancy during October.

BASICS

Operated By: Georgia Dept. of Natural Resources. **Open:** All year. **Site Assignment:** First come, first served. **Registration:** At office. **Fee:** $16–$24. **Parking:** On site.

FACILITIES

Number of RV-only Sites: 55. **Hookups:** Electric, water. **Dump Station:** Yes. **Laundry:** Yes. **Pay Phone:** Yes. **Restrooms and Showers:** Yes. **Fuel:** No. **Propane:** No. **Internal Roads:** Paved. **RV Service:** No. **Market:** In Clarkesville. **Restaurant:** In Clarkesville. **General Store:** On Hwy. 197. **Vending:** Yes. **Swimming:** No. **Playground:** Yes. **Other:** Boat ramp, observation tower, wheelchair-accessible facilities available. **Activities:** Hiking, fishing, canoeing (seasonal). **Nearby Attractions:** Appalachian Trail, Chattahoochee National Forest, Tallulah Gorge State Park.

RESTRICTIONS

Pets: On leash only. **Fires:** Fire ring only. **Alcoholic Beverages:** Not allowed. **Vehicle Maximum Length:** 40 ft.

TO GET THERE

20 mi. north of Clarkesville on GA 197 or 15 mi. west of Clayton on GA 76 and GA 197.

CORDELE   MAP, C-2
Georgia Veterans Memorial State Park

2459-A US 280 West, 31015. T: (229) 276-2371 or (800) 864-7275.

🚐 ★★★★   ▲ ★★★★

Beauty: ★★★★★   **Site Privacy:** ★★★★
Spaciousness: ★★★★★   **Quiet:** ★★★★
Security: ★★★★   **Cleanliness:** ★★★★
Insect Control: ★★★   **Facilities:** ★★★★★

This popular campground, only a few miles from Cordele, has ample sites with moderate hardwood shade. The generally flat landscape is very picturesque and tranquil. RV Camping Areas 1 and 2 (sites 1–53) are arranged by Lake Blackshear, with campsites 1–27 set on the lakefront itself. These are the best sites in the campground, especially sites 25–27 (all are pretty, but site 27 is especially huge and gorgeous). Sites 52 and 53 are particularly large pull-throughs. Camping Area 3 (sites 54–76) is a separate loop set back in the woods; its sites are not as nice as the others. Across the lake are the park's main facilities (the visitor center, a museum, military exhibits, nature trails, etc.); that's also where you'll find tent-camping areas and cottages. This campground has plenty of options for groups, from a fully equipped conference center to a separately reserved, secluded area for group primitive camping.

BASICS

Operated By: Georgia Dept. of Natural Resources. **Open:** All year. **Site Assignment:** First come, first served; can reserve waterfront or non-waterfront. **Registration:** At visitor center. **Fee:** RV, $10.35–$20; tent, $9.15–$18; cottages, $75–$90. **Parking:** At site or in park.

FACILITIES

Number of RV-only Sites: 77. **Hookups:** Electric (30, 50 amps), water, cable TV. **Each Site:** Grills. **Dump Station:** Yes. **Laundry:** Yes. **Pay Phone:** Yes. **Restrooms and Showers:** Yes. **Fuel:** Nearby. **Propane:** Nearby. **Internal Roads:** Paved. **RV Service:** No. **Market:** In Codele. **Restaurant:** In Cordele. **General Store:** Yes. **Vending:** Yes. **Swimming:** Yes. **Playground:** Yes. **Other:** 10 cottages. **Activities:** Nature trail, golf, boating, waterskiing, fishing, model-airplane flying, Frisbee/disc golf. **Nearby Attractions:** Warner Robins Air Museum, Chehaw Wild Animal Park. **Additional Information:** Cordele Chamber of Commerce, (229) 273-1668 or www.cordele-crisp-chamber.com.

RESTRICTIONS

Pets: On leash only. **Fires:** Fire ring only. **Alcoholic Beverages:** At sites only. **Vehicle Maximum Length:** 50 ft.

TO GET THERE

The park is 9 mi. west of I-75 (Exit 101) near Cordele on US 280.

CUMMING MAP, A-1
Bald Ridge

reserve america

4100 Bald Ridge Rd., 30041. T: (770) 889-1591 or (877) 444-6777; www.reserveamerica.com.

★★★★   ★★★★

Beauty: ★★★★★	Site Privacy: ★★★★
Spaciousness: ★★★★★	Quiet: ★★★★
Security: ★★★★★	Cleanliness: ★★★★★
Insect Control: ★★★	Facilities: ★★★

This extraordinarily well-manicured campground is situated in a nice suburban to rural area about 30 miles northeast of Atlanta. The sites vary from shady to open, with gorgeous views, though not a great deal of privacy, at lakefront sites 39–53. We also recommend lakefront sites 70–72, which offer lovely views and are also fairly secluded. Avoid sites 81 and 82 if possible, as they are adjacent to the sewer, and keep in mind noisy boats when choosing a site near the water. Lake Sidney Lanier is host to several Corps of Engineers campgrounds, and Bald Ridge is the flagship, with facilities to accommodate RVs and tents quite well (although the restrooms are nicer at a couple of the other campgrounds). With a combination of back-in and some pull-through sites, the extremely large, paved sites also include a sizable gravel picnic and tent area. Between the gates and general seclusion, security here is excellent, and it's a wonderful spot for families.

BASICS
Operated By: U.S. Army Corps of Engineers. **Open:** Mar.–Oct. **Site Assignment:** Reservations accepted. **Registration:** At park entry station. **Fee:** $22–$24. **Parking:** On site.

FACILITIES
Number of RV-only Sites: 82. **Hookups:** Electric (30, 50 amps), water, sewer. **Each Site:** Picnic table, grill, fire pits. **Dump Station:** Yes. **Laundry:** Yes. **Pay Phone:** Yes. **Restrooms and Showers:** Yes. **Fuel:** Nearby. **Propane:** Nearby. **Internal Roads:** Paved. **RV Service:** No. **Market:** In Cumming. **Restaurant:** In Cumming. **General Store:** Nearby. **Vending:** Soft drinks. **Swimming:** Yes. **Playground:** Yes. **Other:** Boat ramp. **Activities:** Boating, fishing, swimming. **Nearby Attractions:** Lake Lanier Island water park & golf course. **Additional Information:** Cumming–Forsyth County Chamber of Commerce, (770) 887-6461 or www.forsythchamber.org.

RESTRICTIONS
Pets: On leash only. **Fires:** Fire ring only. **Alcoholic Beverages:** Not allowed. **Vehicle Maximum Length:** No limit. **Other:** 14-day stay limit; 3 vehicles per site; 8 people per site.

TO GET THERE
Take Hwy. 400N to Exit 16. Turn right on Pilgrim Mill Rd., then turn right on Sinclair Shores Rd. Turn left on Bald Rich Rd., which ends at the campground.

ELBERTON MAP, B-2
Bobby Brown State Park

2509 Bobby Brown State Park Rd., 30635. T: (706) 213-2046 or (800) 864-7275; www.gastateparks.org.

★★★★   ★★★

Beauty: ★★★★	Site Privacy: ★★
Spaciousness: ★★★	Quiet: ★★★★
Security: ★★★★★	Cleanliness: ★★★★
Insect Control: ★★★★	Facilities: ★★★

One of several camping areas located on the Georgia–South Carolina border, Bobby Brown State Park is situated on what was once the historic boomtown of Petersburg, established in 1798. Now campers come to the 665-acre park to relax and take part in the many activities available here, including fishing, boating, swimming, and hiking. Water and electric hookups are available at the park's 61 sites, which are a mix of pull-throughs and back-ins. When compared to other state parks, these sites are a bit small, but they are still larger than those at many private campgrounds. If you want premium access to the Broad River, pay $2 more and stay at sites 3–13, but look to see if site 60 is open—it's arguably one of the best in the park. Visitors who get the itch to explore will want to check out Pioneer Nancy Hart's Cabin or the Granite Museum.

BASICS
Operated By: Georgia Dept. of Natural Resources. **Open:** All year. **Site Assignment:** Reservations or first come, first served. **Registration:** At main office. **Fee:** $18–$20. **Parking:** 2 vehicles per site.

FACILITIES
Number of RV-only Sites: 61. **Number of Tent-only Sites:** Undesignated sites. **Hookups:** Electric (20, 30, 50 amps), water. **Each Site:** Picnic table, grill, fire ring, lantern pole. **Dump Station:** Yes. **Laundry:** Yes. **Pay Phone:** Yes. **Restrooms and Showers:** Yes. **Fuel:** No. **Propane:** No. **Internal Roads:** Paved. **RV Service:** 22 mi. **Market:** 22 mi. **Restaurant:** 10 mi. **General Store:** No. **Vending:** Soft drinks. **Swimming:** Yes. **Playground:** Yes. **Activities:** Hiking trails, boat launch, 72,000-acre lake, fishing pier, canoes, pedal boats. **Nearby Attractions:** Pioneer Nancy Hart's Cabin, Granite Museum.

RESTRICTIONS
Pets: On leash (6 ft. or less) only. **Fires:** Fire ring only. **Alcoholic Beverages:** At sites only. **Vehicle Maximum Length:** 35 ft. **Other:** 14-day stay limit.

TO GET THERE
From I-85, exit at Hwy. 175 and go to Elberton. Then take Hwy. 72 east 15 mi. Turn right on Bobby Brown State Park Rd. Go 7 mi. to the park entrance.

ELKO MAP, C-2
Twin Oaks RV Park

305 Hwy. 26 East., 31025. T: (478) 987-9361; www.twinoaksrvpark.com.

★★★   n/a

Beauty: ★★★★	Site Privacy: ★★★
Spaciousness: ★★★	Quiet: ★★★
Security: ★★★	Cleanliness: ★★★★
Insect Control: ★★★★	Facilities: ★★

In the center of the state, this private campground has a rural feel despite its proximity to I-75. The RV park itself boasts huge sites and welcomes big rigs, but not tents. Among its pluses are modern restrooms and showers, shade at almost all sites, and RV-friendly facilities. Most of the 76 sites are pull-throughs, with each site having gravel and a nice grassy spot. The whole place is landscaped, pretty, and pleasant, and there is even a little green between some of the sites. Security may be a concern due to the nearby interstate traffic and the lack of a gate, however. Recreation at the RV park is available, and there is plenty in Perry to keep the whole family entertained. With the possible exception of the highway noise, we agree with the park's advertisement: this is a "quiet country" vacation spot, good for families and all ages.

BASICS
Operated By: Maryann & Keith Hueback. **Open:** All year. **Site Assignment:** First come, first served. **Registration:** At camp office. **Fee:** RV, $24; tent, $11. **Parking:** In campground.

FACILITIES
Number of RV-only Sites: 72. **Hookups:** Electric (30, 50 amps), water, sewer, Internet, phone. **Each Site:** Gravel w/ concrete patio, picnic table. **Dump Station:** Yes. **Laundry:** Yes. **Pay Phone:** Yes. **Restrooms and Showers:** Yes. **Fuel:** No. **Propane:** Yes. **Internal Roads:** Gravel. **RV Service:** No. **Market:** In Perry. **Restaurant:** 1 mi. **General Store:** Across from park. **Vending:** No. **Swimming:** Yes. **Playground:** No. **Activities:** Horseshoes, volleyball, basketball. **Nearby Attractions:** Andersonville, fairground, Civil War Museum, Plains, Jimmy Carter Museum.

RESTRICTIONS
Pets: On leash only. **Fires:** At some sites. **Alcoholic Beverages:** At sites only. **Vehicle Maximum Length:** No limit.

TO GET THERE
Take I-75 south from Atlanta to Exit 127. The campground is just below Perry, 0.2 mi. east, on Hwy. 26.

FARGO MAP, D-2
Stephen Foster State Park

17515 Hwy. 122, 31631. T: (912) 637-5274; www.gastateparks.org; www.floridastateparks.org/stephenfoster/default.cfm.

★★★★★   ★★★★★

Beauty: ★★★★★	Site Privacy: ★★★★★
Spaciousness: ★★★★★	Quiet: ★★★★★
Security: ★★★★★	Cleanliness: ★★★★★
Insect Control: ★★	Facilities: ★★★

The extremely remote location of Stephen C. Foster State Park means that its campground is extraordinarily peaceful and serene. The park is the main Georgia entrance to the Okefenokee Swamp and

related Okefenokee National Wildlife Refuge. Eight of the sites are pull-throughs and the rest are back-ins. Campsites are huge, densely shaded, and wooded for offering plenty of privacy. The natural scenery and wildlife are the obvious attractions here, and all that prevents this campground from getting five stars in beauty are the occasional intrusions of telephone lines and unsightly utility buildings. Even so, the quiet blackwater of the swamp, the stately cypress groves, and the hanging curtains of Spanish moss still make this one of the prettiest campgrounds in the region. Families often walk the grounds at night to watch the droves of wild deer that wander placidly by. Be sure to bring insect repellent and mosquito netting, since the swampy conditions are heaven for all manner of bloodsuckers.

BASICS

Operated By: Georgia Dept. of Natural Resources. **Open:** All year. **Site Assignment:** First come, first served. **Registration:** At office. **Fee:** $18–$22 (Mar.–May); $15–$17 (all other months). **Parking:** On site.

FACILITIES

Number of RV-only Sites: 49. **Number of Tent-only Sites:** 17. **Hookups:** Electric (20, 30 amps), water. **Each Site:** Picnic table, grill. **Dump Station:** Yes. **Laundry:** Yes. **Pay Phone:** Yes. **Restrooms and Showers:** Yes. **Fuel:** No. **Propane:** No. **Internal Roads:** Paved. **RV Service:** No. **Market:** In Ernest. **Restaurant:** In Ernest. **General Store:** Yes. **Vending:** No. **Swimming:** No. **Playground:** Yes. **Activities:** Fishing, boating, canoeing. **Nearby Attractions:** Okefenokee Swamp, Suwanee Canal Recreational Area, Laura S. Walker State Park.

RESTRICTIONS

Pets: On leash only. **Fires:** Allowed. **Alcoholic Beverages:** Sites only. **Vehicle Maximum Length:** 50 ft.

TO GET THERE

Take US 441 to Fargo. Go 18 mi. on Hwy. 177N to the state park.

FLOVILLA
Indian Springs State Park

MAP, B-2

reserve america

678 Lake Clark Rd., 30216. T: (770) 504-2277 or (800) 864-7275; www.reserveamerica.com.

🚐 ★★★★	⛺ ★★★★
Beauty: ★★★★	Site Privacy: ★★★★★
Spaciousness: ★★★★★	Quiet: ★★★★
Security: ★★★★	Cleanliness: ★★★★
Insect Control: ★★★	Facilities: ★★★

Campers with a penchant for history will want to visit Indian Springs State Park, believed to be the oldest park in the nation. The park has 88 sites for RVs, trailers, and tents, as well as 30 more primitive sites for tents only. All the sites are pull-throughs, and include electrical, water, and cable hookups. The area is nicely shaded, with pines and the occasional hardwood. Each sight has ample space in which to relax, but the phone lines running through the park

and the well-used outhouses detract from the overall beauty. Those wishing to explore can find a spring house built by the Civilian Conservation Corps. The Creek Native Americans used this spring to heal the ill and impart vigor to the healthy. Today, visitors can participate in a number of activities, including swimming, fishing, and boating. Nearby points of interest include the Jarrell Plantation State Historic Site and the Historic Indian Springs Hotel.

BASICS

Operated By: Georgia Dept. of Natural Resources. **Open:** All year. **Site Assignment:** Sites assigned based on vehicle size. **Registration:** At camp office. **Fee:** RV, $22; tent, $20; parking fee, $2. **Parking:** In campground. $2 parking fee.

FACILITIES

Number of Multipurpose Sites: 88. **Hookups:** Electric (30 amps), water, cable TV. **Each Site:** Picnic table, fire pit. **Dump Station:** Yes. **Laundry:** Yes. **Pay Phone:** No. **Restrooms and Showers:** Yes. **Fuel:** 0.75 mi. **Propane:** 5 min. to Jackson. **Internal Roads:** Paved. **RV Service:** 30 mi. **Market:** 5 mi. in Jackson. **Restaurant:** 5 mi. in Jackson. **General Store:** Outside park. **Vending:** Soft drinks. **Swimming:** Beach. **Playground:** 4 playgrounds. **Other:** Nature trail, museum. **Activities:** Pedal boats, fishing, swimming, boating, golf. **Nearby Attractions:** Jarrell Plantation State Historic Site, High Falls State Park, Piedmont National Wildlife Refuge, Historic Indian Springs Hotel.

RESTRICTIONS

Pets: On leash only. **Fires:** Subject to seasonal bans. **Alcoholic Beverages:** Inside tent; in moderation. **Vehicle Maximum Length:** No limit.

TO GET THERE

From I-75 S., take Exit 205 to Jackson. Proceed south on Hwy. 42 to the park. From I-75 N., take Exit 188 and proceed north on Hwy. 42. The park is approximately 15 mi. from the interstate.

FLOWERY BRANCH
Chestnut Ridge Campground

MAP, A-2, B-2

reserve america

6515 Chestnut Ridge Rd., 30542. T: (770) 967-6710; www.reserveamerica.com.

🚐 ★★★★★	⛺ ★★★★★
Beauty: ★★★★★	Site Privacy: ★★★★★
Spaciousness: ★★★★★	Quiet: ★★★★★
Security: ★★★★★	Cleanliness: ★★★★★
Insect Control: ★★★★	Facilities: ★★★

Another gorgeous campground in the Lake Lanier resort area (see profiles for Shoal Creek in Buford and Lake Lanier Islands), Chestnut Ridge sits on a small peninsula in an upscale residential neighborhood. Campsites are large and shaded, and many have screening foliage between them. Most sites are fairly close together; campsites 1–13 have the most elbow room, while sites 23–29 are the most secluded. As with other properties in this Army

Corps of Engineers–managed area, boat noise is often the only downside; ask attendants for recommendations about the quietest sites. Chestnut Ridge is most often full on weekends. This campground offers little more than nice accommodations, as most visitors come for lake activities and water sports. However, there's plenty to do in the area, since Lake Lanier has 43 day-use parks, ten marinas, and nine state, county, and city parks.

BASICS

Operated By: U.S. Army Corps of Engineers. **Open:** Apr. 26–Sept. 10. **Site Assignment:** 60% reservable; 40% first come, first served. **Registration:** At park-entry station. **Fee:** $16–$24, plus day-use fees. **Parking:** On site.

FACILITIES

Number of RV-only Sites: 85. **Hookups:** Electric (30, 50 amps), water. **Each Site:** Grills, fire pits, picnic table. **Dump Station:** Yes. **Laundry:** Yes. **Pay Phone:** Yes. **Restrooms and Showers:** Yes. **Fuel:** Nearby. **Propane:** Nearby. **Internal Roads:** Paved. **RV Service:** No. **Market:** In Flowery Branch. **Restaurant:** In Flowery Branch. **General Store:** Nearby. **Vending:** No. **Swimming:** Beach. **Playground:** Yes. **Other:** Boat launch. **Activities:** Boating, lake swimming, fishing. **Nearby Attractions:** Lake Lanier Island water park & golf course. **Additional Information:** City of Flowery Branch, (770) 967-6371, or www.cityoffflowerybranch.org.

RESTRICTIONS

Pets: On leash only. **Fires:** Fire ring only. **Alcoholic Beverages:** Not allowed. **Vehicle Maximum Length:** No limit. **Other:** 14-day stay limit.

TO GET THERE

From Atlanta, take I-85N to I-985. Take Exit 8 and turn left onto Hwy. 347, turn right onto McEver Rd., and turn left on Gaines Ferry Rd. Then turn right onto Chestnut Ridge Rd., which ends at the campground.

FORTSON
Blanton Creek Park

MAP, C-1

1516 Bartletts Ferry Rd., 31808. T: (706) 643-7737 or (888) GPC-LAKE; www.georgiapower.com/gpclake.

🚐 ★★★★	⛺ ★★★
Beauty: ★★★★★	Site Privacy: ★★★★
Spaciousness: ★★★★	Quiet: ★★★★★
Security: ★★★★★	Cleanliness: ★★★
Insect Control: ★★★	Facilities: ★★★

Blanton Creek Park is one of numerous Georgia Power–owned campgrounds scattered across the state. This lakeside property has an unusual layout. The hilly terrain rolls down to the shores of Lake Harding, and the roads and campsites form terraces on the hillside. The overall effect is quite lovely, and the only real aesthetic downside to the campground are the less-than-clean facilities (the bathrooms were particularly gross on our visit). Assuming that gets taken care of, there's little to fault in the large campsites set in gorgeous woods. If you're looking for a good pull-through, there aren't many to choose from; however, site 7 is a nice one, and site 12 is even better. Sites 44–47 have fantastic lake views. The tent area here has a nice views, too, but it's really too crowded to recommend.

BASICS

Operated By: Georgia Power Company. **Open:** Apr.–Sept. **Site Assignment:** Reservations accepted. **Registration:** At office. **Fee:** RV, $16; tent, $14; day-use area, $3. **Parking:** In campground.

FACILITIES

Number of RV-only Sites: 43. **Number of Tent-only Sites:** 8. **Hookups:** Electric. **Each Site:** Picnic tables, grills. **Dump Station:** Yes. **Laundry:** Yes. **Pay Phone:** Yes. **Restrooms and Showers:** Yes. **Fuel:** No. **Propane:** No. **Internal Roads:** Paved & gravel. **RV Service:** In Columbus. **Market:** In Columbus. **Restaurant:** In Columbus. **General Store:** No. **Vending:** Soft drinks. **Swimming:** Lake only. **Playground:** Yes. **Other:** Group wilderness camping. **Activities:** Boating, fishing, hiking, bird-watching. **Nearby Attractions:** Calloway Gardens, Pine Mountain, Franklin D. Roosevelt State Park. **Additional Information:** Georgia Power, (888) GPC-LAKE.

RESTRICTIONS

Pets: On leash only; 2 pet max. **Fires:** Grill only. **Alcoholic Beverages:** Not allowed. **Vehicle Maximum Length:** 40 ft. **Other:** Big rigs welcome, call ahead for details.

TO GET THERE

From I-185, take Exit 21 and go 0.25 mi. west on Hwy. 116, then 3.5 mi. west on Hwy. 103, then 1 mi. south on Lick Skillet Rd.

GREENSBORO   MAP, B-2
Old Salem

1530 Old Salem Rd., 30642. T: (706) 467-2850 or (888) GPC-LAKE; www.georgiapower.com/gpclake.

🚐 ★★★	🏕 ★★★
Beauty: ★★★	Site Privacy: ★★★
Spaciousness: ★★★	Quiet: ★★★
Security: ★★★★★	Cleanliness: ★★★★
Insect Control: ★★★★	Facilities: ★★★

The most elaborate of Georgia Power's campgrounds on Lake Oconee (see the following profile for Parks Ferry), Old Salem focuses mostly on lake activities and water sports. This campground is quite popular, and the large number of children and vehicles can make it less than tranquil. Campsites vary in size, but most are acceptably large; all are nicely wooded. The best campsites by far are 85, 87, 89, and 91, with 91 leading the pack. All of these are extremely choice and hard to get due to their lakeside setting and close proximity to the campers-only boat dock. Families might prefer sites 78–80, which are adjacent to the beach house and playground.

BASICS

Operated By: Georgia Power Company. **Open:** Mar. 1–Oct. 30. **Site Assignment:** First come, first served; reservations accepted. **Registration:** At office. **Fee:** $14–$16. **Parking:** In campground.

FACILITIES

Number of RV-only Sites: 92. **Number of Tent-only Sites:** 57. **Hookups:** Electric (20, 30, 50 amps), water. **Each Site:** Picnic table & grill. **Dump Station:** Yes. **Laundry:** Yes. **Pay Phone:** Yes. **Restrooms and Showers:** Yes. **Propane:** No. **Internal Roads:** Paved. **RV Service:** No. **Market:** Nearby. **Restaurant:** Nearby. **General Store:** No. **Vending:** Soft drinks. **Swimming:** Yes. **Playground:** Yes. **Other:** Boat ramp. **Activities:** Swimming, fishing, boating, volleyball. **Nearby Attractions:** Iron Horse, museum, golf course, & Green County Courthouse. **Additional Information:** Green County Chamber of Commerce, (800) 886-5253 www.greeneccoc.org.

RESTRICTIONS

Pets: Allowed. **Fires:** Allowed. **Alcoholic Beverages:** Not allowed. **Vehicle Maximum Length:** No limit. **Other:** Big rigs welcome.

TO GET THERE

From the junction of I-20 Exit 130 and Hwy. 44: go 7 mi. southwest on Hwy. 44, then 0.75 mi. southeast on Linger Longer Rd., then 1 mi. southwest on paved road. Follow signs.

GREENSBORO   MAP, B-2
Parks Ferry

1491 Parks Mill Rd., 30642. T: (706) 453-4308.

🚐 ★★★★	🏕 ★★★
Beauty: ★★★★	Site Privacy: ★★
Spaciousness: ★★★	Quiet: ★★★★
Security: ★★★★★	Cleanliness: ★★★★
Insect Control: ★★★★	Facilities: ★★★

One of several Georgia Power campgrounds on Lake Oconee (see the preceding profile of Old Salem), Parks Ferry is a tight triple loop of campsites set next to the lake and a tiny "wildlife habitat." This property is not as nice as nearby Old Salem, and its long sites are a bit sandwiched together. However, it's also not as crowded as its Oconee sibling, which translates to a bit more quiet and overall privacy. A forest of hardwoods on the grounds also makes the place more attractive than it might otherwise be. A small beach and boat facilities make Parks Ferry a viable alternative when other Lake Oconee campgrounds are overwhelmed with visitors.

BASICS

Operated By: Georgia Power Company. **Open:** Mar.–Sept. **Site Assignment:** First come, first served; reservations accepted. **Registration:** At gatehouse. **Fee:** RV, $16; tent, $14. **Parking:** On site.

FACILITIES

Number of RV-only Sites: 53. **Number of Tent-only Sites:** 40. **Hookups:** Electric, water. **Each Site:** Grill, picnic, fire pit. **Dump Station:** Yes. **Laundry:** Yes. **Pay Phone:** Yes. **Restrooms and Showers:** Yes. **Fuel:** No. **Propane:** No. **Internal Roads:** Paved. **RV Service:** 10 mi. **Market:** 3 mi. to Publix. **Restaurant:** 3 mi. **General Store:** 3 mi. **Vending:** Soft drinks. **Swimming:** Beach. **Playground:** Yes. **Activities:** Beachfront, boat ramp, volleyball, horseshoes. **Nearby Attractions:** Iron Horse, museum, Green County Courthouse, golf course. **Additional Information:** Green County Chamber of Commerce, (800) 886-5253 or www.greeneccoc.org.

RESTRICTIONS

Pets: On leash only. **Fires:** Fire ring only. **Alcoholic Beverages:** Not allowed. **Vehicle Maximum Length:** 40 ft. **Other:** Big rigs welcome.

TO GET THERE

From I-20 Exit 130, go right on Hwy. 44 5.5 mi. and turn right on Kerry Station Rd. Continue 3.5 mi., turn left on Parkshill Rd., and continue 1 mi. to the park on your right.

HARTWELL   MAP, A-2
Hart State Park

330 Hart State Park Rd., 30643. T: (706) 376-8756 or (800) 864-7275; www.gastateparks.org.

🚐 ★★★★	🏕 ★★★★
Beauty: ★★★★	Site Privacy: ★★★★
Spaciousness: ★★★★	Quiet: ★★★
Security: ★★★★	Cleanliness: ★★★★
Insect Control: ★★★	Facilities: ★★★★

The 55,590-acre Hartwell Reservoir is the main attraction at Hart State Park Campground. Anglers can fish for largemouth and hybrid bass, striper, black crappie, bream, rainbow trout, and wall-eyed pike in the reservoir's waters, and the campground's boat ramp and six docks make water access easy. Both the size and overall privacy of these campsites vary immensely. Sites 28–37 are a bit more spacious than most, and they have decent shade and good lake views. The sites are mainly pull-throughs. The adjacent sites 56–58 are not level enough to suit most RVers. A few nature trails lace the edge of the property, and a multiuse trail for hiking and biking offers a good jaunt south of the campground. No visit to the area could possibly be complete with a pilgrimage to nearby Elberton, the "Granite Capital of the World."

BASICS

Operated By: Georgia Dept. of Natural Resources. **Open:** All year. **Site Assignment:** First come, first served. **Registration:** At park-entry station. **Fee:** RV, $15–$19; tent, $11–$15; reservation fee for picnic shelters, $25. **Parking:** On site.

FACILITIES

Number of RV-only Sites: 50. **Number of Tent-only Sites:** 25. **Hookups:** Electric (20, 30, 50 amps), water, sewer. **Each Site:** Picnic, fire ring, grill, lantern pole. **Dump Station:** Yes. **Laundry:** Yes. **Pay Phone:** Yes. **Restrooms and Showers:** Yes. **Fuel:** No. **Propane:** No. **Internal Roads:** Paved. **RV Service:** 30 mi. **Market:** 5 mi. to Hartwell. **Restaurant:** 5 mi. to Hartwell. **General Store:** 5 mi. to Hartwell. **Vending:** Yes. **Swimming:** Seasonal. **Playground:** Yes. **Other:** Picnic shelters, pontoon boats, cottages, canoes, pedal boats, boat ramps. **Activities:** Hiking, fishing, biking, boating, swimming beach, Cricket Theater. **Nearby Attractions:** Hartwell Golf Club, Cateechee Golf Club, Tugaloo State Park, Granite Capital of World, Hartwell Lake & Dam. **Additional Information:** Hart County Chamber of Commerce, (706) 376-8590 or www.hart-chamber.org.

RESTRICTIONS

Pets: On leash only. **Fires:** Fire ring only. **Alcoholic Beverages:** At sites only. **Vehicle Maximum Length:** 40 ft. **Other:** No entry after 11 p.m.

TO GET THERE

From Hartwell, drive north on Hwy. 29. Turn left on Ridge Rd. and go 2 mi. to the park.

HARTWELL — MAP, A-2
Payne's Creek

reserve america

P.O. Box 278, 30643-0298. T: (877) 444-6777 or (706) 376-4788; www.reserveamerica.com.

★★★★★ ▲ ★★★★★

Beauty: ★★★★★	Site Privacy: ★★★★★
Spaciousness: ★★★★★	Quiet: ★★★★
Security: ★★★★★	Cleanliness: ★★★★
Insect Control: ★★★★	Facilities: ★★★

Situated on the Georgia–South Carolina border, this lakeside campground is in easy striking distance from I-85, yet remains fairly remote. Incredibly large sites lie throughout the grounds. Heavy vegetation between sites offers great privacy, and all but a few are on the water. The best of these sites—20, 21, 23, 27–29, 34, and 35—offer wide, beautiful views of the lake. Both back-ins and pull-throughs are available, though the preferred areas have large, circular pull-throughs. No developed sites are designated tents-only, though there is a nearby primitive area. A boat ramp provides a great opportunity to access the nearly 56,000-acre Hartwell Lake, and those wishing to see a working power plant can visit the Hartwell Power plant a few miles away.

BASICS

Operated By: U.S. Army Corps of Engineers. **Open:** May–Sept. **Site Assignment:** Reservation only. **Registration:** By phone or at the Web site, at least 2 days in advance. **Fee:** $16–$18. **Parking:** At site or in designated areas.

FACILITIES

Number of Tent-only Sites: Undesignated sites. **Number of Multipurpose Sites:** 44. **Hookups:** Electric (20, 30, 50 amps), water, sewer. **Dump Station:** Yes. **Laundry:** No. **Pay Phone:** Yes. **Restrooms and Showers:** Yes. **Fuel:** No. **Propane:** No. **Internal Roads:** Paved. **RV Service:** In Hartwell. **Market:** In Hartwell. **Restaurant:** In Hartwell. **General Store:** No. **Vending:** No. **Swimming:** Lake. **Playground:** Yes. **Activities:** Boating, swimming. **Nearby Attractions:** Marinas, boat slips, rentals.

RESTRICTIONS

Pets: On leash (6 ft. or less) only. **Fires:** Fire rings or grills; burn only fallen or purchased wood. **Alcoholic Beverages:** Not allowed. **Vehicle Maximum Length:** 60 ft. **Other:** 14-day stay limit; no guns or fireworks.

TO GET THERE

From I-85, take Exit 177. Proceed south on Hwy. 77 5 mi. Follow directional signs the last 10 mi. to the campground.

HARTWELL — MAP, A-2
Watsadler

reserve america

286 Watsadler Rd., 30643. T: (888) 893-0678; www.reserveamerica.com.

★★★★ ▲ ★★★★

Beauty: ★★★★★	Site Privacy: ★★★★
Spaciousness: ★★★	Quiet: ★★★★
Security: ★★★★	Cleanliness: ★★★★
Insect Control: ★★★	Facilities: ★★★

Another U.S. Army Corps of Engineers property, Watsadler is one of several campgrounds resting on the shores of Hartwell Lake (but this is the only one open year-round). You'd expect this remote property to be dead quiet, but the large number of vehicles in the park tends to create a lot of background noise. Site size varies from fair to huge, with shade ranging from slight to heavy. A few campsites are extremely private, but most are not. Lakeside sites 9 and 10 are among the exceptions, boasting not only a good amount of screening foliage, but also a lot of room and fantastic lake views. Site 5 is also quite picturesque. The July Fourth fireworks here are said to be particularly impressive.

BASICS

Operated By: U.S. Army Corps of Engineers. **Open:** All year. **Site Assignment:** Reservations accepted. **Registration:** At office. **Fee:** $18–$42. **Parking:** On site.

FACILITIES

Number of Multipurpose Sites: 50. **Hookups:** Electric (50 amps), water, sewer. **Each Site:** Fire pit. **Dump Station:** Yes. **Laundry:** No. **Pay Phone:** Yes. **Restrooms and Showers:** Yes. **Fuel:** No. **Propane:** No. **Internal Roads:** Paved. **RV Service:** In Hartwell. **Market:** In Hartwell. **Restaurant:** In Hartwell. **General Store:** No. **Vending:** No. **Swimming:** No. **Playground:** Yes. **Other:** Boat ramp, courtesy dock. **Activities:** Inquire at campground. **Nearby Attractions:** Clemson University, Hartwell Dam, July 4th fireworks. **Additional Information:** Hart County Chamber of Commerce, (706) 376-8590 or www.hart-chamber.org.

RESTRICTIONS

Pets: On leash only. **Fires:** Fire ring only. **Alcoholic Beverages:** Not allowed. **Vehicle Maximum Length:** Call ahead for details. **Other:** 14-day stay limit.

TO GET THERE

From I-85, take Exit 177 onto Hwy. 77 toward Hartwell. In Hartwell, take Hwy. 29N toward Anderson, SC. The campground is 4 mi. outside of Hartwell.

HELEN — MAP, A-2
Unicoi State Park

1788 Hwy. 356, 30545. T: (706) 878-3982; www.gastateparks.org.

 ★★★★ ▲ ★★★★

Beauty: ★★★★★	Site Privacy: ★★★★
Spaciousness: ★★★★	Quiet: ★★★★
Security: ★★★★	Cleanliness: ★★★★
Insect Control: ★★★★	Facilities: ★★★★

Platform camping and walk-in tent sites are only some of the camping possibilities found in this 1,023-acre state park. RVers will find comfort in the 52 back-in sites with water, electric, and sewer hookups. Gorgeous hardwoods and pines tower over most of the sites, and though the camping areas are beautiful throughout, the most notable areas are those near Big Brook Spur. Weekend visitors should plan ahead, as the park often fills up. Even weekday camping here is not a solitary experience. Though the alpine village of Helen and the Dahlonega Gold Museum lie within easy driving distance, visitors will want to remain in the park and take advantage of its offerings as well. Activities include hiking, biking, fishing, and canoeing, and the on-site restaurant and conference center provide resources for groups of all sizes.

BASICS

Operated By: Georgia Dept. of Natural Resources. **Open:** All year. **Site Assignment:** Reservations; credit card or check for first night's stay; make payment 10 days prior to arrival. **Registration:** At front desk at main lodge. **Fee:** Full hookup, $24, RV (electric/water), $22; tent (electric/water), $20; walk-in tent, $14. **Parking:** On site. Walk-ins park in parking lot.

FACILITIES

Number of RV-only Sites: 52. **Number of Tent-only Sites:** 48. **Hookups:** Electric (30 amps), water, sewer. **Each Site:** Grill, picnic table, tent pad, fire ring. **Dump Station:** Yes. **Laundry:** Yes. **Pay Phone:** Yes. **Restrooms and Showers:** Yes. **Fuel:** No. **Propane:** No. **Internal Roads:** Paved. **RV Service:** 9 mi. to Cleveland. **Market:** 3 mi. to Helen. **Restaurant:** On site. **General Store:** Yes. **Vending:** Yes. **Swimming:** Lake. **Playground:** Yes. **Other:** Programs, tours, lake on site, conference center on site. **Activities:** Hiking, mountain biking, fishing, swimming, boating, tennis. **Nearby Attractions:** Anna Ruby Falls, Dahlonega Gold Museum, Appalachian Trail. **Additional Information:** (800) 858-8027.

RESTRICTIONS

Pets: On leash (6 ft. or less) only. **Fires:** Fire ring only. **Alcoholic Beverages:** Allowed. **Vehicle Maximum Length:** 40 ft. **Other:** 14-day stay limit.

TO GET THERE

Take I-85N to I-195 N., which becomes Hwy. 365. At the second light, turn left onto Hwy. 384. At end of the road, turn right onto Hwy. 75. 1 mi. north of Helen, take a right onto Hwy. 356 and follow signs to the campground.

JACKSON — MAP, B-2
High Falls State Park

76 High Falls Park Dr., 30233. T: (478) 993-3053 or (800) 864-7275; www.gastateparks.org.

 ★★★★ ▲ ★★★★

Beauty: ★★★★ Site Privacy: ★★★
Spaciousness: ★★★★ Quiet: ★★
Security: ★★★ Cleanliness: ★★★★
Insect Control: ★★★ Facilities: ★★★★

In spite of its proximity to I-75, this park has a real rural feel to it. RVers and tent campers share all 112 sites, which have full hookups available. Moderately wooded with tall hardwoods, most sites have ample shade, though the limited underbrush reduces privacy. Those wishing to fall asleep to the sound of rushing water should camp in Area 2, situated next to the Towaliga River. Rigs needing lots of space should head for Loop B (sites 82–90). It's more open here, but the bathhouse is nice. For a more secluded experience, look to Area 1 (sites 109–122). The curious will find trails that wind past ruins in this former industrial town. Canoes and paddleboats are available to explore High Falls Lake. But, if it has been rainy, you may want to just stare at the water rushing over the park's namesake.

BASICS

Operated By: Georgia Dept. of Natural Resources. **Open:** All year. **Site Assignment:** Reservations available. **Registration:** At camp office. **Fee:** $20–$22. **Parking:** In campground.

FACILITIES

Number of Multipurpose Sites: 112. **Hookups:** Electric (30, 50 amps), water. **Each Site:** Grill, picnic table. **Dump Station:** Yes. **Laundry:** Yes. **Pay Phone:** Yes. **Restrooms and Showers:** Yes. **Fuel:** No. **Propane:** No. **Internal Roads:** Paved. **RV Service:** No. **Market:** Across the street from park. **Restaurant:** Across the street from park. **General Store:** Across the street from park. **Vending:** Soft drinks. **Swimming:** Pool. **Playground:** Yes. **Activities:** Hiking, fishing, canoe, mini-golf, boating (open Memorial Day–Labor Day). **Nearby Attractions:** Jarrell Plantation State Historic Site, Indian Springs State Park, Piedmont National Wildlife Refuge, Oconee National Forest.

RESTRICTIONS

Pets: On leash only. **Fires:** Allowed. **Alcoholic Beverages:** Not allowed. **Vehicle Maximum Length:** 40 ft. **Other:** 2 camping units per site.

TO GET THERE

The park is 1.8 mi. east of I-75, Exit 198, at High Falls Rd.

JEKYLL ISLAND   MAP, D-3
Jekyll Island Campground

reserve america

1197 Riverview Dr., 31527.
T: (912) 635-3021 or (866) 658-3021;
www.jekyllisland.com/accomodations/camping.asp.

🚐 ★★★★   ⛺ ★★★★

Beauty: ★★★★ Site Privacy: ★★★
Spaciousness: ★★★★ Quiet: ★★★★
Security: ★★★★ Cleanliness: ★★★★
Insect Control: ★★★ Facilities: ★★★

Located in a historic resort community, Jekyll Island campground offers spectacular views of the ocean and shoreline. Covered with gorgeous live oak and pine trees, the area has a wonderfully serene and laid-back vibe. Since the sites vary greatly in size, we recommend sites J7, J11, H15, and H16, as they are the most spacious and secluded. The back tent areas of the campground are generally much nicer. The facilities on the campground are satisfactory but basic. Georgia's mild winters make the campground a perfect winter destination. The campground is more crowded in the spring and summer, and therefore we recommend that you call in advance for availability during these times. Security at Jekyll Island is mediocre, but the campground does have the advantage of being secluded.

BASICS

Operated By: Private operator. **Open:** All year. **Site Assignment:** Reservations accepted. **Registration:** At office. **Fee:** Pull-throughs, $30; back-ins, $26; tent, $19–$23; daily parking fee (day use only), $3. **Parking:** On site. 2 vehicles per site.

FACILITIES

Number of RV-only Sites: 166. **Number of Tent-only Sites:** 41. **Hookups:** Electric, water, sewer, cable TV. **Each Site:** Picnic table, fire ring. **Dump Station:** Yes. **Laundry:** Yes. **Pay Phone:** Yes. **Restrooms and Showers:** Yes. **Fuel:** No. **Propane:** Yes. **Internal Roads:** Paved. **RV Service:** No. **Market:** In Brunswick. **Restaurant:** In Brunswick. **General Store:** Yes. **Vending:** Yes. **Swimming:** No. **Playground:** No. **Activities:** Biking, golfing, fishing, tennis. **Nearby Attractions:** Sea turtle walks, nature center, carriage tours, historic district, beaches. **Additional Information:** Jekyll Island CVB, www.jekyllisland.com or (877) 453-5955.

RESTRICTIONS

Pets: On leash only. **Fires:** Allowed. **Alcoholic Beverages:** At sites only. **Vehicle Maximum Length:** No limit. **Other:** $3 daily parking fee for day use only; 2 vehicles per site.

TO GET THERE

Take I-95 to Exit 29. Follow the signs on US 17 10 mi. and turn right onto Drowning Musgrove Causeway (GA 520). The Jekyll Island Welcome Center is 4 mi. on the left.

LAKE LANIER   MAP, B-2
ISLANDS
Lake Lanier Islands

7000 Holiday Rd., 30518. T: (770) 932-7270 or (800) 840-5253; www.lakelanierislands.com.

🚐 ★★★★   ⛺ ★★★★

Beauty: ★★★★★ Site Privacy: ★★★
Spaciousness: ★★★★ Quiet: ★★★★
Security: ★★★★★ Cleanliness: ★★★★
Insect Control: ★★★★ Facilities: ★★★★★

This huge property is a complete vacation destination. Lake Lanier Islands is spread over the eponymous clumps of land in Lake Lanier, a U.S. Army Corps of Engineers project that has many recreational options of its own. Like the other ten campgrounds on the lake (see profiles of Shoal Creek in Buford and Chestnut Ridge in Flowery Branch), boat noise is always a factor for campers; ask attendants for recommendations on quieter campsites. Most sites are well shaded, and some have screening foliage; size varies greatly. In contrast to some nearby campgrounds that are entirely lake-focused, Lake Lanier Islands has several other choices for campers—two golf clubs, an equestrian center, mountain bike rentals, a waterpark, and more. If you want to explore the surrounding area, the region offers 43 day-use parks, ten marinas, and nine state, county, and city parks.

BASICS

Operated By: Winston Beaver, Manager. **Open:** All year. **Site Assignment:** First come, first served; reservations accepted. **Registration:** At campground office. **Fee:** $31–$40. **Parking:** On site.

FACILITIES

Number of RV-only Sites: 271. **Number of Tent-only Sites:** 31. **Hookups:** Electric, water, sewer. **Each Site:** Picnic areas. **Dump Station:** Yes. **Laundry:** Yes. **Pay Phone:** Yes. **Restrooms and Showers:** Yes. **Fuel:** No. **Propane:** Yes. **Internal Roads:** Paved. **RV Service:** 4 mi. **Market:** 7 mi. **Restaurant:** Less than 7 mi. **General Store:** Yes. **Vending:** No. **Swimming:** No. **Playground:** Yes. **Other:** Full golf course, boat ramp. **Activities:** Boating, beach, waterpark, wave pool, equestrian center, mountain biking. **Nearby Attractions:** Lake Lanier Islands Resort.

RESTRICTIONS

Pets: On leash only. **Fires:** Fire ring only. **Alcoholic Beverages:** Not allowed. **Vehicle Maximum Length:** No limit. **Other:** 2 vehicles per family.

TO GET THERE

From Atlanta, take I-85N to I-985N (Exit 113). Take Exit 8 (Friendship Rd.), and turn left. Continue 4 mi. to the campground.

LAKE PARK   MAP, D-2
Eagles Roost RV Resort

5465 Mill Store Rd., 31636. T: (229) 559-5192; www.eaglesroostresort.com.

🚐 ★★★★   ⛺ ★★★

Beauty: ★★★★ Site Privacy: ★★★
Spaciousness: ★★★ Quiet: ★★★★★
Security: ★★★★ Cleanliness: ★★★★★
Insect Control: ★★★★ Facilities: ★★★

Located right off I-75, just a few miles from the Florida state line, this park offers convenience as well as all the amenities of a top-notch vacation spot. Surrounded by gorgeous hardwoods draped in Spanish moss, the Eagle's Roost offers its guests the tranquility of a rural setting, along with a myriad of activities inside and outside the park. There is a swimming pool, playground and a rec room for the kids inside the campground itself. Nearby, guests can enjoy Georgia's Wild Adventures or Reed Bingham State Park. Section A, or the Club Deluxe area, is our pick for the best spots at the Eagle's Roost, since internal roads are paved and each site is equipped with a concrete pad. Of the 42 available spots in this section, sites 34 through 42 are the most beautiful, with plenty of surrounding moss-covered hardwoods. For families with children, however, our pick for the best spots would have to be sites 5, 6, and 7, since they are closest to the pool, playground, and store. The sites in the B and C sections are sub-par to those in the A section, being closer together and with roads of packed sand rather than asphalt. Overall, this is an attractive, well-run facility. However, our advice to anyone planning to travel in this area is to do so in the early to mid-spring, as this part of Georgia is nearly unbearable when summer is in full swing.

BASICS

Operated By: Terry Herndon. **Open:** All year. **Site Assignment:** First come, first served. **Registration:** At office. **Fee:** $27.95–$29.95. **Parking:** On site.

FACILITIES

Number of RV-only Sites: 120. **Number of Tent-only Sites:** Undesignated sites. **Hookups:** Electric (30, 50 amps), water, cable TV. **Each Site:** Picnic table. **Dump Station:** Yes. **Laundry:** Yes. **Pay Phone:** Yes. **Restrooms and Showers:** Yes. **Fuel:** No. **Propane:** Yes. **Internal Roads:** Paved. **RV Service:** Nearby. **Market:** Yes. **Restaurant:** Nearby. **General Store:** Yes. **Vending:** Yes. **Swimming:** Yes. **Playground:** Yes. **Other:** Shuffleboard, horseshoes, Suwannee River State Park. **Activities:** Wild Adventures Park, Stephen C. Foster Park, Georgia Agrirama. **Nearby Attractions:** Suwannee River State Park.

RESTRICTIONS

Pets: On leash only. **Fires:** Not allowed. **Alcoholic Beverages:** Allowed. **Vehicle Maximum Length:** No restriction.

TO GET THERE

From I-75 Exit 5, go northbound and take a right onto Frontage Rd. at the first light. The campground is 1 mi. on left.

LAKEMONT
Rabun Beach Campground
MAP, A-2

5320 Lake Rabun Rd., 30552. T: (706) 782-3320; www.fs.fed.us/conf.

🚐 ★★★★	🏕 ★★★★★
Beauty: ★★★★★	Site Privacy: ★★★★★
Spaciousness: ★★★★★	Quiet: ★★★★★
Security: ★★★★	Cleanliness: ★★★★
Insect Control: ★★★★★	Facilities: ★★

Those wanting a beautiful and secluded camping experience in rural Georgia will do well to visit Rabun Beach. A gravel road leads campers to 80 sites (5 of which are tent-only). Most of the RV-friendly sites, with water and electric hookups, are back-ins, but a few are pull-throughs. Though the entire area is attractive, sites 49 and 53 are truly gorgeous. No sites are situated directly on Lake Rabun, but all are within easy walking distance. Visitors have their pick of sites during the week, but even on busy weekends visitors will have little problem finding one of the many spacious and well-shaded sites unoccupied. Not far from this extraordinary campground is Tallulah Gorge State Park, sometimes referred to as the Grand Canyon of the southeast, and a 1.3-mile trail leads to 50-foot Angel Falls.

BASICS

Operated By: Federal government. **Open:** May–Oct. **Site Assignment:** First come, first served. **Registration:** At camp office; no reservations; cash or check only. **Fee:** $12–$20. **Parking:** In campground.

FACILITIES

Number of RV-only Sites: 75. **Number of Tent-only Sites:** 5. **Hookups:** Electric (20 amps), water. **Each Site:** Grill, picnic table, tent pad, lantern post. **Dump Station:** Yes. **Laundry:** Yes. **Pay Phone:** Yes. **Restrooms and Showers:** Yes. **Fuel:** No. **Propane:** No. **Internal Roads:** Gravel. **RV Service:** No. **Market:** 6 mi. **Restaurant:** 2 mi. **General Store:** No. **Vending:** No. **Swimming:** Beach. **Playground:** No. **Other:** Lake on site. **Activities:** Hiking, swimming, boating, fishing. **Nearby Attractions:** Angel Falls, Tallulah Gorge overlook. **Additional Information:** Rabun County Civic Center, (706) 212-2149.

RESTRICTIONS

Pets: On leash only. **Fires:** Fire ring only. **Alcoholic Beverages:** Allowed, but not in excess. **Vehicle Maximum Length:** 35 ft.

TO GET THERE

From Hwy. 441 in Clayton, go 2 mi. and turn right on the Wiley Connector. Go 0.1 mi. and turn left on Old Hwy. 441. Go 2 mi. and turn right on Lake Rabun Rd. The campground is 4 mi. ahead on the right.

LAVONIA
Tugaloo State Park
MAP, A-2

1763 Tugaloo State Park Rd., 30553. T: (706) 356-4362 or (800) 864-7275; www.gastateparks.org.

🚐 ★★★	🏕 ★★★
Beauty: ★★★★	Site Privacy: ★★★
Spaciousness: ★★★	Quiet: ★★★
Security: ★★★★★	Cleanliness: ★★★
Insect Control: ★★★	Facilities: ★★★

Between the lovely pine stand and the views of Hartwell Lake, beauty is the major draw of this state park campground. Located in the northeast corner of the state, the campground feels quite rural despite its proximity to I-85. And it is well guarded, making this one of the region's more secure spots for camping. Unfortunately, the restrooms are lousy, and the facilities are lacking in general. But the nearby recreation opportunities and the natural setting help make this an attractive spot nonetheless. With roughly equal numbers of back-in and pull-through sites, the campground sits on a peninsula, and the sites closest to the water are recommended, naturally. The sites, all gravel, vary greatly in size, but are all pretty and wooded. Fishing—especially for largemouth bass—and water sports make this a fun, if noisy, campground that is excellent for families. Keeping in mind the larger crowds in warmer weather, due to the allure of the water, this park offers a pleasant stay in a tent or RV.

BASICS

Operated By: Georgia Dept. of Natural Resources. **Open:** All year. **Site Assignment:** Reservations accepted; first-come, first-serve sites available. **Registration:** At camp office. **Fee:** RV, $18–$21; tent, $8–$18. **Parking:** In campground.

FACILITIES

Number of Multipurpose Sites: 108. **Hookups:** Electric (30 amps), water, sewer, cable TV. **Each Site:** Picnic shelter, fire ring. **Dump Station:** Yes. **Laundry:** Yes. **Pay Phone:** Yes. **Restrooms and Showers:** Yes. **Fuel:** No. **Propane:** No. **Internal Roads:** Paved. **RV Service:** Referral. **Market:** No. **Restaurant:** No. **General Store:** Yes. **Vending:** Yes. **Swimming:** Yes. **Playground:** Yes. **Other:** Swimming beach, tennis court, cottages, picnic shelter. **Activities:** Fishing, boating, hiking, volleyball, horseshoes, mini-golf. **Nearby Attractions:** Ty Cobb Museum, Victoria Bryant State Park & Golf Course, Tallulah Gorge State Park, Hartwell Dam.

RESTRICTIONS

Pets: On leash only. **Fires:** Fire ring only. **Alcoholic Beverages:** At sites. **Vehicle Maximum Length:** 35 ft.

TO GET THERE

Take I-85 to Exit 173. Follow the signs to Gerrard Rd. Turn right and go 1.5 mi. to Hwy. 328. Turn left and proceed 3.3 mi. to the park.

LINCOLNTON
Elijah Clark State Park
MAP, B-2

2959 McCormick Hwy., 30817. T: (706) 359-3458 or (800) 864-7275; www.gastateparks.org.

🚐 ★★★★	🏕 ★★★★
Beauty: ★★★★	Site Privacy: ★★★
Spaciousness: ★★★	Quiet: ★★★
Security: ★★★★★	Cleanliness: ★★★★
Insect Control: ★★★	Facilities: ★★★★

Named after the frontiersman and Revolutionary War hero Elijah Clark, this is one of the more popular state parks in the area. Expect lots of running kids, buzzing boats, and other noises associated with large camps. RVers and tent campers have a choice of 165 sites. Most of the sites have some shade but with very little undergrowth. In Campground 1, sites 38 and 53 are gorgeous, 56 is quite secluded, and 23–31 have lovely open views (though all are a bit crowded). Campground 2 has some sites that are quite shady (108–115) and some with nice views (116–118). Be sure to avoid all sites near boat ramps, especially during summer weekends. The park offers hiking, swimming, and fishing thanks to Clarks Hill Lake, as well as a museum depicting colonial life. Several annual events, including an arts and crafts festival and a bluegrass festival, mean potential visitors should call well in advance.

BASICS

Operated By: Georgia Dept. of Natural Resources. **Open:** All year. **Site Assignment:** Reservations. **Registration:** At camp office. **Fee:** $20–$22. **Parking:** 2 vehicles per site; $2 parking pass required.

FACILITIES

Number of RV-only Sites: 165. **Hookups:** Electric (50 amps), water, cable TV. **Each Site:** Picnic table, fire pit. **Dump Station:** Yes, 2. **Laundry:** Yes. **Pay Phone:** Yes. **Restrooms and Showers:** Yes. **Fuel:** 2 mi. **Propane:** 2 mi. **Internal Roads:** Paved & gravel. **RV Service:** House calls available. **Market:** In Martins Crossroads. **Restaurant:** 7 mi. **General Store:** Small camp store. **Vending:** Soft drinks. **Swimming:** Yes. **Playground:** Yes. **Other:** 3rd weekend in Oct.—Old-timer's Festival, boat ramps. **Activities:** Boating, waterskiing, fishing, museum tours, hiking, miniature golf, swimming, volleyball, shuffleboard. **Nearby Attractions:** Mistletoe State Park, Bobby Brown State Park, historic Washington, Clarks Hill Dam.

RESTRICTIONS

Pets: On leash only. **Fires:** Fire ring only. **Alcoholic Beverages:** Not allowed. **Vehicle Maximum Length:** 40 ft.

TO GET THERE

7 mi. northeast of Lincolnton on US 378.

MCRAE   MAP, C-2
Little Ocmulgee State Park

P.O. Drawer 149, 31055. T: (229) 868-7474 or (800) 864-7275; www.gastateparks.org.

🚐 ★★★★	⛺ ★★★★
Beauty: ★★★★★	Site Privacy: ★★★
Spaciousness: ★★★★	Quiet: ★★★★
Security: ★★★★	Cleanliness: ★★★★
Insect Control: ★★★	Facilities: ★★★★★

A small park created by private land donations and the work of the Civilian Conservation Corps, Little Ocmulgee State Park offers a pleasant retreat from the more popular (and populated) campgrounds in the area. The lodge is the center of activity here, and only lodge and cottage guests can use its swimming pool (though its restaurant is open to everyone, of course). However, you don't need the pool when you can just take a dip in the lake, which has its own pleasant little beach. Because it's a fairly low-key place, most campers seem to visit here to stroll along the nature trail or to tee off on the 18-hole golf course. Be sure to keep moving on the trail, though—the path passes near a buzzard rookery, and stationary campers might draw some interested, circling birds above.

BASICS

Operated By: Georgia Dept. of Natural Resources. **Open:** All year. **Site Assignment:** First come, first served; reservations accepted. **Registration:** At lodge prior to set up. **Fee:** $19–$21. **Parking:** On site; $2 parking fee.

FACILITIES

Number of RV-only Sites: 55. **Hookups:** Electric (30, 50 amps), water, cable TV; 15 full-hookup sites. **Each Site:** Fire pit. **Dump Station:** Yes. **Laundry:** Yes. **Pay Phone:** Yes. **Restrooms and Showers:** Yes. **Fuel:** No. **Propane:** No. **Internal Roads:** Paved. **RV Service:** No. **Market:** 2 mi. in McRae. **Restaurant:** At lodge. **General Store:** No. **Vending:** Yes. **Swimming:** Yes. **Playground:** Yes. **Activi-**

ties: Fishing, boating, beach area, tennis, nature trails, mini-golf, pedal boats, canoes. **Nearby Attractions:** Georgia Veterans State Park & Golf Course, General Coffee State Park & Heritage Farm, Jefferson Davis Memorial State Historic Site.

RESTRICTIONS

Pets: On leash (6 ft. or less) only. **Fires:** Fire ring only. **Alcoholic Beverages:** Allowed, cups only at the beach. **Vehicle Maximum Length:** 40 ft. (min. length is 20 ft.).

TO GET THERE

The park is 2 mi. north of McRae via US 319 and US 441.

NICHOLLS   MAP, C-2
General Coffee State Park

46 John Coffee Rd., 31554. T: (912) 384-7082 or (800) 864-7275; www.gastateparks.org.

🚐 ★★★★	⛺ ★★★★
Beauty: ★★★★★	Site Privacy: ★★★★
Spaciousness: ★★★★★	Quiet: ★★★★★
Security: ★★★★	Cleanliness: ★★★★
Insect Control: ★★★	Facilities: ★★★★★

Approximately 6 miles from Douglas, this rural park includes Seventeen Mile River, which creates six small lakes as it winds through a Cypress swamp. The variety of foliage includes pines and hardwoods draped with Spanish moss. The park was donated to the state by a group of Coffee County citizens in 1970 and was named after General John Coffee, a planter, U.S. congressman, and military leader. In addition to camping, it offers several exhibits at Heritage Farm, including a tobacco barn, a cane mill, and, yes, barnyard animals as well. With comfortable, gravel pull-through sites, the campground has a relatively serene, spacious feel. Both multipurpose camping Areas 1 and 2 are loops, and Area 1 includes a grassy field and playground, although the playground at the picnic area is much nicer. There are separate tent areas, but the facilities overall make both tent and RV camping quite pleasant here. This is a secure spot, largely due to the rural setting and sparse crowds, good for families and privacy.

BASICS

Operated By: Georgia Dept. of Natural Resources. **Open:** All year. **Site Assignment:** First come, first served; reservations accepted. **Registration:** Inside main gate. **Fee:** $16–$24. **Parking:** On site.

FACILITIES

Number of Multipurpose Sites: 50. **Hookups:** Electric (30 amps), water. **Each Site:** Picnic table & fire ring. **Dump Station:** Yes. **Laundry:** Yes. **Pay Phone:** Yes. **Restrooms and Showers:** Yes. **Fuel:** No. **Propane:** No. **Internal Roads:** Paved & Gravel. **RV Service:** No. **Market:** No. **Restaurant:** No. **General Store:** Snacks in the office. **Vending:** Soft drinks. **Swimming:** Memorial Day–Labor day. **Playground:** Yes. **Other:** Amphitheater. **Activities:** Hiking, nature programs, fishing, canoeing. **Nearby Attractions:** Historical farm w/ live animals. **Additional Information:** (800) 864-PARK.

RESTRICTIONS

Pets: On leash (6 ft. or less) only. **Fires:** Allowed. **Alcoholic Beverages:** Not allowed. **Vehicle Maximum Length:** No limit. **Other:** $2 parking pass per vehicle.

TO GET THERE

From Hwy. 221, exit at Hwy. 32, and turn right at the Keystone Dr. entrance after the train tracks.

OAKMAN   MAP, A-1
Doll Mountain Campground

reserve america

P.O. Box 96, 30732. T: (706) 276-4413; www.reserveamerica.com.

🚐 ★★★★★	⛺ ★★★★★
Beauty: ★★★★★	Site Privacy: ★★★★★
Spaciousness: ★★★★★	Quiet: ★★★★★
Security: ★★★★	Cleanliness: ★★★★
Insect Control: ★★★★★	Facilities: ★★★

Doll Mountain Campground is an excellent property located on the shores of Carter Lake, itself an outdoor-activity paradise. There are several camping and recreation areas to choose from on the lake, and Doll Mountain is among the nicest. Most campsites are very spacious, and all are heavily wooded. However, because the sites are strung out along a thin spit of land projecting into the lake, almost all sites have beautiful lake views. Sites 1, 2, 4, 6, and 7 are small, pretty pull-throughs, but they are not as secluded as the other sites. Sites 15, 15A, and 16 are somewhat cramped and distastefully close to the dump station. The best location by far is the loop containing sites 39–46; site 45 is particularly gorgeous. Doll Mountain's sites also vary a bit in terms of overall privacy; some don't have much, but others are some of the most secluded we've seen.

BASICS

Operated By: U.S. Army Corps of Engineers. **Open:** Apr.–Oct. **Site Assignment:** Reservations preferred. **Registration:** At camp office. **Fee:** $14–$20. **Parking:** On site.

FACILITIES

Number of RV-only Sites: 39. **Number of Tent-only Sites:** 25. **Hookups:** Electric (30, 50 amps), water. **Each Site:** Picnic table, fire pit. **Dump Station:** Yes. **Laundry:** Yes. **Pay Phone:** Yes. **Restrooms and Showers:** Yes. **Fuel:** Nearby. **Propane:** No. **Internal Roads:** Paved. **RV Service:** Yes. **Market:** In Ellijay. **Restaurant:** In Ellijay. **General Store:** No. **Vending:** Soft drinks. **Swimming:** Yes. **Playground:** Yes. **Activities:** Basketball, boating, amphitheater, hiking, swimming. **Nearby Attractions:** Battleground, Lake Chattahoochee.

RESTRICTIONS

Pets: On leash only. **Fires:** In designated areas only. **Alcoholic Beverages:** At sites only. **Vehicle Maximum Length:** 35 ft. **Other:** 2-day min. on weekends.

To Get There

From Ellijay, travel 11 mi. southwest on Hwy. 382. Follow signs to campground.

OAKMAN — MAP, A-1
Woodring Branch Campground

reserve america

5026 Woodring Branch Rd., P.O. Box 96, 30732. T: (706) 276-6050 or (877) 444-6777; www.reserveamerica.com; carters.sam.usace.army.mil.

🚐 ★★★★★   ⛺ ★★★★★

Beauty: ★★★★★   Site Privacy: ★★★★★
Spaciousness: ★★★★★   Quiet: ★★★★★
Security: ★★★★★   Cleanliness: ★★★★
Insect Control: ★★★★   Facilities: ★★★

This Corps of Engineers Campground is exceptionally beautiful and quiet, with most sites very close to the shores of Carters Lake. A very rural spot in the northwest corner of the state, this campground boasts huge wooded sites, with some foliage in between. All of the sites are back-ins, with paved RV and car spaces, fine (pea-sized) gravel pads for tents, picnic tables, and so on. Almost every site has a gorgeous lake view, and the most amazing is from site 35. Site 31 is especially secluded, although its view is not as stunning, and 17 is the most impressively huge. Don't let the spacious, peaceful atmosphere fool you, however. There is plenty of recreation to choose from, including water sports. The beauty and privacy make this a great spot for couples, but families will also enjoy the space and activities.

BASICS

Operated By: U.S. Army Corps of Engineers. **Open:** Apr. 7–Oct 28; or all year. **Site Assignment:** First come, first serve available but limited; reservations accepted. **Registration:** At campground. **Fee:** $14–$20. **Parking:** Yes.

FACILITIES

Number of RV-only Sites: 31. **Number of Tent-only Sites:** 11. **Hookups:** Electric (30, 50 amps), water. **Each Site:** Tent pad, picnic table. **Dump Station:** Yes. **Laundry:** Yes. **Pay Phone:** Yes. **Restrooms and Showers:** Yes. **Fuel:** No. **Propane:** No. **Internal Roads:** Paved. **RV Service:** No. **Market:** In Chatsworth. **Restaurant:** In Chatsworth. **General Store:** No. **Vending:** Soft drinks. **Swimming:** Yes. **Playground:** Yes. **Other:** Boat ramp. **Activities:** Boating, hiking trails, water-skiing, fishing. **Nearby Attractions:** Antiques shopping, outlet mall, Cherokee Indian Museum, Fort Mountain State Park, apple orchards.

RESTRICTIONS

Pets: On leash only. **Fires:** In designated areas. **Alcoholic Beverages:** At sites only. **Vehicle Maximum Length:** 40 ft.

To Get There

From Ellijay, travel west on Hwy. 282. Follow signs approximately 4 mi. to the campground.

PERRY — MAP, C-2
Fair Harbor RV Park and Campground

515 Marshallville Rd., 31069. T: (877) 988-8844 or (877) 988-8844; www.fairharborrvpark.com.

🚐 ★★★★   ⛺ n/a

Beauty: ★★★★   Site Privacy: ★★
Spaciousness: ★★   Quiet: ★★★★
Security: ★★★   Cleanliness: ★★★★
Insect Control: ★★★★   Facilities: ★★★

Not far from the Georgia National Fairgrounds, Fair Harbor provides a nice, underdeveloped camping experience just 0.2 miles from I-75. The 100-acre park has 150 RV sites, with about 100 pull-throughs. The 30, densely wooded, tent-only sites are well removed from the rest of the area and have water and electric hookups. Though less shady, the RV sites are quite large, which provides a bit of privacy. For a quieter experience, campers should choose sites closer to the tent-only area. Breakfast is served Tuesday through Saturday. Campers may want to visit during the Georgia National Livestock Show and Rodeo in February as well as tor during the Georgia State Fair in August, but plan ahead as the park fills quickly.

BASICS

Operated By: Tim McCord & Kirk Morris. **Open:** All year. **Site Assignment:** Reservations or first come, first served. **Registration:** At camp office. **Fee:** $11–$22. **Parking:** In campground.

FACILITIES

Number of RV-only Sites: 150. **Number of Tent-only Sites:** 30. **Hookups:** Electric (20, 30, 50 amps), water, sewer, cable TV, phone. **Each Site:** Picnic table, grill. **Dump Station:** Yes. **Laundry:** Yes. **Pay Phone:** Yes. **Restrooms and Showers:** Yes. **Fuel:** No. **Propane:** Yes. **Internal Roads:** Paved, sites gravel. **RV Service:** 15 minutes. **Market:** In Perry. **Restaurant:** Less than 1 mi. **General Store:** Limited. **Vending:** No. **Swimming:** No. **Playground:** No. **Other:** Breakfast Tue.–Sat.; RV storage available, walking trails on property. **Activities:** Pond fishing, horseshoes. **Nearby Attractions:** Georgia Music Hall of Fame, the Hay House, Andersonville National Cemetery, Massee Lane Gardens, Museum of Aviation, Georgia Agricenter & fairgrounds. **Additional Information:** Lodge seats 125 people.

RESTRICTIONS

Pets: On leash only. **Fires:** Allowed. **Alcoholic Beverages:** Allowed. **Vehicle Maximum Length:** No limit.

To Get There

Take I-75 Exit 135. Go 0.1 mi. west to campground.

PINE MOUNTAIN — MAP, B-1
F. D. Roosevelt State Park

2970 Hwy. 190, 31822. T: (706) 663-4858 or (800) 864-7275; www.gastateparks.org.

🚐 ★★★★   ⛺ ★★★★

Beauty: ★★★★   Site Privacy: ★★★★
Spaciousness: ★★★★   Quiet: ★★★
Security: ★★★★   Cleanliness: ★★★★
Insect Control: ★★★   Facilities: ★★★★

In west-central Georgia, this state park is—you guessed it—all about Franklin D. Roosevelt. Actually, the park also has the nature thing going for them, with its hiking and horseback-riding trails amongst hardwoods and pines and its fishing on the lovely Lake Delanor. Despite its secluded, rural setting, the campground stays busy on holidays and weekends. We suggest going during the off-season if you seek quiet. There are both back-in and pull-through sites, mostly gravel. Although most sites are plenty shady, there is little if any foliage between them. We recommend Campground 5 for its privacy and huge pull-throughs. The great lake views are in Campground 1 at sites 3 and 4. In Campground 2, sites 33–41 are nicely wooded. The best tent camping is in Campground 3, since it is more wooded, private, and unpaved. This park's natural beauty and the historical interest of nearby attractions make this spot appeal to families and all ages.

BASICS

Operated By: Georgia Dept. of Natural Resources. **Open:** All year. **Site Assignment:** Reservations accepted. **Registration:** At camp office. **Fee:** $18–$20. **Parking:** In campground.

FACILITIES

Number of Multipurpose Sites: 140. **Hookups:** Electric (50 amps), water. **Each Site:** Picnic area. **Dump Station:** Yes. **Laundry:** Yes (on weekends). **Pay Phone:** No. **Restrooms and Showers:** Yes. **Fuel:** No. **Propane:** No. **Internal Roads:** Paved. **RV Service:** No. **Market:** No. **Restaurant:** No. **General Store:** Open on weekends. **Vending:** No. **Swimming:** Pool (open Memorial Day–Labor Day). **Playground:** Yes. **Activities:** Hiking, biking, fishing, boating, horseback riding. **Nearby Attractions:** Little White House State Park, Sprewell Bluff State Park, West Point Lake.

RESTRICTIONS

Pets: On leash only. **Fires:** In designated areas. **Alcoholic Beverages:** At sites only. **Vehicle Maximum Length:** 40 ft.

To Get There

The park is located just off I-185 near Callaway Gardens, west of Warm Springs on Hwy. 190, and south of Pine Mountain off US 27.

RICHMOND HILL — MAP, C-3
Fort McAllister State Historic Park

3894 Fort McAllister Rd., 31324. T: (912) 727-2339; www.gastateparks.org.

🚐 ★★★★   ⛺ ★★★★

Beauty: ★★★★★   Site Privacy: ★★★★
Spaciousness: ★★★★★   Quiet: ★★★★★
Security: ★★★★   Cleanliness: ★★★★
Insect Control: ★★★   Facilities: ★★★★

Not far from the Georgia coast on the banks of the Great Ogeechee River, campers at Fort McAllister will find a place to rest their heads among Civil War history. The 53 RV sites and 12 tent-only sites lie beneath the giant live oaks that grow in this former battlefield. Water and electric hookups are available in this first-come, first-serve campground. Tours of the fort and a Civil War museum are possible, just call for reservations.

BASICS

Operated By: Georgia Dept. of Natural Resources. **Open:** All year. **Site Assignment:** First come, first served. **Registration:** At museum office. **Fee:** RV, $20; tent, $18. **Parking:** On site.

FACILITIES

Number of RV-only Sites: 53. **Number of Tent-only Sites:** 12. **Hookups:** Electric (30 amps), water. **Each Site:** Grill, picnic table. **Dump Station:** Yes. **Laundry:** Yes. **Pay Phone:** Yes. **Restrooms and Showers:** Yes. **Fuel:** Nearby. **Propane:** Nearby. **Internal Roads:** Paved; sites grass & gravel. **RV Service:** In Richmond Hill. **Market:** 10 mi. **Restaurant:** Nearby. **General Store:** No. **Vending:** Soft drinks. **Swimming:** No. **Playground:** Yes. **Activities:** Hiking, picnicking, saltwater fishing, canoeing, kayaking. **Nearby Attractions:** Civil War museum, fort tours (call for reservations). **Additional Information:** www.gastateparks.org.

RESTRICTIONS

Pets: On leash & attended. **Fires:** Fire ring only. **Alcoholic Beverages:** At sites only. **Vehicle Maximum Length:** No limit.

TO GET THERE

Take I-95 Exit 90. Go 10 mi. east to Georgia Spur 144. Turn left, then go until the road dead-ends at the park (4.4 mi.).

RICHMOND HILL   MAP, C-3
Savannah South KOA

4915 US 17 South, 31324. T: (912) 756-3396 or (800) 562-8741; www.koa.com.

🚐 ★★★   ⛺ ★★★

Beauty: ★★★★   Site Privacy: ★★★
Spaciousness: ★★★   Quiet: ★★★★
Security: ★★★   Cleanliness: ★★★★
Insect Control: ★★★ Facilities: ★★★

Located in a suburban setting, this campground contains sites that are small but attractive. The area is mostly shaded with pine trees, with a few open sites scattered throughout the campground. For the nature lover, the campground has a 35-acre fishing lake that also contains hundreds of ducks, geese, swans, and egrets. The sites closest to the lakefront are by far the prettiest. However, the sites do not offer much privacy. We recommend visiting Savanna South in the fall or the spring when the weather is most pleasant. Reservations are preferred for this KOA campground. However, the campground's security measures are lacking, so be mindful.

BASICS

Operated By: Private operator. **Open:** All year. **Site Assignment:** First come, first served. **Regis-** tration: At office. **Fee:** $27–$36. **Parking:** On site.

FACILITIES

Number of RV-only Sites: 130. **Number of Tent-only Sites:** 10. **Hookups:** Electric (50 amps), water, modem, cable TV. **Each Site:** Picnic table. **Dump Station:** Yes. **Laundry:** Yes. **Pay Phone:** Yes. **Restrooms and Showers:** Yes. **Fuel:** No. **Propane:** Yes. **Internal Roads:** Paved. **RV Service:** No. **Market:** In Richmond Hill. **Restaurant:** In Richmond Hill. **General Store:** Yes. **Vending:** Yes. **Swimming:** Pool. **Playground:** Yes. **Activities:** Fishing, boating, bird-watching, basketball, shuffleboard, game room, golfing, 35-acre lake. **Nearby Attractions:** Savannah, Fort Stewart, Fort McAllister State Historic Park. **Additional Information:** Richmond Hill CVB, (912) 756-2676 or www.richmondhillcvb.org.

RESTRICTIONS

Pets: Must be on leash. **Fires:** Designated areas only. **Alcoholic Beverages:** Not allowed. **Vehicle Maximum Length:** No limit.

TO GET THERE

From I-95 take Exit 87 to US 17 South and turn south. The campground is 0.5 mi. on left.

RINGGOLD   MAP, A-1
KOA–Chattanooga South

199 KOA Blvd., 30736. T: (706) 937-4166 or (800) 562-4167; www.koakampgrounds.com/where/tn/42125.

🚐 ★★★   ⛺ ★★

Beauty: ★★★★   Site Privacy: ★★★
Spaciousness: ★★★   Quiet: ★★★★
Security: ★★★   Cleanliness: ★★★
Insect Control: ★★★★ Facilities: ★★★

Whether Civil War enthusiasts or just families on vacation, campers will find this KOA park offers a relaxing camp experience within easy reach of Chattanooga. A mix of gravel and paved roads provides access to the sites, some of which have tent pads. The prettiest and shadiest sites are located on the east side, near the pet kennel. A minimal understory limits privacy, but campers have some room to move about, as sites are medium to large in size. All sites are pull-throughs. Those wishing to remain in the campground will find an outdoor theater, volleyball court, basketball court, and horseshoe pits. Campers venturing beyond the park can visit Civil War battlefields (Chickamauga and Chattanooga National Military Park) or the Tennessee Aquarium, Ruby Falls, or the Tennessee Valley Railroad.

BASICS

Operated By: KOA. **Open:** All year. **Site Assignment:** Reservations accepted. **Registration:** At camp office. **Fee:** $25–$50. **Parking:** In campground.

FACILITIES

Number of RV-only Sites: 65. **Number of Tent-only Sites:** 21. **Hookups:** Electric (30, 50 amps), water. **Each Site:** Picnic table, fire pit. **Dump Station:** Yes. **Laundry:** Yes. **Pay Phone:** Yes. **Restrooms and Showers:** Yes. **Fuel:** Yes. **Propane:** Yes. **Internal Roads:** Paved & gravel. **RV Service:** Yes. **Market:** 3 mi. in Chattanooga. **Restaurant:** 3 mi. in Chattanooga. **General Store:** Yes. **Vending:** No. **Swimming:** Yes. **Playground:** Yes. **Activities:** Volleyball, basketball, horseshoes, game room. **Nearby Attractions:** Tennessee Aquarium, Ruby Falls, outlet malls, Rock City, Lost Sea, area flea markets, *Southern Belle* riverboat.

RESTRICTIONS

Pets: On leash only. **Fires:** At sites. **Alcoholic Beverages:** At sites only. **Vehicle Maximum Length:** No limit.

TO GET THERE

From I-75, take the Battlefield Pkwy./Fort Oglethorpe exit and proceed west on Hwy. 2 300 yards to the camp entrance on right.

RISING FAWN   MAP, A-1
Cloudland Canyon State Park

122 Cloudland Canyon Park Rd., Hwy. 2 Box 150, 30738. T: (706) 657-4050 or (800) 864-7275; www.gastateparks.org.

🚐 ★★★★   ⛺ ★★★★★

Beauty: ★★★★★   Site Privacy: ★★★★★
Spaciousness: ★★★★★   Quiet: ★★★★
Security: ★★★★★   Cleanliness: ★★★★
Insect Control: ★★★★ Facilities: ★★★★

Cloudland is one of the most scenic parks in Georgia. The 2,200-acre park has 75 sites with an additional 30 primitive tent sites. All of the back-in sites are huge, while the size of the pull-throughs varies greatly. Still, the entire area is gorgeous and heavily wooded, providing great privacy between sites, some of which are quite large and secluded. The nearby town of Trenton provides supplies to the forgetful camper. Tennis and swimming are available, but the hiking trails take visitors to the park's centerpiece—the canyon, which varies in depth between 800 and nearly 2,000 feet. Those who come to relax at Cloudland may still hear the call of Rock City, a private attraction located close by. Visitors may even want to zip up to Chattanooga, where a myriad of activities await, including the Tennessee Aquarium and the Chattanooga Choo Choo.

BASICS

Operated By: Georgia Dept. of Natural Resources. **Open:** All year. **Site Assignment:** Reservations preferred. **Registration:** At camp office. **Fee:** $10–$25. **Parking:** 2 vehicles per site.

FACILITIES

Number of RV-only Sites: 75. **Number of Tent-only Sites:** 30. **Hookups:** Electric (30 amps), water. **Each Site:** Picnic table, fire pit. **Dump Station:** Yes. **Laundry:** Yes. **Pay Phone:** Yes. **Restrooms and Showers:** Yes. **Fuel:** No. **Propane:** No. **Internal Roads:** Paved. **RV Service:** No. **Market:** In Trenton. **Restaurant:** In Trenton. **General Store:** No. **Vending:** Soft drinks. **Swimming:** No. **Playground:** Yes. **Other:** Waterfall trails. **Activities:** Hiking, backpacking, tennis. **Nearby Attractions:** Chief Van House State Historic Site, Ruby Falls, Incline Railway, Lookout Mountain, Tennessee Aquarium, Chickamunga National Battlefield, Chattanooga.

RESTRICTIONS

Pets: On leash only. **Fires:** At sites. **Alcoholic Beverages:** Allowed, in a cup. **Vehicle Maximum Length:** No limit.

To Get There

The campground is located 8 mi. east of Trenton on GA 136 and I 59, or 18 mi. northwest of Lafayette via GA 136.

RUTLEDGE   MAP, B-2
Hard Labor Creek State Park

Knox Chapel Rd., 30663.
T: (706) 557-3001 or (800) 864-7275;
www.gastateparks.org/info/hardlabor.

🚐 ★★★★   ▲ ★★★★

Beauty: ★★★★★	Site Privacy: ★★★★
Spaciousness: ★★★★	Quiet: ★★★★
Security: ★★★★	Cleanliness: ★★★★
Insect Control: ★★★	Facilities: ★★★★★

Named either by slaves working in nearby fields or by Indians who thought the creek was difficult to ford, Hard Labor Creek State Park conjures up very different associations these days. The park's golf course is known as a good value, offering a pro shop, driving range, and unlimited weekday play packages. Campsite sizes vary, but most are spacious and nicely wooded. Five campsites are pull-throughs. The campground is thickly wooded and abuts a swimming beach on the small but pleasant Lake Brantley. Lakeside sites 50 and 51 have nice water views, and sites 22 and 27 are pleasantly secluded; site 42 is a particularly nice pull-through. The area has a beaver pond and is said to be thickly populated with deer and fox squirrels. Nearby, campers can visit Stone Mountain or the Oconee National Forest. There's also a large on-site horse stable with special campsites for equestrians, as well as access to multiuse trails open to both horses and hikers.

BASICS

Operated By: Georgia Dept. of Natural Resources. **Open:** All year. **Site Assignment:** Reservations only. **Registration:** At camp office. **Fee:** Tent/trailer/RV, $20–$24; cottage, $85–$100. **Parking:** 2 vehicles per site.

FACILITIES

Number of Multipurpose Sites: 63. **Hookups:** Electric (30 amps), water, cable TV in cottages. **Each Site:** Picnic table, grill, fire ring. **Dump Station:** Yes. **Laundry:** Yes. **Pay Phone:** Yes. **Restrooms and Showers:** Yes. **Fuel:** No. **Propane:** No. **Internal Roads:** Paved. **RV Service:** 20 mi. **Market:** 5 mi. **Restaurant:** 5 mi. **General Store:** 15 mi. **Vending:** No. **Swimming:** Lake (no lifeguard). **Playground:** Yes. **Activities:** Beach area, golf, hiking trails, horse stable, boat rentals, fishing. **Nearby Attractions:** Stone Mountain, Oconee National Forest, Athens, Panola Mountain State Conservation Park, historic Madison, Charlie Elliott Wildlife Center.

RESTRICTIONS

Pets: On leash only. **Fires:** Fire ring only. **Alcoholic Beverages:** Allowed. **Vehicle Maximum Length:** No limit. **Other:** 14-day stay limit.

To Get There

(2 mi. north of Rutledge.) Take I-20 to Exit 105 into Rutledge and proceed 3 mi. on Fairplay Rd.

SAUTEE   MAP, A-2
Cherokee Campground

45 Bethel Rd., 30571.
T: (706) 878-2267 or (888) 878-2268;
www.helenga.org/cherokeecampground.

🚐 ★★★   ▲ ★★

Beauty: ★★★	Site Privacy: ★★★
Spaciousness: ★★★	Quiet: ★★★
Security: ★★★★	Cleanliness: ★★★★
Insect Control: ★★★★	Facilities: ★★

The sites of this private campground are small but sufficient, with some shade provided by young trees. The absence of underbrush allows easy walking between sites but does little for privacy. Nine of the sites are pull-throughs, while 16 sites are back-ins. Tenters will enjoy soft-mulch tent pads, and all visitors can listen to live music performed on weekends during peak season. This private campground may not have astounding views, but its proximity to the area's cultural and outdoor activities is a plus. Unicoi State Park, the Appalachian Trail, Anna Ruby Falls, and Brasstown Bald provide some of the outdoor fun. Those wanting an Old World experience can drive to nearby Helen, where German crafts and food are readily available in this Alpine-theme town. Reserve far in advance if you intend to camp during the annual Oktoberfest (mid-September through the beginning of November).

BASICS

Operated By: Phil Sheridan. **Open:** All year. **Site Assignment:** First come, first served; reservations accepted. **Registration:** At camp office. **Fee:** Full hookup, $20; no hookup, $18; tent, $15; cable, $2. **Parking:** In campground.

FACILITIES

Number of RV-only Sites: 18. **Number of Tent-only Sites:** 10. **Number of Multipurpose Sites:** 7. **Hookups:** Electric (15, 30, 50 amps), water, sewer, phone, cable TV. **Each Site:** Picnic table. **Dump Station:** Yes. **Laundry:** Yes. **Pay Phone:** Yes. **Restrooms and Showers:** Yes. **Fuel:** No. **Propane:** No. **Internal Roads:** Paved. **RV Service:** 15 mi. **Market:** 5 mi. **Restaurant:** 1 mi. **General Store:** Yes. **Vending:** No. **Swimming:** No. **Playground:** No. **Other:** Pavilion available. **Activities:** Hiking, trout fishing, horseback riding. **Nearby Attractions:** Anna Ruby Falls, Appalachian Trail, whitewater rafting, Brasstown Bald.

RESTRICTIONS

Pets: On leash only. **Fires:** Allowed. **Alcoholic Beverages:** Allowed. **Vehicle Maximum Length:** No limit.

To Get There

Take I-85 northbound to GA 985 North. Continue on GA 985 N to mile marker 42 (GA 384). Turn left onto GA 384 and travel approximately 16 mi. to deadend (GA 75). Turn right on GA 75 through Helen, GA. Continue to GA 356 and turn right. Continue on GA 356 to mile marker 5. Turn right onto Bethel Rd. and follow the signs to Cherokee Campground.

SAVANNAH   MAP, C-3
Skidaway Island State Park

52 Diamond Causeway, 31411-1102.
T: (912) 598-2300 or (800) 864-7275;
www.gastateparks.org/info/skidaway.

🚐 ★★★★★   ▲ ★★★★★

Beauty: ★★★★★	Site Privacy: ★★★★★
Spaciousness: ★★★★★	Quiet: ★★★★★
Security: ★★★★	Cleanliness: ★★★★
Insect Control: ★★★	Facilities: ★★★

Historic Savannah is the cultural anchor of this state park, and the rich, diverse physical environment makes it a stunner for nature lovers as well. It is a glorious, beautiful place that offers fresh and salt water, oodles of wildlife viewing, and plenty of natural variety in the park's forest portions. It is an urban to suburban setting, so sites near the main road are not recommended. The sites are indeed quite large and attractive, with Spanish moss dripping from the trees above. All sites are pull-throughs, with pine-straw and packed-dirt ground cover. Especially huge are sites 1–10, and exceptionally gorgeous are 55, 57, and 59. The only turn-off here are the yucky facilities, but if you can tolerate that, the beauty and privacy more than make up for it. Savannah is a large enough town to provide entertainment for all travelers, and the campground itself is good for families and all ages. For history and/or nature nuts, this is a supreme vacation spot.

BASICS

Operated By: Georgia Dept. of Natural Resources. **Open:** All year. **Site Assignment:** Reservations accepted. **Registration:** At camp office. **Fee:** $22–$24. **Parking:** 2 vehicles per site.

FACILITIES

Number of Multipurpose Sites: 88. **Hookups:** Electric (30 amps), water, cable TV. **Each Site:** Picnic table. **Dump Station:** Yes. **Laundry:** Yes. **Pay Phone:** Yes. **Restrooms and Showers:** Yes. **Fuel:** Nearby. **Propane:** No. **Internal Roads:** Paved. **RV Service:** No. **Market:** In Savannah. **Restaurant:** In Savannah. **General Store:** No. **Vending:** Yes. **Swimming:** Yes. **Playground:** Yes. **Activities:** Hiking, nature trail, bird-watching, swimming, museum & interpretive center. **Nearby Attractions:** Wormsloe State Historic Site, Fort McAllister State Historic Park, Fort Morris State Historic Site, Skidaway Marine Institute, historic Savannah, Tybee Island beaches.

RESTRICTIONS

Pets: On 6-ft leash. Accompanied by owner at all times. **Fires:** At sites, w/in fire rings. **Alcoholic Beverages:** Not allowed. **Vehicle Maximum Length:** No limit.

To Get There

From I-16 in Savannah, take Exit 164A (I516/Lynes Pkwy.), which merges with DeReene Ave. Turn right on Waters Ave. and go straight ahead to Diamond Causeway. Park will be first left between two churches after crossing drawbridge.

Idaho

A visit to Idaho is a journey into time, with much of the country looking exactly as it did for Lewis and Clark and early Native American tribes. Endless swaths of western white pine blanketing majestic mountains seem to prop up the sky. As you wander into the backcountry wilderness, it's not hard to imagine that you're the first human to have ventured into these remote and startling places. The number of Idaho parks, both state and private, and the diversity of Idaho's landscape offer a full spectrum of experience for all outdoor enthusiasts. From campsites accessible only by foot, where you're reminded that toilets are a modern amenity, to comfortable RV campgrounds, it's nearly impossible to escape the feeling of being immersed in wilderness.

As you journey to your camping destinations, take the opportunity to appreciate the views provided by the Gem State. In the north, you might visit **Lake Coeur d'Alene** or **Lake Pend Oreille,** the largest lake in Idaho, or you could motor along the **Lake Coeur d'Alene Scenic Byway,** making sure to rest your wheels for a spell at a scenic lookout—you may be fortunate enough to glimpse an eagle soaring along an updraft. Take the **Northwest Passage Scenic Byway** to recapture moments of Lewis and Clark along 191 miles of their trail and venture into **Hells Canyon,** the deepest in the nation at 7,900 feet, where you can experience the sheer cliffs from water's edge. RV campers will enjoy a stop in **Kamiah,** where the motor-home community is strong. In central Idaho, make a stop in the **Clear Lake Region,** where you can stay at one of many Lewis and Clark Expedition campsites. Explore the area alone or take a guided tour or horseback or mountain bike ride through the remote territories. If you're into the awe-inspiring, drive the **Salmon River Scenic Byway,** with its sprawling views of the **Sawtooth Mountains** and **Grand Tetons,** for a dazzling array of vistas unlike any in the country.

Venturing east and southward, watch as the Idaho landscape transforms itself—subtle desert colors begin to emerge and contrast with the deep evergreen. Ride the **Mesa Falls Scenic Byway** through the **Targhee National Forest,** where glimpses of rushing waterfalls will beg for your attention. The **Bear Lake–Caribou Byway** takes you south past **Bear Lake** and **Minnetonka Caves,** and to the **Lava Hot Springs** established by the Bannock and Shoshone tribes. Farther south is the **Fort Hall Indian Reservation** and the semi-desert town of Pocatello, home to **Idaho State University.** Move farther south along the **Thousand Springs Scenic Byway,** where you can visit the **City of Rocks.** Here, 60-foot granite pillars reach skyward like stalagmites from a cave floor. Nearby, the **Albion Mountain Range** provides a limitless variety of hiking, climbing, and wildlife-viewing experiences. Drive west along **Hells Canyon Scenic Byway,** which is short but steep, and visit southwest Idaho's monumental **Bruneau Sand Dunes,** with sand peaks reaching 400 feet in height—the tallest dunes in North America. Choose a campsite in the **Payette National Forest** and enjoy the extensive hiking, biking, and fishing opportunities there. Wherever you travel in the 43rd state, Idaho is sure to satisfy your spirit for adventure and quest for beauty if you are out for more than just the average camping experience.

Campground Profiles

AHSAHKA   MAP, B-1
Dent Acres Recreation Area

reserve america

North Fork Dr., P.O. Box 48, 83520.
T: (208) 476-1261; www.reserveamerica.com.

🚐 ★★★   ⛺ ★★★★

Beauty: ★★★★	Site Privacy: ★★★
Spaciousness: ★★★	Quiet: ★★★★
Security: ★★★★	Cleanliness: ★★★
Insect Control: ★★★	Facilities: ★★★

Dent Acres Recreation Area sits on the east side of the Dworshak Reservoir, 19 miles northeast of Orofino. The Dworshak Dam is the largest straight-axis dam in North America and its reservoir has 54 miles of tree-lined shore. This 500-acre recreation area offers 50 full-hookup campsites situated in an open meadow. The campgrounds consist of an S configuration offering both shaded and open sites. The elevation of the park is 1,600 feet, offering warm summer days and cool nights. Most sites are spacious and private, both pull-throughs and back-ins. Dent Acres Recreation Area offers trophy-level fishing (kokanee salmon, small mouth bass, and rainbow trout), 18 miles of hiking trails, and 100 additional primitive campsites that can be accessed only by boat. The park also has a full marina with boat dump. Park rangers and a camp attendant are on duty 24 hours a day to provide campers necessary assistance.

BASICS

Operated By: U.S. Army Corps of Engineers (Walla Walla District). **Open:** Recreation area, year-round; campground, Apr.–Nov. **Site Assignment:** 60% of the campsites are reservable. **Registration:** W/ camp attendant. **Fee:** $10–$16; cash, check, unless using the reservation service. **Parking:** At site.

FACILITIES

Number of Multipurpose Sites: 50. **Hookups:** Electric (20, 30 amps), water, sewer. **Each Site:** Picnic table, fire pit. **Dump Station:** Yes. **Laundry:** No. **Pay Phone:** Yes. **Restrooms and Showers:** Yes. **Fuel:** 20 mi. in Orofino (except by boat & then Big Eddy Marina approx. 5 mi. down the res. **Propane:** 20 mi. in Orofino. **Internal Roads:** Paved. **RV Service:** 20 mi. south in Orofino. **Market:** 20 mi. south in Orofino. **Restaurant:** 17 mi. south in Orofino. **General Store:** No. **Vending:** Inquire at campground. **Swimming:** Reservoir (no lifeguard). **Playground:** Yes. **Other:** Boat launch, floating marine dump, group shelters, weather station, camp attendant, boat parking. **Activities:** Fishing (kokanee salmon, small mouth bass, rainbow trout), hunting (elk, deer, black bear, cougar), boating, waterskiing, cross-country skiing, 18 miles of hiking trails, backpacking, mountain biking. **Nearby Attractions:** Dworshak State Park, Dworshak National Steelhead Fish Hatchery, Clearwater County Museum, Lewis & Clark National Historic Trail. **Additional Information:** There are 100 primitive sites surrounding the Dworshak Reservoir, accessible only by boat, featuring picnic tables, fire pits, & vaulted toilets. Orofino Chamber of Commerce, (208) 476-4335, www.orofino.com.

RESTRICTIONS

Pets: On 6-ft. leash only. **Fires:** Fire pit only (fires sometimes prohibited due to weather; ask park official before starting any fire). **Alcoholic Beverages:** Allowed. **Vehicle Maximum Length:** Some sites up to 50 ft. **Other:** Max. 8 people per site, 14-day stay limit.

TO GET THERE

Hwy. 12 to Orofino; in Orofino there are signs to the Dworshak Reservoir Visitor Center. Please stop and obtain a map of the reservoir and recreation area. They will direct you to the area. The roads leading into the recreation area are narrow and curvy. It is 19 mi. from the visitors center to the recreation area. Please note the visitor center closes most days at 4 p.m.

ASHTON   MAP, C-3
Riverside—
Caribou-Targhee National Forest

reserve america

Box 858, 83420. T: (208) 652-7442; www.reserveamerica.com.

🚐 ★★★★   ⛺ ★★★★

Beauty: ★★★★	Site Privacy: ★★★
Spaciousness: ★★★★	Quiet: ★★★
Security: ★★★★	Cleanliness: ★★★★
Insect Control: ★★★★	Facilities: ★

The elevation is 6,200 feet. The campground is composed of three loops—A, B, and C. Loop A stretches along Henry's Fork of the Snake River, with most camping sites adjacent to the river. The parking aprons are paved and there is little shade. Loop B meanders away from the river through a stand of scattered lodgepole pine. The tables and grills are on cement pads next to paved parking aprons. Many of the sites are pull-throughs. Loop C has the most-rustic camping sites, with no cement or pavement to be found. This loop enjoys the most shade, however, from mature pines. The sound of the river can be heard throughout the campground. Firewood is available for a fee. Nature walks are offered on the weekends; check the fee board for subject, time, and place. Riverside is located within the Caribou-Targhee National Forest, which occupies over 3 million acres and stretches across southeastern Idaho, from the Montana, Utah, and Wyoming borders. The Targhee National Forest is full of crystal-clear water and breathtaking vistas patched together by rolling fields of golden grain and dark-green potato plants. With such a variety in topography, the recreational opportunities found in the Targhee National Forest are equally varied and numerous. From water-skiing on Palisades Reservoir to floating down the Buffalo River; to hiking trails that challenge the body and renew the spirit; to miles and miles of rivers, streams, and creeks for the angler; to wildlife viewing and the forest's natural beauty, all await the visitor.

BASICS

Operated By: U.S. Forest Service. **Open:** May 11–Oct. 1. **Site Assignment:** Reservations must be made at least 7 days in advance. **Registration:** At office. **Fee:** Single, $12; double, $24. **Parking:** At park.

FACILITIES

Number of Multipurpose Sites: 180. **Hookups:** None. **Each Site:** Call ahead. **Dump Station:** No. **Laundry:** No. **Pay Phone:** 8 mi. **Restrooms and Showers:** Yes. **Fuel:** 8 mi. **Propane:** 8 mi. **Internal Roads:** Paved. **RV Service:** No. **Market:** No. **Restaurant:** No. **General Store:** 8 mi. **Vending:** No. **Swimming:** No. **Playground:** No. **Activities:** Hiking, fishing, wildlife viewing.

RESTRICTIONS

Pets: Pets must be restrained or on a leash at all times while in developed recreation areas. **Fires:** In fire rings, stoves, grills, or fireplaces provided for that purpose. **Alcoholic Beverages:** Not allowed. **Vehicle Maximum Length:** 35 ft. **Other:** No ATVs allowed.

TO GET THERE

From Ashton, Idaho, travel north on Hwy. 20 for 15 mi., take Riverside Campground turnoff, travel 1 mi. to campground entrance.

ATHOL   MAP, A-1
Farragut State Park

13550 East Hwy. 54, 83801. T: (208) 683-2425; www.idahoparks.org.

🚐 ★★★   ⛺ ★★★★

Beauty: ★★★★	Site Privacy: ★★★
Spaciousness: ★★★	Quiet: ★★★★
Security: ★★★★	Cleanliness: ★★★
Insect Control: ★★★★	Facilities: ★★★

Farragut State Park once served as a vital stop along the Pony Express route and was later purchased by the US Navy, which transformed it into the second-largest navel-training center in the world. Located only 14 miles north of Coeur d'Alene, this 4,000-acre state park is a perfect retreat, set in a forest of lodgepole pine, Douglas fir, white pine, and western red cedar. Farragut State Park has five camping areas with 219 sites altogether. Its Snowberry Campground offers 44 hookup sites, with over 18 pull-throughs situated in a forest atmosphere. The eastern portion of the park is positioned on Idaho's largest lake, Lake Pend Oreille, with depths of 1,150 feet. The surrounding forest and mountain peaks are home to white-tail deer, black bear, coyote, and bald eagle. The elevation is 2,054 feet, offering crisp mornings and comfortable days. Each camping area has a camp host and day-use areas, and the marina gates are locked at 10 p.m.

BASICS

Operated By: Idaho Dept. of Parks and Recreation. **Open:** All year. **Site Assignment:** Reservations are recommended in summer; $6 nonrefundable fee, which must be paid 5 days prior to arrival. **Registration:** At visitor center. **Fee:** Full hookup, $22; No hookup, $17; electric, $16; $3 per vehicle for day use only. **Parking:** At site. $3 per vehicle for day use only.

FACILITIES

Number of RV-only Sites: 44. **Number of Multipurpose Sites:** 175. **Hookups:** Electric (30 amps), water. **Each Site:** Picnic table, fire pit. **Dump Station:** Yes. **Laundry:** No. **Pay Phone:** Yes. **Restrooms and Showers:** Yes. **Fuel:** No. **Propane:** No. **Internal Roads:** Mostly paved, some gravel. **RV Service:** 11 mi. south in Coeur d'Alene. **Market:** In Athol. **Restaurant:** In Athol. **General Store:** No. **Vending:** Yes. **Swimming:** Lakefront swimming. **Playground:** Yes. **Other:** Visitor Center Park Museum, picnic areas, swimming area, model-airplane/glider flying field, boat launch & dock, amphitheater, Boy Scout monument, view points w/ coin-op. binoculars. **Activities:** Swimming, fishing (rainbow trout, bull trout, kokanee, machinaw, perch, blue gill, bass), boating, whitewater rafting, hiking, biking, hard-path trails, volleyball, horseshoe pits, horseback riding, 18-hole golf course, shooting range. **Nearby Attractions:** Silverwood Theme Park, Lake Coeur d'Alene Cruises, Museum of North Idaho, Wild Water (water park). **Additional Information:** Coeur d'Alene Chamber of Commerce, (208) 664-3194 or (877) 782-9232 or www.coeurdalene.org.

RESTRICTIONS

Pets: On 6-ft. leash only or confined, not tied to trees or vegetation, always attended. **Fires:** Fire pit only (fires may be prohibited due to weather; ask park official before starting any fire). **Alcoholic Beverages:** Allowed. **Vehicle Maximum Length:** 60 ft. **Other:** Max. 8 people per site, 14-day stay limit, group camps available, check-out 1 p.m.; tents must be pitched on tent pads; extra-vehicle fee of $5 per night.

TO GET THERE

15 mi. north of Coeur d'Alene or 17 mi. south of sandpoint off of Hwy. 95, turn west on Hwy. 54, park is directly off of Hwy. 54.

ATHOL   MAP, A-1
Silverwood RV Park

North 27843 Hwy. 95, 83801. T: (208) 683-3400/139; www.silverwood4fun.com.

🚐 ★★★	🏕 ★★★
Beauty: ★★★	Site Privacy: ★★★
Spaciousness: ★★★	Quiet: ★★★
Security: ★★★	Cleanliness: ★★★
Insect Control: ★★★	Facilities: ★★★

If you are looking for a great time and enjoy the thrill of a roller coaster or a water flume, this is the park for you. Silverwood RV Park is operated in conjunction with Silverwood Theme Park, one of the Northwest's largest amusement parks, just north of Coeur d'A-lene. The RV park is located adjacent to the theme park's main parking lot and offers discount admissions for its patrons. The campground consists of six wagon-wheel loops of 10–12 sites per loop, plus one larger main loop also with sites. The park offers both back-in and pull-through grass sites with paved trailer pads. The campground is clean and functional, with laundry and a convenience store. Silverwood campground's main function is to provide comfortable alternative lodging for the theme park customers. Security is handled through the main theme park, and the campground operates near full capacity all summer.

BASICS

Operated By: Silverwood Theme Park. **Open:** May 1–Oct. 12. **Site Assignment:** By reservation. **Registration:** At RV office/general store. **Fee:** $22.68. **Parking:** At site.

FACILITIES

Number of Multipurpose Sites: 126. **Hookups:** Electric (30 amps), water, sewer. **Each Site:** Picnic table. **Dump Station:** Yes. **Laundry:** Yes. **Pay Phone:** Yes. **Restrooms and Showers:** Yes. **Fuel:** No. **Propane:** No. **Internal Roads:** Gravel. **RV Service:** In Coeur D'Alene. **Market:** In Athol. **Restaurant:** In Athol. **General Store:** Yes. **Vending:** Soft drinks. **Swimming:** No. **Playground:** No. **Other:** Owned in conjunction w/ Silverwood Theme Park. **Activities:** Fishing, hiking, rafting, volleyball, horseshoe pits. **Nearby Attractions:** Silverwood Theme Park, Museum of North Idaho, Wild Waters, Farragut State Park, Boulder Beach Water Park. **Additional Information:** Silverwood Theme Park tickets sold at a discount, (208) 683-3400, www.silverwood4fun.com. Coeur d'Alene area Chamber of Commerce & Visitor's Center, (208) 664-3194, (877) 782-9232, www.coeurdalene.org.

RESTRICTIONS

Pets: On leash only, may not be left in RVs or tied (Kickaboo Dog & Cat Boarding available in town, (208) 683-3210). **Fires:** No open fires allowed. **Alcoholic Beverages:** In moderation. **Vehicle Maximum Length:** No limit. **Other:** Discounted admission tickets to Silverwood Theme Park.

TO GET THERE

15 mi. north of Coeur d'Alene, on Hwy. 95.

CASCADE   MAP, C-1
Arrowhead Mountain Village

P.O. Box 337, 83611. T: (208) 382-4534.

🚐 ★★★★	🏕 ★★★
Beauty: ★★★★	Site Privacy: ★★★
Spaciousness: ★★	Quiet: ★★★★
Security: ★★★★	Cleanliness: ★★★★
Insect Control: ★★★★	Facilities: ★★★★

Located just within the Cascade city limits, this 115-site RV park is like a home to many returning seasonal visitors. Arrowhead Mountain Village is a pristine community catering to its guests. It offers full amenities, craft classes, totem-pole carving, and many other scheduled activities. Sites are comfortably spaced and most are shaded. The majority of the sites are pull-through, with a few back-ins along the Payette River. The river runs along the southern portion of the property, offering great fishing and non-motorized boating. The park provides a fish-cleaning area and boat ramp. There is a central fire pit on the riverbank, available for campfires. The Cascade Reservoir is only a few miles north, attracting water-skiers, jet skiers, and serious fishermen. Perch, Coho salmon, and rainbow trout are only a few of the many fish found in the reservoir. A constant breeze comes from the adjacent mountains, making summer days very pleasant.

BASICS

Operated By: Gerald Patterson, owner. **Open:** May 1–Oct. 1. **Site Assignment:** Reservations recommended and held w/ credit card. **Registration:** At camp office. **Fee:** RV, $29; tent, $20; per 2 people; extra person, $3; children under 6 free. **Parking:** At site.

FACILITIES

Number of RV-only Sites: 114. **Number of Tent-only Sites:** 5. **Hookups:** Electric (30, 50 amps), water, sewer, cable TV. **Each Site:** Picnic tables. **Dump Station:** Yes. **Laundry:** Yes. **Pay Phone:** Yes. **Restrooms and Showers:** Yes. **Fuel:** Across the street. **Propane:** No. **Internal Roads:** Gravel. **RV Service:** RV supplies located in general store or 12 mi. North in Lake Fork. **Market:** In Cascade. **Restaurant:** In Cascade. **General Store:** Yes. **Vending:** Soft drinks. **Swimming:** No. **Playground:** Yes. **Other:** 3 yurts (circular, Mongolian-style tent), pet area, boat launch & parking, cabins, flower garden, butterfly garden, rec hall, pavilion, fish-cleaning house, secure storage yard. **Activities:** Archery, horseshoes, craft classes, carving classes, ice-cream socials, many scheduled activities, fishing (perch, rainbow trout, Coho salmon), hiking, boating, water skiing, snowmobiling, golf, basketball, skeet shooting, horseback trips. **Nearby Attractions:** Hot Springs, Idaho Historical Railroads. **Additional Information:** Cascade Chamber of Commerce, (208) 382-3833, www.cascadeid.com.

RESTRICTIONS

Pets: On leash only. **Fires:** No open fires allowed; 1 central fire pit. **Alcoholic Beverages:** Allowed. **Vehicle Maximum Length:** No limit.

TO GET THERE

Located directly off of Hwy. 55, within the city limits of Cascade.

CASCADE   MAP, C-1
Water's Edge RV Resort

P.O. Box 1018, 83611. T: (208) 382-3120 or (800) 574-2038; www.watersedgervpark.com.

🚐 ★★★★	🏕 ★★★
Beauty: ★★★★	Site Privacy: ★★★
Spaciousness: ★★★	Quiet: ★★★★
Security: ★★★★	Cleanliness: ★★★★★
Insect Control: ★★★★	Facilities: ★★★★★

Located on the beautiful Payette River and only a few short miles from the Cascade Reservoir, Water's Edge RV Resort is the ideal location for water-sport enthusiasts. Water's Edge offers free canoeing and kayaking from its own riverfront beach. There are 92 lakes and 169 streams in a 50-mile radius with trophy sockeye, Chinook, and rainbow trout. The campground itself offers level gravel sites, with all the amenities, beautifully landscaped common areas, and a brand-new covered picnic pavilion. Water's Edge is famous for its evening campfires on the beach and the hot, fresh cinnamon rolls on summer weekend mornings. And Cascade is known for its cool mountain breeze, which makes summer days pleasant and evenings cool. In winter, the Cascade area offers miles of cross-country skiing and snowmobile trails.

BASICS

Operated By: Ashley and Katrin Thompson, owners. **Open:** May–Oct. **Site Assignment:** Reservations recommended and held w/ credit card. **Registration:** At camp office. **Fee:** $27; each additional person, $2. **Parking:** At site.

FACILITIES

Number of RV-only Sites: 125. **Number of Tent-only Sites:** 10. **Hookups:** Electric (30, 50 amps), water, sewer, cable TV, phone, Internet. **Each Site:** Picnic table. **Dump Station:** Yes. **Laundry:** Yes. **Pay Phone:** Yes. **Restrooms and Showers:** Yes. **Fuel:** No. **Propane:** Yes. **Internal Roads:** Gravel, in excellent condition. **RV Service:** 12 mi. north in Lake Fork. **Market:** In Cascade. **Restaurant:** In Cascade. **General Store:** No. **Vending:** Yes. **Swimming:** Riverfront swimming. **Playground:** No. **Other:** 2 pavilions w/ grills, 2 riverfront fire pits, private riverfront beach (Payette River), cabins, covered picnic area, rec hall w/ kitchen area, free canoes & kayaks, fax & copier service, cinnamon rolls on Sat. morning in the summer. **Activities:** Canoeing, kayaking, beach volleyball, horseshoes, paddleboats, evening campfires, bird-watching, fishing (rainbow trout, perch, Coho salmon), river nature walks, sailing, biking, hiking, windsurfing, whitewater rafting, skeet trap shoots. **Nearby Attractions:** Lake Cascade State Park. **Additional Information:** Cascade Chamber of Commerce, (208) 382-3833, www.cascadeid.com; Snowbank Outfitter, (208) 382-4872; Big Creek Wilderness Outfitter, (208) 382-4872.

RESTRICTIONS

Pets: On leash only; restrictions on certain breeds. **Fires:** In central fire pits only. **Alcoholic Beverages:** Allowed. **Vehicle Maximum Length:** 40 plus.

TO GET THERE

Directly off Hwy. 55 on the north side of Cascade.

CHALLIS
Challis Hot Springs   MAP, C-2

HC 63 Box 1779, 83226. T: (208) 879-4442; www.scenicriver.com.

🚐 ★★★★	▲ ★★★★★
Beauty: ★★★★	Site Privacy: ★★★★
Spaciousness: ★★★★	Quiet: ★★★★
Security: ★★★★	Cleanliness: ★★★★
Insect Control: ★★★★	Facilities: ★★★★

Nestled between the Lost River Range and Salmon River Mountains, this rustic campground is the perfect place to get away from the hubbub of city life. This campground makes a great base camp from which to explore a number of Idaho's spectacular resources, including the Frank Church River of No Return Wilderness, the Salmon River, and the Rocky Mountains. Wildlife frequently pass through the campgrounds, and the Salmon River, which is in easy walking distance, provides a great place to wet some lines. Most of the sites are back-ins with only 2 pull-throughs available. Though the campground is remote, campers can find most amenities in the town of Challis, including food, auto parts, and banking. Challis, the seat of Custer County, is still the area's economic center of mines, ranches, and farms. This area is still known as one of the richest mineral belts in North America.

BASICS

Operated By: Jon Campbell, Mgr. **Open:** All year. **Site Assignment:** By reservation; 50% deposit required. **Registration:** At camp office. **Fee:** Tent, $18–$23; RV, $23 per 2 people, extra person $6. **Parking:** At site.

FACILITIES

Number of RV-only Sites: 30. **Number of Tent-only Sites:** 10. **Number of Multipurpose Sites:** 2. **Hookups:** Electric (30 amps), water, sewer. **Each Site:** Picnic table, fire pit. **Dump Station:** Yes. **Laundry:** No. **Pay Phone:** Yes. **Restrooms and Showers:** Yes. **Fuel:** 3 mi. in Challis. **Propane:** 3 mi. in Challis. **Internal Roads:** Paved. **RV Service:** 3 mi. in Challis. **Market:** 3 mi. in Challis. **Restaurant:** Gourmet meals served once a week on site, & some Dutch-oven cooking, otherwise 3 mi. in Challis. **General Store:** Yes, basic snacks available. **Vending:** No. **Swimming:** Yes. **Playground:** No. **Other:** Natural hot-water swimming pool open year-round, hot mineral pool, driving range, Dutch-oven cooking, rafting outfitters, horseback outfitters, fly-fishing school. **Activities:** Swimming, fly fishing, rafting, golf, driving range. **Nearby Attractions:** Scenic drives, many recreational outfitters. **Additional Information:** Challis Chamber of Commerce, (208) 879-2771.

RESTRICTIONS

Pets: On leash only. **Fires:** Fire pit only (fires may be restricted due to dry weather; always ask management before starting any open fire). **Alcoholic Beverages:** Allowed. **Vehicle Maximum Length:** No limit. **Other:** Complimentary breakfast included.

TO GET THERE

Challis is at the junction of Hwy. 75 and Hwy. 93. From there go 3 mi. east on Hwy. 93 and turn left on Challis Hot Springs Rd.; this road will dead-end into the property. (There are excellent signs directing you into this property.)

COEUR D'ALENE
Coeur d'Alene KOA RV, Tent, and Kabin Resort   MAP, A-1

East 10700 Wolf Lodge Bay Rd., 83814. T: (208) 664-4471 or (800) 562-2609; www.koa.com/where/id/12106.

🚐 ★★★	▲ ★★★
Beauty: ★★★★	Site Privacy: ★★★
Spaciousness: ★★★	Quiet: ★★★★
Security: ★★★	Cleanliness: ★★★
Insect Control: ★★★★	Facilities: ★★★★

Positioned on the side of Coeur d'Alene Mountain and adjacent to Lake Coeur d'Alene, KOA RV, Tent, and Kabin Resort is ideal for recreation. The park is located directly off I-90, only 9 miles east of Coeur d'Alene. The campground offers 86 RV sites and 19 cabins terraced up the side of Coeur d'Alene Mountain, with 79 tent sites and 2 tepees in the valley. The grounds are nicely landscaped and the view is spectacular. Sites, however, are relatively close together. The 20 pull-through sites offer little shade although the camp has a fair amount of pine and willow trees. All sites are gravel and many are difficult to maneuver. A bird and wildlife sanctuary is found in the basin of the valley. The weather can change in the blink of an eye; evenings are cool. This KOA offers two adult-only hot tubs and kayaking from a boat dock. The campground is patrolled.

BASICS

Operated By: David and Karen Striker. **Open:** Apr. 15–Sept. 30. **Site Assignment:** Reservations recommended, 50% deposit. **Registration:** At camp store. **Fee:** RV, $34–$41; tent, $27; cash, credit card, check. **Parking:** At site, very little extra.

FACILITIES

Number of RV-only Sites: 65. **Number of Tent-only Sites:** 25. **Hookups:** Electric (30 amps), water, sewer. **Each Site:** Picnic table, grill, fire pit. **Dump Station:** Yes. **Laundry:** Yes. **Pay Phone:** Yes. **Restrooms and Showers:** Yes. **Fuel:** No. **Propane:** Yes. **Internal Roads:** Gravel, in good condition. **RV Service:** 9 mi. west in Coeur d'Alene. **Market:** 9 mi. west in Coeur d'Alene. **Restaurant:** Steak house on the north frontage road about 0.5 mi., or in Coeur d'Alene. **General Store:** Yes, w/ snacks & homemade pizza. **Vending:** In general store. **Swimming:** Heated pool & 2 hot tubs (seasonal). **Playground:** Yes. **Other:** Amphitheater, camp kitchen, tepees, cabins, nonmotorized boat launch, kayak rentals, game room. **Activities:** Outside movies, paddleboat, canoeing, kayaking, fishing, mini-golf, horseshoes, horseback riding, hiking, bike trails, swimming, golf, bird-watching, gaming. **Nearby Attractions:** Silverwood Theme Park, Wild Water Slides, Silver Mountain Gondola ride, shopping, seaplane & helicopter rides, museums, parasailing, casinos. **Additional Information:** Coeur d'Alene Chamber of Commerce, (208) 664-3194, (877) 782-9232, www.coeurdalene.org.

RESTRICTIONS

Pets: On 6-ft. leash only, cleaned up after, always attended or a fee will be imposed; not allowed in any building or the pool area; pet walk provided. **Fires:** Fire pit only (fires may be prohibited during dry weather). **Alcoholic Beverages:** Allowed. **Vehicle Maximum Length:** 70 ft. **Other:** Free modem access.

TO GET THERE

The campground is 8 mi. east of Coeur d'Alene. From Hwy. 90 take Exit 22 and go 0.5 mi. south.

COEUR D'ALENE   MAP, A-1
Idaho Panhandle National Forest

3815 Schreiber Way, 83815-8363.
T: (208) 765-7223 or (208) 664-2318;
www.fs.fed.us/outernet/ipnf.

🚐 ★★★   ▲ ★★★★

Beauty: ★★★★★   Site Privacy: ★★★★
Spaciousness: ★★★★   Quiet: ★★★★★
Security: ★★★   Cleanliness: ★★★
Insect Control: ★★   Facilities: ★★

Camping in the Panhandle Idaho National Forest is for all outdoor enthusiasts, especially those who seek breathtaking views and pristine lakes and rivers. Most of the sites are accessible by cars and RVs (some even by boat), but this camping experience is relatively rustic for the most part. There are both pull-throughs and back-ins available. Whether you want to do some serious outdoor recreation or just to hang out under the pines (fir, spruce, cedar, and hemlock, to name a few) and breathe the delicious northwest air, the beauty of this national forest will not disappoint. For the most part, you will find level parking spots at the campsites, but be prepared to do some research to choose the most practical site for your style of camping. These rural, quiet campgrounds will provide you with a private, gorgeous wonderland. Rock climbing, hiking, hunting, fishing, and other such diversions will keep you busy.

BASICS

Operated By: U.S. Forest Service. **Open:** May–Sept.; skiing available in winter. **Site Assignment:** Prepay w/ credit card at time of reservation. **Registration:** At registration kiosk or camp host's trailer. **Fee:** Family site, $8.65. **Parking:** At site.

FACILITIES

Number of Multipurpose Sites: 100. **Hookups:** Water. **Each Site:** Level parking spurs (most are paved), picnic table, grated fire pit. **Dump Station:** In several locations throughout the forest. **Laundry:** No. **Pay Phone:** No. **Restrooms and Showers:** Restrooms, mostly w/ vaulted toilets; no showers. **Fuel:** No. **Propane:** No. **Internal Roads:** Most are paved, some gravel. **RV Service:** Couer d'Alene. **Market:** Groceries in almost every small community w/in the forest. **Restaurant:** Plenty of restaurants & a nice variety of dining. **General Store:** No. **Vending:** No. **Swimming:** No, but many areas on the rivers & lakes open to public; many natural hot springs. (Use caution: many of the hot springs are too hot for swimming & will cause second- & third-degree burns.) **Playground:** No. **Other:** Many sites on lakes & rivers, excellent boating & blue-ribbon fishing. **Activities:** Hiking, mountain biking, fishing (Priest Lake, Lake Pend Oreille, St. Joe River), boating, waterskiing, swimming, lakefront beaches, backpacking, mountaineering, motorized-bike trailheads, cross-country skiing, hunting. **Nearby Attractions:** Museum of North Idaho, Silverwood Theme Park, Stateline & Speedway, Fort Sherman Museum, Hells Canyon. **Additional Information:** North Idaho Visitors Center, (888) 333-3737.

RESTRICTIONS

Pets: On leash only. **Fires:** Fire ring only (the forest may prohibit open fires due to weather conditions; always check w/ a ranger or camp host before starting any fires). **Alcoholic Beverages:** Allowed. No boisterous behavior, & campers must clean up all bottles, cups, etc., before leaving the campsite. **Vehicle Maximum Length:** Sites vary in size; the campgrounds on the national reservation service are better equipped to handle larger RVs. **Other:** 14-day stay limit. Campers must bring their own garbage bags.

TO GET THERE

I-90 passes right through the middle of the Idaho Panhandle National Forest. Coeur d'Alene is on I-90, acting as a hub for forest access.

COOLIN   MAP, A-1
Priest Lake State Park

314 Indian Creek Park Rd., 83821-9076. T: (208) 443-2200; www.idahoparks.org/parks/priest.html.

🚐 ★★★   ▲ ★★★

Beauty: ★★★★   Site Privacy: ★★★
Spaciousness: ★★★   Quiet: ★★★
Security: ★★★★   Cleanliness: ★★★
Insect Control: ★★★★   Facilities: ★★★

If you are looking for abundance, spectacular scenery, and cool summer days, then Priest Lake State Park is the vacation spot for you. Priest Lake State Park offers two fully equipped campgrounds situated on a 19-mile lake of crystal-clear water. The campgrounds are under canopies of mature cedars and hemlocks that open to the panoramic view of Priest Lake and the Selkirk Mountain Range. Each site is comfortable in size and offers a sense of privacy. There are both pull-through and back-in sites available, as well as packed-sand trailer pads. Some sites are more level than others, and rain does seem to cause minor flooding. The area is home to diverse wildlife, such as bears and moose, and it is wise to leave all food packed in a safe and secure place outside your sleeping area. The campground is open year-round, with utilities functioning from spring until late fall. Activities differ with each season—from waterskiing in the summer to snowmobiling and cross-country skiing in winter. The park is fully staffed with park officials on duty around the clock.

BASICS

Operated By: Idaho State Parks. **Open:** Indian Creek, all year; Lionhead, seasonally. **Site Assignment:** First come, first served; reservations recommended Memorial Day–Labor Day for Indian Creek. **Registration:** At headquarters building. **Fee:** Electric/water, $18; water, $16; no hookup, $12. **Parking:** $30 extra-vehicle fee.

FACILITIES

Number of Multipurpose Sites: 151. **Hookups:** Electric (30 amps), water at both campgrounds. **Each Site:** Picnic table, fire pit. **Dump Station:** Yes. **Laundry:** Yes. **Pay Phone:** Yes. **Restrooms and Showers:** Yes. **Fuel:** Yes (also boat fuel). **Propane:** No. **Internal Roads:** Paved & dirt. **RV Service:** No.

Market: No. **Restaurant:** In Coolin. **General Store:** Yes, at Indian Creek. **Vending:** In general store. **Swimming:** Lake. **Playground:** No. **Other:** Amphitheater, marina, picnic area, cabins, picnic shelters, day-use area. **Activities:** Fishing, swimming, boating, volleyball, basketball, horseshoes, guided walks, picking huckleberries, evening summer programs; skiing, ice-fishing, & snowmobiling in winter. **Nearby Attractions:** Lionhead, hiking trails. **Additional Information:** Idaho State Parks & Recreation, (208) 334-4199.

RESTRICTIONS

Pets: On 6-ft. leash only. **Fires:** Fire pit only (fires may be prohibited due to dry weather; check w/ park officials before starting any fire). **Alcoholic Beverages:** Allowed, if used w/ good judgment & in moderation. **Vehicle Maximum Length:** 50 ft. **Other:** 15-day stay limit.

TO GET THERE

From N US 95 to N US 2 to ID 57, then follow signs into the park.

EDEN   MAP, D-2
Anderson Camp

1188 East US 99, 83325.
T: (208) 825-9800 or (888) 480-9400; www.andersoncamp.com.

🚐 ★★★★   ▲ ★★★

Beauty: ★★★   Site Privacy: ★★★
Spaciousness: ★★★   Quiet: ★★★
Security: ★★★   Cleanliness: ★★★
Insect Control: ★★★★   Facilities: ★★★

This facility is more aptly described as a resort for campers rather than just a basic campground. Excellently maintained, the RV sites are spacious, with full hookups provided. For those who like to "rough it," a beautiful, open tent area is provided, with convenient access to laundry and shower facilities. Even though this campground is larger than most we've seen, it still provides adequate privacy to guests, as well as lots of peace and quiet. But this vacation spot's most attractive characteristic is its huge variety of activities. The water slide, mini-golf, and game room are just a few on a long list. This park is a very popular spot, so be sure to make a reservation.

BASICS

Operated By: Mike and Pat O'Sullivan. **Open:** All year. **Site Assignment:** By reservation. **Registration:** At camp office. **Fee:** $19; each additional person, $2. **Parking:** At site.

FACILITIES

Number of RV-only Sites: 110. **Number of Tent-only Sites:** Undesignated sites. **Hookups:** Electric (30, 50 amps), water, sewer. **Each Site:** Picnic table & fire ring. **Dump Station:** Yes. **Laundry:** Yes. **Pay Phone:** Yes. **Restrooms and Showers:** Yes. **Fuel:** Yes. **Propane:** Yes. **Internal Roads:** Gravel, in good condition. **RV Service:** Next door. **Market:** Yes. **Restaurant:** Cafe, pizzeria, and snack bar. **General Store:** Yes. **Vending:** Yes. **Swimming:** 2 pools, one wading pool. **Playground:** Yes. **Other:** Natural hot-water swimming pool, gas station, game room, large hall, fruit trees in season, homemade pizza. **Activities:** Swimming, basketball, 18-hole mini-golf, square dancing, skiing, hiking, horseback riding, volleyball. **Nearby Attractions:** Trout farms, Herrett Center, shopping. **Additional Information:** Twin Falls Chamber of Commerce, (208) 733-3974.

RESTRICTIONS

Pets: On leash only. **Fires:** No open fires; there is 1 central fire ring & a few grills. **Alcoholic Beverages:** Allowed. **Vehicle Maximum Length:** No limit.

TO GET THERE

Take I-84 to Exit 182.

GLENNS FERRY   MAP, D-1
Carmela Winery and Golf Course

1289 West Madison, P.O. Box 790, 83623. T: (208) 366-7531 or (208) 366-2313; www.carmelawinery.com.

🚐 ★★★   ⛺ ★★

Beauty: ★★★   Site Privacy: ★★★
Spaciousness: ★★★   Quiet: ★★★★★
Security: ★★★   Cleanliness: ★★★
Insect Control: ★★★   Facilities: ★★★

This tiny RV campground set between the Carmela Winery and Three Island Crossing State Park is little more than a cluster of hookup sites and a dump station. Two of its 15 sites are pull-throughs. The campground is patronized almost exclusively by campers visiting the winery grounds, which, in addition to the fermented-grape-juice concern, sports a golf course, gift shop, bar, and excellent restaurant. There are no restrooms at the campground itself, but you can use those at the winery's stone château across the street; showers are available at the nearby state park for $2. This is definitely just a stop-over while visiting the winery or passing through.

BASICS

Operated By: Roger Jones. **Open:** All year. **Site Assignment:** By reservation or walk-in. **Registration:** At the Stone Château (the main building at the winery). **Fee:** $16. **Parking:** At site.

FACILITIES

Number of Multipurpose Sites: 15. **Hookups:** Electric (30 amps), water. **Each Site:** Some picnic tables. **Dump Station:** Yes. **Laundry:** No. **Pay Phone:** Yes. **Restrooms and Showers:** None in the campground area; restrooms across the street at the Stone Château (winery); showers for $2 at the state park next door. **Fuel:** No. **Propane:** No. **Internal Roads:** Gravel, in good condition. **RV Service:** Limited local service. **Market:** In town. **Restaurant:** On site; excellent restaurant at the Stone Château. **General Store:** Gift shop only. **Vending:** No. **Swimming:** No. **Playground:** No, but large recreation area & playground at the state park next door. **Other:** Winery, restaurant, bar, banquet & conference rooms, gift shop, golf course. **Activities:** Wine tasting, golf. **Nearby Attractions:** Three Island Crossing State Park, Oregon Trail History & Education Center, Glenns Ferry Museum, Elk Farm. **Additional Information:** Glenns Ferry Chamber of Commerce, (208) 366-7345.

RESTRICTIONS

Pets: On leash only. **Fires:** No open fires. **Alcoholic Beverages:** Allowed. **Vehicle Maximum Length:** 45 ft.

TO GET THERE

I-84 to Glenns Ferry exit; follow signs; winery is next door to Three Island State Park.

GLENNS FERRY   MAP, D-1
Three Island Crossing State Park

1083 South Three Island Park Dr., 83623. T: (208) 366-2394; www.idahoparks.org/parks/threeislandcrossing.

🚐 ★★★★   ⛺ ★★★

Beauty: ★★★★   Site Privacy: ★★★
Spaciousness: ★★★   Quiet: ★★★★
Security: ★★★★   Cleanliness: ★★★★
Insect Control: ★★★★   Facilities: ★★★

Three Island Crossing State Park is situated on the Oregon Trail, where early travelers moving west would cross the Snake River. You can see trail ruts and remnants of artifacts along the riverbank. Located a few miles from I-84 in Glenns Ferry, this 513-acre park represents a piece of early American history. The park also is home to the Oregon Trail History and Education Center, where the Snake River crossings are reenacted annually. The campground offers two loops of large, shaded, relatively private sites as well as large common areas of green grass. The park also offers a more primitive area with tepees. A day-use area has a riverfront swimming beach, picnic area, and grills. Both back-in and pull-through sites are paved and level. This park is located in high desert, so the days are warm and the nights are cool. Park officials and rangers are on duty 24 hours a day and are there to assist.

BASICS

Operated By: Idaho Dept. of Parks and Recreation. **Open:** All year. **Site Assignment:** First come, first served in off-season. **Registration:** At visitor center. **Fee:** Hookup, $16; double campsite, $30; cabin, $35; extra-vehicle fee, $4. **Parking:** At site.

FACILITIES

Number of Multipurpose Sites: 100. **Hookups:** Electric (20, 30 amps), water. **Each Site:** Picnic table, grated fire pit, grill. **Dump Station:** Yes. **Laundry:** No. **Pay Phone:** Yes. **Restrooms and Showers:** Yes. **Fuel:** No. **Propane:** No. **Internal Roads:** Paved. **RV Service:** No. **Market:** In Glenns Ferry. **Restaurant:** In Glenns Ferry or next door at the Carmela Vineyard. **General Store:** No. **Vending:** No. **Swimming:** No. **Playground:** Yes. **Other:** Amphitheater, Oregon Trail History & Education Center, picnic shelters, grills, riverfront beach (Snake River), group picnic shelter. **Activities:** Fishing, hiking, weekend campfire program, swimming, guided nature walks. **Nearby Attractions:** Glenns Ferry Historical Museum, Carmela Winery & Golf Club. **Additional Information:** Idaho Dept. of Parks & Recreation, (208) 334-4199; Glenns Ferry Chamber of Commerce, (208) 366-7345, www.cyberhighway.net/~gfcity; Oregon Trail river-crossing reenactment takes place the second weekend in Aug.

RESTRICTIONS

Pets: On leash only, not allowed in beach areas. **Fires:** Fire pit only. **Alcoholic Beverages:** Allowed. **Vehicle Maximum Length:** No limit. **Other:** Max. 8 people per site, 14-day stay limit, fireworks not allowed.

TO GET THERE

I-84 to Exit 120; take a left, then take a left on First Ave., right on Commercial St., right on Madison Ave., left into park; follow signs.

GRANDJEAN   MAP, C-1
Sawtooth Lodge

130 North Haines, 83712. T: (208) 259-3331 (May 15–Oct. 14) or (208) 344-2437 (Oct. 15–May 14); www.sawtoothlodge.com.

🚐 ★★★   ⛺ ★★★★

Beauty: ★★★★   Site Privacy: ★★★
Spaciousness: ★★★   Quiet: ★★★★
Security: ★★★   Cleanliness: ★★★
Insect Control: ★★★   Facilities: ★★★

Situated in the Sawtooth National Forest, Sawtooth Lodge is a favorite destination among outdoor enthusiasts. Opened in 1927, Sawtooth Lodge offers a great place to relax and enjoy the serene beauty of the surrounding wilderness. Ponderosa pines, spruce, and huckleberries give background to a lovely meadow available for tent camping. The RV campground is a simple row of grass back-in sites, with towering mature pines that give privacy to some sites. Well-maintained trails and majestic mountains envelope the property. The swimming-pool water is from a natural hot spring. The south fork of the Payette River and Trail Creek make for great fly fishing. Mornings are crisp, with cool mountain air that warms as the day progresses. Nights are chilly after sunset. Fresh home-style meals are served daily in the lodge, with ice-cream potatoes as a favorite desert. Cabins are available for you, and a boarding barn is available for your horse.

BASICS

Operated By: Rodney and Linda Lockett. **Open:** Memorial Day weekend–Oct. 15. **Site Assignment:** Reservations highly recommended; 2-night minimum on weekends, 3-night minimum over holidays. **Registration:** At camp lodge. **Fee:** $10–$12. **Parking:** At site.

FACILITIES

Number of RV-only Sites: 22. **Number of Tent-only Sites:** Undesignated sites. **Hookups:** Electric (20 amps, but for lights only), water, sewer. **Each Site:** Picnic tables. **Dump Station:** Yes. **Laundry:** No. **Pay Phone:** Yes. **Restrooms and Showers:** Yes. **Fuel:** 15 mi. south at the Sourdough Lodge. **Propane:** Yes. **Internal Roads:** Dirt & gravel. **RV Service:** Boise. **Market:** 40 mi. east in Stanley. **Restaurant:** In lodge, but w/ dinner reservations. **General Store:** Yes. **Vending:** No. **Swimming:** Natural hot-spring water. **Playground:** No. **Other:** Lodge w/ cafe, barn, cabins, lovely open meadow. **Activities:** Fishing (trout & cutthroat), whitewater rafting, hiking, horseback riding, backpacking, mountain biking. **Nearby Attractions:** Natural hot springs, Sawtooth National Recreation Area. **Additional Information:** Stanley-Sawtooth Chamber of Commerce, (208) 744-3411 or (800) 878-7950, www.stanleycc.org.

RESTRICTIONS

Pets: On leash only (you may bring your horse, call about use of barn & fees). **Fires:** In grills only; there is a central fire pit (fire may be prohibited due to weather conditions; ask management before starting any fire). **Alcoholic Beverages:** Allowed. **Vehicle Maximum Length:** No limit.

TO GET THERE

Hwy. 21 between Lowman and Stanley in Grandjean. There is a sign right at the cross guards where they close parts of Hwy. 21 in the winter. Grandjean is 6 mi. back a narrow dirt road. Feel free to get a map of the Sawtooth Recreational area from either the Lowman or Stanley ranger station.

HAGERMAN   MAP, D-2
High Adventure River Tours, RV Park, and Store

1211 E 2350 S, 83332. T: (208) 837-9005; www.inidaho.com.

🚐 ★★★	🏕 ★★★
Beauty: ★★★	Site Privacy: ★★★
Spaciousness: ★★★★	Quiet: ★★★
Security: ★★★★	Cleanliness: ★★★★
Insect Control: ★★★	Facilities: ★★★★

High Adventure River Tours RV Park and Store is conveniently located off I-84 in Hagerman. It specializes in rafting trips and river tours of the Snake River and Snake River Canyon Area. The campground is located on level ground, with nice green grass, behind a small store/outfitter. The campground is configured into rows, with the first row being an open lawn for tent camping. There are no trees on the tent lawn, and spaces are not divided out. The RV sites are all pull-throughs with level gravel parking spurs, divided by nice-size lawns and the occasional shade tree. Hagerman is half way between Twin Falls and Boise. There are some wonderful geological finds in the area and excellent fishing. The staff at High Adventure River Tours RV Park and Store are friendly and inviting.

BASICS

Operated By: Private operator. **Open:** Year-round. **Site Assignment:** By reservations or first come, first served. **Registration:** At camp store. **Fee:** RV, $22–$28; tent, $5–$28. **Parking:** At site.

FACILITIES

Number of RV-only Sites: 27. **Number of Tent-only Sites:** 12. **Hookups:** Electric (20, 30, 50 amps), water, sewer. **Each Site:** Picnic table. **Dump Station:** Yes. **Laundry:** Yes. **Pay Phone:** Yes. **Restrooms and Showers:** Yes. **Fuel:** No. **Propane:** Yes. **Internal Roads:** Gravel, in good condition. **RV Service:** In Wendall. **Market:** In Wendall. **Restaurant:** New Dutch Oven Grill Café. **General Store:** Yes. **Vending:** Yes. **Swimming:** No. **Playground:** Yes. **Other:** River-tour outfitter. **Activities:** Rafting, river tours (Snake River), fishing, boating, hik-

ing, horseshoes, kayaking, and bird-watching. **Nearby Attractions:** Hagerman Fossil Beds National Monument, Snake River Canyon, Blue Heart Springs, Box Canyon Springs, the Heron Rookery. **Additional Information:** Hagerman Valley Chamber of Commerce, (208) 837-9131.

RESTRICTIONS

Pets: On leash only. **Fires:** Grill only. **Alcoholic Beverages:** Allowed. **Vehicle Maximum Length:** 100 ft.

TO GET THERE

I-84 to Exit 147 (Malad Gorge State Park).

IDAHO FALLS   MAP, D-4
Falls Campground

1440 Lindsay Blvd., 83402. T: (800) 562-7644 or (208) 523-3362; www.koa.com.

🚐 ★★★	🏕 ★★★
Beauty: ★★★	Site Privacy: ★★★
Spaciousness: ★★★	Quiet: ★★★★
Security: ★★★★	Cleanliness: ★★★★
Insect Control: ★★★	Facilities: ★★★

This KOA campground, located in Idaho Falls, is one of the cleanest parks we've seen. The roads are gravel, but in excellent condition, and the facilities are well maintained. We preferred the RV sites over the tent sites in terms of beauty, but both were spacious, private, and quiet. The park offers all the amenities for our convenience, including a laundry on the premises. The range of activities is adequate to entertain the whole family, with the usual fishing, playground, and horseshoes, but the thing we liked best was the hot tub and sauna. For sports fans, Idaho Falls is home to a minor league baseball team, and there are several area golf courses.

BASICS

Operated By: Private operator. **Open:** May 26–Sept. 15. **Site Assignment:** No-shows will be charged $20; $10 fee will apply if you change or cancel. **Registration:** At camp store. **Fee:** Tent, $10–$20 per person; RV, $35 per 2 people; $2 each additional person. **Parking:** At site.

FACILITIES

Number of Multipurpose Sites: 130. **Hookups:** Electric (20, 30, 50 amps), water, sewer. **Each Site:** Picnic table. **Dump Station:** Yes. **Laundry:** Yes. **Pay Phone:** Yes. **Restrooms and Showers:** Restrooms are available; however, no showers are provided. **Fuel:** No. **Propane:** Yes. **Internal Roads:** Gravel, in good condition. **RV Service:** In town. **Market:** In town. **Restaurant:** There are many restaurants in town, including several national chains. **General Store:** Yes. **Vending:** Store. **Swimming:** Yes, w/ hot tub & sauna. **Playground:** Yes. **Other:** Cabins, hot tub, sauna, snack bar. **Activities:** Game room, playground, fishing, mini-golf, horseshoes, volleyball, basketball, boating. **Nearby Attractions:** Golf, professional baseball team, indoor aquatic center, pari-mutuel horse racing, zoo, museums. **Additional Information:** Idaho Falls Chamber of Commerce, (208) 523-1010.

RESTRICTIONS

Pets: On leash only. **Fires:** Grill only. **Alcoholic Beverages:** Allowed. **Vehicle Maximum Length:** 80 ft. **Other:** No vehicles on grassy meadows.

TO GET THERE

I-15 Exit 119 E 0.2 mi. to Lindsay.

ISLAND PARK   MAP, C-3
Henry's Lake State Park

3917 E 5100 N, 83429. T: (208) 558-7532; www.idahoparks.org/parks/henryslake.

🚐 ★★★	🏕 ★★★
Beauty: ★★★	Site Privacy: ★★★
Spaciousness: ★★★	Quiet: ★★★
Security: ★★★★	Cleanliness: ★★★
Insect Control: ★★★	Facilities: ★★

This beautiful park is surrounded on three sides by the Continental Divide in the rugged Targhee National Forest. The larger Island Park area offers almost every kind of outdoor recreation imaginable, in any season, including hiking, snowmobiling, cross-country skiing, ATV-riding, snowshoeing, hunting, biking, and more. And if you want still more options, Yellowstone National Park is just 15 miles to the east. The Henry's Lake campground itself is nice but unremarkable, although that doesn't really matter–you'll spend most of your time marveling at the scenery. Trout fishing is the main draw here; angling choices include Henry's Lake and the nearby Henry's Fork, Madison River, and Gallatin River. A boat ramp and docks are available for campers' use, but boaters should be careful of choppy water on the lake caused by occasionally unpredictable high winds. A 3-mile hiking trail originates from the campground.

BASICS

Operated By: Private operator. **Open:** May–Labor Day. **Site Assignment:** First come, first served. **Registration:** At camp office. **Fee:** Standard, $12; serviced site, $16; cabins, $35. **Parking:** At site.

FACILITIES

Number of Multipurpose Sites: 44. **Hookups:** Electric (20, 30 amps), water, sewer. **Each Site:** Picnic table, grated fire pit. **Dump Station:** Yes. **Laundry:** No. **Pay Phone:** Yes. **Restrooms and Showers:** Yes. **Fuel:** No. **Propane:** No. **Internal Roads:** Paved. **RV Service:** Mobile RV service. **Market:** In town. **Restaurant:** In town. **General Store:** No. **Vending:** No. **Swimming:** No. **Playground:** No. **Other:** Fish-cleaning station is available. **Activities:** Fishing (rainbow trout, cutthroat, brook), hiking, golf, biking. **Nearby Attractions:** Yellowstone National Park 16 miles east, Red Rock Lakes National Wildlife Refuge, Mesa Falls Scenic Byway. **Additional Information:** Idaho Dept. of Parks & Recreation, (208) 334-4199.

RESTRICTIONS

Pets: On leash only, not allowed in beach areas. **Fires:** Inquire at campground. **Alcoholic Beverages:** Inquire at campground. **Vehicle Maximum Length:** Call ahead for details. **Other:** $4/day vehicle fee.

TO GET THERE

From Hwy. 20 out of Idaho Falls go north approx. 80 mi. until you see park signs; go 2.5 mi. west to the entrance.

ISLAND PARK   MAP, C-3
Red Rock RV and Camping Park

3707 Red Rock Rd., 83429. T: (800) 473-3762 or (208) 558-7442; www.8004redrock.com.

🚐 ★★★★   ▲ ★★★★

Beauty: ★★★★★   Site Privacy: ★★★
Spaciousness: ★★★   Quiet: ★★★★
Security: ★★★★   Cleanliness: ★★★★
Insect Control: ★★★   Facilities: ★★★

Only 20 miles from the western gateway to Yellowstone Park, Red Rock is situated in a pristine valley that offers panoramic views of the many 8,000–10,000-foot mountains in the area. Thirty-two of its 54 sites are pull-throughs. Sites are grassy and have some privacy from their being spaced about 50 feet apart. Adjacent to Targhee National Forest and Henry's Lake State Park, Red Rock is a great base camp for every outdoor activity imaginable. It's common to spot hawks, but moose are less often seen. For cycling enthusiasts, the Great Western Bike Trail borders the park. A working dude ranch with weekly rodeos is close by, and there's plenty of scenic driving for those who don't want to cozy to the many amenities available at Red Rock. Farther afield, history buffs can visit Montana's Virginia City and Nevada City. Visitors wishing for a more "civilized" day trip can travel south to Island Park.

BASICS

Operated By: Gordon Glenn. **Open:** May 15–Sept. 20. **Site Assignment:** By reservation. **Registration:** At general store. **Fee:** Full hookup, $21; each additional person, $2. **Parking:** At site.

FACILITIES

Number of RV-only Sites: 54. **Number of Tent-only Sites:** 6. **Hookups:** Electric (30, 50 amps), water, sewer. **Each Site:** Picnic table, fire pit. **Dump Station:** Yes. **Laundry:** Yes. **Pay Phone:** Yes. **Restrooms and Showers:** Yes. **Fuel:** No. **Propane:** No. **Internal Roads:** Gravel, in good condition. **RV Service:** Mobile RV service. **Market:** 3 mi. in Island Park. **Restaurant:** The Model Ranch next door, or Island Park. **General Store:** Limited general store. **Vending:** No. **Swimming:** No. **Playground:** Yes. **Other:** Fish photo gallery, Internet data port in the office for checking e-mail only, swings, tetherball, horseshoes. **Activities:** Blue-ribbon trout fishing, boating, hiking, biking, bird- & wildlife-watching. **Nearby Attractions:** Meadow Vue Ranch, Lake Henry, Yellowstone National Park, Red Rock Lakes National Wildlife Refuge, The Great Western Bike Trail, Mesa Falls Scenic Byway. **Additional Information:** www.8004redrock.com.

RESTRICTIONS

Pets: On leash only. **Fires:** Grill or fire pits only. **Alcoholic Beverages:** Allowed. **Vehicle Maximum Length:** No limit. **Other:** Internet included in all RV sites.

TO GET THERE

From Hwy. 20 in Island Park turn west at mile marker 398, follow signs on Red Rock Rd., approx. 5 mi.

JEROME   MAP, D-2
Twin Falls-Jerome KOA

5431 US 93, 83338. T: (800) 562-4169 or (208) 324-4169; www.koa.com.

🚐 ★★★   ▲ ★★★

Beauty: ★★★   Site Privacy: ★★★
Spaciousness: ★★★   Quiet: ★★★
Security: ★★★   Cleanliness: ★★★
Insect Control: ★★★   Facilities: ★★★

This KOA isn't as nice as some we have visited but is clean and well maintained. RV and tent sites are medium sized but have some privacy, and the park itself is quiet. Some RV sites offer full hookups, and all sites come equipped with a picnic table and grill. What this campground lacks in beauty, it makes up for in amenities. Over and above the usual park activities, this KOA offers a hot tub, sauna, camp kitchen, and snack bar. Nearby, guests can try several more adventurous pastimes, like fishing on the Snake River, rafting, mountain biking, or waterskiing. If you visit, be sure to call ahead: this KOA campground is "reservation only."

BASICS

Operated By: Robert Tanner. **Open:** All year. **Site Assignment:** By reservations w/ a credit card. **Registration:** At camp store. **Fee:** Cabin, $45–$75; RV, $28–$40; tent, $23–$29. **Parking:** No extra parking.

FACILITIES

Number of RV-only Sites: 70. **Number of Tent-only Sites:** 22. **Hookups:** Electric (20, 30, 50 amps), water, sewer, cable TV. **Each Site:** Picnic table, grill. **Dump Station:** Yes. **Laundry:** Yes. **Pay Phone:** Yes. **Restrooms and Showers:** Yes. **Fuel:** No, in town. **Propane:** Yes. **Internal Roads:** Gravel, in good condition. **RV Service:** 5 mi. west in Twin Falls. **Market:** In Twin Falls. **Restaurant:** On site or in town. **General Store:** Yes. **Vending:** Yes. **Swimming:** Yes, w/ hot tub and sauna. **Playground:** Yes. **Other:** 6 cabins, sauna, hot tub, camp kitchen, snack bar, & fitness room. **Activities:** Mini-golf, horseshoes, games, fishing, rafting, hiking, mountain biking, waterskiing, boating, ice-cream socials, paddleboats, and swimming. **Nearby Attractions:** Snake River, many outfitters, gold panning. **Additional Information:** Twin Falls Chamber of Commerce, (208) 733-3974.

RESTRICTIONS

Pets: On leash only. **Fires:** Grill only. **Alcoholic Beverages:** Allowed. **Vehicle Maximum Length:** 90 ft. **Other:** During summer season, on-site cafe serves breakfast & dinner.

TO GET THERE

From I-84 Exit 173, go 1 mi. north on US 93.

KETCHUM   MAP, C-2
Sawtooth National Recreation Area

HC 64 Box 8291, 83340. T: (208) 727-5000 or (208) 727-5000; www.fs.fed.us/r4/sawtooth.

🚐 ★★★   ▲ ★★★★

Beauty: ★★★★★   Site Privacy: ★★★★
Spaciousness: ★★★★   Quiet: ★★★★★
Security: ★★★   Cleanliness: ★★★
Insect Control: ★★   Facilities: ★★

This campground is located in the heart of Sawtooth National Forest. The forest sprawls over two million acres, covers four mountain ranges, has over 40 peaks with an elevation greater than 10,000 feet, and offers a scenic landscape in any direction. In a forest with over 300 mountain lakes and several major rivers, this campground has endless opportunities for fishing, bird-watching, and viewing wildlife. The RV sites are quite peaceful and spacious, but the campground's facilities are not very good. The best selling point for this campground is clearly location, location, location. Campers considering coming here should note that this recreation area is very large and has very few gas stations. The campgrounds are open from May to September and we recommend that you make reservations in advance.

BASICS

Operated By: U.S. Forest Service. **Open:** May 26–Sept. 17. **Site Assignment:** Several are by reservation, (877) 444-6777, or self-serve; reservations must be made 4 days in advance. **Registration:** At registration kiosk or camp host's trailer. **Fee:** $13–$26. **Parking:** At site.

FACILITIES

Number of Multipurpose Sites: 33. **Hookups:** Water. **Each Site:** Level parking spurs (most are paved), picnic table, grated fire pit. **Dump Station:** Dumps in several locations throughout the forest. **Laundry:** Laundry facilities in the towns of Hailey, Ketchum, Lowman, Sawtooth City, Stanley, Sunbeam, Redfish, Challis, Salmon, & Mackay. **Pay Phone:** No. **Restrooms and Showers:** Restrooms, mostly w/ vaulted toilets. **Fuel:** The Sawtooth National Recreation Area is very large, w/ very few areas to fuel, even fewer places w/ diesel. **Propane:** Inquire at campground. **Internal Roads:** Most are paved. **RV Service:** Ketchum-Sun Valley. **Market:** Groceries in almost every small community w/in the forest. **Restaurant:** Restaurants throughout the area; excellent dinning in the Ketchum-Sun Valley. **General Store:** No. **Vending:** No. **Swimming:** No, but many areas on the rivers & lakes open to public for swimming; natural hot springs. (Use caution: many hot springs are too hot for swimming & will cause second- & third-degree burns.) **Playground:** No. **Other:** Horse camps. **Activities:** Hiking, mountain biking, fishing, skiing, horseback riding, backpacking, mountaineering, cross-country skiing, mountain climbing, kayaking. **Nearby Attractions:** Trail Creek Canyon, Sun Valley, Sawtooth Fish Hatchery, and three official Scenic Byways. **Additional Information:** Central Idaho Rockies Assoc.

RESTRICTIONS

Pets: On leash only. **Fires:** Fire ring only (the forest service may prohibit open fires due to weather conditions; always check w/ a ranger or camp host before starting any fires). **Alcoholic Beverages:** Allowed. **Vehicle Maximum Length:** Sites vary in size, the campgrounds on the national reservation service are better equipped to handle larger RVs. **Other:** 14-day stay limit; sheep located on the campground, so watch your pets.

TO GET THERE

The main roads in the recreation area are Hwy. 21 and Hwy. 75.

LEWISTON   MAP, B-1
Aht-Wy Plaza RV Park

17818 Nez Perce Rd., 83501. T: (208) 750-0231 or (208) 750-0231.

🚐 ★★★   ⛺ ★★

Beauty: ★★★   Site Privacy: ★★★
Spaciousness: ★★   Quiet: ★★★
Security: ★★★   Cleanliness: ★★★
Insect Control: ★★★★   Facilities: ★★★

Aht-Wy Plaza RV Park offers visitors to the Lewiston area a comfortable place to rest. This simple yet well-maintained RV park is conveniently located off Hwy. 95 on the Nez Perce Reservation, only 5 miles southeast of Lewiston. The campground offers level gravel and grass sites with varying degrees of shade provided by elm, sycamore, and maple trees. Five of its 33 sites are pull-throughs. The tent area has just been expanded, so the foliage is young and there is little shade. The Clearwater River runs parallel to the property just across the highway. That property is the site for occasional sighting of deer and elk, with more frequent sightings of geese, duck, and pheasants. The Aht Wy Plaza offers Clearwater River Casino (next door) and free shuttle service to the casino, as well as to Lapwai, Lewiston, and Clarkston. There are many nearby attractions, including the Nez Perce Historical Society Museum. Summers are warm during the day and cool in the evening; first snow is normally sometime in October. The park has a camp host in residence.

BASICS

Operated By: Nez Perce Tribal Enterprises. **Open:** All year. **Site Assignment:** By reservation or first come, first served. **Registration:** At camp office. **Fee:** $12–$20. **Parking:** At site.

FACILITIES

Number of RV-only Sites: 33. **Number of Tent-only Sites:** 15. **Number of Multipurpose Sites:** 8. **Hookups:** Electric (20, 30, 50 amps), water, sewer, some phone. **Each Site:** Picnic table, grill. **Dump Station:** Yes. **Laundry:** Yes. **Pay Phone:** Very Few. **Restrooms and Showers:** Yes. **Fuel:** Yes (next door). **Propane:** Yes (next door). **Internal Roads:** Gravel. **RV Service:** In Lewiston. **Market:** In Lewiston. **Restaurant:** Yes, next door. **General Store:** No. **Vending:** Yes. **Swimming:** Pool. **Playground:** No. **Activities:** Fishing, hiking, swimming, whitewater rafting, hunting, skiing, gambling. **Nearby Attractions:** Hells Canyon, The Nez Perce National Histor-

ical Park & Museum, Clearwater River Casino. **Additional Information:** Lewiston Chamber of Commerce, (208) 743-3531 or (800) 473-3543, www.lewistonchamber.org.

RESTRICTIONS

Pets: Allowed, must be on leash. **Fires:** Fire pit only. **Alcoholic Beverages:** Allowed. **Vehicle Maximum Length:** No limit.

TO GET THERE

5 mi. south of Lewiston on Hwy. 95/12.

LEWISTON   MAP, B-1
Hells Gate State Park

5100 Hells Gate Rd., 83501. T: (208) 799-5015 (office) or (208) 799-5016 (marina); www.idahoparks.org.

🚐 ★★★★   ⛺ ★★★

Beauty: ★★★   Site Privacy: ★★★
Spaciousness: ★★★★   Quiet: ★★★
Security: ★★★★   Cleanliness: ★★★★
Insect Control: ★★★★   Facilities: ★★★

Hells Gate State Park is a 960-acre facility located in the city limits of Lewiston. Hells Gate offers 96 campsites, in three circular loops. The sites are spacious and well shaded, with both pull-throughs and back-ins available. The Snake River runs along the west side of the property and also serves as the boundary line between Idaho and Washington. Many campsites have a view of the river. The campground area is not as quiet as most since Washington Hwy. 129 runs directly across the river. Hells Gate offers a full-service marina with boat fuel and marine dump. Hells Gate is the opening to the Hells Canyon National Recreation Area. At 9,393 feet, Hells Canyon is the deepest gorge in North America and surpasses even the Grand Canyon. Jet-boat tours of the canyon leave from the park's marina. Hells Gate is known for its moderate weather and has an elevation of only 733 feet. Camp rangers and camp host are available 24 hours a day, with day-use areas closing at 10 p.m. Quiet hours are strictly enforced.

BASICS

Operated By: Idaho State Parks. **Open:** All year. **Site Assignment:** By reservation; reserve sites May 1–Sept. 30.; $6 nonrefundable reservation fee. **Fee:** Hookup, $16; no hookup, $12; cabin, $35; extra vehicle fee, $5; cash, check. **Parking:** At site.

FACILITIES

Number of RV-only Sites: 93. **Number of Multipurpose Sites:** 28. **Hookups:** Electric (20, 30, 50 amps), water. **Each Site:** Picnic table, grated fire pit. **Dump Station:** Yes. **Laundry:** Yes. **Pay Phone:** Yes. **Restrooms and Showers:** Yes. **Fuel:** Boat fuel only. **Propane:** No. **Internal Roads:** Paved. **RV Service:** In Lewiston. **Market:** In Lewiston. **Restaurant:** In Lewiston. **General Store:** Yes. **Vending:** Yes. **Swimming:** No. **Playground:** Yes. **Other:** 2 amphitheaters, counsel ring, covered pavilions, Riverside conference room, marina. **Activities:** Hells Canyon jet-boat tours, fishing, boating, picnicking, interpretive programs, swimming, volleyball. **Nearby Attractions:** Nez Perce National Historical Park. **Additional Information:** www.idahoparks.org.

RESTRICTIONS

Pets: On leash only. **Fires:** Fire pit only (fires may be prohibited due to weather, ask park officials before starting any fire). **Alcoholic Beverages:** Allowed, but no kegs. **Vehicle Maximum Length:** No limit. **Other:** Max. 15 days in a 30-day period.

TO GET THERE

From Hwy. 95 take Hwy. 12 toward Walla Walla, WA. Just before the bridge going into Washington make a left on Snake River Ave. (Hwy. 505); the park is 2.5 mi. on the right.

LUCILE   MAP, B-1
Prospector's Gold RV Park and Campground

P.O. Box 313, 83542. T: (208) 628-3773.

🚐 ★★★★   ⛺ ★★★

Beauty: ★★★★   Site Privacy: ★★★★
Spaciousness: ★★★★   Quiet: ★★★★★
Security: ★★★★   Cleanliness: ★★★★★
Insect Control: ★★★★   Facilities: ★★★★★

Prospector's Gold is small in comparison to some other campgrounds we've visited, but none of the others can compete with the service here. The scenery is breath-taking and the facilities are exceptionally well kept. All of the sites are medium to large, quiet, and with ample privacy. The facilities available on site are clean and more than adequate for anyone's needs. Activities center around the outdoors and include fishing, hunting (elk and deer), and panning for gold. There is a riverfront beach and a nearby outfitter for those who want to try whitewater rafting. Just remember that reservations are required.

BASICS

Operated By: Tucker and Gay Lindsey. **Open:** All year. **Site Assignment:** By reservation. **Registration:** At camp office. **Fee:** RV, $18–$20; tent, $4 per person. **Parking:** At site.

FACILITIES

Number of Multipurpose Sites: 50. **Hookups:** Electric (30, 50 amps), water, sewer. **Each Site:** Picnic table. **Dump Station:** Yes. **Laundry:** No. **Pay Phone:** No. **Restrooms and Showers:** Yes. **Fuel:** 9 mi. south in Riggins. **Propane:** In Riggins. **Internal Roads:** Gravel, in good condition. **RV Service:** Limited service in Riggins. **Market:** In Riggins. **Restaurant:** In the area & in Riggins. **General Store:** No. **Vending:** Yes. **Swimming:** Riverfront beach. **Playground:** Yes. **Other:** Northwest Voyageurs rafting outfitters, contacts for jet-boat trip, video rental. **Activities:** Gold panning, fishing (salmon), hunting (deer & elk), horseshoes, volleyball, rafting, boating. **Nearby Attractions:** Scenic drives, Hells Canyon, Riggins, many outfitters, whitewater rafting. **Additional Information:** Riggins Chamber of Commerce, (208) 628-3778.

RESTRICTIONS

Pets: On leash only. **Fires:** No open fires. **Alcoholic Beverages:** Allowed. **Vehicle Maximum Length:** No limit.

TO GET THERE

Located at mile marker 204 on US 95.

LUCILE — MAP, B-1
Riverfront Gardens RV Park

HCO 1 Box 15, 83542. T: (208) 628-3777.

🚐 ★★★★★   ⛺ ★★★★

Beauty: ★★★★★	Site Privacy: ★★★★
Spaciousness: ★★★★	Quiet: ★★★★
Security: ★★★★	Cleanliness: ★★★★★
Insect Control: ★★★★	Facilities: ★★★★★

Riverfront Gardens RV Park is an incredible work of art. Home of Stan and Norma Moore, this spectacular property could grace the cover of *Home and Garden Magazine*. The owners and horticulture students from the university in Boise have formally landscaped the entire campground. If fact, the grounds are so elegant you might want to bring along your best linen and china for dinner on the beach. All the sites are grass, with large shade trees strategically placed for optimal shade and growth. There is a riverfront beach area with a gazebo, fully equipped with a grill. The surrounding area is high desert, with very dry summers and cool winters. The Little Salmon River is famous for its Chinook Salmon. There are many fishing and rafting outfitters in the Riggins area, and great hunting in the fall.

BASICS

Operated By: Stan and Norma Moore. **Open:** All year. **Site Assignment:** First come, first served or by reservation. **Registration:** Self-serve envelopes at the entrance. **Fee:** RV, $22; tent, $20; cash. **Parking:** Very limited.

FACILITIES

Number of RV-only Sites: 38. **Number of Tent-only Sites:** 38. **Hookups:** Electric (30 amps), water, sewer. **Each Site:** Some picnic tables. **Dump Station:** No. **Laundry:** No. **Pay Phone:** No. **Restrooms and Showers:** Yes. **Fuel:** No. **Propane:** No. **Internal Roads:** Gravel, in excellent condition. **RV Service:** 11 mi. south in Riggins. **Market:** 11 mi. south in Riggins. **Restaurant:** South to Riggins or North White Bird, there a snack shop/cafe in Lucile. **General Store:** No. **Vending:** No. **Swimming:** Riverfront beach. **Playground:** No. **Other:** Formal flower gardens, gazebo, riverfront beach, fax/copier service, wheelchair accessible. **Activities:** Fishing (steelhead fishing Sept.–Mar.; bass, sturgeon, & trout year-round), hunting (elk, deer, black bear, cougar, turkey, pheasant, chukar), whitewater rafting, jet skiing. **Nearby Attractions:** Boat launch 0.25 mi., Hells Canyon National Recreation Area, Salmon River. **Additional Information:** Salmon River Chamber of Commerce, (208) 628-3778, www.rigginsidaho.com; cfriend@ctcweb.net.

RESTRICTIONS

Pets: On leash only. **Fires:** Fire pit only. **Alcoholic Beverages:** Allowed. **Vehicle Maximum Length:** No limit.

TO GET THERE

Directly off Hwy. 95 at mile marker 210.5, 11 mi. north of Riggins.

MCCALL — MAP, C-1
Payette National Forest

800 West Lakeside Ave., P.O. Box 1026, 83638. T: (208) 634-0700; www.fs.fed.us/r4/payette.

🚐 ★★★   ⛺ ★★★★

Beauty: ★★★★★	Site Privacy: ★★★★
Spaciousness: ★★★★	Quiet: ★★★★★
Security: ★★★	Cleanliness: ★★★
Insect Control: ★★	Facilities: ★★

Rustic camping, clean air, dramatic terrain, and stunning photo opportunities give campers at Payette many things to enjoy and to brag about to their friends. Many campsites in this national forest accommodate RVs, and all sites are tent-friendly. Most sites have a paved parking spot, but facilities run from primitive to basic—and we do mean basic. Surrounded by two deep river canyons, this remote area varies in altitude and climate. It ranges from hot desert grasslands to conifer forests to snow-capped peaks. Here you can enjoy cross-country skiing, hiking, rock climbing, hunting, fishing, and lots of outdoor recreation. Plan ahead, bring a good camera, and expect to find quiet, privacy, and beauty that has become legendary.

BASICS

Operated By: U.S. Forest Service. **Open:** Most areas available May–Sept. **Site Assignment:** Several are by reservation, (877) 444-6777 or www.recreation.gov; reservable 240 days in advance, or self-serve. **Registration:** At registration kiosk or camp host's trailer. **Fee:** Standard & serviced, $16; cabin, $35. **Parking:** At site.

FACILITIES

Number of Multipurpose Sites: There 22 campgrounds in the Payette National Forest, 6–32 sites each. **Hookups:** 20, 30, 50 amps. **Each Site:** Level parking spurs (most are paved), picnic table, grated fire pit. **Dump Station:** Dumps are located throughout the forest. **Laundry:** In the small communities scattered throughout the forest but not at the individual campgrounds. **Pay Phone:** No. **Restrooms and Showers:** Restrooms mostly w/ vaulted toilets; no showers. **Fuel:** The Payette National Forest is a very large area w/ very few places to fuel, even fewer w/ diesel. **Propane:** Inquire at campground. **Internal Roads:** Most are paved. **RV Service:** McCall. **Market:** Groceries in almost every small community w/in the forest. **Restaurant:** Very few, mostly cafe/grills & pizza. **General Store:** Nature Store. **Vending:** No. **Swimming:** No, but many areas on the rivers & lakes open to public for swimming; natural hot springs. (Use caution: many hot springs are too hot for swimming & will cause second- & third-degree burns.) **Playground:** No. **Other:** Horse camps (1 commercial horse camp in Idaho City), Boise River, Payette River. **Activities:** Hiking, mountain biking (6 trailheads), fishing, skiing, horseback riding (27 trailheads), backpacking, mountaineering, motorized-bike trailheads, cross-country skiing. **Nearby Attractions:** Arrowrock Reservoir, Anderson Ranch Reservoir, Idaho Historical Museum, Boise Zoo, Ponderosa State Park. **Additional Information:** McCall

Recreation Report, (208) 634-0409; Idaho Fish & Game, (208) 634-8137; McCall Area Chamber of Commerce, (208) 634-7631; Weiser Area Chamber of Commerce, (208) 549-0452.

RESTRICTIONS

Pets: On leash only. **Fires:** Fire ring only (the forest may prohibit open fires due to weather conditions; always check w/ a ranger or camp host before starting any fires). **Alcoholic Beverages:** Allowed. **Vehicle Maximum Length:** Sites vary in size; the campgrounds on the national reservation service are better equipped to handle larger RVs. **Other:** 14-day stay limit.

TO GET THERE

From McCall, travel north to the Hwy. 55 junction with Hwy. 95, where the fifth ranger district office is located (in the city of New Meadows). The New Meadows Ranger District lands are bisected by Hwy. 95 as it heads north to Riggins, ID. Follow signs to the national forest.

MCCALL — MAP, C-1
Ponderosa State Park

P.O. Box 89, 83638. T: (208) 634-2164; www.idahoparks.org.

🚐 ★★★   ⛺ ★★★

Beauty: ★★★	Site Privacy: ★★★
Spaciousness: ★★	Quiet: ★★★
Security: ★★★★	Cleanliness: ★★★
Insect Control: ★★★	Facilities: ★★★

Ponderosa State Park, named for the 150-foot-tall ponderosa pines that inhabit the diverse 1,400-acre area, is known as one of Idaho's favorite recreational spots. It is a sanctuary for wildlife and a nesting ground for the osprey and the bald eagle. The park is on a large peninsula in the Payette Lake, with a public beach on its north end. The campground is the center of activity, with sites both primitive and developed. It is shaded by evergreens, and the ground is level. Sites are fairly close together, and the park reaches full capacity during the summer months. Most sites are laid out in three loops, paved, and offer electricity. The park offers a large variety of activities for patrons of all ages, including paved walking paths, scheduled activities, and an education center. The weather is cool in the spring and fall, with dry, warm summers. The park is fully staffed around the clock. A camp host and rangers are always available to assist.

BASICS

Operated By: Idaho Dept. of Parks and Recreation. **Open:** State park, all year; campgrounds, Memorial Day weekend—the first snow (after Labor Day). **Site Assignment:** Reservations recommended; $6 non-refundable fee to be paid 5 days prior to arrival. **Registration:** At visitor center. **Fee:** Electric/water, $16; water, $12; plus reservation fee. **Parking:** At site.

FACILITIES

Number of Multipurpose Sites: 137. **Hookups:** Electric (20, 30 amps), water. **Each Site:** Picnic table, grated fire pit. **Dump Station:** Yes. **Laundry:** No. **Pay Phone:** Yes. **Restrooms and Showers:** Yes.

Fuel: No. **Propane:** No. **Internal Roads:** Paved. **RV Service:** In McCall. **Market:** In McCall. **Restaurant:** In McCall. **General Store:** No. **Vending:** Yes. **Swimming:** Lake (no lifeguard). **Playground:** Yes. **Other:** 2 yurts (a circular, Mongolian-style domed tent 20 ft. in diameter w/ a plywood floor, insulated & heated in the winter, sleeps 4–6 people), group picnic shelters, boat ramp, lakefront swimming. **Activities:** Fishing, hiking, biking, boating, horseshoes, volleyball, cross-country skiing, golf, interpretive programs, guided nature walks, hard-path trail, youth programs for children 6–12. **Nearby Attractions:** Culture Center Museum, Meadow Creek natural hot springs, Brundage Mountain Ski Resort, scenic chairlifts, outdoor concerts, Cascade Reservoir, Payette Lake. **Additional Information:** McCall Chamber of Commerce & Visitor Bureau, (208) 634-7631 or (800) 260-5130, www. mccall-idchamber.org.

RESTRICTIONS

Pets: On 6-ft. leash only. **Fires:** Fire pit only (fires may be prohibited due to weather; ask park officials before starting any fire). **Alcoholic Beverages:** Allowed. **Vehicle Maximum Length:** Some spaces are up to 80 ft. **Other:** Max. 8 people per site, 14-day stay limit; group camps available.

TO GET THERE

Located 108 mi. north of Boise on Hwy. 55, you will need to follow signs once in McCall.

MOUNTAIN HOME   MAP, D-1
Bruneau Dunes State Park

27068 Sand Dune Rd., 83647. T: (208) 366-7919; www.idahoparks.org.

🚐 ★★★★   ▲ ★★★

Beauty: ★★★	Site Privacy: ★★★
Spaciousness: ★★★	Quiet: ★★★★
Security: ★★★★	Cleanliness: ★★★★
Insect Control: ★★★★	Facilities: ★★★

Bruneau Dunes State Park is home to the largest single sand dune in North America, with a peak 470 feet above the lake surface. Located in the high desert, Bruneau Dunes receives less than 10 inches of rain a year and has temperatures that range from over 100° in summer to well below 0° in winter. The park offers a unique feature, an observatory, as well as fascinating geological formations. There are two camping areas with electricity and water, both circular. The older campsite offers better shade and some covered picnic tables, while the newer area offers larger pull-through sites and 50-amp hookups. However, the trees have not had time to mature. Primitive campsites are set near the park's horse corral for campers who wish to use the park's equestrian trails. There are day-use areas in the park as well as great bluegill and large-mouth bass fishing in the lakes. The Natural Science Center and Observatory offers interpretive programs by reservation.

BASICS

Operated By: Idaho State Parks. **Open:** All year. **Site Assignment:** Upon registration. **Registration:** At visitor center. **Fee:** Hookup, $16; no hookup, $12; cabin, $35; $4 per vehicle per night; cash, check. **Parking:** At site.

FACILITIES

Number of RV-only Sites: 98. **Number of Tent-only Sites:** 16. **Hookups:** Electric (30, 50 amps), water. **Each Site:** Picnic table, grill or grated fire pit. **Dump Station:** Yes. **Laundry:** No. **Pay Phone:** Yes. **Restrooms and Showers:** Yes. **Fuel:** No. **Propane:** No. **Internal Roads:** Paved. **RV Service:** In Mountain Home. **Market:** In Mountain Home. **Restaurant:** In Mountain Home. **General Store:** No. **Vending:** No. **Swimming:** No. **Playground:** Yes. **Other:** Horse corral, picnic area, Bruneau Dunes State Park Astronomical Complex & Natural Science Center, interpretive services, nonmotorized boat dock. **Activities:** Hiking, fishing, equestrian trails, picnicking, volleyball area, sky watching. **Nearby Attractions:** 1 hour from Boise. **Additional Information:** Idaho Dept. of Parks & Recreation, (208) 334-4199.

RESTRICTIONS

Pets: On leash only. **Fires:** Fire pit only. **Alcoholic Beverages:** Allowed. **Vehicle Maximum Length:** No limit. **Other:** 14-day stay limit.

TO GET THERE

From I-84 take Exit 90, bear right onto US 30 (Sunset Strip), south on SR 51, left (east) on SR 78; go about 3.4 mi. and turn right into park.

NORTH FORK   MAP, C-2
Rivers Fork Inn

P.O Box 68, 83466. T: (208) 865-2301; www.riversforkinn.com.

🚐 ★★★★★   ▲ n/a

Beauty: ★★★★★	Site Privacy: ★★★★
Spaciousness: ★★★★	Quiet: ★★★★★
Security: ★★★★	Cleanliness: ★★★★★
Insect Control: ★★★	Facilities: ★★★★★

Twenty-five miles south of the Montana–Idaho line, the small Rivers Fork Inn is in the Salmon National Forest. This quaint eight-site campground is hands down Idaho's most naturally beautiful full-hookup campground. Its eight sites are in a row and lined up just yards from the bank of the Salmon River. From the veranda of the inn's log lodge, guests can view the North Fork River merge with the Salmon River and view the Salmon National Forest's mountains. Both rivers are famous for their fishing, and there are several fishing, hunting, and rafting outfitters in the area. The Joseph Pass Ski Resort is only a few miles north and has wonderful winter snow skiing. The small hotel at this campground is resort quality. The owners are quite affable people, maintain the property meticulously, and live there year-round.

BASICS

Operated By: Ken and Elaine Wilcox. **Open:** All year. **Site Assignment:** By reservation or walk-in. **Registration:** At lodge. **Fee:** $24. **Parking:** At site.

FACILITIES

Number of RV-only Sites: 8. **Hookups:** Electric (30, 50 amps), water, sewer. **Each Site:** Some sites have tables. **Dump Station:** No. **Laundry:** No. **Pay Phone:** Yes. **Restrooms and Showers:** No; campground was build for self-contained RVs, there

are restrooms in the lodge. **Fuel:** In North Fork about 3 mi. **Propane:** In North Fork about 3 mi. **Internal Roads:** Gravel, in good condition. **RV Service:** Limited local service. **Market:** In town. **Restaurant:** In North Fork. **General Store:** No. **Vending:** Yes. **Swimming:** No. **Playground:** No. **Other:** Large lodge, 8-room motel, all sites sit on the river. **Activities:** Mountain biking, hiking, fishing (property is on the Salmon River & backs up to the Salmon National Forest). **Nearby Attractions:** Whitewater rafting, fishing tours, float trips, skiing both cross-country & downhill (10 mi. to the ski resorts). There are several outfitters in the area. **Additional Information:** Salmon Valley Chamber of Commerce, (208) 756-2100.

RESTRICTIONS

Pets: On leash only. **Fires:** No open fires. **Alcoholic Beverages:** Allowed. **Vehicle Maximum Length:** 45 ft.

TO GET THERE

Located at mile marker 326 on US 93 North in North Fork, Idaho.

OROFINO   MAP, B-1
Dworshak State Park

P.O. Box 2028, 83544. T: (208) 476-5994 or (866) 634-3246; www.idahoparks.org.

🚐 ★★★   ▲ ★★★★

Beauty: ★★★★	Site Privacy: ★★★
Spaciousness: ★★★	Quiet: ★★★★
Security: ★★★	Cleanliness: ★★★
Insect Control: ★★★	Facilities: ★★

Located on the west side of the Dworshak Reservoir, Dworshak State Parks offers a spectacular secluded setting of pine forest and open meadows. This 105-campsite park is seated alongside the Dworshak Reservoir with many walk-in tent sites right on the bank. The Dworshak Dam is the largest straight-axis dam in North America and its reservoir has 54 miles of tree-lined shore. The campground consists of three circular loops offering both shaded and open sites. The elevation of the park is 1,600 feet, translating into warm summer days and cool nights. Most sites are spacious and private, providing both pull-through and back-in sites. Dworshak State Park offers trophy fishing, miles of hiking trails, and a full-service group camp. The park also offers weekend interpretive programs throughout the spring and summer in a large outdoor amphitheater. Park rangers and camp host are on duty 24 hours a day to assist.

BASICS

Operated By: Idaho Dept. of Parks and Recreation. **Open:** All year; electric/water Apr.–Oct. **Site Assignment:** Some sites are reservable; $6 nonrefundable fee. **Registration:** At entrance gate or see camp hosts. **Fee:** Standard, $12; serviced, $16; cabins, $35. **Parking:** At site.

FACILITIES

Number of RV-only Sites: 45. **Number of Tent-only Sites:** 20. **Number of Multipurpose Sites:** 40. **Hookups:** Electric (20, 30 amps), water. **Each Site:** Picnic table, fire pit. **Dump Station:** Yes. **Laundry:** No. **Pay Phone:** Yes. **Restrooms and**

Showers: Yes. Fuel: No. Propane: No. Internal Roads: The main roads are paved, some of the campground loops are gravel. RV Service: 25 mi. south in Orofino. Market: 25 mi. south in Orofino. Restaurant: 25 mi. south in Orofino. General Store: No. Vending: No. Swimming: Reservoir. Playground: Yes. Other: Marina, boat launch, boat parking, floating boat dump (shared w/ the U.S. Army Corps of Engineers), group picnic shelter, dry storage, Three Meadows Group Area w/ cabins, lodge, & kitchen facilities. Activities: Fishing (kokanee salmon, smallmouth bass, rainbow trout), weekend interpretive programs, hiking, swimming, boating, waterskiing, jet skiing. Nearby Attractions: Hunting (no hunting on state park property), Dent Acres Recreational Area, Dworshak National Steelhead Fish Hatchery, Clearwater County Museum, Lewis & Clark National Historic Trail. Additional Information: Idaho Dept. of Parks & Recreation, (208) 334-4199; Orofino Chamber of Commerce, (208) 476-4335, www.orofino.com.

RESTRICTIONS

Pets: On 6-ft. leash only. Fires: Fire pit only (fires may be prohibited due to weather; ask park official before starting any fire). Alcoholic Beverages: Allowed. Vehicle Maximum Length: 50 ft. Other: Max. 8 people per site; 14-day stay limit; group camps available; $4 extra-vehicle fee per night.

TO GET THERE

Take Hwy. 12, 40 mi. east of Lewiston into Orofino. Stop at the visitor center or ranger station in Orofino, they will give you a map of the Dworshak reservoir and direct you to the park. The park is 26 mi. north of Orofino on the west side of the reservoir; the road is paved but narrow and curvy.

OSBURN   MAP, A-1
Blue Anchor RV Park

300 W Mullan Ave., P.O. Box 645, 83849.
T: (208) 752-3443 or (877) 590-7275;
www.blueanchorrv.mustbehere.com.

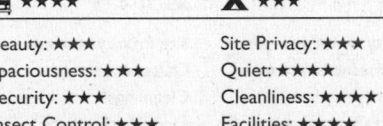

Beauty: ★★★	Site Privacy: ★★★
Spaciousness: ★★★	Quiet: ★★★
Security: ★★★	Cleanliness: ★★★
Insect Control: ★★★	Facilities: ★★★

Tucked into the hills of Northern Idaho, Blue Anchor RV Park is great for a cozy hideaway. The campground is abundant in evergreens providing shade and gorgeous scenery. The spring and summer months are the best time to visit because of the stunning foliage and warmer temperatures. The 15 pull-through RV sites are grassy and average in size compared to others in the area. Just off Exit 57 of I-90, this campground is easily accessible. Surprisingly, there is a range of attractions broad enough to appeal to all age groups in the nearby small town of Osburn.

BASICS

Operated By: Jim. Open: Fall, spring, and summer. Site Assignment: Reservations recommended. Registration: At general store. Fee: $22–$25. Parking: At site.

FACILITIES

Number of RV-only Sites: 60. Number of Tent-only Sites: 10. Hookups: Electric (30, 50 amps), water, sewer, phone, modem, cable TV. Each Site: Picnic table. Dump Station: Yes. Laundry: Yes. Pay Phone: Yes. Restrooms and Showers: Yes. Fuel: 0.25 mi. by I-90. Propane: 0.25 mi. by I-90. Internal Roads: Paved. RV Service: Limited service in Pinehurst, 15 mi. Market: In Osburn. Restaurant: In Osburn. General Store: No. Vending: Yes. Swimming: No. Playground: Yes. Other: Data port, river access. Activities: Volleyball, skiing, hiking nature trails, fishing, basketball, recreation area. Nearby Attractions: Wallace Melodrama Theatre, mining town tours & museums, Silver Mt. Ski Resort, many outfitters, ATV festival, Coeur d'Alene Bike Trail, Hiawatha Bike Trail, Cataldo Mission, Huckleberry Festival. Additional Information: Idaho Tourism, (800) 635-7820.

RESTRICTIONS

Pets: On leash only. Fires: Not allowed. Alcoholic Beverages: Allowed. Vehicle Maximum Length: 100 ft. Other: Discounts for Good Sam & AAA members.

TO GET THERE

Exit 57 off I-90; follow signs.

PINEHURST   MAP, A-1
Kellogg/Silver Valley KOA

801 North Division, 83850. T: (208) 682-3612 or (800) 562-0799; www.koa.com.

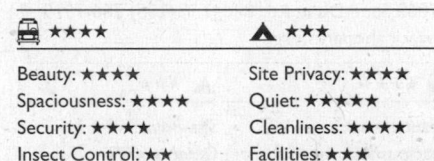

Beauty: ★★★	Site Privacy: ★★★
Spaciousness: ★★★	Quiet: ★★★★
Security: ★★★	Cleanliness: ★★★★
Insect Control: ★★★	Facilities: ★★★★

The Kellogg/Silver Valley KOA is only a few miles from the historic Silver Valley and directly off I-90. This well-manicured campground offers a full array of services, from cable TV and Internet access to fishing and miniature golf. A small stocked stream runs through the campground, adding ambiance. The campground is a completely gated community and patrons must have a code to enter the camping area. Campsites are moderate in size, with gravel parking spurs. The farther back you go into the campground area, the smaller and closer together its sites get. There are 22 pull-through sites, with limited room for extra-large big rigs. The area around the campground is full of silver-mining history and has wonderful fishing and hiking and several museums. Summer days are warm and almost always windy.

BASICS

Operated By: Kent and Kathy Edlund. Open: Apr. 15–Oct. 15. Site Assignment: By reservations w/ credit card. Registration: At camp store. Fee: RV, $22–$34; tent, $15–$28 per 2 people; each additional person, $3; children under 5 stay free. Parking: At site.

FACILITIES

Number of Multipurpose Sites: 57. Hookups: Electric (30, 50 amps), water, sewer, cable TV, phone, modem data port. Each Site: Picnic table, grated fire pit. Dump Station: Yes. Laundry: Yes. Pay Phone: Yes. Restrooms and Showers: Yes. Fuel: Next door. Propane: Next door. Internal Roads: Gravel, in good condition, some paved. RV Service: Inquire at campground. Market: In Pinehurst. Restaurant: In town. General Store: Yes. Vending: Yes. Swimming: Heated pool, hot tub. Playground: Yes. Other: 6 cabins, 1 pond-front cottage, paddleboat dock, day-use area. Activities: Fishing, games, bikes, nature walks, fun cycles, paddleboats, croquet, golf. Nearby Attractions: Coeur d'Alene National Forest, Wallace, Idaho–Silver Capital of the World, Silverwood Theme Park, Idaho Panhandles, mountain-bike trails, Silver Mountain. Additional Information: Kellogg Chamber of Commerce, (208) 784-0821.

RESTRICTIONS

Pets: On leash only. Not permitted in the swimming-pool area. Fires: Fire pit only. Alcoholic Beverages: Allowed. Vehicle Maximum Length: 70 ft. w/ tow. Other: Special holiday rates, KOA discount.

TO GET THERE

60 mi. east of Spokane, 30 mi. east of Coeur d'Alene, get on I-90, take Exit 45.

PLUMMER   MAP, A-1
Heyburn State Park

1291 Chatcolet Rd., 83851. T: (208) 686-1308 or (866) 634-3246; www.idahoparks.org/parks/heyburn.html.

Beauty: ★★★★	Site Privacy: ★★★★
Spaciousness: ★★★★	Quiet: ★★★★★
Security: ★★★★	Cleanliness: ★★★★
Insect Control: ★★	Facilities: ★★★

Heyburn State Park was created from the Coeur d'Alene Indian Reservation by an act of Congress on April 28, 1908. It is the oldest State Park in the Pacific Northwest. The lakes provide an abundance of fish, the marsh areas are filled with waterfowl, and the heavily timbered slopes and open meadows are ideal for deer, bears, and upland birds. Bird-watching is terrific at Heyburn, with osprey and blue heron as common as sparrows elsewhere. Trails for hikers or horseback riders are shaded by 400-year-old ponderosa pines. Heyburn has three campgrounds with sites that range from full hookup to primitive camping. The sites provide the ultimate get away, as they are quiet, spacious, and clean. The campgrounds are open year-round and sites are available on a first-come, first-serve basis.

BASICS

Operated By: Idaho Dept. of Parks and Recreation. Open: All year. Site Assignment: First come, first served. Registration: At registration kiosk or entrance gate. Fee: Standard, $12; serviced, $16; cabins, $35. Parking: At site.

FACILITIES

Number of Multipurpose Sites: 55. Hookups: Electric (30 amps), water, sewer. Each Site: Level parking spurs, picnic table, grated fire pit. Dump Station: Yes. Laundry: No. Pay Phone: Yes.

Restrooms and Showers: Yes. **Fuel:** In the Rocky Point Day-Use Area. **Propane:** In town. **Internal Roads:** Most are paved. **RV Service:** St. Maries. **Market:** 5 mi. east in Plummer. **Restaurant:** Plummer or St. Maries. **General Store:** Marina Store. **Vending:** No. **Swimming:** Lakefront beach. **Playground:** No. **Other:** Boat launch, boat rentals, interpretive center, public docks, amphitheater, boat moorage, boat sewage station, cabins, group shelters. **Activities:** Hiking, boating, fishing, swimming, interpretive programming, audio scenic drives (pick tapes up at local ranger station), biking, beaches, cruiseboat adventures. **Nearby Attractions:** Garnet digging, St. Joe's river, rafting & fishing outfitters. **Additional Information:** St. Maries Chamber of Commerce, (208) 245-3563.

RESTRICTIONS

Pets: On leash, not allowed on waterfront. **Fires:** Fire ring only (the forest service may prohibit open fires due to weather conditions, check w/ a ranger or camp host before starting any fires). **Alcoholic Beverages:** Allowed. **Vehicle Maximum Length:** 45 ft. **Other:** $4 per vehicle.

TO GET THERE

From Hwy. 95, campground is 5 mi. east of Plummer.

WHITE BIRD   MAP, B-1
Swiftwater RV Park and Store

HC 01 Box 24, 83554. T: (208) 839-2700 or (888) 291-5065.

🚐 ★★★★   ⛺ ★★★

Beauty: ★★★★★	Site Privacy: ★★★★
Spaciousness: ★★★	Quiet: ★★★★
Security: ★★★★	Cleanliness: ★★★★★
Insect Control: ★★★★	Facilities: ★★★★

Swiftwater RV Park and Store is located in the Salmon River Valley, 8 miles south of Grangeville. This quiet park has beautifully landscaped level sites, with 8 pull-throughs and 19 back-ins. Situated in an open meadow on the banks of the Salmon River, the park has an attractive gazebo, with fire pit and grill, overlooking the riverfront beach. The town of White Bird is located on the Lewis and Clark Trail. In 1805 Meriwether Lewis became the first white man to visit the Salmon River Valley. Swiftwater RV Park is surrounded by sites with great recreational appeal or historic interest. The area is home to many species of wildlife and offers trophy fishing and hunting. The weather is dry in this high-desert area. Summer days can be very warm, and summer evenings very cool. The owners live on the property.

BASICS

Operated By: Mark and Jamie Mortenson. **Open:** All year. **Site Assignment:** Reservations recommended. **Registration:** At general store, located on the second floor. **Fee:** $15–$30; each additional person, $3. **Parking:** At site.

FACILITIES

Number of Tent-only Sites: Undesignated sites. **Hookups:** Electric (30, 50 amps), water, sewer, satellite TV, phone, Internet. **Each Site:** Some picnic tables. **Dump Station:** Yes. **Laundry:** Yes. **Pay Phone:** Yes. **Restrooms and Showers:** Yes. **Fuel:** No. **Propane:** Yes. **Internal Roads:** Gravel. **RV Service:** 8 mi. north in Grangeville. **Market:** No. **Restaurant:** 1 mi. north. **General Store:** Yes. **Vending:** Yes. **Swimming:** River. **Playground:** No. **Other:** TV room, gazebo w/ gas grill, central fire pit, Salmon River beachfront, well-stocked grocery store available. **Activities:** Fishing (chinook salmon, sockeye, rainbow trout, & perch), hiking, hunting, backpacking. **Nearby Attractions:** Rafting, skiing, snowmobiling, Hells Canyon, Jet boating, kayaking, canoeing, guided hunting & fishing expeditions. **Additional Information:** www.swiftwaterrvpark.com.

RESTRICTIONS

Pets: Allowed. **Fires:** Fire pits and grills only. **Alcoholic Beverages:** Allowed. **Vehicle Maximum Length:** 55 ft.

TO GET THERE

From mile marker 222 on Hwy. 95 at White Bird take Hammer Creek turnoff; campground is 0.5 mi. on the left.

WINCHESTER   MAP, B-1
Winchester Lake State Park

P.O. Box 186, 83555. T: (208) 924-7563 or (866) 634-3246; www.idahoparks.org/parks/winchester.html.

🚐 ★★★★   ⛺ ★★★

Beauty: ★★★★	Site Privacy: ★★★
Spaciousness: ★★★	Quiet: ★★★
Security: ★★★★	Cleanliness: ★★★★
Insect Control: ★★★★	Facilities: ★★★★

Located in the Nez Perce Indian Reservation, Winchester Lake State Park is a beautiful 418-acre park on a 103-acre lake at the foot of the Craig Mountains. The park offers modern camping facilities and yurt rentals. The campsites are configured in three loops on the west side of the lake. Campsites are both back-in and pull-through, with sites in loop A on the lake shaded by Douglas firs and ponderosa pines. The park offers boating, fishing (rainbow trout), hiking trails, and biking trails in the summer; cross-country skiing, ice skating, and ice fishing in the winter. In addition, the park conducts educational programs and guided walks. Many different types of wildlife inhabit the park. Park staff, along with seasonal volunteer hosts, are available to assist.

BASICS

Operated By: Idaho Dept. of Parks & Recreation. **Open:** All year. **Site Assignment:** Reserve May 1–Oct. 1. **Registration:** At park office or self-registration box at entrance gate. **Fee:** Serviced, $26; hookup, $16; no hookup, $12. **Parking:** Yes, but there is an extra vehicle fee of $4.

FACILITIES

Number of RV-only Sites: 50. **Number of Tent-only Sites:** 23. **Hookups:** Electric, water. **Each Site:** Picnic table, grated fire pit. **Dump Station:** Yes. **Laundry:** No. **Pay Phone:** Yes. **Restrooms and Showers:** Yes. **Fuel:** No. **Propane:** No. **Internal Roads:** Paved. **RV Service:** No. **Market:** In Winchester. **Restaurant:** In Winchester. **General Store:** No. **Vending:** No. **Swimming:** No. **Playground:** Yes. **Other:** 4 yurts, lake side picnic area, nonmotorized boat ramp, amphitheater. **Activities:** Fishing, picnicking, boating, hiking, wildlife viewing, winter skiing, ice skating, and ice fishing. **Nearby Attractions:** Inquire at campground. **Additional Information:** Idaho Dept. of Parks & Recreation, (208) 334-4199.

RESTRICTIONS

Pets: On leash only; dogs are not allowed on waterfront or day-use area of the park. **Fires:** Fire pits or grills only. **Alcoholic Beverages:** At sites only. **Vehicle Maximum Length:** 60 ft. **Other:** 15-day stay limit in a 30-day period; small boats allowed, gasoline engine–powered boats not permitted.

TO GET THERE

From US 95 head right on US 95 business, then right on Camas St.; follow signs to park.

Illinois

The "Land of Lincoln" has a welcome blend of history and outdoor activities, along with much more to keep anyone happy. Bordered on almost all sides by water, Illinois is awash with water sports as well as crammed full of timelessness, the unusual fare of uniquely American backroad peculiarities, and Midwestern hospitality. The 21st state's name is derived from the word *Illini,* which represents a confederation of the Cahokia, Kaskaskia, Michigamea, Moingwena, Peoria, and Tamaroa Indian tribes.

Illinois is divided into six distinct regions, each of which plays a role in the geographical diversity and multifaceted splendor of the Prairie State.

The western region and its cultural amenities are most thoroughly accessed by Great River Road, which traverses the entire 550-mile stretch of the western border of Illinois. Along this route are the **Joseph Smith Historic Center** in Nauvoo, wine-making country, and **Galesburg,** home to poet Carl Sandburg, whose ashes are scattered by his request under the town's **Remembrance Rock.** Every year since 1953, the hog capital of the world, **Kewanee,** has hosted its annual pork festival, including the world's largest pork-chop barbecue. While here, head over to the Union Federal Savings and Loan to see if otters still reside inside the bank.

The southwest region is home to **Cahokia Mounds,** the country's only prehistoric Native American heritage city in Collinsville, which is also home to the world's largest bottle of catsup. Belleville's **National Shrine of Our Lady of the Snows** is the country's largest outdoor shrine.

Traveling counterclockwise takes you to the southern region, where the magnificent **Garden of the Gods** in **Shawnee National Forest** will leave you breathless. The Ohio and Mississippi Rivers meet in Cairo, where **Horseshoe Lake** and **Union County Wildlife Refuge** attract one of the nation's largest gatherings of geese each winter. Rend Lake, which is 19,000 acres, also antes up the full spectrum of outdoor recreation.

Middle Fork River, in the central region, is Illinois's only designated scenic waterway and home to several lake-studded state parks. In Springfield, the **Lincoln Home National Historic Site** provides ample invitation into the life of Honest Abe. Here you can also see the 30-foot statue named **"The Rail Splitter"** of a clean-shaven young Lincoln wielding his ax. Although the town of **Metropolis** serves as a shrine to **Superman,** the concurrent resident **Big John** grocery clerk statue makes even the largest Man of Steel monument look a toddler in comparison. See how the Amish introduced their simple and modest way of life in **Arcola,** where you can visit the town's interpretive center. The twin cities of Champaign/Urbana, separated by a single street, share the **University of Illinois** and the **John Philip Sousa Library and Museum.** Not far away lies the nation's first highway, **National Road.**

The Chicagoland region is a small but culturally saturated plop of land fronting Lake Michigan where you can shop to your heart's content or stuff yourself with a panoramic vista of four states in the 1000-foot-high **John Hancock Observatory.** Nearby Berwyn houses the sculptural oddity made up of eight cars impaled on a 40-foot spike, otherwise known as **"The Spindle,"** by Dustin Shuler. Oak Park showcases the **Frank Lloyd Wright Home and Studio,** where the architect's love for the prairie is evident in his creations. The **Field Museum** is home to Sue, the largest and most complete T. rex fossil ever found. But if it's burgers you have on your mind, feel free to call ahead and make an appointment to tour the museum of the first **McDonald's,** located in Des Plaines.

Full circle, the northern region hosts seasonally transformed waterfalls, horseback riding, and sweeping canyons at **Starved Rock State Park** in Utica. More outdoor activities abound and historic sites come alive along the many miles of the **I&M Canal State Trail.** Once the largest Mississippi River port north of St. Louis, Galena has a vibrant downtown and some of the finest period architecture in the Midwest. "Dedicated to all farmers and ag-related business folks who have lived through the Agricultural Crash of the 1980s" is the **Agricultural Crash Monument,** an actual airplane sticking out of the ground in La Salle. Not far from there is a group of stone markers, the Norwegian Settlers State Memorial, commemorating those who fled their native land in search of religious autonomy.

Campground Profiles

AMBOY
Green River Oaks Camping Resort
MAP, A-2

1442 Sleepy Hollow Rd., 61310.
T: (815) 857-2815; www.greenriveroaks.com.

🚐 ★★★★　　　　▲ ★★★★

Beauty: ★★★★	Site Privacy: ★★★★
Spaciousness: ★★★★	Quiet: ★★★★
Security: ★★★★	Cleanliness: ★★★★
Insect Control: ★★	Facilities: ★★★★

A river runs through Green River Oaks, located 3 miles southwest of Amboy. Two creeks also meander through the campground, and giant oaks and pines help account for its beauty and its name. Two heated pools are an unusual plus, but swimming is not allowed in Arrow Lake. A schedule of events is always posted so campers can know what's going on. Arranged in a series of loops, the campground offers mostly grassy sites with an average site width of 35 feet. All sites are back-in and most are shady. More than half the sites are occupied by seasonal residents. Seasonal sites are clumped together in sections—one sizable group by each pool. The remaining RV sites are in rows by themselves. Tent sites are in a separate area with privacy and more grassy and shady surroundings.

BASICS
Operated By: The Ciaccios. **Open:** Early May–mid-Oct. **Site Assignment:** Reservations required w/ 1-night deposit; refunds w/ 7-day notice plus $5 fee. **Registration:** At campground office. **Fee:** $40; cash, check, credit card. **Parking:** At site.

FACILITIES
Number of Tent-only Sites: 10. **Number of Multipurpose Sites:** 225. **Hookups:** Electric (30 amps), water, sewer. **Each Site:** Picnic table. **Dump Station:** Yes. **Laundry:** Yes. **Pay Phone:** Yes. **Restrooms and Showers:** Yes. **Fuel:** No. **Propane:** Yes. **Internal Roads:** Paved, in good condition. **RV Service:** No. **Market:** 3 mi. southwest in Amboy. **Restaurant:** 3 mi. southwest in Amboy. **General Store:** Yes. **Vending:** No. **Swimming:** 2 pools. **Playground:** Yes. **Other:** Sports court, tennis courts, 18-hole mini-golf, softball field, shuffleboard, horseshoes, fishing lake, family center. **Activities:** Swimming, fishing, lumberjack breakfasts on weekends (Memorial Day through Labor Day), planned weekend activities. **Nearby Attractions:** Flea markets, Amboy Depot Museum, wood carvings at Amboy City Park East, scenic drive, bike trail. **Additional Information:** Blackhawk Waterways CVB, (800) 678-2108.

RESTRICTIONS
Pets: On leash only, must be quiet, cleaned up after. **Fires:** Fire pit only or in designated areas. **Alcoholic Beverages:** Allowed. **Vehicle Maximum Length:** 38 ft. **Other:** 3-night min. on holidays, w/ all 3 nights paid at least 1 month in advance.

TO GET THERE
From I-88 take the Sugar Grove Hwy. 30 West Exit. Go to Hwy. 52, turn south to Main St. in downtown Amboy. Turn west and go to the west end of town. Take Rockyford Rd. to the left, go 3 mi. to Sleepy Hollow Rd., and turn right into Green River Oaks. Sleepy Hollow Rd. has poor shoulders.

AMBOY
O'Connell's Yogi Bear Jellystone Park Camp-Resort
MAP, A-2

reserve america

970 Green Wing Rd., P.O. Box 200, 61310.
T: (815) 857-3860; www.jellystoneamboy.com.

🚐 ★★★★　　　　▲ ★★★★

Beauty: ★★★★	Site Privacy: ★★★★
Spaciousness: ★★★★	Quiet: ★★★★
Security: ★★★★★	Cleanliness: ★★★★
Insect Control: ★★	Facilities: ★★★★

O'Connell's Yogi Bear Jellystone Park Camp-Resort is a destination. Folks come to visit because they know they can count on a clean, secure campground with enough recreation and programs to wear anyone out. Campers are escorted to their sites when they arrive or can opt for express check-in on Fridays for reservations paid in full in advance. A rolling, grassy campground with shaded and open sites, O'Connell's is a rural facility, 5 miles east of Amboy, laid out in a series of loops. The typical site width for the 275 pull-throughs is 40 feet. Tent sites are away from RVs and offer more shade and privacy. Because the campground is so large, it features multiple facilities, such as three outdoor pools, three spas, three kiddie pools, three Laundromats, and five large restroom/shower combinations. Laundromats and showers are open 24 hours a day. Security is tops owing to a locked entrance gate with gate codes and regular patrols of the area. To ensure safety and quiet, the enforced speed limit is 7 mph, quiet hours are from 11 p.m. to 7 a.m., no bicycle riding is permitted after dusk, and visitor check-out time is 11 p.m.

BASICS
Operated By: Manufactured Homes Corp. (MHC). **Open:** Mid Apr.–mid Oct. **Site Assignment:** Reservations w/ 1-night deposit; refund (minus $10) or a certificate of credit for full amount of deposit w/ 14-day notice; holiday weekends require pre-pay 1 month in advance and a 3-night minimum; 2-night minimum for weekends; V, MC, D, checks accepted. **Registration:** At campground office. **Fee:** Midweek: full hookup, $41; no hookup, $37; Weekends and holidays: full hookup, $51; no hookup, $47. **Parking:** At site.

FACILITIES
Number of RV-only Sites: 635. **Number of Tent-only Sites:** 250. **Hookups:** Electric (30, 50 amps), water, sewer. **Each Site:** Picnic table. **Dump Station:** Yes. **Laundry:** Yes. **Pay Phone:** Yes. **Restrooms and Showers:** Yes. **Fuel:** No. **Propane:** Yes. **Internal Roads:** Gravel, in good condition. **RV Service:** Yes. **Market:** 5 mi. west in Amboy. **Restaurant:** 5 mi. west in Amboy. **General Store:** Yes. **Vending:** Yes. **Swimming:** 3 pools. **Playground:** Yes. **Other:** 2 lakes, spas, kiddie pools, mini-golf, soccer & softball fields, snack bar, ranger station, game room, pavilion, banquet center, swimming beach, horseshoes, movies, Green River, hiking trails, RV sales, golf-cart rentals, drive-in movie theater. **Activities:** Swimming, fishing, hiking, hay wagon rides, boating (rental kayak & paddleboats available), planned daily activities, Sun. church services. **Nearby Attractions:** Flea markets, festivals, Amboy Depot Museum, wood carvings at Amboy City Park East, scenic drive, bike trail. **Additional Information:** Blackhawk Waterways CVB, (800) 678-2108.

RESTRICTIONS
Pets: On leash only, not allowed in rental units. **Fires:** Fire pit only. **Alcoholic Beverages:** Allowed. **Vehicle Maximum Length:** No limit. **Other:** Spa for 18 years & older.

TO GET THERE
From junction Hwy. 52 and Main St., drive 1.5 mi. east on Main St., then 2.5 mi. southeast on Shaw Rd., then 1 mi. north on Green Wing Rd. Roads are wide and well maintained, with good shoulders.

CASEY
Casey KOA
MAP, C-3

1248 East 1250th Rd., P.O. Box 56, 62420. T: (217) 932-5319 or (800) 562-9113; www.koa.com.

🚐 ★★★★　　　　▲ ★★★★

Beauty: ★★★★	Site Privacy: ★★★★
Spaciousness: ★★★★	Quiet: ★★★★
Security: ★★★★	Cleanliness: ★★★★★
Insect Control: ★★	Facilities: ★★★★

The owners of the Casey KOA wax the campground's restroom floors. That's an indication of the attention to detail shown at the campground. Arranged in a series of loops, the campground offers an average site width of 30 feet, along with 50 pull-throughs. Each site is level, has a tree, and offers a good combination of gravel for an RV and grass for the picnic table. A major plus is the short distance and easy access from the interstate. Traveling campers will find this a good place for an overnight stay—it is a popular stopping-off point for people going to Branson, which is one day away. Located 3 miles north of Casey, the campground also is a good destination in itself, because of its recreation facilities and planned activities. Owners sell RVs and offer onsite service. The best RV site is 11 because it is close to the pool, rec room, and other activities. The most popular site for tent campers is 53 because it is more private and tenters can walk to the lake.

BASICS
Operated By: Glenn and Cathy Klinkman. **Open:** Mar. 1–Oct. 31. **Site Assignment:** Reservations accepted w/ 1-night deposit; refunded for cancellations w/ 48-hour notice, or 2-week notice for holidays. **Registration:** At campground office. **Fee:** $25–$35; 2 people. **Parking:** At site.

FACILITIES

Number of RV-only Sites: 69. **Number of Tent-only Sites:** 10. **Hookups:** Electric (20, 30, 50 amps), water, sewer. **Each Site:** Picnic table, fire ring. **Dump Station:** Yes. **Laundry:** Yes. **Pay Phone:** Yes. **Restrooms and Showers:** Yes. **Fuel:** No. **Propane:** Yes. **Internal Roads:** Gravel, in good condition. **RV Service:** Yes. **Market:** 3 mi. south in Casey. **Restaurant:** 3 mi. south in Casey. **General Store:** Yes. **Vending:** No. **Swimming:** Yes. **Playground:** Yes. **Other:** Game room, stocked fishing lake, horseshoes, basketball, volleyball. **Activities:** Fishing, boating (rental rowboats & paddleboats available), Sun. pancake breakfast, weekly planned activities. **Nearby Attractions:** Amish country, Lincoln log cabin, antique malls, golf course, outlet shopping. **Additional Information:** Arthur Information Center, (800) 722-6474.

RESTRICTIONS

Pets: On leash only. **Fires:** Fire ring only. **Alcoholic Beverages:** Allowed. **Vehicle Maximum Length:** 70 ft.

TO GET THERE

From I-70 and Hwy. 49 junction, take Exit 129, drive 0.25 mi. north on Hwy. 49, then 0.25 mi. west on CO 1250 N. Roads are wide and well maintained; all except the county road have broad shoulders.

CHEBANSE   MAP, B-3
Kankakee South KOA

425 East 6000 South Rd., 60922.
T: (815) 939-4603 or (800) 562-4192;
www.koa.com, www.kankakeesouthkoa.com.

🚐 ★★★   ⛺ ★★★

Beauty: ★★★   Site Privacy: ★★★
Spaciousness: ★★★   Quiet: ★★★★
Security: ★★★   Cleanliness: ★★★
Insect Control: ★★   Facilities: ★★★

KOA Kankakee South offers the best of both worlds—easy access to the interstate, yet a quiet location off the main highway. Six miles south of Kankakee, the campground is shielded from road noise by a row of oak trees and bushes. Farm fields ring the campground. Quiet hours are enforced from 11 p.m. to 7 a.m. The speed limit is a strict 4 mph. Laid out in a series of loops, the campground has gravel, shaded RV sites. The typical site width is 30 feet, and 50 sites offer pull-through access. Only an hour from Chicago, the campground attracts many Chicagoans looking for some country peace. The best RV sites are in row 40, because these offer concrete pads and sewer hookups. Tent sites are located in a back area, where they have more privacy, greenery, and quiet. Security is good, with an owner who lives on the site and offers regular campground patrols.

BASICS

Operated By: Rob and Julie Bruno. **Open:** Apr. 1–Oct. 31. **Site Assignment:** Reservations suggested w/ credit card; refund w/ 24-hour notice. **Registration:** At campground office. **Fee:** Tent, $20–$27; RV, $25–$32; 2 adults. **Parking:** At site.

FACILITIES

Number of RV-only Sites: 60. **Number of Tent-only Sites:** 15. **Hookups:** Electric (20, 30 amps), water, sewer. **Each Site:** Picnic table, fire ring. **Dump Station:** Yes. **Laundry:** Yes. **Pay Phone:** Yes. **Restrooms and Showers:** Yes. **Fuel:** No. **Propane:** Yes. **Internal Roads:** Gravel, in good condition. **RV Service:** No. **Market:** 6 mi. north in Kankakee. **Restaurant:** 6 mi. north in Kankakee. **General Store:** Yes. **Vending:** Soft drinks. **Swimming:** Yes. **Playground:** Yes. **Other:** Pool table, basketball court, volleyball, sports field, video games, picnic shelter. **Activities:** Swimming. **Nearby Attractions:** Golf, canoe trips, Fri. night stockcar races, scenic drive, antique mall, skydiving, Model Railroad Museum. **Additional Information:** Kankakee County CVB, (900) 74-RIVER, www.kanakeecountyvisitorcenter.com.

RESTRICTIONS

Pets: On leash only. **Fires:** Fire ring only. **Alcoholic Beverages:** At sites only. **Vehicle Maximum Length:** 70 ft.

TO GET THERE

Take Exit 308 off I-57 onto US 45/32. Drive 3 mi. south on US 45/52, then 0.5 mi. east on East 6000 South Rd. to Kankakee South KOA. Roads are wide and well maintained, with decent shoulders.

EFFINGHAM   MAP, C-3
Camp Lakewood RV Park

1217 West Rickelman Ave., 62401.
T: (217) 342-6233 or (800) 961-1198;
www.camplakewoodcampground.com.

🚐 ★★★   ⛺ ★★★

Beauty: ★★★   Site Privacy: ★★★★
Spaciousness: ★★★★   Quiet: ★★★★
Security: ★★★★   Cleanliness: ★★★★
Insect Control: ★★   Facilities: ★★★

Camp Lakewood has many good things going for it, but it doesn't offer swimming. For campers who expect that as a normal part of their camping recreation, it may be hard to do without. Located on the north shores of Lake Pauline, 1 mile north of Effingham, the campground has 55 pull-throughs, and the typical site width is 25 feet. Sites are generally gravel and shady. Camp Lakewood is conveniently located near the interstate and city restaurants, shopping, and movies. Security is good, with owners who live on the grounds, providing regular patrols, and city police nearby who keep an eye on the property. Campers are given a good first impression when escorted to their sites instead of just being handed a map with a red line indicating where to go. Tent sites are set off in a more primitive area. The price also is right; very economical for such a clean campground in a good location. But for some campers all the positive aspects might not balance out that one missing element—swimming.

BASICS

Operated By: Kirk and Donna Maupin. **Open:** Mar. 1–Nov. 30. **Site Assignment:** Reservations recommended; guaranteed by MC, V, D; debit cards

---

accepted; no personal checks. **Registration:** At campground office. **Fee:** $26. **Parking:** At site.

FACILITIES

Number of RV-only Sites: 67. **Hookups:** Electric (30, 50 amps), water, sewer, cable TV, Wi-Fi. **Each Site:** Picnic table, fire ring. **Dump Station:** Yes. **Laundry:** Yes. **Pay Phone:** Yes. **Restrooms and Showers:** Yes. **Fuel:** No. **Propane:** No. **Internal Roads:** Gravel, in good condition. **RV Service:** No. **Market:** 1 mi. south in Effingham. **Restaurant:** 1 mi. south in Effingham. **General Store:** Yes. **Vending:** No. **Swimming:** No. **Playground:** Yes. **Other:** Boat ramp, game room, fishing dock, horseshoes. **Activities:** Fishing, boating. **Nearby Attractions:** Golf, mini-golf, movie theater, marina, art galleries, restaurants. **Additional Information:** Effingham CVB, (800) 772-0750.

RESTRICTIONS

Pets: On leash only, kept quiet, picked up after. **Fires:** Fire ring only. **Alcoholic Beverages:** At sites only. **Vehicle Maximum Length:** No limit.

TO GET THERE

From I-57 and I-70, take Effingham Exit 160. Turn north on Hwy. 33/32. Go about 0.25 mi. to Ford Ave. and turn right. Follow signs 1 mi. to Camp Lakewood Campground. Roads are wide and well maintained, with broad shoulders.

GALENA   MAP, A-1, A-2
Palace Campgrounds

11357 Hwy. 20 West, 61036. T: (815) 777-2466;
www.palacecampground.com.

🚐 ★★★★   ⛺ ★★★★

Beauty: ★★★★   Site Privacy: ★★★★
Spaciousness: ★★★★   Quiet: ★★★
Security: ★★★★   Cleanliness: ★★★★
Insect Control: ★★   Facilities: ★★★★

Palace Campgrounds is a rural campground that is rapidly becoming an urban campground as the city of Galena grows out to meet it. That means the campground is surrounded by city amenities such as restaurants and gas stations. A restaurant and hotel/motel is located next door. Bordered by farm fields in the back, the campground features rolling hills, woods, and a tree-lined road. The typical site width is 28 feet. Laid out in a series of loops, the campground has gravel sites for RVs and grassy ones for tents. Some RV sites are open, others shady, and there are eight double pull-through sites. Free fishing is available at the four-acre pond. Tent sites are off by themselves, away from RVs in a more secluded, natural area. The campground is fenced, with one major entrance/exit road. Speed bumps on interior roads keep traffic speeds down.

BASICS

Operated By: Teenie McCarthy. **Open:** Apr. 1–Nov. 1. **Site Assignment:** No reservations for tent camping; 2-night minimum weekends, 3-night minimum holidays w/ 1-night deposit; 10-day cancellation policy; cash and checks only. **Registration:** At campground office. **Fee:** Full hookup, $29; water/electric, $27; electric, $25; no hookup, $19. **Parking:** At site.

FACILITIES

Number of RV-only Sites: 133. **Number of Tent-only Sites:** 100. **Hookups:** Electric (30, 50 amps), water, sewer. **Each Site:** Picnic table, fire ring. **Dump Station:** Yes. **Laundry:** Yes. **Pay Phone:** No. **Restrooms and Showers:** Yes. **Fuel:** No. **Propane:** No. **Internal Roads:** Gravel, in good condition, some blacktop. **RV Service:** No. **Market:** Next door. **Restaurant:** 2 doors down. **General Store:** No. **Vending:** Yes. **Swimming:** Yes. **Playground:** Yes. **Other:** Basketball, snack bar, arcade, mini-golf, rec hall, pool table, outdoor movies, wading pool, sports field, horseshoes. **Activities:** Swimming, fishing, Sat. night hayrides, planned weekend activities. **Nearby Attractions:** Historic Galena, go-cart track, golf, riverboat casino, antique shops, fishing, flea markets, trail rides, cave tours, mountain resort, Alpine slide & chair lift rides. **Additional Information:** Galena/Jo Davies County CVB, (800) 747-9377.

RESTRICTIONS

Pets: On leash only. **Fires:** Fire ring only. **Alcoholic Beverages:** Allowed. **Vehicle Maximum Length:** 40 ft. **Other:** Must be at least 21 to reserve a site.

TO GET THERE

From the west edge of Galena, drive 1 mi. west on US 20. US 20 has no shoulders and there is a steep hill coming out of Galena.

GENESEO   MAP, A-2
Geneseo Campground

22978 IL 82, 61254. T: (309) 944-6465; www.fulltiming-america.com/geneseo.

🚐 ★★★★   ▲ ★★★

Beauty: ★★★★	Site Privacy: ★★★
Spaciousness: ★★★	Quiet: ★★★★
Security: ★★★★	Cleanliness: ★★★★
Insect Control: ★★	Facilities: ★★★★

A rural campground adjacent to the historic Hennepin Canal, Geneseo Campground offers grassy, mostly shaded sites. The campground has mostly pull-through sites with only four back-ins and a typical site width of 24 feet. Rustic cabins with air-conditioning are a popular plus. Along with being a quiet spot, the biggest thing Geneseo Campground has going for it is its location adjacent to the Hennepin Canal. Listed in the National Register of Historic Places, the canal joins the Mississippi and Illinois rivers. There are 32 of the original 33 locks still visible on the canal. Located within walking distance of the campground is one of the five locks restored to working condition and one of the six remaining aqueducts that carry the Hennepin across larger rivers and streams. You can rent a canoe or kayak for a Hennepin Canal trip that begins and ends at the campground. Fully watered, the canal also is a good fishing spot.

BASICS

Operated By: Craig and Shari Weber. **Open:** Apr. 1–Oct. 31. **Site Assignment:** Reservations w/ 1-night deposit on holidays; refund w/ 7-day notice. **Registration:** At campground office. **Fee:** Full hookup w/ 50 amps, $25; full hookup w/ 30 amps, $23; electric/water, $20; no hookup, $18. **Parking:** At site.

FACILITIES

Number of RV-only Sites: 63. **Number of Tent-only Sites:** 12. **Hookups:** Electric (20, 30, 50 amps), water, sewer, phone. **Each Site:** Picnic table, fire ring. **Dump Station:** Yes. **Laundry:** Yes. **Pay Phone:** Yes. **Restrooms and Showers:** Yes. **Fuel:** No. **Propane:** Yes. **Internal Roads:** Gravel, in good condition. **RV Service:** No. **Market:** 2 mi. south in Geneseo. **Restaurant:** 2 mi. south in Geneseo. **General Store:** Yes. **Vending:** Soft drinks. **Swimming:** No. **Playground:** Yes. **Other:** Sports field, horseshoes, rental cabins, rec room, fishing stream, badminton, hiking trails, volleyball. **Activities:** Fishing, canoeing & kayaking (rental canoes & kayaks available), hiking. **Nearby Attractions:** Victorian architecture, antiques, arts & crafts, golf, Grand Illinois Trail, Hennepin Canal, Bishop Hill, John Deere Museum, Rock Island Arsenal, riverboat cruises, casinos, Niabi Zoo, Wacky Waters, Geneseo Historical Museum, community swimming pool. **Additional Information:** Henry County Tourism Council, (309) 937-1255.

RESTRICTIONS

Pets: On leash only. **Fires:** Fire ring only. **Alcoholic Beverages:** Allowed w/ responsible, of-age use. **Vehicle Maximum Length:** No limit.

TO GET THERE

From junction of I-80 and Hwy. 82, take Exit 19 and drive 1.25 mi. north on Hwy. 82. Follow blue camping signs through town, pick up Hwy. 82 again, and drive 2 mi. north. Roads are wide and well maintained, with some narrow shoulders.

GOODFIELD   MAP, B-2
Yogi Bear's Jellystone Park

P.O. Box 92, 61742. T: (309) 965-2224 or (800) 558-2954; www.jellystonegoodfield.com.

🚐 ★★★★   ▲ ★★★★

Beauty: ★★★	Site Privacy: ★★★★
Spaciousness: ★★★★	Quiet: ★★★★
Security: ★★★★★	Cleanliness: ★★★★
Insect Control: ★★★	Facilities: ★★★★

Located 20 miles northwest of Bloomington, Goodfield's Yogi Bear's Jellystone Park Resort offers open and shaded grassy sites on a rolling terrain. Arranged in a series of loops, the rural campground has a typical site width of 30 feet with 15 pull-throughs. The campground offers separate sections for about 100 seasonal campers. Primitive areas for tent campers are scattered around the perimeter of the campground, offering more privacy and natural beauty. Most popular tent sites are by the lake and by the ravine. Best RV sites are 113–122 because they are pull-throughs with small trees for shade. Safety measures include a speed limit of 5 mph, no bike riding after dark, and some restrictions for children. Quiet hours are between 10:30 p.m. and 8 a.m., visitors must leave by 10 p.m., and no generators are allowed in the campground. The owners live on site and a guard helps control access and makes regular patrols of the campgrounds.

BASICS

Operated By: Bruce and Kathy Watkins. **Open:** All year. **Site Assignment:** Reservations w/ 1-night deposit; refunds (minus $10) w/ 7-day notice; 3-day minimum on most holidays. **Registration:** At campground office or over phone. **Fee:** Full hookup, $28–$36; water/electric, $26–$33; no hookup, $19–$26. **Parking:** At site, 2 cars max., extra cars are $5 each.

FACILITIES

Number of RV-only Sites: 387. **Number of Tent-only Sites:** 200. **Hookups:** Electric (30, 50 amps), water, sewer. **Each Site:** Picnic tables, fire sites. **Dump Station:** Yes. **Laundry:** Yes. **Pay Phone:** No. **Restrooms and Showers:** Yes. **Fuel:** No. **Propane:** Yes. **Internal Roads:** Gravel, in fair condition. **RV Service:** No. **Market:** 7 mi. north in Eureka. **Restaurant:** 1.5 mi. south in Goodfield. **General Store:** Yes. **Vending:** Yes. **Swimming:** Yes. **Playground:** Yes. **Other:** Stocked fishing lake, mini-golf, bocce ball court, volleyball, horseshoes, softball, rec hall, clubhouse, hiking trails, boat dock, pedal carts. **Activities:** Swimming, fishing, hiking, boating (rental paddleboats & rowboats available), planned weekend activities. **Nearby Attractions:** Horse racing track, historic sites, museums, art galleries, antique shops, zoo, casino, golf, Prairie Aviation Museum, dinner theater, Factory Outlet Mall. **Additional Information:** Bloomington-Normal Area CVB, (800) 433-8226.

RESTRICTIONS

Pets: On leash only, quiet, cleaned up after. Use designated dog walk area. **Fires:** Fire pit only. **Alcoholic Beverages:** At sites only. **Vehicle Maximum Length:** 65 ft.

TO GET THERE

From junction of I-74 and Hwy. 117, take Exit 112 and drive 1 mi. north on Hwy. 117, then 0.75 mi. east on Timberline Rd. Roads are wide and well maintained, with broad shoulders.

GRANITE CITY   MAP, C-2
Granite City KOA

3157 West Chain of Rocks Rd., 62040. T: (618) 931-5160 or (800) 562-5861; www.koa.com.

🚐 ★★★★   ▲ ★★★

Beauty: ★★★	Site Privacy: ★★★
Spaciousness: ★★★	Quiet: ★★★★
Security: ★★★★	Cleanliness: ★★★★
Insect Control: ★★	Facilities: ★★★★

It's sort of a trade-off. At Granite City KOA, you are 11 miles north of downtown St. Louis on historic Hwy. 66. It's an easy place to use as a base for all the wonderful St. Louis area attractions. But, since it is in the city limits, you cannot have a campfire at Granite City KOA. You can use a grill for cooking but no open fires are permitted in the city limits. Granite City KOA does have a lot of other amenities going for it, though. A rural/urban campground laid out in a series of loops, Granite City KOA offers mostly wooded, grassy, or gravel, level sites. There are few open sites available. The typical site width is 35 feet, and there are 70 pull-throughs. A secluded area set aside for tents is shaded with big elm and maple trees, offering privacy. There are no scheduled activities. With all St. Louis has to offer, most campers don't seem to mind.

BASICS

Operated By: Cuvar Family. **Open:** Mar. 15–Nov. 1. **Site Assignment:** Reservations accepted w/ 1-night deposit; refund w/ 48-hour notice. Walk-ins welcome; MC, V, D accepted. **Registration:** At campground office. **Fee:** RV, $29–$34; tent, $22–$24; cash, credit card. **Parking:** At site.

FACILITIES

Number of RV-only Sites: 80. **Number of Tent-only Sites:** 15. **Hookups:** Electric (20, 30, 50 amps), water, sewer. **Each Site:** Picnic table. **Dump Station:** Yes. **Laundry:** Yes. **Pay Phone:** Yes. **Restrooms and Showers:** Yes. **Fuel:** No. **Propane:** Yes. **Internal Roads:** Gravel, in good condition. **RV Service:** No. **Market:** 3 mi. south in Granite City. **Restaurant:** 3 mi. south in Granite City. **General Store:** Yes. **Vending:** No. **Swimming:** Yes. **Playground:** Yes. **Other:** Basketball, horseshoes, rental cabins, recreation field, pavilion. **Activities:** Swimming. **Nearby Attractions:** St. Louis Arch, raceway, bike trails, historic sites, museums, zoo, riverboat gambling, Six Flags, Busch Stadium, Laclede's Landing. **Additional Information:** St. Louis Convention & Visitors Commission, (800) 916-0040.

RESTRICTIONS

Pets: On leash only. **Fires:** Grills only. No campfires. **Alcoholic Beverages:** Allowed. **Vehicle Maximum Length:** 40 ft.

TO GET THERE

From junction I-270 and Hwy. 3, take Exit 3A, drive 0.25 mi. south on Hwy. 3, then 0.5 mi. east on Chain of Rocks Rd. Roads are wide and well maintained, with broad shoulders.

KNOXVILLE   MAP, B-2
Galesburg East Best Holiday Trav-L-Park

1081 US 150 East, 61448. T: (309) 289-2267; www.allcampgrounds.com/galesburgeast.

🚐 ★★★★   ▲ ★★★

Beauty: ★★★	Site Privacy: ★★★
Spaciousness: ★★★	Quiet: ★★★★
Security: ★★★★★	Cleanliness: ★★★★
Insect Control: ★★	Facilities: ★★★★

Located in a secluded country setting with farm fields around it, Galesburg East Best Holiday Trav-L-Park offers a quiet, secure facility. With easy access from the highway, the campground has level spots shaded with poplar, ash, and maple trees. The campground offers sites with an average width of 25 feet as well as 55 pull-throughs. Tent sites are somewhat separated from RVs and offer more shade and grass. Campers often stay at Galesburg East to do genealogy work in the area and enjoy the local festivals. A welcome touch in the hot summer is the air-conditioned laundry and store. Security is tops thanks to lights on buildings, security cameras, owners who live on the property, and regular patrols of the campground,

which is 7 miles east of Galesburg.

BASICS

Operated By: Stan and Judy Herrick. **Open:** Apr. 1–Oct. 31. **Site Assignment:** Reservations w/ 1-night deposit; refund w/ 24-hour notice. **Registration:** At office. **Fee:** Full hookup w/ 50 amps, $26; full hookup w/ 30 amps, $21; tent, $15; based on 2 people; extra adult, $2; extra child (6–17 yrs), $1. **Parking:** At site.

FACILITIES

Number of RV-only Sites: 58. **Number of Tent-only Sites:** 10. **Hookups:** Electric (30, 50 amps), water, sewer. **Each Site:** Picnic table, portable fire rings available. **Dump Station:** Yes. **Laundry:** Yes. **Pay Phone:** Yes. **Restrooms and Showers:** Yes. **Fuel:** No. **Propane:** Yes. **Internal Roads:** Gravel, in fair condition. **RV Service:** Next door. **Market:** 7 mi. west in Galesburg. **Restaurant:** 3 mi. west in Knoxville. **General Store:** Yes. **Vending:** No. **Swimming:** Yes. **Playground:** Yes. **Other:** Fishing pond, lounge w/ TV, enclosed shelter, heated swimming pool. **Activities:** Fishing. **Nearby Attractions:** Carl Sandburg's birthplace, Bishop Hill Swedish colony, scenic drive, golf, railroad museum, Wolf Covered Bridge spanning Spoon River. **Additional Information:** Galesburg Area CVB, (309) 343-1194.

RESTRICTIONS

Pets: On leash only, cleaned up after. **Fires:** Fire ring only. **Alcoholic Beverages:** At sites only. Not permitted in buildings. **Vehicle Maximum Length:** 45 ft.

TO GET THERE

From Exit 54 on US 150, drive 5 mi. east to the campground. Roads are wide and well maintained, with broad shoulders.

LENA   MAP, A-2
Lena KOA

10982 West Hwy. 20, 61048. T: (815) 369-2612 or (800) 562-5361; www.lenakoa.com.

🚐 ★★★   ▲ ★★★

Beauty: ★★★	Site Privacy: ★★★
Spaciousness: ★★★	Quiet: ★★★★
Security: ★★★★★	Cleanliness: ★★★★★
Insect Control: ★★	Facilities: ★★★

Surrounded by cornfields and woods, Lena KOA is a quiet family campground just 1 mile north of Lena. The typical site width is 27 feet, and the campground has 30 pull-throughs. There is a mixture of wooded and open sites. A Kamping Kitchen, with three cooking stations with sinks and electric stoves, plus six picnic tables, provides cooking and eating facilities for campers to use. Tent sites are grassy, with wooden platforms for tents. RV sites are grassy, with gravel pads for RVs. The best RV sites are M6–11, because they are long sites offering easy in and out; L1–5, because they are away from the road and closer to the woods; and I1–5, because they are long, level, have 50 amps electricity, and a variety of trees. Tent sites are spacious and level, with a short walk to restrooms and showers. Campers are escorted to their sites when they check in. Security is good thanks to an owner who lives on the grounds, a

staffed office from 8 a.m. to 9 p.m., enforced quiet time from 10 p.m. to 7 a.m., and regular patrols of the campground.

BASICS

Operated By: Joe and Diane Long. **Open:** Apr. 1–Nov 1. **Site Assignment:** Reservations w/ 1-night deposit; refund (minus $5) w/ 2-day notice; 20-week notice required for holidays. **Registration:** At campground office. **Fee:** RV, $25–$40; tent, $20–$30; based on 2 people. **Parking:** At site.

FACILITIES

Number of RV-only Sites: 83. **Number of Tent-only Sites:** 5. **Hookups:** Electric (30, 50 amps), water, sewer, Internet. **Each Site:** Picnic table, fire ring. **Dump Station:** Yes. **Laundry:** Yes. **Pay Phone:** Yes. **Restrooms and Showers:** Yes. **Fuel:** No. **Propane:** Yes. **Internal Roads:** Gravel, in good condition. **RV Service:** No. **Market:** 1 mi. north in Lena. **Restaurant:** 1 mi. north in Lena. **General Store:** Yes. **Vending:** Yes. **Swimming:** Yes. **Playground:** Yes. **Other:** Video arcade, rec room, volleyball, horseshoes, basketball, sports field, pavilion, Kamping Kitchen, cabins, cottages. **Activities:** Swimming, biking (rental low-rider bikes available), planned activities on Sat. **Nearby Attractions:** Lena Area Historical Museum, Stagecoach Trail, Field of Dreams movie site, Stephenson–Black Hawk Trail, cheese companies, golf, casino. **Additional Information:** Stephenson County CVB, (815) 223-1357.

RESTRICTIONS

Pets: On leash only. **Fires:** Fire ring only. **Alcoholic Beverages:** At sites only. **Vehicle Maximum Length:** 45 ft.

TO GET THERE

From junction of Hwy. 73 and US 20, drive 0.25 mi. east on US 20. US 20 has no shoulders so be careful turning into the campground.

LITCHFIELD   MAP, C-2
Rainmaker Campground

865 Rainmaker Tr., 62056. T: (217) 532-6370.

🚐 ★★★   ▲ ★★

Beauty: ★★★	Site Privacy: ★★★
Spaciousness: ★★★	Quiet: ★★★★
Security: ★★★★★	Cleanliness: ★★★★
Insect Control: ★★	Facilities: ★★★

The fourth generation of campers are now visiting Rainmaker Campground, 6 miles east of Litchfield. And the same owners are there who started it almost four decades ago. Prices must not have changed much over those years because the campground is a real bargain—$10 for an RV or tent site. Seasonal campers have taken up 140 of the sites and seem to spend considerable time fixing up their second homes with flowers, shrubs, and decorations. The owners don't charge storage if RVs are left year-round on the site. The campground is a destination. Very few RVs would drive those country roads just for an overnight place to stay. The drive is pretty but the winding, narrow roads can get tiresome. RV sites are gravel, with a choice of open or shaded. Typical site width is 25 feet, and there are five pull-throughs in front of the shower facility. Those are the most popular RV sites. Tent campers can use any of the RV sites which puts them at a bit of a disadvantage if they want privacy. The family campground has solid security measures—owners who live on the grounds, regular patrols, a security camera, and an access gate that is locked from 11 p.m. to 6 a.m.

BASICS

Operated By: Rex and June Brawley and Ed and Wendy Wuttke. **Open:** Apr. 1–Oct. 31. **Site Assignment:** Reservations suggested; no deposit. **Registration:** At campground office. **Fee:** RV, $20; tent, $15. **Parking:** At site.

FACILITIES

Number of RV-only Sites: 220. **Number of Tent-only Sites:** 8. **Hookups:** Electric (20, 30 amps), water, sewer. **Each Site:** Picnic table, fire ring. **Dump Station:** Yes. **Laundry:** No. **Pay Phone:** No. **Restrooms and Showers:** Yes. **Fuel:** No. **Propane:** Yes. **Internal Roads:** Paved/gravel, in good condition. **RV Service:** Yes. **Market:** 6 mi. west in Litchfield. **Restaurant:** 6 mi. west in Litchfield. **General Store:** Yes. **Vending:** No. **Swimming:** Lake. **Playground:** Yes. **Other:** Fishing pond, Lake Yeager, nature trails, horseshoes, volleyball, tetherball, basketball, bait, boat ramp, boat dock, rec hall, pavilion, adults room, recreation field. **Activities:** Swimming, fishing, boating, hiking, Sun. church services, planned weekend activities. **Nearby Attractions:** Golf, drive-in theater, nature conservation area, Sportsman's Family Fun Park, nature trails, water sports, swimming. **Additional Information:** Central Illinois Tourism Development Office, (217) 525-7980.

RESTRICTIONS

Pets: On leash only. **Fires:** Fire ring only. **Alcoholic Beverages:** Allowed. **Vehicle Maximum Length:** No limit.

TO GET THERE

From junction of I-55 and Hwy. 16, take Exit 52, drive 5.5 mi. east on Hwy. 16, then 4 mi. northwest on Parsons. The country roads are very winding and narrow at times.

MAHOMET
Tin Cup RV Park
MAP, B-3

1715 Tin Cup Rd., 61853. T: (217) 586-3011.

🚐 ★★★	🏕 ★★★
Beauty: ★★★	Site Privacy: ★★★
Spaciousness: ★★★	Quiet: ★★★★
Security: ★★★★	Cleanliness: ★★★★
Insect Control: ★★★	Facilities: ★★★

At first glance, Tin Cup RV Park looks like a golf course. The slopes of the grassy campground are so well maintained they could be a golf green. Located in the small town of Mahomet, 8 miles west of Champaign, the campground offers a country setting just down the road from the Champaign Country Forest Preserve. A favorite with golfers, the campground also has an updated golf driving range with a ball dispenser. Most sites offer shade with mature trees. Typical site width is 30 feet, and the campground has 18 pull-throughs. Laid out in a series of loops, the campground has mostly gravel pads on grassy sites for RVs. Best RV sites are 33–40

because they are spacious and well shaded and offer easy access. Primitive sites are set aside in three acres of woods where RVs aren't allowed to camp. The tent sites are promoted as being unlimited but could probably accommodate an estimated 700 tent campers. However, the tent area is never filled up so tent campers have a bit more privacy and rustic surroundings. Security is good with a co-owner who lives on the premises and provides regular patrols of the area. Set back from the road, the campground is quiet. Many campers probably spend their days at the nearby 18-hole golf course.

BASICS

Operated By: Stephen Robinson. **Open:** All year. **Site Assignment:** Reservations; no deposit; cash, checks, credit cards accepted. **Registration:** At campground office. **Fee:** Full hookup, $27; tent site, $15. **Parking:** At site.

FACILITIES

Number of RV-only Sites: 65. **Number of Tent-only Sites:** 700. **Hookups:** Electric (20, 30 amps), water, sewer. **Each Site:** Picnic table, fire ring. **Dump Station:** Yes. **Laundry:** No. **Pay Phone:** Yes. **Restrooms and Showers:** Yes. **Fuel:** No. **Propane:** Yes. **Internal Roads:** Paved/gravel, in good condition. **RV Service:** No. **Market:** 0.5 mi. west on Mahomet. **Restaurant:** 0.5 mi. west on Mahomet. **General Store:** No. **Vending:** Yes. **Swimming:** No. **Playground:** Yes. **Other:** Golf driving range w/ ball dispenser, sports field. **Activities:** None on site. **Nearby Attractions:** Golf course, fishing lakes, swimming area, Early American Museum, University of Illinois, hiking trails, paved bike trails. **Additional Information:** Mahomet Chamber of Commerce, (217) 586-3165.

RESTRICTIONS

Pets: On leash only. **Fires:** Fire ring only. **Alcoholic Beverages:** At sites only. **Vehicle Maximum Length:** 40 ft.

TO GET THERE

From junction of I-57 and I-74, take Exit 174 and drive 5 mi. northwest on I-74, then 0.5 mi. north on Prairie View Rd., then 0.5 mi. west on Tincup Rd. Roads are wide and well maintained, with broad shoulders.

MARSHALL
Lincoln Trail State Park
MAP, C-3

16985 East 1350th Rd., 62441. T: (217) 826-2222; www.dnr.state.il.us.

🚐 ★★★	🏕 ★★★★
Beauty: ★★★★	Site Privacy: ★★★★
Spaciousness: ★★★★	Quiet: ★★★★
Security: ★★★★	Cleanliness: ★★★★
Insect Control: ★★	Facilities: ★★★

Officially dedicated in 1958, Lincoln Trail State Park was named after the trail Abraham Lincoln's family followed en route from Indiana to Illinois in 1831. With 3,000 markers showing the way, the trail winds through Kentucky, Indiana, and Illinois. Located 5 miles south of Marshall, the 1,023-acre park centers around the 146-acre Lincoln Trail Lake. Two campgrounds, Plainview and Lakeside, offer amenities,

including mostly gravel, open sites with 16 pull-throughs. For those who wish to be attuned to nature without the distractions of modern conveniences, Lakeside Campground also includes a camping area for tents. Tent sites offer more privacy, grass, and shade. A full-service concession stand near the boat docks offers a wide variety of refreshments and supplies, as well as boat and dock rentals. The Beech Tree Trail is just a half-mile long, extending from the boat dock parking lot and concession stand, past the large picnic shelter, and on to the campground. The trail includes a series of stairways and foot bridges, which provide an excellent view of the beech maple forest contained within the nature preserve. Now, if only Lincoln Trail State Park had someplace nice to swim.

BASICS

Operated By: State of Illinois. **Open:** All year. **Site Assignment:** First come, first served. **Registration:** At campground office. **Fee:** Electric, $15; no electric/primitive, $8. **Parking:** At site.

FACILITIES

Number of RV-only Sites: 208. **Number of Tent-only Sites:** 24. **Hookups:** Electric (20, 30, 50 amps). **Each Site:** Picnic table, fire ring. **Dump Station:** Yes. **Laundry:** No. **Pay Phone:** No. **Restrooms and Showers:** Yes. **Fuel:** No. **Propane:** No. **Internal Roads:** Paved, in good condition. **RV Service:** No. **Market:** 5 mi. north in Marshall. **Restaurant:** On site. **General Store:** No. **Vending:** No. **Swimming:** No. **Playground:** Yes. **Other:** Lincoln Trail Lake, boat ramp, boat dock, hiking trails, wheelchair-accessible sites, bait available, picnic shelters. **Activities:** Fishing, hiking, boating (rental motorboats, canoes, paddleboats, & rowboats available). **Nearby Attractions:** The Archer House former stagecoach stop, Clark County Museum, Stone Arch Bridges, hunting, Amish country, antique shops, golf. **Additional Information:** Central Illinois Tourism Development Office, (217) 525-7980.

RESTRICTIONS

Pets: On leash only. **Fires:** Fire ring only. **Alcoholic Beverages:** Allowed. **Vehicle Maximum Length:** 60 ft. **Other:** 2-week stay limit.

TO GET THERE

From junction US 40 and Hwy. 1, drive 5 mi. south on Hwy. 1, then 1 mi. west on Blacktop Rd. Roads are wide and well maintained, with good shoulders.

MILLBROOK
Yogi Bear's Jellystone Park
MAP, A-3

reserve america

8574 Millbrook Rd., 60536. T: (800) GET-YOGI; www.jellystonechicago.com.

🚐 ★★★★	🏕 ★★★★
Beauty: ★★★★	Site Privacy: ★★★
Spaciousness: ★★	Quiet: ★★
Security: ★★★★	Cleanliness: ★★★
Insect Control: ★★★	Facilities: ★★★★

Kids have a wonderfull time in this heavily treed park, riding their bikes, taking the wagon rides with Yogi while singing songs throughout the camp, and joining in with the many other activities offered throughout the day—from cartoons in the morning to a movie at night, there is always something to do. A new play gym for the kids is a welcome recent addition to a somewhat-aging plaground. The pools sometimes get overcrowded and may not always be perfect blue. The campground seem to host a lot of seasonal people, and although the restrooms are clean, there is only one bathroom for the whole park. Owners are always around, and the staff is friendly and energetic. There is a well-stocked ranger station and easy access to a Wal-mart nearby for last-minute items. Be forewarned that the roads in the park are narrow and may be hard to maneuver through with a big rig.

BASICS

Operated By: Mike Ciero. **Open:** All year. **Site Assignment:** Reservations recommended. **Fee:** Campsite, $31–$51; cabin, $63–$105.

FACILITIES

Number of Multipurpose Sites: 415. **Hookups:** 224 sites w/ electric, sewer; 165 w/ electric; free Wi-Fi. **Dump Station:** Yes. **Laundry:** Yes. **Pay Phone:** Yes. **Restrooms and Showers:** Yes. **Fuel:** No. **Propane:** No. **Internal Roads:** Gravel. **General Store:** Camp store. **Vending:** Yes. **Swimming:** Yes. **Playground:** Yes. **Other:** Kiddie pool, spa, pavilion, snack bar, Wi-Fi. **Activities:** Fishing, supervised children's activities.

RESTRICTIONS

Pets: On leash, attended only. **Fires:** Allowed.

TO GET THERE

40 mi. southwest of Chicago.

MULBERRY GROVE — MAP, C-2
Cedarbrook RV Park and Campgrounds

1109 Mulberry Grove Rd., 62262.
T: (618) 326-8865; www.cedarbrookrvpark.com.

🚐 ★★★★   ⛺ ★★★★

Beauty: ★★★★   Site Privacy: ★★★★
Spaciousness: ★★★   Quiet: ★★★★
Security: ★★★★★   Cleanliness: ★★★★★
Insect Control: ★★   Facilities: ★★★★

Not only are the restrooms at Cedarbrook RV and Camper Park very clean, they are also decorated: scatter rugs lay on the floor, a fan supplies cooling breezes, and a fancy bottle of liquid soap adorns the sink. The owners obviously care. The secluded wilderness setting 8 miles west of Vandalia features nine pull-through sites—the most popular with RVs—and an average site width of 25 feet. A wooded ravine and a small lake for fishing and swimming add to the amenities, but there are no scheduled activities. RV sites are generally gravel, with a mixture of sunny and shady places. Tent sites are more primitive and grassy. The campground has a gate for security, owners who live on the grounds, and regular patrols of the area.

BASICS

Operated By: Spencer and Barbara Gobus. **Open:** Apr. 1–Oct. 31. **Site Assignment:** Reservations w/ 1-night deposit; 72-hr. cancellation notice required;

no refunds on no-show reservations. **Registration:** At campground office. **Fee:** Full hookup, $22–$26; tent w/ electricity, $17; no hookup, $15. Based on family of 4; $2 for each extra person above 5 years old. **Parking:** At site.

FACILITIES

Number of RV-only Sites: 60. **Number of Tent-only Sites:** 6. **Hookups:** Electric (30, 50 amps), water, sewer, Wi-Fi. **Each Site:** Picnic table, fire ring. **Dump Station:** Yes. **Laundry:** Yes. **Pay Phone:** No. **Restrooms and Showers:** Yes. **Fuel:** No. **Propane:** Yes. **Internal Roads:** Gravel, in good condition. **RV Service:** No. **Market:** 9 mi. east in Vandalia. **Restaurant:** 1 mi. north in Mulberry Grove. **General Store:** Yes. **Vending:** No. **Swimming:** Yes. **Playground:** Yes. **Other:** Small lake, clubhouse w/ complete kitchen, Wi-Fi, 3 rental cabins. **Activities:** Volleyball, horseshoes, fishing and boating in lake. **Nearby Attractions:** Carlyle Lake, biggest man-made lake in Illinois; Vandalia, first capitol of Illinois; scenic drives. **Additional Information:** Crawford County Tourism Council, (800) 445-7006.

RESTRICTIONS

Pets: On leash only. **Fires:** Fire ring only. **Alcoholic Beverages:** At site. **Vehicle Maximum Length:** No limit.

TO GET THERE

From I-70, take Exit 52, drive 1 mi. south. Roads are wide and well maintained, with broad shoulders.

OAKWOOD — MAP, B-3
Kickapoo State Recreation Area

10906 Kickapoo Park Rd., 61858.
T: (217) 442-4915; www.dnr.state.il.us.

🚐 ★★★   ⛺ ★★★★

Beauty: ★★★★   Site Privacy: ★★★
Spaciousness: ★★★   Quiet: ★★★★
Security: ★★★★   Cleanliness: ★★★
Insect Control: ★★   Facilities: ★★★

Easily reached by I-74, Kickapoo State Park has a wealth of natural beauty and outdoor activities. Oddly, that is not how it all started. Once a scarred wasteland ravaged by strip-mine operations, Kickapoo State Park's 2,842 acres now provide an outdoor playground with something to appeal to every member of the family. For campers, Kickapoo has two major campgrounds for tent and RV camping. Campers occupying electrical sites are required to pay for the availability of electricity even if the service is not used. A limited number of walk-in sites are available for primitive campers. Sites are level and mostly shaded with a variety of maple, oak, and ash trees. The park is said to be the first in the nation built on strip-mined land and one of the first to be subsidized through public contributions. The spoil piles and mine pits left behind after nearly a century of mining (1850–1940) were the base from which nature had to recover to transform Kickapoo State Park into the outdoor playground it is today. The park has 22 deep-water ponds providing a total of 221 acres of water for boaters, canoeists, and anglers.

BASICS

Operated By: State of Illinois. **Open:** All year. **Site Assignment:** Some sites available for reservations; 1-night deposit, plus $5 fee; refund w/ 3-day notice. **Registration:** At campground office or by mail. **Fee:** Class A (showers & electricity), $15; Class B (showers), $10. **Parking:** At site.

FACILITIES

Number of RV-only Sites: 101. **Number of Multipurpose Sites:** 75. **Hookups:** Electric (30, 50 amps). **Each Site:** Picnic table, fire ring. **Dump Station:** Yes. **Laundry:** No. **Pay Phone:** No. **Restrooms and Showers:** Yes. **Fuel:** No. **Propane:** No. **Internal Roads:** Paved, in good condition. **RV Service:** No. **Market:** 1 mi. south in Oakwood. **Restaurant:** Cafe on site. **General Store:** No. **Vending:** No. **Swimming:** No. **Playground:** Yes. **Other:** Vermilion River, lakes, ponds, horseshoes, boat ramp, shelters, hiking trails, mountain bike trails. **Activities:** Fishing, boating (rental nonmotorized boats available), canoeing, hiking, hunting, scuba diving. **Nearby Attractions:** Danville Stadium, Vermilion County Museum, Middle Fork National Scenic River, Vermilion County War Museum Society, antique stores, arts & crafts. **Additional Information:** Danville Area CVB, (800) 383-4386.

RESTRICTIONS

Pets: On leash only. **Fires:** Fire ring only. **Alcoholic Beverages:** Not permitted in campgrounds. **Vehicle Maximum Length:** 60 ft. **Other:** 2-week stay limit. Electric trolling motors only on boats.

TO GET THERE

From Oakwood, drive 0.5 mi. north on New Town Rd. Roads are wide and well maintained, with mostly broad shoulders.

OREGON — MAP, A-2
Lake LaDonna Family Campground

1302 South Harmony Rd., 61061.
T: (815) 732-6804; www.lakeladonna.com.

🚐 ★★★   ⛺ ★★★

Beauty: ★★★   Site Privacy: ★★★
Spaciousness: ★★★   Quiet: ★★★
Security: ★★★★   Cleanliness: ★★★
Insect Control: ★★   Facilities: ★★★

Campers often stop and ask if they have to be veterans to stay at Lake LaDonna Family Campground. They don't, of course. But the campground is dedicated to veterans and has the nation's first Vietnam Memorial Wall. The 80-foot wall was built in 1982 by the owner, himself a Vietnam vet whose limp attests to his war injuries. Flags fly everywhere, POW and MIA signs are prominently displayed, and military branch symbols are affixed to RVs and campers. Special memorial services also are held several times a year to honor veterans. Laid out in a series of loops, the campground has well-shaded grassy and gravel sites. The average site width is 28 feet, with 50 pull-throughs. The campground has 135 seasonal campers. The campground's white-sand beach and spring-fed lake are its biggest draws. The lake has a 16-foot waterfall, a boardwalk with huge thatched huts for shade, a diving board, and a life guard on duty.

BASICS

Operated By: Lamont Gaston. **Open:** Apr. 15–Oct. 15. **Site Assignment:** Reservation required for weekends; 2-night minimum weekends, 3-night minimum holidays; credit card required to hold reservation (AE, D, MC, V). 1-week cancellation policy; half refund for less than 1-week notice; no refund for less than 24-hour notice. **Registration:** At campground office. **Fee:** $27. **Parking:** At site.

FACILITIES

Number of RV-only Sites: 351. **Number of Tent-only Sites:** 6. **Hookups:** Electric (20, 30 amps), water. **Each Site:** Picnic table. **Dump Station:** Yes. **Laundry:** No. **Pay Phone:** No. **Restrooms and Showers:** Yes. **Fuel:** No. **Propane:** No. **Internal Roads:** Paved, in good condition. **RV Service:** No. **Market:** 5 mi. north in Oregon. **Restaurant:** 5 mi. north in Oregon. **General Store:** Yes. **Vending:** No. **Swimming:** Beach. **Playground:** Yes. **Other:** Manmade lake, beach, rope swing dock, boardwalk, basketball court, lodge, video-game arcade, pool tables, pinball, juke box, fast-food restaurant, amphitheater. **Activities:** Swimming, planned activities. **Nearby Attractions:** Go-carts, mini-golf, bumper boats, ultralight flying lessons, shooting gallery, 4 state parks, paddlewheel boat, 48-ft. tall Black Hawk statue overlooking Rock River. **Additional Information:** Northern Illinois Tourism Development Office, (815) 547-3740.

RESTRICTIONS

Pets: On leash only. **Fires:** Fire pit only. **Alcoholic Beverages:** Allowed. **Vehicle Maximum Length:** 40 ft.

TO GET THERE

From Hwy. 64 west, turn left at the third stoplight (Hwy. 2) in Oregon. Continue south to edge of town. Follow signs to White Pines State Park by turning right onto Pines Rd. Continue on Pines Rd., following signs to White Pines State Park. Two mi. before the state park, turn right off Pines Rd. onto Harmony Rd. Lake LaDonna is 0.5 mi. on left on Harmony Rd., marked by a large, lighted sign. Road is well maintained, with sufficient shoulders.

PITTSFIELD   MAP, C-1
Pine Lakes Camping and Fishing Resort

reserve america

1405 Lakeview Heights, 62363. T: (877) 808-7463 or (217) 285-6719; www.reserveamerica.com.

🚐 ★★★★   ⛺ ★★★★

Beauty: ★★★★	Site Privacy: ★★★★
Spaciousness: ★★★★	Quiet: ★★★★
Security: ★★★★	Cleanliness: ★★★★
Insect Control: ★★	Facilities: ★★★★

Pine Lakes Camping and Fishing Resort in Pittsfield has natural beauty—to begin with, 45-acre Pine Lake with a pretty shoreline, a ravine, and sandy swimming beach. The campground also has little touches to add to its scenic attractions—flower gardens, flower boxes, large wooden carvings, and a totem pole. Laid out in a series of loops, the campground offers a typical site width of 35 feet and has 16 pull-throughs. RV sites are a mixture of grass and gravel. Many RV sites have concrete pads and picnic tables covered with wooden canopies. RVs have a choice of shady or open sites. A primitive site for tents offers more privacy, trees, and grass. The best RV sites are in the 400 section along the lake, and the heavily shaded 100 section. The speed limit is 7.5 mph, no bicycles or golf carts are allowed after dark (bike helmets are encouraged), and each vehicle must exhibit a camper or visitor pass. Security and noise regulations are enforced. Bug zappers are not permitted and quiet hours are 11 p.m. to 8 a.m. Children must be on their site during quiet hours unless accompanied by an adult. A security gate guards the entrance to the campground, and the area is patrolled.

BASICS

Operated By: Jim and Marsha. **Open:** All year; limited winter facilities. **Site Assignment:** Reservations w/ 1-night deposit; refunds (minus $10 w/ 14-day notice; cancellations w/in 3–14 days will be issued credit for current season; 2-night minimum, 3-night minimum holiday weekends; MC, V, D. **Registration:** At campground office. **Fee:** Full hookup w/ cable, $30–$34; no hookup, $16–$20. **Parking:** At site, for 1 vehicle. Overflow parking available.

FACILITIES

Number of RV-only Sites: 153. **Number of Tent-only Sites:** 50. **Hookups:** Electric (20, 30, 50 amps), water, sewer, cable TV. **Each Site:** Picnic table, fire ring. **Dump Station:** Yes. **Laundry:** Yes. **Pay Phone:** Yes. **Restrooms and Showers:** Yes. **Fuel:** No. **Propane:** Yes. **Internal Roads:** Paved/gravel, in good condition. **RV Service:** Nearby. **Market:** 0.5 mi. south in Pittsfield. **Restaurant:** 0.5 mi. south in Pittsfield. **General Store:** Yes. **Vending:** Yes. **Swimming:** Beach. **Playground:** Yes. **Other:** Pine Lake, sandy swimming beach, arcade, fish-cleaning building, tetherball, horseshoes, volleyball, basketball, hiking trail, outdoor movies, bait shop. **Activities:** Swimming, fishing (no license required), boating (rental rowboats, canoes, kayaks, & paddleboats), rental golf carts, hiking, planned activities. **Nearby Attractions:** Hunting, horseback riding, golf, antique shops, craft shops, ostrich farm, genealogy resources, apple orchard, boating, bowling, drive-in. **Additional Information:** Western Illinois Tourism Development Office, (309) 837-7460.

RESTRICTIONS

Pets: On leash only. **Fires:** Fire ring only. **Alcoholic Beverages:** At sites only. **Vehicle Maximum Length:** No limit. **Other:** Pole fishing only, limit 4 catfish & 4 bass a day; no private boats or motors allowed; no boats on water before dawn or after dusk; swimming beach open 10 a.m.–dusk.

TO GET THERE

From junction of I-72/US 36 and Pittsfield/New Salem Rd., take Exit 31 and drive 4.5 mi. south on Pittsfield/New Salem Rd. Roads are wide and well maintained, with broad shoulders.

ROCKFORD   MAP, A-2
Rock Cut State Park

7318 Harlem Rd., 61111. T: (815) 885-3311; www.dnr.state.il.us.

🚐 ★★★   ⛺ ★★★★

Beauty: ★★★★	Site Privacy: ★★★
Spaciousness: ★★★	Quiet: ★★★
Security: ★★★★★	Cleanliness: ★★★★
Insect Control: ★★	Facilities: ★★★

Chiseled out of the state's far northern region, Rock Cut State Park got its name from the blasting operations that railroad crews conducted during the 1859 construction of the Kenosha–Rockford Rail Line. It's an area of rolling plains and two lakes. Pierce Lake, with 162 acres, is a retreat for people wanting to fish, ice fish, or ice skate. The 50-acre Olson Lake is especially for swimmers. Laid out in a series of one-way loops, the wilderness campground, 2 miles north of Loves Park, offers grassy sites for tent campers and gravel pads for RVs with hookups. Sitting on a point overlooking Pierce Lake, site 20 is the most popular for tents. Reservations are not accepted for the site so campers often start arriving around noon, looking to see if the site will be vacated at the 3 p.m. check-out time. For RVs, the 400 loop of sites on the even side are the most popular because of the trees and privacy. The campground has a mix of shady and open sites for RVs but offers no pull-throughs. Security is excellent with a gate that is locked at 10 p.m. and regular patrols of the grounds. A big sign at the entrance warns visitors "Don't get locked in" because the park closes at 10 p.m. Rock Cut has speed bumps as well as speed checked by radar. The campground is very serious about its one-way entrance and exit—nails will chew up the tires of any vehicle that tries to go the wrong way.

BASICS

Operated By: State of Illinois. **Open:** All year. **Site Assignment:** Reservations w/ 1-night deposit plus $5 fee; refund (minus $5) w/ 3-day notice. **Registration:** At campground office. **Fee:** Electric, $20; no electric, $12. **Parking:** At site.

FACILITIES

Number of RV-only Sites: 220. **Number of Tent-only Sites:** 60. **Hookups:** Electric (30, 50 amps). **Each Site:** Picnic table, grill. **Dump Station:** Yes. **Laundry:** No. **Pay Phone:** No. **Restrooms and Showers:** Yes. **Fuel:** No. **Propane:** No. **Internal Roads:** Paved, in good condition. **RV Service:** No. **Market:** 2 mi. south in Loves Park. **Restaurant:** On site. **General Store:** Yes. **Vending:** Yes. **Swimming:** Beach. **Playground:** Yes. **Other:** Pierce Lake, Olson Lake, swimming beach, hiking trails, boat launch, equestrian trails, fishing pier, concession stand, bait shop. **Activities:** Fishing, swimming, hiking, boating (rental rowboats & paddleboats). **Nearby Attractions:** Museums, BMX track, bowling, golf, nature preserve, tennis, Magic Waters, horseback riding, theater, speedway, antique & art shops. **Additional Information:** Rockford Area CVB, (800) 521-0849.

RESTRICTIONS

Pets: On leash only. **Fires:** Grill only; ground fires not allowed. **Alcoholic Beverages:** Not allowed. **Vehicle Maximum Length:** 40 ft. **Other:** 2-week stay limit.

TO GET THERE

From junction of US 51 and Hwy. 173, drive 3 mi. west on Hwy. 173. Roads are wide and well maintained, with good shoulders.

SAVANNA   MAP, A-2
Mississippi Palisades State Park

16327 A IL 84, 61074. T: (815) 273-2731; www.dnr.state.il.us.

🚐 ★★★   ⛺ ★★★★

Beauty: ★★★★	Site Privacy: ★★★★
Spaciousness: ★★★★	Quiet: ★★★★
Security: ★★★★	Cleanliness: ★★★★
Insect Control: ★★	Facilities: ★★

Palisades is the word used to describe a line of lofty, steep cliffs usually seen along a river. Mississippi Palisades, 3 miles north of Savanna, handsomely lives up to its name. Caves are evident, as are dangerous sink holes—limestone caves that go straight down. Atop the bluffs, erosion has carved intriguing rock formations, such as Indian Head and Twin Sisters, which bear keen resemblance to a pair of human figures. With sites in both shaded and open areas, the campground is in demand. Because of its popularity, reservations are not accepted. RV sites have gravel pads and are generally open; 12 are pull-throughs. The best RV site is 64, on the corner of a one-way road and away from tent campers. The best tent site is 25, private and grassy and located over the edge of a hill so no headlights hit it. Three primitive walk-in sites are also tucked into Mississippi Palisades. By hiking about 0.5 miles, you'll be able to enjoy rustic camping along the park's serene northern trails. Natural beauty abounds, but Mississippi Palisades sure could use a good swimming spot.

BASICS

Operated By: Illinois Dept. of Natural Resources. **Open:** All year. **Site Assignment:** First come, first served; no reservations. **Registration:** At campground office. **Fee:** (May 1–Nov.1) electric, $15; tent, $10; (Nov.1–May 1) electric, $13; no electric, $8. **Parking:** At site.

FACILITIES

Number of RV-only Sites: 110. **Number of Tent-only Sites:** 137. **Hookups:** Electric (20, 30, 50 amps). **Each Site:** Picnic table, fire ring. **Dump Station:** Yes. **Laundry:** No. **Pay Phone:** Yes. **Restrooms and Showers:** Yes. **Fuel:** No. **Propane:** No. **Internal Roads:** Paved, in good condition. **RV Service:** No. **Market:** 3 mi. south in Savanna. **Restaurant:** 3 mi. south in Savanna. **General Store:** Yes, open during the summer. **Vending:** No. **Swimming:** No. **Playground:** Yes. **Other:** Mississippi River, boat ramp, boat dock, hiking trails. **Activities:** Fishing, boating, hiking, hunting, nature

programs, slide shows. **Nearby Attractions:** Antique mall, marinas, Savanna-Sabula Bridge, playhouse, scenic drives, golf. **Additional Information:** Northern Illinois Tourism Development Office, (815) 547-3740.

RESTRICTIONS

Pets: On leash only. **Fires:** Fire ring only. **Alcoholic Beverages:** Not allowed. **Vehicle Maximum Length:** No limit. **Other:** 2-day stay limit in a 30-day period.

TO GET THERE

From junction of US 52 and SR 84, drive 2 mi. north on SR 84. Park is 3 mi. north of Savanna. The state road is narrow and winding, with limited shoulders.

SECOR   MAP, B-2
Hickory Hills Campground

973 CR 2250 East, 61771. T: (888) 801-4469; www.hickoryhillcamp.com.

🚐 ★★★   ⛺ ★★★

Beauty: ★★★	Site Privacy: ★★★
Spaciousness: ★★★	Quiet: ★★★★
Security: ★★★★	Cleanliness: ★★★★
Insect Control: ★★	Facilities: ★★★

Hickory Hills Campground is what it sounds like—a grassy rural facility with a lot of trees. The typical site width is 25 feet, and the campground has 12 pull-throughs. About half of the sites are occupied by seasonal campers. Located 4 miles west of El Paso, the campground is level, with a mix of grassy and gravel sites along with shady or open ones. Many campers are repeats who come for the family atmosphere and recreation. Safety measures are enforced, including a 5 mph speed limit. Anyone driving a golf cart must be licensed and all golf carts must be insured if they are driven on the road. Quiet time is 10 p.m. to 8 a.m. on weekdays and midnight to 8 a.m. on weekends. The campground has one entrance road and owners who live on site providing a regular patrol of the campgrounds.

BASICS

Operated By: Bryan and Vicki Outinen. **Open:** Apr. 1–Nov 1. **Site Assignment:** Reservations w/o deposit; holiday weekends require 1-night deposit; personal checks accepted; no credit cards. **Registration:** At campground office. **Fee:** $26. **Parking:** At site.

FACILITIES

Number of RV-only Sites: 179. **Number of Tent-only Sites:** 110. **Hookups:** Electric (20, 30, 50 amps), water, sewer. **Each Site:** Picnic table, fire ring. **Dump Station:** Yes. **Laundry:** Yes. **Pay Phone:** Courtesy phone. **Restrooms and Showers:** Yes. **Fuel:** No. **Propane:** Yes. **Internal Roads:** Gravel, in good condition. **RV Service:** No. **Market:** 4 mi. east in El Paso. **Restaurant:** 4 mi. east in El Paso. **General Store:** Yes. **Vending:** No. **Swimming:** Yes. **Playground:** Yes. **Other:** Mini-golf, rec hall, video games, horseshoes, volleyball, basketball, fishing stream, hiking trails, sports field, shuffleboard. **Activities:** Swimming, fishing, hiking, planned weekend activities. **Nearby Attractions:** Nature center, zoo,

museum, casino, antique shops, art galleries, botanical garden, golf. **Additional Information:** Peoria Area CVB, (800) 747-0302.

RESTRICTIONS

Pets: On leash only. **Fires:** Fire ring only. **Alcoholic Beverages:** Allowed. **Vehicle Maximum Length:** No limit.

TO GET THERE

From junction of I-39 and US 24, take Exit 14, drive 4 mi. west on US 24, then 0.25 mi. south on a county road. Roads are wide and well maintained, with adequate shoulders.

SPRINGFIELD   MAP, B-2
Double J. Campground

9683 Palm Rd., 62629. T: (217) 483-9998; www.doublejcampground.com.

🚐 ★★★★   ⛺ ★★★★

Beauty: ★★★	Site Privacy: ★★★★
Spaciousness: ★★★	Quiet: ★★★★
Security: ★★★★	Cleanliness: ★★★★
Insect Control: ★★	Facilities: ★★★★

Located 15 minutes from downtown Springfield, the campground is a popular spot for folks enjoying the area's historical attractions. The campground also gets many repeat campers who come mainly for the facilities and activities. Arranged in a series of loops, the campground offers a rural setting with mostly pull-through sites. Typical site width is 30 feet, and sites are a mixture of gravel and grass. Most sites are wooded and shady but some are open. RVs favor the sites in the 90s section because they are pull-throughs and offer 50 amps electricity. Tent sites are fairly isolated from the general campground, offering more privacy, grass, and trees. Security is good, with owners who live on the grounds, regular patrols, and the presence of state police from headquarters 2 miles away.

BASICS

Operated By: Jerry and Jeri Francis. **Open:** Apr. 1–Oct 31. **Site Assignment:** Reservations w/ 1-night deposit; no refunds; cash, checks, credit cards accepted. **Registration:** At campground office. **Fee:** $28. **Parking:** At site.

FACILITIES

Number of RV-only Sites: 136. **Number of Tent-only Sites:** 14. **Hookups:** Electric (30, 50 amps), water, sewer, Wi-Fi. **Each Site:** Picnic table, fire rings at most sites. **Dump Station:** Yes. **Laundry:** Yes. **Pay Phone:** Yes. **Restrooms and Showers:** Yes. **Fuel:** No. **Propane:** Yes. **Internal Roads:** Gravel, in good condition. **RV Service:** Yes. **Market:** 5 mi. west in Chatham. **Restaurant:** 5 mi. west in Chatham. **General Store:** Yes, country store and RV parts. **Vending:** No. **Swimming:** Yes. **Playground:** Yes. **Other:** Mini-golf, tennis, rec room, baseball, basketball, Wi-Fi. **Activities:** Swimming, planned weekend activities. **Nearby Attractions:** Lincoln-related historical sites, Illinois State Museum, Frank Lloyd Wright home, scenic drive, bike trail, golf, state fair, Lake Springfield, Hensen Robinson Zoo. **Additional Information:** Springfield CVB, (800) 545-7300.

RESTRICTIONS

Pets: On leash. **Fires:** Fire pit only. **Alcoholic Beverages:** Allowed. **Vehicle Maximum Length:** No limit; big rig friendly.

TO GET THERE

On I-55 Frontage Rd., 1 mi. south of Springfield, between Exits 88 and 83. Roads are wide and well maintained, with broad shoulders.

SPRINGFIELD   MAP, B-2
Mr. Lincoln's Campground

3045 Stanton St., 62703. T: (217) 529-8206.

🚐 ★★★   ▲ ★★★

Beauty: ★★★   Site Privacy: ★★★
Spaciousness: ★★★   Quiet: ★★★
Security: ★★★★   Cleanliness: ★★★★
Insect Control: ★★   Facilities: ★★★

Location is everything, and Mr. Lincoln's Campground sure has it. This urban campground in Springfield is in the midst of more historical sites and recreational opportunities than most other facilities dream of. First and foremost, the area is filled with Abraham Lincoln attractions. The campground also is on the bus line to downtown and the White Oaks Mall. In addition to being the only campground in Lincoln's hometown, the facility also offers the area's largest RV center with parts and service. The campground is laid out in a series of loops, with 30 feet the typical site width. All RV sites have gravel pads, some are shady, and others open. There are 15 pull-throughs. The tent area is separated from RVs and offers more shade and privacy. Because it has a large yard, 51 is the best RV site. All tent sites are similar—secluded, quiet, and tree-lined. The campground has good security measures including a manager staying on the premises, regular staff patrols, one entrance/exit, and patrols by city police. The campground also is completely fenced.

BASICS

Operated By: Sue Johnson. **Open:** All year. **Site Assignment:** Reservations highly recommended; 1-night deposit for special events and holidays; refund w/ 24-hour notice; MC, V, D, personal checks accepted. **Registration:** At campground office. **Fee:** Full hookup, $27. **Parking:** At site.

FACILITIES

Number of RV-only Sites: 42. **Number of Tent-only Sites:** 108. **Hookups:** Electric (30, 50 amps), water, sewer, cable TV. **Each Site:** Picnic table, fire ring. **Dump Station:** Yes. **Laundry:** Yes. **Pay Phone:** No. **Restrooms and Showers:** Yes. **Fuel:** No. **Propane:** Yes. **Internal Roads:** Gravel, in fair condition. **RV Service:** Yes. **Market:** 1 mi. west. **Restaurant:** 0.5 mi. in either direction. **General Store:** Yes. **Vending:** Yes. **Swimming:** No. **Playground:** No. **Other:** Horseshoes, sauna, sports field, movies, RV parts, Internet access, DVDs, accessory store. **Activities:** Local tours. **Nearby Attractions:** Lincoln historical sites, golf, theaters, shopping center, antique malls, lake, universities, walking tours, Old State Capitol, Museum of Funeral Customs, zoo,

botanical gardens, wildlife sanctuary. **Additional Information:** Springfield CVB, (800) 545-7300.

RESTRICTIONS

Pets: On leash only. **Fires:** Fire ring only. **Alcoholic Beverages:** Allowed. **Vehicle Maximum Length:** No limit.

TO GET THERE

From junction of I-55 and Stevenson Dr., take Exit 94 and drive 1 mi. west on Stevenson Dr., then 1 block north on Stanton St. Roads are wide and well maintained, with broad shoulders.

SYCAMORE   MAP, A-2
Sycamore RV Resort

reserve america

375 East North Ave., 60178. T: (815) 895-5590; www.reserveamerica.com.

🚐 ★★★   ▲ n/a

Beauty: ★★★   Site Privacy: ★★★
Spaciousness: ★★★   Quiet: ★★★★
Security: ★★★   Cleanliness: ★★★★
Insect Control: ★★   Facilities: ★★★

Sycamore RV Resort is surprisingly quiet, especially since it is located right in the town of Sycamore. Surrounded on three sides by water and woods, the campground has a natural buffer to keep out urban noises. The owners also enforce rules to keep the peace. Beach hours are 11 a.m. to 6 p.m. and no scheduled activities are planned. The campground also does not allow motorcycle campers or tent campers. All fishing in the two lakes is catch-and-release only and stops at dusk. Laid out in a series of loops, the campground has a typical site width of 30 feet and 14 pull-throughs. RVs park in a level gravel site with a choice of trees or open. Most popular RV sites are 22–46 because they are located along the lake. The campground tends to be crowded and reservations are recommended. Sycamore's annual pumpkin festival in October and other town activities and attractions are located within walking distance.

BASICS

Operated By: Dale and Anita Cappel. **Open:** All year. **Site Assignment:** Reservations suggested w/ credit card; MC, V, personal checks accepted. **Registration:** At campground office. **Fee:** $25–$28. **Parking:** At site.

FACILITIES

Number of RV-only Sites: 86. **Hookups:** Electric (30, 50 amps), water, sewer, phone, Internet. **Each Site:** Picnic table, fire ring. **Dump Station:** Yes. **Laundry:** Yes. **Pay Phone:** Yes. **Restrooms and Showers:** Yes (coin-op.). **Fuel:** No. **Propane:** Yes. **Internal Roads:** Gravel, in good condition. **RV Service:** No. **Market:** 3 blocks in Sycamore. **Restaurant:** 2 blocks in Sycamore. **General Store:** Yes. **Vending:** Soda. **Swimming:** Beach. **Playground:** No. **Other:** 2 spring-fed lakes, swimming beach, boat rentals, sports field, volleyball. **Activities:** Swimming, fishing, boating (rental paddleboats & rowboats).

Nearby Attractions: Golf, speedway, nature trail, Northern Illinois University, historic district walking tour. **Additional Information:** Northern Illinois Tourism Development Office, (815) 547-3740.

RESTRICTIONS

Pets: On leash only. **Fires:** Fire ring only. **Alcoholic Beverages:** At sites only. **Vehicle Maximum Length:** No limit. **Other:** No tent camping; no camping motorcyclists.

TO GET THERE

From junction of Hwy. 64 and Hwy. 23, drive 4 blocks north on Hwy. 23, then 200 yards east on East North Ave. Roads are wide and well maintained, with adequate shoulders.

UTICA   MAP, A-2
LaSalle-Peru KOA

756 North 3150th Rd., 61373. T: (800) 562-9498 or (815) 667-4988; www.koa.com.

🚐 ★★★★   ▲ ★★★★

Beauty: ★★★★   Site Privacy: ★★★
Spaciousness: ★★★   Quiet: ★★★★
Security: ★★★★   Cleanliness: ★★★★★
Insect Control: ★★   Facilities: ★★★

LaSalle-Peru KOA is a clean, quiet campground out in the country. No highway noise or passing trains disturb the setting. Located one-and-a-half hours from Chicago, the campground is a popular getaway for city dwellers wanting some peace and quiet, along with good recreation facilities. Quiet hours are enforced between 10 p.m. and 7 a.m. Bicycle riding is not allowed after dark, and generators are not permitted at any time. Another rule enforcing the quiet time requires that pets be confined in an enclosed vehicle or tent at night. If campers leave the campground, they must take their pets with them. Sites are mostly grassy and shady, with a common width of 30 feet. Laid out in a series of loops, the campground has 40 pull-through sites. The laundry uses soft water, and the camp store offers rental videos. TV reception varies between excellent and poor. Prime time reception is usually better. Tent sites offer some privacy from RVs, grass, and shade from tall oak trees.

BASICS

Operated By: Dave and Linda Waszak. **Open:** Apr. 1–Oct. 31. **Site Assignment:** Reservations recommended; no deposit required. **Registration:** At campground office. **Fee:** RV, $29–$37; tent, $25–$28. **Parking:** At site.

FACILITIES

Number of RV-only Sites: 65. **Number of Tent-only Sites:** 40. **Hookups:** Electric (30, 50 amps), water, sewer. **Each Site:** Picnic table, fire ring. **Dump Station:** Yes. **Laundry:** Yes. **Pay Phone:** Yes. **Restrooms and Showers:** Yes. **Fuel:** No. **Propane:** No. **Internal Roads:** Gravel, in good condition. **RV Service:** No. **Market:** 4 mi. south in Utica. **Restaurant:** 2 mi. south in Utica. **General Store:** Yes. **Vending:** Yes. **Swimming:** Yes. **Playground:** Yes. **Other:** Small fishing creek, game room, horseshoes, recreation field, badminton, volleyball, heated pool,

Internet access available for fee. **Activities:** Swimming, fishing, planned weekend activities. **Nearby Attractions:** Antique shops, golf, stock car races, horseback riding, I & M Canal State Trail, LaSalle County Historical Society, Matthiessen State Park, Starved Rock State Park. **Additional Information:** Heritage Corridor Visitors Bureau, (800) 926-2262.

RESTRICTIONS

Pets: On leash only. **Fires:** Fire ring only. **Alcoholic Beverages:** Allowed. **Vehicle Maximum Length:** 70 ft. **Other:** No visitors. Everyone must be a registered guest. If friends or family are visiting, they must register on a separate campsite.

TO GET THERE

From junction of I-80 and SR 178, take Exit 81, drive north 1.5 mi. on SR 178 to North 3150th Rd., then drive west 0.5 mi. Roads are wide and well maintained, with broad shoulders.

VANDALIA   MAP, C-2
Okaw Valley Kampground

R.R. 2 Box 55A, 1325 Boley Rd., 62418.
www.okawvalley.com.

🚐 ★★★   ⛺ ★★★

Beauty: ★★★★	Site Privacy: ★★★★
Spaciousness: ★★★★	Quiet: ★★★
Security: ★★★	Cleanliness: ★★★★
Insect Control: ★★	Facilities: ★★★

A partially shaded campground on rolling terrain 5 miles east of Vandalia, Okaw Valley Campground is a popular overnight destination with travelers passing through on I-70. The campground is located 330 miles, or about a day's drive, from Branson. The typical site width is 30 feet, and the campground has 25 pull-throughs. Arranged in a series of loops, the rural campground offers both shady and open sites, with mostly gravel spots for RVs. There is a section for tent sites away from RVs, as well as a primitive tent site featuring more grass, trees, and privacy. A five-acre lake allows boating and fishing but no swimming. No license is required to fish in the lake; the catch is mostly bass, catfish, and bluegill. The TV lounge and Laundromat are open 24 hours a day. A service sink on the north wall outside the washrooms is provided for washing pots, pans, and dishes. A 5 mph speed limit is enforced, as is a 10 p.m. to 7 a.m. quiet time.

BASICS

Operated By: Jim and Elizabeth Klotz. **Open:** Apr. 1–Oct. 31. **Site Assignment:** Reservations w/ 1-night deposit; refunds w/ 24-hour notice. **Registration:** At campground office. **Fee:** Full hookup, $25; water/electric, $22; electric, $20; no hookup, $16. Based on 2 adults, 2 children. Extra adult, $2; extra child over 3, $1.50. **Parking:** At site.

FACILITIES

Number of Multipurpose Sites: 52. **Hookups:** Electric (20, 30 amps), water, sewer. **Each Site:** Picnic table, fire ring. **Dump Station:** Yes. **Laundry:** Yes. **Pay Phone:** No. **Restrooms and Showers:** Yes. **Fuel:** No. **Propane:** No. **Internal Roads:** Gravel, in good condition. **RV Service:** No. **Market:** 3 mi. east in Brownstown. **Restaurant:** 5 mi. west in Vandalia. **General Store:** Yes. **Vending:** No. **Swimming:** Yes. **Playground:** Yes. **Other:** Lake, volleyball, basketball, TV lounge, game room, boat dock, rec room, sports field, pavilion. **Activities:** Swimming, fishing, boating (rental paddleboats & rowboats), biking, planned activities. **Nearby Attractions:** Vandalia State House, Fayette County Museum, Steam Engine Museum, golf, roller skating, stock car races, Alwerdt's Gardens. **Additional Information:** Vandalia Chamber of Commerce, (618) 283-2728.

RESTRICTIONS

Pets: On leash only. **Fires:** Fire ring only. **Alcoholic Beverages:** Allowed. **Vehicle Maximum Length:** No limit.

TO GET THERE

From junction of I-70 and US 40, take Exit 68 and drive 1,000 feet north on US 40, then 0.25 mi. west on frontage road. Roads are wide and well maintained, with broad shoulders.

WEST YORK   MAP, C-3
Hickory Holler Campground

9876 East 2000th Ave., 62478. T: (618) 563-4779; www.woodalls.com/a/01008_hickoryholler.html.

🚐 ★★★   ⛺ ★★★

Beauty: ★★★	Site Privacy: ★★★★
Spaciousness: ★★★★	Quiet: ★★★★
Security: ★★★★	Cleanliness: ★★★★
Insect Control: ★★★	Facilities: ★★★

A quiet, rural campground (8 miles north of West Union) with an emphasis on Christian activities, Hickory Holler Campground offers spacious, peaceful surroundings. The typical site width is 40 feet, with grassy sites and a good mixture of shaded and open areas. As the name implies, Hickory Holler is blessed with mature hickory trees. Gospel sing-alongs are held in an old remodeled cattle barn, and nightly campfires offer community get-togethers. Despite the absence of a swimming pool, the campground offers a lot of varied activities and clean surroundings for a low fee (the $14 rate is about half what other area campgrounds charge). Primitive sites for tent campers feature trees and privacy from RV campers. Security lights, an owner who lives on the grounds, and regular patrols add to campground security.

BASICS

Operated By: Tom and Leola Guyer. **Open:** All year. **Site Assignment:** Reservations w/ 1-night deposit; refunds w/ 24-hour notice. **Registration:** At campground office. **Fee:** Water/electric, $14; water/electric/sewer, $15. **Parking:** At site.

FACILITIES

Number of RV-only Sites: 80. **Number of Tent-only Sites:** 20. **Hookups:** Electric (30, 50 amps), water, sewer. **Each Site:** Picnic table, fire ring. **Dump Station:** Yes. **Laundry:** Yes. **Pay Phone:** No. **Restrooms and Showers:** Yes. **Fuel:** No. **Propane:** No. **Internal Roads:** Gravel, in good condition. **RV Service:** No. **Market:** 12 mi. south in Robinson. **Restaurant:** 7 mi. north in West Union. **General Store:** No. **Vending:** No. **Swimming:** No. **Playground:** Yes. **Other:** Mini-golf, rec hall, video games, pool table, 2 lakes. **Activities:** Fishing, boating (rental paddleboats available), nightly community campfires, monthly gospel sing-alongs, talent night. **Nearby Attractions:** Crawford County Historical Museum, military museum, Lincoln Trail College, parks. **Additional Information:** Springfield CVB, (800) 545-7300.

RESTRICTIONS

Pets: On leash only. **Fires:** Fire ring only. **Alcoholic Beverages:** Not allowed. **Vehicle Maximum Length:** 40 ft.

TO GET THERE

From Marshall, drive 18 mi. south on Hwy. 1 to Annapolis Rd. Drive 4 mi. west on Annapolis Rd. to Hickory Holler Campground. Roads are wide and well maintained, with broad shoulders.

Indiana

Home of American icons like James Dean and the Indy 500, the Hoosier State offers unique treats from its "crossroads of America." For starters, the world-famous **Indianapolis Motor Speedway** boasts some of the fastest speeds, smoothest racecars, and most skilled drivers in the racing world. For almost 90 years the world has converged in Speedway to watch the legendary Indy 500. Today, after years of being an exclusively Formula One track, the Motor Speedway has succumbed to the overwhelming popularity of NASCAR and hosts the **Brickyard 400** in August in addition to several seasonal stock-car races. The **Hall of Fame Museum** is impressive as well—featuring over 70 cars year-round, as well as traveling exhibits. Downtown Indianapolis is home to some of the Midwest's most beautiful architecture and several museums. Campers who might find so much concrete and burning rubber a bit daunting can still find plenty of refuge in the city—Indianapolis also is home to 113 city parks, including the 250-acre **White River State Park** right in the heart of the city.

Of course, there's plenty to see outside of Indianapolis. A prime example is the continuously changing artwork seen at the Indiana Dunes. Authorized by Congress as a national lakeshore in 1966, the **Indiana Duns** runs 25 miles along southern Lake Michigan. The park contains 15,000 acres of beach, sand dunes, bog, wetlands, woodland forests, a Canadian homestead from the 1830s, and a early 20th-century farmhouse. Botanically inclined travelers might note that Indiana Dunes is ranked seventh among national parks in native plant diversity. There are almost 1,500 vascular plant species within the park—90 of which are on Indiana's threatened or endangered list. Hikers will enjoy the park's many trails in addition to the challenge of hiking along the dunes. **Wolf Park** in Lafayette is a nonprofit education and research facility that specializes in interpack and individual wolf behavior. Open to the public from May through November, Wolf Park has several seminars (that are rather pricey for casual tourists) dealing with how these fascinating creatures eat, live, and communicate. On Saturday nights throughout the year, Wolf Park has Howl Night. For $5 (less for kids) you can listen—or howl along—to the wolves in their natural habitat. The scenic hills of 195,000-acre **Hoosier National Forest** are perfect for hiking. See the many species of coral and prehistoric ocean life in the fossil bed at **Falls of the Ohio State Park** in Clarksville, or enjoy the unusual limestone formations and waterfalls at **McCormick's Creek State Park,** east of Spencer. The short life of James Dean is celebrated in his hometown of Fairmount, where the *Rebel Without a Cause* star was born and buried.

Spelunking is special in Indiana, where an electric boat takes visitors through **Bluespring Caverns** in Bedford. Hear the story of how Marengo Cave was discovered by two youngsters, or see the cave where Daniel Boone's brother, Squire, is buried in Corydon. Rent a pontoon boat and cruise Bloomington's **Lake Monroe** to catch a glimpse of a nesting bald eagle, or head to Madison to experience the timeless treasure of this beautifully preserved river town. Auburn's history as a luxury-car manufacturing town is recalled at the **Auburn Cord Duesenberg Museum,** and Columbus has architectural landmarks designed by masters, including I. M. Pei.

French Lick and next-door neighbor West Baden were early resorts and health centers because of abundant artesian springs. Take a ride on the historic 1920s railroad and visit the amazing **West Baden Springs Hotel,** whose domed atrium was once considered the Eighth Wonder of the World. In Nashville, the area's beauty led to the establishment of an artists' colony that still thrives today, along with the **Little Nashville Opry,** which showcases top country music stars. Remnants of a utopian community draw visitors to **New Harmony,** and the nation's first theme park thrills families at **Holiday World and Splashin' Safari** in Santa Claus. Home to one of the world's largest Amish communities, Shipshewana also has what is said to be the biggest flea market in America.

Campground Profiles

BEDFORD
Hardin Ridge— Hoosier National Forest
MAP, C-2

reserve america

811 Constitution Ave., 47421. T: (812) 837-9453; www.reserveamerica.com.

🚐 ★★★★   ⛺ ★★★★

Beauty: ★★★★
Spaciousness: ★★★★
Security: ★★★★
Insect Control: ★★★★

Site Privacy: ★★★
Quiet: ★★★
Cleanliness: ★★★★
Facilities: ★★★

The 1,200-acre Hardin Ridge recreational complex is located on the shores of Monroe Reservoir. Located just southeast of Bloomington, the area is easily accessible from State Highway 446. The area offers camping, picnicking, boat launching, swimming, nature walks, and interpretive programs in a forested environment. All sites are shaded and private. Facilities provided include hardened tent pads, water fountains, telephones, hot showers, flush toilets, boat launch, playground, and picnic area. Hardin Ridge is located within the Hoosier National Forest, in the hills of south central Indiana, and provides a wide mix of opportunities and resources for people to enjoy. Rolling hills, back-country trails, and rural crossroad communities make this small but beautiful forest a favorite. Forest managers work with the public to develop a shared vision of how this 200,000-acre forest should be managed. The challenge is to provide a forest with the values and benefits people want while protecting the unique ecosystems on the Hoosier National Forest.

BASICS

Operated By: U.S. Forest Service. **Open:** Apr. 13–Oct. 28. **Site Assignment:** Reservations must be made at least 4 days in advance. **Registration:** At office. **Fee:** Single, $15–$21; cabin, $45. **Parking:** At park.

FACILITIES

Number of Multipurpose Sites: 345. **Hookups:** None. **Each Site:** Fire ring. **Dump Station:** No. **Laundry:** No. **Pay Phone:** Yes. **Restrooms and Showers:** Yes. **Fuel:** No. **Propane:** No. **Internal Roads:** Paved. **RV Service:** No. **Market:** No. **Restaurant:** No. **General Store:** Nearby. **Vending:** No. **Swimming:** Yes. **Playground:** Yes. **Activities:** Biking, boating, hiking, horseshoes.

RESTRICTIONS

Pets: Pets must be restrained or on a leash at all times while in developed recreation areas. **Fires:** In fire rings, stoves, grills, or fireplaces provided for that purpose. **Alcoholic Beverages:** Not allowed. **Vehicle Maximum Length:** Call ahead.

TO GET THERE

From Bedford go 7 mi. east on US 50. Go north on SR 446 for 12 mi. Turn west on Chapel Hill Rd. Go 2 mi. to Hardin Ridge Recreation Area. From Bloomington 46 and 446 intersection, go 14 mi.

BEDFORD
Indian Celina Lake— Hoosier National Forest
MAP, C-2

south on SR 446. Turn west on Chapel Hill Rd. (See Web site for further directions).

reserve america

811 Constitution Ave., 47421. T: (812) 843-4880; www.reserveamerica.com.

🚐 ★★★★   ⛺ ★★★★

Beauty: ★★★★
Spaciousness: ★★★★
Security: ★★★★
Insect Control: ★★★★

Site Privacy: ★★★
Quiet: ★★★
Cleanliness: ★★★★
Facilities: ★★★★

The Indian and Celina Recreation Area is a tranquil getaway in the midst of the Hoosier National Forest. The recreation area contains Celina Lake (164 ac.) and Indian Lake (152 ac.). It is located 3 miles south of Interstate 64, off State Highway 37. The recreation area offers camping, electric motor boating, fishing, and hiking, as well as an interesting historical site. Indian Celina Lake is located within the Hoosier National Forest, in the hills of south central Indiana, and provides a wide mix of opportunities and resources for people to enjoy. Rolling hills, back-country trails, and rural crossroad communities make this small but beautiful forest a favorite. Forest managers work with the public to develop a shared vision of how this 200,000-acre forest should be managed. The challenge is to provide a forest with the values and benefits people want while protecting the unique ecosystems on the Hoosier National Forest.

BASICS

Operated By: U.S. Forest Service. **Open:** Feb. 1–Nov. 30. **Site Assignment:** Reservations must be made at least 4 days in advance. **Registration:** At office. **Fee:** Single, $15–$18; double, $27–$32. **Parking:** At park.

FACILITIES

Number of Multipurpose Sites: 82. **Hookups:** None. **Each Site:** Call ahead. **Dump Station:** No. **Laundry:** No. **Pay Phone:** Yes. **Restrooms and Showers:** Yes. **Fuel:** No. **Propane:** No. **Internal Roads:** Paved. **RV Service:** No. **Market:** No. **Restaurant:** No. **General Store:** Nearby. **Vending:** No. **Swimming:** Yes. **Playground:** Yes. **Activities:** Biking, fishing, hiking, hunting.

RESTRICTIONS

Pets: Pets must be restrained or on a leash at all times while in developed recreation areas. **Fires:** In fire rings, stoves, grills, or fireplaces provided for that purpose. **Alcoholic Beverages:** Not allowed. **Vehicle Maximum Length:** Call ahead. **Other:** No horses are allowed in this campground.

TO GET THERE

Located 3 mi. south of I-64 off IN 37 in Perry County.

BEDFORD
Tipsaw Lake— Hoosier National Forest
MAP, C-2

reserve america

811 Constitution Ave., 47421. T: (812) 843-4890; www.reserveamerica.com.

🚐 ★★★★   ⛺ ★★★★

Beauty: ★★★★
Spaciousness: ★★★★
Security: ★★★★
Insect Control: ★★★★

Site Privacy: ★★★★
Quiet: ★★★
Cleanliness: ★★★★
Facilities: ★★★

The Tipsaw recreational complex is located on the shores of the 131-acre Tipsaw Lake. Tipsaw includes 35 individual sites divided into two shady campground loops. There are more than 5 miles of predominantly single-track mountain-biking trail circling the lake. This is a great route on which to introduce novices to Indiana's fational forest. The grades are relatively easy; there are a couple of moderate climbs, and the lake stays in view much of the ride. After the ride, go for a swim, angle for fish, or simply relax at your campsite—then ride some more. Trail surface is single-track, double-track, and forest road. Tipsaw Lake is located within the Hoosier National Forest, in the hills of south central Indiana, and provides a wide mix of opportunities and resources for people to enjoy. Rolling hills, backcountry trails, and rural crossroad communities make this small but beautiful forest a favorite. Forest managers work with the public to develop a shared vision of how this 200,000-acre forest should be managed. The challenge is to provide a forest with the values and benefits people want while protecting the unique ecosystems on the Hoosier National Forest.

BASICS

Operated By: U.S. Forest Service. **Open:** Apr. 1–Oct. 12. **Site Assignment:** Reservations must be made at least 4 days in advance. **Registration:** At office. **Fee:** Single, $12. **Parking:** At park.

FACILITIES

Number of Multipurpose Sites: 59. **Hookups:** Yes. **Each Site:** Call ahead. **Dump Station:** No. **Laundry:** No. **Pay Phone:** Yes. **Restrooms and Showers:** Yes. **Fuel:** No. **Propane:** No. **Internal Roads:** Paved. **RV Service:** No. **Market:** No. **Restaurant:** No. **General Store:** Yes. **Vending:** No. **Swimming:** Yes. **Playground:** No. **Activities:** Boating, fishing, hiking, horse shoes, hunting, horseback riding.

RESTRICTIONS

Pets: Pets must be restrained or on a leash at all times while in developed recreation areas. **Fires:** In fire rings, stoves, grills, or fireplaces provided for that purpose. **Alcoholic Beverages:** Not allowed. **Vehicle Maximum Length:** Call ahead. **Other:** Electric motors are allowed only on the lake. No horses in the campground.

TO GET THERE
Located 6 mi. south of I-64 and 17 mi. north of Tell City, Indiana on IN 37.

BLOOMINGTON MAP, C-2
Lake Monroe Village Recreation Resort

8107 South Fairfax Rd., 47401. T: (812) 824-CAMP; www.lakemonroevillage.com.

🚐 ★★★★   ⛺ ★★★★

Beauty: ★★★★
Spaciousness: ★★★★
Security: ★★★★
Insect Control: ★★

Site Privacy: ★★★★
Quiet: ★★★★
Cleanliness: ★★★★
Facilities: ★★★★

Arriving at Lake Monroe Village Recreation Resort, visitors are greeted with a smile and escorted on a tour of the facilities. Campers have a choice of any available sites and are allowed to see them before choosing. Located 8 miles southeast of Bloomington, the campground has 30 seasonal campers, 25 pull-through sites, and a typical site width of 24 feet. Laid out in a series of loops, the rural campground offers open and shaded sites. The chlorine-free pool uses electronic purification. Other water recreation choices are an adults-only hot tub and a baby pool. Security measures include surveillance cameras and gates at the entrance and exit. Speed limit is 5 mph and quiet times are from 11 p.m. to 8 a.m. Little touches such as stone walls used as terraces between some sites add to the beauty and quietness of the campground.

BASICS
Operated By: Sandy and Nelson Cicchitto. **Open:** All year. **Site Assignment:** Reservations w/ 1-night deposit; refund w/ 7-day notice. **Registration:** At campground office. **Fee:** $28.75–$42; cash, check, credit card. **Parking:** At site.

FACILITIES
Number of RV-only Sites: 125. **Number of Tent-only Sites:** 50. **Hookups:** Electric (20, 30, 50 amps), water, sewer. **Each Site:** Picnic table, fire ring. **Dump Station:** Yes. **Laundry:** Yes. **Pay Phone:** Yes. **Restrooms and Showers:** Yes. **Fuel:** No. **Propane:** Yes. **Internal Roads:** Gravel, in good condition. **RV Service:** No. **Market:** 6 mi. north in Bloomington. **Restaurant:** 1.5 mi. north in Fairfax. **General Store:** Yes. **Vending:** Yes. **Swimming:** Yes. **Playground:** Yes. **Other:** Pavilion, baseball, hot tub, volleyball, basketball, horseshoes, rec hall, rental cabins, badminton, sports field. **Activities:** Swimming. **Nearby Attractions:** Lake Monroe, Indiana University, golf, antiques, arts & crafts, boating, fishing, museums, historic homes, bike park, speedway, horseback riding, wineries. **Additional Information:** Bloomington/Monroe County CVB, (800) 800-0037.

RESTRICTIONS
Pets: On leash only. **Fires:** Fire ring only. **Alcoholic Beverages:** At sites only. **Vehicle Maximum Length:** No limit.

TO GET THERE
From junction of Hwy. 45 and Hwy. 31, drive 6 mi. south on Hwy. 37, then 1.8 mi. east on Smithville Rd., then 1.25 mi. south on Fairfax Rd. Roads are wide and well maintained, with broad shoulders.

BRISTOL MAP, A-2
Eby's Pines Campground

reserve america

14583 SR 120, 46507. T: (574) 848-4583; www.reserveamerica.com.

🚐 ★★★★   ⛺ ★★★★

Beauty: ★★★★
Spaciousness: ★★★★
Security: ★★★
Insect Control: ★★

Site Privacy: ★★★★
Quiet: ★★★★
Cleanliness: ★★★★
Facilities: ★★★★

Harry Eby was a conservationist with a particular fondness for trees. Campers can now enjoy his legacy at Eby's Pines Campground, located 3 miles east of Bristol. Most of the trees, of course, are pines—white pine, scotch pine, and red pine. Laid out in a series of loops, the campground sites are level, mostly shaded and grassy, with gravel parking spots. The typical site width is 40 feet; there are 96 seasonal campers and 35 pull-through sites. Best RV spots are 71–76 because they are located by the fishing pond, shower facilities, and swimming pools. The best tent sites are in the Poplars section because they are surrounded by poplar trees and have privacy from RVs. For being so close to the interstate, the campground is surprisingly quiet and peaceful, with the pines, the ponds, and the Little Elkhart River providing a natural buffer. At one time a tree farm, the campground has a nicely equipped camp store and Amish hand-built, rustic log camping cabins that can be rented. A large 2,400-square-foot heated pool has a double tube slide, water umbrella, and—most importantly—a certified lifeguard on duty.

BASICS
Operated By: Barry Lang. **Open:** Apr. 1–Oct. 31. **Site Assignment:** Reservations w/ 1-night deposit; refunds (minus $8) w/ 48-hour notice. **Registration:** At campground office. **Fee:** $24–$36; cash, MC, V. **Parking:** At site.

FACILITIES
Number of RV-only Sites: 330. **Number of Tent-only Sites:** 13. **Hookups:** Electric (30, 50 amps), water, sewer. **Each Site:** Picnic table, fire ring. **Dump Station:** Yes. **Laundry:** Yes. **Pay Phone:** Yes. **Restrooms and Showers:** Yes. **Fuel:** No. **Propane:** Yes. **Internal Roads:** Paved/gravel, in good condition. **RV Service:** No. **Market:** 3 mi. west in Bristol. **Restaurant:** 3 mi. west in Bristol. **General Store:** Yes. **Vending:** Yes. **Swimming:** Yes. **Playground:** Yes. **Other:** Basketball, tennis, volleyball, roller skating, horseshoes, rec room, video games, rental cabins, fishing pond, hiking trail, spa pool, pavilion, sports field. **Activities:** Swimming, fishing, hiking, scheduled weekend activities. **Nearby Attractions:** Amish country, Shipshewana Flea Market, golf, RV History Museum, antique shops, arts & crafts shops, museums, historic homes, Notre Dame University. **Additional Information:** Amish Country/Elkhart County Visitors Center, (800) 860-5949.

RESTRICTIONS
Pets: On leash only. **Fires:** Fire ring only. **Alcoholic Beverages:** At sites only. **Vehicle Maximum Length:** No limit.

TO GET THERE
From junction of I-80/90 (Indiana Turnpike) and Hwy. 13, take Exit 101 and drive 1 mi. south on Hwy. 13, then 3 mi. west on Hwy. 120. Roads are wide and well maintained, with broad shoulders.

CLOVERDALE MAP, C-2
Cloverdale RV Park

2789 East CR 800 South, 46120. T: (888) 298-0035 or (765) 795-3294.

🚐 ★★★   ⛺ ★★★

Beauty: ★★★
Spaciousness: ★★★
Security: ★★★★
Insect Control: ★★

Site Privacy: ★★★
Quiet: ★★★★
Cleanliness: ★★★★
Facilities: ★★★

Cloverdale RV Park is a nice, quiet, comfortable place to stay and hosts many return campers. That's why reservations are strongly recommended. Laid out in a series of loops, the campground has all pull-throughs and a typical site width of 35 feet. This rural campground 2 miles north of Cloverdale has a fishing pond but doesn't allow swimming or boating. Regulations to keep the campground quiet and safe are strictly enforced. Quiet times are between 9 p.m. and 8 a.m., and children must be accompanied by an adult in public areas at all times. The campground has an 8 mph speed limit, which might be better set at 5 mph—children camping are more concerned about play than about watching for cars. Security measures include one entrance; an exit is closed at night so vehicles have to drive by the office to enter. Owners live on site and provide regular patrols.

BASICS
Operated By: Cher Nickerson. **Open:** All year. **Site Assignment:** Reservations accepted w/ 1-night deposit; refund w/ 48-hour notice. **Registration:** At campground office. **Fee:** Full hookup, $26; water/electric, $24; tent, $12; cash, check, V, MC. **Parking:** At site.

FACILITIES
Number of RV-only Sites: 52. **Number of Tent-only Sites:** 20. **Hookups:** Electric (30 amps), water, sewer, phone. **Each Site:** Picnic table, fire ring. **Dump Station:** Yes. **Laundry:** Yes. **Pay Phone:** Yes. **Restrooms and Showers:** Yes. **Fuel:** No. **Propane:** No. **Internal Roads:** Gravel, in good condition. **RV Service:** No. **Market:** 2 mi. south in Cloverdale. **Restaurant:** 2 mi. south in Cloverdale. **General Store:** Yes. **Vending:** Yes. **Swimming:** No. **Playground:** Yes. **Other:** Rec room, fax & copy service, fishing pond, horseshoes, basketball, nature trail, coin games, sports field. **Activities:** Fishing, hiking. **Nearby Attractions:** Covered bridges, raceway, antiques, Victory Field, zoo, Cataract Falls. **Additional Information:** Putnam County CVB, (800) 829-4639.

RESTRICTIONS
Pets: On leash only. **Fires:** Fire ring only. **Alcoholic Beverages:** At sites only. **Vehicle Maximum Length:** No limit. **Other:** No clotheslines permitted.

TO GET THERE

From junction of I-70 and US 231, take Exit 41, drive 0.8 mi. north on US 231 to CR 800S, then drive east 0.5 mi. Roads are wide and well maintained, with broad shoulders.

COLUMBUS MAP, C-2
Woods–Waters

8855 South 300 West, 47201. T: (800) 799-3928 or (812) 342-1619; www.woodsnwaters.com.

🚐 ★★★★   ⛺ ★★★★

Beauty: ★★★★   Site Privacy: ★★★★
Spaciousness: ★★★★   Quiet: ★★★★
Security: ★★★★   Cleanliness: ★★★★★
Insect Control: ★★   Facilities: ★★★★

Woods–Waters offers a quiet country setting close to the interstate and other attractions. Located 5 miles south of Columbus, the rural campground has level gravel sites with a typical site width of 35 feet. The campground has 15 seasonal campers and 30 pull-throughs. Situated in a forest, the campground is well maintained and decorated with flowers as well as a wishing well and a wooden swing. The bathrooms are not only extremely clean but also brightened with wallpaper, artificial flowers, framed paintings, and plenty of mirrors over the sink, along with a full-length mirror on the wall. A well-stocked camp store with friendly folks makes it an even more pleasant place. Security and safety measures are good with a 5 mph speed limit, quiet hours from 8 p.m. to 7 a.m., a year-round resident manager, and three deputy sheriffs who are seasonal campers at the campground.

BASICS
Operated By: Larry and Betty York. **Open:** All year. **Site Assignment:** Reservations w/ credit card; refund w/ 24-hour notice. **Registration:** At campground office. **Fee:** $20–$28; cash, check, V, MC, D. **Parking:** At site.

FACILITIES
Number of RV-only Sites: 100. **Number of Tent-only Sites:** 10. **Hookups:** Electric (30, 50 amps), water, sewer. **Each Site:** Picnic table, fire ring. **Dump Station:** Yes. **Laundry:** Yes. **Pay Phone:** Yes. **Restrooms and Showers:** Yes. **Fuel:** No. **Propane:** Yes. **Internal Roads:** Gravel, in good condition. **RV Service:** No. **Market:** 5 mi. north in Columbus. **Restaurant:** 5 mi. north in Columbus. **General Store:** Yes. **Vending:** No. **Swimming:** Yes. **Playground:** Yes. **Other:** Game room, movies, clubhouse, lounge, coin games, pavilion, nature trail, fishing lake, basketball, badminton, sports field, volleyball, horseshoes. **Activities:** Swimming, fishing, hiking, scheduled weekend activities. **Nearby Attractions:** Columbus architecture tour, museums, historic homes, golf, Brown County & Nashville, crafts shops, antiques, Indianapolis Zoo, Indy 500. **Additional Information:** Columbus Area Visitor Center, (800) 468-6564.

RESTRICTIONS
Pets: On leash only. **Fires:** Fire ring only. **Alcoholic Beverages:** At sites only. **Vehicle Maximum Length:** No limit.

TO GET THERE

From junction of I-65 and Hwy. 58 (Ogilville), take Exit 64, drive 0.5 mi. west on Hwy. 58, then 1 mi. south on CR 300W. Roads are wide and well maintained, with broad shoulders, except for CR 300W, which has narrow shoulders.

CRAWFORDSVILLE MAP, B-2
Crawfordsville KOA

1600 Lafayette Rd., 47933. T: (765) 362-4190; www.koa.com.

🚐 ★★★★   ⛺ ★★★★

Beauty: ★★★★   Site Privacy: ★★★★
Spaciousness: ★★★★   Quiet: ★★★
Security: ★★★★   Cleanliness: ★★★★
Insect Control: ★★   Facilities: ★★★★

Crawfordsville KOA is conveniently located, clean, and secure. It also offers spacious spots, almost all of which are pull-throughs, with a typical site width of 48 feet. Laid out in a series of loops, the rural campground offers a choice of shady or open, grassy or gravel sites. Large patches of iris and peonies brighten the campgrounds, as do shrubs and other landscaping. Located 2 miles north of Crawfordsville, the campground is convenient to several popular local festivals—Feast of the Hunters Moon, Strawberry Festival, Covered Bridge Festival, to name a few—so be sure there is an open space if you know when you want to stay there. Easy access and good roads pull a lot of travelers from the interstate looking for a night's rest. Security is good with one entrance road and owners who live on site.

BASICS
Operated By: Richard Nelson. **Open:** Mar. 15–Nov. 15. **Site Assignment:** Reservations accepted w/o deposit. **Registration:** At campground office. **Fee:** $21–$34; cash, check, credit card. **Parking:** At site.

FACILITIES
Number of RV-only Sites: 60. **Number of Tent-only Sites:** 7. **Hookups:** Electric (30, 50 amps), water, sewer, cable TV, Wi-Fi. **Each Site:** Picnic table, fire ring. **Dump Station:** Yes. **Laundry:** Yes. **Pay Phone:** Yes. **Restrooms and Showers:** Yes. **Fuel:** No. **Propane:** Yes. **Internal Roads:** Paved/gravel, in good condition. **RV Service:** Yes. **Market:** 2 mi. south in Crawfordsville. **Restaurant:** 2 mi. south in Crawfordsville. **General Store:** Yes. **Vending:** Yes. **Swimming:** Yes. **Playground:** Yes. **Other:** RV supply store, rec room, horseshoes, pavilion, volleyball, coin games, sports field, rental cabins. **Activities:** Swimming. **Nearby Attractions:** Ben Hur Museum, antiques, Old Jail Museum, 42 covered bridges, golf, canoe trips. **Additional Information:** Crawfordsville CVB, (800) 866-3973.

RESTRICTIONS
Pets: On leash only. **Fires:** Fire ring only. **Alcoholic Beverages:** Allowed. **Vehicle Maximum Length:** 40 ft.

TO GET THERE
From junction of I-74 and US 231, take Exit 34, then drive 1 mi. south on US 231. Roads are wide and well maintained, with good shoulders.

FREMONT MAP, A-3
Yogi Bear's Jellystone Park Camp-Resort

140 Lane 201, 46737. T: (260) 833-1114 or (800) 375-6063; www.jellystonesbest.com.

🚐 ★★★★   ⛺ ★★★★

Beauty: ★★★★   Site Privacy: ★★★★
Spaciousness: ★★★★   Quiet: ★★★★
Security: ★★★★★   Cleanliness: ★★★★★
Insect Control: ★★★   Facilities: ★★★★★

The campground's name indicates that it is a resort, and that is a good way to describe Yogi Bear's Jellystone Park Camp-Resort at Barton Lake. Located 7 miles west of Fremont, the campground offers enough activities to keep families happily busy for days. With its snack bar and well-stocked camp store, it is possible for campers to come, park their vehicles, and not leave the campground for little errands. Campers have a choice of open or shady spots, with 35 feet being the typical site width. Sites are generally grassy with concrete patios. The facility has 216 seasonal campers and 50 pull-through sites. Swimmers have a choice of a sandy beach at Barton Lake, a heated outdoor pool, or an indoor solarium pool. Tent campers can choose a rustic area with more greenery and privacy from RVs, or tents may be put on any of the RV sites. Security is tops with a locked card-coded gate, surveillance cameras, regular patrols, and owners who live on site.

BASICS
Operated By: The Barry and Corcimiglia families. **Open:** Apr. 15–Nov. 1. **Site Assignment:** Reservations w/ 1-night deposit; full deposit for holidays; refund w/ 7-day notice minus $7. **Registration:** At campground office. **Fee:** $29–$52; cash, credit card. **Parking:** At site.

FACILITIES
Number of RV-only Sites: 500. **Number of Tent-only Sites:** 30. **Hookups:** Electric (30, 50 amps), water, sewer. **Each Site:** Picnic table, fire ring. **Dump Station:** Yes. **Laundry:** Yes. **Pay Phone:** Yes. **Restrooms and Showers:** Yes. **Fuel:** No. **Propane:** Yes. **Internal Roads:** Paved, in excellent condition. **RV Service:** Yes. **Market:** 7 mi. east in Fremont. **Restaurant:** 7 mi. east in Fremont. **General Store:** Yes. **Vending:** Yes. **Swimming:** Yes. **Playground:** Yes. **Other:** Fishing lake, rental cabins, spa, snack bar, volleyball, basketball, arcade building, horseshoes, mini-golf, boat launch, rec hall, pavilion, sandy beach. **Activities:** Swimming, fishing, boating (rental rowboats, paddleboats available), movies, scheduled activities. **Nearby Attractions:** Outlet shopping malls, water slide, Amish area, flea market, amusement park, car museum, lakes, golf, antiques, arts & crafts shops. **Additional Information:** Amish County/Elkhart County Visitors Center, (800) 860-5949.

RESTRICTIONS
Pets: On leash only. **Fires:** Fire ring only. **Alcoholic Beverages:** At sites only. **Vehicle Maximum Length:** No limit. **Other:** Campfires must be extinguished by midnight.

TO GET THERE

From I-80/90 (Indiana Turnpike), take Exit 144 to Hwy. 120, drive 3.25 mi. west on Hwy. 120, then 0.5 mi. north on CR 300W. Roads are wide and well maintained, with broad shoulders.

GRANGER   MAP, A-2
South Bend East KOA
Camping Resort

50707 Princess Way, 46530. T: (574) 277-1335 or (800) 562-2470.

🚐 ★★★★   ⛺ ★★★★

Beauty: ★★★★   Site Privacy: ★★★★
Spaciousness: ★★★★   Quiet: ★★★★
Security: ★★★★★   Cleanliness: ★★★★★
Insect Control: ★★   Facilities: ★★★★

Little touches add up to some pleasing results at the South Bend East KOA Camping Resort in the town of Granger, Indiana. Pink rose bushes are planted to help conceal a propane tank; framed pictures and artificial flowers brighten the restrooms; and clean, private shower rooms have lights that turn on when the door is closed. An urban campground with level shaded sites, the facility has 40 pull-throughs, a typical site width of 24 feet, and no seasonal campers. The rec room is modem friendly for computer users. A 5 mph speed limit is enforced for safety and to prevent vehicles from kicking up dust. Security measures include owners who live on site, a traffic control gate, and surveillance cameras. A list of campground guidelines is nicely worded with more than a list of the usual "no's." Instead, the campground requests, "We don't want any of our trees or guests strangled, so please no clotheslines." If campers are not satisfied within one hour of check in, registration fees are refunded.

BASICS

Operated By: Thomas Jetzer and Patricia Schenk. **Open:** Mar. 15–Nov. 20. **Site Assignment:** Reservations w/ 1-night deposit; refund w/ 7-day notice. **Registration:** At campground office. **Fee:** $24–$37; cash, check, credit card. **Parking:** At site.

FACILITIES

Number of RV-only Sites: 58. **Number of Tent-only Sites:** 25. **Hookups:** Electric (30, 50 amps), water, sewer, cable TV, Wi-Fi. **Each Site:** Picnic table, fire ring. **Dump Station:** Yes. **Laundry:** Yes. **Pay Phone:** Yes. **Restrooms and Showers:** Yes. **Fuel:** No. **Propane:** Yes. **Internal Roads:** Paved/gravel, in good condition. **RV Service:** No. **Market:** 2 blocks in Granger. **Restaurant:** 2 blocks in Granger. **General Store:** Yes. **Vending:** Yes. **Swimming:** Yes. **Playground:** Yes. **Other:** Game room, basketball, volleyball, horseshoes, mini-golf, nature trail, rental cabins, pavilion w/ kitchen, coin games, badminton, sports field, adults room, rental lodges. **Activities:** Swimming, hiking, scheduled weekend activities. **Nearby Attractions:** College Football Hall of Fame, golf, Studebaker National Museum, Notre Dame University, zoo, Amish acres, RV museum, Shipshewana Flea Market, antiques, St. Mary's College, historic homes. **Additional Information:** South Bend/Mishawaka CVB, (800) 282-2330.

RESTRICTIONS

Pets: On leash only. **Fires:** Fire ring only. **Alcoholic Beverages:** Allowed at site only. **Vehicle Maximum Length:** No limit.

TO GET THERE

From junction of I-80/90 (Indiana Turnpike), take Exit 83 and drive 0.5 mi. to Hwy. 23, then 2 mi. north on Hwy. 23, then 0.3 mi. north on Princess Way. Roads are wide and well maintained, with broad shoulders.

HOWE   MAP, A-3
Twin Mills Camping Resort

1675 West SR 120, 46746. T: (260) 562-3212; www.twinmills.net.

🚐 ★★★★   ⛺ ★★★★

Beauty: ★★★★   Site Privacy: ★★★★
Spaciousness: ★★★★   Quiet: ★★★★
Security: ★★★★★   Cleanliness: ★★★★
Insect Control: ★★★   Facilities: ★★★★

Twin Mills Camping Resort has the beauty and paved roads of a state park, along with the facilities of a private resort. The result is a winning combination for campers. Located 2 miles east of Howe, the campground has wooded and open sites with a typical site width of 35 feet. Each site is plainly marked with a white pole and red number sign. Mature pine trees and other greenery add to the privacy, quiet, and attractiveness. Laid out in a series of loops, the campground has 280 seasonal and 42 pull-through sites. Most popular sites are in Campers Cove, which is close to the activities. A full-time recreation director keeps the activities going. A 5 mph speed limit and one-way roads help with safety. Security measures are tops with a key-card gate, one entrance/exit road, owners who live on site, surveillance cameras, and regular patrols of the campground.

BASICS

Operated By: Diversified Investments. **Open:** Apr. 15–Oct. 15. **Site Assignment:** Reservations w/ full deposit; refund (minus $25) w/ 45-day notice; camping credit w/ 8–44-day notice. **Registration:** At campground office. **Fee:** $39.50; off-season, $16; cash, check, credit card. **Parking:** At site.

FACILITIES

Number of RV-only Sites: 559. **Number of Tent-only Sites:** 10. **Hookups:** Electric (30 amps), water, sewer, Wi-Fi. **Each Site:** Picnic table, fire ring. **Dump Station:** Yes. **Laundry:** Yes. **Pay Phone:** Yes. **Restrooms and Showers:** Yes. **Fuel:** No. **Propane:** Yes. **Internal Roads:** Paved, in good condition. **RV Service:** No. **Market:** 2 mi. east in Howe. **Restaurant:** 2 mi. east in Howe. **General Store:** Yes. **Vending:** Yes. **Swimming:** Yes. **Playground:** Yes. **Other:** Lake beach, mini-golf, biking & hiking trails, shuffleboard, basketball, horseshoes, volleyball, game room, coin games, rec hall, rental cabins, pavilion, nature lookout, boat dock, badminton. **Activities:** Swimming, hiking, fishing, boating (rental rowboats, canoes available), scheduled weekend activities. **Nearby Attractions:** Amish community, flea market, antique mall, auto museum, golf, arts &

---

crafts, Borkholder Dutch Village. **Additional Information:** LaGrange County CVB, (800) 254-8090.

RESTRICTIONS

Pets: On leash only. **Fires:** Fire ring only. **Alcoholic Beverages:** At sites only. **Vehicle Maximum Length:** No limit.

TO GET THERE

From junction of I-80/90 and Hwy. 9, take Exit 121, drive 2.5 mi. south on Hwy. 9, then 1.75 mi. west on Hwy. 120. Roads are wide and well maintained, with broad shoulders.

KENDALLVILLE   MAP, A-3
Bixler Lake Campground

1615 Lake Park Dr., P. O. Box 516, 46755. T: (260) 347-9941 or (260) 347-1064.

🚐 ★★★   ⛺ ★★★

Beauty: ★★★   Site Privacy: ★★★
Spaciousness: ★★★   Quiet: ★★★
Security: ★★★   Cleanliness: ★★★
Insect Control: ★★   Facilities: ★★★

Located in the woods and wilds, yet close to town and separated by a 120-acre lake, Bixler Lake Campground is a popular spot with local campers and with groups that can be in adjoining sites. Despite the lengthy directions, Bixler Lake Campground is easy to find with signs to point the way. But much of the access travel must be done on residential streets, which can be narrow, with inadequate shoulders. The campground offers a choice of grassy or gravel sites, shady or open, and 14 pull-throughs. Rates are surprisingly low and discounts are given to groups with ten units or more. The campground offers wheelchair-accessible restrooms and showers. Security is good with a check-in point and patrols by local officers.

BASICS

Operated By: Kendallville Parks and Recreation Dept. **Open:** Apr. 30–Oct. 15. **Site Assignment:** Reservations accepted w/o deposit. **Registration:** At campground office. **Fee:** $14.85–$17.50; cash, check. **Parking:** At site.

FACILITIES

Number of RV-only Sites: 80. **Number of Tent-only Sites:** 20. **Hookups:** Electric (20, 30, 50 amps), water. **Each Site:** Picnic table, fire ring. **Dump Station:** Yes. **Laundry:** No. **Pay Phone:** Yes. **Restrooms and Showers:** Yes. **Fuel:** No. **Propane:** No. **Internal Roads:** Paved/gravel, in good condition. **RV Service:** No. **Market:** 2 mi. west in Kendallville. **Restaurant:** 2 mi. west in Kendallville. **General Store:** No. **Vending:** Yes. **Swimming:** No. **Playground:** Yes. **Other:** Fishing lake, swimming beach, boat launch, fishing piers, volleyball, duck pond, nature trails, observation platforms, herb garden, butterfly plots, bee-keeping display, recreation field, tennis court. **Activities:** Fishing, swimming, boating (rental paddleboats available), scheduled weekend activities. **Nearby Attractions:** Windmill museum, golf, nation's 2nd largest genealogy library, Lincoln Museum, zoo, Auburn Cord Duesenberg Museum. **Additional Information:** Fort Wayne/Allen County CVB, (800) 767-7752.

RESTRICTIONS

Pets: On leash only. **Fires:** Fire ring only. **Alcoholic Beverages:** Not allowed. **Vehicle Maximum Length:** 36 ft. **Other:** 14-day stay limit.

TO GET THERE

From junction of US 6 and US 3, drive 1.3 mi. east on US 6 to Fair St., then 0.4 mi. south to Wayne St., 500 feet east to Park Ave., and finally 0.4 mi. south to Lake Park Dr. Roads are well maintained residential streets, some narrow, with poor shoulders.

LAFAYETTE   MAP, B-2
Lafayette AOK Campground

225 East 300 South, 47909. T: (765) 474-5030; www.aokcampgrounds.com.

🚐 ★★★★   ⛺ ★★★★

Beauty: ★★★	Site Privacy: ★★★
Spaciousness: ★★★	Quiet: ★★★
Security: ★★★★	Cleanliness: ★★★★
Insect Control: ★★	Facilities: ★★★★

It is no typo and your eyes aren't playing tricks. This is the Lafayette AOK Campground, not a KOA, but that is a common misconception. Campers often think they are pulling into a KOA. Laid out in a series of loops, the Lafayette AOK offers a choice of shaded or open sites in a rolling terrain. The typical site width is 30 feet and the campground has mostly pull-through sites and 50 seasonal sites. The best RV sites are in the first row in the campground which offers easier access and more trees. The best tent sites are in a corner of the grounds with more woods, shade, and privacy. A 5 mph speed limit is enforced as are quiet times from 10 p.m. to 8 a.m. No outside clotheslines are permitted, but laundry facilities are open 24 hours a day. Security includes one entrance/exit road, a manager living on site, and seasonal campers who keep an eye on their area.

BASICS

Operated By: Ted Riehle. **Open:** All year. **Site Assignment:** Reservations w/ 1-night deposit; refund w/ 24-hour notice. **Registration:** At campground office. **Fee:** $15–$24.75; cash, check, credit card. **Parking:** At site.

FACILITIES

Number of RV-only Sites: 76. **Number of Tent-only Sites:** 150. **Hookups:** Electric (20, 30, 50 amps), water, sewer, cable TV, phone. **Each Site:** Picnic table. **Dump Station:** Yes. **Laundry:** Yes. **Pay Phone:** Yes. **Restrooms and Showers:** Yes. **Fuel:** No. **Propane:** Yes. **Internal Roads:** Paved/gravel, in good condition. **RV Service:** No. **Market:** 0.25 mi. north in Lafayette. **Restaurant:** 0.25 mi. east in Lafayette. **General Store:** Yes. **Vending:** Yes. **Swimming:** Yes. **Playground:** Yes. **Other:** Coin games, pool table, exercise machines, horseshoes, recreation field, rec hall, game room, hiking trails, creek. **Activities:** Swimming, hiking. **Nearby Attractions:** Tippecanoe Battlefield, Wolf Park, Fort Quiatenon, golf, Purdue University, museums, historic homes, antiques, Indiana Beach amusement park. **Additional Information:** Greater Lafayette CVB, (800) 872-6648.

RESTRICTIONS

Pets: On leash only. **Fires:** Fire ring only. **Alcoholic Beverages:** Allowed. **Vehicle Maximum Length:** No limit.

TO GET THERE

From junction of I-65 and Hwy. 38, take Exit 168, drive 1.25 mi. west on Hwy. 38, then 4 mi. west on CR 475E and CR 350S, then 0.5 mi. north on old US 231, then 6 mi. west on CR 300S. Roads are wide and well maintained, with broad shoulders.

MADISON   MAP, C-3
Clifty Falls State Park

2221 Clifty Dr., 1501 Green Rd., 47250. T: (812) 273-8885 or (866) 622-6746; www.in.gov/dnr, www.camp.in.gov.

🚐 ★★★   ⛺ ★★★★

Beauty: ★★★★	Site Privacy: ★★★
Spaciousness: ★★★	Quiet: ★★★★
Security: ★★★★	Cleanliness: ★★★★
Insect Control: ★★	Facilities: ★★★

It's easy to see where Clifty Falls State Park got its name. With four plunging waterfalls, 70-foot gorges, sheer cliffs, and a narrow valley, Clifty Falls shows the awesome forces of nature at work. The park is popular with campers who like to hike in the area. Winter and spring hiking show the falls at their best. July through November offer meager falls and the easiest hiking in Clifty Creek's wonderful stone bed. A muddy, rock-strewn 600-foot tunnel piercing the hillside beneath Oak Grove is the most prominent remnant of the Madison and Indianapolis Railroad, begun in 1852 and abandoned in bankruptcy. It is passable on foot with flashlight. Security is good, with passes needed to enter the campground and a ranger on patrol. Despite the lack of water hookups and laundry, Clifty Falls has a dedicated following of campers, both RV and tents. There are 45 pull-through sites. The natural beauty, the programs, and the security are the main draws.

BASICS

Operated By: Indiana Dept. of Natural Resources. **Open:** May–Oct. **Site Assignment:** Reservations w/ full deposit; refunds (minus $10) w/ 24-hour notice. **Registration:** At campground office. **Fee:** $17–$28; check, credit card. **Parking:** At site.

FACILITIES

Number of RV-only Sites: 103. **Number of Tent-only Sites:** 60. **Hookups:** Electric (30 amps). **Each Site:** Picnic table, fire ring. **Dump Station:** Yes. **Laundry:** No. **Pay Phone:** Yes. **Restrooms and Showers:** Yes. **Fuel:** No. **Propane:** No. **Internal Roads:** Paved, in good condition. **RV Service:** No. **Market:** 1 mi. east in Madison. **Restaurant:** 1 mi. east in Madison. **General Store:** No. **Vending:** No. **Swimming:** Yes. **Playground:** Yes. **Other:** Nature center, inn w/ indoor swimming pool, picnic shelters, tennis court. **Activities:** Swimming, hiking, guided nature walks, summer weekday programs & evening activities offered by naturalist. **Nearby Attractions:** Scenic drives, golf, historic Madison, Ohio River, Lanier State Historic Site, vineyards, marina. **Additional Information:** Madison Area CVB, (800) 559-2956.

RESTRICTIONS

Pets: On leash only. **Fires:** Fire rings, grills only. **Alcoholic Beverages:** At sites only. **Vehicle Maximum Length:** No limit. **Other:** 14-day stay limit.

TO GET THERE

From Madison, drive 1 mi. west on IN 56/62. Roads are generally wide and well maintained. Shoulders are often poor. The area is popular for its scenic, hilly, winding roads but they can be difficult to maneuver.

MARION   MAP, B-3
Sports Lake Camping Resort

7230 East 400 South, 46953. T: (765) 998-2558; www.sportslakecampground.com.

🚐 ★★★   ⛺ ★★★

Beauty: ★★★	Site Privacy: ★★★
Spaciousness: ★★★	Quiet: ★★★★
Security: ★★★★	Cleanliness: ★★★
Insect Control: ★★	Facilities: ★★★

With two golf courses nearby, Sports Lake Camping Resort is a popular campground for golfers and other sports enthusiasts. Located 2 miles east of Gas City, the campground also offers many recreational opportunities on site. Not surprisingly, about half the sites are occupied by seasonal campers and only two full hookups spots remain. A heavily wooded lakeside campground in a secluded rural area, Sports Lake offers a common site width of 30 feet with 25 pull-throughs. A 5 mph speed limit is strictly enforced and motorists who try to enter the exit will find their tires in trouble from a one-way apparatus. Security features include an electric gate that is closed from 10 p.m. to 8 a.m. The owner lives nearby and helper campers also assist in keeping an eye on the campground. About the only noise is what drifts over from the Friday night races nearby. Best spots for RVs are 1A–10A because they are larger pull-throughs. Favorite sites for tent campers are in the woods.

BASICS

Operated By: Ryan and Danielle Richards. **Open:** Seasonal, Apr. 15–Oct. 15; overnight, May–Sept. **Site Assignment:** Reservations accepted w/ 1-night deposit; no refunds. **Registration:** At campground office. **Fee:** Full hookup, $25; water/electric, $22; cash, check. **Parking:** At site.

FACILITIES

Number of Multipurpose Sites: 160. **Hookups:** Electric (20, 30 amps), water, sewer. **Each Site:** Picnic table, fire ring. **Dump Station:** Yes. **Laundry:** No. **Pay Phone:** No. **Restrooms and Showers:** Yes. **Fuel:** No. **Propane:** No. **Internal Roads:** Gravel, in fair condition. **RV Service:** No. **Market:** 2 mi. west in Gas City. **Restaurant:** 2 mi. west in Gas City. **General Store:** Yes. **Vending:** Yes. **Swimming:** Yes. **Playground:** Yes. **Other:** Rec hall, pavilion, fishing lake, mini-golf, shuffleboard, badminton, sports field, horseshoes. **Activities:** Swimming, fishing, boating (rental rowboats, paddleboats available), scheduled weekend activities. **Nearby Attractions:** James Dean's hometown, golf, antiques, museums, Mississinewa Battlefield. **Additional Information:** Grant County CVB, (800) 662-9474.

RESTRICTIONS

Pets: On leash only. **Fires:** Fire ring only. **Alcoholic Beverages:** At sites only. **Vehicle Maximum Length:** No limit. **Other:** Visitors must park in the lot outside & pay $1 each to visit; no swimming in the lake.

TO GET THERE

From junction of I-69 and Hwy. 22, take Exit 59, drive 0.5 mi. east on Hwy. 22, then 1 mi. north on CR 700E, then 0.25 mi. east on CR 400S. Roads are wide and well maintained, with narrow shoulders in spots.

MONTICELLO   MAP, B-2
Yogi Bear's Jellystone Park at Indiana Beach

reserve america

2882 N.W. Shafer Dr., 47960.
T: (574) 583-8646 or (888) 811-9644;
www.jellystoneindianabeach.com.

🚐 ★★★★   ⛺ ★★★★

Beauty: ★★★★	Site Privacy: ★★
Spaciousness: ★★★	Quiet: ★★★
Security: ★★★★★	Cleanliness: ★★★★
Insect Control: ★★★	Facilities: ★★★★

This is one of our favorite places to camp. Shuttle bus takes you right over to the boardwalk for the kids to play. On holiday weekends it may be a bit noisy, but it is still a fun place to camp. There are planned children's activities throughout the day. The campground runs a ferry system to town and a tram shuttle to the nearby amusement park every half hour; camping includes a free shuttle ride and admittance to the amusement park. (Make sure you carry your campground pass with you, or they will not let you ride.) The pool is super, though it offers no shade and can get very crowded. There is also a swimming beach, minature golf, batting cages, go-carts, water park, and restaurants in the immediate area. A well-stock camp store is on the premises. The park is well maintained and kept very tidy. The grounds are immaculately clean, as are the bath houses and the restrooms. The showers are the push-button style, which may be a bit of a nuisance. There are laundry facilities at the bath houses for $1.25. The park is big-rig friendly. Main roads are paved, others are gravel. All sites are gravel and level pull-throughs. Each site is plenty wide and has a grass area and a table. Sites vary from fully shaded to totally in the open. Security patrols on golf carts are visible throughout the park, but they are not intrusive. The campground is very quiet at night.

BASICS

Operated By: Indiana Beach. **Open:** May–Sept. **Site Assignment:** Reservations by phone or in person; no guarantee for specific sites. **Registration:** Sun.–Thurs., 8 a.m.–9 p.m.; Fri. & Sat., 8 a.m.–11 p.m.; off-season hours vary. **Fee:** Water/electric/sewer, $40; water/electric, $35; also available: red carpet sites, barebone cabins & deluxe cabins; all sites include 2 adults & 2 children under 17 years of age.

Cabins sleep 6 people. **Parking:** 1 car per site; additional fee per extra car, $2.

FACILITIES

Number of Multipurpose Sites: 135. **Hookups:** Electric (30, 50 amps), TV cable. **Each Site:** Picnic table, fire ring w/ adjustable grill, TV cable. **Dump Station:** Yes. **Laundry:** Yes. **Pay Phone:** Yes. **Restrooms and Showers:** Yes. **Fuel:** No. **Propane:** No. **Internal Roads:** Gravel. **RV Service:** 20 mi. in Brookston, IN. **Market:** 3 mi. in Monticello. **Restaurant:** 0.5 mi. at Indiana Beach Amusement Park. **General Store:** Camp store. **Vending:** Yes. **Swimming:** Yes, heated pool and beach. **Playground:** Yes. **Activities:** Scheduled children's activities during peak season. Pavilion, volleyball net, miniature golf, water splash pad, arcade. **Nearby Attractions:** Indiana Beach Amusement Park (Monticello, IN), Tippecanoe Country Club (Monticello, IN), Lake Shafer & Lake Freeman, Fair Oaks (Rensennler, IN), Monon Connection Train Museum (Monon, IN), Grissom Air Museum (Peru, IN). **Additional Information:** Great Monticello Visitors Bureau, www.monticelloin.com; Yogi Bear's Jellystone Park, www.campjellystone.com.

RESTRICTIONS

Pets: On leash at all times and cleaned up after. Adults must walk their dogs. **Fires:** Allowed until midnight. **Alcoholic Beverages:** At site only. **Vehicle Maximum Length:** Sites are 50 ft. by 60 ft. **Other:** 2-night min. stay on weekends, 3-night min. stay on holiday weekends; additional $5/night for holiday weekends.

TO GET THERE

Located 4 mi. north of junction of Hwy. 24 and Sixth St. (NW Shafer Dr.). Entrance is on the left just past Indiana Beach North entrance.

NASHVILLE   MAP, C-2
The Last Resort RV Park and Campground

2248 East SR 46, 47448. T: (812) 988-4675;
www.lastresortrvpark.com.

🚐 ★★★★   ⛺ ★★★★

Beauty: ★★★★	Site Privacy: ★★★★
Spaciousness: ★★★★	Quiet: ★★★★
Security: ★★★★	Cleanliness: ★★★★
Insect Control: ★★	Facilities: ★★★★

Location is everything, and The Last Resort RV Park and Campground has a prime spot. The Last Resort is in the midst of beautiful Brown County, 2.5 miles east of Nashville, Indiana, but it offers the peacefulness and beauty of a woodland setting. Situated atop a hill and surrounded by ravines, the campground has both open and shaded sites that are level and grassy, with gravel parking spots. Laid out in a loop, the campground has 16 seasonals, 18 pull-through sites, and a typical site width of 35 feet. Nice touches include private shower stalls, each with a door and a curtain. Speed limit is 5 mph, quiet hours are 10 p.m. to 8 a.m.; generators are not permitted at any time. Sites 114–117 are popular because they back up into the woods and are away from the main activity. Security includes one entrance/exit road and an on-site manager. The campground is particularly lovely when autumn foliage is showing peak colors.

BASICS

Operated By: Frank and Dot Moser. **Open:** Apr. 1–Nov. 1. **Site Assignment:** Reservations w/ 1-night deposit; refund w/ 7-day notice, minus $5. **Registration:** At campground office. **Fee:** $23–$29; cash, check, credit card. **Parking:** At site.

FACILITIES

Number of RV-only Sites: 80. **Number of Tent-only Sites:** 36. **Hookups:** Electric (30, 50 amps), water, sewer, cable TV. **Each Site:** Picnic table, fire ring. **Dump Station:** Yes. **Laundry:** Yes. **Pay Phone:** Yes. **Restrooms and Showers:** Yes. **Fuel:** No. **Propane:** Yes. **Internal Roads:** Gravel, in good condition. **RV Service:** No. **Market:** 2.5 mi. west in Nashville. **Restaurant:** 2.5 mi. west in Nashville. **General Store:** Yes. **Vending:** Yes. **Swimming:** Yes. **Playground:** Yes. **Other:** Rec room, horseshoes, recreation field, pavilion, coin games, basketball, hiking trails. **Activities:** Swimming, hiking, scheduled weekend activities. **Nearby Attractions:** Brown County State Park, Nashville artist colony w/ more than 350 specialty shops, scenic drives, winter skiing, Little Nashville Opry, golf, Indiana University. **Additional Information:** Brown County CVB, (800) 753-3255.

RESTRICTIONS

Pets: On leash. **Fires:** Fire ring only. **Alcoholic Beverages:** At sites. **Vehicle Maximum Length:** No limit.

TO GET THERE

From junction of I-65 and Hwy. 46, take Exit 68, drive 14 mi. west on Hwy. 46. Roads are wide and well maintained, with broad shoulders.

ORLAND   MAP, A-3
Manapogo Park

5495 W 760N, 46776. T: (260) 833-3902;
www.manapogo.com.

🚐 ★★★★   ⛺ ★★★★

Beauty: ★★★	Site Privacy: ★★★★
Spaciousness: ★★★★	Quiet: ★★★★
Security: ★★★★	Cleanliness: ★★★★
Insect Control: ★★★	Facilities: ★★★★

A wooded, grassy campground, Manapogo Park centers around 425-acre Lake Pleasant. Located 4 miles east of Orland, Indiana, the campground has a typical site width of 50 feet. The campground has 247 seasonal campers and no pull-through sites. A five mph speed limit is enforced for vehicles and bicycles. Bicycles may not be ridden after sundown, and motorcycles may be used only for entering or leaving the campground, when idle speed is required. A separate section for tent campers allows more greenery and privacy from RVs. Overnight sites are generally placed together instead of being scattered throughout the park's seasonals. Security measures include entrance gates that require a $5 deposit fee for cards, refundable upon return of the card. The campground owner lives on site and provides regular patrols.

BASICS

Operated By: John West. **Open:** 3rd week in Apr.–1st week in Oct. **Site Assignment:** Reservations w/ 1-night deposit; refund (minus $5) w/ 5-day notice. **Registration:** At campground office. **Fee:** $19–$32. **Parking:** At site.

FACILITIES

Number of RV-only Sites: 304. **Number of Tent-only Sites:** 15. **Hookups:** Electric (30, 50 amps), water, sewer, Wi-Fi. **Each Site:** Picnic table, fire ring. **Dump Station:** Yes. **Laundry:** Yes. **Pay Phone:** Yes. **Restrooms and Showers:** Yes. **Fuel:** Yes. **Propane:** Yes. **Internal Roads:** Paved/gravel, in good condition. **RV Service:** No. **Market:** 4 mi. west in Orland. **Restaurant:** 4 mi. west in Orland. **General Store:** Yes. **Vending:** Yes. **Swimming:** No. **Playground:** Yes. **Other:** Lake Pleasant, swimming beach, pavilion, boat piers, boat ramp, basketball, volleyball, shuffleboard, horseshoes, rental cabins, fish-cleaning station, rec room, coin games. **Activities:** Swimming, fishing, boating (rental fishing boats, paddleboats, canoes available), scheduled weekend activities. **Nearby Attractions:** Golf, Shipshewana flea market, factory outlet stores, amusement park, car museum, go-cart raceway, antiques, arts & crafts shops. **Additional Information:** Amish County/Elkhart County Visitors Center, (800) 860-5949.

RESTRICTIONS

Pets: On leash only; walking of pets in park is not allowed; pets must be carried or transported in vehicle to the designated walking area near the dump station. **Fires:** Fire ring only. **Alcoholic Beverages:** Allowed, but must be kept in covered container if taken off campsite. **Vehicle Maximum Length:** 40 ft. **Other:** No golf carts or mopeds permitted, except for park staff.

TO GET THERE

From junction of Hwy. 327 and Hwy. 120, drive 3.25 mi. east on Hwy. 120, then 0.75 mi. north on CR 650W, then 1 mi. east on CR 760N. Roads are wide and well maintained, with broad shoulders, except for a narrow section and steep curve on CR 760N.

PERU   MAP, B-2
Honey Bear Hollow Campground

4252 West 200 N, 46970. T: (765) 473-4342; www.campindiana.com/campgrounds/honeybear.html.

🚐 ★★★★	🏕 ★★★★
Beauty: ★★★	Site Privacy: ★★★★
Spaciousness: ★★★★	Quiet: ★★★★
Security: ★★★★	Cleanliness: ★★★★
Insect Control: ★★★	Facilities: ★★★★

The entryway to Honey Bear Hollow Campground lets guests know that the owners care about the facility. A small pond and water display along with flowers and other greenery add a nice welcoming touch. Well-tended flower barrels also decorate bathroom entrances. Laid out in a series of loops, the campground has a typical site width of 30 feet with 50 seasonal campers and 55 pull-through sites for all overnight campers. Located 4 miles north of Peru,

Indiana, the campground has a well-stocked camp store and is surrounded by woods. Sites are mostly shady and grassy with gravel pads to park on. Quiet time is 11 p.m. to 8 a.m. and there is a curfew for children under age 18. Security measures include an alarm system, one entrance/exit and owners who live on site.

BASICS

Operated By: Bob and Toni Billetz. **Open:** All year. **Site Assignment:** Reservations w/ 1-night deposit; refund (minus $5) w/ 7-day notice; no refunds on holiday weekends. **Registration:** At campground office. **Fee:** $17–$27; cash, check, credit card. **Parking:** At site.

FACILITIES

Number of RV-only Sites: 105. **Number of Tent-only Sites:** 5. **Hookups:** Electric (30, 50 amps), water. **Each Site:** Picnic table, fire ring. **Dump Station:** Yes. **Laundry:** Yes. **Pay Phone:** Courtesy. **Restrooms and Showers:** Yes. **Fuel:** No. **Propane:** Yes. **Internal Roads:** Gravel, in good condition. **RV Service:** No. **Market:** 4 mi. south in Peru. **Restaurant:** 4 mi. south in Peru. **General Store:** Yes. **Vending:** Yes. **Swimming:** Yes. **Playground:** Yes. **Other:** Rec hall, pavilion, fishing pond, mini-golf, horseshoes, volleyball, game room, disc golf course, cartoons & video games. **Activities:** Swimming, fishing, scheduled weekend activities. **Nearby Attractions:** Grissom Air Museum, historic homes, golf, Big Top Circus & Hall of Fame Museum, antiques, arts & crafts shops. **Additional Information:** Howard County CVB, (800) 837-0971.

RESTRICTIONS

Pets: On leash only. **Fires:** Fire ring only. **Alcoholic Beverages:** At sites only. **Vehicle Maximum Length:** No limit. **Other:** No fireworks of any kind, including sparklers, are permitted.

TO GET THERE

From junction of US 31 and Bypass US 24, go 1 mi. north on US 31, then 1.25 mi. west on CR 200N. Roads are wide and well maintained, with broad shoulders, except for CR 200N, which is narrow, with small shoulders.

PLYMOUTH   MAP, A-2
Yogi Bear's Jellystone Park Camp-Resort

7719 Redwood Rd., 46563. T: (574) 936-7851, Ext. 25/26; www.jellystoneparkplymouth.com.

🚐 ★★★★	🏕 ★★
Beauty: ★★★	Site Privacy: ★★★★
Spaciousness: ★★★★	Quiet: ★★★★
Security: ★★★★	Cleanliness: ★★★★
Insect Control: ★★	Facilities: ★★★★

Yogi Bear's Jellystone Park Camp-Resort is owned by the people who live there, the Marshall County Membership Corp. That helps keep the campground well maintained and attractive. People take pride in what they own. For example, lights in the main bathroom are triggered to come on when someone comes in; the water faucet in the sink releases a certain amount of water when a person's hands are under it.

Those measures are both convenient and energy saving. The facilities also are very clean and nicely decorated. A 5.5 mph speed limit is enforced, and campers are warned: "If you exceed the speed limit at Yogi Bear, you'll find yourself walking." Laid out in a series of loops, the campground has 946 owner/campers, leaving 150 sites for visitors and 32 spots in the primitive tent area, which is used only on Labor Day weekend. Located 4 miles west of Plymouth, Indiana, the campground has ten pull-through sites and a typical site width of 40 feet. Security measures are excellent with a controlled gate entry system and 24-hour security on the premises.

BASICS

Operated By: Marshall County Membership Corp. **Open:** May 1–Oct. 1. **Site Assignment:** Reservations w/ 1-night deposit; refund (minus 10%) w/ 10-day notice. **Registration:** At campground office. **Fee:** $35; cash, check, credit card. **Parking:** At site.

FACILITIES

Number of RV-only Sites: 1096. **Number of Tent-only Sites:** 32. **Hookups:** Electric (30 amps), water, sewer. **Each Site:** Picnic table, fire ring. **Dump Station:** Yes. **Laundry:** Yes. **Pay Phone:** Yes. **Restrooms and Showers:** Yes. **Fuel:** No. **Propane:** Yes. **Internal Roads:** Paved/gravel, in good condition. **RV Service:** No. **Market:** 3 mi. east in Plymouth. **Restaurant:** Cafe. **General Store:** Yes. **Vending:** Yes. **Swimming:** Yes. **Playground:** Yes. **Other:** Snack bar, game room, fishing pond, pavilion, rec hall, rental cabins, tennis, basketball, mini-golf, horseshoes, adults room, recreation field, coin games, wading pool, boat dock. **Activities:** Swimming, fishing, boating (rental kayaks & paddleboats available), scheduled activities. **Nearby Attractions:** Golf, Amish Acres, Culver Military Academy, University of Notre Dame, Studebaker Museum, College Football Hall of Fame, Trail of Courage, antiques, arts & crafts, historic homes. **Additional Information:** Marshall County CVB, (800) 626-5353.

RESTRICTIONS

Pets: On leash only. **Fires:** Fire ring only. **Alcoholic Beverages:** At sites only. **Vehicle Maximum Length:** No limit. **Other:** Roller skates, skateboards, & roller blades are not allowed.

TO GET THERE

From junction of Hwy. 17/US 31 and US 30, drive 4 mi. west on US 30. Roads are wide and well maintained, with broad shoulders.

ROCHESTER   MAP, A-2
Lakeview Campground

7781 East 300 North, 46975. T: (574) 353-8114 or (800) 838-9760; www.lakeviewcampingfun.com.

🚐 ★★★	🏕 ★★★
Beauty: ★★★★	Site Privacy: ★★★★
Spaciousness: ★★★★	Quiet: ★★★★
Security: ★★★★	Cleanliness: ★★★
Insect Control: ★★★	Facilities: ★★★

Campers don't have to worry about getting a lakefront site at Lakeview Campground. Each site is on Barr Lake. Located 7 miles northeast of Rochester,

Indiana, the campground has a surprising amount of shade for lakefront sites. Laid out in a half loop, the campground has a typical site width of 30 feet, with 45 seasonal and 8 pull-through sites. Lakeview is well maintained, with freshly painted buildings, a mowed bank that goes down to a small creek, and a colorful mini-golf setup with a little teepee, windmill, log cabin, bridge, and other gizmos to offer challenge. Tents have a separate area with more greenery and privacy from RVs. Security includes one entrance/exit road, surveillance cameras, and owners who live on site. Quiet hours are 11 p.m. to 8 a.m.

BASICS

Operated By: Jim, Roberta, and Jeff Bever. **Open:** Apr. 15–Oct. 15. **Site Assignment:** Reservations w/o deposit. **Registration:** At campground office. **Fee:** $18–$28; cash, check, credit card. **Parking:** At site.

FACILITIES

Number of RV-only Sites: 105. **Number of Tent-only Sites:** 25. **Hookups:** Electric (30 amps), water, sewer. **Each Site:** Picnic table, fire ring. **Dump Station:** Yes. **Laundry:** No. **Pay Phone:** No. **Restrooms and Showers:** Yes. **Fuel:** No. **Propane:** No. **Internal Roads:** Gravel, in good condition. **RV Service:** No. **Market:** 7 mi. southwest in Rochester. **Restaurant:** 7 mi. southwest in Rochester. **General Store:** Yes, limited. **Vending:** Yes. **Swimming:** No. **Playground:** Yes. **Other:** Barr Lake, swimming beach, mini-golf, pavilion, volleyball, basketball, hiking trails, rec hall, badminton, sports field, fish-cleaning house. **Activities:** Swimming, fishing, boating (rental rowboats, canoes, paddleboats available), hiking, scheduled weekend activities. **Nearby Attractions:** Golf, outlet stores, Rounds Barn Museum, Fulton County Museum, antiques, Living History Village. **Additional Information:** Fulton County Historical Society, (219) 223-4436.

RESTRICTIONS

Pets: On leash only. **Fires:** Fire ring only. **Alcoholic Beverages:** Allowed. **Vehicle Maximum Length:** No limit.

TO GET THERE

From junction of Hwy. 31 and Hwy. 14, drive 6.5 mi. east on Hwy. 14 to Athens, then 3 mi. north on CR 650E, then 1 mi. east on CR 300N. Roads are wide and well maintained, with broad shoulders.

SANTA CLAUS   MAP, D-2
Lake Rudolph Campground and RV Resort

78 North Holiday Blvd., 47579. T: (877) 478-3657 or (812) 937-4458; www.lakerudolph.com.

🚐 ★★★★	🏕 ★★★★
Beauty: ★★★	Site Privacy: ★★★
Spaciousness: ★★★	Quiet: ★★★
Security: ★★★★	Cleanliness: ★★★★
Insect Control: ★★	Facilities: ★★★★

A touch of Christmas lives year-round at Lake Rudolph Campground and RV Resort. Located in the small Indiana town of Santa Claus, Lake Rudolph got its name from, of course, the famed red-nosed reindeer. Sections of the two big loops are named Dasher, Kringer, and Prancer. Next door to Holiday World Theme Park and Splashin' Safari Water Park, the campground is a summertime favorite with folks who like to be a free shuttle ride or a ten-minute walk from their campsite and the amusement park. The spacious, forested campground with its southern Indiana hills features beautiful fall foliage and a quieter refuge when the theme park starts closing down after Labor Day. The best sites for RVs are 2, 11, 17, 35, 37, 39, and 92 in the Dasher section because they are easier to back in (two pull-through sites are available). Sites have gravel pads with a grassy area; no two lots are the same. Tenters favor sites 125–130 in the Dasher section for the huge pine, maple, and oak trees. The freezing temperatures, snow, and lack of on-site water make Lake Rudolph a good-weather option for all but the most hardy—or those who want to experience Santa Claus in his true element.

BASICS

Operated By: Koch Development Corp. **Open:** Apr. 1–Dec. 1. **Site Assignment:** Reservations w/ 1-night deposit; refunds w/ 48-hour notice; nonrefundable deposit on credit card; 10-day notice on RV and cabin rentals. **Registration:** At campground headquarters. **Fee:** $20–$42; cabin, $85–$152; RV rental, $60–$128; cash, credit card. **Parking:** At sites or at headquarters parking lot.

FACILITIES

Number of RV-only Sites: 200. **Number of Tent-only Sites:** 40. **Hookups:** Electric (30, 50 amps), water, sewer, Wi-Fi. **Each Site:** Fire ring, picnic table. **Dump Station:** Yes. **Laundry:** Yes. **Pay Phone:** Yes. **Restrooms and Showers:** Yes. **Fuel:** No. **Propane:** Yes. **Internal Roads:** Paved, in good condition. **RV Service:** No. **Market:** 0.25 mi. west in Santa Claus. **Restaurant:** 0.25 mi. west in Santa Claus. **General Store:** Yes. **Vending:** Yes. **Swimming:** Yes. **Playground:** Yes. **Other:** Game room, billiard room, basketball, horseshoes, volleyball, nature trail, fishing lake, mini-golf, free shuttle to Holiday World Theme Park & Splashin' Safari Water Park, cabin rentals, RV rentals. **Activities:** Fishing, bingo, occasional cookouts, special Halloween weekends w/ hay rides & other activities. **Nearby Attractions:** Holiday World Theme Park & Splashin' Safari Water Park, golf, Santa Claus post office, Lincoln Boyhood National Memorial, caves, Lincoln State Park, Young Abe Lincoln Outdoor Drama. **Additional Information:** Santa Claus–Lincoln City Area Visitors Bureau, (800) GO-SANTA.

RESTRICTIONS

Pets: Leash only (not in rentals). **Fires:** Fire rings, grills only. **Alcoholic Beverages:** At sites only. **Vehicle Maximum Length:** 40 ft. **Other:** Rentals 2-night min. stay, holiday weekends 3-day min. stay.

TO GET THERE

Take Exit 63 off I-64, travel 7 mi. south on SR 162, turn right at Holiday World parking lot, then go 200 yards and turn right into campgrounds. Roads are wide and well maintained.

SCOTTSBURG   MAP, D-2
Yogi Bear's Jellystone Park

4577 W. IN 56, 47170. T: (800) 437-0566 or (812) 752-7046; www.campindiana.com/yogi.

🚐 ★★★★	🏕 ★★★★
Beauty: ★★★★	Site Privacy: ★★★
Spaciousness: ★★★	Quiet: ★★★
Security: ★★★★	Cleanliness: ★★★
Insect Control: ★★★	Facilities: ★★★★

All sites at this Yogi Bear Jellystone Park are all level and well kept up. The entire park is very clean and well maintained, including the restrooms and showers. The swimming pool is nice in summer, and the lake is very large, with lots of fish; no fishing license is required. Many planned activities for the kids are offered on weekends. However, the roads may be too narrow for big rigs to navigate, and some sites may be hard to get in and out. Additionally, you can hear the neverending sound of trains passing by. The staff is very helpful and friendly, and the security is reasonable.

BASICS

Open: All year. **Site Assignment:** Reservations recommended. **Registration:** At ranger station. **Fee:** RV/tent, $26–$35.

FACILITIES

Number of Multipurpose Sites: 94. **Hookups:** Electric (20, 30, 50 amps), sewer. **Dump Station:** Yes. **Laundry:** Yes. **Pay Phone:** Yes. **Restrooms and Showers:** Yes. **Fuel:** No. **Propane:** Yes. **Internal Roads:** Gravel. **General Store:** Camp store. **Vending:** Yes. **Swimming:** Yes. **Playground:** Yes. **Activities:** Stocked fishing lake, rowboat & paddleboat rentals.

RESTRICTIONS

Pets: On leash, attended only. **Fires:** Allowed.

TO GET THERE

Located off I-65 in Scottsburg, 4 mi. west on Hwy. 56 toward Salem, 30 mi. to Louisville, 80 mi. to Indianapolis.

THORNTOWN   MAP, B-2
Old Mill Run Park

8544 West 690 North, 46071. T: (765) 436-7190; www.frontiernet.net/~oldmill.

🚐 ★★★★	🏕 ★★★★
Beauty: ★★★★	Site Privacy: ★★★★
Spaciousness: ★★★★	Quiet: ★★★★
Security: ★★★★	Cleanliness: ★★★★
Insect Control: ★★★	Facilities: ★★★★

Little touches like coordinated wallpaper in the bathrooms, an entrance way decorated with day lilies, and a mill water fountain make this campground stand out. Mature trees and newly planted ones are mingled to ensure future shade. Campers have a choice of open or shaded areas and all pull-through sites. Laid out in a series of loops, Old Mill Run Camp has 197 seasonal campers and a separate section for tents. The average site width is 35 feet and sites are mostly grassy with patios. As a family campground located 1 mile west of Thorntown, Old Mill doesn't allow alcohol at any activities or facilities, including walking around the park with it. Quiet hours are 11 p.m. to 7 a.m. Clotheslines are not permitted in the park, nor are mopeds, four-wheelers, or motorized bikes. Electric golf carts are permitted for seasonal campers age 21 and up. The best RV sites are 216–248 because they are bigger and offer cable TV and cement pads. The best tent sites are P13–P24 because they are behind the pond and provide more green space and privacy. A security patrol, an owner who lives on site, and one entrance/exit to the campground help assure campers' safety.

BASICS

Operated By: Ralph and Sandy Christman. **Open:** Apr. 1–Oct. 15. **Site Assignment:** Reservations w/o deposit. **Registration:** At campground office. **Fee:** Cash, check, credit card. **Parking:** At site.

FACILITIES

Number of RV-only Sites: 322. **Number of Tent-only Sites:** 25. **Hookups:** Electric (30, 50 amps), water, sewer, cable TV, phone. **Each Site:** Picnic table, fire ring. **Dump Station:** Yes. **Laundry:** Yes. **Pay Phone:** Yes. **Restrooms and Showers:** Yes. **Fuel:** No. **Propane:** Yes. **Internal Roads:** Gravel/paved, in good condition. **RV Service:** No. **Market:** 9 mi. east in Lebanon. **Restaurant:** 1 mi. east in Thorntown. **General Store:** Yes. **Vending:** No. **Swimming:** Yes. **Playground:** Yes. **Other:** Mini-golf, horseshoes, rental cabin, rally area, shelter house, 2 fishing ponds, hot tub, 5-hole golf course, basketball, volleyball, shuffleboard, Sugar Creek, coin games, sports field, badminton. **Activities:** Swimming, fishing, scheduled activities, Sun. church services. **Nearby Attractions:** Indianapolis Zoo, Children's Museum, Indianapolis Motor Speedway, antiques, museums, historic sites. **Additional Information:** Boone County Chamber of Commerce, (765) 482-1320.

RESTRICTIONS

Pets: On leash only. **Fires:** Fire ring only. **Alcoholic Beverages:** At sites only. **Vehicle Maximum Length:** No limit. **Other:** Limit of 6 fish per day.

TO GET THERE

From I-65W, take Exit 146, drive 6.5 mi. west on Hwy. 47, then 1 mi. north on CR 825W. Roads are wide and well maintained, with broad shoulders.

VERSAILLES   MAP, C-3
Versailles State Park

1387 E US 50, P. O. Box 205, 47042.
T: (812) 689-6424 or (866) 622-6746;
www.in.gov/dnr or www.camp.in.gov.

 ★★★   ★★★

Beauty: ★★★★
Spaciousness: ★★★
Security: ★★★★
Insect Control: ★★
Site Privacy: ★★★
Quiet: ★★★
Cleanliness: ★★★★
Facilities: ★★★

At 5,905 acres, Versailles State Park is the second-largest state park in Indiana. It also has the second busiest state park swimming pool, a 25-meter pool with a 100-foot waterslide. In peak summer, the park, campgrounds, and pool are overrun with visitors. Hillsides with limestone outcroppings, ravines, upland wooded areas, fields, and a 230-acre lake help make this one of the state's prettiest parks. October is a peak time for fall foliage, as well as the annual Bluegrass Festival. At the entrance to the park, you can drive over Busching Bridge, one of the two remaining covered bridges in Ripley County. Located 2 miles east of Versailles, Indiana, the park is one of the few state parks to offer horseback riding. The horseback trails are open year-round but the saddle barn is open only April through October. The park also has more than 6 miles of scenic hiking trails marked for skilled and beginning hikers. All camping sites will accommodate both RVs and tents. Security measures are strict, with passes needed to enter the campground; the area is patrolled by rangers.

BASICS

Operated By: Indiana Dept. of Natural Resources. **Open:** All year. **Site Assignment:** Reservations by phone (866) 622-6746 or online at www.camp.in.gov. **Registration:** At campground office. **Fee:** $17–$25; entry fees: in-state, $4–$5; out-of-state, $7; check, credit card. **Parking:** At site.

FACILITIES

Number of Multipurpose Sites: 220. **Hookups:** Electric (30 amps). **Each Site:** Picnic table, fire ring. **Dump Station:** Yes. **Laundry:** No. **Pay Phone:** Yes. **Restrooms and Showers:** Yes. **Fuel:** No. **Propane:** No. **Internal Roads:** Paved, in good condition. **RV Service:** No. **Market:** 2 mi. west in Vincennes. **Restaurant:** 2 mi. west in Vincennes. **General Store:** Yes. **Vending:** No. **Swimming:** Yes. **Playground:** Yes. **Other:** Boat ramp (only electric trolling motors permitted), nature center, picnic shelters. **Activities:** Hiking, fishing, boating (rental rowboats, paddleboats, & canoes available), summer weekday programs, nature walks & evening activities offered by naturalist. **Nearby Attractions:** Scenic drives, 27-mi. Hoosier Hills Bicycle Route, golf, Ripley County Historical Society. **Additional Information:** Ripley County Tourism Bureau, (888) 747-3827.

RESTRICTIONS

Pets: On leash only. **Fires:** Fire rings, grills only. **Alcoholic Beverages:** At sites only. **Vehicle Maximum Length:** No limit. **Other:** 14-day stay limit.

TO GET THERE

From junction of US 421 and US 50, drive 1 mi. east on US 50. Roads are wide and well maintained, with adequate shoulders.

WOLCOTTVILLE   MAP, A-3
Gordon's Camping

9500 South 600E, 46795. T: (260) 351-3383 or (260) 436-6823; www.gordonscamping.com.

🚐 ★★★   ▲ ★★★

Beauty: ★★★
Spaciousness: ★★★
Security: ★★★★★
Insect Control: ★★
Site Privacy: ★★★
Quiet: ★★★
Cleanliness: ★★★★
Facilities: ★★★

Calling itself "the cure for summertime blues," Gordon's Camping has enough recreation and activities to keep most anyone happy. Located 35 miles north of Kendallville, the campground also is convenient to many attractions. So, not surprisingly, Gordon's is popular. Offering wooded sites on rolling terrain, Gordon's has 200 pull-throughs and some sites as large as 50 feet wide. Sites are mostly shady and grassy. The best sites for tents are along the pond in the Black Willow section where it is quieter and more natural. The best sites for RVs are in the Black Walnut and Tulip Tree sections because they are pull-throughs, offer 50 amps electricity, and feature more shade. Security is tops with a traffic-control gate requiring a pass, owners who live on site, and regular patrols of the campground.

BASICS

Operated By: Jerry and Sandi Bubb. **Open:** Mid-May–mid-Oct. **Site Assignment:** First come, first served. **Registration:** At campground office. **Fee:** $28; cash, check, credit card. **Parking:** At site.

FACILITIES

Number of RV-only Sites: 300. **Hookups:** Electric (20, 30, 50 amps), water. **Each Site:** Picnic table & fire rings for rent. **Dump Station:** Yes. **Laundry:** No. **Pay Phone:** No. **Restrooms and Showers:** Yes. **Fuel:** No. **Propane:** Yes. **Internal Roads:** Paved/gravel, in good condition. **RV Service:** No. **Market:** 8 mi. south in Kendallville. **Restaurant:** 8 mi. south in Kendallville. **General Store:** Yes. **Vending:** No. **Swimming:** Yes. **Playground:** Yes. **Other:** Mini-golf, hiking trails, pavilion, basketball, volleyball, horseshoes, kids' fishing pond, coin games, wading pool, sports field. **Activities:** Swimming, boating (rental rowboats available), biking (rental bikes available), church services, scheduled activities, rental cabins. **Nearby Attractions:** Golf, Auburn Cord Duesenberg Museum, zoo, nation's 2nd largest genealogy library, windmill museum. **Additional Information:** Fort Wayne/Allen County CVB, (800) 767-7752.

RESTRICTIONS

Pets: On leash only. **Fires:** Open. **Alcoholic Beverages:** Allowed. **Vehicle Maximum Length:** No limit.

TO GET THERE

From junction of US 20 and Hwy. 3, drive 7 mi. south on Hwy. 3, then 1.25 mi. east on CR 600S. Roads are well maintained but narrow with adequate shoulders.

Iowa

If the state of Iowa registers at all to nonresidents, it comes across as an endless field of corn where little other than farming ever happens. Yet to view the Hawkeye State solely in this light is to ignore the many cultural and historical contributions Iowa has made to the nation.

Before Europeans settled in Iowa, a number of Native American tribes lived in the area, including the Sauk, Mesquakie, Sioux, Potawatomi, Otoe, and Missouri; and before them, prehistoric ancestors roamed along the banks of the Mississippi River. In 1673, French explorers Louis Joliet and Father Jacques Marquette were the first Europeans to set foot in Iowa. As in other parts of the United States, pioneers soon came flooding into the state, displacing the native populations. Despite the lack of trees, pioneers remained to discover a land with exceedingly rich soil. As settlement proceeded, the Hawkeye State became a melting pot of cultures. Between 1860 and 1870, the population nearly doubled due to an influx of European immigrants, the majority of which were German. Most of these people came to farm, but interestingly a thriving coal industry also emerged, once making Iowa the major coal producer for the United States.

The state has had its share of hard times. The coal industry collapsed in the early 1900s, leaving many towns deserted, and the stock market crash of 1929 led to many farmers losing their land. In spite of these setbacks, the citizens and the economy of Iowa ultimately prospered: today the state is the number one producer of corn and pork in the country.

Visitors to Iowa will find much to enjoy, including historic frontier forts, authentic American farms, and culturally rich cities.

In the southeast corner of the 29th state, near Cedar Rapids (the second-largest city), campers can visit the **Amana Colonies,** founded 150 years ago by Germans seeking religious freedom. Other sites include **Ushers Ferry Historic Village,** the **National Czech and Slovak Museum,** and the **Indian Creek Nature Center,** which has more than 11 miles of trails. For a taste of what the future will hold, Trekkers are recommended to visit the future birthplace of James T. Kirk, captain of the starship *Enterprise,* in Riverdale, where his "ancestors" put on the **Trek Fest** every year in anticipation of the captain's March 21, 2233, birthday. About 50 miles away in Davenport, visitors can see the **Davenport Museum of Art's Grant Wood collection** as well as the **Adler Theater,** once part of the RKO theater chain. Outdoor enthusiasts will admire the many opportunities offered by the **Upper Mississippi River National Wildlife and Fish Refuge,** which runs along the state's eastern border.

The northeast section of Iowa stands in sharp contrast to the rest of the state. Instead of rolling hills and farmlands, this region, often referred to as Little Switzerland, has large forested swaths of land amid its rugged geography. Outdoor enthusiasts will find much to do here, including paddling opportunities on the Turkey, Upper Iowa, and Volga rivers. The access to the Mississippi also made this a valuable location for prehistoric Native Americans, as visitors will discover at the **Effigy Mounds National Monument.** For travelers seeking more cosmopolitan fare, Cedar Falls/Waterloo hosts many festivals, including the **Cedar Basin Jazz Festival** and **College Hill Arts Festival.** Once you're on the road, it might be fitting to check out the **National Hobo Convention** in Britt the second week of August, or at least visit the hobo museum.

Though lacking in major metropolitan areas, northwest Iowa has plenty to offer. There are numerous state parks and recreation areas within the Natural Lakes region, which was shaped by glacial activity thousands of years ago. **Gull Point State Park** and the **Lost Island Prairie Wetland Nature Center** are two recommended sites. Most winter outdoor activities center around cross-country skiing or snowmobile riding; during the summer, visitors should seek out the **Inkpaduta Canoe Trail,** which follows the meandering Little Sioux River.

One of the geographically richest regions in the state, the Loess Hills, is located in the southwest section of the state. Not rich enough? A trip to Audubon will reveal the world's largest bull, Albert. Those wanting to see what the Iowa landscape looked like before European settlement should visit **Neal Smith National Wildlife Reserve,** where tall-grass prairie is being reintroduced along with natural herds of buffalo and other critters. Don't forget, the capital also offers numerous options for fun and recreation, including the **Des Moines Art Center,** the **historic Jordan House,** and the **Iowa Historical Museum.**

Campground Profiles

ADEL   MAP, B-2
Des Moines West KOA

3418 L Ave., 50003. T: (515) 834-2729 or (800) KOA-2181; www.koa.com.

🚐 ★★★   ⛺ ★★★

Beauty: ★★★	Site Privacy: ★★★
Spaciousness: ★★★	Quiet: ★★★★
Security: ★★★★	Cleanliness: ★★★★
Insect Control: ★★★	Facilities: ★★★

Seventeen miles outside Des Moines and conveniently located directly off I-80 is the West Des Moines KOA. This KOA offers its patrons full amenities, a separate tent area, and all pull-through sites. Each site has a level parking area and a small grass lawn. The campground is nicely landscaped and offers some shade. Hot coffee is served daily, just in time for an early morning dip in the pool. The area is rich in history, with numerous places to visit, such as the Blank Park Zoo, the botanical center, and the now-famous bridges of Madison County. The staff is friendly and helpful, and the park offers excellent security. The park is open year-round, but remember to pack according to the season; Iowa is bitterly cold and windy in the winter.

BASICS

Operated By: David and Patricia Kimmel. **Open:** All year. **Site Assignment:** By reservation w/ credit card. **Registration:** At camp store. **Fee:** RV, $22–$28.50; tent, $19; for 2 people; additional guests, $2; children under 5 free. **Parking:** At site.

FACILITIES

Number of RV-only Sites: 220. **Number of Tent-only Sites:** 80. **Hookups:** Electric (20, 30, 50 amps), water, sewer. **Each Site:** Picnic table. **Dump Station:** Yes. **Laundry:** Yes. **Pay Phone:** Yes. **Restrooms and Showers:** Yes. **Fuel:** No, in Adel or West Des Moines. **Propane:** Yes. **Internal Roads:** Paved, in good condition. **RV Service:** In West Des Moines. **Market:** 10 mi. in Castana, IA. **Restaurant:** In West Des Moines. **General Store:** Yes. **Vending:** No. **Swimming:** Yes. **Playground:** Yes. **Other:** Cabins, fishing pond. **Activities:** Fishing, swimming, horseshoes. **Nearby Attractions:** Living History Farms, State Capitol, John Wayne birthplace, Blank Park Zoo, botanical center, art & science center, Valley West Mall. **Additional Information:** West Des Moines Chamber of Commerce, (515) 225-6009.

RESTRICTIONS

Pets: On leash. **Fires:** No open fires. **Alcoholic Beverages:** Allowed. **Vehicle Maximum Length:** No limit. **Other:** $2 extra to run heat or A/C.

TO GET THERE

From I-80 Exit 106, go north 1 mi. on paved CR P-58.

CEDAR FALLS   MAP, B-3
Black Hawk Park

2410 West Lone Tree Rd., 50613. T: (319) 266-6813 or (319) 266-0328; www.co.black-hawk.ia.us/depts/conservation.html.

🚐 ★★★★   ⛺ ★★★★

Beauty: ★★★★	Site Privacy: ★★★
Spaciousness: ★★★	Quiet: ★★★★
Security: ★★★★	Cleanliness: ★★★
Insect Control: ★★★	Facilities: ★★

Named after Chief Black Hawk of the Sauk Indian Tribe, Black Hawk Park is one of the largest county parks in the state. The park is part of a conservation area over 1,300 acres in size with a 142-site modern campground, complete with restroom facilities and showers. The sites are comfortable and well shaded by mature oak and other hardwoods. The park roads are paved, and there are large sites, both pull-throughs and back-ins. Activities here include archery, a rifle range, and public hunting and fishing. There are even boat ramps. A full-time residential staff person and a host family are available to assist campers. The natural setting is a combination of woodland and prairie with a constant breeze.

BASICS

Operated By: Black Hawk County Conservation Board. **Open:** All year; weather permitting. **Site Assignment:** First come, first served and a few sites by reservation. **Registration:** At registration kiosk. **Fee:** $11–$17. **Parking:** At site.

FACILITIES

Number of Multipurpose Sites: 142. **Hookups:** Electric (20, 30, 50 amps), water. **Each Site:** Picnic table, fire pit. **Dump Station:** Yes. **Laundry:** No. **Pay Phone:** No. **Restrooms and Showers:** Yes. **Fuel:** No, in Cedar Falls. **Propane:** No, in Cedar Falls. **Internal Roads:** Paved, in good condition. **RV Service:** In Cedar Falls. **Market:** In Cedar Falls. **Restaurant:** In Cedar Falls. **General Store:** No. **Vending:** No. **Swimming:** No. **Playground:** Yes. **Other:** 2 cabins, primitive camping, picnic shelters. **Activities:** Recreation trails, boating, rifle & pistol range, archery range, hunting, fishing, water activities, winter activities, ice fishing. **Nearby Attractions:** Sturgis Falls Celebrations, University of Northern Iowa Museum, the Grout Museums, Cedar Valley Nature Trail. **Additional Information:** Cedar Falls Chamber of Commerce, (319) 266-3593.

RESTRICTIONS

Pets: On leash. **Fires:** Fire pit only. **Alcoholic Beverages:** Allowed, no hard liquor. **Vehicle Maximum Length:** No limit.

TO GET THERE

From Cedar Falls where US 218 and SR 58 meet, go north a little more than 1.7 mi. Turn left on East Lone Tree Rd and continue about 2.5 mi. to the campground.

CLERMONT   MAP, A-4
Skip-A-Way

3825 Harding Rd., 52135. T: (800) 728-1167; www.skipawayresort.com.

🚐 ★★★★   ⛺ ★★★

Beauty: ★★	Site Privacy: ★★
Spaciousness: ★★	Quiet: ★★★
Security: ★★★	Cleanliness: ★★★
Insect Control: ★★★	Facilities: ★★★★

With a little imagination and some foresight, Skip and Bev Baker have created a camper's playground at Skip-A-Way Resort. The hosts' aim to make your stay comfortable and fun is accomplished by providing a full range of amenities and a number of family and community activities. Enjoy a round of miniature golf, a game of Norwegian horseshoes, or a leisurely float down the Turkey River after an afternoon of fishing on Quarry Lake. Saturday evenings can be spent in the lodge watching a movie with other campers or bouncing through the campground on a wagon ride. Other scheduled events change each year and may include anything from square dancing to eating contests. For a truly unusual experience, spend a night in the rustic 1800s log cabin that is available for rent. With an eye for improvement, the owners continue to upgrade their campground with landscaping, fresh paint, and added sites, making it increasingly popular. While walk-ins are welcome, it is best to reserve a site early, especially on holiday weekends. Certainly, the highlight of a stay here is the hosts eagerness to help guests have fun.

BASICS

Operated By: Skip and Bev Baker. **Open:** May 1–Oct. 15. **Site Assignment:** Reservations accepted. **Registration:** Call for reservations, otherwise at lodge. **Fee:** $14–$21. **Parking:** At site.

FACILITIES

Number of RV-only Sites: 67. **Number of Tent-only Sites:** 15. **Number of Multipurpose Sites:** 10. **Hookups:** Electric (20, 30, 50 amps), water, sewer. **Each Site:** None. **Dump Station:** Yes. **Laundry:** Yes. **Pay Phone:** No. **Restrooms and Showers:** Yes. **Fuel:** No. **Propane:** Yes. **Internal Roads:** Gravel. **RV Service:** No. **Market:** No. **Restaurant:** Yes. **General Store:** Yes. **Vending:** No. **Swimming:** Yes. **Playground:** Yes. **Other:** Lake & river access. **Activities:** Mini-golf, fishing (need license on river, but not for lake), swimming, boating, weekend movies. **Nearby Attractions:** 1800s log cabin for rent, Echo Valley Speedway.

RESTRICTIONS

Pets: On leash. **Fires:** Fire ring only. **Alcoholic Beverages:** Allowed. **Vehicle Maximum Length:** No limit.

TO GET THERE

From Hwy. 18, take Exit 3825. The campground is visible from the road.

GUTHRIE   MAP, B-2
Springbrook State Park

2437 160th Rd., 50115. T: (641) 747-3591.

🚐 ★★★★   ⛺ ★★★★

Beauty: ★★★   Site Privacy: ★★★★
Spaciousness: ★★★★   Quiet: ★★★★
Security: ★★★★   Cleanliness: ★★★
Insect Control: ★★★   Facilities: ★★

If you're a serious outdoorsman, this park will suit your needs well. Operated by the Iowa Department of Natural Resources, it is open all year and is well maintained. The sites for both RVs and tents are very nice, being spacious, private, and quiet. Some of the RV sites have electric and water hookups, and all of the sites are equipped with a picnic table and grated fire pit. Activities within the park include fishing, boating, and hiking. There is also swimming, biking, waterskiing, and wind surfing in the summer. Nearby, visitors will find a golf course and river fishing. Reservations are not required.

BASICS
Operated By: Iowa Dept. of Natural Resources. **Open:** All year. **Site Assignment:** First come, first served. **Registration:** Self-registration at entrance gate. **Fee:** Prime season, $11–$16; off season; $6–$13. **Parking:** At site.

FACILITIES
Number of RV-only Sites: 81. **Number of Multipurpose Sites:** 40. **Hookups:** Electric (20, 30 amps), water. **Each Site:** Picnic table, grated fire pits. **Dump Station:** Yes. **Laundry:** No. **Pay Phone:** Yes. **Restrooms and Showers:** Yes. **Fuel:** In town. **Propane:** In town. **Internal Roads:** Paved, in good condition. **RV Service:** In Des Moines. **Market:** In Guthrie. **Restaurant:** Several in the area. **General Store:** No. **Vending:** No. **Swimming:** Lakefront beach. **Playground:** Yes. **Other:** 6 cabins, enclosed picnic shelters, boat ramps, boat rentals, beach, fishing dock, large group camp w/ kitchen, dinning hall, & meeting rooms. **Activities:** Fishing (walleye, muskie, yellow bass), boating, jet skiing, waterskiing, wind surfing, swimming, miles of trails, in-line skating, hiking, biking in the summer. Part of The Central Iowa State Park Bike Route. **Nearby Attractions:** River fishing, golf. **Additional Information:** Panora Chamber of Commerce, (641) 755-3300.

RESTRICTIONS
Pets: Dogs on leash. **Fires:** Fire ring only. **Alcoholic Beverages:** Beer & wine only in sites. **Vehicle Maximum Length:** No limit. **Other:** No metal detectors in campground; max of 6 people to a site.

TO GET THERE
From I-80 Exit 86 go north on SR 25 about 20 mi. (you will go through Guthrie Center) and east on SR 384 about 3 mi. into park.

JOHNSTON   MAP, B-2
Saylorville Lake

5600 NW 78th Ave., 50131. T: (515) 276-4656 or (515) 964-0672; www.saylorvillelake.org.

🚐 ★★★★   ⛺ ★★★★

Beauty: ★★★★   Site Privacy: ★★★★
Spaciousness: ★★★★   Quiet: ★★★★
Security: ★★★   Cleanliness: ★★★
Insect Control: ★★★   Facilities: ★★★

Approximately 10 miles north of Des Moines is the U.S. Army Corps of Engineers Saylorville Lake Project. This 5,950-acre area is a wonderful recreation haven for outdoor enthusiasts. It features four campgrounds with over 500 camping sites. Camping sites have level paved parking pads, and there is a variety of amenities, including full hookups on some sites. Modern restrooms and showers can be found in all the camping areas. There are over 25 miles of biking trails, in addition to hiking and cross-country ski trails. Boating and fishing are among the favorite activities with the project offering a full-service marina, repair, and fuel. There is a year-round visitor center, and camping reservations are recommended. The area is a combination of woodland and prairie, and all the campsites are well groomed. There is a registration gate at the entrance to each camping area staffed by seasonal volunteers or corps employees.

BASICS
Operated By: U.S. Army Corps of Engineers. **Open:** Park, year-round; campgrounds, May–Sept. **Site Assignment:** 60% reservable, remainder are first come, first served; call the National Recreation reservation service, (877) 444-6777. **Registration:** At entrance gate, or registration kiosk. **Fee:** $12–$24; based on day of the week & amenities. **Parking:** At site.

FACILITIES
Number of Multipurpose Sites: 588. **Hookups:** Electric (20, 30, 50 amps), water, sewer. **Each Site:** Picnic table, paved trailer pad, fire pit. **Dump Station:** Yes. **Laundry:** No. **Pay Phone:** Yes. **Restrooms and Showers:** Yes. **Fuel:** No. **Propane:** No. **Internal Roads:** Paved, in good condition. **RV Service:** In Des Moines. **Market:** In Des Moines. **Restaurant:** In Des Moines. **General Store:** Yes. **Vending:** Yes. **Swimming:** 2 beaches. **Playground:** Yes. **Other:** 2 beaches, 3 boat ramps, picnic shelters, scheduled activities. **Activities:** Softball, bike trails, hiking trails, fishing, volleyball, horseshoes, swimming, boating, waterskiing, jet skiing, playground, horse trails, golf, winter recreation, scheduled activities, & nature program. **Nearby Attractions:** State capital, Historical Museum, botanical center, Des Moines zoo, Des Moines Science Center. **Additional Information:** West Des Moines Chamber of Commerce, (515) 225-6009.

RESTRICTIONS
Pets: On leash only (6 ft. max.). **Fires:** In approved places only. **Alcoholic Beverages:** Allowed, w/ discretion. **Vehicle Maximum Length:** 45 ft. **Other:** 50% discount w/ Golden Age or Golden Access passport.

TO GET THERE
From I-35 Exit 96 go west on NE 126th Ave. 7.2 mi., then turn left on NW Sheldahl Dr. Go 0.5 mi. and continue south on N. 3rd St.; 1 mi. later turn right on SR 415; go about 5 mi. and follow the signs to the park or visitors center.

KELLOGG   MAP, B-3
Kellogg RV Park

1570 Hwy. 224 South, P.O. Box 380, 50135. T: (641) 526-8535.

🚐 ★★★   ⛺ n/a

Beauty: ★★★   Site Privacy: ★★★
Spaciousness: ★★★   Quiet: ★★★
Security: ★★★   Cleanliness: ★★★
Insect Control: ★★★   Facilities: ★★★

Directly off I-80 halfway between Grinnell and Newtown, is the Kellogg Campground. Set in the backdrop of a small service station and adjacent to a large crop of corn, this small campground gives you the feeling of home. The campsites are arranged in a loop with a few in the center. All the campsites are pull-through, large, level, and have gravel parking pads. Shaded by large, mature maple trees, most of the sites are pull-throughs and come with a barbecue grill. The lawn is plush and well kept, and the area is clean. The restrooms and showers are located in the mini-mart (the Kellduff 5 and 10), and all campground patrons receive a $.10 per gallon discount on fuel. The campground is simple, warm, and a nice place to relax from a long day's drive. There is a small cafe in the mini-mart as well as basic supplies. The weather varies from season to season, but sun and bug protection are always a good idea.

BASICS
Operated By: Richard Wenndt. **Open:** All year. **Site Assignment:** First come, first served. **Registration:** At mini-mart. **Fee:** $11. **Parking:** At site.

FACILITIES
Number of RV-only Sites: 23. **Hookups:** Electric (20, 30, 50 amps), water. **Each Site:** Picnic table, grill, light post. **Dump Station:** Yes. **Laundry:** No. **Pay Phone:** Yes. **Restrooms and Showers:** Yes. **Fuel:** Yes. **Propane:** No. **Internal Roads:** Gravel, in good condition. **RV Service:** 21 mi. in Marshalltown. **Market:** 8 mi. in either Grinnell or Newtown. **Restaurant:** On site or in Grinnell or Newton. **General Store:** Yes. **Vending:** At the mini-mart on property. **Swimming:** No. **Playground:** Yes. **Activities:** Playground, walking, bicycling. **Nearby Attractions:** Inquire at campground. **Additional Information:** Grinnel Chamber of Commerce, (641) 236-6555; Marshaltown Chamber of Commerce, (641) 792-5545.

RESTRICTIONS
Pets: On leash. **Fires:** Grill only. **Alcoholic Beverages:** Allowed. **Vehicle Maximum Length:** No limit.

TO GET THERE
From I-80, take Exit 173 and go north on SR 224 about 0.2 mi. to the Kellduff 5 and 10.

NORTH LIBERTY   MAP, B-3, B-4
Colony Country Campground

1275 Forevergreen Rd., 52317. T: (319) 626-2221.

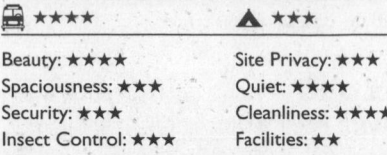

🚐 ★★★★	🏕 ★★★
Beauty: ★★★★	Site Privacy: ★★★
Spaciousness: ★★★	Quiet: ★★★★
Security: ★★★	Cleanliness: ★★★★
Insect Control: ★★★	Facilities: ★★

This family-owned campground is centrally located to many east Iowa points of interest, such as the Hoover Historical Site and the Amana Colonies. The staff is friendly and more than willing to provide helpful tips on which attractions are worth visiting. The grounds are well kept, with meticulously groomed gravel roads and flowered grassy plots throughout. Most sites are tight and may be difficult to maneuver for oversized rigs. Many sites provide both privacy and shade. With plenty of activities on site, such as basketball, volleyball, and horseshoes, leisure time at Colony Country is relaxing and plentiful.

BASICS

Operated By: Private operator. **Open:** Apr.–Nov. 30. **Site Assignment:** By reservations or first come, first served. **Registration:** At camp store. **Fee:** RV, $22; tent, $15; per 4 people. **Parking:** At site.

FACILITIES

Number of Multipurpose Sites: 45. **Hookups:** Electric (20, 30 amps), water, sewer. **Each Site:** Picnic table. **Dump Station:** Yes. **Laundry:** Yes. **Pay Phone:** Yes. **Restrooms and Showers:** Yes. **Fuel:** No. **Propane:** No. **Internal Roads:** Gravel, in good condition. **RV Service:** In town. **Market:** In town. **Restaurant:** Many restaurants in town. **General Store:** Yes. **Vending:** Store. **Swimming:** Yes, w/ hot tub & sauna. **Playground:** Yes. **Other:** Cabins, hot tub, sauna, snack bar, central Internet data port. **Activities:** Basketball, volleyball, playground. **Nearby Attractions:** Hoover Historic Site, Amana Colonies, Kalona & Iowa City/Coralville area. **Additional Information:** Iowa City Chamber of Commerce, (319) 337-9637.

RESTRICTIONS

Pets: On leash. **Fires:** Grill only. **Alcoholic Beverages:** Allowed. **Vehicle Maximum Length:** Big rigs welcome (60 ft.).

TO GET THERE

I-15 Exit 119 E. Go 0.1 mi. to Lindsay.

ONAWA   MAP, B-1
Lewis and Clark State Park

21914 Park Loop, 51040. T: (712) 423-2829.

🚐 ★★★	🏕 ★★★
Beauty: ★★★	Site Privacy: ★★★
Spaciousness: ★★★	Quiet: ★★★
Security: ★★★	Cleanliness: ★★★
Insect Control: ★★★	Facilities: ★★★

Located in an "ox bow" on the Blue Lake, Lewis and Clark State Park is a delightful place to relax and enjoy a small piece of American history. In August of 1804, Lewis and Clark explored this area, making note of its natural beauty. The park features 81 camping sites, all with electrical hookups, along the lakeshore. Most sites have level parking pads and are back-ins, though there are 13 pull-throughs. The foliage is splendid in the spring, and the wind off the lake is crisp. The park, officially part of the Lewis and Clark National Trail, celebrates the Lewis and Clark Festival around the second weekend in June, so call in advance for details and schedules. There are numerous activities available, including self-guided nature trails and a large lodge that's great for family gatherings. The park is well staffed and maintained. Winds in the area can be strong.

BASICS

Operated By: Iowa Dept. of Natural Resources. **Open:** All year. **Site Assignment:** First come, first served. **Registration:** Self-registration at kiosks. **Fee:** $13–$16. **Parking:** At site.

FACILITIES

Number of Multipurpose Sites: 82. **Hookups:** Electric (20, 30 amps), water, sewer. **Each Site:** Picnic table, fire pit, trailer pad. **Dump Station:** Yes. **Laundry:** Yes. **Pay Phone:** No. **Restrooms and Showers:** Yes. **Fuel:** No. **Propane:** No. **Internal Roads:** Paved, in good condition. **RV Service:** 33 mi. northwest in South Sioux City. **Market:** In Onawa. **Restaurant:** In Onawa. **General Store:** No. **Vending:** Yes. **Swimming:** No. **Playground:** Yes. **Other:** Beach, boat ramp, covered picnic tables, historic site. **Activities:** Fishing, hiking, biking, horseshoes, swimming, water activities, hunting. **Nearby Attractions:** The Kiwanis Railroad Depot Museum Complex, The Monona County Historical Museum, Lewis & Clark Festival. **Additional Information:** Onawa Chamber of Commerce, (712) 423-1801.

RESTRICTIONS

Pets: On leash. **Fires:** Allowed in fire pits only. **Alcoholic Beverages:** Allowed, no hard liquor. **Vehicle Maximum Length:** No limit.

TO GET THERE

From I-29, take Exit 112 and go west on SR 175. Turn right on SR 324 and continue to the park.

ONAWA   MAP, B-1
Onawa/Blue Lake KOA

21788 Dogwood Ave., 51040. T: (712) 423-1633; www.koa.com.

🚐 ★★★★	🏕 ★★★★
Beauty: ★★★★	Site Privacy: ★★★★
Spaciousness: ★★★★	Quiet: ★★★★
Security: ★★★★	Cleanliness: ★★★★
Insect Control: ★★★★	Facilities: ★★★★

Set in a rural area in the heart of the Loess Hills in western Iowa is the Onawa/Blue Lake KOA. This campground is situated on a 250-acre lake with excellent bass fishing and waterskiing. The campground offers large pull-through sites under a canopy of large oaks and other mature deciduous trees. It provides a full array of amenities and activities, such as boating and swimming. The campground takes part in Lewis and Clark Festival activities in June, and there are fireworks over the lake on the 4th of July. The KOA is conveniently located near a public golf course, a museum complex, and one of the most beautiful scenic byways in the country. The campground is well kept, and the service is friendly and helpful. It can be very windy, so don't forget your skin protection.

BASICS

Operated By: Terry and Linda Bearce. **Open:** Apr. 15–Oct. 15. **Site Assignment:** By reservation; credit card required; otherwise first come, first served. **Registration:** At camp store. **Fee:** RV, $22.50–$31; tent, $18; for 2 people, $2 per additional guest, children under 6 free. **Parking:** At site.

FACILITIES

Number of RV-only Sites: 47. **Number of Tent-only Sites:** 11. **Number of Multipurpose Sites:** 54. **Hookups:** Electric (20, 30, 50 amps), water, sewer. **Each Site:** Picnic table, grated fire pits. **Dump Station:** Yes. **Laundry:** Yes. **Pay Phone:** No. **Restrooms and Showers:** Yes. **Fuel:** No. **Propane:** Yes. **Internal Roads:** Gravel. **RV Service:** 32 mi. in Sioux City. **Market:** In Onawa. **Restaurant:** In Onawa. **General Store:** Yes. **Vending:** Yes. **Swimming:** Yes. **Playground:** Yes. **Other:** Cabins, fishing docks, boat rentals. **Activities:** Fishing, swimming, horseshoes, rowboating, paddleboating, basketball, volleyball. **Nearby Attractions:** Onawa Aquatic Center Monona County Historical Complex/Depot Museum, Monona County Arboretum, Loess Hills. **Additional Information:** Onawa Chamber of Commerce, (712) 423-1801.

RESTRICTIONS

Pets: On leash. **Fires:** Fire pit only. **Alcoholic Beverages:** Allowed. **Vehicle Maximum Length:** No limit. **Other:** 30-day stay limit.

TO GET THERE

From I-29 Exit 112, merge west onto SR 175 and go about 1 mi. Turn left on Dogwood Ave. and continue 1 mi.

ROCKFORD   MAP, A-3
George Wyatt Park

1 St. NW, 50468. T: (641) 756-3618; www.netins.net/ricweb/community/rockford/rockford.htm.

🚐 ★★★	🏕 ★★★
Beauty: ★★★	Site Privacy: ★★★
Spaciousness: ★★★	Quiet: ★★★★
Security: ★★★	Cleanliness: ★★★
Insect Control: ★★	Facilities: ★★★

George Wyatt Park, not to be confused with George Wyatt State Park, is a delightful small city park in the town of Rockford. This charming little park is located on the Shell Rock River at the edge of town. The campground is simple, with grass sites and mature trees, and overlooks the river. The park offers a small boat ramp for nonmotorized boats and a lovely picnic area. There are also clean restroom facilities and warm showers. The price is great, and the town is full of charm and history. The area is known for its fossil beds, and there is a public pool and golf course in town. This is a wonderful hideaway and a great value. The Rockford Fire Department is right next door, and although the city maintains the park, you could not ask for better security or nicer people.

BASICS

Operated By: City of Rockford, Denny Ginther Manager. **Open:** All year, weather permitting. **Site Assignment:** First come, first served. **Registration:** Self-registration. **Fee:** Electric, $8; no hookup, $7. **Parking:** At site.

FACILITIES

Number of RV-only Sites: 8. **Number of Multi-purpose Sites:** 16. **Hookups:** Electric (20, 30, 50 amps), water. **Each Site:** Some picnic tables. **Dump Station:** Yes. **Laundry:** No. **Pay Phone:** No. **Restrooms and Showers:** Yes. **Fuel:** No. **Propane:** No. **Internal Roads:** Paved & gravel. **RV Service:** 26 mi. in Hanlontown. **Market:** In Rockford. **Restaurant:** In Rockford. **General Store:** No. **Vending:** No. **Swimming:** Public pool in town. **Playground:** Yes. **Other:** Small boat ramp, picnic area, river access. **Activities:** Fishing, hiking, biking. **Nearby Attractions:** The Rockford Fossil Beds, Rockfort Public Pool, golf, Iowa Trolley Park, Aladdin's Castle. **Additional Information:** Charles City Chamber of Commerce, (641) 228-4234.

RESTRICTIONS

Pets: On leash. **Fires:** In approved areas. **Alcoholic Beverages:** Allowed. **Vehicle Maximum Length:** No limit.

TO GET THERE

From Madison City on US 65, go east 9 mi. to US 18, then south on CR-S70 another 5 mi. Follow the signs to the city park.

WAUKEE   MAP, B-2
Timberline Campground

3165 Ashworth Rd., 50263. T: (515) 987-1714; www.timberlineiowa.com.

🚐 ★★★   ▲ ★★★

Beauty: ★★★	Site Privacy: ★★★
Spaciousness: ★★★	Quiet: ★★★
Security: ★★★	Cleanliness: ★★★
Insect Control: ★★★	Facilities: ★★★

Timberline Campground is a comfortable and relaxing getaway, conveniently located on the outskirts of Des Moines, less than 2 miles from I-80. It offers over 40 acres of scenic woodland, with mature shade trees and nature trails full of different wildlife. The campground provides a large selection of amenities, including a RV wash barn and an ice-cream shop. There is a large pool, a full playground, and a rec room with games. The campsites are a nice size, 60 of them level pull-throughs. The campground has many nearby attractions, such as the botanical center, the Blank Park Zoo, and the bridges of Madison County. The weather can be windy, so you will likely need sunscreen. The staff is kind and the atmosphere family-friendly. All visitors must register in the office and security is tight.

BASICS

Operated By: Dick and Deborah Christensen. **Open:** Apr.–Nov. **Site Assignment:** By reservation; credit card and 1-night deposit required. **Registration:** At general store. **Fee:** $18–$29; cash, credit card, check. **Parking:** At site.

FACILITIES

Number of RV-only Sites: 100. **Number of Tent-only Sites:** 16. **Hookups:** Electric (20, 30, 50 amps), water, sewer, phone. **Each Site:** Picnic table. **Dump Station:** Yes. **Laundry:** Yes. **Pay Phone:** No. **Restrooms and Showers:** Yes. **Fuel:** No. **Propane:** Yes. **Internal Roads:** Gravel, in good condition. **RV Service:** In Des Moines. **Market:** In Des Moines. **Restaurant:** In Des Moines. **General Store:** Yes. **Vending:** Yes. **Swimming:** Yes. **Playground:** Yes. **Other:** 3 camping cabins, pavilion, RV wash, game room. **Activities:** Swimming, playground, horseshoes, basketball. **Nearby Attractions:** State capitol & historical museum, botanical center, art center, zoo, Sugar Creek golf course. **Additional Information:** West Des Moines Chamber of Commerce, (515) 225-6009.

RESTRICTIONS

Pets: On leash (no large, aggressive breeds). **Fires:** Fire pit only. **Alcoholic Beverages:** Allowed. **Vehicle Maximum Length:** 45 ft.

TO GET THERE

From I-80 Exit 117, go 1 mi. north and 0.5 mi. east; there are signs to follow.

Kansas

Kansas isn't what you might think: cornfields and tornado country with nothing to see. Although there are rows upon rows of maize and the occasional seasonal twister, there's also much more available to visitors than you might guess by looking over the guardrail as you speed down Interstate 70. If you turn off the main routes, you'll come across an honest vision of America trying to make it one day at a time in the ominously encroaching shadow of same-as-everywhere megamarts and fast-food chains.

On the brighter side, and just like every other state in the country but maybe more so, Kansas is home to much of that which flies in the face of the mundane. For example, **Prairie Dog Town** in the Logan County seat of Oakley is where you go to get your picture taken next to a five-legged cow.

Obviously, Kansas is a small-town state, which is good news for campers, because this makes for a lot of quiet rural nights out under the stars. Though Kansas has its share of overnighters, many campgrounds are in rural areas where you're as likely to encounter a horse as a human being. For outdoor enthusiasts, nearly every county has a state fishing lake open to anglers and campers alike. For starters, try the main three largest lakes in the 34th state: **Turtle Creek Reservoir, Cheney Reservoir,** and **Waconda Lake.** To steal a glimpse at what Kansas life was like in the 19th century, mosey on over to **Dodge City** or **Meade** or **Coffeyville,** where the museums that remain offer tourists a chance to relive a slice of Midwestern history. Ever wondered what may have inspired President Abraham Lincoln to grow a beard? The letter written by a young girl named Grace Bedell Billings to Abe suggesting he sport a facial coif, as well as the president's reply letter, have been reproduced in a bronze monument in the town square of **Delphos,** Ottawa County.

Back to the fleeting present and to experience Kansas in real time, visit the large cities of **Wichita, Kansas City,** and **Topeka.** The eateries, museums, and the arts make these cities convenient destinations on a cross-Kansas trek. Spend a few days in these urban centers to soak up some culture, then hit the road and into the special out-of-the-way places Kansas has to offer. The **Amish community of Yoder,** the logic-defying rock formations at **Monument Rocks National Landmark,** and **"the living ghost town" of Elk Falls** are all grand examples of what it means to have seen the state. However, if none of these options sound esoteric enough, you might want to consider taking a trip over to Rush County to visit the **Barbed Wire Museum** in Lacrosse.

One highway slogan sums it up: "Drive through Kansas and you'll miss it."

Campground Profiles

ABILENE MAP, B-3
Covered Wagon RV Resort

803 South Buckeye, 67410. T: (800) 864-4053 or (785) 263-2343; www.coveredwagonrvpark.com.

🚐 ★★★★★   ⛺ ★★★★★

Beauty: ★★★★	Site Privacy: ★★★★
Spaciousness: ★★★★	Quiet: ★★★★
Security: ★★★	Cleanliness: ★★★★
Insect Control: ★★★★	Facilities: ★★★★

Two dramatically different experiences await RVers at this park, depending on which portion of the park you find yourself parked in. Those parked close to the house will find a forested campsite with level, grassy sites and plenty of (deciduous) tree coverage. Sites 26–31 at the edge of the park are treed-off from the rest of the sites and face a grassy field under a canopy of trees. Site 7 would make a particularly nice tent site due to the protection of trees. However, sites 52–57 sit on an open gravel/grassy strip at the edge of the property with no coverage whatsoever. Adding insult to injury, a row of storage units faces this landing strip, degrading the visual aesthetic even further. For an enjoyable stay, insist on a site closer to the house.

BASICS

Operated By: Rick and Caron Lewis. **Open:** All year. **Site Assignment:** Upon registration, reservations w/ credit card; 24-hour cancellation policy. **Registration:** At house, late arrivals use drop box. **Fee:** $15–$25; V, MC, D; $1 discount for cash, check. **Parking:** At site.

FACILITIES

Number of RV-only Sites: 35. **Hookups:** Electric (30, 50 amps), water, sewer, phone, cable TV. **Each Site:** Picnic table, tree. **Dump Station:** Yes. **Laundry:** Yes. **Pay Phone:** Yes. **Restrooms and Showers:** Yes. **Fuel:** No. **Propane:** Yes. **Internal Roads:** Gravel. **RV Service:** No. **Market:** 1 mi. **Restaurant:** 0.25 mi. **General Store:** No. **Vending:** No. **Swimming:** Pool. **Playground:** Yes. **Other:** Accepts horses, makes reservations for lunch/dinner in town or for tours, horseshoes. **Activities:** Swimming, basketball, tennis, volleyball at nearby Eisenhower Park. **Nearby Attractions:** Dwight D. Eisenhower Presidential Center, Greyhound Hall of Fame, antique doll museum. **Additional Information:** Abilene Chamber of Commerce, (913) 263-1770.

RESTRICTIONS

Pets: On leash only. **Fires:** Grill only. **Alcoholic Beverages:** At sites. **Vehicle Maximum Length:** No limit.

TO GET THERE

From I-70, take Exit 275. Turn south onto Hwy. 15, then drive 2.3 mi. The entrance is on the right. Park behind the house to go to the office.

ATWOOD MAP, A-1
Linis Park at Lake Atwood

4th St. and Lake Rd., 67730. T: (785) 626-3020 or (785) 626-9503.

🚐 ★★★   ⛺ ★★

Beauty: ★★★	Site Privacy: ★★★
Spaciousness: ★★★	Quiet: ★★★★
Security: ★★★	Cleanliness: ★★★★
Insect Control: ★★★★	Facilities: ★★★

Campsites are located in a strip a few hundred feet away from the edge of the lake. With the lake to the northwest, a cute pavilion, and a romantic lit walkway around the circumference of the lake, the campground is pretty, with a quiet, small-town park atmosphere. Sites 1–4 are situated on the paved parking lot (with grass behind), while 5–9 are all grass. All sites are open back-ins with full hookups. Tent sites are located between the RV sites and the lake, in a large, open grassy field with virtually unlimited sites. Be forewarned of the hot-rod rally that occurs May 18–20, as sites fill up quickly. Sites 1 and 9, being end sites, have much more space than all the others. (There is a 10th water hookup and space for another vehicle next to site 9 that isn't rented out, but it seems hard to believe someone might not take advantage of it in the busy season.) While the restroom and showers are in the park, all other services (such as phone and vending) are located at the Vista mart.

BASICS

Operated By: Lion's Club. **Open:** All year. **Site Assignment:** First come, first served. **Registration:** At Vista mart 6 a.m.–midnight. **Fee:** RV, $15; $5 refundable key deposit; tents free. **Parking:** At site.

FACILITIES

Number of RV-only Sites: 9. **Number of Tent-only Sites:** Undesignated sites. **Hookups:** Electric (20, 30, 50 amps), water, sewer. **Each Site:** Grill, picnic table, tree. **Dump Station:** No (sewer at all sites). **Laundry:** Yes. **Pay Phone:** Yes. **Restrooms and Showers:** Yes. **Fuel:** Yes. **Propane:** No. **Internal Roads:** Paved. **RV Service:** No. **Market:** 6 blocks. **Restaurant:** 2 blocks. **General Store:** Yes. **Vending:** Yes. **Swimming:** No. **Playground:** Yes. **Other:** Fishing lake, lit walkway around lake. **Activities:** Fishing, 9-hole golf, softball, basketball, volleyball, boating. **Nearby Attractions:** Lake Atwood 10 mi. race, Hayden Nature Trail, Atwood Country Club & Golf Course. **Additional Information:** Atwood Chamber of Commerce, (785) 626-9630.

RESTRICTIONS

Pets: On leash. **Fires:** Grill only. **Alcoholic Beverages:** At sites. **Vehicle Maximum Length:** No limit.

TO GET THERE

From Hwy. 36 and 4th St. in town, turn north onto 4th St. At the end of the block, turn left onto Lake Rd., then take the immediate right into the park. Select a spot, then walk to the Coastal/Vista gas station on the south side of Hwy. 36 and 4th St. to register.

BELLEVILLE MAP, A-3
Evergreen Acres RV Park

1880 Elm Rd., 66935. T: (785) 987-5544.

🚐 ★★★★   ⛺ ★★★★

Beauty: ★★★★★	Site Privacy: ★★★
Spaciousness: ★★★	Quiet: ★★★★★
Security: ★★★★	Cleanliness: ★★★★★
Insect Control: ★★★★	Facilities: ★★★★

This isolated campground offers an authentic farm experience in a beautiful pastoral setting. Traffic noise is supplanted by the croaking of frogs, the calling of birds, and the sighing of the wind. Large mature evergreens shield the campground from the road and add to the verdant beauty. The campground is divided into two sections: one near the house, one barely a quarter mile away by the lake. (To get to the second section, continue on the road just past the authentic functional barn with the authentic functional cows, take the first left turn, then again the immediate left and turn onto the white gravel driveway.) The lake is located at the second section, but in fact the better sites are closer to the house. Sites near the lake (1–10) are a little more tightly crammed together and are lined up in a single row. Sites at the house are more scattered (offering more privacy) and contain more trees. All sites are grassy and level pull-throughs, however, and the least desirable site is located in the campground you have to go to when all the spaces at Evergreen Acres are full.

BASICS

Operated By: Henry and Mildred Blecha. **Open:** All year; lake area may close for winter. **Site Assignment:** Upon registration. **Registration:** At office. **Fee:** RV, $12; tent, $7; check, no credit cards. **Parking:** At site.

FACILITIES

Number of RV-only Sites: 15. **Number of Tent-only Sites:** Undesignated sites. **Hookups:** Electric (30 amps), water, sewer. **Each Site:** Picnic table. **Dump Station:** No (sewer at all sites). **Laundry:** No. **Pay Phone:** Yes. **Restrooms and Showers:** Yes. **Fuel:** No. **Propane:** No. **Internal Roads:** Gravel. **RV Service:** No. **Market:** 4 mi. north to Chester, Nebraska. **Restaurant:** 4 mi. north to Chester, Nebraska. **General Store:** No. **Vending:** No. **Swimming:** No. **Playground:** Yes. **Other:** Lake. **Activities:** Fishing. **Nearby Attractions:** Pawnee Indian museum. **Additional Information:** Belleville Chamber of Commerce, (913) 527-5519.

RESTRICTIONS

Pets: On leash, cleaned up after. **Fires:** Stoves only. **Alcoholic Beverages:** At sites. **Vehicle Maximum Length:** No limit.

TO GET THERE

From the junction of Hwy. 36 and Hwy. 81, travel north on Hwy. 81 for 9.5 mi., then turn East onto a gravel road. Follow this road 0.8 mi., then turn left at the sign into the entrance. Keep left to go to the office.

COLBY
MAP, A-1
Bourquin's RV Park, Horse Stables, Cabins & Old Depot Restaurant

155 East Willow, I-70 Frontage Rd., Colby 67701.
T: (785) 462-3300; www.colbycamp.com.

★★★　　★★

Beauty: ★★★	Site Privacy: ★★
Spaciousness: ★★	Quiet: ★★★★
Security: ★★★★	Cleanliness: ★★★
Insect Control: ★★★	Facilities: ★★★

Conveniently close (half a mile) to town, this campground is still far enough removed to avoid most of the lights and noise. Most sites are back-in, with the possibility of pull-throughs in the inner circle of the loop (requiring pulling out over a strip of grass that looks like it can take it—and has). Sites are not well shaded, so the summer sun could prove a little overwhelming—as could a strong spring rain or windstorm. The Prairie Art Museum to the north offers a cute view of a miniaturized church, barn, and windmill. Unmarked tent sites are off in the northwest corner, next to a charming red one-room schoolhouse with several large shrubs; they are equally unprotected and sit next to a road. Tenters might optimally give this campground a miss and continue on to Oakley or Goodland. The best RV sites are 19–36, which lie on the outside of the loop away from town-side, and next to open land and a pond to the east. The least desirable sites are 37–48, which are squashed together and share tables and grills.

BASICS
Operated By: Dan & Shirley Bourquin. **Open:** RV park open year-round (winter months use drop box). **Site Assignment:** First come, first served. **Registration:** In office, late arrivals use drop box; verbal reservations OK. **Fee:** RV, $24–$26; tent, $15; cabin, $65; horse accommodation, $15. **Parking:** At site.

FACILITIES
Number of RV Sites: 50. **Number of Tent-only Sites:** Undesignated sites. **Hookups:** Electric (30, 50 amps), water, sewer, cable TV, Wi-Fi. **Each Site:** Table, grill, trees. **Dump Station:** Yes. **Laundry:** Yes. **Pay Phone:** Yes. **Restrooms and Showers:** Yes. **Fuel:** Nearby. **Propane:** Nearby. **Internal Roads:** Gravel, good condition. **RV Service:** Cummins, Caterpillar, Detroit Diesel. **Market:** 0.5 mi. to Colby. **Restaurant:** On site (Old Depot Restaurant, restored 120-year-old Union Pacific Railroad Depot). **General Store:** Yes. **Vending:** No. **Swimming:** Indoor, at Colby Community College; outdoor, downtown. **Playground:** Nearby. **Other:** Groups welcome; RV washing permitted; homemade organic foods; horse stables, cabins, quiet tearoom, living room with high-definition TV, musical DVDs and jams. **Activities:** Bluegrass festival in July, Road Run, car races some Sun. evenings, Picnic in the Park every Thu. in summer, rodeos, fall celebration. **Nearby Attractions:** Prairie Museum of Art & History, KSU Agricultural Experiment Station, Colby Community College. **Additional Information:** Prairie Museum of Art & History, Northwest Research Extension Center.

RESTRICTIONS
Pets: On leash, cleaned up after. **Fires:** In grill only. **Alcoholic Beverages:** At sites. **Vehicle Maximum Length:** None.

TO GET THERE
From I-70, take Exit 54 and drive north on Country Club Dr., about 200 ft. Turn left onto Frontage Rd. (also called Willow) and follow it 0.5 mi. to the entrance.

CONCORDIA
MAP, A-3
Brome Ridge RV Park

1043 North 140th Rd., 66901. T: (785) 243-4539.

★★★★★　　★★★★

Beauty: ★★★★	Site Privacy: ★★★
Spaciousness: ★★★	Quiet: ★★★
Security: ★★★★	Cleanliness: ★★★★
Insect Control: ★★★★	Facilities: ★★★★

This campground is charming and picturesque. Along the drive into the campground are several items of country kitsch ("Coyote Crossing" sign, animal statuettes) that are—surprisingly—tastefully done. Trees line the drive half of the way down, while the rest of the grounds open up to reveal scenes of rural Kansas: rolling hills, farms, cows, and a large pond. Indeed, the entire park feels like it's on a farm. All RV sites are level and grassy pull-throughs situated on a giant loop. While it is hard to think of a "least desirable site" in the campground, site 1 does sit right at the tip of the loop and may therefore receive more internal traffic than a camper would care for. But it's still not bad! Sites 18–20 are slightly nicer than others due to their size and proximity to a large open field. Please note that the hot and cold water knobs were inverted—there really is hot water, you just have to turn it to maximum blue (cold) instead of red (hot).

BASICS
Operated By: Stan and Maxine Van Meter. **Open:** All year. **Site Assignment:** First come, first served. **Registration:** At self-pay station. **Fee:** Full, $19.50; RV, $17; 30 amp, $10; tent, $10. **Parking:** At site.

FACILITIES
Number of RV-only Sites: 19. **Number of Tent-only Sites:** Undesignated sites. **Hookups:** Electric (30, 50 amps), water, sewer, Internet available. **Each Site:** Picnic table, deciduous shrub. **Dump Station:** No (sewer at all sites). **Laundry:** Yes. **Pay Phone:** No. **Restrooms and Showers:** Yes. **Fuel:** No. **Propane:** No. **Internal Roads:** Paved & gravel, in good condition. **RV Service:** No. **Market:** 7 mi. to Concordia. **Restaurant:** 7 mi. to Concordia. **General Store:** No. **Vending:** No. **Swimming:** No. **Playground:** Yes. **Other:** Storm shelter, cabins, pond, catering, club house w/ kitchenette. **Activities:** Hunting, fishing. **Nearby Attractions:** Brown Grand Theatre, Cloud County Historical Museum, Republican River. **Additional Information:** Concordia Chamber of Commerce, (785) 243-4290.

RESTRICTIONS
Pets: On leash, cleaned up after. **Fires:** Grill, fire rings. **Alcoholic Beverages:** At sites. **Vehicle Maximum Length:** No limit.

TO GET THERE
From Hwy. 81, drive 7 mi. south of Concordia. Between mile markerss 195 and 196, turn west at the sign into the entrance. Follow the drive to the self-pay station.

COUNCIL GROVE
MAP, B-3
Council Grove Lake

Hwy. 2 Box 110, 66846.
T: (877) 444-6777 or (620) 767-5195;
www.naturalkansas.org/council.htm.

★★★★★　　★★★★★

Beauty: ★★★★★	Site Privacy: ★★★★
Spaciousness: ★★★★★	Quiet: ★★★★★
Security: ★★★★	Cleanliness: ★★★★
Insect Control: ★★	Facilities: ★★★

Eight different campgrounds surround the lake, with sites ranging from lakeside to higher ground. All sites are spacious, level, and grassy, with some as big as 100 by 100 feet. Although there are too many campsites to enumerate, several distinguish themselves as particularly nice. Sites 21–26 on the peninsula in Ritchie Cove and 1–13 on a strip by the waterfront, for example, have spectacular views of the sunset. All campgrounds have a wilderness feel, and if you come on a weekday in spring, you may get the whole place to yourself! A wonderful destination for a fun-filled stay of any length. There are 38 total pull-through sites.

BASICS
Operated By: U.S. Army Corps of Engineers. **Open:** All year. **Site Assignment:** First come, first served; reservations accepted w/ credit card; $10 cancellation fee, 1-night fee if less than 3-day notice. **Registration:** At self-pay station. **Fee:** $10–$16. **Parking:** At site, additional parking available.

FACILITIES
Number of RV-only Sites: 180. **Hookups:** Electric (30, 50 amps), water, sewer. **Each Site:** Covered picnic table, fire pit/grill, trees. **Dump Station:** Yes. **Laundry:** No. **Pay Phone:** No. **Restrooms and Showers:** Yes. **Fuel:** No. **Propane:** No. **Internal Roads:** Paved. **RV Service:** No. **Market:** 2 mi. to Council Grove. **Restaurant:** 2 mi. to Council Grove. **General Store:** Yes. **Vending:** Yes. **Swimming:** Lake. **Playground:** Yes. **Activities:** Fishing, swimming, boating, waterskiing, hunting. **Nearby Attractions:** July 4th fireworks in town, Kay Mission State Historic Site. **Additional Information:** Council Grove Chamber of Commerce, (316) 767-5413.

RESTRICTIONS
Pets: On leash. **Fires:** Fire ring only. **Alcoholic Beverages:** At sites. **Vehicle Maximum Length:** No limit. **Other:** No fireworks.

TO GET THERE
From the junction of Hwy. 56 and Hwy. 57/177 in town, take Hwy. 57/177 2 mi. north, then turn left at the sign for Council Grove Lake. Follow the road 1.3 mi. across the lake, then cross the intersection to arrive at the office. (You may also go to any campsite and then to a self-pay station.)

DODGE CITY   MAP, B-1, B-2
Watersports Campground and RV Park

500 East Cherry St., 67801.
T: (620) 225-8044 or (620) 225-9003;
www.watersportscampground.com.

🚐 ★★★★   ▲ ★★★

Beauty: ★★★   Site Privacy: ★★★
Spaciousness: ★★★   Quiet: ★★★★
Security: ★★★★   Cleanliness: ★★★★
Insect Control: ★★★   Facilities: ★★★★

This popular RV park sits just west of the lake from which its name derives. (The RV park on the east side of the lake is for members only.) Sites 31–52 have an attractive view of the lake, but 51 and 52 are very close to the playground. Full hookup pull-throughs 1–10 face open grassy land with an attractive row of trees at the far end. Site 31 has extra space to the north side, while site 38 is known among visitors as the best site, presumably for its commanding view of the lake. Sites may be a little cramped for larger rigs (45–50 feet long), and spare vehicles may have to be parked crosswise in a space. Tents can be pitched on the well-manicured lawn that extends between the RV park and the lake.

BASICS
Operated By: Deana Vogel. **Open:** All year. **Site Assignment:** At registration, verbal reservations OK except for holidays. **Registration:** At office, late arrivals use slot in door. **Fee:** $17; utility, $1; water is free; no credit cards. **Parking:** At site.

FACILITIES
Number of RV-only Sites: 56. **Number of Tent-only Sites:** Undesignated sites. **Hookups:** Electric (30, 50 amps), water, sewer, cable TV & modem hookup in office. **Each Site:** Tree, picnic table. **Dump Station:** Yes. **Laundry:** Yes. **Pay Phone:** Yes. **Restrooms and Showers:** Yes. **Fuel:** No. **Propane:** Yes. **Internal Roads:** Dirt/gravel. **RV Service:** No. **Market:** 4 blocks. **Restaurant:** 10 blocks. **General Store:** Yes. **Vending:** Yes. **Swimming:** Lake. **Playground:** Yes. **Other:** Courtesy van to Boot Hill, lifeguard, walking path. **Activities:** Swimming, fishing, pool table, video games, self-guiding tours. **Nearby Attractions:** Boot Hill, Fort Dodge, Home of Stone. **Additional Information:** Dodge City Chamber of Commerce, (316) 227-3119.

RESTRICTIONS
Pets: No rottweilers, Dobermans, or pit bulls. **Fires:** Fire pit only. **Alcoholic Beverages:** At sites. **Vehicle Maximum Length:** 45 ft.

TO GET THERE
From the junction of Hwy. 50 and 2nd Ave. in town, turn south at the light onto 2nd Ave., then drive 0.5 mi. and turn left onto Cherry St. Take Cherry St. 0.4 mi. to the end and follow the dirt road to the right to go to the office.

FARLINGTON   MAP, C-4
Crawford State Park

1 Lake Rd., 66734. T: (620) 362-3671;
www.kdwp.state.ks.us/pmforum/crawford.html.

🚐 ★★★★★   ▲ ★★★★★

Beauty: ★★★★★   Site Privacy: ★★★★★
Spaciousness: ★★★★★   Quiet: ★★★★★
Security: ★★★   Cleanliness: ★★★★★
Insect Control: ★★★   Facilities: ★★★

Campsites around this lake are enormous (some 100 by 100 feet) and vary from waterfront to higher up and set into woods. There are four separate camping areas, several nature trails, a mountain biking/hiking trail, as well as scads of picnic and water-use areas. Some of these areas (evening Breeze Point, Osage Bluff, Cherokee Landing, Lonesome point) offer primitive camping (and toilets) only. All RV sites are back-in only but spacious and private enough to make up for this small inconvenience. Washrooms are surprisingly clean but sparse—possibly a drive away from some campsites. This campground is a great destination to bring the kids.

BASICS
Operated By: Kansas Dept. of Wildlife and Parks. **Open:** All year. **Site Assignment:** First come, first served. **Registration:** At office or self-pay station. **Fee:** Full hookup, $7.50; campsite, $7; vehicle fee, $5.50. **Parking:** At site.

FACILITIES
Number of RV-only Sites: 72. **Number of Tent-only Sites:** 35. **Hookups:** Electric (30 amps), water; no water Oct. 15–Apr. 1. **Each Site:** Picnic table, fire pit/grill, trees. **Dump Station:** Yes. **Laundry:** Yes. **Pay Phone:** Yes. **Restrooms and Showers:** Yes. **Fuel:** No. **Propane:** No. **Internal Roads:** Paved. **RV Service:** No. **Market:** 10 mi. to Farlington. **Restaurant:** 10 mi. to Farlington. **General Store:** No. **Vending:** Yes. **Swimming:** Lake. **Playground:** Yes. **Other:** Boat ramp, amphitheater. **Activities:** Boating, swimming, fishing, hiking. **Nearby Attractions:** Fort Scott. **Additional Information:** Girard Chamber of Commerce, (620) 724-4715.

RESTRICTIONS
Pets: On leash. **Fires:** Fire pits; subject to seasonal bans. **Alcoholic Beverages:** Beer only. **Vehicle Maximum Length:** No limit. **Other:** 1 vehicle/site, boat registration.

TO GET THERE
From the junction of Hwy. 57 and Hwy. 7, turn north onto Hwy. 7 and drive 8.7 mi. Turn right at the sign onto 710 Ave. and continue 1 mi. to the entrance.

FORT SCOTT   MAP, B-4
Fort Scott Campground

2162 Native Rd., 66701. T: (800) 538-0216 or (620) 223-3440.

🚐 ★★★★★   ▲ ★★★★

Beauty: ★★★★   Site Privacy: ★★★
Spaciousness: ★★★   Quiet: ★★★★
Security: ★★★   Cleanliness: ★★★★★
Insect Control: ★★★   Facilities: ★★★

A very cute, tidy campground with 40 pull-throughs and 10 back-ins. An average site measures 24 by 70 feet, leaving a potentially restricted area around some bigger rigs. However, the ambiance is virtually unbeatable, more than making up for possible space shortages. This is the kind of campground you want to take a walk around as soon as you arrive, just to take in the natural beauty. Sites are very clearly labeled with attractive wooden signs. Many sites have two or more trees, increasing the impression of privacy. Site 33 is slightly encroached upon by signs, and 34 (which may not be assigned) appears to be part of a through-road. Any other sites really can't be beat. As an added bonus, end site 42 seems to have inherited some extra space, and 16 (closest to the fishing pond and cow pasture) has a wide-open east side. One glaring exception to this pristine idyll is the swing sets, which are rusted and unstable looking. A safer bet for kids are the teeter-totter and merry-go-round. The tent site to the north of the office offers thick grass, mature shade trees, and almost unlimited number of spaces. A sure bet for campers of any stripe!

BASICS
Operated By: Jack and Ruth Jaro. **Open:** All year; limited services Nov. 16–Feb. 28. **Site Assignment:** First come, first served or by registration; verbal reservations OK; 48-hour cancellation policy. **Registration:** At office, late arrivals use drop box. **Fee:** RV, $19; full, $17; water/electric, $12 winter; check, V, MC, AE. **Parking:** At site.

FACILITIES
Number of RV-only Sites: 50. **Number of Tent-only Sites:** 15. **Hookups:** Electric (30, 50 amps), water, sewer. **Each Site:** Picnic table, trees. **Dump Station:** Yes. **Laundry:** Yes. **Pay Phone:** No. **Restrooms and Showers:** Yes. **Fuel:** No. **Propane:** No. **Internal Roads:** Gravel. **RV Service:** No. **Market:** 4 mi. in Fort Scott. **Restaurant:** 0.25 mi. **General Store:** Yes. **Vending:** No. **Swimming:** Pool. **Playground:** Yes. **Other:** Stocked fishing pond, free firewood, 1 cabin, central fire ring, pet walk area, video games. **Activities:** Fishing, volleyball, horseshoes, pool. **Nearby Attractions:** Fort Scott. **Additional Information:** Fort Scott Chamber of Commerce, (316) 223-3566.

RESTRICTIONS
Pets: On leash, always attended, cleaned up after. **Fires:** Fire ring or grill. **Alcoholic Beverages:** Prefer cans (due to pool). **Vehicle Maximum Length:** 70 ft. **Other:** Some pool restrictions.

TO GET THERE
From the junction of Hwy. 69 and Hwy. 54, take Hwy. 64 west 0.5 mi., turn north immediately at the sign. Follow the road 0.4 mi., then turn right into the entrance and take the second right to the office.

GOODLAND
MAP, A-1
Goodland KOA

1114 East Hwy. 24, 67735. T: (800) 562-5704 or (785) 890-5701; www.koa.com.

🚐 ★★★★   ⛺ ★★★

Beauty: ★★	Site Privacy: ★★★
Spaciousness: ★★★	Quiet: ★★★
Security: ★★★	Cleanliness: ★★★★
Insect Control: ★★★★	Facilities: ★★★★★

Located just off the highway, this campground is an easy-on, easy-off stop. Most campsites have at least two trees, with other trees scattered around the campground, lending a back-to-nature feel. Back-in sites 66–71 have a more than normal number of trees, which gives them woodsy feel. The east side of the campground is partitioned off from neighboring land by dense vegetation, and an open grassy field lies to the north. In addition, cute landscaping using shrubs, flower beds, and several tree trunk carvings liven up the grounds. On the downside, there is unattractive commercial development to the west, but not enough to detract terribly from the environment. Laundry and restroom/shower facilities are large, well lit, and immaculate. Some sites in the 28–42 area are not clearly marked, making their location a minor hassle. Overall, however, this is a convenient and enjoyable stay.

BASICS

Operated By: Dale and Wally Neill. **Open:** Mar. 15–Nov. 1. **Site Assignment:** Upon registration; reservations w/ credit card or check to hold; 24-hour cancellation policy. **Registration:** At office, late arrivals use drop box. **Fee:** $17–$29. **Parking:** At site only.

FACILITIES

Number of RV-only Sites: 51. **Number of Tent-only Sites:** 17. **Hookups:** Electric (30, 50 amps), water, sewer, cable TV. **Each Site:** Picnic table, some fire grills. **Dump Station:** Yes. **Laundry:** Yes. **Pay Phone:** Yes. **Restrooms and Showers:** Yes. **Fuel:** No. **Propane:** No. **Internal Roads:** Gravel/dirt. **RV Service:** No. **Market:** 1.5 mi. (into Goodland). **Restaurant:** 0.25 mi. (into Goodland). **General Store:** Yes. **Vending:** No. **Swimming:** Pool. **Playground:** Yes. **Other:** 4 cabins, dog walk area. **Activities:** Mini-golf, horseshoes, basketball. **Nearby Attractions:** 18-hole golf course, Goodland High Plains Museum. **Additional Information:** Goodland Chamber of Commerce, (913) 899-7130.

RESTRICTIONS

Pets: On leash only. **Fires:** Grill only. **Alcoholic Beverages:** At sites. **Vehicle Maximum Length:** No limit.

TO GET THERE

From I-70, take Exit 19, turn north onto Hwy. 24, and follow it 0.8 mi. The entrance is on the right.

GRANTVILLE
MAP, B-4
Topeka KOA

3366 KOA Rd., 66429. T: (800) 562-8717 or (785) 246-3419; www.koa.com.

🚐 ★★★★★   ⛺ ★★★

Beauty: ★★★★	Site Privacy: ★★★
Spaciousness: ★★★	Quiet: ★★★★
Security: ★★★★	Cleanliness: ★★★★★
Insect Control: ★★★★	Facilities: ★★★★★

This campground has the feeling of being lost in the woods. The land in front of the office is undeveloped, and Area A (in back) is surrounded on three sides by undeveloped land. There is, accordingly, no highway noise; however, trains pass close enough to be heard from all over the campground. Sites are grassy, with 36 level pull-throughs in Area B. Area A has some slope—all sites but end site 26 seem to require jacks. However, this is the nicer area of the campground if you can tolerate some slope. Area B has longer but narrower sites: 25 feet vs. 30 feet in Area A. Area B is also open to office, road, and pool traffic. The best sites are 25 and 26 in Area A, as they are level and in the prettiest part of the park. Sites 1 and 2 are the least desirable, being close to the office, to the parking lot, and to a garbage dumpster. The tent area is a long strip of grass at the front of the property. Sites are separated by a small length of wooden fencing providing better privacy. Although located a fair distance outside of the metropolis of Topeka, this campground is worth the trip and offers a relaxing, quiet stay in the middle of the woods.

BASICS

Operated By: Private operator. **Open:** Apr 1–Nov. 15; otherwise, limited services. **Site Assignment:** Upon registration; credit card to reserve site; cancel before 4 p.m. the day before arrival for refund. **Registration:** At office, late arrivals use drop box. **Fee:** $18–$29. **Parking:** At site.

FACILITIES

Number of RV-only Sites: 36. **Number of Tent-only Sites:** 11. **Hookups:** Electric (15, 30, 50 amps), water, sewer. **Each Site:** Picnic table, grill or fire pit, tree at selected sites. **Dump Station:** Yes. **Laundry:** Yes. **Pay Phone:** No. **Restrooms and Showers:** Yes. **Fuel:** No. **Propane:** No. **Internal Roads:** Gravel. **RV Service:** No. **Market:** 2 mi. to Topeka. **Restaurant:** 2 mi. to Topeka. **General Store:** Yes. **Vending:** Yes. **Swimming:** Pool. **Playground:** Yes. **Other:** Pond, cabins, rec room, antique shop. **Activities:** Golf, shopping, visiting museums, sightseeing, swimming. **Nearby Attractions:** Combat Air Museum, Gage Park, Kansas Center for Historical Research, State Capitol, Ward-Meade Park, golf course, antique malls, casinos. **Additional Information:** Topeka CVB, (800) 235-1030.

RESTRICTIONS

Pets: On leash only, cleaned up after. **Fires:** Fire ring only. **Alcoholic Beverages:** At sites. **Vehicle Maximum Length:** No limit.

TO GET THERE

From the junction of I-70 and Hwy. 75, take Exit 358 and drive 9 mi. to Easton Hwy. 24. Take the Hwy. 24 east exit, then turn left at the KOA sign (at mile marker 374) onto KOA Rd. Follow the gravel drive 1.3 mi. through a residential area and over the bridge. The entrance is on the right, north of 31st St.

SYLVAN GROVE
MAP, B-2, B-3
Lucas Park Campground

4860 Outlet Blvd., 67481. T: (785) 658-2551; www.reserveamerica.com.

🚐 ★★★★   ⛺ ★★★★

Beauty: ★★★★★	Site Privacy: ★★
Spaciousness: ★★	Quiet: ★★★★
Security: ★★★★	Cleanliness: ★★★★
Insect Control: ★★★	Facilities: ★★★

In the Post Rock Country of Central Kansas, Lucas Park Campground on Wilson Lake offers great appeal to the sports lovers, anglers, recreationists, or those who just want to enjoy the beauty and serenity of the lake. Nestled in the Saline River valley is Lake Wilson. Wilson Lake, located on the Saline River, controls a drainage area of 1,917 square miles. The grassland drainage basin above Wilson makes it one of the clearest lake in Kansas. With 9,000 acres of water and 100 miles of shoreline, it has become one of the most popular recreation areas in central Kansas. Historic Wilson Dam was constructed during 1918–1925 as part of the World War I effort. Wilson Lake contains 15,500 acres of surface water and is 15.5 miles long. The waters below Wilson are known as the Smallmouth Capital of the World for the trophy smallmouth bass caught there. This Group Camp has 15 campsites with utility hookups included and can only accommodate a maximum of 15 camper trailers. No more than one camping unit is permitted per utility site. No live music or sound systems are permitted. A special-event permit is required in order to exceed these limits.

BASICS

Operated By: U.S. Army Corps of Engineers. **Open:** All year. **Site Assignment:** Reservations must be made at least 4 days in advance. **Registration:** At office. **Fee:** Single, $6–$18; group, $50–$100. **Parking:** At site.

FACILITIES

Number of Multipurpose Sites: 388. **Hookups:** Yes. **Dump Station:** Yes. **Laundry:** No. **Pay Phone:** Yes. **Restrooms and Showers:** Yes. **Fuel:** No. **Propane:** No. **Internal Roads:** Paved, gravel. **RV Service:** No. **Market:** No. **Restaurant:** No. **General Store:** No. **Vending:** No. **Swimming:** Yes. **Playground:** Yes. **Activities:** Boating, fishing, hiking.

RESTRICTIONS

Pets: Pets must be restrained or on a leash at all times while in developed recreation areas. **Fires:** In fire rings, stoves, grills, or fireplaces provided for that purpose. **Alcoholic Beverages:** Not allowed. **Vehicle Maximum Length:** Call ahead. **Other:** No more than 1 camping unit is permitted per utility site. No live music or sound systems are permitted. No ATVs or ORVs allowed.

TO GET THERE
From I-70, take Exit 206/Wilson. Travel north 9 mi. on Hwy. 232, then left in to Lucas Park.

HIAWATHA · MAP, A-4
Country Squire Motel and RV Park

2000 West Oregon St., 66434. T: (785) 742-2877.

🚐 ★★★ · ▲ ★★

Beauty: ★★★	Site Privacy: ★★★
Spaciousness: ★★★	Quiet: ★★★
Security: ★★★★	Cleanliness: ★★★★★
Insect Control: ★★★★	Facilities: ★★★★

Despite its proximity to urban amenities, this campground has a definite rural feel. Trees line the east and west perimeters and block off most of the road to the south. In addition, a visually appealing chunk of pine forest blocks view of the office from the RV park. To the west is a large, open grassy field. The north is slightly less attractive, with a ball park that can become noisy during games. Campsites are situated on a loop, with back-in sites around the perimeter. All sites are grassy and level, with trees close to the edges. Two exceptions to this are sites 15 and 16, which are not close to any trees and consequently have an open, almost vulnerable feel. The most favorable is site 1 (which is surrounded on two sides by trees), followed by odd-number sites 3–11 (which are away from both the road and the ball park and face a grassy field with trees at the opposite end). Tucked behind the motel buildings, the campground is well away from motel traffic. Tenting sites occupy the tip of the island, with enough space to comfortably fit 10–12 tents. Five large trees (four deciduous) provide enough shelter for a comfortable tent stay.

BASICS
Operated By: Leland and Carla Oplinger. **Open:** All year. **Site Assignment:** Depends on availability. **Registration:** At office, late arrivals ring bell. **Fee:** RV, $10; hookup, $2; cable, $1; tent, $5–$7. **Parking:** At site.

FACILITIES
Number of RV-only Sites: 16. **Number of Tent-only Sites:** 1. **Hookups:** Electric (30, 50 amps), water, sewer, cable TV. **Each Site:** Picnic table. **Dump Station:** Yes. **Laundry:** No. **Pay Phone:** No. **Restrooms and Showers:** Yes. **Fuel:** No. **Propane:** No. **Internal Roads:** Gravel. **RV Service:** No. **Market:** 1 mi. **Restaurant:** 1 mi. **General Store:** No. **Vending:** Yes. **Swimming:** No. **Playground:** No. **Other:** Free coffee. **Nearby Attractions:** Old town clock, Davis Memorial, flea markets, casinos, golf course. **Additional Information:** Hiawatha Chamber of Commerce, (785) 742-7136.

RESTRICTIONS
Pets: On leash. **Fires:** Stove or grill only. **Alcoholic Beverages:** At sites. **Vehicle Maximum Length:** No limit.

TO GET THERE
From Hwy. 36, turn north onto Oregon St. (West exit). Continue 0.3 mi. on Oregon St.—the entrance is on the right-hand side, slightly east (across the road) from the water tower.

HUTCHINSON · MAP, B-3
Melody Acres Campground

1009 East Blanchard, 67501. T: (620) 665-5048.

🚐 ★★★★ · ▲ ★★★★

Beauty: ★★★★	Site Privacy: ★★★★
Spaciousness: ★★★★	Quiet: ★★★
Security: ★★★	Cleanliness: ★★★
Insect Control: ★★★	Facilities: ★★★

This cute campground lined by cedars on the east, is forested to the west, with a line of mature shade trees to the north, giving it a real forested feel. Most camping sites have at least one tree, although some too small to provide any real shade. Tent sites, by contrast, are right in the middle of the treed area providing lots of overhead protection and a real middle-of-the-forest ambiance. While the campgrounds are clean, the restroom/shower facility is a little dingy. The unfinished cement floors and peeling paint make the facilities feel more like a storage area than a comfortable washroom. The most convenient sites are the 15 pull-throughs (1–10 and others in the bizarrely numbered scheme) in the middle of the loop, while the prettiest are the back-ins (8–19 and A–G) that abut the forested area. All sites are level and grassy, with pull-throughs an enormous 45 by 100 feet. (The back-ins are equally wide but not as long.) Sites C and D have a particularly pleasing mulberry tree overhanging them.

BASICS
Operated By: Judy Mitchell. **Open:** All year. **Site Assignment:** First come, first served; verbal reservations OK. **Registration:** At office, late arrivals pay in morning. **Fee:** $10–$21. **Parking:** At site.

FACILITIES
Number of RV-only Sites: 32. **Number of Tent-only Sites:** Undesignated sites. **Hookups:** Electric (30, 50 amps), water, sewer. **Each Site:** Some picnic tables. **Dump Station:** Yes. **Laundry:** Yes. **Pay Phone:** No. **Restrooms and Showers:** Yes. **Fuel:** No. **Propane:** No. **Internal Roads:** Gravel. **RV Service:** No. **Market:** 1 mi. to Hutchinson. **Restaurant:** 1 mi. to Hutchinson. **General Store:** No. **Vending:** Yes. **Swimming:** No. **Playground:** No. **Other:** Storm shelter. **Activities:** Viewing IMAX films, visiting museums. **Nearby Attractions:** Kansas Cosmosphere & Space Center, Reno County Museum, Salt Mine Museum. **Additional Information:** Hutchinson Chamber of Commerce, (316) 662-3391.

RESTRICTIONS
Pets: No dogs over 20 lbs in park, all pets leashed. **Fires:** Subject to seasonal bans. **Alcoholic Beverages:** At sites. **Vehicle Maximum Length:** 70 ft.

TO GET THERE
From the junction of Hwy. 61 and Hwy. 50, go 0.25 mi. west on Hwy. 50. Take the first right turn into the entrance and drive through the campground to the office.

INDEPENDENCE · MAP, C-4
Elk City State Park

4825 Squaw Creek Rd, 67301. T: (620) 331-6295; www.kdwp.state.ks.us.

🚐 ★★★★ · ▲ ★★★★★

Beauty: ★★★★★	Site Privacy: ★★★★
Spaciousness: ★★★★	Quiet: ★★★★★
Security: ★★★	Cleanliness: ★★★★★
Insect Control: ★★★	Facilities: ★★★

This campground is another of the many attractive state parks in Kansas. Sites are well-groomed, located close to the water's edge as well as farther away. Those farther away tend to be more open, with more trees closer to the edge of the lake. (For this reason, tenters may want to consider a site close to the water for the increased shelter.) Most sites are back-ins, with 45 pull-throughs. Sites fill up quickly for major holidays (Memorial Day, July 4th, Labor Day), so get there early in the day to ensure a spot for yourself.

BASICS
Operated By: Kansas Dept. of Wildlife and Parks. **Open:** All year. **Site Assignment:** First come, first served. **Registration:** At office. **Fee:** $7–$18, $5/day vehicle permit; credit card. **Parking:** At site, plenty of additional parking.

FACILITIES
Number of RV-only Sites: 150. **Number of Tent-only Sites:** 56. **Hookups:** Electric (30, 50 amps), water, sewer. **Each Site:** Picnic table, fire pit/grill, trees. **Dump Station:** Yes. **Laundry:** Yes. **Pay Phone:** Yes. **Restrooms and Showers:** Yes. **Fuel:** No. **Propane:** No. **Internal Roads:** Paved. **RV Service:** No. **Market:** 5 mi. to Independence. **Restaurant:** 5 mi. to Independence. **General Store:** No. **Vending:** No. **Swimming:** Lake. **Playground:** Yes. **Other:** Wildlife. **Activities:** Fishing, swimming, boating, waterskiing, hiking, hunting. **Nearby Attractions:** Little House on the Prairie, Riverside Park. **Additional Information:** Independence Chamber of Commerce, (316) 331-1890.

RESTRICTIONS
Pets: On leash only. **Fires:** Fire ring only. **Alcoholic Beverages:** At sites. **Vehicle Maximum Length:** No limit.

TO GET THERE
From the junction of Hwy. 75 and Hwy. 160 (Main St. and 10th St. in town), go west on Hwy. 160 for 1.7 mi. Turn right onto Peter Pan Rd. Go 1 mi. north on this road (which turns into CR 3525), then turn left onto CR 4800. Continue west to the office or to a pay station.

LAWRENCE · MAP, B-4
Lawrence/Kansas City KOA

1473 Hwy. 40, 66044. T: (800) 562-3708 or (785) 842-3877; www.lawrencekoa.com.

🚐 ★★★★ · ▲ ★★★★

Beauty: ★★★	Site Privacy: ★★★★
Spaciousness: ★★★★	Quiet: ★★★
Security: ★★★★	Cleanliness: ★★★
Insect Control: ★★★★	Facilities: ★★★★★

This campground is surrounded by seven acres of undeveloped land to the north and a sod farm with lush green grass to the east. Flowering trees and flowers planted in surprising nooks add color and charm to the grounds. All sites are grassy, level pull-throughs located on loops that are separated by rows of trees. Already packed with features, this campground promises exciting additional services. The best time to come is when the flowers and trees are in bloom. Keep in mind, however, the NASCAR schedule and be sure to cancel well in advance, if necessary, to avoid losing your deposit during these busy times.

BASICS

Operated By: Ralph and Kim Newell. **Open:** All year. **Site Assignment:** Upon registration; credit card for reservation; 24-hour cancellation policy; 1-week for race weekends. **Registration:** At store, late arrivals select site from map & use drop box. **Fee:** RV, $27; tent, $20. **Parking:** At site, additional parking available.

FACILITIES

Number of RV-only Sites: 69. **Number of Tent-only Sites:** 26. **Hookups:** Electric (30, 50 amps), water, sewer. **Each Site:** Picnic table, fire pit, trees, Wi-Fi. **Dump Station:** Yes. **Laundry:** Yes. **Pay Phone:** Yes. **Restrooms and Showers:** Yes. **Fuel:** No. **Propane:** Yes. **Internal Roads:** Paved/dirt. **RV Service:** Yes. **Market:** 2 mi. into Lawrence. **Restaurant:** 0.5 mi. into Lawrence. **General Store:** Yes. **Vending:** Yes. **Swimming:** Pool. **Playground:** Yes. **Other:** Game room, cabins, group meeting room, dog walk area, cycling/running trail. **Activities:** Volleyball, basketball, badminton, canoe trips, tetherball. **Nearby Attractions:** NASCAR track, golf course, Kansas City. **Additional Information:** Lawrence Chamber of Commerce, (913) 865-4411.

RESTRICTIONS

Pets: On leash, not left outside, cleaned up after. **Fires:** Fire pit only. **Alcoholic Beverages:** At sites. **Vehicle Maximum Length:** No limit. **Other:** Pay attention to speed limits, no parking on grass; no clotheslines.

TO GET THERE

From the junction of I-70 and Hwy. 59, drive 0.5 mi. north on 59, veer right (east) onto Hwy. 24, and follow Hwy. 24 for 0.2 mi. Take the first right at the KOA sign into the entrance. Follow the driveway to the end to register at the store.

MANHATTEN   MAP, B-3
Tuttle Creek State Park

5800A River Pond Rd., 66502. T: (785) 539-7941; www.wp.state.ks.us.

🚐 ★★★★★	⛺ ★★★★★
Beauty: ★★★★	Site Privacy: ★★★★★
Spaciousness: ★★★★★	Quiet: ★★★★★
Security: ★★★★	Cleanliness: ★★★★★
Insect Control: ★★★	Facilities: ★★★★

Located to the northwest of Manhatten, this humungous state park (1,100-plus acres) offers four camping areas with grassy sites on large loops. Like other state parks, this campground offers a variety of sites, from waterfront to woodsy. The River Pond campground, for example, offers some spacious, well-groomed pull-throughs (100), although the back-ins (sites 71–104) are a little more pressed together. Tenters should be aware that some sites offer no protection in case of rain. The best time of year to come is after the spring rains, when the deciduous trees are in leaf. Regardless of your tastes and preferences, there is certain to be something for everyone.

BASICS

Operated By: Kansas Dept. of Wildlife and Parks. **Open:** All year. **Site Assignment:** First come, first served; 10 reservable sites; must have credit card to hold, no refunds. **Registration:** At office or self-pay station. **Fee:** Varies; $5/day vehicle permit; add $2 for prime sites indicated by red. **Parking:** At site.

FACILITIES

Number of RV-only Sites: 140. **Hookups:** Electric (30, 50 amps), water. **Each Site:** Picnic table, fire pit, trees. **Dump Station:** Yes. **Laundry:** No. **Pay Phone:** Yes. **Restrooms and Showers:** Yes. **Fuel:** No. **Propane:** No. **Internal Roads:** Paved. **RV Service:** No. **Market:** 3 mi. to Manhattan. **Restaurant:** 3 mi. to Manhattan. **General Store:** Yes. **Vending:** Yes. **Swimming:** Lake. **Playground:** Yes. **Other:** Boat ramp, group picnic shelters, fish-cleaning station, canoe rentals. **Activities:** Swimming, boating, waterskiing, windsurfing, cycling, hiking, softball, hunting. **Nearby Attractions:** Flint Hills, Riley County Historical Museum, Wonder Workshop. **Additional Information:** Manhattan CVB, (800) 759-0134.

RESTRICTIONS

Pets: On 10-ft. leash. **Fires:** In rings or grills. **Alcoholic Beverages:** Beer only. **Vehicle Maximum Length:** No limit. **Other:** $5 per day vehicle permit.

TO GET THERE

From the junction of Hwy. 24 and Hwy. 13, turn east onto Hwy. 13 and drive 1.8 mi. Take the tricky right turn at the sign (this may be problematic for larger rigs) and follow the road 1 mi. to the office or self-pay station. Alternately, take Hwy. 24 0.5 mi. east from the junction with Hwy. 13 and turn left at the sign. This takes you away from the office, but avoids the hair-pin turn.

MARQUETTE   MAP, B-3
Venango Park

105 Riverside Dr., 67464. T: (785) 546-2294; www.reserveamerica.com.

🚐 ★★★★	⛺ ★★★★
Beauty: ★★★	Site Privacy: ★★★
Spaciousness: ★★★	Quiet: ★★★★★
Security: ★★★★★	Cleanliness: ★★★★
Insect Control: ★★★	Facilities: ★★★

Located on the Smoky Hill River in central Kansas approximately 30 miles southwest of Salina, Kanopolis Lake is one of the oldest lakes in Kansas surrounded be vast open prairie. The area offers many recreational opportunities as well as fishing and hunting. A variety of game animals such as pheasant, quail, prairie chicken, whitetail, turkey, waterfowl, rabbit, and squirrel can be found here. The Smoky Hill River valley is the scenic setting for Kanopolis Lake. The best hiking and wildlife viewing are in the Horsethief Canyon area at the north end of the lake. Hundreds of migrating waterfowl can be seen in spring and fall. Look for geese, mergansers, pintails, wigeons, shovelers, teal, mallards, gadwalls, buffle-heads, and goldeneyes. Watch for collared lizards, Texas horned lizards, six-lined racerunners, Great Plains skinks, and other reptiles. In grassland areas mule deer, horned larks, meadowlarks, and kingbirds are common. Beaver and raccoon live along the waterways. Watch for turkeys and prairie dogs in the state park area. In open woodlands and croplands watch for white-tailed deer, pheasants, bobwhite quail, and coyotes. In winter, bald eagles are commonly seen flying over the lake, and turkey vultures can be seen in summer. Prairie wildflowers such as purple poppy mallow, prairie spiderwort, yucca, prairie wild rose, butterfly milkweed, and blue false indigo, along with little bluestem and grasses, are only a few of the 423 species of plants that can be found along the Buffalo Track Canyon Nature Trail. The Cheyenne sandstone formation, up to 100 feet thick in places, makes the walls of the canyon. It has been sculpted by wind and water over the ages into various caves, spires, and rugged escarpments that invite rock scrambling!

BASICS

Operated By: U.S. Army Corps of Engineers. **Open:** All year. **Site Assignment:** Reservations must be made at least 4 days in advance. **Registration:** At office. **Fee:** Single, $4–$18. **Parking:** At site.

FACILITIES

Number of Multipurpose Sites: 736. **Hookups:** Yes. **Dump Station:** Yes. **Laundry:** No. **Pay Phone:** Yes. **Restrooms and Showers:** Yes. **Fuel:** No. **Propane:** No. **Internal Roads:** Paved. **RV Service:** No. **Market:** No. **Restaurant:** No. **General Store:** No. **Vending:** No. **Swimming:** Yes. **Playground:** Yes. **Activities:** ATV, wildlife viewing.

RESTRICTIONS

Pets: Pets must be restrained or on a leash at all times while in developed recreation areas. **Fires:** In fire rings, stoves, grills, or fireplaces provided for that purpose. **Alcoholic Beverages:** Not allowed. **Vehicle Maximum Length:** Call ahead.

TO GET THERE

From Salina, KS, take Hwy. 140 19 mi. west to Hwy. 141. Travel 12 mi. south on Hwy. 141, then 0.5 mi west on paved road; look for signs to the park.

NORTON   MAP, A-2
Prairie Dog State Park

RR 431, 67654. T: (785) 877-2953; www.kdwp.state.ks.us.

🚐 ★★★★	⛺ ★★★★★
Beauty: ★★★★	Site Privacy: ★★★★
Spaciousness: ★★★★★	Quiet: ★★★★★
Security: ★★★★	Cleanliness: ★★★★
Insect Control: ★★★	Facilities: ★★★

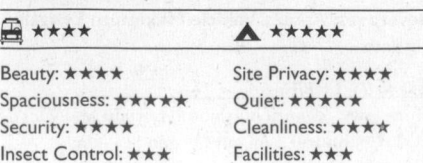

Named for the prairie dog town at the entrance, this park is renowned for the excellent fishing it provides in the Sebelius Reservoir. Best in the spring or fall, the park is extremely crowded during the summer, and especially so for the holidays. Sites are grassy and open, averaging 60 feet long and up to 65 feet wide, with both back-ins and pull-throughs. Despite the number of new trees planted, sites do not benefit from their shade. Branded Cedar sites W1–W6 have a commanding view of the lake and proximity to the showers, while Meadowlark campsites have fire pits and are situated right on the lake. Tenting areas are separated from the RV sites and also offer fire pits. This park is a beautiful alternative to the overnight RV spots in town, with only slightly fewer facilities.

BASICS

Operated By: Camp Hosts Ray and Leta Koel. **Open:** All year. **Site Assignment:** First come, first served; 8 reservable sites. **Registration:** At office or self-pay stations. **Fee:** Call ahead for rates. **Parking:** At site.

FACILITIES

Number of RV-only Sites: 58. **Number of Tent-only Sites:** 139. **Hookups:** Electric (30, 50 amps), water. **Each Site:** Picnic table, tree, some lantern poles. **Dump Station:** Yes. **Laundry:** No. **Pay Phone:** No. **Restrooms and Showers:** Yes. **Fuel:** Yes. **Propane:** Yes. **Internal Roads:** Paved/gravel. **RV Service:** No. **Market:** 6 mi. to Norton. **Restaurant:** 6 mi. to Norton. **General Store:** No. **Vending:** Yes. **Swimming:** Lake. **Playground:** Yes. **Other:** Boat ramp, renovated adobe home, 1-room schoolhouse, marina concessions, picnic shelters, some free firewood. **Activities:** Fishing, boating, swimming, waterskiing, archery, wildlife-watching, fireworks over lake on July 4th w/ free watermelon. **Nearby Attractions:** Gallery of Also Rans (First State Bank building). **Additional Information:** Norton Chamber of Commerce, (785) 877-2501.

RESTRICTIONS

Pets: On leash only. **Fires:** Grill only. **Alcoholic Beverages:** Not allowed (kegs w/ a permit). **Vehicle Maximum Length:** No limit. **Other:** No washing of vehicles or boats.

TO GET THERE

From the junction of Hwy. 283 and Hwy. 36, turn west onto Hwy. 36 and drive 4.3 mi. through the town of Norton. Turn right at the sign for the park onto Hwy. 261 and drive 1 mi. to the office or to a self-pay station.

OAKLEY   MAP, B-1
High Plains Camping

462 US 83, 67748. T: (785) 672-3538 or (888) 446-3507; www.highplainscamping.com.

🚐 ★★★★   ⛺ ★★★★

Beauty: ★★★★	Site Privacy: ★★★
Spaciousness: ★★★	Quiet: ★★★★
Security: ★★★	Cleanliness: ★★★★
Insect Control: ★★★★	Facilities: ★★★

Despite its proximity to the commercial area of Oakley (half a mile), this campground retains a secluded feel. Laid out on loops, sites are spacious, open, and grassy, with both back-ins and pull-throughs. Average sites are 30 feet wide, although several (M1, M10, M11, D12) seem short-changed for space. Sites M1–M10 feel slightly as if they were in a fishbowl for all to look at, but M12–M20 are more removed and private. The best sites are D13–17 and E13–17, which are more secluded but have a convenient proximity to facilities. The tent area is fenced off from the RV sites, next to a large open field. Although the unmarked sites lack overhead protection, this campground is a better bet for tenters than the campground in nearby Colby.

BASICS

Operated By: M. Arlington. **Open:** All year. **Site Assignment:** Reservation accepted and recommended. **Registration:** At office, late arrivals use drop box. **Fee:** $15–$26. **Parking:** At site.

FACILITIES

Number of RV-only Sites: 86. **Number of Tent-only Sites:** Undesignated sites. **Hookups:** Electric (30, 50 amps), water, sewer. **Each Site:** Picnic table, shade tree. **Dump Station:** Yes. **Laundry:** Yes. **Pay Phone:** Yes. **Restrooms and Showers:** Yes. **Fuel:** Yes. **Propane:** Yes. **Internal Roads:** Gravel & paved. **RV Service:** No. **Market:** 1 mi. in Oakley. **Restaurant:** Next door. **General Store:** Yes. **Vending:** No. **Swimming:** Pool (Memorial Day–Labor Day). **Playground:** Yes. **Other:** Mini-golf, discount at Conoco gas station w/ valid RV park receipt. **Activities:** Golf, horseshoes, volleyball, video games. **Nearby Attractions:** Monument Rocks, Fick Fossil & History Museum, Prairie Dog Town. **Additional Information:** Oakley Chamber of Commerce, (913) 672-4862.

RESTRICTIONS

Pets: On leash only. **Fires:** Grill only. **Alcoholic Beverages:** At sites. **Vehicle Maximum Length:** No limit.

TO GET THERE

From I-70, take Exit 70, then turn south onto Hwy. 83. Drive 0.2 mi. on Hwy. 83 and take the first right after the I-70 junction. Go straight into the entrance.

PERRY   MAP, B-4
Old Town

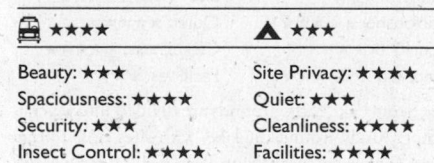

HC 61 Box 238, 66073-9717. T: (785) 597-5144; www.reserveamerica.com.

🚐 ★★★★   ⛺ ★★★★

Beauty: ★★★	Site Privacy: ★★★
Spaciousness: ★★★	Quiet: ★★★★
Security: ★★★★	Cleanliness: ★★★★
Insect Control: ★★★	Facilities: ★★★

Great fishing can be found in the area around Old Town Park at Perry Lake. Crappie and catfish are routinely caught along the shoreline and near the adjacent Highway 92. Located conveniently near the cities of Topeka, Lawrence, and Kansas City, Perry Lake boasts a wide variety of recreational opportunities. The lake is proud to host the 30-mile Perry Lake National Recreational Hiking Trail, renowned for its rugged terrain. Other trails include an equestrian trail, ATV and motorcycle trail, mountain-bike trail, and interpretative hiking trails. Sightseers will revel in the breathtaking panoramic views found throughout the lake area. Several wetland areas provide home to many species of birds. In addition, Perry Lake is host to several camping facilities that contain sites suitable for tent campers to those with recreational vehicles. Each park contains boat ramps and easy shoreline access for fisherman. Two marinas are located at Perry Lake and provide a full assortment of marine services. Several of the nearby communities host restaurants and historical attractions. Nonelectric sites are located in open, flat expanses of the park, and electric sites are located in a more shaded loop. This park is popular with those who enjoy fishing and a relaxing camping experience.

BASICS

Operated By: U.S. Army Corps of Engineers. **Open:** May 1–Sept. 30. **Site Assignment:** Reservations must be made at least 3 days in advance. **Registration:** At office. **Fee:** Single, $12–$16. **Parking:** At site.

FACILITIES

Number of Multipurpose Sites: 282. **Hookups:** Yes. **Dump Station:** Yes. **Laundry:** No. **Pay Phone:** No. **Restrooms and Showers:** Yes. **Fuel:** No. **Propane:** No. **Internal Roads:** Paved. **RV Service:** No. **Market:** No. **Restaurant:** No. **General Store:** Yes. **Vending:** No. **Swimming:** No. **Playground:** Yes. **Activities:** Fishing.

RESTRICTIONS

Pets: Pets must be restrained or on a leash at all times while in developed recreation areas. **Fires:** In fire rings, stoves, grills, or fireplaces provided for that purpose. **Alcoholic Beverages:** Not allowed. **Vehicle Maximum Length:** Call ahead. **Other:** No hunting; ATVs, motorcycles, & golf carts not allowed.

TO GET THERE

From Ozawkie, KS, travel 1.5 mi. east on KS 92. Follow entrance signs.

RUSSELL   MAP, B-2
Triple J Campground

187 Edwards Ave., 67665. T: (785) 483-4826.

🚐 ★★★★   ⛺ ★★★

Beauty: ★★★	Site Privacy: ★★★★
Spaciousness: ★★★★	Quiet: ★★★
Security: ★★★	Cleanliness: ★★★★
Insect Control: ★★★★	Facilities: ★★★★

This campground has 30 pull-throughs that could accommodate all but the largest monster rig on the road without unhooking. Average site size is 40 by 60 feet. The grounds are spacious and open, with a rural feel; an open field and horses in the west corner add to the ambiance. Unmarked tent sites are on a grassy strip that is set away from the RV sites. Trees provide a natural barricade to the neighboring land to the north, and the best sites (even numbers 34–38 and odd numbers 39–47) face this direction. The least favorable sites—still nowhere near a bad spot to end up—are on the east side, facing the distant shopping complex. (The campground is quite removed from this complex, and these sites are offset from the entrance, which gives them extra space and privacy.) RVers will be happy with any available spot; tenters, however, fare a little worse, being closer to the highway and its attendant noise.

BASICS

Operated By: Lana Zorn. **Open:** All year. **Site Assignment:** First come, first served. **Registration:** At office. **Fee:** $12–$20; no credit cards. **Parking:** At site.

FACILITIES

Number of RV-only Sites: 52. **Number of Tent-only Sites:** Undesignated sites. **Hookups:** Electric (30, 50 amps), water, sewer, cable TV & modem. **Each Site:** Picnic table; grill & tree at most sites. **Dump Station:** No (sewer at all sites). **Laundry:** Yes. **Pay Phone:** Yes. **Restrooms and Showers:** Yes. **Fuel:** No. **Propane:** No. **Internal Roads:** Paved/gravel. **RV Service:** No (w/in 1 block). **Market:** 1 block. **Restaurant:** 1 block. **General Store:** Yes. **Vending:** Yes. **Swimming:** No. **Playground:** Yes. **Other:** Storm shelter, data port hookups. **Activities:** Mini-golf, horseshoes, video games. **Nearby Attractions:** Sternberg Museum, Cathedral of the Plains, Garden of Eden sculptures. **Additional Information:** Russell CVB, (800) 658-4686.

RESTRICTIONS

Pets: On leash only, cleaned up after. **Fires:** Grill only. **Alcoholic Beverages:** At sites. **Vehicle Maximum Length:** No limit.

TO GET THERE

From I-70, turn north onto Hwy. 281 and follow it 1 block. The entrance is on the left. Follow the driveway around to the right; the office is across from the mini-golf.

SCOTT CITY   **MAP, B-1**
Camp Lakeside

520 West Scott Lake Dr., 67871.
T: (620) 872-2061.

🚐 ★★★★   🏕 ★★★★★

Beauty: ★★★★	Site Privacy: ★★★★
Spaciousness: ★★★★	Quiet: ★★★★
Security: ★★★	Cleanliness: ★★★★★
Insect Control: ★★★	Facilities: ★★★

The Scott Lake campgrounds are divided into several campgrounds around the lake, with sites close to the water (Lakeside campground) as well as farther up the embankment, with a more woodsy feel (Elm Grove). Sites are laid out on a series of loops, with both pull-throughs and back-ins. All sites are spacious and level, and the lake offers a variety of activities for a day, a week, or even just an afternoon. Rocky outcrops around part of the lake add to the natural beauty, but the lack of water facilities in winter may make this campground too natural for some campers. Those who don't mind roughing it a little

(in winter only) should definitely make a point to stop here—and bring the kids.

BASICS

Operated By: Kansas Dept. of Wildlife and Parks. **Open:** All year. **Site Assignment:** First come, first served. **Registration:** At office or self-pay stations. **Fee:** $7–$18; $5/day vehicle permit. **Parking:** At site.

FACILITIES

Number of RV-only Sites: 60. **Number of Tent-only Sites:** 170. **Hookups:** Electric, water (no water Oct.–Apr.). **Each Site:** Grill. **Dump Station:** Yes. **Laundry:** No. **Pay Phone:** Yes. **Restrooms and Showers:** Yes. **Fuel:** No. **Propane:** No. **Internal Roads:** Paved/gravel. **RV Service:** No. **Market:** 14 mi. to Scott City (limited market on site). **Restaurant:** 14 mi. to Scott City. **General Store:** Yes. **Vending:** Yes. **Swimming:** Lake. **Playground:** Yes. **Other:** Boat ramp, canoe/boat rentals. **Activities:** Boating, fishing, cycling, hiking, horseback riding, hunting. **Nearby Attractions:** El Cuartelego Pueblo ruins. **Additional Information:** Scott City Chamber of Commerce, (316) 872-3525.

RESTRICTIONS

Pets: On leash only. **Fires:** Grill only. **Alcoholic Beverages:** Beer only. **Vehicle Maximum Length:** No limit.

TO GET THERE

From the junction of Hwy. 83 and Hwy. 95, turn north onto Hwy. 95. To go to the office (or a pay station), follow Hwy. 95 to West Scott Lake Drive, and turn left into the office parking lot. To get to other pay stations and campsites, turn right onto East Scott Lake Drive and drive 2.5 mi.

STOCKTON   **MAP, A-2**
Webster State Park

1210 Nine Rd., 67669. T: (785) 425-6775.

🚐 ★★★★   🏕 ★★★

Beauty: ★★★★	Site Privacy: ★★★★
Spaciousness: ★★★★	Quiet: ★★★★★
Security: ★★★	Cleanliness: ★★★★
Insect Control: ★★★	Facilities: ★★★

Sites in this campground vary from water's edge to farther up the embankment. Thus the camper can experience woods, beach, and park all in one. All sites are level and grassy, averaging 50 by 60 feet in size (some pull-throughs are even longer), situated on a series of large loops and some grid sites. The reservoir itself is surrounded by reeds (at the water's edge) and fields with short pines. Sites close to the water generally have more trees, while those away from the water are more open. While parking is available at each of the sites, there is enough additional parking (for day use) to accommodate extra vehicles. Facilities are clean but a hike away from some campsites. Overall, this is a fun, family-oriented destination with plenty of activities for kids and grandparents alike.

BASICS

Operated By: Kansas Dept. of Wildlife and Parks. **Open:** All year. **Site Assignment:** First come, first served; 18 reservable sites, can be reserved 2 weeks

in advance by check or credit card or 1 week in advance in person, no refunds. **Registration:** At station or self-pay sites (Apr. 1–Sept. 30 self-pay only). **Fee:** Campsite, $7; 1 utility, $5.50; 2 utilities, $7.50; 3 utilities, $9.50; add $2 for prime sites marked in red. **Parking:** At site.

FACILITIES

Number of RV-only Sites: 72. **Number of Tent-only Sites:** 100. **Hookups:** Electric (20, 30, 50 amps), water. **Each Site:** Picnic table, fire pit, trees; some lantern poles, some free firewood. **Dump Station:** Yes. **Laundry:** No. **Pay Phone:** Yes. **Restrooms and Showers:** Yes. **Fuel:** No. **Propane:** No. **Internal Roads:** Paved. **RV Service:** No. **Market:** 9 mi. to Stockton. **Restaurant:** 9 mi. to Stockton. **General Store:** No. **Vending:** Yes. **Swimming:** Lake. **Playground:** Yes. **Other:** Picnic shelters, fishing dock, fish-cleaning station, wildlife. **Activities:** Swimming, fishing, baseball, boating, hiking, volleyball, horseshoes. **Nearby Attractions:** Webster Reservation Wildlife Area. **Additional Information:** Stockton Chamber of Commerce & Economic Development: (785) 425-6162.

RESTRICTIONS

Pets: On leash only. **Fires:** Grill or pits. **Alcoholic Beverages:** Beer only. **Vehicle Maximum Length:** 60 ft.

TO GET THERE

From the junction of Hwy. 183 and Hwy. 24, turn north onto Hwy. 24 and drive 9 mi. The entrance is on the left (past the overpass). Follow the road to the office or to a self-pay station. (The turnoff for Webster Reservoir onto Hwy. 283 leads to the Goose Flats camping area.)

SYLVAN GROVE   **MAP, B-2, B-3**
Minooka Park

reserve america

4860 Outlet Blvd., 67481. T: (785) 658-2551; www.reserveamerica.com.

🚐 ★★★★   🏕 ★★★★

Beauty: ★★★★	Site Privacy: ★★★
Spaciousness: ★★★	Quiet: ★★★★★
Security: ★★★★★	Cleanliness: ★★★★
Insect Control: ★★★	Facilities: ★★★

In the Post Rock Country of central Kansas, Minooka Park Campground on Wilson Lake offers great appeal to sports lovers, anglers, recreationists, or those who just want to enjoy the beauty and serenity of the area. Wilson Lake, located on the Saline River, controls a drainage area of 1,917 square miles. The grassland drainage basin above Wilson makes it one of the clearest lake in Kansas. With 9,000 acres of water and 100 miles of shoreline, it has become one of the most popular recreation areas in central Kansas. Historic Wilson Dam was constructed between 1918–1925 as part of the World War I effort. Wilson Lake contains 15,500 acres of surface water and is 15.5 miles long. The waters below Wilson are known as the Smallmouth Capital of the World for the trophy smallmouth bass caught there. Whitetail Ridge offers five primitive walk-in campsites for those who like to get off the beaten path. These sites are located from 0.1 to 0.25 miles from the parking area and include a covered picnic table, fire ring, and lantern post. This primitive setting provides an excellent opportunity for traditional camping and for viewing local wildlife.

BASICS

Operated By: U.S. Army Corps of Engineers. **Open:** All year. **Site Assignment:** Reservations accepted Apr. 15–Sept. 30. **Registration:** At office. **Fee:** Single, $12–$18; double, $24–$36; group, $20–$150. **Parking:** At site.

FACILITIES

Number of Multipurpose Sites: 552. **Hookups:** Yes. **Dump Station:** Yes. **Laundry:** No. **Pay Phone:** Yes. **Restrooms and Showers:** Yes. **Fuel:** No. **Propane:** No. **Internal Roads:** Paved. **RV Service:** No. **Market:** No. **Restaurant:** No. **General Store:** No. **Vending:** No. **Swimming:** Yes. **Playground:** Yes.

RESTRICTIONS

Pets: Pets must be restrained or on a leash at all times while in developed recreation areas. **Fires:** In fire rings, stoves, grills, or fireplaces provided for that purpose. **Alcoholic Beverages:** Not allowed. **Vehicle Maximum Length:** Call ahead. **Other:** No ATVs or ORVs allowed.

TO GET THERE

From I-70 Exit 199 go north on Dorrance Road 7 miles.

WAKEENEY   MAP, B-2
Wakeeney KOA Kampground

P.O. Box 170, 67672. T: (800) 562-2761 or (785) 743-5612; www.koa.com.

🚐 ★★★★   ▲ ★★★

Beauty: ★★★	Site Privacy: ★★★★
Spaciousness: ★★★★	Quiet: ★★★
Security: ★★★★	Cleanliness: ★★★★★
Insect Control: ★★★	Facilities: ★★★★★

This campground features modern, clean, and tastefully decorated facilities. All sites are level and grassy, the majority (all except those in C area) being pull-throughs. Sites and rows are clearly marked, and site sizes average 30 by 62 feet (up to 80 feet). The playground and pool facilities are well away from camping sites. Tent sites are likewise separated from the RV sites by the internal road and from each other by a half-length of wood fencing. The back-ins in the C area face a screen of trees but are closest to the highway. Site 75 in the southeast corner faces two unattractive sheds and a slightly crumbling fence. Besides this minor insult to the senses, you really can't go wrong with any site, nor can the facilities be beat. There is definitely a site to fit all preferences: large shade tree, proximity to the restroom facilities, to the pool, etc.

BASICS

Operated By: Greg and Michelle Dunagen. **Open:** Mar. 15–Nov. 15. **Site Assignment:** Upon registration; reservations w/ credit card; cancel same day.

Registration: At office, late arrivals use drop box. **Fee:** RV, $22–$28; tent $17–$19. **Parking:** At site.

FACILITIES

Number of RV-only Sites: 79. **Number of Tent-only Sites:** 13. **Hookups:** Electric (30, 50 amps), water, sewer. **Each Site:** Picnic table, tree. **Dump Station:** Yes. **Laundry:** Yes. **Pay Phone:** Yes. **Restrooms and Showers:** Yes. **Fuel:** No. **Propane:** Yes. **Internal Roads:** Dirt/gravel. **RV Service:** No. **Market:** 1 mi. to Wakeeney. **Restaurant:** 2 blocks. **General Store:** No. **Vending:** Yes. **Swimming:** Pool. **Playground:** Yes. **Other:** 3 cabins. **Activities:** Volleyball. **Nearby Attractions:** Cedar Bluff State Park, Castle rock. **Additional Information:** Wakeeney Chamber of Commerce, (913) 743-2077.

RESTRICTIONS

Pets: On leash. **Fires:** Grill only. **Alcoholic Beverages:** At sites. **Vehicle Maximum Length:** No limit.

TO GET THERE

From I-70, take Exit 127 and turn south onto Hwy. 283. Go 100 yards on Hwy. 283 onto the frontage road, which dead-ends at the KOA entrance.

WICHITA   MAP, C-3
USI RV Park

2920 East 33rd North, 67219. T: (800) 782-1531 or (316) 838-8699; www.usirvpark.com.

🚐 ★★★★   ▲ n/a

Beauty: ★★	Site Privacy: ★★
Spaciousness: ★★★	Quiet: ★★★
Security: ★★★★	Cleanliness: ★★★★★
Insect Control: ★★★★	Facilities: ★★★★

This popular park consists of gravel and grassy sites laid out in strips 25 feet wide and long enough to accommodate almost any rig. Most sites are pull-throughs with very little grass—there is slightly more grass at the sites around the perimeter. The most favorable sites are in the A area, which boasts trees (sites 6–8 are especially nice), more grass, and proximity to the restrooms. Sites 13–14 are jammed between the office and a garage and seem to have been added as an afterthought. All facilities are fantastically clean, and there are separate phone and data port rooms, which give excellent privacy. While the wooden fence around the west side does a fine job of blocking out the view of neighboring land, there is a storage area to the southeast and a large radio antenna due north that detract from the setting.

BASICS

Operated By: Sheila Wagner. **Open:** All year. **Site Assignment:** Upon registration; reservations strongly recommended; credit card to hold site; for shorter stay, cancel w/in 24 hours; for longer stay, w/in 5 days. **Registration:** At office, late arrivals use drop box. **Fee:** $22–$25. **Parking:** At site.

FACILITIES

Number of RV-only Sites: 75. **Hookups:** Electric (30, 50 amps), water, sewer. **Each Site:** Picnic table, tree. **Dump Station:** Yes. **Laundry:** Yes. **Pay Phone:** Yes. **Restrooms and Showers:** Yes. **Fuel:**

No. **Propane:** Yes. **Internal Roads:** Gravel. **RV Service:** No. **Market:** 3 mi. east. **Restaurant:** 3 mi. east. **General Store:** Yes. **Vending:** Yes. **Swimming:** No. **Playground:** Yes. **Other:** Data ports, rec room, storm shelter. **Activities:** Sightseeing, shopping. **Nearby Attractions:** Wichita Gardens, Sedgwick County Zoo, Indian Center Museum, Wichita Art Museum, Wichita Center for the Arts, Omnisphere & Science Center, Wichita Greyhound Park. **Additional Information:** Wichita Chamber of Commerce, (316) 265-7771, Wichita CVB, (800) 288-9424.

RESTRICTIONS

Pets: 2 pets per vehicle; must sign pet agreement. **Fires:** Not allowed. **Alcoholic Beverages:** No kegs. **Vehicle Maximum Length:** No limit. **Other:** 10-year age limit of vehicle.

TO GET THERE

From Hwy. 135 (southbound Exit 10, northbound Exit 10A), turn east onto Hwy. 96 and go 1 mi. Take the Hillside exit and turn left onto Hillside Rd., then make an immediate left after the overpass onto 33rd St. Drive 1 block and turn right at the sign.

WILLIAMSBURG   MAP, B-4
Homewood RV Park

2161 Idaho Rd., 66095. T: (785) 242-5601.

🚐 ★★★★   ▲ ★★★

Beauty: ★★★★	Site Privacy: ★★★
Spaciousness: ★★★	Quiet: ★★★
Security: ★★★	Cleanliness: ★★★★
Insect Control: ★★★	Facilities: ★★★★

This campground, one corner of a 55-acre farm, is a very pretty and convenient stopover from the highway, and proprietor Betty is friendly and full of life. (If interested, ask to see historical family photos.) The park is ringed on all sides by trees, some of them flowering. There is a small picnic area in a stand of woods bordering the farmland, and an unused (and somewhat unattractive) pond to the north. The audible traffic noise is quickly forgotten in the natural surroundings. Sites 1–3, 10–13, and 17 have particularly nice rustic views, while sites 16, 16b (unmarked), and 17 are off the main loop and back into woods, beyond which lies only farmland. Slightly less desirable sites are 1 (a little too close to the restrooms) and 15 (tip of an island in the loop, and slightly cut off). Tent sites are unmarked, but adequate both in number and in overhead protection. All sites are back-ins.

BASICS

Operated By: Larry and Betty Shaffer. **Open:** All year. **Site Assignment:** Upon registration. **Registration:** At office, verbal reservations OK. **Fee:** $12–$18. **Parking:** At site.

FACILITIES

Number of RV-only Sites: 24. **Number of Tent-only Sites:** Undesignated sites. **Hookups:** Electric (30, 50 amps), water, sewer, some phone. **Each Site:** Trees, some picnic tables. **Dump Station:** Yes. **Laundry:** Yes. **Pay Phone:** Yes. **Restrooms and Showers:** Yes. **Fuel:** No. **Propane:** No. **Internal Roads:**

Gravel. **RV Service:** No. **Market:** 8 mi. to Ottawa. **Restaurant:** 8 mi. to Ottawa. **General Store:** No. **Vending:** No. **Swimming:** No. **Playground:** No. **Other:** Walking trail, library, dog walk area, country & western singer. **Activities:** Impromptu dinners. **Nearby Attractions:** Rail Trail, architecture, antique stores in Ottawa. **Additional Information:** Ottawa Chamber of Commerce, (913) 242-1000.

RESTRICTIONS

Pets: No rottweilers or pit bulls. **Fires:** Grill or fire ring. **Alcoholic Beverages:** At sites. **Vehicle Maximum Length:** 70 ft. **Other:** No hunting, no swimming in pond, no children near pond, children must be accompanied by an adult at all times.

TO GET THERE

From I-35, take Exit 176, then turn north and go 1 block to the entrance on the right. Keep left to go to the office.

Kentucky

The state of Kentucky has a rich historical heritage going back to colonial times and earlier. Thousands of years before Europeans came to America, regions in western Kentucky along the Ohio and Mississippi Rivers were inhabited by bands of ancient mound-building Native Americans. Later, tribes of Shawnee, Iroquois, Delaware, and Chickasaw lived in the area as well. Many of these tribes fought or were allied with American pioneers during skirmishes and wars before and during the American Revolution. Many frontiersmen established settlements in eastern and central Kentucky. One of these was **Boonesborough** on the Kentucky River about 45 miles east of present-day **Harrodstown,** founded by the famous **Daniel Boone.**

Following the American Revolution, Kentucky became the 15th state of the Union. Native American claims to Kentucky were erased in 1818, when the last Chickasaw lands in the western part of the state were acquired by the U.S. government. In the years leading up to the Civil War, large portions of Kentucky were cleared for farming, especially for tobacco. As the agricultural industry kicked into high gear and steamboats appeared, the city of Louisville (located on the Ohio River) became the state's principal trade center.

Kentucky was sharply divided at the outbreak of the Civil War, having strong pro-slavery and pro-Union factions. Though Kentucky's government declared itself neutral, both armies moved through this state. Several large battles were fought there early in the war. Eventually, both the Confederacy and Union claimed Kentucky as an ally (there was a star for the state on both governments' flags).

Today, Kentucky has become known for its thriving urban centers as well as its rich natural beauty. Downtown **Louisville** is a marvel. Nestled on the Ohio River, Louisville is one of the few urban areas that truly blends with its natural environment. Sports fans will be eager to note that this is the hometown of **Muhammad Ali** (and the boulevard that bears his name) and the **Louisville Slugger** factory. Hipper travelers will want to check out **Bardstown Road** and its assemblage of unique record stores, restaurants, boutiques, and karaoke bars. **Lexington** (home of the University of Kentucky) and **Bowling Green** share the same urban/natural synergy as Louisville but with their own pleasant variations.

Natural beauty is a large part of Kentucky's appeal—and there's no shortage of it! **Land Between the Lakes** is a 40-mile-long nature conservation area bordered by **Kentucky Lake** (whose state resort is quite popular among water sports enthusiasts) and **Lake Barkley.** **Mammoth Cave National Park** is the matriarch of Kentucky's many spelunking adventures—get information on all of them online at www.mammothcave.com. If you spend the night in **Cave City,** spend it at the **Wigwam Village Motel.** The **Cumberland Gap** is 800,000 acres of splendid outdoor majesty. **Daniel Boone National Forest** is home to **Cumberland Falls** and an accompanying resort. Called the "Niagara of the South," Cumberland Falls has a 125-foot-wide curtain that cascades 60 feet down into a rocky gorge. On clear nights lit by a full moon, you might see the moonbow created by mist from the falls.

Needless to say, history buffs will be delighted by Kentucky's wealth of Civil War history—including Confederate President Jefferson Davis's birthplace (Fairview) and **Blue Lick Battlefield State Resort**—which has been home to not only battles but prehistoric mammoths, Daniel Boone, and a popular health resort.

Travelers who might want to take a break from "roughing it" in favor of something more refined might want to check out the **Maker's Mark Distillery** near Loretto. Visitors literally walk through the meticulous process of creating this fine Kentucky bourbon. Visitors (at their own expense) can even add the traditional wax seal to their own bottle of bourbon. Of course, the **Kentucky Derby** at **Louisville's Churchill Downs** comes in May in all of its mint julep–soaked glory.

With Kentucky being the Bluegrass State, there's plenty of great music just about everywhere you go. Several great festivals occur throughout the year—even a cursory glance online will yield so many results that you should have no problem in squeezing some pickin' into your itinerary.

Throughout the state, you can find miles of trails, acres of lakes, and uncountable rivers, streams, mountains, and forests that make great places to park an RV or pitch a tent.

Campground Profiles

BARDSTOWN   MAP, B-2
My Old Kentucky Home State Park

reserve america

Hwy. 49, P. O. Box 323, 40004-0323.
T: (502) 348-3502 or (888) 459-7275;
www.reserveamerica.com.

🚐 ★★★★   ⛺ ★★★★

Beauty: ★★★★   Site Privacy: ★★★
Spaciousness: ★★★   Quiet: ★★
Security: ★★★   Cleanliness: ★★★★
Insect Control: ★★★★   Facilities: ★★★★

Though its proper name is Federal Hill Mansion, this park is known as "My Old Kentucky Home" because of its centerpiece immortalized in Stephen Foster's ballad of the same name. Visiting My Old Kentucky Home is a religious pilgrimage for many Kentuckians. For others, it's a fascinating way to learn about lifestyles of the aristocracy in antebellum Kentucky. The campground is just around the corner from the mansion. It's fairly attractive, with ample-sized sites. All sites are paved, with back-in parking. Though the campground would be a lot nicer without the telephone lines, sites are shaded by gorgeous mature trees. Our favorite sites, 19 and 21, enjoy views of the state park golf course. The campground is located in the heart of Bardstown and has no gates, making security fair. For less crowded touring, avoid My Old Kentucky Home on summer and holiday weekends.

BASICS

Operated By: State of Kentucky. **Open:** Year-round; hookups limited in winter. **Site Assignment:** Reservations suggested through www.reserve america.com, at parks.ky.gov, or (888) 459-7275. **Registration:** At campground office. **Fee:** $20; primitive, $12; up to 6 people; seniors/AAA, 10% off. **Parking:** On site.

FACILITIES

Number of RV-only Sites: 39. **Number of Tent-only Sites:** 15. **Hookups:** Electric (30 amps), water. **Each Site:** Picnic table & grill/fire ring. **Dump Station:** Yes. **Laundry:** Nearby. **Pay Phone:** No. **Restrooms and Showers:** Yes. **Fuel:** No. **Propane:** No. **Internal Roads:** Paved. **RV Service:** No. **Market:** Nearby. **Restaurant:** Nearby. **General Store:** Nearby. **Vending:** No. **Swimming:** No. **Playground:** Yes. **Activities:** Picnicking, golfing, tennis, outdoor drama, Christmas Candlelight tours. **Nearby Attractions:** Amphitheater, house museum.

RESTRICTIONS

Pets: On leash. **Fires:** Fire ring only. **Alcoholic Beverages:** Not allowed. **Vehicle Maximum Length:** No limit. **Other:** Check out at 2 p.m.

TO GET THERE

Located in Bardstown on US 150.

BENTON   MAP, A-1 INSET
Sportsman's Anchor Resort and Marina

12888 US 68 East, 42025.
T: (270) 354-8493 or (800) 326-3625;
www.anchorresortandmarina.com.

🚐 ★★★   ⛺ ★★★

Beauty: ★★★★   Site Privacy: ★★★
Spaciousness: ★★   Quiet: ★★★
Security: ★★★   Cleanliness: ★★★★
Insect Control: ★★★   Facilities: ★★★

Sportsman's Anchor is located in a remote though touristy area on Ruff Creek, a branch of Kentucky Lake. The RV sites are a bit small and on top of each other (no understory adds to lack of privacy), but those with boats will appreciate the adjacent full-service marina. The 15 tent-only primitive sites have more elbow room, and they are very attractive, especially for a private campground. The entire campground is shaded by pines and hardwood trees. However, there are no waterside sites, though the creek can be seen through the trees. There are not a lot of activities on the grounds—a pool and playground are located at the entrance—but Land Between the Lakes Recreation Area is only a five-minute drive away. There, visitors can hike, boat, ride horses, bike, or hunt.

BASICS

Operated By: Raymond and Lynn Meyers. **Open:** Seasonal. **Site Assignment:** Upon registration. **Registration:** At office. **Fee:** Full hookup, $27; water/electric, $25; tent, $18; based on 2 people; extra person, $4. **Parking:** On site.

FACILITIES

Number of RV-only Sites: 49. **Hookups:** Electric, water, sewer, cable TV. **Each Site:** Picnic table. **Dump Station:** Yes. **Laundry:** Yes. **Pay Phone:** No. **Restrooms and Showers:** Yes. **Fuel:** No (Gas dock in progress). **Propane:** No. **Internal Roads:** Gravel. **RV Service:** 15 mi. north. **Market:** Yes. **Restaurant:** 1 mi. **General Store:** Yes. **Vending:** No. **Swimming:** Yes (seasonal). **Playground:** Yes. **Other:** Gift shop, country store, rental cottages. **Activities:** Game room, shuffleboard, fishing, boat rentals. **Nearby Attractions:** Kentucky Dam Village State Park, Land Between the Lakes. **Additional Information:** Park Manager.

RESTRICTIONS

Pets: On leash; not in rental units. **Fires:** Small on site (no fire rings). **Alcoholic Beverages:** In covered container only. **Vehicle Maximum Length:** 40 ft.

TO GET THERE

From I-24 East take Exit 25A at Purchase Pkwy. Go south to Hwy. 68 exit and turn left, staying on Hwy. 68 about 14 mi. to resort. From I-24 West take Exit 65; go west on Hwy. 68, 33 mi. to resort.

BURKESVILLE   MAP, C-2
Dale Hollow Lake State Resort Park

reserve america

6371 State Park Rd., 42717-9728.
T: (270) 433-7431 or (800) 325-2282;
www.reserveamerica.com.

🚐 ★★★★   ⛺ ★★★★

Beauty: ★★★★★   Site Privacy: ★★
Spaciousness: ★★★   Quiet: ★★★★
Security: ★★★★★   Cleanliness: ★★★★★
Insect Control: ★★★   Facilities: ★★★★

Known for its clear, clean waters, Dale Hollow Lake attracts scuba divers, waterskiers, and anglers. With a former world record for smallmouth bass, the lake is hailed as one of the best fishing spots in the Southeast. Other catches include crappie, bream, muskie, walleye, and four more bass species. The campground is laid out on 18 cul-de-sacs containing eight sites each. Though sites are small, the campground feels open due to its layout and lack of understory. A few areas enjoy shade, but most lack trees. Parking pads are paved, back-in style. The equestrian camping area is the prettiest. If you left your horse at home, try areas L and N, which offer shady trees. Lucky for campers, there's a swimming pool at the campground. Remote and gated, this campground is very safe. Avoid Dale Hollow Lake on busy holiday weekends.

BASICS

Operated By: State of Kentucky. **Open:** Apr. 1–Oct. 31; 24 sites open all year w/ limited facilities. **Site Assignment:** Reservations suggested through www.reserveamerica.com or at (888) 459-7275. **Registration:** At camp office. **Fee:** $20–$22. **Parking:** On site.

FACILITIES

Number of Multipurpose Sites: 144. **Hookups:** Electric (15, 30, 50 amps), water. **Each Site:** Fire ring, table. **Dump Station:** Yes. **Laundry:** Yes. **Pay Phone:** Yes. **Restrooms and Showers:** Yes. **Fuel:** 3 mi. **Propane:** 9 mi. **Internal Roads:** Paved. **RV Service:** No. **Market:** No. **Restaurant:** Dining, 3 meals at the lodge. **General Store:** Yes. **Vending:** Yes. **Swimming:** Yes. **Playground:** Yes. **Other:** Public swimming lake, 24 equestrian camping sites. **Activities:** Skiing, fishing, boating hiking, scuba diving, biking, amphitheater, golf. **Nearby Attractions:** Nature trails, Tomkind Field, Cordell Hall, Alvin York's birthplace.

RESTRICTIONS

Pets: On leash. **Fires:** Fire ring only. **Alcoholic Beverages:** Not allowed. **Vehicle Maximum Length:** No limit. **Other:** Check out 2 p.m.

TO GET THERE

From I-65, exit at Cumberland parkway (Exit No. 43) and take KY 90 east at Glasgow. Take KY 90 to KY 449 south to KY 1206 to the State Park.

BURNSIDE MAP, C-3
General Burnside Island State Park

reserve america

8801 South Hwy. 27, P. O. Box 488, 42519-0488.
T: (606) 561-4104 or (606) 561-3625;
www.reserveamerica.com.

🚐 ★★★★ ⛺ ★★★★

Beauty: ★★★★ Site Privacy: ★★★★
Spaciousness: ★★★★ Quiet: ★★★★
Security: ★★★★ Cleanliness: ★★★★
Insect Control: ★★★ Facilities: ★★★★

General Burnside Island's campground rests on gentle, verdant hills and offers uncommonly tidy sites. Though site size varies, most are larger than average. About a dozen sites are totally open, but the rest are shaded by lovely mature trees. Many enjoy a measure of privacy. Sites offer paved, back-in style parking. Families should head for sites 1–4, right next to the playground. Other RV campers should try sites 30, 31, or 88, which are secluded. Very shady sites include 74 and 76. General Burnside Island is accessible by a bridge across 50, 000-acre Lake Cumberland and boasts excellent amenities. A well-appointed marina aids fishermen in their quest for crappie and largemouth, smallmouth, and striped bass. The park is incredibly isolated, making security good. Visit any time except summer holidays—there's plenty of elbow room on the island.

BASICS
Operated By: State of Kentucky. **Open:** Apr. 1–Oct. 31. **Site Assignment:** Reservations suggested through www.reserveamerica.com or at (888) 459-7275. **Registration:** At camp entrance. **Fee:** Electric, $18–$20; tent, $12. **Parking:** Site plus limited overflow parking.

FACILITIES
Number of RV-only Sites: 94. **Number of Tent-only Sites:** 16. **Hookups:** Electric, water. **Each Site:** Picnic table, fire ring. **Dump Station:** Yes. **Laundry:** Yes. **Pay Phone:** Yes. **Restrooms and Showers:** Yes. **Fuel:** No (8 mi., Somerset). **Propane:** No (8 mi., Somerset). **Internal Roads:** Paved. **RV Service:** No. **Market:** No. **Restaurant:** 4 mi. in Burnside. **General Store:** No. **Vending:** Soda. **Swimming:** Yes. **Playground:** Yes. **Other:** Boat rentals at the marina. **Activities:** Boating and fishing on Lake Cumberland, golf. **Nearby Attractions:** Cumberland State Resort Park, Cumberland Falls. **Additional Information:** Somerset CVB, (800) 642-6287.

RESTRICTIONS
Pets: On leash, no tying to trees or bushes, clean up after. **Fires:** Fire ring only. **Alcoholic Beverages:** Not publicly displayed. **Vehicle Maximum Length:** No limit. **Other:** Firearms & fireworks not allowed.

TO GET THERE
From Somerset, go 8 mi. south on US 27 and turn left at General Burnside sign.

CADIZ MAP, C-1
Lake Barkley State Resort Park

reserve america

3500 State Park Rd., P. O. Box 700, 42211-0790.
T: (270) 924-1131 or (800) 325-1708;
www.reserveamerica.com.

🚐 ★★★★ ⛺ ★★★★

Beauty: ★★★★★ Site Privacy: ★★★★
Spaciousness: ★★★★ Quiet: ★★★★
Security: ★★★ Cleanliness: ★★★★
Insect Control: ★★★ Facilities: ★★★★★

There are an abundance of campgrounds to choose from in western Kentucky. Campers wishing to pamper themselves should visit Lake Barkley. Located close to the Land Between the Lakes Recreation Area, Lake Barkley has 78 RV sites with water and electric hookups. The sites are larger than average, and a gorgeous forest surrounds the campground. What's intriguing is the number of activities available, both on site and off. The heart of the resort is the Fitness Center, where Nautilus machines and fitness cycles await, preceding an inviting sauna and massage. There is also an indoor heated pool for the winter months. Those desiring more outdoors-oriented activities can fish, swim, or waterski on Lake Barkley, practice their aim at the local trapshoot range, or enjoy over nine miles of hiking trails. This is a popular place; the lodge and cottages book nearly a year in advance—RVs have a distinct advantage as there are no advance reservations.

BASICS
Operated By: State of Kentucky. **Open:** Apr. 1–Nov. 1. **Site Assignment:** Reservations suggested through www.reserveamerica.com or at (888) 459-7275. **Registration:** At office. **Fee:** Water/electric, $17–$19; electric, $12–$14. **Parking:** On site.

FACILITIES
Number of Multipurpose Sites: 78. **Hookups:** Electric (15 amps), water. **Each Site:** Picnic table. **Dump Station:** Yes. **Laundry:** Yes. **Pay Phone:** Courtesy phone. **Restrooms and Showers:** Yes. **Fuel:** No. **Propane:** No. **Internal Roads:** Paved. **RV Service:** No. **Market:** Nearby at lodge. **Restaurant:** Nearby at lodge. **General Store:** No. **Vending:** Soda. **Swimming:** Beach nearby. **Playground:** Yes. **Other:** Fitness center, heated indoor pool, racquetball court, tanning beds, rental cottages. **Activities:** Fishing, boating, lake swimming, golf, tennis, hiking, mountain biking. **Nearby Attractions:** Jefferson Davis Monument State Historic Site.

RESTRICTIONS
Pets: On leash. **Fires:** Fire pit only. **Alcoholic Beverages:** Not allowed. **Vehicle Maximum Length:** 54 ft. (varies according to site).

TO GET THERE
29 mi. west of Hopkinsville. Take US 68 west to KY 1489.

CAMPBELLSVILLE MAP, B-2, C-2
Green River Lake State Park

reserve america

179 Park Office Rd., 42718. T: (270) 465-8255;
www.reserveamerica.com.

🚐 ★★★★ ⛺ ★★★★

Beauty: ★★★ Site Privacy: ★★★
Spaciousness: ★★★ Quiet: ★★★
Security: ★★★ Cleanliness: ★★★★
Insect Control: ★★★ Facilities: ★★★★

Enjoy lakeside fun at the campground on the shores of the 8,200-acre lake at Green River Lake State Park. If you're a fan of water sports, you're sure to find something to fit the bill, with a sand beach along the lake's edge and a nearby marina offering rental houseboats, ski boats, jet skis, and pontoon boats. After a day on the lake, relax on the lakeshore campground and enjoy a beach just for campers. If you're more of a land-lubber, you'll have your pick of a variety of other activities, such as miniature golf, hiking, mountain biking, and horseback riding. Fresh air and good times couldn't be better than in this 156-site campground. A grocery, a dump station, and two central service buildings with showers, restrooms, and a laundry facility are available. For "reel" excitement enjoy a day of fishing at Green River Lake. Both the avid angler and the beginning fisherman will enjoy the challenge of fishing for white, largemouth, smallmouth, and Kentucky bass, bluegill, crappie, and muskie.

BASICS
Operated By: Kentucky State Parks. **Open:** Mar. 1–Oct. 31. **Site Assignment:** Reservations can be made up to 12 months in advance. **Registration:** At office. **Fee:** Single, $12–$30. **Parking:** At site.

FACILITIES
Number of Multipurpose Sites: 280. **Hookups:** Yes. **Dump Station:** Yes. **Laundry:** Yes. **Pay Phone:** Yes. **Restrooms and Showers:** Yes. **Fuel:** W/in 10 mi. **Propane:** Yes. **Internal Roads:** Paved. **RV Service:** No. **Market:** Yes. **Restaurant:** W/in 10 mi. **General Store:** Yes. **Vending:** Yes. **Swimming:** Yes. **Playground:** Yes. **Activities:** Amphitheater, biking, boating, fishing, hiking, horseback riding, jet skiing, jogging/running, picnicking, mini-golf, volleyball, waterskiing, wildlife viewing.

RESTRICTIONS
Other: Longer min.-night stays are required at most campgrounds during holiday periods.

TO GET THERE
Green River Lake State Park is 85 mi. from Louisville and Lexington. From Campbellsville, take Hwy. 55 south 4 mi.; turn on Hwy. 1061 and go 2 mi. to park entrance. From Bowling Green travel 90 mi. to Exit 43/Cumberland Pkwy. Take Exit 49/Hwy. 55 north through Columbia 15 mi.; turn on Hwy. 1061 and go 2 mi. to park entrance.

CARLISLE   MAP, B-3
Blue Licks Battlefield State Resort Park

reserve america

10299 Maysville Rd., 40311. T: (859) 289-5507; www.reserveamerica.com.

🚐 ★★★★   ⛺ ★★★★

Beauty: ★★★   Site Privacy: ★★★
Spaciousness: ★★★   Quiet: ★★★★
Security: ★★★★   Cleanliness: ★★★★
Insect Control: ★★★   Facilities: ★★★★

Throughout history, the salt springs at Blue Licks State Park have attracted prehistoric animals, Indians, and pioneers such as the legendary Daniel Boone. Many 19th-century southerners came to the area seeking the rejuvenation of the therapeutic, bubbling waters. Blue Licks is more widely known, however, as the site of the last Revolutionary War battle in Kentucky. In 1782, Kentuckians engaged Indians and British soldiers near the Licking River. Outnumbered, Kentucky suffered great losses, including one of Boone's sons. Boone's words, "Enough of honour cannot be paid," are inscribed on the monument dedicated to the fallen soldiers in the Battle of Blue Licks. Enjoy the great outdoors year-round at the campground featuring 51 campsites with utility hookups, a dump station, and a central service building with showers and restrooms. A junior Olympic-size pool is a great place to meet friends during the summer. An 18-hole mini-golf course, open seasonally, is perfect for family entertainment. Contact the park to determine whether the course is open during your stay.

BASICS
Operated By: Kentucky State Parks. **Open:** All year. **Site Assignment:** Reservations can be made up to 12 months in advance. **Registration:** At office. **Fee:** Single, $12–$24. **Parking:** At site.

FACILITIES
Number of Multipurpose Sites: 57. **Hookups:** Yes. **Dump Station:** Yes. **Laundry:** Yes. **Pay Phone:** No. **Restrooms and Showers:** Yes. **Fuel:** Less than 1 mi. **Propane:** No. **Internal Roads:** Paved. **RV Service:** No. **Market:** Less than 1 mi. **Restaurant:** Yes. **General Store:** Yes. **Vending:** No. **Swimming:** Yes. **Playground:** Yes. **Activities:** Art & museum, biking, bird-watching, boating, fishing, picnicking, mini-golf, sightseeing, stargazing, volleyball.

RESTRICTIONS
Other: Longer min.-night stays are required at most campgrounds during holiday periods.

TO GET THERE
From Lexington, KY, take Exit 113 from I-75. Turn left onto US 68E/US 27N/Paris Bypass Rd. Continue to follow US 68E/Paris Bypass Rd. Turn left onto Millersburg Rd./US 68 BR/Carlisle Rd. Continue to follow Millersburg Rd. Millersburg Rd. becomes US 68. Turn slight left onto US 68E/KY 36E. Continue to follow US 68E to park.

CARROLLTON   MAP, A-2
General Butler State Resort Park

reserve america

1608 Hwy. 227, 41008-0325. T: (502) 732-4384 or (866) 462-8853; www.reserveamerica.com.

🚐 ★★★★   ⛺ ★★★

Beauty: ★★★★   Site Privacy: ★★★
Spaciousness: ★★★   Quiet: ★★★
Security: ★★★   Cleanliness: ★★★★
Insect Control: ★★★★★   Facilities: ★★★

Named for William Orlando Butler, a Carrollton veteran of the War of 1812 and the American–Mexican War, General Butler State Resort Park has a pretty campground just outside of Carrollton. Set in a pleasant stretch of river valley at the confluence of the Kentucky and Ohio rivers (and on the shores of the 30-acre Butler Lake), the park is well forested with oaks and a variety of other trees. Campsites vary in size, and the parking areas are somewhat small, but the space between sites is usually acceptable. Lakeside campsites 55–59 and 86 are the most secluded and attractive. However, though Butler Lake has a swimming beach accessible to campers, swimming is contingent upon lifeguard availability. Also, the lake was noticeably overgrown with algae when we visited. Regardless, the variety of on-site activities make this campground a popular choice for families.

BASICS
Operated By: Kentucky State Parks. **Open:** Apr. 1–Oct. 31. **Site Assignment:** Reservations suggested through www.reserveamerica.com or at (888) 459-7275. **Registration:** At camp gate. **Fee:** Standard electric, $20–$22; nonpeak times, $12. **Parking:** On site.

FACILITIES
Number of Multipurpose Sites: 111. **Hookups:** Electric, water. **Each Site:** Table, fire ring. **Dump Station:** Yes. **Laundry:** Yes. **Pay Phone:** Courtesy phone. **Restrooms and Showers:** Yes. **Fuel:** No. **Propane:** No. **Internal Roads:** Paved. **RV Service:** No. **Market:** No. **Restaurant:** Yes, at lodge. **General Store:** No. **Vending:** Drinks. **Swimming:** Limited, at lodge. **Playground:** Yes. **Other:** Rental paddleboats, canoes, rowboats, & surf bikes, Butler-Turpin House, rental cottages. **Activities:** Nature trail, boat dock, golf course for fee. **Nearby Attractions:** Historic Carrollton, Outlet Shopping. **Additional Information:** www.carrolltonky.com.

RESTRICTIONS
Pets: On leash. **Fires:** Fire ring only. **Alcoholic Beverages:** Not allowed. **Vehicle Maximum Length:** No limit.

TO GET THERE
44 mi. northeast of Louisville. Take I-71 to Carrollton, Exit 44, go 3 mi. to campground.

CAVE CITY   MAP, C-2
Yogi Bear's Jellystone Park

reserve america

1002 Mammoth Cave Rd., 42127. T: (270) 773-3840 or (800) 523-1854; www.reserveamerica.com.

🚐 ★★★   ⛺ ★★★

Beauty: ★★★★   Site Privacy: ★★
Spaciousness: ★★★   Quiet: ★★★
Security: ★★★   Cleanliness: ★★★★
Insect Control: ★★★★   Facilities: ★★★★

Located three miles from the Entrance to Mammoth Cave National Park, Yogi's is a good choice for families with small children. The marvelous national park includes the world's largest surveyed cave plus vast acres of rolling hills above it. The cave was used by people as early as 2000 B.C., when prehistoric Americans mined for minerals. This isn't the most attractive Jellystone Park we've seen, but it has the kind of family-friendly amenities folks expect from Yogi, including a duck pond. Sites tend to be long and narrow and larger than average. Most sites offer pull-through, gravel parking. Choose from sites in Area A, which is more level, or Area B, which contains more spacious sites. Avoid this touristy area on summer and holiday weekends. And watch your valuables, as there are no gates at this bustling campground.

BASICS
Operated By: Kay and Bill Pott. **Open:** All year. **Site Assignment:** First come, first served except weekends and holidays for tents; reservations required for RV sites; 2-night minimum, 3-night minimum on holidays. **Registration:** At ranger station. **Fee:** Peak season rates: water/electric/sewer/TV, $43.25; water/electric/sewer, $41.25; water/electric, $37.19; primitive tent, $26.75. **Parking:** On site.

FACILITIES
Number of RV-only Sites: 150. **Number of Tent-only Sites:** 60. **Hookups:** Electric (20, 30, 50 amps), water, sewer, TV. **Each Site:** Picnic table, fire ring. **Dump Station:** Yes. **Laundry:** Yes. **Pay Phone:** During peak season only. **Restrooms and Showers:** Yes. **Fuel:** No. **Propane:** Yes. **Internal Roads:** Paved & gravel. **RV Service:** No. **Market:** No. **Restaurant:** No. **General Store:** Yes. **Vending:** Soda. **Swimming:** Yes. **Playground:** Yes. **Other:** Water slide, cabins, free Wi-Fi. **Activities:** Planned events, nature hikes, mini-golf, basketball, softball, outdoor big-screen movies. **Nearby Attractions:** Mammoth Cave National Park, wax museum, antique shops, Alpine Slide Fun Park, Dinosaur World. **Additional Information:** Checks are only accepted 2 weeks or more prior to arrival.

RESTRICTIONS
Pets: On leash, cleaned up after, barking controlled. Not allowed in rental cabins. **Fires:** Fire ring only. **Alcoholic Beverages:** At site only. **Vehicle Maximum Length:** No limit.

TO GET THERE

Take Cave City Exit No. 53 off I-65 and go 1 mi. west on Hwy. 70 to the park.

CORBIN — MAP, C-3
Cumberland Falls State Resort Park

reserve america

7351 Hwy. 90, 40701-8857. T: (606) 528-4121 or (800) 325-0063; www.reserveamerica.com.

🚐 ★★★   ⛺ ★★★

Beauty: ★★★★	Site Privacy: ★★★
Spaciousness: ★★★	Quiet: ★★★
Security: ★★★★	Cleanliness: ★★★
Insect Control: ★★★	Facilities: ★★★★

The campgrounds at Cumberland Falls aren't the tidiest we've ever seen, but they're reasonably attractive. Though site size varies, most are adequate. In the main campground, parking is paved. The nicest sites, 126–137, surround the cul-de-sac at the rear of the campground and offer back-in style parking. Sites 111–155 are downright plain. The smaller campground near the swimming pool is less developed and more attractive. Here, 13 sites with gravel parking line a shady mountain ridge. Known as the Niagara of the South, Cumberland Falls measures 125 feet in width and plunges 60 feet into the Cumberland River. Folks flock to the waterfall on full moon, when its mist creates a spectacular moon-bow. Park offerings, including numerous planned activities, are outstanding. To see the sights without hordes of people around you, try to plan a mid-week full-moon visit. Security is good at this remote park.

BASICS

Operated By: Kentucky State Parks. **Open:** Apr.–Oct. **Site Assignment:** Reservations suggested through www.reserveamerica.com or at (888) 459-7275. **Registration:** At camp store, after-hours register next morning. **Fee:** Electric, $17–$19; tent, $12. **Parking:** At site (2 cars), in parking lot.

FACILITIES

Number of RV-only Sites: 28. **Number of Tent-only Sites:** 50. **Hookups:** Electric (20, 30, 50 amps), water. **Each Site:** Picnic table, fire ring w/ grill. **Dump Station:** Yes. **Laundry:** Yes. **Pay Phone:** Yes. **Restrooms and Showers:** Yes. **Fuel:** No. **Propane:** Yes. **Internal Roads:** Paved. **RV Service:** 15 mi. in Corbin. **Market:** 15 mi. in Corbin. **Restaurant:** Park restaurant. **General Store:** Yes. **Vending:** Yes. **Swimming:** Yes. **Playground:** Yes. **Other:** Lodge, meeting room, Bob Blair Museum, stables, picnic areas, & pavilion. **Activities:** Fishing, boating, canoeing, rafting, nature trails, tennis, horseshoes, shuffleboard, bird-watching, guided equestrian trails, naturalist & recreation programs in summer, square dancing. **Nearby Attractions:** Cumberland, Eagle, Yahoo & Dog Slaughter Falls, Daniel Boone National Forest, Berea Crafts Center, White Hall State Historic Site, Fort Boonesborough State Park, Colonel Har-

land Sanders Café & Museum. **Additional Information:** Corbin Chamber of Commerce, (606) 528-6390.

RESTRICTIONS

Pets: On leash only. **Fires:** Fire ring only. **Alcoholic Beverages:** Cannot be publicly displayed. **Vehicle Maximum Length:** 36 ft. (sites vary). **Other:** 14-day stay limit, quiet hours enforced after 11 p.m.

TO GET THERE

From I-75, take Exit 15 (from the south) or 25 (from the north) and head west on US 25. Drive 7 mi. until merging w/ Hwy. 90. Drive another 7–8 mi. to the park, and the campground is on the left.

DAWSON SPRINGS — MAP, C-1
Pennyrile Forest State Resort Park

reserve america

20781 Pennyrile Lodge Rd., 42408-9212. T: (270) 797-3421 or (800) 325-1711; www.reserveamerica.com.

🚐 ★★★★   ⛺ ★★★★

Beauty: ★★★★	Site Privacy: ★★★
Spaciousness: ★★★	Quiet: ★★★★★
Security: ★★★★	Cleanliness: ★★★★
Insect Control: ★★★★	Facilities: ★★★★★

This campground is set in one of the most lush and beautiful forests in western Kentucky. Despite its relative closeness to the highway, the property has a remote and rural feel. Campsites are of moderate size and all have at least partial shade. With a huge range of on-site activities, Pennyrile Forest is a big hit with families; expect large crowds of children. There's plenty for everyone to do, including good fishing on Pennyrile Lake for bluegill, channel catfish, crappie, and largemouth bass. If you're done with water sports, seven hiking trails weave their way through the forested hills around the lake, ranging from easy, level rambles to more rugged hikes. Both a nine-hole regulation golf course and a quirky mini-golf course are available for campers' use.

BASICS

Operated By: Kentucky State Parks. **Open:** Apr.–Oct. **Site Assignment:** Reservations suggested through www.reserveamerica.com or at (888) 459-7275. **Registration:** At lodge or store. **Fee:** Standard electric, $17–$19 in peak season. **Parking:** On site.

FACILITIES

Number of Multipurpose Sites: 68. **Hookups:** Electric (15, 20, 30, 50 amps), water during season. **Each Site:** Table, grill. **Dump Station:** Yes. **Laundry:** Yes. **Pay Phone:** No. **Restrooms and Showers:** Yes. **Fuel:** No. **Propane:** No. **Internal Roads:** Paved. **RV Service:** No. **Market:** 3 mi. on Hwy 109. **Restaurant:** Yes. **General Store:** Yes. **Vending:** Soda. **Swimming:** Yes. **Playground:** Yes. **Other:** Public beach, nature trails, canoe & paddleboat rentals, rental cottages. **Activities:** Golf course for fee, mini-golf for fee, boat dock, fishing, tennis, basket-

ball. **Nearby Attractions:** Trail of Tears.

RESTRICTIONS

Pets: On leash. **Fires:** Fire ring only. **Alcoholic Beverages:** Not publicly displayed. **Vehicle Maximum Length:** No limit.

TO GET THERE

20 mi. northeast of Hopkinsville on KY 109 North from western Kentucky Pkwy., exit at Dawson Springs and take KY 103 south, 9 mi. to campground.

DUNMOR — MAP, C-1
Lake Malone State Park

reserve america

P.O. Box 93, 42339. T: (270) 657-2111; www.reserveamerica.com.

🚐 ★★★★   ⛺ ★★★★

Beauty: ★★★	Site Privacy: ★★★
Spaciousness: ★★★	Quiet: ★★★★★
Security: ★★★★★	Cleanliness: ★★★★
Insect Control: ★★★	Facilities: ★★★★

Spanning 788 lake acres, Lake Malone captures Kentucky's beauty in a small package. The lake is enclosed by dramatic 50-foot sandstone bluffs rising above the water's edge and surrounded by hardwood forests. The park has a campground, marina, beach, and hiking trail. Discover the beautiful landscape of Lake Malone State Park on the 1.5-mile Laurel Trail. This easy-rated hiking trail provides picturesque views of many rock walls, once used as shelters by Native Americans. Mountain laurel, holly, dogwood, and wildflowers provide a rich tapestry of native flora. Natural wonders abound in this secluded wilderness! Enjoy a symphony of starlight and a chorus of nature camping amid the great outdoors! Over 100 primitive sites are available for tent camping. Twenty campsites are equipped with electric and water hookups to accommodate recreational vehicles. A central service building in the campground offers showers, restrooms, and a laundry; and for completed camping convenience, campsites have grills and picnic tables.

BASICS

Operated By: Kentucky State Parks. **Open:** Apr. 10–Oct. 31. **Site Assignment:** Reservations can be made up to 12 months in advance. **Registration:** At office. **Fee:** Single, $17–$19. **Parking:** At site.

FACILITIES

Number of Multipurpose Sites: 77. **Hookups:** Yes. **Dump Station:** No. **Laundry:** Yes. **Pay Phone:** Yes. **Restrooms and Showers:** Yes. **Fuel:** Yes. **Propane:** No. **Market:** No. **Restaurant:** More than 10 mi. **General Store:** Yes. **Vending:** No. **Swimming:** Yes. **Playground:** Yes. **Activities:** Boating, canoeing, fishing, hiking, horseshoes, jet skiing, jogging/running, photography, picnicking, waterskiing, volleyball, wildlife viewing.

RESTRICTIONS

Other: Longer min.-night stays are required at most campgrounds during holiday periods.

TO GET THERE

Lake Malone is 22 mi. south of Central City. From the Western Kentucky Pkwy. exit at Central City, take US 431 to KY 973 and follow signs to the park. From Greenville, take 181 south to KY 973 and go 5 mi. to park.

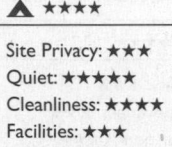

14500 Falls of Rough , 40119-6313.
T: (270) 879-4304; www.reserveamerica.com.

🚐 ★★★★   ⛺ ★★★★

Beauty: ★★★★   Site Privacy: ★★★
Spaciousness: ★★★   Quiet: ★★★★★
Security: ★★★★★   Cleanliness: ★★★★
Insect Control: ★★★   Facilities: ★★★

Cave Creek Campground has 86 sites, boat launching ramp, dump station, pit restrooms, potable water and telephone. Rough River Lake lies within the "Clifty" area of the Pennyroyal Region of Kentucky. A wide variety of recreational opportunities and facilities has been provided for visitor enjoyment by the Corps and the Commonwealth of Kentucky. Visitation at the lake now exceeds 2 million visitor days annually. At Rough River Lake many visitors enjoy seeing the historic Green Farm nearby, consisting of about 3,000 acres, a large ancestral home, an old water-powered mill and store, and a 18-hole golf course, Lafayette Green. The original land grant went to former Kentucky Supreme Court Justice Benjamin Sebastian, who was a co-conspirator with Aaron Burr. George Washington once owned part of the land. Be sure to enjoy some of Cave Creek's water recreation activities choose from boating, fishing, or swimming.

BASICS

Operated By: U.S. Army Corps of Engineers. **Open:** Apr. 20–Sept. 15. **Site Assignment:** Reservations must be made at least 2 days in advance. **Registration:** At office. **Fee:** Single, $9–$13. **Parking:** At site.

FACILITIES

Number of Multipurpose Sites: 246. **Hookups:** None. **Dump Station:** Yes. **Laundry:** No. **Pay Phone:** Yes. **Restrooms and Showers:** Yes. **Fuel:** No. **Propane:** No. **Internal Roads:** Paved. **RV Service:** No. **Market:** No. **Restaurant:** No. **General Store:** No. **Vending:** No. **Swimming:** No. **Playground:** Yes. **Activities:** Boating.

RESTRICTIONS

Pets: Pets must be restrained or on a leash at all times while in developed recreation areas. **Fires:** In fire rings, stoves, grills, or fireplaces provided for that purpose. **Alcoholic Beverages:** Not allowed. **Vehicle Maximum Length:** Call ahead. **Other:** No ORVs allowed.

TO GET THERE

From Elizabethtown, KY, travel the Western KY Pkwy. to the Leitchfield exit, then north on Hwy. 259 to Hwy. 54. Travel west on Hwy. 54 for 11 mi. to Hwy. 79, then 6 mi. to Hwy. 736. Go 2 mi. east on Hwy. 736 to the campground entrance.

14500 Falls of Rough Rd., 40119-6313.
T: (270) 257-8139 or (270) 257-2061;
www.reserveamerica.com.

🚐 ★★★   ⛺ ★★★

Beauty: ★★★★   Site Privacy: ★★★
Spaciousness: ★★★   Quiet: ★★★
Security: ★★★★   Cleanliness: ★★★★
Insect Control: ★★★   Facilities: ★★★

North Fork Park lies in the northern area of the Pennyroyal Region of Kentucky, a place where ancient sandstone, shale, and limestone cliffs abound. This is also the land of caves, and Mammoth Cave lies about 40 miles to the south. North Fork Park is rural in the extreme; if you aren't content to enjoy the peepers and birds while camping here, you'll feel quite isolated. You'll have plenty to do if you enjoy hiking, boating, and swimming. Be sure to provision yourself well—it is a long drive to pick up anything forgotten. There are only a few pull-through sites in this 107-site park, with electric and water hookups available at most sites. The best views can be had from sites 6–11, though 86–88 have nice views too.

BASICS

Operated By: U.S. Army Corps of Engineers. **Open:** Mid-Apr.–mid-Sept. **Site Assignment:** Reservation at least 2 weeks in advance, (877) 444-6777. **Registration:** At toll house. **Fee:** $16–$21. **Parking:** In designated areas.

FACILITIES

Number of Multipurpose Sites: 106. **Hookups:** Electric (50 amps), water. **Each Site:** Picnic table, grill. **Dump Station:** Yes. **Laundry:** No. **Pay Phone:** No. **Restrooms and Showers:** Yes. **Fuel:** No. **Propane:** No. **Internal Roads:** Paved. **RV Service:** No. **Market:** No. **Restaurant:** No. **General Store:** No. **Vending:** No. **Swimming:** Beach. **Playground:** Yes. **Activities:** Boating, hiking, horseshoes, special events. **Nearby Attractions:** Mammoth Caves, Limestone Cliffs. **Additional Information:** (502) 257-8139.

RESTRICTIONS

Pets: On leash. **Fires:** Only in designated areas. **Alcoholic Beverages:** Not allowed. **Vehicle Maximum Length:** 64 ft.

TO GET THERE

The campground is 70 mi. southwest of Louisville, KY. Take US 60, go 10 mi. to Harred, KY. Go 9 mi. west on Hwy. 79 to the campground entrance.

450 Lodge Rd., 40119-6100. T: (270) 257-2311 or (800) 325-1713; www.reserveamerica.com.

🚐 ★★★   ⛺ ★★★

Beauty: ★★★★   Site Privacy: ★★★
Spaciousness: ★★★   Quiet: ★★★★
Security: ★★★★★   Cleanliness: ★★★★
Insect Control: ★★★★   Facilities: ★★★★

Situated on 4,860-acre Rough River Lake, this state resort park runs a marina with 150 rental slips. Fishermen head back to shore with Kentucky bass, bluegill, channel catfish, crappie, and rough fish. Unique park facilities include a 3,200-foot airstrip, air camp, and shuttle service to the lodge. Though the attractive campground lines the Rough River, sites don't enjoy water views. There are both back-in and pull-through sites, with patchy gravel parking. Most sites are well shaded, but there is little undergrowth to provide privacy between sites. Sites are larger than average. RV campers should head for one of the 33 pull-through sites, 32–66. Tent campers should head for site 4 or 5, at the end of a pretty little spur. This park rarely fills to capacity, so it's an excellent destination for all but the busiest holiday weekends. Visit in spring to enjoy dogwood and redbud blooms. Security is excellent at this isolated park.

BASICS

Operated By: Kentucky State Parks. **Open:** Apr. 1–Oct. 31. **Site Assignment:** Reservations suggested through www.reserveamerica.com or at (888) 459-7275. **Registration:** At office. **Fee:** Electric, $20–$22; tent, $12. **Parking:** Camp Site and Main Lodge.

FACILITIES

Number of RV-only Sites: 32. **Hookups:** Electric (15, 20, 35 amps), water, sewer. **Each Site:** Fire ring. **Dump Station:** Yes. **Laundry:** Yes. **Pay Phone:** No. **Restrooms and Showers:** Yes. **Fuel:** No. **Propane:** No. **Internal Roads:** Paved & gravel. **RV Service:** No. **Market:** No. **Restaurant:** Yes. **General Store:** Nearby. **Vending:** Yes. **Swimming:** Beach. **Playground:** Yes. **Other:** Public beach, air camp for aviators. **Activities:** Marina fishing, nature trail, golf, mini-golf, recreation courts, tennis, basketball. **Nearby Attractions:** Manmade Falls antique shops, outdoor theatre.

RESTRICTIONS

Pets: On leash. **Fires:** Fire ring only. **Alcoholic Beverages:** Not allowed. **Vehicle Maximum Length:** Call ahead for details. **Other:** 14-day stay limit. Can be extended w/ management's approval.

TO GET THERE

Located on KY 79. From Western Kentucky Pkwy., Exit KY 79 north from Caneyville or exit on KY 259 north at Leithfield and travel 18 mi. to park via KY 54 from Leithfield.

FALMOUTH — MAP, A-3
Kincaid Lake State Park

reserve america

565 Kincaid Park Rd., 41040-9203.
T: (859) 654-3531; www.reserveamerica.com.

🚐 ★★★   ⛺ ★★★

Beauty: ★★★	Site Privacy: ★★
Spaciousness: ★★★	Quiet: ★★★
Security: ★★★★	Cleanliness: ★★★★
Insect Control: ★★★	Facilities: ★★★★★

Located near the historic town of Falmouth, Kincaid Lake is a quaint state park tucked far from any major development and noise. Tent-only sites, which outnumber RV sites, are mainly primitive. The RV sites are fairly close together, but some of them are pretty deep. Phone lines running throughout the campground detract from its beauty. The shadiest and most tranquil area of the campground can be found at sites 42–52. All of these sites are back-ins and have electric and water hookups during the season. Activities include boating on Kincaid Lake (rentals available), hiking along the parks nature trail, as well as swimming and mini-golf. Those who brig a fishing rod will be pleased with the large population of keeper- and trophy-sized largemouth bass. The Licking River is also nearby; a livery rents boats for interested parties.

BASICS
Operated By: Kentucky State Parks. **Open:** All year; limited staff in winter. **Site Assignment:** Reservations suggested through www.reserve america.com or at (888) 459-7275. **Registration:** At camp office. **Fee:** Standard electric, $20–$22 in peak season. **Parking:** On site.

FACILITIES
Number of RV-only Sites: 84. **Number of Tent-only Sites:** 125. **Hookups:** Electric (20, 30, 50 amps), water. **Each Site:** Picnic table. **Dump Station:** Yes. **Laundry:** Yes. **Pay Phone:** Yes. **Restrooms and Showers:** Yes. **Fuel:** Yes. **Propane:** Yes. **Internal Roads:** Paved. **RV Service:** No. **Market:** Yes. **Restaurant:** No. **General Store:** Yes. **Vending:** Soda. **Swimming:** Yes (fee). **Playground:** Yes. **Other:** Amphitheater, 9-hole golf course. **Activities:** Boat rental, fishing, mini-golf (fee), hiking, tennis, athletic multicourses. **Nearby Attractions:** Historic Falmouth, Kincaid regional Theatre. **Additional Information:** Park Manager (Jeff P. Auchter).

RESTRICTIONS
Pets: On leash. **Fires:** Fire ring only. **Alcoholic Beverages:** Not allowed. **Vehicle Maximum Length:** No limit. **Other:** 14-day stay limit, unless w/ permission of park management.

TO GET THERE
48 mi. southeast of Covington. Take I-275 East to US 27 South to Falmouth and KY 159 to the park.

FRANKFORT — MAP, B-3
Lake Barkley State Resort Park

reserve america

P.O. BOX 790, 42211. T: (270) 924-1131; www.reserveamerica.com.

🚐 ★★★★   ⛺ ★★★★

Beauty: ★★★	Site Privacy: ★★
Spaciousness: ★★	Quiet: ★★★★★
Security: ★★★★★	Cleanliness: ★★★★
Insect Control: ★★★	Facilities: ★★★★

World-class Lake Barkley lodge, designed by Edward Durrell Stone, seems to have just emerged naturally from the wooded shoreline that surrounds it. The grand scale, post-and-beam wood construction features 3.5 acres of glass offering outstanding views of Lake Barkley. In addition to the outdoor pool overlooking the lake, the resort has a heated indoor pool. Our fitness center offers executive treatment with Nautilus equipment, fitness cycles, a weight room, racquet ball court, tanning beds, sauna, whirlpool and fitness trainers. In addition to accommodations in the main lodge, the resort has the secluded Little River Lodge and several cottage styles to choose from. The 18-hole, par-71 Boots Randolph golf course is a challenge for even the most avid of golfers. Resort guests can also enjoy a spacious campground, full-service marina, a lighted airstrip, and trails for hiking and mountain biking. Find delight in the outdoors in the campground. The campground has 78 sites with utility hookups, a dump station, and two central service buildings with showers and restrooms.

BASICS
Operated By: Kentucky State Parks. **Open:** Apr. 1–Oct. 31. **Site Assignment:** Reservations can be made up to 12 months in advance. **Registration:** At office. **Fee:** Single, $12–$19. **Parking:** At site.

FACILITIES
Number of Multipurpose Sites: 79. **Hookups:** Yes. **Dump Station:** Yes. **Laundry:** Yes. **Pay Phone:** Yes. **Restrooms and Showers:** Yes. **Fuel:** Yes. **Propane:** No. **Internal Roads:** Paved. **RV Service:** No. **Market:** W/in 10 mi. **Restaurant:** Yes. **General Store:** Yes. **Vending:** Yes. **Swimming:** Yes. **Playground:** Yes. **Activities:** Amphitheater, archery, biking, bird-watching, boating, fishing, golfing, horseshoes, jet skiing, jogging/running, photography, picnicking, waterskiing, stargazing, tennis, volleyball, wildlife viewing.

RESTRICTIONS
Other: Longer min.-night stays are required at most campgrounds during holiday periods.

TO GET THERE
Lake Barkley State Resort Park is located 8 mi. west of Cadiz on US 68. Take Exit 65 off I-24 onto US 68. Head west 15 mi. to the entrance of the park.

GILBERTSVILLE — MAP, A-1
Kentucky Dam Village State Resort Park

reserve america

P.O. Box 69, 42044. T: (270) 362-4271; www.reserveamerica.com.

🚐 ★★★★   ⛺ ★★★★

Beauty: ★★★	Site Privacy: ★★★
Spaciousness: ★★★	Quiet: ★★★★
Security: ★★★★	Cleanliness: ★★★★
Insect Control: ★★★	Facilities: ★★★★

Kentucky Dam Village is one of three state resort parks near Land Between the Lakes National Recreation Area, a 170,000-acre wooded peninsula bound by Kentucky Lake and Lake Barkley. The abundance of water offers uncrowded cruising, waterskiing, and fishing. With its wide choice of accommodations, excellent marina, and fine dining, Kentucky Dam Village State Resort Park is one of Kentucky's most popular resorts. Relax in one of the cottages or in the main lodge with private balconies or patios overlooking Kentucky Lake. If golf is your game, stay at the Village Green Inn, next to the 18-hole golf course. The park's campground offers 221 paved campsites with water and electricity hookups, a grocery store, two dump stations, and four central service buildings with showers and restrooms. For location of the campground, check our site map. Fishing enjoyment never ceases at Kentucky Dam Village! With an abundance of largemouth, smallmouth, Kentucky and white bass, bluegill, channel and blue catfish, crappie, and sauger, Kentucky Lake is the perfect year-round vacation spot for the avid angler!

BASICS
Operated By: Kentucky State Parks. **Open:** All year. **Site Assignment:** Reservations can be made up to 12 months in advance. **Registration:** At office. **Fee:** Single, $12–$22. **Parking:** At site.

FACILITIES
Number of Multipurpose Sites: 217. **Hookups:** Yes. **Dump Station:** Yes. **Laundry:** Yes. **Pay Phone:** W/in 10 mi. **Restrooms and Showers:** Yes. **Fuel:** Yes. **Propane:** W/in 10 mi. **Internal Roads:** Paved. **RV Service:** No. **Market:** Yes. **Restaurant:** Yes. **General Store:** Yes. **Vending:** No. **Swimming:** Yes. **Playground:** Yes. **Activities:** Bird-watching, boating, fishing, golfing, jet skiing, jogging/running, picnicking, sail boating, waterskiing, stargazing, tennis, volleyball, wildlife viewing.

RESTRICTIONS
Other: Longer min.-night stays are required at most campgrounds during holiday periods.

TO GET THERE
Exit 27 off I-24 onto US 62 east, to Hwy. 282 north. Campground will be about 0.5 mi. on right.

GLASGOW   MAP, C-2
The Narrows at Barren River Lake

11088 Finney Rd., 42141-9642. T: (270) 646-3094 or (270) 646-2055.

🚐 ★★★★   ⛺ ★★★★

Beauty: ★★★★   Site Privacy: ★★★
Spaciousness: ★★★★   Quiet: ★★★★
Security: ★★★★★   Cleanliness: ★★★
Insect Control: ★★★   Facilities: ★★★

This campground is a bit disappointing compared to other superb U.S. Army Corps of Engineers campgrounds in the Southeast. Though attractive, parts of the campground need maintenance work. There are weeds popping up through the gravel parking pads. Campsites are larger than average, with back-in parking. Some are well shaded, while others are more open. If you have a big rig, your site choices may be limited, as pad length varies. Our favorites are in Area B. Sites 31 and 32 boast lake views and ample shade. For tent campers, sites 1, 2, 43, 45, 47, 49, and 50 have no hookups but nestle into the woods and offer seclusion. Remote and gated, the campground has outstanding security. Fishing in Barren River Lake affords shots at bluegill; channel catfish; crappie; rough fish; and largemouth, white, and hybrid striped bass. In the area, many commercial marinas and bait shops cater to fishermen. Avoid Barren River Lake on busy summer holidays and weekends.

BASICS

Operated By: U.S. Army Corps of Engineers. **Open:** Mid-Apr.–mid-Sept. **Site Assignment:** Reservations suggested through www.reserve america.com or at (888) 459-7275. **Registration:** At fee station. **Fee:** $20. **Parking:** On site.

FACILITIES

Number of Multipurpose Sites: 90. **Hookups:** Electric (50 amps), water. **Each Site:** Picnic table, fire ring, work table. **Dump Station:** Yes. **Laundry:** Yes. **Pay Phone:** No. **Restrooms and Showers:** Yes. **Fuel:** No. **Propane:** No. **Internal Roads:** Paved. **RV Service:** No. **Market:** Nearby. **Restaurant:** Nearby. **General Store:** Nearby. **Vending:** No. **Swimming:** Beach. **Playground:** Yes. **Activities:** Fishing, boating, swimming in lake. **Nearby Attractions:** Buckhorn Dam Overlook, Mammoth Cave National Park.

RESTRICTIONS

Pets: On leash. **Fires:** Only in designated areas. **Alcoholic Beverages:** Not allowed. **Vehicle Maximum Length:** No limit. **Other:** Max 6 people per site.

TO GET THERE

From Glasgow, take Hwy. 31 east for 10 mi.; turn right on 1318. Follow the signs.

GREENUP   MAP, B-4
Greenbo Lake State Resort Park

reserve america™

HC 60 Box 52, 41144-9517. T: (606) 473-7324 or (800) 325-0083; www.reserveamerica.com.

🚐 ★★★   ⛺ ★★★

Beauty: ★★★★   Site Privacy: ★★
Spaciousness: ★★★   Quiet: ★★★
Security: ★★★★   Cleanliness: ★★★★
Insect Control: ★★★   Facilities: ★★★★★

The attractive campground at Greenbo Lake is laid out in three spurs and a loop adjacent to Claylick Creek. There are average-sized sites with paved, back-in parking. With woods flanking the campground, some sites enjoy cool shade, while others are totally open. Privacy is minimal. For families we recommend sites 29 and 30 near the wash house and playground. For tent campers, we recommend 16 and 17, tucked into the back of the primitive area. Security is passable; there are no gates, but the park is remote. Visit during the week in the summertime. This park's myriad recreation draws massive crowds. Children love the corkscrew water slide at the swimming pool. The state park is also a hiking haven, with 25 miles of easy-to-challenging hiking. With two largemouth-bass records, fishing in the 225-acre Greenbo Lake is excellent.

BASICS

Operated By: Kentucky State Parks. **Open:** All year. **Site Assignment:** Reservations suggested through www.reserveamerica.com or at (888) 459-7275. **Registration:** At check-in station. **Fee:** Electric, $20–$22; no electric, $12; tent, $12. **Parking:** At site (2 cars), in parking lot.

FACILITIES

Number of Tent-only Sites: 35. **Number of Multipurpose Sites:** 63. **Hookups:** Electric (30 amps), water. **Each Site:** Picnic table, grill, fire ring, asphalt pad. **Dump Station:** Yes. **Laundry:** Yes. **Pay Phone:** Yes. **Restrooms and Showers:** Yes. **Fuel:** No. **Propane:** No. **Internal Roads:** Paved. **RV Service:** 10 mi. in Greenup. **Market:** 5–10 mi. in Greenup. **Restaurant:** Park restaurant. **General Store:** Yes. **Vending:** Yes. **Swimming:** Yes (Memorial Day–Labor Day). **Playground:** Yes. **Other:** Lodge, marina, picnic area, & shelters. **Activities:** Water sports (no jet ski), canoe, pontoon, paddleboat, rowboat, & motorboat rentals, fishing, hiking trails, mini-golf, tennis, basketball, bicycle rentals, summer organized activities, waterslide. **Nearby Attractions:** Golf course, Jesse Stuart birthplace, Kentucky Highlands Museum & Discovery Center, Paramount Arts Center, McConnell House, Carter Caves & Grayson Lake State Parks. **Additional Information:** Boyd/Greenup Counties Chamber of Commerce, (606) 324-5111.

RESTRICTIONS

Pets: On leash only. **Fires:** At sites, fire rings, only. **Alcoholic Beverages:** Allowed in cup, not original container. **Vehicle Maximum Length:** 45 ft. (sites vary). **Other:** 14-day stay limit, no ATVs.

TO GET THERE

From I-64, take Exit 172 and drive 18 mi. north on KY 1. Turn left onto KY 1711/State Park Rd. and the campground is 3 mi. on the left.

HARDIN   MAP, A-1 INSET
Kenlake State Resort Park

reserve america™

542 Kenlake Rd., 42048-9737. T: (270) 474-2211 or (800) 325-0143; www.reserveamerica.com.

🚐 ★★★★   ⛺ ★★★★

Beauty: ★★★★   Site Privacy: ★★★★
Spaciousness: ★★★★   Quiet: ★★★★
Security: ★★★★   Cleanliness: ★★★★
Insect Control: ★★★   Facilities: ★★★★★

Located minutes from the 170,000-acre Land Between the Lakes National Recreation Area, the campground at Kenlake State Resort Park rests on the western shore of Kentucky Lake. You don't have to be a boat enthusiast to visit, but water activities are a significant reason people come here. The 90 back-in sites (each with water and electric hookups) have small parking areas, but the space in between sites is more than adequate. There are only three pull-through sites available. There are only a few waterfront sites (62–69 and 24–29); they are pretty but the ground is not level. The campground is separated from the rest of the resort by Hwy. 68, so while the resort offers tennis, golfing, and some hiking, you might as well visit Land Between the Lakes since you have to get in your car anyway. The resort is host to several festivals throughout the year, including the Hot August Blues Festival and the Aurora County Festival.

BASICS

Operated By: State of Kentucky. **Open:** Apr. 1–Oct. 31. **Site Assignment:** Reservations suggested through www.reserveamerica.com or at (888) 459-7275. **Registration:** At entrance building. **Fee:** Electric, $18–$20; no electric, $16; in peak season. **Parking:** In designated areas assigned, must have car pass/visitor pass visible.

FACILITIES

Number of RV-only Sites: 50. **Number of Tent-only Sites:** 40. **Hookups:** Electric (20, 30, 50 amps), water, sewer. **Each Site:** Picnic table, fire ring. **Dump Station:** Yes. **Laundry:** Yes. **Pay Phone:** No. **Restrooms and Showers:** Yes. **Fuel:** 1.5 mi. **Propane:** 1.5 mi. **Internal Roads:** Paved. **RV Service:** No. **Market:** No, 0.5 mi. **Restaurant:** Yes. **General Store:** No. **Vending:** No. **Swimming:** Yes. **Playground:** Yes. **Other:** Meeting rooms. **Activities:** Fishing, boating, golf, tennis, nature trails, planned recreation. **Nearby Attractions:** Kentucky Dam Village SRP, Hardin Southern Railway, The Homeplace 1850, North-South Trail. **Additional Information:** State of Kentucky, (859) 384-3522.

RESTRICTIONS

Pets: On leash. **Fires:** Fire ring only. **Alcoholic Beverages:** Not allowed. **Vehicle Maximum Length:** No limit. **Other:** No firearms or fireworks.

TO GET THERE

40 mi. southeast of Paducah. Going east on I-24, exit to the Purchase Pkwy., then exit on US 68 east, going west on I-24. Take the Cadiz exit to US 68/KY 80 west.

HENDERSON   MAP, B-1
John James Audubon State Park

reserve america

3100 US 41 North, P.O. Box 576, 42419-0576. T: (270) 826-2247; www.reserveamerica.com.

🚐 ★★★   ⛺ ★★★

Beauty: ★★★★   Site Privacy: ★★★
Spaciousness: ★★★   Quiet: ★★
Security: ★★   Cleanliness: ★★★★
Insect Control: ★★★★ Facilities: ★★★★

Audubon State Park, a little green oasis in the city of Henderson, maintains nice sports facilities including a nine-hole golf course and fishing on the park's small lake. Anglers are rewarded with largemouth bass, bluegill, and catfish. Henderson residents are proud to know that John James Audubon lived here. Today, over 20 species of warblers visit the state park every spring. The campground is laid out in one large loop with three partitions. RV sites 1–28 and tent sites 8T–17T abut the highway and are not recommended. Quieter sites include RV sites 40–63 and tent sites 1T–7T. Site size and distance between sites vary, but most are adequate. Parking is paved, back-in style, with four pull-through sites. Almost all sites are well shaded by sycamore, cottonwood, and other species. There are no gates at this urban campground, making security iffy. Visit during the week to avoid summer crowds.

BASICS

Operated By: Kentucky State Parks. **Open:** All year. Staff available Apr. 1–Oct. 31. **Site Assignment:** Reservations suggested through www.reserveamerica.com or at (888) 459-7275. **Registration:** At entrance kiosk, self-register after hours. **Fee:** Peak season: standard electric, $18–$20; tent w/ water, $16; tent, $12. **Parking:** At site (2 cars).

FACILITIES

Number of RV-only Sites: 69. **Number of Tent-only Sites:** 10. **Hookups:** Electric (30 amps), water. **Each Site:** Picnic table, grill, fire ring. **Dump Station:** Yes. **Laundry:** Yes. **Pay Phone:** No. **Restrooms and Showers:** Yes. **Fuel:** No. **Propane:** No. **Internal Roads:** Paved. **RV Service:** 8 mi. in Evansville, IN. **Market:** 0.25 mi. **Restaurant:** W/in 1 mi. in Henderson. **General Store:** 0.5 mi. in Henderson. **Vending:** Yes. **Swimming:** No. **Playground:** Yes. **Other:** John James Audubon Museum & Nature Center, meeting rooms, picnic area & shelters, boat dock (trolling motors only). **Activities:** 9-hole golf course, pro shop, club & cart rentals, fishing, paddleboat rentals, canoe & hydrobike rentals, hiking trails, tennis (seasonal), ropes challenge course (w/ facilitator only), interpretive & recreation programs year-round. **Nearby Attractions:** Ellis Park Race Course, Aztar Casino Riverboat, Audubon Mill Park,

Wesselman Woods Nature Preserve, Angel Mounds Prehistoric Native American Site. **Additional Information:** Henderson Tourism Commission, (270) 826-3128; Evansville CVB, (800) 433-3025, www.evansvillecvb.org.

RESTRICTIONS

Pets: On leash only. No pets on trails except designated pet trail. **Fires:** Fire ring only. **Alcoholic Beverages:** Not allowed. **Vehicle Maximum Length:** 45 ft. (sites vary). **Other:** 14-day stay limit.

TO GET THERE

From the Pennyrile Pkwy., drive north until it merges w/ US 41. The park is 1.5 mi. north on the right.

JAMESTOWN   MAP, C-2
Lake Cumberland State Resort Park

reserve america

5465 State Park Rd., 42629-7801. T: (270) 343-3111 or (800) 325-1709; www.reserveamerica.com.

🚐 ★★★★   ⛺ ★★★★

Beauty: ★★★★   Site Privacy: ★★★★
Spaciousness: ★★★★   Quiet: ★★★
Security: ★★★   Cleanliness: ★★★★
Insect Control: ★★★   Facilities: ★★★★★

Set on a large peninsula protruding into the 50,250-acre Lake Cumberland, this extremely popular state resort park offers plenty to do and has an upscale feel. Unfortunately, the large crowds make for a hectic atmosphere, and they also somewhat overwhelm the staff's efforts to keep the campground clean. Many families means many children, as well as lots of cars, trucks, and other vehicles. Though campsite size varies, most sites are large, some quite close together. Some sites have both a nice forest canopy as well as screening ground foliage for privacy. The prettiest campsites are 19–21, 38, and 72–75. An unsightly telephone wire runs right through the loop of sites 49–52. Generally, the most visually attractive sites are not as level as others. The large lake means that all varieties of boating and water sports take up most campers' time here, but there are also various sports activities and a four-mile loop nature trail.

BASICS

Operated By: State of Kentucky. **Open:** Apr.–Nov. **Site Assignment:** Reservations suggested through www.reserveamerica.com or at (888) 459-7275. **Registration:** At entrance gate. **Fee:** Peak season: electric, $20–$22; no electric, $12–$14. **Parking:** On site.

FACILITIES

Number of RV-only Sites: 113. **Number of Tent-only Sites:** 34. **Hookups:** Electric (20 amps), water. **Each Site:** Picnic table, fire ring. **Dump Station:** Yes. **Laundry:** Yes. **Pay Phone:** Yes. **Restrooms and Showers:** Yes. **Fuel:** 5 mi. **Propane:** 5 mi. **Internal Roads:** Paved. **RV Service:** No. **Market:** Yes. **Restaurant:** Yes. **General Store:** Yes. **Vend-**

ing: Yes. **Swimming:** Yes. **Playground:** Yes. **Activities:** Golf, game room, mini-golf, stables, hiking, fishing. **Nearby Attractions:** Wolf Creek Dam & Fish Hatchery.

RESTRICTIONS

Pets: On leash. **Fires:** Fire ring only. **Alcoholic Beverages:** Not allowed. **Vehicle Maximum Length:** No limit.

TO GET THERE

Located 45 min. west of Somerset. Take Cumberland Pkwy. to US 127.

LEXINGTON   MAP, B-3
Kentucky Horse Park Campground

reserve america

4089 Iron Works Pkwy., 40511. T: (859) 259-4257 or (800) 370-6416; www.reserveamerica.com.

🚐 ★★★   ⛺ ★★★

Beauty: ★★★★   Site Privacy: ★★
Spaciousness: ★★★   Quiet: ★★★
Security: ★★   Cleanliness: ★★★★
Insect Control: ★★★★ Facilities: ★★★★

Beautiful Kentucky Horse Park rests on 1,200 acres of verdant rolling horse pasture enclosed and subdivided by 30 miles of pristine white fence. The park's mission is multifold. It's a working horse farm, educational facility (with two superb museums and two theaters), competition venue, and tasteful theme park. Children can pet ponies and enjoy a number of exhibitions and shows. The flat campground is passably attractive, with spruce fir and pine shading the sites. It's laid out in two concentric figure 8s, with sites in the rear (160–171 and 29–41) enjoying views of the polo fields. Medium-sized sites feature paved, back-in style parking, with short parking pads. The campground is convenient to restaurants in Lexington and outlet mall shopping in Georgetown. Security is marginal at this giant campground with no gates. Visit during the week for less crowded touring, but avoid weekdays in late spring when armies of school children invade.

BASICS

Operated By: Kentucky Tourism Development Cabinet. **Open:** All year; no water, Nov. 1–Apr. 1. **Site Assignment:** Reservations suggested at www.reserveamerica.com or call (888) 459-7275. **Registration:** At trading post, host makes rounds after hours. **Fee:** Peak season: standard electric, $27–$30; tent, $15–$18; tent w/ electricity, $20–$23. **Parking:** At site (2 cars), in parking lot.

FACILITIES

Number of Tent-only Sites: Undesignated sites. **Number of Multipurpose Sites:** 260. **Hookups:** Electric (20, 30, 50 amps), water. **Each Site:** Picnic table, fire ring, paved pad. **Dump Station:** Yes. **Laundry:** Yes. **Pay Phone:** Yes. **Restrooms and Showers:** Yes. **Fuel:** No. **Propane:** No. **Internal Roads:** Paved. **RV Service:** 5 mi. in Lexington. **Market:** 10 mi. in Georgetown. **Restaurant:** Park

Restaurant, w/in 4 mi. **General Store:** Camp store, 10 mi. in Georgetown (Wal-Mart). **Vending:** Yes. **Swimming:** Yes. **Playground:** Yes. **Other:** Pavilion, museum, gallery, gift shop. **Activities:** Horse drawn tours, riding shows, events, square dancing (occasional), tennis, croquet, volleyball, basketball, horseshoes. **Nearby Attractions:** Aviation Museum of Kentucky, Keeneland Race Course, Lexington Center/ Rupp Arena, Mary Todd Lincoln House, Thoroughbred Center, University of Kentucky. **Additional Information:** Lexington CVB, (800) 845-3959, www.visitlex.com.

RESTRICTIONS

Pets: On leash only. **Fires:** Fire ring only. **Alcoholic Beverages:** Not allowed. **Vehicle Maximum Length:** 45 ft. **Other:** 14-day stay limit.

TO GET THERE

From I-75 (2 mi. north of the junction w/ I-64), take Exit 120. The park is immediately on the east and the campground is on the east side of the park.

LONDON
Grove—Daniel Boone National Forest
MAP, C-3

London Ranger District, 40744. T: (606) 864-4163; www.reserveamerica.com.

🚐 ★★★★   ⛺ ★★★★

Beauty: ★★★	Site Privacy: ★★★
Spaciousness: ★★★★	Quiet: ★★★
Security: ★★★★	Cleanliness: ★★★★
Insect Control: ★★★★	Facilities: ★★

Grove Campground, located along the Cumberland Plateau in the Appalachian foothills of eastern Kentucky, is situated on a wooded ridge above Laurel River Lake, a 5,600-acre lake within the Daniel Boone National Forest. The forest encompasses over 706,000 acres of mostly rugged terrain. The land is characterized by steep forested ridges dissected by narrow ravines and over 3,400 miles of sandstone cliffs. These lands are federally managed to provide the nation with a sustained yield of natural resources, including wood, water, forage, and wildlife. Recreation opportunities are an added bonus. Millions of visitors come to enjoy the scenic beauty and abundant wildlife that the forest has to offer. Cave Run Lake and Laurel River Lake are popular attractions. Other special areas include the Red River Gorge Geological Area, Natural Arch Scenic Area, Clifty Wilderness, Beaver Creek Wilderness, and five wildlife management areas. Over 600 miles of trails provide a quiet escape to more remote places within the forest. Hikers, equestrians, and other trail users enjoy the 269-mile Sheltowee Trace National Recreation Trail that extends the entire length of the Daniel Boone. Hundreds of miles of winding rivers and streams provide the finishing touch in outdoor beauty. There are high cliffs in the area—exercise caution, especially with children.

BASICS

Operated By: U.S. Forest Service. **Open:** Apr. 13–Oct. 28. **Site Assignment:** Reservations must be made at least 3 days in advance. **Registration:** At office. **Fee:** Single, $20; double, $36. **Parking:** At park.

FACILITIES

Number of Multipurpose Sites: 42. **Hookups:** None. **Each Site:** Call ahead. **Dump Station:** Yes. **Laundry:** No. **Pay Phone:** No. **Restrooms and Showers:** Yes. **Fuel:** No. **Propane:** No. **Internal Roads:** Paved. **RV Service:** No. **Market:** No. **Restaurant:** No. **General Store:** Less than 5 mi. **Vending:** No. **Swimming:** No. **Playground:** No. **Activities:** Hiking.

RESTRICTIONS

Pets: Pets must be restrained or on a leash at all times while in developed recreation areas. **Fires:** In fire rings, stoves, grills, or fireplaces provided for that purpose. **Alcoholic Beverages:** Not allowed. **Vehicle Maximum Length:** Call ahead. **Other:** No livestock allowed. No ATVs or ORVs in campground. No motorized vehicles allowed off roads. No refunds for bad weather.

TO GET THERE

Take Exit 25 from I-75 at Corbin, KY. Take US 25W west 5 mi. Turn right on KY 1193 for 2 mi. Turn right on FS 558. Go 3 mi. to campground.

LONDON
Levi Jackson State Park
MAP, C-3

998 Levi Jackson Mill Rd., 40744-8944. T: (606) 878-8000; www.reserveamerica.com.

🚐 ★★★★   ⛺ ★★★★

Beauty: ★★★★	Site Privacy: ★★★
Spaciousness: ★★★	Quiet: ★★★★
Security: ★★★★	Cleanliness: ★★★★
Insect Control: ★★★	Facilities: ★★★★

Levi Jackson Wilderness Road offers diverse family recreation, including a large swimming pool with a water slide and an 18-hole mini-golf course. Traversing the park, the Wilderness Road is believed by many historians to be the most significant trail in the westward flow of English colonists. Lucky hikers can retrace the steps of Daniel Boone. The pretty campground is laid out in many small areas containing both back-in and pull-through sites. Sites have paved parking and are larger than average. Most sites are shady, while a few are open. Many sites are lovely, especially the larger pull-throughs. There are 23 pull-through sites. We particularly fancy sites in Area D, which enjoy a dense tree canopy. Parents, keep your children away from the vexing, ugly, old, and rusty barbed-wire fence that runs the length of the campground. Security is passable—there are no gates at this small-town campground. Avoid this park on summer weekends and holidays.

BASICS

Operated By: Kentucky State Parks. **Open:** All year. **Site Assignment:** Reservations suggested through

www.reserveamerica.com or at (888) 459-7275. **Registration:** At camp store, after-hours register next day (honor system in winter). **Fee:** Peak season: standard electric, $21–$23; tent w/ water, $18; tent, $12. **Parking:** At site (2 cars), in parking lot.

FACILITIES

Number of Multipurpose Sites: 146. **Hookups:** Electric (20, 30, 50 amps), water. **Each Site:** Picnic table, fire ring. **Dump Station:** Yes. **Laundry:** Yes. **Pay Phone:** Yes. **Restrooms and Showers:** Yes. **Fuel:** No. **Propane:** No. **Internal Roads:** Paved. **RV Service:** 3 mi. in London. **Market:** W/in 5 mi. in London. **Restaurant:** W/in 5 mi. in London. **General Store:** Yes. **Vending:** Beverages. **Swimming:** Yes (free). **Playground:** Yes. **Other:** Rec room, Mountain Life Museum, McHargue's Grist Mill (operational summertime), picnic areas, gazebo, amphitheater, bird sanctuary. **Activities:** Mini-golf, hiking trails, horseshoes, basketball, summer organized activities. **Nearby Attractions:** Daniel Boone Motocross Park, Renfro Valley Entertainment Center, Berea Crafts Center, White Hall State Historic Site, Fort Boonesborough State Park, Colonel Harland Sanders Café & Museum. **Additional Information:** London Chamber of Commerce, (606) 864-4789.

RESTRICTIONS

Pets: On leash only. **Fires:** Fire ring only. **Alcoholic Beverages:** Restricted. **Vehicle Maximum Length:** 60 ft. (sites vary). **Other:** 14-day stay limit.

TO GET THERE

From I-75, take Exit 38 and drive 3 mi. east on Hwy. 192. Turn south on US 25 and drive 2 mi. to the first traffic light. Turn left onto KY 1006. Drive 1.5 mi. into the campground.

LOUISA
Yatesville Lake State Park
MAP, B-4

P.O. Box 767, 41230. T: (606) 673-1492; www.reserveamerica.com.

🚐 ★★★★   ⛺ ★★★★

Beauty: ★★★	Site Privacy: ★★★
Spaciousness: ★★★	Quiet: ★★★★
Security: ★★★★	Cleanliness: ★★★★
Insect Control: ★★★	Facilities: ★★★★

Yatesville Lake State Park has a variety of campsites to suit anyone's idea of "roughing it," including double-wide sites for two RVs as well as boat-in, primitive sites. The 2,300-acre lake offers good bluegill, bass, and crappie fishing. Yatesville Lake provides plenty of room to skim the waves or catch some rays in your favorite cruise craft, be it a houseboat, pontoon, speed boat, or jet ski. The Yatesville Marina, named the nation's Most Outstanding Project in 1999 by the States Outdoor Boating Association, offers everything boaters and fishers need for lake fun. Back on shore, enjoy challenging play on the park's 18-hole par-71 Eagle Ridge golf course. The course, built on mountainous terrain, features dramatic views and is part of the Kentucky state park system's signature series of golf courses. Relax in the scenic lakeside setting of the park's 47-site campground. Opened in 1999, the Pleasant Ridge Campgrounds has 27 full-hookup campsites and 20 primitive campsites—16 boat-in and 4 hike-in sites. The campground also has a playground facility, nature trails, laundry room, restrooms and showers, and a dump station. The boat-in sites are maintained by a service road, and three restroom facilities are spaced alongside. The sites are only accessible via boat, but the seclusion and lakeside access are worth it. The hike-in sites are in the regular campground but set back into the woods with no electricity. The setting pays off in communion with nature. The campground also has the park system's first double RV campsites in which two recreational vehicles may park side by side. The Yatesville campground was named among the best campgrounds in all of Kentucky and Tennessee by Menasha Ridge Press.

BASICS

Operated By: Kentucky State Parks. **Open:** All year. **Site Assignment:** Reservations can be made up to 12 months in advance. **Registration:** At office. **Fee:** Single, $12–$23. **Parking:** At site.

FACILITIES

Number of Multipurpose Sites: 47. **Hookups:** Yes. **Dump Station:** Yes. **Laundry:** Yes. **Pay Phone:** Yes. **Restrooms and Showers:** Yes. **Fuel:** Yes. **Propane:** More than 10 mi. **Internal Roads:** Paved. **RV Service:** No. **Market:** No. **Restaurant:** More than 10 mi. **General Store:** Yes. **Vending:** Yes. **Swimming:** Yes. **Playground:** Yes. **Activities:** Bird-watching, boating, canoeing, golfing, hiking, jet skiing, photography, picnicking, mini-golf, sightseeing, waterskiing, stargazing, wildlife viewing.

RESTRICTIONS

Other: Longer min.-night stays are required at most campgrounds during holiday periods.

TO GET THERE

Follow US 23 to Louisa, KY, then take KY 32 west 5 mi. to the junction of KY 32 and KY 3215. KY 3215 leads directly into the state park campground.

LUCAS   MAP, C-2
Barren River Lake State Resort Park

reserve america

1149 State Park Rd., 42156-9709.
T: (270) 646-2151 or (800) 325-0057;
www.reserveamerica.com.

🚐 ★★★★   ▲ ★★★★

Beauty: ★★★★	Site Privacy: ★★★
Spaciousness: ★★★★	Quiet: ★★★★
Security: ★★★★★	Cleanliness: ★★★★
Insect Control: ★★★	Facilities: ★★★★★

The campground at Barren River Lake lies in graceful rolling hills surrounded by woods. The pretty campground contains back-in and pull-through sites with paved parking. Pull-through sites are often huge and open. Some, like 79A and 79B, enjoy views of a green hillside. Back-in sites tend to be average sized and shadier. Our favorite back-in sites numbered in the 80s and 90s. Security is very good, with gates at the campground entrance. Barren River Lake offers outstanding recreational facilities, including a marina with rental slips (100 open and 40 covered). The lake supports bluegill, channel catfish, crappie, rough fish, and largemouth, white, and hybrid striped bass. The park's many planned events climax with the annual Glasgow Highland Games in June. Approximately 35 miles north of the park, Mammoth Cave National Park makes an excellent day trip. Avoid this popular state park on summer holidays and weekends.

BASICS

Operated By: State of Kentucky. **Open:** Apr. 1–Oct. 31. **Site Assignment:** Reservations suggested through www.reserveamerica.com or at (888) 459-7275. **Registration:** At office. **Fee:** Standard electric, $18–$20. **Parking:** On site.

FACILITIES

Number of Multipurpose Sites: 99. **Hookups:** Electric (20, 30 amps), water. **Each Site:** Picnic table, grill. **Dump Station:** Yes. **Laundry:** Yes. **Pay Phone:** Yes. **Restrooms and Showers:** Yes. **Fuel:** 3.5 mi. in Lucas. **Propane:** 3.5 mi. in Lucas. **Internal Roads:** Paved. **RV Service:** No. **Market:** Nearby. **Restaurant:** Yes. **General Store:** Yes. **Vending:** Yes. **Swimming:** Beach. **Playground:** Yes. **Activities:** Basketball, golf, nature trails, horseback riding, boating, recreation programs. **Nearby Attractions:** Dale Hollow Lake, Old Mulkey historic site, Mammoth Cave. **Additional Information:** U.S. Army Corps of Engineers, (606) 642-3308.

RESTRICTIONS

Pets: On leash. **Fires:** Fire ring only. **Alcoholic Beverages:** Not allowed. **Vehicle Maximum Length:** Varies. **Other:** No firearms.

TO GET THERE

From Bowling Green, take I-65 north to the Cumberland Pkwy. and drive east, then go south on US 31 East to the park.

MAMMOTH CAVE   MAP, C-2
Mammoth Cave National Park

P.O. Box 7, 42259. T: (270) 758-2180 or
(800) 967-2283; www.nps.gov/maca/home.htm.

🚐 ★★★★★   ▲ ★★★★★

Beauty: ★★★★★	Site Privacy: ★★★★
Spaciousness: ★★★★★	Quiet: ★★★★
Security: ★★★★★	Cleanliness: ★★★★★
Insect Control: ★★★	Facilities: ★★★★

Fascinating Mammoth Cave has seen plenty of adventure during its 4000-year relationship with humans. Tour guides are full of anecdotes about the characters who've contributed to the cave's colorful history—of course, many of these folks were just trying to make a buck. With over 345 miles of mapped passages, it's the longest cave in the world. Above ground, the rolling woodlands within the park contain 70 miles of multiuse trails. The beautiful Headquarters Campground is laid out in three loops, with paved back-in and pull-through sites. Site size is ample, with pull-through sites tending to be larger than back-in sites. Most sites enjoy a fair amount of seclusion. Sites 65–83, on the second loop, are pretty and quiet. Sites 26–34 are also quite nice looking but may be noisy. Situated near a noisy road, sites 1–10 and 11–21 should be avoided. The campground is remote and gated, making it ultrasafe. Visit during the week in the summer.

BASICS

Operated By: National Park Service. **Open:** Mar.–Oct. **Site Assignment:** Reservations available at (800) 967-2283 or online at reservations.nps.gov. **Registration:** At entrance kiosk. **Fee:** Primitive, $17. **Parking:** In designated areas.

FACILITIES

Number of Multipurpose Sites: 106. **Hookups:** None. **Each Site:** Picnic table, fire grate. **Dump Station:** Yes. **Laundry:** Yes. **Pay Phone:** Yes. **Restrooms and Showers:** Yes (coin-op). **Fuel:** Yes. **Propane:** Yes. **Internal Roads:** Paved. **RV Service:** No. **Market:** No. **Restaurant:** Nearby. **General Store:** Yes. **Vending:** No. **Swimming:** No. **Playground:** No. **Activities:** Hiking, horseback riding, fishing, spelunking. **Nearby Attractions:** Mammoth Cave, water slides, golfing.

RESTRICTIONS

Pets: On leash. **Fires:** Only in designated areas. **Alcoholic Beverages:** Allowed. **Vehicle Maximum Length:** 40 ft. **Other:** Mopeds & motorcycles only on improved roads. Check out at 11 a.m.

TO GET THERE

From north on I-65, Exit 53. From south on I-65, Exit 48.

MAMMOTH CAVE   MAP, C-2
Nolin Lake State Park

reserve america

2998 Briar Creek Rd, 42259. T: (270) 286-4240;
www.reserveamerica.com.

🚐 ★★★   ▲ ★★★★

Beauty: ★★★	Site Privacy: ★★★
Spaciousness: ★★★	Quiet: ★★★★★
Security: ★★★★★	Cleanliness: ★★★★
Insect Control: ★★★	Facilities: ★★★★

Nolin Lake State Park, one of Kentucky's newest state parks located on the northern edge of Mammoth Cave National Park, is home to Nolin Lake. With over 330 acres of rolling hills and lush green forest and Nolin Lake's 5,795 acres, Nolin Lake State Park has lots to offer. From boating and fishing to hiking, biking, and other outdoor activities, visitors to Lake Nolin will find lots of things to do. Relax on the sandy beaches along the shores of Nolin Lake, enjoy a picnic or barbecue in the picnic area or cast your line on Nolin Lake and catch bass, walleye, catfish and crappie. Spend the day on Nolin Lake or exploring miles of trails around the lake and then settle down in the camping area for a night under the stars or in your camper. Nolin Lake Campground features 32 campsites with water and electricity, 20 primitive sites, a restroom/shower building, laundry facilities, and a dump station. A playground is located by the sites. Three sites have been adapted for the disabled.

BASICS

Operated By: Kentucky State Parks. **Open:** Apr. 1–Oct. 31. **Site Assignment:** Reservations can be made up to 12 months in advance. **Registration:** At office. **Fee:** Single, $12–$23. **Parking:** At site.

FACILITIES

Number of Multipurpose Sites: 93. **Hookups:** Yes. **Dump Station:** Yes. **Laundry:** Yes. **Pay Phone:** No. **Restrooms and Showers:** Yes. **Fuel:** W/in 10 mi. **Propane:** W/in 10 mi. **Internal Roads:** Paved. **RV Service:** No. **Market:** Yes. **Restaurant:** W/in 10 mi. **General Store:** Yes. **Vending:** No. **Swimming:** Yes. **Playground:** Yes. **Activities:** Birdwatching, boating, fishing, hiking, jogging/running, photography, picnicking, waterskiing, snorkeling, stargazing.

RESTRICTIONS

Other: Longer min.-night stays are required at most campgrounds during holiday periods.

TO GET THERE

Nolin Lake is north of Mammoth Cave from KY 728 and KY 1827; or 45 mi. southeast of Rough River Dam State Resort Park from KY 259 to KY 728 and KY 1827.

MIDDLESBORO   MAP, C-3
Wilderness Road Campground at Cumberland Gap National Historical Park

US 25 East, 40965. T: (606) 248-2817.

🚐 ★★★★★   ▲ ★★★★★

Beauty: ★★★★★   Site Privacy: ★★★★★
Spaciousness: ★★★★★   Quiet: ★★★★★
Security: ★★★★   Cleanliness: ★★★★
Insect Control: ★★★★   Facilities: ★★★★

Millions of years of wind and water carved this natural gap in the Appalachian Mountains. It was first used by migrating animals, then by Native Americans, and more recently by frontiers-people headed to settle the American West. Historians estimate that 12,000 settlers passed through Cumberland Gap by the end of the American Revolution. Learn about these folks, including Daniel Boone, who shaped the gap's history, at the visitor's center in Kentucky. The national historic park straddles the Kentucky–Virginia border and dips into Tennessee at its southern tip. The beautiful Wilderness Road campground is actually in Virginia. Sites are commodious. With plenty of space and foliage between them, sites are also secluded. Campsites feature gravel, back-in parking under a canopy of oak, poplar, and hickory. Our favorite sites, E1, E2, E4, and F9, are extremely private. The campground at Cumberland Gap is fairly remote, making it safe. Visit the park during the week for less-crowded touring.

BASICS

Operated By: National Park Service. **Open:** All year. **Site Assignment:** First come, first served.

Registration: At ranger station or visitor center. **Fee:** Electric, $17; no electric, $12. **Parking:** On site.

FACILITIES

Number of RV-only Sites: 41. **Number of Tent-only Sites:** 119. **Hookups:** Electric (50 amps). **Each Site:** Picnic table & fire pit. **Dump Station:** Yes. **Laundry:** No. **Pay Phone:** Yes. **Restrooms and Showers:** Yes. **Fuel:** Nearby. **Propane:** Nearby. **Internal Roads:** Paved. **RV Service:** No. **Market:** Nearby. **Restaurant:** Nearby. **General Store:** Nearby. **Vending:** No. **Swimming:** No. **Playground:** No. **Activities:** Hiking & horseback riding trails. **Nearby Attractions:** Abraham Lincoln Museum, Pine Mountain State Park, Museum of Appalachia, antique shops.

RESTRICTIONS

Pets: On leash. **Fires:** Fire ring only. **Alcoholic Beverages:** At site only. **Vehicle Maximum Length:** 37 ft. **Other:** 8 person max. per site, 4 tent max. per site.

TO GET THERE

From I-75 in Kentucky, exit on Hwy. 25E at Corbin; park is 50 mi. south of Corbin on 25E. From I-75 in Tennessee, exit on Hwy. 63 at Jacksboro/La Follette, proceed east to Hwy. 25E, then north on Hwy. 25E 2 mi. to park. From I-81 in Tennessee, exit on 25E at Morristown, TN; the park is 50 mi. northwest on 25E.

MOREHEAD   MAP, B-3
Twin Knobs Recreation Area

reserve america

5195 KY 801 South Morehead, 40351. T: (606) 784-8816 or (606) 780-7818; www.reserveamerica.com.

🚐 ★★★★★   ▲ ★★★★★

Beauty: ★★★★★   Site Privacy: ★★★★★
Spaciousness: ★★★★★   Quiet: ★★★★★
Security: ★★★★★   Cleanliness: ★★★★
Insect Control: ★★★   Facilities: ★★★

Gorgeous Twin Knobs Recreation Area includes quite a few sites with gorgeous views of 8,270-acre Cave Run Lake. Anglers know the lake for its muskie, but it also supports largemouth bass, bluegill, crappie, and catfish. The lake lies within the northern tip of giant Daniel Boone National Forest, which maintains 115 miles of multiuse trails in this district alone. The campground at Twin Knobs is incredibly spacious, with dense undergrowth providing a lush barrier between sites. Most sites are shaded by various hardwoods. Some parking is on pavement, while other parking is on fine gravel. All sites offer back-in parking. Large groups looking for double sites should head for J9 and J10. Gorgeous lakefront sites include D9, D11, and D13, F22–F28, and I7–I9. Elegant loop B is tucked into the woods and offers the most secluded sites. Security is excellent—the campground is remote and gated. Avoid Twin Knobs on busy summer holidays.

BASICS

Operated By: Recreation Resource Management. **Open:** Mar. 18–Nov. 1. **Site Assignment:** Some sites reservable through www. reserveamerica.com w/ $9 fee; other sites first come, first served. **Registration:** At entrance station. **Fee:** Double, $24; single, $16; $4 extra for electric; $5 extra for full hookup. **Parking:** On site.

FACILITIES

Number of RV-only Sites: 216. **Hookups:** Electric (50 amps). **Each Site:** Picnic table, grill, fire ring. **Dump Station:** Yes. **Laundry:** Yes. **Pay Phone:** Yes. **Restrooms and Showers:** Yes. **Fuel:** No. **Propane:** No. **Internal Roads:** Paved. **RV Service:** Nearby. **Market:** No. **Restaurant:** No. **General Store:** Yes. **Vending:** No. **Swimming:** Beach. **Playground:** No. **Other:** Large sandy beach, launch ramp. **Activities:** Hiking, volleyball, lake swimming, boating, fishing, weekly amphitheater programs. **Nearby Attractions:** Cave Run Lake, Minor E. Clark Fish Hatchery, Clear Creek Furnace. **Additional Information:** (606) 784-6428.

RESTRICTIONS

Pets: On leash. **Fires:** Grill only. **Alcoholic Beverages:** Not allowed. **Vehicle Maximum Length:** 42 ft.

TO GET THERE

From I-64 take Exit 133 and go south on KY 801. Campground is 9 mi. on right.

OLIVE HILL   MAP, B-4
Carter Caves State Resort Park

reserve america

344 Caveland Dr., 41164. T: (606) 286-4411; www.reserveamerica.com.

🚐 ★★★★   ▲ ★★★★

Beauty: ★★★   Site Privacy: ★★★
Spaciousness: ★★★   Quiet: ★★★
Security: ★★★   Cleanliness: ★★★★
Insect Control: ★★★   Facilities: ★★★★

Beneath the forested hills of this resort, nature has hidden more than 20 twisting caverns. Visit Cascade Cave, where you'll discover a 30-foot underground waterfall. A must-see while you're at Carter Caves is X Cave, where, for millions of years, nature has formed luminous stone fans, pipes, and spirals. Above ground, enjoy a relaxing game of golf on our nine-hole golf course, canoeing, hiking, horseback riding and mountain biking on 20 miles of single and multiuse trails. Two group camp buildings located in our primitive campground are available for reservation. Each building contains six bunk beds without mattresses. Linens are not provided. Guests will need to bring their own bedding. Each building is equipped with electrical plugs and lights and accommodates up to 12 people. Enjoy the great outdoors year-round! The campground features 89 campsites with utilities, a dump station, and two central service buildings with restrooms and showers.

BASICS

Operated By: Kentucky State Parks. **Open:** All year. **Site Assignment:** Reservations can be made up to 12 months in advance. **Registration:** At office. **Fee:** Single, $12–$24. **Parking:** At site.

FACILITIES

Number of Multipurpose Sites: 124. **Hookups:** Yes. **Dump Station:** Yes. **Laundry:** Yes. **Pay Phone:** W/in 10 mi. **Restrooms and Showers:** Yes. **Fuel:** W/in 10 mi. **Propane:** Yes. **Internal Roads:** Paved. **RV Service:** No. **Market:** W/in 10 mi. **Restaurant:** Yes. **General Store:** Yes. **Vending:** Yes. **Swimming:** Yes. **Playground:** Yes. **Activities:** Archery, biking, bird-watching, boating, canoeing, fishing, golfing, hiking, horseback riding, jogging/running, nature study, picnicking, photography, mini-golf, rock climbing, sightseeing, stargazing, tennis, volley.

RESTRICTIONS

Other: Longer min.-night stays are required at most campgrounds during holiday periods.

TO GET THERE

Take I-64 to Exit 161. Turn east onto US 60 for 2 mi. Then turn left onto N. KY 182. Park entrance is 3 mi. from turning north onto Hwy. 182.

OLIVE HILL MAP, B-4
Grayson Lake State Park

reserve america

314 Grayson Lake Park Rd., 41164-9213. T: (606) 474-9727; www.reserveamerica.com.

🚐 ★★★   ⛺ ★★★

Beauty: ★★★★	Site Privacy: ★★★
Spaciousness: ★★★	Quiet: ★★★
Security: ★★★★	Cleanliness: ★★★★
Insect Control: ★★★★	Facilities: ★★★

Grayson Lake's geology, terrain, and scenery make this a particularly striking place to camp, even though the property is fairly mediocre overall. A walled canyon of sandstone bluffs looms over the lake's waters. Historically, Shawnee and Cherokee Indians camped in the area while hunting, and European frontiersman used the cliffs as a source of flint and saltpeter (an ingredient of gunpowder). A short nature trail allows one to view the distinctive flora and rock formations of the area. Most of the campsites are open, with a few well shaded; all are medium-sized. Sites 13, 14, and 27 are pretty and shaded, while sites 29–32 are completely open. Site 57 is a nice, big pull-through. Lots of children were in evidence when we visited, and it looks like the campground might serve as a sort of local teen hangout.

BASICS

Operated By: Kentucky State Parks. **Open:** Apr. 1–Oct. 31. **Site Assignment:** Reservations suggested through www.reserveamerica.com or at (888) 459-7275. **Registration:** At check-in station. **Fee:** Standard electric, $20–$22. **Parking:** On site.

FACILITIES

Number of Multipurpose Sites: 71. **Hookups:** Electric (50 amps), water. **Each Site:** Table, fire ring.

Dump Station: Yes. **Laundry:** Yes. **Pay Phone:** Yes. **Restrooms and Showers:** Yes. **Fuel:** No. **Propane:** No. **Internal Roads:** Paved. **RV Service:** Ashland, 45 minutes. **Market:** Small grocery 2 mi. **Restaurant:** Grayson, 12 mi. **General Store:** No. **Vending:** Yes. **Swimming:** Beach. **Playground:** Yes. **Other:** Marina (4 mi. away), beach open Memorial Day–Labor Day. **Activities:** Boating, hiking, golf course. **Nearby Attractions:** Carter Caves State Resort Park, Greenbo Lake.

RESTRICTIONS

Pets: On leash. **Fires:** Fire ring only. **Alcoholic Beverages:** Not allowed. **Vehicle Maximum Length:** No limit. **Other:** 14-day stay limit.

TO GET THERE

Take I-64 to the Grayson Exit 172, go south on KY 7 through the town of Grayson. Park is 12 mi. from I-64.

PRESTONSBURG MAP, B-4
Jenny Wiley State Resort Park

reserve america

75 Theatre Ct., 41653-9799. T: (606) 886-2711 or (800) 325-0142; www.reserveamerica.com.

🚐 ★★★   ⛺ ★★★

Beauty: ★★★★	Site Privacy: ★★
Spaciousness: ★★★	Quiet: ★★★
Security: ★★★★	Cleanliness: ★★★
Insect Control: ★★	Facilities: ★★★★

Jenny Wiley State Resort Park offers excellent recreational facilities in the hills of eastern Kentucky. The park roads follow the shoreline of Dewey Lake, which supports largemouth and hybrid striped bass, bluegill, catfish, and crappie. There are 10 miles of hiking trails in the park, with 60 more miles in the surrounding countryside. It's a shame the campground isn't as pretty as the rest of the park. Sites are laid out on four spurs and are frighteningly similar. Each square, mid-sized site features paved, back-in parking. Sites are totally open to each other, with woods behind them providing partial shade. Since the sites are all the same, choose your site based on location. Jenny Wiley State Park stages musicals and hosts festivals all summer long, keeping the campground busy. It's best to plan a mid-week trip to avoid the crowds. Security is excellent—the park is gated and rural.

BASICS

Operated By: Kentucky State Parks. **Open:** Apr. 1–Oct. 31. **Site Assignment:** Reservations suggested through www.reserveamerica.com or at (888) 459-7275. **Registration:** A campground. **Fee:** Electric, $20–$22; tent, $12. **Parking:** In designated areas.

FACILITIES

Number of RV-only Sites: 111. **Number of Tent-only Sites:** 30. **Hookups:** Electric (20, 30, 50 amps), water. **Each Site:** Picnic shelter, table, fire ring. **Dump Station:** Yes. **Laundry:** Yes. **Pay Phone:** Yes. **Restrooms and Showers:** Yes. **Fuel:** 5 mi. **Propane:** 5 mi. **Internal Roads:** Paved. **RV Service:** No. **Market:** Yes. **Restaurant:** No. **General**

Store: Yes. **Vending:** Yes. **Swimming:** Yes. **Playground:** Yes. **Other:** Hiking, nature, mountain bike trails, fishing, boating, golfing. **Activities:** Inquire at campground. **Nearby Attractions:** Breaks Interstate Park, Grave of Jenny Wiley, Pioneer Village, Tunder Ridge, The Samuel May House. **Additional Information:** U.S. Army Corps of Engineers, (606) 642-3308.

RESTRICTIONS

Pets: On leash. **Fires:** Fire ring only. **Alcoholic Beverages:** Not allowed. **Vehicle Maximum Length:** No limit.

TO GET THERE

From I-64 West take the Mountain Pkwy. exit. From I-64 East take the US 23 South exit. From I-75 take the Daniel Boone Pkwy. exit. From I-75 south, take the I-64 East exit. Campground is in Prestonburg, off US 23/460 on KY 3.

RICHMOND MAP, B-3
Fort Boonesborough State Park

reserve america

4375 Boonesborough Rd., 40475-9316. T: (859) 527-3131; www.reserveamerica.com.

🚐 ★★★   ⛺ ★★★

Beauty: ★★★★	Site Privacy: ★★
Spaciousness: ★★★	Quiet: ★★
Security: ★★★	Cleanliness: ★★★★
Insect Control: ★★★	Facilities: ★★★

Here's a rhetorical question: Why build a campground next to a sewage treatment plant? Suffice to say that the campground at Fort Boonesborough would be much more desirable without the aforementioned eyesore. The campground is situated on a gentle hill partially shaded by mature hardwoods. Mid-sized sites offer paved, back-in parking (there is one pull-through), and the campground feels claustrophobic due to its popularity. The shadiest sites, in the back of the campground, include 61–74 and 137–139. Security is okay—there are no gates, but the park is in a rural location. Park facilities are excellent. Fort Boonesborough is a reconstruction based on the fort built here by Daniel Boone and Richard Henderson in the 1770s. Costumed guides and artisans perform demonstrations. Fishing on the Kentucky River is also available. Catches include bluegill, bass, and catfish. Avoid Fort Boonesborough on summer holidays and weekends.

BASICS

Operated By: Kentucky State Parks. **Open:** All year. **Site Assignment:** Reservations suggested through www.reserveamerica.com or at (888) 459-7275. **Registration:** At entrance booth, night arrival register next morning. **Fee:** Electric, $23–$25 during peak season; tent, $12. **Parking:** At site, in parking lot.

FACILITIES

Number of Multipurpose Sites: 167. **Hookups:** Electric (20, 30, 50 amps), water. **Each Site:** Picnic table, grill, fire rings in primitive area. **Dump Station:** Yes. **Laundry:** Yes. **Pay Phone:** No. **Restrooms and Showers:** Yes. **Fuel:** No.

Propane: Yes. **Internal Roads:** Paved. **RV Service:** 25 mi. in Lexington. **Market:** 8 mi. in Winchester. **Restaurant:** 0.25 mi. **General Store:** Camp store. **Vending:** Yes. **Swimming:** Yes (seasonal, w/ waterslide). **Playground:** Yes. **Other:** Rec building, gift shop, meeting room, picnic shelters, boat ramp. **Activities:** Fishing, mini-golf, nature trails, seasonal organized activities. **Nearby Attractions:** Boone Station State Historic Site, Natural Bridge State Resort Park, Daniel Boone National Forest, 15 mi. to Lexington. **Additional Information:** Lexington CVB (800) 845-3959, www.visitlex.com.

RESTRICTIONS

Pets: On leash only. **Fires:** Fire ring only. **Alcoholic Beverages:** Not allowed. **Vehicle Maximum Length:** No limit. **Other:** 14-day stay limit.

TO GET THERE

From I-75, take Exit 95 and drive 5.5 mi. northeast on KY 627. Turn right on KY 388 and the campground is on the left. From I-64, take Exit 94/Winchester onto KY 1958 for 3 mi., then drive 8 mi. southwest on KY 627. Turn left on KY 388.

SALT LICK MAP, B-3
Zilpo—Daniel Boone National Forest

P.O. Box 218, 4037101. T: (606) 768-2722; www.reserveamerica.com.

🚐 ★★★★　　🏕 ★★★★

Beauty: ★★★★	Site Privacy: ★★★
Spaciousness: ★★★	Quiet: ★★★
Security: ★★★★	Cleanliness: ★★★★
Insect Control: ★★★★	Facilities: ★★★

The campground is very scenic and located on a peninsula in the middle portion of Cave Run Lake. Zilpo is located within the Daniel Boone National Forest, along the Cumberland Plateau in the Appalachian foothills of eastern Kentucky. The forest encompasses over 706,000 acres of mostly rugged terrain. The land is characterized by steep forested ridges dissected by narrow ravines and over 3,400 miles of sandstone cliffs. These lands are federally managed to provide the nation with a sustained yield of natural resources, including wood, water, forage, and wildlife. Recreation opportunities on the national forest are an added bonus. The conservation management of natural resources and recreation provides significant economic, environmental, and social benefits in the public interest. Millions of visitors come to enjoy the scenic beauty and abundant wildlife that the forest has to offer. Cave Run Lake and Laurel River Lake are popular attractions on the forest. Other special areas include the Red River Gorge Geological Area, Natural Arch Scenic Area, Clifty Wilderness, Beaver Creek Wilderness, and five wildlife management areas. Over 600 miles of trails provide a quiet escape to more remote places within the forest. Hikers, horseback riders, and other trail users get back to nature along the 269-mile Sheltowee Trace National Recreation Trail that extends the entire length of the Daniel Boone. Hundreds of miles of winding rivers and streams provide the finishing touch in outdoor beauty. Come and discover what you've been missing.

BASICS

Operated By: U.S. Forest Service. **Open:** Mar. 23–Oct. 31. **Site Assignment:** Reservations must be made at least 4 days in advance. **Registration:** At office. **Fee:** Single, $16.96–$26.50; double, $25.44–$34.98. **Parking:** At park.

FACILITIES

Number of Multipurpose Sites: 314. **Hookups:** Yes. **Each Site:** Call ahead. **Dump Station:** No. **Laundry:** No. **Pay Phone:** Yes. **Restrooms and Showers:** Yes. **Fuel:** No. **Propane:** No. **Internal Roads:** Paved. **RV Service:** No. **Market:** No. **Restaurant:** No. **General Store:** Yes. **Vending:** No. **Swimming:** Yes. **Playground:** No. **Activities:** Boating, hiking, horseback riding, nature programs.

RESTRICTIONS

Vehicle Maximum Length: Call ahead. **Other:** No refunds due to inclement weather.

TO GET THERE

Coming on I-64 from Lexington, KY, take Exit 123, US 60 east of Salt Lick, KY. Turn right on Road 211 and follow signs to campground. Coming on I-64 from Ashland, take Exit 133 to Farmers, on Road 801. Turn right on US 60 to Salt Lick and left on Road 21 (check Web site for further directions).

SASSAFRAS MAP, C-4
Carr Creek State Park

Hwy. 15, P.O. Box 249, 41759-0249. T: (606) 642-4050; www.reserveamerica.com.

🚐 ★★★★　　🏕 ★★★★

Beauty: ★★★★★	Site Privacy: ★★
Spaciousness: ★★★★	Quiet: ★★★★
Security: ★★★★	Cleanliness: ★★★★
Insect Control: ★★★★	Facilities: ★★★

The flat, pretty campground at Carr Creek State Park rests in an Appalachian Mountain valley. It offers large sites with paved, back-in parking. Each site also has either a gravel or paved picnic area. Most sites are open to each other, with pleasant woods surrounding the campground. The campground is laid out in two loops, with the nicest sites in the back. Sites 14, 16, 18, 20, 22, and 23 are partially shady, with views of the mountains. The state park offers a full-service marina and fishing on a 750-acre lake. Common catches include bass, crappie, and walleye. Carr Creek is so isolated, we thought we would never arrive. But it's definitely worth the drive. Though there is no gate, security is fine. Avoid the park on holiday weekends. Otherwise, these cool mountain highlands are a good summer destination.

BASICS

Operated By: Kentucky State Parks. **Open:** Apr. 1–Oct. 31. **Site Assignment:** Reservations suggested through www.reserveamerica.com or at (888) 459-7275. **Registration:** At office. **Fee:** Electric, $19–$21. **Parking:** Designated areas.

FACILITIES

Number of RV-only Sites: 39. **Hookups:** Electric (30, 50 amps), water. **Each Site:** Picnic table. **Dump Station:** Yes. **Laundry:** Yes. **Pay Phone:** Yes. **Restrooms and Showers:** Yes. **Fuel:** 1 mi. **Propane:** 1 mi. **Internal Roads:** Paved. **RV Service:** No. **Market:** No. **Restaurant:** No. **General Store:** No. **Vending:** Yes. **Swimming:** Beach area. **Playground:** Yes. **Activities:** Fishing, boating, hiking, pontoons, theatre. **Nearby Attractions:** Inquire at campground.

RESTRICTIONS

Pets: On leash. **Fires:** Fire ring only. **Alcoholic Beverages:** Not allowed. **Vehicle Maximum Length:** No limit.

TO GET THERE

From Hazard on KY 15, Carr Creek is located 15 mi. south.

SCOTTSVILLE MAP, C-2
Tailwater Recreation Area at Barren River Lake

701 Tailwater Rd., 42164. T: (270) 622-7732 or (270) 646-2055; www.reserveamerica.com.

🚐 ★★★★　　🏕 ★★★

Beauty: ★★★★	Site Privacy: ★★★
Spaciousness: ★★★★	Quiet: ★★★★
Security: ★★★★	Cleanliness: ★★★★
Insect Control: ★★★	Facilities: ★★★

The campground at the Tailwater Recreation Area was designed with the avid angler in mind. Most of the 49 sites are right on the water, and those that aren't lie nearby. Most of these sites are long and narrow, and while the trees provide ample shade throughout, the minimal ground cover reduces the privacy between sites. There are only two pull-through sites. If campers can snag it, site 5 is one of the best in the area; it is huge, has one of the only two pull-throughs, and a gorgeous view. Though the campground can get quite crowded on summer weekends, it seldom fills up. Besides fishing, in-camp activities include horseshoes and hiking.

BASICS

Operated By: U.S. Army Corps of Engineers. **Open:** Mid-Apr.–mid-Sept. **Site Assignment:** Reservations suggested through www.recreation.gov or at (877) 444-6777. **Registration:** At fee station. **Fee:** $15; check, V, MC, AE, D. **Parking:** On site.

FACILITIES

Number of RV-only Sites: 49. **Hookups:** Electric (30, 50 amps), water. **Each Site:** Picnic table, grill. **Dump Station:** Yes. **Laundry:** No. **Pay Phone:** No. **Restrooms and Showers:** Yes. **Fuel:** Nearby. **Propane:** Nearby. **Internal Roads:** Paved. **RV Service:** No. **Market:** Nearby. **Restaurant:** Nearby. **General Store:** Nearby. **Vending:** Soda. **Swimming:** Nearby. **Playground:** Yes. **Activities:** Fishing, boating, horseshoes, hiking. **Nearby Attractions:** Barren River Lake State Resort.

RESTRICTIONS

Pets: On leash. **Fires:** Only in designated areas. **Alcoholic Beverages:** Not allowed. **Vehicle Maximum Length:** 45 ft.

TO GET THERE

From Glasgow, take Hwy. 31E south for 4 mi.; turn right on 252. Go 8 mi. and cross the dam. The Tailwater entrance road is at the south end of the dam.

SLADE   MAP, B-3
Natural Bridge State Resort Park

reserve america

2135 Natural Bridge Rd., 40376-9701.
T: (606) 663-2214 or (800) 325-1710;
www.reserveamerica.com.

🚐 ★★★   ▲ ★★★

Beauty: ★★★★   Site Privacy: ★★
Spaciousness: ★★★   Quiet: ★★★
Security: ★★★★   Cleanliness: ★★★★
Insect Control: ★★★★★ Facilities: ★★★★

It's a shame that the campgrounds at Natural Bridge are so mediocre, given the natural beauty of the land in this part of the Daniel Boone National Forest. With the campgrounds squeezed into tight mountain hollers, sites are on the small side of average. What's more, this park is extremely popular and the campgrounds stay full all summer. Sites offer gravel, back-in parking. Shadiness varies. We recommend shady RV sites in the back of the Whittleton Campground, particularly A33–A35. For tent campers, we like sites in the primitive area, numbered C4–C10. The state park's namesake is a giant sandstone arch. Nearby, the Red River Gorge contains a plethora of rock-climbing routes catering to novices and experts. The Red River is known for gorgeous canoeing as well as Class II–III whitewater. Security is passable at this isolated state park. Visit in spring or fall if you value solitude.

BASICS

Operated By: State of Kentucky. **Open:** Apr. 1–Oct. 31. **Site Assignment:** Reservations suggested through www.reserveamerica.com or at (888) 459-7275. **Registration:** At booth at campground entry. **Fee:** Electric/water, $24–$26; electric, $18–$20; no electric, $12–$14; tent, $12. **Parking:** In designated areas.

FACILITIES

Number of Multipurpose Sites: 86. **Hookups:** Electric (30, 50 amps), water. **Each Site:** Picnic table, fire rings. **Dump Station:** Yes. **Laundry:** Yes. **Pay Phone:** Yes. **Restrooms and Showers:** Yes. **Fuel:** Nearby. **Propane:** Nearby. **Internal Roads:** Paved. **RV Service:** No. **Market:** No. **Restaurant:** No. **General Store:** Nearby. **Vending:** Soda. **Swimming:** Yes. **Playground:** Nearby. **Other:** Nature center. **Activities:** Fishing, mini-golf, hiking. **Nearby Attractions:** Buckhorn Lake State Resort Park.

RESTRICTIONS

Pets: On leash. **Fires:** Fire ring only. **Alcoholic Beverages:** Not allowed. **Vehicle Maximum Length:** No limit. **Other:** Check out at 1 p.m.

TO GET THERE

I-64 East to Exit 98 onto Bert T. Combs Mountain Pkwy. East. Take KY 11 Exit 33 toward Slade/Beattyville. Keep right at the fork in the ramp. Merge onto KY 11. Park is 0.33 mi.

TAYLORSVILLE   MAP, B-2
Taylorsville Lake State Park

reserve america

Taylorsville Lake State Park, 40071.
T: (502) 477-8713; www.reserveamerica.com.

🚐 ★★★★   ▲ ★★★★

Beauty: ★★★   Site Privacy: ★★★
Spaciousness: ★★★   Quiet: ★★★★
Security: ★★★★   Cleanliness: ★★★★
Insect Control: ★★★   Facilities: ★★★★

Taylorsville Lake State Park is a wrangler's and angler's dream come true. The park sits on 3,050-acre Taylorsville Lake, where anglers can vie for bass, bluegill, and crappie. The 1,200-acre park encompasses some of the most beautiful riding country around, not far away from Kentucky's biggest city. The campground at Taylorsville Lake offers 42 campsites for RVs, and horse-lovers can sleep under the stars with their equine pals at one of ten camp sites set up specifically for horse camping. The park also offers over 16 miles of trails for hiking, horseback riding, and biking. Camp out in Taylorsville Lake's beautiful countryside in a 45-site RV campground. Sites have water and electric and use the same service building with laundry. A day on the lake is a glorious opportunity at Taylorsville Lake! Rent a marina fishing boat and cast for bass, bluegill, or crappie; schedule cruising time on one of the marina's pontoon boats, or launch your own from four launching ramps.

BASICS

Operated By: Kentucky State Parks. **Open:** All year. **Site Assignment:** Reservations can be made up to 12 months in advance. **Registration:** At office. **Fee:** Single, $12–$23; equestrian, $12–$25. **Parking:** At site.

FACILITIES

Number of Multipurpose Sites: 70. **Hookups:** Yes. **Dump Station:** Yes. **Laundry:** Yes. **Pay Phone:** W/in 10 mi. **Restrooms and Showers:** Yes. **Fuel:** W/in 10 mi. **Propane:** W/in 10 mi. **Internal Roads:** Paved. **RV Service:** No. **Market:** W/in 10 mi. **Restaurant:** W/in 10 mi. **General Store:** Yes. **Vending:** Yes. **Swimming:** No. **Playground:** Yes. **Activities:** Bird-watching, boating, fishing, hiking, horseback riding, jet skiing, jogging/running, sightseeing, waterskiing, volleyball, walking.

RESTRICTIONS

Other: Longer min.-night stays are required at most campgrounds during holiday periods.

TO GET THERE

From I-64 east, take Exit 32 south. Take Hwy. 55 south to KY 44 east to KY 248 east.

UNION   MAP, A-3
Big Bone Lick State Park

reserve america

3380 Beaver Rd., 41091-9627. T: (859) 384-3522 or (859) 384-3495; www.reserveamerica.com.

🚐 ★★★★   ▲ ★★★★

Beauty: ★★★★   Site Privacy: ★★
Spaciousness: ★★★   Quiet: ★★★
Security: ★★★★★   Cleanliness: ★★★★
Insect Control: ★★★   Facilities: ★★★★

The institutional-looking campground at Big Bone Lick is not gorgeous, but it's pleasant. Set on a large, gentle hill, the campground features average-sized sites with minimal privacy. Some sites are shady, but the campground is open enough that you can easily see one end from the other. Sites offer paved, back-in parking. Many of the parking pads are short. Our favorite sites, 25–29, are on a cul-de-sac at the end of the campground. Fascinating Big Bone Lick State Park, the birthplace of American vertebrate paleontology, was a swamp at the end of the Ice Age. Prehistoric animals, such as giant mammoths, mastodons, ground sloths, and bison, were attracted by the swamp's salt and minerals, became trapped in the quagmire, and died. Their remains fossilized, leaving paleontologists a treasure trove of bones to study. Located near Cincinnati, this park stays busy all summer. Visit during the week, or in spring or fall. Security is excellent.

BASICS

Operated By: State of Kentucky. **Open:** All year; most water turned off Nov. 1–Mar. 31. **Site Assignment:** Reservations suggested through www.reserveamerica.com or at (888) 459-7275. **Registration:** At campground store. **Fee:** Standard electric, $22–$24 during peak season. **Parking:** On site.

FACILITIES

Number of Multipurpose Sites: 62. **Hookups:** Electric (30 amps), water. **Each Site:** Grill, water, picnic table. **Dump Station:** Yes. **Laundry:** Yes. **Pay Phone:** Yes. **Restrooms and Showers:** Yes. **Fuel:** 5 mi. **Propane:** 5 mi. **Internal Roads:** Paved. **RV Service:** No. **Market:** No. **Restaurant:** No. **General Store:** Yes. **Vending:** Soda. **Swimming:** Yes. **Playground:** Yes. **Other:** Observation deck, museum store, small fishing lake, shelter rentals. **Activities:** Miniature golf, fishing, basketball, tennis, softball fields, nature trails, nature center, visitor's center w/ mastodon exhibit, bison herd. **Nearby Attractions:** Inquire at campground. **Additional Information:** State of Kentucky, (859) 384-3522.

RESTRICTIONS

Pets: On leash. **Fires:** Fire ring only. **Alcoholic Beverages:** Not publicly displayed. **Vehicle Maximum Length:** 38 ft. (varies according to site). **Other:** No hunting, rappelling, rock climbing, motorized vehicles & bikes, collecting or digging for artifacts.

TO GET THERE

22 mi. southwest of Covington I-75, go south to KY 338, off US 42/127 and I-71/I-75.

Louisiana

Louisiana is one of America's great cultural melting pots. The state's famous festivals are a lively way for visitors to immerse themselves in the local culture. **Mardi Gras** is the crown jewel of Louisiana festivals. From town to town, folks celebrate Mardi Gras in unique ways. Many cities, including **Shreveport-Bossier City,** feature family-oriented Mardi Gras celebrations. Other noteworthy festivals include **Cajun Fun Fest, New Orleans Jazz & Heritage Festival,** and the **Louisiana Folklife Festival.** Call (800) 947-6711 for a statewide calendar of fairs and festivals.

Throughout history, varied peoples have affected Louisiana history and traditions. Native American habitation dates back thousands of years. Learn about these ancient cultures at various mounds and archaeological sights, including **Poverty Point State Historic Site.** Today, the Tunica-Biloxi, Coushatta, and other tribes make rich contributions to the state's economy and culture.

Louisiana has many points of interest for the music lover. In 20th-century New Orleans, the roots of jazz came alive in **Congo Square.** That tradition lives on in the form of dozens of jazz clubs in and around the **French Quarter.** For those who would prefer to keep in the quarter, **Storyville** and **The Maison Bourbon Jazz Club** are all guaranteed to show you a good time. Clubs outside of the Quarter can be a little hard for the novice New Orleans tourist to find—but don't be daunted. A variety of club listings (and maps) to several of New Orleans best clubs can be found at www.satchmo.com. The New Orleans Jazz Festival packs 'em in every year with acts both indigenous and world renowned. Travelers who find themselves in **Ferriday** might want to stop by the **Jerry Lee Lewis Family Museum.** The home of Lewis' sister, Frankie Jean, visitors will be overwhelmed at the vast amount of "Killer" memorabilia. On your way out, feel free to pick up something for the road at the drive-thru liquor store attached to the house. **Ernie K-Doe's "Mother In Law" Lounge** is an off the wall, self-made shrine dedicated to the New Orleans–born singer and his most famous song.

Folks from outside of Louisiana aren't always aware of the state's Hispanic influences. Even before Hernando de Soto arrived in 1541, other Spanish explorers had seen the mouth of the Mississippi. The present-day Isleños community of **St. Bernard Parish** preserve their heritage at the **Isleños Museum.** Vestiges of Spanish colonial culture are also evident throughout New Orleans' famous historic districts.

Louisiana is famous for its Cajun culture, which arose from the great **Acadian Diaspora of 1755.** This tragic phase in Cajun history was brought about when the British tried to force French-speaking colonists in New Brunswick and Nova Scotia to renounce Catholicism. When families refused, they were forced to flee. Great numbers of Acadians made their way to southern Louisiana, where their culture thrives. Learn about Acadian culture at numerous museums, including **Acadian Village** in Lafayette.

No discussion of Louisiana is complete without mentioning the food—it's fabulous. Even if you're heading to Louisiana for primitive tent camping, make plans to stop at one of the state's fine Cajun or seafood restaurants. A number of excellent guidebooks detail Louisiana cuisine.

Louisiana (and New Orleans) is so rich with cultural activities that it's pointless to try to mention them all here. Besides, there are several books and online guides that can help whittle down your tourist options. What we are concerned with is the Louisiana's many beautiful natural habitats and out-of-the-way attractions that are so easily eclipsed by this remarkable state's bustling nightlife.

Close to New Orleans, history buffs can stand the same ground as Andrew Jackson when he defeated British forces during the War of 1812. **Fort Pike** is also the first of the **Third System** fortifications—a group of brick structures that were built to protect the Gulf Coast from future sea-bearing attacks. **Fontainebleau State Park** is home to a sugar mill built in 1829 by Bernard de Marigny de Mandeville, who named the area after a forest near Paris. The park is also habitat to 400 species of birds—making it a must for bird-watchers. Louisiana's dozens of other parks, campgrounds, and bed-and-breakfasts are all perfect ways to enjoy Louisiana's rich diversity without the impedance of a hangover.

Campground Profiles

ANACOCO   MAP, B-1
South Toledo Bend State Park

reserve america

120 Bald Eagle Rd., 71403. T: (888) 398-4770;
www.reserveamerica.com.

🚐 ★★★★   ⛺ ★★★★

Beauty: ★★★   Site Privacy: ★★★★
Spaciousness: ★★★★   Quiet: ★★★
Security: ★★★   Cleanliness: ★★★★
Insect Control: ★★★   Facilities: ★★★★

Pleasantly located on several small bluffs that extend over and into the Toledo Bend Reservoir, South Toledo Bend State Park offers a scenic waterfront view from many vantage points. While the reservoir is nationally recognized as a destination for bass-fishing tournaments, visitors to the park can also enjoy other outdoor recreational activities such as hiking, cycling, bird-watching, camping, and enjoying the many forms of wildlife in the area. The area also is a common nesting ground for the bald eagle, which feeds from the plentiful supply of freshwater fish—including largemouth bass, catfish, bream, and white perch—found in the reservoir. The avid fisher can set out onto the reservoir at the two-lane boat ramp area, to also enjoy a freshly caught dinner. Guests will be able to learn about local animal and plant life at the park's visitor center, with exhibits designed to increase awareness of these species and their role in the environment. An open-air breezeway leads out to the observation deck and a majestic view of the reservoir lake and nearby islands. A 3,000-foot surfaced nature trail provides an opportunity for all visitors to explore the area around the visitor center and the RV camping areas. Also nestled among the trees near the visitor center are several picnic tables, so visitors can enjoy a lunch or snack while enjoying their day at South Toledo Bend State Park.

BASICS
Operated By: Louisiana State Parks. **Open:** All year. **Site Assignment:** Reservations can be made up to 16 weeks in advance. **Registration:** At office. **Fee:** Single, $12–$18; cabin, $90; meeting room, $150. **Parking:** 2 vehicles per site.

FACILITIES
Number of Multipurpose Sites: 81. **Hookups:** Yes. **Dump Station:** Yes. **Laundry:** Yes. **Pay Phone:** Yes. **Restrooms and Showers:** Yes. **Fuel:** No. **Propane:** No. **Internal Roads:** Paved. **RV Service:** Yes. **Market:** No. **Restaurant:** No. **General Store:** Yes. **Vending:** Yes. **Swimming:** Yes. **Playground:** No. **Activities:** Hiking, boating, nature center, fishing, swimming, biking, wildlife.

RESTRICTIONS
Pets: Pets are not allowed in any buildings, including cabins lodges. **Vehicle Maximum Length:** Call ahead.

TO GET THERE
South Toledo Bend State Park is located in Sabine Parish, off LA 191, 16 mi. west of Anacoco. To get to South Toledo Bend State Park from I-20, take LA 171 south to Anacoco; turn west onto LA 111/392, then north onto LA 191. Turn west onto Bass Haven Rd.; the park entrance is 0.5 mi. on the left. To get to the park from I-10/Baton Rouge area, take US 190 to I-49 north to Alexandria; take LA 28 west to Leesville; turn north on LA 171 to Anacoco. For traffic traveling on I-10 from the Lake Charles area, take LA 171 north from Lake Charles into Anacoco.

BASTROP   MAP, A-2
Chemin-A-Haut State Park

reserve america

14656 State Park Rd., 71220-7078.
T: (888) 677-2436; www.reserveamerica.com.

🚐 ★★★★   ⛺ ★★★★

Beauty: ★★★★   Site Privacy: ★★★★
Spaciousness: ★★★★   Quiet: ★★★★
Security: ★★★★   Cleanliness: ★★★★
Insect Control: ★★★★   Facilities: ★★★

Chemin-A-Haut offers one attractive camping loop. Site size is ample, though privacy varies. The most secluded sites are 11, 12, and 14, in the back of the campground. Though distance between sites varies, all are large and comfortably spaced. Mature trees, including oak, hickory, and pine, shade the campground, and undergrowth provides privacy between sites. Sites feature paved back-in parking. Chemin-A-Haut is situated on high bluffs overlooking Bayou Bartholomew and offers a paved walking trail along the water. The large playground and wading pool are a hit with younger children. Older children can cast a line into Big Slough Lake, on the eastern edge of the park. Avoid Chemin-A-Haut on summer and holiday weekends. Summer weather isn't necessarily torturous, so the park makes a good mid-week summertime destination. Security is excellent at this very rural location. Gates are locked at night.

BASICS
Operated By: State of Louisiana Dept. of Culture, Recreation, and Tourism. **Open:** All year. **Site Assignment:** First come, first served; reservations can be held w/ V or MC by calling (888) 677-1400; $10 fee if cancelled 15 days or more before the first reserved day; if cancelled 14 days or less to the first reserved day, then the fee is 1-night's rental of all reserved items. **Registration:** At main office. **Fee:** RV/tent, $16; Golden Access card, 50% off. **Parking:** 3 cars per site or 2 cars and 1 RV.

FACILITIES
Number of Multipurpose Sites: 26. **Hookups:** Electric (30 amps), water. **Each Site:** Tent pad, fire ring, grill, picnic table, lantern hook. **Dump Station:** Yes. **Laundry:** Yes. **Pay Phone:** Yes. **Restrooms and Showers:** Yes. **Fuel:** No. **Propane:** No. **Internal**

Roads: Paved. **RV Service:** 15 mi. south in Bastrop. **Market:** 7 mi. south in Log Cabin. **Restaurant:** 15 mi. south in Bastrop. **General Store:** 15 mi. south in Bastrop. **Vending:** Beverages. **Swimming:** Yes. **Playground:** Yes. **Other:** Hiking trails, baseball field, boat launch, group lodging. **Activities:** Boat renting, hiking, fishing, field games. **Nearby Attractions:** Poverty Point State Commemorative Area, Lake D'Arbonne State Park, Handy Brake National Wildlife Refuge, Georgia Pacific Wildlife Management Area, Lake Claiborne State Park, Caney Creek Lake State Park. **Additional Information:** Bastrop-Morehouse Tourism Commission, (318) 281-3794.

RESTRICTIONS
Pets: On leash only. **Fires:** Fire ring only. **Alcoholic Beverages:** At site only. **Vehicle Maximum Length:** 60 ft. **Other:** 15-day stay limit; be familiar w/ all alligator precautions.

TO GET THERE
From Bastrop take US 425 north 10 mi. Turn right onto LA 2229 (State Park Rd.).

BRAITHWAITE   MAP, C-3, C-4
St. Bernard State Park

P.O. Box 534, 70092. T: (888) 677-7823;
www.reserveamerica.com.

🚐 ★★★★   ⛺ ★★★★

Beauty: ★★★★   Site Privacy: ★★★
Spaciousness: ★★★★   Quiet: ★★★★
Security: ★★★★   Cleanliness: ★★★★
Insect Control: ★★   Facilities: ★★★

St. Bernard is situated around a series of man-made lagoons and provides a habitat for alligators, turtles, and other wetlands wildlife. The Mississippi River is across Hwy. 39 from the park, and Chalmette National Historic Park is nearby. Less than one hour from downtown New Orleans, St. Bernard is popular with folks from the Crescent City. It should be avoided on holiday and festival weekends, especially Jazz Fest. Visit in early April or in the fall if you value tranquility. St. Bernard offers one camping loop, with sites partially shaded by a variety of trees. We like the shadier sites, including 16, 22, 45, and 46. Site privacy is not exceptional. Site size varies immensely. Some are 90 feet from their neighbors, while others are only 25 feet from neighbors. All sites offer paved back-in parking. Remote and gated, St. Bernard offers excellent security.

BASICS
Operated By: State of Louisiana, Dept. of Culture, Recreation, and Tourism. **Open:** All year. **Site Assignment:** First come, first served; reservations can be made w/ a V or MC; $12 deposit; call (888) 677-1400; $12 cancellation fee. **Registration:** At ranger station. **Fee:** $16; Golden Access Card, 50% off. **Parking:** 2 vehicles per site, overflow parking available.

FACILITIES·

Number of Multipurpose Sites: 51. **Hookups:** Electric (30 amps), water. **Each Site:** Picnic table, fire ring, concrete patio, grill. **Dump Station:** Yes. **Laundry:** Yes. **Pay Phone:** Yes. **Restrooms and Showers:** Yes. **Fuel:** No. **Propane:** No. **Internal Roads:** Paved. **RV Service:** 5 mi. west in Chalmette. **Market:** Convenience store 0.5 mi. north, grocery 2 mi. west. **Restaurant:** 1 mi. west. **General Store:** K-Mart is 7 mi. west in Chalmette. **Vending:** Beverages. **Swimming:** Yes (Memorial Day–Labor Day). **Playground:** Yes. **Other:** Trails, field for athletics, pavilion. **Activities:** Hiking, boating, & fishing less than a mile from the State Park. **Nearby Attractions:** Bayou Sagnette State Park, Fairview Riverside State Park, Louisiana State Museum, New Orleans & the Historic French Quarter, Chalmette Battlefield-Jean Lafitte National Historic Park & Preserve, Isleno Cultural Center-Jean Lafitte National Historic Park & Preserve, San Bernardo Scenic Byway, Bayou Sauvage National Wildlife Refuge. **Additional Information:** St. Bernard Parish Tourist Commission (888) 278-2054.

RESTRICTIONS

Pets: Leash only, 5 ft. max. **Fires:** Fire ring only. **Alcoholic Beverages:** Allowed. **Vehicle Maximum Length:** 50 ft.

TO GET THERE

From I-10 get on 510 (Hwy. 47) toward Chalmette. Go 6 mi. to the intersection of Hwy. 46 and turn left. Go 7 mi. to Hwy. 39 and turn right to go south. Go 0.5 mi. and the entrance is on the left.

CHATHAM   MAP, A-2
Jimmie Davis State Park
at Caney Lake

S.R. No. 1209, 71226. T: (888) 677-2263; www.reserveamerica.com.

🚐 ★★★★   ⛺ ★★★★

Beauty: ★★★★★	Site Privacy: ★★★★
Spaciousness: ★★★★★	Quiet: ★★★★
Security: ★★★★★	Cleanliness: ★★★★★
Insect Control: ★★★	Facilities: ★★★

Jimmie Davis State Park features a lovely camping area, with sites laid out along the lakeshore. Sites vary in size. Shadiness also varies—though most sites are shaded by pine and other species, sites 13–17 are quite open. All sites offer paved back-in parking. Few sites offer privacy. The nicest waterfront sites include 38, 40, 42, 43, and 45. However, the crown jewel is site 54, with its knockout view of the lake. Boasting numerous record catches, Caney Lake is bass fishin' heaven. The park maintains two boat launches and a fishing pier as well as an attractive swimming beach. Even though it's off the beaten path, the park is very popular and should be avoided on summer holidays and weekends. Security is excellent. Gates are attended during the day and locked at night.

BASICS

Operated By: State of Louisiana Dept. of Culture, Recreation, and Tourism. **Open:** All year. **Site Assignment:** First come, first served; reservations can be held w/ V or MC; call (888) 677-1400; 1-night cancellation fee. **Registration:** At main office. **Fee:** Premium waterfront, $18; improved, $16; Golden Access card, 50% off. **Parking:** 2 cars or 1 RV and 1 car per site, overflow parking available.

FACILITIES

Number of Multipurpose Sites: 73. **Hookups:** Electric (30 amps), water. **Each Site:** Tent pad, grill, fire ring, picnic table. **Dump Station:** Yes. **Laundry:** Yes. **Pay Phone:** Yes. **Restrooms and Showers:** Yes. **Fuel:** No. **Propane:** No. **Internal Roads:** Paved. **RV Service:** 35 mi. northeast in West Monroe. **Market:** 6 mi. east in Chatham. **Restaurant:** 6 mi. east in Chatham. **General Store:** 15 mi. west in Jonesboro. **Vending:** No. **Swimming:** No. **Playground:** No. **Other:** Fishing pier, pavilions, boat launch. **Activities:** Picnicking, fishing, boating (bring your own). **Nearby Attractions:** Poverty Point State Commemorative Area, Lake D'Arbonne State Park, Historic Town of Chatham, Lake Claiborne State Park, Jackson Bienville Wildlife Management Area. **Additional Information:** Monroe-West Monroe CVB.

RESTRICTIONS

Pets: On leash only. **Fires:** Fire ring. **Alcoholic Beverages:** Allowed (none on beach). **Vehicle Maximum Length:** Approximately 72 ft. **Other:** 15-day stay limit; no 3- or 4-wheelers allowed.

TO GET THERE

From Jonesboro go east on LA 4 for 12.8 mi. then turn right onto Lakeshore Dr. State Park Rd. 1209 is on the right, 20 mi. ahead.

DELHI   MAP, A-2, A-3
Poverty Point Reservoir
State Park

1500 Poverty Point Parkway, 71232. T: (800) 474-0392; www.reserveamerica.com.

🚐 ★★★★   ⛺ ★★★★

Beauty: ★★★	Site Privacy: ★★★
Spaciousness: ★★★	Quiet: ★★★★
Security: ★★★★	Cleanliness: ★★★★
Insect Control: ★★★	Facilities: ★★★★

The 2,700-acre man-made lake that is the center piece for Poverty Point Reservoir State Park offers visitors an outlet for a variety of water-sport activities and a scenic backdrop for waterfowl migration each spring and fall. The site name is derived from a nearby Native American site consisting of complex earthworks and artifacts. Dubbed the Poverty Point culture, its people settled on the banks of Bayou Macon, near what is now the community of Epps, between 1400 and 700 B.C. Park guests are only 20 minutes away from Poverty Point State Historic Site for day trips to what has become a focal point for

archaeological research since the mid-20th century. The fish and wildlife species inhabiting or migrating through the reservoir are numerous. Anglers can fish the lake year-round for largemouth bass, black crappie, blue gill, and channel catfish. The region falls within the Mississippi Flyway for many winged species. Depending on the season, visitors will see cormorants, ducks, geese, and pelicans. Special attention should be given to any Louisiana black bear sightings on or near the reservoir. The eastern edge of the park, along Bayou Macon, contains attractive bear habitat, and visitors are cautioned to keep all exterior cabin areas and day-use areas cleared of accessible food products and refuse. Bear-proof containers are provided for waste disposal throughout the park. The two four-lane boat launches, one at the North Marina Complex and one at the South Landing, provide access to the water. A fish-cleaning station is provided at each launch area for visitor use. Four two-bedroom lodges will each sleep ten people and rent for $90 per night. Lodges provide full kitchen, bathroom, screened porches, and open deck. Bed linens, basic kitchen utensils, and dishware are provided with each unit. Visitors must bring their own towels. A covered boat dock is provided for lodge guests on the southwest shoreline across from the lodge area.

BASICS

Operated By: Louisiana State Parks. **Open:** All year. **Site Assignment:** Reservations can be made up to 16 weeks in advance. **Registration:** At office. **Fee:** Single, $16–$18; lodge, $125. **Parking:** 2 vehicles per site.

FACILITIES

Number of Multipurpose Sites: 65. **Hookups:** Yes. **Dump Station:** No. **Laundry:** No. **Pay Phone:** Yes. **Restrooms and Showers:** Yes. **Fuel:** No. **Propane:** No. **Internal Roads:** Paved. **RV Service:** Yes. **Market:** No. **Restaurant:** No. **General Store:** Yes. **Vending:** Yes. **Swimming:** Yes. **Playground:** No. **Activities:** Boating, canoeing, fishing, hiking, picnicking, swimming, waterskiing, nature/activity center.

RESTRICTIONS

Pets: Pets are not allowed in any buildings, including cabins lodges. **Vehicle Maximum Length:** Call ahead.

TO GET THERE

The site is 3 mi. north of Delhi with separate South Landing and North Marina Complex entrances off LA 17. Travelers heading east or west on I-20 take the Delhi exit and go north.

DOYLINE   MAP, A-1
Lake Bistineau State Park

106 Park Rd., 71023. T: (888) 677-2478; www.reserveamerica.com.

🚐 ★★★★   ⛺ ★★★★

Beauty: ★★★★★   Site Privacy: ★★★★
Spaciousness: ★★★★★   Quiet: ★★★★★
Security: ★★★★   Cleanliness: ★★★★
Insect Control: ★★★   Facilities: ★★★★

The campground at Lake Bistineau consists of one attractive loop. Many sites have lovely views of the lake with its elegant cypress and tupelo trees. Seven sites offer pull-through parking. The rest offer back-in. Parking is paved. Some sites are huge, including number 26, a pull-through with a lake view. Others are close together and offer little privacy. Lake Bistineau is a 200-year-old man-made lake, first created when a goliath log jam caused the Red River to flood. In 1935, a permanent dam was constructed and the lake was enlarged. It now supports black crappie, largemouth bass, yellow bass, bullheads, blue gill, and red ear sunfish. The state park is divided into two areas, each with its own boat launch and swimming pool. The campground is in Area 1. Visit Lake Bistineau in late spring or fall for pleasant weather. Avoid the park on summer weekends and holidays.

BASICS

Operated By: Sate of Louisiana Dept. of Culture, Recreation, and Tourism. **Open:** All year. **Site Assignment:** First come, first served; hold reservation w/ V or MC; call (877) 226-7652; 48-hour cancellation policy; 1-night cancellation fee. **Registration:** At main office. **Fee:** Premium, $18; improved, $16; Golden Access Card, 50% off. **Parking:** 2 cars or 1 car and 1 RV per site. Overflow parking available.

FACILITIES

Number of Multipurpose Sites: 67. **Hookups:** Electric (20, 30 amps), water. **Each Site:** Tent pad, fire ring, picnic table, lantern hook varies. **Dump Station:** Yes. **Laundry:** Yes. **Pay Phone:** Yes. **Restrooms and Showers:** Yes. **Fuel:** No. **Propane:** No. **Internal Roads:** Paved. **RV Service:** 30 mi. northwest in Shreveport. **Market:** 6 mi. north in Doyline. **Restaurant:** 10 mi. north in Doyline. **General Store:** 10 mi. north in Doyline. **Vending:** Beverages. **Swimming:** Yes. **Playground:** Yes. **Other:** Group lodge, boat launch, athletic field, boat rental. **Activities:** Nature trails, boating, swimming. **Nearby Attractions:** Nearby Attractions: Lake Claiborne State Park, Historic Town of Minden, Kisatche National Forest-Caney Lakes Recreation Area, Trails End Public Golf Course, Loggy Bayou Wildlife Management Area, Ambrose Mountain, Driskoll Mountain, Mt. Lebanon, Bodcau Wildlife Management Area. **Additional Information:** Shreveport/Bossier Convention & Tourist Bureau (888) 45-VISIT.

RESTRICTIONS

Pets: On leash only. **Fires:** Fire ring only. **Alcoholic Beverages:** Allowed. **Vehicle Maximum Length:** Approximately 40 ft. **Other:** No fireworks, acquaint yourself w/ all alligator precautions.

TO GET THERE

From Shreveport, take I-20 East to Exit 33 (Haughton/Filmore). Go to the right then take an immediate left on Hwy. 3227, which dead-ends into Hwy. 164. Take a right on 164 and go about 4–5 mi. until you reach the town of Doyline. Take a right at the flashing caution light (Hwy. 163). Keep straight about 8 mi. Look for Lake Bistineau State Park Area sign to the right. Turn left to enter main gate. Stop at park office on right for further instructions.

FARMERVILLE   MAP, A-2
Lake D'Arbonne State Park

reserve america

3628 Evergreen Rd., 71241. T: (888) 677-5200; www.reserveamerica.com.

🚐 ★★★★   ⛺ ★★★★

Beauty: ★★★★★   Site Privacy: ★★★★
Spaciousness: ★★★★   Quiet: ★★★★
Security: ★★★★★   Cleanliness: ★★★★★
Insect Control: ★★★   Facilities: ★★★

The beautiful campground at Lake D'Arbonne is situated in two loops with a fishing pier and boat dock at the campground. The campground is shaded by a lovely stand of loblolly pines and sites feature paved, back-in parking. Most sites are larger than average, with a little greenery providing privacy barriers between sites. Sites 24, 28, 44, and 45 enjoy lake views but are less secluded than some others. For elbow room, head to site 20. The lake is home to gorgeous cypress stands as well as record catches of crappie and bass. The park's well-kept fishing facilities augment the fishing experience. This park is also popular with road bikers due to its roads winding through shady hills. Avoid Lake D'Arbonne on summer holidays and weekends and during hot July and August. This rural park locks its gates at night, making security excellent.

BASICS

Operated By: State of Louisiana Dept. of Culture, Recreation, and Tourism. **Open:** All year. **Site Assignment:** First come, first served; hold reservations w/ MC or V; call (888) 677-1400. 15-day cancellation policy; cancellation fee is 1-day's rental of all reserved items. **Registration:** At entrance station. **Fee:** $18–$16; Golden Access card discount. **Parking:** 2 cars or 1 RV and 1 car per site, extra parking available.

FACILITIES

Number of Multipurpose Sites: 58. **Hookups:** Electric (30 amps), water. **Each Site:** Picnic table, lantern hook, tent pad, grill, fire ring. **Dump Station:** Yes. **Laundry:** Yes. **Pay Phone:** Yes. **Restrooms and Showers:** Yes. **Fuel:** No. **Propane:** No. **Internal Roads:** Paved. **RV Service:** 30 mi. southeast in West Monroe. **Market:** 5 mi. east in Farmerville. **Restaurant:** 5 mi. east in Farmerville. **General Store:** 5 mi. east in Farmerville. **Vending:** No. **Swimming:** Yes. **Playground:** Yes. **Other:** Nature trails, tennis courts, fishing piers, volleyball court, horseshoe court. **Activities:** Nature trails, fishing clinic (call for more information), Easter egg hunt, hay rides, tennis, fishing, picnicking, volleyball, horseshoe. **Nearby Attractions:** Kisatchie National Forest-Corney Lakes Recreation Area, Lincoln Parish Park, Georgia Pacific Wildlife Management Area, Handy Brake National Wildlife Refuge, Louisiana Pur-chase Gardens (Berstein Park). **Additional Information:** Union Parish Tourist Commission Bernice, (318) 285-9333.

RESTRICTIONS

Pets: On leash only. **Fires:** Fire ring only. **Alcoholic Beverages:** At site only. **Vehicle Maximum Length:** Approximately 72 ft. **Other:** 15-day stay limit; no 3- or 4-wheelers allowed.

TO GET THERE

From Farmerville take LA 2 approximately 5 mi. west on the left side.

GARDNER   MAP, B-2
Kincaid Lake Recreation Area

Kisatchie National Forest, 9912 Hwy. 28 West, 71409. T: (318) 793-9427; www.southernregion.fs.fed.us/kisatchie.

🚐 ★★★★★   ⛺ ★★★★★

Beauty: ★★★★★   Site Privacy: ★★★★
Spaciousness: ★★★★★   Quiet: ★★★★★
Security: ★★★★   Cleanliness: ★★★★★
Insect Control: ★★★   Facilities: ★★★★

The campgrounds at Kincaid Lake Recreation Area are gorgeous. Here, large sites are shaded by a variety of lovely southern yellow pine and other upland hardwoods. Dense growth provides privacy between most sites. All sites feature paved back-in parking. Most of the sites don't have views of the water in summertime, but site 23 has a gorgeous water view in wintertime. We also like site 29, which is gargantuan. Kisatchie National Forest is not one contiguous tract. Rather, the forest consists of five land units in central and northern Louisiana. Kincaid Lake area includes large group and day-use facilities. The man-made lake is stocked with sun perch, bass, and catfish. Security is very good here—gates are locked at night during the summer. Summers are extremely hot and humid in southern Louisiana. For the nicest weather, visit in spring or fall.

BASICS

Operated By: U.S.D.A. Forest Service. **Open:** All year. **Site Assignment:** First come, first served; no reservations. **Registration:** Self-reservation at fee box. **Fee:** Double, $20; regular, $15. **Parking:** At sites, limit 2 vehicles.

FACILITIES

Number of Multipurpose Sites: 41. **Hookups:** Electric (30 amps), water. **Each Site:** Picnic table, lantern post, fire ring. **Dump Station:** Yes. **Laundry:** No. **Pay Phone:** No. **Restrooms and Showers:** Yes. **Fuel:** No. **Propane:** No. **Internal Roads:** Paved. **RV Service:** 13 mi. east in Alexandria. **Market:** 13 mi. east in Alexandria. **Restaurant:** 6 mi. east in Tunks. **General Store:** 5 mi. north in Gardner. **Vending:** No. **Swimming:** No. **Playground:** No. **Other:** Picnic pavilions, trails, boat launch, boat dock, fishing pier, swimming beach. **Activities:** Picnicking, road biking, mountain biking, hiking, nature study, swimming, fishing, boating, automobile touring. **Nearby Attractions:** Louisiana Cowboy Town, Frogmore Cotton Plantation & Gins, Tunica-Biloxi Indian Museum, casinos, Hodges Gardens.

Additional Information: Alexandria/Pineville Area CVB, (800) 551-9546.

RESTRICTIONS

Pets: On leash only. **Fires:** Fire ring only. **Alcoholic Beverages:** Allowed. **Vehicle Maximum Length:** 65 ft.

TO GET THERE

From Alexandria, drive west in LA 28 for 13 mi. Turn left onto LA 121 and drive south for 0.5 mi. Turn right onto FS 279 and drive south for 6 mi. Turn onto FS 205, which leads to the campground.

GRAND ISLE · · · · · · · · · · · · · MAP, C-3, C-4
Grand Isle State Park

reserve america

Admiral Craig Dr., 70358. T: (225) 787-2559; www.reserveamerica.com.

🚐 ★★★   ⛺ ★★★★

Beauty: ★★★   Site Privacy: ★
Spaciousness: ★★★   Quiet: ★★★
Security: ★★★★★   Cleanliness: ★★★
Insect Control: ★★   Facilities: ★★★

Grand Isle's 400-foot fishing pier, ponds, and lagoons provide excellent fishing opportunities. Deep-sea fishing off of Grand Isle is extraordinary, and commercial guide services abound. Birdwatchers appreciate the variety of wetland habitats found at Grand Isle. The campgrounds at Grand Isle are smaller than average, with gravel parking for tent campers. All sites are back-in parking, with the exception of 49 pull-throughs. Sites are totally open, so come equipped with awnings, umbrellas, and sunscreen. Since all sites are bland, choose your site based on proximity to the beach. Tent campers have better choices; primitive camping is allowed on the beautiful beach. Security is excellent at Grand Isle. The park is excruciatingly remote and it's gated. Avoid Grand Isle in late summer, when it's horribly hot. Also, be sure to arm yourself with insect repellent.

BASICS

Operated By: Louisiana State Parks. **Open:** All year. **Site Assignment:** No reservations for tent/beach sites. **Registration:** At camp office. **Fee:** $18 per night per vehicle; Golden Access, 50% discount; V, MC, cash, money order, LA check. **Parking:** Sites plus overflow.

FACILITIES

Number of RV-only Sites: 49. **Number of Tent-only Sites:** 76. **Hookups:** Electric (30, 50 amps), water. **Each Site:** Picnic table, fire ring. **Dump Station:** Yes. **Laundry:** No. **Pay Phone:** Yes. **Restrooms and Showers:** Yes. **Fuel:** No. **Propane:** No. **Internal Roads:** Paved & gravel. **RV Service:** 100 mi. **Market:** 3 mi. **Restaurant:** 3 mi. **General Store:** 3 mi. **Vending:** In the Park. **Swimming:** No. **Playground:** No. **Other:** Fishing piers, fish-cleaning station. **Activities:** Fishing, crabbing, birding, swimming, nature trail, gulf beaches. **Nearby Attractions:** Fishing rodeos in Grand Isle, charter boats, Wisner Wildlife Management Area, Fort Liv-

ingston, 2 hours to New Orleans. **Additional Information:** Grand Isle Tourist Commission (985) 787-2997.

RESTRICTIONS

Pets: On leash only. **Fires:** Small okay. **Alcoholic Beverages:** Allowed; no glass containers. **Vehicle Maximum Length:** No limit.

TO GET THERE

From US 90 (New Orleans), take LA 1 south to Grand Isle, where Hwy. 1 becomes Admiral Craik Dr. The State Park is on the far east end of the island.

HOMER · · · · · · · · · · · · · · · MAP, A-1, A-2
Lake Claiborne State Park

reserve america

225 State Park Rd., 71040. T: (888) 677-2524; www.reserveamerica.com.

🚐 ★★★★   ⛺ ★★★★

Beauty: ★★★★★   Site Privacy: ★★★★
Spaciousness: ★★★★   Quiet: ★★★★
Security: ★★★★★   Cleanliness: ★★★★
Insect Control: ★★★   Facilities: ★★★★

Swimming, fishing, bird-watchinging, boating of all kinds, waterskiing, camping, hiking, or just plain relaxing and enjoying the unsurpassed natural beauty—Lake Claiborne State Park has it all. For fishermen, the freshwater lake is lavishly stocked with largemouth bass, bluegill sunfish, channel catfish, black crappie, striped bass, chain pickerel, bream, and white perch. The lake itself has a surface area of 6,400 acres. One of the most popular activities for visitors is swimming at the park's sandy beach situated on an inlet of the lake and protected from boats and waterskiers. Ecologists and sportsmen alike hail the lake's excellent water quality. The woods of Lake Claiborne are home to a wide variety of wildlife. Lovely nature trails and a scenic overlook allow you to appreciate the beauty of the area at your own pace. Nature tours are offered on a regular basis, and a park naturalist is available to present nature-based programs and give guided hikes.

BASICS

Operated By: State of Louisiana, Dept. of Culture, Recreation, and Tourism. **Open:** All year. **Site Assignment:** First come, first served; reservations can be made w/ V, MC, D, AE; call (877) 226-7652; no out of state checks allowed; cancellation fee is 1-night's rate. **Registration:** At entrance station. **Fee:** RV/tent, $12–$18; Golden Access card discount. **Parking:** 2 vehicles per site, overflow parking available.

FACILITIES

Number of Multipurpose Sites: 87. **Hookups:** Electric (30, 50 amps), water. **Each Site:** Picnic table, grill, fire ring, some have lantern hook, tent pad. **Dump Station:** Yes. **Laundry:** Yes. **Pay Phone:** Yes. **Restrooms and Showers:** Yes. **Fuel:** No. **Propane:** No. **Internal Roads:** Paved. **RV Service:** 12 mi. northwest in Homer. **Market:** 12

mi. northwest in Homer. **Restaurant:** 12 mi. northwest in Homer. **General Store:** 15 mi. northwest in Homer. **Vending:** No. **Swimming:** No. **Playground:** Yes. **Other:** Group lodging, boat launch, fishing pier, primitive canoe camp sites available, nature trails. **Activities:** Guided/unguided hiking trails, fishing, boating of all kinds, waterskiing, nature-based programs. **Nearby Attractions:** Poverty Point State Historic Site, Lake Bistineau State Park, Lake D'Arbonne State Park, historic town of Homer, Lincoln Parish Park, Kisatchie National Forest–Caney Lakes Recreation Area, Jimmie Davis State Park at Caney Lake, Jackson Bienville Wildlife Management Area, Georgia Pacific Wildlife Management Area. **Additional Information:** Homer Chamber of Commerce.

RESTRICTIONS

Pets: On leash only. **Fires:** Ring only. **Alcoholic Beverages:** Allowed. **Vehicle Maximum Length:** 60 ft. **Other:** 15-day stay limit.

TO GET THERE

From the intersection of Hwy. 79 and Hwy. 146 in Homer, go southeast on Hwy. 146 for 7 mi.; the park entrance will be on the left.

INDEPENDENCE · · · · · · · · · · MAP, B-3
Indian Creek Campground and RV Park

53013 West Fontana Rd., 70443. T: (985) 878-6567.

🚐 ★★★   ⛺ ★★★

Beauty: ★★★   Site Privacy: ★★★
Spaciousness: ★★★   Quiet: ★★★
Security: ★★★   Cleanliness: ★★★
Insect Control: ★★★   Facilities: ★★★

Indian Creek offers shady sites situated in numerous small sections. Though privacy varies, most sites are on the small side. All sites feature gravel parking. There are both back-in and pull-through sites. Our favorite sites are 86–91, small, wooded, pull-throughs. Families should ask for a site in the front of the park, near the playground, wash house, and other amenities. There's plenty to keep kids busy here, but we don't recommend Indian Creek as a vacation destination. It's better used as a convenient stop over. There are plenty of shops and restaurants nearby. Unfortunately, Indian Creek had an unpleasant smell while we were there. Stay away from southeastern Louisiana in late summer, when the heat and humidity are oppressive. Security is fair. There are no gates, but Indian Creek is in a quiet area.

BASICS

Operated By: Bob and Kathy Albright. **Open:** All year. **Site Assignment:** First come, first served or by reservation. **Registration:** At office in store, 9 a.m.–8 p.m. Sun.–Thurs., 9 a.m.–10 p.m. Fri. & Sat. **Fee:** RV, $33; primitive, $19; holidays, $22.50; $5 per extra person, max. 7 people. **Parking:** Sites plus overflow.

FACILITIES

Number of RV-only Sites: 184. **Number of Tent-only Sites:** 100. **Hookups:** Electric (30 amps), water, some sewer. **Each Site:** Picnic table, grills available. **Dump Station:** Yes. **Laundry:** Yes. **Pay Phone:** Yes. **Restrooms and Showers:** Yes. **Fuel:** No. **Propane:** Yes. **Internal Roads:** Gravel. **RV Service:** On call. **Market:** Yes. **Restaurant:** 5 mi. **General Store:** 10 mi. (Wal-Mart), 2 mi. (Piggly Wiggly). **Vending:** Beverages. **Swimming:** Yes. **Playground:** 2. **Activities:** Fishing pond (catch & release), hiking & biking trails, basketball court, volleyball, horseshoes, paddle-boat & canoe rentals, scheduled activities on weekends. **Nearby Attractions:** Global Wildlife, swamp tours, alligator farm, Aquarium of the Americas, 55 mi. to New Orleans. **Additional Information:** Tangipahoa Parish Tourist Commission, (504) 542-7520; New Orleans CVB, (800) 672-6124.

RESTRICTIONS

Pets: On leash only. **Fires:** Allowed. **Alcoholic Beverages:** Allowed. **Vehicle Maximum Length:** 55–60 ft. **Other:** Quiet hours enforced.

TO GET THERE

From I-55, take Exit 41, go 1,000 feet west on Hwy. 40 to Fontana Rd. Turn left, campground is 1.5 mi. on the right.

KINDER   MAP, B-2
Grand Casino Coushatta Luxury RV Resort at Red Shoes Park

777 Coushatta Dr., P.O. Box 1510, 70648. T: (888) 867-8727 or (888)-77-GRAND; www.gccoushatta.com.

🚐 ★★★★   ⛺ n/a

Beauty: ★★★   Site Privacy: ★★
Spaciousness: ★★★   Quiet: ★★★★
Security: ★★★★   Cleanliness: ★★★★★
Insect Control: ★★★★   Facilities: ★★★★

The Coushatta Tribe of Louisiana run an extremely tidy campground on a flat piece of land behind their Grand Casino. The swimming pool and other facilities are spotless as well. The drawback here is the overly sanitized landscaping. There are no mature trees to break the park's visual monotony. The campground consists of two main areas which flank a picturesque fishing pond. Sites are larger than average but are neither shady nor private. Each site has paved parking, a paved patio, and a grassy plot. Most sites are pull-through style (128). Couples seeking solitude should try for lakeside sites 24–39. Families with children should score a site close to the pool. Security is very good. The park is gated 24/7, but there is no fence around the campground. Avoid southern Louisiana in sticky, hot late summer. For the mildest weather, visit in spring or fall.

BASICS

Operated By: Grand Casino Coushatta. **Open:** All year. **Site Assignment:** First come, first served; reservations can be held w/ a major credit card; call (888) 677-1400; specific sites may not be reserved; 24-hour cancellation policy; no refund for less than 24-hour notice. **Registration:** At main lodge. **Fee:** Weekends, $18.95 plus tax; weekdays, $14.95 plus tax. **Parking:** 2 vehicles per site, overflow parking available.

FACILITIES

Number of Multipurpose Sites: 158. **Hookups:** Electric (30, 50 amps), water. **Each Site:** Fire ring, picnic table. **Dump Station:** Yes. **Laundry:** Yes. **Pay Phone:** Yes. **Restrooms and Showers:** Yes. **Fuel:** No. **Propane:** No. **Internal Roads:** Paved. **RV Service:** On call. **Market:** 7 mi. south in Kinder. **Restaurant:** 1 mi. **General Store:** 17 mi. north in Oakdale. **Vending:** Beverage, snacks. **Swimming:** Yes. **Playground:** Yes. **Other:** Internet hookup in the main lodge, pier, athletic courts, small group chalets. **Activities:** Volleyball, paddleboating, tennis, shuffleboard, horseshoes, fishing, basketball. **Nearby Attractions:** Grand Casino. **Additional Information:** Avoyelles Commission of Tourism, (800) 833-4195.

RESTRICTIONS

Pets: On leash only. **Fires:** Fire ring that is located behind the main lodge (not 1 per site). **Alcoholic Beverages:** Allowed. **Vehicle Maximum Length:** No limit.

TO GET THERE

Get off I-10 onto Hwy. 165 (Exit 44) north. The park entrance is 35 mi. north on the left side.

LAKE CHARLES   MAP, C-1
Sam Houston Jones State Park

reserve america

107 Sutherland Rd., 70611. T: (888) 677-7264; www.reserveamerica.com.

🚐 ★★★★   ⛺ ★★★★

Beauty: ★★★★   Site Privacy: ★★★
Spaciousness: ★★★★   Quiet: ★★★★
Security: ★★★★   Cleanliness: ★★★★
Insect Control: ★★★   Facilities: ★★★

This suburban park is nestled into the West Fork of the Calcasieu River, where it meets the Houston River. Park boat launches provide access to the Gulf of Mexico as well as the river system. Within the park, a series of lagoons provides refuge for alligators, ducks, and geese. Known as one of the finest bird-watching areas in the state, the park is a home to migratory waterfowl in the spring. There are two camping areas at Sam Houston Jones: Area 1 includes pretty sites lining a lagoon (tent sites 16–19 and RV sites 12–21 are especially attractive), while Area 2 may be a better choice for families (sites 35 and 37 are near the playground). All sites are shaded by a variety of trees, including cypress in low-lying areas. There are back-in and pull-through sites. Some sites offer gravel parking, others offer paved. Sites are larger than average, but not very private. Gates lock at night, making security good. Avoid muggy late summer in southern Louisiana.

BASICS

Operated By: State of Louisiana Dept. of Culture, Recreation, and Tourism. **Open:** All year. **Site Assignment:** By reservation and first come first served; reservations held w/ V or MC; call (888) 677-1400; 15-day cancellation policy; cancellation fee is 1-night's rent of all reserved items. **Registration:** At entrance station. **Fee:** RV, $16–$18; tent, $16; primi-

tive, $1; Golden Access card, 50% off. **Parking:** 2 cars per site, overflow parking lot.

FACILITIES

Number of Tent-only Sites: 19. **Number of Multipurpose Sites:** 62. **Hookups:** Electric (20, 30 amps), water; 20 RV w/ electric, water, sewer. **Each Site:** Fire ring, tent pad, some sites have picnic tables. **Dump Station:** Yes. **Laundry:** No. **Pay Phone:** Yes. **Restrooms and Showers:** Yes. **Fuel:** No. **Propane:** No. **Internal Roads:** Paved. **RV Service:** 15 mi. in West Lake. **Market:** 10 mi. north in Moss Bluff. **Restaurant:** 10 mi. north in Moss Bluff. **General Store:** 10 mi. north in Moss Bluff. **Vending:** No. **Swimming:** No. **Playground:** Yes. **Other:** Group lodge, boat launch, nature trails. **Activities:** Boating, hiking, children's weekend nature activities, picnicking, fishing. **Nearby Attractions:** Creole Nature Trail National Scenic Byway, Sabine National Wildlife Refuge, Cameron Prairie National Wildlife Refuge, Lacassine National Wildlife Refuge, Rockefeller Wildlife Refuge. **Additional Information:** Southwest Louisiana/Lake Charles CVB, (800) 456-SWLA.

RESTRICTIONS

Pets: On leash. **Fires:** Fire ring only. **Alcoholic Beverages:** Allowed. **Vehicle Maximum Length:** No limit. **Other:** 15-day stay limit.

TO GET THERE

From I-10, take Exit No. 33 in Lake Charles. Go north on Hwy. 171. At the first light in Moss bluff take a left onto 378. Take a right onto Sam Houston Jones Pkwy.

MADISONVILLE   MAP, B-3
Fairview-Riverside State Park

reserve america

119 Fairview Dr., 70447. T: (985) 845-3318 or (888) 677-3247; www.reserveamerica.com.

🚐 ★★★   ⛺ ★★★

Beauty: ★★★★   Site Privacy: ★★★
Spaciousness: ★★★   Quiet: ★★★
Security: ★★★   Cleanliness: ★★★
Insect Control: ★★★   Facilities: ★★★

The nice-looking campground at Fairview-Riverside offers mid-sized sites shaded by moss-laden oaks and other hardwoods. There is little foliage to provide privacy between sites. All parking is paved, back-in style. For shade, we like sites near the front of the campground. Popular sites in the back enjoy river views. Fairview-Riverside is an elegant little park nestled into a bend in the Tchefuncte River. Fishing, crabbing, and boating are favorite pastimes here. The historic Otis House (ca. 1880) serves as an elegant reminder of Frank Otis, who, upon his death, donated the park's land to the state in 1961. When we arrived, we were greeted by one of the park's lovely peacocks. Avoid southeastern Louisiana in late summer, when heat and humidity are unbearable. Security is fair at this suburban park; the entrance is gated, but there is no fence around the park.

BASICS

Operated By: Louisiana State Parks. **Open:** All year. **Site Assignment:** First come, first served. **Registration:** At park entrance, Sun.-Thurs., 6 a.m.–9 p.m.; Fri. & Sat., 6 a.m.–10 p.m. **Fee:** $12–$18; max. 6 people; Golden Access, 50% discount. **Parking:** Sites, parking areas.

FACILITIES

Number of RV-only Sites: 81. **Number of Tent-only Sites:** 20. **Hookups:** Electric (30, 50 amps), water. **Each Site:** Picnic table, grill, fire ring, lantern poles on tent sites. **Dump Station:** Yes. **Laundry:** Yes. **Pay Phone:** Yes. **Restrooms and Showers:** Yes. **Fuel:** 0.5 mi. **Propane:** No. **Internal Roads:** Paved. **RV Service:** 30 mi. **Market:** 3 mi. **Restaurant:** 1 mi. **General Store:** 10 mi. **Vending:** No. **Swimming:** No. **Playground:** Yes. **Other:** Boat launch. **Activities:** Fishing, waterskiing & water sports, rental pavilions, Otis House Museum, walking trail. **Nearby Attractions:** Fontainebleau State Park, Fort Pike State Commemorative Area, Tammany Trace trail for bicycling, hiking, horseback riding, New Orleans. **Additional Information:** New Orleans CVB, (800) 672-6124; Slidell CVB, (504) 646-6426.

RESTRICTIONS

Pets: On leash only. **Fires:** Fire rings, grills only. **Alcoholic Beverages:** Allowed. **Vehicle Maximum Length:** No limit. **Other:** 15-day stay limit.

TO GET THERE

From the east, take I-12 Exit 59 at Mandeville (from the west Exit 57). Take Hwy. 190 south to Hwy. 22. Go west 5 mi., the park is on the right. From New Orleans, take the Causeway/Hwy. 190 north to Hwy. 22.

MANDEVILLE — MAP, B-3
Fontainebleau State Park

reserve america

62883 Hwy. 1089, 70448. T: (504) 624-4443 or (888) 677-3668; www.reserveamerica.com.

🚐 ★★★★   ⛺ ★★★★

Beauty: ★★★★   Site Privacy: ★★★★
Spaciousness: ★★★★★   Quiet: ★★★★
Security: ★★★★   Cleanliness: ★★★★
Insect Control: ★★★   Facilities: ★★★

Built on a former sugar plantation, Fontainebleau harbors the ruins of an 1829 sugar mill. The park is situated on Lake Pontchartrain, between Bayou Castine and Cane Bayou. Fishermen may try their luck on the lakeshore or on a two-acre brackish pond. The Tammany Trace, an 18-mile multiuse "rail to trail" conversion, is also near the park. The campgrounds at Fontainebleau feature many attractive sites and a few beautiful sites. There are two main areas, "Improved" and "Unimproved." In the improved area, there are huge pull-through sites with refreshing shade cover, including loblolly pine. Dense foliage provides privacy between some sites. The unimproved area contains more hardwoods, such as sweet gum and live oak, and is preferable for

tent campers. Security is very good at this suburban park, and gates are locked at night. Avoid southern Louisiana in boiling-hot late summer.

BASICS

Operated By: Louisiana State Parks. **Open:** All year. **Site Assignment:** By reservation and first come, first served. **Registration:** At ranger station, Sun.–Thurs., 7 a.m.–9 p.m.; Fri. & Sat., 7 a.m.–10 p.m. **Fee:** $12–$18; Golden Access discount; cash, LA check, V, MC. **Parking:** Sites plus lots.

FACILITIES

Number of RV-only Sites: 132. **Number of Tent-only Sites:** 200. **Hookups:** Electric (most 30, some 50 amps), water. **Each Site:** Picnic table (all developed sites, most primitive), grill or fire ring (all developed sites, some primitive). **Dump Station:** Yes. **Laundry:** Yes. **Pay Phone:** Yes. **Restrooms and Showers:** Yes. **Fuel:** No. **Propane:** No. **Internal Roads:** Paved. **RV Service:** In Mandeville. **Market:** 2.5 mi. in Mandeville. **Restaurant:** 2.5 mi. in Mandeville. **General Store:** No. **Vending:** Beverages. **Swimming:** Yes. **Playground:** Yes. **Other:** Sailboat launch (shallow). **Activities:** Beach on Lake Pontchartrain, fishing pond, bicycle trail, nature trail, hiking trail, boardwalk, interpretive ranger programs weekends. **Nearby Attractions:** Swamp tours, antique shopping in Ponchatoula, Tammany Trace bicycling & equestrian trails, Pearl River Wildlife Management Area, New Orleans. **Additional Information:** New Orleans CVB, (800) 672-6124.

RESTRICTIONS

Pets: On leash only. **Fires:** At sites only. **Alcoholic Beverages:** Allowed. **Vehicle Maximum Length:** No limit. **Other:** 15-day stay limit, then 7 days out.

TO GET THERE

From New Orleans, take the Causeway north, across Lake Pontchartrain, then take the first exit onto US 190 East. The park is on the right in 6 mi. From I-12, take Exit 65, then drive 3.5 mi. south to the traffic light at US 190. Turn left and the park is on the right in 2.5 mi.

MINDEN — MAP, A-1
Caney Lakes Recreation Area

Kisatchie National Forest, 3288 Hwy. 795, 71040. T: (318) 927-2061; www.southernregion.fs.fed.us/kisatchie.

🚐 ★★★★   ⛺ ★★★★

Beauty: ★★★★★   Site Privacy: ★★★★★
Spaciousness: ★★★★★   Quiet: ★★★★★
Security: ★★★★   Cleanliness: ★★★★
Insect Control: ★★★   Facilities: ★★★

The beautiful campground at Caney Lakes Recreation Area includes giant sites with paved back-in parking. Sites are partially shaded by loblolly and short leaf pine and other species. However, growth is not too thick, a blessing that allows campers to enjoy gorgeous water views. On the Turtle Slide tent loop, we especially like waterfront sites 10, 11, 13, and 15. On the Beaver Dam RV loop, we like waterfront sites 10–15. The Caney Lakes area consists of a number of lakes offering excellent fishing for bass, crappie, bluegill,

sand bass, and catfish. Boat launches and docks are available at nearby day-use areas. There is also a seven-mile hiking trail. The area is popular in autumn, when its rolling hills are resplendent with color. Visit on weekdays in summer and fall. Security is very good at Caney—the campground is remote and gated.

BASICS

Operated By: Federal Government, Caney Ranger District. **Open:** All year. **Site Assignment:** First come, first served. **Registration:** Self-register at fee box. **Fee:** RV, $10; tent, $5. **Parking:** At sites.

FACILITIES

Number of RV-only Sites: 28. **Number of Tent-only Sites:** 21. **Hookups:** Electric (30 amps), water. **Each Site:** Picnic table, fire ring, grill, RV pads, tent pads. **Dump Station:** Yes. **Laundry:** No. **Pay Phone:** Yes. **Restrooms and Showers:** Yes. **Fuel:** No. **Propane:** No. **Internal Roads:** Paved. **RV Service:** 7 mi. south in Minden. **Market:** 7 mi. south in Minden. **Restaurant:** 7 mi. south in Minden. **General Store:** 7 mi. south in Minden. **Vending:** No. **Swimming:** No. **Playground:** Yes. **Other:** Hiking trails, volleyball net, boat ramp, dock, swimming beach, picnic area. **Activities:** Hiking, fishing, boating, waterskiing, picnicking. **Nearby Attractions:** Inquire at campground. **Additional Information:** Minden Chamber of Commerce.

RESTRICTIONS

Pets: On leash only. **Fires:** Allowed. **Alcoholic Beverages:** Allowed. **Vehicle Maximum Length:** 50 ft.

TO GET THERE

From Shreveport or Monroe take the Minden/Dubberly exit. Turn left onto Hwy. 79. Keep straight through the traffic light. Follow the signs.

SPRINGFIELD — MAP, B-3
Tickfaw State Park

reserve america

27225 Patterson Rd., 70462-8906. T: (225) 294-5020 or (877) 226-7652; www.reserveamerica.com.

🚐 ★★★★   ⛺ ★★★★

Beauty: ★★★★★   Site Privacy: ★★★★
Spaciousness: ★★★★★   Quiet: ★★★★★
Security: ★★★★★   Cleanliness: ★★★★
Insect Control: ★★★   Facilities: ★★★

Bordered on the southwest side by the Tickfaw River, this state park is popular with canoeists. Lucky visitors spot snowy egrets and great blue herons along the river. Convenient to both Baton Rouge and New Orleans, Tickfaw is extremely popular with Louisiana residents. In the area, folks enjoy pick-your-own strawberry, blackberry, and blueberry farms. The campground features huge, beautiful RV sites with varying degrees of shade. All parking is paved, back-in style, with extremely long pads. Shade and privacy vary from site to site. The tent camping area at Tickfaw is fabulous, with shady woods and a little foliage between most sites. We especially liked tent sites 37, 39, 41, 43, and 47. The wash houses at Tickfaw are nice and spacious. Avoid southern Louisiana when heat and humidity become oppressive in late summer. Security is excellent at Tickfaw—the park is remote and gated.

BASICS

Operated By: Louisiana State Parks. **Open:** All year. **Site Assignment:** First come, first served and reservations. **Registration:** At fee station at park entrance, Sun.–Thurs., 7 a.m.–9 p.m.; Fri. & Sat., 7 a.m.–10 p.m. **Fee:** Electric/water, $16; tent, $12; Golden Access, 50% off. **Parking:** Sites plus overflow.

FACILITIES

Number of RV-only Sites: 30. **Number of Tent-only Sites:** 20. **Hookups:** Electric (20, 30, 50 amps), water. **Each Site:** Picnic table, grill/fire ring, lantern post, tent pad (tent sites only). **Dump Station:** Yes. **Laundry:** Yes. **Pay Phone:** Yes. **Restrooms and Showers:** Yes. **Fuel:** No. **Propane:** No. **Internal Roads:** Paved. **RV Service:** No. **Market:** 4 mi. **Restaurant:** 20 minutes to Hammond. **General Store:** No. **Vending:** Yes. **Swimming:** No. **Playground:** No. **Activities:** Canoe rentals, fishing, elevated boardwalks, nature center w/ guided hikes & children's activities, hiking trails. **Nearby Attractions:** Turtle & alligator tours, Ponchatoula Historic District, Fairview-Riverside State Park, Global Wildlife Park, 35 mi. to Baton Rouge, 50 mi. to New Orleans. **Additional Information:** Livingston Parish Tourist Commission, New Orleans CVB, (800) 672-6124

RESTRICTIONS

Pets: No pets, except in campers. **Fires:** At sites, rings only (firewood from ground only, no cutting). **Alcoholic Beverages:** Allowed. **Vehicle Maximum Length:** Varies. **Other:** Speed limit enforced, Rangers always on duty.

TO GET THERE

From I-12, take Exit 32 Albany/Springfield, then go south on LA 43 for 2 mi., merge w/ LA 42, and go 1 more mi. to the center of Springfield. At the only traffic light, turn right (west) on LA 1037, and go 6 mi. to Patterson Rd. (from Woodland Baptist Church). Turn left (south) 1.2 mi. to the park entrance.

ST. JOSEPH   MAP, A-3
Lake Bruin State Park

reserve america

Hwy. 1 Box 183, 71366. T: (318) 766-3530 or (877) 226-7652; www.reserveamerica.com.

🚐 ★★★★   ⛺ ★★★★

Beauty: ★★★★★	Site Privacy: ★★★
Spaciousness: ★★★	Quiet: ★★★★
Security: ★★★★	Cleanliness: ★★★★
Insect Control: ★★	Facilities: ★★★★

The pretty campground at this small state park is a real treat. Campers enjoy a view of Lake Bruin, an oxbow lake, formerly part of the Mississippi River. Fishing is excellent here—launches, docks, and three piers support fishing and the quest for crappie, bluegill, and largemouth bass. The lakeshore is lined with cypress trees, and the sunset over the lake is absolutely gorgeous. The campground is laid out in two areas, each with its own bathhouse. Sites are not outstanding in size or other features. However, the views of Lake Bruin are outstanding. Sumptuous lakefront campsites include numbers 1–20. All sites offer paved back-in style parking, with only one pull-through site. Elegant moss-covered oaks shade campsites but provide little privacy. Lake Bruin State Park is remote and gated, making it extra secure. Visit in spring or fall for the best weather and the best bass fishin'.

BASICS

Operated By: Louisiana State Parks. **Open:** All year. **Site Assignment:** First come, first served; reservations accepted. **Registration:** At park entrance, Sun.–Thurs., 6 a.m.–9 p.m.; Fri. & Sat., 6 a.m.–10 p.m. **Fee:** $12–$18; Golden Access, 50% discount; cash, LA check, V, MC. **Parking:** Sites plus overflow.

FACILITIES

Number of Multipurpose Sites: 25. **Hookups:** Electric (50 amps), water. **Each Site:** Picnic table, grill, fire ring. **Dump Station:** Yes. **Laundry:** Yes. **Pay Phone:** Yes. **Restrooms and Showers:** Yes. **Fuel:** No. **Propane:** No. **Internal Roads:** Paved. **RV Service:** 90 mi. in Monroe. **Market:** 3 mi. in St. Joseph. **Restaurant:** 3 mi. in St. Joseph. **General Store:** 45 mi. in Winnsboro. **Vending:** No. **Swimming:** No. **Playground:** Yes. **Other:** Boat launch. **Activities:** Lake swimming, fishing (boat or pier). **Nearby Attractions:** Winter Quarters Commemorative area & Plantation Home, Natchez Trace, Vicksburg casinos, National Military Park. **Additional Information:** St. Joseph Mayor's Office, (318) 766-3713.

RESTRICTIONS

Pets: On leash only. **Fires:** At sites, rings only. **Alcoholic Beverages:** Allowed. **Vehicle Maximum Length:** 45 ft.

TO GET THERE

From I-20, take US 65 south to LA 128. Turn left (east), then at LA 606 turn left (north). Turn right on LA 604, campground is on the left. From the south, take US 65 north and turn right (east) on LA 128.

ST. MARTINVILLE   MAP, C-2
Lake Fausse Pointe State Park

reserve america

5400 Levee Rd., 70582. T: (888) 677-7200; www.reserveamerica.com.

🚐 ★★★★   ⛺ ★★★★

Beauty: ★★★★★	Site Privacy: ★★★★
Spaciousness: ★★★★★	Quiet: ★★★★★
Security: ★★★★★	Cleanliness: ★★★★
Insect Control: ★★★	Facilities: ★★★

At 6,000 acres, Lake Fausse Point is one of Louisiana's larger state parks. The park is situated on a peninsula on Lake Fausse Point. Inside the park is a system of streams, complete with canoe trails. The park also maintains walking and hiking trails with varying difficulty levels. The park is built on former swampland. The park is adjacent to the Atchafalaya Basin, a huge swamp that once covered most of the land between the Mississippi River and Bayou Teche. The flat campground consists of two areas along Barrow Pit Canal. Boat docks at the campgrounds provide convenient access to local waters. Sites are large and lovely. Each site features paved back-in parking plus a gravel picnic area. A variety of hardwoods shade the campground. Unfortunately, there is little foliage between sites. The nicest sites, 27–33, have gorgeous water views and are closest to the docks. Security is excellent at this ultra-remote park. Avoid this area in July and August—the heat and humidity are unbearable.

BASICS

Operated By: State of Louisiana Dept. of Culture, Recreation, and Tourism. **Open:** All year. **Site Assignment:** First come, first served; reservations held w/ V or MC; call (877) 226-7652. 15-day cancellation policy; cancellation fee is 1-day's rental for all reserved items for late cancellations and $10 for 15-day cancellations. **Registration:** At main office. **Fee:** $12–$18; Golden Access card, 50% discount. **Parking:** At site.

FACILITIES

Number of Multipurpose Sites: 50. **Hookups:** Electric (20, 30 amps), water. **Each Site:** Tent pad, fire ring, grill, lantern hook, picnic table. **Dump Station:** Yes. **Laundry:** Yes. **Pay Phone:** Yes. **Restrooms and Showers:** Yes. **Fuel:** No. **Propane:** No. **Internal Roads:** Paved. **RV Service:** 40 mi. west in Lafayette. **Market:** 18 mi. west in St. Martinville. **Restaurant:** 18 mi. west in St. Martinville. **General Store:** 10 mi. west in Cotau Holmes. **Vending:** Beverages. **Swimming:** No. **Playground:** Yes. **Other:** Volleyball net, athletic fields, nature trails, boat launch. **Activities:** Business retreats, canoe swamp tours, volleyball, basketball, hiking, fishing, backpacking trails where tent camping is available on the trail, overnight canoe rides where tent camping is available, children's activities. **Nearby Attractions:** Cypremort Point State Park, Longfellow-Evangeline State Historic Site, historic town of St. Martinville, historic town of New Iberia, plantations along Bayou Teche. **Additional Information:** St. Martin Parish Tourist Commission, (888) 565-5939.

RESTRICTIONS

Pets: On leash only. **Fires:** Fire ring only. **Alcoholic Beverages:** Allowed. **Vehicle Maximum Length:** 62 ft. **Other:** No swimming; 15-day stay limit.

TO GET THERE

From I-10 going south toward Lafayette, take Breaux Bridge Town exit. Turn right onto Hwy. 31 going south and go to St. Martinville. Turn left in St. Martinville onto Hwy. 96 and drive for 3.5 mi. Turn right onto Hwy. 679, drive for 4.3 mi., and then turn left onto Hwy. 3083. Turn right onto Levee Rd. and the park will be 8 mi. south on the right.

VILLE PLATTE   MAP, B-2
Chicot State Park

3469 Chicot Park Rd., 70586. T: (888) 677-2442 or (337) 363-2403; www.reserveamerica.com.

🚐 ★★★★★   ▲ ★★★★★

Beauty: ★★★★★	Site Privacy: ★★★★★
Spaciousness: ★★★★★	Quiet: ★★★★★
Security: ★★★★★	Cleanliness: ★★★★
Insect Control: ★★★★	Facilities: ★★★

Chicot State Park is adjacent to the Louisiana State Arboretum, which offers educational strolls through 300 acres of mature beech-magnolia forest. The Arboretum is home to diverse plants, showcasing species that usually grow in other parts of the state. Chicot State Park maintains extensive fishing, boating, and swimming facilities along the shore of Lake Chicot. There are two camping areas at Chicot. We fell in love with the beautiful South Landing Campground—it's newer and with bigger sites. All of the sites are shaded by gorgeous trees and feature paved back-in parking. Some sites are exceptionally large and many are extremely secluded. In South Landing, the largest sites include 24, 26, and 76. Sites 74 and 75 enjoy a gorgeous view of the lake with its majestic cypress and tupelo. Park gates are locked at night, making Chicot extra secure. This area is unbearably hot and humid in late summer. Visit in spring or fall.

BASICS

Operated By: State of Louisiana Dept. of Culture, Recreation, and Tourism. **Open:** All year. **Site Assignment:** First come, first served; reservation can be made w/ V or MC; call (888) 226-7652. 15-day cancellation policy; cancellation fee is 1-day's rental of campsite for late cancellations or $10 for 15-day cancellations. **Registration:** At main office at the south entrance. **Fee:** $16; Golden Access card, 50% off. **Parking:** 2 cars or 1 RV and 1 car, overflow parking available.

FACILITIES

Number of RV-only Sites: 208. **Number of Tent-only Sites:** 25. **Hookups:** Electric (20, 30 amps), water. **Each Site:** Tent pad at tent sites only, fire ring, grill, picnic table. **Dump Station:** Yes. **Laundry:** Yes. **Pay Phone:** No. **Restrooms and Showers:** Yes. **Fuel:** No. **Propane:** No. **Internal Roads:** Paved. **RV Service:** 6 mi. south in Ville Platte. **Market:** 4 mi. south in Ville Platte. **Restaurant:** 4 mi. south in Ville Platte. **General Store:** 8 mi. south in Ville Platte. **Vending:** Beverages. **Swimming:** Yes. **Playground:** Yes. **Other:** Nature trails, boat launch, group lodge. **Activities:** Fishing (Florida bass), picnicking, hiking, boating. **Nearby Attractions:** Louisiana State Arboretum, Prairie Acadian Cultural Center–Jean Lafitte National Historical Park & Reserve, Acadian Town of Ville Platte; historic town of Opelousas, historic town of Washington, Zydeco Cajun Prairie Scenic Byway, Liberal Theatre/City of Eunice, Thistlethwaite Wildlife Management Area.

Additional Information: Acadia Parish Convention & Visitors Commission, (877) 783-2109.

RESTRICTIONS

Pets: On leash only. **Fires:** Fire ring only. **Alcoholic Beverages:** Allowed. **Vehicle Maximum Length:** Approximately 65 ft. **Other:** 15-day stay limit; no gray water on the ground.

TO GET THERE

Coming from the north on I-49, exit on LA 106 south. Turn left off LA 106 onto LA 3042 south. Continue to the main entrance.

WESTWEGO   MAP, C-3
Bayou Segnette State Park

7777 Westbank Expressway, 70094. T: (504) 736-7140 or (888) 677-2296; www.reserveamerica.com.

🚐 ★★★   ▲ ★★★

Beauty: ★★★★	Site Privacy: ★★★
Spaciousness: ★★★★	Quiet: ★★★
Security: ★★★	Cleanliness: ★★★★
Insect Control: ★★	Facilities: ★★★

Bayou Segnette lies at the conjunction of two kinds of wetland: swamp and marsh. Plentiful bird species include red-winged blackbirds, Mississippi kites, and bald eagles. Located 30 miles from New Orleans, across the Mississippi River, this suburban park is convenient if you're touring the city on a weekend. However, it's not convenient to New Orleans when rush-hour traffic climaxes. Avoid the New Orleans area during festivals, when the city is zoo-like, and late summer, when the heat is unbearable. Security is good here—gates are locked at night. The flat yet attractive campground offers commodious sites. Most sites have at least a little shade and all parking is paved, back-in style. Privacy varies greatly. We recommend sites 13, 15, 62, and 100 for seclusion. Site 7 is recommended for families with children—it's next to the playground and wash house. Site 81 is extra shady.

BASICS

Operated By: Louisiana State Parks. **Open:** All year. **Site Assignment:** Reservations accepted w/ 1-night deposit; call (888) 677-2296; V, MC, cash, in-state checks; 2-week cancellation notice required for full refund, otherwise $10 fee. **Registration:** At campground office. **Fee:** $12; Golden Access card discount. **Parking:** 2 vehicles per site and parking lots.

FACILITIES

Number of Multipurpose Sites: 98. **Hookups:** Electric, water. **Each Site:** Picnic table, fire ring w/ grill. **Dump Station:** Yes. **Laundry:** Yes. **Pay Phone:** Yes. **Restrooms and Showers:** Yes. **Fuel:** No. **Propane:** No. **Internal Roads:** Paved. **RV Service:** No. **Market:** No. **Restaurant:** 0.5 mi. east. **General Store:** 0.5 mi. east. **Vending:** No. **Swimming:** Yes. **Playground:** Yes. **Other:** Boat landing,

wave pool. **Activities:** Hiking, fishing. **Nearby Attractions:** French Quarter, Audubon Zoo & Botanical Gardens, Aquarium of the Americas, Paddlewheel Boats, Superdome, National D-Day Museum. **Additional Information:** New Orleans CVB, (504) 566-5005.

RESTRICTIONS

Pets: On leash only. **Fires:** At site only. **Alcoholic Beverages:** Allowed. **Vehicle Maximum Length:** 50 ft. **Other:** Quiet hours enforced.

TO GET THERE

From New Orleans, take US 90 west over the Greater New Orleans Bridge, which turns into the West Bank Expressway. Continue 8 mi. to flashing caution light and take a left on Drake Ave. There is a sign for the park.

ZWOLLE   MAP, B-1
North Toledo Bend State Park

2907 North Toledo Park Rd., 71486. T: (888) 677-6400; www.crt.state.la.us.

🚐 ★★★★★   ▲ ★★★★★

Beauty: ★★★★★	Site Privacy: ★★★★★
Spaciousness: ★★★★★	Quiet: ★★★★★
Security: ★★★★	Cleanliness: ★★★★★
Insect Control: ★★★	Facilities: ★★★★

This gorgeous park is situated on a peninsula jutting into massive Toledo Bend Reservoir. Across the reservoir is Texas' Sabine National Forest. At North Toledo Bend, recreation revolves around fishing for largemouth bass, catfish, and crappie. For landlubbers, there's a nature trail and an Olympic-sized swimming pool. Although the terrain consists of rolling hills, the campground is pretty flat. The beautiful campground is laid out in two loops containing huge sites. Sites are shaded by a variety of tree species dominated by pine. Privacy is provided by greenery between sites. All parking is paved back-in style, with the exception of six pull-through sites. The most private sites are 29–34. We also like sites 13 and 14, which have partial water views. Avoid North Toledo Bend on holiday weekends and during hot late summer. Otherwise, the campground rarely fills up, making it a good destination for an early summer weekend. Security is excellent at this remote park.

BASICS

Operated By: State of Louisiana Dept. of Culture, Recreation, and Tourism. **Open:** All year. **Site Assignment:** First come, first served; reservations held w/ V, MC; call (877) 226-7652; no out-of-state checks accepted; cancellation fee is $10 or 1-night's rent, whichever is largest. **Registration:** At park office. **Fee:** $12; Golden Access card discount. **Parking:** 2 vehicles per site.

FACILITIES

Number of Multipurpose Sites: 63. **Hookups:** Electric (30, 50 amps), water. **Each Site:** Tent pad, lantern hook, fire ring, picnic table. **Dump Station:** Yes. **Laundry:** Yes. **Pay Phone:** Yes. **Restrooms and Showers:** Yes. **Fuel:** No. **Propane:** No. **Internal Roads:** Paved. **RV Service:** 50 mi. east in Natchitoches. **Market:** 8 mi. east in Zwolle. **Restaurant:** 9 mi. east in Zwolle. **General Store:** 20 mi. east in Many. **Vending:** Yes. **Swimming:** Yes. **Playground:** Yes. **Other:** Boat launch, fishing pier, athletic field, nature trails, group lodging. **Activities:** Field activities, fishing, picnicking, hiking. **Nearby Attractions:** Fort Jesup State Commemorative Area, Mansfield State Commemorative Area, Rebel State Commemorative Area, Los Adaes State Commemorative Area, Historic town of Natchitoches, Cane River Country, Kisatchie

National Forest-Longleaf Vista National Recreation Trail, Sabine Wildlife Refuge, National Fish Hatchery & Aquarium. **Additional Information:** Sabine Parish Tourist & Recreation Commission/Toledo Bend Country, (800) 358-7802.

RESTRICTIONS

Pets: On leash only. **Fires:** Fire ring only. **Alcoholic Beverages:** Allowed. **Vehicle Maximum Length:** No limit. **Other:** 15-day stay limit.

TO GET THERE

From I-49, exit onto Hwy. 6 and go west 30 mi. to Many. Turn right on to Hwy. 171, going north. After passing through the town of Zwolle, take a left onto Hwy. 482. Turn left onto Hwy. 3229. The entrance to the park is on the left.

Maine

Six moose, four rabbits, a Native American gravesite, and a little bit of Canada. That's what we saw on our campground-to-campground road trip from **Rangeley Lake** to the **Moose River.** (They don't call Maine's Rte. 16 "Moose Alley" for nothing!) From there, we followed the silvery-blue glimmer of **Moosehead Lake** to spectacular **Lily Bay,** where **Mount Kineo** rises out of a sea (OK, lake) of blue. We took the long way around the lake, because, at 117 square miles, every way is the long way, and we set up camp along the shore. Just another day of camping in Maine.

As camping grounds go, Maine is outrageously attractive. Just when you think you've seen the most incredible vista of rockbound coastline, pine-shrouded mountain, or sea-meets-sky, you take another turn in the road and see something even more ahh-inspiring. We are understating this. Good news for campers: Maine boasts more than 200 places to take it all in. These vary widely, from upscale camping resorts like **Point Sebago** and **Megunticook-by-the-Sea** with golf courses and gourmet coffee, to rustic retreats (and in Maine, when they say rustic, they mean "the generator goes out at 11 p.m."). Some are so remote, the road in is six suspension-testing miles long; ask 'em if they have a Web site, and they'll snort, "We don't even have a phone."

Everybody heads to the south coast and midcoast regions, and for good reason: the beaches and the lobster shacks are there. Count on plenty of traffic in summer, and woe to those who show up in July or August, on a weekend, without reservations! Keep driving, though, and the glories of **Downeast Maine** and **Acadia** await, with a landscape that rivals the most beautiful anywhere.

True Maine insiders know, however, that some of the best camping spots in the state are far from the Atlantic. **The Sebago Lake–Long Lake** chain, in the western lakes and mountains region, offers wonderful lakeside camping, along with boating (many campgrounds offer rentals, or BYOB), fishing, and even paddle-wheeler trips. This is camping like you remember it from your childhood, complete with those allowance-busting snack bars. (Hint: come in the fall for the **Fryeburg Fair,** among the best events in Maine.) Heading north, **South Arm (at Richardson Lake), Eustis** (where you'll find an amazing stand of towering red pines, where Benedict Arnold once trod), and **Chain of Ponds** are well worth seeking out. (Just check out our best list.) The **Jackman-Moose River** area, nudging Canada, is a paradise for sports-loving campers, and everybody who's ever been there loves **Greenville,** a taste of Montana near Moosehead Lake. Then there's **Katahdin,** and **Caribou**—enough said. Just know that the south coast of Maine is only the beginning.

Campground Profiles

ABBOT VILLAGE   MAP, C-2
Balsam Woods Campground

112 Pond Rd., 04406. T: (207) 876-2731; www.balsamwoods.com.

🚐 ★★★★   ▲ ★★

Beauty: ★★★	Site Privacy: ★★★
Spaciousness: ★★★★	Quiet: ★★★★
Security: ★★★★	Cleanliness: ★★★
Insect Control: ★★★★	Facilities: ★★★

Located just 18 miles south of outdoorsy Greenville and Moosehead Lake, Balsam Woods (despite its name) has a totally different vibe. Set in tiny Abbot Village, almost dead-center in the state, the campground has a rural, countryside feel. Freshly mown grass surrounds a swimming pool and playground area, dotted with picnic tables. Sites in the center of the park are open and grassy, while those at the perimeter are wooded with pines, with plenty of shrubbery buffer for privacy. The sites are all back-in, with the exception of three pull-throughs. The property connects with a hiking trail, and the owners will point you toward berry bushes if you want to pick some fresh fruit for dinner. Nothing goes better with Maine blueberries than lobster, and they'll sell you some here. (Shouldn't every Maine campground have its own lobster pound?) Best sites, with hookups, are F3 through 5, and F7, 9, 10, and 11, backing up into the pines. Tenters might find the campsites here too exposed. In any event, avoid the privies (ugh!), and plan to hike up to the nice, clean restroom behind the rec hall.

BASICS
Operated By: Milon and Peggy Fuller. **Open:** Memorial Day–Oct. **Site Assignment:** Reservations recommended; 1-night deposit required for stays of less than 1 week; 25% deposit for stays of 1 week or longer; refunds for cancellations w/ 14-day notice. **Registration:** At office. **Fee:** $25; based on family of 4; V, MC, no checks. **Parking:** At site.

FACILITIES
Number of RV-only Sites: 50. **Hookups:** Electric (30 amps), water. **Each Site:** Picnic table, fire ring. **Dump Station:** Yes. **Laundry:** Yes. **Pay Phone:** Yes. **Restrooms and Showers:** Yes. **Fuel:** Wood. **Propane:** Yes. **Internal Roads:** Gravel, in good condition. **RV Service:** No. **Market:** 10 mi. south. **Restaurant:** 18 mi. north. **General Store:** Yes. **Vending:** No. **Swimming:** Yes. **Playground:** Yes. **Other:** Rec hall. **Activities:** Hiking, berry picking, horseshoes, volleyball, planned activities. **Nearby Attractions:** Appalachian Trail, Moosehead Lake, S.S. Katahdin steamboat cruises, Moosehead Marine Museum, Eveleth-Crafts-Sheridan Historical House, Lily whitewater rafting, boating, fishing. **Additional Information:** Moosehead Lake Region Chamber of Commerce, (207) 723-4443.

RESTRICTIONS
Pets: Must be leashed, quiet, & cleaned up after. Must not be left unattended. **Fires:** Fire ring only. **Alcoholic Beverages:** Allowed. **Vehicle Maximum Length:** 45 ft. **Other:** Max. of 6 people per campsite.

TO GET THERE
From junction of Hwy. 15 and Hwy. 16, go 1 mi. north on Hwy. 15, then 3 mi. west on Pond Rd. Campground entrance is on the left.

ANDOVER   MAP, C-1
South Arm Campground

P.O. Box 310, 04216. T: (207) 364-5155 or (207) 364-5154; www.southarm.com.

🚐 ★★★★★   ▲ ★★★★★

Beauty: ★★★★★	Site Privacy: ★★★★
Spaciousness: ★★	Quiet: ★★★★
Security: ★★★★	Cleanliness: ★★★
Insect Control: ★★	Facilities: ★★★

The owner calls it "Maine's most beautiful campground." No argument here. Set amidst a 1,000-acre wilderness area in western Maine, the campground nudges the south arm of Richardson Lake, with mountains providing a backdrop. Seventeen miles of lakes are accessible here; adventurous campers can choose from remote sites along the lake, reachable only by boat or canoe. The main campground is on a peninsula, with 65 wooded sites set in a loop. At least half of these are on the beach and waterfront. These prime sites require a two-night stay, but you'd want to stay that long anyway. It's a long haul to this campground, and it takes a couple of days to explore the waterways and soak in all the beauty here. Sites 1–51 (odd numbers) are shore side. They're all great, but sites 29A and 29B are set back a bit, with amazing views. Site 31 is beautiful, too. These get snapped up quickly. Off the beach, we like sites 2–12 and especially site 24, near the point. Book early for July and August, but don't even consider June, when black flies are out in force. Rainy days, borrow a book, puzzle, game, or novel.

BASICS
Operated By: Scott Mitchell. **Open:** 1 week after Memorial Day–2 weeks after Labor Day. **Site Assignment:** Reservations recommended; 1-night deposit required; check or cash accepted; refunds for cancellation w/ 1-month notice; 2-night minimum stay; 3 days on holiday weekends. **Registration:** At office. **Fee:** $24–$32; 2 adults & their children under age 18; wilderness site, $5 per family/couple; no credit cards. **Parking:** At site, $3 per car.

FACILITIES
Number of RV-only Sites: 65. **Hookups:** Electric (30 amps), water; generator goes off at 11 p.m., comes back on at 7 a.m. **Each Site:** Picnic table, fireplace. **Dump Station:** Yes. **Laundry:** Yes. **Pay Phone:** No. **Restrooms and Showers:** Yes, coin-op. **Fuel:** No. **Propane:** Yes. **Internal Roads:** Gravel, in fair condition. **RV Service:** No. **Market:** 15 mi. south. **Restaurant:** 15 mi. south. **General Store:** Yes. **Vending:** No. **Swimming:** No. **Playground:** No. **Other:** Marina, boat ramp, dock. **Activities:** Appalachian Trail hiking, fishing (licenses available), lake swimming, boating (rentals available), boat cruises, planned activities. **Nearby Attractions:** Coose Canyon, White Mountain National Forest, historical museums. **Additional Information:** River Valley Chamber of Commerce, (207) 364-3241.

RESTRICTIONS
Pets: Must be leashed, quiet, & cleaned up after. Must not be left unattended. Current rabies vaccination certificate required. **Fires:** Fire ring only. **Alcoholic Beverages:** At sites only. **Vehicle Maximum Length:** 35 ft. **Other:** 2-night min. stay for waterfront & beach sites (remote or other sites are available by the day); 3-night min. on holidays.

TO GET THERE
From junction of Hwy. 5 and Hwy. 120, go 0.5 mi. east on Hwy. 120, then 11 mi. north on South Arm Rd. Campground entrance is on the left.

APPLETON   MAP, C-2
Sennebec Lake Campground

100 Lodge Ln., 04862. T: (207) 785-4250 or (888) 878-5647; www.reserveamerica.com.

🚐 ★★★★   ▲ ★★★

Beauty: ★★★★	Site Privacy: ★★★
Spaciousness: ★★★	Quiet: ★★★★
Security: ★★★★	Cleanliness: ★★★★★
Insect Control: ★★★	Facilities: ★★★★

This neat, well-kept campsite is set in a rural area in mid-coast Maine, about 12 miles northwest of Camden. It may not be on the ocean, but it's a great spot, with grassy, terraced sites overlooking Lake Sennebec. RV sites are side-by-side along the lakefront; wooded site 72 (electric and water) is the nicest, in our view. Lakeside sites include sites 62 through 73 and 74 through 80. Sites are mostly back-ins. Tent sites are walk-in, with a footpath leading over a stream to a secluded, piney grove. Best tent sites are 94 and 95; beware of lumpy site 93. There's a sandy beach with a float, and they sell bait and fishing gear if you want to have a go at the lake's bass, perch, and pickerel population. We'd be tempted to rent a canoe and paddle around the placid lake. A lodge, overlooking the lake, is the venue for Saturday night dances with live bands. This campground makes a dandy centralized base for Maine adventures.

BASICS
Operated By: Lorraine and John Bender. **Open:** June 16–Sept. 4. **Site Assignment:** Reservations recommended; 50% deposit required; refunds for cancellation w/ 14-day notice, minus $10; 7% Maine lodging tax. **Registration:** At office. **Fee:** $20–$42; 2 adults & up to 3 children under age 18; V, MC. **Parking:** At site.

FACILITIES
Number of RV-only Sites: 96. **Number of Tent-only Sites:** 10. **Hookups:** Electric (30 amps), water, sewer, modem access. **Each Site:** Picnic table, fireplace. **Dump Station:** Yes. **Laundry:** Yes. **Pay Phone:** Yes. **Restrooms and Showers:** Yes. **Fuel:** No. **Propane:** Yes. **Internal Roads:** Paved, in good

condition. **RV Service:** No. **Market:** 3 mi. south.
Restaurant: 3 mi. south. **General Store:** Yes.
Vending: Yes. **Swimming:** No. **Playground:** Yes.
Other: Rec hall, boat ramp, arcade. **Activities:** Lake
swimming, fishing (license required), boating (rentals
available), basketball, volleyball, planned activities.
Nearby Attractions: Camden (12 mi. southeast, w/
its harbor, galleries, museums, & shops), windjammer
fleet, Penobscot Bay cruises, Conway Homestead &
Mary Cramer Museum (18th-century restored farmhouse & gardens), Camden Hills State Park, Merryspring Park, Owl's Head Transportation Museum,
golf. **Additional Information:** Union Chamber of
Commerce, (207) 785-3200.

RESTRICTIONS

Pets: Must be leashed, quiet, & cleaned up after. Must
not be left unattended. **Fires:** Fire ring only. **Alcoholic Beverages:** At sites only. **Vehicle Maximum
Length:** 45 ft. **Other:** 2-night min. stay required in
July & Aug.; 3-night min. stay required on holiday
weekends.

TO GET THERE

From junction of Hwy. 17 and Hwy. 131, go 3 mi.
north on Hwy. 131. Campground entrance is on
the right.

BANGOR   MAP, C-2
Paul Bunyan Campground

1862 Union St., 04401. T: (207) 941-1177 or (207)
947-3734; www.paulbunyancampground.com.

🚐 ★★★   ▲ ★★

Beauty: ★★★	Site Privacy: ★★★
Spaciousness: ★★★	Quiet: ★★★
Security: ★★★	Cleanliness: ★★★
Insect Control: ★★★	Facilities: ★★★

Of the two campgrounds off the interstate in the
Bangor area (also see Pleasant Hill Campground),
this one is livelier and a bit noisier, attracting a regular clientele of families during summer weekends and
weeklong vacations. The campground offers plenty
of entertainment, live bands and DJs, potluck dinners and parades, ice-cream socials, contests, and
tournaments. There's also free pancake breakfast for
campers every Sunday morning throughout the summer. Come fall, the campground calms down a bit,
hosting more one-night travelers. The campground
feels spacious due to the surrounding fields and
expansive public areas, but individual sites are average to small in size. There's a small, separate tent-
only area along the road; pull-through, full hookup
sites are clustered in the open field toward the back
of the campground. There's a pond on the property,
aptly dubbed Babe's Bathtub. Don't expect much: it's
barely more than a mosquito incubator, but small
kids have fun tossing stones and navigating paddleboats around its tiny perimeter.

BASICS

Operated By: Dennis and Shirley Hachey. **Open:**
Apr.–Nov. **Site Assignment:** Reservations suggested; 1-night deposit required for stays of 3 days or
less, $40 for 4 or more days; 2-week cancellation pol-
icy w/ $5 fee; MC, V, checks. **Registration:** At office
or by mail. **Fee:** Full hookup (50 amps), $27; 30

amps, $24; water/electric, $19.50; no hookup, $15;
based on 2 adults & 2 children. **Parking:** At site.

FACILITIES

Number of RV-only Sites: 52. **Number of Tent-
only Sites:** 18. **Hookups:** Electric (30, 50 amps),
water, sewer. **Each Site:** Picnic table, fire ring.
Dump Station: Yes. **Laundry:** Yes. **Pay Phone:** Yes.
Restrooms and Showers: Yes. **Fuel:** No.
Propane: Yes. **Internal Roads:** Dirt, gravel, paved
(fair). **RV Service:** No. **Market:** Bangor, 2 mi.
Restaurant: No. **General Store:** Yes. **Vending:**
No. **Swimming:** Yes. **Playground:** Yes. **Other:**
Small pond, paddleboat rentals, picnic shelter, game
room, sports field. **Activities:** Swimming, live enter-
tainment, potluck dinners, planned activities, chil-
dren's programs, hayrides, socials. **Nearby
Attractions:** Bangor, Bar Harbor, Acadia National
Park, Maine coast. **Additional Information:** Bangor
Regional Chamber of Commerce, 519 Maine St., P.O.
Box 1443, Bangor, ME 04402, (207) 947-0307,
www.bangorregion.com.

RESTRICTIONS

Pets: Must be on a leash, never left unattended. **Fires:**
Grill, stoves, fire rings only. **Alcoholic Beverages:** At
site only. **Vehicle Maximum Length:** 40 ft.

TO GET THERE

From I-95, Exit 47, go 2.8 mi. west on Hwy. 222
(Union St.); campground is on the left.

BAR HARBOR   MAP, C-3
Bar Harbor Campground

409 ME 3, 04609. T: (207) 288-5185;
www.barharborcamping.com.

🚐 ★★★★★   ▲ ★★★★★

Beauty: ★★★★★	Site Privacy: ★★★★
Spaciousness: ★★★★	Quiet: ★★★★
Security: ★★★	Cleanliness: ★★★★
Insect Control: ★★★	Facilities: ★★★

This is the closest campground to Bar Harbor and
one of the prettiest in the area. They like to keep it
simple here: all sites are first come, first served.
Campers can drive through the campground and
select their site and then register. You might have a
difficult time choosing; there are plenty of spacious,
private spots with sweeping views of Frenchman's
Bay. In fact, the entire campground has a roomy,
expansive feel. There's a large secluded area for tents
and small pop-ups (we like the woodsy privacy in the
S loop) and a cluster of tent-only ocean view sites
(Q1, Q2, and R1–4 are especially nice.) Water and
electric sites and full hookups are scattered throughout, many with ocean views. We especially like the
swimming pool area at this campground, set high on
an point, overlooking the Maine coastline.

BASICS

Operated By: Craig Robbins. **Open:** Memorial
Day–Columbus Day. **Site Assignment:** First come,
first served; cash only. **Registration:** At office. **Fee:**
Full hookup, $27; water/electric, $25; no hookup,
$20. **Parking:** At site.

FACILITIES

Number of RV-only Sites: 155. **Number of Tent-
only Sites:** 145. **Hookups:** Electric (30, 50 amps),

water, sewer. **Each Site:** Picnic table, fire ring.
Dump Station: Yes. **Laundry:** Yes. **Pay Phone:** Yes.
Restrooms and Showers: Yes (coin-op). **Fuel:** No.
Propane: Yes. **Internal Roads:** Paved, gravel
(good). **RV Service:** No. **Market:** Bar Harbor, 4 mi.
Restaurant: No. **General Store:** Yes. **Vending:**
Yes. **Swimming:** Yes. **Playground:** Yes. **Other:**
Ocean frontage, game room, TV room. **Activities:**
Swimming, horseshoes, shuffleboard, basketball.
Nearby Attractions: Bar Harbor, Acadia National
Park. **Additional Information:** Acadia National
Park, P.O. Box 177, Bar Harbor, ME 04609, (207) 288-
3338, www.nps/gov/acad. Also, Acadia Information
Center, P.O. Box 139, Mount Desert, ME 04660, (207)
667-8550 or (800) 358-8550, www.acadiainfo.com.

RESTRICTIONS

Pets: Must be on a leash, never left unattended.
Fires: Grill, stoves, fire rings only. **Alcoholic Beverages:** At site only. **Vehicle Maximum Length:** No
limit. **Other:** No skateboards or rollerblades
allowed.

TO GET THERE

From junction Hwy. 102 and Hwy. 3, go south 5
mi. on Hwy. 3; campground is on the left.

BAR HARBOR   MAP, C-3
Bar Harbor KOA

136 C.R., 04609. T: (207) 288-3520;
www.koa.com.

🚐 ★★★★★   ▲ ★★★★

Beauty: ★★★★	Site Privacy: ★★★
Spaciousness: ★★★	Quiet: ★★★
Security: ★★★	Cleanliness: ★★★★
Insect Control: ★★★	Facilities: ★★★★

This pretty property, a stone's throw from Bar Harbor and Acadia National Park, boasts 3,500 feet of
oceanfront with stunning panoramic views of the
rocky Maine coastline. We love to sit on the oceanfront patio and watch the sun slip to the other side of
the world while seals play on off-shore rocks.
Another nicety: the campground serves up a traditional fresh lobster dinner nightly during the summer. Campers can rent kayaks on site to explore area
waters and coves or sign up for a guided excursion. A
variety of tours are available from the campground,
ranging from a few hours to all day. There's a rocky
oceanfront beach for tide pooling and toe dunking,
too. There are plenty of oceanfront sites, a separate
tent-only area in the trees, and level, open RV sites
clustered near the front, many with ocean views.

BASICS

Operated By: Tom and Stacy Brooks. **Open:** May
10–Oct. 20. **Site Assignment:** Reservations
accepted year-round, recommended July–Aug.;
1-night deposit required; 48-hour cancellation w/ $5
fee; MC, V, checks. **Registration:** At office or online.
Fee: $30–$60. **Parking:** At site, 1 vehicle per site.

FACILITIES

Number of RV-only Sites: 201. **Number of Tent-
only Sites:** 31. **Hookups:** Electric (30 amps), water,
sewer, modem, cable. **Each Site:** Picnic table, fire
ring. **Dump Station:** Yes. **Laundry:** Yes. **Pay
Phone:** Yes. **Restrooms and Showers:** Yes (coin-

op). **Fuel:** No. **Propane:** Yes. **Internal Roads:** Paved, gravel (good). **RV Service:** No. **Market:** Bar Harbor, 2 mi. **Restaurant:** No. **General Store:** Yes. **Vending:** No. **Swimming:** Yes. **Playground:** Yes. **Other:** Ocean frontage, beach, game room, kayak rentals & guided kayak excursions, boat launch area, sunset viewing patio, free bus shuttle to Bar Harbor, pop-up rentals. **Activities:** Swimming, boating, lobster bakes, basketball, volleyball, badminton, horseshoes. **Nearby Attractions:** Bar Harbor, Acadia National Park. **Additional Information:** Acadia National Park, P.O. Box 177, Bar Harbor, ME 04609, (207) 288-3338, www.nps/gov/acad. Also, Acadia Information Center, P.O. Box 139, Mount Desert, ME 04660, (207) 667-8550 or (800) 358-8550, www.acadiainfo.com.

RESTRICTIONS

Pets: Must be on a leash, never left unattended. Only 2 dogs per site. **Fires:** Grill, stoves, fire rings only. **Alcoholic Beverages:** At site only. **Vehicle Maximum Length:** 43 ft.

TO GET THERE

From junction of Hwy. 3, Hwy. 102, and Campground Rd., go southwest on Campground Rd.

BAR HARBOR MAP, C-3
Hadley's Point Campground

33 Hadley Point Rd., 04609. T: (207) 288-4808; www.hadleyspoint.com.

🚐 ★★★	🏕 ★★★
Beauty: ★★★	Site Privacy: ★★★
Spaciousness: ★★★	Quiet: ★★★
Security: ★★★	Cleanliness: ★★★★
Insect Control: ★★★	Facilities: ★★★

This campground, just four miles from the Acadia National Park entrance, is a clean, pleasant base for campers visiting the area. There are plenty of nearby attractions and activities and a public saltwater beach within walking distance of the campground. The plain-Jane property offers minimal frills (swimming pool, laundry, ultra clean restrooms and showers) but you'll have a choice of sites. There's a separate tent-only area with wooded sites and adequate room and privacy. Other sites are located in an open field, ringed in a circle; these don't offer much privacy but they're good for campers who like sunny, open spaces. The staff is exceptionally friendly and come Sunday there's no need to head into town for church, if you're so inclined: church service is held each week at the campground throughout July and August.

BASICS

Operated By: Robert and Suzanne Baker. **Open:** May 15–Oct. 15. **Site Assignment:** Reservations suggested July–Aug.; $30 deposit for stays of less than 5 days, $60 deposit for stays of 5 days or more; 48-hour cancellation policy, minus $5; no refunds on holiday weekends; MC, V, checks. **Registration:** At office. **Fee:** Full hookup, $35; water/electric, $30; no hookup, $22; based on party of 4. **Parking:** At site.

FACILITIES

Number of RV-only Sites: 155. **Number of Tent-only Sites:** 45. **Hookups:** Electric (20, 30 amps),

water, sewer. **Each Site:** Picnic table, fire ring. **Dump Station:** Yes. **Laundry:** Yes. **Pay Phone:** Yes. **Restrooms and Showers:** Yes (coin-op). **Fuel:** No. **Propane:** Yes. **Internal Roads:** Mostly paved. **RV Service:** No. **Market:** Bar Harbor, 5 mi. **Restaurant:** No. **General Store:** Yes. **Vending:** Yes. **Swimming:** Yes. **Playground:** Yes. **Other:** Sun. church service on site. **Activities:** Swimming, horseshoes, shuffleboard. Some scheduled events throughout the year. **Nearby Attractions:** Bar Harbor, Acadia National Park. **Additional Information:** Acadia National Park, P.O. Box 177, Bar Harbor, ME 04609, (207) 288-3338, www.nps/gov/acad; Acadia Information Center, P.O. Box 139, Mount Desert, ME 04660, (207) 667-8550 or (800) 358-8550, www.acadiainfo.com.

RESTRICTIONS

Pets: Must be on a leash, never left unattended. **Fires:** Grill, stoves, fire rings only. **Alcoholic Beverages:** At site only. **Vehicle Maximum Length:** No limit.

TO GET THERE

From junction Hwy. 102 and Hwy. 3, go east 3 mi. on Hwy. 3, then north 0.25 mi. on Hadley Point Rd.; the campground is on the right.

BAR HARBOR MAP, C-3
Mount Desert Narrows

reserve america

1219 ME 3, 04609. T: (207) 288-4782 or (866) 780-4782; www.reserveamerica.com.

🚐 ★★★★★	🏕 ★★★★★
Beauty: ★★★★★	Site Privacy: ★★★★
Spaciousness: ★★★	Quiet: ★★★
Security: ★★★	Cleanliness: ★★★★★
Insect Control: ★★★	Facilities: ★★★★★

This oceanfront campground is one of the most popular in the Bar Harbor/Acadia National Park area for both RVers and tenters, offering modern facilities, a great location, and pretty scenery. You'll find 2,100 feet of shoreline, plenty of oceanfront and ocean view sites, on-site recreation, and a free bus shuttle to downtown Bar Harbor. Tenters have their own 25-acre section (first come, first served) and several prime oceanfront sites with sweeping views (sites 14 and 15 are favorites.) Tent site 30 at the end of a point on the shoreline also offers great views and plenty of space. Full-hookup sites are set side-by-side near the front of the campground. There are also a handful of water and electric sites and water only sites on the ocean, too. If you're looking for a water and electric hookup, sites 88–94 on the shoreline, can't be beat.

BASICS

Operated By: Pat Stanley, owner. **Open:** May–Oct. 25. **Site Assignment:** Reservations accepted year-round, suggested July–Aug.; 2-night minimum stay; 3-night minimum on holiday weekends; holidays are prepaid and nonrefundable; oceanfront sites require 3-night minimum in July and Aug.; basic tenting sites are first come, first served only. $50 deposit for 2

nights, $100 for 3 nights, $150 for 4–7 nights, $200 for 8 or more nights; 30-day cancellation policy minus $10; MC, V, D, checks for reservations; no checks upon arrival. **Registration:** At office. **Fee:** Full hookup, $38–$55; Prices may vary, call ahead for details. **Parking:** At site.

FACILITIES

Number of RV-only Sites: 239. **Number of Tent-only Sites:** 130. **Hookups:** Electric (20, 30, 50 amps), water, sewer, cable TV, modem. **Each Site:** Picnic table, fire ring. **Dump Station:** Yes. **Laundry:** Yes. **Pay Phone:** Yes. **Restrooms and Showers:** Yes. **Fuel:** No. **Propane:** Yes. **Internal Roads:** Gravel, some paved. **RV Service:** No. **Market:** Bar Harbor, 4 mi. **Restaurant:** No. **General Store:** Yes. **Vending:** Yes. **Swimming:** Yes. **Playground:** Yes. **Other:** Ocean frontage, entertainment pavilion, game room, shuttle bus service to Bar Harbor, canoe rentals, boat launch. **Activities:** Swimming, boating, horseshoes, basketball, volleyball, planned activities, hayrides, movies, storytelling, & more. **Nearby Attractions:** Bar Harbor, Acadia National Park. **Additional Information:** Acadia National Park, P.O. Box 177, Bar Harbor, ME 04609, (207) 288-3338, www.nps/gov/acad. Also, Acadia Information Center, P.O. Box 139, Mount Desert, ME 04660, (207) 667-8550 or (800) 358-8550, www.acadiainfo.com.

RESTRICTIONS

Pets: Must be on a leash, never left unattended. **Fires:** Grill, stoves, fire rings only. **Alcoholic Beverages:** At site only. **Vehicle Maximum Length:** No limit.

TO GET THERE

From junction Hwy. 102 and Hwy. 3, go east 1.5 mi. on Hwy. 3; campground is on the left.

BASS HARBOR MAP, C-3
Bass Harbor Campground

Hwy. 102A, 04653. T: (207) 244-5857 or (800) 327-5857; www.bassharbor.com.

🚐 ★★★	🏕 ★★★★
Beauty: ★★★	Site Privacy: ★★★
Spaciousness: ★★★	Quiet: ★★★★
Security: ★★★★	Cleanliness: ★★★
Insect Control: ★★	Facilities: ★★★

Loyal campers return to Bass Harbor Campground year after year, using it as a base to explore Acadia National Park and the surrounding area. Most come for a week or two and appreciate the peace and quiet of the campground, away from the hustle, bustle, and traffic in the Bar Harbor area. Livin' is easy and slower here; days are spent visiting Bass Harbor Lighthouse, biking and hiking area paths, or taking day trips to Acadia National Park attractions. Full-hookups sites are set in rows behind the office and pool area; water and electric and tent sites (some with platforms) are off a loop road in the woods. There's also a separate tent-only area across the street with shaded sites and its own bathhouse and showers.

BASICS

Operated By: Mike and Sue Clayton. **Open:** Memorial Day–Columbus Day. **Site Assignment:**

Reservations suggested in July–Aug.; 1-night deposit, 14-day cancellation policy w/ $10 fee; MC, V, D, AE, checks; deposit required. **Registration:** At office. **Fee:** $28–$45; for 2 adults; $4 per extra adult; kids stay free. **Parking:** At site.

FACILITIES

Number of RV-only Sites: 94. **Number of Tent-only Sites:** 36. **Hookups:** Electric (20, 30, 50 amps), water, sewer, cable TV, modem. **Each Site:** Picnic table, fire ring. **Dump Station:** Yes. **Laundry:** Yes. **Pay Phone:** Yes. **Restrooms and Showers:** Yes. **Fuel:** No. **Propane:** Yes. **Internal Roads:** Gravel, dirt (good). **RV Service:** No. **Market:** Bass Harbor, 1 mi. **Restaurant:** No. **General Store:** Yes. **Vending:** No. **Swimming:** Yes. **Playground:** Yes. **Other:** Cabin & trailer- & motor-home rentals. **Activities:** Swimming, basketball, kayaking, bird-watching, hiking, nature cruises, scuba diving. **Nearby Attractions:** Bar Harbor, Acadia National Park. **Additional Information:** Acadia National Park, P.O. Box 177, Bar Harbor, ME 04609, (207) 288-3338, www.nps/gov/acad. Also, Acadia Information Center, P.O. Box 139, Mount Desert, ME 04660, (207) 667-8550 or (800) 358-8550, www.acadiainfo.com.

RESTRICTIONS

Pets: Must be on a leash, cleaned up after, never left unattended. **Fires:** Grill, stoves, fire rings only. **Alcoholic Beverages:** At site only. **Vehicle Maximum Length:** No limit. **Other:** No skateboards in campground.

TO GET THERE

From junction Hwy. 102 and Hwy. 102A, in Southwest Harbor, go south 5 mi. on Hwy. 102A; campground is on the right.

BOOTHBAY   MAP, D-2
Little Ponderosa Campground

159 Wiscasset Rd., 04537. T: (207) 633-2700; www.littleponderosa.com.

🚐 ★★★★   ▲ ★

Beauty: ★★★★	Site Privacy: ★★★
Spaciousness: ★★★	Quiet: ★★★★
Security: ★★★★★	Cleanliness: ★★★★
Insect Control: ★★★★★	Facilities: ★★★★

Mini-golf and a snack bar—two sure signs that Little Ponderosa caters to the family crowd. Of all the campgrounds in the Boothbay area, this one has the most child-friendly vibe. Saturday night concerts, ice-cream-sundae nights (Sundays), and nondenominational church services are among the happenings here. Then, there's nearby Boothbay Harbor, a great place to hang out, eat, shop, and take a boat cruise. This nicely wooded campground is set on a tidal inlet, with a small, squishy-bottomed beach (wear your water shoes) and a swim raft. About one-third of the campsites are situated along the waterfront. Campsites are grass and gravel, set in a loop. The two tent-only sites are fairly exposed; we'd opt for a water/electric site, perhaps 17, 18, or 19, offering more privacy and better views. The best full-hookup sites are 63 through 65, backed into the woods. There are 10 pull-through sites and 89 back-in sites. We'd skip site 4, since it's right by the beach path.

And Little Ponderosa gets extra points for aggressive insect management: they've installed six "mosquito magnets" to rid the place of pesky pests.

BASICS

Operated By: Jeff and Allison Lowell. **Open:** May 15–Oct. 15. **Site Assignment:** Reservations recommended; 1-night deposit required. **Registration:** At office. **Fee:** $21–$31; for 2 adults & 2 children; V, MC, D. **Parking:** At site.

FACILITIES

Number of RV-only Sites: 95. **Number of Tent-only Sites:** 2. **Hookups:** Electric (20, 30 amps), water, sewer, modem access. **Each Site:** Picnic table, fire ring. **Dump Station:** Yes. **Laundry:** Yes. **Pay Phone:** Yes. **Restrooms and Showers:** Yes, coin-op. **Fuel:** No. **Propane:** Yes. **Internal Roads:** Gravel, in good condition. **RV Service:** No. **Market:** 4 mi. south. **Restaurant:** 2 mi. south. **General Store:** Yes. **Vending:** No. **Swimming:** No. **Playground:** Yes. **Other:** Mini-golf, rec hall. **Activities:** Swimming, fishing (no license required), volleyball, horseshoes, boating (canoe & kayak rentals available), planned activities. **Nearby Attractions:** Boothbay Railway Village, Maine Resources Aquarium, Boothbay Harbor restaurants, shops & galleries, deep-sea fishing, whale-watching cruises, golf. **Additional Information:** Boothbay Harbor Region Chamber of Commerce, (207) 633-2353 or (800) 266-8422.

RESTRICTIONS

Pets: Must be leashed, quiet, & cleaned up after. Must not be left unattended. **Fires:** Fireplaces only. **Alcoholic Beverages:** At sites only. **Vehicle Maximum Length:** 40 ft. **Other:** Ask on arrival.

TO GET THERE

Take Maine Turnpike to Exit 9, then take I-95 to Hwy. 1 in Brunswick (Exit 22). Stay on Hwy. 1 through Wiscasset, then turn right on Hwy. 27 south to Boothbay Harbor Region. Campground is 5 mi. on the right.

BOOTHBAY HARBOR   MAP, D-2
Shore Hills Campground

553 Wiscasset Rd., 04537. T: (207) 633-4782; www.shorehills.com.

🚐 ★★★   ▲ ★★★

Beauty: ★★★	Site Privacy: ★★★★
Spaciousness: ★★★	Quiet: ★★★
Security: ★★★★★	Cleanliness: ★★★★
Insect Control: ★★★	Facilities: ★★★

"It's very quiet—that's why I keep coming," says Peggy, a happy camper at Shore Hills. That sums it up. Although this wooded coastal campground is only four miles from bustling, touristy Boothbay Harbor, all is quiet here. The far western edge of this campground sits on the Cross River. The river runs south to the sea. From site 84, guests can take a woodsy walk to the marsh and "fishing rocks," a great spot to cast a line or just gaze out to the river, where there's bound to be a paddler or two. (Nice touch here: use of canoes is free.) Most sites are back-in, but there are 14 pull-throughs with excellent buffer for privacy. The Family Circle area is wide open, suitable for the largest rigs, while sites 66 and

67 are closest to the water. Site 57, for tenting, boasts awesome views, while hillside site 11 overlooks the marsh, very nice. Some tent sites offer a crushed-rock surface for good drainage in case of rain. All sites have water. Another great feature here, if you hate cruising for a parking place: they'll shuttle-bus you to Boothbay Harbor. This peaceful place caters to an older clientele, many of whom (like Peggy) have been coming for years.

BASICS

Operated By: Neal and Jean. **Open:** Apr. 15–Columbus Day. **Site Assignment:** Reservations recommended; $30 deposit required; refunds for cancellations w/ 7-day notice. **Registration:** At office and by mail from online form. **Fee:** $26–$32; for 2 adults & 2 children; no credit cards. **Parking:** At site.

FACILITIES

Number of RV-only Sites: 85. **Number of Tent-only Sites:** 20. **Hookups:** Electric (30, 50 amps), water, sewer, cable TV. **Each Site:** Picnic table, fire ring. **Dump Station:** Yes. **Laundry:** Yes. **Pay Phone:** Yes. **Restrooms and Showers:** Yes, coin-op. **Fuel:** No. **Propane:** Yes. **Internal Roads:** Paved & gravel, in good condition. **RV Service:** No. **Market:** 4 mi. south. **Restaurant:** 4 mi. south. **General Store:** Yes. **Vending:** Yes. **Swimming:** Yes. **Playground:** Yes. **Other:** Rec hall. **Activities:** Saltwater river fishing, boating (canoes available), swimming (at high tide), horseshoes. **Nearby Attractions:** Boothbay Railway Village, Maine Resources Aquarium, Boothbay Harbor restaurants, shops & galleries, deep-sea fishing, whale-watching cruises, golf. **Additional Information:** Boothbay Harbor Region Chamber of Commerce, (207) 633-2353 or (800) 266-8422.

RESTRICTIONS

Pets: Must be leashed, quiet, & cleaned up after. Must not be left unattended. **Fires:** Fire ring only. **Alcoholic Beverages:** At sites only. **Vehicle Maximum Length:** No limit. **Other:** 3-day min. stay on holidays.

TO GET THERE

From Portland, take 295 north to Coastal Hwy. 1 for 47 mi. From Edgecomb, take Hwy. 27 south 8 mi. to campground, on right.

BROWNFIELD   MAP, D-1
Woodland Acres Camp 'N' Canoe

33 Woodland Acres Dr., 04010. T: (207) 935-2529; www.woodlandacres.com.

🚐 ★★★★   ▲ ★★★

Beauty: ★★★	Site Privacy: ★★★
Spaciousness: ★★★★★	Quiet: ★★★★★
Security: ★★★	Cleanliness: ★★★★
Insect Control: ★★	Facilities: ★★★

Just 25 miles from North Conway, New Hampshire, and 45 miles from Portland, this Western Lakes–area campground is a perfect choice for Saco-bound paddlers. The Saco River is a mecca for canoe and kayak enthusiasts, offering a blend of leisurely floats and short stretches of rapids (depending on the trip you choose) and scenery that includes clay cliffs and covered bridges. This peaceful riverfront campground is a great base for exploring the river. Sites are gravel, mostly wooded back-ins, and the choicest spots (94 through 104, even numbers) sit alongside the river. If those are taken, ask for something among sites 47 through 50, or 13 and 14, nice and quiet. The paddling is the thing here, and these folks know what they're doing. Bring your own boat and you can launch it here, or they'll shuttle you to a put-in point on another part of the river. Or, rent one of their canoes or kayaks and have them set you up on a trip lasting two hours or two days (an overnight and wilderness camping along the river) or something in between.

BASICS

Operated By: Chris and Susan Gantick. **Open:** May 15–Oct. 15. **Site Assignment:** Reservations recommended; 50% deposit required; full payment required for holiday weekends (3-night minimum); refunds for cancellations w/ 14-day notice, minus $5; 2-night minimum on weekends. **Registration:** At office. **Fee:** $30–$34 per night for 2 adults & children under age 18; V, MC, D. **Parking:** At sites or as designated.

FACILITIES

Number of RV-only Sites: 40. **Number of Tent-only Sites:** 20. **Number of Multipurpose Sites:** 50. **Hookups:** Electric (20, 30, 50 amps), water, sewer. **Each Site:** Picnic table, fireplace. **Dump Station:** Yes. **Laundry:** Yes. **Pay Phone:** Yes. **Restrooms and Showers:** Yes, coin-op. **Fuel:** No. **Propane:** Yes. **Internal Roads:** Gravel (sandy), in good condition. **RV Service:** No. **Market:** 18 mi. west, in North Conway, NH. **Restaurant:** 7 mi. north, in Fryeburg. **General Store:** Yes. **Vending:** No. **Swimming:** No. **Playground:** Yes. **Other:** Boat ramp, rec hall. **Activities:** Paddling, fishing (license available at general store). **Nearby Attractions:** Narramissic 19th-century working farm, Shawnee Peak Ski Area (hiking, mountain biking), outlet shopping (North Conway, NH). **Additional Information:** Bridgton Lakes Region Chamber of Commerce, (207) 647-3472.

RESTRICTIONS

Pets: Leashed, quiet, & cleaned up after. Must not be left unattended. $2.50 per dog per day. **Fires:** Fireplaces only. **Alcoholic Beverages:** At site only. **Vehicle Maximum Length:** 40 ft. **Other:** 7-night min. stay required for river sites during July & Aug.

TO GET THERE

From Maine Turnpike, take Exit 11 to Hwy. 202 to Hwy. 115 west for 3 mi. Connect w/ Hwy. 35S at junction of Hwy. 302 for 9 mi. Turn right onto Hwy. 25 west for 2 mi., then go right onto Hwy. 113 north. Follow Hwy. 113 north 23 mi. into Brownfield. Head right onto Hwy. 160. Campground is 0.5 mi. on the left, just before green iron bridge.

BRUNSWICK   MAP, D-1
Thomas Point Beach

29 Meadow Rd., 04011. T: (207) 725-6009 or (877) TPB-4321; www.thomaspointbeach.com.

 ★★★★   ★★★

Beauty: ★★★★   Site Privacy: ★★
Spaciousness: ★★   Quiet: ★★
Security: ★★★★★   Cleanliness: ★★★★★
Insect Control: ★★★   Facilities: ★★★★★

If this pretty oceanfront spot looks familiar, maybe you've been here before, say, sitting on the lawn at the annual Bluegrass Festival, or the Maine Arts Festival, or, perhaps, the tartaned goings-on of the Maine Highland Games. Set on Thomas Bay in midcoast Maine, between the towns of Brunswick and Bath, this property is stunning. Manicured green lawns slope to a tidal beach, flanked by lofty pines. No wonder this is a popular site for big community events and festivals. Thomas Point was an old salting bay used by native people; some of the old salt stones still exist. The property also features odd historic bits like the totem pole from the 1964 World's Fair (when Alaska became a state), millstones, and the handsome old cupola from St. Mary's Church. The public areas, including a pine-paneled rec hall and bathhouse, are extra-nice. Look for pretty wooded campsites to the right of the main lodge; sites 1 through 3 (RVs only) are among the best. Sites 1 through 64 are set along the marsh, with plenty of tall pines but little privacy; another camping area is located on the other, more forested side of the property. Among these, tent site L is a super spot. This whole area, including sites B through M, give or take, are quiet and wooded. Sites are mostly back-in, but there are 35 pull-through sites.

BASICS

Operated By: Patricia Crooker. **Open:** Mid-May–Oct. **Site Assignment:** Reservations recommended; 1-night deposit required; full payment due for weekends and holidays; refunds for cancellations w/ 7-day notice, minus $10. **Registration:** At office. **Fee:** $20–$25; for 2 adults & 2 children under age 12; additional older child/adult, $5 per night; shipping/handling fee of $2.50 added to telephone charges; V, MC. **Parking:** At site.

FACILITIES

Number of RV-only Sites: 75. **Hookups:** Electric (20, 30 amps), water. **Each Site:** Picnic table, fire ring. **Dump Station:** Yes. **Laundry:** Yes. **Pay Phone:** Yes. **Restrooms and Showers:** Yes (coin-op). **Fuel:** No. **Propane:** No. **Internal Roads:** Paved, in good condition. **RV Service:** No. **Market:** 7 mi. east. **Restaurant:** 7 mi. east. **General Store:** Yes. **Vending:** Yes. **Swimming:** No. **Playground:** Yes. **Other:** Rec hall. **Activities:** Ocean swimming, ball field. **Nearby Attractions:** Reid State Park, Popham Beach State Park, Morse Mountain Sanctuary, Maine Maritime Museum, Bowdoin College Museum of Art, Peary-MacMillan Arctic Museum, deep-sea fishing. **Additional Information:** Chamber of Commerce of the Bath-Brunswick Region, (207) 725-8797 or (207) 443-9751, www.midcoastmaine.com.

RESTRICTIONS

Pets: Registered "camping" pets under 25 lbs., no pets during public events. **Fires:** Fire ring only. **Alcoholic Beverages:** At sites only. **Vehicle Maximum Length:** No limit. **Other:** 14-day stay limit.

TO GET THERE

From junction of Hwy. 1 and Hwy. 24, go 3.75 mi. south on Hwy. 24, then 0.5 mi. southeast on Board Rd., then 0.5 mi. east on Meadow Rd. Campground entrance is on the right.

CAMDEN   MAP, C-2
Camden Hills State Park

280 Belfast Rd., 04843. T: (207) 236-3109 or (207) 236-0849 (off-season); www.campwithme.com.

🚐 ★★★   ⛺ ★★★★★

Beauty: ★★★★★   Site Privacy: ★★★
Spaciousness: ★★★★   Quiet: ★★★
Security: ★★★★★   Cleanliness: ★★★★★
Insect Control: ★★★   Facilities: ★★★★

Psst. Want to enjoy some of the best views in Maine, or (we'll go out on a limb here) all of New England? Camp here, and drive or hike to the summit of 800-foot Mt. Battie. From there, climb 26 steps up a stone tower for panoramic views of Penobscot Bay, dotted with sailboats and gem-like islands. You'll feel like you're on top of the (very gorgeous) world. Look for the Edna St. Vincent Millay poem etched on a rock here, inspired by this spot. There are 25 miles of hiking trails here, including another mountain summit, Mt. Megunticook, elevation 1380 feet. Bring those hiking boots. On one side of the park is Mt. Battie; on the other side is the camping area. Some sites are woody, others are open and grassy. Some, alas, are stony. Site 60L, known as the "Honeymoon Suite," is huge and secluded. For tenting, we like sites 75M through 81M, on the far side of the property; 75M and 81M are real beauties. Of all 107 sites, 101 are back-in and only 6 are pull-through. Good features include nice countertops and baby-changing stations in the ladies' restroom. Bad features are the black flies, who take over in May.

BASICS

Operated By: Maine Dept. of Conservation, Bureau of Parks and Lands. **Open:** May 15–Oct. 31. **Site Assignment:** In spring and fall, camping is first come, first served; in summer, reservations accepted starting on first business day in Jan.; from June 15 to the night before Labor Day, sites may be reserved for a min. of 2 nights and up to 2 weeks; reservations recommended in July and Aug., at least 2 weeks in advance; full payment charged to credit card when reservation is processed; refund w/ $15 fee; 24 sites are nonreservable and available first come, first served. **Registration:** At office and online. **Fee:** Maine residents, $15; nonresidents, $20; plus $2 fee if reserved in advance; V, MC. **Parking:** At sites and hikers lot only.

FACILITIES

Number of Multipurpose Sites: 107. **Hookups:** None. **Each Site:** Picnic table, fire ring. **Dump Station:** Yes. **Laundry:** No. **Pay Phone:** Yes. **Restrooms and Showers:** Yes. **Fuel:** No. **Propane:** No. **Internal Roads:** Gravel, in good condition. **RV Service:** No. **Market:** 2 mi. south. **Restaurant:** 2 mi. south. **General Store:** No. **Vending:** No. **Swimming:** No. **Playground:** Yes. **Activities:** Hiking (25 mi. of trails), scenic drive or hike to summit of Mt. Battie. **Nearby Attractions:** Camden galleries, museums & shops, windjammer fleet, Penobscot Bay cruises, Conway Homestead &

Mary Cramer Museum (18th-century restored farmhouse & gardens), Camden Hills State Park, Merryspring Park, Owl's Head Transportation Museum, golf, ocean swimming. **Additional Information:** Rockport-Camden-Lincolnville Chamber of Commerce, (207) 236-4404 or (800) 223-5459.

RESTRICTIONS

Pets: Must be leashed, quiet, & cleaned up after. Must not be left unattended. **Fires:** Fireplaces only. **Alcoholic Beverages:** Not allowed. **Vehicle Maximum Length:** No limit.

TO GET THERE

From junction of Hwy. 105 and Hwy. 1, go 2 mi. northeast on Hwy. 1. Campground entrance is on the left.

CANAAN   MAP, C-2
Skowhegan/Canaan KOA

P.O. Box 87, 04924. T: (207) 474-2858 or (800) 562-7571; www.koa.com.

🚐 ★★★★   ▲ ★★★

Beauty: ★★★★	Site Privacy: ★★★
Spaciousness: ★★★	Quiet: ★★★
Security: ★★★	Cleanliness: ★★★★★
Insect Control: ★★★	Facilities: ★★★

This woodsy campground in central Maine is a perfect base for exploring Maine's western lakes and mountains or mid-coastal beaches. There's also whitewater rafting, top-notch stream and lake fishing, hiking and biking, and plenty of good antiquing nearby. The country setting, spread over 60 acres, is pleasant in the summer (try blueberry picking along the trails) and gorgeous in the fall, when the mountains and valleys are awash in fiery hues. Hiking and biking trails take off from the property and, during the summer, there are planned activities to keep families happy. Facilities are white-glove clean, staff helpful and friendly, and atmosphere decidedly low-key. There are 58 spacious pull-throughs and a separate tent-only area, nestled in the woods. The campground is a pleasant great woods getaway and jumping off point for lots of outdoor recreation.

BASICS

Operated By: Don Cloutier. **Open:** May 7–Oct. 17. **Site Assignment:** Reservations not required; credit card will hold site, 2-week cancellation notice for cabins, 48-hour notice on tent or RV sites; holidays no refund. **Registration:** At office. **Fee:** Full hookup, $28; water/electric, $26; no hookup, $20, based on 2 adults & 2 children under 10; additional adult, $5; additional child, $3. **Parking:** At site.

FACILITIES

Number of RV-only Sites: 86. **Number of Tent-only Sites:** 14. **Hookups:** Electric (20, 30, 50 amps), water, sewer, cable TV, modem, Wi-Fi. **Each Site:** Picnic table, fire ring. **Dump Station:** Yes. **Laundry:** Yes. **Pay Phone:** Yes. **Restrooms and Showers:** Yes. **Fuel:** No. **Propane:** Yes. **Internal Roads:** Gravel, dirt (good). **RV Service:** No. **Market:** Skowhegan, 10 mi. **Restaurant:** Yes. **General Store:** Yes. **Vending:** Yes. **Swimming:** Yes. **Playground:** Yes. **Other:** Game room, TV room, sports

fields, pavilion, nature trails, bike rentals, cabin rentals. **Activities:** Swimming, hiking, biking, softball, volleyball, basketball, horseshoes, badminton, planned activities, including socials, contests, & group hikes. **Nearby Attractions:** Western mountains & lakes, mid-coast parks & beaches, Bangor. **Additional Information:** Skowhegan Area Chamber of Commerce, 10 Russell St., Skowhegan, ME 04976, (207) 474-3621, www.skowheganchamber.com.

RESTRICTIONS

Pets: Must be on a leash, never left unattended. **Fires:** Grill, stoves, fire rings only. **Alcoholic Beverages:** At site only. **Vehicle Maximum Length:** No limit.

TO GET THERE

From I-95, Exit 36, go north 6 mi. on Hwy. 201, then north 7 mi. on Hwy. 23, then 0.6 mi. east on Hwy. 2; campground is on the right.

CASCO   MAP, D-1
Point Sebago Golf and Beach Resort

261 Point Sebago Rd., 04015. T: (207) 655-3821 or (800) 655-1232; www.pointsebago.com.

🚐 ★★★★   ▲ ★★★

Beauty: ★★★★	Site Privacy: ★★
Spaciousness: ★★★★	Quiet: ★★
Security: ★★★★★	Cleanliness: ★★★★★
Insect Control: ★★★	Facilities: ★★★★★

One look at busy Chippy's Pavilion on the beach, and you'd swear you were at a theme park. "Number 32, your onion rings are ready," a voice chirps over the P.A. system. Meanwhile, groups of T-shirt-clad counselors are lining up small fry for scooter races. Just another summer day at Point Sebago, set on southwestern Maine's Lake Sebago, where adults can play golf on one of the finest courses in the state, while the kids chum around with their own kind in an award-winning program, from 9 to 5, if you choose. Kids' programs are split into five groups, by age, and supervised by 40 energetic young counselors. And if you think the fun stops when night falls, you've never been to Point Sebago's Vaudeville Night or the family bonfire. So what's the camping like? Sites are shaded, gravel, and mostly back-in; size and levelness vary. Tents and RVs are intermingled; we noticed that their rental units get the prime spots. If you like to be near the action, sites 801 to 811 are good for RVers, while sites along Red Rd., numbered 601 to 621, are pretty and wooded. Sites 901 to 929 back up into woods and seem fairly quiet. The campground is sprawling, people are everywhere, and the place smells like French fries, not wood smoke. But, how often do you find a camping place with a cybercafe, and great golf?

BASICS

Operated By: Larry and Anna Gould. **Open:** May 1–Oct. 31. **Site Assignment:** Reservations recommended; opens up for following year in mid-June 50% deposit w/in 10 days of making reservation; refund for cancellation w/ 45-day notice prior to arrival,

minus $25. **Registration:** At office. **Fee:** $216–$413 per week (during Family Value Weeks) or $364–$455; V, MC, D. **Parking:** At site.

FACILITIES

Number of RV-only Sites: 250. **Hookups:** Electric (20, 30, 50 amps), water, sewer. **Each Site:** Picnic table, fireplace. **Dump Station:** Yes. **Laundry:** Yes. **Pay Phone:** Yes. **Restrooms and Showers:** Yes. **Fuel:** No. **Propane:** Yes. **Internal Roads:** Gravel, in good condition. **RV Service:** Yes. **Market:** 5 mi. west. **Restaurant:** Yes. **General Store:** Yes. **Vending:** Yes. **Swimming:** No. **Playground:** Yes. **Other:** Cyber cafe, marina, golf (championship course). **Activities:** Lake swimming, golf, tennis, archery, boating (rentals available), boat cruises aboard the Point Sebago Princess, fishing (licenses available), waterskiing (lessons available), mini-golf, basketball, ball field, shuffleboard, children's program. **Nearby Attractions:** Golf, mini-golf, seaplane rides, boat cruises, Songo River Queen paddleboat, Douglas Mountain hiking, Sebago Lake State Park, outlet shopping (North Conway, NH). **Additional Information:** Naples Business Assoc., (207) 693-3285.

RESTRICTIONS

Pets: Only in one's own unit (not in rentals) & in specific areas. **Fires:** Fireplaces only. **Alcoholic Beverages:** At site only. **Vehicle Maximum Length:** 48 ft. **Other:** 7-day min. stay in peak season (third week of June through Labor Day).

TO GET THERE

From Maine Turnpike, take Exit 8; travel 22 mi. on Hwy. 302 to Point Sebago Rd.; proceed left to resort.

EAST ORLAND   MAP, C-2
Balsam Cove

Hwy. 102A, Back Ridge Rd., 04431. T: (207) 469-7771 or (800) 469-7771; www.balsamcove.com.

🚐 ★★★   ▲ ★★★

Beauty: ★★★	Site Privacy: ★★★
Spaciousness: ★★★	Quiet: ★★★★
Security: ★★★★	Cleanliness: ★★★
Insect Control: ★★★	Facilities: ★★★

This modest campground, located midway between Bucksport and Ellsworth (within an hour's drive to Acadia National Park), offers relaxed lakeside camping. Families enjoy the sandy beach area and the warm, shallow waters. There are boats to rent for paddling and fishing and, at night, a campground bonfire for roasting marshmallows. The long drive into the campground, a mile off busy Hwy. 1, helps keep the atmosphere subdued and quiet. Sites are a bit helter-skelter placed in rows and loops throughout the property. There are larger pull-through sites near the front of the campground and a handful of beachfront and water view sites. Families may like sites 14–19 across from the swimming area and playground. One of two campgrounds in the area on pristine Toddy Pond (also see Whispering Pines), Balsam Cove offers a few more facilities (laundry, general store) but less rustic charm.

BASICS

Operated By: Sharon and Charlie Young. **Open:** Memorial Day–Sept. **Site Assignment:** Reservations suggested July–Aug.; 50% deposit required; 14-day cancellation policy w/ $10 fee; MC, V, D, checks. **Registration:** At office. **Fee:** Full hookup, $24; waterfront (20 amps), $24; waterfront (no hookup), $21; wooded (30 amps), $21; wooded (20 amps), $19; wooded (no hookup), $18, based on 2 adults & 2 children under 18. **Parking:** At site.

FACILITIES

Number of RV-only Sites: 56. **Number of Tent-only Sites:** 4. **Hookups:** Electric (30 amps), water. **Each Site:** Picnic table, fire ring. **Dump Station:** Yes. **Laundry:** Yes. **Pay Phone:** Yes. **Restrooms and Showers:** Yes. **Fuel:** No. **Propane:** No. **Internal Roads:** Gravel (good). **RV Service:** No. **Market:** Bucksport, 6 mi. **Restaurant:** No. **General Store:** Yes. **Vending:** Yes. **Swimming:** No. **Playground:** Yes. **Other:** Lake frontage, beach, rowboat, canoe & paddleboat rentals, docks, boat ramp, rec room, group tent area, cabin rentals. **Activities:** Swimming, boating, fishing, basketball, horseshoes. **Nearby Attractions:** Deer Isle Peninsula, Bar Harbor, Acadia National Park. **Additional Information:** Bucksport Bay Area Chamber of Commerce, P.O. Box 1880, 263 Main St., Bucksport, ME, 04416-1880, (207) 469-6818; Acadia Information Center, P.O. Box 139, Mount Desert, ME, 04660 (207) 667-8550 or (800) 358-8550, www.acadiainfo.com.

RESTRICTIONS

Pets: Must be on a leash, never left unattended. No pets allowed on waterfront sites. 1 pet per site, some breeds not allowed. **Fires:** Grill, stoves, fire rings only. **Alcoholic Beverages:** At site only. **Vehicle Maximum Length:** 35 ft.

TO GET THERE

From junction of Hwy. 1 and Hwy. 15 (in East Orland), go north 1.7 mi. on Hwy. 1, then south 1.5 mi. on Back Ridge Rd.; campground is 1 mi. east on entrance road.

EAST ORLAND
Whispering Pines
MAP, C-2

US 1, P.O. Box 91, 04431. T: (207) 469-3443; www.campmaine.com/whisperingpines.

🚐 ★★★	🛖 ★★★
Beauty: ★★★★	Site Privacy: ★★★★
Spaciousness: ★★★★	Quiet: ★★★★★
Security: ★★★★	Cleanliness: ★★★
Insect Control: ★★★	Facilities: ★★

This small lakeside campground, within commuting distance to Deer Isle Peninsula to the south and Acadia National Park to the north, oozes old-fashioned charm. A stay here is akin to visiting family and friends at their summer cottage and owners Dwight and Sandy Gates do everything they can to make you feel at home. The rustic, woodsy setting, along the shores of Toddy Pond, is scenic and tranquil: birds sing in the pines, loons call at dusk, beavers and otters frolic in the water. "Pond" is a misnomer; it runs 9.7 miles long and 130 feet deep. Relaxing is a top activity here, but there's swimming and boating, and the fishing for landlocked salmon, lake trout, and bass is good. ("We're not an entertainment center," owner Sandy readily admits.) There is a handful of seasonal renters, an older clientele who come for the natural setting and peace and quiet. But there are plenty of sites to rent on a nightly basis. Most sites are clustered in the woods but there are a few on the water. Sites are mostly back-in. Roomy sites B4 and B5, next to the beach, are most popular and are often booked a year in advance.

BASICS

Operated By: Dwight and Sandy Gates. **Open:** Memorial Day–Sept. 30. **Site Assignment:** Reservations suggested; $35 deposit; 1-week cancellation policy; no credit cards, checks accepted. **Registration:** At office. **Fee:** $24; for 2 adults; $1 each child; $2 for electricity; $1 for sewer; $3 extra adult. **Parking:** At site.

FACILITIES

Number of Tent-only Sites: 7. **Number of Multipurpose Sites:** 45. **Hookups:** Electric (20 amps), water, sewer. **Each Site:** Picnic table, fire ring. **Dump Station:** Yes. **Laundry:** No. **Pay Phone:** No. **Restrooms and Showers:** Yes. **Fuel:** No. **Propane:** No. **Internal Roads:** Gravel, dirt (fair). **RV Service:** Yes. **Market:** Bucksport, 6 mi. **Restaurant:** No. **General Store:** No. **Vending:** No. **Swimming:** No. **Playground:** Yes. **Other:** Lake frontage, beach, dock, picnic area, game room, canoe, rowboats & bicycles to use (free). **Activities:** Swimming, fishing, boating, volleyball, horseshoes. **Nearby Attractions:** Deer Isle Peninsula, Bar Harbor, Acadia National Park. **Additional Information:** Bucksport Bay Area Chamber of Commerce, P.O. Box 1880, 263 Main St., Bucksport, ME, 04416-1880, (207) 469-6818; Acadia Information Center, P.O. Box 139, Mount Desert, ME 04660, (207) 667-8550 or (800) 358-8550, www.acadiainfo.com.

RESTRICTIONS

Pets: Must be on a leash, never left unattended, no more than 2 dogs. **Fires:** Grill, stoves, fire rings only. **Alcoholic Beverages:** At site only. **Vehicle Maximum Length:** No limit.

TO GET THERE

From junction of Hwy. 1 and Hwy. 15 (in East Orland), go north 2 mi. on Hwy. 1; campground is on the right.

ELLSWORTH
Branch Lake Camping Area
MAP, C-2

180 Hansons Landing Rd., 04605. T: (207) 667-5174; www.campmaine.com.

🚐 ★★★	🛖 ★★★
Beauty: ★★★	Site Privacy: ★★★
Spaciousness: ★★★	Quiet: ★★★
Security: ★★★	Cleanliness: ★★★
Insect Control: ★★★	Facilities: ★★★

This small lakeside campground is located halfway between Ellsworth and Bangor and a short drive to Bar Harbor and Acadia National Park. Set on the shores of ten-mile-long, spring-fed Branch Lake, the campground is a quiet getaway with pretty views of the crystal-clear lake dotted with rocky, pine-covered islands. Bring your boat (there's dock space if you reserve early) or rent a canoe from the campground. The campground's 175 feet of lake frontage includes a swimming beach and fishing pier. The sites are set randomly throughout the campground, tucked here and there under the trees and around scattered boulders; larger sites are angled in rows, farthest away from the beach area. Tenters may be frustrated. The separate tent area is tiny and has a view of the cluster of RV sites. Sites are mostly back-in; there are only six pull-throughs.

BASICS

Operated By: Dick and Brenda Graves. **Open:** May 15–Oct. 15. **Site Assignment:** Reservations suggested; 1-night deposit, 7-day cancellation policy, 2-night minimum July–Aug.; no credit cards accepted. **Registration:** At office. **Fee:** $25; tent, $18. **Parking:** At site.

FACILITIES

Number of RV-only Sites: 45. **Number of Tent-only Sites:** 5. **Number of Multipurpose Sites:** 10. **Hookups:** Electric (30 amps), water, sewer. **Each Site:** Picnic table, fire ring. **Dump Station:** Yes. **Laundry:** No. **Pay Phone:** Yes. **Restrooms and Showers:** Yes (coin-op). **Fuel:** No. **Propane:** No. **Internal Roads:** Gravel, dirt (fair). **RV Service:** No. **Market:** Ellsworth, 8 mi. **Restaurant:** No. **General Store:** Yes. **Vending:** Yes. **Swimming:** No. **Playground:** Yes. **Other:** Lake frontage, beach, boat launch, boat dock, boat & canoe rentals. **Activities:** Swimming, boating, fishing, horseshoes, potluck dinners. **Nearby Attractions:** Bangor, Bar Harbor, Acadia National Park. **Additional Information:** 180 Hansons Landing, Ellsworth 04605, (207) 667-5174.

RESTRICTIONS

Pets: Must be on a leash, never left unattended. 2 dogs per site; some breeds not allowed (pit bulls, rottweilers). **Fires:** Grill, stoves, fire rings only. **Alcoholic Beverages:** At site only. **Vehicle Maximum Length:** 50 ft.

TO GET THERE

From junction Hwy. 1 and 1A (in Ellsworth), go northwest 10 mi. on Hwy. 1A, then southwest (left) 0.5 mi. on Winkumpaugh Rd., then south 1 mi. on Hanson Landing Rd.; campground is on the left.

ELLSWORTH
Lamoine State Park
MAP, C-2

23 State Park Rd., 04605. T: (207) 667-4778.

🚐 ★★★	🛖 ★★★★
Beauty: ★★★★	Site Privacy: ★★★
Spaciousness: ★★★★	Quiet: ★★★★
Security: ★★★	Cleanliness: ★★★★
Insect Control: ★★★	Facilities: ★★★

The view of the ocean, the cool ocean breezes (even on the muggiest summer afternoons), the potent scents of evergreen forest blended with the salty tang of the ocean, and the aroma of wood smoke drifting as the day draws to an end all help to make Lamoine State Park an excellent campground selection. The whole gestalt here is that of being on a windswept, oceanside bluff—which you are. The camping sites, like the park itself, run the gamut from sunny, breezy, spacious, and open and to densely forested, isolated, and tiny. Either way, you can't lose. All sites are back-in. There's a short path down to the water right across from site 49; and there's also the one-mile Loop Trail for those in need of a little exercise. Take a moment after you've set up your campsite to sit back, draw in a deep breath, and enjoy the sights, sounds, and scents of this oceanside campground.

BASICS

Operated By: Maine Dept. of Conservation. **Open:** Mid-May–mid-Oct. **Site Assignment:** By reservation or first come, first served. **Registration:** At ranger station. **Fee:** $15–$20; additional $2 per night for reservations. **Parking:** At site.

FACILITIES

Number of Multipurpose Sites: 62. **Hookups:** None. **Each Site:** Picnic table, fire ring. **Dump Station:** No. **Laundry:** No. **Pay Phone:** Yes. **Restrooms and Showers:** Yes. **Fuel:** No. **Propane:** No. **Internal Roads:** Gravel. **RV Service:** No. **Market:** No. **Restaurant:** No. **General Store:** No. **Vending:** No. **Swimming:** No. **Playground:** Yes. **Other:** Boat launch. **Activities:** Boating, swimming, saltwater fishing. **Nearby Attractions:** Arcadia National Park, area lighthouses.

RESTRICTIONS

Pets: On leash. **Fires:** Fire ring only. **Alcoholic Beverages:** At site. **Vehicle Maximum Length:** 35 ft. **Other:** Max. 6 people per party, 14-day stay limit during the summer.

TO GET THERE

The campground is on ME Hwy. 184, 8 mi. southeast from Ellsworth.

ELLSWORTH   MAP, C-2
Patten Pond Camping Resort

reserve america

1470 Bucksport Rd., Rte. 1 & 3, 04605.
T: (207) 667-7600 or (877) 667-7376;
www.reserveamerica.com.

🚐 ★★★★★	⛺ ★★★
Beauty: ★★★★	Site Privacy: ★★★
Spaciousness: ★★★	Quiet: ★★★
Security: ★★★★	Cleanliness: ★★★★★
Insect Control: ★★★★	Facilities: ★★★★★

This lively, modern camping resort, a half-hour from Bar Harbor and Acadia National Park, offers an array of activities and top-notch facilities. It's located on pretty Patten Pond, a crystal-clear freshwater lake dotted with rocky islands and flanked by pine-tree forests. There's a sandy stretch of beach, a favorite hangout at the campground, with a fishing pier, boat dock, and viewing/sunning deck. When campers are not on the lake, they're buzzing about the campground, taking part in a host of activities: live entertainment, movies, kids' programs, Sunday morning church services, lobster bakes, and more. Most campers use the resort as a base to explore the area,

near enough to major attractions but far enough from the summer traffic and commotion of the Bar Harbor area. Sites are uniform throughout the campground, most with three-way hookups, set side-by-side in rows. (No sites are on the water.) There's a separate tenting area that backs up to sparse woods.

BASICS

Operated By: Pat Stanley. **Open:** May–Oct. **Site Assignment:** Reservations accepted year-round; suggested July–Aug.; 2-night minimum, 3 nights on holiday weekends; $50 deposit for 3 nights, $75 for 4–7 nights, $100 for 8 nights or more; 14-day cancellation policy w/ $10 fee. Holidays are paid in full and nonrefundable; MC, V, D, checks accepted for reservations; no checks upon arrival. **Registration:** At office. **Fee:** Full hookup (best, 50 amps), $40 peak, $29 early & late summer; full hookup (50 amps), $35–$28; full hookup (best, 30 amps), $32–$26; full hookup (30 amps), $29–$24; water & electric, $26–$20; best tent, $20–$17; tent, $18–$15, based on 2. **Parking:** At site.

FACILITIES

Number of RV-only Sites: 80. **Number of Tent-only Sites:** 35. **Number of Multipurpose Sites:** 30. **Hookups:** Electric (30, 50 amps), water, sewer, modem, cable TV, Wi-Fi. **Each Site:** Picnic table, fire ring. **Dump Station:** Yes. **Laundry:** Yes. **Pay Phone:** Yes. **Restrooms and Showers:** Yes. **Fuel:** No. **Propane:** Yes. **Internal Roads:** Gravel, dirt (good). **RV Service:** No. **Market:** Ellsworth, 9 mi. **Restaurant:** No. **General Store:** Yes. **Vending:** No. **Swimming:** No. **Playground:** Yes. **Other:** Lake frontage, beach, fishing pier, dock, paddleboat, sailboat, kayak & canoe rentals, entertainment pavilion, cabin, cottage & apartment rentals, gift store, game room, modem center, car rentals on site. **Activities:** Swimming, boating, fishing, basketball, volleyball, planned activities, including live entertainment, children's programs, lobster bakes. **Nearby Attractions:** Bar Harbor, Acadia National Park. **Additional Information:** Ellsworth Area Chamber of Commerce, P.O. Box 267, Ellsworth, ME 04605, (207) 667-5584; Acadia Information Center, P.O. Box 139, Mount Desert, ME 04660, (207) 667-8550 or (800) 358-8550, www.acadiainfo.com.

RESTRICTIONS

Pets: Must be on a leash, never left unattended. **Fires:** Grill, stoves, fire rings only. **Alcoholic Beverages:** At site only. **Vehicle Maximum Length:** No limit.

TO GET THERE

From junction Hwy. 1 and Hwy. 1A (in Ellsworth), go southwest 7.5 mi. on Hwy. 1; campground is on the left.

EUSTIS   MAP, C-1
Cathedral Pines

Hwy. 27, P.O. Box 146, 04936. T: (207) 246-3491; www.eustismaine.com/pines/.

🚐 ★★★★★	⛺ ★★★★★
Beauty: ★★★★★	Site Privacy: ★★★★★
Spaciousness: ★★★★★	Quiet: ★★★★
Security: ★★★★	Cleanliness: ★★★★
Insect Control: ★★★★	Facilities: ★★★

Northern California has its redwoods; here in Eustis, Maine, the cathedral pines are famous for their lofty beauty. Happily, campers can enjoy this enchanted setting. Located in the rural western corner of the state, just 26 miles south of the Canadian border, Cathedral Pines is a nonprofit campground, and one of the most scenic in all of New England. Funds go to the towns of Stratton and Eustis, who operate the park. The tall, virgin stand of Norway (red) pines is set on the shores of Flagstaff Lake, where there's a private beach for campers, a public beach, and a picnic area. This site was one of Benedict Arnold's stops during his ill-fated march to Quebec City in 1775. The sand and gravel sites are canopied by the gorgeous pines, with buffer provided by low-growing shrubbery. Campsites are set in loops, including a separate area for tents (no water and electric); tent site 69, on the lake, is stunning. Among the water/electric sites, sites 13, 15, 16, 17, and 18 are nice, big, and lakeside. The sites are mostly back-in; there are only two pull-through sites. Three-way hookup sites are situated near the campground's entrance. All sites are widely spaced, spacious, and private, not to mention jaw-droppingly beautiful. Don't miss this one.

BASICS

Operated By: Stratton-Eustis Development Corp. **Open:** May 15–Oct. 1. **Site Assignment:** Reservations recommended; no reservations accepted for less than a 2-night stay; must pay in full w/in 10 days of making reservation; 48-hour cancellation policy; credit for future stay only. **Registration:** At office. **Fee:** $15–$20; for 4 people; V, MC. **Parking:** At site.

FACILITIES

Number of RV-only Sites: 115. **Number of Tent-only Sites:** 13. **Hookups:** Electric (30 amps), water, sewer. **Each Site:** Picnic table, fireplace. **Dump Station:** Yes. **Laundry:** Yes. **Pay Phone:** Yes. **Restrooms and Showers:** Yes. **Fuel:** No. **Propane:** No. **Internal Roads:** Paved, in good condition. **RV Service:** No. **Market:** 4 mi. south. **Restaurant:** 4 mi. south. **General Store:** Yes. **Vending:** Yes. **Swimming:** No. **Playground:** Yes. **Other:** Boat ramp, rec hall. **Activities:** Lake swimming, fishing (need license), hiking on Appalachian Trail, bicycling, boating (rentals available). **Nearby Attractions:** Moose watching, Arnold Trail (follows Benedict Arnold's route to Quebec City), Dead River Historical Society Museum, golf, Bigelow Mountain. **Additional Information:** Flagstaff Area Business Assoc., (207) 246-4221, www.eustismaine.com.

RESTRICTIONS

Pets: Must be leashed, quiet, & cleaned up after. Must not be left unattended. Not allowed in buildings or beaches. $10 refundable deposit required. **Fires:** Fireplaces only. **Alcoholic Beverages:** Allowed. **Vehicle Maximum Length:** 40 ft. **Other:** 3-night min. stay on holidays, payable in advance.

TO GET THERE

From Maine Turnpike, take Exit 12 (Auburn) to Hwy. 4 north. Connect w/ Hwy. 27 north in Farmington; follow to Eustis. Campground is on the right. (Total mileage from turnpike is 90 mi.)

EUSTIS MAP, C-1
Natanis Point Campground

HC 73 Box 270, 04936. T: (207) 297-2694 or (207) 645-5207 (winter); www.natanispoint.com.

🚐 ★★★ ▲ ★★

Beauty: ★★★★	Site Privacy: ★★★★
Spaciousness: ★★★	Quiet: ★★★★
Security: ★★★	Cleanliness: ★★★★
Insect Control: ★★★	Facilities: ★★★

We were all set to overlook this tiny, rustic campground, just six miles south of the Canadian border. But, we couldn't, once we realized one could camp here, on the Chain of Ponds, and wake up to gorgeous views of deep-blue water, flanked by pine-sloped mountains. Wooded campsites are set on two loops, overlooking Round Pond and Natanis Pond. All sites are back-in. We recommend the Natanis Pond side for best views, especially site 6. Sites 3 through 9 are fabulous; you couldn't be closer to the water unless you slept on your boat. Speaking of which, you can park your boat right alongside your tent or RV and roll it in when you're ready. Sites 32 through 44 are farthest from the water. (Look for the Natanis Memorial just behind site 9; read about the legend of Natanis, a Native American female trapper, in the campground office.) The owners say this campground is at its best in fall, when the foliage season kicks in; however, the cold comes early here, and they drain the water pipes and close the bathhouse in early Oct. Rates drop to $10 per night.

BASICS

Operated By: Ken and Sharon Thomas. **Open:** May 15–Oct. 15. **Site Assignment:** Reservations recommended for weekends; 50% deposit required; 1-week cancellation policy. **Registration:** At office. **Fee:** $16; for 1 to 4 people; V, MC. **Parking:** At site.

FACILITIES

Number of Tent-only Sites: 4. **Number of Multipurpose Sites:** 57. **Hookups:** Water. **Each Site:** Picnic table, fire ring. **Dump Station:** Yes. **Laundry:** No. **Pay Phone:** Yes. **Restrooms and Showers:** Yes. **Fuel:** No. **Propane:** No. **Internal Roads:** Gravel, in good condition. **RV Service:** No. **Market:** 5 mi. north. **Restaurant:** 5 mi. north. **General Store:** Yes. **Vending:** No. **Swimming:** No. **Playground:** Yes. **Other:** Supper building (rec hall). **Activities:** Fishing (license required), pond swimming, boating (kayak & canoe rentals available), volleyball, ATV trails, planned activities. **Nearby Attractions:** Arnold Trail (follows Benedict Arnold's route to Quebec City), Dead River Historical Society Museum, Flagstaff Lake, golf, Bigelow Mountain. **Additional Information:** Flagstaff Area Business Assoc., (207) 246-4221, www.eustismaine.com.

RESTRICTIONS

Pets: Must be leashed, quiet, & cleaned up after. Must not be left unattended, aggressive breeds are not allowed. **Fires:** Fire ring only. **Alcoholic Beverages:** At sites only. **Vehicle Maximum Length:** 35 ft.

TO GET THERE

From Maine Turnpike, take Exit 12 (Auburn) to Hwy. 4 north. Connect w/ Hwy. 27 north in Farmington; follow Hwy. 27 north to Eustis. Stay on Hwy. 27 for 17 mi., heading north. Campground is on the left.

FREEPORT MAP, D-1
Cedar Haven

39 Baker Rd., 04032. T: (207) 865-6254 or (800) 454-3403; www.campmaine.com/cedarhaven.

🚐 ★★★ ▲ ★★★

Beauty: ★★★	Site Privacy: ★★★
Spaciousness: ★★★	Quiet: ★★★
Security: ★★★	Cleanliness: ★★★
Insect Control: ★★★	Facilities: ★★★

This woodsy campground is just two miles from touristy downtown Freeport, but campers feel worlds away. The modest, family-oriented property has a large sports field, a small (0.25-acre) spring-fed swimming pond (usually full of tiny tots at the end of long summer's day) and roomy sites. Sites are mostly back-in. Tenters will especially enjoy the shaded, private, hillside sites offering a natural-setting getaway from the busy Freeport area. (Site 38 set back in the woods is a favorite.) Big-rig drivers will find four large-size, full-hookup sites and extra wide roads for convenience. Most campers spend the day exploring the area (and outlet shopping) and breathe a heavy sigh of relief by the time they reach their site. Nothing fancy here—just a little peace and quiet.

BASICS

Operated By: Private operator. **Open:** May–Oct. **Site Assignment:** Reservations suggested; hold w/ credit card during peak season; no-shows charged 1-night fee; MC, V, D, checks, no AE. **Registration:** At office. **Fee:** Full hookup, $32; water/electric, $26; no hookup, $21.50, based on 2 adults & 2 children under 18. **Parking:** At site.

FACILITIES

Number of RV-only Sites: 48. **Number of Tent-only Sites:** 10. **Hookups:** Electric (30 amps), water, sewer, cable TV at selected sites. **Each Site:** Picnic table, fire ring, trash barrel. **Dump Station:** Yes. **Laundry:** Yes. **Pay Phone:** Yes. **Restrooms and Showers:** Yes (coin-op). **Fuel:** No. **Propane:** Yes. **Internal Roads:** Gravel (good). **RV Service:** No. **Market:** Freeport, 2 mi. **Restaurant:** No. **General Store:** Yes. **Vending:** No. **Swimming:** No. **Playground:** Yes. **Other:** Sports field, game room, mini-golf, spring-fed pond, beach, cabin rental, group area. **Activities:** Swimming, horseshoes, mini-golf, volleyball, basketball. **Nearby Attractions:** Freeport, outlet shopping, mid-coast parks & beaches. **Additional Information:** Freeport Merchants Assoc., 23 Depot St., Freeport, ME 04032-0452, (207) 865-1212 or (800) 865-0881, www.freeportusa.com.

RESTRICTIONS

Pets: Must be on a leash, never left unattended. **Fires:** Grill, stoves, fire rings only. **Alcoholic Beverages:** At site only. **Vehicle Maximum Length:** No limit.

TO GET THERE

From I-95, take Exit 22; bear right on Hwy. 125/136 for 0.5 mi, then turn right on Hwy. 125 for 0.5 mi, then right on Baker Rd.; campground is on the left.

FREEPORT MAP, D-1
Desert Dunes of Maine Campground

95 Desert Rd., 04032. T: (207) 865-6962; www.desertofmaine.com.

🚐 ★★★ ▲ ★★★

Beauty: ★★★	Site Privacy: ★★★
Spaciousness: ★★★	Quiet: ★★★
Security: ★★★	Cleanliness: ★★★
Insect Control: ★★★	Facilities: ★★★

This is the only campground we know of in New England that sits next to—and on top of—a desert. The owners of the campground also own the adjacent Desert of Maine attraction, a unique natural phenomenon drawing close to 50,000 visitors each year. Guided safari and walking tours take visitors across vast sandy dunes. There's a museum, sand art classes, and gemstone hunts for children. Campers have free access to the attraction and most take advantage of it. At the campground, sites are scattered in the trees or up on hills. There's a handful of very nice tent-only sites in the woods with plenty of room and privacy. For extra seclusion, book site T8, the honeymoon site, deep in the woods, set apart from the others. There are also a number of spacious wooded pull-through sites. There are 27 back-in sites. Though the campground is relatively small, just 50 sites spread on ten acres, it often feels busy. Not only do tourists funnel through the office/gift store in route to the attraction but the front of the campground, including the picnic area, is often taken over by buses of visitors.

BASICS

Operated By: Sid and Carolyn Dobson. **Open:** May–mid Oct. **Site Assignment:** Reservations suggested; 1-night deposit; 30-day cancellation policy w/ $5 charge; MC, V, D, AE, no checks. **Registration:** At office. **Fee:** Full hookup, $36; water/electric, $28; no hookup, $21, based on 2 people per site, additional person in RV, $5; additional person in tent, $7; children ages 3–12, $2; ages 13–16, $3. **Parking:** At site.

FACILITIES

Number of RV-only Sites: 45. **Number of Tent-only Sites:** 10. **Hookups:** Electric (20, 30 amps), water, sewer, modem. **Each Site:** Picnic table, fire ring. **Dump Station:** Yes. **Laundry:** Yes. **Pay Phone:** No. **Restrooms and Showers:** Yes (coin-op). **Fuel:** No. **Propane:** Yes. **Internal Roads:** Gravel, dirt (good). **RV Service:** No. **Market:** Freeport, 6 mi. **Restaurant:** No. **General Store:** Yes. **Vending:** No. **Swimming:** Yes. **Playground:** No. **Other:** Free access to Desert of Maine & discount on tours, group area, picnic area, nature trails. **Activities:** Swimming, horseshoes. **Nearby Attractions:** Desert of Maine, Freeport, mid-coast parks & beaches. **Additional Information:** Freeport Merchants Assoc., 23 Depot St., Freeport, ME 04032-0452, (207) 865-1212 or (800) 865-0881, www.freeportusa.com.

RESTRICTIONS

Pets: Must be on a leash, never left unattended. **Fires:** Grill, stoves, fire rings only. **Alcoholic Beverages:** At site only. **Vehicle Maximum Length:** No limit.

TO GET THERE

From I-95, Exit 19, go west 2 mi. on Desert Rd.; campground is on the left.

GREENVILLE   MAP, B-2
Lily Bay State Park

13 Myrle's Way, 04441. T: (800) 332-1501 or (207) 287-3824 ; www.state.me.us/doc/parks/ reservations.

🚐 ★★★★   ⛺ ★★★

Beauty: ★★★★★	Site Privacy: ★★★★★
Spaciousness: ★★★★★	Quiet: ★★★★
Security: ★★★	Cleanliness: ★★★
Insect Control: ★★	Facilities: ★

I've waited my whole career for this, says Lily Bay State Park general manager Andy Haskell, spreading his arms to encompass his surroundings. It's easy to see why he's got a big grin on his face. Haskell's realm is a spectacular natural area set on the eastern shore of Moosehead Lake, the largest lake in New England. From the lake, campers look out toward mountain vistas all around, including Mt. Kineo, which seems to spring from the lake itself, rising 800 feet above the water. Campsites are set in two loops, both on the lake. There's Dunn Point, good for families because it's a close walk to the beach and playground, and Rowell Cove, which offers several walk-in tent sites. Sites are back-in with the exception of one pull-through. Plus, at Rowell Cove, tent sites are set closer to the water. Among the choicest sites at Rowell Cove are 20L and 21L, directly on the lake and roomy enough for 30 foot campers. Lake-view sites at Dunn Point are those numbered 210, 211, 213, 214, and 215, and 218, 220, 221, and 222. You'll hear the haunting cry of loons at night. If you've brought a kayak or canoe, paddle out to Sugar Island (open to the public). If you can handle wilderness camping, it doesn't get better than Lily Bays

BASICS

Operated By: Maine Dept. of Conservation, Bureau of Parks and Lands. **Open:** May 15–Columbus Day. **Site Assignment:** In spring and fall, first come, first served. In summer, reservations open on the first business day in Feb.; refunds w/ $15 fee; 17 sites are nonreservable and available first come, first served; call the reservations line to cancel a reservation more than 3 days in advance; if cancelling less than 3 days in advance, call the park directly. **Registration:** At office. **Fee:** Maine residents, $14; nonresidents, $19; plus $2 fee reserved in advance; V, MC. **Parking:** At site.

FACILITIES

Number of Tent-only Sites: 22. **Number of Multipurpose Sites:** 68. **Hookups:** None. **Each Site:** Picnic table, fireplace. **Dump Station:** Yes. **Laundry:** No. **Pay Phone:** Yes. **Restrooms and Showers:** Yes. **Fuel:** No. **Propane:** No. **Internal Roads:** Gravel, in good condition. **RV Service:** No.

Market: 9 mi. southwest, in Greenville. **Restaurant:** 9 mi. southwest, in Greenville. **General Store:** No. **Vending:** Yes. **Swimming:** Yes. **Playground:** Yes. **Other:** Boat ramps, boat docks. **Activities:** Lake swimming, shoreline hiking trail w/ interpretive signage, volleyball, boating, picnicking, fishing. **Nearby Attractions:** Moosehead Lake, S.S. Katahdin steamboat cruises, Moosehead Marine Museum, Eveleth-Crafts-Sheridan Historical House, Lily whitewater rafting, boating, fishing, moose watching at Lazy Tom Bog, lots of hiking!. **Additional Information:** Moosehead Lake Region Chamber of Commerce, (207) 695-2702.

RESTRICTIONS

Pets: Must be leashed, quiet, & cleaned up after. Must have rabies vaccination certificate. Not allowed on beach. **Fires:** Fireplaces only. **Alcoholic Beverages:** Not allowed. **Vehicle Maximum Length:** 35 ft. **Other:** 2-week stay limit between last Sat. in June & last Sat. in Aug.

TO GET THERE

From Greenville, go 9 mi. northeast on Lily Bay Rd. (also called Kodjako Rd.). Campground is on the left.

HERMON   MAP, C-2
Pleasant Hill RV Park and Campground

45 Mansell Rd., 04401. T: (207) 848-5127; www.pleasanthillcampground.com.

🚐 ★★★   ⛺ ★★★

Beauty: ★★★	Site Privacy: ★★★
Spaciousness: ★★★	Quiet: ★★★
Security: ★★★	Cleanliness: ★★★
Insect Control: ★★★	Facilities: ★★★

The name says it all: friendly and pleasant, this rural campground, just outside of Bangor, attracts a wide variety of clientele, from family campers who return year after year for a weekend away to off-the-road travelers in and out in a day. It's situated just a few miles off the main interstate, an hour or so from Acadia National Park and en route to the Canadian Maritime Provinces, making it a favorite stopover for tourists needing a place to lay their heads for the night. Campers find a helpful staff, clean, maintained grounds and a choice of sunny or shaded sites. Pull-through, full hookups are set side-by-side off the main campground road; water and electric sites and tent sites are set in loops nestled in woods or in open, sunny fields. Families will find enough to keep little ones entertained for an evening or two: besides the swimming pool, there's a stocked fishing pond, modest mini-golf course, and game room on site.

BASICS

Operated By: Montford family. **Open:** May 1–Columbus Day. **Site Assignment:** First come, first served; call for reservations to reserve a specific site only; 1-night deposit; 2 week cancellation policy w/ $10 fee; MC, V, D, checks. **Registration:** At office. **Fee:** Full hookup, $35.50 (50 amps); $31 (30 amps); water/electric (50 amps) $32.50; water only (tent), $20; trailer rentals available, $70. **Parking:** At site.

FACILITIES

Number of RV-only Sites: 84. **Number of Tent-only Sites:** 21. **Hookups:** Electric (30, 50 amps), water, sewer. **Each Site:** Picnic table, fire ring. **Dump Station:** Yes. **Laundry:** Yes. **Pay Phone:** Yes. **Restrooms and Showers:** Yes. **Fuel:** No. **Propane:** Yes. **Internal Roads:** 90% paved, 10% gravel. **RV Service:** No. **Market:** Bangor, 5 mi. **Restaurant:** No. **General Store:** Yes. **Vending:** No. **Swimming:** Yes. **Playground:** Yes. **Other:** Rec hall, mini-golf, stocked fishing pond, adult reading lounge, pavilion. **Activities:** Swimming, fishing, horseshoes, volleyball, mini-golf, basketball. **Nearby Attractions:** Bangor, Bar Harbor, Acadia National Park, Maine coast. **Additional Information:** Bangor Regional Chamber of Commerce, 519 Maine St., P.O. Box 1443, Bangor, ME 04402, (207) 947-0307, www.bangorregion.com.

RESTRICTIONS

Pets: On leash, never unattended. **Fires:** Grill, stoves, fire rings only. **Alcoholic Beverages:** At site only. **Vehicle Maximum Length:** No limit.

TO GET THERE

From I-95, Exit 184, go 5 mi. west on Hwy. 222 (Union St.); campground is on the left.

MEDWAY   MAP, B-2
Katahdin Shadows

Hwy. 157, P.O. Box 606, 04460. T: (207) 746-9349 or (800) 794-5267; www.katahdinshadows.com.

🚐 ★★★★   ⛺ ★★★★★

Beauty: ★★★★★	Site Privacy: ★★★★
Spaciousness: ★★★★	Quiet: ★★★★
Security: ★★★★	Cleanliness: ★★★★
Insect Control: ★★★	Facilities: ★★★★

We love this plush oasis nestled in the vast northern Maine woods, just outside of Baxter State Park. Outdoor enthusiasts have miles of hiking trails, canoeing, whitewater rafting, and some of the best fishing in Maine right outside their doorsteps. The ultra-friendly campground owners provide plenty of tips and information and will set campers up with outdoor adventure guide and shuttle service. Guided fishing trips take off directly from the campground. Most campers come to play in the great outdoors but save plenty of time for relaxing around the campground. There are lots of nice facilities here: swimming pool, lounges, sports fields, function hall, and more. On summer weekends, kids can join in a number of planned activities. Tenters looking for quiet and solitude will appreciate "the jungle," a separate, secluded area with plenty of privacy. RVers will like sites 51–56, with full hookups, easy access, and lots of shade. Sites are mostly back-in; there are eight pull-throughs. The campground also rents hutniks (8 by 8 wooded shelters with roll-down doors) and cabins. Added bonus: the campground stays open year-round with miles of cross-country, snowshoe, and snowmobile trails accessible from the property.

BASICS

Operated By: David and Theresa Violette. **Open:** All year. **Site Assignment:** Reservations suggested July–Aug.; 1-night deposit; 7-day cancellation policy;

MC, V, D, checks. 2-night minimum on holiday weekends; $5 per additional person 18 and up. **Registration:** At office. **Fee:** Full hookup, $26; water/electric, $24; no hookup, $21, based on 2 adults & 2 children. **Parking:** At site.

FACILITIES

Number of RV-only Sites: 80. **Number of Tent-only Sites:** 30. **Number of Multipurpose Sites:** 20. **Hookups:** Electric (30, 50 amps), water, sewer. **Each Site:** Picnic table, fire ring. **Dump Station:** Yes. **Laundry:** Yes. **Pay Phone:** Yes. **Restrooms and Showers:** Yes. **Fuel:** No. **Propane:** Yes. **Internal Roads:** Gravel, dirt (good). **RV Service:** No. **Market:** Medway (w/in walking distance). **Restaurant:** No. **General Store:** Yes. **Vending:** Yes. **Swimming:** Yes. **Playground:** Yes. **Other:** Game room, sports fields, adult lounge, function hall, guided fishing trips, boat rentals, planned activities, guide & shuttle service to whitewater rafting, kayaking & canoeing. **Activities:** Swimming, boating, fishing, hiking, whitewater rafting, guided excursions. **Nearby Attractions:** Baxter State Park, Penobscot River, Gulf Hagas, Allagash River, Mattawamkeag Wilderness Park, Katahdin Iron Works. **Additional Information:** Katahdin Area Chamber of Commerce, 1029 Central St., Millinocket, Maine 04462, (207) 723-4443, www.katahdinmaine.com.

RESTRICTIONS

Pets: On leash; never left unattended. **Fires:** Grill, camp stoves, fire rings only. **Alcoholic Beverages:** At site only. **Vehicle Maximum Length:** No limit.

TO GET THERE

From I-95, Exit 56, go 1.7 mi. west on Hwy. 157; campground is on the right.

NEW HARBOR   MAP, D-2
Sherwood Forest Campsite

Pemaquid Beach, P.O. Box 189, 04554. T: (800) 274-1593 or (207) 677-3642.

🚐 ★★★	🏕 ★★★
Beauty: ★★★	Site Privacy: ★★★
Spaciousness: ★★★	Quiet: ★★★★
Security: ★★★	Cleanliness: ★★★★
Insect Control: ★★★	Facilities: ★★★

In the party mood? Keep going. "Go to Lake Pemaquid Campground!" owner Marilyn Stooky advises. "You won't be happy here." This wooded campground, about a half-hour's drive from Boothbay Harbor on Maine's mid-coast, is located in the Pemaquid Beach area but sits inland from the ocean. If you prefer "quiet and woodsy" to "crowded and beachy," you'll be quite content here. This campground has been in the same family for 23 years, with a younger generation poised to take over. Sites are grassy and set in a loop that starts just beyond the pool, store, and pavilion area, which is bordered by four cabins. Sites are heavily wooded and nicely buffered for privacy; sunlight filters through the dense canopy of foliage on bright summer days. Sites 15E and F, facing a small pond, are pretty, but stay away from 15H, alongside a big brush pile when we visited. Site 15D2 is nestled in woodlands and very private. Sites 9A and 9B sit in a wooded glen, nicely

situated. There are eight pull-through sites and the rest are back-in. Among the tent sites, the owner recommends sites B, C, and D, set on a cul-de-sac; we like nicely shaded site 43, which backs into the woods. Outbuildings are fairly rustic, but changes may come as the kids take over.

BASICS

Operated By: Gary and Marilyn Stooky. **Open:** May 1–Oct. 1. **Site Assignment:** Reservations recommended; $25 deposit required; refunds for cancellations w/ 1-week notice, minus $5. **Registration:** At office. **Fee:** $20–$26 for 2 adults & 2 children; no credit cards. **Parking:** At site.

FACILITIES

Number of RV-only Sites: 49. **Number of Tent-only Sites:** 13. **Hookups:** Electric (15, 20, 30 amps), water. **Each Site:** Picnic table, fire ring. **Dump Station:** Yes. **Laundry:** Yes. **Pay Phone:** Yes. **Restrooms and Showers:** Yes, coin-op. **Fuel:** No. **Propane:** No. **Internal Roads:** Gravel, in good condition. **RV Service:** No. **Market:** 1 mi. east. **Restaurant:** 1 mi. east. **General Store:** Yes. **Vending:** Yes. **Swimming:** Yes. **Playground:** Yes. **Other:** Cabin rentals. **Activities:** Swimming, basketball, boating (may add rentals; pending). **Nearby Attractions:** Pemaquid Point Lighthouse, Boothbay Railway Village, Maine Resources Aquarium, Boothbay Harbor restaurants, shops & galleries, deep-sea fishing, whale-watching cruises, golf. **Additional Information:** Damariscotta Info Bureau, (207) 563-3176.

RESTRICTIONS

Pets: Must be leashed, quiet, & cleaned up after. Must not be left unattended. $1 charge per dog per day. **Fires:** Fireplaces only. **Alcoholic Beverages:** Allowed. **Vehicle Maximum Length:** No limit. **Other:** 3-day min. stays on July 4th weekend, Old Bristol Days (in Aug., call to confirm dates), & Labor Day.

TO GET THERE

From Bus. Hwy. 1 and Hwy. 130 in Damariscotta, go 12 mi. south on Hwy. 130, then 0.75 mi. west on Snowball Hill Rd., then 800 ft. south on Pemaquid Tr. Entrance is on the left.

OLD ORCHARD BEACH   MAP, D-1
Old Orchard Beach Campground

27 Ocean Park Rd., 04064. T: (207) 934-4477; www.gocamping.com.

🚐 ★★★	🏕 ★★★★
Beauty: ★★★	Site Privacy: ★★★
Spaciousness: ★★★	Quiet: ★★★
Security: ★★★★★	Cleanliness: ★★★
Insect Control: ★★★	Facilities: ★★★

Location, just off the highway and minutes from Old Orchard Beach, makes this campground popular with travelers exploring the southern coast of Maine. Families come for weekends and week-long stays to vacation at popular Old Orchard Beach. The price is right (particularly when compared to some beach area resorts) and there's the added convenience of the campground shuttle bus. Campers can avoid parking

fees and traffic hassles. The campground has modest facilities: clean restrooms and free showers, two pools, and a kid-friendly arcade room. Most hookup sites are set side-by-side in rows, flanked by woods for shade and privacy. There's a large wooded wilderness area for open tenting (no numbered sites) set in a dense forest apart from the others. Be forewarned: this area is sometimes a magnet for partying groups.

BASICS

Operated By: Daigle family. **Open:** May–Columbus Day. **Site Assignment:** Reservations suggested; $25 deposit; 14-day cancellation policy w/ $10 fee; 3-night minimum for holiday weekends; MC, V, D; checks accepted as deposits but not upon arrival. **Registration:** At office, online or by mail (using online form). **Fee:** Full hookup, $39; water/electric, $36; no hookup, $32, based on family of 2; additional adults, $7; additional children, ages 3–17, $5. **Parking:** At site.

FACILITIES

Number of RV-only Sites: 150. **Number of Tent-only Sites:** 150. **Hookups:** Electric (20, 30 amps), water, sewer. **Each Site:** Picnic table, fire ring. **Dump Station:** Yes. **Laundry:** Yes. **Pay Phone:** Yes. **Restrooms and Showers:** Yes. **Fuel:** No. **Propane:** Yes. **Internal Roads:** Gravel, dirt (good). **RV Service:** No. **Market:** Saco, 5 mi. **Restaurant:** No. **General Store:** Yes. **Vending:** No. **Swimming:** Yes. **Playground:** Yes. **Other:** Rec hall, bus shuttles to the beach. **Activities:** Swimming, basketball, horseshoes, volleyball. **Nearby Attractions:** Old Orchard Beach, southern coastal parks & beaches, Portland. **Additional Information:** Old Orchard Beach Chamber of Commerce, First St., Old Orchard Beach, ME 04064, (207) 934-2500 or (800) 365-9386, www.oldorchardbeachmaine.com.

RESTRICTIONS

Pets: Must be on a leash, never left unattended. Only adults can walk dogs in campground. **Fires:** Grill, stoves, fire rings only. **Alcoholic Beverages:** At site only. **Vehicle Maximum Length:** No limit.

TO GET THERE

From junction Maine Turnpike and I-195, Exit 5, go 2 mi. east on I-195, then east 1,500 feet on Hwy. 5; campground is on the right.

OLD ORCHARD BEACH   MAP, D-1
Powder Horn Family Camping Resort

Hwy. 98, P.O. Box 366, 04064. T: (207) 934-4733 or (800) 934-7038; www.mainecampgrounds.com.

🚐 ★★★★	🏕 ★★★
Beauty: ★★★	Site Privacy: ★★★
Spaciousness: ★★★	Quiet: ★★
Security: ★★★★★	Cleanliness: ★★★★★
Insect Control: ★★★	Facilities: ★★★★★

This giant-size resort in southern Maine is a popular summer vacation destination for New England campers. If you're looking to get away from it all, this is not the place to go. Powder Horn is chockfull of nonstop activities and crowds of vacationing families. It's located just minutes from rollicking Old Orchard

Beach (the campground offers shuttle bus service to the beach and downtown area), but the pace doesn't slow or calm down much at the campground. The three-pool complex, adjacent to the sports fields and mini-golf course, is a hub of activity, especially late afternoon and evening when campers return for the day. There are almost 500 sites, so there's plenty of choice. A number of sites are set in open meadows, with full and partial sun throughout the day. Others, including an open tent-only area, are tucked in oak and pine groves toward the back of the campground, away from the busy front recreation/office area.

BASICS

Operated By: David and Glenna Ahearn. **Open:** Memorial Day–Columbus Day. **Site Assignment:** Reservations suggested, $50 deposit; 7-day cancellation policy w/ $10 fee; MC, V, D, no checks. **Registration:** At office. **Fee:** $32–$45. **Parking:** At site, 1 vehicle per site; extra vehicles, $3.

FACILITIES

Number of RV-only Sites: 442. **Number of Tent-only Sites:** 56. **Hookups:** Electric (20, 30, 50 amps), water, sewer, cable TV, modem. **Each Site:** Picnic table, fire ring. **Dump Station:** Yes. **Laundry:** Yes. **Pay Phone:** Yes. **Restrooms and Showers:** Yes. **Fuel:** No. **Propane:** Yes. **Internal Roads:** Paved (good). **RV Service:** No. **Market:** Full-service store on the premises. **Restaurant:** Yes. **General Store:** Yes. **Vending:** No. **Swimming:** Yes. **Playground:** Yes. **Other:** Game room, shuttle bus to beach, hot tubs, adult lounge, rec room, 18-hole mini-golf course, L.L. Bean, whale watching, waterslides, stock car racing. **Activities:** Swimming, horseshoes, shuffleboard, basketball, mini-golf, planned activities, including children's programs, arts & crafts, contests, live entertainment, dances, socials, & more. **Nearby Attractions:** Old Orchard Beach, southern coast parks & beaches, Portland. **Additional Information:** Old Orchard Beach Chamber of Commerce, First St., Old Orchard Beach, ME 04064, (207) 934-2500 or (800) 365-9386, www.oldorchardbeach maine.com.

RESTRICTIONS

Pets: Must be on a leash, never left unattended. **Fires:** Grill, stoves, fire rings only. **Alcoholic Beverages:** At site only. **Vehicle Maximum Length:** No limit. **Other:** Fire out/quiet time at 11 p.m. No minibikes, skateboards, roller skates, or scooters.

TO GET THERE

From junction Maine Turnpike and I-195, Exit 5, go east 1.2 mi. on I-195, then north 3 mi. on Hwy. 1, then east 2 mi. on Hwy. 98; campground is on the left.

OLD ORCHARD BEACH
Wild Acres
MAP. D-1

reserve america

179 Saco Ave., 04064. T: (207) 934-2535; www.reserveamerican.com or www.mainecamping.com.

🚐 ★★★★   ⛺ ★★★★

Beauty: ★★★   Site Privacy: ★★★
Spaciousness: ★★★   Quiet: ★★
Security: ★★★★   Cleanliness: ★★★★
Insect Control: ★★★   Facilities: ★★★★

This is one of southern Maine's bustling mega camping resorts, with more than 500 sites, crowds, and activities galore. Wild Acres is the closest campground to Old Orchard Beach and offers direct ocean access for walking, swimming, and sunbathing. On the property, you'll find more activities than you could possibly do in a weekend, or perhaps even a week. There are three swimming pools (two adult and one kiddie pool), three hot tubs, an 18-hole mini-golf course, and weekend entertainment. The adult lounge features pool tables, big-screen TV, and a fieldstone fireplace. Kids have their own rec hall. The landscaping throughout the campground has received special attention (we like the small ponds and fountains scattered throughout the property), and the owner has left several undeveloped areas, adding to the natural ambiance of the resort. Sites are good-sized, shaded or in the open. Fifty pull-through, full-hookup sites are set side-by-side near the front of the resort. The tent-only section is nestled in the back of the property, closest to the ocean walk access, with its own nearby pool and playground area.

BASICS

Operated By: Rick Ahearn. **Open:** Memorial Day–Labor Day. **Site Assignment:** Reservations suggested; $50 credit card deposit; 7-day cancellation policy w/ $10 fee; no minimum Memorial Day weekend; 3-night minimum July 4th and Labor Day; MC, V, D, no checks. **Registration:** At office, by phone, mail or email. **Fee:** Full hookup, $43–$48; water/electric, $37–$40; no hookup, $30–$34, based on 2 people, additional adults, $7; children ages 3–21, $3. **Parking:** At site.

FACILITIES

Number of RV-only Sites: 450. **Number of Tent-only Sites:** 25. **Hookups:** Electric (30, 50 amps), water, sewer, cable TV, modem. **Each Site:** Picnic table, fire ring. **Dump Station:** Yes. **Laundry:** Yes. **Pay Phone:** Yes. **Restrooms and Showers:** Yes. **Fuel:** No. **Propane:** No. **Internal Roads:** Paved. **RV Service:** No. **Market:** Saco, 2 mi. **Restaurant:** No. **General Store:** Yes. **Vending:** Yes. **Swimming:** Yes. **Playground:** Yes. **Other:** Hot tubs, rec hall, adult lounge, nature trails, stocked fishing pond, 18-hole mini-golf course, entertainment pavilion, access to ocean & beach, tennis courts, arcade center, shuttle service. **Activities:** Swimming, fishing, beachcombing, tennis, mini-golf, horseshoes, shuffleboard, volleyball. **Nearby Attractions:** Old Orchard Beach, Portland, southern coastal parks & beaches. **Additional Information:** Old Orchard Beach Chamber of Commerce, First St., Old Orchard Beach, ME 04064, (207) 934-2500 or (800) 365-9386, www.oldorchardbeachmaine.com.

RESTRICTIONS

Pets: Must be on a leash, never left unattended. Some breeds not allowed. **Fires:** Grill, stoves, fire rings only. **Alcoholic Beverages:** At site only. **Vehicle Maximum Length:** No limit. **Other:** Skateboards & rollerblades not allowed.

TO GET THERE

From Maine Turnpike and I-195, Exit 5, go east 2 mi. on I-195, then east 1.5 mi. on Hwy. 5; campground is on the right.

ORR'S ISLAND
Orr's Island Campground
MAP, D-1

44 Bond Point Rd., 04066. T: (207) 833-5595; www.orrsisland.com.

🚐 ★★★★   ⛺ ★★★★

Beauty: ★★★★★   Site Privacy: ★★★★
Spaciousness: ★★★★★   Quiet: ★★★★★
Security: ★★★★★   Cleanliness: ★★★★
Insect Control: ★★★   Facilities: ★★★

Orr's Island is quite far out into Casco Bay, but the drive out from Brunswick and over Great Island will melt away any stress. Once you've set up your campsite, take a moment to walk around and drink in the views of Muscongus Bay, Harpswell Cove, and Reed Cove. Close your eyes and feel the breezes and the sunlight washing over you. The open camping sites up on North Bluff offer a view of Harpswell Sound and many feature small stands of trees separating them from their neighbors. Plus, from North and South Bluff, you'll have access to the shore for beachcombing, hanging out on the rocks, or swimming if you're cast of sturdy Scandinavian stock. The Cove Rd. lettered sites are perfectly situated for tents and kayaks—what a stellar combination. After a night spent in one of these sites, you'll have that pleasant ache in your lungs from the fresh salt air.

BASICS

Operated By: The Bond Family. **Open:** Memorial Day–mid-Sept. **Site Assignment:** Reservations or first come, first served; 2-night minimum for advance reservations. **Registration:** At office. **Fee:** $24–$35. **Parking:** At site.

FACILITIES

Number of RV-only Sites: 70. **Hookups:** Electric (30 amps), water, sewer. **Each Site:** Fire ring, picnic table. **Dump Station:** Yes. **Laundry:** Yes. **Pay Phone:** Yes. **Restrooms and Showers:** Yes. **Fuel:** No. **Propane:** No. **Internal Roads:** Gravel. **RV Service:** No. **Market:** 0.5 mi. north on Hwy. 24. **Restaurant:** No. **General Store:** Ice, soft drinks, camping supplies. **Vending:** No. **Swimming:** No. **Playground:** Yes. **Other:** Recreational equipment can be borrowed. **Activities:** Swimming, boating, canoe rental, wild berry picking, bird-watching, games & books. **Nearby Attractions:** L. L. Bean, Boothbay Harbor, movie theater, Reid Sate Park, Popham Beach, Eagle Island. **Additional Information:** Boothbay Harbor Region Chamber of Commerce, (207) 633-2353 or (800) 266-8422.

RESTRICTIONS

Pets: On leash. **Fires:** Fire ring only. **Alcoholic Beverages:** Allowed. **Vehicle Maximum Length:** 35 ft. **Other:** Advance reservations require a 2-night stay.

TO GET THERE

Take Exit 22 off of Hwy. 95. This will put you on Hwy. 1 between Brunswick and Bath. From Hwy. 1 take the Cooks Corner exit for Orr's and Bailey Island. Take Hwy. 24 (straight ahead at the traffic light). Follow Hwy. 24 the rest of the way. Crossing the first bridge puts you on Great Island. Crossing the second bridge puts you on Orr's Island. Turn right on to Bond Point Rd. (our entrance). A large white ship's wheel (our logo) will be at the turn onto Bond Point Rd. We are 2 mi. from the Orr's Island Bridge, or a total of 11 mi. from Cooks Corner.

PALMYRA　　　　　　MAP, C-2
Palmyra Golf and RV Resort

147 Lang Hill Rd., 04965. T: (207) 938-5677; www.palmyra-me.com.

🚐 ★★★★★　　　▲ ★★

Beauty: ★★★　　　　Site Privacy: ★★★
Spaciousness: ★★★　　Quiet: ★★★
Security: ★★★★　　　Cleanliness: ★★★★★
Insect Control: ★★★★　Facilities: ★★★★★

If you like to golf, you're going to love this campground in central Maine, with its own 18-hole 72-par course, pro shop, and clubhouse on the premises. Located off the interstate, just south of Bangor, this campground caters to large motor home and RV travelers who enjoy a pampered camping experience. Local golfers use the public course but campers get a discount. There's a driving range and pitch and putt center, too. You'll have a choice of roomy, bigger-than-average open sites, all set in rows off the campground's long, one-way streets. There's also a separate loop of shaded sites behind the office and recreation area. Campers tend to prefer sites 1–15. There's plenty of room to spread out in this campground, and the hilly, terraced terrain and views of the golf course add to its expansiveness and beauty.

BASICS

Operated By: Cayer family. **Open:** May 15–Oct. 15. **Site Assignment:** Reservations suggested; no deposit required (if you don't show by 6:30 p.m. of scheduled day of arrival, they rent space); MC, V, D. **Registration:** At office. **Fee:** Full hookup, $24; water/electric (50 amps), $23; (30 amps), $21.50. **Parking:** At site.

FACILITIES

Number of RV-only Sites: 91. **Number of Tent-only Sites:** 4. **Hookups:** Electric (30, 50 amps), water, sewer. **Each Site:** Picnic table, fire ring, light. **Dump Station:** Yes. **Laundry:** Yes. **Pay Phone:** Yes. **Restrooms and Showers:** Yes. **Fuel:** No. **Propane:** No. **Internal Roads:** Paved, gravel (good). **RV Service:** No. **Market:** Palmyra, 2 mi. **Restaurant:** Yes. **General Store:** Yes. **Vending:** No. **Swimming:** Yes. **Playground:** No. **Other:** 18-hole golf course, pro shop, clubhouse, driving range, function hall, group area. **Activities:** Golf, swimming, horseshoes, volleyball, shuffleboard. **Nearby Attractions:** Bangor. **Additional Information:** Bangor Regional Chamber of Commerce, 519 Maine St., P.O.

Box 1443, Bangor, ME 04402, (207) 947-0307, www.bangorregion.com.

RESTRICTIONS

Pets: On leash, never left unattended. **Fires:** Grill, stoves, fire rings only. **Alcoholic Beverages:** At site only. **Vehicle Maximum Length:** No limit.

TO GET THERE

From I-95, Exit 39, go west 3 mi. on Hwy. 2; campground is on the right.

PERU　　　　　　　MAP, C-1
Honey Run Beach and Campground

456 East Shore Rd., 04290. T: (207) 562-4913; www.honeyruncampground.com.

🚐 ★★★★　　　▲ ★★

Beauty: ★★★　　　　Site Privacy: ★★
Spaciousness: ★★★★　Quiet: ★★★★
Security: ★★★★★　　Cleanliness: ★★★★★
Insect Control: ★★★　Facilities: ★★★

Located in a small lakeside community just east of Rumford, Honey Run Beach and Campground was formerly more geared to seasonal campers. It is now much more of a vacation destination. Just a handful of sites are seasonal now. A pavilion is in place for groups and the family-reunion set. Campsites (suitable for big rigs) dot a big, grassy field surrounded by woods. Woodsy sites ring the perimeter of the property, and there are even a few primitive tent sites "up the mountain," as owner Jeff Lennox puts it. OK, so it's not really a mountain, but a climb up the hill would make a dandy work-out and leg-stretch for the road-weary RVer! Another good selling point here: a short but wide, private sandy beach on sparkling Worthley Pond, located across the street. There's enough space for a few sun-bathers, plus some picnic tables and rental canoes and kayaks; good for taking a peek at the houses surrounding the pond and playing the "Would you ever want to move here?" game.

BASICS

Operated By: Jeff Lennox. **Open:** Memorial Day–Labor Day. **Site Assignment:** Reservations suggested; deposit of first night's fee required; refund for cancellations w/ 14-day notice. **Registration:** At office. **Fee:** Electric (30 amps)/water, $28; w/ sewer, $30; tent, $22; electric (20 amps)/water, $24; electric (50 amps)/water, $55; 7% lodging tax applies. **Parking:** At site.

FACILITIES

Number of Tent-only Sites: 39. **Number of Multipurpose Sites:** 79. **Hookups:** Electric (30, 50 amps), water, sewer. **Each Site:** Picnic table, fire ring. **Dump Station:** Yes. **Laundry:** Yes. **Pay Phone:** Yes. **Restrooms and Showers:** Yes. **Fuel:** No. **Propane:** No. **Internal Roads:** Gravel, in good condition. **RV Service:** No. **Market:** 12 mi. north. **Restaurant:** 12 mi. north. **General Store:** Yes. **Vending:** Yes. **Swimming:** Yes. **Playground:** Yes. **Other:** Rec hall w/ pavilion. **Activities:** Lake swimming, hiking (on hillside trails behind campground), boating (canoe & kayak rentals available). **Nearby**

Attractions: Norland's Living History Museum, Appalachian Trail hiking, Black Mountain, Pennacook Falls, Santa's Village, Mt. Blue State Park. **Additional Information:** River Valley Chamber of Commerce, (207) 364-3241.

RESTRICTIONS

Pets: Must be leashed, quiet, & cleaned up after. Must not be left unattended. **Fires:** Fire ring only. **Alcoholic Beverages:** At sites only. **Vehicle Maximum Length:** No limit. **Other:** Ask on arrival.

TO GET THERE

Take Maine Turnpike to Exit 12 (Auburn). Follow Hwy. 4 north to Hwy. 108 west. Follow Hwy. 108 for 11 mi., then turn left at Worthley Pond and campground sign. Campground is 3.5 mi. in.

PHIPPSBURG　　　　MAP, D-1, D-2
Meadowbrook Camping

33 Meadowbrook Rd., 04562. T: (207) 443-4967 or (800) 370-CAMP; www.meadowbrookme.com.

🚐 ★★★★　　　▲ ★★★

Beauty: ★★　　　　　Site Privacy: ★★
Spaciousness: ★★　　Quiet: ★★★
Security: ★★★　　　Cleanliness: ★★★★★
Insect Control: ★★★　Facilities: ★★★

This mid-coast campground, located just five miles south of Bath, is wildly popular with RVers, who don't seem to care that the ocean is nowhere in sight. Matter of fact, one of Maine's nicest stretches of sand, Popham Beach State Park, is but a ten-mile-drive away, and if you can't wait to swim, there's always the campground's heated pool, surely warmer than the North Atlantic! (About that pool, we think some umbrellas would be a nice touch.) And should you want a shore dinner, you don't have to leave; they sell lobsters, clams, and corn, daily, and will cook it up for you for no extra charge. Campsites, set in loops, are gravel, of varying size. The largest RV sites are in an open, grassy area near the (funky) rec hall and pool area; head farther back into the property, and sites are wooded, nudging toward cliffs and a beaver pond. Sites 77 through 82 overlook a marsh; stay away from 82 if you're tenting, though, since it's on a downhill slope that would be a real mess in the rain. Site 35 is great, with a long approach to a woodsy spot on a hill; site 33 offers great cliffside views, as well, edging a wooded area. Among the tent sites, we'd go for site 73, near the nature trail, built on a platform.

BASICS

Operated By: TLM Enterprises. **Open:** May 1–Oct. 1. **Site Assignment:** Reservations recommended; for less than 1-week stay, full fee required for deposit; for stays of more than 1 week, 10% deposit required; refunds for cancellations w/in 7 days, minus $10. **Registration:** At office. **Fee:** $20–$26; per family; V, MC, D, AE. **Parking:** At site.

FACILITIES

Number of RV-only Sites: 90. **Number of Tent-only Sites:** 10. **Hookups:** Electric (15, 20, 30, 50 amps), water. **Each Site:** Picnic table, fireplace.

Dump Station: Yes. **Laundry:** Yes. **Pay Phone:** Yes. **Restrooms and Showers:** Yes. **Fuel:** No. **Propane:** Yes. **Internal Roads:** Gravel, in good to fair condition. **RV Service:** No. **Market:** 5 mi. north. **Restaurant:** 5 mi. north. **General Store:** Yes. **Vending:** No. **Swimming:** Yes. **Playground:** Yes. **Other:** Rec hall, mini-golf. **Activities:** Swimming, mini-golf, mile-long nature trail, basketball, shuffleboard, horseshoes. **Nearby Attractions:** Popham Beach State Park, Morse Mountain Sanctuary, Maine Maritime Museum, Bowdoin College Museum of Art, Peary-MacMillan Arctic Museum, deep-sea fishing. **Additional Information:** Chamber of Commerce of the Bath-Brunswick Region, (207) 725-8797 or (207) 443-9751, www.midcoastmaine.com.

RESTRICTIONS

Pets: Must be leashed, quiet, & cleaned up after. Must not be left unattended. **Fires:** Fireplaces only. **Alcoholic Beverages:** At sites only. **Vehicle Maximum Length:** No limit. **Other:** 1 vehicle per site.

TO GET THERE

From Hwy. 1 in Bath, take Popham Beach exit, Hwy. 209. Follow for 2.5 mi., heading south, to Winnegance Store, then turn right and go 3 mi. to campground. Entrance is on right.

POLAND SPRING   MAP, D-1
Poland Spring Campground

Connor Ln., P.O. Box 409n, 04274.
T: (207) 998-2151; www.polandspringcamp.com.

🚐 ★★★   ⛺ ★★

Beauty: ★★★	Site Privacy: ★★★
Spaciousness: ★★★	Quiet: ★★★★
Security: ★★★★	Cleanliness: ★★★★★
Insect Control: ★★★	Facilities: ★★★

The nicest feature of this Western Lakes–area campground: it sits on a pretty, forested pond, dotted with islands. Three-mile-long Lower Range Pond, sandy-bottomed, provides a great swimming hole for campers here. While there isn't much of a beach, the buoyed swimming area is plenty big. Bonus: if you don't like lake swimming, there's a pool. The campground itself is shaded with pines and mixed hardwoods, and campsites are level and woodsy. Birdwatchers will admire the loons and blue heron that are common here, as well as the eagles that soar overhead quite often. This campground is better-tended, and the campsites more prepared than what you'll find at neighboring Two Lakes Camping Area (see listing.) The friendly owners take care of the details that make all the difference: plenty of trash barrels, an inviting picnic grove overlooking the pond, and a nice booklet for campers, chock-full of information about the local area, dining, shopping, and attractions. Campsites are set on spoke-like roads, surrounding the activity pod of rec hall, office, store, restrooms, laundry, game room, and so on. It's quiet, child-friendly, and appealing.

BASICS

Operated By: David and Tami Wight. **Open:** May 1–Columbus Day. **Site Assignment:** Reservations recommended; $30 deposit required for weekends; $40 for week-long stay; refunds for cancellation w/ 7-day notice, minus $5. **Registration:** At office. **Fee:** $19–$28; for 2 adults & up to 3 children; V, MC, D, debit cards. **Parking:** At site.

FACILITIES

Number of RV-only Sites: 21. **Number of Tent-only Sites:** 11. **Number of Multipurpose Sites:** 100. **Hookups:** Electric (20, 30 amps), water, sewer. **Each Site:** Picnic table, fire ring. **Dump Station:** Yes. **Laundry:** Yes. **Pay Phone:** Yes. **Restrooms and Showers:** Yes, coin-op. **Fuel:** No. **Propane:** Yes. **Internal Roads:** Gravel, in good condition. **RV Service:** No. **Market:** 5 mi. north. **Restaurant:** 1 mi. north; 8 mi. south. **General Store:** Yes. **Vending:** No. **Swimming:** Yes. **Playground:** Yes. **Other:** Game room, adult rec room, boat dock. **Activities:** Fishing (licenses available), lake swimming, boating (rentals available), volleyball, planned activities. **Nearby Attractions:** Sabbathday Lake shaker village, Maine Wildlife Park, tourmaline gem mines, golf, hiking at Range Pond State Park. **Additional Information:** Androscoggin County Chamber of Commerce, (207) 783-2249, www.androscoggincounty.com.

RESTRICTIONS

Pets: Must be leashed, quiet, & cleaned up after. Must not be left unattended. Not allowed in pool, lake, & public areas. **Fires:** Fireplaces only. **Alcoholic Beverages:** Allowed. **Vehicle Maximum Length:** 40 ft. **Other:** 2-night min. stay on weekends in July & Aug.; 3-night min. on holidays.

TO GET THERE

From the Maine Turnpike, take Exit 11 (Gray.) Follow Hwy. 26 north for 12 mi. Turn right on Connor Ln. Entrance is at end of road, 0.5 mi.

RANGELEY   MAP, C-1
Rangeley Lake State Park

HC 32 P.O. Box 5000, 04970. T: (207) 864-3858 or (207) 624-6080 (off-season).

🚐 ★★★★   ⛺ ★★★★★

Beauty: ★★★★	Site Privacy: ★★★★
Spaciousness: ★★★★	Quiet: ★★★★
Security: ★★★★★	Cleanliness: ★★★★
Insect Control: ★★	Facilities: ★★★

Set in Maine's western mountains region, an area famous for rugged beauty and great fishing, this state park draws nature-loving campers from New England and beyond. The town of Rangeley has several boat rental outfits; bring your boat to the campground and you can launch it for free. Don't forget the fishing license. You'll want to have a go at the trout and land-locked salmon in this icy-cold lake. Should you wish to brave the waters yourself, there's a grassy hill with granite stairs that lead to a marked off, somewhat pebbly swimming area. Campsites are set in a loop on the lakeside, at the opposite end of the park from the day-use area, beach, and boat launch. Well-spaced back-ins offering plenty of privacy, sites are heavily wooded with spruce and fir. Some campsites have footpaths through the trees that lead to the lake. Most desirable sites (closest to the water) are 11M through 21L, even numbers. Letters refer to size of site; S is small, M is medium, and so on. Site 42X (as in extra-large) is very private, set off by itself way back in the woods. Besides all the natural beauty you could wish for, this campground boasts another winning attribute, not to be taken lightly in a state park: great showers!

BASICS

Operated By: Maine Dept. of Conservation, Bureau of Parks and Lands. **Open:** May 15–Sept. 30. **Site Assignment:** In spring and fall, first come, first served. In summer, reservations open on the first business day in Jan.; from June 15 to the night before Labor Day, sites may be reserved for a min. of 2 nights and up to 2 weeks; full payment charged to credit card when reservation is processed; refund w/ $15 fee; 10 sites are nonreservable and available first come, first served; call the reservations line to cancel a reservation more than 3 days in advance; if canceling less than 3 days in advance, call the park directly. **Registration:** At office. **Fee:** Maine residents, $15; nonresidents, $20; plus $2 fee if reserved in advance; V, MC. **Parking:** At sites and designated lots only.

FACILITIES

Number of Multipurpose Sites: 50. **Hookups:** None. **Each Site:** Fire ring. **Dump Station:** Yes. **Laundry:** No. **Pay Phone:** Yes. **Restrooms and Showers:** Yes. **Fuel:** No. **Propane:** No. **Internal Roads:** Gravel & paved, in good condition. **RV Service:** No. **Market:** 7 mi. northwest. **Restaurant:** 7 mi. northwest. **General Store:** No. **Vending:** Yes. **Swimming:** No. **Playground:** Yes. **Other:** Boat ramps & slips. **Activities:** Lake swimming, boating, fishing (need license; available in town), ball field, volleyball, horseshoes, hiking, picnicking. **Nearby Attractions:** Wilhelm Reich Museum, moose watching, golf, scenic flights, Appalachian Trail hiking. **Additional Information:** Rangeley Lakes Region Chamber of Commerce, (207) 864-5364 or (800) MT-LAKES.

RESTRICTIONS

Pets: Must be leashed, quiet, & cleaned up after. Must not be left unattended. **Fires:** Fireplaces only. **Alcoholic Beverages:** Not allowed. **Vehicle Maximum Length:** 40 ft. **Other:** 2-week stay limit between last week in June & Labor Day.

TO GET THERE

From junction of Hwy. 16 and Hwy. 4, go 4 mi. south on Hwy. 4, then 5 mi. west on S. Shore Dr., then 1 mi. north to campground.

RAYMOND   MAP, D-1
Kokatosi Campground

635 Webbs Mills Rd., 04071.
T: (207) 627-4642 or (800) 9-CAMPIN;
kokatosi.maine.com.

🚐 ★★★   ⛺ ★★★

Beauty: ★★★	Site Privacy: ★
Spaciousness: ★★	Quiet: ★★★
Security: ★★★★★	Cleanliness: ★★★★
Insect Control: ★★	Facilities: ★★★

Whether you're looking for a ride on an antique "Hooterville" fire engine or prefer a freshwater cruise on an eight-seater "Patio Boat," Kokatosi's the place.

Located in the Western Lakes region of southwest Maine, on five-mile-long Crescent Lake, this campground offers a "summer camp for families" experience. In fact, this lake-dotted, woodsy area is chock-a-block with summer camps. Most campers can't resist paddling or motoring to Tenney River, a mile-and-a-half away, then on to Panther Pond. The fishing is said to be pretty good, too. The campground offers a rather communal experience; you're bound to get to know your neighbors, since sites don't have much buffer between them (only boulders, in some cases.) About 50 percent of the sites are seasonal, but the transient sites are closest to the beach. RV sites 25, 26, and 28 overlook the lake. Some of the tent sites have platforms and canopies, providing a tree-house effect perched over the lake. Sites 4 through 7 and 11 are among them. A nicely done rec hall is the scene for country bands and potluck suppers.

BASICS

Operated By: Todd Southwick. **Open:** May 15–Columbus Day. **Site Assignment:** Reservations recommended; 50% deposit required; must pay in full for holiday weekends; refund w/ cancellation and 30-day notice, minus $10; no refunds for holiday weekends. **Registration:** At office. **Fee:** $32–$39; for 2 adults & 2 children under age 18; V, MC. **Parking:** At sites and designated lot (tenters).

FACILITIES

Number of RV-only Sites: 145. **Number of Tent-only Sites:** 17. **Hookups:** Electric (20, 30 amps), water, sewer. **Each Site:** Picnic table, fire ring. **Dump Station:** Yes. **Laundry:** Yes. **Pay Phone:** Yes. **Restrooms and Showers:** Yes. **Fuel:** No. **Propane:** Yes. **Internal Roads:** Gravel, in good condition. **RV Service:** No. **Market:** 10 mi. east. **Restaurant:** 10 mi. east. **General Store:** Yes. **Vending:** Yes. **Swimming:** No. **Playground:** Yes. **Other:** Rec hall, boat dock, trailer rentals. **Activities:** Lake swimming, fishing (license required), boating (rentals available, including 14-ft. motorboats), volleyball, bocce, horseshoes, planned activities. **Nearby Attractions:** Golf, mini-golf, seaplane rides, boat cruises, Songo River Queen paddleboat, Douglas Mountain hiking, Sebago Lake State Park, outlet shopping (N. Conway, NH). **Additional Information:** Gray Business Assoc., (207) 657-7000.

RESTRICTIONS

Pets: Must be leashed, quiet, & cleaned up after. Not allowed on beach or in buildings. **Fires:** Fireplaces only. **Alcoholic Beverages:** Allowed. **Vehicle Maximum Length:** No limit. **Other:** 2-day min. stay required; 3-day min. on holidays.

TO GET THERE

From junction of Hwy. 302 and Hwy. 85, go 6 mi. northeast on Hwy. 85. Campground entrance is on the right.

ROCKPORT   MAP, D-2
Camden Hills RV Resort

Hwy. 90, 04856. T: (207) 236-2498 or (888) 842-0592; www.camdenhillsrv.com.

 ★★★   ★★

Beauty: ★★★	Site Privacy: ★★★
Spaciousness: ★★★	Quiet: ★★★★★
Security: ★★★	Cleanliness: ★★★★★
Insect Control: ★★★	Facilities: ★★★

"We know where to get the freshest, best, and cheapest lobster around!" they whisper conspiratorially at Camden Rockport Camping, and if that's not a selling point, we don't know what is. This quiet, peaceful family campground is located near the bustling seaport towns of Camden and Rockport (thus the name) in mid-coast Maine. You'd never know you were a hop and a skip from tourist-filled streets, shops, and galleries, though. This campground is the quietest one around (quieter than nearby Megunticook by the Sea), since it's off the beaten track—Hwy. 1—a bit. The campsites are grassy back-ins, with good shade trees dotting the big-rig area. Even the tent sites are grassy. They're not completely level, though. Ask for tent site 14, very private and wooded with white birch. The campground is neat as a pin, and boasts nice touches like fresh flowers in the restroom and a rec hall with a kitchen and book exchange. There are 13 pull-throughs.

BASICS

Operated By: John and Lori Alexander. **Open:** June 15–Oct. 19. **Site Assignment:** Reservations recommended, especially in July and Aug.; deposit required, $50 for 3 nights or less, $100 for 4 or more; refund for cancellation w/ 7-day notice, minus $15. **Registration:** At office. **Fee:** $22–$38; for 2 adults & 2 children under age 18; no credit cards. **Parking:** At site.

FACILITIES

Number of RV-only Sites: 44. **Number of Tent-only Sites:** 8. **Hookups:** Electric (30, 50 amps), water, sewer, cable TV. **Each Site:** Picnic table, fire ring. **Dump Station:** Yes. **Laundry:** Yes. **Pay Phone:** Yes. **Restrooms and Showers:** Yes. **Fuel:** No. **Propane:** Yes. **Internal Roads:** Gravel, in good condition. **RV Service:** No. **Market:** 3 mi. east. **Restaurant:** 3 mi. east. **General Store:** Yes. **Vending:** Yes. **Swimming:** Yes. **Playground:** Yes. **Other:** Rec hall (under renovation), clubhouse, hot tub. **Activities:** Basketball, ball field, horseshoes, volleyball. **Nearby Attractions:** Camden galleries, museums & shops), windjammer fleet, Penobscot Bay cruises, Conway Homestead & Mary Cramer Museum (18th-century restored farmhouse & gardens), Camden Hills State Park, Merryspring Park, Owl's Head Transportation Museum, golf, ocean swimming. **Additional Information:** Rockport-Camden-Lincolnville Chamber of Commerce, (207) 236-4404 or (800) 223-5459.

RESTRICTIONS

Pets: Must be leashed, quiet, & cleaned up after. Must not be left unattended. **Fires:** Fire ring only. **Alcoholic Beverages:** At sites only. **Vehicle Maximum Length:** No limit. **Other:** No electric heaters. 2-night min. stay on weekends in July & Aug.; 3-night min. stay during Maine Lobster Festival (early Aug.).

TO GET THERE

From the north junction of Hwy. 1 and Hwy. 90, go 2 mi. southwest on Hwy. 90. Campground entrance is on the left.

ROCKPORT   MAP, D-2
Megunticook Campground
by the Sea

Hwy. 1, P.O. Box 375, 04856. T: (207) 594-2428 or (800) 884-2428; www.campgroundbythesea.com.

🚐 ★★★★   ⛺ ★★★

Beauty: ★★★★★	Site Privacy: ★★★
Spaciousness: ★★	Quiet: ★★★
Security: ★★★	Cleanliness: ★★★★★
Insect Control: ★★★	Facilities: ★★★★★

As you're enjoying a lobster bake on the oceanfront deck, watching a Maine windjammer schooner sail past on Penobscot Bay, one question might cross your mind: "This is camping?" Oh, yeah, this is camping at Megunticook, a camping resort on mid-coast Maine, just three miles south of Camden. Want freshly brewed Green Mountain coffee, or pizza delivered to your site? Perhaps a harbor tour on a Downeast cruiser? No problem. Other nice touches include a pool area with a picket fence surrounding it, not that ugly chain-link stuff. A waterfront deck is graced with a tumble of gardens and seating, the perfect place to watch the world—or local lobstermen—go by. Admire Indian Island lighthouse in the distance. A row of rental cabins sits close to busy Hwy. 1; we'd head back as far as possible, away from the road and toward the ocean. RV sites 46–49, near Vernah Brook, fill the bill. Tent sites are set way back, toward the water, nicely level with good surfacing for drainage. Tent site 81 is huge, while site 87 boasts the most privacy and is closest to the water. There are 60 pull-throughs and 10 back-ins. This is a classic Maine beauty spot.

BASICS

Operated By: Megunticook Campground by the Sea. **Open:** May 15–Columbus Day. **Site Assignment:** Reservations recommended July–Oct.; deposit of 1-night fee required; refunds for cancellation w/ 7-day notice, minus $15. **Registration:** At office. **Fee:** $28–$45; for 2 adults & 2 children; V, MC, D. **Parking:** At site.

FACILITIES

Number of RV-only Sites: 66. **Number of Tent-only Sites:** 20. **Hookups:** Electric (20, 30, 50 amps), water, sewer, cable TV, phone. **Each Site:** Picnic table, fire ring. **Dump Station:** Yes. **Laundry:** Yes. **Pay Phone:** Yes. **Restrooms and Showers:** Yes. **Fuel:** No. **Propane:** No. **Internal Roads:** Gravel, in good condition. **RV Service:** No. **Market:** 2.5 mi. north. **Restaurant:** 3 mi. north. **General Store:** Yes. **Vending:** Yes. **Swimming:** Yes. **Playground:** Yes. **Other:** Game room, sport field, lobster bakes. **Activities:** Biking (rentals available), kayaking (rentals available), boat cruises on *Loriander*, swimming, ball field, croquet, horseshoes, badminton. **Nearby Attractions:** Camden galleries, museums, & shops, windjammer fleet, Penobscot Bay cruises, Conway Homestead & Mary Cramer Museum (18th-century restored farmhouse & gardens), Camden Hills State Park, Merryspring Park, Owl's Head Transportation Museum, golf. **Additional Information:** Rockport-Camden-Lincolnville Chamber of Commerce, (207) 236-4404 or (800) 223-5459.

RESTRICTIONS

Pets: Must be leashed, quiet, & cleaned up after. Must not be left unattended. **Fires:** Fireplaces only. **Alcoholic Beverages:** At sites only. **Vehicle Maximum Length:** No limit. **Other:** 2-night min. stay required on weekends in July & Aug.; 3-night min. stay required on holiday weekends & Aug. 1–5 (Maine Lobster Festival).

TO GET THERE

From junction of Hwy. 1 and Hwy. 90 in Rockport, go 2 mi. south on Hwy. 1. Campground is on the left.

SACO — MAP, D-1
Saco/Portland South KOA

814A Portland Rd., 04072. T: (207) 282-0502 or (800) 562-1886; www.sacokoa.com.

🚐 ★★★★★ ⛺ ★★★★

Beauty: ★★★	Site Privacy: ★★★
Spaciousness: ★★★	Quiet: ★★★★
Security: ★★★★★	Cleanliness: ★★★★★
Insect Control: ★★★	Facilities: ★★★★

This woodsy campground is just two miles from Old Orchard Beach and many of southern Maine's best parks and attractions and offers a natural, quiet escape from the summer masses. Ultra clean facilities, a family-friendly atmosphere, and lots of added conveniences make this property a favorite with locals and out-of-town travelers alike. Most sites are tucked in a shady, cool virgin forest; tent sites are nestled under old growth pine trees. There are 49 pull-through sites. Recreation fields, pool, office and pavilion areas are clustered in front. We like the porch off the office cabin, with rockers and benches overlooking the pool and playground. The campground also offers discounted tickets to area attractions. Before heading out for the day, feast on a wild blueberry pancake breakfast, offered each day at the campground. Spaghetti dinners and assorted desserts are available in the evening.

BASICS

Operated By: Nancy and Larry Babyak. **Open:** May–Oct. **Site Assignment:** Reservations suggested; a 1-night deposit is required; 48-hour cancellation policy; MC, V, no checks. **Registration:** At office. **Fee:** RV $28.80–$46; tent, $26.10–$39. **Parking:** At site.

FACILITIES

Number of RV-only Sites: 96. **Number of Tent-only Sites:** 22. **Hookups:** Electric (20, 30, 50 amps), water, sewer, cable TV. **Each Site:** Picnic table, fire ring. **Dump Station:** Yes. **Laundry:** Yes. **Pay Phone:** Yes. **Restrooms and Showers:** Yes. **Fuel:** No. **Propane:** Yes. **Internal Roads:** Gravel, dirt (good). **RV Service:** No. **Market:** Old Orchard Beach, 2 mi. **Restaurant:** Yes. **General Store:** Yes. **Vending:** Yes. **Swimming:** Yes. **Playground:** Yes. **Other:** Pavilion, game room, cabin rentals, discount tickets to area attractions. **Activities:** Swimming, basketball, volleyball, horseshoes, TV/movie room. **Nearby Attractions:** Old Orchard Beach, southern coast parks & beaches, Portland, Funtown Theme Park, lighthouses. **Additional Information:** Old

Orchard Beach Chamber of Commerce, First St., Old Orchard Beach, ME 04064, (207) 934-2500 or (800) 365-9386, www.oldorchardbeachmaine.com.

RESTRICTIONS

Pets: Must be on a leash, never left unattended. **Fires:** Grill, stoves, fire rings only. **Alcoholic Beverages:** At site only. **Vehicle Maximum Length:** No limit.

TO GET THERE

From main turnpike (I-95), take Exit 5 (I-95), go 1.2 mi. east on I-95, take Exit 2B (1N). Go north 1.6 mi on Hwy. 1, turn left at campground sign.

SCARBOROUGH — MAP, D-1
Bayley's

275 Pine Point Rd., 04074. T: (207) 883-6043; www.bayleys-camping.com.

🚐 ★★★★★ ⛺ ★★★★

Beauty: ★★★	Site Privacy: ★★★
Spaciousness: ★★★	Quiet: ★
Security: ★★★★★	Cleanliness: ★★★★
Insect Control: ★★★	Facilities: ★★★★★

This mega-resort campground in southern coastal Maine is one of the largest in New England. It's a sprawling family resort, spread over 200 acres, with activities to keep everyone entertained. There's professional entertainment four nights a week: bands play, comedians joke, jugglers juggle. There are three swimming pools, three ponds, a full-service restaurant (lobsters anyone?), mini-golf, sports fields, and nonstop planned activities morning to night. If that's not enough, campers can hop on the free double-decker bus and head to Old Orchard Beach, only a few minutes away. This is probably the best bargain in southern coastal Maine. With 500+ sites, you'll have plenty to choose from. There are 270 back-in and 30 pull-through sites. If you're driving a large motor home, the A and C sites are best—shaded, level, and easy to pull in and out. They're close to the front office, pool, theater, and restaurant. If you want more privacy, try the V section. If you're a tenter who prefers to get away from the action, there's a wilderness area in the back of the property. Nature trails, fishing ponds, mini-golf, sports fields, and another pool are back even farther and make up one of Maine's largest outdoor activity centers.

BASICS

Operated By: Fred and Kathleen Bayley. **Open:** Apr. 28–Oct. 15. **Site Assignment:** Reservations suggested; stays of 4 days or less must be paid in full; $150 deposit for longer stays; 30-day cancellation policy w/ $25 fee 3-night minimum for Memorial Day and Labor Day weekends; 4-night minimum for July 4th holiday; MC, V, no checks. **Registration:** At office. **Fee:** Full hookup (cable/TV/AC), $55–$60; full hookup (no AC), $50–$55; water/electric/cable TV (Bayley's Best), $48–$53; water/electric/cable TV, $41; no hookup, $40–$45; amp service, additional $3. **Parking:** At site, 1 vehicle per site (additional vehicle, $5/day).

FACILITIES

Number of RV-only Sites: 300. **Number of Tent-only Sites:** 100. **Hookups:** Electric (30, 50 amps), water, sewer, cable TV, modem. **Each Site:** Picnic

table, fire ring. **Dump Station:** Yes. **Laundry:** Yes. **Pay Phone:** Yes. **Restrooms and Showers:** Yes. **Fuel:** No. **Propane:** Yes. **Internal Roads:** Gravel (good). **RV Service:** No. **Market:** Old Orchard Beach, 2 mi. **Restaurant:** Yes. **General Store:** Yes. **Vending:** Yes. **Swimming:** Yes. **Playground:** Yes. **Other:** 3 ponds (2 stocked fishing ponds), boat dock, hot tubs, mini-golf course, boat rentals, outdoor theater, nature trails, bike rentals, complimentary beach bus, trailer rentals, game room, rec hall, sports fields. **Activities:** Swimming, boating, fishing, mini-golf, basketball, volleyball, horseshoes, live entertainment, planned activities, including children's games, fishing derbies, contests, dinners & more. **Nearby Attractions:** Old Orchard Beach, Portland, southern coastal parks & beaches. **Additional Information:** Old Orchard Beach Chamber of Commerce, First St., Old Orchard Beach, ME 04064, (207) 934-2500 or (800) 365-9386, www.oldorchardbeachmaine.com.

RESTRICTIONS

Pets: Must be on a leash, never left unattended. Pets not allowed in activity areas; only adults may walk pets in the campground. **Fires:** Grill, stoves, fire rings only, out by 11 p.m. **Alcoholic Beverages:** At site only. **Vehicle Maximum Length:** No limit. **Other:** No children allowed in hot tubs.

TO GET THERE

From Maine Turnpike (Exit 5) and I-195, go east 1.2 mi. on I-195, then north 5 mi. on Hwy. 1, then east (right) 3 mi. on Hwy. 9 (Pine Point Rd.); campground is on right.

SCARBOROUGH — MAP, D-1
Wassamki Springs

56 Saco St., 04074. T: (207) 839-4276; www.wassamkisprings.com.

🚐 ★★★★ ⛺ ★★★

Beauty: ★★★★	Site Privacy: ★★★
Spaciousness: ★★★	Quiet: ★★★
Security: ★★★	Cleanliness: ★★★★
Insect Control: ★★★	Facilities: ★★★★

Vacationing families and Maine's summer tourists clamor to this Portland-area activity-based campground. We like that the campground is only a few minutes from Maine's largest city (with restaurants, galleries, and historic sites) with quick access to southern coastal beaches, cruises, and attractions. But, if you stay here, you don't have to be in the hub of it all. The property flanks a 30-acre private lake and campers have their own mile-long sandy beach and warm, crystal-clear swimming waters. There are boat rentals, family hayrides, group bonfires, and planned activities to keep things entertaining. There's also a trout-stocked fishing pond popular with kids and parents alike. Facilities are clean and modern and campers have a choice of sites: lakefront, shaded, or open (though a little over half of the campground is taken by seasonal renters.) Tent-only sites are few (nine) and tucked back away from the lake.

BASICS

Operated By: Hillock family. **Open:** May–Columbus Day. **Site Assignment:** Reservations suggested

July–Aug.; $10 daily deposit; holiday weekends paid in full; 2-week cancellation policy; no refunds for holiday weekends; MC, V, D; checks accepted for deposit but not upon arrival; must pay in full for 2 nights or less. **Registration:** At office. **Fee:** Full hookup (50 amps), $46; full hookup, $41; water/electric, $39; no hookup, $24; based on 2 adults & up to 4 children. **Parking:** At site.

FACILITIES

Number of RV-only Sites: 151. **Number of Tent-only Sites:** 9. **Hookups:** Electric (30, 50 amps), water, sewer, phone, modem. **Each Site:** Picnic table, fire ring. **Dump Station:** Yes. **Laundry:** Yes. **Pay Phone:** Yes. **Restrooms and Showers:** Yes. **Fuel:** No. **Propane:** Yes. **Internal Roads:** Gravel, dirt (good). **RV Service:** No. **Market:** Scarborough, 0.5 mi. **Restaurant:** Yes. **General Store:** Yes. **Vending:** Yes. **Swimming:** No. **Playground:** Yes. **Other:** Lake frontage, beach, boat rentals, stocked fishing pond, pavilion, game room, sports fields, planned activities. **Activities:** Swimming, boating, fishing, volleyball, horseshoes, basketball, softball. **Nearby Attractions:** Portland, Casco Bay, coastal beaches, Freeport. **Additional Information:** Greater Portland Area Chamber of Commerce, 60 Pearl St., Portland, ME 04101, (207) 772-2811, www.portlandregion.com.

RESTRICTIONS

Pets: Must be on a leash; never left unattended. **Fires:** Grill, camp stoves, fire rings only. **Alcoholic Beverages:** At site only. **Vehicle Maximum Length:** No limit.

TO GET THERE

From I-95 and Exit 7A, go 4 mi. west on Hwy. 22, then 0.2 mi. east on Saco St.; campground is on the left.

SEARSPORT   MAP, C-2
Searsport Shores Camping Resort

216 West Main St., 04974. T: (207) 548-6059; www.campocean.com.

 ★★★★★    ★★★★★

Beauty: ★★★★★	Site Privacy: ★★★★
Spaciousness: ★★★★	Quiet: ★★★★
Security: ★★★★	Cleanliness: ★★★★★
Insect Control: ★★★★	Facilities: ★★★★★

This midcoastal Maine campground, boasting 1,200 feet of scenic ocean shoreline, is one of the top in New England. The views of rocky coastline, picturesque coves, Sears Island (the largest uninhabited, undeveloped island in the state) and open ocean are spectacular. Campers have a long stretch of private beaches to enjoy, ranging from rocky tide pools to water smoothed pebbles to soft sand. Keep meandering and you'll run into Moose Lake State Park, just down the coast, within walking distance from the campground. The grounds include ocean-viewing decks and sitting areas, arbors and trellis, and artistic wood carvings. Facilities are top-notch, including modern restrooms and showers, a large rec hall with a library lending area, an array of musical instru-

ments, and an indoor play area for young children. There are hiking and biking trails, kayak and canoe rentals, and a list of planned activities, including old-fashioned lobster bakes on the beach, guided nature walks, children's programs, and more. Sites are spacious and include a separate, large adult-only tenting area overlooking the ocean, affectionately dubbed the "honeymoon suite."

BASICS

Operated By: Rosalie and Zaban Koltookian. **Open:** May 15–Oct. 15. **Site Assignment:** Reservations suggested July–Aug.; 50% deposit for stays less than 1 week, $100 deposit for stays of 1 week or more; 14-day cancellation policy w/ a 1-night fee; sites must be paid in full for holiday weekends and are nonrefundable; MC, V, D, checks. **Registration:** At office. **Fee:** Water/electric (premium), $42; water/electric (oceanview), $38; no hookup (premium ocean), $32; (ocean tent), $27. **Parking:** At site.

FACILITIES

Number of RV-only Sites: 10. **Number of Tent-only Sites:** 30. **Number of Multipurpose Sites:** 70. **Hookups:** Electric (30 amps), water. **Each Site:** Picnic table, fire ring. **Dump Station:** Yes. **Laundry:** Yes. **Pay Phone:** Yes. **Restrooms and Showers:** Yes. **Fuel:** No. **Propane:** Yes. **Internal Roads:** Gravel (good). **RV Service:** No. **Market:** Searsport, 1 mi. **Restaurant:** No. **General Store:** Yes. **Vending:** Yes. **Swimming:** No. **Playground:** Yes. **Other:** Ocean frontage, beaches, rec hall, library, patios, ocean-viewing sitting areas, group area, biking & walking trails, canoe & kayak rentals, guided kayak lessons & tours, guided tours of Acadia National Park, interpretive walks on the beach. **Activities:** Swimming, fishing, boating, beachcombing, nature walks, baseball, volleyball, horseshoes, basketball, guided tours, planned activities, including potluck suppers, lobster bakes, live entertainment, craft classes, treasure hunts, & more. **Nearby Attractions:** Bucksport, Searsport, Maine coastal beaches, Deer Isle Peninsula, Bar Harbor, Acadia National Park. **Additional Information:** Searsport Economic Development Committee, Reservoir St., Searsport, ME 04974, (207) 548-7255, www.searsportme.com; Acadia Information Center, P.O. Box 139, Mount Desert, ME 04660, (207) 667-8550 or (800) 358-8550, www.acadiainfo.com.

RESTRICTIONS

Pets: Must be on a leash, never left unattended. 1 pet per site only. **Fires:** Grill, stoves, fire rings only. **Alcoholic Beverages:** At site only. **Vehicle Maximum Length:** 75 ft.

TO GET THERE

From junction Hwy. 1 and Hwy. 3 (in Belfast), go north 5 mi. on Hwy. 1; campground is on the right.

SOUTHPORT   MAP, D-2
Gray Homestead Oceanfront Campground

21 Homestead Rd., 04576. T: (207) 633-4612; www.graysoceancamping.com.

 ★★★★    ★★★★

Beauty: ★★★★	Site Privacy: ★★
Spaciousness: ★★★	Quiet: ★★★
Security: ★★★	Cleanliness: ★★★★
Insect Control: ★★★	Facilities: ★★

Finally, a Boothbay-area campground with ocean views! Gray Homestead was once a boarding house for the wealthy; now, the property—still owned by the Gray family—includes a cottage, two apartments, and a small wooded campground. "People either love it or hate it," says Rachel, a campground employee. "There's nothing to do here, just nature." Big, beautiful nature, as in the Atlantic Ocean. Sounds good to us. There are kayaks, for poking around the peninsula, and owner Steve has a lobster boat. He'll catch lobsters and cook 'em for you or lend you a big pot so you can do it yourself. While the campground offers awesome ocean views and all campsites are a brief walk to the shore, sites tend to be small (and wet, when we visited), better for smaller RVs and pop-ups than tent camping. Site 17C, overlooking the water, is woodsy, with wonderful views. Oceanfront sites go first, naturally. Sites 9A and 9B are pretty, and set back in the woods, while sites 29A through C are nicely secluded for tenters. Sites 23 and 24 (water and electric) are good choices for RVers. Campers are drawn to the rocky point—great for fishing or just basking in the sun.

BASICS

Operated By: Steve and Suzanne Gray. **Open:** May 1–Columbus Day. **Site Assignment:** Reservations recommended; 50% deposit required; no refunds for cancellation, but will issue credit for future stay. **Registration:** At office. **Fee:** $21–$32 per campsite; no credit cards. **Parking:** At site.

FACILITIES

Number of Multipurpose Sites: 40. **Hookups:** Electric (20, 30 amps), water. **Each Site:** Picnic table, fire ring. **Dump Station:** Yes. **Laundry:** Yes. **Pay Phone:** Yes. **Restrooms and Showers:** Yes, coinop. **Fuel:** No. **Propane:** No. **Internal Roads:** Gravel, in good condition. **RV Service:** No. **Market:** 4.5 mi. north. **Restaurant:** 2 mi. north. **General Store:** No. **Vending:** Yes. **Swimming:** Yes. **Playground:** Yes (swings). **Other:** Cottage Rentals, Oceanfront Apts. **Activities:** Boating (kayak rentals), fishing. **Nearby Attractions:** Boothbay Railway Village, Maine Resources Aquarium, Boothbay Harbor restaurants, shops, & galleries, deep-sea fishing, whale-watching cruises, golf. **Additional Information:** Boothbay Harbor Region Chamber of Commerce, (207) 633-2353 or (800) 266-8422.

RESTRICTIONS

Pets: Must be leashed, quiet, & cleaned up after. Must not be left unattended. **Fires:** Fire ring only. **Alcoholic Beverages:** At sites only. **Vehicle Maximum Length:** 40 ft. **Other:** 3-day min. stay on holidays.

TO GET THERE

From Maine Turnpike, take Exit 9 to Coastal Hwy. 1, then take Exit 22 for Brunswick/Bath. Follow Hwy. 1 through Bath and Wiscasset to Hwy. 27 south. Follow Hwy. 27 to Boothbay Harbor; stay on Hwy. 27 through Boothbay to Southport. At second bridge, take a left onto Hwy. 238. Campground is 2 mi. on left.

SOUTHWEST HARBOR
Smuggler's Den Campground

MAP. C-3

Hwy. 102, P.O. Box 787, 04679.
T: (207) 244-3944 or (877) 244-9033;
www.smugglersdencampground.com.

🚐 ★★★   ⛺ ★★★★

Beauty: ★★★
Spaciousness: ★★★★
Security: ★★★★
Insect Control: ★★★

Site Privacy: ★★★
Quiet: ★★★★
Cleanliness: ★★★★
Facilities: ★★★

We like the fact that once we park our car at this campground we never have to get in it again until we leave to go home. There are several hiking trails accessible from the campground, including trails to Long Pond and Echo Lake (one of the best places to swim in the area!) You can walk into lovely Southwest Harbor, if you like, where you'll find supplies, restaurants, galleries, shops, and more. Live lobsters are for sale at the campground store! It's a great base to explore the quiet side of Mount Desert Island and Acadia National Park. We like the airy, sunny sites with views across open fields and mountains in distance. There's a separate group camping area, nestled in the trees, with plenty of elbow room and privacy. The sites are mostly back-ins with the exception of three pull-throughs.

BASICS

Operated By: Damaris Smith. **Open:** Memorial Day–Columbus Day. **Site Assignment:** Reservations suggested July–Aug.; accepted for 2 nights or longer; 50% deposit required; 14-day cancellation policy w/ $15 fee; MC, V, and checks. **Registration:** At office. **Fee:** Full hookup, $49; water/electric, $35; no hookup, $28; based on 4 people per site, over 12 years old. **Parking:** At site.

FACILITIES

Number of RV-only Sites: 70. **Number of Tent-only Sites:** 30. **Hookups:** Electric (20, 30, 50 amps), water, sewer. **Each Site:** Picnic table, fire ring. **Dump Station:** Yes. **Laundry:** Yes. **Pay Phone:** Yes. **Restrooms and Showers:** Yes. **Fuel:** No. **Propane:** Yes. **Internal Roads:** Paved. **RV Service:** No. **Market:** Southwest Harbor, 0.5 mi. **Restaurant:** No. **General Store:** Yes. **Vending:** Yes. **Swimming:** Yes. **Playground:** Yes. **Other:** Hiking trails, sports field, cabin rentals, group camping area. **Activities:** Swimming, hiking, horseshoes. **Nearby Attractions:** Bar Harbor, Acadia National Park. **Additional Information:** Acadia National Park, P.O. Box 177, Bar Harbor, ME 04609 (207) 288-3338, www.nps/gov/acad. Also, Acadia Information Center, P.O. Box 139, Mount Desert, ME 04660, (207) 667-8550 or (800) 358-8550, www.acadiainfo.com.

RESTRICTIONS

Pets: On a leash, never left unattended. **Fires:** Grill, stoves, fire rings only. **Alcoholic Beverages:** At site only. **Vehicle Maximum Length:** No limit.

TO GET THERE

From junction Hwys. 3, 198, and 102, go south 9.5 mi. on Hwy. 102; campground is on right.

SOUTHWEST HARBOR
White Birches Campground

MAP. C-3

195 Seal Cove Rd., 04679. T: (207) 244-3797 or (888) 716-0727; www.mainecamper.com.

🚐 ★★★   ⛺ ★★★

Beauty: ★★★
Spaciousness: ★★★★
Security: ★★★
Insect Control: ★★★

Site Privacy: ★★★
Quiet: ★★★
Cleanliness: ★★★
Facilities: ★★★

This modest, no-frills campground sits on the doorstep of Acadia National Park, 20 minutes from Bar Harbor and only minutes from Echo Lake, Southwest Harbor, and other major sights and attractions. Hiking, biking, kayaking, and swimming are nearby. Most campers use it as a quiet—and economical—base to explore the area. The campground is best for tenters and small pop-up trailer campers who like privacy and elbow room and won't miss the planned activities and evening entertainment offered at other area campgrounds. The campground is divided by Seal Cove Rd. with sites on both sides. Each area offers wooded, back-in sites, tucked under pine trees. We like the extra room and privacy of the B loop sites, on the opposite side of the street from the office, pool, and play area. Sites 9B–11B are especially nice. But, these sites are also across the street from the campground's only restrooms and showers, an inconvenient distance away.

BASICS

Operated By: Ronald, Jaylene, Melody, and Colton Sanborn. **Open:** May 15–Oct. 15. **Site Assignment:** Reservations accepted year-round, suggested July–Aug.; 1-night nonrefundable deposit required for reservation; MC, V, and checks. **Registration:** At office. **Fee:** Water/electric, $30; no hookup, $27; based on 2 adults & 2 children under 16. **Parking:** At site, 1 vehicle per site.

FACILITIES

Number of RV-only Sites: 25. **Number of Tent-only Sites:** 35. **Hookups:** Electric (20, 30, 50 amps), water. **Each Site:** Picnic table, fire ring. **Dump Station:** Yes. **Laundry:** Yes. **Pay Phone:** No. **Restrooms and Showers:** Yes. **Fuel:** No. **Propane:** No. **Internal Roads:** Gravel, dirt (good). **RV Service:** No. **Market:** Southwest Harbor, 1.5 mi. **Restaurant:** No. **General Store:** Yes. **Vending:** Yes. **Swimming:** Yes. **Playground:** Yes. **Other:** Cabin rentals. **Activities:** Swimming, tetherball, basketball. **Nearby Attractions:** Bar Harbor, Acadia National Park. **Additional Information:** Acadia National Park, P.O. Box 177, Bar Harbor, ME 04609, (207) 288-3338, www.nps/gov/acad. Also, Acadia Information Center, P.O. Box 139, Mount Desert, ME 04660, (207) 667-8550 or (800) 358-8550, www.acadiainfo.com.

RESTRICTIONS

Pets: Must be on a leash, never left unattended. **Fires:** Grill, stoves, fire rings only. **Alcoholic Beverages:** At site only. **Vehicle Maximum Length:** 35 ft.

TO GET THERE

From junction Hwy. 3 and Hwy. 102/198, go east 10.5 mi. on Hwy. 102 (toward Southwest Harbor), then south (right) 1.2 mi. on Seal Cove Rd.; the campground is on the left.

STEEP FALLS
Acres of Wildlife

MAP, D-1

Hwy. 113/11, 04085. T: (207) 675-CAMP; www.acresofwildlife.com.

🚐 ★★★★   ⛺ ★★★★

Beauty: ★★★★
Spaciousness: ★★★★
Security: ★★★★★
Insect Control: ★★★

Site Privacy: ★★★
Quiet: ★★★
Cleanliness: ★★★
Facilities: ★★★★

The long gravel approach to this campground might scare some campers off. To others, it's a sign that they're getting away from it all. Indeed, this southwestern Maine campground, a half-hour from Portland, is its own world of family fun. In summer, the activity schedule is virtually nonstop (we like the water-balloon slingshot contest); meanwhile, down at Rainbow Lake, there's swimming, tubing, boating, and fishing, and mini-golf up by the playground and ball field, and a mammoth arcade. Hard to believe this place was once a turkey farm. In that spirit, they still bake turkey pies, but you're more like to see a moose than a turkey lurking around these acres. The fresh baked goods (mostly made here) are a big draw. Savvy muffin-mavens order their breakfast goodies the night before. Campsites (gravel) are clustered around the lake, with a couple rows of seasonal sites set back into the woods. The sites are mostly back-in, with the exception of about six pull-throughs. Some tent sites are located in a woodsy wilderness area, as well. We like two-way hookup sites W5 through 8, on the lake, and 61A (if you miss out on the lakeside sites.) Water-only sites B6 through B22 (even numbers) are also lakeside, and really nice.

BASICS

Operated By: Baptista family. **Open:** May 1–Columbus Day. **Site Assignment:** Reservations recommended; for stays of less than 1 week in summer, reserve 30 days in advance; 50% deposit required w/ reservation; refunds for cancellations w/ 30-day notice, minus $15. **Registration:** At office. **Fee:** $24–$38; for 2 adults & up to 3 children under age 18; V, MC, D, AE. **Parking:** At site (2 cars allowed) or designated lot.

FACILITIES

Number of Tent-only Sites: 30. **Number of Multipurpose Sites:** 220. **Hookups:** Electric (20, 30 amps), water, sewer, cable TV. **Each Site:** Picnic table, fireplace. **Dump Station:** Yes. **Laundry:** Yes. **Pay Phone:** Yes. **Restrooms and Showers:** Yes. **Fuel:** No. **Propane:** Yes. **Internal Roads:** Gravel, in good condition. **RV Service:** No. **Market:** 1 mi. east, in Standish. **Restaurant:** Yes. **General Store:** Yes. **Vending:** Yes. **Swimming:** No. **Playground:** Yes. **Other:** Mini-golf, pub, restaurant, rec hall. **Activities:** Fishing (no license required), lake swimming, boating (rentals available), volleyball, basketball, ball field, bocce, planned activities. **Nearby Attractions:** Songo River Queen paddle wheeler cruise, Sebago Lake State Park, hiking at Douglas Hill, Willbrook Antique Museum, Jones Gallery Glass Museum, Portland.

Additional Information: Bridgton Lakes Region Chamber of Commerce, (207) 647-3472.

RESTRICTIONS

Pets: Must be leashed, quiet, & cleaned up after. Must not be left unattended. Charge is $5 per night in season. **Fires:** Fireplaces only. **Alcoholic Beverages:** Allowed. **Vehicle Maximum Length:** 35 ft. **Other:** 3-night min. stay during holiday weekends.

TO GET THERE

From Maine Turnpike, take Exit 7A, go left, and follow signs to Hwy. 22/114 North (Gorham) on your left. In Gorham, take Hwy. 25W on your left, to Hwy. 113, on the right. Go 6 mi. on Hwy. 113 to campground entrance, then 3 mi. on gravel entrance road.

TRENTON
Narrows Too
MAP, C-2

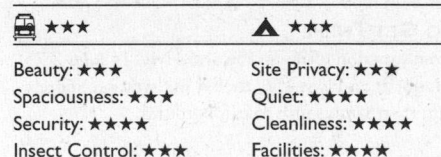

1150 Bar Harbor Rd., 04605. T: (207) 667-4300 or (866) 917-4300; www.reserveamerica.com.

🚐 ★★★★★   ⛺ ★★★★

Beauty: ★★★★	Site Privacy: ★★★
Spaciousness: ★★★	Quiet: ★★★
Security: ★★★	Cleanliness: ★★★★★
Insect Control: ★★★	Facilities: ★★★★★

In an area blessed with a multitude of fine campgrounds, this oceanfront property remains a standout, especially for campers who like a lot of activities and facilities on site. It has a busy, bustling atmosphere full of families, young couples, and retirees on vacation, here to explore Acadia National Park and the surrounding area. There's plenty to do at the campground: magic shows and movies in the evenings, mini-golf, swimming, and more; most activities and sports fields are clustered in the front of the campground. Head toward the back of the site and you'll have splendid views of the ocean. Days are typically quiet when most campers leave to visit area attractions (there's a free shuttle bus service from the campground to downtown Bar Harbor) but by late afternoon the campground is a hive of activity. You'll have a choice of sites, most are back-in, sunny and open, and many have expansive ocean views. There is a cluster of cabins and shaded sites in the woods that offer more privacy (sites 203–206 are favorites), and a separate tenting circle. As expected, most popular sites are on the ocean (sites 311–314 are particularly nice.)

BASICS

Operated By: Pat Stanley. **Open:** Memorial Day–Columbus Day. **Site Assignment:** Reservations accepted year-round, recommended July–Aug.; all sites require 2-night minimum and 3-night minimum on holiday weekends; holidays are paid in full and nonrefundable; oceanfront sites require 3-night minimum in July and Aug.; $50 deposit for 2 nights, $100 for 3 nights, $150 for 4–7 nights, $200 for 8 or more nights; 30-day cancellation policy minus $10; MC, V, D, checks for reservations; no checks upon arrival. **Registration:** At office. **Fee:** $20–$60; depending on the season. **Parking:** At site.

FACILITIES

Number of RV-only Sites: 120. **Number of Tent-only Sites:** 12. **Hookups:** Electric (20, 30, 50 amps), water, sewer, cable TV, modem. **Each Site:** Picnic table, fire ring. **Dump Station:** Yes. **Laundry:** Yes. **Pay Phone:** Yes. **Restrooms and Showers:** Yes. **Fuel:** No. **Propane:** Yes. **Internal Roads:** Gravel, dirt (good). **RV Service:** No. **Market:** Trenton, 1.5 mi. **Restaurant:** No. **General Store:** Yes. **Vending:** No. **Swimming:** Yes. **Playground:** Yes. **Other:** Ocean frontage, rec room, entertainment center, exercise room, reading room, mini-golf, free shuttle bus service to Bar Harbor, cabin rentals, modem in office. **Activities:** Swimming, volleyball, basketball, horseshoes, mini-golf, live entertainment & planned activities, including children's programs, arts & crafts, movies, & more. **Nearby Attractions:** Bar Harbor, Acadia National Park. **Additional Information:** Bar Harbor Chamber of Commerce, (207) 208-5103.

RESTRICTIONS

Pets: Must be on a leash, never left unattended. **Fires:** Grill, stoves, fire rings only. **Alcoholic Beverages:** At site only. **Vehicle Maximum Length:** 45 ft.

TO GET THERE

From junction Hwy. 230 and Hwy. 3, go east 200 feet on Hwy. 3; campground is on the left.

WATERFORD
Papoose Pond Resort and Campground
MAP, D-1

700 Norway Rd., 04088. T: (207) 583-4470; www.papoosepondresort.com.

🚐 ★★★★★   ⛺ ★★

Beauty: ★★★	Site Privacy: ★★★
Spaciousness: ★★★★	Quiet: ★★
Security: ★★★★	Cleanliness: ★★★★
Insect Control: ★★★	Facilities: ★★★★

The sign at the bathhouse says it all: "Do not use bathhouse sinks for water balloons"! This is definitely a family scene, with a rousing schedule of canoe trips, hayrides, and nightly entertainment. "We're like Beaver Cleaver-Ville," says owner Bill Strauss. Set on an 80-acre pond in Western Maine, complete with antique carousel, this place evokes a wholesome, early-1960s feel. The only thing lacking: moms with bouffant hair-dos. Three generations of families have been coming here to splash in the pond, take out the paddleboats, and roast marshmallows around the campfire. The prime lakeside spots are taken by rental cabins, although BS (beachside) sites 14 through 16, with electric and water, are pretty sweet. Forget the other end of the beach, though; BS sites 4 through 8, plus two on the end, are fairly exposed. Surprise: there's a whole section of campsites across the street and nestled into the woods. For the sake of peace, quiet, and privacy, we'd opt for any of these, especially sites HB 14 through 16 (they're huge) and HBHM 1 through 11 (ultra-private). This is definitely a destination campground, great fun for kids.

BASICS

Operated By: Strauss family. **Open:** Mid-May–Columbus Day. **Site Assignment:** Reserva-

tions recommended and open 1 year in advance; 50% deposit due for reservations; payment in full due if staying less than 1 week; refunds for cancellation w/ 30-day notice, minus $15; $5 fee charged for each reservation change. **Registration:** At office. **Fee:** $18–$58; V, MC, D. **Parking:** At site.

FACILITIES

Number of Tent-only Sites: 10. **Number of Multipurpose Sites:** 170. **Hookups:** Electric (20, 30 amps), water, sewer, modem. **Each Site:** Picnic table, fireplace. **Dump Station:** Yes. **Laundry:** Yes. **Pay Phone:** Yes. **Restrooms and Showers:** Yes. **Fuel:** No. **Propane:** No. **Internal Roads:** Gravel, in good condition. **RV Service:** No. **Market:** 15 mi. south, in Norway. **Restaurant:** Yes. **General Store:** Yes. **Vending:** Yes. **Swimming:** Yes. **Playground:** Yes. **Other:** Rec hall, game room, mini-golf, carousel. **Activities:** Mini-golf, lake swimming, tennis, boating (rentals available), fishing, basketball, volleyball, shuffle-board, horseshoes, carousel rides, planned daily activities. **Nearby Attractions:** Mt. Sabattus (hiking), outlet shopping (North Conway, NH). **Additional Information:** Bridgton Lakes Region Chamber of Commerce, (207) 647-3472.

RESTRICTIONS

Pets: Must be leashed, quiet, & cleaned up after. Must be under control at all times. Not allowed on beach. **Fires:** Fire ring only. **Alcoholic Beverages:** At sites only. **Vehicle Maximum Length:** No limit. **Other:** 3-night min. on Memorial Day & Labor Day weekends.

TO GET THERE

From Maine Turnpike, take Exit 11 (Gray). From Gray, take Hwy. 26 north to Norway, then Hwy. 118 for 10 mi. west to campground.

WELD
Mount Blue State Park
MAP, C-1

299 Center Hill Rd., 04285. T: (207) 585-2347 or (207) 585-2261 (off-season).

🚐 ★★★   ⛺ ★★★

Beauty: ★★★	Site Privacy: ★★★
Spaciousness: ★★★	Quiet: ★★★★
Security: ★★★★	Cleanliness: ★★★★
Insect Control: ★★★	Facilities: ★★★★

Gold-panning on the Swift River? Moonlight owl walks? Intriguing ranger-led programs like these are just part of the appeal at this state park, located in mountainous western Maine. The park is split into two areas: a beach and camping area on Lake Webb, and, 14 miles away, 3167-foot Mt. Blue, reachable via hiking trails. If you like to hike, this is your kind of place, with a variety of hikes for all abilities (ask rangers for suggestions.) Campsites are set in three back-in loops, with trails leading to the narrow, sandy beach and big, roped-off swim area. If you're tenting, inquire about a level one, like site 70L; some are pretty bumpy here. Most sites are set far back from the road. Some, like site 22L, even boast their own furnishings—nice, flat boulders that make perfect chairs. Lots of fallen logs are left to nature to deal with here, but campsites are mostly cleared. Site 104X (as in extra-large) has a nice approach and is great for big rigs. Friday and Saturday evening ranger programs in the amphitheater are worth attending. There's only one shower room at this park, but at least it has plenty of showers.

BASICS

Operated By: Maine Dept. of Conservation, Bureau of Parks and Lands. **Open:** June 15–Labor Day. **Site Assignment:** In spring and fall, first come, first served. In summer, reservations open on the first business day in Jan.; from June 15 to the night before Labor Day, sites may be reserved for a min. of 2 nights and up to 2 weeks; full payment charged to credit card when reservation is processed; refund w/ $15 fee; 26 sites are nonreservable and available first come, first served; call the reservations line to cancel a reservation more than 3 days in advance; if canceling less than 3 days in advance, call the park directly. **Registration:** At office. **Fee:** Maine residents, $15; nonresidents, $20; plus $2 fee if reserved in advance; V, MC. **Parking:** At sites or assigned lots.

FACILITIES

Number of Multipurpose Sites: 136. **Hookups:** None. **Each Site:** Picnic table, fireplace. **Dump Station:** Yes. **Laundry:** No. **Pay Phone:** Yes. **Restrooms and Showers:** Yes. **Fuel:** No. **Propane:** No. **Internal Roads:** Gravel, in good condition. **RV Service:** No. **Market:** 14 mi. southeast. **Restaurant:** 14 mi. southeast. **General Store:** No. **Vending:** Yes. **Swimming:** No. **Playground:** Yes. **Other:** Boat ramp, amphitheater, nature center. **Activities:** Bicycling, mountain biking, hiking (multi-use trail & nature trail), boating (rentals available), volleyball, basketball, moose watching, interpretive programs. **Nearby Attractions:** Mt. Blue (14 mi.), other day hikes. **Additional Information:** Greater Farmington Chamber of Commerce, (207) 778-4215.

RESTRICTIONS

Pets: Must be leashed, quiet, & cleaned up after. Must not be left unattended. Not allowed on beach. **Fires:** Fire ring only. **Alcoholic Beverages:** Not allowed. **Vehicle Maximum Length:** 38 ft. **Other:** 2-week stay limit between last week in June & Labor Day.

TO GET THERE

From junction of Hwy. 156 and Hwy. 142, go 2.75 mi. north on Hwy. 156, then 4 mi. west on Shore Rd., then 1 mi. south to campground.

WELLS
Sea-Vu Campground

MAP, D-1

Hwy. 1, 1733 Post Rd., 04090. T: (207) 646-7732; www.sea-vucampground.com.

🚐 ★★★	⛺ ★★★
Beauty: ★★★	Site Privacy: ★★★
Spaciousness: ★★★	Quiet: ★★★
Security: ★★★★★	Cleanliness: ★★★★
Insect Control: ★★★	Facilities: ★★★

This southern-coast campground, with quick and easy access to area parks, beaches, and attractions, boasts picturesque views of the Atlantic Ocean and Wells Harbor. Up front, there's a small fitness area where early morning classes are held throughout the summer. Several rows of seasonal renters stretch from the front office area toward the water. Most sites don't have much of a view but there is a nice seating area overlooking the wide expanse of tidal marshes, inlets, and open ocean. All sites are back-in. The handful of tent-only sites have ocean views, nestled in a grassy, shaded area in the back. Most campers don't demand much from their stay at Sea-Vu: a clean, friendly place to set up home away from home so they can explore the region. Sea-Vu delivers that.

BASICS

Operated By: Dave and Elaine Talevi. **Open:** May 12–Oct. 15. **Site Assignment:** Reservations suggested; full deposit for 3 nights or less, one-half deposit for 4 nights or more; 14-day cancellation policy; no refunds for holiday reservations; MC, V, D, no checks. **Registration:** At office. **Fee:** Full hookup, $41; no hookup (water nearby), $32; based on 2 people; additional person, $4. **Parking:** At site.

FACILITIES

Number of RV-only Sites: 60. **Number of Tent-only Sites:** 6. **Hookups:** Electric (30, 50 amps), water, sewer, cable TV. **Each Site:** Picnic table, fire ring. **Dump Station:** Yes. **Laundry:** Yes. **Pay Phone:** Yes. **Restrooms and Showers:** Yes (coin-op). **Fuel:** No. **Propane:** Yes. **Internal Roads:** Paved, gravel (good). **RV Service:** Yes. **Market:** Wells, 1 mi. **Restaurant:** Yes. **General Store:** Yes. **Vending:** Yes. **Swimming:** Yes. **Playground:** Yes. **Other:** Game room, fitness center, 18-hole mini-golf course, sports field. **Activities:** Swimming, mini-golf, basketball, volleyball, horseshoes. **Nearby Attractions:** Old Orchard Beach, Wells Harbor, Ogunquit, Kennebunkport, southern coast parks & beaches, Portland. **Additional Information:** Wells Chamber of Commerce, 136 Post Rd., Hwy. 1, Wells, ME 04090, (207) 646-2451, www.wellschamber.org.

RESTRICTIONS

Pets: Must be on a leash, never left unattended. **Fires:** Grill, stoves, fire rings only. **Alcoholic Beverages:** At site only. **Vehicle Maximum Length:** No limit.

TO GET THERE

From junction Maine Turnpike and Hwy. 109, Exit 2, go east 1.5 mi. on Hwy. 109, then north 0.4 mi. on Hwy. 1; campground is on the right.

WELLS
Wells Beach Resort Campground

MAP, D-1

reserve america

1000 Post Rd., 04090. T: (207) 646-7570 or (800) 640-2267; www.reserveamerica.com.

🚐 ★★★★	⛺ ★★★
Beauty: ★★	Site Privacy: ★★★
Spaciousness: ★★★	Quiet: ★★
Security: ★★★	Cleanliness: ★★★★
Insect Control: ★★★	Facilities: ★★★★

This is one of the nicest campgrounds in the popular Wells Beach area, boasting super clean facilities, modern hookups and level sites, and plenty of amenities for kids and grownups alike—all this in the heart of Maine's southern coastal resort area. What you don't find at the campground is within easy walking distance: fast-food franchises, local restaurants, movie theaters, factory outlet shops, beaches, and more. We like the poolside laundry with an outdoor sitting area and the small fitness room for early morning workouts. There's a choice of open and shaded sites; tent sites come with water, electric, and cable TV and are set in the back, flanked by trees. There are 70 back-in sites and 180 pull-through sites. Don't expect much privacy or quiet; it's a busy, activity-oriented place, swarming with southern coastal Maine tourists and vacationing families.

BASICS

Operated By: Griffin family. **Open:** May 15–Oct. 15. **Site Assignment:** Reservations suggested; $100 deposit for stays of 3 days or less, $200 deposit for 4 days or more, in full for holiday stays; 14-day cancellation policy w/ $15 fee; MC, V, D, no checks. **Registration:** At office. **Fee:** Full hookup (20, 30, 50 amps), $59; water/electric/cable/sewer, $53; tent, $38; Summer weekends & holidays may be higher, based on 2 people; additional person, ages 4 & older, $6. **Parking:** At site, 1 vehicle per site.

FACILITIES

Number of RV-only Sites: 210. **Number of Tent-only Sites:** 28. **Hookups:** Electric (20, 30, 50 amps), water, sewer, cable TV, modem. **Each Site:** Picnic table, fire ring. **Dump Station:** Yes. **Laundry:** Yes. **Pay Phone:** Yes. **Restrooms and Showers:** Yes. **Fuel:** No. **Propane:** No. **Internal Roads:** Paved. **RV Service:** No. **Market:** Wells, 0.5 mi. **Restaurant:** No. **General Store:** Yes. **Vending:** Yes. **Swimming:** Yes. **Playground:** Yes. **Other:** Fitness center, rec hall, sports fields., 18-hole mini-golf course, pavilion, Wells Trolley Car stop. **Activities:** Swimming, bocce ball, mini-golf, volleyball, basketball, horseshoes, shuffleboard. **Nearby Attractions:** Old Orchard Beach, Wells Harbor, Ogunquit, Kennebunkport, southern coast parks & beaches, Portland. **Additional Information:** Wells Chamber of Commerce, 136 Post Rd., Hwy. 1, Wells, ME 04090, (207) 646-2451, www.wellschamber.org.

RESTRICTIONS

Pets: Must be on a leash, never left unattended. Pets are not allowed on tent sites, 2 pet max. **Fires:** Grill, stoves, fire rings only. **Alcoholic Beverages:** At site only. **Vehicle Maximum Length:** No limit.

TO GET THERE

From junction Maine Turnpike and Hwy. 109 (Exit 2), go east 1.5 mi. on Hwy. 109, then south 1.4 mi. on Hwy. 1; campground is on the right.

WISCASSET
Chewonki Campgrounds

MAP, D-2

P.O. Box 261, 04578. T: (207) 882-7426 or (800) 465-7747; www.chewonkicampground.com.

🚐 ★★★★	⛺ ★★★★
Beauty: ★★★★★	Site Privacy: ★★
Spaciousness: ★★★★	Quiet: ★★
Security: ★★★	Cleanliness: ★★★★
Insect Control: ★★	Facilities: ★★★★

Wiscasset calls itself "Maine's Prettiest Village." If you'd like to check out the veracity of that statement, or simply want a pleasant, centralized base for exploring mid-coast Maine, consider this inviting campground. Run by the Brackett family for 25 years, and currently managed by sisters Ann and Pamela, Chewonki Campgrounds overlooks a saltwater inlet of Montsweag Bay. It's a really pretty spot, with rolling hillsides leading to salt marsh and sea. Watery nooks and crannies beckon paddlers. (When we visited, a large group of kayakers were tent-camping here.) The grassy sites are spacious, with mature trees providing a measure of privacy for some. Sites 10, 10A, and 10B (no hookups) are right on the water, but the best views, we think, are from sites 13 through 16 (water and electricity), overlooking the salt marsh. Most of the sites are back-in with the exception of nine pull-throughs. Flower plantings add to the sense that this campground is well cared-for; plus, everything from the saltwater-filtered pool area to the restrooms is superclean. A downside here: there's a small airport nearby, so you're bound to hear aircraft overhead during the day. By night, they stop flying, so it's peaceful. One look at the star-filled sky, and you'll feel far from the urban hustle and bustle.

BASICS

Operated By: Pamela D. Brackett and Ann Brackett Beck. **Open:** Mid-May–mid-Oct. **Site Assignment:** Reservations recommended; 1-month advance booking in July and Aug. recommended; for a stay of 3 days or less, the deposit is equal to the amount charged for 1-night stay; for a stay of 4–7 days, the deposit is equal to the amount charged for 2 days; refunds for cancellation w/ 21-day notice, minus $15. **Registration:** At office. **Fee:** $28–$41; V, MC. **Parking:** At site, 1 car limit.

FACILITIES

Number of RV-only Sites: 10. **Number of Tent-only Sites:** 10. **Number of Multipurpose Sites:** 27. **Hookups:** Electric (20, 30 amps), water, sewer. **Each Site:** Picnic table, fire ring. **Dump Station:** Yes. **Laundry:** No. **Pay Phone:** Yes. **Restrooms and Showers:** Yes, coin-op. **Fuel:** No. **Propane:** No. **Internal Roads:** Gravel, in good condition. **RV Service:** No. **Market:** 2 mi. north. **Restaurant:** 1.5 mi. south. **General Store:** Yes. **Vending:** No. **Swimming:** Yes. **Playground:** Yes. **Other:** Rec hall, tennis courts, boat ramp (for small craft), hot tub except in June & July. **Activities:** Boating (canoe & kayak rentals), swimming, volleyball, croquet, nature walk, one-hole golf course. **Nearby Attractions:** Historic village of Wiscasset, Pemaquid Point lighthouse, art museums, Old Jail, boat cruises, deep-sea fishing, antique shops, flea markets. **Additional Information:** Wiscasset Regional Business Assoc., (207) 882-4600, www.wiscassetmaine.com.

RESTRICTIONS

Pets: Must be leashed, quiet, & cleaned up after. Must not be left unattended. **Fires:** Fire ring only. **Alcoholic Beverages:** At sites only. **Vehicle Maximum Length:** No limit. **Other:** 3-day min. stay on holidays.

TO GET THERE

From Maine Turnpike, take Exit 9, Hwy. 95 and Hwy. 1 to Bath. Follow 7 mi. to Hwy. 144, then turn right. Follow signs to campground, 1.5 mi. on right.

YORK HARBOR   MAP, D-1
Libby's Oceanside Camp

Hwy. 1A, P.O. Box 40, 03911. T: (207) 363-4171.

🚐 ★★★★	🏕 ★★
Beauty: ★★★★	Site Privacy: ★★
Spaciousness: ★★	Quiet: ★★★
Security: ★★★	Cleanliness: ★★★★★
Insect Control: ★★★★	Facilities: ★★★

Never mind that the sites are a bit tight and that you won't have much privacy: this campground has one of the finest pieces of real estate on the southern coast. Just down the road are multimillion-dollar houses; their owners don't have any better views than campers at Libby's. The campground boasts 1,100 feet of ocean frontage, with unsurpassed views of beaches, harbors, coves, and open ocean. On clear days, you can see Nubble Lighthouse, one of the most photographed sights in Maine. There are 45 oceanfront sites. All sites are back-in. Many are taken by seasonal renters but the owners have been freeing up more and more each year for the transient crowd. There's access to a rocky beach on one end of the campground, a great place for tide pooling at low tide. At high tide, locals come down with their fishing rods. When we were there, they were casting for stripers from the beach. When you've had enough of "roughing it," head to upscale York Harbor or nearby Ogunquit for gallery hopping and gourmet meals.

BASICS

Operated By: Davidson family. **Open:** May 15–Oct. 15. **Site Assignment:** Reservations accepted for 1-week stays only, Sun.–Sun.; shorter stays are first come, first served; $100 deposit for each week reserved; 14-day cancellation policy; MC, V, D, no checks. **Registration:** At office. **Fee:** Oceanfront sites, $60; all other sites, $50; amp, $2; cable TV, $1.50; based on 2 adults & 2 children under 16, or 3 adults (all sites include sewer, water, & 30-amp electric). **Parking:** At site.

FACILITIES

Number of RV-only Sites: 85. **Number of Tent-only Sites:** 10. **Hookups:** Electric (20, 30, 50 amps), water, sewer, cable TV. **Each Site:** Picnic table. **Dump Station:** No. **Laundry:** Yes. **Pay Phone:** No. **Restrooms and Showers:** Yes. **Fuel:** No. **Propane:** No. **Internal Roads:** Paved. **RV Service:** Yes. **Market:** York Harbor, 1 mi. **Restaurant:** No. **General Store:** No. **Vending:** Yes. **Swimming:** No. **Playground:** No. **Other:** Hot tub, ocean frontage, beach, activity room. **Activities:** Swimming, saltwater fishing, beach combing, tide pooling. **Nearby Attractions:** Yok Harbor, York beaches, southern coast parks & beaches, Portsmouth. **Additional Information:** Yorks Chamber of Commerce, One Stonewall Ln., York, ME 03909, (207) 363-4422 or (800) 639-2442, www.yorkme.org.

RESTRICTIONS

Pets: Must be on a leash, never left unattended. No pets allowed on the beach; only 2 pets allowed per site. **Fires:** Grill, stoves, fire rings only. **Alcoholic Beverages:** At site only. **Vehicle Maximum Length:** No limit.

TO GET THERE

From I-95, Exit 4, go east 0.3 mi. on connector road, then south 0.3 mi. on Hwy. 1, then north 3 mi. on Hwy. 1A; campground is on the right.

Maryland

Dubbed "America in Miniature" by a *National Geographic* reporter in the 1920s, Maryland boasts the green **Allegheny Mountains** to the west as well as the tranquil **Chesapeake Bay** and white-sand **Atlantic** beaches along its eastern shore. Consider the culture-rich, metropolitan cities of **Baltimore** and nearby **Washington, D.C.,** along with myriad historic small towns, and you can see that the reporter's view of the Old Line State remains accurate.

Cascading streams, hiking trails, lakes ideal for boating, and slopes meant for skiing are prevalent in western Maryland in the Allegheny Mountains. **Deep Creek Lake,** Maryland's largest man-made body of water at six square miles, is a haven for water sports in warmer months. **Wisp Ski and Golf Resort** has more than two dozen slopes and an 18-hole golf course. Part of the **Chesapeake and Ohio Canal National Historical Park,** which includes the **C&O Canal National Park Exhibit Center** as well as its boat replica and **Paw Paw Tunnel** in Cumberland, illustrates Maryland's glorious canal era. Though Gettysburg is known as the Civil War's bloodiest battle, more than 23,000 men were killed in **Antietam** on September 17, 1862—the deadliest single day in the Civil War. More than 350 monuments, plaques, and battlefield maps along eight miles of paved roadways detail the battle's story. The visitor center even houses a museum and a 26-minute movie about the bloodbath.

Shaped by Northern and Southern traditions, Baltimore served as the nation's capital for two months when Philadelphia was invaded by British troops during the American Revolution. In 1814, when the British attacked **Baltimore,** defenders of **Fort McHenry** withstood the naval bombardment for 25 hours. When the British ceased fire and gave up, Francis Scott Key noticed the massive American flag still flying above the fort, and this inspired him to compose "The Star-spangled Banner." Today, the **Fort McHenry National Monument and Historic Shrine** is restored to its War of 1812 appearance. Narrated cruises depart from the fort and explore the surrounding area. Baseball fans will appreciate the **Baltimore Orioles** at **Camden Yards** and the **Babe Ruth Birthplace and Baseball Center.** The **Edgar Allan Poe House,** the **National Aquarium,** and the **Star-spangled Banner Flag House and 1812 Museum** are other recommended sites. Founded in 1649, the state capitol of **Annapolis** is best experienced by **Three Centuries Tours,** which offers walking tours of the **U.S. Naval Academy** and the historic district led by guides dressed in colonial attire.

In 1791, Maryland officials donated land that became Washington, D.C. There are many interesting attractions, towns, and sites in the Maryland counties that border our nation's capital. Frederick is a historic town where museums capture the lives of Civil War heroine Barbara Fritchie and Key. **Olde Towne Gaithersburg,** the **Clara Barton National Historic Site** in **Glen Echo, Andrews Air Force Base,** and the **NASA/Goddard Space Flight Visitor Center** are certainly worth exploring before or after venturing to Washington.

Southern Maryland is the most naturally pristine region in the state. Cliffs rise above fossil-strewn beaches. Lighthouses guard the waters of the **Chesapeake Bay,** and the fishing is rewarding in the **Patuxent** and **Potomac Rivers. St. Mary's City,** the area's capital until 1694, features an outdoor museum at the site of the first capitol. The living history complex includes a reconstructed **1676 State House,** a 17th-century tobacco plantation, and a 17th-century inn. Inside the dense forests of 1460-acre **Calvert Cliffs State Park,** about 600 species of fossils have been discovered around the jutting cliffs overlooking Chesapeake Bay.

Charming villages and towns dot the landscape of Maryland's eastern shore, **Delmarva,** which is bordered by the Chesapeake Bay and Atlantic Ocean. **Ocean City,** home to white-sand beaches, the annual **White Marlin Open Fishing Tournament,** the world's largest billfishing competition, a three-mile boardwalk, and the **Jolly Roger and Trimpers Amusement Parks,** is Maryland's only Atlantic Coast resort town. Although you can wax up your board and hit the waves in the morning and evening, two surfing beaches are designated per day in season while lifeguards are on duty. Many visitors come here not just for the ocean but also to explore the **Assateague Island National Seashore,** a 37-mile barrier strand off the eastern shore; large populations of wild ponies, Sitka deer, and peregrine falcons reside there. (Stopping to pet or feed the untamed equines is not recommended.) The eastern shore is also Maryland's blue-crab country. This scavenger's succulent meat is the essential dish at any of the countless seafood houses along Maryland's coast and makes for the world's best crab cakes.

Bring your appetite for wonder and allot extra travel time for the seventh state—its beauty has entranced many visitors into making Maryland their home.

Campground Profiles

ABINGDON   MAP, A-3
Bar Harbor RV Park and Marina

reserve america

4228 Birch Ave., 21009. T: (800) 351-CAMP or (410) 679-0880; www.reserveamerica.com.

🚐 ★★★★   ▲ n/a

Beauty: ★★★★★	Site Privacy: ★★★★
Spaciousness: ★★★★	Quiet: ★★★★
Security: ★★★★	Cleanliness: ★★★★
Insect Control: ★★★★	Facilities: ★★★★

Situated on a densely forested peninsula on the Bush River along Chesapeake Bay, Bar Harbor RV Park and Marina is a half-hour northeast of Baltimore's Inner Harbor. The marina, where bald eagles and great blue herons gracefully glide, has boat slips and rowboat, kayak, and paddleboat rentals. Campers who bring their own boat can venture by water to Chesapeake Bay ports, including Baltimore and Annapolis. Sites are shaded and feature full hookups and patios. Some sites are located on the waterfront, and other are away from the water. The swimming pool is surrounded with vibrant wildflowers and lush plants. When we were here, many campers were basking in the sun by the pool and casting their lines into Bush River. The aforementioned paddleboat and kayak rentals are also popular.

BASICS

Operated By: Phil and Jonn Schaefer. **Open:** All year. **Site Assignment:** Reservations accepted (MC, V, cash, or check will hold site, received at least 3 weeks in advance); walk-ins accepted; refund (minus $10) w/ 6-day notice; less than 6 days, 1-night fee; 31-day notice required for holidays, subject to 3-night cancellation charge. **Registration:** At campground office. **Fee:** $39–$42; cash, check, V, MC. **Parking:** At site.

FACILITIES

Number of RV-only Sites: 93. **Hookups:** Electric (30, 50 amps), cable TV, phone. **Each Site:** Fire ring, picnic table. **Dump Station:** Yes. **Laundry:** Yes. **Pay Phone:** Yes. **Restrooms and Showers:** Yes. **Fuel:** No. **Propane:** Yes. **Internal Roads:** Gravel & paved, in good condition. **RV Service:** No. **Market:** W/in 2 mi. **Restaurant:** W/in 2 mi. **General Store:** Yes. **Vending:** Yes. **Swimming:** Yes. **Playground:** Yes. **Other:** Bush River. **Activities:** Canoeing, boating, kayaking, boat rentals, fishing, game room, rec hall. **Nearby Attractions:** Baltimore, Camden Yards, Chesapeake Bay, Inner Harbor, Baltimore Zoo, National Aquarium, U.S. Naval Academy, Annapolis, Washington, D.C. **Additional Information:** Baltimore Area Convention Visitors Assoc., (800) 343-3468, www.baltimore.org.

RESTRICTIONS

Pets: On leash only. Under 35 lbs. **Fires:** At site. **Alcoholic Beverages:** At site. **Vehicle Maximum Length:** 40 ft. **Other:** No tents or screen rooms.

TO GET THERE

From I-95, take Exit 80 and go 1.5 mi. south on Hwy. 543, 2 mi. west on US 40, 0.75 mi. south on Long Bar Rd., and 0.5 mi. east on Baker Ave. Entrance is on the left.

BERLIN   MAP, C-4
Bayside Campground and Oceanside Campground

Assateague Island National Seashore, 7206 National Seashore Ln., 21811. T: (410) 641-3030 or (800) 365-2267; www.nps.gov/asis/index.htm, reservations.nps.gov.

🚐 ★★★   ▲ ★★★★

Beauty: ★★★★★	Site Privacy: ★★★★
Spaciousness: ★★★★	Quiet: ★★★★★
Security: ★★★★★	Cleanliness: ★★★★
Insect Control: ★★★	Facilities: ★★★

Operated by the National Park Service, Assateague Island National Seashore has two campgrounds—Bayside and Oceanside. Oceanside walk-in tent sites are provided for tenters who wish to camp 100–200 feet from parking areas. Centrally located facilities include chemical toilets, cold-water showers, and drinking water. Before exploring the island, visit the national park's visitor center, where exhibits and aquariums describe the barrier island environment. Be aware that the barrier island environment can be harsh if you are not prepared. Bring firewood, sunscreen, insect repellent, screen tents for shade, insect protection, and long tent stakes to anchor tents in the sand and wind. Assateague Island National Seashore in Maryland and the Chincoteague National Wildlife Refuge in Virginia (which is located on the island) are federal fee areas. The $5 entrance fee is in effect year-round. Also, be sure to observe the wildlife from a distance, especially the renowned Chincoteague ponies, which are known to bite and kick.

BASICS

Operated By: National Park Service. **Open:** All year. **Site Assignment:** Reservations accepted (may be made up to 5 months in advance); Oct. 16–Apr. 14, first come, first served; Apr. 15–Oct. 15, reservations accepted for all campsites. **Registration:** At campground office. **Fee:** Oct.16–Apr.14, $16; Apr.15–Oct.15, $20; V, MC, D. **Parking:** At designated area.

FACILITIES

Number of RV-only Sites: 128. **Number of Tent-only Sites:** 24. **Hookups:** None. **Each Site:** Picnic table. Some have fire rings, others have grills. **Dump Station:** Yes. **Laundry:** No. **Pay Phone:** Yes. **Restrooms and Showers:** Yes. **Fuel:** No. **Propane:** No. **Internal Roads:** Paved, in good condition. **RV Service:** No. **Market:** W/in 7 mi. **Restaurant:** W/in 7 mi. **General Store:** No. **Vending:** No. **Swimming:** Yes. **Playground:** No. **Other:** Assateague Island National Seashore. **Activities:** Saltwater swimming and fishing, hiking trails boating, canoeing. **Nearby Attractions:** Assateague State Park, Chincoteague National Wildlife Refuge. **Additional Information:** Maryland Office of Tourism Development, (800) 543-1036, www.mdisfun.org.

RESTRICTIONS

Pets: On leash only. **Fires:** At site only. **Alcoholic Beverages:** Alcohol permitted. **Vehicle Maximum Length:** 40 ft. **Other:** 14-day stay limit.

TO GET THERE

From Hwy. 376, go 4 mi. southeast on Hwy. 611 and 2 mi. south on Bayberry Drive. Follow signs to campground.

CLARKSBURG   MAP, A-2
Little Bennett Regional Park Campground

23701 Frederick Rd., 20871. T: (301) 972-9222; www.mc-mncppc.org.

🚐 ★★★   ▲ ★★★★

Beauty: ★★★★	Site Privacy: ★★★★
Spaciousness: ★★★★	Quiet: ★★★★
Security: ★★★★	Cleanliness: ★★★★
Insect Control: ★★★★	Facilities: ★★★

Located in northern Montgomery County, 30 miles north of Washington, D.C., in Clarksburg, the 3,700 forested acres of Little Bennett Regional Park are set amid the tributaries of Little Bennett Creek. The campground has 91 sites, 25 of which have electric hookups. Sites are situated in five back-in loops. Loops D and E, at the north end, are near the amphitheater, laundry facility, nature center, horseshoe pits, and volleyball court. A central dump station is available for self-contained units, but there are no individual water or sewer connections. More than 14 miles of hiking and horseback riding trails wander throughout the park. During winter months, the trails are used as cross-country ski trails. A camp store is combined with the registration office. Soda, ice cream, ice, snacks, and souvenirs are available. Little Seneca Lake, five miles away in Black Hill Regional Park, also offers boating and fishing.

BASICS

Operated By: Montgomery County. **Open:** Apr. 1–Oct. 31. **Site Assignment:** Reservations and walk-ins accepted; reservations w/ full nonrefundable deposit. **Registration:** At campground office. **Fee:** $18–$26; V, MC. **Parking:** At site.

FACILITIES

Number of RV-only Sites: 25. **Number of Tent-only Sites:** 66. **Hookups:** Electric (30 amps). **Each Site:** Picnic table & grill. **Dump Station:** Yes. **Laundry:** Yes. **Pay Phone:** Yes. **Restrooms and Showers:** Yes. **Fuel:** No. **Propane:** No. **Internal Roads:** Paved, in good condition. **RV Service:** No. **Market:** W/in 2 mi. **Restaurant:** W/in 2 mi. **General Store:** Yes. **Vending:** No. **Swimming:** No. **Playground:** Yes. **Other:** Little Bennett Creek. **Activities:** Hiking, horseback trails, horseshoes, volleyball, rec fields, planned activities on weekends. **Nearby Attractions:** Black Hill Regional Park, Baltimore, Washington, D.C. **Additional Information:**

Maryland Office of Tourism Development, (800) 543-1036, www.mdisfun.org.

RESTRICTIONS

Pets: On leash only. **Fires:** Group fire ring. **Alcoholic Beverages:** No alcohol permitted. **Vehicle Maximum Length:** 45 ft. **Other:** 14-day stay limit.

TO GET THERE

From I-270, take Exit 18 and go 0.5 mi. northeast on Hwy. 121, 0.5 mi. north on Hwy. 355, then follow the posted signs. Entrance is on the right.

COLLEGE PARK   MAP, B-2
Cherry Hill Park

9800 Cherry Hill Rd., 20740. T: (800) 801-6449 or (301) 937-7116; www.cherryhillpark.com.

🚐 ★★★★   ▲ ★★★★

Beauty: ★★★★   Site Privacy: ★★★★
Spaciousness: ★★★★   Quiet: ★★★★
Security: ★★★★   Cleanliness: ★★★★
Insect Control: ★★★★   Facilities: ★★★★★

Located about seven miles north of Washington, D.C., Cherry Hill Park is convenient (via city bus) to the Washington Area Metrorail (subway), which can take campers to the attractions in our nation's capital; Gray Line tour buses also stop here in season. One of the finest parks in Maryland and the mid-Atlantic, Cherry Hill has two swimming pools, a sauna, a whirlpool, and a large-screen TV lounge (with crackling fireplace in winter). The open and shaded sites are level, and 350 have full hookups. Cherry Hill accommodates 35 pull-throughs. The park is also within a half-hour drive of Baltimore and Annapolis. In nearby College Park, campers can visit the College Park Aviation Museum, located at the world's oldest operating airport; Greenbelt Park, a 1,100-acre wooded area operated by the National Park Service; and the NASA/Goddard Visitor Center, where rockets, capsule, and other space-related items are displayed.

BASICS

Operated By: Private operator. **Open:** All year. **Site Assignment:** Reservations accepted ($25 deposit required); walk-ins accepted; refund w/ 48-hour notice. **Registration:** At campground office. **Fee:** $48–$60; V, MC, D. **Parking:** At site.

FACILITIES

Number of RV-only Sites: 400. **Number of Tent-only Sites:** 50. **Hookups:** Electric (30, 50 amps), water, cable TV, phone, sewer. **Each Site:** Fire ring, picnic table. **Dump Station:** Yes. **Laundry:** Yes. **Pay Phone:** Yes. **Restrooms and Showers:** Yes. **Fuel:** No. **Propane:** Yes. **Internal Roads:** Gravel & paved, in good condition. **RV Service:** Yes. **Market:** W/in 2 mi. **Restaurant:** On premises. **General Store:** Yes. **Vending:** Yes. **Swimming:** Yes. **Playground:** Yes. **Other:** Dog-walking service, RV superstore, fishing pond. **Activities:** Swimming, game room, rec hall, sauna, whirlpool, pond fishing, mini-golf, basketball, planned activities, movies, hiking trails, volleyball. **Nearby Attractions:** Baltimore, Annapolis, Washington, D.C., College Park Aviation Museum, Greenbelt Park, NASA/Goddard Visitor Center, University of Maryland. **Additional Information:** Maryland

Office of Tourism Development, (800) 543-1036, www.mdisfun.org.

RESTRICTIONS

Pets: On leash only. **Fires:** At site. **Alcoholic Beverages:** At site. **Vehicle Maximum Length:** 50 ft. **Other:** $2 for extra vehicle; 1 car permitted w/ RV.

TO GET THERE

From I-95, take Exit 25 and go 0.1 mi. south on US 1 and 1 mi. west on Cherry Hill Rd. Entrance is on the left.

CRISFIELD   MAP, C-3
Janes Island State Park

26280 Alfred Lawson Dr., 21817. T: (410) 968-1565 or (888) 432-2267; www.dnr.state.md.us.

🚐 ★★★   ▲ ★★★★

Beauty: ★★★★   Site Privacy: ★★★★
Spaciousness: ★★★★   Quiet: ★★★★
Security: ★★★★★   Cleanliness: ★★★★
Insect Control: ★★★★   Facilities: ★★★★

Mostly surrounded by Chesapeake Bay and its inlets, Janes Island State Park features a developed mainland section (where the campground is located) and a portion accessible only by boat. With miles of isolated shoreline and marshes, Janes Island is a place where tranquility reigns. The most exciting part of Janes Island State Park is the canoe trails, which cover 2,900 acres of marshes, beaches, and highlands. Most of the waterways are protected from wind and currents, providing ideal conditions for canoeists of all skill levels. The yellow trail leads to Tangier Sound and the secluded beaches on the west side of the island. Overall, there are six marked trails, all of which begin and end at the marina and boat launch near the campground. Boat slips are available to campers for a small fee. The campground itself is situated along Daugherty Creek Canal. Sites are primarily in three clusters near the water, but not directly along it. All sites are mostly back-in, but there are three pull-through sites.

BASICS

Operated By: State of Maryland. **Open:** Apr. 28–Oct. 30. **Site Assignment:** Reservations accepted (must be paid in full at time of booking when using credit card); walk-ins accepted; refund w/ 24-hour notice (minus $6 per night); late cancellations subject to 1-night fee and $6 per night. **Registration:** At campground office. **Fee:** $25–$30; V, MC. **Parking:** At site.

FACILITIES

Number of Multipurpose Sites: 104. **Hookups:** Electric (30 amps). **Each Site:** Fire ring, picnic table. **Dump Station:** Yes. **Laundry:** Yes. **Pay Phone:** Yes. **Restrooms and Showers:** Yes. **Fuel:** No. **Propane:** No. **Internal Roads:** Paved, in good condition. **RV Service:** No. **Market:** W/in 2 mi. **Restaurant:** W/in 2 mi. **General Store:** Yes. **Vending:** Yes. **Swimming:** No. **Playground:** Yes. **Other:** Canoe trails. **Activities:** Swimming, fishing, boating, canoeing, boat rentals, planned activities. **Nearby Attractions:** Smith Island and Tangier Island boat cruises, Chesapeake Bay. **Additional Information:**

Crisfield Area Chamber of Commerce, (410) 968-2500, www.crisfield.org.

RESTRICTIONS

Pets: Not allowed. **Fires:** Fire ring only. **Alcoholic Beverages:** At site only. **Vehicle Maximum Length:** 35 ft. **Other:** 14-day stay limit.

TO GET THERE

Take Hwy. 413 to Plantation Rd., then to Alfred Lawson Dr.

CUMBERLAND   MAP, C-1, C-2 INSET
Rocky Gap State Park

12500 Pleasant Valley Rd., 21530. T: (301) 722-1480 or (888) 432-2267; www.dnr.state.md.us.

🚐 ★★★★   ▲ ★★★★

Beauty: ★★★★★   Site Privacy: ★★★★
Spaciousness: ★★★★   Quiet: ★★★★★
Security: ★★★★★   Cleanliness: ★★★★
Insect Control: ★★★★   Facilities: ★★★★★

Consisting of 3,000 acres of stunning ridges, valleys, and mountain peaks near Cumberland in western Maryland, Rocky Gap State Park has it all—rugged hiking and mountain biking trails, kayaking and whitewater rafting, fishing and boating on 243-acre Lake Habeeb, the Rocky Gap Lodge and Golf Resort, and a 278-site campground. The lake is fed by Rocky Gap Run, which winds through a mile-long gorge with jutting cliffs, overlooks, and a hemlock forest dense with rhododendron. The campground, where sites are clustered around nine loops, is located at the northeast side of Lake Habeeb. Pets are permitted at the two Ridge loops—one at the northeast tip of the campground and the other at the southeast side. The Rocky Gap Lodge and Golf Resort is at the opposite end of Lake Habeeb. The resort consists of a 220-room lodge, a full-service restaurant overlooking the lake, and an 18-hole Jack Nicklaus–designed golf course.

BASICS

Operated By: State of Maryland. **Open:** Apr. 28–Oct. 23. **Site Assignment:** Reservations and walk-ins accepted; refunds (minus $6 per night) given w/ 24-hour notice; late cancellations are subject to 1-night fee plus $6 per night. **Registration:** At campground office. **Fee:** $25–$30; V, MC. **Parking:** At site.

FACILITIES

Number of RV-only Sites: 30. **Number of Tent-only Sites:** 248. **Hookups:** Electric (20 amps). **Each Site:** Fire ring, picnic table. **Dump Station:** Yes. **Laundry:** Yes. **Pay Phone:** Yes. **Restrooms and Showers:** Yes. **Fuel:** No. **Propane:** No. **Internal Roads:** Paved, in good condition. **RV Service:** No. **Market:** W/in 6 mi. **Restaurant:** On premises. **General Store:** Yes. **Vending:** Yes. **Swimming:** Yes. **Playground:** Yes. **Other:** Lake Habeeb, Rocky Gap Lodge & Golf Resort. **Activities:** Lake swimming and fishing, boat rentals, canoeing, planned activities, hiking trails, golf, kayaking, biking. **Nearby Attractions:** Fort Cumberland Trail, Green Ridge State Forest, The Narrows, George Washington's headquarters, History House, Western Maryland Scenic Railroad, Western Maryland Station Center, Toll Gate House.

Additional Information: Allegany County CVB, (800) 50-VISIT, www.mdmountainside.com.

RESTRICTIONS

Pets: Allowed in 2 designated loops. **Fires:** At site. **Alcoholic Beverages:** No alcohol permitted. **Vehicle Maximum Length:** 29 ft. **Other:** Pets & fires may not be left unattended.

TO GET THERE

From Cumberland, go 6 mi. east on US 40. Follow signs to park and campground.

DENTON   MAP, B-3
Martinak State Park

137 Deep Shore Rd., 21629. T: (410) 820-1668 or (888) 432-2267; www.dnr.state.md.us.

🚐 ★★★★   ▲ ★★★★

Beauty: ★★★★	Site Privacy: ★★★★
Spaciousness: ★★★★	Quiet: ★★★★
Security: ★★★★★	Cleanliness: ★★★★
Insect Control: ★★★★	Facilities: ★★★★

Located on the Choptank River and Watts Creek, two miles east of Denton and Maryland's eastern shore, Martinak State Park is surrounded by hardwood and pine forests. A Chesapeake Bay Sportfishing License is required to fish the tidal waters of the river and creek, which teem with bass, perch, sunfish, and catfish. The park has a boat launch, and canoes are available for rent during the summer. Situated north of Watts Creek, the 63-site campground has two loops; the 30 sites of Loop B have electric hookups. A hiking trail winds near the campgrounds and leads to the creek. A well-maintained bathhouse is centrally located in each loop. Though there are no water hookups, a dump station is available for trailer use. Potable water is located around each loop. Martinak rents four camper cabins, as well as a full-service cabin which overlooks the Choptank River and is available year-round.

BASICS

Operated By: State of Maryland. **Open:** Apr. 14–Sept. 25. **Site Assignment:** Reservations recommended (full payment due at time of booking if using credit card); walk-ins accepted; refunds (minus $6 per night) given w/ 24-hour notice; late cancellations are subject to 1-night fee plus $6 per night. **Registration:** At campground office. **Fee:** $20–$25; V, MC. **Parking:** At site.

FACILITIES

Number of RV-only Sites: 60. **Number of Tent-only Sites:** 3. **Hookups:** Electric (20 amps). **Each Site:** Fire ring, picnic table. **Dump Station:** Yes. **Laundry:** No. **Pay Phone:** Yes. **Restrooms and Showers:** Yes. **Fuel:** No. **Propane:** No. **Internal Roads:** Paved, in good condition. **RV Service:** No. **Market:** W/in 3 mi. **Restaurant:** W/in 3 mi. **General Store:** No. **Vending:** No. **Swimming:** No. **Playground:** Yes. **Other:** Choptank River. **Activities:** Fishing, canoeing, canoe rentals, planned activities, hiking trails. **Nearby Attractions:** Chesapeake Bay, Museum of Rural Life, Chesapeake Bay Maritime Museum, C&D Canal Museum, Plumpton Park Zoo. **Additional Information:** Maryland Office of

Tourism Development, (800) 543-1036, www.mdisfun.org.

RESTRICTIONS

Pets: Not allowed. **Fires:** At site. **Alcoholic Beverages:** At site. **Vehicle Maximum Length:** 40 ft. **Other:** 14-day stay limit.

TO GET THERE

From the business center in Denton, go 1 mi. south on Hwy. 404 and 0.75 mi. on Deep Shore Rd. Entrance is on the left. Follow signs to campground.

ELLICOTT CITY   MAP, A-2
Patapsco Valley State Park

8020 Baltimore National Pike, 21043. T: (410) 461-5005 or (888) 432-2267; www.dnr.state.md.us.

🚐 ★★★   ▲ ★★★★

Beauty: ★★★★	Site Privacy: ★★★★
Spaciousness: ★★★★	Quiet: ★★★★
Security: ★★★★★	Cleanliness: ★★★★
Insect Control: ★★★★	Facilities: ★★★

Stretching 32 miles along the Patapsco River, Patapsco Valley State Park covers 14,000 acres and includes five developed recreational areas, two of which have campgrounds. The Hollofield campground offers tent and RV sites, some of which have electric hookups; the Hilton campground is for tents only. The Patapsco River flows to the Port of Baltimore and empties into the Chesapeake Bay, offering good fishing and boating. Campers can see the Thomas Viaduct, the world's longest multiple-arched stone railroad bridge; walk across the swinging bridge, a 300-foot suspension walkway over the river; hike to Bloede's Dam, the world's first internally housed hydroelectric dam; and gaze at the Patapsco Valley from an overlook near the Hollofield area campground. Pets are prohibited in the Hilton campground, but there is a "pet loop" at the south end of the Hollofield campground. Most of the Hollofield sites are situated in a circle surrounding the camp store, restrooms, and showers.

BASICS

Operated By: State of Maryland. **Open:** Apr.–Oct. **Site Assignment:** Reservations (must be paid in full at time of booking when using credit card); walk-ins accepted; refunds (minus $6 per night) given w/ 24-hour notice; late cancellations are subject to 1-night fee plus $6 per night. **Registration:** At campground office. **Fee:** $20–$25; V, MC. **Parking:** At site.

FACILITIES

Number of Multipurpose Sites: 73. **Hookups:** Electric (20 amps). **Each Site:** Fire ring, picnic table. **Dump Station:** Yes. **Laundry:** No. **Pay Phone:** Yes. **Restrooms and Showers:** Yes. **Fuel:** No. **Propane:** No. **Internal Roads:** Gravel, in good condition. **RV Service:** No. **Market:** W/in 3 mi. **Restaurant:** W/in 3 mi. **General Store:** Yes. **Vending:** No. **Swimming:** Yes. **Playground:** Yes. **Other:** Patapsco River. **Activities:** Canoeing, river fishing, hiking trails, sports field, bicycling, tubing. **Nearby Attractions:** Cider Mill Farm, Ellicott City B&O Railroad Station Museum. **Additional Information:**

Howard County Tourism Council, (800) 288-TRIP, www.howardcountymdtour.com.

RESTRICTIONS

Pets: In Hollofield area pet loop. No pets at Hilton area campground. **Fires:** At site. **Alcoholic Beverages:** At site. **Vehicle Maximum Length:** 40 ft.

TO GET THERE

From I-695, take Exit 15 and go 3 mi. west on US 40. Follow signs to Hollofield camping area.

FREDERICK   MAP, A-2
Gambrill State Park

6430 Gambrill State Park Rd., 21702. T: (301) 293-4170 or (888) 432-2267; www.dnr.state.md.us.

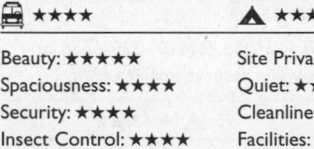

🚐 ★★★★   ▲ ★★★★

Beauty: ★★★★★	Site Privacy: ★★★
Spaciousness: ★★★★	Quiet: ★★★★
Security: ★★★★	Cleanliness: ★★★★
Insect Control: ★★★★	Facilities: ★★★

Gambrill State Park is best visited in the spring, when Catoctin Mountain's dogwoods and mountain laurels are in bloom. Of course, considering the breathtaking views in this northwest Maryland park, any time is a good time to see Gambrill. Three native stone overlooks on the 1,600-foot-high summit of High Knob offer the most stunning vistas, midway between the Mason-Dixon Line and the Potomac River. Two separate areas of Gambrill provide recreational facilities and activities. The Rock Run area, where the campground can be found, is located at the park entrance. The High Knob area is located at the top of Catoctin Mountain. The campground has one major loop with sites surrounding the bathhouse. Six sites have electric hookups, and all sites are back-in. A small pond at the campground has largemouth bass, bluegill, and channel catfish. There are 13 miles of wooded trails, mostly loops that return to the trailhead parking lot just north of the campground on Gambrill Park Rd.

BASICS

Operated By: State of Maryland. **Open:** Apr.–Oct. **Site Assignment:** Reservations (full payment required at time of booking when using credit card); walk-ins accepted; refunds (minus $6 per night) given w/ 24-hour notice; late cancellations are subject to 1-night fee plus $6 per night. **Registration:** At campground office. **Fee:** $20–$25; V, MC. **Parking:** At site.

FACILITIES

Number of RV-only Sites: 30. **Number of Tent-only Sites:** 5. **Hookups:** Electric (20 amps). **Each Site:** Fire ring, picnic table. **Dump Station:** Yes. **Laundry:** No. **Pay Phone:** Yes. **Restrooms and Showers:** Yes. **Fuel:** No. **Propane:** No. **Internal Roads:** Paved, in good condition. **RV Service:** No. **Market:** W/in 6 mi. **Restaurant:** W/in 6 mi. **General Store:** No. **Vending:** No. **Swimming:** No. **Playground:** Yes. **Other:** Fishing pond. **Activities:** Fishing, planned activities. **Nearby Attractions:** Monocacy National Battlefield, Brunswick Museum, Barbara Fritchie House and Museum, Francis Scott Key Museum, Rose Hill Manor Children's Museum. **Additional Information:** Tourism Council of

Frederick, (800) 999-3613, www.co.frederick.md.us/tour/tourpage.html.

RESTRICTIONS

Pets: On leash only. **Fires:** At site. **Alcoholic Beverages:** At site. **Vehicle Maximum Length:** 30 ft. **Other:** 14-day stay limit.

TO GET THERE

From Frederick, go 6 mi. northwest on US 40 and 0.5 mi. north on Gambrill Pk. Rd. to the Rock Run area. Follow signs to campground.

FREELAND   MAP, A-2
Morris Meadows Recreation Farm

reserve america

1523 Freeland Rd., 21053. T: (410) 329-6636 or (800) 643-7056; www.reserveamerica.com.

🚐 ★★★★★   ▲ ★★★★★

Beauty: ★★★★★	Site Privacy: ★★★★
Spaciousness: ★★★★	Quiet: ★★★★
Security: ★★★★★	Cleanliness: ★★★★
Insect Control: ★★★★	Facilities: ★★★★★

Located in northern Maryland between Baltimore and Harrisburg (PA), Morris Meadows Recreation Farm is just a few miles south of the Pennsylvania border. In fact, Morris Meadows is central to Baltimore, Washington, D.C., and Annapolis in Maryland, and Gettysburg, Lancaster, and Hershey in Pennsylvania. Morris Meadows is an ideal base for visiting attractions in these cities, but the campground itself is one of the best in the mid-Atlantic. A hiking and biking trail winds through Morris Meadow's rolling hills, and caboose tours are given of the 300-acre farm. Campers have their choice of open and wooded sites, including 75 pull-throughs. The grounds are well manicured, and facilities here are extremely clean. The museum of antiques and artifacts is truly a treat for both adults and children. The items on display were collected by Clyde and Virginia Morris, among them the Morris family's first recorded land deed, which is written on goat skin and dated December 4, 1793.

BASICS

Operated By: Morris family. **Open:** All year. **Site Assignment:** Reservations accepted ($35 off for 7-night stay); walk-ins accepted. **Registration:** At campground office. **Fee:** $23–$52; V, MC. **Parking:** At site.

FACILITIES

Number of RV-only Sites: 250. **Number of Tent-only Sites:** 12. **Hookups:** Electric (20, 30, 50 amps), water, cable TV, phone. **Each Site:** Fire ring, picnic table. **Dump Station:** Yes. **Laundry:** Yes. **Pay Phone:** Yes. **Restrooms and Showers:** Yes. **Fuel:** No. **Propane:** Yes. **Internal Roads:** Paved, in good condition. **RV Service:** No. **Market:** W/in 4 mi. **Restaurant:** W/in 4 mi. **General Store:** Yes. **Vending:** Yes. **Swimming:** Yes. **Playground:** Yes. **Other:** Museum of antiques & artifacts, caboose tours, fishing pond. **Activities:** Pond fishing, mini-golf, game room, rec hall, driving range, basketball, movies, tennis, planned activities, horseshoes, hiking and biking trails,

volleyball. **Nearby Attractions:** Baltimore, Camden Yards, Chesapeake Bay, Inner Harbor, Baltimore Zoo, National Aquarium, U.S. Naval Academy, Annapolis, Washington, D.C. **Additional Information:** Baltimore Area Convention Visitors Assoc., (800) 343-3468, www.baltimore.org.

RESTRICTIONS

Pets: On leash only. **Fires:** At site. **Alcoholic Beverages:** At site. **Vehicle Maximum Length:** No limit.

TO GET THERE

From I-83, take Exit 36 and go 0.25 mi. west on Hwy. 439, 1 mi. north on Hwy. 45, and 3 mi. west on Freeland Rd. Entrance is on the left.

GRANTSVILLE   MAP, C-1 INSET
Big Run State Park

349 Headquarters Ln., 21536. T: (301) 895-5453 or (888) 432-2267; www.dnr.state.md.us.

🚐 ★★★   ▲ ★★★★

Beauty: ★★★★	Site Privacy: ★★★★
Spaciousness: ★★★★	Quiet: ★★★★
Security: ★★★★	Cleanliness: ★★★★
Insect Control: ★★★	Facilities: ★★★

Situated near the mouth of the Savage River Reservoir in Garrett County, 300-acre Big Run State Park is ideal for campers longing for a rustic outdoor experience. The campground has no showers or electric hookups, and there is no camp store or dump station. Surrounded by the 52,800-acre Savage River State Forest, the park has a boat launch where campers can venture to the Savage River Reservoir. Big Run is the trailhead for Monroe Run, a six-mile pathway that winds through the state forest. Located two miles south of the Pennsylvania border on the western tip of Maryland, Grantsville is also home to the Casselman Bridge, a single-span stone arch built over the Casselman River in 1813. If campers long for more outdoor adventure, Big Run is near New Germany State Park, which is also located within the Savage River State Forest and has a 13-acre lake, hiking trails, and a 30-site campground with cabins. All sites are back-in with the exception of one pull-through.

BASICS

Operated By: State of Maryland. **Open:** All year. **Site Assignment:** First come, first served only. **Registration:** At campground office. **Fee:** $15; V, MC, check. **Parking:** At site.

FACILITIES

Number of Multipurpose Sites: 30. **Hookups:** None. **Each Site:** Fire ring, picnic table. **Dump Station:** No. **Laundry:** No. **Pay Phone:** No. **Restrooms and Showers:** Restrooms, no showers. **Fuel:** No. **Propane:** No. **Internal Roads:** Paved, in good condition. **RV Service:** No. **Market:** W/in 5 mi. **Restaurant:** W/in 5 mi. **General Store:** No. **Vending:** No. **Swimming:** No. **Playground:** Yes. **Other:** Savage River Reservoir. **Activities:** Lake and stream fishing, boating, canoeing, hiking trails. **Nearby Attractions:** Casselman Bridge, Savage River State Forest, Spruce Forest Artisan Village, New Germany State Park. **Additional Information:** Garrett County Chamber of Commerce, (301) 334-1948, www.garrettchamber.com.

RESTRICTIONS

Pets: On leash only. **Fires:** At site. **Alcoholic Beverages:** Alcohol permitted. **Vehicle Maximum Length:** 29 ft.

TO GET THERE

From I-68, take Exit 22 and go south on Chestnut Ridge Rd. to New Germany Rd. Follow to Big Run Rd. Follow signs to campground, which is 16 mi. from the I-68 exit.

GREENSBORO   MAP, B-3
Holiday Park Campground

P.O. Box 277, 21639. T: (410) 482-6797; www.holidaypark.com.

🚐 ★★★★   ▲ ★★★★

Beauty: ★★★★	Site Privacy: ★★★★
Spaciousness: ★★★★	Quiet: ★★★★
Security: ★★★★★	Cleanliness: ★★★★
Insect Control: ★★★★	Facilities: ★★★★

A family-friendly campground with four playgrounds and three pavilions, Holiday Park Campground is situated on the Del-Mar-Va Peninsula at the headwaters of the Choptank River, which flows into Chesapeake Bay in eastern Maryland. Located in Greensboro, Holiday Park offers spacious shaded sites, including 23 pull-throughs. A large game room is stocked with video games, pool tables, and ping pong tables. The swimming pool is large and well maintained. Campers can paddle on the Choptank in a canoe or a kayak, or just fish the river. Holiday Park is less than five miles west of the Delaware border and about a half-hour drive from Dover, Delaware's capital city. The Delaware Archaeology Museum and the Museum of Small Town Life are intriguing family-oriented attractions in Dover. Tours are offered at the circa-1792 Old State House, which is the second-oldest seat of government in continuous use.

BASICS

Operated By: Private operator. **Open:** Apr. 1–Nov. 15. **Site Assignment:** Reservations and walk-ins accepted; refunds (minus $2) w/ 2-day notice. **Registration:** At campground office. **Fee:** $37.50–$46; V, MC. **Parking:** At site.

FACILITIES

Number of RV-only Sites: 200. **Number of Tent-only Sites:** 150. **Number of Multipurpose Sites:** 150. **Hookups:** Electric (20, 30, 50 amps), water, cable TV. **Each Site:** Fire ring, picnic table. **Dump Station:** Yes. **Laundry:** Yes. **Pay Phone:** No. **Restrooms and Showers:** Yes. **Fuel:** No. **Propane:** Yes. **Internal Roads:** Paved & dirt, in good condition. **RV Service:** No. **Market:** W/in 5 mi. **Restaurant:** W/in 2 mi. **General Store:** Yes. **Vending:** Yes. **Swimming:** Yes. **Playground:** Yes. **Other:** 3 concrete-floored pavilions, Choptank River. **Activities:** Fishing, canoeing, kayaking, mini-golf, rec hall, game room, basketball, shuffleboard, planned activities on weekends, movies, tennis, sports field, badminton, hiking trails, horseshoes, volleyball. **Nearby Attractions:** Choptank River, Del-Mar-Va Peninsula, Chesapeake Bay, Dover (DE), Museum of Small Town Life, Old State House, Delaware

Archaeology Museum. **Additional Information:** Maryland Office of Tourism Development, (800) 543-1036, www.mdisfun.org.

RESTRICTIONS

Pets: On leash only. **Fires:** At site. **Alcoholic Beverages:** At site. **Vehicle Maximum Length:** 50 ft.

TO GET THERE

From Hwy. 313, go 0.25 mi. east on Hwy. 314, 0.1 mi. north on Wothers Rd., 0.75 mi. east on Boyce Mill Rd., and 2 mi. north on Drapers Mill Rd. Entrance is on the left.

HAGERSTOWN   MAP, A-1
Fort Frederick State Park

11100 Fort Frederick Rd., 21711. T: (301) 842-2155 or (888) 432-2267; www.dnr.state.md.us.

🚐 ★★★   ▲ ★★★★

Beauty: ★★★★	Site Privacy: ★★★
Spaciousness: ★★★	Quiet: ★★★★
Security: ★★★★	Cleanliness: ★★★★
Insect Control: ★★★★	Facilities: ★★★

Fort Frederick State Park adjoins the Potomac River, and the Chesapeake and Ohio Canal passes through park grounds. Built in 1756, Fort Frederick was unique because of its large size and strong stone wall. Most other forts of the period were built of wood and earth. Camping at the park is a rustic experience as there are no electric hookups, showers, or dump station. Located at the south end of the park between Big Pool (a lake) and the Potomac River, the campground does have a store. Also, souvenirs and food are sold at Captain Wort's Sutler Shop at the visitors center, where campers can rent rowboats and canoes for use in Big Pool only. The fort is north of the campground and is accessible by road. Exploring the park by foot is simple with two marked pathways, the 0.75-mile Plantation Trail and the 0.3-mile Wetlands Trail.

BASICS

Operated By: State of Maryland. **Open:** Mar. 5–Oct. 23. **Site Assignment:** Reservations accepted May 1–Sept. 30; remaining dates are first come, first served; refunds (minus $6 per night) given w/ 24-hour notice; late cancellations are subject to 1-night fee plus $6 per night. **Registration:** At campground office. **Fee:** $15; cash, check. **Parking:** At site.

FACILITIES

Number of RV-only Sites: 29. **Hookups:** None. **Each Site:** Fire ring, picnic table. **Dump Station:** No. **Laundry:** No. **Pay Phone:** Yes. **Restrooms and Showers:** Restrooms, no showers. **Fuel:** No. **Propane:** No. **Internal Roads:** Paved, in good condition. **RV Service:** No. **Market:** W/in 10 mi. **Restaurant:** W/in 8 mi. **General Store:** Yes. **Vending:** No. **Playground:** Yes. **Other:** Fort Frederick. **Activities:** Hiking trails, biking, boating, canoeing, boat rentals, fishing, historical tours. **Nearby Attractions:** Fort Frederick, Antietam National Battlefield, Hagerstown Roundhouse Museum, Washington County Museum of Fine Arts, Harper's Ferry (WV), Chesapeake and Ohio Canal National Historical Park. **Additional Information:** Hagerstown/Washington County Tourism Office, (800) 228-7829, www.marylandmemories.org.

RESTRICTIONS

Pets: On leash only. **Fires:** At site. **Alcoholic Beverages:** At site. **Vehicle Maximum Length:** 35 ft. **Other:** 14-day stay limit.

TO GET THERE

From Hagerstown, go 18 mi. west on I-70 to Exit 12 and 1 mi. south on Hwy. 56. Follow signs to the campground.

HAGERSTOWN   MAP, A-1
Greenbrier State Park

21843 National Pike, 21713. T: (301) 791-4767 or (888) 432-2267; www.dnr.state.md.us.

🚐 ★★★★   ▲ ★★★★

Beauty: ★★★★	Site Privacy: ★★★
Spaciousness: ★★★★	Quiet: ★★★★
Security: ★★★★	Cleanliness: ★★★★
Insect Control: ★★★★	Facilities: ★★★★

Ten miles east of Hagerstown, Greenbrier State Park is highlighted by an impressive network of hiking trails and the 42-acre Greenbrier Lake. Greenbrier is nestled in the Appalachian Mountains, and a portion of the Appalachian Trail enters the eastern edge of the park on Bartman's Hill, or South Mountain. Visitors can rent rowboats and canoes at a boat launch on the Greenbrier River. Greenbrier also has a beach and a lifeguard-monitored swimming area. The campground is located south of Greenbrier Lake, and sites are arranged in four loops, each with bathhouses. This campground—which has a dump station, a store, and showers—offers more amenities than the camping area at Fort Frederick State Park. The Dogwood Loop, which is the southernmost cluster of sites, offers the most solitude. All sites on the Cedar Loop, which is near several hiking trails and a hunting area, have electric hookups. A lakeside hiking trail sprouts from the Ash Loop.

BASICS

Operated By: State of Maryland. **Open:** Mar. 29–Oct. 29. **Site Assignment:** Reservations accepted (full payment due at time of booking when using credit card); walk-ins accepted; refunds (minus $6 per night) given w/ 24-hour notice; late cancellations are subject to 1-night fee plus $6 per night. **Registration:** At campground office. **Fee:** $25–$30; V, MC. **Parking:** At site.

FACILITIES

Number of Multipurpose Sites: 165. **Hookups:** Electric (20 amps). **Each Site:** Fire ring, picnic table. **Dump Station:** Yes. **Laundry:** No. **Pay Phone:** Yes. **Restrooms and Showers:** Yes. **Fuel:** No. **Propane:** No. **Internal Roads:** Gravel & paved, in good condition. **RV Service:** No. **Market:** W/in 6 mi. **Restaurant:** W/in 4 mi. **General Store:** Yes. **Vending:** Yes. **Playground:** Yes. **Other:** Greenbrier Lake, cabin rentals. **Activities:** Lake fishing and swimming, boating, canoeing, boat rentals, hiking trails, planned activities. **Nearby Attractions:** Fort Frederick, Antietam National Battlefield, Hagerstown Roundhouse Museum, Washington County Museum of Fine Arts, Harper's Ferry (WV), Chesapeake and Ohio Canal National Historical Park. **Additional Information:** Hagerstown/Washington County Tourism Office,

(800) 228-7829, www.marylandmemories.org.

RESTRICTIONS

Pets: Not allowed. **Fires:** At site. **Alcoholic Beverages:** Alcohol permitted except on beach. **Vehicle Maximum Length:** 29 ft. **Other:** 14-day stay limit.

TO GET THERE

From Hagerstown, go 8 mi. east on US 40. Follow signs to campground.

HAGERSTOWN   MAP, A-1
Snug Harbor KOA

11759 Snug Harbor Ln., 21795. T: (301) 223-7571 or (800) 562-7607; www.koa.com.

🚐 ★★★★   ▲ ★★★★

Beauty: ★★★★	Site Privacy: ★★★
Spaciousness: ★★★	Quiet: ★★★★
Security: ★★★★★	Cleanliness: ★★★★
Insect Control: ★★★★	Facilities: ★★★★

Nestled on the banks of the historic Conococheague Creek in the rolling hills of western Maryland, Snug Harbor KOA is convenient to several history-rich Civil War sites, including Gettysburg, Harper's Ferry (WV), and Antietam National Battlefield. Campers have their choice of open and shaded sites, some of which are situated along the creek. There are 20 pull-throughs and 43 full-hookup sites. Guests can cast their lines and paddle a canoe on the creek. The campground has a heated pool, a mini-golf course, and wooded hiking trails. A portion of the Appalachian Trail passes near the campground. There are also hiking trails along the Chesapeake and Ohio Canal National Park, and at Fort Frederick and Greenbrier state parks. Of course, many campers use this KOA as a base to visit Civil War sites at Antietam, Harper's Ferry, and even Gettysburg.

BASICS

Operated By: John and Judi Durham. **Open:** Mar. 15–Dec. 3. **Site Assignment:** Reservations accepted (1-night deposit required); walk-ins accepted; refund (minus $5) w/ 48-hour notice. **Registration:** At campground office. **Fee:** $28–$48; V, MC, AE, D. **Parking:** At site.

FACILITIES

Number of RV-only Sites: 92. **Number of Tent-only Sites:** 17. **Hookups:** Electric (20, 30, 50 amps), water, Wi-Fi. **Each Site:** Fire ring, picnic table. **Dump Station:** Yes. **Laundry:** Yes. **Pay Phone:** Yes. **Restrooms and Showers:** Yes. **Fuel:** No. **Propane:** Yes. **Internal Roads:** Paved & dirt, in fair condition. **RV Service:** No. **Market:** W/in 3 mi. **Restaurant:** W/in 3 mi. **General Store:** Yes. **Vending:** Yes. **Swimming:** Yes. **Playground:** Yes. **Other:** Conococheague Creek, cabin rentals. Haunted house in Oct. **Activities:** Boating, canoeing, canoe rentals, river fishing, mini-golf, rec hall, game room, badminton, planned activities on weekends, hiking trails, volleyball, horseshoes. **Nearby Attractions:** Fort Frederick, Antietam National Battlefield, Hagerstown Roundhouse Museum, Washington County Museum of Fine Arts, Harper's Ferry (WV), Chesapeake and Ohio Canal National Historical Park, Gettysburg. **Additional Information:**

Hagerstown/Washington County Tourism Office, (800) 228-7829, www.marylandmemories.org.

RESTRICTIONS

Pets: On leash only, under control. **Fires:** At site. **Alcoholic Beverages:** At site. **Vehicle Maximum Length:** 60 ft. **Other:** No refunds; credits are given.

TO GET THERE

From I-81, go 1.5 mi. west on I-70, 0.25 mi. south on Hwy. 63, 2.5 mi. west on Kemps Mill Rd. Entrance is on the right.

HAGERSTOWN   MAP, A-1
Yogi Bear's Jellystone Park

16519 Lappans Rd., 21795. T: (301) 223-7117 or (800) 421-7116; www.jellystonemaryland.com.

🚐 ★★★★   ⛺ ★★★★

Beauty: ★★★★   Site Privacy: ★★★★
Spaciousness: ★★★★   Quiet: ★★★★★
Security: ★★★★   Cleanliness: ★★★★
Insect Control: ★★★★   Facilities: ★★★★★

Located in western Maryland near Hagerstown, Yogi Bear's Jellystone Park at Williamsport/Hagerstown was named the chain's facility of the year in 2000. The wealth of recreational activities—and the cleanliness and appearance of the facilities—indicate why this honor was bestowed. Though this park is not located along the water like nearby Snug Harbor KOA, it does have 50-plus acres of forest and meadow trails for hiking and biking. 50 spacious pull-through sites are located at the northeast side of the campground. A wooded tent-only area is situated at the northwest end. If you prefer to camp near most of the activity centers, the sites along Deer Trail, Piney Woods, and Jellystone Parkway are recommended. This campground has a nice selection of well-maintained cabins for those without an RV or tent. Overall, 60 sites accommodate double and triple slideouts. Guided bus tours of our nation's capital embark from the campground on Saturdays and Sundays in season.

BASICS

Operated By: Vicki and Ron Vitkun. **Open:** All year. **Site Assignment:** Reservations accepted (1-night deposit required; 3-night minimum on holiday weekends); walk-ins accepted. **Registration:** At campground office. **Fee:** $20–$72; V, MC, D. **Parking:** At site.

FACILITIES

Number of RV-only Sites: 131. **Number of Tent-only Sites:** 28. **Hookups:** Electric (30, 50 amps), water, cable TV. **Each Site:** Fire ring, picnic table. **Dump Station:** Yes. **Laundry:** Yes. **Pay Phone:** Yes. **Restrooms and Showers:** Yes. **Fuel:** No. **Propane:** Yes. **Internal Roads:** Gravel & paved, in good condition. **RV Service:** No. **Market:** W/in 3 mi. **Restaurant:** W/in 3 mi. **General Store:** Yes. **Vending:** Yes. **Swimming:** Yes. **Playground:** Yes. **Other:** Cabin rentals, Washington, D.C. tours. **Activities:** Kiddie pool plus swimming pool, game room, rec hall, basketball, mini-golf, bike rentals, planned activities, movies,

hiking trails, horseshoes, volleyball. **Nearby Attractions:** Fort Frederick, Antietam National Battlefield, Hagerstown Roundhouse Museum, Washington County Museum of Fine Arts, Harper's Ferry (WV), Chesapeake and Ohio Canal National Historical Park, Gettysburg. **Additional Information:** Hagerstown/Washington County Tourism Office, (800) 228-7829, www.marylandmemories.org.

RESTRICTIONS

Pets: On leash only. No pets permitted in cabins. **Fires:** At site. **Alcoholic Beverages:** At site. **Vehicle Maximum Length:** No limit.

TO GET THERE

From I-81, go 1 mi. east on Hwy. 68. Entrance is on the right.

HAVRE DE GRACE   MAP, A-3
Susquehanna State Park

3318 Rocks Chrome Hill Rd., 21084. T: (410) 557-7994 or (888) 432-2267; www.dnr.state.md.us.

🚐 ★★★   ⛺ ★★★★

Beauty: ★★★★   Site Privacy: ★★★
Spaciousness: ★★★   Quiet: ★★★★
Security: ★★★★   Cleanliness: ★★★★
Insect Control: ★★★★   Facilities: ★★★

Located along the densely forested Susquehanna River Valley at Chesapeake Bay, Susquehanna State Park is home to some of the most popular mountain biking trails in Maryland. Overall, there are 15 miles of marked trails in the park. The boat launch offers access to the river and the headwaters of Chesapeake Bay. Pike, perch, bass, catfish and carp are abundant in the Susquehanna. The campground is divided into the Beechnut and Acorn loops, both of which surround bathhouses with hot showers. Six sites on the Acorn loop have electric hookups. The remnants of the Susquehanna Tidewater Canal can be seen as it parallels the river from Havre de Grace to Wrightsville (PA). Tours of the Rock Run Historic Area are conducted May to September. Susquehanna State Park is also home to the privately operated Steppingstone Museum, which includes exhibits of antique farm implements, a woodwright's shop, a blacksmith shop, a decoy carving shop, and a restored farm house.

BASICS

Operated By: State of Maryland. **Open:** Apr. 28–Sept. 25. **Site Assignment:** Reservations accepted (2-night minimum Memorial Day–Labor Day); walk-ins accepted. **Registration:** At campground office. **Fee:** $20–$25; V, MC. **Parking:** At site.

FACILITIES

Number of RV-only Sites: 69. **Hookups:** Electric (20 amps). **Each Site:** Fire ring, picnic table. **Dump Station:** Yes. **Laundry:** No. **Pay Phone:** Yes. **Restrooms and Showers:** Yes. **Fuel:** No. **Propane:** No. **Internal Roads:** Paved, in good condition. **RV Service:** No. **Market:** W/in 4 mi. **Restaurant:** W/in 4 mi. **General Store:** No. **Vending:** No. **Swimming:** No. **Playground:** Yes. **Other:** Susquehanna River, Steppingstone Museum. **Activities:** River fishing and swimming, planned activities,

historic buildings, boating, canoeing, hiking trails. **Nearby Attractions:** Concord Point Lighthouse, Decoy Museum, Chesapeake Bay, Baltimore, Wilmington (DE). **Additional Information:** Havre de Grace Chamber of Commerce, (800) 851-7756, www.hdstourism.com.

RESTRICTIONS

Pets: On leash only. **Fires:** At site. **Alcoholic Beverages:** At site. **Vehicle Maximum Length:** 29 ft. **Other:** 14-day stay limit.

TO GET THERE

From Havre de Grace, go 3 mi. north on Hwy. 155. Follow signs to the campground.

LOTHIAN   MAP, B-3
Duncan's Family Campground

5381 Sands Rd., 20711. T: (410) 741-9558 or (800) 222-2086; www.duncansfamilycampground.com.

🚐 ★★★★   ⛺ ★★★★

Beauty: ★★★   Site Privacy: ★★
Spaciousness: ★★★   Quiet: ★★★
Security: ★★★★   Cleanliness: ★★★★
Insect Control: ★★★★   Facilities: ★★★★

Located a half-hour southeast of Washington, D.C., Duncan's Family Campground is also a half-hour southwest of Annapolis and less than an hour south of Baltimore. Campsites are wooded, and there are 200 pull-throughs. This is a campground that caters to families. Duncan's makes it easy for campers to reach Washington, D.C. The campground offers a shuttle to the nearby DC Metrorail. Also, tour buses depart for DC directly from Duncan's. If you do not take the guided bus tour from the campground, there are numerous guided tours of DC available in the city. Taking either the bus tour from Duncan's or the shuttle to the Metrorail is recommended. Driving in DC is often challenging to say the least, especially for a first-time visitor.

BASICS

Operated By: Private operator. **Open:** All year. **Site Assignment:** Reservations accepted (1-night deposit required); walk-ins accepted. **Registration:** At campground office. **Fee:** $24–$44; V, MC. **Parking:** At site.

FACILITIES

Number of RV-only Sites: 147. **Number of Tent-only Sites:** 99. **Hookups:** Electric (20, 30, 50 amps), water, sewer; 120 full hookups, cable TV, Wi-Fi. **Each Site:** Picnic tables, grills. **Dump Station:** Yes. **Laundry:** Yes. **Pay Phone:** Yes. **Restrooms and Showers:** Yes. **Fuel:** No. **Propane:** Yes. **Internal Roads:** Gravel & paved, in good condition. **RV Service:** No. **Market:** W/in 8 mi. **Restaurant:** W/in 7 mi. **General Store:** Yes. **Vending:** Yes. **Swimming:** Yes. **Playground:** Yes. **Other:** Washington, D.C. tours, free shuttle to Metrorail. **Activities:** Swimming, kiddie pool, game room, rec hall, mini-golf, basketball, movies, planned activities on weekends, horseshoes, volleyball, hiking trails. **Nearby Attractions:** Washington, D.C., Six Flags, Chesapeake Bay, Baltimore, Annapolis, U.S. Naval Academy. **Additional Information:** Maryland Office of Tourism Development, (800) 543-1036, www.mdisfun.org.

RESTRICTIONS

Pets: On leash only. Small pets only. **Fires:** At site. **Alcoholic Beverages:** At site, under control. **Vehicle Maximum Length:** 40 ft.

TO GET THERE

From US 301, go 2 mi. southeast on Hwy. 4, 0.5 mi. on Hwy. 408, and 0.25 mi. north on Sands Rd. Entrance is on the right.

NANTICOKE   MAP, C-3
Roaring Point Waterfront Campground

2316 Nanticoke Wharf Rd., P.O. Box 80, 21840. T: (410) 873-2553; www.roaringpoint.com.

🚐 ★★★★   ⛺ ★★★★

Beauty: ★★★★	Site Privacy: ★★
Spaciousness: ★★★	Quiet: ★★★
Security: ★★★★	Cleanliness: ★★★★
Insect Control: ★★★★	Facilities: ★★★★

Overlooking the Nanticoke River and Tangier Sound, secluded Roaring Point Waterfront offers shaded sites along the waterfront and in a grassy area near the playgrounds, bathhouse, and laundry facilities. The sites are all back-in. Some tent sites have a waterfront view of Tangier Sound, where campers can swim and fish. Crab is king in Maryland, and Roaring Point rents crabbing equipment for use on the 135-foot-long fishing and crabbing pier. Though Roaring Point does not have a swimming pool, it does have a sandy beach and saltwater swimming area. Also, there are many biking-friendly roads in the area surrounding the campground, but be sure to bring your own wheels. The campground rents boats, but not bicycles. Roaring Point is about 15 miles southwest of Salisbury, near points of interest like the Salisbury Zoo and Furnace Town—an 1840s village with blacksmith, broom-making shops, and other historic structures.

BASICS

Operated By: Private operator. **Open:** Apr. 1–Nov. 1. **Site Assignment:** Reservations accepted (deposit of one-third of total fee required); walk-ins accepted; refunds (minus fee for checks w/ 1-week notice); no cash refunds. **Registration:** At campground office. **Fee:** $25–$40; V, MC, D, check. **Parking:** At site.

FACILITIES

Number of Tent-only Sites: 25. **Number of Multipurpose Sites:** 150. **Hookups:** Electric (30, 50 amps), water, sewer; 82 full hookups. **Each Site:** Fire ring, picnic table. **Dump Station:** Yes. **Laundry:** Yes. **Pay Phone:** Yes. **Restrooms and Showers:** Yes. **Fuel:** No. **Propane:** Yes. **Internal Roads:** Gravel, in good condition. **RV Service:** No. **Market:** W/in 3 mi. **Restaurant:** W/in 5 mi. **General Store:** Yes. **Vending:** Yes. **Swimming:** No. **Playground:** Yes. **Other:** Nanticoke River, Tangier Sound. **Activities:** Saltwater swimming and fishing, boating, rowboat and sailboat rentals, basketball, planned activities on weekends, volleyball, hiking trails, horseshoes, badminton, game room, rec hall. **Nearby Attractions:** Smith Island and Tangier Island boat cruises, Ward

Museum of Wildfowl Art, Furnace Town, Salisbury City Zoo, Assateague Island National Seashore, Chincoteague National Wildlife Refuge, Chesapeake Bay, Ocean City. **Additional Information:** Maryland Office of Tourism Development, (800) 543-1036, www.mdisfun.org.

RESTRICTIONS

Pets: On leash only. **Fires:** Fire ring only. **Alcoholic Beverages:** At site. **Vehicle Maximum Length:** 40 ft. **Other:** 2 vehicles in addition to camping unit allowed per campsite; additional vehicles must be parked in storage area.

TO GET THERE

From US 50, go 22 mi. south on Hwy. 349. Entrance is on the right.

OAKLAND   MAP, C-1
Deep Creek Lake State Park

898 State Park Rd., 21561. T: (301) 387-5563 or (888) 432-2267; www.dnr.state.md.us.

🚐 ★★★★   ⛺ ★★★★

Beauty: ★★★★	Site Privacy: ★★★
Spaciousness: ★★	Quiet: ★★★★
Security: ★★★★	Cleanliness: ★★★★
Insect Control: ★★★★	Facilities: ★★★★

Located at the southernmost end of Meadow Mountain on the far western tip of Maryland, Deep Creek Lake State Park features a mile of shoreline along 3,900-acre Deep Creek Lake, the largest lake in Maryland. A boat launch, swimming area, and picnicking area are located along the shore in the park. Meadow Mountain campground is located at the southwest end of the park, near lots of hiking trails and within a short drive of Deep Creek Lake. Sites are clustered around four main loops, each with a bathhouse. The sites are all back-in. The Deep Creek Lake Discovery Center, an interpretive environmental museum, is nestled on the shore of Deep Creek Lake in the park. The Discovery Center offers hands-on exhibits that showcase the fauna, wildlife, and cultural and historical heritage of western Maryland. Garrett County, where Deep Creek Lake is located, boasts the highest peak in Maryland—3,360-foot Backbone Mountain.

BASICS

Operated By: State of Maryland. **Open:** Apr. 28–Oct. 16. **Site Assignment:** Reservations and walk-ins accepted; refunds (minus $6 per night) given w/ 24-hour notice; late cancellations are subject to 1-night fee plus $6 per night. **Registration:** At campground office. **Fee:** $25–$30; V, MC. **Parking:** At site.

FACILITIES

Number of RV-only Sites: 60. **Number of Tent-only Sites:** 52. **Hookups:** Electric (30 amps). **Each Site:** Fire ring & picnic table, lantern post. **Dump Station:** Yes. **Laundry:** No. **Pay Phone:** Yes. **Restrooms and Showers:** Yes. **Fuel:** No. **Propane:** No. **Internal Roads:** Paved, in good condition. **RV Service:** No. **Market:** W/in 9 mi. **Restaurant:** W/in 9 mi. **General Store:** No. **Vending:** No. **Swimming:** Yes. **Playground:** Yes. **Other:** Deep Creek Lake Discovery Center. **Activities:** Lake swimming and fishing, hiking trails, boating,

canoeing, rowboat rentals, planned activities. **Nearby Attractions:** Backbone Mountain, Garrett State Forest, Potomac State Forest, Swallow Falls State Park. **Additional Information:** Garrett County Chamber of Commerce, (301) 334-1948, www.garrettchamber.com.

RESTRICTIONS

Pets: Allowed in designated loops. **Fires:** Fire ring only. **Alcoholic Beverages:** At site. **Vehicle Maximum Length:** 28 ft. **Other:** 14-day stay limit.

TO GET THERE

From Oakland, go 10 mi. north on US 219 and 2 mi. northeast on Glendale Bridge Rd. Follow signs to campground.

OCEAN CITY   MAP, C-4
Frontier Town Campground

P.O. Box 691, 21843-0691. T: (410) 641-0880 or (800) 228-5590; www.frontiertown.com.

🚐 ★★★★   ⛺ ★★★★

Beauty: ★★★★★	Site Privacy: ★★
Spaciousness: ★★★	Quiet: ★★★
Security: ★★★★★	Cleanliness: ★★★★
Insect Control: ★★★★	Facilities: ★★★★★

Perched along Sinepuxent Bay five minutes from Assateague Island National Seashore, Frontier Town Campground is hands-down the mid-Atlantic's finest family-oriented campground. The campground alone would be attractive to visitors, but Frontier Town also includes a water park, a 38-acre wild west town, and an immaculately landscaped mini-golf course. Sites along AA, BB, and Z lanes are situated on the bay. Sites at the northern end are near the swimming pool, lagoon, marina, basketball and volleyball courts, and the crabbing and fishing pier. The Wild West Show encompasses a 38-acre, circa-1860 recreated western town, with shops, eateries, stage coach, and steam-train rides, water park, horseback rides for adults and pony rides for youngsters, gun fights and bank holdups, and Native American ceremonial dancing among other activities. Cowboy Mini-Golf features 18 holes amid a setting of waterfalls and flowers. Lastly, there's a free shuttle from the campground to Ocean City and Assateague Island beaches.

BASICS

Operated By: Private operator. **Open:** Apr. 15–Oct. 22. **Site Assignment:** Reservations recommended ($45 per site, $25 in spring and fall); walk-ins accepted; refund w/ 7-day notice. **Registration:** At campground headquarters. **Fee:** $25–$53; V, MC. **Parking:** At site.

FACILITIES

Number of RV-only Sites: 475. **Number of Tent-only Sites:** 75. **Hookups:** Electric (30, 50 amps), water, cable TV. **Each Site:** Fire ring, picnic table. **Dump Station:** Yes. **Laundry:** Yes. **Pay Phone:** Yes. **Restrooms and Showers:** Yes. **Fuel:** No. **Propane:** Yes. **Internal Roads:** Gravel & paved, in fair condition. **RV Service:** No. **Market:** W/in 4 mi. **Restaurant:** On premises. **General Store:** Yes. **Vending:** Yes. **Swimming:** Yes. **Playground:** Yes. **Other:** Frontier Town Water Park, Frontier Town Wild West Show. **Activities:** Wading pool and swimming pool, boating, canoeing, kayaking, motor boat rentals, mini-golf, saltwater fishing, shuffleboard, basketball, hiking trails, volleyball, horseshoes, planned activities, movies. **Nearby Attractions:** Ocean City boardwalk attractions and beaches, Assateague Island National Seashore, Chincoteague National Wildlife Refuge, golf courses. **Additional Information:** Ocean City Chamber of Commerce, (410) 213-0552, www.oceancity.org.

RESTRICTIONS

Pets: On leash only; must have valid rabies tags. **Fires:** At site; 8 a.m.–midnight. **Alcoholic Beverages:** At site, under control. **Vehicle Maximum Length:** 45 ft. **Other:** Quiet time 11 p.m.–8 a.m.; do not leave pets or fires unattended.

TO GET THERE

From Hwy. 528, go 1 mi. west on US 50 and 4 mi. south on Hwy. 611. Entrance is on the left.

SCOTLAND   MAP, C-3
Point Lookout State Park

P.O. Box 48, 11175 Point Lookout Rd., 20687. T: (301) 872-5688 or (888) 432-2267; www.dnr.state.md.us.

🚐 ★★★★   ▲ ★★★★

Beauty: ★★★★	Site Privacy: ★★★
Spaciousness: ★★★	Quiet: ★★★★
Security: ★★★★	Cleanliness: ★★★★
Insect Control: ★★★	Facilities: ★★★★

Situated on a peninsula at the confluence of the Potomac River and Chesapeake Bay, southern Maryland's Point Lookout State Park is a haven for water sports and Civil War history. A lighthouse, built in 1830 and now owned by the U.S. Navy, still sits at the tip of the point. The original earthworks and recreated structures of Civil War–era Fort Lincoln are on the river shore near Cornfield Harbor. Of the campground's 143 wooded sites, 26 have full hookups—a pleasant convenience at a park with so many recreational and historical points of interest. Campsites are arranged on five loops which are nestled between Point Lookout Creek (west), Tanner's Creek (east), and Lake Conoy (south). Point Lookout has three fishing areas, including a 710-foot fishing pier; there's also a boat launch, boat rentals, and several hiking trails.

BASICS

Operated By: State of Maryland. **Open:** All year. **Site Assignment:** Reservations and walk-ins accepted; refunds (minus $6 per night) given w/ 24-hour notice; late cancellations are subject to 1-night fee plus $6 per night. **Registration:** At campground office. **Fee:** $25–$40; V, MC. **Parking:** At site.

FACILITIES

Number of RV-only Sites: 143. **Number of Tent-only Sites:** 3. **Hookups:** Electric (20, 30 amps); 26 full hookups. **Each Site:** Fire ring, picnic table. **Dump Station:** Yes. **Laundry:** Yes. **Pay Phone:** Yes. **Restrooms and Showers:** Yes. **Fuel:** No. **Propane:** No. **Internal Roads:** Paved, in good condition. **RV Service:** No. **Market:** W/in 5 mi. **Restaurant:** W/in 5 mi. **General Store:** Yes. **Vending:** No. **Swimming:** Yes. **Playground:** Yes. **Other:**

Potomac River, Chesapeake Bay, 2 creeks, lake, cabins, pavilion, cottages. **Activities:** Saltwater and freshwater fishing, boating, canoeing, boat rentals, freshwater swimming, hiking trails, planned activities. **Nearby Attractions:** Point Lookout Lighthouse, Civil War Museum, Confederate Cemetery, Potomac River, Chesapeake Bay, Washington, D.C. **Additional Information:** Maryland Office of Tourism Development, (800) 543-1036, www.mdisfun.org.

RESTRICTIONS

Pets: In designated loops. **Fires:** At site. **Alcoholic Beverages:** At site. **Vehicle Maximum Length:** 45 ft. **Other:** 14-day stay limit.

TO GET THERE

From Scotland's business center, go 4 mi. south on Hwy. 5. Follow signs to the campground.

THURMONT   MAP, A-2
Cunningham Falls State Park

14039 Catoctin Hollow Rd., 21788. T: (301) 271-7574 or (888) 432-2267; www.dnr.state.md.us.

🚐 ★★★   ▲ ★★★★

Beauty: ★★★★	Site Privacy: ★★★★
Spaciousness: ★★★★	Quiet: ★★★★
Security: ★★★★	Cleanliness: ★★★★
Insect Control: ★★★	Facilities: ★★★★

Nestled in northern Maryland's Catoctin Mountains, Cunningham Falls State Park is named for its 78-foot cascading waterfall, located a half-mile from Big Hunting Creek in the park's Houck Area and accessible by the Falls Trail. There are two main developed sections at Cunningham Falls, the Houck Area and the Manor Area. Camping areas are located in both; Houck has 119 sites and Manor has 31 sites. Each loop has a bathhouse with showers and flush toilets. Campsites with electric hookups are situated in Addison Run Circle and Deer Spring Branch Circle in the Houck Area, and at sites 6–10 and 15–21 in the Manor Area. Drinking water spigots are placed throughout each loop. A dump station is located in the Houck Area near the camp office. There are nine hiking trails which venture through Cunningham Falls and Catoctin Mountain National Park. Big Hunting Creek offers catch-and-release trout fishing and boating.

BASICS

Operated By: State of Maryland. **Open:** May 1–Oct. **Site Assignment:** Reservations accepted May 1–Oct.; full deposit (cash, credit card); refunds (minus $6 per night) given w/ 24-hour notice; late cancellations are subject to 1-night fee plus $6 per night. **Registration:** At campground office. **Fee:** $25–$30; V, MC. **Parking:** At site.

FACILITIES

Number of Multipurpose Sites: 149. **Hookups:** Electric (30 amps). **Each Site:** Fire ring, picnic table. **Dump Station:** Yes. **Laundry:** No. **Pay Phone:** Yes. **Restrooms and Showers:** Yes. **Fuel:** No. **Propane:** No. **Internal Roads:** Paved, in good condition. **RV Service:** No. **Market:** W/in 3 mi. **Restaurant:** W/in 3 mi. **General Store:** Yes. **Vending:** Yes. **Swimming:** Yes. **Playground:** Yes. **Other:** Catoctin Furnace, Cunningham Falls. **Activities:**

Lake swimming and fishing, boating, canoe rentals, hiking trails, planned activities. **Nearby Attractions:** Catoctin Mountain National Park, Frederick, Monocacy National Battlefield, Francis Scott Key Museum, Harper's Ferry, Hagerstown. **Additional Information:** Tourism Council of Frederick County, (800) 999-3613, www.co.frederick.md.us.

RESTRICTIONS

Pets: Permitted in Manor Area only. **Fires:** At site. **Alcoholic Beverages:** At site. **Vehicle Maximum Length:** 30 ft. **Other:** 14-day stay limit.

TO GET THERE

To reach the Houck Area from Thurmont, go 3 mi. west on Hwy. 77 and follow signs. To reach the Manor Area from Thurmont, go 3 mi. south on US 15 and follow signs.

WHALEYVILLE   MAP, C-4
Fort Whaley Campground

11224 Dale Rd., 21872. T: (410) 641-9785; www.fortwhaley.com.

🚐 ★★★★   ▲ ★★★★

Beauty: ★★★★	Site Privacy: ★★★
Spaciousness: ★★★	Quiet: ★★★
Security: ★★★★	Cleanliness: ★★★★
Insect Control: ★★★★	Facilities: ★★★★

The sister park to Frontier Town Campground, Fort Whaley Campground is located in Whaleyville, about ten miles northwest of Ocean City. Fort Whaley campers are granted free admission to Frontier Town's water park and discounted admission to the wild west town. Like Frontier Town, Fort Whaley has a western theme. The swimming pool, mini-golf course, clubhouse and arcade, store, and office are near the park entrance. Sites along E Circle on Rayne Lake are our favorites. The lake is at the eastern end, and three clusters of sites are nearby. Primitive sites along G Lane and water and electric sites on A Lane are closest to most of the activity centers. Fort Whaley is a 15-minute drive from Ocean City's boardwalk attractions and beaches.

BASICS

Operated By: Private operator. **Open:** All year. **Site Assignment:** Reservations accepted ($75 deposit required, $25 for spring and fall); walk-ins accepted; refund w/ 7-day notice. **Registration:** At campground office. **Fee:** $31–$73; V, MC. **Parking:** At site.

FACILITIES

Number of RV-only Sites: 133. **Number of Tent-only Sites:** 32. **Hookups:** Electric (30, 50 amps), water, cable TV. **Each Site:** Fire ring, picnic table. **Dump Station:** Yes. **Laundry:** Yes. **Pay Phone:** Yes. **Restrooms and Showers:** Yes. **Fuel:** No. **Propane:** Yes. **Internal Roads:** Gravel & paved, in good condition. **RV Service:** No. **Market:** W/in 3 mi. **Restaurant:** W/in 3 mi. **General Store:** Yes. **Vending:** Yes. **Swimming:** Yes. **Playground:** Yes. **Other:** Fishing pond, free admission to Frontier Water Park, cabins available. **Activities:** Pond fishing, mini-golf, game room, rec hall, paddleboat rentals, basketball, shuffleboard, volleyball, horseshoes, movies, planned activities on weekends, sports field. **Nearby Attractions:**

Ocean City boardwalk attractions and beaches, Assateague Island National Seashore, Chincoteague National Wildlife Refuge, Rehoboth Beach (DE). **Additional Information:** Ocean City Chamber of Commerce, (410) 213-0552, www.oceancity.org.

RESTRICTIONS

Pets: On leash only, valid rabies tags required. **Fires:** At site. **Alcoholic Beverages:** At site. **Vehicle Maximum Length:** 45 ft. **Other:** Pets & fires may not be left unattended.

TO GET THERE

From US 50, go 0.25 mi. south on Hwy. 610. Entrance is on the left.

WILLIAMSPORT   MAP, A-1
Yogi Bear's Jellystone Park

16519 Lappans Rd., 21795. T: (800) 421-7116 or (301) 223-7117; www.reserveamerica.com.

🚐 ★★★★   ▲ ★★★★

Beauty: ★★★★	Site Privacy: ★★★★
Spaciousness: ★★★★	Quiet: ★★★★
Security: ★★★★	Cleanliness: ★★★★
Insect Control: ★★★★	Facilities: ★★★★

This is a very kid-friendly campground with numerous daily activities, so it gets completely packed on weekends. An older, heavily wooded area offers lots of privacy and quiet but may be more difficult to navigate because of large boulders and trees, while the newer sites are level and easily navigated but offer no shade or privacy. The campground is very clean and well maintained, all facilities are in good condition, and the staff is friendly and ready to help. Imagine the whole family racing down the 400-foot waterslides, playing a game of "down and dirty" kickball, and cooking dinner over an open fire. In the evening, you can practice your putting on the 18-hole minigolf course, kick up your heels at the street dance, or just sit back and enjoy the outdoor movie theater.

BASICS

Operated By: Ron and Vicki Vitkun. **Open:** All year. **Site Assignment:** Site requests accepted but not guaranteed. **Registration:** At ranger station;

night registration available after hours. **Fee:** Campsite, $20–$54; cabin, $50–$165; maximum 6 people per site; summer fee per person, $7 (includes all amenities). **Parking:** Limit 2 vehicles per site.

FACILITIES

Number of Multipurpose Sites: 185. **Hookups:** Water, electric (30, 50 amps), sewer, cable, wireless Internet. **Each Site:** Picnic table, fire ring. **Dump Station:** Yes. **Laundry:** Yes. **Pay Phone:** Yes. **Restrooms and Showers:** Yes. **Fuel:** No. **Propane:** Yes. **Internal Roads:** Paved, gravel. **RV Service:** 2 mi. south. **Market:** 5 mi. north. **Restaurant:** 5 mi north in Hagerstown. **General Store:** Yes. **Vending:** Yes. **Swimming:** 2 pools, 1 wading pool, 2- 400ft water slides. **Playground:** Yes. **Activities:** Planned activities daily in summer, weekends Apr–May and Sept–Nov., pedal carts, 22 ft. inflatable slide, moon bounce, hiking trails, mini-golf, basketball court, horseshoes, outdoor movie theater, snack bar. **Additional Information:** www.marylandmemories.com.

RESTRICTIONS

Pets: On leash only. **Fires:** Allowed in fire rings provided. **Alcoholic Beverages:** At site only. **Vehicle Maximum Length:** 80 ft. **Other:** Some monthly sites available.

TO GET THERE

From I-81, take Exit 1 in Maryland, Hwy. 68, go 1 mi. east, park is on your right.

WOODBINE   MAP, A-2
Ramblin' Pines Family Campground

801 Hoods Mill Rd., 21797. T: (410) 795-5161 or (800) 550-TREE; www.ramblinpines.com.

🚐 ★★★★   ▲ ★★★★

Beauty: ★★★★	Site Privacy: ★★★
Spaciousness: ★★★★	Quiet: ★★★★
Security: ★★★★★	Cleanliness: ★★★★
Insect Control: ★★★★	Facilities: ★★★★

Located about 45 minutes north of Washington, D.C., a half-hour west of Baltimore, and 20 minutes east of Frederick, Ramblin' Pines Family Campground is the type of park you prefer when looking for a sightseeing home base. The campground is in a

rural, tranquil area, and guests have their choice of wooded and open sites, each of which is equipped with a full hookup. Ramblin' Pines can accommodate 15 pull-throughs. Most people know about the multitude of attractions in Washington, D.C., and Baltimore; though lesser known, Frederick is an interesting city in its own right. Monocacy National Battlefield, located three miles south of the town, offers tours at the site of a Union victory in 1864.

BASICS

Operated By: Private operator. **Open:** All year. **Site Assignment:** Reservations accepted (2-night minimum on weekends, 3-night minimum on holiday weekends); walk-ins accepted; 1-night deposit; partial refund w/ 2-day notice. **Registration:** At campground office. **Fee:** $30–$42.50; V, MC. **Parking:** At site.

FACILITIES

Number of RV-only Sites: 200. **Number of Tent-only Sites:** 12. **Hookups:** Electric (30, 50 amps), water, phone, sewer, TV. **Each Site:** Fire ring, picnic table. **Dump Station:** Yes. **Laundry:** Yes. **Pay Phone:** No. **Restrooms and Showers:** Yes. **Fuel:** No. **Propane:** Yes. **Internal Roads:** Gravel & paved, in good condition. **RV Service:** No. **Market:** W/in 3 mi. **Restaurant:** W/in 3 mi. **General Store:** Yes. **Vending:** Yes. **Swimming:** Yes. **Playground:** Yes. **Other:** Fishing pond, cabin rentals, exercise room. **Activities:** Swimming, pond fishing, mini-golf, basketball, game room, lodge hall, shuffleboard, planned activities on weekends, hiking trails, volleyball, sports field, horseshoes. **Nearby Attractions:** Frederick, Baltimore, Hagerstown, Harper's Ferry (WV), Washington, D.C., Annapolis, Gettysburg. **Additional Information:** Maryland Office of Tourism Development, (800) 543-1036, www.mdisfun.org.

RESTRICTIONS

Pets: On leash only. **Fires:** Fire ring only. **Alcoholic Beverages:** At site, under control. **Vehicle Maximum Length:** 60 ft.

TO GET THERE

From I-70, take Exit 76 and go 2.5 mi. north on Hwy. 97 and 0.5 mi. northwest on Hoods Mill Rd. Entrance is on the left.

Massachusetts

What's really special about camping in Massachusetts? No matter where you choose to settle in for the night, you're never too far from history, cultural landmarks, museums, or the bustle of city life. It takes less than four hours to drive the width of the state—unless you're amazingly unlucky in traffic—so you could wake up in a woodsy rural campground in the **Berkshire Hills** and arrive in **Boston** in time for lunch. Here's a tip: ditch the rig first, and take the car into the city—all the better to navigate those cow paths turned cobblestone streets! Happily, there are several campgrounds within a 30-mile radius of Boston. Some offer bus tours of the city, and others are located near the commuter rail line, should you choose not to brave city traffic.

Although Massachusetts may not have a huge number of commercial campgrounds, those that do exist are generally clean and well-kept. Also, they tend to be clustered near desirable places to visit. For example, **Cape Ann Camp Site,** in **Gloucester,** overlooks the salt marshes of the **North Shore** and is a bike ride away from a lovely ocean beach. Fishing villages and art colonies are nearby, and so are whale-watching tours and sunset boat cruises. **Salem** is close as well, and the threat of an old-fashioned witch trial is always a good tool for quelling a traveler's unruly companions. All in all, it's a dandy place to enjoy some seaside ambiance.

Cape Cod is home to numerous campgrounds, some chockful of amenities, others all swaying sea boats and salt air. Even **Martha's Vineyard** is home to a campground—the aptly named **Martha's Vineyard Family Campground.** Located only 1.5 miles from the **Vineyard Haven** ferry terminal, it's a 45-minute ferry ride from **Woods Hole** across the **Vineyard Sound.** On arriving, travelers can rent bikes, mopeds, and autos to explore the island. Seventy-five miles of paved bike trails cross the island, and during the season, buses run every 30 minutes. Those wanting to bring along their own transportation will find that the ferry will accommodate most cars and trailers. The scenery is lovely, and nearby shops and restaurants help pass the time. Besides being surrounded by some of the most dazzling scenery in New England, campers on the Cape and islands are enjoying it all at a bargain (a word not heard frequently in these parts!).

The fact is, some of the most prime real estate in Massachusetts is open to campers. Twenty-eight state parks offer camping, and the settings are truly spectacular. Just steps away from **Buzzard's Bay,** settle in for the night behind a sand dune at one of Massachusett's most historical campsites, **Horseneck Beach State Reservation.** Farther north, **Salisbury Beach** offers nearly 500 campsites hugging the Atlantic Coast. These are wildly popular, so make a reservation early. Reservations for any state campground can be made by calling the same toll-free number (877) I-CAMP-MA (422-6762). Cyber-savvy travelers can make online reservations at www.state.ma.us/dem/forparks.htm.

For a totally different experience, check out the hidden gems in the western part of the state, the arts-and-theater mecca known as the **Berkshires.** Settled in the late 1700s, the Berkshires is a hilly region about 120 miles east of Boston. Comprised of 30 small, mainly rural towns, this area is classic New England. An upscale three-story building, lodging, and dining complex on 17 rural acres, the **1896 House** is a swank place to visit while exploring the Berkshires. Made up of two motels, a historic barn, and a renowned tavern and restaurant, the 1896 House is one of the nicest bed-and-breakfasts in all the East. Summer travelers should check out the **Tanglewood Jazz Festival**—a three-day event that has brought some in some pretty big names, including Dave Brubeck, Sonny Rollins, and Diana Krall. Besides all the culture you could ask for, this region offers wonderful hiking and paddling, plus glorious state parks. Deeply wooded, dotted with sapphire ponds, these campgrounds are a great choice for tent campers or RVers with self-contained units, who consider a pristine natural setting to be the ultimate amenity.

The camping season in Massachusetts generally runs from Memorial Day to Columbus Day.

Campground Profiles

BALDWINVILLE — MAP, A-2
Lake Dennison Recreation Area

reserve america

86 Winchendon Rd., 01436. T: (978) 939-8962; www.reserveamerica.com.

🚐 ★★★★   ⛺ ★★★★

Beauty: ★★★	Site Privacy: ★★★
Spaciousness: ★★★	Quiet: ★★★
Security: ★★	Cleanliness: ★★★★
Insect Control: ★★★	Facilities: ★★★

Located in North Central Massachusetts, 4,221-acre Lake Dennison offers wonderful wooded camping on the shores of an 85-acre lake as well as swimming, fishing, and a boat ramp for canoes and other non-power boats. The park also offers 50 miles of mountain biking trails in the adjacent Birch Hill Wildlife Management Area. Winter activities include snowmobiling and cross-country skiing. Whether swimming and boating in Lake Dennison, camping on its shores or on the shores of Beamon Pond, canoeing the Millers River to King Philip Rock, exploring the forest—this area is indeed a gem. With three habitat types—oak/hickory, northern hardwood, and pine—the 4,000 acres of forest are home to diverse wildflowers and birds. Lake Dennison is a section of the U.S. Army Corps of Engineers Birch Hill Flood Control Project. The DCR, via Otter River State Park staff, manages 4,221 acres of Corp land for recreational use. Located in Winchendon, the park has 150 campsites. There is a swimming beach on Lake Dennison.

BASICS
Operated By: Massachusetts State Parks. **Open:** May 24–Sept. 3. **Site Assignment:** Reservations can be made up to 6 months in advance. **Registration:** At office. **Fee:** Single, $12–$14; group, $25. **Parking:** 2 vehicles per campsite.

FACILITIES
Number of Multipurpose Sites: 153. **Hookups:** None. **Dump Station:** W/in 10 mi. **Laundry:** No. **Pay Phone:** W/in 10 mi. **Restrooms and Showers:** Yes. **Fuel:** No. **Propane:** No. **Internal Roads:** Paved. **RV Service:** No. **Market:** No. **Restaurant:** No. **General Store:** No. **Vending:** No. **Swimming:** Yes. **Playground:** No. **Activities:** Cross-country skiing, fishing, snowmobiling.

RESTRICTIONS
Pets: Keep pets leashed (10-ft. leash max.) at all times. Proof of rabies vaccination is required. Pets are never to be left unattended. **Fires:** Campfires in designated fireplaces. **Alcoholic Beverages:** Alcoholic beverages are prohibited in all MA state parks & campgrounds. **Other:** Quiet hours are 10 p.m.–7 a.m. No unnecessary or disturbing noise at any time. Equipment is limited to 2 tents or 1 camping vehicle & 1 small tent per site. Tents are limited to 300 square feet of combined floor space. Massachusetts law requires that children age 16 and under wear a helmet when bicycling.

TO GET THERE
From the east: Take Hwy. 2 west to Exit 20 then right on Baldwinville Rd. to the end. Go right onto Hwy. 202 north 3.7 mi. to park entrance on left. Look for 2nd Lake Dennison sign. From the west: Take Hwy. 2 east to Exit 19. Take Hwy. 202 north 7.5 mi. to park entrance on left. Look for 2nd Lake Dennison sign.

BALDWINVILLE — MAP, A-2
Otter River State Forest

reserve america

86 Winchendon Rd., 01436. T: (978) 939-8962; www.reserveamerica.com.

🚐 ★   ⛺ ★★★

Beauty: ★★★★	Site Privacy: ★★★
Spaciousness: ★★★	Quiet: ★★★★
Security: ★★★	Cleanliness: ★★★★★
Insect Control: ★★	Facilities: ★★

Located in a rural area along Hwy. 2, northwest of Boston, Otter River State Forest is notable as the first state forest established in Massachusetts (1915). Criss-crossed with rivers and streams, this wilderness area offers a clutch of campsites clustered near Beamon Pond. Along with its sister campground, Lake Dennison State Recreation Area, to the north, Otter River is a pleasant place to overnight near the beginning of the Mohawk Trail, a 63-mile scenic drive (and former Native American footpath) that officially starts in Orange. Heavily wooded, and very quiet, Otter River offers good hiking, including a section of the Ware River Rail Trail. Beamon Pond has a small, sandy beach and a concrete fishing bridge. Ranger programs, including kids' crafts, games, nature walks, movies, and bike rides, are run on weekends in summer. Lacking hookups, this campground is best for tent campers and pop-ups. Campsites are mostly gravel, softened with pine needles. Least-desirable sites are numbers 73–78, as they're small and close to the road. Sites 1–27 are open only to self-contained RVs. Site 62 is a great spot, near the beach, as is 81, very secluded on a dead end, but near the beach and showers and a water faucet. There's not a lot of action here, but this campground is a pleasant short-term nature escape, especially if combined with a visit to Lake Dennison State Recreation Area.

BASICS
Operated By: Massachusetts State Forests and Parks. **Open:** May 1–Columbus Day. **Site Assignment:** Reservations recommended; reserve up to 6 months in advance by calling Reserve America at (877) I-CAMP-MA or online at www.reserveamerica.com. About 20% of campsites are nonreservable and first come, first served; to change arrival or departure date, or site type, call at least 3 days prior to arrival date; $10 cancellation/transfer fee. **Registration:** At contact station. **Fee:** Massachusetts residents, $12; nonresidents, $14; V, MC. **Parking:** At site.

FACILITIES
Number of Multipurpose Sites: 85. **Hookups:** None. **Each Site:** Picnic table, fireplace. **Dump Station:** No. **Laundry:** No. **Pay Phone:** Yes. **Restrooms and Showers:** Yes. **Fuel:** No. **Propane:** No. **Internal Roads:** Paved, good condition. **RV Service:** No. **Market:** 5 mi. north, in Winchendon. **Restaurant:** 5 mi. north, in Winchendon. **General Store:** No. **Vending:** No. **Swimming:** Yes. **Playground:** No. **Other:** Interpretive Center. **Activities:** Hiking, nature walks, campfire programs, fishing, swimming. **Nearby Attractions:** Lake Dennison State Recreation Area, Mohawk Trail scenic drive. **Additional Information:** Central Massachusetts Tourist Council, (508) 755-7400, www.worcester.org.

RESTRICTIONS
Pets: Must be leashed & cleaned up after. Must not be left unattended. Proof of rabies vaccination required. **Fires:** Fireplaces only. **Alcoholic Beverages:** Not allowed. **Vehicle Maximum Length:** Sites are fairly small, & best for pop-ups & small rigs. **Other:** 14 cumulative day stay limit between Memorial Day & Labor Day.

TO GET THERE
Follow Hwy. 2 west to Exit 20 (Baldwinville Rd.) to Hwy. 202 north; follow signs.

BOURNE — MAP, B-4
Bay View Campgrounds

260 MacArthur Blvd., 02532. T: (508) 759-7610; www.bayviewcampground.com.

🚐 ★★★★   ⛺ ★★

Beauty: ★★★★	Site Privacy: ★★★
Spaciousness: ★★★★	Quiet: ★★
Security: ★★★★	Cleanliness: ★★★★★
Insect Control: ★★★	Facilities: ★★★★★

Located on the Upper Cape, just beyond the Bourne Bridge (one of two bridges that connect Cape Cod to the mainland), Bay View is about 60 percent seasonal. Don't let that put you off, though. This is a great spot for RV campers (tenters might find its location near the busy roadway a bit noisy) who want to enjoy the Cape Cod experience without driving the length of the Cape. They also sell tickets here for ferry boats to Martha's Vineyard and Nantucket, a nice convenience. Campsites are level, spacious, and semi-shaded; sites 155 through 160 are especially pleasant, and backed by woods. Number 59 is another good choice, big and level. We'd skip site 169, an elevated site with views of other RV's roofs. There's plenty to do here, from daily planned activities to a really elaborate, state-of-the-art arcade. Nice touches make a difference, including vanity lights around mirrors and a baby-changing table in the ladies' room, and good signage and trash bag dispensers throughout the campground. One quibble: the $10 per person guest fee is pretty pricey. Chalk it up to the desirability of the Cape.

BASICS

Operated By: Bay View Campground Inc. **Open:** May 1–Oct. 15. **Site Assignment:** Reservations recommended; call to reserve after Jan. 10; secure reservation w/ a nonrefundable deposit on V or MC; if stay is less than 1 week, a 1-night deposit is required; otherwise, 1-night deposit per week of stay; full balance required upon arrival in cash, traveler's checks, or credit card. **Registration:** At office. **Fee:** $34–$45; based on 2 adults; additional children under age 18, $3; additional adult, $10; V, MC. **Parking:** At site.

FACILITIES

Number of RV-only Sites: 425. **Hookups:** Electric (20, 30 amps), water, sewer, cable TV, modem (in office). **Each Site:** Picnic table, fireplace. **Dump Station:** Yes. **Laundry:** Yes. **Pay Phone:** Yes. **Restrooms and Showers:** Yes, coin-op. **Fuel:** No. **Propane:** Yes. **Internal Roads:** Paved, in good condition. **RV Service:** No. **Market:** 3 mi. north. **Restaurant:** Yes. **General Store:** Yes (snack bar). **Vending:** Yes. **Swimming:** Yes (2–3). **Playground:** Yes. **Other:** Rec hall, tennis courts, ice-cream parlor, coffee center. **Activities:** Swimming, tennis, volleyball, basketball, shuffleboard, horseshoes, ball field, planned activities. **Nearby Attractions:** Cape Cod beaches, boating, fishing, antique shops, golf, scenic bike paths, ferries to Martha's Vineyard & Nantucket. **Additional Information:** Cape Cod Chamber of Commerce, (888) 33-CAPECOD or (508) 362-3225, www.capecod-chamber.org.

RESTRICTIONS

Pets: Must be leashed, quiet, & cleaned up after. Current rabies certificate required upon request. **Fires:** At sites only. **Alcoholic Beverages:** Allowed. **Vehicle Maximum Length:** 40 ft. **Other:** 2-night min. stay required on weekends between Memorial Day & Labor Day. 3-night min. stay on holidays. 7-night min. on July 4th week. 4-night min. stay in season, 2-night min. stay out of season. No motorcycles or mopeds operated in park.

TO GET THERE

Take I-195 or I-495 to Hwy. 25, go over Bourne Bridge and continue 1 mi. on Hwy. 28 south. Campground entrance is on the right.

BREWSTER   MAP, B-4
Nickerson State Park

Hwy. 6A, 3488 Main St., 02631. T: (508) 896-3491; www.reserveamerica.com.

  ★★   ▲ ★★★★

Beauty: ★★★★★   Site Privacy: ★★★
Spaciousness: ★★★★   Quiet: ★★★★
Security: ★★★★   Cleanliness: ★★★
Insect Control: ★★★★   Facilities: ★★★

Self-sufficient, energetic types will adore this state park, located in the mid-Cape area of Cape Cod. You won't find hookups, but you will find acres of piney woods, more reminiscent of the Berkshires than the Cape. The woodsy landscape is dotted with eight freshwater kettle ponds, formed when glaciers retreated from the Cape more than 10,000 years ago. Ponds are stocked with land-locked trout and salmon; marked bike trails connect with 25-mile Cape Cod Rail Trail (rail trail users can park for free). Deep-blue Flax Pond, with a sandy beach, is great for swimming and boating. Hiking trails lead to the beach. For the winter tenting crowd, the park offers yurts (available all year). Campsites are grouped in seven areas. Area 4 is heavily used, since it's close to the beach; sites 41 through 51 (odd numbers) are pretty, and backed by pines. Area 3 is hilly, and not as desirable as Area 2, which boasts wooded water views (especially sites 112 through 120). You'd think the farthest-back camping areas, 6, 6X, and 7 would be quietest, but you'd be wrong; that tends to be Party Central in summer. There are only five pull-though sites and the rest are back-ins.

BASICS

Operated By: Massachusetts State Forests and Parks. **Open:** Apr.–Oct. **Site Assignment:** Reservations required; reserve up to 6 months in advance by calling Reserve America at (877) I-CAMP-MA or online at www.reservamerica.com; to change arrival or departure date, or site type, call at least 3 days prior to arrival date; $10 cancellation/transfer fee; no refunds for amounts less than $5. **Registration:** At headquarters. **Fee:** Massachusetts residents, $15; nonresidents, $17; V, MC. **Parking:** At sites or designated parking lots.

FACILITIES

Number of Tent-only Sites: 350. **Number of Multipurpose Sites:** 50. **Hookups:** Water. **Each Site:** Picnic table, fireplace. **Dump Station:** Yes. **Laundry:** No. **Pay Phone:** Yes. **Restrooms and Showers:** Yes. **Fuel:** No. **Propane:** No. **Internal Roads:** Paved, in good condition. **RV Service:** No. **Market:** 1 mi. east. **Restaurant:** Yes (snack bar). **General Store:** Yes. **Vending:** No. **Swimming:** Yes. **Playground:** Yes. **Other:** Nature center, amphitheater, boat rentals, bike rentals. **Activities:** Pond swimming, fishing (catch & release) in Higgins Pond, bicycling, boating, hiking. **Nearby Attractions:** Golf, biking (Cape Cod Rail Trail), ocean swimming, pond swimming, boating, tennis, antiquing. **Additional Information:** Cape Cod Chamber of Commerce, (508) 862-0700 or (888) 33-CAPECOD, www.capecodchamber.org.

RESTRICTIONS

Pets: Must be leashed & cleaned up after. Must not be left unattended. Proof of rabies vaccination required. Not allowed on Flax Pond swimming beach. **Fires:** Fire ring only. **Alcoholic Beverages:** Not allowed. **Vehicle Maximum Length:** 35 ft. **Other:** Must renew by 8 p.m. the night prior to your sched-

uled check-out; 14 cumulative day stay limit between Memorial Day & Labor Day.

TO GET THERE

Take Hwy. 6 east to Exit 12. Go left off the ramp. Park is 2 mi. ahead on the left.

BREWSTER   MAP, B-4
Sweetwater Forest

676 Hwy. 124 (Harwich Rd.), P.O. Box 1797, 02631. T: (508) 896-3773; www.sweetwaterforest.com.

🚐 ★★★   ▲ ★★★★

Beauty: ★★★★   Site Privacy: ★★★
Spaciousness: ★★★★   Quiet: ★★★★
Security: ★★★★   Cleanliness: ★★★
Insect Control: ★★★   Facilities: ★★★

Conveniently located in a desirable area of the mid–Cape Cod, this is the most inviting private campground around. (Brewster is also home to terrific Nickerson State Park.) It has a pleasant feel; campers are greeted with tumbles of blue hydrangea and well-tended plantings, and a winding entrance road skirting oak trees and lofty pines. Set amidst 60 acres of woodland, the property includes Snow's Pond, with a fishing dock and small swimming area. For cyclists, the best feature here may well be the bike path connecting with the Cape Cod Rail Trail, a paved 25-mile bike path. Rental rowboats and canoes add to the recreation possibilities. Families will have a good time here. Seasonal sites are grouped together to the left of the entrance. Among the rest, sites C6–10 (electric and water) are big, level, and wooded, while site C28B is so big, you could put a house on it. Some tent sites are set alongside a retired cranberry bog. Sites B13–16 are close to a restroom, and a short walk to the pond.

BASICS

Operated By: Jim Rylander. **Open:** Apr.–Nov.; reservations only in winter. **Site Assignment:** Reservations recommended; can reserve 1 year in advance and online; $30 deposit required; $15 refund if cancellation occurs 2 weeks in advance of scheduled arrival. **Registration:** At office. **Fee:** $27–$30; for 2 adults, plus unmarried children under 18; V, MC, D. **Parking:** At site.

FACILITIES

Number of RV-only Sites: 250. **Hookups:** Electric (30 amps), water, sewer, cable TV. **Each Site:** Picnic table, fireplace. **Dump Station:** Yes. **Laundry:** No. **Pay Phone:** Yes. **Restrooms and Showers:** Yes. **Fuel:** No. **Propane:** Yes. **Internal Roads:** Gravel, in good condition. **RV Service:** Limited. **Market:** 3 mi. east. **Restaurant:** 5 mi. east. **General Store:** Yes. **Vending:** Yes. **Swimming:** No. **Playground:** Yes. **Other:** Rec lodge, mini-golf. **Activities:** Boating (rowboat & canoe rentals), hiking, basketball, biking (access to Cape Cod Rail Trail), horseshoes, fishing, planned activities. **Nearby Attractions:** Ocean beaches, freshwater swimming, boating, golf, antiques, Cape Cod Museum of Natural History, charter boat fishing trips, whale-watching cruises. **Additional Information:** Cape Cod Chamber of Commerce, (508) 862-0700 or (888) 33-CAPECOD, www.capecodchamber.org.

RESTRICTIONS

Pets: Must be leashed. Must not be left unattended. Proof of rabies vaccination required. Dog boarding service available. **Fires:** Fireplaces only. **Alcoholic Beverages:** Allowed. **Vehicle Maximum Length:** No limit. **Other:** 2-night min.; 3-night min. on holidays.

TO GET THERE

From Sagamore Bridge, enter Hwy. 6. Follow Hwy. 6 to Exit 10, Hwy. 124. Turn left off ramp, heading north toward Brewster on Hwy. 124. Follow Hwy. 124 for 2.8 mi. Look for the sign on the left to the campground entrance.

CHARLEMONT   MAP, A-1
Mohawk Trail State Forest

reserve america

Hwy. 2, P.O. Box 7, 01339. T: (413) 339-5504; www.reserveamerica.com.

🚐 ★★   ⛺ ★★★★

Beauty: ★★★★	Site Privacy: ★★
Spaciousness: ★★★	Quiet: ★★
Security: ★★★	Cleanliness: ★★★
Insect Control: ★★	Facilities: ★★★

This rustic area, set in the Berkshire Hills in Western Massachusetts, is Bear Country. They've had bear sightings here, so it's wise to heed the advice on the bear flyer you get when you enter the park. The best campsites here are set on the banks of the Cold River. Snag one of these, and you can listen to the rushing water as you drift off to sleep (provided bear nightmares don't keep you awake). The sites are all back-in, on gravel, and they are close together but buffered by trees. Campsites are set on two loops running alongside the river, with a little string of nonreservable sites at the end of the road. Of the nonreservable sites, numbers 15–22 are nice and close to the river, while 18 and 41 are both good, roomy options for an RV. Sites 46 and 47 are dandy for tenters, with the advantage of an end-of-the-road location. The farther you head back from the river, though, the farther you get from Hwy. 2 and the hum of traffic. Reserve a site numbered 23–35 if quiet, not water views, are your priority. The showers—just one set serves all, alas— are located near site 24. This is primarily a family camping area, but whitewater paddlers take over when the dam is released. Be sure to grab a trail map when you enter the park; this is a superb area for hiking, with good views from Totem Trail overlook.

BASICS

Operated By: Massachusetts State Forests and Parks. **Open:** Mid-Apr.–mid-Oct. **Site Assignment:** Reservations recommended; reserve up to 6 months in advance by calling Reserve America at (877) I-CAMP-MA or online at www.reserveamerica.com; 10 sites nonreservable and first come, first served; to change arrival or departure date, or site type, call at

least 3 days prior to arrival date; $10 cancellation/ transfer fee; no refunds for amounts less than $5. **Registration:** At office. **Fee:** Massachusetts residents, $12; nonresidents, $14; V, MC. **Parking:** At site.

FACILITIES

Number of Multipurpose Sites: 56. **Hookups:** None. **Each Site:** Picnic table, fireplace. **Dump Station:** Yes. **Laundry:** No. **Pay Phone:** Yes. **Restrooms and Showers:** Yes. **Fuel:** No. **Propane:** No. **Internal Roads:** Gravel, in good condition. **RV Service:** No. **Market:** 4 mi. east, in Charlemont. **Restaurant:** 4 mi. east, in Charlemont. **General Store:** No. **Vending:** Yes. **Swimming:** Yes. **Playground:** No. **Activities:** Canoeing, picnicking, hiking, fishing, swimming, interpretive programs, bicycling. **Nearby Attractions:** Mass MOCA (Museum of Contemporary Art), Clark Art Museum, Natural Bridge, Bridge of Flowers. **Additional Information:** Berkshire Hills Visitors Bureau, (413) 443-9186 or (800) 237-5747, www.berkshires.org.

RESTRICTIONS

Pets: Must be leashed & cleaned up after. Must not be left unattended. Proof of rabies vaccination required. **Fires:** Fireplaces only. **Alcoholic Beverages:** Not allowed. **Vehicle Maximum Length:** 35 ft. **Other:** 14 cumulative day stay limit between Memorial Day & Labor Day.

TO GET THERE

From I-91, take Exit 26 (Hwy. 2) west to Charlemont. Campground is 4 mi. west of Charlemont Center; entrance is on the right.

CHESTER   MAP, A-1
Walker Island Camping

No. 27 Hwy. 20, 01011. T: (413) 354-2295; www.walkerIsland.com.

🚐 ★★★★   ⛺ ★★

Beauty: ★★★	Site Privacy: ★★
Spaciousness: ★★★	Quiet: ★★★
Security: ★★	Cleanliness: ★★★
Insect Control: ★★	Facilities: ★★

This family-friendly campground is located in the Berkshire Hills region of Western Massachusetts. Dead-center in the place is, of all things, a small island, home to a mini-golf course, a small beach, a slightly worse-for-wear kiddie playground, and a sports court for bocce, horseshoes, and shuffleboard. Trout-stocked Walker Brook flows around the island, and offers its own recreation possibilities, including fishing and tubing. The brook, abundant trees, and rocky ledges lend a serene aspect to an otherwise rather cluttery place. Campsites are back-in, set on three levels, becoming more "wild" the higher you go. On the upper level, campsites are tucked into ledges, offering plenty of seclusion. (Warning: the restrooms are the nonflush type up there.) Site 68 is a super tent site if you like privacy, while RV sites 49–54, near the back entrance, are among the most inviting. There's a lot going on, plus kids everywhere, making this a very different scene than you'll encounter at one of the numerous state park camping areas in the region. Still, it's homey and easy going.

BASICS

Operated By: Shawn Myrick. **Open:** Apr. 28–Oct. 15 (2006), normally May 2–Oct. 31. **Site Assignment:** Reservations recommended; 1-night deposit due w/ reservation; deposits are refundable w/ minimum of 1-week notice. **Registration:** At office. **Fee:** Full hookup, $32; water/electric, $29; tent, $27; extra adult, $6; extra child, $3; V, MC. **Parking:** At site.

FACILITIES

Number of Multipurpose Sites: 90. **Hookups:** Electric (30 amps), water, sewer, cable TV. **Each Site:** Picnic table, fire ring. **Dump Station:** Yes. **Laundry:** Yes. **Pay Phone:** Yes. **Restrooms and Showers:** Yes. **Fuel:** No. **Propane:** Yes. **Internal Roads:** Gravel, in good condition. **RV Service:** No. **Market:** 25 mi. east or west. **Restaurant:** 3 mi. east. **General Store:** Yes. **Vending:** No. **Swimming:** Yes. **Playground:** Yes. **Other:** Rec hall, game room, mini-golf. **Activities:** Swimming, mini-golf, tubing, shuffleboard, hiking, fishing, planned activities. **Nearby Attractions:** Norman Rockwell Museum, Tanglewood (music), Jacob's Pillow (dance), Six Flags New England theme park, waterfalls, summer theater, Chesterfield Gorge, golf, horseback riding, boating. **Additional Information:** Berkshire Hills Visitors Bureau, (413) 443-9186 or (800) 237-5747, www.berkshires.org.

RESTRICTIONS

Pets: Must be leashed, quiet, & cleaned up after. Must not be left unattended. **Fires:** Fireplaces only. **Alcoholic Beverages:** Allowed. **Vehicle Maximum Length:** 40 ft. **Other:** Quiet hours 10 p.m.–8 a.m.

TO GET THERE

From I-90 (Massachusetts Turnpike), take Exit 3, turn right and proceed for 2 mi. Turn right onto Hwy. 20, heading west. Follow Hwy. 20 for 17 mi. to Chester. Campground entrance is on the right.

CLARKSBURG   MAP, A-1
Clarksburg State Park

reserve america

1199 Middle Rd., 01247. T: (413) 664-8345; www.reserveamerica.com.

🚐 ★★   ⛺ ★★★★★

Beauty: ★★★★★	Site Privacy: ★★★★
Spaciousness: ★★★	Quiet: ★★★
Security: ★★	Cleanliness: ★★★★
Insect Control: ★★	Facilities: ★★★

Set in the far northwest corner of the state, nudging the Vermont border, this densely forested camping area is beautiful, with secluded, well-spaced campsites. The good looks even extend to the restrooms, which are nicely landscaped (with usable mirrors, a rarity at state parks) thanks to a recent park beautification program. One of the nicest features here is sparkling Mauserts Pond, a day-use area for swimming, fishing, and picnicking. Campsites are arrayed in a loop near the south end of the pond, but not directly on the waterfront. A scenic hiking trail skirts the pond, great for wildlife watching. The most enticing feature of this park may well be its proximity to the Appalachian Trail. Hikers come here when they want to trek the A.T. and Mt. Greylock (the highest point in the state), the park supervisor tells us. They prefer to camp here rather than at primitive Mt. Greylock so they can take advantage of creature comforts, like hot showers and running water. Only four sites are big enough for 36-footers, so plan ahead. Sites boasting excellent water views include 2, 4, 6, 8, 24, and 25.

BASICS

Operated By: Massachusetts State Forests and Parks. **Open:** Memorial Day–Columbus Day, perhaps later; call ahead. **Site Assignment:** Reservations may be made up to 6 months in advance by calling Reserve America at (877) I-CAMP-MA or online at www.reserveamerica.com; 10 sites are first come, first served; to change arrival or departure date, or site type, call at least 3 days prior to arrival date; $10 cancellation/transfer fee; no refunds for amounts less than $5. **Registration:** At office. **Fee:** Massachusetts residents, $12; nonresidents, $14; V, MC, D, check. **Parking:** At site.

FACILITIES

Number of RV-only Sites: 22. **Number of Tent-only Sites:** 22. **Hookups:** None. **Each Site:** Picnic table, fireplace. **Dump Station:** No. **Laundry:** No. **Pay Phone:** Yes. **Restrooms and Showers:** Yes. **Fuel:** No. **Propane:** No. **Internal Roads:** Paved, in good condition. **RV Service:** No. **Market:** 3 mi. south, in North Adams. **Restaurant:** 3 mi. south, in North Adams. **General Store:** 1 mi. **Vending:** No. **Swimming:** No. **Playground:** No. **Other:** Pavilion. **Activities:** Swimming, fishing, picnicking, hiking. **Nearby Attractions:** Mass MOCA (contemporary art museum), Appalachian Trail. **Additional Information:** Berkshire Hills Visitors Bureau, (413) 443-9186 or (800) 237-5747, www.berkshires.org.

RESTRICTIONS

Pets: Must be leashed & cleaned up after. Must not be left unattended. Proof of rabies vaccination required. **Fires:** Fireplaces only. **Alcoholic Beverages:** Not allowed. **Vehicle Maximum Length:** 36 ft. **Other:** 14 cumulative day stay limit between Memorial Day & Labor Day.

TO GET THERE

Follow Hwy. 8 north to Middle Rd. in Clarksburg; follow signs.

DENNISPORT MAP, B-4
Campers Haven RV Resort

reserve america

184 Old Wharf Rd., 02639. T: (508) 398-2811; www.reserveamerica.com.

🚐 ★★★	🏕 n/a
Beauty: ★★	Site Privacy: ★★
Spaciousness: ★★	Quiet: ★★
Security: ★★★★★	Cleanliness: ★★★★
Insect Control: ★★★	Facilities: ★★

This mid-Cape campground, located on the beach road in Dennisport, has bragging rights to a major amenity: a private sandy beach on Nantucket Sound, right across the street from the campground. Never mind that it's a little, fenced-off thing—it's a beach, with a nice swath of swimmable water which, they say, averages a toasty 80 degrees in the summer. Beyond that, the campground offers open, grassy sites for RVs (no tenting), mostly back-in. Many sites are seasonal. Nice touch: if you're in a class A or class C motor home with no car in tow, they'll shuttle you to local restaurants and ferries. A plethora of planned activities, like sing-alongs and ice-cream socials, plus an on-site snack bar, make this a destination park. But, all the attractions of Hyannis, the Cape's biggest town, are just 12 miles away. For all that, it plays to an older crowd. We'd suggest another Cape campground if you have kids in tow.

BASICS

Operated By: Paul and Elaine Peterson. **Open:** May 1–Columbus Day. **Site Assignment:** Reservations recommended; 50% deposit required; reservations of 2 nights or less and holidays require payment in full in advance; deposits for cancellations are refundable, minus $15, w/ 2-week notice. **Registration:** At office. **Fee:** $46–$56; for 2 adults & 2 children; July 4th & Labor Day weekend, $52–$62; 3-night minimum; V, MC, AE. **Parking:** At sites or by permission only (w/ extra charge).

FACILITIES

Number of RV-only Sites: 244. **Hookups:** Electric (30, 50 amps), water, sewer, cable TV. **Each Site:** None. **Dump Station:** Yes. **Laundry:** Yes. **Pay Phone:** Yes. **Restrooms and Showers:** Yes. **Fuel:** No. **Propane:** No. **Internal Roads:** Paved, in good condition. **RV Service:** No. **Market:** 3 mi. west. **Restaurant:** No. **General Store:** Yes. **Vending:** Yes. **Swimming:** No. **Playground:** Yes. **Other:** Rec hall (pavilion), mini-golf, adult clubhouse w/ exercise equipment & hot tub. **Activities:** Swimming (private ocean beach), horseshoes, mini-golf, basketball, shuffleboard, bocce, planned activities. **Nearby Attractions:** JFK Hyannis Museum, Cape Cod Rail Trail, golf, fishing, ferries to islands. **Additional Information:** Cape Cod Chamber of Commerce, (508) 862-0700 or (888) 33-CAPECOD, www.capechamber.org.

RESTRICTIONS

Pets: No dogs allowed June 25 to Labor Day. Limit one dog per site when allowed. No outdoor cats. **Fires:** Not allowed. **Alcoholic Beverages:** Allowed. **Vehicle Maximum Length:** 40 ft. **Other:** No smoking in any of the buildings.

TO GET THERE

Take Hwy. 6 to Exit 8. Turn right onto Hwy. 134 and go to the end. Turn left onto Lower County Rd. and go 0.5 mi. to Old Wharf Rd. (Look closely; signs are on stone road posts and devilishly hard to read.) Turn right and go 1 mi. to campground, on left.

EAST FALMOUTH MAP, B-4
Cape Cod Campresort

reserve america

176 Thomas Landers Rd., 02536. T: (508) 548-1458; www.reserveamerica.com.

🚐 ★★★	🏕 ★★★
Beauty: ★★★	Site Privacy: ★★
Spaciousness: ★★★	Quiet: ★★★
Security: ★★★★★	Cleanliness: ★★★
Insect Control: ★★	Facilities: ★★★

This campground is actually three entities: a camping club, a camping co-op with some transient and seasonal sites, and the Cape Cod Campresort, with sites available specifically for transient use. Everybody shares the amenities, including a swimming pool, kiddie pool, and clubhouse; otherwise, everybody sticks to their area (marked by signage). There's a small beach, with a swimming area, on Round Pond. It's a nice-looking place, with campsites nestled in cool pines. Sites are grassy and back-in, carpeted with pine needles. The tenting area is off to one side, just to the right of the office, with tents clustered in a pine grove off a skinny gravel road. Tent site E is especially nice. Among the RV sites, 98 and 99 are very private and set off the road. Site 76 is a winner, too, backed up into the woods. There's not much buffer between campsites. Another quibble: where are the umbrellas alongside the well-used pool area? Compared to nearby Sippewissett Campground (see listing), this one offers more activities for families and a bit more breathing room.

BASICS

Operated By: Cape Cod Campresort. **Open:** May 1–Oct. 15. **Site Assignment:** Reservations recommended; 30% deposit required; no refunds for cancellations occurring 7 days or less prior to scheduled arrival date. **Registration:** At office. **Fee:** $28–$34; based on 2 people; extra adult, $8 per night; extra child under age 15, $4 per night; V, MC. **Parking:** At sites and designated parking lots only.

FACILITIES

Number of RV-only Sites: 200. **Hookups:** Electric (30, 50 amps), water, sewer. **Each Site:** Picnic table, fireplace. **Dump Station:** Yes. **Laundry:** No. **Pay Phone:** Yes. **Restrooms and Showers:** Yes. **Fuel:** No. **Propane:** No. **Internal Roads:** Gravel, in good condition. **RV Service:** No. **Market:** 2 mi. east. **Restaurant:** 5 mi. east. **General Store:** Yes. **Vending:** Yes. **Swimming:** Yes. **Playground:** Yes. **Other:** Rec hall. **Activities:** Ball field, swimming, horseshoes, boating (boat rentals). **Nearby Attractions:** Ferries to Martha's Vineyard, Woods Hole aquarium, ocean beaches, Nobska Lighthouse, golf. **Additional Information:** Cape Cod Chamber of Commerce, (508) 862-0700 or (888) 33-CAPECOD, www.capecod chamber.org.

RESTRICTIONS

Pets: Must be leashed, quiet, & cleaned up after. Proof of rabies vaccination required. $4 charge per day.

Fires: Fire ring only. **Alcoholic Beverages:** Allowed. **Vehicle Maximum Length:** No limit; over 30 ft. incurs extra charge of $1 per ft. per night. **Other:** All visitors must register upon entering the park.

TO GET THERE

From Bourne Bridge, take Hwy. 28S (second turn off rotary) to next rotary; continue on 28S, then take second exit to Thomas Landers Rd. Take left off ramp. Campground is exactly 2.7 mi. on the right.

EAST OTIS　　　　MAP, B-1
Tolland State Forest

reserve america

P.O. Box 342, 410 Tolland Rd., 01029.
T: (413) 269-6002; www.reserveamerica.com.

🚐 ★★★★　　　　🔺 ★★★★

Beauty: ★★★	Site Privacy: ★★★
Spaciousness: ★★	Quiet: ★★★★
Security: ★★★★	Cleanliness: ★★★★
Insect Control: ★★★	Facilities: ★★★★

The centerpiece of this state forest, located in the rolling southern Berkshire Hills, is the 1,065-acre Otis Reservoir. The lake provides a wide variety of recreational activities. A public boat-launch ramp is available, popular with fishermen seeking out trout and bass in the lake's depths. A unique and popular destination during the summer is the campground, located on a scenic and wooded peninsula. Also available is a day-use area with sandy beach and several multiuse trails. Because of its elevation atop the undulating Southern Berkshire Plateau, the woodlands of Tolland State Forest are dominated by northern hardwoods. But Otis Reservoir, one of the largest water bodies in western Massachusetts at 1,065 acres, forms the focal point for numerous anglers, hunters, campers, off-road-vehicle users, and others who visit. Hunting is open (in season) for all types of game, including turkey, bear, and deer. The trail system is little used by hikers—quite a contrast to the heavily utilized recreation areas—making a sojourn to this property, which imparts a wilderness feeling, rewarding and enjoyable.

BASICS

Operated By: Massachusetts State Parks. **Open:** May 11–Oct. 8. **Site Assignment:** Reservations can be made up to 6 months in advance. **Registration:** At office. **Fee:** Single, $12–$14. **Parking:** 2 vehicles per campsite.

FACILITIES

Number of Multipurpose Sites: 93. **Hookups:** None. **Dump Station:** Yes. **Laundry:** No. **Pay Phone:** Yes. **Restrooms and Showers:** Yes. **Fuel:** No. **Propane:** No. **Internal Roads:** Paved. **RV Service:** No. **Market:** No. **Restaurant:** No. **General Store:** No. **Vending:** No. **Swimming:** Yes. **Playground:** No. **Activities:** Biking, boating, canoeing, fishing, hiking, hunting, interpretive programs, picnicking.

RESTRICTIONS

Pets: Keep pets leashed (10-ft. leash max.) at all times. Proof of rabies vaccination is required. Pets are never to be left unattended. **Fires:** Campfires in designated fireplaces. **Alcoholic Beverages:** Alcoholic beverages are prohibited in all MA state parks & campgrounds. **Other:** Quiet hours are 10 p.m.–7 a.m. No unnecessary or disturbing noise at any time. Equipment is limited to 2 tents or 1 camping vehicle & 1 small tent per site. Tents are limited to 300 square feet of combined floor space. Massachusetts law requires that children age 16 and under wear a helmet when bicycling.

TO GET THERE

From the east: Massachusetts Turnpike Exit 3 (Westfield). Follow Hwy. 10-202 South to Hwy. 20. Proceed west on Hwy. 20 for about 6 mi. Turn left onto Hwy. 23 west. Follow Hwy. 23 west through Blandford into Otis. About 1 mi. past the Otis town line, turn left onto West Shore Rd., then left onto Tolland Rd. Follow signs. From north or south: Hwy. 8 to Otis. Take Reservoir Rd. to Tolland Rd. Follow signs.

EAST TAUNTON　　　　MAP, B-3
Massasoit State Park

reserve america

1361 Middleboro Ave., 02718. T: (508) 822-7405; www.reserveamerica.com.

🚐 ★★★★　　　　🔺 ★★★★

Beauty: ★★★★	Site Privacy: ★★★
Spaciousness: ★★★★★	Quiet: ★★★★
Security: ★★★	Cleanliness: ★★★
Insect Control: ★★★	Facilities: ★★★

Located about 40 miles south of Boston, this campground boasts a unique feature for a state park: water and electrical hookups. This may explain why campers tend to make a vacation of it and stay for a whole two weeks. Very popular with local urban dwellers, Massasoit State Park is a cool oasis on a sweltering summer day. Pine carpeted, the gravel and grassy campsites are set in four loops, designated by alphabet. Areas E and G, with hookups, have frontage on Middle Pond. The pond offers a rocky, grassy beach with a small, unguarded swimming area. Site E5 is huge, great for RVs. Section H is for self-contained camping units (no restrooms), while section C has no electrical hookups. Sites C2 and C3 are fairly secluded tent sites, with good proximity to a restroom. (Shy guys take note: the men's showers are open, not curtained.) There's a nice picnic grove, and fishing, on Big Bearhole Pond (off J Rd.) A hiking trail leads to this peachy spot. Trivia tidbit: Stall Island, on park property, was one of Elizabeth Pole's farms. It is said that she traded "a jackknife and a pot of beans" to Native Americans for 5,000 acres of land in 1637.

BASICS

Operated By: Massachusetts State Forests and Parks. **Open:** Mid-Apr.–Columbus Day. **Site Assign-**

ment: Reservations recommended; reserve up to 6 months in advance by calling Reserve America at (877) I-CAMP-MA or online at www.reservamerica.com; 15 sites are first come, first served; to change arrival or departure date, or site type, call at least 3 days prior to arrival date; $10 cancellation/transfer fee; no refunds for amounts less than $5. **Registration:** At park headquarters. **Fee:** Massachusetts residents (w/ electric), $13; nonresidents (w/ electric), $15; V, MC. **Parking:** At site.

FACILITIES

Number of Multipurpose Sites: 126. **Hookups:** Electric (20 amps), water, sewer available. **Each Site:** Picnic table, fireplace. **Dump Station:** Yes. **Laundry:** No. **Pay Phone:** Yes. **Restrooms and Showers:** Yes. **Fuel:** No. **Propane:** No. **Internal Roads:** Paved, in good condition. **RV Service:** No. **Market:** 3 mi. north on Hwy. 44. **Restaurant:** 4–5 mi. northeast. **General Store:** No. **Vending:** No. **Swimming:** Yes. **Playground:** No. **Other:** Boat ramp. **Activities:** Hiking, horse trails, bicycling, fishing (MA license available in Middleboro), swimming. **Nearby Attractions:** Edaville Railroad, Battleship Cove, New Bedford Whaling Museum, Plimoth Plantation, Cranberry World Visitors Center, Pilgrim Hall Museum, Fuller Museum of Art. **Additional Information:** Plymouth County CVB, (508) 747-0100 or (800) 231-1620, www.plymouth-1620.com.

RESTRICTIONS

Pets: Must be leashed, quiet, & cleaned up after. Current rabies vaccination certificate required. Posted areas are off-limits to pets. **Fires:** Fireplaces only. **Alcoholic Beverages:** Not allowed. **Vehicle Maximum Length:** 40 ft. **Other:** 14 cumulative day stay limit between Memorial Day & Labor Day.

TO GET THERE

Follow Hwy. 24 south to Hwy. 44 (Exit 13); heading east, follow signs on Hwy. 44 to campground.

ERVING　　　　MAP, A-2
Erving State Forest

200 East Main St., Rte. 2A, 01344.
T: (978) 544-3939 or (978) 544-7745;
www.reserveamerica.com.

🚐 ★★　　　　🔺 ★★★

Beauty: ★★★★	Site Privacy: ★★
Spaciousness: ★★	Quiet: ★★★
Security: ★★★	Cleanliness: ★★★★
Insect Control: ★★	Facilities: ★★

Great find: a camping area that stays open into October, for the leaf-peeping crowd. The Mohawk Trail is great route for fall color tours, so this campground couldn't be handier. Right off Hwy. 2, it's got a great approach: a winding, tree-lined road bordered with lush ferns. Gravel sites are set on both sides of Camp Rd., backed by forest. The centerpiece of the state park is pretty Laurel Lake, stocked with brook trout. There are a few private cottages on the waterfront, but no campsites; campers stay at sites on the other side of the main road, and walk a short distance to picnic areas along the shore. There's a nice beach for campers, and a big buoyed swimming area, complete with lifeguards (sometimes). Campsites here are not as nice as the surrounding area, but they're adequate, mostly measuring 30 by 30 feet, with mature trees as a buffer between them. Sites 11 and 12 offer a good amount of privacy, since they're spaced far apart. A nice feature here: engaging interpretive programs, such as "Serpent Session" (local snakes) and "Beginning Birding." A not-so-nice feature: no showers—that's why this park charges only $8 or $10 per night.

BASICS

Operated By: Massachusetts State Forests and Parks. **Open:** May–Oct. **Site Assignment:** Reservations may be made up to 6 months in advance by calling Reserve America at (877) I-CAMP-MA or online at www.reserveamerica.com; 15 sites are first come, first served; to change arrival or departure date, or site type, call at least 3 days prior to arrival date; $10 cancellation/transfer fee; no refunds for amounts less than $5. **Registration:** At office. **Fee:** Massachusetts residents, $8; nonresidents, $10; V, MC. **Parking:** At site.

FACILITIES

Number of Multipurpose Sites: 29. **Hookups:** None. **Each Site:** Picnic table, fireplace. **Dump Station:** No. **Laundry:** No. **Pay Phone:** Yes. **Restrooms and Showers:** Yes (nonflush), no showers. **Fuel:** No. **Propane:** No. **Internal Roads:** Paved, in good condition. **RV Service:** No. **Market:** 5 mi. east or west. **Restaurant:** 5 mi. east or west. **General Store:** No. **Vending:** No. **Swimming:** No. **Playground:** No. **Other:** Boat ramp, nature center. **Activities:** Swimming, hiking, boating, fishing (need MA license, available at Wal-Mart in Orange), interpretive programs. **Nearby Attractions:** Mohawk Trail scenic drive, Bridge of Flowers (Shelburne), Historic Deerfield. **Additional Information:** Mohawk Trail Association, (413) 743-8127, www.mohawktrail.com.

RESTRICTIONS

Pets: Must be leashed & cleaned up after. Must not be left unattended. Proof of rabies vaccination required. **Fires:** Fireplaces only. **Alcoholic Beverages:** Not allowed. **Vehicle Maximum Length:** 20 ft. **Other:** 14 cumulative day stay limit between Memorial Day & Labor Day.

TO GET THERE

Take Hwy. 2 west to Erving Center. Take immediate left on Church St., exit right, and follow signs.

FLORIDA   MAP, A-1
Savoy Mountain State Forest

260 Central Shaft Rd., 01247. T: (413) 663-8469; www.reserveamerica.com.

 ★★★★   ▲ ★★★★

Beauty: ★★★   Site Privacy: ★★★
Spaciousness: ★★★   Quiet: ★★
Security: ★★★   Cleanliness: ★★★★
Insect Control: ★★★   Facilities: ★★★

Savoy Mountain State Forest makes it easy to leave the everyday world behind. Scenic North and South Ponds, with wooded edges and hills rising in the distance, offer tranquil places to fish, picnic, and swim. 45 campsites and one group site are located in an old apple orchard. Four log cabins overlook South Pond, available for year-round rental. Over 50 miles of wooded trails invite year-round recreational access to spectacular natural features. Hike the Bog Pond Trail, with its floating bog islands. Or climb up Spruce Hill on the Busby Trail for breathtaking views, especially during fall foliage and hawk migration. Be sure to visit Tannery Falls (and nearby Parker Brook Falls), where Ross Brook flows through a deep chasm, and then cascades over 50 feet to a clear pool below. Savoy Mountain State Forest is located atop the Hoosac Mountain Range in northwestern Massachusetts. The Hoosac Range is an extension of the Green Mountains of Vermont and is the first mountain barrier encountered rising west of the Connecticut River Valley. "Hoosac" is an Algonquin word meaning "place of stones." Settlement of these remote towns of Florida and Savoy by farmers began in the early 19th century. The construction of the Hoosac Tunnel (1851–75) for railroad transportation created a momentary population boom. After its completion the tunnel workers left. Many moved down in the valley to Adams or North Adams to work in the woolen mills, or headed west to join in the great land rush for better farmland. Savoy Mountain State Forest was created in 1918 with the purchase of 1,000 acres of this abandoned farmland. During the 1930s the Civilian Conservation Corps (CCC) reforested much of this area with Norway and blue spruce and built new concrete dams at Bog, Burnett, and Tannery Pond to replace older dams. Today, apple trees interspersed throughout the campground and stonewalls are some reminders of the once vibrant farming history.

BASICS

Operated By: Massachusetts State Parks. **Open:** All year. **Site Assignment:** Reservations can be made up to 6 months in advance. **Registration:** At office. **Fee:** Single, $12–$14; group, $25; cabin, $30. **Parking:** 2 vehicles per campsite.

FACILITIES

Number of Multipurpose Sites: 50. **Hookups:** Yes. **Dump Station:** No. **Laundry:** No. **Pay Phone:** Yes. **Restrooms and Showers:** Yes. **Fuel:** No. **Propane:** No. **Internal Roads:** Paved. **RV Service:** No. **Market:** No. **Restaurant:** No. **General Store:** No. **Vending:** No. **Swimming:** No. **Playground:** No. **Activities:** Biking, boating, canoeing, fishing, hiking, hunting, interpretive programs, picnicking, cross-country skiing, snowmobiling.

RESTRICTIONS

Pets: Pets are not allowed at Savoy Mountain cabins, yurts, Boston Harbor Islands or WBNERR camping areas. **Fires:** Campfires in designated fireplaces. **Alcoholic Beverages:** Alcoholic beverages are prohibited in all MA state parks & campgrounds. **Other:** Quiet

hours are 10 p.m.–7 a.m. No unnecessary or disturbing noise at any time. Equipment is limited to 2 tents or 1 camping vehicle & 1 small tent per site. Tents are limited to 300 square feet of combined floor space. Bears are regular visitors to this campground. Bears are wild and can be dangerous. To protect your family and your property, keep all food, coolers, and cooking supplies and equipment in your vehicle when not in use. Massachusetts law requires that children age 16 and under wear a helmet when bicycling.

TO GET THERE

From the east: Follow Hwy. 2 west to the town of Florida. Turn left onto Central Shaft Rd. Follow the signs to the campground on the right after the day-use area parking lot. From the west: Follow Hwy. 2 east to the town of Florida. Turn right onto Central Shaft Rd. Follow the signs to the campground on the right after the day-use area parking lot.

FOXBORO   MAP, B-3
Normandy Farms Family Camping Resort

72 West St., 02035. T: (508) 543-7600; www.normandyfarms.com.

🚐 ★★★★★   ▲ ★★★

Beauty: ★★★★★   Site Privacy: ★★★
Spaciousness: ★★★★   Quiet: ★★★★★
Security: ★★★★   Cleanliness: ★★★★
Insect Control: ★★★★★   Facilities: ★★★★★

Wow. The facilities at this four-season camping resort are really something. The timber-beamed rec center is reminiscent of a ski lodge, complete with an 18-plus adult loft and arcade. The lodge overlooks a lovely pool area with two pools. Elsewhere, there's yet another pool and two hot tubs. Campsites are, mostly, located in an open, grassy field, beautifully landscaped and surrounded by woods. The nicest full-hookup sites, backing up into the woods, are 801 through 807, 901 through 908, and 1001 through 1008. Test sites are shaded and set around the perimeter of the park. Best tent sites are T1 through T10, located near the fishing pond. Anywhere, though, there's not much privacy for tenters. This place speaks more to the RVer who's looking for some frills, not a wilderness-seeking tenter. There are lots of daily activities going on in the summer and during holiday weekends all year, from an Elvis Tribute to ice-cream socials. Most of these are free. (Free swim lessons and free water aerobics classes are a nice touch.) The campground runs guided bus trips to the Cape and Boston (30 miles south), very popular with campers.

BASICS

Operated By: Daniels family. **Open:** All year. **Site Assignment:** Reservations recommended; may be made by phone, mail, e-mail, or online; reservations line opens Mar. 15 for bookings for the following year; for holidays, book 1 year in advance; for summer weekends, book at least 1 month in advance; 2-day minimum required weekends; 3- to 4-day stay required holiday weekends; deposit required w/in 3 weeks of reservation; secure w/ cash, traveler's checks, checks, or credit cards; refunds for cancellation received 1 week prior to scheduled arrival date. **Registration:** At office. **Fee:** $35–$66 (late May to Labor Day); V, MC, D. **Parking:** At sites and designated lots only.

FACILITIES

Number of RV-only Sites: 400. **Number of Tent-only Sites:** 23. **Hookups:** Electric (20, 30, 50 amps), water, sewer. **Each Site:** Picnic table, fire ring. **Dump Station:** Yes. **Laundry:** Yes. **Pay Phone:** Yes. **Restrooms and Showers:** Yes. **Fuel:** No. **Propane:** Yes. **Internal Roads:** Paved, in good condition. **RV Service:** Yes. **Market:** 6 mi. east, in Mansfield. **Restaurant:** Yes. **General Store:** Yes. **Vending:** Yes. **Swimming:** Yes (3). **Playground:** Yes. **Other:** Hot tubs, rec lodge, 18-hole Frisbee golf course. **Activities:** Guided tours to Boston, Newport, & Cape Cod, swimming, fishing, volleyball, soccer field, horseshoes, basketball, planned activities. **Nearby Attractions:** Tweeter Center for the Performing Arts (concerts), Gillette Stadium (football), Edaville Railroad, Plimoth Plantation, Cranberry World Visitors Center, Pilgrim Hall Museum. **Additional Information:** Plymouth County CVB, (508) 747-0100 or (800) 231-1620, www.plymouth-1620.com.

RESTRICTIONS

Pets: Must be leashed & cleaned up after. May not be left unattended. **Fires:** Fire ring only. **Alcoholic Beverages:** Allowed. **Vehicle Maximum Length:** 45 ft. **Other:** Visitors must pay a fee & are not allowed to bring their pets in.

TO GET THERE

From Boston, take I-93 south to Exit 2, then I-95 south to Exit 9. Take Hwy. 1 south for 6.7 mi. to Thurston St. Turn left onto Thurston. Campground is 1.4 mi. on the right.

GLOUCESTER MAP, A-3
Cape Ann Camp Site

80 Atlantic St., 01930. T: (978) 283-8683; www.capeanncampsite.com.

🚐 ★★★★	🏕 ★★★
Beauty: ★★★★★	Site Privacy: ★★★★
Spaciousness: ★★★★	Quiet: ★★★★
Security: ★★★	Cleanliness: ★★★
Insect Control: ★★	Facilities: ★★★

Located about an hour's drive north of Boston, this coastal campground overlooks the Jones River salt marsh and the briny bays of the Atlantic Ocean. Salt air, sand dunes, and sea oats beckon at Wingaersheek Beach, a mile away. The lower area of the campground is reserved for sizable RVs; beyond that, a series of loop roads winds up a hill through a woodsy, boulder-studded camping area. Designated areas are set aside for tent campers. Secluded site 330 is a superb choice for tenters, offering the ultimate room-with-a-view: a footpath leads to a rocky ledge with sweeping views of the river, estuaries, and East Gloucester shoreline. For smaller RVs, the electricity-only sites 215E to 217E are pleasant and out-of-the-way. Don't expect much in the way of amenities here; it's just the basics. But the campground's natural beauty and its superb location make up for the lack of

frills. During the day, everyone heads out to the beach or to take in the sights on Cape Ann. Among the options: Gloucester's Rocky Neck, the oldest artists' colony in America, and the arts-flavored town of Rockport—home of the most-painted, most-photographed fishing shack anywhere, Motif #1.

BASICS

Operated By: Matz family. **Open:** May 1–Nov. 1. **Site Assignment:** Reservations recommended; reserve by phone beginning in Apr.; $30 deposit due w/ reservation. Personal checks accepted for deposit only. **Registration:** At office. **Fee:** $25–$30; per day, per car, up to 2 people; additional person, $2–$8 per day; V, MC. **Parking:** At sites only. 1 vehicle per site.

FACILITIES

Number of RV-only Sites: 125. **Number of Tent-only Sites:** 125. **Hookups:** Electric (30, 50 amps), water, sewer. **Each Site:** Picnic table, fireplace. **Dump Station:** Yes. **Laundry:** No. **Pay Phone:** Yes. **Restrooms and Showers:** Yes, coin op. **Fuel:** No. **Propane:** No. **Internal Roads:** Paved & gravel, good condition. **RV Service:** No. **Market:** 0.5 mi. west. **Restaurant:** 2 mi. south off Hwy. 128. **General Store:** Yes. **Vending:** No. **Swimming:** Ocean swimming. **Playground:** No. **Other:** Metered showers, modem in a central location. **Activities:** Swimming at ocean beach, saltwater fishing (no license needed), bike riding. **Nearby Attractions:** Wingaersheek Beach (1 mi. east; discounted parking permit available at campground office), Hammond Castle Museum, whale-watching boat trips, antiquing, Bearskin Neck artists' colony. **Additional Information:** North of Boston CVB, (978) 977-7760 or (800) 742-5306, www.northofboston.org.

RESTRICTIONS

Pets: Must be leashed, quiet, & cleaned up after. Must have rabies vaccination certificate. **Fires:** Fireplaces only. **Alcoholic Beverages:** At sites only. **Vehicle Maximum Length:** 45 ft. **Other:** 3-night min. stay for Fri. arrivals; June 15–Labor Day, 2-night min. stay for Sat. arrivals; may require 4-day min. stay on July 4th & Labor Day weekends. Walk-ins OK if space is available.

TO GET THERE

Take Hwy. 128 North to Exit 13. Go northeast on Concord St. for 0.7 mi., then turn right onto Atlantic St. Campground is located 0.5 mi. east; entrance is on the left.

GRANVILLE MAP, B-1
Granville State Forest

323 West Hartland Rd., 01034. T: (413) 357-6611; www.reserveamerica.com.

🚐 ★★★★	🏕 ★★★★
Beauty: ★★★	Site Privacy: ★★★★
Spaciousness: ★★★★	Quiet: ★★★★★
Security: ★★★★★	Cleanliness: ★★★★
Insect Control: ★★★	Facilities: ★★

Located along the southern border of Massachusetts in the towns of Granville and Tolland, this 2,426-acre state forest borders Connecticut's 9,152-acre Tunxis State Forest, creating a sense of tranquil remoteness. This extensive rolling terrain was once the hunting and fishing ground of the Tunxis tribe, later becoming open farmland and pastures, and now slowly reverting back into a northern hardwood-conifer forest. This regeneration has created a rich mix of natural and semi-natural communities where wildlife viewing can be excellent. Hints of former human occupation remain, such as an old apple orchard and horticultural plantings at an abandoned home site along West Hartland Road. Endowed with a fine reptile and amphibian population, Granville is also a wonderful place to look for mammals and their signs. Coyote, red fox, raccoon, beaver, and numerous smaller creatures abound. Woodland and wetland birds are abundant also. Old fields and meadows of flowering plants host bees, butterflies, beetles, and other winged insects. In 1749 the first English pioneer to this area, Samuel Hubbard, settled along the banks of the river now bearing his name. Enjoy a walk along the Hubbard River as it cascades through natural rock formations forming pools and waterfalls, dropping a rapid 450 feet in 2.5 miles. Recreation at Granville includes a wooded camping area with toilet and shower facilities, offering access to nearby regional tourist attractions. Other popular activities include bird-watching, wildlife viewing, snowshoeing, and mountain biking.

BASICS

Operated By: Massachusetts State Parks. **Open:** May 24–Sept. 3. **Site Assignment:** Reservations can be made up to 6 months in advance. **Registration:** At office. **Fee:** Single, $12–$14. **Parking:** 2 vehicles per campsite.

FACILITIES

Number of Multipurpose Sites: 22. **Hookups:** None. **Dump Station:** No. **Laundry:** No. **Pay Phone:** Yes. **Restrooms and Showers:** Yes. **Fuel:** No. **Propane:** No. **Internal Roads:** Paved. **RV Service:** No. **Market:** No. **Restaurant:** No. **General Store:** No. **Vending:** No. **Swimming:** No. **Playground:** No. **Activities:** Biking, fishing, hiking, horseback riding, hunting, cross-country skiing, snowmobiling.

RESTRICTIONS

Pets: Keep pets leashed (10-ft. leash max.) at all times. Proof of rabies vaccination is required. Pets are never to be left unattended. **Fires:** Campfires in designated fireplaces. **Alcoholic Beverages:** Alcoholic beverages are prohibited in all MA state parks & campgrounds. **Other:** Quiet hours are 10 p.m.–7 a.m. No unnecessary or disturbing noise at any time. Equipment is limited to 2 tents or 1 camping vehicle & 1 small tent per site. Tents are limited to 300 square feet of combined floor space. Bears are regular visitors to this campground. Bears are wild and can be dangerous. To protect your family and your property, keep all food, coolers, and cooking supplies and equipment in your vehicle when not in use.

Massachusetts law requires that children age 16 and under wear a helmet when bicycling.

To Get There

From the east: Take the Massachusetts Turnpike (Hwy. 90) to Exit 3 (Westfield). Turn right onto Hwy. 10/202 south to Hwy. 57 west to Granville, MA. Go through the center of Granville for 6 mi. Turn left onto West Hartland Rd. From the west: Take the Massachusetts Turnpike to Exit 2 (Lee). Follow Hwy. 20 east to Hwy. 8 south. Follow Hwy. 8 to Hwy. 57 east. After entering the Town of Granville, go 0.5 mi. to West Hartland Rd. on the right. Turn right onto West Harland Rd. Campground will be on the left 0.5 mi. after the park headquarters.

GRANVILLE   MAP, B-1
Prospect Mountain Campground

1349 Main Rd., 01034. T: (413) 357-6494 or (888) 550-4762; www.prospectmtncampground.com.

🚐 ★★★   ⛺ ★★★

Beauty: ★★★	Site Privacy: ★★★★
Spaciousness: ★★★★	Quiet: ★★★★★
Security: ★★★	Cleanliness: ★★★★
Insect Control: ★★	Facilities: ★★★★

Located in the rural town of Granville, southwest of Springfield and nudging the Connecticut border, this is a handy base camp for area attractions. Six Flags New England, the region's largest theme park, is a half-hour drive east, and the campground offers good discounts on admission tickets. ($14 off adult ticket prices, at press time.) Sodom Mountain Campground, in Southwick (see listing), is closer, and they, too, offer steeply discounted tickets to Six Flags. The trade-off here: impeccably maintained facilities, with nice touches like tent platforms, a nice kiddie playscape, private, bug-free (!) showers, and umbrellaed tables around the swimming pool. Instead of mountain hiking, a la Sodom Mountain, this campground has walking trails and really gets into the theme stuff, with pig roasts and "Survivor" weekends. The campground boasts a nice spot, at a 1300-foot elevation, with lots of trees and two fishing ponds. The sites are mostly back-in, but there are about six pull-through sites. The gravel sites are set in loops, with tent sites set at the far end of the property. Tent site T15, on Gaintner Pond, is nice, while the water and electric sites along Peter's Pond, especially sites 64 and 65, are inviting.

Basics

Operated By: Ann Schlosser. **Open:** May 1–Oct. 15. **Site Assignment:** Reservations recommended; 50% deposit required on credit card. No-shows will be charged; refunds for cancellations w/ 2-week notice. **Registration:** At office. **Fee:** $30–$42 for 2 adults & any children under 17; V, MC, AE, D. **Parking:** At site.

Facilities

Number of RV-only Sites: 225. **Hookups:** Electric (30, 50 amps), water, sewer. **Each Site:** Picnic table, fire ring. **Dump Station:** Yes. **Laundry:** Yes. **Pay Phone:** Yes. **Restrooms and Showers:** Yes.

Fuel: No. **Propane:** Yes. **Internal Roads:** Gravel, in good condition. **RV Service:** No. **Market:** 11 mi. east, in Southwick. **Restaurant:** 11 mi. east, in Southwick. **General Store:** Yes. **Vending:** Yes. **Swimming:** Yes. **Playground:** Yes. **Other:** Rec hall. **Activities:** Swimming, volleyball, basketball, nature trail, paddleboats, planned activities, themed weekends, shuffle board, bocce ball. **Nearby Attractions:** Six Flags New England theme park, Basketball Hall of Fame, Southwick Motocrosse 338, Big E (Eastern States Exposition) fair, late Sept. **Additional Information:** Greater Springfield CVB, (413) 755-1343, www.valleyvisitor.com.

Restrictions

Pets: Must be leashed, quiet, & cleaned up after. Must not be left unattended. Not allowed in cabins or rental trailers. **Fires:** Fire ring only. **Alcoholic Beverages:** At sites only. **Vehicle Maximum Length:** 40 ft. **Other:** 3-night min. stay required on holidays.

To Get There

Take I-90 (Massachusetts Turnpike) to Exit 3, Westfield. Turn right onto Hwy. 10 and 202, follow into Southwick Center. In town, take a right at second light onto Hwy. 57 west. Follow Hwy. 57 into center of Granville (6.5 mi.). Continue on 57W for another 4.1 mi. Campground is directly off Hwy. 57, on the left.

HINGHAM   MAP, A-3
Boston Harbor Islands

Building 45, 349 Lincoln St., 02043. T: (781) 740-1605; www.reserveamerica.com.

🚐   ⛺ ★★★★

Beauty: ★★★	Site Privacy: ★★
Spaciousness: ★★	Quiet: ★★
Security: ★★	Cleanliness: ★★★★
Insect Control: ★★★	Facilities: ★★

This 17-island state park is part of the 34-island Boston Harbor Islands National Park Area. They are a wonderful natural resource, only 45 minutes by ferry from downtown Boston. Seventeen of the islands are managed the Department of Conservation and Recreation (DCR). Six of the 17 islands, and Webb State Park, a 36-acre peninsula in Weymouth, are staffed and open for public use daily during the summer and weekends in the spring and fall. Visitors to the park enjoy shell and slate beaches, easy hiking paths, old hay fields gone wild with bayberry, raspberry, and elderberry, and old roadways to historic foundations and forts. Shade is found at picnic sites, trailside benches, and on wooded trails. There are many historic and scenic harbor vistas such as Dorchester, Quincy, Hull, and Hingham Bays, the Blue Hills, Boston's skyline, 34 islands, and outward to Massachusetts Bay. Resident Park Managers/ Interpreters live on-island during the visiting season. They provide island supervision, give island tours, and offer ongoing educational programs and special events. Check Boston Harbor

Islands for schedules of island openings and special event listings.

Basics

Operated By: Massachusetts State Parks. **Open:** May 24–Sept. 3. **Site Assignment:** Reservations can be made up to 6 months in advance. **Registration:** At office. **Fee:** Single, $8–$10; group, $25. **Parking:** 2 vehicles per campsite.

Facilities

Number of Multipurpose Sites: 52. **Hookups:** None. **Dump Station:** No. **Laundry:** No. **Pay Phone:** No. **Restrooms and Showers:** Yes. **Fuel:** No. **Propane:** No. **Internal Roads:** Paved. **RV Service:** No. **Market:** No. **Restaurant:** No. **General Store:** No. **Vending:** No. **Swimming:** Yes. **Playground:** No. **Activities:** Boating, canoeing, fishing, hiking, hunting, interpretive programs, picnicking.

Restrictions

Pets: Pets are not allowed at Savoy Mountain cabins, yurts, Boston Harbor Islands or WBNERR camping areas. **Fires:** Campfires in designated fireplaces. Open fires are not allowed above high-tide line. Fresh water is not available. **Alcoholic Beverages:** Alcoholic beverages are prohibited in all MA state parks & campgrounds. **Other:** Quiet hours are 10 p.m.–7 a.m. No unnecessary or disturbing noise at any time. Equipment is limited to 2 tents or 1 camping vehicle & 1 small tent per site. Tents are limited to 300 square feet of combined floor space. Bears are regular visitors to this campground. Bears are wild and can be dangerous. To protect your family and your property, keep all food, coolers, and cooking supplies and equipment in your vehicle when not in use. Massachusetts law requires that children age 16 and under wear a helmet when bicycling.

To Get There

Boston Harbor Islands are passenger boat access only. Ferry service is available from the Fore River Shipyard on Hwy. 3A Quincy, MA and at Long Wharf, Boston. Due to the economy and availability of overnight parking, campers are encouraged to depart from the Fore River Shipyard on Hwy. 3A Quincy. For directions, park information, and current ferry schedules, go to www.bostonislands.com or call park information at (617) 223-8666. Private boaters may off load passengers and equipment at the dock but must anchor off shore out of the main fairway. A dinghy is available on Grape and Bumpkin Islands for access to anchored vessels. Private boaters use USCG chart 13270.

HINGHAM   MAP, A-3
Wompatuck State Park

Union St., 02043. T: (781) 749-7160; www.reserveamerica.com.

🚐 ★★★★   ⛺ ★★★★

Beauty: ★★★	Site Privacy: ★★★★★
Spaciousness: ★★★	Quiet: ★★★★
Security: ★★★★	Cleanliness: ★
Insect Control: ★★★★	Facilities: ★★★

This is the closest campground to Boston where campers can enjoy a wilderness experience. Located on the South Shore of Massachusetts, about 19 miles from the city, Wompatuck State Park is a favorite of cycling enthusiasts. The park offers 10 miles of paved bike paths and another 30 miles or so of unpaved multiuse (bike, hike, horseback) trails, winding through lush forests and alongside freshwater ponds. Campsites are set in two areas, one with electric hookups (Camping Area 2), one without (Camping Area 1). Sites along the perimeter road, backed by woodlands, offer the most privacy, especially C-1 through C-14 (with electric hookups). Nearby, sites E-15, 17, and 19, are also nice, and near the restrooms. In general, the sites in Camping Area 2 are set back farther from the road, more shaded, and more secluded than those in Area 1. Tent campers can use either one. A nice feature of this park is the abundance of fresh water, available at stone washbasins and water fountains scattered throughout the park. There's also collectible spring water, available at Mt. Blue Spring. (Avoid heavily trafficked campsite X-9, nearest the hiking trail to the spring.) A not-so-nice feature: the restrooms, where a recent visit revealed missing mirrors, overflowing waste cans, and a lack of toilet paper.

BASICS

Operated By: Massachusetts State Forests and Parks. **Open:** Mid-Apr.–mid-Oct. **Site Assignment:** Reservations recommended; reserve up to 6 months in advance by calling Reserve America at (877) I-CAMP-MA or online at www.reserveamerica.com; 65 sites are first come, first served; to change arrival or departure date, or site type, call at least 3 days prior to arrival date; $10 cancellation/transfer fee; no refunds for amounts less than $5. **Registration:** At office. **Fee:** Massachusetts residents, $10–$12; non-residents, $12–$14; electric utility add $3; water/sewer add $2; V, MC. **Parking:** At site.

FACILITIES

Number of RV-only Sites: 262. **Hookups:** Electric (20 amps). **Each Site:** Picnic table, fireplace w/ grill top. **Dump Station:** Yes. **Laundry:** No. **Pay Phone:** Yes. **Restrooms and Showers:** Yes. **Fuel:** No. **Propane:** No. **Internal Roads:** Paved, in good condition. **RV Service:** No. **Market:** 2.5 mi. north. **Restaurant:** 3.5 mi. north. **General Store:** No. **Vending:** Yes. **Swimming:** No. **Playground:** No. **Other:** Boat ramp. **Activities:** Hiking, bicycling, mountain biking, interpretive programs. **Nearby Attractions:** Boston attractions, golf, South Shore Music Circus (outdoor concerts). **Additional Information:** Greater Boston CVB, (617) 536-4100 or (888) SEE-BOSTON, www.bostonusa.com.

RESTRICTIONS

Pets: Must be leashed & cleaned up after. Must not be left unattended. Proof of rabies vaccination required. **Fires:** Fireplaces only. **Alcoholic Beverages:** Not allowed. **Vehicle Maximum Length:** 30 ft. **Other:** 2-night min. stay required between Memorial Day & Labor Day. 14 cumulative day stay limit between Memorial Day & Labor Day. No swimming.

TO GET THERE

Follow Hwy. 3 to Exit 14; then take Hwy. 228

north (left) into Hingham. Turn right on Free St. to campground entrance.

HINGHAM MAP, A-3
Wompatuck State Park

Union St., 02043. T: (781) 749-7160; www.reserveamerica.com.

🚐 ★★★★   ⛺ ★★★★

Beauty: ★★★   Site Privacy: ★★★
Spaciousness: ★★   Quiet: ★★
Security: ★★   Cleanliness: ★★★★
Insect Control: ★★★   Facilities: ★★★★

Located just a 35-minute drive from downtown Boston, Wompatuck State Park offers 262 wooded campsites (140 of them with electricity), 12 miles of paved bicycle trails, and many miles of wooded bridle paths and hiking trails. The park is very popular with trailer campers: electrical and water hookups are available. Fishing is allowed in the Cohasset Reservoir. A boat ramp is provided for car-top boats, but no boat trailers, please. One of the most notable features of the Park is Mt. Blue Spring, which is a popular source of fresh drinking water. Visitors can help themselves for free. The park is named for an Indian chief the local colonists knew as Josiah Wompatuck. In 1665, Chief Wompatuck deeded the park and the surrounding land to the English settlers. During WWII the park was used as an ammunition depot by the U.S. military. The trails in Wompatuck offered varied riding experiences to area mountain bikers. Wompatuck is bisected by Union Street. In the past most of the off road bicycling was done on the right side of Union Street, where the majority of the park's unbroken woodland exists. But, over the past several years the park's staff, aided by area mountain bikers, has been hard at work creating an entirely new network of single track trails on the left side of the park in some areas recently reacquired by the state.

BASICS

Operated By: Massachusetts State Parks. **Open:** Apr. 13–Oct. 28. **Site Assignment:** Reservations can be made up to 6 months in advance. **Registration:** At office. **Fee:** Single, $12–$17. **Parking:** 2 vehicles per campsite.

FACILITIES

Number of Multipurpose Sites: 262. **Hookups:** Yes. **Dump Station:** Yes. **Laundry:** No. **Pay Phone:** Yes. **Restrooms and Showers:** Yes. **Fuel:** No. **Propane:** No. **Internal Roads:** Paved. **RV Service:** No. **Market:** No. **Restaurant:** No. **General Store:** No. **Vending:** No. **Swimming:** No. **Playground:** No. **Activities:** Biking, boating, fishing, hiking, horseback riding, hunting, interpretive programs, cross-country skiing, snowmobiling.

RESTRICTIONS

Pets: Keep pets leashed (10-ft. leash max.) at all times. Proof of rabies vaccination is required. Pets are never to be left unattended. **Fires:** Campfires in des-

ignated fireplaces. **Alcoholic Beverages:** Alcoholic beverages are prohibited in all MA state parks & campgrounds. **Other:** Quiet hours are 10 p.m.–7 a.m. Please, no unnecessary or disturbing noise at any time. Equipment is limited to 2 tents or 1 camping vehicle & 1 small tent per site. Tents are limited to 300 square feet of combined floor space.

TO GET THERE

From the south and Cape Cod: Take Hwy. 3 north to Exit 14 and the intersection with Hwy. 228. Follow Hwy. 228 north about 5 mi. to Free St. on the right. Turn right onto Free St. 1 mi. to the park entrance on the right. The camping area is 1.5 mi. into the park on the right. From the north and Boston: Follow Hwy. 3 south to Exit 14 and the intersection with Hwy. 228. Follow Hwy. 228 north about 5 mi. to the intersection with Free St. on the right. Turn right onto Free St. and follow it 1 mi. to the park entrance on the right. The camping area is 1.5 mi. into park on the right.

LANESBOROUGH MAP, A-1
Mt. Greylock State Reservation

30 Rockwell Rd. P.O. Box 138, 01237. T: (413) 499-4262; www.reserveamerica.com.

🚐 ★★★★   ⛺ ★★★★

Beauty: ★★★   Site Privacy: ★★★
Spaciousness: ★★★   Quiet: ★★★★★
Security: ★★★★★   Cleanliness: ★★★★
Insect Control: ★★★   Facilities: ★

At 3,491 feet, Mount Greylock is the highest peak in Massachusetts. Acquired by the Commonwealth in 1898, it became Massachusetts' first state park. Arriving at the summit by foot-trail or auto road you may see a panorama of five states, visit the Veterans War Memorial Tower, or relax in rustic Bascom Lodge, which offers overnight accommodations and meals. The reservation has over 70 miles of trails, including a section of the Appalachian National Scenic Trail. The campground on Sperry Road offers 35 campsites and five group campsites. Also available are five remote trailside backpack shelters, picnic sites, and a pavilion. Click here to see a panoramic view from the summit of Mount Greylock at dawn. Great hiking opportunities abound in the immediate area of Mount Greylock. Greylock Glen features challenging trails up the steep eastern side of the mountain. Nearby Taconic Trail State Park (no facilities available) on the Massachusetts–New York state border and the Phelps Trail provide access to the Taconic Crest Trail, a 35-mile-long foot path.

BASICS

Operated By: Massachusetts State Parks. **Open:** All year. **Site Assignment:** Reservations can be made up to 6 months in advance. **Registration:** At office. **Fee:** Single, $8–$10; group, $25. **Parking:** 2 vehicles per campsite.

FACILITIES

Number of Multipurpose Sites: 40. **Hookups:** None. **Dump Station:** No. **Laundry:** No. **Pay Phone:** W/in 10 mi. **Restrooms and Showers:** Yes. **Fuel:** No. **Propane:** No. **Internal Roads:** Paved. **RV Service:** No. **Market:** No. **Restaurant:** No. **General Store:** No. **Vending:** W/in 10 mi. **Swimming:** No. **Playground:** No. **Activities:** Biking, hiking, interpretive programs, picnicking.

RESTRICTIONS

Pets: Keep pets leashed (10-ft. leash max.) at all times. Proof of rabies vaccination is required. Pets are never to be left unattended. **Fires:** Campfires in designated fireplaces. **Alcoholic Beverages:** Alcoholic beverages are prohibited in all MA state parks & campgrounds. **Other:** Quiet hours are 10 p.m.–7 a.m. No unnecessary or disturbing noise at any time. Equipment is limited to 2 tents or 1 camping vehicle & 1 small tent per site. Tents are limited to 300 square feet of combined floor space. Bears are regular visitors to this campground. Bears are wild and can be dangerous. To protect your family and your property, keep all food, coolers, and cooking supplies and equipment in your vehicle when not in use. The nearest water source in this park is 2 mi. from the campground. Emergency phone service is 6 mi. (public phone). Massachusetts law requires that children age 16 and under wear a helmet when bicycling.

TO GET THERE

Take Massachusetts Turnpike (Hwy. 90) to Exit 2 (Lee). Turn right onto Hwy. 20 to Hwy. 7 north toward Lenox and Pittsfield. Follow Hwy. 7 north through Pittsfield to the Town of Lanesborough. Take right onto North Main St., follow signs. Go 1.8 mi. to the visitor center. The campground is on Sperry Rd. 7.8 mi. The park entrance will be on the right.

LEE   MAP, A-1
October Mountain State Forest

317 Woodland Rd., 01238. T: (413) 243-1778; www.reserveamerica.com.

🚐 ★★★	⛺ ★★★
Beauty: ★★	Site Privacy: ★★★
Spaciousness: ★★★	Quiet: ★★
Security: ★★★	Cleanliness: ★★★
Insect Control: ★★	Facilities: ★★★

Set on a sunny hillside in the center of Berkshire County, this campground is a good base for enjoying the area's numerous cultural attractions. Tanglewood Music Festival is just six miles away, so this campground offers visitors the chance to hear music under the stars, then return to the park to sleep under the stars (well, sort of). October Mountain also boasts several miles of hiking paths, including a section of the famous Appalachian Trail. A favorite footpath leads to Schermerhorn Gorge; others lead to lakes and (minor) mountain summits. Trailer sites are set in a loop near the campground entrance. These are mostly open, level, and grassy, with just a bit of shade. Tent sites are grouped together on the second level of the camping area. Site 46 is very secluded and close to the restroom; site 40 is also a good, end-of-the-road spot. Stay clear of site 34, on the third level, where an old tank detracts from the beauty of the space. One downside of this park: off-road vehicles are allowed to use the multiuse trails. They're gone by evening, so this shouldn't disturb anyone's sleep. Also, a nearby power plant makes a humming noise. This is most audible near the entrance of the park and the trailer sites and shouldn't bother tenters, who are sited farther back on the second and third levels of the park. (Trivia note: October Mountain is the largest state forest in Massachusetts.)

BASICS

Operated By: Massachusetts State Forests and Parks. **Open:** Mid-May–mid-Oct. **Site Assignment:** Reservations recommended; reserve up to 6 months in advance by calling Reserve America at (877) I-CAMP-MA or online at www.reserveamerica.com; 10 sites are first come, first served; to change arrival or departure date, or site type, call at least 3 days prior to arrival date; $10 cancellation/transfer fee; no refunds for amounts less than $5. **Registration:** At office. **Fee:** Massachusetts residents, $10–$15; non-residents, $12–$17; electric/water/sewer, $3; V, MC. **Parking:** At site.

FACILITIES

Number of RV-only Sites: 46. **Hookups:** None. **Each Site:** Picnic table, fireplace. **Dump Station:** Yes. **Laundry:** No. **Pay Phone:** Yes. **Restrooms and Showers:** Yes. **Fuel:** No. **Propane:** No. **Internal Roads:** Paved, in good condition. **RV Service:** No. **Market:** 2 mi. east, in Lee. **Restaurant:** 2 mi. east, in Lee. **General Store:** No. **Vending:** No. **Swimming:** No. **Playground:** No. **Other:** Boat ramp. **Activities:** Hiking, fishing, ATV riding. **Nearby Attractions:** Tanglewood, Jacob's Pillow (dance). **Additional Information:** Berkshire Hills Visitors Bureau, (413) 443-9186 or (800) 237-5747, www.berkshires.org.

RESTRICTIONS

Pets: Must be leashed & cleaned up after. Must not be left unattended. Proof of rabies vaccination required. **Fires:** Fireplaces only. **Alcoholic Beverages:** Not allowed. **Vehicle Maximum Length:** 30 ft. **Other:** Pets are not allowed in buildings.

TO GET THERE

From I-90 (Massachusetts Turnpike), take Exit 2, Hwy. 20 west. Turn right on Center St., follow signs.

LITTLETON   MAP, A-3
Boston Northwest/Minuteman KOA

P.O. Box 2122, 264 Ayer Rd., 01460. T: (877) 677-0042; www.minutemancampground.com.

🚐 ★★★★	⛺ ★★★★

Beauty: ★★★★★	Site Privacy: ★★★
Spaciousness: ★★★	Quiet: ★★★
Security: ★★★★	Cleanliness: ★★★★★
Insect Control: ★★★	Facilities: ★★★★

A scenic drive it's not. As you head west on Hwy. 2-A, a quarry-lined industrial corridor, you may well be wondering why you'd ever consider camping in such an unlikely area. Then, you spot the KOA sign and pull into a road flanked by tall white pines. Trees never looked so good! And so it is at Boston Northwest/Minuteman KOA campground, about an hour's drive west of Boston. Not only do the trees provide shade for campsites, but they help muffle the sound of traffic. The heart of the campground is the familiar KOA A-frame with an office, convenience store (very complete, with everything from supplies to souvenirs to rental videos), laundry facility, and restrooms. A pool and a rec hall are situated nearby. From there, five streets branch out, with a total of 100 campsites. This is definitely an RV camper's scene; all pull-through sites, just nine sites are designated for tenters, although 25 are multiuse. Seven cabins are sprinkled throughout the property. The park-like setting, plus the pool and (nice) playground make this a good choice for day-tripping families, especially those with the battle sites at Lexington and Concord on their itineraries.

BASICS

Operated By: Ted and Maureen Nussdorfer. **Open:** Apr. 28–Oct. 15. **Site Assignment:** Reservations taken all year; special requests should be made in advance; smaller units can typically book w/in 1 week of arrival date. **Registration:** At office. **Fee:** $26.50–$37 for 2 adults; extra adult, $6; extra child over age 5, $2; discounted rates w/ KOA Value Card; V, MC, D. **Parking:** At site.

FACILITIES

Number of RV-only Sites: 91. **Number of Tent-only Sites:** 9. **Hookups:** Electric (20, 30, 50 amps), water, sewer. **Each Site:** Picnic table, fire ring. **Dump Station:** Yes. **Laundry:** Yes. **Pay Phone:** Yes. **Restrooms and Showers:** Yes. **Fuel:** No. **Propane:** Yes. **Internal Roads:** Paved & gravel, good condition. **RV Service:** No. **Market:** 4 mi. east. **Restaurant:** 1 mi. west. **General Store:** Yes. **Vending:** No. **Swimming:** Yes. **Playground:** Yes. **Other:** Rec hall, rental cabins. **Activities:** Volleyball, horseshoes, videos, planned activities, pool tables. **Nearby Attractions:** Lexington & Concord historic sites, golf, mini-golf. **Additional Information:** Greater Merrimack Valley CVB, (978) 459-6150 or (800) 443-3332, www.lowell.org.

RESTRICTIONS

Pets: Must be leashed, quiet, & cleaned up after. Must not be left unattended. Use enclosed dog-walk area. **Fires:** Fire ring only. **Alcoholic Beverages:** At sites only. **Vehicle Maximum Length:** 40 ft. **Other:** No limit on number of days stayed.

TO GET THERE

Take I-495 to Exit 30. Go west on Hwy. 2A and Hwy. 110 for 2.5 mi. Campground is on the left.

MONTEREY   MAP, A-1, B-1
Beartown State Forest

reserve america

69 Blue Hill Rd. P.O. Box 97, 01245.
T: (413) 528-0904; www.reserveamerica.com.

🚐 ★★★★   ⛺ ★★★★

Beauty: ★★★		Site Privacy: ★★★★	
Spaciousness: ★★★★		Quiet: ★★★★	
Security: ★★★★		Cleanliness: ★★★★	
Insect Control: ★★★		Facilities: ★★★	

Beartown State Forest has two distinctly different worlds between the summer and winter. During the warm months the pristine 35-acre Benedict Pond attracts swimmers, boaters, and fishermen. An extensive network of trails on over 12,000 acres offers visitors a chance to glimpse deer, bear, bobcat, fisher, and other wildlife, including the park's namesake, the Black Bear. Brooks, beaver ponds, rich deciduous forest, flowering shrubs and wildflowers, and fall foliage are plentiful. The Appalachian Trail passes near Benedict Pond and offers spectacular wooded views. The other half of the year the forest becomes a winter wonderland, where visitors on cross-country skis, snowshoes, or snowmobiles can explore a snow-covered wilderness. The 1.5-mile Benedict Pond Loop Trail is a must in any season. Year-round camping is also available. Nearby, on US 7 in Great Barrington, Fountain Pond State Park and Monument Mountain (The Trustees of Reservations) offer a variety of hiking trails and breathtaking views any time of year.

BASICS
Operated By: Massachusetts State Parks. **Open:** All year. **Site Assignment:** Reservations can be made up to 6 months in advance. **Registration:** At office. **Fee:** Single, $8–$10. **Parking:** 2 vehicles per campsite.

FACILITIES
Number of Multipurpose Sites: 12. **Hookups:** None. **Dump Station:** No. **Laundry:** No. **Pay Phone:** Yes. **Restrooms and Showers:** Yes. **Fuel:** No. **Propane:** No. **Internal Roads:** Paved. **RV Service:** No. **Market:** No. **Restaurant:** No. **General Store:** No. **Vending:** No. **Swimming:** Yes. **Playground:** No. **Activities:** Biking, boating, canoeing, fishing, hiking, horseback riding, hunting, picnicking, cross-country skiing, snowmobiling.

RESTRICTIONS
Pets: Keep pets leashed (10-ft. leash max.) at all times. Proof of rabies vaccination is required. Pets are never to be left unattended. **Fires:** Campfires in designated fireplaces. **Alcoholic Beverages:** Alcoholic beverages are prohibited in all MA state parks & campgrounds. **Other:** Quiet hours are 10 p.m.–7 a.m. No unnecessary or disturbing noise at any time. Equipment is limited to 2 tents or 1 camping vehicle & 1 small tent per site. Tents are limited to 300 square feet of combined floor space. Bears are regular visitors to this campground. Bears are wild and can be dangerous. To protect your family and your property, keep all food, coolers, and cooking supplies and equipment in your vehicle when not in use. Massachusetts law requires that children age 16 and under wear a helmet when bicycling.

TO GET THERE
From the MA Turnpike (Rte. 90): Take Exit 2 to Hwy. 102 west to Hwy. 7 south. Follow Hwy. 7 to Hwy. 23 east to Monterey (Blue Hill Rd.). Follow the brown signs to the campground.

NORTH ANDOVER   MAP, A-3
Harold Parker State Forest

reserve america

1951 Turnpike Rd., 01845. T: (978) 686-3391 or (877) I-CAMP-MA; www.reserveamerica.com.

🚐 ★★   ⛺ ★★★★

Beauty: ★★★★		Site Privacy: ★★★★	
Spaciousness: ★★★★		Quiet: ★★★★★	
Security: ★★★		Cleanliness: ★★★	
Insect Control: ★★		Facilities: ★★	

About 25 miles north of Boston, 3,500-acre Harold Parker State Forest offers a taste of the wilderness with easy access to big-city attractions. A drive into the forest reveals a mix of hardwoods and fragrant pine, studded with nine ponds. Ninety campsites are arrayed in a loop, just to the west of jalapeño-shaped Frye Pond. The most popular sites, for good reason, are those on the waterfront (63–87). If those are taken, site 15 is a good choice, located up a small hill and away from the road. Steer clear of sites 52, 54, and 56 if you need proximity to a restroom. Once settled in, you'll enjoy the rustic setting and woodsy hiking trails. (Ask for a trail map when you come in.) If you've brought a kayak or canoe, don't miss a sunset paddle on Frye Pond. The campground opens in mid-April, but April tends to be muddy around here. Also beware of mid-May, black-fly season. Given the lack of facilities, Harold Parker State Forest is best-suited for tent campers or self-sufficient RVers looking for a back-to-nature escape. It makes a great base for campers who want to play tourist in bustling Boston and the North Shore, then return to the tranquility of woods and water.

BASICS
Operated By: Massachusetts State Forests and Parks. **Open:** Mid-Apr.–mid-Oct. **Site Assignment:** Reserve up to 6 months in advance by calling (877) I-CAMP-MA or online at www.reserveamerica.com; if you cancel or change dates or type of site, call (877) 422-6762 at least 3 days prior to arrival; $10 cancellation/transfer fee. Walk-ins welcome if space is available; best time to try is after 11 a.m. check-out period. **Registration:** At office. **Fee:** Massachusetts residents, $12; nonresidents, $14; accessible sites available; V, MC. **Parking:** At site.

FACILITIES
Number of RV-only Sites: 91. **Hookups:** None. **Each Site:** Picnic table, fireplace, grills (to come). **Dump Station:** Yes. **Laundry:** No. **Pay Phone:** Yes. **Restrooms and Showers:** Yes. **Fuel:** No. **Propane:** No. **Internal Roads:** Paved, in good condition. **RV Service:** No. **Market:** 5 mi. east in Middleton. **Restaurant:** 5 mi. east in Middleton. **General Store:** No (firewood for sale at campground office). **Vending:** No. **Swimming:** No. **Playground:** Planned. **Other:** Ball field, basketball court (planned), small beach. **Activities:** 25 mi. of multiuse trails (hiking, biking, bridle), fishing (license required), canoeing, pond swimming, hunting (limited; mostly in fall). **Nearby Attractions:** Witchcraft & maritime-related attractions in Salem, Peabody-Essex Museum, whale-watching boat trips out of Gloucester, Salem, and Newburyport, Lexington & Concord, Boston. **Additional Information:** North of Boston CVB, (978) 977-7760 or (800) 742-5306, www.northofboston.org.

RESTRICTIONS
Pets: Must be leashed, quiet, & cleaned up after. Rabies vaccination certificate required. **Fires:** Fireplaces only. **Alcoholic Beverages:** Not allowed. **Vehicle Maximum Length:** No limit. **Other:** 14-day max. cumulative stay Memorial Day–Labor Day.

TO GET THERE
Take Hwy. 495 to Exit 42E to Hwy. 114W; follow signs to forest. Go right at camping sign, left at first stop sign. Pass residential area; go left onto Jenkins Rd. Camp office will be on your right.

OAKHAM   MAP, A-2
Pine Acres Family Camping Resort

203 Bechan Rd., 01068. T: (508) 882-9509 or (866) 571-6048; www.pineacresresort.com.

🚐 ★★★★★   ⛺ ★★★★★

Beauty: ★★★★★		Site Privacy: ★★★	
Spaciousness: ★★★		Quiet: ★★★★	
Security: ★★★★★		Cleanliness: ★★★★★	
Insect Control: ★★		Facilities: ★★★★★	

This wonderfully appealing campground is located almost dead-center in the state, 15 miles from Worcester and about 50 miles west of Boston. Amidst a small-town New England landscape, this campground is a destination in itself. Set on a pine-shrouded hillside above 70-acre Lake Dean, it's a mini resort-land, with everything from tennis and boating to gourmet coffee and live entertainment. (Even waterskiing, if you bring your own boat.) Operated for 41 years by the Packard family, this place sets the standard, combining natural beauty with loads of amenities and small touches that add up: a porta-potty by the beach, a dog walk, stone fire rings (not the rusty jobs that are all too prevalent.) Campsites are set on loop roads, off a center pod with a lodge, rec hall, store, and so on. About half are seasonal. Site 137, on a hill overlooking the lake, is a fine choice, while sites 78 and 79 face the beach. Ditto sites 89, 93, and 93A. Sites H10 and H11, near wilderness trails, are good for hikers, while site 105, among the tent sites, offers a wooded spot on a hill with lake views. We'd pass on the M sites; too close to the hub of activity. Tip: Don't forget the bug juice!

BASICS

Operated By: Oakham Pine Acres, Inc. **Open:** All year. **Site Assignment:** Reservations recommended; 3-week advance notice is good; can reserve online; 50% deposit required; holiday weekends require 3-night minimum and payment in full w/ reservation; will try to honor specific site requests but cannot guarantee site requests for stays of less than 1 week; refund given for cancellations w/ 30-day notice, minus $10; if cancelling less than 30 days but at least 7 days prior to arrival, payments will be used as credit for future stay. **Registration:** At office. **Fee:** $25–$50 per family, w/ up to 3 unmarried children under age 18; V, MC, D. **Parking:** At sites and designated lots only.

FACILITIES

Number of RV-only Sites: 300. **Hookups:** Electric (20, 30, 50 amps), water, sewer, cable TV, modems. **Each Site:** Picnic table, fire ring. **Dump Station:** Yes. **Laundry:** Yes. **Pay Phone:** Yes. **Restrooms and Showers:** Yes, coin-op. **Fuel:** No. **Propane:** Yes. **Internal Roads:** Paved & gravel, in good condition. **RV Service:** Yes. **Market:** 3 mi. south on Hwy. 148. **Restaurant:** Yes. **General Store:** Yes. **Vending:** Yes. **Swimming:** Yes. **Playground:** Yes. **Other:** Boat ramp, rec hall, adult lounge, tennis court, mini-golf. **Activities:** Fishing (need MA license, available in Rutland), tennis, boating (rentals available), volleyball, horseshoes, ball field, hiking, planned activities. In winter, cross-country skiing, skating, snowmobiling, ice fishing. **Nearby Attractions:** Old Sturbridge Village living history museum, Worcester Art Museum, Worcester Centrum (events), New England Science Center, Quabbin Reservoir, Higgins Armory Museum, Brimfield Flea Markets, apple orchards, golf. **Additional Information:** Central Massachusetts Tourist Council, (508) 775-7400, www.worcester.org.

RESTRICTIONS

Pets: Must be leashed, quiet, & cleaned up after. Must not be left unattended. **Fires:** Fire ring only. **Alcoholic Beverages:** Allowed. **Vehicle Maximum Length:** 40 ft. **Other:** Children must be supervised at all times.

TO GET THERE

From Boston, take Massachusetts Turnpike (I-90) west to Exit 10 (Auburn), then Hwy. 20W. Turn right onto Hwy. 56N, go through Leicester, then left onto Hwy. 122N, and left again onto Hwy. 148S. Watch for campground signs on Hwy. 148.

PITTSFIELD   MAP, A-1
Pittsfield State Forest

reserve america

1041 Cascade St, 01201. T: (413) 442-8992; www.reserveamerica.com.

🚐 ★★★   ⛺ ★★★★

Beauty: ★★★★★   Site Privacy: ★★★
Spaciousness: ★★★   Quiet: ★★★★
Security: ★★★★   Cleanliness: ★★★
Insect Control: ★★   Facilities: ★★★

If you don't mind doing without some creature comforts (namely, flush toilets and showers), you'll appreciate the wonderful natural features at this pristine state park located at the far Western edge of the state (Berkshire County.) From late May into June, 65 acres of wild azaleas bloom into a sea of pink blossoms. Two camping areas are clustered nearby, surrounding Berry Pond, the highest natural water body in Massachusetts at 2,150 feet. Fishing enthusiasts have discovered the pond, while hikers enjoy the vista from the top of Berry Mountain, a great place for sunset-watching. Great tent sites in this area include site 7, with good pond views, and sites 9–12, which are roomy, flat, and wooded. The only toilet here is pit-style (nonflush). Follow the loop road, running alongside Parker Brook, and you'll reach the second set of campsites, grouped near a flush toilet. These are pretty and woodsy as well, but set a bit closer together than those at Berry Pond, with less buffer between sites. Site 18 is big but not very secluded. Hiking trails wind through a variety of forest, and beckon visitors to escape into the woods.

BASICS

Operated By: Massachusetts State Forests and Parks. **Open:** Late May–mid-Oct. **Site Assignment:** Reservations may be made up to 6 months in advance by calling Reserve America at (877) I-CAMP-MA or online at www.reserveamerica.com; some sites are first come, first served; to change arrival or departure date, or site type, call at least 3 days prior to arrival date; $10 cancellation/transfer fee; no refunds for amounts less than $5. **Registration:** At office. **Fee:** Massachusetts residents, $12; nonresidents, $14; Parker Brook area, $5; Berry Pond area, $5 (no flush toilets); V, MC. **Parking:** At site.

FACILITIES

Number of RV-only Sites: 5. **Number of Tent-only Sites:** 26. **Hookups:** None. **Each Site:** Picnic table, fireplace. **Dump Station:** No. **Laundry:** No. **Pay Phone:** Yes. **Restrooms and Showers:** Yes, no showers. **Fuel:** No. **Propane:** No. **Internal Roads:** Paved & gravel, good to fair condition. **RV Service:** No. **Market:** 5 mi. east. **Restaurant:** 5 mi. east. **General Store:** No. **Vending:** Soda. **Swimming:** Pond. **Playground:** No. **Other:** Nature center. **Activities:** Hiking (including wheelchair-accessible trail), swimming (in Lulu Pond), bicycling, fishing, horseback riding, interpretive programs. **Nearby Attractions:** Tanglewood (music), Jacob's Pillow (dance), Mt. Greylock, Norman Rockwell Museum. **Additional Information:** Berkshire Hills Visitors Bureau, (413) 443-9186 or (800) 237-5747, www.berkshires.org.

RESTRICTIONS

Pets: Must be leashed & cleaned up after. Must not be left unattended. Proof of rabies vaccination required. **Fires:** Fireplaces only. **Alcoholic Beverages:** Not allowed. **Vehicle Maximum Length:** None. **Other:** Paved trail ideal for those in a wheelchair.

TO GET THERE

From the Massachusetts Turnpike (I-90), take Exit 2. At the junction of Hwy. 7 and Hwy. 20, go west on Hwy. 20. Take West St. to Cascade St. Follow signs.

PLYMOUTH   MAP, B-4
Pinewood Lodge

190 Pinewood Rd., 02360.
T: (508) 746-3548;
www.pinewoodlodge.com.

🚐 ★★★★★   ⛺ ★★★★★

Beauty: ★★★   Site Privacy: ★★
Spaciousness: ★★★★   Quiet: ★★★★
Security: ★★★★   Cleanliness: ★★★★★
Insect Control: ★★★★★   Facilities: ★★★★

The tasteful white wooden sign that welcomes guests to Pinewood Lodge is a harbinger of things to come. Run by the Saunders family since 1962 (now operated by the great-grandchildren), this campground is the nicest one in the Plymouth area. Families who stay here while exploring Plimoth Plantation, ten miles away, won't be disappointed. Set amidst the pines on Pinewood Lake, at the end of a dead-end road, the campground boasts 3,000 feet of lake frontage. A private beach is buoyed off for swimming; near the beach there's a playground and rental rowboats and canoes. With its bustling rec room (nice feature: a piano) and activities galore (air hockey tournaments, a pots-and-pans parade), Pinewood Lodge is a destination resort. In summer, that is; in fall, retirees replace kids on bikes and the mood changes completely. Campsites are mostly wooded, carpeted with pine needles, and set fairly close together. Avoid the sites along the main road (beginning with letter D) and head to the East and West Park areas (beginning with letter S). Nicest sites for tents is the small colony on the opposite side of the park, numbers 14 through 21. Fees are comparable to other area campgrounds, although they charge extra per child, but Pinewood Lodge offers more in the way of cleanliness, amenities, and attention to detail.

BASICS

Operated By: Saunders family. **Open:** May 1–Oct. 1. **Site Assignment:** Reservations recommended; deposit required equal to 1-night stay; $50 deposit required for holiday stay; deposits refunded w/ 2-week notice only; $5 fee applies to cancelled or shortened stays. **Registration:** At office. **Fee:** $20–$38; based on 2 people; extra children age 13-plus, $10; 12 & under, $4; V, MC. **Parking:** At sites and parking lots.

FACILITIES

Number of RV-only Sites: 230. **Number of Tent-only Sites:** 20. **Hookups:** Electric (20, 30, 50 amps), water, sewer. **Each Site:** Picnic table, ring. **Dump Station:** Yes. **Laundry:** Yes. **Pay Phone:** Yes. **Restrooms and Showers:** Yes, coin-op. **Fuel:** No. **Propane:** Yes. **Internal Roads:** Paved & gravel, in good condition. **RV Service:** Yes. **Market:** 5 mi. east, in Plymouth. **Restaurant:** Yes. **General Store:** Yes. **Vending:** No. **Swimming:** No. **Playground:** Yes. **Other:** Rec hall. **Activities:** Fishing, swimming, boating (rentals available), canoeing, basketball, planned activities. **Nearby Attractions:** Plimoth Plantation, whale-watching cruises, scenic harbor cruises, Mayflower II, Plymouth National Wax Museum, Pilgrim Hall Museum, winery, Ocean Spray

Cranberry World, tours, winery. **Additional Information:** Destination Plymouth, (800) USA-1620 or www.visit-plymouth.com.

RESTRICTIONS

Pets: Not allowed. **Fires:** Fire ring only. **Alcoholic Beverages:** Allowed. **Vehicle Maximum Length:** No limit. **Other:** 3-night min. stay required on holiday weekends; 5-night min. on 4th of July.

TO GET THERE

Take Hwy. 3 south to Hwy. 44, Exit 6B. Take Hwy. 44 west 3 mi. to Pinewood Rd., turn left to campground entrance.

ROCHESTER   MAP, B-3
Outdoor World— Gateway to Cape Cod

90 Stevens Rd., P.O. Box 217, 02770.
T: (508) 763-5911 or (800) 588-2221;
www.campoutdoorworld.com.

🚐 ★★★★   ⛺ ★★

Beauty: ★★★★	Site Privacy: ★★★
Spaciousness: ★★★	Quiet: ★★★★
Security: ★★★★★	Cleanliness: ★★★★
Insect Control: ★★★	Facilities: ★★★★★

Located about 55 miles south of Boston and 20 miles from the Cape Cod Canal, this membership park is nestled in tall pines at the end of a dead-end road. This is a big-rig country—you might even see five-wheelers here—so tent campers are likely to feel dwarfed in these surroundings. But RVers will find plenty to like, from pull-through sites to natural beauty to nice touches, like big umbrellas at poolside. And how often do you find tennis courts at a campground? There's a nice spot to get away from it all, too; a couple of picnic tables overlooking Leonard's Pond, at the end of Whitehorse Rd. (The rusted-out grills at several campsites are a downer, though.) Campsites are set in three sections, with A and B sections closest to the entrance and activities areas, and C section set back, near the tennis courts, basketball court, playground, and, at the very end, the pond and overflow sites. Among the nicest, in our view, are sites A42 through A47, which back up into the woods but are an easy walk to the snack bar, pool, and other facilities. Tent sites are clustered just behind the A section. With so much to do, families will be happy here, in this very resort-like property.

BASICS

Operated By: Resorts U.S.A. **Open:** Mid-Apr.–mid-Oct. **Site Assignment:** Outdoor World is a membership park; call (800) 222-5557 for information on arranging a visit or to reserve a campsite. **Registration:** At office. **Fee:** $25 per family; V, MC, D, AE. **Parking:** At site.

FACILITIES

Number of RV-only Sites: 180. **Number of Tent-only Sites:** 8. **Hookups:** Electric (30, 50 amps), water, sewer. **Each Site:** Picnic table, fire ring, grill. **Dump Station:** No. **Laundry:** Yes. **Pay Phone:** Yes. **Restrooms and Showers:** Yes. **Fuel:**

No. **Propane:** Yes. **Internal Roads:** Gravel, in good condition. **RV Service:** No. **Market:** 5 mi. east. **Restaurant:** Yes. **General Store:** Yes. **Vending:** Yes. **Swimming:** Yes. **Playground:** Yes. **Other:** Game room, rec hall, tennis courts. **Activities:** Tennis, swimming, volleyball, softball, bocce, shuffleboard, horseshoes, canoeing, kayaking, planned activities. **Nearby Attractions:** Edaville Railroad, berry picking, golf, outlet shopping, Plymouth attractions. **Additional Information:** Bristol County CVB, (508) 997-1250 or (800) 288-6263, www.bristol-county.org.

RESTRICTIONS

Pets: Must be leashed, quiet, & cleaned up after. Not permitted in buildings, pavilions, or pool & lake areas. Must not be left unattended. **Fires:** Fireplaces only. **Alcoholic Beverages:** Allowed; must be in a cup when carried off site. **Vehicle Maximum Length:** No limit. **Other:** Max. 10 people per campsite (including visitors) at any time.

TO GET THERE

Take I-495 south to junction of Hwy. 58, Exit 2. Turn right and go to traffic light where Hwy. 58 becomes County Rd. Continue south on County Rd. 1.5 mi. to High St. Turn right on High St. and go another 1.5 mi. to Stevens Rd. Turn left onto Stevens Rd., follow signs 0.5 mi. to campground entrance.

SAGAMORE BEACH   MAP, B-4
Scusset Beach State Reservation Camping Area

reserve america

140 Scusset Beach Rd., 02562. T: (508) 888-0859; www.reserveamerica.com.

🚐 ★★★   ⛺ ★★★★

Beauty: ★★★★	Site Privacy: ★★★
Spaciousness: ★★★★	Quiet: ★★★★
Security: ★★★★★	Cleanliness: ★★★
Insect Control: ★★★	Facilities: ★★

Set on Cape Cod Bay on the Upper Cape, Scusset Beach State Reservation is the quietest camping place in the area. The public beach is reachable via a long, looping road; the camping area is set back from the shore, behind the bathhouse, snack bar, and parking lot. The grassy, back-in RV sites are fairly open; scattered low trees provide some buffer between sites, but not much shade. The worst RV sites are numbers 80 through 91, located on an open field right next to the beach parking lot. Anything set back (lower numbers) is much better. Tent sites are surprisingly secluded. While the tent sites (grouped together) are a stroll from the beach, they're tucked away down walking paths, roomy and very private. Each tent site is surrounded by trees. If you're an RVer, don't count on an evening 'round the fire, unless you've brought a camp stove; only the tent sites have fireplaces. Only one restroom serves all. This place is low on the frills meter,

unless you consider a Cape Cod beach the ultimate amenity.

BASICS

Operated By: Massachusetts State Forests and Parks. **Open:** Apr.–Columbus Day. **Site Assignment:** Reservations recommended; reserve up to 6 months in advance by calling ReserveAmerica at (877) I-CAMP-MA or online at www.reservamerica.com; to change arrival or departure date, or site type, call at least 3 days prior to arrival date; $10 cancellation/transfer fee; no refunds for amounts less than $5. **Registration:** At office. **Fee:** Massachusetts residents, $15; nonresidents, $17; V, MC. **Parking:** At sites or parking lots only.

FACILITIES

Number of RV-only Sites: 98. **Number of Tent-only Sites:** 5. **Hookups:** Electric (20, 30 amps), water. **Each Site:** Picnic table (fireplaces at tent sites only). **Dump Station:** Yes. **Laundry:** No. **Pay Phone:** No. **Restrooms and Showers:** Yes. **Fuel:** No. **Propane:** No. **Internal Roads:** Paved, in good condition. **RV Service:** No. **Market:** 4–5 mi. west in Bourne. **Restaurant:** 2 mi. south. **General Store:** No. **Vending:** No. **Swimming:** No. **Playground:** No. **Other:** Interpretive center, fishing pier. **Activities:** Swimming (in Cape Cod Bay), bicycling, volleyball, planned activities. **Nearby Attractions:** Boating, fishing, antique shops, golf, scenic bike paths, ferries to Martha's Vineyard & Nantucket. **Additional Information:** Cape Cod Chamber of Commerce, (888) 33-CAPECOD or (508) 362-3225, www.capecodchamber.org.

RESTRICTIONS

Pets: Must be leashed, quiet, & cleaned up after. Current rabies vaccination certificate required. Posted areas are off-limits to pets. **Fires:** Fireplaces at tent sites only. **Alcoholic Beverages:** Not allowed. **Vehicle Maximum Length:** 40 ft. **Other:** 14 cumulative day stay limit between Memorial Day & Labor Day.

TO GET THERE

Follow Hwy. 3 to Sagamore Bridge traffic circle, then follow signs to campground.

SALISBURY   MAP, A-3
Black Bear Family Campground

54 Main St., 01952. T: (978) 462-3183; www.blackbearcamping.com.

🚐 ★★★★   ⛺ ★★

Beauty: ★★★	Site Privacy: ★★★
Spaciousness: ★★	Quiet: ★★★★
Security: ★★★	Cleanliness: ★★★★
Insect Control: ★★★	Facilities: ★★★★

Despite the menacing appearance of the black-bear sculpture at the entrance, the Chouinard family welcomes campers who like a few amenities with their outdoor experience. Although it is located near Salisbury Beach State Reservation (see listing), this campground offers a completely different experience. The trappings at this suburban campground include two swimming pools, a nice playground area, and a 1950s-style rec hall with a pool table and video games. The campground owners operate a pizza shop/bakery next door. The campground is located just south of the New Hampshire border, near the junctions of I-95 and Hwy. 1, so it's a handy base for exploring Portsmouth, New Hampshire, and Hampton Beach, and it's only three miles from Salisbury Beach. (Bonus: there's a free trolley to the beaches.) Some campsites are shaded, some are open, and some look to be fairly permanent. If your list of campground qualifications reads "quiet, family-friendly, and easily accessible from the highway," Black Bear Family Campground will meet your needs squarely.

BASICS

Operated By: Chouinard family. **Open:** May 15–Sept. 30. **Site Assignment:** Reservations accepted year-round; reservations recommended July & Aug.; for 7 nights or less, payment due in full or 1-week deposit; refunds only w/ cancellation 2 weeks prior to arrival date; first come, first served on a space-available basis (limited number of sites available for less than 1 week). **Registration:** At office. **Fee:** $30–$42; based on 2 people; extra adult, $5; extra child under age 18, $1; V, MC. **Parking:** At site. Only 1 car per site.

FACILITIES

Number of RV-only Sites: 225. **Number of Tent-only Sites:** 25. **Hookups:** Electric (30, 50 amps), water, sewer, modem. **Each Site:** Picnic table, fire ring. **Dump Station:** Yes. **Laundry:** Yes. **Pay Phone:** Yes. **Restrooms and Showers:** Yes, coin op. **Fuel:** No. **Propane:** No. **Internal Roads:** Gravel, in good condition. **RV Service:** No. **Market:** 1 mi. north. **Restaurant:** Yes. **General Store:** No. **Vending:** No. **Swimming:** Yes. **Playground:** Yes. **Other:** Rec hall. **Activities:** Volleyball, basketball, horseshoes, shuffleboard, pool table, arcade games. **Nearby Attractions:** Ocean beaches, whale-watching cruises, Salisbury Beach amusement area, deep-sea fishing charters, golf. **Additional Information:** North of Boston CVB, (978) 977-7760 or (800) 742-5306, www.northofboston.org.

RESTRICTIONS

Pets: Small pets permitted if leashed at all times & cleaned up after. **Fires:** Fire ring only. **Alcoholic Beverages:** Sites only. **Vehicle Maximum Length:** No limit. **Other:** 2-week stay limit for tent campers.

TO GET THERE

From I-95, take Exit 60. At first set of lights, take a left. Campground entrance is 200 feet on the left.

SALISBURY   MAP, A-3
Salisbury Beach State Reservation

reserve america

P.O. Box 5303, 01952. T: (978) 462-4482 or (877) I-CAMP-MA; www.reserveamerica.com.

🚐 ★★★★★   ⛺ ★★★

Beauty: ★★★★★   Site Privacy: ★★★
Spaciousness: ★★★★   Quiet: ★★★
Security: ★★★   Cleanliness: ★★★★
Insect Control: ★★★   Facilities: ★★★

If this stretch of beach wasn't owned by the state, it would be chock-a-block with high-rise hotels. No wonder Salisbury Beach State Reservation is a favorite of beach-loving campers. It's an ahh-inspiring panoramic vista of sandy shore, lapped by the sparkling waters of the North Atlantic. Located 40 miles north of Boston, at the northeast border of Massachusetts, Salisbury Beach is a destination campground. Why leave when there's a four-mile ocean beach (swimming permitted), a one-mile river beach, a boardwalk for strolling, fishing gear for rent, and ranger programs in the evenings (in season)? Whether you choose a site alongside the Merrimack River, or a spot near the ocean beach, it's hard to go wrong here. Like a suburban subdivision, campsites are set in rows on "streets" labeled A–H and W–Z, within the park's perimeter loop road. With this set-up, there's not a lot of privacy. Tent campers are likely to feel rather exposed. Sites are grassy, with little shade. The campground is immaculate and well maintained. You can't beat $20 (or less) per night for an oceanfront setting, and clean restrooms to boot. While the honky-tonk action of Salisbury Beach (go-carts, skee-ball, dance clubs) is right up the street, it's easy to leave it all behind here.

BASICS

Operated By: Massachusetts State Forests and Parks. **Open:** Mid-Apr.–mid-Nov.; limited winter camping available. **Site Assignment:** Reserve up to 6 months in advance by calling (877) I-CAMP-MA or online at www.reserveamerica.com; if you cancel or change dates or type of site, call (877) 422-6762 at least 3 days prior to arrival; $10 cancellation/transfer fee; full payment w/ credit card or check required, 30 days prior to arrival; cancellation fee is $10; 20% of campsites reserved for walk-ins. **Registration:** At office. **Fee:** Massachusetts residents (w/ electric), $17(w/out, $15); nonresidents, $20–$17; V, MC. **Parking:** At site.

FACILITIES

Number of RV-only Sites: 484. **Hookups:** Electric (15, 20 amps), water. **Each Site:** Picnic table, fireplace. **Dump Station:** Yes. **Laundry:** No. **Pay Phone:** Yes. **Restrooms and Showers:** Yes. **Fuel:** No. **Propane:** No. **Internal Roads:** Paved, in good condition. **RV Service:** No. **Market:** 4 mi. west. **Restaurant:** Several w/in 1 mi. **General Store:** Yes. **Vending:** Yes. **Swimming:** Yes. **Playground:**

Yes. **Other:** Boat ramp, boardwalk. **Activities:** Evening ranger programs, swimming, boating, canoeing, fishing in ocean & Merrimack River (ocean fishing prohibited 10 a.m.–5 p.m.; rentals & bait available, no license needed). **Nearby Attractions:** Pirate's Fun Park (amusement rides), golf, go-cart track, whale watch boat cruises (out of Newburyport), scenic tours. **Additional Information:** North of Boston CVB, (978) 977-7760 or (800) 742-5306, www.northofboston.org.

RESTRICTIONS

Pets: Must be leashed & cleaned up after. Must not be left unattended. Proof of rabies vaccination required at check-in. No pets allowed on ocean, beach, or in restrooms. **Fires:** Fireplaces only. **Alcoholic Beverages:** Not allowed. **Vehicle Maximum Length:** 28 ft. **Other:** 14 cumulative day stay limit between Memorial Day & Labor Day.

TO GET THERE

From junction of I-95 and Hwy. 110, head east on Hwy. 110 to Hwy. 1-A North. Follow signs to state reservation.

SANDWICH   MAP, B-4
Peters Pond Park Family Camping

185 Cotuit Rd., P.O. Box 999, 02563. T: (508) 477-1775; www.peterspond.com.

🚐 ★★★★   ⛺ ★

Beauty: ★★   Site Privacy: ★★★
Spaciousness: ★★★   Quiet: ★★
Security: ★★★★★   Cleanliness: ★★★★
Insect Control: ★★   Facilities: ★★★★

This bustling family campground is just seven miles from the Sagamore Bridge, one of two bridges marking the "entrance" to the vacationland of Cape Cod. And it's definitely a vacation scene here, complete with nightly campfires, a party tent, and kids whooping it up on aqua bikes and paddleboats. The big drawing card here is a 137-acre spring-fed pond, stocked with salmon, trout, and bass, with a nice, sandy beach. (There are actually two beaches, but one is too small to bother with.) Another nice feature: the campground abuts the Rebel Lot Conservation Area, offering good hiking trails. Campsites, with an average width of 40 feet, are set on small side streets, village-like, off a main road. Not quite half the sites are seasonal. A good number of these are set at the far end of the campground. Sites are lined with pine needles or cedar chips and are very level. Best sites on the pond are C21 and 22. Other than those sites, we'd skip the C loop, though; it's pretty crowded. Nice touch: campers get a handy booklet with campground info and map, discounted tickets to area attractions, restaurant menus, etc.

BASICS

Operated By: Morgan Management, LLC. **Open:** Patriot's Day (mid-Apr.)–Columbus Day. **Site Assignment:** Reservations recommended; call the Sun. before for weekend reservations during summer season; for each week of camping, a 2-night deposit is required (3-night deposit for holiday weekends);

deposit secures reservation; checks and credit cards OK for deposit; cancellation notice of 2 weeks required for refunds, minus service charge. **Registration:** At office. **Fee:** $32–$71; includes up to 4 people; V, MC. **Parking:** At site.

FACILITIES

Number of RV-only Sites: 452. **Number of Tent-only Sites:** 60. **Hookups:** Electric (20, 30, 50 amps), water, sewer, cable TV, modem. **Each Site:** Picnic table. **Dump Station:** Yes. **Laundry:** Yes. **Pay Phone:** Yes. **Restrooms and Showers:** Yes, coin-op. **Fuel:** No. **Propane:** Yes. **Internal Roads:** Paved, in good condition. **RV Service:** No. **Market:** 1 mi. north. **Restaurant:** Yes (snack bar). **General Store:** Yes. **Vending:** Yes. **Swimming:** Lake swimming. **Playground:** Yes. **Other:** Rec hall, boat ramp. **Activities:** Lake swimming, boating (rental row-boats, paddleboats, kayaks, aqua cycles), fishing, basketball, ball field, hiking, shuffleboard, volleyball, horseshoes, planned activities. **Nearby Attractions:** Thornton Burgess Museum, Sandwich Glass Museum, Aptucxet Trading Post, ocean beaches, golf. **Additional Information:** Cape Cod Chamber of Commerce, (888) 33-CAPECOD; (508) 862-0700, www.capecodchamber.org.

RESTRICTIONS

Pets: Pets welcome from opening day until July 1 & from Labor Day until closing. Spruce St. camping area can campers w/ pets during July & Aug. Must be leashed; must have rabies vaccination certificate. Must be kept on site in July & Aug. **Fires:** No open fires. **Alcoholic Beverages:** At sites only. **Vehicle Maximum Length:** None. **Other:** 3-day min. stay on holidays.

TO GET THERE

Take Hwy. 3 south to Sagamore Bridge. From bridge, follow Hwy. 6 to Exit 2, Hwy. 130. Turn right, go 3 mi. Turn left at first set of lights, Quaker Meeting House Rd. Turn right at next set of lights (Cotuit Rd.). Then head south 0.5 mi. to campground, on right.

SANDWICH   MAP, B-4
Shawme-Crowell State Forest

reserve america

42 Main St. (Rte. 130), 02563-0621.
T: (508) 888-0351; www.reserveamerica.com.

🚐 ★★★★　　　▲ ★★★★

Beauty: ★★★	Site Privacy: ★★★
Spaciousness: ★★	Quiet: ★★
Security: ★★★	Cleanliness: ★★★★
Insect Control: ★★★	Facilities: ★★★

Shawme-Crowell State Park is situated on Cape Cod next to the Sagamore Bridge. Though the campground is in a forest, you are not far from the Cape Cod Bay and the air can turn quite salty depending on where the wind comes from. Naturally, Shawme-Crowell is the best starting point for a ride on the bike path along the Cape Cod canal. More than 15 miles of roads and trails provide hiking and equestrian access to over 700 acres of pitch-pine and scrub-oak landscape. The campground has 285 sites, and open-air campfires are allowed at the wooded tent and RV (no hookups) sites. Yurt camping is also available. Heated restroom and shower facilities are welcome by visitors on chilly mornings. Sites vary from medium-sized to outright large, especially in Area 1—in some cases you are unlikely to even see your neighbors through the trees. Though Route 6 is not far, traffic noise is not a nuisance (unless your site is in the southern part of Area 2, where you are closer to the road), and the staff is generally friendly and helpful. Campers also get access to free day use at Scusset Beach. Shawme-Crowell is much less-known than Nickerson State Park: even if you don't have a reservation, and if you arrive early, you can probably land one of the first-come, first-served sites.

BASICS

Operated By: Massachusetts State Parks. **Open:** All year. **Site Assignment:** Reservations can be made up to 6 months in advance. **Registration:** At office. **Fee:** Single, $12–$14; group, $25; yurt, $30–$40. **Parking:** 2 vehicles per campsite.

FACILITIES

Number of Multipurpose Sites: 286. **Hookups:** None. **Dump Station:** Yes. **Laundry:** No. **Pay Phone:** Yes. **Restrooms and Showers:** Yes. **Fuel:** No. **Propane:** No. **Internal Roads:** Paved. **RV Service:** No. **Market:** No. **Restaurant:** No. **General Store:** No. **Vending:** No. **Swimming:** No. **Playground:** Yes. **Activities:** Hiking.

RESTRICTIONS

Pets: Keep pets leashed (10-ft. leash max.) at all times. Proof of rabies vaccination is required. Pets are never to be left unattended. **Fires:** Campfires in designated fireplaces. **Alcoholic Beverages:** Alcoholic beverages are prohibited in all MA state parks & campgrounds. **Other:** Quiet hours are 10 p.m.–7 a.m. Please, no unnecessary or disturbing noise at any time. Equipment is limited to 2 tents or 1 camping vehicle & 1 small tent per site. Tents are limited to 300 square feet of combined floor space. Massachusetts law requires that children age 16 and under wear a helmet when bicycling.

TO GET THERE

From the north: Take Hwy. 3 south to the Sagamore Bridge and Hwy. 6 east. Follow Hwy. 6 east over the bridge to Exit 2 and the intersection with Hwy. 130 in Sandwich. Follow Hwy. 130 into Sandwich and follow the State Forest signs 3 mi. to the park entrance on the left. From the west: Take Hwy. 495 south to the intersection with Hwy. 6 east. Follow Hwy. 6 east along the Cape Cod Canal to the intersection with Hwy. 3 and the Sagamore Bridge Rotary. Follow Hwy. 6 east over the Sagamore Bridge to Exit 2 in Sandwich. Follow Hwy. 130 into Sandwich and follow the signs 3 mi. to the park entrance on the left.

SAVOY   MAP, A-1
Shady Pines Campground

547 Loop Rd., 01256. T: (413) 743-2694; www.shadypinescampground.com.

🚐 ★★★★　　　▲ ★★★

Beauty: ★★★	Site Privacy: ★★★
Spaciousness: ★★★★★	Quiet: ★★
Security: ★★★★★	Cleanliness: ★★★★
Insect Control: ★★	Facilities: ★★★

Amidst the rolling hills and farmlands of the Berkshires in Western Massachusetts, this campground is a hub of activity. There's often something going on in the adult lounge—perhaps a polka-and-pierogi fest (as when we visited), complete with live entertainment. (Full bar, too.) It's not just a couples scene, though; the fenced-in playground is school-yard sized. Spacious campsites ring a grassy, open area with a ball park, pavilion, swimming pool, and playground. Adjacent to the pavilion is a ten-acre safari field! Somehow, they manage to keep this huge property nicely mown and landscaped; a nice touch is the sand-and-limestone coating on the roads. No mud or dust here. Campsites are semi-wooded or open. Tent sites are clustered in the far right-hand corner of the property, near some rental cabins. These, and RV sites 197 through 202, are in close proximity to walking trails leading to Savoy Mountain. A unique feature here: piped-in music in restrooms. All in all, a livelier scene than at nearby Peppermint Park Campground (see listing) and—certainly—Windsor State Park.

BASICS

Operated By: Steve and Diane Daniels. **Open:** All year. **Site Assignment:** Reservations recommended; send 1-night deposit to reserve; 3-night minimum holiday weekends; reservation will be accepted only w/ payment in full. **Registration:** At office. **Fee:** $27; 2 people; extra children aged 15–18, $3 per day; age 7–14, $3 per day; V, MC. **Parking:** At site.

FACILITIES

Number of RV-only Sites: 150. **Hookups:** Electric (20 amps), water. **Each Site:** Picnic table, fireplace. **Dump Station:** Yes. **Laundry:** Yes. **Pay Phone:** Yes. **Restrooms and Showers:** Yes, coin-op. **Fuel:** No. **Propane:** No. **Internal Roads:** Gravel, in good condition. **RV Service:** No. **Market:** Yes. **Restaurant:** Yes. **General Store:** Yes. **Vending:** No. **Swimming:** Yes. **Playground:** Yes. **Other:** Rec hall, game room, adult lounge (18 & up). **Activities:** Swimming, walking trails, horseshoes, ball field, planned activities. **Nearby Attractions:** Mt. Greylock, Tanglewood (outdoor concerts), Natural Bridge, Western Gateway Heritage State Park, Mass MOCA (Contemporary Arts museum), Clark Art Institute, Jacob's Pillow (dance). **Additional Information:** Berkshire Hills Visitors Bureau, (413) 443-9186 or (800) 237-5747, www.berkshires.org.

RESTRICTIONS

Pets: Must be leashed & cleaned up after. Must not be left unattended. Walk dogs in woods, away from campsites. **Fires:** Fireplaces only. **Alcoholic Beverages:** Allowed. **Vehicle Maximum Length:** None. **Other:** No motorcycles.

TO GET THERE

From junction of Hwy. 8A and Hwy. 116, go 3 mi. southeast on Hwy. 116, then 0.25 mi. north on Loop Rd. Campground entrance is on the right.

SAVOY/FLORIDA   MAP, A-1
Savoy Mountain State Forest

260 Central Shaft Rd., 01247. T: (413) 663-8469; www.reserveamerica.com.

🚐 ★★	⛺ ★★★★
Beauty: ★★★★	Site Privacy: ★★★
Spaciousness: ★★★	Quiet: ★★★★
Security: ★★★	Cleanliness: ★★★
Insect Control: ★★	Facilities: ★★

A ranger at another state park, with 30 years' experience in the system, deems Savoy Mountain his absolute favorite. It's easy to see why. Located in the Berkshire Hills of Western Massachusetts, this park offers wonderful diversity, with waterfalls, balanced rocks, and scenic vistas galore. Campsites are located in an old apple orchard, which fills the air with scent in springtime. Wooded hills rise in the distance, while fields of mountain laurel are studded with sparkling ponds. Recreational activities include hiking (60 miles of trails), pond swimming, or fishing in trout-stocked North Pond. Campsites, set in a loop, are mostly open and grassy, all back-ins and bordered by trees. Sites 13 through 18, nearest the beach at South Pond, fill up quickly, as do the three nice-looking rustic cabins. Site 43 is fairly open, but near the restroom. Number 29 is very wooded, while sites 21, 22, and 23 are set back for ample privacy. This park offers an inviting wilderness getaway for tent campers and pop-up RVs but note that it's located in bear country (and we saw evidence of same), so practice bear-safe camping.

BASICS

Operated By: Massachusetts State Forests and Parks. **Open:** Mid-May–Columbus Day. **Site Assignment:** Reservations recommended; reserve up to 6 months in advance by calling ReserveAmerica at (877) I-CAMP-MA or online at www.reserveamerica .com; 36 campsites are reservable; 9 are nonreservable and first come, first served; to change arrival or departure date, or site type, call at least 3 days prior to arrival date; $10 cancellation/transfer fee; no refunds for amounts less than $5. **Registration:** At office. **Fee:** Massachusetts residents, $12; nonresidents, $14; log cabins, $30; V, MC. **Parking:** At site.

FACILITIES

Number of Multipurpose Sites: 45. **Hookups:** None. **Each Site:** Picnic table, fireplace. **Dump Station:** No. **Laundry:** No. **Pay Phone:** Yes. **Restrooms and Showers:** Yes. **Fuel:** No. **Propane:** No. **Internal Roads:** Paved, in good condition. **RV Service:** No. **Market:** 0.7 mi. north. **Restaurant:** 5 mi. west. **General Store:** No. **Vending:** Yes. **Swimming:** No. **Playground:** No. **Other:**

Boat ramp, nature center. **Activities:** Swimming, boating (no gas-powered engines), interpretive programs, fishing. **Nearby Attractions:** Mt. Greylock, Tanglewood (outdoor concerts), Natural Bridge State Park, Western Gateway Heritage State Park, Mass MOCA (contemporary art), Clark Art Institute, Jacob's Pillow (dance). **Additional Information:** Berkshire Hills Visitors Bureau, (413) 443-9186 or (800) 237-5747, www.berkshires.org.

RESTRICTIONS

Pets: Must be leashed & cleaned up after. Must not be left unattended. Proof of rabies vaccination required. **Fires:** Fireplaces only. **Alcoholic Beverages:** Not allowed. **Vehicle Maximum Length:** 25–30 ft. **Other:** 14 cumulative day stay limit between Memorial Day & Columbus Day.

TO GET THERE

Follow Hwy. 2 west through Florida, then bear left on Central Shaft Rd. Head 4 mi. south on Central Shaft Rd. to campground entrance.

SOUTH CARVER   MAP, B-4
Myles Standish State Forest

Cranberry Rd., P.O. Box 66, 02366.
T: (508) 866-2526; www.reserveamerica.com.

🚐 ★★	⛺ ★★★
Beauty: ★★★★★	Site Privacy: ★★★★
Spaciousness: ★★★★	Quiet: ★★★★★
Security: ★★★	Cleanliness: ★★★
Insect Control: ★★	Facilities: ★★★

It's not easy trying to find it—those helpful blue RV road signs seem to be missing at key points along the route—but this immense state forest is worth sleuthing out. Just 40 miles from Boston, Myles Standish State Forest is the largest remaining pine barrens zone in New England and one of the largest public open spaces in Massachusetts. Soaring pitch pines, scrub oak, and plantations of white and red pine make this a real wilderness escape. Dozens of gem-like ponds dot the landscape. Campsites are clustered near the ponds, with the best ones overlooking Barrett Pond. Camp near Fearing Pond, though, and you get the benefit of a swimming hole; plus, the pond is stocked with trout. White-tailed deer and red and grey fox can also be found roaming the campground. Sites 18 and 19 are spectacular; best for RVs are sites 28, 34, and 35, all flat, wooded, and wide, offering great views of Fearing Pond. Beyond swimming and fishing, the park offers more than 90 miles of biking and hiking trails (15 paved for biking) and nature programs daily in season, perhaps a wildflower walk or edible-plant hike. At nearly 18,000 acres, the park is big and difficult to navigate. Pay close attention to your map, or you may end up, as we did, face-to-face with the MCI Plymouth correctional facility, located, curiously enough, on park property.

BASICS

Operated By: Massachusetts State Forests and Parks. **Open:** Mid-Apr.–Columbus Day. Fully open, Memorial Day–Labor Day; sites limited in off-season. **Site Assignment:** Reservations recommended; reserve up to 6 months in advance by calling ReserveAmerica at (877) I-CAMP-MA or online at www.reserveamerica.com; some sites are nonreservable and first come, first served; arrive before 11 a.m. to get on waiting list; to change arrival or departure date, or site type, call at least 3 days prior to arrival date; $10 cancellation/transfer fee; no refunds for amounts less than $5. **Registration:** At office. **Fee:** Massachusetts residents, $12; nonresidents, $14; V, MC. **Parking:** At sites and parking lots near trailheads.

FACILITIES

Number of RV-only Sites: 425. **Hookups:** None. **Each Site:** Picnic table, fireplace. **Dump Station:** Yes. **Laundry:** No. **Pay Phone:** Yes. **Restrooms and Showers:** Yes. **Fuel:** No. **Propane:** No. **Internal Roads:** Gravel, in good condition. **RV Service:** No. **Market:** 5 mi. north, in Plymouth. **Restaurant:** 5 mi. north, in Plymouth. **General Store:** No. **Vending:** No. **Swimming:** No. **Playground:** No. **Other:** Interpretive center. **Activities:** Bicycling, boating (no gas-powered engines), hiking, swimming in Fearing Pond & College Pond, fishing (trout-stocked Fearing Pond), interpretive programs, wildlife watching (endangered turtles are seen at East Head Reservoir). **Nearby Attractions:** Plimoth Plantation, whale-watching cruises, scenic harbor cruises, Mayflower II, Plymouth National Wax Museum, Pilgrim Hall Museum, winery, Ocean Spray Cranberry World, tours, winery, Edaville Railroad. **Additional Information:** Destination Plymouth, (800) USA-1620 or www.visit-plymouth.com.

RESTRICTIONS

Pets: Must be leashed & cleaned up after. Must not be left unattended. Proof of rabies vaccination required. **Fires:** Fireplaces only. **Alcoholic Beverages:** Not allowed. **Vehicle Maximum Length:** 30 ft. **Other:** 14 cumulative day stay limit between Memorial Day & Labor Day.

TO GET THERE

From Hwy. 3, take Exit 5; head west on Long Pond Rd. Follow signs to campground; turn right on Alden Rd.

SOUTHWICK   MAP, B-1, B-2
Sodom Mountain Campground

P.O. Box 702, 233 Loomis St., 01077.
T: (413) 569-3930;
www.sodommountain.com.

🚐 ★★★	⛺ ★★★
Beauty: ★★★	Site Privacy: ★★★
Spaciousness: ★★★	Quiet: ★★★★
Security: ★★★★★	Cleanliness: ★★
Insect Control: ★★	Facilities: ★★

Heading to Six Flags New England theme park or other attractions in the Springfield area? This campground is a convenient base. Located 12 miles east of Six Flags, it's the closest campground to the park, other than Southwick Acres (owned by the same family but geared more to seniors and seasonal campers than Sodom Mountain.) Another selling point: they offer discounted tickets to Six Flags—sizable discounts on adult admissions, we found. Factor in your savings on a couple of adult tickets to Six Flags, and it's like you're getting a night of camping for free. Not into wild rides and the whole theme-park scene? The campground is located alongside Sodom Mountain, offering marked hiking trails for all abilities. We also sleuthed out Southwick's town beach, on South Pond, with a sandy-bottomed, life-guarded swimming area and lots of picnic tables. The campground offers wooded and open sites, with some pull-throughs. Sites 67A and B are nicest for tents, while site 105 is a shady spot for RVs. The G section is the nicest overall, in our view. The restroom (one serves all) is very basic. Check out the peacock pen near the entrance.

BASICS

Operated By: LaFrance family. **Open:** May 1–Columbus Day. **Site Assignment:** Reservations recommended, especially weekends; 1-night deposit required; refunds for cancellations w/ 2-week notice, minus $7. **Registration:** At office. **Fee:** $26–$40; 2 adults/2 children; V, MC. **Parking:** At site.

FACILITIES

Number of RV-only Sites: 165. **Number of Tent-only Sites:** 15. **Hookups:** Electric (30, 50 amps), water, sewer. **Each Site:** Picnic table, fire ring. **Dump Station:** Yes. **Laundry:** Yes. **Pay Phone:** Yes. **Restrooms and Showers:** Yes, coin-op. **Fuel:** No. **Propane:** Yes. **Internal Roads:** Gravel, in good condition. **RV Service:** No. **Market:** 4.1 mi. south on Hwy. 202. **Restaurant:** 4.1 mi. south on Hwy. 202. **General Store:** Yes. **Vending:** Yes. **Swimming:** Yes. **Playground:** Yes. **Other:** Lodge, game room. **Activities:** Swimming, hiking, shuffleboard, basketball, volleyball. **Nearby Attractions:** Six Flags New England theme park, Basketball Hall of Fame, Southwick Motocrosse 338, Big E (Eastern States Exposition) fair, late Sept., Southwick Town Beach at South Pond. **Additional Information:** Greater Springfield CVB, (413) 755-1343, www.valleyvisitor.com.

RESTRICTIONS

Pets: Must be leashed, quiet, & cleaned up after. Must not be left unattended. Current rabies certificate required. **Fires:** Fire ring only. **Alcoholic Beverages:** At sites or in lodge only. **Vehicle Maximum Length:** 40 ft. **Other:** 2-night min. stay required June–Aug.; 3-night min. plus advance payment in full for holidays.

TO GET THERE

From I-90 (Massachusetts Turnpike), take Exit 3. Follow Hwy. 202 south to Southwick Center. Go through town, then take Hwy. 57 west 3 mi. to South Loomis St. Take a left on South Loomis for 0.25 mi. to campground, on right.

30 River Rd., P.O. Box 600, 01566.
T: (508) 347-9570 or (508) 347-2336;
www.jellystonesturbridge.com.

🚐 ★★★★   ⛺ ★★★

Beauty: ★★★	Site Privacy: ★
Spaciousness: ★★	Quiet: ★★
Security: ★★★★★	Cleanliness: ★★★★
Insect Control: ★★★	Facilities: ★★★★★

If the presence of costumed characters Yogi, Cindy, and Boo Boo Bear don't convince you, perhaps the all-day schedule of kids' activities will—the emphasis here is on family fun. Open year-round, the campground offers nonstop action in summer months, from mini-golf to movies to ice-cream-eating contests. Some parents escape to the Bear's Den, a post-and-beam style lounge with a stone fireplace. Campsites are arranged in a series of loops, with the far end devoted to rental cabins. There are 15 pull-through sites. The camping area is heavily wooded, but there's not much buffer between sites. Two fairly spacious, pretty sites are 739 and 740, although they're a good trek from the beach, pool, and main building activity hub. The nicest tent sites, grouped together here, are 266 and 267, relatively secluded and leafy, also close to restrooms, laundry, and the aqua center. (Waterslides, a pool and hot tub; they charge extra for these.) This park is on the pricey side, but you get lots of activity, good security, and clean facilities for your money.

BASICS

Operated By: James Leaming, manager. **Open:** All year. **Site Assignment:** Reservations recommended; 50% deposit required; refund for cancellation w/ 7-day notice minus $5. **Registration:** At office. **Fee:** Memorial Day–Labor Day, $48–$58; off-season $26–$29.75; extra charge, holiday weekends & weekends in July–Aug. Rates are for 2 adults at site, per day; extra charge of $3 for children; $5–$9 for extra adult. Packages available, MC, D. **Parking:** At site and designated parking areas only.

FACILITIES

Number of RV-only Sites: 359. **Number of Tent-only Sites:** 40. **Hookups:** Electric (20, 30 amps), water, sewer, cable TV. **Each Site:** Picnic tables, fire rings. **Dump Station:** Yes. **Laundry:** Yes. **Pay Phone:** Yes. **Restrooms and Showers:** Yes. **Fuel:** No. **Propane:** Yes. **Internal Roads:** Paved & gravel, in fair condition. **RV Service:** No. **Market:** 1 mi. north in Sturbridge. **Restaurant:** Yes. **General Store:** Yes. **Vending:** Yes. **Swimming:** Yes. **Playground:** Yes. **Other:** Mini-golf, aqua center (water slide, hot tub), lounge, game room, petting zoo. **Activities:** Lake swimming, fishing (no license required), boating, pony rides. **Nearby Attractions:** Old Sturbridge Village living history museum. **Additional Information:** Plymouth County CVB, (800) 231-1620, www.plymouth-1620.com.

RESTRICTIONS

Pets: Must be leashed, quiet, & cleaned up after. Unattended pets should be left inside trailers. **Fires:**

Fire ring only. **Alcoholic Beverages:** Allowed. **Vehicle Maximum Length:** None. **Other:** Air-conditioners & electric heaters not allowed unless prior arrangements are made w/ office.

TO GET THERE

From junction of I-84 and Hwy. 20, go 1 mi. west on I-84 to Exit 2, then 0.25 mi. on River Rd. Campground entrance is on the right.

19 Mashapaug Rd., 01566. T: (508) 347-7156;
www.campoutdoorworld.com.

🚐 ★★★★   ⛺ ★★★

Beauty: ★★★★	Site Privacy: ★★
Spaciousness: ★★★★	Quiet: ★★★
Security: ★★★★	Cleanliness: ★★★★★
Insect Control: ★★★	Facilities: ★★★★★

Step into the piney lodge or the indoor pool and hot-tub area, and you'd think you were on the property of a resort hotel. Such is the oh-so-luxe life that awaits the happy camper at Outdoor World, a membership resort owned by Resorts USA. Set on Pioneer Lake, the resort employs a social director, who arranges things like live music, storyteller visits, and events like a cardboard boat race, chili cook-off, and theme weekends. Campsites ring the lake, with the nicest spots right on the water, including RV sites S6–S14 (even numbers) and S21–S23, the most secluded of the bunch. Ask for tent site S18A for best views. Sites B1–B5 are lovely, as well. Steer clear of sites near the busy lodge and pool area. The full-hookup sites are more exposed and more tightly packed together than the others. Only two are pull-through. Sites aren't terribly spacious, but campers are generally quiet here, and the wooded surroundings provide a peaceful quality. It's a far less rollicking, more adult atmosphere than that of nearby Jellystone Park.

BASICS

Operated By: Resorts USA. **Open:** All year. **Site Assignment:** Outdoor World is a membership park; call (800) 222-5557 for information on arranging a visit, or to reserve a campsite. **Registration:** At office. **Fee:** Standard, $59–$61; economy, $53–$55; no extra charge for additional person; V, MC, D, AE. **Parking:** At site or designated parking areas.

FACILITIES

Number of RV-only Sites: 93. **Number of Tent-only Sites:** 5. **Hookups:** Electric (30, 50 amps), water, sewer, cable TV. **Each Site:** Picnic table, fire ring. **Dump Station:** Yes. **Laundry:** Yes. **Pay Phone:** Yes. **Restrooms and Showers:** Yes. **Fuel:** No. **Propane:** Yes. **Internal Roads:** Gravel, in good condition. **RV Service:** No. **Market:** 5 mi. north in Sturbridge. **Restaurant:** 5 mi. north in Sturbridge or 1 mi. south. **General Store:** Yes. **Vending:** Yes. **Swimming:** Yes (indoor). **Playground:** Yes. **Other:** Mini-golf, game room, lounge, hot tub, beach, boat house. **Activities:** Lake swimming, boating (canoes, rowboats, paddleboats), lake fishing, mini-golf, basketball, volleyball, horseshoes, hiking trails, movies, planned activities. **Nearby**

Attractions: Old Sturbridge Village living history museum. **Additional Information:** Plymouth County CVB, (800) 231-1620, www.plymouth-1620.com.

RESTRICTIONS

Pets: On leash; pets must accompany owner when leaving campsite or trailer. Owners must clean up after pets. **Fires:** Fire pit only. **Alcoholic Beverages:** Allowed. **Vehicle Maximum Length:** 35 ft. **Other:** Limit 10 people per campsite.

TO GET THERE

Take the Massachusetts Turnpike west to I-84 (Exit 9); follow I-84 to MA Exit 1 and turn left off exit. Take first right onto Mashapaug Rd. to campground entrance.

STURBRIDGE   MAP, B-2
Wells State Park

Walker Mountain Rd., Rte. 49, P.O. Box 602, 01566. T: (508) 347-9257; www.reserveamerica.com.

🚐 ★★   ⛺ ★★★★★

Beauty: ★★★★★	Site Privacy: ★★★★
Spaciousness: ★★★★	Quiet: ★★★★★
Security: ★★★	Cleanliness: ★★★★
Insect Control: ★★	Facilities: ★★★

Among the several campgrounds in the Sturbridge area, this one is the wilderness option. If you can do without hookups, you'll enjoy the Old New England beauty of this property. Criss-crossed with stone walls, Wells State Park is a true beauty spot, heavily wooded with a mix of maples and other deciduous trees. Other natural features include a beaver lodge and dam, vernal pools, and a sandy-bottomed pond. The hiking here is exceptional, offering 9.5 miles of marked scenic trails. The 1.5-mile hike to Carpenter's Rocks leads to a cliff face with east-facing views of the park. Interpretive programs include wildflower walks and beaver pond tours. Campsites are set on upper and lower loops, with each loop surrounding a grassy playing field. The lower loop is closest to Walker Pond. On the upper loop, site 51 is spacious and secluded, as is 27, a campsite set far from the road. The best sites on the lower loop feature water views. Sites 15 and 16 are close together, but near the water. Site 19 is a good waterfront RV site, with pull-through access. A couple of waterfront sites are held for walk-ins and not reservable, so it may be possible, with luck, to get a prime spot here without planning ahead.

BASICS

Operated By: Massachusetts State Forests and Parks. **Open:** May 5–Oct. 8. **Site Assignment:** Reserve up to 6 months in advance through Reserve America by calling (877) I-CAMP-MA or online at www.reserveamerica.com; to change your reservation or site type, or to cancel, call at least 3 days prior to arrival date; $10 cancellation/transfer fee; no refunds for amounts less than $5; 2-night minimum required

on weekends. **Registration:** At park headquarters. **Fee:** Massachusetts residents, $12; nonresidents, $14; V, MC. **Parking:** At site and parking lot only.

FACILITIES

Number of RV-only Sites: 58. **Number of Tent-only Sites:** 2. **Hookups:** None. **Each Site:** Picnic table, fireplace w/ grill, lantern pole. **Dump Station:** Yes. **Laundry:** No. **Pay Phone:** Yes. **Restrooms and Showers:** Yes. **Fuel:** No. **Propane:** No. **Internal Roads:** Gravel, in good condition. **RV Service:** No. **Market:** 2.3 mi. east in Sturbridge. **Restaurant:** 2.3 mi. east in Sturbridge. **General Store:** No. **Vending:** Yes. **Swimming:** Yes. **Playground:** No. **Other:** Interpretive center. **Activities:** Swimming in Walker Pond, beach, ball fields, basketball court, hiking, biking, equestrian trails, fishing, interpretive programs for children (must be accompanied by an adult). **Nearby Attractions:** Old Sturbridge Village living history museum, Brimfield Flea Markets (various weekends). **Additional Information:** Plymouth County CVB, (508) 747-0100 or (800) 231-1620, www.plymouth-1620.com.

RESTRICTIONS

Pets: Pets must be leashed & cleaned up after. Proof of rabies vaccination required. Do not leave pets unattended. **Fires:** Fireplaces only. **Alcoholic Beverages:** Not allowed. **Vehicle Maximum Length:** 35 ft. **Other:** 14 cumulative day stay limit between Memorial Day & Labor Day.

TO GET THERE

Take I-90 (Massachusetts Turnpike) to Hwy. 20 East. Follow Hwy. 20E to Hwy. 49N, following signs to park access road. Park entrance is 1 mi. north on Hwy. 49 (third left).

TOWNSEND   MAP, A-2, A-3
Willard Brook State Forest

reserve america™

595 Main St., 01474. T: (978) 386-7146; www.reserveamerica.com.

🚐 ★★★★   ⛺ ★★★★

Beauty: ★★★	Site Privacy: ★★★
Spaciousness: ★★	Quiet: ★★★★
Security: ★★★★	Cleanliness: ★★★★
Insect Control: ★★★	Facilities: ★★★

Willard Brook State Forest contains 2,597 acres and is located in the towns of Ashby and Townsend, 50 miles from Boston. Here you can find the character and feeling of forests usually found much farther west in the state, with a tumbling brook, a quick water amid groves of classic New England woods, and 21 campsites spread beneath a pine canopy. A wide variety of activities is offered, including swimming, walking, hiking, birding, fishing, horseback riding, and winter trail sports. The Department of Conservation and Recreation (DCR) of Massachusetts and the Friends of Willard Brook organization (FOWB) collaborated on a trails grant to build a new trail connecting Damon Pond Campground of Willard Brook

State Forest to Pearl Hill State Park in West Townsend. With assistance from DCR personnel, Trailwrights of New Hampshire, the Student Conservation Association workers, and FOWB volunteers, the trail is now open for all to enjoy. It's four-miles long, and you should plan up to three hours or more to hike the entire trail in good conditions.

BASICS

Operated By: Massachusetts State Parks. **Open:** May 24–Sept. 3. **Site Assignment:** Reservations can be made up to 6 months in advance. **Registration:** At office. **Fee:** Single, $8–$10. **Parking:** 2 vehicles per campsite.

FACILITIES

Number of Multipurpose Sites: 21. **Hookups:** None. **Dump Station:** No. **Laundry:** No. **Pay Phone:** Yes. **Restrooms and Showers:** Yes. **Fuel:** No. **Propane:** No. **Internal Roads:** Paved. **RV Service:** No. **Market:** No. **Restaurant:** No. **General Store:** No. **Vending:** No. **Swimming:** Yes. **Playground:** No. **Activities:** Biking, fishing, hiking, horseback riding, hunting, interpretive programs, picnicking, cross-country skiing, snowmobiling.

RESTRICTIONS

Pets: Keep pets leashed (10-ft. leash max.) at all times. Proof of rabies vaccination is required. Pets are never to be left unattended. **Fires:** Campfires in designated fireplaces. **Alcoholic Beverages:** Alcoholic beverages are prohibited in all MA state parks & campgrounds. **Vehicle Maximum Length:** Trailers longer than 20 ft. may have difficult maneuvering into their site. **Other:** Quiet hours are 10 p.m.–7 a.m. No unnecessary or disturbing noise at any time. Equipment is limited to 2 tents or 1 camping vehicle & 1 small tent per site. Tents are limited to 300 square feet of combined floor space. Massachusetts law requires that children age 16 and under wear a helmet when bicycling.

TO GET THERE

From the northeast: Take Hwy. 495 to Littleton; take the Hwy. 119 exit. Follow Hwy. 119 west 21 mi. through West Townsend to the campground on the left. From the west: Follow Hwy. 2 east to Hwy. 31 north in Fitchburg. Follow Hwy. 31 north through Fitchburg to the Town of Ashby and the intersection with Hwy. 119 east. Follow Hwy. 119 east 0.5 mi. to the campground entrance on the right. From the east: Take Hwy. 2 west to Fitchburg and Hwy. 13 north. Follow Hwy. 13 north to Hwy. 119 west in West Townsend. Turn left onto Hwy. 119. Follow Hwy. 119 4 mi. to the park entrance on the left.

WALES   MAP, B-2
Oak Haven Family Campground

P.O. Box 166, 22 Main St., 01081. T: (413) 245-7148; www.oakhavencampground.com.

🚐 ★★★★   ⛺ ★

Beauty: ★★★	Site Privacy: ★★★
Spaciousness: ★★★★	Quiet: ★★★
Security: ★★★	Cleanliness: ★★★★
Insect Control: ★★★	Facilities: ★★★

Wooded, grassy, and set in a rural area between Worcester and Springfield, Oak Haven has become a summer home-away-from-home for its 80 or so seasonal campers. Campers who join them for the weekend or the week will quickly sense the low-key camaraderie here. Street signs reflect a sense of humor; there's Snob Hill and Rowdy Rd., for example. A comedy hypnotist is likely to show up on the activities schedule. There's an activities director on board to plan kids' stuff. Site sizes vary; some are open, some are shaded. All are back-in and fairly spacious. Campsites are set in a loop, with the smallest numbers closest to the entrance. Higher numbers are in back, near a good-sized ball field. There are only two restrooms, so you can bet that's where the tenters are, although this campground attracts far more RVers than tenters. The ambiance of the place is wholesome and well maintained. Bonus for flea market mavens and collectors: this campground is just five minutes away from Brimfield Flea Markets, New England's largest antique flea market. Events are held on various weekends during spring, summer, and fall.

BASICS

Operated By: Alan & Penny Jalbert. **Open:** May 1–Oct. 15. **Site Assignment:** Reservations accepted year-round; 1-night deposit required except holidays & Shriner's Benefit weekend, which must be paid in full 1 month in advance; full refund, less $10 fee, for reservations cancelled before 7 days. **Registration:** At office. **Fee:** $30–$32; based on 2 people, 1 camping unit, & 2 vehicles. Extra adult (18 years & up), $5; children (age 6 & up), $1; air-conditioning or electric heat, $3 per day; MC, V. **Parking:** At site.

FACILITIES

Number of RV-only Sites: 140. **Hookups:** Electric (20, 30, 50 amps), water, sewer. **Each Site:** Picnic table, fireplace. **Dump Station:** Yes. **Laundry:** Yes. **Pay Phone:** Yes. **Restrooms and Showers:** Yes (coin-op). **Fuel:** No. **Propane:** Yes. **Internal Roads:** Gravel, in good condition. **RV Service:** No. **Market:** 10 mi. east, in Sturbridge, & 10 mi. west, in Palmer. **Restaurant:** In Sturbridge & Palmer. **General Store:** Yes. **Vending:** Yes. **Swimming:** Yes. **Playground:** Yes. **Other:** Rec hall. **Activities:** Baseball, swimming, volleyball, horseshoes. **Nearby Attractions:** Old Sturbridge Village, Brimfield Flea Markets (various weekends), Norcross Wildlife Sanctuary. **Additional Information:** Greater Springfield CVB, (800) 723-1548, www.valleyvisitor.com.

RESTRICTIONS

Pets: Max. 2 dogs per campsite. Dogs must be kept on leash & picked up after. Dogs should not be left unattended. **Fires:** Grill, camp stoves, fireplaces only. **Alcoholic Beverages:** At site only. **Vehicle Maximum Length:** None. **Other:** 3-night min. stay required on holiday weekends.

TO GET THERE

From I-90 (Massachusetts Turnpike), take Exit 9 (Sturbridge) to US 20 west. At the center of Brimfield, take SR 19S, 4.5 mi. to center of Wales. Campground will be on your left.

WAQUOIT   MAP, B-4
Waquoit Bay National Estuarine Research Reserve

reserve america

149 Waquoit Hwy., 02536. T: (508) 457-0495; www.reserveamerica.com.

🚐 ★★★★   ⛺ ★★★★

Beauty: ★★★   Site Privacy: ★★★
Spaciousness: ★★   Quiet: ★★
Security: ★★   Cleanliness: ★★★★
Insect Control: ★★★   Facilities: ★

The Waquoit Bay National Estuarine Research Reserve (WBNERR) is located on the south shore of Cape Cod, Massachusetts, in the towns of Falmouth and Mashpee. It encompasses some 3,000 acres of open waters, barrier beaches, marshlands, and uplands. Land components include Washburn Island, South Cape Beach State Park, property surrounding the Quashnet River and Reserve Headquarters. The Waquoit Bay NERR is part of the National Estuarine Research Reserve System, which presently includes 25 sites in 20 states and Puerto Rico. Each site represents a different coastal region. The Waquoit Bay Reserve is representative of the Northern Virginian biogeographic region, from Chesapeake Bay to Cape Cod. WBNERR is co-funded and co-managed by the National Oceanic and Atmospheric Administration's Office of Ocean and Coastal Resource Management, Estuarine Reserves Division and by the Massachusetts Department of Conservation and Recreation. Our main office is open to the public Monday through Friday from 10 am to 4 pm, closed holidays. Stop by to find out more about our programs!

BASICS

Operated By: Massachusetts State Parks. **Open:** May 11–Oct. 8. **Site Assignment:** Reservations can be made up to 6 months in advance. **Registration:** At office. **Fee:** Single, $8–$10; group, $25. **Parking:** 2 vehicles per campsite.

FACILITIES

Number of Multipurpose Sites: 11. **Hookups:** None. **Dump Station:** No. **Laundry:** No. **Pay Phone:** No. **Restrooms and Showers:** No. **Fuel:** No. **Propane:** No. **RV Service:** No. **Market:** No. **Restaurant:** No. **General Store:** No. **Vending:** No. **Swimming:** Yes. **Playground:** No. **Activities:** Boating, fishing, hiking.

RESTRICTIONS

Pets: Keep pets leashed (10-ft. leash max.) at all times. Proof of rabies vaccination is required. Pets are never to be left unattended. **Fires:** No open fires are allowed on the island. Please bring a portable stove using man-made fuels or a charcoal grill. **Alcoholic Beverages:** Alcoholic beverages are prohibited in all MA state parks & campgrounds. **Other:** Quiet hours are 10 p.m.–7 a.m. Please, no unnecessary or disturbing noise at any time. Equipment is limited to 2 tents or 1 camping vehicle & 1 small tent per site. Tents are

limited to 300 square feet of combined floor space. Access to the Washburn Island Campground is by boat only. Camping on Washburn Island is a primitive camping experience. There is no water on the island. Ticks are present on Washburn Island, please check yourself thoroughly.

TO GET THERE

From Boston: Follow Hwy. 3 south to Sagamore Bridge/Cape Cod Canal. Follow Hwy. 6 east over the bridge to Exit 2 and the intersection with Hwy. 130. Follow Hwy. 130 south to Great Neck Rd. in Mashpee. Just after the Flume restaurant, bear right to the Mashpee Rotary. Halfway around the rotary take Hwy. 28 North. Take a left on a small road immediately after Edwards Boat Yard (4 mi. from the Mashpee Rotary). Parking is only available in a large town administered parking area adjacent to the intersection of Hwy. 28. From Providence/West: Follow Hwy. 495 or Hwy.195 to Hwy. 25. Hwy. 25 crosses over the Bourne Bridge and becomes Hwy. 28. Follow Hwy. 28 south to Hwy. 151. Follow Hwy. 151 to the Mashpee Rotary. Halfway around the rotary take Hwy. 28 north. Take a left on a small road immediately after Edwards Boat Yard (4 mi. from the Mashpee Rotary). Parking is only available in a large town administered parking area adjacent to the intersection of Hwy. 28.

WEST SUTTON   MAP, B-2
The Old Holbrook Place

114 Manchaug Rd., 01590-1141.
T: (508) 865-5050.

🚐 ★★★★   ⛺ ★★

Beauty: ★★★★   Site Privacy: ★★★
Spaciousness: ★★★   Quiet: ★★★★
Security: ★★★★   Cleanliness: ★★★
Insect Control: ★★★   Facilities: ★★★★

Located just south of Worcester on 350-acre Lake Manchaug, The Old Holbrook Place is a tiny gem of a campground. Operating the property since 1946, now on their third generation of guests, the Nelsons are delightfully friendly hosts (Mrs. Nelson was making a shell necklace for a camper kid when we visited), typical of the character here). The property includes a small picnic grove and a hilly, three-sided sandy beach and swim area with raft. One side is a shallow, baby's crib (wading beach). Campsites are set along both sides of the camp road, with some along the lake and some along the road. About half are seasonal sites (blessedly lacking in lawn art). The best tent site is at Big Rock, alongside a boulder. Among the waterfront sites, numbers 16 and 17 boast the best views and get nice breezes off the lake. They're close to restrooms, but right next to the boat launch. Site 26 is nice, too, facing a marshy area of the lake. Although the picnic area and beach are open for day use, campers use a private restroom (you get a key upon check-in.) Other nice features: books and puzzles to swap, and nice park benches at waters' edge.

BASICS

Operated By: Nelson family. **Open:** Memorial Day–Labor Day. **Site Assignment:** Reservations recommended, at least 2 weeks in advance; will try to honor site requests; 1-night deposit required; deposit is refundable if cancellation is made a week in advance, and if site can be rented. **Registration:** At office. **Fee:** $18–$25 per family (parents & unmarried children); no credit cards. **Parking:** At site.

FACILITIES

Number of RV-only Sites: 66. **Hookups:** Electric (20 amps), water, sewer. **Each Site:** Picnic table, fire ring. **Dump Station:** Yes. **Laundry:** No. **Pay Phone:** Yes. **Restrooms and Showers:** Yes. **Fuel:** No. **Propane:** No. **Internal Roads:** Gravel, in good condition. **RV Service:** No. **Market:** 2 mi. west. **Restaurant:** 4 mi. east. **General Store:** Yes. **Vending:** No. **Swimming:** Lake swimming. **Playground:** No. **Other:** Boat ramp. **Activities:** Boating (rentals available), lake swimming. **Nearby Attractions:** New England Science Center, Ecotarium, Worcester Art Museum, outlet shopping. **Additional Information:** Central Massachusetts Tourist Council, (508) 755-7400, www.worcester.org.

RESTRICTIONS

Pets: Must be leashed & cleaned up after. Not allowed on the beach. **Fires:** Fire ring only. **Alcoholic Beverages:** Allowed. **Vehicle Maximum Length:** 30 ft. **Other:** Visitors must register upon entering the park.

TO GET THERE

From Hwy. 395, take Exit 4A, onto Sutton Ave. Head east 3.6 mi., then take second right (after passing white church) to Manchaug Rd. Campground is exactly 1 mi. in from Central Tpk. (Sutton Ave.), on Manchaug Rd. (Second campground you pass.)

WEST TOWNSEND   MAP, A-2
Pearl Hill State Park

105 New Fitchburg Rd., 01474. T: (978) 597-2850; www.reserveamerica.com.

🚐 ★★★★	🏕 ★★★★
Beauty: ★★★	Site Privacy: ★★★
Spaciousness: ★★★	Quiet: ★★★★
Security: ★★★★	Cleanliness: ★★★★
Insect Control: ★★★	Facilities: ★★

Pearl Hill's campground offers some of the largest and most private campsites in Massachusetts, all beneath a canopy of stately pines. Served by a modern bathhouse, Pearl Hill offers exceptional woodland camping. This 1,000-acre park is open on a seasonal basis from Memorial Day through Labor Day. Pearl Hill's campground offers some of the largest and most private campsites in Massachusetts, all beneath a canopy of stately pines. There are 51 campsites served by a nice bathhouse, and a day-use area that includes a five-acre pond created by the seasonal damming of Park Hill Brook, with a beach area on the pond. The area offers miles of hiking trails, abundant swimming opportunities, and great antiquing. There is a trail connecting Damon Pond of Willard Brook State Forest to Pearl Hill State Park. It's four-miles long, and you should plan up to three hours or more to hike the entire trail in good conditions.

BASICS

Operated By: Massachusetts State Parks. **Open:** May 24–Oct. 8. **Site Assignment:** Reservations can be made up to 6 months in advance. **Registration:** At office. **Fee:** Single, $12–$14. **Parking:** 2 vehicles per campsite.

FACILITIES

Number of Multipurpose Sites: 50. **Hookups:** None. **Dump Station:** No. **Laundry:** No. **Pay Phone:** Yes. **Restrooms and Showers:** Yes. **Fuel:** No. **Propane:** No. **Internal Roads:** Paved. **RV Service:** No. **Market:** No. **Restaurant:** No. **General Store:** No. **Vending:** No. **Swimming:** W/in 10 mi. **Playground:** No. **Activities:** Biking, hiking, horseback riding.

RESTRICTIONS

Pets: Keep pets leashed (10-ft. leash max.) at all times. Proof of rabies vaccination is required. Pets are never to be left unattended. **Fires:** Campfires in designated fireplaces. **Alcoholic Beverages:** Alcoholic beverages are prohibited in all MA state parks & campgrounds. **Other:** Quiet hours are 10 p.m.–7 a.m. No unnecessary or disturbing noise at any time. Equipment is limited to 2 tents or 1 camping vehicle & 1 small tent per site. Tents are limited to 300 square feet of combined floor space. Massachusetts law requires that children age 16 and under wear a helmet when bicycling.

TO GET THERE

From the northeast: Take Hwy. 495 to Littleton and the intersection with Hwy. 119 west. Follow Hwy. 119 west 19 mi. to West Townsend. Turn left (south) on New Fitchburg Rd. Follow New Fitchburg Rd. 1.5 mi. to the park entrance on the right. From the west: Follow Hwy. 2 east to Hwy. 31 north in Fitchburg. Follow Hwy. 31 North through Fitchburg to the Town of Ashby and the intersection with Hwy. 119 east. Follow Hwy. 119 east 2.5 mi. to New Fitchburg Rd. in West Townsend. Turn right on New Fitchburg Rd. The park entrance is 1.5 mi. on the right. From the east: Take Hwy. 2 west to Leominster and Hwy. 13 north. Follow Hwy. 13 north to Hwy. 119 west in West Townsend. Turn left onto Hwy. 119. Turn left onto New Fitchburg Rd. The park entrance is 1.5 mi. on the right.

WESTFORD   MAP, A-3
Wyman's Beach Family Campground

48 Wyman's Beach Rd., 01886. T: (978) 692-6287; www.wymanscamping.com.

🚐 ★★★★	🏕 ★★★★
Beauty: ★★★	Site Privacy: ★★★
Spaciousness: ★★	Quiet: ★★★★
Security: ★★	Cleanliness: ★★★
Insect Control: ★★★★★	Facilities: ★★★

Time seems to have stood still at Wyman's Beach campground, 30 miles northwest of Boston. Generations of kids have splashed in sandy-bottomed Long Sought-for Pond, known as, simply, "the lake." RVers and tent campers join seasonal campers and cabin-dwellers to relax here on a small campers-only beach, or with the public at a day-use beach. The campground has the feeling of a lakeside resort, with a snack bar, horseshoe pit, playground, even an activity director who leads the kids in arts-and-crafts projects, and theme nights—perhaps a 1950s party (perfect), Hawaiian Night, or bingo. Site sizes vary; some are 25 feet wide, some as big as 60 by 55 feet or so. The most-requested, most-secluded RV site is 81, on a hill, and semi-secluded 117. Best tent sites by far are 129 and 130, roomy and away from the action. Count on plenty of kids, and grandkids, running around, especially on holiday weekends. Sites are grass, back-in, and mostly shaded, set on short side streets and loop streets off the main road. Wyman's Beach campground offers a pleasant lakeshore experience and a central location, with easy access to Lexington and Concord and Boston.

BASICS

Operated By: Wyman family. **Open:** Early May–early Sept. **Site Assignment:** Reserve 2 weeks in advance, by phone or online; 2-night deposit required; refund w/ 2-week notice prior to arrival date. **Registration:** At office. **Fee:** $32–$45; based on 2 adults per site; each child over 5, add $2 per day; V, MC, D. **Parking:** At site.

FACILITIES

Number of RV-only Sites: 200. **Hookups:** Electric (30, 50 amps), water, sewer. **Each Site:** Picnic table, fire ring. **Dump Station:** Yes. **Laundry:** Yes. **Pay Phone:** Yes. **Restrooms and Showers:** Yes, coin op. **Fuel:** No. **Propane:** Yes. **Internal Roads:** Paved & gravel, good condition. **RV Service:** No. **Market:** 5 mi. south. **Restaurant:** 2 mi. west on Hwy. 40. **General Store:** Yes. **Vending:** Yes. **Swimming:** 2 beaches. **Playground:** Yes. **Other:** Rec hall. **Activities:** Pond swimming, arcade games, horseshoes, bocce, volleyball, basketball, shuffleboard, planned activities. **Nearby Attractions:** Butterfly Place, Lowell National Historic Park. **Additional Information:** Greater Merrimack Valley CVB, (978) 459-6150 or (800) 443-3332, www.lowell.org.

RESTRICTIONS

Pets: Must be leashed, quiet, & cleaned up after. Must not be left unattended. **Fires:** Fire ring only. **Alcoholic Beverages:** At sites only. **Vehicle Maximum Length:** 40 ft.

TO GET THERE

From I-495, take Exit 35 (Hwy. 3N) 4 mi. to Hwy. 40 (Exit 33.) Head west 2.6 mi. to Dunstable Rd. Go north 0.8 mi. Campground is on right.

WESTPORT POINT — MAP, B-3
Horseneck Beach State Reservation

John Reed Rd., 02791. T: (508) 636-8817 or (508) 636-8816 (off-season); www.reserveamerica.com.

🚐 ★★★   ⛺ ★★★

Beauty: ★★   Site Privacy: ★★
Spaciousness: ★★   Quiet: ★★
Security: ★★   Cleanliness: ★
Insect Control: ★★★   Facilities: ★★★

Nudging the Rhode Island border to the west and jutting into Buzzards Bay, Horseneck Beach offers a sublime seacoast setting, with campsites directly on the beach or nestled behind sand dunes. Windswept sea oats and rosa rugosa add to the allure. While the campers' beach is rather rocky, campers get free access to the wide, sandy, public beach to the north. There's not much here in the way of amenities (savvy campers know to bring their own firewood, or they'll have to travel 16-plus miles to the nearest supermarket to get it), and the restrooms can be really grungy (due to staffing shortages, they say.) There are 200 total sites, 100 are back-ins and 100 are pull-throughs. The seaside location is the draw here. Several campsites are directly on the beach, or right across the road from it, but they can get windy. These sites aren't so good for tenters, but fine for RVers, who sort of parallel-park into them. Even-numbered sites 54–82 sit right on the water's edge; odd-numbered sites 55–81 face the water, too, although the road runs between the campsites and the beach. Avoid site 77; it's oddly tiny. For tenters, sites 97 and 99 sit right behind a dune, but close to the restrooms and beach path. You're never far from the water here.

BASICS
Operated By: Dept. of Conservation and Recreation, Massachusetts State Parks. **Open:** Mid-May–mid-Oct. **Site Assignment:** Reservations recommended; reserve up to 6 months in advance by calling ReserveAmerica at (877) I-CAMP-MA or online at www.reserveamerica.com; to change arrival or departure date, or site type, call at least 3 days prior to arrival date; $10 cancellation/transfer fee. **Registration:** At office. **Fee:** Massachusetts residents, $15; nonresidents, $17; V, MC. **Parking:** At site.

FACILITIES
Number of Multipurpose Sites: 100. **Hookups:** None. **Each Site:** Picnic table, fireplace. **Dump Station:** Yes. **Laundry:** No. **Pay Phone:** Yes. **Restrooms and Showers:** Yes. **Fuel:** No. **Propane:** No. **Internal Roads:** Paved, in good condition. **RV Service:** No. **Market:** 16.3 mi. north, on Hwy. 88N. **Restaurant:** Yes (snack bar at public beach). **General Store:** No. **Vending:** No. **Swimming:** Ocean swimming. **Playground:** Yes. **Other:** Boat ramp, nature center. **Activities:** Swimming (ocean beach), basketball, volleyball, saltwater fishing, interpretive programs, Jr. Ranger program. **Nearby Attractions:** Winery, New Bedford Whaling Museum, Cape Cod. **Additional Information:** Bristol County CVB, (800) 288-6263, www.bristol-county.org.

RESTRICTIONS
Pets: On leash, quiet, & cleaned up after. Rabies vaccination certificate required. Beach & swimming areas are off-limits to pets. **Fires:** Fireplaces only. **Alcoholic Beverages:** Not allowed. **Vehicle Maximum Length:** None. **Other:** 14-day stay limit between Memorial Day & Labor Day.

TO GET THERE
Take I-95 west to Hwy. 88, Exit 10 south. Follow Hwy. 88 south for 10 mi. to state reservation. Campground entrance is just past main entrance on right.

WILLIAMSBURG — MAP, A-1
D A R State Forest

555 East St., 01096. T: (413) 268-7098; www.reserveamerica.com.

🚐 ★★★★   ⛺ ★★★★

Beauty: ★★★   Site Privacy: ★★★
Spaciousness: ★★★   Quiet: ★★★★★
Security: ★★★★★   Cleanliness: ★★★★
Insect Control: ★★★   Facilities: ★★

The Daughters of the American Revolution (DAR) donated 1,020 acres to the Commonwealth for a state forest in 1929. Since then more than 750 additional acres have been acquired to include Upper and Lower Highland lakes, which offer a popular swimming beach, shady picnic area, and a group picnic pavilion. Located in the eastern foothills of the Berkshires, 15 miles of mixed-use trails through northern hardwood-conifer forest are awaiting you. Possessing great wildlife diversity, extensive northern hardwood forest, swamps, lakes, and ponds, DAR State Forest is a wonderful place for a day of walking, nature study, and panoramic vistas. Because most of the area lies above 1,400 feet elevation, the growing season is curtailed; this has a profound influence on the plants and animals that live here. Stands of red spruce and bunchberry and boggy pockets give clues to the northern character of this forest. A lookout tower on high Moore Hill (1,697 feet) rewards you with a magnificent 360-degree view of the surrounding wooded ridges, including the nearby Chapelbrook Ledges. Unmistakable evidence of earlier agriculture stands in the form of rock walls and old cellar holes found in this maturing beech/maple/hemlock woodland. Climb the Goshen fire tower for spectacular views of the Connecticut River Valley and into five states. The campground offers 51 wooded campsites featuring modern comfort stations with showers and a private beach. Wheelchair-accessible campsites are also available. In summer other activities include nonmotorized boating, hiking, fishing, horseback riding (bring your horse), and mountain biking. In winter, ice fishing, skating, cross-country skiing, snowshoeing, and snowmobiling are popular.

BASICS
Operated By: Massachusetts State Parks. **Open:** All year. **Site Assignment:** Reservations can be made up to 6 months in advance. **Registration:** At office. **Fee:** Single, $12–$14; group, $25. **Parking:** 2 vehicles per campsite.

FACILITIES
Number of Multipurpose Sites: 52. **Hookups:** None. **Dump Station:** No. **Laundry:** No. **Pay Phone:** W/in 10 mi. **Restrooms and Showers:** Yes. **Fuel:** No. **Propane:** No. **Internal Roads:** Paved. **RV Service:** No. **Market:** No. **Restaurant:** No. **General Store:** No. **Vending:** No. **Swimming:** Yes. **Playground:** No. **Activities:** Biking, boating, canoeing, fishing, hiking, horseback riding, interpretive programs, picnicking, cross-country skiing, snowmobiling.

RESTRICTIONS
Pets: Keep pets leashed (10-ft. leash max.) at all times. Proof of rabies vaccination is required. Pets are never to be left unattended. **Fires:** Campfires in designated fireplaces. **Alcoholic Beverages:** Alcoholic beverages are prohibited in all MA state parks & campgrounds. **Other:** Quiet hours are 10 p.m.–7 a.m. No unnecessary or disturbing noise at any time. Equipment is limited to 2 tents or 1 camping vehicle & 1 small tent per site. Tents are limited to 300 square feet of combined floor space. Bears are regular visitors to this campground. Bears are wild and can be dangerous. To protect your family and your property, keep all food, coolers, and cooking supplies and equipment in your vehicle when not in use. Massachusetts law requires that children age 16 and under wear a helmet when bicycling.

TO GET THERE
From the north: Take Hwy. 91 south to Hwy. 2 west, Greenfield exit. Follow Hwy. 2 west to Hwy. 112 south. Follow Hwy. 112 south 10 mi. to park entrance on left. From the south: Take Hwy. 91 north to Exit 19 in Northampton. Hwy. 9 west to Goshen. Turn right onto Hwy. 112 north. Park entrance is 1 mi. on the right. From east and west: MA Turnpike (Hwy. 90) to Exit 4 and Hwy. 91 north. Hwy. 91 north to Exit 19 in Northampton. Follow Hwy. 9 west to Goshen. Turn right onto Hwy. 112 north. The park entrance is 1 mi. on right.

WINDSOR — MAP, A-1
Windsor State Forest

River Rd., 01270. T: (413) 684-0948; www.reserveamerica.com.

🚐 ★★★★   ⛺ ★★★★

Beauty: ★★★   Site Privacy: ★★★
Spaciousness: ★★   Quiet: ★★★★★
Security: ★★★★★   Cleanliness: ★★★★
Insect Control: ★★★   Facilities: ★★★★

Deep in the rolling hills of the Berkshire highlands, Windsor State Forest's cascading waterfall at Windsor Jambs stands out for its spectacular beauty.

Windsor Jambs Brook plunges through a 25-foot-wide gorge, with 80-foot-high granite walls rising on either side; a beautiful and refreshing place to visit. The popular day-use area along the Westfield River offers a 100-foot sandy beach for swimming with wooded picnic sites. Twenty-four limited-service campsites are also available (no showers or flush toilets). Trails and old dirt roads that wind through the The Bush are favored by hikers, cross-country skiers, and snowmobiles. Fishermen and hunters are also welcome. Twenty miles northeast of Pittsfield, this day hike travels between the two properties. Tour mixed woods, plantations, and wet meadow bottoms, crisscrossing Steep Bank Brook to visit the rocky gorge of Windsor Jambs. Special attractions are the tranquil woods, rocky brooks, cascades, gorge, and the sightings of turkey, porcupine, and deer. Don't forget you are in black-bear country. Never physically confront, feed, torment, or throw anything at bears. Take appropriate precautions with food so as not to attract bears.

BASICS

Operated By: Massachusetts State Parks. **Open:** May 24–Sept. 3. **Site Assignment:** Reservations can be made up to 6 months in advance. **Registration:** At office. **Fee:** Single, $8–$10; group, $25. **Parking:** 2 vehicles per campsite.

FACILITIES

Number of Multipurpose Sites: 24. **Hookups:** None. **Dump Station:** No. **Laundry:** No. **Pay Phone:** Yes. **Restrooms and Showers:** Yes. **Fuel:** No. **Propane:** No. **Internal Roads:** Paved. **RV Service:** No. **Market:** No. **Restaurant:** Yes. **General Store:** No. **Vending:** No. **Swimming:** Yes. **Playground:** No. **Activities:** Biking, fishing, hiking, horseback riding, hunting, picnicking.

RESTRICTIONS

Pets: Keep pets leashed (10-ft. leash max.) at all times. Proof of rabies vaccination is required. Pets are never to be left unattended. **Fires:** Campfires in designated fireplaces. **Alcoholic Beverages:** Alcoholic beverages are prohibited in all MA state parks & campgrounds. **Other:** Quiet hours are 10 p.m.–7 a.m. No unnecessary or disturbing noise at any time. Equipment is limited to 2 tents or 1 camping vehicle & 1 small tent per site. Tents are limited to 300 square feet of combined floor space. Bears are regular visitors to this campground. Bears are wild and can be dangerous. To protect your family and your property, keep all food, coolers, and cooking supplies and equipment in your vehicle when not in use. Massachusetts law requires that children age 16 and under wear a helmet when bicycling.

TO GET THERE

From the east: Massachusetts Turnpike (Hwy. 90) to Exit 4 (Hwy. 91, Holyoke) Follow Hwy. 91 north to Exit 19 and the intersection with Hwy. 9 in Northampton. Follow Hwy. 9 west to West Cummington. Turn right into the village of West Cummington. Turn north on River Rd. The forest begins after 4 mi. From the north and Hwy. 116: Follow Hwy. 116 to Savoy. Go 0.5 mi. east of the town center then turn south on River Rd. Follow River Rd. 3 mi. to the campground entrance on the left.

Michigan

RVers and campers alike should find the recreational opportunities that Michigan has to offer too tempting to resist. Home to two national forests, two national lakeshores, and a national park, Michigan shares its Great Lakes and nearly 100 state parks, as well as magnificent sand dunes, with residents and visitors alike. Despite the more than 100 lighthouses guarding the Spartan State's shores, 38,000 square miles of Great Lakes bottomlands remain the final resting place of more than 3,000 shipwrecks, attracting scuba divers and encouraging glass-bottomed boat tours.

In the Motor City of Detroit, Henry Ford and his Model T gave highway travelers the wheels to hit the road. However, if it's an entertaining history lesson you seek, the **Henry Ford Museum** and **Greenfield Village** in Dearborn are the places to be. The state is also home to the original "Big Mac"—the **Mackinac Bridge,** which joins Michigan's **Lower Peninsula** to its rugged, more undisturbed **Upper Peninsula.** Ironically, **Mackinac Island** enforces a no-cars ban on its picturesque shores. A ferry, catamaran, or plane is available to access the tiny island, especially to marvel at the **1887 Grand Hotel** and its sweeping 600-foot-long white veranda capped by a sky-blue ceiling. While touring the Upper Peninsula, adventure seekers may want to take a shot at scaling the 26th state's highest peak, **Mount Arvon,** which stands at 1,978 feet.

Culture, oddity, and nature abound any time of the year. For a taste of the state's Dutch heritage, stop by Holland, where shopkeepers still scrub cobblestone sidewalks; a 200-year-old, ten-story Dutch windmill, **DeZwaan,** still twirls; and a profusion of color dazzles visitors each May during **Tulip Time Festival.** To get a feel for Munich, head to **Frankenmuth,** home of Bronner's **Christmas Wonderland.** With a showroom larger than four football fields, Bronner's is said to be the world's most expansive Christmas shop. Travelers near Crystal City in August can take part in the town's **Humongous Fungus Festival,** dedicated to the 37-acre, 1,500-year-old underground fungus that inhabits **Iron County Forest.**

The cereal capital of the world, **Battle Creek,** showcases breakfast food history through its interactive museum, **Kelloggs Cereal City USA,** where the wonders of marketing tickle your peripherals and a factory tour rewards you with the crunchy breakfast foods, hot from the mill. **Petoskey** draws rock hounds seeking stone remnants of an extinct coral that inhabited the shallow waters there 350 million years ago. In **Cheboygan,** one of the Great Lakes' largest cattail marshes serves as a nesting site for 54 bird species.

In **Lac Labelle,** there is a particular beach along the **Keweenaw Peninsula** where the **Singing Sands of Bete Gris** can be magically brought to song with a circular motion of the hand on the beach. Good luck taking some home for show and tell—once removed, the sand loses its voice and can only be heard in that location. For something you can take with you, head to the town of **Lennon,** otherwise known as the lawn ornament capital of the United States, for a glimpse of gaud and Americana, not to mention the opportunity to score some neighbor-annoying yard decor.

In **Sault Ste. Marie,** directly across the pond from Ontario, huge freighters pass through the town's greatest attraction, the **Soo Locks.** Come winter, ice-fishing shacks sprout up all over the Michigan waterways like igloos as anglers chip away the frozen wet stuff in hopes of bringing in a fresh catch.

With a name that means "heaven," **Ishpeming** has become a well-known ski center, as well as home to the world's largest working chain saw at **Da Yoopers Tourist Trap.** As the largest island in Lake Superior, **Isle Royale** is 98 percent wilderness, where even games of tag are discouraged to help retain as much of the quiet solitude as possible. An invitation to Michigan's natural beauty doesn't get much more personal and reflective than this.

Campground Profiles

ALBION
Rockey's Campground

MAP, D-2

19880 27-1/2 Mile Rd., 49224.
T: (877) 762-5397 or (517) 857-2200;
www.michcampgrounds.com/rockeys.

🚐 ★★★★   ⛺ ★★★

Beauty: ★★★★   Site Privacy: ★★★★
Spaciousness: ★★★★   Quiet: ★★★★
Security: ★★★★   Cleanliness: ★★★★
Insect Control: ★★★★   Facilities: ★★★

A rural campground on a chain of five lakes, Rockey's Campground is located about 6.5 miles south of Albion. The secluded campground offers open or shaded sites, with a typical site width of 35 feet. The campground has 50 seasonal campers and only one pull-through site. A large building is available for groups, and a cement boat ramp is popular with boaters. Sites are level and grassy with gravel pads. The best sites are those closest to the water. Be aware that no large dogs are permitted. Facilities are very clean and well maintained. About half the sites are occupied by seasonals, and many other regulars return year after year, so reservations are recommended. For security measures, owners and staff members seem to keep a close watch on the campground while also being friendly and helpful.

BASICS

Operated By: Brian & Vicki Mead. **Open:** May 15–Oct. 1. **Site Assignment:** Reservations w/ 1-night deposit; refund (minus $5) w/ 7-day notice. **Registration:** At campground office. **Fee:** Tent, $25; cabins, $39; cash, check. **Parking:** At site.

FACILITIES

Number of RV-only Sites: 100. **Hookups:** Electric (20, 30 amps), water. **Each Site:** Picnic table, fire ring. **Dump Station:** Yes. **Laundry:** No. **Pay Phone:** Yes. **Restrooms and Showers:** Yes. **Fuel:** No. **Propane:** Yes. **Internal Roads:** Gravel, in good condition. **RV Service:** Yes. **Market:** 5 mi. south in Albion. **Restaurant:** 1 mi. north. **General Store:** Camp store. **Vending:** Yes. **Swimming:** Pool, beach. **Playground:** Yes. **Other:** Bass Lake, sandy beach, lake swimming, game room, mini-golf, boat ramp, sports field, horseshoes, rental cottage. **Activities:** Swimming, fishing, boating (rental rowboats, canoes available), scheduled weekend activities. **Nearby Attractions:** Whitehouse Nature Center, antiques, Albion's Historic Walkway, Albion College Observatory, Bobbitt Visual Arts Center, children's museum, Star Commonwealth, golf, Brueckner Museum & Gladstone Cottage, Westwood Mall. **Additional Information:** Greater Albion Chamber of Commerce, (517) 629-5533.

RESTRICTIONS

Pets: On leash, no large dogs, no pets in cabins. **Fires:** Fire ring only. **Alcoholic Beverages:** Allowed. Keep glass bottles at own site. **Vehicle Maximum Length:** No limit. **Other:** Entrance gate closes at 11 p.m. Must be 21 or older to rent campsite.

TO GET THERE

From the junction of I-94 and 28 Mile Rd., take Exit 121 (Albion exit) and drive 6.7 mi. north on 28 Mile Rd. to campground. Follow signs. Roads are mostly wide and well maintained, with adequate shoulders.

ALLEGAN
Tri-Ponds Family Camp Resort

MAP, D-1

3687 Dumont Rd., 49010. T: (269) 673-4740.

🚐 ★★★★   ⛺ ★★★★

Beauty: ★★★   Site Privacy: ★★★★
Spaciousness: ★★★★   Quiet: ★★★★
Security: ★★★★   Cleanliness: ★★★★
Insect Control: ★★★★   Facilities: ★★★★

Circling several small ponds in Allegan, Tri-Ponds Family Camp Resort offers open and shaded campsites. Sites are level with a typical site width of 35 feet. The campground has 26 seasonal campers and eight pull-through sites. An activities and crafts director is on staff and worship services are held on Sunday. No license is necessary to fish in the ponds. The campground is well maintained and clean, with a great deal of attention put into keeping bathrooms and shower facilities in tip-top shape. Security is good with owners who make sure the campground is safe and quiet for campers.

BASICS

Operated By: Paul and Dotty VanDrunen. **Open:** May 1–Oct. 31. **Site Assignment:** Reservations required (1-night deposit); refund w/ 2-week notice. **Registration:** At campground office. **Fee:** Modern, $28; rustic $23; cabin, $65; cash, check, credit card. **Parking:** At site.

FACILITIES

Number of RV-only Sites: 86. **Number of Tent-only Sites:** 15. **Hookups:** Electric (30 amps), water, sewer. **Each Site:** Picnic table, fire ring. **Dump Station:** Yes. **Laundry:** Yes. **Pay Phone:** Yes. **Restrooms and Showers:** Yes. **Fuel:** No. **Propane:** No. **Internal Roads:** Paved, in good condition. **RV Service:** No. **Market:** 2 mi. **Restaurant:** 2 mi. **General Store:** Yes. **Vending:** Yes. **Swimming:** Yes. **Playground:** Yes. **Other:** Pond, swimming beach, rec hall, horseshoes, petting zoo, hiking trails, volleyball, sports field, activities & craft director. **Activities:** Swimming, fishing, family fun, scheduled activities. **Nearby Attractions:** Golf, antiques, bowling, horseback riding, Old Jail Museum, orchards, parks, Allegan State Game Area, arts & crafts, skiing. **Additional Information:** Allegan Area Chamber of Commerce, (616) 673-2479.

RESTRICTIONS

Pets: On leash only. **Fires:** Fire ring only. **Alcoholic Beverages:** Not allowed. **Vehicle Maximum Length:** No limit.

TO GET THERE

From the junction of Hwys. M 40/M 89 and 36th St. (4 mi. northwest of town), go north 2.2 mi. on 36th St. to Dumont Rd., then northwest 0.5 mi.

Roads are mostly wide and well maintained, with narrow shoulders in places. Dumont Rd. is paved but in only fair condition.

ALLENDALE
River Pines RV Park and Campground

MAP, A-3 INSET

reserve america

8275 Warner, 49401. T: (616) 895-6601 or (906) 884-4600; www.reserveamerica.com.

🚐 ★★★★   ⛺ ★★★★

Beauty: ★★★★   Site Privacy: ★★★★
Spaciousness: ★★★★   Quiet: ★★★★
Security: ★★★★   Cleanliness: ★★★★
Insect Control: ★★★★   Facilities: ★★★★

A little gem along the Ontonagon River, River Pines RV Park and Campground offers great facilities with sparkling-clean restrooms. Located outside Ontonagon, the campground has open or shaded level sites, with a typical site width of 35 feet. Laid out in a series of loops, the campground has 30 pull-through sites. A separate tent section in the woods allows more green space and privacy. A four-season campground, River Pines features easy access to 500 miles of snowmobile trails and five major ski hills within a 60-mile radius. Winter group housing available in the main building for those frigid, snowy Michigan winters. The best RV sites are in the pine tree section. Walleye and salmon fishing are popular in the river by the campground. With only 32 sites, reservations are strongly recommended from June through September. Security includes owners who live on the site and keep a close watch on the campground.

BASICS

Operated By: Dan & Donna Bowen. **Open:** All year. **Site Assignment:** Reservations w/ 1-night deposit; refund w/ 7-day notice; credit cards w/ 24-hour notice. **Registration:** At campground office. **Fee:** $24–$36; cash, check, credit card. **Parking:** At site.

FACILITIES

Number of RV-only Sites: 30. **Number of Tent-only Sites:** 2. **Hookups:** Electric (20, 30, 50 amps), water, sewer, phone, cable TV. **Each Site:** Picnic table, fire ring. **Dump Station:** Yes. **Laundry:** Yes. **Pay Phone:** Yes. **Restrooms and Showers:** Yes. **Fuel:** No. **Propane:** Yes. **Internal Roads:** Gravel, in good condition. **RV Service:** No. **Market:** 1 mi. east in Ontonagon. **Restaurant:** 1 mi. east in Ontonagon. **General Store:** Yes, limited. **Vending:** Yes. **Swimming:** Yes. **Playground:** Yes. **Other:** Rec hall, coin games, boat dock, fishing river, basketball, badminton, sports field, horseshoes, volleyball, wheelchair accessibility. **Activities:** Fishing, boating (rental canoe, rowboats, paddleboats, motorboats available). **Nearby Attractions:** Ontonagon River, 45 waterfalls, Porcupine Mountains State Park, sailing, backpacking, hiking, Presque Isle Falls, Lake of the Clouds, golf, antiques, arts & crafts, Ontonagon County Historical Museum. **Additional Information:** Ontonagon County Chamber of Commerce, (906) 884-4735.

RESTRICTIONS

Pets: On leash only. No pets in any building area. **Fires:** Fire ring only. **Alcoholic Beverages:** Allowed. **Vehicle Maximum Length:** No limit. **Other:** Quiet time at 10 p.m.

TO GET THERE

From the junction of US 45 and Hwy. 64, drive 0.25 mi. south on Hwy. 64, then 0.5 mi. east on River Rd. Roads are mostly wide and well maintained, with adequate shoulders.

ALPENA — MAP, B-3
Campers Cove RV Park

5005 Long Rapids Rd., 49707. T: (989) 356-3708; www.camperscovecampground.com.

🚐 ★★★★ ⛺ ★★★★

Beauty: ★★★★	Site Privacy: ★★★★
Spaciousness: ★★★★	Quiet: ★★★★
Security: ★★★★	Cleanliness: ★★★★
Insect Control: ★★★	Facilities: ★★★★

Located on a lake 7 miles west of Alpena, Campers Cove RV Park has 45 waterfront sites. Sites are mostly grassy and shaded with a typical site width of 50 feet. Some sites have places to tie up boats on the inland waterway for easy access to Thunder Bay River. A sauna is available by request only and takes half an hour to heat. No children under age 13 are permitted in the sauna unless accompanied by an adult. The indoor heated pool has adults-only swim times. Laid out in a series of loops, the campground has level sites with 15 seasonal campers and 16 pull-throughs. Rustic tent sites are in a separate area with more green space and privacy. Speed limit is 5.6 mph and quiet times are 11 p.m. to 8 a.m. Security measures include one entrance/exit road, owners who live on site, and regular patrols of the campground.

BASICS

Operated By: Mark & Judy Hall. **Open:** May 1–Oct. 31. **Site Assignment:** Reservations w/ $25 deposit; refund (minus $5) w/ 15-day notice; deposits made a year in advance are nonrefundable. **Registration:** At campground office. **Fee:** $20–$32; cash, check, credit card. **Parking:** At site.

FACILITIES

Number of Multipurpose Sites: 85. **Hookups:** Electric (20, 30, 50 amps), water, sewer, cable TV, phone. **Each Site:** Picnic table, fire ring. **Dump Station:** Yes. **Laundry:** Yes. **Pay Phone:** Yes. **Restrooms and Showers:** Yes. **Fuel:** No. **Propane:** Yes. **Internal Roads:** Paved/gravel, in good condition. **RV Service:** No. **Market:** 7 mi. east in Alpena. **Restaurant:** 7 mi. east in Alpena. **General Store:** Seasonal. **Vending:** Yes. **Swimming:** Seasonal. **Playground:** Yes. **Other:** Lake Winyah, sauna, game room, TV lounge, pavilion, mini-golf, shuffleboard, basketball, volleyball, nature area, stocked fishing pond, badminton, sports field, coin games, boat ramp, boat dock. **Activities:** Swimming, boating (rental canoes, kayaks, paddleboats, & rowboats avail-

able), biking (rental bicycles, fun cycles, & electric scooters available), fishing. **Nearby Attractions:** Wildlife sanctuary, planetarium, golf, museums, historic homes, dinosaur gardens, charter boat fishing, lighthouses, beaches, underwater park, diving, rock hound areas, sinkholes, antiques. **Additional Information:** Alpena Area CVB, (800) 4-ALPENA.

RESTRICTIONS

Pets: On leash only. **Fires:** Fire ring only. **Alcoholic Beverages:** Allowed. **Vehicle Maximum Length:** No limit.

TO GET THERE

From the junction of US 23 and Long Rapids Rd., drive 6 mi. west on Long Rapids Rd. (Johnson St.). Roads are wide and well maintained, with broad shoulders.

BELMONT — MAP, C-2
Grand Rogue Campgrounds, Canoe, and Tube Livery

6400 West River Dr., 49306. T: (616) 361-1053; www.grandrogue.com.

🚐 ★★★★ ⛺ ★★★★

Beauty: ★★★★	Site Privacy: ★★★★
Spaciousness: ★★★★	Quiet: ★★★★
Security: ★★★★	Cleanliness: ★★★★
Insect Control: ★★★★	Facilities: ★★★

Located on the Grand and Rogue rivers in Belmont, Rogue River Campgrounds Canoe and Tube Livery is minutes away from Grand Rapids attractions. Sites are back-in, grassy, and partly shaded with a typical site width of 40 feet. The campground is adjacent to an 18-hole golf course and lighted driving range. Located in a secluded lake and riverside setting, the campground offers canoe and tube trips from one to four hours long. Be aware that alcohol is not permitted on paddle sport trips. The campground also has a tour train that runs along the river and through 75 acres of wooded trails. A large pavilion is available for use to campers. Campground staff is friendly and helpful, escorting campers to sites upon check-in. They will help park the camping unit or park it for you.

BASICS

Operated By: Tom & Joan Briggs. **Open:** May–Sept. **Site Assignment:** Reservations w/ $30 deposit; refund (minus $2) w/ 5-day notice; no show, no call, no refund. **Registration:** At campground office. **Fee:** Hookup, $32.50; no hookup, $24; rustic, $18.50; cash, check, credit card. **Parking:** At site.

FACILITIES

Number of Multipurpose Sites: 110. **Hookups:** Electric (20, 30 amps), water, phone. **Each Site:** Picnic table, fire ring. **Dump Station:** Yes. **Laundry:** Yes. **Pay Phone:** Yes. **Restrooms and Showers:** Yes. **Fuel:** No. **Propane:** No. **Internal Roads:** Gravel, in good condition. **RV Service:** No. **Market:** 3 mi. **Restaurant:** 3 mi. **General Store:** Yes, limited. **Vending:** Yes. **Swimming:** Small lake. **Playground:** Yes. **Other:** Lake, river, pavilion, horseshoes, sports field, boat ramp, float trips, golf, basketball, hiking trails, volleyball. **Activities:** Swim-

ming, fishing, boating (rental canoes, kayaks available), scheduled weekend activities. **Nearby Attractions:** Gerald B. Ford Museum, Fredrick Meijer Gardens, zoo, Michigan Adventure Amusement Park, Roger B. Chaffee Planetarium, golf, tennis, rivers & lakes, antiques, Wooden Shoe Factory. **Additional Information:** Grand Rapids/Kent County CVB.

RESTRICTIONS

Pets: On leash only. **Fires:** Fire ring only. **Alcoholic Beverages:** Not on river activities. **Vehicle Maximum Length:** No limit.

TO GET THERE

From north junction of I-96 and US 131, take Exit 91 and drive 1.5 mi. north on US 131, then 4 mi. east on West River Dr. Roads are mostly wide and well maintained, with adequate shoulders.

BENZONIA — MAP, B-1
Vacation Trailer Park

2080 Benzie Hwy., 49616. T: (231) 882-5101 or (800) 482-5101; www.vacationtrailer.com.

🚐 ★★★★ ⛺ ★★★

Beauty: ★★★★	Site Privacy: ★★★★
Spaciousness: ★★★★	Quiet: ★★★★
Security: ★★★★	Cleanliness: ★★★★
Insect Control: ★★★★	Facilities: ★★★★

Nestled into the natural beauty of the Betsie River, Vacation Trailer Park offers camping and activities on the designated scenic river. Located less than a mile from West Benzonia, the campground is rolling and grassy with a typical site width of 30 feet. Vacation Trailer Park has 20 seasonal campers and five pull-through sites with a choice of open or shaded. A canoe livery service lets you rent a canoe and paddle down the Betsie River right past your camp site. The best sites for RVs are right on the river. Tents are permitted on any sites except the river ones to prevent erosion and problems with water pipes. Vacation Trailer Sales is located only 100 yards up the road and carries a complete line of RV parts and accessories. The campground general store also has a nice selection of fishing and hunting supplies. The campground provides 24-hour security with night managers on site and regular patrols of the campground.

BASICS

Operated By: Bill & Betty Workman. **Open:** All year. **Site Assignment:** Reservations w/ 1-night deposit; no refund but camping credit for 1 year. **Registration:** At campground office. **Fee:** Campsite, $26–$30.50; cabin/trailer, $75; cash, check, credit card. **Parking:** At site.

FACILITIES

Number of Multipurpose Sites: 100. **Hookups:** Electric (20, 30, 50 amps), water, sewer, cable TV. **Each Site:** Picnic table, fire ring. **Dump Station:** Yes. **Laundry:** Yes. **Pay Phone:** Yes. **Restrooms and Showers:** Yes. **Fuel:** No. **Propane:** No. **Internal Roads:** Gravel, in good condition. **RV Service:** Yes. **Market:** 0.25 mi. north in West Benzonia. **Restaurant:** 0.25 mi. north in West Benzonia. **General Store:** Yes. **Vending:** Yes. **Swimming:** Yes. **Playground:** Yes. **Other:** Betsie River, rec room, coin games, boat docks, fishing guide, fish-cleaning station, basketball, badminton, horseshoes, canoe launch area, rental RVs, rental cabins, hiking trails, volleyball, sports field. **Activities:** Swimming, hiking, fishing, boating (rental canoes, kayaks available), float trips. **Nearby Attractions:** Lake Michigan, Crystal Mountain, Point Betsie Lighthouse, marinas, golf, downhill ski runs, snowmobile & cross-country ski trails, antiques, arts & crafts, Benzie Area Historical Museum, Gwen Frostic Prints. **Additional Information:** Benzie Area Visitors Bureau, (800) 882-5801.

RESTRICTIONS

Pets: On leash only. **Fires:** Fire ring only. **Alcoholic Beverages:** At sites only. **Vehicle Maximum Length:** No limit.

TO GET THERE

From south junction of Hwy. 115 and US 31, drive 1 mi. north on US 31. Roads are wide and well maintained, with broad shoulders.

BRECKENRIDGE   MAP, C-2
River Ridge Campground

1989 West Pine River Rd., 48615.
T: (800) 647-2267 or (989) 842-5184;
www.michcampgrounds.com/riverridge.

🚐 ★★★★   ⛺ ★★★★

Beauty: ★★★★	Site Privacy: ★★★★
Spaciousness: ★★★★	Quiet: ★★★★
Security: ★★★★	Cleanliness: ★★★★
Insect Control: ★★★★	Facilities: ★★★★

A wooded campground with some open sites on Pine River, River Ridge Campground offers two important camping ingredients—quiet and cleanliness. Located in Breckenridge, the campground also has a scenic river and plenty of activities to keep campers happy. Good fishing can be found in the river or the spring-fed pond, where no license is required. Campsites are level with a typical site width of 30 feet. There are 30 seasonal campers and ten pull-through sites. The best sites are alongside the river. Swimmers have a choice between the heated pool, pond, or river. An added water plus is the spa. Security includes a traffic control gate and owners who keep a close watch on the campground.

BASICS

Operated By: Dan & Louella Staley. **Open:** May 1–Oct. 15. **Site Assignment:** Reservations w/ 1-night deposit; refund w/ 7-day notice. **Registration:** At office. **Fee:** Water/electric/sewer, $30; water/electric, $26; tent, $24; check, credit card. **Parking:** At site.

FACILITIES

Number of RV-only Sites: 150. **Number of Tent-only Sites:** 12. **Hookups:** Electric (20, 30, 50 amps), water, sewer, phone. **Each Site:** Picnic table, fire ring. **Dump Station:** Yes. **Laundry:** No. **Pay Phone:** Yes. **Restrooms and Showers:** Yes. **Fuel:** No. **Propane:** Yes. **Internal Roads:** Gravel, in good condition. **RV Service:** No. **Market:** 6 mi. north. **Restaurant:** 6 mi. north. **General Store:** Yes, limited. **Vending:** No. **Swimming:** Yes. **Playground:** Yes. **Other:** Pine River, rec hall, pavilion, coin games, spa, basketball, badminton, sports field, horseshoes, volleyball, rental cabins. **Activities:** Swimming, fish-

ing, boating (rental kayaks, paddleboats, tubes available). **Nearby Attractions:** Bowling, mini-golf, hiking trails, outdoor concert park, farmers' market, Alden B. Down Home & Studio, Chippewa Nature Center, Dow Gardens, antiques, arts & crafts, golf, casino. **Additional Information:** Midland County CVB, (888) 464-3526.

RESTRICTIONS

Pets: On leash only; indoor pets only. **Fires:** Fire ring only. **Alcoholic Beverages:** At sites only. **Vehicle Maximum Length:** No limit.

TO GET THERE

M 46 to Meridian Rd., turn north 0.1 mi. to Pine River Rd. at Gordonville, then turn left 4.75 mi. to camp. Or take M 20 to Meridian Rd., turn south 3.25 mi. to Pine River Rd., then 4.75 mi. to camp. From Breckenridge, turn north on McClellend Rd. 8 mi., turn right on Pine River 2 mi., follow signs. Roads are mostly wide and well maintained, with narrow shoulders in spots.

BROOKLYN   MAP, D-2
Greenbriar RV Park and
Golf Course

14820 Wellwood, 49230. T: (517) 592-6943;
www.michcampgrounds.com/greenbriar.

🚐 ★★★★   ⛺ ★★★

Beauty: ★★★★	Site Privacy: ★★★
Spaciousness: ★★★	Quiet: ★★★★
Security: ★★★★	Cleanliness: ★★★★
Insect Control: ★★★★	Facilities: ★★★

The name says it all. Greenbriar RV Park and Golf Course offers camping with an 18-hole golf course and watered fairways. Located five minutes from Michigan International Speedway in Brooklyn, the campground is also near Wampler's Lake and Irish Hills attractions. With a rolling, grassy terrain, the campground offers a choice of open or shaded sites with a typical site width of 30 feet. There are ten pull-throughs and 15 seasonals. A children's fishing pond provides catch-and-release fishing. Golf and camping packages are available. A pavilion and clubhouse are comfortable gathering spots. Facilities are clean and well maintained. Grounds are nicely landscaped and mowed, as would be expected for a golf course.

BASICS

Operated By: Arthur & Thelma Babian. **Open:** Apr. 1–Nov. 1. **Site Assignment:** Reservations w/ 1-night deposit; refund (minus $5) w/ 7-day notice; 3–5 night minimum stay. **Registration:** At campground office. **Fee:** Water/electric, $27; primitive, $20; cash, check, credit card. **Parking:** At site.

FACILITIES

Number of RV-only Sites: 82. **Number of Tent-only Sites:** 18. **Hookups:** Electric (20, 30, 50 amps), water. **Each Site:** Picnic table, fire ring. **Dump Station:** Yes. **Laundry:** Yes. **Pay Phone:** Yes. **Restrooms and Showers:** Yes. **Fuel:** No. **Propane:** No. **Internal Roads:** Gravel, paved, in good condition. **RV Service:** No. **Market:** 1 mi. **Restaurant:** 1 mi. **General Store:** Yes. **Vending:** Yes. **Swimming:** Yes. **Playground:** Yes. **Other:** 18-

hole golf course, clubhouse, children's fishing pond, pavilion, game room, putting green, basketball, horseshoes, volleyball, sports field. **Activities:** Golf, swimming, fishing. **Nearby Attractions:** Irish Hills, Michigan International Speedway, Irish Hills Towers, Mystery Hill, Prehistoric Forest, St. Joseph's Shrine, Stagecoach Stop, Cambridge Historical Park, Hidden Lake Gardens, state parks, antiques. **Additional Information:** Jackson County Visitors Bureau, (517) 764-4440.

RESTRICTIONS

Pets: On leash only. **Fires:** Fire ring only. **Alcoholic Beverages:** Allowed. **Vehicle Maximum Length:** No limit. **Other:** Only allowed 1 unit per site.

TO GET THERE

From the junction of US 12 and Hwy. 124, drive 1.5 mi. north on Hwy. 124 to Wellwood Rd. Irish Hills 1 mi. off US 12 (north of Hayes State Park) on M 124 on corner of Wellwood and M 124. Follow signs. Roads are wide and well maintained, with broad shoulders.

BUCHANAN   MAP, D-1
Fuller's Resort and
Campground on Clear Lake

1622 East Clear Lake Rd., 49107.
T: (269) 695-3785; www.fullersresort.com.

🚐 ★★★   ⛺ ★★★

Beauty: ★★★★	Site Privacy: ★★★
Spaciousness: ★★★	Quiet: ★★★★
Security: ★★★★	Cleanliness: ★★★
Insect Control: ★★★★	Facilities: ★★★

Fuller's Resort and Campground on Clear Lake offers a quiet country setting. Located in Buchanan, the campground has 110 seasonal campers, so it is best to make reservations. Sites are level and mostly shaded, with four pull-throughs and a typical site width of 30 feet. The campground features an eight-acre spring-fed lake with 400 feet of clean sandy beach. The best sites are closest to the lake. A primitive area for tents offers more green space and privacy. A rental log cabin nestled in the woods features a fieldstone fireplace. Two modern cottages can be rented right on the lakeside. A shaded picnic area is a nice addition. A family-oriented campground under strict supervision, Fuller's Resort boasts 16 flavors of ice cream at its concession stand.

BASICS

Operated By: Jeff & Rene McNeil. **Open:** Apr. 15–Oct. 15. **Site Assignment:** Reservations w/ 1-night deposit; refund (minus $5) w/ 2-day notice. **Registration:** At campground office. **Fee:** Water/electric, $22–$25; primitive, $18–$20; cash, check, credit card. **Parking:** At site.

FACILITIES

Number of RV-only Sites: 140. **Number of Tent-only Sites:** 30. **Hookups:** Electric (20, 30 amps), water, sewer. **Each Site:** Picnic table, fire ring. **Dump Station:** Yes. **Laundry:** Yes. **Pay Phone:** Yes. **Restrooms and Showers:** Yes. **Fuel:** No. **Propane:** Yes. **Internal Roads:** Gravel, in good condition. **RV Service:** No. **Market:** 3 mi. **Restaurant:**

Ice-cream store. **General Store:** Yes. **Vending:** Yes. **Swimming:** Lake. **Playground:** Yes. **Other:** Clear Lake, sandy beach, rental log cabins & cottages, recreation barn, coin games, boat ramp, basketball, sports field, horseshoes, volleyball. **Activities:** Swimming, fishing, boating (rental rowboats, canoes, & paddleboats available), scheduled weekend activities. **Nearby Attractions:** Amish Acres, golf, antiques, Berrien County Museum, Deer Forest, Bear Cave, Apple Valley Market, nature center, zoo, Kamm's Brewery, museums, Andrews University. **Additional Information:** Buchanan Area Chamber of Commerce, (616) 695-3291.

RESTRICTIONS

Pets: Not allowed. **Fires:** Fire ring only. **Alcoholic Beverages:** Not allowed in overnight camping areas. **Vehicle Maximum Length:** No limit.

TO GET THERE

From the junction of US 12 and Bakertown Rd., drive 2 mi. north on Bakertown Rd., then 1 mi. west on Elm Valley, then 1 mi. northwest on East Clear Lake Rd. Roads are mostly wide and in fair condition, with narrow shoulders in spots.

BYRON   MAP, D-3
Myers Lake United Methodist Campground

10575 Silver Lake Rd., 48418. T: (800) 994-5050; www.michcampgrounds.com/myerslake.

🚐 ★★★   ▲ ★★★

Beauty: ★★★★	Site Privacy: ★★★★
Spaciousness: ★★★★	Quiet: ★★★★
Security: ★★★★	Cleanliness: ★★★
Insect Control: ★★★	Facilities: ★★★

Located on the banks of a 100-acre lake in Byron, Myers Lake United Methodist Campground offers good, clean family fun in a quiet rural facility. The campground features family, group, and church camping in an alcohol-free environment. Sites are mostly grassy and shaded, with a typical site width of 30 feet. The campground has only 18 water and electric sites; the rest are electric-only, so reservations are recommended. The best RV sites are the lake-view ones with 50-amp electricity and water hookups. The sites overlook the clear, spring-fed lake and nature trail. Special sites with 20-amp electricity for tenters, overlooking the lake and outdoor chapel, are also available on holiday weekends. The lake has a 75-hp limit. Centrally located near the cities of Brighton, Flint, and Lansing, the campground is owned by the United Methodist Church, but is open to the public. Basic safety and security rules are enforced, but few campers seem to need to be reminded. Church services are held on Sunday.

BASICS

Operated By: Detroit Conference, The United Methodist Church. **Open:** May 1–Oct. 15. **Site Assignment:** Reservations w/ 1-night deposit; refund (minus $5) w/ 3-day notice. **Registration:** At campground office. **Fee:** Lakeview, $30–$35; family, $24–$27; group, $23–$27; tent, $27; cash, check, credit card. **Parking:** At site.

FACILITIES

Number of RV-only Sites: 120. **Number of Tent-only Sites:** 6. **Hookups:** Electric (20, 30, 50 amps), water. **Each Site:** Picnic table, fire ring. **Dump Station:** Yes. **Laundry:** Yes. **Pay Phone:** Yes. **Restrooms and Showers:** Yes. **Fuel:** No. **Propane:** Yes. **Internal Roads:** Gravel, in good condition. **RV Service:** No. **Market:** 5 mi. **Restaurant:** 5 mi. **General Store:** Yes. **Vending:** Yes. **Swimming:** No. **Playground:** Yes. **Other:** Myers Lake, sandy beach, rec hall, pavilion, coin games, boat dock, boat ramp, basketball, sports field, horseshoes, volleyball, tetherball, softball, rental cabins. **Activities:** Swimming, fishing, boating (rental pontoons, rowboats, kayaks, & paddleboats available), scheduled weekend activities. **Nearby Attractions:** Children's Museum, Crossroads Village & Huckleberry Railroad, Genesee Belle cruises, Flint Cultural Center, Genesee Recreation Area, Alfred P. Sloan Museum, Flint Institute of Arts, Longway Planetarium, golf, antiques, arts & crafts. **Additional Information:** Flint Area CVB, (800) 253-5468.

RESTRICTIONS

Pets: On leash only. **Fires:** Fire ring only. **Alcoholic Beverages:** Not allowed. **Vehicle Maximum Length:** No limit.

TO GET THERE

From the junction of US 23 and Silver Lake Rd., take Linden-Fenton Exit 79 and drive 10 mi. west on Silver Lake Rd. Road is mostly wide and well maintained, with narrow shoulders in places.

CADILLAC   MAP, C-2
Camp Cadillac

10621 East 34 Rd., 49601. T: (231) 775-9724; www.campcadillac.com.

🚐 ★★★★   ▲ ★★★★

Beauty: ★★★★	Site Privacy: ★★★★
Spaciousness: ★★★★	Quiet: ★★★★
Security: ★★★★	Cleanliness: ★★★★
Insect Control: ★★★★	Facilities: ★★★★

Adjacent to state forest land, Camp Cadillac has the privacy and feel of a park with the conveniences of a modern campground. Located 2 miles east of Cadillac, the campground offers level, grassy, and mostly shaded sites with a typical site width of 45 feet. Laid out in a series of loops, the rural campground has nine pull-through sites. A large roster of activities, including the popular barrel train and petting zoo, makes this a favorite spot for families. Friendly owners, sparkling-clean restrooms, and a nice family atmosphere keep campers coming back. Many people also use Camp Cadillac as a base to enjoy all the area has to offer. The best RV sites are by the pool and facilities. The best tent sites are in the more wooded, private areas. Security measures include owners who live on site and keep a close watch on the campground.

BASICS

Operated By: Tim & Angie Vaughan. **Open:** Apr. 15–Oct. 15. **Site Assignment:** Reservations w/ 1-night deposit; refund (minus $5) w/ 7-day notice. **Registration:** At campground office. **Fee:**

Water/electric/sewer, $30.50–$35; tent, $25; cabin, $62; cash, check, credit card. **Parking:** At site.

FACILITIES

Number of RV-only Sites: 105. **Number of Tent-only Sites:** 10. **Hookups:** Electric (20, 30, 50 amps), water, sewer, phone. **Each Site:** Picnic table, fire ring. **Dump Station:** Yes. **Laundry:** Yes. **Pay Phone:** Yes. **Restrooms and Showers:** Yes. **Fuel:** No. **Propane:** Yes. **Internal Roads:** Gravel, in good condition. **RV Service:** No. **Market:** 2 mi. west in Cadillac. **Restaurant:** 2 mi. west in Cadillac. **General Store:** Yes, limited. **Vending:** Yes. **Swimming:** Yes. **Playground:** No. **Other:** Clam River, petting zoo, rec hall, coin games, pond fishing, basketball, movies, badminton, sports field, horseshoes, hiking trails, volleyball, rental cabins, rental RVs. **Activities:** Swimming, hiking, fishing, scheduled activities. **Nearby Attractions:** Johnny's Wild Game & Fish Park, golf, hunting, bike path, walkway, scenic drives, pontoon boat rides, natural history museum, Shay Steam Locomotive, historic walking tour, antiques, arts & crafts, Shrine of the Pines. **Additional Information:** Cadillac Area Visitors Bureau, (800) 225-2537.

RESTRICTIONS

Pets: None. **Fires:** Fire ring only. **Alcoholic Beverages:** At sites only. **Vehicle Maximum Length:** No limit. **Other:** No extra tents on same site.

TO GET THERE

From north junction of Hwy. 55 and US 131, drive 2.4 mi. north on US 131, then 2 mi. east on East Boon Rd./E 34 Rd. Roads are mostly wide and well maintained, with adequate shoulders.

CEDAR SPRINGS   MAP, C-2
Lakeside Camp Park

13677 White Creek Ave., 49319. T: (616) 696-1735; www.michcampgrounds.com/lakeside.

🚐 ★★★★   ▲ ★★★

Beauty: ★★★★	Site Privacy: ★★★★
Spaciousness: ★★★★	Quiet: ★★★★
Security: ★★★★	Cleanliness: ★★★★
Insect Control: ★★★★	Facilities: ★★★★

Located 17 miles north of Grand Rapids, Lakeside Camp Park offers convenience and easy access from the interstate. In a suburban setting, the campground features a five-acre private lake with a nice sandy swimming beach and off-shore raft and fishing dock. The lake is stocked annually with trout, bass, catfish, perch, and panfish. No fishing license is required. Laid out in a series of loops, the campground has grassy, level lakeside sites with a typical site width of 30 feet. Sites offer a choice of open or shaded, with nine pull-throughs and 62 seasonal campers in an area apart from daily or weekend campers. The best sites are closest to Lake Waller. A recreation building has seating for 80 and can be used by small or large groups camping at Lakeside. A speed limit of 7.5 mph is enforced and owners keep a close watch on the campground for security.

BASICS

Operated By: Richard & Diane Lupico. **Open:** May 1–Oct. 5. **Site Assignment:** Reservations w/ 1-night deposit; refund w/ 2-week notice; 24-hr. cancellation

---

policy. **Registration:** At campground office. **Fee:** Full hookup, $28.50; electric/water, $25.50; cash, check, credit card. **Parking:** At site.

FACILITIES

Number of RV-only Sites: 146. **Hookups:** Electric (20, 30 amps), water, sewer. **Each Site:** Picnic table, fire ring. **Dump Station:** No. **Laundry:** Yes. **Pay Phone:** Yes. **Restrooms and Showers:** Yes. **Fuel:** No. **Propane:** No. **Internal Roads:** Gravel, in good condition. **RV Service:** No. **Market:** Groceries/supplies. **Restaurant:** One block. **General Store:** Yes. **Vending:** Yes. **Swimming:** Yes. **Playground:** Yes. **Other:** Waller Lake, swimming beach, volleyball, basketball, game room, golf range, coin games, pavilion, boat ramp, badminton, sports field. **Activities:** Swimming, fishing, boating (rental rowboats, kayaks, & paddleboats available), scheduled weekend activities. **Nearby Attractions:** Grand Rapids, golf, botanical gardens, pro baseball, Van Andel Museum, Gerald Ford Museum, Old Kent Baseball Stadium, antiques. **Additional Information:** Cedar Springs Chamber of Commerce, (616) 696-3260.

RESTRICTIONS

Pets: On leash only; no aggressive breeds. **Fires:** Fire ring only. **Alcoholic Beverages:** Allowed. **Vehicle Maximum Length:** No limit.

TO GET THERE

The campground is 17 mi. north of Grand Rapids. Take US 131 to Cedar Springs Exit 104. Go east 300 ft. to 1st traffic light. Turn right and go 0.5 mi. to the campground. Roads are wide and well maintained, with adequate shoulders.

CEDARVILLE   MAP, A-2
Cedarville RV Park Campground

634 Grove St., 49719. T: (906) 484-3351; www.cedarvilleparkrv.com.

🚐 ★★★★   ⛺ ★★★★

Beauty: ★★★★   Site Privacy: ★★★
Spaciousness: ★★★   Quiet: ★★★★
Security: ★★★★   Cleanliness: ★★★★
Insect Control: ★★★★   Facilities: ★★★★

Located on the shores of Lake Huron in the midst of Les Cheneaux Islands, Cedarville RV Park Campground offers beautiful views. The campground also has seven deep-water docks and 35 other boat docks, as well as a boat launch. A fish-cleaning building helps give the campground its sparkling facilities. Just three blocks away from downtown Cedarville, the campground offers level, mostly open sites, with a typical site width of 25 feet. The campsites are all back-in and there are 12 seasonal campers. Reservations are recommended during prime vacation time since the campground is a popular spot with water sports enthusiasts, as well as campers visiting the local attractions. Security measures include owners who live on site and keep a close watch on the campground. Although they won't tolerate any misbehavior, owners are very friendly and helpful.

BASICS

Operated By: Jon & Sharrie Steinbach. **Open:** May 1–Oct. 15. **Site Assignment:** Reservations w/ 1-night deposit; refund (minus $7.50) w/ 1-week

---

notice. **Registration:** At campground office. **Fee:** $27–$33; cash, check, credit card. **Parking:** At site.

FACILITIES

Number of RV-only Sites: 53. **Number of Tent-only Sites:** 2. **Hookups:** Electric (20, 30, 50 amps), water, sewer. **Each Site:** Picnic table, fire ring. **Dump Station:** Yes. **Laundry:** Yes. **Pay Phone:** Yes. **Restrooms and Showers:** Yes. **Fuel:** No. **Propane:** No. **Internal Roads:** Gravel, in good condition. **RV Service:** No. **Market:** 3 blocks. **Restaurant:** 3 blocks. **General Store:** No. **Vending:** Yes. **Swimming:** Lake. **Playground:** No. **Other:** Lake Huron, rec hall, boat dock, boat ramp, rental cabins, fish-cleaning building. **Activities:** Swimming, fishing, boating (rental rowboats & kayaks available). **Nearby Attractions:** Castle Rock, Mackinac Bridge, Mackinac Island, Mackinaw City, Deer Ranch, golf, casino, Fort De Baude Indian Museum, Marquette Mission Park & Museum of Ojibwa Culture, New France Discovery Center & Father Marquette National Memorial, Soo Locks, Ft. Millimackinac, Tahqomen Falls. **Additional Information:** St. Ignace Tourism Assoc., (800) 338-6660.

RESTRICTIONS

Pets: On leash only. **Fires:** Fire ring only. **Alcoholic Beverages:** At camp site only. **Vehicle Maximum Length:** 35,000 lbs. or 43 ft.

TO GET THERE

From the junction of I-75 and Hwy. 134, take Exit 359 and drive 17 mi. east on Hwy. 134 through Cedarville, then 1 block south on Lake St. Roads are well maintained, with adequate shoulders.

CHAMPION   MAP, A-3 INSET
Michigamme Shores Campground Resort

Hwy. 41 W, 49814. T: (906) 339-2116; www.michigammeshores.com.

🚐 ★★★★   ⛺ ★★★★

Beauty: ★★★★   Site Privacy: ★★★★
Spaciousness: ★★★★   Quiet: ★★★★
Security: ★★★★   Cleanliness: ★★★★
Insect Control: ★★★★   Facilities: ★★★★

Michigamme Shores Campground Resort has a great location—2.5 miles west of Champion, on the shores of Lake Michigamme, in the heart of Upper Michigan's moose country. Facilities are very clean and well maintained, showing close attention to detail. Sites are mostly gravel and shaded, with a typical site width of 30 feet and ten pull-throughs. A separate area for tents provides more green space and privacy. The best sites are close to the lake. Lake Michigamme encompasses 4,360 acres, or almost 7 square miles. The lake has more than 20 islands and depths of 50 feet. Michigamme Shores is the closest resort to moose country, and winter sports enthusiasts can catch cross-country ski trails right at the campground. Miles of groomed trails through the UP's snow-covered backcountry are available for snowmobiling or skiing. Hunters have access to some of the best hunting in the UP. Hikers can enjoy the wilderness and a bevy of animals and birds.

BASICS

Operated By: Woody & Pat Taylor. **Open:** May 1–Oct 15. **Site Assignment:** Reservations w/ 1-night deposit; refund w/ 2-week notice. **Registration:** At campground office. **Fee:** $24–$43; cash, check, credit card. **Parking:** At site.

FACILITIES

Number of RV-only Sites: 60. **Number of Tent-only Sites:** 10. **Number of Multipurpose Sites:** 15. **Hookups:** Electric (20, 30, 50 amps), water, sewer. **Each Site:** Picnic table, fire ring. **Dump Station:** No. **Laundry:** Yes. **Pay Phone:** Yes. **Restrooms and Showers:** Yes. **Fuel:** No. **Propane:** Yes. **Internal Roads:** Paved, in good condition. **RV Service:** No. **Market:** 2 mi. east in Champion. **Restaurant:** Pizza in camp store. **General Store:** Yes. **Vending:** Yes. **Swimming:** Beach. **Playground:** Yes. **Other:** Michigamme Lake, sandy beach, rec hall, coin games, basketball, tennis, badminton, sports field, horseshoes, hiking trails, volleyball, boat dock. **Activities:** Swimming, fishing, boating (rental canoes, rowboats, motorboats, pontoons, paddleboats available), hiking. **Nearby Attractions:** Walking tours, historical museum, Marquette Maritime Museum, Presque Isle Park, Upper Peninsula Children's Museum, golf, waterfalls, ghost towns, Pictured Rocks National Lakeshore, rock hounding, Copper Harbor & Keweenaw Peninsula. **Additional Information:** Marquette County CVB.

RESTRICTIONS

Pets: On leash only. **Fires:** Fire ring only. **Alcoholic Beverages:** Allowed. **Vehicle Maximum Length:** No limit.

TO GET THERE

The campground is 2.5 mi. west of Champion on US 41 W. Roads are wide and well maintained, with broad shoulders.

CHEBOYGAN   MAP, B-2
Waterways Campground

9575 M33 Hwy., P.O. Box 262, 49721. T: (231) 627-7066; www.michcampgrounds.com/waterways.

🚐 ★★★   ⛺ ★★★

Beauty: ★★★   Site Privacy: ★★★
Spaciousness: ★★★   Quiet: ★★★★
Security: ★★★★   Cleanliness: ★★★★
Insect Control: ★★   Facilities: ★★★

One of the newest campgrounds on the inland waterway, Waterways Campground is nestled on the shores of the Cheboygan River. Located 2 miles south of Cheboygan, the campground offers level sites arranged in upper and lower levels. Sites are grassy with gravel parking spots and have a typical site width of 30 feet. The campground has 11 seasonal campers, mostly open sites, and nine pull-throughs. Bouquets of fresh-cut flowers in the clean bathroom are a nice touch. Apple trees are scattered around the property, which is located across from a marina. A tent area is separate from RVs and offers more privacy and green space. The best RV sites are 42–50 because they are in the back of the campground, offer full hookup, and have cable TV. The speed limit is 5 mph and security measures include one entrance/exit road, one-way streets, owners who live on site, and regular campground patrols.

BASICS

Operated By: Ron & Jan Ramsey. **Open:** May 1–Nov. 1. **Site Assignment:** Reservations w/ 1-night deposit; refund w/ 48-hour notice. **Registration:** At campground office. **Fee:** $25–$27; cash, check, credit card. **Parking:** At site.

FACILITIES

Number of RV-only Sites: 50. **Number of Tent-only Sites:** Undesignated sites. **Hookups:** Electric (30, 50 amps), water, sewer, cable TV. **Each Site:** Picnic table, fire ring. **Dump Station:** Yes. **Laundry:** Yes. **Pay Phone:** Yes. **Restrooms and Showers:** Yes. **Fuel:** No. **Propane:** Yes. **Internal Roads:** Gravel, in good condition. **RV Service:** No. **Market:** 2 mi. north in Cheboygan. **Restaurant:** 2 mi. north in Cheboygan. **General Store:** Yes. **Vending:** No. **Swimming:** No. **Playground:** Yes. **Other:** Cheboygan River, horseshoes, game room, recreation field, boat ramp, boat dock, basketball, badminton, hiking trails, volleyball. **Activities:** Fishing, boating (rental pontoon, rowboats, paddleboats available), scheduled weekend activities. **Nearby Attractions:** Cheboygan Opera House, golf, archery range, Cross of the Woods Shrine, Mackinaw City, Mackinac Island, museums, antiques, beaches, state & city parks, 42 mi. of continuous inland waterway, minutes from Cheboygan's shopping & restaurants. **Additional Information:** Cheboygan Area Chamber of Commerce, (800) 968-3302.

RESTRICTIONS

Pets: On leash only; large or multiple pets must have prior approval. **Fires:** Fire ring only. **Alcoholic Beverages:** Allowed. **Vehicle Maximum Length:** No limit.

TO GET THERE

I-75 from the south, Exit 313; I-75 from the north, Exit 326 or 322 to the junction of M 27 and M 33; go 0.25 mi. south on M 33, on the Cheboygan River. Roads are wide and well maintained, with broad shoulders.

CLYDE   MAP, D-3
Fort Trodd Family Campground Resort

6350 Lapeer Rd., 48049. T: (810) 987-4889; www.forttrodd.com.

🚐 ★★★★	🏕 n/a
Beauty: ★★★★	Site Privacy: ★★★★
Spaciousness: ★★★★	Quiet: ★★★★
Security: ★★★★	Cleanliness: ★★★★★
Insect Control: ★★★★★	Facilities: ★★★★

A campground can't get much more convenient than Fort Trodd Family Campground Resort, just a stone's throw from I-69. The grassy campground is nicely landscaped with a typical site width of 30 feet. Situated beside a 40-acre, spring-fed lake, the campground has three swimming beaches. The lake is stocked with largemouth bass and northern pike.

Air-conditioned camping cabins for rent on an island are a nice addition. Located 6 miles west of Port Huron, the campground has 65 seasonal sites and 26 pull-throughs. Sites are a mix of paved, gravel, or grass with open or shade. Be aware that no tents are allowed. Facilities are sparkling clean and well maintained. A group camping area is available with a pavilion. Security measures include a card-coded security gate.

BASICS

Operated By: Tom & Kathy Hess. **Open:** May 1–Oct. 31. **Site Assignment:** Reservations w/ 1-night deposit; refund w/ 7-day notice. **Registration:** At campground office. **Fee:** Pay in seasons: 5 months, $2,205; 6 months, $2,605; cash, check, credit card. **Parking:** At site.

FACILITIES

Number of RV-only Sites: 185. **Hookups:** Electric (20, 30, 50 amps), water, sewer. **Each Site:** Picnic table, fire ring. **Dump Station:** Yes. **Laundry:** Yes. **Pay Phone:** Yes. **Restrooms and Showers:** Yes. **Fuel:** No. **Propane:** No. **Internal Roads:** Paved, in good condition. **RV Service:** No. **Market:** 2 blocks. **Restaurant:** 2 blocks. **General Store:** Yes. **Vending:** Yes. **Swimming:** Yes. **Playground:** Yes. **Other:** Lake Tomka, 3 swimming beaches, rental cabin, pavilion, rec hall, coin games, basketball, shuffleboard, tennis, badminton, sports field, horseshoes, hiking trials, volleyball. **Activities:** Swimming, hiking, fishing, boating (rental canoes, kayaks, paddleboats available), scheduled weekend activities. **Nearby Attractions:** Parks, Fort Gratiot Lighthouse, Huron Lightship Museum, historic district, antiques, arts & crafts, golf, Port Huron Museum, Canadian International Border. **Additional Information:** Blue Water Area CVB, (800) 852-4242.

RESTRICTIONS

Pets: On leash only. **Fires:** Fire ring only. **Alcoholic Beverages:** Allowed. **Vehicle Maximum Length:** No limit. **Other:** No tents allowed.

TO GET THERE

From the junction of I-69 and Barth Rd., take Exit 194 and drive 500 feet north on Barth Rd. Roads are wide and well maintained, with broad shoulders.

COLDWATER   MAP, D-2
Waffle Farm Campground

790 North Union Rd., 49036. T: (517) 278-4315; www.wafflefarm.com.

🚐 ★★★★	🏕 ★★★★
Beauty: ★★★★	Site Privacy: ★★★★
Spaciousness: ★★★★	Quiet: ★★★★
Security: ★★★★	Cleanliness: ★★★★
Insect Control: ★★	Facilities: ★★★★

A lakeside campground with open and shaded sites, Waffle Farm Campground got its name from the owner's grandmother, Myra Waffle, who started the camping business in 1925 with primitive camping and two wooden boats for rent. The campsites are now spread over more than 1.5 miles of water frontage, mainly Craig Lake and part of Morrison Lake. The two lakes are part of a group totaling over

---

1,074 acres, known as the Randall-Morrison Chain. The campground has 240 seasonal campers, 25 pull-throughs, and a typical site width of 30 feet. Seasonal campers are mostly in a separate area from other campsites. Tent campers have a section with more green space and privacy. Quiet hours are 11 p.m. to 8 a.m. Speed limit is 10 mph, a bit fast for a family campground. Security includes a guard on weekends.

BASICS

Operated By: Loyd Green Jr. & Family. **Open:** Apr. 15–Oct. 15. **Site Assignment:** Reservations w/ $20 deposit; refund (minus $5) w/ 7-day notice. **Registration:** At campground office. **Fee:** Lakefront, $27–$30; off-lake, $24–$28; cash, check. **Parking:** At site.

FACILITIES

Number of Multipurpose Sites: 376. **Hookups:** Electric (20, 30, 50 amps), water, sewer. **Each Site:** Picnic table, fire spot. **Dump Station:** Yes. **Laundry:** No. **Pay Phone:** Yes. **Restrooms and Showers:** Yes. **Fuel:** Yes. **Propane:** Yes. **Internal Roads:** Gravel & dirt, in very good condition. **RV Service:** No. **Market:** 3 mi. south in Coldwater. **Restaurant:** 3 mi. south in Coldwater. **General Store:** Large. **Vending:** Yes. **Swimming:** Lake, beach. **Playground:** Yes. **Other:** Lake, swimming beach, pavilion, arcade, mini-golf, driving range, fish-cleaning stand, club area, boat ramp, boat landing, rental cottages, rec room, sports field, hiking trails. **Activities:** Swimming, fishing, hiking, boating (rental rowboats, paddleboats available). **Nearby Attractions:** Bowling, golf, summer theater, Branch County Historical Society, antiques, drive-in theaters, motor speedway, historic homes, museums, arts & crafts shops. **Additional Information:** Branch County Tourism Bureau, (800) 968-9333.

RESTRICTIONS

Pets: On leash only. **Fires:** Permitted on ground. **Alcoholic Beverages:** Allowed. **Vehicle Maximum Length:** No limit.

TO GET THERE

From the junction of I-69 and US 12, drive 3.5 mi. north on I-69, take Exit 16, then 2.75 mi. west on Jonesville Rd., then 0.75 mi. north on Union City Rd. Easy access off I-69, Exit 16 Jonesville Rd. Roads are well maintained, with broad shoulders.

DECATUR   MAP, D-1
Leisure Valley Campground

40851 CR 669, 49045. T: (269) 423-7122; www.leisurevalley.com.

🚐 ★★★★	🏕 ★★★
Beauty: ★★★★	Site Privacy: ★★★★
Spaciousness: ★★★★	Quiet: ★★★★
Security: ★★★★	Cleanliness: ★★★★
Insect Control: ★★★★	Facilities: ★★★★

A grassy campground with open and shaded sites, Leisure Valley Campground is located 3 miles south of Decatur. Sites are level with a typical site width of 35 feet. The campground has 30 seasonal campers. A clubhouse with a kitchen is available. Campsites are adjacent to a small lake and five ponds. The lake is stocked with bass, bluegill, and perch. The best campsites are closest to the water. A small island is a nice picnic spot. Facilities are very clean and well maintained, and the owners provide security for this quiet, family-oriented place.

BASICS

Operated By: Gale & Josie Congdon. **Open:** Apr. 1–Oct. 31. **Site Assignment:** Reservations w/ 1-night deposit; refund (minus $5) w/ 7-day notice. **Registration:** At campground office. **Fee:** Full hookup, $30; water/electric, $27; tent, $24; cash, check. **Parking:** At site.

FACILITIES

Number of RV-only Sites: 108. **Hookups:** Electric (20, 30 amps), water, sewer, phone. **Each Site:** Picnic table, fire ring. **Dump Station:** Yes. **Laundry:** Yes. **Pay Phone:** Yes. **Restrooms and Showers:** Yes. **Fuel:** No. **Propane:** Yes. **Internal Roads:** Gravel, pavement. **RV Service:** No. **Market:** 2 mi. north in Decatur. **Restaurant:** 2 mi. north in Decatur. **General Store:** Yes. **Vending:** Yes. **Swimming:** Yes. **Playground:** Yes. **Other:** Swimming lake, rec hall, pavilion, coin games, boat dock, mini-golf, basketball, shuffleboard, badminton, horseshoes, volleyball, hiking trails, rental trailers. **Activities:** Swimming, fishing, boating (rental canoes, rowboats, paddleboats available), scheduled weekend activities, hiking. **Nearby Attractions:** Golf, stock car racing, winery tours, playhouses, Palisades Nuclear Plant, Deer Forest, antiques, arts & crafts. **Additional Information:** Decatur Chamber of Commerce, (616) 423-7014.

RESTRICTIONS

Pets: On leash only. **Fires:** Fire ring only. **Alcoholic Beverages:** Allowed. **Vehicle Maximum Length:** No limit.

TO GET THERE

From the junction of Hwy. 51 and George St., drive 3 mi. south on George St., then 0.25 mi. west on Valley Rd. Roads are mostly wide and well maintained, with adequate shoulders. Access road is in fair condition.

DECATUR   MAP, D-1
Oak Shores Campground

86882 CR 215, 49045. T: (269) 423-7370; www.michcampgrounds.com/oakshores.

🚐 ★★★★   ▲ ★★★★

Beauty: ★★★	Site Privacy: ★★★★
Spaciousness: ★★★★	Quiet: ★★★★
Security: ★★★★	Cleanliness: ★★★
Insect Control: ★★★★	Facilities: ★★★★

Located on a private 75-acre lake in Decatur, Oak Shores Campground offers a choice of sites ranging from full sun to full shade. Sites are level and grassy with a typical site width of 30 feet. There are 95 seasonal campers and 10 pull-through sites. The best sites are closest to Knickerbocker Lake. A separate primitive tent area provides more green space and privacy. Along with other playgrounds, Oak Shores offers a fenced-in Little Tykes playground with more size-appropriate equipment. A large rec hall is available for

dancing and club activities. Owners provide security measures and try to make sure the campground maintains a peaceful, family-oriented atmosphere. From all the camping families that keep returning, their efforts must be working.

BASICS

Operated By: Joe & Mary Lou Schantz. **Open:** Apr. 15–Oct. 15. **Site Assignment:** Reservations suggested; 1-night deposit required; refund (less $10) w/ 7-day notice. **Registration:** At campground office. **Fee:** $34–$30; cabins, $80–$115; cash, check, credit card. **Parking:** At site.

FACILITIES

Number of Multipurpose Sites: 240. **Hookups:** Electric (30, 50 amps), water, sewer, phone. **Each Site:** Picnic table, fire ring. **Dump Station:** Yes. **Laundry:** Yes. **Pay Phone:** Yes. **Restrooms and Showers:** Yes. **Fuel:** No. **Propane:** Yes. **Internal Roads:** Paved. **RV Service:** No. **Market:** 5 mi. **Restaurant:** 5 mi. **General Store:** Yes. **Vending:** Yes. **Swimming:** Yes. **Playground:** Yes. **Other:** Knickerbocker Lake, sandy beach, coin games, rental cabins & travel trailers, sports field, whirlpool, game room, adult game room, pavilion, tennis, shuffleboard, rec hall, horseshoes, volleyball, basketball. **Activities:** Swimming, fishing, boating (rental canoes, kayaks, rowboats, paddleboats available), scheduled weekend activities. **Nearby Attractions:** Golf, stock car racing, winery tours, playhouses, Palisades Nuclear Plant, Deer Forest, antiques, arts & crafts. **Additional Information:** Decatur Chamber of Commerce, (616) 423-7014.

RESTRICTIONS

Pets: None. **Fires:** Fire ring only. **Alcoholic Beverages:** Allowed. **Vehicle Maximum Length:** No limit. **Other:** No firewood brought into campground.

TO GET THERE

Take I-94 to Exit 56. Go south on M 51 about 10 mi., then north on CR 215 for 0.25 mi. Roads are mainly wide and well maintained, with adequate shoulders.

DECATUR   MAP, D-1
Timber Trails RV Park

84981 47-1/2 St., 49045. T: (269) 423-7311; www.michcampgrounds.com/timbertrails.

🚐 ★★★   ▲ ★★★★

Beauty: ★★★★	Site Privacy: ★★★★
Spaciousness: ★★★★	Quiet: ★★★★
Security: ★★★★	Cleanliness: ★★★★
Insect Control: ★★★★	Facilities: ★★★

With lakefront sites on the 289-acre Lake of the Woods, Timber Trails RV Park offers a full slate of water activities. Located in the Lower Peninsula 7 miles north of Decatur, the campground is just a few miles from Lake Michigan. Campsites are level and grassy with a choice of open or shade. The best sites are on the lakefront. The typical site width is 30 feet, and the campground has three pull-through sites. Group RV and tent sites are available. Facilities are clean and well maintained, and the location is scenic.

Those facts are all the good news. The bad news is that most of the campsites are taken by seasonal campers. About 25 sites are available for nonseasonal campers, so reservations are recommended. Note that pets are not allowed.

BASICS

Operated By: Gary & Deborah Douqlas. **Open:** May 1–Sept. 30. **Site Assignment:** Reservations w/ 1-night deposit; refund w/ 14-day notice. **Registration:** At campground office. **Fee:** Water/electric, $28; cash, check, credit card. **Parking:** At site.

FACILITIES

Number of Multipurpose Sites: 147. **Hookups:** Electric (20, 30 amps), water. **Each Site:** Picnic table, fire ring. **Dump Station:** Yes. **Laundry:** Yes. **Pay Phone:** Yes. **Restrooms and Showers:** Yes. **Fuel:** No. **Propane:** Yes. **Internal Roads:** Gravel, in good condition. **RV Service:** No. **Market:** 6 mi. north in Decatur. **Restaurant:** 6 mi. north in Decatur. **General Store:** Yes, limited. **Vending:** Yes. **Swimming:** Yes. **Playground:** Yes. **Other:** Lake of the Woods, sandy beach, volleyball, horseshoes, shuffleboard, game room, boat dock, sports field, badminton, boat slips. **Activities:** Swimming, fishing, boating (rental rowboats, canoes, paddleboats available). **Nearby Attractions:** Golf, stock car racing, winery tours, playhouses, Palisades Nuclear Plant, Deer Forest, antiques, arts & crafts. **Additional Information:** Decatur Chamber of Commerce, (616) 423-7014.

RESTRICTIONS

Pets: Not allowed. **Fires:** Fire ring only. **Alcoholic Beverages:** Allowed. **Vehicle Maximum Length:** No limit.

TO GET THERE

From I-94 take Exit 56; go south 7 mi. Go through Decatur past McDonald's. Travel 1 mi. to first road on the right; turn right and go 0.5 mi. to entrance on right. Roads are mostly wide and well maintained, with broad shoulders.

DORR   MAP, D-1
Hungry Horse Campground

2016 142nd St., 49323. T: (616) 681-9836; www.hungryhorsecampground.com.

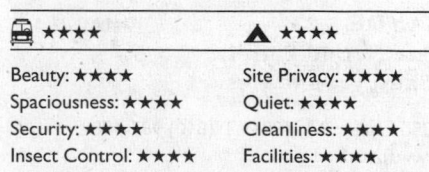

🚐 ★★★★   ▲ ★★★★

Beauty: ★★★★	Site Privacy: ★★★★
Spaciousness: ★★★★	Quiet: ★★★★
Security: ★★★★	Cleanliness: ★★★★
Insect Control: ★★★★	Facilities: ★★★★

Located 15 miles south of Grand Rapids in Dorr, Hungry Horse Campground offers a quiet rural setting. Laid out in a series of loops, the campground has level, grassy sites with a choice of open or shade. The typical site width is 30 feet, and the campground has 30 seasonal campers and 31 pull-through sites. Hungry Horse is nicely landscaped with flower beds, hanging baskets, and many perennial and annual flowers. Someone has a green thumb and spends a great deal of time keeping the grounds in tip-top shape. The playground with wooden structures is a nice addition. A heated wading pool is also popular with smaller youngsters. Rules are enforced to keep the campground well maintained and quiet. For example, long hair on swimmers in the swimming pool must be braided or tied back. Bicycles can be ridden on campground roads only, and quiet hours are enforced from 10 p.m. to 8 a.m. Motorcycles and all-terrain vehicles can't be ridden in the campgrounds. A 10-mph speed limit is enforced but seems a bit high for such a family-oriented facility.

BASICS

Operated By: Norm & Nancy Fifelski. **Open:** May 1–Oct. 1. **Site Assignment:** Reservations w/ 1-night deposit; refund (minus $10) w/ 4-day notice. **Registration:** At campground office. **Fee:** Water/electric/sewer, $30; water/electric, $25; primitive, $7; cash, check, credit card. **Parking:** At site.

FACILITIES

Number of RV-only Sites: 85. **Number of Tent-only Sites:** 5. **Hookups:** Electric (20, 30 amps), water, sewer. **Each Site:** Picnic table, fire ring. **Dump Station:** Yes. **Laundry:** Yes. **Pay Phone:** Yes. **Restrooms and Showers:** Yes. **Fuel:** No. **Propane:** Yes. **Internal Roads:** Paved/gravel, in good condition. **RV Service:** No. **Market:** 3 mi. east. **Restaurant:** 3 mi. east. **General Store:** Yes. **Vending:** Yes. **Swimming:** Yes. **Playground:** Yes. **Other:** Pavilion, rec room, shuffleboard, badminton, sports field, horseshoes, hiking trails, volleyball, coin games, wading pool. **Activities:** Swimming, hiking, scheduled weekend activities. **Nearby Attractions:** Gerald B. Ford Museum, Fredrick Meijer Gardens, zoo, Michigan Adventure Amusement Park, Roger B. Chaffee Planetarium, golf, tennis, rivers & lakes, antiques, Wooden Shoe Factory. **Additional Information:** Grand Rapids/Kent County CVB, (800) 678-9859.

RESTRICTIONS

Pets: On leash only. **Fires:** Fire ring only. **Alcoholic Beverages:** At sites only. **Vehicle Maximum Length:** No limit.

TO GET THERE

Located 15 minutes south of Grand Rapids off US 131 and 20 minutes east of Lake Michigan. Roads are wide and well maintained, with adequate shoulders.

ELK RAPIDS   MAP, B-2
Honcho Rest RV Resort

8988 Cairn Hwy., 49629. T: (231) 264-8548.

🚐 ★★★	🏕 n/a
Beauty: ★★★	Site Privacy: ★★★
Spaciousness: ★★★	Quiet: ★★★
Security: ★★★★	Cleanliness: ★★★★
Insect Control: ★★★★	Facilities: ★★★

Located on the east shore of Bass Lake in Elk Rapids, Honcho Rest Resort offers a choice of shaded or open sites with a typical site width of 30 feet. Honcho Rest has 25 seasonal campers and two pull-through sites. Campsites have cement pads and patios. Across the street is a nine-hole golf course and Elk Lake. One mile away is Lake Michigan. The campground is clean and well maintained with seasonal spots also kept attractive. The number of sea-

sonal campers does seem to continue growing, so reservations are recommended. Security measures are good, with a main gate that is closed from 11 p.m. to 6 a.m.

BASICS

Operated By: Robert & Johanna Wilder. **Open:** May 1–Oct. 15. **Site Assignment:** Reservations w/ 1-night deposit; refund w/ 24-hour notice. **Registration:** At campground office. **Fee:** $35–$40; cash, check, credit card. **Parking:** At site.

FACILITIES

Number of RV-only Sites: 50. **Hookups:** Electric (20, 30, 50 amps), water, sewer, cable TV. **Each Site:** Picnic table, fire ring. **Dump Station:** Yes. **Laundry:** Yes. **Pay Phone:** Yes. **Restrooms and Showers:** Yes. **Fuel:** No. **Propane:** Yes. **Internal Roads:** Gravel, in good condition. **RV Service:** No. **Market:** 2 blocks. **Restaurant:** 2 blocks. **General Store:** No. **Vending:** No. **Swimming:** No. **Playground:** Yes. **Other:** Bass Lake, boat dock, sports field. **Activities:** Swimming, fishing, boating (rental rowboats, canoes available). **Nearby Attractions:** Golf course, Lake Michigan, Elk Lake, marina, Guntzviller's Spirit of the Woods Museum, antiques, arts & crafts, fishing, swimming, water sports. **Additional Information:** Elk Rapids Chamber of Commerce, (231) 264-8202.

RESTRICTIONS

Pets: On leash only. **Fires:** Fire ring only. **Alcoholic Beverages:** Allowed. **Vehicle Maximum Length:** No limit. **Other:** No tents allowed.

TO GET THERE

From US 31 in Elk Rapids, go east at stoplight (Ames St.). At 1.25 mi. turn on Cairn Hwy. Watch for sign on left. The campground is located on the east shore of Bass Lake. Roads are wide and well maintained, with adequate shoulders.

FENWICK   MAP, C-2
Snow Lake Kampground

644 East Snow Lake Rd., 48834. T: (989) 248-3224.

🚐 ★★★★	🏕 ★★★★
Beauty: ★★★★	Site Privacy: ★★★★
Spaciousness: ★★★★	Quiet: ★★★★
Security: ★★★★	Cleanliness: ★★★★
Insect Control: ★★★★	Facilities: ★★★★

Located 28 miles from Grand Rapids in Fenwick, Snow Lake Kampground is a Christian family resort. The rural campground has open or shaded sites with a typical site width of 40 feet. The campground has 200 seasonal campers so reservations are recommended. Sites are mostly gravel with 25 pull-throughs. A rally area features a bathhouse and an enclosed pavilion. Facilities are very clean and well maintained. A nice touch is a kiddie pool for youngsters who might be too small for the regular heated pool. Sunday church services are held in the Little Church in the Wildwood. The best sites are those closest to Snow Lake. Owners keep a close watch on the campground and provide security measures. Without being nagging or intrusive, owners also

enforce guidelines to keep Snow Lake Kampground a clean, quiet, safe, family-oriented facility.

BASICS

Operated By: Ronald & Marie Sellers. **Open:** May 1–Oct. 1. **Site Assignment:** Reservations w/ 1-night deposit; refund w/ 5-day notice. **Registration:** At campground office. **Fee:** $24–$33; cash, check, credit card. **Parking:** At site.

FACILITIES

Number of RV-only Sites: 252. **Number of Tent-only Sites:** 5. **Hookups:** Electric (20, 30, 50 amps), water, sewer, phone. **Each Site:** Picnic table, fire ring. **Dump Station:** Yes. **Laundry:** Yes. **Pay Phone:** Yes. **Restrooms and Showers:** Yes. **Fuel:** No. **Propane:** No. **Internal Roads:** Gravel, paved in good condition. **RV Service:** No. **Market:** 3 mi. north. **Restaurant:** Yes. **General Store:** Yes. **Vending:** Yes. **Swimming:** Yes. **Playground:** Yes. **Other:** Snow Lake, rec room, coin games, wading pool, boat dock, mini-golf, basketball, shuffleboard, sports field, horseshoes, volleyball, pavilion. **Activities:** Swimming, fishing, boating (rental rowboats, kayaks, paddleboats available), scheduled weekend activities. **Nearby Attractions:** Gerald R. Ford Museum, Fredrick Meijer Gardens, zoo, Michigan Adventure Amusement Park, Roger B. Chaffee Planetarium, golf, tennis, rivers & lakes, antiques, Wooden Shoe Factory. **Additional Information:** Grand Rapids/Kent County CVB, (800) 678-9859.

RESTRICTIONS

Pets: On leash only. Some breeds not allowed. **Fires:** Fire ring only. **Alcoholic Beverages:** Only at campsite. **Vehicle Maximum Length:** 40 ft. **Other:** Campers must be age 21 or accompanied by an adult.

TO GET THERE

From the junction of Hwy. 57 and Hwy. 66, drive 3 mi. south on Hwy. 66, then 0.75 mi. east on Snow Lake Rd. Roads are mostly wide and well maintained, with adequate shoulders.

FRANKENMUTH   MAP, C-3
Frankenmuth Jellystone Park

reserve america

1339 Weiss St., 48734. T: (989) 652-6668; www.frankenmuthjellystone.com.

🚐 ★★★★	🏕 ★★★★
Beauty: ★★★★	Site Privacy: ★★★★
Spaciousness: ★★★★	Quiet: ★★★★
Security: ★★★★★	Cleanliness: ★★★★★
Insect Control: ★★★	Facilities: ★★★★★

Located in the heart of the number-one tourist attraction in Michigan, Frankenmuth Jellystone Park is a popular spot with reservations recommended. A bonus is that it's possible to park at the campground and walk to many attractions. It is 1,000 yards to Bronner's Christmas Wonderland and 0.75 miles to most shopping areas. There are sidewalks from the park to downtown. Laid out in a series of loops, sites are mostly open, level, and grassy with concrete pads or gravel to park on. The campground has no seasonal campers. The typical site width is 30 feet, and there are 48 pull-through sites. Cleanliness and security are tops. Security measures include a card-coded gate, ranger patrols, and an owner who lives on site. The downside to the campground's convenient location is that it must abide by city ordinances concerning campfires. So if you enjoy spending a quiet evening by your private campfire, this is not the place. Campers are welcome to use charcoal or gas grills at their sites, but wood campfires are permitted only in designated rings off the sites. Community campfire rings are located between the rec hall and bathrooms and next to the pool.

BASICS

Operated By: Erv Banes. **Open:** All year. **Site Assignment:** Reservations w/ $35 deposit; refund (minus $5) w/ 7-day notice. **Registration:** At campground office. **Fee:** Campsite, $34–$44; trailer, $100–$110; cash, credit card. **Parking:** At site.

FACILITIES

Number of RV-only Sites: 250. **Number of Tent-only Sites:** 20. **Hookups:** Electric (20, 30, 50 amps), water, sewer. **Each Site:** Picnic table. **Dump Station:** Yes. **Laundry:** Yes. **Pay Phone:** Yes. **Restrooms and Showers:** Yes. **Fuel:** No. **Propane:** Yes. **Internal Roads:** Paved, in great condition. **RV Service:** No. **Market:** Next door. **Restaurant:** Next door. **General Store:** Yes. **Vending:** Yes. **Swimming:** Yes. **Playground:** Yes. **Other:** Game room, hot tub, activity room, rec hall, snack bar, mini-golf, pavilion, rental cabins, coin games, basketball, badminton, movies, horseshoes, volleyball. **Activities:** Swimming, scheduled activities. **Nearby Attractions:** Bronner's Christmas Wonderland, golf, paddlewheel boat, winery, antiques, arts & crafts, Bavarian shops, cheese haus, Michigan's Own Military & Space Museum. **Additional Information:** Frankenmuth Chamber of Commerce, (800) FUN-TOWN.

RESTRICTIONS

Pets: On leash only. **Fires:** Designated community fire rings only. **Alcoholic Beverages:** At sites only. **Vehicle Maximum Length:** No limit. **Other:** Children under age 16 not permitted in hot tub. Limit of 1 guest family per site per day. Guests are not permitted on holiday & Halloween event weekends.

TO GET THERE

From the junction of I-75 and M 83 (Birch Run Rd.), take Exit 136, drive 2 mi. east on Birch Run Rd., drive 5 mi. north on Gera Rd., drive 1 block north on Weiss St. Roads are wide and well maintained, with broad shoulders.

FRANKENMUTH   MAP, C-3
Pine Ridge RV Campground

11700 Gera Rd., 48415. T: (989) 624-9029.

🚐 ★★★	🔺 n/a
Beauty: ★★★	Site Privacy: ★★★
Spaciousness: ★★★★	Quiet: ★★★★
Security: ★★★★	Cleanliness: ★★★★
Insect Control: ★★	Facilities: ★★★

Located about 4 miles south of Frankenmuth, Pine Ridge RV Campground has the benefit of being conveniently close to "Little Bavaria" without being restricted under city campfire codes. Individual campsites are permitted to have wood campfires in fire rings. Laid out in a series of loops, the campground is mostly shaded with mature trees. Sites are grassy with gravel parking spots. The campground has 150 pull-through sites and no seasonal campers. Tents are not permitted. The best site is 61, but it is often reserved a year or two in advance. This end site has a beautiful yard with tall trees, offers pull-through access, and is a quiet spot. Site 147 is also popular because it is across from the clubhouse. The typical site width is 40 feet. Security measures are great, with a card-coded gate, a manager who lives on site, and regular patrols of the campground.

BASICS

Operated By: Norman Wooten. **Open:** Apr. 1–Nov. 1. **Site Assignment:** Reservations suggested or first come, first served; 1-night deposit required; refund w/ 7-day notice. **Registration:** At campground office. **Fee:** $32; cash, check, credit card. **Parking:** At site.

FACILITIES

Number of RV-only Sites: 201. **Hookups:** Electric (20, 30, 50 amps), water, sewer. **Each Site:** Picnic table, fire ring. **Dump Station:** Yes. **Laundry:** Yes. **Pay Phone:** Yes. **Restrooms and Showers:** Yes. **Fuel:** No. **Propane:** Yes. **Internal Roads:** Paved/gravel, in good condition. **RV Service:** No. **Market:** Walking distance. **Restaurant:** Walking distance. **General Store:** No. **Vending:** No. **Swimming:** No. **Playground:** Yes. **Other:** Pavilion, rec hall, basketball, volleyball. **Activities:** Sports, picnics. **Nearby Attractions:** Bronner's Christmas Wonderland, golf, paddlewheel boat, winery, antiques, arts & crafts, Bavarian shops, cheese haus, Michigan's Own Military & Space Museum. **Additional Information:** Frankenmuth Chamber of Commerce, (800) FUN-TOWN.

RESTRICTIONS

Pets: On leash only. **Fires:** Fire ring only. **Alcoholic Beverages:** At sites only. **Vehicle Maximum Length:** No limit. **Other:** No tents allowed.

TO GET THERE

From I-75, take Birch Run Exit 136. Drive east on Birch Run Rd., follow signs to Frankenmuth, turn north on M 83, drive 0.25 mi. to Pine Ridge RV. Roads are wide and well maintained, with broad shoulders.

FREDERIC   MAP, B-2
Trails Campground

4066 Old 27 N., 49733. T: (989) 348-8692.

🚐 ★★★	🔺 ★★★
Beauty: ★★★	Site Privacy: ★★★
Spaciousness: ★★★	Quiet: ★★★★
Security: ★★★★	Cleanliness: ★★★★★
Insect Control: ★★	Facilities: ★★

Trails Campground offers a quiet little place at a low price. It has few activities, but the campground is very clean and would be a nice spot to stay while enjoying all the recreational opportunities in the Au Sable River area. Laid out in a series of loops, the campground offers grassy, level sites with a choice of shade or open. There are 18 seasonal campers and no pull-through sites. Mature white pines, red pines, aspens, and maples add a woodland effect. Located 2 miles south of Frederic, the campground has well-maintained, decorated bathrooms, including shower stalls with woodland scenes and nice wooden counters. The best tent sites are in the back against the woods, where there is more privacy and green space. Security measures include one entrance/exit road and owners who live on site and patrol the campground.

BASICS

Operated By: Jim & Ruth Thompson. **Open:** All year. **Site Assignment:** Reservations w/ no deposit. **Registration:** At campground office. **Fee:** $18–$24; cash, check. **Parking:** At site.

FACILITIES

Number of RV-only Sites: 40. **Number of Tent-only Sites:** 23. **Hookups:** Electric (20 amps), water. **Each Site:** Picnic table, fire ring. **Dump Station:** Yes. **Laundry:** Yes. **Pay Phone:** No. **Restrooms and Showers:** Yes. **Fuel:** No. **Propane:** No. **Internal Roads:** Dirt & gravel, in good condition. **RV Service:** No. **Market:** 8 mi. south in Grayling. **Restaurant:** 2 mi. north in Frederic. **General Store:** No. **Vending:** No. **Swimming:** No. **Playground:** Yes. **Other:** Horseshoes, volleyball. **Nearby Attractions:** Au Sable River, fishing, canoeing, hunting, Wellington Farm Park, state parks, golf, fish hatchery, bowling, antiques, arts & crafts. **Additional Information:** Grayling Area Visitors Council, (800) 937-8837.

RESTRICTIONS

Pets: On leash only. **Fires:** Fire ring only. **Alcoholic Beverages:** Allowed. **Vehicle Maximum Length:** 40 ft.

TO GET THERE

Tale I-75 to Exit 259 (M 93), then west about 2 mi. to stop sign. Turn north (old Hwy. 27) then go about 3 mi. The park is located on the right. Roads are wide and well maintained, with broad shoulders.

GAYLORD   MAP, B-2
Gaylord Michaywe Wilderness Resort

5101 Campfires Pkwy., 49735. T: (989) 939-8723; www.gaylordkoa.com.

🚐 ★★★	🔺 ★★★
Beauty: ★★★	Site Privacy: ★★★
Spaciousness: ★★★	Quiet: ★★★
Security: ★★★★	Cleanliness: ★★★
Insect Control: ★★	Facilities: ★★★

Nestled in 80 acres of birch, aspen, and pine, Gaylord Michaywe is bordered by the north branch of the Au Sable River. Laid out in a series of loops, the campground has 40 pull-through sites and a typical site width of 35 feet. The campground offers level, shaded, riverside sites. A 5-mph speed limit is strictly enforced with first-time offenders kicked out. "Kids always have right of way," campground rules state. Quiet hours are from 10 p.m. to 8 a.m. In season, campers can pick morel mushrooms, wild strawberries, raspberries, blueberries, and blackberries on the property. Security includes a traffic control gate, one entrance/exit, an owner who lives on site, and regular patrols of the campground.

BASICS

Operated By: Dave & Georganne Hornaceks. **Open:** Apr. 28–Oct. 29. **Site Assignment:** Reservations w/ 1-night deposit; refund w/ 7-day notice. **Registration:** At entrance gate. **Fee:** $25–$33; cash, check, credit card. **Parking:** At site.

FACILITIES

Number of Multipurpose Sites: 100. **Hookups:** Electric (50 amps), water, sewer. **Each Site:** Picnic table, fire ring. **Dump Station:** Yes. **Laundry:** Yes. **Pay Phone:** Yes. **Restrooms and Showers:** Yes. **Fuel:** No. **Propane:** Yes. **Internal Roads:** Gravel, in good condition. **RV Service:** No. **Market:** In Alpine Village of Gaylord. **Restaurant:** In Alpine Village of Gaylord. **General Store:** Yes. **Vending:** Yes. **Swimming:** Yes. **Playground:** 2. **Other:** Au Sable River, golf driving nets, rental cabins, mini-golf, basketball, volleyball, rental cabins, game room, child-sitting service, horseshoes, shuffleboard, sports field, hiking trails. **Activities:** Swimming, fishing, scheduled weekend activities. **Nearby Attractions:** Golf, bowling, ice skating, Bottle Cap Museum, canoeing, horseback riding, elk viewing, Otsego County Historical Museum, antiques. **Additional Information:** Gaylord Area Information Center, (800) 345-8621.

RESTRICTIONS

Pets: On leash only. **Fires:** Fire ring only. **Alcoholic Beverages:** At sites only. **Vehicle Maximum Length:** 50 ft.

TO GET THERE

Take I-75 (Exit 279), then travel 2 mi. south on old Hwy. 27, then 0.5 mi. east on Charles Brink Rd. (follow signs). Roads are wide and well maintained, with broad shoulders.

GRAND HAVEN — MAP, C-1
Yogi Bear's Jellystone Park Camp-Resort

reserve america

10990 US 31, 49417. T: (616) 842-9395 or (800) 828-1453; www.ghjellystone.com.

🚐 ★★★★   ⛺ ★★★★

Beauty: ★★★★		Site Privacy: ★★★★
Spaciousness: ★★★★		Quiet: ★★★★
Security: ★★★★		Cleanliness: ★★★★
Insect Control: ★★★★		Facilities: ★★★★

Beautiful 286-site park on 45 acres of white pines, oaks, maples, and poplars providing large comfortable sites to accommodate large rigs but still cozy enough for the small campers. Offers a wonderful family environment of fun and memories. Whether you are an RV park enthusiast, enjoy the comfort of a cabin in the woods, or just like to tent camp and sleep in the great outdoors, Jellystone Park is a good option. Activities available include swimming, mini-golf, hay rides, tennis, volleyball, fishing, hiking, and appearances from Yogi Bear™ and friends.

BASICS

Operated By: Andy, Jane, & June Eaton. **Open:** Apr. 20–Oct. 1. **Site Assignment:** Reservations recommended; requests taken but not guaranteed; cancellation fee & lost deposit 7–14 days prior to arrival. **Registration:** At front gate/ranger station; security gate closed at 10 p.m.; security personnel checks gate periodically for late check-ins. **Fee:** RV, $43–$59; tent, $32–$43; pool/playground sites, add $2; includes 2 adults/2 children, each additional person, $3–$8; limit 8 people per site; V, MC. **Parking:** Limit 2 cars per site; overflow parking available for fee.

FACILITIES

Number of Multipurpose Sites: 286. **Hookups:** Electric (20, 50 amps), sewer. **Each Site:** Picnic table, fire pit. **Dump Station:** Yes. **Laundry:** Yes. **Pay Phone:** No. **Restrooms and Showers:** Yes. **Fuel:** No. **Propane:** Yes. **Internal Roads:** 40% paved; 60% gravel. **RV Service:** 12 mi. south in Holland; limited on-call RV service. **Market:** 5 mi. north in Grand Haven. **Restaurant:** 1 mi. north in Grand Haven. **General Store:** Camp store. **Vending:** Yes. **Swimming:** Pool & baby pool. beaches 2–3 mi. **Playground:** Yes. **Other:** Volleyball, horseshoes, sand-based playground, pavilion, shuffleboard, golf-cart & bike rentals, kiddie rides, bumper boats, mini-golf, go-carts, planned activities, basketball court. **Nearby Attractions:** Michigan's Adventure Water Park, Grand Haven Lighthouse, Veldheer Tulip Farm, Coast Guard, Musical Fountain, Boating, Kirk Park County Park, Grand Haven State Park, Beaches, Sand Dunes, Museums, Shopping, Boardwalk, Submarine tours. **Additional Information:** Grand Haven Chamber of Commerce, (616) 842-4910.

RESTRICTIONS

Pets: On leash only. Not allowed in rental units. **Fires:** Allowed. **Alcoholic Beverages:** At site only. **Vehicle Maximum Length:** 70 ft. **Other:** Monthly & seasonal rates available. Gate card required for entry to security gate.

TO GET THERE

From Grand Haven, take US 31 south to Lake Michigan Drive (M 45). Go 0.1 mi. past M 45 on US 31 and turn left into the park. From Holland, take US 31 north about 12 mi. with entrance to campground on the right just before Lake Michigan Drive. From Grand Rapids, take M 45 (Lake Michigan Drive) west to US 31, go south 0.1 mi. and turn left into the park entrance.

GRAYLING — MAP, B-2
River Park Campground and Trout Pond

2607 Peters Rd., 49738. T: (989) 517-9092; www.riverparkcampground.com.

🚐 ★★★★   ⛺ ★★★

Beauty: ★★★		Site Privacy: ★★★★
Spaciousness: ★★★★		Quiet: ★★★★
Security: ★★★★		Cleanliness: ★★★★
Insect Control: ★★★★		Facilities: ★★★

Surrounded by hundreds of acres of state land, River Park Campground and Trout Pond is located on the east branch of the Au Sable River in Grayling. The campground offers level, grassy, shaded spots with a wealth of pine, maple, and oak trees. The typical site width is 40 feet. River Park has 40 seasonal campers and no pull-through sites. Laid out in a series of loops, the campground has a separate area for tent campers with more green space and privacy. The trout pond is stocked two or three times each summer with rainbow trout. No throwbacks are allowed—you have to keep what you catch and pay 40 cents per inch for the fish. Most of the trout measure from 10 inches up to 21 inches. River Park is open year-round and attracts winter enthusiasts who like being able to snowmobile from their campsite or ski out of the campground. Water is turned off at individual campsites during the winter, but the bathhouse is kept heated and open. Security includes owners who live on site, one entrance/exit road, and regular camp patrols.

BASICS

Operated By: Dennis & Maureen Fyock. **Open:** All year. **Site Assignment:** Reservations w/ 1-night deposit; refund w/ 7-day notice. **Registration:** At campground office. **Fee:** Water/electric, $28; electric, $25; primitive, $16; cash, check, credit card. **Parking:** At site.

FACILITIES

Number of RV-only Sites: 58. **Number of Tent-only Sites:** 10. **Hookups:** Electric (30 amps), water. **Each Site:** Picnic table, fire ring. **Dump Station:** Yes. **Laundry:** Yes. **Pay Phone:** Yes. **Restrooms and Showers:** Yes. **Fuel:** No. **Propane:** Yes. **Internal Roads:** Paved, in good condition. **RV Service:** No. **Market:** 6 mi. south in Grayling. **Restaurant:** 6 mi. south in Grayling. **General Store:** Yes, limited. **Vending:** No. **Swimming:** No. **Playground:** Yes. **Other:** Au Sable River, shuffleboard, horseshoes, rec hall, sports field, coin games, basketball, shuffleboard, fishing pond. **Activities:** Swimming, fishing. **Nearby Attractions:** Wellington Farm Park, state parks, golf, fish hatchery, bowling, antiques, arts & crafts, fishing, canoeing, hunting. **Additional Information:** Grayling Area Visitors Council, (800) 937-8837.

RESTRICTIONS

Pets: On leash only. Some breeds not allowed. **Fires:** Fire ring only. **Alcoholic Beverages:** Allowed. **Vehicle Maximum Length:** No limit.

TO GET THERE

From I-75 north, take Exit 259. Turn right and go 3 mi. to Bobcat Tail; turn right 2 mi. to campground. Roads are wide and well maintained, with broad shoulders.

GRAYLING
MAP, B-2
Yogi Bear's Jellystone Park Camp-Resort

370 West Four Mile Rd., 49738. T: (989) 348-2157; www.michcampgrounds.com/yogibears.

★★★★   ★★★

Beauty: ★★★★   Site Privacy: ★★★★
Spaciousness: ★★★★   Quiet: ★★★★
Security: ★★★★   Cleanliness: ★★★★
Insect Control: ★★★★   Facilities: ★★★★

With easy access to the interstate and a widely recognized name, Yogi Bear's Jellystone Park Camp-Resort in Grayling, is a popular stopping spot. The campground also is a destination for families because of its large roster of recreational activities. Located in a wooded, rural setting, the campground is laid out in a series of loops and offers grassy, mostly shaded sites. The typical site width is 45 feet, and the campground has 130 seasonal campers and no pull-through sites. Quiet hours are enforced from 11 p.m. to 8 a.m. and the campground doesn't allow ATVs anywhere in the campground or on adjacent private property. Security measures include a 5-mph speed limit, one entrance/exit road, owners who live on site, and patrols of the campground.

BASICS
Operated By: Tim & Lori Weismiller. **Open:** May 1–Sept. 31. **Site Assignment:** Reservations w/ 1-night deposit; refund w/ 4-day notice. **Registration:** At campground office. **Fee:** $34–$40; cash, check, credit card. **Parking:** At site.

FACILITIES
Number of Sites: 230. **Hookups:** Electric (20, 30, 50 amps), water, sewer. **Each Site:** Picnic table, fire ring. **Dump Station:** Yes. **Laundry:** Yes. **Pay Phone:** Yes. **Restrooms and Showers:** Yes. **Fuel:** No. **Propane:** No. **Internal Roads:** Dirt, in good condition. **RV Service:** No. **Market:** Yes. **Restaurant:** 10 mi. north in Grayling. **General Store:** Yes. **Vending:** Yes. **Swimming:** Yes. **Playground:** Yes. **Other:** Mini-golf, coin games, outdoor cartoon theater, shuffleboard, horseshoes, rec hall, game room, sports field, rental cabins, hiking trails, horseshoes. **Activities:** Swimming, hiking, scheduled activities. **Nearby Attractions:** Au Sable River, fishing, canoeing, hunting, Wellington Farm Park, state parks, golf, fish hatchery, bowling, antiques, arts & crafts, horseback riding. **Additional Information:** Grayling Area Visitors Council, (800) 937-8837.

RESTRICTIONS
Pets: None. **Fires:** Fire ring only. **Alcoholic Beverages:** At sites only. **Vehicle Maximum Length:** 32 ft.

TO GET THERE
From the junction of I-75 and Four Mile Rd., take Exit 251 and drive 4.5 mi. east on Four Mile Rd. Roads are wide and well maintained, with broad shoulders.

HARRISON
MAP, C-2
Countryside Campground

805 Byfield Dr., 48625. T: (989) 539-5468.

★★★   ★★

Beauty: ★★★   Site Privacy: ★★★
Spaciousness: ★★★   Quiet: ★★★
Security: ★★★★   Cleanliness: ★★★★
Insect Control: ★★   Facilities: ★★★

Located 1 mile west of Harrison, Countryside Campground has a nice combination of town conveniences and country peacefulness. Laid out in a series of loops, the campground has four seasonal campers, 20 pull-through sites, and a typical site width of 35 feet. A major plus is the campground's proximity to 20 lakes within 20 miles. Situated on rolling hills with a forest of pine trees, the campground offers a choice of shaded or open spots. Sites are grassy and level. The best sites are 14–24 because they surround a wooded area and offer more privacy. Pull-through sites also are popular because of their convenience. Families with children often prefer sites 8–13 located near the playground and swimming pool. Security measures include one-way roads past the office and owners who keep a close eye on the campground.

BASICS
Operated By: Bob & Sylvia Kern. **Open:** May 1–Oct. 15. **Site Assignment:** Reservations w/ 1-night deposit; refund w/ 2-week notice. **Registration:** At campground office. **Fee:** $25–$30; cash, check, credit card. **Parking:** At site.

FACILITIES
Number of Sites: 50. **Hookups:** Electric (30 amps), water, sewer. **Each Site:** Picnic table, fire ring. **Dump Station:** Yes. **Laundry:** Yes. **Pay Phone:** Yes. **Restrooms and Showers:** Yes. **Fuel:** No. **Propane:** No. **Internal Roads:** Gravel & pavement, in good condition. **RV Service:** No. **Market:** Yes, limited. **Restaurant:** 2 blocks. **General Store:** Yes. **Vending:** Yes. **Swimming:** Yes. **Playground:** Yes. **Other:** Rental cabins, horseshoes, volleyball, basketball, badminton, sports field, rental bikes. **Activities:** Swimming, sports, biking. **Nearby Attractions:** Golf, casino, river rafting, hunting, hiking, canoeing, boating, fishing, museums, antiques, Amish area. **Additional Information:** Clare County CVB, (800) 715-3550.

RESTRICTIONS
Pets: On leash only. **Fires:** Fire ring only. **Alcoholic Beverages:** At sites only. **Vehicle Maximum Length:** No limit.

TO GET THERE
From the junction of Business 27 and Hwy. 61 in Harrison, drive 0.75 mi. west on Hwy. 61/Main St., then 0.25 mi. north on Byfield Dr. Roads are wide and well maintained, with broad shoulders.

HARRISON
MAP, C-2
Wilson State Park

910 North First St., 48625. T: (989) 539-3021 or (800) 447-2757; www.michigandnr.com/parksandtrails/parksandtrailsinfo.

 ★★★    ★★★★

Beauty: ★★★★   Site Privacy: ★★★
Spaciousness: ★★★   Quiet: ★★★
Security: ★★★★   Cleanliness: ★★★
Insect Control: ★★★   Facilities: ★★

Located in Harrison, Wilson State Park is known for its sandy beach on Budd Lake and its muskie fishing. The campground also is unusual because it is in town and provides easy access to local attractions, restaurants, and shops. The campground is right across the street from the county fairground. Reservations are a must during fair time (the last weekend of July and first week of August). Sites are grassy and mostly shaded with no seasonal campers and four pull-through sites. The best sites for RVs are 25 because it is big, 125 because it overlooks the lake, and 134 because it is a pull-through close to the beach. Tents are permitted on any sites. Because of the lake and woods, the campground is quiet despite its location off such a busy street. Park rangers also ensure that the noise level at campsites is kept down so as not to disturb other campers. Security is tops with one entrance/exit road, a state park sticker required on vehicles, and regular patrols by park rangers and county police.

BASICS
Operated By: State of Michigan. **Open:** Apr. 1–Dec. 1. **Site Assignment:** Reservations are accepted w/ a $2 fee; refund w/ 48-hour notice. **Registration:** At campground office. **Fee:** $20–$23; cash, check, credit card. **Parking:** At site.

FACILITIES
Number of RV-only Sites: 160. **Hookups:** Electric (30 amps). **Each Site:** Picnic table, fire ring. **Dump Station:** Yes. **Laundry:** No. **Pay Phone:** No. **Restrooms and Showers:** Yes. **Fuel:** No. **Propane:** No. **Internal Roads:** Paved/gravel, in good condition. **RV Service:** No. **Market:** Next door. **Restaurant:** Next door. **General Store:** No. **Vending:** Yes. **Swimming:** Yes. **Playground:** Yes. **Other:** Budd Lake, swimming beach, pavilion, boating ramp, fishing lake, horseshoes, volleyball, recreation field, rental cabin. **Activities:** Swimming, fishing, boating. **Nearby Attractions:** Golf, casino, river rafting, hunting, hiking, canoeing, museums, antiques, Amish area. **Additional Information:** Clare County CVB, (800) 715-3550.

RESTRICTIONS
Pets: On leash only. **Fires:** Fire ring only. **Alcoholic Beverages:** At sites only. **Vehicle Maximum Length:** 40 ft. **Other:** 15-day stay limit.

TO GET THERE
From US 27, take the Harrison exit, drive 3.5 mi. west. Roads are wide and well maintained, with broad shoulders.

HASTINGS   MAP, D-2
Whispering Waters Campground and Canoe Livery

1805 North Irving Rd., 49058.
T: (800) 985-7019 or (269) 945-5166;
www.michcampgrounds.com/whisperingwaters.

🚐 ★★★★   ⛺ ★★★★

Beauty: ★★★★	Site Privacy: ★★★★
Spaciousness: ★★★★	Quiet: ★★★★
Security: ★★★★	Cleanliness: ★★★★
Insect Control: ★★★★	Facilities: ★★★★

A river runs through it. Whispering Waters Campground and Canoe Livery is a wooded rolling campground on the high bank of the Thornapple River. Located in South Central Michigan in Hastings, the campground offers level, mostly shaded sites with a typical site width of 35 feet. The campground has 20 seasonal campers and 20 pull-through sites. A tent area on the river offers more green space and privacy. No motors are permitted on the river. A huge front porch at the campground building is a nice gathering spot, as is a commons area that features comfortable chairs, a microwave, TV, and library. Basic regulations for safety and security are enforced, including no alcohol on the river. The campground also doesn't tolerate rowdy behavior.

BASICS

Operated By: Roger & Uta Vilmont. **Open:** Apr. 25–Sept. 29. **Site Assignment:** Reservations 15 or more days prior; $5 per site; first night nonrefundable. **Registration:** At campground office. **Fee:** Water/electric/sewer, $35; water/electric, $31; rustic, $25; cabin, $60; cash, check, credit card. **Parking:** At site.

FACILITIES

Number of RV-only Sites: 115. **Number of Tent-only Sites:** 3. **Hookups:** Electric (20, 30, 50 amps), water, sewer, phone. **Each Site:** Picnic table, fire ring. **Dump Station:** Yes. **Laundry:** Yes. **Pay Phone:** Yes. **Restrooms and Showers:** Yes. **Fuel:** No. **Propane:** Yes. **Internal Roads:** Gravel & dirt, in good condition. **RV Service:** No. **Market:** 3 mi. **Restaurant:** 3 mi. **General Store:** Yes. **Vending:** Yes. **Swimming:** Yes. **Playground:** Yes. **Other:** Thornapple River, swimming beach, rec room, pavilion, shuffleboard, badminton, sports field, horseshoes, hiking trails, volleyball, rental cabins, adults room. **Activities:** Swimming, fishing, hiking, boating (rental canoes available), scheduled weekend activities. **Nearby Attractions:** Riding ranch, golf, hot air ballooning, Gilmore Car Museum, Cheesbrough Rake Factory, Gun Lake, skydiving school, state parks, Kalamazoo Air Zoo, Historic Charleton Park Village & Museum. **Additional Information:** Barry County Chamber of Commerce, (616) 945-2454.

RESTRICTIONS

Pets: On leash only. **Fires:** Fire ring only. **Alcoholic Beverages:** At sites only. Not near river. **Vehicle Maximum Length:** No limit.

TO GET THERE

From Grand Rapids, take M 37 25 mi. south of Woodland Mall; go left on Irving Rd. From Hastings, go 4 mi. north on M 37 to Irving Rd., then right 0.25 mi. to camp. Follow signs. Roads are mostly wide and well maintained, with adequate shoulders.

HILLMAN   MAP, B-3
Jack's Landing Resort

20836 Tennis Rd., 49746. T: (517) 742-4370;
www.jackslanding.com.

🚐 ★★★   ⛺ ★★★

Beauty: ★★★★	Site Privacy: ★★★
Spaciousness: ★★★	Quiet: ★★★
Security: ★★★★	Cleanliness: ★★★
Insect Control: ★★★	Facilities: ★★★

Located 7 miles southeast of Hillman, Jack's Landing Resort has a beautiful view of Fletcher Pond. But don't let the name fool you. The "pond" offers 9,000 acres of premier fishing for pike, bass, and panfish. Wildlife viewing includes sights of eagles, osprey, loons, and many ducks. The campground has level open or shaded sites. It has no pull-throughs. From January 4–March 18, the campground offers ice fishing, with heated ice fishing shanties and a snow plow to keep the area open. The best RV site is 25 because it offers 50-amp hookup. The best tent site is 44 because it is set back in the woods and offers more privacy. Security measures include a 5-mph speed limit, one entrance/exit road, an owner who lives on site, and occasional campground patrols.

BASICS

Operated By: Dean & Annie Robinson. **Open:** May 1–Oct. 31. **Site Assignment:** Reservations w/ 1-night deposit; refund w/ 7-day notice. **Registration:** At campground office. **Fee:** Electric/water, $25; electric, $20; rustic, $15; cash, check, credit card. **Parking:** At site.

FACILITIES

Number of RV-only Sites: 14. **Number of Tent-only Sites:** 16. **Hookups:** Electric (20, 30, 50 amps), water. **Each Site:** Picnic table, fire ring. **Dump Station:** Yes. **Laundry:** No. **Pay Phone:** Yes. **Restrooms and Showers:** Yes. **Fuel:** Yes. **Propane:** Yes. **Internal Roads:** Gravel, some pavement in fair condition. **RV Service:** No. **Market:** 7 mi. west in Hillman. **Restaurant:** On site. **General Store:** Yes. **Vending:** Yes. **Swimming:** No. **Playground:** Yes. **Other:** Fletcher Pond, marina, bar, rental cabins, lodge rooms, boat slips, boat launch, sports field, horseshoes, hiking trails, fish-cleaning hut. **Activities:** Fishing, swimming, boating (rental motorboats, pontoons available), hiking, billiards. **Nearby Attractions:** Golf, charter boat fishing, Lake Huron, elk viewing, Pigeon River Country State Forest, lighthouses, antiques, shipwreck sanctuary, museums, historic homes. **Additional Information:** Hillman Area Chamber of Commerce, (989) 742-3739.

RESTRICTIONS

Pets: On leash only. **Fires:** Fire ring only. **Alcoholic Beverages:** Allowed. **Vehicle Maximum Length:** No limit.

TO GET THERE

From the junction of Hwy. 451 and Hwy. 32, drive 2 mi. east on Hwy. 32, then 5 mi. south on Jack's Landing Rd. The highway is wide and well maintained, with broad shoulders, but Jack's Landing Rd. is bumpy gravel.

HOLLAND   MAP, D-1
Oak Grove Resort Campgrounds

2011 Ottawa Beach Rd., 49424. T: (616) 399-9230;
www.michcampgrounds.com/oakgrove.

🚐 ★★★★   ⛺ n/a

Beauty: ★★★★	Site Privacy: ★★★★
Spaciousness: ★★★★	Quiet: ★★★★
Security: ★★★★	Cleanliness: ★★★★★
Insect Control: ★★★★	Facilities: ★★★★

Oak Grove Resort Campground fills the wish list many campers have of the ideal spot to visit. Located within walking distance of Lake Macatawa and Lake Michigan beaches, the Holland campground is in the midst of a wealth of vacation recreation. Oak Grove itself is sparkling clean, well arranged, friendly, secure, and a pleasure to visit. Beautiful landscaping touches such as flowers, shrubs, and mowed sites show close attention to detail. A large 24 by 50 heated pool and hot tub are a nice treat for those not ready to jump into the cold waters of Lake Michigan. The campground is also 1 mile before Holland State Park and offers access to miles of paved bike trails. Sites are level, wooded, and mostly shaded, with a typical site width of 35 feet. All sites have full hookups, and there are 80 seasonal campers. Mid-May brings the annual Tulip Festival, a glorious event that means reservations are strongly recommended for the campground. Be aware that no tents are allowed. Also note that the office building is closed on Sunday and that the security gate closes each night at 10.

BASICS

Operated By: Ron & Betty, Rod & Maria VandenBerg. **Open:** Apr. 29–Oct. 10. **Site Assignment:** 5-night stay required for campsite reservation and/or camping cabins. **Registration:** At campground office. **Fee:** Site, $40–$45; cabin, $70–$90; cash, check, credit card. **Parking:** At site.

FACILITIES

Number of RV-only Sites: 135. **Hookups:** Electric (30, 50 amps), water, sewer, cable TV. **Each Site:** Picnic table, fire ring. **Dump Station:** Yes. **Laundry:** Yes. **Pay Phone:** Yes. **Restrooms and Showers:** Yes. **Fuel:** No. **Propane:** Yes. **Internal Roads:** Paved, in good condition. **RV Service:** No. **Market:** 2 blocks. **Restaurant:** 2 blocks. **General Store:** Yes. **Vending:** Yes. **Swimming:** Yes. **Playground:** Yes. **Other:** Rec hall, hiking trails, rental cabins, whirlpool, horseshoes, basketball. **Activities:** Swimming, hiking, basketball, game room. **Nearby Attractions:** Lake Macatawa, Lake Michigan, bike trails, Cappon House Museum, De Klomp Wooden Shoe & Delftware Factory, Dutch Village, Holland Museum, tulip gardens, Windmill Island, antiques, arts & crafts. **Additional Information:** Holland Area CVB, (800) 506-1299.

RESTRICTIONS

Pets: On leash only. **Fires:** Fire ring only. **Alcoholic Beverages:** Not allowed. **Vehicle Maximum Length:** No limit. **Other:** No tents allowed.

TO GET THERE

From the junction of US 31 and Lakewood Blvd., drive 1.5 mi. west on Lakewood Blvd., then 1.5 mi. west on Douglas, then 3 mi. west on Ottawa Beach Rd. Roads are mostly wide and well maintained, with adequate shoulders.

HOLLY   MAP, D-3
Yogi Bear's Jellystone Park Camp-Resort

7072 East Grange Hall Rd., 48442.
T: (248) 634-8621 or (800) 442-YOGI;
www.michcampgrounds.com/jellystone-holly.

🚐 ★★★★	⛺ ★★★
Beauty: ★★★	Site Privacy: ★★★★
Spaciousness: ★★★★	Quiet: ★★★★
Security: ★★★★	Cleanliness: ★★★★
Insect Control: ★★	Facilities: ★★★★

Easy access off I-75 is a major draw for this campground, as is a long list of activities provided for campers. An activities director keeps fun times rolling with a creative list of activities for all ages. One unusual activity invites visitors to "fine-tune" their campers by comparing notes on how to repair or fix up a camper and where to visit, when to camp, and what to see. Located 3 miles east of Holly, Yogi Bear's Jellystone Park of Holly offers shaded grassy sites with gravel parking spots. Laid out in a series of loops, the campground has 30 seasonal campers, 40 pull-through sites, and a typical site width of 30 feet. The campground is open all year but has limited winter facilities and would appeal to only the hardiest campers. One time it might be fun to brave the cold would be for the annual Dickens Olde Fashioned Christmas Festival in Holly during weekends in late November and throughout December. But be prepared for frigid weather and possible snow. The speed limit is 7.5 mph and quiet times are 11 p.m. to 8 a.m.

BASICS

Operated By: Leon & Sandy Sterling. **Open:** Apr.–Dec. **Site Assignment:** Reservations w/ 1-night deposit; refund (minus $5) w/ 7-day notice. **Registration:** At campground office. **Fee:** $40; cash, credit card. **Parking:** At site.

FACILITIES

Number of RV-only Sites: 146. **Number of Tent-only Sites:** 40. **Hookups:** Electric (20, 30, 50 amps), water. **Each Site:** Picnic table, fire ring, barbecues. **Dump Station:** Yes. **Laundry:** Yes. **Pay Phone:** Yes. **Restrooms and Showers:** Yes. **Fuel:** No. **Propane:** Yes. **Internal Roads:** Paved/gravel, in good condition. **RV Service:** No. **Market:** 3 mi. west in Holly. **Restaurant:** 3 mi. west in Holly. **General Store:** Yes. **Vending:** Yes. **Swimming:** Yes. **Playground:** Yes. **Other:** Arcade, mini-golf, rental cabins, kiddie train, bumper boats, T. rex, bounce house, power wheels, basketball, rental

bikes, horseshoes, movies, activities director, adults' room. **Activities:** Swimming, scheduled activities. **Nearby Attractions:** Children's museum, Huckleberry Railroad, paddle wheeler, museums, Longway Planetarium, Flint River, antiques, golf, arts & crafts. **Additional Information:** Holly Chamber of Commerce, (248) 634-1900.

RESTRICTIONS

Pets: On leash only. Not in cabin. **Fires:** Fire ring only. **Alcoholic Beverages:** Allowed. **Vehicle Maximum Length:** No limit. **Other:** Checks not accepted at check-in.

TO GET THERE

From I-75 (north- or southbound), take Exit 101 (Grange Hall Rd). Go east right next to the Sunoco gas station. From US 23 (north- or southbound), take Exit 79 (Silver Lake Pkwy.). Travel east 10 mi., then cross over I-75. Roads are wide and well maintained with broad shoulders.

HOPKINS   MAP, D-1
East Lake Camping

3091 Weick Dr., 49328. T: (269) 793-7177;
www.eastlakecamping.com.

🚐 ★★★	⛺ ★★★
Beauty: ★★★★	Site Privacy: ★★★
Spaciousness: ★★★	Quiet: ★★★★
Security: ★★★★	Cleanliness: ★★★★
Insect Control: ★★★	Facilities: ★★★

Located midway between Grand Rapids, Holland, and Kalamazoo, East Lake Camping offers family camping in the hills around East Lake. The quiet country setting outside Hopkins features camping sites from rustic to full hookups. The campground has open and shaded sites on a hilly terrain. The best sites are closest to the large lake. East Lake Camping has 59 seasonal campers, a typical site width of 30 feet, and seven pull-through sites. Chapel services are offered on Sunday. The lake has a nice sandy beach for swimmers and is a good place to fish and boat. Owners enforce basic regulations to keep the campground safe, quiet, and family-oriented, while still maintaining a friendly atmosphere.

BASICS

Operated By: Greg & Catherine Miller. **Open:** May 1–Oct. 1. **Site Assignment:** Reservations w/ 1-night deposit; refund (minus $5) w/ 7-day notice. **Registration:** At campground office. **Fee:** $25; cash, check, credit card. **Parking:** At site.

FACILITIES

Number of RV-only Sites: 109. **Number of Tent-only Sites:** 1. **Hookups:** Electric (20, 30, 50 amps), water, sewer. **Each Site:** Picnic table, fire ring. **Dump Station:** Yes. **Laundry:** Yes. **Pay Phone:** Yes. **Restrooms and Showers:** Yes. **Fuel:** No. **Propane:** No. **Internal Roads:** Gravel, in good condition. **RV Service:** No. **Market:** 1 mi. **Restaurant:** 1 mi. **General Store:** Yes. **Vending:** Yes. **Swimming:** Lake. **Playground:** Yes. **Other:** East Lake, sandy beach, pavilion, coin games, rec room, basketball, shuffleboard, sports field, horseshoes, boat

ramp, boat dock, volleyball, hiking trail, rental RVs, rental cabin. **Activities:** Swimming, hiking, fishing, boating (rental rowboats, kayaks, paddleboats available), scheduled weekend activities. **Nearby Attractions:** Gerald R. Ford Museum, Fredrick Meijer Gardens, zoo, Michigan Adventure Amusement Park, Roger B. Chaffee Planetarium, golf, tennis, rivers & lakes, antiques, Wooden Shoe Factory. **Additional Information:** Grand Rapids/ Kent County CVB, (800) 678-9859.

RESTRICTIONS

Pets: On leash only. **Fires:** Fire ring only. **Alcoholic Beverages:** Allowed. **Vehicle Maximum Length:** 35 ft.

TO GET THERE

From US 131, take Wayland Exit 64 and drive 3 mi. west on 135th Ave., then 2.5 mi. south on 18th St., then 2.5 mi. west on 130th Ave. to Weick Dr. Roads are mostly wide and well maintained, with narrow shoulders in spots.

HOUGHTON LAKE   MAP, C-2
Houghton Lake Travel Park

370 Cloverleaf Ln., 48629.
T: (989) 422-3931 or (800) 659-9379;
www.houghtonlaketravelpark.com.

🚐 ★★★	⛺ ★★★
Beauty: ★★★	Site Privacy: ★★★
Spaciousness: ★★★	Quiet: ★★★★
Security: ★★★★	Cleanliness: ★★★★
Insect Control: ★★	Facilities: ★★★

Houghton Lake Travel Park offers easy access to Michigan's largest inland lake. Houghton Lake is 10 miles long and 6 miles wide, with a 31-mile shoreline. The campground offers open, level sites. All sites are pull-throughs and there are 21 seasonal campers. Tent sites are in a rustic section with more green space and privacy. A tradition of the travel park, located 12 miles south of Frederic, is the train ride. Sports enthusiasts and vacationers have replaced the loggers and commercial anglers who once were the vital elements of Houghton Lake. The village is the core of a year-round resort area that borders the lake. Summer brings boaters and water-skiers. Winter attracts snow skiers. Fishing knows no season. The rural campground closes in October, so it is not available for the winter season of ice fishing and snowmobiling.

BASICS

Operated By: Ron & Jo Seim. **Open:** Apr. 1–Oct. 31. **Site Assignment:** Reservations w/ 1-night deposit; refund w/ 7-day notice. **Registration:** At campground office. **Fee:** $25–$35; cash, check, credit card. **Parking:** At site.

FACILITIES

Number of RV-only Sites: 60. **Number of Tent-only Sites:** 20. **Hookups:** Electric (20, 30, 50 amps), water, sewer. **Each Site:** Picnic table, fire ring. **Dump Station:** Yes. **Laundry:** Yes. **Pay Phone:** Yes. **Restrooms and Showers:** Yes. **Fuel:** No. **Propane:** Yes. **Internal Roads:** Gravel, in good condition. **RV Service:** No. **Market:**

12 mi. north in Frederic. **Restaurant:** 12 mi. north in Frederic. **General Store:** Yes. **Vending:** Yes. **Swimming:** Yes. **Playground:** Yes. **Other:** Rec room, rental cabins, sports field, horseshoes, volleyball. **Activities:** Swimming. **Nearby Attractions:** Houghton Lake, fishing, golf, amusement parks, mini-golf, Merritt Speedway, firemen's memorial, antiques, arts & crafts. **Additional Information:** Houghton Lake Chamber of Commerce, (800) 248-5253.

RESTRICTIONS

Pets: On leash only. **Fires:** Fire ring only. **Alcoholic Beverages:** Allowed. **Vehicle Maximum Length:** No limit.

TO GET THERE

One block east of US 127 on M 55 turn south off M 55 at Cloverleaf Lane. From I-75, take M 55 (18 mi.) through Houghton Lake, past state police post to Cloverleaf Lane. Roads are wide and well maintained, with broad shoulders.

HOUGHTON LAKE   MAP, C-2
Sandyoak RV Park

2757 Owens Rd., 48629. T: (989) 366-5555.

🚐 ★★★★	⛺ n/a
Beauty: ★★★	Site Privacy: ★★★
Spaciousness: ★★★★	Quiet: ★★★★
Security: ★★★★	Cleanliness: ★★★★
Insect Control: ★★	Facilities: ★★★★

Located in the town of Houghton Lake, Sandyoak RV Park is a resort with camping lots for sale or rent. No tents are allowed. The campground has 183 seasonal campers and no pull-through sites. Laid out in a series of loops, the park has an indoor heated pool, two heated bathhouses, and two laundries. Sites are mostly grassy and shaded with a typical site width of 40 feet. A large clubhouse with kitchen facilities is available for gatherings. Speed limit is 10 mph, a bit high, especially in the playground areas. Most permanent sites are well maintained and decorated. To keep the park attractive, the association has a rule that the sales and rental agent has the right to refuse the registration of any trailer that would be "detrimental to the general appearance" of the park. They also have the right to instruct that such trailers must be removed from the park by the owner.

BASICS

Operated By: Sandyoak Village Assoc. **Open:** All year. **Site Assignment:** Reservations w/ 1-night deposit; refund w/ 2-week notice. **Registration:** At campground office. **Fee:** $25–$30; cash, check. **Parking:** At site.

FACILITIES

Number of RV-only Sites: 227. **Hookups:** Electric (30, 50 amps), water, sewer, cable TV. **Each Site:** Picnic table, fire ring. **Dump Station:** No. **Laundry:** Yes. **Pay Phone:** No. **Restrooms and Showers:** Yes. **Fuel:** No. **Propane:** No. **Internal Roads:** Paved, in good condition. **RV Service:** No. **Market:** 1 block. **Restaurant:** 1 block. **General Store:** No. **Vending:** Yes. **Swimming:** Yes. **Playground:** Yes. **Other:** Clubhouse, horseshoes, shuffleboard, basketball, sales office, spa, rec hall, game room, recreation

field, hiking trails. **Activities:** Swimming, hiking, scheduled activities. **Nearby Attractions:** Houghton Lake, fishing, golf, amusement parks, mini-golf, Merritt Speedway, Firemen's Memorial, antiques, arts & crafts. **Additional Information:** Houghton Lake Chamber of Commerce, (800) 248-5253.

RESTRICTIONS

Pets: On leash only; max. of 2 per site. Some breeds not allowed. **Fires:** Fire rings only; must be extinguished w/ water before retiring for night. **Alcoholic Beverages:** At sites only. **Vehicle Maximum Length:** No limit. **Other:** Children under age 12 not permitted in hot tub. No tents allowed.

TO GET THERE

From the junction of US 27 and Hwy. 55, drive 6 mi. east on Hwy. 55 (West Houghton Lake Dr.), then 1 block south on Owens Dr. Roads are wide and well maintained, with broad shoulders.

HOUGHTON LAKE   MAP, C-2
Wooded Acres Family Campground

997 Federal Ave., 48629. T: (989) 422-3413; www.michcampgrounds.com/woodedacres.

🚐 ★★★★	⛺ ★★★
Beauty: ★★★	Site Privacy: ★★★
Spaciousness: ★★★	Quiet: ★★★
Security: ★★★★	Cleanliness: ★★★★
Insect Control: ★★	Facilities: ★★★★

Located in a large resort area in Houghton Lake, Wooded Acres Family Campground offers open and secluded sites in a wooded area. Laid out in a series of loops, the campground has 30 seasonal campers, 30 pull-through sites and a typical site width of 30 feet. The best RV sites are 77–88 because they offer full hookups. The best tent site is 14 because it is well shaded, large, and offers more privacy. Security measures include one entrance/exit, owners who live on site, and campground patrols. As the name indicates, Wooded Acres has a wealth of trees and enforces rules to keep them. Cutting any standing timber or vegetation is prohibited. If a tree branch is in the way of a camper, staff employees should be notified to deal with the problem. Violation of the regulation results in a $100 fine. For safety and quietness, snowmobiles, motorcycles, scooters, mopeds, and three- and four-wheelers are not allowed to be ridden in the park. Golf carts also are prohibited, except for use by elderly people or those with disabilities. The campground is well maintained and features an antique John Deere tractor theme.

BASICS

Operated By: Dave & Tina Dietzel. **Open:** All year. **Site Assignment:** Reservations w/ 1-night deposit; refund (minus $5) w/ 7-day notice. **Registration:** At campground office. **Fee:** Pull-through, $31; water/electric, $26; rustic, $21; cash, check, credit card. **Parking:** At site.

FACILITIES

Number of RV-only Sites: 72. **Number of Tent-only Sites:** 30. **Hookups:** Electric (30, 50 amps),

water, sewer. **Each Site:** Picnic table, fire ring. **Dump Station:** Yes. **Laundry:** Yes. **Pay Phone:** No. **Restrooms and Showers:** Yes. **Fuel:** No. **Propane:** Yes. **Internal Roads:** Gravel, in good condition. **RV Service:** No. **Market:** 2 mi. north in Houghton Lake. **Restaurant:** 2 mi. north in Houghton Lake. **General Store:** Yes, limited. **Vending:** No. **Swimming:** Yes. **Playground:** Yes. **Other:** Pavilion, rental cabin, game room, basketball, volleyball, shuffleboard, horseshoes, fishing pond, sports field. **Activities:** Swimming, fishing. **Nearby Attractions:** Houghton Lake, fishing, amusement parks, mini-golf, Merritt Speedway, golf, firemen's memorial, antiques, arts & crafts. **Additional Information:** Houghton Lake Chamber of Commerce, (800) 248-5253.

RESTRICTIONS

Pets: On leash only. **Fires:** Fire ring only. **Alcoholic Beverages:** Allowed. **Vehicle Maximum Length:** 40 ft.

TO GET THERE

From US 127, exit at M 55 East Houghton Lake. Turn right or south at the second stoplight, which is Loxley Rd. Go 1.5 mi. to the stop sign at Federal Ave. Roads are wide and well maintained, with broad shoulders.

INDIAN RIVER   MAP, B-2
Indian River RV Resort and Campground

561 North Straits Hwy., 49749.
T: (888) 792-CAMP or (231) 238-0035;
www.indianrivercampground.com

🚐 ★★★★	⛺ ★★★★
Beauty: ★★★★ .	Site Privacy: ★★★★
Spaciousness: ★★★★	Quiet: ★★★★
Security: ★★★★	Cleanliness: ★★★★★
Insect Control: ★★★★★	Facilities: ★★★★

Just minutes from I-75, Indian River RV Resort and Campground offers convenience in the heart of the Inland Waterways and the gateway to Mackinaw City. Located in Indian River, the campground offers shaded level sites with a typical site width of 45 feet. Sites are mostly gravel with all pull-throughs. Tent sites are in an area offering more green space and privacy. A large pavilion is handy for groups and family gatherings. Facilities are so sparkling clean that they must be attended to more often than the customary once a day. Owners provide security and enforce simple regulations to keep the campground safe, quiet, and comfortable, while still being friendly.

BASICS

Operated By: Don & Nancy Schlickau. **Open:** Apr.–Oct. **Site Assignment:** Reservations w/ 1-night deposit; refund w/ 2-week notice; if cancelled 7 days or less, 1-night camping fee. **Registration:** At campground office. **Fee:** $38–$55; cash, check, credit card. **Parking:** At site.

FACILITIES

Number of RV-only Sites: 74. **Number of Tent-only Sites:** 77. **Hookups:** Electric (20, 30, 50 amps), water, sewer, cable TV. **Each Site:** Picnic table, fire ring. **Dump Station:** Yes. **Laundry:** Yes. **Pay Phone:** Yes. **Restrooms and Showers:** Yes. **Fuel:** No. **Propane:** Yes. **Internal Roads:** Gravel, in good condition. **RV Service:** No. **Market:** Less than 1 mi. **Restaurant:** Less than 1 mi. **General Store:** Yes. **Vending:** Yes. **Swimming:** Yes. **Playground:** Yes. **Other:** Pavilion, rental cabins, coin games, rec hall, horseshoes, basketball, volleyball, badminton, sports field, hiking trials. **Activities:** Swimming, hiking, scheduled weekend activities. **Nearby Attractions:** Mackinac Island, golf, casino, Cross in the Woods, Lake Michigan, beaches, dunes, ferry, Old Mill Creek State Historic Park, Fort Michilimackinac, antiques, scenic drives, arts & crafts, Mackinac Bridge, Mackinac Bridge Museum. **Additional Information:** Greater Mackinaw City Area Chamber of Commerce, (800) 814-0160.

RESTRICTIONS

Pets: On leash only. Must keep quiet. **Fires:** Fire ring only. No higher than 1.5 ft. high. **Alcoholic Beverages:** Allowed. **Vehicle Maximum Length:** 45 ft. **Other:** Pavilion (holds 100 people).

TO GET THERE

From the junction of I-75 north and Hwy. 27, take Exit 313 and drive 1.5 mi. north on Hwy. 27. Roads are wide and well maintained, with broad shoulders.

INDIAN RIVER   MAP, B-2
Yogi Bear's Jellystone Park Camp-Resort

reserve america

2201 East M-68, 49749. T: (231) 238-8259; www.reserveamerica.com.

🚐 ★★★★	⛺ ★★★★
Beauty: ★★★★	Site Privacy: ★★★★
Spaciousness: ★★★★	Quiet: ★★★★
Security: ★★★★★	Cleanliness: ★★★★
Insect Control: ★★★★	Facilities: ★★★★

Campers usually know what they will find when they pull into a Yogi Bear's Jellystone Park. Facilities and security are top-notch. Activities are abundant and well organized. Restrooms and showers are sparkling clean, and the grounds are well maintained. But the Indian River Yogi Bear's has an extra surprise. The heated swimming pool is in the shape of Michigan with a road map on the bottom. That nice touch shows the attention to detail this campground pays to make a visit special. The campground offers level, wooded sites with a typical site width of 30 feet. There are 36 pull-through sites. Tent sites are in a rustic area with more green space and privacy. The campground is in the heart of Northern Michigan with all its attractions, and reservations are strongly recommended. Rangers are on hand for security and to answer questions or lend a helping hand to campers.

BASICS

Operated By: Clark & Barbara Tallman & Fred Jana. **Open:** May 15–Sept. 15. **Site Assignment:** Reservations w/ 1-night deposit; refund (minus $5)

w/ 7-day notice. **Registration:** At campground office. **Fee:** Full hookup, $41; water/electric, $36; electric, $32; rustic, $28; cash, check, credit card. **Parking:** At site.

FACILITIES

Number of RV-only Sites: 156. **Number of Tent-only Sites:** 24. **Hookups:** Electric (20, 30, 50 amps), water, sewer. **Each Site:** Picnic table, fire ring. **Dump Station:** Yes. **Laundry:** Yes. **Pay Phone:** Yes. **Restrooms and Showers:** Yes. **Fuel:** No. **Propane:** Yes. **Internal Roads:** Paved/gravel, in good condition. **RV Service:** No. **Market:** 3 mi. west in Indian River. **Restaurant:** 3 mi. west in Indian River. **General Store:** Yes. **Vending:** Yes. **Swimming:** Yes. **Playground:** Yes. **Other:** Mini-golf, nature trails, pavilion, outdoor theater, tetherball, horseshoes, bocce ball, volleyball, shuffleboard, game room, rental cabins, basketball, activities director, snack bar, coin games, sports field. **Activities:** Swimming, hiking, scheduled activities. **Nearby Attractions:** Mackinac Island, golf, casino, Cross in the Woods, Lake Michigan, beaches, dunes, ferry, Old Mill Creek State Historic Park, Fort Michilimackinac, antiques, scenic drives, arts & crafts, Mackinac Bridge, Mackinac Bridge Museum. **Additional Information:** Greater Mackinaw City Area Chamber of Commerce, (888) 455-8100.

RESTRICTIONS

Pets: On leash only. **Fires:** Fire ring only. **Alcoholic Beverages:** Allowed. **Vehicle Maximum Length:** 40 ft.

TO GET THERE

From I-75, take Indian River Exit 310, drive 4 mi. east on Hwy. 68. Roads are wide and well maintained, with broad shoulders.

INTERLOCHEN   MAP, B-1, B-2
Interlochen State Park

M 137, 49643. T: (231) 276-9511; www.michigan.gov/dnr.

🚐 ★★★	⛺ ★★★★
Beauty: ★★★★	Site Privacy: ★★★
Spaciousness: ★★★	Quiet: ★★★★
Security: ★★★★	Cleanliness: ★★★
Insect Control: ★★★	Facilities: ★★

Established in 1919, Interlochen State Park was the first campground in Michigan's state park system. The campground, 14 miles southwest of Traverse City, is nestled among one of the state's few remaining stands of virgin pine. Located between two lakes, the park offers a rustic campground with 72 sites along Green Lake and a modern campground with 428 sites at Duck Lake. In addition to enjoying a natural setting, water sports, and recreation, campers can attend summer concerts given by premier entertainers next door at Interlochen National Music Camp. Walking trails lead from the campground to the cultural center. Modern campsites with electricity at Duck Lake have restrooms with flush toilets. The Duck Lake campground offers two loops of campsites on each side of the day-use area with its park store, volleyball, video arcade, beach, and swimming area. But boat launch ramps are provided on

both lakes. As usual, the restrooms could be better maintained. The tree-lined shores of Green Lake offers rustic camping. Duck Lake sites are mostly gravel, with a typical site width of 30 feet and five pull-through sites. Security is great, with a 24-hour attendant and regular campground patrols.

BASICS

Operated By: State of Michigan. **Open:** Apr. 15–Nov. 1. **Site Assignment:** Reservations w/ 1-night deposit; refund (minus $5) w/ 1-week notice; call (800) 44-PARKS. **Registration:** At campground office. **Fee:** RV, $20; tent, $9; state park sticker fee, $4/day or $20/season. **Parking:** At site.

FACILITIES

Number of RV-only Sites: 428. **Number of Tent-only Sites:** 72. **Hookups:** Electric (30 amps). **Each Site:** Picnic table, fire pits. **Dump Station:** Yes. **Laundry:** No. **Pay Phone:** Yes. **Restrooms and Showers:** Yes. **Fuel:** No. **Propane:** No. **Internal Roads:** Paved & gravel, in good condition. **RV Service:** No. **Market:** 4 mi. **Restaurant:** 4 mi. **General Store:** Cafe. **Vending:** Yes. **Swimming:** Yes. **Playground:** Yes. **Other:** Duck Lake, Green Lake, coin games, swimming beach, boat ramp, horseshoes, game room, sports field, display of 1890s logging era items. **Activities:** Swimming, fishing, boating (rental rowboats available), volleyball, hiking. **Nearby Attractions:** Canoe livery, Grand Traverse Bay, Sleeping Bear Sand Dunes, casino, golf, outlet mall, cherry orchards, winter sports, Old Mission, museums, wineries. **Additional Information:** Interlochen Chamber of Commerce, (231) 276-7141.

RESTRICTIONS

Pets: On leash only. Some breeds not allowed. **Fires:** Fire ring only. Out at midnight. **Alcoholic Beverages:** Allowed. **Vehicle Maximum Length:** No limit. **Other:** 15-day stay limit.

TO GET THERE

Located 15 mi. southwest of Traverse City on M 137. Take US 31 west of Traverse City for 7 mi. to Interlochen, then go south on M 137 for 2 mi. Roads are wide and well maintained, with adequate shoulders.

ITHACA   MAP, C-2
Just-In-Time Campgrounds

8421 E. Pierce Rd., 48847. T: (989) 875-2865; www.justintimecampground.net.

🚐 ★★★	⛺ ★★★
Beauty: ★★★	Site Privacy: ★★★
Spaciousness: ★★★	Quiet: ★★★
Security: ★★★	Cleanliness: ★★★
Insect Control: ★★	Facilities: ★★★

Just-In-Time Campgrounds is a beautiful little nook about 7 miles east of Ithaca. An abundance of trees and a spring-fed lake add to the rural setting. But a sandpit across from the lake stands out like a sore thumb. The campground offers a choice of shaded or open sites, some backing up into the woods or situated right on the lake. Nicely maintained grass adds to the beauty. The campground has 29 seasonal campers and no pull-through sites. No license is needed for fishing in Lake Earl. No gas-powered motors are permitted on the lake, and the campground has only a few boats to rent, so it is best to bring your own, including required life preservers. Be aware that the water outside the roped-in swimming area is very deep and dangerous. No swimming or wading is permitted outside the roped-in area. No lifeguard is on duty, and swimmers are urged to never swim alone. Children must always be accompanied by an adult when swimming. No pets are allowed at the campground.

BASICS

Operated By: Keith & Shelly Roosa, Everett & Roxanne Hathaway. **Open:** May 1–Oct. 15. **Site Assignment:** Reservations w/ 1-night deposit; refunds w/ 7-day notice; on holidays, no refunds w/ 7-day notice unless site can be rented (minus $4 fee). **Registration:** At campground office. **Fee:** Cabin, $38; electric/water/sewer, $29; electric/water, $26; rustic, $15; cash, check, credit card. **Parking:** At site.

FACILITIES

Number of RV-only Sites: 58. **Hookups:** Electric (20, 30 amps), water, sewer. **Each Site:** Picnic table, fire ring. **Dump Station:** Yes. **Laundry:** Yes. **Pay Phone:** No. **Restrooms and Showers:** Yes. **Fuel:** No. **Propane:** Yes. **Internal Roads:** Gravel, in good condition. **RV Service:** No. **Market:** 7 mi. west in Ithaca. **Restaurant:** 7 mi. west in Ithaca. **General Store:** Yes, limited. **Vending:** Yes. **Swimming:** Yes. **Playground:** Yes. **Other:** Lake Earl, swimming beach, rental cabins, water trampoline. **Activities:** Swimming, fishing, boating (electric motors only, rental rowboats available), weekend activities. **Nearby Attractions:** Golf, hiking, horseback riding, charter boats, historic downtown, antiques, arts & crafts, museums. **Additional Information:** Travel Michigan, (888) 784-7328.

RESTRICTIONS

Pets: Not permitted. **Fires:** Fire ring only. **Alcoholic Beverages:** At campsite only. **Vehicle Maximum Length:** 40 ft.

TO GET THERE

From the junction of US 27 and Washington Rd., drive 7 mi. east on Washington Rd., then 2 mi. south on Ransom, then 0.5 mi. east on Pierce Rd. Roads are wide and well maintained, with broad shoulders, except for Pierce Rd., which is a rough gravel surface.

KIMBALL   MAP, D-3
Port Huron KOA

5111 Lapeer Rd., 48074. T: (810) 987-4070 or (800) 562-0833; www.koa.com/where/mi/22220/.

🚐 ★★★★	⛺ ★★★★
Beauty: ★★★★	Site Privacy: ★★★★
Spaciousness: ★★★★	Quiet: ★★★
Security: ★★★★★	Cleanliness: ★★★★
Insect Control: ★★★★	Facilities: ★★★★★

Just a stone's throw from the Canadian border, Port Huron KOA is a combination amusement park/campground. Located 5 miles west of Port Huron, the campground has enough activities to keep anyone hopping from morning into the night. Many activities like hayrides, train rides, and movies are free but many others will need a ready supply of coins. Air-conditioned restrooms, a western town, and two swimming pools are nice touches, as are the one- to six-passenger rental bikes. Sites are mostly level with a choice of open or heavily shaded. The campground has 56 pull-throughs and a typical site width of 42 feet. A separate area for tents allows for more privacy and green space. The best sites depend on what the goal of the camper is—if it's to enjoy all the activities with children, then sites close to the recreation are best; if it's to get some peace and commune with nature, then stay as far away from the recreation as possible.

BASICS

Operated By: Howard & Shirley Stein. **Open:** Apr. 15–Oct. 31. **Site Assignment:** Reservations w/ 1-night deposit; refund w/ 2-week notice. **Registration:** At campground office. **Fee:** RV, $26–$60; tent, $15–$34; cash, check, credit card w/ 48 hours notice. **Parking:** At site.

FACILITIES

Number of Multipurpose Sites: 294. **Hookups:** Electric (60 amps), water, sewer, phone, cable TV. **Each Site:** Picnic table, fire pit. **Dump Station:** Yes. **Laundry:** Yes. **Pay Phone:** Yes. **Restrooms and Showers:** Yes. **Fuel:** No. **Propane:** No. **Internal Roads:** Paved/gravel, in good condition. **RV Service:** No. **Market:** 1 mi. **Restaurant:** 1 mi. **General Store:** Yes. **Vending:** Yes. **Swimming:** Yes. **Playground:** Yes. **Other:** Adventure golf, batting cages, bumper boats, game room, western town, go-cart track, soccer, tennis, in-line skating rink, sports shop, Pursuit Park Paint Ball, rental cottages, train rides, pavilion, coin games, sports field, horseshoes, hiking trails. **Activities:** Swimming, hiking, scheduled activities, movies. **Nearby Attractions:** Parks, Fort Gratiot Lighthouse, Huron Lightship Museum, historic district, antiques, arts & crafts, golf, Port Huron Museum, Canadian International Border. **Additional Information:** Blue River Area CVB, (800) 852-4242.

RESTRICTIONS

Pets: On leash only. **Fires:** Fire ring only. **Alcoholic Beverages:** Allowed. **Vehicle Maximum Length:** 45 ft. **Other:** Wi-Fi.

TO GET THERE

Located 5 mi. west of Port Huron. From I-94: Take Exit 262, travel north 8 mi. to Lapeer Rd., then east 0.25 mi. From I-69: Take Exit 196, travel north 0.5 mi. to Lapeer Rd., then east 0.25 mi. Roads are mostly wide and well maintained, with adequate shoulders.

LAKE LEELANAU   MAP, B-1
Lake Leelanau RV Park

3101 Lake Shore Dr., 49653. T: (231) 256-7236; www.lakeleelanaurvpark.com.

🚐 ★★★★	⛺ ★★★
Beauty: ★★★★	Site Privacy: ★★★★
Spaciousness: ★★★★	Quiet: ★★★★
Security: ★★★★	Cleanliness: ★★★★
Insect Control: ★★★★	Facilities: ★★★★

Check out all the boats and fishing gear at Lake Leelanau RV Park and you'll know one of the main draws for this campground. Located on 700 feet of frontage on the shores of Lake Leelanau, the campground offers easy access to 21 miles of clear waters for boating, fishing, and other water activities. The campground also has a boat launch, gas pump, and 98 boat docks available for rent. A safe sandy beach with a large, shallow swimming area attracts big and little swimmers. Sites are mostly grassy and scattered among trees. Lakefront sites are mostly open and grassy with a concrete pad and patio. Laid out in a series of loops, the campground has a typical site width of 30 feet, 116 seasonal campers, and 15 pull-through sites. Paved roads make it easy to maneuver RVs and boat trailers in the campground. An extra is the free pipe organ concerts every Sunday evening, played on the 3,576-pipe, 62-rank pipe organ right in the office.

BASICS

Operated By: Donald & Marilyn Wilson. **Open:** May 1–Oct. 15. **Site Assignment:** Reservations w/ 1-night deposit; refund (minus $5) w/ 14-day notice. **Registration:** At campground office. **Fee:** Summer/holidays, $40–$49; off-season, $13 less/day; cash, check, credit card. **Parking:** At site.

FACILITIES

Number of RV-only Sites: 244. **Hookups:** Electric (20 amps), water, sewer, cable TV. **Each Site:** Picnic table, fire ring. **Dump Station:** Yes. **Laundry:** Yes. **Pay Phone:** Yes. **Restrooms and Showers:** Yes. **Fuel:** Yes. **Propane:** Yes. **Internal Roads:** Paved, in good condition. **RV Service:** No. **Market:** 3 mi. **Restaurant:** 3 mi. **General Store:** No. **Vending:** Yes. **Swimming:** Yes. **Playground:** Yes. **Other:** Lake Leelanau, sandy beach, badminton, sports field, horseshoes, volleyball, boat dock, boat ramp, marina. **Activities:** Swimming, fishing, boating (rental motorboats, pontoons, canoes, paddleboats, Seadoos available), scheduled activities. **Nearby Attractions:** Historic Fishtown, orchards, wineries, Manitou Island, excursion boats, Sleeping Bear Sand Dunes, beaches, golf, casino, Interlochen Music Camp. **Additional Information:** Leelanau Peninsula Chamber of Commerce, (231) 256-9895.

RESTRICTIONS

Pets: On leash only. **Fires:** Fire ring only. **Alcoholic Beverages:** Allowed. **Vehicle Maximum Length:** 40 ft.

TO GET THERE

From the junction of Hwy. 204 and CR 643, drive 3.5 mi. south on CR 643. Roads are mostly wide and well maintained, with adequate shoulders.

LUDINGTON   MAP, C-1
Crystal Lake Best Holiday
Trav-L-Park

1884 West Hansen Rd., 49454. T: (231) 757-4510.

🚐 ★★★★	⛺ ★★★
Beauty: ★★★	Site Privacy: ★★★★
Spaciousness: ★★★★	Quiet: ★★★★
Security: ★★★★	Cleanliness: ★★★★
Insect Control: ★★★★	Facilities: ★★★★

A rural lakeside campground near Ludington, Crystal Lake Best Holiday Trav-L-Park offers secluded sites with a choice of shade or open. The typical site width is 30 feet. There are 30 seasonal campers and no pull-through sites. A nice plus is that children camp free. The wooded campground also has a very clean, tiled bathroom which must see more than the usual once-a-day cleaning. The lake has a nice sandy walk-out beach, that is also kept very clean. The best sites, of course, are as close to the lake as possible. Security measures include owners who keep a close watch on the campground to make sure it stays a clean, quiet, family-oriented facility. Their efforts seem to be working.

BASICS

Operated By: City of Crystal Falls. **Open:** Apr. 1–Nov. 1. **Site Assignment:** Reservations w/ 1-night deposit; refund (minus $5) w/ 7-day notice. **Registration:** At front gate. **Fee:** $32; cash, check, credit card. **Parking:** At site.

FACILITIES

Number of RV-only Sites: 160. **Hookups:** Electric (20, 30 amps), water, sewer. **Each Site:** Picnic table, fire ring. **Dump Station:** Yes. **Laundry:** Yes. **Pay Phone:** Yes. **Restrooms and Showers:** Yes. **Fuel:** No. **Propane:** Yes. **Internal Roads:** Paved/gravel, in good condition. **RV Service:** No. **Market:** 3 mi. west. **Restaurant:** 3 mi. west. **General Store:** Yes. **Vending:** Yes. **Swimming:** Yes. **Playground:** Yes. **Other:** Crystal Lake, sandy beach, rec hall, coin games, boat dock, fishing lake, mini-golf, basketball, badminton, sports field, horseshoes, hiking trails, volleyball, snack bar, ice-cream parlor. **Activities:** Swimming, hiking, fishing, boating (rental rowboats, canoes, kayaks, paddleboats), scheduled weekend activities. **Nearby Attractions:** Lake Michigan, Pere Marquette River, harbor, SS *Badger* cruises, beaches, dunes, antiques, scenic drives, arts & crafts, White Pine Village, golf, tennis, charter fishing, lighthouse, seaplane rides. **Additional Information:** Ludington Area CVB, (231) 845-0324, www.ludington.org.

RESTRICTIONS

Pets: On leash only. **Fires:** Fire ring only. **Alcoholic Beverages:** Allowed. **Vehicle Maximum Length:** Inquire ahead. **Other:** Historic Town.

TO GET THERE

From west junction of US 10 and US 31, drive 3 mi. east on US 10/31, then 1.5 mi. north on Stiles Rd. and 0.5 mi. east on Hansen Rd. Roads are generally wide and well maintained, with narrow shoulders in spots.

LUDINGTON　　　MAP, C-1
Poncho's Pond

5335 West Wallace Rd., 49431. T: (888) 308-6602; www.poncho.com.

 ★★★★★　　 ★★★★

Beauty: ★★★★		Site Privacy: ★★★★★
Spaciousness: ★★★★★		Quiet: ★★★★
Security: ★★★★★		Cleanliness: ★★★★★
Insect Control: ★★★★★		Facilities: ★★★★★

Poncho's Pond has a well-deserved reputation as a quality place to stay. Located in Ludington, only 2 miles from Lake Michigan beaches, Poncho's isn't content to rest on its laurels. The friendly owners keep a close watch on maintenance and are always looking for ways to improve the campground. Cleanliness is tops as are the lighted, paved roads. The campground boasts two pools—one for children and families, the other for adults, along with an adult spa. Laid out in a series of loops, the campground has a typical site width of 35 feet, 55 seasonal campers, and 85 pull-through sites. Located in the center of the park is a pleasant three-acre pond stocked with fish to keep young anglers happy. Sites are mostly open and level, with the most popular ones being by the pond. Each lot has cable TV at no extra charge. For security, owners live on site and make sure the campground is secure. Even though the owners of Poncho's Pond and nearby Vacation Station have the same last name, they are not related. Both have top-notch facilities.

BASICS

Operated By: Robert Smith Jr. & Carol Smith. **Open:** Apr. 1–Oct. 31. **Site Assignment:** Reservations w/ 1-night deposit; refund w/ 7-day notice. **Registration:** At campground office. **Fee:** $35–$40; cash, check, credit card. **Parking:** At site.

FACILITIES

Number of RV-only Sites: 202. **Number of Tent-only Sites:** 8. **Hookups:** Electric (30, 50 amps), water, sewer, cable TV, phone. **Each Site:** Picnic table, fire ring. **Dump Station:** Yes. **Laundry:** Yes. **Pay Phone:** Yes. **Restrooms and Showers:** Yes. **Fuel:** No. **Propane:** Yes. **Internal Roads:** Paved, in good condition. **RV Service:** Yes. **Market:** 2 blocks. **Restaurant:** 2 blocks. **General Store:** Yes. **Vending:** Yes. **Swimming:** Yes. **Playground:** Yes. **Other:** Pond, rec hall, pavilion, coin games, spa, basketball, movies, badminton, sports field, horseshoes, volleyball, club house. **Activities:** Swimming, fishing, boating (rental paddleboats available), scheduled activities. **Nearby Attractions:** Lake Michigan, Pere Marquette River, harbor, SS Badger cruises, illuminated cross, beaches, dunes, antiques, scenic drives, arts & crafts, White Pine Village, golf, tennis, charter fishing, lighthouse, seaplane rides. **Additional Information:** Ludington Area CVB, (877) 420-6618.

RESTRICTIONS

Pets: On leash only. **Fires:** Fire ring only. **Alcoholic Beverages:** Allowed. **Vehicle Maximum Length:** 45 ft.

TO GET THERE

Take US 31 north to the first Ludington exit (S. Pere Marquette Rd./Old US 31), turn left on S. taking you straight into Poncho's Pond. Roads are wide and well maintained, with broad shoulders.

LUDINGTON　　　MAP, C-1
Vacation Station RV Park

4895 West US 10, 49431. T: (877) 856-0390; www.vacationstationrvpark.com.

🚐 ★★★★★　　⛺ ★★★★

Beauty: ★★★★		Site Privacy: ★★★★★
Spaciousness: ★★★★★		Quiet: ★★★★★
Security: ★★★★★		Cleanliness: ★★★★★
Insect Control: ★★★★★		Facilities: ★★★★★

Ask a camping family to create their dream campground, and this might be it. That's what the Smith family did in 1997. Vacation Station RV Park in Ludington offers the tops in convenience, clean facilities, and activities. Plus, the owners are friendly and want campers to enjoy their stay. Located on one of the state's most beautiful shorelines, the campground has a quiet, natural setting with a neighborhood feel. Adjacent to a family fun park, the campground is within walking distance of restaurants and shopping. Vacation Station has lighted paved roads, a choice of open or shaded sites, and exceptionally clean restrooms and showers. A nice touch is flowers in the restrooms and attention to detail that means more than a daily cleaning. The rural campground has a typical site width of 40 feet, 50 seasonal campers in a secluded area away from overnight campers, and 17 pull-through sites. A clubhouse overlooks a private pond with a fountain. Security includes an on-site manager and regular patrols of the campground.

BASICS

Operated By: The Smith family. **Open:** Apr. 1–Oct. 31. **Site Assignment:** Reservations w/ credit card; refund (minus $5) w/ 7-day notice. **Registration:** At campground office. **Fee:** Apr.–May, $39; May–Sept., $47; Sept.–Oct., $39; cash, check, credit card. **Parking:** At site.

FACILITIES

Number of RV-only Sites: 150. **Hookups:** Electric (20, 30, 50 amps), water, sewer, phone, cable TV. **Each Site:** Picnic table, fire ring. **Dump Station:** No. **Laundry:** Yes. **Pay Phone:** Yes. **Restrooms and Showers:** Yes. **Fuel:** No. **Propane:** Yes. **Internal Roads:** Paved, in good condition. **RV Service:** No. **Market:** Across the street. **Restaurant:** Across the street. **General Store:** Yes. **Vending:** Yes. **Swimming:** Yes. **Playground:** Yes. **Other:** Fishing pond, snack bar, game room, adult spa, rec hall, coin games, basketball, movies, badminton, sports field, horseshoes, volleyball. **Activities:** Swimming, boating, fishing, (rental paddleboats available), scheduled activities. **Nearby Attractions:** Lake Michigan, Pere Marquette River, harbor, SS *Badger* cruises, illuminated cross, beaches, dunes, antiques, scenic drives, arts & crafts, White Pine Village, golf, tennis, charter fishing, lighthouse, seaplane rides. **Additional Information:** Ludington Area CVB, (877) 420-6618.

RESTRICTIONS

Pets: On leash only. **Fires:** Fire ring only. **Alcoholic Beverages:** At sites only. **Vehicle Maximum Length:** No limit.

TO GET THERE

From west junction of US 31/10, drive 0.9 mi. west on US 10. Roads are wide and well maintained, with broad shoulders.

MACKINAW CITY   MAP, A-2
Mackinaw Mill Creek Camping

P.O. Box 728, 49701. T: (231) 436-5584; www.campmackinaw.com.

🚐 ★★★★   ⛺ ★★★★

Beauty: ★★★★	Site Privacy: ★★★★
Spaciousness: ★★★★	Quiet: ★★★★
Security: ★★★★	Cleanliness: ★★★★
Insect Control: ★★★★	Facilities: ★★★★

The beautiful view of Mackinac Bridge is reason enough to try this campground. But there is so much more to make a camper happy. Located in Mackinaw City, Mackinaw Mill Creek Camping has more than 1 mile of shoreline, which means more campers get lakeside spots. Just five minutes from Mackinac Island ferry docks, the campground offers free shuttles to the ferries. Laid out in a series of loops, the campground has level, grassy sites. It offers a choice of shaded or open sites, with a typical site width of 25 feet. There are 20 seasonal campers and no pull-through sites. Reservations are recommended, especially on busy weekends. Quiet time from 10 p.m. to 9 a.m. is enforced, with no generators allowed at any time in the campground. Speed limit is 5 mph. Security measures include a manager who lives on site and provides regular patrols of the campground.

BASICS

Operated By: Richard & Rose Rogala. **Open:** May 1–Oct. 31. **Site Assignment:** Reservations w/ 1-night deposit; refund w/ 7-day notice. **Registration:** At campground office. **Fee:** $20–$35; cash, check, credit card. **Parking:** At site.

FACILITIES

Number of RV-only Sites: 525. **Number of Tent-only Sites:** 75. **Hookups:** Electric (30 amps), water, sewer, Internet. **Each Site:** Picnic table, fire ring. **Dump Station:** Yes. **Laundry:** No. **Pay Phone:** Yes. **Restrooms and Showers:** Yes. **Fuel:** No. **Propane:** Yes. **Internal Roads:** Paved/gravel, in good condition. **RV Service:** No. **Market:** 2 mi. north in Mackinaw City. **Restaurant:** 2 mi. north in Mackinaw City. **General Store:** Yes. **Vending:** Yes. **Swimming:** Yes. **Playground:** Yes. **Other:** Lake Huron, rental cabins, rec hall, basketball, boat pier, foot bridge, mini-golf, coin games, sports field, hiking trails, badminton. **Activities:** Swimming, fishing, boating, hiking, local tours. **Nearby Attractions:** Mackinac Island, golf, casino, Lake Michigan, beaches, Olde Mill State Historic Park, Fort Michilimackinac, antiques, scenic drives, arts & crafts, Mackinac Bridge, Mackinac Bridge Museum. **Additional Information:** Greater Mackinaw City Area Chamber of Commerce, (888) 455-8100.

RESTRICTIONS

Pets: On leash only. **Fires:** Fire ring only. **Alcoholic Beverages:** At sites only. **Vehicle Maximum Length:** No limit. **Other:** No camping motorcyclists. Do not feed seagulls, Canada geese or swans as their droppings may damage the finish on cars or campers.

TO GET THERE

From I-75, take Exit 338 and drive 0.2 mi. south past Ramada Inn, then 2.5 mi. east and south on US 23. Roads are wide and well maintained, with broad shoulders.

MACKINAW CITY   MAP, A-2
Tee Pee Campground

11262 West US 23, 49701. T: (231) 436-5391; www.teepeecampground.com.

🚐 ★★★★   ⛺ ★★★★

Beauty: ★★★★	Site Privacy: ★★★★
Spaciousness: ★★★★	Quiet: ★★★★
Security: ★★★★	Cleanliness: ★★★★
Insect Control: ★★★	Facilities: ★★★

Location is everything, and Tee Pee Campground has a terrific location. On Lake Huron in Mackinaw City, the campground has an excellent view of Mackinac Bridge and Mackinac Island. Some lucky campers can be lulled to sleep by the sounds of the lake lapping the shore. Nightly beach campfires give a friendly atmosphere to the campground, owned by the same family since 1969. Tee Pee is a ten-minute walk from downtown attractions. Laid out in a horseshoe, the campground offers level, mostly shaded sites, a typical site width of 35 feet, six pull-through sites, and eight seasonal campers. Another plus is free shuttle service to ferry boats and a casino. The most popular sites are close to the lake. Reservations are recommended, especially for busy weekends. Quiet hours starting at 10 p.m. are enforced, as is a 5-mph speed limit. Security includes a resident manager and regular camp patrols.

BASICS

Operated By: Gene & Jo Cooley. **Open:** May 15–Oct. 15. **Site Assignment:** Reservations w/ 1-night deposit; refund (minus $5) w/ 48-hour notice. **Registration:** At campground office. **Fee:** Hookup (30 amp), $31; hookup (20 amp), $28; based on 4 people per site; each extra person, $3; cash, check, credit card. **Parking:** At site.

FACILITIES

Number of RV-only Sites: 100. **Hookups:** Electric (20, 30 amps), water. **Each Site:** Picnic table, fire ring. **Dump Station:** Yes. **Laundry:** No. **Pay Phone:** Yes. **Restrooms and Showers:** Yes. **Fuel:** No. **Propane:** No. **Internal Roads:** Gravel, pavement, in good condition. **RV Service:** No. **Market:** 0.5 mi. northwest in Mackinaw City. **Restaurant:** 0.5 mi. northwest in Mackinaw City. **General Store:** Yes, limited. **Vending:** Yes. **Swimming:** Yes. **Playground:** Yes. **Other:** Lake Huron, swimming beach, rec room, coin games, basketball, badminton, sports field, volleyball, horseshoes, bonfire pit, boat dock. **Activities:** Swimming, fishing, boating, local tours. **Nearby Attractions:** Mackinac Island, golf, casino, Lake Michigan, beaches, dunes, ferry, Old Mill Creek State Historic Park, Fort Michilimackinac, antiques, scenic drives, arts & crafts, Mackinac Bridge & Museum. **Additional Information:** Greater Mackinaw City Area Chamber of Commerce, (888) 455-8100.

RESTRICTIONS

Pets: On leash only. **Fires:** Fire ring only. **Alcoholic Beverages:** Allowed. **Vehicle Maximum Length:** 38 ft.

TO GET THERE

Campground is 0.5 mi. south of Mackinaw City on US 23 and Lake Huron. I-75 northbound: take Exit 337, go to US 23, turn right, go .5 mi. south. I-75 southbound: take Exit 338, follow signs for US 23. Roads are wide and well maintained, with broad shoulders.

MANISTIQUE   MAP, A-1
Indian Lake Travel Resort

202 South Country Rd. 455, 49854. T: (906) 341-2807.

🚐 ★★★★   ⛺ ★★★

Beauty: ★★★★	Site Privacy: ★★★★
Spaciousness: ★★★★	Quiet: ★★★★
Security: ★★★★	Cleanliness: ★★★★
Insect Control: ★★★★	Facilities: ★★★★

Located 6 miles west of Manistique, in the heart of the Hiawatha National Forest, Indian Lake Travel Resort is popular for its water attractions. Surrounded by trees, the campground is also quiet and clean. Situated on the southwest shore of Indian Lake, the campground has level, mowed-grass sites with a choice of open or shaded. A safe sandy beach is a nice spot for swimming. The typical site width is 35 feet. The campground has seven seasonal campers and four pull-through sites. The campground charges no fee to launch boats of registered guests. The best sites are closest to Indian Lake. Rates at about $15 are very reasonable for such a popular tourism area.

BASICS

Operated By: Richard & Caroline Ellis. **Open:** May 1–Oct. 30. **Site Assignment:** Reservations w/ 1-night deposit; refund w/ 7-day notice. **Registration:** At campground office. **Fee:** $20–$23; cash, check. **Parking:** At site.

FACILITIES

Number of RV-only Sites: 58. **Hookups:** Electric (20, 30 amps), water, sewer. **Each Site:** Picnic table, fire ring, sewer, water/electric hookup. **Dump Station:** Yes. **Laundry:** Yes. **Pay Phone:** Yes. **Restrooms and Showers:** Yes. **Fuel:** No. **Propane:** Yes. **Internal Roads:** Gravel, in good condition. **RV Service:** No. **Market:** 3 mi. **Restaurant:** 3 mi. **General Store:** Yes, limited. **Vending:** Yes. **Swimming:** Yes. **Playground:** Yes. **Other:** Indian Lake, rec hall, sandy beach, boat ramp, badminton, sports field, horseshoes, hiking trails, volleyball, boat dock. **Activities:** Swimming, fishing, boating (rental rowboats available). **Nearby Attractions:** Lake Michigan, lighthouse, maritime museum, golf, fish hatchery, state parks, antiques, Seney Wildlife Refuge, Big Spring, Siphon Bridge, ATV trails, casino, scenic drive. **Additional Information:** Schoolcraft County Chamber of Commerce, (906) 341-5010.

RESTRICTIONS

Pets: On leash only. **Fires:** Fire ring only. **Alcoholic Beverages:** Allowed. **Vehicle Maximum Length:** No limit.

TO GET THERE

From the junction of US 2 and Hwy. 149, drive 3.75 mi. northwest on Hwy. 149, then 0.5 mi.

north on CR 455. Roads are mostly wide and well maintained, with adequate shoulders.

MARSHALL   MAP, D-2
Tri-Lakes Trails Campground

219 Perrett Rd., 49068. T: (269) 781-2297.

🚐 ★★★   ⛺ ★★★

Beauty: ★★★★   Site Privacy: ★★★
Spaciousness: ★★★★   Quiet: ★★★
Security: ★★★★   Cleanliness: ★★★★
Insect Control: ★★★   Facilities: ★★★

Tri-Lakes Trails Campground has the natural beauty and economic price to make it a popular place for campers who may prefer the tradeoffs of amenities for price and more natural ambiance. The public announcement service is a noisy distraction on a quiet day. Located 5 miles south of Marshall, Tri-Lake Trails has three lakes and a nice nature trail through virgin timber. Sites are open, shaded, and grassy, with 160 seasonals and no pull-through sites. The typical site width is 40 feet, most popular spots are by the lake. Speed limit is 6 mph. The entrance to the campground is beautiful, like a state park with a good road and woods on both sides. A sign along the way does note that "if you don't like rules and common courtesy, please turn around here."

BASICS
Operated By: Jack & Jean Gladstone, Jack & Doris Sebring, Bob & Faye Sebring. **Open:** May 1–Oct. 1. **Site Assignment:** First come, first served or reservations w/ 1-night deposit; refund w/ 7-day notice. **Registration:** At camp office. **Fee:** $25–$32; cash, check. **Parking:** At site.

FACILITIES
Number of RV-only Sites: 250. **Number of Tent-only Sites:** 22. **Hookups:** Electric (30,50 amps), water. **Each Site:** Picnic table, fire ring. **Dump Station:** Yes. **Laundry:** No. **Pay Phone:** Yes. **Restrooms and Showers:** Yes. **Fuel:** No. **Propane:** No. **Internal Roads:** Mostly paved, in great condition. **RV Service:** No. **Market:** 5 mi. north in Marshall. **Restaurant:** 5 mi. north in Marshall. **General Store:** No. **Vending:** Yes. **Swimming:** Yes. **Playground:** Yes. **Other:** Lake, pond, swimming beach, pavilion, activity barn, hiking trails, shuffleboard, mini-golf, horseshoes, recreation field, boat dock, badminton, volleyball. **Activities:** Swimming, fishing, boating (rental rowboats available), scheduled weekend activities. **Nearby Attractions:** Historic homes, golf, antiques, arts & crafts shops, museums. **Additional Information:** Marshall Area Chamber of Commerce, (800) 877-5163.

RESTRICTIONS
Pets: On leash only, cleaned up after, some breeds not allowed. **Fires:** Fire ring only. **Alcoholic Beverages:** Allowed in moderation at site. **Vehicle Maximum Length:** 35 ft. **Other:** No scooters, skateboards, or in-line skates permitted. Small motors only on lake.

TO GET THERE
From the junction of I-94 and I-69, drive 5.75 mi. south on I-69, take Exit 32, then 1.25 mi. east on F

Dr. South, then 0.25 mi. south on Old US 27, then 0.75 mi. west on Perrett Rd. Roads are wide and well maintained, with generally good shoulders, but entrance is through a residential neighborhood. Campground signs ask campers to limit trips through neighborhood and also to be aware of speed traps.

MEARS   MAP, C-1
Sandy Shores Campground and Resort

8595 West Silver Lake Rd., 49436. T: (231) 873-3003; www.sandyshorescampground.com.

🚐 ★★★★   ⛺ ★★★

Beauty: ★★★★   Site Privacy: ★★★★
Spaciousness: ★★★★   Quiet: ★★★★
Security: ★★★★   Cleanliness: ★★★★
Insect Control: ★★★★   Facilities: ★★★★

Located in a sand dune recreation area in Mears, Sandy Shores Campground and Resort is a wonderful spot to enjoy all the area activities. Right next to Silver Lake State Park, the campground is on a good fishing lake with a large sandy beach for swimming. Sites are level and grassy with a choice of open or shade. The typical site width is 40 feet. The campground has 140 seasonal campers and 11 pull-through sites. Restrooms and showers are very clean and well maintained, which must be the result of more than once-a-day attention. Reservations are recommended since about two-thirds of the campground is filled with seasonal campers. Security measures are top-notch, with owners who live on the premises. The campground's central location in the midst of such a popular resort area also means that local law enforcement officials will be patrolling.

BASICS
Operated By: Jerry & Chris Klepper. **Open:** May 1–Oct. 1. **Site Assignment:** Reservations w/ 1-night deposit; refund (minus $5) w/ 7-day notice. **Registration:** At campground office. **Fee:** Full hookup, $39; water/electric, $34; cash, check, credit card. **Parking:** At site.

FACILITIES
Number of RV-only Sites: 210. **Hookups:** Electric (30 amps), water, sewer. **Each Site:** Picnic table, fire ring. **Dump Station:** Yes. **Laundry:** Yes. **Pay Phone:** 2 locations. **Restrooms and Showers:** Yes. **Fuel:** No. **Propane:** Yes. **Internal Roads:** Paved/gravel, in good condition. **RV Service:** No. **Market:** Less than 1 mi. **Restaurant:** Less than 1 mi. **General Store:** Yes. **Vending:** Yes. **Swimming:** Yes. **Playground:** Yes. **Other:** Silver Lake, badminton, volleyball, boat dock, marina, rental cottage. **Activities:** Swimming, fishing, boating (rental rowboats, canoes, sailboats, paddleboats available). **Nearby Attractions:** Lake Michigan, sand dunes, state parks, golf, fruit farms, harbor, riverboats, lighthouse, antiques, gemstone factory, arts & crafts. **Additional Information:** Oceana County Tourism Bureau, (616) 873-3982.

RESTRICTIONS
Pets: On leash only. **Fires:** Fire ring only. **Alcoholic**

Beverages: Allowed. **Vehicle Maximum Length:** No limit.

TO GET THERE
10 mi. west of US 31 exits Shelby and Hart. Roads are well maintained, with adequate shoulders.

MEARS   MAP, C-1
Yogi Bear's Jellystone Park at Silver Lake

reserve america

8239 West Hazel Rd., 49436. T: (231) 873-4502 or (800) 558-2954; www.silverlakejellystone.com, www.reserveamerica.com.

🚐 ★★★★   ⛺ ★★★★

Beauty: ★★★   Site Privacy: ★★★★
Spaciousness: ★★★★   Quiet: ★★★
Security: ★★★★   Cleanliness: ★★★★
Insect Control: ★★★★   Facilities: ★★★★

Located near a large sand dune area and next door to an amusement center, Yogi Bear's Jellystone Park at Silver Lake has enough activities to keep anyone busy. The campground itself boasts a big slate of things to do. Just a quarter-mile away is Silver Lake, 1 mile is the dunes, and 2 miles away is Lake Michigan Beach and a lighthouse. Next door are a slide, go-carts, adventure golf, bumper boats, an arcade, and dune buggy rentals. The campground offers open or shaded sites with a typical site width of 40 feet. There are 40 seasonal campers. Restrooms and showers are cleaned often to keep up with all the children and sand lovers. The heated pool is a refreshing change from the cold Lake Michigan swimming beach. Security measures include regular campground patrols. Reservations are strongly recommended.

BASICS
Operated By: Craig & Lorie Cihak. **Open:** Apr. 15–Oct. 15. **Site Assignment:** Reservations w/ 1-night deposit; refund w/ 30-day notice; cancellation fee, $10. **Registration:** At campground office. **Fee:** Full hookup, $15–$43; electric, $15–$39; rustic, $15–$36. **Parking:** At site.

FACILITIES
Number of RV-only Sites: 200. **Number of Tent-only Sites:** 23. **Hookups:** Electric (20, 30 amps), water, sewer, phone. **Each Site:** Picnic table, fire ring. **Dump Station:** Yes. **Laundry:** Yes. **Pay Phone:** Yes. **Restrooms and Showers:** Yes. **Fuel:** No. **Propane:** No. **Internal Roads:** Paved/gravel, in good condition. **RV Service:** No. **Market:** 1 mi. **Restaurant:** 1 mi. **General Store:** Yes. **Vending:** Yes. **Swimming:** Yes. **Playground:** Yes. **Other:** Rec hall, pavilion, coin games, fishing pond, mini-golf, basketball, shuffleboard, movies, horseshoes, volleyball, rental trailers, rental cabins, sports field. **Activities:** Swimming, fishing, scheduled activities. **Nearby Attractions:** Lake Michigan, sand dunes, state parks, golf, fruit farms, harbor, riverboats, lighthouse, antiques, gemstone factory, arts & crafts. **Additional Information:** Oceana County Tourism Bureau, (616) 873-3982.

RESTRICTIONS

Pets: On leash only. No pets in rental units. **Fires:** Fire ring only. **Alcoholic Beverages:** Allowed. **Vehicle Maximum Length:** No limit.

TO GET THERE

From US 31, take Hart exit and drive 5.5 mi. west on Polk Rd./56th Ave./Fox Rd., then 0.5 mi. west on Hazel Rd. Roads are wide and well maintained, with adequate shoulders.

MIDLAND   MAP, C-2
Valley Plaza RV Park

5221 Bay City Rd., 48642. T: (800) 262-0006; www.valleyplazaresort.com/old/rvpark.cfm.

🚐 ★★★   ⛺ n/a

Beauty: ★★★	Site Privacy: ★★★★
Spaciousness: ★★★★	Quiet: ★★★
Security: ★★★★	Cleanliness: ★★★★
Insect Control: ★★★★	Facilities: ★★★★

Campers can get spoiled at Valley Plaza RV Park with all the luxury features in the recreation complex. Located 5 miles south of Midland, the campground is behind a recreation complex that includes a motel, restaurant, theater, bowling alley, health club, tanning beds, indoor mini-golf, arcade, and more. This is not an out-in-the-country kind of campground. It is more like an open space with trees that still have a bunch of growing to do to provide shade. Sites are mostly open with a typical site width of 30 feet. There are 12 seasonal campers and 55 pull-through sites. The campground has a three-acre lake with a sandy beach and seasonal water sports. Sites are within a well-illuminated and fenced area, ensuring privacy. Be aware that no tents are permitted. Many campers come to enjoy the facilities at the campground as well as those at the recreation complex. Security is tops with a security patrol that keeps a close eye on the area.

BASICS

Operated By: Jason Raponis. **Open:** Mar. 1–Nov. 23. **Site Assignment:** Reservations w/ 1-night deposit; refund (minus $5) w/ 7-day notice. **Registration:** At campground office. **Fee:** $25–$31; cash, check, credit card. **Parking:** At site.

FACILITIES

Number of RV-only Sites: 77. **Hookups:** Electric (30, 50 amps), water, sewer. **Each Site:** Picnic table, fire pit, grill, patio. **Dump Station:** Yes. **Laundry:** Yes. **Pay Phone:** Yes. **Restrooms and Showers:** Yes. **Fuel:** Yes. **Propane:** Yes. **Internal Roads:** Paved, in good condition. **RV Service:** No. **Market:** 5 mi. north in Midland. **Restaurant:** Yes. **General Store:** Yes. **Vending:** Yes. **Swimming:** Yes. **Playground:** Yes. **Other:** Lake, rec hall, pavilion, coin games, wading pool, sauna, whirlpool, fishing pond, mini-golf, basketball, badminton, horseshoes, volleyball, boat dock, adults' room, sports field. **Activities:** Swimming, fishing, boating (rental paddleboats, kayaks available), scheduled activities. **Nearby Attractions:** Bowling, mini-golf, hiking trails, outdoor concert park, farmers' market, Alden B. Down Home & Studio, Chippewa Nature Center, Dow Gardens, antiques,

arts & crafts, golf, casino. **Additional Information:** Midland County CVB, (888) 464-3526.

RESTRICTIONS

Pets: On leash only. **Fires:** Fire ring only. **Alcoholic Beverages:** Allowed. **Vehicle Maximum Length:** No limit. **Other:** No tents allowed.

TO GET THERE

From the junction of I-75 and US 10, take Exit 162B and drive 10 mi. west on US 10 to Bay City Rd. exit, then drive 0.1 mi. west on Bay City Rd. Roads are wide and well maintained, with broad shoulders.

MILAN   MAP, D-3
KC Campground

14048 Sherman Rd., 48160. T: (734) 439-1076; www.kccampgroundmilan.com.

🚐 ★★★   ⛺ ★★★

Beauty: ★★★	Site Privacy: ★★★
Spaciousness: ★★★	Quiet: ★★★
Security: ★★★★	Cleanliness: ★★★
Insect Control: ★★★	Facilities: ★★★

A rural campground with mostly shaded sites in a grassy meadow, KC Campground is located 3 miles east of Milan. The best sites are along a very small pond used for swimming. The campground has a typical site width of 30 feet, with 20 seasonal campers and 15 pull-through sites. Laid out in a series of loops, the campground has separate tent areas with more green space and privacy. Quiet time between 10 p.m. and 8 a.m. is enforced, and no motorcycles, minibikes, or ATVs are allowed. Reservations are recommended during the annual Milan Bluegrass Festival in August. The festival draws top names in Bluegrass entertainment. Security measures at the campground include an owner and manger who live on site, one entrance/exit road, and regular patrols of the campground.

BASICS

Operated By: Mark & Peggy Ann Gaynier. **Open:** Apr. 1–Oct. 31. **Site Assignment:** Reservations w/ 1-night deposit; refund w/ 72-hour notice. **Registration:** At campground office. **Fee:** Electric/water, $25; tent, $20; cash, check, credit card. **Parking:** At site.

FACILITIES

Number of RV-only Sites: 100. **Number of Tent-only Sites:** 50. **Hookups:** Electric (20, 30 amps), water. **Each Site:** Picnic table, fire ring. **Dump Station:** Yes. **Laundry:** No. **Pay Phone:** No. **Restrooms and Showers:** Yes. **Fuel:** No. **Propane:** Yes. **Internal Roads:** Gravel, in good condition. **RV Service:** No. **Market:** 3 mi. west in Milan. **Restaurant:** 3 mi. west in Milan. **General Store:** Yes, limited. **Vending:** Yes. **Swimming:** Yes. **Playground:** Yes. **Other:** Swimming pond, rec hall, volleyball, basketball, horseshoes, sports field. **Activities:** Swimming. **Nearby Attractions:** Golf, Cabela's, Cedar Point, Toledo Center of Science & Industry, Greenfield Village, Monroe County Historical Museum, River Raisin Battlefield, Sauders Farm & Craft Village, zoo, Yankee Air museum, antiques. **Additional Information:** Monroe County Convention & Tourism Bureau, (800) 252-3011.

RESTRICTIONS

Pets: On leash only. **Fires:** Fire ring only. **Alcoholic Beverages:** At sites only. **Vehicle Maximum Length:** 54 ft.

TO GET THERE

From US 23 take Exit 25 and go 2 mi. to Plank Rd. Go southeast 2 mi. to Sherman Rd., then left on Sherman 0.25 mi. to campground. Roads are mostly wide and well maintained, but Plank Rd. has narrow shoulders, and the access road is bumpy, with gravel.

MONROE   MAP, D-3
Harbortown RV Resort

reserve america

14931 LaPlaisance Rd., 48161. T: (734) 384-4700; www.reserveamerica.com.

🚐 ★★★★   ⛺ ★

Beauty: ★★★	Site Privacy: ★★★
Spaciousness: ★★★	Quiet: ★★
Security: ★★★★★	Cleanliness: ★★★★★
Insect Control: ★★★★★	Facilities: ★★★★★

Opened in spring of 2000, Harbortown RV Resort is a state-of-the-art facility in Monroe that includes Time Out Family Recreation Center. Bring plenty of coins for the activities. Offering easy access from I-75, the campground is only 1 mile from Lake Erie and all its water sports. Laid out in a series of loops, the campground offers level, open, paved sites with a typical site width of 30 feet. There are 80 pull-throughs. Facilities are squeaky clean. A full-time staff must be at work constantly to keep the campground in such tip-top shape. Security is great; it doesn't seem likely anyone would enter or exit without being seen. Tents are permitted, but there is no separate section for them. Tent campers must pay the regular fee for an RV site. Harbortown seems like a campground of the future. There are several opportunities for improvement, however. One would be the addition of propane for sale; it's not easy to find nearby. Another would be the need for some shade trees; that will come with time when the landscaping has a chance to mature. The last is the installation of a hedge or other sound buffer next to the train tracks bordering one edge of the campground.

BASICS

Operated By: Private operator. **Open:** All year. **Site Assignment:** Reservations w/ 1-night deposit; refund w/ 48-hour notice. **Registration:** At campground office. **Fee:** Premier, $39; water/electric, $33; cabins, $130; cash, check, credit card. **Parking:** At site.

FACILITIES

Number of Multipurpose Sites: 250. **Hookups:** Electric (20, 30, 50 amps), water, sewer, phone, cable TV. **Each Site:** Picnic table, fire ring. **Dump Station:** Yes. **Laundry:** Yes. **Pay Phone:** Yes. **Restrooms and Showers:** Yes. **Fuel:** No. **Propane:** No. **Internal Roads:** Paved, in good condition. **RV Service:** No. **Market:** Next door. **Restaurant:** Next door. **General Store:** Yes. **Vending:** Yes. **Swimming:** Yes. **Playground:** Yes.

Other: Rec hall, coin games, mini-golf, movies, horseshoes, volleyball, go-carts, 18-hole golf course, sports field, rental cabins, batting cages, modem access available. **Activities:** Swimming, scheduled activities. **Nearby Attractions:** Cabela's, outlet mall, Lake Erie, Vietnam War Memorial, Heck Park, historic tours, Monroe County Historical Museum, River Raisin Battlefield Visitor Center, antiques, arts & crafts, Navarre-Anderson Trading Post Complex. **Additional Information:** Monroe County Convention & Tourism Bureau, (800) 252-3011.

RESTRICTIONS

Pets: On leash only. **Fires:** Fire ring only. **Alcoholic Beverages:** Allowed. **Vehicle Maximum Length:** No limit.

TO GET THERE

From the junction of I-75 and LaPlaisance Rd., take Exit 11 and drive 0.5 mi. west on LaPlaisance Rd. Roads are wide and well maintained, with broad shoulders.

MONTAGUE   MAP, C-1
Trailway Campground

4540 Dowling St., 49437. T: (231) 894-4903.

🚐 ★★★★   ▲ ★★★★

Beauty: ★★★   Site Privacy: ★★★
Spaciousness: ★★★   Quiet: ★★★★
Security: ★★★★   Cleanliness: ★★★★
Insect Control: ★★★★   Facilities: ★★★

Although the campground offers little activities of its own, it does provide a fish-cleaning hut and complimentary fish freezing. That tells you what the major draw is. Jerry's Campground in Montague is across from beautiful White Lake and two blocks from the public boat launch. It is also at the south end of the Montague/Hart Bike Trail. Most people use Jerry's Campground as a base to enjoy area activities. Golf is nearby, and shops and dining are within walking distance. A campground in town, Jerry's has mostly open, flat, grassy sites with a typical site width of 30 feet. The campground has 25 seasonal campers and 21 pull-through sites. Quiet hours from 10 p.m. to 7 a.m. are enforced. Security measures are good, with patrols and local police always close at hand.

BASICS

Operated By: The City of Montague. **Open:** Late Apr.–mid Oct. **Site Assignment:** Reservations w/ 1-night deposit; refund w/ 2-week notice. **Registration:** At campground office or by phone. **Fee:** $25; cash, check. **Parking:** At site.

FACILITIES

Number of RV-only Sites: 51. **Number of Tent-only Sites:** 4. **Hookups:** Electric (30, 50,110 amps), water, sewer, cable TV. **Each Site:** Picnic table. **Dump Station:** Yes. **Laundry:** No. **Pay Phone:** No. **Restrooms and Showers:** Yes. **Fuel:** No. **Propane:** Yes. **Internal Roads:** Gravel, in good condition. **RV Service:** No. **Market:** 1 mi. **Restaurant:** Walking distance. **General Store:** Next door. **Vending:** Yes. **Swimming:** No. **Playground:** Yes. **Other:** Pavilion, horseshoes, fish-cleaning station. **Activities:** None. **Nearby Attractions:** Lake Michigan, White Lake, marinas, Michigan's Adventure Amusement Park, White River Lighthouse Museum, golf, bike trail, mini-golf, world's largest weather vane. **Additional Information:** White Lake Area Chamber of Commerce, (800) 879-9702.

RESTRICTIONS

Pets: On leash only. **Fires:** Common fire pit available. **Alcoholic Beverages:** Allowed in moderation. **Vehicle Maximum Length:** No limit.

TO GET THERE

From north: take US 31 south to Fruitvale Rd. (B86 Exit), go right on Fruitvale Rd. to the 4-way stop. Turn left at the stop onto Water St. and continue for 3.5 mi. to the traffic light in downtown. Roads are wide and well maintained, with broad shoulders.

MORAN   MAP, A-2
Brevort Lake Campground—
Hiawatha National Forest

reserve america

120 Campground Rd., 49760. T: (906) 292-0098; www.reserveamerica.com.

🚐 ★★★★   ▲ ★★★★

Beauty: ★★★★   Site Privacy: ★★★
Spaciousness: ★★★★   Quiet: ★★★
Security: ★★★★   Cleanliness: ★★★★
Insect Control: ★★★★   Facilities: ★★★

Brevort Lake is located 15 minutes from the Mackinac Bridge. This 4,400-acre all-sports lake is surrounded by 85 percent federal land, making it a very popular and one of the larger lakes in this area. Stretching 7 miles from end to end, it is a good-size lake filled with many different fish specie, perfect for the fisherman at heart, including northern pike, yellow perch, bluegills, sunfish, muskies, ciscoes, rock bass, bowfin, long-nose gar, white sucker, carp, black crappie, walleye, smallmouth bass, largemouth bass, hybrid bluegill, pumpkin-seed sunfish, rainbow trout, brook trout, smelt, brown and black bullhead. There was a walleye reef put in on the north side of the lake in the early 1990s and just recently modified to enhance the fish quality of this lake. Also, if you are a history buff, a self-guided tour will allow you to go back in time and/or memory to days of the Great Depression, when folks were hungry and jobs were few. Young men looked to the newly created Civilian Conservation Corps (CCC) as an opportunity to earn money to help feed their families. In creating the CCC, President Franklin D. Roosevelt saw it as a way to put such men to work and, at the same time, revitalize the country's ravaged natural resources. Much of the CCC's work centered on national forests like the Hiawatha (it was then the Marquette National Forest). On the St. Ignace Ranger District (former Moran Ranger District) are a number of CCC sites, including camps, work projects, and plantations. Some of the work done at Brevort Lake Campground included a bathhouse, log shelters, toilets, wells, tables, bulletin boards, and fireplaces. A gravel road from US 2 to the park area was also constructed. Improvements to those facilities have been made by St. Ignace Ranger District personnel.

BASICS

Operated By: U.S. Forest Service. **Open:** May 11–Oct. 1. **Site Assignment:** 2-night minimum; 3-night minimum on holidays. **Registration:** At office. **Fee:** Single, $14. **Parking:** At park.

FACILITIES

Number of Multipurpose Sites: 68. **Hookups:** None. **Each Site:** Fire pit, picnic table. **Dump Station:** Yes. **Laundry:** No. **Pay Phone:** Yes. **Restrooms and Showers:** Yes. **Fuel:** No. **Propane:** No. **Internal Roads:** Paved. **RV Service:** No. **Market:** No. **Restaurant:** No. **General Store:** No. **Vending:** No. **Swimming:** Yes. **Playground:** No. **Activities:** Biking, boating, canoeing, fishing, wildlife viewing.

RESTRICTIONS

Pets: Pets must be restrained or on a leash at all times while in developed recreation areas. **Fires:** In fire rings, stoves, grills, or fireplaces provided for that purpose. **Alcoholic Beverages:** Not allowed. **Vehicle Maximum Length:** Call ahead. **Other:** Please do not bring firewood from home.

TO GET THERE

Campground is located 20 mi. west of St. Ignace. From US 2, turn north on Brevort Camp Rd. (FR 3108), right at FR 3473 to the campground entrance.

MT. PLEASANT   MAP, C-2
Shardi's Hide-Away

340 North Loomis Rd., 48858. T: (989) 773-4268.

🚐 ★★★   ▲ ★★★

Beauty: ★★★   Site Privacy: ★★★
Spaciousness: ★★★   Quiet: ★★★
Security: ★★★   Cleanliness: ★★★
Insect Control: ★★   Facilities: ★★★

A rural campground in a semiwooded setting, Shardi's Hide-Away is located 6 miles east of Mount Pleasant. Sites are level, mostly shaded and with a typical site width of 25 feet. There are no seasonal campers and the campground has eight pull-through sites. The campground is a popular place for deer hunters and campers who enjoy mushroom and berry picking. The playground features a big wooden boat and a jeep, which are hits with youngsters. The 10-mph speed limit is rather high, but traffic generally travels slower because of the gravel and dirt road. Reservations are highly recommended during festival times—April for the Maple Syrup Festival, May for the Highland Scottish Festival, July for the Bluegrass Festival and Antique Engine Show, and August for the Isabella County Fair.

BASICS

Operated By: The Miller Family. **Open:** All year. **Site Assignment:** Reservations w/ 1-night deposit; no refunds. **Registration:** At campground office. **Fee:** $16–$24; cash, check, credit card. **Parking:** At site.

FACILITIES

Number of RV-only Sites: 102. **Number of Tent-only Sites:** 10. **Hookups:** Electric (20, 30, 50 amps), water, sewer. **Each Site:** Picnic table, fire ring. **Dump Station:** Yes. **Laundry:** No. **Pay Phone:** Yes. **Restrooms and Showers:** Yes. **Fuel:** No. **Propane:** No. **Internal Roads:** Gravel/dirt, in fair condition. **RV Service:** No. **Market:** 6 mi. west in Mt. Pleasant. **Restaurant:** 6 mi. west in Mt. Pleasant. **General Store:** Yes. **Vending:** No. **Swimming:** Yes. **Playground:** Yes. **Other:** Pavilion, rental cabins, hiking trails, shuffleboard, volleyball, horseshoes, sand hill, basketball, tetherball, fishing pond, badminton, recreation field. **Activities:** Swimming, fishing, hiking. **Nearby Attractions:** Casino, horse & car race tracks, golf, canoeing, tubing, fishing, antiques, farmers' market. **Additional Information:** Mt. Pleasant Area CVB, (800) 772-4433.

RESTRICTIONS

Pets: On leash only. **Fires:** Fire ring only. **Alcoholic Beverages:** Allowed at sites only. **Vehicle Maximum Length:** No limit.

TO GET THERE

From the junction of US 27 and Hwy. 20, drive 3.5 mi. east on Hwy. 20, then 2.5 mi. north on Loomis Rd. Roads are wide and well maintained, with broad shoulders, except for Loomis Rd., which is a rough gravel surface.

MUNISING   MAP, A-1
Wandering Wheels Campground

P.O. Box 419, 49862. T: (906) 387-1580

🚐 ★★★★   ▲ ★★★

Beauty: ★★★★	Site Privacy: ★★★★
Spaciousness: ★★★★	Quiet: ★★★★
Security: ★★★★	Cleanliness: ★★★★
Insect Control: ★★★★	Facilities: ★★★★

Wandering Wheels Campground, 3.5 miles east of Munising, is surrounded by scenic attractions and activities. The campground is quite nice in and of itself. Sites are level, secluded, and mostly wooded. About half are grassy and half are dirt. The typical site width is 40 feet and the campground has 44 pull-through sites. Free showers in the sparkling-clean facilities are a nice plus. Wandering Wheels also has camping cabins with gas fireplaces that cost about $50 to $60 for up to four persons, which is cheaper than most motels and far more pleasant. Reservations are recommended for the campsites and cabins. Security is good, with owners keeping a close eye on the campground.

BASICS

Operated By: William Ramsey, Jr. **Open:** May 1–Oct. 15. **Site Assignment:** Reservations w/ 1-night deposit; refund w/ 7-day notice. **Registration:** At campground office. **Fee:** In season, $15.95–$26.95; out of season, $14.95–$15.95; cash, check, credit card. **Parking:** At site.

FACILITIES

Number of RV-only Sites: 92. **Number of Tent-only Sites:** 12. **Hookups:** Electric (20, 30, 50 amps), water, sewer, phone, cable TV. **Each Site:** Picnic table, fire ring. **Dump Station:** Yes. **Laundry:** Yes. **Pay Phone:** Yes. **Restrooms and Showers:** Yes. **Fuel:** No. **Propane:** Yes. **Internal Roads:**

Gravel, in good condition. **RV Service:** No. **Market:** Less than 1 mi. **Restaurant:** Next door. **General Store:** Yes. **Vending:** Yes. **Swimming:** Yes. **Playground:** Yes. **Other:** Rec room, coin games, basketball, badminton, sports field, horseshoes, volleyball, rental cabins. **Activities:** Swimming, sports. **Nearby Attractions:** Waterfalls, Pictured Rocks National Lakeshore, golf, Alger Underwater Preserve, boat tours, shipwreck tours, glass-bottom boat tours, snowmobiling. **Additional Information:** Munising Visitors Bureau, (906) 387-2138.

RESTRICTIONS

Pets: On leash only. **Fires:** Fire ring only. **Alcoholic Beverages:** Allowed at site only. **Vehicle Maximum Length:** No limit.

TO GET THERE

From town, drive 3.5 mi. east on Hwy. 28. Roads are wide and well maintained w/ broad shoulders.

NILES   MAP, D-1
Spaulding Lake Campground

2305 Bell Rd., 49120. T: (269) 684-4445 or (269) 684-1760.

🚐 ★★★★   ▲ ★★★

Beauty: ★★★★	Site Privacy: ★★★★
Spaciousness: ★★★★	Quiet: ★★★★
Security: ★★★★	Cleanliness: ★★★★
Insect Control: ★★★★	Facilities: ★★★★

On the Indiana/Michigan border in Niles, Spaulding Lake Campground is a good base to cover a wide area, including Amish country in Northern Indiana. The campground has three man-made ponds, one for swimming and two for fishing. Just 5 miles north of South Bend, Spaulding Lake is the closest campground to Notre Dame. No fishing license is required at the spring-fed stocked pond. Sites are level and grassy, with a typical site width of 30 feet. The campground has 15 seasonal campers and 44 pull-through sites. Be aware that the campground does not permit alcohol anywhere on the premises. The campground and facilities are clean and well maintained. Rules and security measures are enforced. The goal is a family-oriented campground where people feel comfortable camping. Spaulding Lake Campground is always busy, so the owners must be achieving their goal.

BASICS

Operated By: Nolan & Virginia Spaulding. **Open:** Apr. 1–Oct. 31. **Site Assignment:** First come, first served or reservations w/ 1-night deposit; refund (minus $5) w/ 7-day notice. **Registration:** At campground office. **Fee:** $25–$27 (2 people); cash, check. **Parking:** At site.

FACILITIES

Number of RV-only Sites: 106. **Number of Tent-only Sites:** 14. **Hookups:** Electric (20, 30, 50 amps), water, sewer, cable TV, phone. **Each Site:** Picnic table, fire ring. **Dump Station:** Yes. **Laundry:** Yes. **Pay Phone:** Yes. **Restrooms and Showers:** Yes. **Fuel:** No. **Propane:** No. **Internal Roads:** Gravel, in good condition. **RV Service:** No.

Market: 3 mi. **Restaurant:** 3 mi. **General Store:** Yes. **Vending:** Yes. **Swimming:** Yes. **Playground:** Yes. **Other:** Swimming lake, fishing lake, rec hall, coin games, trout stream, basketball, shuffleboard, badminton, sports field, pavilion, horseshoes, volleyball, hiking trails, modem hookup in office. **Activities:** Swimming, fishing, hiking. **Nearby Attractions:** Amish Country, Fort St. Joseph Museum, historic homes, antiques, arts & crafts, Fernwood Botanic Garden & Nature Center, Notre Dame. **Additional Information:** Four Flags Area Council on Tourism, (269) 684-7444.

RESTRICTIONS

Pets: On leash only. **Fires:** Fire ring only. **Alcoholic Beverages:** Not allowed. **Vehicle Maximum Length:** No limit. **Other:** No outside firewood permitted.

TO GET THERE

From the junction of US 12 and Hwy. 51, drive 0.25 mi. south on Hwy. 51, then 2 mi. east on Bell Rd. Roads are generally wide and well maintained, with adequate shoulders.

ORTONVILLE   MAP, D-3
Clearwater Campground

1140 South M-15, 48462. T: (248) 627-3820.

🚐 ★★★   ▲ ★★★

Beauty: ★★★	Site Privacy: ★★★
Spaciousness: ★★★	Quiet: ★★★
Security: ★★★★	Cleanliness: ★★★
Insect Control: ★★★	Facilities: ★★★

A lakeside campground with open and shaded sites, Clearwater Campground is located in Ortonville. Laid out in a series of loops, the campground has a typical site width of 25 feet. It has 30 seasonal campers and eight pull-through sites. All sites have full hookup, and tents are not allowed on any of the full-hookup sites. Tents are permitted only in the primitive area, which offers more green space and privacy. Quiet time from 10 p.m. to 8 a.m. is enforced, as is a 5-mph speed limit. No minibikes, off-road bikes, or similar vehicles are permitted in the park. The campground also has a rule that any RV that is detrimental to the appearance of the park may be refused registration. The campground manager decides what constitutes a detrimental appearance. Security measures include a resident manager and a gate that requires a card pass to enter.

BASICS

Operated By: Mike & Christie Neadow & Mark & Michaelanne Reis. **Open:** Apr. 15–Oct. 15. **Site Assignment:** Reservations w/ 1-night deposit; refund w/ 7-day notice. **Registration:** At camp office. **Fee:** Up to $50; cash, check. **Parking:** At site.

FACILITIES

Number of RV-only Sites: 209. **Number of Tent-only Sites:** 15. **Hookups:** Electric (30, 50 amps), water, sewer, cable TV, phone. **Each Site:** Picnic table, fire ring. **Dump Station:** No. **Laundry:** Yes. **Pay Phone:** Yes. **Restrooms and Showers:** Yes. **Fuel:** No. **Propane:** Yes. **Internal Roads:** Paved, in good condition. **RV Service:** No. **Market:** 0.25 mi. north in Ortonville. **Restaurant:** Across the street. **General Store:** Yes, limited. **Vending:** Yes. **Swimming:** Yes. **Playground:** Yes. **Other:** Swimming lake, pavilion, mini-golf, sports field, horseshoes. **Activities:** Swimming, fishing, boating (electric motors only), scheduled weekend activities. **Nearby Attractions:** Children's Museum, Huckleberry Railroad, paddle wheeler, museums, Longway Planetarium, Flint River, antiques, golf, arts & crafts. **Additional Information:** Holly Chamber of Commerce, (248) 634-1900.

RESTRICTIONS

Pets: On leash only; 1 pet per site. **Fires:** Fire ring only. **Alcoholic Beverages:** Allowed. **Vehicle Maximum Length:** No limit. **Other:** Tents permitted only on primitive sites.

TO GET THERE

From the junction of I-75 and Hwy. 15, take Exit 91 and drive 6.2 mi. north on Hwy. 15. Roads are wide and well maintained, with broad shoulders.

PENTWATER   MAP, C-1
Whispering Surf Camping Resort

7070 South Lakeshore Dr., 49449. T: (231) 869-5050; www.denaliseed.com/wsurf.html.

🚐 ★★★   ▲ ★★★★

Beauty: ★★★★	Site Privacy: ★★★★
Spaciousness: ★★★★	Quiet: ★★★★
Security: ★★★★	Cleanliness: ★★★★
Insect Control: ★★★★	Facilities: ★★★

One of Michigan's oldest continuously operating resorts, Whispering Surf Camping Resort got its start in 1913. But the campground is not outdated. Full hookups and modern facilities are available, along with free hot showers. Located 4 miles north of Pentwater, between Bass Lake and Lake Michigan, Whispering Surf is forested with oak, pine, and white birch trees. Tucked in the North Woods, the campground offers shaded sites and a private beach. Sites are mostly grassy with a typical site width of 35 feet. There are 20 seasonals that maintain their sites nicely. It's an 8-mile walk to Lake Michigan and its white "singing sands." The campground has a rustic tent area for more green space and privacy. A fishing license is required to fish in the lake. The turn-of-the-century pavilion is now used for recreation and as a meeting place for groups. It is one of the few such pavilions remaining in Michigan.

BASICS

Operated By: Reginald Yaple. **Open:** May 15–Oct. 15. **Site Assignment:** Reservations w/ 1-night deposit; refund w/ 2-week notice. **Registration:** At campground office. **Fee:** $26; cash, check, credit card. **Parking:** At site.

FACILITIES

Number of RV-only Sites: 65. **Number of Tent-only Sites:** 20. **Hookups:** Electric (20, 30 amps), water, sewer. **Each Site:** Picnic table, fire ring. **Dump Station:** Yes. **Laundry:** No. **Pay Phone:** Yes. **Restrooms and Showers:** Yes. **Fuel:** No. **Propane:** No. **Internal Roads:** Gravel, in good condition. **RV Service:** No. **Market:** 1 mi. **Restaurant:** 1 mi. **General Store:** Yes, limited. **Vending:**

Yes. **Swimming:** Yes. **Playground:** Yes. **Other:** Bass Lake, boat dock, game room, rec hall, pavilion, coin games, swimming beach, horseshoes, boat ramp. **Activities:** Swimming, fishing, boating (rental canoe, paddleboats available), scheduled weekend activities. **Nearby Attractions:** Hart-Montague Bike Trail, state parks, White Pine Village, Rose Hawley Museum, lighthouses, Shrine of the Pines, English Double-Decker Bus Tour, historic homes, antiques, Lake Michigan Carferry. **Additional Information:** Pentwater Chamber of Commerce, (231) 869-4150.

RESTRICTIONS

Pets: On leash only. **Fires:** Fire ring only. **Alcoholic Beverages:** Consumed inconspicuously at site. **Vehicle Maximum Length:** No limit.

TO GET THERE

From north junction US 31 and Business US 31, drive 0.6 mi. west on Business US 31, then 1 mi. north on Lake Shore Dr. Roads are mostly wide and well maintained, with adequate shoulders.

PETERSBURG   MAP, D-3
Monroe County KOA/ Toledo North

US 23, Exit 9, 49270. T: (734) 856-4972 or (800) 562-7646; www.koa.com/where/mi/22105.

🚐 ★★★★   ▲ ★★★★

Beauty: ★★★★	Site Privacy: ★★★★
Spaciousness: ★★★★	Quiet: ★★★★
Security: ★★★★	Cleanliness: ★★★★★
Insect Control: ★★★	Facilities: ★★★★

Nestled in maple, oak, and pine trees, Monroe County KOA Kampground is 9 miles north of the Ohio line. Sites are grassy and mostly shaded. Laid out in a series of loops, the campground has a typical site width of 35 feet and 47 pull-through sites. There are no seasonal campers. A two-acre sandy-beach swimming lake is a popular draw. The beach is cleaned and dragged several times a week. The lake has two aerators putting oxygen in the lake year-round. Quiet hours are from 11 p.m. to 7 a.m., when no radio, TV, or voices are to be heard beyond each camping site. No subwoofers on car stereos are allowed at any time. No golf carts or generators are allowed. Security includes traffic control gates and owners who live on the site and provide campground patrols.

BASICS

Operated By: Ray & Donna Crots. **Open:** Apr. 18–Oct. 19. **Site Assignment:** Reservations w/ $50 deposit; refund (less half) w/ 48-hour notice. **Registration:** At campground office. **Fee:** RV, $31–$55; tent $27–$50; cash, check, credit card. **Parking:** At site.

FACILITIES

Number of RV-only Sites: 230. **Number of Tent-only Sites:** 50. **Hookups:** Electric (20, 30, 50 amps), water, sewer. **Each Site:** Picnic table, fire ring. **Dump Station:** Yes. **Laundry:** Yes. **Pay Phone:** Yes. **Restrooms and Showers:** Yes. **Fuel:** No. **Propane:** Yes. **Internal Roads:** Gravel, in good condition. **RV Service:** No. **Market:** 5 mi. south in

Lambertville. **Restaurant:** 5 mi. south in Lambertville. **General Store:** Yes. **Vending:** Yes. **Swimming:** Yes. **Playground:** Yes. **Other:** Rec hall, fishing lake, mini-golf, shuffleboard, tetherball, basketball, horseshoes, baseball, trout pond, volleyball, club room, rental cabins, waterslides, sandy beach, coin games, food wagon. **Activities:** Swimming, fishing, boating (rental rowboats, canoes, kayaks, paddleboats available), schedule weekend activities. **Nearby Attractions:** Golf, Cabela's, Cedar Point, Toledo Center of Science & Industry, Greenfield Village, Monroe County Historical Museum, River Raisin Battlefield, Sauder Farm & Craft Village, Toledo Zoo, Yankee Air Museum, antiques. **Additional Information:** Monroe County Convention & Tourism Bureau, (800) 252-3011.

RESTRICTIONS

Pets: Leash only, $2 extra. **Fires:** Fire rings only; must be extinguished by 11 p.m. **Alcoholic Beverages:** At sites only. **Vehicle Maximum Length:** 40 ft.

TO GET THERE

From the junction of US 23 and Hwy. 50, drive 9 mi. south on US 23, then 200 yards southeast on Summerfield Rd., then 10 yards east on Tunnicliffe Rd. Roads are wide and well maintained, with broad shoulders.

PETERSBURG   MAP, D-3
Pirolli Park

6030 Sylvania-Petersburg Rd., 49270. T: (734) 279-1487; www.pirollipark.com.

🚐 ★★★   ▲ ★★★

Beauty: ★★★	Site Privacy: ★★★
Spaciousness: ★★★	Quiet: ★★★
Security: ★★★★	Cleanliness: ★★★
Insect Control: ★★★	Facilities: ★★★

When leaving Pirolli Park, visitors are not only bade farewell and asked to drive safely, they are also given directions to US 23. Every major stop also has signs directing travelers to the main road. More campgrounds should pick up on that useful idea. Laid out in a series of loops, the campground has 45 seasonal campers, 20 pull-through sites and a typical site width of 30 feet. Sites are level and mostly shaded. Located 2 miles south of Petersburg, the campground does not allow outside firewood to be brought into the area because of infectious tree diseases such as Dutch Elm Disease and because of gypsy moths. Firewood is for sale at the campground. Scheduled activities include such creative themes as cowboys-and-Indians weekend (where children make their own Native American headdress and get a Native American name), grandparents weekend, and law enforcement weekends. Security includes one entrance/exit road, owners who live on site, and regular campground patrols.

BASICS

Operated By: James & Pat Pirolli. **Open:** All year. **Site Assignment:** First come, first served or reservations w/ 1-night deposit; refund w/ 7-day notice. **Registration:** At camp office. **Fee:** $26–$29; check, credit. **Parking:** At site.

FACILITIES

Number of RV-only Sites: 200. **Number of Tent-only Sites:** 50. **Hookups:** Electric (20, 30, 50 amps), water, sewer. **Each Site:** Picnic table, fire ring. **Dump Station:** Yes. **Laundry:** Yes. **Pay Phone:** Yes. **Restrooms and Showers:** Yes. **Fuel:** No. **Propane:** Yes. **Internal Roads:** Paved/gravel, in good condition. **RV Service:** No. **Market:** 2 mi. north in Petersburg. **Restaurant:** 2 mi. north in Petersburg. **General Store:** Yes, well equipped, also sells beer, wine & liquor. **Vending:** No. **Swimming:** Yes. **Playground:** Yes. **Other:** Swimming lake, fishing lake, sports field, horseshoes, volleyball, pavilion, rec hall, driving range, pavilion. **Activities:** Swimming, fishing, scheduled weekend activities. **Nearby Attractions:** Golf, Cabela's, Cedar Point, Toledo Center of Science & Industry, Greenfield Village, Monroe Co. Historical Museum, River Raisin Battlefield, Sauder Farm & Craft Village, Toledo Zoo, Yankee Air Museum, antiques. **Additional Information:** Monroe County Convention & Tourism Bureau, (800) 252-3011.

RESTRICTIONS

Pets: Leash only, no rottweilers, chows, pit bulls, Dobermans, German Shepherds are allowed. **Fires:** Fire ring only. **Alcoholic Beverages:** At sites only. **Vehicle Maximum Length:** 50 ft. (call ahead for details).

TO GET THERE

From the junction of US 23 and Summerfield Rd., take Exit 9, drive 0.25 mi. north on Summerfield Rd., then 1.5 mi. west on Teal Rd., then 1.5 mi. southwest on Ida Center Rd., then 0.25 mi. south on Sylvania-Petersburg Rd. Roads are generally wide and well maintained, with broad shoulders, sometimes becoming narrow shoulders.

PETERSBURG	MAP, D-3
Totem Pole Park	

16333 Lulu Rd., 49270. T: (800) 227-2110 or (734) 279-2110.

🚐 ★★★   🏕 ★★★

Beauty: ★★★		Site Privacy: ★★★
Spaciousness: ★★★		Quiet: ★★★★
Security: ★★★★		Cleanliness: ★★★★
Insect Control: ★★		Facilities: ★★★

A rural campground with open and shaded sites, Totem Pole Park is located 3 miles east of Petersburg. Laid out in a series of loops, the campground has 70 seasonal campers, 26 pull-through sites, and a typical site width of 35 feet. A nice playground features a wooden train and wooden fort. No motors are allowed on the lake, nor are metal, wooden or fiberglass boats. The lake area closes at dark. Most popular RV sites are the 26 pull-throughs. The best tent sites are 120–130 which are grassy and wooded, and offer more privacy. The speed limit is 5 mph, and no off-road vehicles such as motorcycles and ATVs are allowed. The campground adjoins state game land and offers a sandy bottom lake for swimming. Security includes one entrance/exit road and owners who live on site and offer patrols of the campground.

BASICS

Operated By: Carl & Joyce Laming. **Open:** Mid Apr.–mid Oct. **Site Assignment:** Reservations w/ 1-night deposit; refund (minus $5) w/ 7-day notice. **Registration:** At campground office. **Fee:** Electric (50 amp), $33; electric (30 amp), $29; no hookup, $27; cash, check, credit card. **Parking:** At site.

FACILITIES

Number of RV-only Sites: 130. **Number of Tent-only Sites:** Undesignated sites. **Hookups:** Electric (30, 50 amps), water, sewer. **Each Site:** Picnic table, fire ring. **Dump Station:** Yes. **Laundry:** No. **Pay Phone:** Yes. **Restrooms and Showers:** Yes. **Fuel:** No. **Propane:** No. **Internal Roads:** Gravel, in good condition. **RV Service:** No. **Market:** 10 mi. north in Dundee. **Restaurant:** 3 mi. west in Petersburg. **General Store:** Yes. **Vending:** Yes. **Swimming:** Yes. **Playground:** Yes. **Other:** Swimming beach, pond fishing, basketball, horseshoes, sand volleyball, rental cabins, shuffleboard, pavilion, sports field. **Activities:** Swimming, fishing, hayrides, canoeing, scheduled weekend activities. **Nearby Attractions:** Golf, Cabela's, Cedar Point, Toledo Center of Science & Industry, Greenfield Village, Monroe Co. Historical Museum, River Raisin Battlefield, Sauders Farm & Craft Village, zoo, Yankee Air Museum, antiques, Michigan International Speedway. **Additional Information:** Monroe County Convention & Tourism Bureau, (800) 252-3011.

RESTRICTIONS

Pets: On leash only. **Fires:** Fire ring only. **Alcoholic Beverages:** At sites only. **Vehicle Maximum Length:** No limit. **Other:** Family-oriented campground.

TO GET THERE

Located 9 mi. north of Ohio line on US 23. Northbound: Exit 9, west on Summerfield Rd. to Lulu Rd. Southbound: Exit 13 turn right, go to Summerfield Rd., turn left, go to Lulu Rd. Follow signs; campground is only 3 mi. from either exit. Summerfield Rd. is paved but bumpy; Lulu Rd. has a rough gravel surface.

PETOSKEY	MAP, B-2
Petoskey KOA	

1800 North US 31, 49770. T: (800) 933-1574 or (231) 347-0005; www.petoskeykoa.com.

🚐 ★★★★★   🏕 ★★★★

Beauty: ★★★★★		Site Privacy: ★★★★★
Spaciousness: ★★★★★		Quiet: ★★★★★
Security: ★★★★★		Cleanliness: ★★★★★
Insect Control: ★★★★★		Facilities: ★★★★★

In a vacation wonderland, Petoskey KOA is a camper's dream. Facilities are top-notch, cleanliness is A+, activities are varied and many, security and safety measures are excellent, and the folks who run the campground are friendly and hardworking. Campers return again and again to this Petoskey campground and begin to feel part of the Rose family. Laid out in a series of loops, the campground offers level, open, and shaded sites in sloping and level terrain. There are 31 pull-through sites. Nice

landscaping and attention to detail make Petoskey KOA a pleasure to see. No mats or carpets are permitted on grass or ground to keep the area nice. A recreation and activities director has a wealth of programs, including nature programs to educate as well as entertain. A gazebo kitchen with electric cooking burners, sinks, and picnic tables is a welcome facility for campers. A Fun Bus makes it easy to catch the shuttle and leave your car at home or parked with the camper. Security measures include a card-coded gate. A speed limit of 5 mph is enforced.

BASICS

Operated By: The Rose family. **Open:** Apr. 27–Oct. 13. **Site Assignment:** Reservations w/ 1-night deposit; refund w/ 2-week notice; credit cards for 1-night stays, w/ 24-hour notice & one-half deposit cancellation fee. **Registration:** At campground office. **Fee:** $30–$37; cash, check, credit card. **Parking:** At site.

FACILITIES

Number of RV-only Sites: 200. **Number of Tent-only Sites:** 6. **Hookups:** Electric (20, 30, 50 amps), water, sewer, phone, cable TV. **Each Site:** Picnic table, fire ring, grill, patios. **Dump Station:** Yes. **Laundry:** Yes. **Pay Phone:** Yes. **Restrooms and Showers:** Yes. **Fuel:** No. **Propane:** Yes. **Internal Roads:** Paved/gravel, in good condition. **RV Service:** No. **Market:** 3 mi. in Petosky. **Restaurant:** 3 mi. in Petosky. **General Store:** Yes. **Vending:** Yes. **Swimming:** Yes. **Playground:** Yes. **Other:** Hot tub, horseshoes, rec hall, sports field, rental cabins, game room, movies, rental cottages, coin games, volleyball, nature classes, recreation & activities director, local tours, rental cottages, shuttle bus, rental cars. **Activities:** Swimming, scheduled activities, bingo, scavenger hunts. **Nearby Attractions:** Golf, marina, go-carts, bike trails, horseback riding, Lake Michigan Beach, Mackinac Island, casino, Tunnel of Trees Drive, historic Bay View, Little Traverse Bay, antiques, Little Traverse Historical Museum. **Additional Information:** Petoskey/Harbor Springs/Boyne County Visitors Bureau, (800) 845-2828.

RESTRICTIONS

Pets: On leash only. **Fires:** Fire ring only. **Alcoholic Beverages:** Allowed. **Vehicle Maximum Length:** No limit.

TO GET THERE

From the junction of Hwy. 119 and US 31, drive 1 mi. north on US 31. Roads are wide and well maintained, with broad shoulders.

QUINCY	MAP, D-2
Cottonwood Resort	

219 Wildwood Beach Rd., 49082. T: (517) 639-4415.

🚐 ★★★★   🏕 ★★★★

Beauty: ★★★★		Site Privacy: ★★★
Spaciousness: ★★★		Quiet: ★★★★
Security: ★★★		Cleanliness: ★★★★
Insect Control: ★★		Facilities: ★★★

Marble Lake is the centerpiece of Cottonwood Resort, located 8 miles southeast of Coldwater. The lake leads into Branch County's Chain of Lakes, offering 2,500 acres of water in six lakes for fishing and water activities. A rural campground with shaded level sites, Cottonwood has 87 of its sites occupied by seasonal campers, leaving 6 for short-term campers. The typical site width is 25 feet, and the campground has four pull-throughs. Quiet time is 11 p.m. to 7 a.m., and the speed limit is 5 mph. The campground offers easy access from the interstate, but be sure to check that a site is available before planning to stop. Owners live on site to help with security measures.

BASICS

Operated By: Barney & Eunice Pohl, Roy, Darla, Bailey, & Halle Pohl. **Open:** May 1–Oct. 15. **Site Assignment:** Reservations w/ 1-night deposit; refund w/ 7-day notice. **Registration:** At campground office. **Fee:** $25–$32; cash, check. **Parking:** At site.

FACILITIES

Number of RV-only Sites: 93. **Number of Tent-only Sites:** 4. **Hookups:** Electric (30 amps), water, sewer. **Each Site:** Picnic table, fire ring. **Dump Station:** Yes. **Laundry:** No. **Pay Phone:** Yes. **Restrooms and Showers:** Yes. **Fuel:** No. **Propane:** No. **Internal Roads:** Gravel, in good condition. **RV Service:** No. **Market:** 8 mi. northwest in Coldwater. **Restaurant:** 8 mi. northwest in Coldwater. **General Store:** Yes. **Vending:** Yes. **Swimming:** Yes. **Playground:** Yes. **Other:** Marble Lake, swimming beach, rental cottages, horseshoes, rec hall, video games, volleyball, boat ramp, sports field. **Activities:** Swimming, fishing, boating (rental fishing boats available). **Nearby Attractions:** Bowling, golf, summer theater, Branch County Historical Society, antiques, drive-in theaters, motor speedway, historic homes, museums, arts & crafts shops. **Additional Information:** Branch County Tourism Bureau, (800) 969-9333.

RESTRICTIONS

Pets: On leash only. **Fires:** Fire ring only. **Alcoholic Beverages:** Allowed. **Vehicle Maximum Length:** No limit.

TO GET THERE

From the junction of I-69 and US 12, drive 4.75 mi. east on US 12, then 2.25 mi. south on Main St. and Ray Quincy Rd., then 1 mi. west on Wildwood Rd. Roads are wide and well maintained, with broad shoulders.

RAPID RIVER   MAP, A-1
Whitefish Hill RV Park and Campground

8455 US 2, 49878. T: (800) 476-6515; www.whitefishhill.com.

🚐 ★★★	🏕 ★★
Beauty: ★★★	Site Privacy: ★★★
Spaciousness: ★★★	Quiet: ★★★
Security: ★★★	Cleanliness: ★★★★
Insect Control: ★★★★	Facilities: ★★★

An RV area in a mobile home park, Whitefish Hill RV Park and Campground is just 1.5 miles from

---

access waters to Little Bay De Noc. Located 2 miles east of Rapid River, the campground offers open, level, grassy sites with eight pull-throughs. The typical site width is 30 feet. A nice benefit is facilities that are open 24 hours a day. The focal point of the park is an old barn that houses an office, showers, small kitchen, and activity room. The campground is a popular base for fishing and hunting. Whitefish Hill opens earlier in the season and stays open later than many other campgrounds, which makes it handy for outdoor enthusiasts who want a home base that is modern rather than rustic. Security includes owners who live on site and keep an eye on the campground.

BASICS

Operated By: Ed & Pat Violette. **Open:** Apr. 30–Nov. 30. **Site Assignment:** Reservations w/ 1-night deposit; refund w/ 7-day notice; credit cards w/ 10-day notice. **Registration:** At campground office. **Fee:** $26 for 2 people; cash, check, MC, V, D. **Parking:** At site.

FACILITIES

Number of RV-only Sites: 23. **Number of Tent-only Sites:** 2. **Hookups:** Electric (30, 50 amps), water, sewer, cable TV, phone. **Each Site:** Picnic table, fire ring. **Dump Station:** Yes. **Laundry:** Yes. **Pay Phone:** Yes. **Restrooms and Showers:** Yes. **Fuel:** No. **Propane:** Yes. **Internal Roads:** Paved/gravel, in good condition. **RV Service:** No. **Market:** 1 mi. **Restaurant:** 1 mi. **General Store:** No. **Vending:** Yes. **Swimming:** Yes. **Playground:** Yes. **Other:** Game room, rental RVs, sports field, horseshoes, basketball, sauna, fish-cleaning station, charter fishing, firewood available, modem hookup in rec room. **Activities:** Fishing, hunting. **Nearby Attractions:** Little Bay De Noc, fishing, swimming, boating, scenic drives, Lake Michigan, Delta County Historical Museum, Sandpoint Lighthouse, antiques, arts & crafts. **Additional Information:** Delta County Area Chamber of Commerce, (888) 335-8264.

RESTRICTIONS

Pets: On leash only. **Fires:** Fire ring only. **Alcoholic Beverages:** Allowed. **Vehicle Maximum Length:** No limit.

TO GET THERE

From US 2 and US 41, drive 2.5 mi. east on US 2 (look for red historic barn). Roads are wide and well maintained, with adequate shoulders.

RIVERSIDE   MAP, D-1
Coloma/St. Joseph KOA

3527 Coloma Rd., 49084. T: (269) 849-3333; www.koa.com.

🚐 ★★★★	🏕 ★★★★
Beauty: ★★★	Site Privacy: ★★★
Spaciousness: ★★★★	Quiet: ★★★★
Security: ★★★★	Cleanliness: ★★★★
Insect Control: ★★★★	Facilities: ★★★★

With easy interstate access and a big roster of activities, Benton Harbor/St. Joseph KOA is a popular camping spot. Reservations are recommended, especially for busy weekends and peak season. The area is

---

known for having a festival almost every summer and early fall weekend. The campground offers level, grassy sites with a choice of open or shaded. The typical site width is 45 feet. The campground has 12 seasonal campers and 18 pull-through sites. A small pond offers a chance to dunk a worm, but don't count on catching much. Lake Michigan is only five minutes away, with great fishing and other water activities. The hot tub is a nice touch, but sometimes it gets crowded. Quiet time is enforced beginning at 11 p.m., and rowdy people can be ejected. Security is also good with regular patrols and owners who keep a close watch on the campground. The goal is to have a nice, family-oriented campground, and it seems to be working at Benton Harbor/St. Joseph KOA.

BASICS

Operated By: Ginter & Ursela Bansen. **Open:** Apr. 15–Oct. 15. **Site Assignment:** Reservations w/ 1-night deposit; refunds (minus $5) w/ 3-day notice. **Registration:** At campground office. **Fee:** $30–$38; cash, check, credit card. **Parking:** At site.

FACILITIES

Number of Multipurpose Sites: 125. **Hookups:** Electric (50 amps), water, sewer. **Each Site:** Picnic table, fire ring. **Dump Station:** Yes. **Laundry:** Yes. **Pay Phone:** Yes. **Restrooms and Showers:** Yes. **Fuel:** No. **Propane:** Yes. **Internal Roads:** Paved, in good condition. **RV Service:** No. **Market:** Fruit market. **Restaurant:** 3 mi. west. **General Store:** Yes. **Vending:** Yes. **Swimming:** May 26–Sept.5 & hot tub. **Playground:** Yes. **Other:** Fishing pond, sauna, hot tub, rental cabins, tennis, basketball, volleyball, shuffleboard, mini-golf, movies, rec hall, badminton, sports field, hiking trails, horseshoes. **Activities:** Swimming, fishing, hiking, scheduled activities. **Nearby Attractions:** Lake Michigan, fruit farms, charter boats, golf, Deer Forest, Curious Kids' Museum, Krasl Art Center, nature center, wineries, atomic plants, tennis, historic walking tour, antiques, arts & crafts. **Additional Information:** St. Joseph Today, (616) 982-0032.

RESTRICTIONS

Pets: On leash only. **Fires:** Fire ring only. **Alcoholic Beverages:** Allowed. **Vehicle Maximum Length:** 80 ft.

TO GET THERE

From I-94 use Exit 34, then 4 mi. north on I-196 use Exit 4, east 200 yards. Roads are wide and well maintained, with broad shoulders.

ROSCOMMON   MAP, B-2
Higgins Hills RV Park

3800 West Federal Hwy., 48653. T: (800) 478-8151 or (989) 275-8151; www.michcampgrounds.com/higginshills.

🚐 ★★★★	🏕 ★★★★
Beauty: ★★★★	Site Privacy: ★★★★
Spaciousness: ★★★★	Quiet: ★★★★
Security: ★★★★	Cleanliness: ★★★★
Insect Control: ★★★★	Facilities: ★★★★

Location is everything, and Higgins Hills RV Park certainly has it. With easy access to I-75 and US 27, the campground is in a large lake resort area. Year-round activities abound, and Higgins Hills is open all year with limited facilities in the winter. One mile east of Higgins Hills, the campground offers level, shaded sites with a typical site width of 30 feet. There are 35 seasonal campers and 32 pull-through sites. The campground has abundant natural hardwoods and pine trees, deer, and other wildlife. It's only minutes to Higgins Lake and Au Sable River, and there are groomed snowmobile trails as well as cross-country and downhill skiing. The campground also is home to the Michigan Snowshoe Center, which offers a large selection of snowshoes and sporting equipment. Facilities are very clean, and owners provide on-site security.

BASICS

Operated By: The Carr family. **Open:** All year. **Site Assignment:** Credit card required for reservations w/ 72-hour cancellation policy. **Registration:** At campground office. **Fee:** $25–$28 (2 people); each additional person, $3; cash, check, credit card. **Parking:** At site.

FACILITIES

Number of RV-only Sites: 98. **Number of Tent-only Sites:** 8. **Hookups:** Electric (20, 30 amps), water, sewer, phone. **Each Site:** Picnic table, fire ring. **Dump Station:** Yes. **Laundry:** Yes. **Pay Phone:** Yes. **Restrooms and Showers:** Yes. **Fuel:** No. **Propane:** Yes. **Internal Roads:** Gravel, in good condition. **RV Service:** No. **Market:** 5 mi. **Restaurant:** 1 mi. **General Store:** Full-service store. **Vending:** Yes. **Swimming:** Yes. **Playground:** Yes. **Other:** Rec room, coin games, basketball, shuffleboard, badminton, sports field, volleyball, horseshoes, hiking trails, rental cabins, rental RVs. **Activities:** Hiking, scheduled weekend activities. **Nearby Attractions:** Higgins Lake, Au Sable River, fishing, canoeing, hunting, Wellington Farm Park, state parks, golf, fish hatchery, bowling, antiques, arts & crafts. **Additional Information:** Higgins Lake-Roscommon Chamber of Commerce, (989) 275-8760.

RESTRICTIONS

Pets: Leash only, no aggressive breeds. **Fires:** Fire ring only. **Alcoholic Beverages:** At site only. **Vehicle Maximum Length:** No limit. **Other:** 8 people per site max., 2 units per site max.

TO GET THERE

From I-75, Exit 244, Higgins Hills is 1 mi. west. From US 127, Military Rd. exit, Higgins Hills is 4.5 mi. east. Roads are wide and well maintained, with adequate shoulders.

SAULT STE. MARIE   MAP, A-2
Soo Locks Campground and RV Park

1001 East Portage Ave., 49783. T: (906) 632-3191.

🚐 ★★★★   ⛺ ★★★

Beauty: ★★★   Site Privacy: ★★★
Spaciousness: ★★★   Quiet: ★★★★
Security: ★★★★   Cleanliness: ★★★★
Insect Control: ★★★★   Facilities: ★★★

Watch the freighters travel through Soo Locks from your campsite at Soo Locks Campground and RV Park in Sault Ste. Marie. With sites on St. Mary's River, the facility is the closest campground to the locks. Sites are mostly open and grassy, with a typical site width of 25 feet. Campers can walk to the locks and watch ships pass through. Restaurants and other facilities are within one block. The campground has nine pull-through sites. Complimentary coffee is a nice welcoming touch. Facilities are very clean and well maintained, and owners provide good security. The best sites are closest to the river. Be aware that the area can be quite cold in May and in October when the campground is open. The camping experience is definitely worth it, but be sure to bring plenty of warm blankets and clothing if camping during those times.

BASICS

Operated By: Bob & Helen Collia. **Open:** May 1–Oct. 20. **Site Assignment:** Reservations w/ 1-night deposit; refund (minus $5) w/ 2-week notice. **Registration:** At campground office. **Fee:** $22–$30; cash, check, credit card. **Parking:** At site.

FACILITIES

Number of RV-only Sites: 100. **Hookups:** Electric (30 amps), water. **Each Site:** Picnic table, fire ring. **Dump Station:** Yes. **Laundry:** Yes. **Pay Phone:** Yes. **Restrooms and Showers:** Yes. **Fuel:** No. **Propane:** No. **Internal Roads:** Paved, gravel, in good condition. **RV Service:** No. **Market:** 1 block. **Restaurant:** 1 block. **General Store:** Yes. **Vending:** Yes. **Swimming:** No. **Playground:** Yes. **Other:** St. Mary's River, boat dock, rec room, coin games, adults room w/ complimentary coffee. **Activities:** Fishing, boating, boat tours. **Nearby Attractions:** Soo Locks, Locks Park Historic Walkway, Johnston Homestead, Museum Ship Valley Camp, River of History Museum, dinner cruises, boat tours, Tower of History, casino. **Additional Information:** Sault Area Chamber of Commerce & Convention & Bureau, (906) 632-3301.

RESTRICTIONS

Pets: On leash only. Some breeds not allowed. **Fires:** Fire ring only. **Alcoholic Beverages:** At site. **Vehicle Maximum Length:** No limit.

TO GET THERE

From the junction of I-75 and Easterday, take Exit 394 and drive 0.1 mi. west on Easterday, then 3 mi. north and east on Portage. Roads are wide and well maintained, with adequate shoulders.

SMYRNA   MAP, C-2
Double R Ranch Camping Resort

4424 Whites Bridge Rd., 48809. T: (800) 734-3575 or (877) 794-0520; www.doublerranch.com.

🚐 ★★★★   ⛺ ★★★★

Beauty: ★★★★   Site Privacy: ★★★★
Spaciousness: ★★★★   Quiet: ★★★★
Security: ★★★★   Cleanliness: ★★★★
Insect Control: ★★★★   Facilities: ★★★★

Double R Ranch Camping Resort is a ranch, resort, and campground with so much going for it, it's hard to know where to start. As a resort, it has a full slate of activities, like two heated swimming pools as well as a river and a variety of water sports. As a ranch, it has horses and one of West Michigan's best trail rides over hills, along forest paths, and fording streams, plus a bunkhouse where guests can enjoy the Wild West without roughing it. As a campground, it features camping by the river. Sites are mostly grassy and level, with a typical site width of 40 feet. The campground has ten seasonal sites and ten pull-throughs. Located 20 miles from Grand Rapids, the campground has a choice of open or shaded sites. The best sites are the wooded ones along Flat River. The Ironhorse golf course alone draws plenty of golfers with its 3,365-yard championship golf course.

BASICS

Operated By: Richard & Mary Reeves. **Open:** May 1–Sept. 15. **Site Assignment:** Reservations w/ $25 deposit; refund w/ 2-week notice; extra charge for early arrival. **Registration:** At campground office. **Fee:** $30 (2 people); each additional person, $3; cash, check, credit card. **Parking:** At site.

FACILITIES

Number of RV-only Sites: 100. **Hookups:** Electric (30 amps), water, sewer. **Each Site:** Picnic table, fire ring. **Dump Station:** Yes. **Laundry:** Yes. **Pay Phone:** Yes. **Restrooms and Showers:** Yes. **Fuel:** No. **Propane:** No. **Internal Roads:** Gravel, in good condition. **RV Service:** No. **Market:** 2 mi. **Restaurant:** 2 mi. **General Store:** Yes. **Vending:** Yes. **Swimming:** Yes. **Playground:** Yes. **Other:** Flat River, rec hall, rec room, coin games, boat ramp, float trips, basketball, horseback riding trails, badminton, sports field, horseshoes, hiking trails, volleyball, snack bar, adult lounge, rental chalets, motel, 9-hole golf course. **Activities:** Swimming, fishing, golf, hiking, boating (rental canoes available), horseback riding (rental horses available), tubing, scheduled weekend activities. **Nearby Attractions:** Gerald Ford Museum, Fredrick Meijer Gardens, zoo, Michigan Adventure Amusement Park, Roger B. Chaffee Planetarium, golf, tennis, rivers & lakes, antiques, Wooden Shoe Factory. **Additional Information:** Grand Rapids/Kent County CVB, (800) 678-9859.

RESTRICTIONS

Pets: On leash only. **Fires:** Fire ring only. **Alcoholic Beverages:** Allowed at camp site only. **Vehicle Maximum Length:** No limit.

TO GET THERE

Take West River Dr. exit from Hwy. 131 at Comstock Park East to M 44. Turn north on M 44. Follow M 44 to Belding to White Bridge Rd. Turn south on White Bridge, 2.5 mi. to Double R Ranch. Roads are wide and well maintained, with adequate shoulders.

ST. IGNACE   MAP, A-2
Castle Rock Mackinac Trail Campark

2811 Mackinac Trail, 49781.
T: (800) 333-8754 or (906) 643-9222;
www.stignace.com/lodging/castlecamp.

🚐 ★★★★   ⛺ ★★★★

Beauty: ★★★★   Site Privacy: ★★★★
Spaciousness: ★★★★   Quiet: ★★★★
Security: ★★★★   Cleanliness: ★★★★
Insect Control: ★★★★   Facilities: ★★★★

The sunsets alone are worth a night at Castle Rock Mackinac Trail Campark. Sites are nestled between landscaped trees on Lake Huron with half a mile of lake frontage in view of Mackinac Island. Campsites are available on or off the beach. Castle Rock provides the only beach camping on Lake Huron with a Mackinac Island view. The campground features 2,000 feet of sandy beach. Sites are level and grassy with a typical site width of 30 feet. There are seven pull-throughs and a choice of open or shaded. Less than a mile from the St. Ignace city limits, the campground is next to a federal forest with trails and bird-watching. A nearby casino and a ferry service for Mackinac Island offer free shuttle service from the campground. The most popular sites are on the beach. Reservations are strongly recommended. Security includes careful watches of the campground, along with the assistance of local law officials, if necessary.

BASICS
Operated By: Charles & Delores Muscott. **Open:** May 15–Oct. 10. **Site Assignment:** Reservations w/ $20 deposit; refund w/ 3-day notice. **Registration:** At campground office. **Fee:** $19–$24; cash, check, credit card. **Parking:** At site.

FACILITIES
Number of RV-only Sites: 95. **Number of Tent-only Sites:** 15. **Hookups:** Electric (20, 30, 50 amps), water, sewer. **Each Site:** Picnic table, fire ring. **Dump Station:** Yes. **Laundry:** Yes. **Pay Phone:** Yes. **Restrooms and Showers:** Yes. **Fuel:** No. **Propane:** No. **Internal Roads:** Paved/gravel, in good condition. **RV Service:** No. **Market:** 2 blocks. **Restaurant:** 2 blocks. **General Store:** Yes. **Vending:** No. **Swimming:** Yes. **Playground:** Yes. **Other:** Sandy beach, rec room, fishing pond, coin games, boat ramp, boat dock, badminton, sports field, horseshoes, volleyball, free casino shuttle, free ferry shuttle. **Activities:** Swimming, fishing, boating, local tours. **Nearby Attractions:** Castle Rock, Mackinac Bridge, Mackinac Island, Mackinaw City, Deer Ranch, ice arena, golf, casino, Fort De Baude Indian Museum, Marquette Mission Park & Museum of Ojibwa Culture, New France Discovery Center & Father Marquette National Memorial, Soo Locks, Fort Michilimackinac, Tahqomenon Falls. **Additional Information:** St. Ignace Tourism Assoc., (800) 338-6660.

RESTRICTIONS
Pets: On leash only. **Fires:** Fire ring only. **Alcoholic Beverages:** Allowed. **Vehicle Maximum Length:** No limit.

TO GET THERE
Located 4 mi. north of the Mackinac Bridge. From I-75, Exit 348, go right 0.25 block, then left onto Mackinac Trail; it's 4 blocks to park entrance. Roads are wide and well maintained, with broad shoulders.

ST. IGNACE   MAP, A-2
Foley Creek Campground— Hiawatha National Forest

reserve america

3103 N. Mackinac Trail, 49781. T: (906) 643-8403; www.reserveamerica.com.

🚐 ★★★★   ⛺ ★★★★

Beauty: ★★★★   Site Privacy: ★★★
Spaciousness: ★★★   Quiet: ★★★
Security: ★★★★   Cleanliness: ★★★★
Insect Control: ★★★★   Facilities: ★

The Foley Creek Campground is only 3 miles from the St. Ignace city limits and is an excellent campground for visitors to use as a home base. St. Ignace has a variety of recreational opportunities for your enjoyment: the Father Marquette National Memorial, the Ojibwa Museum, and ferry services to historic Mackinac Island. There are also organization-sponsored activities, good restaurants, golfing, sandy beaches, and interesting shops. Your visit to St. Ignace will be a memorable one. Foley Creek Campground is located within the Hiawatha National Forest and contains 850 miles of perennial streams, a majority of which is considered trout habitat and half of which serves as spawning and rearing habitat for anadromous fish species. There are 77 miles of Great Lakes shoreline. Certain areas of the shoreline provides unique habitat for some rare plant species. There are five river systems with established canoe trails, including the Whitefish, Sturgeon River, Indian River, Carp River (all federally designated Wild and Scenic River), and the Au Train. There are a total of 287 lakes contained within the forest boundaries, which total 20,834 acres. There are 378 miles of nonmotorized trails and 318 miles of motorized trails. There are 24 developed campgrounds, 17 dispersed campsites, and 18 primitive campgrounds throughout the forest.

BASICS
Operated By: U.S. Forest Service. **Open:** May 11–Oct. 1. **Site Assignment:** Reservations must be made at least 3 days in advance. **Registration:** At office. **Fee:** Single, $12. **Parking:** At park.

FACILITIES
Number of Multipurpose Sites: 212. **Hookups:** None. **Each Site:** Picnic table, fire ring. **Dump Station:** No. **Laundry:** No. **Pay Phone:** No. **Restrooms and Showers:** Yes. **Fuel:** No. **Propane:** No. **Internal Roads:** Paved. **RV Service:** No. **Market:** No. **Restaurant:** No. **General Store:** No. **Vending:** No. **Swimming:** No. **Playground:** No. **Activities:** Biking, bird-watching, hiking, photog

RESTRICTIONS
Pets: Pets must be restrained or on a leash at all times while in developed recreation areas. **Fires:** In fire rings, stoves, grills, or fireplaces provided for that purpose. **Alcoholic Beverages:** Not allowed. **Vehicle Maximum Length:** Call ahead. **Other:** Do not bring firewood from home.

TO GET THERE
From the Mackinac Bridge, continue north on I-75 to Exit 352. Turn right after 1 block and right on the Mackinac Trail (H 63) south 2 mi. to the campground on the east side of Mackinac Trail.

ST. IGNACE   MAP, A-2
St. Ignace/Mackinac Island KOA

1242 US 2 West, 49781. T: (906) 643-9303 or (800) 562-0534; www.simikoa.com.

🚐 ★★★★   ⛺ ★★★★

Beauty: ★★★★   Site Privacy: ★★★★
Spaciousness: ★★★★   Quiet: ★★★★
Security: ★★★★   Cleanliness: ★★★★★
Insect Control: ★★★★   Facilities: ★★★★

Located in the heart of Michigan vacationland, St. Ignace-Mackinac Island KOA offers easy access to I-75 and quality facilities. Sites are grassy, wooded, and secluded, with a typical site width of 50 feet; there are 80 pull-throughs. Campers are greeted with a travel info packet when they register, and the friendly staff is very helpful in recommending local attractions. The campground has its own attractions—a free Indian museum and a wildlife zoo featuring a live fox, bobcat, peacock, and deer. Campers are invited to hand-feed the deer and take photos. The campground also offers free shuttles to the island ferries and casino. A separate rustic tent area provides more green space and privacy. Campground facilities are very clean, and landscaping shows extra attention to detail.

BASICS
Operated By: Private operator. **Open:** May 1–Oct. 31. **Site Assignment:** Reservations w/ 1-night deposit; refund w/ 3-day notice. **Registration:** At office. **Fee:** RV, $36–$42; tent, $26; check, credit. **Parking:** At site.

FACILITIES
Number of RV-only Sites: 140. **Number of Tent-only Sites:** 60. **Hookups:** Electric (20, 30 amps), water, sewer, phone. **Each Site:** Picnic table, fire ring. **Dump Station:** Yes. **Laundry:** Yes. **Pay Phone:** Yes. **Restrooms and Showers:** Yes. **Fuel:** No. **Propane:** No. **Internal Roads:** Gravel, in good condition. **RV Service:** No. **Market:** 2 mi. **Restaurant:** 1 mi. **General Store:** Yes. **Vending:** Yes. **Swimming:** Yes. **Playground:** Yes. **Other:** Rec room, coin games, rental cabins, mini-golf, badminton, sports field, hiking trails. **Activities:** Swimming, hiking, local tours, free shuttle to ferry & casino. **Nearby Attractions:** Castle Rock, Mackinac Island, Mackinaw City, Deer Ranch, ice arena, golf, casino, Fort De Baude Indian Museum, Marquette Mission Park & Museum of Ojibwa Culture, New France Discovery Center & Father Marquette National Memorial, Soo Locks, Fort Michilimackinac, Tahquamenon

Falls. **Additional Information:** St. Ignace Tourism Assoc., (800) 338-6660.

RESTRICTIONS

Pets: Leash only, cleaned up after. **Fires:** Fire ring only. **Alcoholic Beverages:** Allowed. **Vehicle Maximum Length:** No limit.

TO GET THERE

From Mackinac Bridge: northbound I-75, take Exit 344B (southbound I-75, Exit 344) then go 2.5 mi. west on US 2. Roads are wide and well maintained, with broad shoulders.

THOMPSON   MAP, A-1
Driftwood Shores Resort and RV Park

14045 Yager Rd., 49854. T: (800) 788-3111; www.wmallory.com.

🚐 ★★★★   ⛺ n/a

Beauty: ★★★★   Site Privacy: ★★★★
Spaciousness: ★★★★   Quiet: ★★★★
Security: ★★★★   Cleanliness: ★★★★★
Insect Control: ★★★★★   Facilities: ★★★

For the right kind of camper, Driftwood Shores Resort and RV Park is a sparkling gem. Located on Lake Michigan 6 miles west of Manistique, the campground offers 500 feet of shoreline and a sandy beach with complimentary float tubes. The campground caters to campers ages 55 and up but is open to anyone. What campers won't find are coin games, playgrounds, and activities aimed at children. What campers will find is peaceful surroundings, great fishing and birding, and benches, swings, and gliders overlooking the lake. The sites are mostly back-ins, but there are about five pull-through sites. Campers also are welcome to complimentary videos and all the free driftwood they can burn. The campground got its name from the wealth of driftwood that continues to wash up on its shores. The driftwood is the legacy of a sawmill that used to be nearby in the 1880s. It closed in the 1930s, but the driftwood keeps coming, enough for campers to take home as souvenirs, artists to gather up for painting and carving, and still enough left over for campfires. A huge stone fireplace is available for everyone to enjoy. Security measures include owners who live on site and offer regular patrols of the campground.

BASICS

Operated By: Bill & Diane Mallory. **Open:** May 1–Oct. 31; weather permitting. **Site Assignment:** Reservations w/ full pay; refund w/ 2-week notice. **Registration:** At campground office. **Fee:** $25; cash, check, credit card. **Parking:** At site.

FACILITIES

Number of RV-only Sites: 15. **Hookups:** Electric (30, 50 amps), water. **Each Site:** Picnic table, fire ring. **Dump Station:** Yes. **Laundry:** Yes. **Pay Phone:** No. **Restrooms and Showers:** Yes. **Fuel:** No. **Propane:** No. **Internal Roads:** Gravel, in good condition. **RV Service:** No. **Market:** 6 mi. **Restaurant:** 6 mi. **General Store:** No. **Vending:** No. **Swimming:** No. **Playground:** No. **Other:** Lake Michigan, rocky beach, sports field, rental cabins,

rental lodge rooms. **Activities:** Swimming, fishing. **Nearby Attractions:** Lighthouse, maritime museum, golf, fish hatchery, state parks, antiques, Seney Wildlife Refuge, Big Spring, Siphon Bridge, snowmobile trails, casino, scenic drive. **Additional Information:** Schoolcraft County Chamber of Commerce, (906) 341-5010.

RESTRICTIONS

Pets: On leash only. **Fires:** Fire ring only. **Alcoholic Beverages:** Allowed. **Vehicle Maximum Length:** No limit. **Other:** No tent camping.

TO GET THERE

Turn onto Little Harbor Rd. at the US 2/149 Caution light at the Thompson Outpost. Go 0.2 mi on Little Harbor, turn toward the lake on Thompson Rd. and you will see Driftwood Shores. Roads are mainly wide and well maintained, with adequate shoulders.

TIPTON   MAP, D-2
Ja Do Campground

5603 US 12, 49287. T: (517) 431-2111; www.michcampgrounds.com/jado.

🚐 ★★★   ⛺ ★★★

Beauty: ★★★   Site Privacy: ★★★★
Spaciousness: ★★★★   Quiet: ★★★★
Security: ★★★★   Cleanliness: ★★★★
Insect Control: ★★★★   Facilities: ★★★

Nestled in rolling hills in Tipton, Ja Do Campground offers open and shaded sites with a typical site width of 50 feet. Laid out in a series of loops, the campground has primitive sites with more green space and privacy for tent campers. The campground has 30 seasonal campers. A stocked fishing pond set in the woods has a nature trail leading to it. Quiet hours are 11 p.m. to 7 a.m., when all children must be at sites. No loud music is allowed at any time. Motorcycles, ATVs, minibikes, and scooters cannot be ridden in the campground. No bike riding is allowed after dark. Speed limit is 10 mph, a bit high for such a family-friendly campground. Security is good, with owners keeping a close watch.

BASICS

Operated By: Doug & Kay Miller. **Open:** May 1–Oct. 15. **Site Assignment:** Reservations w/ 1-night deposit; refund (minus $5) w/ 5-day notice. **Registration:** At campground office. **Fee:** Electric/water, $25; rustic, $22; cash, check, credit card. **Parking:** At site.

FACILITIES

Number of RV-only Sites: 100. **Number of Tent-only Sites:** 30. **Hookups:** Electric (30, 50 amps), water, sewer, phone. **Each Site:** Picnic table, fire ring. **Dump Station:** Yes. **Laundry:** Yes. **Pay Phone:** Yes. **Restrooms and Showers:** Yes. **Fuel:** No. **Propane:** Yes. **Internal Roads:** Gravel, in good condition. **RV Service:** No. **Market:** 1 mi. **Restaurant:** 1 mi. **General Store:** Yes, limited. **Vending:** Yes. **Swimming:** No. **Playground:** Yes. **Other:** Pond, basketball, horseshoes, hiking trails, volleyball. **Activities:** Fishing, hayrides, glow parades. **Nearby Attractions:** Michigan International Speedway, Irish Hills, golf, Mystery Hill, mini-golf, waterskiing, Prehis-

toric Forest, museums, St. Joseph's Shrine, Stagecoach Stop USA, Irish Hills Towers. **Additional Information:** Lenawee Conference & Visitors Bureau, (800) 682-6580.

RESTRICTIONS

Pets: On leash only. **Fires:** Fire ring only. **Alcoholic Beverages:** No public display of alcohol. **Vehicle Maximum Length:** 40 ft.

TO GET THERE

US 12 Irish Hills 5 mi. west of M 52, 6 mi. east of M 50. Roads are wide and well maintained, with adequate shoulders.

TRAVERSE CITY   MAP, B-1
Holiday Park Campground

4860 US 31 South, 49864. T: (231) 943-4410; www.michcampgrounds.com/holidaypark.

🚐 ★★★★   ⛺ ★★★★

Beauty: ★★★★   Site Privacy: ★★★★
Spaciousness: ★★★★   Quiet: ★★★★
Security: ★★★★   Cleanliness: ★★★★
Insect Control: ★★★★   Facilities: ★★★★

Nestled in a forest on the shores of Silver Lake, Holiday Park Campground offers quiet, level campsites with a choice of open or shade. Laid out in a loop, the campground has a typical site width of 35 feet, with 15 pull-throughs. Located 7 miles south of Traverse City, the campground is open year-round with limited facilities in the winter. The best sites are on the lakefront—sites 66–75—which have full hookups. Other sites also are available on the lake, where campers can see some grand sunsets. A sandy beach offers nice swimming. Facilities are clean and well maintained and feature such landscaping touches as a split-rail fence and flower beds.

BASICS

Operated By: Michigan Airstreamers Park Assoc. **Open:** Apr. 1–Nov. 1. **Site Assignment:** Reservations w/ 1-night deposit; refund w/ 7-day notice. **Registration:** At camp office. **Fee:** Lakefront, $47; wooded, $42; pines, $38; off-season, $32; check, V, MC, D. **Parking:** At site.

FACILITIES

Number of RV-only Sites: 170. **Hookups:** Electric (20, 30, 50 amps), water, sewer. **Each Site:** Picnic table, fire ring. **Dump Station:** Yes. **Laundry:** Yes. **Pay Phone:** Yes. **Restrooms and Showers:** Yes. **Fuel:** No. **Propane:** Yes. **Internal Roads:** Paved, in good condition. **RV Service:** No. **Market:** 3 mi. **Restaurant:** 3 mi. **General Store:** Yes. **Vending:** No. **Swimming:** Yes. **Playground:** Yes. **Other:** Silver Lake, sandy beach, boat ramp, boat dock, basketball, badminton, horseshoes, volleyball, sports field. **Activities:** Swimming, fishing, boating (rental rowboats, kayaks, paddleboats). **Nearby Attractions:** Grand Traverse Bay, Interlochen Music Camp, Sleeping Bear Sand Dunes, casinos, golf, outlet mall, cherry orchards, beaches, winter sports, Old Mission, parks, replica schooner, museums, wineries. **Additional Information:** Traverse City CVB, (800) 872-8377.

RESTRICTIONS

Pets: On leash only. **Fires:** Fire ring only. **Alcoholic Beverages:** Allowed. **Vehicle Maximum Length:** 40 ft.

TO GET THERE

Located at the south end of Silver Lake on Hwy. US 31, 7 mi. south of Traverse City and 6 mi. east of Interlochen. Roads are wide and well maintained, with adequate shoulders.

TRAVERSE CITY   MAP, B-1
Timber Ridge Campground

4050 Hammond Rd., 49686.
T: (800) 909-2327 or (231) 947-2770;
www.michcampgrounds.com/timberridge.

🚐 ★★★★   ⛺ ★★★★

Beauty: ★★★★	Site Privacy: ★★★★
Spaciousness: ★★★★	Quiet: ★★★★
Security: ★★★★	Cleanliness: ★★★★
Insect Control: ★★★★	Facilities: ★★★★

A secluded resort campground 6 miles east of Traverse City, Timber Ridge Campground offers gently rolling terrain. Sites are level and mostly shaded, with a typical site width of 30 feet. The campground has 43 pull-throughs and tent sites that have more green space and privacy. A lodge with a color TV, games, and fireplace is a nice amenity, especially in the winter when the area can get very cold and snow-covered. Open all year with limited facilities in the winter, the campground offers winter sports such as lighted ski trails. Timber Ridge also conducts learn-to-ski cross-country clinics throughout the season. The property borders over 60,000 acres of state land and trail systems for biking, hiking, and cross-country skiing. Reservations are recommended, particularly in July during the annual Traverse City Cherry Festival.

BASICS

Operated By: Private operator. **Open:** All year. **Site Assignment:** Reservations w/ 1-night deposit; refund (minus $10) w/ 5-day notice. **Registration:** At office. **Fee:** Water/electric/sewer, $45; water/electric, $38; rustic, $26; check, credit. **Parking:** At site.

FACILITIES

Number of RV-only Sites: 227. **Number of Tent-only Sites:** 29. **Hookups:** Electric (20, 30 amps), water, sewer, phone. **Each Site:** Picnic table, fire ring. **Dump Station:** Yes. **Laundry:** Yes. **Pay Phone:** Yes. **Restrooms and Showers:** Yes. **Fuel:** No. **Propane:** Yes. **Internal Roads:** Paved/gravel, in good condition. **RV Service:** No. **Market:** 2 mi. **Restaurant:** 2 mi. **General Store:** Yes. **Vending:** Yes. **Swimming:** Yes. **Playground:** Yes. **Other:** Wading pool, rec hall, pavilion, coin games, mini-golf, basketball, shuffle ball, movies, badminton, sports field, horseshoes, hiking trails, volleyball, rental cabins. **Activities:** Swimming, hiking, scheduled activities, winter sports. **Nearby Attractions:** Grand Traverse Bay, Interlochen Music Camp, Sleeping Bear Sand Dunes, casinos, golf, outlet mall, cherry orchards, beaches, winter sports, Old Mission, parks, replica schooner, museums, wineries. **Additional Information:** Traverse City CVB, (800) 872-8377.

RESTRICTIONS

Pets: On leash only. **Fires:** Fire ring only. **Alcoholic Beverages:** Not allowed. **Vehicle Maximum Length:** No limit. **Other:** 24-hour security.

TO GET THERE

From south junction of US 31 and Hwy. 72, drive 5 mi. east on Hwy. 31/72, then 2 mi. south on Four Mile Rd., then 2 mi. east on Hammond Rd. Roads are mostly wide and well maintained, with narrow shoulders in places.

TRAVERSE CITY   MAP, B-1
Traverse City South KOA

9700 M-37, 49620. T: (800) 562-0280 or (800) 562-0280; www.traversecitykoa.com.

🚐 ★★★★   ⛺ ★★★★

Beauty: ★★★★	Site Privacy: ★★★★
Spaciousness: ★★★★	Quiet: ★★★★
Security: ★★★★	Cleanliness: ★★★★
Insect Control: ★★★★	Facilities: ★★★★

Located 15 miles south of Traverse City, the Traverse City South KOA is a family campground in a quiet country setting. Sites are level and grassy with a choice of open or shaded. The typical site width is 30 feet, and the campground has eight pull-throughs. Restrooms are very clean; someone must check on them more than the usual once a day to keep them so spiffy. A wading pool is a popular spot with toddlers and their parents. The campground is a good base for Traverse City attractions, but it is also a destination campground for families. Owners keep a close watch on the campground for security and safety measures, but they are also friendly and helpful and seem to enjoy what they are doing.

BASICS

Operated By: Dave, Cathy, Stacy & Jamie Kuebler. **Open:** May 1–Oct. 15. **Site Assignment:** Reservations w/ 1-night deposit; refund w/ 2-week notice. **Registration:** At campground office. **Fee:** $25–$39; cash, check, credit card. **Parking:** At site.

FACILITIES

Number of RV-only Sites: 110. **Hookups:** Electric (20, 30, 50 amps), water, sewer, phone. **Each Site:** Picnic table, fire ring. **Dump Station:** Yes. **Laundry:** Yes. **Pay Phone:** Yes. **Restrooms and Showers:** Yes. **Fuel:** No. **Propane:** Yes. **Internal Roads:** Gravel, in good condition. **RV Service:** No. **Market:** 3 mi. south in Buckley. **Restaurant:** 3 mi. south in Buckley. **General Store:** Yes. **Vending:** Yes. **Swimming:** Yes. **Playground:** Yes. **Other:** Rec room, rental cabins, wading pool, coin games, basketball, movies, badminton, sports field, horseshoes, volleyball, snack bar, petting farm, hiking trails, snack bar. **Activities:** Swimming, hiking, scheduled activities. **Nearby Attractions:** Grand Traverse Bay, Interlochen Music Camp, Sleeping Bear Sand Dunes, casinos, golf, outlet mall, cherry orchards, beaches, winter sports, Old Mission, parks, replica schooner, museums, wineries. **Additional Information:** Traverse City CVB, (800) 872-8377.

RESTRICTIONS

Pets: On leash only. **Fires:** Fire ring only. **Alcoholic Beverages:** Allowed. **Vehicle Maximum Length:** No limit.

TO GET THERE

From the junction of US 31 and Hwy. 37, drive 10 mi. south on Hwy. 37. Roads are wide and well maintained, with broad shoulders.

WATERS   MAP, B-2
Headwaters Camping and Cabins

11687 Headwaters Court, 49797.
T: (989) 705-2066.

🚐 ★★★   ⛺ ★★★

Beauty: ★★★	Site Privacy: ★★★★
Spaciousness: ★★★★	Quiet: ★★★★
Security: ★★★★	Cleanliness: ★★★★★
Insect Control: ★★	Facilities: ★★★

Headwaters Court Camping and Cabins offers level, grassy sites with gravel parking spots on Bradford Lake. Located 2 miles south of Water, the campground also shows what a little creativity can do to brighten bathrooms. A "stone" floor and little critters painted on the walls make Headwaters' bathrooms more attractive and outdoorsy. Laid out in one big loop, the campground has five seasonals and seven pull-through sites. Sites are mostly open, with some situated right on a canal so boats can be left docked conveniently close to campsites. A welcoming extra is a free pancake breakfast every Sunday during the summer. Speed limit is 5 mph, and quiet hours are 10 p.m. to 9 a.m. Snowmobiling is a popular sport at the campground during winter. Security measures include one entrance/exit road, owners who live on site, and regular patrols of the campground.

BASICS

Operated By: Steve & Kimi Kwapis. **Open:** All year. **Site Assignment:** Reservations w/ 1-night deposit; refund w/ 7 day notice. **Registration:** At campground office. **Fee:** Water/electric/sewer, $25; cash, check, credit card. **Parking:** At site.

FACILITIES

Number of RV-only Sites: 89. **Number of Tent-only Sites:** 4. **Hookups:** Electric (30, 50 amps), water, sewer. **Each Site:** Picnic table, fire ring. **Dump Station:** Yes. **Laundry:** No. **Pay Phone:** No. **Restrooms and Showers:** Yes. **Fuel:** No. **Propane:** No. **Internal Roads:** Gravel, in good condition. **RV Service:** No. **Market:** 2 mi. north in Waters. **Restaurant:** 2 mi. north in Waters. **General Store:** No. **Vending:** Yes. **Swimming:** No. **Playground:** Yes. **Other:** Bradford Lake, swimming beach, boat ramp, volleyball, horseshoes, shuffleboard, boat dock, rental cabins, pavilion,. **Activities:** Swimming, fishing, boating, scheduled weekend activities. **Nearby Attractions:** Au Sable River, golf, bowling, ice skating, Bottle Cap Museum, canoeing, horseback riding, elk viewing, antiques, arts & crafts. **Additional Information:** Grayling Area Visitors Council, (800) 937-8837.

RESTRICTIONS

Pets: Leash only, proof of immunizations required. No large breeds. **Fires:** Fire ring only. **Alcoholic**

Beverages: Allowed. **Vehicle Maximum Length:** No limit. **Other:** No check-in after 10 p.m.

TO GET THERE

From I-75, take Exit 270, drive 0.25 mi. west on Marlett Rd., then 2 mi. south on Old 27, then 0.1 mi. west on Headwaters Court. Roads are wide and well maintained, with broad shoulders.

ZEELAND — Dutch Treat Camping and Recreation

MAP, D-1

10300 Gordon, 49464. T: (616) 772-4303.

🚐 ★★★★   ▲ ★★★

Beauty: ★★★	Site Privacy: ★★★★
Spaciousness: ★★★★	Quiet: ★★★★
Security: ★★★★	Cleanliness: ★★★★
Insect Control: ★★★★	Facilities: ★★★★

Right in the heart of vacationland, Dutch Treat Camping in Zeeland offers level sites by a small pond. The campground has level sites with a choice of open or shaded sites and a typical site width of 35 feet. There are 15 seasonal campers, 34 pull-through sites and 31 back-in sites. Rustic tent sites offer more green space and privacy. During May, millions of beautiful tulips provide a floral display in this western Michigan city settled by Dutch immigrants. Reservations are recommended during the annual tulip festival. Dutch Treat facilities are clean and well maintained. Most sites are grassy, but some gravel ones are available. A large deck around the heated pool is a nice bonus. A large recreation shelter is heated or air-conditioned and provides a welcome spot during extreme weather. Church services are offered on Sundays. Owners make sure the campground is well monitored to maintain a friendly family atmosphere.

BASICS

Operated By: Nelson Riemersma. **Open:** Apr. 1–Nov. 1. **Site Assignment:** Reservations w/ 1-night deposit; refund (minus $5) w/ 72-hour notice. **Registration:** At campground office. **Fee:** $35; cash, check, credit card. **Parking:** At site.

FACILITIES

Number of RV-only Sites: 105. **Number of Tent-only Sites:** 15. **Hookups:** Electric (20, 30, 50 amps), water, sewer, phone. **Each Site:** Picnic table, fire ring. **Dump Station:** Yes. **Laundry:** Yes. **Pay Phone:** Yes.

Restrooms and Showers: Yes. **Fuel:** No. **Propane:** No. **Internal Roads:** Paved, in good condition. **RV Service:** No. **Market:** 2 blocks. **Restaurant:** 2 blocks. **General Store:** Yes, limited. **Vending:** Yes. **Swimming:** Yes. **Playground:** Yes. **Other:** Pond, horseshoes, rec hall, sports field, coin games, basketball, badminton, volleyball, game room, modem hookup in office. **Activities:** Swimming, fishing, boating (rental paddleboats available). **Nearby Attractions:** Lake Macatawa, Lake Michigan, bike trails, Cappon House Museum, De Klomp Wooden Shoe & Delftware Factory, Dutch Village, Holland Museum, tulip gardens, Windmill Island, antiques, arts & crafts. **Additional Information:** Holland Area CVB, (800) 506-1299.

RESTRICTIONS

Pets: On leash only. **Fires:** Fire ring only. **Alcoholic Beverages:** Allowed. **Vehicle Maximum Length:** No limit.

TO GET THERE

From the junction of Hwy. 31 and East/West Business I-196, drive 2.2 mi. east on I-96, then 0.25 mi. east on Gordon. Roads are wide and well maintained, with broad shoulders.

Minnesota

The "Land of 10,000 lakes" isn't just bragging. In fact, Minnesota actually has more than 15,000 lakes and ample access to just about any known water-related activity. It also is the reputed home of Babe the Blue Ox, sidekick to legendary lumberman Paul Bunyan. Don't be surprised to see Babe and Paul statues along the roadsides throughout your adventure along the roads of the 32nd state.

A little bit of history resides in a lot of Minnesota. One of the last remaining colonies of eastern timberwolves in the continental United States can be found at **Voyageurs National Park.** To appreciate the hardships the state's settlers faced, visit the museum in **Walnut Grove** dedicated to and with memorabilia from resident Laura Ingalls Wilder, author of the *Little House on the Prairie* books. For history, towns like **New Ulm** have an unmistakable European accent in their shops, restaurants, festivals, and breweries. Shoppers flock from around the world for the welcome distractions located within the gargantuan **Mall of America** in Bloomington.

The birthplace of the snowmobile, the Gopher State contains more than 15,000 miles of rideable trails in most of its 66 state recreation areas, making winter a popular outdoor season. Ice fishing keeps boredom at bay, even for the least dedicated of anglers. One of the first rivers in the nation to be granted the Wild and Scenic designation, the **St. Croix** retains an outstandingly beautiful shoreline. To preserve the natural beauty of the area, the **Boundary Waters Canoe Area Wilderness,** part of **Superior National Forest,** has banned motorized boats on most of its more than 2,500 lakes. **Bemidji's Paul Bunyan Bike Trail** is a popular route for bicycling, skating, and snowmobiling. For what has recently been named one of the best fall color drives in the nation, travelers lured by the changing leaves can take a tour along the **Edge of the Wilderness National Scenic Byway.**

For a broad sampling of the eccentric, Minnesota ranks high on the list of states teeming with the unusual as well as the unique. The **Runestone Museum** is located in Alexandria, which also claims to be the birthplace of America, where mystery surrounds the 200-pound rock found in a Minnesota farmer's field in 1898. Carvings on the rock tell the tale of a Viking voyage that ended in tragedy in 1362. Known as **Spam Town USA,** Austin pays homage to its world-famous meat product at the **Hormel Spam Museum,** and in Duluth, an unusual elevator bridge is 386 feet long and spans the canal entrance to **Duluth Harbor.** Located near the navigational headwaters of the Mississippi River, the city of **Grand Rapid** was the birthplace of **Judy Garland** and offers its own yellow brick road to her historic home. **The Mayo Clinic in Rochester** is known for its advanced technologies and pioneering discoveries in the world of medicine. The **Twin Cities** pull their fair share of credit in Minnesota's charm department. Minneapolis is home not only to the country's longest running dinner theater, the **Old Log Theater,** but also to the country's largest dinner theater, **Chanhassan,** as well. The city's sculpture garden doesn't do too shabbily either, and it is considered the biggest in the world. St. Paul, almost named Pig's Eye after the French Canadian whiskey trader Pierre Parrant, who led the original settlers there, happens to be home to the world's largest stucco snowman. A trip to **Darwin** will reveal the world's largest ball of twine made by one man; as testament to the popularity of the sport in the state, one of the world's largest hockey sticks, complete with puck, stands in **Eveleth.**

Whether you have a week or three months to take in the gems of the state, any impression you leave Minnesota with will be an unforgettable and lasting one.

Campground Profiles

ALBERT LEA — MAP, D-2
Hickory Hills Campground

15694 717th Ave., 56007. T: (507) 852-4555;
www.hickoryhillscampground.com.

🚐 ★★★   ⛺ ★★

Beauty: ★★★   Site Privacy: ★★★
Spaciousness: ★★★   Quiet: ★★★★
Security: ★★★★   Cleanliness: ★★★
Insect Control: ★★★   Facilities: ★★★

This is a well-managed campground. Showers and restrooms are modern, and the campground area is regularly weeded and mowed. Located in a rural area with shaded, wooded sites, the campground is off the beaten path and has little outside noise. The only noise would be whatever the campers bring with them, and the owners try to keep that to a minimum. Sites are generally 30 by 60 with about 12 pull-through sites. At 35 by 84, the swimming pool is bigger than those at most campgrounds. Sites 1 and 10 are the most popular RV sites because they are the first in the park, located near the playground, and offer easy access to campground amenities. Tent sites are separated from RVs, but not enough to provide much privacy. With one entrance/exit and owners who live on site and patrol the area, security is very good. Also, it would be hard to imagine anyone driving all the way out to Hickory Hills on those gravel roads for any reason other than camping.

BASICS
Operated By: Bill & Kay Rask. **Open:** Apr. 15–Oct. 11; limited services after Oct. 11. **Site Assignment:** Reservations accepted; nonrefundable deposit, $20. **Registration:** At campground office. **Fee:** $20–$28; cash, check, credit card. **Parking:** At site.

FACILITIES
Number of RV-only Sites: 18. **Number of Tent-only Sites:** 3. **Hookups:** Electric (30, 50 amps), water. **Each Site:** Picnic table, fire ring. **Dump Station:** Yes. **Laundry:** Yes. **Pay Phone:** Yes. **Restrooms and Showers:** Yes. **Fuel:** No. **Propane:** No. **Internal Roads:** Gravel, rough in some spots. **RV Service:** No. **Market:** 7 mi. north in Albert Lea. **Restaurant:** 7 mi. north in Albert Lea. **General Store:** Yes. **Vending:** No. **Swimming:** Yes. **Playground:** Yes. **Other:** Hiking trail, horseshoes, game room, recreation field, volleyball, mini-golf, fire place, lounge. **Activities:** Swimming, hiking, scheduled activities on weekends & holidays such as karaoke, treasure hunt, sock hop dance, hog roast. **Nearby Attractions:** Lake, Freeborn County Museum & Historical Village, Story Lady Doll & Toy Museum, golf, aquatic center. **Additional Information:** Albert Lea-Freeborn County CVB, (900) 345-8414.

RESTRICTIONS
Pets: Leash only, clean up after. **Fires:** Fire ring only. **Alcoholic Beverages:** Allowed. **Vehicle Maximum Length:** No limit.

TO GET THERE
From the junction of I-90 and Hwy. 13/69, take Exit 154 and drive 9.75 mi. south on Hwy. 69, then follow signs for 1.5 mi. on gravel roads. Gravel roads are wide but rough in spots.

ALBERT LEA — MAP, D-2
Hickory Hills Campground

15694 717th Ave., 56007. T: (507) 852-4555;
www.hickoryhillscampground.com.

🚐 ★★★   ⛺ ★★

Beauty: ★★★   Site Privacy: ★★★
Spaciousness: ★★★   Quiet: ★★★★
Security: ★★★★   Cleanliness: ★★★
Insect Control: ★★★   Facilities: ★★★

This is a well-managed campground. Showers and restrooms are modern, and the campground area is regularly weeded and mowed. Located in a rural area with shaded, wooded sites, the campground is off the beaten path and has little outside noise. The only noise would be whatever the campers bring with them, and the owners try to keep that to a minimum. Sites are generally 30 by 60 with about 12 pull-through sites. At 35 by 84, the swimming pool is bigger than those at most campgrounds. Sites 1 and 10 are the most popular RV sites because they are the first in the park, located near the playground, and offer easy access to campground amenities. Tent sites are separated from RVs, but not enough to provide much privacy. With one entrance/exit and owners who live on site and patrol the area, security is very good. Also, it would be hard to imagine anyone driving all the way out to Hickory Hills on those gravel roads for any reason other than camping.

BASICS
Operated By: Bill and Kay Rask. **Open:** Apr. 15–Oct. 11; limited services after Oct. 11. **Site Assignment:** Reservations accepted; non-refundable deposit, $20. **Registration:** At campground office. **Fee:** $20–$28; cash, check, credit card. **Parking:** At site.

FACILITIES
Number of RV-only Sites: 18. **Number of Tent-only Sites:** 3. **Hookups:** Electric (30, 50 amps), water. **Each Site:** Picnic table, fire ring. **Dump Station:** Yes. **Laundry:** Yes. **Pay Phone:** Yes. **Restrooms and Showers:** Yes. **Fuel:** No. **Propane:** No. **Internal Roads:** Gravel, rough in some spots. **RV Service:** No. **Market:** 7 mi. north in Albert Lea. **Restaurant:** 7 mi. north in Albert Lea. **General Store:** Yes. **Vending:** No. **Swimming:** Yes. **Playground:** Yes. **Other:** Hiking trail, horseshoes, game room, recreation field, volleyball, mini-golf, fire place, lounge. **Activities:** Swimming, hiking, scheduled activities on weekends & holidays such as karaoke, treasure hunt, sock hop dance, hog roast. **Nearby Attractions:** Lake, Freeborn County Museum & Historical Village, Story Lady Doll & Toy Museum, golf, aquatic center. **Additional Information:** Albert Lea-Freeborn County CVB, (900) 345-8414.

RESTRICTIONS
Pets: Leash only, clean up after. **Fires:** Fire ring only. **Alcoholic Beverages:** Allowed. **Vehicle Maximum Length:** No limit.

TO GET THERE
From the junction of I-90 and Hwy. 13/69, take Exit 154 and drive 9.75 mi. south on Hwy. 69, then follow signs for 1.5 mi. on gravel roads. Gravel roads are wide but rough in spots.

ALTURA — MAP, D-3
Lazy D Campground

18248 CR 39, RR 1 Box 252, 55910. T: (507) 932-3098; www.lazyd-camping-trailrides.com.

🚐 ★★★   ⛺ ★★★★

Beauty: ★★★★   Site Privacy: ★★★★
Spaciousness: ★★★★   Quiet: ★★★★
Security: ★★★   Cleanliness: ★★★
Insect Control: ★★   Facilities: ★★★

A river runs through Lazy D Campground. And it's filled with trout. That's one reason the campground is popular. Another is that is offers horseback rides and other equestrian treats and the horses are on site. Located in the wilderness bluff country on the Middle Branch of the Whitewater River, the campground has spacious (40 by 50 the smallest), level, grassy sites. RV and tent sites are both available alongside the stream. The campground is mowed and the spring-fed water flows fast so mosquitoes aren't a problem. What is a problem for some is the lack of pull-through sites.

BASICS
Operated By: Mark & Betty Thoreson. **Open:** Apr. 15–late Nov. **Site Assignment:** Reservations w/ 1-night deposit; refunds w/ 7-day notice. **Registration:** At campground office. **Fee:** $22–$30; cash, check, credit card. **Parking:** At site.

FACILITIES
Number of RV-only Sites: 108. **Number of Tent-only Sites:** 6. **Hookups:** Electric (20, 30, 50 amps), water. **Each Site:** Picnic table, fire ring. **Dump Station:** Yes. **Laundry:** Yes. **Pay Phone:** Yes. **Restrooms and Showers:** Yes. **Fuel:** No. **Propane:** No. **Internal Roads:** Gravel, in good condition. **RV Service:** No. **Market:** 8 mi. north in St. Charles. **Restaurant:** 2 mi. north in Elba. **General Store:** Yes. **Vending:** Yes. **Swimming:** Yes. **Playground:** Yes. **Other:** Game room, volleyball, basketball, tetherball, horseshoes, antique carriage museum, trout stream, recreation field. **Activities:** Fishing, swimming, horseback riding (horses on site), pony rides, hayrides, trail rides, inner tubing, covered wagon rides. **Nearby Attractions:** Aquatic center, golf, fire tower, hiking trails, beach, Historic Marnach House. **Additional Information:** Rochester CVB, (800) 634-8277.

RESTRICTIONS
Pets: On leash only. **Fires:** Fire ring only. **Alcoholic Beverages:** Allowed. **Vehicle Maximum Length:** No limit.

TO GET THERE

From the junction of I-90 and Hwy. 74, take Exit 233, drive 8.5 mi. north on Hwy. 74, then 150 yards west on CR 39.

ALTURA   MAP, D-3
Whitewater State Park

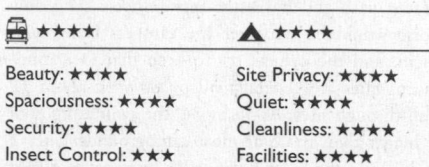

Hwy. 1 Box 256, 19041 Hwy. 74, 55910. T: (507) 932-3007; www.reserveamerica.com.

🚐 ★★   ⛺ ★★★★

Beauty: ★★★★   Site Privacy: ★★★★
Spaciousness: ★★★★   Quiet: ★★★★
Security: ★★★★   Cleanliness: ★★★
Insect Control: ★★   Facilities: ★★

Established in 1919, Whitewater State Park is one of the most popular Minnesota state parks because of its dolomite cliffs, trout streams, hardwood forests, and noticeable lack of mosquitoes. The absence of the pesky insects isn't because of vigilant spraying. Rather, it is the result of the fast-moving streams that don't give mosquitoes a chance to breed. Located 2 miles south of Elba, the campground's screens of trees and plants keep it naturally quiet. Do note that the park gate is closed from 10 p.m. to 8 a.m., except to registered campers, and quiet time begins at 10 p.m. The RV sites are mostly grassy and shady, with five pull-throughs. Size width varies from 15 to 30 feet. In addition to 55 tent camping sites, Whitewater also has four hike-in sites and a primitive area that can accommodate 100 tent campers. Tent campers have an edge at this wilderness campground: the tent sites outnumber the RV sites. Although rattlesnake sightings are rare, reptiles do live within the park. Hikers should report any sightings to the park office.

BASICS

Operated By: State of Minnesota. **Open:** All year. **Site Assignment:** Reservations w/ 1-night deposit plus $8.50 nonrefundable fee; refunds (minus $5 & $7.25 fees) w/ 3-day notice. **Registration:** At campground office. **Fee:** $18–$22; cash, check, credit card. **Parking:** At site.

FACILITIES

Number of RV-only Sites: 47. **Number of Tent-only Sites:** 63. **Hookups:** Electric (20, 30, 50 amps). **Each Site:** Picnic table, fire ring. **Dump Station:** Yes. **Laundry:** No. **Pay Phone:** Yes. **Restrooms and Showers:** Yes. **Fuel:** No. **Propane:** No. **Internal Roads:** Paved, gravel, in good condition. **RV Service:** No. **Market:** 2 mi. north in Elba. **Restaurant:** 2 mi. north in Elba. **General Store:** No. **Vending:** Yes. **Swimming:** Yes. **Playground:** No. **Other:** Whitewater River, swimming beach, volleyball, horseshoes, hiking trails, ski touring trails, naturalist interpretive center, visitor center, wheelchair-accessible fishing pier. **Activities:** Hiking, fishing, swimming, cross-country ski trails, interpretive programs. **Nearby Attractions:** Mayo Clinic, art center, Mayowood Mansion, golf, Olmsted County History Center, Root River State Trail, scenic drives. **Additional Information:** Rochester CVB, (800) 634-8277.

RESTRICTIONS

Pets: On leash only. **Fires:** Fire ring only. **Alcoholic Beverages:** Not allowed. **Vehicle Maximum Length:** 50 ft. **Other:** Vehicle permits of $25 per year or $7 per day are required to enter all Minnesota state parks; 14-day stay limit.

TO GET THERE

From Elba, drive 2 mi. south on Hwy. 74. Roads are wide and well maintained, with broad shoulders.

AUSTIN   MAP, D-3
Beaver Trails Campgrounds

21943 630th Ave., No. 1, 55912. T: (507) 584-6611 or (800) 245-6281; www.beavertrails.com.

🚐 ★★★★   ⛺ ★★★★

Beauty: ★★★   Site Privacy: ★★★★
Spaciousness: ★★★★   Quiet: ★★★★
Security: ★★★★   Cleanliness: ★★★
Insect Control: ★★   Facilities: ★★★★

Beaver Trails Campgrounds is four campgrounds in one. The Lodge Area is where the action is and is a favorite with families and children. As a result, it is a little noisier and crowded. The Quiet Area offers large sites (30 by 78), plenty of grass and trees, and some primitive sites. The Group Area can accommodate any size group and features pavilions for gatherings. The wooded Trails End Area has pack-in sites, chemical toilets, and plenty of solitude. It would be the best pick for tent campers. The campground is blessed with grassy, level sites, each with its own tree. A big bonus for RV campers is that most of the sites are pull-throughs. It may have been unusual, but at the time of our visit, one of the campground's toilets was out of order and another wouldn't flush. With a campground this size, having two unusable toilets isn't pleasant.

BASICS

Operated By: Bill & Carol Sheely. **Open:** Apr. 15–Oct. 1. **Site Assignment:** Reservations w/ $20 deposit. **Registration:** At campground office. **Fee:** $34–$41; cash, check, credit card. **Parking:** At site.

FACILITIES

Number of RV-only Sites: 300. **Number of Tent-only Sites:** 20. **Hookups:** Electric (30, 50 amps), water, sewer. **Each Site:** Picnic table, fire ring. **Dump Station:** Yes. **Laundry:** Yes. **Pay Phone:** Yes. **Restrooms and Showers:** Yes. **Fuel:** No. **Propane:** Yes. **Internal Roads:** Gravel/paved, in good condition. **RV Service:** No. **Market:** 8 mi. west in Austin. **Restaurant:** 8 mi. west in Austin. **General Store:** Yes. **Vending:** Yes. **Swimming:** Yes. **Playground:** Yes. **Other:** Dance hall, shuffleboard, game room, ping-pong room, volleyball, meeting room, big screen TV, pavilion, hiking trails, badminton, horseshoes, snack bar, small animal zoo, outdoor stage, mini-golf, fish pond, coin games, wading pool. **Activities:** Swimming, fishing, canoeing (rental canoes & paddleboats available), movies, activities every weekend, such as karaoke, line dancing, Christmas in July, kids' crafts, train rides, story time. **Nearby Attractions:** Nature center, historical center, cave, Spam Museum, historic homes, skate park, golf, bowling, snowmobile trails, speedway, hockey

rink. **Additional Information:** Austin CVB, (800) 444-5713.

RESTRICTIONS

Pets: On leash only. **Fires:** Fire ring only. **Alcoholic Beverages:** Allowed. **Vehicle Maximum Length:** No limit.

TO GET THERE

From the junction of US 218 and I-90, drive 7.5 mi. east on I-90, take Exit 187, drive 25 yards south on CR 20. Roads are wide and well maintained, with broad shoulders.

BEMIDJI   MAP, B-2
Bemidji KOA

510 Bright Star Rd. NW, 56601. T: (218) 444-7562 or (800) KOA-1742; www.bemidjikoa.com.

🚐 ★★★★   ⛺ ★★★★

Beauty: ★★★★   Site Privacy: ★★★★
Spaciousness: ★★★★   Quiet: ★★★★
Security: ★★★★   Cleanliness: ★★★★
Insect Control: ★★★   Facilities: ★★★★

Located in the heart of the Northwoods county, 2 miles west of Bemidji, this KOA has five area lakes within 4 miles. Tall pine, spruce, fir, and white birch trees offer shade. The campground has 28 pull-throughs, and the typical site width is 20 feet. The RV sites have a gravel pad for parking. Laid out in a loop, the rural campground has a well-stocked store and a 24-hour laundry. Primitive tent sites are situated away from the RV sites in a wooded area. Summer temperatures are generally cool with daytime highs in the 70s and 80s. It can snow in May and October. The owner lives on site and offers regular patrols. As a friendly touch, the campground shows free movies every night and offers free popcorn in the pavilion. Every morning, free coffee is offered in the store.

BASICS

Operated By: Keith & Mary Davidson. **Open:** May 1–Oct. 15. **Site Assignment:** Reservations w/ 1-night deposit; refund w/ 2-day notice; $5 cancellation fee. **Registration:** At campground office. **Fee:** $30; cash, credit card. **Parking:** At site.

FACILITIES

Number of RV-only Sites: 65. **Number of Tent-only Sites:** 15. **Hookups:** Electric (30, 50 amps), water, sewer, cable TV. **Each Site:** Picnic table, fire ring. **Dump Station:** Yes. **Laundry:** Yes. **Pay Phone:** Yes. **Restrooms and Showers:** Yes. **Fuel:** No. **Propane:** Yes. **Internal Roads:** Gravel, in good condition. **RV Service:** No. **Market:** 2 mi. east in Bemidji. **Restaurant:** 2 mi. east in Bemidji. **General Store:** Yes. **Vending:** No. **Swimming:** Yes. **Playground:** Yes. **Other:** Mini-golf, video game room, book exchange, badminton, sports field, horseshoes, hiking trails, volleyball, rental cabins. **Activities:** Swimming, hiking, biking (rental bikes available), scheduled weekend activities. **Nearby Attractions:** Mississippi River, Paul Bunyan & Babe the Blue Ox statues, amusement parks, waterslide, logging camp, fishing, golf. **Additional Information:** Bemidji Area Tourist Information, (800) 458-2223.

RESTRICTIONS

Pets: On leash only. **Fires:** Fire ring only. **Alcoholic Beverages:** Allowed. **Vehicle Maximum Length:** No limit.

TO GET THERE

From the junction of US 71 and US 2, drive 2.5 mi. west on US 2. Road is wide and well maintained, with broad shoulders.

BENA   MAP, B-2
Nodak Lodge

15080 Nodak Dr., 56626. T: (800) 752-2758 or (218) 665-2226; www.nodaklodge.com.

🚐 ★★★   ▲ ★★

Beauty: ★★★   Site Privacy: ★★★
Spaciousness: ★★★   Quiet: ★★★
Security: ★★★   Cleanliness: ★★★
Insect Control: ★★   Facilities: ★★★

A lakeside RV area in a mobile home park, Nodak Lodge offers water recreation activities galore with fishing as a highlight. Charter boats and whole- or half-day launch fishing is available as are fishing guides. The marina features a large harbor with plenty of docking space and has boat rentals, a fish-cleaning house, gas, oil, and live bait. Dock boys are on hand to assist in the marina area and will clean and package a daily catch for a small fee. As often happens in a popular campground, all the full-hookup sites are occupied by seasonals. The sites are grassy, level, and open with few trees, and the typical site width is 30 feet. There are no scheduled activities at this campground. The best RV site is B3 because it is bigger and has shade. Tent campers will like Nodak Lodge for its outdoor activities but might not like being clumped with RVs and mobile homes.

BASICS

Operated By: Roger & Melissa Crokaer. **Open:** May 1–Oct. 1. **Site Assignment:** Reservations, no deposit necessary. **Registration:** At campground office. **Fee:** $25; for 4 people; cash, check, credit card. **Parking:** At site.

FACILITIES

Number of Tent-only Sites: 10. **Number of Multipurpose Sites:** 10. **Hookups:** Electric (30 amps), water. **Each Site:** Picnic table, fire ring. **Dump Station:** Yes. **Laundry:** Yes. **Pay Phone:** No. **Restrooms and Showers:** Yes. **Fuel:** No. **Propane:** No. **Internal Roads:** Dirt, in fair condition. **RV Service:** No. **Market:** 20 mi. east in Deer River. **Restaurant:** 20 mi. east in Deer River. **General Store:** Yes. **Vending:** No. **Swimming:** Yes. **Playground:** Yes. **Other:** Lake Winnibigoshish, tanning bed, marina, boat docks, fish-cleaning house, lodge, snack bar, game room, sports field, horseshoes, volleyball. **Activities:** Fishing, swimming, boating (rental motor boats, canoes & paddleboats available). **Nearby Attractions:** Hunting, hiking, mountain biking, fish-angling houses, fish-spearing houses, snowmobile trails, cross-country & downhill skiing. **Additional Information:** Grand Rapids CVB, (800) 472-6366.

RESTRICTIONS

Pets: Leash only, $10 fee per day. **Fires:** Fire ring only. **Alcoholic Beverages:** Allowed. **Vehicle Maximum Length:** No limit.

TO GET THERE

From the junction of CR 8 and US 2, drive 0.5 mi. west on US 2. Roads are wide and well maintained, with broad shoulders.

BRAINERD   MAP, C-2
Don and Mayva's Crow Wing Lake Campground

2393 Crow Wing Camp Rd., 56401. T: (218) 829-6468; www.brainerd.net/~cwcamp.

🚐 ★★★★   ▲ ★★★★

Beauty: ★★★★   Site Privacy: ★★★★
Spaciousness: ★★★★   Quiet: ★★★★
Security: ★★★★   Cleanliness: ★★★★
Insect Control: ★★   Facilities: ★★★★

Nestled in 40 wooded acres on the shores of 400-acre Crow Wing Lake, Don and Mayva's Crow Wing Lake Campground offers plenty of mature oak tree shade, grassy sites, and RV locations with large concrete patios. The camp store is well stocked, including a snack bar and bait section. The campground has 40 seasonal sites, leaving 60 for visiting campers. The typical site width is 30 feet, and the campground has 27 pull-throughs. While tent campers are definitely in the minority, they are provided with separate grassy, wooded sites. Started in 1970 by the Kottkes, the campground is well organized and well maintained. Concrete patios and designated parking spots help keep the grass in good condition. Campground security is ensured with only one entrance road that passes the office, owners who live on site, and a regular area patrol. Quiet hours—which means no radios, generators, or loud voices—are strictly enforced from 10 p.m. to 8 a.m., even on weekends. Reservations are strongly recommended as the campground fills up quickly on weekends and holidays. Weekday camping is recommended for those who like to avoid the crowds.

BASICS

Operated By: Don & Mayva Kottke. **Open:** May 1–Oct. 1. **Site Assignment:** Reservations accepted w/ $50 deposit; refunds (minus $5) w/ 7-day notice; 2-night minimum on weekends; 3-night minimum on holidays. **Registration:** At campground office. **Fee:** $37–$47; cash, check, credit card. **Parking:** At site.

FACILITIES

Number of RV-only Sites: 90. **Number of Tent-only Sites:** 10. **Hookups:** Electric (30, 50 amps), water, sewer. **Each Site:** Picnic table, fire ring. **Dump Station:** Yes. **Laundry:** Yes. **Pay Phone:** Yes. **Restrooms and Showers:** Yes. **Fuel:** Yes. **Propane:** No. **Internal Roads:** Gravel, in good condition. Paved entrance & exit roads. **RV Service:** No. **Market:** 10 mi. north in Brainerd. **Restaurant:** 5 mi. south in Port Ripley. **General Store:** Yes. **Vending:** Yes. **Swimming:** Yes. **Playground:** Yes. **Other:** Crow Wing Lake, fish-cleaning house, boat launch, disc golf, bank shot basketball, shuffleboard, badminton, softball, horseshoes, volleyball, nature trail, rec room, coin games. **Activities:** Swimming, hiking, fishing, boating (rental motorboats, canoes, paddleboats, rowboats, pontoon boats available). **Nearby Attractions:** Raceway, casino, golf, Mille Lacs Indian Museum, Paul Bunyan Amusement Center, antiques stores, art galleries, historic homes, Lindbergh State Park, Lindbergh Home & Interpretive Center. **Additional Information:** Brainerd Lakes Area Chamber of Commerce, (800) 450-2838.

RESTRICTIONS

Pets: On leash only. **Fires:** Fire ring only. **Alcoholic Beverages:** Allowed. **Vehicle Maximum Length:** No limit.

TO GET THERE

From the junction of Hwys 18, 371, and 210, drive 11.5 mi. south on Hwy. 371. Roads are wide and well maintained, with broad shoulders.

BRAINERD   MAP, C-2
Sullivan's Resort and Campground

7685 CR 127, 56401. T: (888) 829-5697; www.sullivansresort.com.

🚐 ★★★★   ▲ ★★★★

Beauty: ★★★★   Site Privacy: ★★★★
Spaciousness: ★★★★   Quiet: ★★★★
Security: ★★★★   Cleanliness: ★★★★
Insect Control: ★★★★   Facilities: ★★★★

Take a look at beautiful North Long Lake and the clean facilities at Sullivan's Resort and Campground, and you'll know why so many campers find their way to this spot located just 3.5 miles from the Paul Bunyan State Trail. The trail's first 50 miles are paved for bicycling, hiking, and skating. The campground's North Long Lake is 7 miles long and 3 miles wide, with 5,998 acres of clean, clear water. Shallow, sandy shores make the lake ideal for children and adults who like to play in the water. To accent the natural water attractions, Sullivan's also has a heated indoor pool, a sauna, and a hot tub. Sullivan's has 16 seasonal campers, so reservations are recommended for those who wish to camp on the remaining sites. The campground has partly shaded sites on grassy, level ground along the lake. The typical site width is 30 feet, and there are no pull-throughs available.

BASICS

Operated By: Lowell & Dee Sullivan. **Open:** May 1–Oct. 1. **Site Assignment:** Reservations w/ $50 nonrefundable deposit. **Registration:** At campground office. **Fee:** $36–$42; cash, check, V, MC. **Parking:** At site. 1 car per site. Extra cars must be registered & parked in extra parking area.

FACILITIES

Number of RV-only Sites: 50. **Hookups:** Electric (30 amps), water, sewer. **Each Site:** Picnic table, fire ring. **Dump Station:** No. **Laundry:** Yes. **Pay Phone:** Yes. **Restrooms and Showers:** Yes. **Fuel:** No. **Propane:** Yes. **Internal Roads:** Gravel, in good condition. **RV Service:** No. **Market:** 8 mi. east in Brainerd. **Restaurant:** 8 mi. east in Brainerd. **General Store:** Yes. **Vending:** No. **Swimming:** Yes. **Playground:** Yes. **Other:** North Long Lake, hot tub, rec room, coin games, boat dock, boat ramp, fish-cleaning house, sandy beach, fish-freezing service, shuffleboard, horseshoes, volleyball, recreation field, rental cabins, large retreat home. **Activities:** Fishing, swimming, boating (rental kayaks, pontoons, motorboats, canoes, paddleboats available). **Nearby Attractions:** Paul Bunyan Bike Trail, cross-county skiing, snowmobiling, Brainerd International Raceway, antiques, arts & crafts, Crow Wing County Historical Society Museum, golf, Paul Bunyan Amusement Center. **Additional Information:** Brainerd Lakes Area Chamber of Commerce, (800) 450-2838.

RESTRICTIONS

Pets: Not allowed. **Fires:** Fire ring only. **Alcoholic Beverages:** Allowed. **Vehicle Maximum Length:** No limit. **Other:** Tents & screen houses must be moved every 2–3 days on the same site; doormats & rugs not allowed on site.

TO GET THERE

From the junction of Hwy. 210 and Hwy. 371, drive 7.5 mi. north on Hwy. 371, then 2.25 mi. northeast on CR 115, then 1 mi. east on CR 127. Roads are mostly wide and well maintained, with adequate shoulders.

BRANDON   MAP, C-1
Kamp Kappy Family Resort and Campgrounds

13110 Devils Lake Rd. NW, 56315.
T: (320) 524-2225.

🚐 ★★★   ▲ ★★★★

Beauty: ★★★★   Site Privacy: ★★★
Spaciousness: ★★★★   Quiet: ★★★★
Security: ★★★★   Cleanliness: ★★★
Insect Control: ★★   Facilities: ★★★

Third and fourth generations are now visiting the almost 100-year-old Kamp Kappy. Located on Devils Lake 1.5 miles north of Brandon, the campground has no highway or trains running by it to disturb the quiet. The only noise is what campers bring with them, and the owners work to keep that minimal. Part of a chain of lakes leading to the Minnesota River, Devils Lake is a 300-acre natural lake. Because the lake is small and stocked well, it is a relatively easy lake to fish, even in weather that would typically keep folks off most other lakes. The campground offers a fish-cleaning house with three sinks and plenty of freezer space for daily catches. The sandy swimming beach gradually slopes out to a swim dock, and the swimming area is marked with buoys. Sites are level, grassy, and shaded in this wooded lakeside campground. The typical site width is 40 feet, and the best RV sites are 1A and 2A because they provide slightly bigger pull-through spaces. Tent campers have a separate area overlooking the lake that is protected by an unobtrusive security light. With one dead-end access road, owners who live on the campground, and regular campground patrols, campers are likely to feel quite safe.

BASICS

Operated By: Ray & Sharalyn Berndt. **Open:** May 1–Oct. 1. **Site Assignment:** Reservations w/ 1-night deposit; refunds (minus $15) w/ 30-day notice. **Registration:** At campground office. **Fee:** $20–$30; cash, check, credit card. **Parking:** At site.

FACILITIES

Number of RV-only Sites: 50. **Number of Tent-only Sites:** 14. **Hookups:** Electric (15, 20, 30 amps), water, sewer. **Each Site:** Picnic table, fire ring. **Dump Station:** Yes. **Laundry:** No. **Pay Phone:** Yes. **Restrooms and Showers:** Yes. **Fuel:** Yes. **Propane:** No. **Internal Roads:** Gravel, in good condition. **RV Service:** No. **Market:** 1.5 mi. south in Brandon. **Restaurant:** 1.5 mi. south in Brandon. **General Store:** Yes. **Vending:** Yes. **Swimming:** No. **Playground:** Yes. **Other:** Devils Lake, sandy beach, Ray's R/C Land (radio-control hobby shop), horseshoes, volleyball, badminton, basketball, rec room, fish-cleaning facility, pavilion, boat ramp, boat dock, sports field. **Activities:** Swimming, fishing, boating (rental motorboats, pontoons, canoes & paddleboats available). **Nearby Attractions:** Golf, tennis, Runestone Museum, Fort Alexandria Agricultural Exhibit. **Additional Information:** Alexandria Lakes Area Chamber of Commerce, (800) 245-2539.

RESTRICTIONS

Pets: Leash only, $10 per pet per stay. **Fires:** Fire ring only. **Alcoholic Beverages:** Allowed. **Vehicle Maximum Length:** 35 ft.

TO GET THERE

From the junction of I-94 and CR 7, take Exit 90 and drive 4 mi. north on CR 7, then 0.5 mi. west on access road. Roads are wide and well maintained, with adequate shoulders.

CASS LAKE   MAP, B-2
Stony Point Resort Campground and RV Park

5510 US 2 NW, P.O. Box 318, 56633.
T: (800) 332-6311 or (218) 335-6311;
www.stonyptresortcasslake.com.

🚐 ★★★★   ▲ ★★★★

Beauty: ★★★★   Site Privacy: ★★★★
Spaciousness: ★★★★   Quiet: ★★★★
Security: ★★★★   Cleanliness: ★★★★
Insect Control: ★★★   Facilities: ★★★★

Known as the Little Venice of the North, Stony Point has a 2,000-foot winding boat canal. that keeps campers in close proximity to their boats. The campground is located 2 miles east of Cass Lake, which is connected with seven other lakes. This is a nice stop for avid boaters. Located on the lake, the campsites are mostly shaded, level, and grassy with concrete patios. The typical site width is 35 feet, and there are 30 pull-throughs. The campground also has mobile homes and many seasonals. Tent sites are in a separate area for more privacy. The restaurant and lounge offers a complete menu and salad bar, as well as catering services for picnics and other events. The marina offers fish-cleaning, fish freezing, and fish packing. Security measures are good with owners who live on site, regular patrols, and surveillance cameras.

BASICS

Operated By: Cheryl Gangelhoff, Karen & Jim Bowley. **Open:** May 1–Oct. 15. **Site Assignment:** Reservations w/ 1-night deposit; refunds w/ 7-day notice. **Registration:** At campground office. **Fee:** $20–$28.50; cash, check, credit card. **Parking:** At site.

FACILITIES

Number of RV-only Sites: 165. **Number of Tent-only Sites:** 10. **Hookups:** Electric (30, 50 amps), water, sewer. **Each Site:** Picnic table, fire ring. **Dump Station:** Yes. **Laundry:** Yes. **Pay Phone:** Yes. **Restrooms and Showers:** Yes. **Fuel:** Yes. **Propane:** Yes. **Internal Roads:** Gravel, in good condition. **RV Service:** No. **Market:** 2 mi. west in Cass Lake. **Restaurant:** On site. **General Store:** Yes. **Vending:** Yes. **Swimming:** No. **Playground:** Yes. **Other:** Lake, boat canal, rec room, marina, concrete patios, restaurant & bar, video games, pavilion, recreation field, basketball, badminton, horseshoes, hiking trails, volleyball, fish-cleaning house. **Activities:** Swimming, boating (rental pontoon boats, kayaks, canoes, paddleboats, motorboats available), hiking, fishing, hunting. **Nearby Attractions:** Lakes, Native American burial grounds, logging museum, wildlife park, scenic drives, golf, tennis, bingo, casino, summer theater. **Additional Information:** Bemidji Area Tourist Information Center, (800) 458-2223, ext. 100.

RESTRICTIONS

Pets: On leash only. **Fires:** Fire ring only. **Alcoholic Beverages:** Allowed. **Vehicle Maximum Length:** No limit.

TO GET THERE

From the junction of Hwy. 371 and US 2, drive 2 mi. east on US 2. Roads are wide and well maintained, with broad shoulders.

CLOQUET   MAP, B-3
Cloquet/Duluth KOA

1381 Carlton Rd., 55720. T: (800) KOA-9506 or (218) 879-5726.

🚐 ★★★★   ▲ ★★★

Beauty: ★★   Site Privacy: ★★★
Spaciousness: ★★★   Quiet: ★★★★
Security: ★★★★   Cleanliness: ★★★★
Insect Control: ★★   Facilities: ★★★★

Travelers on their way through the Cloquet and Duluth area are often pleased to find the Cloquet/Duluth KOA. It is very clean, offers good facilities, and is conveniently located near major roads. It is not much of a destination campground, however. Campers don't stop here planning to spend several days at the campground. The activities are rather skimpy, and it doesn't provide much in the way of natural beauty. Sites are level, open, and shaded, and 30 feet is the average site width. Most RV sites are gravel, and 27 are pull-throughs. The most requested RV sites are 1 to 10 because they offer full hookup and pull-through access. Tent sites are scattered throughout the campground. Security is provided by owners who live on the grounds providing regular patrols, and local police also keep an eye on the campground.

BASICS

Operated By: Bill, Barbara, Bob, & Linde Higton. **Open:** May 1–Oct. 15. **Site Assignment:** Reservations w/ 1-night deposit; refunds w/ 2-day notice. **Registration:** At campground office. **Fee:** $23–$40; cash, check, credit card. **Parking:** At site; 1 vehicle & 1 RV per site.

FACILITIES

Number of RV-only Sites: 50. **Number of Tent-only Sites:** 12. **Hookups:** Electric (30, 50 amps), water, sewer. **Each Site:** Picnic table, fire ring. **Dump Station:** Yes. **Laundry:** Yes. **Pay Phone:** Yes. **Restrooms and Showers:** Yes. **Fuel:** No. **Propane:** Yes. **Internal Roads:** Gravel, in good condition. **RV Service:** No. **Market:** 1 mi. south in Cloquet. **Restaurant:** 3 mi. south in Cloquet. **General Store:** Yes. **Vending:** Yes. **Swimming:** Yes. **Playground:** Yes. **Other:** Hot tub, pool, horseshoes, volleyball, game room, badminton, basketball, rec hall, recreation field, TV room. **Activities:** Swimming, biking (rental bikes available), Sat. night hayride, weekly ice-cream social, pancake breakfast on Sun. **Nearby Attractions:** Zoo, train museum, harbor cruises, casino, paper mill tour, train rides, charter fishing, agate hounding, mansion tours, canal park. **Additional Information:** Cloquet Area Chamber of Commerce, (800) 554-4350.

RESTRICTIONS

Pets: On leash only; no more than 2 per site. **Fires:** Fire ring only. **Alcoholic Beverages:** Allowed. **Vehicle Maximum Length:** 40 ft.

TO GET THERE

From the junction of I-35 and Hwy. 45, take Exit 239 and drive 2 mi. south on Hwy. 45, then 0.25 mi. west on CR 3. Roads are wide and well maintained, with broad shoulders.

COKATO LAKE — MAP, C-2
Cokato Lake Campground

2945 CR 4 SW, 55321. T: (320) 286-5779; www.cokatolakecampground.com.

🚐 ★★★★ ▲ ★★★★

Beauty: ★★★★	Site Privacy: ★★★★
Spaciousness: ★★★★	Quiet: ★★★★
Security: ★★★★	Cleanliness: ★★★★
Insect Control: ★★	Facilities: ★★★★

Located beside Cokato Lake on a hilly terrain, this campground offers mostly shaded, grassy sites with a typical site width of 25 feet. There are 12 pull-through sites, and some open spots for campers concerned about satellite TV reception. Laid out in a series of loops, the campground has 100 seasonal campers. Quiet hours are enforced from 11 p.m. to 8 a.m. when all children must remain at sites and radios must be off. Mini-bikes, ATVs, and gas golf carts are not allowed on the grounds. The swimming pool is closed on Mondays for maintenance. The speed limit is 10 mph, rather high for a family campground, and campers are asked to limit driving after dark. Security includes owners who live on site and a security gate.

BASICS

Operated By: Turning Point Investments. **Open:** May 1–Oct. 1. **Site Assignment:** Reservations w/ $50 deposit; refunds (minus $10) w/ 2-week notice. **Registration:** At campground office. **Fee:** $29–$37; cash, check, credit card. **Parking:** At site.

FACILITIES

Number of RV-only Sites: 202. **Number of Tent-only Sites:** 23. **Hookups:** Electric (20, 30, 50 amps), water, sewer. **Each Site:** Picnic table, fire ring. **Dump Station:** Yes. **Laundry:** Yes. **Pay Phone:** Yes. **Restrooms and Showers:** Yes. **Fuel:** No. **Propane:** Yes. **Internal Roads:** Gravel, in good condition. **RV Service:** No. **Market:** 3 mi. south in Cokato. **Restaurant:** 3 mi. south in Cokato. **General Store:** Yes. **Vending:** Yes. **Swimming:** Yes. **Playground:** Yes. **Other:** Rental cabins & cottages, chapel, Cokato Lake, game room, mini-golf, tennis, softball, volleyball, rec hall, pavilion, boat ramp, boat dock. **Activities:** Swimming, fishing, boating (rental rowboats, canoes, paddleboats & motorboats available), scheduled weekend activities. **Nearby Attractions:** Charles A. Lindbergh House & History Center, Ellingson Car Museum, Minnesota Baseball Hall of Fame, St. John's Benedictine Abbey, golf, antiques, arts & crafts shops. **Additional Information:** St. Cloud Area CVB, (800) 264-2940.

RESTRICTIONS

Pets: On leash only. **Fires:** Fire ring only. **Alcoholic Beverages:** Allowed. **Vehicle Maximum Length:** 40 ft.

TO GET THERE

From the junction of US 12 and CR 4, drive 3 mi. northeast on CR 4. Roads are wide and well maintained, with broad shoulders.

DETROIT LAKES — MAP, B-1
Country Campground

13639 260th Ave., 56501. T: (800) 898-7901 or (218) 847-9621; www.lakesnet.net/ccdl.

🚐 ★★★★ ▲ ★★★★

Beauty: ★★★★	Site Privacy: ★★★★
Spaciousness: ★★★★	Quiet: ★★★★
Security: ★★★★	Cleanliness: ★★★★
Insect Control: ★★★★	Facilities: ★★★

Little touches are what make Country Campground such an inviting place to stay. The entrance is welcoming with a trellis, old wagon-wheel, flowers, and statues of friendly critters. Other bits of landscaping around the campground are also pleasant. Located 1 mile south of Detroit Lakes, which has a mile-long beach, Country Campground offers level, grassy sites along Glawe Lake. The typical site width is 40 feet, and there are 15 pull-through sites. A well-organized gift shop with dolls, wood carvings, ceramics, and handblown glass is a plus. Another attraction is a fenced-in children's area complete with swing sets, sandbox, and toys. A dock with a love seat swing is a popular spot. Security measures include owners who keep a close watch on the campground.

BASICS

Operated By: Elwood & Lois Orner. **Open:** May 1–Oct. 1. **Site Assignment:** Reservations w/ 1-night deposit; refund w/ 7-day notice. **Registration:** At campground office. **Fee:** $25; cash, check, credit card. **Parking:** At site.

FACILITIES

Number of RV-only Sites: 30. **Number of Tent-only Sites:** 4. **Hookups:** Electric (30, 50 amps), water, sewer. **Each Site:** Picnic table, fire ring. **Dump Station:** Yes. **Laundry:** Yes. **Pay Phone:** No. **Restrooms and Showers:** Yes. **Fuel:** No. **Propane:** Yes. **Internal Roads:** Gravel, in good condition. **RV Service:** No. **Market:** 1 mi. north in Detroit Lakes. **Restaurant:** 1 mi. north in Detroit Lakes. **General Store:** Yes, limited. **Vending:** Yes. **Swimming:** No. **Playground:** Yes. **Other:** Pavilion, fishing lake, recreation building, softball, basketball, horseshoes, volleyball, lounge, gift shop, croquet. **Activities:** Fishing, boating (paddleboats & canoes available). **Nearby Attractions:** Swimming, golf, 2 amusement parks, boating, snowmobiling, cross-country skiing, downhill skiing, Becker County Museum, 412 lakes, scenic drives, Tamarac National Wildlife Refuge. **Additional Information:** Detroit Lakes Regional Chamber of Commerce & Tourism Bureau, (800) 542-3992.

RESTRICTIONS

Pets: On leash only. **Fires:** Fire ring only. **Alcoholic Beverages:** At site only. **Vehicle Maximum Length:** No limit.

TO GET THERE

From the north: Take US 59 south to the intersection of US 10. Continue south 2 mi. to the intersection of Becker CR 6. Turn left onto Becker CR 6 and go 0.5 mi. Stop, or you'll be introduced to one of the area's most popular attractions—Detroit Lake. Turn right at the stop sign onto Becker CR 22 and go 1 mi. until you just pass the Lakeview General Store on your left. Bear left at the curve onto 260th Ave. and continue 0.75 mi. Look to your left. Roads are mostly wide and well maintained, with adequate shoulders.

FARIBAULT — MAP, D-2, D-3
Camp Faribo

21851 Bagley Ave., 55021. T: (800) 689-8453 or (507) 332-8453; www.exploreminnesota.com/lodging/2291.html.

🚐 ★★★★ ▲ ★★★

Beauty: ★★★★	Site Privacy: ★★★
Spaciousness: ★★★	Quiet: ★★★★
Security: ★★★★	Cleanliness: ★★★★
Insect Control: ★★★★	Facilities: ★★★★

An open, grassy campground with level sites, Camp Faribo is a handy camping spot if you plan to visit nearby attractions. Many campers come year after year to visit area attractions and to enjoy the activities at the campground. Camp Faribo is about 45 minutes from the Mall of America and the Minnesota Zoo and is close to ten lakes. The campground has a typical site width of 25 feet and has 20 pull-throughs. With only nine seasonal campers, the campground has plenty of room for visitors. The most popular sites are close to the heated swimming pool and the facilities. The owners keep a close watch on the campground to keep it quiet and family oriented.

BASICS

Operated By: Bob & Lori Bruns. **Open:** Apr. 1–Oct. 24. **Site Assignment:** Reservations w/ 1-night deposit; refund w/ 14-day notice. **Registration:** At campground office. **Fee:** $26–$30; cash, check, credit card. **Parking:** At site.

FACILITIES

Number of RV-only Sites: 71. **Number of Tent-only Sites:** Undesignated sites. **Hookups:** Electric (20, 30, 50 amps), water, sewer. **Each Site:** Picnic table, fire ring. **Dump Station:** Yes. **Laundry:** Yes. **Pay Phone:** Yes. **Restrooms and Showers:** Yes. **Fuel:** No. **Propane:** Yes. **Internal Roads:** Gravel, in good condition. **RV Service:** No. **Market:** 2 mi. north. **Restaurant:** 2 mi. north. **General Store:** Yes. **Vending:** Yes. **Swimming:** Yes. **Playground:** Yes. **Other:** Rec hall, coin games, sports field, horseshoes, volleyball, modem hookup, video games, billiards, air hockey. **Activities:** Swimming, bike rentals ($2.50–$3.50). **Nearby Attractions:** Historic walking tours, Alexander Faribault House, Episcopal Cathedral, Faribault Woolen Mill, Ivan Whillock Studio, Rice County Museum of History, Mall of America, Minnesota Zoo, 10 lakes. **Additional Information:** Faribault Area Chamber of Commerce, (800) 658-2354.

RESTRICTIONS

Pets: On leash only. **Fires:** Fire ring only. **Alcoholic Beverages:** Allowed. **Vehicle Maximum Length:** No limit.

TO GET THERE

From the junction of I-35 and Hwy. 60, take Exit 56, drive 500 ft. east on Hwy. 60, then 1.5 mi. south on Western Ave. Roads are wide and well maintained, with adequate shoulders.

GRAND RAPIDS   MAP, B-2
Sugar Bay Campground/Resort

21812 Moose Point Rd., 55721. T: (218) 326-8493; www.sugarbaycampgroundresort.com.

🚐 ★★★   ▲ ★★

Beauty: ★★★★	Site Privacy: ★★★
Spaciousness: ★★★★	Quiet: ★★★★
Security: ★★★★	Cleanliness: ★★★★
Insect Control: ★★	Facilities: ★★★

Campers who have seen the campground exit sign on the highway often pull in to Sugar Bay frustrated and tired. Since the state won't post a mileage sign for the campground, many campers who have turned off hoping to find a convenient night's rest are often a bit angry. It is almost a 14-mile trip from the highway to the campground. But it is worth it for a quiet night's sleep. The campground is small, well maintained, and clean. Sites are level, grassy, and some are shady with four pull-throughs, 19 back-ins, and a typical site width of 40 feet. Baby trees are planted around the site. The Pokegama Lake campground features water activities and draws many repeat customers because of them. Bait and groceries are not sold at Sugar Bay, so be sure to take what you need, or you might have to drive 20 miles round-trip to get it.

BASICS

Operated By: Jim & Sandy Holasek. **Open:** May 11–Oct. 1. **Site Assignment:** Reservations w/ $20 nonrefundable deposit. **Registration:** At campground office. **Fee:** $21–$24; cash, check. **Parking:** At site.

FACILITIES

Number of RV-only Sites: 23. **Hookups:** Electric (20, 30 amps), water, sewer. **Each Site:** Picnic table,

fire ring. **Dump Station:** Yes. **Laundry:** No. **Pay Phone:** No. **Restrooms and Showers:** Yes. **Fuel:** Yes. **Propane:** No. **Internal Roads:** Gravel, in good condition. **RV Service:** No. **Market:** 10 mi. east in Grand Rapids. **Restaurant:** 8 mi east in Grand Rapids. **General Store:** No. **Vending:** No. **Swimming:** No. **Playground:** No. **Other:** Pokegama Lake, boat ramp, boat dock, horseshoes, cement patios, marina. **Activities:** Swimming, fishing, boating (rental motorboats, paddleboats & pontoons available). **Nearby Attractions:** Golf, Forest History Center, Otasca Heritage Center, Judy Garland Birthplace, Children's Discovery Museum. **Additional Information:** Grand Rapids Convention & Visitors Center, (800) 472-6366.

RESTRICTIONS

Pets: Leash only, restricted to campsite. **Fires:** Fire ring only. **Alcoholic Beverages:** Allowed. **Vehicle Maximum Length:** 40 ft.

TO GET THERE

From the junction of US 2 and US 169S, drive 7.5 mi. south on US 169, then 6 mi. west and north on CR 17, then 0.25 mi. east on CR 239. Roads are wide and well maintained, with broad shoulders.

HINCKLEY   MAP, C-2, C-3
Grand Casino Hinckley RV Resort

Hwy. 3 Box 14, 777 Lady Luck Dr., 55037. T: (800) 995-GRAND or (800) 468-3517; www.grandcasinosminnesota.com.

🚐 ★★★★★   ▲ n/a

Beauty: ★★★	Site Privacy: ★★★
Spaciousness: ★★★	Quiet: ★★★★
Security: ★★★★★	Cleanliness: ★★★★★
Insect Control: ★★	Facilities: ★★★★★

Grand Casino Hinckley RV Resort is the best money can buy. A full-time cleaning staff keeps the restrooms, showers, grounds, and other facilities spotless. The interior roads are better than you find in some towns. The grass is manicured like a golf course. The recreation options are excellent and suited to all ages. The security is outstanding—the campground office is open 24 hours a day, the campgrounds are well lit and patrolled, and access is through a manned locked gate, where visitors need an access code to enter. If you want to gamble and enjoy the pool and other amenities, it is well worth a visit. The Grand Casino Hinckley is open 24 hours a day, with blackjack tables and more than 2,000 slot machines, big-name entertainment acts from Las Vegas to Nashville, four restaurants, and an all-you-can-eat buffet. But if you want to sit under a shade tree and commune with nature, this is not the place. Laid out in a series of loops, the campground is basically a big paved field with baby trees. The typical site width is 35 feet. All sites have full hookup, and all sites are back-ins. Tent campers are out of luck. Tents are allowed only as an auxiliary unit.

BASICS

Operated By: The Mille Lacs Band of Ojibwe. **Open:** All year. **Site Assignment:** Reservation w/ 1-night deposit; refund w/ 7-day notice. **Registration:** At campground office. **Fee:** In-season,

$19.95–$22.95; off-season, $12.95; cash, check, credit card. **Parking:** At site.

FACILITIES

Number of RV-only Sites: 271. **Hookups:** Electric (20, 30, 50 amps), water, sewer, cable TV, Wi-Fi. **Each Site:** Picnic table, fire ring, light, patio. **Dump Station:** Yes. **Laundry:** Yes. **Pay Phone:** Yes. **Restrooms and Showers:** Yes. **Fuel:** No. **Propane:** No. **Internal Roads:** Paved, in excellent condition. **RV Service:** No. **Market:** 2 mi. west in Hinckley. **Restaurant:** Next door. **General Store:** Yes. **Vending:** Yes. **Swimming:** Yes. **Playground:** Yes. **Other:** Casino, free shuttle to casino, lodge, performers in outdoor amphitheater & Silver Sevens Lounge, volleyball, horseshoes, game room, Kids Quest Activity Center, rec room, whirlpool, golf, badminton, video games, shuffleboard, basketball, recreation field. **Activities:** Gambling, swimming, golf. **Nearby Attractions:** Fire Museum, state trails, scenic drives, flea market, antiques shops, historical sites. **Additional Information:** Hinckley CVB, (800) 996-4566.

RESTRICTIONS

Pets: On leash only. **Fires:** Fire ring only. **Alcoholic Beverages:** Allowed. **Vehicle Maximum Length:** 63 ft. **Other:** Tents permitted as an auxiliary unit only.

TO GET THERE

From the junction of I-35 and Hwy. 48, drive 1 mi. east on Hwy. 48. Roads are wide and well maintained, with broad shoulders.

HINCKLEY   MAP, C-2, C-3
St. Croix State Park

reserve america

30065 St. Croix Park Rd., 55037. T: (320) 384-6591; www.reserveamerica.com.

🚐 ★★   ▲ ★★★★

Beauty: ★★★★	Site Privacy: ★★★★
Spaciousness: ★★★★	Quiet: ★★★★
Security: ★★★★	Cleanliness: ★★★
Insect Control: ★★	Facilities: ★★

Located 15 miles east of Hinckley, St. Croix State Park is Minnesota's largest. Situated along the St. Croix River, the park covers over 33,000 acres of forests, meadows, marshes, and streams. The park was established in 1943 after being developed by the National Park Service as a demonstration area. It lives up to its reputation as a popular recreational spot. The park offers 127 miles of hiking trails, 75 miles of horse trails, 6 miles of paved trails, 80 miles of groomed snowmobile trails, and 6 miles of ski trails. The RV sites are gravel and rather small at 15 by 60. They are mostly shaded with no pull-through sites available. Tent sites include two pack-in sites, ten primitive canoe campsites, and a primitive group camp for up to 200 campers. Tent campers have more room and privacy in their wilderness setting.

BASICS

Operated By: State of Minnesota. **Open:** All year. **Site Assignment:** Full reservation costs must be paid in advance along w/ a nonrefundable $8.50 service charge; refunds (minus $5 & $8.50 fees) w/ 7-day notice. **Registration:** At campground office. **Fee:** $18–$22; cash, check, credit card. **Parking:** At site.

FACILITIES

Number of RV-only Sites: 42. **Number of Tent-only Sites:** 170. **Hookups:** Electric (30 amps). **Each Site:** Picnic table, fire ring. **Dump Station:** Yes. **Laundry:** No. **Pay Phone:** Yes. **Restrooms and Showers:** Yes. **Fuel:** No. **Propane:** No. **Internal Roads:** Paved/gravel, in good condition. **RV Service:** No. **Market:** 22 mi. north in Hinckley. **Restaurant:** 22 mi. north in Hinckley. **General Store:** Yes. **Vending:** Yes. **Swimming:** No. **Playground:** Yes. **Other:** Lake w/ sandy beach, hiking trail, bike trail, interpretive center, horse camp area, enclosed picnic shelter, canoe landings. **Activities:** Swimming, fishing, hiking, boating (rental canoes available), biking (rental bikes available), year-round interpretive programs. **Nearby Attractions:** Casino, Fire Museum, golf, state trails, scenic drives, flea market, antique shops, historical sites. **Additional Information:** Hinckley CVB, (800) 996-4566.

RESTRICTIONS

Pets: On leash only. **Fires:** Fire ring only. **Alcoholic Beverages:** Not allowed. **Vehicle Maximum Length:** 66 ft. **Other:** Vehicle permits of $25 per year or $7 per day are required to enter all Minnesota state parks; 14-day stay limit.

TO GET THERE

From the junction of I-35 and Hwy. 48, take the Hinckley exit, drive 15 mi. east on Hwy. 48, then 5 mi. south on CR 22. Roads are wide and well maintained, with broad shoulders.

HOUSTON   MAP, D-3
Money Creek Haven

18502 County 26, 55943. T: (507) 896-3544; www.moneycreekhaven.com.

🚐 ★★★	🏕 ★★★
Beauty: ★★★	Site Privacy: ★★★
Spaciousness: ★★★★	Quiet: ★★★
Security: ★★★	Cleanliness: ★★★
Insect Control: ★★	Facilities: ★★★

The campsite celebrated its 40th birthday in 2002. About half the sites at Money Creek Haven are occupied by seasonals. The on-site restaurant serves several hundred people every morning with a big country breakfast. The restaurant offers mostly fast-food the rest of the day. The campground offers primarily shaded, grassy sites in a rural setting. The typical site size is 50 by 50 with a mix of back-in and pull-through sites. The best sites for RVs are in the B section, which offers full hookups, easy access, lots of shade, and a location by the pool. Tents are not well screened for privacy from RV campers. Be aware that no one is allowed in the swimming pool after dark.

BASICS

Operated By: Wayne Fitting. **Open:** Apr. 15–Oct. 15. **Site Assignment:** Reservations w/ 1-night deposit; refunds w/ 7-day notice. **Registration:** At camp office. **Fee:** $18–$25; cash, check, credit card. **Parking:** At site.

FACILITIES

Number of RV-only Sites: 185. **Number of Tent-only Sites:** 12. **Hookups:** Electric (20, 30 amps), water, sewer. **Each Site:** Picnic table, fire ring. **Dump Station:** Yes. **Laundry:** Yes. **Pay Phone:** Yes. **Restrooms and Showers:** Yes. **Fuel:** No. **Propane:** No. **Internal Roads:** Paved/gravel, in good condition. **RV Service:** No. **Market:** 6 mi. south in Houston. **Restaurant:** On site. **General Store:** Yes. **Vending:** No. **Swimming:** Yes. **Playground:** Yes. **Other:** Game room w/ video & pool tables, horseshoes, volleyball, fishing pond, badminton, hiking trails, recreation field. **Activities:** Swimming, fishing, hiking. **Nearby Attractions:** Golf, snowmobile, farm tours, art & antiques shops, scenic drives, nature center. **Additional Information:** Bluff Country Regional CVB, (800) 428-2030.

RESTRICTIONS

Pets: On leash only. **Fires:** Fire ring only. **Alcoholic Beverages:** Allowed. **Vehicle Maximum Length:** 50 ft. **Other:** No ATVs.

TO GET THERE

From the junction of I-90 and Hwy. 76, drive 8 mi. south on Hwy. 76, then 0.25 mi. west on Hwy. 26. Roads are wide and well maintained, with broad shoulders.

ISLE   MAP, C-2
South Isle Family Campground

39002 Hwy. 47, 56342. T: (320) 676-8538; www.southislecampground.com.

🚐 ★★★	🏕 ★★★
Beauty: ★★★	Site Privacy: ★★★
Spaciousness: ★★★	Quiet: ★★★
Security: ★★★	Cleanliness: ★★★
Insect Control: ★★	Facilities: ★★★

Family owned and operated since 1991, South Isle Family Campground is located 2 miles south of Isle. The rural campground is surrounded by woods, marshland, and prairie grass areas. The typical campsite width is 40 feet, and the campground has 20 pull-throughs. However, all the full-hookup sites are occupied by seasonals. Sites are grassy and shaded to semishaded. A separate area for tent campers offers privacy and more natural amenities. The campground is known for its R/C airplane airstrip where hobbyists can fly their radio-controlled airplanes and curious bystanders can watch.

BASICS

Operated By: Wally & Sue Heise. **Open:** Apr. 21–Oct. **Site Assignment:** Reservations w/ $35 deposit, $75 deposit on holiday weekends; refund (minus $5) w/ 7-day notice. **Registration:** At campground office. **Fee:** $22–$35; cash, credit card. **Parking:** At site.

FACILITIES

Number of RV-only Sites: 120. **Number of Tent-only Sites:** 0. **Hookups:** Electric (20, 30, 50 amps), water. **Each Site:** Picnic table, fire ring. **Dump Station:** Yes. **Laundry:** No. **Pay Phone:** No. **Restrooms and Showers:** Yes. **Fuel:** No. **Propane:** No. **Internal Roads:** Gravel, in good

condition. **RV Service:** No. **Market:** Yes. **Restaurant:** 2 mi. north in Isle. **General Store:** 2 mi. north in Isle. **Vending:** No. **Swimming:** Yes. **Playground:** Yes. **Other:** Kids' fishing pond w/ free paddleboat to use, horseshoes, disc golf course, shuffleboard, nature trails, basketball, volleyball, softball, tetherball, badminton, TV lounge & video game area. **Activities:** Swimming, hiking, scheduled weekend activities. **Nearby Attractions:** Golf, Mille Lacs Lake, Soo Line Bicycle Trail, Mille Lacs Grand Casino, craft & antiques shops, museums, Father Hennepin State Park. **Additional Information:** Mille Lacs Area Tourism Council, (888) 350-2692.

RESTRICTIONS

Pets: Leash only; 1 dog per site. Additional dog, $2.50/day. **Fires:** Fire ring only. **Alcoholic Beverages:** Allowed. **Vehicle Maximum Length:** No limit. **Other:** Daily rates are based on 2 people; children under age 4 are free; additional children are $2 per day; additional adults are $4 per day; visitors are $4 per day.

TO GET THERE

From town, drive 2 mi. south on Hwy. 47. Road is in good shape.

KELLIHER   MAP, B-2
Rogers' Campground and RV Park

49690 Rogers Rd. NE, 56650. T: (218) 647-8262; www.rogerscg.net.

🚐 ★★★	🏕 ★★★
Beauty: ★★★	Site Privacy: ★★★
Spaciousness: ★★★	Quiet: ★★★
Security: ★★★	Cleanliness: ★★★
Insect Control: ★★★	Facilities: ★★★

Located on the Upper Red Lake in Kelliher, Rogers' Campground provides lakeside access. The remote campground offers mostly open campsites that enjoy the lakeside breeze. More shaded sites are offered in the back. The typical site width is 25 feet. Laid out in a series of loops, the campground has four pull-through sites and 20 seasonal campers. Shotley Brook winds its way through the center of the campground, making many on-the-water campsites. Over 800 feet of sandy beach is available on Upper Red Lake, a very shallow lake with no drop-off, making it a nice swimming beach. A private concrete boat ramp and protected harbor add to the boating activities. To protect the peace and quiet, as well as the abundant wildlife—including an active eagle's nest on the property—no ATVs are allowed in the campground. Although only the most hardy would want to camp in northern Minnesota during the winter, the campground provides some wintertime amenities. Available for rent are several cabins and ice-fishing shacks. Owners also have three snowplows to make the campground passable for winter campers.

BASICS

Operated By: Jerry & Joani Barthel. **Open:** All year. **Site Assignment:** Reservations w/ 1-night deposit; refund (minus $5) w/ 2-week notice. **Registration:** At campground office. **Fee:** $24; cash, check, credit card. **Parking:** At site.

FACILITIES

Number of RV-only Sites: 74. **Number of Tent-only Sites:** 5. **Hookups:** Electric (20, 30 amps), water, sewer. **Each Site:** Picnic table, fire ring. **Dump Station:** Yes. **Laundry:** Yes. **Pay Phone:** Yes. **Restrooms and Showers:** Yes. **Fuel:** No. **Propane:** No. **Internal Roads:** Gravel, in good condition. **RV Service:** No. **Market:** 14 mi. southeast in Kelliher. **Restaurant:** 14 mi. southeast in Kelliher. **General Store:** Yes, limited. **Vending:** Yes. **Swimming:** No. **Playground:** Yes. **Other:** Upper Red Lake, swimming beach, hiking trails, fish-cleaning house, sports field, croquet, pavilion, tetherball, volleyball, basketball, horseshoes, rec room, boat dock, boat ramp, badminton, rental houses. **Activities:** Swimming, fishing, hiking, boating (rental tubes, paddleboats & kayaks available), scheduled weekend activities. **Nearby Attractions:** Mississippi River, Paul Bunyan & Babe the Blue Ox statues, water parks, waterslide, logging camp, fishing, golf, antiques, arts & crafts. **Additional Information:** Bemidji Area Tourist Information, (800) 458-2223.

RESTRICTIONS

Pets: On leash only. **Fires:** Fire ring only. **Alcoholic Beverages:** Allowed. **Vehicle Maximum Length:** No limit.

TO GET THERE

From the junction of CR 36 and Hwy. 72, drive 9 mi. north on Hwy. 72, then 5 mi. west on CR 23, then 0.75 mi. north on access road. Roads are mostly wide and well maintained, with adequate shoulders.

LANESBORO   MAP, D-3
Eagle Cliff Campground and Lodging

Hwy. 1 Box 344, 55949. T: (507) 467-2598; www.eaglecliff-campground.com.

🚐 ★★★	🏕 ★★★★
Beauty: ★★★★	Site Privacy: ★★★
Spaciousness: ★★★	Quiet: ★★★★
Security: ★★★★	Cleanliness: ★★★★★
Insect Control: ★★	Facilities: ★★★

Located in a valley with bluffs rising on one side and the Root River running on another, Eagle Cliff Campground and Lodging is a great place for river activities. It has a useful rinse area to keep the river water and dirt out of spotless showers and bathroom facilities. The wilderness campground has no scheduled activities or swimming pool, thereby allowing the river to be the center of recreation. All sites are grassy and level, and there are no gravel or paved sites. Many RV sites are open with young trees too little to provide shade. The typical site width is 45 feet with a dozen pull-throughs. A special section by the river has been set aside for tent campers, and, unlike many campgrounds, Eagle Cliff has more tent sites than RV sites. Visiting during the week would be best because the campground quickly fills on weekends. Reservations are recommended.

BASICS

Operated By: Naber family. **Open:** Apr. 1–Dec. 1. **Site Assignment:** Reservations w/ 1-night deposit;

refunds w/ 2-week notice. **Registration:** At campground office. **Fee:** $18–$27; cash, check, credit card. **Parking:** At site.

FACILITIES

Number of RV-only Sites: 62. **Number of Tent-only Sites:** 88. **Hookups:** Electric (20, 30, 50 amps), water, sewer. **Each Site:** Picnic table, fire ring. **Dump Station:** Yes. **Laundry:** Yes. **Pay Phone:** Yes. **Restrooms and Showers:** Yes. **Fuel:** No. **Propane:** No. **Internal Roads:** Gravel, in good condition. **RV Service:** No. **Market:** 3 mi. west in Lanesboro. **Restaurant:** 3 mi. west in Lanesboro. **General Store:** Yes. **Swimming:** No. **Playground:** Yes. **Other:** River rinse-off area, game room, horseshoes, volleyball, canoe landing, recreation field. **Activities:** Hunting, fishing, boating (rental kayaks, canoes & tubes available), biking (rental bikes available), hiking. **Nearby Attractions:** Golf, scenic drives, petting zoo, Amish tours. **Additional Information:** Lanesboro Office of Visitor Information, (800) 944-2670.

RESTRICTIONS

Pets: On leash only. You will be charged if your dog digs holes. **Fires:** Fire ring only. **Alcoholic Beverages:** Allowed. **Vehicle Maximum Length:** 40 ft. **Other:** No check-in after 11 p.m.

TO GET THERE

From the junction of US 52 and Hwy. 16, drive 9 mi. east on Hwy. 16.

LITTLE FALLS   MAP, C-2
Charles A. Lindbergh State Park

reserve america

1615 Lindbergh Dr. S., 56345. T: (320) 616-2525 or (866) 85-PARKS; www.reserveamerica.com.

🚐 ★★	🏕 ★★★★
Beauty: ★★★★	Site Privacy: ★★★★
Spaciousness: ★★★★	Quiet: ★★★★
Security: ★★★★	Cleanliness: ★★★
Insect Control: ★★	Facilities: ★★

This state park was established in 1931 when 110 acres were donated to the state in memory of Charles A. Lindbergh, Sr. World renowned for his trans-Atlantic solo flight in 1927, Lindbergh lived his boyhood years in the house by the park overlooking the Mississippi River. Water and woodland activities are a major attraction in the state park. The Pike Creek meanders through and empties into the Mississippi River in the southern part of the park. Located 1.5 miles south of Little Falls, the campground's sites are mostly shaded and level with back-ins and no pull-throughs. The most popular RV sites are 1, 3, 7, 9, 10, 11, and 12 because they offer electricity and are next to Pike Creek. Tent sites are in a separate loop. Also, there is one hike-in site and one site available by canoe. Security is great with one access road, a security gate which is closed from 10 p.m. to 8 a.m. except to registered campers, and regular patrols by park rangers and city police.

BASICS

Operated By: State of Minnesota. **Open:** All year. **Site Assignment:** First come, first served; reserva-

tions accepted in summer w/ $8.50 nonrefundable fee. **Registration:** At campground office. **Fee:** $18–$22; cash, check, credit card. **Parking:** At site.

FACILITIES

Number of RV-only Sites: 15. **Number of Tent-only Sites:** 23. **Hookups:** Electric (30 amps). **Each Site:** Picnic table, fire ring. **Dump Station:** Yes. **Laundry:** No. **Pay Phone:** Courtesy phone. **Restrooms and Showers:** Yes. **Fuel:** No. **Propane:** No. **Internal Roads:** Paved, in good condition. **RV Service:** No. **Market:** 1.5 mi. north in Little Falls. **Restaurant:** 1.5 mi. north in Little Falls. **General Store:** 1.5 mi. north in Little Falls. **Vending:** No. **Swimming:** No. **Playground:** Yes. **Other:** Picnic area, enclosed shelters, hiking & skiing trails, boat ramp, ranger station. **Activities:** Fishing, hiking, boating (rental canoes available). **Nearby Attractions:** Charles A. Lindbergh House State Historic Site, Weyerhaeuser Museum, Minnesota Military Museum, Pine Grove Park & Zoo, bowling, golf, horseback riding, tennis. **Additional Information:** Little Falls CVB, (800) 325-5916.

RESTRICTIONS

Pets: On leash only. **Fires:** Fire ring only. **Alcoholic Beverages:** 3.2% beer only. **Vehicle Maximum Length:** 50 ft. **Other:** Vehicle permits of $25 per year or $7 per day are required to enter all Minnesota state parks; 14-day stay limit.

TO GET THERE

From the junction of Hwy. 27 and CR 52, drive 1.5 mi. southwest on CR 52. Roads are wide and well maintained, with broad shoulders.

MOOSE LAKE   MAP, C-3
Red Fox Campground and RV Park

P.O. Box 10, 55767. T: (218) 485-0341.

🚐 ★★★	🏕 ★★★
Beauty: ★★★	Site Privacy: ★★★
Spaciousness: ★★★	Quiet: ★★★
Security: ★★★★	Cleanliness: ★★★
Insect Control: ★★	Facilities: ★★★

Red Fox Campground and RV Park offers easy access from I-35, 2 miles south of Moose Lake. But it also is easy to drive past it. The campground is located behind a Conoco gas station, which serves as a convenience and fast-food store for campers. The campground features a typical site width of 30 feet, but the sites are long. Site 34 is 100 feet long, and sites 19 and 20 are 90 feet long. The shortest site length is 45 feet. Sites are level, shady, and grassy with 11 pull-throughs. A separate tent site sets tent campers off from RVs for more privacy. The campground has very good security measures—a manager lives on site, visitors must leave by 10 p.m., and city police patrol the grounds regularly.

BASICS

Operated By: Sherri & Ron Graves. **Open:** May 15–Oct. 15. **Site Assignment:** Reservations accepted w/ $15 deposit; refund (minus $3) w/ 1-week notice. **Registration:** At campground office. **Fee:** $19–$23; cash, check. **Parking:** At site.

FACILITIES

Number of RV-only Sites: 36. **Number of Tent-only Sites:** 15. **Hookups:** Electric (30, 50 amps), water. **Each Site:** Picnic table, fire ring. **Dump Station:** Yes. **Laundry:** Yes. **Pay Phone:** No. **Restrooms and Showers:** Yes. **Fuel:** No. **Propane:** No. **Internal Roads:** Gravel, narrow but good condition. **RV Service:** No. **Market:** 2 mi. north in Moose Lake. **Restaurant:** 2 mi. north in Moose Lake. **General Store:** No. **Vending:** No. **Swimming:** No. **Playground:** Yes. **Other:** Pond w/ sandy beach, basketball, recreation building, putting green, horseshoes, group picnic area, hiking trails, volleyball, mini-golf. **Activities:** Swimming, fishing, hiking. **Nearby Attractions:** Casinos, state park, whitewater rafting, bike trails, golf, bowling, State Agate Center. **Additional Information:** Duluth Convention & Visitors Center, (800) 438-5884.

RESTRICTIONS

Pets: On leash only. **Fires:** Fire ring only. **Alcoholic Beverages:** At sites only. **Vehicle Maximum Length:** No limit.

TO GET THERE

From the junction of I-35 and Hwy. 73, take Exit 214, drive 500 ft. west behind Conoco gas station. Road is wide and well maintained, with broad shoulders.

NISSWA   MAP, C-2
Fritz's Resort and Campground

P.O. Box 803, 56468. T: (218) 568-8988; www.fritzsresort.com.

🚐 ★★★★   ▲ ★★

Beauty: ★★★★	Site Privacy: ★★★
Spaciousness: ★★★	Quiet: ★★★
Security: ★★★★	Cleanliness: ★★★★
Insect Control: ★★	Facilities: ★★★★

Fritz's Resort and Campground offers easy access and a nice roster of activities, as many campers have already discovered. All but 25 RV sites are occupied by seasonal campers. Call ahead to be sure a site is open before pulling in. Also be aware that pets are not allowed from Memorial Day to Labor Day. The rural campground is well organized in a series of loops with level, shaded sites, cement patios, and 15 pull-throughs. The typical site width is 25 feet. Tent campers are sort of left out with only three sites available, but they are well shaded. Being so close to the highway, 2.5 miles north of Nisswa, it's inevitable that traffic noise would creep in a bit. Lake Edna is a beautiful attraction, and the beach is groomed every morning by a maintenance team to keep it that way. The best RV sites are 1–4 around the rec hall because they are pull-throughs and roomy at 60 by 100. Security is good with owners who live on site, a regular campground patrol, and city police driving through the area.

BASICS

Operated By: Richard & Jane Geike. **Open:** May 1–Oct. 10. **Site Assignment:** Reservations w/ $40 deposit; no refund. **Registration:** At campground office. **Fee:** $36; cash, check, credit card. **Parking:** At site.

FACILITIES

Number of RV-only Sites: 75. **Hookups:** Electric (30, 50 amps), water, sewer. **Each Site:** Picnic table, fire ring. **Dump Station:** Yes. **Laundry:** Yes. **Pay Phone:** No. **Restrooms and Showers:** Yes. **Fuel:** Yes. **Propane:** Yes. **Internal Roads:** Paved, in good condition. **RV Service:** No. **Market:** 2.5 mi. south in Nisswa. **Restaurant:** 2.5 mi. south in Nisswa. **General Store:** Yes. **Vending:** No. **Swimming:** Yes. **Playground:** Yes. **Other:** Lake Edna, sandy beach, rec hall, pool tables, Ping-Pong, shuffleboard, 9-hole golf course, snack bar, adult room, fish-cleaning house, tennis court. **Activities:** Swimming, fishing, boating (rental motorboats, pontoons, canoes, paddleboats available). **Nearby Attractions:** Cross-country skiing, snowmobiling, raceway, Crow Wing County Historical Society, Paul Bunyan Amusement Center, Paul Bunyan Trail. **Additional Information:** Brainerd Lakes Area Chamber of Commerce, (800) 450-2838.

RESTRICTIONS

Pets: Pets will be allowed in campgrounds only before Memorial Day weekend & after Labor Day; $3 per day for each pet. **Fires:** Fire ring only. **Alcoholic Beverages:** Allowed. **Vehicle Maximum Length:** No limit.

TO GET THERE

From Nisswa, drive 1.5 mi. north on Hwy. 371.

NISSWA   MAP, C-2
Upper Cullen Resort and Campground

P.O. Box 72, 56468. T: (218) 963-2249 or (888) 872-8553; www.uppercullen.com.

🚐 ★★★   ▲ ★★★

Beauty: ★★★	Site Privacy: ★★★
Spaciousness: ★★★	Quiet: ★★★★
Security: ★★★★	Cleanliness: ★★★
Insect Control: ★★	Facilities: ★★★

A rural lakeside facility, Upper Cullen Resort and Campground is a peaceful family place. Located on the eastern shore of Upper Cullen Lake, 5 miles east of Nisswa, the secluded, heavily wooded campground features nature in abundance. Arranged in a series of loops, the campground has well-shaded level sites and four pull-throughs. The quiet surroundings and outdoor activities would probably appeal to tent campers. But there is no area set off for tents; tent sites are interspersed among RVs. Security is good, with only one entrance to the campground, owners who live on site, and regular patrols. Reservations are recommended as the campground is very popular in June, July, and August.

BASICS

Operated By: Bruce & Donna Galles. **Open:** May 1–Oct. 1. **Site Assignment:** Reservations w/ 2-night deposit; refund if site rerented, office fee of $25. **Registration:** At campground office. **Fee:** $31–$33; cash, check, credit card. **Parking:** At site.

FACILITIES

Number of RV-only Sites: 43. **Hookups:** Electric (20, 30 amps), water, sewer. **Each Site:** Picnic table, fire ring, water, electric. **Dump Station:** Yes. **Laundry:** Yes. **Pay Phone:** Yes. **Restrooms and Showers:** Yes. **Fuel:** Yes. **Propane:** No. **Internal Roads:** Gravel, narrow but in good condition. **RV Service:** No. **Market:** 5 mi. west in Nisswa. **Restaurant:** 5 mi. west in Nisswa. **General Store:** Yes. **Vending:** No. **Swimming:** No. **Playground:** Yes. **Other:** Upper Cullen Lake, sandy beach, horseshoes, shuffleboard, badminton, volleyball, basketball, tetherball, boat ramp, game room, nature trails, boat ramp, boat dock. **Activities:** Swimming, fishing, boating (rental motorboats, canoes, paddleboats & pontoons), hayrides, scheduled activities. **Nearby Attractions:** Cross-country skiing, snowmobiling, raceway, Crow Wing County Historical Society Museum, Paul Bunyan Amusement Center, Paul Bunyan Trail. **Additional Information:** Brainerd Lakes Area Chamber of Commerce, (800) 450-2838.

RESTRICTIONS

Pets: Not allowed. **Fires:** Fire ring only. **Alcoholic Beverages:** Allowed. **Vehicle Maximum Length:** 40 ft.

TO GET THERE

From downtown Nisswa, drive 2.25 mi. east on CR 18, then 2.5 mi. north on Old Hwy. 18. Roads are wide and well maintained, with broad shoulders.

OGILVIE   MAP, C-2
Hilltop Family Campground

2186 Empire St., 56358. T: (320) 272-4300; www.hilltopcampground.com.

🚐 ★★★   ▲ ★★★

Beauty: ★★★	Site Privacy: ★★★
Spaciousness: ★★★★	Quiet: ★★★★
Security: ★★★	Cleanliness: ★★★
Insect Control: ★★	Facilities: ★★★

Located 6 miles south of Ogilvie, Hilltop Family Campground offers spacious, wooded sites near a lake. The typical site width is 40 feet. Tent campers can use any sites, but there is no primitive area. The general store has limited stock, and all of the full-hookup sites are occupied by the 80 seasonals. Laid out in a series of loops, the campground has grassy sites—there are no concrete RV pads—and shade from Norway pines and other hardwood trees. The rural campground has 12 pull-through sites. Day visitors pay a $3 fee and must leave by 10 p.m. Quiet hours, including no radio playing, are between 11 p.m. and 8 a.m. No one under age 16 is allowed in the spa pool or spa area. Also, children under 14 must be accompanied by an adult at the swimming pool. Although the campground speed limit is 10 mph, the owners ask that campers walk instead of drive around the campground because of children playing.

BASICS

Operated By: John & Dot Forrest. **Open:** May 1–Oct. 1. **Registration:** At campground office. **Parking:** At site.

FACILITIES

Number of RV-only Sites: 125. **Number of Multipurpose Sites:** 18. **Hookups:** Electric (30, 50 amps), water. **Each Site:** Picnic table, fire ring. **Dump Station:** Yes. **Laundry:** Yes. **Pay Phone:**

No. **Restrooms and Showers:** Yes. **Fuel:** No. **Propane:** No. **Internal Roads:** Gravel, in fair condition. **RV Service:** No. **Market:** 6 mi. south to Ogilvie. **Restaurant:** 6 mi. south to Ogilvie. **General Store:** Yes. **Vending:** No. **Swimming:** Yes. **Playground:** Yes. **Other:** Fish-cleaning house, boat parking, rec hall, library, snack area, electronic games, pool table, spa tub, volleyball, basketball, softball, horseshoes, hiking trails. **Activities:** Swimming, hiking. **Nearby Attractions:** Fishing & boating across road on Ann Lake, golf. **Additional Information:** St. Cloud Area CVB, (800) 264-2940.

RESTRICTIONS

Pets: Leash only, $3 per pet per day. **Fires:** Fire ring only. **Alcoholic Beverages:** Allowed. **Vehicle Maximum Length:** No limit.

TO GET THERE

From the junction of Hwy. 23 and Hwy. 47, drive 5 mi. north on Hwy. 47, then 0.75 mi. east on CR 90, then 0.25 mi. south on Empire St. Roads are narrow and in fair condition, with narrow shoulders.

ORTONVILLE — MAP, C-1
Lakeshore RV Park and Fruit Farm

39445 Lakeshore RV Park Rd., 56278.
T: (800) 9for-FUN; www.lakeshorervpark.com.

🚐 ★★★★   ▲ ★★★★

Beauty: ★★★★	Site Privacy: ★★★★
Spaciousness: ★★★★	Quiet: ★★★★
Security: ★★★★	Cleanliness: ★★★★★
Insect Control: ★★★★	Facilities: ★★★★

A winning combination for campers is at Lakeshore RV Park and Fruit Farm. Located 3 miles north of Ortonville, the campground on the shores of Big Stone Lake offers level, prepared sites in a working apple orchard. The campground has a typical site width of 30 feet, 13 back-in and 65 pull-through sites with a choice of open or shaded. Cleanliness is tops and it's a pleasure to see such sparkling restroom facilities. Apples are available to be picked starting in September. A separate primitive area for tents allows more green space and privacy. The mini-golf course is unusually challenging, with such toughies as Adam's Rib and the Apple and the Worm in the Dutchman's Rock Garden. Security measures are good with owners who keep a close eye on the campground to make sure it is quiet, clean, and family-oriented.

BASICS

Operated By: Lakeshore RV Park Inc. **Open:** Apr. 15–Oct. 1. **Site Assignment:** Reservations w/ 1-night deposit; refund w/ 3-week notice (minus 10% fee). **Registration:** At campground office. **Fee:** $24.95; cash, check, credit card. **Parking:** At site.

FACILITIES

Number of RV-only Sites: 44. **Number of Tent-only Sites:** 10. **Hookups:** Electric (30, 50 amps), water, sewer. **Each Site:** Picnic table, fire ring. **Dump Station:** No. **Laundry:** Yes. **Pay Phone:** Courtesy phone. **Restrooms and Showers:** Yes. **Fuel:** No. **Propane:** Yes. **Internal Roads:** Gravel, in good condition. **RV Service:** No. **Market:** 3 mi. south in Ortonville. **Restaurant:** 3 mi. south in

Ortonville. **General Store:** Yes, limited. **Vending:** No. **Swimming:** Yes. **Playground:** Yes. **Other:** Big Stone Lake, arcade, hot tub, boat ramp, train rides, rec room, mini-golf, pavilion, sports field, volleyball, boat dock. **Activities:** Swimming, fishing, boating (rental excursion boat, bumper boats, pontoons, charter fishing, paddleboats available). **Nearby Attractions:** Golf, excursion boats, scenic drives, antiques, arts & crafts, wildlife refuge, mahogany granite quarries. **Additional Information:** Big Stone Lake Area Chamber of Commerce, (800) 568-5722.

RESTRICTIONS

Pets: On leash only. **Fires:** Fire ring only. **Alcoholic Beverages:** Allowed. **Vehicle Maximum Length:** No limit.

TO GET THERE

From the junction of US 12 and Hwy. 7, drive 3 mi. north on Hwy. 7. Roads are wide and well maintained, with broad shoulders.

PARK RAPIDS — MAP, B-2
Itasca State Park

reserve america™

36750 Main Park Dr., 56470. T: (218) 266-2100 or (866) 857-2757; www.reserveamerica.com.

🚐 ★★★   ▲ ★★★★

Beauty: ★★★★	Site Privacy: ★★★★
Spaciousness: ★★★	Quiet: ★★★★
Security: ★★★★	Cleanliness: ★★★
Insect Control: ★★	Facilities: ★★★

Itasca State Park really offers two campgrounds— Bear Paw Campground along the shores of Lake Itasca and Pine Ridge Campground, originally the 1930s Civilian Conservation Corps Camp. Both campgrounds have shady, back-in sites with a typical site size of 15 by 60 feet. Some sites have 40-foot widths. During the off season, Pine Ridge Campground is open for rustic winter camping with pit toilets; water is available at the park headquarters. For those looking for solitude, 11 year-round back-country campsites are accessible via 1- to 5-mile hikes. These sites offer fire rings and pit toilets but no water supply, and campers must carry out their garbage. Itasca also offers group camps with a staff cabin, dining hall with kitchen, modern toilet facility, and a tent area for up to 75 people. What Itasca State Park lacks in camping amenities, it makes up for in beauty and recreational opportunities.

BASICS

Operated By: State of Minnesota. **Open:** May 15–Oct. 15. **Site Assignment:** Reservations w/ 1-night deposit; refund (minus $5) w/ 3-day notice; nonrefundable $8.50 reservation fee is charged per camping reservation. **Registration:** At campground office. **Fee:** $15–$22; day park fee, $7; season permit, $25; cash, check, credit card. **Parking:** At site.

FACILITIES

Number of RV-only Sites: 100. **Number of Tent-only Sites:** 135. **Hookups:** Electric (20, 30 amps). **Each Site:** Picnic table, fire ring. **Dump Station:** Yes. **Laundry:** No. **Pay Phone:** Yes. **Restrooms**

and Showers: Yes. **Fuel:** No. **Propane:** No. **Internal Roads:** Paved/gravel, in good condition. **RV Service:** No. **Market:** 3 mi. north to Lake Itasca. **Restaurant:** Douglas Lodge at park. **General Store:** No. **Vending:** Yes. **Swimming:** No. **Playground:** Yes. **Other:** Hiking trails, hostel, sandy beach, bike trail, several lakes, lodges, cabins, tour boat, gift shop, visitor center, lodge, amphitheater, boat landing, fire tower, interpretive center. **Activities:** Swimming, fishing, hiking, biking, (rental bikes available), boating (rental pontoons, paddleboat, canoe & fishing boats available), naturalist programs, workshops. **Nearby Attractions:** Scenic drives, historic sites. **Additional Information:** Minnesota Office of Tourism, (800) 657-3700.

RESTRICTIONS

Pets: On leash only. **Fires:** Fire ring only. **Alcoholic Beverages:** Not allowed. **Vehicle Maximum Length:** 60 ft. **Other:** 14-day stay limit.

TO GET THERE

From Park Rapids, drive 20 mi. north on US 71. Road is in fair condition, with often narrow shoulders.

PARK RAPIDS — MAP, B-2
Vagabond Village

23801 Green Pines Rd., 56470. T: (218) 732-5234; www.vagabondvillage.com.

🚐 ★★★★   ▲ ★★★★

Beauty: ★★★★	Site Privacy: ★★★★
Spaciousness: ★★★★	Quiet: ★★★★
Security: ★★★★	Cleanliness: ★★★★
Insect Control: ★★★	Facilities: ★★★

Surrounded by birch and pine trees, Vagabond Village Campground overlooks Potato Lake with views of hills and water. Located 8 miles north of Park Rapids, the campground has level, mostly open sites with a typical site width of 50 feet. Laid out in a series of loops, Vagabond Village has ten pull-through sites and 35 seasonal campers. Most RVs prefer the bigger sites near the facilities. Tents usually like F section best, because it is more private with green space and separated from RVs. Several outside shelters are popular for group gatherings and family reunions. A nice soda fountain serves old-fashioned ice cream and other treats. Security measures include owners who live on site, regular campground patrols, a gate, and surveillance cameras.

BASICS

Operated By: The Nelson family. **Open:** May 11–Oct. 1. **Site Assignment:** Reservation w/ $40 deposit; refund (minus $10) w/ 15-day notice. **Registration:** At campground office. **Fee:** $33–$36; cash, check. **Parking:** At site.

FACILITIES

Number of RV-only Sites: 116. **Number of Tent-only Sites:** 10. **Hookups:** Electric (30, 50 amps), water, sewer. **Each Site:** Picnic table, fire ring. **Dump Station:** Yes. **Laundry:** Yes. **Pay Phone:** Yes. **Restrooms and Showers:** Yes. **Fuel:** No. **Propane:** Yes. **Internal Roads:** Gravel/dirt, in good condition. **RV Service:** Yes. **Market:** 8 mi. south in Park Rapids. **Restaurant:** 8 mi. south in Park Rapids. **General**

Store: Yes, limited. **Vending:** No. **Swimming:** Yes. **Playground:** Yes. **Other:** Potato Lake, volleyball, hiking trails, horseshoes, sports field, badminton, tennis, rec hall, pavilion, boat ramp, boat dock, croquet, game room, soda fountain, pavilions. **Activities:** Swimming, fishing, boating (rental motorboats, pontoons, paddleboats, canoes available), hiking, scheduled weekend activities. **Nearby Attractions:** Itasca State Park, tennis, horseback riding, golf, go-carts, Heartland Trail, antiques, historic sites, arts & crafts shops. **Additional Information:** Park Rapids Area Chamber of Commerce, (800) 247-0054.

RESTRICTIONS

Pets: On leash only. **Fires:** Fire ring only. **Alcoholic Beverages:** Allowed. **Vehicle Maximum Length:** 50 ft.

TO GET THERE

From the junction of Hwy. 34 and US 71, drive 7.25 mi. north on US 71, then 6 mi. east on CR 40, then 0.5 mi. on access road. Roads are wide and well maintained, with broad shoulders.

PINE CITY   MAP, C-3
Pokegama Lake RV Park and Golf Course

19193 Island Resort Rd., 55063. T: (800) 248-6552 or (320) 629-6552; www.woischkes.com.

🚐 ★★★   ⛺ ★★★

Beauty: ★★★	Site Privacy: ★★★
Spaciousness: ★★★	Quiet: ★★★
Security: ★★★★	Cleanliness: ★★★★
Insect Control: ★★	Facilities: ★★★

Pokegama Lake RV Park and Golf Course is a nice family place with many activities. In fact, it is so popular that 97 of the full-hookup sites are taken by seasonals. That leaves 15 full-hookup sites and 26 with water and electric for visiting RVs. Reservations are strongly recommended for the campground 6 miles north of Pine City. Most people come for the golfing, swimming, fishing, and boating. The fish-cleaning house is located away from campers—but yet is convenient—and is kept very clean with a garbage disposal at the bottom of the fish-cleaning counter. Campsites are both open and wooded with 30 pull-throughs. The typical site width is 25 feet with the campground laid out in a series of loops. A welcome respite for adults is a modular adult recreation center that does not allow anyone under age 18.

BASICS

Operated By: Bill & Shirl Woischke. **Open:** May 1–Oct. 1. **Site Assignment:** Reservations w/ $20 deposit; refund w/ 7-day notice; 3-night minimum on holiday weekends w/ $40 deposit; refund w/ 14-day notice. **Registration:** At campground office. **Fee:** $22–$26; cash, check, credit card. **Parking:** At site.

FACILITIES

Number of RV-only Sites: 38. **Hookups:** Electric (30, 50 amps), water, sewer. **Each Site:** Picnic table, fire ring. **Dump Station:** Yes. **Laundry:** No. **Pay Phone:** No. **Restrooms and Showers:** Yes. **Fuel:** No. **Propane:** No. **Internal Roads:** Paved, in good condition. **RV Service:** No. **Market:** 6 mi. south in

Pine City. **Restaurant:** 0.5 mi. south in Pokegama Lake. **General Store:** Limited. **Vending:** No. **Swimming:** Yes. **Playground:** Yes. **Other:** Pokegama Lake, lounge area w/ color TV, rec room, video games, pool tables, screened picnic shelter, adult recreation center, horseshoes, volleyball, basketball, fish-cleaning house, boat harbor, boat ramps, boat docks, 9-hole golf. **Activities:** Golfing, swimming, fishing, boating skiing, scheduled activities on holiday weekends. **Nearby Attractions:** North West Company Fur Post, supper club in walking distance, antiques shops, scenic drives, museum. **Additional Information:** Pine City Area Chamber of Commerce, (320) 629-3861.

RESTRICTIONS

Pets: On leash only. **Fires:** Fire ring only. **Alcoholic Beverages:** At sites only. **Vehicle Maximum Length:** 40 ft.

TO GET THERE

From the junction of I-35 and CR 11, take Exit 171 and drive 4 mi. west on CR 11, then 1 block south on access road. Roads are wide and well maintained, with broad shoulders.

PINE RIVER   MAP, B-2
Riverview RV Park

3040 16th Ave. SW, 56474. T: (218) 587-4112.

🚐 ★★★   ⛺ ★★★

Beauty: ★★★	Site Privacy: ★★★
Spaciousness: ★★★	Quiet: ★★★★
Security: ★★★★	Cleanliness: ★★★★
Insect Control: ★★	Facilities: ★★

Riverview RV Park has two big natural attractions going for it—the Pine River and the Paul Bunyan Trail. Riverview RV Park is the closest campground—right across the street—to the 100-mile-long trail that runs from Brainerd to Bemidji. The trail is popular for biking, in-line skating, jogging, walking, and snowmobiling. Located 2 miles south of Pine River, the campground also offers easy access to the river. Canoes can be rented at the campground, for a trip that starts in the Arvig Creek that flows through the campground and leads into the Pine River and then into White Fish Lake. RV sites are grassy with cement patios and mostly shaded by pine, oak, and elm trees. The typical site width is 30 feet and the campground has three pull-throughs. Tent sites are separate from RVs and provide more privacy and shade. The best RV sites are 1–9 because they are on the east side and get better satellite TV reception, and sites 11, 19, and 20 because they are on the west side and get more shade in the afternoon. Firewood is provided free. Think maybe a small washer and dryer could be squeezed in somewhere?

BASICS

Operated By: Jeff & Marilyn Chlebecek. **Open:** May 1–Oct. 1. **Site Assignment:** Reservations w/ no deposit. **Registration:** At campground office. **Fee:** $17.50–$24. **Parking:** At site.

FACILITIES

Number of RV-only Sites: 26. **Number of Tent-only Sites:** 4. **Hookups:** Electric (30 amps), water, sewer. **Each Site:** Picnic table, fire ring. **Dump Sta-

tion:** Yes. **Laundry:** No. **Pay Phone:** No. **Restrooms and Showers:** Yes. **Fuel:** No. **Propane:** No. **Internal Roads:** Gravel, in fair condition. **RV Service:** No. **Market:** 2 mi. north in Pine River. **Restaurant:** 2 mi. north in Pine River. **General Store:** No. **Vending:** No. **Swimming:** No. **Playground:** Yes. **Other:** Rec hall, Ping-Pong, pool table, horseshoes, volleyball, badminton. **Activities:** Fishing, canoeing (rental canoes available), biking. **Nearby Attractions:** Paul Bunyan Trail, Paul Bunyan Amusement Center, raceway, Crow Wing County Historical Society, cross-country skiing, snow. **Additional Information:** Pine River Area Chamber of Commerce, (800) BUNYAN.

RESTRICTIONS

Pets: On leash only. **Fires:** Fire ring only. **Alcoholic Beverages:** Allowed. **Vehicle Maximum Length:** No limit.

TO GET THERE

From the junction of Hwy. 371 and CR 44, drive 0.25 mi. east on CR 44. Roads are wide and well maintained, with broad shoulders.

PIPESTONE   MAP, D-1
Pipestone RV Campground

919 North Hiawatha Ave., 56164. T: (507) 825-2455; www.pipestonervcampground.com.

🚐 ★★★   ⛺ ★★★

Beauty: ★★★	Site Privacy: ★★★
Spaciousness: ★★★	Quiet: ★★★
Security: ★★★★	Cleanliness: ★★★
Insect Control: ★★	Facilities: ★★★

Pipestone RV Campground offers level, grassy sites with crushed stone for RV pads. The typical site width is 35 feet and the rural campground has 31 pull-throughs. A fully stocked camp store also features complimentary morning coffee and a good selection of souvenirs and crafts. Most of the sites are shaded with tall oak trees. The most popular RV sites are 1 to 24 because they offer full service. Tenters favor sites in the back, where it is more rustic and away from RVs. Located in Pipestone, the campground doesn't have any seasonal campers. It does offer large camping tepees for rent that kids seem to love to sleep in with their parents. Security is good, with owners who live on the premises and regular patrols by city police.

BASICS

Operated By: Kevin & Ronda McGinty. **Open:** Apr.–Oct. **Site Assignment:** Reservations recommended; refunds w/ 24-hour notice. **Registration:** At campground office. **Fee:** $17.60–$25.85; cash, check, credit card. **Parking:** At site.

FACILITIES

Number of RV-only Sites: 66. **Number of Tent-only Sites:** 13. **Hookups:** Electric (20, 30, 50 amps), water, sewer, cable TV, Wi-Fi. **Each Site:** Picnic table, fire ring. **Dump Station:** Yes. **Laundry:** Yes, air-conditioned. **Pay Phone:** Yes. **Restrooms and Showers:** Yes. **Fuel:** No. **Propane:** No. **Internal Roads:** Gravel, in good condition. **RV Service:** No. **Market:** 7 blocks south in Pipestone. **Restaurant:** 7 blocks south in Pipestone. **General Store:** Yes.

Vending: No. **Swimming:** Yes. **Playground:** Yes. **Other:** Horseshoes, rental tepees, volleyball, tetherball, enclosed pavilion, rec hall, sports field. **Activities:** Swimming. **Nearby Attractions:** Across the street from Pipestone National Monument & Hiawatha Pageant Grounds, antiques, crafts. **Additional Information:** Pipestone Area CVB, (800) 336-6125; (507) 825-3316.

RESTRICTIONS

Pets: On leash only. **Fires:** Fire ring only. **Alcoholic Beverages:** Allowed. **Vehicle Maximum Length:** No limit. **Other:** Children under age 17 free.

TO GET THERE

From the junction of Hwy. 23 and Hwy. 30, drive 0.25 mi. west on Hwy. 30, then 1.25 mi. north on Hiawatha Ave. Roads are wide and well maintained, with broad shoulders.

PRESTON   MAP, D-3
Hidden Valley Campground

Hwy. 1, Box 56, 55965. T: (507) 765-2467.

🚐 ★★★   ⛺ ★★★

Beauty: ★★★★	Site Privacy: ★★★
Spaciousness: ★★★★	Quiet: ★★★★
Security: ★★★★	Cleanliness: ★★★★
Insect Control: ★★	Facilities: ★★

Located on the edge of Preston, Hidden Valley Campground has two major recreation attractions going for it—the Root River and the 65-mile-long Root River Bike Trail. Nestled in a valley of willows, oaks, and pines, the campground is bordered by a well-stocked trout stream. In the same family since 1968, the campground is kept wooded and shady by a tree-planting program which sees about 50–100 trees planted every year. Laid out in a series of loops, the campground has mostly grassy, shady, large sites with no pull-through sites. The typical site width is 50 feet. The most popular RV sites are the 16 along the river. Tent sites are separate from RVs, in a more wooded, primitive area that offers more privacy. About 3.5 miles of hiking trails take hikers through the pine woods and ravines to the bluff. Quiet and security measures are good, with a 10 p.m. quiet time, an owner who lives on site, regular patrols, plus swing-throughs from city police and county sheriff deputies. Changes are being implemented that should improve campground facilities, including a central building, more services, and more sites.

BASICS

Operated By: Luke & Rachel Schieffelbein, Scott & Denise Hamson. **Open:** Apr. 15–Oct. 15. **Site Assignment:** Monthly/seasonal campground only. **Registration:** At campground office. **Fee:** Monthly, $300; season, $1,000; cash, check. **Parking:** At site.

FACILITIES

Number of RV-only Sites: 30. **Hookups:** Electric (30 amps), water. **Each Site:** Picnic table, fire ring. **Dump Station:** Yes. **Laundry:** No. **Pay Phone:** No. **Restrooms and Showers:** Yes. **Fuel:** No. **Propane:** No. **Internal Roads:** Gravel, in good condition. **RV Service:** No. **Market:** 0.5 mi. west in Preston. **Restaurant:** 0.5 mi. west in Preston. **General Store:** No. **Vending:** No. **Swimming:** No.

Playground: Yes. **Other:** Root River, swimming beach, sports field, horseshoes, volleyball, hiking trails, basketball. tetherball, softball. **Activities:** Swimming, fishing, canoeing (rental canoes available), hiking. **Nearby Attractions:** State park, Amish community, scenic drives, historic sites, antiques & crafts shops. **Additional Information:** Preston Area Tourism Assoc., (888) 845-2100.

RESTRICTIONS

Pets: On leash only. **Fires:** Fire pit only. **Alcoholic Beverages:** Allowed. **Vehicle Maximum Length:** No limit.

TO GET THERE

From north junction of Hwy. 16 and US 52, drive 2 mi. south on Hwy. 16/US 52 to bridge, then 0.25 mi. north on gravel road. Roads are wide and well maintained, with good shoulders.

PRESTON   MAP, D-3
Old Barn Resort

Hwy. 3, Box 57, 55965. T: (800) 552-2512 or (507) 467-2512, ext 1; www.barnresort.com.

🚐 ★★★★   ⛺ ★★★★

Beauty: ★★★★	Site Privacy: ★★★★
Spaciousness: ★★★	Quiet: ★★★★
Security: ★★★★	Cleanliness: ★★★★
Insect Control: ★★	Facilities: ★★★★

A big four-story white barn is the hub for the Old Barn Resort. Built in 1884 by Edward Allis of Allis-Chalmers, the barn was restored in 1988 to house a bar and grill, banquet rooms, and a 44-bed hostel. The campground is located in a scenic valley in Historic Bluff County, right on the Root River State Trail. The campsites are mostly open and level with a typical site width of 30 feet. A few pull-through sites are available. Favorite sites for RVs are A4 and A19 because they are on the ends and quieter. Tent campers like F1 and G1 because they offer more shade. The heated pool is a nice combination of indoor/outdoor, with a roof that lets the sunshine in and sides that can be opened for an outdoor feeling. The Old Barn books up quickly and recommends reservations be made three to four months in advance for holidays and two nights in advance for summer weekends.

BASICS

Operated By: Doug & Shirley Brenna. **Open:** Apr. 1–Nov. 1. **Site Assignment:** Reservations accepted w/ 1-night deposit; refund w/ 2-week notice (minus $5); reservations require 2-night minimum on weekends & 3-night minimum on holidays. **Registration:** At campground office. **Fee:** $22–$30; cash, check, credit card. **Parking:** At site.

FACILITIES

Number of RV-only Sites: 130. **Number of Tent-only Sites:** 40. **Hookups:** Electric (30, 50 amps), water, sewer. **Each Site:** Picnic table, fire ring. **Dump Station:** Yes. **Laundry:** Yes. **Pay Phone:** Yes. **Restrooms and Showers:** Yes. **Fuel:** No. **Propane:** No. **Internal Roads:** Gravel, in fair condition. **RV Service:** No. **Market:** 3 mi. southwest in Preston. **Restaurant:** On site. **General Store:** Yes. **Vending:** Yes. **Swimming:** Yes. **Playground:** Yes.

Other: Golf course, Root River, hiking trail, game room, horseshoe, volleyball, basketball, sports field. **Activities:** Hiking, golf, swimming, fishing, biking (rental bikes available), boating (rental canoes & inner tubes available). **Nearby Attractions:** State park, Amish community, scenic drives, historic sites, antiques & crafts shops. **Additional Information:** Preston Area Tourism Assoc., (888) 845-2100.

RESTRICTIONS

Pets: On leash only. **Fires:** Fire ring only. **Alcoholic Beverages:** Allowed. **Vehicle Maximum Length:** No limit. **Other:** No ATVs.

TO GET THERE

From the junction of US 52 and CR 17 (Apple Orchard Rd.) at west edge of town, drive 3 mi. east on CR 17, then 1 mi north on gravel road. Gravel road is bumpy, in fair condition.

RICHMOND   MAP, C-2
El Rancho Mañana

27302B Ranch Rd., 56368. T: (320) 597-2740; www.camperm.com.

🚐 ★★★★   ⛺ ★★★★

Beauty: ★★★★	Site Privacy: ★★★★
Spaciousness: ★★★★	Quiet: ★★★★
Security: ★★★★★	Cleanliness: ★★★★
Insect Control: ★★	Facilities: ★★★★

El Rancho Mañana Campground features 120 large grassy sites designed for traditional family camping from tents to RVs. Sites vary from full service (50-amp electricity and water), prime (30-amp electricity and water) to basic (water in the area). El Rancho Mañana has a variety of large versatile group sites. All sites include a picnic table and a fire ring. Sixty sites are pull-through and 60 sites are back-in.

BASICS

Operated By: Ward family. **Open:** May 4–Oct. 5. **Site Assignment:** Reservations w/ 2-night deposit; refunds w/ 2-week notice; cancellation w/in 2 weeks w/ $5 fee. **Registration:** At campground office. **Fee:** $17.50–$42; cash, check, credit card. **Parking:** At site.

FACILITIES

Number of RV-only Sites: 115. **Number of Tent-only Sites:** 30. **Hookups:** Electric (30, 50 amps), water, sewer. **Each Site:** Picnic table, fire ring. **Dump Station:** Yes. **Laundry:** Yes. **Pay Phone:** Yes. **Restrooms and Showers:** Yes. **Fuel:** Yes. **Propane:** Yes. **Internal Roads:** Gravel/dirt, in good condition. **RV Service:** No. **Market:** 6 mi. south in Richmond. **Restaurant:** 6 mi. south in Richmond. **General Store:** Yes. **Vending:** Yes. **Swimming:** Yes. **Playground:** Yes. **Other:** Rec hall, horse stables, game room, hiking trails, horse trails, horseshoes, volleyball, baseball, sandy swimming beach, Long Lake, shelter, boat landing, boat docks, mountain biking trails, badminton. **Activities:** Swimming, fishing, boating (rental rowboats, pontoons, canoes, paddleboats available), hayrides, hiking, mountain biking, horseback riding (rental horses available), planned activities. **Nearby Attractions:** Golf, historic sites, museums, Minnesota Baseball Hall of Fame, antiques shops, art galleries. **Additional Information:** St. Cloud Area CVB, (800) 264-2940.

RESTRICTIONS

Pets: On leash only. **Fires:** Fire ring only. **Alcoholic Beverages:** At sites only. **Vehicle Maximum Length:** No limit. **Other:** A $20 deposit or driver's license in return for a security card to operate security gate. Deposit or license will be returned at time of departure.

TO GET THERE

From the junction of I-94 and CR 9, take Exit 153 and drive 8.5 mi. south on CR 9, then 0.5 mi. east on Manana Rd., then 2 mi. north on Ranch Rd. Roads are wide and well maintained, with good shoulders. Ranch Rd. is rough gravel and can stir up a lot of dust.

ROCHESTER — MAP, D-3
Rochester KOA

5232 65th Ave. SE, 55904. T: (800) 562-5232 or (507) 288-0785; www.koa.com.

★★★★ ▲ ★★

Beauty: ★★★	Site Privacy: ★★★★
Spaciousness: ★★★★	Quiet: ★★★★
Security: ★★★★	Cleanliness: ★★★★★
Insect Control: ★★	Facilities: ★★★★

Rochester KOA is a nice, clean, well-run, friendly, safe place to stay. It is not particularly pretty, but that is not the owners' fault. They have done what they could to make it attractive, including having exceptionally clean bathrooms. But the natural beauty just isn't there. The open, rural campground is conveniently located just a quarter mile from I-90 and features level sites mostly 30 feet wide. The most popular sites are 4–16 with full hookup. A separate grassy tent site offers privacy, but tents must be moved daily by noon to protect the grass. The campground is mostly used for overnight stays by RVs on their way to or from somewhere. For that, it fits the need perfectly.

BASICS

Operated By: Roger & Barb Philip. **Open:** Mar. 15–Oct. 31. **Site Assignment:** Reservations accepted w/ 1-night deposit; refund (minus $5) w/ 2-day notice, 1-week notice on holidays. **Registration:** At campground office. **Fee:** $23–$35; cash, credit card. **Parking:** At site.

FACILITIES

Number of RV-only Sites: 73. **Number of Tent-only Sites:** 20. **Hookups:** Electric (30 amps), water, sewer. **Each Site:** Picnic table, fire ring. **Dump Station:** Yes. **Laundry:** Yes. **Pay Phone:** Yes. **Restrooms and Showers:** Yes. **Fuel:** No. **Propane:** Yes. **Internal Roads:** Gravel, in good condition. **RV Service:** No. **Market:** 6 mi. north in Rochester. **Restaurant:** 6 mi. north in Rochester. **General Store:** Yes. **Vending:** Yes. **Swimming:** Yes. **Playground:** Yes. **Other:** Volleyball, basketball, badminton, game room, horseshoes, rec hall, recreation field. **Activities:** Swimming, no scheduled activities except an ice-cream social on Sat. nights Memorial Day–Labor Day. **Nearby Attractions:** Mayo Clinic, park, art center, Mayowood Mansion, Olmsted County History Center, Root River State Trail, scenic drive, shopping center. **Additional Information:** Rochester CVB, (800) 634-8277.

RESTRICTIONS

Pets: On leash only. **Fires:** Fire ring only. **Alcoholic Beverages:** Allowed. **Vehicle Maximum Length:** No limit. **Other:** Adult visitor fee, $5; children, $2.50.

TO GET THERE

From the junction of I-90 and US 52, take Exit 218, drive 0.25 mi. south on US 52, then 500 ft. east on 54th St. SE, then 100 ft. north on 65th Ave. Roads are wide and well maintained, with broad shoulders.

ROYALTON — MAP, C-2
Two Rivers Park

5116 145th St NW, 56373. T: (320) 584-5125.

★★★★ ▲ ★★★★

Beauty: ★★★★	Site Privacy: ★★★★
Spaciousness: ★★★★	Quiet: ★★★★
Security: ★★★★	Cleanliness: ★★★★
Insect Control: ★★	Facilities: ★★★

Two Rivers Park is located 3 miles south of Royalton, on a peninsula formed by the waters of the Mississippi and Platte rivers. Not surprisingly, the campground is popular for water activities, especially its inner tube float trips. Starting with a shuttle bus trip to the beginning point, you can lean back in a huge inner tube and float 3.5 miles back to the park through the beautiful Platte River Valley. The relaxing trip takes about two hours and costs $7 a person, children ages 5 and under are free. Laid out in a series of loops, the landscaped campground offers grassy shaded sites with 25 pull-throughs. The typical site width is among the largest in any campground—60 feet. From waterfront to high bluff and whispering pine sites, tent campers have a wonderful choice of places. Security and safety measures are good—the campground has one access road and owners live on site and provide regular patrols. Quiet time is from 11 p.m. to 8 a.m., visitors must leave by 10 p.m., the playground closes at dusk, no bike riding after dark, and children must be on site by 10 p.m. The posted speed limit is "as fast as a child can walk." With all it has going for it, the campground has one pesky flaw—no laundry facilities for all those wet and dirty clothes from river activities.

BASICS

Operated By: Shorty Spohn. **Open:** May 1–Oct. 15. **Site Assignment:** Reservations w/ $60 deposit (2 nights); 3-night minimum on holiday weekends; refunds (minus $5) w/ 7-day notice. **Registration:** At campground office. **Fee:** $24–$36; cash, check, credit card. **Parking:** At site.

FACILITIES

Number of RV-only Sites: 110. **Number of Tent-only Sites:** 20. **Hookups:** Electric (20, 30, 50 amps), water. **Each Site:** Picnic table, fire ring. **Dump Station:** Yes. **Laundry:** No. **Pay Phone:** No. **Restrooms and Showers:** Yes. **Fuel:** No. **Propane:** Yes. **Internal Roads:** Paved/gravel, in good condition. **RV Service:** No. **Market:** 3 mi. north in Royalton.

Restaurant: 3 mi. north in Royalton. **General Store:** Yes. **Vending:** Yes. **Swimming:** No. **Playground:** Yes. **Other:** Game room, tubing shuttle bus, volleyball, mini-golf, badminton, basketball, croquet, disc golf, boat launch, recreation field, shelter building, boat ramp, horseshoes, hiking trails. **Activities:** Fishing, river swimming, boating, agate hunting, inner tube float trips, shuffleboard, volleyball. **Nearby Attractions:** Golf, zoo, bowling, roller skating, waterslide, museums, tennis, skeet shoot, game farm, go-cart tracks. **Additional Information:** Little Falls CVB, (800) 325-5916.

RESTRICTIONS

Pets: On leash only. **Fires:** Fire ring only. **Alcoholic Beverages:** Allowed. **Vehicle Maximum Length:** No limit. **Other:** No Jet skis, personal watercraft allowed. Kids under age 18 free.

TO GET THERE

From the junction of US 10 and CR 40, drive 100 ft. southwest on CR 40, then 1 mi. south on CR 73, then 0.5 mi. west on 145th St. Roads are wide and well maintained, with good shoulders.

SAVAGE — MAP, C-2
Town and Country Campground

12630 Boone Ave. South, 55378. T: (952) 445-1756; www.townandcountrycampground.com.

★★★★ ▲ ★★★★

Beauty: ★★★★	Site Privacy: ★★★★
Spaciousness: ★★★★	Quiet: ★★★★
Security: ★★★★	Cleanliness: ★★★★
Insect Control: ★★★★	Facilities: ★★★★

Town and County Campground in Savage, has done a good job of providing "city close and country quiet." Conveniently located 18 miles southwest of Minneapolis, Town and Country is surprisingly quiet and homey for being so close to a metro area. Attractive landscaping, including bushes and flowers, adds to the welcoming atmosphere. There's even Eagle Creek for quiet walks and a big shade tree on the playground—a nice change from campgrounds whose playgrounds are sitting right out in the broiling sun. Sites are level, grassy, shaded, or open with a typical site width of 35 feet. Laid out in a series of loops, the campground has 15 pull-through sites and five seasonal campers. Security is great with owners who keep a close eye on the site. A speed limit of 5 mph is enforced, as is quiet time from 10 p.m. to 7 a.m. Be aware that campfires are not permitted on individual sites, but there is a community fire ring available with wood provided.

BASICS

Operated By: David & Jill Olmstead. **Open:** Apr. 1–Nov. 1; limited winter reservations. **Site Assignment:** Reservations w/ $25 deposit; refund w/ 48-hour notice. **Registration:** At campground office. **Fee:** $20–$34; cash, check, credit card, V, MC, D. **Parking:** At site; 1 car per site only.

FACILITIES

Number of RV-only Sites: 82. **Number of Tent-only Sites:** 14. **Hookups:** Electric (20, 30, 50 amps), water, sewer, phone, cable TV, Wi-Fi. **Each Site:** Picnic table, portable fire pits. **Dump Station:** Yes.

Laundry: Yes. **Pay Phone:** Yes. **Restrooms and Showers:** Yes. **Fuel:** No. **Propane:** No. **Internal Roads:** Paved, in good condition. **RV Service:** No. **Market:** Couple of blocks. **Restaurant:** Couple of blocks. **General Store:** Yes, limited. In office. **Vending:** Yes. **Swimming:** Yes. **Playground:** Yes. **Other:** Spa, game room, storm shelter, sports field, stream, coin games, basketball. **Activities:** Swimming. **Nearby Attractions:** Mall of America, Minnesota Zoo, Mississippi River cruises, casino, Minnesota Children's Zoo, Murphy's Landing Historic Village, Fort Snelling State Park, horse racing, auto racing, antiques, gold, horseback riding, Valley Fair. **Additional Information:** Greater Minneapolis Convention & Visitors Assoc., (800) 445-7412.

RESTRICTIONS

Pets: On leash only; extra fee of $1 per dog. **Fires:** In community fire ring or portable fire pit. **Alcoholic Beverages:** At site only. **Vehicle Maximum Length:** No limit. **Other:** Motorcycles & motorbikes not to be ridden, except to & from site.

TO GET THERE

From the junction of I-35W and Hwy. 13S, take Exit 3B and drive 4.5 mi. west on Hwy. 13S, then 500 ft. south on Hwy. 13, then 0.5 mi. west on 126th St. to Boone Ave. Roads are mostly wide and well maintained, with adequate shoulders.

ST. CLOUD   MAP, C-2
St. Cloud Campground and RV Park

2491 2nd St. SE, 56304. T: (800) 690-7045 or (320) 251-4463; www.stcloudcampground.com.

🚐 ★★★★   ⛺ ★★★★

Beauty: ★★★★	Site Privacy: ★★★★
Spaciousness: ★★★★	Quiet: ★★★★
Security: ★★★★★	Cleanliness: ★★★★★
Insect Control: ★★★	Facilities: ★★★★

St. Cloud Campground and RV Park plays host to many camping club rallies. That's one indication of what a well run, popular facility it is. Another indication is to visit, drive through, stay, and see why it is one of the best in the state. Laid out in a series of loops, the campground offers a mix of gravel and grassy, shaded and open RV sites with a typical site width of 30 feet and 40 pull-throughs at 35 by 70. As campers check in, a guide escorts them to their site, shows them where the hookup is, and makes sure the sewer site is correctly attached to the RV. Just a little over a mile outside St. Cloud, the campground is in a quiet country setting. Tent campers have several different sites separated from RVs, as well as a primitive area offering more room and privacy. Security is tops with an owner who lives on site, regular patrols, Workkampers who live in each row of campsites and keep an eye on their area, and county sheriff patrols coming through for rounds.

BASICS

Operated By: Chris & Deb Thell. **Open:** Apr. 1–Oct. 15. **Site Assignment:** Reservations w/ $25 deposit or credit card; full refund w/ 48-hour notice. **Registration:** At campground office. **Fee:** $23.75–$29.75; cash, check, credit card. **Parking:** At site.

FACILITIES

Number of RV-only Sites: 90. **Number of Tent-only Sites:** 7. **Hookups:** Electric (30, 50 amps), water, sewer, Wi-Fi. **Each Site:** Picnic table, fire ring. **Dump Station:** Yes. **Laundry:** Yes. **Pay Phone:** Yes. **Restrooms and Showers:** Yes. **Fuel:** No. **Propane:** Yes. **Internal Roads:** Gravel, in good condition. **RV Service:** No. **Market:** 2 mi. west in St. Cloud. **Restaurant:** 2 mi. west in St. Cloud. **General Store:** Yes. **Vending:** No. **Swimming:** Yes. **Playground:** Yes. **Other:** Hiking trails, volleyball, basketball, badminton, croquet, lodge, book exchange, pool table, electronic games, heated rally center building w/ kitchenette, game room. **Activities:** Swimming, hiking. **Nearby Attractions:** Charles A. Lindbergh House & History Center, Ellingson Car Museum, Minnesota Baseball Hall of Fame, Munsinger Gardens & Clemens Gardens, Stearn's County Heritage Center, St. John's Benedictine Abbey. **Additional Information:** St. Cloud Area CVB, (800) 264-2940.

RESTRICTIONS

Pets: On leash only. **Fires:** Fire ring only. **Alcoholic Beverages:** Allowed. **Vehicle Maximum Length:** No limit.

TO GET THERE

From the junction of US 10 and Hwy. 23, drive 1 block east on Hwy. 23 to lights at 14th Ave., drive south 1 block, then east 1 mi. Roads are wide and well maintained, with broad shoulders.

TAYLORS FALLS   MAP, C-3
Camp Waub-O-Jeeg

2185 Chisago St., 55084. T: (651) 465-5721; www.taylorsfalls.com/waubojeeg.html.

🚐 ★★★   ⛺ ★★★★

Beauty: ★★★	Site Privacy: ★★★★
Spaciousness: ★★★★	Quiet: ★★★★
Security: ★★★★	Cleanliness: ★★★
Insect Control: ★★	Facilities: ★★

Once you get there, Camp Waub-O-Jeeg is a nice quiet place to stay. But driving an RV on some of those roads is a bit tricky. CR 16 is wide and well maintained with mostly broad shoulders, but it is a curvy scenic road. The real test is the steep narrow hill leading from the campground office into the campground. Since the campground is atop a hill, the main access road is paved but it is steep, narrow, and winding with a pull-off lane in case a vehicle is coming down while another is going up. Very narrow, rough, gravel roads lead into the campsites. But it really feels like camping once you arrive. Sites are secluded on wooded, rolling terrain with level, prepared shaded spots. The typical site width is 20 feet with the majority being pull-throughs. The sites seem bigger and more private because of all the trees surrounding them. Tent campers in particular will appreciate the privacy and wilderness setting. Security measures are good with a gate that is closed at night, owners who live on site and patrol, and regular patrols by local police. Located 5 miles west of Taylors Falls, the campground got its unusual name from a brave Chippewa war leader born about 1747.

BASICS

Operated By: Jon & Nou Gamble. **Open:** Apr. 15–Oct. 15. **Site Assignment:** Reservations w/ 1-night deposit; refund w/ 48-hour notice. **Registration:** At campground office. **Fee:** $22–$28; cash, check, credit card. **Parking:** At site.

FACILITIES

Number of RV-only Sites: 50. **Number of Tent-only Sites:** 20. **Hookups:** Electric (30 amps), water. **Each Site:** Picnic table, fire ring. **Dump Station:** Yes. **Laundry:** No. **Pay Phone:** No. **Restrooms and Showers:** Yes. **Fuel:** No. **Propane:** No. **Internal Roads:** Gravel, in fair condition. **RV Service:** No. **Market:** 5 mi. east in Taylors Falls. **Restaurant:** 5 mi. east in Taylors Falls. **General Store:** Yes. **Vending:** Yes. **Swimming:** No. **Playground:** Yes. **Other:** St. Croix River, pavilion, shuffleboard, badminton, horseshoes, hiking trail, volleyball. **Activities:** Swimming, fishing, hiking. **Nearby Attractions:** Scenic drives, Wild Mountain, art shops, antiques stores, historic homes, skiing, snowboarding, Wildlife Educational Center, golf, rock climbing. **Additional Information:** Taylors Falls Chamber of Commerce, (800) 447-4958.

RESTRICTIONS

Pets: On leash only. **Fires:** Fire ring only. **Alcoholic Beverages:** At sites only. **Vehicle Maximum Length:** 30 ft.

TO GET THERE

From the junction of Hwy. 95 and CR 16, drive 2 mi. north on CR 16.

TAYLORS FALLS   MAP, C-3
Interstate State Park

reserve america

P.O. Box 254, 55084. T: (651) 465-5711; www.reserveamerica.com.

🚐 ★★   ⛺ ★★★★

Beauty: ★★★★★	Site Privacy: ★★
Spaciousness: ★★	Quiet: ★★★
Security: ★★★★	Cleanliness: ★★★
Insect Control: ★★	Facilities: ★★

Few private campgrounds can compete with the natural beauty of city, state, and national parks. Interstate State Park is one of the most beautiful in Minnesota. However, few public parks can compete with the facilities offered at private campgrounds—such as water and sewer hookups, laundry, general store, and heated swimming pool. That's the case with Interstate State Park. And enough campers must find the beauty and recreational activities more important than the comfort amenities because this campground is often packed. Folks know a good thing when they see it. Established in 1895, it is the oldest state park in both Wisconsin and Minnesota, and is located on the border of Taylors Falls in Minnesota and St. Croix Falls in Wisconsin. The park is best known for the towering rocky gorge that forms the dalles of the river and for the glacial potholes that are the deepest in the world. Laid out in a loop, the campground offers shady, level, back-in sites—no pull-throughs. Both RV and tent sites are right on the river, with sites 5–23 offering the best view. Swimming is prohibited because of the drop-offs, deep channel, and strong current.

BASICS

Operated By: State of Minnesota. **Open:** Mar. 1–Dec. 1. **Site Assignment:** Reservations w/ full-stay fee plus $8.50 nonrefundable service charge; refunds (minus $5 & $8.50 fees) w/ 30-day notice; if less than 30-day notice, refund (minus fees & less first night). **Registration:** At campground office. **Fee:** $22; cash, check, credit card. **Parking:** At site.

FACILITIES

Number of RV-only Sites: 22. **Number of Tent-only Sites:** 15. **Hookups:** Electric (20, 30 amps). **Each Site:** Picnic table, fire ring. **Dump Station:** Yes. **Laundry:** No. **Pay Phone:** Yes. **Restrooms and Showers:** Yes. **Fuel:** No. **Propane:** No. **Internal Roads:** Paved, in good condition. **RV Service:** No. **Market:** 2 mi. north in Taylors Falls. **Restaurant:** 2 mi. north in Taylors Falls. **General Store:** No. **Vending:** Yes. **Swimming:** No. **Playground:** No. **Other:** St. Croix River, nature store, picnic shelters, hiking trail, visitor center, volleyball. **Activities:** Fishing, hiking, boating (rental canoes available). **Nearby Attractions:** Scenic drives, Wild Mountain, art shops, antiques stores, historic homes, skiing, snowboarding, Wildlife Educational Center, golf, rock climbing. **Additional Information:** Taylors Falls Chamber of Commerce, (800) 447-4958.

RESTRICTIONS

Pets: On leash only. **Fires:** Fire ring only. **Alcoholic Beverages:** Not allowed. **Vehicle Maximum Length:** 45 ft. **Other:** Vehicle permits of $25 per year or $7 per day are required to enter all Minnesota state parks; 14-day stay limit.

TO GET THERE

From Taylors Falls, drive 1.5 mi. south on US 8. Road is wide and well maintained, with broad shoulders.

TENSTRIKE   MAP, B-2
Summer Haven RV Resort

10647 Clydesdale Cir. NE, RR 1, Box 28, 56683.
T: (218) 586-2842 or (866) 586-2842;
www.summerhavenrvresort.com.

🚐 ★★★★   ▲ ★★★★

Beauty: ★★★★   Site Privacy: ★★★★
Spaciousness: ★★★★   Quiet: ★★★★
Security: ★★★★   Cleanliness: ★★★★
Insect Control: ★★★★   Facilities: ★★★★

Overlooking Gull Lake just north of Bemidji, this campground offers 3,000 feet of lakeshore. Sites are grassy with a choice of open or shaded areas. The typical site width is a generous 45 feet, and the campground has six pull-throughs. Naturally, the best camping spots are closest to the water. Fishing is a popular pastime here, and a clean, screened-in fish-cleaning house is located on site. Restroom and laundry facilities are very clean. Priding itself on being a quiet, family-oriented campground, Summer Haven takes measures to keep the facility

safe and comfortable. The owners keep a close watch on the campground and set the mood for a friendly stay.

BASICS

Operated By: Steve & Nancy, Duane & Donna. **Open:** May 15–Oct. 15. **Site Assignment:** Reservations w/ 1-night deposit; refund w/ 30-day notice. **Registration:** At campground office. **Fee:** Full hookup, $35; cash, check. **Parking:** At site.

FACILITIES

Number of Multipurpose Sites: 135. **Hookups:** Electric (20, 30, 50 amps), water, sewer. **Each Site:** Picnic table, fire ring. **Dump Station:** Yes. **Laundry:** Yes. **Pay Phone:** No. **Restrooms and Showers:** Yes. **Fuel:** Yes. **Propane:** Yes. **Internal Roads:** Gravel, in good condition. **RV Service:** No. **Market:** 5 mi. south. **Restaurant:** 5 mi. south. **General Store:** Yes. **Vending:** Yes. **Swimming:** Yes. **Playground:** Yes. **Other:** Gull Lake, boat ramp, fish-cleaning house, rec room, coin games, horseshoes, shuffleboard, badminton, volleyball, sports field. **Activities:** Swimming, fishing, boating (rental fishing boats, canoes, paddleboats, rowboats available), scheduled weekend activities. **Nearby Attractions:** Mississippi River, Paul Bunyan & Babe the Blue Ox statues, amusement parks, waterslide, logging camp, fishing, golf, antiques, arts & crafts. **Additional Information:** Bemidji Area Tourist Information, (800) 458-2223.

RESTRICTIONS

Pets: On leash only; $2.50 per day per pet. **Fires:** Fire ring only. **Alcoholic Beverages:** Allowed. **Vehicle Maximum Length:** No limit.

TO GET THERE

From west junction of US 2 and US 71, drive 10.5 mi. north on US 71, then 6 mi. north on CR 23. Roads are mostly wide and well maintained, with narrow shoulders in spots.

WABASHA   MAP, D-3
Pioneer Campsite

130 Pioneer Dr., 64739 140th Ave., 55981.
T: (651) 565-2242.

🚐 ★★★   ▲ ★★★

Beauty: ★★★   Site Privacy: ★★★
Spaciousness: ★★★   Quiet: ★★★
Security: ★★★   Cleanliness: ★★★
Insect Control: ★★   Facilities: ★★★

A rural campground with access to the Mississippi River, Pioneer Campsite is 4.5 miles east of Wabasha. The campground offers a choice of shaded or open, grassy or sandy sites, with a typical site width of 35 feet. There are 25 pull-through sites and 183 seasonal campers. The grounds are somewhat hilly with plenty of trees, lots of birds, and bird feeders. "Behold the beauty of the Lord," a campground sign says. Church services are offered on Sundays. Laid out in a series of loops, Pioneer Campsites has a separate area for tent campers for more green space and privacy. Security measures include owners who live on site and provide patrols of the campgrounds.

BASICS

Operated By: Logan Camping, Inc. **Open:** Apr. 15–Oct. 15. **Site Assignment:** Reservations w/o deposit. **Registration:** At campground office. **Fee:** $25–$30; cash, check. **Parking:** At site.

FACILITIES

Number of RV-only Sites: 233. **Number of Tent-only Sites:** 7. **Hookups:** Electric (20, 30, 50 amps), water, sewer. **Each Site:** Picnic table, fire ring. **Dump Station:** Yes. **Laundry:** No. **Pay Phone:** No. **Restrooms and Showers:** Yes. **Fuel:** No. **Propane:** No. **Internal Roads:** Paved/gravel, in good condition. **RV Service:** No. **Market:** 4.5 mi. west in Wabasha. **Restaurant:** 4.5 mi. west in Wabasha. **General Store:** Yes, limited. **Vending:** No. **Swimming:** Yes. **Playground:** Yes. **Other:** Rec hall, recreation game, coin games, river, mini-golf, basketball, sports field, horseshoes, hiking trails, volleyball, boat ramp. **Activities:** Swimming, hiking, fishing, boating (rental canoes, rowboats available). **Nearby Attractions:** Mississippi River, toy museum, golf, Arrowhead Bluffs Museum, antiques, historic sites, arts & crafts shops. **Additional Information:** Wabasha Area Chamber of Commerce, (800) 565-4158.

RESTRICTIONS

Pets: On leash only. **Fires:** Fire ring only. **Alcoholic Beverages:** Allowed. **Vehicle Maximum Length:** No limit. **Other:** Children stay free w/parents.

TO GET THERE

From the junction of Hwy. 60 and US 61, drive 4 mi. south on US 61, then watch for signs. Roads are wide and well maintained, with broad shoulders.

WALKER   MAP, B-2
Shores of Leech Lake
Campground and Marina

6616 Morriss Point Rd. NW, 56484.
T: (218) 547-1819; www.shoresofleechlake.com.

🚐 ★★★★   ▲ ★

Beauty: ★★★★   Site Privacy: ★★★
Spaciousness: ★★★   Quiet: ★★★★
Security: ★★★★   Cleanliness: ★★★
Insect Control: ★★★   Facilities: ★★★★

The best sites in Shores of Leech Lake Campground and Marina are on the water—not just the shoreline but on the actual lake itself. Covered boat slips with water and electric hookups make this a wonderful place for people who want to camp on their boats. Some of the 20- to 30-foot floating bungalows have homesteaded this harbor for more than a decade. Nestled deep in the Chippewa National Forest, Leech Lake is the third largest lake in Minnesota. Except for the eagles, mosquitoes, deer, bears, and fireflies who make their home here, midweek sailors often have this 20-mile-wide, 23-mile-long body of water to themselves. Many lakefront campground sites are occupied by seasonal campers. Sites have a typical width of 30 feet, are shaded and level with eight pull-throughs. Only one site is set aside for tent campers. The campground located 3 miles north of Walker, has a full-service marina with gas, bait, ice, marine power, pump-out station, boat, and motor rentals. A comfortable lodge offers sandwiches, pizza, beer, wine, and free coffee.

BASICS

Operated By: Mitch & Mara Loomis. **Open:** May 1–Oct. 15. **Site Assignment:** Reservations for 3-night min. w/ 1-night deposit; refund w/ 14-day notice or will incur 2-night charges. **Registration:** At campground office. **Fee:** $41; cash, check, credit card. **Parking:** At site.

FACILITIES

Number of RV-only Sites: 47. **Number of Tent-only Sites:** 1. **Hookups:** Electric (30 amps), water, sewer, cable TV, phone, Wi-Fi. **Each Site:** Picnic table, fire ring. **Dump Station:** Yes. **Laundry:** Yes. **Pay Phone:** Yes. **Restrooms and Showers:** Yes. **Fuel:** Yes. **Propane:** No. **Internal Roads:** Paved. **RV Service:** No. **Market:** 2.5 mi. south in Walker. **Restaurant:** 2.5 mi. south in Walker. **General Store:** Yes. **Vending:** Yes. **Swimming:** No. **Playground:** Yes. **Other:** Leech Lake, fish-cleaning house, sandy beach, basketball court, hiking trails, boat ramp, boat dock, rec room, lodge. **Activities:** Swimming, biking, fishing, boating, hiking, (rental canoes, sailboats, paddleboats, motorboats available). **Nearby Attractions:** Golf, hunting, bird-watching, snowmobiling, skiing, horseback rides, antiques & crafts stores, Museum of Natural History, Sugar Point Battle Monument, Itasca State Park. **Additional Information:** Leech Lake Area Chamber of Commerce, (800) 833-1118.

RESTRICTIONS

Pets: Leash only, $4 fee per night. **Fires:** Fire ring only. **Alcoholic Beverages:** Allowed. **Vehicle Maximum Length:** No limit.

TO GET THERE

From the junction of Hwy. 34 and Hwy. 200/371, drive 2.5 mi. north on Hwy. 371, then 0.5 mi. east on access road. Roads are wide and well maintained, with good shoulders.

WASECA
Kiesler's Campground

MAP, D-2

P.O. Box 503B, 56093. T: (800) 533-4642, ext. 4 or (507) 835-3179; www.kieslers.com.

🚐 ★★★★　　🏕 ★★★★

Beauty: ★★★★	Site Privacy: ★★★★
Spaciousness: ★★★★	Quiet: ★★★★
Security: ★★★★	Cleanliness: ★★★★
Insect Control: ★★	Facilities: ★★★★

If you played from sunup to sundown, you probably wouldn't run out of things to do at Kiesler's Campground. Recreation choices are everywhere, including a 2,000-square-foot heated swimming pool with a gigantic enclosed slide and a heated wading pool,

along with a nice lake for fishing and swimming. A wood chip base on the playground makes it both cleaner for children and less painful if they fall. Laid out in a series of loops, the rural campground offers a tree on every site, gravel pads for RVs, and a typical site width of 40 feet. Not surprisingly, Kiesler's has 80 seasonal campers. Surprisingly, it has only ten pull-throughs. Although tents can be put on any site, most tenters seem to prefer the east area of the park, which is more wooded and away from RVs. Security measures are good, with owners who live on site, regular patrols, and a traffic control gate that requires a pass to enter.

BASICS

Operated By: The Kieslers. **Open:** Apr. 15–Oct. 1. **Site Assignment:** Reservations w/ $50 deposit, $70 on holidays; refund (minus $5) w/ 7-day notice. **Registration:** At campground office. **Fee:** $30–$42; cash, check, credit card. **Parking:** At site.

FACILITIES

Number of RV-only Sites: 280. **Number of Tent-only Sites:** 17. **Hookups:** Electric (30, 50 amps), water, sewer, cable TV, Wi-Fi. **Each Site:** Picnic table, fire ring. **Dump Station:** Yes. **Laundry:** Yes. **Pay Phone:** Yes. **Restrooms and Showers:** Yes. **Fuel:** No. **Propane:** Yes. **Internal Roads:** Gravel, in good condition. **RV Service:** No. **Market:** 1.5 mi. west in Waseca. **Restaurant:** W/in walking distance. **General Store:** Yes. **Vending:** Yes. **Swimming:** Yes. **Playground:** Yes. **Other:** Volleyball, shuffleboard, horseshoes, mini-golf, game room, basketball, wading pool, hiking trails, recreation building, boat docks, lake. **Activities:** Swimming, fishing, hiking, boating (rental motorboats available), scheduled weekend activities. **Nearby Attractions:** Cabela's, golf, antique & craft shops, Mall of America, Farmamerica. **Additional Information:** Owatonna Area Convention & Tourism, (800) 423-6466.

RESTRICTIONS

Pets: Leash only but encourage campers to leave pets at home. **Fires:** Fire ring only. **Alcoholic Beverages:** Allowed. **Vehicle Maximum Length:** 40 ft. **Other:** All visitors must register as day campers at $4 per person per day.

TO GET THERE

From the junction of US 14 and Hwy. 13, drive east 1.5 mi. Roads are wide and well maintained, with broad shoulders.

WINONA
Winona KOA

MAP, D-3

Hwy. 6, Box 18, 55987. T: (507) 454-2851 or (800) 562-0843.

🚐 ★★★　　🏕 ★★★

Beauty: ★★★	Site Privacy: ★★★
Spaciousness: ★★★	Quiet: ★★★
Security: ★★★	Cleanliness: ★★★
Insect Control: ★★	Facilities: ★★★

Located in hilly country 8 miles south of Winona, the Winona KOA is a rural campground with sites on three levels of the hillside. A metal staircase leads up to the office and playroom. The third tier of campsites has a steep hill going up to it. The different levels of campground allow for more privacy and a better view. The campground attracts a lot of local campers—there are 27 seasonal campers—as well as travelers on their way to the Wisconsin Dells. Campsites are generally shady with mature oak trees, level, and grassy. The typical site width is 30 feet and the campground has 12 pull-throughs. Most sites have gravel pads for RVs. Tent sites have more trees, grass, and greenery. For security, the owners live on site and patrols the campground.

BASICS

Operated By: Tom & Connie Burkhard. **Open:** Apr. 15–Oct. 15. **Site Assignment:** Reservations w/ $10 deposit, $20 for holidays; refund w/ 3-day notice (minus $5). **Registration:** At campground office. **Fee:** $21–$33; cash, check, credit card. **Parking:** At site.

FACILITIES

Number of RV-only Sites: 75. **Number of Tent-only Sites:** 30. **Hookups:** Electric (20, 30, 50 amps), water. **Each Site:** Picnic table, fire ring. **Dump Station:** Yes. **Laundry:** Yes. **Pay Phone:** Yes. **Restrooms and Showers:** Yes. **Fuel:** No. **Propane:** Yes. **Internal Roads:** Paved/gravel, in good condition. **RV Service:** No. **Market:** 8 mi. north in Winona. **Restaurant:** 4 mi. south in Pickwick. **General Store:** Yes. **Vending:** Yes. **Swimming:** Yes. **Playground:** Yes. **Other:** Mississippi River, rec room, pavilion, boat ramp, boat dock, sports field, hiking trails, horseshoes, volleyball, marina. **Activities:** Swimming, fishing, hiking, boating (rental canoes available), planned weekend activities. **Nearby Attractions:** Museums, Polish Cultural Institute, golf, boating, aquatic center, antiques shops, art galleries, ice arena. **Additional Information:** Winona CVB, (800) 657-4972.

RESTRICTIONS

Pets: On leash only. **Fires:** Fire ring only. **Alcoholic Beverages:** Allowed. **Vehicle Maximum Length:** No limit.

TO GET THERE

From the junction of Hwy. 43 and US 61/14, drive 6 mi. south and east on US 61/14. Roads are wide and well maintained, with broad shoulders.

Mississippi

Visitors to Mississippi will more than likely not be surprised at the breadth of cultural heritage within an arm's reach at any given spot on the state's map.

Think of the Magnolia State's geography in terms of five regions: the hills region lies in the northeast corner of the state and is traced on the eastern side by the **Tennessee-Tombigbee Waterway.** The flatter-than-a-pancake delta in the northwestern part of the state is bounded by the **Mississippi River** on its western side. The capital/river region in the southwest corner of the state contains the historically and culturally significant cities of **Natchez, Vicksburg,** and **Jackson.** The central-eastern pines region contains prairies and hills as well as evergreen forests. Finally, the coastal region of the southeast enjoys a tourism boom due to its newly established gaming industry.

The **Natchez Trace Parkway** may have originated as many as 8,000 years ago as a migratory path for buffalo, which ran from the lower expanses of the Mississippi River up to what is now Tennessee. Eventually the route was heavily utilized by the Chickasaw, Choctaw, and other Native American tribes; however, its heyday existed during the period from roughly 1785 to 1820, when Kaintuck boatmen headed back north on foot after cashing in their wares and river transportation. The Trace is designated and maintained as a scenic parkway featuring campgrounds; biking, hiking, and horse trails; and interpretive programs.

The depth and isolation of the South has a tendency to obscure the massive amount of talent Mississippi has contributed to the art world. The little town of **Drew,** considered by musicologists worldwide as the home of the delta blues, was the birthplace of such luminaries as Robert Johnson, Son House, Howlin' Wolf, Louise Johnson, and Willie Brown. For its literary talent, Mississippi lays claim to the works of such writers as Eudora Welty, Nobel Prize laureate William Faulkner, and *Native Son* author Richard Wright. Even the father of country music, "the singing brakeman" Jimmie Rodgers, has a museum honoring him in his hometown of **Meridian.**

Mississippi historical sites span centuries. The **Phau Indian Mounds** in the northeast corner of the state were maintained by ancient nomadic Indians until roughly 1200. **Natchez** at one time was purported to have the most millionaires outside of New York City. Many of Natchez's pre–Civil War buildings were spared desecration in the Civil War because of the city's early surrender to the Union forces. Scores of these historic buildings and lavish mansions are open for touring today.

Confederate president Jefferson Davis grew up near **Woodville** in southern Mississippi and retired to **Biloxi,** where a memorial shrine is now dedicated to him (after he was acquitted of federal treason charges).

The fortified port city of **Vicksburg** was the focus of one of the bloodiest and most dramatic campaigns of the Civil War. In spring and summer 1863, battles were fought at various sites in west-central Mississippi. The campaign culminated in the 47-day siege of Vicksburg and its capitulation on July 4, 1863. With this victory, the Union gained control of the lower Mississippi River while severing Confederate transport and communication with Louisiana, Arkansas, and Texas. Learn more at the 1,700-acre **Vicksburg National Military Park.** While you're there, be sure to take in the relics stored in the **Old Courthouse Museum;** of special and bizarre interest is its minié ball exhibit. It is purported that a round shot at a young Confederate soldier went through him in a not-so-pleasant place and into the equivalent spot on a young woman standing very close by. Remarkably, both lived. Not too soon after, and by some otherworldly laws of nature, the woman found out she was pregnant.

Outdoors enthusiasts will find plenty to do in Mississippi at such places as **Beinville National Forest, De Soto National Forest,** and **Gulf Islands National Seashore.** Freshwater fishing, boating, skiing, and swimming can be had on some of the most surprisingly gorgeous lakes in the southeast. There is also deep-sea fishing in the Gulf, as well as an abundance of hunting, trails, and paddling. Golfers also fare well in Mississippi, where casinos have complemented respected older courses with some challenging, contemporary holes. The state parks system offers, among a few to choose from, one of the top ten "best new affordable public courses" in the country according to *Golf Digest.*

If you've the time to do some serious exploring in Mississippi, there are numerous recommended destinations and curiosities that more than amply represent a generous slice of what the state has to offer. Laurel's **National Anvil Shooting Contest,** a pastime that dates back to the Civil War, is a hoot if explosions and flying heavy metal are your thing. The only petrified forest located east of the Mississippi River is located in **Flora.** Elvis Presley's birthplace as well as the **Elvis Presley Center and Museum** can be visited in **Tupelo.** An even more intimate and personal brush with the King can be experienced at the 24-hour, seven-days-a-week tribute to the **King at Graceland Too** in **Holly Springs.**

Campground Profiles

BAY ST. LOUIS   MAP, D-2
Casino Magic RV Park

reserve america

711 Casino Magic Dr., 39520. T: (800) 5-MAGIC-5; www.reserveamerica.com.

🚐 ★★★★   ▲ n/a

Beauty: ★★★★   Site Privacy: ★★★
Spaciousness: ★★★★   Quiet: ★★★★
Security: ★★★★   Cleanliness: ★★★★
Insect Control: ★★★★   Facilities: ★★★★

Attractive Casino Magic has large sites laid out in two loops that flank the office and washhouse. Few sites are shady. Sites 45, 47, 49, and 50 are shady and roomy, with nice views of the golf course. Sites 4, 5, 7, and 9 enjoy a pleasant view of marshy bayou with ducks and water lilies. All sites feature paved parking, and most have back-in parking. Guests either walk to the casino or take the free 24-hour shuttle. The campground is about 1 mile from a beach on Bay St. Louis and about 15 miles from beaches on the Gulf of Mexico. Bay St. Louis is an energetic little town with plenty of dining and entertainment. There are no gates at Casino Magic, but the park is patrolled by casino security personnel 24 hours a day. Avoid southern Mississippi in the hot, humid summer months.

BASICS
Operated By: Casino Magic. **Open:** All year. **Site Assignment:** Sites assigned; reservations strongly recommended, credit card deposit; 24-hour cancellation notice required for refund; reservations held until 6 p.m. **Registration:** At office (24-hours weekends), latecomers check for instructions at office. **Fee:** $29; cash, V, MC, AE, D; Players Club discounts. **Parking:** At sites, not on grass.

FACILITIES
Number of RV-only Sites: 100. **Hookups:** Electric (30, 50 amps), water, sewer, cable TV. **Each Site:** Grill, picnic table. **Dump Station:** Yes. **Laundry:** Yes. **Pay Phone:** Yes. **Restrooms and Showers:** Yes. **Fuel:** No. **Propane:** No. **Internal Roads:** Paved. **RV Service:** On-call mechanic. **Market:** 0.5 mi. **Restaurant:** Several at the casino. **General Store:** 15 mi. in Gulfport. **Vending:** Yes. **Swimming:** No. **Playground:** No. **Other:** Boat launch, pavilion. **Activities:** Free shuttle to casinos (walking distance), The Bridges 18-hole golf course. **Nearby Attractions:** John C. Stennis Space Center, Gulfport boat & bayou tours, Marine Life Oceanarium, Wildlife Management Areas, Bay St. Louis antiques shopping. **Additional Information:** Mississippi Gulf Coast CVB, (228) 896-6699.

RESTRICTIONS
Pets: On leash only. **Fires:** Grill only. **Alcoholic Beverages:** At site only. **Vehicle Maximum Length:** 45 ft. **Other:** 1-week stay limit. No tent camping.

TO GET THERE
Take I-10 Exit 13, MS 43/603 toward Bay St. Louis for 6 mi. to US 90 east for 2 mi. then left at Blue Meadow for 0.5 mi., then right on Casino Magic Dr. Follow signs.

BILOXI   MAP, D-3
Mazalea Travel Park

8220 West Oaklawn Rd., 39532. T: (228) 392-8575 or (800) 877-8575.

🚐 ★★★★   ▲ ★★★

Beauty: ★★★★   Site Privacy: ★★★★
Spaciousness: ★★★★   Quiet: ★★★★
Security: ★★   Cleanliness: ★★★★
Insect Control: ★★   Facilities: ★★

Mazalea is 9 miles from the beach and 8 miles from outlet malls. There are over a dozen casinos in Biloxi and scores of restaurants. Tourist attractions include Beauvoir, the retirement home of Jefferson Davis, and art galleries and museums. The campground is adjacent to I-10, making it a cinch to tool around Biloxi. However, this urban locale is cause for security concerns given the park's lack of gates. Snowbirds like to winter at Mazalea, and families flock here in the spring, summer, and fall. Try to visit in spring or fall in order to avoid the heat.

BASICS
Operated By: Williams family. **Open:** All year. **Site Assignment:** Sites usually assigned; reservations recommended, no deposit; receive credit toward future stay w/ early departure. **Registration:** At camp store. **Fee:** $25–$30; cash, check, V, MC, D. **Parking:** At site, in parking lot.

FACILITIES
Number of RV-only Sites: 134. **Number of Tent-only Sites:** 5. **Hookups:** Electric (30, 50 amps), water, sewer, cable TV. **Each Site:** Picnic table. **Dump Station:** Yes. **Laundry:** Yes. **Pay Phone:** Yes. **Restrooms and Showers:** Yes. **Fuel:** No. **Propane:** Yes. **Internal Roads:** Paved. **RV Service:** 7 mi. east in D'Iberville. **Market:** Camp store, Wal-Mart 5 mi. east in D'Iberville. **Restaurant:** 3 mi. west in Gulfport. **General Store:** Camp store, Wal-Mart 5 mi. east in D'Iberville. **Vending:** Yes. **Swimming:** No. **Playground:** Yes. **Other:** Activities building, public boat ramp, his/hers dressing rooms, RV supplies. **Activities:** Shuffleboard, horseshoes, winter potluck gatherings. **Nearby Attractions:** Biloxi casinos, museums, outlet shopping, beach w/in 8 mi. **Additional Information:** Mississippi Gulf Coast CVB, (228) 896-6699.

RESTRICTIONS
Pets: 2 small dogs or 2 small cats. **Fires:** Not allowed. **Alcoholic Beverages:** At site only. No glass bottles. **Vehicle Maximum Length:** 45 ft.

TO GET THERE
From I-10, take Exit 41 (Woolmarket Rd.). The campground is 300 yards south on the right.

BILOXI   MAP, D-3
Parker's Landing

7577 East Oaklawn Rd., 39532. T: (228) 392-7717; www.parkerslandingpark.com.

🚐 ★★★★   ▲ ★★★

Beauty: ★★★★   Site Privacy: ★★★
Spaciousness: ★★★   Quiet: ★★★
Security: ★★★   Cleanliness: ★★★★
Insect Control: ★★   Facilities: ★★★

Convenient to numerous casinos, restaurants, and tourist attractions, Parker's Landing is located 8 miles from the beach in Biloxi. This tidy, urban campground straddles Parker's Creek and maintains a boat ramp. This park doesn't offer the wide assortment of entertainment facilities found at many private campgrounds. There are two camping areas. The older section includes midsized sites, which are long, thin, and sandwiched together. Some sites in the older section are open. Others, including sites 64–76 and 50–58, are nicely shaded by pine, cedar, and oak. Newer sites across the creek are completely open and provide parking for two additional vehicles at each site. All parking is paved, and there are pull-through and back-in sites. Parker's Landing is adjacent to I-10 and has no gates, making security marginal. Try to plan a visit for spring or fall.

BASICS
Operated By: Elva & Dennis O'Brian. **Open:** All year. **Site Assignment:** Reservations recommended; call (228) 392-7717; credit-card deposit; 3-day cancellation policy for refund on holidays. **Registration:** At office. **Fee:** $18–$25; cash, check, V, MC, AE. **Parking:** At sites & in parking lot. No parking on grass.

FACILITIES
Number of RV-only Sites: 130. **Number of Tent-only Sites:** 5. **Number of Multipurpose Sites:** 12. **Hookups:** Electric (30, 50 amps), water, sewer, cable TV. **Each Site:** Picnic table. **Dump Station:** No. **Laundry:** Yes. **Pay Phone:** Yes. **Restrooms and Showers:** Yes. **Fuel:** No. **Propane:** Yes. **Internal Roads:** Paved. **RV Service:** 7 mi. east in D'Iberville. **Market:** Camp store, Wal-Mart 5 mi. east in D'Iberville. **Restaurant:** 5 mi. east in D'Iberville. **General Store:** 5 mi. east in D'Iberville, gift shop. **Vending:** Beverages. **Swimming:** Yes. **Playground:** No. **Other:** Fire rings by the creek, boat ramp, banquet hall, lodge, gift shop, cable TV, clubhouse. **Activities:** Creek fishing, swimming, picnics. **Nearby Attractions:** Biloxi casinos, Beauvoir Jefferson Davis home, museums, outlet shopping, beach w/in 7 mi. **Additional Information:** Mississippi Gulf Coast CVB, (228) 896-6699.

RESTRICTIONS
Pets: On leash only. No guard dogs. **Fires:** Creek side fire rings only. **Alcoholic Beverages:** Allowed. **Vehicle Maximum Length:** 45 ft.

TO GET THERE

From I-10, take Exit 41 (Woolmarket Rd.). The campground is just south of the interstate on the right.

COLDWATER   MAP, A-2
Arkabutla Lake, South Abutment Campground

3905 Arkabutla Dam Rd., 38618. T: (662) 562-6261 or (877) 444-6777; www.recreation.gov.

🚐 ★★★★★   🏕 ★★★★★

Beauty: ★★★★★	Site Privacy: ★★★★★
Spaciousness: ★★★★★	Quiet: ★★★★★
Security: ★★★	Cleanliness: ★★★★★
Insect Control: ★★★	Facilities: ★★★

Often less crowded than Enid and Sardis Lakes, Arkabutla Lake also has extensive recreational facilities. Fishermen find catfish, bream, white bass, black bass, and some of the largest crappie in the southeast. All three campgrounds at Arkabutla have nice-looking, commodious sites. We prefer the South Abutment campground; it is the least frequented of the three and has the most spacious washhouse. Sites at south Abutment are shady, and most are secluded. All campsites at Lake Arkabutla have paved parking. There are two pull-throughs at Hernando Point; other sites offer back-in parking. Security at this rural recreation area is fair; gates do not lock, but law enforcement patrols throughout the night.

BASICS

Operated By: U.S. Army Corps of Engineers. **Open:** All year. **Site Assignment:** First come, first served; reservations accepted through the National Recreation Reservation Service (NRRS) at (877) 444-6777 or www.recreation.gov; reservations can be made up to 240 days in advance, full payment required upon making reservation; credit card preferred (V, MC, D, AE), or pay by money order if at least 21 days in advance of arrival; $10 fee for cancellation or change of site or dates; cancellation w/in 3 days of arrival charged first night, no-show charged $20 plus first night. **Registration:** At entrance stations. **Fee:** $8–$10; V, MC, D. **Parking:** At site.

FACILITIES

Number of Tent-only Sites: 3. **Number of Multi-purpose Sites:** 77. **Hookups:** Electric (20, 30 amps), water. **Each Site:** Picnic table, grill, fire ring. **Dump Station:** Yes. **Laundry:** No. **Pay Phone:** Yes. **Restrooms and Showers:** Yes. **Fuel:** No. **Propane:** No. **Internal Roads:** Paved. **RV Service:** 40 mi. north in Memphis. **Market:** 15 mi. southeast in Coldwater. **Restaurant:** 5 mi. south in Arkabutla. **General Store:** 15 mi. southeast in Coldwater. **Vending:** Yes. **Swimming:** Yes. **Playground:** Yes. **Other:** Boat launch, 36,000 acres, beaches, primitive equestrian trails, picnic areas & shelters, nature trails. **Activities:** Fishing, hunting, swimming, hiking, windsailing, volleyball, fall festival. **Nearby Attractions:** Attractions in Tunica & Memphis; Beale St., Mud Island, Graceland. **Additional Information:** Hernando Chamber of Commerce, (662) 429-9055; or Senatobia Chamber of Commerce, (662) 562-8715.

RESTRICTIONS

Pets: On leash only. **Fires:** At sites only. **Alcoholic Beverages:** Not allowed. **Vehicle Maximum Length:** No limit.

TO GET THERE

From I-55, take Exit 271 (Coldwater) and go west on MS 306 for 2 mi. Turn left onto US 51 and go south for 1 mi. to Coldwater. At the 4-way stop, turn right and go west on Scenic Hwy. 304 for 10 mi. to Arkabutla, where 304 turns north. Continue 5 mi. to the Main Dam and office.

COLLINSVILLE   MAP, C-3
Twiltley Branch Camping Area

reserve america

Okatibee Lake, 9200 Hamrick Rd. North, 39325. T: (601) 626-8068 or (601) 626-8431; www.reserveamerica.com.

🚐 ★★★★   🏕 ★★★★

Beauty: ★★★★★	Site Privacy: ★★★
Spaciousness: ★★★★	Quiet: ★★★★
Security: ★★★★★	Cleanliness: ★★★★
Insect Control: ★★★★	Facilities: ★★★★

Twiltley Branch is preferable to nearby Okatibee Water Park campground for both tent and RV campers. There are plenty of activities for all ages at Okatibee Lake, including a water park. About 4,000 acres of forest are available for hunting. The attractive campground features large to huge sites shaded by loblolly pine, black gum, and various oak species. Parking is on gravel and back-in style. The exceptions are three huge, paved pull-throughs. There is little foliage to provide privacy between sites. Two loops have hookups. Although all lakefront sites are pretty, sites 32–36 on the Black Gum Loop are exceptional for their size and shadiness. The Cypress Loop has no hookups, but it is near a lovely stand of cypress.

BASICS

Operated By: U.S. Army Corps of Engineers. **Open:** All year. **Site Assignment:** First come, first served; 38 sites available for reservation through the National Recreation Reservation Service (NRRS) at (877) 444-6777 or www.recreation.gov; reservations can be made up to 240 days in advance, full payment required upon making reservation; credit card preferred (V, MC, D, AE), or pay by money order if at least 21 days in advance of arrival; $10 fee for cancellation or change of site or dates; cancellation w/in 3 days of arrival charged first night, no-show charged $20 plus first night. **Registration:** At gatehouse, no late registration. **Fee:** Waterfront, $16; nonwaterfront, $14; primitive tent, $10. Fees include 8 people. **Parking:** At site, in parking lot.

FACILITIES

Number of Multipurpose Sites: 61. **Hookups:** Electric (30, 50 amps), water. **Each Site:** Picnic table, fire ring, grill, lantern pole. **Dump Station:** Yes. **Laundry:** Yes. **Pay Phone:** Yes. **Restrooms and Showers:** Yes. **Fuel:** No. **Propane:** No. **Internal Roads:** Paved. **RV Service:** 10 mi. south in Meridian. **Market:** 3 mi. west in Collinsville. **Restaurant:**

10 mi. south in Meridian. **General Store:** 3 mi. west in Collinsville. **Vending:** Beverages. **Swimming:** Yes. **Playground:** Yes. **Other:** Boat ramps, boat rentals at marina, foot trails, Okatibee Water Park (lodge, playground, waterslide, beaches, picnic shelter), beaches, picnic facilities, scenic overlook, amphitheater. **Activities:** Swimming, waterskiing, bank fishing, hunting, boating, picnicking, hiking, photography. **Nearby Attractions:** Mississippi Grand Opera House, Dunn's Falls in Enterprise, Bonita Lakes City Park & golf course, Sam Dale Historic Site. **Additional Information:** Meridian Chamber of Commerce, (601) 693-1306.

RESTRICTIONS

Pets: Leash only (no pets on the beach). **Fires:** Fire ring only. **Alcoholic Beverages:** Allowed, at sites only (not allowed on the beach). **Vehicle Maximum Length:** No limit. **Other:** 2-week stay limit w/in 30 days, limit 8 people per campsite. Security provided.

TO GET THERE

From I-20, take Exit 150 and drive north on Hwy. 19 for 8.5 mi. Turn right onto Twitley Branch Rd. and drive 2 mi. to Hamrick Rd. Turn right and drive about 0.75 mi. to the park entrance.

COLUMBUS   MAP, B-3
Blue Bluff

reserve america

3606 W. Plymouth Rd., 39701-9504. T: (662) 369-2832 or (877) 444-6777; www.reserveamerica.com.

🚐 ★★★★   🏕 ★★★★

Beauty: ★★★★	Site Privacy: ★★★★
Spaciousness: ★★★★	Quiet: ★★★
Security: ★★★★★	Cleanliness: ★★★★
Insect Control: ★	Facilities: ★★★

Named for the 80-foot clay and limestone bluffs bordering the park on the eastern side, the campground at Blue Bluff is quite attractive. The campground is laid out in two loops. Most sites are spacious, but sites found in pairs feel small and exposed. Gorgeous tree cover provides shade to all sites. A few sites are secluded, but most are open to their neighbors. The most secluded sites (good honeymoon suites) are 53 and 65. Sites 66–92 include some waterfront sites with nice views. Site 45 wins the beauty pageant with its breathtaking view. Sites 1–32, while nicely wooded, tend to be closer together than the rest. Most sites offers back-in parking; all parking is paved.

BASICS

Operated By: U.S. Army Corps of Engineers. **Open:** Reservation season, Mar. 1–Sept. 15; walk-ins, Sept. 16–Feb. 28. **Site Assignment:** First come, first served; reservations accepted through the National Recreation Reservation Service (NRRS) at (877) 444-6777 or www.recreation.gov; reservations can be made up to 240 days in advance, full payment required upon making reservation; credit card preferred (V, MC, D, AE), or pay by money order if at least 21 days in advance of arrival; $10 fee for cancellation or change of site or dates; cancellation w/in 3 days of arrival charged first night, no-show charged $20 plus first night. **Registration:** At gatehouse or night-access lane. **Fee:** Waterfront or sewer, $18; basic, $16. **Parking:** At site, limit 2 vehicles per site, $3 fee for extra vehicles.

FACILITIES

Number of Multipurpose Sites: 92. **Hookups:** Electric (30, 50 amps), water, 2 w/ sewer. **Each Site:** Picnic table, fire ring, grill, lantern post, impact pad. **Dump Station:** Yes. **Laundry:** Yes. **Pay Phone:** Yes. **Restrooms and Showers:** Yes. **Fuel:** No. **Propane:** No. **Internal Roads:** Paved. **RV Service:** 1.5 mi. northwest in Aberdeen. **Market:** 1.5 mi. northwest in Aberdeen. **Restaurant:** 1.5 mi. northwest in Aberdeen. **General Store:** 1.5 mi. northwest in Aberdeen. **Vending:** Beverages. **Swimming:** Yes. **Playground:** Yes. **Other:** Boat launch, fishing piers, boat ramp, boat docks, fish-cleaning station, picnic shelters. **Activities:** Swimming beach, hiking trail, volleyball & tennis courts. **Nearby Attractions:** Aberdeen Pilgrimage Antebellum home tours, Blue Bluff River Festival. **Additional Information:** Aberdeen Visitors Bureau, (662) 369-9440.

RESTRICTIONS

Pets: Leash only, not allowed in buildings. **Fires:** Fire ring only. Must be completely extinguished. **Alcoholic Beverages:** Allowed (no glass bottles), no alcohol on beach. **Vehicle Maximum Length:** No limit. **Other:** Title 36 regulations posted.

TO GET THERE

From Columbus, drive 30 mi. north on US 45 to Aberdeen. In downtown Aberdeen, at the intersection of Commerce and Meridian, turn northeast onto Meridian. Cross the railroad tracks and the bridge, then take the first right. The campground is on the left.

COLUMBUS MAP, B-3
DeWayne Hayes Campground

reserve america

7934 Barton Ferry Rd., 39701. T: (662) 434-6939 or (877) 444-6777; www.reserveamerica.com.

🚐 ★★★★   ⛺ ★★★★

Beauty: ★★★★★	Site Privacy: ★★★
Spaciousness: ★★★★★	Quiet: ★★★★
Security: ★★★★★	Cleanliness: ★★★★
Insect Control: ★	Facilities: ★★★

This area was named after Pfc. Loyd DeWayne Hayes, who died at the age of 20 while helping with preparations for the Tennessee-Tombigbee Waterway. Although less wooded, DeWayne Hayes campground has nicer waterfront sites than nearby Town Creek. Sites on the right-hand side of the main road often have water views. The nicest of these are sites 3–36 and 70–92. Site 91 is exceptionally lovely. All sites are large with ample space between neighbors. All are nicely shaded, although there is little privacy between sites. Parking is paved, and most sites are back-ins. Of the pull-throughs, lackluster number 66 is the largest. Day-use facilities are extensive at this

rural recreation area. Prepare for monster mosquitoes, and avoid visiting during hot, humid late summer. Excellent destinations when the weather is mild, the campgrounds along the Tennessee-Tombigbee Waterway rarely fill to capacity. Gates lock at night, making this park extremely secure.

BASICS

Operated By: U.S. Army Corps of Engineers. **Open:** All year. **Site Assignment:** First come, first served; reservations accepted through the National Recreation Reservation Service (NRRS) at (877) 444-6777 or www.recreation.gov; reservations can be made up to 240 days in advance, full payment required upon making reservation; credit card preferred (V, MC, D, AE), or pay by money order if at least 21 days in advance of arrival; $10 fee for cancellation or change of site or dates; cancellation w/in 3 days of arrival charged first night, no-show charged $20 plus first night. **Registration:** At gatehouse. **Fee:** $16–$20. **Parking:** At site, limit 2 vehicles, $3 fee for extra vehicles.

FACILITIES

Number of Tent-only Sites: 10. **Number of Multipurpose Sites:** 100. **Hookups:** Electric (50 amps), water, 25 w/ sewer. **Each Site:** Picnic table, fire ring, concrete pad, grill, lantern pole. **Dump Station:** Yes. **Laundry:** Yes. **Pay Phone:** Yes. **Restrooms and Showers:** Yes. **Fuel:** No. **Propane:** No. **Internal Roads:** Paved. **RV Service:** 5 mi. east in Columbus. **Market:** 7 mi. east in Columbus. **Restaurant:** 5 mi. east in Columbus. **General Store:** 5 mi. east in Columbus. **Vending:** Beverages. **Swimming:** Yes. **Playground:** Yes. **Other:** Boat launch, fish-cleaning station, picnic shelters, group campfire ring, wildlife viewing area, water sport theme park. **Activities:** Cypress Swamp Nature Trail, swimming beach, fishing, volleyball, tennis, hiking. **Nearby Attractions:** Columbus & West Point w/in 5 mi., Mississippi State University, Tombigbee National Forest, Lake Lowndes State Park. **Additional Information:** Columbus Chamber of Commerce, (662) 327-7796.

RESTRICTIONS

Pets: On leash only. **Fires:** Fire ring only. **Alcoholic Beverages:** Allowed. **Vehicle Maximum Length:** No limit.

TO GET THERE

From Columbus, take US 45 north for 4 mi. to the junction of MS 50 and MS 373. Turn left and follow MS 373 north for 1.5 mi. to Stenson Creek Rd. and turn left. Drive 2 mi. to Barton's Ferry Rd. Turn left to the entrance.

COLUMBUS MAP, B-3
Lake Lowndes State Park

3319 Lake Lowndes Rd., 39702. T: (662) 328-2110; www.mdwfp.com.

🚐 ★★★   ⛺ ★★★

Beauty: ★★★★	Site Privacy: ★★★
Spaciousness: ★★★	Quiet: ★★★
Security: ★★★	Cleanliness: ★★★★
Insect Control: ★★	Facilities: ★★★★

Situated on 150-acre Lake Lowndes, this state park offers an interesting variety of activities. The small lake is stocked with catfish, crappie, bass, and bream. The campground consists of three main loops situated in a shady stand of trees dominated by loblolly pine and various oak species. Site size is average, and there is little foliage between sites to provide privacy. All parking is back-in–style and paved. The nicest sites are situated along the lake. There is only one washhouse serving 50 sites, so we anticipate lines for potties on crowded holiday weekends. Located 6 miles from Columbus, home of Mississippi State University, this campground is busier on fall football weekends. Try visiting in late spring when Mississippi weather is at its best. Security is fair at this rural park, where gates were not locked and night-time patrolling was sporadic when we visited.

BASICS

Operated By: Mississippi Dept. of Wildlife, Fisheries & Parks. **Open:** All year. **Site Assignment:** First come, first served; reservations accepted, $15 1-night deposit, nonrefundable. **Registration:** Ranger makes rounds in the evening. **Fee:** Full hookup, $20 (first night $15 w/ reservation); water/electric, $14; tent, $9; seniors & disabled, $9; cash, V, MC, D. **Parking:** At site, in lot.

FACILITIES

Number of RV-only Sites: 50. **Number of Tent-only Sites:** 12. **Hookups:** Electric (30, 50 amps), water, some w/ sewer. **Each Site:** Picnic table, grill. **Dump Station:** Yes. **Laundry:** Yes. **Pay Phone:** Yes. **Restrooms and Showers:** Yes. **Fuel:** No. **Propane:** No. **Internal Roads:** Paved. **RV Service:** 20 mi. north in Columbus. **Market:** Camp store (in season only), 1 mi. west in Columbus. **Restaurant:** 1 mi. west in Columbus. **General Store:** Camp store (in season only), 2.5 mi. north in Columbus. **Vending:** Yes. **Swimming:** Yes. **Playground:** Yes. **Other:** Pool table, Ping-Pong table, nature trail, picnic sites, swimming beach, bike trail, equestrian trail, visitor center, meeting rooms, video games, marina, boat ramp. **Activities:** Disc golf, walking track, boat rentals, tennis, volleyball, basketball, soccer, softball, fishing. **Nearby Attractions:** Over 100 antebellum homes, Historic Downtown Columbus, river ferry, Tennessee-Tombigbee Waterway, art & family festivals, Mississippi University for Women, Mississippi State University. **Additional Information:** Columbus Visitor Information, (662) 329-1191.

RESTRICTIONS

Pets: On leash only. **Fires:** Campsites, in fire pits only. **Alcoholic Beverages:** Not allowed. **Vehicle Maximum Length:** No limit. **Other:** Very busy during MSU football season.

TO GET THERE

Take I-82 to Columbus. Take the Least Oaks exit and drive south on MS 69. Turn east onto Lake Lowndes Rd. The park is 10 mi. southeast of Columbus. 6 mi. southeast of Columbus off MS 69.

COLUMBUS
Town Creek Campground

reserve america

3606 West Plymouth Rd., 39701.
T: (662) 327-2142 or (662) 494-4885;
www.reserveamerica.com.

🚐 ★★★★   ⛺ ★★★★

Beauty: ★★★★   Site Privacy: ★★★★
Spaciousness: ★★★★★   Quiet: ★★★★★
Security: ★★★★   Cleanliness: ★★★★★
Insect Control: ★   Facilities: ★★★

Yet another lovely impoundment of the Tennessee-Tombigbee River system, Columbus Lake offers excellent fishing, and Town Creek Recreation Area offers excellent amenities for anglers. Within the recreation area, small Kennedy Lake provides additional fishing opportunities, as well as a sandy swimming beach with sundeck. Many campsites boast serene lake views. Site size varies, with lakefront sites often smaller than their upland counterparts. Some sites are totally shady and secluded, while others are only partially shaded and open to neighbors. The campground is laid out in two loops and a spur with paved, back-in parking spaces. There are six attractive pull-through sites in the back of the campground. Other beautiful sites include 34, 36, 70, 71, 75, and 83–94. At this very rural campground, security is fine. However, mosquitoes are extremely annoying along the low-lying Tenn-Tom Waterway. Bring plenty of insect repellent. Avoid this area in steamy late summer.

BASICS

Operated By: U.S. Army Corps of Engineers.
Open: All year. **Site Assignment:** 60% reservable, 40% first come, first served; reservation season Mar. 1–Sept. 15; walk-ins Sept. 16–Feb. 28; refunds must be requested no later than 14 days prior to arrival. **Registration:** At office. **Fee:** Premium, $18; water, $16; family tent, $10. **Parking:** At site, 2-vehicle limit. Extra vehicles, $3 each.

FACILITIES

Number of RV-only Sites: 100. **Number of Tent-only Sites:** 10. **Hookups:** Electric (30, 50 amps). **Each Site:** Concrete pads, lantern posts, grills, fire ring, picnic table, access to boat ramp. **Dump Station:** Yes. **Laundry:** Yes. **Pay Phone:** Yes. **Restrooms and Showers:** Yes. **Fuel:** No. **Propane:** No. **Internal Roads:** Paved. **RV Service:** 10 mi. **Market:** Nearby. **Restaurant:** Nearby. **General Store:** Nearby. **Vending:** Yes. **Swimming:** Yes. **Playground:** Yes. **Other:** Fish-cleaning station, disabled-accessible, bike trails, boat launch ramp. **Activities:** Swim beach, multiuse park fields, picnic pavilions, nature & hiking trails, biking.

RESTRICTIONS

Pets: On leash only. **Fires:** Fire ring only. **Alcoholic Beverages:** Allowed but not on beach. **Vehicle Maximum Length:** No limit. **Other:** 24-hour attendant.

TO GET THERE

From Columbus, take Hwy. 45 N to junction with Hwy. 50 W, turn left, follow Hwy. 50 W past Hwy. 50 Waterway Bridge. Intersection is 2 mi. west of bridge. Turn north, follow signs.

DENNIS   MAP, A-3
Piney Grove Campground

reserve america

82 Bay Springs Resource Rd., 38859.
T: (662) 728-1134; www.reserveamerica.com.

🚐 ★★★★   ⛺ ★★★★

Beauty: ★★★★★   Site Privacy: ★★★★
Spaciousness: ★★★★★   Quiet: ★★★★
Security: ★★★★★   Cleanliness: ★★★★★
Insect Control: ★   Facilities: ★★★

Piney Grove is typical of the U.S. Army Corps of Engineers campgrounds found along the Tennessee-Tombigbee Waterway; it has incredibly beautiful campsites. All sites are commodious, with ample shade provided by loblolly pine and various hardwoods. Most campsites are afforded plenty of privacy by screening foliage. The peninsular campground contains sites in three main areas. With views of Bay Springs Lake, the area containing sites 55–81 boasts some of the most gorgeous sites in the state. Secluded and picturesque, sites 64 and 75 are absolutely fabulous. All sites have paved parking and a large gravel picnic area. Most sites are back-in. There are 11 pull-through sites, the nicest of which is number 113. Situated in the rural, rolling hills of northeast Mississippi, this park locks its gates at night, making it extremely secure. Rarely crowded, it's safe to visit here on summer weekends if you can stand the heat and mosquitoes.

BASICS

Operated By: U.S. Army Corps of Engineers.
Open: Mar. 25–Nov. 13. **Site Assignment:** First come, first served; reservations accepted through the National Recreation Reservation Service (NRRS) at (877) 444-6777 or www.recreation.gov; reservations can be made up to 240 days in advance, full payment required upon making reservation; credit card preferred (V, MC, D, AE), or pay by money order if at least 21 days in advance of arrival; $10 fee for cancellation or change of site or dates; cancellation w/in 3 days of arrival charged first night, no-show charged $20 plus first night. **Registration:** At gatehouse, gate locks at 10 p.m. **Fee:** Waterfront, $18; nonwaterfront, $16; 8 people max. **Parking:** At site, limit 3 vehicles, fee for extra vehicles.

FACILITIES

Number of RV-only Sites: 141. **Number of Multipurpose Sites:** 141. **Hookups:** Electric (20, 30, 50 amps), water. **Each Site:** Grill, picnic table, fire ring, lantern pole. **Dump Station:** Yes. **Laundry:** Yes. **Pay Phone:** No. **Restrooms and Showers:** Yes. **Fuel:** No. **Propane:** No. **Internal Roads:** Paved. **RV Service:** 30 mi. east in Red Bay, AL. **Market:** 25 mi. west in Booneville. **Restaurant:** 25 mi. west in Booneville. **General Store:** 25 mi. west in Booneville. **Vending:** Beverages. **Swimming:** Yes. **Playground:** Yes. **Other:** Boat ramp, fishing piers, fish-cleaning station, amphitheater, swimming beach, picnic shelter. **Activities:** Multiuse game courts, nature trails, fishing, swimming, campfire programs in-season. **Nearby Attractions:** Tishomingo State Park, Brices Cross Roads National Battlefield Site, Chickasaw Village, Tupelo, Birthplace of Elvis Presley, Tennessee-Tombigbee Waterway. **Additional Information:** Tupelo CVB, (662) 842-4521.

RESTRICTIONS

Pets: On leash only. Not in swimming area. **Fires:** Grills, fire rings. **Alcoholic Beverages:** Not allowed. **Vehicle Maximum Length:** Sites vary. **Other:** 14-day stay limit.

TO GET THERE

From the junction of Hwy. 4 and Hwy. 30 east in Booneville, MS, take Hwy. 30 east 11 mi. to Burton, turn right on CR 3501. Follow CR 3501 for 3 mi. and turn left at the sign for Piney Grove Recreation Area.

DENNIS   MAP, A-3
Whitten Park Campground

reserve america

82 Bay Springs Resource Rd., 38838.
T: (662) 862-5414 or (662) 862-7070;
www.reserveamerica.com.

🚐 ★★★★   ⛺ ★★★★

Beauty: ★★★★★   Site Privacy: ★★★★
Spaciousness: ★★★★   Quiet: ★★★★★
Security: ★★★★★   Cleanliness: ★★★★★
Insect Control: ★★   Facilities: ★★★

Whitten Park is extremely pretty. The campground is laid out in three loops, each of which has a few waterfront sites. Sites 10, 11, and 12 have pretty water views. Close to the playground, 27 and 28 are excellent choices for families. Sites 42 and 46, the only pull-throughs at Whitten Park, are extremely large. Parking is paved, and sites are shaded by dense woods with foliage providing site privacy. On the property, the Jamie L. Whitten Historical Center features exhibits on the area's economic development. One focus is the Tennessee-Tombigbee Waterway, the largest U.S. Army Corps of Engineers project in history. Built mainly for navigation, the "Ten-Tom" connects the lower Tennessee Valley to the Gulf of Mexico, is five times longer than the Panama Canal, and required moving one-third more earth. Security is excellent at this remote, gated campground. This campground rarely fills up, making it a good choice for summer weekend camping.

BASICS

Operated By: U.S. Army Corps of Engineers.
Open: All year. **Site Assignment:** First come, first served; reservations accepted through the National Recreation Reservation Service (NRRS) at (877) 444-6777 or www.recreation.gov; reservations can be made up to 240 days in advance, full payment required upon making reservation; credit card preferred (V, MC, D, AE), or pay by money order if at least 21 days in advance of arrival; $10 fee for cancellation or change of site or dates; cancellation w/in 3 days of arrival charged first night, no-show charged

$20 plus first night. **Registration:** At gatehouse, gate locks at 10 p.m. **Fee:** Waterfront, $18; nonwaterfront, $16; fee includes 8 people; cash, personal check, V, MC, D, AE. **Parking:** At sites, in parking lots.

FACILITIES

Number of Multipurpose Sites: 61. **Hookups:** Electric (30, 50 amps), water. **Each Site:** Picnic table, fire ring, grill, lantern pole. **Dump Station:** Yes. **Laundry:** Yes. **Pay Phone:** Yes. **Restrooms and Showers:** Yes. **Fuel:** No. **Propane:** No. **Internal Roads:** Paved. **RV Service:** 25 mi. east in Red Bay. **Market:** 2 mi. south in Fulton. **Restaurant:** 2 mi. south in Fulton. **General Store:** Wal-Mart 2 mi. south in Fulton. **Vending:** Beverages. **Swimming:** Yes. **Playground:** Yes. **Other:** Boat ramp, fish-cleaning station, fishing piers, boat docks, picnic shelters, information center, Jamie L. Whitten Historical Center. **Activities:** Multiuse courts, swimming (swimming beach for campground use only), fishing, nature trails. **Nearby Attractions:** Bean's Ferry Pottery, Tennessee-Tombigbee Waterway, Elvis Presley Birthplace in Tupelo, Tupelo National Battlefield, Oren Dunn Museum. **Additional Information:** Tupelo CVB, (800) 533-0611.

RESTRICTIONS

Pets: On leash only. **Fires:** Fire ring only. **Alcoholic Beverages:** Not allowed. **Vehicle Maximum Length:** No limit. **Other:** Title 36 regulations posted. No dumping gray water allowed.

TO GET THERE

From US 78, take Hwy. 25 south (Exit 104). Go north 200 yards, then turn left on Access Rd. at first traffic light. Go north 4 mi. The campground is on the left side of the road, inside the Jamie L. Whitten Historical Center and Park.

ENID   MAP, A-2
Chickasaw Hill Campground

reserve america

P.O. Box 10, 38927-0010. T: (662) 563-4571; www.reserveamerica.com.

🚐 ★★★★   ⛺ ★★★★

Beauty: ★★★	Site Privacy: ★★
Spaciousness: ★★	Quiet: ★★★★
Security: ★★★★	Cleanliness: ★★★★
Insect Control: ★★★	Facilities: ★★★

Enid Lake is one of four lakes in Northern Mississippi and is located on the Yocona River, is known for its family camping facilities. Enid offers many recreational activities such as boating, swimming, waterskiing, camping, picnicking, hiking, nature photography, environmental interpretive programs and a horseback riding trail. Two of the most popular activities at Enid Lake are fishing and hunting. Enid is famous for its resources, particular white crappie, bass, and catfish. Enid Lake annually hosts many crappie and bass tournaments. Crappie is king in this reservoir. Since 1957, a 5-pound, 3-ounce white crappie holds the world record. The average crappie is 1 pound, while largemouth bass average 3 pounds! Channel cats and flatheads are also available. All sites

have electrical hookups and water. Other amenities include shower houses, boat ramp, playground, swimming beach, hiking trail, large picnic shelter, amphitheater, and a dump station.

BASICS

Operated By: U.S. Army Corps of Engineers. **Open:** All year. **Site Assignment:** Reservations must be made at least 3 days in advance. **Registration:** At office. **Fee:** Single, $8–$12. **Parking:** At site.

FACILITIES

Number of Multipurpose Sites: 118. **Hookups:** Yes. **Dump Station:** Yes. **Laundry:** No. **Pay Phone:** No. **Restrooms and Showers:** Yes. **Fuel:** Yes. **Propane:** No. **Internal Roads:** Paved. **RV Service:** No. **Market:** No. **Restaurant:** No. **General Store:** No. **Vending:** No. **Swimming:** Yes. **Playground:** Yes. **Other:** Campground may be closed due to flooding starting in mid-Apr. & opening mid-July. All equipment must fit on the site pad. **Activities:** Boating, swimming, fishing, hunting, waterskiing, camping, picnicking, hiking, nature photography, environmental interpretive programs & horseback riding trail.

RESTRICTIONS

Pets: Pets must be restrained or on a leash at all times while in developed recreation areas. **Fires:** In fire rings, stoves, grills, or fireplaces provided for that purpose. **Alcoholic Beverages:** Not allowed. **Vehicle Maximum Length:** Call ahead.

TO GET THERE

From I 55: Take Exit 233 14 mi south of Batesville to Enid Dam Rd. (CR 36). Go 1 mi. to the Enid Lake Field Office. From the Enid Lake Field Office, go north 3 mi. on Chapel Hill Rd., then go east on Pope Water Valley Rd. for 7 mi. and then south on Chickasaw Rd. 1.5 mi. to the campground.

ENID   MAP, A-2
Wallace Creek Campground

reserve america

P.O. Box 10, 38927-0010. T: (662) 563-4571; www.reserveamerica.com.

🚐 ★★★★   ⛺ ★★★★

Beauty: ★★★★	Site Privacy: ★★★★
Spaciousness: ★★★★	Quiet: ★★★★
Security: ★★★	Cleanliness: ★★★★★
Insect Control: ★★★★	Facilities: ★★★

The Enid Lake area includes verdant rolling hills, blue water, and extensive recreational facilities. Fishing is spectacular here—Enid Lake holds the world's record for largest crappie. With the newest washhouses and largest sites, Wallace Creek is the most appealing campground at Enid Lake. A few choice sites, including 26, 28, 41, 71, 90, 91, and 92, have views of the lake. All campsites at Wallace Creek are spacious and shady, though few are secluded. All parking is paved. Most sites offer back-in parking. Security at Wallace Creek is fair; the campground is very close to I-55, and there are no locked gates at night, although rangers patrol regularly and Enid is in a rural location.

BASICS

Operated By: U.S. Army Corps of Engineers. **Open:** All year. **Site Assignment:** Reservations must be made at least 4 days in advance. **Registration:** At office. **Fee:** Single, $8–$15. **Parking:** At site.

FACILITIES

Number of Tent-only Sites: 16. **Number of Multipurpose Sites:** 99. **Hookups:** Electric (50 amps), water. **Each Site:** Picnic table, grill, fire ring, lantern pole. **Dump Station:** Yes. **Laundry:** No. **Pay Phone:** Yes. **Restrooms and Showers:** Yes. **Fuel:** No. **Propane:** No. **Internal Roads:** Paved. **RV Service:** 21 mi. south in Grenada. **Market:** 13 mi. north Batesville. **Restaurant:** 1 mi. at Enid Dam. **General Store:** 1 mi. at Enid Dam. **Vending:** No. **Swimming:** Yes. **Playground:** Yes. **Other:** Boat launches, motorcycle trail, picnic shelters, amphitheater, swimming beach, scenic overlook, information center. **Activities:** Fishing, boating (boat rentals at State Park), swimming, hiking, equestrian trail, waterskiing, horseback-riding trail. **Nearby Attractions:** George Payne Cossar State Park, Holly Springs National Forest, attractions in Oxford, Tunica & Memphis, medical facility. **Additional Information:** Panola Partnership/ Chamber of Commerce, (662) 563-3126.

RESTRICTIONS

Pets: On leash only. **Fires:** Fire ring only. **Alcoholic Beverages:** Allowed (dry county for beer, wet for liquor). **Vehicle Maximum Length:** No limit. **Other:** Title 36 regulations posted. Large, covered picnic shelters, $30 per day.

TO GET THERE

From I-55, take Exit 233, 14 mi. south of Batesville, then go east on CR 36 2.5 mi. and follow signs to Wallace Creek Campground.

GRENADA   MAP, B-2
North Graysport Campground

reserve america

Grenada Lake, P.O. Box 903, 38901-0903. T: (662) 226-5911 or (662) 226-1679; www.reserveamerica.com.

🚐 ★★★★   ⛺ ★★★★

Beauty: ★★★★	Site Privacy: ★★★★
Spaciousness: ★★★★	Quiet: ★★★
Security: ★★★	Cleanliness: ★★★★
Insect Control: ★★★	Facilities: ★★★★

The 63,000-acre Grenada Lake is the largest lake in Mississippi, and there is plenty of recreation available here. Stop by the Visitor Center (located on scenic Hwy. 333) to get information on what's available. The North Graysport Campground is one of nine on Grenada Lake. It offers generous sites, with lovely shade provided by mature loblolly pine, short-leaf pine, red cedar, and various oak species. However, there is little privacy between sites. All parking is paved, back-in style. There are no waterfront sites, and many sites are far from the washhouses. Opt for a site near the "facilities." Security is fair at this rural campground that doesn't lock its gates at night. Also, the campground gets incredibly crowded in the summer and should be avoided particularly on holiday weekends.

BASICS

Operated By: U.S. Army Corps of Engineers in conjunction w/ Mississippi Dept. of Wildlife, Fisheries & Parks. **Open:** All year. **Site Assignment:** First come, first served; reservations accepted for 3-night min., family sites subject to nonrefundable 1-night deposit; refunds must be requested no later than 14 days prior to arrival. **Registration:** At gatehouse. **Fee:** $10. **Parking:** At site (preferably not to exceed 3 vehicles).

FACILITIES

Number of Multipurpose Sites: 51. **Hookups:** Electric (30, 50 amps), water. **Each Site:** Picnic table, grill, fire ring, lantern pole, some tent pads. **Dump Station:** Yes. **Laundry:** No. **Pay Phone:** No. **Restrooms and Showers:** Yes. **Fuel:** No. **Propane:** No. **Internal Roads:** Paved. **RV Service:** 5 mi. south in Grenada. **Market:** 7 mi. south in Grenada. **Restaurant:** 7 mi. south in Grenada. **General Store:** 8 mi. south in Grenada (Wal-Mart). **Vending:** Beverages. **Swimming:** No. **Playground:** No. **Other:** Boat launches, picnic area, visitor center, picnic shelters. **Activities:** Several swimming beaches, fishing, boating, amphitheater. **Nearby Attractions:** Historic Grenada, walking & driving tours, Confederate Cemetery, Cocchuma Archery Range, Hugh White State Park. **Additional Information:** Grenada Tourism Commission, (800) 373-2571.

RESTRICTIONS

Pets: On leash only. Some breeds not allowed. **Fires:** Fire ring only. **Alcoholic Beverages:** Allowed. **Vehicle Maximum Length:** 50 ft.

TO GET THERE

Exit I-55 on Hwy. 8, drive east 15 mi. to flashing light at Gore Springs. Turn left 4 mi. across the lake, follow signs.

HATTIESBURG   MAP, D-2
Paul B. Johnson State Park

319 Geiger Lake Rd., 39401. T: (601) 582-7721; www.mdwfp.com.

🚐 ★★★★	⛺ ★★★★
Beauty: ★★★★	Site Privacy: ★★★
Spaciousness: ★★★	Quiet: ★★★★
Security: ★★★★	Cleanliness: ★★★★
Insect Control: ★★★★	Facilities: ★★★

Paul B. Johnson State Park offers back-in campsites situated in one area and 22 pull-through sites in another area. We recommend the back-in area. The pull-through area is crowded and far less attractive. For a nice view of 300-acre Lake Geiger, try back-in sites 15-18 and 65, 67, 69, 71, 77, 78, 80, 85, and 84. These sites are shaded by a variety of tree species, including loblolly, longleaf, and short-leaf pine. All parking is paved. Less than two hours from New Orleans, this park is popular with Crescent City–slickers and should be avoided on summer holidays and weekends. In the summer, this park

becomes so hot and humid that you could steam veggies on your car hood. Although the park's surroundings are rural, Hattiesburg businesses are only 15–20 miles away. Park gates are not locked at night, but rangers patrol regularly.

BASICS

Operated By: Mississippi Dept. of Wildlife, Fisheries & Parks. **Open:** All year; office closed Christmas. **Site Assignment:** Some first come, first served; designated sites available for reservation, w/ $15 nonrefundable 1-night deposit. **Registration:** Ranger checks in. **Fee:** Full hookup, $16; water/electric, $14; primitive tent site or seniors, $10; entrance fee, $3. **Parking:** At site, limit 2 vehicles.

FACILITIES

Number of RV-only Sites: 108. **Number of Tent-only Sites:** 25. **Hookups:** Electric (30, 50 amps), water; sewer at 50 sites. **Each Site:** Picnic table, grill. **Dump Station:** Yes. **Laundry:** Yes. **Pay Phone:** Yes. **Restrooms and Showers:** Yes. **Fuel:** No. **Propane:** No. **Internal Roads:** Paved. **RV Service:** 22 mi. north in Hattiesburg. **Market:** 15 mi. north in Hattiesburg. **Restaurant:** 3.5 mi. north in Hattiesburg. **General Store:** 15 mi. north in Hattiesburg. **Vending:** Yes. **Swimming:** Yes. **Playground:** Yes. **Other:** Boat ramp, lake beach, picnic pavilions, group camp, group camp swim area. **Activities:** Fishing, swimming, paddleboat rentals in-season, fishing boat & canoe rentals year-round, water sports, nature trail, playing fields, beach, disc golf. **Nearby Attractions:** Historic Hattiesburg, Camp Shelby Armed Forces Museum, Black Creek, Wildlife Management Areas, University of Southern Mississippi. **Additional Information:** Hattiesburg Chamber of Commerce, (601) 268-3220.

RESTRICTIONS

Pets: 6-ft. leash only. **Fires:** Allowed. **Alcoholic Beverages:** Not allowed. **Vehicle Maximum Length:** 40 ft. **Other:** No metal detectors. Busy during USM football season.

TO GET THERE

From I-59, take Exit 59 (Lucedale/Mobile/Hwy. 98E). Drive 3.5 mi. on Hwy. 98 east to the Hwy. 49/Mississippi Gulf Coast exit. Take Hwy. 49 south 8.5 for mi. The park is on the right.

JACKSON   MAP, C-2
LeFleur's Bluff State Park

2140 Riverside Dr., 39202. T: (601) 987-3923 or (601) 987-3985; www.mdwfp.com.

🚐 ★★★★	⛺ ★★★★
Beauty: ★★★★	Site Privacy: ★★★★
Spaciousness: ★★★★	Quiet: ★★★★
Security: ★★★★	Cleanliness: ★★★★
Insect Control: ★	Facilities: ★★★★★

This family-oriented park is building the state's largest playground. A small fishing lake is stocked with bass, bream, catfish, and crappie. The campground is attractive, although you can see suburban neighborhoods from your campsite. Site size is ample, and there are plenty of shady loblolly pines. Parking is on back-in, paved pads. About half of the

sites are lakefront. Of these, 6, 7, 12, and 14 are recommended because of their views and proximity to the washhouses. All sites are situated on one loop. Security is very good at this suburban state park; gates are locked at night and attended during the day. When we visited, we were eaten by mosquitoes, and the rangers told us that ants and bees are also problematic. Bring insect repellent.

BASICS

Operated By: Mississippi Dept. of Wildlife, Fisheries & Parks. **Open:** All year; frequent closings in spring due to flooding; closed Thanksgiving, Christmas, & New Year's Day. **Site Assignment:** First come, first served; 5 sites available for reservation for 2-night min., $15 nonrefundable 1-night deposit. **Registration:** At gatehouse; ranger checks in (code required to enter after gate closes—call ahead). **Fee:** $14–$20; seniors & disabled, $11. **Parking:** At site, in parking lot, limit 2 vehicles.

FACILITIES

Number of Multipurpose Sites: 30. **Hookups:** Electric (50 amps), water. **Each Site:** Picnic table, grill. **Dump Station:** Yes. **Laundry:** No. **Pay Phone:** Yes. **Restrooms and Showers:** Yes. **Fuel:** No. **Propane:** No. **Internal Roads:** Gravel, limestone. **RV Service:** 6 mi. west in Jackson. **Market:** 2 mi. north in Jackson. **Restaurant:** 1 mi. east in Flowood. **General Store:** 3 mi. north in Jackson. **Vending:** Beverages. **Swimming:** No. **Playground:** Yes. **Other:** Clubhouse, picnic area & pavilion, lodge, meeting rooms. **Activities:** Fishing (trolling motors only), boat rentals year-round, nature trails, 9-hole golf course, driving range, tennis, disc golf. **Nearby Attractions:** Jim Buck Ross Mississippi Agriculture & Forestry Museum, National Agricultural Aviation Museum, Mississippi Governors Mansion, Museum of Art, Natural Science Museum, Mississippi Sports Hall of Fame, Old Capital Museum. **Additional Information:** Jackson CVB, (800) 354-7695 or (601) 960-1891; www.visitjackson.com.

RESTRICTIONS

Pets: On leash only. **Fires:** Allowed. **Alcoholic Beverages:** Not allowed. **Vehicle Maximum Length:** 50 ft. **Other:** Very good security.

TO GET THERE

From I-55, take Exit 98B and drive east on Lakeland Dr. to the second traffic light. Turn right, and the campground is straight ahead.

MORTON   MAP, C-2
Roosevelt State Park

2149 Hwy. 13 South, 39117. T: (601) 732-6316; www.mdwfp.com.

🚐 ★★★★★	⛺ ★★★★★
Beauty: ★★★★★	Site Privacy: ★★★★★
Spaciousness: ★★★★★	Quiet: ★★★★★
Security: ★★★	Cleanliness: ★★★★
Insect Control: ★★	Facilities: ★★★★★

Set in the rolling hills of Bienville National Forest, Roosevelt State Park is one of the most beautiful state parks in Mississippi. The park has plenty of recreation for families. The 160-acre Shadow Lake is stocked with bream, crappie, bass, and catfish. Waterskiing is allowed in summertime, making the park noisier during the day. Commodious sites are shaded by lovely loblolly pine and other species. Plenty of foliage provides privacy between sites. Campsites feature back-in, paved parking. Both camping areas have drop-dead gorgeous lakefront sites. At the old campground, sites 13–15 and 24–28 are choice. At the new campground, snag a site in the 40s, 50s, 80s, or 90s. Security is fair at rural Roosevelt State Park. There are no gates, and the park is close to I-20, but rangers cruise regularly. Folks from Jackson reach the park in under one hour, making it extremely popular. If you're looking for nice weather and solitude, visit in spring or fall.

BASICS

Operated By: Mississippi Dept. of Wildlife, Fisheries, & Parks. **Open:** All year. **Site Assignment:** Most sites first come, first served; limited sites available for reservation w/ $15 nonrefundable 1-night deposit. **Registration:** At gate, after-hours ranger will check in. **Fee:** Full hookup, $16; water/electric, $14; primitive tent, $10; cash, check, V, MC. **Parking:** At site, in lot.

FACILITIES

Number of Multipurpose Sites: 109. **Hookups:** Electric (30, 50 amps), water, 28 sites w/ sewer. **Each Site:** Picnic table, grill, burn-out area. **Dump Station:** Yes. **Laundry:** Yes. **Pay Phone:** Yes. **Restrooms and Showers:** Yes. **Fuel:** No. **Propane:** No. **Internal Roads:** Paved. **RV Service:** 32 mi. west in Jackson. **Market:** 2 mi. north in Morton. **Restaurant:** 12 mi. east in Forest. **General Store:** 12 mi. east in Forest. **Vending:** Yes. **Swimming:** Seasonal. **Playground:** Yes. **Other:** Full-time catering service for groups, picnic area, pavilions, meeting rooms, group lodge, lodge, picnic facilities, gift shop, amphitheater, waterslide, tennis court, mini-golf. **Activities:** Fishing, fishing boat & paddleboat rentals in-season, waterslide, swimming, waterskiing, tennis, softball, nature trail, video games. **Nearby Attractions:** Bienville National Forest, several wildlife management areas, Shockaloe riding trails, Natchez Trace National Scenic Trail. **Additional Information:** Morton Chamber of Commerce, (601) 732-6135.

RESTRICTIONS

Pets: On leash only. **Fires:** At sites only (except under burn ban). **Alcoholic Beverages:** Not allowed. **Vehicle Maximum Length:** 32 ft. **Other:** Great view of Bienville National Forest.

TO GET THERE

The park is located 32 mi. east of Jackson. From I-20, take Exit 77 and head north on MS 13 for 0.25 mi. The entrance to the park is on the left.

NATCHEZ — MAP, C-1
Plantation Park

1 Frederick Rd., 39120. T: (601) 442-5222; www.plantationrvpark.com.

🚐 ★★★   ⛺ n/a

Beauty: ★★★   Site Privacy: ★★★
Spaciousness: ★★★   Quiet: ★★★
Security: ★★★   Cleanliness: ★★★
Insect Control: ★★   Facilities: ★★

This quiet, semiresidential RV park is conveniently located if you plan to tour historic Natchez. Just before the Civil War, over half of the millionaires in the United States had homes in Natchez. Most of these antebellum mansions survived the war and are open for touring in the spring and fall. Call the Natchez Convention and Visitors Bureau, and plan to visit while the tours are in progress. Plantation Park offers midsized sites with plenty of shade, but there is little privacy between sites. All sites offer paved back-in parking. Most of the overnight sights are parallel to Mississippi Hwy. 61. The nicest sites are even numbers 20–30, which are quieter than the other overnight sites. Security at Plantation is fair to good; there is no gate, but the park is in a rural area. Since the swimming pool is the only recreational facility, there's not much here to keep children occupied.

BASICS

Operated By: Plantation Park. **Open:** All year. **Site Assignment:** First come, first served; reservations accepted w/ 1-night deposit (by check, no credit cards), cancel 2 weeks in advance for refund (less $5 fee). **Registration:** At office, latecomers register next morning. **Fee:** RV (50 amp), $25; RV (30 amp), $21; tent, $15. **Parking:** At site.

FACILITIES

Number of Multipurpose Sites: 45. **Hookups:** Electric (30, 50 amps), water, sewer, cable TV. **Each Site:** Picnic table, concrete patio. **Dump Station:** Yes. **Laundry:** Yes. **Pay Phone:** No. **Restrooms and Showers:** Yes. **Fuel:** No. **Propane:** No. **Internal Roads:** Paved. **RV Service:** 63 mi. east in McComb. **Market:** Camp store, 3 mi. north in Natchez. **Restaurant:** 3 mi. north in Natchez. **General Store:** Camp store, Wal-Mart 5 mi. west in Natchez. **Vending:** Beverages. **Swimming:** Yes. **Playground:** No. **Activities:** Swimming, visit historic sights. **Nearby Attractions:** Historic downtown Natchez, Grand Village of the Natchez Indians, Natchez Trace National Scenic Trail, Jefferson Military College. **Additional Information:** Natchez Visitor Reception Center, (800) 647-6724 or (601) 446-6345, www.natchez.ms.us.

RESTRICTIONS

Pets: On leash only. **Fires:** At campsite. **Alcoholic Beverages:** Allowed. **Vehicle Maximum Length:** 70 ft. **Other:** No tent camping

TO GET THERE

From junction of US 65/84/98 and US 61, go 3.75 mi. south on US 61. RV park entrance is on the left.

OCEAN SPRINGS — MAP, D-3
Camp Journey's End

7501 Hwy. 57, 39564. T: (228) 875-2100; www.campjourneys-end.com.

🚐 ★★★★   ⛺ ★★★

Beauty: ★★★★   Site Privacy: ★★★
Spaciousness: ★★★★   Quiet: ★★★★
Security: ★★★   Cleanliness: ★★★★
Insect Control: ★★★★   Facilities: ★★★

This is an attractive campground with an uncommonly welcoming staff. On property is "Liberty," a 350-year old live oak tree. Adjacent to the park is Fort Bayou River with its speckled trout. The park maintains a boat ramp and dock. Camp Journey's End is 7 miles from the beach and within 35 miles of the casinos, attractions, and restaurants in Biloxi. The campground is one large grid, featuring midsized sites and back-in parking. Popular sites 62–73 and 80–91 have paved parking. Other sites may have grass, gravel, or sand parking. Most sites are partially shady, while a few are totally open. Shady sites include 58–61, 74–79, and 99–108. Bathhouses are nicer than average. Camp Journeys End is popular with retirees during the winter and families during the summer and spring. Plan an autumn visit to avoid crowds. The park is right next to I-20 and has no gate; security is not fantastic.

BASICS

Operated By: Craig & Linda Orrison. **Open:** All year. **Site Assignment:** First come, first served; reservations accepted, credit-card deposit; no charge w/ 24-hour notice of cancellation; call for long-term stays. **Registration:** At office. **Fee:** $26.75–$29.96 for 2 people; additional children, $2; adults, $3. **Parking:** At site, in parking lot.

FACILITIES

Number of Multipurpose Sites: 110. **Hookups:** Electric (30, 50 amps), water, sewer, cable TV. **Each Site:** Picnic tables at most sites, grills, fire rings on request. **Dump Station:** Yes. **Laundry:** Yes. **Pay Phone:** Yes. **Restrooms and Showers:** Yes. **Fuel:** No. **Propane:** Yes. **Internal Roads:** Paved. **RV Service:** On call. **Market:** Camp store, 5 mi. south in Ocean Springs. **Restaurant:** Barbecue on site, 1 mi. south in Ocean Springs. **General Store:** Camp store, 5 mi. south in Ocean Springs. **Vending:** Yes. **Swimming:** Yes. **Playground:** Yes. **Other:** Boat launch, 18 mi. of waterway, pier, duck pond, fitness center, kayak rentals. **Activities:** Fishing, boating, horseshoes, basketball, seasonal organized activities, swimming, volleyball, badminton. **Nearby Attractions:** Ocean Springs art museums, 11 mi. to Biloxi casinos, Beauvoir Jefferson Davis home, 60 mi. to Mobile, 90 mi. to New Orleans, golf courses, art galleries. **Additional Information:** Mississippi Gulf Coast CVB, (228) 896-6699.

RESTRICTIONS

Pets: On leash only. Fenced pet area. **Fires:** Fire ring only. **Alcoholic Beverages:** Allowed. **Vehicle Maximum Length:** 40 ft. **Other:** Free cable TV 50 ft. from service area.

TO GET THERE

The campground is 11 mi. east of Biloxi and 20 mi. west of the Alabama state line. From I-10, take Exit 57. Drive north on MS 57 for 0.25 mi. to the campground.

OCEAN SPRINGS   MAP, D-3
Davis Bayou Campground

Gulf Islands National Seashore, 3500 Park Rd., 39564. T: (228) 875-3962; www.nps.gov.

🚐 ★★★★   ⛺ ★★★★

Beauty: ★★★★	Site Privacy: ★★★
Spaciousness: ★★★★	Quiet: ★★★★
Security: ★★★★	Cleanliness: ★★★
Insect Control: ★★	Facilities: ★★★

Gulf Islands National Seashore consists of 11 geographically distinct units stretching from West Ship Island, MS to Santa Rosa Island, FL. Davis Bayou Recreation Area nestles into the suburban mainland and has no beach. Visitors enjoy the bayou via the boat ramp and fishing pier. The beach is 4 miles away at Ocean Springs. The small, very pretty campground consists of two loops. The smaller loop (sites 11–19) contains the nicest sites. Sites 12 and 13 are especially gorgeous. These sites are afforded shade and privacy by ample woods, and they include views of the salt marsh. Most sites are wooded with little foliage between them. Site size varies widely, but all are adequate. Parking is paved and back-in–style. Coastal Mississippi can be excruciatingly hot in the summer. Try to plan a visit in spring or fall. Patrolled by rangers all night, security at this national park is good.

BASICS

Operated By: National Park Service. **Open:** All year. **Site Assignment:** First come, first served; Golden Age Passports, 50% discount. **Registration:** At office or self-registration. **Fee:** Electric, $16; water only, $14; cash, personal check, V, MC, D. **Parking:** At sites & parking areas. Parking is extremely limited.

FACILITIES

Number of Multipurpose Sites: 52. **Hookups:** Electric (30, 50 amps), water. **Each Site:** Picnic table, grill. **Dump Station:** Yes. **Laundry:** No. **Pay**

Phone: Yes. **Restrooms and Showers:** Yes. **Fuel:** No. **Propane:** No. **Internal Roads:** Paved. **RV Service:** No. **Market:** No. **Restaurant:** 0.5 mi. west. **General Store:** 1.5 mi. east. **Vending:** No. **Swimming:** No. **Playground:** Yes. **Other:** Boat launches, visitor center, fishing pier, picnic area. **Activities:** Fishing, boating, kayaking, walking trails, bicycle trails; no swimming due to alligators. **Nearby Attractions:** Beaches, museums, boat tours, 4 mi. to Biloxi casinos, 75 mi. to New Orleans. **Additional Information:** Mississippi Gulf Coast CVB, (228) 896-6699.

RESTRICTIONS

Pets: On leash only. **Fires:** Grill only. No ground fires. **Alcoholic Beverages:** Allowed (no glass containers). **Vehicle Maximum Length:** 45 ft. **Other:** No swimming due to alligators.

TO GET THERE

From the west, take I-10 to Ocean Springs and exit at Tucker Rd. Take Tucker Rd. south 5–7 mi. to US 90. Head east (left) on US 90 and proceed 5–7 mi. The park is on the right, and the campground is 2 mi. inside the Seashore area on the right. From the east, take I-10 to the Fontainebleau exit. Take MS 57 south to US 90 west, and the Seashore is on the left.

TOOMSUBA   MAP, C-3
Meridian East Toomsuba KOA

3953 KOA Campground Rd., 39364.
T: (601) 632-1684 or (800) 562-4202;
www.koa.com/where/ms/24120.

🚐 ★★★   ⛺ ★★★

Beauty: ★★★★	Site Privacy: ★★★
Spaciousness: ★★★	Quiet: ★★★★
Security: ★★★	Cleanliness: ★★★★
Insect Control: ★★★	Facilities: ★★★

Situated in a shady grove dominated by loblolly pine, this is an incredibly attractive KOA. Sites at this rural campground are midsized and offer gravel parking. Roughly 25 of the sites are pull-through parking. The prettiest RV campsites (sites 26–29) are the shady back-ins flanking the group tent area. All of the tent sites are nice looking, and some have tent pads. Children will especially like the pool, waterslide, and other recreation here. In Meridian, children will enjoy the historic Dentzel Carousel, which

has been in operation since 1909. Although there is no gate, this KOA is off the beaten path, making security fair. Avoid visiting Meridian during the hot, humid southern summer. Also avoid this campground on holiday weekends, when its facilities make it popular with families.

BASICS

Operated By: Christine & Lionel Waldman. **Open:** All year. **Site Assignment:** Sites assigned; reservations recommended in summer & holidays; credit-card deposit required for reservation; cancel by 4 p.m. the day before arrival for refund. **Registration:** At store, self-registration at night. **Fee:** RV, $24–$32; tent, $21–$26; cabins, $39–$55. **Parking:** At site, in parking lot.

FACILITIES

Number of Tent-only Sites: 16. **Number of Multipurpose Sites:** 43. **Hookups:** Electric (30, 50 amps), water, sewer. **Each Site:** Picnic table, fire ring, (tent sites have tent pads). **Dump Station:** Yes. **Laundry:** Yes. **Pay Phone:** Courtesy phones. **Restrooms and Showers:** Yes. **Fuel:** No. **Propane:** Yes. **Internal Roads:** Gravel. **RV Service:** 12 mi. southwest in Meridian. **Market:** Grocery on site, supermarket 12 mi. southwest in Meridian. **Restaurant:** Snack bar on site & 12 mi. southwest in Meridian. **General Store:** On site & 12 mi. southwest in Meridian. **Vending:** No. **Swimming:** Yes. **Playground:** Yes. **Other:** Pavilion, snack bar. **Activities:** 550-ft. ground waterslide, game room, horseshoes, tetherball, basketball. **Nearby Attractions:** Jimmie Rodgers Museum, Peavey Museum, antebellum homes, Highland Park, Dentzel Carousel, Dunn's Falls in Enterprise, Hamasa Shrine Temple Theater. **Additional Information:** Meridian Chamber of Commerce, (601) 693-1306.

RESTRICTIONS

Pets: Leash only (cleanup enforced). **Fires:** At tent sites only. **Alcoholic Beverages:** Allowed, sites only. **Vehicle Maximum Length:** 73 ft. (sites vary). **Other:** Visitors must register at the office.

TO GET THERE

From I-59 and 20, take Exit 165 (Toomsuba), go south 1.5 mi., then turn right on KOA Campground Rd.; go 0.5 mi. on right to KOA.

Missouri

Many visitors come to Kansas City for the casinos, amusement parks, or a dash of culture; but for RVers, **Kansas City** is the place to go for top-notch resorts. Although some travelers pine for a photo of the **Arch** in **St. Louis,** for others Missouri means **Branson.** Home to dozens of theaters that host big-name entertainers in extravagant shows, Branson has had a tradition of live music since the 1950s. Today, the town that was once a well-kept secret is now one of the entertainment capitals of the country. With more than 80 shows performed in over 40 theaters year-round, there is bound to be a show that will get a rise out of campers of all ages and tastes. If you want to relax before a big night out, **Lake Tanycom** and **Table Rock** are also close by for some of the best trout and bass fishing in the state. These are all legitimate destinations, but so much more of Missouri lies in the natural places—and you don't have to tunnel underground in the Cave State to find them.

The **Trail of Tears State Park** near **Cape Girardeau** is de rigueur for anyone wishing to understand the state's history. Bikers as well as history buffs will be interested in the **Katy Trail**—a 225-mile-long trail built along the corridor of the Missouri–Kansas–Texas railroad. From **St. Charles** (where the trail begins) to **Booneville,** the Katy Trail travels along the same route chosen by Lewis and Clark as their historic trek through America's unknown wild passed through Missouri. If you really do want to visit a cave, adventurous spelunkers have over 5,000 to choose from. For the less-experienced cave explorer, 22 of Missouri's caves have guided tours. **Meramec State Park** near **Sullivan** is a fine place to look for hidden adventure. While you're there, don't forget to check out **Meramec Cavern**—the former hideout of outlaw Jesse James!

In **Saco** (where it is illegal to wear weird hats that might frighten children or animals), you'll find a not-so-hidden treasure that covers much of the southeastern part of the state: the **Mark Twain National Forest.** Similarly evident is the **Ozark State Mountains** region, where scenic hills offer free roller-coaster rides. Missouri has 90 state lakes and more than 30 rivers—each dotted by towns both modern and nostalgic. The **Harry S. Truman Reservoir** is an enormous complex of lakes that will appeal to water sports enthusiasts, anglers, and campers. Also of note is the **Lake of the Ozarks**—which, covering over 54,000 acres, offers one of Missouri's most inspirational glimpses of fall. You don't have to go to the big cities in Missouri to enjoy this state; its green places have as much to offer as its metropolitan centers.

But if you are looking for sophisticated delights that are still a bit off the beaten path, **Columbia** (located between St. Louis and Kansas City) embodies the scenic and cultural diversity that travelers have come to expect from this charming state. Columbia's nine-block downtown offers a nice variety of fine dining establishments and wineries as well as plenty of restaurants of a more relaxed character. Kids are sure to be delighted by the **Downtown Twilight Festivals,** which are held in June and September and feature petting zoos, clowns, music, and the work of local artists. The **Annual Heritage Festival** features the handiwork of artisans from the late 19th- and early 20th centuries, not to mention plenty of food, storytelling, and music. For those more interested in modern times, the **Columbia Festival of the Arts** features over 40 live performances offering dance, theater, music, and the visual arts. Check with the **Columbia Convention and Visitors Bureau** for more information; call (800) 652-0987.

CAMERON   MAP, A-1
Down Under Camp Resort

8074 NE County Hwy. H, 64493.
T: (816) 632-3695; www.campdownunder.com.

🚐 ★★★★   ⛺ ★★★★★

Beauty: ★★★★	Site Privacy: ★★★
Spaciousness: ★★★	Quiet: ★★★★★
Security: ★★★★★	Cleanliness: ★★★★
Insect Control: ★★★★	Facilities: ★★★★

Sites in this huge campground are scattered, undeveloped spaces with a grass-and-gravel mix and a fair number of trees. Sites A1–A5, north of Kanga Lake, are full-hookup back-ins. Site 27 is a large (90 feet) pull-through, while 28–28 are much smaller (30–45 feet). These sites are mostly open, without the cover of shade trees. Sites 60–69 are 70-foot pull-throughs with little shade. A small gazebo lies next to site 65. Sites 70–74, 81, and 82 are 30-foot back-ins that lie right next to the pool. These sites see a large amount of foot traffic. The best sites in the campground are 87–100 and 120, which are located right on the lake. They are grassy and without much shade (except for 96 and 97). These sites are 45-foot back-ins, although a larger rig could overhang slightly, due to the sites' open end. Sites 104–110 are open grassy sites that face lush vegetation. They are very nice, but the grassy strip they lie on suffers from some degree of slope, and campers will have to take time to level their rig. The nicest tent sites are T3–T5, which lie right on the lake (but also on the entrance road). The grass here is very suitable for tenting. The showers are clean and spacious, if a little primitive. The restrooms are also clean, and, on the whole, the facilities are quite comfortable. A fun campground that offers activities for the whole family in a pleasant environment.

BASICS

Operated By: Bonnie Beck. **Open:** All year; limited services Apr.–Nov. **Site Assignment:** Reservations recommended (credit card or check required); refunds (minus $10) w/ 7-day notice; notice of less than 7 days, lose 1-night deposit. **Registration:** At office; late arrivals use drop box. **Fee:** RV (full), $30; water/electric, $28; electric, $25; tent, $22; check, V, MC. **Parking:** At site.

FACILITIES

Number of RV-only Sites: 120. **Number of Tent-only Sites:** 26. **Hookups:** Electric (20, 30, 50 amps), water, sewer. **Each Site:** Picnic table, grill. **Dump Station:** Yes. **Laundry:** Yes. **Pay Phone:** No. **Restrooms and Showers:** Yes. **Fuel:** No. **Propane:** Yes. **Internal Roads:** Gravel. **RV Service:** No. **Market:** 8 mi. west. **Restaurant:** 8 mi. west. **General Store:** Yes. **Vending:** Yes. **Swimming:** Pool. **Playground:** Yes. **Other:** RV parts, modem, lake, mini-golf, pavilion, snack bar, game room, cabin on lake. **Activities:** Fishing, paddleboating, swimming, shuffleboard. **Nearby Attractions:** Worlds of Fun. **Additional Information:** Cameron Chamber of Commerce, (816) 632-2005.

RESTRICTIONS

Pets: On leash, cleaned up after. **Fires:** Grill only. **Alcoholic Beverages:** At sites. **Vehicle Maximum Length:** No limit. **Other:** No fireworks, children under age 14 years in pool must be supervised by adult w/in pool fence.

TO GET THERE

From I-35 (Exit 48), turn east onto Hwy. 69 and go 2.5 mi. Turn right onto H and go 1.1 mi. Turn right at the sign into the entrance.

CAPE GIRARDEAU   MAP, C-4
Trail of Tears State Park (Mississippi River and Lake Boutin Campgrounds)

429 Moccasin Springs, 63755. T: (573) 334-1711 or (877) 422-6766; www.mostateparks.com.

🚐 ★★★★   ⛺ ★★★★★

Beauty: ★★★★	Site Privacy: ★★★★
Spaciousness: ★★★★	Quiet: ★★★★★
Security: ★★★★★	Cleanliness: ★★★
Insect Control: ★★★★	Facilities: ★★★

This state park contains the only campground in Missouri that lies on the Mississippi River (named, appropriately, Mississippi River Campground), as well as one primitive campground (Boutin Campground). The Mississippi River Campground has electric sites close to the river bank. Sites 4–10 back to the river. Site 13 is a handicapped site that lies in a corner against a forested backdrop. Sites 14–19 back to woods as well, and are all well shaded. There is only one unisex toilet in this campground and the bathhouse is within 0.25 mi. Boutin Campground has forested primitive sites. Site 20 is by far the longest pull-through (140 feet). Site 30 is located across from the bathhouse and the Camp Hosts, which is normally a benefit, but the dump station is also right next to it. Sites 47, 51, 52, and 54 are more isolated, being located at the end of a roundabout in the internal road. Boutin is a wonderful campground with a historical element that families will appreciate, and with plenty of recreational facilities appreciated by any camper.

BASICS

Operated By: Missouri Dept. of Natural Resources. **Open:** All year. **Site Assignment:** Reservations & walk-ins accepted. **Registration:** At office; fees also collected by Camp Hosts. **Fee:** RV (full), $17; water/electric, $15; tent, $8; check, V, MC, D. Off-season: RV, $13; water/electric, $12; tent, $7. **Parking:** At site.

FACILITIES

Number of RV-only Sites: 18. **Number of Tent-only Sites:** 35. **Hookups:** Electric (30 amps), water, sewer. **Each Site:** Picnic table, fire pit. **Dump Station:** Yes. **Laundry:** Yes. **Pay Phone:** Yes. **Restrooms and Showers:** Yes. **Fuel:** No. **Propane:** No. **Internal Roads:** Paved. **RV Service:** No. **Market:** 15 mi. south. **Restaurant:** 15 mi. south. **General Store:** No. **Vending:** No. **Swimming:** Lake. **Playground:** Yes. **Other:** Boat ramp, exhibits. **Activities:** Fishing, boating, swimming, hiking, tours. **Nearby Attractions:** Trail of Tears, Bollinger Mill State Historic Site, Cape Rock. **Additional Information:** Cape Girardeau CVB, (800) 777-0068, (573) 335-1631.

RESTRICTIONS

Pets: On leash, cleaned up after. **Fires:** Grill only. **Alcoholic Beverages:** At sites. **Vehicle Maximum Length:** No limit. **Other:** Gates locked at 10 p.m.

TO GET THERE

From the junction of Broadway and Hwy. 177 in town, turn north onto Hwy. 177 and go 11.8 mi. (Be sure to turn right at the 11.7 mi. mark.) Take first right into park.

CARTHAGE   MAP, C-1, C-2
Ballard's Campground

13965 Ballard Loop, 64836. T: (417) 359-0359.

🚐 ★★★   ⛺ ★★★

Beauty: ★★★★	Site Privacy: ★★★★
Spaciousness: ★★★★	Quiet: ★★★
Security: ★★★★★	Cleanliness: ★★★★
Insect Control: ★★★★	Facilities: ★★★

While the highway passes on one side of this campground, the three other sides are surrounded by forest, giving it a natural, almost wilderness, feel. Ballard's is arranged in three rows of paired sites that are slightly tiered but level. Sites 1–6, 13–18, and 21–26 are 85-foot pull-throughs, while 7–12 and 19–20 are 75-foot pull-throughs. Most sites are very well shaded, but 10 and 25 are exceptions. Outside sites 12, 22, 24, and 26 seem a little short on space. They require parking at the edge of the internal road and sharing the picnic space on the far side of the neighboring site. Site 7 is close to the fishing pond, and site 12 is at the edge of the property, which makes it a little more private. The nicest site is probably 21—everything just seems to coalesce nicely here: it is well shaded, grassy, far from the entrance, and facing mostly forest. The tent area is in a large open space next to the pond, with trees around the perimeter. The grass is very nice, but there is little shade or protection from the elements. The restrooms are spacious and mostly clean, with modern facilities. A nice campground that feels farther away from it all than its convenient location belies.

BASICS

Operated By: William & Wanda Goff. **Open:** All year. **Site Assignment:** First come, first served; no reservations. **Registration:** At office; late arrivals pay in morning. **Fee:** Full hookup, $17; water/electric, $15; electric, $13; check, credit cards. **Parking:** At site.

FACILITIES

Number of RV-only Sites: 30. **Number of Tent-only Sites:** Undesignated sites. **Hookups:** Electric (30, 50 amps), water, sewer, Wi-Fi. **Each Site:** Picnic table, fire pit. **Dump Station:** Yes. **Laundry:** Yes. **Pay Phone:** No. **Restrooms and Showers:** Yes. **Fuel:** No. **Propane:** Yes. **Internal Roads:** Gravel. **RV Service:** No. **Market:** 5 mi. north. **Restaurant:**

2 mi. south. **General Store:** Yes. **Vending:** Yes. **Swimming:** No. **Playground:** No. **Other:** Fishing pond w/ pavilion. **Activities:** Fishing (catch & release). **Nearby Attractions:** Precious Moments Chapel. **Additional Information:** Carthage CVB, (417) 358-2373.

RESTRICTIONS

Pets: On leash only, cleaned up after. **Fires:** Grill only. **Alcoholic Beverages:** At sites. **Vehicle Maximum Length:** No limit.

TO GET THERE

From I-44, take Exit 18A. On the south side of the highway overpass, go 0.3 mi. on 59 south.

CHILLICOTHE   MAP, A-2
McCullough Park Campground

13248 Liv 216, 64601. T: (660) 646-2795.

🚐 ★★★★   ⛺ ★★★★

Beauty: ★★★★★	Site Privacy: ★★★★
Spaciousness: ★★★★★	Quiet: ★★★★★
Security: ★★★★★	Cleanliness: ★★★★
Insect Control: ★★★★★	Facilities: ★★★

Most sites in this campground are forested, making for cooler summer days. The main campground is in the wooded area to the north of the office. This is a slice of forest with a farm flavor. (None of the sites are designated by anything other than an open area with an electrical outlet for several sites, and the owners often provide extension cords for additional electric sites, so a description of individual sites is neither possible nor helpful in this case.) The undeveloped sites to the east of the office are tenter or pop-up heaven, but not convenient for large rigs or tows. Larger RVs should head toward the "big rig section" on the hill to the northwest of the office. It's an open field with trees around the perimeter and huge sites with room for wide turns. Again, the sites are not numbered, but are indicated by the presence of the hookups. Tenting is unlimited in lush, beautiful grass and a thick forest canopy overhead. The restroom is smallish but comfortable and clean. With the exception of the bluegrass festival held here every year, this is a quiet campground secluded in the woods. It is absolutely a haven for tenters, and the section for large RVs ensures that all campers can enjoy their stay here.

BASICS

Operated By: Pat McCullough. **Open:** All year; limited service Nov.–Mar. **Site Assignment:** Upon registration; verbal reservations OK. **Registration:** At office; late arrivals select available site & pay in the morning. **Fee:** RV (full), $18; water/electric, $15; tent, $12; check, no credit cards. **Parking:** At site.

FACILITIES

Number of Multipurpose Sites: 100. **Hookups:** Electric (30 amps), water, sewer. **Each Site:** Ask owners for table. **Dump Station:** Yes. **Laundry:** No. **Pay Phone:** No. **Restrooms and Showers:** Yes. **Fuel:** No. **Propane:** No. **Internal Roads:** Gravel. **RV Service:** No. **Market:** 5 mi. south. **Restaurant:** 5 mi. south. **General Store:** No. **Vending:** No. **Swimming:** No. **Playground:** No.

Other: Firewood. **Activities:** Special events (including bluegrass festival), old-time harvest. **Nearby Attractions:** Pershing State Park, Poosey Conservation Area, Bunch Hollow Conservation Area. **Additional Information:** Chillicothe Area Chamber of Commerce, (660) 646-4050.

RESTRICTIONS

Pets: On leash only, cleaned up after. **Fires:** Grill only. **Alcoholic Beverages:** At sites, restricted during events. **Vehicle Maximum Length:** 40 ft.

TO GET THERE

From the junction of Hwy. 36 and Hwy. 65, turn north onto Hwy. 65 and go 7.4 mi. Turn right onto the gravel road and go 0.3 mi. Turn left at the sign into the entrance.

CLINTON   MAP, B-2
Harry S. Truman Dam and Reservoir

Sparrowfoot Park, 150 SE 450 Rd., 64735. T: (877) 444-6777, (660) 438-7317, or (660) 438-2216 (visitor center); www.recreation.gov.

🚐 ★★★★   ⛺ ★★★★

Beauty: ★★★★	Site Privacy: ★★★★
Spaciousness: ★★★	Quiet: ★★★★
Security: ★★★★	Cleanliness: ★★★★
Insect Control: ★★★★	Facilities: ★★★

A lakeside campground, this park has sites laid out in two large loops. Loop A itself has two loops in a figure 8. Most sites in this loop are somewhat shaded, but not forested. Sites on the inside of the loop back to dense vegetation, while sites on the outside back to more open vegetation. Sites A13 and A14 are entirely unshaded. Prime sites closest to the lake include A15–A21, of which A17–A19 have the best views. Site A22, a 90-foot pull-through, is just across from A20 and A21 but does not include the prime-site price tag. Site 33 is just as close to the toilets as 32, but likewise does not cost as much as the more expensive site. Sites 28–48 back to other sites and are thus less private. Sites along the northeast edge and 16–21 do not back to any other sites. Site A50 is a 105-foot pull-through, and sites A59–62 are closest to the restrooms in the second loop of Loop A. In Loop B, site B1 is a prime site due to its proximity to the restrooms, but is much too close to the road for comfort. Even-numbers 2–16 back to dense vegetation, which makes them very attractive. Sites B15, 18, and 20 are just as close to the water access area as B16, 17, and 19, but are not priced like prime sites. Sites B19 and 20 may, in fact, suffer from an inordinate amount of passing foot traffic. The restrooms and showers are basic but functional. During off-season, only pit toilets are available—no showers, flush toilets, or laundry. Overall, an attractive campground that offers plenty of recreation facilities and pleasant spots for campers.

BASICS

Operated By: U.S. Army Corps of Engineers. **Open:** All year; limited services Oct. 16–Apr. 14. **Site Assignment:** Reservations & walk-ins accepted; refund (minus $10) w/ 3-day notice; notice

of less than 3 days subject to $10 & 1-night charge. **Registration:** At office; late arrivals select available site from sign-in sheet in booth & pay in the morning. **Fee:** Premium RV, $18; electric, $16; tent, $12; V, MC, AE, D, DC. **Parking:** At site.

FACILITIES

Number of RV-only Sites: 93. **Number of Tent-only Sites:** 19. **Hookups:** Electric (20, 30 amps). **Each Site:** Picnic table, fire pit, lantern pole. **Dump Station:** Yes. **Laundry:** Yes. **Pay Phone:** No. **Restrooms and Showers:** Yes. **Fuel:** No. **Propane:** No. **Internal Roads:** Paved. **RV Service:** No. **Market:** 5 mi. to Clinton. **Restaurant:** 5 mi. to Clinton. **General Store:** No. **Vending:** No. **Swimming:** Lake. **Playground:** Yes. **Other:** Picnic area, beach. **Activities:** Fishing, boating, swimming, ATV riding. **Nearby Attractions:** Henry County Museum & Cultural Arts Center. **Additional Information:** Clinton Chamber of Commerce, (660) 885-8168.

RESTRICTIONS

Pets: On leash only, cleaned up after. **Fires:** Grill only. **Alcoholic Beverages:** At sites. **Vehicle Maximum Length:** No limit.

TO GET THERE

From the junction of Hwy. 7 and Hwy. 13 by hospital, turn south onto Hwy. 13 and go 7 mi. Turn left onto southeast 450 and go 1.2 mi. Turn right at the sign into the entrance.

COLUMBIA   MAP, B-2
Cottonwoods RV Park

5170 N. Oakland Gravel Rd., 65202. T: (573) 474-2747.

🚐 ★★★★★   ⛺ ★★★★

Beauty: ★★★★	Site Privacy: ★★★★
Spaciousness: ★★★★	Quiet: ★★★★
Security: ★★★★★	Cleanliness: ★★★★★
Insect Control: ★★★★	Facilities: ★★★★★

Like most RV parks in the area, Cottonwoods does not offer much shade. This is where the similarity with most other campgrounds ends, however, as this is a fantastic, upscale resort that will appeal to all RV campers. It features extremely well-tended landscaping, with grass and trees on three sides and buildings to the east. Strips of grassy sites run east to west, with monthlies (1–23) located at the southern end. All sites are 27 feet wide, and overnight spaces are 60–65 feet, 64 site pull-throughs. (Sites 70–97 are doubles that meet end to end and measure 110 feet—slightly less than the rest of the sites.) Although it is difficult to pick a "best" site, campers may prefer the middle area (roughly 32–43, 52–63, 74–80, 87–93), as it is farthest from the entry road, does not face any buildings, has very nice trees and grass, and is close to the restrooms. Tent sites are at the entrance of the park. They have beautiful grass but—again—no shade, and feel somewhat like an afterthought in an RV park. Restrooms and showers are exceptionally clean and comfortable. This RV park caters to the upscale urban camper. It is extremely comfortable by any standards, and campers of any kind will enjoy a stay here.

BASICS

Operated By: Buster & Loretta Caudle. **Open:** All year. **Site Assignment:** Upon registration; credit card required for reservation, 24-hour cancellation policy. **Registration:** At office; late arrivals use drop box. **Fee:** RV (50 amp), $28.50; (30 amp), $26; water/electric, $25; tent, $14; check, V, MC, D. **Parking:** At site.

FACILITIES

Number of RV-only Sites: 97. **Number of Tent-only Sites:** 20. **Hookups:** Electric (20, 30, 50 amps), water, sewer. **Each Site:** Picnic table. **Dump Station:** Yes. **Laundry:** Yes. **Pay Phone:** Yes. **Restrooms and Showers:** Yes. **Fuel:** No. **Propane:** Yes. **Internal Roads:** Gravel. **RV Service:** No. **Market:** 2 mi. south. **Restaurant:** 3 mi. south. **General Store:** Yes. **Vending:** Yes. **Swimming:** Pool. **Playground:** Yes. **Other:** Meeting room, game room, antique mall, gift shop, modem, pool table, exercise equipment, pet walk, small & large pavilions. **Activities:** Biking, hiking, basketball, horseshoes, swimming. **Nearby Attractions:** Katy Trail State Park, Rockbridge State Park. **Additional Information:** Columbia Chamber of Commerce, (573) 875-1231.

RESTRICTIONS

Pets: On leash only, cleaned up after. **Fires:** Grill only. **Alcoholic Beverages:** At sites. **Vehicle Maximum Length:** No limit. **Other:** No refunds.

TO GET THERE

From I-70 (Exit 128A), turn north to Hwy. 63. Go 3 mi., then turn right onto Oakland Gravel Rd. Turn right off the ramp, then left onto Starke Ln. Go 0.4 mi., then turn right at the sign into the entrance.

DANVILLE   MAP, B-3
Kan-Do Kampground RV Park

99 Hwy. TT, 63361. T: (573) 564-7993.

🚐 ★★★★★   ⛺ ★★★★★

Beauty: ★★★★	Site Privacy: ★★★★
Spaciousness: ★★★★	Quiet: ★★★★
Security: ★★★★	Cleanliness: ★★★★★
Insect Control: ★★★★	Facilities: ★★★★

This campground is laid out in a loop, with all sites on the outside and a large grassy field on the inside. All sites are pull-throughs, some of them enormous (11 is 140 feet, 2–9 and 15–26 are 120 feet), and all well shaded. In fact, you really can't go wrong with any site in the park. Sites with full hookups are located along the south side of the campground. Sites 1 and 27–29 are seasonal. Tent sites are equally well shaded and have a mix of grass, gravel, and dirt. The restroom is small but immaculate. Kan-Do is a campground that all campers will enjoy, and spacious enough to meet the demands of any sized rig.

BASICS

Operated By: Drew & Kathy Elias. **Open:** All year. **Site Assignment:** Upon registration; credit card required for reservation (V, MC); 48-hour cancellation policy. **Registration:** At office; late arrivals use

---

drop box. **Fee:** RV (50 amp), $27; (30 amp), $22; tent, $17–$18. **Parking:** At site.

FACILITIES

Number of RV-only Sites: 50. **Number of Tent-only Sites:** 12. **Hookups:** Electric (30, 50 amps), water, sewer, Wi-Fi. **Each Site:** Picnic table, fire pit. **Dump Station:** No (sewer at all sites). **Laundry:** Yes. **Pay Phone:** No. **Restrooms and Showers:** Yes. **Fuel:** No. **Propane:** Yes. **Internal Roads:** Gravel. **RV Service:** No. **Market:** 7 mi. northeast. **Restaurant:** 5 mi. east. **General Store:** Yes. **Vending:** No. **Swimming:** Pool. **Playground:** Yes. **Other:** Fishing pond, recreation fields, pavilion. **Activities:** Volleyball, swimming, fishing. **Nearby Attractions:** Graham Cave State Park. **Additional Information:** Columbia Chamber of Commerce, (573) 874-1132.

RESTRICTIONS

Pets: On leash, cleaned up after. **Fires:** Grill only. **Alcoholic Beverages:** At sites. **Vehicle Maximum Length:** No limit.

TO GET THERE

From I-70 (Exit 170), turn north onto Hwy. 161 and then take the first left onto West Service Rd. at the dead-end sign. Go 1 mi., then turn right at the sign into the entrance.

DONIPHAN   MAP, C-3
Rocky River Resort

304 West Jefferson, 63935. T: (800) 748-7672 or (573) 996-7171; www.rockyriverresort.com.

🚐 ★★★★   ⛺ ★★★★

Beauty: ★★★★	Site Privacy: ★★★★
Spaciousness: ★★★★	Quiet: ★★★
Security: ★★★★★	Cleanliness: ★★★
Insect Control: ★★★★	Facilities: ★★★

Hidden in the forest, Doniphan has wooded, grassy back-ins and pull-throughs, as well as a tenting area. This campground abuts the Current River, and the focus is squarely on float trips. Sites 1–18 are 60 by 55-foot back-ins along the entrance road. Sites 6–9 are located across from a play area, and 13–15 are across from a pavilion, which may increase traffic past these sites. Sites 19–34 are situated around the "Teardrop" area. These are 50-foot back-ins, best for tenters or smaller RVs (such as pop-ups), as the dirt road can be difficult to navigate. Closest to the river access area are sites 23–27. The rest of the sites (35–51) are forested, comfortable, and spacious. Site 35, across from the Snack Shack, has one open side that is not forested. The tenting area is secluded and close to the river on the western edge of the campground. The restrooms are reasonably modern and clean, aside from paint flaking off the floors. There are several porta-potties throughout the campground in addition to the restrooms. A fun campground geared toward floating on the river; a great destination for families.

BASICS

Operated By: Rocky River Inc. **Open:** All year. **Site Assignment:** Upon registration; credit card or check deposit for reservation (credit, but no refunds,

---

given). **Registration:** At office; late arrivals select available site & pay in the morning. **Fee:** RV, $17.50–$18.50; tent, $10; check, V, MC, AE, D. **Parking:** At site.

FACILITIES

Number of RV-only Sites: 40. **Number of Tent-only Sites:** 8. **Hookups:** Electric (30, 50 amps), water, sewer, cable TV. **Each Site:** Picnic table, fire pit. **Dump Station:** Yes. **Laundry:** No. **Pay Phone:** Yes. **Restrooms and Showers:** Yes. **Fuel:** No. **Propane:** No. **Internal Roads:** Gravel. **RV Service:** No. **Market:** 0.25 mi. east. **Restaurant:** 0.25 mi. east. **General Store:** Yes. **Vending:** Yes. **Swimming:** No. **Playground:** Yes. **Other:** Tube rentals. **Activities:** Tubing. **Nearby Attractions:** Current River. **Additional Information:** Doniphan Chamber of Commerce: (573) 996-2212.

RESTRICTIONS

Pets: On leash, cleaned up after, no pit bulls or Rottweilers. **Fires:** Grill only. **Alcoholic Beverages:** At sites, no bottles. **Vehicle Maximum Length:** No limit. **Other:** 2 vehicles per site, visitors must check in.

TO GET THERE

From the junction of Hwy. 21 and Hwys. 142 and 160, go 0.85 mi. west on 21/142/160. Take last left turn on east side of bridge and go 0.35 mi. on Jefferson (which is not signed). Turn right at the sign into the entrance.

EAGLEVILLE   MAP, A-2
I-35 RV Park

Exit 106, P.O. Box 56, 64442. T: (660) 867-3377.

🚐 ★★★   ⛺ ★★★

Beauty: ★★★	Site Privacy: ★★★
Spaciousness: ★★	Quiet: ★★★
Security: ★★★★	Cleanliness: ★★★
Insect Control: ★★★★	Facilities: ★★

Sites in this campground are laid out in one big loop, with pull-throughs in a strip on the west side, and back-ins in a strip on the east side. Pull-through sites range 75–85 feet in length and average 22 feet in width. Back-ins are 45 feet long before the site begins to slope. Site 1 is next to the office, and may receive registration traffic passing by. Sites 7 and 8 are closest to the restrooms, while 9 and 10 are closest to the entrance. The nicest site is 18, closest to a tree with a seat below it. The tenting area is to the south, near the restrooms. There is good grass cover for these sites, and a communal fire pit. The restrooms are primitive but decent. The shower is a cement room with plastic sheeting that renders it waterproof. Some campers may find this setup a little bizarre and uncomfortable. With residences to the west and north and a semiindustrial area to the east, this campground has a slightly urban feel, but the pretty farmland to the south makes up somewhat for the lacking beauty. Overall, an acceptable stay but not an important destination.

BASICS

Operated By: Michael & Betty Sanchez. **Open:** All year. **Site Assignment:** First come, first served;

---

verbal reservations OK. **Registration:** At office; late arrivals use drop box. **Fee:** RV (pull-through), $17.50; (back-in), $15; tent, $12; check. **Parking:** At site.

FACILITIES

Number of RV-only Sites: 20. **Number of Tent-only Sites:** Undesignated sites. **Hookups:** Electric (20, 30, 50 amps), water, sewer. **Dump Station:** Yes. **Laundry:** No. **Pay Phone:** Courtesy. **Restrooms and Showers:** Yes. **Fuel:** No. **Propane:** Yes. **Internal Roads:** Gravel. **RV Service:** No. **Market:** Next door. **Restaurant:** 3 blocks east. **General Store:** RV supplies. **Vending:** No. **Swimming:** No. **Playground:** Yes. **Other:** Snack shop, RV supplies, close to town square, covered picnic pavilion. **Activities:** Horseshoes. **Nearby Attractions:** Grand Trace Conservation Area. **Additional Information:** Cameron Chamber of Commerce, (816) 632-2005.

RESTRICTIONS

Pets: On leash, cleaned up after. **Fires:** In communal fire ring. **Alcoholic Beverages:** At sites. **Vehicle Maximum Length:** No limit. **Other:** Pay before occupying site.

TO GET THERE

From I-35 (Exit 106), turn west and go 0.2 mi. Turn left at the sign into the entrance.

EMINENCE   MAP, C-3
Jacks Fork Campground

P.O. Box 188, 65466. T: (800) JACKSFORK or (573) 858-3221; www.jacksforkcanoe.com.

🚐 ★★★★   ⛺ ★★★★★

Beauty: ★★★★		Site Privacy: ★★★★
Spaciousness: ★★★★★		Quiet: ★★★
Security: ★★★★		Cleanliness: ★★★
Insect Control: ★★★		Facilities: ★★★★

This natural campground lies along a river and is geared toward floating and canoe trips. Sites 1–21 are in a forested strip along the entrance road. These grassy sites have water and electricity, and back to lush vegetation. Along the same entrance road, sites 22–29 are much more open and not quite as nice as the first 21 sites. Grassy sites with no hookups, sites 37–40, 46, and 47 lie along the river. They contain lots of vegetation and a fair number of trees, which makes them quite comfortable. One row back from the river, sites 41–45 are spacious and with lots of shade. Similar to these are sites 50–55 in another row farther back. Pull-through sites with river access include 41–45. Sites 102–129 are in a loop at the north end of the campground. Of these, sites 105–108 are right on the river, 114–115 are in a shaded corner, while 129 contains a little stand of young trees that give some amount of shade. Right at the entrance to the loop are sites 102, 127, and 128. They are right under a number of shade trees, but all other sites in this loop are very open. The restrooms are in an aging wooden building, the showers are coin-operated. Jacks Fork makes for a decent stay for RVers who can snag a site with hookups (or don't mind going without electricity and using their facilities), and is a great place for tenters to camp.

BASICS

Operated By: Gene & Eleanor Maggard. **Open:** Apr. 15–Oct. 15. **Site Assignment:** Depends on site availability; credit card required for reservations; full refund w/ 8-day notice, credit certificates only under 8 days; reservation (by phone) w/ $7 fee (per person, per night). (V, MC, D, AE). **Registration:** At office; late arrivals pick available site & settle in the morning. **Fee:** Full hookup, $10; electric, $7; water, $1; per person, $6–$8. **Parking:** At site.

FACILITIES

Number of RV-only Sites: 75. **Number of Tent-only Sites:** 80. **Hookups:** Electric (20, 30, 50 amps), water, sewer. **Each Site:** Picnic table, grill, trees. **Dump Station:** Yes. **Laundry:** No. **Pay Phone:** Yes. **Restrooms and Showers:** Yes. **Fuel:** No. **Propane:** No. **Internal Roads:** Gravel. **RV Service:** No. **Market:** 0.5 mi. to Eminence. **Restaurant:** 0.5 mi. to Eminence. **General Store:** Yes. **Vending:** Yes. **Swimming:** River. **Playground:** Yes. **Other:** Cabins, pavilion. **Activities:** Swimming, canoeing, volleyball, fishing. **Nearby Attractions:** Angenvine Conservation Area, Peck Ranch Conservation Area, Ozarck National Scenic Riverways, Mark Twain National Forest. **Additional Information:** Eminence Chamber of Commerce, (573) 226-3318.

RESTRICTIONS

Pets: On leash, cleaned up after. **Fires:** Grill only. **Alcoholic Beverages:** At sites. **Vehicle Maximum Length:** No limit. **Other:** Campground divided into noisy & quiet sections. No ATVs, fireworks, dirt bikes.

TO GET THERE

From the junction of Hwy. 19 and Hwy. 106, go 0.4 mi. east on Hwy. 106. Turn left at the sign into the campground.

GRAVOIS MILLS   MAP, B-2
Gravois Creek Campground

P.O. Box 167, 65037. T: (800) 573-CAMP or (573) 372-3211; www.gravoiscreek.com.

🚐 ★★★★   ⛺ ★★★★★

Beauty: ★★★★★		Site Privacy: ★★★
Spaciousness: ★★★		Quiet: ★★★★
Security: ★★★★★		Cleanliness: ★★★★
Insect Control: ★★★★		Facilities: ★★★★

Gravois Creek is a rural campground with a wilderness feel and very attractive landscaping, including grape vines on a trellis in front of the restrooms, flowering trees, and woods on all four sides. The creek lies to the northeast and is accessible from the campground. Most sites are shaded, making this an exceptional camping area. Sites 1–4 are 75-foot pull-throughs, 7–13 are larger (85 feet) and well shaded, and 15–22 are even bigger (90 feet) and hidden amidst trees. Down by the creek are sites suitable for tents or pop-ups. Sites farthest to the east are electric sites wrapped by bushes and hidden under shade trees. For tenters and those RVs that can fit, this is an excellent place to camp. The area to the north of the office—a beautiful grassy field with loads of shade—is strictly for tents (no cars allowed). The showers are

individual units, and the restrooms are small but very clean. This campground is a shade-lovers' paradise (a rare thing in the area).

BASICS

Operated By: The Beckers. **Open:** Mar.–Nov. **Site Assignment:** Depends on site availability; credit card required for reservation, 48-hour cancellation policy. **Registration:** At office; late arrivals use drop box. **Fee:** RV (full), $23.50; tent, $17; check, V, MC, D. **Parking:** At site.

FACILITIES

Number of RV-only Sites: 35. **Number of Tent-only Sites:** Undesignated sites. **Hookups:** Electric (30, 50 amps), water, sewer. **Each Site:** Picnic table, grill or fire pit. **Dump Station:** Yes. **Laundry:** Yes. **Pay Phone:** No. **Restrooms and Showers:** Yes. **Fuel:** No. **Propane:** No. **Internal Roads:** Gravel. **RV Service:** No. **Market:** 2 mi. south. **Restaurant:** 1 mi. south. **General Store:** Yes. **Vending:** Yes. **Swimming:** Stream. **Playground:** Yes. **Other:** Cabins, firewood, pet area, creek. **Activities:** Fishing, swimming. **Nearby Attractions:** Free public boat ramp. **Additional Information:** Lake of The Ozarks West Chamber of Commerce, (573) 374-5500.

RESTRICTIONS

Pets: On leash, cleaned up after, not in cabins. **Fires:** Grill only. **Alcoholic Beverages:** At sites. **Vehicle Maximum Length:** No limit. **Other:** No fireworks.

TO GET THERE

From the north city limits, go 1.7 mi. north on Hwy. 5. Turn right at the sign into the entrance.

HANNIBAL   MAP, A-3
Injun Joe Campground

14113 Clemens Dr., 63459. T: (573) 985-3581 or (573) 985-9910; www.hanmo.com/clemslanding.

🚐 ★★★★   ⛺ ★★★★

Beauty: ★★★★		Site Privacy: ★★★
Spaciousness: ★★★		Quiet: ★★★
Security: ★★★★★		Cleanliness: ★★★
Insect Control: ★★★★		Facilities: ★★★★

A sure hit with families, Injun Joe offers swimming, go-carts, plays, and many more recreation facilities. Most sites are back-ins, with an average size of 55 feet; there are ten pull-throughs. Sites 8–35 are laid out in a loop and back to woods as do sites 101–107. Sites 130–133 are located along the entrance road and may receive more passing traffic. Site 107 is in the farthest corner, with pleasant views to two sides. Sites 139–144 back to sites 1–7 so closely that detract from the privacy of both sets of sites. The tenting area is a large field with quite a number of trees. There is a picnic shelter and decent grass covering. Most natural and woodsy is the area to the southwest. The restroom is extremely small for such a large campground, with one toilet for every 45 RV campers. It is clean and modern, but you may have to wait in line for a while during the morning rush hour. It is hard not to have a great time in Injun Joe, and families would do well to spend a few days enjoying the recreation facilities on offer.

BASICS

Operated By: Clarence & Ann Steinman. **Open:** All year. **Site Assignment:** Upon registration; credit card or check required for reservation, 2-week cancellation policy; refund minus $12. **Registration:** At office. **Fee:** RV (full), $23; water/electric, $22.50; tent, $20; check, no credit cards on registration. **Parking:** At site.

FACILITIES

Number of RV-only Sites: 118. **Number of Tent-only Sites:** Undesignated sites. **Hookups:** Electric (20, 30, 50 amps), water, sewer. **Each Site:** Picnic table on concrete slab, grill. **Dump Station:** Yes. **Laundry:** Yes. **Pay Phone:** Yes. **Restrooms and Showers:** Yes. **Fuel:** No. **Propane:** Yes. **Internal Roads:** Gravel. **RV Service:** No. **Market:** 2 mi. south. **Restaurant:** On site. **General Store:** Yes. **Vending:** No. **Swimming:** Pool. **Playground:** Yes. **Other:** Dog walk, lakes, go-carts, waterslide, mini-golf, batting cage, amphitheater, game room. **Activities:** Fishing, swimming, plays, go-carting. **Nearby Attractions:** Mark Twain Cave, Sawyer's Creek Fun Park, Riverview Park, Mark Twain Outdoor Theater. **Additional Information:** Hannibal CVB, (573) 221-2477.

RESTRICTIONS

Pets: On leash, cleaned up after. **Fires:** Grill only. **Alcoholic Beverages:** At sites. **Vehicle Maximum Length:** 40 ft. **Other:** No ATVs.

TO GET THERE

From the junction of Hwy. 36 and Hwy. 61, turn south onto Hwy. 61 and go 6.5 mi. Turn right. (Look for the statue and sign for Clemens Landing.) Go 2 blocks past the residences into the campground.

HAYTI MAP, C-4
Hayti-Portageville KOA

2824 MO State East Outer Rd., 63873. T: (800) 562-1508 or (573) 359-1580; www.koa.com.

🚐 ★★★★   ⛺ ★★★★

Beauty: ★★★	Site Privacy: ★★★★
Spaciousness: ★★★★	Quiet: ★★★
Security: ★★★★	Cleanliness: ★★★★★
Insect Control: ★★★★	Facilities: ★★★★★

This campground is surrounded on three sides by agricultural land (with the highway on the fourth side), which lends it a rural feel. A large number of trees throughout the park make the sites comfortable, even when the sun is boring down. Situated in five rows, sites are a combination of gravel and grass, with a predominance of pull-throughs. Sites 1–7 are 45-foot back-ins close to the playground area. The rest of the sites are 70–75-foot pull-throughs, whose desirability more or less depends on personal taste (proximity to restrooms, etc.). Several exceptionally good sites are the end sites (31, 41, 39, 49) of the last two rows, as these are farthest from the highway and seem to have more space. The tent sites are located in the southwest corner on grassy ground cover and have loads of trees. The tenting area is so spacious that each tent can be pitched under a different tree.

The laundry is small but clean and contains an exercise bike. The restrooms are very clean, and the showers (individual units) are immaculate and have air-conditioning. A very comfortable campground with great facilities.

BASICS

Operated By: Gary & Deborah Carnie. **Open:** All year. **Site Assignment:** Upon registration; credit card required for reservations; 1-night deposit; refund w/ 24-hour notice. **Registration:** At office; late arrivals use drop box. **Fee:** RV, $5–$31; tent, $20–$24. **Parking:** At site.

FACILITIES

Number of RV-only Sites: 49. **Number of Tent-only Sites:** 20. **Hookups:** Electric (30, 50 amps), water, sewer, Wi-Fi. **Each Site:** Picnic table, grill. **Dump Station:** Yes. **Laundry:** Yes. **Pay Phone:** Yes. **Restrooms and Showers:** Yes. **Fuel:** No. **Propane:** Yes. **Internal Roads:** Gravel. **RV Service:** No. **Market:** 7 mi. north or south. **Restaurant:** 7 mi. north or south. **General Store:** Yes. **Vending:** Yes. **Swimming:** Pool. **Playground:** Yes. **Other:** Cabins, game room, snack bar, kitchen, modem. **Activities:** Swimming. **Nearby Attractions:** Mississippi River. **Additional Information:** Hayti Chamber of Commerce, (573) 359-0632.

RESTRICTIONS

Pets: On leash, cleaned up after, no vicious breeds (pit bulls, Rottweilers) outside of vehicles. **Fires:** Fire ring only. **Alcoholic Beverages:** At sites. **Vehicle Maximum Length:** 82 ft. **Other:** No smoking in buildings.

TO GET THERE

From I-55, take Exit 27. Turn onto the service road on the east side of the highway (East Outer Rd.) and go 3 mi. Turn left at the sign into the campground.

HERMITAGE MAP, B-2
Damsite

reserve america™

Rte. 2 Box 2160, 65668-9509. T: (417) 745-2244; www.reserveamerica.com.

🚐 ★★★★   ⛺ ★★★★

Beauty: ★★★	Site Privacy: ★★★
Spaciousness: ★★★	Quiet: ★★★★
Security: ★★★★	Cleanliness: ★★★★
Insect Control: ★★★	Facilities: ★★★

The clear water of Pomme de Terre Lake and the rolling Ozark hills provide an excellent setting for camping, picnicking, swimming, fishing, hunting, or almost any outdoor recreational activity. Pomme de Terre Lake, with its 7,790 surface acres and 113 miles of shoreline, is well known for excellent fishing combined with panoramic scenery. Pomme de Terre Lake is located in South-West Missouri at the confluence of Lindley Creek and the Pomme de Terre River (for which it is named). The lake is located in southern Hickory and northern Polk counties, about 50 miles north of Springfield, Missouri. The name is

---

French and translates to "apple of the earth" or potato. The lake is part of a series of lakes in the Osage River Basin designed and constructed by the U.S. Army Corps of Engineers for flood control. Construction began in 1957 and was complete in 1961 at a cost of $14,946,784. Storage of water began on October 29, 1961 and the multipurpose pool was reached on June 15, 1963.

BASICS

Operated By: U.S. Army Corps of Engineers. **Open:** All year. **Site Assignment:** Reservations must be made at least 3 days in advance. **Registration:** At office. **Fee:** Single, $12–$22. **Parking:** At site.

FACILITIES

Number of Multipurpose Sites: 437. **Hookups:** Yes. **Dump Station:** Yes. **Laundry:** Yes. **Pay Phone:** No. **Restrooms and Showers:** Yes. **Fuel:** No. **Propane:** No. **Internal Roads:** Paved. **RV Service:** No. **Market:** No. **Restaurant:** No. **General Store:** No. **Vending:** No. **Swimming:** Yes. **Playground:** Yes. **Activities:** Amphitheater, picnicking, fishing, hunting.

RESTRICTIONS

Pets: Pets must be restrained or on a leash at all times while in developed recreation areas. **Fires:** In fire rings, stoves, grills, or fireplaces provided for that purpose. **Alcoholic Beverages:** Not allowed. **Vehicle Maximum Length:** Call ahead. **Other:** Sites 1–47, 70, 73–76, T01–T07 closed until further notice.

TO GET THERE

From Springfield MO: Take US 65 north 60 mi. to Preston MO. Take Hwy. 54 west to Hermitage, MO. Take Hwy. 254/64 south to Carsons Corner, take Hwy. 254 west toward the Dam. The entrance to Damsite Park is on the south side of 254.

HERMITAGE MAP, B-2
Wheatland Park

reserve america™

Rte. 2 Box 2160, 65668. T: (417) 282-5267; www.reserveamerica.com.

🚐 ★★★★   ⛺ ★★★★

Beauty: ★★★★	Site Privacy: ★★★★
Spaciousness: ★★★★	Quiet: ★★★★★
Security: ★★★★★	Cleanliness: ★★★★
Insect Control: ★★★	Facilities: ★★★

The clear water of Pomme de Terre Lake and the rolling Ozark hills provide an excellent setting for camping, picnicking, swimming, fishing, hunting or almost any outdoor recreational activity. Pomme de Terre Lake with its 7,790 surface acres and 113 miles of shoreline is well known for excellent fishing combined with panoramic scenery.

BASICS

Operated By: U.S. Army Corps of Engineers. **Open:** All year. **Site Assignment:** Reservations must be made at least 3 days in advance. **Registration:** At office. **Fee:** Single, $12–$20; group, $20. **Parking:** At site.

FACILITIES

Number of Multipurpose Sites: 256. **Hookups:** Yes. **Dump Station:** Yes. **Laundry:** No. **Pay Phone:** No. **Restrooms and Showers:** Yes. **Fuel:** No. **Propane:** No. **Internal Roads:** Paved. **RV Service:** No. **Market:** No. **Restaurant:** No. **General Store:** No. **Vending:** No. **Swimming:** Yes. **Playground:** Yes. **Activities:** Boating, fishing, hunting, picnicking.

RESTRICTIONS

Pets: Pets must be restrained or on a leash at all times while in developed recreation areas. **Fires:** In fire rings, stoves, grills, or fireplaces provided for that purpose. **Alcoholic Beverages:** Not allowed. **Vehicle Maximum Length:** Call ahead.

TO GET THERE

From Springfield: Take Hwy. 13N to Bolivar, then travel Hwy. 83E/N past Elkton to Hwy. 254. Follow Hwy. 254E to The Triangle and take CR 205S. Follow signs to park.

KIRKSVILLE   MAP, A-2
Thousand Hills State Park

20431 MO 157, 63501. T: (660) 665-6995 or (800) 334-6946; www.mostateparks.com.

🚐 ★★★★   🏕 ★★★★

Beauty: ★★★★	Site Privacy: ★★★
Spaciousness: ★★★	Quiet: ★★★★
Security: ★★★★	Cleanliness: ★★★★
Insect Control: ★★★★	Facilities: ★★★

Campground 1 has grassy sites (mostly back-ins) that back to forest. This is a large, popular place, and sites go quickly during high season. They range from 30 feet to more than 80 feet. Sites 28–35 are located on a separate road from the others, affording a little more privacy. Sites 36, 48, 50, 57, and 58 are paved pull-throughs. Site 66 is closest to the bathhouse. Campground 3 is smaller and not quite as popular. Site 13 is located right at the entrance, which makes it less desirable. Contrary to this, sites 15–17 are located on a separate road and are thus more private. Site 18 is a large pull-through. The restroom here is less developed than the bathhouse in campground 1, but still decent. This campground makes a wonderful destination for RVers and campers who wish to recreate on the water or learn about the local natural environment.

BASICS

Operated By: Missouri Dept. of Natural Resources. **Open:** All year (limited services Nov.–Mar.). **Site Assignment:** First come, first served; reservations are accepted w/ $8.50 deposit; refund (minus $5). **Registration:** Ranger will collect fees at site. **Fee:** RV $7–$17; check, no credit cards. **Parking:** At site.

FACILITIES

Number of RV-only Sites: 42. **Number of Tent-only Sites:** 15. **Hookups:** Electric (30, 50 amps). **Each Site:** Picnic table, grill, lantern post. **Dump Station:** Yes. **Laundry:** No. **Pay Phone:** Yes. **Restrooms and Showers:** Yes. **Fuel:** No. **Propane:** No. **Internal Roads:** Paved. **RV Service:** No. **Market:** Junction of Hwys. 6 & 63. **Restaurant:**

Junction of Hwys. 6 & 63. **General Store:** Yes. **Vending:** Yes. **Swimming:** Lake. **Playground:** Yes. **Other:** Amphitheater, cabins, petroglyphs, picnic area, mountain-biking trails, boat rentals, fishing licenses. **Activities:** Fishing, boating, swimming, hiking, mountain biking, nature activities. **Nearby Attractions:** Still National Osteopathic Museum, Big Creek, Sugar Creek. **Additional Information:** Kirksville Area Chamber: (660) 665-3766.

RESTRICTIONS

Pets: On leash, cleaned up after. **Fires:** Grill only. **Alcoholic Beverages:** At sites. **Vehicle Maximum Length:** No limit.

TO GET THERE

From the junction of Hwy. 63 and Hwy. 6, turn west onto Hwy. 6 and go 3.3 mi. Turn left onto Hwy. 157. Go 1.7 mi. to first campground.

LESTERVILLE   MAP, C-3
Parks Bluff Campground

P.O. Box 24, 63654. T: (573) 637-2290; www.parksbluff.com.

🚐 ★★★   🏕 ★★★★

Beauty: ★★★★	Site Privacy: ★★★
Spaciousness: ★★★	Quiet: ★★★★★
Security: ★★★★★	Cleanliness: ★★★★
Insect Control: ★★★★	Facilities: ★★★

Campers looking for fun on the river or in an ATV have come to the right place, but those who are looking for a quiet time should probably look elsewhere. (One indication of this is that quiet time begins at midnight.) Sites 1–4 and A–K are located in an open field surrounded by bushes and trees. These sites can accommodate a rig of any size, but cannot be pulled through unless the campground were completely empty. Most other electric sites are in a forested patch just off the Mud Pit (used for four-wheeling). Sites 23–30 are 60-foot back-ins adjacent to the pit. Across the internal road are loads of tenting spaces. These are mostly dirt with some grass, and back thick vegetation. Many of the sites have short paths that lead to the river. There is also unlimited tenting possible along the southeast edge of the property by the river's edge. The restroom building is primitive, but the facilities are decent; the three showers are all open. Parks Bluff is geared more toward tenters than RVs (view the lack of hookups other than electric), but anyone in search of fun on the river will enjoy their stay here.

BASICS

Operated By: Jayme Parks. **Open:** May–Sept. **Site Assignment:** RV sites upon registration, tent sites first come, first served; credit card or check deposit for reservation; refund (minus $3) w/ 7-day notice. **Registration:** At office; late arrivals check in w/ guard at gate. **Fee:** Adult, $6; child, $3; electric, $6; water, $6; V, MC, D. **Parking:** At site.

FACILITIES

Number of RV-only Sites: 40. **Number of Tent-only Sites:** Undesignated sites. **Hookups:** Electric (30 amps). **Each Site:** Picnic table, fire pit. **Dump Station:** Yes. **Laundry:** No. **Pay Phone:** No.

Restrooms and Showers: Yes. **Fuel:** No. **Propane:** No. **Internal Roads:** Gravel. **RV Service:** No. **Market:** 9 mi. to Centerville. **Restaurant:** Less than 1 mi. west. **General Store:** Yes. **Vending:** No. **Swimming:** River. **Playground:** No. **Activities:** Floating, 4-wheeling, volleyball. **Nearby Attractions:** Black River, Johnsons Shut-Ins State Park, Taum Sauk State Park. **Additional Information:** Missouri Dept. of Natural Resources, (800) 334-6946.

RESTRICTIONS

Pets: On leash, cleaned up after. **Fires:** Grill only. **Alcoholic Beverages:** At sites, no glass. **Vehicle Maximum Length:** No limit. **Other:** No vehicles in river. Midnight quiet hour. No ATVs, dirt bikes, or fireworks.

TO GET THERE

From the junction of Hwy. 49 north and Hwy. 21/49/72, turn east onto Hwy. 21/49/72 and go 2.8 mi. Turn right at the sign into the entrance.

MACON   MAP, A-2
Long Branch Lake State Park

28615 Visitors Center Rd., 63552. T: (660) 773-5229; www.mostateparks.com.

🚐 ★★★★   🏕 ★★★★★

Beauty: ★★★★★	Site Privacy: ★★★★
Spaciousness: ★★★★	Quiet: ★★★★★
Security: ★★★★★	Cleanliness: ★★★★
Insect Control: ★★★★	Facilities: ★★★★

Sites in this campground are divided between electric and primitive. Those with electrical hookups are numbered 1–40, and those without any hookups, 41–83. Most sites are 65-foot back-ins. Sites located on the outside of the loop are open, while those on the inside are more forested. Site 1 is right next to the entrance, 10 is next to the restrooms. Sites 12 and 13 and 19 and 20 are doubles. The nicest site is 52, which is located at the end of a roundabout, surrounded by lush vegetation, and offers views of the lake. Site 53, also secluded, is adjacent to a lake access area, and 78–80 are next to a boat access area. Sites 54–62 are walk-in tent sites hidden in thick woods. Site 30 is a long (120 feet) pull-through located next to the entrance for easy access. Site 40, all on its own, is located near the entrance and the RV dump. The restrooms and showers are clean, roomy, and modern. This is a great campground for those who like to get out into the wild, but it also offers modern amenities for maximum comfort.

BASICS

Operated By: Missouri Dept. of Natural Resources. **Open:** All year; limited facilities Nov.–Mar. 31. **Site Assignment:** First come, first served; no reservations. **Registration:** On-season, fees collected at sites; off-season, pay in drop-box. **Fee:** Electric, $12–$14; basic, $7–$8; check, V, MC, D. **Parking:** At site.

FACILITIES

Number of RV-only Sites: 65. **Number of Tent-only Sites:** 18. **Hookups:** Electric (30, 50 amps), water. **Each Site:** Picnic table, fire pit, lantern pole.

Dump Station: Yes. **Laundry:** No. **Pay Phone:** Yes. **Restrooms and Showers:** Yes. **Fuel:** No. **Propane:** No. **Internal Roads:** Paved. **RV Service:** No. **Market:** 4.5 mi. east. **Restaurant:** 3 mi. east. **General Store:** Yes. **Vending:** Yes. **Swimming:** Lake. **Playground:** Yes. **Activities:** Fishing, boating, swimming, hiking. **Nearby Attractions:** Thomas Hill Reservoir. **Additional Information:** Chamber of Commerce., (660) 385-5627.

RESTRICTIONS

Pets: On 6-ft. leash, cleaned up after. **Fires:** Grill only. **Alcoholic Beverages:** At sites. **Vehicle Maximum Length:** No limit. **Other:** Max. 6 people/site.

TO GET THERE

From the junction of Hwy. 63 and Hwy. 36, turn west onto Hwy. 36 and go 2.1 mi. Exit to the right at the sign, then take the first left onto Visitor Center Rd. and turn right off the exit.

MOBERLY   MAP, A-2
Thompson Campground

Rothwell Park Rd., 65270. T: (660) 670-4522 or (660) 263-6757.

🚐 ★★★   ▲ ★★★

Beauty: ★★★★	Site Privacy: ★★★
Spaciousness: ★★★	Quiet: ★★★★★
Security: ★★★★★	Cleanliness: ★★★
Insect Control: ★★★★	Facilities: ★★★

This park has RV sites in a strip of 12 spaces, with two RVs designated per site. None of the sites are numbered. Sounds confusing? The setup is apparently just as confusing to the people who run the park, as they are not even sure of the number of RVs the park can accommodate. Nonetheless, this is a nice little park surrounded on three sides by woods, and is worth the minor hassle the site numbers may cause. Although sites are 90 feet in length, the slope from which nearly all of them suffer cuts the usable length down to about 70 feet. (Sites to the south are more level, but are adjacent to stored equipment and piles of miscellaneous stuff.) The tenting area is just as confusing as the RV section. In fact, there is no indication anywhere of the location of the tent area. It is, for the record, just to the north of the internal road, facing the RV sites. The thick grass and tree coverage make for comfortable camping, but the primitive toilet and lack of sink and showers are a severe drawback for tenters—as are the almost inescapable security lights. (Still, at this price, who can complain?) Police and ranger patrols ensure that the campground is secure throughout the night. Thompson is nicer for RVs than for tents, although the cheap price makes it worthwhile for any camper on a budget.

BASICS

Operated By: City of Moberly. **Open:** All year. **Site Assignment:** First come, first served; no reservations. **Registration:** Ranger will collect fees at site. **Fee:** Water/electric, $8; tent, $3; check, cash. **Parking:** At site.

FACILITIES

Number of RV-only Sites: 36. **Number of Tent-only Sites:** Undesignated sites. **Hookups:** Electric

---

(30 amps), water. **Each Site:** Picnic table. **Dump Station:** Yes. **Laundry:** No. **Pay Phone:** No. **Restrooms and Showers:** Restrooms; no shower. **Fuel:** No. **Propane:** No. **Internal Roads:** Gravel. **RV Service:** No. **Market:** 1 mi. northeast. **Restaurant:** 1 mi. northeast. **General Store:** No. **Vending:** No. **Swimming:** Pool. **Playground:** Yes. **Other:** Jogging trails, group shelters, lake, pool, recreation field, boat ramp. **Activities:** Fishing, boating, swimming, field sports, basketball, archery. **Nearby Attractions:** Mark Twain Birthplace State Historic Area. **Additional Information:** Chamber of Commerce Moberly Area, (660) 263-6070.

RESTRICTIONS

Pets: On leash, cleaned up after. **Fires:** Grill only. **Alcoholic Beverages:** At sites, subject to public drinking ordinance if outside sites. **Vehicle Maximum Length:** No limit.

TO GET THERE

From the junction of Hwy. 63 and Hwy. 24, turn west on Hwy. 24 and go 3 mi. Turn right onto Rothwell Park Rd. Turn right at the sign into the entrance.

MONETT   MAP, C-2
Pine Trails RV Ranch

40 Hwy. 60, 65708. T: (417) 235-8682.

🚐 ★★★★   ▲ n/a

Beauty: ★★★★	Site Privacy: ★★★★★
Spaciousness: ★★★★	Quiet: ★★★★
Security: ★★★★★	Cleanliness: ★★★★★
Insect Control: ★★★★	Facilities: ★★

This small RV park in the pine trees has 80 by 33-foot pull-throughs laid out in two rows. To the northeast is forest, and to the northwest are open fields creating a very quiet and peaceful atmosphere. Site 1 is slightly easier to get in and out of. (This is true of the lower numbers in general.) Site 21 has a larger grassy area than other sites, but, in general, all the sites are of a uniform quality. Unabashedly oriented toward older folks, this campground provides a very low-key and quiet place to camp.

BASICS

Operated By: Charles & Yvonne Swartz. **Open:** Apr. 1–Dec. 31; open all year upon request. **Site Assignment:** Upon registration; verbal reservations OK. **Registration:** At office; late arrivals use drop box. **Fee:** RV, $19; check, no credit cards. **Parking:** 1 vehicle per site. Overflow parking available.

FACILITIES

Number of RV-only Sites: 21. **Hookups:** Electric (30, 50 amps), water, sewer, phone hookups are your responsibility for extended stays. **Each Site:** Picnic table. **Dump Station:** Yes. **Laundry:** No. **Pay Phone:** Yes. **Restrooms and Showers:** Yes. **Fuel:** No. **Propane:** No. **Internal Roads:** Gravel. **RV Service:** No. **Market:** 3 mi. west. **Restaurant:** 3 mi. west. **General Store:** No. **Vending:** No. **Swimming:** No. **Playground:** Yes. **Other:** Modem, picnic area, close to attractions, pet walk area. **Activities:** Hiking, shows (in Branson), fishing, boating. **Nearby Attractions:** Roaring River State Park, Mark Twain National Forest, Branson, Springfield. **Additional**

Information: Monett Chamber of Commerce, (417) 235-7919.

RESTRICTIONS

Pets: On leash, cleaned up after. **Fires:** In common fire ring. **Alcoholic Beverages:** At sites. Not during quiet hours (10 p.m.–8 a.m.). **Vehicle Maximum Length:** 50 ft. **Other:** Keep satellite dish on gravel. No tent camping.

TO GET THERE

From the junction of Hwy. 37 and Hwy. 60, turn east onto Hwy. 60 and go 3 mi. Turn left at the sign into the entrance.

MONROE CITY   MAP, A-3
Mark Twain Landing

reserve america

42819 Landing Lane, 63456. T: (573) 735-9422; www.marktwainlanding.com, www.reserve america.com.

🚐 ★★★★   ▲ ★★★★

Beauty: ★★★★	Site Privacy: ★★★
Spaciousness: ★★	Quiet: ★★
Security: ★★★	Cleanliness: ★★★
Insect Control: ★★★	Facilities: ★★★★

This is a very wooded, beatiful campground, with lots of shade and wildlife everywhere. Almost all the sites are shaded and the surrounding campground area is heavily forested. The sites are roomy and well spaced apart, with a real sense of privacy. While some are reservable, many are not. The roads and sites are paved but narrow in some places. The campground is beautifully maintained, and the restrooms and showers were clean while we were there. Water and dump station are available, and there are several playgrounds and swimming-beach facilities. There is a marina with a store and small restaurant on site, but they serve boaters and do not carry RV-related items. You can rent a small fishing motorboat for a small fee at Mark Twain Lake. Also closeby are the Mark Twain birthplace and Clarence Cannon Dam and Visitors Center. The staff is helpful, and the security is good, with frequent patrols by park rangers.

BASICS

Operated By: Legacy RV Resorts. **Open:** All year. **Site Assignment:** First come, first served; reservations accepted. **Registration:** At office. **Fee:** RV, $33; tent, $20; fee includes 4 people. **Parking:** Limit 2 vehicles per site.

FACILITIES

Number of Multipurpose Sites: 228. **Hookups:** Full hookup (30, 50 amps), cable. **Each Site:** Picnic table. **Dump Station:** Yes. **Laundry:** Yes. **Pay Phone:** Yes. **Restrooms and Showers:** Yes. **Fuel:** Yes. **Propane:** Yes. **Internal Roads:** Paved. **RV Service:** 10 mi. east of Monroe City. **Market:** 6 mi. northeast in Monroe City. **Restaurant:** On site. **General Store:** Convenience store. **Vending:** Yes. **Swimming:** Pool & water park. **Playground:** Yes. **Activities:** Fishing, paddleboats, mini-golf, amusement

---

rides, water park, restaurant. **Nearby Attractions:** Mark Twain Lake, Hannibal. **Additional Information:** Monroe City Chamber of Commerce.

RESTRICTIONS

Pets: On leash only. **Fires:** Allowed. **Alcoholic Beverages:** Allowed. **Vehicle Maximum Length:** 50 ft. **Other:** Seasonal, monthly, daily.

TO GET THERE

From Monroe City: Take US 36 east to J. Travel south on Hwy. J for 7.9 mi. From Hannibal: Go west on US 36 for 20 mi. to Hwy. J., then south on J for 7.9 mi.

MOUNTAIN GROVE
MAP. C-2. C-3

Missouri Park Campground

2325 Missouri Park Dr., 65711.
T: (417) 926-4104 or (417) 926-5550;
www.missouriparkcampground.com.

🚐 ★★★★   ⛺ ★★★★

Beauty: ★★★★ **Site Privacy:** ★★★★
Spaciousness: ★★★ **Quiet:** ★★★★
Security: ★★★★ **Cleanliness:** ★★★★
Insect Control: ★★★★ **Facilities:** ★★★★

This campground has a combination of overnight RV spaces and mobile homes. Sites 1–9 are right at the entrance. These are 90-foot gravel pull-throughs just south of the mobile-home area. Site 2 has some shade, but the others in this strip are all open. The rest of the RV sites lie west, in a forested area, with sites 1–10 being the most forested. Sites 2, 4, and 6 are 95–120-foot pull-throughs; 16 and 18 are also very long. The back-ins in this area range from 35 to 45 feet in length. (Most of the sites are not numbered, which makes it difficult to find the proper site, especially in the northern part of the loop, 12–18.) The tenting area is a large grassy field that can take any number of tents. The grass cover is healthy, but because the area is slightly sloped, tenting in some areas becomes difficult; there is also a lack of shade in the entire field. The restrooms are clean and comfortable, with air-conditioning, new countertops, and new tile on the floor. A woodsy, comfortable campground.

BASICS

Operated By: Paul & Christine Gasperson. **Open:** All year; limited services Jan.–Feb. **Site Assignment:** Depends on site availability; verbal reservations OK; no deposit. **Registration:** At office; late arrivals use drop box. **Fee:** Full, $22; check, no credit cards. **Parking:** At site.

FACILITIES

Number of RV-only Sites: 30. **Number of Tent-only Sites:** Undesignated sites. **Hookups:** Electric (30, 50 amps), water, sewer. **Each Site:** Picnic table, fire ring. **Dump Station:** No (sewer at all sites). **Laundry:** Yes. **Pay Phone:** Yes. **Restrooms and Showers:** Yes. **Fuel:** No. **Propane:** No. **Internal Roads:** Gravel. **RV Service:** No. **Market:** 3 mi. to Exit 95. **Restaurant:** 3 mi. to Exit 95. **General Store:** Yes. **Vending:** No. **Swimming:** Pool. **Playground:** No. **Other:** Fishing lake, game room w/

pool table. **Activities:** Swimming, fishing, hiking. **Nearby Attractions:** Laura Ingalls Wilder's Home, Mark Twain NF. **Additional Information:** Mountain Grove Chamber of Commerce, (417) 926-4135.

RESTRICTIONS

Pets: On leash, cleaned up after. **Fires:** Grill only. **Alcoholic Beverages:** At sites. **Vehicle Maximum Length:** No limit.

TO GET THERE

From Hwy. 60, take west Bus. 60, go north over the highway overpass, and take the service road 1.2 mi. Turn right onto Missouri Park Dr. and then left into the campground.

OAK GROVE
MAP, B-2

Kansas City East KOA

303 NE 3rd St., P.O. Box 191, 64075.
T: (800) 562-7507 or (816) 690-6660;
www.koa.com.

🚐 ★★★★   ⛺ ★★★

Beauty: ★★★ **Site Privacy:** ★★★
Spaciousness: ★★★ **Quiet:** ★★★
Security: ★★★★ **Cleanliness:** ★★★★
Insect Control: ★★★★ **Facilities:** ★★★★

This campground has several rows of large pull-throughs (60): 1–10 are unshaded 70-foot sites, 18–26 are unshaded 54-foot sites, and 27–33 are shaded 90-foot sites. Sites 42–47 are head-to-head pull-throughs along the east edge. These sites are well shaded, but as a consequence of being doubles, they offer less room and privacy. Sites 54–68 along the south edge are back-ins that back to trees and other vegetation. These are mostly well-shaded sites. Sites 71–73 are located in the shaded northwest corner and are comfortable and grassy. Sites T1 and T2 are located in the southeast corner, and back to a hedge. They have decent grass and cool shade. Other tent sites (38–41) are located to the north of sites 42–43. The restrooms and showers are somewhat old but still clean and comfortable. Although slightly better for RVers than for tents, this campground is a decent stay with loads of facilities for all.

BASICS

Operated By: Mary & Melvin Lueck. **Open:** All year. **Site Assignment:** Depends on site availability; credit card required for reservation (charged 1 night); refund (minus $5) w/ 48-hour notice. **Registration:** At office; late arrivals use drop box in laundry. **Fee:** RV, $28–$29; tent $20–$2; V, MC, D. **Parking:** At site.

FACILITIES

Number of RV-only Sites: 73. **Number of Tent-only Sites:** 24. **Hookups:** Electric (30, 50 amps), water, sewer, Wi-Fi. **Each Site:** Picnic table, fire pit. **Dump Station:** Yes. **Laundry:** Yes. **Pay Phone:** Yes. **Restrooms and Showers:** Yes. **Fuel:** No. **Propane:** Yes. **Internal Roads:** Gravel. **RV Service:** No. **Market:** Less than 1 mi. southwest. **Restaurant:** Less than 1 mi. southwest. **General Store:** Yes. **Vending:** Yes. **Swimming:** Pool. **Playground:** Yes. **Other:** Mini-golf, dog walk, cabins, game room, pool table, horseshoes. **Activities:** Vol-

leyball, basketball, swimming. **Nearby Attractions:** Worlds of Fun, Truman Library, Truman Home, casinos. **Additional Information:** CVB of Greater Kansas City, (800) 767-7700, (816) 221-5242.

RESTRICTIONS

Pets: On leash, cleaned up after. **Fires:** Grill only. **Alcoholic Beverages:** At sites. **Vehicle Maximum Length:** 75 ft.

TO GET THERE

From I-70 (Exit 28), turn north onto H and go 0.25 mi. Turn right onto 3rd St. and go 2 blocks to the entrance on the right.

PECULIAR
MAP, B-1

Peculiar Park Place

22901 SE Outer Rd., 64078. T: (816) 779-6300;
www.gocampingamerica.com.

🚐 ★★★★★   ⛺ n/a

Beauty: ★★★★ **Site Privacy:** ★★★★
Spaciousness: ★★★★ **Quiet:** ★★★
Security: ★★★★★ **Cleanliness:** ★★★★★
Insect Control: ★★★★ **Facilities:** ★★★★

Although only open since August 2000, this RV park is already a beautiful place to camp. The landscaping includes rocks, plants, trees, brick, and wood on the office building, and a bricked patio and stenciled cement table for each site. Sites 1–10 are 75-foot pull-throughs that have a very nice view of the highway and the woods beyond. Sites 11 and 12 are located in a beautiful grassy spot with an attractive rock retaining wall behind, while 13–18 back to woods, also with very pleasant landscaping. Sites 19–28 are 90-foot unshaded pull-throughs that overlook sites 1–10 and share the same view. Sites 29–34 are 70-foot pull-throughs, 39–51 are 90-foot pull-throughs. Like 13–18, 35–38 also back to some nice woods. The restrooms are absolutely top-notch—some of the best of any campground on the road. They are tiled, modern, and at least as comfortable as at home. Although tenters will have to find another place to camp, RVers would be well advised to mark this park on their itinerary. It is the nicest RV park in the Kansas City area and is destined only to get better.

BASICS

Operated By: Frosty & Gail. **Open:** All year. **Site Assignment:** Upon registration; verbal reservations OK; no deposit. **Registration:** At office; late arrivals call phone number on door 24 hrs. **Fee:** RV (full), $25; check, no credit cards. **Parking:** At site.

FACILITIES

Number of RV-only Sites: 60. **Hookups:** Electric (20, 30, 50 amps), water, sewer, Wi-Fi. **Each Site:** Picnic table, brick patio, fire pit. **Dump Station:** Yes. **Laundry:** Yes. **Pay Phone:** Yes. **Restrooms and Showers:** Yes. **Fuel:** No. **Propane:** Yes. **Internal Roads:** Gravel. **RV Service:** No. **Market:** 2 mi. west. **Restaurant:** 2 mi. west. **General Store:** No. **Vending:** No. **Swimming:** No. **Playground:** No. **Other:** Pet walk, gift shop, gazebo; planned facilities include pavilion, bandstand, putting green, dance floor, hot tub. **Activities:** Wildlife viewing, hiking, potlucks.

Nearby Attractions: Branson, Kansas City. **Additional Information:** CVB of Greater Kansas City, (800) 767-7700, (816) 221-5242.

RESTRICTIONS

Pets: On leash, cleaned up after, small or medium-sized dogs only. **Fires:** Grill only. **Alcoholic Beverages:** At sites. **Vehicle Maximum Length:** No limit.

TO GET THERE

From Hwy. 71 (Peculiar Exit), turn east onto J and take first right after highway off-ramp onto East Outer Rd. Go 1.5 mi. and turn left at the sign into the entrance.

PERRYVILLE MAP, B-4
Perryville/Cape Girardeau KOA

89 KOA Ln., 63775. T: (800) 562-5304 or (573) 547-8303; www.koa.com.

🚐 ★★★★★   ▲ ★★★★★

Beauty: ★★★★   Site Privacy: ★★★★
Spaciousness: ★★★   Quiet: ★★★
Security: ★★★★   Cleanliness: ★★★★★
Insect Control: ★★★★   Facilities: ★★★★★

Sites in this campground are arranged in rows A–K. All rows but A and B are hidden amongst shade trees, which makes them more desirable. There are 80 pull-throughs and 12 back-ins. Row A contains 65-foot pull-throughs, rows B–J have 72-foot pull-throughs. Sites A1 and B1 are next to a residence, and C1 and D1 are next to an unattractive shed. Sites J4 and J5 and F1 have large pieces of electrical hardware that encroach on their space. Sites F8 and F9 and E9 and E10 are less shaded than others around them. Aside from these few shortcomings, you really can't go wrong with any of the sites in this park. For a more wilderness feel, try rows H–K. They are less developed and are farther back in the woods. Row K has 52-foot back-ins that back to the forest surrounding the campground. The best sites in any row (especially C–J) are close to the middle (for example, 3–6). Tent sites are 45 feet wide, with plenty of depth, grassy, and forested—ideal for a tenter. The restrooms are clean, spacious, and very private. This campground is comfortable for any style of camping and offers plenty to do. A great place to bring kids.

BASICS

Operated By: Garry & Deborah Ingram. **Open:** Mar. 1–Dec. 20. **Site Assignment:** Depends on site availability; verbal reservations OK; 1-night deposit. **Registration:** At office; late arrivals use drop box. **Fee:** RV (full), $28.95–$32; water/electric, $27.95; tent, $25; in-state check, V, MC, D. **Parking:** At site.

FACILITIES

Number of RV-only Sites: 92. **Number of Tent-only Sites:** 10. **Hookups:** Electric (30, 50 amps), water, sewer, telephone, Wi-Fi. **Each Site:** Picnic table, grill. **Dump Station:** Yes. **Laundry:** Yes. **Pay Phone:** Courtesy. **Restrooms and Showers:** Yes. **Fuel:** No. **Propane:** Yes. **Internal Roads:** Gravel. **RV Service:** No. **Market:** 1 mi. east. **Restaurant:** 1 mi. east. **General Store:** Yes. **Vending:** Yes. **Swimming:** Pool. **Playground:** Yes. **Other:** Mini-golf, cabins, pavilions, pet walk, game room, sun deck,

accommodates groups, fishing pond, hiking trails. **Activities:** Campfires, Sat. kids' events, Christmas in July, fishing (catch & release). **Nearby Attractions:** Hometown of Popeye the Sailor (Chester, IL), Historic St. Genevieve (oldest town west of the Mississippi), St. Mary's seminary. **Additional Information:** Perryville Chamber of Commerce, (573) 547-6062.

RESTRICTIONS

Pets: On leash, cleaned up after. **Fires:** Grill only. **Alcoholic Beverages:** At sites. **Vehicle Maximum Length:** 100 ft. **Other:** Catch & release fishing.

TO GET THERE

From I-55 (Exit 129), turn west onto Hwy. 51 and take the first right after the highway overpass (Outer Rd. North). Go 1.4 mi., then turn left at the sign into the entrance.

PHILLIPSBURG MAP, B-2
Lebanon KOA

18376 Campground Rd., 65722. T: (800) KOA-3424 or (417) 532-3422; www.koa.com.

🚐 ★★★★   ▲ ★★★★

Beauty: ★★★★   Site Privacy: ★★★★
Spaciousness: ★★★   Quiet: ★★★★
Security: ★★★★   Cleanliness: ★★★★★
Insect Control: ★★★★   Facilities: ★★★★★

Long pull-throughs are the name of the game in this campground. There is no need to unhook any towed vehicles, as there is sure to be a site that can accommodate the longest rigs on the road. Sites 16–19B (RV sites start at 16) are 70 feet long, while the neighboring ones (in the 20s–40s) average 75 feet. Sites 50–52 are the big boys of the campground, measuring 100–120 feet. Site 52—the longest and very well shaded—is the nicest in the entire campground. Site 50 is unshaded and therefore less desirable. Tent sites have crushed gravel inside a tent pad surrounded by logs, and nice thick grass. Unfortunately, there is little shade offered to tent sites. (Tent sites T1–T3, along the entrance road, are shaded, but receive all the incoming and outgoing traffic from the campground.) Billing itself as an overnight park, this campground with easy on/off access from the highway offers much more than that label might suggest. In fact, it's nice enough for an extended stay for either RVers or tenters.

BASICS

Operated By: Robert & Sandra Ebling. **Open:** Mar. 1–Dec. 15. **Site Assignment:** Upon registration; credit card required for reservation; 48-hour cancellation policy (by 4 p.m. the day before); $5 fee for cancellation. **Registration:** At office; late arrivals use drop box. **Fee:** RV, $25–30; tent, $20–22; check, V, MC, D. **Parking:** At site.

FACILITIES

Number of RV-only Sites: 40. **Number of Tent-only Sites:** 15. **Hookups:** Electric (50 amps), water, sewer, Wi-Fi. **Each Site:** Picnic table, fire pit. **Dump Station:** Yes. **Laundry:** Yes. **Pay Phone:** Yes. **Restrooms and Showers:** Yes. **Fuel:** No. **Propane:** Yes. **Internal Roads:** Gravel. **RV Service:** Next door. **Market:** 7 mi. east. **Restaurant:** 4

mi. east. **General Store:** Yes. **Vending:** No. **Swimming:** Pool. **Playground:** Yes. **Other:** Cabins, video games, modem, fishing hole. **Activities:** Basketball, volleyball, ping pong, breakfasts & dinners, ice-cream socials on weekends, fishing. **Nearby Attractions:** Branson, Springfield, Mansfield, Meramec Caverns, Laura Ingalls Wilder Home, Bennett Springs State Park. **Additional Information:** Lebanon Chamber of Commerce, (417) 588-3256.

RESTRICTIONS

Pets: On leash, cleaned up after. **Fires:** Grill only. **Alcoholic Beverages:** At sites. **Vehicle Maximum Length:** 100 ft.

TO GET THERE

From I-44 (Exit 123), turn south and take the first left after the highway ramp onto Outer Rd. East. Go 0.25 mi. and turn right at the sign into the entrance.

PLATTE CITY MAP, A-1
Basswood Country Inn and RV Resort

reserve america

15880 Interurban Rd., 64079. T: (800) 242-2775 or (816) 858-5556; www.basswoodresort.com.

🚐 ★★★★★   ▲ ★★★★

Beauty: ★★★★   Site Privacy: ★★★
Spaciousness: ★★★   Quiet: ★★★★
Security: ★★★★★   Cleanliness: ★★★★★
Insect Control: ★★★★   Facilities: ★★★★★

Rarely does an RV "resort" live up to the excellence its name promises. However, Basswood is an exception; it's a smooth operation and a guaranteed great stay for both RVers and tenters. Besides the usual facilities, there are stocked fishing lakes, modem access, and room at the inn for those who need a change of pace. The two areas named "Tent A" and "Tent B" on the map handed out to you are misleading—these are all RV spaces. There are only 28 pull-through sites. Tent A has 51-foot cement slabs in pull-through sites, while Tent B has 30-foot gravel back-ins. Of these sites, 8 and 21 are particularly well shaded. South of this is the real tenting area. These are grassy, shaded sites, very comfortable for tents. Site A is above the lake and across the interior road, B and C are right on the lake. These are the best tent sites, as they are closest to the lake and more isolated. Sites D–T are in rows to the west of this area. These are grass-and-dirt sites but lack any real shade. (There are only decorative trees and shrubs.) Sites D–L on the east side are 33 by 45 feet, while M–T are 25 by 36 feet. The big-rig area is located to the extreme west, in a hollow surrounded by trees and dirt cliffs. Sites 75 and 76 are 35-foot back-ins, but the rest of the sites are much larger. Sites 77–97 and 120–129 are 75 by 30-foot gravel pull-throughs. The restrooms are individual units with shower, toilet, and sink. They are all very modern, extremely comfortable, and with air conditioning. Received "National Park of the Year" award for a medium-sized park.

BASICS

Operated By: Legacy Inc. **Open:** All year. **Site Assignment:** Upon registration; credit card required for reservation, 7-day cancellation policy; $30 deposit; refund minus $5. **Registration:** At office; late arrivals knock on night window. **Fee:** $22–$38. **Parking:** At site.

FACILITIES

Number of RV-only Sites: 159. **Number of Tent-only Sites:** 20. **Hookups:** Electric (30, 50 amps), water, sewer, phone. **Each Site:** Picnic table, grill, fire pit. **Dump Station:** No (sewer at all sites). **Laundry:** Yes. **Pay Phone:** Yes. **Restrooms and Showers:** Yes. **Fuel:** No. **Propane:** Yes. **Internal Roads:** Gravel/paved. **RV Service:** On-call. **Market:** 6 mi. west. **Restaurant:** 5 mi. west. **General Store:** Yes. **Vending:** Yes. **Swimming:** Pool. **Playground:** Yes. **Other:** Athletic field, meeting facilities, fishing lakes, games, cottage, inn, trails, covered picnic shelter, modem. **Activities:** Fishing, boating, swimming, hiking. **Nearby Attractions:** Alldredge Orchards, Guy B. Park Conservation Area, Platte Falls Conservation Area, Pumpkins Etc., Fulk's Tree Farm, Shiloh Springs Golf Course. **Additional Information:** Platte City Chamber of Commerce: www.plattecitymo.com.

RESTRICTIONS

Pets: On leash, cleaned up after. **Fires:** Grill only. **Alcoholic Beverages:** At sites. **Vehicle Maximum Length:** 70 ft. **Other:** No washing or working on vehicles.

TO GET THERE

From I-29 (Exit 18), turn east onto Hwy. 92 and go 3.5 mi. Turn left onto Winan Ave. and go 1.7 mi. to the stop sign. Turn left onto Interurban Hwy. and go 0.3 mi. Turn left at the sign onto Basswood Lake Rd. and drive up to the office.

POTOSI   MAP, B-3
Council Bluff Recreation Area— Mark Twain National Forest

reserve america

16251 MO 21, 63664. T: (573) 766-0043; www.reserveamerica.com.

🚐 ★★★★   ▲ ★★★★

Beauty: ★★★	Site Privacy: ★★★
Spaciousness: ★★★★	Quiet: ★★★
Security: ★★★★	Cleanliness: ★★★★
Insect Control: ★★★★	Facilities: ★

Council Bluffs Recreation Area is built around the 440-acre Council Bluffs Lake on the Big River. Opened in 1985, Wild Boar Ridge Campground is a group of campsites strung along the spine of a forested Ozark ridge above the lake. Stretching over a mile-long ridge instead of being crammed into the tight cluster we've come to expect in public campgrounds, sites in Wild Boar Campground are comfortably spaced. All have ample level space for tents. Although many sites are large enough for RVs, lack of hookups keeps most RVs away. When a behemoth does show up, good spacing between sites and thick woods between camps keep things private and peaceful. The Mark Twain National Forest is located in southern and central Missouri, and extends from the St. Francois Mountains in the southeast to dry rocky glades in the southwest, from the prairie lands along the Missouri River to the nation's most ancient mountains in the south. Clear spring-fed rivers and streams, rocky bluffs, pastoral views, and shaded trails all welcome visitors to explore and enjoy the beauty of the renowned Ozarks.

BASICS

Operated By: U.S. Forest Service. **Open:** May 1–Oct. 14. **Site Assignment:** Reservations must be made at least 4 days in advance. **Registration:** At office. **Fee:** Single, $8; double, $16; group, $25. **Parking:** At park.

FACILITIES

Number of Multipurpose Sites: 104. **Hookups:** None. **Each Site:** Call ahead. **Dump Station:** No. **Laundry:** No. **Pay Phone:** No. **Restrooms and Showers:** Yes. **Fuel:** No. **Propane:** No. **Internal Roads:** Paved. **RV Service:** No. **Market:** No. **Restaurant:** No. **General Store:** No. **Vending:** No. **Swimming:** Yes. **Playground:** No. **Activities:** Hiking.

RESTRICTIONS

Pets: Pets must be restrained or on a leash at all times while in developed recreation areas. **Fires:** In rings and grill provided for that purpose. **Alcoholic Beverages:** Not allowed. **Vehicle Maximum Length:** Call ahead.

TO GET THERE

From Potosi, take Hwy. P south 10 mi. to junction C Hwy. Right on C Hwy. for 0.125 mi. to junction DD Hwy. Turn left on DD Hwy. and go 5 mi. to recreation area entrance.

REVERE   MAP, A-3
Battle of Athens State Historical Site Campground

R.R. 1 Box 26, 63465. T: (660) 877-3871; www.mostateparks.com/athens.htm.

🚐 ★★★★   ▲ ★★★★

Beauty: ★★★★	Site Privacy: ★★★★
Spaciousness: ★★★★	Quiet: ★★★★
Security: ★★★★	Cleanliness: ★★★★
Insect Control: ★★★★	Facilities: ★★

Located southwest of the historical site, this campground has all forested sites located in lush vegetation. Sites are back-ins that average 65–75 feet. Sites 1–4 are located on a separate road that branches off the main road right at the entrance. Sites 1 and 4 are the nicest in the campground, as they are more secluded than the others. Sites 14 and 18 are very close together and lack privacy. Sites 26 and 27 are doubles, best suited for groups that need two adjacent sites. The three restrooms in the campground all have pit toilets and no showers or running water. An attractive campground, but rather short on facilities—especially for tent campers.

BASICS

Operated By: Missouri Dept. of Natural Resources. **Open:** All year. **Site Assignment:** First come, first served; no reservations. **Registration:** Camp host will collect fees at sites. **Fee:** $7–$17; cash, check. **Parking:** At site.

FACILITIES

Number of RV-only Sites: 15. **Number of Tent-only Sites:** 14. **Hookups:** Electric (30 amps). **Each Site:** Picnic table, fire pit. **Dump Station:** No. **Laundry:** No. **Pay Phone:** Yes. **Restrooms and Showers:** Restrooms; no shower. **Fuel:** No. **Propane:** No. **Internal Roads:** Paved. **RV Service:** No. **Market:** 10 mi. to Farmington. **Restaurant:** 10 mi. to Farmington. **General Store:** No. **Vending:** No. **Swimming:** No. **Playground:** Yes. **Other:** Lake. **Activities:** Fishing, boating, hiking. **Nearby Attractions:** Des Moines River, Mark Twain Birthplace Museum, Thousand Hills. **Additional Information:** Kirksville Chamber of Commerce, (660) 665-3766.

RESTRICTIONS

Pets: On leash, cleaned up after. **Fires:** Grill only. **Alcoholic Beverages:** At sites. **Vehicle Maximum Length:** No limit.

TO GET THERE

From the junction of Hwy. 81 and Hwy. CC, turn east onto Hwy. CC and go 4 mi. Turn left onto gravel road and continue to park entrance.

ROLLA   MAP, B-3
Silver Mines— Mark Twain National Forest

reserve america

401 Fairgrounds Rd, 65401. T: (573) 364-4621; www.reserveamerica.com.

🚐 ★★★★   ▲ ★★★★

Beauty: ★★★	Site Privacy: ★★★
Spaciousness: ★★★	Quiet: ★★★
Security: ★★★★	Cleanliness: ★★★★
Insect Control: ★★★★	Facilities: ★★

Silver Mines Recreation Area, named for actual silver mines, active in the 1920s but long since played out, is located on the banks of the St. Francis River. Whitewater enthusiasts from around the world bring their kayaks to enjoy the challenges of the river during the White Water Festival and spring high water. There is a 1-mile-long trail along each side of the river. From Turkey Creek Picnic Area, a 1.2-mile trail to the north leads to Millstream Garden Conservation Area, managed by the Missouri Department of Conservation. Silver Mines is located within the Mark Twain National Forest is located in southern and central Missouri, and extends from the St. Francois Mountains in the southeast to dry rocky glades in the southwest, from the prairie lands along the Missouri River to the nation's most ancient mountains in the south. Clear spring-fed rivers and streams, rocky bluffs, pastoral views and shaded trails all welcome visitors to explore and enjoy the beauty of the renowned Ozarks.

BASICS

Operated By: U.S. Forest Service. **Open:** Mar. 1–Oct. 14. **Site Assignment:** Reservations must be made at least 4 days in advance. **Registration:** At office. **Fee:** Single, $8–$15; double, $16–$30; group, $25–$100. **Parking:**.

FACILITIES

Number of Multipurpose Sites: 109. **Hookups:** None. **Each Site:** Picnic table, lantern post, fire ring. **Dump Station:** No. **Laundry:** No. **Pay Phone:** No. **Restrooms and Showers:** Yes. **Fuel:** No. **Propane:** No. **Internal Roads:** Paved. **RV Service:** No. **Market:** No. **Restaurant:** No. **General Store:** No. **Vending:** No. **Swimming:** Yes. **Playground:** No. **Activities:** Fishing, hiking, kayaking.

RESTRICTIONS

Pets: Pets must be restrained or on a leash at all times while in developed recreation areas. **Fires:** In fire rings, stoves, grills, or fireplaces provided for that purpose. **Alcoholic Beverages:** Not allowed. **Vehicle Maximum Length:** 40 ft.

TO GET THERE

In Shell Knob, take MO YY east 2.8 mi. to campground sign (FS 1083). Turn left onto FS 1083 and go 0.7 mi. to campground.

SEDALIA   MAP, B-2
Countryside Adult/ Senior RV Park

5464 South Limit Ave., 65301. T: (660) 827-6513.

🚐 ★★★   ⛺ n/a

Beauty: ★★★★	Site Privacy: ★★★
Spaciousness: ★★★	Quiet: ★★★
Security: ★★★★	Cleanliness: ★★★★
Insect Control: ★★★★	Facilities: ★★★

The owners of this campground are normally out during the day, but sites available for overnighters are posted on the door to the office. Sites 19–22, 27, and 28 are (at least nominally) pull-throughs. It is, however, difficult to see how sites 21–25 could be pull-throughs without driving over the grassy patch that borders them on one side (and looks more like landscaping than a driveway). Sites are on a large gravel area and measure 100 feet in length. Sites 1–13, on the east side, back to woods and residences. Sites 14–20 are against the southern edge and back to woods and the office. The large open field to the northwest that looks so enticing is used only during the summer fair in Sedalia. Overnighters must select from open sites on the gravel. The restrooms are individual units that include showers. These are all very clean and comfortable. This campground is a decent stop for overnighters, although many may wish they could camp out on the grass instead.

BASICS

Operated By: Linda Alcorn. **Open:** Mar. 15–Nov. 15. **Site Assignment:** Reservations required; 1-night deposit; 48-hour cancellation. **Registration:** At house. **Fee:** RV (full), $25; water/electric, $23. **Parking:** At site.

FACILITIES

Number of RV-only Sites: 27. **Hookups:** Electric (30, 50 amps), water, sewer. **Each Site:** Picnic table. **Dump Station:** Yes. **Laundry:** Yes. **Pay Phone:** Yes. **Restrooms and Showers:** Yes. **Fuel:** No. **Propane:** No. **Internal Roads:** Gravel. **RV Service:** No. **Market:** Less than 5 mi. north. **Restaurant:** Less than 5 mi. north. **General Store:** No. **Vending:** No. **Swimming:** No. **Playground:** No. **Other:** Modem hookup, pavilion. **Activities:** Self-guiding tours. **Nearby Attractions:** Bothwell Lodge, Silver Dollar City. **Additional Information:** Sedalia Area Chamber of Commerce, (800) 827-5295, (660) 826-2222.

RESTRICTIONS

Pets: On leash, cleaned up after. **Fires:** Grill only. **Alcoholic Beverages:** At sites. **Vehicle Maximum Length:** No limit.

TO GET THERE

From the junction of Hwy. 50 and Hwy. 65, turn south onto Hwy. 65 and go 2.8 mi. Turn right at the sign into the entrance and follow the gravel drive around to the house.

SPRINGFIELD   MAP, C-2
Travelers Park Campground

425 South Trailview Rd., 65802. T: (417) 866-4226.

🚐 ★★★★   ⛺ ★★★★

Beauty: ★★★★★	Site Privacy: ★★★★
Spaciousness: ★★★★★	Quiet: ★★★
Security: ★★★★	Cleanliness: ★★★★
Insect Control: ★★★★	Facilities: ★★★

This campground is surrounded by trees, and some of the sites have tree cover, providing desirable shade in the summer months. Sites are unnumbered, making it a little hard to figure out which site is which. Four RV sites in the northwest corner are completely forested, which makes them very desirable. On the north side of the campground are 72-foot back-ins that back to fields with a natural, "wild" feel. There are 30 pull-through sites. Five sites in the middle of the campground are 90–110-foot pull-throughs with loads of space. The two westernmost sites are well shaded and are some of the most desirable sites in the entire park. In the southeast corner are RV sites in an open field that can accommodate rigs of any size. In the same corner are tent sites with exceptionally nice grass and a number of large shade trees.

BASICS

Operated By: Winfred & Maxine Short. **Open:** All year. **Site Assignment:** Upon registration; verbal reservations OK. **Registration:** At office; late arrivals select available site & pay in the morning or use drop box. **Fee:** RV, $20; tent, $15; checks, no credits cards. **Parking:** At site.

FACILITIES

Number of RV-only Sites: 33. **Number of Tent-only Sites:** Undesignated sites. **Hookups:** Electric (30 amps), water, sewer. **Each Site:** Picnic table. **Dump Station:** No (sewer at all sites). **Laundry:** Yes. **Pay Phone:** No. **Restrooms and Showers:** Yes. **Fuel:** No. **Propane:** No. **Internal Roads:** Gravel. **RV Service:** Next door. **Market:** 4 mi. east.

Restaurant: 4 mi. east. **General Store:** No. **Vending:** No. **Swimming:** Pool. **Playground:** No. **Other:** Game room. **Activities:** Golf. **Nearby Attractions:** Bass Pro Shop, golf course, tours, Dy Center, Fantastic Caverns, Japanese Stroll Garden. **Additional Information:** Springfield CVB Tourist Information Center, (800) 678-8767, (417) 881-5300.

RESTRICTIONS

Pets: On leash, cleaned up after. **Fires:** Grill only. **Alcoholic Beverages:** At sites. **Vehicle Maximum Length:** 42 ft. **Other:** See rule sheet upon arrival.

TO GET THERE

From I-44 (Exit 72), on west side of Hwy. overpass, take the first left onto Outer Rd. and go 0.5 mi. The campground is at the end of this dead-end road.

ST. JAMES   MAP, B-3
Pheasant Acres

20279 Hwy. 8, 65559. T: (573) 265-5149.

🚐 ★★★★   ⛺ ★★★★

Beauty: ★★★★★	Site Privacy: ★★★★★
Spaciousness: ★★★★	Quiet: ★★★★★
Security: ★★★★★	Cleanliness: ★★★★★
Insect Control: ★★★★	Facilities: ★★

RV sites in this campground are back-ins that range from 36 to 54 feet in length and are 35 feet wide. Sites 1–10 are in a strip along the west side. These sites are well shaded and back to a line of trees. In front of these spaces is a grassy field with some lovely flowers, bushes, and other vegetation. Site 10 has a large amount of space and is farthest from the entrance. Sites 12–18 are located on the inner loop of the internal road. All of these sites are quite decent. Sites 19–21 lie between the restrooms and a barn. They are a little less roomy, but back to woods and are otherwise comfortable. The tenting area lies under magnificent oaks and has a thick grass cover. The area is surrounded on two sides by woods, but, on the downside, there is some slope. The restrooms are located in a mobile home near the tenting area. It is very clean and comfortable, and the showers even have a large dry area for clothes and a towel.

BASICS

Operated By: Chuck & Diana Kesler. **Open:** All year. **Site Assignment:** Depends on site availability; verbal reservations OK. **Registration:** At office; late arrivals use drop box. **Fee:** RV (full), $18; electric, $15; tent, $12. **Parking:** At site.

FACILITIES

Number of RV-only Sites: 20. **Number of Tent-only Sites:** 5. **Hookups:** Electric (30 amps), water, sewer. **Each Site:** Picnic table, grill. **Dump Station:** No (sewer at 15 sites). **Laundry:** No. **Pay Phone:** No. **Restrooms and Showers:** Yes. **Fuel:** No. **Propane:** No. **Internal Roads:** Gravel. **RV Service:** No. **Market:** 5 mi. west. **Restaurant:** 2 mi. east or west. **General Store:** No. **Vending:** No. **Swimming:** No. **Playground:** No. **Other:** Borders conservation area, wood, pavilion. **Activities:** Hiking, float trips, basketball. **Nearby Attractions:** Wineries, Maramec Spring Park, Maramec

Museum. **Additional Information:** Rolla Chamber of Commerce, (573) 364-3577.

RESTRICTIONS

Pets: On leash, cleaned up after. **Fires:** Grill only. **Alcoholic Beverages:** At sites. **Vehicle Maximum Length:** 40 ft. **Other:** Quiet enforced.

TO GET THERE

From I-44 (Exit 195), turn south and go 6 mi. on Hwy. 8. Turn left at the sign into the entrance. (Campers would be advised to drive slowly, as the sign is small and the entrance a little narrow.)

STOCKTON   MAP, B-2
Orleans Trail

reserve america

16435 E. Stockton Lake Dr., 65785.
T: (417) 276-6948; www.reserveamerica.com.

🚐 ★★★★   ⛺ ★★★★

Beauty: ★★★   Site Privacy: ★★★
Spaciousness: ★★★   Quiet: ★★★★★
Security: ★★★★★   Cleanliness: ★★★★
Insect Control: ★★★   Facilities: ★★★

Orleans Trail Campground is located on Stockton Lake in southwest Missouri. The Stockton Lake area offers many recreational opportunities, including fishing, hunting, camping, sailing, boating, and scuba diving. Stockton Lake, one of the Ozarks' best-kept secrets, is located on the Sac River in Southwest Missouri, tucked into the foothills of the scenic Ozark Mountain range. Its pristine waters are home to several species of fish, including small- and large-mouth bass, crappie, white bass, walleye, catfish, and sunfish, to name a few. In addition to great fishing, Stockton Lake is a popular choice for the sailing enthusiast. Orleans Trail Park consists of a campground with 118 campsites, three shower houses, two dump stations, boat ramp, and a swimming beach. A group camp area is available with 12 electric sites, and a small shelter house. Five of the basic sites are located in the south campground near the equestrian trailhead, where horses can be kept. The Orleans Trail Marina is located nearby with camping and full marina services available.

BASICS

Operated By: U.S. Army Corps of Engineers. **Open:** May 12–Sept. 10. **Site Assignment:** Reservations must be made at least 3 days in advance. **Registration:** At office. **Fee:** Single, $10–$12; group, $85–$110. **Parking:** At site.

FACILITIES

Number of Multipurpose Sites: 444. **Hookups:** Yes. **Dump Station:** Yes. **Laundry:** No. **Pay Phone:** Yes. **Restrooms and Showers:** Yes. **Fuel:** No. **Propane:** No. **Internal Roads:** Paved, gravel. **RV Service:** No. **Market:** No. **Restaurant:** No. **General Store:** No. **Vending:** No. **Swimming:** Yes. **Playground:** No. **Activities:** Fishing, hunting, camping, sailing, boating, scuba diving.

RESTRICTIONS

Pets: Pets must be restrained or on a leash at all times while in developed recreation areas. **Fires:** In fire rings, stoves, grills, or fireplaces provided for that purpose. **Alcoholic Beverages:** Not allowed. **Vehicle Maximum Length:** Call ahead.

TO GET THERE

From Stockton, take Hwy. 39 south 0.5 mi. to RB Road; east 0.5 mi.; right on Blake St., 0.5 mi. to park area.

SULLIVAN   MAP, B-3
Native Experience Ecosystem Base Camp

1451 East Springfield, 63080. T: (573) 468-8750.

🚐 ★★★★   ⛺ ★★★★★

Beauty: ★★★★   Site Privacy: ★★★★
Spaciousness: ★★★★   Quiet: ★★★★
Security: ★★★★★   Cleanliness: ★★★★★
Insect Control: ★★★★   Facilities: ★★★★★

More than just a campground, Native Experience is a philosophy. Proprietor Keith Campbell envisions creating a natural and ecologically sustainable campground where travelers and adventurers converge for shared experiences. The campground is situated on Historic Rte. 66 and close to a number of recreation areas, which attracts travelers and adventurers alike. All sites are well shaded, with grassy sites laid out in a loop. There are 20 pull-through sites. Sites 1–17 are 75-to-100-foot pull-throughs (the largest are sites 10–17). Sites 19 and 20 are even longer, at 120 feet and 80 feet respectively. Running in a row from north to south, sites 24–36 are 50 by 36-foot back-ins. (Sites 22 and 23 can pull through if the opposite site is vacant.) The tenting area is north of RV site 36. Surrounded by woods, the area is also well forested and protects tenters from both sun and rain. All tent sites are located on the inside of the looped interior road. Campers are encouraged to enjoy a "native experience" in Sullivan, and should feel free to ask the knowledgeable owner about natural recreation opportunities in the area.

BASICS

Operated By: Keith Campbell. **Open:** Earth Day (Apr. 23)–Halloween (Oct. 31). **Site Assignment:** Depends on site availability; verbal reservations OK. **Registration:** At office; late arrivals use drop box (honor system). **Fee:** RV (full), $25; electric, $20; tent, $15; backpack, $10. **Parking:** At site.

FACILITIES

Number of RV-only Sites: 36. **Number of Tent-only Sites:** 20. **Hookups:** Electric (30 amps), water, sewer. **Each Site:** Picnic table, fire pit. **Dump Station:** Yes. **Laundry:** Yes. **Pay Phone:** Yes. **Restrooms and Showers:** Yes. **Fuel:** No. **Propane:** No. **Internal Roads:** Gravel, natural. **RV Service:** No. **Market:** 2 mi. west (at I-44). **Restaurant:** 2 mi. west (at I-44). **General Store:** No. **Vending:** No. **Swimming:** Pool. **Playground:** Yes. **Other:** Dog walk, cabin, caving, adventure tours, outfitting, base camp for skydivers. **Activities:** Caving,

swimming, hiking, kayaking, biking, skydiving, adventure tours. **Nearby Attractions:** Meremac State Park, Rte. 66. **Additional Information:** Sullivan Area Chamber of Commerce, (573) 468-3314.

RESTRICTIONS

Pets: On leash, cleaned up after. **Fires:** Grill only. **Alcoholic Beverages:** At sites. **Vehicle Maximum Length:** No limit. No semis. **Other:** No ATVs/dirt bikes, no generators.

TO GET THERE

From I-44 (Exit 226), turn south onto Hwy. 185 and go 0.25 mi. Turn left onto Service Rd. (first left after gas station complex) and go 1.4 mi. Turn left at the sign into the entrance (Historic Rte. 66).

VAN BUREN   MAP, C-3
Alley Spring

reserve america

P.O. Box 490, 63965. T: (573) 323-4236;
www.reserveamerica.com.

🚐 ★★★★   ⛺ ★★★★

Beauty: ★★★★   Site Privacy: ★★★★
Spaciousness: ★★★★   Quiet: ★★★
Security: ★★★★★   Cleanliness: ★★★★
Insect Control: ★★★   Facilities: ★★★

There are many water recreational activities available at Big Spring National park ranging from canoeing to tubing and swimming. Fishing is also a very popular. The town of Eminence is 5 miles east and offers restaurants, outdoor supplies, horseback riding, and canoe rental concessionaires. Historic and picturesque Alley Mill and the scenic Alley Spring are nearby. A short walk from the campground leads to a popular swimming area on the Jacks Fork River. The river is crystal clear and spring fed, cool and refreshing on a hot summer day. The campground has flush toilets and free hot showers available. Ranger-led campfire programs are offered in the campground amphitheater during the summer months. Ranger-led interpretive activities are available at the historic Alley Mill. Alley was home, farm, and school for people who lived here a century ago. Dances, baseball games, and roller skating were all part of Alley's busier days. John Knotts purchased the 80-acre site in 1902 and diversified the enterprises to include a well-stocked store and blacksmith shop. The milling operation was expanded to include cornmeal production as well as flour. Alley's school in 1903 had an enrollment of 42 students. Church services were also held at the schoolhouse. Conrad Hug became the owner in 1912, and made Alley one of Missouri's first resorts, known as Crystal Spring Town Site. Glider swings for tourists were scattered around the spring and July Fourth was one of many festive celebrations. We may not know their names, but the story of Alley wouldn't be complete without mentioning the farmers who brought grain and timber to be milled. It is easy to imagine a "spit and whittle club," as folks swapped fishing tales and caught up on local news. There were an even earlier people at

Alley, yet the records of their lives are vague. Archeological evidence suggests that Native Americans camped throughout the area. Alley Spring with its natural abundance of fresh water and game was used as a camp some ten thousand years ago! A mill was vital to community life, where grain was ground to provide the daily bread. The present building was constructed during 1893-1894 by George Washington McCaskill as a merchant mill. It was larger than most mills in the Jacks Fork area and replaced an earlier mill on this same site that was built by 1868. Originally unpainted, it was first painted white with green trim, then later the famous red color associated with Alley Mill today.

BASICS

Operated By: National Park Service. **Open:** All year. **Site Assignment:** Reservations must be made at least 7 days in advance; reservations accepted Apr. 15–Oct. 15. **Registration:** At registration office. **Fee:** Single, $14–$17; double, $30; group, $50–$100. **Parking:** At site.

FACILITIES

Number of Multipurpose Sites: 343. **Hookups:** None. **Each Site:** Call ahead. **Dump Station:** Yes. **Laundry:** No. **Pay Phone:** No. **Restrooms and Showers:** Yes. **Fuel:** No. **Propane:** No. **Internal Roads:** Paved. **RV Service:** No. **Market:** 5 mi. east. **Restaurant:** 6 mi. east. **General Store:** No. **Vending:** No. **Swimming:** Yes. **Playground:** No. **Activities:** Amphitheater, biking, bird-watching, boating, campfire programs, canoeing, fishing, hiking, horseback riding, hunting, photography, scuba diving, sightseeing, tubing, waterskiing, wildlife viewing, wind surfing.

RESTRICTIONS

Pets: Pets must be on a leash at all times. **Fires:** Allowed; Campfire Program. **Alcoholic Beverages:** Not allowed. **Vehicle Maximum Length:** Varies; call ahead. **Other:** All equipment must fit on site pad.

TO GET THERE

Alley Spring Campground is located 5 mi. west of Eminence. From the east on US 60, turn north on MO 19 in Winona. Continue north 12 mi. to Eminence. From Eminence, Alley Spring Campground is 5 min. west of MO 106. From Mountain View, go 19 mi. east on US 60 and turn north on CR E. Go north on CR E for 10 mi. to MO 106. Then, turn west on MO 106 and travel 2 mi. The Alley Spring Campground is on the south side of MO 106.

VAN BUREN   MAP, C-3
Big Spring Campground

reserve america

P.O. Box 490, 63965. T: (573) 323-4236; www.reserveamerica.com.

🚐 ★★★★   ⛺ ★★★★

Beauty: ★★★★   Site Privacy: ★★★★
Spaciousness: ★★★★   Quiet: ★★★★
Security: ★★★★★   Cleanliness: ★★★★
Insect Control: ★★★   Facilities: ★★★

Big Spring Campground is open year-round, but water is shut off Oct. 30–Apr. 15 to prevent frozen pipes. In off-season, campers will be directed to an open restroom or vault toilet, which may be a short distance from their campsite. Group sites are also closed in the off-season. There is no sewer hookup, but a dump station is available at the campground entrance. Canoeing, tubing, swimming, and fishing are popular activities here. The town of Van Buren is four miles north and offers restaurants, outdoor supplies, and tube-and-canoe rental concessionaires. The scenic Big Spring is nearby. Big Spring is the largest freshwater spring in North America and produces an outflow of 280 million gallons a day. The river is crystal clear and spring fed, cool and refreshing on a hot summer day. Ranger-led campfire programs are offered in the campground amphitheater during summer months, and Picnic Pavilion reservations are accepted year-round. Quiet hours are from 10 p.m. to 6 a.m.

BASICS

Operated By: National Park Service. **Open:** All year. **Site Assignment:** Reservations must be made 7 days in advance. **Registration:** At registration office. **Fee:** Family, $14; electric, $17; group, $100 (up to 45 people). **Parking:** At site.

FACILITIES

Number of Multipurpose Sites: 123. **Hookups:** Water, electric (50 amps). **Each Site:** Picnic table, fire ring. **Dump Station:** Yes. **Laundry:** No. **Pay Phone:** No. **Restrooms and Showers:** Yes, Apr. 15–Oct. 15. **Fuel:** No. **Propane:** No. **Internal Roads:** Paved. **RV Service:** No. **Market:** 4 mi. north. **Restaurant:** 5 mi. north. **General Store:** No. **Vending:** No. **Swimming:** Yes. **Playground:** No. **Activities:** Bird-watching, boating, campfire programs, canoeing, fishing, hiking, hunting, sightseeing, tubing, wildlife viewing. **Other:** Picnic pavilion, group sites, amphitheater.

RESTRICTIONS

Pets: Pets must be on a leash at all times. **Fires:** In ring; campfire program. **Alcoholic Beverages:** Not allowed. **Vehicle Maximum Length:** Varies; call ahead. **Other:** Group campsites are tent camping only, except at Round Spring, and are closed Oct. 30–Apr. 15. Water systems are turned off Oct. 30–Apr. 15. Diving from river bluffs is dangerous & can result in injury or death.

TO GET THERE

Big Spring Campground is located 4 mi. south of the town of Van Buren. Turn south on MO 103 and continue south for 4 mi. to the Big Spring unit of the park.

VAN BUREN   MAP, C-3
Round Spring

reserve america

P.O. Box 490, 63965. T: (573) 323-4236; www.reserveamerica.com.

🚐 ★★★★   ⛺ ★★★★

Beauty: ★★★★   Site Privacy: ★★★★
Spaciousness: ★★★★   Quiet: ★★★★
Security: ★★★★★   Cleanliness: ★★★★
Insect Control: ★★★   Facilities: ★★★★

Long before there was an Ozark National Scenic River ways, Missourians realized Round Spring was a treasure. In 1924 this scenic jewel near the banks of the Current River became one of Missouri's first state parks. Named for the shape of the pool from which it flows, Round Spring wells gently from the earth at a rate of 26 million gallons daily, flows through a fissure in the wall surrounding its pool, and meanders into the Current River. The main campground at Round Spring is beautiful. For a well-developed campground it's a surprisingly laid-back place. Sites are a little close together, but landscaping and thick woods make things feel fairly private. It's built into a hillside above the river, with many sites terraced above or below the camp road, thus creating a more isolated atmosphere. The paved road eliminates dust and the annoying crunch of tires on gravel.

BASICS

Operated By: National Park Service. **Open:** All year. **Site Assignment:** Reservations must be made 7 days in advance. **Registration:** At registration office. **Fee:** Parking: At site.

FACILITIES

Number of Multipurpose Sites: 234. **Hookups:** Yes. **Each Site:** Call ahead. **Dump Station:** Yes. **Laundry:** No. **Pay Phone:** No. **Restrooms and Showers:** Yes. **Fuel:** No. **Propane:** No. **Internal Roads:** Paved. **RV Service:** No. **Market:** No. **Restaurant:** 16 mi. south. **General Store:** No. **Vending:** No. **Swimming:** Yes. **Playground:** No. **Activities:** Amphitheater, biking, bird-watching, boating, campfire programs, canoeing, fishing, hiking, horseback riding, hunting, kayaking, photography, sightseeing, swimming, tubing, wildlife viewing.

RESTRICTIONS

Pets: Pets must be on a leash at all times. **Fires:** Allowed; Campfire Program. **Alcoholic Beverages:** Not allowed. **Vehicle Maximum Length:** Varies; call ahead. **Other:** Quiet hours 10 p.m.–6 a.m.; group sites are available in walk-in season only.

TO GET THERE

Round Spring Campground is located 16 mi. north of the town of Eminence on MO Hwy. 19.

WARSAW   MAP, B-2
Berry Bend Campground

reserve america

15968 Truman Rd., 65355-9603.
T: (660) 438-7318; www.reserveamerica.com.

🚐 ★★★★   ⛺ ★★★★

Beauty: ★★★★   Site Privacy: ★★
Spaciousness: ★★   Quiet: ★★
Security: ★★   Cleanliness: ★★★★
Insect Control: ★★★   Facilities: ★★★

Berry Bend Campground is located on the Osage Arm of Truman Reservoir, 9 miles southwest of Warsaw, Missouri. The park is covered with oak-hickory forest and is essentially a peninsula in a bend of the Osage River. The area is divided in half by a causeway with a campground and swimming beach to the south and a boat ramp, group picnic shelter, and equestrian area to the north. The park and surrounding area have interesting topography and natural beauty. Several campsites are offered with various hookups such as water and electric. Harry S. Truman Lake is located adjacent to the Lake of the Ozarks, a short drive north of Branson, Truman features excellent fishing, hunting, camping, hiking, and boating opportunities. Truman Lake also offers a regional visitor center and power plant exhibit area. Rugged hills, scenic bluffs, hardwood forest, and prairie offer some of the best scenery in the state.

BASICS

Operated By: U.S. Army Corps of Engineers. **Open:** All year. **Site Assignment:** Reservations must be made at least 4 days in advance. **Registration:** At office. **Fee:** Single, $16–$18. **Parking:** At site.

FACILITIES

Number of Multipurpose Sites: 538. **Hookups:** Yes. **Dump Station:** Yes. **Laundry:** Yes. **Pay Phone:** Yes. **Restrooms and Showers:** Yes. **Fuel:** No. **Propane:** No. **Internal Roads:** Paved. **RV Service:** No. **Market:** No. **Restaurant:** No. **General Store:** No. **Vending:** No. **Swimming:** Yes. **Playground:** Yes. **Activities:** Fishing, hunting, swimming, boating.

RESTRICTIONS

Pets: Pets must be restrained or on a leash at all times while in developed recreation areas. **Fires:** In fire rings, stoves, grills, or fireplaces provided for that purpose. **Alcoholic Beverages:** Not allowed. **Vehicle Maximum Length:** Call ahead.

TO GET THERE

Located in St. Clair County 10 mi. west of Warsaw. From Z Hwy., travel 2 mi. south on the Berry Bend Access Rd.

WARSAW   MAP, B-2
Berry Bend Equestrian Campground

reserve america

Rte. 2 Box 29A, 65355-9603. T: (660) 438-7317; www.reserveamerica.com.

🚐 ★★★★   ⛺ ★★★★

Beauty: ★★★   Site Privacy: ★★★
Spaciousness: ★★★   Quiet: ★★★
Security: ★★★   Cleanliness: ★★★★
Insect Control: ★★★   Facilities: ★★★

Berry Bend Equestrian Campground is located at Harry S. Truman Lake, which is forested with rocky hills and bluffs. The Berry Bend Equestrian Campground is an excellent fishing location. Visitors enjoy fishing, hunting, swimming, and boating. There are white-tailed deer and turkey and other animals and birds that live in and around the Berry Bend area, including raccoons, skunks, squirrels, turkey vultures, hawks, and ospreys, and during the winter months bald eagles can be seen. Harry S. Truman Lake is located adjacent to the Lake of the Ozarks, a short drive north of Branson. Truman features excellent fishing, hunting, camping, hiking, and boating opportunities. Truman Lake also offers a regional visitor center and power plant exhibit area. Rugged hills, scenic bluffs, hardwood forest and prairie offer some of the best scenery in the state. Berry Bend Equestrian Park is limited to equestrian users. Equestrian riders will find several miles of trails. Riders utilizing the trail for the day should access the trails from the Berry Bend #1 Picnic Shelter area. The trails are for hikers and equestrian use only.

BASICS

Operated By: U.S. Army Corps of Engineers. **Open:** All year. **Site Assignment:** Reservations must be made at least 4 days in advance. **Registration:** At office. **Fee:** Single, $16–$18; group, $25. **Parking:** At site.

FACILITIES

Number of Multipurpose Sites: 294. **Hookups:** Yes. **Dump Station:** Yes. **Laundry:** Yes. **Pay Phone:** Yes. **Restrooms and Showers:** Yes. **Fuel:** No. **Propane:** No. **Internal Roads:** Gravel. **RV Service:** No. **Market:** No. **Restaurant:** No. **General Store:** No. **Vending:** No. **Swimming:** Yes. **Playground:** Yes. **Activities:** Horseback riding, wildlife viewing.

RESTRICTIONS

Pets: Dogs must be on a 6-ft. leash. Campers must have their own horse. **Fires:** In fire rings, stoves, grills, or fireplaces provided for that purpose. **Alcoholic Beverages:** Not allowed. **Vehicle Maximum Length:** Call ahead.

TO GET THERE

Located in Benton County 10 mi. west of Warsaw. From Z Hwy., travel 2 mi. south on the Berry Bend Access Rd. For more information about Truman Lake, call (660) 438-7317.

WARSAW   MAP, B-2
Bucksaw Campground

reserve america

15968 Truman Rd., 65355-9603.
T: (660) 438-7318; www.reserveamerica.com.

🚐 ★★★★   ⛺ ★★★★

Beauty: ★★★   Site Privacy: ★★★
Spaciousness: ★★★   Quiet: ★★★★
Security: ★★★★   Cleanliness: ★★★★
Insect Control: ★★★   Facilities: ★★★★

Bucksaw Campground is located on the Grand River Arm of Truman Reservoir, 11 miles southeast of Clinton, Missouri, near Harry S. Truman Lake. The campground has a lot of trees and open grass areas. Bucksaw Point Marina is located within the park area. The Bucksaw area is an excellent fishing location. Popular activities include fishing, hunting, camping, swimming, and boating. Animals that live in and around the area include whitetail deer, turkeys, raccoons, skunks, squirrels, turkey vultures, hummingbirds, hawks, and ospreys. Bald eagles can be seen in the winter months. The Harry S. Truman Llake area is forested, with rocky hills and rock bluffs extending into the lake. This is the birthplace home of the only Missourian ever elected President of the United States—Harry S Truman.

BASICS

Operated By: U.S. Army Corps of Engineers. **Open:** All year. **Site Assignment:** Reservations must be made at least 4 days in advance. **Registration:** At office. **Fee:** Single, $6. **Parking:** At site.

FACILITIES

Number of Multipurpose Sites: 622. **Hookups:** Yes. **Dump Station:** Yes. **Laundry:** Yes. **Pay Phone:** Yes. **Restrooms and Showers:** Yes. **Fuel:** No. **Propane:** No. **Internal Roads:** Paved. **RV Service:** No. **Market:** No. **Restaurant:** No. **General Store:** No. **Vending:** No. **Swimming:** Yes. **Playground:** Yes. **Activities:** Fishing, hunting, camping, swimming, boating.

RESTRICTIONS

Pets: Pets must be restrained or on a leash at all times while in developed recreation areas. **Fires:** In fire rings, stoves, grills, or fireplaces provided for that purpose. **Alcoholic Beverages:** Not allowed. **Vehicle Maximum Length:** Call ahead.

TO GET THERE

Located in Henry County 13 mi. southeast of Clinton, MO. From Hwy. 7, travel south 3 mi. on Hwy. U. Stay on the paved road and follow signs into the campground.

WARSAW   MAP, B-2
Sparrowfoot

reserve america

Rte. 2 Box 29A, 65355-9603. T: (660) 438-7317;
www.reserveamerica.com.

🚐 ★★★★   ⛺ ★★★★

Beauty: ★★★★   Site Privacy: ★★★
Spaciousness: ★★★   Quiet: ★★★★
Security: ★★★★   Cleanliness: ★★★★
Insect Control: ★★★   Facilities: ★★★★

Sparrowfoot Park is located at Harry S. Truman Lake in a mixed forest and grassland area with some rocky bluffs extending into the lake. The area is an excellent catfish and crappie fishing location. Harry S. Truman Lake is located adjacent to the Lake of the Ozarks, a short drive north of Branson. Truman features excellent fishing, hunting, camping, hiking, and boating opportunities. Truman Lake also offers a regional visitor center and power plant exhibit area. Rugged hills, scenic bluffs, hardwood forest, and prairie offer some of the best scenery in the state. The lake was named after Harry S. Truman, the 33rd President of the United States (1945–53). Popular activities include fishing, hunting, camping, swimming, and boating. In addition to the 48 campsites, the park also has three reservable day-use group shelters. There are white-tailed deer and turkey and other animals and birds that live in and around the Sparrowfoot area, including raccoons, skunks, squirrels, turkey vultures, hummingbirds, hawks, and ospreys. Bald eagles can be seen during the winter months.

BASICS
Operated By: U.S. Army Corps of Engineers.
Open: All year. **Site Assignment:** Reservations must be made at least 4 days in advance. **Registration:** At office. **Fee:** Single, $12–$18; group, $20. **Parking:** At site.

FACILITIES
Number of Multipurpose Sites: 326. **Hookups:** Yes. **Dump Station:** Yes. **Laundry:** Yes. **Pay Phone:** Yes. **Restrooms and Showers:** Yes. **Fuel:** No. **Propane:** No. **Internal Roads:** Paved, gravel. **RV Service:** No. **Market:** No. **Restaurant:** No. **General Store:** No. **Vending:** No. **Swimming:** Yes. **Playground:** Yes. **Activities:** Fishing, hunting, camping, swimming, boating.

RESTRICTIONS
Pets: Pets must be restrained or on a leash at all times while in developed recreation areas. **Fires:** In designated areas. **Alcoholic Beverages:** Not allowed. **Vehicle Maximum Length:** Call ahead.

TO GET THERE
Located in Henry County, about 4 mi. southeast of Clinton. From Hwy. 13, travel about 1 mi. east on SE 450 Rd. and follow signs into the park.

WARSAW   MAP, B-2
Talley Bend

reserve america

Rte. 2 Box 29A, 65355-9603. T: (417) 644-2446;
www.reserveamerica.com.

🚐 ★★★★   ⛺ ★★★★

Beauty: ★★★   Site Privacy: ★★★
Spaciousness: ★★★   Quiet: ★★★★★
Security: ★★★★★   Cleanliness: ★★★★
Insect Control: ★★★   Facilities: ★★★★

Talley Bend Campground is located at Harry S. Truman Lake. The park is forested with rocky hills and rock bluffs extending into the lake. Harry S. Truman Lake is located adjacent to the Lake of the Ozarks, a short drive north of Branson. Truman features excellent fishing, hunting, camping, hiking, and boating opportunities. Truman Lake also offers a regional visitor center and power plant exhibit area. Rugged hills, scenic bluffs, hardwood forest, and prairie offer some of the best scenery in the state. The lake was named after Harry S. Truman, the 33rd President of the United States (1945–53). The Talley Bend area is an excellent cat fishing location. Visitors enjoy fishing, hunting, and boating. Animals that live in and around the Talley Bend area include white-tailed deer, turkey, raccoons, skunks, squirrels, turkey vultures, hummingbirds, hawks, and ospreys.

BASICS
Operated By: U.S. Army Corps of Engineers.
Open: All year. **Site Assignment:** Reservations must be made at least 4 days in advance. **Registration:** At office. **Fee:** Single, $6–$18. **Parking:** At site.

FACILITIES
Number of Multipurpose Sites: 396. **Hookups:** Yes. **Dump Station:** Yes. **Laundry:** Yes. **Pay Phone:** Yes. **Restrooms and Showers:** Yes. **Fuel:** No. **Propane:** No. **Internal Roads:** Paved, gravel. **RV Service:** No. **Market:** No. **Restaurant:** No. **General Store:** No. **Vending:** No. **Swimming:** No. **Playground:** Yes. **Activities:** Fishing, hunting, boating.

RESTRICTIONS
Pets: Pets must be restrained or on a leash at all times while in developed recreation areas. **Fires:** In fire rings, stoves, grills. **Alcoholic Beverages:** Not allowed. **Vehicle Maximum Length:** Call ahead.

TO GET THERE
Located in St. Clair County about 13 mi. northeast of Osceola. From Hwy. 13, travel east on Hwy. C for 6 mi. Follow signs into the campground.

WARSAW   MAP, B-2
Thibaut Point

reserve america

Rte. 2 Box 29A, 65355-9603. T: (660) 438-7317;
www.reserveamerica.com.

🚐 ★★★★   ⛺ ★★★★

Beauty: ★★★   Site Privacy: ★★★
Spaciousness: ★★★   Quiet: ★★★★★
Security: ★★★★★   Cleanliness: ★★★★
Insect Control: ★★★   Facilities: ★★★★

Thibaut Point Park is located at Harry S. Truman Lake. The park is forested with rocky hills and rock bluffs extending into the lake. Harry S. Truman Lake is located adjacent to the Lake of the Ozarks, a short drive north of Branson. Truman features excellent fishing, hunting, camping, hiking, and boating opportunities. Truman Lake also offers a regional visitor center and power plant exhibit area. Rugged hills, scenic bluffs, hardwood forest, and prairie offer some of the best scenery in the state. The lake was named after Harry S. Truman, the 33rd President of the United States (1945–53). The Thibaut Point area is an excellent fishing location. In addition to the campsites, three group camps and two day-use group shelters may be reserved. Popular activities include fishing, hunting, swimming, and boating. There are white-tailed deer and turkey and other animals and birds that live in and around the Thibaut Point area, including raccoons, skunks, squirrels, turkey vultures, hummingbirds, hawks, and ospreys. During the winter months, bald eagles can be seen.

BASICS
Operated By: U.S. Army Corps of Engineers.
Open: All year. **Site Assignment:** Reservations must be made at least 4 days in advance. **Registration:** At office. **Fee:** Single, $6–$18; group, $50–$100. **Parking:** At site.

FACILITIES
Number of Multipurpose Sites: 150. **Hookups:** Yes. **Dump Station:** Yes. **Laundry:** Yes. **Pay Phone:** Yes. **Restrooms and Showers:** Yes. **Fuel:** No. **Propane:** No. **Internal Roads:** Paved, gravel. **RV Service:** No. **Market:** No. **Restaurant:** No. **General Store:** No. **Vending:** No. **Swimming:** Yes. **Playground:** No. **Activities:** Boating, fishing, hiking, hunting, wildlife viewing.

RESTRICTIONS
Pets: Pets must be restrained or on a leash at all times while in developed recreation areas. **Fires:** In fire rings, stoves, grills. **Alcoholic Beverages:** Not allowed. **Vehicle Maximum Length:** Call ahead. **Other:** All equipment must fit on the site pad. Vehicles park in developed areas only.

TO GET THERE
Located in Benton County, 8 mi. north of Warsaw. From Hwy. 65, travel west on Hwy. T for 3 mi., turn south on Road 218 (road is gravel) and follow for 1 mi.

WILLIAMSVILLE   MAP, C-3
Lake Wappapello State Park

HC 2 Box 102, 63967.
T: (573) 297-3232 or (800) 334-6946;
www.mostateparks.com/lakewappapello.htm.

🚐 ★★★★	⛺ ★★★★★
Beauty: ★★★★★	Site Privacy: ★★★★★
Spaciousness: ★★★★★	Quiet: ★★★★★
Security: ★★★★★	Cleanliness: ★★★★
Insect Control: ★★★	Facilities: ★★★★

This state park offers two campgrounds—one by the lake and the other perched on a ridge in the woods. All sites in the lakeside campground are grassy, shaded sites with cement slabs and a view of the lake. Closest to the lake are 57, 58, 63, 65, and 67–73. Sites 55 and 74 are farthest from the lake and have more of a forested feel than a lakeside feel. Sites 65, 71, 74, and 79 are 75-foot pull-throughs. Sites 61 and 62 are 60-foot doubles. The rideside campground has 60-foot gravel back-ins that back to forest as well as some colossal (110 feet) pull-throughs, such as 38. The east side of this campground has a partial view of the lake, while the west side is pure forest. Sites 7 and 8 are doubles. The remotest sites are 23 and 24, which are located at the end of a roundabout. Lake Wappapello State Park offers the best of both worlds: forest and lakeside sites. Both those wishing to play in the water and those wishing to relax in the shade will find it an appealing campsite.

BASICS

Operated By: Missouri Dept. of Natural Resources. **Open:** All year; limited services Nov.–Mar. **Site Assignment:** Reservations, call (877) 422-6766; walk-ins accepted. **Registration:** Fees will be collected by ranger or pay at office. **Fee:** Water/electric, $14; tent, $8; check, V, MC, D. **Parking:** At site, do not park on grass (boat or trailer OK).

FACILITIES

Number of Multipurpose Sites: 81. **Hookups:** Electric (30, 50 amps). **Each Site:** Picnic table, grill, lantern post. **Dump Station:** Yes. **Laundry:** Yes. **Pay Phone:** Yes. **Restrooms and Showers:** Yes. **Fuel:** No. **Propane:** No. **Internal Roads:** Paved. **RV Service:** No. **Market:** 18 mi. to Poplar Bluff. **Restaurant:** 5 mi. to Chaonia Landing. **General Store:** Limited. **Vending:** No. **Swimming:** Lake. **Playground:** Yes. **Other:** 3 boat ramps, 8 cabins, amphitheater, firewood, picnic shelters, horse trails, hiking trails. **Activities:** Fishing, boating, swimming, horseback riding, hiking. **Nearby Attractions:** Lake Wappapello. **Additional Information:** Poplar Bluff Chamber of Commerce, (573) 785-7761.

RESTRICTIONS

Pets: On leash, cleaned up after. **Fires:** Grill only. **Alcoholic Beverages:** At sites, no glass bottles. **Vehicle Maximum Length:** No limit. **Other:** No fireworks, no digging, no metal detectors, no hunting, visitors must leave by 10 p.m., no breaking of tree limbs.

TO GET THERE

From the junction of Hwy. 67 and Hwy. 172, turn east onto Hwy. 172 and go 8 mi. The office is on the left.

Montana

As with much of the United States, Montana was first inhabited by Native Americans, including the Arapaho, Assiniboine, and Cheyenne. French trappers made inroads into the land as early as 1740, followed some years later by the Lewis and Clark expedition in 1805.

Most of what is now Montana was turned over to the United States in the Louisiana Purchase of 1803. The Jesuits and various trading companies attempted to form permanent settlements here, but not until gold was discovered in the 1860s did great numbers of people begin to settle in the area. The open land in the eastern parts of the state drew another type of pioneer who helped settle the land—cattle farmers.

The settling of Montana was difficult. Native Americans did not give up their land willingly; pioneers appropriating Native American land were under constant threat of raids, which did not abate until the Wounded Knee Massacre in 1890. Settlers then caused their own strife, as rancher fought rancher during the infamous range wars in the late 1800s.

In the twentieth century, drilling for oil joined mining as a major source of revenue for the state, but people also recognized the need to preserve natural resources. In addition to **Glacier National Park,** many state parks and historic sites were created to preserve Montana's natural and cultural heritage.

Montana is made up of six different regions, each with a distinct history and recreational offerings. The most western region, glacier country, is home to Glacier National Park, the **Flathead Indian Reservation,** and the town of **Missoula,** seen by many as the cultural, retail, and medical hub of western Montana. Home of the **University of Montana,** Missoula is the gateway to the **Flathead** and **Bitterroot valleys.**

The adjacent gold country is similar in geography to glacier country. The many mountains and valleys create a beautiful landscape, and numerous recreational possibilities abound, from hiking the **Continental Divide Trail** to skiing down spectacular slopes. The two largest towns in this region, **Butte** and **Helena** (the capital), originated as mining towns. Many attractions in this area still reflect that heritage, including Butte's **World Museum of Mining,** where visitors can see an authentic reproduction of an 1890s mining camp and can visit the numerous ghost towns around Helena.

To the west of Gold Country is Montana's most famous region, **Yellowstone** country. Although over 4 million people visit the nation's first national park each year, few venture north of the park, much to their loss. Those who do will find **Bozeman.** Located in the Gallatin Valley, this city is a significant agricultural center as well as home to the largest university in Montana's system. Several annual festivals enliven this college town, including the **Montana Winter Fair** and the **Sweet Pea Festival.** The region also hosts two key ski resorts—**Bridger Bowl** and **Big Sky.**

For those interested in raft trips, **Russell** country is the place to visit. Rivers of all difficulty are paddled here, including the **Madison, Gallatin, Yellowstone,** and the river that carried Lewis and Clark across the state, the **Missouri.** Lewis and Clark's progress west was stymied at the "great falls" along the Missouri, site now of Montana's third largest city. **Great Falls** is known as the Electric City for its many hydroelectric dams. While here, visitors can swing by the **Lewis and Clark National Historic Trail Interpretive Center** or by **Malmstrom Air Force Base,** location of the nation's first **Minuteman Missile Complex.**

Much of Lewis and Clark's journey through Montana passed through the **Missouri River Country.** This region is home to **Fort Belknap** and **Fort Peck Indian reservations** as well as the 1.1-million-acre **Charles M. Russell National Wildlife Refuge.** Also known as the **Montana Badlands,** this area was once a lush wetland where dinosaurs roamed, but the land now provides a wealth of fossils from the dry landscape.

Located in the southeastern part of the state, **Custer** country is probably most famous for one of the worst U.S. military defeats. The **Battle of Little Bighorn,** sometimes referred to as Custer's Last Stand, took place not far from present-day **Billings.** While other towns arose (and died) because of mining, Billings's existence is due to the railroad. Today it is a major shipping point for cattle and other agricultural products as well as home of **Montana State University–Billings.** Cultural offerings include the **Yellowstone Art Museum** and the **Western Heritage Museum.**

ALDER   MAP, C-2
Alder/Virginia City KOA

Hwy. 287, 0.25 mi. east of Alder, 59710.
T: (406) 842-5677 or (800) 562-1898;
www.koa.com.

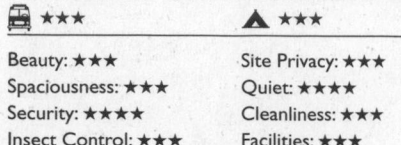

★★★   ▲ ★★★

Beauty: ★★★	Site Privacy: ★★★
Spaciousness: ★★★	Quiet: ★★★★
Security: ★★★★	Cleanliness: ★★★
Insect Control: ★★★	Facilities: ★★★

Over one hundred years ago, people visited this valley for one reason—gold. Not far from this KOA campground, Alder Gulch was one of the largest producers of gold in Montana. Modern-day visitors can still pan for gold or search for semi-precious stones while using this campground as a base. This campground is small, with 32 RV sites (hookups include electric, water, sewer, and some phones) and 18 tent-only sites. The sites are all grass, and all are pull-through sites. A daily pancake breakfast and ice-cream social are available, and Sundays are steak nights. Several accessible rivers means outstanding fishing, and the campground is located in the heart of elk country—good news for hunters. Those leaning more toward history may want to visit nearby Virginia and Nevada City. Visitors can wander through an historic log-cabin village, or take an "historic" stage coach or steam engine ride through the landscape. Several festivals and gatherings occur locally, including Gold Rush Fever Days and the Cowboy and Indian Western Antique & Collectible Trade Show, so reservations are recommended far in advance.

BASICS

Operated By: Ed & Andy. **Open:** All year. **Site Assignment:** Reservations (800) 562-1898. **Registration:** At general store. **Fee:** RV, $28–$32; tent, $20. **Parking:** At site.

FACILITIES

Number of RV-only Sites: 32. **Number of Tent-only Sites:** 18. **Hookups:** Electric (20, 30, 50 amps), water, sewer, phone. **Each Site:** Picnic tables, grated fire pits. **Dump Station:** Yes. **Laundry:** Yes. **Pay Phone:** Yes. **Restrooms and Showers:** Yes. **Fuel:** Yes. **Propane:** Yes. **Internal Roads:** Gravel. **RV Service:** Sheridan. **Market:** Sheridan. **Restaurant:** On-site (seasonal). **General Store:** Yes. **Vending:** In store. **Swimming:** No. **Playground:** Yes. **Other:** 1 cabin. **Activities:** Fishing (rainbow & brown trout), volleyball, horseshoes, hiking, rock hunting, pond, hunting (elk, whitetail & mule deer, antelope, bear, moose, mountain goat, Rocky Mountain big-horn sheep). **Nearby Attractions:** 9 mi. west of Virginia City, Nevada City, Museums, gold panning, tours. **Additional Information:** Virginia City Chamber of Commerce, (800) 829-2969.

RESTRICTIONS

Pets: On leash. **Fires:** Fire pit only. **Alcoholic Beverages:** Allowed. **Vehicle Maximum Length:** No limit.

TO GET THERE

Located 0.25 mi. east of Alder on Hwy. 287.

BELT   MAP, B-2
Fort Ponderosa Family Campground and RV Park

568 Armington Rd., P. O. Box 425, 59412.
T: (406) 277-3232.

★★★★   ▲ ★★★

Beauty: ★★★★	Site Privacy: ★★★
Spaciousness: ★★★	Quiet: ★★★★
Security: ★★★★	Cleanliness: ★★★★
Insect Control: ★★★★	Facilities: ★★★★

Fort Ponderosa Family Campground and RV Park is conveniently located directly off I-90 in Belt. The campground is situated on seven acres, with large shade trees and a blue ribbon trout stream. The campsites are level, gravel, and offer both pull-through and back-in sites. The grass is green and well kept. In addition to the campsites, there are several mobile homes as well as the owner's home. Facilities include a large playground, pavilion, five-hole golf coarse, and room for children to play and ride bicycles. While it is well used, the campground is nice and peaceful. The community of Belt is a short drive from Great Falls, and there are a variety of outdoor activities in the area. Summer days are warm, the evenings cool, and the owner offers delightful conversation.

BASICS

Operated By: Dana Ratliff. **Open:** May 1–Dec. 1. **Site Assignment:** By reservation. **Registration:** At camp office. **Fee:** RV, $22–$25; tent, $20. **Parking:** At site.

FACILITIES

Number of RV-only Sites: 42. **Hookups:** Electric (30, 50 amps), water, sewer. **Each Site:** Picnic table. **Dump Station:** Yes. **Laundry:** Yes. **Pay Phone:** Yes. **Restrooms and Showers:** Yes. **Fuel:** No. **Propane:** Yes. **Internal Roads:** Gravel, in good condition. **RV Service:** 20 mi. west in Great Falls. **Market:** 2 mi. in town. **Restaurant:** 2 mi. in town. **General Store:** Limited w/ gift shop. **Vending:** In store. **Swimming:** No. **Playground:** Yes. **Other:** 2 covered pavilions, 1 w/ barbecue, gift shop. **Activities:** Mini-golf, swimming in Belt Creek, fishing (German, brown, & rainbow trout). **Nearby Attractions:** More fly fishing, fishing guide services, float trips, horseback riding, Smith River, Fort Benton, Great Falls, Sluice Box hiking Area, Clark National Forest, Memorial Falls. **Additional Information:** Great Falls Chamber of Commerce, (406) 761-4434.

RESTRICTIONS

Pets: On leash. **Fires:** Fire ring only. **Alcoholic Beverages:** Allowed. **Vehicle Maximum Length:** No limit.

TO GET THERE

20 mi. southeast on Hwys. 87/89 (Armington Jct.), then 1 mi. north (follow signs).

BILLINGS   MAP, B-3
Yellowstone River RV Park and Campground

309 Garden Ave., 59101.
T: (406) 259-0878 or (800) 654-0878;
www.yellowstonerivercampground.com.

★★★★   ▲ ★★★

Beauty: ★★★★	Site Privacy: ★★★★
Spaciousness: ★★★★	Quiet: ★★★★
Security: ★★★★	Cleanliness: ★★★★
Insect Control: ★★★	Facilities: ★★★

Often called the "Magic City," Billings is where the rustic adventure of the Wild West and the conveniences of a modern city converge. The town provides a number of activities for the passing traveler. The city is surrounded by six mountain ranges and offers a fine view of Montana scenery. Located on the Yellowstone River, this campground is beautifully landscaped, the sites are arranged in rows, and most are shaded by cottonwoods. Sites are spacious, and the RV sites are separated from the tent sites, but with little distinction. The nice lawn, clean surroundings, and quiet stillness contribute to a pleasing experience. If you're lucky, you may spot deer at this peaceful campground. River access and a nature trail compliment the campground, and amenities make this a more than comfortable stay. A large on-site antiques display is a unique addition for avid collectors and curious visitors. Be sure to visit historical area attractions to give yourself a taste of the area's rich past.

BASICS

Operated By: Doug & Judy Barnes. **Open:** Apr.–Oct. **Site Assignment:** Reservations recommended. **Registration:** At general store. **Fee:** RV, $31; tent, $28; per 2 people, extra person, $4. **Parking:** At site.

FACILITIES

Number of RV-only Sites: 85. **Number of Tent-only Sites:** 21. **Hookups:** Electric (20, 30, 50 amps), water, sewer. **Each Site:** Picnic table. **Dump Station:** Yes (2). **Laundry:** Yes. **Pay Phone:** Yes. **Restrooms and Showers:** Yes. **Fuel:** Less than 1 mi. **Propane:** Less than 1 mi. **Internal Roads:** Gravel. **RV Service:** Local service. **Market:** Locally. **Restaurant:** Several possibilities in Billings. **General Store:** Yes. **Vending:** No. **Swimming:** Yes. **Playground:** Yes. **Other:** Arcade, gift shop, river access, Internet data port, recreation area, 3 camping cabins. **Activities:** Nature walk, fishing, horseshoes. **Nearby Attractions:** Little Bighorn Battlefield National Monument, Pompeys Pillar National Historic Landmark, Beartooth Mountain Pass/Red Lodge, Bighorn Canyon National Recreation Area/Yellowtail Dam. **Additional Information:** Billings Chamber of Commerce, (406) 245-4111.

RESTRICTIONS

Pets: On leash only. **Fires:** No open fires. **Alcoholic Beverages:** Allowed. **Vehicle Maximum Length:** No limit.

TO GET THERE

From I-90 Exit 450, go west on SR 3 (S 27th St.) 0.2 mi., then left onto State Ave., left on to Sugur

Ave., left onto Garden Ave. (Total distance from I-90 is 3 mi.)

BOZEMAN MAP, C-2
Bozeman KOA

81123 Gallatin Rd., 59718. T: (406) 587-3030 or (800) 562-3036; www.koa.com.

🚐 ★★★　　🏕 ★★

Beauty: ★★★　　Site Privacy: ★★★
Spaciousness: ★★★　　Quiet: ★★★
Security: ★★★★　　Cleanliness: ★★★
Insect Control: ★★★　　Facilities: ★★★

This campground is located 7 miles southwest of Bozeman on Hwy. 191S, and it offers neither a purely wilderness experience nor a purely citified experience. A view of distant mountains, a trickling creek behind the on-site cabins, and a small collection of mature trees characterize the nature experience here, but it is quite accessible to the city. This campground works best as a base camp to explore Bozeman and the surrounding area. Nearby Gallatin Canyon provides some favored hiking, and proximity to Yellowstone Park, Lewis and Clark Caverns, and Red Rock Mine makes for some nice day trips. The 100 RV sites are more spacious than the 22 tent sites, and the tent sites sit cramped together, offering little privacy or shade. Sites L6–L11 and M1–M4 are arranged in rows, and all sites are grassy. Keep in mind that Bozeman is home to Montana State University, so avoid the area during graduation, unless of course, you are attending the graduation.

BASICS
Operated By: The Linde family. **Open:** All year. **Site Assignment:** By reservation. **Registration:** At camp store. **Fee:** RV, $20–$42; tent, $18–$28; per 2 people; extra person, $3; children under age 5 free. **Parking:** At site.

FACILITIES
Number of RV-only Sites: 87. **Number of Tent-only Sites:** 34. **Hookups:** Electric (30, 50 amps), water, sewer. **Each Site:** Picnic table. **Dump Station:** Yes. **Laundry:** Yes. **Pay Phone:** Yes. **Restrooms and Showers:** Yes. **Fuel:** No. **Propane:** Yes. **Internal Roads:** Gravel, in good condition. **RV Service:** In Bozeman. **Market:** In town. **Restaurant:** Several in town. **General Store:** Yes. **Vending:** In store. **Swimming:** Bozeman Natural Hot Springs. **Playground:** Yes. **Other:** Cabins, camper kitchen, creek. **Activities:** Swimming (next door), horseshoes, volleyball, basketball, fun cycles, mountain biking, fishing, hiking. **Nearby Attractions:** Museum of the Rockies, Yellowstone Park, Lewis & Clark Caverns. **Additional Information:** Bozeman Chamber of Commerce, (406) 586-5421.

RESTRICTIONS
Pets: On leash. **Fires:** Fire pit only. **Alcoholic Beverages:** Allowed. **Vehicle Maximum Length:** No limit.

TO GET THERE
From I-90 Exit 298, go 7 mi. south on Hwy. 85.

CAMERON MAP, C-2
Madison River Cabins and RV

1403 Hwy. 287 North, 59720. T: (406) 682-3030; www.madison-river.com.

🚐 ★★★★　　🏕 ★★★★

Beauty: ★★★★★　　Site Privacy: ★★★
Spaciousness: ★★★　　Quiet: ★★★★
Security: ★★★★　　Cleanliness: ★★★★★
Insect Control: ★★★★　　Facilities: ★★★★★

A small but quaint family-run campground, Madison River Cabins and RV is nestled in the beautiful Madison Valley directly on the banks of the Madison River. This park makes for a very cozy, romantic getaway or a great base for serious anglers. The campground is within easy reach of many famous trout streams—Madison, Gallatin, Beaverhead, and Henry's Fork rivers. Each of the 12 unique cabins and RV sites has no shade, but they do offer great views of the adjacent Madison River and the distant mountains. The sites are level, have gravel parking spurs with some grassy areas, and have full-hookups with back-in and pull-through sites available. The Madison Bend Store offers a variety of fishing supplies, licenses, and a large assortment of groceries. In addition, it houses the laundry facilities and restrooms. The restrooms and showers are the cleanest and best maintained of any campground in the state. Madison River Cabins and RV is less than an hour from the west entrance to Yellowstone National Park.

BASICS
Operated By: Papoose Creek LLC. **Open:** Jun. 1–Sept. 30. **Site Assignment:** By reservation or first come, first served. **Registration:** At fly shop. **Fee:** RV, $25. **Parking:** At site.

FACILITIES
Number of RV-only Sites: 9. **Number of Tent-only Sites:** Undesignated sites. **Hookups:** Electric (30 amps), water, sewer. **Each Site:** Picnic table. **Dump Station:** No. **Laundry:** Yes. **Pay Phone:** Yes. **Restrooms and Showers:** Yes. **Fuel:** No, 6 mi. south. **Propane:** No, 6 mi. south. **Internal Roads:** Gravel, in good condition. **RV Service:** No. **Market:** 35 mi. in either direction. **Restaurant:** Steak house next door. **General Store:** Madison Bend: rustic lodge fly shop w/ fishing tack, supplies, gift items, groceries, & wine cellar. **Vending:** No. **Swimming:** No. **Playground:** Activity field. **Other:** 12 fully furnished & unique cabins, all cabins & RV sites overlook the Madison River, restaurant next door. **Activities:** Fly fishing & riverfront activities. **Nearby Attractions:** More fly fishing, fishing guide services, float trips, horseback riding, Yellowstone National Park, golf, hot springs, Historic Virginia City, Yellowstone. **Additional Information:** Virginia City Chamber of Commerce, (406) 646-7701.

RESTRICTIONS
Pets: No leashes, pick up after. **Fires:** Fire ring only. **Alcoholic Beverages:** Allowed. **Vehicle Maximum Length:** None.

TO GET THERE
On Hwy. 287 north between Ennis and West Yellowstone, mile marker 14.

CARDWELL MAP, B-2
Cardwell Store and RV Park

770 Hwy. 2 East, 59721. T: (406) 287-5092.

🚐 ★★★　　🏕 ★★★

Beauty: ★★★　　Site Privacy: ★★★★
Spaciousness: ★★★★　　Quiet: ★★★★
Security: ★★★　　Cleanliness: ★★★
Insect Control: ★★★　　Facilities: ★★★

Cardwell Store and RV Park is located between Whitehall and Three Forks, directly off I-90. This simple campground is great for overnight stays. It offers extra-large, spacious pull-through sites arranged in a horseshoe configuration. Each site is well shaded by cottonwoods, junipers, golden willows, and apple trees. They each have a level, gravel parking spur, full hookups, and a light post. To the east of the RV sites is a separate tent area with water and one cabin on the bank of a nice-size stocked fishing pond. Deer, moose, and raccoons share the campground with paying guests, as well. There is a large day-use and picnic area, with lots of room for children to play. The grounds are well kept, and the restrooms are clean. The campground has a large store, with fuel and movies to rent for the evening. The staff is friendly and inviting. There are many attractions in the area, including the Lewis and Clark Caverns.

BASICS
Operated By: Kipp & Dawn Huckaba. **Open:** All year; water is off Nov.–Feb. 28. **Site Assignment:** By reservation or walk-in. **Registration:** At camp store. **Fee:** RV, $20–$22 per unit; tent, $10. **Parking:** At site.

FACILITIES
Number of RV-only Sites: 36. **Number of Tent-only Sites:** 10. **Hookups:** Electric (30, 50 amps), water, sewer. **Each Site:** Picnic table, light post. **Dump Station:** Yes. **Laundry:** Yes. **Pay Phone:** Yes. **Restrooms and Showers:** Yes. **Fuel:** Yes. **Propane:** Yes. **Internal Roads:** Gravel, in good condition. **RV Service:** 30 mi. west in Butte. **Market:** Whitehall. **Restaurant:** In Whitehall. **General Store:** Yes. **Vending:** Store. **Swimming:** No. **Playground:** No. **Other:** All pull-through sites, 1 cabin, stocked fishing pond, recreation area, picnic area, 1 tepee, movie rentals, regulation-size soccer field. **Activities:** Hiking, biking, fishing (trout), volleyball, soccer, horseshoes, small casino. **Nearby Attractions:** Lewis & Clark Caverns State Park, Madison Buffalo Jump State Park, Museum of the Rockies, Deer Lodge NF, hunting & fishing outfitters. **Additional Information:** Whitehall Chamber of Commerce, (406) 287-2260.

RESTRICTIONS
Pets: On leash. **Fires:** Tent area only. **Alcoholic Beverages:** Allowed. **Vehicle Maximum Length:** None. **Other:** Group max 5 to a site.

TO GET THERE
I-90 Exit 256 on the east frontage road.

CHOTEAU   MAP, B-2
Choteau KOA

85 MT 221, 59422. T: (406) 466-2615 or
(800) 562-4156; www.koa.com.

🚐 ★★★   ⛺ ★★★

Beauty: ★★★   Site Privacy: ★★★
Spaciousness: ★★★   Quiet: ★★★★
Security: ★★★★   Cleanliness: ★★★
Insect Control: ★★★   Facilities: ★★★

Located 20 miles east of the Rocky Mountains on
the Rocky Mountain Front, Choteau KOA is a great
base camp for exploring the area. All sites are pull-
through and are fairly well shielded from each other,
creating some privacy. Campers are in easy reach of
the 1-million-acre Bob Marshall Wilderness and the
Teton Spring Creek Bird Preserve. Those interested
in dinosaurs should visit the Old Trail Museum in
town, where visitors learn about the vast inland sea
that covered this area 80 million years ago; if time
permits, go on a dinosaur dig at Egg Mountain,
available June through August.

BASICS

Operated By: Shane & Gerri Boyle. **Open:** Mar.
15–Dec. 1. **Site Assignment:** By reservation. **Registration:** At camp store. **Fee:** RV, $22–$35; tent,
$18–$22; per 2 people; extra person, $2; children
under age 3 stay free. **Parking:** At site.

FACILITIES

Number of RV-only Sites: 55. **Hookups:** Electric
(20, 30, 50 amps), water, sewer. **Each Site:** Picnic
tables, fire pits. **Dump Station:** Yes. **Laundry:** Yes.
Pay Phone: Yes. **Restrooms and Showers:** Yes.
Fuel: 1 mi. in town. **Propane:** No. **Internal Roads:**
Gravel. **RV Service:** Limited service in town. **Mar-
ket:** In town. **Restaurant:** In town. **General
Store:** Yes. **Vending:** Yes. **Swimming:** Public pool
(less than 1 mi.). **Playground:** 2 playgrounds.
Other: 3 cabins, 3 tepees, tent village, data port.
Activities: Mini-golf, horseshoes, large common
area for games, game room, 9-hole golf course next
door. **Nearby Attractions:** Fishing (Eureka Lake,
Teton River), dinosaur digs, Bob Marshall Wilderness
Complex, Old Trail Museum, Teton Spring Creek Bird
Preserve. **Additional Information:** Choteau
Chamber of Commerce, (800) 823-3866.

RESTRICTIONS

Pets: On leash. **Fires:** Fire ring (fires may be prohibited due to dry weather; please ask management
before starting any open fires). **Alcoholic Beverages:** Allowed. **Vehicle Maximum Length:** No
limit.

TO GET THERE

From I-15 Exit 290, go west on US-89 for 40 mi.,
then bear right (west) on US-287 and follow in to
Choteau. From Choteau, go east at the blinking
light, 0.75 mi. on Hwy. 221.

COLUMBIA FALLS   MAP, A-1
La Salle RV Park

5618 Hwy. 2 West, 59912. T: (406) 892-4668 or
(877) 894-4178; www.lasallervpark.com.

🚐 ★★★   ⛺ ★★★

Beauty: ★★★   Site Privacy: ★★★
Spaciousness: ★★★   Quiet: ★★★★
Security: ★★★★   Cleanliness: ★★★★
Insect Control: ★★★★   Facilities: ★★★

Conveniently located off Hwy. 2 about 5 miles
southwest of Columbia Falls, the La Salle RV Park is
a comfortable, clean, and well-maintained campground with excellent service and friendly smiles.
The seven-acre property is divided into three areas:
RV, tent, and cabins. The main entrance road is
paved and loops around several rows of RV sites.
Each RV site has a lush lawn and a level gravel parking pad, with 25 pull-through sites available. The
tent area is in the back of the property with large sites
divided by well-kept shrubs. In addition, there are
five simple sleeping cabins. The campground is only
14 miles outside of Kalispell and 15 miles from the
west entrance to Glacier National Park. The camping
prices are one of the most reasonable in the area. The
days are warm in the summer and evenings are cool.
The owners live year-round on site and are always
there to assist.

BASICS

Operated By: Sandra, Wayne & Mitch Johnson.
Open: All year. **Site Assignment:** Reservations
recommended May–Sept., held w/ credit card. **Registration:** At office/general store. **Fee:** RV, $24; tent,
$16; per 2 people; extra person, $2; cash, credit,
check. **Parking:** At site.

FACILITIES

Number of RV-only Sites: 52. **Number of Tent-
only Sites:** 8. **Hookups:** Electric (20, 30, 50 amps),
water, sewer. **Each Site:** Picnic table, grated fire pits
(tent sites, cabins). **Dump Station:** No. **Laundry:**
Yes. **Pay Phone:** No. **Restrooms and Showers:**
Yes. **Fuel:** 2 mi. northeast in Columbia Falls.
Propane: 2 mi. northwest in Columbia Falls. **Internal Roads:** Paved & gravel. **RV Service:** 11 mi.
south in Kalispell. **Market:** 2 mi. northeast in Columbia Falls. **Restaurant:** 2 mi. northeast in Columbia
Falls. **General Store:** Yes. **Vending:** Yes. **Swimming:** No. **Playground:** Yes. **Other:** 4 cabins, lobby
w/ TV & Internet. **Activities:** Volleyball, basketball,
horseshoes, group outings. **Nearby Attractions:**
Glacier National Park 20 mi., waterslides, go-cart
tracks, fishing (rainbow trout, whitefish), Hungry
Horse Dam, Whitefish Lake, boating, whitewater rafting, golfing. **Additional Information:** Columbia
Falls Area Chamber of Commerce, (406) 892-2072.

RESTRICTIONS

Pets: On leash only. **Fires:** Fire pit only; fires may be
prohibited due to weather; please ask management
before starting any fire. **Alcoholic Beverages:** At
site. **Vehicle Maximum Length:** 65 ft.

TO GET THERE

11 mi. northeast of Kalispell directly off Hwy. 2.

CONRAD   MAP, A-2
Pondera RV Park

120 7th Ave., 59425. T: (406) 278-5724;
www.conradrv.com.

🚐 ★★★   ⛺ ★★

Beauty: ★★★   Site Privacy: ★★★
Spaciousness: ★★★   Quiet: ★★★
Security: ★★★   Cleanliness: ★★★
Insect Control: ★★★   Facilities: ★★★

Pondera RV Park is located in the center of Conrad,
across from the city park. Pondera RV Park is a full-
service facility with all the amenities looked for in an
RV park. The sites are level and gravel with six pull-
through sites available. There is some grass and a few
shade trees. Sites are close together and there are a
few mobile homes. The area seems fairly quiet, and
the park across the street has several activities: an
Olympic-size public pool, large playground, tennis
courts, and picnic areas. The campground is convenient to local restaurants, shopping, and repair. The
Lewis and Clark Trail runs through Conrad, and the
campground is not far from Glacier National Park,
Great Falls, or Lake Holter Recreation Area. The area
is very dry in the summer, and the days can be very
warm. This campground is not staffed during the
day, and the owners show up around 4 p.m. There is
a number on the bulletin board for emergencies.

BASICS

Operated By: Lew & Carol Jones. **Open:** All year.
Site Assignment: By reservation or first come, first
served. **Registration:** At camp office. **Fee:** $20–$22
per unit. **Parking:** At site.

FACILITIES

Number of RV-only Sites: 48. **Number of Tent-
only Sites:** 10. **Hookups:** Electric (30 amps), water,
sewer, cable TV, phone. **Each Site:** Some picnic
tables. **Dump Station:** Yes. **Laundry:** Yes. **Pay
Phone:** Yes. **Restrooms and Showers:** Yes. **Fuel:**
Less than 1 mi. **Propane:** Less than 1 mi. **Internal
Roads:** Gravel, in good condition. **RV Service:** Limited local service. **Market:** In town. **Restaurant:** In
town. **General Store:** No. **Vending:** Yes. **Swimming:** Public pool (across the street). **Playground:**
Located across the street in city park. **Other:** Internet data port, across from the Conrad Municipal
Park: pavilions, grills, tennis. **Activities:** Park, pool,
tennis, volleyball, horseshoes. **Nearby Attractions:**
Golf, bowling, movies, dinosaur digs, hiking, fishing, an
hour drive to Glacier National Park, community theater, horseback riding. **Additional Information:**
Conrad Chamber of Commerce, (406) 278-7791.

RESTRICTIONS

Pets: On leash. **Fires:** No open fires. **Alcoholic
Beverages:** Allowed. **Vehicle Maximum Length:**
50 ft.

TO GET THERE

Take Exit 339 off I-15 and enter Conrad. Follow
Main St. 11 blocks. Turn right on 7th. Go 1.5
blocks and look to your left.

CORAM   MAP, A-1
North American RV Park and Yurt Village

P.O. Box 83, 10784 Hwy. 2 East, 59913.
T: (406) 387-5800 or (800) 704-4266;
www.northamericanrvpark.com.

🚐 ★★★   ⛺ ★★

Beauty: ★★★   Site Privacy: ★★★
Spaciousness: ★★★   Quiet: ★★★★
Security: ★★★   Cleanliness: ★★★
Insect Control: ★★★★   Facilities: ★★★★

Located a few miles from the west entrance of Glacier National Park in the small community of Coram is the North American RV Park. This campground is ideal for those campers looking for a convenient base camp with up-to-date modern amenities. North America RV Park offers its patrons a clean, well-maintained facility with large, gravel, pull-through sites at the base of a huge mountain. There are few trees and little shade, but the satellite television reception is great. There is plenty of additional parking, and this campground caters to extra-large motor coaches with tows. The tent sites lie along the back of the property in a sparsely grassy area by the mountain. The campground also has two rental yurts. Since this campground is in a valley with few trees, summer days can be very warm, though the evenings tend to be very cool. The park office is open daily and there are also camp hosts to assist with any needs that may arise.

BASICS

Operated By: Ronnie & Theresa Baker. **Open:** Apr.–Oct. **Site Assignment:** Reservations recommended. **Registration:** At camp office. **Fee:** RV, $20–$33; tent, $19.26; per 4 people; extra person, $3; Good Sam Club; cash, credit, check. **Parking:** At site.

FACILITIES

Number of RV-only Sites: 89. **Number of Tent-only Sites:** 2. **Hookups:** Electric (30, 50 amps), water, sewer, cable TV, phone. **Each Site:** Picnic table. **Dump Station:** Yes. **Laundry:** Yes. **Pay Phone:** Yes. **Restrooms and Showers:** Yes. **Fuel:** In Coram or West Glacier. **Propane:** In Coram or West Glacier. **Internal Roads:** Gravel. **RV Service:** 14 mi. southwest in Columbia Falls. **Market:** In Coram or West Glacier. **Restaurant:** In Coram or West Glacier. **General Store:** Yes. **Vending:** Yes. **Swimming:** No. **Playground:** Yes. **Other:** 2 yurts (a circular, Mongolian-style domed tent w/ a plywood floor, sleeps 4–6 people). **Activities:** Picnic area, volleyball, horseshoes, North American Wildlife Museum. **Nearby Attractions:** Glacier National Park, House of Mystery, Hungry Horse Dam, golf, fishing tours, whitewater rafting, helicopter tours. **Additional Information:** Columbia Falls Area Chamber of Commerce, (406) 892-2072.

RESTRICTIONS

Pets: On leash only. **Fires:** Fire pit only. Fires may be prohibited due to dry weather; ask management before starting any fires. **Alcoholic Beverages:** Allowed. **Vehicle Maximum Length:** No limit.

TO GET THERE

Off US 2 about 5 mi. south of West Glacier.

CUT BANK   MAP, A-2
Shady Grove RV Park and Campground

P.O. Box 691, 59427. T: (406) 336-2475;
www.northerntel.net/~shdygrov/.

🚐 ★★★   ⛺ ★★★

Beauty: ★★★   Site Privacy: ★★★
Spaciousness: ★★★   Quiet: ★★★★★
Security: ★★★★   Cleanliness: ★★★★
Insect Control: ★★★★   Facilities: ★★★

Located on the east side of Glacier National Park in the flat farmland of Montana is Shady Grove RV Park and Campground. The air is sweet and the grass is green. There are beautiful mature maples, oaks, and pines surrounding the property, which houses squirrels and raccoons, and feelings of home and family pervade the campground. The campsites form a circular perimeter around the property, with the Bomars' home in the center. There are clean and well-maintained facilities, as well as a small playground. All the sites are back-in but roomy in size and length. The most preferable are the tent sites on lush grass that are well spaced for privacy. The park is a wonderful place to enjoy the stars on a cloudless night. The weather is typical of high desert, and is very dry in the summer. There are no open fires allowed in the campground. For extra security, the gates are closed in the evening. It is 30 miles to the east entrance of Glacier National Park.

BASICS

Operated By: Larry & Carole Bomar. **Open:** May 1–Oct. 1. **Site Assignment:** Reservations recommended, held w/ credit card. **Registration:** Larry & Carole's home. **Fee:** RV, $20; tent, $14; per 2 people; extra adult, $2; children ages 3–12, $1; under age 3 stay free; cash & check only. **Parking:** At site.

FACILITIES

Number of RV-only Sites: 19. **Number of Tent-only Sites:** 10. **Hookups:** Electric (20, 30 amps), water, sewer. **Each Site:** Picnic table. **Dump Station:** No. **Laundry:** No. **Pay Phone:** Yes. **Restrooms and Showers:** Yes. **Fuel:** 6 mi. east in Cut Bank. **Propane:** 6 mi. east in Cut Bank. **Internal Roads:** Gravel. **RV Service:** 100 mi. in Great Falls. **Market:** 6 mi. east in Cut Bank. **Restaurant:** 6 mi. east in Cut Bank. **General Store:** No. **Vending:** Drinks & ice available at owners' home. **Swimming:** No. **Playground:** Yes. **Activities:** Play area, horseshoes, large open field great for playing ball. **Nearby Attractions:** Glacier National Park. **Additional Information:** www.visitmontana.com.

RESTRICTIONS

Pets: Leash only, some large breed restrictions. **Fires:** No open fires. **Alcoholic Beverages:** In campers only. **Vehicle Maximum Length:** No limit.

TO GET THERE

Directly off Hwy. 2, 6 mi. west of Cut Bank.

DEER LODGE   MAP, B-2
Indian Creek RV Campground

745 Maverick Ln., 59722.
T: (406) 846-3848 or (800) 294-0726;
www.indiancreekcampground.net.

🚐 ★★★   ⛺ ★★★

Beauty: ★★★★   Site Privacy: ★★★
Spaciousness: ★★★   Quiet: ★★★
Security: ★★★★   Cleanliness: ★★★
Insect Control: ★★★   Facilities: ★★★

Indian Creek RV Campground is a great location for travelers with extra-large motorcoaches or towed vehicles. Situated in the scenic Deer Lodge area, this park is less than an hour away from Yellowstone National Park. The campground offers level sites with 40 pull-throughs available, 50-amp service, modem service, and cable TV. There is a large recreation lodge with laundry, very well-maintained restrooms, and lounge. The campground sits on the banks of the Yellowstone River, and the view is spectacular. The staff is friendly and welcoming, and the climate is dry and breezy. In addition to Yellowstone, the Deer Lodge area has fine dining, shopping, hot springs, and much more. This is a wonderful place to mountain bike or hike. Indian Creek has a tendency to fill up early, so reservations are highly recommended.

BASICS

Operated By: Fickler Oil Company. **Open:** Apr. 15–Oct. 15. **Site Assignment:** By reservation. **Registration:** At camp office. **Fee:** RV, $21; tent, $14. **Parking:** At site.

FACILITIES

Number of RV-only Sites: 50. **Number of Tent-only Sites:** Undesignated sites. **Hookups:** Electric (50 amps), water, sewer, cable TV. **Each Site:** Picnic table. **Dump Station:** Yes. **Laundry:** Yes. **Pay Phone:** Yes. **Restrooms and Showers:** Yes. **Fuel:** Next door. **Propane:** Yes. **Internal Roads:** Gravel, in good condition. **RV Service:** Mobile service from Butte. **Market:** In town. **Restaurant:** In town. **General Store:** Small w/ a few drinks. **Vending:** In store. **Swimming:** No. **Playground:** Activity field, horseshoe pit. **Activities:** Hiking, biking, enjoying views of Mt. Powell. **Nearby Attractions:** Grant-Kohrs Ranch National Historic Site, the Old Montana Prison Museum Complex, casino. **Additional Information:** Deer Lodge Chamber of Commerce, (406) 846-2094.

RESTRICTIONS

Pets: On leash, designated walking area. **Fires:** No open fires. **Alcoholic Beverages:** Allowed. **Vehicle Maximum Length:** No limit.

TO GET THERE

From I-90 Exit 184, go west on I-90 Bus 0.25 mi., make a left on Access Rd., follow signs 0.5 mi. down access road to 745 Maverick Ln.

Reserve your campsite online at www.ReserveAmerica.com

ELMO
MAP, A-1
Arrowhead RV Park and Marina

76076 Hwy. 93, 59915. T: (406) 849-5545 or (866) 808-1902

🚐 ★★★   ⛺ ★★★

Beauty: ★★★★   Site Privacy: ★★★
Spaciousness: ★★★   Quiet: ★★★★
Security: ★★★★   Cleanliness: ★★★★★
Insect Control: ★★★★   Facilities: ★★★★

Situated on Flathead Lake, the largest natural freshwater lake west of the Mississippi, Arrowhead Resort is a perfect retreat if you are looking for a quiet atmosphere in a pristine setting. Flathead Lake is fed by melting glaciers in the nearby Glacier National Park. Only 15 miles north of Polson, Arrowhead Resort overlooks Chief Cliff Mountain and Wild Horse Island. Arrowhead Resort is a delightfully manicured resort offering 28 pull-through grass sites, a swimming beach, and a marina. The breeze off the lake creates pleasant summer days and cool evenings. The proprietors live on site throughout the season and are there to assist in any way.

BASICS
Operated By: Ray & Shannon Geiser. **Open:** May 1–Sept. 30. **Site Assignment:** Reservations recommended, $16.50 nonrefundable deposit if less than 1 week, $25 deposit for more than 1 week. **Registration:** At camp office. **Fee:** RV, $26–$34; tent, $16. **Parking:** At site.

FACILITIES
Number of RV-only Sites: 28. **Number of Tent-only Sites:** 2. **Hookups:** Electric (30, 50 amps), water, sewer. **Each Site:** Picnic table, some grills. **Dump Station:** Yes. **Laundry:** Yes. **Pay Phone:** Office phone. **Restrooms and Showers:** Yes. **Fuel:** 1 mi. in Elmo. **Propane:** 1 mi. in Elmo. **Internal Roads:** Gravel. **RV Service:** 25 mi. north in Kalispell. **Market:** 13 mi. south in Polson. **Restaurant:** 13 mi. south in Polson. **General Store:** No. **Vending:** In office: drinks & ice. **Swimming:** Lake. **Playground:** No. **Other:** Marina, boat launch, boat rentals. **Activities:** Fishing, boating, waterskiing, jet skiing, parasailing. **Nearby Attractions:** Charter fishing trips, hunting, hiking, backpacking, Flathead Lake State Park. **Additional Information:** Polson Chamber of Commerce, (406) 883-5971.

RESTRICTIONS
Pets: On leash only. **Fires:** Fire pit only. **Alcoholic Beverages:** Allowed. **Vehicle Maximum Length:** No limit.

TO GET THERE
Located on Hwy. 93, 13 mi. north of Polson at the 76 mile marker.

GLENDIVE
MAP, B-4
Glendive RV Park and Campground

201 California St., 59330. T: (406) 377-6721; www.glendivervpark.com.

🚐 ★★★   ⛺ ★★★

Beauty: ★★★   Site Privacy: ★★★
Spaciousness: ★★★   Quiet: ★★★
Security: ★★★   Cleanliness: ★★★
Insect Control: ★★★   Facilities: ★★★

Located 33 miles west of the North Dakota border, Glendive offers the last bit of civilization before leaving the sprawling desertlike scenery of eastern Montana. Just a quick exit from I-94, this campground might be a convenient stop as you journey to the next state. The chain-link fence, hodgepodge of buildings, and patchy grass found at the entrance are not aesthetically pleasing, but, luckily, the campsites are not located in close view. Sites 1–18 are arranged in three rows and are the farthest from the interstate. However, they are not as spacious as sites 19–52, which are arranged in a horseshoe pattern. The inner horseshoe, sites 19–31, hug the playground, and sites 19 and 33 catch any incoming traffic. All sites are pull-through. The separate tent area places tent campers closest to the interstate and hides them among occasional trees and sparse ground cover. Not far from the camp, Makoshika State Park, (Makoshika is the Sioux name for "badlands"), captures the subtle desert scenery of sandstone and sage, and is an interesting contrast to the Yellowstone experience. If you happen through during spring, be sure to catch the annual Buzzard Days festival celebrating the return of the turkey vultures.

BASICS
Operated By: Larry Phillips. **Open:** Mar. 1–Oct. 15. **Site Assignment:** By reservation or first come, first served; reservation recommended. **Registration:** At camp office. **Fee:** RV, $22–$26; tent, $14; per 2 people; extra person charge, $2; children under age 5 stay free. **Parking:** At site.

FACILITIES
Number of RV-only Sites: 51. **Number of Tent-only Sites:** 5. **Hookups:** Electric (20, 30, 50 amps), water, sewer, phone, Internet. **Each Site:** Picnic tables, fire pits. **Dump Station:** Yes. **Laundry:** Yes. **Pay Phone:** Yes. **Restrooms and Showers:** Yes. **Fuel:** Less than 1 mi. **Propane:** No. **Internal Roads:** Gravel, in good condition. **RV Service:** Miles City (70 mi.). **Market:** In town, 3–5 mi. **Restaurant:** On site. **General Store:** Yes. **Vending:** No. **Swimming:** Yes. **Playground:** Yes. **Other:** On the Yellowstone River, 2 cabins w/ refrigerators, hot plates, running water, air-conditioning, cable TV, exercise bar, Internet data port. **Activities:** Horseshoes, basketball, volleyball, swimming, fishing, badminton. **Nearby Attractions:** Yellowstone River, boating, fishing, agate hunting, Makoshika State Park, self-guided walking tour of Glendive's downtown historic district. **Additional Information:** Glendive Chamber of Commerce, (406) 365-5601.

RESTRICTIONS
Pets: On leash. **Fires:** Fire pit only. **Alcoholic Beverages:** Not allowed. **Vehicle Maximum Length:** No limit.

TO GET THERE
North of I-94 Exit 215; you can see campground from the interstate.

HARDIN
MAP, B-3
Hardin KOA

R.R. 1, 59034. T: (406) 665-1635 or (800) 562-1635; www.koa.com.

🚐 ★★★   ⛺ ★★★

Beauty: ★★★   Site Privacy: ★★★
Spaciousness: ★★★   Quiet: ★★★★
Security: ★★★★   Cleanliness: ★★★★
Insect Control: ★★   Facilities: ★★★

Hardin KOA is the perfect place for campers who have a taste for history. Within easy driving distance is Pompey's Pillar, a large, solitary plateau offering panoramic views of the surrounding countryside. The remnants of Native American pictographs can be found here, as well as the signature of Captain William Clark of Lewis and Clark fame. Also nearby is the Little Bighorn National Monument, site of the brutal battle between Custer's Seventh Cavalry and the Sioux Indians. The 58 pull-through RV sites and ten tent-only sites lie on mostly flat ground with minimal shade. Activities within camp include swimming, horseshoes, volleyball, and nightly movies during the summer. This camp fills up quickly during Little Big Horn Days each summer, so call ahead.

BASICS
Operated By: Sandra Biery. **Open:** Apr. 1–Oct. 31. **Site Assignment:** By reservation or first come, first served. **Registration:** At camp store. **Fee:** RV, $25.50–$32; tent, $18; per 2 people; extra person, $5; children under 3 free; children 5–17, $1. **Parking:** At site.

FACILITIES
Number of RV-only Sites: 56. **Number of Tent-only Sites:** 10. **Hookups:** Electric (30, 50 amps), water, sewer, cable TV. **Each Site:** Picnic table. **Dump Station:** Yes. **Laundry:** Yes. **Pay Phone:** Yes. **Restrooms and Showers:** Yes. **Fuel:** No. **Propane:** Yes. **Internal Roads:** Gravel, in good condition. **RV Service:** In Billings. **Market:** In town, 2 mi. **Restaurant:** There are several in town, 2 mi. **General Store:** Yes. **Vending:** No. **Swimming:** Yes w/ hot tub. **Playground:** Yes. **Other:** 6 cabins, hot tub, snack bar, nightly summer barbecues. **Activities:** Swimming, horseshoes, volleyball, basketball, nightly summer movies. **Nearby Attractions:** Fishing (Big Horn River), Big Horn Nat'l Monument, Little Big Horn Days Jun. 20–25. **Additional Information:** Hardin Chamber of Commerce, (406) 665-1672.

RESTRICTIONS
Pets: On leash. **Fires:** Fire pit only. **Alcoholic Beverages:** Allowed. **Vehicle Maximum Length:** None.

TO GET THERE
I-90 Exit 495, go north 1.5 mi. on Hwy. 47.

HELENA   MAP, B-2
Helena Campground and RV Park

5820 North Montana Ave., 59602. T: (406) 458-4714; www.helenacampgroundrvpark.com.

🚐 ★★★   ⛺ ★★

Beauty: ★★★   Site Privacy: ★★★
Spaciousness: ★★★★   Quiet: ★★★
Security: ★★★   Cleanliness: ★★★★
Insect Control: ★★★★   Facilities: ★★★

Welcome to the capital city of Helena. The Helena Campground and RV Park is a mere 3 miles outside the city limits and is a comfortable vacation spot for those visitors wishing to visit the city and surrounding area. The campground is configured in rows containing both pull-through and back-in sites, which are well groomed with trailer pads. Tent sites have nice lawn areas, but are small with little privacy. There is also a tent corral with electricity and water, and a few cabins. During the peak season, patrons may enjoy an all-you-can-eat breakfast, ice-cream socials, and a dip in the pool. Canyon Ferry and Hauser Lakes are close by with tours and boating. The weather in Helena is dry and warm in the summer, with temperatures dropping in the evening. The campground has good security with someone always on the clock.

BASICS
Operated By: Robert Dunlop. **Open:** Mar. 1–Oct. 31. **Site Assignment:** By reservation, w/ 1-night deposit; $5 cancellation fee. **Registration:** At camp office. **Fee:** RV, $25–$32; tent, $25; per 2 people; extra person, $7.50; children under age 3 free; AC/heat, $2.50 extra per night. **Parking:** Yes; extra vehicle, $5.

FACILITIES
Number of RV-only Sites: 100. **Number of Tent-only Sites:** 29. **Hookups:** Electric (30, 50 amps), water, sewer. **Each Site:** Picnic tables, some grills, some fire pits. **Dump Station:** Yes. **Laundry:** Yes. **Pay Phone:** Yes. **Restrooms and Showers:** Yes. **Fuel:** In Helena. **Propane:** In Helena. **Internal Roads:** Paved & gravel. **RV Service:** In Helena. **Market:** In Helena. **Restaurant:** In Helena. **General Store:** Yes. **Vending:** General store. **Swimming:** Yes (very large, Memorial Day–Labor Day). **Playground:** Yes. **Other:** All tent sites have water, 3 cabins, tent village, rec room, breakfast. **Activities:** Game room, swimming, fun cycles. **Nearby Attractions:** State Capitol Building, Holter Museum of Art, Boulder Hot Springs, St. Helena Cathedral, Elkhorn Ghost Town, Holter Lake & Recreation Area. **Additional Information:** Helena Chamber of Commerce, (406) 444-2654, (800) 743-5362 or www.helenachamber.com.

RESTRICTIONS
Pets: On leash. **Fires:** Fire pits or grills only. Fires may be restricted due to dry weather; ask management before starting any fire. **Alcoholic Beverages:** Allowed on site. **Vehicle Maximum Length:** No limit.

TO GET THERE
From I-15, take Lincoln Rd. Exit 200 (SR 279) west, take a left onto Montana Ave. Park is located 3 mi. down on your right.

HUNGRY HORSE   MAP, A-1
Canyon RV and Campground

9540 Hwy. 2 East, P. O. Box 7, 59919. T: (406) 387-9393; www.montanacampground.com.

🚐 ★★★   ⛺ ★★★

Beauty: ★★★★   Site Privacy: ★★★
Spaciousness: ★★   Quiet: ★★★★
Security: ★★★★   Cleanliness: ★★★★
Insect Control: ★★★   Facilities: ★★★

Only ten minutes away from the western entrance to Glacier National Park on the Flat Head River is Canyon RV and Campground. Canyon RV and Campground enjoys river frontage, great for trout fishing, and panoramic views of the snow-capped mountains. It is conveniently located near many of the attractions in the Hungry Horse–West Glacier area, including golf, the Hungry Horse Dam, and glacier helicopter tours. The campground is configured in a large loop with both back-in and pull-through sites. Sites, however, are relatively close together and tent sites lack privacy and shade. The air is crisp and dry, but be prepared for the cold any day of the year. The foliage is spectacular in the late spring to early summer, and the sunsets are magnificent. The owners stay on property during the operating season and are there to assist in any way.

BASICS
Operated By: Steve & Dee Brown. **Open:** May 1–Sept. 30. **Site Assignment:** Reservations held w/ credit card. **Registration:** At general store. **Fee:** RV, $21–$30; tent, $21; per 2 people; extra person, $3; cash, check. **Parking:** At site.

FACILITIES
Number of RV-only Sites: 51. **Number of Tent-only Sites:** 15. **Hookups:** Electric (20, 30, 50 amps), water, sewer. **Each Site:** Picnic table, some grills. **Dump Station:** Yes. **Laundry:** No. **Pay Phone:** Yes. **Restrooms and Showers:** Yes. **Fuel:** In Hungry Horse. **Propane:** In Hungry Horse. **Internal Roads:** Gravel. **RV Service:** Mobile service in Hungry Horse. **Market:** In Hungry Horse. **Restaurant:** In Hungry Horse. **General Store:** Yes. **Vending:** General store. **Swimming:** No. (No swimming in the Flathead River). **Playground:** No. **Other:** 6 cabins & 1 tepee, central fire ring. **Activities:** Fishing (bull trout, whitefish, rainbow trout), horseshoes, hiking. **Nearby Attractions:** Glacier National Park, House of Mystery, North American Wildlife Museum, go-carts, helicopter tours, whitewater rafting, fishing tours. **Additional Information:** Columbia Falls Area Chamber of Commerce, (406) 892-2072.

RESTRICTIONS
Pets: On leash only. **Fires:** Fire ring only. Fires may be prohibited due to dry weather, ask management before starting any fire. **Alcoholic Beverages:** No alcoholic beverages allowed. **Vehicle Maximum Length:** No limit.

TO GET THERE
Directly off Hwy. 2 in Hungry Horse, 18 mi. northeast of Kalispell.

HUNGRY HORSE   MAP, A-1
Mountain Meadow Campground

9125 Hwy. 2 East, 59919. T: (406) 387-9125; www.mmrvpark.com.

🚐 ★★★★★   ⛺ ★★★★

Beauty: ★★★★★   Site Privacy: ★★★★
Spaciousness: ★★★★   Quiet: ★★★★★
Security: ★★★★   Cleanliness: ★★★★★
Insect Control: ★★★★   Facilities: ★★★★★

Welcome to one of the most beautiful and pristine campgrounds in Montana. Located only a few short miles from the west entrance to Glacier National Park and the Hungry Horse Dam is Mountain Meadow Campground. High atop a mountain peak with a spectacular view of the Glacier Mountains, one finds cozy wooded camping sites, cabins with all the modern luxuries of a full-service campground, and the rustic ambiance only nature can share. Large Douglas firs, cedars, spruce, and pines canopy each site, and along with the wild roses scattered throughout the park, lend a sweet aroma to the air. Bald eagle sightings are not rare here, along with more common woodpeckers, deer, elk, and moose. The roads are wide, the sites are large, most are pull-through, and the trees are well groomed. Tent sites are secluded and private. There is a large well-stocked fishing pond and large picnic area. The air is crisp and the breeze is inviting. Several nice restaurants are in walking distance as well as outfitters and helicopter tours. The office is staffed daily and security is good.

BASICS
Operated By: Dan & Sue Hussion. **Open:** May 1–Oct. 1. **Site Assignment:** Reservations recommended w/ credit card. **Registration:** At general store. **Fee:** RV, $30–$32; tent, $22–$24; per 2 people; extra child, $1.50; adult, $5; cash, credit, check. **Parking:** At site.

FACILITIES
Number of RV-only Sites: 50. **Number of Tent-only Sites:** 10. **Hookups:** Electric (30, 50 amps), water, sewer. **Each Site:** Picnic table, grated fire pits. **Dump Station:** Yes. **Laundry:** Yes. **Pay Phone:** Yes. **Restrooms and Showers:** Yes. **Fuel:** In Coram. **Propane:** In Coram. **Internal Roads:** Gravel. **RV Service:** 10 mi. southwest in Columbia Falls. **Market:** In town, 0.5 mi. **Restaurant:** In town, 0.5 mi. **General Store:** Yes. **Vending:** Yes. **Swimming:** No. **Playground:** Yes. **Other:** 3 cabins, stocked rainbow trout lake overlooking the mountains, swings, modem hookup in the office. **Activities:** Fishing (rainbow trout), swing, hiking, biking. **Nearby Attractions:** 9 mi. from Glacier National Park, Hungry Horse Dam, Lion Lake, horseback riding, fly-fishing tours, whitewater rafting, helicopter tours. **Additional Information:** Columbia Falls Area Chamber of Commerce, (406) 892-2072.

RESTRICTIONS
Pets: On leash only. **Fires:** Fire pit only. Fires may be prohibited due to weather; ask management before starting any fires. **Alcoholic Beverages:** Allowed. **Vehicle Maximum Length:** None.

TO GET THERE
Located directly off Hwy. 2 in Hungry Horse.

Reserve your campsite online at www.ReserveAmerica.com

HUNGRY HORSE   MAP, A-1
Timber Wolf Resort

9105 Hwy. 2 East, P. O. Box 190800, 59919.
T: (406) 387-9653 or (877) 846-9653;
www.timberwolfresort.com.

🚐 ★★★★   ▲ ★★★★

Beauty: ★★★★★   Site Privacy: ★★★
Spaciousness: ★★★   Quiet: ★★★★★
Security: ★★★★   Cleanliness: ★★★★
Insect Control: ★★★★   Facilities: ★★★★★

Nestled in a 20-acre forest only 9 miles from the west entrance to Glacier National Park, Timber Wolf Resort is a true jewel. Timber Wolf offers a full-service campground with excellent amenities, including a beautiful large gazebo with three barbecue grills, bike rentals, and a playground. The campground has hiking trails and bike trails that connect to those in Glacier National Park. Timber Wolf offers large gravel sites, both pull-through and back-in, with a natural forest floor and shade. In addition, they offer 15 beautiful camping cabins, a small bed-and-breakfast, and wonderfully secluded tent sites. The campground, while offering large sites, is not designed for huge (45-foot plus) RVs. The resort is open year-round and the owners reside on the property. The winters are long, cold, and snowy, and the summers too short, but beautiful.

BASICS

Operated By: Rob & Tracy Elek. **Open:** Apr.–Oct. **Site Assignment:** Reservations recommended. **Registration:** At general store or at the Eleks' residence. **Fee:** RV, $20–$30; tent, $15–$20; cash, credit, check. **Parking:** At site.

FACILITIES

Number of RV-only Sites: 24. **Number of Tent-only Sites:** 10. **Hookups:** Electric (30, 50 amps), water, sewer. **Each Site:** Picnic table, grated fire pits. **Dump Station:** No. **Laundry:** No. **Pay Phone:** Yes. **Restrooms and Showers:** Yes. **Fuel:** In Hungry Horse. **Propane:** In Hungry Horse. **Internal Roads:** Gravel. **RV Service:** 10 mi. southwest in Columbia Falls. **Market:** In Hungry Horse. **Restaurant:** In Hungry Horse. **General Store:** Yes. **Vending:** Yes. **Swimming:** No. **Playground:** Yes. **Other:** Large gazebo w/ 3 gas barbecues, bed & breakfast, cabins. **Activities:** Hiking, horseshoes. **Nearby Attractions:** 9 mi. from Glacier National Park, Hungry Horse Dam, House of Mystery, helicopter tours, fly fishing (bull trout, rainbow trout), whitewater rafting, cross-country skiing, Big Mountain Ski Resort. **Additional Information:** Columbia Falls Area Chamber of Commerce, (406) 892-2072.

RESTRICTIONS

Pets: Leash only (please note that the owners have a beautiful, well-behaved, & friendly retriever that has free reign of the property, but guests' pets must be on leash). **Fires:** Fire pit only. Fires may be prohibited due to weather; please ask management before starting any fires. **Alcoholic Beverages:** Allowed. **Vehicle Maximum Length:** 40 ft.

TO GET THERE

Located directly off Hwy. 2 in Hungry Horse, 20 mi. northeast of Kalispell.

KALISPELL   MAP, A-1
Flathead Lake State Park

490 North Meridian, 59901. T: (406) 752-5501 or (406) 849-5255; www.fwp.state.mt.us/parks.

🚐 ★★★   ▲ ★★★

Beauty: ★★★★   Site Privacy: ★★★
Spaciousness: ★★★   Quiet: ★★★
Security: ★★★★   Cleanliness: ★★★
Insect Control: ★★★   Facilities: ★★★

The Flathead Lake State Park consists of six areas and five campgrounds around the outer circumference of Flathead Lake. Flathead Lake is one of the largest natural lakes in the world with the Flathead River as its major tributary. Montana's Department of Fish, Wildlife and Parks operates these park units as well as several islands around this magnificent lake. The campgrounds are semideveloped with paved parking pads and great waterfront access. Finley Point is the only waterfront site with hookups. All the sites are large back-in parking spaces. Yellow Bay is intended for tent camping only. It is the smallest and most private of the areas, with only five camping sites. Each of the areas has entrance gates, water access, boat ramps, and someone on staff or a host at all times. The weather is cool in the evening and there is always a breeze.

BASICS

Operated By: Montana Fish, Wildlife & Parks. **Open:** All year. **Site Assignment:** First come, first served; no reservations. **Registration:** At park entrance. **Fee:** $12–$15, depending on residency & campsite. **Parking:** At site.

FACILITIES

Number of RV-only Sites: 16. **Number of Tent-only Sites:** 4. **Number of Multipurpose Sites:** 40. **Hookups:** Electric (30 amps), water (Finley Point Campground only). **Each Site:** Picnic table, fire pit or grill. **Dump Station:** In Wayfarers. **Laundry:** No. **Pay Phone:** In Wayfarers & Big Arm. **Restrooms and Showers:** Yes, but only in Wayfarers, Yellow Bay, & Big Arm (these are coin-operated showers, 25 cents per 3 min.). **Fuel:** No. **Propane:** No. **Internal Roads:** Paved. **RV Service:** Kalispell. **Market:** Polson or Kalispell. **Restaurant:** Polson or Kalispell. **General Store:** No. **Vending:** No. **Swimming:** Lake. **Playground:** No. **Other:** Group camping, interpretive programs, boat launches, covered picnic areas, horse trails, Wild Horse Island accessible by boat. **Activities:** Swimming, fishing, hiking, waterskiing. **Nearby Attractions:** Ninepipes Museum, North America Wildlife Museum, Glacier National Park. **Additional Information:** Polson Chamber of Commerce, (406) 883-5970.

RESTRICTIONS

Pets: On leash. **Fires:** In approved pits grills. **Alcoholic Beverages:** Allowed. **Vehicle Maximum Length:** 51 ft. **Other:** 7-day stay limit; you may purchase a MT state passport, which waives entrance fees.

TO GET THERE

The Flathead State Park Units each have their own entrance. The entrances are all located around the perimeter of Flathead Lake. They are located either off US 93 or SR 35. For exact directions to the campground or area of your choice, please visit the Web site.

LIBBY   MAP, A-1
Rexford Beach—
Kootenai National Forest

reserve america™

1101 Hwy. 2 West, 59923. T: (406) 293-6211; www.reserveamerica.com.

🚐 ★★★★   ▲ ★★★★

Beauty: ★★★   Site Privacy: ★★★★
Spaciousness: ★★★★   Quiet: ★★★
Security: ★★★★   Cleanliness: ★★★★
Insect Control: ★★★★   Facilities: ★★★

Rexford Bench Campground is located on the Kootenai National Forest in northwest Montana. At an elevation of 2,500 feet, the campground encompasses 25 acres. There are 54 campsites to choose from. Drinking water and restrooms are provided. Lake Koocanusa offers many activities including fishing, swimming, and boating. Rexford Bench Campground is located within the Kootenai National Forest on the Northwest corner of Montana and the Northeast corner of Idaho on the Canadian border. Providing abundant recreation and a wealth of natural resources, the Kootenai is a perfect place to relax and enjoy your National Forests! Campers will find many miles of backcountry roads available to access the forest. Some areas are closed to motorized vehicles in order to protect wildlife and watershed values, offering recreational opportunities for hiking or horseback riding. Many developed campgrounds are located throughout the forest, as well as unlimited dispersed camping areas available. Mountain bikers will find many miles of trails to enjoy with spectacular views. The winter snows typically melt in April and May, although some high-country areas aren't accessible until June. Wildflowers are at their peak May through July. In August and September, berries ripen and many people enjoy picking huckleberries as a family activity. Fall brings the turning of the larch to a golden yellow and the sounds of elk bugling, marking the beginning of hunting season for deer, elk, moose, bears, and other big game species. Those seeking a novel way to enjoy the forest may enjoy reserving a fire lookout with commanding views of the surrounding terrain.

BASICS

Operated By: U.S. Forest Service. **Open:** May 7–Sept. 23. **Site Assignment:** Reservations must be made at least 4 days in advance. **Registration:** At office. **Fee:** Single, $10. **Parking:** At park.

FACILITIES

Number of Multipurpose Sites: 60. **Hookups:** None. **Each Site:** Call ahead. **Dump Station:** Yes. **Laundry:** No. **Pay Phone:** Yes. **Restrooms and Showers:** Yes. **Fuel:** No. **Propane:** No. **Internal Roads:** Paved. **RV Service:** No. **Market:** No.

Restaurant: No. **General Store:** No. **Vending:** No. **Swimming:** Yes. **Playground:** No. **Activities:** Fishing, hiking.

RESTRICTIONS

Pets: Pets must be restrained or on a leash at all times while in developed recreation areas. **Fires:** In fire rings, stoves, grills, or fireplaces provided for that purpose. **Alcoholic Beverages:** Not allowed. **Vehicle Maximum Length:** 75 ft.

TO GET THERE

Located in northwest Montana near the Canadian/US border. 7 mi. west of US 93 Eureka, MT on Hwy. 37, near the community of Rexford.

LIVINGSTON   MAP, C-2
Paradise Valley KOA

163 Pine Creek Rd., 59047. T: (406) 222-0992 or (800) 562-2805; www.koa.com.

🚐 ★★★   ▲ ★★★

Beauty: ★★★★★	Site Privacy: ★★★
Spaciousness: ★★★	Quiet: ★★★★
Security: ★★★★	Cleanliness: ★★★
Insect Control: ★★★	Facilities: ★★★★

The drive on I-90 to this KOA offers a pleasant combination of Montana's subtly sloping hills, expansive plains, distant cragged mountains, and towering pines, marking a transition in the journey toward Yellowstone National Park. On your way into Paradise Valley, you'll pass a sign that reads, "Don't get the gumps. It's only a few more bumps to KOA." Rest assured your camping experience here will keep you gump-free. Located 8 miles south of Livingston, the campground is nestled at the foot of the Absaroka Mountains on the banks of the winding Yellowstone River. This KOA provides well-maintained, semiprivate sites surrounded by huge cottonwood, Douglas fir, and quaking aspen. Pull-through and back-in sites are available. The campground offers the usual KOA comforts complete with morning coffee and inexpensive breakfasts. Yellowstone is a short 35 miles away, but you might find yourself tempted to enjoy the area attractions: challenge yourself to a whitewater rafting trip, enjoy a quiet fly-fishing adventure, or hike one of the scenic trails.

BASICS

Operated By: Terry & Diane Devine. **Open:** May 1–Oct. 15. **Site Assignment:** By reservation. **Registration:** At camp store. **Fee:** RV, $22–$38; tent, $18–$22; per 2 people; extra person, $2.50; children under 7 free. **Parking:** At site.

FACILITIES

Number of RV-only Sites: 47. **Number of Tent-only Sites:** 22. **Hookups:** Electric (30, 50 amps), water, sewer. **Each Site:** Picnic table. **Dump Station:** Yes. **Laundry:** Yes. **Pay Phone:** Yes. **Restrooms and Showers:** Yes. **Fuel:** No. **Propane:** Yes. **Internal Roads:** Gravel, in good condition. **RV Service:** In Bozeman. **Market:** In town. **Restaurant:** Several in town. **General Store:** Yes. **Vending:** In store. **Swimming:** Indoor w/ hot tub. **Playground:** Yes. **Other:** 23 cabins, 1 cottage, hot tub, snack bar, pavilion. **Activities:** Swimming, horse-

shoes, volleyball, basketball, fun cycles, mountain biking, rafting (outfitters next door). **Nearby Attractions:** Yellowstone National Park, scenic drives, horseback riding, hot springs, guided park tours, fly-fishing trips, Yellowstone Gateway Museum. **Additional Information:** Livingston Chamber of Commerce, (406) 222-0850.

RESTRICTIONS

Pets: On leash. **Fires:** Fire pit only. **Alcoholic Beverages:** Allowed. **Vehicle Maximum Length:** 95 ft.

TO GET THERE

I-90 Exit 333 toward Yellowstone, go south 10 mi. on Hwy. 89 to Yellowstone Rd.

LIVINGSTON   MAP, C-2
Yellowstone's Edge RV Park

3502 Hwy. 89, 59047. T: (406) 333-4036 or (800) 865-7322; www.mtrv.com.

🚐 ★★★★★   ▲ ★★★★

Beauty: ★★★★	Site Privacy: ★★★★
Spaciousness: ★★★★	Quiet: ★★★★★
Security: ★★★★	Cleanliness: ★★★★★
Insect Control: ★★★★	Facilities: ★★★★★

As its name implies, Yellowstone's Edge RV Park is situated on the Yellowstone River, one of the longest free-flowing rivers in the United States and a great fly-fishing destination to boot. The park's 81 RV sites are shaded by maples, oaks, and pines, and they have great views of the river and surrounding landscape. Sites are close together, but with many return folks, this means the park is quite a friendly and neighborly place. Raccoons and squirrels are among some of the permanent residents, with deer sighted occasionally. The RV sites are divided evenly between pull-through and back-in, with electric, water, sewer, and phone hookups available. The river-view sites at this campground are the favorites among guests. This is a great alternative to staying in Yellowstone, which is only a 35-mile drive south. Other activities within easy driving distance include Chico Hot Springs, Museum of the Rockies, Lewis and Clark Caverns, and Virginia City. Staying closer to camp, campers have the option to hike, fish, mountain bike, or play volleyball.

BASICS

Operated By: Chan & Pam Libbey. **Open:** May 1–Oct. 10. **Site Assignment:** By reservation. **Registration:** At camp store. **Fee:** RV, $36; per 2 people. No tents. **Parking:** At site.

FACILITIES

Number of RV-only Sites: 81. **Number of Tent-only Sites:** 0. **Hookups:** Electric (30, 50 amps), water, sewer, phone. **Each Site:** Picnic table. **Dump Station:** No, all sites are on sewers. **Laundry:** Yes. **Pay Phone:** Yes. **Restrooms and Showers:** Yes. **Fuel:** 5 mi. south in Immigrant. **Propane:** Yes. **Internal Roads:** Gravel, in good condition. **RV Service:** In Bozeman. **Market:** In Livingston. **Restaurant:** There are several toward Bozeman. **General Store:** Yes. **Vending:** Yes. **Swimming:** No. **Playground:** No. **Other:** Large lodge, rec room, game room, 1

river suite, central fire ring, modem. **Activities:** Hiking, fishing (Yellowstone River), mountain biking, volleyball, game room, book exchange. **Nearby Attractions:** 36 mi. from the North Gate to Yellowstone National Park, scenic drives, horseback riding, hot springs, guided park tours, fly-fishing trips, Yellowstone Gateway Museum. **Additional Information:** Livingston Chamber of Commerce, (406) 222-0850.

RESTRICTIONS

Pets: On leash. **Fires:** No open fires. **Alcoholic Beverages:** Allowed. **Vehicle Maximum Length:** Up to 90 ft. w/tow.

TO GET THERE

Directly off Hwy. 89 in S. Livingston.

POLSON   MAP, B-1
Polson/Flathead Lake KOA

200 Irvine Flats Rd., 59860. T: (406) 883-2151 or (800) 562-2130; www.flatheadlakekoa.com.

🚐 ★★★★★   ▲ ★★★★

Beauty: ★★★★★	Site Privacy: ★★★
Spaciousness: ★★★	Quiet: ★★★★
Security: ★★★★	Cleanliness: ★★★★★
Insect Control: ★★★★	Facilities: ★★★★★

Built atop a hill, peering over the Flathead Lake is the Polson/Flathead Lake KOA. The view is magnificent and the air is crisp and cool. This KOA offers exceptional service and a lovely, clean, and well maintained property. Campsites offer level, gravel camping spurs, both back-in and pull-through, some lawn, and a terrific panoramic view of the Mission Mountains. There is a separate tent area, and if you prefer, there are sites in a tent village with water. The Polson KOA has a charming pool, spa, and snack bar. The Polson Koa is conveniently located to Glacier National Park and the National Bison Range. The Polson area has several places to rent boats or Jet Skis and offers outfitter services. The Flathead Lake is one of the largest naturally fed lakes in the country and offers recreation for every member of the family.

BASICS

Operated By: Paul & Carlisa London. **Open:** Apr. 15–Oct. 15. **Site Assignment:** By reservation. **Registration:** At camp store. **Fee:** RV, $27–$60; tent, $19–$28; per 2 people; extra person, $5; children under 6 stay free. **Parking:** At site.

FACILITIES

Number of RV-only Sites: 52. **Number of Tent-only Sites:** 6. **Hookups:** Electric (30, 50 amps), water, sewer. **Each Site:** Picnic table. **Dump Station:** Yes. **Laundry:** Yes. **Pay Phone:** Yes. **Restrooms and Showers:** Yes. **Fuel:** No. **Propane:** Yes. **Internal Roads:** Gravel, in good condition. **RV Service:** Limited in town. **Market:** In town. **Restaurant:** There are several in town. **General Store:** Yes. **Vending:** In store. **Swimming:** Indoor w/ hot tub. **Playground:** Yes. **Other:** 6 cabins, 1 cottage, hot tub, snack bar, pavilion, camp kitchen, tent village, central fire ring, adult-only hot tub, pancake breakfast weekends & holidays. **Activities:** Swimming, horseshoes, volleyball, day tours. **Nearby Attractions:** Flathead Lake, great fishing &

boating, boat rental, Wild Horse Island, several museums, short drive to Glacier National Park, *The Polson Princess* (50-ft. tour boat), whitewater float trips, guided fishing trips. **Additional Information:** Polson Chamber of Commerce, (406) 883-5969.

RESTRICTIONS

Pets: On leash. **Fires:** Fire pit only. **Alcoholic Beverages:** Allowed. **Vehicle Maximum Length:** Limited sites for very large RVs.

TO GET THERE

Half-mi. north of Polson, just off Hwy. 93.

SILVER STAR   MAP, C-2
Jefferson River Guest Ranch and Campground

5162 MT 41, 59751. T: (406) 684-5225 or (888) 474-8377; www.thejeffersonrivercamp.com.

🚐 ★★★   ⛺ ★★★★★

Beauty: ★★★★	Site Privacy: ★★★
Spaciousness: ★★★	Quiet: ★★★
Security: ★★★★	Cleanliness: ★★★★
Insect Control: ★★★★	Facilities: ★★★

Less than 30 miles from historic Virginia City, this campground is a beautiful 75-acre working ranch. Located on the Jefferson River, there are 15 RV sites. For tenters, the ranch offers open tenting most anywhere on the ranch. If you left your RV or tent at home, two fully furnished cabins are available for rent (probably best to call ahead for reservations, especially in summer). Scattered with cottonwoods, willows, and pines, this campground attracts the occasional moose, elk, deer, and pheasant. The friendly folks who own the campground also own the Four Rivers Fishing Company. The campground, located on a half-mile stretch of the scenic and trout-rich Jefferson River, is a prime stop for trout fishermen.

BASICS

Operated By: Greg Smith. **Open:** Apr. 1–Nov. 1. **Site Assignment:** By reservation, open tenting. **Registration:** At camp office or self-registration. **Fee:** RV, $30; tent, $20. **Parking:** At site.

FACILITIES

Number of RV-only Sites: 15. **Number of Tent-only Sites:** Undesignated sites. **Hookups:** Electric (30, 50 amps), water, sewer. **Each Site:** Picnic table, fire pits. **Dump Station:** Yes. **Laundry:** Yes, at the courtesy of the host. **Pay Phone:** Courtesy phone available. **Restrooms and Showers:** Yes. **Fuel:** About 2 mi. in Silver Star. **Propane:** Next door. **Internal Roads:** Combination of gravel & packed dirt. **RV Service:** In Butte. **Market:** In Twin Bridges. **Restaurant:** 10 mi. in either direction. **General Store:** Next door. **Vending:** Yes. **Swimming:** River. **Playground:** No. **Other:** Located on Jefferson River. **Activities:** Blue-ribbon fly fishing, quilting, book exchange, mountain biking. **Nearby Attractions:** Horseback riding, Virginia City, hunting, gold panning, biking. **Additional Information:** Whitehall Chamber of Commerce, (406) 287-2260.

RESTRICTIONS

Pets: On leash only. **Fires:** Fire pit only. Fires may be prohibited due to dry weather; ask management

before starting any fire. **Alcoholic Beverages:** Allowed. **Vehicle Maximum Length:** 40 ft. **Other:** 14-day stay limit Memorial Day–Labor Day.

TO GET THERE

Located between I-90 and I-15 on Hwy. 41.

ST. MARY   MAP, A-1
Johnson's Campground and RV Park

HC 72 10 Star Rte., 59417-9701. T: (406) 732-4207; www.johnsonsofstmary.com/services/campground/campground.htm.

🚐 ★★★   ⛺ ★★★

Beauty: ★★★	Site Privacy: ★★★
Spaciousness: ★★★	Quiet: ★★★★
Security: ★★★	Cleanliness: ★★★
Insect Control: ★★★	Facilities: ★★★

Upon a hilltop directly adjacent to the east entrance to Glacier National Park is Johnson Campground and RV Park. East of the Continental Divide, the St. Mary's area offers a diversified high desert terrain and hot summer days. The campground sits atop a large hill overlooking the peaks of Logan Pass and circles back down the hill into a small grass and sand valley where there are several tent sites. The larger RV sites are located on top of the hill in an open clearing with a panoramic view of Glacier. All sites are pull-through. The internal roads are gravel and dirt, which may hinder mobility into sites provided for smaller RVs and fifth wheelers. The campground has a very natural appearance and sites tend to be a bit rustic. In addition to the campground, there is a cafe, a covered picnic area with a grill, and a small motel. Someone is always on staff to assist with any need.

BASICS

Operated By: Johnson family. **Open:** Mid-May–late Sept. **Site Assignment:** Reservations recommended w/ 1-night deposit. **Registration:** At general store. **Fee:** RV, $21–$37.45; tent, $19.26; per 2 people, extra person, $5; children under 12, $2.50; cash, credit, check; members of Good Sam. **Parking:** At site.

FACILITIES

Number of RV-only Sites: 42. **Number of Tent-only Sites:** 75. **Number of Multipurpose Sites:** 40. **Hookups:** Electric (20, 30 amps), water, sewer. **Each Site:** Picnic table, some fire pits. **Dump Station:** Yes. **Laundry:** Yes. **Pay Phone:** Yes. **Restrooms and Showers:** Yes. **Fuel:** Next door. **Propane:** Yes. **Internal Roads:** Gravel. **RV Service:** 50 mi. west in Kalispell. **Market:** 1 mi. southeast in St. Mary. **Restaurant:** Yes. **General Store:** Yes. **Vending:** Yes. **Swimming:** No. **Playground:** Yes. **Other:** 1 cabin, covered pavilion w/ kitchen facilities & 2 barbecue grills, small motel, cafe. **Activities:** Horseshoe pit, hiking, biking. **Nearby Attractions:** Glacier National Park (east entrance), hiking, backpacking, guided tours of the park, interpretive programs, helicopter tours, balloon tours. **Additional Information:** www.glacierinfo.com, click on St. Mary.

RESTRICTIONS

Pets: On leash only. **Fires:** Fire pit only. Fires may be prohibited due to weather; please ask management

before starting any fire. **Alcoholic Beverages:** At site only. **Vehicle Maximum Length:** Call ahead for details.

TO GET THERE

Located in the heart of St. Mary on Hwy. 89, 0.25 mi. from the east entrance to Glacier National Park, (15 mi. northwest of Browing).

ST. MARY   MAP, A-1
St. Mary-Glacier Park KOA

106 West Shore, 59417. T: (406) 732-4122 or (800) 562-1504; www.goglacier.com, www.koa.com.

🚐 ★★★   ⛺ ★★★

Beauty: ★★★	Site Privacy: ★★★
Spaciousness: ★★★	Quiet: ★★★★
Security: ★★★	Cleanliness: ★★★★
Insect Control: ★★★	Facilities: ★★★★

Directly at the east gate of Glacier and Waterton International Parks sits St. Mary KOA. The campground is an ideal base for families wishing to visit the national parks. Scenic Going-to-the-Sun Road is only a few miles away. St. Mary-Glacier Park KOA is a full-service modern campground with all the amenities, including canoe, paddleboat, and kayak rentals. There are barbecue dinners in the evenings and pancakes for breakfast. The campground is large, but sites are small with little privacy between. Tent sites are in fields of aspen but a fair walk from the facilities. There is a nice hot tub with a spectacular mountain view. However, it is close to the dump. The weather is warm and dry in the summer on the eastern side of the Continental Divide. The altitude is high, so the air may seem a bit thin. The view is spectacular and the staff is friendly.

BASICS

Operated By: Will & Susan Brook. **Open:** May 1–Sept. 30. **Site Assignment:** Reservations recommended, held w/ credit card. **Registration:** At gift shop. **Fee:** RV, $28–$50; tent, $22–$23; plus 10% tax per 2 people; KOA value card 10% discount; cash, credit. **Parking:** At site.

FACILITIES

Number of RV-only Sites: 60. **Number of Tent-only Sites:** 64. **Number of Multipurpose Sites:** 10. **Hookups:** Electric (30, 50 amps), water, sewer. **Each Site:** Picnic table, some grated fire pits. **Dump Station:** Yes. **Laundry:** Yes. **Pay Phone:** Yes. **Restrooms and Showers:** Yes. **Fuel:** No. **Propane:** Yes. **Internal Roads:** Gravel. **RV Service:** 126 mi. southeast in Great Falls. **Market:** In St. Mary. **Restaurant:** In St. Mary or on the property. **General Store:** Yes. **Vending:** General store. **Swimming:** No, but 2 hot tubs. **Playground:** Yes. **Other:** 25 camp cabins, 2 cottages, game room, gift shop, outdoor barbecue restaurant, 2 hot tubs, canoe rental, bike rental, car rental, group sites, Internet data port in the gift shop. **Activities:** Fish (rainbow trout), canoe, bike, hike, game room, horseshoes, volleyball. **Nearby Attractions:** Glacier National Park (2 mi. from east entrance), hiking trails, mountain bike trails, horseback riding, nightly interpretive programs in Glacier. **Additional Information:** www.goglacier.com, www.koa.com.

RESTRICTIONS

Pets: On leash only. **Fires:** Fire pit only (fires may be prohibited due to weather; please ask camp staff before starting any fire). **Alcoholic Beverages:** Allowed. **Vehicle Maximum Length:** No limit.

TO GET THERE

From Hwy. 89 in St. Mary, look for huge KOA sign; turn down West Shore, and the KOA sits on the right hand side 1 mi. down.

ST. REGIS	MAP, B-1
Campground St. Regis	

44 Frontage Rd. West, 59866. T: (406) 649-2470 or (888) 247-8734; www.campgroundstregis.com.

🚐 ★★★★   ⛺ ★★★★

Beauty: ★★★★★	Site Privacy: ★★★★
Spaciousness: ★★★★	Quiet: ★★★★
Security: ★★★★	Cleanliness: ★★★★★
Insect Control: ★★★★	Facilities: ★★★★

Campground St. Regis is conveniently located off I-90 on the frontage road in St. Regis. This family-oriented campground is nestled in a wooded setting, offering activities for all. Campground St. Regis is surrounded by mountains and is only a few miles from the St. Regis River. Elk, deer, and even a few bears have been spotted here. This campground offers large, spacious, ponderosa pine and maple–shaded sites with some pull-throughs as long as 75 ft. They provide a large heated pool, game room, and video rentals. The weather offers summer days averaging in the 70s and evenings in the low 40s. There are two golf courses in the area, along with whitewater rafting, horseback riding, hunting, antiques stores, and lots of fishing. St. Regis is the western gateway to the National Bison Range and the Flathead Lake Area.

BASICS

Operated By: Lisa & Mitch Hollingsworth. **Open:** All year. **Site Assignment:** Reservations recommended. **Registration:** At general store. **Fee:** RV, $23; tent, $18. **Parking:** At site.

FACILITIES

Number of Multipurpose Sites: 75. **Hookups:** Electric (20, 30, 50 amps), water, sewer, phone, Internet. **Each Site:** Picnic table, some fire pits. **Dump Station:** Yes. **Laundry:** Yes. **Pay Phone:** Yes. **Restrooms and Showers:** Yes. **Fuel:** 1 mi. in St. Regis. **Propane:** Yes. **Internal Roads:** Gravel. **RV Service:** In St. Regis, 1 mi. **Market:** In St. Regis, 1 mi. **Restaurant:** In St. Regis, 1 mi. **General Store:** Yes. **Vending:** No. **Swimming:** Yes (Memorial Day–Labor Day). **Playground:** Yes. **Other:** Game room, video rental, fax service, horse boarding (must make reservations). **Activities:** Swimming, horseshoes, biking, hiking. **Nearby Attractions:** Fishing (St. Regis River or Flathead Lake), boating, hunting, golf, whitewater rafting, casinos. **Additional Information:** Montana Visitors Information, (406) 841-2870.

RESTRICTIONS

Pets: On leash only. **Fires:** Fire pit only. **Alcoholic Beverages:** Allowed. **Vehicle Maximum Length:** No limit.

TO GET THERE

I-90 Exit 33, go north to 4-way and turn left onto Mullan Rd. Go 0.75 mi. and turn left on Little Joe Rd. Go 0.5 mi. and turn right on Frontage Rd.; campground is 0.5 mi. on right. There are excellent signs directing you from interstate exit.

ST. REGIS	MAP, B-1
Nugget RV Resort	

105 Old Hwy. 10 East, 59866. T: (406) 649-2122 or (888) 800-0125; www.nuggetrvresort.com.

🚐 ★★★★★   ⛺ ★★★

Beauty: ★★★★	Site Privacy: ★★★★
Spaciousness: ★★★★	Quiet: ★★★★
Security: ★★★★	Cleanliness: ★★★★★
Insect Control: ★★★	Facilities: ★★★★★

Conveniently located on the frontage road directly off I-90 in St. Regis, the Nugget RV Resort is a unique experience. The facility is well maintained and clean. They offer all the modern amenities, including a pool and driving range. There is a historic mining camp on the property to visit. There is a camping kitchen, snack bar, and Wi-Fi throughout. The sites are a combination of grass and gravel. The weather is comfortable in the summer and cold in the winter. There is someone on security duty around the clock. The owners have gone out of their way to make this resort truly memorable.

BASICS

Operated By: Jim & Shirley Shotwell. **Open:** Mar. 1–Nov. 1. **Site Assignment:** Reservations recommended during summer & holiday seasons; reservations can be made from Web site w/ online form. **Registration:** At general store. **Fee:** RV, $27–$30; tent, $21–$24; cabin, $45–$55; per 2 people; extra person, $3; Good Sam discount available. **Parking:** At site.

FACILITIES

Number of RV-only Sites: 50. **Number of Tent-only Sites:** 10. **Hookups:** Electric (30, 50 amps), water, sewer, Wi-Fi. **Each Site:** Picnic tables; most have fire pits. **Dump Station:** Yes. **Laundry:** Yes. **Pay Phone:** Courtesy phone. **Restrooms and Showers:** Yes. **Fuel:** 1 mi. in St. Regis. **Propane:** Yes. **Internal Roads:** Gravel. **RV Service:** 1 hour in Missoula. **Market:** In St. Regis. **Restaurant:** In St. Regis. **General Store:** Yes. **Vending:** General store. **Swimming:** Yes (Memorial Day–Labor Day). **Playground:** Yes. **Other:** Cabins, camp kitchen w/grill & microwave, historic mining camp (tent area), snack bar, Wi-Fi, mini casino. **Activities:** Driving range, nature trails, fishing, hunting, swimming, horseshoe pits. **Nearby Attractions:** St. Regis River, golf, Flathead Lake, horseback riding, Hiawatha Bike Trail, National Bison Range, Clark Fork River. **Additional Information:** Montana Visitors Information, (406) 649-2290.

RESTRICTIONS

Pets: On leash only. Off-leash area available. **Fires:**

Fire pit only. **Alcoholic Beverages:** Allowed. **Vehicle Maximum Length:** No limit.

TO GET THERE

From I-90 Exit 33 in St. Regis, go north to 4-way stop, turn right on Frontage Rd. Nugget RV Resort is 1 mi. on your left.

THREE FORKS	MAP, B-2
Three Forks KOA	

15 KOA Rd., 59752. T: (406) 285-3611 or (800) 562-9752; www.koa.com.

🚐 ★★★★   ⛺ ★★★

Beauty: ★★★★	Site Privacy: ★★★
Spaciousness: ★★★	Quiet: ★★★
Security: ★★★★	Cleanliness: ★★★★
Insect Control: ★★★	Facilities: ★★★★

Nestled in a panoramic setting, this KOA is a very pleasant park indeed. The maple and oak–shaded RV and tent sites are adequately sized, with lovely views of the countryside. Squirrels are commonplace at this campsite, and deer have been known to wander into the park occasionally. Security is above average and the grounds are well maintained. Each site offers parking, picnic tables, and fire pits, and some RV sites with full hookups. The campground also offers a good many family activities, including a petting zoo, ice-cream parlor, and a pool table. For those guests on a working vacation, data ports are available. Nearby, there are golf courses, the Lewis and Clark Caverns, and the Headwater Heritage Museum, just to list a few. Reservations are recommended, however, because finding a place in the peak season is difficult.

BASICS

Operated By: Tom Glorvigen. **Open:** Apr. 15–Oct. 15. **Site Assignment:** Reservations recommended. **Registration:** At general store. **Fee:** RV, $20–$34; tent, $20; per 2 people; extra person, $3. **Parking:** At site.

FACILITIES

Number of RV-only Sites: 56. **Number of Tent-only Sites:** 21. **Hookups:** Electric (30, 50 amps), water, sewer. **Each Site:** Picnic tables, fire pits. **Dump Station:** Yes. **Laundry:** Yes. **Pay Phone:** Yes. **Restrooms and Showers:** Yes. **Fuel:** 1 mi. by I-90. **Propane:** 1 mi. by I-90. **Internal Roads:** Gravel. **RV Service:** 32 mi. in E. Bozeman. **Market:** 3 mi. in Three Forks. **Restaurant:** In town. **General Store:** Yes. **Vending:** No. **Swimming:** Yes w/ slide. **Playground:** Yes. **Other:** 4 cabins, petting zoo (chickens & horses), ice cream, data port. **Activities:** Volleyball, pool table, nature trails, fishing w/ water access. **Nearby Attractions:** Headwater Heritage Museum, golf, Lewis & Clark Caverns, the Madison, Jefferson, & Missouri rivers, hunting, float trip outfitters. **Additional Information:** Montana Visitors Info, (406) 649-2290.

RESTRICTIONS

Pets: On leash only. **Fires:** Fire pit only. **Alcoholic Beverages:** Allowed. **Vehicle Maximum Length:** No limit.

TO GET THERE
From I-90 Exit 274, follow signs to KOA, less than 1 mi.

WEST GLACIER · MAP, A-1
Glacier Campground

P.O. Box 447, 59936. T: (406) 387-5689 or (888) 387-5689; www.glaciercampground.com.

🚐 ★★★★ 　　　 ⛺ ★★★★

Beauty: ★★★★★	Site Privacy: ★★★★
Spaciousness: ★★★★	Quiet: ★★★★
Security: ★★★★	Cleanliness: ★★★★★
Insect Control: ★★★★	Facilities: ★★★

Just outside the gates of Glacier National Park is Glacier Campground. This delightful campground is nestled in a mountain clearing surrounded by 40 acres of wooded area. The surrounding trees provide shelter for rabbits and squirrels. Bears may also be spotted here occasionally. The air is crisp and the view is spectacular. The campground consists of 175 wooded sites that are private, spacious, and large enough for easy mobility. Sites are both back-in and pull-through, with gravel parking pads. The natural fir and pines stand tall, and overhanging branches do not seem to be a problem. Tent sites are private and offer a rustic ambiance. The campground is convenient to numerous lakes and rivers, restaurants, ski resorts, and other area activities. The weather is typical of high-altitude areas, with dramatic temperature drops in the evening. The campground is staffed around the clock, with the office and lodge open daily.

BASICS
Operated By: George & Kathleen Flint. **Open:** May 15–Sept. 30. **Site Assignment:** Reservations recommended, held w/ credit card. **Registration:** At camp office. **Fee:** RV, $20–$26; tent, $19; per 2 people; extra child ages 5–11, $1; extra adult, $1.50; cash, credit, check. **Parking:** At site.

FACILITIES
Number of RV-only Sites: 50. **Number of Tent-only Sites:** 50. **Number of Multipurpose Sites:** 75. **Hookups:** Electric (20, 30 amps), water. **Each Site:** Picnic tables, grated fire pits. **Dump Station:** Yes. **Laundry:** Yes. **Pay Phone:** Yes. **Restrooms and Showers:** Yes. **Fuel:** In West Glacier. **Propane:** Yes. **Internal Roads:** Mostly paved, some well-graded gravel. **RV Service:** Ask in office. **Market:** In West Glacier. **Restaurant:** Yes. **General Store:** Yes. **Vending:** No. **Swimming:** No. **Playground:** Yes. **Other:** Pavilion w/ kitchen facilities, 5 cabins, level tent pads, beautiful rustic Lodge w/ round central fireplace & rec room, large-screen TV, area where large dogs may run. **Activities:** Horseshoes, volleyball, basketball, picnic area. **Nearby Attractions:** Glacier National Park, world class fly-fishing (Dolly Varden trout, eastern brook trout, western slope native cutthroat, bull trout), whitewater rafting, helicopter tours, scenic drives, fishing tours, horseback riding, House of Mystery, North American Wildlife Museum. **Additional Information:** Columbia Falls Area Chamber of Commerce, (406) 892-2072, Glacier National Park (406) 888-7800, or www.areaparks.com.

RESTRICTIONS
Pets: On leash only. **Fires:** Fire pit only. Fires may be restricted due to dry weather; ask management before starting any fire. **Alcoholic Beverages:** Allowed. **Vehicle Maximum Length:** None.

TO GET THERE
Located directly off Hwy. 2 in West Glacier.

WEST GLACIER 　 MAP, XX-00
Glacier National Park

Park Headquarters, 59936. T: (406) 888-7800 or (406) 888-7898; www.nps.gov/glac/home.htm.

🚐 ★★★ 　　　 ⛺ ★★★★

Beauty: ★★★★★	Site Privacy: ★★★
Spaciousness: ★★★	Quiet: ★★★
Security: ★★★★	Cleanliness: ★★★★
Insect Control: ★★★★	Facilities: ★★★★

Welcome to one of America's most pristine and biodiverse parks. Glacier National Park stretches over a million acres, crosses the Continental Divide, and is home to over 1,000 species of plants and some of the largest and smallest animals found below the Arctic Circle. Glacier National Park offers over 1,000 campsites in varying terrain. You may choose the mature western red cedar and hemlock forests found in the west to rolling grasslands and aspens found in the east. In order to preserve the natural setting and protect its wildlife inhabitants, Glacier National Park does not offer full-hookup facilities. There are several dump stations located throughout the park. Most of Glacier's campgrounds are designed in loops, with an amphitheater somewhere in the middle offering evening interpretive programs. The weather in Glacier National Park varies from the east to the west, with more rain in the west and warmer days in the east. Temperatures in the summer average high 70s for the day and drop into the low 40s during the evening. Remember, however, it can snow any day of the year. Camp hosts attend to most campground areas, and rangers are on duty 24 hours a day.

BASICS
Operated By: U.S. National Park Service. **Open:** All year; most campsites open May–Sept. 30; primitive winter camping available. **Site Assignment:** 2 of the 13 campgrounds are reservable (Fish Creek on the west & St. Mary on the east); the rest are first come, first served; (800) 365-2267 or reservations.nps.gov. **Registration:** Register at information bulletin board for the selected campground, only pay 1 night at a time (see camp host for assistance). **Fee:** $12–$17; cash, check. **Parking:** At site.

FACILITIES
Number of Multipurpose Sites: 1328. **Hookups:** Water. **Each Site:** Picnic table, grated fire pits. **Dump Station:** Yes. **Laundry:** Yes, located at the Swift Current Motor Inn in the Many Glacier area of the park, also in West Glacier & St. Mary right outside the park gate. **Pay Phone:** Yes, in designated service areas but not individual campgrounds. **Restrooms and Showers:** Restrooms in all campgrounds (many w/ flush toilets). Showers may be taken at the Swiftcurrent Motor Inn in the Many Glacier Area, or the Rising Sun Motor Inn in the Rising Sun Area. **Fuel:** There is no fuel in the park; you may purchase fuel in West Glacier (west entrance) or St. Mary (east entrance), also in Babb, MT; Waterton, Alberta; Browning, MT. **Propane:** No. **Internal Roads:** Paved, gravel, & dirt. **RV Service:** In West Glacier. **Market:** Apgar, Lake McDonald, West Glacier, St. Mary, or Waterton. **Restaurant:** There are 8 restaurants located in the park, or West Glacier & St. Mary. **General Store:** There are 10 gift shops/camp stores in the area. **Vending:** In designated service areas, but not in individual campgrounds. **Swimming:** Lakes & streams. **Playground:** No. **Other:** Several boat launches, boat rentals (Lake McDonald, Apgar, Many Glaciers, Two Medicine), picnic areas, amphitheaters, 6 hotels, 10 gift shops, camera & film development shop, 3 visitor centers, many more primitive hike-in campsites, ATM machines (Apgar). **Activities:** Scenic boat tours (Lake McDonald, Many Glacier, Rising Sun, Two Medicine), 700 mi. of maintained hiking trails & backpacking (permit required), bicycling (permitted only on roadways), horseback riding (Many Glacier & Lake McDonald). **Nearby Attractions:** Whitewater rafting, balloon rides, helicopter tours. **Additional Information:** www.glacierparkinc.com, www.americanparks.net/glaciernationalpark.htm.

RESTRICTIONS
Pets: Leashed, or crated only. Pets are not permitted on trails, along lakeshores, or in backcountry. **Fires:** Fire pit only (fires may be restricted due to dry weather; ask park official before starting any fire). **Alcoholic Beverages:** Allowed w/ discretion. **Vehicle Maximum Length:** Apgar, 40 ft.; Many Glacier, Fish Creek, St. Mary, Two Medicine, 35 ft.; Avalanche, 26 ft.; Sprague Creek, 21 ft. (no tow-in units). **Other:** 7-day stay limit per campsite; 8 people max. per site; no more than 2 tents per site; group sites available; special bike-camping sites available for $3 per night per person.

TO GET THERE
West entrance is located off Hwy. 2 in West Glacier, 23 mi. northeast of Kalispell; east entrance is located off Hwy. 89 in St. Mary, 17 mi. north of Browning. You may also enter the park in Waterson, Alberta, or off Hwy. 89 in Babb, MT.

WEST YELLOWSTONE 　MAP, C-2
Yellowstone Park/ West Entrance KOA

P.O. Box 348, 3305 Targhee Pass Hwy., 59758. T: (406) 646-7606 or (800) 562-7591; www.yellowstonekoa.com.

🚐 ★★★★ 　　　 ⛺ ★★★

Beauty: ★★★★	Site Privacy: ★★★
Spaciousness: ★★★	Quiet: ★★★
Security: ★★★★	Cleanliness: ★★★★
Insect Control: ★★★	Facilities: ★★★★

The perfect base camp for exploring Yellowstone's 2 million acres, Yellowstone Park KOA offers 166 RV sites and 73 tent-only sites within 6 miles of the west entrance. Back-in and pull-through sites are available. The paved road provides easy access throughout the grounds. Pancake breakfast and a chuck wagon dinner are available daily in season (mid-June to Labor Day). There's not much campers can't do outside of camp, including hiking, whitewater rafting, and horseback riding. Camp activities include mini-golf, basketball, and horseshoes. Bike rentals are also available. Nearby attractions include the Yellowstone IMAX Theater, Grizzly Discovery Center and Wolf Preserve, and Museum of Yellowstone. An indoor pool and spa provide comfort for those relaxing after a day of adventuring.

BASICS

Operated By: Steve & Laurel Linde. **Open:** May 22–Oct. 1. **Site Assignment:** Reservations highly recommended. **Registration:** At general store. **Fee:** RV, $47; tent, $36. **Parking:** At site.

FACILITIES

Number of RV-only Sites: 166. **Number of Tent-only Sites:** 73. **Number of Multipurpose Sites:** 3. **Hookups:** Electric (30, 50 amps), water, sewer. **Each Site:** Picnic table, grated fire pits, some concrete patios. **Dump Station:** Yes. **Laundry:** Yes. **Pay Phone:** Yes. **Restrooms and Showers:** Yes. **Fuel:** No. **Propane:** Yes. **Internal Roads:** Paved. **RV Service:** Local service. **Market:** West Yellowstone. **Restaurant:** West Yellowstone (pancake breakfast & barbecue dinners served on site). **General Store:** Yes. **Vending:** Yes. **Swimming:** Indoor pool & hot tub. **Playground:** Yes. **Other:** 58 cabins, camping kitchen, gifts, fresh fudge, Internet data port. **Activities:** Mini-golf, fun cycle & bike rentals, fishing, basketball, game room, Yellowstone tours. **Nearby Attractions:** Yellowstone National Park, IMAX, Museums, Grizzly Discovery Center, whitewater rafting, Teton Aviation Center, Yellowstone Historic Center. **Additional Information:** West Yellowstone Chamber of Commerce, (406) 646-7701.

RESTRICTIONS

Pets: On leash. **Fires:** Fire pit only. **Alcoholic Beverages:** Allowed. **Vehicle Maximum Length:** No limit.

TO GET THERE

From West Yellowstone, go east 5 mi. on US 20 to the campground entrance.

WHITE SULPHUR SPRINGS   MAP. B-2
Conestoga Campground

P.O. Box 869, 59645. T: (406) 547-3890 or (888) 898-5386; www.ccmemberships.com.

🚐 ★★★	🏕 ★★★
Beauty: ★★★	Site Privacy: ★★★
Spaciousness: ★★★	Quiet: ★★★★
Security: ★★★★	Cleanliness: ★★★
Insect Control: ★★★	Facilities: ★★★

This privately owned campground is surrounded by the Big Belt, Little Belt, and Castle Mountains, and offers some of the most magnificent views in North America. While the site facilities are average, the campground's strongest selling point is its location. The campground is nestled between Yellowstone National Park and Glacier National Park, and provides easy access to these national treasures. The

campground is also in close proximity to the world-famous Smith River along with numerous mountain lakes and streams filled with various species of fish. The locals boast that this unspoiled pine and fir–filled part of Montana has more elk and deer than people. There are more than 860 miles of hiking trails in seven mountain ranges. The campground is open from April through November, and reservations can be made by phone.

BASICS

Operated By: Fred & Merianne Steinback. **Open:** May 1–Nov. 15. **Site Assignment:** By reservation. **Registration:** At camp office. **Fee:** $30 per 2 people; extra person, $3; members: special rate plan. **Parking:** At site.

FACILITIES

Number of RV-only Sites: 41. **Number of Tent-only Sites:** Undesignated sites. **Hookups:** Electric (20, 30, 50 amps), water, sewer. **Each Site:** Picnic tables. **Dump Station:** Yes. **Laundry:** Yes. **Pay Phone:** Yes. **Restrooms and Showers:** Yes. **Fuel:** No, 1 mi. in town. **Propane:** No. **Internal Roads:** Gravel. **RV Service:** Limited service in Townsend. **Market:** In town. **Restaurant:** In town. **General Store:** Yes. **Vending:** Yes. **Swimming:** No. **Playground:** Yes. **Other:** Trout pond, all pull-through sites 25 by 80 ft., water in tent area, free shuttle service to many area activities. **Activities:** Games, picnicking, fishing. **Nearby Attractions:** Golf, teen center, hot mineral baths, many fishing & rafting outfitters, big-game hunting, skiing, boating, several museums, Old Fort Logan. **Additional Information:** Meagher County Chamber of Commerce, (406) 547-2250.

RESTRICTIONS

Pets: On leash. **Fires:** No open fires. **Alcoholic Beverages:** Allowed. **Vehicle Maximum Length:** No limit. **Other:** This is a special membership RV park; refer to their Web site or call for more information.

TO GET THERE

66 mi. from I-90 Exit 340, head northeast on US 89 for 57 mi., then go north on US 12 for 9 mi., left onto SR 360, go 0.25 mi. and left or south on 8th Ave. SW to entrance.

WHITEFISH   MAP, A-1
Whitefish-Kalispell North

5121 Hwy. 93S, 59937. T: (406) 862-4242 or (800) 562-8734; www.glacierparkkoa.com.

🚐 ★★★★	🏕 ★★★★
Beauty: ★★★★	Site Privacy: ★★★
Spaciousness: ★★★	Quiet: ★★★
Security: ★★★★	Cleanliness: ★★★★
Insect Control: ★★★★	Facilities: ★★★★★

Whitefish-Kalispell is a superb campground with amenities and activities for the entire family. Nestled in a scenic forest atmosphere 2 miles south of Whitefish, this campground is located in the Rocky Mountains, near Glacier National Park, the Flathead River, Whitefish Lake, and Big Mountain Ski Resort. The campground offers large comfortable sites, both pull-through and back-in. Tent sites are available in the woods or on a more open lawn area. The park

features a large family entertainment center with an indoor/outdoor pool, game room, and pizzeria. The area is famous for its skiing and fishing, and has an abundance of hiking and biking trails (the campground rents bikes). In addition, the campground has ten cabins and a huge recreation hall that accommodates up to 500 people. The weather is cool through late June, so remember to pack warm. The campground offers 24-hour security and the staff is very friendly. Summers fill up quickly, so make reservations as far in advance as possible.

BASICS

Operated By: Walt Staves. **Open:** All year. **Site Assignment:** Reservations recommended Apr.–Oct., held w/ credit card. **Registration:** At general store. **Fee:** RV, $37; tent, $26; per 2 people; extra adult, $4; children under age 17 stay free; KOA Value card discount & Good Sam honored; cash, credit, check. **Parking:** At site.

FACILITIES

Number of RV-only Sites: 15. **Number of Tent-only Sites:** Undesignated sites. **Hookups:** Electric (30, 50 amps), water, sewer. **Each Site:** Picnic table, fire pits. **Dump Station:** No. **Laundry:** Yes, at the courtesy of the host. **Pay Phone:** Courtesy phone available. **Restrooms and Showers:** Yes. **Fuel:** About 2 mi. in Silver Star. **Propane:** Yes. **Internal Roads:** Gravel & packed dirt. **RV Service:** In Butte. **Market:** In Whitefish. **Restaurant:** Buffalo Bob's Pizza Place on property; also in Kalispell or Whitefish. **General Store:** Yes. **Vending:** In restaurant or general store. **Swimming:** Yes, indoor w/child wading pool (open year-round). **Playground:** Yes. **Other:** Recreation center w/ game room, 10 cabins, hot tub, restaurant. **Activities:** Paddleboats, volleyball, horseshoes, basketball, fun cycles, game room, hiking. **Nearby Attractions:** Big Mountain Ski Resort, Whitefish Lake, 18 mi. from Glacier National Park, boating, fishing (whitefish, cutthroat), cross-country skiing, snowmobile trails, waterskiing, windsurfing. **Additional Information:** Whitefish Chamber of Commerce, (406) 862-3501.

RESTRICTIONS

Pets: On leash only. **Fires:** Fire pit only. Fires may be prohibited due to dry weather; ask management before starting any fire. **Alcoholic Beverages:** Allowed. **Vehicle Maximum Length:** 40 ft. **Other:** 14-day stay limit Memorial Day–Labor Day.

TO GET THERE

Located directly off Hwy. 93, 4 mi. south of Whitefish.

WHITEHALL   MAP, B-2
Pipestone Campground

41 Bluebird Ln., 59759. T: (406) 287-5224 or (888) 287-5224; www.pipestonervpark.com.

🚐 ★★★	🏕 ★★★
Beauty: ★★★	Site Privacy: ★★★
Spaciousness: ★★★	Quiet: ★★★★
Security: ★★★	Cleanliness: ★★★
Insect Control: ★★★	Facilities: ★★★

Located 16 miles east of Butte, just off I-90, Pipestone Campground has 75 sites that offer a mix of pull-throughs and back-ins, some with complete hookups. The grounds are mostly open with a few scattered trees that provide little shade. Visitors will want to make sure to take advantage of the outdoor hot tub with a view of the snow-capped mountains. Activities such as horseshoes, swimming, tetherball and volleyball can help pass the time. Those wanting to explore Butte will find several museums and interpretive centers dedicated to mining, including the World Museum of Mining, the Mineral Museum, and the Anselmo Mine Yard.

BASICS

Operated By: Dan & Dianna Graves. **Open:** Apr. 1–Oct. 15. **Site Assignment:** Reservations accepted. **Registration:** At general store. **Fee:** RV, $22–$32; tent, $20; extra adult, $2; ages 5 & under, free. **Parking:** At site.

FACILITIES

Number of RV-only Sites: 75. **Number of Tent-only Sites:** Undesignated sites. **Hookups:** Electric (20, 30, 50 amps), water, sewer, phone. **Each Site:** Picnic tables, some fire pits. **Dump Station:** Yes. **Laundry:** Yes. **Pay Phone:** Yes. **Restrooms and Showers:** Yes. **Fuel:** No. **Propane:** Yes. **Internal Roads:** Gravel, in good condition. **RV Service:** 18 mi. west in Butte. **Market:** 5 mi. east in Whitehall. **Restaurant:** 5 mi. east in Whitehall. **General Store:** Yes. **Vending:** Yes. **Swimming:** Yes. **Playground:** Yes. **Other:** Cabins, RV wash, game room, mail service, large adult spa, Internet data port on pay phone. **Activities:** Swimming, campfires, volleyball, tetherball, horseshoes. **Nearby Attractions:** Fishing (rainbow trout), hunting, float trips, fishing tours. **Additional Information:** Whitehall Chamber of Commerce, (406) 287-2260.

RESTRICTIONS

Pets: On leash. **Fires:** Fire pit only. Fires may be restricted due to weather; ask management before starting any open fires. **Alcoholic Beverages:** Allowed. **Vehicle Maximum Length:** 45 ft.

TO GET THERE

I-90 Exit 241, 16 mi. east of Butte, can be seen from interstate.

WOLF CREEK MAP, XX-00
Lake Holter Recreation Area

1383 Beartooth Rd., 59648. T: (406) 452-3622; www.mt.blm.gov.

🚐 ★★★　　　　　　🔺 ★★★

Beauty: ★★★	Site Privacy: ★★★
Spaciousness: ★★★	Quiet: ★★★
Security: ★★★	Cleanliness: ★★★
Insect Control: ★★★	Facilities: ★★★

Approximately 35 miles north of Helena, the highlight of this recreation area is its proximity to Holter Lake. With 56 grassy sites located on the lake, there is a good chance you might be able to enjoy some lakefront camping. The area provides plenty of opportunity for recreational activities, including hiking, horseback riding, and fishing. Gravel access and interior roads, scant landscaping, a propensity for high winds, and sparsely wooded surrounding hills make this campground wanting of scenery. However, this might well be a worthwhile stop for any avid fisher. Lake Holter, located on the Missouri River, is home to walleye, and the "Mighty Mo," known worldwide for its dry fly-fishing, runs wild with brown and rainbow trout. This is definitely a destination spot for a pleasing fishing experience.

BASICS

Operated By: U.S. Bureau of Land Management. **Open:** Mid-may–mid-Oct. **Site Assignment:** First come, first served. **Registration:** Self-serve. **Fee:** $10 per unit. **Parking:** At site.

FACILITIES

Number of Multipurpose Sites: 140. **Hookups:** Water. **Each Site:** Picnic tables, fire pits. **Dump Station:** No. **Laundry:** No. **Pay Phone:** Yes. **Restrooms and Showers:** Restrooms only. **Fuel:** No. **Propane:** No. **Internal Roads:** Gravel. **RV Service:** Limited local service. **Market:** In town. **Restaurant:** Next door. **General Store:** No. **Vending:** No. **Swimming:** Beach at the lake. **Playground:** Yes. **Other:** Lake access, covered pavilion, lodge, 3 designated swimming areas, 2 multilaned boat ramps, docks w/ about 60 slips. **Activities:** Swimming, fishing, boating, jet skiing, waterskiing. **Nearby Attractions:** Several vacation ranches, blue-ribbon fishing, the state capital, horseback riding, natural hot springs, ghost towns, Helena. **Additional Information:** Helena Chamber of Commerce, (406) 442-4120.

RESTRICTIONS

Pets: On leash. **Fires:** Fire pit only. **Alcoholic Beverages:** Allowed. **Vehicle Maximum Length:** No limit. **Other:** 7-day stay limit.

TO GET THERE

Take Exit 226 at Wolf Creek and follow Recreation Frontage Rd. northeast about 3 mi., then 2 mi. east on gravel road.

Nebraska

The best way to get the full experience of Nebraska, America's gateway to the West, is by motorcoach, bike, or a good horse are Fur traders once navigated through this high plains state to avoid the mountain passes of Colorado as they ventured toward the Pacific. Nebraska was also used for the first transcontinental railroad, as well as the Pony Express. In many ways, the 37th state is a living museum. Every scenic byway tells a story and adds another piece to the puzzle of our American heritage. From the **Great Platte River Road Archway** to the famous **Oregon Trail Chimney Rock** landmark, the state's rich history comes alive.

Today, the Cornhusker State is broken into seven distinct regions; clockwise from the northwest: panhandle, sandhills, Lewis and Clark, metro, pioneer country, frontier trails, and prairie lakes. Tackling these regions on the road becomes less of a challenge and more of a moving classroom when experienced through the lens of Nebraska's nine major historical routes. The **Heritage Highway,** which scoops along the south of the state on Highway 136, offers a personal interaction with the **Oregon Trail.** To the north and east on Highway 75 lies the **Lewis and Clark Scenic Byway,** where the state's oldest settlements of **Fort Atkinson, Decatur,** and **South Sioux City** bubble over with the past. Darting back west along the northern ridge of Nebraska is the **Outlaw Trail Scenic Byway** along Highway 12, a corridor once notorious for its horse thieves, scofflaws, and the lawmen who fought them. In the far northwest corner on Highway 20, the **Bridges to Buttes Byway** leads you through the **Nebraska National Forest,** the largest hand-planted forest in the country, out onto land teeming with prehistoric fossils and immense views. Dipping south from there is the **385-Gold Rush Byway,** named for the discovery of the shiny stuff, unfortunately at the expense of the Sioux Indians' land, in the Black Hills. Highways 26/92's **Western Trails Historic and Scenic Byway** is home to **Buffalo Bill Cody** and **Lake McConaughy,** Nebraska's largest reservoir. The somewhat isolated **Platte River Scenic Trails Byway** on Highway 30 crosses the 100th meridian, and for bird-watchers, Highway 2, on the **Sandhills Journey Scenic Byway,** empties out onto **Grande Island.** From there, the **Loup Rivers Scenic Byway** careens southward along Highways 91/11 into the easygoing, beckoning heartland.

Nebraska is also an outdoor enthusiast's paradise—its rivers and streams offer a variety of options. Whether you enjoy paddling, rafting, waterskiing, or basking on the dock, there is a waterway for you. If you're a serious angler, the waters of Nebraska are full of walleye, trout, and bass. If you prefer to go green and are looking for a wide-open scenic route, hundreds of miles of biking and equestrian trails await you. Pedal complete sections of the **Cowboy Trail** linking **Norfolk** and **Chadron,** the longest **Rails to Trails** endeavor in the country at 321 miles, or cycle along the **Platte River.** Professional outfitters abound throughout, and the state parks make wonderful base camps.

Make no mistake, there is a refined side of Nebraska as well—one devoted to the fine arts, offering art museums, sculpture gardens, symphonies, and theater. If you are traveling west on the **Heritage Highway** through the southern portion of the state, a recommended stop-off is the **Willa Cather Heritage Museum and Educational Foundation** in **Red Cloud** for a glimpse into the life and legacy of one of the country's most noted literary contributors. Of bizarre interest for all you philatelists heading down the **Lewis and Clark Scenic Byway** may be the world's largest ball of stamps, weighing in at 600 pounds, in the **Boy's Town** visitor center located in West Omaha.

No matter how you approach the state, recreational camping remains the best way to experience the adventures Nebraska has to offer. Although the majority of full-service campgrounds are located off Interstate 80, you have to venture away from the major roads to fully appreciate the landscape and history. For impressive vistas of sweeping natural beauty, Nebraska state parks and recreation areas are some of the best in the country.

Campground Profiles

ASHLAND
Eugene T. Mahoney State Park

MAP, B-4

28500 West Park Hwy., 68003. T: (402) 944-2523; www.ngpc.state.ne.us/parks/guides/parksearch/etmaquatic.asp.

🚐 ★★★   ▲ ★★★

Beauty: ★★★   Site Privacy: ★★★
Spaciousness: ★★★   Quiet: ★★★★
Security: ★★★★   Cleanliness: ★★★
Insect Control: ★★★   Facilities: ★★

Offering large, shaded sites near Owen Marina Lake, camping in Eugene T. Mahoney State Park can be enjoyed year-round. It is easily accessible due to its I-80 location midway between Lincoln and Omaha. For campers who don't want to travel far for activities, this is the place to be, with everything from a waterslide to a virtual reality game room within the park. Winter recreation pursuits include ice-skating from November through March in the Pavilion, fishing in the 10-acre, trout-stocked US West Lake, and downhill sledding. The centrally located theater provides family fun with melodramas that run from Memorial Day weekend through early November. Next door to the park is the Strategic Air and Space Museum, the nation's foremost facility of its kind, with aircraft and missile exhibits.

BASICS
Operated By: Nebraska Game & Parks Commission. **Open:** All year. **Site Assignment:** First come, first served. **Registration:** At self-serve registration kiosks. **Fee:** $15; depends on site & amenities, plus vehicle entrance fee. **Parking:** At site.

FACILITIES
Number of RV-only Sites: 149. **Hookups:** Electric (20, 30 amps), water. **Each Site:** Picnic tables, fire pit. **Dump Station:** Yes; there is also a boat pump out on the marina. **Laundry:** Yes. **Pay Phone:** Yes. **Restrooms and Showers:** Yes. **Fuel:** Boat fuel only at the marina. **Propane:** No. **Internal Roads:** Paved. **RV Service:** 17 mi. in Elkhorn. **Market:** In Ashland. **Restaurant:** Peter Kiewit Lodge on site, the marina, or in Ashland. **General Store:** The marina is open Memorial Day through Labor Day. **Vending:** Yes. **Swimming:** Yes. **Playground:** Yes. **Other:** 51-cabin, 40-room lodge w/ full-service restaurant, waterslide, hiking trails, 10 picnic shelters, 1 w/ electricity, fish-cleaning station, full-service marina, Kountz Memorial Theater, observation tower, visitor center, indoor activity center, boat rentals. **Activities:** Swimming, waterslide, mini-golf, boating, fishing, hiking, arts & crafts, rock climbing simulator, indoor playground, hunting simulator, ball simulator, ice-skating, picnics, driving range. **Nearby Attractions:** Gavins Point Dam, Lewis & Clark Visitor Center, The National Fish Hatchery, Lakeview Golf Course. **Additional Information:** Gretna Chamber of Commerce, (402) 332-3535.

RESTRICTIONS
Pets: On leash. **Fires:** Grill or fire pits only. **Alcoholic Beverages:** No alcoholic beverages allowed. **Vehicle Maximum Length:** 45 ft.

TO GET THERE
From I-80 Exit 426, go northwest on W. Park Hwy., then bear right on Park Dr.

CHADRON
Chadron State Park

MAP, A-1

15951 Hwy. 385, 69337-7353. T: (308) 432-6167; www.chadron.com/csp.php.

🚐 ★★★   ▲ ★★★

Beauty: ★★★   Site Privacy: ★★★
Spaciousness: ★★★   Quiet: ★★★★
Security: ★★★★   Cleanliness: ★★★
Insect Control: ★★★   Facilities: ★★

Situated near the Nebraska National Forest, Chadron State Park guarantees exceptional scenery. The fees are very reasonable, and there are no reservations required. The sites for both RVs and tents are average sized, with picnic tables and fire pits. The campground offers only adequate privacy, but there's lots of peace and quiet. Ponderosa pines are the main source of shade, and turkey and deer have been spotted in the park. As for activities available, Chadron has some very unusual and interesting pastimes for the family. There is an old-time fur trade demonstration, and arts and crafts, as well as archery, tennis, and a buffalo stew cookout by appointment. Nearby, guests will find the Dawes County Historical Museum, biking, and golf.

BASICS
Operated By: Nebraska Game & Parks Commission. **Open:** All year. **Site Assignment:** First come, first served. **Registration:** At self-serve registration kiosks. **Fee:** $3–$12; depends on site & amenities, plus vehicle entrance fee. **Parking:** At site.

FACILITIES
Number of RV-only Sites: 70. **Number of Tent-only Sites:** 18. **Hookups:** Electric (20, 30 amps), water. **Each Site:** Picnic tables, fire pit. **Dump Station:** Yes. **Laundry:** Yes. **Pay Phone:** Yes. **Restrooms and Showers:** Yes. **Fuel:** No. **Propane:** No. **Internal Roads:** Paved. **RV Service:** In town. **Market:** In town. **Restaurant:** There is a large variety of restaurants in town. **General Store:** Yes. **Vending:** Yes. **Swimming:** Yes. **Playground:** Yes. **Other:** 22 cabins, hiking trails, biking trails, horseback riding, fishing pond, large picnic shelter w/ electricity, several hundred picnic tables & grills. **Activities:** Archery, horseback riding, fur trade demonstration, arts & crafts, Jeep rides, volleyball, tennis, fishing, buffalo stew cookouts by appointment. **Nearby Attractions:** Museum of the fur trade, Nebraska National Forest, Dawes County Historical Museum, biking, golf. **Additional Information:** Chadron Chamber of Commerce, (308) 432-4401.

RESTRICTIONS
Pets: On leash. **Fires:** Grill or fire pits only. **Alcoholic Beverages:** No alcoholic beverages allowed. **Vehicle Maximum Length:** 45 ft.

TO GET THERE
From Chadron, take south Hwy. 385 8.4 mi., then turn right onto park road.

CRAWFORD
Fort Robinson State Park

MAP, A-1

P.O. Box 392, 69339-0392. T: (308) 665-2900; www.ngpc.state.ne.us.

🚐 ★★★   ▲ ★★★

Beauty: ★★★   Site Privacy: ★★★
Spaciousness: ★★★   Quiet: ★★★★
Security: ★★★★   Cleanliness: ★★★
Insect Control: ★★★   Facilities: ★★

Fort Robinson State Park is a place of Western tradition, made famous by men such as Walter Reed and Red Cloud. The fort was established in 1874 as an active military post and remained so for the next 74 years. Today, Fort Robinson State Park is a living museum. Train, horseback, and jeep tours help tell of this Western heritage. The park greets its visitors with resort-like accommodations with lodging and modern camping available. The internal roads are paved, and the campground offers large, paved camping spurs, well separated from neighbors. The park works hard at keeping the facilities clean and the lawn manicured. A variety of activities takes place in the park and the surrounding area. Camping is on a first-come, first-served basis, so be sure to arrive early in order to get a site. There is full restaurant service in the Fort Robinson Inn during the summer. All visitors must register at the entrance gate and pay an entrance fee.

BASICS
Operated By: Nebraska Game & Parks Commission. **Open:** Park, year-round; camping, Apr.–Nov. **Site Assignment:** First come, first served. **Registration:** At self-serve registration kiosks. **Fee:** $11–$19; depends on site & amenities, plus vehicle entrance fee. **Parking:** At site.

FACILITIES
Number of RV-only Sites: 100. **Number of Tent-only Sites:** 25. **Hookups:** Electric (30, 50 amps), water. **Each Site:** Picnic tables, fire pit. **Dump Station:** Yes. **Laundry:** Yes. **Pay Phone:** Yes. **Restrooms and Showers:** Yes. **Fuel:** No. **Propane:** No. **Internal Roads:** Paved. **RV Service:** 60 mi. in Scottsbluff. **Market:** In Crawford. **Restaurant:** At the lodge, or Sutler's Store on site (Memorial Day through Labor Day) or in town. **General Store:** Yes, Sutler's Store, Memorial Day–Labor Day. **Vending:** Yes. **Swimming:** Yes. **Playground:** Yes. **Other:** 35 cabins, 22-room lodge w/ restaurant, hiking trails, 4 picnic shelters, one w/ electricity, Fort Robinson Museum, trailside museum, meeting facilities, historic tours, bike rentals, more than 100 picnic tables & grills, modern horse stable (boarding available). **Activities:** Swimming, boating, fishing, hiking, horseback riding (22,000 acres of horse trails), Jeep rides, craft center, horse-drawn tour train, stagecoach rides, pony rides, rodeo. **Nearby Attractions:** None. **Additional Information:** Chadron Chamber of Commerce, (308) 432-4401.

RESTRICTIONS
Pets: On leash. **Fires:** Grill or fire pits only. **Alcoholic Beverages:** No alcoholic beverages allowed. **Vehicle Maximum Length:** No limit.

TO GET THERE
Off US 20 about 3 mi. west of Crawford.

CROFTON   MAP, A-3
Lewis and Clark State Recreation Area

54731 897 Rd., 43349 South Dakota Hwy. 52, 68730-3290. T: (605) 668-2985; www.ngpc.state.ne.us.

🚐 ★★★   ▲ ★★★

Beauty: ★★★	Site Privacy: ★★★
Spaciousness: ★★★	Quiet: ★★★★
Security: ★★★★	Cleanliness: ★★★
Insect Control: ★★★	Facilities: ★★

Straddling the northeast border with South Dakota, Lewis and Clark Lake offers a good place to fish and relax. On the Nebraska side of the lake, the recreation area is roughly divided into five parts. If you're lucky, you'll spot deer or turkeys. Oaks and cottonwoods are spread throughout all five areas, with robins and blue jays flitting between each. The Weigand-Burbach area is the most developed, featuring most of the campsites (electric hookups, pull-throughs, some tent camping, etc.), a full-service marina, convenience store, swimming beach, and other amenities. This is the first choice of most campers. Bloomfield is smaller and more secluded, with about 30 campsites with electric hookups, modern and primitive restrooms, and a boat ramp; this is an acceptable second option if the Weigand-Burbach area is full or you just want fewer neighbors. The Miller Creek and South Shore areas are primitive camping only, offering basic restrooms and boat ramps. The Deep Water area is nothing more than an access point with a parking lot.

BASICS
Operated By: Nebraska Game & Parks Commission. **Open:** All year. **Site Assignment:** First come, first served; check Web site for online registration. **Registration:** At self-serve registration kiosks; a few sites are reservable. **Fee:** $14–$16; plus vehicle entrance fee. **Parking:** At site.

FACILITIES
Number of RV-only Sites: 366. **Number of Tent-only Sites:** 45. **Number of Multipurpose Sites:** 50. **Hookups:** Electric (30, 50 amps). **Each Site:** Picnic tables, fire pit. **Dump Station:** Yes; there is also a boat pump out on the marina. **Laundry:** No. **Pay Phone:** Yes. **Restrooms and Showers:** Yes. **Fuel:** Boat fuel only at the marina. **Propane:** No. **Internal Roads:** Paved. **RV Service:** 10 mi. in Yankton, SD. **Market:** In Yankton, SD. **Restaurant:** There is one restaurant in Crofton, but there are several in Yankton, SD. **General Store:** The marina is open Memorial Day through Labor Day. **Vending:** No. **Swimming:** Yes. **Playground:** Yes. **Other:** Swimming beach, 10 cabins, 4 boat ramps, 6 docks, 6 boat slips, boat fuel, marina, fish-cleaning station, picnic shelter w/ electricity, more than 200 picnic table & grills. **Activities:** Fishing, picnicking, swimming, boating. **Nearby Attractions:** Gavins Point Dam, Lewis & Clark Visitor Center, the National Fish Hatchery, Lakeview Golf Course. **Additional Information:** Bloomfield City Clerk, (402) 373-4396.

RESTRICTIONS
Pets: On leash. **Fires:** Grill or fire pits only. **Alcoholic Beverages:** No alcoholic beverages allowed. **Vehicle Maximum Length:** 50 ft.

TO GET THERE
From Crofton, drive north on Hwy. 121 7 mi., then 4 mi. west on 54C. Park entrance is on the right.

HASTINGS   MAP, B-3
Hastings Campground

302 East 26th St., 68901. T: (402) 462-5621.

🚐 ★★★   ▲ ★★★

Beauty: ★★★	Site Privacy: ★★★
Spaciousness: ★★★	Quiet: ★★★
Security: ★★★★	Cleanliness: ★★★
Insect Control: ★★★	Facilities: ★★★

Located on the north edge of town, Hastings Campground has a semirural location situated among the cornfields. The 48 spacious RV sites have hookups available, and the 15 tent-only sites round out the campground's offerings. There isn't any shade, but the owners planted maples, oaks, cottonwoods, and elms to improve this campground for future years. Geese and ducks are common here, with Sandhill Cranes stopping by in the spring and summer months. There are numerous outdoor recreation areas within easy driving distance (many located along the I-80 corridor), though most are fairly small. Hastings's main draws are its cultural and sports offerings. Numerous softball tournaments occur here, including the state championships, and the nearby Champions Sports and Recreation Center offers fun for the family as well as fitness buffs. Hastings also has the only symphony between Lincoln and Denver, and the Hastings Museum offers explorations into cultural and natural history, as well as an IMAX theater and planetarium. And those who remember drinking Kool-Aid as kids will by happy to know that the sweet summer concoction got its start here.

BASICS
Operated By: Bill & Dorothy Gilliland. **Open:** All year. **Site Assignment:** By reservation, held on credit card. **Registration:** At camp office. **Fee:** RV, $23–$25; tent, $17.36; cash, credit, check. **Parking:** At site.

FACILITIES
Number of RV-only Sites: 48. **Number of Tent-only Sites:** 15. **Hookups:** Electric (20, 30, 50 amps), water, sewer, cable TV. **Each Site:** Picnic tables. **Dump Station:** Yes. **Laundry:** Yes. **Pay Phone:** Yes. **Restrooms and Showers:** Yes. **Fuel:** No. **Propane:** No. **Internal Roads:** Gravel. **RV Service:** On site or 25 mi. in Grand Island. **Market:** In town. **Restaurant:** In town. **General Store:** Yes. **Vending:** Yes. **Swimming:** Yes; also 2 hot tubs. **Playground:** Yes. **Other:** TV room, RV wash, wildflower garden, arcade room, 3 cabins, horseshoes, storm shelter. **Activities:** Swimming, coin games, horseshoes. **Nearby Attractions:** Hastings Fun Park, IMAX, Pioneer Village, Great Platte River Road Monument, Kool-Aid Museum. **Additional Information:** Hastings Chamber of Commerce, (402) 462-4159.

RESTRICTIONS
Pets: On leash. **Fires:** Grill or fire pits only. **Alcoholic Beverages:** At site. **Vehicle Maximum Length:** No limit.

TO GET THERE
From I-80 Exit 312, go south on US 34 14.6 mi., turn left into South Shore Dr., and continue east on CR 80 (East 26th St.) about 300 yards.

NIOBRARA   MAP, A-3
Niobrara State Park

P.O. Box 226, 89261 522 Ave., 68760-0226. T: (402) 857-3373; www.ngpc.state.ne.us.

🚐 ★★★   ▲ ★★★★

Beauty: ★★★	Site Privacy: ★★★
Spaciousness: ★★★	Quiet: ★★★★
Security: ★★★★	Cleanliness: ★★★
Insect Control: ★★★	Facilities: ★★

Niobrara State Park is situated at the confluence of the Niobrara and Missouri rivers on Nebraska's northeastern border. Visitors at this park have an opportunity to sample a wide range of outdoor recreation, including horseback trail rides, hiking, and fishing. The park offers numerous opportunities to observe wildlife such as white-tailed deer, wild turkeys, beavers, muskrats, and mink. The camping area extends along 3 miles of an extremely hilly, winding, one-way road, and it's interspersed with stands of elm, hackberry, and ash. Many sites are situated on elevated hills adjacent to the Niobrara River and primarily offer back-in sites. The park is open year-round, although modern facilities, including cabins, are open from mid-April through mid-November. Reservations for all campsites may be made up to one year in advance.

BASICS
Operated By: Nebraska Game & Parks Commission. **Open:** All year. **Site Assignment:** First come, first served. **Registration:** At self-serve registration kiosks. **Fee:** $6–$13; plus vehicle entrance fee. **Parking:** At site.

FACILITIES
Number of RV-only Sites: 69. **Number of Tent-only Sites:** 50. **Hookups:** Electric (20, 30, 50 amps), water. **Each Site:** Picnic tables, fire pit. **Dump Station:** Yes. **Laundry:** Yes. **Pay Phone:** Yes. **Restrooms and Showers:** Yes. **Fuel:** No. **Propane:** No. **Internal Roads:** Paved. **RV Service:** 30 mi. in Yankton, SD. **Market:** In town. **Restaurant:** In town. **General Store:** No. **Vending:** Yes. **Swimming:** Yes. **Playground:** Yes. **Other:** 19 cabins, hiking trails, 9 picnic shelters, 2 w/ electricity, more than 160 acres open for horseback riding, more than 100 picnic tables & grills, 3 boat ramps, mountain bike trails, hiking trails. **Activities:** Swimming, boating, fishing, hiking, horseback riding (160 acres of horse trails), guided float trips. **Nearby Attractions:** Smith Falls, golf, Ashfall State Historic Site. **Additional Information:** Creighton Area Chamber of Commerce, (402) 358-3737.

RESTRICTIONS
Pets: On leash. **Fires:** Grill or fire pits only. **Alcoholic Beverages:** No alcoholic beverages allowed. **Vehicle Maximum Length:** 45 ft.

To Get There

The campground is about 3 mi. west of Niobrara on SR 12.

PONCA
Ponca State Park
MAP, A-4

88090 Spur 26-E, P. O. Box 688, 68770.
T: (402) 755-2284; www.ngpc.state.ne.us.

🚐 ★★★   ▲ ★★★

Beauty: ★★★★	Site Privacy: ★★★
Spaciousness: ★★★	Quiet: ★★★★
Security: ★★★★	Cleanliness: ★★★
Insect Control: ★★★	Facilities: ★★

As you would expect from a state-operated park in this area, Ponca State Park is well run and situated in the midst of gorgeous scenery with a variety of bushes and trees, and occasionally guests will discover a fox or raccoon exploring the campground. The fees are very reasonable, and the available sites medium sized. Even though the camping area is fairly large, the sites still afford privacy and quiet for all guests. Eight pull-through sites are available. The biggest surprise regarding this park is the list of activities. Over and above the usual, Ponca offers golf, archery, waterskiing, hunting, and a special fishing clinic for the children on Sundays. The surrounding area isn't a disappointment either. Nearby, visitors to the park can hike the Lewis and Clark Trail; hunt deer, turkey, or duck; or stop by the Mid-America Air Museum. Overall, this is a wonderful place to stay, and reservations are not required.

BASICS

Operated By: Nebraska Game & Parks Commission. **Open:** All year. **Site Assignment:** First come, first served at Turkey Ridge; reservations required at Oak Gluff. **Registration:** At camp office. **Fee:** Hookup, $12–$13; no hookup, $9; plus vehicle fee. **Parking:** At site.

FACILITIES

Number of RV-only Sites: 73. **Number of Tent-only Sites:** 72. **Number of Multipurpose Sites:** 10. **Hookups:** Electric (30, 50 amps). **Each Site:** Picnic tables, fire ring. **Dump Station:** Yes. **Laundry:** No. **Pay Phone:** Yes. **Restrooms and Showers:** Yes. **Fuel:** No. **Propane:** No. **Internal Roads:** Paved in good condition. **RV Service:** 14 mi. in Sioux City. **Market:** Local or Sioux City. **Restaurant:** There are 2 restaurants in Ponca, or Sioux City. **General Store:** No. **Vending:** Yes. **Swimming:** Yes (no swimming in river). **Playground:** Yes. **Other:** Lodge, 14 modern cabins, covered picnic shelters, boat ramps, scenic overlook, horse barn, horse trails, hiking trails, biking trails, golf course. **Activities:** Swimming, horseback riding, fishing, hiking, organized activities Memorial Day weekend through Labor Day, children's fishing clinics on Sun., archery range, outdoor education naturalist programs. **Nearby Attractions:** Missouri River; Lewis & Clark Trail w/ 17 mi. of hiking trails; deer, pheasant, duck, & turkey hunting; Mid-America Air Museum, Sgt. Floyd River Museum. **Additional Information:** www.ngpc.state.ne.us.

RESTRICTIONS

Pets: On 6-ft. leash. **Fires:** Fire ring only. **Alcoholic Beverages:** No alcoholic beverages allowed in the state park. **Vehicle Maximum Length:** 45 ft.

To Get There

From I-29 Exit 144B, go west on US 75, which becomes US 20. Turn right on SR 12. Go 12.5 mi. and follow signs into park (campground is 32.5 mi. from Sioux City and I-29).

RAYMOND
Branched Oak State Recreation Area
MAP, B-4

12000 W Branched Oak Rd., 68428.
T: (402) 783-3400; www.ngpc.state.ne.us.

🚐 ★★★   ▲ ★★★

Beauty: ★★★	Site Privacy: ★★★
Spaciousness: ★★★	Quiet: ★★★★
Security: ★★★★	Cleanliness: ★★★
Insect Control: ★★★	Facilities: ★★

The largest of the Salt Valley areas, Branched Oak has nine camping areas spread out around a lake that stretches for almost 4 miles. Sites in the campground are set in a straight line overlooking the lake. Trees are behind the sites, but they're too far away to provide much in the way of shade. Visitors with horses can use the 3-mile multiuse trail on the south side of Branched Oak Lake and camp with their horses in Area 3. The 800-acre dog trail (about 1 mile from Area 9) has championship events, so call ahead for a schedule to avoid the crowds. Anglers will enjoy the variety of fish found in the lake, including bluegill, largemouth bass, and catfish. The recreation area is also classified as a wildlife management area, so hunters arrive in the fall to hunt pheasants, quail, doves, and ducks.

BASICS

Operated By: Nebraska Game & Parks Commission. **Open:** All year. **Site Assignment:** First come, first served; reservation sites up to 1 year in advance. **Registration:** At self-serve registration kiosks, or by reservation ($3 fee). **Fee:** $4–$17; plus vehicle entrance fee. **Parking:** At site.

FACILITIES

Number of RV-only Sites: 206. **Number of Tent-only Sites:** 287. **Number of Multipurpose Sites:** 71. **Hookups:** Electric (20, 30, 50 amps), water. **Each Site:** Picnic tables, fire pit. **Dump Station:** Yes. **Laundry:** No. **Pay Phone:** Yes. **Restrooms and Showers:** Yes (in areas 1, 4, 11). **Fuel:** Yes. **Propane:** Yes. **Internal Roads:** Paved. **RV Service:** in Lincoln. **Market:** in Lincoln. **Restaurant:** On site at the Marina or in Lincoln. **General Store:** Yes, at the Marina. **Vending:** Yes. **Swimming:** No. **Playground:** Yes. **Other:** 9 boat ramps, 49 fishing piers, 41 picnic shelters w/ more than 600 picnic tables & grills. **Activities:** Fishing (walleye, blue gill, blue catfish, largemouth bass), boating, waterskiing, hiking, biking. **Nearby Attractions:** Lincoln, Nebraska; shopping, golf, museums, movies. **Additional Information:** Lincoln Chamber of Commerce, (402) 436-2350.

RESTRICTIONS

Pets: On leash. **Fires:** Grill or fire pits only. **Alcoholic Beverages:** No alcoholic beverages allowed. **Vehicle Maximum Length:** None.

To Get There

From I-80 Exit 388, go north on SR 103 5.5 mi., then east on US 34 1 mi. Take NW 140 St. 6 mi. and then turn right (east) onto West Branched Oak Rd. 1.6 mi. Follow signs into park.

REPUBLIC CITY
Hunter Cove
MAP, C-3

Rte. 1 Box 123A , 68971-9742. T: (308) 799-2105; www.reserveamerica.com.

🚐 ★★★★   ▲ ★★★★

Beauty: ★★★★	Site Privacy: ★★★
Spaciousness: ★★★	Quiet: ★★
Security: ★★	Cleanliness: ★★★★
Insect Control: ★★★	Facilities: ★★★

Hunter Cove Park is located on Harlan County Lake near Republican City, Nebraska. Harlan County Lake, with a normal pool surface of 13,250 acres, is the second largest lake in Nebraska. It is located in the south-central part of the state, 7 miles from the Nebraska–Kansas state line. Considered some of the best fishing in Nebraska, Harlan County Lake is about 9 miles long and has 75 miles of shoreline. The corps maintains six established campgrounds, with the entire project open to public access. Truly a sportsman's paradise, Harlan County is also home to excellent pheasant, quail, dove, duck, goose, and turkey hunting, along with the furbearers raccoon, coyote, and bobcat, as well as white-tailed and mule deer hunting. During the winter months, hundreds of bald eagles stop over at the lake on their annual migration. Eight parks around the lake have been developed to provide a wide variety of recreation opportunities to area visitors. The corps maintains six established campgrounds with services ranging from full electrical hookups and modern shower buildings to random tent campsites and privies. There are 19 pull-through sites at Hunter Cove with a minimum length of 100 feet that can accommodate longer trailers. Electrical hookups have been increased to 50 amps. Hunter Cove park is located on a hard-surfaced road on the eastern end of the lake.

BASICS

Operated By: U.S. Army Corps of Engineers. **Open:** Apr. 1–Nov. 30. **Site Assignment:** Reservations must be made at least 4 days in advance. **Registration:** At office. **Fee:** Single, $10–$16. **Parking:** At site.

FACILITIES

Number of Multipurpose Sites: 479. **Hookups:** Yes. **Dump Station:** Yes. **Laundry:** Yes. **Pay Phone:** Yes. **Restrooms and Showers:** Yes. **Fuel:** No. **Propane:** No. **Internal Roads:** Paved. **RV Service:** No. **Market:** No. **Restaurant:** No. **General Store:** No. **Vending:** No. **Swimming:** No. **Playground:**

Yes. **Other:** No off-road driving. No ATVs allowed in park areas. **Activities:** Fishing, boating.

RESTRICTIONS

Pets: Pets must be restrained or on a leash at all times while in developed recreation areas. **Fires:** In fire rings, stoves, grills, or fireplaces provided for that purpose. **Alcoholic Beverages:** Not allowed. **Vehicle Maximum Length:** Call ahead.

TO GET THERE

From Republican City, take Hwy. 136, turn south on Berrigan Rd., and travel 1.25 mi. to intersection of Road B. Travel west 1 mi. to park entrance on south side of the road.

REPUBLICAN CITY   MAP, C-3
Methodist Cove

Rte. 1 Box 123A, 68971-9742. T: (308) 799-2105; www.reserveamerica.com.

🚐 ★   ▲ ★★★★

Beauty: ★★★	Site Privacy: ★★★
Spaciousness: ★★★	Quiet: ★★★★
Security: ★★★★	Cleanliness: ★★★★
Insect Control: ★★★	Facilities: ★★★★

Methodist Cove Park is located on Harlan County Lake by Alma, Nebraska. Harlan County Lake, with a normal pool surface of 13,250 acres, is the second largest lake in Nebraska. It is located in the south-central part of the state, 7 miles from the Nebraska–Kansas state line. Considered some of the best fishing in Nebraska, Harlan County Lake is about 9 miles long and has 75 miles of shoreline. The corps maintains six established campgrounds, with the entire project open to public access. Truly a sportsman's paradise, Harlan County is also home to excellent pheasant, quail, dove, duck, goose, and turkey hunting, along with the furbearers raccoon, coyote, and bobcat, as well as white-tailed and mule deer hunting. During the winter months, hundreds of bald eagles stop over at the lake on their annual migration. Methodist Cove park is located on a black-top road near the west end of the lake, 2 miles east of Alma, Nebraska. There are 155 campsites and two group areas; 49 sites offer electrical hookups.

BASICS

Operated By: U.S. Army Corps of Engineers. **Open:** Apr. 1–Nov. 30. **Site Assignment:** Reservations must be made at least 4 days in advance. **Registration:** At office. **Fee:** Single, $10–$14; group, $50. **Parking:** At site.

FACILITIES

Number of Multipurpose Sites: 444. **Hookups:** Yes. **Dump Station:** Yes. **Laundry:** No. **Pay Phone:** No. **Restrooms and Showers:** Yes. **Fuel:** No. **Propane:** No. **Internal Roads:** Paved. **RV Service:** No. **Market:** No. **Restaurant:** No. **General Store:** No. **Vending:** No. **Swimming:** No. **Playground:** Yes. **Activities:** Bird-watching.

RESTRICTIONS

Pets: Pets must be restrained or on a leash at all times while in developed recreation areas. **Fires:** In

fire rings, stoves, grills, or fireplaces provided for that purpose. **Alcoholic Beverages:** Not allowed. **Vehicle Maximum Length:** Call ahead.

TO GET THERE

From Alma: On Hwy. 183, turn east on South St. and travel 2.5 mi. Park entrance on south side of the road.

SCOTTSBLUFF   MAP, B-1
Scottsbluff Chimney Rock KOA

180037 KOA Dr., 69361. T: (800) 562-0845 or (308) 635-3760; www.koa.com.

🚐 ★★★   ▲ ★★★

Beauty: ★★★	Site Privacy: ★★★
Spaciousness: ★★	Quiet: ★★★★
Security: ★★★★	Cleanliness: ★★★
Insect Control: ★★★	Facilities: ★★★

This KOA is rather small by comparison to others we've visited, but it still offers all the amenities of the larger campgrounds. The scenery is not spectacular by any means, but the property is pleasant and fairly clean. The RV and tent sites are small to average, but despite this fact, they still manage to provide a little privacy and a lot of quiet. Quite a few of the RV sites offer full hookups, and all sites come with picnic tables, grills, and fire pits. All sites are pull-through. As a bonus to the guests, amenities on the premises include a data port, game room, recreation room, and nature trails. Nearby, visitors can enjoy the Agate Fossil Beds, Fort Laramie, North Platte Valley Museum, or the local zoo.

BASICS

Operated By: Private operator. **Open:** Apr. 15–Oct. **Site Assignment:** By reservation. **Registration:** At camp office. **Fee:** RV, $20–$26; tent, $16–$18; per 2 people; cash, credit, check. **Parking:** At site.

FACILITIES

Number of RV-only Sites: 38. **Number of Tent-only Sites:** 6. **Number of Multipurpose Sites:** 17. **Hookups:** Electric (20, 30, 50 amps), water, sewer. **Each Site:** Picnic tables, grills, fire pits. **Dump Station:** Yes. **Laundry:** Yes. **Pay Phone:** No. **Restrooms and Showers:** Yes. **Fuel:** No. **Propane:** Yes. **Internal Roads:** Combination of gravel & pavement. **RV Service:** Local service. **Market:** Local. **Restaurant:** Local. **General Store:** Yes. **Vending:** Yes. **Swimming:** Yes. **Playground:** Yes. **Other:** Cabins, nature trail, Internet data port, rec room. **Activities:** Game room, swimming, volleyball, basketball, horseshoes. **Nearby Attractions:** Scottsbluff National Monument, Agate Fossil Beds, North Platte Valley Museum, Fort Laramie, the zoo. **Additional Information:** Gothenburg Chamber of Commerce, (308) 537-3505.

RESTRICTIONS

Pets: On leash. **Fires:** Fire pit only. **Alcoholic Beverages:** Allowed. **Vehicle Maximum Length:** 40 ft.

TO GET THERE

From I-80 Exit 59, take SR 17 north 0.2 mi. to SR 19. Follow SR 19 for 2 mi., then go north on US 30 0.3 mi. to US 385. Follow US 385 40 mi., then take US 26 west another 42 mi. to KOA.

WATERLOO   MAP, B-4
Two Rivers State Recreation Area

27702 F St., 68069-7012. T: (402) 359-5165; www.outdoornebraska.com.

🚐 ★★★   ▲ ★★★

Beauty: ★★★	Site Privacy: ★★★
Spaciousness: ★★★	Quiet: ★★★★
Security: ★★★★	Cleanliness: ★★★
Insect Control: ★★★	Facilities: ★★

Adjacent to the Platte River just off NE 92 near Venice, Two Rivers State Recreation Area offers a wide range of back-in campsites in five campgrounds, with primitive camping in two areas and sites for small groups in a third. Campgrounds are located near the river or one of the five ponds. This is a popular spot for canoe-campers traveling the 55-mile segment of the Platte River. Due to the location, most sites enjoy peace and quiet with deer, rabbits, and foxes often spotted. For campers who enjoy fishing, this is one of the few spots in the state that offer trout fishing. A wheelchair-accessible pier is provided. Railroad buffs will delight in ten cabooses donated by the Union Pacific Railroad, remodeled and restored, and now used as lodging in the park.

BASICS

Operated By: Nebraska Game & Parks Commission. **Open:** All year. **Site Assignment:** First come, first served. **Registration:** At self-serve registration kiosks. **Fee:** $11–$17; depends on site & amenities, plus vehicle entrance fee. **Parking:** At site.

FACILITIES

Number of RV-only Sites: 93. **Number of Tent-only Sites:** 39. **Number of Multipurpose Sites:** 63. **Hookups:** Electric (20, 30 amps), water. **Each Site:** Picnic tables, fire pit. **Dump Station:** Yes. **Laundry:** No. **Pay Phone:** Yes. **Restrooms and Showers:** Yes. **Fuel:** No. **Propane:** No. **Internal Roads:** Paved. **RV Service:** Local service. **Market:** In town. **Restaurant:** In town. **General Store:** Yes. **Vending:** Yes. **Swimming:** Swimming beach w/ showers. **Playground:** Yes. **Other:** 10 Union Pacific train cabooses converted into cabins (no pets in cabooses), hiking trails, 3 picnic shelters, 2 w/ electricity, more than 100 picnic tables & grills, boat ramps, 7 lakes, Platte River access, pull & take trout lake, mountain bike trails, hikin. **Activities:** Swimming, boating, fishing, hiking. **Nearby Attractions:** Strategic Air Command Museum. **Additional Information:** Elkhorn Chamber of Commerce, (402) 289-2678.

RESTRICTIONS

Pets: On leash. **Fires:** Grill or fire pits only. **Alcoholic Beverages:** Not allowed. **Vehicle Maximum Length:** 45 ft.

TO GET THERE

From I-80 Exit 445 (in Omaha) go west on US 275 10.8 mi.; US 275 becomes SR 92, so continue 2 mi., then turn left on CR 96 (S. 26th St.). Go 1 mi. and turn right onto CR 49 (F St.) into park.

Nevada

Nevada is much more than just **Las Vegas,** though the state has no shortage of casino RV parks combining parking-lot camping and hookups with buffets, entertainment, and gaming. Within an hour of Las Vegas, nature lovers can begin experiencing another Nevada, where livestock and wild burros wander across roads, ancient Native American petroglyphs hide among red rock formations, and the fossils of giant fish dinosaurs preserved at **Berlin-Ichthyosaur State Park** remind you that parts of this mining state were underwater at one time.

High mountains and high deserts present winter sports opportunities, the best known being around **Lake Tahoe** and **Carson City.** High elevations also mean summer opportunities to escape the searing desert heat outside the air-conditioned casinos, though weekend reservations are highly recommended if you intend to beat the locals fleeing Las Vegas for the cool juniper and pine forests of **Spring Mountains National** and **Lee Canyon Recreation Areas.** For those looking for a unique antithesis to Las Vegas and an escape back to a world where consumer culture holds little value and creativity and self-sufficiency and neighborliness become the utmost priority, abandon your bags and take a chunk of time to fully immerse yourself into the **Black Rock Desert Wilderness** experience known worldwide as the **Burning Man Festival.** Every year the week before Labor Day and the weekend including, this barren playa of gypsum and talc attracts hundreds of thousands and becomes a city unto itself—perhaps the largest in the world—and then disappears without a trace.

The Silver or Sagebrush State has 200 isolated mountain ranges snaking north and south among its equally numerous desert valleys. Small government campgrounds and attractive lakes and reservoirs present summer recreation and winter possibilities like helicopter skiing and ice fishing. There are numerous amenities and hookups in cities like **Fallon, Hawthorne, Winnemucca, Ely,** and **Elko,** where every January the nation's oldest cowboy poetry festival wrangles up rustic balladeers from around the country. But the best of the northern and central mountain ranges are the province of self-sufficient campers seeking out the more primitive campgrounds to experience nature in all its raw ruggedness and isolated beauty. A charmer of the **Pony Express Territory** is the **Great Basin National Park,** home of the ancient bristlecone pines, and **Wheeler Peak,** the second highest point in the state.

The folded, rippled, uplifted, and otherwise intriguingly contorted and colorfully banded sedimentary and metamorphic mountain ranges are more than just geologic curiosities. Indeed, camping in the 36th state is often a history lesson in the Old West, particularly the boom-and-bust economics of mining. A pathetic failure of a gold miner named Samuel Clemens turned it into literary gold under his pseudonym, Mark Twain, in his book *Roughing It.* Though Nevada's many working mines produce everything from gypsum and copper to silver and gold, there is a widespread legacy of old gold, silver, mercury, and tungsten mines and ghost towns near places as far-flung as **Beatty, Tonopah, Gabbs, Ely, Elko, Pioche,** and the capital, Carson City.

Nevada is also a state with incredible man-made lakes. **Lake Mead,** the largest man-made lake in the Western Hemisphere (thanks to the Hoover Dam), which happens to be one of the seven man-made wonders of the world, and **Lake Mohave,** south of Las Vegas, are popular for fishing, houseboats, and water sports. Both of these destination sites are part and parcel of the **Lake Mead National Recreation Area,** which has beaches, marinas, and campgrounds. Natural lakes in the middle of the desert are not a mirage. **Walker Lake** is a still-shrinking remnant of ancient **Lake Lahontan,** which once filled Nevada's desert valleys and left ancient Native Americans living along a shoreline that is now mountaintops. Out about 90 miles north of Las Vegas on NV 375, dubbed "Extraterrestrial Highway," is a government-restricted lake—the über-top-secret military facility known as Groom Lake or Area 51. According to reports, most of the government's top-secret aircraft are constructed and flown out of the dry lake bed base here in the pioneer territory. If you happen into the road's lone town of **Rachel,** stop by the **Little A'Le'Inn** for a bite and listen to some curious stories from the locals about UFOs or just plain weird activities occurring in the area and skies overhead.

Campground Profiles

AMARGOSA VALLEY MAP, D-2
Longstreet Inn, Casino, RV Park, and Golf Club

HCR 70, P.O. Box 559, 89020. T: (775) 372-1777; www.longstreetinn.com.

🚐 ★★★ ▲ ★★

Beauty: ★★★
Site Privacy: ★★★★
Spaciousness: ★★★★
Quiet: ★★★★
Security: ★★★★
Cleanliness: ★★★★★
Insect Control: ★★★★
Facilities: ★★★★★

An isolated stopping post for those crossing Death Valley Junction, Longstreet is far enough from Beatty's RV parks on US 95 to provide relative solitude. The 25-foot-wide spaces are meant to accommodate anything on the road and snag Furnace Creek traffic. The gravel RV park, with its few scraggly trees, looks out over a small golf course toward Death Valley's Funeral Mountains. Sharp eyes can detect the ridge where the old Tidewater and Tonopah Railroad ran. The casino, with its pool and large free-form rock firewater reservoir (often mistaken for the pool), acts as a protective backdrop and is the source of all amenities here. Nearby Ash Meadows National Wildlife Refuge, designated a "Wetland of International Importance," contains "fossil water," an endangered pup fish, and 24 plant and animals found nowhere else in the world. There are no tables or grills (fire hazard), and tent campers need air mattresses.

BASICS
Operated By: Longstreet Inn, Casino, RV Park & Golf Club. **Open:** All year. **Site Assignment:** First come, first served. **Registration:** At hotel front desk in casino. **Fee:** $20; V, MC, AE, D, DC, CB. **Parking:** At site.

FACILITIES
Number of RV-only Sites: 50. **Hookups:** Electric (50 amps), water, sewer, cable TV, phone (16 sites). **Each Site:** Varies. **Dump Station:** Yes. **Laundry:** Yes. **Pay Phone:** Yes. **Restrooms and Showers:** Yes. **Fuel:** No. **Propane:** No. **Internal Roads:** Gravel, dusty but good. **RV Service:** No. **Market:** In casino. **Restaurant:** In casino. **General Store:** Yes. **Vending:** Yes. **Swimming:** Hotel pool. **Playground:** No. **Other:** 9-hole par-28 golf course, Jacuzzi. **Activities:** Gambling. **Nearby Attractions:** Death Valley, Ash Meadows National Wildlife Refuge. **Additional Information:** Ash Meadows NWR, (775) 372-5435.

RESTRICTIONS
Pets: On leash under owner's control. **Fires:** Not allowed. **Alcoholic Beverages:** Allowed. **Vehicle Maximum Length:** No limit.

TO GET THERE
From junction of US 95 at Lathrop Wells, go 7 mi. south on NV 373.

AUSTIN MAP, B-2
Berlin Ichthyosaur State Park

HC Box 61200, 89310. T: (775) 964-2440; www.park.nv.gov.

🚐 ★★★ ▲ ★★★★

Beauty: ★★★★
Site Privacy: ★★★★★
Spaciousness: ★★★
Quiet: ★★★★★
Security: ★★★★
Cleanliness: ★★★★
Insect Control: ★★★
Facilities: ★★★

An unusual combination of ghost town and aquatic dinosaur fossil site, Berlin Ichthyosaur State Park is relatively remote, even by Nevada standards. Nevada mining towns have a history of boom and bust, with miners carting off the scarce wood and moving to the next site when the ore plays out. What makes Berlin unique is the intact nature of the town. Summer weekends the rangers even run some of the old mining equipment. The ichthyosaur fossils were first exposed by erosion, not miners, and the 50-foot-long specimens in the fossil shelter are among the world's largest. The campsites pose a back-in challenge for trailers, but each site is very private and screened from the others by tall junipers and pines. Seven miles to the north along a gravel road, the historic mercury-mining town of Ione clings to life with a few prospectors, a bar, and several RV sites with hookups.

BASICS
Operated By: Nevada State Parks. **Open:** All year. **Site Assignment:** First come, first served; group reservations required. **Registration:** At self-pay fee station. **Fee:** $12; cash, check. **Parking:** At site.

FACILITIES
Number of RV-only Sites: 140. **Hookups:** None. **Each Site:** Sheltered table, grill, fire ring. **Dump Station:** Yes. **Laundry:** No. **Pay Phone:** No. **Restrooms and Showers:** No showers. **Fuel:** No. **Propane:** No. **Internal Roads:** Gravel. **RV Service:** No. **Market:** Tonopah, 77 mi. **Restaurant:** Gabbs, 23 mi. **General Store:** No. **Vending:** No. **Swimming:** No. **Playground:** No. **Other:** Drinking water (mid-Apr.–Oct.). **Activities:** Fossil, mine- & ghost-town exploration. **Nearby Attractions:** Ghost towns. **Additional Information:** Ione Mercantile (RV hookups), (775) 847-0571.

RESTRICTIONS
Pets: On leash. **Fires:** Allowed (in designated fire containers or commercial stoves/fireplaces only). **Alcoholic Beverages:** Allowed. **Vehicle Maximum Length:** 25 ft. **Other:** No horses w/o permit, no metal detectors, no loaded firearms, no wood gathering.

TO GET THERE
From Gabbs, go 23 mi. east on NV 844 (last 4 mi. are gravel).

BAKER MAP, B-3
Lower and Upper Lehman Creek Campgrounds

100 Great Basin National Park, 89311. T: (775) 234-7331; www.nps.gov/grba.

🚐 ★★★★ ▲ ★★★★★

Beauty: ★★★★★
Site Privacy: ★★★★★
Spaciousness: ★★★★
Quiet: ★★★★★
Security: ★★★★
Cleanliness: ★★★★
Insect Control: ★★★
Facilities: ★

One of the eight least visited national parks in the nation, Great Basin offers four campgrounds, which fill up only on weekends and holidays like Memorial Day, Labor Day, Fourth of July, and Utah Pioneer Days (July). Lower Lehman campsites offer ample privacy where the desert sagebrush, greasewood, and rabbitbrush give way to evergreen pines and aspens in this vast park that includes alpine meadows, cool streams, Lehman Caves, and 19th-century mining remnants like Osceola Ditch. Lower Lehman Creek (six pull-through sites) and sites 1–8 of Upper Lehman Creek are best for RVs and trailers. Upper Lehman has tent-only sites, and the road narrows too much for all but the smallest trailers on the secluded loop with sites 17–24. Wheeler Peak Campground, farther up a steep (8% grade) scenic road, is not recommended for long vehicles. However, 4 miles of sagebrush-lined dirt road lead to Baker Campground, which has seven pull-through sites.

BASICS
Operated By: National Park Service. **Open:** All year. **Site Assignment:** First come, first served. **Registration:** At self-pay fee station. **Fee:** $12; cash, check. **Parking:** At site.

FACILITIES
Number of RV-only Sites: 35. **Hookups:** Water available during summer. **Each Site:** Table, fire ring. **Dump Station:** Yes. **Laundry:** No. **Pay Phone:** Yes (visitor center). **Restrooms and Showers:** No showers. **Fuel:** No. **Propane:** No. **Internal Roads:** Gravel, rough w/ ruts, pot holes. **RV Service:** No. **Market:** Baker, 5 mi. **Restaurant:** Baker, 5 mi. (Park cafe has limited hours.) **General Store:** No. **Vending:** No. **Swimming:** No. **Playground:** No. **Other:** Ranger-led summer programs. **Activities:** Cave tours, horseback riding, trails, mountain biking on roads, fishing in Baker & Johnson lakes. **Nearby Attractions:** Baker Archaeological Site, Johnson Lake Mining District. **Additional Information:** White Pine Chamber of Commerce, (775) 289-8877; Great Basin Assoc., (775) 234-7270.

RESTRICTIONS
Pets: On leash under owner's physical control at all times; not on trails. **Fires:** Allowed only in metal fire rings; no collecting of firewood (firewood sold in Baker 24 hrs/day). **Alcoholic Beverages:** Allowed. **Vehicle Maximum Length:** No limit. **Other:** No fireworks, no ATVs, no dirt bikes.

TO GET THERE
From junction of NV 487 and 488 in Baker, go 5 mi. west on NV 488.

BEATTY
Bailey's Hot Springs

MAP, C-2

US 95, 89003. T: (775) 553-2395.

 ★★★   ▲ ★★★

Beauty: ★★★   Site Privacy: ★★★★
Spaciousness: ★★★★   Quiet: ★★★★
Security: ★★★   Cleanliness: ★★★
Insect Control: ★★★ Facilities: ★★

One of five RV parks in Beatty, Bailey's is the only campground with hot springs (available for day-use visitors), though it is also farthest from the casinos and markets. Beatty's RV parks are all along the highway, but traffic is relatively light at night. All sites are pull-through. Tent campers on the lawns here are protected by reeds and can fall asleep to the sound of running creek water (which irrigates local farms). The campground is shady, breezy, and friendly. Most here are regulars and word-of-mouth customers stopping for a night or two of hot-spring use, coming and going from Death Valley. The adjacent corral houses the owner's breeding horses, and the view across the highway is BLM land (OK to hike) and Death Valley mountain ranges. Only weekly customers get sewer hookups because of the high water table from the spring and the underground Amargosa River.

BASICS
Operated By: Sharon Patton. **Open:** All year. **Site Assignment:** First come, first served. **Registration:** At office (an RV). **Fee:** RV, $18; tent, $16. **Parking:** At site.

FACILITIES
Number of RV-only Sites: 14. **Number of Tent-only Sites:** Undesignated sites. **Hookups:** Electric (30 amps), water. **Each Site:** Varies. **Dump Station:** No. **Laundry:** No. **Pay Phone:** No. **Restrooms and Showers:** Yes. **Fuel:** No. **Propane:** No. **Internal Roads:** Gravel, good. **RV Service:** No. **Market:** Beatty, 5 mi. **Restaurant:** Beatty, 5 mi. **General Store:** No. **Vending:** No. **Swimming:** Hot springs. **Playground:** No. **Other:** Central picnic area w/ barbecue. **Activities:** Soaking in hot springs. **Nearby Attractions:** Death Valley, Rhyolite ghost town, Amargosa Valley, Goldfield, 3 casinos. **Additional Information:** Beatty Chamber of Commerce, (775) 553-2424.

RESTRICTIONS
Pets: On leash under owner's control. **Fires:** None permitted. **Alcoholic Beverages:** Allowed. **Vehicle Maximum Length:** None. **Other:** High water table limits sewage discharge.

TO GET THERE
Go 5 mi. north of Beatty on US 95.

BOULDER BASIN
Callville Bay

MAP, D-3

Lake Mead National Recreation Area, 601 Nevada Hwy., 89005. T: (702) 293-8906; www.nps.gov/lame/home.html, www.callvillebay.com.

 ★★★   ▲ ★★★

Beauty: ★★★★   Site Privacy: ★★★
Spaciousness: ★★★   Quiet: ★★★★
Security: ★★★★   Cleanliness: ★★★★
Insect Control: ★★★ Facilities: ★★★★

A 589-slip boating and water recreation site on the huge desert lake created when the Hoover Dam was built, Callville Bay offers access to Lake Mead and proximity to Las Vegas Territory casinos. Low desert foothills sprinkled with willows and mesquite surround the campsites, which are jammed close together and separated from each other by tall poisonous oleanders (watch young kids closely). The occasional vulture, coyote, and roadrunner can be seen in the foothills, also. The nearby marina offers ample facilities and rentals for water fun. RV hookups can be found across the street at Callville Bay Resort (operated by Forever Resorts; (800) 255-5561), which caters to mobile-home residents. A word of warning: Though near the lake, the area is still desert, and summer temperatures in locked vehicles can reach 130° F in 30 minutes. So don't leave pets in locked vehicles. For more impressive desert scenery and red rocks, continue east on NV 167 toward Echo Bay or head inland to Valley of Fire State Park.

BASICS
Operated By: National Park Service. **Open:** All year. **Site Assignment:** First come, first served. **Registration:** At self-pay station at entrance. **Fee:** $10; Golden Age/Access, $5. **Parking:** At site.

FACILITIES
Number of RV-only Sites: 80. **Hookups:** Electric, water, sewer. **Each Site:** Sheltered table, grill. **Dump Station:** Yes. **Laundry:** Yes. **Pay Phone:** Yes. **Restrooms and Showers:** Yes. **Fuel:** Yes. **Propane:** Yes. **Internal Roads:** Paved, good condition. **RV Service:** No. **Market:** At nearby marina. **Restaurant:** At nearby marina. **General Store:** Yes. **Vending:** Yes. **Swimming:** Lake (at own risk). **Playground:** No. **Other:** Boat & houseboat rentals, launch ramp, yacht club, trailer village. **Activities:** Boating, fishing. **Nearby Attractions:** Las Vegas, Hoover Dam, Lost City Museum, Valley of Fire State Park. **Additional Information:** Callville Bay Resort, (702) 565-8958 or (800) 255-5561; Alan Bible Visitor Center (NPS), (702) 293-8990.

RESTRICTIONS
Pets: On leash under handler's control. **Fires:** Grills only, no ground fires. **Alcoholic Beverages:** Allowed at site. **Vehicle Maximum Length:** Not specified. **Other:** 30-day stay limit, noon checkout, 8 people & 2 vehicles or 4 motorcycles per site.

TO GET THERE
From North Las Vegas, go east on Lake Mead Blvd. (NV 147) 12 mi., then northeast on NV 167 (Northshore Scenic Dr.) for 8 mi. and south at Callville Bay turnoff 4 mi.

BOULDER CITY
Boulder Beach

MAP, D-3

601 Nevada Hwy., 89005. T: (702) 293-8907; www.nps.gov/lame/home.html.

 ★★★   ▲ ★★★

Beauty: ★★★★★   Site Privacy: ★★★★
Spaciousness: ★★★   Quiet: ★★★★★
Security: ★★★   Cleanliness: ★★★★★
Insect Control: ★★★★ Facilities: ★★

Boulder Beach shares the same scenic Lake Mead desert landscape as Las Vegas Bay, which is 7 miles to the north along the Lakeshore Scenic Drive. The park's Alan Bible Visitor Center is 9 miles southwest and Hoover Dam is 5 miles southeast, making this an especially good choice for first-time visitors getting acquainted with the area. Unlike Las Vegas Bay, there is swimming here. South of Hoover Dam the waters flow through Black Canyon, a prime bighorn sheep viewing area, and become Lake Mohave. Another 20 miles south on US 93 (a route leading to the South Rim of the Grand Canyon) is Willow Beach, a 1,500-year-old Native American trading site known for petroglyphs and fine fishing. Those wanting Boulder Beach with hookups can check into the adjacent Lakeshore Trailer Village (see appendix), which has 80 "transient" spaces with cable TV among the 215 mobile homes.

BASICS
Operated By: National Park Service. **Open:** All year. **Site Assignment:** First come, first served. **Registration:** At self-pay entrance fee station. **Fee:** $5–$20. **Parking:** At site.

FACILITIES
Number of Multipurpose Sites: 150. **Hookups:** None. **Each Site:** Table, grill. **Dump Station:** Yes. **Laundry:** No. **Pay Phone:** Yes. **Restrooms and Showers:** Yes (shower fee at trailer village). **Fuel:** No (boat fuel only). **Propane:** No. **Internal Roads:** Paved, good. **RV Service:** No. **Market:** Boulder City, 6 mi. **Restaurant:** Boulder City, 6 mi. **General Store:** Yes. **Vending:** Yes. **Swimming:** Lake (at own risk). **Playground:** No. **Other:** Boat launch, motel, partial wheelchair access. **Activities:** Boating, fishing. **Nearby Attractions:** Lake Mead, Las Vegas, Henderson, Hoover Dam, Boulder City. **Additional Information:** Lake Mead Resort, (800) 752-9669, (702) 293-3484; Lake Mead Cruises, (702) 293-6180.

RESTRICTIONS
Pets: On leash under owner's control. **Fires:** Allowed. **Alcoholic Beverages:** Allowed. **Vehicle Maximum Length:** 30 ft. **Other:** 30-day stay limit.

TO GET THERE
From Boulder City, go 6 mi. northeast on NV 166 (Lakeshore Rd.).

CALIENTE
Young's RV Park

MAP, C-3

P.O. Box 84, 1350 S. Front St., 89008. T: (775) 726-3418.

 ★★★★   ▲ ★★★★

Beauty: ★★★★   Site Privacy: ★★★★
Spaciousness: ★★★★   Quiet: ★★★★
Security: ★★★★   Cleanliness: ★★★★
Insect Control: ★★★★ Facilities: ★★★

For travelers between Las Vegas and Great Basin National Park on US 93, Young's is the only intermediate stop with full hookups. Young's is also a popular stopping place for migrating snowbirds, who like the poplar, cottonwood, and elm trees, as well as the grass strips between the three gravel rows. Tent campers share a large grassy area with a few tables. The campground can be a bit tricky to locate, as the sign for the dirt turnoff road on the southwest edge of Caliente says "Young's" in tiny black letters easily missed. Look instead for the big blue letters saying "RV Park" above the large red arrow to spot the turnoff. About half the park's business comes from the sign, whose tiny white letters advertise full hookups and showers. Except for the Union Pacific train rumbling through at night, it is fairly quiet because highway traffic slows to 25 mph entering town.

BASICS

Operated By: Chad & Brenda Young. **Open:** All year. **Site Assignment:** First come, first served. **Registration:** At office. **Fee:** RV, $16; tent, $10. **Parking:** At site.

FACILITIES

Number of RV-only Sites: 27. **Number of Tent-only Sites:** Undesignated sites. **Hookups:** Electric (20, 30 amps), water, sewer. **Each Site:** Table. **Dump Station:** Yes. **Laundry:** Yes. **Pay Phone:** Yes. **Restrooms and Showers:** Yes. **Fuel:** No. **Propane:** No. **Internal Roads:** Gravel, good. **RV Service:** No. **Market:** Caliente. **Restaurant:** Caliente. **General Store:** No. **Vending:** No. **Swimming:** No. **Playground:** No. **Activities:** Historic buildings tour. **Nearby Attractions:** Several state parks, Pioche Boot Hill Cemetery, Caliente train depot. **Additional Information:** Caliente Chamber of Commerce, (775) 726-3129; Nevada Div. of State Parks Regional Visitors Center, (775) 728-4460.

RESTRICTIONS

Pets: On leash under owner's control. **Fires:** Allowed. **Alcoholic Beverages:** Allowed. **Vehicle Maximum Length:** None.

TO GET THERE

From US 93 near the bridge at the southwest outskirts of Caliente, turn down the gravel road running between the BLM building and the Lincoln County shops.

CARSON CITY   MAP, B-1
Davis Creek Regional Park

25 Davis Creek Rd., 89704. T: (775) 849-0684; www.visitrenotahoe.com/plan_your_trip/ outdoors/parks_beaches/regional_parks/.

🚐 ★★★★   ▲ ★★★★

Beauty: ★★★★   Site Privacy: ★★★★
Spaciousness: ★★★★   Quiet: ★★★
Security: ★★★   Cleanliness: ★★★★
Insect Control: ★★★   Facilities: ★★

An attractive area where pine forests meet sagebrush desert on the eastern slope of the Sierra Nevada Mountains in the Washoe Valley north of Carson City, Davis Creek Regional Park features a picnic area surrounding a three-acre pond. The pond, used for ice-skating in winter, was once an ice source for Virginia City. The park, once part of the 4,000-acre Winters Ranch known for its racetrack and horse breeding in the early 1900s, has separate North and South Campgrounds for tents and RVs that can be reserved by groups. All sites are pull-throughs. Granite boulders line the perimeter, tall ponderosa pines provide shade and whiffs of vanilla scent, and pine needles carpet the campground. The Ophir Creek Trail leads from the campground through steep canyons, mountain creeks, and boulder fields to Price Lake and Tahoe Meadows. Reno's gaming and entertainment is only 21 miles away.

BASICS

Operated By: Washoe County Parks & Recreation Dept. **Open:** All year. **Site Assignment:** First come, first served; group reservations. **Registration:** At self-pay fee station. **Fee:** $11–$15; cash, check. **Parking:** At site.

FACILITIES

Number of RV-only Sites: 19. **Number of Tent-only Sites:** 44. **Hookups:** None. **Each Site:** Table, fire ring. **Dump Station:** Yes. **Laundry:** No. **Pay Phone:** Yes. **Restrooms and Showers:** Yes. **Fuel:** No. **Propane:** No. **Internal Roads:** Paved, excellent. **RV Service:** No. **Market:** Carson City, 12 mi. **Restaurant:** Carson City, 12 mi. **General Store:** No. **Vending:** No. **Swimming:** Pool at Bowers Mansion Regional Park (1 mi.). **Playground:** No. **Other:** Wheelchair-accessible site, amphitheater, pond. **Activities:** Horseback riding, fishing, boating, ice skating. **Nearby Attractions:** Bowers Mansion, Lake Tahoe. **Additional Information:** Carson Valley Chamber of Commerce & Visitors Authority, (800) 727-7677, www.carsonvalleynv.org.

RESTRICTIONS

Pets: On leash under owner's control. **Fires:** Allowed (only in fire pits, no fires when danger is high in summer). **Alcoholic Beverages:** Allowed. **Vehicle Maximum Length:** 30 ft. **Other:** No firearms or patio torches, food must be locked from bears, no amplified music.

TO GET THERE

Go 12 mi. north from Carson City on US 395 and 0.5 mi. southwest on Old US 395.

CARSON CITY   MAP, B-1
Washoe Lake State Park

4855 East Lake Blvd., 89704. T: (775) 687-4319; www.state.nv.us/stparks.

🚐 ★★★★   ▲ ★★★★

Beauty: ★★★★   Site Privacy: ★★★★★
Spaciousness: ★★★★   Quiet: ★★★★
Security: ★★★★   Cleanliness: ★★★★
Insect Control: ★★★★   Facilities: ★★★

Six-foot-tall sagebrush teeming with quail and sand dunes stand between the two campground loops and Washoe Lake, while the backdrop is forested mountains in one direction and low rocky hills that turn golden in summer in the other. Loop B (sites 25–49) is at a slightly higher elevation than Loop A (sites 1–24) and has more glimpses of the lake over the sand dunes. A few tables are sheltered, but the mostly small trees have yet to grow tall enough to provide much shade. Site 37 is wheelchair accessible and one of the few sites with a tall cottonwood tree for shade and a good lake view. The lake's willows and cattails were used for basketry by the Washo Indians thousands of years ago and provide a good migratory bird-watching habitat today. Carson City is 5 miles south and Reno only 18 miles to the north.

BASICS

Operated By: Nevada State Parks. **Open:** All year. **Site Assignment:** First come, first served; group area requires reservations. **Registration:** At self-pay fee station. **Fee:** $12; cash, check. **Parking:** At site.

FACILITIES

Number of RV-only Sites: 47. **Number of Tent-only Sites:** 3. **Hookups:** None. **Each Site:** Table, fire ring. **Dump Station:** Yes. **Laundry:** No. **Pay Phone:** Yes. **Restrooms and Showers:** Yes. **Fuel:** No. **Propane:** No. **Internal Roads:** Paved, excellent. **RV Service:** No. **Market:** Carson City, 6 mi. **Restaurant:** Carson City, 6 mi. **General Store:** No. **Vending:** No. **Swimming:** Lake. **Playground:** No. **Other:** Boat launch, windsocks, equestrian viewing areas, day-use picnic tables & grills, 2 boat ramps. **Activities:** Hang gliding, fishing, hunting, boating, bird-watching, golf, horseback riding, hiking. **Nearby Attractions:** Virginia City, historic areas, museums. **Additional Information:** Carson City Chamber of Commerce, (775) 882-1565, www.carsoncitychamber.com.

RESTRICTIONS

Pets: On leash at all times (except in wetlands during hunting season). **Fires:** Allowed (in grills only, no wood collection, firewood sold). **Alcoholic Beverages:** Allowed. **Vehicle Maximum Length:** None. **Other:** 7-day stay limit per 30-day period.

TO GET THERE

From US 395 Exit 42 north of Carson City, go 2 mi. east on East Lake Blvd.

COTTONWOOD COVE MAP, D-3
Cottonwood Cove

P.O. Box 123, 89046. T: (702) 297-1464; www.nps.gov/lame/home.html.

🚐 ★★★★   ▲ ★★★★★

Beauty: ★★★★★   Site Privacy: ★★★★★
Spaciousness: ★★★★   Quiet: ★★★★★
Security: ★★★★★   Cleanliness: ★★★★★
Insect Control: ★★★   Facilities: ★★★★★

Like Katherine near Bullhead City, Arizona, Cottonwood Cove is a very popular Lake Mohave destination that begins filling up on Thursday for long weekends. At peak times, consider a reservation at the Forever Resorts (phone (800) 255-5561; www.foreverresorts.com) trailer village (30-, 50-amp hookups) and camp out amongst the mobile homes. Tent campers will like having a whole loop area of their own, an unusual arrangement in the Lake Mead National Recreation Area. The gray desert beauty and solitude of the location should provide solace against holiday crowds. The ranger station has a cactus garden with several cholla species and a good display of area history, ranging from local railroad spikes to minerals. It is only 14 miles (west) to Searchlight and a roadside casino with 10-cent coffee. Like the rest of the Lake Mead National Recreation Area, Lake Mohave life revolves around the water and boating.

BASICS

Operated By: National Park Service. **Open:** All year. **Site Assignment:** First come, first served. **Registration:** At self-pay entrance fee station. **Fee:** $21–$26. **Parking:** At site.

FACILITIES

Number of RV-only Sites: 100. **Number of Tent-only Sites:** 45. **Hookups:** Electric, water, sewer. **Each Site:** Table, fire pit. **Dump Station:** Yes. **Laundry:** Yes. **Pay Phone:** Yes. **Restrooms and Showers:** Yes. **Fuel:** Yes. **Propane:** Yes. **Internal Roads:** Paved, good. **RV Service:** No. **Market:** At marina. **Restaurant:** At marina. **General Store:** Yes. **Vending:** Yes. **Swimming:** Lake (at own risk). **Playground:** No. **Other:** Boat launch, motel. **Activities:** Boating, canoeing, fishing, volleyball, shuffleboard, horseshoes. **Nearby Attractions:** Laughlin. **Additional Information:** Cottonwood Cove Marina & Resort, (702) 297-1464, www.foreverresorts.com.

RESTRICTIONS

Pets: On leash under owner's control. **Fires:** Allowed. **Alcoholic Beverages:** Allowed in moderation; problems will result in arrest. **Vehicle Maximum Length:** 30 ft. **Other:** No loaded firearms or fireworks, do not disturb plants/rocks/archaeological features.

TO GET THERE

Take NV 164 between Laughlin and Las Vegas, and at Searchlight go east 14 mi. on Cottonwood Cove Rd.

ELKO
Valley View RV Park   MAP, A-3

6000 East Idaho St. (Hwy. 40 East), 89801.
T: (775) 753-9200.

🚐 ★★★   ▲ ★★★

Beauty: ★★★   Site Privacy: ★★★
Spaciousness: ★★★★   Quiet: ★★★
Security: ★★★★   Cleanliness: ★★★★
Insect Control: ★★★★   Facilities: ★★★★

Just down the road from the Hilton and the bare gravel Double Dice RV Park, Valley View at least offers some attractive patches of grass, a friendly family feel, and the best campsite prices in town. The word of mouth here is good, and repeat customers stop by regularly for three to five days. Families settling in for longer stays let their kids pick up the school bus at the bus stop in front. The owners are amiable, and Valley View seems like a friendly little town where people have the time to stop and chat. There is some noise from the nearby highway, but the trees provide an offset, and a snack bar should soon be in operation to lessen the need for trips into town. Back-in and pull-through sites are available. All in all, a pleasant alternative to Nevada's prevalent casino RV parking lots and about as good as they come in this remote area.

BASICS

Operated By: Private operator. **Open:** All year. **Site Assignment:** First come, first served. **Registration:** At office. **Fee:** RV, $15; tent, $10; V, MC. **Parking:** At site.

FACILITIES

Number of RV-only Sites: 74. **Number of Tent-only Sites:** Undesignated sites. **Hookups:** Electric (30, 50 amps), water, sewer, phone (modem), satellite TV. **Each Site:** Grills, tables in tent area only. **Dump Station:** Yes. **Laundry:** Yes. **Pay Phone:** No. **Restrooms and Showers:** Yes. **Fuel:** No. **Propane:** No. **Internal Roads:** Paved, good. **RV Service:** No. **Market:** Elko, 3 mi. **Restaurant:** Elko, 1 mi. **General Store:** No. **Vending:** No. **Swimming:** No. **Playground:** No. **Other:** Mail delivery, school-bus pickup, dog walk. **Activities:** Fishing, hunting, biking, golf, baseball, bird-watching. **Nearby Attractions:** Ruby Mountains, Lamoille Canyon, Jarbridge Wilderness, ghost towns. **Additional Information:** Elko Chamber of Commerce, (775) 738-7135, www.elkonevada.com.

RESTRICTIONS

Pets: On leash or contained at all times. **Fires:** Allowed. **Alcoholic Beverages:** Allowed. **Vehicle Maximum Length:** 55 ft. **Other:** Children must have adult supervision at all times.

TO GET THERE

From US I-80 Exit 303, go 3 mi. east on Idaho St. (Hwy. 40).

ELY
Ward Mountain Campground   MAP, B-3

reserve america

350 8th St., 825 Avenue East, 89301.
T: (702) 289-3031; www.reserveamerica.com.

🚐 ★★★★   ▲ ★★★★★

Beauty: ★★★★★   Site Privacy: ★★★★★
Spaciousness: ★★★★   Quiet: ★★★★
Security: ★★★★   Cleanliness: ★★★★
Insect Control: ★★★   Facilities: ★★

When the hunger for open space is strong enough that Ely's rustic KOA and Valley View (no relation to the one in Elko) RV Parks and even the free promo hookups at the Holiday Inn casino will no longer do, Ward Mountain's large, wide (site 29 is 38 feet wide and 126 feet long) spaces deep in the pines and junipers may be the perfect remedy. Large RVs have their own private loop (sites 22–29) with a huge parking area near the South Trailhead. Two loops with smaller sites are on either side of the RV loop. Though Ward Mountain is popular for group picnics, it rarely reaches 50% occupancy (usually at Ely special events). Typically, a half dozen campers a night share the three loops, which are on the German and Swiss tourist routes for doing the national parks between San Francisco and Denver.

BASICS

Operated By: Humboldt-Toiyabe National Forests Ely Ranger District. **Open:** Jun.–Sept. **Site Assignment:** First come, first served; day-use picnic area reservations. **Registration:** At self-pay fee station. **Fee:** $8; cash, check. **Parking:** At site.

FACILITIES

Number of RV-only Sites: 17. **Hookups:** Water. **Each Site:** Table, grill, fire ring. **Dump Station:** No.

Laundry: No. **Pay Phone:** No. **Restrooms and Showers:** No showers, pit toilets. **Fuel:** No. **Propane:** No. **Internal Roads:** Gravel, well maintained. **RV Service:** No. **Market:** Ely, 6 mi. **Restaurant:** Ely, 6 mi. **General Store:** No. **Vending:** No. **Swimming:** No. **Playground:** Yes. **Other:** Amphitheater, baseball field. **Activities:** Baseball, hiking, biking, horseback riding. **Nearby Attractions:** Ward Charcoal Ovens, Cave Lake State Park, Great Basin National Park, museum, historic railroad. **Additional Information:** White Pine County Chamber of Commerce, (702) 289-8877.

RESTRICTIONS

Pets: On leash under owner's control. **Fires:** Allowed. **Alcoholic Beverages:** Allowed. **Vehicle Maximum Length:** 126 ft. **Other:** 14-day stay limit, no saddle or pack animals, no water Oct. 16–May 20.

TO GET THERE

From Ely, go 6 mi. southwest on US 6 and 1 mi. on gravel road (FR 10439) turnoff.

FALLON
Silver Springs Beach   MAP, B-1

Lahontan State Recreation Area,
16799 Lahontan Dam Rd, 89406.
T: (775) 577-2226 or (775) 867-3500;
www.state.nv.us/stparks.

🚐 ★★★   ▲ ★★★★

Beauty: ★★★★   Site Privacy: ★★★★
Spaciousness: ★★★★   Quiet: ★★★★
Security: ★★★★   Cleanliness: ★★★★
Insect Control: ★★★   Facilities: ★★★

A 17-mile-long reservoir with 69 miles of shoreline, Lahontan State Recreation Area offers unlimited beach camping on the sand right up to the water's edge and a small number of designated sites shaded by tall cottonwood trees. Beach 7 has designated campsites, some with lake views and a few large enough to accommodate any vehicle on the road. Large diesel trucks have camped here, and there is no limit on what can be driven onto the beaches. However, the undesignated beach camping sites have no facilities other than restrooms, not even shade. Just beyond Beach 7 the pavement ends and a sign says "Where the pavement ends and the fun begins," which is where a vendor offers horse rides across Lahontan's varied terrain. Additional designated campsites are available about 25 miles northeast on the Carson River near Lahontan Dam and the park headquarters in Fallon.

BASICS

Operated By: Nevada State Parks. **Open:** All year. **Site Assignment:** First come, first served. **Registration:** At entrance kiosk. **Fee:** $10–$15; V, MC. **Parking:** At site.

FACILITIES

Number of RV-only Sites: 29. **Hookups:** None. **Each Site:** Picnic table, fire ring at developed sites. **Dump Station:** Yes. **Laundry:** No. **Pay Phone:** Yes, credit card only. **Restrooms and Showers:** Yes. **Fuel:** No. **Propane:** No. **Internal Roads:** Paved, excellent. **RV Service:** No. **Market:** Lahontan, 1 mi.

Restaurant: Silver Springs, 5 mi. **General Store:** No. **Vending:** No. **Swimming:** Lake. **Playground:** No. **Other:** Boat launch, wheelchair-accessible site. **Activities:** Boating, water sports, bird-watching. **Nearby Attractions:** Virginia City, Carson City, Reno, Sand Mountain Rec Area, Fort Churchill State Park. **Additional Information:** Silver Springs Chamber of Commerce, (775) 577-4336.

RESTRICTIONS

Pets: On leash. **Fires:** Allowed. **Alcoholic Beverages:** Allowed. **Vehicle Maximum Length:** No limit. **Other:** No ATVs.

TO GET THERE

From junction of US 50 and Alt 95, go 4 mi. south on US Alt 95 and 1.5 mi. east on Fir St.

HENDERSON   MAP, D-3
Las Vegas Bay Campground

601 Nevada Hwy., 89005.
T: (702) 293-8907 or (702) 293-8990;
www.nps.gov/archive/lame/maplvbcamp.htm.

🚐 ★★★   ▲ ★★★

Beauty: ★★★	Site Privacy: ★★★
Spaciousness: ★★★	Quiet: ★★★
Security: ★★★	Cleanliness: ★★★★★
Insect Control: ★★★★	Facilities: ★★

A small, very relaxing campground, Las Vegas Bay combines Lake Mead water recreation with nearness to the Henderson and Las Vegas casino strips. The 650-slip marina does not rent houseboats or allow swimming, but many campsites have marina or lake views. Landscaping is the Lake Mead National Recreation Area standard of palms, oleanders, and eucalyptus. The gray desert backdrop is greened up some by the creosote bush, desert wash plant, rabbit brush, brittle brush, and mesquite. Kangaroo rats and jackrabbits call this campsite home, with the occasional big-horn sheep or coyote visit. One loop houses both tents and RVs, so a steady hum of diesel generators can often be heard until the quiet hours, 10 p.m. to 6 a.m. There are plenty of picnic tables to make this part of a day trip from Las Vegas, possibly stopping off at the Ethel M chocolate factory and cactus garden en route to Hoover Dam.

BASICS

Operated By: National Park Service. **Open:** All year. **Site Assignment:** First come, first served. **Registration:** At self-pay entrance fee station. **Fee:** $10. **Parking:** At site.

FACILITIES

Number of RV-only Sites: 86. **Hookups:** None. **Each Site:** Table, grill. **Dump Station:** Yes. **Laundry:** No. **Pay Phone:** Yes. **Restrooms and Showers:** Yes. **Fuel:** No. **Propane:** No. **Internal Roads:** Paved, good. **RV Service:** No. **Market:** Henderson, 8 mi. **Restaurant:** At marina. **General Store:** Yes. **Vending:** No. **Swimming:** No. **Playground:** No. **Other:** Boat ramp. **Activities:** Fishing, boating. **Nearby Attractions:** Lake Mead, Las Vegas, Henderson, Hoover Dam. **Additional Information:** Las Vegas Bay Marina, (702) 565-9111.

RESTRICTIONS

Pets: On leash under owner's control. **Fires:** Allowed. **Alcoholic Beverages:** Allowed. **Vehicle Maximum Length:** Not specified. **Other:** 15-day stay limit.

TO GET THERE

From Henderson, go 9 mi. northeast on NV 146.

LAKE TAHOE   MAP, B-1
Zephyr Cove RV Park
and Campground

760 Hwy. 50, 89448. T: (775) 589-4981 or
(800) 238-2463; www.zephyrcove.com.

🚐 ★★★★   ▲ ★★★★

Beauty: ★★★★	Site Privacy: ★★★★
Spaciousness: ★★★★	Quiet: ★★★★
Security: ★★★★	Cleanliness: ★★★★
Insect Control: ★★★★	Facilities: ★★★★

A National Forest Service campground that stretches far back from the trolley stop fronting US 50, Zephyr Cove's coveted boulder-strewn, walk-in tent sites require that foodstuffs be locked from black bears that roam across the street from beaches and water recreation. Pull-through sites book up quickly and are closest to the highway, which means more road noise and lake views. There are also good lake views from the 47 walk-in tent sites, especially 45–53, but 32–43 and 54–57 are more secluded among the campground's tall ponderosa pine trees. The drive-in tent sites, 1–10, and RV sites like 117–120 are also attractively situated among the tall ponderosa pines and boulders. Weekends, particularly in summer, the campground books solid and reservations are a necessity. Besides Lake Tahoe's casinos, Zephyr Cove Resort has beaches, an operational Mississippi River Paddleboat, the *M.S. Dixie II,* stables with horses, and a restaurant across the street from the campground.

BASICS

Operated By: Aramark. **Open:** All year. **Site Assignment:** First come, first served; reservations advised. **Registration:** At office/trailer at entrance. **Fee:** RV, $53; tent, $27; V, MC, AE. **Parking:** At site; parking areas for walk-in tent sites.

FACILITIES

Number of RV-only Sites: 94. **Number of Tent-only Sites:** 57. **Hookups:** Electric (30, 50 amps), water, sewer, cable TV, phone (modem, unlimited Internet). **Each Site:** Table, fire pit, "bear-proof" food lockers. **Dump Station:** Yes. **Laundry:** Yes. **Pay Phone:** Yes. **Restrooms and Showers:** Yes. **Fuel:** No. **Propane:** Yes. **Internal Roads:** Paved, good. **RV Service:** No. **Market:** Stateline, 2 mi. **Restaurant:** Across the street. **General Store:** Yes. **Vending:** Yes. **Swimming:** Lake. **Playground:** No. **Other:** Cabins, lodge accommodations, stables, marina, Mississippi River paddleboat. **Activities:** Boating, fishing, horseback riding, winter sports, gambling. **Nearby Attractions:** Incline Village ski slopes. **Additional Information:** Forest Service (Lake Tahoe), www.r5.fs.fed.us/ltbmu; Lake Tahoe Visitors Authority, (530) 544-5050, www.virtualtahoe.com.

RESTRICTIONS

Pets: On leash under owner's control. **Fires:** Allowed (no higher than 1 ft. above fire ring or after 11 p.m., $50 fine for ground fires, firewood for sale). **Alcoholic Beverages:** Allowed. **Vehicle Maximum Length:** No limit. **Other:** No kegs, loud music, or generators.

TO GET THERE

At the Zephyr Cove stoplight on US 50.

LAS VEGAS   MAP, D-3
Red Rock Canyon Campground

HCR 33 Box 5500, 89124. T: (702) 515-5350;
www.nv.blm.gov/redrockcanyon/
activities/camping.htm.

🚐 ★★★   ▲ ★★★★

Beauty: ★★★★	Site Privacy: ★★★★
Spaciousness: ★★★★	Quiet: ★★★★
Security: ★★★★	Cleanliness: ★★★★
Insect Control: ★★★	Facilities: ★★

Watch for wildlife when driving Blue Diamond Road between Las Vegas and Red Rock Canyon, as cottontail rabbits, wild horses, and burros dart onto the highway in this National Conservation Area that is so incongruously close to the glitzy Vegas strip. During the sizzling summer months, only about 25% of 13 Mile Campground's loops are open. Nevertheless, people come here to camp in the cool evening hours and leave to do their hiking by 6 a.m., before the desert temperatures once again soar. Tent campers will appreciate the 25 walk-in sites and the level gray gravel pads widely dispersed among the low desert scrub, though red-rock views are lacking. The visitor center has vending machines, a botanical display, and excellent exhibits explaining the shallow sea origins of nearby gypsum mines and how the area's stunning red rocks formed from 180-million-year-old iron oxide–tinged sand dunes.

BASICS

Operated By: Bureau of Land Management. **Open:** All year. **Site Assignment:** First come, first served; 5 group sites require advance reservation. **Registration:** At self-pay fee station. **Fee:** $10; cash, check. **Parking:** At site; parking area for walk-in sites.

FACILITIES

Number of RV-only Sites: 70. **Number of Tent-only Sites:** 10. **Hookups:** None. **Each Site:** Table, grill, fire ring. **Dump Station:** No. **Laundry:** No. **Pay Phone:** No. **Restrooms and Showers:** No showers. **Fuel:** No. **Propane:** No. **Internal Roads:** Gravel, good. **RV Service:** No. **Market:** Las Vegas, 6 mi. **Restaurant:** Las Vegas, 6 mi. **General Store:** No. **Vending:** No. **Swimming:** No. **Playground:** No. **Other:** Visitor center, gift shop. **Activities:** Horseback riding, biking, rock climbing, hiking. **Nearby Attractions:** Las Vegas casinos, Mount Charleston Nat'l Forest, Lake Mead Recreation Area, national forests. **Additional Information:** Friends of Red Rock Canyon, (702) 255-8743.

RESTRICTIONS

Pets: On leash under owner's control. **Fires:** Allowed (no open fires). **Alcoholic Beverages:** Allowed.

Vehicle Maximum Length: 40 ft. **Other:** Do not feed or touch wild burros (they kick & bite).

TO GET THERE

From Las Vegas, go 20 mi. west on NV 159 (Blue Diamond Rd.).

LAUGHLIN   MAP, D-3
Riverside RV Park

PMB 500, 89029. T: (800) 227-3849 or (702) 298-2535; www.riversideresort.com.

🚐 ★★★   ⛺ n/a

Beauty: ★★★	Site Privacy: ★★★★
Spaciousness: ★★★★	Quiet: ★★★★
Security: ★★★★	Cleanliness: ★★★★
Insect Control: ★★★	Facilities: ★★★★

Across the street from Don Laughlin's Riverside Resort Hotel and Casino, at the north edge of Casino Drive, across the river from Bullhead City, Arizona, is a nicely terraced alternative to the informal camping prevalent in casino parking lots here. Scattered about the terrace are eucalyptus and some mulberry trees, and the occasional roadrunner and coyote can be spotted, too. The terraces add a sense of privacy and a view but are too unstable for walking or child's play. However, children can use two swimming pools and play the latest coin games in the casino kids' arcade. Cable TV, phone, and modem hookups are among the other comforts. Besides casino entertainment, outlet stores and a bank are next door. Sellouts are the rule when special events come to town, so reservations are advised three weeks in advance (no cancellation penalties). Bullhead City across the river also has several conventional RV parks to choose from, albeit sans casinos, and there are more isolated casino RV parks north and south of here (see appendix).

BASICS

Operated By: Don Laughlin's Riverside Resort Hotel & Casino. **Open:** All year. **Site Assignment:** First come, first served; reservations highly recommended. **Registration:** At office. **Fee:** $23–$25; V, MC, AE, D. **Parking:** At site.

FACILITIES

Number of RV-only Sites: 740. **Hookups:** Electric (30, 50 amps), cable TV, water, sewer. **Each Site:** Varies. **Dump Station:** Yes. **Laundry:** Yes. **Pay Phone:** Yes. **Restrooms and Showers:** Yes. **Fuel:** Nearby. **Propane:** Yes. **Internal Roads:** Paved, excellent condition. **RV Service:** No. **Market:** Next door. **Restaurant:** Yes (across street, at casino). **General Store:** No. **Vending:** Yes. **Swimming:** Hotel pool. **Playground:** No. **Other:** Boat ramp, casino shuttles. **Activities:** Casino has bowling, movies, auto museum, Kids Kastle. **Nearby Attractions:** Casinos, outlet stores, river boating, fishing. **Additional Information:** Laughlin Visitor Center, (702) 298-3321 or (800) 4-LAUGHLIN.

RESTRICTIONS

Pets: 2 per rig; must be kept attended on leash. **Fires:** In approved containers only. **Alcoholic Beverages:** Nevada state law prevails. **Vehicle Maximum Length:** Not specified. **Other:** Firearms & firecrackers prohibited.

TO GET THERE

From Laughlin Civic Dr. and Colorado River bridge, go 0.25 mi. south on Casino Dr.

LEE CANYON   MAP, D-3
RECREATION AREA
McWilliams and Dolomite Campgrounds

reserve america

Toiyabe National Forest, SR 156, 89124. T: (702) 515-5400 or (800) 328-6226; www.reserveamerica.com.

🚐 ★★★★   ⛺ ★★★★

Beauty: ★★★★	Site Privacy: ★★★★★
Spaciousness: ★★★★	Quiet: ★★★★★
Security: ★★★★	Cleanliness: ★★★★★
Insect Control: ★★★★	Facilities: ★

When summer temperatures are hitting 110° F in Las Vegas, the locals are fleeing to their reserved sites here under the tall ponderosa pines for long, cool (77–85° F) three-day mountain weekends. In winter, this Humboldt Toiyabe National Forest area is a bustling ski and snowboard resort. At McWilliams, 1–9 are double sites reservable for families (240 days in advance); loop sites 26–40 are reservable single sites; sites 10–25 on a long hilly straightaway are first come, first serve. Both McWilliams and Dolomite Campgrounds are exceptionally well maintained by Thousand Trails Inc. under a special-use permit granted by the Humboldt Toiyabe National Forest. A totally separate entity, National Recreation Reservation Service, handles phone and Internet reservations. For tent-site reservations, request McWilliams, which has only a few 34-foot sites. Big vehicles do best at adjacent Dolomite (20 reservable sites), which accommodates 40-foot vehicles.

BASICS

Operated By: Thousand Trails Inc. **Open:** May–Sept., weather permitting. **Site Assignment:** First come, first served; weekend, holiday reservations advised. **Registration:** At self-pay entrance fee station. **Fee:** $13; triple site, $30; double site, $20. **Parking:** At site.

FACILITIES

Number of RV-only Sites: 70. **Hookups:** None. **Each Site:** Table, fire ring, grill. **Dump Station:** No. **Laundry:** No. **Pay Phone:** Yes. **Restrooms and Showers:** Showers (coin-op). **Fuel:** No. **Propane:** No. **Internal Roads:** Paved, good condition. **RV Service:** No. **Market:** Las Vegas, 35 mi. **Restaurant:** Kyle Canyon, 15 mi. **General Store:** No. **Vending:** No. **Swimming:** No. **Playground:** No. **Other:** Double & triple sites, helicopter pad, large picnic areas nearby. **Activities:** Boating, skiing, winter sports. **Nearby Attractions:** Las Vegas, Mount Charleston trails, Lee Canyon Ski & Snowboard Resort. **Additional Information:** Humboldt Toiyabe National Forest, (702) 873-8800, www.fs.fed.us.htnf.

RESTRICTIONS

Pets: On leash at all times. **Fires:** Allowed (firewood sold). **Alcoholic Beverages:** Allowed (no boisterous behavior). **Vehicle Maximum Length:** 34 ft. (McWilliams), 40 ft. (Dolomite). **Other:** $5 per extra vehicle at family sites, no tree chopping.

TO GET THERE

From US 95 20 mi. north of Las Vegas, go west 15 mi. on NV 156 (Lee Canyon Rd.).

OVERTON   MAP, D-3
Echo Bay

Lake Mead National Recreation Area, 601 Nevada Hwy., 89005. T: (702) 293-8907 or (702) 394-4966; www.nps.gov/lame/home.html.

🚐 ★★★   ⛺ ★★★★★

Beauty: ★★★★	Site Privacy: ★★★★
Spaciousness: ★★★★	Quiet: ★★★★
Security: ★★★★	Cleanliness: ★★★★
Insect Control: ★★	Facilities: ★★★★

Echo Bay has become the northernmost tent campground along Lake Mead. The RV park has large pull-through and back-in sites. More RV sites are also available 18 miles north at Overton Beach Resort. Echo Bay is a good place to stake tents because it combines access to water fun on Lake Mead with nearness to the red-rock formations of Valley of Fire State Park. Two widely separated loops (designated upper and lower) function like separate campgrounds with their own entrances and fee stations. The lower loop has several advantages. It is closer to the marina, has taller oleanders between sites, shady cottonwood and olive trees, and a ranger station perched on a ledge overlooking the campground. The upper loop has smaller oleanders, eucalyptus, small olives, and palms.

BASICS

Operated By: National Park Service. **Open:** All year. **Site Assignment:** First come, first served. **Registration:** At self-pay entrance fee station. **Fee:** $10 entrance fee for 7 days. **Parking:** At site.

FACILITIES

Number of RV-only Sites: 155. **Hookups:** None. **Each Site:** Fire ring. **Dump Station:** Yes. **Laundry:** Yes. **Pay Phone:** Yes. **Restrooms and Showers:** Yes (shower fee at trailer village). **Fuel:** No. **Propane:** No. **Internal Roads:** Paved, excellent. **RV Service:** No. **Market:** At marina. **Restaurant:** At marina. **General Store:** No. **Vending:** No. **Swimming:** Lake (at own risk). **Playground:** No. **Other:** Houseboat & watercraft rentals, motel. **Activities:** Boating, fishing. **Nearby Attractions:** Las Vegas, Hoover Dam, Lost City Museum (Overton), Valley of Fire State Park. **Additional Information:** Lake Mead Visitor Center (NPS), (702) 293-8990; Seven Crowns Resorts, (702) 394-4000.

RESTRICTIONS

Pets: On leash under owner's control. **Fires:** Allowed (in grills only). **Alcoholic Beverages:** Allowed; disorderly conduct or public intoxication will result in arrest. **Vehicle Maximum Length:** Not specified. **Other:** 30-day stay limit.

TO GET THERE

From junction of NV 147 and 167, go 32 mi. northeast on NV 167 and then 5 mi. east on Echo Bay Rd.

OVERTON — MAP, D-3
Echo Bay Resort RV Park

4 mi. off North Shore Rd., 89040. T: (702) 394-4000 or (800) 752-9669; www.sevencrown.com/lakes/ lake_mead/echo_bay/index.htm.

🚐 ★★★★   ⛺ n/a

Beauty: ★★★★   Site Privacy: ★★★★
Spaciousness: ★★★★   Quiet: ★★★★
Security: ★★★★   Cleanliness: ★★★★
Insect Control: ★★★   Facilities: ★★★★

Pleasant desert living among eucalyptus trees best sums up Echo Bay RV Park, which is geared for larger rigs that don't fit into the nearby Echo Bay campground. Some sites have views of Lake Mead, and the nearby marina beckons with water play rentals ranging from houseboats and fishing gear to water skis, sea-doos, and knee boards. The sites lack tables and grills, but most people are too busy at the lake to even notice the occasional bighorn sheep wandering into the RV park for water during the day. It is harder to miss the wild burros wandering in at night. The campground is farther from the water than the one at Overton Beach Marina. But Echo Bay RV Park has a rustic charm that makes Overton seem like a lakeside parking lot.

BASICS

Operated By: Seven Crowns Resorts. **Open:** All year. **Site Assignment:** First come, first served; reservations advised for peak times. **Registration:** At motel. **Fee:** $14–$20; V, MC, AE. **Parking:** At site.

FACILITIES

Number of RV-only Sites: 36. **Hookups:** Electric (30, 50 amps), water, sewer. **Each Site:** Wood posts. **Dump Station:** Yes. **Laundry:** Yes. **Pay Phone:** Yes. **Restrooms and Showers:** Yes. **Fuel:** No. **Propane:** Yes. **Internal Roads:** Paved, weathered. **RV Service:** No. **Market:** No. **Restaurant:** At Echo Bay Marina. **General Store:** At Echo Bay Marina. **Vending:** Yes. **Swimming:** No. **Playground:** No. **Other:** Houseboat, watercraft & water-sport rentals, moorage slips, dry storage, motel, airstrip. **Activities:** Boating, fishing. **Nearby Attractions:** Las Vegas, Lost City Museum (Overton), Roger Springs, Valley of Fire State Park. **Additional Information:** Lake Mead Visitor Center (NPS), (702) 293-8990, www.nps.gov/lame/ home.html.

RESTRICTIONS

Pets: On leash under owner's control. **Fires:** Allowed only w/ approved fire ring; must bring your own. **Alcoholic Beverages:** Allowed. **Vehicle Maximum Length:** 45 ft.

TO GET THERE

From junction of NV 147 and 167, go 32 mi. northeast on NV 167 and then 5 mi. east on Echo Bay Rd.

OVERTON — MAP, D-3
Overton Beach Marina

HCR 30 Box 70, 89040. T: (702) 394-4040; www.overtonbeachmarina.net.

🚐 ★★★★   ⛺ n/a

Beauty: ★★★★   Site Privacy: ★★★★
Spaciousness: ★★★★   Quiet: ★★★★
Security: ★★★★   Cleanliness: ★★★★
Insect Control: ★★★   Facilities: ★★★★

Well run by a National Park Service concessionaire inside Lake Mead National Recreation Area, the Overton Beach Marina RV park is a boater's paradise. The campground itself is down a short road (dirt and paved patches alternate) separated by a quarter-mile stretch of swimming beach and a boat launch from the busy marina, where there is a store, gas station, fish cleaner, restaurant, lounge, motel, and ranger station. The middle of the three rows of RV sites accommodates the largest vehicles. There are 13 pull-through sites, and the remaining sites are back-in. Each site is attractively separated by a low wooden fence and has its own cottonwood tree. Sheep and coyote are known to be around the campground. Many sites also enjoy at least a partial lake view. Most sites also have room to park a trailer with a boat. Indeed, life here centers around the lake and lovely marina. It is hard to go wrong here, but best to call ahead and reserve a site.

BASICS

Operated By: Overton Beach Marina. **Open:** All year. **Site Assignment:** First come, first served; reservations accepted. **Registration:** At marina store. **Fee:** $21; V, MC. **Parking:** At site.

FACILITIES

Number of RV-only Sites: 41. **Hookups:** Electric, water, sewer, phone. **Each Site:** Table, grill, cottonwood tree, low wood fence. **Dump Station:** Yes. **Laundry:** Yes. **Pay Phone:** Yes. **Restrooms and Showers:** Yes. **Fuel:** Yes. **Propane:** Yes. **Internal Roads:** Pavement, worn in spots. **RV Service:** No. **Market:** Overton, 8 mi. **Restaurant:** At Marina. **General Store:** Yes. **Vending:** No. **Swimming:** Lake (at own risk). **Playground:** No. **Other:** Houseboat, boat & slip rentals, launch ramp, fish cleaner, motel, boat storage. **Activities:** Boating, fishing. **Nearby Attractions:** Lost City Museum, Valley of Fire State Park. **Additional Information:** Lake Mead Visitor Center (NPS), (702) 293-8990.

RESTRICTIONS

Pets: On leash under handler's control. **Fires:** Grill only. **Alcoholic Beverages:** Allowed. **Vehicle Maximum Length:** 65 ft.

TO GET THERE

From junction of NV 167 and 169, go 4 mi. south on Overton Beach Rd.

PANACA — MAP, C-3
Cathedral Gorge State Park

P.O. Box 176, 89042. T: (775) 728-4460; www.state.nv.us/stparks.

🚐 ★★★★   ⛺ ★★★★

Beauty: ★★★★   Site Privacy: ★★★★
Spaciousness: ★★★★   Quiet: ★★★★
Security: ★★★★   Cleanliness: ★★★★
Insect Control: ★★★   Facilities: ★★

Though mostly an overnight stop because the turnoff is right off US 93, Cathedral Gorge is beautifully surrounded by white, tan, and buff colored eroding clay and siltstone cliffs and spires from a million-year-old lakebed known as the Panaca Formation. The badland cliffs are fronted by desert scrub loaded with black-tailed jackrabbits and the occasional rattler. Snowbirds on their spring and fall migration journeys often stop here. If your timing is lucky, snag one of the two large pull-through sites (the other 20 sites are mostly 24–30 feet). With Russian olive trees providing shade, this is actually a very relaxing stop and far enough from the highway that noise is not a factor. Advantages to overnighters include being nearer to historic towns (Caliente, Pioche, Panaca) and the main highway (US 93) than either Echo Canyon or Spring Valley State Parks, which require roundtrips down NV 322.

BASICS

Operated By: Nevada State Parks. **Open:** All year. **Site Assignment:** First come, first served; group site reservation only. **Registration:** At self-pay entrance fee station. **Fee:** $14. **Parking:** At site.

FACILITIES

Number of RV-only Sites: 22. **Hookups:** None. **Each Site:** Sheltered table, grill. **Dump Station:** Yes. **Laundry:** No. **Pay Phone:** Yes. **Restrooms and Showers:** Yes. **Fuel:** No. **Propane:** No. **Internal Roads:** Gravel, good. **RV Service:** No. **Market:** Panaca, 2 mi. **Restaurant:** Panaca, 2 mi. **General Store:** No. **Vending:** No. **Swimming:** No. **Playground:** No. **Other:** Wheelchair accessible. **Activities:** Bird-watching, picnicking, hiking. **Nearby Attractions:** Bullionville Cemetery, Caliente, Pioche, Echo Canyon, Spring Valley, Kershaw/Ryan State Park in Caliente. **Additional Information:** Panaca District Ranger, (775) 728-4467.

RESTRICTIONS

Pets: On leash, under owner's control. **Fires:** Allowed (bring own firewood). **Alcoholic Beverages:** Allowed if quiet & not drunk. **Vehicle Maximum Length:** 40 ft. **Other:** No guns.

TO GET THERE

Go 2 mi. north of Panaca to park turnoff.

PIOCHE — MAP, C-3
Spring Valley State Park

Star Rte. Box 201, 89043. T: (775) 962-5102; www.state.nv.us/stparks.

🚐 ★★★★   ⛺ ★★★★★

Beauty: ★★★★★   Site Privacy: ★★★★★
Spaciousness: ★★★★   Quiet: ★★★★★
Security: ★★★★   Cleanliness: ★★★
Insect Control: ★★   Facilities: ★★

Horsethief Gulch Campground is the most developed of Spring Valley State Park's two campgrounds, with 36 sites just west of Eagle Valley Reservoir, where paved NV 322 ends after winding through several miles of tall gray spires reminiscent of Great

Basin National Park to the north. Two miles north of Horsethief Gulch via a dirt road is the primitive six-site Ranch Campground (tables, grills, restroom). Many RVs skip the park fees altogether and park on nearby BLM land (a big turnout loop just before the paved road ends), mooching free showers at the park while swimming, fishing, and boating at the reservoir. The upper loop at Horsethief Gulch has a large pull-through site and is particularly private thanks to many large junipers (a source of rot-resistant wood in Nevada's early days) growing among the single-leaf piñons (edible nuts), big sagebrush (state flower), and rubber rabbitbrush (winter jackrabbit food).

BASICS

Operated By: Nevada State Parks. **Open:** All year. **Site Assignment:** First come, first served; group site reservations. **Registration:** At self-pay entrance fee station. **Fee:** $13–$15. **Parking:** At site.

FACILITIES

Number of Multipurpose Sites: 42. **Hookups:** None. **Each Site:** Sheltered table, grill, fire ring. **Dump Station:** Yes. **Laundry:** No. **Pay Phone:** Yes. **Restrooms and Showers:** Yes. **Fuel:** No. **Propane:** No. **Internal Roads:** Gravel, good. **RV Service:** No. **Market:** Pioche, 18 mi. **Restaurant:** Pioche, 18 mi. **General Store:** No. **Vending:** No. **Swimming:** Reservoir (at own risk). **Playground:** No. **Other:** Boat launch, fish-cleaning station, 2 wheelchair-accessible sites. **Activities:** Boating, fishing, hiking. **Nearby Attractions:** Pioche, Echo Canyon, Cathedral Gorge. **Additional Information:** Pioche Chamber of Commerce, (775) 962-5544.

RESTRICTIONS

Pets: On leash under owner's control. **Fires:** Allowed. **Alcoholic Beverages:** Allowed. **Vehicle Maximum Length:** 40 ft. **Other:** Firewood collection prohibited.

TO GET THERE

From Pioche, go 18 mi. northeast on NV 322 through the town of Ursine until the paved road ends.

RACHEL   MAP, C-3
Quik-Pik Mini Mart and Campground

HCR 61 Box 23, 89001. T: (775) 729-2529.

🚐 ★★★   ▲ ★★★

Beauty: ★★★   Site Privacy: ★★★★
Spaciousness: ★★★★   Quiet: ★★★★
Security: ★★★★   Cleanliness: ★★★★
Insect Control: ★★★★   Facilities: ★★

The only stopping place on the Extraterrestrial Highway (NV 375), so named because it leads the world in UFO sightings, the 22-year-old town of Rachel is a major motorcycle stopping place, as heading west the next gas is 110 miles away in Tonopah. Rachel's 3,000 acres of high-protein alfalfa trucked to California dairies are overshadowed by its proximity to Area 51. ET buffs believe that the U.S. government's super-secret weapons development center around usually dry Groom Lake houses the remains of space aliens from the 1947 Roswell, New Mexico,

crash. The lady and her son running the store, gas station, and RV park are skeptics, but they'll sell you alien T-shirts and souvenirs to take home. The trailer park itself has 22 spots filled by permanent residents. The 10 available pull-through spaces across from the Rachel Senior Center Thrift Store are gravel with a bit of desert brush.

BASICS

Operated By: Fay Day. **Open:** All year. **Site Assignment:** First come, first served. **Registration:** At mini-mart. **Fee:** $12–$15. **Parking:** At site.

FACILITIES

Number of RV-only Sites: 10. **Hookups:** Electric (20, 30 amps), water, sewer. **Each Site:** Gravel. **Dump Station:** No. **Laundry:** Yes. **Pay Phone:** Yes. **Restrooms and Showers:** Yes. **Fuel:** Yes. **Propane:** No. **Internal Roads:** Gravel, good. **RV Service:** No. **Market:** At mini-mart (limited; Tonopah, 110 mi.). **Restaurant:** In Rachel. **General Store:** Yes. **Vending:** No. **Swimming:** No. **Playground:** No. **Activities:** UFO watching. **Nearby Attractions:** Area 51. **Additional Information:** Little A'Le Inn, (702) 729-2515.

RESTRICTIONS

Pets: On leash under owner's control. **Fires:** Not allowed. **Alcoholic Beverages:** Allowed. **Vehicle Maximum Length:** Any size.

TO GET THERE

From triple junction of US 93 and NV 318 and 375, go west 36 mi. on NV 375.

SILVER SPRINGS   MAP, B-1
Fort Churchill State Historic Park

1000 Hwy. 95A, 89429. T: (775) 577-2345; parks.nv.gov/fc.htm.

🚐 ★★★   ▲ ★★★★

Beauty: ★★★★   Site Privacy: ★★★★
Spaciousness: ★★★★   Quiet: ★★★★
Security: ★★★★   Cleanliness: ★★★★
Insect Control: ★★★★   Facilities: ★★★

After three white male kidnappers were killed and their outpost burned by local Native Americans to free two of their girls held hostage, a volunteer group of white settlers declared all-out war and were routed near Pyramid Lake in 1860. Government troops were called in from California, and Fort Churchill was constructed to guard the Pony Express and serve as a base for anti–Native American expeditions. Fort Churchill was abandoned in 1869, and all that remains now are some old adobe ruins that can be explored, a cemetery, some relics, and an interpretive center. A scenic trail network connecting with Lahontan State Recreation Area is an ongoing state project. The campground at Fort Churchill, which is reached via a gravel road crossing a one-lane wood bridge, has large cottonwood trees shading widely dispersed campsites with good views of the surrounding low rolling hills and cattle grazing in pastures.

BASICS

Operated By: Nevada State Parks. **Open:** All year. **Site Assignment:** First come, first served; group

reservation required. **Registration:** At self-pay fee station. **Fee:** $12; cash, check. **Parking:** At site.

FACILITIES

Number of RV-only Sites: 20. **Hookups:** None. **Each Site:** Table, fire ring. **Dump Station:** Yes. **Laundry:** No. **Pay Phone:** Yes. **Restrooms and Showers:** No showers. **Fuel:** No. **Propane:** No. **Internal Roads:** Gravel, good. **RV Service:** No. **Market:** Lahontan, 5 mi. **Restaurant:** Silver Springs, 9 mi. **General Store:** No. **Vending:** Yes. **Swimming:** No. **Playground:** No. **Other:** Museum, cemetery, wheelchair-accessible site. **Activities:** Boating, water sports, horseback riding, bird-watching, hunting. **Nearby Attractions:** Virginia City, Carson City, Reno, Buckland Station. **Additional Information:** Lyon County Information Center, (775) 463-2246, www.tele-net.net/lyontour.

RESTRICTIONS

Pets: On leash. **Fires:** Allowed (only in fire rings, bring own firewood or approved stove). **Alcoholic Beverages:** Allowed. **Vehicle Maximum Length:** 30 ft. **Other:** Do not climb on the ruins; 14-day stay limit.

TO GET THERE

From junction of US 50 and Alt 95, go 8 mi. south on Alt 95 and 1 mi. west on Old Fort Churchill Rd.

SPRING MOUNTAIN NATIONAL RECREATION AREA   MAP, D-3
Hilltop Campground

HCR 38, 4701 North Torrey Pines Dr., 89130. T: (702) 515-5400 or (800) 328-6226; www.reserveamerica.com.

🚐 ★   ▲ ★★★★

Beauty: ★★★★★   Site Privacy: ★★★★★
Spaciousness: ★★   Quiet: ★★★★★
Security: ★★★★   Cleanliness: ★★★★
Insect Control: ★★★★   Facilities: ★

Midway between Lee Canyon and Kyle Canyon on a twisting mountain highway with gnarled bristlecone pines and spectacular views into distant canyons, Hilltop Campground is the most remote area campground and the only one with showers (coin-operated; often inoperative). The entrance from NV 158 forks, with one road leading to Spring Mountain Youth Camp Correctional Facility and the adjacent Hilltop Exit sporting a warning sign for the tire shredders that will ruin the day of those entering the wrong way. Like Lee Canyon, 60% of the sites among the gnarled hillside pines here are reserved in advance on hot Vegas weekends. Sites have either forest views or views deep into the valleys below. Reserve sites 9–11,13,14, and 16–18 for the best valley views (not for those afraid of heights). Sites 25–30 (no reservations) are among the most private looking into the forest. Nearby Mahogany Grove has two group sites.

BASICS

Operated By: Thousand Trails Inc. **Open:** May 15–Oct. 15, weather permitting. **Site Assignment:**

First come, first served. **Registration:** At self-pay entrance fee station. **Fee:** $15; triple site, $35; double site, $25. **Parking:** At site.

FACILITIES

Number of RV-only Sites: 35. **Hookups:** None. **Each Site:** Table, grill, fire ring. **Dump Station:** No. **Laundry:** No. **Pay Phone:** No. **Restrooms and Showers:** Yes. **Fuel:** No. **Propane:** No. **Internal Roads:** Paved, excellent condition. **RV Service:** No. **Market:** Las Vegas, 35 mi. **Restaurant:** Kyle Canyon, 6 mi. **General Store:** No. **Vending:** No. **Swimming:** No. **Playground:** No. **Other:** Tire shredders at exit. **Activities:** Archery range, hiking, horseback riding. **Nearby Attractions:** Mount Charleston, Lee Canyon, Las Vegas. **Additional Information:** Humboldt Toiyabe National Forest, (702) 873-8800, www.fs.fed.us.htnf; Spring Mountains Assoc., (702) 896-7213.

RESTRICTIONS

Pets: On leash under owner's control. **Fires:** Allowed. **Alcoholic Beverages:** Allowed. **Vehicle Maximum Length:** 25 ft. **Other:** No fireworks.

TO GET THERE

From junction of US 95 and NV 157 north of Las Vegas, go 17 mi. west on NV 157 and then 6 mi. northwest on NV 158.

SPRING MOUNTAIN NATIONAL RECREATION AREA   MAP, D-3
Kyle Canyon and Fletcher View Campgrounds

reserve america

HCR 38, P.O. Box 451, 89124. T: (702) 515-5400 or (800) 328-6226; www.reserveamerica.com.

🚐 ★★★★	🏕 ★★★★
Beauty: ★★★★	Site Privacy: ★★★★★
Spaciousness: ★★★★	Quiet: ★★★★
Security: ★★★★	Cleanliness: ★★★★
Insect Control: ★★★	Facilities: ★

Nestled alongside a dry creek bed with shady oaks and ponderosa pines, Kyle Canyon and Fletcher View campgrounds are closer to Las Vegas than Hilltop, Dolomite, and McWilliams campgrounds. All five campgrounds attract the same weekenders seeking to beat the Vegas summer heat by fleeing to the mountains. The dozen Fletcher View sites are very spread out, relatively spacious (most can squeeze in 36–40-foot vehicles), and cannot be reserved in advance. By contrast, 10 of the 25 Kyle Canyon sites, which are closer together, can be reserved and often are booked up well in advance (beginning Friday night) on summer weekends. Picnics are also popular, and the visitor center has hiking. Less than a mile down the road is Kyle Canyon RV Camp, which lacks toilets but can hold 15 self-contained vehicles as an overflow area or be reserved as a group area.

BASICS

Operated By: Thousand Trails Inc. **Open:** Apr. 1–Oct. 17, weather permitting. **Site Assignment:** First come, first served; 60% of sites reservable. **Registration:** At self-pay entrance fee station. **Fee:** $14. **Parking:** At site.

FACILITIES

Number of RV-only Sites: 13. **Hookups:** None. **Each Site:** Table, grill, fire ring. **Dump Station:** No. **Laundry:** No. **Pay Phone:** Yes. **Restrooms and Showers:** No showers. **Fuel:** No. **Propane:** No. **Internal Roads:** Gravel, good. **RV Service:** No. **Market:** Las Vegas, 23 mi. **Restaurant:** Kyle Canyon. **General Store:** No. **Vending:** No. **Swimming:** No. **Playground:** No. **Other:** Wheelchair-accessible sites, hotel, picnic area. **Activities:** Hiking, winter sports. **Nearby Attractions:** Lee Canyon Ski Area, Mount Charleston, Las Vegas. **Additional Information:** Humboldt Toiyabe National Forest, (702) 873-8800, www.fs.fed.us.htnf; Spring Mountains Assoc., (702) 896-7213.

RESTRICTIONS

Pets: On leash under owner's control. **Fires:** Allowed. **Alcoholic Beverages:** Allowed. **Vehicle Maximum Length:** 36 ft.

TO GET THERE

From junction of US 95 and NV 157 north of Las Vegas, go 18 mi. west on NV 157.

WINNEMUCCA   MAP, A-1, A-2
Hi-Desert RV Park

5575 East Winnemucca Blvd., 89445. T: (775) 623-4513 or (800) 699-3959.

🚐 ★★★★	🏕 ★★★★
Beauty: ★★★★	Site Privacy: ★★★★
Spaciousness: ★★★★	Quiet: ★★★★
Security: ★★★★	Cleanliness: ★★★★
Insect Control: ★★★★	Facilities: ★★★★

Winnemucca is a good stopping place between Reno and Salt Lake City or Boise, and Hi-Desert is an attractive alternative to the casino parking lots. Poplar and walnut trees provide shade, grassy strips separate each site, and attractive white-bulb fixtures sit atop black lamp poles. The highway is nearby, but the rustling of tree leaves in the wind helps muffle the occasional motorcycle or truck at this well-maintained park. The tent area is grass and conveniently located near the store and pool. The gift shop has an interesting selection of knives sheathed in python, alligator, and rattlesnake skin cases, plus gambling machines to satisfy casino urges. Heading east there is not another good RV park until Elko, as Battle Mountain has been suffering from low gold prices and the miners living in the RV parks there have moved on.

BASICS

Operated By: Connie Sasser. **Open:** All year. **Site Assignment:** First come, first served; reservations advised May–Aug. **Registration:** At office. **Fee:** RV, $25; tent, $18; V, MC, AE, D. **Parking:** At site.

FACILITIES

Number of RV-only Sites: 132. **Number of Tent-only Sites:** 11. **Hookups:** Electric (20, 30, 50 amps), water, sewer, cable TV. **Each Site:** Table. **Dump Station:** Yes. **Laundry:** Yes. **Pay Phone:** Yes. **Restrooms and Showers:** Yes. **Fuel:** No. **Propane:** Yes. **Internal Roads:** Paved, good. **RV Service:** No. **Market:** Winnemucca, 2 mi. **Restaurant:** Winnemucca, 0.3 mi. **General Store:** Yes. **Vending:** Yes. **Swimming:** Pool. **Playground:** Yes. **Other:** Grills in tent area, dog walk, free shuttle to town, whirlpool, tetherball, volleyball, horseshoes. **Activities:** Golf, bowling, gambling, hunting, fishing, biking. **Nearby Attractions:** Buckaroo Hall of Fame, Paradise Valley. **Additional Information:** Winnemucca Convention Center, (775) 623-5071, (800) 962-2638, www.winnemucca.com.

RESTRICTIONS

Pets: On leash under owner's control. **Fires:** Allowed (no open fires, only in grills). **Alcoholic Beverages:** Allowed. **Vehicle Maximum Length:** 61 ft. **Other:** Children must be under adult supervision & in campsites by 10 p.m.

TO GET THERE

From US I-80, take Exit 180 west 0.8 mi.

New Hampshire

From coastal beaches, freshwater lakes, northern forests, rolling hills and valleys, and towering mountains, New Hampshire offers campers a diverse landscape rich in scenic beauty and cultural heritage. The state boasts more than 150 private campgrounds, ranging from rustic sites to resort-style properties, as well as some of the finest state parks in the nation. Visitors to the Granite State can set up camp on an ocean beach or along the shorelines of a pristine lake; you can camp amid acres of dense pine forest dotted with meandering rivers, cascades, and waterfalls or in the shadows of New England's tallest mountains. Campgrounds can also be found near the state's top tourist attractions and just outside its bustling cities and resort towns.

The southwest region of the state, dominated by **Mount Monadnock,** is often called New Hampshire's quiet corner. Frequently cited as the most climbed mountain in the world, Mount Monadnock has long been an attraction for those searching for a bit of serenity. Even Henry David Thoreau and Ralph Waldo Emmerson hiked Monadnock and remarked on its spiritual and environmental significance. Hikers of all experience levels will enjoy the dozen or so trails around the mountain (**White Cross** and **White Dot** are two of the most popular), which are all graded by difficulty. Campers will find scenic backroads leading to woodlands, lakes, valley villages, and historic sites. It's the perfect place to get away from it all. Travelers who enjoy searching the arcane should skip over to nearby Hinsdale, where they will find a house plastered with license plates.

The New Hampshire lakes region, nestled in the center of the state, is dotted with 273 lakes and ponds, including **Lake Winnipesaukee,** the state's largest. As expected, campers in this region will find that recreation centers around the water: fishing, swimming, and boating are popular pursuits. The region also boasts several random but no less entertaining attractions, including a **Shaker village, railroads, the Mount Washington Observatory,** and a temporary tattoo parlor (the tattoos are temporary, not the parlor)!

The south-central region of the state is home to its largest cities: **Manchester, Nashua,** and **Concord,** where campers have museums, theaters, and shopping malls to visit. Just outside the cities, campgrounds are nestled in a rural landscape of rolling hills, fields, and farms.

Campground choices abound in the popular northern White Mountains region. The 780,000-acre **White Mountain National Forest** dominates most of the area. The **Kancamagus National Scenic Byway** is a must for those looking for a pleasant drive. Though only 28 miles long, "the Kanc" takes about an hour or so to completely navigate and climbs to nearly 3,000 feet up Mount Kancamagus. While on the eastern half of the drive, keep a lookout for the **Rocky Gorge Scenic area,** a great example of erosion at its finest. One can see where the Swift River has slowly and surely created a narrow passage through solid stone. Rock climbers with plenty of time on their hands (and feet) should explore a few of the region's 48 4,000ers (mountains exceeding 4,000 feet), including 6,288-foot **Mount Washington,** which is the tallest mountain in the Northeast. Rockheads will also want to take note of the dozen or so AMC huts that dot the region. AMC huts are a great place to take a break, warm up, and stock up on snacks and supplies. Hikers can also spend the night but will want to make a reservation (call (603) 466-2727 for information, reservations, and rates). Also, there are more than 100 waterfalls and thousands of miles of rivers, streams, and trails. Campers have a delightful blend of **busy resort towns** (like **North Conway, Lincoln,** and **North Woodstock**), quaint villages, and wide expanses of back-to-nature wilderness to explore. Campgrounds in the area run the gamut from small, tucked-away properties to spacious, amenity-laden resorts.

New Hampshire has a mere 18 miles of Atlantic coastline and only one state park campground with oceanfront property. But several top-notch campgrounds are clustered in surrounding inland towns, some set in rural areas, others along freshwater rivers and tidal marshlands. All have quick access to the **historic seaport city of Portsmouth,** ocean beaches and parks (much of the coastline is public land), and popular seacoast attractions.

Another fun trip: Outside of Concord is a little town by the name of **Weare.** Ask a resident where they're from and they'll respond, "Weare." Trump them by not repeating the question.

One very nice bonus for campers visiting small and condensed New Hampshire: No matter where you set up camp, the mountains, lakes, cities, attractions, and ocean are just a short drive away.

Campground Profiles

ALBANY MAP, C-3
Jigger Johnson Campground

Kancamagus Hwy., 03818. T: (603) 447-2116;
www.fs.fed.us/r9/white.

🚐 ★★★ ⛺ ★★★★

Beauty: ★★★★ Site Privacy: ★★★★
Spaciousness: ★★★★ Quiet: ★★★★
Security: ★★★★ Cleanliness: ★★★★
Insect Control: ★★★ Facilities: ★★★

Jigger Johnson is the largest campground on the Kancamagus, and the only campground along the Kanc that has coin-operated hot showers. Most of the sites along the northeastern end of the campground, near the banks of the Swift River, are spacious and set amid fairly dense forest. There is a series of interpretive programs on Saturday evenings throughout the summer, focusing on a particular aspect of the local flora and fauna, and the campground is very close to some classic White Mountain hiking. The trail that leads down to the banks of the Swift River intersects with a trail that runs along the backside of the campground. Bird-watchers would enjoy the soothing sounds of songbirds along the path. This mellow trail follows the Swift both upstream and downstream for quite a distance, passing some beautiful bends in the river and traveling through delightful aromatic groves of birch, maple, and pine. It's a great hike to do with kids because it's relatively flat, and there are all sorts of wonderful things to see and experience.

BASICS

Operated By: U.S. Forest Service. **Open:** Mid-May–mid-Oct. **Site Assignment:** First come, first served; no reservations. **Registration:** Select site, then pay at self-service fee station. **Fee:** $20. **Parking:** At site.

FACILITIES

Number of Multipurpose Sites: 76. **Hookups:** None. **Each Site:** Fire ring, picnic table. **Dump Station:** No. **Laundry:** No. **Pay Phone:** No. **Restrooms and Showers:** Yes. **Fuel:** No. **Propane:** No. **Internal Roads:** Paved. **RV Service:** No. **Market:** No. **Restaurant:** No. **General Store:** No. **Vending:** No. **Swimming:** Yes. **Playground:** No. **Activities:** Fishing, hiking, scenic byway, swimming. **Nearby Attractions:** Historic Russell-Colbath, an 1830s homestead. **Additional Information:** North Conway Chamber of Commerce, (603) 356-3171.

RESTRICTIONS

Pets: On leash. **Fires:** Fire ring only. **Alcoholic Beverages:** At site. **Vehicle Maximum Length:** Varies. **Other:** 8 people per site; 14-day stay limit; 2 vehicles; $5 charge for 2nd vehicle.

TO GET THERE

From Lincoln, follow Kancamagus Hwy. to campground on left. From Conway, follow Kancamagus Hwy. to campground on right, shortly after Bear Notch Rd., also on right.

ASHLAND MAP, C-2
Ames Brook Campground

104 Winona Rd., 03217. T: (603) 968-7998;
www.amesbrook.com.

🚐 ★★★ ⛺ ★★★

Beauty: ★★★ Site Privacy: ★★★
Spaciousness: ★★★ Quiet: ★★★★
Security: ★★★ Cleanliness: ★★★
Insect Control: ★★★ Facilities: ★★★

If all you're looking for is a clean, pleasant base to explore the New Hampshire Lakes region and beyond, you can't go wrong here. This rural campground, minutes from downtown Ashland and Lake Winnipesaukee, has flat sites, rectangular sandy swatches laid out in a row, all carved out of the woods. Filled with maple, oak, and pine trees, this woody area is inhabited by deer, skunk, fox, and the occasional bear. Alas, the campground doesn't have much of a personality; a row of semi-permanent-looking seasonals crowd the front of the campground; farther back in the woods, you'll find the narrow, barely-there Ames Brook winding through a small section of the campground. There are 9 pull-through sites at the campground, and the remaining sites are back-in. Campers' favorite sites are located near the bathrooms and around the lake. If you like to sleep to the sound of babbling water, request sites numbers 50 to 52. A small row of full-hookup sites is also along the brook. We like the library of books and magazines the owners keep in the office and laundromat area—nice touch. The campground offers a quieter, more natural setting than its neighbor, Yogi Bear's Jellystone Park, but with fewer activities and facilities.

BASICS

Operated By: Barbara Marion. **Open:** Mid-May–Oct. 31. **Site Assignment:** Reservations suggested, one-half of scheduled stay required as deposit; must cancel w/in 21 days of visit; MC, V accepted; personal checks not accepted. **Registration:** At office. **Fee:** Full hookup, $34; water/electric, $31; no hookup, $30; based on 2 adults; children 10–17 years, additional $3; extra adult, $10. **Parking:** At site, 1 vehicle per site.

FACILITIES

Number of RV-only Sites: 86. **Number of Tent-only Sites:** 4. **Hookups:** Electric (30, 50 amps), water, sewer, cable TV. **Each Site:** Table, fire ring. **Dump Station:** Yes. **Laundry:** Yes. **Pay Phone:** No. **Restrooms and Showers:** Yes. **Fuel:** No. **Propane:** Yes. **Internal Roads:** Gravel, dirt (fair). Entrance paved. **RV Service:** No. **Market:** Ashland, 1 mi. **Restaurant:** Yes. **General Store:** Yes. **Vending:** No. **Swimming:** Yes. **Playground:** Yes. **Other:** Small book library, game room, activities hall. **Activities:** Swimming, croquet, basketball, volleyball, horseshoes, fishing. **Nearby Attractions:** Lake Winnipesaukee, Squam Lake, Weirs Beach, outlet shopping, antiquing, quick access to the White Mountain area. **Additional Information:** Greater Laconia/Weirs Beach Chamber of Commerce, 11 Veterans Square, Laconia, NH 03246, (603) 524-5531.

RESTRICTIONS

Pets: Must be on a leash, never left unattended, max. 2. **Fires:** Grill, stoves, fire rings only. **Alcoholic Beverages:** At site only. **Vehicle Maximum Length:** No limit. **Other:** 2 tents or 1 trailer per site; no boats parked on site but may be parked in lot.

TO GET THERE

From I-93, Exit 24, go 0.75 mi. south on Hwy. 3, then 0.25 mi. south on Hwy. 132, then 0.5 mi. south on Winona Rd. Campground is on the right.

ASHLAND MAP, C-2
Yogi Bear's Jellystone Park

35 Jellystone Park, 03256. T: (603) 968-9000;
www.jellystonenh.com.

🚐 ★★★★ ⛺ ★★

Beauty: ★★ Site Privacy: ★★
Spaciousness: ★★ Quiet: ★★
Security: ★★★ Cleanliness: ★★★★
Insect Control: ★★★ Facilities: ★★★★★

If you're looking for a little peace and quiet, don't even think about coming here. This franchise property is a "happening place" for campers who like a jam-packed, bustling schedule of activities and very close neighbors. The campground features major events throughout the summer, with concerts, dances, parades, contests, and a daily schedule of arts and crafts, hayrides, workshops, and bingo. Whew! We get tired just reading the list and watching the families scurry from event to event. Most sites are small back-ins and in the open, with little privacy, but beautiful maple, pine, and hardwood trees surround the area. The property is set on the pretty Pemigawasset River, but an annoying and unattractive fence separates you from the view. There's a small beach area and a fishing dock. But, if you want to get away from it all, you'll have to rent a boat and paddle the river. Otherwise, let the kids go meet Yogi and Booboo while you join the country line dancing lessons—right before the ice-cream social! Lots of people, especially families, love this place.

BASICS

Operated By: Diane & Wayne Kleckcamp. **Open:** Memorial Day–Columbus Day. **Site Assignment:** Reservations strongly urged; full deposit for 2–3 day stay, 50% for longer stays; refunds w/ 14-day notice. MC, V, D, & personal checks accepted in advance; cabins require payment in full & notice 60 days in advance. **Registration:** At office. **Fee:** Full hookup, $60; water/electric, $56; based on 2 people per site; children, ages 2–17, $2; grandparents, $6; additional adults, $28. **Parking:** At site, 1 vehicle per site.

FACILITIES

Number of RV-only Sites: 255. **Number of Multipurpose Sites:** 255. **Hookups:** Electric (20, 30, 50 amps), water, sewer. **Each Site:** Table, fire ring. **Dump Station:** Yes. **Laundry:** Yes. **Pay Phone:** Yes.

Restrooms and Showers: Yes (coin-op). **Fuel:** No. **Propane:** No. **Internal Roads:** Paved (good). **RV Service:** No. **Market:** Ashland, 2 mi. **Restaurant:** Yes. **General Store:** Yes. **Vending:** Yes. **Swimming:** Yes. **Playground:** Yes. **Other:** Water playground, hot tub, river frontage, boat dock, indoor & outdoor theaters, teen rec hall, arcade, canoe, rowboat, & kayak rentals, 19-hole mini-golf, day-trip information center, babysitting referral service, ice-cream shop, cabin rentals. **Activities:** Swimming, fishing, boating, basketball, mini-golf, horseshoes, shuffleboard, volleyball, softball, bocce ball, planned activities including dance workshops, arts & crafts, concerts, live entertainment, hayrides, movies, & more. **Nearby Attractions:** Lake Winnipesaukee, Squam Lake, Weirs Beach, outlet shopping, antiquing, quick access to the White Mountain area. **Additional Information:** Greater Laconia/Weirs Beach Chamber of Commerce, 11 Veterans Square, Laconia, NH 03246, (603) 524-5531.

RESTRICTIONS

Pets: Strongly discouraged; must be on a leash, never left unattended & not allowed in most public areas. **Fires:** Grill, stoves, fire rings only. **Alcoholic Beverages:** Must be in cup or glass if carried off site. **Vehicle Maximum Length:** No limit.

TO GET THERE

From I-93, Exit 23, go 0.5 mi. east on Hwy. 104, then 4 mi. north on Hwy. 132; campground is on the left.

BARRINGTON   MAP, D-3
Ayers Lake Farm Campground and Cottages

557 Hwy. 202, 03825. T: (603) 335-1110 or (603) 332-5940; www.ucampnh.com/ayerslake.

🚐 ★★★   ⛺ ★★★★

Beauty: ★★★★	Site Privacy: ★★★
Spaciousness: ★★★	Quiet: ★★★★
Security: ★★★★★	Cleanliness: ★★★★
Insect Control: ★★★	Facilities: ★★★

When we first drove up to the campground, we thought we'd arrived at a very pretty New England country inn. The office is in a beautiful, historic farmhouse, with sweeping lawns and gardens reaching to the water. The campground itself is just south of the farmhouse, with nearly all the sites nestled in a semicircle along the shoreline. There's a pretty beach on Ayers Lake, and 15 secluded acres of pine forest, fields, and shorefront. It's located between New Hampshire's mountains and ocean, only a short 30- to 45-minute drive to either if you'd like to explore. But you'll be tempted to stay put. That's the good news. The bad news: Only a few sites are available on any given night throughout the season; most are taken by returning seasonal renters who obviously love this place. Call ahead and see if you get lucky. Also, check into the campground's more secluded cottage rentals on the property.

BASICS

Operated By: Bedford family. **Open:** May 20–Sept. 20. **Site Assignment:** Reservations suggested, 50% deposit, 3 days paid in advance for holiday weekends, 2-week notice for refund of deposit. **Registration:**

At farmhouse/office. **Fee:** Waterside, $40; waterfront, $38; full hookup, $34; no hookup, $30. **Parking:** At site, 2 vehicle max.

FACILITIES

Number of RV-only Sites: 46. **Number of Tent-only Sites:** 6. **Hookups:** Electric (20, 30, 50 amps), water, sewer. **Each Site:** Picnic table, fire ring. **Dump Station:** Yes. **Laundry:** Yes. **Pay Phone:** Yes. **Restrooms and Showers:** Yes. **Fuel:** No. **Propane:** No. **Internal Roads:** Dirt (good). **RV Service:** No. **Market:** Barrington, 5 mi. **Restaurant:** No. **General Store:** No. **Vending:** Soda. **Swimming:** Yes. **Playground:** Yes. **Other:** Lake frontage, beach, boat ramp, cottage rentals, canoe & rowboat rentals, sports field, wood & ice available. **Activities:** Swimming, boating, fishing, horseshoes. **Nearby Attractions:** New Hampshire seacoast beaches, historic town of Portsmouth, quick access to Lakes Region, antiquing, Blue Job Mountain. **Additional Information:** Barrington Chamber of Commerce, P.O. Box 363, Barrington, NH 03825, (603) 664-2200; also visit www. seacoastnh.com.

RESTRICTIONS

Pets: Must be on a leash, cleaned up after, never left unattended. Pets are not allowed on beach or playground. **Fires:** Grill, stoves, fire rings only. **Alcoholic Beverages:** At site only. **Vehicle Maximum Length:** 38 ft. **Other:** No power boats can be landed, launched, grounded, or docked in the campground. No fireworks.

TO GET THERE

From junction Hwy. 16 (Spaulding Turnpike) take Exit 13 and go 5 mi. southwest on US 202; campground is on the right.

BARRINGTON   MAP, D-3
Barrington Shores

70 Hall Rd., 03825. T: (603) 664-9333; www.barringtonshores.com.

🚐 ★★★★   ⛺ ★★★

Beauty: ★★★★	Site Privacy: ★★★
Spaciousness: ★★★	Quiet: ★★★
Security: ★★★★★	Cleanliness: ★★★★
Insect Control: ★★★	Facilities: ★★★

Remember busy summer days spent at the lakeside cottage? There was boating, and fishing, and races to the raft. In the evening, there were bonfires and marshmallow roasts. If you're looking for that classic lake vacation, for a fraction of the cost, head to Barrington Shores. This hilly campground on pretty Swain's Lake offers freshwater lake swimming, fishing, boating, and lots of planned activities. There are plenty of lake views from the tiered sites, two large, sandy beaches, boat ramp (many campers bring their own), and dock. This is a busy place with a festive atmosphere, perfect for hot, summer days. The roads are a bit of a maze, but we like the sandy sites and fieldstone fire pits. Try to avoid sites 116 and 117 right off a road, but 121 and 122 on the lake and with water and electric hookups are especially nice; sites 69–73, with full service, overlook the lake and have a bit of room around them.

BASICS

Operated By: Don & Gail Ziemba. **Open:** Mid-May–late Sept. **Site Assignment:** Reservations recommended; holiday weekends & 2-night stays or less requires payment in full; longer stays require a 50% deposit; 2-week notice for full refund, less $10 fee. **Registration:** At office. **Fee:** $35–$45; based on 2 adults & up to 3 children under 18; additional child, $3 per night; additional adult, $12 per night. **Parking:** At site; 1 vehicle per site.

FACILITIES

Number of RV-only Sites: 137. **Number of Tent-only Sites:** 5. **Hookups:** Electric (20, 30, 50 amps), water, sewer, cable TV, phone, Wi-Fi. **Each Site:** Picnic table, fireplace. **Dump Station:** Yes. **Laundry:** Yes. **Pay Phone:** Yes, w/ Internet modem. **Restrooms and Showers:** Yes. **Fuel:** No. **Propane:** Yes. **Internal Roads:** Dirt, gravel (fair). **RV Service:** No. **Market:** Lee, 2 mi. **Restaurant:** No. **General Store:** Yes. **Vending:** No. **Swimming:** Yes. **Playground:** Yes. **Other:** Game room, safari field for rallies, 2 lakeside beaches, cottage & cabin rentals. **Activities:** Boat rentals, basketball, fishing, swimming, planned activities on weekends, fishing. **Nearby Attractions:** New Hampshire & southern Maine beaches, Portsmouth, factory outlet shopping, golf courses, water park, Strawbery Banke historic museum, Seacoast Science Center, antiques shops. **Additional Information:** Barrington Chamber of Commerce, P.O. Box 363, Barrington, NH 03825, (603) 664-2200; also visit www.seacoastnh.com.

RESTRICTIONS

Pets: Must be on a leash, cleaned up after, never left unattended. No pets in cottage or cabins. **Fires:** Grill, stoves, fire rings. **Alcoholic Beverages:** At site only. **Vehicle Maximum Length:** 40 ft. **Other:** No bicycle riding or swimming after dark. No motorized children's toys.

TO GET THERE

From I-95, take Spaulding Turnpike (Hwy. 16) in Portsmouth to Exit 6W (Hwy. 4). Follow Hwy. 4 to Lee traffic circle and the junction of Hwy. 4 and Hwy. 125. Take Hwy. 125 north 2.5 mi.; take left onto Beauty Hill Rd. Go 1 mi., take left onto Hall Rd., 1 mi. to campground.

CAMBRIDGE   MAP, A-3
Umbagog Lake State Campground

reserve america

Rte. 26, 03579. T: (603) 482-7795 or (603) 271-3628; www.reserveamerica.com.

🚐 ★★★   ⛺ ★★★★

Beauty: ★★★★	Site Privacy: ★★★★
Spaciousness: ★★★★	Quiet: ★★★★
Security: ★★★★	Cleanliness: ★★★
Insect Control: ★★	Facilities: ★★

This unique, rustic campground in New Hampshire's Great North Woods region offers wilderness sites on remote islands, in addition to its woodsy, lakeside base camp. If you're looking to get away from it all and enjoy a more natural wilderness experience, this campground has plenty to offer. The base camp is situated on the shores of still-wild Lake Umbagog and is popular with canoeists, kayakers, and anglers. In recent years, outdoor enthusiasts have come for its peace and quiet and wildlife watching. Herons, osprey, loons, moose, deer, beavers, and bald eagles are often spotted. The base camp includes 30 spacious sites, and all sites are back-in, clustered in loops from the shoreline. For a more private, remote camping experience, reserve one of the island sites. Transportation, for a nominal fee, can be arranged to these sites, though to really appreciate this spot, you'll want to explore in your own boat.

BASICS

Operated By: New Hampshire Division of Parks & Recreation. **Open:** Mid-May–mid-Oct. **Site Assignment:** Reservations suggested & must be made through central reservations, (603) 271-3628; reservations must be made at least 7 days in advance; $5 nonrefundable fee for each reservation; 24-hour cancellation policy w/ $10 fee. MC, V, D; no personal checks. **Registration:** At office. **Fee:** $24–$29. **Parking:** At site, no parking at remote wilderness sites (boat access only).

FACILITIES

Number of Tent-only Sites: 34. **Hookups:** Water, electric. **Each Site:** Picnic table, fire ring. **Dump Station:** Yes. **Laundry:** Dryer. **Pay Phone:** Yes. **Restrooms and Showers:** Yes (coin-op). **Fuel:** Boat fuel. **Propane:** No. **Internal Roads:** Dirt, gravel (fair). **RV Service:** No. **Market:** Errol, 7 mi. **Restaurant:** No. **General Store:** Yes. **Vending:** No. **Swimming:** Beach. **Playground:** No. **Other:** Boat launch, boat slips, canoe rentals, cabin rentals, transportation to remote sites. **Activities:** Swimming, boating, fishing, wildlife watching. **Nearby Attractions:** Connecticut Lakes, Rangley & Saddleback Mountain area of Maine. **Additional Information:** North Country Chamber of Commerce, P.O. Box 1, Colebrook, NH 03576, (603) 237-8939 or Northern White Mountains Chamber of Commerce, 164 Main St., P.O. Box 298, Berlin, NH 03570, (603) 752-6060.

RESTRICTIONS

Pets: In designated areas only; must be on a leash; never left unattended. **Fires:** Grill, camp stoves, fire rings only. **Alcoholic Beverages:** At site only. **Vehicle Maximum Length:** No limit. **Other:** 30 wilderness campsites are accessible by water only; transportation available.

TO GET THERE

From junction of Hwy. 16 and Hwy. 26 (in Errol), go east 7 mi. on Hwy. 26; campground is on the left.

CHICHESTER MAP, D-2, D-3
Hillcrest Family Campground

78 Dover Rd., 03258. T: (603) 798-5124; www.ucampnh.com/hillcrest.

 ★★★★   ★★★★

Beauty: ★★★
Spaciousness: ★★★★
Security: ★★★★★
Insect Control: ★★★

Site Privacy: ★★★★
Quiet: ★★★
Cleanliness: ★★★★★
Facilities: ★★★★★

The living is easy at this central New Hampshire campground, one of the prettiest in the area. It also offers plenty of conveniences, including a centralized location and on-site amenities. The hilly campground site features towering pine tree woods and a picturesque pond with a sandy cove beach. Scenic nature trails allow families to explore the wild and possibly spot a few deer. The mostly shaded sites, nestled in the woods, are adequately spaced (about 30 feet in average width) and level. There are 36 back-in sites and 8 pull-through. The campground is popular with families, who enjoy the organized activities, the large, modern pool, fishing and boating on the pond, and nature trails. Tenters will like the private and spacious Honeymoon site or No. 10, overlooking the pond. There's also a safari field for larger groups with its own pavilion and recreational hall. Forget your gear? Rent one of the eight heated cabins flanking the front of the campground. During the busy summer months, there's a plethora of planned activities to keep you busy, including dances, dinners, children's activities and games, hayrides, fishing tournaments, bingo, and more.

BASICS

Operated By: Bob Cavacco. **Open:** May–mid Oct. **Site Assignment:** Reservations recommended; 1-night deposit required; 1-week cancellation notice. **Registration:** At office. **Fee:** Full hookup w/ cable, $33; water/electric w/ cable, $31; water/electric, $30; no hookup, $28. **Parking:** At site.

FACILITIES

Number of RV-only Sites: 50. **Number of Tent-only Sites:** 10. **Hookups:** Electric (20, 30 amps), water, sewer, cable TV. **Each Site:** Picnic table, fire ring. **Dump Station:** Yes. **Laundry:** Yes. **Pay Phone:** Yes. **Restrooms and Showers:** Yes (coin-op). **Fuel:** No. **Propane:** No. **Internal Roads:** Paved, gravel (good). **RV Service:** Less than 1 mi. down road. **Market:** Epsom, 2 mi. **Restaurant:** No. **General Store:** Yes. **Vending:** No. **Swimming:** Yes. **Playground:** Yes. **Other:** Small pond, group area, mini-golf, rec room, arcade, boat rentals, nature trails, pavilion, cabin rentals. **Activities:** Swimming, boating, fishing, volleyball, badminton, mini-golf, horseshoes, organized activities throughout July–Aug., including arts & crafts, contests, dances, hayrides, dinners, bingo, & more. **Nearby Attractions:** Concord, NH International Speedway, quick access to Lakes Region & Seacoast area, antiquing. **Additional Information:** Greater Concord Chamber of Commerce, 244 North Main St., Concord, NH 03301-5078, (603) 224-2508.

RESTRICTIONS

Pets: Must be on a leash, never left unattended. **Fires:** Grill, stoves, & fire rings only. Out by midnight. No higher than knee. **Alcoholic Beverages:** At site only, ages checked. **Vehicle Maximum Length:** Up to 50 ft.

TO GET THERE

From 93, take Exit 15 east, go 5 mi. Campground is on the left.

CHOCORUA MAP, C-3
Chocorua Camping Village

893 White Mountain Hwy., Hwy. 16, 03817. T: (603) 323-8536 or (888) 237-8642; www.chocoruacamping.com.

★★★★   ★★★★

Beauty: ★★★★
Spaciousness: ★★★★
Security: ★★★★★
Insect Control: ★★★

Site Privacy: ★★★★
Quiet: ★★★
Cleanliness: ★★★★
Facilities: ★★★★★

A pretty setting on the shores of Moore's Pond and the Chocorua River, a central locale, 30 minutes to North Conway and the White Mountains, and an award-winning activities program have made this campground a top choice for families vacationing in the area. There's plenty to do at the campground: swimming and boating on the pond, hiking the 4 miles of nature paths, and biking the trails throughout the property. There are also lots of sports, free movies in the small theater, and planned activities three times a day. Kids have a wide choice of entertainment, from flower planting, mushroom hunts, and arts and crafts to bonfires, sing-alongs, and parades. For more sedate pleasures, there's a piano in the rec hall, lending library, and a deck and picnic area overlooking the pond. All of the terraced campground sites are generously spaced; as expected, waterfront sites are the most popular.

BASICS

Operated By: Shirley & Lee Spencer. **Open:** May–Columbus Day. **Site Assignment:** Reservations suggested; deposit of one-half fee required, 7-day cancellation policy w/ 10% fee. MC, V, & personal checks accepted. **Registration:** At office. **Fee:** Full hookup & waterfront, $59; water/electric, $39; no hookup, $32; based on 2 adults, 2 children, 1 vehicle & 1 sleeping unit. **Parking:** At site.

FACILITIES

Number of RV-only Sites: 126. **Number of Tent-only Sites:** 4. **Hookups:** Electric (20, 30, 50 amps), water, sewer. **Each Site:** Picnic table, fire ring. **Dump Station:** Yes. **Laundry:** Yes. **Pay Phone:** Yes. **Restrooms and Showers:** Yes (coin-op). **Fuel:** No. **Propane:** Yes. **Internal Roads:** Gravel, dirt (good). **RV Service:** Outside service available on request. **Market:** Ossipee, 2 mi. **Restaurant:** No. **General Store:** Yes. **Vending:** Yes. **Swimming:** Yes. **Playground:** Yes. **Other:** Lake & river frontage, group safari area, rec hall, movie theater, craft shop, nature trails, cabin rentals, game room, rowboat & canoe rentals. **Activities:** Swimming, fishing, boating, basketball, volleyball, horseshoes, hiking, planned activities including arts & crafts, nature walks, day hikes, sing-alongs, movies, & more. **Nearby Attractions:** Attitash Bear Peak, Story Land, Conway Scenic Railroad, North Conway, quick access to White Mountains. **Additional Information:** Greater Conway Village Area Chamber of Commerce, P.O. Box 1019, Conway, NH 03818, (603) 447-2639; also Mount Washington Valley Chamber of Commerce, P.O. Box 2300, North Conway, NH 03860, (800) 521-2137.

RESTRICTIONS

Pets: Must be on a leash, never left unattended. No rottweilers, pit bulls, Dobermans, German shepherds; one dog per site. **Fires:** Grill, stoves, fire rings only. **Alcoholic Beverages:** At site only. **Vehicle Maximum Length:** 35 ft. **Other:** Ask on arrival.

TO GET THERE

From the junction of Hwy. 25 and Hwy. 16, go 3 mi. north on Hwy. 16; campground is on the right.

CONWAY   MAP, B-3
Passaconaway Campground

Hwy. 12/Kancamagus Hwy., 03812.
T: (603) 447-2166; www.fs.fed.us/r9/white.

🚐 ★★★   ▲ ★★★★

Beauty: ★★★★	Site Privacy: ★★★★★
Spaciousness: ★★★★	Quiet: ★★★★
Security: ★★★★	Cleanliness: ★★★★
Insect Control: ★★★	Facilities: ★★★

Of all the campgrounds along the Kancamagus, Passaconaway is probably most conducive to RVs, though there are no hookups. The spacious sites are well suited to larger groups or families with kids, and the relatively central location along the Kancamagus Highway puts you in a good spot if you're not sure what part of the Kanc you want to explore first. You'll be close to Rocky Gorge, Sabbaday Falls, the Swift River picnic area, and the myriad trailheads spread out along the length of this superlative stretch of road. The forest separating the individual sites at Passaconaway is fairly dense, which provides a nice sense of seclusion and helps make this an extremely quiet campground. All you'll hear is an occasional vehicle zipping past on the Kanc and the soft rush of the wind in the evergreens, punctuated by the chatter of the forest birds and animals. There's a trailhead right next to site 18; the campground host is located at site 19.

BASICS

Operated By: U.S. Forest Service. **Open:** Mid-May–mid-Oct. **Site Assignment:** First come, first served; no reservations. **Registration:** Select site, then pay at self-service fee station. **Fee:** $18. **Parking:** At site.

FACILITIES

Number of RV-only Sites: 33. **Hookups:** None. **Each Site:** Fire ring, picnic table. **Dump Station:** No. **Laundry:** No. **Pay Phone:** No. **Restrooms and Showers:** Restrooms, no showers. **Fuel:** No. **Propane:** No. **Internal Roads:** Paved. **RV Service:** No. **Market:** No. **Restaurant:** No. **General Store:** No. **Vending:** No. **Swimming:** No. **Playground:** No. **Activities:** Fishing, hiking, picnicking, scenic byway. **Nearby Attractions:** Historic Russell-Colbath, an 1830s homestead. **Additional Information:** North Conway Chamber of Commerce, (603) 356-3171.

RESTRICTIONS

Pets: On leash. **Fires:** Fire ring only. **Alcoholic Beverages:** At site. **Vehicle Maximum Length:** Varies. **Other:** 8 people per site; 14-day stay limit, 2 vehicles; $5 charge for 2nd vehicle.

TO GET THERE

Passaconaway Campground is almost in the center of the Kancamagus Hwy. From Lincoln, follow the Kancamagus Hwy. 16 mi. to campground on left. From Conway, follow Kancamagus Hwy. 15 mi. to campground on right.

DEERING   MAP, D-2
Oxbow Campground

8 Oxbow Rd., 03244. T: (603) 464-5952;
www.ucampnh.com/oxbow.

🚐 ★★★   ▲ ★★★

Beauty: ★★★★	Site Privacy: ★★★★
Spaciousness: ★★★★	Quiet: ★★★
Security: ★★★★★	Cleanliness: ★★★
Insect Control: ★★★	Facilities: ★★★

This peaceful, outdoors-oriented campground in southwestern New Hampshire, less than a mile from downtown Hillsboro, is a favorite among local campers and vacationing families, especially in August during the Lobster Fest. There are three brook-fed ponds on the property: a three-acre, boating pond (people-powered boats only), a one-acre, sandy bottom swimming pond, and a 0.3-acre catch and release stocked fishing pond (no license needed). Sites on the property vary from deeply wooded with pines and maples for those who like privacy to open and secluded for sun worshipers. All sites have plenty of space; there are 18 back-in and 4 pull-through sites with an average width of about 55 feet. More than 140 acres of the campground are open for hiking. Along these hiking trails, raccoons, deer, and moose can be spotted. The Welcome Hall is especially nice, with reading and video libraries, puzzle making and card-playing tables. The Pine Pavilion, on the beach overlooking the swimming pond, is also a favorite gathering spot.

BASICS

Operated By: Thomas Irving. **Open:** May 1–Oct. 15. **Site Assignment:** Reservations suggested; 1–7 day stay, $30 deposit; 1–9 week stay, $100 deposit; whole season, $200; 3-day min. on holiday weekends; over 7-day cancellation notice, full refund; under 7 days, no refund on holidays & refund less $30 on nonholidays. MC, V, personal checks accepted. **Registration:** At office. **Fee:** Full hookup, $32; electric, $25; waterfront site, $3 extra; based on 2 adults & 2 children under 18. **Parking:** At site.

FACILITIES

Number of RV-only Sites: 103. **Number of Tent-only Sites:** 13. **Hookups:** Electric (20, 30, 50 amps), water, sewer, cable TV, phone. **Each Site:** Picnic table, fire ring. **Dump Station:** No. **Laundry:** Yes. **Pay Phone:** Yes. **Restrooms and Showers:** Yes (coin-op). **Fuel:** No. **Propane:** Yes. **Internal Roads:** Gravel, dirt (fair). **RV Service:** No. **Market:** Hillsboro, 0.5 mi. **Restaurant:** No. **General Store:** Yes. **Vending:** No. **Swimming:** Pond. **Playground:** Yes. **Other:** 3 ponds, beach areas, rec hall, pavilion, sports field, hiking trails, cabin rentals. **Activities:** Swimming, fishing, boating, shuffleboard, volleyball, basketball, horseshoes, planned activities on summer weekends. **Nearby Attractions:** Hillsboro, Con-

cord, state parks, lakes & fishing streams. **Additional Information:** Greater Concord Chamber of Commerce, 244 North Main St., Concord, NH 03301-5078, (603) 224-2508.

RESTRICTIONS

Pets: Must have up-to-date vaccinations, kept on a leash, never left unattended, picked up after. **Fires:** Grill, stoves, fire rings only. **Alcoholic Beverages:** No more than one beverage per person open at any time. **Vehicle Maximum Length:** 45 ft.

TO GET THERE

From junction Hwys. 202, 9, and 149, go south 0.75 mi. on Hwy. 149; campground is on the left.

EAST WAKEFIELD   MAP, C-3
Lake Ivanhoe Inn and Camping Resort

631 Acton Ridge Rd., 03830. T: (603) 522-8824;
www.lakeivanhoe.com.

🚐 ★★★   ▲ ★★★

Beauty: ★★★	Site Privacy: ★★★
Spaciousness: ★★★★	Quiet: ★★★★
Security: ★★★	Cleanliness: ★★★
Insect Control: ★★★	Facilities: ★★

If your idea of the perfect getaway is to get away from it all, this campground could be for you. (Though within an hour's drive, you can be in the White Mountains or on the seacoast of Maine.) This campground, set off the main drag, is pleasantly quiet and relaxing. There's a small historic inn on the property and a 100-foot-long private, sandy beach across the street for campers. About half the campground is taken by summer seasonal renters who seem content with the slow life: a morning paddle on the lake, an afternoon nap, bingo at night. Lake pleasures seem to dominate, here. There's swimming, boating, and fishing on spring-fed 120-acre Lake Ivanhoe, one of 11 lakes in the Wakefield area. Facilities are clean but basic (chemical toilets). Seasonal renters and large rigs are placed up front, while tenters head to the shaded, back portion of the property.

BASICS

Operated By: Ann & Tony Bettencourt. **Open:** Mid-May–Columbus Day. **Site Assignment:** Reservations suggested, 50% deposit required, 14-day notice for refund of deposit; 2-night min. weekends. MC, V, & personal checks accepted. **Registration:** At office. **Fee:** $31–$38. **Parking:** At site.

FACILITIES

Number of RV-only Sites: 69. **Number of Tent-only Sites:** 6. **Hookups:** Electric (20, 30 amps), water, sewer, cable TV, modem. **Each Site:** Picnic table, fire ring. **Dump Station:** Yes. **Laundry:** Yes. **Pay Phone:** Yes. **Restrooms and Showers:** Yes. **Fuel:** No. **Propane:** Yes. **Internal Roads:** Dirt, gravel (fair). **RV Service:** No. **Market:** Wakefield, 1 mi. **Restaurant:** No. **General Store:** Yes. **Vending:** No. **Swimming:** Beach. **Playground:** Yes. **Other:** Lake frontage & beach, canoe & paddleboat rentals, adult rec hall, game room, sports field, safari area. **Activities:** Swimming, boating, horseshoes, badminton, volleyball, shuffleboard, planned activities on weekends including hayrides, bingo, socials. **Nearby Attractions:** Lake Winnipesaukee, Lakes Region attractions. **Additional Information:** Lakes Region Assoc., Hwy. 104, P.O. Box 430, New Hampton, NH 03252, (603) 744-8664.

RESTRICTIONS

Pets: Must be on a leash, never left unattended. Pets are not allowed on the beach or in tent areas. Only one pet per site. **Fires:** Grill, stoves, fire rings only. **Alcoholic Beverages:** At site only. Must be of age. **Vehicle Maximum Length:** No limit.

TO GET THERE

From junction Hwy. 16 and Wakefield Rd., go 0.5 mi. east on Wakefield Rd. to Hwy. 153, then 2.5 mi. north to Acton Ridge Rd., then 1.2 mi. east; campground is on the left.

EPSOM   MAP, D-3
Circle 9 Ranch

Windymere Dr., P.O. Box 282, 03234.
T: (603) 736-9656; www.circle9campground.com.

🚐 ★★★★★   ⛺ ★★

Beauty: ★★	Site Privacy: ★★
Spaciousness: ★★★	Quiet: ★★
Security: ★★★★★	Cleanliness: ★★★★★
Insect Control: ★★★★	Facilities: ★★★★★

If you're looking for a hootin' and hollerin' time, head to Circle 9, New Hampshire's nod to the west. This popular campground, minutes from downtown Concord and the New Hampshire International Speedway, features live country and western music every Saturday night in its well-known entertainment and commercial bingo center. If you don't meet your fellow campers on the dance floor, you surely will at the campsite, where big rigs are perched side-by-side in an open central area. There's not a lot of space at individual sites; average width is about 20 feet. We prefer the more private, shaded sites in the back of the campground, clustered around two small ponds or in the woods—and farthest away from the dance hall. Site No. 59 is popular with tenters. You'll find all the amenities here, but not a lot of peace and quiet. Come here for the location and the action.

BASICS

Operated By: Norman Gentry. **Open:** All year. **Site Assignment:** Reservations recommended; MC, V, D, AE, personal checks accepted; sites must be paid in full during July & Aug.; 7-day cancellation policy. **Registration:** At office. **Fee:** $25–$69. **Parking:** At site, 1 vehicle per site.

FACILITIES

Number of RV-only Sites: 113. **Number of Tent-only Sites:** 12. **Hookups:** Electric (50 amps), water, sewer, cable TV, Internet access. **Each Site:** Picnic table, fire ring. **Dump Station:** Yes. **Laundry:** Yes. **Pay Phone:** Yes. **Restrooms and Showers:** Yes (coin-op). **Fuel:** No. **Propane:** No. **Internal Roads:** Paved, gravel (good). **RV Service:** Some service available. **Market:** Epsom, 1 mi. **Restaurant:** Only on Sat. **General Store:** Yes. **Vending:** No. **Swimming:** Yes. **Playground:** Yes. **Other:** Adult-only hot tub, large entertainment center, live country music & western band performances, rec hall, arcade,

function hall, pond, safari area. **Activities:** Sat. night concerts & dances, basketball, pond fishing, swimming, horseshoes, commercial bingo. **Nearby Attractions:** Concord, NH International Speedway, quick access to Lakes Region & Seacoast area, antiquing. **Additional Information:** Greater Concord Chamber of Commerce, 244 North Main St., Concord, NH 03301-5078, (603) 224-2508.

RESTRICTIONS

Pets: Must be on a leash, never left unattended, cleaned up after. No dogs allowed w/ visitors. **Fires:** Grill, stoves, fire rings only. **Alcoholic Beverages:** At site & at entertainment center. **Vehicle Maximum Length:** 65 ft.

TO GET THERE

From junction of Hwys. 2/202 and 28, go south 0.25 mi. on Hwy. 28, then south 0.25 mi. to Windymere Dr.; the campground is on the right.

EPSOM   MAP, D-3
Epsom Valley Campground

990 Suncook Valley Hwy., 03234.
T: (603) 736-9758 or (978) 658-4396 (winter); www.ucampnh.com/epsomvalley.

🚐 ★★★   ⛺ ★★★

Beauty: ★★★	Site Privacy: ★★★
Spaciousness: ★★★	Quiet: ★★★★
Security: ★★★	Cleanliness: ★★★★
Insect Control: ★★	Facilities: ★★★

You'll find none of the thrills and frills of some of the more modern campgrounds at Epsom Valley. Come here to settle in the woods, swim in the Suncook River, cast a lure in a rock-strewn river pool. Shaded sites are set under tall pine trees about 25 feet from one another. Not a lot of room, but the woods offer some privacy. There are also a number of open, grassy sites for those who prefer the sun. Four pull-through sites are available. Activities are centered around simple pleasures: paddling a canoe on the river, fishing from the banks, tossing horseshoes, or playing a game of mini-golf. Most visitors will take time to explore the area; the campground is centrally located, an hour's drive from the seacoast, New Hampshire Lakes Region, or the mountains. Holiday and race weeks (New Hampshire International Speedway in Loudon is just up the road) are busy, and the atmosphere becomes a bit more bustling and noisy, especially with groups filling the campground's Safari Field area.

BASICS

Operated By: John & Dwyna Arvanitis. **Open:** Memorial Day–Oct. 12. **Site Assignment:** Reservations suggested; 2-day min. during holiday weekends & race weeks.; credit cards accepted; deposit at your discretion. **Registration:** At office. **Fee:** Full hookup, $28; water/electric, $25; no hookup, $23; based on 2 adults, 2 children. **Parking:** At site, 1 vehicle per site.

FACILITIES

Number of RV-only Sites: 67. **Number of Tent-only Sites:** 3. **Hookups:** Electric (20, 30 amps), water, sewer. **Each Site:** Picnic table, fire ring. **Dump Station:** Yes. **Laundry:** Yes. **Pay Phone:** Yes.

Restrooms and Showers: Yes (coin-op). **Fuel:** No. **Propane:** No. **Internal Roads:** Gravel, dirt (fair). **RV Service:** Chichester, 2 mi. **Market:** Epsom, 1 mi. **Restaurant:** No. **General Store:** No. **Vending:** No. **Swimming:** Yes. **Playground:** Yes. **Other:** Recreational field, baseball diamond, mini-golf course, canoe & paddleboat rentals, safari field. **Activities:** Fishing, swimming, horseshoes, volleyball, canoeing, potluck dinners on weekends. **Nearby Attractions:** NH International Speedway, Concord, quick access to Lakes Region & Seacoast area, antiquing, Anheuser-Busch brewery, Christa McAuliffe Planetarium. **Additional Information:** Greater Concord Chamber of Commerce, 244 North Main St., Concord, NH 03301-5078, (603) 224-2508.

RESTRICTIONS

Pets: Must be on a leash, never left unattended, not allowed on beach. One pet per site. **Fires:** Grill, stoves, fire rings only. **Alcoholic Beverages:** At site only. **Vehicle Maximum Length:** 40 ft.

TO GET THERE

From junction Hwys. 4/202 and 28, go 0.25 mi. north on Hwy. 28; campground is on the right.

EPSOM   MAP, D-3
Lazy River Campground

427 Goboro Rd., 03234. T: (603) 798-5900.

🚐 ★★★   ⛺ ★★★

Beauty: ★★★	Site Privacy: ★★★
Spaciousness: ★★★	Quiet: ★★★★
Security: ★★★	Cleanliness: ★★★
Insect Control: ★★	Facilities: ★★★

One of the clusters of campgrounds in the Concord area, this rural, riverside property offers more activities than its neighbor up the street (Epsom Valley) and a bit more space to roam. However, it lacks some of its neighbor's picturesque, woodsy scenery. There's swimming in the Suncook River, or take a dip in one of the two pools (one of them is a children's pool). On holiday weekends, families join in a host of activities, including dances, water balloon tosses, and arts and crafts. You have a choice of wooded, open field sites or riverfront sites. We like site No. 1 on the river, or site No. 91A, which is larger than most. (The average site width is about 35 feet, so all have a bit of space around them.) If you're traveling in a group, try to rent sites 53–58. These campsites are set off by themselves, situated on a point along the river. This campground, as most in the area, fills up fast during the popular Loudon race car weeks. If you're looking to miss the crowds, avoid these summer events (times vary); if you're heading to the races, reserve well in advance, often up to a year.

BASICS

Operated By: Kenneth Smith. **Open:** May–Sept. **Site Assignment:** Reservations recommended; 2-day min. during holiday weekends & race week; 1-night deposit required, no fee for cancellation. MC, V, & personal checks accepted. **Registration:** At office. **Fee:** Full hookup, $28; water/electric, $24; based on 2 adults & 3 children. **Parking:** At site, 1 vehicle per site.

FACILITIES

Number of RV-only Sites: 109. **Hookups:** Electric (20, 30 amps), water, sewer. **Each Site:** Picnic table, fire ring. **Dump Station:** Yes. **Laundry:** Yes. **Pay Phone:** No. **Restrooms and Showers:** Yes (coin-op). **Fuel:** No. **Propane:** No. **Internal Roads:** Dirt (fair). **RV Service:** No, w/in 3 mi. **Market:** Epsom, 0.5 mi. **Restaurant:** Epsom, 0.5 mi. **General Store:** Yes. **Vending:** No. **Swimming:** Yes. **Playground:** Yes. **Other:** Rec hall, arcade, riverfront beach, group area. **Activities:** Volleyball, fishing, swimming, horseshoes, Ping-Pong, pool, planned activities on holiday weekends including dances, contests, arts & crafts. **Nearby Attractions:** Concord, NH International Speedway, quick access to New Hampshire Lakes Region & Seacoast areas, antiquing. **Additional Information:** Greater Concord Chamber of Commerce, 244 North Main St., Concord, NH, 03301-5078, (603) 224-2508.

RESTRICTIONS

Pets: Must be on a leash, never left unattended. **Fires:** Grill, stoves, fire rings only. **Alcoholic Beverages:** At site only. **Vehicle Maximum Length:** 35 ft.

TO GET THERE

From junction of Hwys. 4/202 and 28, go 2 mi. north on Hwy. 28, then 0.5 mi. east on Depot Rd.; campground is on the right.

EXETER   MAP, D-3
Exeter Elms Family Riverside Campground

reserve america

188 Court St., 03833. T: (603) 778-7631 or (866) 778-7631; www.reserveamerica.com.

🚐 ★★★   ⛺ ★★★★

Beauty: ★★★	Site Privacy: ★★★★
Spaciousness: ★★★★	Quiet: ★★★★
Security: ★★★★★	Cleanliness: ★★★
Insect Control: ★★	Facilities: ★★★

We like the spacious, woodsy feel of this campground, set far off the main road along the Exeter River. The level sites are spacious and private; average width is about 50 feet and most are nestled in trees for extra seclusion with river frontage or views. Many waterfront sites have banks that drop off into deep water, so parents with young children may have to keep an eye out; but we particularly like the fact that, unlike some campgrounds, here, there are no annoying, unattractive fences to detract from the natural beauty of the setting. The campground offers a separate wooded tent-only area, but, if you prefer sun and open spaces, you'll have plenty to choose from, too. You'll find a variety of campground activities, plus fishing and canoeing on the river. The town of Portsmouth and the seacoast region is less than a half-hour's drive away.

BASICS

Operated By: Eric & Carol Waleryszak. **Open:** May 15–Sept. 15. **Site Assignment:** Reservations recommended; 50% deposit; refund given if cancelled 2 weeks prior to check-in, minus 10%; 3-day min. on Memorial Day & Labor Day weekends; 4-day min. over July 4th. **Registration:** At office. **Fee:** Full

hookup, $39; water/electric; $37; tent, $27. **Parking:** At site.

FACILITIES

Number of RV-only Sites: 202. **Number of Tent-only Sites:** 60. **Hookups:** Electric (15, 30, 50 amps), water, sewer. **Each Site:** Picnic table, fire ring. **Dump Station:** Yes. **Laundry:** Yes. **Pay Phone:** Yes. **Restrooms and Showers:** Yes (coin-op). **Fuel:** No. **Propane:** No. **Internal Roads:** Dirt, gravel (good). **RV Service:** No. **Market:** Exeter, 3 mi. **Restaurant:** No. **General Store:** Yes. **Vending:** Soda. **Swimming:** Yes. **Playground:** Yes. **Other:** Game room, boat rentals, 1-mi. river frontage w/ access & beach area, recreation field. **Activities:** Swimming, fishing, boating, planned activities w/ full-time rec. director, volleyball, basketball, shuffleboard. **Nearby Attractions:** New Hampshire & southern Maine beaches, Portsmouth, Exeter, factory outlet shopping, golf courses, water park, Strawbery Banke historic museum, Seacoast Science Center, antique shops. **Additional Information:** Exeter Area Chamber of Commerce, 120 Water St., Exeter, NH 03833, (603) 772-2411; also visit www.seacoastnh.com.

RESTRICTIONS

Pets: Must be on a leash, never left unattended, cleaned up after, not allowed at canoe docking area or in campground buildings. **Fires:** Grill, stoves, fire rings only. **Alcoholic Beverages:** At site only. **Vehicle Maximum Length:** 40 ft. **Other:** No ATVs.

TO GET THERE

From junction Hwy. 111 and Hwy. 108, go 1.5 mi. south on Hwy. 108 to entrance; campground is on the left. From I-95, Exit 1, go left on Hwy. 107. Take a right onto Hwy. 150, go 4 mi., then take a right onto Hwy. 108 north; campground is on the right.

FRANCONIA   MAP, B-2
Cannon Mountain RV Park

reserve america

Franconia Notch State Park, US 18, 03580. T: (603) 823-8800 or (603) 271-3628; www.cannonmt.com.

🚐 ★★★★   ⛺ n/a

Beauty: ★★★★	Site Privacy: ★★★
Spaciousness: ★★★	Quiet: ★★★
Security: ★★★	Cleanliness: ★★★★
Insect Control: ★★★	Facilities: ★★★★

The campground itself is meager, only seven sites, all back-in, stuck in a row at the back of a parking lot. Yet, if you want to camp here you better reserve a spot well in advance—up to a year! The setting, in Franconia Notch State Park, is gorgeous, surrounded by beautiful maple and birch trees. You'll camp at the base of pristine Echo Lake, elevation 1,931 feet, surrounded by views of Mt. Lafayette and Cannon Mountain. From here, you can walk to the shoreline for boating, swimming, and fishing, take an aerial tram ride to the 4,180-foot summit of Cannon Mountain, visit the New England Ski Museum and the Old Man in the Mountain Museum, and access a handful of popular hiking trails. You can also walk to

the Cannon Mountain Ski Resort facilities, including its cafeteria, shops, and restaurant. The campground is open year-round (though there's no electric or water hookups after mid-October). Reserve now for next year.

BASICS

Operated By: New Hampshire Division of Parks & Recreation. **Open:** All year. **Site Assignment:** Reservations suggested & must be made through central reservation office, (603) 271-3628); reservations must be made at least 3 days in advance; $5 nonrefundable fee for each reservation; 24-hour cancellation fee w/ $10 fee. MC, V, D; no personal checks. **Registration:** At office. **Fee:** $29. **Parking:** At site.

FACILITIES

Number of RV-only Sites: 7. **Hookups:** Electric (20, 30 amps), water, sewer. **Each Site:** Picnic table, fire ring. **Dump Station:** Yes. **Laundry:** No. **Pay Phone:** Nearby (0.5 mi.). **Restrooms and Showers:** Open during day. Closed at night. **Fuel:** No. **Propane:** No. **Internal Roads:** Gravel (good). **RV Service:** No. **Market:** Franconia, 3 mi. **Restaurant:** Cafeteria at tramway, 0.2 mi. **General Store:** No. **Vending:** No. **Swimming:** Beach. **Playground:** No. **Other:** Access to Franconia Notch State Park & Cannon Ski Resort facilities, boat launch. **Activities:** Swimming, boating, fishing, skiing, hiking, aerial tram. **Nearby Attractions:** Franconia Notch State Park, White Mountains attractions. **Additional Information:** Franconia Notch Chamber of Commerce, P.O. Box 780, Franconia, NH 03580, (800) 237-9007.

RESTRICTIONS

Pets: Not allowed. **Fires:** Fire ring only. **Alcoholic Beverages:** At site only. **Vehicle Maximum Length:** No limit.

TO GET THERE

Take Exit 34C off Franconia Notch Pkwy./I-93, then 0.8 mi. to large sign.

FRANCONIA   MAP, B-2
Lafayette Campground

reserve america

Franconia Notch State Park, I-93, Exit 34A, 03580. T: (603) 823-9513; www.franconianotch statepark.com/lafayette.html.

🚐 ★   ⛺ ★★★★★

Beauty: ★★★★	Site Privacy: ★★★★
Spaciousness: ★★★★	Quiet: ★★★
Security: ★★★	Cleanliness: ★★★
Insect Control: ★★	Facilities: ★★

This rustic state park campground sits in gorgeous Franconia Notch State Park, surrounded by mountains, streams, and hiking trails. It's best for campers who like to rough it a bit; tenters and pop-up trailers take up the majority of sites. The campground draws lots of outdoorsy types and backpackers who come to play in the mountains. There are several popular hiking trails that leave directly from the campground and state park attractions; The Basin, Profile Lake, Old Man in the Mountains, and The Flume are all close by. The woodsy sites, set on hilly terrain and along the Pemigewasset River, are generously spaced with plenty of privacy but no hookups.

BASICS

Operated By: New Hampshire Division of Parks & Recreation. **Open:** Mid-May–mid-Oct. **Site Assignment:** Reservations suggested. Half the sites can be reserved, half are first come, first served; call Reservation Center (603) 271-3628 Jan.–early Oct., Mon.–Fri., or via e-mail, www.nhparks.state.nh.us; payment due w/in 7 days of making reservation; each reservation is subject to $5 nonrefundable fee; refund requests must be received in writing by the reservation office w/in 14 days of scheduled arrival & are handled on a case-by-case basis, subject to a $10 handling fee & may be subject to a penalty of 1-night fee. MC, V; no personal checks. **Registration:** At office. **Fee:** $19; based on 2 adults & children under 18; each additional adult is half the site fee w/ max. of 4 adults per site. **Parking:** At site, 2 cars max.

FACILITIES

Number of Multipurpose Sites: 97. **Hookups:** None. **Each Site:** Picnic table, fire ring. **Dump Station:** Yes. **Laundry:** No. **Pay Phone:** Yes. **Restrooms and Showers:** Yes (coin-op). **Fuel:** No. **Propane:** Yes. **Internal Roads:** Dirt, gravel (fair). **RV Service:** No. **Market:** Lincoln, 7 mi. **Restaurant:** No. **General Store:** Yes. **Vending:** Soda. **Swimming:** No. **Playground:** No. **Other:** River frontage, hiking trails. **Activities:** Swimming, hiking. **Nearby Attractions:** Franconia Notch State Park, White Mountains. **Additional Information:** Franconia Notch Chamber of Commerce, P.O. Box 780, Franconia, NH 03580, (800) 237-9007.

RESTRICTIONS

Pets: Not allowed. **Fires:** Grill, stoves, fire rings only. **Alcoholic Beverages:** At site only, must be of age. **Vehicle Maximum Length:** No limit.

TO GET THERE

Take Lafayette Campground Exit off southbound I-93, between exits 39A and 34B.

GILFORD   MAP, C-2
Ellacoya State Beach and RV Park

reserve america

Hwy. 11, P.O. Box 7163, 03246.
T: (603) 293-7821 or (603) 271-3628;
www.nhstateparks.com/ellacoya.html.

🚐 ★★★   ⛺ n/a

Beauty: ★★★	Site Privacy: ★★★
Spaciousness: ★★★	Quiet: ★★★
Security: ★★★★★	Cleanliness: ★★★
Insect Control: ★★★	Facilities: ★★★

Come summer, it seems that everyone in New Hampshire (and beyond) wants to get on Lake Winnipesaukee, the state's largest lake. Camping here is one way to do it. This small RV campground sits on the southwest shore of the lake and boasts a 600-foot-long sandy beach, with views of the surround-

---

ing Sandwich and Ossipee mountains. Campers must share the space with hordes of day visitors, but come sunset, you'll have it—and the spectacular views—to yourself. Sites all have three-way hookups and are set in rows; amenities are basic (bathhouse, small camp store, showers). But it's tough to beat this shoreline location in the heart of the Lakes Region.

BASICS

Operated By: New Hampshire Division of Parks & Recreation. **Open:** May–Oct. **Site Assignment:** Reservations required & must be made through central reservation office, (603) 271-3628; reservations must be made at least 4 days in advance; $3 nonrefundable fee for each reservation; 24-hour cancellation policy minus $10. MC, V; no personal checks. **Registration:** At office. **Fee:** Full hookup, $42. **Parking:** At site, 3 vehicles max.

FACILITIES

Number of RV-only Sites: 38. **Hookups:** Electric (20, 30 amps), water, sewer. **Each Site:** Picnic table. **Dump Station:** No. **Laundry:** Yes. **Pay Phone:** Yes. **Restrooms and Showers:** Yes. **Fuel:** No. **Propane:** No. **Internal Roads:** Gravel, dirt (fair). **RV Service:** No. **Market:** Laconia, 5 mi. **Restaurant:** No. **General Store:** Yes. **Vending:** No. **Swimming:** Yes. **Playground:** No. **Other:** Lake frontage, beach, boat launch. **Activities:** Swimming, boating, fishing, volleyball. **Nearby Attractions:** Weirs Beach, Lakes Region attractions. **Additional Information:** Greater Laconia/Weirs Beach Chamber of Commerce, 11 Veterans Square, Laconia, NH 03246, (603) 524-5531.

RESTRICTIONS

Pets: Must be on leash, supervised. Not permitted on beach. **Fires:** In communal fire pit only. **Alcoholic Beverages:** At site only. **Vehicle Maximum Length:** No limit. **Other:** No tents allowed.

TO GET THERE

From I-93, take Exit 20 onto Hwy. 3 to Wards Laconia, then take Hwy. 11 4 mi. to campsite.

GLEN   MAP, B-3
Glen Ellis Family Campground

Rte. 302, P.O. Box 397, 03838. T: (603) 383-4567; www.glenelliscampground.com.

🚐 ★★★★★   ⛺ ★★★★★

Beauty: ★★★★★	Site Privacy: ★★★★
Spaciousness: ★★★★★	Quiet: ★★★★
Security: ★★★★★	Cleanliness: ★★★★★
Insect Control: ★★★	Facilities: ★★★★★

This is top-notch, upscale camping at its finest. Here, campers have the beauty, scenery, and economics of outdoor living with the comforts, amenities, and services of a resort. Glen Ellis is one of our favorite places to camp. The campground, in New Hampshire's picturesque White Mountains area, lies in the shadows of the Presidential mountain range, nestled between the Ellis and Saco rivers. Facilities, including a large pool, sports fields, laundromat (open to the public), store, playground, and tennis courts are top-of-the-line, immaculate, and finely landscaped. There are sweeping fields and spacious public areas, offering lots of room to romp and roam. Sites are spacious too, many with river

---

frontage, offering both shade and sun at each site. There are two riverfront beaches for dunks in cool mountain waters (the pool is heated), a few planned activities on Saturday evenings, and White Mountain attractions and outdoor activities at your doorstep. Set your camp on river site 56, our favorite (if you'd like hookups, look at sites 86–100 on the Saco River or 33–51 on the Ellis River), and you won't want to leave.

BASICS

Operated By: Rich & Dick Goff. **Open:** Memorial Day–Columbus Day. **Site Assignment:** Reservations suggested, 1-night deposit; 14-day cancellation policy. **Registration:** At office. **Fee:** Waterfront, $28; other, $24; electric, AC, & sewer, $2 each; based on 2 adults & children under 18. **Parking:** At site.

FACILITIES

Number of RV-only Sites: 130. **Number of Tent-only Sites:** 73. **Hookups:** Electric (30 amps), water, sewer. **Each Site:** Picnic table, fire ring. **Dump Station:** Yes. **Laundry:** Yes. **Pay Phone:** Yes. **Restrooms and Showers:** Yes (coin-op). **Fuel:** No. **Propane:** No. **Internal Roads:** Gravel, dirt (good). **RV Service:** No. **Market:** Glen, 0.5 mi. **Restaurant:** No. **General Store:** Yes. **Vending:** No. **Swimming:** Yes. **Playground:** Yes. **Other:** Rec hall, river frontage & beaches on 2 rivers, tennis courts, sports fields. **Activities:** Swimming, tubing, basketball, volleyball, baseball, tennis, planned activities on Sat. evening during summer. **Nearby Attractions:** Storyland, Santa's Village, Six Gun City, White Mountains, North Conway, Flume Gorge, Hobo Railroad. **Additional Information:** Mount Washington Valley Chamber of Commerce, P.O. Box 2300, North Conway, NH 03860, (800) 521-2137.

RESTRICTIONS

Pets: No dogs allowed, full-time campers only. **Fires:** Grill, stoves, fire rings only. **Alcoholic Beverages:** At site only. **Vehicle Maximum Length:** No limit. **Other:** Quiet time 10 p.m.–8 a.m.

TO GET THERE

From I-93, take Exit 23 onto Hwy. 104 East. Then travel north on Hwy. 3, then to Hwy. 25 East to Hwy. 16 North. Follow Hwy. 16N all the way through North Conway to Glen. At the intersection of Hwy. 16N and Hwy. 302 West, continue straight on Hwy. 302 West for 0.25 miles. Glen Ellis is located just past Patches Market on the left. From I-95, get off at the Portsmouth exit, onto the Spaulding Turnpike. It automatically goes onto Hwy. 16 North. Follow the direction above from Hwy. 15 in Glen.

GREENFIELD   MAP, D-2
Greenfield State Park Campground

Forest Rd., 03047.
T: (603) 547-3497 or (603) 271-3628;
www.nhstateparks.org/parkspages/
greenfield/grnfld.html.

🚐 ★★★   ⛺ ★★★★★

Beauty: ★★★★ Site Privacy: ★★★★
Spaciousness: ★★★★ Quiet: ★★★
Security: ★★★ Cleanliness: ★★★
Insect Control: ★★★ Facilities: ★★★

If you like a lot of elbow room and a woodsy, natural setting, you can't beat this lovely state park campground in southern New Hampshire. The wind in the trees, the heavy smell of pine, a crystal clear lake and plenty of room to roam are enticing features of this 401-acre oasis. Deer, moose, and hawks are regulars here, and red foxes have been spotted by some guests. We like the extra large sites, all nestled in the oaks and pines, and the separate "campers beach." Day visitors and picnickers have their own lakefront area, which means campers don't have to share their own slice of sandy beach and swimming area on pretty Otter Lake. Some favorite sites are 33, 36, 38, 220–226. Bring your hiking boots and fishing poles: There are nature trails meandering through the woods and skirting Beaver, Mud, and Hogback Ponds, and canoes for rent at the lakeside general store.

BASICS

Operated By: New Hampshire Division of Parks & Recreation. **Open:** May–Columbus Day. **Site Assignment:** Reservations suggested, must be made at least 3 days in advance; full payment due, plus $3 nonrefundable fee; 7-day cancellation policy; some sites not reservable but available first come, first served. MC, V, D accepted; no personal checks. **Registration:** At office. **Fee:** $19; based on 2 adults & dependent children under 18; each additional adult is half the site fee. **Parking:** At site, 2 cars per site.

FACILITIES

Number of RV-only Sites: 252. **Hookups:** None. **Each Site:** Picnic table, fire ring. **Dump Station:** Yes. **Laundry:** No. **Pay Phone:** Yes. **Restrooms and Showers:** Yes (coin-op). **Fuel:** No. **Propane:** No. **Internal Roads:** Paved, gravel, dirt (good). **RV Service:** No. **Market:** Greenfield, 1 mi. **Restaurant:** No. **General Store:** Yes. **Vending:** Yes. **Swimming:** Yes. **Playground:** No. **Other:** Lake frontage, beach, nature trails, boat launch, boat rentals. **Activities:** Swimming, boating, fishing, hiking. **Nearby Attractions:** Manchester, Concord, Monadnock State Park. **Additional Information:** Manchester Chamber of Commerce, 889 Elm St., Manchester, NH 03101, (603) 434-7438 or Greater Peterborough Chamber of Commerce, P.O. Box 401, Peterborough, NH 03458, (603) 924-7234.

RESTRICTIONS

Pets: Pets are allowed on designated sites only. Must be on a leash, never left unattended. **Fires:** Grill, stoves, fire rings only. **Alcoholic Beverages:** At site only. **Vehicle Maximum Length:** No limit.

TO GET THERE

From junction of Hwy. 31 and Hwy. 136, go west 0.5 mi. on Hwy. 136; campground is on the right.

HAMPTON BEACH   MAP, D-3
Hampton Beach State RV Park

Rte. 1A, P.O. Box 606, 03871.
T: (603) 926-8990 or (603) 271-3628;
www.nhstateparks.org/parkspages/
hampton/hampton.html.

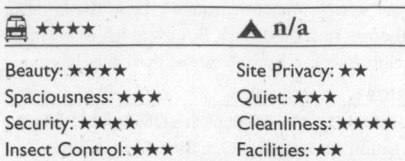

🚐 ★★★★   ⛺ n/a

Beauty: ★★★★ Site Privacy: ★★
Spaciousness: ★★★ Quiet: ★★★
Security: ★★★★ Cleanliness: ★★★★
Insect Control: ★★★ Facilities: ★★

The New Hampshire seacoast is a mere 18 miles long (though full of fine state parks and beaches along the way), and this is the only campground on its shoreline. This state park campground, for RVs only, offers few conveniences and fewer comforts. The sites are basic; RVs are set side-by-side on open gravel sites with little privacy and no shade. The office is in a public-works-style building that sits next to a huge parking lot, used for overflow campsites (no hookups in this area.) But the view! Cast your eyes to the east and you'll see swaying sea grasses, a stretch of sugar white beach, and the Atlantic Ocean beyond. To your south is a wide, picturesque tidal inlet. There are sandy paths to the beach and to the state park next door (with a store, restrooms, and cold showers.) Smack dab on Hampton Beach, you can't beat the locale—or the price—of this real estate. You'll need to reserve one year in advance to get a site for anytime during the summer months.

BASICS

Operated By: NH Division of Parks & Recreation. **Open:** May–Thanksgiving. **Site Assignment:** Reservations required through Reservation Center at (603) 271-3628; reservations can also be requested online at www.nhparks.state.nh.us; 2-night min. w/ reservations, 3 nights on holiday weekends & for a max. of 14 days in a 30-day period during prime season; overflow area accommodates 18 RVs (no hookups) on a first-come, first-served basis. MC, V. **Registration:** At office. **Fee:** Full hookup, $42. **Parking:** At site.

FACILITIES

Number of RV-only Sites: 28. **Hookups:** Electric (30 amps), water, sewer. **Each Site:** Picnic table, fire ring. **Dump Station:** No. **Laundry:** No. **Pay Phone:** Yes. **Restrooms and Showers:** No. **Fuel:** No. **Propane:** No. **Internal Roads:** Gravel (good). **RV Service:** No. **Market:** Hampton, 1 mi. **Restaurant:** Seabrook. **General Store:** Yes. **Vending:** No. **Swimming:** Yes, beach. **Playground:** No. **Other:** Boat ramp, direct access to ocean, pavilion & state park adjacent to campground. **Activities:** Ocean swimming, fishing, beach-combing. **Nearby Attractions:** Hampton Beach, whale watching, saltwater fishing, Portsmouth, New Hampshire oceanfront state parks. **Additional Information:** Hampton Beach Chamber of Commerce, 490 Lafayette Rd., Hampton, NH 03843, (603) 926-8717; also NH Division of Parks & Recreation, P.O. Box 1856, Concord, NH, 03302-1856, (603) 271-3556, fax (603) 271-2629, www.nhparks.state.nh.us.

RESTRICTIONS

Pets: Must be on a leash, never left unattended. **Fires:** Grill, stoves, fire rings only. **Alcoholic Beverages:** Not permitted. **Vehicle Maximum Length:** No limit. **Other:** There are often high winds in this area. Use of awnings, fires, and so on, may be restricted. No tents or pop-ups.

TO GET THERE

From I-95 take Exit 2, Hwy. 101 east toward Hampton Beach. Follow signs to Hampton Beach. Campground is located on Hwy. 1A just south of the main part of Hampton Beach near the Seabrook-Hampton town line.

HAMPTON FALLS   MAP, D-3
Wakeda Campground

Hwy. 88, 03844. T: (603) 772-5274;
www.wakedacampground.com.

🚐 ★★★   ⛺ ★★★

Beauty: ★★★ Site Privacy: ★★★
Spaciousness: ★★★ Quiet: ★★★
Security: ★★★★ Cleanliness: ★★★
Insect Control: ★★★ Facilities: ★★★

This family-friendly campground on the New Hampshire seacoast offers the best of two worlds: far enough from the crowds and traffic of seacoast beaches and attractions but close enough (only 20–30 minutes) for convenient day trips. The ride back and forth is pleasant, too: you'll pass farms, you-pick-it-orchards, and the sprawling lawns and meandering fieldstone walls of new and historic homes. The campground is a mile off the road, with its own large neighborhood of seasonal renters and vacationing families. It's quiet (especially considering that there are more than 400 sites here) and spread out. The campground is shaded by pines and various hardwoods, full of birds and squirrels, and deer have been known to wander into Wakeda as well. The kids will like the 18-hole mini-golf course but miss not having a swimming pool. The adults will appreciate the small hut serving coffee with bagels and donuts on the weekends (nice touch, we think). There's a variety of sites, open and shaded, all about the same size (average width is about 35 feet). If you like a bit more privacy and extra space, consider sites 32–47 and 16 East.

BASICS

Operated By: Terry Savage, Jan Humbleton, & Karen Bark. **Open:** May 15–Oct. 1. **Site Assignment:** Reservations suggested; no deposit required. MC, V, personal checks accepted. **Registration:** At office. **Fee:** Full hookup 50 amps, $38.50; full 30 amps, $32.50; water 30 amps, $30.50; water 20 amps, $27.50; no hookup, $25. All fees based on 2 adults & 3 children or less. **Parking:** At site.

FACILITIES

Number of RV-only Sites: 300. **Number of Tent-only Sites:** 50. **Hookups:** Electric (20, 50 amps), water, sewer. **Each Site:** Picnic table, fire ring. **Dump Station:** Yes. **Laundry:** Yes. **Pay Phone:** Yes. **Restrooms and Showers:** Yes (coin-op). **Fuel:** No. **Propane:** No. **Internal Roads:** Paved, gravel (good). **RV Service:** No. **Market:** Exeter, 2 mi. **Restaurant:** Yes, small coffee shop. **General Store:** Yes. **Vending:** No. **Swimming:** No. **Playground:** Yes. **Other:** Pavilion, 18-hole mini-golf course, game room, arcade, group facilities, camping cabins, half-court basketball. **Activities:** Mini-golf, horseshoes, volleyball, badminton, basketball, planned activities (ice-cream bar, pancake breakfasts) on weekends. **Nearby Attractions:** Portsmouth, seacoast beaches including Hampton Beach, whale watching, saltwater fishing. **Additional Information:** Hampton Beach Chamber of Commerce, 490 Lafayette Rd., Hampton, NH 03843, (603) 926-8717.

RESTRICTIONS

Pets: Must be on a leash, never left unattended. **Fires:** Grill, stoves, fire rings only. **Alcoholic Beverages:** At site only. **Vehicle Maximum Length:** 44 ft.

TO GET THERE

From south on I-95, take Exit 1 (Kingston-Seabrook). Bear right off ramp; turn left at Hwy. 1. Go 1.5 mi. and take a left on Hwy. 88; campground is 4 mi. on left.

HENNIKER MAP, D-2
Keyser Pond Campground

47 Old Concord Rd., 03242. T: (800) 272-5221; www.keyserpond.com.

🚐 ★★★   ⛺ ★★★

Beauty: ★★★★	Site Privacy: ★★★
Spaciousness: ★★★	Quiet: ★★★
Security: ★★★	Cleanliness: ★★★★
Insect Control: ★★★	Facilities: ★★★

This relaxed and friendly campground in the south-central region of New Hampshire is one of two favorites in the area. (Also see Mile-Away listing.) Both are very popular with families, but this is our pick of the two. We like the low-key, slow-paced style of this woodsy destination, sitting on the shores of pretty Keyser Pond. We also like the views from the large, sandy beach and from the waterfront sites: glistening waters surrounded by rolling hills carpeted in dense pine forests. (There is little development along the shoreline.) Moose and grey herrings share this beautiful campground with the human guests. Days are spent pursuing old-fashioned pleasures, like swim races to a raft, canoe paddles, early morning fishing outings, and marshmallow roasts and sing-alongs around the communal campfire circle. There are planned activities and socials offered on summer weekends, too.

BASICS

Operated By: Jolly Kimball. **Open:** May 15–Oct. 15. **Site Assignment:** Reservations suggested, 1-night deposit, 3-day cancellation policy; MC, V, D accepted, no personal checks. **Registration:** At office. **Fee:** Full hookup/waterfront, $37; waterfront, $35; full hookup, $32; water/electric, $25; water, $25; based on 2 adults & their children under 18. **Parking:** At site. Only 1 car per campsite. More parking in other parking lot.

FACILITIES

Number of RV-only Sites: 118. **Number of Tent-only Sites:** 9. **Hookups:** Electric (20, 30 amps), water, sewer. **Each Site:** Picnic table, fire ring. **Dump Station:** Yes. **Laundry:** Yes. **Pay Phone:** Yes. **Restrooms and Showers:** Yes (coin-op). **Fuel:** No. **Propane:** Yes. **Internal Roads:** Gravel (good). **RV**

Service: No. **Market:** Henniker, 4.5 mi. **Restaurant:** No. **General Store:** Yes. **Vending:** No. **Swimming:** Beach. **Playground:** Yes. **Other:** Lake frontage, beach, boat rentals, mini-golf course, rec hall, trailer rentals. **Activities:** Swimming, boating, fishing, horseshoes, shuffleboard, volleyball, badminton, planned activities on summer weekends. **Nearby Attractions:** Henniker, Concord, Lakes Region. **Additional Information:** Greater Concord Chamber of Commerce, 244 North Main St., Concord, NH 03301-5078, (603) 224-2508 or New London/Lake Sunapee Region Chamber of Commerce, P.O. Box 532, New London, NH 03257, (603) 536-6575.

RESTRICTIONS

Pets: Must be on a leash, never left unattended. **Fires:** Grill, stoves, fire rings only. **Alcoholic Beverages:** At site only; no glass containers in rec room or on beach. **Vehicle Maximum Length:** No limit.

TO GET THERE

From I-89 north, take Exit 5. Go 3.5 mi., then turn left onto Old Concord Rd. From the west, take Hwy. 9 to Old Concord Rd.

HENNIKER MAP, D-2
Mile-Away Campground

41 Old West Hopkinton Rd., NH 202-9, 03242. T: (603) 428-7616 or (800) 787-4679; www.mileaway.com.

🚐 ★★★★   ⛺ ★★★

Beauty: ★★★	Site Privacy: ★★★
Spaciousness: ★★★	Quiet: ★★★
Security: ★★★	Cleanliness: ★★★★
Insect Control: ★★★	Facilities: ★★★

This well-kept, woodsy campground in the south-central region of New Hampshire is one of two favorites in the area (also see Keyser Pond Campground listing). Both are popular with families and great places to stay. Mile-Away is located on state-stocked French's Pond (trout anglers may want to pack their fly rods) with a picturesque sandy beach area and a long, shallow slope perfect for young swimmers. There are boat rentals and plenty of planned activities offered on weekends throughout the summer. This campground is one of the few in the state that stay open throughout the winter months, with cross-country and snowmobile trails accessible from the property, ice-skating on the pond, and alpine skiing nearby. There are several summer seasonal renters, most clustered near the rec hall and office and toward the beach area. The rest of the sites, mostly shaded with water and electric hookups, are scattered in loops on good-sized lots (average width is about 50 feet), with two pull-through sites available.

BASICS

Operated By: Robert French. **Open:** All year. **Site Assignment:** Reservations suggested, 1-night deposit; no shows forfeit deposit; cash & personal checks accepted. **Registration:** At office. **Fee:** Full hookup, $35; water/electric, $28; based on 4 people. **Parking:** At site.

FACILITIES

Number of RV-only Sites: 160. **Number of Tent-only Sites:** 14. **Hookups:** Electric (20, 50 amps),

water, sewer, cable. **Each Site:** Picnic table, fire ring. **Dump Station:** Yes. **Laundry:** Yes. **Pay Phone:** No. **Restrooms and Showers:** Yes (coin-op). **Fuel:** No. **Propane:** Yes. **Internal Roads:** Gravel, dirt (good). **RV Service:** No. **Market:** Henniker, 3 mi. **Restaurant:** Henniker, 3 mi. **General Store:** Yes. **Vending:** No. **Swimming:** Beach. **Playground:** Swing sets. **Other:** Pond, beach, boat dock, boat rentals, mini-golf, rec hall, game room, pavilion, safari field. **Activities:** Swimming, boating, fishing, hiking, ice-skating, cross-country skiing, snowmobiling, shuffleboard, basketball, horseshoes, mini-golf, badminton, volleyball, planned activities on summer weekends, including socials, bingo, crafts & games, live bands. **Nearby Attractions:** Henniker, Lake Sunapee. **Additional Information:** Greater Concord Chamber of Commerce, 244 North Main St., Concord, NH 03301-5078, (603) 224-2508 or New London/Lake Sunapee Region Chamber of Commerce, P.O. Box 532, New London, NH 03257, (603) 536-6575.

RESTRICTIONS

Pets: Must be on a leash, never left unattended. **Fires:** Grill, stoves, fire rings only. **Alcoholic Beverages:** At site only. **Vehicle Maximum Length:** Specify when making reservations.

TO GET THERE

From junction of I-89 and Hwy. 202 (Exit 5), go west 5 mi. on Hwy. 202, then northeast 1 mi. on Old West Hopkinton Rd.; campground is on the left.

LACONIA MAP, C-2
Campton Campground—
White Mountain National Forest

reserve america

719 N. Main St., 03246. T: (603) 528-8721; www.reserveamerica.com.

🚐 ★★★★   ⛺ ★★★★

Beauty: ★★★★	Site Privacy: ★★★★
Spaciousness: ★★★★	Quiet: ★★★
Security: ★★★★	Cleanliness: ★★★★
Insect Control: ★★★★	Facilities: ★

Campton Campground is located within the White Mountain National Forest and is a special and wonderful place to visit throughout the year. There are campgrounds, hiking trails, scenic drives, historic places, and plenty of space to just sit back and relax. Whether you stay for a while or just pass through, we hope you will enjoy your national forest and all it has to offer. The White Mountain National Forest is a forest contained within the White Mountains. It was initially established in 1918. Most of the forest is in New Hampshire; a small part crosses the border into Maine. While often casually referred to as a park, this is a national forest, used not only for hiking, camping, and skiing, but also for logging and other limited commercial purposes. The White Mountain National Forest is the only national forest located in either New Hampshire or Maine. More than 100 miles of the Appalachian Trail traverse the White Mountains National Forest.

BASICS

Operated By: U.S. Forest Service. **Open:** Apr. 13–Oct. 12. **Site Assignment:** Reservations must be made at least 7 days in advance. **Registration:** At office. **Fee:** Single, $18; group, $40–$100. **Parking:** At park.

FACILITIES

Number of Multipurpose Sites: 158. **Hookups:** None. **Each Site:** Call ahead. **Dump Station:** No. **Laundry:** No. **Pay Phone:** No. **Restrooms and Showers:** Yes. **Fuel:** No. **Propane:** No. **Internal Roads:** Gravel. **RV Service:** No. **Market:** No. **Restaurant:** No. **General Store:** No. **Vending:** No. **Swimming:** No. **Playground:** No. **Activities:** Nature programs & interpretive programs.

RESTRICTIONS

Pets: Pets must be restrained or on a leash at all times while in developed recreation areas. **Fires:** In fire rings, stoves, grills, or fireplaces provided for that purpose. **Alcoholic Beverages:** Prohibited.

TO GET THERE

From Hwy. 93, take Exit 28 and follow Hwy. 49 (Mad River Rd.) east 2 mi.

LACONIA   MAP, C-2
Gunstock Mountain Resort Campground

reserve america

Area Rd. Hwy. 11A, P.O. Box 1307, 03247. T: (603) 293-4341 or (800) 486-7862/502; www.gunstock.com.

🚐 ★★★★   ▲ ★★★★

Beauty: ★★★★	Site Privacy: ★★★
Spaciousness: ★★★	Quiet: ★★★
Security: ★★★★	Cleanliness: ★★★★
Insect Control: ★★★	Facilities: ★★★★★

Within a few minutes' drive are three mountain ranges, dozens of sparkling lakes (including the Granite State's largest—Lake Winnipesaukee), and a slew of attractions. But there's no need to ever leave the campground property; we rarely venture out once we've pounded in the stakes. Outside your doorstep (or tent flap) is a top-notch year-round resort, complete with a mountain sports center, equestrian center, swimming pools, skate park, archery center, restaurant, and more. In winter, there's cross-country and downhill skiing, tubing, nature programs, and snowshoeing. The property also boasts several ponds and a good-sized lake surrounded by pines and maples. Turkey and deer are some of the more elusive year-round residents, but if you're lucky you may spot one or two. The campground is large, with more than 250 sites, and often bustling with activity (especially during New Hampshire's popular Race Weeks held in the summer). Sites are set in rows; the lakeview sites are the prettiest, if you can get one.

BASICS

Operated By: Belknap. **Open:** Memorial Day–Columbus Day; Dec.–Mar. **Site Assignment:** Reservations suggested & can be made 1 year in advance;

reservations require a 2-night stay, $20 nonrefundable deposit; holiday stays must be paid in advance & may require 3-night min. MC, V, D, AE; no personal checks. **Registration:** At office. **Fee:** Full hookup, $35; water/electric, $30; no hookup, $25. **Parking:** At site.

FACILITIES

Number of RV-only Sites: 111. **Number of Tent-only Sites:** 159. **Hookups:** Electric (20, 30 amps), water, sewer. **Each Site:** Picnic table, fire ring. **Dump Station:** Yes. **Laundry:** Yes. **Pay Phone:** Yes. **Restrooms and Showers:** Yes. **Fuel:** No. **Propane:** Yes. **Internal Roads:** Paved, gravel, dirt (good). **RV Service:** No. **Market:** Gilford, 4 mi. **Restaurant:** No. **General Store:** Yes. **Vending:** Yes. **Swimming:** Yes. **Playground:** Yes. **Other:** Mountain sports center, mountain bike center, skate park, equestrian center, group areas, conference center, ski resort, trails, rec hall, ponds & lake access, cabin rentals. **Activities:** Swimming, boating, hiking, horseback riding, archery, biking, alpine & cross-country skiing, planned programs. **Nearby Attractions:** Lake Winnipesaukee, Lakes region attractions. **Additional Information:** Greater Laconia/Weirs Beach Chamber of Commerce, 11 Veterans Square, Laconia, NH 03246, (603) 524-5531 or Meredith Area Chamber of Commerce, P.O. Box 732, Meredith, NH 03253-0732, (603) 279-6121.

RESTRICTIONS

Pets: Must be on a leash; never left unattended. Rabies certificate required. **Fires:** Grill, camp stoves, fire rings only. **Alcoholic Beverages:** At site only. **Vehicle Maximum Length:** 40 ft.

TO GET THERE

From junction of Hwy. 16 (Spaulding Turnpike) and Hwy. 11, go 15 mi. north on Hwy. 11, then 12 mi. north on Hwy. 11A; Gunstock Campground is on the left.

LANCASTER   MAP, B-2
Mountain Lake Campground

Hwy. 3, P.O. Box 475, 03584. T: (603) 788-4509; www.allroutes.to/mountainlake.

🚐 ★★★   ▲ ★★★

Beauty: ★★★	Site Privacy: ★★★
Spaciousness: ★★★	Quiet: ★★★★
Security: ★★★★	Cleanliness: ★★★★
Insect Control: ★★★	Facilities: ★★★

This Lancaster campground in the northern White Mountains, close to Santa's Village, Franconia Notch State Park, and other popular attractions, is suited to families who prefer a quieter lakeside locale. Situated on the pristine 25-acre Mountain Lake, campers have access to a sandy beach, two boat docks, and rental boats (paddleboats, canoes, and kayaks). Campers can also bring their own boats, though no power motors are allowed on the lake. Fishing for perch, bass, pickerel, and sunfish is good and a favorite pastime at the campground. Families will enjoy the short nature trail that runs through the property, skirting a frog pond and tadpole stream. There's also a giant-size chess and checker game to play, sports fields, and a rec hall. Level RV sites are set on a hill; the tent area is below toward the lake.

There are a number of waterfront sites with water and electric hookups (sites 76-80 are favorites); site 23 is nicely tucked in the woods for extra privacy. We'd stay away from sites 1-15, if you can; they're too close to the road for our liking. Looking for something different? You can rent the tepee on site; the rustic cabins are nice, too.

BASICS

Operated By: Bob & Maria Cummings. **Open:** May 1–Oct. 31. **Site Assignment:** Reservations suggested July–Aug., 1-night deposit, 7-day cancellation policy; MC, V, & personal checks accepted. **Registration:** At office. **Fee:** Full hookup, $39.50; water/electric, $34; no hookup, $30. **Parking:** At site.

FACILITIES

Number of Multipurpose Sites: 100. **Hookups:** Electric (30, 50 amps), water, sewer, cable TV. **Each Site:** Picnic table, fire ring. **Dump Station:** Yes. **Laundry:** Yes. **Pay Phone:** Courtesy phone. **Restrooms and Showers:** Yes. **Fuel:** No. **Propane:** Yes. **Internal Roads:** Dirt, gravel, & paved (good). **RV Service:** No. **Market:** Lancaster, 4 mi. **Restaurant:** No. **General Store:** Yes. **Vending:** No. **Swimming:** Yes. **Playground:** Yes. **Other:** Lake frontage, beach, boat rentals, boat docks, rec hall, cabin rentals, videos & board games for rent. **Activities:** Swimming, boating, fishing, shuffleboard, basketball, volleyball, horseshoes, life-size chess & checkers. **Nearby Attractions:** Santa's Village, Six Gun City, Storyland, White Mountains, Franconia Notch State Park. **Additional Information:** Northern White Mountains Chamber of Commerce, 164 Main St., P.O. Box 298, Berlin, NH 03570, (603) 752-6060, also Franconia Notch Chamber of Commerce, P.O. Box 780, Franconia, NH 03580, (800) 237-9007.

RESTRICTIONS

Pets: Pets allowed w/ restrictions. Ask for more information. **Fires:** Grill, stoves, fire rings only. **Alcoholic Beverages:** Permitted. **Vehicle Maximum Length:** 40 ft.

TO GET THERE

From junction of Hwy. 3 and Hwy. 2, go south 4 mi. on Hwy. 3; campground is on the right.

LANCASTER   MAP, B-2
Roger's Campground

10 Roger's Campground Rd., 03584. T: (603) 788-4885; www.rogerscampground.com.

🚐 ★★★★   ▲ ★★★

Beauty: ★★★★	Site Privacy: ★★★
Spaciousness: ★★★	Quiet: ★★
Security: ★★★★★	Cleanliness: ★★
Insect Control: ★★★	Facilities: ★★★★★

Located halfway between Lancaster and Jefferson in the scenic northern White Mountains area, Roger's is New Hampshire's largest campground with 400 sites (not including a large safari group area). The backdrop is splendid: rolling foothills, forested valleys and craggy summits of the Presidential mountain range surround the campground. There are plenty of nearby attractions and outdoor activities at your doorstep, but most campers come to stay put for awhile. This is a destination campground with lots of on-site facilities: hot tub, swimming pool with waterslide, kiddie pool, tennis courts, mini-golf, nature trails, on-site restaurant, and a host of planned activities and live entertainment. Kids will love the huge barn-turned-arcade/billiards room and upstairs TV room. RV sites are all pull-throughs, set side-by-side in rows of grassy sites. The tenting area is separate, set behind the pool and motel area, backed by woods. We find the campsites and some facilities a bit bedraggled; it'd all look better with a little sprucing up.

BASICS

Operated By: Crosby Peck/Interlocks Property North. **Open:** Mid-May–mid-Oct. **Site Assignment:** Reservations suggested, one-half of stay required for deposit, 30-day cancellation policy, MC, V, D, AE, & personal checks accepted. **Registration:** At office. **Fee:** Full hookup, $35; water/electric, $25; electric, $24; no hookup, $23; based on 2 people; additional adult, $5; additional child, $3. **Parking:** At site.

FACILITIES

Number of RV-only Sites: 350. **Number of Tent-only Sites:** 110. **Hookups:** Electric (30 amps), water, sewer, Wi-Fi. **Each Site:** Picnic table, fire ring. **Dump Station:** Yes. **Laundry:** Yes. **Pay Phone:** Yes. **Restrooms and Showers:** Yes. **Fuel:** No. **Propane:** Yes. **Internal Roads:** Paved. **RV Service:** Yes. **Market:** Lancaster, 3 mi. **Restaurant:** Yes. **General Store:** Yes. **Vending:** Yes. **Swimming:** Yes. **Playground:** Yes. **Other:** Cabin & trailer rentals, on-site motel, mini-golf, arcade, waterslide, rec hall, TV room, hot tub, wading pool, tennis courts, safari field, nature trail, sports field. **Activities:** Swimming, tennis, hiking, softball, volleyball, mini-golf, basketball, shuffleboard, horseshoes. **Nearby Attractions:** Santa's Village, Six Gun City, Storyland, White Mountains, Franconia Notch State Park. **Additional Information:** Northern White Mountains Chamber of Commerce, 164 Main St., P.O. Box 298, Berlin, NH 03570, (603) 752-6060, also Franconia Notch Chamber of Commerce, P.O. Box 780, Franconia, NH 03580, (800) 237-9007.

RESTRICTIONS

Pets: Must be on a leash, never left unattended. Pets are not allowed in rental units. **Fires:** Grill, stoves, fire rings. **Alcoholic Beverages:** At site only. **Vehicle Maximum Length:** No limit.

TO GET THERE

From junction of Hwy. 2 and Hwy. 3, go 2 mi. east on Hwy. 2; campground is on the right.

LEBANON   MAP, C-1
Mascoma Lake Campground

92 US 4A, 03766. T: (603) 448-5076 or (800) 769-7861; www.mascomalake.com.

🚐 ★★★★   ▲ ★★★★

Beauty: ★★★★	Site Privacy: ★★★
Spaciousness: ★★★	Quiet: ★★★
Security: ★★★	Cleanliness: ★★★
Insect Control: ★★★	Facilities: ★★★★

If you're in the mood for old-fashioned pleasures (think sunsets across the lake, early morning canoe paddles, and sing-alongs around a bonfire), you'll enjoy your stay at this lakeside campground. It's situated in the "quiet corner" of New Hampshire (though there are plenty of those!) straddling the Vermont border. Campground activity centers around pretty Mascoma Lake, with plenty of boating (there are canoe, kayak, and paddleboat rentals), swimming, fishing, and lots of lounging on the sandy beach. Campsites are terraced, many overlooking the lake, with a bit of elbow room; average site width is about 35 feet. Type A, active types can happily stay busy with planned events on the weekend and sports activities, or a trip to nearby attractions (covered bridges, Quechee Gorge, and antiquing are favorites).

BASICS

Operated By: Paul & Jane Raymond. **Open:** Early May–mid Oct. **Site Assignment:** Reservations suggested; 1-night stays & holiday weekends paid in full; 7-day cancellation policy w/ $10 fee; less than 7-day cancellation gets a 50% refund, or no refund on holidays & weekends; inclement weather is not acceptable for cancellation. MC, V. **Registration:** At office. **Fee:** Full hookup, $35; water/electric, $28; no hookup, $25. **Parking:** At site.

FACILITIES

Number of RV-only Sites: 82. **Number of Tent-only Sites:** 13. **Hookups:** Electric (20, 30, 50 amps), water, sewer, cable. **Each Site:** Picnic table, fire ring. **Dump Station:** Yes. **Laundry:** Yes. **Pay Phone:** Yes. **Restrooms and Showers:** Yes. **Fuel:** No. **Propane:** Yes. **Internal Roads:** Gravel, dirt (good). **RV Service:** Yes. **Market:** Lebanon, 3 mi. **Restaurant:** No. **General Store:** Yes. **Vending:** Yes. **Swimming:** Yes. **Playground:** Yes. **Other:** Lake frontage, beach, rec hall, boat dock, boat rentals, sports field, planned activities, cabin rentals. **Activities:** Swimming, boating, fishing, hiking, bingo, karaoke, horseshoes. **Nearby Attractions:** Hanover, Dartmouth, Sunapee, Quechee Gorge, covered bridges, antiquing, 23-mile trail for biking & hiking. **Additional Information:** Greater Lebanon Chamber of Commerce, 2 Whipple Place, P.O. Box 97, Lebanon, NH 03766, (603) 448-1203.

RESTRICTIONS

Pets: Must be on a leash; never left unattended. No vicious breeds. Must pick up after pets. **Fires:** Grill, camp stoves, fire rings only. **Alcoholic Beverages:** At site only. **Vehicle Maximum Length:** 42 ft. **Other:** Lake.

TO GET THERE

From I-89 and Exit 17, go east 2 mi. on Hwy. 4, then south 0.75 mi. on Hwy. 4A; campground is on right.

LINCOLN   MAP, B-2
Hancock Campground

Kancamagus Hwy., 03251. T: (603) 447-5448.

🚐 ★★★   ▲ ★★★

Beauty: ★★★★	Site Privacy: ★★★
Spaciousness: ★★★★	Quiet: ★★★★
Security: ★★★	Cleanliness: ★★★★
Insect Control: ★★★	Facilities: ★★★

Hancock Campground is one of two along the Kancamagus that is open all year, and great for those looking to ski on the cheap, with a dash of added adventure. Most all the sites are nicely forested, fairly spacious, well spaced apart, and set within a beautiful birch grove. Right across the street from Hancock is a trail that takes you up and over Potash Knob and Big Coolidge Mountain. Hancock is the campground on the Kancamagus that is closest to civilization, only 5 miles east of Lincoln, where you can grab a pizza or see a movie if you need a little diversion. Another diversionary tactic is to take the short path to the East Branch of the Pemigewasset River (between sites 43 and 45 on the outer side of the loop) and drop a hook in the water. There are also a few spots where you can drop yourself in the water, but be careful. Even late in the summer, that water can be mighty chilly.

BASICS

Operated By: U.S. Forest Service. **Site Assignment:** First come, first served; no reservations. **Registration:** Select site, then pay at self-service fee station. **Fee:** $20. **Parking:** At site, $5 for a 2nd vehicle.

FACILITIES

Number of RV-only Sites: 35. **Number of Tent-only Sites:** 21. **Hookups:** None. **Each Site:** Fire ring, picnic table. **Dump Station:** No. **Laundry:** No. **Pay Phone:** No. **Restrooms and Showers:** Yes. **Fuel:** No. **Propane:** No. **Internal Roads:** Gravel. **RV Service:** No. **Market:** No. **Restaurant:** No. **General Store:** No. **Vending:** No. **Swimming:** Short walk from site. **Playground:** No. **Other:** Unique swimming hole, Upper Lady's Bath. **Activities:** Swimming, fishing, hiking, picnicking, scenic byway. **Nearby Attractions:** Whale's Tale Water Park, White Mountain Motor Sports Park, Lost River Reservation. **Additional Information:** Lincoln-Woodstock Chamber of Commerce, (603) 745-6621, www.lincolnwoodstock.com.

RESTRICTIONS

Pets: On leash. **Fires:** Fire ring only. **Alcoholic Beverages:** At site. **Vehicle Maximum Length:** Varies. **Other:** 8 people per site; 14-day stay limit; 2 vehicles, $5 charge for 2nd vehicle.

TO GET THERE

From Lincoln, follow Kancamagus Hwy. to campground on right. It's the first campground you'll come to. From Conway, follow Kancamagus Hwy. west to Hancock campground on left. From this side, it will be the last campground you come to.

LISBON   MAP, B-2
Littleton/Lisbon KOA

2154 Hwy. 302, 03585. T: (603) 838-5525 or (800) 562-5836; www.koa.com.

🚐 ★★★★   ▲ ★★★

Beauty: ★★★	Site Privacy: ★★★
Spaciousness: ★★★	Quiet: ★★★
Security: ★★★	Cleanliness: ★★★★★
Insect Control: ★★★	Facilities: ★★★★

This campground is a popular stopover and weekend destination for travelers exploring the scenic Franconia

Notch area and beyond. Upon check-in, campers are given a helpful brochure detailing six one-day itineraries, all within an hour of the campground. Conveniently located, the Littleton/Lisbon KOA also offers some nice touches: an adults-only hot tub, frontage on the Ammonoosuc River with swimming holes and pebble beaches (bring your own tubes or kayaks; stocked fishing with license, too), white-glove clean bath facilities, and—our favorite—meal delivery! The campground owners work with a local Italian restaurant (pizza, sandwiches, pasta, salads); pick from the menu in the office, and the campground will deliver your meal for a nominal fee. Large pull-through sites are clustered in the middle of the property, while tent-only sites back up to the trees and the river. Full hookups are contained in a small loop behind the office and store. All sites are very tidy and uniform.

BASICS

Operated By: Jane & Steve Jesseman. **Open:** First weekend in May–mid-Oct. **Site Assignment:** Reservations suggested July–Aug., 1-night deposit, 48-hour cancellation policy, 3-day min. on holiday weekends, MC, V, D, AE, & personal checks accepted. **Registration:** At office. **Fee:** Full hookup, $35–$38; water/electric, $33–$36; no hookup, $29–$32; based on 2 adults; additional child, 17 years & under, $5; additional adult, $7. Call ahead to confirm. **Parking:** At site.

FACILITIES

Number of RV-only Sites: 43. **Number of Tent-only Sites:** 17. **Hookups:** Electric (20, 30 amps), water, sewer, cable TV, modem. **Each Site:** Picnic table, fire ring. **Dump Station:** Yes. **Laundry:** Yes. **Pay Phone:** Yes. **Restrooms and Showers:** Yes. **Fuel:** No. **Propane:** Yes. **Internal Roads:** Gravel (good). **RV Service:** Yes. **Market:** Littleton & Lisbon, 5 mi. **Restaurant:** Littleton & Lisbon, 5 mi. **General Store:** Yes. **Vending:** No. **Swimming:** Yes. **Playground:** Yes. **Other:** Adults-only hot tub, river frontage, bike rentals, cabin rentals. **Activities:** Swimming, fishing, horseshoes, basketball, mini-golf. **Nearby Attractions:** White Mountains, Franconia Notch State Park. **Additional Information:** Littleton Area Chamber of Commerce, P.O. Box 105, 120 Main St., Littleton, NH 03561, (603) 444-6561; Franconia Notch Chamber of Commerce, P.O. Box 780, Franconia, NH 03580, (800) 237-9007.

RESTRICTIONS

Pets: Must be on a leash, never left unattended. No overly aggressive pets. **Fires:** Grill, stoves, fire rings only. **Alcoholic Beverages:** At site only. **Vehicle Maximum Length:** No limit.

TO GET THERE

From I-91, Exit 17, go east 18 mi. on Hwy. 302. Campground is on right.

LITTLETON   MAP, B-2
Crazy Horse Campground

788 Hilltop Rd., 03561. T: (603) 444-2204 or (800) 639-4107; www.ucampnh.com/crazyhorse.

🚐 ★★★   ⛺ ★★★★

Beauty: ★★★★   Site Privacy: ★★★
Spaciousness: ★★★   Quiet: ★★★★

Security: ★★★★   Cleanliness: ★★★★
Insect Control: ★★★   Facilities: ★★★

Looking to get away from it all? This White Mountain–area campground offers a picturesque, serene escape, especially appealing to tent campers and outdoor enthusiasts. That's not to say there isn't lots to do in the area: From here you can visit Franconia Notch State Park attractions or head east to the busy North Conway area—easy day trips, if you're looking for some action. But you might be tempted to stay close to the campground, where you'll find hiking and biking trails, planned activities, and a number of nature programs conducted throughout the summer by the New Hampshire Audubon Society. Also nearby is 12-mile-long Moore Lake, with a sandy beach, canoe rentals, and good fishing. The tent-only area is separate and remote, tucked in the woods, with the White Mountains as a backdrop (sites C88–96 are especially nice). Full-hookup sites for larger rigs are clustered in loops near the front, with plenty of shade and level ground. Also, great pop-up sites with water and electric hookups.

BASICS

Operated By: Barbara & Joseph DiPierre. **Open:** All year. **Site Assignment:** Reservations suggested; 1-night deposit, 48-hour cancellation policy, 4-day cancellation policy for holiday weekends. MC, V, personal checks accepted. **Registration:** At office. **Fee:** Full hookup, $29–$31; water/electric, $27; no hookup, $24. **Parking:** At site.

FACILITIES

Number of RV-only Sites: 125. **Number of Tent-only Sites:** 40. **Hookups:** Electric (30, 50 amps), water, sewer, modem. **Each Site:** Picnic table, fire ring. **Dump Station:** Yes. **Laundry:** Yes. **Pay Phone:** Emergency phone in office. **Restrooms and Showers:** Yes. **Fuel:** No. **Propane:** Yes. **Internal Roads:** Gravel, dirt (fair). **RV Service:** Yes. **Market:** Littleton, 2 mi. **Restaurant:** No. **General Store:** Yes. **Vending:** Yes. **Swimming:** Yes. **Playground:** Yes. **Other:** Boat rentals, rec hall, pavilion, lake access, trailer, tepee & lean-to rentals. **Activities:** Swimming, boating, fishing, volleyball, horseshoes, basketball, biking, hiking, planned activities, NH Audubon programs, winter activities on-site including skiing, snowmobiling. **Nearby Attractions:** White Mountain attractions, Franconia State Park, Crawford Notch, Week State Park, Mount Washington Cog Railway, Flume Gorge. **Additional Information:** Littleton Area Chamber of Commerce, P.O. Box 105, 120 Main St., Littleton, NH 03561, (603) 444-6561.

RESTRICTIONS

Pets: Must be on a leash; never left unattended; current rabies certificate. Pets not allowed in rental units. **Fires:** Grill, camp stoves, fire rings only. **Alcoholic Beverages:** At site only. **Vehicle Maximum Length:** No limit. **Other:** Helmets required for bikes.

TO GET THERE

From junction of I-93 and Hwy. 135 (Exit 43), go south 100 yards on Hwy. 135, then northwest (right) 1 mi. on Hwy. 135/18, then north (right) 1.5 mi. on Hilltop Rd.; campground is on the right.

MEREDITH   MAP, C-2
Clearwater Campground

26 Campground Rd., 03253. T: (603) 279-7761; www.clearwatercampground.com.

🚐 ★★★   ⛺ ★★★

Beauty: ★★★★   Site Privacy: ★★★
Spaciousness: ★★★   Quiet: ★★★
Security: ★★★★★   Cleanliness: ★★★★
Insect Control: ★★★★   Facilities: ★★★★

This centrally located Lakes Region campground, just minutes off the highway, is a water lover's paradise. The property bumps up to pretty Pemigewasset Lake, with its own sandy beach, boat launch, slips, and dock. There's plenty of recreation off the water, too, with planned activities, play areas, a rec room, and more. It's easier to get to a number of popular attractions in the area and to explore the region from this base. Still, many campers, especially those with kids in tow, are content to stick around and enjoy the lake and campground activities. Most of the sites are on nicely wooded lots that loop off the main roads; only a handful have water views. The most requested site is site 125, next to a huge granite boulder. It's very picturesque, but we found it a bit busy, next to the docks and beach area. Bigger rigs should consider the Meredith Woods RV resort across the street, owned by the same family.

BASICS

Operated By: John & Sue Mackie. **Open:** May 19–Oct. 10. **Site Assignment:** Reservations recommended, $125 per week deposit required for holiday period; 3 nights or less require full payment in advance; cancellation policy: deposits refunded up to 1 week before arrival; min. stays often required during summer & holiday weekends; V, MC, D, AE, & personal checks accepted. **Registration:** At office. **Fee:** Electric/water/sewer/cable, $42; electric/water, $39; no hookup, $39; May 19–June 15 (excluding Memorial Day weekend) & Sept. 4–Oct. 9, fees are $20–$28 per night. **Parking:** At site, max. of 2 vehicles.

FACILITIES

Number of RV-only Sites: 146. **Number of Tent-only Sites:** 4. **Hookups:** Electric (20, 30, 50 amps), water, sewer, cable TV. **Each Site:** Picnic table, fire ring, trash barrel. **Dump Station:** Yes. **Laundry:** Yes. **Pay Phone:** Yes. **Restrooms and Showers:** Yes. **Fuel:** No. **Propane:** No. **Internal Roads:** Gravel (good). **RV Service:** No. **Market:** Meredith, 2 mi. **Restaurant:** No. **General Store:** Yes. **Vending:** No. **Swimming:** Beach. **Playground:** Yes. **Other:** Lake frontage, beach area, self-guided nature walk, boat rentals, boat dock, launching & slips, recreation pavilion, trailer & cabin rentals, rec rooms w/ library, arcade games, TV. **Activities:** Swimming, boating, Ping-Pong, shuffleboard, planned activities. **Nearby Attractions:** Lake Winnepesaukee, Squam Lake, Weirs Beach, scenic railroad, golf courses, hiking trails. **Additional Information:** Meredith Area Chamber of Commerce, P.O. Box 732, Meredith, NH, 03253-0732, (603) 279-6121 or Lakes Region Assoc., Hwy. 104, P.O. Box 430, New Hampton, NH 03252, (603) 744-8664.

RESTRICTIONS

Pets: Must be on a leash, never left unattended, picked up after. Not permitted on beach. **Fires:** Grill, stoves, fire rings only. **Alcoholic Beverages:** At site. **Vehicle Maximum Length:** 35 ft. **Other:** No motorcycles.

TO GET THERE

From I-93, Exit 23 (Meredith); go 3 mi. east on Hwy. 104; campground is on the right.

MEREDITH   MAP, C-2
Harbor Hill Camping Area

189 Hwy. 25 East, 03253. T: (603) 279-6910; www.hhcamp.com.

🚐 ★★★   ⛺ ★★★★

Beauty: ★★★   Site Privacy: ★★★★
Spaciousness: ★★★★   Quiet: ★★★★
Security: ★★★★★   Cleanliness: ★★★★
Insect Control: ★★★   Facilities: ★★★

Location, location, location. You can't beat Harbor Hill's location if you want to explore New Hampshire's popular Lakes Region. The campground is a short distance to the shores of Squam Lake (where *On Golden Pond* was filmed), Lake Winnipesaukee (New Hampshire's largest freshwater lake), and rollicking Weirs Beach. It's especially popular with families who want a quiet, relaxing place to come home to after a day of exploring area beaches and attractions.

BASICS

Operated By: Chuck & Barbara Palm. **Open:** Memorial Day–Columbus Day. **Site Assignment:** Reservations suggested, 50% deposit, 3-day deposit for holiday weekends; for cancellations made less than 7 days before scheduled arrival, the deposit is held as rain check for future stay w/in same year subject to availability & a $10 fee. MC, V, personal checks accepted. **Registration:** At office. **Fee:** Full hookup, $34; water/electric, $30; no hookup, $28. **Parking:** At site, 1 vehicle per site.

FACILITIES

Number of RV-only Sites: 122. **Number of Tent-only Sites:** 18. **Hookups:** Electric (20, 30, 50 amps), water, sewer. **Each Site:** Picnic table, fire ring. **Dump Station:** No. **Laundry:** Yes. **Pay Phone:** Yes. **Restrooms and Showers:** Yes (coin-op). **Fuel:** No. **Propane:** Yes. **Internal Roads:** Paved, gravel (good). **RV Service:** Yes. **Market:** Meredith, 2 mi. **Restaurant:** Meredith, 2 mi. **General Store:** Yes. **Vending:** No. **Swimming:** Yes. **Playground:** Yes. **Other:** Rec hall, arcade, cabin rentals, sport court. **Activities:** Swimming, basketball, shuffleboard. **Nearby Attractions:** Lake Winnipesaukee, Squam Lake, Weirs Beach, fishing, boating, quick access to White Mountain area. **Additional Information:** Meredith Chamber of Commerce, P.O. Box 732, Meredith, NH, 03253-0732, (603) 279-6121.

RESTRICTIONS

Pets: Must be on a leash, never left unattended, cleaned up after. 1 pet per site. Not allowed in rental sites. Vaccination papers must be available. **Fires:**

Grill, stoves, fire rings. **Alcoholic Beverages:** At site only. **Vehicle Maximum Length:** 40 ft.

TO GET THERE

From Hwy. 93 Exit 23, take Hwy. 104 east. Go 12 mi. to Hwy. 3, then left on Hwy. 3 to Hwy. 25 east; campground is 1.5 mi. on right.

MEREDITH   MAP, C-2
Meredith Woods

26 Campground Rd., 03253. T: (603) 279-5449; www.meredithwoods.com.

🚐 ★★★★   ⛺ n/a

Beauty: ★★★   Site Privacy: ★★★
Spaciousness: ★★★   Quiet: ★★★
Security: ★★★★★   Cleanliness: ★★★★
Insect Control: ★★★★★   Facilities: ★★★★★

This year-round RV park is a miniature gated neighborhood of rigs. It's RV heaven, smack-dab in the middle of New Hampshire's popular Lakes Region. You won't find much in the way of scenic beauty at this campground: all sites are level, gravel or sandy plots, flanked by a few trees and bushes scattered in between for foliage and privacy. It's all very clean and orderly, albeit a bit bland. The most extraordinary feature of this park is the large (and plush, by campground standards) recreational center with a heated indoor pool and hot tub, TV social room, and game room. All the facilities are modern. Another bonus: Meredith Woods campers have access to the beach, boating, and all other programs and facilities at Clearwater Campground, across the street (but not vice versa).

BASICS

Operated By: Mackie family. **Open:** All year. **Site Assignment:** Reservations recommended, $125 deposit per week of scheduled stay; reservations of 3 nights or less & holiday reservations require full payment in advance; deposits are refundable up to 7 days of arrival. **Registration:** At office. **Fee:** Summer, $42; winter, $28–$38; based on 2 adults & 3 children under age of 18; additional adults, $10; additional children, $1. **Parking:** At site, 4 vehicles per site.

FACILITIES

Number of RV-only Sites: 102. **Hookups:** Electric (20, 30, 50 amps), water, sewer, cable TV, phone. **Each Site:** Picnic table, fire ring, trash can. **Dump Station:** No, all sites have sewer. **Laundry:** Yes. **Pay Phone:** Yes. **Restrooms and Showers:** Yes. **Fuel:** No. **Propane:** No. **Internal Roads:** Paved (good). **RV Service:** No. **Market:** Meredith, 2 mi. **Restaurant:** No. **General Store:** Yes. **Vending:** No. **Swimming:** Yes. **Playground:** Yes. **Other:** indoor pool & hot tub, TV social room & game room, boat docking by reservation, canoe rack space available; guests also have use of all activities & facilities at Clearwater Campground, across the street, including lake frontage, beach area. **Activities:** Swimming, boating, hiking, Ping-Pong, shuffleboard, planned activities. **Nearby Attractions:** Lake Winnipesaukee, Squam Lake, Weirs Beach, quick access to White Mountain region. **Additional Information:** Meredith Area Chamber of Commerce, P.O. Box 732, Meredith, NH 03253-0732, (603) 279-6121.

RESTRICTIONS

Pets: Must be on a leash, never left unattended, picked up after. Not allowed on beach. **Fires:** Grill, stoves, fire rings only. **Alcoholic Beverages:** At site only. **Vehicle Maximum Length:** 40 ft. **Other:** Limit of 7 people per site on an overnight basis, no more than 4 of whom can be adults; limit of 1 RV per site.

TO GET THERE

From I-93, Exit 23 (Meredith), go 3 mi. east on Hwy. 104; campground is on the left.

MILTON   MAP, C-3
Mi-Te-Jo Campground

111 Mi-Te-Jo Rd., P. O. Box 830, 03851. T: (603) 652-9022; www.mi-te-jo.com.

🚐 ★★★★★   ⛺ ★★★★★

Beauty: ★★★★★   Site Privacy: ★★★★
Spaciousness: ★★★★   Quiet: ★★★
Security: ★★★★★   Cleanliness: ★★★★★
Insect Control: ★★★   Facilities: ★★★★★

This top-notch lakeside campground, less than one hour from the White Mountains to the north and ocean beaches to the east, is a real gem. There's lots of easy day trips from here, but there is little reason to leave. In fact, most campers rent summer sites a week at a time, Saturday to Saturday. This is a true destination/vacation campground, with plenty of outdoor pleasures. There are two sandy beaches on Northeast Pond. "Pond" is an understatement: 770 acres of fresh water feed into another 371-acre pond. Swimming and fishing are top pursuits, and many campers choose to bring their own boats to park in slips or at the docks ($5-per-day charge). There are lots of nice sites on the water (sites A–D are especially nice); sites 111, 112, and 0 are favorites, too, overlooking the lake. But you really can't go wrong here. Landscaping throughout the campground is well done, with planted flowers and natural tall pines adding to its overall beauty. This campground attracts a lot of visitors, but some of the more elusive are the porcupines, foxes, and moose—more patient human guests may be lucky enough to catch a glimpse of these creatures. The facilities are clean, modern, and top-of-the-line.

BASICS

Operated By: Gary & Susan Marique. **Open:** May 15–Oct. 15. **Site Assignment:** Reservations recommended; required July–Aug., 50% deposit, cancel w/in 14 days to avoid $20 fee; cash, personal checks accepted. **Registration:** At office. **Fee:** Premium (full hookup), $41; premium (water/electric), $36; vacation (full hookup), $36; vacation (water/electric), $31; based on 2 adults & their children ages 18 & under. **Parking:** At site.

FACILITIES

Number of RV-only Sites: 201. **Hookups:** Electric (30, 50 amps), water, sewer, cable TV, Wi-Fi. **Each Site:** Picnic table, fire ring. **Dump Station:** Yes. **Laundry:** Yes. **Pay Phone:** Yes. **Restrooms and Showers:** Yes. **Fuel:** No. **Propane:** Yes. **Internal Roads:** Dirt (good). **RV Service:** No. **Market:** Milton, 1 mi. **Restaurant:** Milton, 1 mi. **General Store:** Yes. **Vending:** Yes. **Swimming:** Yes.

Playground: Yes. **Other:** 2 beaches, 1,900 ft. of lake frontage, tennis court, ball field, pavilion, rec hall, boat slips, docks, cabin rentals, canoe, kayak & paddleboat rentals, arcade. **Activities:** Swimming, boating, fishing, bocce, horseshoes, basketball, volleyball, tennis. **Nearby Attractions:** New Hampshire seacoast, Portsmouth, quick access to Lakes Region & Lake Winnipesaukee, antiquing, hiking. **Additional Information:** Lakes Region Assoc., Hwy. 104, P.O. Box 430, New Hampton, NH 03252, (603) 744-8664, fax (603) 744-8659, or visit www.lakesregion.org.

RESTRICTIONS

Pets: Must be on a leash, never left unattended. Pets are not allowed on the beaches or in cabins. **Fires:** Grill, stoves, fire rings only. **Alcoholic Beverages:** Responsible consumption. **Vehicle Maximum Length:** No limit. **Other:** Sites are limited to 7 campers of which only 4 may be adults; 1 RV per site.

TO GET THERE

From Hwy. 16 (Spaulding Turnpike), take Exit 17. Go 0.75 mi. east on Hwy. 75, then 3.25 mi. north on Hwy. 125. Turn right on Townhouse Rd.; the campground is 1 mi. on the left.

MOULTONBORO   MAP, C-2
Long Island Bridge Campground

29 Long Island Rd., 03254. T: (603) 253-6053; www.ucampnh.com/longislandbridge.

🚐 ★★★   ▲ ★★★

Beauty: ★★★★	Site Privacy: ★★★
Spaciousness: ★★★	Quiet: ★★★★
Security: ★★★	Cleanliness: ★★★
Insect Control: ★★★	Facilities: ★★★

Here's your chance to get your own slice of pricey Lake Winnipesaukee waterfront real estate, if only for a few nights. This campground rests on the shores of New Hampshire's largest (and very popular) freshwater lake. Only 15 minutes from Center Harbor, the campground is nestled in a cove, away from the hustle and bustle of many of the busier spots on the lake. (Note: The campground is next to a large marina, so you're likely to see some boat traffic.) Campers have access to a lovely, sandy stretch of beach and, if you reserve well in advance, a choice of sites along the shore facing picturesque Long Island and the setting sun. The rest of the sites and facilities are on a hilly terrace across the street. You won't see much, if any, of the lake from these sites (and those with water views have already been snatched up by long-time seasonal renters), but most of the available sites are spacious and ringed with trees for privacy. There are some open, grassy sites, too, for those who prefer the sun. We like the waterfront sites the best, of course, but sites 55, 55A, and 55B are roomy and private. This campground is a great base from which to explore the area and enjoy the lake.

BASICS

Operated By: Watson family. **Open:** May 15–Oct. 15. **Site Assignment:** Reservations suggested, 1-night deposit, refunded on a 2-week notice; cash, personal checks only. **Registration:** At office. **Fee:** Full hookup, $30; water/electric, $25; no hookup, $23;

waterfront, $32–$35, based on 1 family (parents & unmarried children) per site. **Parking:** At site.

FACILITIES

Number of RV-only Sites: 100. **Number of Tent-only Sites:** 12. **Hookups:** Electric (20, 30 amps), water, sewer. **Each Site:** Picnic table, fire ring. **Dump Station:** Yes. **Laundry:** Yes. **Pay Phone:** Yes. **Restrooms and Showers:** Yes (coin-op). **Fuel:** No. **Propane:** No. **Internal Roads:** Dirt (fair). **RV Service:** No. **Market:** Moultonborough, 7 mi. **Restaurant:** No. **General Store:** Yes. **Vending:** Yes. **Swimming:** Yes. **Playground:** Yes. **Other:** Lake frontage, beach, boat rentals. **Activities:** Swimming, boating, fishing, basketball, volleyball, horseshoes. **Nearby Attractions:** Lake Winnipesaukee, Squam Lake, Weirs Beach, outlet shopping, antiquing. **Additional Information:** Wolfeboro Chamber of Commerce, P.O. Box 547, 32 Central Ave., Wolfeboro, NH 03894, (603) 569-2200.

RESTRICTIONS

Pets: Must be on a leash, never left unattended, cleaned up after. Pets not allowed at waterfront sites or beach area (pets are generally not encouraged here). **Fires:** Grill, stoves, fire rings only, out by midnight. **Alcoholic Beverages:** At site only. **Vehicle Maximum Length:** No limit.

TO GET THERE

From the junction of Hwy. 3 and Hwy. 25 (in Meredith), go 10 mi. northeast on Hwy. 25, then 6.5 mi. south on Moultonboro Neck Rd.; the campground is on the left.

NEW BOSTON   MAP, D-2
Friendly Beaver Campground

Old Coach Rd., 03070. T: (603) 487-5570; www.friendlybeaver.com.

🚐 ★★★★★   ▲ ★★★

Beauty: ★★★	Site Privacy: ★★★
Spaciousness: ★★★	Quiet: ★★★
Security: ★★★★	Cleanliness: ★★★★★
Insect Control: ★★★	Facilities: ★★★★★

We love the facilities at this southern New Hampshire campground; they rival many high-end resorts. A stay at Friendly Beaver is certainly not "roughing it." There's a three-pool outdoor complex, including a children's pool, sports pool (water basketball, anyone?), swim pool, and hot tubs. Next door is the adults-only rec hall and indoor pool complex. Kids have their own rec hall—a huge space with an upstairs activity area, large-screen TV, and games. There are plenty of planned activities for adults and children throughout summer weekends, too. Despite the size and resort-style facilities, the campground remains quite friendly, almost quaint. Seasonal renters are spread throughout the major areas of the campground; transient campers are clustered in a separate circle (full hookups available) in open, sunny sites. Special note: The campground is open year-round, with nearby skiing, ice fishing, and snowmobiling in the winter.

BASICS

Operated By: Christine & Tom Quirk. **Open:** All year. **Site Assignment:** Reservations suggested, full

payment required as deposit if less than 30 days away; 3-night min. during holidays; 14-day cancellation notice, w/ $10 fee; 7- to 13-day notice, camping credit for the same year, 6-day notice or less, no refund or credit. MC,V, personal checks accepted for deposit; no personal checks accepted upon arrival. **Registration:** At office. **Fee:** Full hookup, $38; water/electric, $35; no hookup, $33; based on 2 adults & 2 children under 18. **Parking:** At site.

FACILITIES

Number of RV-only Sites: 166. **Number of Tent-only Sites:** 7. **Hookups:** Electric (30, 50 amps), water, sewer. **Each Site:** Picnic table, fire ring. **Dump Station:** Yes. **Laundry:** Yes. **Pay Phone:** Yes. **Restrooms and Showers:** Yes. **Fuel:** No. **Propane:** No. **Internal Roads:** Gravel, dirt (good). **RV Service:** No. **Market:** Goffstown, 15 mi. **Restaurant:** No. **General Store:** Yes. **Vending:** Yes. **Swimming:** Yes. **Playground:** Yes. **Other:** Adult rec hall & lounge, game room, hiking, biking & snowmobiling trails, outdoor patios & decks, hot tubs, sports field, pavilion. **Activities:** Swimming, basketball, volleyball, horseshoes, hiking, biking, snowmobiling, planned activities, including pony rides, arts & crafts, children's programs, socials, contests, dances, live entertainment, & more. **Nearby Attractions:** Manchester, Concord, Crotched Mountain. **Additional Information:** Manchester Chamber of Commerce, 889 Elm St., Manchester, NH 03101, (603) 434-7438.

RESTRICTIONS

Pets: Must be on a 6-ft. leash, never left unattended, cleaned up after. **Fires:** Grill, stoves, fire rings only. **Alcoholic Beverages:** At site & in rec hall only. Must be of age. **Vehicle Maximum Length:** No limit.

TO GET THERE

From the junction of Hwys. 77, 136, and 13, go south 100 feet on Hwy. 13, then west 2 mi. on Old Coach Rd.; campground is on the right.

NEW HAMPTON   MAP, C-2
Twin Tamarack

Hwy. 104, P.O. Box 121, 03256. T: (603) 279-4387; www.ucampnh.com/twintamarack.

🚐 ★★★★   ▲ ★★★

Beauty: ★★★	Site Privacy: ★★★
Spaciousness: ★★★	Quiet: ★★
Security: ★★★★★	Cleanliness: ★★★★
Insect Control: ★★★	Facilities: ★★★★

This large, activity-oriented campground in the Lakes Region is popular with families and groups. On warm, sunny days, campers gather around the pool, located up front next to the recreational hall and office. Or they head across the street to the sandy beach area on Pemigewasset Lake to swim in spring-fed waters or go boating. Evenings are filled with special events and activities (movies, music, and socials). There's Ping-Pong, video games, pool, hayrides, fishing contests, and more to keep even the most active in your brood busy and happy. The boulder-strewn, hilly grounds and scattered woods add visual interest, but don't expect too much privacy.

Many sites are small, close to the road, and each other. But it's a "more the merrier" attitude here, perfect for social, friendly campers and traveling groups. Eleven pull-through sites are available.

BASICS

Operated By: Laura & John Osuchowski. **Open:** Memorial Day–Columbus Day. **Site Assignment:** Reservations suggested, take credit card to reserve site & charges 1-night fee if cancelled 2 weeks before arrival unless site is resold. MC, V, D, personal checks not accepted on arrival but can be used to reserve site. **Registration:** At office. **Fee:** Full hookup, $36; water/electric, $32; based on family of 4 or 2 adults. **Parking:** At site.

FACILITIES

Number of Multipurpose Sites: 256. **Hookups:** Electric (30, 50 amps), water, sewer. **Each Site:** Picnic table, fire ring. **Dump Station:** Yes. **Laundry:** Yes. **Pay Phone:** No. **Restrooms and Showers:** Yes. **Fuel:** No. **Propane:** Small bottles. **Internal Roads:** Gravel, dirt (good). **RV Service:** No. **Market:** New Hampton, 3 mi. **Restaurant:** No. **General Store:** Yes. **Vending:** No. **Swimming:** Yes. **Playground:** Yes. **Other:** Outdoor hot tub, sports courts, canoe & boat rentals, lake access, boat launch, rec room, arcade, free Wi-Fi in rec hall. **Activities:** Swimming, boating, fishing, basketball, horseshoes, volleyball, planned activities, including arts & crafts, fishing derbies, movies, hayrides, dances & socials. **Nearby Attractions:** Lake Winnipesaukee, Squam Lake, Weirs Beach, quick access to White Mountain region. **Additional Information:** Greater Laconia/Weirs Beach Chamber of Commerce, 11 Veterans Square, Laconia, NH 03246, (603) 524-5531.

RESTRICTIONS

Pets: Must be on a leash, never left unattended. **Fires:** Grill, stoves, fire rings only. **Alcoholic Beverages:** At site only. **Vehicle Maximum Length:** 45 ft. **Other:** Motorcycles not allowed.

TO GET THERE

From I-93, take Exit 23. Go 2.5 mi. east on Hwy. 104; campground is on the left.

NEWPORT MAP, C-1
Crow's Nest Campground

529 South Main St., 03773. T: (603) 863-6170; www.crowsnestcampground.com.

🚐 ★★★		🏕 ★★★	
Beauty: ★★★		Site Privacy: ★★★	
Spaciousness: ★★★		Quiet: ★★★	
Security: ★★★		Cleanliness: ★★★	
Insect Control: ★★★		Facilities: ★★★	

Located in the Lake Sunapee region, Crow's Nest Campground is a favorite with families and anglers in the summer and snowmobilers and skiers in the winter. It is one of the few campgrounds in New Hampshire that remains open when the mercury drops. The property flanks the meandering Sugar River, with plenty of spots for trout fishing and hot summer day dunks. (Those who prefer a less natural swimming experience can take advantage of the campground's heated pool and kid-friendly wading pool.) There's

also a spring-fed pond on the property. In winter, there's downhill and cross-country skiing nearby, sledding, and snowmobiling (trails are directly accessible from the campground). You'll have a choice of open, wooded, pond, and riverfront sites. The more primitive tent sites are located near the pond with a convenient footpath to the river. Full-hookup sites are set in rows near the front of the campground with easy access to the rec hall and office (both heated in the winter). This campground offers 4 pull-through sites. Our favorites sites are 56–65, with water and electric hookups, set on the riverbank.

BASICS

Operated By: Howie & Kathy Neuberger. **Open:** May 15–Oct. 15; Dec 1–Apr. 1. **Site Assignment:** Reservations suggested; stay of 1 night requires full deposit; 2 or more nights, 50% deposit; holiday stays paid in full; 14-day cancellation policy w/ $10 fee; no refunds for holiday stays. MC, V, D, AE, personal checks accepted. **Registration:** At office. **Fee:** Full hookup 50 amps, $36; full hookup 30 amps, $33; water/electric (riverfront) $34; water/electric, $30; no hookup, $27, based on 2 adults & 3 children. **Parking:** At site.

FACILITIES

Number of RV-only Sites: 108. **Number of Tent-only Sites:** 12. **Hookups:** Electric (20, 30, 50 amps), water, sewer, modem, Wi-Fi. **Each Site:** Picnic table, fire ring. **Dump Station:** Yes. **Laundry:** Yes. **Pay Phone:** Yes. **Restrooms and Showers:** Yes (coin-op). **Fuel:** No. **Propane:** Yes. **Internal Roads:** Gravel, dirt (good). **RV Service:** No. **Market:** Newport, 2 mi. **Restaurant:** No. **General Store:** Yes. **Vending:** No. **Swimming:** Yes. **Playground:** Yes. **Other:** Pond & river frontage, group area, mini-golf, bike rentals, sports fields, rec hall, RV, cabin & tent rentals, planned activities, including arts & crafts, socials, & themed weekends. **Activities:** Swimming, fishing, basketball, biking, mini-golf, badminton, horseshoes, volleyball, snowmobiling. **Nearby Attractions:** Lake Sunapee, Dartmouth, Hanover. **Additional Information:** Greater Lebanon Chamber of Commerce, 2 Whipple Place, P.O. Box 97, Lebanon, NH 03766, (603) 448-1203.

RESTRICTIONS

Pets: Must be on a leash; never left unattended. No pets in rental units. **Fires:** Grill, camp stoves, fire rings only. **Alcoholic Beverages:** At site only. **Vehicle Maximum Length:** No limit.

TO GET THERE

From the junction of I-89 and Hwy. 103 (Exit 9), go west 22 mi. on Hwy. 103, then south 2 mi. on Hwy. 10; campground is on the right.

NORTH WOODSTOCK MAP, B-2
Lost River Valley Campground

951 Lost River Rd., 03262. T: (603) 745-8321 or (800) 370-5678; www.lostriver.com.

🚐 ★★★★		🏕 ★★★★★	
Beauty: ★★★★		Site Privacy: ★★★★★	
Spaciousness: ★★★★★		Quiet: ★★★★	
Security: ★★★★★		Cleanliness: ★★★★★	
Insect Control: ★★★		Facilities: ★★★★	

We've dubbed this campground "The Rivers Run Through It." Located on the site of a turn-of-the-20th-century lumber mill (an authentic waterwheel still churns), the scenic property is surrounded on three sides by national forest and situated between the Lost River and Walker Brook. It's hard to believe that you're only minutes off the highway and near many of New Hampshire's White Mountains and Franconia Notch State Park attractions. The large, mostly back-in sites have been sensitively carved out of the boulder-strewn setting, many with river or popular brook frontage, and wooded with maple and birch forest. Bears and moose have been spotted in Lost River Valley, and the lucky, patient camper may spot them. Recreation areas, including a swimming pond, beach area, playground, and sports fields, are situated across the street. Crossing the street may be an issue for families with small children, but the setup keeps the campground sites quiet, more natural, and pristine. You'll go to sleep to the sound of running waters.

BASICS

Operated By: Jim Kelley. **Open:** May 15–Columbus Day. **Site Assignment:** First come, first served w/ reservations accepted for 3-night stay or longer, 3-day deposit or 50% for stays of a week or more, 14-day cancellation policy w/ $15 fee; MC, V, D; personal checks accepted for advance reservations only. **Registration:** At office. **Fee:** Full hookup, $33.50; water/electric: (wooded), $27.50; (brook front), $31.50; water only: (wooded), $23.50; (brook front), $27.50; based on 2 adults per site, 1 camp unit & 1 car per site, additional children, ages 17 & under, $2; additional adult, $8. **Parking:** At site.

FACILITIES

Number of RV-only Sites: 100. **Number of Tent-only Sites:** 32. **Hookups:** Electric (20, 30, 50 amps), water, sewer. **Each Site:** Picnic table, fire ring, water. **Dump Station:** Yes. **Laundry:** Yes. **Pay Phone:** Yes. **Restrooms and Showers:** Yes. **Fuel:** No. **Propane:** Yes. **Internal Roads:** Dirt, gravel (good). **RV Service:** No. **Market:** North Woodstock, 4 mi. **Restaurant:** No. **General Store:** Yes. **Vending:** No. **Swimming:** Beach. **Playground:** Yes. **Other:** River frontage, beach area, kayak & paddleboat rentals, rec hall, TV/reading room, game room, sports court, tennis court. **Activities:** Swimming, boating, fishing, badminton, tennis, basketball, volleyball. **Nearby Attractions:** Franconia Notch State Park, The Flume, Lost River Gorge, Clark's Trading Post, hiking, biking. **Additional Information:** Lincoln-Woodstock Chamber of Commerce, P.O. Box 358, Kancamagus Hwy., Lincoln, NH 03251, (603) 745-6621; Franconia Notch Chamber of Commerce, P.O. Box 780, Franconia, NH 03580, (800) 237-9007.

RESTRICTIONS

Pets: Must be on a leash, never left unattended. Not allowed in cabins. **Fires:** Grill, stoves, fire rings only. **Alcoholic Beverages:** At site only. **Vehicle Maximum Length:** 32 ft.

TO GET THERE

From I-93, take Exit 32. Go 3.5 mi. west on Hwy. 112; campground is on the left.

NOTTINGHAM   MAP, D-3
Pawtuckaway State Park Campground

128 Mountain Rd., 03290.
T: (603) 895-3031 or (603) 271-3628;
www.nhstateparks.org/parkspages/
pawtuckaway/pawtckcmp.html.

🚐 ★★★   ⛺ ★★★★★

Beauty: ★★★★	Site Privacy: ★★★★
Spaciousness: ★★★★	Quiet: ★★★
Security: ★★★	Cleanliness: ★★★★
Insect Control: ★★★	Facilities: ★★★

This state park gem in the south-central region of New Hampshire is one of our favorite lakeside destinations. Woods and water dominate the scenery and outdoor activities. Hemlock- and oak-forested, primitive-style campsites are clustered on islands dotting pristine Pawtuckaway Lake. Our favorites are the sites on Horse Island (check out sites 16, 41–46, and 67–69 on the island points with great water views), but you can hardly go wrong here—all are spacious and private. This is a popular spot for day visitors; we like that overnight campers have a separate area, removed from the daytime crowds and school and scout groups. There are boat rentals for exploring the lake (fishing is decent, too) and miles of hiking trails. Pack a lunch and head to the top of 908-foot South Mountain, with great views from its summit fire tower. Or walk the Fundy Trail bordering Burnhams Marsh in early morning or evening for a glimpse of beavers, deer, moose, and great herons.

BASICS

Operated By: New Hampshire Division of Parks & Recreation. **Open:** Mid-May–Columbus Day. **Site Assignment:** Reservations suggested by calling Reservation Center (603) 271-3628 Jan.–early Oct.; reservations must be made 7 days in advance, paid in full; 7-day cancellation policy w/ $3 fee; some sites first come, first served; MC, V, D; no personal checks. **Registration:** At office. **Fee:** Most sites, $27; Big Island (inland), $19; based on 2 adults & dependent children under 18. **Parking:** At site, 2 vehicle max.

FACILITIES

Number of RV-only Sites: 19. **Hookups:** None. **Each Site:** Picnic table, fire ring. **Dump Station:** No. **Laundry:** No. **Pay Phone:** Yes. **Restrooms and Showers:** Yes (coin-op). **Fuel:** No. **Propane:** Yes. **Internal Roads:** Dirt, gravel (good). **RV Service:** No. **Market:** Raymond, 4 mi. **Restaurant:** No. **General Store:** Yes. **Vending:** No. **Swimming:** Yes. **Playground:** No. **Other:** Lake frontage, beach, boat rentals, boat launch, hiking trails, group areas. **Activities:** Swimming, hiking, biking, boating, fishing. **Nearby Attractions:** Concord, Manchester, coastal beaches & attractions. **Additional Information:** Greater Concord Chamber of Commerce, 244 North Main St., Concord, NH 03301-5078, (603) 224-2508 or Manchester Chamber of Commerce, 889 Elm St., Manchester, NH 03101, (603) 434-7438.

RESTRICTIONS

Pets: Not permitted. **Fires:** In grill, stoves, fire rings. **Alcoholic Beverages:** At site. **Vehicle Maximum Length:** Varies. **Other:** Quiet hours 10 p.m.–7 a.m.

TO GET THERE

From the junction of Hwy. 101 and Hwy. 107 (Exit 5 in Raymond), go north 3.5 mi. on Hwy. 107, then 0.2 mi. west on Hwy. 27, then 1 mi. north on Hwy. 156; campground is on the left, a few mi. in.

RAYMOND   MAP, D-3
Pine Acres RV Resort

reserve america

74 Freetown Rd., P.O. Box 1017, 03077. T: (603) 895-2519; www.pineacresrecreation.com.

🚐 ★★★★★   ⛺ ★★★★

Beauty: ★★★★	Site Privacy: ★★★
Spaciousness: ★★★	Quiet: ★★★
Security: ★★★★	Cleanliness: ★★★
Insect Control: ★★★	Facilities: ★★★★★

This busy, action-packed campground is a mini-resort, popular with vacationing families. It's within a half-hour's drive to New Hampshire's coastal beaches to the east and the Lakes Region to the north. But why leave? Most campers don't; they stay to play on the on-site waterslides, swim, fish and boat in the pond, order burgers, fries, and sundaes from Big Daddy's snack bar, and join in nonstop activities (think bingo, hayrides, karaoke, crafts, races, contests). This large campground has a natural side, too, as it flanks the pretty Lamprey River. There's a good-sized sandy beach and a wide, still-water section of the river. Most sites are nicely shaded and spaced about 30 feet from one another. Tenters will like sites A1–A4 near the beach. There are cabin and RV rentals on-site.

BASICS

Operated By: Morgan Management. **Open:** Apr. 15–Oct. 28. **Site Assignment:** Reservations recommended; full hookups, 6-night min. July & Aug.; water/electric, 3 night min.; 21-day cancellation policy; full credit for next season or refund (minus $50); less than 21-day notice, no refund, no credit. **Registration:** At office. **Fee:** Full hookup, $41; water/electric, $38; no hookup, $33; weekends & holidays an additional $5 per night; based on family of 5 (2 adults, 3 children). **Parking:** At site, 2 vehicles per site.

FACILITIES

Number of RV-only Sites: 403. **Hookups:** Electric (20, 30, 50 amps), water, sewer. **Each Site:** Picnic table, fire ring. **Dump Station:** Yes. **Laundry:** Yes. **Pay Phone:** Yes. **Restrooms and Showers:** Yes (coin-op). **Fuel:** No. **Propane:** Yes. **Internal Roads:** Paved. **RV Service:** Yes. **Market:** Raymond, 2 mi. **Restaurant:** Yes. **General Store:** Yes. **Vending:** Yes. **Swimming:** Lake. **Playground:** Yes. **Other:** Dual flume waterslide, 18-hole mini-golf, river frontage, beach area, boat rentals, teen rec hall, adult rec hall, trailer & cabin rentals, full-time activities director. **Activities:** Swimming, boating, basketball, horseshoes, softball, volleyball, lake & river fishing, planned activities, special themed weekends. **Nearby Attractions:** Beaches, Portsmouth, Strawbery Banke museum. **Additional Information:** Greater Portsmouth Chamber, P.O. Box 239, Portsmouth, NH 03801, (603) 436-3988; also visit www.seacoastnh.com.

RESTRICTIONS

Pets: Must be on a leash, never left unattended. **Fires:** Grill, stoves, fire rings only. **Alcoholic Beverages:** At site only. **Vehicle Maximum Length:** 40 ft. **Other:** Helmets required for bicycle riders under age 16.

TO GET THERE

From the junction of Hwy. 101 and Hwy. 107/102, go south 1 mi. on Hwy. 107/102; campground is on the left.

RICHMOND   MAP, D-1
Shir-Roy Camping Area

100 Athol Rd., 03470. T: (603) 239-4768; www.ucampnh.com/shir-roy.

🚐 ★★★   ⛺ ★★★★

Beauty: ★★★★	Site Privacy: ★★★
Spaciousness: ★★★	Quiet: ★★★★
Security: ★★★	Cleanliness: ★★★
Insect Control: ★★★	Facilities: ★★★

This woodsy, rustic campground on pretty, 42-acre, spring-fed Wheeler Pond has been around since 1956. The first time we visited, it was a cool summer night (not unusual for New England) and a warm, roaring log fire was burning in the massive fieldstone fireplace in the main building. This is also where the office and recreational room are housed and where the popular campground potluck dinners are held. Walk out the door, and footsteps away is a 200-foot sandy beach, a kiddie playground, and boats to rent. At night, bring a long stick and marshmallows to roast; there are campfires on the beach. Sounds like summer camp, huh? It feels like it, too. This rustic gem always takes us back to nostalgic, carefree summer days of our youth. Today, families return to share a similar experience with their children and grandchildren. Most of the sites are tucked into the woods, scattered in pods behind the recreation area. Only a handful of sites have lake views, but most are only a short walk away from the beach. The most spacious and private sites are in the "R" section, nestled in the northwest corner of the property. Of the campgrounds in the quiet Monadnock region of New Hampshire, this one is our sentimental favorite.

BASICS

Operated By: Shirley Heise. **Open:** May 15–Oct. 15. **Site Assignment:** Reservations suggested, 50% deposit or min. 3-day deposit for holiday weekends; 14-day cancellation notice for return of deposit; cash & personal checks only. **Registration:** At office. **Fee:** Full hookup, $29; electric only, $28; no hookup, $23; based on 1 family (2 adults & unmarried children) per site. **Parking:** At site, 1 vehicle per site.

FACILITIES

Number of RV-only Sites: 106. **Number of Tent-only Sites:** 2. **Hookups:** Electric (20, 30, 50 amps), water, sewer. **Each Site:** Picnic table, fire ring. **Dump Station:** Yes. **Laundry:** Yes. **Pay Phone:** Yes. **Restrooms and Showers:** Yes. **Fuel:** No. **Propane:** No. **Internal Roads:** Gravel, dirt (fair). **RV Service:** No. **Market:** Winchester, 7 mi. **Restaurant:** No. **General Store:** Yes. **Vending:** No. **Swimming:** Lake. **Playground:** Yes. **Other:**

Rec hall, 200 ft. of frontage on spring-fed pond, beach, dock, canoe, rowboat & paddleboat rentals, trailer rentals, group camping area, game room, athletic field. **Activities:** Swimming, fishing, boating, volleyball, horseshoes, potluck suppers, square dancing, holiday events. **Nearby Attractions:** Mount Monadnock, historic towns of Keene, Jaffrey, & Peterborough, covered bridges, hiking, antiquing. **Additional Information:** Greater Keene Chamber of Commerce, 48 Central Square, Keene, NH 03431, (603) 352-1303.

RESTRICTIONS

Pets: Must be on a leash, never left unattended. **Fires:** Grill, stoves, fire rings only. **Alcoholic Beverages:** At site only. **Vehicle Maximum Length:** No limit.

TO GET THERE

From the junction of Hwy. 10 and Hwy. 119 (in Winchester), go 6 mi. east on Hwy. 119, then 0.5 mi. south on Hwy. 32; the campground is on the left.

SOUTH HAMPTON MAP, D-3
Tuxbury Pond Campground

88 Whitehall Rd., 03827. T: (603) 394-7660 or (800) 585-7660; www.tuxburypond.com.

🚐 ★★★★ ⛺ ★★★

Beauty: ★★★★	Site Privacy: ★★★
Spaciousness: ★★★	Quiet: ★★★
Security: ★★★★★	Cleanliness: ★★★★
Insect Control: ★★★	Facilities: ★★★★★

This high-energy, action-packed campground is a magnet for vacationing families and a longtime favorite among repeat summer visitors. Located in the popular Hampton Beach area, there's plenty to do on and off this property. The campground is located on a freshwater pond with swimming, boat rentals, and fishing. There's a boat ramp, too, and some campers bring their own boats in tow. (There's a 40-horsepower limit.) Sports fields, rec rooms, mini-golf, two swimming pools, and a variety of planned activities keep youngsters busy while parents relax. There's even a snack bar on the premises for quick meals and munchies. There are many seasonal sites and lots of big rigs, all for campers drawn to the campground for its many facilities and recreation.

BASICS

Operated By: Robert Peterson. **Open:** May 1–Oct. 15. **Site Assignment:** Seasonal only. **Registration:** At office. **Fee:** Seasonal sites start at $2,550. **Parking:** At site.

FACILITIES

Number of RV-only Sites: 235. **Hookups:** Electric (20, 30, 50 amps), water, sewer, cable TV, modem in office. **Each Site:** Picnic table, fire ring. **Dump Station:** Yes. **Laundry:** Yes. **Pay Phone:** Yes. **Restrooms and Showers:** Yes. **Fuel:** No. **Propane:** Yes. **Internal Roads:** Gravel, dirt (good). **RV Service:** Yes. **Market:** South Hampton, 3 mi. **Restaurant:** Yes. **General Store:** Yes. **Vending:** Yes. **Swimming:** Yes. **Playground:** Yes. **Other:** Pond, beach, boat rentals, game room, rec hall, mini-golf, pavilion, group area, sports fields, snack bar &

restaurant. **Activities:** Swimming, boating, fishing, mini-golf, softball, basketball, volleyball, horseshoes, planned activities. **Nearby Attractions:** Hampton Beach, Massachusetts's North Shore, Portsmouth, coastal beaches. **Additional Information:** Hampton Beach Area Chamber of Commerce, 490 Lafayette Rd., Hampton, NH 03843, (603) 926-8717.

RESTRICTIONS

Pets: Must be on a leash; never left unattended. **Fires:** Grill, camp stoves, fire rings only. **Alcoholic Beverages:** At site only. **Vehicle Maximum Length:** 40 ft.

TO GET THERE

From the junction of I-495 and Hwy. 150 (Exit 54 in Amesbury, MA), go 0.8 mi. north on Hwy. 150, then 0.5 mi. northwest on Highland St., then 1.5 mi. west on Lions Mouth Rd., then 1 mi. north on Newton Rd.; campground is on the left.

TAMWORTH MAP, C-2, C-3
Tamworth Camping Area

Depot Rd., P. O. Box 99, 03886. T: (603) 323-8031 or (800) 274-8031; www.tamworthcamping.com.

🚐 ★★★ ⛺ ★★★★

Beauty: ★★★	Site Privacy: ★★★
Spaciousness: ★★★★	Quiet: ★★★
Security: ★★★★★	Cleanliness: ★★★
Insect Control: ★★★	Facilities: ★★★

This pretty riverside campground has been around since 1967 and keeps on improving. Just 30 minutes from popular North Conway and White Mountain area attractions, the campground is close enough for convenient day trips, yet away from the hustle and bustle. It boasts about 1,900 feet of Swift River frontage and a pretty, sandy-bottom swimming area perfect for fishing, wading, and river tubing. The 18 river sites, with water and electric hookups, are the most spacious and scenic; reserve them early. We especially like sites 8, 10, and 12. Most sites are back-in, but 4 pull-through sites are offered. There's also an open group-tent area, nestled in a meadow filled with blueberries and views of Mount Whittier and the Ossipee Mountains. Families also like the weekend activities that may include arts and crafts, make-your-own-sundae parties, hayrides, and more. Beavers, hawks, and bears may occasionally be spotted by patient and lucky guests.

BASICS

Operated By: Dana & Laurie Bonica. **Open:** May 15–Columbus Day. **Site Assignment:** Reservations suggested; 2-night min. for riverfront sites; 50% deposit, 100% deposit for holiday weekends & motorcycle rally weeks; 14-day cancellation policy w/ $5 fee. MC, V, D, personal checks accepted. **Registration:** At office. **Fee:** Full hookup $38; water/electric $34; water/electric on river, $38; water, $29; no hookup, $27. **Parking:** At site.

FACILITIES

Number of RV-only Sites: 87. **Number of Tent-only Sites:** 13. **Hookups:** Electric (20, 30 amps), water, sewer. **Each Site:** Picnic table, fire ring. **Dump Station:** Yes. **Laundry:** Yes. **Pay Phone:** Yes. **Restrooms and Showers:** Yes (coin-op).

Fuel: No. **Propane:** By weight only. **Internal Roads:** Gravel (good). **RV Service:** No. **Market:** Ossipee, 6 mi. **Restaurant:** No. **General Store:** Yes. **Vending:** No. **Swimming:** River, beach. **Playground:** Yes. **Other:** Rec hall, pavilion, group area, crafts cabin, lending library, 9-hole mini-golf course, sports field, barnyard w/ animals. **Activities:** Swimming, volleyball, basketball, horseshoes, softball, shuffleboard, badminton, fishing, planned activities, including arts & crafts, hayrides, dances, & more. **Nearby Attractions:** Attitash Bear Peak, Weirs Beach, Story Land, Conway Scenic Railroad, North Conway, quick access to White Mountains. **Additional Information:** Greater Conway Village Area Chamber of Commerce, P.O. Box 1019, Conway, NH 03818, (603) 447-2639.

RESTRICTIONS

Pets: Must be on a leash, never left unattended, cleaned up after. **Fires:** Grill, stoves, fire rings only. **Alcoholic Beverages:** In a responsible manner. **Vehicle Maximum Length:** No limit. **Other:** Ask on arrival.

TO GET THERE

From the junction of Hwy. 25 and Hwy. 16, go 0.5 mi. north on Hwy. 16 to Depot Rd., then 3 mi. west; campground is on the left.

TAMWORTH MAP, C-2, C-3
White Lake State Park Campground

Hwy. 16, 03886. T: (603) 323-7350 or (603) 271-3628; www.nhstateparks.org/parkspages/whitelake/whitelakecmp.html.

🚐 ★ ⛺ ★★★★★

Beauty: ★★★★★	Site Privacy: ★★★★
Spaciousness: ★★★★	Quiet: ★★★
Security: ★★★★★	Cleanliness: ★★★★
Insect Control: ★★★	Facilities: ★★

This is New Hampshire's most popular state park and campground for several good reasons. First, there's the lake: gorgeous White Lake, clear, sandy-bottomed, and ringed by picturesque mountains. The state owns all the property you can see surrounding the lake, so there's no development. The shallow, gradually sloping swimming area is popular with families with young children. There's also a lifeguard on duty. The campground sites are rustic (no hookups) but spacious and private, nestled in trees; a handful are on the water. Sites are divided into two separate campground pods, one on each side of the beach and park picnic and day-use area. Both have paths to the large, natural-sand beach. There's also a 2-mile walking trail around the lake through the Pitch Pine National Natural Landmark, one of the most virginal stands of northern pitch pines in North America. The park offers showers, restrooms, and a bathhouse; these are uncommonly nice for state park campground facilities. Only downside: This gets plenty of day-use visitors, so the beach can get crowded.

BASICS

Operated By: New Hampshire Division of Parks & Recreation. **Open:** Mid-May–Columbus Day. **Site Assignment:** Reservations are suggested, but 30 sites are first come, first served; call Reservation Center (603) 271-3628 Jan.–early Oct., Mon.–Fri., or via e-mail, www.nhparks.state.nh.us; payment is due w/in 7 days of making reservation; MC, V accepted. **Registration:** At office. **Fee:** $19; water view, $27; based on 2 adults & children under 18; each additional adult is half the site fee; max. 4 adults per site. **Parking:** At site.

FACILITIES

Number of RV-only Sites: 25. **Hookups:** None. **Each Site:** Picnic table, fire ring. **Dump Station:** Yes. **Laundry:** No. **Pay Phone:** Yes. **Restrooms and Showers:** Yes (coin-op). **Fuel:** No. **Propane:** No. **Internal Roads:** Gravel (good). **RV Service:** No. **Market:** Tamworth, 1 mi. **Restaurant:** Tamworth, 1 mi. **General Store:** Yes. **Vending:** No. **Swimming:** Yes. **Playground:** Yes. **Other:** Lake frontage, beach, lifeguards, kayak, canoe & kayak rentals, playfield, hiking trails. **Activities:** Swimming, hiking, boating, picnicking. **Nearby Attractions:** North Conway, White Mountains, Crawford Notch Scenic Railroad, outlet shopping. **Additional Information:** Greater Conway Village Area Chamber of Commerce, P.O. Box 1019, Conway, NH 03818, (603) 447-2639.

RESTRICTIONS

Pets: Not allowed. **Fires:** Grill, stoves, fire rings only. **Alcoholic Beverages:** At site. **Vehicle Maximum Length:** No limit. **Other:** No loud car stereos.

TO GET THERE

From the junction of Hwy. 16 and Hwy. 25, go north 1.25 mi.; campground is on the left.

TWIN MOUNTAIN   MAP, B-2
Beech Hill Campground and Cabins

970 Hwy. 302 West, P.O. Box 129, 03595.
T: (603) 846-5521; www.beechhill.com.

🚐 ★★★★   ⛺ ★★★★★

Beauty: ★★★★	Site Privacy: ★★★★★
Spaciousness: ★★★★★	Quiet: ★★★★
Security: ★★★★	Cleanliness: ★★★
Insect Control: ★★★	Facilities: ★★★★

We love the spaciousness, privacy, and location of this campground in the White Mountains. Beech Hill caters to folks who like to explore area attractions during the day and return to a lot of elbow room, outdoor scenery, an indoor pool, and planned activities in the evening. The campground is also a favorite with hikers who want to have some of New Hampshire's best trails nearby (including trails to the summit of Mount Washington, New England's highest peak). Each site is surrounded by trees for privacy; the tent-only sites are especially roomy and secluded. Our favorites: sites 26A–26D. But really, you can't go wrong here.

BASICS

Operated By: Jason & Mary Sullivan. **Open:** May 15–Oct. 15. **Site Assignment:** Reservations suggested, 1-night deposit, 10-day cancellation policy; MC, V, personal checks accepted. **Registration:** At office. **Fee:** Full hookup, $38; water/electric, $33; no hookup, $28; based on 2 adults & 3 children under 14. **Parking:** At site.

FACILITIES

Number of RV-only Sites: 93. **Number of Tent-only Sites:** 38. **Hookups:** Electric (15, 30 amps), water, sewer, cable TV. **Each Site:** Picnic table, fire ring. **Dump Station:** Yes. **Laundry:** Yes. **Pay Phone:** Yes. **Restrooms and Showers:** Yes. **Fuel:** No. **Propane:** Yes. **Internal Roads:** Dirt, gravel (good). **RV Service:** No. **Market:** Littleton, 12 mi. **Restaurant:** No. **General Store:** Yes. **Vending:** No. **Swimming:** Yes. **Playground:** Yes. **Other:** Rec hall, game room, hiking trails, cabin rentals. **Activities:** Swimming, basketball, volleyball, planned activities on summer weekends, tubing. **Nearby Attractions:** White Mountains, Franconia Notch State Park, Cannon Mountain Aerial Tram, The Flume, Whale's Tale. **Additional Information:** Franconia Notch Chamber of Commerce, P.O. Box 780, Franconia, NH 03580, (800) 237-9007; also Twin Mountain Chamber of Commerce, (800) 245-TWIN.

RESTRICTIONS

Pets: Must be on a leash, never left unattended. Not allowed in cabins. **Fires:** Grill, stoves, fire rings only. **Alcoholic Beverages:** At site only. **Vehicle Maximum Length:** No limit.

TO GET THERE

From the junction of Hwy. 3 and Hwy. 302, go west 1.8 mi. on Hwy. 302; campground is on the right.

TWIN MOUNTAIN   MAP, B-2
Living Water Campground

100 Hwy. 302 East, P.O. Box 158, 03595.
T: (603) 846-5513; www.livingwatercampground.com.

🚐 ★★★   ⛺ ★★★★

Beauty: ★★★★	Site Privacy: ★★★★
Spaciousness: ★★★	Quiet: ★★★★★
Security: ★★★★★	Cleanliness: ★★★★★
Insect Control: ★★★	Facilities: ★★★

This campground is clean, clean, clean, in more ways than one. "Alcohol-free camping, Experience the Difference!" is their motto, and the owners go the extra mile to ensure a "clean, quiet, family atmosphere." Rules are heavily enforced: absolutely no alcohol, no pets, no radios, no rowdy behavior, quiet time—and they mean quiet—by 10 p.m. "We're only after a niche market, and when they find us, they like it," says owner Jack Catalano. They're very upfront and forward about the rules when taking reservations and when campers check in. If you like a few wine coolers or bottle of ale around the campfire, you better look elsewhere. The calm Twin Mountain campground attracts four-legged guests as well, and the lucky camper may spot deer or beavers. The campground is located in the center of popular White Mountain attractions set along the Ammonoosuc River. Most families head out during the day to explore the area and return in late afternoon to wade in the river, swim in the pool, and watch the sun set over the mountains. Both open, grassy sites and apple-, cherry-, and maple-shaded sites are available; full hookups are clustered in a half-circle behind the office. The most popular sites among guests are those on the riverfront. All sites are back-in.

BASICS

Operated By: Jack Catalano. **Open:** All year. **Site Assignment:** Reservations suggested, 1-night deposit, 48-hour cancellation policy; MC, V, no personal checks. **Registration:** At office. **Fee:** Full hookup, $33; water/electric 30 amps, $33; water/electric 20 amps, $30; no hookup, $28; riverfront site, add $2; based on 2 persons, additional child age 4–11, $1; additional child age 12–17, $2; additional adult, family member, $6. **Parking:** At site. 1 vehicle per site. Additional parking in other lot.

FACILITIES

Number of RV-only Sites: 10. **Number of Tent-only Sites:** 35. **Hookups:** Electric (30 amps), water, sewer. **Each Site:** Picnic table, fire ring. **Dump Station:** Yes. **Laundry:** Yes. **Pay Phone:** No. **Restrooms and Showers:** Yes (coin-op). **Fuel:** Yes. **Propane:** No. **Internal Roads:** Gravel (good). **RV Service:** No. **Market:** Whitefield, 9 mi. **Restaurant:** Yes. **General Store:** Yes. **Vending:** No. **Swimming:** Yes. **Playground:** Yes. **Other:** Rec hall, river frontage, on-site motel. **Activities:** Swimming, fishing, tetherball, basketball, badminton, volleyball, horseshoes. **Nearby Attractions:** White Mountains, Franconia Notch State Park, AML hiking trails. **Additional Information:** Franconia Notch Chamber of Commerce, P.O. Box 780, Franconia, NH 03580, (800) 237-9007; Twin Mountain Chamber of Commerce, (800) 245-TWIN.

RESTRICTIONS

Pets: Not allowed. **Fires:** Grill, stoves, fire rings only. **Alcoholic Beverages:** Not allowed. **Vehicle Maximum Length:** No limit. **Other:** Restrictions strongly enforced: musical instruments & singing must be kept at low volumes & not permitted after 10 p.m. or before 7 a.m.; radios, TVs, CD players, etc. permitted only w/ earphones; minibikes, scooters, ATVs not permitted.

TO GET THERE

From the junction of Hwy. 3 and Hwy. 302, go east 1,000 feet on Hwy. 302; campground is on the right.

TWIN MOUNTAIN   MAP, B-2
Twin Mountain KOA

327 Hwy. 115, P. O. Box 148, 03595.
T: (603) 846-5559 or (800) 562-9117; www.twinmountainkoa.com, www.twinmtnkoa.com.

🚐 ★★★★   ⛺ ★★★

Beauty: ★★★★	Site Privacy: ★★★
Spaciousness: ★★★	Quiet: ★★★★
Security: ★★★	Cleanliness: ★★★★★
Insect Control: ★★★	Facilities: ★★★★

The last time we visited this White Mountain area campground was in the fall, and the surrounding forest of towering pine, poplar, maple, and birch was ablaze with fiery autumn hues. The summit of Mount Washington, visible from our site, had a fresh dusting of powdery white snow. You'll have wonderful mountain views, quick access to outdoor activities (biking, hiking, rock climbing, fishing, boating), and plenty of on-site amenities (swimming pool, planned activities, free movies) at this franchise campground. Most campers explore the surrounding area attractions (check out the popular moose-watching tours in nearby Gorham) before returning to the campground in late afternoon. The facilities and sites are ultraclean, and the atmosphere friendly and relaxed. This site offers 6 pull-through sites and 22 back-ins. For something different, reserve the "kamping kaboose." Where else can you camp in an authentic 19th-century train caboose?

BASICS

Operated By: Barbara & Steve Rabesa. **Open:** May 15–Oct. 15. **Site Assignment:** Reservations suggested; 1-night deposit, holiday weekends paid in full; 7-day cancellation policy w/ $5 fee. MC,V, AE, D. **Registration:** At office. **Fee:** Full hookup, $32–$45; water/electric, $29–$35; no hookup, $24–$35; based on 2 people; additional adult, $6–$10; additional children, ages 3-17, $2–$4. **Parking:** At site; 1 car per site.

FACILITIES

Number of RV-only Sites: 28. **Number of Tent-only Sites:** 16. **Number of Multipurpose Sites:** 25. **Hookups:** Electric (30, 50 amps), water, sewer, cable TV, modem, Wi-Fi. **Each Site:** Picnic table, fire ring. **Dump Station:** Yes. **Laundry:** Yes. **Pay Phone:** Yes. **Restrooms and Showers:** Yes. **Fuel:** No. **Propane:** Yes. **Internal Roads:** Gravel, dirt (good). **RV Service:** No. **Market:** Twin Mountain, 2 mi. **Restaurant:** No. **General Store:** Yes. **Vending:** No. **Swimming:** Yes. **Playground:** Yes. **Other:** Rec hall, amphitheater, nature trails, cabin & caboose rentals, group area. **Activities:** Swimming, hiking, biking, volleyball, badminton, horseshoes. **Nearby Attractions:** Moose tours, fishing, boating, Storyland, Conway Scenic Railroad, Mount Washington Auto Rd. **Additional Information:** Twin Mountain Chamber of Commerce, Twin Mountain, NH 03595, (800) 245-TWIN.

RESTRICTIONS

Pets: Must be on a leash, never left unattended. Pets not allowed in rental units. **Fires:** Grill, stoves, fire rings only. **Alcoholic Beverages:** At site. **Vehicle Maximum Length:** No limit.

TO GET THERE

From the junction of Hwy. 3 and Hwy. 302, go north 2 mi. on Hwy. 3, then north 1 mi. on Hwy. 115; campground is on the right.

TWIN MOUNTAIN   MAP, B-2
Twin Mountain Motor Court and RV Park

554 Hwy. 3 North, P. O. Box 104, 03595.
T: (603) 846-5574 or (800) 332-8946;
www.twinmountainmotorcourtrvpark.com.

🚐 ★★★	🅰 n/a
Beauty: ★★★	Site Privacy: ★★★
Spaciousness: ★★★	Quiet: ★★★★
Security: ★★★	Cleanliness: ★★★★
Insect Control: ★★★	Facilities: ★★★

If you're a self-contained big-rig driver looking for ease and convenience, this campground is a great base when traveling in the White Mountains area. Large 25 by 85–foot sites, all pull-throughs, cater to large RVs; sites are easy to pull in and out of, and all have four-way hookups. Outside, you'll find panoramic views of the mountains, including Mount Washington, Twin Mountains, and Mount Haystack. There's an outdoor swimming pool for a refreshing dip at the end of the day, or head to the Ammon-oosuc River, which flanks the rear of the campground. Bring your fishing rod; the Ammon-oosuc is famous for its elusive trout.

BASICS

Operated By: Roger & Cheryl Gorbich. **Open:** May 1–Nov. 1. **Site Assignment:** Reservations suggested, 7-day cancellation policy for holidays, otherwise 3-day policy; MC,V; personal checks not accepted. **Registration:** At office. **Fee:** Full hookup, $32. **Parking:** At site.

FACILITIES

Number of RV-only Sites: 18. **Hookups:** Electric (30 amps), water, sewer, cable TV, modem. **Each Site:** Picnic table. **Dump Station:** No. **Laundry:** Yes. **Pay Phone:** Emergency phone. **Restrooms and Showers:** No. **Fuel:** No. **Propane:** No. **Internal Roads:** Gravel (good). **RV Service:** No. **Market:** Whitefield, 8 mi. **Restaurant:** No. **General Store:** Yes. **Vending:** Soda. **Swimming:** Yes. **Playground:** Yes. **Other:** River frontage, hiking trails, rec hall, cottage rentals. **Activities:** Swimming, hiking, badminton, horseshoes, basketball, volleyball. **Nearby Attractions:** White Mountains, Franconia Notch State Park, Log Railway. **Additional Information:** Franconia Notch Chamber of Commerce, P.O. Box 780, Franconia, NH 03580, (800) 237-9007; Twin Mountain Chamber of Commerce, (800) 245-TWIN.

RESTRICTIONS

Pets: Must be on a leash, never left unattended, cleaned up after. Pets not allowed in cottages. **Fires:** Allowed in first-come, first-served portable pits. **Alcoholic Beverages:** At site only. **Vehicle Maximum Length:** No limit.

TO GET THERE

From the junction of Hwy. 302 and Hwy. 3, go 1 mi. south on Hwy. 3; campground is on the right.

WARREN   MAP, C-2
Moose Hillock Campground

96 Batchelder Brook Rd., Rte. 118 North, 03279.
T: (603) 764-5294; www.moosehillock.com.

🚐 ★★★★★	🅰 ★★★★★
Beauty: ★★★	Site Privacy: ★★★★★
Spaciousness: ★★★★★	Quiet: ★★★
Security: ★★★	Cleanliness: ★★★★
Insect Control: ★★★	Facilities: ★★★★★

Campers with kids in tow will find everything they need—and more!—at this action-packed, family-friendly campground. This place is always squirming with smiling kids—zipping down the waterslide at the themed "Blue Lagoon" swimming pool, fishing the stocked pond, shooting pool, playing games in the large post-and-beam barn turned rec hall, or joining in the organized games, treasure hunts, and arts-and-crafts activities. Nearby are miles of mountain biking and hiking trails. (Two trails leave right from the campground.) Most families come to stay and play and (for the adventurous) to climb nearby Mount Moosilauke, one of New Hampshire's 4,000-footers. Facilities are top-notch, and most sites are adequately spaced for elbow room and privacy. Families with young children tend to cluster around the lower loop, close to the pool and playground. RVers wanting more privacy and peace and quiet should select one of the very large full-hookup sites that back up to the national forest, where bear and deer have occasionally been spotted. Most RV sites are back-in. Tenters have their own woodsy, private area.

BASICS

Operated By: Ed & Robin Paradis. **Open:** Mid-May–Columbus Day. **Site Assignment:** Reservations suggested; deposit of full amount for stays of 3 days or less, 50% for stays of 1 week or longer; 14-day cancellation policy w/ $5 fee; reservations cancelled 7–14 days prior to scheduled arrival receive 50% of deposit; no refunds for cancellations w/ less than 7-day notice. MC,V, personal checks accepted. **Registration:** At office. **Fee:** Full hookup (midweek), $43; (Fri., Sat. & holidays), $54; water/electric, $39.50–$50.50; no hookup, $33–$44. **Parking:** At site.

FACILITIES

Number of RV-only Sites: 200. **Number of Tent-only Sites:** 20. **Hookups:** Electric (20, 30, 50 amps), water, sewer. For seasonal, cable TV. **Each Site:** Picnic table, fire ring. **Dump Station:** Yes. **Laundry:** Yes. **Pay Phone:** Yes. **Restrooms and Showers:** Yes (coin-op). **Fuel:** No. **Propane:** Yes. **Internal Roads:** Dirt, gravel (fair). **RV Service:** No. **Market:** Warren, 5 mi. **Restaurant:** Yes. **General Store:** Yes. **Vending:** Yes. **Swimming:** Yes. **Playground:** Yes. **Other:** Rec hall, game room, cabin rentals, pavilion, Chapel service, river access, stocked fishing pond, nature trails. **Activities:** Swimming, volleyball, horseshoes, tetherball, basketball, fishing, hiking, planned activities including live entertainment, arts & crafts, contests, socials, & more. **Nearby Attractions:** White Mountains, Franconia Notch State Park, Mount Moosilauke. **Additional Information:** Lincoln-Woodstock Chamber of Commerce, P.O. Box 358, Kancamagus Hwy., Lincoln, NH 03251, (603) 745-6621; also Franconia Notch Chamber of Commerce, P.O. Box 780, Franconia, NH 03580, (800) 237-9007.

RESTRICTIONS

Pets: Must be on a leash, never left unattended. **Fires:** Grill, stoves, fire rings only. **Alcoholic Beverages:** At site only. **Vehicle Maximum Length:** No limit.

TO GET THERE

From I-93, take Exit 26. Go 25 mi. northwest on Hwy. 25 to Hwy. 1·18, then north 1 mi. to campground road; campground is 0.5 mi. ahead.

WEARE
Cold Springs Camp Resort

MAP, D-2

reserve america

62 Barnardhill Rd., 03281. T: (603) 529-2528; www.coldspringscampresort.com.

🚐 ★★★★★   ⛺ ★★★★

Beauty: ★★★	Site Privacy: ★★★
Spaciousness: ★★★	Quiet: ★★★
Security: ★★★★★	Cleanliness: ★★★★★
Insect Control: ★★★	Facilities: ★★★★★

This high-energy, activity-based campground is one of the top choices for families in the southern New Hampshire region. This is primarily a destination campground. Though the mountains to the north and ocean to the east are just an hour-and-a-half drive away, most folks are content to stay put once they've set up camp. They come to Cold Springs for a quick getaway, to relax at their sites, take part in weekend activities, and use the facilities. There really is no need to leave: everything we wanted was right here. The three-pool complex, complete with hot tubs and waterfall, is the action spot at this property. There's an adult-only pool, a family fun pool for all ages, and another for folks six years and older. There's also a beach area along a slow-moving river if you prefer a more natural and tranquil setting. About half the sites located in the back of the campground are taken by seasonal renters. But there are plenty more to choose from if you wish to come for the weekend or week. Sites are fairly uniform in size and appearance. All are set in level, gravel clearings flanked by trees with an average width of about 25 feet. Most sites are back-in, but a few pull-through sites are available. Tenters have few choices, but we liked sites 147 and 148, set in the woods and backing up to a small (often dry in the summer) creek.

BASICS

Operated By: Bob Silva. **Open:** May–early Oct. **Site Assignment:** Reservations suggested, 1-night deposit, holiday stays paid in full, 7-day cancellation policy w/ $20 fee. MC, V, D accepted, no personal checks. **Registration:** At office. **Fee:** Full hookup (w/ cable), $46; full hookup, $44; water/electric, $42; based on 2 people; additional adult, $7; additional children under 16, $3. **Parking:** At site.

FACILITIES

Number of RV-only Sites: 400. **Number of Tent-only Sites:** 10. **Hookups:** Electric (30, 50 amps), water, sewer, cable TV, phone, Wi-Fi. **Each Site:** Picnic table, fire ring. **Dump Station:** Yes. **Laundry:** Yes. **Pay Phone:** Yes. **Restrooms and Showers:** Yes (coin-op). **Fuel:** No. **Propane:** Yes. **Internal Roads:** Paved (good). **RV Service:** Yes. **Market:** Weare, 1 mi. **Restaurant:** Yes. **General Store:** Yes. **Vending:** Yes. **Swimming:** Yes. **Playground:** Yes. **Other:** Hot tubs, river frontage, beach, pavilions, adult, teen & children's rec halls, trailer rentals. **Activities:** Swimming, shuffleboard, basketball, volleyball, horseshoes, planned activities, including children's & adult programs, contests, socials, dances, live entertainment, & more. **Nearby Attractions:** Manchester, Concord, Mall of New Hampshire. **Additional Information:** Man-

chester Chamber of Commerce, 889 Elm St., Manchester, NH 03101, (603) 434-7438.

RESTRICTIONS

Pets: Must be on a leash, never left unattended, cleaned up after. Pets are not allowed in beach area, rental trailers or cabins. **Fires:** Grill, stoves, fire rings only. **Alcoholic Beverages:** Allowed. **Vehicle Maximum Length:** No limit (sites vary).

TO GET THERE

From the junction of Hwy. 149 and Hwy. 114, go southeast 1 mi. on Hwy. 114, then east 0.25 mi. on Barnard Hill Rd.; campground is on the right.

WENTWORTH
Pine Haven Campground

MAP, C-2

Hwy. 25, P.O. Box 43, 03282. T: (603) 786-2900 or (800) 370-PINE; www.pinehavencampground.net.

🚐 ★★★★   ⛺ ★★★★

Beauty: ★★★★	Site Privacy: ★★★★
Spaciousness: ★★★★	Quiet: ★★★
Security: ★★★★	Cleanliness: ★★★★
Insect Control: ★★★	Facilities: ★★★★

If you like the sound of rustling woods and moving waters, you're going to love this pristine campground at the base of the White Mountains. It sits in the quiet and quaint Wentworth area, halfway between popular Lincoln and North Woodstock, with 3,000 feet of frontage on the South Branch of the Baker River. There's a classic river swimming hole for dunks in the clear, cold mountain waters; there's also a heated pool. Families not only flock here for the scenery and clean outdoor living, but also for the daily activities offered throughout July and August. These are moonlight swims, horseshoe tournaments, archery, hayrides, crafts, and more. Sites are spacious and nicely tucked in the woods for privacy. Tenters have choice spots along the river; M5 and M6 are our favorites, as is R1. The campground is popular with climbers who come to scale the giant boulders and rock walls in Rumney.

BASICS

Operated By: Rebele family. **Open:** May 15–Oct. 15. **Site Assignment:** Reservations highly suggested, payment in full for stays of 3 days or less; or 3-day deposit for longer stays; must cancel w/in 14 days of arrival for deposit refund minus $10; 2-night min. July & Aug. **Registration:** At office. **Fee:** Full hookup, $35; water/electric, $33; no hookup, $29; based on 2 adults & their children under 18. **Parking:** At site.

FACILITIES

Number of RV-only Sites: 77. **Number of Tent-only Sites:** 18. **Hookups:** Electric (30, 50 amps), water, sewer, Wi-Fi. **Each Site:** Picnic table, fire ring. **Dump Station:** Yes. **Laundry:** Yes. **Pay Phone:** Yes. **Restrooms and Showers:** Yes. **Fuel:** No. **Propane:** Yes. **Internal Roads:** Dirt, gravel (good). **RV Service:** Down the road, 5 mi. **Market:** Rumney, 5 mi. **Restaurant:** Rumney, 5 mi. **General Store:** Yes. **Vending:** No. **Swimming:** Heated pool. **Playground:** Yes. **Other:** Rec hall, river frontage, river swimming, game room, computer center w/ cable modem access & Wi-Fi. **Activities:** Swimming, boating, full-court basketball, horseshoes, planned activities including arts & crafts, hayrides, moonlight swims,

game nights, softball field. **Nearby Attractions:** Quick access to White Mountains & Lakes Region, hiking, rock climbing, antiquing. **Additional Information:** Baker Valley Tourist Board, www.bakerriver.com.

RESTRICTIONS

Pets: Must be on a leash, never left unattended, no overly aggressive dogs. Must get prior approval. **Fires:** Grill, stoves, fire rings only. **Alcoholic Beverages:** At site only. **Vehicle Maximum Length:** 40 ft.

TO GET THERE

On I-93, take Exit 26. Go 12 mi. west on Hwy. 25; campground is on the left. From I-91 in Vermont, take Exit 15. Take a right off ramp, left onto Hwy. 5, right over bridge to NH, right onto Hwy. 10, left on Hwy. 25A, right on Hwy. 25, 3 mi. to campgrounds.

WENTWORTH
Swain Brook Campground

MAP, C-2

Beech Hill Rd., P.O. Box 157, 03282. T: (603) 764-5537; www.swainbrook.com.

🚐 ★★★★   ⛺ ★★★★★

Beauty: ★★★★★	Site Privacy: ★★★★
Spaciousness: ★★★★	Quiet: ★★★★
Security: ★★★★	Cleanliness: ★★★★
Insect Control: ★★★	Facilities: ★★★★

Nature lovers and outdoor enthusiasts will think they've died and gone to heaven when they check into this modest campground in New Hampshire's quiet countryside. You'll be about 12 miles from a major city (Plymouth to the southeast and Lincoln to the northeast) but at the doorstep of your own private nature preserve. The campground encompasses 417 acres—65 acres of campground and 352 acres of forest, waterfalls, cascades, and swimming holes. There are 4 miles of hiking trails on the property, with mountain vistas, rest areas, and fishing and swimming spots along the way. Swain Brook is the largest of five mountain brooks in the campground, dropping 520 feet in elevation over a 1.6-mile stretch. Elevation on the property ranges from 650 feet to 1,290 feet, so bring your hiking boots—and your fishing pole, as the deep hole at the bottom of Freedom Falls is a favorite with campground anglers. The rustic wilderness sites are our favorites, though RV campers will find a cluster of nicely spaced, shaded back-in sites near the front of the campground.

BASICS

Operated By: Swain Brook Campground, Inc. **Open:** May–Oct. **Site Assignment:** Reservations suggested; 14-day cancellation policy w/ $10 fee. MC, V; no personal checks. **Registration:** At office. **Fee:** Water/electric (on brook), $33; water/electric, $30; no hookup, $30; (on pond or brook), $22; based on 2 adults & 2 children. **Parking:** At site.

FACILITIES

Number of RV-only Sites: 23. **Number of Tent-only Sites:** 30. **Hookups:** Electric (30 amps), water, sewer. **Each Site:** Picnic table, fire pit. **Dump Station:** Yes. **Laundry:** No. **Pay Phone:** Yes. **Restrooms and Showers:** Yes (coin-op). **Fuel:** No. **Propane:** No. **Internal Roads:** Gravel (fair). **RV**

Service: No. **Market:** Warren, 3 mi. **Restaurant:** No. **General Store:** Yes. **Vending:** No. **Swimming:** Wading in brook. **Playground:** Yes. **Other:** Nature park, trails, river & pond frontage, swimming holes, mini-golf, trailer, tent rentals, library, rec hall. **Activities:** Swimming, hiking, biking, mini-golf, horseshoes, tetherball, full-court basketball. **Nearby Attractions:** Lincoln, Plymouth, North Woodstock, Mount Moosilauke, Franconia State Park, Warren Fish Hatchery & Wildlife Center, Norway Pines Speedway, Whale's State Water Park, Appalachian Trail. **Additional Information:** Lincoln-Woodstock Chamber of Commerce, P.O. Box 358, Kancamagus Hwy., Lincoln, NH 03251, (603) 745-6621 or Greater Plymouth Chamber of Commerce, P.O. Box 65, Plymouth, NH 03264, (800) 386-3678.

RESTRICTIONS

Pets: Must be on a leash, never left unattended, cleaned up after. **Fires:** Grill, stoves, fire rings only. **Alcoholic Beverages:** At site only. **Vehicle Maximum Length:** 34 ft. **Other:** No motorcycles allowed. Quiet hours 10 p.m.–8 a.m.

TO GET THERE

From the junction of I-93 and Hwy. 25 (Exit 26), go west 16.5 mi. on Hwy. 25, then west 1 mi. on Beech Hill Rd.; campground is on the left.

WEST OSSIPEE	MAP, C-3
Westward Shores	

110 Nichols Rd., 03890. T: (603) 539-6445; www.wwscamp.com.

🚐 ★★★★   ⛺ ★

Beauty: ★★★	Site Privacy: ★★★
Spaciousness: ★★★	Quiet: ★★★
Security: ★★★★★	Cleanliness: ★★★
Insect Control: ★★★	Facilities: ★★★★

This destination getaway rests on the shores of Ossipee Lake, with 1,800 feet of natural sandy beach and a full-service marina on-site. Watery pleasures—swimming, boating, and fishing—reign here. You'll find all the supplies you need, including a fleet of boats to rent. Fishing for bass, perch, salmon, and trout is a big draw; Lovell River, one of New England's top trout streams, flows into Ossipee Lake. Families like the gradually sloping, sandy swimming area and the planned activities throughout the summer months. There's also a large rec hall for dances, bingo, and socials, and tennis courts (free to campers). This year-round destination welcomes snowmobilers, cross-country skiers, and ice-fishers in the winter. You'll have to reserve early to get a site in the summer; most are taken by seasonal renters, so only about 20 are reserved for overnighters. We especially like this campground in the fall, when the surrounding mountain ranges and valleys are ablaze with color, and the lake is still warm enough to enjoy.

BASICS

Operated By: Charlie Smith. **Open:** All year. **Site Assignment:** Reservations required, 1-night

deposit, 24-hour cancellation policy. MC, V, personal checks accepted. **Registration:** At gatehouse. **Fee:** $40; all sites have full hookup. **Parking:** At site.

FACILITIES

Number of RV-only Sites: 260. **Hookups:** Electric (20, 30 amps), water, sewer, cable TV. **Each Site:** Picnic table, fire ring. **Dump Station:** Yes. **Laundry:** No. **Pay Phone:** Yes. **Restrooms and Showers:** Yes (coin-op). **Fuel:** No. **Propane:** No. **Internal Roads:** Dirt, gravel (good). **RV Service:** No. **Market:** Ossipee, 2 mi. **Restaurant:** No. **General Store:** Yes. **Vending:** No. **Swimming:** Beach. **Playground:** Yes. **Other:** Rec hall, marina, launching ramp, boat slips, lake frontage, private beach, boat rentals (including power boats, Jet skis, pontoons), cabin rentals, game room, tennis courts, pavilion. **Activities:** Swimming, boating, fishing, snowmobiling, ice skating, tennis, basketball, volleyball, planned activities including arts & crafts, children's games, socials. **Nearby Attractions:** North Conway, White Mountains. **Additional Information:** Greater Conway Village Area Chamber of Commerce, P.O. Box 1019, Conway, NH 03818, (603) 447-2639; also Mount Washington Valley Chamber of Commerce, P.O. Box 2300, North Conway, NH 03860, (800) 521-2137.

RESTRICTIONS

Pets: Must be on a leash, never left unattended. **Fires:** Grill, stoves, fire rings only. **Alcoholic Beverages:** At site only. **Vehicle Maximum Length:** 32 ft.

TO GET THERE

From the junction of Hwy. 25 and Hwy. 16, go 8 mi. north on Hwy. 16; campground is on the right.

New Jersey

Though New Jersey is the most densely populated state in the Union with more than 1,000 people per square mile, that figure is misleading. Two-thirds of the population live in the northern section of the state, most within 30 miles of New York City. Much of the Garden State is composed of tree-lined 18th-century towns, more than 800 lakes and ponds, and 100-plus rivers and streams, many of which are bustling with trout. The Jersey Shore includes beautifully preserved **Cape May** and longtime touristy resort areas **Atlantic City** and **Ocean City.**

The shore of the third state stretches about 130 miles from Cape May in the south to **Sandy Hook** in the north. **Avon, Spring Lake, Bay Head,** and **Point Pleasant Beach** are among the resort towns splayed along the coast. The nation's oldest seashore resort, Cape May is surrounded by the **Atlantic Ocean** and **Delaware Bay.** The entire town is a **National Historic Landmark,** with more than 600 Victorian homes and buildings adorning the streets. Cape May has 4 miles of beaches, a 1.5-mile promenade, and a 3-block area dedicated to shopping, dining, and relaxing. There are several guided tours in Cape May that take visitors along the beaches and through historic homes. If you discover a shiny rock on the shores of Delaware Bay, you've most likely got a Cape May diamond; unfortunately, it's not a real diamond but actually pure quartz shaped and polished by the surf. Each year, millions of migratory birds make their way to **Cape May Point State Park,** where the 157-foot **Cape May Lighthouse,** circa 1859, is open for tours.

Even before the casinos opened their doors here in 1977, **Atlantic City** had already made its name as a popular resort. Now it's one of the country's most sought-out destinations, with more than 37 million visitors annually. The boardwalk at Atlantic City was the first structure of its kind; Alexander Boardman commissioned the walkway of wooden planks, originally called Boardman's walk and later shortened to the term "boardwalk." From the **Trump Taj Mahal** and **Trump Plaza** to the **Sands** and **Ballys Park Place,** Atlantic City has a wide selection of casinos and hotels, most of which are located along the boardwalk, complemented by a multitude of restaurants, shops, and dazzling attractions. Highlights include the **Atlantic City Historical Museum** and the amusements on **Steel Pier.** The sparkling $300 million **Atlantic City Convention Center** has a 12,000-room hotel, shops, theaters, and eateries, and plays host to the **Miss America Pageant** every September. Other Atlantic City attractions include **Storybook Land,** an amusement park with more than 50 children's storybook-themed buildings, and **Lucy the Elephant** in Margate, the world's largest pachyderm at six-stories tall. Built in 1881, she is also the world's only elephant-shaped museum declared a National Historic Landmark.

Other Jersey Shore areas include Sandy Hook, home to the **Lifesaving Museum** and **Fort Hancock** and **Sandy Hook Museum;** the **Highlands,** where the twin towers of **Twin Lights Historic Site** were erected in 1862; **Monmouth Park,** the famous thoroughbred race track; and **Ocean Grove,** a town with well-preserved Victorian homes and buildings.

Northern New Jersey is anchored by the old industrial towns of **Hoboken** and **Jersey City,** but a surprising amount of the region is rural. The majority of it lies in the **Skylands,** which includes the **Delaware Water Gap National Recreation Area** and the 7,200-acre **Great Swamp National Wildlife Refuge.** The **Appalachian Trail** passes through the **Delaware Water Gap,** which stretches for 37 miles on both sides of the **Delaware River,** forming the border of New Jersey and Pennsylvania. Though Hoboken and Jersey City are not exactly meccas of tourism, the latter is home to 1,200-acre **Liberty State Park,** which faces the Statue of Liberty and boasts stunning views of lower Manhattan. Central New Jersey sports **Princeton,** home of **Princeton University** and **Princeton Battlefield State Park; Camden,** located across the Delaware River from Philadelphia; **New Brunswick,** where **Rutgers University** is situated; and **Trenton,** the state's gold-domed capital.

In southeast New Jersey, the Pine Barrens include the 100,000-acre **Wharton State Forest,** the 40,000-acre **Edwin B. Forsythe National Wildlife Refuge,** and **Batsto Village,** a restored 19th-century settlement.

Whether it is a date with a one-armed bandit, a trek through a scenic pass, or a spot in the sand you've come for, New Jersey spells it out for you and then some.

Campground Profiles

ABSECON HIGHLANDS MAP. D-2, D-3
Shady Pines Camping Resort

443 South 6th Ave., 08201.
T: (609) 652-1516 or (800) 352-4917;
www.beachcomber.com/nj/camping/atlan/
shadepin.html.

🚐 ★★★★   ▲ n/a

Beauty: ★★★★   Site Privacy: ★★
Spaciousness: ★★   Quiet: ★★★
Security: ★★★★   Cleanliness: ★★★★
Insect Control: ★★★★   Facilities: ★★★★

Every site has a full hookup at Shady Pines Camping Resort, located 6 miles north of Atlantic City's casinos, boardwalk, and beach. As the name implies, sites are shaded by mature pines. The terrain here is flat and sandy, and sites are spacious and level. There are seven pull-through sites available. Campers can rent economy cars at Shady Pines and join the 37 million annual visitors who flock to the row of casinos along the beach. The boardwalk features amusement piers lined with shops, eateries, museums, and entertainment. If you need a break from the ringing of slot machines and the crowds along the boardwalk, head to the Edwin B. Forsythe National Wildlife Refuge, a 40,000-acre sanctuary with interpretive trails and a self-guided driving tour route. As exhilarating as Atlantic City can be, after a while it's a relief to leave the city and surround yourself with the sounds of nature.

BASICS

Operated By: Jay & Carol Waters. **Open:** Mar. 1–Nov. 1. **Site Assignment:** Reservations accepted (7-day notice required for refund), walk-ins accepted. **Registration:** At campground office. **Fee:** $39; V, MC. **Parking:** At site.

FACILITIES

Number of RV-only Sites: 140. **Hookups:** Electric (20, 30 amps), phone. **Each Site:** Fire ring, picnic table. **Dump Station:** Yes. **Laundry:** Yes. **Pay Phone:** Yes. **Restrooms and Showers:** Yes. **Fuel:** No. **Propane:** Yes. **Internal Roads:** Paved, in good condition. **RV Service:** Nearby, 1.5 mi. **Market:** W/in 1 mi. **Restaurant:** W/in 1 mi. **General Store:** No. **Vending:** Yes. **Swimming:** Yes. **Playground:** Yes. **Other:** Rentals cars available. **Activities:** Swimming, shuffleboard, horseshoes, rec hall. **Nearby Attractions:** Atlantic City casinos, boardwalk, & beach. **Additional Information:** Atlantic City Convention Visitors Authority, (800) ACVISIT, www.atlanticcitynj.com.

RESTRICTIONS

Pets: On leash only. **Fires:** At site. **Alcoholic Beverages:** At site. **Vehicle Maximum Length:** 40 ft.

TO GET THERE

From US 9, go 1.5 mi. west on US 30 and 1.5 mi. north on 6th Ave. Entrance is on the left.

ANDOVER MAP, A-2
Panther Lake Camping Resort

6 Panther Lake Rd., 07821. T: (973) 347-4440 or (800) 543-2056; njcamping.com/panther.

🚐 ★★★★   ▲ ★★★★

Beauty: ★★★★   Site Privacy: ★
Spaciousness: ★★   Quiet: ★★★
Security: ★★★★   Cleanliness: ★★★★
Insect Control: ★★★★   Facilities: ★★★★

The 45-acre Panther Lake is the centerpiece of Panther Lake Camping Resort in northern New Jersey. The 160-acre campground is adorned with forests and meadows on the rolling hills of the New Jersey Skylands region, so there are open and wooded sites, including 300 full hookups. The lake, complete with sandy beach, is situated on the southwest side of the campground, while the pond and swimming pool are in the southeast section. Clusters of sites are located along and near both areas as well as between the two. An adults-only whirlpool is located next to the swimming pool. The 70,000-acre Delaware Water Gap National Recreation Area and the 7,000-acre Great Swamp National Wildlife Refuge offer excellent hiking, fishing, boating, and other recreational opportunities. A day trip to New York City is feasible from Panther Lake; the Big Apple is about a 1.5-hour drive east.

BASICS

Operated By: Private operator. **Open:** Apr. 1–Nov. 1. **Site Assignment:** Reservations & walk-ins accepted. **Registration:** At campground office. **Fee:** Daily, $35; weekly, $30–$48; V, MC. **Parking:** At site.

FACILITIES

Number of RV-only Sites: 400. **Number of Tent-only Sites:** 35. **Hookups:** Electric (15, 20, 30 amps), water, cable TV. **Each Site:** Picnic table, fire ring. **Dump Station:** Yes. **Laundry:** Yes. **Pay Phone:** Yes. **Restrooms and Showers:** Yes. **Fuel:** No. **Propane:** Yes. **Internal Roads:** Gravel & paved, in good condition. **RV Service:** No. **Market:** W/in 5 mi. **Restaurant:** W/in 3 mi. **General Store:** Yes. **Vending:** Yes. **Swimming:** Yes. **Playground:** Yes. **Other:** Panther Lake. **Activities:** Lake swimming, lake & pond fishing, boating, canoeing, boat rentals, mini-golf, rec hall, game room, shuffleboard, tennis, planned activities on weekends, horseshoes, volleyball. **Nearby Attractions:** Delaware Water Gap National Recreation Area, Great Swamp National Wildlife Refuge, Duke Gardens, Lakota Wolf Preserve, Space Farms Zoo & Museum. **Additional Information:** Skylands Tourism Council of New Jersey, (800) 4SKYLAND, www.state.nj.us/travel.

RESTRICTIONS

Pets: On leash only. **Fires:** At site only. **Alcoholic Beverages:** At site only. **Vehicle Maximum Length:** 40 ft. **Other:** Check-in & check-out time is 2 p.m.

TO GET THERE

From CR 517, go 1.5 mi. south on US 206. Entrance is on the left.

BAYVILLE MAP, C-3
Cedar Creek Campground

1052 Hwy. 9, 08721. T: (732) 269-1413; www.cedarcreeknj.com.

🚐 ★★★★   ▲ ★★★★

Beauty: ★★★★   Site Privacy: ★★★
Spaciousness: ★★★   Quiet: ★★★★
Security: ★★★★   Cleanliness: ★★★★
Insect Control: ★★★★   Facilities: ★★★★

Located on the eastern side of central New Jersey, Cedar Creek Campground is close to both the Atlantic Ocean and the Pine Barrens—home to one million acres of pine forests. Of course, location is not the only amenity at Cedar Creek. The campground has an on-site canoe livery, and there are guided canoe and kayak excursions on Barnegat Bay and along Cedar Creek. Wooded sites on sandy terrain are spacious. There are 20 pull-throughs and 100 full-hookup sites. Island Beach State Park is a short drive away across Barnegat Bay. The park is situated along the Atlantic Ocean and features 1,900 acres of sand dunes, saltwater marshes, and freshwater bogs. A canoe float on Barnegat Bay and Cedar Creek, a hike at Island Beach State Park, and a drive through the Pine Barrens will change your impression of New Jersey for the better.

BASICS

Operated By: Debra Fleming. **Open:** All year. **Site Assignment:** Reservations recommended, walk-ins accepted. **Registration:** At campground office. **Fee:** RV, $38–$49; tent, $32–$42; trailer, $135; cabin, $125; V, MC. **Parking:** At site.

FACILITIES

Number of RV-only Sites: 220. **Number of Tent-only Sites:** 45. **Hookups:** Electric (20, 30, 50 amps), water, phone. **Each Site:** Fire ring, picnic table. **Dump Station:** Yes. **Laundry:** Yes. **Pay Phone:** Yes. **Restrooms and Showers:** Yes. **Fuel:** No. **Propane:** Yes. **Internal Roads:** Gravel & paved, in good condition. **RV Service:** No. **Market:** W/in 2 mi. **Restaurant:** W/in 2 mi. **General Store:** Yes. **Vending:** Yes. **Swimming:** Yes. **Playground:** Yes. **Other:** Cabin & RV rentals. **Activities:** Canoeing, kayaking, planned activities on weekends, game room, rec hall, badminton, horseshoes, volleyball. **Nearby Attractions:** Island Beach State Park, Toms River, Barnegat Light Museum, Deep Cut Gardens, Six Flags Great Adventure & Wild Safari, Longstreet Farm, Point Pleasant Beach. **Additional Information:** Shore Region Tourism Council, (732) 544-9300, www.state.nj.us/travel.

RESTRICTIONS

Pets: On leash only. **Fires:** At site. **Alcoholic Beverages:** At site. **Vehicle Maximum Length:** No limit. **Other:** Pets may not be left unattended.

TO GET THERE

From Garden State Pkwy., take Exit 80 and go 5 mi. south on US 9. Follow signs to entrance.

BRANCHVILLE   MAP, A-2
Harmony Ridge Campground

23 Risdon Dr., 07826. T: (973) 948-4941;
www.harmonyridge.com.

🚐 ★★★   ▲ ★★★★

Beauty: ★★★★   Site Privacy: ★★★
Spaciousness: ★★★   Quiet: ★★★★
Security: ★★★★   Cleanliness: ★★★★★
Insect Control: ★★★★   Facilities: ★★★

Perched in the Kittatiny Mountains in northern New Jersey, the 160-acre Harmony Ridge Campground includes colorful flower gardens, three lakes, and several hiking trails. Chances are you will see a deer, wild turkey, raccoon, or bald eagle—or maybe a few of each. Some sites are clustered around the three lakes, including island sites in the center of the eastern lake. Tent sites are located on the western side of the campground. The office resembles an old-fashioned barn, complete with antique farm tools. The volleyball court is lined with sand brought from Cape May. The Space Wild Animal Farm and Museum is located about 10 miles north in Sussex. Here, you will find a zoo and a village of buildings stocked with historic exhibits, including antique cars, motorcycles, carriages, and wagons.

BASICS
Operated By: Ed Risdon. **Open:** All year. **Site Assignment:** Reservations accepted (cancellations w/ at least 72-hour notice will receive credit valid for 1 year depending on availability), walk-ins accepted. **Registration:** At campground office. **Fee:** $15/night per person; V, MC, AE. **Parking:** At site.

FACILITIES
Number of RV-only Sites: 225. **Number of Tent-only Sites:** 50. **Hookups:** Electric (20, 30 amps), water. **Each Site:** Stone fireplace. **Dump Station:** Yes. **Laundry:** Yes. **Pay Phone:** Yes. **Restrooms and Showers:** Yes. **Fuel:** No. **Propane:** Yes. **Internal Roads:** Gravel, in fair condition. **RV Service:** Yes, limited. **Market:** W/in 2 mi. **Restaurant:** W/in 2 mi. **General Store:** Yes. **Vending:** Yes. **Swimming:** Yes. **Playground:** Yes. **Other:** Pond. **Activities:** Pond swimming & fishing, game room, mini-golf, basketball, shuffleboard, badminton, volleyball, horseshoes, hiking trails, rec hall. **Nearby Attractions:** Appalachian Trail, Waterloo Village, Delaware Water Gap National Recreation Area, Space Wild Animal Farm & Museum, High Point State Park, Stokes State Forest, Kittatiny Mountains. **Additional Information:** Skylands Tourism Council of New Jersey, (800) 4SKYLAND, www.state.nj.us/travel.

RESTRICTIONS
Pets: On leash only, under control. **Fires:** At site. **Alcoholic Beverages:** At site. **Vehicle Maximum Length:** No limit.

TO GET THERE
From CR 521, go 0.5 mi. north on US 206, 2 mi. east and south on CR 636, and 1 mi. east on Mattison Reservoir Ave. Entrance is on the left.

BRANCHVILLE   MAP, A-2
Kymer's Camping Resort

69 Kymer Rd., 07826. T: (973) 875-3167 (office) or (800) 526-2267 (reservations); www.njcamping.com.

🚐 ★★★★   ▲ ★★★★

Beauty: ★★★★   Site Privacy: ★★
Spaciousness: ★★★   Quiet: ★★★★
Security: ★★★★   Cleanliness: ★★★★
Insect Control: ★★★★   Facilities: ★★★★

Like Harmony Ridge Campground, Kymer's Camping Resort is nestled in the Kittatiny Mountains, close to the Appalachian Trail. The 200-acre campground is similar in size to Harmony Ridge, and both places offer similar amenities and clean facilities. While Harmony Ridge has waterfront sites on three lakes, Kymer's has a lake with no waterfront sites. What Kymer's does have is a vast menu of recreational opportunities, including mini-golf, tennis, and basketball. On weekends, Kymer's is often the scene of special events such as bingo and country and western music entertainment. Most full-hookup sites are situated at the north end of the campground, while a small cluster of sites is located in the center. The group of sites with water and electric hookups on the western side is secluded from the rest of the campground; these sites are near the lake, swimming pool, store, and most activity centers. For outdoor adventure, nearby Stokes State Forest is located on the Kittatiny Ridge. The mountain view is spectacular from Sunrise Mountain, and the natural gorge Tillman Ravine can be found in the southern part of the forest.

BASICS
Operated By: Kymer family. **Open:** Apr. 1–Oct. 31. **Site Assignment:** Reservations accepted (2-night min.), walk-ins accepted. **Registration:** At campground office. **Fee:** $34; V, MC. **Parking:** At site.

FACILITIES
Number of RV-only Sites: 250. **Hookups:** Electric (20, 30 amps), water. **Each Site:** Picnic table, fire ring. **Dump Station:** Yes. **Laundry:** Yes. **Pay Phone:** Yes. **Restrooms and Showers:** Yes. **Fuel:** No. **Propane:** No. **Internal Roads:** Gravel & paved, in good condition. **RV Service:** No. **Market:** W/in 5 mi. **Restaurant:** W/in 5 mi. **General Store:** Yes. **Vending:** Yes. **Swimming:** Yes. **Playground:** Yes. **Other:** Pond. **Activities:** Fishing, rec hall, game room, swimming, mini-golf, planned activities on weekends, tennis, basketball, sports field, horseshoes, volleyball. **Nearby Attractions:** Waterloo Village, Appalachian Trail, High Point State Park & Franklin Mineral Museum, Delaware Water Gap National Recreation Area, Space Wild Animal Farm & Museum, Stokes State Forest, Kittatiny Mountains. **Additional Information:** Skylands Tourism Council of New Jersey, (800) 4SKYLAND, www.state.nj.us/travel.

RESTRICTIONS
Pets: On leash only. **Fires:** At site. **Alcoholic Beverages:** At site. **Vehicle Maximum Length:** 35 ft. **Other:** Quiet time 11 p.m.–7 a.m.

TO GET THERE
From I-80, take Exit 34B and go 16 mi. north on SR 15, 2 mi. north on SR 206, 5 mi. northeast on CR 519, and 1 mi. west on Kymer Rd. Entrance is on the right.

BUENA   MAP, C-2
Buena Vista Camping Park

775 Harding Hwy., 08310. T: (856) 697-5555; www.bvcp.com.

🚐 ★★★★   ▲ ★★★★

Beauty: ★★★★   Site Privacy: ★
Spaciousness: ★★   Quiet: ★★★
Security: ★★★★★   Cleanliness: ★★★★
Insect Control: ★★★★   Facilities: ★★★★

Centrally located between Atlantic City and Philadelphia, Buena Vista Camping Park is a place that kids—and kids at heart—will not want to leave. In addition to a miniature zoo with exotic animals, the 175-acre campground features a 40-foot double waterslide, a spacious swimming pool, a kiddie pool, and a mini-golf course. Just those would keep most children entertained, but Buena Vista offers much more for families. An amusement area features child-friendly carnival rides, a trampoline, and a 30-foot "dry" slide. Admission is free at the campground's antique museum, which is stocked with old cars, farm equipment, and artifacts. Most sites provide little privacy, but they are situated under mature woodlands, so there is plenty of shade on sticky summer days. Seventy pull-through sites are available. Buena Vista's variety of fun things for the family to do compensate for the lack of privacy the sites offer. Buena Vista is located about 30 miles northwest of Atlantic City—away from the crowds, but close enough if boardwalk excitement is your goal.

BASICS
Operated By: Morgan Management. **Open:** All year. **Site Assignment:** Reservations & walk-ins accepted. **Registration:** At campground office. **Fee:** $41–$43; cabin, $75–$95; vinyl suite, $99–$109; cabin suite, $109–$119; V, MC, personal check. **Parking:** At site.

FACILITIES
Number of RV-only Sites: 700. **Hookups:** Electric (20, 30, 50 amps), water, phone. **Each Site:** Fire ring, picnic table. **Dump Station:** Yes. **Laundry:** Yes. **Pay Phone:** Yes. **Restrooms and Showers:** Yes. **Fuel:** No. **Propane:** Yes. **Internal Roads:** Gravel & paved, in good condition. **RV Service:** No. **Market:** W/in 4 mi. **Restaurant:** W/in 4 mi. **General Store:** Yes. **Vending:** Yes. **Swimming:** Yes. **Playground:** Yes. **Other:** Waterslide, cabin rentals. **Activities:** Wading pool, lake swimming, boat rentals, pond fishing, mini-golf, zoo, basketball, shuffleboard, game room, rec hall, movies, sports field, hiking trails, volleyball. **Nearby Attractions:** Atlantic City, Ocean City, Cape May, Philadelphia. **Additional Information:** Greater Atlantic City Region Tourism, (609) 652-7777, www.state.nj.us/travel.

RESTRICTIONS
Pets: On leash only. **Fires:** At site. **Alcoholic Beverages:** At site. **Vehicle Maximum Length:** 40 ft.

TO GET THERE

From Hwy. 54, go 0.1 mi. east on Hwy. 40. Entrance is on the left.

CAPE MAY   MAP, D-2
Beachcomber Camping Resort

reserve america

462 Seashore Rd., 08204.
T: (609) 886-6035 or (800) 233-0150
(reservations); www.reserveamerica.com or
www.beachbercamp.com.

🚐 ★★★★★   ⛺ ★★★★★

Beauty: ★★★★   Site Privacy: ★★
Spaciousness: ★★   Quiet: ★★★
Security: ★★★★★   Cleanliness: ★★★★★
Insect Control: ★★★★   Facilities: ★★★★★

Four miles north of Cape May, and the same distance south of Wildwoods, Beachcomber is the premier park in southern New Jersey. On the New Jersey Cape, Beachcomber has two spring-fed lakes for fishing and swimming, three adult pools, and three kiddie pools. An adults-only clubhouse, playground, and two Laundromats are some of the other amenities. Site offerings range from water and electric hookups for pop-up campers and tents to the "Ultra VIP" site area, which accommodates RVs up to 48 feet long and includes full hookups, a concrete pad, a lamp post, and a fence. These sites are close to the resort's central activity hub. All sites are back-in. Classic car and motorcycle shows and remote-controlled boat and dune buggy races are among the events hosted here.

BASICS

Operated By: Brodesser family. **Open:** Apr. 15–Oct. 1. **Site Assignment:** Reservations recommended (3-day min. July & Aug. & on holiday weekends), walk-ins accepted. **Registration:** At campground office. **Fee:** $21–$51; V, MC, D. Check Web site for details. **Parking:** At site.

FACILITIES

Number of RV-only Sites: 530. **Number of Tent-only Sites:** 60. **Hookups:** Electric (30, 50, 100 amps), water, cable TV, phone. **Each Site:** Fire ring, picnic table, electric, water. **Dump Station:** No. **Laundry:** Yes. **Pay Phone:** Yes. **Restrooms and Showers:** Yes. **Fuel:** No. **Propane:** Yes. **Internal Roads:** Gravel & paved, in good condition. **RV Service:** No. **Market:** W/in 1.5 mi. **Restaurant:** W/in 1.5 mi. **General Store:** Yes. **Vending:** Yes. **Swimming:** Yes. **Playground:** Yes. **Other:** Private lake, lakefront & wilderness cabin rentals, wireless Internet access, golf-cart rentals, paddleboat rentals. **Activities:** Lake swimming & fishing, boat rentals, wading pool, 3 swimming pools, basketball, shuffleboard, planned activities, movies, horseshoes, volleyball, game room, rec hall, kayaking. **Nearby Attractions:** Historic Cape May boat & walking tours, Victorian Cape May, Point Lighthouse & Park, Cold Spring Village, Cape May beaches, Wildwood amusement parks, Cape May County Park & Zoo, Cape May–Lewes (DE) Ferry, Atlantic City. **Additional Information:** Cape May County Chamber, (609) 884-9562, www.capemaycountychamber.com.

RESTRICTIONS

Pets: On leash only, I pet per site. **Fires:** At site. **Alcoholic Beverages:** Not permitted at campground. **Vehicle Maximum Length:** 48 ft. **Other:** Pets may not be left unattended.

TO GET THERE

From Hwy. 47, go 1 mi. south on US 9 and follow signs to entrance, which is on the left.

CAPE MAY   MAP, D-2
Cape Island Resort

709 Hwy. 9, 08204. T: (800) 437-7443 or
(609) 884-5777; www.capeisland.com.

🚐 ★★★★   ⛺ ★★★★

Beauty: ★★★★   Site Privacy: ★★★★
Spaciousness: ★★★   Quiet: ★★★★
Security: ★★★★★   Cleanliness: ★★★★★
Insect Control: ★★★★   Facilities: ★★★★

Cape Island Campground has 475 sites situated on 175 acres; many of these sites are separated by shrubbery, so campers have plenty of privacy. Few parks in southern New Jersey offer as much privacy as Cape Island. Overall, there are 310 full hookups and 17 pull-throughs. Since Cape May is a major tourist destination, parking can be a hassle at many of the attractions. The Cape May Seashore Line Railroad, which has a stop across from the campground, transports passengers from Cape May Court House across the Cape May Canal to the city of Cape May. Cape Island is also across the street from Cold Spring Historic Village, a replica circa-1870 living farm village. Cape May Point Lighthouse is also nearby, as are the beaches. The Cape May–Lewes (DE) Ferry takes passengers on a 16-mile, 70-minute voyage across Delaware Bay. Be sure to take your Dramamine before embarking if oceangoing travel makes you sick. Believe us, you will not regret it.

BASICS

Operated By: Private operator. **Open:** May 1–Nov. 1. **Site Assignment:** Reservations recommended, walk-ins accepted. **Registration:** At campground office. **Fee:** $26–$38; V, MC. **Parking:** At site.

FACILITIES

Number of RV-only Sites: 455. **Number of Tent-only Sites:** 20. **Hookups:** Electric (20, 30 amps), water, phone. **Each Site:** Picnic table, fire ring. **Dump Station:** Yes. **Laundry:** Yes. **Pay Phone:** Yes. **Restrooms and Showers:** Yes. **Fuel:** No. **Propane:** Yes. **Internal Roads:** Gravel, in good condition. **RV Service:** Yes. **Market:** W/in 0.5 mi. **Restaurant:** W/in 0.25 mi. **General Store:** Yes. **Vending:** Yes. **Swimming:** Yes. **Playground:** Yes. **Other:** Pavilion. **Activities:** Game room, rec hall, swimming, wading pool, mini-golf, basketball, shuffleboard, planned activities, tennis, horseshoes, sports field, volleyball. **Nearby Attractions:** Historic Cape May boat & walking tours, Victorian Cape May, Point Lighthouse & Park, Cold Spring Village, Cape May beaches, Wildwood amusement parks, Cape May County Park & Zoo, Cape May–Lewes (DE) Ferry, Atlantic City. **Additional Information:** Cape May Chamber of Commerce, (609) 884-9562, www.capemaychamber.com.

RESTRICTIONS

Pets: On leash only. **Fires:** At site. **Alcoholic Beverages:** At site. **Vehicle Maximum Length:** No limit. **Other:** Pets may not be left unattended.

TO GET THERE

From Hwy. 109, go 0.5 mi. north on US 9. Entrance is on the right.

CAPE MAY   MAP, D-2
Holly Shores Campground and RV Resort

reserve america

491 Hwy. 9, 08204. T: (609) 886-1234 or
(877) 49-HOLLY; www.hollyshores.com.

🚐 ★★★★   ⛺ ★★★★

Beauty: ★★★★   Site Privacy: ★
Spaciousness: ★★   Quiet: ★★★
Security: ★★★★   Cleanliness: ★★★★
Insect Control: ★★★★   Facilities: ★★★★

Holly Shores is situated between Cape May and the Wildwoods. Along with lots of recreational activities, the campground has a full menu of themed weekends and special events throughout the season, including our favorite—the Gilligan's Island Survivor's Weekend, when campers dress as their favorite character. Call us old-fashioned, but we prefer Mary Ann over Ginger. Keep in mind that the swimming pool area, store, game room, and basketball courts are at the southern end, while the tennis, volleyball, and bocce ball courts, as well as the nature trail, are at the northern end. Sites along the pool loop are ideal if you prefer to be near most of the activity centers. Maples and pines shade some sites, and raccoons have been seen here. The campground has 181 full hookups but no pull-throughs. Cape May Point Lighthouse and Victorian Cape May are among our favorite attractions in the area, about 4 miles south of Holly Shores.

BASICS

Operated By: Robinson family. **Open:** Apr. 14–Oct. 31. **Site Assignment:** Reservations accepted (stay 6 nights, get 7th night free), walk-ins accepted. **Registration:** At campground office. **Fee:** Call or visit Web site for pricing details. **Parking:** At site.

FACILITIES

Number of RV-only Sites: 300. **Hookups:** Electric (20, 30, 50 amps), water, sewer, cable TV; 181 full hookups. **Each Site:** Fire ring, picnic table. **Dump Station:** Yes. **Laundry:** Yes. **Pay Phone:** Yes. **Restrooms and Showers:** Yes. **Fuel:** No. **Propane:** Yes. **Internal Roads:** Paved, in good condition. **RV Service:** No. **Market:** W/in 2 mi. **Restaurant:** W/in 2 mi. **General Store:** Yes. **Vending:** Yes. **Swimming:** Yes. **Playground:** Yes. **Other:** Shuffleboard courts are lighted. **Activities:** Swimming, wading pool, whirlpool, game room, rec hall, shuffleboard, tennis, planned activities, movies, horseshoes, hiking trails, sports field, volleyball, basketball. **Nearby Attractions:** Historic Cape May boat & walking tours, Victorian Cape May, Point Lighthouse & Park, Cold Spring Village, Cape May beaches, Wildwood amusement parks, Cape May

County Park & Zoo, Cape May–Lewes (DE) Ferry, Atlantic City. **Additional Information:** Cape May Chamber of Commerce, (609) 884-9562, www.capemaychamber.com.

RESTRICTIONS

Pets: On leash only. **Fires:** At site. **Alcoholic Beverages:** At site. **Vehicle Maximum Length:** 50 ft. **Other:** Pets may not be left unattended.

TO GET THERE

From Hwy. 47, go 1.25 mi. south on US 9. Entrance is on the left.

CAPE MAY MAP, D-2
Seashore Campsites

reserve america

720 Seashore Rd., 08204. T: (609) 884-4010 or (800) 313-2267; www.reserveamerica.com.

🚐 ★★★★ ⛺ ★★★★

Beauty: ★★★★	Site Privacy: ★
Spaciousness: ★★	Quiet: ★★★
Security: ★★★★	Cleanliness: ★★★★
Insect Control: ★★★★	Facilities: ★★★★

Wooded sites, a heated pool, and a filtered lake solely for swimming are among the features of Seashore Campsites, located close to the beaches in Cape May. Seashore has its own beach at the lake; the campground is open all year, but facilities are only fully operational April 15 to October 31. Like most campgrounds in the Cape May area, July and August are the busiest months at Seashore. Three-night stays are required during this time. If you do not like crowds but want to see Cape May during warmer months, consider visiting in June or September. The restored homes of Victorian Cape May are nearby, and there are several tours that detail the history behind these homes. Cold Spring Village, another attraction close to the campground, re-creates an 1870 south Jersey farm village, where blacksmiths, weavers, potters, broom makers, and bakers ply their trades.

BASICS

Operated By: Private operator. **Open:** Apr. 15–Oct. 31. **Site Assignment:** Reservations accepted (recommended July & Aug., when there is 3-night min.), walk-ins accepted. **Registration:** At campground office. **Fee:** Apr. 15–30, $20; Apr. 30–May 26, $24–$28; May 26–29, $37–$44; May 29–June 16, $24–$28; June 16–Sept. 4, $37–$44; Sept. 4–Oct. 16, $24–$28; Oct. 16–Oct. 31, $20. **Parking:** At site.

FACILITIES

Number of RV-only Sites: 632. **Number of Tent-only Sites:** 68. **Hookups:** Electric (20, 30, 50 amps), water, cable TV. **Each Site:** Fire ring, picnic table. **Dump Station:** Yes. **Laundry:** Yes. **Pay Phone:** Yes. **Restrooms and Showers:** Yes. **Fuel:** No. **Propane:** Yes. **Internal Roads:** Paved, in good condition. **RV Service:** No. **Market:** W/in 1 mi. **Restaurant:** W/in 1 mi. **General Store:** Yes. **Vending:** No. **Swimming:** Yes. **Playground:** Yes. **Other:** Filtered swimming lake. **Activities:** Tennis, basketball, lake swimming, waterslide, mini-golf, badminton, horseshoes, volleyball, rec halls, shuffleboard, planned activi-

ties, movies, game room. **Nearby Attractions:** Cape May boat & walking tours, Point Lighthouse & Park, Cold Spring Village, beaches, amusement parks, Cape May County Park & Zoo, Cape May–Lewes (DE) Ferry, Atlantic City. **Additional Information:** Cape May Chamber, (609) 884-9562, www.capemaychamber.com.

RESTRICTIONS

Pets: On leash. Proof of shots required for pets. **Fires:** At site. **Alcoholic Beverages:** Not allowed. **Vehicle Maximum Length:** 40 ft.

TO GET THERE

From Hwy. 47, go 3 mi. south on US 9, 0.1 mi. west over train tracks and 0.1 mi. north on Hwy. 626. Entrance is on the left.

CAPE MAY MAP. D-2
COURT HOUSE
Big Timber Lake Family Camping Resort

reserve america

116 Swainton-Goshen Rd., P. O. Box 366, 08210. T: (609) 465-4456 or (800) 542-CAMP; www.reserveamerica.com or www.bigtimberlake.com.

🚐 ★★★★ ⛺ ★★★★

Beauty: ★★★★	Site Privacy: ★★
Spaciousness: ★★	Quiet: ★★★
Security: ★★★★	Cleanliness: ★★★★
Insect Control: ★★★★	Facilities: ★★★★

Two freshwater lakes—one for swimming and the other for fishing—adorn the grounds of Big Timber Lake Family Camping Resort, located in Cape May Court House near the ocean beaches. Only one family is allowed to stay at each site. A small cluster of full-hookup sites are situated along the southwestern end of the swimming lake. The fishing lake, which is just north of the swimming lake, borders the basketball, shuffleboard, and bocce ball courts, as well as the horseshoe pits. Though no sites are directly on the fishing lake, several sites are within sight of it. Located northwest of Cape May, Cape May Court House is home to the Cape May County Park and Zoo. The town, like Cape May, has its share of immaculate Victorian-style homes. The nearby Leaming's Run Gardens has 20 acres of lush lawns, ponds, and gardens, each with a different theme.

BASICS

Operated By: Menz family. **Open:** Apr. 15–Oct. 15. **Site Assignment:** Reservations accepted (deposit required to hold site), walk-ins accepted. **Registration:** At campground office. **Fee:** $38.25–$53; V, MC, D. **Parking:** At site.

FACILITIES

Number of RV-only Sites: 515. **Number of Tent-only Sites:** 100. **Hookups:** Electric (20, 30, 50 amps), water, cable TV, phone. **Each Site:** Fire ring, picnic table. **Dump Station:** Yes. **Laundry:** Yes. **Pay Phone:** Yes. **Restrooms and Showers:** Yes. **Fuel:** No. **Propane:** Yes. **Internal Roads:** Gravel & paved, in good condition. **RV Service:** No. **Market:** W/in 2 mi. **Restaurant:** W/in 2 mi. **General Store:** Yes.

Vending: Yes. **Swimming:** No. **Playground:** Yes. **Other:** Cabin rentals, fishing pond, RV rentals. **Activities:** Pond fishing, game room, mini-golf, sports field, rec hall, basketball, shuffleboard, movies, volleyball, badminton. **Nearby Attractions:** Cape May County Historical Museum, Cape May County Park & Zoo, Leaming's Run Gardens, Historic Cape May boat & walking tours, Victorian Cape May, Point Lighthouse & Park, Cold Spring Village, Cape May beaches, Wildwood amusement parks, Cape May–Lewes (DE) Ferry, Atlantic City. **Additional Information:** Cape May County Chamber of Commerce, (609) 465-7181, www.cmccofc.com.

RESTRICTIONS

Pets: On leash only. **Fires:** At site. **Alcoholic Beverages:** At site. **Vehicle Maximum Length:** No limit. **Other:** No guests permitted after 10 p.m. unless prior arrangement is made w/ office.

TO GET THERE

From Garden State Pkwy., take Exit 13 and go 0.5 mi. west, 1 mi. south on US 9, and 1 mi. west on CR 646. Entrance is on the right.

CAPE MAY MAP. D-2
COURT HOUSE
Hidden Acres Campground

1142 West Hwy. 83, 08210. T: (609) 624-9015 or (800) 874-7576; www.hiddenacrescampground.com.

🚐 ★★★★ ⛺ ★★★★

Beauty: ★★★★	Site Privacy: ★★★
Spaciousness: ★★★	Quiet: ★★★★
Security: ★★★★	Cleanliness: ★★★★
Insect Control: ★★★★	Facilities: ★★★★

Located between Cape May Court House and Clermont, Hidden Acres is an ideal base for exploring Cape May, the Wildwoods, and even Atlantic City. Set amid forests of pine and laurel, Hidden Acres features 300 shaded sites on flat, sandy ground. Half of the sites offer full hookups, while the other half have water and electric hookups. The Atlantic Ocean is less than 10 minutes away, but you do not have to leave the campground to enjoy the water. Hidden Acres has a filtered swimming lake and a white-sanded beach. Few people leave Cape May without strolling along the beach and visiting the 157-foot-tall Cape May Lighthouse, which was built in 1859. We recommend that, before you leave the Cape May area, you take a whale-watching cruise. Cape May Whale Watcher guarantees the sighting of a whale or dolphin; if you do not see either, you receive credit for another trip.

BASICS

Operated By: Joyce Springer. **Open:** Apr. 15–Oct. 12. **Site Assignment:** Reservations and walk-ins accepted (3-day min. on holidays). **Registration:** At office. **Fee:** $35–$38; V, MC, D. **Parking:** At site.

FACILITIES

Number of RV-only Sites: 200. **Number of Tent-only Sites:** 100. **Hookups:** Electric (20, 30, 50 amps), water, sewer, cable TV; 100 full hookups. **Each Site:** Picnic table, fire ring. **Dump Station:** Yes. **Laundry:** Yes. **Pay Phone:** No. **Restrooms**

and Showers: Yes. **Fuel:** No. **Propane:** Yes. **Internal Roads:** Paved & dirt, in fair condition. **RV Service:** No. **Market:** W/in 2 mi. **Restaurant:** W/in 0.5 mi. **General Store:** Yes. **Vending:** No. **Swimming:** Yes. **Playground:** Yes. **Other:** Freshwater lake w/ beach. **Activities:** Lake swimming, basketball, shuffleboard, mini-golf, game room, rec hall, horseshoes, badminton. **Nearby Attractions:** Cape May County Historical Museum, Cape May County Park & Zoo, Leaming's Run Gardens, Historic Cape May boat & walking tours, Victorian Cape May, Point Lighthouse & Park, Cold Spring Village, Cape May beaches, Wildwood amusement parks, Cape May–Lewes (DE) Ferry, Atlantic City. **Additional Information:** Cape May County Chamber of Commerce, (609) 465-7181, www.cmccofc.com.

RESTRICTIONS

Pets: On leash. **Fires:** At site. **Alcoholic Beverages:** At site. **Vehicle Maximum Length:** No limit. **Other:** 35 ft.

TO GET THERE

From US 9, go 0.5 mi. west on Hwy. 83. Entrance is on the right.

CAPE MAY COURT HOUSE   MAP. D-2
North Wildwood Camping Resort

240 West Shell Bay Ave., 08210.
T: (609) 465-4440 or (800) 752-4882
(reservations); www.nwcamp.com.

🚐 ★★★★　　　⛺ ★★★★

Beauty: ★★★★	Site Privacy: ★
Spaciousness: ★★	Quiet: ★★★
Security: ★★★★★	Cleanliness: ★★★★
Insect Control: ★★★★	Facilities: ★★★★

Located 10 minutes north of Cape May, North Wildwood Camping Resort is just a few minutes from Stone Harbor and North Wildwood beaches. A well-kept park with wooded sites on flat, sandy grounds, North Wildwood does not have the same variety of recreational facilities as some campgrounds in the area. Campers looking for a clean and comfortable place to stay while visiting Cape May and the Wildwoods—those who do not require filtered swimming lakes, fishing ponds, and multiple pools—will find North Wildwood to their liking. This does not mean the campground is without recreation, as it does have a pool and athletic courts. All of the activity centers (including the pool) are located along Shell Bay Ave. at the southern end of North Wildwood. Full-hookup sites stretch from the center to the far western end. Primitive, wooded tent sites are located at the far north end of the campground near the paintball field. Thirteen pull-through sites are available.

BASICS

Operated By: Richard & Bonnie Lynch. **Open:** Apr. 1–Oct. 15. **Site Assignment:** Reservations recommended (3-night min. required July & Aug. & on holiday weekends), walk-ins accepted. **Registration:** At campground office. **Fee:** May 25–Sept. 3, $37–$94; off-season, half price per site per night; cabin, $65. **Parking:** At site. 1 vehicle per site.

FACILITIES

Number of RV-only Sites: 260. **Number of Tent-only Sites:** 120. **Hookups:** Electric (20, 30 amps), water, cable TV. **Each Site:** Fire ring, picnic table. **Dump Station:** Yes. **Laundry:** Yes. **Pay Phone:** Yes. **Restrooms and Showers:** Yes. **Fuel:** No. **Propane:** Yes. **Internal Roads:** Gravel & paved, in fair condition. **RV Service:** Yes. **Market:** W/in 2 mi. **Restaurant:** W/in 2 mi. **General Store:** Yes, limited. **Vending:** Yes. **Swimming:** Yes. **Playground:** Yes. **Other:** Pavilion. **Activities:** Tennis, horseshoes, shuffleboard, rec hall, planned activities, swimming. **Nearby Attractions:** Cape May County Historical Museum, Cape May County Park & Zoo, Leaming's Run Gardens, Historic Cape May boat & walking tours, Victorian Cape May, Point Lighthouse & Park, Cold Spring Village, Cape May beaches, Wildwood amusement parks, Cape May–Lewes (DE) Ferry, Atlantic City. **Additional Information:** Cape May County Chamber of Commerce, (609) 465-7181, www.cmccofc.com.

RESTRICTIONS

Pets: On leash. **Fires:** At site. **Alcoholic Beverages:** At site. **Vehicle Maximum Length:** No limit. **Other:** Pets & fires must be attended at all times.

TO GET THERE

From Garden State Pkwy., take Exit 9 and go 1 mi. west on Shell Bay Ave. Entrance is on the right.

CHATSWORTH   MAP, C-2
Wading Pines Camping Resort

85 Godfrey Bridge Rd., 08019. T: (609) 726-1313 or (888) 726-1313; www.wadingpines.com.

🚐 ★★★★　　　⛺ ★★★★

Beauty: ★★★★	Site Privacy: ★★
Spaciousness: ★★★	Quiet: ★★★★
Security: ★★★★★	Cleanliness: ★★★★
Insect Control: ★★★★	Facilities: ★★★★

Located deep in the million-acre Pine Barrens—or Pinelands, if you prefer—Wading Pines Camping Resort is situated along the Wading River. The campground has a private hiking and picnicking island ("Fantasy Island") on the river; campers can also fish in the river or the stocked pond, or swim in the river and the pool. Children are entertained by the "Jersey Devil," the campground train that winds around Wading Pines. A cluster of inviting back-in full-hookup sites surrounds the fishing lake on the southeast side. The row of sites at the far western end of the campground (away from the activity centers) is also pleasant. Some sites that border the fishing lake are also along the river, though there are no sites on the river near Fantasy Island. The island is accessed by footbridge or swimming from the beach. Activity centers, including the swimming pool and the riverside beach, are situated on the northeast end of the campground.

BASICS

Operated By: Mark & Margie Rogers. **Open:** Mar. 1–Dec. 15. **Site Assignment:** Reservations accepted (2-night min. on weekends), walk-ins accepted. **Registration:** At campground office. **Fee:** $50–$70; V, MC, AE, D. **Parking:** At site.

FACILITIES

Number of RV-only Sites: 300. **Number of Tent-only Sites:** 17. **Hookups:** Electric (20, 30 amps), water, cable TV, phone. **Each Site:** Fire ring, picnic table. **Dump Station:** Yes. **Laundry:** Yes. **Pay Phone:** Yes. **Restrooms and Showers:** Yes. **Fuel:** No. **Propane:** Yes. **Internal Roads:** Dirt, in good condition. **RV Service:** No. **Market:** W/in 9 mi. **Restaurant:** W/in 7 mi. **General Store:** Yes. **Vending:** Yes. **Swimming:** Yes. **Playground:** Yes. **Other:** Stocked fishing lake, train rides. **Activities:** Swimming, volleyball, canoeing, kayaking, canoe & kayak rentals, game room, rec hall, lake & river fishing, basketball, planned activities on weekends, shuffleboard, tennis, movies, horseshoes, badminton, hiking trails. **Nearby Attractions:** Pine Barrens, Wading River, Island Beach State Park, Atlantic City, Barnegat Lighthouse State Park, wineries, NJ State Aquarium, Six Flags Great Adventure. **Additional Information:** New Jersey Office of Travel & Tourism, (800) JERSEY7, www.state.nj.us/travel.

RESTRICTIONS

Pets: On leash only, not in cabin area. Proof of rabies vaccination required. **Fires:** At site. **Alcoholic Beverages:** At site. **Vehicle Maximum Length:** 45 ft.

TO GET THERE

From Hwy. 72, go 13 mi. south on CR 563 and 0.75 mi. north at campground sign. Entrance is on the left.

CLARKSBORO   MAP, C-1
Timberlane Campground

117 Timberlane Rd., 08020. T: (856) 423-6677; www.timberlanecampground.com.

🚐 ★★★★　　　⛺ ★★★★

Beauty: ★★★	Site Privacy: ★★
Spaciousness: ★★	Quiet: ★★★
Security: ★★★★	Cleanliness: ★★★★
Insect Control: ★★★★	Facilities: ★★★★

A suburban campground where ducks and swans gracefully paddle on a shimmering pond, Timberlane Campground is located in Clarksboro, about 15 minutes from Independence Hall and other history-rich attractions in downtown Philadelphia. Covering 20 acres, Timberlane offers open and wooded sites, including 70 pull-throughs. This is an ideal base for a family vacation in Philadelphia. The lounge has a TV and a fireplace. Not all the fun near Timberlane is limited to Philly. In Camden, the New Jersey State Aquarium contains one of the nation's largest open ocean tanks. At the aquatic nursery, you can touch sharks, stingrays, and starfish in special tanks. Literature buffs will want to visit the Walt Whitman House State Historic Site; it was the poet's last residence before his death in 1892.

BASICS

Operated By: Delores Goess. **Open:** All year. **Site Assignment:** Reservations recommended, walk-ins accepted. **Registration:** At campground office. **Fee:** $24–$38; V, MC. **Parking:** At site.

FACILITIES

Number of RV-only Sites: 14. **Number of Tent-only Sites:** 81. **Hookups:** Electric (20, 30, 50 amps), water, cable TV. **Each Site:** Picnic table & fire ring. **Dump Station:** Yes. **Laundry:** Yes. **Pay Phone:** Yes. **Restrooms and Showers:** Yes. **Fuel:** No. **Propane:** Yes. **Internal Roads:** Gravel & paved, in good condition. **RV Service:** Yes. **Market:** W/in 1.5 mi. **Restaurant:** W/in 1.5 mi. **General Store:** RV supplies. **Vending:** Yes. **Swimming:** Yes. **Playground:** Yes. **Other:** Cabin rentals, batting cages. **Activities:** Game room, rec hall, pond fishing, basketball, shuffleboard, horseshoes, kiddie pool. **Nearby Attractions:** Philadelphia, New Jersey State Aquarium, Sesame Place, Delaware Memorial Bridge, Garden State Race Track, Rutgers University. **Additional Information:** Delaware River Region Tourism, (856) 414-0805, www.state.nj.us/travel.

RESTRICTIONS

Pets: On leash only. No pets permitted in cabins. **Fires:** At site. **Alcoholic Beverages:** At site. **Vehicle Maximum Length:** No limit.

TO GET THERE

From I-295, take Exit 18 and go 0.75 mi. east on Timberlane Rd. Entrance is on the right.

CLERMONT — MAP, D-2
Driftwood Camping Resort

1955 Shore Rd. Hwy. 9, 08210. T: (609) 624-1899 or (800) 624-3743; www.driftwoodrvcenter.com.

🚐 ★★★★	🏕 ★★★★
Beauty: ★★★	Site Privacy: ★
Spaciousness: ★★★	Quiet: ★★★
Security: ★★★★★	Cleanliness: ★★★★
Insect Control: ★★★★	Facilities: ★★★★

From Driftwood Camping Resort, casino tours embark for Atlantic City about 40 miles north, but you do not need to leave the campground for excitement. Located midway between Atlantic City and Cape May, Driftwood has a wide selection of shaded sites, including primitive tent sites and 400 full hookups. The campground's freshwater lake has a soft-sand beach. Linksters will enjoy the Pine Barrens Golf Club, a beautiful 27-hole course named one of the "Top 10 New Golf Courses in America" by *The Golfer Magazine* in 1997. Driftwood has an RV sales and service center with new motorhomes, park models, fifth wheels, and travel trailers, and they stock a large inventory of RV parts and accessories. Driftwood is a short drive from attractions and beaches in the Wildwoods and Cape May, both of which are less than a half-hour drive south.

BASICS

Operated By: Robertson family. **Open:** Apr. 15–Oct. 15. **Site Assignment:** Reservations accepted (1-night deposit required), walk-ins accepted. **Registration:** At campground office. **Fee:** $28–$36; V, MC, AE, D. **Parking:** At site.

FACILITIES

Number of RV-only Sites: 680. **Number of Tent-only Sites:** 20. **Hookups:** Electric (20, 30, 50 amps), water, sewer, cable TV, phone. **Each Site:** Fire ring.

picnic table. **Dump Station:** Yes. **Laundry:** Yes. **Pay Phone:** Yes. **Restrooms and Showers:** Yes. **Fuel:** No. **Propane:** Yes. **Internal Roads:** Paved & dirt, in fair condition. **RV Service:** Yes. **Market:** W/in 3 mi. **Restaurant:** W/in 3 mi. **General Store:** Yes. **Vending:** Yes. **Swimming:** Yes. **Playground:** Yes. **Other:** Private lake w/ beach, RV & cabin rentals. **Activities:** Lake swimming, pool, 3 playgrounds, basketball, tennis, rec hall, game room, horseshoes, volleyball, casino tours. **Nearby Attractions:** Cape May County Historical Museum, Cape May County Park & Zoo, Leaming's Run Gardens, Historic Cape May boat & walking tours, Victorian Cape May, Point Lighthouse & Park, Cold Spring Village, Cape May beaches, Wildwood amusement parks, Cape May–Lewes (DE) Ferry, Atlantic City. **Additional Information:** Cape May County Chamber of Commerce, (609) 465-7181, www.cmccofc.com.

RESTRICTIONS

Pets: On leash only, under control. **Fires:** At site. **Alcoholic Beverages:** At site. **Vehicle Maximum Length:** 40 ft.

TO GET THERE

From Hwy. 83, go 0.25 mi. south on US 9. Entrance is on the right.

COLUMBIA — MAP, A-2
Camp Taylor Campground

85 Mount Pleasant Rd., 07832. T: (908) 496-4333 or (800) 545-9662; www.camptaylor.com.

🚐 ★★★★	🏕 ★★★★
Beauty: ★★★★	Site Privacy: ★★★★
Spaciousness: ★★★★	Quiet: ★★★★★
Security: ★★★★	Cleanliness: ★★★★
Insect Control: ★★★★	Facilities: ★★★★

Adjacent to the 72,000-acre Delaware Water Gap National Recreation Area, Camp Taylor Campground is situated on 350 acres of densely forested mountain ridges in the northern New Jersey Skylands region. The Delaware Water Gap is accessible from hiking trails at the campground, and the Appalachian Trail is nearby. One of the most fascinating campground attractions anywhere is Camp Taylor's Lakota Wolf Preserve, where you can observe packs of tundra, timber, and Arctic wolves. Informal talks about the wolves are presented, and guided wildlife photography sessions are available. Sites are located on both sides of Mount Pleasant Rd., though most sites are on the northern side. All RV sites are back-in. The row of sites near the wildlife pens are popular, especially if you do not mind the occasional howling of wolves. A cluster of primitive tenting sites is on the northwest side, secluded from the rest of the campground.

BASICS

Operated By: Taylor family. **Open:** All year. **Site Assignment:** Reservations accepted (required Oct. 15–May 1), walk-ins accepted. **Registration:** At front building. **Fee:** $20–$25; V, MC, AE, D. **Parking:** At site.

FACILITIES

Number of RV-only Sites: 100. **Number of Tent-only Sites:** 50. **Hookups:** Electric (20, 30 amps),

water. **Each Site:** Picnic table, fire ring. **Dump Station:** Yes. **Laundry:** No. **Pay Phone:** Yes. **Restrooms and Showers:** Yes. **Fuel:** No. **Propane:** Yes. **Internal Roads:** Gravel, in good condition. **RV Service:** No. **Market:** W/in 2 mi. **Restaurant:** W/in 4 mi. **General Store:** Yes, limited. **Vending:** Yes. **Swimming:** Yes. **Playground:** Yes. **Other:** Lakota Wolf Preserve located on the premises. **Activities:** Lake swimming (no fishing), game room, rec hall, volleyball, hiking trails, boat rentals, mini-golf, planned activities on weekends, badminton, sports field. **Nearby Attractions:** Lakota Wolf Preserve, Hope Historic Village, Delaware Water Gap, High Point State Park, Land of Make Believe, Space Farms Zoo & Museum. **Additional Information:** Skylands Tourism Council of New Jersey, (800) 4SKYLAND, www.state.nj.us/travel.

RESTRICTIONS

Pets: 1 pet per site, leashed. **Fires:** At site. **Alcoholic Beverages:** At site. **Vehicle Maximum Length:** 40 ft.

TO GET THERE

From I-80, go 3.5 mi. north on Hwy. 94, 0.5 mi. west on Benton Rd., 0.2 mi. north on Frog Pond Rd., 1.5 mi. north on Wishing Well Rd., and 0.5 mi. south on Mount Pleasant Rd. Entrance is on the right.

EGG HARBOR CITY — MAP, C-2
Holly Acres RV Park

218 Frankfurt Ave., 08215. T: (609) 965-2287 or (800) 2 RVCAMP; www.kiz.com/bestholiday.

🚐 ★★★★	🏕 n/a
Beauty: ★★★★	Site Privacy: ★★★
Spaciousness: ★★★	Quiet: ★★★★
Security: ★★★★★	Cleanliness: ★★★★
Insect Control: ★★★★	Facilities: ★★★★

Located about 20 miles northwest of Atlantic City, Holly Acres RV Park is a short drive to the casino and the boardwalk attractions, yet it is far enough away to avoid the crowds. The RV-only campsites are open and wooded, with back-in and pull-through sites available. The pool and arts and crafts center are located near the office close to the entrance. A cluster of sites in the center of the campground is near the pool, mini-golf course, and most of the other activity centers. The fishing pond is nestled amid fragrant pines at the northern end of Holly Acres. Renault Winery is a short drive from the campground, as is Historic Smithville, a restored 18th-century village where streets are lined with specialty shops and eateries. Horse-drawn carriage rides, train rides, and an old-fashioned carousel are among the attractions. Animal lovers will enjoy the Marine Mammal Stranding Center and Museum and the Edwin B. Forsythe National Wildlife Refuge.

BASICS

Operated By: Holiday Trav-L-Park. **Open:** May 1–Sept. 30. **Site Assignment:** Reservations accepted ($25 for 2-night stay), walk-ins accepted. **Registration:** At campground office. **Fee:** $28–$33; V, MC, D. **Parking:** At designated area.

FACILITIES

Number of RV-only Sites: 175. **Hookups:** Electric (20, 30, 50 amps), water, cable TV. **Each Site:** Picnic table, fire ring. **Dump Station:** Yes. **Laundry:** Yes. **Pay Phone:** Yes. **Restrooms and Showers:** Yes. **Fuel:** No. **Propane:** No. **Internal Roads:** Gravel, in good condition. **RV Service:** No. **Market:** W/in 4 mi. **Restaurant:** W/in 3 mi. **General Store:** Yes. **Vending:** Yes. **Swimming:** Yes. **Playground:** Yes. **Other:** Fishing pond, pavilion. **Activities:** Pond fishing, blueberry picking, rec hall, game room, swimming, wading pool, mini-golf, shuffleboard, planned activities on weekends, volleyball, badminton, horseshoes. **Nearby Attractions:** Atlantic City, Story Book Land, Sea Life Museum, Edwin B. Forsythe National Wildlife Refuge. **Additional Information:** Greater Atlantic City Region Tourism, (800) VISIT-NJ, www.state.nj.us/travel.

RESTRICTIONS

Pets: On leash. **Fires:** At site. **Alcoholic Beverages:** At site. **Vehicle Maximum Length:** No limit. **Other:** Mini-bikes & motor bikes not permitted.

TO GET THERE

From Hwy. 50, go 2 mi. east on US 30 and 1.5 mi. north on Frankfurt Ave. Entrance is on the left.

ELMER   MAP, C-2
Yogi Bear's Jellystone Camp-Resort at Tall Pines Resort

reserve america

49 Beal Rd., 08318. T: (800) 252-2890 or (856) 451-7479; www.reserveamerica.com or www.tallpines.com

🚐 ★★★★   ⛺ ★★★★

Beauty: ★★★★	Site Privacy: ★★
Spaciousness: ★★★	Quiet: ★★★
Security: ★★★★★	Cleanliness: ★★★★
Insect Control: ★★★★	Facilities: ★★★★★

Spacious, shaded sites under towering pines define the landscape of Yogi Bear's Jellystone Camp-Resort at Tall Pines Resort. The campground is located in Elmer—about 40 miles south of Philadelphia—yet Tall Pines is still a comfortable drive to Atlantic City, the Wildwoods, and Cape May. Children will like the playground, hayrides, and fire engine rides. Most of the activity centers—including the pool, mini-golf course, and camp store—are in the middle of the campground. Conveniently, the lake is along Cohansey Creek, providing campers with ample water-related activities in one area. A cluster of full-hookup sites and water-electric sites are on the southwest side of the lake. A row of primitive tent sites is a short distance from the lake on Cohansey Creek. Tall Pines also has lodges, chalets, and cottages for rent.

BASICS

Operated By: Rick & Leigh Frederick. **Open:** All year. **Site Assignment:** Reservations and walk-ins accepted (required in July & Aug. & holiday weekends). **Registration:** At campground office. **Fee:** Call or visit Web site for pricing details. **Parking:** At site.

FACILITIES

Number of RV-only Sites: 262. **Number of Tent-only Sites:** 8. **Hookups:** Electric (20, 30 amps), water, cable TV. **Each Site:** Fire ring, picnic table. **Dump Station:** Yes. **Laundry:** Yes. **Pay Phone:** Yes. **Restrooms and Showers:** Yes. **Fuel:** No. **Propane:** Yes. **Internal Roads:** Dirt, in good condition. **RV Service:** No. **Market:** W/in 8 mi. **Restaurant:** W/in 6 mi. **General Store:** Yes. **Vending:** Yes. **Swimming:** Yes. **Playground:** Yes. **Other:** Lake Jellystone. **Activities:** Lake swimming & fishing, stream fishing, wading pool, boating, canoeing, kayaking, boat rentals, mini-golf, basketball, planned activities, movies, bike rentals, horseshoes, badminton, volleyball, hiking trails, sports field. **Nearby Attractions:** Philadelphia, New Jersey State Aquarium, Delaware River, Delaware Bay, Wildwoods, Cape May, Atlantic City. **Additional Information:** Delaware River Region Tourism, (856) 414-0805, www.state.nj.us/travel.

RESTRICTIONS

Pets: On leash only. No pets in rental units. **Fires:** At site. **Alcoholic Beverages:** At site. **Vehicle Maximum Length:** 40 ft.

TO GET THERE

From Hwy. 40, go 6 mi. southwest on CR 635 and a half-mi. east on Beal Rd. Entrance is on right.

HOPE   MAP, A-2
Triplebrook Family Camping Resort

58 Honey Run Rd., 07825. T: (888) 343-CAMP or (908) 459-4079; www.triplebrook.com.

🚐 ★★★★   ⛺ ★★★★

Beauty: ★★★★	Site Privacy: ★★★
Spaciousness: ★★★★	Quiet: ★★★★★
Security: ★★★★	Cleanliness: ★★★★
Insect Control: ★★★★	Facilities: ★★★★

Chickens fly (or at least attempt to fly) and cow dung is art at Triplebrook Family Camping Resort in Hope—and campers flock here to see both. Located in the Kittatiny Mountains, Triplebrook is set on a 250-acre working farm 7 miles from the Delaware Water Gap National Recreation Area in the New Jersey Skylands. Many sites are wooded, and most are situated at the northern end. The campground hosts several entertaining special events throughout the year, including Hillbilly Weekend, the International Chicken Flying Meet, and Bovine Day. On Bovine Day, cow-dung sculpting and cow-chip throwing contests are held. On any day, campers can see chickens, emus, horses, and other farm animals, and watch feedings. The campground's trading post is stocked with groceries, sundries, and RV and camping supplies.

BASICS

Operated By: Brenda & George James. **Open:** Apr. 29–Oct. 22; seasonal. **Site Assignment:** Reservations required Dec. 1–Mar. 31; walk-ins accepted in other months; 2-night min. required for reservations. **Registration:** At campground office. **Fee:** Campsites, $30–$38; cabin, $60–$70; V, MC, AE, D, personal check. **Parking:** At site.

FACILITIES

Number of RV-only Sites: 217. **Hookups:** Electric (20, 30, 50 amps), water, sewer, limited phone; 110 full hookups. **Each Site:** Picnic table. **Dump Station:** Yes. **Laundry:** Yes. **Pay Phone:** Yes. **Restrooms and Showers:** Yes. **Fuel:** No. **Propane:** Yes. **Internal Roads:** Gravel & paved, in fair condition. **RV Service:** Yes. **Market:** W/in 4 mi. **Restaurant:** W/in 4 mi. **General Store:** Yes. **Vending:** Yes. **Swimming:** Yes. **Playground:** Yes. **Other:** Cabin rentals. **Activities:** Basketball, tennis, game room, sports field, rec hall, canoeing, kayaking, fishing, mini-golf, movies, hiking trails, boat rentals. **Nearby Attractions:** Delaware Water Gap National Recreation Area, Appalachian Trail, Land of Make Believe, Lakota Wolf Preserve, Space Wild Animal Farm, Moravian Village of Hope. **Additional Information:** Skylands Tourism Council of New Jersey, (800) 4SKYLAND, www.state.nj.us/travel.

RESTRICTIONS

Pets: Not allowed. **Fires:** At site. **Alcoholic Beverages:** At site. **Vehicle Maximum Length:** No limit. **Other:** No electric bug zappers.

TO GET THERE

From I-80, take Exit 12 and go 1 mi. south on CR 521, 3 mi. west on CR 609, 1 mi. north on Nightingale Rd., and 0.5 mi. east on Honey Run Rd. Entrance is on the left.

JACKSON   MAP, C-2
Butterfly Camping Resort

360 Butterfly Rd., 08527. T: (732) 928-2107; www.butterflycamp.com.

🚐 ★★★★   ⛺ ★★★★

Beauty: ★★★★	Site Privacy: ★★★
Spaciousness: ★★	Quiet: ★★
Security: ★★★★	Cleanliness: ★★★★
Insect Control: ★★★★	Facilities: ★★★★

Adjacent to Butterfly Bogs State Wildlife Refuge, Butterfly Camping Resort attracts many visitors because of its proximity to Six Flags Great Adventure Theme Park and Wild Safari. The campground offers discount tickets to Six Flags for its guests. Butterfly features private, shaded sites, including eight pull-throughs. The activity centers are located near the entrance at the southern end. There are four long clusters of sites stretching south to north. Six Flags features a 350-acre drive-through safari with more than 1,200 free-roaming animals from six continents and a 125-acre theme park with roller coasters, rides, and live shows. Island Beach State Park is about 20 minutes east of Butterfly Camping Resort. This unspoiled barrier beach separating Barnegat Bay from the Atlantic Ocean is a must-see, with 1,900 acres of sand dunes, freshwater bogs, and saltwater marshes.

BASICS

Operated By: Don & Patty Letho. **Open:** Apr. 1–Oct. 31. **Site Assignment:** Reservations accepted (3-night min. on holiday weekends), walk-ins accepted. **Registration:** At campground store. **Fee:** Campsite, $42–$47; cabin, $67–$94; V, MC. **Parking:** At site. 1 vehicle per site.

FACILITIES

Number of RV-only Sites: 135. **Number of Tent-only Sites:** 70. **Hookups:** Electric (20, 30, 50 amps), water, sewer, phone available. **Each Site:** Fire ring, picnic table. **Dump Station:** Yes. **Laundry:** Yes. **Pay Phone:** Yes. **Restrooms and Showers:** Yes. **Fuel:** No. **Propane:** Yes. **Internal Roads:** Gravel & dirt, in good condition. **RV Service:** No. **Market:** W/in 2.5 mi. **Restaurant:** W/in 2.5 mi. **General Store:** Yes. **Vending:** Yes. **Swimming:** Yes. **Playground:** Yes. **Other:** Cabin rentals, modem hookups, firewood & ice available. **Activities:** Lake fishing, boating, canoeing, kayaking, mini-golf, basketball, volleyball, badminton, horseshoes, sports field, shuffleboard, game room, rec hall, planned activities, movies. **Nearby Attractions:** Six Flags Great Adventure & Wild Safari, Island Beach State Park, Barnegat Light Museum, Deep Cut Gardens, Longstreet Farm, Atlantic Ocean beaches. **Additional Information:** Shore Region Tourism Council, (732) 544-9300, www.state.nj.us/travel.

RESTRICTIONS

Pets: On leash only. **Fires:** At site. **Alcoholic Beverages:** At site. **Vehicle Maximum Length:** No limit. **Other:** Fires may not be left unattended; no pit bulls, Dobermans, or rottweilers allowed.

TO GET THERE

From I-195, take Exit 21 and go 3.5 mi. south on CR 527, 5.25 mi. east on CR 528, and 0.5 mi. north on Butterfly Rd. Entrance is on the left.

JACKSON   MAP, C-2
Indian Rock RV Resort and Campground

920 West Veterans Hwy. (Hwy. 528), 08527. T: (732) 928-0034 or (800) 442-4954 (NJ only); www.indianrockresort.com.

🚐 ★★★★   ⛺ ★★★★

Beauty: ★★★★	Site Privacy: ★★
Spaciousness: ★★	Quiet: ★★★★
Security: ★★★★★	Cleanliness: ★★★★
Insect Control: ★★★★	Facilities: ★★★★

Located within an hour's drive from midtown Manhattan, Philadelphia, and the Jersey Shore, Indian Rock RV Resort and Campground is a good base for day trips to the aforementioned areas and nearby Six Flags. A snack bar is open on weekends, and the campground store is well stocked. Sites here are spacious and set among pine and oak trees; most of the sites are east and north of the activity centers, though a cluster of sites near the entrance is convenient to the children's catch-and-release fishing pond. During October, Indian Rock becomes a "frightening" place with its Jersey Devil Hayride. Country-western line dancing is held every Friday night from 8 p.m. to midnight on the expansive dance floor. Even the beginner's lessons offered on the first Friday of each month could not help us move any better, but perhaps they can help you.

BASICS

Operated By: Private operator. **Open:** All year; limited winter facilities. **Site Assignment:** Reserva-

---

tions accepted, walk-ins accepted. **Registration:** At campground office. **Fee:** $36–$63; V, MC, AE. **Parking:** At site.

FACILITIES

Number of RV-only Sites: 60. **Hookups:** Electric (20, 30 amps), water, sewer, phone; 90 full hookups. **Each Site:** Fire ring, picnic table. **Dump Station:** Yes. **Laundry:** Yes. **Pay Phone:** Yes. **Restrooms and Showers:** Yes. **Fuel:** No. **Propane:** Yes. **Internal Roads:** Dirt, in fair condition. **RV Service:** No. **Market:** W/in 5 mi. **Restaurant:** W/in 5 mi. **General Store:** Yes. **Vending:** Yes. **Swimming:** Yes. **Playground:** Yes. **Other:** Cabin rentals. **Activities:** Pond fishing, game room, pool, mini-golf, basketball, planned activities on weekends, movies, badminton, hiking trails, volleyball, rec hall, arts & crafts center. **Nearby Attractions:** Six Flags Great Adventure & Wild Safari, Island Beach State Park, Barnegat Light Museum, Deep Cut Gardens, Longstreet Farm, Atlantic Ocean beaches. **Additional Information:** Shore Region Tourism Council, (732) 544-9300, www.state.nj.us/travel.

RESTRICTIONS

Pets: Under 25 pounds, at campsite. **Fires:** At site. **Alcoholic Beverages:** At site. **Vehicle Maximum Length:** 40 ft. **Other:** Fires must be out by midnight.

TO GET THERE

From I-95, take Exit 16B and go 1 mi. southeast on CR 537, 4.5 mi. south on CR 571, and 1.5 mi. west on CR 528. Entrance is on the right.

JACKSON   MAP, C-2
Timberland Lake Campground

P.O. Box 48, 08527. T: (732) 928-0500 or (609) 758-2235; www.timberlandlakecampground.com.

🚐 ★★★★   ⛺ ★★★★★

Beauty: ★★★	Site Privacy: ★★★
Spaciousness: ★★★	Quiet: ★★★★
Security: ★★★★★	Cleanliness: ★★★★
Insect Control: ★★★★	Facilities: ★★★

A five-acre lake is the centerpiece of Timberland Lake Campground, which is located in Jackson (not to be confused with Timberlane Campground in Clarksboro). Sites are set on the eastern and western sides of the lake, which is wide at the southern end but narrows to the north. The fishing pier is located at the southern end, across the lake from the beach, the store, and most of the activity centers. A cluster of sites here is ideal for campers who want to be near the action, but we recommend the lakeside sites on both sides of the lake at the northern end. These are more spacious and more peaceful, since they are away from the activity centers. This campground offers 20 pull-through sites. Timberland Lake offers three-, four-, and five-night packages, as well as discounted tickets to Six Flags. In late March, Timberland Lake offers a free camping weekend for guests who rake leaves for two hours (advance reservations required).

BASICS

Operated By: Kathy Elliott. **Open:** Mar. 1–Dec. 1. **Site Assignment:** Reservations accepted (1-night

---

deposit required), walk-ins accepted. **Registration:** At campground office. **Fee:** $34; V, MC, D, personal check. **Parking:** At site.

FACILITIES

Number of RV-only Sites: 200. **Hookups:** Electric (20, 30, 50 amps), water, phone, cable TV. **Each Site:** Fire ring, picnic table. **Dump Station:** Yes. **Laundry:** No. **Pay Phone:** Yes. **Restrooms and Showers:** Yes. **Fuel:** No. **Propane:** Yes. **Internal Roads:** Dirt, in fair condition. **RV Service:** Yes. **Market:** W/in 1 mi. **Restaurant:** W/in 1 mi. **General Store:** Yes. **Vending:** Yes. **Swimming:** Yes. **Playground:** Yes. **Other:** Timberland Lake. **Activities:** Canoeing, kayaking, boat rentals, lake fishing, mini-golf, game room, planned activities, movies, hiking trails, horseshoes, shuffleboard, volleyball, rec hall. **Nearby Attractions:** Six Flags Great Adventure & Wild Safari, Island Beach State Park, Barnegat Light Museum, Deep Cut Gardens, Longstreet Farm, Atlantic Ocean beaches. **Additional Information:** Shore Region Tourism Council, (732) 544-9300, www.state.nj.us/travel.

RESTRICTIONS

Pets: On leash only, at campsite. **Fires:** At site until midnight. **Alcoholic Beverages:** At site. **Vehicle Maximum Length:** No limit.

TO GET THERE

From I-195, take Exit 16 and go 3 mi. west on CR 537, 0.25 mi. south on Hawkins Rd., and 0.5 mi. east on Reed Rd. Entrance is on the right.

JACKSON   MAP, C-2
Tip Tam Camping Resort

301 Brewers Bridge Rd., 08527. T: (877) TIP-TAMI or (732) 363-4036; www.tiptam.com.

🚐 ★★★★   ⛺ ★★★★

Beauty: ★★★★	Site Privacy: ★
Spaciousness: ★★	Quiet: ★★★★
Security: ★★★★★	Cleanliness: ★★★★
Insect Control: ★★★★	Facilities: ★★★★

Featuring shaded sites in a colorful grove, Tip Tam Camping Resort offers discount tickets and packages to nearby Six Flags in Jackson. Most sites have full hookups, though the campground does not accommodate pull-throughs. RVers with big rigs may be more satisfied with Butterfly Camping Resort or Timberland Lake Campground, both of which accommodate pull-throughs. Children are kept happy with swimming races, scavenger and treasure hunts, mini-golf tournaments, and coloring contests. Team trivia matches, children's Olympics, candy bar bingo, and weekends honoring mothers and fathers on their respective holidays are also hosted at Tip Tam. With planning, a memorable family vacation can include a day each at Six Flags, Philly, New York City, Island Beach State Park, Cape May, and the Wildwoods.

BASICS

Operated By: Guglielmelli family. **Open:** Apr. 15–Sept. 30. **Site Assignment:** Reservations accepted (10-day cancellation notice required, 3-night min. on holiday weekends), walk-ins accepted. **Registration:** At campground office. **Fee:** $40–$43; V, MC, D. **Parking:** At site.

FACILITIES

Number of RV-only Sites: 200. **Number of Tent-only Sites:** 15. **Hookups:** Electric (20, 30 amps), water, sewer, cable TV. **Each Site:** Fire ring, picnic table. **Dump Station:** Yes. **Laundry:** Yes. **Pay Phone:** Yes. **Restrooms and Showers:** Yes. **Fuel:** No. **Propane:** Yes. **Internal Roads:** Gravel & paved, in fair condition. **RV Service:** No. **Market:** W/in 1.5 mi. **Restaurant:** W/in 1.5 mi. **General Store:** Yes. **Vending:** No. **Swimming:** Yes. **Playground:** Yes. **Other:** Amphitheater, cabin rentals. **Activities:** Game room, 2 rec halls, 2 pools, planned activities, mini-golf, volleyball, horseshoes, shuffleboard, basketball, sports field. **Nearby Attractions:** Six Flags Great Adventure & Wild Safari, Island Beach State Park, Barnegat Light Museum, Deep Cut Gardens, Longstreet Farm, Atlantic Ocean beaches. **Additional Information:** Shore Region Tourism Council, (732) 544-9300, www.state.nj.us/travel.

RESTRICTIONS

Pets: At site only. No pets permitted in rental units. **Fires:** At site. **Alcoholic Beverages:** At site. **Vehicle Maximum Length:** 35 ft.

TO GET THERE

From I-195, take Exit 21 and go 0.25 mi. south on CR 527, 6 mi. east on CR 526, and 2 mi. south on Brewers Bridge Rd. Entrance is on the left.

MARMORA   MAP, D-2
Whippoorwill Campground

reserve america

810 South Shore (US 9), 08223. T: (609) 390-3458 or (800) 424-8275; www.reserveamerica.com.

🚐 ★★★★   ⛺ ★★★★

Beauty: ★★★★	Site Privacy: ★★
Spaciousness: ★★	Quiet: ★★★
Security: ★★★★★	Cleanliness: ★★★★
Insect Control: ★★★★	Facilities: ★★★★

Located 3 miles from Ocean City, Whippoorwill Campground offers level, wooded sites and a family atmosphere. Most of the nonseasonal sites are nestled in the center of the campground around a bathhouse and laundry facility. All are back-in and offer moderate privacy due to well-spaced sites. The Olympic-sized swimming pool is located across from the camp store and office northwest of the entrance, but most of the activity centers, including basketball, volleyball, and tennis courts, are positioned on the southeast side near Hwy. 9. From the Work Party Weekend in early April (when campers earn a free stay by performing clean-up tasks for four hours) to the Pig Roast Finale in early September, Whippoorwill has several entertaining theme weekends. If you like canned meat, the Spam Fest will whet your appetite with an assortment of creative dishes. If you have a more discriminating palate, there are lots of eateries along the 2-mile boardwalk in Ocean City.

BASICS

Operated By: Tom & Cindy Swank. **Open:** Apr. 1–Oct. 31. **Site Assignment:** Reservations recommended; 2-night min. required; 3-night min. during

holidays; payment in full required for holiday weekends; walk-ins accepted. **Registration:** At campground office. **Fee:** Campsite, $45; cabin, $80; V, MC, D. **Parking:** At site. 1 vehicle per site.

FACILITIES

Number of RV-only Sites: 288. **Number of Tent-only Sites:** 50. **Hookups:** Electric (20, 30, 50 amps), water, sewer, cable TV; 226 full hookups. **Each Site:** Fire ring, picnic table. **Dump Station:** Yes. **Laundry:** Yes. **Pay Phone:** Yes. **Restrooms and Showers:** Yes. **Fuel:** No. **Propane:** Yes. **Internal Roads:** Paved, in good condition. **RV Service:** No. **Market:** W/in 15 mi. **Restaurant:** W/in 15 mi. **General Store:** Yes. **Vending:** Yes. **Swimming:** Yes. **Playground:** Yes. **Other:** Cabin rentals. Internet available. **Activities:** Tennis, volleyball, game room, planned activities, basketball, horseshoes, rec hall, kiddie pool. **Nearby Attractions:** Ocean City boardwalk & beaches, Atlantic City, Cape May, the Wildwoods. **Additional Information:** New Jersey Office of Travel Tourism, (800) JERSEY7, www.state.nj.us/travel.

RESTRICTIONS

Pets: On leash, attended, cleaned up after. No pets permitted in rental units. **Fires:** At site. **Alcoholic Beverages:** No alcohol permitted. **Vehicle Maximum Length:** 40 ft.

TO GET THERE

From Garden State Pkwy., take Exit 25 and go 1 block west and 1.5 mi. south on US 9. Entrance is on the right.

MAYS LANDING   MAP, D-2
Winding River Campground

6752 Weymouth Rd., 08330. T: (609) 625-3191; www.windingrivercamping.com.

🚐 ★★★★   ⛺ ★★★★

Beauty: ★★★★	Site Privacy: ★★★
Spaciousness: ★★★	Quiet: ★★★★
Security: ★★★★	Cleanliness: ★★★★
Insect Control: ★★★★	Facilities: ★★★★

Egg Harbor River cuts through Winding River Campground, where sites are set among mature, lush woodlands near Mays Landing in southern New Jersey. Most sites have full hookups. Cooled by a gentle breeze beneath a forested canopy, campers can relax on lawn chairs beside the river. Winding River is a half-hour from the boardwalk and beaches of Atlantic City. Ocean City, the Wildwoods, and Cape May are located to the south. The allure of Egg Harbor River is what draws many campers to Winding River. The campground has a swimming pool, but outdoor enthusiasts head for the river, where canoes, kayaks, and inner tubes are available for rent. Guided canoe floats ranging from two to six hours depart from Winding River. Adirondack-style cabins are available for campers without RVs and tents. The rustic-looking cabins have two double-decker, built-in bunks, restrooms, a kitchen, and a screened dining area.

BASICS

Operated By: Al & Therese Horsey. **Open:** May 1–Oct. 15. **Site Assignment:** Reservations accepted (2-night min.; 3-night min. on holiday weekends), walk-ins accepted. **Registration:** At campground

office. **Fee:** Campsite, $32–$34; cabin, $75–$95; V, MC, D. **Parking:** At site.

FACILITIES

Number of RV-only Sites: 133. **Number of Tent-only Sites:** 29. **Hookups:** Electric (30 amps), water, sewer; 105 full hookups. **Each Site:** Fire ring, picnic table. **Dump Station:** Yes. **Laundry:** Yes. **Pay Phone:** Yes. **Restrooms and Showers:** Yes. **Fuel:** No. **Propane:** Yes. **Internal Roads:** Dirt, in fair condition. **RV Service:** No. **Market:** W/in 8 mi. **Restaurant:** W/in 4 mi. **General Store:** Yes. **Vending:** No. **Swimming:** Yes. **Playground:** Yes. **Other:** Cabin rentals. **Activities:** Tubing, canoeing, kayaking, boating, badminton, game room, river fishing, basketball, rec hall, volleyball, planned activities on weekends. **Nearby Attractions:** Atlantic City, Cape May, Ocean City, Story Book Land, the Wildwoods. **Additional Information:** Greater Atlantic City Region Tourism, (609) 652-7777, www.state.nj.us/travel.

RESTRICTIONS

Pets: On leash only. No pets in rental units. **Fires:** At site in fire ring. **Alcoholic Beverages:** At site. **Vehicle Maximum Length:** 39 ft. **Other:** No motorcycles.

TO GET THERE

From Hwy. 50 and Hwy. 40 in Mays Landing, go 4 mi. north on CR 559. Entrance is on the right.

MAYS LANDING   MAP, D-2
Yogi Bear's Jellystone Park Camp-Resort

reserve america

1079 West 12th Ave., 08330. T: (800) 355-0264 or (609) 476-2811; www.atlanticcityjellystone.com.

🚐 ★★★★   ⛺ ★★★★

Beauty: ★★★★	Site Privacy: ★★
Spaciousness: ★★	Quiet: ★★★
Security: ★★★★	Cleanliness: ★★★★
Insect Control: ★★★★	Facilities: ★★★★

In Mays Landing, located a half-hour northwest of Atlantic City, Yogi Bear's Jellystone Park Camp-Resort and Winding River Campground are the two main camping choices. Both campgrounds are clean and well maintained, but each serves a different purpose. With its Egg Harbor River location and amenities, Winding River is a destination in itself. Though it has some recreation options, Jellystone is best used as a base for trips to Atlantic City, Ocean City, Cape May, and Philadelphia. Shower and restroom facilities are extremely clean here. The campground has open and wooded sites on flat ground. Rental units include cabins (with ceiling fans and cable TV) and trailers with room for six people. Themed events include the "No Talent Needed Weekend," when daring campers attempt to sing, dance, and perform. Audience members recommend we stick to writing and forgo a career in stand-up comedy.

BASICS

Operated By: Yogi Bear's Jellystone Park. **Open:** All year. **Site Assignment:** Reservations accepted

(7-day notice required for refund, less $10 fee), walk-ins accepted. **Registration:** At campground office. **Fee:** RV/tent, $45; cabin, $100; trailer, $200; V, MC, D. **Parking:** At site.

FACILITIES

Number of RV-only Sites: 130. **Number of Tent-only Sites:** 20. **Hookups:** Electric (20, 30, 50 amps), water, sewer, cable TV, phone. **Each Site:** Fire ring, picnic table. **Dump Station:** Yes. **Laundry:** Yes. **Pay Phone:** Yes. **Restrooms and Showers:** Yes. **Fuel:** No. **Propane:** Yes. **Internal Roads:** Gravel & dirt, in fair condition. **RV Service:** No. **Market:** W/in 3 mi. **Restaurant:** W/in 2 mi. **General Store:** Yes. **Vending:** Yes. **Swimming:** Yes. **Playground:** Yes. **Other:** Cabin & trailer rentals. **Activities:** Pond fishing, kiddie pool, game room, rec hall, mini-golf, basketball, planned activities, movies, horseshoes, badminton, volleyball. **Nearby Attractions:** Atlantic City, Cape May, Ocean City, Story Book Land, the Wildwoods. **Additional Information:** Greater Atlantic City Region Tourism, (609) 652-7777, www.state.nj.us/travel.

RESTRICTIONS

Pets: On leash only. **Fires:** At site. **Alcoholic Beverages:** At site. **Vehicle Maximum Length:** 40 ft. **Other:** Pets not permitted in rental units.

TO GET THERE

From Hwy. 40, go 0.5 mi. south on Hwy. 50, 4 mi. west on 11th Ave., 0.25 mi. north on Beach St., and 0.1 mi. east on 12th Ave. Entrance is on the right.

NEW GRETNA — MAP, C-2
Timberline Lake Camping Resort

P.O. Box 278, 08224. T: (609) 296-7900; www.timberlinelake.com.

🚐 ★★★★   ⛺ ★★★

Beauty: ★★★★	Site Privacy: ★★★
Spaciousness: ★★★★	Quiet: ★★★★
Security: ★★★★★	Cleanliness: ★★★★
Insect Control: ★★★★	Facilities: ★★★★

Located about 20 miles northwest of the 24-hour excitement of Atlantic City, Timberline Lake Camping Resort is nestled in the Pine Barrens around a 30-acre private lake. Some sites are open, but many are wooded and lakeside. The campground can accommodate 10 pull-throughs. Canoes and kayaks are available for rent. Families flock to the TV lounge, which has a deck and a playroom. Timberline's location north of Atlantic City is convenient to the boardwalk and the casinos, as well as the scenery of Island Beach State Park, an unspoiled barrier island separating Barnegat Bay from the Atlantic Ocean. The park boasts more than 1,900 acres of sand dunes, saltwater marshes, and freshwater bogs.

BASICS

Operated By: Private operator. **Open:** May 1–Oct. 13; winter seasonals only. **Site Assignment:** By reservation & first come, first served. **Registration:** At campground office. **Fee:** Campsite, $32; cabin, $59; RV, $94; V, MC. **Parking:** At site.

FACILITIES

Number of RV-only Sites: 158. **Hookups:** Electric (20, 30, 50 amps), water, cable TV, phone. **Each Site:** Fire ring, picnic table. **Dump Station:** Yes. **Laundry:** Yes. **Pay Phone:** Yes. **Restrooms and Showers:** Yes. **Fuel:** No. **Propane:** No. **Internal Roads:** Dirt, in good condition. **RV Service:** No. **Market:** W/in 8 mi. **Restaurant:** W/in 4 mi. **General Store:** Yes. **Vending:** Yes. **Swimming:** Yes. **Playground:** Yes. **Other:** Timberline Lake. **Activities:** Lake swimming & fishing, basketball, rec hall, game room, boating, canoeing, kayaking, boat rentals, planned activities on weekends, volleyball, horseshoes. **Nearby Attractions:** Atlantic City, Barnegat Light Museum, Island Beach State Park, Story Book Land, Edwin B. Forsythe National Wildlife Refuge. **Additional Information:** Greater Atlantic City Region Tourism, (800) VISIT-NJ or (609) 777-0885, www.state.nj.us/travel.

RESTRICTIONS

Pets: On leash only. Proof of rabies shots required. **Fires:** At site. **Alcoholic Beverages:** At site. **Vehicle Maximum Length:** 35 ft.

TO GET THERE

From US 9, go 4 mi. west on CR 679. Entrance is on the left.

NEWTON — MAP, A-2
Green Valley Beach Family Campground

68 Phillips Rd., 07860. T: (973) 383-4026; www.greenvalleybeach.com.

🚐 ★★★★   ⛺ ★★★★

Beauty: ★★★★	Site Privacy: ★
Spaciousness: ★★	Quiet: ★★★★
Security: ★★★★★	Cleanliness: ★★★★
Insect Control: ★★★★	Facilities: ★★★★

Located in the foothills of the Kittatiny Mountains in northwest New Jersey's Sussex County, Green Valley Beach Family Campground is convenient to lots of family-oriented attractions, including Space Farms Zoo and Museum and Wild West City. Of course, with a 3.5-acre lake for fishing and swimming, an Olympic-sized swimming pool, and a rec hall where live entertainment is hosted and free movies are shown, there is plenty to do without leaving the grounds. Ideal for families who want to be in the center of the action, a cluster of sites is situated between a pond and the lake on the southwest end of the campground. The pool fronts the lake near the entrance. The recreation hall and the pavilion border the lake. Full-hookup sites at the northwest tip offer the most privacy away from activity centers. The Delaware Water Gap National Recreation Area is a 15-minute drive to the west. Green Valley is also near Skylands Park, home of the New Jersey Cardinals, the St. Louis Cardinals Single-A affiliate in the New York–Penn League.

BASICS

Operated By: Private operator. **Open:** Apr. 15–Oct. 15. **Site Assignment:** Reservations accepted (2-night min. required on weekends, 3 nights on holiday weekends), walk-ins accepted. **Registration:** At campground office. **Fee:** $32; V, MC, D. **Parking:** At site.

FACILITIES

Number of RV-only Sites: 235. **Number of Tent-only Sites:** 15. **Hookups:** Electric (15, 20, 30 amps), water, sewer, cable TV, phone. **Each Site:** Fire ring, picnic table. **Dump Station:** Yes. **Laundry:** Yes. **Pay Phone:** Yes. **Restrooms and Showers:** Yes. **Fuel:** No. **Propane:** Yes. **Internal Roads:** Gravel & paved, in good condition. **RV Service:** No. **Market:** W/in 4 mi. **Restaurant:** W/in 2 mi. **General Store:** Yes. **Vending:** Yes. **Swimming:** Yes. **Playground:** Yes. **Other:** Private lake. **Activities:** Lake fishing & swimming, game room, rec hall, canoeing, kayaking, boat rentals, planned activities, sports field, horseshoes, volleyball. **Nearby Attractions:** Delaware Water Gap National Recreation Area, Village of Waterloo, Sterling Hill Mine, Wild West City, Kittatiny Valley State Park, Lakota Wolf Preserve, Land of Make Believe, Space Farms Zoo & Museum, Great Swamp National Wildlife Refuge. **Additional Information:** Skylands Tourism Council of New Jersey, (800) 4SKY-LAND, www.state.nj.us/travel.

RESTRICTIONS

Pets: On leash only, attended, cleaned up after. **Fires:** At site. **Alcoholic Beverages:** At site. **Vehicle Maximum Length:** 35 ft. **Other:** All daily visitors must leave the campground by 10 p.m.

TO GET THERE

From US 206, go 0.5 mi. west on CR 611 and follow signs 1 mi. south to the entrance, which is on the left.

OCEAN VIEW — MAP, D-2
Frontier Campground

84 Tyler Rd., 08230. T: (609) 390-3649 or (800) 277-4109; www.frontiercampground.com.

🚐 ★★★★   ⛺ ★★★★

Beauty: ★★★★	Site Privacy: ★★★
Spaciousness: ★★★	Quiet: ★★★★
Security: ★★★★	Cleanliness: ★★★★
Insect Control: ★★★★	Facilities: ★★★★

Located between Ocean City and Sea Isle City on the Jersey Cape, Frontier Campground is a short drive from the ocean beaches. Adorned with evergreens, hardwoods, and wild laurel, the campground is also a half-hour north of Cape May and a half-hour south of Atlantic City. Frontier offers wooded and open sites amid rolling hills. Tall shrubs separate many sites, offering good privacy. Recreational opportunities are minimal here; most campers stay at Frontier because the facilities are clean and well maintained, and the campground is centrally located between Atlantic City, Ocean City, the Wildwood, and Cape May. Ocean City is the closest of these destinations at about 10 miles north of Frontier. Actually an island nestled between Great Egg Harbor and the Atlantic Ocean, Ocean City has 8 miles of beaches and 2-plus miles of boardwalk and related points of interest. The boardwalk sports various attractions and amusements, including an enclosed auditorium.

BASICS

Operated By: George Reagan. **Open:** Mid-Apr.–mid-Oct. **Site Assignment:** Reservations recommended (1-night deposit required), walk-ins accepted. **Registration:** At A-frame house. **Fee:** Campsite, $25–$32; tree house camping, $85 (w/ $50 deposit); V, MC, AE, D. **Parking:** At site.

FACILITIES

Number of RV-only Sites: 196. **Number of Tent-only Sites:** 9. **Hookups:** Electric (20, 30, 50 amps), water, sewer, cable TV, phone. **Each Site:** Fire ring, picnic table. **Dump Station:** Yes. **Laundry:** Yes. **Pay Phone:** Yes. **Restrooms and Showers:** Yes. **Fuel:** No. **Propane:** Yes. **Internal Roads:** Dirt, in good condition. **RV Service:** No. **Market:** W/in 1 mi. **Restaurant:** W/in 1 mi. **General Store:** Yes. **Vending:** Yes. **Swimming:** Yes. **Playground:** Yes. **Other:** Furnished tree houses available for rent. **Activities:** Rec hall, saltwater fishing, basketball, badminton, horseshoes, volleyball. **Nearby Attractions:** Ocean City, Atlantic City, the Wildwoods, Cape May. **Additional Information:** New Jersey Office of Travel Tourism, (800) JERSEY7, www.state.nj.us/travel.

RESTRICTIONS

Pets: Not allowed. **Fires:** At site. **Alcoholic Beverages:** Not allowed. **Vehicle Maximum Length:** 40 ft.

TO GET THERE

From Garden State Pkwy., take Exit 25 and go 3.5 mi. west on Hwy. 631 and 1.5 mi. south on Hwy. 616. Entrance is on the right.

OCEAN VIEW MAP, D-2
Ocean View Resort Campground

2555 Hwy. 9, P. O. Box 607, 08230.
T: (609) 624-1675; www.ovresort.com.

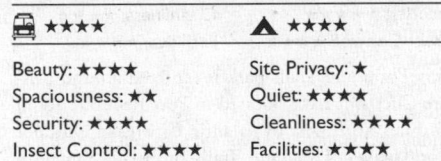

🚐 ★★★★   ⛺ ★★★★

Beauty: ★★★★	Site Privacy: ★
Spaciousness: ★★★	Quiet: ★★★
Security: ★★★★★	Cleanliness: ★★★★
Insect Control: ★★★★	Facilities: ★★★★★

At Ocean View Resort Campground, more than 1,175 sites are set in groves of oak, cedar, and pine on 180 acres, just outside of Ocean View, south of Atlantic City, and north of Cape May. The boardwalk and beaches of Ocean City are 10 minutes away; Atlantic City and Cape May are each about a half-hour drive. Yet Ocean View Resort campers can be entertained without leaving the grounds. You can swim, ride a pedal boat, or bask in the sun on the sandy beach at the spring-fed Trail's End Lake. Or you can fish for largemouth bass and hybrid striped bass at Greenbriar Pond. Kids flock to the fully equipped playground and the game room building with video games, pool tables, air hockey, and skee ball. The expansive club house hosts craft shows, flea markets, movies, and dances. Each of Ocean View's sites has full hookups. Most are wooded, and some are situated along the lake. Obviously, with more than 1,175 sites on 180 acres, privacy is at a minimum, though the sites are spacious.

BASICS

Operated By: Private operator. **Open:** Apr. 11–Oct. 13; open weekends only in Apr., May, & after Labor Day. **Site Assignment:** Reservations recommended; July–Aug., 3-night min.; walk-ins accepted.

Registration: At campground office. **Fee:** Campsite, $39–$52; lake area, $49–$62; deluxe, $49–$62; cabin (1 room), $66–$86; cabin (2 rooms), $93–$113; V, MC, D. **Parking:** At site.

FACILITIES

Number of RV-only Sites: 1,175. **Number of Tent-only Sites:** 40. **Hookups:** Electric (20, 30, 50 amps), sewer, cable TV, phone. **Each Site:** Fire ring, picnic table. **Dump Station:** No. **Laundry:** Yes. **Pay Phone:** Yes. **Restrooms and Showers:** Yes. **Fuel:** No. **Propane:** Yes. **Internal Roads:** Paved, in good condition. **RV Service:** Yes. **Market:** W/in 3 mi. **Restaurant:** W/in 3 mi. **General Store:** Yes. **Vending:** Yes. **Swimming:** Yes. **Playground:** Yes. **Other:** Freshwater lake w/ beaches, stocked fishing pond, pool, tram, boat storage. **Activities:** Lake swimming, wading pool, game room, rec hall, pedal-boat rentals, boating, pond fishing, mini-golf, basketball, shuffleboard, planned activities, movies, tennis, badminton, sports field, volleyball. **Nearby Attractions:** Ocean City, Atlantic City, the Wildwoods, Cape May. **Additional Information:** New Jersey Office of Travel Tourism, (800) JERSEY7, www.state.nj.us/travel.

RESTRICTIONS

Pets: On leash only. **Fires:** At site. **Alcoholic Beverages:** At site. **Vehicle Maximum Length:** 40 ft. **Other:** No motor bikes or buses permitted.

TO GET THERE

From Garden State Pkwy., take Exit 17 and go 0.25 mi. west on CR 625 and 0.25 mi. north on US 9. Entrance is on the left.

OCEAN VIEW MAP, D-2
Outdoor World—Lake and Shore Campground

545 Corson Tavern Rd., 08230. T: (800) 222-5557; www.campoutdoorworld.com.

🚐 ★★★★   ⛺ ★★★★

Beauty: ★★★★	Site Privacy: ★★★
Spaciousness: ★★★	Quiet: ★★★★
Security: ★★★★	Cleanliness: ★★★★
Insect Control: ★★★★	Facilities: ★★★★★

Central to Cape May, the Wildwoods, Ocean City, and Atlantic City, Outdoor World—Lake and Shore Campground is located outside of Ocean View near the Jersey Shore. Outdoor World campgrounds are typically clean and well maintained, and this one is no different. All but 25 sites have full hookups. Recreational opportunities are plentiful here, with options like mini-golf, an indoor water park, outdoor pool, kiddie pool, whirlpool, and a 12-acre lake for fishing and swimming. Pedal boats are also available for rent. The campground has a full slate of special events throughout the year. Lake and Shore is about 10 minutes north of another Outdoor World campground, Sea Pines, which has similar recreational facilities and site features. Both are good bases for Jersey Shore vacations. Lake and Shore is a few minutes closer to Ocean City and Atlantic City, while Sea Pines is a few minutes closer to the Wildwoods and Cape May. This is a membership-only campground, but a maximum of two stays may be taken advantage of without purchasing a membership.

BASICS

Operated By: Outdoor World. **Open:** All year. **Site Assignment:** Reservations required; 2-week notice for the public, no advance notice required for Outdoor World members. **Registration:** At campground office. **Fee:** $34–$40; V, MC, AE, D. **Parking:** At designated area.

FACILITIES

Number of RV-only Sites: 426. **Number of Tent-only Sites:** 25. **Hookups:** Electric (30, 50 amps), cable TV, phone. **Each Site:** Fire ring, picnic table. **Dump Station:** Yes. **Laundry:** Yes. **Pay Phone:** Yes. **Restrooms and Showers:** Yes. **Fuel:** No. **Propane:** Yes. **Internal Roads:** Paved & dirt, in good condition. **RV Service:** No. **Market:** W/in 3 mi. **Restaurant:** W/in 3 mi. **General Store:** Yes. **Vending:** Yes. **Swimming:** Yes. **Playground:** Yes. **Other:** Private lake, indoor water park. **Activities:** Lake fishing & swimming, wading pool, whirlpool, canoeing, kayaking, pedal boat rentals, game room, rec hall, mini-golf, basketball, shuffleboard, planned activities, horseshoes, hiking trails, sports field, volleyball. **Nearby Attractions:** Ocean City, Atlantic City, the Wildwoods, Cape May. **Additional Information:** New Jersey Office of Travel Tourism, (800) JERSEY7, www.state.nj.us/travel.

RESTRICTIONS

Pets: On leash only. **Fires:** At site. **Alcoholic Beverages:** At site, under control. **Vehicle Maximum Length:** No limit. **Other:** Pets may not be left unattended.

TO GET THERE

From Garden State Pkwy., take Exit 17 and go 0.25 mi. west on CR 625, 0.5 mi. north on US 9, 1 mi. west on CR 550, and 0.25 mi. north on Corson Tavern Rd. Look for posted sign.

OCEAN VIEW MAP, D-2
Sea Grove Camping Resort

2665 Hwy. 9, Box 603, 08230. T: (609) 624-3529 or (800) 432-6629; www.seagroveresort.com.

🚐 ★★★★   ⛺ ★★★★

Beauty: ★★★★	Site Privacy: ★
Spaciousness: ★★	Quiet: ★★★★
Security: ★★★★	Cleanliness: ★★★★
Insect Control: ★★★★	Facilities: ★★★★

Though the beaches of Sea Isle City are a short drive away, and Ocean City is about 15 minutes to the north, sometimes a simple afternoon by the pool is what you want on a vacation. Unlike many of the campgrounds in the Ocean View/Sea Isle City area, Sea Grove does not have a private lake. Many campers head for Sea Isle City's beaches when they are not by the pool. Sea Grove's sites are wooded, but none accommodate pull-throughs. Sea Grove has one- and two-bedroom cabins and park models for rent if you choose to leave your RV or tent at home. If you decide to visit Cape May, a 20-minute drive to the south, hop aboard the Cape May–Lewes (DE) Ferry. The 16-mile, 70-minute journey across Delaware Bay leads to Lewes, which is not far from Rehoboth Beach.

BASICS

Operated By: Private operator. **Open:** Apr. 1–Nov. 1. **Site Assignment:** Reservations accepted; 1-night deposit required, 3-night min. required on holiday weekends & Jun. 22–Sept. 3; walk-ins accepted. **Registration:** At campground office. **Fee:** Visit Web site or call for pricing details. **Parking:** At site.

FACILITIES

Number of RV-only Sites: 182. **Number of Tent-only Sites:** 8. **Hookups:** Electric (20, 30, 50 amps), water, sewer, cable TV. **Each Site:** Picnic table. **Dump Station:** Yes. **Laundry:** Yes. **Pay Phone:** Yes. **Restrooms and Showers:** Yes. **Fuel:** No. **Propane:** Yes. **Internal Roads:** Gravel & paved, in good condition. **RV Service:** No. **Market:** W/in 3 mi. **Restaurant:** W/in 3 mi. **General Store:** Yes. **Vending:** Yes. **Swimming:** Yes. **Playground:** Yes. **Other:** Cabin & park model rentals. **Activities:** Swimming, horseshoes, volleyball, rec hall, game room, planned activities, sports field, horseshoes. **Nearby Attractions:** Ocean City, Atlantic City, the Wildwoods, Cape May. **Additional Information:** New Jersey Office of Travel Tourism, (800) JERSEY7, www.state.nj.us/travel.

RESTRICTIONS

Pets: On leash only. **Fires:** At site. **Alcoholic Beverages:** At site. **Vehicle Maximum Length:** 35 ft. **Other:** No camping motorcycles allowed.

TO GET THERE

From CR 550, go 0.5 mi. north on US 9. Entrance is on the left.

PORT REPUBLIC MAP, D-2, D-3
Thousand Trails—Chestnut Lake

631 Chestnut Neck Rd., 08241.
T: (609) 652-1005 or (800) 288-7245;
www.thousandtrails.com.

🚐 ★★★★   ⛺ ★★★★

Beauty: ★★★★		Site Privacy: ★★★
Spaciousness: ★★★		Quiet: ★★★★
Security: ★★★★★		Cleanliness: ★★★★
Insect Control: ★★★★		Facilities: ★★★★

This Thousand Trails park is centered around pristine Chestnut Lake, located in Port Republic about 15 miles northwest of Atlantic City. Like Outdoor World parks, Thousand Trails properties are clean and well maintained. And like most Thousand Trails parks, Chestnut Lake is in a rural location secluded from the hustle and bustle of Jersey Shore tourism. The campground accommodates 102 pull-throughs, and most sites are open. The lake is the focus of activity during warmer months. Chestnut Lake is about a 20-minute drive from Atlantic City's boardwalk, beaches, and casinos. Storybook Land—which features 50-plus buildings and displays depicting children's stories, live animals, rides, and a playground area—is also about 20 minutes away in Atlantic City. The Edwin B. Forsythe National Wildlife Refuge is only a 10-minute drive from the campground. This 40,000-acre refuge includes an 8-mile drive through wetlands and uplands where more than 200 species of birds may be observed.

BASICS

Operated By: Thousand Trails. **Open:** May 1–Oct. 15. **Site Assignment:** By reservation & first come, first served. **Registration:** At campground office. **Fee:** $35 per vehicle; V, MC, AE, D. **Parking:** At site.

FACILITIES

Number of RV-only Sites: 175. **Hookups:** Electric (30 amps), water. **Each Site:** Grill & picnic table. **Dump Station:** Yes. **Laundry:** Yes. **Pay Phone:** Yes. **Restrooms and Showers:** Yes. **Fuel:** No. **Propane:** Yes. **Internal Roads:** Gravel & paved, in good condition. **RV Service:** No. **Market:** W/in 8 mi. **Restaurant:** W/in 6 mi. **General Store:** Yes. **Vending:** Yes. **Swimming:** Yes. **Playground:** Yes. **Other:** Chestnut Lake. **Activities:** Swimming, canoeing, kayaking, fishing, mini-golf, basketball, shuffleboard, horseshoes, rec hall, game room. **Nearby Attractions:** Ocean City, Atlantic City, the Wildwoods, Cape May. **Additional Information:** New Jersey Office of Travel Tourism, (800) JERSEY7, www.state.nj.us/travel.

RESTRICTIONS

Pets: On leash only. **Fires:** At site. **Alcoholic Beverages:** At site. **Vehicle Maximum Length:** No limit. **Other:** No swimming in lake.

TO GET THERE

From Garden State Pkwy., take Exit 48 and turn right onto US 9, follow it 0.25 mi., then go 0.5 mi. west on CR 575. Entrance is on the right.

SUSSEX MAP, A-2
Beaver Hill Campground

120 Big Spring Rd., 07461. T: (800) 229-CAMP or (973) 827-0670; www.beaverhill.com.

🚐 ★★★★   ⛺ ★★★★

Beauty: ★★★★		Site Privacy: ★★
Spaciousness: ★★★		Quiet: ★★★★
Security: ★★★★		Cleanliness: ★★★★
Insect Control: ★★★★		Facilities: ★★★★

Located in the Skylands region of northern New Jersey, where the Kittatiny Mountains offer a contrast to the Jersey Shore beaches, Beaver Hill Campground has shaded sites amid well-manicured lawns. If you are fortunate, you will arrive at Beaver Hill during the Hawaiian Luau weekend when campers dance Hawaiian style and partake in a pig roast. Beaver Hill is near several interesting family-oriented attractions, such as Space Farms Zoo and Museum, a combination of exotic animals and historical museums; Sterling Hill Mine, where tours of a former zinc mine are offered; Mountain Creek, a water park; and Wild West City, which re-creates a 19th-century town in—you guessed it—the Wild West. The campground is also a short drive from Skylands Park, home of the New Jersey Cardinals, the Single-A affiliate of the St. Louis Cardinals.

BASICS

Operated By: Private operator. **Open:** May 1–Nov. 15. **Site Assignment:** Reservations accepted (3-day min. on holiday weekends). **Registration:** At log cabin. **Fee:** Campsite, $32–$38; trailer, $75; seasonal, $2,500; V, MC, D. **Parking:** At site.

FACILITIES

Number of RV-only Sites: 135. **Hookups:** Electric (20, 30, 50 amps), water, phone. **Each Site:** Fire ring, picnic table. **Dump Station:** Yes. **Laundry:** Yes. **Pay Phone:** Yes. **Restrooms and Showers:** Yes. **Fuel:** No. **Propane:** Yes. **Internal Roads:** Paved & dirt, in good condition. **RV Service:** No. **Market:** W/in 3 mi. **Restaurant:** W/in 1 mi. **General Store:** Yes. **Vending:** No. **Swimming:** Yes. **Playground:** Yes. **Other:** RV rentals, fishing pond, game room, firewood, modem service, party pavilion. **Activities:** Pond fishing, game room, rec hall, basketball, sports field, mini-golf, planned activities on weekends, hiking trails, badminton, volleyball, horseshoe pits. **Nearby Attractions:** Delaware Water Gap National Recreation Area, Village of Waterloo, Sterling Hill Mine, Wild West City, Kittatiny Valley State Park, Lakota Wolf Preserve, Land of Make Believe, Space Farms Zoo & Museum, Great Swamp National Wildlife Refuge. **Additional Information:** Skylands Tourism Council of New Jersey, (800) 4 SKYLAND, www.state.nj.us/travel.

RESTRICTIONS

Pets: On leash only, $1 extra per night. **Fires:** At site. **Alcoholic Beverages:** At site. **Vehicle Maximum Length:** 40 ft. **Other:** Fires & pets may not be left unattended.

TO GET THERE

From CR 565, go 3 mi. south on Hwy. 23, 1 mi. south on Hwy. 94, 2 mi. west on Beaver Spring Run Rd., and 0.5 mi. south on Big Spring Rd. Entrance is on the left.

SUSSEX MAP, A-2
Pleasant Acres Farm Campground

61 DeWitt Rd., 07461. T: (800) 722-4166 or (973) 875-4166; www.pleasantacres.com.

🚐 ★★★★★   ⛺ n/a

Beauty: ★★★★★		Site Privacy: ★★★
Spaciousness: ★★★★		Quiet: ★★★★
Security: ★★★★★		Cleanliness: ★★★★
Insect Control: ★★★★		Facilities: ★★★★★

Guests at Pleasant Acres Farm Campground typically do not make the rounds to the many nearby attractions; they are too busy enjoying the campground itself. A working farm where campers can pet baby animals, participate in pig chases and cow milking, and take a horse-drawn hayride around the lush hills, Pleasant Acres is one of our favorite places in the mid-Atlantic. Sites are open and shaded; no tents are permitted, except for RV campers who want to pitch a tent on their site. Meals, entertainment, and recreation are included in the basic campsite price here. Though the farm attractions are a big draw, Pleasant Acres also has an Olympic-sized swimming pool, a kiddie pool, a mini-golf course, a three-acre fishing lake, basketball and volleyball courts, and several nature trails in the mountains. Scheduled free meals are offered on weekdays in July and August. You can work up an appetite shearing sheep and chasing pigs.

BASICS

Operated By: Richard Denman. **Open:** All year. **Site Assignment:** Reservations recommended ($20 deposit required, 3-night min. required on holiday weekends), walk-ins accepted. **Registration:** At campground office. **Fee:** $42; V, MC, D, AE. **Parking:** At site.

FACILITIES

Number of RV-only Sites: 300. **Hookups:** Electric (20, 30, 50 amps), water, sewer, phone; 289 full hookups. **Each Site:** Fire ring, picnic table. **Dump Station:** Yes. **Laundry:** Yes. **Pay Phone:** Yes. **Restrooms and Showers:** Yes. **Fuel:** No. **Propane:** Yes. **Internal Roads:** Paved, in good condition. **RV Service:** Yes. **Market:** W/in 4 mi. **Restaurant:** W/in 4 mi. **General Store:** Yes. **Vending:** Yes. **Swimming:** Yes. **Playground:** Yes. **Other:** Working farm, fishing pond. **Activities:** Swimming, wading pool, whirlpool, fishing, mini-golf, basketball, planned activities, movies, sports field, volleyball, horseshoes, hiking trails, pig chases, cow milking, hiking trails. **Nearby Attractions:** Delaware Water Gap National Recreation Area, Village of Waterloo, Sterling Hill Mine, Wild West City, Kittatinny Valley State Park, Lakota Wolf Preserve, Land of Make Believe, Space Farms Zoo & Museum, Great Swamp National Wildlife Refuge. **Additional Information:** NJ Campground Owners Association, (609) 465-8444.

RESTRICTIONS

Pets: On leash only. **Fires:** At site. **Alcoholic Beverages:** At site. **Vehicle Maximum Length:** 40 ft. **Other:** No tents are permitted, though RV campers can use a tent on their site.

TO GET THERE

From Hwy. 284, go 5 mi. north on Hwy. 23 and 1 mi. east on DeWitt Rd. Entrance is on the left.

SWAINTON   MAP, D-2
Outdoor World—
Sea Pines Campground

1535 Hwy. 9 North, 08210. T: (609) 465-4517 or (800) 222-5557; www.campoutdoorworld.com.

🚐 ★★★★   ⛺ ★★★★

Beauty: ★★★★★		Site Privacy: ★★	
Spaciousness: ★★		Quiet: ★★★★	
Security: ★★★★		Cleanliness: ★★★★	
Insect Control: ★★★★		Facilities: ★★★★★	

Located south of Outdoor World's Lake and Shore Campground near Sea Isle City, Outdoor World—Sea Pines Campground features wooded sites, 300 of which have full hookups. There are no pull-through sites. Like at most Outdoor World campgrounds, there are a wide assortment of recreational opportunities. Campers can fish and kayak in the private lake, take a dip in the swimming pool, and play mini-golf. Sea Pines does not have an indoor water park, as Lake and Shore does. With the glitz of Atlantic City, the tradition of Ocean City, and the Victorian charm of Cape May, the Wildwoods are sometimes forgotten by travelers making vacation plans to the Jersey Shore. However, Wildwood's 2-mile-long boardwalk is scenic and inviting, as is the 5-mile-long beach it shares with neighboring North Wildwood and Wildwood Crest.

BASICS

Operated By: Outdoor World. **Open:** May 15–Oct. 12. **Site Assignment:** By reservation & first come, first served. **Registration:** At campground office. **Fee:** $30 per family; V, MC, AE, D; call ahead. **Parking:** At site.

FACILITIES

Number of RV-only Sites: 541. **Number of Tent-only Sites:** 8. **Hookups:** Electric (30, 50 amps), water, sewer; 300 full hookups. **Each Site:** Fire ring, picnic table. **Dump Station:** Yes. **Laundry:** Yes. **Pay Phone:** Yes. **Restrooms and Showers:** Yes. **Fuel:** No. **Propane:** Yes. **Internal Roads:** Gravel & dirt, in good condition. **RV Service:** No. **Market:** W/in 3 mi. **Restaurant:** W/in 3 mi. **General Store:** Yes. **Vending:** Yes. **Swimming:** Yes. **Playground:** Yes. **Other:** Private lake. **Activities:** Swimming, lake fishing, wading pool, canoeing, kayak, boat rentals, rec hall, game room, mini-golf, basketball, shuffleboard, planned activities, movies, sports field, horseshoes, volleyball. **Nearby Attractions:** Wildwoods boardwalk & beaches, Ocean City, Cape May, Cape May County Park & Zoo, Victorian Cape May tours, Historic Cold Spring Village, Cape May–Lewes (DE) Ferry, Atlantic City. **Additional Information:** New Jersey Office of Travel Tourism, (800) JERSEY7, www.state.nj.us/travel.

RESTRICTIONS

Pets: On leash only. **Fires:** At site. **Alcoholic Beverages:** At site. **Vehicle Maximum Length:** 40 ft.

TO GET THERE

From Garden State Pkwy., take Exit 13 and go 0.25 mi. west on CR 601 and 0.25 mi. south on US 9. Entrance is on the right.

TUCKERTON   MAP, C-3
Atlantic City North
Family Campground

Stage Rd., P.O. Box 242, 08087. T: (609) 296-9163 or (888) 229-9776; www.members.aol.com/campacn.

🚐 ★★★★   ⛺ ★★★★

Beauty: ★★★★		Site Privacy: ★★	
Spaciousness: ★★		Quiet: ★★★★	
Security: ★★★★		Cleanliness: ★★★★	
Insect Control: ★★★★		Facilities: ★★★★	

Set in the Pine Barrens of New Jersey, 15 minutes west of Long Beach Island and a half-hour north of Atlantic City, Atlantic City North Family Campground is ideal for visitors who want to experience both sides of the Jersey Shore. The campground provides free passes to Long Beach Island in season and a free van service to Atlantic City to campers who stay at least two nights. For dog owners, a dog-walking path winds around the outskirts of the campground. The swimming pool and the main building—which houses the camp store, rec hall, lounge, restrooms, showers, laundry room, and snack bar—are located west of the campground's main entrance. Sites surround the pool and main building in circular rows.

Other site clusters are located east of the main entrance. These sites are more spacious and are away from the activity centers. Tent sites are located at the far western end, beyond the circular rows of RV sites that surround the pool and main building.

BASICS

Operated By: Private operator. **Open:** All year. **Site Assignment:** Reservations accepted (2-night min. July & Aug.), walk-ins accepted. **Registration:** At campground office. **Fee:** Campsite, $25–$35; cabin, $55–$70; V, MC, D. **Parking:** At site.

FACILITIES

Number of RV-only Sites: 119. **Number of Tent-only Sites:** 33. **Hookups:** Electric (30, 50 amps), water, phone. **Each Site:** Fire ring, picnic table. **Dump Station:** Yes. **Laundry:** Yes. **Pay Phone:** Yes. **Restrooms and Showers:** Yes. **Fuel:** No. **Propane:** Yes. **Internal Roads:** Gravel, in good condition. **RV Service:** No. **Market:** W/in 4 mi. **Restaurant:** W/in 4 mi. **General Store:** Yes. **Vending:** Yes. **Swimming:** Yes. **Playground:** Yes. **Other:** Cabin rentals. **Activities:** Swimming, wading pool, mini-golf, basketball, rec hall, game room, shuffleboard, planned activities, movies, horseshoes, badminton, hiking trails, volleyball. **Nearby Attractions:** Long Beach Island; Atlantic City casinos, boardwalk, & beach. **Additional Information:** Atlantic City Convention Visitors Authority, (800) AC-CENTER, www.atlanticcitynj.com.

RESTRICTIONS

Pets: On leash only. **Fires:** At site. **Alcoholic Beverages:** At site. **Vehicle Maximum Length:** 40 ft. **Other:** Max. of 1 camping unit & 6 people per campsite.

TO GET THERE

From Garden State Pkwy., take Exit 58 and go about 50 ft. east on CR 539, 4 mi. south on Poormans Pkwy., and 0.5 mi. east on Stage Rd. Entrance is on the right.

WEST CAPE MAY   MAP, D-2
The Depot Travel Park

800 Broadway, 08204. T: (609) 884-2533.

🚐 ★★★★   ⛺ ★★★★

Beauty: ★★		Site Privacy: ★	
Spaciousness: ★★		Quiet: ★★	
Security: ★★★★		Cleanliness: ★★★★	
Insect Control: ★★★★		Facilities: ★★★★	

If you are looking for a campground with loads of swimming pools, sports courts, clubhouses, and private lakes, the Depot Travel Park in West Cape May is not for you. This campground has little on-site recreation, but it is located just blocks from Cape May's beaches, shops, and historic district. Sunbathing, ocean swimming, fishing, sightseeing boats, seafood restaurants, antiques and gift shops, and the boardwalk are all a few minutes away on foot. Cape May Beach is 1 mile away, and the Washington Street Victorian Mall, with three blocks of charming shops and sidewalk cafes, is within a few blocks of the Depot. Sites are open and offer little privacy; a cluster of sites surrounds a small wooded area at the northern end of the campground.

BASICS

Operated By: Glen Reeve. **Open:** May 1–Sept. 30. **Site Assignment:** Reservations accepted (full payment due upon check-in), walk-ins accepted. **Registration:** At campground office. **Fee:** $27.75; 2 adults, 2 children; no credit cards accepted. **Parking:** At site.

FACILITIES

Number of RV-only Sites: 150. **Hookups:** Electric (20, 30 amps), water. **Each Site:** Picnic table. **Dump Station:** Yes. **Laundry:** No. **Pay Phone:** Yes. **Restrooms and Showers:** Yes. **Fuel:** No. **Propane:** Yes. **Internal Roads:** Paved, in good condition. **RV Service:** No. **Market:** W/in 0.25 mi. **Restaurant:** W/in 0.25 mi. **General Store:** No. **Vending:** No. **Swimming:** Yes. **Playground:** Yes. **Other:** Located near the beach & Victorian Cape May. **Activities:** Horseshoes. **Nearby Attractions:** Victorian Cape May tours, Cape May beaches, Cape May–Lewes (DE) Ferry, Historic Cold Spring Village, Cape May County Park & Zoo. **Additional Information:** Cape May Chamber of Commerce, (609) 884-5508, www.capemaychamber.com.

RESTRICTIONS

Pets: On leash only. **Fires:** At site. **Alcoholic Beverages:** No alcohol permitted. **Vehicle Maximum Length:** No limit. **Other:** No cleaning of fish permitted on campground premises, no washing of vehicles allowed, electric heaters & electric water heaters not allowed.

TO GET THERE

From Hwy. 109, go 0.2 mi. west on US 9 and 2 mi. south on Seashore Rd. Entrance is on the right.

WEST CREEK   MAP, C-3
Sea Pirate Campground

Hwy. 9, P.O. Box 271, 08092. T: (800) 822-CAMP or (609) 296-7400; www.seapiratecamp.com.

🚐 ★★★★   ⛺ ★★★★

Beauty: ★★★★	Site Privacy: ★★★
Spaciousness: ★★★★	Quiet: ★★★★
Security: ★★★★★	Cleanliness: ★★★★
Insect Control: ★★★★	Facilities: ★★★★

Located 8 miles west of Long Beach Island and about a half-hour north of Atlantic City near West Creek, Sea Pirate Campground definitely caters to families. The park has a fishing pond stocked with bass, basketball and volleyball courts, and an assortment of scheduled activities, including ceramics, arts and crafts, and hayrides. Campers can rent a 14- or 16-foot John boat to explore the creek, which winds through a natural estuary leading into Little Egg Harbor Bay. Most of the activity centers—including the pool, basketball court, and softball field—are located near the entrance. A building housing the arcade, game room, and store is near the center. Sites are located across the street from the ice-cream parlor, snack bar, and activity centers, as well as all around the arcade building. Wooded sites near the fishing pond at the northwestern tip of the campground are recommended for campers who crave solitude.

BASICS

Operated By: Private operator. **Open:** May 1–Oct. 1. **Site Assignment:** Reservations accepted (4-night min. June 26–Labor Day), walk-ins accepted. **Registration:** At campground office. **Fee:** Call or see Web site for pricing details. **Parking:** At site.

FACILITIES

Number of RV-only Sites: 193. **Number of Tent-only Sites:** 6. **Hookups:** Electric (20, 30, 50 amps), water, sewer, cable TV, phone. **Each Site:** Fire ring, picnic table. **Dump Station:** Yes. **Laundry:** Yes. **Pay Phone:** Yes. **Restrooms and Showers:** Yes. **Fuel:** No. **Propane:** Yes. **Internal Roads:** Gravel, in good condition. **RV Service:** No. **Market:** W/in 5 mi. **Restaurant:** W/in 5 mi. **General Store:** Yes. **Vending:** No. **Swimming:** Yes. **Playground:** Yes. **Other:** RV & cabin rentals, fishing pond, crabbing area, lending library, access to buses to & from Atlantic City. **Activities:** Swimming, boating, canoeing, kayaking, boat rentals, rec hall, game room, fishing, basketball, planned activities, movies, sports field, volleyball, horseshoes. **Nearby Attractions:** Long Beach Island; Atlantic City casinos, boardwalk, beaches, Six Flags Great Adventure. **Additional Information:** Atlantic City Convention Visitors Authority, (800) ACVISIT, www.atlanticcitynj.com.

RESTRICTIONS

Pets: On leash only; attended. **Fires:** At site. Must be kept small. **Alcoholic Beverages:** No alcohol permitted. **Vehicle Maximum Length:** 40 ft. **Other:** Pets & fires may not be left unattended.

TO GET THERE

From Hwy. 72, go 5 mi. south on US 9. Entrance is on the left.

New Mexico

The epitome of the Southwest, New Mexico is striking, with its contrasting colors of purple blooms in the desert, shocking red chilies, brown adobe houses, and yellow-and-black Native American blankets for sale in the marketplace. Known as "the Land of Enchantment," sunbaked New Mexico attracts millions of tourists with its stark, delicate beauty and countless adventures.

For a quick visual into this living gallery, call to mind the brilliant desert paintings of Georgia O'Keeffe. But with all of the natural beauty that awaits, we invite you to resist lingering in the galleries.

Natural wonders are abundant in the form of undeveloped caves, spectacular rock formations, and lava flows. After a day of hiking, melt the day away in one of the many natural hot springs. Numerous ancient and Spanish colonial ruins set New Mexico apart from other states. For a look at the past, you can find anything from 11th-century Pueblo ruins to 13th-century cliff dwellings. If you would rather drive through this multicolored palette, then take one of 27 historic and scenic byways that showcase New Mexico in all its glory. Or maybe you would prefer to take in the view from overhead. Hot-air balloon flights can be found statewide, and in October, Albuquerque is host to the **Kodak International Balloon Fiesta.** If that's not daring enough for you, then you should head to the city of **Hobbs.** This is the best place in the state for soaring and hang gliding, where many world records for both distance and altitude have been set.

Outdoor sports and recreation offer endless fun for the entire family. Smooth-road biking and rough mountain-terrain biking have been tested by the many cycling enthusiasts who call this state home. An abundance of trails, caves, and canyons are awaiting those who enjoy hiking, caving, or climbing. Horse lovers will be happy to know that horseback riding and rodeos are plentiful and easy to find. Riding stables are located throughout the state, and special events are always on the docket. Wildlife gazing is also a fun sport in these parts. The patient observer can expect to see elk, deer, quail, dove, pheasant, waterfowl, and the lesser-known pronghorn, javeling, oryx, Persian ibex, and Barbary sheep. Anglers can find a wide variety of species like trout, bass, panfish, catfish, walleye, and northern pike. If golf is your forte, there is a wide variety of courses to choose from, making it easy to find the links best suited to your style of play.

With its diverse geography, this state offers not only desert territory but also a plethora of opportunities for water and winter sports. For water lovers, there is scuba diving, parasailing, kayaking, catamaran sailing, windsurfing, swimming, sailing, waterskiing, rafting, canoeing, bass tournaments, pontoon boat cruising, and dragboat races. The wild **Rio Grande** is the river of choice for the experienced whitewater enthusiast, while the **Rio Chama** is for beginners who like to take it slow. Several outfitters offer guided overnight and day tours through this stretch. For folks who prefer dry sports, the land sailor can harness the wind to skim waterless lakebeds on three-wheeled wind racers west of **Lordsburg,** home of the **Great Overland Landsail Races.** Sandsurfing on plastic saucers is another unique activity on the dunes at **White Sands National Monument** near **Alamogordo.**

The snow enthusiast can find ten downhill ski areas, including world-class **Taos Ski Valley,** that offer a wide range of skiing and snowboarding terrain. Other winter sports in the area are snow skating, snow biking, tubing, cross-country skiing, and snowmobiling. Scattered among the mountains are a few maintained ponds and lakes that are great for ice-skaters to play hockey or hone their figure-skating skills. Most of these attractions are generally served by well-maintained roads that lead to exciting and scenic camping opportunities.

Whether you stay for a week or a winter, you need not look too far to find fun for the entire family, because in this state it's around every corner. Just like chilies in your salsa, New Mexico will pleasantly surprise you with its flavor and spice.

Campground Profiles

ABIQUIU   MAP, A-2
Riana Campground

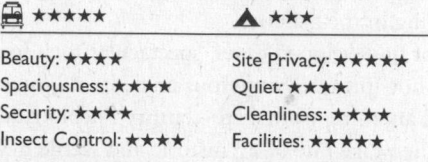

Abiquiu Lake Project Office, P.O. Box 290, 87510.
T: (505) 685-4371 or (505) 685-4561;
www.reserveamerica.com.

🚐 ★★★★   ⛺ ★★★★★

Beauty: ★★★★★   Site Privacy: ★★★★
Spaciousness: ★★★★   Quiet: ★★★★★
Security: ★★★★   Cleanliness: ★★★★
Insect Control: ★★★★   Facilities: ★★

Laid out in several loops, Riana offers sites above the
reservoir—some with excellent views. Sites 1–15 are
mostly 60- to 75-foot back-ins with electric
hookups. These sites have extra space for a boat or
second vehicle. Sites 9 and 10 are pull-throughs
(actually "pull-alongsides") that are 90 feet in length.
Sites 13 and 15 have the best views but are just above
the playground. Sites 16–30 are located in a fenced-
in parking area. Each site is 36 by 30 feet with a
camping area beside. The fences make it difficult for
larger rigs to back into some of these sites (such as
25–30). Sites 16 and 17 are pull-throughs similar to
9 and 10. Sites 18–20 have the best views. The
remaining sites are primitive or walk-in sites. The RV
sites are 45- to 55-foot back-ins with wonderful
views of the reservoir. Sites 40–54 are walk-in tent
sites inside a fenced-in area. Each site has a 12 by 12-
foot crushed gravel pad for a tent. Sites 47–50 have
nice desert views. There are portable toilets for tenters' use in this area. Riana is a pretty (but rather
primitive) campground that offers lake recreation
and fun for the entire family.

BASICS
Operated By: U.S. Army Corps of Engineers.
Open: Apr. 15–Oct. 15. **Site Assignment:** Half of
sites first come, first served; reservations made
through ReserveAmerica for the other half at
www.recreation.gov, (877) 444-6777. **Registration:**
At gate; camp host will come around to sites in
morning in case of late arrivals. **Fee:** Water/electric,
$14; primitive $10; walk-in tent $5; check, V, MC, AE,
D. **Parking:** At site, overflow parking.

FACILITIES
Number of RV-only Sites: 30. **Number of Tent-
only Sites:** 15. **Hookups:** Electric (30, 50 amps),
water. **Each Site:** Covered picnic table, grill, lantern
pole. **Dump Station:** Yes. **Laundry:** No. **Pay
Phone:** No. **Restrooms and Showers:** Yes. **Fuel:**
No. **Propane:** No. **Internal Roads:** Mostly paved.
RV Service: No. **Market:** 8 mi. south to Abiquiu.
Restaurant: 8 mi. south to Abiquiu. **General Store:**
No. **Vending:** No. **Swimming:** Reservoir. **Play-
ground:** Yes. **Other:** Picnic area. **Activities:** Fishing,
boating, swimming, hiking. **Nearby Attractions:**
Ghost Ranch Conference Center, Georgia O'Keeffe
house in Abiquiu. **Additional Information:** Española
Chamber of Commerce, (505) 753-2831.

RESTRICTIONS
Pets: On leash, cleaned up after. **Fires:** Grill only.
Alcoholic Beverages: At sites. **Vehicle Maxi-
mum Length:** 40 ft.

TO GET THERE
From the junction of Hwy. 84 and Hwy. 96 (about
7 mi. north of town), turn west onto Hwy. 96 and
go 1.3 mi. Turn right at the sign into the entrance.

ALAMOGORDO   MAP, C-2
Alamogordo Roadrunner Campground

412-24th St., 88310. T: (877) 437-3003 or (505)
437-3003; www.roadrunnercampground.com.

🚐 ★★★★★   ⛺ ★★★

Beauty: ★★★★   Site Privacy: ★★★★★
Spaciousness: ★★★★   Quiet: ★★★★
Security: ★★★★   Cleanliness: ★★★★
Insect Control: ★★★★   Facilities: ★★★★★

This campground boasts beautiful landscaping as
well as mountain vistas to the east (especially sites
48–63). A small section of ratty fencing to the south
that conceals a mobile-home park does insult the
view but can be mostly ignored. The 38 pull-
throughs are level and long (60 by 30 feet), while
back-ins are a spacious 32 by 30 feet. The smaller
back-ins close to the pool (65–67) have nice grass and
trees and are still pleasant spots to camp. Tent sites are
away from the RV sites, along the southwest side of
the office on a strip of grass with plenty of tree coverage. However, parking is directly behind the sites,
where a row of RVs in storage compete for space. The
laundry facility is large, clean, and modern, with lots
of machines, loads of space, and a raft of magazines.
Restrooms are also large, clean, well lit, and tastefully
decorated. Playground facilities are well maintained
and safe. Overall, this is a great destination in a great
location for visiting the White Sands National Monument, and even Carlsbad Caverns and Mexico.

BASICS
Operated By: Ken & Judy Bonnell. **Open:** All year.
Site Assignment: Upon registration; credit card
required for reservation, 24-hour cancellation policy
or charged 1-night fee plus $5. **Registration:** At
office; late arrivals use drop box. **Fee:** RV, $24–$29;
tent, $19. **Parking:** At site.

FACILITIES
Number of RV-only Sites: 65. **Number of Tent-
only Sites:** 10. **Hookups:** Electric (15, 30, 50 amps),
water, sewer, cable TV, Wi-Fi. **Each Site:** Cement
table, cement privacy wall, tree, lamp, grill. **Dump
Station:** Yes. **Laundry:** Yes. **Pay Phone:** Yes.
Restrooms and Showers: Yes. **Fuel:** No.
Propane: Yes. **Internal Roads:** Paved. **RV Service:**
No. **Market:** 1 mi. **Restaurant:** 2 blocks. **General
Store:** Yes. **Vending:** No. **Swimming:** Pool. **Play-
ground:** Yes. **Other:** 2 cabins, pool open May
15–Sept. 15. **Activities:** Swimming. **Nearby Attrac-
tions:** White Sands National Monument, White
Sands Missile Range/Trinity site, Texas, Mexico. **Addi-**

tional Information: Alamogordo Chamber of
Commerce, (800) 826-0294, (505) 437-6120.

RESTRICTIONS
Pets: On leash. **Fires:** Grills. **Alcoholic Beverages:**
At sites. **Vehicle Maximum Length:** 40 ft.

TO GET THERE
From Hwy. 54/70 (White Sands Blvd.), turn east
onto 24th St. in town. Go 0.2 mi. on 24th St., then
turn right at the sign into the entrance. The office
lies straight ahead.

ALBUQUERQUE   MAP, B-1, B-2
Albuquerque Central KOA

12400 Skyline Rd. NE, 87123. T: (505) 296-2729 or
(800) 562-7781; www.koa.com.

🚐 ★★★★   ⛺ ★★★

Beauty: ★★★   Site Privacy: ★★★
Spaciousness: ★★★   Quiet: ★★★
Security: ★★★★   Cleanliness: ★★★★★
Insect Control: ★★★★   Facilities: ★★★★★

This is an enormous campground with rows and rows
of RV sites. Sites 1–15 are 35-foot sites that back to a
fence and residential area. D row, which contains the
best sites (28–44), is in the middle of the campground, away from the road and the highway on the
other side. Sites 33–36 are close to the restrooms, and
35 is well shaded. The rows containing sites 45–74
are in the second-best area. West of this area is a sea of
RVs: five rows of RV sites (81–169) packed in
together. Sites 81–88, along the southwest fence, are
60-foot back-ins. Sites 98–148 are 70 by 33–foot
pull-throughs—large enough for any rig, but placed
like dozens of pawns on a chessboard. Sites 149–169
are 30-foot back-ins along the west wall that back to
apartments close by. End sites on the north side (113
and 130) are close to both the pet run and the highway, and are therefore less desirable. The "Tent Village" is a fenced-in dirt area with one shade tree.
While it might work out if a large group were camping together, it feels cramped for campers who do not
know each other. There are, in fact, two tenting areas,
one of which has a shaded bench and table per tent
site, and one that does not. Neither is particularly
roomy, and campers may feel hemmed in by the fencing. This is a gigantic campground, and one may feel
somewhat like an anonymous log moving through a
sawmill. The facilities, however, are clean and comfortable, and the campground offers a safe and comfortable (if crowded) environment.

BASICS
Operated By: Milt Dudley. **Open:** All year. **Site
Assignment:** Upon registration; credit card
required for reservation; 48-hour cancellation policy.
Registration: At office; late arrivals use drop box.
Fee: RV full hookup 50 amp, $44; full hookup 30
amp, $42; water/electric, $37; tent, $28; V, MC, AE, D.
Parking: At site.

FACILITIES
Number of RV-only Sites: 206. **Number of Tent-
only Sites:** 25. **Hookups:** Electric (30, 50 amps),

water, sewer, Wi-Fi, telephone. **Each Site:** Picnic table. **Dump Station:** Yes. **Laundry:** Yes. **Pay Phone:** Yes. **Restrooms and Showers:** Yes. **Fuel:** No. **Propane:** Yes. **Internal Roads:** Paved. **RV Service:** Mobile. **Market:** 0.25 mi. north. **Restaurant:** 0.25 mi. north. **General Store:** Yes. **Vending:** Yes. **Swimming:** Pool. **Playground:** Yes. **Other:** Cabin, modem, 1 phone site, rec hall, mini-golf, video games, RV rentals, spa. **Activities:** Swimming, golf. **Nearby Attractions:** Balloon Fiesta (first Sun. in Oct.). **Additional Information:** Albuquerque Chamber of Commerce, (505) 764-3700.

RESTRICTIONS

Pets: On leash, cleaned up after. **Fires:** Grill only. **Alcoholic Beverages:** At sites. **Vehicle Maximum Length:** 80 ft.

TO GET THERE

From I-40 (Exit 166), turn south onto Juan Tabo Blvd. and go 0.25 mi. Turn left onto Skyline Rd. and go 0.35 mi. Turn left at the sign into the entrance.

ANGEL FIRE   MAP, A-2
Sierra Bonita Cabins and RV Park

P.O. Box 963, 87710. T: (800) 942-1556 or (505) 387-5508; www.sierrabonita.com.

🚐 ★★★★   ⛺ ★★★★

Beauty: ★★★★★	Site Privacy: ★★★
Spaciousness: ★★★	Quiet: ★★★★
Security: ★★★★	Cleanliness: ★★★★★
Insect Control: ★★★★	Facilities: ★★★

This park consists of one strip of open-ended back-ins. The open field in which these sites are located allows for any size rig. Most sites are 22 feet wide and back to the road about 50 feet away. Site 1, in the northwest corner, is closest to the bathhouse. Site 11 in the southwest corner seems a little cramped (there is a fence on one side). The park is located in a valley, which means that sunrise is slightly later and sunset slightly earlier—this may make for a chilly morning or evening. The location is absolutely gorgeous, with forested hills on all sides. The lucky and patient camper may spot elk, deer, foxes, and black bears. The park abuts a fishing area that guests may use. The showers are individual unisex units that are very clean and comfortable. The restrooms are also individual units, and likewise very clean. This park is much more secluded than the RV park in town, although it requires a longer drive to get to. However, the drive is absolutely worth the extra effort, and this is a campground that many people return to year after year.

BASICS

Operated By: Dale, Kelly, & Jeanie Powell. **Open:** May 15–Oct. 15. **Site Assignment:** First come, first served; credit card required for reservation, 1-night deposit; no refund of deposit upon cancellation. **Registration:** At office; late arrivals select available site & pay in the morning. **Fee:** Water/electric, $14.95; check, V, MC, D. **Parking:** At site.

FACILITIES

Number of RV-only Sites: 10. **Hookups:** Electric (20, 30 amps), water. **Each Site:** Picnic table, fire pit. **Dump Station:** Yes. **Laundry:** Yes. **Pay Phone:**

No. **Restrooms and Showers:** Yes. **Fuel:** No. **Propane:** No. **Internal Roads:** Dirt. **RV Service:** No. **Market:** 17 mi. north or south. **Restaurant:** 17 mi. north or south. **General Store:** Yes. **Vending:** No. **Swimming:** No. **Playground:** No. **Other:** Cabins, group shelter. **Activities:** Fishing, scenic drives through Coyote Creek Canyon. **Nearby Attractions:** Harold Brock fishing area, Coyote Creek State Park. **Additional Information:** New Mexico State Parks Division, (888) NM-PARKS.

RESTRICTIONS

Pets: On leash, cleaned up after. **Fires:** Grill only. **Alcoholic Beverages:** At sites, not in group shelter. **Vehicle Maximum Length:** No limit.

TO GET THERE

From the junction of Hwy. 64 and Hwy. 434, turn south onto Hwy. 434 and go 10.8 mi. Turn right at the junction with Hwy. 120 to stay on Hwy. 434 and go a further 8.2 mi. The office is on the right, up a flight of stairs.

ARTESIA   MAP, C-3
Artesia RV Park

201 Hermosa Dr., 88210. T: (505) 746-6184; www.artesiarvpark.com.

🚐 ★★★★   ⛺ ★★★

Beauty: ★★	Site Privacy: ★★★★★
Spaciousness: ★★★★★	Quiet: ★★★★
Security: ★★★★★	Cleanliness: ★★★★★
Insect Control: ★★★★	Facilities: ★★★

This is a rather simple but comfortable campground with open gravel spaces divided into undefined rows. Sites 1–5 to the northwest average 45 by 34 feet. Sites 6–13 (in two rows) are also 45 feet in length. Site 13 is located against a shed, which makes it less desirable, but 10 has a trellis with plants growing up it, and 9 and 12 have trees. (The trees that dot the park are not large enough to provide shade, but add to the overall attractiveness.) Sites B1–10 and A1–10 in the middle of the park are doubles about 75 feet long but only 12 feet wide. End sites A6 and B10 are the widest (30 feet), since they do not share a site. Site 14 in the southwest corner is adjacent to a wooden storage shed, and is thus less desirable. Sites 16–21 along the southern edge are for long-term residents. The tent area is a grassy strip to the east of the RV sites. While there are a few covered tables and two grills, it is obvious that this park is more RV-than tent-oriented. The horseshoes at one end of the tent area could make for a rude awakening to an unlucky tent camper on that side. The restrooms and showers are wonderfully clean and extremely spacious. This is a park that RVers will enjoy thoroughly, although tenters may wish to move on.

BASICS

Operated By: Ken Otte. **Open:** All year. **Site Assignment:** Upon registration; verbal reservations OK. **Registration:** At office; late arrivals use drop box. **Fee:** RV (full), $22–$24; tent, $10; check, V, MC, D. **Parking:** At site.

FACILITIES

Number of RV-only Sites: 42. **Number of Tent-only Sites:** 2. **Hookups:** Electric (30, 50 amps),

water, sewer, cable TV, phone. **Each Site:** Picnic table, grill. **Dump Station:** Yes. **Laundry:** Yes. **Pay Phone:** No. **Restrooms and Showers:** Yes. **Fuel:** No. **Propane:** No. **Internal Roads:** Gravel. **RV Service:** No. **Market:** 3 mi. west. **Restaurant:** Nearby. **General Store:** Yes, RV supplies. **Vending:** Soda. **Swimming:** No. **Playground:** No. **Other:** Modem, pet walk. **Activities:** Tours to Carlsbad Caverns, horseshoes. **Nearby Attractions:** Brantly Lake State Park, Carlsbad Caverns, Roswell. **Additional Information:** Artesia Chamber of Commerce, (505) 746-2744.

RESTRICTIONS

Pets: On leash, cleaned up after. **Fires:** Grill only. **Alcoholic Beverages:** At sites. **Vehicle Maximum Length:** 40 ft.

TO GET THERE

From the junction of Hwy. 82 and Hwy. 285, turn south onto Hwy. 285 and go 1 mi. to Hermosa Drive. Turn right onto Hermosa Dr. and go 0.1 mi. Turn left at the sign into the entrance.

BUCKHORN   MAP, C-1
Buckhorn RV Park

7656 Hwy. 180 West, 88025. T: (505) 535-2995.

🚐 ★★★★   ⛺ ★★★

Beauty: ★★★	Site Privacy: ★★★
Spaciousness: ★★★	Quiet: ★★★★
Security: ★★★★	Cleanliness: ★★★★
Insect Control: ★★★★	Facilities: ★★

Sites in this campground are laid out in two rows and numbered 1–10 and A–I. All sites in this field are open-ended, roughly 90 feet long. There are mobile homes around the entire perimeter of this campground. Sites on the east side (A–I) are 24 feet wide pull-throughs under willow trees. Site I is next to a mobile home. The nicest sites are A–C, as they are closest to the restrooms and away from the mobile homes. On the west side, sites 1–10 are open-ended, 20-foot-wide back-ins. These sites are entirely unshaded and not as nice as the pull-through spaces. Site 10 lies next to some buildings. The restrooms are small but clean and comfortable. This is a decent stop for a short stay, and is conveniently located near some interesting areas, such as the Catwalk.

BASICS

Operated By: Dave & Polli Morgan. **Open:** All year. **Site Assignment:** First come, first served; verbal reservations OK. **Registration:** At house or store; late arrivals use drop box at manager's house. **Fee:** RV (full), $15; tent, $7; check, no credits cards. **Parking:** At site.

FACILITIES

Number of RV-only Sites: 19. **Number of Tent-only Sites:** Undesignated sites. **Hookups:** Electric (30, 50 amps), water, sewer. **Dump Station:** No (sewer at all sites). **Laundry:** Yes. **Pay Phone:** Yes. **Restrooms and Showers:** Yes. **Fuel:** No. **Propane:** No. **Internal Roads:** Gravel. **RV Service:** No. **Market:** 10 mi. to Gila. **Restaurant:** 0.25 mi. **General Store:** 0.25 mi. **Vending:** Yes. **Swimming:** No. **Playground:** No. **Activities:** Bird-watching, fishing, hiking. **Nearby Attractions:**

Mogollon ghost town, Glenwood Catwalk, Bill Evans Lake, Silver City. **Additional Information:** Silver City Grant County Chamber of Commerce, (505) 538-3785.

RESTRICTIONS

Pets: On leash, cleaned up after. **Fires:** Grill only. **Alcoholic Beverages:** At sites. **Vehicle Maximum Length:** No limit.

TO GET THERE

From Hwy. 180, 0.25 mi. west of the town sign, on the south side of the highway.

CAPULIN   MAP, A-3
Capulin RV Park

P.O. Box 68, 88414. T: (505) 278-2921; www.capulinrvpark.com.

🚚 ★★★   ⛺ ★★★

Beauty: ★★★	Site Privacy: ★★★
Spaciousness: ★★	Quiet: ★★★
Security: ★★★★	Cleanliness: ★★★★
Insect Control: ★★★★	Facilities: ★★★

This campground has one row of back-ins and one row of pull-throughs. Sites 1–10 are 60-foot back-ins along the north edge that back to trees behind which is the highway. Sites 11–29 are 50-foot pull-throughs that can pull in sideways for extra space if one site is not large enough. Eastern end site 11 has the most space (33 feet wide) compared to the others (15 feet wide). Sites 13, 14, 15, and 16 share large shade trees. All other pull-through sites are unshaded, except for 29, which is right up against a copse of trees. (In fact, it is so close that the space is somewhat cramped because of its location.) Tenting is possible wherever there is grass (which is mostly to the south or east, next to sites 11 or 12). While the grass cover is quite adequate, the campground itself is not really tent-oriented, and there are no other facilities (such as table or fire pit) for tenters' use. The restrooms are clean and comfortable. This campground is a very nice spot to stay for a few days, and the Capulin Volcano National Monument is well worth checking out.

BASICS

Operated By: Chance & Joni Hall. **Open:** All year. **Site Assignment:** First come, first served; verbal reservations or e-mail OK. **Registration:** At office; late arrivals use drop box. **Fee:** RV (30, 50 amps), $21; tent, $13; cash, check, MC, V. **Parking:** At site.

FACILITIES

Number of RV-only Sites: 30. **Number of Tent-only Sites:** Undesignated sites. **Hookups:** Electric (30, 50 amps), water, sewer; 14 full hookup. **Each Site:** Picnic tables. **Dump Station:** Yes. **Laundry:** Yes. **Pay Phone:** 1 block. **Restrooms and Showers:** Yes. **Fuel:** No. **Propane:** No. **Internal Roads:** Gravel. **RV Service:** No. **Market:** 0.25 mi. west. **Restaurant:** 0.25 mi. west. **General Store:** Capulin Country Store/Restaurant (0.25 mi. west). **Vending:** No. **Swimming:** No. **Playground:** No. **Other:** Cards & picnicking in the garage. Slide-outs welcome. **Activities:** Cards, hiking, swimming, boating, fishing in the area. **Nearby Attractions:** Sugarite Canyon State Park, Capulin Volcano National Monument, Folsom Man Site, Clayton Lake State

Park. **Additional Information:** Raton Chamber of Commerce, (800) 638-6161.

RESTRICTIONS

Pets: On leash, cleaned up after. **Fires:** Grill only. **Alcoholic Beverages:** At sites. **Vehicle Maximum Length:** No limit.

TO GET THERE

From the junction of Hwy. 325 and Hwy. 87/64, turn east onto Hwy. 87/64 and go 0.1 mi. Turn right at the sign into the entrance.

CARLSBAD   MAP, C-3
Carlsbad RV Park and Campground

4301 National Parks Hwy., 88220. T: (505) 885-6333 or (888) 8RV-PARK (888-878-7275); www.carlsbadrvpark.com.

🚚 ★★★★   ⛺ ★★★

Beauty: ★★★	Site Privacy: ★★★★
Spaciousness: ★★★★	Quiet: ★★★★
Security: ★★★★	Cleanliness: ★★★★★
Insect Control: ★★	Facilities: ★★★★★

Located on the southwest side of town (toward the caverns as you leave Carlsbad), this campground has got it all: pool, laundry, RV servicing, and activities galore. On top of that, facilities are super-clean and spacious. Sites are level and long (60 feet), with some extra-wide spaces (45 feet) for slide-outs, and all are pull-through. Most RV sites have trees, with the exception of A4–A6. End site B31 is perhaps the most desirable site, with a large shade tree, extra space, and an easy in/out. Tent sites are level but with a thin grass coverage. Tent sites 33 and 39 have good, large trees, and the unmarked site in the extreme northeast corner has extra room, being on the end of a row and backing onto a grassy field. Normal tent sites are 40 by 40 feet, a comfortable size. However, tent sites would be greatly improved if the trees were away from the road instead of right up against it. Owners of large dogs will be happy with the three-acre off-leash area, where horses have even been let out to roam! Large camping groups can likewise be accommodated with the meeting room that can hold more than 100 people and includes a kitchen. Carlsbad makes a wonderful stop for those exploring the caverns or making their way to Texas or even Mexico.

BASICS

Operated By: Jim & Mary Crozier. **Open:** All year. **Site Assignment:** Upon registration; verbal reservations OK, necessary in summer; 24-hour cancellation policy. **Registration:** At office; late arrivals use drop box. **Fee:** Call for rates; MC, V. **Parking:** At site.

FACILITIES

Number of RV-only Sites: 20. **Number of Tent-only Sites:** 40. **Hookups:** Electric (30, 50 amps), water, sewer, cable TV, Wi-Fi. **Each Site:** Picnic table, grill. **Dump Station:** Yes. **Laundry:** Yes. **Pay Phone:** Yes. **Restrooms and Showers:** Yes. **Fuel:** No. **Propane:** No. **Internal Roads:** Gravel, in good condition. **RV Service:** Next door. **Market:** 1.5 mi. in Carlsbad. **Restaurant:** 3 blocks. **General Store:** Yes. **Vending:** Yes. **Swimming:** Heated indoor pool.

Playground: Yes. **Other:** Cabins, rec room, group meeting room (100-plus person) w/ kitchen, dog walk, free charcoal & gas grills, RV storage, jukebox. **Activities:** Summer holiday potlucks, Ping-Pong, video games, swimming, air hockey. **Nearby Attractions:** Carlsbad Caverns, Sitting Bull Falls, Living Desert. **Additional Information:** Carlsbad CVB, (800) 221-1224, (505) 887-6516.

RESTRICTIONS

Pets: On leash. **Fires:** Fire rings or grills. **Alcoholic Beverages:** Allowed. **Vehicle Maximum Length:** 60 ft.

TO GET THERE

From the junction of Hwy. 62/180 and Hwy. 285, go 1.7 mi. south on Hwy. 62/180. Turn west at the sign into the campground. The office is straight ahead.

CHAMA   MAP, A-2
Rio Chama RV Park

182 North NM 17, P.O. Box 706, 87520. T: (505) 756-2303.

🚚 ★★★★★   ⛺ ★★★★★

Beauty: ★★★★★	Site Privacy: ★★★★★
Spaciousness: ★★★★	Quiet: ★★★★
Security: ★★★★★	Cleanliness: ★★★★
Insect Control: ★★★	Facilities: ★★

This lovely campground is loaded with trees, sits next to the Rio Chama River, and has beautiful RV and tent sites. The Cumbres and Toltec Scenic Railway passes within a stone's throw of the east border—which may or may not be an attraction to some campers. (There is only one run per day, entailing two passes of the campground.) Pretty much any site is highly desirable, with the possible exception of A6, which is right at the entrance. Site 39 has no shade tree but receives shade from the trees in neighboring sites. Pull-throughs are a good 65 feet in length, while back-ins average 42 feet. All sites are nearly 30 feet in width, which makes them comfortably spacious. The tenting area is absolutely gorgeous: it contains lush grass, large sites, and plenty of trees. A barbed-wire fence runs the length of the area, making it quite secure. Site 5 is the least desirable, as it contains a telephone pole and the communal wash basin. Any other tent site is well worth the price of admission. This campground is a popular destination—many seniors return year after year to meet old friends—and justifiably so.

BASICS

Operated By: Margie & Russ Patterson. **Open:** May–Oct. 15. **Site Assignment:** Upon registration; for reservations, write to the campground between Oct. & May, call between May & Oct. **Registration:** At office; late arrivals wake up manager for site assignment. **Fee:** RV, $20–$26; tent $13; V, MC. **Parking:** At site.

FACILITIES

Number of RV-only Sites: 78. **Number of Tent-only Sites:** 14. **Hookups:** Electric (30, 50 amps), water, sewer. **Each Site:** Picnic table, fire ring/grill, many trees. **Dump Station:** Yes. **Laundry:** No. **Pay Phone:** Yes. **Restrooms and Showers:** Yes. **Fuel:**

No. **Propane:** No. **Internal Roads:** Gravel. **RV Service:** No. **Market:** 2 mi. into Chama. **Restaurant:** 0.25 mi. **General Store:** No. **Vending:** No. **Swimming:** No. **Playground:** No. **Other:** Rio Chama River, covered shelter & stage, RV storage, notice board, railroad passes park (twice daily). **Activities:** Potlucks, ice-cream socials, coffee & doughnuts on weekends, horseback riding, fishing, volleyball, Ping-Pong, horseshoes. **Nearby Attractions:** Cumbres & Toltec Scenic Railroad, Rio Chama River. **Additional Information:** Chama Valley Chamber of Commerce, (800) 477-0149, (505) 756-2306.

RESTRICTIONS

Pets: On leash, cleaned up after, always attended outside. **Fires:** In ring/grill between 4–10 p.m. **Alcoholic Beverages:** At sites. **Vehicle Maximum Length:** 60 ft. **Other:** No generators.

TO GET THERE

From the junction of Hwy. US 84/64 and Hwy. 17, go 1.8 mi. north on Hwy. 17. Turn right (east) at the sign into the campground entrance. The office is in a boxcar on the right.

CIMARRON   MAP, A-3
Ponil Campground

Hwy. 64, P.O. Box 323, 87714. T: (505) 376-2700.

🚐 ★★★★   ⛺ ★★★

Beauty: ★★★★	Site Privacy: ★★★
Spaciousness: ★★★	Quiet: ★★★★
Security: ★★★★★	Cleanliness: ★★★★★
Insect Control: ★★★★	Facilities: ★★★★

There is a tangible feeling of community among campers in Ponil. The sites in this park contribute to this feeling, as they are not all clearly delineated, and there is not a lot of space between them. However, there are spaces to accommodate a rig of any size. Sites in the northeast corner (in a somewhat separated nook) are very well shaded. Sites along the north and northwest edge back to trees. Sites in the southwest (along the entrance) back to an open grassy field where deer and elk are seen in the morning. These sites can pull through. The space around them is enough for each camper to do his or her own thing, but also lends itself to meeting and interacting with neighbors—one of the best reasons to travel. Tenting is possible in the open field in front of the house. There is one large tree and a hedge along the perimeter of the property that blocks out the road. This is a favorite destination for Cub Scouts and for RVers who wish to meet other campers in a lovely and quiet setting.

BASICS

Operated By: Kathy & Stanley Jones, Rosene & Kit Gunter. **Open:** All year. **Site Assignment:** Depends on site availability; verbal reservations OK. **Registration:** At manager's trailer; late arrivals select available site & pay in the morning. **Fee:** RV (full), $20; tent, $10; check, no credits cards. **Parking:** At site.

FACILITIES

Number of RV-only Sites: 36. **Number of Tent-only Sites:** Undesignated sites. **Hookups:** Electric (30 amps), water, sewer. **Each Site:** Picnic tables. **Dump Station:** Yes. **Laundry:** Yes. **Pay Phone:** Yes.

Restrooms and Showers: Yes. **Fuel:** No. **Propane:** No. **Internal Roads:** Gravel. **RV Service:** No. **Market:** 1.5 mi. south. **Restaurant:** 1 mi. south. **General Store:** No. **Vending:** No. **Swimming:** No. **Playground:** Yes. **Other:** Rec room, screened pavilion. **Activities:** Singing twice weekly, hiking, wildlife viewing, craft classes. **Nearby Attractions:** Cimarron Canyon State Park, Maxwell National Wildlife Reserve, Ponil River at edge of campground. **Additional Information:** Cimarron Chamber of Commerce, (505) 376-2417.

RESTRICTIONS

Pets: On leash, cleaned up after. **Fires:** Grill only. **Alcoholic Beverages:** At sites. **Vehicle Maximum Length:** No limit.

TO GET THERE

From the junction of Hwy. 58 and Hwy. 64, turn east onto Hwy. 64 and go 1 mi. Turn left at the sign into the entrance.

CLAYTON   MAP, A-3
Meadowlark KOA

P.O. Box 366, 903 South 5th St., 88415. T: (800) 562-9507 or (505) 374-9508; www.koa.com.

🚐 ★★★★   ⛺ ★★★★

Beauty: ★★★★	Site Privacy: ★★★★
Spaciousness: ★★★★	Quiet: ★★★★
Security: ★★★★	Cleanliness: ★★★★★
Insect Control: ★★★★	Facilities: ★★★★

The sites in Meadowlark KOA are enormous (easily 100 feet in length) and are able to accommodate a rig of any size. They are level, open, and grassy, with decent space (30 feet) between each one. The campground is surrounded by trees (except to the south), but there are not a lot of shade trees within the campground itself. The best RV sites are end sites 7, 14, 21, 27, and 33, which are endowed with larger trees and much more space. The least desirable sites are the back-ins along the eastern edge—not only because they are smaller (24 by 30 feet) and require backing in, but because they are close to the dog walk area. Indeed, sites 109 and 110 (100 and 101 on the map) are right on top of the dog walk area and contain a pooper scooper and trash bin. Sites 50–80 to the north are also less desirable, as they contain unsightly stumps (one has to wonder why the trees were cut down!) and are closer to the manager's house and the office buildings. Tent sites along the western edge are situated in front of a row of trees (which supply a canopy of shade) and are a roomy 24 by 40 feet. Those tent sites at the north side of the campground have much smaller trees and back to a residential area, which makes them not nearly as nice as the former. The restroom and showers are modern, spacious, and spotless. They are simply, but nicely, decorated. The laundry is likewise clean and roomy. This is a campground that is worthwhile finding, whether camping in an RV or a tent.

BASICS

Operated By: Seth & Nicole Richards. **Open:** All year. **Site Assignment:** Upon registration; credit card required for reservation, 48-hour cancellation

policy. **Registration:** At office; late arrivals use drop box. **Fee:** RV, $24–$32; tent, $16–$22. **Parking:** At site.

FACILITIES

Number of RV-only Sites: 65. **Number of Tent-only Sites:** 12. **Hookups:** Electric (30, 50 amps), water, sewer, cable TV, Wi-Fi. **Each Site:** Picnic table, grill, shrubs for privacy. **Dump Station:** Yes. **Laundry:** Yes. **Pay Phone:** Yes. **Restrooms and Showers:** Yes. **Fuel:** No. **Propane:** Yes. **Internal Roads:** Gravel. **RV Service:** No. **Market:** 8 blocks northwest. **Restaurant:** 6 blocks northwest. **General Store:** Yes. **Vending:** No. **Swimming:** No. **Playground:** Yes. **Other:** 2 cabins, game room, pet walk area. **Activities:** Hiking, tetherball. **Nearby Attractions:** Clayton State Park, Capulin Mountain National Monument, dinosaur tracks. **Additional Information:** Clayton Chamber of Commerce, (505) 374-9253.

RESTRICTIONS

Pets: On leash, cleaned up after. **Fires:** Grill only. **Alcoholic Beverages:** At sites. **Vehicle Maximum Length:** 100 ft.

TO GET THERE

From the junction of Hwy. 56/64/402 and Hwy. 87, go 0.7 mi. south on Hwy. 87 (east). Turn left at the sign onto Spruce, and go 0.35 mi. to the entrance. Turn right at the sign.

CLOVIS   MAP, B-3
Ideal RV Park

1051 CR 311, 88101. T: (505) 791-3177 or (505) 799-2315.

🚐 ★★★   ⛺ n/a

Beauty: ★★★	Site Privacy: ★★★
Spaciousness: ★★★★	Quiet: ★★★★
Security: ★★★	Cleanliness: ★★★
Insect Control: ★★★	Facilities: ★★★

Ideal is a shady campground with loads of trees: there are trees at nearly every site, and a row of trees along the north perimeter, beyond which lies agricultural land. The downside are the mobile homes to the east and along part of the south side–they detract about as much as the trees add. Sites are 60-foot-long pull-throughs, 33 feet wide, level and grassy. However, most sites are not clearly marked: only those closest to the laundry have numbers. The laundry facility is large and well lit, with a cute row of flowers planted around the outside. The restrooms within are clean except for the floors (including inside the showers), which, during our visit, were peeling paint and in need of a scrub. The site that could be 14 (6 sites east of the laundry on the north side) has a nice tree and a little extra space. The least desirable sites are on the ends closest to the mobile homes—again, unnumbered.

BASICS

Operated By: Rickey & Mindy Boddy. **Open:** All year. **Site Assignment:** First come, first served; verbal reservations OK. **Registration:** At office; late arrivals use drop box. **Fee:** Full, $14; tent, $8. **Parking:** At site.

FACILITIES

Number of RV-only Sites: 20. **Number of Tent-only Sites:** 3. **Hookups:** Electric (30, 50 amps), water, sewer. **Each Site:** Tree. **Dump Station:** No (sewer at all sites). **Laundry:** Yes. **Pay Phone:** No. **Restrooms and Showers:** Yes. **Fuel:** No. **Propane:** No. **Internal Roads:** Gravel. **RV Service:** No. **Market:** 7 mi. east to Clovis. **Restaurant:** 7 mi. east to Clovis. **General Store:** 0.5 mi. **Vending:** No. **Swimming:** No. **Playground:** No. **Other:** Close to Cannon Air Force Base. **Activities:** Clovis Music Festival. **Nearby Attractions:** Blackwater Draw Museum. **Additional Information:** Clovis/Curry County Chamber of Commerce, (505) 763-3435.

RESTRICTIONS

Pets: On leash. **Fires:** In grills/pits, unless burn ban in effect. **Alcoholic Beverages:** At sites. **Vehicle Maximum Length:** No limit.

TO GET THERE

From the junction of Hwy. 70 and Hwy. 60/84, turn west onto Hwy. 60/84 (first street north of the bridge) and drive 7.2 mi. to Hwy. 311. Turn right onto Hwy. 311 and drive 0.5 mi., then turn right at the sign into the entrance. The office is on the right.

COLUMBUS   MAP, D-1
Pancho Villa State Park

400 Hwy. 9 W, P. O. Box 450, 88029. T: (505) 531-2711 or (877) 664-7787; www.nmparks.com.

🚐 ★★★★★	🏕 ★★★★

Beauty: ★★★★★	Site Privacy: ★★★★★
Spaciousness: ★★★★★	Quiet: ★★★★
Security: ★★★★	Cleanliness: ★★★★
Insect Control: ★★★★	Facilities: ★★★

Columbus is a small town, and despite proximity to the highway and the town, the park still retains a desert-wilderness feel. On top of this, the park management obviously puts a lot of work into maintenance, which brings out the beauty of the natural environment. Large rigs will love this park, as all but four sites are pull-throughs—and those four are large enough (60 feet) to "parallel park" instead of backing in, if so desired. Sites 1–4 are 150-foot pull-throughs along the eastern edge of the campground (by the highway). Sites 22–25 are the same, but across an internal drive, and 26–34 are farther south. Sites 5–10 are located on a gigantic, open gravel road that can fit any rig in practically any direction. Sites 10–16 are nicer than the eastern side, since they are farther from the highway. Sites 58–61 are developed back-in sites (no electricity) that measure 60 by 60 feet. The best area to camp in is the western side, as it is farther from the highway and the entrance. However, any site in this park is a beautiful place to camp. Tent sites are located on a patch of thick grass that looks rather out of place in this desert campground but offers nice camping. The restrooms are attractively modeled and both clean and spacious. This is a wonderful campground with natural sites that tenters and RVers will enjoy.

BASICS

Operated By: New Mexico State Park Division. **Open:** All year. **Site Assignment:** First come, first served; reservations by credit card or check, no refunds. **Registration:** At pay station. **Fee:** Water/electric, $14; developed, $10; primitive, $8; check, no credit cards. **Parking:** At site.

FACILITIES

Number of RV-only Sites: 80. **Number of Tent-only Sites:** Undesignated sites. **Hookups:** Electric (20, 30 amps), water. **Each Site:** Picnic table, fire pit. **Dump Station:** Yes. **Laundry:** No. **Pay Phone:** Yes. **Restrooms and Showers:** Yes. **Fuel:** No. **Propane:** No. **Internal Roads:** Paved & gravel. **RV Service:** No. **Market:** 0.5 mi. east. **Restaurant:** 0.5 mi. east. **General Store:** 0.5 mi. east. **Vending:** No. **Swimming:** No. **Playground:** Yes. **Other:** Rec hall, picnic pavilion, botanical gardens, museum. **Activities:** Tours to Mexico, rock hounding. **Nearby Attractions:** Mexico, El Paso, Rockhound State Park. **Additional Information:** New Mexico State Parks Division, (888) NM-PARKS.

RESTRICTIONS

Pets: On leash, cleaned up after; 10 ft. max. leash. **Fires:** In grills & fire pits. **Alcoholic Beverages:** At sites. **Vehicle Maximum Length:** No limit.

TO GET THERE

From the junction of Hwy. 11 and Hwy. 9, turn southwest onto Hwy. 9 and go 0.1 mi. Turn left at the sign into the entrance.

DATIL   MAP, B-1
Eagle Guest Ranch

P.O. Box 68, 87821. T: (505) 772-5612.

🚐 ★★★★	🏕 ★★

Beauty: ★★★★	Site Privacy: ★★★★
Spaciousness: ★★★★	Quiet: ★★★★
Security: ★★★★	Cleanliness: ★★★
Insect Control: ★★★★	Facilities: ★★

This RV park is located behind a cafe, motel, gas station, and crafts store. The campground is very undeveloped, with grass and dirt spaces. Some of the sites (especially 1–4) are overgrown with weeds, and the campground itself needs a good picking-up. Sites 1–14 are 45-foot back-ins laid out along the highway. Sites 1–3 are very well shaded, site 10 is unshaded, and sites 7 and 8 are used by long-term residents. Pull-throughs include 15 and 16 (40 feet) and 20–22 (150 feet). Sites 12, 14, 17, and 18 can be used as pull-throughs if the accompanying site is unoccupied. Sites 24 and 25 are 75-foot back-ins, and 26 is a well shaded 45-foot pull-through. Both 25 and 26 have a rather rough road. Tenting is possible wherever there is grass (which is pretty much anywhere around the campground), but a shade tree is hard to come by. As there are no showers, tenters will have a rougher time than self-contained units. Likewise, the restrooms in the store are closed after 9 p.m. and all day Sunday. There are many campgrounds in the area, but they do not offer hookups. In fact, this may very well be the only campground within 50 miles to offer hookups of any kind. Tenters may have a better stay at a national forest campground, as these are sure to provide showers.

BASICS

Operated By: Carol Coker. **Open:** All year. **Site Assignment:** First come, first served; no reservations. **Registration:** At store; late arrivals select available site & pay in the morning. **Fee:** RV (full), $12; tent, $12; V, MC, AE, D, DC, CB. **Parking:** At site.

FACILITIES

Number of RV-only Sites: 25. **Number of Tent-only Sites:** Undesignated sites. **Hookups:** Electric (20, 50 amps), water, sewer. **Each Site:** None. **Dump Station:** No. **Laundry:** No. **Pay Phone:** Yes. **Restrooms and Showers:** No (restrooms in store). **Fuel:** Yes. **Propane:** No. **Internal Roads:** Gravel. **RV Service:** No. **Market:** On site. **Restaurant:** On site. **General Store:** Yes. **Vending:** No. **Swimming:** No. **Playground:** No. **Other:** Cafe, motel, gas station. **Activities:** Rock-climbing, fishing, boating, hunting. **Nearby Attractions:** Thompson Canyon, VLA, Quemado Lake. **Additional Information:** Socorro Chamber of Commerce, (505) 835-0424.

RESTRICTIONS

Pets: On leash, cleaned up after. **Fires:** Grill only. **Alcoholic Beverages:** At sites. **Vehicle Maximum Length:** No limit.

TO GET THERE

Located at the intersection of Hwy. 12 and Hwy. 60 in Datil.

DEMING   MAP, C-1
Wagon Wheel RV Park

2801 East Motel Dr., 88030. T: (505) 546-8650.

🚐 ★★★★	🏕 ★★★

Beauty: ★★★	Site Privacy: ★★★
Spaciousness: ★★★★	Quiet: ★★★
Security: ★★★★	Cleanliness: ★★★
Insect Control: ★★★★	Facilities: ★★★

Laid out in three rows of sites, this campground has very attractive landscaping using bushes, trees, and flowers. Sites 1–11 are 45-foot back-ins in the southeast corner. Site 12 is secluded by trees and a fence and has good shade. In the eastern row, sites 13–28 are 60-foot pull-throughs. Sites in the northern section (21–28) are bare gravel. Sites 29–51 in the middle row are open-ended pull-throughs averaging 60 by 21 feet. Site 29, in front of the office, may receive registration traffic. Sites 31, 34, and 39 are very well shaded. Sites in the northern section (44–51) are bare gravel. The western row (sites 56–72) has back-ins along the fence (sites 56–63) and 60-foot pull-throughs (64–72). All sites can be used for tenting, although 1–12 are probably the best. The rec room and hot tub are comfortable, although the campground gets crowded in winter, and you may have to wait to use these facilities. The restrooms are OK but could use a deep cleaning. Priding itself on being the least expensive campground in the area, this is a very nice destination for RVers for a short stay or even over the winter.

BASICS

Operated By: Dan Wagner. **Open:** All year. **Site Assignment:** Depends on availability; verbal reservations OK. **Registration:** At office; late arrivals use drop box. **Fee:** RV (full), $12; tent, $12; check, no credit cards. **Parking:** At site.

FACILITIES

Number of RV-only Sites: 73. **Hookups:** Electric (20, 30, 50 amps), water, sewer, cable TV, phone. **Each Site:** Picnic table. **Dump Station:** No (sewer at all sites). **Laundry:** Yes. **Pay Phone:** Yes. **Restrooms and Showers:** Yes. **Fuel:** No. **Propane:** No. **Internal Roads:** Gravel. **RV Service:** No. **Market:** 1.25 mi. west. **Restaurant:** Less than 0.25 mi. west. **General Store:** Yes, limited. **Vending:** Yes. **Swimming:** No (Jacuzzi). **Playground:** No. **Other:** RV supplies, clubhouse w/ kitchen, game room, movies, gift shop, modem. **Activities:** Planned activities in winter, rock hounding, hiking. **Nearby Attractions:** Rockhound State Park, City of Rocks State Park. **Additional Information:** Deming Chamber of Commerce, (505) 546-2674.

RESTRICTIONS

Pets: On leash, cleaned up after. **Fires:** Grill only. **Alcoholic Beverages:** At sites (not in clubhouse). **Vehicle Maximum Length:** No limit.

TO GET THERE

From I-10 (Exit 85), turn south onto Motel Dr. and go 1.2 mi. Turn right at the sign into the entrance.

DWYER · MAP, C-1
Faywood Hot Springs

165 Hwy. 61, HC 71 Box 1240, 88034.
T: (505) 536-9663; www.faywood.com.

🚐 ★★★★   ⛺ ★★★★★

Beauty: ★★★★★	Site Privacy: ★★★★★
Spaciousness: ★★★★★	Quiet: ★★★★★
Security: ★★★★★	Cleanliness: ★★★★★
Insect Control: ★★★★	Facilities: ★★★

Let's put this out upfront: this natural campground in the desert wilderness will most likely appeal to folks with an adventurous heart. The public clothing-optional areas are certainly not for everyone. That being said, it's a wonderful campground with beautiful, if undeveloped, sites somewhat scattered about the property. Sites 7–16 are pull-throughs located along the northern edge. Site 7 is located next to the caretaker's mobile home. Site 10 is extra wide (40 feet compared to 21 feet). One of the nicest spots, 18, lacks shade but is an extremely large back-in that commands a gorgeous view. Sites 23–26 in the southwest corner are surrounded by vegetation and are therefore very private. Tent sites 4–6 are sandy sites surrounded by vegetation. These are the nicest, most private sites. The other tent sites are mixed in amongst the RV sites. The restrooms are pit toilets scattered around the campground, and the shower is outdoors, only partially concealed. This campground may appeal most to tenters and the adventurous Airstream crowd but is a beautiful slice of desert wilderness that should not be missed.

BASICS

Operated By: Wanda Fuselier. **Open:** All year. **Site Assignment:** First come, first served; credit card required for reservation, 2-day cancellation policy. **Registration:** At office; no late arrivals, gate locked

at 10 p.m. **Fee:** RV (1 person), $24; RV (2 people), $34; tent (1 person), $18; tent (2 people), $29; additional adult, $15; additional child, $10; V, MC. **Parking:** At site.

FACILITIES

Number of RV-only Sites: 21. **Number of Tent-only Sites:** 12. **Hookups:** Electric (20, 30, 50 amps), water, sewer. **Each Site:** Picnic tables. **Dump Station:** Yes. **Laundry:** No. **Pay Phone:** No. **Restrooms and Showers:** Yes. **Fuel:** No. **Propane:** No. **Internal Roads:** Gravel. **RV Service:** No. **Market:** Convenience store 12 mi. north to Hurley, supermarket 24 mi. north or south. **Restaurant:** 12 mi. north to Hurley. **General Store:** No. **Vending:** No. **Swimming:** No (hot springs). **Playground:** No. **Other:** 1,200 acres of hiking, drinks & some grocery items, cabins, tepee, shaded picnic pavilion, clothing required/optional areas. **Activities:** Horseback riding, birding, hiking, biking, stargazing. **Nearby Attractions:** City of Rocks State Park, Gila National Monument, Las Cruces. **Additional Information:** Deming Chamber of Commerce, (505) 546-2674.

RESTRICTIONS

Pets: On leash, cleaned up after. **Fires:** Grill only. **Alcoholic Beverages:** At sites. **Vehicle Maximum Length:** No limit.

TO GET THERE

From the junction of Hwy. 180 and Hwy. 61, go north on Hwy. 61 1.6 mi. Turn left onto a very nondescript gravel road (with small sign) and follow it to the office.

EAGLE NEST · MAP, A-2
West Lake RV Park

HCR 71, P.O. Box 6, 87718. T: (505) 377-PARK.

🚐 ★★★★   ⛺ n/a

Beauty: ★★★★	Site Privacy: ★★★
Spaciousness: ★★	Quiet: ★★★★
Security: ★★★★	Cleanliness: ★★★★★
Insect Control: ★★★★	Facilities: ★

This campground is located in a valley surrounded by mountains, with lake views and access to the lake. Elk, bears, wild turkeys, and eagles may be spotted by campers with patience and keen eyes. Sites are laid out in a semicircle around the perimeter of the property. There are open-ended back-ins, but they're limited to about 45 by 25 feet. Sites 1–12 are located along the wooden fence to the north. Site 1 is quite small (30 by 25 feet), and 11–13, in the corner, seem somewhat hemmed in. Sites 13–18 are laid out along the east side, overlooking the lake. These sites (minus 13 and 18) are the nicest sites. Sites 19–28, along the south side, overlook fields, cabins, and the lake. Sites 18 and 19 are slightly blocked by one another. In an area with a number of RV parks, this campground offers nice lake views. Any one of the RV parks in the area is a great place to be when the weather elsewhere is climbing into the 90s, as this place stays cool all year.

BASICS

Operated By: Phil & Glenda Lenz. **Open:** May 1–Oct. 1. **Site Assignment:** Depends on site availability; verbal reservations OK. **Registration:** At

office; late arrivals select available site & pay in the morning. **Fee:** RV, $22; check, no credits cards. **Parking:** At site.

FACILITIES

Number of RV-only Sites: 28. **Hookups:** Electric (30, 50 amps), water, sewer, phone. **Each Site:** Covered picnic table. **Dump Station:** No (sewer at all sites). **Laundry:** Yes. **Pay Phone:** Courtesy phone. **Restrooms and Showers:** No. **Fuel:** No. **Propane:** No. **Internal Roads:** Gravel. **RV Service:** No. **Market:** 12 mi. to Angel Fire. **Restaurant:** 1.5 mi. east. **General Store:** In Angel Fire. **Vending:** No. **Swimming:** No. **Playground:** No. **Other:** Covered pavilion, views, cool weather, firewood available. **Activities:** Fishing, boating, fish fry Fri., potlucks. **Nearby Attractions:** Cimarron Canyon State Park, DAV Vietnam Veterans National Memorial. **Additional Information:** Eagle Nest Chamber of Commerce, (505) 377-2420.

RESTRICTIONS

Pets: On leash, cleaned up after. **Fires:** In common grill, fire pit. **Alcoholic Beverages:** At sites. **Vehicle Maximum Length:** 42 ft.

TO GET THERE

From the junction of Hwy. 38 and Hwy. 64, turn west onto Hwy. 64 and go 1.5 mi. Turn left at the sign into the entrance.

EL MORRO · MAP, B-1
Ancient Way Café and Outpost

HC 61 Box 44, 87321. T: (505) 783-4612; www.elmorro-nm.com.

🚐 ★★★   ⛺ ★★★★

Beauty: ★★★★	Site Privacy: ★★★
Spaciousness: ★★★★	Quiet: ★★★★
Security: ★★★★	Cleanliness: ★★★
Insect Control: ★★★★	Facilities: ★★★

This is a wilderness campground with the highway directly to the north. Sites are not all numbered, and the only distinction between a tent or RV site is the existence or lack of hookups. Sites 1 and 3 are 60-foot back-ins that back slightly into the woods. Sites 2 and 4 are 45-foot back-ins that are slightly sloped. Sites on the inside of the loop are 54-foot back-ins (including 7). The site farthest west on the outside of the loop (possibly 9) is a 65-foot back-in. Site 10 is the largest, at 75 feet. This is a dirt back-in with trees around the site, but the site itself is not shaded. Sites 15 and 16 are overgrown with weeds. Sites that back to the highway include 10, 16, and 19, as well as some unnumbered sites on the north side of the loop. Tent sites include three in the southwest corner, on the inside of the loop. Tent site 35 is the best, as it offers a space under a tree. Neither the roads nor the sites themselves are in especially good condition. The sites are mostly dirt, and many are overgrown. On the plus side, there are excellent views of a rocky outcropping, and the campground is located only 1 mile from the El Morro National Monument.

BASICS

Operated By: Private operator. **Open:** All year. **Site Assignment:** First come, first served; no reservations. **Registration:** In cafe; late arrivals select available site & pay in the morning. **Fee:** RV (full), $20; tent, $10; V, MC. **Parking:** At site.

FACILITIES

Number of RV-only Sites: 25. **Number of Tent-only Sites:** 6. **Hookups:** Electric (20, 30 amps), water, sewer. **Each Site:** Picnic table. **Dump Station:** No. **Laundry:** No. **Pay Phone:** Yes. **Restrooms and Showers:** Yes. **Fuel:** No. **Propane:** No. **Internal Roads:** Gravel/dirt. **RV Service:** No. **Market:** Small, 5 mi. southwest; large, 15 mi. to Vine Hill. **Restaurant:** Yes. **General Store:** No. **Vending:** No. **Swimming:** No. **Playground:** No. **Other:** Cafe serving breakfast, lunch, & dinner; cabins; trails. **Activities:** Hiking, caving. **Nearby Attractions:** El Morro National Monument, Bandera Crater & Ice Caves, Cibola National Forest. **Additional Information:** Grants Chamber of Commerce, (505) 287-4802.

RESTRICTIONS

Pets: On leash, cleaned up after. **Fires:** Grill only; no open fires. **Alcoholic Beverages:** At sites. **Vehicle Maximum Length:** No limit.

TO GET THERE

From I-40 (Exit 81), turn southwest onto Hwy. 53 and go 40 mi. Turn left at the sign (near mile marker 46) into the entrance.

ELEPHANT BUTTE   MAP, C-2
Lakeside RV Park

107 Country Club Blvd., P.O. Drawer 981, 87935. T: (800) 808-5848 or (505) 744-5996; www.lakesiderv.com.

🚐 ★★★★★   ⛺ n/a

Beauty: ★★★★	Site Privacy: ★★★★★
Spaciousness: ★★★★★	Quiet: ★★★★
Security: ★★★★★	Cleanliness: ★★★★★
Insect Control: ★★★★	Facilities: ★★★★

This RV park is not only the closest park to the lake, but it's a beautiful place to camp to boot. Laid out in three tiers, the park uses natural desert landscaping (rocks, cacti) to beautiful effect. In the lowest tier, sites 2–8 are open-ended back-ins (roughly 55 by 22 feet) situated around the office. The uppermost tier contains sites large enough for a vehicle and boat. These open-ended pull-throughs (sites 20–26 and 36–41) are about 70 by 30 feet. Sites 27–30 are 45-foot back-ins. Sites 42–50 deserve special mention, as they are located around the Native Garden, a gorgeous display of aloe, rocks, and cacti. Of these sites, 44 and 47 have the best shade. These are by far the most beautiful sites in the park. In the middle tier are 54-foot back-ins that back to either a fence and the first tier (on the west side) or to a hedge and the road (on the east side). Two hosts live in the campground, ensuring that the park remains secure at all times. The restrooms are absolutely spotless and nicely decorated. The showers are likewise clean and very comfortable. This is an RV park that deserves a special visit, not only for the surrounding beauty, but also for the care and maintenance given to the park itself.

BASICS

Operated By: Jim & Lynn Claxton. **Open:** All year. **Site Assignment:** Upon registration; credit

card required for reservation, refund w/ 48-hour notice. **Registration:** At office; late arrivals select available site & pay in the morning. **Fee:** Back-ins, $21–$23; pull-throughs, $25–$29; check, V, MC. **Parking:** At site.

FACILITIES

Number of RV-only Sites: 70. **Hookups:** Electric (30, 50 amps), water, sewer, cable TV, Wi-Fi. **Each Site:** None. **Dump Station:** Yes. **Laundry:** Yes. **Pay Phone:** Yes. Courtesy. **Restrooms and Showers:** Yes. **Fuel:** No. **Propane:** No. **Internal Roads:** Gravel. **RV Service:** No. **Market:** 5 mi. to Truth or Consequences. **Restaurant:** 0.5 mi. to Elephant Butte. **General Store:** No. **Vending:** No. **Swimming:** Lake. **Playground:** No. **Other:** Lounge, phone hookups, barbecue pits. **Activities:** Organized activities (in winter), potlucks, doughnuts on Wed. morning, boating, fishing, swimming. **Nearby Attractions:** Ghost towns, Truth or Consequences, Elephant Butte State Park. **Additional Information:** Elephant Butte Chamber of Commerce, (505) 744-9101.

RESTRICTIONS

Pets: On leash, cleaned up after, no barking. **Fires:** Grill only. **Alcoholic Beverages:** At sites. **Vehicle Maximum Length:** No limit.

TO GET THERE

From I-25 (Exit 83): from the east side of the highway, go straight east on Hwy. 195 3.6 mi. Turn right onto Country Club Blvd. and go 0.1 mi. Turn right onto Water Ave. and take the first right into the park.

ESPAÑOLA   MAP, A-2
Cottonwood RV Park

62 Sombrillo Rd., 87532. T: (505) 747-4777 or (505) 231-2334; www.cottonwoodrv.com.

🚐 ★★★   ⛺ ★★★

Beauty: ★★★★	Site Privacy: ★★★
Spaciousness: ★★★	Quiet: ★★★★
Security: ★★★★★	Cleanliness: ★★★
Insect Control: ★★★★	Facilities: ★★★

RV sites in this campground are laid out in one continuous row from the entrance at the south end to the farthest site to the north. They are, however, broken up into three tiers, with a fourth tier for tents right at the entrance. Sites 1–12 on the first tier are 30-foot sites (1–6 are pull-throughs, 7–12 are back-ins). All spaces are 25 feet wide. Sites 2 and 10 are well shaded; site 12 lies next to and above a house. On the second tier, site 13 is used by a long-term guest, and 14 is the smallest site at 40 feet. The rest of the sites are 70-foot pull-throughs. Sites 17–20 have the best shade. Site 22 has only 45 feet of usable space before it begins to slope. On the lowest tier, site 23 requires an excruciatingly tight turn on the sloped road from the second tier and should be avoided by larger rigs. Sites 30–33 share a large shade tree, and 30 is the overall nicest (and shadiest) site. Site 32 looks unusable, and the tree there prevents site 31 from being a true pull-through. This level is the nicest area, as it is surrounded by vegetation and offers the most shade. The tent sites are located in a dirt area sheltered by cottonwoods. There is one barbecue grill and a

cement fire pit with seats for communal use. The restrooms need a good cleaning, and the stalls (at least in the men's room) do not have doors. This campground is equally nice for tenters as for RVers.

BASICS

Operated By: Art Martinez. **Open:** All year. **Site Assignment:** Upon registration; credit card required for reservation, 48-hour cancellation policy. **Registration:** At office; late arrivals select available site & pay in the morning. **Fee:** RV (full), $19.95–$21.95; tent, $14; check, V, MC, D. **Parking:** At site.

FACILITIES

Number of RV-only Sites: 40. **Number of Tent-only Sites:** Undesignated sites. **Hookups:** Electric (30, 50 amps), water, sewer, Wi-Fi. **Each Site:** None. **Dump Station:** No (sewer at all sites). **Laundry:** Yes. **Pay Phone:** Yes. **Restrooms and Showers:** Yes. **Fuel:** No. **Propane:** No. **Internal Roads:** Gravel. **RV Service:** No. **Market:** 4 mi. north. **Restaurant:** 0.5 mi. **General Store:** No. **Vending:** Yes. **Swimming:** No. **Playground:** No. **Other:** Discount on meal or free margarita upon registration. **Activities:** Fishing, gambling, visiting pueblos. **Nearby Attractions:** Pueblos, Santa Fe Opera, casinos. **Additional Information:** Española Chamber of Commerce, (505) 753-2831.

RESTRICTIONS

Pets: On leash, cleaned up after. **Fires:** Grill only. **Alcoholic Beverages:** At sites. **Vehicle Maximum Length:** 50 ft. **Other:** Hair salon & health spa on site.

TO GET THERE

Hwy. 84/285, 0.5 mi. south of Española.

GALLUP   MAP, B-1
USA RV Park

3900 E. Hwy. 66, 87301. T: (505) 863-5021; www.usarvpark.com.

🚐 ★★★★   ⛺ ★★★

Beauty: ★★★	Site Privacy: ★★★★
Spaciousness: ★★★★	Quiet: ★★★★
Security: ★★★★★	Cleanliness: ★★★★★
Insect Control: ★★★★	Facilities: ★★★★★

This campground is laid out in five rows of pull-throughs with two rows of tent sites behind them and one row of back-ins along the eastern wall. Sites 1–12 and 15–30 are 70-foot gravel sites, slightly shorter (60 feet) on the ends. Sites 31–48 are 65-foot sites, while 49–69 and 70–91 are slightly shorter (54 feet and 60 feet). Back-ins 122–141 are 30-foot sites, best suited for pop-ups or vans. The best RV sites are those on the eastern edge (1, 15, 31, 49, and 70), as these face into trees and hills beyond. The tent sites at the end of the park are 24 by 27–foot open sites. Trees are mostly small and scarce. The best tent sites are 23 and 25, which share a larger tree. The restrooms and showers are exceptionally clean and comfortable. The electric eye at the gate alerts the owners of all incoming guests, ensuring the safety of the park. This is a very comfortable campground that campers of all types will enjoy.

BASICS

Operated By: Gene Dolney. **Open:** All year. **Site Assignment:** Upon registration; verbal reservations OK. **Registration:** At office. **Fee:** RV, $30–$52; tent, $21–$33; check, V, MC. **Parking:** At site.

FACILITIES

Number of RV-only Sites: 120. **Number of Tent-only Sites:** 16. **Hookups:** Electric (30, 50 amps), water, sewer, cable TV, telephone. **Each Site:** Picnic table. **Dump Station:** Yes. **Laundry:** Yes. **Pay Phone:** Yes. Courtesy. **Restrooms and Showers:** Yes. **Fuel:** No. **Propane:** Yes. **Internal Roads:** Paved. **RV Service:** No. **Market:** 1 mi. west. **Restaurant:** On site. **General Store:** Yes. **Vending:** No. **Swimming:** Pool. **Playground:** Yes. **Other:** Cabins, modem. **Activities:** Swimming, rodeos, American Indian dances. **Nearby Attractions:** Historic Rte. 66, Red Rock State Park, Inter-Tribal Indian Ceremonial. **Additional Information:** Gallup McKinley City Chamber of Commerce, (505) 722-2228.

RESTRICTIONS

Pets: On 6-ft. leash, cleaned up after, use dog walk. **Fires:** Grill only. **Alcoholic Beverages:** At sites. **Vehicle Maximum Length:** 84 ft. **Other:** No groups.

TO GET THERE

From I-40 (Exit 16), turn east onto Hwy. 66 and go 1 mi. Turn right at the sign into entrance.

GRANTS   MAP, B-1
Lavaland RV Park

1901 East Santa Fe Ave., 87020. T: (505) 287-8665; www.lavalandrvpark.com.

🚐 ★★★★   ⛺ ★★★

Beauty: ★★★★	Site Privacy: ★★★★
Spaciousness: ★★★★	Quiet: ★★★
Security: ★★★★	Cleanliness: ★★★★
Insect Control: ★★★★	Facilities: ★★★

Sites in Lavaland are laid out in four rows. Sites are 60 feet long and 30 feet wide. Sites 1–11 are back-ins along the western edge that back to a retaining wall with trees and a fence. Sites 11 and 12 at the end do not have shade trees. In the middle of the campground, sites 12–27 and 28–39 are pull-throughs. Site 39 is located next to the dump station and is thus less desirable. On the east side, sites 40–51 face the highway and hills in the distance. These pull-throughs as well as the road they lie on are rougher in spots (especially 48) than the other rows of pull-throughs. The tenting area is in the southeast corner by the entrance. These dirt sites have nice desert views, and some are shaded by ponderosa pines. Rabbits and quail are full-time residents here and share the campground with paying guests. The restrooms and showers are clean, but there is no window, so the room is pitch black when the light is not on. (Be sure to turn on the light before the door closes!) Lavaland is an attractive campground that will appeal to many campers–a little better to RVers than to tenters.

BASICS

Operated By: Fidel & Leticia Duenas. **Open:** All year. **Site Assignment:** Upon registration; credit card required for reservation, 48-hour cancellation policy. **Registration:** At office; late arrivals use drop box. **Fee:** RV (full), $17; tent, $15; V, MC, D. **Parking:** At site.

FACILITIES

Number of RV-only Sites: 51. **Number of Tent-only Sites:** Undesignated sites. **Hookups:** Electric (30, 50 amps), water, sewer, cable TV. **Each Site:** Picnic table, grill. **Dump Station:** Yes. **Laundry:** Yes. **Pay Phone:** Yes. **Restrooms and Showers:** Yes. **Fuel:** No. **Propane:** No. **Internal Roads:** Gravel. **RV Service:** No (minor repairs). **Market:** 0.25 mi. at I-40. **Restaurant:** 0.25 mi. at I-40. **General Store:** Small, limited. **Vending:** No. **Swimming:** No. **Playground:** No. **Other:** Studio rooms, gift shop, video games. **Activities:** Caving, hiking. **Nearby Attractions:** Visitor center w/in walking distance, Mine Museum, ice caves, Acoma Sky City, Cibola National Forest, seniors' center next to park. **Additional Information:** Grants Chamber of Commerce, (505) 287-4802.

RESTRICTIONS

Pets: On leash, cleaned up after, no big dogs allowed. **Fires:** Grill only. **Alcoholic Beverages:** At sites. **Vehicle Maximum Length:** No limit.

TO GET THERE

From I-40 (Exit 85), from the south side of the highway, turn south and take the first right onto Jurassic Ct., then take the first right into the campground.

HOBBS   MAP, C-3
Harry McAdams Park

5000 Jack Gomez Blvd., 88240. T: (505) 392-5845.

🚐 ★★★   ⛺ ★★★★

Beauty: ★★★★	Site Privacy: ★★★★
Spaciousness: ★★★★	Quiet: ★★★★
Security: ★★★★	Cleanliness: ★★★★
Insect Control: ★★★	Facilities: ★★

Six miles northwest of Hobbs, near the College of the Southwest, the Harry McAdams Park is divided into north and south, each with a different flavor. The north campground is more primitive with regard to hookups (only three sites have full hookups), but contains the restroom facilities and sits on prettier grounds. Sites are 54-foot back-ins with enough space on all sides to accommodate a large family with children. Sites inside the loop share an interior common grounds, while those on the outside of the loop back onto an expansive grassy area. Site 9 on the outside loop is situated somewhat away from the rest and backs onto a field that runs toward the day area a few hundred yards away. The grass is lush and extremely well maintained—be forewarned that crews get under way early to avoid the hot sun of afternoon. The restroom facilities are acceptably clean and spacious, with showers in a separate curtained-off area. The south campground is an open field with a strip of sites down a central road. The field is humongous but does receive some airplane noise. Campsites here are more minimalist, with a table and young tree that does not provide shade. (An exception is the tree in sites 21/23.) These pull-through sites, virtually unlimited in size, are not your traditional pull-throughs: when leaving, you pull out into the field, turn around, and come back through your site. The south campground rates lower on beauty and quiet, and would rate higher on facilities due to the hookups, although the restrooms are a block away in the north campground. For those seeking a quiet escape (and can forgo full hookups for a night), Harry McAdams (especially the north side) is an extremely pleasant and comfortable place to stay.

BASICS

Operated By: City of Hobbs. **Open:** All year. **Site Assignment:** First come, first served. **Registration:** At self-pay station. **Fee:** Full hookup, $15. **Parking:** At site.

FACILITIES

Number of RV-only Sites: 47. **Hookups:** Electric (30 amps), water, sewer. **Each Site:** North campground: Picnic shelter w/ table, trees, grill; south campground: picnic table. **Dump Station:** Yes. **Laundry:** No. **Pay Phone:** Yes. **Restrooms and Showers:** Yes. **Fuel:** No. **Propane:** No. **Internal Roads:** Paved, in perfect condition. **RV Service:** No. **Market:** 4 mi. in Hobbs. **Restaurant:** 2 mi. toward Hobbs. **General Store:** No. **Vending:** No. **Swimming:** No. **Playground:** Yes. **Other:** 2 trout-stocked ponds, day-use area. **Activities:** Volleyball, horseshoes, fishing. **Nearby Attractions:** Blackwater Draw Museum, Old Fort Sumner Museum, Billy the Kid Museum. **Additional Information:** Hobbs Chamber of Commerce, (800) 658-6291, (505) 397-3202.

RESTRICTIONS

Pets: On leash. **Fires:** Grill only. **Alcoholic Beverages:** At sites. **Vehicle Maximum Length:** No limit. **Other:** No generators; 1 camp vehicle, plus 1 other vehicle per site.

TO GET THERE

From Hwy. 18 (between Hobbs and Lovington), turn west onto Jack Gomez. (Much more visible than the street sign are the 2 signs at the street entrance on the west side for the Hobbs Industrial Air Park.) Go 0.8 mi. on Jack Gomez behind a police station, then turn right into the campground. All guests must register at the pay station here. To get to the south campground, continue on Jack Gomez through the stop sign and into the area marked Hobbs Army Air Base. Make the first left into the campground, then return to the north campground to register.

JEMEZ SPRINGS   MAP, A-2
Trail's End RV Park

37695 Hwy. 126, 87025. T: (505) 829-4072; www.trailsendrv.com.

🚐 ★★★★★   ⛺ ★★★★★

Beauty: ★★★★★	Site Privacy: ★★★★★
Spaciousness: ★★★★★	Quiet: ★★★★★
Security: ★★★★★	Cleanliness: ★★★★★
Insect Control: ★★★★★	Facilities: ★★

Trail's End offers the only full hookups in the area. But even if that weren't the case, it would well be worth a visit. The area is gorgeous, and the campground takes full advantage of the forest where it lies. Sites are left in a natural condition, and there are flowers planted among the pines. Sites 1–7 are gravel back-ins located up-slope from the office. Site 1 is one of the longest, at 55 feet. Smaller sites (30 feet) include 3–9. Sites 8–17 are located along the southern side. Of these, 11 is a 70-foot pull-through (of which only 60 feet are usable, due to the slope), and 17 is likewise quite long (65 feet). Sites 12, 13, and 15 are 45-foot back-ins. Closest to the entrance (which makes for the easiest in and out), but also located just off the highway is site 16, which is a 60-foot pull-through. (Some of the sites have a slightly smaller usable length due to the slope.) Tenting is possible in sites 18 and 19, but, with 50,000 acres of national forest surrounding the campground and offering free camping, even the owner asks why a tenter would pay to camp. This is an absolutely gorgeous campground that is not to be missed by RVers.

BASICS

Operated By: Steve McMahon. **Open:** May 15–Oct. 12. **Site Assignment:** Upon registration; verbal reservations OK. **Registration:** At office; no arrivals after 9 p.m. **Fee:** RV (full), $25; tent, $23; check, no credits cards. **Parking:** At site.

FACILITIES

Number of RV-only Sites: 14. **Number of Tent-only Sites:** 2. **Hookups:** Electric (30 amps), water, sewer, Wi-Fi. **Each Site:** Picnic table, fire ring. **Dump Station:** No (sewer at all sites). **Laundry:** No. **Pay Phone:** No. **Restrooms and Showers:** Toilet; no shower. **Fuel:** No. **Propane:** No. **Internal Roads:** Gravel. **RV Service:** No. **Market:** 1 mi. south. **Restaurant:** 1 mi. south. **General Store:** No. **Vending:** No. **Swimming:** No. **Playground:** Yes. **Other:** Surrounded by national forest. **Activities:** Fishing, hiking, horseback riding, hunting. **Nearby Attractions:** Soda Dam, Santa Fe, Albuquerque, hot springs, Fenton Lake State Park, Santa Fe National Forest, Jemez Pueblo, Zia Pueblo. **Additional Information:** Los Alamos Chamber of Commerce, (505) 662-8105.

RESTRICTIONS

Pets: On leash, cleaned up after. **Fires:** Grill only. **Alcoholic Beverages:** At sites. **Vehicle Maximum Length:** 38 ft. **Other:** No children 5–18.

TO GET THERE

From the junction of Hwy. 550 and Hwy. 4, turn north onto Hwy. 4 and go 26.5 mi. (8.1 mi. north of Jemez Springs National Monument). Turn left onto Hwy. 126 and go 5 mi. to the campground.

LAS CRUCES   MAP, C-2
Best View RV Park

814 Weinrich Rd., 88007. T: (800) 562-1627 or (505) 526-6555; www.lascrucescampgrounds.com.

🚐 ★★★★★   ⛺ ★★★★

Beauty: ★★★★		Site Privacy: ★★★	
Spaciousness: ★★★		Quiet: ★★★★	
Security: ★★★★★		Cleanliness: ★★★★	
Insect Control: ★★★★		Facilities: ★★★★★	

Southwest of Las Cruces and toward the airport, this campground commands a view of the town with its agricultural areas, plentiful trees, and the Organ Pipe Mountain behind that really lives up to its name. The campground is laid out in a giant L shape, with back-ins around the perimeter and pull-throughs inside. Pull-throughs average 62 feet in length, with sites 60–61 slightly longer (65 feet), which makes them among the best sites available—certainly for longer rigs. Back-ins are roughly the same length as pull-throughs, although there are some much smaller sites to accommodate vans/pop-ups near the tent and cabin area. All sites are level and mostly open. The tent area is short of tables and grills, with only a bare ground covering of grass. (Grass does not grow well in the area.) However, there are enough trees for ample protection from above. Tent sites are generally flat, with a slight slope in sites 75 and 80. The second tent (and RV) area near the cabins is close to the road, with the attendant traffic sounds. The southwest corner above the cabins contains a slightly scruffy residence, but that is the only detraction from the beauty of this campground. The restroom and shower facilities are quite clean. Overall, this is a great camping experience for both RVers and tenters, with a "best view" from nearly all of the sites.

BASICS

Operated By: Steve Perry. **Open:** All year. **Site Assignment:** Upon registration; reservations require credit card; 48-hour cancellation. **Registration:** At office; late arrivals use drop box. **Fee:** Full, $28–$35; water/electric, $24; tent, $22. **Parking:** At site.

FACILITIES

Number of RV-only Sites: 79. **Number of Tent-only Sites:** 12. **Hookups:** Electric (30, 50 amps), water, sewer. **Each Site:** Picnic table, grill, tree. **Dump Station:** Yes. **Laundry:** Yes. **Pay Phone:** Yes. **Restrooms and Showers:** Yes. **Fuel:** No. **Propane:** Yes. **Internal Roads:** Paved, gravel. **RV Service:** No. **Market:** 5 mi. northeast to Las Cruces. **Restaurant:** 5 mi. northeast to Las Cruces. **General Store:** Yes. **Vending:** No. **Swimming:** Pool (May–Sept.). **Playground:** Yes. **Other:** 4 acres RV storage, 4 cabins, dog walk. **Activities:** Hiking. **Nearby Attractions:** White Sands National Monument, Mesilla, City of Rocks State Park, Gila Cliff Dwellings. **Additional Information:** Las Cruces CVB, (800) 343-7827, (505) 541-2444.

RESTRICTIONS

Pets: On leash, cleaned up after. **Fires:** Grill only. **Alcoholic Beverages:** At sites. **Vehicle Maximum Length:** No limit.

TO GET THERE

From I-10, Exit 135. From I-25, Exit 6, follow SR 20 west 7 mi.

LOGAN   MAP, B-3
Ute Lake State Park

P.O. Box 52, 88426. T: (877) 664-7787 or (505) 487-2284 or (888) NM-PARKS; www.nmparks.com.

🚐 ★★★   ⛺ ★★★

Beauty: ★★★		Site Privacy: ★★★★★	
Spaciousness: ★★★★★		Quiet: ★★★★	
Security: ★★★★		Cleanliness: ★★★	
Insect Control: ★★★		Facilities: ★★	

There are two campgrounds (Zia and Yucca) in this desert-setting state park. Zia Campground is closest to the office and contains the reservable sites. The outside of this looped campground contains 95-foot pull-throughs (all odd numbers), while the inside contains 35-foot back-ins (all even numbers), which are separated one from the other by large boulders and trees. Sites with the best lake views are 11, 13, and 15. Those closest to the restrooms are 17, 18, 20, and 21. To the south of this loop is an area of primitive sites that offer sheltered picnic tables and grills. The southernmost sites are grassy, shaded, and open to the lake. (The rest of the sites are open to the blazing sun.) Yuccan Campground has absolutely the largest pull-throughs you'll ever see (165 by 65 feet)—obviously built with the boater in mind. Sites are in two rows along a gravel drive. Sites on the south side (57–72) have a view of the lake and are closest to the lake access area (by 72), but there is no boat ramp there. Instead, this road provides access to the dispersed tent camping along the bank of the lake. While there is no shade nor grass, the upside is that you can practically roll out of your tent into the lake if you want. The bathhouse, located east of Yucca Campground, is clean, comfortable, and very spacious. Both campgrounds are visited occasionally by deer, antelope, quail, and ducks. There are farther campgrounds on the north and south sides of the lake, but the two described are easier to access and enjoyable for anyone looking for fun on a lake.

BASICS

Operated By: New Mexico State Park Division. **Open:** May 15–Sept. 15. **Site Assignment:** First come, first served; reservations by credit card or check, no refunds. **Registration:** At pay station. **Fee:** Developed, $10; primitive, $8; hookup, $4; check, V, MC, D. **Parking:** At site.

FACILITIES

Number of RV-only Sites: 77. **Number of Tent-only Sites:** 57. **Hookups:** Electric (30 amps), water. **Each Site:** Picnic table, grill, fire pit. **Dump Station:** Yes. **Laundry:** No. **Pay Phone:** No. **Restrooms and Showers:** Yes. **Fuel:** No. **Propane:** No. **Internal Roads:** Mixed. **RV Service:** No. **Market:** 2.5 mi. east. **Restaurant:** 2.5 mi. east. **General Store:** Yes. **Vending:** No. **Swimming:** Lake. **Playground:** Yes. **Other:** Trails, boat ramp, baseball field. **Activities:** Fishing, boating, swimming, hiking. **Nearby Attractions:** Ute Lake, dinosaur museum. **Additional Information:** State Park Office, (505) 487-2284.

RESTRICTIONS

Pets: On leash, cleaned up after. **Fires:** Grill only. **Alcoholic Beverages:** At sites, no glass containers. **Vehicle Maximum Length:** No limit.

TO GET THERE

From the junction of Hwy. 54 and Hwy. 540, turn west onto Hwy. 540 and go 2.4 mi. Turn left at the sign into the entrance.

LORDSBURG   MAP, C-1
Lordsburg KOA

1501 Lead St., 88045. T: (800) 562-5772 or
(505) 542-8003; www.koa.com.

🚐 ★★★★   ▲ ★★★★

Beauty: ★★★   Site Privacy: ★★★★★
Spaciousness: ★★★★★   Quiet: ★★★
Security: ★★★★   Cleanliness: ★★★★★
Insect Control: ★★★★   Facilities: ★★★★★

This campground with mountain views in all directions offers all 60-foot (or larger) pull-throughs laid out in eight rows. Rows 1 and 2 (sites 1–4 and 14–17) are open-ended sites that can easily accommodate 60 feet and are 33 feet wide. These sites are closest to the facilities. Rows 4–7 are slightly larger than 60 feet and contain the remotest sites to the southwest. (The single remotest site is 54 in row 7.) Row 8 runs perpendicular to rows 1–7 on the south edge of the property. The longest pull-throughs (90 feet) are located in this row. Of these sites, the least desirable are 5 (faces a mobile home) and 9 (faces a dumpster). Sites 58–63, along the north edge, are electric sites only. These are grassier, however, and quite nice. Tent sites occupy sites 1–3 of row 3 and T4 of row 4. These walled-in sites are 33 by 22 feet and offer a square of dirt for a tent. Site 3 has the communal wash basin and trash receptacle. There is also group tenting along the north edge by the cabins. A camping kitchen for tenters is located next to the basketball court. Lordsburg is a very nice campground that both RVers and tenters will enjoy.

BASICS

Operated By: Marin & Naty. **Open:** All year. **Site Assignment:** Upon registration; credit card required for reservation, 24-hour cancellation policy. **Registration:** At office; late arrivals use drop box. **Fee:** RV, $24–$30; tent, $20–$22; check, V, MC, D. **Parking:** At site.

FACILITIES

Number of RV-only Sites: 62. **Number of Tent-only Sites:** 5. **Hookups:** Electric (30, 50 amps), water, sewer, cable TV, Wi-Fi. **Each Site:** Picnic table (tent sites: picnic table, grill, lantern pole). **Dump Station:** Yes. **Laundry:** Yes. **Pay Phone:** Yes. **Restrooms and Showers:** Yes. **Fuel:** No. **Propane:** Yes. **Internal Roads:** Gravel. **RV Service:** No. **Market:** Less than 0.25 mi. on Main Street. **Restaurant:** Less than 0.25 mi. on Main Street. **General Store:** Yes. **Vending:** Yes. **Swimming:** Pool. **Playground:** Yes. **Other:** Dog walk, cabins, covered pavilion, rec room. **Activities:** Swimming, basketball, badminton, horseshoes, hiking, visiting ghost towns. **Nearby Attractions:** Shakespeare Ghost Town, Gila National Forest. **Additional Information:** Lordsburg-Hidalgo Chamber of Commerce, (505) 542-9864.

RESTRICTIONS

Pets: On leash, cleaned up after. **Fires:** Grill only. **Alcoholic Beverages:** At sites. **Vehicle Maximum Length:** 70 ft.

TO GET THERE

From I-10 (Exit 22), from the south side of the highway, go 1 block south on Main to Maple St. and turn right. Follow Maple (which curves to the left) and go 0.3 mi. Continue straight on into the campground.

MAYHILL   MAP, C-2
Rio Penasco RV Camp

P.O. Box 47, 2180 Rio Penasco Rd., 88339.
T: (505) 687-3715.

🚐 ★★★★★   ▲ ★★★★

Beauty: ★★★★   Site Privacy: ★★★
Spaciousness: ★★★   Quiet: ★★★★★
Security: ★★★★   Cleanliness: ★★★★★
Insect Control: ★★★   Facilities: ★★★★

Just to the south of Mayhill, Rio Penasco is surrounded on all sides by trees and verdant hills along the entire eastern perimeter. Laid out as a giant circle with rows cut inside, the campground boasts gigantic (70-feet-long) pull-throughs as well as a few back-ins around the office area. (These are the least desirable sites, assigned last when the park is full. Sites 3 and 4 are especially prone to registration traffic, being smack dab in front of the office.) The best site by a long shot is 13, which is a huge pull-through well apart from the rest, under an enormous willow, and open to the hills and creek to the east. Second place goes to 9, which is similar in every way to 13, but is sided by site 8, which detracts only slightly from its desirability. Sites are all a level grassy/gravel mix, long enough to accommodate pretty much anything, but a little on the narrow side (22 feet wide). Should this concern you at all, however, the restroom and laundry facilities will ease your mind a hundredfold. These are the nicest restroom facilities you are likely to find on your journey—no matter where you are destined. Tastefully decorated with handicrafts, they are carpeted, immaculate, and as comfortable as those at home. Likewise, the laundry facility is spacious and clean, and contains a small, carpeted rec room with sofa, table, games, puzzles, magazines, and more handicrafts. Situated in a gorgeous setting in the tiny mountain town of Mayhill near Cloudcroft, this campground is a splendid destination for return visits.

BASICS

Operated By: John & Emily Nutt. **Open:** All year. **Site Assignment:** Depends on availability; credit card or check for reservations, reservations required June–Aug. **Registration:** At office; late arrivals use drop box or settle in morning. **Fee:** RV, $17. **Parking:** At site.

FACILITIES

Number of RV-only Sites: 33. **Hookups:** Electric (30 amps), water, sewer, cable, Wi-Fi. **Each Site:** Picnic table. **Dump Station:** No (sewer at all sites). **Laundry:** Yes. **Pay Phone:** Yes. **Restrooms and Showers:** Yes. **Fuel:** No. **Propane:** Yes. **Internal Roads:** Gravel, in good condition. **RV Service:** No. **Market:** 1 mi. to Mayhill. **Restaurant:** 1 mi. to Mayhill. **General Store:** Yes. **Vending:** No. **Swimming:** No. **Playground:** No. **Other:** RV supplies, creek, pavilion, rec room. **Activities:** Nightly entertainment in pavilion, fishing, games. **Nearby Attractions:** Cloudcroft, Weed (historic logging town). **Additional Information:** Cloudcroft Chamber of Commerce, (505) 682-2733.

RESTRICTIONS

Pets: On leash, cleaned up after; no barking. **Fires:** Grill or fire ring in pavilion. **Alcoholic Beverages:** Not allowed. **Vehicle Maximum Length:** No limit. **Other:** Christian atmosphere (no swearing).

TO GET THERE

From the junction of Hwy. 82 and Hwy. 130 (Rio Penasco Rd.), turn west onto Rio Penasco Rd., cross bridge and take the first left at the sign into the campground. (This turn may be a little tricky for large rigs. For those wishing to avoid the turn, there is another entrance/exit just to the west of this one.) The office is to the right of the first entrance.

MIMBRES   MAP, C-1
Mountain Spirits RV Park

NM Hwy. 35, P.O. Box 2539, 88049.
T: (505) 536-3797.

🚐 ★★★★   ▲ ★★★★

Beauty: ★★★★   Site Privacy: ★★★★
Spaciousness: ★★★   Quiet: ★★★★
Security: ★★★★   Cleanliness: ★★★★
Insect Control: ★★★★   Facilities: ★★

All sites in this campground are 72 by 24–foot pull-throughs laid out in a straight line bordering the highway 60 feet away. There are mountain views to the north and south. Most sites are quite well shaded. Site 3 is extra wide to accommodate a long-term guest. Site 11 is closest to the bathhouse. There are Camp Hosts in sites 8 and 9. End site 20 is next to mobile homes, but end site 1 has a fence, extra space, and larger trees, making it the most desirable site. Tenting is possible in sites 12 and 13, which are roped off from RVs. These sites have fine gravel and sparse grass, and loads of shade from trees. There is also an open tenting area to the southwest. The restrooms and showers are in a carpeted mobile home, and are both clean and very comfortable. This campground makes a very nice stop for both RVers and tenters.

BASICS

Operated By: Robert Klossner. **Open:** All year. **Site Assignment:** First come, first served; verbal reservations OK. **Registration:** At pay station at entrance. **Fee:** RV 50 amps, $20; RV 30 amps, $18; tent, $5; check, no credits cards. **Parking:** At site.

FACILITIES

Number of RV-only Sites: 17. **Number of Tent-only Sites:** 2. **Hookups:** Electric (30, 50 amps), water, sewer, phone. **Each Site:** Garbage can. **Dump Station:** No (sewer at all sites). **Laundry:** Yes. **Pay Phone:** No. **Restrooms and Showers:** Yes. **Fuel:** No. **Propane:** On site. **Internal Roads:** Gravel. **RV Service:** No. **Market:** 25 mi. to Silver City. **Restaurant:** 0.5 mi. north. **General Store:** No. **Vending:** No. **Swimming:** No. **Playground:** No. **Activities:** Hiking, scenic drives. **Nearby Attractions:** Gila Cliff Dwellings National Monument, Gila National Forest. **Additional Information:** Silver City Grant County Chamber of Commerce, (505) 538-3785.

RESTRICTIONS

Pets: On leash, cleaned up after. **Fires:** Grill only. **Alcoholic Beverages:** At site. **Vehicle Maximum Length:** No limit.

TO GET THERE

From the junction of Hwy. 180 and Hwy. 152, turn north onto Hwy. 152 and go 13 mi. east. Turn left onto Hwy. 35 and go 1.5 mi. Turn left at the sign into the entrance.

MOUNTAINAIR   MAP, B-2
Manzano Mountains State Park

HC 66 Box 202, 87036. T: (505) 847-2820 or (505) 344-7240 (off season); www.nmparks.com.

🚐 ★★★★   ▲ ★★★★

Beauty: ★★★★★   Site Privacy: ★★★★★
Spaciousness: ★★★★   Quiet: ★★★★★
Security: ★★★★   Cleanliness: ★★★★★
Insect Control: ★★★★   Facilities: ★★

Laid out in a loop, this small campground is located in a forest at the foot of the Manzano Mountains. Sites are all back-ins, ranging from 30 feet (1 and 3) to 70 feet (6). Some sites (1, 6, 7, 10, and 12) have covered shelters, while others (11–16) offer electrical hookups. Site 7 seems particularly spacious, as does 16. Sites 9 and 10 are next to the access for overflow camping, which is normally closed, but may increase traffic by these two sites when open. Site 8 is a 60-foot site, completely hidden in trees. Sites 4 and 5 are tent-only sites, but a tenter would be happy at any of these sites. Although the sites are not grassy, nearly all offer overhanging tree cover, making tenting comfortable in this park. The restrooms are clean and modern. The nearby Red Canyon National Forest campground (accessed by turning right at the entrance to this state park) is only slightly larger at around 50 sites but offers no hookups. Tenters may find it an acceptable alternative, but RVers will prefer the Manzano Mountains campground due to the electrical hookups.

BASICS

Operated By: New Mexico State Park Division. **Open:** All year. **Site Assignment:** First come, first served; reservations at (877) 664-7787. **Registration:** At pay station. **Fee:** Electric, $14; developed, $10; primitive, $8; check, no credit cards. **Parking:** At site.

FACILITIES

Number of Multipurpose Sites: 45. **Hookups:** Electric (20, 30 amps). **Each Site:** Picnic table, grill, fire pit. **Dump Station:** Yes. **Laundry:** No. **Pay Phone:** No. **Restrooms and Showers:** Yes. **Fuel:** No. **Propane:** No. **Internal Roads:** Gravel. **RV Service:** No. **Market:** Small: Manzano, 3 mi.; large: Sturgess, 26 mi. **Restaurant:** 13 mi. to Mountainair. **General Store:** No. **Vending:** No. **Swimming:** No. **Playground:** No. **Other:** Group shelter, backs to national forest. **Activities:** Hiking, visiting ruins, horseshoes. **Nearby Attractions:** Salinas Pueblo Ruins. **Additional Information:** New Mexico State Parks Division, (888) NM-PARKS.

RESTRICTIONS

Pets: On leash, cleaned up after. **Fires:** Grill only. **Alcoholic Beverages:** At sites. **Vehicle Maximum Length:** No limit.

TO GET THERE

From the junction of Hwy. 60 and Hwy. 55, turn north onto Hwy. 55 and go 12.4 mi. Turn left onto Hwy. 131 and go 2.4 mi. Continue straight ahead to enter the park.

PORTALES   MAP, B-3
Wagon Wheel RV Park

42699 US 70, 88130. T: (505) 356-3700.

🚐 ★★★   ▲ ★★

Beauty: ★★★   Site Privacy: ★★★
Spaciousness: ★★★   Quiet: ★★★
Security: ★★★★   Cleanliness: ★★★★
Insect Control: ★★★   Facilities: ★★★

On the wall outside the restrooms is a collage of notes from previous satisfied customers attesting to their contentment with this quiet and "peaseful" campground. The grounds are quite clean and peaceful, although some traffic noise from the highway does reach the park. The campground is laid out in two rows, the lettered strip sporting more grass and thus being generally a little nicer. While most trees are too thin to provide shade, the tree at sites 7 and 8 is an exception. Sites are level pull-throughs that vary in length from 45 to 56 feet. Site 11 is at the shortest extreme (45 feet) and has no tree, making it the least desirable RV site. Tent sites in the southeast corner have good grass, and the possible use of a row of small trees along the back fence. Behind these sites is a pleasant farm with geese and a pond. The restrooms are reasonably clean and comfortable with a nice wood decor. The campground, likewise, is comfortable and clean, but may not quite live up to the letters it boasts on the walls.

BASICS

Operated By: Birl & Sue Gray. **Open:** All year. **Site Assignment:** First come, first served. **Registration:** At office; late arrivals use drop box (most often no one in office); verbal reservations OK. **Fee:** RV (full), $17; check, no credit cards. **Parking:** At site.

FACILITIES

Number of RV-only Sites: 14. **Hookups:** Electric (20, 30, 50 amps), water, sewer. **Each Site:** Most have trees, some picnic tables. **Dump Station:** No. **Laundry:** No. **Pay Phone:** No. **Restrooms and Showers:** Yes. **Fuel:** No. **Propane:** No. **Internal Roads:** Gravel, some paved; in good condition. **RV Service:** No. **Market:** 2.5 mi. southwest. **Restaurant:** 5 mi. southwest. **General Store:** No. **Vending:** No. **Swimming:** No. **Playground:** No. **Other:** Basketball hoop. **Activities:** Basketball. **Nearby Attractions:** Blackwater Draw Museum. **Additional Information:** Roosevelt County Chamber of Commerce, (800) 635-8036, (505) 356-8541.

RESTRICTIONS

Pets: On leash, cleaned up after, no barking, not tied up outside. **Fires:** Grill only. **Alcoholic Beverages:** At sites. **Vehicle Maximum Length:** 55 ft. **Other:** No generators; park vehicle only in front of or behind RV.

TO GET THERE

From the junction of Hwy. 70 and Hwy. 206 in town, drive 4.2 mi. north on Hwy. 70. Turn east at the sign (at mile marker 427) into the campground. The office is at the entrance. The campground is also 18 mi. south of Clois on Hwy. 70.

PREWITT   MAP, B-1
Bluewater Lake State Park

P. O. Box 3419, 87045. T: (505) 876-2391; www.nmparks.com.

🚐 ★★★★   ▲ ★★★★★

Beauty: ★★★★★   Site Privacy: ★★★★
Spaciousness: ★★★★★   Quiet: ★★★★★
Security: ★★★★   Cleanliness: ★★★★
Insect Control: ★★★★   Facilities: ★★★

There are four major campgrounds in this state park (Canyonside, Lakeside, Northpoint, and Creek Overlook), offering everything from waterfront camping to hillside sites with a view. Canyonside Campground, to the southeast of the ranger station, has the only electric sites in the park. Reservable sites are E1–E6, which are 57-foot back-ins. The Campground host is located at E7. Sites E9 and E10 are doubles (75 feet and 60 feet), while E11 and E13 are huge (100-foot and 150-foot) pull-throughs. This campground also has the only showers. Lakeside Campground (which ought really to be called "Lake Overlook") has primitive sites with a view (although Pinon Cliff Campground is better). The road in is rough and steep—no place for a large RV. Northpoint Campground likewise has primitive sites and a rough road that ends at the lake. There is no real road between sites. For the best views (but, again, primitive sites), go to Creek Overlook Campground. This campground offers dirt sites amid trees. There are beautiful vistas of rocky bluffs, the grassy creek area, and woods below. The restrooms and showers (in Canyonside Campground) are clean and decently large. This state park caters to tenters, but RVers who don't mind forgoing water and sewer hookups (let alone cable!) will enjoy the beautiful views and outdoor recreation opportunities this park affords.

BASICS

Operated By: New Mexico State Park Division. **Open:** All year. **Site Assignment:** First come, first served; reservations by credit card or check, no refunds. **Registration:** At pay station. **Fee:** Electric, $14; developed, $10; primitive, $8; check, no credit cards. **Parking:** At site.

FACILITIES

Number of RV-only Sites: 14. **Number of Tent-only Sites:** 106. **Hookups:** Electric (20, 30 amps). **Each Site:** Picnic table, fire pit. **Dump Station:** Yes. **Laundry:** No. **Pay Phone:** Yes. **Restrooms and Showers:** Yes. **Fuel:** No. **Propane:** No. **Internal Roads:** Paved. **RV Service:** No. **Market:** 25 mi. in Grants. **Restaurant:** 25 mi. in Grants. **General Store:** No. **Vending:** No. **Swimming:** No. **Playground:** Yes. **Other:** Boat ramp. **Activities:** Fishing, boating, swimming, hiking. **Nearby Attractions:** Red Rock State Park. **Additional Information:** New Mexico State Parks Division, (888) NM-PARKS.

RESTRICTIONS

Pets: On leash, cleaned up after. **Fires:** Grill only. **Alcoholic Beverages:** At sites. **Vehicle Maximum Length:** No limit.

TO GET THERE

From I-40 (Exit 63), turn south onto Hwy. 412 and go 8 mi. to the entrance of the park.

RATON   MAP, A-3
Summerlan RV Park

1900 Cedar St., 87740. T: (505) 445-9536.

🚐 ★★★★   ▲ ★★★

Beauty: ★★★
Site Privacy: ★★★
Spaciousness: ★★★
Quiet: ★★★
Security: ★★★★
Cleanliness: ★★★★
Insect Control: ★★★★
Facilities: ★★★★

Sites in this campground are laid out in Rows A, B, and C. Western-end sites (A1 and 2, B1 and 2, C1 and 2) share large shade trees. Sites B9, C5–8, and C15 are well shaded, but A4–8 are mostly unshaded. Rows A and B are pull-throughs, while Row C has only back-ins. Tenting is possible behind the RV sites. (There is a bridge between the two areas at site C9.) There is thick grass, but not much shade. There is, however, a covered pavilion for tenters' use. The restrooms are simple, with painted cement walls, but quite clean and spacious. This is a decent campground for a short stay, and there is long-term RV storage for those who do not want to haul their rig back home at the end of the season. Tenters will also enjoy this campground, although the addition of shade trees would make the tenting experience much better.

BASICS

Operated By: Buddy, Linda, & Tim Bryant. **Open:** All year. **Site Assignment:** Upon registration; credit card required for reservation, 24-hour cancellation policy. **Registration:** At office; late arrivals use drop box. **Fee:** RV (full), $25.50; tent, $15; check preferred; V, MC, D. **Parking:** At site.

FACILITIES

Number of RV-only Sites: 45. **Number of Tent-only Sites:** Undesignated sites. **Hookups:** Electric (30, 50 amps), water, sewer, cable TV. **Each Site:** Picnic tables. **Dump Station:** No (sewer at all sites). **Laundry:** Yes. **Pay Phone:** No. **Restrooms and Showers:** Yes. **Fuel:** No. **Propane:** Yes. **Internal Roads:** Gravel, paved. **RV Service:** Yes. **Market:** 0.75 mi. west. **Restaurant:** 2 blocks. **General Store:** No. **Vending:** No. **Swimming:** No. **Playground:** No. **Other:** Storage, covered pavilion. **Activities:** Horseshoes, hiking. **Nearby Attractions:** Sugarite Canyon State Park, Capulin Volcano National Monument, NRA Whittington Center. **Additional Information:** Raton Chamber of Commerce, (505) 376-2417.

RESTRICTIONS

Pets: On leash, cleaned up after. **Fires:** Grill only. **Alcoholic Beverages:** At sites. **Vehicle Maximum Length:** 45 ft.

TO GET THERE

From I-25 (Exit 451), from the east side of the highway, take the immediate right into 1900 Cedar St. and go 0.2 mi. Turn right at the sign into the entrance.

RODEO   MAP, D-1
Rodeo RV Park and Country Store

P.O. Box 272, 88056. T: (505) 557-2510 or (505) 557-2266.

🚐 ★★★   ▲ ★★

Beauty: ★★★
Site Privacy: ★★★
Spaciousness: ★★★★
Quiet: ★★★★
Security: ★★★★★
Cleanliness: ★★★★
Insect Control: ★★★★
Facilities: ★★★

This campground consists of an open gravel lot next to a residence and a store. Laid out in a single row, sites are open-ended pull-throughs that can accommodate a rig of any length, but are only 18 feet wide. Site 9 lies closest to the entrance (next to a fence and stored equipment), while site 1 is farthest from the entrance. There are a number of vehicles, along with stored equipment, scattered about the campground, making it less attractive. Tenting is possible anywhere, as there is crushed gravel all around the campground. This campground is OK for an overnight stay for RVers, but the motel right next door (that also has RV spaces) might be better for tenters. It is only slightly more expensive ($1 more for tenters, $2 more for RVers), and of roughly the same quality.

BASICS

Operated By: Marianne & Edward Gullot. **Open:** All year. **Site Assignment:** First come, first served; verbal reservations OK. **Registration:** At store; late arrivals select available site & pay in the morning. **Fee:** RV (full), $14; tent, $4; check, V, MC, D. **Parking:** At site.

FACILITIES

Number of RV-only Sites: 9. **Number of Tent-only Sites:** Undesignated sites. **Hookups:** Electric (20, 30 amps), water, sewer. **Each Site:** None. **Dump Station:** No (sewer at all sites). **Laundry:** No. **Pay Phone:** No. **Restrooms and Showers:** Yes. **Fuel:** Yes. **Propane:** No. **Internal Roads:** Gravel. **RV Service:** No (some small repairs). **Market:** Yes. **Restaurant:** On site. **General Store:** Yes. **Vending:** Yes. **Swimming:** No. **Playground:** No. **Activities:** World-class bird-watching, hiking, hunting. **Nearby Attractions:** Chiracahua Gallery, Wachuka Mountains, Geronimo Surrender Monument, Wonderland of Rock, Natural History Museum Research Center. **Additional Information:** Lordsburg-Hidalgo Chamber of Commerce, (505) 542-9864.

RESTRICTIONS

Pets: On leash, cleaned up after. **Fires:** Grill only. **Alcoholic Beverages:** At sites. **Vehicle Maximum Length:** No limit.

TO GET THERE

From the junction of Hwy. 9 and Hwy. 80, turn south onto Hwy. 80 and go 5.8 mi. into Rodeo. Turn left at the sign into the entrance.

ROSWELL   MAP, C-3
Trailer Village RV Campground

1706 East 2nd, 88201. T: (505) 623-6040.

🚐 ★★★   ▲ ★★

Beauty: ★★★
Site Privacy: ★★★
Spaciousness: ★★★★
Quiet: ★★★★
Security: ★★★★
Cleanliness: ★★★★
Insect Control: ★★★★
Facilities: ★★★

Laid out in an L shape, this campground has back-ins all along the perimeter and a row of pull-throughs in the middle. Sites 1–13 back against a fence and residences. All of these but 5 are well shaded. Sites 14–19 turn the corner toward the southwest. These are 42-foot back-ins against the fence. Sites 20–27 back to a fence along the south side, beyond which lies a farm. Site 27 is a little narrower than other sites and fenced on three sides. Sites 29–45 are smaller back-ins (30 feet) that back to a field beyond the fence. Of these, 30 has the most shade. The pull-through sites in the middle of the park all have a shade tree except 48. End site 46 has a larger grassy area than the other sites. The tent sites are the same as RV sites 1–5. These offer a thin grass covering and little shade. As the name suggests, this "campground" is RV-oriented, but it is not really a camping destination.

BASICS

Operated By: Debbie & Erin McGonagle. **Open:** All year. **Site Assignment:** Depends on site availability; credit card required for reservation, 24-hour cancellation policy. **Registration:** At office; late arrivals use drop box. **Fee:** RV (full hookup), $25; tent (2 people), $15; checks, V, MC. **Parking:** At site.

FACILITIES

Number of RV-only Sites: 53. **Number of Tent-only Sites:** 5. **Hookups:** Electric (30, 50 amps), water, sewer, cable TV, Wi-Fi. **Each Site:** Picnic tables. **Dump Station:** No (sewer at all sites). **Laundry:** Yes. **Pay Phone:** Yes. **Restrooms and Showers:** Yes. **Fuel:** No. **Propane:** No. **Internal Roads:** Gravel. **RV Service:** No. **Market:** 8 blocks west. **Restaurant:** 6 blocks west. **General Store:** 4 blocks west. **Vending:** No. **Swimming:** No. **Playground:** No. **Other:** Modem. **Activities:** Swimming, visiting museums, lake, watching wildlife. **Nearby Attractions:** Bitter Lake National Wildlife Reserve, Bottomless Lakes State Park, International UFO Museum & Research Center, Dragonfly Festival. **Additional Information:** Roswell Chamber of Commerce, (505) 623-5695.

RESTRICTIONS

Pets: On leash, cleaned up after, 2 pets of max. 20 lbs. **Fires:** Grill only. **Alcoholic Beverages:** At sites. **Vehicle Maximum Length:** No limit.

TO GET THERE

From the junction of Hwy. 285 and Hwy. 70/380, turn east onto Hwy. 380 (2nd St. in town) and go 1.4 mi. Turn right at the sign into the entrance.

RUIDOSO   MAP, C-2
Tall Pines RV Park

1800 Sudderth Dr., 88345. T: (877) 957-5233.

🚐 ★★★★   ▲ n/a

Beauty: ★★★★   Site Privacy: ★★★
Spaciousness: ★★★   Quiet: ★★★
Security: ★★★★   Cleanliness: ★★★★
Insect Control: ★★★★   Facilities: ★★★★

This campground is divided into three sections: an upper, middle, and lower tier. The lower tier is located on the same level as the office and entrance. Lower-numbered sites back to woods on the west side and to a fence on the south side. Sites 17–32 are 60-foot back-ins that also back to woods. Sites 33–38 are 45-foot back-ins, and 39–43 are 78-foot pull-throughs. In the middle tier, sites 49 and 50 are slightly secluded in a wooded patch along the road. Site 61, to the west, is also slightly secluded. The sites in this section (61–76) are 75-foot pull-throughs. The lower level is coated by the river and is the nicest area to camp in. Sites 51–57 back to sites in the middle tier, but sites 58–60 back to the river, making these the most desirable sites in the park. The restroom in the rec building is a decent facility, but if you happen to find the one in the laundry, you will not be as pleased. That restroom seems to be an afterthought, stuck in an old furnace room, with one toilet and no sink. This campground is a popular spot for campers, and choice sites may be occupied by guests staying for several weeks. However, it is definitely worth the trip.

BASICS
Operated By: Private operator. **Open:** All year; peak season, May 1–Oct. 31. **Site Assignment:** Upon registration; credit card required for reservation, 48-hour cancellation policy. **Registration:** At office; late arrivals use drop box. **Fee:** RV, $37–$38 ($33 w/ discount); check, V, MC, AE, D. **Parking:** At site, lots of extra parking.

FACILITIES
Number of RV-only Sites: 74. **Hookups:** Electric (30, 50 amps), water, sewer, cable TV. **Each Site:** None. **Dump Station:** Yes. **Laundry:** Yes. **Pay Phone:** Yes. **Restrooms and Showers:** Toilets; no shower. **Fuel:** No. **Propane:** No. **Internal Roads:** Gravel. **RV Service:** No. **Market:** 1.5 mi. west. **Restaurant:** Across the street. **General Store:** No. **Vending:** Yes. **Swimming:** No. **Playground:** No. **Other:** Downtown w/in walking distance, modem, rec building. **Activities:** Fishing, golf. **Nearby Attractions:** Casinos, horse races. **Additional Information:** Ruidoso Chamber of Commerce, (505) 257-7395.

RESTRICTIONS
Pets: On leash, cleaned up after. **Fires:** Grill only. **Alcoholic Beverages:** At sites. **Vehicle Maximum Length:** 45 ft.

TO GET THERE
From the junction of Hwy. 70 and Hwy. 48 (Sudderth Dr. in town), turn west onto Sudderth Dr. and go 2.1 mi. Turn right at the sign into the entrance.

SAN ANTONIO   MAP, C-2
Bosque Birdwatcher's RV Park

1481 NM Rd. 1, 87832. T: (505) 835-1366.

🚐 ★★★   ▲ ★★

Beauty: ★★★   Site Privacy: ★★★★
Spaciousness: ★★★★   Quiet: ★★★★★
Security: ★★★★★   Cleanliness: ★★★★
Insect Control: ★★★★   Facilities: ★★★

Surrounded by national wildlife refuge land, this campground has undeveloped (mostly dirt) sites and natural gardens and landscaping, using rocks and local plants. Sites around the house are unnumbered, and finding them can be at times a confusing task. There is one small site behind the house under a shade tree, and one long pull-through under a row of shade trees to the south of the house. These sites are the nicest, as they are very well shaded and have character. The rest of the sites are in a gravel clearing to the west of the house. The south row has 60 by 30-foot pull-throughs, while the north row has larger (90 by 30-foot) sites. The north row has some amount of shade at each site, but the south row is unshaded. Tenting is possible along the north edge of the gravel lot. There is sparse grass and no shade, making for rather barren camping. The restrooms are rather simple but spotless and very comfortable. This is a reasonable stop for RVers, and a great convenience for bird-watchers, but tenters will likely want to move on.

BASICS
Operated By: Jackie & Billy Trujillo. **Open:** All year. **Site Assignment:** Upon registration; verbal reservations OK. **Registration:** At office; late arrivals select available site & pay in the morning. **Fee:** RV 30 amps, $20; RV 50 amps, $23; tent single, $10; tent double, $15; check, no credits cards. **Parking:** At site.

FACILITIES
Number of RV-only Sites: 36. **Number of Tent-only Sites:** Undesignated sites. **Hookups:** Electric (20, 30, 50 amps), water, sewer. **Dump Station:** No (sewer at all sites). **Laundry:** No. **Pay Phone:** No. **Restrooms and Showers:** Yes. **Fuel:** No. **Propane:** No. **Internal Roads:** Gravel. **RV Service:** No. **Market:** 13 mi. north. **Restaurant:** 3 mi. north. **General Store:** No. **Vending:** No. **Swimming:** No. **Playground:** No. **Other:** 2 phone hookups, modem. **Activities:** Bird-watching. **Nearby Attractions:** Bosque del Apache National Wildlife Refuge. **Additional Information:** Socorro Chamber of Commerce, (505) 835-0424.

RESTRICTIONS
Pets: On leash, cleaned up after. **Fires:** Grill only. **Alcoholic Beverages:** At sites. **Vehicle Maximum Length:** No limit.

TO GET THERE
From I-40 (Exit 139), turn east onto Hwy. 380 from the east side of the highway, and go 0.55 mi. Turn right onto Hwy. 1 and go 3.1 mi. (Go 0.1 mi. past the billboard.) Turn right at the sign into the entrance.

SANTA FE   MAP, B-2
Redondo Campground—
Santa Fe National Forest

reserve america

1474 Rodeo Rd., 87505. T: (505) 438-7825; www.reserveamerica.com.

🚐 ★★★★   ▲ ★★★

Beauty: ★★★   Site Privacy: ★★★★
Spaciousness: ★★★   Quiet: ★★★
Security: ★★★★   Cleanliness: ★★★★
Insect Control: ★★★★   Facilities: ★

Redondo Campground–Santa Fe National Forest is a nice local campground. The area offers a variety of recreational opportunities, and the campground managers help ensure visitors have a good time. Some of the finest mountain scenery in the Southwest is found in the 1.6 million acres covered by the Santa Fe National Forest. Elevations rise from 5,300 to 13,103 feet at the summit of Truchas Peak, located within the Pecos Wilderness.

BASICS
Operated By: U.S. Forest Service. **Open:** May 13–Sept. 30. **Site Assignment:** Reservations must be made at least 4 days in advance. **Registration:** At office. **Fee:** Single, $10. **Parking:** At park.

FACILITIES
Number of Multipurpose Sites: 76. **Hookups:** None. **Each Site:** Call ahead. **Dump Station:** No. **Laundry:** No. **Pay Phone:** No. **Restrooms and Showers:** Yes. **Fuel:** No. **Propane:** No. **Internal Roads:** Paved. **RV Service:** No. **Market:** No. **Restaurant:** No. **General Store:** No. **Vending:** No. **Swimming:** No. **Playground:** No.

RESTRICTIONS
Pets: Pets must be restrained or on a leash at all times while in developed recreation areas. **Fires:** In fire rings, stoves, grills, or fireplaces provided for that purpose. **Alcoholic Beverages:** Not allowed. **Vehicle Maximum Length:** 30 ft. **Other:** No ATVs or ORVs allowed. No water available at the Redondo Campground.

TO GET THERE
2 mi. east of La Cueva on NM 4. From the Jemez Ranger Station, go south 7.5 mi. north to the junction of NM 4 and NM 126 at La Cueva. Turn right and continue on NM 4 for 2 mi. to the campground turnoff.

SANTA FE   MAP, B-2
Santa Fe Skies RV Park

14 Browncastle Ranch, 87508. T: (877) 565-0451 or (505) 473-5946; www.santafeskiesrvpark.com.

🚐 ★★★★★   ▲ n/a

Beauty: ★★★★★   Site Privacy: ★★★★
Spaciousness: ★★★★   Quiet: ★★★★★
Security: ★★★★   Cleanliness: ★★★★★
Insect Control: ★★★★   Facilities: ★★★★

Although this campground is relatively new, one thing that will not change as new facilities are added are the gorgeous 360-degree views for which the campground is named. There are, in essence, two mini-campgrounds contained in this park. The first has an RV park feel to it, with sites laid out in rows of gravel strips with a small strip of vegetation. These are 70 by 25–foot pull-throughs. Sites 1–10 are back-ins along the western edge. The second section of this park lies on Yucca and has a more "campground" feel to it. Sites are 45–54 by 42–foot back-ins separated by wild-growing bushes. Sites 1–22 back to a wooden fence. The sites with the best views face north on top of a slight hill on Yucca: 24–28, J, and K. This campground is a destination to return to annually.

BASICS

Operated By: John & Carrie Brown. **Open:** All year. **Site Assignment:** Upon registration; credit card required for reservation (Sept.–Oct.), 48-hour cancellation policy. **Registration:** At office; late arrivals select available site & pay in the morning. **Fee:** RV (pull-through), $31.99; back-in, $29.78; concrete patio, $35.27; check, V, MC. **Parking:** At site.

FACILITIES

Number of RV-only Sites: 98. **Hookups:** Electric (20, 30, 50 amps), water, sewer, instant phone, Wi-Fi. **Each Site:** Picnic tables. **Dump Station:** Yes. **Laundry:** Yes. **Pay Phone:** Courtesy. **Restrooms and Showers:** Yes. **Fuel:** No. **Propane:** Yes. **Internal Roads:** Gravel. **RV Service:** On-call. **Market:** 5 mi. north. **Restaurant:** 5 mi. north. **General Store:** Yes. **Vending:** No. **Swimming:** No. **Playground:** No. **Other:** Modem, views. **Activities:** Tours, shopping, opera, music. **Nearby Attractions:** Hyde Memorial State Park, Tesuque Pueblo, galleries, Georgia O'Keeffe Museum. **Additional Information:** Santa Fe CVB, (800) 777-CITY, (505) 984-6760.

RESTRICTIONS

Pets: On leash, cleaned up after. **Fires:** Gas grills only. **Alcoholic Beverages:** At sites. **Vehicle Maximum Length:** 100 ft. **Other:** No tents.

TO GET THERE

From I-25 (southbound Exit 276, northbound Exit 276A): on the north side of the highway, follow the signs for Hwy. 14, then cross Hwy. 14 and go 0.5 mi. Turn left at the sign into the entrance.

SILVER CITY — MAP, C-1
Manzano's RV Park

103 Flury Ln., 88061. T: (505) 538-0918; www.manzanosrvpark.uswestdex.com.

🚐 ★★★★★   ⛺ n/a

Beauty: ★★★★★	Site Privacy: ★★★★★
Spaciousness: ★★★★★	Quiet: ★★★★★
Security: ★★★★★	Cleanliness: ★★★★★
Insect Control: ★★★★	Facilities: ★★★

In this campground, natural beauty reigns. There are flowers, trees, native plants, and rocks, and the campground itself is surrounded by trees. Site 1, a 90-foot back-in by the entrance, is nicely mostly hidden by bushes. Site 2 is smaller (75 feet) and more open, but has attractive landscaping. Sites 4, 5, 6,

and 7 are pull-throughs that flow into each other and are easily 80 feet each. Sites 8–13 are 60- to 80-foot back-ins. In the middle island, site 14 (on the west side) is laid out along the internal road, and can accommodate a rig of any size. In the southwest corner of the island, site 15 is easily the widest site (45 feet wide) but only 40 feet in length. Site 16, on the other hand, is the shortest pull-through. Sites 17 and 18, located behind the office, are 60-foot back-ins that are situated quite close together. This is a delightfully natural campground that RVers will enjoy much more than the nearby competition. (Tenters, however, may find the KOA the best choice, as Manzano's does not take tents.)

BASICS

Operated By: E. C. Manzano. **Open:** All year. **Site Assignment:** First come, first served; verbal reservations OK. **Registration:** At house; late arrivals select site & pay in the morning. **Fee:** RV, $20; check, no credit cards. **Parking:** At site.

FACILITIES

Number of RV-only Sites: 18. **Hookups:** Electric (30, 50 amps), water, sewer. **Each Site:** Picnic table. **Dump Station:** No (sewer at all sites). **Laundry:** Yes. **Pay Phone:** Yes. **Restrooms and Showers:** Yes. **Fuel:** No. **Propane:** No. **Internal Roads:** Gravel. **RV Service:** Portable service available nearby. **Market:** 1 mi. toward Silver City. **Restaurant:** 1 mi. toward Silver City. **General Store:** No. **Vending:** No. **Swimming:** No. **Playground:** No. **Other:** Quiet, views. **Activities:** Hiking. **Nearby Attractions:** City of Rocks State Park, Gila National Forest. **Additional Information:** Old West Country Chamber of Commerce, (505) 538-0061.

RESTRICTIONS

Pets: On leash, cleaned up after. **Fires:** Grill only. **Alcoholic Beverages:** At sites. **Vehicle Maximum Length:** 45 ft. **Other:** Pick up cigarette butts.

TO GET THERE

From the junction of Hwy. 90 and Hwy. 180, turn east onto Hwy. 180 and go 2.5 mi. Turn south onto Kirkland Rd. and go 0.3 mi. to Flury Ln. Turn right and go 0.4 mi. straight into the campground.

TAOS — MAP, A-2
Monte Bello RV Park

24819 Hwy. 64 West, P. O. Box 2709, 87571. T: (505) 751-0774; www.taosmontebellorvpark.com.

🚐 ★★★★   ⛺ ★★★

Beauty: ★★★★★	Site Privacy: ★★★★
Spaciousness: ★★★★★	Quiet: ★★★
Security: ★★★★	Cleanliness: ★★★★★
Insect Control: ★★★★	Facilities: ★★★★

This campground features three rows of unshaded sites, but they have wonderful views of the mountains and spectacular sunrises and sunsets. Both the campground and the sites themselves are left in a natural state, without being overly developed. All sites are 80 by 40–foot pull-throughs. End site 7 (to the north) has extra space to the side, as does 14, but this latter is next to the playground. Site 19 is next to

the tenting sites. The best sites are on the northern or eastern end (7 and 19), as they are farthest from the highway and have the best views. The tent sites to the northeast are 25 by 40–foot spaces of dirt and sparse grass. Although there are currently only 4 tent sites, more are planned. This campground looks like it will become a top-notch campground when all of the facilities are in place. It is a very nice place to stay.

BASICS

Operated By: John & Concha Torres. **Open:** All year. **Site Assignment:** Depends on availability; credit card required for reservation, $10 deposit, no refund. **Registration:** At store; late arrivals select available site & pay in the morning. **Fee:** RV (full), $29.95; water/electric, $25.95; tent, $15.95; V, MC. **Parking:** At site.

FACILITIES

Number of RV-only Sites: 19. **Number of Tent-only Sites:** 4. **Hookups:** Electric (20, 30, 50 amps), water, sewer. **Each Site:** Picnic table. **Dump Station:** Yes. **Laundry:** Yes. **Pay Phone:** Yes. **Restrooms and Showers:** Yes. **Fuel:** No. **Propane:** No. **Internal Roads:** Gravel. **RV Service:** No. **Market:** 5 mi. to Taos. **Restaurant:** 3 mi. to Taos. **General Store:** Yes. **Vending:** No. **Swimming:** No. **Playground:** Yes. **Other:** Dog walk, walking trail, modem, sunrises/sunsets. **Activities:** Children's activities, skiing, scenic drives, mountain biking, rafting, walking tours, galleries. **Nearby Attractions:** Taos, Rio Grande Gorge Bridge, Taos Pueblo, Kit Carson State Historic Park. **Additional Information:** Taos Chamber of Commerce, (505) 758-3873.

RESTRICTIONS

Pets: On leash, cleaned up after. **Fires:** Grill only. **Alcoholic Beverages:** At sites. **Vehicle Maximum Length:** 80 ft.

TO GET THERE

From the junction of Hwy. 522, 150, and 64, turn west onto Hwy. 64 and go 2.25 mi. Turn right at the sign into the entrance.

TUCUMCARI — MAP, B-3
Mountain Road RV Park

1700 Mountain Rd., 88401. T: (505) 461-9628.

🚐 ★★★   ⛺ ★★★

Beauty: ★★★	Site Privacy: ★★★
Spaciousness: ★★★	Quiet: ★★★★
Security: ★★★★	Cleanliness: ★★★★
Insect Control: ★★★★	Facilities: ★★★

This campground has 4 rows of open-ended pull-throughs. Sites are only about 45 by 28 feet, although rigs can stick out somewhat from there. Sites are mostly of a uniform quality, without much to distinguish one from the other. Site 59 is given over to long-term residents. Site 60 is a little cramped compared to the other sites. The best sites are 50–55, which face mostly fields and are located away from the entrance and the mobile homes. The tent sites are in an area to the southwest. This area has a decent grass covering and two large shade trees for protection from the sun. The adjacent fields make for attractive surroundings. This campground makes for an agreeable overnight stay and is fine for even longer.

BASICS

Operated By: Franklin McCasland. **Open:** All year. **Site Assignment:** Depends on availability; no reservations. **Registration:** At office; late arrivals use drop box. **Fee:** RV (full), $18–$21; tent, $10; check, V, MC, D. **Parking:** At site.

FACILITIES

Number of RV-only Sites: 60. **Number of Tent-only Sites:** 6. **Hookups:** Electric (30, 50 amps), water, sewer. **Each Site:** Picnic table. **Dump Station:** No (sewer at all sites). **Laundry:** Yes. **Pay Phone:** Yes. **Restrooms and Showers:** Yes. **Fuel:** No. **Propane:** No. **Internal Roads:** Gravel. **RV Service:** No. **Market:** Less than 8 mi. to Tucumcari. **Restaurant:** less than 8 mi. to Tucumcari. **General Store:** No. **Vending:** No. **Swimming:** No. **Playground:** Yes. **Other:** RV supplies. **Activities:** Fishing, boating, swimming, hiking, visiting museums, cheese sampling. **Nearby Attractions:** Mesalands Dinosaur Museum, Tucumcari Historical Museum, Tucumcari Mountain Cheese Museum, Conchas Lake State Park. **Additional Information:** Tucumcari Chamber of Commerce, (505) 461-1694.

RESTRICTIONS

Pets: On leash, cleaned up after. **Fires:** Grill only. **Alcoholic Beverages:** At sites. **Vehicle Maximum Length:** No limit.

TO GET THERE

From I-40 (Exit 333): From the north side of the highway, turn north onto Hwy. 54 and go 0.3 mi. Turn left at the sign into the entrance.

WHITE'S CITY   MAP, D-3
White's City RV Park

17 Carlsbad Caverns Hwy., 88268.
T: (800) CAVERNS or (505) 785-2291;
www.whitescity.com.

🚐 ★★★   ⛺ ★★

Beauty: ★★★	Site Privacy: ★★★
Spaciousness: ★★★	Quiet: ★★★★
Security: ★★★★	Cleanliness: ★★★
Insect Control: ★★★★	Facilities: ★★★

Located a block west of the Registration Lobby, this campground is made up of blocks of individual campgrounds, making effectively four different campgrounds. The RV sites closest to the road average 32 by 36 feet in size, for both back-ins and pull-throughs. (Longer sites farther south and west can accommodate vehicles up to 60 feet in length.) Sites are open and level on a gravel lot. Sites J–P sit atop a bit of an embankment but are otherwise level. Sites around the perimeter abut a dried streambed filled with cacti and bushes, and most benefit from a mature shade tree, making these sites (127–142) most desirable. The least desirable sites (R–Y) are situated along the road and exit, and are not clearly labeled. Site R is particularly open to road traffic. Restroom facilities are unisex rooms with an open toilet and shower. The laundry facility is modern and clean, with a counter for folding clothes and table and bench for killing time while your clothes get done. Tent sites, separated from the RV sites by 100 yards, are located on a loop with a grassy field on the interior. Sites on the inside of the loop have ample tree coverage, and those in the middle back to the common area, making them potentially double the size of end sites. Tent sites on the outside of the loop have no trees and are restricted to 30 by 40 feet. The restroom facilities here are less modern and less clean, and the shower is not closed off. The playground area occupies the most lush patch of grass in the entire park, with several large trees providing enough shade for families to picnic while the children play. Tenters may be green with envy at the sight of this patch of grass, but RVers will find this an acceptable base of operations for tours into Carlsbad, or a jumping-off point to Texas and beyond.

BASICS

Operated By: Tom Dugger. **Open:** All year. **Site Assignment:** First come, first served. **Registration:** At registration lobby; late arrivals ring bell. **Fee:** RV/tent, $22.25. **Parking:** At site.

FACILITIES

Number of RV-only Sites: 106. **Number of Tent-only Sites:** 25. **Hookups:** Electric (30 amps), water, sewer. **Each Site:** Picnic table, grill, shared shelter, most have trees. **Dump Station:** No. **Laundry:** Yes. **Pay Phone:** Yes. **Restrooms and Showers:** Yes. **Fuel:** Yes. **Propane:** No. **Internal Roads:** Paved, gravel. **RV Service:** No. **Market:** Yes. **Restaurant:** Yes. **General Store:** Yes. **Vending:** Yes. **Swimming:** Yes. **Playground:** Yes. **Other:** Security gate, post office, shops. **Nearby Attractions:** Carlsbad Caverns. **Additional Information:** Carlsbad CVB, (800) 221-1224, (505) 887-6516.

RESTRICTIONS

Pets: On leash. **Fires:** In grills/pits. **Alcoholic Beverages:** At sites. **Vehicle Maximum Length:** No limit. **Other:** Water park is not part of RV park; admission is $6. No overnight parking w/in 5 mi. radius (if not in campground).

TO GET THERE

From Hwy. 62/180, turn west onto Carlsbad Caverns Hwy., then take the first left into the Old West complex. Register in the Registration Lobby.

New York

For many travelers New York State evokes visions of the bright lights, mammoth skyscrapers, **Broadway** shows, chic restaurants, world-class museums, and nonstop energy of New York City. Yet the Big Apple is just the southeastern tip of its namesake state, which is an outdoor enthusiast's paradise. New York City is a place every American should visit at least once. Of course, one trip will permit you to see only a fraction of what the most populous city in the nation has to offer, but you can at least whet your appetite for another visit. Exploring **Manhattan** can take a week. Your best bet is a comprehensive tour that hits multiple sites.

There are several specialized tours in Manhattan and the other boroughs—**Queens, the Bronx, Staten Island,** and **Brooklyn.** Heading west, **Long Island** is mostly a resort area with white-sand beaches, secluded bays and coves, and thick woods. Prominent Long Island destinations include **Jones Beach State Park; Shelter Island,** home to the **Mashomack Nature Preserve;** the trendy **Hamptons,** a beach retreat for the well-heeled; and **Montauk,** where you will find **Montauk Point State Park** and the 1795 **Montauk Lighthouse.**

Victorian cottages with stone fences, opulent mansions, and small towns define the **Hudson Valley,** the area south of **Albany** that follows the **Hudson River** between the **Catskill Mountains** and the Connecticut border. Heading north from New York City, the lower Hudson Valley includes picturesque and historic towns like **Nyack, Goshen, Tarrytown,** and **West Point,** home of the **U.S. Military Academy.** In the mid–Hudson Valley, the **Samuel F. B. Morse Historic Site** is found near **Poughkeepsie. Hyde Park** features the **Franklin D. Roosevelt Home National Historic Site;** the **Eleanor Roosevelt National Historic Site,** better known as **Val-Kill;** and the **Vanderbilt Mansion National Historic Site.** In the upper Hudson Valley is the classic Americana downtown of **Hudson,** as well as the **Shaker Museum and Library** about 20 miles north.

The name **Catskills** refers to both a mountain range and a region of small towns and resorts north and west of the Hudson Valley. The Hudson River borders the Catskills on the east, and the **Delaware River** on the southwest at the Pennsylvania border. Numerous streams and nature trails make the Catskills a favorite destination for fishing, boating, and hiking. Part of the Appalachians, it includes **Catskill Park and Forest Preserve. Albany,** New York's capital, is near the confluence of the Hudson River and **Mohawk River** in **Mohawk Valley.** Famous for its Victorian homes, pristine gardens, and lavish spas, **Saratoga Springs** hosts **Saratoga Spa State Park.** Located on the banks of **Otsego Lake, Cooperstown** is the home of the **National Baseball Hall of Fame and Museum, Fenimore Art Museum,** and the **Farmers Museum and Village Crossroads.**

Covering 6 million acres, **Adirondack Park** is the main feature of the **Adirondack Mountains** in northern New York. The **Adirondack Forest Preserve** makes up 40 percent of the park, including the state's highest peak, the 5,344-foot **Mount Marcy. Lake George, Lake Champlaign,** and **Lake Placid** are resort areas offering bountiful outdoor activities. **Fort Ticonderoga,** built in 1755, played an integral role in the American Revolution and is located in the **Lake George** area. The village of **Blue Mountain Lake** not only has the 2,000-foot-high peak overlooking the lake, but is also the home of the **Adirondack Museum,** a complex of 22 historic buildings. Located at the head of the **St. Lawrence River** on the U.S.–Canada border and extending more than 50 miles downstream from **Lake Ontario,** the **Thousand Islands** region actually consists of more than 1,800 islands ranging in size from small rocks to 5 miles wide and 20 miles long. **Alexandria Bay** is the main resort town of the Thousand Islands, which also has a multitude of other small towns, state parks, and boat tours. The **Finger Lakes** region encompasses 11 finger-shaped lakes such as **Seneca, Cayuga,** and **Keuka,** as well as countless breathtaking natural sites like the gorges and waterfalls of **Watkins Glen State Park. Syracuse** and **Rochester,** which both have pleasant museums and attractions, are also located near the Finger Lakes.

New York's second-most-visited attraction (after New York City) is **Niagara Falls. Buffalo,** New York's second-largest city, is 20 miles from Niagara Falls. The **Buffalo and Erie County Naval and Military Park,** an assortment of **Frank Lloyd Wright** homes, the **Albright-Knox Art Gallery,** and the **Original American Kazoo Factory** are among the most interesting attractions in Buffalo.

Campground Profiles

ALEXANDRIA BAY   MAP, A-4
Keewaydin State Park

reserve america

P.O. Box 247, 13607. T: (800) 456-CAMP or
(315) 482-3331; www.reserveamerica.com.

🚐 ★★★   ▲ ★★★★

Beauty: ★★★★   Site Privacy: ★★★★
Spaciousness: ★★★★   Quiet: ★★★★
Security: ★★★★   Cleanliness: ★★★★
Insect Control: ★★★★   Facilities: ★★★

Located 1 mile west of Alexandria Bay, Keewaydin State Park is situated along the St. Lawrence River in New York's Thousand Islands region. The park's terrain includes steep, rocky outcroppings between the campground's 41 sites and the shoreline, providing vantage points for watching the oceangoing vessels traversing the St. Lawrence. Keewaydin is a quiet and private campground, especially for tenters. The swimming pool is within walking distance of the campground, and there's a marina and a boat launch for boaters and anglers. Ice fishing, snowshoeing, and cross-country skiing are popular during the winter, when the campground is closed. The Boldt Castle, located on Heart Island, is an interesting side trip from Keewaydin. George C. Boldt, proprietor of the Waldorf-Astoria in New York City, began construction on a turreted stone castle in 1900—a $2.5 million gift to his wife. When Boldt's wife died in 1904, construction was halted and the castle was never finished. Tours of the castle and the grounds are given mid-May–mid-October.

BASICS
Operated By: State of New York. **Open:** Late May–early Sept. **Site Assignment:** Reservations up to 9 months in advance & walk-ins accepted. **Registration:** At campground office. **Fee:** Waterfront, $17; regular, $13; V, MC. **Parking:** At site.

FACILITIES
Number of RV-only Sites: 48. **Hookups:** None. **Each Site:** Picnic table, grill. **Dump Station:** No. **Laundry:** No. **Pay Phone:** Yes. **Restrooms and Showers:** Yes. **Fuel:** No. **Propane:** No. **Internal Roads:** Paved, in good condition. **RV Service:** No. **Market:** W/in 1 mi. **Restaurant:** W/in 2 mi. **General Store:** Yes. **Vending:** Yes. **Swimming:** Yes. **Playground:** Yes. **Other:** Marina & boat launch. **Activities:** Boating, fishing, hiking trails, canoeing, swimming. **Nearby Attractions:** Thousand Islands Skydeck, Lake Ontario, St. Lawrence River, Boldt Castle, Ogdensburg, Oswego, Fort Ontario, H. Lee White Marine Museum. **Additional Information:** St. Lawrence County Chamber of Commerce, (315) 386-4000, slccoc@northnet.org.

RESTRICTIONS
Pets: On leash only, max. length 6 ft. **Fires:** At site. **Alcoholic Beverages:** Alcohol permitted. No kegs/beer balls. **Vehicle Maximum Length:** 35 ft. **Other:** 14-day stay limit.

TO GET THERE
From Alexandria Bay, go 1 mi. west on SR 12. Follow signs to campground.

ANCRAM   MAP, C-5
Lake Taghkanic Campground

reserve america

1528 NY 82, 12502-9731. T: (518) 851-3631; www.reserveamerica.com.

🚐 ★★★★   ▲ ★★★★

Beauty: ★★★   Site Privacy: ★★★
Spaciousness: ★★★   Quiet: ★★★★★
Security: ★★★★★   Cleanliness: ★★★★
Insect Control: ★★★   Facilities: ★★★★

Lake Taghkanic Campground was named in 2005 as one of the Top 100 Campgrounds in the nation by Reserve America. Lake Taghkanic State Park, nestled next to Lake Taghkanic in the rolling hills and lush forests of Columbia County, offers a wonderful variety of recreational activities. The park has tent and trailer campsites and cabin and cottage camping facilities, two beaches, picnic grounds, and a boat launch. In addition, the park has hiking, biking, cross-country skiing, and snowmobile trails. Ice skating and ice fishing are permitted when conditions are appropriate. Bow hunting for deer and turkeys is permitted in season. Located in the middle of rolling hills and a lush green forest, the Lake Taghkanic Campground offers 60 tent and RV sites with 32 of the sites offering platforms. This campground does not have electric hookups. It does have hot showers, flush toilets, potable water, a wheelchair-accessible site, and a recreation building. Located next to the campground are 15 cabins. Across the main road is Lake Taghkanic and its day-use facilities, including swimming at two beaches, car-top boat launch, picnic tables, concession, and bathhouse. There are also 17 lakeside cottages. A nature center offers scheduled talks. Park roads may be bicycled and warm-water fishing is enjoyed in Lake Taghkanic.

BASICS
Operated By: New York State Parks. **Open:** May 11–Oct. 27. **Site Assignment:** Reservations can be made 9 months in advance. **Registration:** At office. **Fee:** Single, $13; cabin, $320–$530; full service, $625–$675. **Parking:** At site.

FACILITIES
Number of Multipurpose Sites: 91. **Hookups:** None. **Dump Station:** W/in 10 mi. **Laundry:** Yes. **Pay Phone:** No. **Restrooms and Showers:** Yes. **Fuel:** No. **Propane:** No. **Internal Roads:** Paved. **RV Service:** No. **Market:** W/in 10 mi. **Restaurant:** W/in 10 mi. **General Store:** W/in 10 mi. **Vending:** Yes. **Swimming:** Yes. **Playground:** Yes. **Activities:** Baseball, basketball, biking, bird-watching, boating, cross-country skiing, fishing, hiking, hunting, ice fishing, ice skating, paddle boating, parasailing, picnicking, sailing, snowmobiling, volleyball.

RESTRICTIONS
Pets: Pets are allowed in the campground w/ proof of vaccination shots; they are restricted to parking lots & hiking trails only. No pets allowed in cabin cottages. Call ahead for details. **Fires:** Permitted in designated fireplaces. **Alcoholic Beverages:** Persons age 21 or over who possess or consume alcoholic beverages must produce adequate identification & proof of age upon request. **Other:** Quiet hours 10 p.m.–7 a.m. are strictly enforced. Firearms, fireworks, tree cutting, & gasoline boat motors are not allowed.

TO GET THERE
Lake Taghkanic is located off the Taconic State Pkwy. Passenger vehicles' entrance to the park is directly off the Taconic State Pkwy., 1 mi. south of Hwy. 82 (Hudson Ancram exit), 6 mi. north of the Jackson Corners exit. The park is 2.5 hours north of New York City. Commercial vehicles and trailers' entrance off Hwy. 82, 3 mi. south of the Town of West Taghkanic, 5 mi. north of Ancram.

AUSABLE CHASM   MAP, A-5
Ausable Chasm Campground

US 9, 12911. T: (866) 782-4276 or
(518) 834-9990; www.ausablechasm.com.

🚐 ★★★   ▲ ★★★

Beauty: ★★★★   Site Privacy: ★★★
Spaciousness: ★★★   Quiet: ★★★★
Security: ★★★★   Cleanliness: ★★★
Insect Control: ★★★★   Facilities: ★★★

Located near the Ausable Chasm in Adirondack Park, Ausable Chasm Campground offers spacious wooded sites, including 80 pull-throughs. This is a popular campground because of its proximity to the Ausable Chasm itself. The multitude of pull-through sites makes this campground convenient for RVers. Families will not be disappointed with the extensive selection of activities here. Facilities here are acceptable but not as well kept as those at the Ausable River Campsite. This campground is ideal for travelers who want to be near the Ausable Chasm boat ride and tour. A 1.5-mile-long gorge, Ausable Chasm ranges from 20 to 50 feet wide, and its rocky walls rise as high as 200 feet above the Ausable River. Tours include a raft ride followed by a 0.75-mile-long self-guided walking tour before reaching the bus for the return trip. Lake Champlain is just 3 miles away from the campground, as are the ferries that carry passengers across the lake to Vermont. Other attractions near the campground include Santa's Workshop, where the magic of Christmas springs to life in rides, shows, and entertainment; High Falls Gorge, overlooking the Ausable River; and Frontier Town, a re-created 19th-century town with action-packed shows and a rodeo.

BASICS
Operated By: Ausable Chasm. **Open:** May 19–Oct. 9. **Site Assignment:** By reservation & first come, first served. **Registration:** At campground office. **Fee:** $25–$30; tent, $18; V, MC, AE. **Parking:** At site.

FACILITIES

Number of RV-only Sites: 103. **Number of Tent-only Sites:** 46. **Hookups:** Electric (20, 30, 50 amps), water. **Each Site:** Fire ring, picnic table. **Dump Station:** Yes. **Laundry:** Yes. **Pay Phone:** Yes. **Restrooms and Showers:** Yes. **Fuel:** No. **Propane:** Yes. **Internal Roads:** Dirt, in fair condition. **RV Service:** No. **Market:** W/in 5 mi. **Restaurant:** W/in 3 mi. **General Store:** Yes. **Vending:** Yes. **Swimming:** Yes. **Playground:** Yes. **Other:** Game room, movies, free showers. **Activities:** Rec room, swimming, mini-golf, shuffleboard, planned activities, tennis, badminton, sports field, horseshoes, hiking trails, volleyball. **Nearby Attractions:** Ausable Chasm, Lake Placid, Lake Champlain, Fort Ticonderoga, ferry to Vermont, Whiteface Mountain, Adirondack Park. **Additional Information:** New York Division of Tourism, (800) CALL-NYS, www.iloveny.state.ny.us.

RESTRICTIONS

Pets: On leash only. **Fires:** At site. **Alcoholic Beverages:** At site. **Vehicle Maximum Length:** No limit.

TO GET THERE

From US 9, go 800 ft. east on Hwy. 373. Entrance is on the left.

AUSTERLITZ   MAP, C-5
Woodland Hills Campground

386 Fog Hill Rd., 12017. T: (518) 392-3557; www.whcg.net.

🚐 ★★★★   ⛺ ★★★

Beauty: ★★★★	Site Privacy: ★★★
Spaciousness: ★★★	Quiet: ★★★★
Security: ★★★★	Cleanliness: ★★★★
Insect Control: ★★★★	Facilities: ★★★★

Nestled in the Berkshires near the Massachusetts border in southeastern New York, Woodland Hills Campground has 206 open and shaded sites, including 149 full hookups—a definite plus for RVers. This is a campground with peaceful surroundings, though many sites offer little privacy. A private lake is located in the center of the campground, and the sites surround it. There are small clusters of sites bordering both sides of the lake, and larger clusters are located away from the lake on all sides of the park. The lake is a serene and peaceful place where campers can rent pedal boats and swim. The campground also has a fishing pond. Woodland Hills is a short drive to Tanglewood and Lebanon Valley Speedway. Catskill Park and Albany are within 40 miles and make interesting day trips for Woodland Hills campers. Consisting of 705,500 acres, Catskill Park boasts some of the wildest terrain south of Maine. The park has more than 200 miles of marked hiking trails. The capitol of New York, Albany is home to the New York State Museum, Schuyler Mansion State Historic Site, and Rensselaerville, among other attractions.

BASICS

Operated By: Rich & Nancy Hreschak. **Open:** May 15–Oct. 8. **Site Assignment:** Reservations

recommended, walk-ins accepted. **Registration:** At campground office. **Fee:** $22–$29; V, MC, D. **Parking:** At site.

FACILITIES

Number of RV-only Sites: 190. **Number of Tent-only Sites:** 16. **Hookups:** Electric (20, 30 amps), water, phone. **Each Site:** Fire ring, picnic table. **Dump Station:** Yes. **Laundry:** Yes. **Pay Phone:** Yes. **Restrooms and Showers:** Yes. **Fuel:** No. **Propane:** Yes. **Internal Roads:** Gravel, in good condition. **RV Service:** No. **Market:** W/in 4 mi. **Restaurant:** W/in 4 mi. **General Store:** Yes. **Vending:** Yes. **Swimming:** Yes. **Playground:** Yes. **Other:** Private lake. **Activities:** Lake swimming, pond fishing, game room, rec hall, boating, canoeing, pedal boat rentals, basketball, playground, badminton, sports field, horseshoes, volleyball. **Nearby Attractions:** Catskill Park, Albany, Lebanon Valley Speedway, Tanglewood, Berkshire Mountains. **Additional Information:** New York Division of Tourism, (800) CALL-NYS, www.iloveny.state.ny.us.

RESTRICTIONS

Pets: Welcome. **Fires:** At site. **Alcoholic Beverages:** At site. **Vehicle Maximum Length:** 40 ft.

TO GET THERE

From I-90, take Exit B-3 and go 2 mi. south on Hwy. 22, 0.5 mi. west on Middle Rd., and 0.75 mi. north on Fog Hill Rd. Entrance is on the left.

AVERILL PARK   MAP, C-5
Alps Family Campground

1928 NY 43, 12018. T: (518) 674-5565.

🚐 ★★★★   ⛺ ★★★★

Beauty: ★★★★	Site Privacy: ★★★
Spaciousness: ★★★	Quiet: ★★★★
Security: ★★★★	Cleanliness: ★★★★
Insect Control: ★★★★	Facilities: ★★★★

Located 15 miles west of the Massachusetts border and about 20 miles southwest of the Vermont border, Alps Family Campground in Averill Park is an ideal base for campers interested in exploring nearby Albany and venturing into Massachusetts and Vermont. This is a clean and quiet campground, and most sites are shaded by mature trees; however, there are only three pull-throughs, which is a minus for RVers on crowded spring and autumn weekends. Open all year, Alps has activities for campers no matter the weather. There's a fishing pond, a swimming pool, basketball and volleyball courts, and hiking trails. Indoors, Alps has a teen center and a game room. The campground also features a spacious adult pavilion with fireplace. During the summer, the campground hosts live entertainment in the courtyard, hayrides, and softball games. In Albany, in addition to the architectural and historical treasures such as the state capitol and the Crailo State Historic Site, visitors can embark on scenic cruises on the Hudson River with Dutch Apple Cruises.

BASICS

Operated By: Ronald Van Fleet. **Open:** All year; winter w/ reservations only. **Site Assignment:** By reservation & first come, first served. **Registra-**

tion: At campground office. **Fee:** Full hookup, $29; water/electric, $26; tent, $23; V, MC, AE. **Parking:** At site.

FACILITIES

Number of RV-only Sites: 79. **Number of Tent-only Sites:** 21. **Hookups:** Electric (20, 30 amps), water, sewer; 40 full hookups. **Each Site:** Fire ring, picnic table. **Dump Station:** Yes. **Laundry:** Yes. **Pay Phone:** Yes. **Restrooms and Showers:** Yes. **Fuel:** Yes. **Propane:** Yes. **Internal Roads:** Gravel, in fair condition. **RV Service:** No. **Market:** W/in 3 mi. **Restaurant:** W/in 3 mi. **General Store:** Yes. **Vending:** Yes. **Swimming:** Yes. **Playground:** Yes. **Other:** Adult pavilion w/ fireplace. **Activities:** Pond & stream fishing, game room, rec hall, swimming, basketball, shuffleboard, planned activities on weekends, badminton, sports field, horseshoes, hiking trails, volleyball. **Nearby Attractions:** Junior Museum, Troy, Albany, New York State Capitol, New York State Museum. **Additional Information:** Albany County CVB, (800) 258-3582, www.albany.org.

RESTRICTIONS

Pets: On leash only. **Fires:** At site. **Alcoholic Beverages:** At site. **Vehicle Maximum Length:** 45 ft. max.

TO GET THERE

From Hwy. 66, go 3 mi. southeast on Hwy. 66/Hwy. 43 and 1.5 mi. southeast on Hwy. 43. Entrance is on the left.

BAINBRIDGE   MAP, C-4
Oquaga Creek State Park

reserve america

5995 City Hwy. 20, 13733. T: (607) 467-4160; www.reserveamerica.com.

🚐 ★★★★   ⛺ ★★★★

Beauty: ★★★	Site Privacy: ★★
Spaciousness: ★★	Quiet: ★★★
Security: ★★★	Cleanliness: ★★★★
Insect Control: ★★★	Facilities: ★★★★

Campers frolic in the wooded shade of this lovely upstate New York retreat. Oquaga Creek State Park is just three hours from New York City and New Jersey, which makes its beach facilities and forested campsites the perfect summer escape. The 55-acre Arctic Lake has a sand beach for swimmers, and anglers can fish for black bass, bullheads, and rainbow trout. The rolling, wooded hills are ideal for winter sledding. Winter visitors can also ice skate or ice fish on the frozen lake and snowshoers and cross-country skiers can explore 6 miles of trails. If you like to camp, 95 sites are available with nearby showers and restrooms. If you don't want to bother to pack a tent and equipment, you may be interested in the full-service accommodation. This cottage provides two bedrooms, a kitchen with a refrigerator, stove, cooking utensils, dishes, silverware, and more. Oquaga Creek State Park offers a disc-golf course that, although it was built in the 1970s, is well maintained.

BASICS

Operated By: New York State Parks. **Open:** All year. **Site Assignment:** Reservations can be made 9 months in advance. **Registration:** At office. **Fee:** Single, $13; full service, $550. **Parking:** Amenity parking.

FACILITIES

Number of Multipurpose Sites: 101. **Hookups:** Yes. **Dump Station:** Yes. **Laundry:** No. **Pay Phone:** No. **Restrooms and Showers:** Yes. **Fuel:** No. **Propane:** No. **Internal Roads:** Paved. **RV Service:** No. **Market:** No. **Restaurant:** No. **General Store:** Yes. **Vending:** Yes. **Swimming:** Yes. **Playground:** Yes. **Activities:** Baseball, basketball, biking, bird-watching, boating, cross-country skiing, fishing, Frisbee golf, hiking, horseshoes, ice fishing, ice skating, paddle boating, sledding, tubing, volleyball.

RESTRICTIONS

Pets: Pets must have valid rabies certificate. Dogs must be kept on 6-ft. leash. **Fires:** Permitted in designated fireplaces. **Alcoholic Beverages:** Persons age 21 or over who possess or consume alcoholic beverages must produce adequate identification & proof of age upon request. **Vehicle Maximum Length:** 40 ft. **Other:** Quiet hours are 10 p.m.–7 a.m. While biking, children must wear helmets. Private boats w/ a permit are allowed on the lake sunrise–sundown. Car-top boats only, no motors.

TO GET THERE

From Binghamton, take Hwy. 88 east to Bainbridge. Follow Hwy. 206 east 4 mi. to Beech Hill Rd. Take a right on Beech Hill Rd.; go 5 mi. to a right on East Afton Rd. to park. From New York City, take Hwy. 17 west to Exit 84 at Deposit. Go north on Hwy. 8 3 mi. Turn on CR 20, follow 9 mi. to the park. From Albany, take the New York State Thruway (I-90) west to Schenectady. Take Exit 25A and follow Hwy. 88 west to Bainbridge exit. Take Hwy. 206 east to Beech Hill Rd. (4 mi. east of Bainbridge). Turn right on Beech Hill Rd.; travel 5 mi. to a right turn on East Afton Rd., then continue to park. From Buffalo, Rochester, and Syracuse, take the New York State Thruway (I-90) east to Exit 36 (junction with I-81). Take I-81 south to Whitney Point exit. Take Hwy. 206 east to Beech Hill Rd. (4 mi. east of Bainbridge). Take a right on Beech Hill Rd.; travel 5 mi. to a right turn on East Afton Rd.; continue to park.

BARKER   MAP, B-2
Golden Hill State Park

reserve america

9691 Lower Lake Rd., 14012. T: (716) 795-3885; www.reserveamerica.com.

🚐 ★★★★   ⛺ ★★★★

Beauty: ★★★	Site Privacy: ★★
Spaciousness: ★★	Quiet: ★★★★
Security: ★★★★	Cleanliness: ★★★★
Insect Control: ★★★	Facilities: ★★★★

Named in 2005 as one of Reserve America's Top Outdoor Locations, Golden Hill State Park was acquired by New York State in 1962. The Thirty Mile Lighthouse, decommissioned by the U.S. Coast Guard in 1958, is part of the park and available for rental year-round. This landmark has a rich history that can be enjoyed by visitors of the park through the Friends of Thirty Mile Point Lighthouse. The lighthouse originally provided keepers and assistant keepers family quarters. Golden Hill Campground offers 55 tent and RV sites, 19 with electric hookup. Potable water is convenient to all sites. There are flush toilets, hot showers, and a scrubbing sink. A picnic area with pavilion is located near the boat launch. Hiking trails meander throughout the park which also allows biking on the campground roads. Campers enjoy horseshoes, a children's playground, and fishing in Lake Ontario. A recreation hall is located near the historic lighthouse. The park permits snowshoeing and snowmobiling in winter. Other activities offered in the park are: a boat launch, biking, fishing, hunting for small game and waterfowl, disc golf, hiking, a nature trail, picnic pavilions, picnic tables, a children's playground, play fields, powerboating, recreation programs, cross-country skiing, snowmobiling, and snowshoeing.

BASICS

Operated By: New York State Parks. **Open:** All year. **Site Assignment:** Reservations can be made 9 months in advance. **Registration:** At office. **Fee:** Single, $13; cabin, $975. **Parking:** Amenity parking.

FACILITIES

Number of Multipurpose Sites: 65. **Hookups:** None. **Dump Station:** Yes. **Laundry:** No. **Pay Phone:** No. **Restrooms and Showers:** Yes. **Fuel:** No. **Propane:** No. **Internal Roads:** Paved. **RV Service:** No. **Market:** W/in 10 mi. **Restaurant:** W/in 10 mi. **General Store:** W/in 10 mi. **Vending:** No. **Swimming:** No. **Playground:** Yes. **Other:** All full-service cottages are smoke free & pet free. **Activities:** Baseball, biking, bird-watching, cross-country skiing, fishing, hiking, interpretive programs, jet skiing, picnicking, powerboating, sailboarding, sailing, snowmobiling, volleyball, waterskiing.

RESTRICTIONS

Pets: Pets must have a valid rabies certificate & be on a leash not longer than 6 feet at all times. **Fires:** Permitted in designated fireplaces. **Alcoholic Beverages:** Persons age 21 or over who possess or consume alcoholic beverages must produce adequate identification & proof of age upon request.

TO GET THERE

Golden Hill is located in Western New York State. The park is located 20 mi. northeast of Lockport. Take Hwy. 104 or Hwy. 18 to Hwy. 269. Turn right on Hwy. 269 to Lower Lake Rd., left at stop sign and go 0.75 mi. to camp entrance. For off-season information, please call (716) 795-3117.

BARRYVILLE   MAP, B-2
Kittatinny Campgrounds

3854 Hwy. 97, 12719. T: (570) 828-2338; www.kittatinny.com.

🚐 ★★★   ⛺ ★★★★

Beauty: ★★★★	Site Privacy: ★★★★
Spaciousness: ★★★★	Quiet: ★★★★
Security: ★★★★	Cleanliness: ★★★★
Insect Control: ★★★★	Facilities: ★★★

Outdoor adventure is the name of the game at Kittatinny Campgrounds. Located close to the Pennsylvania border along the crystal-clear waters of the Delaware River, Kittatinny has more than 320 sites spread over 250 wooded acres. Sites 901–960, located along the Delaware River on the campground's southeastern end, are among the most inviting. Upon request, campers can stay at sites in a nonalcohol section. With the river, a stream teeming with trout, mountain trails to explore, and 250 sites with no hookups, Kittatinny is ideal for tent campers who long to be one with nature. Kittatinny's headquarters is located in Dingman's Ferry, Pennsylvania. The campground in Barryville is convenient to Kittatinny's whitewater rafting trips. Kittatinny also offers relaxing canoe trips, kayak rentals, and tube rentals. For adventure of a different sort, try paintball. Kittatinny's combat fields are situated on a mountaintop and overlook the Delaware River. You can combine adventure with history in Barryville, which is home to the Fort Delaware Museum of Colonial History and the Zane Grey Museum.

BASICS

Operated By: Kittatinny Canoes. **Open:** Apr. 15–Oct. 15. **Site Assignment:** By reservation & first come, first served. **Registration:** At campground headquarters. **Fee:** $12. **Parking:** At site.

FACILITIES

Number of RV-only Sites: 100. **Number of Tent-only Sites:** 250. **Hookups:** Electric (15, 20 amps), water. **Each Site:** Fire ring, picnic table. **Dump Station:** Yes. **Laundry:** Yes. **Pay Phone:** Yes. **Restrooms and Showers:** Yes. **Fuel:** No. **Propane:** Yes. **Internal Roads:** Gravel & paved, in good condition. **RV Service:** No. **Market:** W/in 3 mi. **Restaurant:** W/in 3 mi. **General Store:** Yes. **Vending:** Yes. **Swimming:** Yes. **Playground:** Yes. **Other:** 1,000 canoe rentals, paintball, game room. **Activities:** Canoeing, swimming, boating, river & stream fishing, badminton, sports field, hiking trails, horseshoes, volleyball, rec hall. **Nearby Attractions:** Delaware River, whitewater rafting, Fort Delaware Museum of Colonial History, Zane Grey Museum. **Additional Information:** Kittatinny Canoes, (800) FLOAT-KC, www.kittatinny.com.

RESTRICTIONS

Pets: On leash only. **Fires:** At site. **Alcoholic Beverages:** At site. **Vehicle Maximum Length:** 40 ft.

TO GET THERE

From Hwy. 55, go 2 mi. northwest on Hwy. 97. Entrance is on the right.

BATAVIA
Lei-Ti Campground

MAP, C-2

9979 Francis Rd., 14020. T: (585) 343-8600 or (800) 445-3484; www.leiti.com.

🚐 ★★★★   ⛺ ★★★★

Beauty: ★★★★   Site Privacy: ★★★★
Spaciousness: ★★★★   Quiet: ★★★★
Security: ★★★★   Cleanliness: ★★★★
Insect Control: ★★★★   Facilities: ★★★★

Located in western New York—west of Rochester and east of Buffalo—the Lei-Ti Campground is a haven for recreation. This rural campground has open and shaded sites, including seven pull-throughs and 85 full hookups. The wooded RV and tent sites are especially inviting and more private than the open sites. Lei-Ti RV Sales and Service is located on-site, so RV campers have access to a full-time mechanic. At Lei-Ti, children will enjoy the petting zoo, two playgrounds, hayrides, a mini-golf course, and a video arcade. Lei-Ti Lake has a sandy beach, and boat rentals are available. Birdwatchers and nature enthusiasts will like the nearby Iroquois National Wildlife Refuge, where waterfowl migrate in massive numbers, especially during the spring. The refuge has several hiking trails and scenic overlooks. Since Batavia is quiet in all seasons, some campers use Lei-Ti as a base for ventures to Niagara Falls, located about 40 miles west.

BASICS

Operated By: Private operator. **Open:** All year. **Site Assignment:** Reservations may be made online or by telephone, no walk-ins. **Registration:** At campground office. **Fee:** $25–$31; V, MC, D. **Parking:** At site.

FACILITIES

Number of RV-only Sites: 221. **Number of Tent-only Sites:** 12. **Hookups:** Electric (20, 30 amps), water, phone. **Each Site:** Fire ring, picnic table. **Dump Station:** Yes. **Laundry:** Yes. **Pay Phone:** Yes. **Restrooms and Showers:** Yes. **Fuel:** No. **Propane:** Yes. **Internal Roads:** Gravel & paved, in good condition. **RV Service:** Yes. **Market:** W/in 5 mi. **Restaurant:** W/in 3 mi. **General Store:** Yes. **Vending:** Yes. **Swimming:** Yes. **Playground:** Yes. **Other:** Lei-Ti Lake. **Activities:** Lake swimming, boating, boat rentals, bike rentals, rec hall, equipped pavilion, game room, mini-golf, lake fishing, basketball, canoeing, shuffleboard, planned activities on weekends, movies, tennis, badminton, hiking trails, sports field. **Nearby Attractions:** Batavia Downs, Six Flags Darien Lake, Holland Land Office Museum, Iroquois National Wildlife Refuge, Le Roy House, Niagara Falls, Rochester. **Additional Information:** Genesee County Chamber of Commerce, (800) 622-2686, www.iinc.com/gencounty.

RESTRICTIONS

Pets: On leash only. **Fires:** At site. **Alcoholic Beverages:** At site. **Vehicle Maximum Length:** 45 ft. **Other:** At least 1 person in party must be 21 or older to reserve site.

TO GET THERE

From Hwy. 5, go 2.5 mi. southeast on Hwy. 63, 0.5 mi. south on Shepherd Rd., 0.75 mi. west on Put-nam Rd., and 2 mi. south on Francis Rd. Entrance is on the left.

BATH
Hickory Hills Family Camping Resort

MAP, C-2

reserve america

7531 Mitchellsville Rd., 14810. T: (607) 776-4345 or (800) 760-0947; www.reserveamerica.com or www.hickoryhillcampresort.com.

🚐 ★★★★   ⛺ ★★★★

Beauty: ★★★★   Site Privacy: ★★★
Spaciousness: ★★★   Quiet: ★★★★
Security: ★★★★   Cleanliness: ★★★★★
Insect Control: ★★★★   Facilities: ★★★★★

Located in western New York, Hickory Hills Family Camping Resort is one of the finest and cleanest campgrounds in the mid-Atlantic region. The campground has open and shaded sites, including 35 pull-throughs. Maples, evergreens, and hickories shade this campground and house squirrels and a variety of birds. Sites with water and electric hookups near the pond are ideal for RVers, as are the full-hookup sites scattered about the park. Sites 76–77 and 88–89 are favorites among campers. Tenters will like the "Rustic Village" perched at Hickory Hill's north tip. These sites are in a quiet part of the campground, away from the activity centers. We like any campground that offers therapeutic massage—Hickory Hills has licensed therapists performing deep-tissue massages, sports massages, and Swedish massages, among other options. Campers can also participate in Tai Chi, yoga, water aerobics, and kickboxing. Often, Hickory Hill campers venture to nearby Corning, where the Corning Glass Center features the Corning Museum of Glass, which has more than 25,000 striking objects on display; the Hall of Science and Industry, which explores the glassmaking industry; and the Steuben Factory, where craftspeople transform molten glass into fine crystal. Nature enthusiasts flock to Watkins Glen State Park, a short drive from Hickory Hills. Within the park, Watkins Glen Gorge drops about 400 feet in 2 miles, and features 18 waterfalls and a bridge that spans the glen 165 feet above the water.

BASICS

Operated By: Randy Lehman & Janet Opila-Lehman. **Open:** May 1–Oct. 30. **Site Assignment:** Reservations recommended (1-night deposit required), walk-ins accepted. **Registration:** At campground store. **Fee:** $33–$47; V, MC, D. **Parking:** At site.

FACILITIES

Number of RV-only Sites: 208. **Number of Tent-only Sites:** 3. **Hookups:** Electric (20, 30, 50 amps), water, cable TV. **Each Site:** Picnic tables & fire rings. **Dump Station:** Yes. **Laundry:** Yes. **Pay Phone:** Yes. **Restrooms and Showers:** Yes. **Fuel:** No. **Propane:** Yes. **Internal Roads:** Gravel, in good condition. **RV Service:** No. **Market:** W/in 2 mi. **Restaurant:** W/in 2 mi. **General Store:** Yes. **Vending:** Yes. **Swimming:** Yes. **Playground:** Yes. **Other:** Cabin & cottage rentals. **Activities:** Rec hall, hiking trails, sports field, skating area, mini-golf, pond fishing, basketball, shuffleboard, planned activities, movies, volleyball. **Nearby Attractions:** National Warplane Museum, National Soaring Museum, Sonnenberg Gardens & Mansion, Corning Museum of Glass, Rockwell Museum, Historic Corning, Greyton H. Taylor Wine Museum, Watkins Glen Gorge, Watkins Glen Farm Sanctuary. **Additional Information:** Corning Chamber of Commerce, (607) 936-4686, www.corning-chamber.org.

RESTRICTIONS

Pets: On leash only. **Fires:** At site. **Alcoholic Beverages:** At site. **Vehicle Maximum Length:** No limit. **Other:** 2 vehicles allowed per campsite.

TO GET THERE

From Hwy. 17, take Exit 38 and go 1 mi. east and north on Hwy. 54 and 2 mi. north on Haverling St. Entrance is on the left.

BEAR MOUNTAIN
Sebago Cabins

MAP, D-5

reserve america

7 Lakes Dr., 10911. T: (845) 351-2360; www.reserveamerica.com.

🚐 ★★★★   ⛺ ★★★★

Beauty: ★★★   Site Privacy: ★★★
Spaciousness: ★★★   Quiet: ★★★★★
Security: ★★★★★   Cleanliness: ★★★★
Insect Control: ★★★ Facilities: ★★★★

The Sebago Cabin Camp in Harriman State Park is on Lake Sebago. The camp offers rustic cabins and full-service cottages. Also available are row-boat rentals; beach, biking, and hiking; organized sports; Saturday bonfire; rainy-day movies and activities, play area; recreation hall; and tennis courts. Harriman State Park, located in Rockland and Orange counties, is the second-largest park in the parks system, with 31 lakes and reservoirs, 200 miles of hiking trails, three beaches, two public camping areas, a network of group camps, miles of streams and scenic roads, and scores of wildlife species, vistas, and vantage points.

BASICS

Operated By: New York State Parks. **Open:** Apr. 20–Oct. 8. **Site Assignment:** Reservations can be made 9 months in advance. **Registration:** At office. **Fee:** Cabin, $210–$355; full service, $580–$648. **Parking:** Amenity parking.

FACILITIES

Number of Multipurpose Sites: 40. **Hookups:** None. **Dump Station:** No. **Laundry:** Yes. **Pay Phone:** No. **Restrooms and Showers:** Yes. **Fuel:** No. **Propane:** No. **Internal Roads:** Paved. **RV Service:** No. **Market:** W/in 10 mi. **Restaurant:** Yes. **General Store:** Yes. **Vending:** No. **Swimming:** Yes. **Playground:** Yes. **Activities:** Amphitheater, baseball, basketball, biking, fishing, hiking, picnicking, tennis, volleyball.

RESTRICTIONS

Pets: No pets. **Fires:** Permitted in designated fireplaces. **Alcoholic Beverages:** No alcohol. **Other:** No subletting of sites is permitted at the park. Boat launch sites require a boat permit. Please contact the park for further details.

To Get There

From the Palisades J. H. Pkwy. (north or south) take Exit 16 (Lake Welch Dr.). Take Lake Welch Dr. to 7 Lakes Drive (follow the signs to Sebago Beach). Turn right onto 7 Lakes Drive and make the first left at the traffic divider to go the opposite way. Sebago Beach is just off to the right. Sebago Cabins are about 1 mi. southwest on the right. From Hwy. 17 at Sloatsburg light, turn onto 7 Lakes Drive. Sebago Cabins are exactly 5 mi. northeast on the left side of the road. Sebago Beach is 1 mi. farther north.

BRIDGEWATER   MAP, C-4
Lake Chalet Campground and Motel

Rte. 8 Box 22, 13313. T: (315) 822-6074; www.lakechalet.com.

🚐 ★★★   ▲ ★★★

Beauty: ★★★   Site Privacy: ★★★
Spaciousness: ★★★   Quiet: ★★★★
Security: ★★★★   Cleanliness: ★★★★
Insect Control: ★★★★   Facilities: ★★★

Located between Cooperstown and Utica in central New York, Lake Chalet Campground and Motel is a place where campers fish and swim in a private six-acre lake, cast their lines into a shaded and stocked brook, and explore more than 10,000 acres of forest laced with trails. Lake Chalet has both open and shaded sites; all sites are grassy. Some RV sites overlook the lake. Tent sites are situated in a secluded part of the campground between the lake and a gurgling brook—the perfect relaxing harmony for a peaceful night's sleep. Though there is no swimming pool, Lake Chalet has a spacious, sandy beach where campers can bask in the sun or swim in the lake. There are also log cabins and a Swiss-style efficiency motel overlooking the lake. In nearby Utica, children will like the Utica Zoo and the Children's Museum. Cooperstown is home to the National Baseball Hall of Fame, a must-see for fans of our national pastime. Here, the history of baseball's players, stadiums, teams, and figures are brought to life with interactive displays and lively exhibits.

Basics

Operated By: Joe & Martha Pcola. **Open:** May 1–Oct. 15. **Site Assignment:** By reservation & first come, first served. **Registration:** At campground office. **Fee:** $23.50–$75; V, MC, AE, D. **Parking:** At site.

Facilities

Number of RV-only Sites: 22. **Number of Tent-only Sites:** 24. **Hookups:** Electric (20, 30, 50 amps), water, phone. **Each Site:** Fire ring, picnic table. **Dump Station:** Yes. **Laundry:** Yes. **Pay Phone:** Yes. **Restrooms and Showers:** Yes. **Fuel:** No. **Propane:** No. **Internal Roads:** Gravel, in good condition. **RV Service:** No. **Market:** W/in 2 mi. **Restaurant:** W/in 2 mi. **General Store:** Yes. **Vending:** Yes. **Swimming:** Yes. **Playground:** Yes. **Other:** Slovak Lake. **Activities:** Lake swimming & fishing,

game room, boating, canoeing, pedal-boat rentals, basketball, badminton, horseshoes, volleyball, sports field. **Nearby Attractions:** Bridgewater 1240 BMX Track, National Baseball Hall of Fame, Utica Brewery, Utica Zoo, Erie Canal Village, Turning Stone Casino, Madison Bouckville Antique Fair & Shops, Unadilla International motocross races, Holy Trinity Russian Monastery, Auriesville Martyrs Shrine. **Additional Information:** Oneida County CVB, (315) 724-7221, www.oneidacountycvb.com.

Restrictions

Pets: On leash only. **Fires:** At site. **Alcoholic Beverages:** At site. **Vehicle Maximum Length:** 40 ft.

To Get There

From US 20, go 1 mi. north on Hwy. 8. Entrance is on the left.

BROCTON   MAP, C-1
Lake Erie State Park

reserve america

RD 1, 14716. T: (716) 792-9214; www.reserveamerica.com.

🚐 ★★★★   ▲ ★★★★

Beauty: ★★★   Site Privacy: ★★★
Spaciousness: ★★★   Quiet: ★★★
Security: ★★★   Cleanliness: ★★★★
Insect Control: ★★★   Facilities: ★★★★

Lake Erie State Park was named in 2005 as one of the Top 100 Campgrounds in the nation. High bluffs overlooking Lake Erie provide a breathtaking view for the visitor to the park. Cheek-tingling breezes attract cross-country skiers in winter, while sandy white beaches draw thousands in summer. The campground features a shoreline covering over three quarters of a mile bordering the shallowest of the Great Lakes. Located in the northwest corner of the Allegheny Travel Region, Lake Erie State Park rests on high bluffs overlooking the now gorgeous waters of Lake Erie. Beginning in the mid-1800s, industries dumped their waste into the lake, resulting in devastating amounts of pollution. In the 1960s, the U.S. government in conjunction with Canada, began cleanup efforts. In a lake where swimming was prohibited and the fish population was virtually dead, today it serves as a recreation delight. Visitors to Lake Erie State Park enjoy swimming, sightseeing, fishing, boating, sailing, and more. Whether camping in one of the campsites or one of the cabins offered at this park, the magnificent scenery will capture your attention. Day users can enjoy the swimming and picnic areas with shelters, playgrounds, and hiking trails that are available to the cross-country skiers during the winter months. Lake Erie State Park is recognized as an excellent place for locating rare migratory birds following the lake's edge.

Basics

Operated By: New York State Parks. **Open:** Apr. 27–Oct. 27. **Site Assignment:** Reservations can be made 9 months in advance. **Registration:** At office. **Fee:** Single, $13; cabin, $250. **Parking:** At site.

Facilities

Number of Multipurpose Sites: 112. **Hookups:** Yes. **Dump Station:** Yes. **Laundry:** No. **Pay Phone:** No. **Restrooms and Showers:** Yes. **Fuel:** No. **Propane:** No. **Internal Roads:** Paved. **RV Service:** No. **Market:** Yes. **Restaurant:** No. **General Store:** Yes. **Vending:** No. **Swimming:** Yes. **Playground:** Yes. **Activities:** Fishing, hiking, picnicking, skiing.

Restrictions

Pets: Pets must have proof of current rabies inoculation & must be leashed at all times. **Fires:** Permitted in designated fireplaces. **Alcoholic Beverages:** Persons age 21 or over who possess or consume alcoholic beverages must produce adequate identification & proof of age upon request. **Other:** No tents in the cabin area.

To Get There

From the west on I-90, take Exit 59 to Hwy. 60 north. Left on Hwy. 5. Park is located 6 mi. west of Dunkirk, NY. From the east on I-90, take Exit 60 to Hwy. 394 north. Right on Hwy. 5. Park is located 8.5 mi. east of Westfield, NY.

BYRON   MAP, B-2
Southwoods RV Resort

6749 Townline Rd., P. O. Box 226, 14422. T: (585) 548-9002.

🚐 ★★★★   ▲ ★★★★

Beauty: ★★★★   Site Privacy: ★★
Spaciousness: ★★   Quiet: ★★★
Security: ★★★★   Cleanliness: ★★★★
Insect Control: ★★★★   Facilities: ★★★★

Just minutes from Six Flags Darien Lake and a short drive from Rochester, Southwoods RV Resort has open and wooded sites, including 80 full hookups and 60 pull-throughs. This campground is nestled in a pastoral country setting, but sites offer little privacy. For linksters, there is a six-hole amateur golf course. Southwoods also has a swimming pool and hiking trails, among other recreational activities. Rochester, home to Seneca Park Zoo and the Susan B. Anthony House, is 30 miles east. Niagara Falls is less than an hour's drive west. Some campers use Southwoods as a base to explore nearby Letchworth State Park, called the Grand Canyon of the East by locals. At Letchworth, cliffs rise as high as 600 feet, and there are three waterfalls. Located in Avon, the Genesee Country Village and Museum is an interesting day trip from Southwoods. The re-created village depicts 19th-century life in the Genesee River valley, with 57 period buildings.

Basics

Operated By: T. Chapell. **Open:** 1st weekend in May–3rd weekend in Oct. **Site Assignment:** By reservation & first come, first served. **Registration:** At campground office. **Fee:** Full, $28; regular, $25; weekly, $168; V, MC. **Parking:** At site.

Facilities

Number of RV-only Sites: 144. **Hookups:** Electric (20, 30, 50 amps), water, phone. **Each Site:** Fire ring, picnic table. **Dump Station:** Yes. **Laundry:**

Your Ticket to Great Outdoor Savings!

For only $15, get great savings with some of America's best known brands & save 10% off camping fees*

Access exclusive membership benefits your family can use at home or on your next camping trip!

Become a Member. Join Today!

Visit: www.TheCampingClub.com/Frommers

*$15 purchases a single twelve (12) month membership to The Official Camping Club starting at date of purchase. Camping Club members gain exclusive online access to discounted tickets from Ticketmaster hosted events and 20% off Coleman gear purchased on Coleman.com. Membership also includes Welcome Kit with various one-time use savings coupons totaling $500 in value from a variety of affiliated companies. One-time use savings coupons within the Welcome Kit that are either valid thru August 31st 2007 or December 31st 2007. 10% off camping fees is only valid at participating parks and may not be combined with any other offers or discounts. All discounts, affiliated companies and Camping Club membership benefits may change without notice and The Camping Club and ReserveAmerica is under no obligation to replace or provide equivalent value.

Reserve *your* **Place Under the Stars**™

CAMP HERE AND A THOUSAND OTHER PLACES

www.Recreation.gov

Yes. **Pay Phone:** Yes. **Restrooms and Showers:** Yes. **Fuel:** Yes. **Propane:** Yes. **Internal Roads:** Gravel, in good condition. **RV Service:** No. **Market:** W/in 5 mi. **Restaurant:** W/in 5 mi. **General Store:** Yes. **Vending:** Yes. **Swimming:** Yes. **Playground:** Yes. **Other:** 6-hole golf course. **Activities:** Game room, swimming, rec hall, golf, basketball, planned activities on weekends, badminton, sports field, horseshoes, hiking trails, volleyball. **Nearby Attractions:** Six Flags Darien Lake, Rochester, Seneca Park Zoo, Genesee Country Village & Museum, Niagara Falls, Finger Lakes. **Additional Information:** Greater Rochester Visitors Assoc., (800) 677-7282, www.visitrochester.com.

RESTRICTIONS

Pets: On leash only. **Fires:** At site. **Alcoholic Beverages:** At site. **Vehicle Maximum Length:** No limit.

TO GET THERE

From I-90, take Exit 47 and go 3.5 mi. north on Hwy. 19 and 7 mi. west on Hwy. 262. Entrance is on the left.

CALEDONIA
MAP, C-2
Genesee Country Campground

40 Flint Hill Rd., P.O. Box 100, 14423.
T: (585) 538-4200; www.campingfriend.com/geneseecountrycampground.

🚐 ★★★   ⛺ ★★★

Beauty: ★★★★	Site Privacy: ★★★
Spaciousness: ★★★	Quiet: ★★★★
Security: ★★★★	Cleanliness: ★★★★
Insect Control: ★★★	Facilities: ★★★

Like Southwoods RV Resort, Genesee Country Campground is convenient to Rochester, Niagara Falls, and Letchworth State Park. And, like Southwoods, Genesee Country has a golf course—this one a Par-3. Genesee Country has 100 grassy and wooded sites, 50 of which have electric and water hookups, and 50 of which have no hookups. This campground offers 30 pull-through sites, with the rest being back-ins. Regarding campsites for RVers and tenters, Genesee Country and Southwoods are even—though the nod for recreational facilities goes to Southwoods. Campers looking to cool off on a sweltering summer day should look elsewhere; there is no swimming pool here. Of course, there are plenty of swimming holes to be found in the Finger Lakes region, and Genesee Country is near Six Flags Darien Lake. The campground is not far from Genesee Country Village and Museum in Avon, as well as a multitude of museums in Rochester, including the Rochester Museum and Science Center and the Strong Museum, a family favorite where children can appear on a television screen with Sesame Street characters.

BASICS

Operated By: Edie & Joe Rae. **Open:** May 1–Oct. 31. **Site Assignment:** By reservation & first come, first served. **Registration:** At campground office. **Fee:** $23–$35; V, MC. **Parking:** At site.

FACILITIES

Number of RV-only Sites: 75. **Number of Tent-only Sites:** 50. **Hookups:** Electric (20, 30 amps),

water, phone. **Each Site:** Fire ring, picnic table. **Dump Station:** Yes. **Laundry:** Yes. **Pay Phone:** Yes. **Restrooms and Showers:** Yes. **Fuel:** No. **Propane:** Yes. **Internal Roads:** Gravel, in good condition. **RV Service:** No. **Market:** W/in 3 mi. **Restaurant:** W/in 3 mi. **General Store:** Yes. **Vending:** Yes. **Swimming:** No. **Playground:** Yes. **Other:** Par 3 golf course. **Activities:** Golf, basketball, game room, rec hall, planned activities, sports field, hiking trails, horseshoes. **Nearby Attractions:** Rochester, Niagara Falls, Letchworth State Park, Six Flags Darien Lake, Finger Lakes. **Additional Information:** Greater Rochester Visitors Assoc., (800) 677-7282, www.visitrochester.com.

RESTRICTIONS

Pets: On leash only. **Fires:** At site. **Alcoholic Beverages:** At site. **Vehicle Maximum Length:** 45 ft.

TO GET THERE

From Hwy. 36N in Caledonia, go 3 mi. west on Hwy. 5 and 0.5 mi. northeast on Flint Hill Rd. Entrance is on the left.

CAMBRIDGE
MAP, B-5, B-6
Lake Lauderdale Campground

744 CR 61, 12816. T: (518) 677-8855; www.lakelauderdalecampground.com.

🚐 ★★★★   ⛺ ★★★★

Beauty: ★★★★	Site Privacy: ★★★
Spaciousness: ★★★	Quiet: ★★★★
Security: ★★★★	Cleanliness: ★★★★
Insect Control: ★★★★	Facilities: ★★★★

Located in eastern New York just minutes from the Vermont border, Lake Lauderdale Campground is convenient to many places. Historic and scenic Saratoga Springs and Saratoga National Historical Park are about 20 miles west. Albany is less than an hour's drive southwest. Lake George and the southeastern tip of Adirondack Park is less than an hour's drive northwest. The campground's proximity to several attractions is a consolation for what it doesn't have—a swimming pool or double slideout accommodations. This campground does, however, offer back-in and pull-through sites. Trout fishing in the nearby Battenkill River and the leisurely Battenkill Scenic Train Ride are recommended activities for campers. A short drive from the campground will lead to the springs, mineral baths, and geysers of Saratoga Springs. At Saratoga National Historical Park, visitors can see where American forces defeated the British in two skirmishes in 1777.

BASICS

Operated By: Private operator. **Open:** May 1–Oct. 15. **Site Assignment:** By reservation & first come, first served. **Registration:** At campground office. **Fee:** $22–$29; V, MC. **Parking:** At site.

FACILITIES

Number of RV-only Sites: 60. **Number of Tent-only Sites:** 15. **Hookups:** Electric (20, 30, 50 amps), water, phone. **Each Site:** Fire ring, picnic table. **Dump Station:** Yes. **Laundry:** Yes. **Pay Phone:** Yes. **Restrooms and Showers:** Yes. **Fuel:** No. **Propane:** Yes. **Internal Roads:** Gravel, in fair condition. **RV Service:** Yes. **Market:** W/in 4 mi. **Restau-**

rant: W/in 5 mi. **General Store:** Yes. **Vending:** Yes. **Swimming:** No. **Playground:** Yes. **Other:** Cabin & trailer rentals, pavilion w/ big-screen TV. **Activities:** Game room, basketball, shuffleboard, planned activities on weekends, sports field, horseshoes, badminton, hiking trails, hayrides, volleyball. **Nearby Attractions:** Battenkill Scenic Train Ride, Battenkill River (trout fishing), Saratoga Springs, Saratoga National Historical Park, Arlington & Manchester (VT), Lake George, Albany. **Additional Information:** New York Division of Tourism, (800) CALL-NYS, www.iloveny.state.ny.us.

RESTRICTIONS

Pets: On leash only, under control. **Fires:** At site. **Alcoholic Beverages:** At site. **Vehicle Maximum Length:** No limit.

TO GET THERE

From Hwy. 372, go 4.5 mi. north on Hwy. 22 and 0.75 mi. east on CR 61. Entrance is on the right.

CAMPBELL
MAP, C-3
Camp Bell Campground

8700 SR 415, P.O. Box 466, 14821.
T: (607) 527-3301 or (800) 587-3301; www.campbellcampground.com.

🚐 ★★★★   ⛺ ★★★★

Beauty: ★★★	Site Privacy: ★★
Spaciousness: ★★★★	Quiet: ★★★
Security: ★★★★	Cleanliness: ★★★★
Insect Control: ★★★★	Facilities: ★★★★

Located in New York's Finger Lakes region between Bath and Corning, Camp Bell Campground is nestled outside of the town of Campbell (hence "Camp Bell"). Camp Bell is an ideal place to relax with a group. There are comfortable club facilities, a spacious rec hall, and a 60-foot heated swimming pool. Campers have their choice of open or shaded sites, all which have electric and water hookups. Most sites are spacious, but privacy is limited. RVers like Camp Bell because the park can accommodate any size rig. The glass center of Corning is about 15 miles southeast. The Rockwell Museum, which houses the largest collection of American Western art in the east, is also located in Corning. Watkins Glen State Park and Seneca Lake are about a half-hour's drive to the east. Watkins Glen Gorge is surely a sight to behold, and tour boats offer cruises along Seneca Lake. Seneca Lake is known for its 22 wineries, many of which offer tastings and tours.

BASICS

Operated By: Private operator. **Open:** May 1–Oct. 15. **Site Assignment:** Reservations recommended (especially on holiday weekends), walk-ins accepted. **Registration:** At campground office. **Fee:** $26–$75; V, MC, D. **Parking:** At site.

FACILITIES

Number of RV-only Sites: 96. **Hookups:** Electric (20 amps), water, cable TV, phone. **Each Site:** Fire ring, picnic table. **Dump Station:** Yes. **Laundry:** Yes. **Pay Phone:** Yes. **Restrooms and Showers:** Yes. **Fuel:** No. **Propane:** Yes. **Internal Roads:** Gravel, in good condition. **RV Service:** No. **Market:** W/in 4 mi. **Restaurant:** W/in 4 mi. **General Store:** Yes.

Vending: Yes. **Swimming:** Yes. **Playground:** Yes. **Other:** Cabin rentals, pavilion. **Activities:** Rec hall, game room, sports field, planned activities on weekends, basketball, horseshoes, volleyball, swimming. **Nearby Attractions:** Watkins Glen State Park, Corning Glass Center, Rockwell Museum, Harris Hill Soaring Museum. **Additional Information:** Schuyler County Chamber of Commerce, (800) 607-4552, www.schuylerny.com.

RESTRICTIONS

Pets: On leash only. **Fires:** At site. **Alcoholic Beverages:** At site. **Vehicle Maximum Length:** No limit.

TO GET THERE

From Hwy. 17, take Exit 41 and go 0.5 mi. east on Hwy. 333 and 0.75 mi. northwest on Hwy. 415. Entrance is on the left.

CARMEL MAP, D-5
Clarence Fahnestock Memorial State Park

Rte. 301, 10512. T: (845) 225-7207; www.reserveamerica.com.

🚐 ★★★★	🏕 ★★★★
Beauty: ★★★	Site Privacy: ★★★
Spaciousness: ★★★	Quiet: ★★★
Security: ★★★	Cleanliness: ★★★★
Insect Control: ★★★	Facilities: ★★

Named in 2005 as one of Reserve America's Top Outdoor Locations, Clarence Fahnestock Memorial State Park is a delight for outdoor enthusiasts. This 14,086-acre park, covering land in Putnam and Dutchess counties, boasts hiking trails, a beautiful beach, picnic areas, scenic campground, and abundant opportunities for boating, hunting, fishing, and birding. The park is also home to the Taconic Outdoor Education Center which provides high-quality environmental programming, and Fahnestock Winter Park which includes 15 kilometers of groomed trails for cross-country skiing and snowshoeing, plus an area for sledding. The scenic campground, formed along the park's natural rock ridges, provides alcoves of privacy and tranquility for campers. Each of the campsites has a picnic table and fire ring. Additionally there is an area for RV camping. Although there are no hookups available or dump station, restroom and shower facilities are centrally located to all RV and tent sites. Individuals, as well as larger camping groups, are welcome.

BASICS

Operated By: New York State Parks. **Open:** May 18–Oct. 27. **Site Assignment:** Reservations can be made 9 months in advance. **Registration:** At office. **Fee:** Single, $13. **Parking:** Amenity parking.

FACILITIES

Number of Multipurpose Sites: 86. **Hookups:** None. **Each Site:** Picnic table, barbecue grill, fire ring. **Dump Station:** No. **Laundry:** No. **Pay Phone:** No. **Restrooms and Showers:** Yes. **Fuel:**

No. **Propane:** No. **Internal Roads:** Paved. **RV Service:** No. **Market:** W/in 10 mi. **Restaurant:** W/in 10 mi. **General Store:** W/in 10 mi. **Vending:** No. **Swimming:** No. **Playground:** No. **Activities:** Biking, bird-watching, hiking, horseback riding, interpretive programs, picnicking.

RESTRICTIONS

Pets: Dogs are permitted on sites 70–81. Must be on a leash of no more than 6 ft. Certificate of rabies vaccination required. **Fires:** Permitted in designated fireplaces. **Alcoholic Beverages:** Persons age 21 or over who possess or consume alcoholic beverages must produce adequate identification & proof of age upon request. **Other:** Firearms are not permitted at the park. Quiet hours 10 p.m. to 7 a.m. are strictly enforced. There is swimming Memorial Day weekend–3rd Sun. of Jun. on weekends only. From the 4th Sat. of Jun.–Labor Day there is daily swimming.

TO GET THERE

Taconic Pkwy. to Hwy. 301 west (Cold Spring). Turn right onto Hwy. 301. Campground is 0.25 mi. west of pkwy. on the left.

CASTILE MAP, C-2
Letchworth State Park

reserve america

1 Letchworth State Park, 14427. T: (585) 493-3600 or (800) 456-CAMP; www.reserveamerica.com.

🚐 ★★★	🏕 ★★★
Beauty: ★★★★	Site Privacy: ★★★
Spaciousness: ★★★	Quiet: ★★★★
Security: ★★★★	Cleanliness: ★★★
Insect Control: ★★★	Facilities: ★★★

At Letchworth State Park in western New York, the raging white water of the Genesee River roars through deep canyons and over three waterfalls. No wonder it is called the "Grand Canyon of the East." Sites here are wooded; a separate camping area features cabins for rent. The campground has 270 sites, all of which are back-ins. Seventeen miles of the 14,344-acre park include the Genesee River Gorge. Wildlife includes gigantic evergreen trees, countless birds, and deer. Cliffs rise as high as 600 feet, and one of the three waterfalls is 107 feet high. Overall, 66 miles of hiking trails can be found in the park, which is also a center for fishing, whitewater rafting, and even hot-air ballooning. Breakfast, lunch, and dinner are served at the nearby Glen Iris Inn. The park also has a conference center for group retreats. If you can pull yourself away from the natural splendor, the William Pryor Letchworth Museum displays Native American artifacts and captivating photos of the park.

BASICS

Operated By: State of New York. **Open:** Mid-May–mid-Oct. **Site Assignment:** By reservation & first come, first served. **Registration:** At campground office. **Fee:** $19; V, MC. **Parking:** At designated area.

FACILITIES

Number of Multipurpose Sites: 270. **Hookups:** Electric (20, 30, 50 amps). **Each Site:** Fire ring, picnic table. **Dump Station:** Yes. **Laundry:** Yes. **Pay Phone:** Yes. **Restrooms and Showers:** Yes. **Fuel:** No. **Propane:** No. **Internal Roads:** Paved, in good condition. **RV Service:** No. **Market:** W/in 7 mi. **Restaurant:** W/in 5 mi. **General Store:** Yes. **Vending:** No. **Swimming:** Yes. **Playground:** Yes. **Other:** Cabin rentals. **Activities:** Fishing, swimming, canoeing, rec hall, planned activities, sports field, volleyball, hiking trails. **Nearby Attractions:** Genesee River Gorge, William Pryor Letchworth Museum, Rochester, Genesee Country Village & Museum, Conesus Lake. **Additional Information:** Greater Rochester Visitors Assoc., (800) 677-7282, www.visitrochester.com.

RESTRICTIONS

Pets: On leash only; dogs require rabies certificate. **Fires:** At site. **Alcoholic Beverages:** At site, no kegs. **Vehicle Maximum Length:** 40 ft.

TO GET THERE

From I-390, take Exit 7 and go 2 mi. southwest on Hwy. 408, 2 mi. north on Hwy. 36, and 6 mi. south on the main park road. Entrance is on the left.

CHENANGO FORKS MAP, C-4
Chenango Valley State Park

reserve america

153 State Park Rd., 13746. T: (607) 648-5251; www.reserveamerica.com.

🚐 ★★★★	🏕 ★★★★
Beauty: ★★★★	Site Privacy: ★★★
Spaciousness: ★★★	Quiet: ★★★★
Security: ★★★★	Cleanliness: ★★★★
Insect Control: ★★★	Facilities: ★★★★

Chenango Valley State Park is an ice age wonder. Its two kettle lakes, Lily and Chenango, were created when the last glacier retreated and left behind huge chunks of buried ice which melted to form the lakes, and bog. Birdwatchers may glimpse woodpeckers, nut hatches, warblers, and thrushes along woodland trails and herons, ducks, and kingfishers lakeside. Fishermen will find trout, bass, perch, and bullhead in Chenango Lake. Campers can choose from among campsites or cabins and golfers will appreciate the 18-hole golf course. Ice-skating, sledding, and cross-country ski trails attract visitors in winter.

BASICS

Operated By: New York State Parks. **Open:** Apr. 13–Nov. 7. **Site Assignment:** Reservations can be made 9 months in advance. **Registration:** At office. **Fee:** Single, $13; cabin, $270–$310. **Parking:** Amenity parking.

FACILITIES

Number of Multipurpose Sites: 252. **Hookups:** None. **Dump Station:** Yes. **Laundry:** No. **Pay Phone:** Yes. **Restrooms and Showers:** Yes. **Fuel:** No. **Propane:** No. **Internal Roads:** Paved. **RV Service:** No. **Market:** W/in 10 mi. **Restaurant:** Yes.

General Store: W/in 10 mi. **Vending:** Yes. **Swimming:** Yes. **Playground:** Yes. **Activities:** Baseball, basketball, boating, golf, hiking, mountain biking, picnicking, recreation programs, volleyball.

RESTRICTIONS

Pets: Dogs must have valid rabies certificate & be leashed at all times. **Fires:** Permitted in designated fireplaces. **Alcoholic Beverages:** Persons age 21 or over who possess or consume alcoholic beverages must produce adequate identification & proof of age upon request. **Other:** Bike helmets are required for children under 14 years of age. Rollerblades, roller skates, & skateboards are not allowed at the park. Quiet hours are 10 p.m.–8 a.m.

TO GET THERE

From Buffalo/Rochester: Take I-90 to Exit 46; Hwy. 390 south to Hwy. 17 east to I-81 north. Follow I-81 north to I-88 east, to Exit 3, Port Crane; turn left on Hwy. 369 north 4 mi.

CHERRY VALLEY MAP, C-4
Belvedere Lake Resort

270 Gage Rd., 13320. T: (607) 264-8182; www.belvederelake.com.

🚐 ★★★★ ⛺ ★★★★

Beauty: ★★★★ Site Privacy: ★★★
Spaciousness: ★★★ Quiet: ★★★★
Security: ★★★★ Cleanliness: ★★★★
Insect Control: ★★★★ Facilities: ★★★★

Located about 10 miles northeast of Cooperstown and the National Baseball Hall of Fame and Museum, Belvedere Lake Resort is an ideal base for campers interested in exploring the history of Cooperstown and the natural splendor of Lake Otsego. The 25-acre Belvedere Lake is tranquil and beautiful, and the campground has spacious open and shaded back-in sites. The best sites are situated along the lake. Recreational opportunities include a mini-golf course; a 9-hole, par 3 golf course; fishing, swimming, and boating at the lake; and a petting zoo and playground for the children. Fire truck rides, hayrides, bingo contests, and ice-cream socials are among the special events that are regularly held at Belvedere Lake Resort, which also hosts live entertainment in season. If you are not traveling with your RV or your tent, the campground has seven octagon-shaped, two-bedroom cottages for rent that overlook the lake. Tents are also available.

BASICS

Operated By: Private operator. **Open:** May 5–Oct. 9. **Site Assignment:** By reservation & first come, first served. **Registration:** At campground office. **Fee:** $30–$40; rates for 4 people. **Parking:** At site.

FACILITIES

Number of RV-only Sites: 160. **Hookups:** Electric (20, 30 amps), water, sewer; 125 full hookups. **Each Site:** Fire ring, picnic table. **Dump Station:** Yes. **Laundry:** Yes. **Pay Phone:** Yes. **Restrooms and Showers:** Yes. **Fuel:** No. **Propane:** Yes. **Internal Roads:** Gravel & paved, in good condition. **RV Service:** No. **Market:** W/in 6 mi. **Restaurant:** W/in 6 mi. **General Store:** Yes. **Vending:** Yes. **Swimming:** Yes. **Playground:** Yes. **Other:** Belvedere

Lake, petting zoo. **Activities:** Lake swimming & fishing, boating, canoeing, boat rentals, mini-golf, rec hall, planned activities on weekends, tennis, sports field, hiking trails, horseshoes, volleyball. **Nearby Attractions:** Cherry Valley Museum, National Baseball Hall of Fame & Museum, Farmers Museum & Village Crossroads, Lake Otsego Boat Tours, Fenimore Art Museum. **Additional Information:** Cooperstown Chamber of Commerce, (607) 547-9983, www .cooperstownchamber.org.

RESTRICTIONS

Pets: On leash only. **Fires:** At site. **Alcoholic Beverages:** At site, under control. **Vehicle Maximum Length:** 45 ft. **Other:** No cash refunds.

TO GET THERE

From Hwy. 54, go 4 mi. south on Hwy. 166, 0.5 mi. southeast on Hwy. 165, 0.1 mi. east on CR 57, and 0.75 mi. north on Gage Rd. Entrance is on the left.

CLAYTON MAP, A-3
Canoe-Picnic Point State Park

36661 Cedar Point State Park Dr., 13624. T: (315) 686-3048; www.reserveamerica.com.

🚐 n/a ⛺ ★★★★

Beauty: ★★★ Site Privacy: ★★★★
Spaciousness: ★★★★ Quiet: ★★★
Security: ★★★ Cleanliness: ★★★★
Insect Control: ★★★ Facilities: ★

Canoe-Picnic Point State Park is only reachable by boat, offering a quiet camping experience in a wooded area with plenty of dock space available. Just south of the camping area is Picnic Point, a picnic ground with a beautiful picnic gazebo, shore dinner cooking facility, and dockage. The fishing is excellent.

BASICS

Operated By: New York State Parks. **Open:** May 18–Sept. 2. **Site Assignment:** Reservations can be made 9 months in advance. **Registration:** At office. **Fee:** $10; cabin, $230. **Parking:** At marina—park can only be reached by boat.

FACILITIES

Number of Multipurpose Sites: 28. **Hookups:** None. **Dump Station:** No. **Laundry:** No. **Pay Phone:** No. **Restrooms and Showers:** Yes. **Fuel:** No. **Propane:** No. **Internal Roads:** Paved. **RV Service:** No. **Market:** No. **Restaurant:** No. **General Store:** No. **Vending:** No. **Swimming:** No. **Playground:** No. **Activities:** Boating, fishing, picnicking.

RESTRICTIONS

Pets: Pets are allowed w/ proof of a valid rabies certificate. They must be kept on a leash confining them to the site. **Fires:** Permitted in designated fireplaces. **Alcoholic Beverages:** Persons age 21 or over who possess or consume alcoholic beverages must produce adequate identification & proof of age upon request.

TO GET THERE

For Canoe Point, boat launching, parking, and directions are available at Wellesley Island and Grass Point state parks. Wellesley Island: Take Exit 51 off I-81 and follow signs to Wellesley Island State Park. Grass Point: Take Exit 50 off I-81 to Hwy. 12 west 2 mi.

CLAYTON MAP, A-3
Grass Point Campground

36661 Cedar Point State Park Dr., 13624. T: (315) 686-4472; www.reserveamerica.com.

🚐 ★★★★ ⛺ ★★★★

Beauty: ★★★ Site Privacy: ★★★
Spaciousness: ★★ Quiet: ★★★
Security: ★★★ Cleanliness: ★★★★
Insect Control: ★★★ Facilities: ★★★★

Grass Point State Park is on a point of land that projects into the American Channel of the St. Lawrence River, known for some of the best fishing in the country. The park is a popular spot for campers and day-users, who come to boat, swim, fish, picnic, or just relax. There is a marina and boat launch, an area available for games, and a sandy beach and shallow water that are excellent for children. Grass Point Campground offers a swimming beach, a boat-launch site, dockage, marina, fishing in St. Lawrence River, hunting for waterfowl, picnic tables and shelters, a children's playground, powerboating, hot showers, flush toilets, public telephone, a pet trail, camp store, cross-country skiing during winter, and a long fishing pier that offers fabulous views and an opportunity to fish in deep waters. The fishing site, picnic area, campground, and showers are wheelchair-accessible.

BASICS

Operated By: New York State Parks. **Open:** May 11–Oct. 7. **Site Assignment:** Reservations can be made 9 months in advance. **Registration:** At office. **Fee:** Single, $13; cabin, $500–$700. **Parking:** Amenity parking.

FACILITIES

Number of Multipurpose Sites: 78. **Hookups:** None. **Dump Station:** Yes. **Laundry:** No. **Pay Phone:** No. **Restrooms and Showers:** Yes. **Fuel:** No. **Propane:** No. **Internal Roads:** Paved. **RV Service:** No. **Market:** W/in 10 mi. **Restaurant:** W/in 10 mi. **General Store:** W/in 10 mi. **Vending:** No. **Swimming:** Yes. **Playground:** Yes. **Other:** All full-service cottages are smoke-free & pet-free. **Activities:** Boating, fishing, picnicking.

RESTRICTIONS

Pets: Pets must have a valid rabies certificate & be on a leash not longer than 6 ft. at all times. **Fires:** Permitted in designated fireplaces. **Alcoholic Beverages:** Persons age 21 or over who possess or consume alcoholic beverages must produce adequate identification & proof of age upon request.

TO GET THERE

Grass Point is located off I-81. The park is 1 mi. west of I-81 Exit 50S on Hwy. 12. Winter phone number (315) 654-2522.

CLAYTON   MAP, A-3
Mary Island

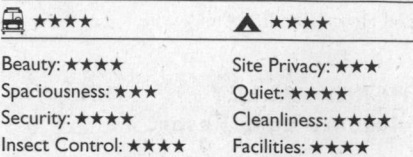

36661 Cedar Point State Park Dr., 13624.
T: (315) 482-9381; www.reserveamerica.com.

🚐 ★★★★	🏕 ★★★★
Beauty: ★★★	Site Privacy: ★★★★★
Spaciousness: ★★★★★	Quiet: ★★★
Security: ★★★	Cleanliness: ★★★★
Insect Control: ★★★	Facilities: n/a

Mary Island is located to the east of Wellesley Island. Access is by boat only from either Grass Point State Park (4 miles over water), or Keewaydin State Park, which is 2 miles from the island. Mary Island State Park comprises 12 heavily wooded acres with steep rocky outcroppings. Twelve waterfront campsites are scattered throughout the park, offering seclusion and spectacular views of the Canadian shore or the shipping channel. Flush toilets and potable water are available but not electric hookups. Access is by boat only with the island providing two floating docks for campers only. Boats may be beached or moored near campsites. The park has a picnic area and several foot trails. A third service dock is provided on the south side with a second service dock nestled in a northeastern cove. High scenic cliffs, quiet seclusion, and excellent fishing waters are the main attractions. Hiking is limited to the island.

BASICS

Operated By: New York State Parks. **Open:** May 18–Sept. 2. **Site Assignment:** Reservations can be made 9 months in advance. **Registration:** At office. **Fee:** Single, $10. **Parking:** At marina—park can only be reached by boat.

FACILITIES

Number of Multipurpose Sites: 13. **Hookups:** None. **Dump Station:** No. **Laundry:** No. **Pay Phone:** No. **Restrooms and Showers:** No. **Fuel:** No. **Propane:** No. **Internal Roads:** Paved. **RV Service:** No. **Market:** W/in 10 mi. **Restaurant:** No. **General Store:** W/in 10 mi. **Vending:** No. **Swimming:** No. **Playground:** No. **Activities:** Boating, fishing, picnicking.

RESTRICTIONS

Pets: Pets are allowed w/ proof of a valid rabies certificate. They must be kept on a leash confining them to the site. **Fires:** Permitted in designated fireplaces. **Alcoholic Beverages:** Persons age 21 or over who possess or consume alcoholic beverages must produce adequate identification & proof of age upon request. **Other:** The only way to get to the park is by boat. Patrons must have at least a 14-ft. motorized boat to access Mary Island.

TO GET THERE

For Mary Island: Boat launching, parking, and directions are available at Keewaydin State Park, which is 1 mi. west of Alexandria Bay off Hwy. 12. Take Exit 50N off I-81 to Hwy. 12 and go 4 mi. Keewaydin State Park will be on your left.

CLEVELAND   MAP, B-4
Lazy K RV Ranch

965 Stonebarn Rd., P.O. Box 507, 13042-0507.
T: (315) 675-8100 or (888) 381-6415;
www.lazykrvranch.com.

🚐 ★★★	🏕 ★★★
Beauty: ★★★★	Site Privacy: ★★★
Spaciousness: ★★★	Quiet: ★★★★
Security: ★★★★	Cleanliness: ★★★★
Insect Control: ★★★★	Facilities: ★★★★

Located near Oneida Lake and 20 miles northeast of Syracuse in north-central New York, Lazy K RV Ranch offers level and wooded campsites on 200 acres of tranquil woodlands accessible by several hiking trails. Ninety-two of the sites handle pull-throughs. Tent sites are located near many of the hiking trails. If you enjoy the water, Lazy K is an ideal place to camp. The campground itself has a 50-acre pond for fishing, rowboating, and canoeing. Two miles away is a boat launch on Oneida Lake. Children will like the well-equipped playground, wagon rides, and the kiddie-sized pool. The outdoor activities and natural splendor of Oneida Lake, the thrill rides of Sylvan Beach Amusement Park, and the history-rich Erie Canal Village are among the attractions close to Lazy K. If you are captivated by the 24-hour excitement of slot machines and craps, Turning Stone Casino is nearby. Operated by the Oneida Indian Nation, Turning Stone was the first legalized gambling casino in New York.

BASICS

Operated By: Lew & Dolores Kraeuter. **Open:** May 15–Oct. 15. **Site Assignment:** Reservations recommended, walk-ins accepted. **Registration:** At campground office. **Fee:** $20–$28; tent, $20. **Parking:** At site.

FACILITIES

Number of RV-only Sites: 100. **Number of Tent-only Sites:** 20. **Hookups:** Electric (15, 30 amps), water, 36 full hookups. **Each Site:** Fire ring, picnic table. **Dump Station:** Yes. **Laundry:** Yes. **Pay Phone:** Yes. **Restrooms and Showers:** Yes. **Fuel:** No. **Propane:** No. **Internal Roads:** Dirt & gravel, in good condition. **RV Service:** No. **Market:** W/in 2 mi. **Restaurant:** W/in 2 mi. **General Store:** Yes. **Vending:** Yes. **Swimming:** Yes. **Playground:** Yes. **Other:** 50-acre pond stocked w/ bass. **Activities:** Pond fishing, game room, rec hall, hiking trails, planned activities on weekends, horseshoes, volleyball. **Nearby Attractions:** Sylvan Beach Amusement Park, Oneida Lake, Stonebarn Castle, Turning Stone Casino, Erie Canal Village, Fort Rickey Children's Discovery Zoo, Syracuse. **Additional Information:** Syracuse CVB, (800) 234-4797, www.visitsyracuse.org.

RESTRICTIONS

Pets: On leash only. **Fires:** At site. **Alcoholic Beverages:** At site. **Vehicle Maximum Length:** No limit. **Other:** Fires are monitored during extended dry weather.

TO GET THERE

From Cleveland, go 2.5 mi. east on Hwy. 49, 0.25 mi. north on Hall Rd., and 0.1 mi. east on Stonebarn Rd. Entrance is on the left.

COOPERSTOWN   MAP, C-4
Cooperstown Beaver Valley Cabins and Campsites

P.O. Box 704, 13326.
T: (800) 726-7314 or (607) 293-7324;
www.beavervalleycampground.com.

🚐 ★★★★	🏕 ★★★★
Beauty: ★★★★	Site Privacy: ★★★
Spaciousness: ★★★	Quiet: ★★★★
Security: ★★★★	Cleanliness: ★★★★
Insect Control: ★★★★	Facilities: ★★★★

Beaver Valley is home to Cooperstown Baseball Camp, which uses the campground's two pristine baseball fields. Nestled amid wooded hills and dotted with open meadows, Beaver Valley has open and shaded sites, 17 of which accommodate pull-throughs. Sites on the south end offer greater privacy than those at the north end. Tent sites along Beaver Pond are ideal. This is a campground where you wish you were a kid. Few children can resist the timber playground, which has a track ride, tire swing, sheltered sandbox, and traditional swings. The centerpiece of the fenced preschool play area is a castle. There is fishing and boating on Beaver Pond Lake, and a fossil pit for aspiring young archeologists. You can even feed carrots to the Sadie the pony and Tannin the cow. Raccoons, beavers, and herons are some of the other more elusive animals present at Beaver Valley. For campers without RVs or tents, Beaver Valley has three modular homes located in a secluded area in the campground. There are also seven one-room cabins situated in a row at the edge of the baseball fields.

BASICS

Operated By: Private operator. **Open:** May 26–Sept. 25. **Site Assignment:** By reservation & first come, first served. **Registration:** At campground office. **Fee:** $31; V, MC. **Parking:** At site.

FACILITIES

Number of RV-only Sites: 95. **Number of Tent-only Sites:** 20. **Hookups:** Electric (20, 30 amps), water, phone. **Each Site:** Fire ring, picnic table. **Dump Station:** Yes. **Laundry:** Yes. **Pay Phone:** Yes. **Restrooms and Showers:** Yes. **Fuel:** No. **Propane:** Yes. **Internal Roads:** Gravel, in good condition. **RV Service:** No. **Market:** W/in 5 mi. **Restaurant:** W/in 5 mi. **General Store:** Yes. **Vending:** Yes. **Swimming:** Yes. **Playground:** Yes. **Other:** Beaver Pond Lake, cabin rentals. **Activities:** Swimming, game room, fishing, boating, canoeing, boat rentals, bike rentals, basketball, planned activities on weekends, sports field, horseshoes, hiking trails, volleyball.

Nearby Attractions: Cooperstown Dreams Park, National Baseball Hall of Fame & Museum, Otsego Lake, Farmers Museum & Village Crossroads, Fenimore Art Museum. **Additional Information:** Cooperstown Chamber of Commerce, (607) 547-9983, www.cooperstownchamber.org.

RESTRICTIONS

Pets: On leash only. Rabies certificate for pet must be presented upon arrival. **Fires:** At site. **Alcoholic Beverages:** At site. **Vehicle Maximum Length:** No limit.

TO GET THERE

From Hwy. 80 in Cooperstown, go 4 mi. south on Hwy. 28 and 2.25 mi. west on Seminary Rd. Entrance is on the left.

COOPERSTOWN   MAP, C-4
Cooperstown KOA

565 Ostrander Rd., 13439.
T: (315) 858-0236 or (800) 562-3402;
www.koa.campgrounds.com/where/ny/32114.

🚐 ★★★★   ⛺ ★★★★

Beauty: ★★★	Site Privacy: ★★
Spaciousness: ★★★	Quiet: ★★★★
Security: ★★★★	Cleanliness: ★★★★
Insect Control: ★★★★	Facilities: ★★★★

Convenient to the National Baseball Hall of Fame and Museum, Otsego Lake, and the history-rich village of Cooperstown, Cooperstown KOA is a comfortable base to visit the many area attractions. Mini-golf, swimming, hiking, and basketball are among the activities at the campground, which is ideal for RVers with 58 pull-throughs and 27 full hookups. Sites are open and shaded, and facilities here are clean. The National Baseball Hall of Fame and Museum, of course, is the destination of many campers here. Our favorite is the exhibit on beloved ballparks, but the displays on baseball's greatest moments, the World Series, and the All-Star Game are about equally fascinating. Did you know that though Pete Rose is banned from the sport and not eligible for the Hall of Fame, baseball's all-time hits leader has a museum devoted to him in Cooperstown? Other area attractions that are inviting to families but not widely known are the Lolly Pop Farm and Petting Zoo, the Petrified Creatures Museum of Natural History, and the Cooperstown Fun Park, home of the Hamburger Hall of Fame.

BASICS

Operated By: KOA. **Open:** Apr. 15–Oct. 31. **Site Assignment:** Reservations recommended, walk-ins accepted. **Registration:** At campground office. **Fee:** $27–$54; V, MC, AE, D. **Parking:** At site.

FACILITIES

Number of RV-only Sites: 106. **Number of Tent-only Sites:** 28. **Hookups:** Electric (20, 30, 50 amps), water, phone. **Each Site:** Fire ring, picnic table. **Dump Station:** Yes. **Laundry:** Yes. **Pay Phone:** Yes. **Restrooms and Showers:** Yes. **Fuel:** No. **Propane:** Yes. **Internal Roads:** Gravel, in good condition. **RV Service:** No. **Market:** W/in 6 mi. **Restaurant:** W/in 8 mi. **General Store:** Yes.

Vending: Yes. **Swimming:** Yes. **Playground:** Yes. **Other:** Cabin rentals, pavilion. **Activities:** Swimming, game room, mini-golf, planned activities on weekends, basketball, movies, badminton, hiking trails, horseshoes, volleyball, rec hall. **Nearby Attractions:** Cooperstown Dreams Park, National Baseball Hall of Fame & Museum, Otsego Lake, Farmers Museum & Village Crossroads, Fenimore Art Museum. **Additional Information:** Cooperstown Chamber of Commerce, (607) 547-9983, www.cooperstownchamber.org.

RESTRICTIONS

Pets: On leash only. **Fires:** At site. **Alcoholic Beverages:** At site. **Vehicle Maximum Length:** 60 ft.

TO GET THERE

From Hwy. 28, go 11 mi. north on Hwy. 80E, 0.5 mi. west on US 20, and 1 mi. north and west on paved road with signs leading to campground. Entrance is on the left.

COOPERSTOWN   MAP, C-4
Cooperstown Shadow Brook Campground

2149 CR 31, 13326. T: (607) 264-8431 or (888) 806-2267; www.cooperstowncamping.com.

🚐 ★★★★★   ⛺ ★★★★★

Beauty: ★★★★★	Site Privacy: ★★★
Spaciousness: ★★★	Quiet: ★★★★
Security: ★★★★	Cleanliness: ★★★★★
Insect Control: ★★★★	Facilities: ★★★★

Featuring 100 sites that surround a spring-fed stocked pond, Cooperstown Shadow Brook Campground is one of the nicest campgrounds in New York, with 20 pull-through sites and 50 sites with accommodations for slide-outs. Though it does not offer the on-site baseball excitement that Beaver Valley does, Shadow Brook has plenty to recommend it. Colorful landscaped grounds, a heated pool with an inviting sun deck, an abundance of activities, clean facilities, and serene mountain scenery are among the features that attract campers here. In the middle of the campground, sites are available on the north and south sides of the pond. If you want to camp near the water but away from the center of the campground and the pond, sites are available along the actual Shadow Brook on the campground's northeast tip. New "cozy cabins" are available for rent as well. Weekend fun includes big-screen movies, hayrides, and dances. The National Baseball Hall of Fame and Museum and Cooperstown Dreams Park are a short drive away.

BASICS

Operated By: Private operator. **Open:** May 19–Oct. 15. **Site Assignment:** Reservations accepted (1-night deposit required), walk-ins accepted. **Registration:** At campground office. **Fee:** $24–$37; V, MC, D. **Parking:** At site.

FACILITIES

Number of RV-only Sites: 90. **Number of Tent-only Sites:** 10. **Hookups:** Electric (20, 30 amps), water, phone. **Each Site:** Fire ring, picnic table. **Dump Station:** Yes. **Laundry:** Yes. **Pay Phone:** Yes.

Restrooms and Showers: Yes. **Fuel:** No. **Propane:** Yes. **Internal Roads:** Paved, in good condition. **RV Service:** No. **Market:** W/in 5 mi. **Restaurant:** W/in 5 mi. **General Store:** Yes. **Vending:** Yes. **Swimming:** Yes. **Playground:** Yes. **Other:** Spring-fed stocked pond, cabin rentals. **Activities:** Game room, rec hall, fishing, planned activities on weekends, movies, dances, boat rentals, sports field, boating. **Nearby Attractions:** Cooperstown Dreams Park, National Baseball Hall of Fame & Museum, Otsego Lake, Farmers Museum & Village Crossroads, Fenimore Art Museum. **Additional Information:** Cooperstown Chamber of Commerce, (607) 547-9983, www.cooperstownchamber.org.

RESTRICTIONS

Pets: On leash only. **Fires:** At site. **Alcoholic Beverages:** At site. **Vehicle Maximum Length:** 40 ft. **Other:** Reservations & 5-night min. stay required Jun. 30–Aug. 22.

TO GET THERE

From Cooperstown, at Main St. take Hwy. 80E and go 10.75 mi. north, 4 mi. east on Hwy. 20, and 1 mi. south on CR 31. Entrance is on the right.

COOPERSTOWN   MAP, C-4
Meadow-Vale Campsites

505 Gilbert Lake Rd., 13810. T: (607) 293-8802 or (800) 701-8802; www.meadow-vale.com.

🚐 ★★★   ⛺ ★★★

Beauty: ★★★★	Site Privacy: ★★★
Spaciousness: ★★★	Quiet: ★★★★
Security: ★★★★	Cleanliness: ★★★★
Insect Control: ★★★	Facilities: ★★★★

Everywhere you look from the grounds of Meadow-Vale Campsites, there are towering woods and rolling green hills, which in the distance resemble a patchwork quilt. Meadow-Vale is a peaceful campground with a 2.5-acre natural lake, where campers can fish and explore with rented canoes and pedal boats. Each RV site has electric and water hookups. Tent sites are located in a wooded area and offer more privacy than RV sites. The campground has a mini-golf course, but if you are a serious golfer, there are three full-size courses in the area. If you still have energy to spare after boating and swimming at Otsego Lake and exploring Cooperstown, you can tackle the physical fitness trail. With 16 exercise stations along the way, you are sure to get a vigorous workout. An expansive croquet court, nature trails, horseshoe pits, and basketball and volleyball courts are other recreational options. Bingo and pot luck suppers are among Meadow-Vale's special events.

BASICS

Operated By: Cecelia & Wayne Schleder. **Open:** May 12–Oct. 9. **Site Assignment:** By reservation & first come, first served. **Registration:** At campground office. **Fee:** RV/cabin, $30; tent, $25; V, MC. **Parking:** At site.

FACILITIES

Number of RV-only Sites: 96. **Number of Tent-only Sites:** 14. **Hookups:** Electric (15, 20, 30 amps), water, phone. **Each Site:** Fire ring, picnic table.

Dump Station: Yes. **Laundry:** Yes. **Pay Phone:** Yes. **Restrooms and Showers:** Yes. **Fuel:** No. **Propane:** Yes. **Internal Roads:** Gravel, in good condition. **RV Service:** No. **Market:** W/in 7 mi. **Restaurant:** W/in 5 mi. **General Store:** Yes. **Vending:** Yes. **Swimming:** Yes. **Playground:** Yes. **Other:** Meadow-Vale Lake. **Activities:** Swimming, boating, boat rentals, pond fishing, pavilion, game room, minigolf, basketball, planned activities on weekends, movies, badminton, sports field, hiking trails, volleyball, canoeing. **Nearby Attractions:** Cooperstown Dreams Park, National Baseball Hall of Fame & Museum, Otsego Lake, Farmers Museum & Village Crossroads, Fenimore Art Museum. **Additional Information:** Cooperstown Chamber, (607) 547-9983, www.cooperstownchamber.org.

RESTRICTIONS

Pets: On leash only. **Fires:** At site. **Alcoholic Beverages:** At site. **Vehicle Maximum Length:** 40 ft.

TO GET THERE

From Hwy. 80, go 2.5 mi. south on Hwy. 28, 7.5 mi. west on CR 11, 4 mi. southwest on CR 14, and 0.25 mi. south on Gilbert Lake Rd. Entrance is on the right.

COOPERSTOWN   MAP, C-4
Yogi Bear's Jellystone Park at Crystal Lake

reserve america

111 East Turtle Lake Rd., 13342. T: (607) 965-8265 or (800) 231-1907; www.cooperstownjellystone.com.

🚐 ★★★★   ⛺ ★★★★

Beauty: ★★★★	Site Privacy: ★★★★
Spaciousness: ★★★	Quiet: ★★★★
Security: ★★★★	Cleanliness: ★★★★★
Insect Control: ★★★★	Facilities: ★★★★

Located centrally between the National Baseball Hall of Fame and Museum in Cooperstown and the National Soccer Hall of Fame in Oneonta (where there is also a Single-A minor league baseball team), Yogi Bear's Jellystone Park at Crystal Lake is certainly an all-star in the franchise's vast league of campgrounds. There are open and shaded sites, including 40 full hookups. The campground's most attractive sites are located along 35-acre Crystal Lake. The lake offers campers fishing and boating opportunities, but no swimming is allowed. Sites on the north side of Crystal Lake offer more privacy than those on the south side, which is near the traffic of County Rd. 17. Full-hookup sites are located on the southeast side of the campground near a nature trail. Non-RVers and tenters need not fret; cabins, cottages, and trailers are available for rent.

BASICS

Operated By: Reinard family. **Open:** May 19–Sept. 10. **Site Assignment:** Reservations recommended (2-night deposit required, 3 on holidays), walk-ins accepted. **Registration:** At campground office. **Fee:** $35–$53; V, MC. **Parking:** At site.

FACILITIES

Number of RV-only Sites: 226. **Number of Tent-only Sites:** 16. **Hookups:** Electric (30, 50 amps), water, phone. **Each Site:** Fire ring, picnic table. **Dump Station:** Yes. **Laundry:** Yes. **Pay Phone:** Yes. **Restrooms and Showers:** Yes. **Fuel:** No. **Propane:** Yes. **Internal Roads:** Paved, in good condition. **RV Service:** No. **Market:** W/in 4 mi. **Restaurant:** W/in 6 mi. **General Store:** Yes. **Vending:** Yes. **Swimming:** Yes. **Playground:** Yes. **Other:** Crystal Lake, cabin rentals, pavilion. **Activities:** Swimming, game room, rec hall, boating, canoeing, boat rentals, lake fishing, basketball, planned activities, movies, bingo, trolley, tennis, badminton, volleyball, hiking trails, sports field, horseshoes. **Nearby Attractions:** National Soccer Hall of Fame, Cooperstown Dreams Park, National Baseball Hall of Fame & Museum, Otsego Lake, Farmers Museum & Village Crossroads, Fenimore Art Museum. **Additional Information:** Cooperstown Chamber of Commerce, (607) 547-9983, www.cooperstownchamber.org.

RESTRICTIONS

Pets: On leash only, under control; 2 pets per campsite. **Fires:** At site. **Alcoholic Beverages:** At site. **Vehicle Maximum Length:** No limit.

TO GET THERE

From Hwy. 28, go 10.75 mi. west on Hwy. 80, 5.75 mi. south on CR 16, 0.75 mi. north on Hwy. 51, and 1 mi. west on CR 17. Entrance is on the left.

COPAKE   MAP, C-5
Oleana Family Campground

2236 CR 7, 12516. T: (518) 329-2811; www.oleanacampground.com.

🚐 ★★★★   ⛺ ★★★★

Beauty: ★★★★	Site Privacy: ★★
Spaciousness: ★★	Quiet: ★★★★
Security: ★★★★★	Cleanliness: ★★★★
Insect Control: ★★★	Facilities: ★★★

Oleana Family Campground is nestled in the Hudson Valley between the Catskill Mountains and the Berkshires, two hours north of New York City and near the Massachusetts and Connecticut borders. All sites here have full hookups, and there are 50 pull-throughs. With 350 sites, Oleana is crowded in some areas, with little privacy. Some sites along Cree Pass at the far north tip of the campground offer more space and some privacy. You can fish and swim in the campground's lake. Children will enjoy the fire truck rides and hayrides. Remember the *Seinfeld* episode when George was bullied by the Van Buren Boys, who named the gang after the eighth President of the United States? Even if you don't, you still may enjoy the Martin Van Buren State Historic Site in nearby Kinderhook. The American Museum of Firefighting in Hudson is also an interesting afternoon venture.

BASICS

Operated By: Bill & Claudia Storey. **Open:** All year. **Site Assignment:** By reservation & first come, first served. **Registration:** At campground office. **Fee:** $28–$35. **Parking:** At site.

FACILITIES

Number of RV-only Sites: 350. **Hookups:** Electric (15, 20, 30 amps), phone. **Each Site:** Fire ring, picnic table. **Dump Station:** Yes. **Laundry:** Yes. **Pay Phone:** Yes. **Restrooms and Showers:** Yes. **Fuel:** No. **Propane:** Yes. **Internal Roads:** Gravel, in good condition. **RV Service:** No. **Market:** W/in 2 mi. **Restaurant:** W/in 2 mi. **General Store:** Yes. **Vending:** Yes. **Swimming:** Yes. **Playground:** Yes. **Other:** Lake. **Activities:** Lake swimming & fishing, boating, planned activities on weekends, volleyball, horseshoes, game room, sports field, rec hall, tennis. **Nearby Attractions:** Catamount Ski Mountain, American Museum of Firefighting, Clermont State Historic Site, Martin Van Buren National Historic Site, golf. **Additional Information:** Columbia County Chamber of Commerce, (800) 724-1846 www.columbiacountyny.org.

RESTRICTIONS

Pets: On leash only. **Fires:** At site. **Alcoholic Beverages:** At site. **Vehicle Maximum Length:** No limit. **Other:** Max. 4 adults per campsite.

TO GET THERE

West of Copake, the campground is located at the junction of Hwy. 7 and Hwy. 7A.

CORINTH   MAP, B-5
Alpine Lake RV Resort

reserve america

78 Heath Rd., 12822-2306. T: (518) 654-6260; www.alpinelakervresort.com.

🚐 ★★★★   ⛺ ★★★★

Beauty: ★★★★	Site Privacy: ★★
Spaciousness: ★★★	Quiet: ★★★★
Security: ★★★★	Cleanliness: ★★★★
Insect Control: ★★★★	Facilities: ★★★★★

Located near Lake George, Lake Luzerne, and Saratoga Springs in the lush Adirondack Forest, Alpine Lake RV Resort is a truly giant campground. Each RV site accommodates double slideouts, and there are 300 pull-throughs. Few sites here offer privacy, but campers do not seem to mind, especially since there is so much to do. The campground's centerpiece is the namesake Alpine Lake, a beautiful private lake where campers can boat, fish, swim, and bask in the sun on a sandy beach. Alpine Lake RV Resort has two swimming pools, two pavilions, lighted tennis courts, hiking trails, a gift shop, and even a day-use kennel, among other amenities. South of Alpine Lake, Saratoga Springs is known for its mineral baths. The Great Escape and Splashwater Kingdom Fun Park is New York's largest theme park, with 120 rides, including roller coasters, a river raft adventure, and a water park. At the Fort William Henry Museum, visitors can see a rebuilt French and Indian War–era stockade.

BASICS

Operated By: Sandwick family. **Open:** May 5–Oct. 15. **Site Assignment:** By reservation & first come, first served. **Registration:** At campground office. **Fee:** $36–$48; V, MC. **Parking:** At site.

FACILITIES

Number of RV-only Sites: 450. **Number of Tent-only Sites:** 50. **Hookups:** Electric (30, 50 amps), cable TV, phone. **Each Site:** Fire ring, picnic table. **Dump Station:** Yes. **Laundry:** Yes. **Pay Phone:** Yes. **Restrooms and Showers:** Yes. **Fuel:** No. **Propane:** Yes. **Internal Roads:** Paved, in good condition. **RV Service:** Yes. **Market:** W/in 3 mi. **Restaurant:** W/in 3 mi. **General Store:** Yes. **Vending:** Yes. **Swimming:** Yes. **Playground:** Yes. **Other:** Alpine Lake. **Activities:** Lake swimming & fishing, game room, rec hall, boating, canoeing, boat rentals, basketball, planned activities on weekends, movies, tennis, sports field, badminton, horseshoes, hiking trails, volleyball. **Nearby Attractions:** Lake George, Saratoga Springs, Lake Luzerne, Prospect Mountain, Fort William Henry, Water Slide World, Great Escape & Splashwater Kingdom Fun Park. **Additional Information:** Lake George Chamber of Commerce, (800) 705-0059, www.lakegeorgevillage.com.

RESTRICTIONS

Pets: On leash only. **Fires:** At site. **Alcoholic Beverages:** At site. **Vehicle Maximum Length:** No limit. **Other:** No skateboards.

TO GET THERE

From Corinth, go 1.25 mi. south on Hwy. 9N and 1.25 mi. east on Heath Rd. Entrance is on the left.

CORNING   MAP, C-3
Ferenbaugh Campsites

4682 SR 414, 14830. T: (607) 962-6193 or (941) 298-9215; www.ferenbaugh.com.

🚐 ★★★★	🏕 ★★★★
Beauty: ★★★★	Site Privacy: ★★★★
Spaciousness: ★★★	Quiet: ★★★★
Security: ★★★	Cleanliness: ★★★★
Insect Control: ★★★★	Facilities: ★★★★

Covering 275 acres and located 5 miles from Corning, Ferenbaugh Campsites is set in a valley bursting with color in the spring and the fall. The campground has many wooded and creekside sites—offering welcomed privacy—and 30 pull-throughs. Campers without RVs or tents will relish the spacious, clean cabins that overlook Post Creek. Ferenbaugh is just a few minutes from the Corning Glass Center. If you are interested in the crafting and history of glass, this is a must-see. The center includes the Corning Museum of Glass, which contains a vast collection of 26,000 glass items; the Hall of Science and Industry, which features hands-on exhibits about technology; and the Steuben Glass Factory, where you can watch glassblowers transform molten glass into gifts and collectibles. In Corning's historic Market Street area, the Rockwell Museum displays a large collection of American Western art.

BASICS

Operated By: Private operator. **Open:** Apr. 15–Oct. 15. **Site Assignment:** By reservation & first come, first served. **Registration:** At campground headquarters. **Fee:** $25–$37; V, MC, D. **Parking:** At site.

FACILITIES

Number of RV-only Sites: 145. **Number of Tent-only Sites:** 18. **Hookups:** Electric (20, 30, 50 amps), water, cable TV, phone. **Each Site:** Fire ring, picnic table. **Dump Station:** Yes. **Laundry:** Yes. **Pay Phone:** Yes. **Restrooms and Showers:** Yes. **Fuel:** No. **Propane:** Yes. **Internal Roads:** Gravel, in good condition. **RV Service:** No. **Market:** W/in 5 mi. **Restaurant:** W/in 5 mi. **General Store:** Yes. **Vending:** Yes. **Swimming:** No. **Playground:** Yes. **Other:** Trout stream, stocked pond. **Activities:** Fishing, mini-golf, hiking trails, game room, sports field, planned activities on weekends, volleyball, badminton, horseshoes. **Nearby Attractions:** Corning Glass Center, Rockwell Museum, Watkins Glen State Park, Watkins Glen International Speedway, Harris Hill Soaring Museum, National War Plane Museum, Seneca Lake wineries. **Additional Information:** Corning Chamber of Commerce, (607) 936-4686, www.corningny.com.

RESTRICTIONS

Pets: On leash only. **Fires:** At site. **Alcoholic Beverages:** At site. **Vehicle Maximum Length:** No limit.

TO GET THERE

From I-86, take Exit 46 and go 5 mi. north on Hwy. 414. Entrance is on the right.

DANSVILLE   MAP, C-2
Sugar Creek Glen Campground

P.O. Box 143W, 14437. T: (585) 335-6294; www.sugarcreekglencampground.com.

🚐 ★★★★	🏕 ★★★★
Beauty: ★★★★★	Site Privacy: ★★★
Spaciousness: ★★★	Quiet: ★★★★
Security: ★★★★	Cleanliness: ★★★★
Insect Control: ★★★★	Facilities: ★★★★

Located in east central New York, Sugar Creek Glen Campground is less than two hours from Niagara Falls, but it has 15 acres of natural beauty on its own grounds. Sugar Creek Glen is in fact a shady glen with five cascading waterfalls, including one that is lighted for nighttime viewing. There are several hiking trails that meander through the glen and offer spectacular views of the waterfalls. Sites are shaded and wooded, and many are along Sugar Creek. RVers and tenters alike can camp in the summer with shelter from the hot sun. Most campers venture here because of the waterfalls and hiking trails, but the campground does have a full menu of family-oriented activities. Sugar Creek Glen is convenient to the Finger Lakes region; Conesus Lake and Canandaigua Lake are closest to the campground. Letchworth State Park with its Genesee River Gorge is a rewarding day trip for campers. The park has three waterfalls, one of which is 107 feet high

BASICS

Operated By: Alice & Bob Klos. **Open:** Apr. 27–Oct. 14. **Site Assignment:** By reservation & first come, first served. **Registration:** At campground office. **Fee:** $25–$28; V, MC. **Parking:** At site.

FACILITIES

Number of RV-only Sites: 105. **Number of Tent-only Sites:** 26. **Hookups:** Electric (15, 30

amps), water. **Each Site:** Fire ring, picnic table. **Dump Station:** Yes. **Laundry:** Yes. **Pay Phone:** Yes. **Restrooms and Showers:** Yes. **Fuel:** No. **Propane:** Yes. **Internal Roads:** Gravel & dirt, in good condition. **RV Service:** No. **Market:** W/in 5 mi. **Restaurant:** W/in 5 mi. **General Store:** Yes. **Vending:** Yes. **Swimming:** Yes. **Playground:** Yes. **Other:** 5 waterfalls on grounds (1 is lighted), cabin rentals. **Activities:** River swimming, game room, rec hall, hiking trails, fishing, basketball, badminton, volleyball. **Nearby Attractions:** Niagara Falls, Letchworth State Park, Finger Lakes, golf. **Additional Information:** Finger Lakes Assoc., (800) 548-4386, www.fingerlakes.org.

RESTRICTIONS

Pets: On leash only. **Fires:** At site. **Alcoholic Beverages:** At site. **Vehicle Maximum Length:** 30 ft.

TO GET THERE

From I-390, take Exit 4 and go about 500 ft. south on Hwy. 36 and 4 mi. southwest on Poag's Hole Rd. Entrance is at the end.

DARIEN CENTER   MAP, C-2
Darien Lakes State Park

reserve america

10289 Harlow Rd., 14040. T: (585) 547-9242; www.reserveamerica.com.

🚐 ★★★★	🏕 ★★★★
Beauty: ★★★	Site Privacy: ★★★
Spaciousness: ★★★	Quiet: ★★★★★
Security: ★★★★★	Cleanliness: ★★★★
Insect Control: ★★★	Facilities: ★★★★

Darien Lakes State Park's terrain is hilly with woodlands, ravines, streams and 12-acre Harlow Lake. The park has a combination of electric and nonelectric sites with heated comfort stations and showers, a sandy beach, playgrounds, fishing for largemouth black bass, hiking and horseback riding trails, picnic areas, and a rustic bridge over the lake channel to Picnic Island. In winter, multiple-use trails are open for hiking, cross-country skiing, and snowmobiling and a maintained and heated building for an outdoor skating rink. Darien also has two picnic shelters available for a fee by reservation only.

BASICS

Operated By: New York State Parks. **Open:** All year. **Site Assignment:** Reservations can be made 9 months in advance. **Registration:** At office. **Fee:** Single, $13. **Parking:** Amenity parking.

FACILITIES

Number of Multipurpose Sites: 142. **Hookups:** Yes. **Dump Station:** Yes. **Laundry:** W/in 10 mi. **Pay Phone:** No. **Restrooms and Showers:** Yes. **Fuel:** No. **Propane:** No. **Internal Roads:** Paved. **RV Service:** No. **Market:** W/in 10 mi. **Restaurant:** W/in 10 mi. **General Store:** W/in 10 mi. **Vending:** No. **Swimming:** Yes. **Playground:** Yes. **Other:** Swimming at beach only on weekends starting Memorial Day–Jun. 25; then daily through Labor Day. **Activities:** Basketball, cross-country skiing, fishing, hiking, hunting, ice skating, picnicking, snowmobiling.

RESTRICTIONS

Pets: Pets are allowed on all sites. A valid rabies certificate is required & they must be kept on a 6-ft. leash at all times. **Fires:** Permitted in designated fireplaces. **Alcoholic Beverages:** Persons age 21 or over who possess or consume alcoholic beverages must produce adequate identification & proof of age upon request. **Other:** Max. 2 vehicles per site.

TO GET THERE

From Buffalo, take Broadway (Hwy. 20) east to Darien. Turn north onto Harlow Rd., go 0.25 mi. north to park entrance. On the New York State Thruway (I-90) take Exit 48A, Hwy. 77 south 6 mi. to Hwy. 20. Go west on Hwy. 20 to first right turn (Harlow Rd.). Go 0.25 mi. north to park entrance.

DARIEN CENTER   MAP, C-2
Skyline Camping Resort

10933 Townline Rd., 14040. T: (585) 591-2021 or (800) 724-3619; www.skylinervresort.com.

🚐 ★★★★   🏕 ★★★★

Beauty: ★★★★	Site Privacy: ★★
Spaciousness: ★★	Quiet: ★★★★
Security: ★★★★★	Cleanliness: ★★★★
Insect Control: ★★★★	Facilities: ★★★★

Located 40 miles east of Niagara Falls and five minutes from Six Flags Darien Lake, Skyline Camping Resort sits atop a ridge in the rolling, forested hills of western New York. Sites are wooded and open. We especially like the privacy and the fragrant aroma around the sites in the Pine Woods area. These shaded sites are situated amid Scotch and Austrian Pine trees. Sites at the northwest side of the pond offer little privacy, but they have a good view of the water and are near activity centers. Campers can fish in the six-acre private pond that teems with largemouth bass. Skyline has a large pavilion for live entertainment, dances, bingo, and movies. Skyline also has an RV sales and service center, so you are in luck if your RV is running rough. In addition to Darien Lake, Six Flags Darien Lake, and Niagara Falls, Buffalo and Rochester are other potential day trip destinations for Skyline campers.

BASICS

Operated By: Tybor family. **Open:** Apr. 28–Oct. 9. **Site Assignment:** By reservation & first come, first served. **Registration:** At campground office. **Fee:** $30–$38; V, MC, D. **Parking:** At site.

FACILITIES

Number of RV-only Sites: 250. **Number of Tent-only Sites:** 25. **Hookups:** Electric (20, 30 amps), water. **Each Site:** Picnic table. **Dump Station:** Yes. **Laundry:** No. **Pay Phone:** Yes. **Restrooms and Showers:** Yes. **Fuel:** No. **Propane:** Yes. **Internal Roads:** Paved & gravel, in good condition. **RV Service:** Yes. **Market:** W/in 3 mi. **Restaurant:** W/in 3 mi. **General Store:** Yes. **Vending:** Yes. **Swimming:** Yes. **Playground:** Yes. **Other:** 6-acre private fishing lake. **Activities:** Fishing, swimming, mini-golf, game room, rec hall, basketball, shuffleboard, planned activities on weekends, tennis, badminton, sports field, horseshoes, volleyball. **Nearby Attractions:** Darien Lake, Six Flags

Darien Lake, Niagara Falls, Rochester, Buffalo. **Additional Information:** New York Division of Tourism, (800) CALL-NYS, www.iloveny.state.ny.us.

RESTRICTIONS

Pets: On leash only. **Fires:** At site. **Alcoholic Beverages:** At site. **Vehicle Maximum Length:** No limit.

TO GET THERE

From Hwy. 77, go 4 mi. east on US 20 and 1 mi. south on Townline Rd. Entrance is on the left.

DAVENPORT   MAP, C-4
Beaver Spring Lake Campground

Hwy. 23, P.O. Box 64, 13750. T: (607) 278-5293 or (866) 377-5293; www.beaverspringlake.com.

🚐 ★★★★   🏕 ★★★★

Beauty: ★★★★	Site Privacy: ★★★
Spaciousness: ★★	Quiet: ★★★★
Security: ★★★★	Cleanliness: ★★★★
Insect Control: ★★★★	Facilities: ★★★★

Located 20 miles southeast of Cooperstown and 15 miles east of Oneonta, Beaver Spring Lake Campground is a tranquil place where campers fish and boat in the 15-acre lake. The campground has 12 pull-throughs among its open and shaded sites. For venturing onto the lake, there are rowboats, pedal boats, and canoes for rent. Beaver Spring Lake also has a game room, a clean and well-equipped pavilion, a swimming pool, and playground, among other facilities. Many campers use Beaver Spring Lake as a base for a visit to Cooperstown—and not just to see the National Baseball Hall of Fame and other baseball attractions. The Fenimore Art Museum houses memorabilia from author James Fenimore Cooper, who wrote *The Last of the Mohicans*.

BASICS

Operated By: Bob & Betty. **Open:** Apr. 15–Oct. 31. **Site Assignment:** By reservation & first come, first served. **Registration:** At campground office. **Fee:** $28–$32; rates for 2 adults & 2 children; V, MC. **Parking:** At site.

FACILITIES

Number of RV-only Sites: 104. **Number of Tent-only Sites:** 20. **Hookups:** Electric (15, 20, 30 amps), water. **Each Site:** Fire ring, picnic table. **Dump Station:** Yes. **Laundry:** Yes. **Pay Phone:** Yes. **Restrooms and Showers:** Yes. **Fuel:** No. **Propane:** Yes. **Internal Roads:** Gravel & dirt, in fair condition. **RV Service:** No. **Market:** W/in 2 mi. **Restaurant:** W/in 2 mi. **General Store:** Yes. **Vending:** Yes. **Swimming:** Yes. **Playground:** Yes. **Other:** Beaver Spring Lake, cabin rentals, pavilion. **Activities:** Fishing, boating, game room, sports field, boat rentals, planned activities on weekends, badminton, horseshoes, volleyball, swimming. **Nearby Attractions:** National Soccer Hall of Fame, Cooperstown Dreams Park, National Baseball Hall of Fame & Museum, Otsego Lake, Farmers Museum & Village Crossroads, Fenimore Art Museum. **Additional Information:** Cooperstown Chamber of Commerce, (607) 547-9983, www.cooperstownchamber.org.

RESTRICTIONS

Pets: On leash only. **Fires:** At site. **Alcoholic Beverages:** At site. **Vehicle Maximum Length:** 40 ft.

TO GET THERE

From Davenport, head east on Hwy. 23. Entrance is on the left.

DEWITTVILLE   MAP, C-1
Chautauqua Heights
Camping Resort

5652 Thumb Rd., 14728. T: (716) 386-3804; www.chautauquahgts.com.

🚐 ★★★★   🏕 ★★★★

Beauty: ★★★★	Site Privacy: ★★★
Spaciousness: ★★★	Quiet: ★★★★
Security: ★★★★★	Cleanliness: ★★★★
Insect Control: ★★★★	Facilities: ★★★★

Chautauqua Heights Camping Resort has 142 open and wooded sites on 150 acres in western New York, near Lake Erie and the Pennsylvania border. With its proximity to Lake Erie and Allegheny State Park, Chautauqua Heights is a haven for outdoor enthusiasts. Each site accommodates a double slide-out, and there are 40 pull-throughs. The campground is a half-mile from Chautauqua Lake and a short drive to the Chautauqua Institution, a 215-acre center for religion, recreation, education, and the arts. The gated institution, designated a National Historic District, began as a Sunday-school-teachers' training camp. About 1,000 people live here year-round, but the population swells to more than 10,000 during the summer. Entertainment and lectures at the amphitheater, performances by the Chautauqua Opera Company at Norton Memorial Hall, and boating and fishing on the lake are among the activities here.

BASICS

Operated By: Bill Perry. **Open:** Apr. 15–Oct. 15. **Site Assignment:** By reservation & first come, first served. **Registration:** At campground office. **Fee:** $21–$35; V, MC, AE, D. **Parking:** At site.

FACILITIES

Number of RV-only Sites: 154. **Number of Tent-only Sites:** 28. **Hookups:** Electric (20, 30, 50 amps), water, phone. **Each Site:** Fire ring, picnic table. **Dump Station:** Yes. **Laundry:** Yes. **Pay Phone:** Yes. **Restrooms and Showers:** Yes. **Fuel:** No. **Propane:** Yes. **Internal Roads:** Gravel, in good condition. **RV Service:** No. **Market:** W/in 1 mi. **Restaurant:** W/in 1 mi. **General Store:** Yes. **Vending:** Yes. **Swimming:** Yes. **Playground:** Yes. **Other:** Cottage & cabin rentals. **Activities:** Swimming, basketball, game room, rec hall, movies, horseshoes, hiking trails, volleyball. **Nearby Attractions:** Chautauqua Institution, *Chautauqua Belle* steamboat, Chautauqua Lake, Midway Park, Allegheny State Park, golf course. **Additional Information:** Chautauqua-Allegheny Region, (800) 242-4569, www.chautauqua-allegheny.org.

RESTRICTIONS

Pets: On leash only. **Fires:** At site. **Alcoholic Beverages:** At site. **Vehicle Maximum Length:** 40 ft. **Other:** Check-in is 4 p.m.; $1 added for early check-in.

TO GET THERE

From Chautauqua, go 0.5 mi. east on Hwy. 430. Entrance is on the left.

DEXTER   MAP, B-3
Black River Bay Campground

P.O. Box 541, 13634-0541. T: (315) 639-3735; www.blackriverbaycamp.com.

🚐 ★★★★   ⛺ ★★★★

Beauty: ★★★★	Site Privacy: ★★
Spaciousness: ★★	Quiet: ★★★★
Security: ★★★★	Cleanliness: ★★★★
Insect Control: ★★★★	Facilities: ★★★★

The raging white water of Black River Canyon. The world-class fishing on Lake Ontario. The natural splendor of the Thousand Islands. Black River Bay Campground is near all of it. Guided whitewater rafting excursions in Black River Canyon start and embark from the campground. Fishing trips on Lake Ontario, which is 1 mile by boat from Black River Bay, lead to dramatic catch stories of muskie, salmon, small and largemouth bass, brown trout and lake trout, and northern pike. We like the campsites located along the Black River, especially sites 16–19, which have a good view of Squaw Island. Alexandria Bay, the resort center of the Thousand Islands, is not far from Black River Bay. Points of interest in the area include the Thousand Islands Skydeck, which offers stunning views of the islands between the spans of the Thousand Islands International Bridge, and Boldt Castle, the 19th-century creation of hotel magnate George C. Boldt.

BASICS

Operated By: Laura Todd. **Open:** May 1–Oct. 15. **Site Assignment:** By reservation & first come, first served. **Registration:** At campground office. **Fee:** Tent, $20; V, MC. **Parking:** At site.

FACILITIES

Number of RV-only Sites: 150. **Number of Tent-only Sites:** 50. **Hookups:** Electric (20, 30 amps), water, sewer, phone; 75 full hookups. **Each Site:** Fire ring, picnic table. **Dump Station:** Yes. **Laundry:** Yes. **Pay Phone:** Yes. **Restrooms and Showers:** Yes. **Fuel:** Yes. **Propane:** Yes. **Internal Roads:** Gravel, in good condition. **RV Service:** No. **Market:** W/in 5 mi. **Restaurant:** W/in 5 mi. **General Store:** Yes. **Vending:** Yes. **Swimming:** No. **Playground:** Yes. **Other:** Boat docks, boat launch, cabin rentals. **Activities:** Boating, canoeing, boat rentals, river fishing, planned activities on weekends, horseshoes, volleyball, game room, rec hall. **Nearby Attractions:** Thousand Islands, Lake Ontario, Black River, St. Lawrence River, Alexandria Bay, American Maple Museum, Long Point State Park. **Additional Information:** Watertown Chamber of Commerce, (315) 788-4400, www.watertownny.com.

RESTRICTIONS

Pets: On leash only. **Fires:** At site. **Alcoholic Beverages:** At site. **Vehicle Maximum Length:** 35 ft. (accommodations made for larger rigs). **Other:** Quiet hours 10 p.m.–7 a.m.

TO GET THERE

From I-81, take Exit 46 and go 6 mi. west on Hwy. 12F and 0.25 mi. on Foster Park Rd. Entrance is on the right.

DOWNSVILLE   MAP, C-4
Bear Spring Mountain

reserve america

East Trout Brook Rd., 13755. T: (607) 865-6989; www.reserveamerica.com.

🚐 ★★★★   ⛺ ★★★★

Beauty: ★★★	Site Privacy: ★★★
Spaciousness: ★★★	Quiet: ★★★★★
Security: ★★★★★	Cleanliness: ★★★★
Insect Control: ★★★	Facilities: ★★

Bear Spring Mountain is located in the western end of the Catskill Forest Preserve offering primitive camping and Launt Pond in all its beauty. The campgrounds beach, boat rental, and multiuse trail system offers fun for all ages. For the horseback-riding enthusiast, Spruce Grove camping and trail system is one-of-a-kind facility in the Catskill region. This region is also known for its excellent hunting and fishing.

BASICS

Operated By: New York State Dept. of Environmental Conservation. **Open:** May 18–Sept. 2. **Site Assignment:** Reservations can be made 9 months in advance. **Registration:** At office. **Fee:** Single, $14. **Parking:** 2 vehicles per site; additional vehicles, extra daily fee & cannot be parked at the site.

FACILITIES

Number of Multipurpose Sites: 41. **Hookups:** None. **Dump Station:** Yes. **Laundry:** No. **Pay Phone:** No. **Restrooms and Showers:** No. **Fuel:** No. **Propane:** No. **Internal Roads:** Paved. **RV Service:** No. **Market:** W/in 10 mi. **Restaurant:** W/in 10 mi. **General Store:** W/in 10 mi. **Vending:** No. **Swimming:** Yes. **Playground:** No. **Activities:** Basketball, biking, bird-watching, boating, canoeing, fishing, hiking, horseback riding, horseshoes, nature study, picnicking, volleyball.

RESTRICTIONS

Pets: Pets are allowed w/ proof of current/valid rabies vaccination. Campers can walk a dog on a leash no longer than 6 feet as long as the dog is under control. Dogs can not be left unattended. Campers are responsible for cleaning up after their pets. **Fires:** Permitted in designated fireplaces. **Alcoholic Beverages:** Persons age 21 or over who possess or consume alcoholic beverages must produce adequate identification & proof of age upon request. **Other:** Possession of fireworks & the operation of chainsaws is strictly forbidden. All boats, including canoes, must be equipped w/ an approved floatation device for each person aboard. Firearms are not allowed in the campground except during the fall or spring hunting season. No motorized boats.

TO GET THERE

Bear Spring Mountain is located in the western Catskills, 5 mi. south of Walton. From the south

---

take Hwy. 17 west to Exit 90 (East Branch), take Hwy. 30 north to Shinhopple, turn left on East Trout Brook Rd.; travel 4–5 mi.; campground on the right. (Launt Pond Loop is 7 mi. from Hwy. 30).

DUANE CENTER   MAP, C-5
Deer River Campsite

CR 14, 12953. T: (518) 483-0060; www.deerrivercampsite.com.

🚐 ★★★★   ⛺ ★★★★

Beauty: ★★★★	Site Privacy: ★★★
Spaciousness: ★★★★	Quiet: ★★★★
Security: ★★★★★	Cleanliness: ★★★★
Insect Control: ★★★★	Facilities: ★★★★★

Located near Malone at the edge of the northern section of Adirondack Park, Deer River Campsite features wooded and spacious sites, some of which accommodate double slideouts and pull-throughs, and some of which are set on the 1.5-mile-wide lake. The campground has clean restrooms and showers, a laundry facility, and a cafe. Campers can fish and swim in the lake. Rowboats, canoes, and pedal boats are available for rent. The 6-million-acre Adirondack Park encompasses New York's largest mountain range, itself ribboned with rippling streams that cut through towering peaks, winding wilderness trails, and unspoiled forests mirrored in shining lakes and ponds. There are 750 miles of marked trails wandering through pine and spruce forests and along the numerous streams and lakes. Whiteface Mountain, Lake Placid, and Saranac Lake are within an hour's drive south of Deer River.

BASICS

Operated By: Janine Paddock. **Open:** May 12–Sept. 24. **Site Assignment:** By reservation & first come, first served. **Registration:** At campground office. **Fee:** $26–$55; V, MC, D. **Parking:** At site.

FACILITIES

Number of RV-only Sites: 78. **Number of Tent-only Sites:** 6. **Hookups:** Electric (30 amps), water, sewer, phone, 12 full hookups. **Each Site:** Fire ring, picnic table. **Dump Station:** Yes. **Laundry:** Yes. **Pay Phone:** Yes. **Restrooms and Showers:** Yes. **Fuel:** No. **Propane:** Yes. **Internal Roads:** Gravel, in good condition. **RV Service:** No. **Market:** W/in 3 mi. **Restaurant:** On premises. **General Store:** Yes. **Vending:** Yes. **Swimming:** Yes. **Playground:** Yes. **Other:** Deer River. **Activities:** Lake swimming & boating, boat rentals, game room, rec hall, lake fishing, basketball, planned activities on weekends, movies, volleyball, hiking trails, horseshoes, sports field, badminton. **Nearby Attractions:** Adirondack Park, Whiteface Mountain, Lake Placid, Saranac Lake, Six Nations Indian Museum, Akwesasne Mohawk Casino, Ausable Chasm, Adirondack Visitors Center, St. Lawrence Seaway Locks, Laura Ingalls Wilder Home. **Additional Information:** New York Division of Tourism—The Adirondacks, (800) 487-6867. www.iloveny.state.ny.us.

RESTRICTIONS

Pets: On leash only. **Fires:** At site. **Alcoholic Beverages:** At site. **Vehicle Maximum Length:** 35 ft. **Other:** Overnight visitors must register by 8 p.m.

TO GET THERE

From Hwy. 30, go 1.5 mi. west on CR 14 (Red Tavern Rd.). Entrance is on the left.

ELMIRA   MAP, C-3
Newtown Battlefield State Park

451 Oneida Rd., 14901. T: (607) 732-6067;
www.reserveamerica.com.

🚐 ★★★★   ⛺ ★★★★

Beauty: ★★★	Site Privacy: ★★★
Spaciousness: ★★★	Quiet: ★★★
Security: ★★★	Cleanliness: ★★★★
Insect Control: ★★★	Facilities: ★

In August of 1779, the peace and tranquility of this forested hill was broken by the boom of cannons, the crack of musket fire, and the yells of Iroquois warriors. The Continental Army was engaged in battle with the British regulars, Loyalist rangers, and 1,000 Iroquois Indian warriors. The battle of Newtown was the decisive clash in one of the largest offensive campaigns of the American Revolution. This expedition, known as the Sullivan-Clinton Campaign, had been regarded as punishment to several tribes among the Six Nations of the Iroquois Confederacy who had sided with the British in the war and had attacked frontier settlements. A stone monument was dedicated at the top of the hill on August 29, 1879, the centennial of the Battle of Newtown. The present granite monument was erected in 1912. During the 1930s, Civilian Conservation Corps crews built and developed many of the present facilities of the park, including a beautiful, rustic lodge. In 1973, Newtown Battlefield Reservation was designated as a historic landmark and placed on the National Register of Historic Places. This historic park offers tent camping as well as cabins.

BASICS

Operated By: New York State Parks. **Open:** May 11–Oct. 7. **Site Assignment:** Reservations can be made 9 months in advance. **Registration:** At office. **Fee:** Single, $13; cabin, $290. **Parking:** Amenity parking.

FACILITIES

Number of Multipurpose Sites: 23. **Hookups:** None. **Dump Station:** Yes. **Laundry:** No. **Pay Phone:** No. **Restrooms and Showers:** No. **Fuel:** No. **Propane:** No. **Internal Roads:** Paved. **RV Service:** No. **Market:** No. **Restaurant:** No. **General Store:** No. **Vending:** No. **Swimming:** No. **Playground:** No.

RESTRICTIONS

Pets: Pets must have current rabies certificate. Pets must be on leash at all times & attended. **Fires:** Permitted in designated fireplaces. **Alcoholic Beverages:** Persons age 21 or over who possess or consume alcoholic beverages must produce adequate identification & proof of age upon request. **Other:** 2 sleeping tents max or 1 camping unit & 1 small tent; 6 people per site. No tents in cabin area. These rules

are strictly enforced. The cabins are rustic & no bedding, cookware, or heat is provided.

TO GET THERE

Call (607) 732-6067 for directions.

ENDICOTT   MAP, C-3
Pine Valley RV Park
and Campground

600 Boswell Hill Rd., 13760. T: (607) 785-6868;
www.pinevalleycampground.com.

🚐 ★★★★   ⛺ ★★★

Beauty: ★★★★	Site Privacy: ★
Spaciousness: ★★	Quiet: ★★★★
Security: ★★★★	Cleanliness: ★★★★
Insect Control: ★★★★	Facilities: ★★★★

Nestled in the rolling hills that overlook Binghamton, Pine Valley RV Park and Campground is located outside of Endicott, which forms the Triple Cities with Binghamton and Johnson City. The open and wooded sites are situated around a six-acre lake in the center of the campground. Sites in sections A and D offer more space than other sections. Privacy is virtually nonexistent here. Sites along the lake are extremely popular. There are 18 golf courses and several shopping malls in the area. Though Pine Valley is located near Endicott, most of the area's attractions are found in Binghamton. Some campers also use Pine Valley as a base for day trips to Cooperstown and Corning.

BASICS

Operated By: Private operator. **Open:** May 1–Oct. 15. **Site Assignment:** Reservations accepted (3-day min. on holiday weekend), walk-ins accepted. **Registration:** At campground office. **Fee:** $22.95–$32.95; V, MC, D. **Parking:** At site.

FACILITIES

Number of RV-only Sites: 102. **Number of Tent-only Sites:** 13. **Hookups:** Electric (20, 30, 50 amps), water, phone. **Each Site:** Fire ring, picnic table. **Dump Station:** Yes. **Laundry:** Yes. **Pay Phone:** Yes. **Restrooms and Showers:** Yes. **Fuel:** No. **Propane:** Yes. **Internal Roads:** Gravel, in fair condition. **RV Service:** No. **Market:** W/in 3 mi. **Restaurant:** W/in 3 mi. **General Store:** Yes. **Vending:** Yes. **Swimming:** Yes. **Playground:** Yes. **Other:** Lodge. **Activities:** Lake swimming & fishing, boat rentals, planned activities on weekends, canoeing, boating, hiking trails, horseshoes, volleyball, sports field. **Nearby Attractions:** Binghamton, Ross Park Zoo, Chenango Valley State Park, Discovery Center of the Southern Tier, Roberson Museum & Science Center, Kopernik Space Education Center, Finch Hollow Nature Center, golf course, bowling. **Additional Information:** Broome County CVB, (800) 836-6740, www.binghamtonevb.com.

RESTRICTIONS

Pets: On leash only. **Fires:** At site. **Alcoholic Beverages:** At site. **Vehicle Maximum Length:** 45 ft. **Other:** Check in/out time is 3 p.m.; early arrivals & late departures are charged $3 per hour.

TO GET THERE

From Hwy. 17, take Exit 67N and go 6 mi. north on Hwy. 26, 1 block northwest on Maple Dr., and 1 mi. west on Boswell Hill Rd. Entrance is on the left. Owners of RVs taller than 12 feet should call for alternative directions.

FAIR HAVEN   MAP, B-3
Fair Haven Beach State Park

Rte. 104A, P.O. Box 16, 13064.
T: (315) 947-5205; www.reserveamerica.com.

🚐 ★★★★   ⛺ ★★★★

Beauty: ★★★	Site Privacy: ★★★
Spaciousness: ★★★	Quiet: ★★★
Security: ★★★	Cleanliness: ★★★★
Insect Control: ★★★	Facilities: ★★★★

Fair Haven Beach State Park has one of the finest public lakefronts in upstate New York, with high bluffs above sandy beaches and hilly woodlands. Inland, there is Sterling Pond, surrounded by campsites and cabins, eight of the latter winterized. Located at Little Sodus Bay along the shores of Lake Ontario—the third-deepest Great Lake at 902 feet and the smallest, spanning a distance of 7,320 square miles—this lovely park offers two separate campgrounds, one along the shores of Sterling Pond and the other on the high bluffs overlooking Lake Ontario. There are 33 cabins tucked into a small area between the two campgrounds. Each campground offers hot showers, flush toilets, and potable water. The park also offers three full-service accommodations that provide guests with a shower, refrigerator, range, microwave, pillows, bedding, cooking utensils, dishes, and coffeemaker. The swimming and fishing are excellent. Rowboats, paddleboats, and canoes are for rent and the park has a boat launch and a recreation building. The recreation building is available for rental.

BASICS

Operated By: New York State Parks. **Open:** All year. **Site Assignment:** Reservations can be made 9 months in advance. **Registration:** At office. **Fee:** Single, $13; cabin, $170–$470; full service, $300–$550. **Parking:** Amenity parking.

FACILITIES

Number of Multipurpose Sites: 221. **Hookups:** None. **Dump Station:** Yes. **Laundry:** No. **Pay Phone:** Yes. **Restrooms and Showers:** Yes. **Fuel:** No. **Propane:** No. **Internal Roads:** Paved. **RV Service:** No. **Market:** W/in 10 mi. **Restaurant:** W/in 10 mi. **General Store:** W/in 10 mi. **Vending:** Yes. **Swimming:** Yes. **Playground:** Yes. **Activities:** Baseball, basketball, biking, bird-watching, boating, canoeing, cross-country skiing, fishing, horseshoes, hunting, jet-skiing, paddle boating, sailboarding, snowmobiling, volleyball, waterskiing.

RESTRICTIONS

Pets: Pet owners must have a current rabies certificate for pets. Pets must be on a 6-ft. leash at all times

& never left unattended. **Fires:** Permitted in designated fireplaces. **Alcoholic Beverages:** Persons age 21 or over who possess or consume alcoholic beverages must produce adequate identification & proof of age upon request. **Other:** No kegs or beer balls; cabins 9 & 12 have no running water Columbus Day–Apr. 15.

TO GET THERE

From the New York State Thruway (I-90) take Exit 40, left on Hwy. 34 north to Hannibal. Turn left at junction to Hwy. 3 South. Go left at junction to Hwy. 104A. Park is on the right side. From Rochester, take Hwy. 104 east to Red Creek, left on Hwy. 104A to Fair Haven. Park is on the left side. From Syracuse, take Hwy. 481 north to Fulton, left at junction to Hwy. 3. Follow Hwy. 3 through Hannibal to Hwy. 104A, left on Hwy. 104A to Fair Haven. Park is on the right side.

FARMINGTON   MAP, C-3
Canandaigua/Rochester KOA

5374 Farmington Town Line Rd., 14425.
T: (800) KOA-0533 or (585) 398-3582;
www.koa.com/where/ny.

🚐 ★★★★   ⛺ ★★★★

Beauty: ★★★	Site Privacy: ★★★
Spaciousness: ★★★	Quiet: ★★★★
Security: ★★★★	Cleanliness: ★★★★
Insect Control: ★★★★	Facilities: ★★★★

The westernmost of the 11 Finger Lakes, Canandaigua Lake is a haven for outdoor recreation, and the Canandaigua/Rochester KOA is an ideal base for it. The campground has open and shaded sites, including 36 pull-throughs. This KOA has a swimming pool, a water park, a fishing pond, pedal boat rentals, and a mini-golf course. Sonnenberg Gardens is a worthy side trip in Canandaigua. The 50-acre Victorian garden estate includes the 1887 mansion, a conservatory, and nine formal gardens. The region is graced with numerous glens and gorges with plunging streams, creating a photographer's paradise. Overall, there are 25 state parks in the Finger Lakes region, and plenty of opportunities for hiking, fishing, and boating, among other diversions. As the name implies, this campground is also near Rochester, about 35 miles southeast.

BASICS

Operated By: KOA. **Open:** Apr. 1–Oct. 31. **Site Assignment:** By reservation & first come, first served. **Registration:** At campground office. **Fee:** RV, $31–$42; tent, $27–$29; V, MC, AE, D. **Parking:** At site.

FACILITIES

Number of RV-only Sites: 90. **Number of Tent-only Sites:** 20. **Hookups:** Electric (20, 30, 50 amps), water, phone. **Each Site:** Picnic tables. **Dump Station:** Yes. **Laundry:** Yes. **Pay Phone:** Yes. **Restrooms and Showers:** Yes. **Fuel:** No. **Propane:** Yes. **Internal Roads:** Gravel, in good condition. **RV Service:** No. **Market:** W/in 4 mi. **Restaurant:** W/in 1 mi. **General Store:** Yes. **Vending:** Yes. **Swimming:** Yes. **Playground:** Yes. **Other:** Cabin rentals, pavilion. **Activities:** Pond fishing, pedal

boat rentals, water park, sports field, mini-golf, game room, rec hall, movies, planned activities on weekends, shuffleboard, horseshoes. **Nearby Attractions:** Canandaigua Lake, Finger Lakes, Finger Lakes Race Track, Sonnenberg Gardens, wineries. **Additional Information:** Finger Lakes Assoc., (800) 548-4386, www.fingerlakes.org.

RESTRICTIONS

Pets: On leash only. **Fires:** At site. **Alcoholic Beverages:** At site. **Vehicle Maximum Length:** 50 ft.

TO GET THERE

From I-90, take Exit 44 and go 4 mi. south on Hwy. 332 and 1 mi. east on Farmington Town Line Rd. Entrance is on the left.

FINEVIEW   MAP, A-3
Wellesley Island State Park

44927 Cross Island Rd., 13640. T: (315) 482-2722; www.reserveamerica.com.

🚐 ★★★★   ⛺ ★★★★

Beauty: ★★★	Site Privacy: ★★
Spaciousness: ★★	Quiet: ★★★★
Security: ★★★★	Cleanliness: ★★★★
Insect Control: ★★★	Facilities: ★★★★

This state park was named in 2005 as one of Reserve America's Top Outdoor Locations, and in 2004 as one of the Top 100 campgrounds in the nation. Wellesley Island State Park has the largest camping complex in the Thousand Islands region. Secluded wilderness sites nestled along the banks of the St. Lawrence River are accessible only by foot or boat. Within this rustic paradise, fishing is excellent—particularly for Muskie in autumn. To accommodate boaters, the park has a full-service marina and four boat launches. A sandy beach on the river offers great swimming and sunbathing, and there is a recreation barn and 9-hole golf course on the island. One of the main attractions of the park is the Minna Anthony Common Nature Center, which includes a museum, varied habitats such as wooded wetlands, 3 miles of shoreline and open granite outcrops, and miles of trails for hiking, cross-country skiing and nature education. The Nature Center provides educational and recreational programs for all ages.

BASICS

Operated By: New York State Parks. **Open:** All year. **Site Assignment:** Reservations can be made 9 months in advance. **Registration:** At office. **Fee:** Single, $13; cabin, $170–$230; full service, $600–$700. **Parking:** Amenity parking.

FACILITIES

Number of Multipurpose Sites: 454. **Hookups:** Yes. **Dump Station:** Yes. **Laundry:** No. **Pay Phone:** Yes. **Restrooms and Showers:** Yes. **Fuel:** No. **Propane:** No. **Internal Roads:** Paved. **RV Service:** No. **Market:** W/in 10 mi. **Restaurant:** W/in 10 mi. **General Store:** W/in 10 mi. **Vending:** Yes. **Swimming:** Yes. **Playground:** Yes. **Activities:** Amphitheater, baseball, biking, bird-watching, boating,

canoeing, cross-country skiing, fishing, golfing, hiking, hunting, interpretive programs, jet skiing, picnicking, powerboating, sailing, volleyball, waterskiing.

RESTRICTIONS

Pets: Pets must have a valid rabies certificate. Pets must also be on a leash no longer than 6 ft. No pets are allowed in the cottages or H area. **Fires:** Permitted in designated fireplaces. **Alcoholic Beverages:** Persons age 21 or over who possess or consume alcoholic beverages must produce adequate identification & proof of age upon request. **Other:** Each site has room for 2 tents or 1 RV. In the F Loop, the primary camping unit must have sewage hookup. Small tents are allowed w/ primary camping unit. C Loop has electric hookups, but no water or sewer hookups. All prime sites are water sites except sites in the F Loop.

TO GET THERE

From I-81 north, cross the TI toll bridge, Exit 51. Follow sign from stop sign to park entrance. From Ontario, Canada, take Hwy. 401 to US Toll Bridge. Take I-81 south to Exit 51. Follow signs from stop sign.

FRANKLINVILLE   MAP, C-2
Triple R Camping Resort and Trailer Sales

3491 Bryant Hill Rd., 14737-9783.
T: (716) 676-3856; www.triplercamp.com.

🚐 ★★★★   ⛺ ★★★★

Beauty: ★★★★	Site Privacy: ★★★
Spaciousness: ★★★	Quiet: ★★★★
Security: ★★★★★	Cleanliness: ★★★★★
Insect Control: ★★★★	Facilities: ★★★★

Situated in the foothills of the Allegheny Mountains in western New York, Triple R Camping Resort is an hour south of Buffalo and Niagara Falls. Two swimming pools, volleyball and basketball courts, a fishing pond, a mini-golf course, and 50 acres of hiking trails through a wooded hillside are among the recreational offerings here. There are also wagon rides and live entertainment on holiday weekends. The open and wooded sites are spacious; there are 14 pull-throughs. Sites 25 through 46 are campers' favorites. RV sites around the pools are very spacious, as are the sites that border the woods near the tenting area, which is nestled amid mature trees and not far from hiking trails. The campground is a short drive from Allegheny State Park, which covers 64,000 acres and is the largest state park in New York. The nearby Seneca-Iroquois National Museum in Salamanca is another interesting attraction. The museum has numerous exhibits on the Seneca Indians, who lived in New York 10,000 years ago.

BASICS

Operated By: Don & Lori Evans. **Open:** Apr. 22–Oct. 10. **Site Assignment:** Reservations recommended (1-night deposit required; reservations required on holiday weekends), walk-ins accepted. **Registration:** At campground office. **Fee:** RV, $80; tent, $30; V, MC, AE, D. **Parking:** At site.

FACILITIES

Number of Multipurpose Sites: 200. **Hookups:** Electric (30, 50 amps), water, sewer, phone, cable TV, 200 full hookups. **Each Site:** Fire ring, picnic table. **Dump Station:** Yes. **Laundry:** Yes. **Pay Phone:** Yes. **Restrooms and Showers:** Yes. **Fuel:** No. **Propane:** Yes. **Internal Roads:** Gravel, in good condition. **RV Service:** Yes. **Market:** W/in 1.5 mi. **Restaurant:** W/in 1.5 mi. **General Store:** Yes. **Vending:** Yes. **Swimming:** Yes. **Playground:** Yes. **Other:** RV rentals, cabin rentals. **Activities:** Game room, sports field, mini-golf, basketball, planned activities on weekends, hiking trails, volleyball, horseshoes, rec hall, fishing, 2 pools. **Nearby Attractions:** Allegheny State Park, Letchworth State Park, Amish country, Freedom Raceway, Seneca-Iroquois National Museum, Ellicottville, antique shopping. **Additional Information:** New York Division of Tourism–Chautauqua-Allegheny, (800) 242-4569, www.iloveny.state.ny.us.

RESTRICTIONS

Pets: On leash only. All dogs must stay inside vehicle or tent at night. **Fires:** At site. **Alcoholic Beverages:** At site. **Vehicle Maximum Length:** No limit.

TO GET THERE

From Hwy. 98, go 1 mi. north on Hwy. 16/98, 1.5 mi. west on Elm St., and 0.3 mi. southwest on Bryant Hill Rd. Entrance is on the left.

FULTONHAM — MAP, C-5
Max V. Shaul State Park

P.O. Box 23 Rte. 30, 12071. T: (518) 827-4711; www.reserveamerica.com.

🚐 ★★★★   ⛺ ★★★★

Beauty: ★★★   Site Privacy: ★★★★
Spaciousness: ★★★★   Quiet: ★★★★★
Security: ★★★★★   Cleanliness: ★★★★
Insect Control: ★★★   Facilities: ★★★

Max V. Shaul State Park is a well-kept secret. Located in the Schoharie Valley at the base of Toe Path Mountain, it is a smaller park, so it is a quiet place to kick back and enjoy shady picnicking, several trails, fishing in the Panther Creek, and watching children play at the playground. The park does allow cross-country skiing in winter. Max V. Shaul State Park is a small, quiet camping area with 30 wooded tent and trailer sites. The park has shady picnic grounds, as well as playing fields, horseshoe pits and a playground. There is a nature and hiking trail, fishing is allowed in Panther Creek and winter visitors can cross-country ski. The park's proximity to Mine Kill State Park opens many more recreational opportunities to campers. Mine Kill State Park overlooks the New York Power Authority's Blenheim-Gilboa Pumped Storage Project's lower reservoir and surrounding hills. The lower reservoir is stocked with rainbow trout, brown trout, bass, walleye, carp, and pan fish, and is ideal for boating, waterskiing, and fishing. Swimming is not allowed in the reservoir, but the park has an Olympic-sized swimming pool, a wading pool, and a diving pool. In winter, visitors enjoy snowshoeing, cross-country skiing, and snowmobiling.

BASICS

Operated By: New York State Parks. **Open:** May 11–Oct. 7. **Site Assignment:** Reservations can be made 9 months in advance. **Registration:** At office. **Fee:** Single, $13. **Parking:** Amenity parking.

FACILITIES

Number of Multipurpose Sites: 30. **Hookups:** None. **Dump Station:** No. **Laundry:** No. **Pay Phone:** Yes. **Restrooms and Showers:** Yes. **Fuel:** No. **Propane:** No. **Internal Roads:** Paved. **RV Service:** No. **Market:** No. **Restaurant:** No. **General Store:** No. **Vending:** No. **Swimming:** No. **Playground:** Yes. **Other:** Permits are required for alcohol use at the park. Permits are required for alcohol use at the park. **Activities:** Baseball, basketball, hiking, picnicking, volleyball.

RESTRICTIONS

Pets: Pets must have proof of current rabies inoculation & be leashed at all times. **Fires:** Permitted in designated fireplaces. **Alcoholic Beverages:** Persons age 21 or over who possess or consume alcoholic beverages must produce adequate identification & proof of age upon request.

TO GET THERE

From New York City, take I-87 north to Kingston. Take Hwy. 28 west to Hwy. 42 north to Hwy. 23 west. Go to Hwy. 30 north to Fultonham. From Albany (and points north), take I-90 to I-88. Exit at Hwy. 30, south to Fultonham. From the east or west, take I-90 west to Fultonville, then take Hwy. 30A south. Hwy. 30A becomes Hwy. 30. Go to Fultonham.

GANSEVOORT — MAP, B-5
Moreau Lake State Park

605 Old Saratoga Rd., 12831. T: (518) 793-0511; www.reserveamerica.com.

🚐 ★★★★   ⛺ ★★★★

Beauty: ★★★   Site Privacy: ★★★
Spaciousness: ★★★   Quiet: ★★★★
Security: ★★★★   Cleanliness: ★★★★
Insect Control: ★★★   Facilities: ★★★★

This campground was named in 2005 as one of Reserve America's Top Outdoor Locations and one of the Top 100 Campgrounds in the nation. Moreau Lake State Park's lake lies amid hardwood forests, pine stands, and rocky ridges. Shady groves of trees shelter picnic grounds and a pavilion overlooking the lake. The sandy beach, nature, hiking and cross-country ski trails, opportunities for boating, fishing, and ice fishing, and proximity to the Saratoga Spring and Lake George areas make the park attractive to visitors. A wooden pavilion with a 120-person capacity and three canvas tents, which can accommodate from 35 to 50 people, may be reserved on a daily basis. In the summer, beach lounges, beach umbrella, and fishing gear can be rented. In the winter, snowshoes are available for rent. Wooded campgrounds are quiet and secluded, offering facilities for group campers as well as 149 tent and trailer sites, but no electric hookups. Car-top boat launching is permitted but no motors are allowed on Moreau Lake. Several fishing docks are available, with one dock located on the day-use side of the park. Campers also enjoy the swimming beach, playground, and shady picnic grove. Flush toilets, hot showers, a scrubbing sink, and potable water are located throughout the campground's five loops. Other amenities include rowboat rental, nature center, hunting grounds, bicycling on park roads, and in winter, cross-country skiing, ice fishing, and snowshoeing.

BASICS

Operated By: New York State Parks. **Open:** May 11–Oct. 7. **Site Assignment:** Reservations can be made 9 months in advance. **Registration:** At office. **Fee:** Single, $13; full service, $325–$530. **Parking:** Amenity parking.

FACILITIES

Number of Multipurpose Sites: 149. **Hookups:** None. **Each Site:** Picnic table, fire ring. **Dump Station:** Yes. **Laundry:** No. **Pay Phone:** Yes. **Restrooms and Showers:** Yes. **Fuel:** No. **Propane:** No. **Internal Roads:** Paved. **RV Service:** No. **Market:** W/in 10 mi. **Restaurant:** W/in 10 mi. **General Store:** W/in 10 mi. **Vending:** Yes. **Swimming:** Yes. **Playground:** Yes. **Other:** Garbage & recyclables must be separated & brought to recycling or refuse center. **Activities:** Boating, canoeing, cross-country skiing, fishing, hiking, horseshoes, hunting, nature center, paddle boating, picnicking, sailboarding, sailing, volleyball.

RESTRICTIONS

Pets: Pets must have proof of a current rabies vaccination & must be on a leash & attended to at all times. **Fires:** Permitted in designated fireplaces. **Alcoholic Beverages:** Persons age 21 or over who possess or consume alcoholic beverages must produce adequate identification & proof of age upon request.

TO GET THERE

From I-87 in NY, take Exit 17S (Adirondack Northway) to Hwy. 9. Travel south on Hwy. 9 0.25 mi. to Old Saratoga Rd. Make a right on Old Saratoga Rd.; park entrance is less than 1 mi. on the right.

GARDINER — MAP, D-5
Yogi Bear's Jellystone Park Camp-Resort at Lazy River

50 Bevier Rd., 12525. T: (845) 255-5193; www.lazyriverny.com.

🚐 ★★★★★   ⛺ ★★★★★

Beauty: ★★★★★   Site Privacy: ★★★
Spaciousness: ★★★   Quiet: ★★★★
Security: ★★★★★   Cleanliness: ★★★★★
Insect Control: ★★★★   Facilities: ★★★★★

Located 90 minutes northwest of New York City in the Mid-Hudson Valley, Yogi Bear's Jellystone Park Camp-Resort at Lazy River has been named one of the top 10 in its chain. The campground has river-front, meadow, and maple-wooded RV sites, 30 of which accommodate pull-throughs. Sites on the river at the east side of the park are away from the noise of the activity centers but have less space than riverfront sites at the center of the park. Most river-front sites are more spacious than the clusters of sites at the center of the campground. Boo Boo's Toddler Playground and the Pirate Ship Play-ground are kid favorites. If you stay on a weekend and savor fresh fruit, you are in luck. On Saturday mornings, a fresh produce wagon travels through-out the campground offering its tempting inven-tory. New York City is a popular day-trip destination for campers. The Franklin D. Roosevelt Home National Historic Site, the Eleanor Roo-sevelt National Historic Site, and the Vanderbilt Mansion National Historic Site—all in the Hyde Park area—are a short drive away. Of course, the highlight for some campers (especially the younger ones) will be the visits from Yogi Bear and Boo Boo.

BASICS

Operated By: John & Heidi Lawrence & Glen & Tammy Bracklow. **Open:** May 2–Oct. 13. **Site Assignment:** Reservations recommended, walk-ins accepted. **Registration:** At campground store. **Fee:** $46–$51; V, MC, D. **Parking:** At site.

FACILITIES

Number of RV-only Sites: 100. **Number of Tent-only Sites:** 9. **Hookups:** Electric (20, 30, 50 amps), water. **Each Site:** Fire ring, picnic table. **Dump Sta-tion:** Yes. **Laundry:** Yes. **Pay Phone:** Yes. **Restrooms and Showers:** Yes. **Fuel:** No. **Propane:** Yes. **Internal Roads:** Gravel, in good con-dition. **RV Service:** Yes, limited. **Market:** W/in 2 mi. **Restaurant:** W/in 3 mi. **General Store:** Yes. **Vend-ing:** Yes. **Swimming:** Yes. **Playground:** Yes. **Other:** Cabin & RV rentals. **Activities:** Volleyball, rec hall, game room, sports field, mini-golf, planned activities, shuffleboard, boating, whitewater rafting, movies, hik-ing trails, river fishing. **Nearby Attractions:** New York City, West Point (U.S. Military Academy), Franklin D. Roosevelt Home National Historic Site, Eleanor Roosevelt National Historic Site, Vanderbilt Mansion National Historic Site, Hudson River tours. **Additional Information:** New York Division of Tourism—Hudson Valley, (800) 762-8687, www.iloveny.state.ny.us.

RESTRICTIONS

Pets: On leash only; only on RV sites, not on tent sites. **Fires:** At site. **Alcoholic Beverages:** At site. **Vehicle Maximum Length:** No limit. **Other:** Fires must be out by 11 p.m.

TO GET THERE

From Hwy. 208, go 2.5 mi. west on Hwy. 44/55, 0.2 mi. south on Albany Post Rd., and 0.5 mi. east on Bevier Rd. Entrance is at the end.

GASPORT   MAP, B-2
Niagara Hartland RV Park and Campground

2383 Hartland Rd., 14067.
T: (716) 795-3812 or (800) 571-4829;
www.niagara-usa.com/accommodations/
canal_camp.html.

🚐 ★★★★   ⛺ ★★★★

Beauty: ★★★★   Site Privacy: ★★★
Spaciousness: ★★★   Quiet: ★★★★
Security: ★★★★   Cleanliness: ★★★★
Insect Control: ★★★★   Facilities: ★★★★

Located in Niagara County near Niagara Falls and Lake Ontario, Niagara Hartland RV Park and Campground offers spacious, grassy sites. There are 75 full hookups and 14 pull-throughs. With the spring-fed lake—where campers can swim, fish, and use rented pedal boats—there is no shortage of out-door recreation. Anglers can also drop their lines in Lake Ontario, which is just 10 miles away. Niagara Falls and its multitude of tours, including the famous Maid of the Mist boat excursion, is about a half-hour drive from Hartland. Devil's Hole State Park offers a good view of the lower falls, and Nia-gara Reservation State Park provides views of the main falls. At Prospect Point, there is a 282-foot-high observation tower. An elevator takes passengers to the gorge below and the Maid of the Mist board-ing point.

BASICS

Operated By: Private operator. **Open:** May 15–Oct. 15. **Site Assignment:** By reservation & first come, first served. **Registration:** At campground office. **Fee:** $23; V, MC, D. **Parking:** At site.

FACILITIES

Number of RV-only Sites: 78. **Number of Tent-only Sites:** 22. **Hookups:** Electric (20, 30, 50 amps), water, phone. **Each Site:** Fire ring, picnic table. **Dump Station:** Yes. **Laundry:** Yes. **Pay Phone:** Yes. **Restrooms and Showers:** Yes. **Fuel:** No. **Propane:** No. **Internal Roads:** Gravel & paved, in good condition. **RV Service:** No. **Market:** W/in 5 mi. **Restaurant:** W/in 4 mi. **General Store:** Yes. **Vending:** Yes. **Swimming:** Yes. **Playground:** Yes. **Other:** Spring-fed lake. **Activities:** Fishing, lake swimming, boating, canoeing, pedal boat rentals, game room, rec hall, planned activities on weekends, bad-minton, sports field, horseshoes, volleyball, basketball. **Nearby Attractions:** Niagara Falls, Lake Ontario, Aquarium of Niagara Falls, Artpark, Devil's Hole State Park, Fort Niagara State Park, Niagara Reserva-tion State Park, Maid of the Mist tours, Prospect Point Observation Tower. **Additional Information:** New York Division of Tourism—Greater Niagara, (800) 338-7890, www.iloveny.state.ny.us.

RESTRICTIONS

Pets: On leash only, under control. **Fires:** At site. **Alcoholic Beverages:** At site. **Vehicle Maximum Length:** No limit.

TO GET THERE

From Hwy. 104, go 3.75 mi. north on Hartland Rd. Entrance is on the right.

GILBOA   MAP, C-5
Country Roads Campground

144 Peaceful Rd., 12076. T: (518) 827-6397;
www.countryroadscampground.com.

🚐 ★★★   ⛺ ★★★

Beauty: ★★★★   Site Privacy: ★★★
Spaciousness: ★★★   Quiet: ★★★★
Security: ★★★★   Cleanliness: ★★★
Insect Control: ★★★★   Facilities: ★★★

Perched on a hilltop in the northern Catskill Mountains—in the skies at an elevation of 2,175 feet—Country Roads Campground is a peaceful campground with an extensive menu of outdoor recreation in the vicinity, including horseback riding, fishing, and hiking. Most of the park features wooded sites, but there are a cluster of open, grassy sites at the southeastern side. Events such as corn roasts, potluck suppers, bingo, and live entertain-ment are hosted in the pavilion. Mine Kill State Park and Mine Kill Falls are a recommended excursion for Country Roads campers. Located on the Hudson River about 50 miles southeast of Gilboar, Catskill is the scene of numerous family-oriented attractions. Choices include the Zoom Flume Waterpark, known as the largest of its kind in the Catskills, and Catskill Game Farm, where children can feed tame deer, antelope, llamas, and other exotic animals.

BASICS

Operated By: Diane & Art Keil. **Open:** May 15–Columbus Day. **Site Assignment:** Reservations recommended, walk-ins accepted. **Registration:** At A-frame house. **Fee:** $25–$28; V, MC, D. **Park-ing:** At site.

FACILITIES

Number of RV-only Sites: 95. **Number of Tent-only Sites:** 25. **Hookups:** Electric (20, 30, 50 amps), water, phone. **Each Site:** Fire ring, picnic table. **Dump Station:** Yes. **Laundry:** Yes. **Pay Phone:** Yes. **Restrooms and Showers:** Yes. **Fuel:** No. **Propane:** Yes. **Internal Roads:** Gravel, in good con-dition. **RV Service:** No. **Market:** W/in 11 mi. **Restaurant:** W/in 3 mi. **General Store:** Yes. **Vend-ing:** Yes. **Swimming:** Yes. **Playground:** Yes. **Activi-ties:** Swimming, whirlpool, game room, rec hall, planned activities on weekends, sports field, bad-minton, horseshoes, volleyball, ping-pong, fishing, hik-ing. **Nearby Attractions:** Catskill Park, Catskill Game Farm, Hunter Mountain, Howe Caverns, Zoom Flume Waterpark, Mine Kill Falls, Carson City Wild West Town, Cooperstown & National Baseball Hall of Fame & Museum. **Additional Information:** Schoharie Chamber of Commerce, (918) 295-7033.

RESTRICTIONS

Pets: On leash only, keep quiet. Rabies vaccination required. **Fires:** At site, confined to fire ring. **Alco-holic Beverages:** At site. **Vehicle Maximum Length:** 40 ft.

TO GET THERE

From intersection of Hwy. 23 and Hwy. 30 (Grande Gorge), go north on Hwy. 30, then 1.75 mi. east on Hwy. 990V. Follow signs 3.25 mi. north. Entrance is on the left.

GLOVERSVILLE   MAP, B-5
Caroga Lake Campground

reserve america™

3043 NY 29A, 12078. T: (518) 835-4241;
www.reserveamerica.com.

🚐 ★★★★   ⛺ ★★★★

Beauty: ★★★   Site Privacy: ★★★
Spaciousness: ★★★   Quiet: ★★
Security: ★★   Cleanliness: ★★★★
Insect Control: ★★★   Facilities: ★★★★

Caroga Lake Campground offers large, level sites to accommodate the smallest tent to the 30-foot RVs. A diversified exercise course with 18 exercise stations wanders through the campground challenging those who enjoy staying physically fit in an outdoor environment. The sandy beach offers a guarded swimming area from mid-June to Labor Day. The campground offers boat, canoe, and kayak rentals to leisurely explore or fish East Caroga Lake. Numerous hiking trails are located nearby. The area offers historic interests from the French and Indian and Revolutionary wars. A par-70, 18-hole municipal golf course is located just minutes north of the campground.

BASICS
Operated By: New York State Parks. **Open:** May 18–Sept. 2. **Site Assignment:** Reservations can be made 9 months in advance. **Registration:** At office. **Fee:** Single, $16. **Parking:** Amenity parking.

FACILITIES
Number of Multipurpose Sites: 161. **Hookups:** None. **Dump Station:** Yes. **Laundry:** No. **Pay Phone:** Yes. **Restrooms and Showers:** Yes. **Fuel:** No. **Propane:** No. **Internal Roads:** Paved. **RV Service:** No. **Market:** W/in 10 mi. **Restaurant:** W/in 10 mi. **General Store:** W/in 10 mi. **Vending:** No. **Swimming:** Yes. **Playground:** No. **Activities:** Boating, fishing, picnicking, waterskiing.

RESTRICTIONS
Pets: Pets are allowed w/ proof of current/valid rabies vaccination. Campers can walk a dog on a leash no longer than 6 feet as long as the dog is under control. Dogs cannot be left unattended. Pets are not allowed in day-use areas, beaches or any structure. **Fires:** Permitted in designated fireplaces. **Alcoholic Beverages:** Persons age 21 or over who possess or consume alcoholic beverages must produce adequate identification & proof of age upon request. **Other:** Quiet hours are 10 p.m.–7 a.m. & are strictly enforced. Campers not listed on the camping permit are not allowed in the facility during these hours. Generators may not be operated during these hours.

TO GET THERE
From the west (Utica/Syracuse): From the New York State Thruway, take Exit 29 in Canajoharie; follow Hwy. 10 north to the intersection of Hwy. 29A. Take a right onto Hwy. 29A going east and the park is about 1 mi. on the right. It is 20 mi. from Thruway exit to the campground.

GRAND ISLAND   MAP, B-1
Niagara Falls KOA

2570 Grand Island Blvd., 14072. T: (800) KOA-0787 or (716) 773-7583; www.koa.com.

🚐 ★★★★   ⛺ ★★★★

Beauty: ★★★★   Site Privacy: ★★
Spaciousness: ★★   Quiet: ★★★
Security: ★★★★   Cleanliness: ★★★★
Insect Control: ★★★★   Facilities: ★★★★

Location is certainly an amenity at Niagara Falls KOA—along with its 462 sites (447 of which are pull-throughs), heated pool, and ponds where campers can fish and pedal boat. Set on Grand Island, this KOA is 7 miles from Niagara Falls and 10 miles from Buffalo. The campground is also next to Fantasy Island, an 80-acre theme park with roller coasters, live shows, a water park, and a Western town. A train at the campground transports passengers to Fantasy Island. There is no shortage of open and shaded sites here. Though Niagara Falls is the main attraction for many campers, a day in nearby Buffalo is worthwhile. New York's second-largest city has several Frank Lloyd Wright houses. The Buffalo and Erie County Botanical Gardens and the Buffalo and Erie County Naval and Military Park are interesting attractions. Maple trees are abundant on the grounds, as well as geese, which attract a lot of attention. Sites are well kept here, but privacy and space are lacking.

BASICS
Operated By: KOA. **Open:** Apr. 1–Oct. 31. **Site Assignment:** By reservation & first come, first served. **Registration:** At campground headquarters. **Fee:** $20–$39; V, MC, D. **Parking:** At site.

FACILITIES
Number of RV-only Sites: 362. **Number of Tent-only Sites:** 100. **Hookups:** Electric (20, 30, 50 amps), water, phone. **Each Site:** Fire ring, picnic table. **Dump Station:** Yes. **Laundry:** Yes. **Pay Phone:** Yes. **Restrooms and Showers:** Yes. **Fuel:** No. **Propane:** Yes. **Internal Roads:** Gravel, in good condition. **RV Service:** No. **Market:** W/in 3 mi. **Restaurant:** W/in 2 mi. **General Store:** Yes. **Vending:** Yes. **Swimming:** Yes. **Playground:** Yes. **Other:** Niagara Falls tours embark from campground. **Activities:** Pond fishing, game room, rec hall, basketball, movies, planned activities, bike rentals, badminton, horseshoes, volleyball. **Nearby Attractions:** Niagara Falls, Buffalo, Fort Niagara State Park, Fantasy Island, Buffalo & Erie County Naval & Military Park, Buffalo Zoological Gardens, Niagara River & Lake Erie boat cruises. **Additional Information:** Niagara Falls CVB, (800) 421-5223, www.nfcvb.com.

RESTRICTIONS
Pets: On leash only, under control. **Fires:** At site. **Alcoholic Beverages:** At site. **Vehicle Maximum Length:** No limit.

TO GET THERE
From I-190, take Exit N19 and go 0.5 mi. east on Whitehaven Rd. and 0.75 mi. north on Hwy. 324. Entrance is on the left.

GREENFIELD PARK   MAP, D-5
Skyway Camping Resort

P.O. Box 194, 12435. T: (845) 647-5747 or (800) 447-5992; www.skywaycamping.com.

🚐 ★★★★★   ⛺ ★★★★★

Beauty: ★★★★★   Site Privacy: ★★★
Spaciousness: ★★★   Quiet: ★★★★
Security: ★★★★★   Cleanliness: ★★★★★
Insect Control: ★★★★★   Facilities: ★★★★★

The Catskill Mountains are just two hours north of New York City, but it seems like a world away. That is the feeling you get at Skyway Camping Resort, 6 miles west of Ellenville near the southeastern edge of Catskill Park. RVers and tenters will feel like they are staying at a resort hotel. The immaculate three-story clubhouse, a well-equipped workout room, an Olympic-sized solar-heated pool and whirlpool, a pond for fishing and boating, and tennis and handball courts are among the amenities at this campground—one of the best in the Catskills. Luxury trailers with full baths rent for $125 a night. Located north and west of the Hudson Valley, the Catskills are bordered by the Hudson and Delaware rivers. Skyway is not far from Minnewaska State Park, which has numerous trails for hiking, biking, cross-country skiing, and snowshoeing. The Fort Delaware Museum of Colonial History in nearby Narrowsburg is open during summer months.

BASICS
Operated By: The London Family. **Open:** May 5–Columbus Day. **Site Assignment:** By reservation & first come, first served. **Registration:** At campground office. **Fee:** $54–$60; V, MC, AE, D. **Parking:** At site.

FACILITIES
Number of RV-only Sites: 145. **Number of Tent-only Sites:** 45. **Hookups:** Electric (20, 30 amps), water, phone, cable TV. **Each Site:** Fire ring, picnic table. **Dump Station:** Yes. **Laundry:** Yes. **Pay Phone:** Yes. **Restrooms and Showers:** Yes. **Fuel:** No. **Propane:** Yes. **Internal Roads:** Gravel & paved, in good condition. **RV Service:** No. **Market:** W/in 5 mi. **Restaurant:** W/in 5 mi. **General Store:** Yes. **Vending:** Yes. **Swimming:** Yes. **Playground:** Yes. **Other:** 3-story clubhouse, professional exercise room. **Activities:** Swimming, whirlpool, tennis, handball, boating, boat rentals, lake fishing, basketball, sports field, badminton, planned activities, hiking trails, volleyball, horseshoes. **Nearby Attractions:** Catskill Park, Lake Superior State Park, Delaware & Hudson Canal Linear Park, Minisink Battleground Park, Stone Arch Bridge Historical Park, Fort Delaware Museum of Colonial History. **Additional Information:** New York Division of Tourism—The Catskills, (800) NYS-CATS, www.iloveny.state.ny.us.

RESTRICTIONS
Pets: On leash only. **Fires:** At site. **Alcoholic Beverages:** At site. **Vehicle Maximum Length:** No limit.

TO GET THERE
From US 209, go 5 mi. west on Hwy. 52 and 1 mi. south on Skyway RV Rd. Entrance is on the left.

HAGUE   MAP, B-5
Rogers Rock Campground

reserve america

Rte. 9N, 9894 Lakeshore Dr., 12836.
T: (518) 585-6746; www.reserveamerica.com.

🚐 ★★★★   ⛺ ★★★★

Beauty: ★★★	Site Privacy: ★★
Spaciousness: ★★	Quiet: ★★★★★
Security: ★★★★★	Cleanliness: ★★★★
Insect Control: ★★★	Facilities: ★★★★

Rogers Rock Campground is located along the northwestern shore of Lake George on Cooks Bay. Lake George is 32 miles long and covers an area of 28,200 acres with a maximum depth of 190 feet. The lake is 3 miles across at the widest point. This popular destination campground offers many tent and RV sites and 10 island sites accessible only by boat. The main campground offers a dump station and trailer sites accommodating RVs up to 40 feet. The restroom amenities include flush toilets, scrubbing sinks, and hot showers. Potable water is throughout the campground except at the island sites. A public telephone is near the ranger's station. Rogers Rock also has group camping facilities. There are two areas known as Association Area and Ballfield. Each allows between 35 and 60 campers. Day-use facilities include a swimming beach, bathhouse, horseshoe pit, sand volleyball court, and a boat launch that includes 30 mooring slots. Lake George is renowned for its population of large and smallmouth bass, landlocked salmon, lake trout, rainbow trout, and northern pike.

BASICS
Operated By: New York State Parks. **Open:** May 4–Oct. 7. **Site Assignment:** Reservations can be made 9 months in advance. **Registration:** At office. **Fee:** Single, $18. **Parking:** Amenity parking.

FACILITIES
Number of Multipurpose Sites: 362. **Hookups:** None. **Dump Station:** Yes. **Laundry:** No. **Pay Phone:** Yes. **Restrooms and Showers:** Yes. **Fuel:** No. **Propane:** No. **Internal Roads:** Paved. **RV Service:** No. **Market:** W/in 10 mi. **Restaurant:** W/in 10 mi. **General Store:** W/in 10 mi. **Vending:** No. **Swimming:** Yes. **Playground:** No. **Activities:** Biking, bird-watching, boating, canoeing, fishing, jet skiing, picnicking, powerboating, sailboarding, sailing, tubing, volleyball, waterskiing.

RESTRICTIONS
Pets: Pets are allowed w/ proof of current/valid rabies vaccination. Dogs must be on a leash no longer than 6 ft. & under control. Dogs cannot be left unattended. Pets are not allowed in day-use areas, beaches, or any structures. **Fires:** Permitted in designated fireplaces. **Alcoholic Beverages:** Persons age 21 or over who possess or consume alcoholic beverages must produce adequate identification & proof of age upon request.

TO GET THERE
From I-87 Exit 25 take Hwy. 8 to Hague. Turn left (north) onto Hwy. 9N. Campground is 3 mi. on right. From I-87 Exit 24 take CR 11 to Hwy.

9N; turn left (north) to Hwy. 9N to Village of Hague. Campground is on the right 3 mi. north of Hague. From Lake George Village take Hwy. 9N north to Hague; continue 3 mi. Campground is on the right.

HAMLIN   MAP, B-2
Hamlin Beach State Park

reserve america

1 Camp Rd., 14464. T: (585) 964-2121; www.reserveamerica.com.

🚐 ★★★★   ⛺ ★★★★

Beauty: ★★★	Site Privacy: ★★★
Spaciousness: ★★★	Quiet: ★★★
Security: ★★★	Cleanliness: ★★★★
Insect Control: ★★★	Facilities: ★★★★

Located about 25 miles west of Rochester, Hamlin Beach State Park offers wonderful views of the expansive Lake Ontario while offering day-use and overnight facilities. The most prominent feature of the park is the bluff area at the west end known as Devil's Nose. Because of dangerous conditions, it is a restricted area, but it remains a landmark for sailors as they pass to the north. Picnicking, camping, fishing, hiking, or biking on over 10 miles of trails and visiting the environmental education center are several other pastimes. Hamlin Beach State Park's clear water, sandy beaches, and 264 tent and trailer campsites bring thousands of visitors to the park each year. The environmental education center in the Yanty Creek Marsh area at the east end of the park has a mile-long self-guided nature trail. In addition, there are 10 miles of hiking and biking trails, as well as snowmobile and cross-country skiing trails. Visitors can launch car-top boats, fish for salmon and trout, and enjoy the picnic facilities.

BASICS
Operated By: New York State Parks. **Open:** May 17–Oct. 8. **Site Assignment:** Reservations can be made 9 months in advance. **Registration:** At office. **Fee:** Single, $13. **Parking:** Amenity parking.

FACILITIES
Number of Multipurpose Sites: 264. **Hookups:** None. **Dump Station:** Yes. **Laundry:** Yes. **Pay Phone:** Yes. **Restrooms and Showers:** Yes. **Fuel:** No. **Propane:** No. **Internal Roads:** Paved. **RV Service:** No. **Market:** W/in 10 mi. **Restaurant:** W/in 10 mi. **General Store:** W/in 10 mi. **Vending:** No. **Swimming:** Yes. **Playground:** Yes. **Other:** Extra charge for additional vehicles & visitors. **Activities:** Baseball, biking, bird-watching, cross-country skiing, fishing, hiking, parasailing, picnicking snowmobiling, tennis.

RESTRICTIONS
Pets: No pets allowed on sites 74–264; pets allowed on sites 1–73. All pets must have a valid rabies certificate & be leashed at all times. **Fires:** Permitted in designated fireplaces. **Alcoholic Beverages:** Persons age 21 or over who possess or consume alcoholic beverages must produce adequate identification & proof of age upon request.

TO GET THERE
Hamlin State Park is located off the New York State Thruway (I-90). From the New York State Thruway, take Exit 47 to Hwy. 19 north to Lake Ontario Pkwy. Go west 2 mi. to park entrance. From Hwy. 490, take Hwy. 390 north to Lake Ontario Pkwy. West. It is 15 mi. to the entrance of Hamlin Beach State Park. Note: 11'3" height restriction on the Pkwy. from Hwy. 390 to Hamlin Beach State Park.

HERKIMER   MAP, B-4
Herkimer Diamond KOA

4626 Hwy. 28 N., 13350.
T: (315) 891-7355 or (800) 562-0897; www.herkimerdiamond.com.

🚐 ★★★★   ⛺ ★★★★

Beauty: ★★★★	Site Privacy: ★★
Spaciousness: ★★	Quiet: ★★★★
Security: ★★★★	Cleanliness: ★★★★
Insect Control: ★★★★	Facilities: ★★★★

Located about 20 miles from the southwest tip of Adirondack Park in Herkimer, Herkimer Diamond KOA is well maintained and offers a lot to do without leaving the area. There is a choice of level open or wooded sites, including 18 pull-throughs. The campground is located on West Canada Creek, where campers can fish and swim. There is also a disc golf area, a mini-golf course, and hiking trails, among other activities. Diamond prospecting is the name of the game at the Herkimer Diamond Mines, which claims it is the only place in the world where you can prospect for diamonds like this. Hammers are provided, but power tools are not permitted, so you have to find your gem through old-fashioned elbow grease. You can also learn about diamonds and minerals at the geological museum or dine at the Crystal Chandelier Restaurant. This KOA can be used as a base for ventures to Adirondack Park, Cooperstown, and Utica.

BASICS
Operated By: KOA. **Open:** Apr. 15–Oct. 31. **Site Assignment:** Reservations recommended (1-night deposit required), walk-ins accepted. **Registration:** At campground office. **Fee:** $23–$39; V, MC, AE, D. **Parking:** At site.

FACILITIES
Number of RV-only Sites: 107. **Number of Tent-only Sites:** 22. **Hookups:** Electric (20, 30, 50 amps), water, cable TV, phone. **Each Site:** Fire ring, picnic table. **Dump Station:** Yes. **Laundry:** Yes. **Pay Phone:** Yes. **Restrooms and Showers:** Yes. **Fuel:** No. **Propane:** Yes. **Internal Roads:** Partially paved, in good condition. **RV Service:** No. **Market:** W/in 7 mi. **Restaurant:** Yes. **General Store:** Yes. **Vending:** Yes. **Swimming:** Yes. **Playground:** Yes. **Other:** Interactive museum, rock & gem gift shop, 16 cabins, 5 cottages. **Activities:** Diamond prospecting, game room, rec hall, sports field, trout fishing, movies, disc golf, mini-golf, horseshoes, hiking trails, volleyball, planned activities on weekends, river swimming. **Nearby Attractions:** Herkimer Diamond Mines, Herkimer Home State Historic Site, Adirondack Park, Utica, National Baseball Hall of Fame &

Museum, Cooperstown, Remington Gun Museum.
Additional Information: Herkimer County Chamber of Commerce, (315) 866-7820, www.herkimer countyinfo.com.

RESTRICTIONS

Pets: On leash only, not in cabins. **Fires:** At site.
Alcoholic Beverages: At site. **Vehicle Maximum Length:** No limit.

TO GET THERE

From Hwy. 5, go 7 mi. north on Hwy. 28. Entrance is on the right.

HINCKLEY   MAP, B-4
Trail's End Campground

438 MacArthur Rd., 13324. T: (315) 826-7220;
www.trailend.com.

🚐 ★★★★   ⛺ ★★★★

Beauty: ★★★★	Site Privacy: ★★★
Spaciousness: ★★	Quiet: ★★★★
Security: ★★★★★	Cleanliness: ★★★★
Insect Control: ★★★★	Facilities: ★★★★

Located in the Adirondack foothills near Old Forge, Trail's End Campground is situated on 7-mile-long Hinckley Lake. This well-kept campground has a beach, a boat launch, and a fishing pond, among other features. Sites alongside the pond and the lake are especially pleasant, and some are shaded by cherry, pine, poplar, oak, and maple trees. Trail's End has just three pull-throughs. Hinckley Lake is the center of attention here; the campground's beach is for campers only Monday–Friday, but it is open to the public on Saturday and Sunday. Trail's End rents boats and ATVs. Raquette Lake and Blue Mountain Lake—both with a variety of hiking, fishing, and boating opportunities—are a short drive away from the campground. Water Safari, in nearby Old Forge, has several slides and pools. The Old Forge Hardware Store offers an entire city block of housewares, books, handmade furniture, and, of course, hardware.

BASICS

Operated By: Private operator. **Open:** May 1–Oct. 15. **Site Assignment:** Reservations recommended. **Registration:** At campground office. **Fee:** $22–$32; V, MC, D. **Parking:** At site.

FACILITIES

Number of RV-only Sites: 78. **Number of Tent-only Sites:** 11. **Hookups:** Electric (15, 20, 30 amps), water. **Each Site:** Fire ring, picnic table. **Dump Station:** Yes. **Laundry:** Yes. **Pay Phone:** Yes. **Restrooms and Showers:** Yes. **Fuel:** No. **Propane:** Yes. **Internal Roads:** Dirt, in good condition. **RV Service:** No. **Market:** W/in 10 mi. **Restaurant:** W/in 3 mi. **General Store:** Yes. **Vending:** Yes. **Swimming:** Yes. **Playground:** Yes. **Other:** Hinckley Lake. **Activities:** Fishing, boating, boat rentals, hiking trails, planned activities on weekends, canoeing, lake swimming, shuffleboard, sports field, horseshoes, volleyball. **Nearby Attractions:** Adirondack Park, Utica Zoo, Adirondack Scenic Railroad, Blue Mountain Lake, Water Safari Water Park, Old Forge. **Additional Information:** New York

Division of Tourism–Adirondacks, (800) 487-6867, www.iloveny.state.ny.us.

RESTRICTIONS

Pets: On leash only; no aggressive breeds. No more than 2 pets per campsite. **Fires:** At site, confined to fire pit. **Alcoholic Beverages:** At site. **Vehicle Maximum Length:** No limit.

TO GET THERE

From Hwy. 12, go 4 mi. east on Hwy. 365 and 3 mi. southeast on CR 151. Follow signs. Entrance is at the end.

HOUGHTON   MAP, C-2
Camping at Mariposa Ponds

7632 Centerville Rd., 14744. T: (585) 567-4211;
www.mariposaponds.com.

🚐 ★★★★.   ⛺ ★★★★

Beauty: ★★★★	Site Privacy: ★★★
Spaciousness: ★★★	Quiet: ★★★★
Security: ★★★★	Cleanliness: ★★★★
Insect Control: ★★★★	Facilities: ★★★★

Butterflies and songbirds share forests of hickory, maple, oak, and beech at Camping at Mariposa Ponds in Houghton, a town about midway between Letchworth State Park and Allegheny State Park in western New York. "Mariposa," the owners tell us, is Spanish for butterfly, and this campground is a haven for these colorful and beautiful creatures. Five butterfly gardens at Mariposa Ponds host plants like butterfly weed, butterfly bush, coreopsis, and purple coneflowers, attracting monarchs, white admirals, fritillaries, and hummingbirds. Hiking trails at the campground meander through lush stands of pines and hardwoods. Largemouth bass, perch, and sunfish are among the residents in the fishing pond. Sites here are open and wooded. The lodge has an indoor swimming pool, a game room, and a landscaped patio. Nearby Moss Lake Nature Sanctuary, operated by the Nature Conservancy, is a bog where fish, turtles, birds, and other wildlife live amid rare carnivorous plants.

BASICS

Operated By: Dave & Trudi Schwert. **Open:** May 1–Oct. 15. **Site Assignment:** Reservations accepted (stay 6 nights, 7th night free), walk-ins accepted. **Registration:** At campground office. **Fee:** $24–$26; V, MC, D. **Parking:** At site.

FACILITIES

Number of RV-only Sites: 73. **Number of Tent-only Sites:** 2. **Hookups:** Electric (30, 50 amps). **Each Site:** Fire ring, picnic table. **Dump Station:** Yes. **Laundry:** No. **Pay Phone:** Yes. **Restrooms and Showers:** Yes. **Fuel:** No. **Propane:** Yes. **Internal Roads:** Gravel, in good condition. **RV Service:** No. **Market:** W/in 4 mi. **Restaurant:** W/in 3 mi. **General Store:** Yes. **Vending:** No. **Swimming:** Yes. **Playground:** Yes. **Other:** Lodge, cabin rentals. **Activities:** Indoor swimming, game room, rec hall, pond fishing, basketball, planned activities on weekends, horseshoes, sports field, hiking trails, volleyball. **Nearby Attractions:** Letchworth State Park, Alle-

gany State Park, Moss Lake Nature Sanctuary, Genesee River, Seneca-Iroquois National Museum. **Additional Information:** New York Division of Tourism–Chautauqua-Allegheny, (800) 242-4569, www.iloveny.state.ny.us.

RESTRICTIONS

Pets: On leash only. No pets in rental cabins. **Fires:** At site. **Alcoholic Beverages:** At site. **Vehicle Maximum Length:** 38 ft.

TO GET THERE

From Hwy. 243, go 3 mi. north on Hwy. 19, 0.25 mi. west on Houghton College Rd., and 1.5 mi. west on Centerville Rd. Entrance is on the right.

IRVING   MAP, C-1
Evangola State Park

reserve america™

Shaw Rd., 14081. T: (716) 549-1802;
www.reserveamerica.com.

🚐 ★★★★   ⛺ ★★★★

Beauty: ★★★	Site Privacy: ★★★
Spaciousness: ★★★	Quiet: ★★★
Security: ★★★	Cleanliness: ★★★★
Insect Control: ★★★	Facilities: ★★★★

Evangola State Park is a 733-acre park opened in 1954. Formerly farmland, the land was used to grow tomatoes, beans, and corn. Evangola's major attraction is its beautiful arc-shaped shoreline and natural sand beach on Lake Erie. Low cliffs of Angola shale line the edge of the beach. In addition to swimming, the park has picnic facilities, baseball and soccer fields, tennis and basketball courts, and 80 campsites. The park has a variety of habitats including lakeshore, woodland, meadow, and wetlands. Wildlife in the park includes white-tailed deer, raccoons, turkey, and red-tailed hawks. Over 100,000 people visit this park each year.

BASICS

Operated By: New York State Parks. **Open:** Apr. 20–Oct. 21. **Site Assignment:** Reservations can be made 9 months in advance. **Registration:** At office. **Fee:** Single, $13; cabin, $270. **Parking:** At park.

FACILITIES

Number of Multipurpose Sites: 80. **Hookups:** Yes. **Dump Station:** Yes. **Laundry:** Yes. **Pay Phone:** No. **Restrooms and Showers:** Yes. **Fuel:** No. **Propane:** No. **Internal Roads:** Gravel. **RV Service:** No. **Market:** No. **Restaurant:** No. **General Store:** Yes. **Vending:** Yes. **Swimming:** Yes. **Playground:** Yes. **Activities:** Baseball, basketball, bird-watching, disc golf, casino, hiking, picnicking, recreation programs, tennis court, volleyball.

RESTRICTIONS

Pets: Pets must have proof of current rabies vaccination. Pets must be kept on 6-ft. leash & never left unattended. **Fires:** Permitted in designated fireplaces. **Alcoholic Beverages:** Persons age 21 or over who possess or consume alcoholic beverages must produce adequate identification & proof of age upon request. **Other:** Quiet hours are 10 p.m.–8 a.m. Management reserves the right to require visitors to park in the park when the campground lots are full. Your auto &/or camping unit must be parked on a gravel driveway or lot where provided. An extension cord may be needed to reach power source.

TO GET THERE

Take the New York State Thruway (I-90) to Silvercreek Exit 58. Take a right on Hwy. 5/20. At a fork in the road, stay to your left on Hwy. 5. It will be 3 mi. to park entrance.

ITHACA   MAP, C-3
Buttermilk Falls State Park

reserve america

105 Enfield Falls Rd., 14850. T: (607) 273-5761; www.reserveamerica.com.

🚐 ★★★★   ⛺ ★★★★

Beauty: ★★★★   Site Privacy: ★★★★★
Spaciousness: ★★★★★   Quiet: ★★★
Security: ★★★   Cleanliness: ★★★★
Insect Control: ★★★   Facilities: ★★★★

Buttermilk Falls State Park takes its name from the foaming cascade formed by Buttermilk Creek as it flows down the steep valley side toward Cayuga Lake. The upper park has a small lake, hiking trails through woodlands and along the gorge and rim, picnic areas, and playing fields. The lower park has a campground, pool, and playing fields, beyond which is Larch Meadows. Larch Meadows is a moist, shady glen and wetland area through which a nature trail winds. Park activities including tours through Buttermilk gorge are offered weekly from the Fourth of July through Labor Day.

BASICS

Operated By: New York State Parks. **Open:** May 11–Oct. 7. **Site Assignment:** Reservations can be made 9 months in advance. **Registration:** At office. **Fee:** Single, $13; cabin, $170. **Parking:** Amenity parking.

FACILITIES

Number of Multipurpose Sites: 53. **Hookups:** None. **Dump Station:** Yes. **Laundry:** No. **Pay Phone:** No. **Restrooms and Showers:** Yes. **Fuel:** No. **Propane:** No. **Internal Roads:** Paved. **RV Service:** No. **Market:** No. **Restaurant:** No. **General Store:** No. **Vending:** No. **Swimming:** Yes. **Playground:** Yes. **Activities:** Bird-watching, fishing, hiking, hunting, interpretive programs, picnicking, sightseeing.

RESTRICTIONS

Pets: Pets must have current rabies certificate. Pets must be on leash & not left unattended. Pets are NOT permitted in the swimming area. **Fires:** Permitted in designated fireplaces. **Alcoholic Beverages:** Persons age 21 or over who possess or consume alcoholic beverages must produce adequate identification & proof of age upon request. **Other:** 2 sleeping tents max or 1 camping unit & 1 small tent, 6 people per site. No tents in cabin area. These rules

are strictly enforced. The cabins are rustic & no bedding, cookware, or heat is provided.

TO GET THERE

Take Hwy. 13 South at city limits. Visit Web site for further directions.

ITHACA   MAP, C-3
Robert H. Treman State Park

reserve america

105 Enfield Falls Rd., 14850. T: (607) 273-3440; www.reserveamerica.com.

🚐 ★★★★   ⛺ ★★★★

Beauty: ★★★★   Site Privacy: ★★
Spaciousness: ★★   Quiet: ★★★
Security: ★★★   Cleanliness: ★★★★
Insect Control: ★★★   Facilities: ★★★

Robert H. Treman State Park features a number of fabulous waterfalls, including the plunging 115-foot Lucifer Falls. The deep, cool, moist gorges of this park are sided by towering rock cliffs. A trail system winds past a dozen falls close enough for refreshing sprays on hot summer days. There is even an opportunity to swim at the basin pool. Robert H. Treman State Park's most treasured attraction is the Enfield Glen, which is a 3-mile gorge of sheer cliff walls with magnificent square corners. Several hiking trails give the visitor an up-close experience with the falls. Swimming is permitted in the fallen pool and is guarded. Bow-hunting for white-tailed deer is permitted in season. The Robert H. Treman Campground is a beautiful area located along the deep cool gorges of Enfield Creek. Flush toilets, scrubbing sink, hot showers, and potable water are convenient for most campers. A picnic and playground area are within the campgrounds.

BASICS

Operated By: New York State Parks. **Open:** Apr. 27–Nov. 24. **Site Assignment:** Reservations can be made 9 months in advance. **Registration:** At office. **Fee:** Single, $13; cabin, $170–$315. **Parking:** Amenity parking.

FACILITIES

Number of Multipurpose Sites: 86. **Hookups:** None. **Dump Station:** No. **Laundry:** No. **Pay Phone:** No. **Restrooms and Showers:** Yes. **Fuel:** No. **Propane:** No. **Internal Roads:** Paved. **RV Service:** No. **Market:** No. **Restaurant:** No. **General Store:** No. **Vending:** No. **Swimming:** Yes. **Playground:** Yes. **Activities:** Bird-watching, fishing, hiking, hunting, picnicking.

RESTRICTIONS

Pets: Pets must have current rabies certificate. Pets must be on a 6-ft. leash & attended at all times. Pets are NOT permitted in the swimming area. **Fires:** Permitted in designated fireplaces. **Alcoholic Beverages:** Persons age 21 or over who possess or consume alcoholic beverages must produce adequate identification & proof of age upon request. **Other:** Cabins are rustic, w/ no bedding, cookware, or heat. No tents in the cabin area are allowed.

TO GET THERE

On Hwy. 13, go 3 mi. south of Ithaca. Turn on to Hwy. 327. The park entrance is about 500 feet away.

ITHACA   MAP, C-3
Spruce Row Campsite and RV Resort

reserve america

2271 Kraft Rd., 14850. T: (607) 387-9225; www.sprucerow.com.

🚐 ★★★★   ⛺ ★★★★

Beauty: ★★★★   Site Privacy: ★
Spaciousness: ★★   Quiet: ★★★
Security: ★★★★   Cleanliness: ★★★★
Insect Control: ★★★★   Facilities: ★★★★

Perched on a hill above the southern end of Cayuga Lake just north of downtown Ithaca, Spruce Row has an even amount of open and secluded sites, four of which handle pull-throughs. Sites along Willow Creek and in the walnut grove are particularly inviting, with seductive apple and maple trees. Though it looks unusual, the swimming pool is roomy and refreshing. Nature walks, hayrides, live entertainment, and the fall pig roast are among the activities hosted at Spruce Row. Cayuga Lake has an abundance of hiking and water sports opportunities. Four state parks—Robert H. Treman, Allan H. Treman, Buttermilk Falls, and Taughannock Falls—are located in the area. Several wineries are situated along the Cayuga Wine Trail, including Six Mile Creek Vineyard in Ithaca. The campuses of Cornell University and Ithaca College overlook Cayuga Lake and are open for tours.

BASICS

Operated By: Harry Weber. **Open:** May 1–Columbus Day. **Site Assignment:** Reservations recommended (1-night deposit required), walk-ins accepted. **Registration:** At campground office. **Fee:** $26–$31; V, MC, D. **Parking:** At site.

FACILITIES

Number of RV-only Sites: 100. **Number of Tent-only Sites:** 18. **Hookups:** Electric (20, 30 amps), water, phone. **Each Site:** Fire ring, picnic table. **Dump Station:** Yes. **Laundry:** No. **Pay Phone:** Yes. **Restrooms and Showers:** Yes. **Fuel:** No. **Propane:** Yes. **Internal Roads:** Gravel & paved, in good condition. **RV Service:** No. **Market:** W/in 2 mi. **Restaurant:** W/in 2 mi. **General Store:** Yes. **Vending:** Yes. **Swimming:** Yes. **Playground:** Yes. **Other:** Cabin & RV rentals. **Activities:** Game room, sports field, boating, boat rentals, pond fishing, planned activities on weekends, mini-golf, bike rentals, basketball, badminton, horseshoes, shuffleboard, hiking trails, volleyball. **Nearby Attractions:** Watkins Glen, Cornell University, Ithaca College, Buttermilk Falls, Taughannock Falls, Cayuga Wine Trail, Sciencenter, Cayuga Lake. **Additional Information:** Ithaca/Tompkins County CVB, (800) 284-8422, www.ithaca.ny.us/commerce.

RESTRICTIONS

Pets: On leash only. Keep dogs in designated dog-walk areas. **Fires:** At site. **Alcoholic Beverages:**

At site. **Vehicle Maximum Length:** No limit.

To Get There

From Hwy. 13, go 7 mi. northwest on Hwy. 96, 0.5 mi. north on Jacksonville Rd., and 1.25 mi. east on Kraft Rd. Entrance is on the right.

KEESEVILLE   MAP, A-5
Ausable River Campsite

P.O. Box 276, 12944. T: (518) 834-9379; www.ausablerivercampsite.com.

🚐 ★★★   ▲ ★★★★

Beauty: ★★★★	Site Privacy: ★★★
Spaciousness: ★★★	Quiet: ★★★
Security: ★★★★	Cleanliness: ★★★★
Insect Control: ★★★★	Facilities: ★★★

The Ausable River Campsite is located on 130 acres along the Ausable River within the Adirondack Park. Most of the 102 sites are open, and there are 12 pull-throughs. Some sites are situated along the river, and campers can even cast their line from their site. The section of tent sites offers the most privacy in the park; RV sites are open. Ceramic classes are offered, movies are shown, and there is an adults-only lounge. Children enjoy the pirate ship playground, but families who like to spend extensive time at a campground may prefer the nearby Ausable Chasm Campground, which has a mini-golf course and a tennis court, among other recreational opportunities. However, Ausable River Campsite's facilities are cleaner, and campers who do not require mini-golf and tennis will be happy. Ausable Chasm is the main draw to the area. A 1.5-mile-long gorge, Ausable Chasm ranges from 20 to 50 feet wide, and its rocky walls rise as high as 200 feet above the Ausable River. Tours include a raft ride followed by a 0.75-mile-long self-guided walking tour before reaching the bus for the return trip. The tour offers stunning views. Be sure to wear comfortable clothing, and be aware that the self-guided walking tour includes many stairs to climb. Ausable River Campsite is also just 3 miles from Lake Champlain and the ferry that transports passengers to Vermont.

Basics

Operated By: Private operator. **Open:** May 13–Oct. 16. **Site Assignment:** Reservations must be made 7 days in advance. **Registration:** At campground office. **Fee:** $20–$31; V, MC. **Parking:** At site.

Facilities

Number of RV-only Sites: 90. **Number of Tent-only Sites:** 12. **Hookups:** Electric (20, 30, 50 amps), water. **Each Site:** Fire ring, picnic table. **Dump Station:** Yes. **Laundry:** Yes. **Pay Phone:** Yes. **Restrooms and Showers:** Yes. **Fuel:** No. **Propane:** No. **Internal Roads:** Gravel, in fair condition. **RV Service:** No. **Market:** W/in 3 mi. **Restaurant:** W/in 3 mi. **General Store:** Yes. **Vending:** Yes. **Swimming:** No. **Playground:** Yes. **Other:** Located on Ausable River. **Activities:** Swimming, canoeing, river & pond fishing, planned activities on weekends, sports field, horseshoes, volleyball. **Nearby Attractions:** Ausable Chasm, Lake Placid, Lake Champlain, Fort Ticonderoga, ferry to Vermont, Whiteface Mountain, Adirondack Park. **Additional**

Information: New York Division of Tourism, (800) CALL-NYS, www.iloveny.state.ny.us.

Restrictions

Pets: On leash only. **Fires:** At site. **Alcoholic Beverages:** At site. **Vehicle Maximum Length:** 40 ft.

To Get There

From I-87, take Exit 34 and go 0.25 mi. west on Hwy. 9N and 0.75 mi. south on entry road. Entrance is on the left.

KEESEVILLE   MAP, A-5
Poke-O-Moonshine Campground

reserve america™

135 Rte. 9, 12944. T: (518) 834-9045; www.reserveamerica.com.

🚐 ★★★★   ▲ ★★★★

Beauty: ★★★	Site Privacy: ★★★
Spaciousness: ★★★	Quiet: ★★★★★
Security: ★★★★★	Cleanliness: ★★★★
Insect Control: ★★★	Facilities: ★★

Poke-O-Moonshine answers the dream of rock climbers everywhere. Boasting clear vertical ledges it provides some of the most difficult climbing opportunities anywhere. As an alternative, take the well-traveled hiking trail to the summit where you will find an old fire tower, and enjoy the panoramic view overlooking the Adirondacks, Canada, and Vermont. Besides climbers, the long, clean, rock face is utilized as breeding habitat by peregrine falcons, a state and federally listed endangered species. Twenty-five campsites will accommodate camping equipment from tents to 30-foot RVs and each site is equipped with a picnic table and fireplace. The rock face of Poke-O-Moonshine can be extremely dangerous for beginning rock climbers. It should be avoided by all but advanced climbers. Human disturbance of peregrine falcons during the breeding season can result in reduced reproductive success. To help ensure that attempts at reproduction on the ledges of Poke-O-Moonshine Mountain are successful, rock climbing routes which would bring individuals close to the nest site (eyrie) are closed between April 1 and mid-August. The base of the cliff, where the routes begin, is posted with department signs warning potential users to stay clear.

Basics

Operated By: New York State Parks. **Open:** May 18–Sept. 2. **Site Assignment:** Reservations can be made 9 months in advance. **Registration:** At office. **Fee:** Single, $12. **Parking:** Amenity parking.

Facilities

Number of Multipurpose Sites: 27. **Hookups:** None. **Dump Station:** No. **Laundry:** No. **Pay Phone:** Yes. **Restrooms and Showers:** Yes. **Fuel:** No. **Propane:** No. **Internal Roads:** Paved. **RV Service:** No. **Market:** No. **Restaurant:** W/in 10 mi. **General Store:** W/in 10 mi. **Vending:** No. **Swimming:** No. **Playground:** No. **Activities:** Biking, hiking, picnicking, rock climbing, wildlife viewing.

Restrictions

Pets: Pets are allowed w/ proof of current/valid rabies vaccination. Campers can walk a dog on a leash no longer than 6 ft. as long as the dog is under control. Dogs cannot be left unattended. Pets are not allowed in day-use areas, on beaches, or in any structure. **Fires:** Permitted in designated fireplaces. **Alcoholic Beverages:** Persons age 21 or over who possess or consume alcoholic beverages must produce adequate identification & proof of age upon request. **Vehicle Maximum Length:** 30 ft. **Other:** Quiet hours are 10 p.m.–7 a.m. & are strictly enforced. Campers not listed on the camping permit are not allowed in the facility during these hours. Generators may not be operated during these hours.

To Get There

Lake I-87 to Exit 33 (Wilsboro and Essex). Go south on Hwy. 9 about 3 mi. There is a sign on the roadside for the park.

LAKE GEORGE   MAP, B-5
Adirondack Camping Village

P.O. Box 406, 43 Finkle Farm Rd., 12845. T: (518) 668-5226; www.adirondackcampingvillage.com.

🚐 ★★★★   ▲ ★★★★

Beauty: ★★★★	Site Privacy: ★★★
Spaciousness: ★★	Quiet: ★★★★
Security: ★★★★★	Cleanliness: ★★★★
Insect Control: ★★★★	Facilities: ★★★★

Located in Adirondack Park at the northern edge of Lake George Village, the Adirondack Camping Village is situated on a forested mountain and has level, open, and wooded sites. Tent sites are located at the campground's northern end. RV sites along the woods where the Possum Run Nature Trail cuts through are private and serene. The campground is within five minutes of Lake George and the village. A heated swimming pool, wading pool, fishing pond, and scenic hiking trails are some of the campground's recreational offerings. The Lake George Trolley stops at the campground and takes passengers to Lake George Village. Boat tours on Lake George are popular. So is swimming at Million Dollar Beach. Water Slide World and the Great Escape and Splashwater Kingdom Fun Park offer thrills for families. The Fort William Henry Museum, a replica of the 1755 stockade, details the area's French and Indian War heritage.

Basics

Operated By: Private operator. **Open:** May 15–Oct. 1. **Site Assignment:** Reservations & walk-ins accepted (10% discount to Canadians). **Registration:** At campground office. **Fee:** $28–$43; V, MC. **Parking:** At site.

Facilities

Number of RV-only Sites: 125. **Number of Tent-only Sites:** 25. **Hookups:** Electric (15, 20, 30 amps), water. **Each Site:** Fire ring, picnic table. **Dump Station:** Yes. **Laundry:** Yes. **Pay Phone:** Yes. **Restrooms and Showers:** Yes. **Fuel:** No. **Propane:** No. **Internal Roads:** Gravel & paved, in good condition. **RV Service:** No. **Market:** W/in 2 mi. **Restaurant:** W/in 2 mi. **General Store:** Yes.

Vending: Yes. **Swimming:** Yes. **Playground:** Yes. **Activities:** Game room, rec hall, swimming, wading pool, basketball, pond fishing, hiking trails, movies, planned activities, sports field, horseshoes, volleyball, shuffleboard. **Nearby Attractions:** Lake George, Fort William Henry Museum, The Great Escape & Splashwater Kingdom Fun Park, Lake George boat tours, Water Slide World, Prospect Mountain, Lake George Battlefield Picnic Area, Lake George Dinner Theater, Lake George Action Park. **Additional Information:** Lake George Chamber of Commerce, (800) 705-0059, www.lakegeorgevillage.com.

RESTRICTIONS

Pets: On leash only. **Fires:** At site. **Alcoholic Beverages:** At site. **Vehicle Maximum Length:** 35 ft.

TO GET THERE

From I-87, take Exit 22 and go 1.5 mi. on US 9. Entrance is on the right.

LAKE GEORGE   MAP, B-5
Lake George Escape
Camping Resort

P.O. Box 431, East Schroon River Rd., 12845. T: (800) 327-3188 or (518) 623-3207; www.lakegeorgeescape.com.

🚐 ★★★★★	⛺ ★★★★★
Beauty: ★★★★	Site Privacy: ★★★
Spaciousness: ★★★	Quiet: ★★★
Security: ★★★★★	Cleanliness: ★★★★★
Insect Control: ★★★★★	Facilities: ★★★★★

In the Adirondacks—and throughout New York—few campgrounds can match the beauty and amenities of the Lake George Escape Camping Resort. Located 6 miles from Lake George Village, Lake George Escape features a large fishing pond and several sites along the Schroon River. Covering 148 acres of woods and meadows and a mile of riverbank, Lake George Escape is a haven for RVers and tenters alike. The RV sites include 50 pull-throughs. The campground has tent sites situated along the pond, the river, and in the towering pine woods. You can fish, swim, or inner tube in the Schroon River, which flows to the Hudson River. Canoes and rowboats are available for rent. You do not have to leave the campground to satisfy your hunger, since the Alfresco serves breakfast, lunch, and dinner. A free shuttle transports campers to attractions in Lake George Village.

BASICS

Operated By: Private operator. **Open:** May 12–Columbus Day. **Site Assignment:** Reservations recommended (1-night deposit for 3 nights or less, $85 for 4 nights or more), walk-ins accepted. **Registration:** At campground office. **Fee:** $19–$46; V, MC, AE, D. **Parking:** At site.

FACILITIES

Number of RV-only Sites: 424. **Number of Tent-only Sites:** 148. **Hookups:** Electric (20, 30, 50 amps), water, cable TV, phone. **Each Site:** Fire ring, picnic table. **Dump Station:** Yes. **Laundry:** Yes. **Pay Phone:** Yes. **Restrooms and Showers:** Yes. **Fuel:** No. **Propane:** Yes. **Internal Roads:** Paved, in good condition. **RV Service:** No. **Market:** W/in 2 mi.

Restaurant: On premises. **General Store:** Yes. **Vending:** Yes. **Swimming:** Yes. **Playground:** Yes. **Other:** Schroon River. **Activities:** River swimming, canoeing, boating, boat rentals, river & pond fishing, mini-golf, shuffleboard, golf, planned activities, movies, tennis, badminton, sports field, horseshoes, hiking trails, volleyball, game room, rec hall. **Nearby Attractions:** Lake George, Fort William Henry Museum, The Great Escape & Splashwater Kingdom Fun Park, Lake George boat tours, Water Slide World, Prospect Mountain, Lake George Battlefield Picnic Area, Lake George Dinner Theater, Lake George Action Park. **Additional Information:** Lake George Chamber of Commerce, (800) 705-0059, www.lakegeorgevillage.com.

RESTRICTIONS

Pets: On leash only, under control. Pets cannot be left unattended at campsite. **Fires:** At site. **Alcoholic Beverages:** At site. **Vehicle Maximum Length:** No limit.

TO GET THERE

From I-87, take Exit 23 and go 0.25 mi. east on Diamond Point Rd. and 0.75 mi. north on E. Schroon River Rd. Entrance is on the left.

LAKE GEORGE   MAP, B-5
Lake George RV Park

74 SR 149 Dept. W, 12845-3501. T: (518) 792-3775; www.lakegeorgervpark.com.

🚐 ★★★★★	⛺ n/a
Beauty: ★★★★★	Site Privacy: ★★★
Spaciousness: ★★★	Quiet: ★★★★
Security: ★★★★★	Cleanliness: ★★★★★
Insect Control: ★★★★★	Facilities: ★★★★★

Like Lake George Escape Camping Resort, the Lake George RV Park is an immaculate campground with beautiful surroundings and a multitude of amenities. Lake George RV Park, however, does not have tent-only sites, though campers can pitch a tent next to their RV. Sites are level and wooded, and there are 250 pull-throughs. The cluster of sites on the western end of the campground is close to the pedal boat and fishing pond, as well as the indoor pool, snack bar, game room, and adult lounge. Sites on the eastern side are near the creek and the athletic area, which includes a softball field, volleyball and basketball courts, and a bocce ball area. There are 3 miles of paved bike trails; bicyclists can also ride trails to Lake George and Glens Falls. A trolley takes passengers from Lake George RV Park to the assortment of Lake George attractions. The campground offers discount tickets to many attractions.

BASICS

Operated By: David King. **Open:** May 4–Oct. 8. **Site Assignment:** Reservations recommended (required for holiday weekends), walk-ins accepted. **Registration:** At office/store. **Fee:** $36–$56 for 2 people; each additional person, $6; V, MC, AE, D. **Parking:** At site.

FACILITIES

Number of RV-only Sites: 390. **Hookups:** Electric (30, 50 amps), cable TV, phone. **Each Site:** Fire ring, picnic table. **Dump Station:** Yes. **Laundry:** Yes.

Pay Phone: Yes. **Restrooms and Showers:** Yes. **Fuel:** No. **Propane:** Yes. **Internal Roads:** Paved, in good condition. **RV Service:** No. **Market:** W/in 4.5 mi. **Restaurant:** W/in 0.5 mi. **General Store:** Yes. **Vending:** Yes. **Swimming:** Yes. **Playground:** Yes. **Other:** RV rentals. **Activities:** 5 swimming pools (one indoor), game room, rec hall, wading pool, pedal boat rentals, pond & stream fishing, basketball, planned activities, movies, badminton, tennis, sports field, horseshoes, hiking trails, volleyball, shuffle board. **Nearby Attractions:** Lake George, Fort William Henry Museum, The Great Escape & Splashwater Kingdom Fun Park, Lake George boat tours, Water Slide World, Prospect Mountain, Lake George Battlefield Picnic Area, Lake George Dinner Theater, Lake George Action Park. **Additional Information:** Lake George Chamber of Commerce, (800) 705-0059, www.lakegeorgevillage.com.

RESTRICTIONS

Pets: On leash only. Pets may not be left unattended. **Fires:** At site, confined to fire ring. **Alcoholic Beverages:** At site. **Vehicle Maximum Length:** No limit.

TO GET THERE

From I-87, take Exit 20 Northway and go 0.75 mi. north on Hwy. 149/US 9 and 0.5 mi. east on Hwy. 149. Entrance is on the right.

LAKE GEORGE   MAP, B-5
Ledgeview Village RV Park

321 SR 149, 12845. T: (518) 798-6621 or (888) 353-5936; www.ledgeview.com.

🚐 ★★★★	⛺ n/a
Beauty: ★★★★	Site Privacy: ★★
Spaciousness: ★★★	Quiet: ★★★★
Security: ★★★★★	Cleanliness: ★★★★
Insect Control: ★★★★	Facilities: ★★★★

Though Ledgeview Village does not have the amenities of nearby Lake George RV Park, Ledgeview is still a good base for exploring the Lake George area. The campsites are spacious, level, and wooded, and there are 17 pull-throughs. No tents are permitted. The store is well stocked; and the Laundromat, restrooms, and showers are clean. The swimming pool, playground, store, and recreational areas are located near the entrance of the park, and sites are situated along the streets behind them. For breathtaking scenery, take a drive along the Veterans Memorial Highway (a toll road) to the top of 2,021-foot-high Prospect Mountain. There are hiking trails and picnic sites at the summit, where you can see Lake George, Vermont's Green Mountains, and New Hampshire's White Mountains.

BASICS

Operated By: Hughes family. **Open:** May 1–Columbus Day. **Site Assignment:** Reservations accepted (2-night deposit required), walk-ins accepted. **Registration:** At campground office. **Fee:** $31–$34; V, MC. **Parking:** At site.

FACILITIES

Number of RV-only Sites: 150. **Hookups:** Electric (30, 50 amps), water, cable TV. **Each Site:** Fire ring, picnic table. **Dump Station:** No. **Laundry:** Yes. **Pay Phone:** Yes. **Restrooms and Showers:** Yes. **Fuel:** No. **Propane:** No. **Internal Roads:** Paved, in good condition. **RV Service:** No. **Market:** W/in 3 mi. **Restaurant:** W/in 2 mi. **General Store:** Yes. **Vending:** Yes. **Swimming:** Yes. **Playground:** Yes. **Other:** Pavilion. **Activities:** Game room, rec hall, basketball, bike rentals, badminton, shuffleboard, volleyball. **Nearby Attractions:** Lake George, Fort William Henry Museum, The Great Escape & Splashwater Kingdom Fun Park, Lake George boat tours, Water Slide World, Prospect Mountain, Lake George Battlefield Picnic Area, Lake George Dinner Theater, Lake George Action Park. **Additional Information:** Lake George Chamber of Commerce, (800) 705-0059, www.lakegeorgevillage.com.

RESTRICTIONS

Pets: Not allowed. **Fires:** At site. **Alcoholic Beverages:** At site. **Vehicle Maximum Length:** No limit. **Other:** No tent camping.

TO GET THERE

From I-87, take Exit 20 Northway and go 0.75 mi. north on Hwy. 149/US 9 and 1.5 mi. east on Hwy. 149. Entrance is on the left.

LAURENS   MAP, C-4
Gilbert Lake State Park

reserve america

18 CCC Rd., 13796. T: (607) 432-2114; www.reserveamerica.com.

🚐 ★★★★	⛺ ★★★★
Beauty: ★★★	Site Privacy: ★★
Spaciousness: ★★	Quiet: ★★★★★
Security: ★★★★★	Cleanliness: ★★★★
Insect Control: ★★★	Facilities: ★★★★

Gilbert Lake State Park lies at the foothills of the Catskills with wonderful views of rolling terrain, a lake, and two small ponds. Twelve miles of trails are open year-round for hikers, mountain bikers, cross-country skiers, and snowmobilers. Other park amenities include camping, fishing, recreation programs, and disc-golf. Gilbert Lake State Park rests on the shores of Gilbert Lake. Despite the small size of the lake, it is a source of great enjoyment to anglers, boaters, and other water-sport enthusiasts. With its location in the foothills of the Catskills, it offers wonderful scenery of hardwood forests reflected in the clear waters of one lake and two ponds. A network of hiking trails leads to secluded fishing spots and wonderful overlooks. Bow hunting is permitted. Gilbert Lake offers two campgrounds and a large cabin area. Both offer potable water, a playground, flush toilets, hot showers, horseshoe pits, and a public phone. The Hill Top campground offers electric hookups.

BASICS

Operated By: New York State Parks. **Open:** May 11–Oct. 7. **Site Assignment:** Reservations can be made 9 months in advance. **Registration:** At office.

Fee: Single, $13; cabin, $310–$395. **Parking:** Amenity parking.

FACILITIES

Number of Multipurpose Sites: 254. **Hookups:** At Hill Top. **Dump Station:** No. **Laundry:** No. **Pay Phone:** Yes. **Restrooms and Showers:** Yes. **Fuel:** No. **Propane:** No. **Internal Roads:** Paved. **RV Service:** No. **Market:** No. **Restaurant:** Yes. **General Store:** No. **Vending:** No. **Swimming:** Yes. **Playground:** Yes. **Activities:** Baseball, basketball, biking, boating, cross-country skiing, disc golf, hiking, horseshoes, hunting, interpretive programs, paddle boating, picnicking, recreation programs, snowmobiling, volleyball.

RESTRICTIONS

Pets: Pets must be on 6-ft. leash & must have proof of rabies vaccination. **Fires:** Permitted in designated fireplaces. **Alcoholic Beverages:** Persons age 21 or over who possess or consume alcoholic beverages must produce adequate identification & proof of age upon request. **Other:** Chainsaws, subletting of camping areas, rollerblades, firearms, & fireworks are not allowed in the park. Campers must be on site before the park closes & visitors must leave by 10 p.m. Water is centrally located. Quiet hours 10 p.m.–7 a.m. Generators may be used between 8 a.m.–5 p.m. & 8–10 p.m. There is an overflow parking area available for third vehicles for a fee.

TO GET THERE

From I-88 take Exit 13. Follow Hwy. 205 north to Laurens. Take CR 12 to park. From Hwy. 51 go to New Lisbon and take CR 12 to park. Follow signs to park.

LEEDS   MAP, C-5
Indian Ridge Campsites

1446 Leeds Athens Rd., 12451. T: (518) 943-3516.

🚐 ★★★	⛺ ★★★
Beauty: ★★★★	Site Privacy: ★★★
Spaciousness: ★★★	Quiet: ★★★★
Security: ★★★★	Cleanliness: ★★★★
Insect Control: ★★★★	Facilities: ★★★★

Near the eastern entrance to the Catskill Mountains resort area, Indian Ridge Campsites are set in a mountain valley overlooking its private pond. Most sites here are wooded, though some are open. There are 12 pull-through sites. Indian Ridge offers a family tenting area. Tent sites here are secluded—even more so than the RV sites, only some of which have privacy. There's a swimming pool, a walking trail, and a children's fishing pond, along with other activities like basketball and volleyball. The Catskill area is an ideal place for children who enjoy animals. Visitors may feed tame deer, antelope, llamas, and other exotic animals (some of which are rare or endangered) at the Catskill Game Farm. Turtles, alligators, and crocodiles are among the featured residents at Ted Martin's Reptile Adventure. The Zoom Flume Waterpark is also a popular family-oriented attraction in Catskill. Outdoor enthusiasts flock to the 287,989-acre Catskill Forest Preserve, where Slide Mountain's peak is the highest point at 4,180 feet. The preserve has hiking trails and three fishing streams.

BASICS

Operated By: Private operator. **Open:** May 1–Oct. 24. **Site Assignment:** By reservation & first come, first served. **Registration:** At campground headquarters. **Fee:** $23–$27; V, MC, AE. **Parking:** At site.

FACILITIES

Number of RV-only Sites: 45. **Number of Tent-only Sites:** 25. **Hookups:** Electric (20, 30 amps), water, phone. **Each Site:** Fire ring, picnic table. **Dump Station:** Yes. **Laundry:** Yes. **Pay Phone:** Yes. **Restrooms and Showers:** Yes. **Fuel:** No. **Propane:** Yes. **Internal Roads:** Gravel, in good condition. **RV Service:** No. **Market:** W/in 3 mi. **Restaurant:** W/in 3 mi. **General Store:** Yes. **Vending:** Yes. **Swimming:** Yes. **Playground:** Yes. **Other:** Children's fishing pond. **Activities:** Pond fishing, game room, rec hall, swimming, basketball, planned activities on weekends, volleyball, horseshoes, badminton, walking trail. **Nearby Attractions:** Catskill Mountains, Catskill Game Farm, Zoom Flume Waterpark. **Additional Information:** Greene County Promotion Dept., (800) 355-CATS, www.greene-ny.com.

RESTRICTIONS

Pets: On leash only, under control. **Fires:** At site. **Alcoholic Beverages:** At site. **Vehicle Maximum Length:** 36 ft.

TO GET THERE

From I-87, take Exit 21 and go 0.25 mi. west on Hwy. 23B and 0.5 mi. north on Forest Hill Ave. Entrance is on the right.

LEROY   MAP, C-2
Lei-Ti, Too! Campground and Recreation Area

8101 Conlon Rd., 14482. T: (585) 768-4883 or (585) 594-2304; www.leiti.com.

🚐 ★★★	⛺ ★★★
Beauty: ★★★★	Site Privacy: ★★★
Spaciousness: ★★	Quiet: ★★★
Security: ★★★	Cleanliness: ★★★★
Insect Control: ★★★★	Facilities: ★★★★

Located about 16 miles southwest of Rochester, Lei-Ti, Too! Campground is known for its proximity to challenging ski slopes and for its tasty sourdough pancakes (served with maple syrup to campers on Sunday mornings). The campground is dotted with apple trees, and there are ten pull-through sites. Frost Ridge has hiking trails on its grounds, but the most inviting outdoor recreation is in the surrounding area. Options include Letchworth State Park, the home of Genesee River Gorge or the "Grand Canyon of the East"; the outdoor recreation of Hamlin Beach State Park; and Genesee County Village and Museum. In Rochester, you can visit the Susan B. Anthony House and the George Eastman House (the founder of Kodak). Frost Ridge is also an hour's drive from Niagara Falls.

BASICS

Operated By: Private operator. **Open:** All year. **Site Assignment:** By reservation & first come, first served. **Registration:** At campground office. **Fee:** $23–$26. **Parking:** At site.

FACILITIES

Number of RV-only Sites: 116. **Number of Tent-only Sites:** 15. **Hookups:** Electric (20, 30, 50 amps), water, phone. **Each Site:** Fire ring, picnic table. **Dump Station:** Yes. **Laundry:** No. **Pay Phone:** Yes. **Restrooms and Showers:** Yes. **Fuel:** No. **Propane:** Yes. **Internal Roads:** Gravel, in good condition. **RV Service:** No. **Market:** W/in 4 mi. **Restaurant:** W/in 5 mi. **General Store:** Yes. **Vending:** Yes. **Swimming:** No. **Playground:** Yes. **Other:** Large recreation building. **Activities:** Game room, rec hall, basketball, sports field, hiking trails, horseshoes. **Nearby Attractions:** Jell-O Museum, Rochester, Lake Ontario, Letchworth State Park, Hamlin Beach State Park, Rochester Museum & Science Center, Genesee Country Village & Museum, Susan B. Anthony House, University of Rochester, George Eastman House, International Museum of Photography & Film. **Additional Information:** Greater Rochester Visitors Assoc., (800) 677-7282, www.visitrochester.com.

RESTRICTIONS

Pets: On leash only. **Fires:** At site. **Alcoholic Beverages:** At site. **Vehicle Maximum Length:** 50 ft.

TO GET THERE

From I-90, take Exit 47 and go 0.5 mi. south on Hwy. 19, 1 mi. east on North Rd., and 0.25 mi. south on Conlon Rd. Entrance is on the left.

LEWISTON   MAP, B-1
Niagara Falls North KOA

1250 Pletcher Rd., 14174.
T: (716) 754-8013 or (800) 562-8715;
www.koa.com/where/ny/32127.

🚐 ★★★★   ⛺ ★★★★

Beauty: ★★★★	Site Privacy: ★
Spaciousness: ★★	Quiet: ★★
Security: ★★★	Cleanliness: ★★★★
Insect Control: ★★★	Facilities: ★★★★

Wooded and peaceful with open and shaded sites. Niagara Falls North KOA serves as an uncrowded home base for campers who want to explore Niagara Falls. There are 40 pull-through sites, site numbers 13 and 38 being most popular. The campground is loaded with maple trees, and raccoons are sighted quite often. Guided tours of Niagara Falls embark from the campground. Niagara Reservation State Park offers views of the falls from several points. The 282-foot-high Prospect Point Observation Tower is adjacent to American Falls, and the elevator transports guests to the famous Maid of the Mist boat tour. Other great views can be found at Whirlpool State Park and Goat Island. Nearby attractions include Fantasy Island, an 80-acre theme park, and the Aquarium at Niagara Falls, where more than 2,000 marine creatures reside. For a fun day trip, take a 90-minute drive to Toronto, where points of interest include Ontario Place, the Canadian National Exhibition, Ontario Science Center, Toronto Zoo, and Casaloma Castle.

BASICS

Operated By: KOA. **Open:** Apr. 15–Oct. 15. **Site Assignment:** By reservation & first come, first served. **Registration:** At campground office. **Fee:** Tent, $25–$32; RV, $31–$45; cabin, $49–$75; trailer, $110–$130; V, MC, D. **Parking:** At site.

FACILITIES

Number of RV-only Sites: 60. **Number of Tent-only Sites:** 18. **Hookups:** Electric (20, 30, 50 amps), water, sewer, phone; 18 full hookups. **Each Site:** Fire ring, picnic table. **Dump Station:** Yes. **Laundry:** Yes. **Pay Phone:** No. **Restrooms and Showers:** Yes. **Fuel:** No. **Propane:** Yes. **Internal Roads:** Gravel, in good condition. **RV Service:** No. **Market:** W/in 3 mi. **Restaurant:** W/in 3 mi. **General Store:** Yes. **Vending:** Yes. **Swimming:** Yes. **Playground:** Yes. **Other:** Cabin rentals. **Activities:** Game room, rec hall, swimming, basketball, bike rentals, horseshoes, volleyball. **Nearby Attractions:** Niagara Falls CVB, (800) 421-5223, www.nfcvb.com. **Additional Information:** Niagara Falls, Aquarium of Niagara Falls, Artpark, Devil's Hole State Park, Fantasy Island, Fort Niagara State Park, Niagara Reservation State Park, Prospect Point Observation Tower, Maid of the Mist tours, Whirlpool State Park.

RESTRICTIONS

Pets: On leash only. **Fires:** At site. **Alcoholic Beverages:** At site. **Vehicle Maximum Length:** No limit.

TO GET THERE

From I-90, take Exit 25B and go 3 mi. north on Robert Moses Pkwy. and 1.75 mi. east on Pletcher Rd. Entrance is on the left.

MASSENA   MAP, A-4
Robert Moses State Park

reserve america

P.O. Box 548, 13662. T: (315) 769-8663;
www.reserveamerica.com.

🚐 ★★★★   ⛺ ★★★★

Beauty: ★★★	Site Privacy: ★★★
Spaciousness: ★★★	Quiet: ★★★
Security: ★★★	Cleanliness: ★★★★
Insect Control: ★★★	Facilities: ★★★★

Robert Moses State Park is located partially on the mainland and partially on Barnhart Island and is located along the St. Lawrence Seaway 3 miles north of Massena. Visitors reach the Barnhart section of the park through a tunnel under the Eisenhower Lock. This beautiful park is home to a variety of wildlife and plant life. Recreational opportunities include a campground and cabins, a boat launch and marina, some of the best fishing in the Northeast, picnic areas, a swimming beach, tennis courts, and a nature museum. The Fire Island portion of the park offers an array of outdoor activities from golfing to swimming and picnicking. The park is open year-round from dawn to dusk. There is an 18-hole pitch-putt-golf course, which is 1,425 yards and par 55. Robert Moses Campground offers visitors an opportunity to view a large variety of flora and fauna, enjoy a multitude of recreation opportunities, and to visit sites along Lake St. Lawrence. Wooded campsites and cabins are located on a small scenic peninsula. There are 168 tent and RV areas, with 36 sites offering electric hookups. A wheelchair-accessible site and path is paved and reservable. Cabins, including the one handicapped cabin, total 15. Playground, flush toilets, hot showers, scrubbing sink, and potable water are conveniently located. The marina and boat launch are enjoyed by the camping community, offering immediate access to excellent fishing waters that support northern pike, walleye, and largemouth and smallmouth bass. Day-use amenities include picnic areas, a swimming beach, tennis courts, 9-hole miniature golf, shuffleboard, and horseshoe pit. Interesting sites include the Long Sault Spillway Dam, Hawking Point Overlook, the Robert Moses Power Dam, and the park's nature center. In winter, visitors enjoy cross-country skiing, ice skating, ice fishing, snowshoeing, and snowmobiling.

BASICS

Operated By: New York State Parks. **Open:** May 25–Oct. 7. **Site Assignment:** Reservations can be made 9 months in advance. **Registration:** At office. **Fee:** Single, $13; cabin, $330. **Parking:** Amenity parking.

FACILITIES

Number of Multipurpose Sites: 233. **Hookups:** None. **Dump Station:** Yes. **Laundry:** No. **Pay Phone:** Yes. **Restrooms and Showers:** Yes. **Fuel:** No. **Propane:** No. **Internal Roads:** Paved. **RV Service:** No. **Market:** W/in 10 mi. **Restaurant:** W/in 10 mi. **General Store:** W/in 10 mi. **Vending:** No. **Swimming:** Yes. **Playground:** No. **Other:** Cabins are 7-day or 14-day reservations (Sat. to Sat. only)! Cabin campers must supply all bed/bath linens & kitchen utensils. **Activities:** Baseball, basketball, biking, bird-watching, canoeing, fishing, hiking, jet skiing, picnicking, powerboating, sailboarding, sailing, tennis, volleyball, waterskiing.

RESTRICTIONS

Pets: Pets must have proof of a current rabies inoculation. Pets must be on a 6-ft. leash or caged at all times. **Fires:** Permitted in designated fireplaces. **Alcoholic Beverages:** Persons age 21 or over who possess or consume alcoholic beverages must produce adequate identification & proof of age upon request.

TO GET THERE

Robert Moses State Park is located 5 mi. from Hwy. 37 on Hwy. 131. Turn at the traffic circle in front of the shopping mall. Follow signs to park entrance and information center. Please note that Robert Moses State Park is located on the St. Lawrence River on the United States/Canada border in northern New York.

MECHANICVILLE   MAP, C-5
Deer Run Campground

reserve america

200 Deer Run Dr. Schagticoke, 12154.
T: (518) 664-2804; www.abdeerrun.com.

🚐 ★★★★★   ⛺ ★★★★

Beauty: ★★★★   Site Privacy: ★★
Spaciousness: ★★★   Quiet: ★★★★
Security: ★★★★★   Cleanliness: ★★★★★
Insect Control: ★★★★   Facilities: ★★★★★

Perched on a green plateau overlooking the Hoosic River, Deer Run Campground is certainly a treasure for families and nature seekers. The grounds are colorful, overflowing with pine and maple trees, and deer sightings are not uncommon. There are three swimming pools and a kiddie pool, plus two enclosed pavilions with fireplaces. The facilities are extremely well maintained and clean. Volleyball, basketball, and bocce ball courts can also be found on the grounds. There are more than 400 sites, 344 of which are pull-throughs to accommodate the largest RVs. Located about 30 miles from the southeast tip of Adirondack Park and about the same distance west of the Vermont and Massachusetts borders, Deer Run is convenient to attractions in Saratoga Springs and Albany. If Deer Run's fresh air and three swimming pools do not refresh you, certainly the mineral baths of Saratoga Spa State Park will.

BASICS
Operated By: Doug & Jacklyn Dyer. **Open:** May 1–Oct. 15. **Site Assignment:** By reservation & first come, first served. **Registration:** At campground office. **Fee:** $35; V, MC. **Parking:** At site.

FACILITIES
Number of Multipurpose Sites: 411. **Hookups:** Electric (30 amps), cable TV, phone. **Each Site:** Fire ring, picnic table. **Dump Station:** Yes. **Laundry:** Yes. **Pay Phone:** Yes. **Restrooms and Showers:** Yes. **Fuel:** No. **Propane:** Yes. **Internal Roads:** Gravel & paved, in good condition. **RV Service:** Yes. **Market:** W/in 3 mi. **Restaurant:** W/in 1 mi. **General Store:** Yes. **Vending:** Yes. **Swimming:** Yes. **Playground:** Yes. **Other:** Fishing pond & animal sanctuary. **Activities:** Fishing, game room, 3 swimming pools, wading pool, movies, planned activities on weekends, mini-golf, basketball, sports field, badminton, hiking trails, volleyball, horseshoes. **Nearby Attractions:** Saratoga Springs, Albany, Adirondack Park, Saratoga Spa State Park, Saratoga National Historical Park. **Additional Information:** Saratoga County Chamber of Commerce, (518) 584-3255, www.saratoga.org.

RESTRICTIONS
Pets: On leash only, rabies certificate required for dogs. **Fires:** At site. **Alcoholic Beverages:** At site. **Vehicle Maximum Length:** No limit. **Other:** No electric heaters permitted.

TO GET THERE
From I-87, take Northway Exit 9 and go 2.25 mi. north on Hwy. 4/Hwy. 32, 1.25 mi. east on Hwy. 67, and 1.5 mi. north on Deer Run Dr. Entrance is on the left.

MEXICO   MAP, B-3
Yogi Bear's Jellystone Park Campground

601 CR 16, 13114. T: (800) 248-7096 or (315) 963-7096; www.jellystonecny.com.

🚐 ★★★★   ⛺ ★★★★

Beauty: ★★★★   Site Privacy: ★★
Spaciousness: ★★   Quiet: ★★★★
Security: ★★★★★   Cleanliness: ★★★★
Insect Control: ★★★★   Facilities: ★★★★

At Yogi Bear's Jellystone Park in Mexico, campers can swim in the pool, test their putting skills on the mini-golf course, and play shuffleboard under the lights, among other activities. Located 35 miles north of Syracuse, the campground is just 2 miles from Lake Ontario, where it has a private boat dock and boat launch. At the campground, there is a lounge for adults and a play room for toddlers. Sites are open and shaded, and there are 15 pull-throughs. The sites are well maintained, but they offer little privacy, and some are cramped. Ideal for a day trip, Syracuse has its share of natural and cultural attractions. Beaver Lake Nature Center, Burnet Park Zoo, the Erie Canal Museum, and New York State Canal cruises are some of the more interesting things to do in the city.

BASICS
Operated By: Yogi Bear's Jellystone Park. **Open:** Apr. 15–Oct. 25. **Site Assignment:** Reservations recommended (2-night min. required on weekends), walk-ins accepted. **Registration:** At campground headquarters. **Fee:** $21–$32; V, MC, D. **Parking:** At site.

FACILITIES
Number of RV-only Sites: 92. **Number of Tent-only Sites:** 32. **Hookups:** Electric (20, 30, 50 amps), water, phone. **Each Site:** Fire ring, picnic table. **Dump Station:** Yes. **Laundry:** Yes. **Pay Phone:** Yes. **Restrooms and Showers:** Yes. **Fuel:** No. **Propane:** Yes. **Internal Roads:** Gravel, in good condition. **RV Service:** No. **Market:** W/in 5 mi. **Restaurant:** W/in 3 mi. **General Store:** Yes. **Vending:** Yes. **Swimming:** Yes. **Playground:** Yes. **Other:** Little Salmon River. **Activities:** River fishing, swimming, rec hall, game room, bike rentals, basketball, shuffleboard, planned activities, movies, sports field, volleyball, horseshoes. **Nearby Attractions:** Lake Ontario, Little Salmon River, Syracuse. **Additional Information:** Syracuse CVB, (800) 234-4797, www.syracusecvb.org.

RESTRICTIONS
Pets: On leash only; 1 pet per site, no aggressive breeds. No pets allowed in rental units. **Fires:** At site. **Alcoholic Beverages:** At site. **Vehicle Maximum Length:** No limit.

TO GET THERE
From I-81, take Exit 34 and go west on to Hwy. 104 into Mexico, turn right onto CR 16, and go 3 mi. Entrance is on the left.

MORRISTOWN   MAP, A-4
Eel Weir State Park

reserve america

P.O. Box 380, 13664. T: (315) 393-1138; www.reserveamerica.com.

🚐 ★★★★   ⛺ ★★★★

Beauty: ★★★   Site Privacy: ★★★
Spaciousness: ★★★   Quiet: ★★
Security: ★★   Cleanliness: ★★★★
Insect Control: ★★★   Facilities: ★★

Eel Weir State Park is smaller than some of the other state parks in the county. This tiny 16-acre park is located on the Oswegatchie River 2 miles from Black Lake and about 8 miles from Ogdensburg. Both waterways are known for excellent bass fishing and are ideal for canoes or rowboats. As it is small and secluded, the park is a perfect place to get away from it all. It offers a mere 34 tent and RV sites with no electric hookups. The sites are located all along the park's only road, which is adjacent to Oswegatchie River, a popular spot with paddle-sport enthusiasts and bass anglers. Several campsites, a picnic pavilion, and restrooms are handicapped accessible. Potable water is available from several locations. A public telephone is located near the beginning of the campground loop. Flush toilets, hot showers, and scrubbing sinks are available, as are a picnic area and pavilion.

BASICS
Operated By: New York State Parks. **Open:** May 25–Sept. 2. **Site Assignment:** Reservations can be made 9 months in advance. **Registration:** At office. **Fee:** Single, $13.

FACILITIES
Number of Multipurpose Sites: 34. **Hookups:** None. **Dump Station:** No. **Laundry:** No. **Pay Phone:** Yes. **Restrooms and Showers:** Yes. **Fuel:** No. **Propane:** No. **Internal Roads:** Paved. **RV Service:** No. **Market:** W/in 10 mi. **Restaurant:** W/in 10 mi. **General Store:** W/in 10 mi. **Vending:** No. **Swimming:** No. **Playground:** No. **Other:** Firearms & weapons are strictly prohibited. **Activities:** Biking, boating, canoeing, fishing, picnicking.

RESTRICTIONS
Pets: Pets must have proof of current rabies inoculation, on a 6-ft. leash, & attended at all times. **Fires:** Permitted in designated fireplaces. **Alcoholic Beverages:** Persons age 21 or over who possess or consume alcoholic beverages must produce adequate identification & proof of age upon request.

TO GET THERE
From Ogdensburg on Hwy. 3, turn onto Hwy. 812. Follow signs to park (it is 6 mi. southeast of Ogdensburg).

NATURAL BRIDGE MAP, B-4
Natural Bridge/Watertown KOA

6081 New York State Rte. 3, 13665.
T: (800) 562-4780 or (315) 644-4880;
www.aticamping.com.

🚐 ★★★★   ⛺ ★★★★

Beauty: ★★★★ | Site Privacy: ★★
Spaciousness: ★★★ | Quiet: ★★★★
Security: ★★★★ | Cleanliness: ★★★★
Insect Control: ★★★★ | Facilities: ★★★★

Set under towering pines, east of Adirondack Park and west of Watertown, Natural Bridge/Watertown KOA is an ideal base for whitewater rafting on the Black River and exploring the Thousand Islands (about 30 miles northwest). Many sites are shaded here, but some are open. The campground accommodates 37 pull-throughs. The swimming pool is located indoors, which is especially welcome when it is cold or raining. Bingo, pancake breakfasts, scavenger hunts, and moonlight madness sales are a sampling of the events. Alexandria Bay, located 30 miles northwest of the campground, is the center for Thousand Islands activities. This is where you will find Boldt Castle, the Thousand Islands Skydeck, and boat tours of the region. Watertown, a short drive west of the campground, is home to Long Point State Park, the American Maple Museum, and Sci-Tech Center, a hands-on science and technology museum for children.

BASICS
Operated By: Francis & Paul Larrivee. **Open:** Apr. 1–Nov. 1. **Site Assignment:** Reservations (3-day cancellation notice required), walk-ins accepted. **Registration:** At campground office. **Fee:** $20–$32; V, MC, D. **Parking:** At site.

FACILITIES
Number of RV-only Sites: 55. **Number of Tent-only Sites:** 13. **Hookups:** Electric (30, 50 amps), water, sewer; 29 full hookups. **Each Site:** Fire ring, picnic table. **Dump Station:** Yes. **Laundry:** Yes. **Pay Phone:** Yes. **Restrooms and Showers:** Yes. **Fuel:** No. **Propane:** Yes. **Internal Roads:** Gravel, in fair condition. **RV Service:** No. **Market:** W/in 10 mi. **Restaurant:** W/in 7 mi. **General Store:** Yes. **Vending:** Yes. **Swimming:** Yes. **Playground:** Yes. **Other:** Cabin rentals. **Activities:** Indoor swimming, game room, rec hall, planned activities on weekends, badminton, sports field, hiking trails, horseshoes, volleyball. **Nearby Attractions:** Thousand Islands boat tours, Boldt Castle, Fort Drum military reservation, whitewater rafting on Black River, Adirondack Park, Alexandria Bay, Long Point State Park, Sci-Tech Center in Watertown. **Additional Information:** New York Division of Tourism–Thousand Islands, (800) 847-5263, www.iloveny.state.ny.us.

RESTRICTIONS
Pets: On leash only. **Fires:** At site. **Alcoholic Beverages:** At site. **Vehicle Maximum Length:** 45 ft.

TO GET THERE
From I-81, take Exit 48 and go 7 mi. east on Hwy. 342, 7 mi. east on Hwy. 3, 5 mi. east on Hwy. 3A, and 6 mi. east on Hwy. 3. Entrance is on the left.

NEW BERLIN MAP, C-4
Hunts Pond State Park

452 Hunts Pond Rd., 13411. T: (607) 859-2249;
www.reserveamerica.com.

🚐 ★★★★   ⛺ ★★★★

Beauty: ★★★ | Site Privacy: ★★★★
Spaciousness: ★★★★ | Quiet: ★★★
Security: ★★★ | Cleanliness: ★★★★
Insect Control: ★★★ | Facilities: n/a

Hunts Pond State Park is located in the Central Travel Region below the small burg of New Berlin. The woodland park sits on the tiny Hunt Pond, which offers a boat launch and 18 primitive campsites. As a pollution-control measure, only nonmotorized watercraft are permitted in the lake. A boat launch is available to visitors. Hunts Pond attracts hunters to its land. The pond also attracts anglers, primitive campers, and winter-sport enthusiasts. There are no developed hiking trails, but adjacent Hunts Pond State Forest is available for visitors to use for hiking, snowmobiling, and cross-country skiing. Hunts Pond State Forest has a diverse landscape of open fields, softwood plantations, hardwood forests, and beaver meadows. When driving through Hunts Pond State Forest, one will see a number of open grassy fields. These fields are maintained as such to provide habitat for numerous wildlife species that inhabit grass and open lands. Other animals rely upon the shelter of wooded areas and use neighboring open areas in which to graze, forage, or hunt. White-tailed deer, wild turkey, ruffed grouse, bluebirds, and many varieties of hawks are commonly seen throughout the forest.

BASICS
Operated By: New York State Parks. **Open:** May 11–Oct. 8. **Site Assignment:** Reservations can be made 9 months in advance. **Registration:** At office. **Fee:** Single, $10. **Parking:** Amenity parking.

FACILITIES
Number of Multipurpose Sites: 21. **Hookups:** None. **Dump Station:** No. **Laundry:** No. **Pay Phone:** No. **Restrooms and Showers:** No. **Fuel:** No. **Propane:** No. **Internal Roads:** Paved. **RV Service:** No. **Market:** No. **Restaurant:** No. **General Store:** No. **Vending:** No. **Swimming:** No. **Playground:** No. **Activities:** Biking, bird-watching, boating, canoeing, cross-country skiing, fishing, ice fishing, picnicking.

RESTRICTIONS
Pets: Pets must have proof of a recent rabies inoculation. Dogs must be on a 6-ft. leash at all times. **Fires:** Permitted in designated fireplaces. **Alcoholic Beverages:** Persons age 21 or over who possess or consume alcoholic beverages must produce adequate identification & proof of age upon request. **Other:** No swimming or wading is allowed in the pond. Car-top boats are allowed in the pond by permit only. Do not park your vehicles on the road.

TO GET THERE
From I-88, exit at Hwy. 23 west to South New Berlin. Turn right at light and follow Hwy. 8 for 2.6 mi. Turn left on Hunts Pond Rd. and go 2.9 mi.; park is on the right. Coming in on Hwy. 8 from the north, go straight through New Berlin, from the light go 5 mi. Turn right on Hunts Pond Rd. and go 2.9 mi. The park is on the right.

NEWCOMB MAP, B-5
Lake Harris Campground

Campsite Rd., 12852. T: (518) 582-2503;
www.reserveamerica.com.

🚐 ★★★★   ⛺ ★★★★

Beauty: ★★★ | Site Privacy: ★★★
Spaciousness: ★★★ | Quiet: ★★★★★
Security: ★★★★★ | Cleanliness: ★★★★
Insect Control: ★★★ | Facilities: ★★★

Lake Harris is fed by the mighty Hudson River in its beginning stages and is sheltered among large hardwood trees which offer splendid color contrasts throughout the year. While the lake offers many watercraft opportunities, many love visiting the visitor interpretive center or the Santanoni Preserve Historic Site, both close by. Lake Harris Campground is located on the northern shore of 275-acre Lake Harris. A number of the sites offer a good degree of privacy. Camping equipment from tents to 40-foot RVs can be accommodated. Lake Harris Campground offers a variety of recreational opportunities including canoeing and boating, fishing, hiking, and bicycling.

BASICS
Operated By: New York State Dept. of Environmental Conservation. **Open:** May 18–Sept. 8. **Site Assignment:** Reservations can be made 9 months in advance. **Registration:** At office. **Fee:** Single, $14. **Parking:** Amenity parking.

FACILITIES
Number of Multipurpose Sites: 93. **Hookups:** None. **Dump Station:** Yes. **Laundry:** No. **Pay Phone:** No. **Restrooms and Showers:** Yes. **Fuel:** No. **Propane:** No. **Internal Roads:** Paved. **RV Service:** No. **Market:** W/in 10 mi. **Restaurant:** W/in 10 mi. **General Store:** W/in 10 mi. **Vending:** No. **Swimming:** Yes. **Playground:** No. **Activities:** Boating, canoeing, fishing, hiking, interpretive programs, jet skiing, picnicking, sailing, waterskiing.

RESTRICTIONS
Pets: Pets are allowed w/ proof of current/valid rabies vaccination. Campers can walk a dog on a leash no longer than 6 feet (under control). Dogs cannot be left unattended. Pets are not allowed in day-use areas, beaches, or any structure. **Fires:** Permitted in designated fireplaces. **Alcoholic Beverages:** Persons age 21 or over who possess or consume alcoholic beverages must produce adequate identification & proof of age upon request. **Other:** Garbage must be taken to a central recycling area at designated times for processing. Clear plastic bags

are required. Quiet hours are 10 p.m.–7 a.m. & are strictly enforced. Possession of firearms, fireworks, or the operation of chainsaws is strictly forbidden.

TO GET THERE

From I-87 (Adirondack Northway), take Exit 29. Go west 18 mi. on Blue Ridge or Boreas Rd. to Hwy. 28 north. Travel west 3.5 mi. to campsite road in Newcomb. From I-90 take Hwy. 12 north to Hwy. 28 north, to Blue Mountain Lake, then Hwy. 28 north through Long Lake to Newcomb.

NORTH HUDSON   MAP, B-5
Yogi Bear's Jellystone Park at Paradise Pines

4035 Blue Ridge Rd., 12855.
T: (518) 532-7493 or (800) 232-5349; www.paradisepines.com.

🚐 ★★★★   ⛺ ★★★★

Beauty: ★★★★   Site Privacy: ★★
Spaciousness: ★★★   Quiet: ★★★
Security: ★★★★   Cleanliness: ★★★★
Insect Control: ★★★★   Facilities: ★★★★

Located along the Schroon River amid the fragrant trees that give the campground its name, Yogi Bear's Jellystone Park at Paradise Pines rests beneath the Adirondack Mountains. Lake George, Lake Placid, Lake Champlain, Ausable Chasm, and the Vermont border are all within an hour's drive. Many sites are shaded by pines, others are open. Not all sites are located along the Schroon River, but riverside sites are quieter. Sites along the river on the campground's southwest side are near activity centers. For more solitude, stay at a riverside site on the northwest side. Campers can swim in the Schroon, and there are rowboats, canoes, and kayaks available for rent. The store here is more like a miniature supermarket, where you can stock your basket and then enjoy a picnic by the river.

BASICS

Operated By: Mike & Gina Lenhard. **Open:** May 1–Oct. 20. **Site Assignment:** Reservations accepted (1-night deposit required for 2-night stay), walk-ins accepted. **Registration:** At campground office. **Fee:** $37–$49; V, MC, D. **Parking:** At designated area.

FACILITIES

Number of RV-only Sites: 125. **Number of Tent-only Sites:** 15. **Hookups:** Electric (30, 50 amps), water, cable TV, phone. **Each Site:** Fire ring, picnic table. **Dump Station:** Yes. **Laundry:** Yes. **Pay Phone:** Yes. **Restrooms and Showers:** Yes. **Fuel:** No. **Propane:** Yes. **Internal Roads:** Gravel & paved, in good condition. **RV Service:** No. **Market:** W/in 3 mi. **Restaurant:** W/in 1 mi. **General Store:** Yes. **Vending:** Yes. **Swimming:** Yes. **Playground:** Yes. **Other:** Schroon River, cabin & trailer rentals. **Activities:** Swimming, game room, rec hall, wading pool, river swimming, whirlpool, canoeing, kayaking, boat rentals, mini-golf, fishing, bike rentals,

basketball, planned activities, movies, shuffleboard, sports field, horseshoes, volleyball. **Nearby Attractions:** Adirondack Park, Lake George, Vermont, Lake Placid, Fort Ticonderoga, Ausable Chasm. **Additional Information:** New York Division of Tourism–Adirondacks, (800) 487-6867, www.iloveny.state.ny.us.

RESTRICTIONS

Pets: On leash only, 1 dog per site, cleaned up after. **Fires:** At site. **Alcoholic Beverages:** At site. **Vehicle Maximum Length:** No limit.

TO GET THERE

From I-87, take Exit 29 and go about 750 ft. east on Blue Ridge Rd. Entrance is on the left.

NORTH JAVA   MAP, C-2
Yogi Bear's Jellystone Park of Western New York

5204 Youngers Rd., 14113. T: (585) 457-9644 or (800) 232-4039; www.wnyjellystone.com.

🚐 ★★★★   ⛺ ★★★★

Beauty: ★★★★   Site Privacy: ★★★
Spaciousness: ★★★   Quiet: ★★★★
Security: ★★★★   Cleanliness: ★★★★
Insect Control: ★★★★   Facilities: ★★★★

Like much of the state, the lush forests and hills of western New York are especially vibrant during the spring and fall. Yogi Bear's Jellystone Park of Western New York is an ideal place to observe this splendor. You can fish and pedal-boat the pond, explore the hilly trails by foot or mountain bike, or take a dip in the heated swimming pool. There is a full slate of activities for both children and adults. The cluster of sites tucked between the fishing pond and the swimming pools on the eastern side are ideal if you prefer proximity to recreation. Sites on the far northern side of the campground are away from the bustle of activity centers. If you don't have an RV or tent, trailers and attractive one-bedroom chalets are available for rent. Letchworth State Park and Conesus Lake are the nearest major natural attractions. Buffalo is about an hour's drive away.

BASICS

Operated By: Scott & Sue Crompton. **Open:** May 1–Oct. 15. **Site Assignment:** Reservations accepted (50% deposit required for 2- & 3-night stays, full deposit required for longer stays), walk-ins accepted. **Registration:** At campground office. **Fee:** $20–$34; V, MC. **Parking:** At site.

FACILITIES

Number of RV-only Sites: 160. **Number of Tent-only Sites:** 40. **Hookups:** Electric (15, 20, 30 amps), water. **Each Site:** Fire ring, picnic table. **Dump Station:** Yes. **Laundry:** Yes. **Pay Phone:** Yes. **Restrooms and Showers:** Yes. **Fuel:** No. **Propane:** Yes. **Internal Roads:** Gravel & paved, in fair condition. **RV Service:** No. **Market:** W/in 3 mi. **Restaurant:** W/in 2 mi. **General Store:** Yes. **Vend-**

ing: Yes. **Swimming:** Yes. **Playground:** Yes. **Other:** Fishing pond. **Activities:** Swimming, boating, pedal-boat rentals, game room, rec hall, fishing, mini-golf, planned activities on weekends, badminton, sports field, horseshoes, hiking trails, volleyball. **Nearby Attractions:** Niagara Falls, Buffalo, Letchworth State Park, Conesus Lake, Lake Erie. **Additional Information:** New York Division of Tourism–Greater Niagara, (800) 338-7890, www.iloveny.state.ny.us.

RESTRICTIONS

Pets: On leash only. Visitors may not bring pets. **Fires:** At site. **Alcoholic Beverages:** At site. **Vehicle Maximum Length:** No limit.

TO GET THERE

From North Java, go 2.25 mi. south on Hwy. 98, 1.5 mi. east on Pee Dee Rd., and 0.75 mi. south on Youngers Rd. Entrance is on the right.

NORTHVILLE   MAP, B-5
Sacandaga Campground

HC-01, Star Rte. 30, Box 104, 12134.
T: (518) 924-4121; www.reserveamerica.com.

🚐 ★★★★   ⛺ ★★★★

Beauty: ★★★★   Site Privacy: ★★
Spaciousness: ★★   Quiet: ★★★★★
Security: ★★★★★   Cleanliness: ★★★★
Insect Control: ★★★   Facilities: ★★★

Situated in a stand of white pine and northern hardwoods on the Sacandaga River, this serene campground offers the camper a wide selection of fishing and hiking on nearby state lands. The campground offers a Junior Naturalist Program, a nature-based program that encourages children to explore the surrounding environment. Sacandaga Campground rests on 125 acres along the Sacandaga River nestled at the foot of several mountains. The site offers 136 tent and RV sites along with a dump station; no electric hookups. Washhouse amenities include flush toilets, a scrubbing sink, and hot showers. Potable water is found sprinkled throughout the park. A public telephone is located adjacent to the ranger's cabin. Several sites are handicapped accessible, including several picnic spots. Fishing is popular in both the Sacandaga River and Lake Algonquin which is 3 miles north of the park. The river supports smallmouth bass, while the lake supports both smallmouth bass and walleye. This campground does not offer a boat launch; however, one is available along the backside of Lake Algonquin. Bicycling and in-line skating are permitted on the campground roads. A very popular activity at this park is tubing the river.

BASICS

Operated By: New York State Parks. **Open:** May 18–Oct. 7. **Site Assignment:** Reservations can be made 9 months in advance. **Registration:** At office. **Fee:** Single, $16. **Parking:** At site.

FACILITIES

Number of Multipurpose Sites: 143. **Hookups:** None. **Dump Station:** Yes. **Laundry:** No. **Pay Phone:** Yes. **Restrooms and Showers:** Yes. **Fuel:** No. **Propane:** No. **Internal Roads:** Paved. **RV Service:** No. **Market:** W/in 10 mi. **Restaurant:** W/in 10 mi. **General Store:** W/in 10 mi. **Vending:** No. **Swimming:** No. **Playground:** No. **Activities:** Biking, bird-watching, fishing, picnicking.

RESTRICTIONS

Pets: Pets are allowed w/ proof of current/valid rabies vaccination. Campers can walk a dog on a leash no longer than 6 feet as long as the dog is under control. Dogs cannot be left unattended. Pets are not allowed in day-use areas, beaches, or any structure. **Fires:** Permitted in designated fireplaces. **Alcoholic Beverages:** Persons age 21 or over who possess or consume alcoholic beverages must produce adequate identification & proof of age upon request. **Other:** Prohibited: beer balls & beer kegs. All campers must wear camper ID bracelets, provided at registration, throughout the stay. No vehicle traffic after midnight. No visitors or day-users after 8 p.m. Quiet hours are 10 p.m.–7 a.m. & are strictly enforced. Campers not listed on the camping permit are not allowed in the facility during these hours. Generators may not be operated during these hours. A recycling center is available for refuse disposal.

TO GET THERE

Take the New York State Thruway to Exit 27 (Amsterdam). Proceed north on Hwy. 30 for 35 mi. Look for the campground entrance sign on the left side of the road.

OLD FORGE — MAP, B-4
Old Forge Camping Resort

3347 SR 28, 13420. T: (315) 369-6011 or (800) CAMPING; www.oldforgecamping.com.

Beauty: ★★★★ Site Privacy: ★★★
Spaciousness: ★★★ Quiet: ★★★★
Security: ★★★★ Cleanliness: ★★★★
Insect Control: ★★★★ Facilities: ★★★★

Located on the western end of Adirondack Park, near the Fulton Chain of Lakes, Old Forge Camping Resort is a year-round campground in the Adirondack Mountains with 123 acres and its own lake. There are 131 sites, only 5 of which are pull-throughs. Sites are spacious and wooded with mostly pine trees, and the campground is within a mile of the village of Old Forge, where 28-mile boat cruises float along the Fulton Chain of Lakes. Though Old Forge does not have a swimming pool, it does have Serene Lake, where campers can swim, fish, or enjoy the water aboard a rented rowboat, canoe, or pedal boat. The nearby Enchanted Forest is a 60-acre water park that also has amusement rides and circus performances. Since the campground is open all year, you can enjoy the winter wonderland in cold months. In the region, there are 500 miles of groomed trails for snowmobiling, cross-country and alpine skiing, and snowshoeing.

BASICS

Operated By: Private operator. **Open:** All year. **Site Assignment:** Reservations recommended (1-night deposit required), walk-ins accepted. **Registration:** At campground office. **Fee:** Tent, $24; full hookup, $33–$43; cabin, $60; cottage, $155; V, MC, D. **Parking:** At site.

FACILITIES

Number of RV-only Sites: 47. **Number of Tent-only Sites:** 205. **Hookups:** Electric (20, 30, 50 amps), water, phone. **Each Site:** Fire rings, picnic tables. **Dump Station:** Yes. **Laundry:** Yes. **Pay Phone:** Yes. **Restrooms and Showers:** Yes. **Fuel:** Yes. **Propane:** Yes. **Internal Roads:** Gravel & paved, in excellent condition. **RV Service:** No. **Market:** W/in 1 mi. **Restaurant:** W/in 1 mi. **General Store:** Yes. **Vending:** Yes. **Swimming:** Yes. **Playground:** Yes. **Other:** Serene Lake. **Activities:** Lake swimming & fishing, basketball, rec hall, game room, boating, boat rentals, movies, horseshoes, hiking trails, volleyball. **Nearby Attractions:** Adirondack Scenic Railroad, Old Forge Lake Cruise, Enchanted Forest & Water Safari, McCauley Mountain, Adirondack Park, Forest Industries Exhibit Hall, Raquette Lake. **Additional Information:** New York Division of Tourism–Adirondacks, (800) 487-6867, www.iloveny.state.ny.us.

RESTRICTIONS

Pets: On leash only. **Fires:** At site. **Alcoholic Beverages:** At site. **Vehicle Maximum Length:** No limit. **Other:** 21 or older to rent sites. 6 persons max. per site.

TO GET THERE

From Old Forge, go 1 mi. north on Hwy. 28. Entrance is on the left.

OXFORD — MAP, C-4
Bowman Lake State Park

745 Bliven Sherman Rd., 13830. T: (607) 334-2718; www.reserveamerica.com.

Beauty: ★★★ Site Privacy: ★★★
Spaciousness: ★★★ Quiet: ★★★★
Security: ★★★★ Cleanliness: ★★★★
Insect Control: ★★★ Facilities: ★★★★

Bowman Lake State Park is a remote sylvan retreat known as "a camper's paradise." Scenic park roads wind through evergreen and hardwood forests to shady campsites. There is a sandy lakefront for swimmers and sunbathers with several picnic areas nearby. The lake is regularly stocked with trout, and bird-watchers can spot as many as 103 species of birds. The park also has a nature center that stocks a self-guiding trail brochure for those who wish to stroll the nature trail around the lake. In winter, snowmobilers and cross-country skiers enjoy outstanding scenery on 8 miles of designated trails.

BASICS

Operated By: New York State Parks. **Open:** All year. **Site Assignment:** Reservations can be made 9 months in advance. **Registration:** At office. **Fee:** Single, $13. **Parking:** Amenity parking.

FACILITIES

Number of Multipurpose Sites: 209. **Hookups:** None. **Dump Station:** Yes. **Laundry:** No. **Pay Phone:** Yes. **Restrooms and Showers:** Yes. **Fuel:** No. **Propane:** No. **Internal Roads:** Paved. **RV Service:** No. **Market:** No. **Restaurant:** Yes. **General Store:** Yes. **Vending:** No. **Swimming:** Yes. **Playground:** Yes. **Other:** Campers must set up & occupy the site. **Activities:** Baseball, basketball, biking, bird-watching, boating, canoeing, cross-country skiing, fishing, hiking, hunting, interpretive programs, nature study, picnicking, snowmobiling, volleyball.

RESTRICTIONS

Pets: Pets must have proof of a recent rabies inoculation. Dogs must be on a 6-ft. leash at all times. **Fires:** Permitted in designated fireplaces. **Alcoholic Beverages:** Persons age 21 or over who possess or consume alcoholic beverages must produce adequate identification & proof of age upon request.

TO GET THERE

From the Syracuse area take Hwy. 81 south to Exit 9 (Marathon). Take Hwy. 221 east to Hwy. 41. Travel on Hwy. 41 through Willett 0.5 mi. and turn left onto Germantown Rd. to McDonough. Go through stop sign to Hwy. 220. Take Hwy. 220 about 7 mi.; follow signs to park.

PAUL SMITHS — MAP, A-5
Meacham Lake Campground

P.O. Box 53, NY 30, 12970. T: (518) 483-5116; www.reserveamerica.com.

Beauty: ★★★ Site Privacy: ★★★
Spaciousness: ★★★ Quiet: ★★★★★
Security: ★★★★★ Cleanliness: ★★★★
Insect Control: ★★★ Facilities: ★★★★

Campers at Meacham Lake are provided with a wide-open view of a truly undeveloped area and can often hear the loon calling in early morning and late evening. This beautiful location rests amid a wondrous mountain environment. Each fall, the forest is a tapestry of unparalleled colors. Aside from a fishermen's paradise, the campground has an activities area complete with environmental interpreters, volleyball, horseshoes, kids' playground, and bathing beach. Meacham Lake Campground is located on the north and west shores of Meacham Lake. The campground represents the only development of this 1,203-acre lake. The campground is in a very scenic area, surrounded by the northern mountains and extensive tracts of wild forest state land. All types of camping units can be accommodated, from small tents to large RVs, on the 224 campsites. The west side offers primitive and walk-in sites, while the main campground will accommodate both tents and RVs.

BASICS

Operated By: New York State Parks. **Open:** May 18–Oct. 7. **Site Assignment:** Reservations can be made 9 months in advance. **Registration:** At office. **Fee:** Single, $16. **Parking:** Amenity parking.

FACILITIES

Number of Multipurpose Sites: 224. **Hookups:** None. **Dump Station:** Yes. **Laundry:** No. **Pay Phone:** Yes. **Restrooms and Showers:** Yes. **Fuel:** No. **Propane:** No. **Internal Roads:** Paved. **RV Service:** No. **Market:** No. **Restaurant:** W/in 10 mi. **General Store:** No. **Vending:** No. **Swimming:** Yes. **Playground:** Yes. **Activities:** Basketball, biking, bird-watching, boating, canoeing, fishing, hiking, interpretive programs, picnicking, powerboating, volleyball.

RESTRICTIONS

Pets: Pets are allowed w/ proof of current/valid rabies vaccination. Campers can walk a dog on a leash no longer than 6 feet as long as the dog is under control. Dogs cannot be left unattended. Pets are not allowed in day-use areas, on beaches, or in any structures. **Fires:** Permitted in designated fireplaces. **Alcoholic Beverages:** Persons age 21 or over who possess or consume alcoholic beverages must produce adequate identification & proof of age upon request. **Other:** Quiet hours are 10 p.m. to 7 a.m. & are strictly enforced. Generators may not be operated during these hours. A recycling center is available for refuse disposal.

TO GET THERE

From Paul Smiths, go 9.5 mi. north on Hwy. 30. From Malone, go 22 mi. south on Hwy. 30.

PHELPS   MAP, C-3
Cheerful Valley Campground

1412 Hwy. 14, 14532. T: (315) 781-1222; www.gocampingamerica.com.

🚐 ★★★★	▲ ★★★★
Beauty: ★★★★	Site Privacy: ★★★
Spaciousness: ★★★	Quiet: ★★★★
Security: ★★★★	Cleanliness: ★★★★
Insect Control: ★★★★	Facilities: ★★★★

Blessed with beautiful weeping willow trees and the serenity of the Canandaigua, Cheerful Valley Campground is located in the Geneva area in the heart of the Finger Lakes region. The campground is nestled in a valley—thus the name Cheerful Valley—where open and shaded sites include 35 pull-throughs. Campers can fish in the river and swim in the spacious pool. Dances and ice-cream socials are among the events held at the party pavilion. Outlet malls are within five minutes of the campground, and Cheerful Valley has occasional on-site flea markets. The Finger Lakes are the main draw here: fishing, boating, and hiking opportunities abound. Cheerful Valley is located on the Canandaigua, and Seneca and Cayuga Lakes are not far. The region boasts several wineries; Applewood Winery is a short drive from

Cheerful Valley. Lake Ontario and Sodus Point and Bay are 18 miles away.

BASICS

Operated By: Carl & Grace Carlson. **Open:** Apr. 15–Oct. 15. **Site Assignment:** By reservation & first come, first served. **Registration:** At campground office. **Fee:** $28–$34; V, MC. **Parking:** At site.

FACILITIES

Number of Multipurpose Sites: 90. **Hookups:** Electric (20, 30 amps), water, phone. **Each Site:** Fire ring, picnic table. **Dump Station:** Yes. **Laundry:** Yes. **Pay Phone:** Yes. **Restrooms and Showers:** Yes. **Fuel:** No. **Propane:** Yes. **Internal Roads:** Gravel & paved, in good condition. **RV Service:** No. **Market:** W/in 2 mi. **Restaurant:** W/in 2 mi. **General Store:** Yes. **Vending:** Yes. **Swimming:** No. **Playground:** Yes. **Other:** Party pavilion. **Activities:** Game room, sports field, rec hall, fishing, shuffleboard, fire truck rides, planned activities, horseshoes, volleyball. **Nearby Attractions:** Rochester, Syracuse, Seneca Lake, Cayuga Lake, Canandaigua Lake, Lake Ontario, Sodus Point & Bay, Finger Lakes outlets. **Additional Information:** New York Division of Tourism—Finger Lakes, (800) 548-4386, www.iloveny.state.ny.us.

RESTRICTIONS

Pets: On leash only. **Fires:** At site. **Alcoholic Beverages:** At site. **Vehicle Maximum Length:** 36 ft.

TO GET THERE

From I-90, take Exit 42 and go 0.5 mi. north on Hwy. 14. Entrance is on the left.

PISECO   MAP, B-5
Little Sand Point Campground

Old Piseco Rd., 12139. T: (518) 548-7585; www.reserveamerica.com.

🚐 ★★★★	▲ ★★★★
Beauty: ★★★	Site Privacy: ★★★
Spaciousness: ★★★	Quiet: ★★★★★
Security: ★★★★★	Cleanliness: ★★★★
Insect Control: ★★★	Facilities: ★★★★

Little Sand Point Campground is a small, linear park stretching a mere 20 acres but offering a full range of outdoor recreation. Located on picturesque Piseco Lake, Little Sand Point Campground offers the seclusion and serenity for family camping. Nestled within the hardwood and conifer trees are 78 large, level campsites with moderate remoteness to one another. Piseco Lake is a good-sized lake, about 8 miles long and 2 miles across, and offers fine fishing, canoeing, sailing, and all types of water sports. There is a concrete boat launch. The fish available include walleye, rainbow trout, brown trout, lake trout, smallmouth bass, brown bullhead, perch, rock bass, and white fish. Numerous hiking trails to challenge the day hiker to the 133-mile-long Northville–Lake Placid Trail are located just minutes away. Piseco Lake is known for the popular hike that begins at

Little Sand Point and climbs to a scenic view from the top of Echo Cliffs on Panther Mountain. A sandy beach offers a guarded swimming area from mid-June to Labor Day.

BASICS

Operated By: New York State Parks. **Open:** May 18–Sept. 2. **Site Assignment:** Reservations can be made 9 months in advance. **Registration:** At office. **Fee:** Single, $16. **Parking:** Amenity parking.

FACILITIES

Number of Multipurpose Sites: 78. **Hookups:** None. **Dump Station:** Yes. **Laundry:** No. **Pay Phone:** Yes. **Restrooms and Showers:** Yes/No. **Fuel:** No. **Propane:** No. **Internal Roads:** Paved. **RV Service:** No. **Market:** W/in 10 mi. **Restaurant:** W/in 10 mi. **General Store:** W/in 10 mi. **Vending:** No. **Swimming:** Yes. **Playground:** No. **Activities:** Biking, boating, canoeing, fishing, jet skiing, paddle boating, picnicking, sailing, waterskiing.

RESTRICTIONS

Pets: Pets are allowed w/ proof of current/valid rabies vaccination. Campers can walk a dog on a leash no longer than 6 ft. as long as the dog is under control. Dogs cannot be left unattended. Pets are not allowed in day-use areas, on beaches, or in any structures. **Fires:** Permitted in designated fireplaces. **Alcoholic Beverages:** Persons age 21 or over who possess or consume alcoholic beverages must produce adequate identification & proof of age upon request. **Other:** Quiet hours 10 p.m. to 7 a.m. & are strictly enforced. Possession of firearms, fireworks, or the operation of chainsaws is strictly forbidden.

TO GET THERE

From the New York State Thruway (I-90), take Exit 27. Follow Hwy. 30 north 50 mi. to village of Speculator. Turn left on Hwy. 8; go 11 mi. to Old Piseco Rd. Turn right, go 7 mi.; campground on left. Also from the New York State Thruway (I-90) take Exit 31 (Utica). Proceed north on Hwy. 8 for 55 mi. to Old Piseco Rd. Turn left, go about 4 mi.; 2nd campground on right.

PISECO   MAP, B-5
Point Comfort Campground

reserve america

Old Piseco Rd., 12139. T: (518) 548-7586; www.reserveamerica.com.

🚐 ★★★★	▲ ★★★★
Beauty: ★★★	Site Privacy: ★★★
Spaciousness: ★★★	Quiet: ★★★★★
Security: ★★★★★	Cleanliness: ★★★★
Insect Control: ★★★	Facilities: ★

Located on picturesque Piseco Lake, Point Comfort offers the camper a number of activities, such as hiking, swimming, and fishing. The campground, developed in the late season of 1929 to provide additional camping to the area, is in the central portion of Adirondack Park at 1,660 feet above sea level. Visitors will find primitive features at Point Comfort

Campground. Only 76 spacious sites are offered for both tent and RV; no electric hookups. Vault toilets and potable water is the extent of the facilities. Campers may use the recycling area and trailer dump station located 2 miles north at Little Sand Point Campground. Irondequoit Bay supports a healthy population of smallmouth bass. A boat launch is offered to anglers. Rowboat and canoe rental may be found at Piseco Lake Lodge. Swimmers will find a guarded beach, beach house, and lakeside picnicking. Approximately 5 miles of hiking trails are easily accessed from the campground. The terrain is basically hills with well-wooded areas consisting of conifers and mixed hardwoods.

BASICS

Operated By: New York State Parks. **Open:** May 18–Sept. 2. **Site Assignment:** Reservations can be made 9 months in advance. **Registration:** At office. **Fee:** Single, $16. **Parking:** Amenity parking.

FACILITIES

Number of Multipurpose Sites: 76. **Hookups:** None. **Dump Station:** No. **Laundry:** No. **Pay Phone:** No. **Restrooms and Showers:** No. **Fuel:** No. **Propane:** No. **Internal Roads:** Paved. **RV Service:** No. **Market:** W/in 10 mi. **Restaurant:** W/in 10 mi. **General Store:** W/in 10 mi. **Vending:** No. **Swimming:** Yes. **Playground:** No. **Activities:** Boating, canoeing, fishing, jet skiing, paddle boating, picnicking, sailing, waterskiing.

RESTRICTIONS

Pets: Pets are allowed w/ proof of current/valid rabies vaccination. Campers can walk a dog on a leash no longer than 6 ft. as long as the dog is under control. Dogs cannot be left unattended. Pets are not allowed in day-use areas, on beaches, or in any structure. **Fires:** Permitted in designated fireplaces. **Alcoholic Beverages:** Persons age 21 or over who possess or consume alcoholic beverages must produce adequate identification & proof of age upon request. **Other:** Quiet hours are 10 p.m. to 7 a.m. & are strictly enforced. Generators may not be operated during these hours. A recycling center is available for refuse disposal. Possession of firearms, fireworks, or the operation of chainsaws is strictly forbidden.

TO GET THERE

From points east on the New York State Thruway (I-90), take Exit 27 (Amsterdam). Follow Hwy. 30 north 50 mi. to the Village of Speculator. Turn left on Hwy. 8 and go about 11 mi. to Old Piseco Rd. Go about 7 mi.; campground entrance on the left. From points west on the New York State Thruway (I-90), take Exit 31 (Utica). Follow Hwy. 30 north 55 mi. to Old Piseco Rd. Turn left and go 1 mi. The campground entrance is on the right.

PISECO   MAP, B-5
Poplar Point Campground

reserve america

Old Piseco Rd., 12139. T: (518) 548-8031; www.reserveamerica.com.

🚐 ★★★★   ⛺ ★★★★

Beauty: ★★★	Site Privacy: ★★★
Spaciousness: ★★★	Quiet: ★★★★★
Security: ★★★★★	Cleanliness: ★★★★
Insect Control: ★★★	Facilities: ★

Located on picturesque Piseco Lake, 15 acre Poplar Point Campground offers the camper the quiet solitude that campers enjoy. The campground is located in the central portion of the Adirondack Park at an elevation of 1,660 feet above sea level. The terrain is basically hills with well-wooded areas consisting of conifers and mixed hardwoods. This campground offers fine fishing, canoeing, sailing, and all watersport opportunities as well as a concrete boat launch. Numerous hiking trails, from day hikes to the 133-mile-long Northville–Lake Placid Trail, are located just minutes away. A natural sand beach offers a guarded swimming area from mid-June to Labor Day. Vault toilets and potable water accompany the tent and RV sites. No electric hookups are available. Anglers enjoy the primitive quiet atmosphere while fishing for smallmouth bass. A boat launch, guarded swimming beach, bathhouse, and several lakeside picnic tables are offered. Piseco Lake Lodge offers boat and canoe rental.

BASICS

Operated By: New York State Parks. **Open:** May 18–Sept. 2. **Site Assignment:** Reservations can be made 9 months in advance. **Registration:** At office. **Fee:** Single, $16. **Parking:** Amenity parking.

FACILITIES

Number of Multipurpose Sites: 24. **Hookups:** None. **Dump Station:** No. **Laundry:** No. **Pay Phone:** No. **Restrooms and Showers:** No. **Fuel:** No. **Propane:** No. **Internal Roads:** Paved. **RV Service:** No. **Market:** W/in 10 mi. **Restaurant:** W/in 10 mi. **General Store:** W/in 10 mi. **Vending:** No. **Swimming:** Yes. **Playground:** No. **Activities:** Boating, canoeing, fishing, hiking, jet skiing, paddle boating, picnicking, sailing, waterskiing.

RESTRICTIONS

Pets: Pets are allowed w/ proof of current/valid rabies vaccination. Campers can walk a dog on a leash no longer than 6 ft. as long as the dog is under control. Dogs cannot be left unattended. Pets are not allowed in day-use areas, on beaches, or in any structures. **Fires:** Permitted in designated fireplaces. **Alcoholic Beverages:** Persons age 21 or over who possess or consume alcoholic beverages must produce adequate identification & proof of age upon request. **Other:** Quiet hours are 10 p.m. to 7 a.m. & are strictly enforced. Campers not listed on the camping permit are not allowed in the facility during these hours. Generators may not be operated during these hours. A recycling center is available for refuse disposal at Little Sand Point Campground.

TO GET THERE

From the New York State Thruway (I-90), take Exit 27 (Amsterdam) and follow Hwy. 30 north 50 mi. to the Village of Speculator. Turn left onto Hwy. 8 and go about 11 mi. to Old Piseco Rd. Turn right about 5 mi. The campground entrance is on the left. Also from the New York State Thruway (I-90) take Exit 31 (Utica) and proceed north on Hwy. 8 about 55 mi. to Old Piseco Rd. Turn left and travel 7 mi. The campground entrance is on the right.

PLATTEKILL   MAP, D-5
Newburgh/New York City
North KOA

119 Freetown Hwy., 12568. T: (845) 564-2836 or (800) 562-7220; www.koa.com.

🚐 ★★★★★   ⛺ ★★★★★

Beauty: ★★★★	Site Privacy: ★★★
Spaciousness: ★★★★	Quiet: ★★★★
Security: ★★★★	Cleanliness: ★★★★
Insect Control: ★★★★	Facilities: ★★★★★

Situated in the Hudson Valley, the 65 forested acres of Newburgh/New York City North KOA offer lovely mountain views, playgrounds, two swimming pools, a fishing pond, and a nature trail. This is the closest KOA campground to New York City, and guided tours of the Big Apple depart from the campground. Campers have their choice of wooded sites, which are spacious and private. There are 24 pull-throughs. The campground even offers a dog-walking service. The Hudson Valley is renowned for its lavish homes and wineries, many of which are open for tours. In nearby Hyde Park, you can see the Franklin D. Roosevelt National Historic Site and the Eleanor Roosevelt National Historic Site. Minnewaska State Park is a short drive away; hiking and bridle trails lead to mountain lakes, waterfalls, and beautiful overlooks. "The Gunks" at Minnewaska is a popular rock-climbing area.

BASICS

Operated By: KOA. **Open:** Apr. 1–Oct. 31. **Site Assignment:** Reservations accepted (2-night min. on weekends), walk-ins accepted. **Registration:** At campground office. **Fee:** RV, $34–$55; tent, $29–$39; V, MC, D. **Parking:** At site.

FACILITIES

Number of RV-only Sites: 140. **Number of Tent-only Sites:** 10. **Hookups:** Electric (20, 30, 50 amps), water, cable TV, phone. **Each Site:** Fire ring, picnic table. **Dump Station:** Yes. **Laundry:** Yes. **Pay Phone:** Yes. **Restrooms and Showers:** Yes. **Fuel:** No. **Propane:** Yes. **Internal Roads:** Paved, in good condition. **RV Service:** No. **Market:** W/in 6 mi. **Restaurant:** W/in 4 mi. **General Store:** Yes. **Vending:** Yes. **Swimming:** Yes. **Playground:** Yes. **Other:** New York City tours. **Activities:** Shuffleboard, mini-golf, planned activities, movies, game room, rec hall, swimming, pond fishing, bike rentals, sports field, badminton, horseshoes, basketball, hiking trails, volleyball.

Nearby Attractions: Newburgh, West Point (U.S. Military Academy), Franklin D. Roosevelt National Historic Site, Eleanor Roosevelt National Historic Site, Washington's Headquarters State Historic Site, Hudson River cruises, New York City. **Additional Information:** Orange County Chamber, (914) 562-5100, www.orangeny.org.

RESTRICTIONS

Pets: On leash only, under control. **Fires:** At site, in fire ring only. **Alcoholic Beverages:** At site. **Vehicle Maximum Length:** No limit.

TO GET THERE

From I-84, take Exit 7N and go 4 mi. north on Hwy. 300, 5 mi. north on Hwy. 32, and 0.5 mi. northeast on Freetown Hwy. Entrance is on left.

PLATTSBURG MAP, A-5
Cumberland Bay State Park

152 Cumberland Head Rd., 12901.
T: (518) 563-5240; www.reserveamerica.com.

🚐 ★★★★   ⛺ ★★★★

Beauty: ★★★★   Site Privacy: ★★★
Spaciousness: ★★★   Quiet: ★★★
Security: ★★★   Cleanliness: ★★★★
Insect Control: ★★★   Facilities: ★★★★

Cumberland Bay State Park, on the west shore of Lake Champlain, is a very popular day-use area because of its large natural sand beach and picnic grounds with tables and grills. The park has 152 campsites, a playground, and playing fields. Cross-country runners frequent the park in the fall. Cumberland Bay is 160 miles east of the Thousand Islands area.

BASICS

Operated By: New York State Parks. **Open:** May 18–Oct. 7. **Site Assignment:** Reservations can be made 9 months in advance. **Registration:** At office. **Fee:** Single, $13. **Parking:** Amenity parking.

FACILITIES

Number of Multipurpose Sites: 152. **Hookups:** None. **Dump Station:** Yes. **Laundry:** No. **Pay Phone:** Yes. **Restrooms and Showers:** Yes. **Fuel:** No. **Propane:** No. **Internal Roads:** Paved. **RV Service:** No. **Market:** No. **Restaurant:** No. **General Store:** Yes. **Vending:** No. **Swimming:** Yes. **Playground:** Yes. **Activities:** Basketball, biking, boating, canoeing, fishing, picnicking, sailboarding, sailing, volleyball.

RESTRICTIONS

Pets: All pets must have proof of currently effective rabies inoculation. Pets must be under constant control either in a cage or on a leash not exceeding 6 ft. in length. Pets are prohibited on the beach in the picnic area. **Fires:** Permitted in designated fireplaces. **Alcoholic Beverages:** Persons age 21 or over who possess or consume alcoholic beverages must produce adequate identification & proof of age upon request. **Other:** Quiet hours are in effect 10 p.m.–7 a.m. Swimming at guarded areas only when lifeguards are on duty. Recycling is mandatory.

TO GET THERE

Cumberland Bay is located off I-87. Take Exit 39 off I-87. Go east on Hwy. 314 toward Vermont. It is 1 mi. to camp entrance, which will be on the right.

POLAND MAP, B-4
West Canada Creek Campsites

12275 SR 28, 13431.
T: (315) 826-7390 or (888) 461-2267;
www.westcanadacreekcampsites.com.

🚐 ★★★★   ⛺ ★★★★

Beauty: ★★★★   Site Privacy: ★★
Spaciousness: ★★   Quiet: ★★★★
Security: ★★★★   Cleanliness: ★★★★
Insect Control: ★★★★   Facilities: ★★★★

West Canada Creek is angler heaven, so it's natural that West Canada Creek Campsites near Poland serves as an angler's sanctuary. Five miles from the southwest tip of Adirondack Park and 10 miles northeast of Utica, the campground is situated along West Canada Creek and features 68 level, open, and shaded sites, including 10 pull-throughs. Bait and licenses are sold at the campground. If you crave something sweet, stroll to the Lil' Caboose Ice Cream Station on the premises. The 24-hour Turning Stone Casino is a short drive from the campground. Utica has a zoo and a children's museum. Cooperstown (home of the National Baseball Hall of Fame and Museum) and Otsego Lake are an hour south of West Canada Creek. We learned that many campers prefer to remain at the campground, though—the fishing at West Canada Creek is that good.

BASICS

Operated By: Private operator. **Open:** Apr. 15–Oct. 15. **Site Assignment:** Reservations accepted (10-day notice required for refunds), walk-ins accepted. **Registration:** At campground office. **Fee:** $22–$45; V, MC. **Parking:** At site.

FACILITIES

Number of RV-only Sites: 56. **Number of Tent-only Sites:** 12. **Hookups:** Electric (20, 30, 50 amps), water, cable TV, phone. **Each Site:** Fire ring, picnic table. **Dump Station:** Yes. **Laundry:** Yes. **Pay Phone:** Yes. **Restrooms and Showers:** Yes. **Fuel:** No. **Propane:** Yes. **Internal Roads:** Gravel, in good condition. **RV Service:** No. **Market:** W/in 10 mi. **Restaurant:** W/in 8 mi. **General Store:** Yes. **Vending:** Yes. **Swimming:** Yes. **Playground:** Yes. **Other:** Ice-cream parlor, West Canada Creek. **Activities:** River swimming & fishing, planned activities on weekends, game room, rec hall, horseshoes, hiking trails, volleyball, badminton, basketball, canoeing, canoe rentals. **Nearby Attractions:** Turning Stone Casino, Utica, Adirondack Park, Herkimer Diamond Mines, Utica Zoo, F.X. Matt Brewing Co., Utica Children's Museum. **Additional Information:** Oneida County CVB, (315) 724-7221, www.oneidacountycvb.com.

RESTRICTIONS

Pets: On leash only; rabies vaccination required. **Fires:** At site. **Alcoholic Beverages:** At site. **Vehicle Maximum Length:** 40 ft.

TO GET THERE

From I-90, take Exit 31 and go 11 mi. north on Hwy. 8. Entrance is on the left.

PORTAGEVILLE MAP, C-2
Four Winds Campground

7350 Tenefly Rd., 14536.
T: (716) 493-2794 or (877) 777-8655;
www.woodalls.com.

🚐 ★★★★   ⛺ ★★★★

Beauty: ★★★★   Site Privacy: ★★★
Spaciousness: ★★   Quiet: ★★★★
Security: ★★★★   Cleanliness: ★★★★
Insect Control: ★★★★   Facilities: ★★★★

Located 3 miles from Letchworth State Park, Four Winds Campground draws campers interested in exploring the Genesee River Gorge, Niagara Falls, Buffalo, or Rochester. This Portageville campground does not have a pool, but there is a pond for fishing and swimming. Four Winds is definitely tranquil enough to hear the gentle wind blow; its rural location is quite peaceful and occasionally attracts deer. Sites are open and partially shaded with a variety of trees, and there are 10 pull-through sites. You can whet your appetite on the campground's hilly and forested hiking trails, but the best hiking is within the 14,344 acres of Letchworth. Bring your camera; there are cliffs that rise as high as 600 feet, plus three waterfalls, one of which is 107 feet high. Rochester is about an hour north of Four Winds. Niagara Falls and Buffalo are a little more than an hour northwest. The campground is also within an hour of Canandaigua Lake and the Finger Lakes region.

BASICS

Operated By: Private operator. **Open:** May 6–Oct. 13. **Site Assignment:** Reservations & walk-ins accepted. **Registration:** At campground office. **Fee:** $25.50–$28.50; V, MC, D. **Parking:** At site.

FACILITIES

Number of RV-only Sites: 125. **Number of Tent-only Sites:** 25. **Hookups:** Electric (20, 30, 50 amps), sewer, phone. **Each Site:** Fire ring, picnic table. **Dump Station:** Yes. **Laundry:** Yes. **Pay Phone:** Yes. **Restrooms and Showers:** Yes. **Fuel:** No. **Propane:** Yes. **Internal Roads:** Gravel, in very good condition. **RV Service:** No. **Market:** W/in 8 mi. **Restaurant:** W/in 6 mi. **General Store:** Yes. **Vending:** Yes. **Swimming:** Yes. **Playground:** Yes. **Other:** Pond. **Activities:** Pond swimming, fishing, game room, rec hall, shuffleboard, planned activities on weekends, hiking trails, volleyball, sports field, horseshoes, hiking trails, volleyball. **Nearby Attractions:** Letchworth State Park, Rochester, Niagara Falls, Buffalo, Conesus Lake, Lake Erie. **Additional Information:** New York Div. of Tourism—Greater Niagara, (800) 338-7890, www.iloveny.state.ny.us.

RESTRICTIONS

Pets: On leash only, under control. **Fires:** At site. **Alcoholic Beverages:** At site. **Vehicle Maximum Length:** 45 ft.

TO GET THERE

From Hwy. 436, go 0.25 mi. north on Hwy. 19A, 1.75 mi. west on Griffith Rd., and 1.25 mi. south on Tenefly Rd. Entrance is on the right.

PULASKI   MAP, B-3
Brennan Beach RV Park

reserve america

80 Brennan Beach, 13142. T: (888) 891-5979 or (315) 298-2242; www.reserveamerica.com or www.brennanbeachrvresort.com.

🚐 ★★★★   ⛺ ★★★★

Beauty: ★★★★   Site Privacy: ★
Spaciousness: ★★   Quiet: ★★★
Security: ★★★★★   Cleanliness: ★★★★
Insect Control: ★★★★   Facilities: ★★★★

Overall, Brennan Beach RV Park has more than 1,100 sites, making it the largest campground in New York and one of the largest in the northeast United States. There are two swimming pools, two recreation halls and a recreation center, two tennis courts, an indoor mini-golf course, shuffleboard courts, playgrounds, and basketball and volleyball courts. Relaxing on the beach is a favorite pastime here, and it is easy to do since the white sands stretch a half-mile. Not all sites here are used at once; there are seasonal sections. You can drop your line in Lake Ontario and the nearby Salmon River. Craft classes and dances are scheduled here, and the campground also offers bingo games and flea markets. This is truly a campground where you can remain on-site for your entire stay—unless you choose to fish in the Salmon River or drive an hour south to Syracuse.

BASICS

Operated By: Private operator. **Open:** May 1–Oct. 15. **Site Assignment:** Reservations accepted (2-night min.), walk-ins accepted. **Registration:** At campground office. **Fee:** $29–$39; V, MC, AE, D. **Parking:** At site.

FACILITIES

Number of RV-only Sites: 400. **Number of Tent-only Sites:** 700. **Hookups:** Electric (20, 30, 50 amps), water, cable TV, phone. **Each Site:** Fire ring, picnic table. **Dump Station:** Yes. **Laundry:** Yes. **Pay Phone:** Yes. **Restrooms and Showers:** Yes. **Fuel:** No. **Propane:** Yes. **Internal Roads:** Gravel & paved, in good condition. **RV Service:** No. **Market:** W/in 5 mi. **Restaurant:** W/in 3 mi. **General Store:** Yes. **Vending:** Yes. **Swimming:** No. **Playground:** Yes. **Other:** Lake Ontario. **Activities:** Lake swimming & fishing, mini-golf, game room, rec hall, boating, basketball, shuffleboard, tennis, horseshoes, volleyball. **Nearby Attractions:** Lake Ontario, Salmon River, Syracuse. **Additional Information:** New York Division of Tourism, (800) CALL-NYS, www.iloveny.state.ny.us.

RESTRICTIONS

Pets: On leash only. **Fires:** At site. **Alcoholic Beverages:** At site. **Vehicle Maximum Length:** No limit.

TO GET THERE

From Hwy. 13, go 1 mi. north on Hwy. 3 and fol-

low signs 0.5 mi. west on entry road. Entrance is on the left.

PULASKI   MAP, B-3
Selkirk Shores State Park

reserve america

7101 NY 3, 13142. T: (315) 298-5737; www.reserveamerica.com.

🚐 ★★★★   ⛺ ★★★★

Beauty: ★★★★   Site Privacy: ★★★
Spaciousness: ★★★   Quiet: ★★★★
Security: ★★★   Cleanliness: ★★★★
Insect Control: ★★★   Facilities: ★★★★

Named in 2005 as one of Reserve America' Top Outdoor Locations, Selkirk Shores State Park is a birders' delight. Over 200 species of birds have been recorded at this park. The migrations tend to follow the shoreline, thereby avoiding the long lake crossing. Raptors are usually seen in early spring. The park is bordered by Lake Ontario to the west, Salmon River to the north, and Grindstone Creek and its marsh to the south. A network of trails wind through the area, offering views of the birds as well as white-tailed deer and other small woodland and marsh animals. Anglers enjoy the huge salmon and steelhead trout populations that migrate up the Salmon River to spawn each fall and winter. Northern pike are the catch during spring and summer. Day-use amenities enjoyed by campers include a boat launch, playground, swimming beach, trails, and a picnic grove with reservable shelters. In winter, cross-country skiing and snowmobiling are enjoyed throughout the park's 980 acres.

BASICS

Operated By: New York State Parks. **Open:** May 3–Oct. 20. **Site Assignment:** Reservations can be made 9 months in advance. **Registration:** At office. **Fee:** Single, $13; cabin, $310–$470; full service, $600. **Parking:** Amenity parking.

FACILITIES

Number of Multipurpose Sites: 185. **Hookups:** Yes. **Dump Station:** Yes. **Laundry:** No. **Pay Phone:** Yes. **Restrooms and Showers:** Yes. **Fuel:** No. **Propane:** No. **Internal Roads:** Paved. **RV Service:** No. **Market:** No. **Restaurant:** No. **General Store:** Yes. **Vending:** No. **Swimming:** Yes. **Playground:** No. **Activities:** Baseball, basketball, biking, bird-watching, boating, canoeing, cross-country skiing, fishing, hiking, jet skiing, picnicking, powerboating, sailing, snowmobiling, volleyball.

RESTRICTIONS

Pets: Pets are welcome; proof of rabies vaccination required. **Fires:** Permitted in designated fireplaces. **Alcoholic Beverages:** Persons age 21 or over who possess or consume alcoholic beverages must produce adequate identification & proof of age upon request. **Other:** Chainsaws, chopping down trees, firearms, fireworks are not allowed at the park. When biking, children under 14 must wear a helmet. Quiet hours are 10 p.m.–7 a.m. Visitors must leave the park by 10 p.m. No substitutions or subletting of campsites or cabins. No skateboards or Rollerblades

to be used in the park. Generators can be excessively loud &/or may omit fumes that can be obnoxious to other campers, especially during meal times. Therefore, operation of generators will be permitted only between 9 a.m.–noon & 8–10 p.m. Excessively loud &/or obnoxious generators will not be allowed.

TO GET THERE

From Syracuse, take I-81 north to Exit 36 (Pulaski). Go north then west on Hwy. 13 through Pulaski to Hwy. 3. Then go south on Hwy. 3 1.5 mi. to the park entrance. From Rochester, take Hwy. 104 east to Hwy. 3. Go north to the park entrance. From Buffalo, take the New York State Thruway (I-90) east to Exit 41 (Seneca Falls). Take Hwy. 414 north to Hwy. 104. Go east on Hwy. 104 to Hwy. 3. Go north on Hwy. 3 to the park entrance. From New York City or Albany, take the New York State Thruway (I-90) west to Exit 34A. Take Hwy. 481 north to I-81. Go north on I-81 to Exit 36 (Pulaski). Take Hwy. 13 to Hwy. 3. Travel south on Hwy. 3 1.5 mi. to park entrance.

QUEENSBURY   MAP, B-5
Lake George Campsite

reserve america

1053 Hwy. 9, 12804. T: (800) 542-2292 or (518) 798-6218; www.lgcamp.com.

🚐 ★★★★   ⛺ ★★★★

Beauty: ★★★★   Site Privacy: ★★★★
Spaciousness: ★★★   Quiet: ★★★★
Security: ★★★★   Cleanliness: ★★★★
Insect Control: ★★★★   Facilities: ★★★★

Located near Lake George Village, Lake George Campsite is the closest campground to the Great Escape and Splashwater Kingdom Fun Park. Billed as New York's largest theme park, the Great Escape has more than 120 rides, live shows, and a storybook-themed children's area. The water park includes a wave pool, waterslides, and Adventure River. Lake George Campsite has fewer activities than other area campgrounds, but its proximity to family-oriented attractions and the village itself makes it an ideal base for a Lake George vacation. The campground, though, does have a swimming pool, a well-stocked store, clean restrooms and showers, and basketball and volleyball courts. There are 175 sites, half of which are secluded, and 75 pull-throughs for long RVs. Tent site 102 is a favorite among campers. Campers may purchase discount tickets to many Lake George attractions, and a bus transports campers to Lake George beaches, boat tours, and other sites. Expect to see lots of white birch here and maybe a bear if you're lucky.

BASICS

Operated By: Private operator. **Open:** All year. **Site Assignment:** Reservations accepted (1-night deposit required), walk-ins accepted. **Registration:** At campground office. **Fee:** Jun. 19–Sept. 5, $32–$42; off-season, $24–$32; V, MC, D. **Parking:** At site.

FACILITIES

Number of RV-only Sites: 125. **Number of Tent-only Sites:** 50. **Hookups:** Electric (20, 30 amps),

water, cable TV, phone. **Each Site:** Fire ring, picnic table. **Dump Station:** Yes. **Laundry:** Yes. **Pay Phone:** Yes. **Restrooms and Showers:** Yes. **Fuel:** No. **Propane:** Yes. **Internal Roads:** Gravel & paved, in good condition. **RV Service:** Yes. **Market:** W/in 2 mi. **Restaurant:** W/in 2 mi. **General Store:** Yes. **Vending:** Yes. **Swimming:** No. **Playground:** Yes. **Activities:** Game room, basketball, horseshoes, volleyball, basketball, rec hall, badminton. **Nearby Attractions:** Lake George, Fort William Henry Museum, The Great Escape & Splashwater Kingdom Fun Park, Lake George boat tours, Water Slide World, Prospect Mountain, Lake George Battlefield Picnic Area, Lake George Dinner Theater, Lake George Action Park. **Additional Information:** Lake George Chamber, (800) 705-0059, www.lakegeorgevillage.com.

RESTRICTIONS

Pets: On leash only. **Fires:** At site. **Alcoholic Beverages:** At site. **Vehicle Maximum Length:** No limit.

TO GET THERE

From I-87S, take Exit 20 and go 1 mi. south on US 9. Entrance is on the right.

RAQUETTE LAKE   MAP, B-4
Tioga Point Campground

General Delivery, 13436.
T: (315) 354-4101;
www.reserveamerica.com.

🚐 ★★★★	🏕 ★★★★
Beauty: ★★★	Site Privacy: ★★★★
Spaciousness: ★★★★	Quiet: ★★★★★
Security: ★★★★★	Cleanliness: ★★★★
Insect Control: ★★★	Facilities: n/a

Tioga Point Campground is a boat-access-only campground which provides great views of Raquette Lake and the surrounding mountains.

BASICS

Operated By: New York State Department of Environmental Conservatoin. **Open:** May 18–Sept. 2. **Site Assignment:** Reservations can be made 9 months in advance. **Registration:** At office. **Fee:** Single, $14. **Parking:** At marina—park can only be reached by boat.

FACILITIES

Number of Multipurpose Sites: 27. **Hookups:** None. **Dump Station:** No. **Laundry:** No. **Pay Phone:** No. **Restrooms and Showers:** No. **Fuel:** No. **Propane:** No. **Internal Roads:** Paved. **RV Service:** No. **Market:** No. **Restaurant:** No. **General Store:** W/in 10 mi. **Vending:** No. **Swimming:** No. **Playground:** No. **Activities:** Boating, fishing, jet skiing, picnicking, powerboating, sailing, waterskiing.

RESTRICTIONS

Pets: Pets are allowed w/ proof of current/valid rabies vaccination. Campers can walk a dog on a leash no longer than 6 ft. as long as the dog is under control. Dogs cannot be left unattended. Pets are not allowed in day-use areas, beaches or any structures.

Fires: Permitted in designated fireplaces. **Alcoholic Beverages:** Persons age 21 or over who possess or consume alcoholic beverages must produce adequate identification & proof of age upon request. **Other:** Quiet hours are 10 p.m.–7 a.m. & are strictly enforced. Campers not listed on the camping permit are not allowed in the facility during these hours. Generators may not be operated during these hours. Possession of firearms, fireworks, or the operation of chainsaws is strictly forbidden.

TO GET THERE

From the Adirondack Northway (I-87): Take Exit 23 at Warrensburg. Follow Hwy. 9 north to Hwy. 28. Go west on Hwy. 28 through the villages of Indian Lake and Blue Mountain Lake to Raquette Lake. Toiga Point is reached by launching boats in center of village.

RAYBROOK   MAP, A-5
Sharp Bridge Campground

P.O. Box 296-NYSDEC, 12977.
T: (518) 532-7538;
www.reserveamerica.com.

🚐 ★★★★	🏕 ★★★★
Beauty: ★★★	Site Privacy: ★★★
Spaciousness: ★★★	Quiet: ★★★★★
Security: ★★★★★	Cleanliness: ★★★★
Insect Control: ★★★	Facilities: ★★

The Sharp Bridge Campground, built in 1920, was one of the first two public campsites built on forest preserve land in the Adirondacks. Its location is best suited for daily hiking excursions in the Adirondack High Peaks, since it is a short distance from some of the most renowned hiking areas in the state. The park offers a variety of recreational opportunities, including canoeing and boating, fishing, hiking, and bicycling. Sharp Bridge Campground rests on 17 acres of land located on the west shore of the Schroon River and offers 40 tent and RV sites. A trailer dump station is provided. Maximum RV length is 20 feet. The campground has pit toilets and showers. Potable water is scattered throughout this riverside campground. Several picnic tables and a picnic pavilion are adjacent to Schroon River. There is also a trail that travels through the hardwood forest stretching down to the river.

BASICS

Operated By: New York State Parks. **Open:** May 18–Sept. 2. **Site Assignment:** Reservations can be made 9 months in advance. **Registration:** At office. **Fee:** Single, $14. **Parking:** Amenity parking.

FACILITIES

Number of Multipurpose Sites: 43. **Hookups:** None. **Dump Station:** Yes. **Laundry:** No. **Pay Phone:** No. **Restrooms and Showers:** Yes. **Fuel:** No. **Propane:** No. **Internal Roads:** Paved. **RV Service:** No. **Market:** No. **Restaurant:** No. **General Store:** No. **Vending:** No. **Swimming:** No. **Playground:** No. **Activities:** Fishing, hiking, picnicking.

RESTRICTIONS

Pets: Pets are allowed w/ proof of current/valid rabies vaccination. Campers can walk a dog on a leash no longer than 6 ft. as long as the dog is under control. Dogs cannot be left unattended. Pets are not allowed in day-use areas, on beaches, or in any structure. **Fires:** Permitted in designated fireplaces. **Alcoholic Beverages:** Persons age 21 or over who possess or consume alcoholic beverages must produce adequate identification & proof of age upon request. **Vehicle Maximum Length:** 20 ft. **Other:** Garbage must be taken to a central recycling area at designated times for processing. Clear plastic bags are required. Quiet hours are 10 p.m.–7 a.m. & are strictly enforced. Campers not listed on the camping permit are not allowed in the facility during these hours. Generators may not be operated during these hours. Possession of firearms, fireworks, or the operation of chainsaws is strictly forbidden.

TO GET THERE

From the north, take I-87 to Exit 30. Proceed south on Hwy. 9 6 mi. Watch for roadside sign on your left. From the south, take I-87 to Exit 29 in North Hudson and turn right (east). Turn left at the next stop sign and travel about 8 mi. The campground will be on your right.

RED CREEK   MAP, B-2
Holiday Harbor Resort
Campground and Marina

9415 Blind Sodus Bay Rd., 13143.
T: (315) 947-5244;
www.lakeontario.net/holidayharbor.

🚐 ★★★★	🏕 ★★★★
Beauty: ★★★★	Site Privacy: ★★
Spaciousness: ★★★	Quiet: ★★★
Security: ★★★★	Cleanliness: ★★★★
Insect Control: ★★★★	Facilities: ★★★★

Located on Lake Ontario's Blind Sodus Bay, Holiday Harbor Resort Campground and Marina is sheltered in a small harbor. The campground includes a 900-foot-long beach on Lake Ontario and a boat ramp and dock along the bay. Grassy bayside sites are popular, and all sites have a view of the lake or the bay. There are eight pull-through sites, with the rest being back-ins. Pines and maples provide most of the shade here. The campground rents rowboats, and guided fishing trips are available. In nearby Fair Haven, you can drive the New York Seaway Trail, a 454-mile roadway that parallels Lake Erie, the Niagara River, the St. Lawrence River, and Lake Ontario. The route passes through villages, towns, and many historic points. Interpretive signs along the way mark 42 different War of 1812 sites. Holiday Harbor is 15 miles southwest of Oswego, where Lake Ontario meets the mouth of the Oswego River. Fair Haven Beach State Park and the Fort Ontario State Historic Site, built by the British in 1755, are among Oswego's attractions.

BASICS

Operated By: Robert Schneider. **Open:** Apr. 1–Oct. 15. **Site Assignment:** Reservations accepted (recommended Jul. & Aug. weekends), walk-ins

accepted. **Registration:** At the old farm house.
Fee: $16–$27; cash, personal check; no credit cards.
Parking: At site.

FACILITIES

Number of RV-only Sites: 100. **Number of Tent-only Sites:** 22. **Hookups:** Electric (15, 20, 30, 50 amps), water, phone. **Each Site:** Fire ring, picnic table. **Dump Station:** Yes. **Laundry:** Yes. **Pay Phone:** Yes. **Restrooms and Showers:** Yes. **Fuel:** No. **Propane:** No. **Internal Roads:** Gravel, in good condition. **RV Service:** No. **Market:** W/in 2.5 mi. **Restaurant:** W/in 2.5 mi. **General Store:** Yes. **Vending:** No. **Swimming:** No. **Playground:** Yes. **Other:** Cottage rentals, boat dock. **Activities:** Game room, video games, rec hall, boat rentals, lake fishing, hiking trails, horseshoes, boating, canoeing, Renaissance Faire. **Nearby Attractions:** Lake Ontario, Oswego, Fair Haven Beach State Park, Syracuse, Rochester. **Additional Information:** Fair Haven Chamber of Commerce, (315) 947-6037, www.fairhavenny.com.

RESTRICTIONS

Pets: On leash only. **Fires:** At site. **Alcoholic Beverages:** At site. **Vehicle Maximum Length:** No limit.

TO GET THERE

From Fair Haven, go 1 mi. west on Hwy. 104A and 3 mi. north on Blind Sodus Bay Rd. Entrance is on the left.

REDWOOD   MAP, A-4
Cedar Island State Park

reserve america

25950 Kring Point Rd., 13679.
T: (315) 482-2444;
www.reserveamerica.com.

🚐 n/a   ⛺ ★★★★

Beauty: ★★★   Site Privacy: ★★★★
Spaciousness: ★★★★   Quiet: ★★★★
Security: ★★★★   Cleanliness: ★★★★
Insect Control: ★★★   Facilities: ★

Located in Chippewa Bay near Hammond, Cedar Island State Park takes up half of the island. The park is favored by people who appreciate quiet boating, fishing, and beautiful scenery. The park's campsites are lightly wooded, with a day-use area and picnic pavilion nearby.

BASICS

Operated By: New York State Parks. **Open:** May 18–Sept. 2. **Site Assignment:** Reservations can be made 9 months in advance. **Registration:** At office. **Fee:** Single, $10. **Parking:** At marina—park can only be reached by boat.

FACILITIES

Number of Multipurpose Sites: 18. **Hookups:** None. **Dump Station:** No. **Laundry:** No. **Pay Phone:** No. **Restrooms and Showers:** Yes/No. **Fuel:** No. **Propane:** No. **Internal Roads:** Paved. **RV Service:** No. **Market:** W/in 10 mi. **Restaurant:** W/in 10 mi. **General Store:** W/in 10 mi. **Vending:** No. **Swimming:** No. **Playground:** No. **Other:**

Cedar Island sites are accessible by boat only, there are no bridges or ferries. Boat rentals available at Wellesley Island State Park Marina. **Activities:** Boating, canoeing, fishing, jet-skiing, picnicking, powerboating, sailing, waterskiing.

RESTRICTIONS

Pets: Pets must have a current rabies certificate & be kept on a 6-ft. leash. **Fires:** Permitted in designated fireplaces. **Alcoholic Beverages:** Persons age 21 or over who possess or consume alcoholic beverages must produce adequate identification & proof of age upon request.

TO GET THERE

For Cedar Island: Boat launching and parking are available at the Chippewa Bay Launch Ramp. From I-81, take Exit 50N and go east on Hwy. 12 for 18 mi. and follow the signs for Cedar Island and Chippewa Bay.

ROSCOE   MAP, D-4
Russell Brook Campsites

101 Russell Brook Rd., 12776.
T: (607) 498-5416;
www.russellbrook.com.

🚐 ★★★   ⛺ ★★★

Beauty: ★★★★   Site Privacy: ★★★
Spaciousness: ★★★   Quiet: ★★★★
Security: ★★★★   Cleanliness: ★★★★
Insect Control: ★★★★ Facilities: ★★★★

High in the Catskill Mountains, Russell Brook Campsites is surrounded by nature's splendor—15,000 acres packed with hiking trails and fishing spots. Located in southeastern New York, Russell Brook is situated on the southwestern tip of Catskill Park. Sites are scattered among tall evergreens along Russell Brook and through the center of the campground. There are two tent-only sections, which are secluded from the RV section. At the campground, anglers can cast their lines into Russell Brook (there are two children's fishing ponds as well). For other challenges, the Beaverkill is just a few minutes away. Willowemoc and Little Beaverkill are both a 10-minute drive from Russell Brook. Binghamton is about an hour west; attractions there include Ross Park Zoo, the Roberson Museum and Science Center, and the Discovery Center of the Southern Tier.

BASICS

Operated By: Doris & Charlie. **Open:** May 1–Dec. 10. **Site Assignment:** Reservations accepted (1-night deposit required), walk-ins accepted. **Registration:** At campground office. **Fee:** Tent, $28; premium, $30; trailer, $30; cabin, $50–$55; V, MC. **Parking:** At site.

FACILITIES

Number of RV-only Sites: 90. **Number of Tent-only Sites:** 50. **Hookups:** Electric (20 amps), water. **Each Site:** Fire ring, picnic table. **Dump Station:** Yes. **Laundry:** Yes. **Pay Phone:** Yes. **Restrooms and Showers:** Yes. **Fuel:** No. **Propane:** Yes. **Internal Roads:** Fair, gravel & dirt roads. **RV Service:** No. **Market:** W/in 3 mi. **Restaurant:** W/in 3 mi. **General Store:** Yes. **Vending:** Yes. **Swimming:** Yes. **Playground:** Yes. **Other:** Russell Brook, fishing

ponds. **Activities:** Fishing, swimming, hiking trails, game room, rec hall, planned activities, basketball, horseshoes. **Nearby Attractions:** Catskill Park, Catskill Fly Fishing Center & Museum, Delaware & Ulster Railway, Delaware County Fair. **Additional Information:** New York Division of Tourism–Catskills, (800) NYS-CATS, www.iloveny.state.ny.us.

RESTRICTIONS

Pets: On leash only. **Fires:** At site. **Alcoholic Beverages:** At site. **Vehicle Maximum Length:** 40 ft. **Other:** Max. 6 people per site.

TO GET THERE

From Hwy. 17, take Exit 93 and go 0.1 mi. west on Old Hwy. 17 and 0.75 mi. on Russell Brook Rd. Entrance is on the left.

SABAEL   MAP, B-5
Lewey Lake

reserve america

General Delivery, 12864.
T: (518) 648-5266;
www.reserveamerica.com.

🚐 ★★★★   ⛺ ★★★★

Beauty: ★★★★   Site Privacy: ★★★
Spaciousness: ★★★   Quiet: ★★★★★
Security: ★★★★★   Cleanliness: ★★★★
Insect Control: ★★★   Facilities: ★★★★

This campground is located in the central portion of the Adirondack Park, on a 90-acre lake and offers secluded, wooded sites. This picturesque campground offers 211 tent and RV sites with no electric hookup, yet it does offer a dump station. Potable water is conveniently located through the campground, which extends to both sides of SR 30. Campers will find the flush toilets, hot showers, and scrubbing sinks centrally located. A swimming beach at Lewey Lake is offered in addition to the adjacent bathhouse, boat launch, and picnic area. A boat launch is also available at Indian Lake, which supports smallmouth bass, northern pike, landlocked salmon, and lake trout. Rowboat and canoe rentals are available from a private concessionaire located within the campground. Bicycling and in-line skating on campground roads is enjoyed by young and old alike. Hiking opportunities include the red-blazed Sucker Brook Trail. Camping at this area was well established before development of a campground began in 1920. Initial camping was at Indian Lake, just north of the present highway bridge, and the campground was known as Lewey Bridge, being named for the hermit and campground resident Louis Seymour. Reachable by only 13 miles of poor roads, the area was initially developed by the Civilian Conservation Corps during the 1930s. Modernization, however, was not attempted until after the development of the present highway.

BASICS

Operated By: New York State Parks. **Open:** May 18–Oct. 7. **Site Assignment:** Reservations can be made 9 months in advance. **Registration:** At office. **Fee:** Single, $16. **Parking:** At site.

FACILITIES

Number of Multipurpose Sites: 211. **Hookups:** None. **Dump Station:** Yes. **Laundry:** No. **Pay Phone:** Yes. **Restrooms and Showers:** Yes. **Fuel:** No. **Propane:** No. **Internal Roads:** Paved. **RV Service:** No. **Market:** W/in 10 mi. **Restaurant:** No. **General Store:** W/in 10 mi. **Vending:** No. **Swimming:** Yes. **Playground:** No. **Activities:** Boating, canoeing, fishing, hiking, picnicking, power-boating, sailing, waterskiing.

RESTRICTIONS

Pets: Pets are allowed w/ proof of current/valid rabies vaccination. Campers can walk a dog on a leash no longer than 6 ft. as long as the dog is under control. Dogs cannot be left unattended. Pets are not allowed in day-use areas, beaches or any structures. **Fires:** Permitted in designated fireplaces. **Alcoholic Beverages:** Persons age 21 or over who possess or consume alcoholic beverages must produce adequate identification & proof of age upon request. **Other:** Quiet hours are 10 p.m.–7 a.m. & are strictly enforced. Possession of firearms, fireworks or the operation of chainsaws is strictly forbidden.

TO GET THERE

From the New York State Thruway (I-90) take Exit 27 (Amsterdam). Go north on Hwy. 30 through the villages of Wells and Speculator. Lewey Lake is 12 mi. north on Hwy. 30 on the right. From the Adirondack Northway (I-87) take Exit 23 at War-rensberg. Take Hwy. 9 north to Hwy. 28 west to Indian Village. Lewey Lake is 12 mi. south of the village of Indian Lake on the right side of Hwy. 30.

SARANAC LAKE   MAP, A-5
Fish Creek Pond Campground

reserve america

Star Rte., Box 75, 12983. T: (518) 891-4560; www.reserveamerica.com.

🚐 ★★★★	⛺ ★★★★
Beauty: ★★★	Site Privacy: ★★★
Spaciousness: ★★★	Quiet: ★★★★★
Security: ★★★★★	Cleanliness: ★★★★
Insect Control: ★★★	Facilities: ★★★★

Fish Creek Pond Campground offers a natural sand shoreline and water access for most campsites. Campers are provided with pristine rivers and ponds accessible to both motorized and nonmotorized boats. Square Pond and Fish Creek Pond (the two bodies of water around which the campground is situated) are open to motor boat usage. Also, motorboat operators can enjoy miles of open water on the Upper Saranac Lake. A trailered boat launch with a small temporary parking area nearby receive steady usage throughout the camping season. Campers seeking nonmotorized boating opportunities are usually referred by the campground staff to the ponds in the Rollins Pond Campground area or the nearby St. Regis Canoe Area (3 miles north of the campground). It is considered by many to be the finest and most attractive of all the Adirondack campgrounds. Campers will find 355 tent and RV sites on 121 acres. RVs are restricted to 40 feet in length. A dump station is offered. Restroom facilities include flush toilets, scrubbing sink, and hot showers. Potable water locations are found scattered about. The campground offers a variety of other recreational opportunities, including an interpreter activity program, canoeing and boating, fishing, hiking, and bicycling.

BASICS

Operated By: New York State Parks. **Open:** Apr. 13–Nov. 10. **Site Assignment:** Reservations can be made 9 months in advance. **Registration:** At office. **Fee:** Single, $18. **Parking:** Amenity parking.

FACILITIES

Number of Multipurpose Sites: 355. **Hookups:** None. **Dump Station:** Yes. **Laundry:** No. **Pay Phone:** Yes. **Restrooms and Showers:** Yes. **Fuel:** No. **Propane:** No. **Internal Roads:** Paved. **RV Service:** No. **Market:** W/in 10 mi. **Restaurant:** W/in 10 mi. **General Store:** W/in 10 mi. **Vending:** No. **Swimming:** Yes. **Playground:** Yes. **Activities:** Amphitheater, basketball, biking, boating, canoeing, fishing, hiking, hunting, interpretive programs, jet skiing, picnicking, powerboating, snowmobiling, volleyball, waterskiing.

RESTRICTIONS

Pets: Pets are allowed w/ proof of current/valid rabies vaccination. Dogs cannot be left unattended. Pets are not allowed in day-use areas, on beaches, or in any structures. **Fires:** Permitted in designated fireplaces. **Alcoholic Beverages:** Persons age 21 or over who possess or consume alcoholic beverages must produce adequate identification & proof of age upon request. **Vehicle Maximum Length:** 40 ft. **Other:** Garbage must be taken to a recycling area at designated times for processing. Clear plastic bags are required. Instructions will be provided directing you in. Possession of firearms, fireworks, or the operation of chainsaws is strictly forbidden. Quiet hours are 10 p.m.–7 a.m. & are strictly enforced. Campers not listed on the camping permit are not allowed in the facility during these hours. Generators may not be operated during these hours. This campground has a 3-day min. stay for reservations.

TO GET THERE

From Saranac Lake, take Hwy. 86 north to Hwy. 186. Where Hwy. 186 ends, take Hwy. 30 south 9 mi. From Tupper Lake, take Hwy. 3/30 north then Hwy. 30 north.

SAUGERTIES   MAP, C-5
Rip Van Winkle Campground

149 Blue Mountain Rd., 12477.
T: (845) 246-8334 or (845) 246-8114;
www.ripvanwinklecampground.com.

🚐 ★★★★	⛺ ★★★★
Beauty: ★★★★	Site Privacy: ★★★
Spaciousness: ★★★★	Quiet: ★★★★
Security: ★★★★★	Cleanliness: ★★★★
Insect Control: ★★★★	Facilities: ★★★★

Rip Van Winkle, legend says, slept somewhere in the Catskills for 20 years. His namesake campground is perfect as a base for Hudson River excursions and outdoor adventures in the Catskills. The campground has a mile of frontage on Plattekill Creek, where campers can swim and fish for trout. There are 20 pull-through sites available, and all sites are heavily wooded with hemlocks. Lucky and patient campers are likely to see raccoons, deer, and owls. Catskill Game Farm and Zoom Flume Waterpark are located in nearby Catskill. The arts colony of Woodstock and the town of Saugerties are not far from Rip Van Winkle. Woodstock was originally chosen as the site for the famous 1969 music festival. When the event grew larger than expected, it was moved 40 miles southwest to a farmer's field outside of Bethel. Cortina Valley Ski Area is in Saugerties, where the Hudson River meets Esopus Creek. The Overlook Observatory, where you can gaze at the stars, is located between Saugerties and Woodstock.

BASICS

Operated By: Private operator. **Open:** May 1–Oct. 1. **Site Assignment:** Reservations accepted (7-day notice required for refund), walk-ins accepted. **Registration:** At campground office. **Fee:** $30–$46; V, MC, D. **Parking:** At site.

FACILITIES

Number of RV-only Sites: 100. **Number of Tent-only Sites:** 50. **Hookups:** Electric (20, 30, 50 amps), water, sewer; 100 full hookups. **Each Site:** Fire ring, picnic table. **Dump Station:** Yes. **Laundry:** Yes. **Pay Phone:** Yes. **Restrooms and Showers:** Yes. **Fuel:** No. **Propane:** Yes. **Internal Roads:** Gravel, in good condition. **RV Service:** No. **Market:** W/in 3 mi. **Restaurant:** W/in 3 mi. **General Store:** Yes. **Vending:** No. **Swimming:** Yes. **Playground:** Yes. **Other:** Plattekill Creek, beach. **Activities:** River fishing & swimming, hiking trails, volleyball, badminton, sports field, horseshoes, croquet, race track w/ radio controlled cars. **Nearby Attractions:** Cortina Valley Ski Area, Opus 40 & Quarryman's Museum, Catskill Park, Catskill Game Farm, Zoom Flume Waterpark, Hudson River, Howe Caverns, Franklin D. Roosevelt National Historic Site, Eleanor Roosevelt National Historic Site. **Additional Information:** New York Division of Tourism–Catskills, (800) NYS-CATS, www.iloveny.state.ny.us.

RESTRICTIONS

Pets: On leash only. **Fires:** At site. **Alcoholic Beverages:** At site. **Vehicle Maximum Length:** 40 ft.

TO GET THERE

From I-87, take Exit 20 and go 0.1 mi. south on Hwy. 32, 2 mi. west on Hwy. 212, and 0.5 mi. north at Centerville Fork on CR 35. Entrance is on the left.

SCHUYLER FALLS   MAP, A-5
Macomb Reservation State Park

reserve america

201 Campsite Rd., 12985. T: (518) 643-9952;
www.reserveamerica.com.

🚐 ★★★★   ⛺ ★★★★

Beauty: ★★★   Site Privacy: ★★★
Spaciousness: ★★★   Quiet: ★★★★★
Security: ★★★★★   Cleanliness: ★★★★
Insect Control: ★★★   Facilities: ★★★★

Macomb Reservation State Park lies just outside the Adirondack Park along the Salmon River's course toward Lake Champlain. Surrounded by state land, the park has a wilderness atmosphere. Visitors can swim in man-made Davis Pond and use nonmotorized boats or fish in the pond or the Salmon River. The park has playing fields, a picnic area, a self-guided nature trail, a hiking trail, and electric and nonelectric wooded campsites. Winter activities include ice skating, cross-country skiing, snowshoeing, and snowmobiling. Macomb Reservation Campground offers 170 tent and RV wooded sites from mid-May through Labor Day, but no electric hookups. There is a large recreation hall with scheduled programs, two baseball diamonds, a car-top boat launch, and a sandy swimming beach and fishing dock in Davis Pond and one at Salmon River. The day-use amenities enjoyed by campers also include a large picnic area with several shelters, a bathhouse, playground, and public phone. Bicycling is permitted on campground roads and cross-country skiing is permitted in winter. The campground has potable water, flush toilets, and hot showers convenient to all.

BASICS

Operated By: New York State Parks. **Open:** May 18–Sept. 2. **Site Assignment:** Reservations can be made 9 months in advance. **Registration:** At office. **Fee:** Single, $13. **Parking:** Amenity parking.

FACILITIES

Number of Multipurpose Sites: 170. **Hookups:** None. **Dump Station:** Yes. **Laundry:** No. **Pay Phone:** Yes. **Restrooms and Showers:** Yes. **Fuel:** No. **Propane:** No. **Internal Roads:** Paved. **RV Service:** No. **Market:** No. **Restaurant:** W/in 10 mi. **General Store:** Yes. **Vending:** No. **Swimming:** No. **Playground:** No. **Activities:** Baseball, boating, canoeing, fishing, hiking, interpretive programs, picnicking, rafting.

RESTRICTIONS

Pets: Pets are allowed w/ proof of current/valid rabies vaccination. Campers can walk a dog on a leash no longer than 6 feet as long as the dog is under control. Dogs cannot be left unattended. Pets are not allowed in day-use areas, on beaches, or in any structures. **Fires:** Permitted in designated fireplaces. **Alcoholic Beverages:** Persons age 21 or over who possess or consume alcoholic beverages must produce adequate identification & proof of age upon request. **Other:** Quiet hours are in effect 10 p.m.–7 a.m.; recycling is mandatory.

TO GET THERE

Macomb Reservation is located off I-87 (Adirondack Northway). From I-87 take Exit 37 near the Champlain Centres. Proceed on Hwy. 3 for 2 mi. to intersection, and bear left onto Hwy. 22B. Continue through Village of Morrisonville, bearing left to Village of Schuyler Falls. At Rock's Store, turn right to Norrisville Rd. Proceed on Norrisville Rd. for 3 mi. Park entrance is on left.

SENECA FALLS   MAP, C-3
Cayuga Lake State Park

reserve america

2678 Lower Lake Rd., 13148. T: (315) 568-5163; www.reserveamerica.com.

🚐 ★★★★   ⛺ ★★★★

Beauty: ★★★   Site Privacy: ★★★★
Spaciousness: ★★★★   Quiet: ★★
Security: ★★   Cleanliness: ★★★★
Insect Control: ★★★   Facilities: ★★★★

Cayuga Lake State Park's terrain is flat at lakeshore, where the beach and sun lawns are, then slopes gently uphill to campsites and cabins. The scenic highlight of the park is its expansive view of Cayuga Lake. In the shallow water near the park, largemouth bass, bullheads, and carp thrive. In deeper water, anglers can catch northern pike, smallmouth bass, lake trout, landlocked salmon, and many other varieties of fish. The park has a boat launch, playground, and playing field. Vacation rentals are also available.

BASICS

Operated By: New York State Parks. **Open:** Jun. 22–Oct. 28. **Site Assignment:** Reservations can be made 9 months in advance. **Registration:** At office. **Fee:** Single, $13; cabin, $190–$315; full service, $700. **Parking:** Amenity parking.

FACILITIES

Number of Multipurpose Sites: 301. **Hookups:** None. **Dump Station:** Yes. **Laundry:** No. **Pay Phone:** Yes. **Restrooms and Showers:** Yes. **Fuel:** No. **Propane:** No. **Internal Roads:** Paved. **RV Service:** No. **Market:** W/in 10 mi. **Restaurant:** W/in 10 mi. **General Store:** W/in 10 mi. **Vending:** No. **Swimming:** Yes. **Playground:** Yes. **Activities:** Baseball, basketball, biking, boating, canoeing, fishing, hiking, jet skiing, picnicking, powerboating, sailboarding, sailing, volleyball, waterskiing.

RESTRICTIONS

Pets: No pets allowed in full-service accommodation at Cayuga Lake. **Fires:** Permitted in designated fireplaces. **Alcoholic Beverages:** Persons age 21 or over who possess or consume alcoholic beverages must produce adequate identification & proof of age upon request. **Other:** No smoking allowed in full-service accommodations at Cayuga Lake. When booking cabins during the peak season the length of stay must be either 7 days or 14 days max.

TO GET THERE

From the New York State Thruway (I-90) take Exit 41, then turn right onto Hwy. 414. At Hwy. 318 take a left to Hwy. 5/20. Make a left on Hwy. 5/20, then turn right onto Hwy. 89. Continue to Cayuga Lake State Park. As Hwy. 89 goes through the park, turn left for the East Camp and right for the West Camp. It is a 15-minute trip from the New York State Thruway.

SPECULATOR   MAP, B-5
Moffitt Beach Campground

reserve america

Page St., 12164. T: (518) 548-7102; www.reserveamerica.com.

🚐 ★★★★   ⛺ ★★★★

Beauty: ★★★   Site Privacy: ★★★
Spaciousness: ★★★   Quiet: ★★★★★
Security: ★★★★★   Cleanliness: ★★★★
Insect Control: ★★★   Facilities: ★★★

Moffitt Beach Campground is located in the central portion of the Adirondack Park on picturesque Sacandaga Lake. At an elevation of 1,730 feet above sea level, the area is generally flat and well wooded with large white pines and hardwoods. This campground offers an interpretive activity program, which provides a high-quality organized recreational and educational awareness experience for both the camper and day user. The programs are provided daily through the months of July and August. Be sure to ask about the Junior Naturalist program for the younger camper. This popular family campground offers large, level sites within the 70- to 80-foot-tall white pine trees to provide a rustic camping ambience. Many of these sites are located on the water's edge. A boat launch aides accessibility to Sacandaga Lake's fine fishing and water-sport opportunities. The campground also offers a guarded natural sand beach from mid-June to Labor Day; a large picnic area with pavilion; and an informal nature trail with information stations.

BASICS

Operated By: New York State Parks. **Open:** May 18–Oct. 7. **Site Assignment:** Reservations can be made 9 months in advance. **Registration:** At office. **Fee:** Single, $18. **Parking:** Amenity parking.

FACILITIES

Number of Multipurpose Sites: 262. **Hookups:** None. **Dump Station:** Yes. **Laundry:** No. **Pay Phone:** No. **Restrooms and Showers:** Yes. **Fuel:** No. **Propane:** No. **Internal Roads:** Paved. **RV Service:** No. **Market:** W/in 10 mi. **Restaurant:** W/in 10 mi. **General Store:** W/in 10 mi. **Vending:** No. **Swimming:** Yes. **Playground:** No. **Activities:** Biking, bird-watching, boating, canoeing, fishing, interpretive programs, paddle boating, picnicking, powerboating, sailing, volleyball, waterskiing.

RESTRICTIONS

Pets: Pets are allowed w/ proof of current/valid rabies vaccination. Campers can walk a dog on a leash no longer than 6 ft. as long as the dog is under control. Dogs cannot be left unattended. Pets are not allowed in day-use areas, on beaches, or in any structure. **Fires:** Permitted in designated fireplaces. **Alcoholic**

Beverages: Persons age 21 or over who possess or consume alcoholic beverages must produce adequate identification & proof of age upon request. **Other:** Beer balls & beer kegs prohibited. All campers must wear camper ID bracelets, provided at registration, throughout the stay. No vehicle traffic after midnight. No visitors or day-users after 8 p.m. Possession of firearms, fireworks, or the operation of chainsaws is strictly forbidden.

TO GET THERE

Moffitt Beach is located off the New York State Thruway. From the Thruway, take Exit 27 at Amsterdam. Go north on Hwy. 30 to Speculator. Go west on Hwy. 8 for 1.5 mi., then turn right on Page St. It is 1 mi. to campground.

ST. JOHNSVILLE   MAP, C-4, C-5
Crystal Grove Diamond Mine and Campground

161 County Hwy. 114, 13452.
T: (518) 568-2914 or (800) KRY-DIAM;
www.crystalgrove.com.

🚐 ★★★★   ⛺ ★★★★

Beauty: ★★★	Site Privacy: ★
Spaciousness: ★★	Quiet: ★★★
Security: ★★★★	Cleanliness: ★★★★
Insect Control: ★★★★	Facilities: ★★★

Set in the foothills of the Adirondacks, Crystal Grove Campground is located adjacent to a mine where—with some work—you may walk away with a sparkling diamond. The prizes are Herkimer diamonds, which are world-famous quartz crystals found only in specific locations in New York State. These unusually clear, brilliant crystals began forming millions of years ago and are highly sought after. Campers can bring their own shovel, hammer, and chisel, or they can rent tools from Crystal Grove. There is also a rock and mineral shop near the mine. Crystal Grove is home to 80 species of birds, and wild flowers blanket the area in season. This is a small campground with just 35 sites (4 pull-throughs), all of which are wooded with maples and ash trees, and located along a stream. The diamond mine is Crystal Grove's main draw, though the campground is not completely devoid of activities. It does have basketball and volleyball courts and a horseshoes pit. About 10 miles from the southern tip of Adirondack Park, Crystal Grove is 30 miles east of Utica and 30 miles north of Cooperstown.

BASICS

Operated By: Private operator. **Open:** Apr. 15–Oct. 15. **Site Assignment:** Reservations recommended (1-night deposit required), walk-ins accepted. **Registration:** At campground office. **Fee:** RV, $29; tent, $22; cabin, $55–$80; V, MC, D. **Parking:** At designated area.

FACILITIES

Number of RV-only Sites: 23. **Number of Tent-only Sites:** 10. **Hookups:** Electric (15, 30 amps), water. **Each Site:** Fire ring, picnic table. **Dump Station:** Yes. **Laundry:** No. **Pay Phone:** Yes. **Restrooms and Showers:** Yes. **Fuel:** No.

Propane: No. **Internal Roads:** Gravel & dirt, in fair condition. **RV Service:** No. **Market:** W/in 10 mi. **Restaurant:** W/in 4 mi. **General Store:** No. **Vending:** No. **Swimming:** No. **Playground:** Yes. **Other:** Crystal Grove Diamond Mine, trout stream on-site. **Activities:** Stream fishing, volleyball, horseshoes, basketball, sports field, rec hall. **Nearby Attractions:** Howe Caverns, Cooperstown, National Baseball Hall of Fame & Museum, Otsego Lake, Remington Gun Museum, Adirondack Park. **Additional Information:** New York Division of Tourism, (800) CALL-NYS, www.iloveny.state.ny.us.

RESTRICTIONS

Pets: On leash only. No pets allowed in mines. **Fires:** At site. **Alcoholic Beverages:** At site. **Vehicle Maximum Length:** 35 ft.

TO GET THERE

From St. Johnsville, go 0.75 mi. on Division St. and 3.75 mi. northeast on Lassellville Rd. Entrance is on the right.

STAATSBURG   MAP, D-5
Mills–Norrie State Park

reserve america.

Old Post Rd., P.O. Box 308, 12580.
T: (845) 889-4646; www.reserveamerica.com.

🚐 ★★★★   ⛺ ★★★★

Beauty: ★★★	Site Privacy: ★★
Spaciousness: ★★	Quiet: ★★★★
Security: ★★★★	Cleanliness: ★★★★
Insect Control: ★★★	Facilities: ★★

Margaret Lewis Norrie State Park adjoins Ogden Mills and Ruth Livingston Mills Memorial State Park and together they comprise more than 1,000 acres. Margaret Lewis Norrie State Park offers a full menu of exhilarating recreational opportunities and activities for visitors of all ages. The numerous trails that thread through the grounds of both Mills and Norrie state parks are ideal for walking, jogging, hiking, cycling, cross-country skiing, and snowshoeing—treating visitors to fabulous views of the Hudson River, which runs directly along the parks' western boundaries. A serene wooded area with glimpses of the river provides an ideal location for camping. There are 48 tent sites and 10 cabins available for rental at the park. RVs are also welcome, but the park does not offer hookup facilities. River access is available for campers with boats at the Norrie Marina, and at the Norrie Environmental Center a variety of nature programs are offered on Saturdays during the summer months. Restroom facilities and showers are located within walking distance. A marina consisting of slip space and a boat-launch ramp is a popular area within the park. There are 145 slips, both fixed pier and floating dock, which are rented on a seasonal basis. Transient boaters are welcome if space allows. The marina also houses showers and a pump-out station.

BASICS

Operated By: New York State Parks. **Open:** May 11–Oct. 28. **Site Assignment:** Reservations can be

made 9 months in advance. **Registration:** At office. **Fee:** Single, $13; cabin, $290. **Parking:** Amenity parking.

FACILITIES

Number of Multipurpose Sites: 58. **Hookups:** None. **Dump Station:** Yes. **Laundry:** No. **Pay Phone:** No. **Restrooms and Showers:** Yes. **Fuel:** No. **Propane:** No. **Internal Roads:** Paved. **RV Service:** No. **Market:** W/in 10 mi. **Restaurant:** No. **General Store:** W/in 10 mi. **Vending:** No. **Swimming:** No. **Playground:** No. **Activities:** Biking, bird-watching, boating, canoeing, cross-country skiing, fishing, golfing, hiking, picnicking, sailing.

RESTRICTIONS

Pets: Dogs allowed in campground; current shot record required. **Fires:** Permitted in designated fireplaces. **Alcoholic Beverages:** Persons age 21 or over who possess or consume alcoholic beverages must produce adequate identification & proof of age upon request. **Other:** Quiet hours are 10 p.m.–7 a.m. Firearms & other weapons are prohibited.

TO GET THERE

Mill-Norrie State Park is located on the east side of the Hudson River, in Dutchess County directly off Hwy. 9 in the Hamlet of Staatsburg. The park is 5 mi. north of the Town of Hyde Park and 5 mi. south of Rhinebeck.

STOW   MAP, C-1
Camp Chautauqua Camping Resort

P. O. Box 100, Rte. 394, 14785.
T: (716) 789-3435 or (800) 578-4849;
www.campchautauqua.com.

🚐 ★★★★★   ⛺ ★★★★★

Beauty: ★★★★★	Site Privacy: ★★★
Spaciousness: ★★★	Quiet: ★★★★
Security: ★★★★★	Cleanliness: ★★★★
Insect Control: ★★★★	Facilities: ★★★★★

Located on Chautauqua Lake in western New York, Camp Chautauqua Camping Resort is one of the nicest in New York and the mid-Atlantic. Some of the 250 sites are located along the shoreline, and all sites are within a five-minute walk of the lake. This is one of New York's finest parks because of its clean facilities and abundant recreational opportunities. RVers are especially catered to, with 114 pull-through sites. The campground has boat rentals, a boat dock, and a beach. The world-famous Chautauqua Institution, a lakeside summer retreat for the arts, education, religion, and recreation, is only minutes away from Camp Chautauqua. You can catch a performance by the Chautauqua Symphony Orchestra and other arts organizations at the amphitheater, listen to a lecture by a well-known speaker, and stroll through Palestine Park, a model of the Holy Land. Fans of *I Love Lucy* will not want to miss the Lucy-Desi Museum in nearby Jamestown. Campers who like hitting the links should bring their clubs to Camp Chautauqua; there are 20 golf courses within 45 minutes of the campground.

BASICS

Operated By: Private operator. **Open:** All year.
Site Assignment: Reservations accepted (traveler's rates available for overnight stays), walk-ins accepted.
Registration: At campground office. **Fee:** $27–$37.50; V, MC, D. **Parking:** At site.

FACILITIES

Number of RV-only Sites: 225. **Number of Tent-only Sites:** 25. **Hookups:** Electric (20, 30, 50 amps), water, cable TV, phone. **Each Site:** Fire ring, picnic table. **Dump Station:** Yes. **Laundry:** Yes. **Pay Phone:** Yes. **Restrooms and Showers:** Yes. **Fuel:** Yes. **Propane:** Yes. **Internal Roads:** Gravel, in good condition. **RV Service:** Yes. **Market:** W/in 3 mi. **Restaurant:** W/in 3 mi. **General Store:** Yes. **Vending:** Yes. **Swimming:** Yes. **Playground:** Yes. **Other:** Boat dock, animal petting farm. **Activities:** Swimming in pool & lake, wading pool, game room, boat rentals, sports field, tennis, basketball, volleyball, horseshoes, boating, fishing, planned activities on weekends, badminton, skiing in the winter. **Nearby Attractions:** Chautauqua Lake, *Chautauqua Belle & Summer Wind* excursion boats, Chautauqua Institution, golf courses. **Additional Information:** New York Division of Tourism, (800) CALL-NYS, www.iloveny.state.ny.us.

RESTRICTIONS

Pets: On leash only. 1 pet per campsite. **Fires:** At site. **Alcoholic Beverages:** At site. **Vehicle Maximum Length:** No limit.

TO GET THERE

From I-86, take Exit 8 and go 3 mi. north on Hwy. 394. Follow signs to campground.

THREE MILE BAY   MAP, A-3, B-3
Long Point State Park

reserve america

7495 State Park Rd., 13693. T: (315) 649-5258; www.reserveamerica.com.

🚐 ★★★★	⛺ ★★★★
Beauty: ★★★	Site Privacy: ★★★
Spaciousness: ★★★	Quiet: ★★★★★
Security: ★★★★★	Cleanliness: ★★★★
Insect Control: ★★★	Facilities: ★★★

Named in 2005 as one of the Top 100 Campgrounds in the nation, Long Point State Park is in a remote area, offering a peaceful, relaxing camping experience. Situated on a peninsula facing Chaumont Bay on Lake Ontario, the park is small and almost completely surrounded by water, with great views from anywhere in the park. Campsites are fairly open and grass-covered, with scattered trees, a playground, and picnic areas. The bay provides a protected harbor for boats, and Lake Ontario offers excellent boating and fishing opportunities. Constant lake breezes keep the park cool and mosquito-free. Long Point on Lake Chautauqua is a moraine, which is a natural deposit left at the end of a glacier. This thickly wooded area rests 1,308 feet above sea level. The lake is known as one of the highest navigable bodies of water in North America. The forest is a combination of beech, maple, spruce, poplar, and oak. Fishing for warm-water species include Muskie, bass, and perch. Powerboating opportunities prevail. Multiuse trails attract hikers, mountain bikers, cross-country skiers, and snowmobilers. Picnicking, playground, swimming beach, a boat launch, showers, and more are offered.

BASICS

Operated By: New York State Parks. **Open:** May 18–Sept. 15. **Site Assignment:** Reservations can be made 9 months in advance. **Registration:** At office. **Fee:** Single, $13. **Parking:** At site.

FACILITIES

Number of Multipurpose Sites: 85. **Hookups:** None. **Dump Station:** Yes. **Laundry:** No. **Pay Phone:** No. **Restrooms and Showers:** Yes. **Fuel:** No. **Propane:** No. **Internal Roads:** Paved. **RV Service:** No. **Market:** W/in 10 mi. **Restaurant:** W/in 10 mi. **General Store:** W/in 10 mi. **Vending:** No. **Swimming:** No. **Playground:** Yes. **Other:** There is a recycling program in effect at the park. No kegs or beer balls allowed on campsites. **Activities:** Basketball, biking, boating, canoeing, fishing, jet skiing, picnicking, powerboating, sailboarding, sailing, volleyball, waterskiing.

RESTRICTIONS

Pets: Pets must have proof of a current rabies inoculation. **Fires:** Permitted in designated fireplaces. **Alcoholic Beverages:** Persons age 21 or over who possess or consume alcoholic beverages must produce adequate identification & proof of age upon request.

TO GET THERE

Take I-81 to Exit 46. Then take Hwy. 12F 6 mi. to Hwy. 180. Turn right. Follow signs to Hwy. 12E. Turn left on Hwy. 12E, go 13 mi. just past Three Mile Bay. Turn left on Hwy. 57 to State Park Rd. Turn left on State Park Rd. It is about 3 mi. to the park.

TRUMANSBURG   MAP, C-3
Taughannock Falls State Park

reserve america

2221 Taughannock Park Rd., 14886.
T: (607) 387-6739; www.reserveamerica.com.

🚐 ★★★★	⛺ ★★★★
Beauty: ★★★★	Site Privacy: ★★★
Spaciousness: ★★★	Quiet: ★★★
Security: ★★★	Cleanliness: ★★★★
Insect Control: ★★★	Facilities: ★★★

Taughannock Falls State Park's namesake waterfall is one of the outstanding natural attractions of the Northeast. Taughannock Falls plunges 215 feet past rocky cliffs that tower nearly 400 feet above the gorge. Gorge and rim trails offer spectacular views from above the falls and from below at the end of the gorge trail. Campsites and cabins overlook Cayuga Lake, with marina, boat launch, and beach nearby. A multiuse trail—hiking, cross-country skiing—winds past sledding slopes and natural skating ponds.

The park also offers organized activities, including tours through the Taughannock Gorge and summer concerts along the lakefront. The spectacular scenery alone draws thousands of campers each year to this campground. In addition, there are 16 cabins (handicapped accessible). Flush toilets, scrubbing sinks, hot showers, and potable water are found throughout the wooded campground. Campers enjoy the park's recreation programs, swimming beach, archery hunting, boat launch, boat rental, concession, and playground. In-line skating is permitted on campground roads. In winter, visitors enjoy cross-country skiing, ice skating, and sledding.

BASICS

Operated By: New York State Parks. **Open:** Mar. 30–Oct. 20. **Site Assignment:** Reservations can be made 9 months in advance. **Registration:** At office. **Fee:** Single, $13. **Parking:** At site.

FACILITIES

Number of Multipurpose Sites: 90. **Hookups:** None. **Dump Station:** Yes. **Laundry:** No. **Pay Phone:** No. **Restrooms and Showers:** Yes. **Fuel:** No. **Propane:** No. **Internal Roads:** Paved. **RV Service:** No. **Market:** W/in 10 mi. **Restaurant:** W/in 10 mi. **General Store:** W/in 10 mi. **Vending:** No. **Swimming:** Yes. **Playground:** No. **Other:** A bridge prevents launch of boats that project more than 6 ft. above water line. Cabins are rustic w/ 4 cots & a refrigerator. No bedding or cooking utensils are provided. Cabins are 7-day or 14-day reservations only. **Activities:** Bird-watching, boating, canoeing, fishing, hiking, jet skiing, picnicking, powerboating, sailboarding, sailing, waterskiing.

RESTRICTIONS

Pets: Pet owners must show a current rabies certificate. **Fires:** Permitted in designated fireplaces. **Alcoholic Beverages:** Persons age 21 or over who possess or consume alcoholic beverages must produce adequate identification & proof of age upon request. **Other:** Boat launch site is not suitable for any type of sailboat.

TO GET THERE

The park is located 8 mi. north of Ithaca on NY 89, along the west side of Cayuga Lake.

VERONA   MAP, B-4
The Villages at Turning Stone RV Park

5218 Patrick Rd., 13478.
T: (800) 771-7711 or (315) 361-7711;
www.turning-stone.com.

🚐 ★★★★★	⛺ n/a
Beauty: ★★★★	Site Privacy: ★
Spaciousness: ★★★	Quiet: ★★★★
Security: ★★★★	Cleanliness: ★★★★★
Insect Control: ★★★★★	Facilities: ★★★★★

Once you arrive on the grounds of the Villages at Turning Stone RV Park, you may not depart until your vacation is over—and you may not leave with your shirt. After all, this lavish destination revolves around action-packed casino games, high-stakes bingo, and prize fights. Nine eateries, a resort hotel,

---

an inn, trendy shops, four golf courses, a driving range and putting green, and an on-site golf academy are just a few of the many facilities available at the casino resort. The park, located 0.5 miles from the casino resort, also has a convenience store and a Laundromat. All sites here are paved and have full hookups, and there are 50 pull-throughs. The cluster of sites at the southeast end of the campground are near the boating pond, store, arcade, and most of the athletic courts. Sites at the far northern tip are quieter and are near the deep-woods hiking trail.

BASICS

Operated By: Villages at Turning Stone. **Open:** Apr. 1–Nov. 30. **Site Assignment:** By reservation & first come, first served. **Registration:** At campground headquarters. **Fee:** $23–$36; V, MC, AE, D. **Parking:** At site.

FACILITIES

Number of RV-only Sites: 175. **Hookups:** Electric (20, 30, 50 amps), cable TV, phone. **Each Site:** Fire ring, picnic table. **Dump Station:** Yes. **Laundry:** Yes. **Pay Phone:** Yes. **Restrooms and Showers:** Yes. **Fuel:** Yes. **Propane:** Yes. **Internal Roads:** Paved, in good condition. **RV Service:** No. **Market:** W/in 2 mi. **Restaurant:** At the resort. **General Store:** Yes. **Vending:** Yes. **Swimming:** Yes. **Playground:** Yes. **Other:** Casino, shops, hotel. **Activities:** Swimming, whirlpool, wading pool, game room, rec hall, pedal boat rentals, pond fishing, golf, driving range, putting green, basketball, planned activities on weekends, movies, tennis, hiking trails, horseshoes. **Nearby Attractions:** Utica, Oneida Lake, Cooperstown, National Baseball Hall of Fame & Museum. **Additional Information:** New York Division of Tourism, (800) CALL-NYS, www.iloveny.state.ny.us.

RESTRICTIONS

Pets: On leash. **Fires:** At site. **Alcoholic Beverages:** At site. **Vehicle Maximum Length:** No limit.

TO GET THERE

From I-90, take Exit 33 and go 1.5 mi. west on Hwy. 365. Entrance is on the right.

WADDINGTON
Coles Creek State Park
MAP, A-4

P.O. Box 442, 13694. T: (315) 388-5636; www.reserveamerica.com.

🚐 ★★★★ 　　　　Ⓐ ★★★★

Beauty: ★★★	Site Privacy: ★★★
Spaciousness: ★★★	Quiet: ★★★
Security: ★★★	Cleanliness: ★★★★
Insect Control: ★★★	Facilities: ★★★★

Coles Creek State Park has wooded and open campsites near a swimming beach on Lake St. Lawrence. The lake is ideal for boating and fishing as well. A marina on the mouth of Coles Creek lies just north of the park entrance. The park also has a playground, playing fields, and a large pavilion.

BASICS

Operated By: New York State Parks. **Open:** May 25–Oct. 7. **Site Assignment:** Reservations can be made 9 months in advance. **Registration:** At office. **Fee:** Single, $13. **Parking:** Amenity parking.

FACILITIES

Number of Multipurpose Sites: 235. **Hookups:** None. **Dump Station:** Yes. **Laundry:** No. **Pay Phone:** Yes. **Restrooms and Showers:** Yes. **Fuel:** No. **Propane:** No. **Internal Roads:** Paved. **RV Service:** No. **Market:** No. **Restaurant:** Yes. **General Store:** Yes. **Vending:** Yes. **Swimming:** Yes. **Playground:** Yes. **Other:** Recycling is mandatory. No dumping gray water on the ground. No swimming from any campsite. **Activities:** Baseball, basketball, biking, bird-watching, boating, cross-country skiing, fishing, hiking, jet skiing, picnicking, sailing, volleyball.

RESTRICTIONS

Pets: Pets must have proof of a current rabies inoculation. Pets must also be caged or leashed at all times. Loop B is pet-free. **Fires:** Permitted in designated fireplaces. **Alcoholic Beverages:** Persons age 21 or over who possess or consume alcoholic beverages must produce adequate identification & proof of age upon request.

TO GET THERE

Coles Creek State Park is 15 mi. west of Massena and 4 mi. east of Waddington along the St. Lawrence River. Signs for the park are located along Hwy. 37.

WARRENSBURG
Lake George/ Schroon Valley Resort
MAP, B-5

1730 Schroon River Rd., 12885. T: (518) 494-2451 or (800) 958-CAMP; www.reserveamerica.com or www.lakegeorgecamping.com.

🚐 ★★★★ 　　　　Ⓐ ★★★★

Beauty: ★★★★★	Site Privacy: ★★
Spaciousness: ★★★	Quiet: ★★★★
Security: ★★★★★	Cleanliness: ★★★★★
Insect Control: ★★★★	Facilities: ★★★★★

Situated along the Schroon River not far from Lake George and Lake George Village, the Lake George/ Schroon Valley Resort is a tranquil campground under white pines, birches, and maples in the Adirondacks. The trees are full of birds, including blue jays, robins, and hummingbirds. Some sites are open; others are wooded and located on the river, where campers fish for northern pike and rainbow trout when not innertubing. Sites on the northeast side are on the river and near many of the recreational facilities. This campground offers 23 pull-through sites. On display is a restored 1931 Covered Wagon RV, which campground managers say was built in Detroit and registered as New York State's first RV trailer. In nearby Lake George Village, you can take a boat tour of the lake, visit Fort William Henry Museum, and frolic at the Great Escape and Splashwater Kingdom Fun Park. The latter has more than 120 rides, including roller

coasters, a storybook-themed children's area, and an expansive water park.

BASICS

Operated By: Private operator. **Open:** Mother's Day–Columbus Day. **Site Assignment:** Reservations accepted (camp 6 nights & 7th night is free), walk-ins accepted. **Registration:** At campground office. **Fee:** $23–$32; V, MC. **Parking:** At site.

FACILITIES

Number of RV-only Sites: 150. **Number of Tent-only Sites:** 35. **Hookups:** Electric (30, 50 amps), sewer. **Each Site:** Fire ring, picnic table. **Dump Station:** Yes. **Laundry:** Yes. **Pay Phone:** Yes. **Restrooms and Showers:** Yes. **Fuel:** No. **Propane:** Yes. **Internal Roads:** Gravel, in good condition. **RV Service:** No. **Market:** W/in 7 mi. **Restaurant:** W/in 7 mi. **General Store:** Yes. **Vending:** Yes. **Swimming:** Yes. **Playground:** Yes. **Other:** Cabin & trailer rentals, Schroon River. **Activities:** Swimming, game room, rec hall, canoeing, float trips, bike rentals, fishing, basketball, planned activities on weekends, movies, badminton, sports field, volleyball, horseshoes, arts & crafts daily, bingo. **Nearby Attractions:** Lake George, Fort William Henry Museum, Great Escape & Splashwater Kingdom Fun Park, Prospect Mountain State Parkway, Lake George boat excursions, Water Slide World, Adirondack Park. **Additional Information:** New York Division of Tourism–Adirondacks, (800) 487-6867, www.iloveny.state.ny.us.

RESTRICTIONS

Pets: On leash only; no aggressive breeds. **Fires:** At site. **Alcoholic Beverages:** At site. **Vehicle Maximum Length:** No limit. **Other:** No refunds for early departures.

TO GET THERE

From I-87, take Exit 24 and go 50 yards east and 0.75 mi. south on Schroon River Rd. Entrance is on the left.

WATERPORT
Lakeside Beach State Park
MAP, B-2

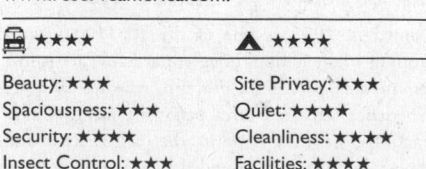

Rte. 18, 14571-9712. T: (585) 682-4888; www.reserveamerica.com.

🚐 ★★★★ 　　　　Ⓐ ★★★★

Beauty: ★★★	Site Privacy: ★★★
Spaciousness: ★★★	Quiet: ★★★★
Security: ★★★★	Cleanliness: ★★★★
Insect Control: ★★★	Facilities: ★★★★

Named in 2005 as one of the Top 100 campgrounds in the nation, Lakeside Beach State Park offers an outstanding panoramic view of Lake Ontario and the surrounding farms and fruit orchards. No swimming is allowed because of the steep banks, but 274 campsites, 4 miles of hiking and biking trails, fishing along the lakefront, picnic grounds, and playing fields bring thousands to the park. Winter activities include hiking, cross-country skiing, and snowmobiling. Each of the 274 campsites offers electrical hookups. Potable water is conveniently located as well as convenient restrooms with hot showers. The park staff offers recreation programs as well as recreation areas, including two ball fields, horseshoe pits, several playgrounds, and two basketball courts. Campers also enjoy picnicking, the on-site laundry facilities, and the camp store. Four miles of multiuse trails are enjoyed by hikers, mountain bikers, and in winter, cross-country skiers. Anglers may fish Lake Ontario.

BASICS

Operated By: New York State Parks. **Open:** Apr. 27–Nov. 5. **Site Assignment:** Reservations can be made 9 months in advance. **Registration:** At office. **Fee:** Single, $13. **Parking:** Amenity parking.

FACILITIES

Number of Multipurpose Sites: 274. **Hookups:** None. **Dump Station:** Yes. **Laundry:** Yes. **Pay Phone:** No. **Restrooms and Showers:** Yes. **Fuel:** No. **Propane:** No. **Internal Roads:** Paved. **RV Service:** No. **Market:** No. **Restaurant:** No. **General Store:** Yes. **Vending:** Yes. **Swimming:** No. **Playground:** Yes. **Activities:** Baseball, basketball, biking, bird-watching, fishing, hiking, hunting, picnicking, snowmobiling, volleyball.

RESTRICTIONS

Pets: Pets must have proof of rabies vaccination & remain on a leash at all times. NO pets in A, B, C, or D loops Pets are allowed in E, F, G loops only. **Fires:** Permitted in designated fireplaces. **Alcoholic Beverages:** Persons age 21 or over who possess or consume alcoholic beverages must produce adequate identification & proof of age upon request. **Other:** Quiet hours are 10 p.m.–7 a.m. No permanent hookups to water spigots. Do not cut trees or branches. No alcohol in kegs or beer balls; no firearms, air rifles, bows & arrows, or slingshots. No loud speakers or stereo equipment. No fish cleaning.

TO GET THERE

On south shore of Lake Ontario, 42 mi. west of Rochester on Hwy. 18 or Lake Ontario State Pkwy., 10 mi. north of Albion, 40 mi. east of Niagara Falls on Hwy. 18.

WATKINS GLEN   MAP, C-3
Watkins Glen/Corning KOA

1710 Hwy. 414 South, 14891.
T: (607) 535-7404 or (800) KOA-7430;
www.watkinsglenkoa.com.

🚐 ★★★★   ⛺ ★★★★

Beauty: ★★★★	Site Privacy: ★★★
Spaciousness: ★★★	Quiet: ★★★★
Security: ★★★★	Cleanliness: ★★★★
Insect Control: ★★★★	Facilities: ★★★★

South of Watkins Glen and Seneca Lake, Watkins Glen/Corning KOA is in the heart of central New York's Finger Lakes region. Amenities are plentiful here. A trout stream cuts through the campground's northern end; campers can fish in the stream and in a stocked pond. From Memorial Day to Labor Day, a breakfast buffet is served on Saturday and Sunday. Thirty-five pull-through sites are available, and there are full-hookup sites at the northern tip of the campground near the trout stream. A cluster of maple-

and evergreen-forested tent sites on the northeast side are a short walk from the fishing pond. Nearby Watkins Glen State Park has 19 waterfalls and stunning canyon views from well-marked trails. Cruises of Seneca Lake embark from the Watkins Glen area. Twenty-two wineries dot the hillsides around the lake, and each of them offer tastings and tours. South of the campground, Corning is home to the Corning Glass Center and historic district with shops and cafes.

BASICS

Operated By: Cam & Paul Friesen. **Open:** Apr. 15–Nov. 1. **Site Assignment:** Reservations recommended (1-night deposit required), walk-ins accepted. **Registration:** At A-frame office. **Fee:** Tent, $29; RV, $34–$50; Kamping Kabin, $52–$75; Kottage, $90–$113; deluxe Kottage, $105–$135; V, MC, AE, D. **Parking:** At site.

FACILITIES

Number of RV-only Sites: 106. **Number of Tent-only Sites:** 9. **Hookups:** Electric (20, 30, 50 amps), water, sewer, cable TV; 56 full hookups. **Each Site:** Fire ring, picnic table. **Dump Station:** Yes. **Laundry:** Yes. **Pay Phone:** Yes. **Restrooms and Showers:** Yes. **Fuel:** No. **Propane:** Yes. **Internal Roads:** Gravel, in good condition. **RV Service:** No. **Market:** W/in 5 mi. **Restaurant:** W/in 5 mi. **General Store:** Yes. **Vending:** No. **Swimming:** Yes. **Playground:** Yes. **Other:** Fishing pond, cabin & cottage rentals. **Activities:** Mini-golf, movies, rec hall, game room, pond fishing, sports field, bike rentals, hiking trails, horseshoes. **Nearby Attractions:** Watkins Glen, Seneca Lake boat cruises, Montour Falls, Watkins Glen State Park, Seneca Lake winery tours, Watkins Glen International Speedway, Corning Glass Center. **Additional Information:** Schuyler County Chamber of Commerce, (800) 607-4552, www.schuylerny.com.

RESTRICTIONS

Pets: On leash only. **Fires:** At site. **Alcoholic Beverages:** At site. **Vehicle Maximum Length:** No limit. **Other:** Check-in & check-out is 1 p.m. for RV, 2 p.m. for cabins & cottages.

TO GET THERE

From Hwy. 14, go 4.5 mi. south on Hwy. 414. Entrance is on the left.

WILMINGTON   MAP, A-5
Lake Placid/
Whiteface Mountain KOA

77 Fox Farm Rd., 12997.
T: (800) 562-0368 or (518) 946-7878;
www.koa.com.

🚐 ★★★★   ⛺ ★★★★

Beauty: ★★★★★	Site Privacy: ★★★★
Spaciousness: ★★★★	Quiet: ★★★★★
Security: ★★★★	Cleanliness: ★★★★
Insect Control: ★★★★	Facilities: ★★★★★

Shaded by behemoth white birches and pines, Lake Placid/Whiteface Mountain KOA is nestled along the Ausable River at the base of Whiteface Mountain in the northeast section of Adirondack Park. Sites are spacious, level, and wooded, and there are 82 pull-

throughs. Bikes are available for rent, as are canoes, kayaks, and tubes for use on the Ausable River. Special events include bingo, movies, and ice-cream socials. With its location at the base of Whiteface Mountain, the campground is near many hiking trails and fishing spots, some of which are accessible from the grounds. Mt. Marcy, New York's highest peak at 5,344 feet, is one of the mountains that surround nearby Lake Placid, a Winter Olympics site. High Falls Gorge and Ausable Chasm are must-see natural treasures nearby. For a refreshing drive, venture along the Whiteface Mountain Memorial Highway, a 5-mile toll road that leads to the peak's summit, where you can see Lake Placid, the St. Lawrence River, and Vermont.

BASICS

Operated By: KOA. **Open:** Apr. 29–Oct. 31. **Site Assignment:** By reservation & first come, first served. **Registration:** At campground office. **Fee:** $69–$278; V, MC, D. **Parking:** At site.

FACILITIES

Number of RV-only Sites: 165. **Number of Tent-only Sites:** 50. **Hookups:** Electric (20, 30, 50 amps), water, cable TV, phone. **Each Site:** Fire ring, picnic table. **Dump Station:** Yes. **Laundry:** Yes. **Pay Phone:** Yes. **Restrooms and Showers:** Yes. **Fuel:** No. **Propane:** Yes. **Internal Roads:** Gravel & dirt, in fair condition. **RV Service:** No. **Market:** W/in 3 mi. **Restaurant:** W/in 1 mi. **General Store:** Yes. **Vending:** Yes. **Swimming:** Yes. **Playground:** Yes. **Other:** Cabin & cottage rentals. **Activities:** Swimming, canoeing, boat rentals, river fishing, mini-golf, basketball, rec hall, game room, bike rentals, planned activities, movies, tennis, hiking trails, horseshoes. **Nearby Attractions:** Lake Placid, Ausable River, Whiteface Mountain, High Falls Gorge, Whiteface Mountain Memorial Highway, Ausable Chasm, Whiteface Mountain Ski Center, Santa's Home Workshop, Lake Placid Center for the Arts. **Additional Information:** Whiteface Mountain Regional Visitors Bureau, (888) WHITEFACE, www.whiteface.net.

RESTRICTIONS

Pets: On leash only. **Fires:** At site. **Alcoholic Beverages:** At site. **Vehicle Maximum Length:** 70 ft.

TO GET THERE

From Hwy. 431, go 2 mi. southwest on Hwy. 86 and 0.25 mi. east on Fox Farm Rd. Entrance is on the left.

WILMINGTON   MAP, A-5
North Pole Campground
and Motor Inn

5644 NY 86, 12997.
T: (800) 245-0228 or (518) 946-7733;
www.northpoleresorts.com.

🚐 ★★★★   ⛺ ★★★★

Beauty: ★★★★★	Site Privacy: ★★★
Spaciousness: ★★★	Quiet: ★★★★★
Security: ★★★★	Cleanliness: ★★★★
Insect Control: ★★★★	Facilities: ★★★★★

Located at the base of Whiteface Mountain along the banks of the Ausable River, North Pole Campground and Motor Inn has two sections for RV and tent campers. The campground's original spot, along the Ausable River, features few sites directly on the river, but all sites are shaded by pines and maples and just a short walk away from the river. Lucky campers may even spot blue herons or woodpeckers. Ducks are frequent visitors, as well. Activity centers are situated near the entrance at the south end. Sites lead north from the campground entrance to the river. North Pole's 100-acre wilderness area is located across the street and features spacious, secluded sites for tenters and pull-through sites for RVers. The network of hiking and mountain biking trails connects to state park trails at Whiteface Mountain. For those without an RV or tent, North Pole has a motel located at the campground, as well as cabins and cottages for rent. Campers can rent rowboats, canoes or pedal boats for use on the Ausable River.

BASICS

Operated By: Carmelitano family. **Open:** All year. **Site Assignment:** By reservation & first come, first served. **Registration:** At campground office. **Fee:** Tent, $23–$26; pop-up, $33–$36; trailer, $35–$38; cabin, $48–$54; cottage, $99–$139; V, MC, D. **Parking:** At site.

FACILITIES

Number of RV-only Sites: 85. **Number of Tent-only Sites:** 40. **Hookups:** Electric (30, 50 amps), water, sewer, cable TV, phone. **Each Site:** Fire ring, picnic table. **Dump Station:** Yes. **Laundry:** Yes. **Pay Phone:** Yes. **Restrooms and Showers:** Yes. **Fuel:** No. **Propane:** Yes. **Internal Roads:** Paved, in good condition. **RV Service:** No. **Market:** W/in 1.5 mi. **Restaurant:** W/in 1 mi. **General Store:** Yes. **Vending:** Yes. **Swimming:** Yes. **Playground:** Yes. **Other:** On-site motel; cabins & cottages available for rent. **Activities:** Swimming, canoeing, boating, boat rentals, rec hall, game room, fishing, mini-golf, basketball, planned activities on weekends, movies, sports field, horseshoes, hiking trails, volleyball. **Nearby Attractions:** Lake Placid, Ausable River, Whiteface Mountain, High Falls Gorge, Whiteface Mountain Memorial Highway, Ausable Chasm, Whiteface Moun-

tain Ski Center, Santa's Home Workshop, Lake Placid Center for the Arts. **Additional Information:** Whiteface Mountain Regional Visitors Bureau, (888) WHITEFACE, www.whiteface.net.

RESTRICTIONS

Pets: On leash only, under control. **Fires:** At site. **Alcoholic Beverages:** At site. **Vehicle Maximum Length:** 50 ft. **Other:** 1 vehicle & 1 camping unit per site.

TO GET THERE

From Hwy. 431, go 0.25 mi. southwest on Hwy. 86. Entrance is on the left.

WOODRIDGE MAP, D-5
Yogi Bear's Jellystone Park at Birchwood Acres

reserve america™

P.O. Box 482, 12789.
T: (845) 434-4743 or (800) 552-4724;
www.nyjellystone.com.

🚐 ★★★★★	🏕 ★★★★★
Beauty: ★★★★★	Site Privacy: ★★
Spaciousness: ★★★	Quiet: ★★★★
Security: ★★★★	Cleanliness: ★★★★★
Insect Control: ★★★★	Facilities: ★★★★★

Located 8 miles west of Ellenville near the southeastern edge of Catskill Park, Yogi Bear's Jellystone Park at Birchwood Acres rivals nearby Skyway Camping Resort. This 150-acre campground has a nice swimming pool and whirlpool and a central sports complex with softball, basketball, paddleball, tennis, shuffleboard, and horseshoes. There is a well-maintained playground, plus wagon rides with Yogi and fire truck rides for the children. The five-acre lake is stocked with bass and bluegill. Campsites are partially wooded. There are 136 double slideout sites, but no pull-throughs. If you want to stay near the

lake, the swimming pool, the adult lounge, basketball and volleyball courts, and other activity centers, we recommend the cluster of sites at the southeast end of the campground. Lodge rentals and RV sites at the northern tip of the campground are away from the activity centers and offer more tranquility.

BASICS

Operated By: Jellystone Park. **Open:** May 1–Oct. 9. **Site Assignment:** By reservation & first come, first served. **Registration:** At campground office. **Fee:** $51–$59; V, MC. **Parking:** At site.

FACILITIES

Number of RV-only Sites: 227. **Number of Tent-only Sites:** 25. **Hookups:** Electric (20, 30 amps), water, phone, cable TV. **Each Site:** Fire ring, picnic table. **Dump Station:** Yes. **Laundry:** Yes. **Pay Phone:** Yes. **Restrooms and Showers:** Yes. **Fuel:** No. **Propane:** Yes. **Internal Roads:** Gravel & paved, in good condition. **RV Service:** No. **Market:** W/in 6 mi. **Restaurant:** W/in 5 mi. **General Store:** Yes. **Vending:** Yes. **Swimming:** Yes. **Playground:** Yes. **Other:** Cabin, lodge & trailer rentals. **Activities:** Swimming, whirlpool, boating, boat rentals, game room, rec hall, lake fishing, movies, shuffleboard, basketball, planned activities, volleyball, tennis, sports field, horseshoes. **Nearby Attractions:** Catskill Park, Minnewaska State Park, Delaware & Hudson Canal Linear Park, Minisink Battleground Park, Stone Arch Bridge Historical Park, Fort Delaware Museum of Colonial History, golf course. **Additional Information:** New York Division of Tourism–The Catskills, (800) NYS-CATS, www.iloveny.state.ny.us.

RESTRICTIONS

Pets: On leash only, under control. 1 pet per site. **Fires:** At site. **Alcoholic Beverages:** At site. **Vehicle Maximum Length:** No limit. **Other:** Quiet time 11 p.m.–8 a.m.

TO GET THERE

From US 209, go 8 mi. west on Hwy. 52 and 0.5 mi. south on Martinfield Rd. Entrance is on the left.

North Carolina

With a wide variety of recreational activities to be had from the western mountain region through the central heartland to the eastern coastal region, North Carolina is a camper's delight.

In the mountain region of North Carolina, you'll find two ranges of the **Southern Appalachians:** the **Blue Ridge Mountains** and the **Great Smoky Mountains.** Here, there are 43 peaks that reach 6,000 feet. **Mount Mitchell,** at 6,684 feet, is the highest peak in the eastern United States. Enjoy your camping experience by engaging in the limitless activities available in the mountains. Fly-fish for trout in the Great Smoky Mountains on **Kerr** or **Falls Lake.** Rock climb or hike at **Table Rock, Looking Glass Rock,** or **Linville Gorge** in **Pisgah National Forest.** Enjoy exciting whitewater rafting on the **Nantahala** and **Pidgeon Rivers.**

Asheville offers plenty for travelers to see and do. Nestled in the **Blue Ridge Mountains,** Asheville's elevation (about 5,000 feet) promises inspirational vistas and comfortable (if occasionally chilly) climates. Autumn travelers will be delighted by one of the longest-running color displays in the country. Culturally minded travelers could easily find themselves overwhelmed by Asheville's myriad of art galleries and boutique shopping. Those wanting a peek at extravagance would do to pay a visit to the 8,000-acre **Biltmore Estate,** featuring the Vanderbilt mansion, a winery, and a 75-acre garden designed by **Frederick Law Olmstead,** the architect who designed Central Park. Couples wishing to enhance the romance of their stay can take a sunset carriage ride that comes complete with a bottle of Biltmore sparkling wine.

Whether approaching or leaving Asheville, it is imperative for travelers to take at least a short jaunt along the **Blue Ridge Parkway.** One of America's most scenic roads, the Blue Ridge Parkway has 252 miles of spectacular views. Along the way, there are plenty of places to pull over and picnic, hike, and camp. There are five campgrounds along the Parkway, so be sure to stop to enjoy some of the outdoor adventure offered in this area. The **Land of Waterfalls** in the Pisgah National Forest offers some breathtaking scenery. Camp in the Great Smoky Mountains or take a scenic ride on the railroad to enjoy unsurpassed views of the area.

Also known as the Piedmont and home of America's first gold rush, the heartland of North Carolina bustles with the state's largest urban areas. Its rolling plains, smooth lakes, meandering rivers, and romantic lagoons provide scenic camping experiences and plenty of water recreation. Be sure to explore the banks and waters of the Lumber River, which is one of North Carolina's four **National Wild and Scenic Rivers.** Boasting 32,500 acres of water, **Lake Norman** provides ample opportunity for campers hoping to swim and boat—which is especially nice on those hot, lazy summer days. The **Roanoke Canal Trail** is also an excellent stop, with its nicely preserved 19th-century canal and seven miles of unique hiking trails that feature views of old bridges and steps carved in the earth.

Venture to North Carolina's coast and its 300 miles of uninterrupted beach and quiet inlets. The history here is rich and inspiring. Sir Walter Raleigh established the first English settlement on **Roanoke Island.** The Wright brothers experienced their first flight on the sandy dunes of **Kitty Hawk** in 1903. The city of **New Bern** is known as the birthplace of **Pepsi,** first marketed as Brad's Drink. Perhaps you can enjoy a sip of the bubbly drink (does it taste different here?) while enjoying a coastal scene comprised of historic lighthouses, islands, and graceful seabirds skimming the surface of the sea. Scuba diving proves to be a particularly unusual experience in the **Graveyard of the Atlantic,** where travelers can explore the remains of over 2,000 ships. On the coast the **Croatan National Forest** offers an excellent stop for campers looking for a wide variety of outdoor activities. The Croatan is also home to unique animal and plant life, including bald eagles and Dionaea musipula—better known as the Venus flytrap! Be sure, too, to visit the **Cape Hatteras National Seashore,** where you can enjoy a number of attractions, including the **Cape Hatteras Lighthouse,** which, at 208 feet tall, is the tallest lighthouse in the country.

Campground Profiles

ALBEMARLE   MAP, B-4
Morrow Mountain State Park

49104 Morrow Mountain Rd., 28001. T: (704) 982-4402; www.ils.unc.edu/parkproject/visit/momo/hone.html.

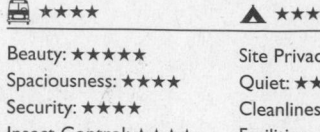

Beauty: ★★★★★   Site Privacy: ★★★
Spaciousness: ★★★★   Quiet: ★★★★
Security: ★★★★   Cleanliness: ★★★★★
Insect Control: ★★★★   Facilities: ★★★★

The campground at Morrow Mountain is situated on gently rolling terrain shaded by pine trees and various hardwoods. Pine straw softens the ground. Many sites enjoy views of pleasant fields, but with little greenery between sites, privacy is minimal. Sites are large, with gravel parking. Most offer back-in parking, though there are couple of pull-through sites. Loop C is recommended for RVs—sites tend to be flatter, with greater maneuverability. Morrow Mountain is the only state park in North Carolina with a swimming pool. For fisher folk, Lake Tillery supports crappie, largemouth bass, striped bass, white bass, perch, bluegill, and catfish. The park is located in the gentle Uwharrie Mountains and includes 16 miles of hiking trails and 16 miles of equestrian trails. When we visited, we saw neither hide nor hair of rangers or staff, making security a bit iffy. But the park is extremely remote. Visit anytime except summer weekends and holidays.

BASICS
Operated By: North Carolina State Parks. **Open:** All year except Christmas. **Site Assignment:** First come, first served; campers can pick desirable site if the site is vacant. **Registration:** At the campsite. **Fee:** No hookup, $15; senior citizens (62 years of age), $10. **Parking:** 2 vehicles per site.

FACILITIES
Number of Multipurpose Sites: 106. **Hookups:** None. **Each Site:** Picnic table, grill. **Dump Station:** Yes. **Laundry:** No. **Pay Phone:** Yes. **Restrooms and Showers:** Yes. **Fuel:** No. **Propane:** No. **Internal Roads:** Paved. **RV Service:** Approx. 30 mi. in Charlotte. **Market:** 7 mi. west in Albemarle. **Restaurant:** 7 mi. west in Albemarle. **General Store:** 8 mi. west in Albemarle. **Vending:** No (concession stand during the summer months). **Swimming:** Yes (Jun. 1–Labor Day). **Playground:** No. **Other:** Group lodging, fishing deck, boat launch, amphitheater, primitive camp sites, cabin rentals, shelters. **Activities:** Boat rental, horseback riding, picnicking, fishing. **Nearby Attractions:** Afro-American Cultural Center, Brem House Artisans Gallery, Charlotte Museum of History, Mint Museum of Art, Paramount's Carowinds Water & Theme Park. **Additional Information:** Charlotte CVB, (704) 334-2282.

RESTRICTIONS
Pets: On leash only; not in buildings or swimming area. **Fires:** Fire ring & in other designated areas. **Alcoholic Beverages:** Not allowed. **Vehicle**

Maximum Length: No limit. **Other:** 6 person max per site.

TO GET THERE
From Albemarle, travel 6 mi. east on NC 740. Follow Morrow Mountain Rd. into the park.

APEX   MAP, B-5
Crosswinds Campground

Jordan Lake State Recreation Area, 280 State Park Rd., 27502. T: (919) 362-0586; www.ils.unc.edu/parkproject/visit/jord/.

Beauty: ★★★★   Site Privacy: ★★★★★
Spaciousness: ★★★★★   Quiet: ★★★★
Security: ★★★★★   Cleanliness: ★★★
Insect Control: ★★★★   Facilities: ★★★

Crosswinds has one advantage over nearby Poplar Point: it's smaller. Otherwise, these two campgrounds are comparable. Crosswinds features incredibly large sites amid hills. And double sites (designed for two families to share) are gargantuan. Sites are densely wooded, with plenty of undergrowth providing privacy between sites. Most sites have back-in parking, though there are a handful of pull-through sites. Parking pads are gravel, and each site has a pea gravel picnic area. Our favorite sites in Area A (18, 19, 22, 46, and 47) have pristine lake views. Families should head for sites 36–39 in Area B, which are convenient to the beach. In Area C, we like sites 19 and 21. Recreation revolves around Jordan Lake, which is known for its teeming crappie, catfish, and bass. Crosswinds locks its gates at night. Though it feels extremely rural, it's only about 20 miles from Raleigh. The campground stays busy in the summer. Visit in spring or fall for solitude.

BASICS
Operated By: N.C. State Parks. **Open:** All year. **Site Assignment:** First come, first served; reservations can be made if staying 7 nights or more, (919) 362-0586; cash & checks accepted; cancel 2 weeks before the arrival date w/o penalty. **Registration:** At campground office. **Fee:** Water/electric, $20; no hookup, $15; senior citizens (62 years of age), $10. **Parking:** 2 vehicles per site, overflow parking available.

FACILITIES
Number of Multipurpose Sites: 177. **Hookups:** Electric (30 amps), water. **Each Site:** Lantern pole, picnic table, grill, trash can. **Dump Station:** Yes. **Laundry:** No. **Pay Phone:** Yes. **Restrooms and Showers:** Yes. **Fuel:** No. **Propane:** No. **Internal Roads:** Paved & gravel. **RV Service:** 6 mi. east in Pittsboro. **Market:** 6 mi. east in Pittsboro. **Restaurant:** 6 mi. in Pittsboro. **General Store:** 1 mi. **Vending:** No. **Swimming:** Yes. **Playground:** No. **Other:** Boat ramps. **Activities:** Fishing, boating, educational activities, hiking, bald eagle watching. **Nearby Attractions:** African American Cultural Complex, North Carolina Art Museum, Mordecai Historic Park, Exploris, JC Raulston Arboretum.

Additional Information: Greater Raleigh CVB, (919) 831-2887.

RESTRICTIONS
Pets: On leash only; not in buildings or swimming areas. **Fires:** Allowed. **Alcoholic Beverages:** Not allowed. **Vehicle Maximum Length:** No limit. **Other:** 2-week stay limit; do not remove plants or animals.

TO GET THERE
From the US 1 and US 64 junction, go west on US 64.

APEX   MAP, B-5
Poplar Point Campground

Jordan Lake State Recreation Area, 280 State Park Rd., 27523. T: (919) 362-0586; www.ncparks.net.

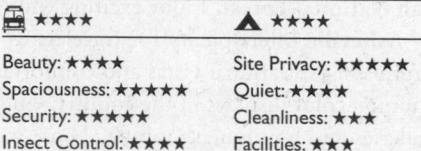

Beauty: ★★★★   Site Privacy: ★★★★★
Spaciousness: ★★★★★   Quiet: ★★★★
Security: ★★★★★   Cleanliness: ★★★
Insect Control: ★★★★   Facilities: ★★★

Mammoth Poplar Point offers sites very much like those at Crosswinds. Both campgrounds feature large sites amongst lovely hills. Most sites are back-in and very shady, with plenty of greenery to provide privacy between neighbors. The majority of parking is back-in style, though there are a few sites with pull-through parking. Parking spaces are gravel, with a pea gravel picnic area at each site. Our favorite lake views are at sites C3–C35, F12, F15, F17, F19. Loop E offers picturesque sites near a small pond (E9, E10, E14, and E15 are the nicest). Tent campers should head to E50–E55. RV campers craving a big, gorgeous pull-through should head for E98. Amenities at Poplar Point are also comparable to those at Crosswinds. However, the beach is more likely to be crowded here because there are so many more sites. Security is good—the campground is gated. To avoid throngs of people, visit mid-week or in spring or autumn.

BASICS
Operated By: N.C. State Parks. **Open:** All year. **Site Assignment:** First come, first served; reservations can be made if staying 7 nights or more, (919) 362-0586; cash & checks accepted; 2-weeks cancellation policy. **Registration:** At campground office. **Fee:** Water/electric, $20; no hookup, $15; senior citizens (62 years of age), $10. **Parking:** 2 vehicles per site, overflow parking available.

FACILITIES
Number of Multipurpose Sites: 580. **Hookups:** Electric (20, 30 amps), water. **Each Site:** Lantern pole, picnic table, fire ring, grill, trash can. **Dump Station:** Yes. **Laundry:** No. **Pay Phone:** Yes. **Restrooms and Showers:** Yes. **Fuel:** No. **Propane:** No. **Internal Roads:** Paved & gravel. **RV Service:** Approx. 6 mi. east in Pittsboro. **Market:** Approx. 6 mi. east in Pittsboro. **Restaurant:** Approx. 6 mi. east in Pittsboro. **General Store:** 1

mi. **Vending:** No. **Swimming:** No. **Playground:** No. **Other:** Boat ramps. **Activities:** Boating, fishing, canoeing, cultural history programs, hiking. **Nearby Attractions:** African American Cultural Complex, North Carolina Art Museum, Mordecai Historic Park, Exploris, JC Raulston Arboretum. **Additional Information:** Greater Raleigh CVB, (919) 831-2887.

RESTRICTIONS

Pets: On leash only. **Fires:** Fire ring only. **Alcoholic Beverages:** Not allowed. **Vehicle Maximum Length:** No limit. **Other:** 2-week stay limit.

TO GET THERE

Go 10 mi. west on US 64 to Wilsonville, then go 2 mi. south on Hwy. 1008.

ASHEVILLE MAP, B-2
Lake Powhatan— Pisgah National Forest

reserve america

375 Wesley Branch Rd., 28806. T: (828) 670-5627; www.reserveamerica.com.

🚐 ★★★★   ⛺ ★★★★

Beauty: ★★★★	Site Privacy: ★★★
Spaciousness: ★★★★	Quiet: ★★★
Security: ★★★★	Cleanliness: ★★★★
Insect Control: ★★★★	Facilities: ★★★★

Lake Powhatan is a very attractive recreation area operated by the Cradle of Forestry in America Interpretive Association under permit from the U.S. Forest Service. Sited well within the Bent Creek Research Forest area, it is one of the more attractive campgrounds in the National Forests within North Carolina. As the name implies, there is a lake (an impoundment of Bent Creek) which includes a fishing pier down by the dam and a nicely maintained sandy swimming beach at the upper end of the lake. (A lifeguard is usually present during the summer months.) Lake Powhatan, located within the Pisgah National Forest, consists of over half a million acres of forest surrounding Mt. Pisgah. The beginnings of the Pisgah National Forest occurred when George Vanderbilt, grandson of railroad baron Cornelius Vanderbilt, assembled property around his growing estate at the confluence of the Swannanoa and French Broad rivers in western North Carolina. As he added to his 125,000 acre estate, one of the acquisitions included Mt. Pisgah. The mountain dominates the Pisgah Ledge, which parallels the French Broad River west of the Biltmore Estate. West of Biltmore, thousands of acres of his Pisgah Forest was managed for the production of timber, water, and other natural resources. These lands were managed first by Gifford Pinchot, forester, conservationist, and first chief of the Forest Service; and later by Dr. Carl Alwin Schenck, a German forester hired by Vanderbilt on Pinchot's recommendation. The area was sold after Vanderbilt's death in 1914 to the U.S. government and became one of the first tracts of the Pisgah National Forest.

BASICS

Operated By: U.S. Forest Service. **Open:** Apr. 1–Nov. 30. **Site Assignment:** Reservations must be made at least 4 days in advance. **Registration:** At office. **Fee:** Single, $17. **Parking:** At park.

FACILITIES

Number of Multipurpose Sites: 97. **Hookups:** None. **Each Site:** Call ahead. **Dump Station:** Yes. **Laundry:** No. **Pay Phone:** Yes. **Restrooms and Showers:** Yes. **Fuel:** No. **Propane:** No. **Internal Roads:** Paved. **RV Service:** No. **Market:** No. **Restaurant:** No. **General Store:** No. **Vending:** No. **Swimming:** Yes. **Playground:** No. **Other:** No boats allowed on lake. **Activities:** Interpretive programs.

RESTRICTIONS

Pets: Pets must be restrained or on a leash at all times while in developed recreation areas. **Fires:** In fire rings, stoves, grills, or fireplaces provided for that purpose. **Alcoholic Beverages:** Not allowed. **Vehicle Maximum Length:** Call ahead.

TO GET THERE

From I-26, take Exit 33 (Old Exit 2), south 2 mi. on NC 191 to the Lake Powhatan Recreation Area sign. Turn right and follow signs to campground.

ASHEVILLE MAP, B-2
Mount Pisgah Campground

reserve america

51 Ranger Dr., 28805. T: (828) 648-2644; www.reserveamerica.com.

🚐 ★★★   ⛺ ★★★★

Beauty: ★★★★	Site Privacy: ★★★
Spaciousness: ★★★★	Quiet: ★★★★
Security: ★★★★★	Cleanliness: ★★★★
Insect Control: ★★★	Facilities: ★★★★

Mt. Pisgah Campground is located on the scenic Blue Ridge Parkway at Milepost 408, near Boone and Blowing Rock, North Carolina. The campground is adjacent to Price Lake. Today on the Blue Ridge Parkway it's possible to rock climb, hang glide, fish for trout, bicycle—almost any activity that doesn't damage the park or endanger other visitors. Campers and hikers alike can meander alongside or cross the Parkway; trails provide a close-up look at some of the most beautiful landscape in the region. Many trails wind their way through unique biological and geological environments. Others lead to historic sites with stories of how people have shaped our heritage. Fishermen who find themselves at a mountaintop park will discover surprisingly good angling.

BASICS

Operated By: National Park Service. **Open:** May 11–Oct. 28. **Site Assignment:** Reservations must be made May 20–Oct 23. **Registration:** At registration office. **Fee:** Call park for fees. **Parking:** At site.

FACILITIES

Number of Multipurpose Sites: 180. **Hookups:** None. **Each Site:** Call ahead. **Dump Station:** Yes. **Laundry:** Yes. **Pay Phone:** No. **Restrooms and

Showers: Yes. **Fuel:** No. **Propane:** No. **Internal Roads:** Paved. **RV Service:** No. **Market:** No. **Restaurant:** Yes. **General Store:** Yes. **Vending:** No. **Swimming:** No. **Playground:** No. **Activities:** Campfire programs, hiking, sightseeing.

RESTRICTIONS

Pets: Pets must be on a leash at all times. **Fires:** Allowed; Campfire Program. **Alcoholic Beverages:** Not allowed. **Vehicle Maximum Length:** Varies; call ahead. **Other:** Food-storage restrictions in effect; no generator use in loop C & D (tent loops).

TO GET THERE

From I-40 west, take Exit 47 to Hwy. 191 south to the Blue Ridge Pkwy. Campground is south on the Pkwy. from Hwy. 191 entrance. Campground is on the right, across from Pisgah Inn. From I-26, take Exit 33 to Hwy. 191 south to Blue Ridge Pkwy. campground is south on the Pkwy. from Hwy. 191 entrance.

BALSAM MAP, B-2
Moonshine Creek Campground

27 Moonshine Cr. Trail, 28707. T: (828) 586-6666; www.moonshinecreekcampground.com.

🚐 ★★★★   ⛺ ★★★★

Beauty: ★★★★★	Site Privacy: ★★★
Spaciousness: ★★★	Quiet: ★★★★
Security: ★★★★	Cleanliness: ★★★★
Insect Control: ★★★★	Facilities: ★★

Balsam is a sweet little town, with restaurants as close as Waynesville and plenty of mountain recreation nearby. The Blue Ridge Parkway intersects the town, making Balsam a good camping choice for motor tourists. Drive east about 10 miles to Richland Balsam, the highest point on the Blue Ridge Parkway (elevation 6,047 feet). The campground offers small, picturesque, back-in sites laid out along Moonshine Creek. Tree cover is lovely, and houses squirrels, birds, and raccoons. Gravel parking pads overwhelm some sites to the extent that there is little natural ground cover. Our favorite creekside sites—14, 16, 18, and 20—are nicely situated but have no grass. Other nice sites include 8, which is more spacious than most, and 9–12. Balsam's cool mountain weather is heavenly in the summer. For the least-hassled touring, plan a mid-week visit. Security is fine here. There is no gate but the park is extremely remote.

BASICS

Operated By: Mack & Janet McDonald. **Open:** Apr.–Nov. **Site Assignment:** Deposit must be received 7 days prior to reservation; 7-day notice on cancellations for refund; V, MC, check, cash, money order. **Registration:** At office. **Fee:** RV, $28–$33; tent, $20. **Parking:** At site.

FACILITIES

Number of RV-only Sites: 59. **Number of Tent-only Sites:** 30. **Hookups:** Electric (30 amps), water, sewer. **Each Site:** Fire ring, picnic table. **Dump Station:** Yes. **Laundry:** Yes. **Pay Phone:** Yes. **Restrooms and Showers:** Yes. **Fuel:** No. **Propane:** Yes. **Internal Roads:** Gravel, entrance is asphalt. **RV Service:** 5 mi. toward Waynesville. **Market:** 5 mi.

toward Waynesville. **Restaurant:** 5 mi. toward Waynesville. **General Store:** Yes. **Vending:** No. **Swimming:** No. **Playground:** Yes. **Other:** Web connection. **Activities:** Planned cookouts, fishing. **Nearby Attractions:** Appalachian Trail, Biltmore House, Blowing Rock, Blue Ridge Pkwy., Cherohala Skyway, Cherokee Bear Zoo, Cherokee Corn Maze, Cherokee Indian Museum, Cherokee Indian Reservation, Chimney Rock Park, Deep Creek tubes, Fields of the Wood, Fontana Lake & Dam, Ghost Town in Maggie Valley, Grand Father Mountain, Great Smoky Mountain National Park, Harra's Cherokee Casino, Joyce Kilmer Memorial Forest, Linville Caverns, Mountain Farm & Museum, Mountain Waters Scenic Byway, Nantahala National Forest, Nantahala River Rafting, Oconaluftee Indian Village, Pisgah National Forest, Santa's Land Fun Park & Zoo, Soco Gardens Zoo, Smoky Mountain Country Club, Tribal Bingo, Tsali Trail, Unto These Hills Outdoor Drama.

RESTRICTIONS

Pets: Allowed. **Fires:** Fire ring only. **Alcoholic Beverages:** At site only. **Vehicle Maximum Length:** No limit.

TO GET THERE

From Cherokee: Drive south on US 441, then northeast on US 74/23. Follow signs to campground.

BLOWING ROCK   MAP, A-3
Julian Price

reserve america™

5580 Shulls Mill Rd., 28605. T: (828) 963-5911; www.reserveamerica.com.

🚐 ★★★★   ▲ ★★★

Beauty: ★★★★	Site Privacy: ★★★
Spaciousness: ★★★★	Quiet: ★★★★
Security: ★★★★★	Cleanliness: ★★★★
Insect Control: ★★★	Facilities: ★★

Julian Price Park Campground is located on the beautiful Blue Ridge Parkway near Boone and Blowing Rock, North Carolina. The campground is adjacent to Price Lake. Today on the Blue Ridge Parkway it's possible to rock climb, hang glide, fish for trout, bicycle—almost any activity that doesn't damage the park or endanger other visitors. Many activities attract campers to Julian Price and the Blue Ridge Parkway, such as the hiking where campers and hikers alike can meander alongside or cross the Parkway. Trails provide a close-up look at some of the most beautiful landscape in the region. Many trails wind their way through unique biological and geological environments. Others lead to historic sites with stories of how people have shaped our heritage. If you are a fisherman at heart you'll find yourself at a mountaintop park, may seem an unlikely place to fish, but just the opposite is true!

BASICS

Operated By: National Park Service. **Open:** May 11–May 28. **Site Assignment:** Reservations must be made 2 days in advance. **Registration:** At registration office. **Fee:** Single, $16. **Parking:** At site.

FACILITIES

Number of Multipurpose Sites: 320. **Hookups:** None. **Each Site:** Call ahead. **Dump Station:** Yes. **Laundry:** No. **Pay Phone:** No. **Restrooms and Showers:** Yes. **Fuel:** No. **Propane:** No. **Internal Roads:** Paved. **RV Service:** No. **Market:** No. **Restaurant:** No. **General Store:** No. **Vending:** No. **Swimming:** No. **Playground:** No. **Other:** All equipment must fit on the site pad. Vehicles park in developed areas only. **Activities:** Campfire programs, canoeing, hiking, sightseeing.

RESTRICTIONS

Pets: Pets must be on a leash at all times. **Fires:** Allowed; Campfire Program. **Alcoholic Beverages:** Not allowed. **Vehicle Maximum Length:** Varies; call ahead.

TO GET THERE

From Asheville, go north on Blue Ridge Pkwy. to milepost 297 (85 mi.). From Hwy. 321 near Boone, enter Blue Ridge Pkwy. and travel south 5 mi.

CAPE HATTERAS   MAP, B-8
Ocracoke

1401 National Park Dr., P.O. Box 675, 27954. T: (252) 928-3841; www.nps.gov/caha.

🚐 ★★★★   ▲ ★★★★

Beauty: ★★★★★	Site Privacy: ★★
Spaciousness: ★★★★	Quiet: ★★★★★
Security: ★★★★★	Cleanliness: ★★★★
Insect Control: ★★★	Facilities: ★

Beautiful Ocracoke campground is bounded by gentle natural dunes and native grasses. It is flatter than the campground at Oregon Inlet, allowing for nicer views. We recommend this quiet campground for tent campers. Ocracoke can be reached by ferry only. Once you're on the island, you can explore the beaches once frequented by Blackbeard, or check out the oldest operating lighthouse in North Carolina (built in 1823). Many sites on the perimeter of the campground are nestled into the dunes. Sites D23, D25, and D27 are especially comfortable for tent campers. RV campers should head for sites B3, D33, D35, and D37, which offer both privacy and long parking pads. If you prefer open sites, there are plenty to choose from. Sites contain back-in parking, paved parking, and grassy areas. Site size is ample, though spacing between sites varies. Security is excellent; Ocracoke Island is nearly deserted at night. Come prepared to battle insects. Visit midweek for peace and quiet.

BASICS

Operated By: National Park Service. **Open:** Apr. 13–Oct. 8. **Site Assignment:** First come, first served only, except May 15–Sept. 17; reservations can be made at (800) 365-CAMP. V, MC, D; if cancelled prior to the date of arrival the fee is $13.65; if cancelled on the day of arrival, the fee is $13.65 plus 1-night fee. **Registration:** At campground office. **Fee:** $20; Golden Age/Access card, 50% off. **Parking:** 2 vehicles per site.

FACILITIES

Number of Multipurpose Sites: 136. **Hookups:** None. **Each Site:** Picnic table, grill. **Dump Station:**

Yes. **Laundry:** No. **Pay Phone:** Yes. **Restrooms and Showers:** Yes (no heated showers). **Fuel:** No. **Propane:** No. **Internal Roads:** Paved. **RV Service:** 1 mi. **Market:** 15 mi. north in Hatteras (must take ferry). **Restaurant:** 15 mi. north in Hatteras (must take ferry). **General Store:** 15 mi. north in Hatteras (must take ferry). **Vending:** No. **Swimming:** No. **Playground:** No. **Activities:** Picnicking, fishing. **Nearby Attractions:** Currituck Beach Lighthouse, Elizabethan Gardens, Engineer Research Development Center, Frisco Native American Museum, Wright Brother's National Monument, Lost Colony. **Additional Information:** Outer Banks Visitor's Bureau, (252) 473-2138.

RESTRICTIONS

Pets: On leash only. **Fires:** In grill on the beach under the high tide line 100 ft. away from vegetation. **Alcoholic Beverages:** Not allowed. **Vehicle Maximum Length:** 35 ft. **Other:** Longer than normal tent stakes are recommended; 2-week stay limit.

TO GET THERE

From Norfolk, Virginia, take 64 south. Turn onto 168 south. 168 turns into 158 and then into NC 12. Stay on NC 12 going south and the campground will be on the left.

CAPE HATTERAS   MAP, B-8
Oregon Inlet

1401 National Park Dr., P.O. Box 675, 27954. T: (252) 473-2111; www.nps.gov/caha.

🚐 ★★★★   ▲ ★★★★

Beauty: ★★★★★	Site Privacy: ★★★
Spaciousness: ★★★★	Quiet: ★★★
Security: ★★★	Cleanliness: ★★★★
Insect Control: ★★★	Facilities: ★

Oregon Inlet is the most attractive of the Cape Hatteras National Seashore campgrounds. It's also the closest to civilization, with quaint private beach houses as little as 2 miles away. The Wright Brothers National Memorial, including the first flight airstrip, is about 20 miles north. The Bodie Island Lighthouse, built in 1872, is just a few miles north of Oregon Inlet. The campground consists of three loops, built amongst pleasant dunes. Sites are large, with some privacy provided by the dunes and grasses. Back-in parking spaces may be paved or packed sand. Our favorite sites, 2, 19, 21, and 23, are the most private because they're recessed into the dunes. We also like sites along the back of loops B and C, which are the farthest from Hwy. 12. Oregon Inlet is the most popular of the National Seashore campgrounds, and should be avoided on busy summer weekends. Security is fair—the gates are not closed at night.

BASICS

Operated By: National Park service. **Open:** Apr. 13–Oct. 8. **Site Assignment:** First come, first served. **Registration:** At entrance station. **Fee:** $20; Golden Age/Access card, 50% off. **Parking:** 2 vehicles per site, overflow parking available.

FACILITIES

Number of Multipurpose Sites: 120. **Hookups:** None. **Each Site:** Picnic table, grill. **Dump Station:**

Yes. **Laundry:** No. **Pay Phone:** Yes. **Restrooms and Showers:** Yes. **Fuel:** No. **Propane:** No. **Internal Roads:** Paved. **RV Service:** 5 mi. north in Nags Head. **Market:** 17 mi. north in Manteo. **Restaurant:** 17 mi. north in Manteo. **General Store:** 17 mi. north in Manteo. **Vending:** No. **Swimming:** No. **Playground:** No. **Other:** Group lodging is available for groups w/ 7–30 members. **Activities:** Picnicking, fishing. **Nearby Attractions:** Currituck Beach Lighthouse, Elizabethan Gardens, Engineer Research Development Center, Frisco Native American Museum, Wright Brother's National monument, Lost Colony. **Additional Information:** Outer Banks Visitor's Bureau, (252) 473-2138.

RESTRICTIONS

Pets: On leash only. **Fires:** Grill only. **Alcoholic Beverages:** Not allowed. **Vehicle Maximum Length:** 35 ft. **Other:** 2-week stay limit.

TO GET THERE

From Norfolk, Virginia take 64 south. Turn onto 168 south. 168 turns into 158 and then into NC 12. Stay on NC 12 going south and the campground will be on the left.

CAROLINA BEACH MAP, C-6
Carolina Beach State Park

P.O. Box 475, 28428. T: (910) 458-8206;
www.ils.unc.edu.

🚐 ★★★★   ▲ ★★★★

Beauty: ★★★★★	Site Privacy: ★★★★★
Spaciousness: ★★★★★	Quiet: ★★★★
Security: ★★★★	Cleanliness: ★★★★
Insect Control: ★★★	Facilities: ★★★

Carolina Beach is a tent camper's dream-come-true. Intrepid RV campers also appreciate the beauty of this campground, even if they must forego hookups for a few days. Sites are commodious and lovely, with a thick understory providing privacy between them. Campsites enjoy the shade of longleaf pine, turkey oak, and live oak. Parking is on gravel and packed sand, and all sites offer back-in parking. The best sites are on the outside of the camping loops. The park is located in a densely developed suburb of Wilmington, at the conjunction of the Cape Fear River and the Intracoastal Waterway. A marina and fishing deck serve anglers and boaters. Swimmers will have to drive a few miles, to the Atlantic Ocean beach at Fort Fisher State Recreation Area. Before you leave Carolina Beach, check out the exhibit on carnivorous plants in the exhibit hall (species found in the park include Venus flytraps, pitcher plants, butterworts, and bladderworts). Security is fair—gates are locked at night, but attended during the day. Avoid visiting on summer weekends.

BASICS

Operated By: N.C. State Parks. **Open:** All year except Christmas. **Site Assignment:** First come, first served. **Registration:** At marina office. **Fee:** $15. **Parking:** 2 vehicles per site.

FACILITIES

Number of Multipurpose Sites: 83. **Hookups:** None. **Each Site:** Picnic table, grill. **Dump Station:** Yes. **Laundry:** Yes. **Pay Phone:** Yes.

Restrooms and Showers: Yes. **Fuel:** Sold for boats only. **Propane:** No. **Internal Roads:** Paved. **RV Service:** 15 mi. north in Wilmington. **Market:** 2 mi. south in Carolina Beach. **Restaurant:** 2 mi. south in Carolina Beach. **General Store:** 2 mi. south in Carolina Beach. **Vending:** Marina store. **Swimming:** No. **Playground:** No. **Other:** Boat launch, trails, group camping areas. **Activities:** Boat rental, picnicking, hiking, fishing. **Nearby Attractions:** Winter boat cruises, Masonboro Sound, Atlantic Ocean. **Additional Information:** Cape Fear Coast CVB, (910) 341-4029.

RESTRICTIONS

Pets: Leash only, not inside buildings. **Fires:** Grill only. **Alcoholic Beverages:** Not allowed. **Vehicle Maximum Length:** Call ahead for details. **Other:** 2-week stay limit; do not remove plants or animals from park.

TO GET THERE

From Wilmington, take NC 421 10 mi. south. Follow signs to entrance.

CARTHAGE MAP, B-5
Heritage–Camping and Recreation

353 Sadler Family Rd, 28327. T: (910) 949-3433;
www.theheritagenc.com.

🚐 ★★★★   ▲ ★★★★

Beauty: ★★★★★	Site Privacy: ★★★★
Spaciousness: ★★★★	Quiet: ★★★★
Security: ★★★★	Cleanliness: ★★★★
Insect Control: ★★★	Facilities: ★★★★

The owners of the Heritage are nice folks. Small and inviting, this campground is preferable to nearby Travel Resorts of America if you're traveling with children. The picturesque lake is outfitted with a fun swimming beach and stocked with game fish. Although the park is in a rural location, the golf courses of Pinehurst and its environs are a short drive away. The campground is laid out in five long rows, including both pull-through and back-in sites. Parking is on packed sand and pine straw. Lovely tree cover includes tall southern pines, dogwood, and various oak species. Privacy is good, with a little foliage between most sites. Sites are on the large side of average. Sites 39 and 40 are excellent—secluded and lakefront. Try not to visit the Heritage during a major golf tournament. Security is fine—there are no gates, but the driveway leading to the campground is about a mile long.

BASICS

Operated By: Faye Sadler. **Open:** All year. **Site Assignment:** Reservations accepted. **Registration:** At office. **Fee:** $22; 2 people. **Parking:** At office.

FACILITIES

Number of RV-only Sites: 57. **Hookups:** Electric (30, 50 amps), water, sewer. **Each Site:** Fire ring. **Dump Station:** Yes. **Laundry:** Dryer only. **Pay Phone:** In office. **Restrooms and Showers:** Yes. **Fuel:** Nearby (3 mi.). **Propane:** Nearby (3 mi.). **Internal Roads:** Gravel. **RV Service:** Nearby. **Market:** Nearby. **Restaurant:** Nearby. **General Store:**

Nearby. **Vending:** Yes. **Swimming:** Yes. **Playground:** Yes. **Other:** Beach by lake w/ swimming area. **Activities:** Fishing, hiking, boating, horseshoes, volleyball, croquet, shuffleboard, basketball, petting farm, hayride w/ history of area. **Nearby Attractions:** Antique shopping.

RESTRICTIONS

Pets: Allowed. **Fires:** Fire ring only. **Alcoholic Beverages:** Not in public areas. **Vehicle Maximum Length:** No limit. **Other:** Children must be attended at all times; check-out is at 2 p.m.

TO GET THERE

From Raleigh: Take US 1 to Vass, turn right at first stoplight onto Union Church Rd., go 4 mi. and turn onto Heritage Farm Rd., go 1 mi. and turn left into The Heritage. From Southern Pines and Rockingham: Take US 1 to Vass, turn left onto Carthage Rd., go 3.5 mi. and turn right onto Heritage Farms Rd., go 0.5 mi. and turn right into The Heritage.

CHEROKEE MAP, B-2
Cherokee KOA

92 KOA Kampground 12D, 28719.
T: (828) 497-9711 or (800) 825-8352;
www.cherokeekoa.com.

🚐 ★★★★   ▲ ★★★

Beauty: ★★★	Site Privacy: ★★★
Spaciousness: ★★★	Quiet: ★★★
Security: ★★★★★	Cleanliness: ★★★
Insect Control: ★★★★	Facilities: ★★★★

The KOA in Cherokee is an attractive campground nestled between the Raven Fork River and a narrow trout pond. Sites are on the small side, and this campground is extremely popular. If you value breathing space, KOA Cherokee is not for you. Sites are mostly shady, with paved parking. There are both back-in and pull-through sites. Our favorite sites are those along the river and pond—they have the prettiest views and tend to be the shadiest. The fishing pond is stocked twice a week in season. The recreational facilities here are very good—and very crowded. With 300 campsites, there should be more than one swimming pool and playground. To avoid the vacationing masses, visit during the week in summer and fall. Security is excellent. With gates attended at all times, the park is nearly impenetrable.

BASICS

Operated By: KOA. **Open:** All year. **Site Assignment:** Reservations required 30 days in advance; pay in full at time of reservation; 3-day cancellation policy & $50 fee. **Registration:** At store. **Fee:** RV, $31.99–$36.99; tent (no hookup), $20–$40; Kamping Kabins, $34–$99. **Parking:** On site.

FACILITIES

Number of RV-only Sites: 300. **Number of Tent-only Sites:** 107. **Hookups:** Electric (30, 50 amps), cable TV. **Each Site:** None. **Dump Station:** Yes. **Laundry:** Yes. **Pay Phone:** Yes. **Restrooms and Showers:** Yes. **Fuel:** Yes. **Propane:** Yes. **Internal Roads:** Paved. **RV Service:** Yes. **Market:** On site. **Restaurant:** On site. **General Store:** Yes. **Vending:** Inquire at campground. **Swimming:** Yes. **Playground:** Yes. **Other:** Hot tubs, fitness center, computer center, data ports, casino shuttle, kiddie pool, pavilions. **Activities:** Tennis, basketball, horseshoes, fishing, white-water rafting, horseback riding. **Nearby Attractions:** Casino, Dollywood.

RESTRICTIONS

Pets: Allowed. **Fires:** Only in designated areas. **Alcoholic Beverages:** Allowed. **Vehicle Maximum Length:** Call ahead for details.

TO GET THERE

Take Cherokee North 441 to park boundary, then take Big Cove Rd.

CHEROKEE   MAP, B-2
Smokemont Campground

107 Park Headquarters Rd., 37738.
T: (865) 436-1200; www.nps.gov/grsm.

🚐 ★★★★   ▲ ★★★★

Beauty: ★★★★	Site Privacy: ★★★
Spaciousness: ★★★★	Quiet: ★★★★
Security: ★★★	Cleanliness: ★★★★
Insect Control: ★★★★★	Facilities: ★★★

Situated in a flat river valley, Smokemont is the largest campground in Great Smoky Mountains National Park. It's popular with hikers, who may choose from day or overnight hikes originating at Smokemont. Anglers enjoy the Oconaluftee River, which runs alongside the campground. Automobile touring is another popular pastime—Smokemont is just a few miles from the southern terminus of the Blue Ridge Parkway. Nearby, the town of Cherokee offers casinos, kitsch, and Native American culture and crafts. The long, slender campground includes a large multipurpose camping area as well as an RV-only loop. Sites are on the large side of average, with paved parking. In the RV-only area, sites have back-in parking. In the multipurpose area, there are both back-in and pull-through sites. Though there are some open sites in the RV loop, most sites are deliciously shady and fairly private. For beauty, the nicest sites are 8–18, in the back of the multipurpose area. Smokemont Campground stays packed on summer and fall weekends. Visit during the week. Security is fair—there are no gates.

BASICS

Operated By: National Park Service. **Open:** All year. **Site Assignment:** First come, first served; reservations accepted May 15–Oct. 31 up to 5 months in advance, w/ full deposit; $13.25 fee w/ at least 24-hour notice, otherwise 1-night plus fee charged; reservations made by calling (800) 365-CAMP or at reservations.nps.gov (personal check, money order, V, D, MC). **Registration:** Self-registration. **Fee:** $17–$20; up to 6 people; 2 tents or 1 tent & 1 RV (cash only for off-season self-registration). **Parking:** At site (2 vehicles).

FACILITIES

Number of RV-only Sites: 43. **Number of Tent-only Sites:** 18. **Hookups:** None. **Each Site:** Picnic table, fire ring, grill, tent pad. **Dump Station:** Yes. **Laundry:** No. **Pay Phone:** Yes. **Restrooms and Showers:** Restrooms, no showers. **Fuel:** No. **Propane:** No. **Internal Roads:** Paved. **RV Service:**

No. **Market:** 8 mi. in Cherokee. **Restaurant:** 8 mi. in Cherokee. **General Store:** 20 mi. in Waynesville. **Vending:** No. **Swimming:** No. **Playground:** No. **Other:** Amphitheater, picnic areas, horse trails, interpretive trails. **Activities:** Hiking, fishing, horseback riding, canoeing, backcountry hiking, ranger programs (seasonal). **Nearby Attractions:** Pisgah National Forest, Eastern Cherokee Indian Reservation, Cataloochee Ski Area, Gatlinburg, Pigeon Forge, Dollywood, Asheville. **Additional Information:** Pigeon Forge Visitor Information, (865) 453-5700; Park Information, (865) 436-1200; Asheville Area Chamber of Commerce, (828) 258-6101.

RESTRICTIONS

Pets: On leash only. **Fires:** Fire ring only. **Alcoholic Beverages:** Allowed. **Vehicle Maximum Length:** 35 ft.

TO GET THERE

From US 441, drive north to Newfound Gap Rd. Smokemont campground is on the right, 4 mi. off the highway.

CHEROKEE   MAP, B-2
Yogi Bear's Jellystone Park in the Smokies

reserve america

317 Galamore Bridge Rd., 28719.
T: (828) 497-9151 or (877) 716-6711;
www.jellystone-cherokee.com.

🚐 ★★★   ▲ ★★★

Beauty: ★★★★	Site Privacy: ★★★
Spaciousness: ★★★	Quiet: ★★★
Security: ★★★★	Cleanliness: ★★★
Insect Control: ★★★★	Facilities: ★★★

This Jellystone resort doesn't offer as much recreation as its Gatlinburg counterpart, but it is attractive and kid-oriented. Planned recreation in the summer and fall includes live bands, fishing contests, and costume parties. The playground and pool are aged, but adequate. The campground includes sites in two main areas, which hug a bend in the Raven Fork River. Sites are on the small side. Parking is on packed dirt, grass, and gravel—it's a bit messy. There are both pull-through and back-in sites. Most sites are nicely shaded. Our favorite sites, 114–134E, line the river. Other nice sites include 213–235, which have full hookups and are large and heavily wooded. Security is fair at Yogi's. There are no gates, but the park is very remote. Avoid Cherokee on summer and fall weekends, when hordes of automobiles create gridlock on Cherokee roads.

BASICS

Operated By: Bruce & Sharon Daughters. **Open:** Mar.–Oct. **Site Assignment:** Reservations accepted, 2-day cancellation notice required for deposit refund. **Registration:** At office. **Fee:** RV, $29–$38; primitive tent, $27. **Parking:** On site.

FACILITIES

Number of Multipurpose Sites: 179. **Hookups:** Electric (20, 30 amps), water, sewer, cable TV. **Each**

Site: Picnic tables, fire ring. **Dump Station:** Yes. **Laundry:** Yes. **Pay Phone:** Yes. **Restrooms and Showers:** Yes. **Fuel:** No. **Propane:** Yes. **Internal Roads:** Gravel. **RV Service:** No. **Market:** No. **Restaurant:** No. **General Store:** Yes. **Vending:** Yes. **Swimming:** Yes. **Playground:** Yes. **Other:** Arcade. **Activities:** Fishing, tubing, horseshoes, theatre, hiking, mountain biking. **Nearby Attractions:** Great Smoky Mountain National Park, Dollywood, Ghost Town in the Sky, Pigeon Forge, Mingo Falls, Museum of Cherokee Indians.

RESTRICTIONS

Pets: Allowed. **Fires:** Fire ring only. **Alcoholic Beverages:** Allowed. **Vehicle Maximum Length:** 46 ft.

TO GET THERE

Take I-40 to Exit No. 27 onto Hwy. 74 west, then to Exit No. 74 onto Hwy. 441 north; 6.5 mi. north of Cherokee. Follow the signs.

DANBURY   MAP, A-4
Hanging Rock State Park

2005 Visitor Center Dr., P. O. Box 278, 27016.
T: (336) 593-8480; www.ncsparks.net.

🚐 ★★★★★   ▲ ★★★★★

Beauty: ★★★★★	Site Privacy: ★★★★★
Spaciousness: ★★★★★	Quiet: ★★★★★
Security: ★★★★★	Cleanliness: ★★★★★
Insect Control: ★★★★	Facilities: ★★★★

Hanging Rock contains 18 miles of easy to strenuous hiking trails, many leading to picturesque waterfalls. There's also a 12-acre lake equipped with a swimming beach for sun-lovers and stocked with bass and bream for fishermen. At the north end of the park, a boat launch provides access to the Dan River for canoeing, tubing, or fishing for smallmouth bass and catfish. The campground is laid out in two loops on a gentle mountain ridge. Campsites are lovely; most are extremely large and secluded. Mature trees shade the sites and dense foliage provides a natural barrier between neighbors. Although the park is very popular, the campground is quiet due to adequate spacing between sites. Sites have gravel back-in parking. We especially like sites 8 and 32 for RVs and sites 1 and 4 for tent campers. Security is excellent. Hanging Rock is extra remote and gated. Avoid this park on busy summer and fall weekends.

BASICS

Operated By: N.C. State Parks. **Open:** All year except Christmas Eve & Christmas Day. **Site Assignment:** First come, first served; pay w/ in-state check or cash. **Registration:** At campsite; camp ranger will come by to register. **Fee:** $10–$15. **Parking:** 2 vehicles per site.

FACILITIES

Number of Multipurpose Sites: 73. **Hookups:** None. **Each Site:** Picnic table, tent pad, fire ring, grill. **Dump Station:** No. **Laundry:** No. **Pay Phone:** Yes. **Restrooms and Showers:** Yes. **Fuel:** No. **Propane:** No. **Internal Roads:** Paved. **RV Service:** Winston-Salem. **Market:** In Danbury approx. 5 mi. northeast. **Restaurant:** In Danbury approx. 5 mi. northeast. **General Store:** In Danbury approx. 5 mi.

northeast. **Vending:** Beverage, snacks, Jun. 1–Labor Day. **Swimming:** Park lake (Jun. 1–Labor Day, extra fee). **Playground:** No. **Other:** Group lodging available, trails. **Activities:** Hiking, rock climbing, picnicking, fishing, natural & cultural history programs, museum exhibits. **Nearby Attractions:** Diggs Gallery at Winton-Salem State University, Historic Bethabara Park, Old Salem. **Additional Information:** Stokes County EDC, (336) 983-8468.

RESTRICTIONS

Pets: Leash only, attended at all times by responsible adult. **Fires:** Fire ring only. **Alcoholic Beverages:** Not allowed. **Vehicle Maximum Length:** Call ahead for details. **Other:** Max 6 people per site, each site must have at least 1 adult (18 or older), all tent must be on tent pads, visitors out of the park by closing time.

TO GET THERE

From Danbury, take Hwy. 889 going north, go approx. 4 mi. and turn left onto Hanging Rock Rd.

EMERALD ISLE   MAP, C-7
Holiday Trav-L-Park Resort

9102 Coast Guard Rd., 28594. T: (252) 354-2250; www.htpresort.com.

🚐 ★★★★   ▲ ★★★

Beauty: ★★★★	Site Privacy: ★★
Spaciousness: ★★	Quiet: ★★★
Security: ★★★★★	Cleanliness: ★★★★★
Insect Control: ★★★	Facilities: ★★★★★

This attractive park is right on the Atlantic Ocean. Holiday Trav-L-Park has extremely nice pools, playgrounds, and other amenities, as well as planned activities in the summer. The most unique amenity is the park's gourmet food and wine shop. Nearby attractions include Fort Macon, a five-sided fort built between 1826 and 1834, and the historic town of Beaufort, including buildings dating back to 1709. The campground is laid out in five long rows of back-in and pull-through sites, terminating at the Atlantic Ocean. Sites in the back, near the ocean, have nice views of the dunes. Landscaping is very tidy, with shady trees in the front of the campground, near the store and pool. Sites are small, with grass parking. Choose your site based on desired location. Security is excellent. Holiday Trav-L-Park is located in an urban resort area, and is conscientious about camper safety. Visit in spring or fall for peace. Avoid the park on crowded summer weekends.

BASICS

Operated By: Watson family. **Open:** Feb. 15–Dec. 5. **Site Assignment:** Reservations recommended, (252) 354-2250. No out-of-state checks allowed; MC, V accepted; 7-day cancellation policy. **Registration:** At check-in station. **Fee:** $25–$85. **Parking:** 2 vehicles per RV site, 1 vehicle per tent, overflow parking available.

FACILITIES

Number of RV-only Sites: 375. **Number of Tent-only Sites:** 30. **Hookups:** Electric (20, 30 amps), water, sewer. **Each Site:** Picnic table. **Dump Station:** Yes. **Laundry:** Yes. **Pay Phone:** Yes.

Restrooms and Showers: Yes. **Fuel:** Yes. **Propane:** Yes. **Internal Roads:** Paved. **RV Service:** 2 mi. west in Cedarpoint. **Market:** 1 mi. **Restaurant:** 1 mi. **General Store:** Yes. **Vending:** Beverage, snacks. **Swimming:** Yes. **Playground:** Yes. **Other:** Rec. hall. **Activities:** Live entertainment, church service, Bible school, kid's cook-out, bingo, sandcastle competitions, arts & crafts, kite flying. **Nearby Attractions:** None. **Additional Information:** Carteret County Tourism Development, (252) 726-8148.

RESTRICTIONS

Pets: On leash only. No pets allowed in tenting area, call for more information, (252) 354-2250. **Fires:** No open fires (bring your own grill). **Alcoholic Beverages:** Allowed. **Vehicle Maximum Length:** 45 ft.

TO GET THERE

Take Hwy. 58 going east through Emerald Isle. Go over the high-rise bridge and at the first stop light after the bridge take a right. The park will be on the left.

FRANKLIN   MAP, B-2
Country Woods RV Park

2887 Georgia Rd., 28734. T: (828) 524-4339; www.kiz.com/countrywoods.

🚐 ★★★★   ▲ n/a

Beauty: ★★★★	Site Privacy: ★★★
Spaciousness: ★★★	Quiet: ★★★★
Security: ★★★★	Cleanliness: ★★★★★
Insect Control: ★★★★	Facilities: ★★★

The friendly owners of Country Woods operate an attractive and extremely tidy park on a terraced mountainside. Sites are small, but picturesque and nicely wooded. Many have wooden decks or concrete patios. Parking is gravel. Most sites feature back-in parking, but there are a few pull-through sites. Our favorite sites are 18, a large pull-through, and 57, a picturesque wooded campsite in the back of the park. Many sites offer views of the surrounding Black Mountains. Though Country Woods' amenities aren't extensive, they are well maintained and inviting. Franklin is a lovely town, with numerous boutiques and fishing and tubing on the Little Tennessee River. Security is fine here—there are no gates, but Franklin is a very nice town. Avoid the mountains on summer and fall weekends. Instead, visit during the week.

BASICS

Operated By: Darold & Marilyn Long. **Open:** Call ahead for details. **Site Assignment:** By reservation & first come, first served. **Registration:** At office. **Fee:** $23. **Parking:** 1 car per site, additional parking if necessary.

FACILITIES

Number of RV-only Sites: 65. **Hookups:** Electric (30 amps), water, sewer, cable TV. **Each Site:** Picnic table, fire ring. **Dump Station:** No. **Laundry:** Yes. **Pay Phone:** Yes. **Restrooms and Showers:** Yes. **Fuel:** No. **Propane:** No. **Internal Roads:** Gravel & paved. **RV Service:** 1.5 mi. northwest in Aberdeen. **Market:** 1.5 mi. northwest in Aberdeen. **Restaurant:** 1.5 mi. northwest in Aberdeen. **General**

Store: 1.5 mi. northwest in Aberdeen. **Vending:** No. **Swimming:** No. **Playground:** No. **Other:** Gathering room, library, clubhouse, walking trails. **Activities:** Horseshoes, park get-togethers. **Nearby Attractions:** Antique shops, gem mining, hiking trails, waterfalls, Scottish Tartan Museum, Franklin Gem Show, Wayah Bald, Great Smoky Mountain National Park, Blue Ridge Pkwy., the town of Cherokee, Harrah's Casino, Biltmore House, Smoky Mountain Train Ride.

RESTRICTIONS

Pets: On leash, cleaned up after. **Fires:** Fire ring only. **Alcoholic Beverages:** At site only. **Vehicle Maximum Length:** 40 ft. **Other:** Motorized bikes may be used for transportation into & out of park only.

TO GET THERE

Located on US 441/23, 2 mi. south of the intersection of 441/23 and Hwy. 64.

FRANKLIN   MAP, B-2
Standing Indian Campground—Nantahala National Forest

Off Forest Development Rd. 67, 28734. T: (828) 524-6441; www.reserveamerica.com.

🚐 ★★★★   ▲ ★★★★

Beauty: ★★★★	Site Privacy: ★★★
Spaciousness: ★★★	Quiet: ★★★
Security: ★★★★	Cleanliness: ★★★★
Insect Control: ★★★★	Facilities: ★★★★

The Nantahala River is born on Standing Indian Mountain just upstream from this outstanding, high-country campground, where cool breezes from the ridgetops temper the warm summer air. With sites on five loops, the campground is spread out and offers the camper varying site conditions. The first loop diffuses along the Nantahala with hemlock-shaded sites isolated by thick stands of rhododendron. Across the river, three loops are spread out in a large, flat area interspersed with large hardwoods that allow plenty of sun and grass to flourish among their ranks. Campground hosts occupy each loop for your safety and convenience. Sixteen water pumps are strategically located throughout the loops, in addition to five comfort stations with flush toilets. Two of the comfort stations have hot showers. There are no electric hookups. You may pick up dead, downed firewood from the surrounding area without a permit. Standing Indian is located within Nantahala National Forest and Nantahala is a Cherokee Indian name purported to mean "Land of the Noonday Sun." It is the largest of the four national forests in North Carolina, lying in the mountains and valleys of western North Carolina with elevations as high as 5,800 feet at Lone Bald in Jackson County, to a low 1,200 feet in Cherokee County along the Tusquitee River and is the home of many western North Carolina waterfalls. The last part of the Mountain Waters Scenic Byway travels through this forest.

BASICS

Operated By: U.S. Forest Service. **Open:** Apr. 1–Nov. 26. **Site Assignment:** Reservations must be made at least 4 days in advance. **Registration:** At office. **Fee:** Single, $14; double, $28. **Parking:** At park.

FACILITIES

Number of Multipurpose Sites: 128. **Hookups:** None. **Each Site:** Call ahead. **Dump Station:** Yes. **Laundry:** No. **Pay Phone:** Yes. **Restrooms and Showers:** Yes. **Fuel:** No. **Propane:** No. **Internal Roads:** Paved. **RV Service:** No. **Market:** No. **Restaurant:** No. **General Store:** Yes. **Vending:** No. **Swimming:** No. **Playground:** No. **Activities:** Amphitheater, fishing, hiking, hunting, photography.

RESTRICTIONS

Pets: Pets must be restrained or on a leash at all times while in developed recreation areas. **Fires:** In fire rings, stoves, grills, or fireplaces provided for that purpose. **Alcoholic Beverages:** Not allowed. **Vehicle Maximum Length:** Call ahead.

TO GET THERE

Take US 64 west from Franklin 12 mi. passing through Winding Stair Gap. Near the bottom of the mountain from the gap, turn left on West Old Murphy Rd. (SR 1448). There is a directional sign for the campground there. (See Web site for further details.)

HENDERSON   MAP, A-6
Hibernia

518 Hibernia Rd., 27537. T: (252) 438-7791; www.ncsparks.net.

🚐 ★★★★★   ⛺ ★★★★★

Beauty: ★★★★★   Site Privacy: ★★★★★
Spaciousness: ★★★★★   Quiet: ★★★★★
Security: ★★★★   Cleanliness: ★★★★★
Insect Control: ★★★   Facilities: ★★★

Hibernia is a gorgeous campground with numerous lakefront sites. Sites are huge, with your choice open sites or heavily wooded sites. Often the open sites provide stunning views of Kerr Lake, the banks of which are fortified with either concrete walls, rocks, or other materials to prevent erosion. Parking is on aged gravel, and the campground includes mostly back-in sites. For RVs we recommend Area 2, which has hookups and a washhouse. Other recommendations are amazingly lovely sites 43 and 44 in Area 1. Recreation at mammoth Kerr Lake revolves around lake swimming, sailing, boating, and fishing for crappie, channel catfish, and various bass species. There are limited footpaths for walkers and hikers. Hibernia is extremely remote, with gates locked at night, making security very good. Visit anytime except for summer holidays and weekends. Also avoid special-event weekends, such as the Governor's Cup Invitational Regatta and various bass tournaments.

BASICS

Operated By: N.C. Division of Parks & Recreation. **Open:** All year except Christmas. **Site Assignment:** First come, first served; reservations can be made at (252) 438-7791; cash & checks accepted; 2-week cancellation policy. **Registration:** At main office at campground. **Fee:** No hookup: $12; senior citizens (age 62 and up), $10. Sites w/electric: $17; senior citizens, $14. **Parking:** 2 vehicles per site.

FACILITIES

Number of Multipurpose Sites: 150. **Hookups:** Electric (30 amps). **Each Site:** Some have picnic table, fire ring, grill. **Dump Station:** Yes. **Laundry:** No. **Pay Phone:** Yes. **Restrooms and Showers:** Yes. **Fuel:** No. **Propane:** No. **Internal Roads:** Paved. **RV Service:** 15 mi. south in Henderson. **Market:** 15 mi. south in Henderson. **Restaurant:** 15 mi. south in Henderson. **General Store:** 2 mi. from park entrance in Henderson. **Vending:** Beverages. **Swimming:** No. **Playground:** Yes. **Other:** Group camping available, boat ramp, trails. **Activities:** Fishing, picnicking, boating, hiking, canoeing, natural & cultural history programs. **Nearby Attractions:** Steele Creek & Satterwhite Point. **Additional Information:** Vance County Tourism, (252) 438-5873.

RESTRICTIONS

Pets: On leash only. **Fires:** Designated areas only. **Alcoholic Beverages:** Not allowed. **Vehicle Maximum Length:** 40 ft. **Other:** 2-week stay limit.

TO GET THERE

From I-85 take Exit 214 and get onto NC 39. Travel approx. 12.5 mi. north on NC 39 and turn right onto Hibernia Rd.

HIGHLANDS   MAP, B-2
Sassafras Gap Campground

5920 Walhalla Rd., 28741. T: (800) 815-2259 or (828) 526-9909.

🚐 ★★★   ⛺ ★★★

Beauty: ★★★   Site Privacy: ★★★
Spaciousness: ★★★   Quiet: ★★★★
Security: ★★★   Cleanliness: ★★★
Insect Control: ★★★★   Facilities: ★★★

This funky little campground is something of an anomaly in the Highlands, a town known for its annual Chamber Music Festival. Down-home Sassafras Gap hosts live bluegrass and folk music events. Adventurous souls should consider a trip down the Chattooga National Wild and Scenic River. The campground offers RV campsites laid out in eight rows descending a hillside. Most sites feature gravel pull-through parking and enjoy a little shade. RV sites at the top of the hill, including 19, 33, 34, 48, and 59, are the prettiest. There are two tent areas in the back of the campground, both of which are shady, secluded, and nice-looking. Although the bathrooms are notably spacious and clean, the landscaping is very untidy, with long grass and patchy gravel. Security is fair—there are no gates, but the campground is in the middle of nowhere. Visit during the week in summer and fall.

BASICS

Operated By: Steve Potts. **Open:** Apr.–Oct. **Site Assignment:** $20 deposit or reserve w/ credit card; MC, V, D, AE, cash, check; must cancel 5 days in advance for refund. **Registration:** At office. **Fee:** $15–$26. **Parking:** At site.

FACILITIES

Number of RV-only Sites: 79. **Number of Tent-only Sites:** 20. **Hookups:** Electric (30, 50 amps), water, sewer, cable TV. **Each Site:** Tables, fire ring, trash pickup. **Dump Station:** No. **Laundry:** Yes. **Pay Phone:** Yes. **Restrooms and Showers:** Yes. **Fuel:** No. **Propane:** No. **Internal Roads:** Paved & gravel. **RV Service:** Yes. **Market:** On site. **Restaurant:** 5 mi. toward Highlands. **General Store:** 5 mi. toward Highlands. **Vending:** Yes. **Swimming:** No. **Playground:** Yes. **Activities:** 2 ponds & pavilion, game room, horseshoes. **Nearby Attractions:** Highland Playhouse, Chattooga National Wild & Scenic River, Highlands Botanical Gardens & Nature Center, whitewater rafting, Whiteside Mountain & Yellow Mountain, tubing, Dry Falls, canoeing, Whitewater Falls, kayaking, Glen Falls, fishing, Foothills Trail, horseback riding, Bartram Trail, golf.

RESTRICTIONS

Pets: On a leash. **Fires:** Fire ring only. **Alcoholic Beverages:** At site only. **Vehicle Maximum Length:** No limit.

TO GET THERE

Located 5 mi. south of Highlands, near the Chattooga National Wild and Scenic River.

JACKSON SPRINGS   MAP, B-5
Travel Resorts of America

1059 Sycamore Ln., 27281. T: (910) 652-5559.

🚐 ★★★★   ⛺ n/a

Beauty: ★★★★★   Site Privacy: ★★
Spaciousness: ★★★   Quiet: ★★★★★
Security: ★★★★   Cleanliness: ★★★★★
Insect Control: ★★★★   Facilities: ★★★★

Travel Resorts of America is a lovely flat campground situated in a stand of towering pine trees with pine straw ground cover. Picturesque Lake Sycamore is stocked with bass. Manicured landscaping adds to the natural beauty of the setting, and recreational amenities are excellent. This park is preferred over the Heritage for couples who seek solitude. It's also closer to most of the golf courses than the Heritage. The campground is laid out in rows of back-in sites, with large, chunky gravel parking pads. Sites are average sized, with little privacy. The most quiet sites, 1–12, are the farthest from Sycamore Lane and the closest to the bath house. Security is fine. There is no gate, but the neighborhood is spotless. Avoid this area during golf tournaments. For the best deals on greens fees and the least crowds, visit in the winter—but prepare for cold weather.

BASICS

Operated By: Travel Resorts of America. **Open:** All year. **Site Assignment:** Reservations required. **Registration:** At office. **Fee:** Call ahead for details. **Parking:** Yes.

FACILITIES

Number of RV-only Sites: 136. **Hookups:** Electric (30, 50 amps), water. **Dump Station:** Yes. **Laundry:** No. **Pay Phone:** Yes. **Restrooms and

Showers: Yes. Fuel: Yes. Propane: Yes. Internal Roads: Paved & gravel. RV Service: Yes. Market: Nearby. Restaurant: Nearby. General Store: Yes. Vending: Inquire at campground. Swimming: Yes. Playground: Yes. Activities: Boating, basketball, fishing. Nearby Attractions: Rockingham Speedway, Stoneybrook Steeplechase, Pinehurst golfing.

RESTRICTIONS

Pets: Allowed. Fires: Only in designated areas. Alcoholic Beverages: Inquire at campground. Vehicle Maximum Length: No limit.

TO GET THERE

From south US I-95, take Hwy. 501 north to Aberdeen, NC. Turn right onto Roseland Rd. Continue until it ends, turn right onto Sycamore Ln., 3 mi. to entrance.

LEXINGTON   MAP, B-4
High Rock Lake Marina and Campground

1013 Wafford Cir., 27292. T: (336) 798-1196 or (800) 382-3239; www.gocampingamerica.com/highroads.

🚐 ★★★★   ▲ ★★★

Beauty: ★★★★★   Site Privacy: ★★★★
Spaciousness: ★★★   Quiet: ★★★
Security: ★★★★   Cleanliness: ★★★★
Insect Control: ★★★   Facilities: ★★★★

This attractive campground is situated on a peninsula on High Rock Lake. Most sites are rented on a seasonal/long term basis, but there are usually a few short-term sites available. Site size is ample, but not huge. Most sites are very shady, and there are often a few trees between sites. Parking is on gravel. There are both pull-through and back-in spaces, and sites are often misrepresented on the park map. Nice looking pull-through sites 77–82 are more likely to be available for short-term campers. Tent sites have a lovely view of the lake, but they are preposterously small and we don't recommend them. The campground offers boat dockage (fees apply), and other excellent amenities for anglers. Fishing in High Rock Lake is excellent, and usually not too crowded. Avoid this campground on summer holidays. Security is fine here—there are no gates, but the campground is rurally located.

BASICS

Operated By: Lynn & Stephany Farquhar, Owners. Open: All year. Site Assignment: Reservations recommended, 2-week cancellation policy. Registration: At office. Fee: RV: daily, $25–$32; weekly, $154–$175. Tent: daily, $21; weekly, $125. Parking: 1 vehicle per site, extra overflow area.

FACILITIES

Number of RV-only Sites: 101. Number of Tent-only Sites: 5. Hookups: Electric (30, 50 amps), water, sewer, cable TV. Each Site: Cable TV, trash pickup, picnic table, fire ring. Dump Station: Yes. Laundry: Yes. Pay Phone: Yes. Restrooms and Showers: Yes. Fuel: Yes. Propane: Yes. Internal Roads: Main paved, some gravel. RV Service: 7 mi., Lexington. Market: 7 mi. Lexington. Restaurant: 7

mi., Lexington. General Store: Yes. Vending: Yes. Swimming: Yes. Playground: Yes. Other: Snack bar, game room, modem hookup. Activities: Fishing pier, boat rental, waterskiing. Nearby Attractions: "RCR Promotions," Welcome Center, NASCAR racing, NC Zoo at Asheboro, Furniture Discovery Center, Furniture Capital of the World. Lexington barbecue festival (Oct.), Historic Old Salem, Southeast Old Thresher's Reunion (Jul.), Carowinds, Emerald Pointe Water Park.

RESTRICTIONS

Pets: On leash only. Fires: Fire ring only. Alcoholic Beverages: Allowed, only covered containers. Vehicle Maximum Length: 50 ft. Other: No bike riding after dark, no skateboards or rollerblades allowed. Disorderly behavior, profanity, any firearms (including licensed concealed weapons), illegal drugs, fireworks, & intoxication are strictly prohibited. No swimming in the lake.

TO GET THERE

From Salisbury take I-85 (US 52) 15 mi. to Exit 91. Exit onto SR 8. Head south on SR 8 for 8 mi.

LINVILLE FALLS   MAP, A-3
Linville Falls Campground

P. O. Box 205, 28647. T: (828) 765-2681; www.reserveamerica.com.

🚐 ★★★★   ▲ ★★★★

Beauty: ★★★   Site Privacy: ★★★
Spaciousness: ★★★★   Quiet: ★★★
Security: ★★★★★   Cleanliness: ★★★★★
Insect Control: ★★★★★   Facilities: ★★★

Linville Falls is an excellent choice for nature nuts. Nearby Linville Gorge Wilderness Area is beloved for its fantastic rock formations and dramatic waterfalls. Grandfather Mountain, a privately owned park that was designed by the United Nations as an International Biosphere Reserve, is about 15 miles north of the campground. Like other Blue Ridge Parkway campgrounds, Linville Falls offers separate tent and RV sites interspersed on two loops. Situated in a flat river valley, most sites are shaded by white pine and a variety of hardwoods. Mountain laurel and rhododendron are scattered throughout the campground, as well. Parking is paved, back-in style. The nicest sites are on Loop A, next to picturesque Linville River. Security is good—there are no gates, but the campground is in a remote location. The Blue Ridge Parkway experiences outrageous traffic on summer and fall weekends. If you can't live without gorgeous fall foliage, tour the parkway midweek.

BASICS

Operated By: National Park Service. Open: Call ahead for details. Site Assignment: First come, first served. Registration: At office. Fee: $18–$30. Parking: Yes.

FACILITIES

Number of RV-only Sites: 35. Number of Tent-only Sites: 50. Hookups: Electric, water, sewer. Each Site: Picnic table, grill, fire ring. Dump Sta-

tion: Yes. Laundry: Yes. Pay Phone: Yes. Restrooms and Showers: Yes. Fuel: No. Propane: No. Internal Roads: Paved. RV Service: No. Market: No. Restaurant: No. General Store: Yes. Vending: Inquire at campground. Swimming: No. Playground: No. Other: Cabin rentals, trailer rentals. Activities: Hiking, fishing, shopping, & water sports nearby. Nearby Attractions: Linville Gorge, Linville Caverns, Gem Mountain, Grandfather Mountain.

RESTRICTIONS

Pets: Allowed. 1 pet per site. Fires: Allowed. Alcoholic Beverages: Inquire at campground. Vehicle Maximum Length: Call ahead for details.

TO GET THERE

Follow the Blueridge Pkwy. to milepost 316.4. Follow signs to campground.

MARION   MAP, B-3
Hidden Valley Campground and Waterpark

1210 Deacon Dr., 28752. T: (828) 652-7208.

🚐 ★★★★   ▲ ★★★★

Beauty: ★★★★   Site Privacy: ★★★
Spaciousness: ★★★★   Quiet: ★★★
Security: ★★★★   Cleanliness: ★★★
Insect Control: ★★★★   Facilities: ★★★★

Hidden Valley is built into a gorgeous mountainside, leading down to a pond. The campground would be exceptionally beautiful, if not for obtrusive telephone lines and poor road conditions. The water park and playground are appreciated by children, and the park is convenient to the quaint towns of Black Mountain and Chimney Rock. Hidden Valley has uncommonly large campsites for a private campground. Some sites are totally open, including our favorite pull-through sites, B9–B13. Others are nicely shaded, including our favorite back-in sites, B1–B8. These back-in sites enjoy a pretty view across the valley. Tent sites T5–T8 are wooded and private. The rest of the tent sites should be avoided. Hidden Valley is extremely popular on summer and fall weekends. For fewer crowds, visit midweek. The campground is only about 3 miles from I-40, but it has a rural feel. There are no gates, making security fair.

BASICS

Operated By: Robin Rovveyrol. Open: Apr. 1–Nov. 1. Site Assignment: Reservations accepted w/ nonrefundable deposit. Registration: At office. Fee: RV, $20–$24; tent, $18; for 2 people; each additional person, $2. Parking: At site.

FACILITIES

Number of RV-only Sites: 62. Number of Tent-only Sites: 9. Hookups: Electric (30 amps), water, sewer. Each Site: Picnic table, grill, fire ring. Dump Station: Yes. Laundry: Yes. Pay Phone: Yes. Restrooms and Showers: Yes. Fuel: No. Propane: No. Internal Roads: Gravel. RV Service: Nearby. Market: Nearby. Restaurant: Nearby. General Store: Yes. Vending: Yes. Swimming: Yes. Playground: Yes. Other: Snack bar. Activities: Waterslide, mini-golf, paddleboats, game room, fishing, volleyball, basketball, horseshoes, shuffleboard. **Nearby Attractions:** Black Mountain, Chimney Rock, Grandfather Mountain, Biltmore Estate.

RESTRICTIONS

Pets: Allowed. **Fires:** Fire ring only. **Alcoholic Beverages:** Not in public areas. **Vehicle Maximum Length:** No limit.

TO GET THERE

Take I-40 to Exit 86, then north on Hwy. 226. Follow the signs 2.5 mi.

MARION   MAP, B-3
Yogi Bear's Jellystone Park

reserve america

1210 Deacon Dr., 28752. T: (828) 652-7208; www.jellystonemarion.com.

🚐 ★★★★   ⛺ ★★★★

Beauty: ★★★★	Site Privacy: ★★★
Spaciousness: ★★	Quiet: ★★
Security: ★★★	Cleanliness: ★★★
Insect Control: ★★★	Facilities: ★★★★

Whether you are an RV park enthusiast, enjoy the comfort of a cabin in the woods, or just like to tent camp and sleep in the great outdoors, Jellystone Park's accommodations, amenities, and activities are topnotch. Amenities and activities include swimming, mini-golf, hay rides, tennis. volleyball, fishing, hiking, and appearances from Yogi Bear™ and friends.

BASICS

Operated By: McCloskey. **Open:** Apr. 1–Oct. 31. **Site Assignment:** Reservations recommended. **Registration:** At store. **Fee:** $25–$36; depending on location.

FACILITIES

Number of Multipurpose Sites: 70. **Hookups:** Water, electric (30 amps), sewer. **Dump Station:** Yes. **Laundry:** Yes. **Pay Phone:** Yes. **Restrooms and Showers:** Yes. **Fuel:** No. **Propane:** Yes. **Internal Roads:** Gravel. **Market:** 6 mi. **Restaurant:** 3 mi. **General Store:** Camp store. **Vending:** Yes. **Swimming:** Yes. **Playground:** Yes. **Activities:** Minigolf, arcade. **Nearby Attractions:** Biltmore Estate.

RESTRICTIONS

Pets: On leash attended only. **Fires:** Allowed. **Alcoholic Beverages:** At site only. **Vehicle Maximum Length:** 65 ft.

TO GET THERE

The site is conveniently located 2.5 mi. off I-40 at Exit 86 between Asheville and Hickory, NC.

MORGANTON   MAP, B-3
Steele Creek Park and Campground

7081 NC 181, 28655. T: (828) 433-5660; www.steelecreekpark.com.

🚐 ★★★★   ⛺ ★★★★

Beauty: ★★★★	Site Privacy: ★★
Spaciousness: ★★★	Quiet: ★★★★
Security: ★★★★	Cleanliness: ★★★★
Insect Control: ★★★★	Facilities: ★★★★

Steel Creek is a lovely campground situated in a flat mountain valley. Sites fan out from a huge, grassy field, and many have lovely views of the surrounding southernmost portion of the Blue Ridge Mountains. Most sites are partially shady. RV sites generally have gravel parking, while tent and pop-up sites usually have grass parking. There are both pull-through and back-in sites. Sites are on the small side, but the setting is so open that we didn't feel penned in. Choose your site based on location and amenities. Families will want to camp closer to the beach, while couples may want to seek a quieter site away from the recreation. Steel Creek has nice recreational facilities, especially for children. The Blue Ridge Parkway is about 15 miles north, and other tourist attractions are within 30 miles. There is no gate, but it's remote. So security is good.

BASICS

Operated By: The Loven family. **Open:** Apr. 1–Oct. 31. **Site Assignment:** First come, first served; reservations for groups only. **Registration:** At main building. **Fee:** $25; per night, up to 2 people, each additional person, $3. **Parking:** On site.

FACILITIES

Number of RV-only Sites: 168. **Number of Tent-only Sites:** 65. **Hookups:** Electric (30, 50 amps), water, sewer. **Each Site:** None. **Dump Station:** Yes. **Laundry:** Yes. **Pay Phone:** Yes. **Restrooms and Showers:** Yes. **Fuel:** No. **Propane:** Yes. **Internal Roads:** Paved. **RV Service:** Morganton. **Market:** Morganton. **Restaurant:** Morganton. **General Store:** Morganton. **Vending:** Yes. **Swimming:** Yes. **Playground:** Yes. **Other:** Beach by creek w/ swimming area. **Activities:** Fishing, game room, horseshoes, mini-golf, waterslide, hiking. **Nearby Attractions:** Mt. Mitchell, Grandfather Mountain, Linville Falls, Linville Cavern, Table Rock.

RESTRICTIONS

Pets: Allowed. **Fires:** Allowed. **Alcoholic Beverages:** Not allowed. **Vehicle Maximum Length:** 45 ft.

TO GET THERE

13 mi. north of Morganton, south on 181 from Linville.

MURPHY   MAP, M-1
Hanging Dog

123 Woodland Dr., 28906. T: (828) 837-5152; www.cs.unca.edu/nfsnc.

🚐 ★★★★   ⛺ ★★★★

Beauty: ★★★★	Site Privacy: ★★★★
Spaciousness: ★★★★	Quiet: ★★★★
Security: ★★★★	Cleanliness: ★★★★
Insect Control: ★★★★	Facilities: ★★★

This attractive campground is laid out in four loops, with grass and gravel back-in parking. Site size is ample but not huge. Many sites offer plenty of shade, compliments of pine and various oak species. Privacy varies, with wooded sites at the end of loop A tending to be the most private. Our favorite sites are on loop B, which offers views of 6,120-acre Hiwassee Lake. The lake is known for catches that include northern pike, bass, and musky. There are also trout streams in the area. Murphy, a charming town, is home to the worthwhile Cherokee County Historical Museum. Security is good at this extremely remote campground. Visit in late spring to enjoy the blooming rhododendrons. Or visit on weekdays in the fall for leaf peeping.

BASICS

Operated By: U.S.D.A. Forest Service. **Open:** May–Oct. **Site Assignment:** First come, first served. **Registration:** Self-registration on site. **Fee:** $8. **Parking:** At site.

FACILITIES

Number of RV-only Sites: 60. **Number of Tent-only Sites:** 9. **Hookups:** None. **Each Site:** Picnic table, fire ring, tent pad, lantern post. **Dump Station:** No. **Laundry:** No. **Pay Phone:** Yes. **Restrooms and Showers:** Yes. **Fuel:** No. **Propane:** No. **Internal Roads:** Paved. **RV Service:** No. **Market:** No. **Restaurant:** No. **General Store:** No. **Vending:** No. **Swimming:** No. **Playground:** No. **Activities:** Boating, hiking, fishing. **Nearby Attractions:** Inquire at campground.

RESTRICTIONS

Pets: Allowed. **Fires:** Fire ring only. **Alcoholic Beverages:** At site. **Vehicle Maximum Length:** 32 ft. **Other:** 14-day stay limit.

TO GET THERE

From Murphy, take Brown Rd. (NC 1326) northwest 5 mi. Turn left at campground sign. The campground is straight ahead.

ROARING GAP   MAP, A-3
Stone Mountain State Park

3042 Frank Pkwy., 28668. T: (336) 957-8185.

🚐 ★★★★   ⛺ ★★★★

Beauty: ★★★★	Site Privacy: ★★★★
Spaciousness: ★★★★	Quiet: ★★★★
Security: ★★★★★	Cleanliness: ★★★★★
Insect Control: ★★★★	Facilities: ★★★★

Stone Mountain State Park is beloved by nature enthusiasts, though it offers a wide range of activities. For the adventurous, there's rock climbing on the park's namesake, a 600-foot gray granite inselberg. Mellower folks can reach the top of Stone Mountain by a short but strenuous hiking trail. Other park activities include trout fishing in mountain streams. The campground consists of two loops, with gravel parking. Sites are shaded by white pine, red maple, and various oak species. A thick understory provides privacy between most sites. Site size is moderate, but there is plenty of space between sites. For tent campers, we recommend sites on the first loop, which tend to be more wooded. For RV campers, we recommend sites 20, 26, and 27, on the second loop. Stone Mountain is extremely secure—it's remote and gates are locked at night. This park stays cool in late summer, making it a great mid-week summer destination.

BASICS

Operated By: State of North Carolina. **Open:** All year. **Site Assignment:** First come, first served; reservations for groups only. **Registration:** At office. **Fee:** $9–$20. **Parking:** On site.

FACILITIES

Number of RV-only Sites: 37. **Number of Tent-only Sites:** 6. **Hookups:** None. **Each Site:** Picnic table, grill, tent pad. **Dump Station:** Yes. **Laundry:** No. **Pay Phone:** Yes. **Restrooms and Showers:** Yes. **Fuel:** No. **Propane:** No. **Internal Roads:** Paved & gravel. **RV Service:** No. **Market:** Nearby. **Restaurant:** Nearby. **General Store:** No. **Vending:** Yes. **Swimming:** No. **Playground:** No. **Other:** Waterfalls, mountain cultural exhibit, Hutchingson Homestead. **Activities:** Trout fishing, rock climbing, hiking. **Nearby Attractions:** Bullhead Stream fishing (permit $12 per section).

RESTRICTIONS

Pets: On leash, max. 6 ft. **Fires:** Allowed. **Alcoholic Beverages:** Not allowed. **Vehicle Maximum Length:** No limit. **Other:** No firearms, no fireworks.

TO GET THERE

From the south: Take US 21 to SR 1002, go 4.5 mi. to John P. Frank Pkwy. From the west: Take NC 18 north and turn right on SR 1002, follow SR 1002 to the John P. Frank Pkwy.

SPRUCE PINE   MAP, A-3
Bear Den Campground

600 Bear Den Mountain Rd., 28777.
T: (828) 765-2888 or (828) 765-2844;
www.bear-den.com.

🚐 ★★★★★	⛺ ★★★★★
Beauty: ★★★★★	Site Privacy: ★★★★★
Spaciousness: ★★★★	Quiet: ★★★★★
Security: ★★★★★	Cleanliness: ★★★★★
Insect Control: ★★★★★	Facilities: ★★★★

Bear Den is fabulous. The campground is laid out in four areas nestled into a mountainside right off the Blue Ridge Parkway. Excellent amenities include five playgrounds and a picturesque swimming lake. There's also fishing in the creek bordering the park. Hikers enjoy easy access to miles of trails managed by the National Park Service and U.S. Forest Service. Sites at Bear Den aren't huge, but most feel very private due to the confluence of natural vegetation and thoughtful landscaping; almost all sites are refreshingly wooded by pines, maples, and oaks with greenery between sites. Tiger lilies are common here. This wooded campground is also home to a variety of birds, rabbits, and raccoons. Lucky campers have even spotted deer and bears. Parking is on pea gravel and there are back-in and pull-through sites. If your rig fits, go for one of the ten pull-through sites, as they tend to be more private. Our favorite sites in areas A and B are those on the outside of the loops. In area D, sites 15 and 16 are huge. Security is fine. There are no gates, but the area is pretty remote. The mountain towns that dot the Blue Ridge Parkway in

this area are uniformly quaint and worth exploring.

BASICS

Operated By: Moody Family. **Open:** Mar.–Nov. **Site Assignment:** 1-night deposit for reservations; 90% of deposit refundable if reservation cancelled 7 days in advance; V, MC, D, AE. **Registration:** At office. **Fee:** $28–$56. **Parking:** At site.

FACILITIES

Number of RV-only Sites: 44. **Number of Tent-only Sites:** 100. **Number of Multipurpose Sites:** 2. **Hookups:** Electric (30 amps), water, sewer. **Each Site:** Fire rings, picnic tables. **Dump Station:** Yes. **Laundry:** Yes. **Pay Phone:** Yes. **Restrooms and Showers:** Yes. **Fuel:** No. **Propane:** Yes. **Internal Roads:** Gravel & paved. **RV Service:** 15 mi. toward Spruce Pine. **Market:** 6 mi. toward Spruce Pine. **Restaurant:** 8 mi. toward Spruce Pine. **General Store:** Yes. **Vending:** Yes. **Swimming:** Yes. **Playground:** Yes. **Other:** Golf cart rentals, store, game room, firewood, ATM, swimming lake, & nature trails. **Activities:** Pool table, basketball, volleyball, horseshoes, badminton, shuffleboard, ping pong, square dancing, Sun. church services, pinball, video games, canoe & paddleboat rentals. **Nearby Attractions:** Gemstone mining, mini-golf, climbing wall, go-carts, Mt. Mitchell, golf, Linville Caverns, Linville Gorge, whitewater rafting, Blue Ridge Pkwy., Grandfather Mountain, Little Switzerland, Museum of NC, fishing, Blowing Rock, Roan Mountain, Tweetsie Railroad.

RESTRICTIONS

Pets: Allowed. **Fires:** Fire ring only. **Alcoholic Beverages:** Not allowed. **Vehicle Maximum Length:** No limit.

TO GET THERE

Going north from junction Hwy. 226, it is 6 mi. to milepost 324.8, Bear Den Mountain Rd. Turn right. Going south from junction Hwy. 221, it is 5.3 mi. to Bear Den Overlook, milepost 323. Travel another 1.8 mi. to Bear Den Mountain Rd. (milepost 324.8). Turn left at small sign.

SPRUCE PINE   MAP, A-3
Linville Falls

reserve america

214 Parkway Maintenance Rd., 28777.
T: (828) 765-7818; www.reserveamerica.com.

🚐 ★★★★	⛺ ★★★
Beauty: ★★★★	Site Privacy: ★★★
Spaciousness: ★★★★	Quiet: ★★★
Security: ★★★★★	Cleanliness: ★★★★
Insect Control: ★★★	Facilities: ★★

Linville Falls Campground, located off the Blue Ridge Parkway at milepost 317, is family oriented, located next to the Linville River. It provides easy access to numerous hiking trails to some of the most beautiful scenery in the Linville Gorge area. Interpretive programs are provided on weekends during the peak recreation season. Fishing opportunities are available on the Linville River. The Blue Ridge Parkway is located near Boone and Blowing Rock, NC. Today on

the Blue Ridge Parkway it's possible to rock climb, hang glide, fish for trout, bicycle—almost any activity that doesn't damage the park or endanger other visitors. Here is a sampling of some of the activities that will help you connect with this special place. There are many activities that attract campers to Julian Price and the Blue Ridge Parkway such as the hiking where campers and hikers alike can meander alongside or cross the Parkway, trails provide a close-up look at some of the most beautiful landscape in the region. Many trails wind their way through unique biological and geological environments. Others lead to historic sites with stories of how people have shaped our heritage. If you are a fisherman at heart you'll find yourself at a mountaintop park, may seem an unlikely place to fish, but just the opposite is true!

BASICS

Operated By: National Park Service. **Open:** Apr. 1–Oct. 23. **Site Assignment:** Reservations must be made 2 days in advance. **Registration:** At registration office. **Fee:** Single, $14–$16. **Parking:** At site.

FACILITIES

Number of Multipurpose Sites: 124. **Hookups:** None. **Each Site:** Call ahead. **Dump Station:** Yes. **Laundry:** No. **Pay Phone:** No. **Restrooms and Showers:** Yes. **Fuel:** No. **Propane:** No. **Internal Roads:** Paved. **RV Service:** No. **Market:** No. **Restaurant:** No. **General Store:** No. **Vending:** No. **Swimming:** No. **Playground:** No. **Other:** Swimming is not allowed. **Activities:** Amphitheater, campfire programs, fishing, hiking, sightseeing, wildlife viewing.

RESTRICTIONS

Pets: Pets must be on a leash at all times. **Fires:** Allowed; Campfire Program. **Alcoholic Beverages:** Not allowed. **Vehicle Maximum Length:** Varies; call ahead.

TO GET THERE

From I-40 east, take Hwy. 221 north to Linville Falls, NC. Enter the Blue Ridge Pkwy. at Linville Falls. Go north 1 mi. to Linville Falls Spur Rd. Campground is 0.5 mi. down the spur road. From Asheville, NC, go north on the Blue Ridge Pkwy. to milepost 317 (65 mi.).

STATESVILLE   MAP, B-3
Midway Campground
and RV Resort

114 Midway Dr., P.O. Box 199B, 28625.
T: (888) 754-4809 or (704) 546-7615;
www.kiz.com/midway.

🚐 ★★★	⛺ ★★★
Beauty: ★★★★	Site Privacy: ★★★
Spaciousness: ★★★	Quiet: ★★★
Security: ★★★	Cleanliness: ★★★★
Insect Control: ★★★★	Facilities: ★★★

Midway is an attractive campground on a hillside sloping down to a fishing pond teeming with catfish. Sites are on the small side, but nicely spaced and shady. Privacy is not optimal. Parking is on gravel. Most parking pads are back-in, but a few very long pull-through sites can accommodate big rigs. The prettiest sites, 19–24, enjoy views of the pond. The pool is large enough for lap swimmers, and recreation areas are also nicely appointed. Midway has no gates, and is close to I-40 in a rural area, making security fair. South of Statesville is mammoth Lake Norman, offering fishing and boating opportunities. Many buildings in downtown Statesville are on the National Register of Historic Places. For the nicest weather, visit Statesville in late spring or fall.

BASICS

Operated By: Randy & Jocelyn Jenkins. **Open:** All year. **Site Assignment:** Reservations are suggested for holidays & weekends; deposit based on length of stay; full refund given on deposit only if cancelled at least 1 week ahead of time; MC, AE, V. **Registration:** At office. **Fee:** RV, $25–$33; tent, $25. **Parking:** Yes.

FACILITIES

Number of RV-only Sites: 60. **Number of Tent-only Sites:** 13. **Hookups:** Electric (20, 30, 50 amps), water, sewer. **Each Site:** Picnic table, fire ring. **Dump Station:** Yes. **Laundry:** Yes. **Pay Phone:** Yes. **Restrooms and Showers:** Yes. **Fuel:** No. **Propane:** Yes. **Internal Roads:** Paved & gravel. **RV Service:** Exit 170 on I-40. **Market:** On site. **Restaurant:** 7 mi. from town. **General Store:** 7 mi. from town. **Vending:** No. **Swimming:** Yes. **Playground:** Yes. **Other:** Game room, ATM machine, modem connection, pavilion, cabin rentals. **Activities:** Basketball, badminton, horseshoes, mini-golf, volleyball, paddleboats, fishing lake, pavilion, Sun. church services. **Nearby Attractions:** Mall. **Additional Information:** Statesville Chamber of Commerce, (704) 873-2892.

RESTRICTIONS

Pets: On leash, attended, not in buildings. **Fires:** Fire ring only. **Alcoholic Beverages:** At site only. **Vehicle Maximum Length:** No limit. **Other:** Quiet hours 11 p.m.–7 a.m.

TO GET THERE

Heading east on I-40, take Exit 162. Turn right. Go 0.25 mi. and turn left on Campground Rd. Go 0.25 mi. to campground. Heading west on I-40, take Exit 162. Turn left and go 0.5 mi. to Campground Rd. Turn left. Go 0.25 mi. to campground.

SWANNANOA   MAP, B-2
Asheville East KOA

2708 Hwy. 70., 28778.
T: (800) KOA-5907 or (828) 686-3121;
www.koakampgrounds.com/where/nc/33116.htm.

🚐 ★★★★	⛺ ★★★★
Beauty: ★★★★	Site Privacy: ★★★★
Spaciousness: ★★★★	Quiet: ★★★
Security: ★★★	Cleanliness: ★★★★
Insect Control: ★★★★	Facilities: ★★★★

The Asheville East KOA is laid out in numerous sections dissected by the Swannanoa River. There are also two ponds adding to the visual appeal of the property. Both the river and the ponds are open for trout fishing (no license required for the ponds). Though site size and privacy vary, most are slightly larger than average. Tree cover ranges from dense to totally open. Parking is on gravel, grass, or dirt, and all sites are back-in style. Our favorite RV sites are found in Section D—these are lakeside, with picturesque views of water lilies. Section G contains shady tent sites. Security is fair; the campground has no gates. Avoid this area on summer and autumn weekends. KOA is a good place to stay if you plan to tour the lovely city of Asheville as well as the wilderness areas east of Black Mountain. A day at the Biltmore Estate, America's largest privately owned home, is worth inflated admissions prices.

BASICS

Operated By: Asheville East KOA. **Open:** All year; limited availability in winter. **Site Assignment:** Reservations recommended; must cancel 7 days in advance during holidays & 2 days in advance during non-holidays to refund deposit; requested campsites not guaranteed; deposit is 1-night rent or credit card. V, MC, local checks, travelers checks, cash. **Registration:** [AQ]. **Fee:** RV, $25–$35. **Parking:** 1 vehicle & camping unit per site. Additional vehicle parking is available.

FACILITIES

Number of Multipurpose Sites: 225. **Hookups:** Electric (20, 30, 50 amps), water, sewer, cable TV. **Each Site:** Picnic table, fire ring. **Dump Station:** Yes. **Laundry:** Yes. **Pay Phone:** Yes. **Restrooms and Showers:** Yes. **Fuel:** No. **Propane:** Yes. **Internal Roads:** Gravel & dirt. **RV Service:** 10 mi. toward Asheville. **Market:** 2 mi. toward Swannanoa. **Restaurant:** 10 mi. toward Ashlie. **General Store:** Yes. **Vending:** Yes. **Swimming:** Yes. **Playground:** Yes. **Activities:** 2 fishing lakes, trout stream, game room, mini-golf, bicycle rentals, pavilion, basketball, horseshoes, boat rentals, paddle boat rentals, walking trail, firewood. **Nearby Attractions:** Maggie Valley, Ridgecrest/Montreat, River Rafting, Horseback Riding, WNC Nature Center, Biltmore Estate, Chimney Rock.

RESTRICTIONS

Pets: Leashed cleaned up after. Not allowed in lodges. **Fires:** Fire ring only. **Alcoholic Beverages:** At site only. **Vehicle Maximum Length:** No limit.

TO GET THERE

From I-40, take Exit 59. Go north 1 block to signal (US-70). Turn right and drive 2 mi. on left.

TABOR CITY   MAP, C-5, C-6
Yogi Bear's Jellystone Park at Daddy Joe's

reserve america

626 Richard Wright Rd., 28463.
T: (910) 653-2155;
www.taborcityjellystone.com.

🚐 ★★★★	⛺ ★★★★
Beauty: ★★★★	Site Privacy: ★★★
Spaciousness: ★★	Quiet: ★★
Security: ★★★★	Cleanliness: ★★★
Insect Control: ★★★	Facilities: ★★★★

This award-winning resort opened in 2001 and is located on 350 acres in a beautiful rural setting near coastal North and South Carolina. It's a quiet, family-oriented destination resort with large, big-rig friendly sites throughout park with Wi-Fi access. All spacious RV sites have concrete pads for the largest of RVs, with 52 pull-through sites. Check our Web site for a virtual tour of the park. Whether you are an RV park enthusiast, enjoy the comfort of a cabin in the woods, or just like to tent camp and sleep in the great outdoors, Jellystone Park's accommodations, amenities, and activities top-notch. Amenities and activities include swimming, mini-golf, hay rides, tennis, volleyball, fishing, hiking, and appearances from Yogi Bear™ and friends.

BASICS

Operated By: Rick Coleman. **Open:** All year. **Site Assignment:** Reservations preferred. **Registration:** At ranger station; hours vary by season; night registration available. **Fee:** $29–$45; includes 4 people; each additional adult, $4; each additional child, $2; extra car fee, $3; first night deposit required for bookings. **Parking:** Limit 2 cars per site, overflow parking available.

FACILITIES

Number of RV-only Sites: 78. **Number of Tent-only Sites:** 8. **Hookups:** Electric (20, 30, 50 amps), water, sewer. **Each Site:** 70 ft. concrete pad, picnic table, grill. **Dump Station:** Yes. **Laundry:** Yes. **Pay Phone:** Yes. **Restrooms and Showers:** Yes. **Fuel:** No. **Propane:** Yes. **Internal Roads:** Gravel. **RV Service:** Camping World: 40 mi. southwest in Myrtle Beach. **Market:** 1 mi. in Tabor City. **Restaurant:** 1 mi. in Tabor City; Grill on Park. **General Store:** Camp store. **Vending:** Yes. **Swimming:** 2 pools, Splash Zone. **Playground:** Yes. **Other:** 9 fishing ponds, hiking trails, bike & golf cart rentals, Wi-Fi. **Activities:** Organized summer activities, water volleyball, horseshoes. **Nearby Attractions:** Myrtle Beach, SC, historic Wilmington, NC, North Carolina beaches. **Additional Information:** Columbus County Tourism, (910) 640-2818.

RESTRICTIONS

Pets: On leash only. **Fires:** Allowed. **Alcoholic Beverages:** At site only. **Vehicle Maximum Length:** 70 ft. **Other:** 2-night min. on weekends. Monthly rentals available. Multi-month available during off-season.

TO GET THERE

Southbound off I-95, take US 74E to NC 410. Go south on NC 410 to US 701, then turn right on US 701S. Travel 0.5 mi. and turn left on Richard Wright Rd. and 0.4 mi. From Myrtle Beach, SC, take SC 31N to SC 9 to US 701N, then US 701 bypass 2 mi. and turn right on Richard Wright Rd. From Wilmington, NC, take US 74W to US 701S, then go 18 mi. to Tabor City and then to Richard Wright Rd. Turn left and go 0.4 mi. to campground.

TUCKASEGEE MAP, B-2
Singing Waters Camping Resort

1006 Trout Creek Rd., 28783.
T: (828) 293-5872;
www.singingwaterscampingresort.com.

🚐 ★★★★   ⛺ ★★★★

Beauty: ★★★★
Site Privacy: ★★★
Spaciousness: ★★★
Quiet: ★★★★
Security: ★★★★
Cleanliness: ★★★★
Insect Control: ★★★★
Facilities: ★★★

This pretty campground is tucked into a wooded mountain valley, with sites alongside bubbling Trout Creek. With an elevation of 3,000 feet, Singing Waters stays cool, making it an excellent summertime destination—just avoid visiting on busy holidays. Their refreshing natural swimming pond is just the thing to escape summer heat. The campground consists of back-in and pull-through sites beautifully shaded by mature white pine, black gum, black walnut, and red oak trees. Singing Waters is also home to a variety of birds, including gold finches, purple wailers, and woodpeckers. Parking, on a mixture of pine bark mulch and pine straw, is luxurious. Sites are medium sized, and greenery like honeysuckle and rhododendron provides privacy. The nicest sites, 28–32, are in the back of the campground along the creek. Two tent sites, 48 and 49, offer raised tent pads and covered picnic tables. More traditional tent camping sites are also available. Security is fine here; there are no gates but the park is off the beaten path. Halfway between Sylva and Cashiers, Singing Waters is in the heart of Pisgah National Forest.

BASICS
Operated By: Cooper family. **Open:** Full hookups, open Mar.–Dec.; partial hookups, open May–Oct. **Site Assignment:** Reservations recommended, (828) 293-5872. V, AE, MC, D; if cancelled w/in 7 days of arrival date, deposit refundable less $10. **Registration:** At registration office. **Fee:** Full hookup (2 people), $28–$30; campsite, $25–$30; each additional child (6–17 years old), $2; each additional adult, $5. **Parking:** 2 vehicles per site, overflow parking available.

FACILITIES
Number of RV-only Sites: 63. **Number of Tent-only Sites:** 10. **Hookups:** Electric (20, 30, 50 amps), water. **Each Site:** Picnic table, fire ring, grill. **Dump Station:** Yes. **Laundry:** Yes. **Pay Phone:** Yes. **Restrooms and Showers:** Yes. **Fuel:** No. **Propane:** No. **Internal Roads:** Gravel. **RV Service:** On call. **Market:** 10 mi. south in Glenville. **Restaurant:** Yes. **General Store:** Yes. **Vending:** Beverages. **Swimming:** Pond (no lifeguard). **Playground:** Yes. **Other:** Pond, basketball court, volleyball net, trails, rec room, pavilion. **Activities:** Hiking, basketball, volleyball, indoor games. **Nearby Attractions:** Blue Ridge Pkwy., Great Smoky Mountains National Park, Nantahala National Forest, Qualla-Cherokee Indian Reservation, Harrah's Cherokee Casino, Great Smoky Mountains Railway, Biltmore Estates, white-water rafting, golf, gem mining, boating & fishing, crafts & antique shops. **Additional Infor-**

mation: Jackson County Chamber of Commerce, (828) 586-2155.

RESTRICTIONS
Pets: On leash only; small pets only. **Fires:** Fire pit only. **Alcoholic Beverages:** At site only. **Vehicle Maximum Length:** 42 ft.

TO GET THERE
On I-40 from Asheville, take Exit 27 onto Smoky Mountain Expressway west. Take Exit 85 and go west. Take a left at the second light and go 17 mi. south on Hwy. 107 to sign for park. Turn left onto Trout Creek Rd. Go 1 mi. east. The entrance is on the right.

WAVES MAP, B-8
Camp Hatteras

reserve america

24798 Hwy. 12, P.O. Box 10, 27968. T: (252) 987-2777; www.reserveamerican.com or www.camphatteras.com.

🚐 ★★★   ⛺ ★★★

Beauty: ★★★
Site Privacy: ★★
Spaciousness: ★★
Quiet: ★★
Security: ★★★★
Cleanliness: ★★★★
Insect Control: ★★★
Facilities: ★★★★

Camp Hatteras is situated on a narrow piece of Hatteras Island and maintains two main camping areas along Hwy. 12, one on each side of the road. The largest area is on the same side as the pool and office, and includes some sites near the Atlantic Ocean. Across the highway, a smaller section includes tent-only sites with pretty views of Pamlico Sound. The recreation and facilities at Camp Hatteras are very nice. Unfortunately, Camp Hatteras offers miserably small campsites, situated in a series of loops. Sites feature paved, back-in parking. There is no shade. Views of the ocean are obscured by dunes. Families should choose their site based on proximity to facilities and the beach. Sites along the perimeter of the park are likely to be a little quieter. Security is very good. The campground is gated and attended at all times. Avoid Hatteras Island on summer holidays and weekends, when masses of people flock here.

BASICS
Operated By: Jett Ferebee. **Open:** All year. **Site Assignment:** Reservations recommended, (252) 987-2777. MC, AE, D, V; no penalty for cancellation 1 week in advance.; if cancelled w/in a week of arrival day then deposit is nonrefundable. **Registration:** At guardhouse. **Fee:** RV, $26.95–$68.95; tent, $24.95–$50.95. **Parking:** 2 vehicle per site, overflow parking available.

FACILITIES
Number of RV-only Sites: 300. **Number of Tent-only Sites:** 60. **Hookups:** RV w/ electric (30, 50 amps), water, sewer, cable TV; tent w/ electric (30, 50 amps), water; 60 sites w/ no hookups. **Each Site:** Picnic table, pad for RV sites. **Dump Station:** No. **Laundry:** Yes. **Pay Phone:** Yes. **Restrooms and Showers:** Yes. **Fuel:** No. **Propane:** No. **Internal**

Roads: Paved. **RV Service:** On call. **Market:** 18 mi. south in Avon. **Restaurant:** 1 mi. **General Store:** K-Mart 32 mi. north in Kill Devil Hills. **Vending:** Beverage, snacks. **Swimming:** Yes. **Playground:** Yes. **Other:** Marina area, boat ramp (small boats), mini-golf course, arcade, pavilion, stocked fishing ponds. **Activities:** Golfing, windsurfing, sailing, shuffleboard, tennis, arcade games, recreational activities, surfing, fishing. **Nearby Attractions:** Elizabethan Gardens, Lost colony Drama, Cape Hatteras Lighthouse, Pea Island National Refuge, NC Aquarium, Wright Brothers Memorial. **Additional Information:** Outer Banks Visitors Bureau, (252) 473-2138.

RESTRICTIONS
Pets: On leash only. **Fires:** On beach only. **Alcoholic Beverages:** At sites only. **Vehicle Maximum Length:** 45 ft. **Other:** Family-oriented park.

TO GET THERE
From Virginia Beach take Hwy. 168 south to Hwy. 158 east. Exit onto Hwy. 12 south. Turn left into park.

WILKESBORO MAP, A-3
Bandits Roost Park

reserve america

W. Kerr Scott Reservoir, 499 Reservoir Rd., 28697-0182. T: (336) 921-3390 or (336) 921-3750; www.reserveamerica.com.

🚐 ★★★★   ⛺ ★★★★★

Beauty: ★★★★★
Site Privacy: ★★★
Spaciousness: ★★★★★
Quiet: ★★★★★
Security: ★★★★★
Cleanliness: ★★★★★
Insect Control: ★★★★
Facilities: ★★★

This gorgeous campground features an amazing tent area. Tent campers are treated to views of W. Kerr Scott Reservoir from huge, secluded sites. RV campers have good choices, too: there are delightfully secluded sites on Loop B, surrounded by white pine, Virginia pine, and oak trees, or choose an open site with a fabulous view of the lake. We like stunning pull-through sites 24–28, which are situated on a peninsula. Sites 32–35 are also very nice. All sites have gravel parking, with pea gravel picnic areas. Though site size varies, most are large. Bandits Roost is extremely remote, and is gated and guarded, making security outstanding. This area experiences mild summers, making it a good destination in spring, summer, and fall. Just avoid visiting on holiday weekends. Near Bandits Roost are day-use areas and the Skyline Marina, which offers boat launches and other fishing facilities. The reservoir is stocked with crappie, bluegill, catfish, and largemouth and striped hybrid bass.

BASICS
Operated By: U.S. Army Corps of Engineers. **Open:** Apr. 1–Oct. 31. **Site Assignment:** 60% of site can be reserved (877) 444-6777, MC, V; other 40% are first come, first served; if cancelled the fee is $10 plus the 1-night fee. **Registration:** At entrance station. **Fee:** RV, $18; tent, $14; Golden Age/Golden Access card, $8/$6. **Parking:** 2 vehicles per site, overflow parking available.

FACILITIES

Number of RV-only Sites: 42. **Number of Tent-only Sites:** 42. **Hookups:** Electric (30 amps), water, at RV site; tent sites w/ no hookups. **Each Site:** Picnic table, fire ring, tent pad, lantern hook. **Dump Station:** Yes. **Laundry:** No. **Pay Phone:** Yes. **Restrooms and Showers:** Yes. **Fuel:** No. **Propane:** No. **Internal Roads:** Paved. **RV Service:** 6 mi. north in Wilkesboro. **Market:** 6 mi. north in Wilkesboro. **Restaurant:** 6 mi. north in Wilkesboro. **General Store:** 5 mi. north in Wilkesboro. **Vending:** No. **Swimming:** Yes. **Playground:** Yes. **Other:** Boating ramp, trails, group lodging. **Activities:** Picnicking, hiking, fishing, basketball, activities in the amphitheater. **Nearby Attractions:** Blue Ridge Pkwy., river rafting. **Additional Information:** Wilkes Chamber of Commerce, (336) 838-8662.

RESTRICTIONS

Pets: On leash only. **Fires:** Fire ring only. **Alcoholic Beverages:** Not allowed. **Vehicle Maximum Length:** No limit. **Other:** Fishing is state regulated 14-day stay limit.

TO GET THERE

From I-77, exit onto 421 north, then exit onto Hwy. 268 going west; the park is 6 mi. on the right.

WILKESBORO   MAP, A-3
Doughton Park Campground

45356 Blue Ridge Pkwy., 28644. T: (336) 372-8568; www.blueridgeparkway.org.

🚐 ★★★★   ⛺ ★★★★

Beauty: ★★★★	Site Privacy: ★★★
Spaciousness: ★★★	Quiet: ★★★
Security: ★★★★	Cleanliness: ★★★★★
Insect Control: ★★★★★	Facilities: ★★★

Doughton Park is the largest recreation area on the Blue Ridge Parkway, and offers plenty of mileage for hikers in the summer and cross-country skiers in the winter. We like the lodge's restaurant for a break from campsite cooking. Nearby, Stone Mountain State Park offers numerous rock-climbing routes to the top of the park's namesake. The campground at Doughton is separated into six loops, some for RV campers, others for tent campers. There are both heavily wooded and more open sites, so take your pick. Sites are average sized, with varying levels of privacy. Tent campers seeking private sites should go for walk-in sites 23–33. RV campers looking for solitude should head to the back of the campground. Though there are no gates, security is excellent at this isolated campground. Even though this is a less-trafficked part of the Blue Ridge Parkway, it's best to visit midweek during summer and fall.

BASICS

Operated By: National Park Service. **Open:** May–Oct. **Site Assignment:** First come, first served. **Registration:** At office. **Fee:** $16. **Parking:** Yes.

FACILITIES

Number of RV-only Sites: 25. **Number of Tent-only Sites:** 110. **Hookups:** None. **Each Site:** Picnic table, fireplace. **Dump Station:** Yes. **Laundry:** No. **Pay Phone:** Yes. **Restrooms and Showers:** Yes. **Fuel:** Yes. **Propane:** No. **Internal Roads:** Paved. **RV Service:** No. **Market:** No. **Restaurant:** Yes. **General Store:** Yes. **Vending:** Inquire at campground. **Swimming:** No. **Playground:** No. **Activities:** Hiking, fishing. **Nearby Attractions:** Cumberland Knob, Brinegar Cabin.

RESTRICTIONS

Pets: Allowed. **Fires:** Allowed. **Alcoholic Beverages:** Inquire at campground. **Vehicle Maximum Length:** Call ahead for details.

TO GET THERE

From intersection of US 21 and Blue Ridge Pkwy., drive south to milepost 239, or from intersection of NC 18 and Blue Ridge Pkwy., drive north to milepost 239.

North Dakota

Although generally considered a Plains state, North Dakota offers varied terrain loaded with unique opportunities for prospective campers to enjoy the outdoors, not to mention some immense diversions for curiosity seekers as well. If camping is the most popular recreational activity within the 39th state, it's safe to say that campers are drawn to North Dakota's unique charms. Whether or not the Cass County city of **Casselton's Largest Stack of Empty Oil Cans** is one of those charms is up to the true adventurer.

In addition to its flat, rolling landscape, North Dakota has five state forests—**Mouse River** in McHenery County, **Sheyenne River** in Ransom County, **Tetrault Woods** in Pembina County, **Homen** in Bottineau County, and, the largest chunk of land in the system, **Turtle Mountain,** also in Bottineau—ideal habitats for primary residents of moose and deer. The state is rich in wildlife and contains more than 60 wildlife refuges, more than any other state. Animals native to the state include wild horses, sheep, bison, white-tail deer, and eagles. In fact, the world's largest buffalo can be seen gazing stoically on the horizon from **Jamestown,** in the south-central county of Stutsman.

North Dakota is divided into three distinct geological areas: the **Missouri Plateau,** the **Red River Valley,** and the **Drift Prairie.** The Missouri Plateau is sculpted with colorful canyons, gorges, ravines, bluffs, and buttes, whereas the Red River Valley and Drift Prairie pan out into the fertile farmlands. Added to the topographical mix are North Dakota's numerous state parks and forests. Most of North Dakota's 18 state parks have camping and picnicking facilities. **Theodore Roosevelt National Park,** in northwestern North Dakota, is one of several national parks found in the state, the newest one of which straddles the the U.S.–Canadian border. Dedicated on July 14, 1993, the **International Peace Garden** in Dunseith, North Dakota, and in Boissevain, Manitoba, is recognized as a genuine symbol of peace between the Lower 48 and our Northern neighbor. For an even more off-the-beaten-path monument, the Pierce County town of **Rugby** has erected a 15-foot stone obelisk at the junction of Routes 2 and 3, declaring its location the geographical center of North America.

North Dakota is also filled with rivers and lakes, 171 to be exact. The major rivers are the **Missouri,** which flows south into the Mississippi, and the **Red,** which forms the border between North Dakota and Minnesota. Naturally, there are countless opportunities for fishing, boating, and bird-watching. It is said that more ducks reproduce in North Dakota than anywhere in the nation.

The state's largest city is **Fargo,** which offers many modern conveniences while maintaining its rustic, Western charm. Fifteen minutes southwest in the somewhat smaller town of **Horace** is North Dakota's **Champion Tree**—a giant cottonwood that stands at more than 100 feet. Other prominent cities include the state capital, **Bismarck; Grand Forks,** home of the **University of North Dakota;** and **Pembina,** home of the newest state historical museum. If it's a historical diversion you desire, head to the far northwest town of **Antler** to see the world's largest historical quilt. Made in 1988 by Leona Tennyson, to celebrate North Dakota's 100th anniversary, the quilt totals 11,390 square feet.

North Dakota is heaven on earth for lovers of the outdoors and stands out as one of the most diverse wildlife areas in the country. In terms of camping, the state's only drawback is its winters, which are cold and long. However, if a little bit of the fluffy white stuff doesn't impede your plans, then North Dakota is the ideal spot for all the standard winter activities, such as snowmobile riding, skiing, snowboarding, ice fishing, sledding, and skating. When it comes to a vast array of unique opportunities, this rectangular state is definitely no square.

Campground Profiles

ARVILLA   MAP, B-4
Turtle River State Park

3084 Park Ave., 58214. T: (701) 594-4445 or
(800) 807-4723 reservations; www.ndparks.com.

🚐 ★★★   ⛺ ★★★

Beauty: ★★★   Site Privacy: ★★★
Spaciousness: ★★★   Quiet: ★★★★
Security: ★★★★   Cleanliness: ★★★
Insect Control: ★★   Facilities: ★★

In the eastern part of the state, not far from Grand
Forks, campers can find a nice mix of river recreation
and mountain fun. Typical of nature-oriented camping in this climate, the time of year absolutely defines
the vacation, with cross-country skiing in winter and
water fun in the summer (mountain bikers ride
whenever they will). This is a family place, and kids
can even borrow fishing gear from the park office to
try their luck in the rainbow trout–stocked Turtle
River. The campground is fairly attractive, with pull-
through sites and varying privacy. The facilities are
nothing special, but are totally adequate for both RV
and tent campers (although facilities are limited during the off-season). We recommend this campground for families.

BASICS

Operated By: North Dakota Parks & Recreation
Dept. **Open:** All year; water is off Oct.–May in the
campground. **Site Assignment:** Camping: first
come, first served (some reservations accepted).
Cabins: by reservation, 14-day cancellation policy.
Picnic shelters/woodland lodge/chalet: by reservation up to 1 year in advance. 1-month cancellation
policy for large facilities. **Registration:** At visitors
center. **Fee:** Electric, $14; no hookup, $8; plus a $5
entrance fee per vehicle or annual park pass ($25).
Parking: At site.

FACILITIES

Number of Multipurpose Sites: 80. **Hookups:**
Electric (30 amps) & water (at certain sites). **Each
Site:** Picnic table, grated fire pit. **Dump Station:**
Yes. **Laundry:** No. **Pay Phone:** Yes. **Restrooms
and Showers:** Yes. **Fuel:** No. **Propane:** No. **Inter-
nal Roads:** Paved. **RV Service:** 22 mi. in Grand
Forks. **Market:** In Larimore. **Restaurant:** In Lari-
more. **General Store:** Visitors center. **Vending:** Yes.
Swimming: No. **Playground:** Yes, several. **Other:**
Paved nature trail, 6 cabins, picnic shelters, 6 mi. of
groomed cross-country ski trails. **Activities:** Hiking,
fishing (rainbow trout), biking, sledding, cross-country
skiing, wildlife viewing, birding, special park programs.
Nearby Attractions: Grand Forks 22 mi. east, golf.
Additional Information: North Dakota Parks &
Recreation Dept., (701) 328-5357.

RESTRICTIONS

Pets: On leash. **Fires:** Fire pits or grills only; fires
may be restricted due to weather conditions; please
ask management before starting any open fires. **Alcoholic Beverages:** Allowed. **Vehicle Maximum
Length:** No limit, pull-through sites.

TO GET THERE

22 mi. west of Grand Forks directly off of Hwy. 2;
there are excellent signs.

BISMARK   MAP, B-2
Bismark KOA

3720 Centennial Rd., 58503. T: (701) 222-2662;
www.koa.com.

🚐 ★★★★★   ⛺ ★★★★★

Beauty: ★★★★★   Site Privacy: ★★★★★
Spaciousness: ★★★★★   Quiet: ★★★★
Security: ★★★★   Cleanliness: ★★★★
Insect Control: ★★★   Facilities: ★★★★

Located just ten minutes from the state capitol, the
Heritage Center, and the museums and art galleries
of Bismarck, this KOA offers a comfortable camping
experience. The 20-acre campground is spacious,
and a nicely wooded area provides both site privacy
and relaxing shade for activity-wearied campers.
Arranged in rows, most sites offer proximity to some
campground amenity. Sites 1–10 border the playing
fields but are close to nearby Centennial Road.
Though they are closest to the frequented dog walk
area, sites 71–78 are on the perimeter of the campground, farthest from the access road, and offer one
of the only views of land without campers. Sites
100–115 offer a similar experience except that the
tent campground occupies the adjacent "wilderness," offering lilacs, honeysuckle, and a variety of
birds. With relatively mild summer temperatures,
Bismarck is a nice family destination. The city
itself provides a busy schedule of summertime
activities, including a softball tournament, rodeo,
United Tribes International Pow-Wow, and Folkfest.
Depending on whether you plan to participate in
the festivities or avoid the crowds, be sure to check
dates for events before making plans to camp.

BASICS

Operated By: Gary & Jimilou Woodard. **Open:**
Apr. 1–Oct. 15. **Site Assignment:** By reservation.
Registration: At general store. **Fee:** RV, $28–$34;
tent, $20–$28; per 2 people; extra person, $3;
under 6, free. **Parking:** Limited, visitors park in a
separate area.

FACILITIES

Number of Multipurpose Sites: 118. **Hookups:**
Electric (20, 30, 50 amps), water, sewer, Wi-Fi. **Each
Site:** Picnic table. **Dump Station:** 2. **Laundry:** Yes.
Pay Phone: Courtesy phone. **Restrooms and
Showers:** Yes, **Fuel:** No, in town. **Propane:** No, in
town. **Internal Roads:** Gravel. **RV Service:** In
town. **Market:** In town. **Restaurant:** In town. **General Store:** Yes. **Vending:** Yes. **Swimming:** Yes.
Playground: 3. **Other:** Picnic shelter, 4 cabins, jogging area, data port by laundry room, basketball
court, volleyball court, tennis court. **Activities:**
Swimming, basketball, volleyball, horseshoes, tennis,
ice-cream socials. **Nearby Attractions:** State Capital, Dakota Zoo, Heritage Center, Museums, golf, Fort
Abraham Lincoln, Lewis & Clark Interpretive Center,

water park. **Additional Information:**
www.koa.com.

RESTRICTIONS

Pets: On leash. **Fires:** No open fires. **Alcoholic
Beverages:** Allowed, at site only. **Vehicle Maximum Length:** No limit.

TO GET THERE

From I-94, take Exit 161 and go north 1 mi. on the
left.

BOTTINEAU   MAP, A-2
Lake Metigoshe State Park

No. 2 Lake Metigoshe State Park Rd., 58318.
T: (701) 263-4651; www.ndparks.com.

🚐 ★★★★   ⛺ ★★★★

Beauty: ★★★★   Site Privacy: ★★★★
Spaciousness: ★★★★   Quiet: ★★★★
Security: ★★★★   Cleanliness: ★★★
Insect Control: ★★★   Facilities: ★★

Situated in the scenic Turtle Mountains on the shores
of Lake Metigoshe, this campground was constructed
by the Works Progress Administration (WPA) in the
1930s. The park's rolling hills, aspen forests, and
small lakes make the site one of the most popular
vacation spots in North Dakota. Lake Metigoshe is
noted for its northern pike, walleye, and perch. The
Old Oak Trail, a National Recreation Trail, is also
found within the park's boundaries. The park has
both modern and primitive camping, as well as picnic
areas. The 38 pull-through and 80 back-in RV sites
are spacious and private, providing a wonderful feeling of tranquility. Winter provides opportunities for
snowmobiling, skating, sledding, and ice fishing. The
park is open year-round, although water is turned off
during the winter months.

BASICS

Operated By: North Dakota Parks & Recreation
Dept. **Open:** All year; water is off Oct.–May (winter)
in the campground. **Site Assignment:** First come,
first served. **Registration:** At entrance gate. **Fee:**
Water/electric, $14; no hookup, $8; plus $5 entrance
fee per vehicle or annual park pass. **Parking:** At site.

FACILITIES

Number of RV-only Sites: 90. **Number of Tent-
only Sites:** 28. **Hookups:** Electric (30 amps), water.
Each Site: Picnic table, grated fire pit. **Dump Station:** Yes. **Laundry:** No. **Pay Phone:** Courtesy
phone. **Restrooms and Showers:** Yes. **Fuel:** No.
Propane: No. **Internal Roads:** Paved. **RV Service:**
90 mi. south in Minot. **Market:** 3 in town. **Restaurant:** Several in town. **General Store:** No. **Vending:** Yes. **Swimming:** Lakefront beach. **Playground:**
Several. **Other:** 3 year-round cabins, group dorms
(total cap.120), kitchen, dining hall & auditorium,
swim beach, boat ramp, fishing dock, picnic shelters,
seasonal naturalist, canoe rentals, warming house,
cross-country ski & snowshoe rentals. **Activities:**
Hiking, fishing (walleye, chinook, trout, pike), boating,
skiing, ice fishing in the winter, wildlife viewing, special
park programs, cross-country skiing, sledding,

mountain biking. **Nearby Attractions:** International Peace Garden, downhill & cross-country ski areas, Peace Garden State Snowmobile Trail, Golf courses, Turtle Mountains, J. Clark Salyer & Lords Lake National Wildlife Refuges, State Scenic Byway. **Additional Information:** North Dakota Parks & Recreation Dept. (701) 328-5357.

RESTRICTIONS

Pets: On leash, but not on beach or public picnic areas. **Fires:** Fire pits or grills only; fires may be restricted due to weather conditions; please ask management before starting any open fires. **Alcoholic Beverages:** At site. **Vehicle Maximum Length:** No limit.

TO GET THERE

14 mi. northeast of Bottineau. From SR 5 go north on Lake Rd. 10.2 mi., make a right on SR 43 6.1 mi., then follow signs into park.

CAVALIER   MAP, A-4
Graham's Island State Park

152 South Duncan Dr., 58301. T: (701) 766-4015 or (800) 807-4723 reservations; www.ndparks.com.

🚐 ★★★★	🏕 ★★★★
Beauty: ★★★★	Site Privacy: ★★★★★
Spaciousness: ★★★★	Quiet: ★★★★
Security: ★★★★	Cleanliness: ★★★
Insect Control: ★★	Facilities: ★★

Of the three state parks on Devils Lake, this is the largest and most developed. Naturally, water sports are a big draw, and you can even do some serious ice fishing for yellow perch in the winter. Other catches in the warmer months may include walleye, northern pike, and white bass. While you're tromping through the oak, ash, elm, and aspen in the surrounding hills, you may partake of some deer, wild turkey, and other small game. Other creatures that occasionally visit Graham's Island include horned owls and bald eagles. The camping facilities are nothing spectacular, but they are certainly sufficient for RVs and tents, with plenty of recreation for all ages—with emphasis on nature appreciation, of course. The 12 back-in and 94 pull-through sites vary in size, and the facilities are more limited in the winter, but with a little planning this would be a lovely destination anytime. The setting is rural, about 9 miles from the town of Devils Lake, and near plenty of other diversions. Security is good and privacy is superb at this campground. Take your parka or your swimsuit and enjoy.

BASICS

Operated By: North Dakota Parks & Recreation Dept. **Open:** All year; water is off Oct.–May in the winter. **Site Assignment:** First come, first served (also in the summer). **Registration:** At entrance gate. **Fee:** Electric, $14; no hookup, $8; plus a $5 entrance fee per vehicle or $25 annual park pass. **Parking:** At site.

FACILITIES

Number of RV-only Sites: 85. **Number of Tent-only Sites:** 21. **Hookups:** Electric (30, 50 amps),

water. **Each Site:** Picnic table, fire rings. **Dump Station:** Yes. **Laundry:** No. **Pay Phone:** Courtesy phone. **Restrooms and Showers:** Yes. **Fuel:** Yes. **Propane:** No. **Internal Roads:** Paved. **RV Service:** Devils Lake. **Market:** Devils Lake. **Restaurant:** Devils Lake. **General Store:** Yes, Grahams Island. **Vending:** No. **Swimming:** No. **Playground:** Yes, several. **Other:** Boat ramp (Grahams Island & Black Tiger Bay), picnic shelter, hiking trails (Grahams Island) & Sivert Thompson Activities Center (Grahams Island), fish-cleaning station. **Activities:** Boating, fishing (walleye, northern pike, perch, & white bass), hiking, biking, self-guided nature tours, interpretive programming, playgrounds, swimming, snowmobiling, cross-country skiing, & ice fishing. **Nearby Attractions:** Fort Totten State Historic Site, Sully's Hill National Game Preserve, Historic Downtown Devils Lake. **Additional Information:** North Dakota Parks & Recreation Dept., (701) 328-5357.

RESTRICTIONS

Pets: On leash. **Fires:** Fire pits or grills only; fires may be restricted due to weather conditions; please ask management before starting any open fires. **Alcoholic Beverages:** Allowed. **Vehicle Maximum Length:** No limit.

TO GET THERE

To get to Grahams Island State Park, take Hwy. 2 north to Hwy. 19 west to Grahams Island Rd. Continue south on Grahams Island Rd. to park entrance.

CAVALIER   MAP, A-4
Icelandic State Park

13571 Hwy. 5, 58220. T: (701) 265-4561 or (800) 807-4723; www.ndparks.com.

🚐 ★★★	🏕 ★★★
Beauty: ★★★	Site Privacy: ★★★
Spaciousness: ★★★	Quiet: ★★★★
Security: ★★★★	Cleanliness: ★★★
Insect Control: ★★	Facilities: ★★

It's not as cold as you think. But, then, neither is Iceland. Actually, this state park celebrates and preserves natural splendor and pioneer history, at the same time providing a good variety of recreation. In the northeastern corner of the state, this rural spot on Lake Renwick offers plenty of water sports, and the northern pike are abundant. In the winter, plan to fish through a hole in the ice (OK, it gets pretty cold). This is a well-rounded campground, with average facilities (that are more limited in the winter), comfortable for RVs and tents, relatively quiet, and secure. The medium-sized pull-through sites offer a decent amount of privacy, and the old oak trees provide a good bit of shade, especially in the picnic area. Family-friendly recreation and wonderful wildlife viewing make this a delightful vacation spot. Depending on the crowd, this is a quiet, remote, secure campground where you can expect a peaceful and fun vacation.

BASICS

Operated By: North Dakota Parks & Recreation Dept. **Open:** All year; water is off Oct.–May in the campground. **Site Assignment:** Some sites by reservation, some first come, first served; reserva-

tions only taken in the summer. **Registration:** At entrance gate. **Fee:** Electric, $14; no hookup, $8; plus a $5 entrance fee per vehicle or annual park pass. **Parking:** At site.

FACILITIES

Number of Multipurpose Sites: 159. **Hookups:** Electric (30 amps), water. **Each Site:** Picnic table, grated fire pit. **Dump Station:** Yes. **Laundry:** No. **Pay Phone:** Yes. **Restrooms and Showers:** Yes. **Fuel:** No. **Propane:** No. **Internal Roads:** Paved. **RV Service:** In Cavalier. **Market:** In Cavalier. **Restaurant:** In Cavalier. **General Store:** No. **Vending:** Yes. **Swimming:** Beach. **Playground:** Yes, several. **Other:** Boat ramp, picnic shelter, visitors center, historic buildings, historic artifacts, meeting room, & 3 cabins. **Activities:** Boating, shore & ice fishing (northern pike), hiking, biking, self-guided nature tours, interpretive programming, playgrounds, swimming, & artifacts exhibits on area's settlement. **Nearby Attractions:** Pembina County Historical Museum, Patton's Isle of Memories, Frostfire Mountain Ski Resort, golf, snowmobile trail, & scenic byway. **Additional Information:** North Dakota Parks & Recreation Dept., (701) 328-5357.

RESTRICTIONS

Pets: On leash. **Fires:** Fire pits or grills only; fires may be restricted due to weather conditions; please ask management before starting any open fires. **Alcoholic Beverages:** Allowed. **Vehicle Maximum Length:** No limit.

TO GET THERE

Icelandic State Park is located 5 mi. west of Cavalier on Hwy. 5.

ECKELSON   MAP, B-4
Prairie Haven

10121 36th St. SE, 58481. T: (701) 646-2267; www.prairie-haven.com.

🚐 ★★★	🏕 ★★★
Beauty: ★★★	Site Privacy: ★★★
Spaciousness: ★★★	Quiet: ★★★
Security: ★★★	Cleanliness: ★★★
Insect Control: ★★★	Facilities: ★★★

The onsite spring-fed lake, more aptly called a pond, compliments the quiet serenity of this park-like campground and offers a quaint experience slightly reminiscent of Thoreau's Walden. The pull-through sites here are spacious and most can accommodate double slide-outs. Though mature trees give ample shade and the uninterrupted grassy sites provide an expanse of pleasing green, the lack of bushes and trees between sites offers little privacy. Perhaps this is a ploy by hosts and owners Biff and Claudine Flowers to encourage guests to make new friends, but if you like eating dinner alone, you may have to venture elsewhere. The rustic architecture of the general store and one-room cabin add to the country ambience of the campground. This campground offers a simple, pleasing experience to RV and tent-campers alike and is a nice overnight stop.

BASICS

Operated By: Biff & Claudine Flowers. **Open:** May–Oct. **Site Assignment:** By reservation. **Registration:** At general store. **Fee:** RV, $22; tent, $18; per 2 people; extra person, $3; under age 6, free. **Parking:** On site.

FACILITIES

Number of Multipurpose Sites: 31. **Hookups:** Electric (20, 30, 50 amps), water, sewer. **Each Site:** Picnic tables. **Dump Station:** Yes. **Laundry:** Yes. **Pay Phone:** Yes. **Restrooms and Showers:** Yes. **Fuel:** Yes. **Propane:** No, 8 mi. in Sandborn. **Internal Roads:** Gravel. **RV Service:** 15 mi. in Jamestown. **Market:** 15 mi. in Jamestown. **Restaurant:** Yes. **General Store:** Yes. **Vending:** Store. **Swimming:** No. **Playground:** Yes. **Other:** Spring-fed lake, 2 cabins. **Activities:** Fishing, basketball, volleyball, horseshoes, boat rental. **Nearby Attractions:** Inquire at campground. **Additional Information:** www.prairie-haven.com.

RESTRICTIONS

Pets: On leash. **Fires:** 1 central fire ring. **Alcoholic Beverages:** Allowed, at site only. **Vehicle Maximum Length:** No limit.

TO GET THERE

From I-94, take Exit 276 (Eckelson) and go south less than 0.25 mi. First turn on the left.

EPPING   MAP, B-1
Lewis and Clark State Park

4904 119th Rd. NW, 58843. T: (701) 859-3071 or (800) 807-4723 reservations; www.ndparks.com.

🚐 ★★★★   ⛺ ★★★★

Beauty: ★★★★	Site Privacy: ★★★★
Spaciousness: ★★★★	Quiet: ★★★★
Security: ★★★★	Cleanliness: ★★★★
Insect Control: ★★★	Facilities: ★★★

A rural spot on an upper bay of the mighty Lake Sakakawea, this state park is of course named for the famous explorers, and you can find commemorations of the Lewis and Clark expedition here and there. In the northwest part of the state, this setting offers a striking view of the rugged buttes of the Badlands. Water sports and wildlife viewing are major draws, and the fishing is terrific as well. In addition to the healthy supply of walleye, sauger, and northern pike, you might occasionally discover a pallid sturgeon or a paddlefish. Lucky campers may spot deer and pheasant, as well. This is a great place for tent and RV camping, with adequate facilities (although they are limited in the winter). There are 18 back-in sites and the rest are pull-through. As is the case with many state parks, this is a beautiful place to spend a vacation, with privacy, space and peace defining the campground, and a great variety of recreation for all ages in and around the park. History buffs and nature lovers alike will love it here.

BASICS

Operated By: North Dakota Parks & Recreation Dept. **Open:** All year; electricity/water off Oct.–May in the campground. **Site Assignment:** By reservation in summer; first come, first served Oct.–Apr.

Registration: At entrance gate. **Fee:** Electric, $14; no hookup, $8; plus a $5 entrance fee per vehicle, or annual park pass. **Parking:** At site.

FACILITIES

Number of Multipurpose Sites: 80. **Hookups:** Electric (30 amps), water. **Each Site:** Picnic table, grated fire pit. **Dump Station:** Yes. **Laundry:** No. **Pay Phone:** No. **Restrooms and Showers:** Yes. **Fuel:** No. **Propane:** No. **Internal Roads:** Paved. **RV Service:** 19 mi. NW of Williston. **Market:** 19 mi. NW of Williston. **Restaurant:** 10 mi. east. **General Store:** Concession stand. **Vending:** No. **Swimming:** No. **Playground:** Yes. **Other:** Fish-cleaning station, picnic shelters, lakefront beach, picnic area w/ grills, nature trails, slip rentals, amphitheater. **Activities:** Hiking, wildlife viewing, special park programs, snow skiing. **Nearby Attractions:** Buffalo Trail Museum, Fort Buford, Fort Union. **Additional Information:** North Dakota Parks & Recreation Dept., (701) 328-5357.

RESTRICTIONS

Pets: On leash. **Fires:** Fire pits or grills only; fires may be restricted due to weather conditions; please ask management before starting any open fires. **Alcoholic Beverages:** Allowed. **Vehicle Maximum Length:** No limit.

TO GET THERE

The park is 19 mi. SE of Williston on Hwy. 1804; turn on CR 15 and it is 3 mi. on the left. There is excellent signage from Hwy. 1804.

GARRISON   MAP, B-2
Fort Stevenson State Park

1252-A 41st. Ave. NW, 58540. T: (701) 337-5576 or (800) 807-4723 reservations; www.ndparks.com.

🚐 ★★★★   ⛺ ★★★★

Beauty: ★★★★	Site Privacy: ★★★★
Spaciousness: ★★★★	Quiet: ★★★★
Security: ★★★★	Cleanliness: ★★★
Insect Control: ★★★	Facilities: ★★

Located in the center of the state, on the eastern end of giant Lake Sakakawea, this park is an angler's paradise. Plenty of other water sports and nature appreciation is available to campers here, but the park hosts several annual fishing tournaments, and is known as the "walleye capital of North Dakota." Accordingly, the fishing-related facilities outshine those in the campground, but both RVs and tents should be comfortable here. Two pull-through sites are available, and the rest are back-ins. Ash, elms, and cottonwoods provide some shade, and the park is scattered with native wildflowers like purple clover, pasque flowers, purple coneflowers, and wild roses. The facilities are more limited in the winter, but the park is fun year-round. Just a few miles from the small town of Garrison, the park is in a rural area, and its remoteness enhances the security as well as the general quiet and privacy. This is a typically lovely campground for a state park, and all ages should enjoy the experience, just so long as you're not trying to escape fishing folks.

BASICS

Operated By: North Dakota Parks & Recreation Dept. **Open:** All year; water is off Oct.–May in the campground. **Site Assignment:** By reservation in summer; first come, first served Oct.–Apr. **Registration:** At entrance gate. **Fee:** Electric, $14; no hookup, $8; plus a $5 entrance fee per vehicle or annual park pass. **Parking:** At site.

FACILITIES

Number of RV-only Sites: 107. **Number of Tent-only Sites:** 35. **Hookups:** Electric (30, 50 amps), water (at certain sites). **Each Site:** Picnic table, grated fire pit. **Dump Station:** Yes. **Laundry:** No. **Pay Phone:** Courtesy phone. **Restrooms and Showers:** Yes. **Fuel:** No. **Propane:** No. **Internal Roads:** Paved. **RV Service:** 4 mi. north in Garrison. **Market:** 4 mi. north in Garrison. **Restaurant:** In Garrison. **General Store:** Yes. **Vending:** No. **Swimming:** Lakefront beach. **Playground:** Yes, several. **Other:** Pavilions w/ grill, 5 cabins, lakefront beach, picnic area w/ grills, meeting facilities, arboretum, prairie dog town, boat rentals. **Activities:** Hiking, fishing (walleye, chinook, trout, pike), boating, skiing, ice fishing in the winter, wildlife viewing, special park programs, cross-country skiing, in-season bow hunting for white-tail deer. **Nearby Attractions:** Broste Rock Museum, White Shield Powwow, golf, tennis, St. Stevensons State Park, Guard House Interpretive Center. **Additional Information:** North Dakota Parks & Recreation Dept., (701) 328-5357.

RESTRICTIONS

Pets: On leash, but not on beach or public picnic areas. **Fires:** Fire pits or grills only; fires may be restricted due to weather conditions; please ask management before starting any open fires. **Alcoholic Beverages:** Allowed. **Vehicle Maximum Length:** No limit. **Other:** 14-day camping limit.

TO GET THERE

Garrison is located on Hwy. 37, and the park is 4 mi. south on CR 15 on Lake Sakakawea's north shore.

JAMESTOWN   MAP, B-3
Frontier Fort Campground

P.O. Box 143, 58401. T: (701) 252-7492.

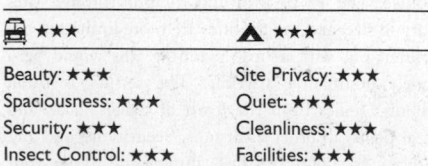

🚐 ★★★   ⛺ ★★★

Beauty: ★★★	Site Privacy: ★★★
Spaciousness: ★★★	Quiet: ★★★
Security: ★★★	Cleanliness: ★★★
Insect Control: ★★★	Facilities: ★★★

Frontier Fort is a solid middle-of-the-road campground attached to a small Western-themed tourist attraction called Frontier Village. Despite Frontier Village's general tackiness, it's hard not to marvel at the World's Largest Buffalo (a 26-foot-tall, 46-foot-long, 60-ton concrete behemoth). There's even a pair of normal-sized live buffalo you can hand-feed behind the gift shop. Depending as it does almost completely on traveling flocks of older RVers, facilities are limited at this campground during the off-season. Fifteen of the campsites are sizable pull-throughs. Besides Frontier Village attractions, there is little to see here.

BASICS

Operated By: Tanata Enterprises Inc. (Charley, Liz, & Jim). **Open:** All year. **Site Assignment:** By reservation or first come, first served. **Registration:** At general store. **Fee:** RV, $24; tent, $12. **Parking:** At site.

FACILITIES

Number of RV-only Sites: 72. **Number of Multipurpose Sites:** 20. **Hookups:** Electric (20, 30, 50 amps), water, sewer. **Each Site:** Picnic table. **Dump Station:** Yes. **Laundry:** Yes. **Pay Phone:** Yes. **Restrooms and Showers:** Yes. **Fuel:** No, but in town. **Propane:** No, but in town. **Internal Roads:** Combination pavement & gravel in good condition. **RV Service:** In town. **Market:** In Jamestown. **Restaurant:** On site and in Jamestown. **General Store:** Yes. **Vending:** Yes. **Swimming:** No. **Playground:** No. **Other:** Bar, buffalo, Village Trader Gift Shoppe. **Activities:** Electronic gaming (adults only). **Nearby Attractions:** Frontier Village, Old West stagecoach ride, dinner theater, zoo, museum.

RESTRICTIONS

Pets: On leash. **Fires:** Fire pits or grills only; fires may be restricted due to weather conditions; please ask management before starting any open fires. **Alcoholic Beverages:** Allowed. **Vehicle Maximum Length:** No limit.

TO GET THERE

From I-94 take Exit 258, Go north on US 281 (about 0.5 mi.) to first stop light, then east on 17th St. Entrance on right.

JAMESTOWN   MAP, B-3
Jamestown KOA Campground

3605 80th Ave. South, 58401-9511. T: (701) 252-6262 or (800) 562-6350; www.koa.com.

🚐 ★★★★	🏕 ★★★★
Beauty: ★★★★	Site Privacy: ★★★★
Spaciousness: ★★★★	Quiet: ★★★★
Security: ★★★★	Cleanliness: ★★★
Insect Control: ★★	Facilities: ★★★

While this KOA offers the usual amenities and abundant opportunities for play, including bocce ball, tetherball, heated pool, and disc golf, it lacks anything particularly unique. Though the RV sites are spacious, the landscaping and design are modest. All RV sites are gravel, most are pull-through, and sites 1–6 are best if you are looking for a nicely shaded spot. Sites 1–18 are closest to the play equipment, and sites 19–36 are closer to the lodge and restrooms. Smart planning places the play area and lodge between the sites and the frontage road to act as a buffer. Tent sites, designated separately from the RV sites, offer the most secluded and wooded experience. A nice feature is a half-mile walking trail on the perimeter of the campground. Jamestown, only 2 miles away, pays homage to the legendary buffalo and frontier spirit with its National Buffalo Museum and the World's Largest Buffalo and Frontier Village. This is a nice overnight stop to someplace else, but is probably not a destination for an extended stay.

BASICS

Operated By: Ann Case. **Open:** May 1–Oct. 1. **Site Assignment:** By reservation (800) 313-6262, held on credit card. **Registration:** At general store. **Fee:** RV, $26–$28; tent, $22; per 2 people, extra person, $3. **Parking:** At site.

FACILITIES

Number of RV-only Sites: 48. **Number of Tent-only Sites:** 20. **Hookups:** Electric (20, 30, 50 amps), water, sewer, cable TV. **Each Site:** Picnic table. **Dump Station:** Yes. **Laundry:** Yes. **Pay Phone:** Courtesy phone. **Restrooms and Showers:** Yes. **Fuel:** No. **Propane:** No. **Internal Roads:** Gravel. **RV Service:** Jamestown, 2 mi. **Market:** Jamestown, 2 mi. **Restaurant:** Jamestown, 2 mi. **General Store:** Yes. **Vending:** Yes. **Swimming:** No. **Playground:** Yes. **Other:** Cabins, game room. **Activities:** Tetherball, disc golf, bocce ball, basketball, horseshoes, & nature walk. **Nearby Attractions:** National Buffalo Museum & live herd, world's largest buffalo & frontier village. **Additional Information:** Jamestown Chamber of Commerce, (701) 252-4830.

RESTRICTIONS

Pets: On leash. **Fires:** Fire pits or grills only; fires may be restricted due to weather conditions; please ask management before starting any open fires. **Alcoholic Beverages:** Allowed. **Vehicle Maximum Length:** No limit.

TO GET THERE

I-94 to Exit 256, then west on South Frontage Rd. 1 mi.

LARIMORE   MAP, B-4
Larimore Dam Recreation Area and Campground

P.O. Box 268, 58251-0268. T: (701) 343-2078.

🚐 ★★★★	🏕 ★★★★
Beauty: ★★★★	Site Privacy: ★★★★
Spaciousness: ★★★★	Quiet: ★★★★
Security: ★★★★	Cleanliness: ★★★★
Insect Control: ★★	Facilities: ★★★

This pretty and well-run campground makes a good headquarters for exploring the nearby Grand Forks area. Anglers will relish the chance to fish for trout, bluegill, bullhead, walleye, and largemouth bass in the waters of the Turtle River. Other recreational options abound, of course. Campers can hike or bike the nature trails; there's even a paved bike path running from the town of Larimore to the dam itself, which makes for a good day trip in either direction. Seasonally, visitors can relax on the campground beach in warmer months, or enjoy snow sledding during the winter.

BASICS

Operated By: Private operator. **Open:** Apr.–late Oct.; depends on weather. **Site Assignment:** By reservation or first come, first served. **Registration:** At general store. **Fee:** $14 w/ hookups. **Parking:** At site.

FACILITIES

Number of Multipurpose Sites: 144. **Hookups:** Electric (20, 30, 50 amps), water, sewer. **Each Site:** Picnic table, fire pit. **Dump Station:** Yes. **Laundry:** Yes. **Pay Phone:** Yes. **Restrooms and Showers:** Yes. **Fuel:** No. **Propane:** No. **Internal Roads:** Combination pavement & gravel in good condition. **RV Service:** Grand Forks, 30 mi. **Market:** In Larimore. **Restaurant:** In Larimore. **General Store:** Yes. **Vending:** Yes. **Swimming:** Beach. **Playground:** Yes. **Other:** Picnic shelters, Myra Arboretum, a gazebo, fishing dock, nature trails. **Activities:** Softball, volleyball, boating, waterskiing, fishing, hiking, swimming, & biking. **Nearby Attractions:** Inquire at campground.

RESTRICTIONS

Pets: On leash. **Fires:** Fire pits or grills only; fires may be restricted due to weather conditions; please ask management before starting any open fires. **Alcoholic Beverages:** Allowed. **Vehicle Maximum Length:** No limit.

TO GET THERE

Located 30 mi. west of Grand Forks on Hwy. 4.

MANDAN   MAP, B-2
Fort Lincoln State Park

4480 Fort Lincoln Rd., 58554. T: (701) 667-6340 or (800) 807-4723 reservations; www.ndparks.com.

🚐 ★★★	🏕 ★★★
Beauty: ★★★	Site Privacy: ★★★
Spaciousness: ★★★	Quiet: ★★★★
Security: ★★★★	Cleanliness: ★★★
Insect Control: ★★	Facilities: ★★

This state park is interesting for both its military and Native American commemorative sites. What with Little Big Horn and Custer battle reminders, and the reconstructed On-A-Slant Indian Village, the cultural history here is intriguing. The view of the Missouri River from the trails is stunning, offering a full panorama in some places. The recreational opportunities include hiking, rainbow trout fishing, and wildlife viewing, with snowmobiling and cross-country skiing in the winter. Campers will find typical facilities for a state park, average-sized back-in sites and decent privacy, comfortable but not luxurious. It is a fairly quiet and secure campground, pleasant and generally peaceful. Keep in mind that facilities are limited in the winter, and bring along a history and/or anthropology friend to enhance your culturally enriching camping vacation.

BASICS

Operated By: North Dakota Parks & Recreation Dept. **Open:** All year; water is off Oct.–May in the campground. **Site Assignment:** By reservation in summer, (800) 807-4723; first come, first served Oct.–Apr. **Registration:** At entrance gate. **Fee:** Electric, $14; no hookup, $8; plus a $5 entrance fee per vehicle or annual park pass. **Parking:** At site.

FACILITIES

Number of Multipurpose Sites: 95. **Hookups:** Electric (30 amps), water. **Each Site:** Picnic table, grated fire pit. **Dump Station:** Yes. **Laundry:** No. **Pay Phone:** Courtesy phone. **Restrooms and**

Showers: Yes. **Fuel:** No. **Propane:** No. **Internal Roads:** Paved. **RV Service:** 7 mi. north in Mandan. **Market:** 7 mi. north in Mandan. **Restaurant:** 7 mi. north in Mandan. **General Store:** No. **Vending:** Yes. **Swimming:** No. **Playground:** Yes, several. **Other:** Gift Store, paved bike trails, 2 cabins, picnic shelters, trail riding concession, state snowmobile trailhead, On-a-Slant Mandan Village Earthlodges & other historical buildings, including the Custer House & commissary, museum, cross-country ski trails. **Activities:** Tours of Fort Lincoln, snowmobiling, hiking, fishing (rainbow trout), biking, sledding, cross-country skiing, wildlife viewing, special park programs. **Nearby Attractions:** Grand Forks 22 mi. east, golf. **Additional Information:** North Dakota Parks & Recreation Dept., (701)328-5357.

RESTRICTIONS

Pets: On leash. **Fires:** Fire pits or grills only; fires may be restricted due to weather conditions; please ask management before starting any open fires. **Alcoholic Beverages:** Allowed. **Vehicle Maximum Length:** No limit.

TO GET THERE

From I-94 Exit 152, go south on Sunset Dr. to Main St.; take a left on Main St. to 6th Ave.; then right on 6th Ave. 7 mi. to Fort Abraham Lincoln State Park.

MINOT
Minot KOA
MAP, B-2

5261 Hwy. 52 East, 58701. T: (701) 839-7400 or (800) 562-7421 reservations; www.koa.com.

🚐 ★★★	⛺ ★★★
Beauty: ★★★	Site Privacy: ★★★
Spaciousness: ★★★	Quiet: ★★★★
Security: ★★★★	Cleanliness: ★★★
Insect Control: ★★	Facilities: ★★★

This campground is really lovely, set in rolling hills and meadowland. The grounds are well manicured and clean, and on-site security is great. Each site is medium to average size, which gives the guests privacy and quiet. The grounds are shaded by elms and cottonwoods, and a variety of birds and rabbits call this campground home. It's somewhat smaller than other KOAs we've seen. However, we don't think this takes away from the campground at all. There are still all the amenities of the larger facilities, even a laundry, but without the crowd you'd find at a big park. There are plenty of things to do on site, as well as in town, but some of the more interesting attractions are Roosevelt Park and Zoo and Pioneer Village.

BASICS

Operated By: Sandy Boe. **Open:** Apr. 15–Oct. 15. **Site Assignment:** By reservation (800) 562-7421. **Registration:** At general store. **Fee:** RV, $22–$29; tent, $19–$23; per 2 people. **Parking:** At site.

FACILITIES

Number of Multipurpose Sites: 66. **Hookups:** Electric (20, 30, 50 amps), water, sewer. **Each Site:** Picnic table. **Dump Station:** Yes. **Laundry:** Yes. **Pay Phone:** Courtesy phone. **Restrooms and Showers:** Yes. **Fuel:** No. **Propane:** No. **Internal Roads:** Gravel. **RV Service:** Minot. **Market:** Minot. **Restaurant:** Several in town. **General Store:** Yes. **Vending:** No. **Swimming:** No, but there is swimming at the Roosevelt Park & Zoo. **Playground:** Yes. **Other:** Game room. **Nearby Attractions:** Roosevelt Park & Zoo, golf, Pioneer Village, mini-golf, go-carts, movies. **Additional Information:** Minot Chamber of Commerce, (701) 852-6000.

RESTRICTIONS

Pets: On leash. **Fires:** Grills only. **Alcoholic Beverages:** Allowed. **Vehicle Maximum Length:** No limit. **Other:** Fire in grills only; strictly enforced.

TO GET THERE

Go 2.25 mi. southeast on Hwy. 52 from Minot. Follow signs to Jamestown.

WILLISTON
Prairie Acres RV Park
MAP, B-1

2008 University Ave., 58801. T: (701) 572-4860.

🚐 ★★★	⛺ n/a
Beauty: ★★★	Site Privacy: ★★★
Spaciousness: ★★★	Quiet: ★★★★
Security: ★★★	Cleanliness: ★★★★
Insect Control: ★★★	Facilities: ★★★

Prairie Acres RV Park is located on the Montana–North Dakota line 1 mile west of Williston, North Dakota. Prairie Acres offers a rural setting overlooking crop fields and summer wildflowers. All of Prairie Acres sites are grass, level, and pull-through, set on a large rectangular open lawn with few trees. The area is great for observing the stars and watching the summer evening lightning. Prairie Acres caters exclusively to people in RVs wishing to escape to a quiet and restful environment; no tenting allowed. Prairie Acres offers full-service hookups with 50-amp receptacles, but there are no public restrooms, showers, or laundry. This is a simple well-groomed campground for those visitors wishing for a comfortable night's sleep. There are no bells and whistles, just friendly people and peace. The spring is cool, and the summer dry. The wind blows constantly.

BASICS

Operated By: Orville C. Loomer. **Open:** May–Oct. **Site Assignment:** First come, first served. **Registration:** At camp office. **Fee:** Call ahead for rates. **Parking:** At site.

FACILITIES

Number of RV-only Sites: 36. **Hookups:** Electric (30, 50 amps), water, sewer. **Dump Station:** Yes. **Laundry:** No. **Pay Phone:** Courtesy phone. **Restrooms and Showers:** No. **Fuel:** No. **Propane:** No. **Internal Roads:** Paved. **RV Service:** 2 mi. in Williston. **Market:** In Williston. **Restaurant:** In Williston. **General Store:** No. **Vending:** No. **Swimming:** No. **Playground:** Yes. **Other:** Large sites, fantastic views. **Activities:** Inquire at campground. **Nearby Attractions:** Fort Union Trading Post National Historic Site, The James Memorial Center for the Visual Arts, Williston Community Center w/ indoor pool, Theodore Roosevelt National Park. **Additional Information:** Williston Area Chamber of Commerce, (701) 572-3767.

RESTRICTIONS

Pets: On leash. **Fires:** No open fires. **Alcoholic Beverages:** Allowed. **Vehicle Maximum Length:** No limit.

TO GET THERE

2 mi. west of Williston on Hwy. 2.

Ohio

With a name meaning "great" in Iroquois, Ohio easily lives up to the assessment lent it by its original inhabitants. Commonly divided into five regions—central, northeast, northwest, southeast, and southwest—the Buckeye State affords residents and visitors alike many distinct opportunities for travel, diversions, sightseeing, and historical insight, regardless of location.

From **Lake Erie** on its northern border to the **Ohio River** on its southern, the Buckeye State offers a treasure trove of water recreation, 74 state parks with 57 campgrounds, and outdoor opportunities galore. At **Mohican State Park** near Mansfield, **Clear Fork River** is stocked with more than 100,000 brown trout for a fishing fantasy. Cleveland has one of the nation's largest park systems, with a 100-mile chain of city parks known as the **Emerald Necklace.** For an adventure seemingly out of place, you can scuba dive adjacent to downtown, where a freshwater reef has been created by the remains of the demolished **Cleveland Municipal Stadium.** In your travels around the city, see if you can find the world's largest rubber stamp, designed by Claes Oldenburg. **Hocking State Forest** and **Hocking Hills State Park** in southern Ohio offers climbing and rappelling on 99 acres of sheer rock faces and challenging cliffs, including ascents from 20 to 120 feet.

Those with different thrill-seeking adventures in mind will find that the Buckeye State spares no detail. In **Sandusky,** the famous 364-acre **Cedar Point Amusement Park,** also known as the roller-coaster capital of the world, features more than 60 rides, not to mention 13 spine-tingling roller coasters. See the stars nightly at the **Akron Civic Theater,** either on the ceiling, where the heavens are astonishingly simulated, or on its concert stage and big screen. At the **Hale Farm and Village**, travel back in time to the mid-1800s, as craftspeople and village residents portray life as it was in Ohio's Western Reserve. Historic **Sauder Village** in **Archbold** and **Roscoe Village** in **Coshocton** likewise celebrate the past.

Called "the most beautiful of America's inland cities" by Winston Churchill, **Cincinnati** saved its famed railroad station, **Union Terminal,** and turned it into several museums and an Omnimax theater. If that doesn't get you going, then be sure to seek out and sample some of the city's world-famous chili, in its unique three- four- or five-way styles. Nearby **Lebanon** evokes a remarkable Colonial atmosphere, and **Waynesville,** known as the antiques capital of the Midwest, is home to the **Ohio Sauerkraut Festival.** In its 100 acres, **Fort Ancient** contains 18,000 feet of earthwork constructed at least 2,000 years ago by the Hopewell Indians as part of their celestial calendar. For the more technologically inclined, learn about Orville and Wilbur Wright's first dreams of flight in the **U.S. Air Force Museum** in **Dayton.**

Hinckley has the dubious honor every March 15 of welcoming home squadron after squadron of buzzards returning from winter in the Smoky Mountains. If you're a budding ornithologist who prefers more variety, about 110 kinds of birds are known to nest in **Hocking Hills State Park** in **Logan. Put-In-Bay** on **South Bass Island** is known for its fish hatcheries, wineries, and caves, and **COSI Toledo** is a hands-on center that makes learning science fun.

Those in search of the more quirky and obscure can be assured that the 17th state has no short supply. For example, for those who can't leave their desks behind, a museum dedicated to pencil sharpeners resides in **Carbon Hill,** and in **Cambridge** there's the **Degenhart Paperweight Museum.** On July 4, **Ashville** celebrates like any other town in the United States, except that its show of lights also includes putting up the world's oldest stoplight at the corners of Walnut and Harrison. For fans of four-wheeled mayhem, the **National Tractor Pull Championships** are held each August in **Bowling Green.** Those seeking a slower pace can take a stroll on the oldest concrete street in America, **Court Avenue,** in **Bellefontaine.**

Campground Profiles

BELLVILLE MAP, B-2
Yogi Bear's Jellystone Park Mansfield

reserve america

SR 546 at Black Rd., 44813. T: (419) 886-CAMP; www.jellystonemansfield.com.

🚐 ★★★   ⛺ ★★★

Beauty: ★★★
Spaciousness: ★★★★
Security: ★★★
Insect Control: ★★★
Site Privacy: ★★★★
Quiet: ★★★★
Cleanliness: ★★★★
Facilities: ★★★

Yogi Bear's Jellystone Park Mansfield, located 8 miles south of Bellville, features rolling terrain along a lake. Laid out in a series of loops, the campground has 80 seasonal campers (some sites in not very good shape), three pull-through sites, and an average site width of 45 feet. Sites are level and grassy, with a choice of shaded or open. The entrance is a nice welcome to the campground with a fence, flowers, and ivy climbing a trellis. Security is provided by owners who live on site. Speed limit is 10.5 mph, high for a Yogi Bear facility. Quiet hours are 11 p.m. to 8 a.m. and minors age 18 and under are not permitted on the park grounds after 7:30 p.m. without adult supervision. Best RV sites are by the lake. Best tent sites are in a rustic area by the woods that affords more green space and privacy.

BASICS

Operated By: Bill Bings. **Open:** Apr. 15–Nov. 1. **Site Assignment:** Reservations w/ 1-night deposit; refund w/ 7-day notice. **Registration:** At campground office. **Fee:** $25–$33; cash, check, credit card. **Parking:** At site.

FACILITIES

Number of RV-only Sites: 175. **Number of Tent-only Sites:** 30. **Hookups:** Electric (30, 50 amps), water, sewer. **Each Site:** Picnic table, fire ring. **Dump Station:** Yes. **Laundry:** Yes. **Pay Phone:** Yes. **Restrooms and Showers:** Yes. **Fuel:** No. **Propane:** Yes. **Internal Roads:** Paved & gravel, in good condition. **RV Service:** No. **Market:** 8 mi. north in Bellville. **Restaurant:** 8 mi. north in Bellville. **General Store:** Yes. **Vending:** Yes. **Swimming:** No. **Playground:** Yes. **Other:** Swimming beach, pavilion, rental cabins, volleyball, game room, outdoor theater, horseshoes, stocked fishing lake, boat ramp, boat dock, recreation field. **Activities:** Swimming, fishing, boating (rental rowboats, canoes & paddleboats available), scheduled activities. **Nearby Attractions:** Amish Country, Mid-Ohio Race Track, golf, Mohican Forest, canoeing, plant tours, Malabar Farm State Park, Living Bible Museum, Richland Carousel Park, ski resorts, Ohio State Reformatory. **Additional Information:** Mansfield-Richland Area Chamber of Commerce, (419) 522-3211.

RESTRICTIONS

Pets: On leash only. **Fires:** Fire ring only. **Alcoholic Beverages:** At sites only. **Vehicle Maximum**

Length: No limit. **Other:** Bass & catfish under 15 inches must be returned to the lake immediately.

TO GET THERE

From the junction of I-71 and Hwy. 97, take Exit 165 and drive 1.5 mi. southeast on Hwy. 97, then 3 mi. west on Mock Rd., then 4 mi. south on Hwy. 546, then 0.25 mi. southwest on Black Rd. Roads are wide and well maintained but have narrow shoulders in spots.

BLUFFTON MAP, B-1
Twin Lakes Park

3506 Township Rd. 34, 45817.
T: (419) 477-5255 or (888) 477-5255; www.camptwinlakesohio.com.

🚐 ★★★   ⛺ ★★★

Beauty: ★★★
Spaciousness: ★★★
Security: ★★★
Insect Control: ★★★
Site Privacy: ★★★
Quiet: ★★★
Cleanliness: ★★★
Facilities: ★★★

A grassy campground on two lakes, Twin Lakes Park offers level, wooded, and open sites. Located 5 miles north of Bluffton, the campground's typical site has a width of 30 feet. There are 50 seasonals and five pull-through sites. Situated near I-75, the campground is subject to some noise from vehicles whizzing past. The best RV sites are by the lake or near the facilities. Tent sites are in a separate area with more greenery and privacy. A flea market, where campers set-up is free, is a popular event that takes place the last Saturday of each month, May through August. Safety measures include a 5.5-mph speed limit and speed bumps. Security includes one entrance/exit through a card-coded gate, owners who live on site, and regular patrols.

BASICS

Operated By: Bob & Elaine Harris. **Open:** All year. **Site Assignment:** Reservations w/ 1-night deposit; no refunds. **Registration:** At office. **Fee:** RV, $26; tent, $22; cash, check, credit card. **Parking:** At site.

FACILITIES

Number of RV-only Sites: 85. **Number of Tent-only Sites:** 10. **Hookups:** Electric (30, 50 amps), water, sewer. **Each Site:** Picnic table, fire ring. **Dump Station:** Yes. **Laundry:** No. **Pay Phone:** Yes. **Restrooms and Showers:** Yes. **Fuel:** No. **Propane:** Yes. **Internal Roads:** Paved, in good condition. **RV Service:** No. **Market:** 5 mi. south in Bluffton. **Restaurant:** 5 mi. south in Bluffton. **General Store:** Yes, limited. **Vending:** Yes. **Swimming:** Yes. **Playground:** Yes. **Other:** Swimming lake, fishing lake, volleyball, horseshoes, shuffleboard, basketball, shelter house, game room, volleyball, sandy beach, sports field, cabin rentals. **Activities:** Swimming, fishing, boating (rental rental rowboats, canoe, paddleboats available), scheduled weekend activities. **Nearby Attractions:** Golf, antiques, museums, historic homes, arts & crafts shops, motor sports park, Children's Garden, skating arena, Neil Armstrong Air & Space Museum, Indian Lake. **Additional Information:** Lima/Allen County CVB, (888) 222-6075.

RESTRICTIONS

Pets: On leash only; $2 for first pet, $3 for additional. Must provide proof of current vaccinations for pets. **Fires:** Fire ring only. **Alcoholic Beverages:** Allowed. **Vehicle Maximum Length:** No limit. **Other:** No hunting of frogs or turtles, limit of 2 bass.

TO GET THERE

From the junction of I-75 and Hwy. 235, take Exit 145 and drive 0.1 mi. south on Hwy. 235, then 0.5 mi. east on Township Rd. 34. The roads are wide and well maintained w/ broad shoulders.

BOWLING GREEN MAP, A-1
Fire Lake Camper Park

13630 West Kramer Rd., 43402.
T: (419) 352-1185 or (888) 879-2267; www.gocampingamerica.com/firelake/index.html.

🚐 ★★★   ⛺ ★★★

Beauty: ★★★
Spaciousness: ★★★
Security: ★★★★
Insect Control: ★★★
Site Privacy: ★★★
Quiet: ★★★
Cleanliness: ★★★★
Facilities: ★★★

A rural campground by an eight-acre lake, Fire Lake Camper Park offers open and shaded sites with easy access to the interstate. Some highway traffic noise can be heard at the far end of the campground. Sites are grassy with gravel pads for parking. The campground has 45 seasonal campers and five pull-through sites. Many sites are right on the lake, and most offer a lake view. A design flaw affecting a number of sites is the positioning of vehicle parking between the lake and the campsites. Typical site width is 30 feet. The campground is adjacent to the Slippery Elm Trail, a 23-mile trail that is free and open to the public for biking, walking, running, skating, horseback riding, and in-line skating. The trail, which is also wheelchair accessible, is a beautiful natural corridor converted from an unused railroad track. Bikes are available for rent at the campground. Security measures include owners who live on site, one entrance/exit road (with an enforced five-mph speed limit), and regular campground patrols.

BASICS

Operated By: Martin & Jennifer Gladieux. **Open:** Mar. 1–Oct. 15. **Site Assignment:** Reservations w/ 1-night deposit; refunds w/ 7-day notice. **Registration:** At campground office. **Fee:** $28–$32; cash, check, credit card. **Parking:** At site.

FACILITIES

Number of RV-only Sites: 96. **Number of Tent-only Sites:** 20. **Hookups:** Electric (30 amps), water. **Each Site:** Picnic table, fire ring. **Dump Station:** Yes. **Laundry:** Yes. **Pay Phone:** Yes. **Restrooms and Showers:** Yes. **Fuel:** No. **Propane:** No. **Internal Roads:** Paved/gravel, in good condition. **RV Service:** No. **Market:** 3 mi. north in Bowling Green. **Restaurant:** 3 mi. north in Bowling Green. **General Store:** Yes. **Vending:** Yes. **Swimming:** No. **Playground:** Yes. **Other:** Lake, swimming beach, rental cabins, basketball, volleyball, pavilion, rec room, boat dock, sports field, rental bikes. **Activities:** Swimming, catch-&-release fishing, boating (rental kayaks & paddleboats available), scheduled weekend activities. **Nearby Attractions:** Bowling Green State University, Slippery Elm Trail, museum, Sauder Historic village, golf, antiques, mill, canal boat, passenger train, Toledo Zoo. **Additional Information:** Greater Toledo CVB, (800) 243-4667.

RESTRICTIONS

Pets: On leash only. **Fires:** Fire ring only. **Alcoholic Beverages:** At sites only. **Vehicle Maximum Length:** No limit.

TO GET THERE

From the junction of I-75 and US 6, take Exit 179 and drive 1.5 mi. west on US 6, then 0.5 mi. south on Hwy. 25, then 0.5 mi. west on Kramer Rd. Roads are wide and well maintained w/ broad shoulders.

BROOKVILLE   MAP, C-1
Dayton Tall Timbers KOA Resort

7796 Wellbaum Rd., 45309.
T: (937) 833-3888 or (800) KOA-3317;
www.koa.com/where/oh/35102.htm.

🚐 ★★★★   ⛺ ★★★

Beauty: ★★★★	Site Privacy: ★★★★
Spaciousness: ★★★★	Quiet: ★★★★
Security: ★★★★★	Cleanliness: ★★★★★
Insect Control: ★★	Facilities: ★★★★★

Dayton Tall Timbers KOA Resort has all the large and small touches that make camping a pleasure. Laid out in a series of loops, the campground is grassy with gravel parking spots and concrete patios. The semiwooded facility offers a choice of open or shaded sites. The typical site width is 30 feet, and the campground has 20 seasonal campers and 150 pull-through sites. Little ponds, gazebos, flowers, brick walkways, benches, and a covered bridge add to the beauty. A well-stocked general store also features craft and souvenir items. A spring-fed fishing lake has bass, bluegill, perch, crappie, and catfish. No minibikes, mopeds or golf carts are allowed. Modest swimwear is required, i.e., no revealing bikinis or thongs. Alcoholic beverages are permitted at campsites, but tables should be kept free of open containers. Speed limit is five mph. Security measures include owners who live on site, one entrance/exit road, and regular campground patrols.

BASICS

Operated By: Rhonda & Joe Landis. **Open:** Apr. 1–Nov. 1. **Site Assignment:** Reservations w/ 1-night deposit; refund (minus $5) w/ 7-day notice. **Registration:** At campground office. **Fee:** RV $37–$52; tent, $29–$39; Kamping Kabin, $59–$85; Kottage/lodge, $115–$145; cash, check, credit card. **Parking:** At site.

FACILITIES

Number of RV-only Sites: 250. **Hookups:** Electric (20, 30, 50 amps), water, sewer, modem. **Each Site:** Picnic table, fire ring. **Dump Station:** Yes. **Laundry:** Yes. **Pay Phone:** Yes. **Restrooms and**

Showers: Yes. **Fuel:** No. **Propane:** Yes. **Internal Roads:** Paved/gravel, in good condition. **RV Service:** No. **Market:** 3 mi. west in Brookville. **Restaurant:** 3 mi. west in Brookville. **General Store:** Yes. **Vending:** Yes. **Swimming:** Yes. **Playground:** Yes. **Other:** Petting zoo, basketball, horseshoes, mini-golf, game room, picnic shelter, hiking trail, volleyball, rental cabins, badminton, fishing lake, coin games, pavilion, sports field. **Activities:** Swimming, boating (rental paddleboats available), fishing, hiking, scheduled activities. **Nearby Attractions:** Golf, US Air Force Museum, Sunwatch Indian Village, Wright Cycle Company Shop, Dayton Art Institute, Packard Museum, historic homes, museums, outdoor drama, Paramount Kings Island Theme Park, Museum of Discovery. **Additional Information:** Dayton & Montgomery County CVB, (800) 221-8235.

RESTRICTIONS

Pets: On leash only. **Fires:** Fire ring only. **Alcoholic Beverages:** At sites only. **Vehicle Maximum Length:** No limit.

TO GET THERE

From the junction of I-70 and Hwy. 49N, take Exit 24 and drive 0.5 mi. north on Hwy. 49, then 0.5 mi. west on Pleasant Plains Rd., then 0.25 mi. south on Wellbaum Rd. Roads are wide and well maintained w/ broad shoulders.

BUCKEYE LAKE   MAP, C-2
Buckeye Lake KOA

P.O. Box 972, 43008.
T: (740) 928-0706 or (800) 562-0792;
www.koakampgrounds.com/where/oh/35101.htm.

🚐 ★★★★   ⛺ ★★★★

Beauty: ★★★★	Site Privacy: ★★★★
Spaciousness: ★★★★	Quiet: ★★★★
Security: ★★★★	Cleanliness: ★★★★
Insect Control: ★★★	Facilities: ★★★★

Located 23 miles east of Columbus, Buckeye Lake KOA offers shady, level sites. The campground has ten seasonals, 102 pull-through sites, and a typical site width of 35 feet. Our favorite RV sites are the full-hookup ones. The best tent sites are in the primitive area at the rear of the campground, with more trees and privacy. Some tenters prefer the sites with full hookup or water and electric, but the tradeoff is a little less privacy and green space. Because it is convenient to the interstate and offers easy access, the campground is popular with campers visiting Columbus attractions. No outside firewood is permitted in the campground in order to prevent tree diseases, but firewood is for sale at the campground. A small gift shop is a nice touch. The campground provides on-site security 24/7.

BASICS

Operated By: Preble Family. **Open:** Apr. 1–Oct. 31. **Site Assignment:** Reservations w/ 1-night deposit; refund w/ 7-day notice. **Registration:** At campground office. **Fee:** $26–$40. **Parking:** At site.

FACILITIES

Number of RV-only Sites: 177. **Number of Tent-only Sites:** 28. **Hookups:** Electric (20, 30, 50 amps),

water, sewer, phone, cable TV. **Each Site:** Picnic table, fire ring. **Dump Station:** Yes. **Laundry:** Yes. **Pay Phone:** Yes. **Restrooms and Showers:** Yes. **Fuel:** No. **Propane:** Yes. **Internal Roads:** Gravel, in good condition. **RV Service:** No. **Market:** 2 mi. south. **Restaurant:** 2 mi. south. **General Store:** Yes. **Vending:** Yes. **Swimming:** Yes. **Playground:** Yes. **Other:** Rec hall, pavilion, coin games, mini-golf, basketball, shuffleboard, movies, badminton, sports field, horseshoes, hiking trails, volleyball, rental cabins. **Activities:** Swimming, hiking, scheduled weekend activities. **Nearby Attractions:** Golf, museums, Columbus Zoo, botanical garden & conservatory, German Village, Ohio Statehouse, COSI Columbus, antiques, Ohio State Univ., museums, historic homes. **Additional Information:** Greater Columbus CVB, (800) 345-4386.

RESTRICTIONS

Pets: On leash only. **Fires:** Fire ring only, no outside wood can be brought in. **Alcoholic Beverages:** At sites only. **Vehicle Maximum Length:** No limit.

TO GET THERE

From the junction of I-70 and Hwy. 79, take Exit 129A, then drive 1.5 mi. south on Hwy. 79. Roads are wide and well maintained w/ broad shoulders.

BUTLER   MAP, B-2
River Trail Crossing

1597 SR 97 East, 44822. T: (419) 883-3888;
www.rivertrailcrossing.com.

🚐 ★★★   ⛺ ★★★

Beauty: ★★★	Site Privacy: ★★★★
Spaciousness: ★★★★	Quiet: ★★★★
Security: ★★★★	Cleanliness: ★★★★
Insect Control: ★★	Facilities: ★★★

Nestled in the foothills of the Appalachian Mountains along Clear Fork River, Blue Lagoon Campground offers level, open sites with a typical site width of 50 feet. Located 3 miles west of Butler, the campground has one seasonal camper and two pull-through areas. A five-mph speed limit and quiet hours between 11 p.m. and 8 a.m. are enforced. The river is stocked by the Ohio Division of Natural Resources with trout and 26 other species of fish. The property is the only full-facility campground with direct access to the Richland B&O Bike Trail, an 18-mile paved multiuse trail. Open year-round during daylight hours and accessible to people with disabilities, the trail is off-limits to motorized vehicles and horseback riding. Security measures at the campground include owners who live on site and locked bathroom facilities. Campers pay a $5 deposit to get a bathroom key.

BASICS

Operated By: David & Linda Chalut. **Open:** May 1–Oct. 15. **Site Assignment:** Reservations w/ 1-night deposit; refund (minus $4) w/ 7-day notice. **Registration:** At campground office. **Fee:** $25–$28; cash, credit card. **Parking:** At site.

FACILITIES

Number of RV-only Sites: 27. **Number of Tent-only Sites:** 17. **Hookups:** Electric (20, 30 amps),

water, sewer. **Each Site:** Picnic table, fire ring. **Dump Station:** Yes. **Laundry:** Yes. **Pay Phone:** No. **Restrooms and Showers:** Yes. **Fuel:** No. **Propane:** Yes. **Internal Roads:** Paved, in good condition. **RV Service:** No. **Market:** 3 mi. east in Butler. **Restaurant:** 3 mi. east in Butler. **General Store:** Yes. **Vending:** No. **Swimming:** No. **Playground:** Yes. **Other:** Swimming pond, fishing river, volleyball, rental cabin, tetherball, horseshoes, basketball. **Activities:** Swimming, fishing. **Nearby Attractions:** Living Bible Museum, Johnny Appleseed Monument, Richland Carousel Park, state forest, covered bridge, Amish country, Mid-Ohio Sports Car Course, golf, antiques, arts & crafts, Kingwood Center. **Additional Information:** Mansfield-Richland Area Chamber of Commerce, (419) 522-3211.

RESTRICTIONS

Pets: Leash only, $1 per pet. **Fires:** Fire rings only; fires must be extinguished before retiring for the night. **Alcoholic Beverages:** Allowed. **Vehicle Maximum Length:** No limit. **Other:** RV outdoor mats larger than 2–3 ft. are not permitted.

TO GET THERE

From the junction of I-71 and Hwy. 97, take Exit 165 and drive 7.7 mi. east on Hwy. 97. Roads are wide and well maintained w/ broad shoulders.

CAMBRIDGE MAP, C-3
Spring Valley Campground

8000 Dozer Rd., 43725. T: (614) 439-9291; www.koa.com.

🚐 ★★★★   ▲ ★★★★

Beauty: ★★★★	Site Privacy: ★★★★
Spaciousness: ★★★★	Quiet: ★★★★
Security: ★★★★	Cleanliness: ★★★★
Insect Control: ★★	Facilities: ★★★

With easy access off the interstate, Spring Valley Campground is surprisingly quiet. The grassy campground is cushioned by beautiful hills and woods. Level sites include 18 pull-throughs and a typical site width of 35 feet. Most sites have oak and maple trees, but there are some open sites. Lucky campers may spot deer and turkey if they're patient. There are also 65 seasonal campers. The well-maintained campground has a five-mph speed limit and quiet time beginning at 11 p.m. Sunday through Friday and at midnight on Saturday. The 3.5-acre lake is stocked with bass, crappie, and bluegill. It also has a beach area, slides, and diving boards, as well as a separate swimming pool. Security includes one entrance/exit road and owners who live on site.

BASICS

Operated By: Hlads family. **Open:** Apr. 1–Nov. 1. **Site Assignment:** Reservations w/ $10 deposit, not refundable or transferable. **Registration:** At campground office. **Fee:** $24–$26; cash, check, credit card. **Parking:** At site.

FACILITIES

Number of RV-only Sites: 170. **Hookups:** Electric (30, 50 amps), water, sewer, cable TV. **Each Site:** Picnic table, fire ring. **Dump Station:** Yes. **Laundry:** No. **Pay Phone:** Yes. **Restrooms and Showers:** Yes. **Fuel:** No. **Propane:** Yes. **Internal Roads:**

Gravel, in good condition. **RV Service:** No. **Market:** 1 mi. in any direction. **Restaurant:** 1 mi. in any direction. **General Store:** Yes. **Vending:** Yes. **Swimming:** Yes. **Playground:** Yes. **Other:** Lake, pavilion, rental cabins, basketball, rec room, coin games, badminton, sports field, horseshoes, hiking trails, volleyball. **Activities:** Swimming, fishing, hiking, scheduled weekend activities. **Nearby Attractions:** State parks, golf, antiques, art glass factories & museums, *Living Word* outdoor drama, museums, Hopalong Cassidy Museum, riding stable, Amish country. **Additional Information:** Cambridge CVB, (800) 933-5480.

RESTRICTIONS

Pets: On leash only. **Fires:** Fire ring only. **Alcoholic Beverages:** Not allowed. **Vehicle Maximum Length:** 45 ft.

TO GET THERE

From the junction of I-77 and I-70, drive 1 mi. west on I-70. Take Exit 178, then 50 yards south on Hwy. 209, then 1 mi. west on Dozer Rd. Roads are wide and well maintained w/ broad shoulders.

COOLVILLE MAP, C-2, C-3
Carthage Gap Campground

22575 Brimstone Rd., 45723.
T: (740) 667-3072;
www.carthagegaprvpark.com.

🚐 ★★★★   ▲ ★★★

Beauty: ★★★★	Site Privacy: ★★★★
Spaciousness: ★★★★	Quiet: ★★★★
Security: ★★★★	Cleanliness: ★★★★
Insect Control: ★★	Facilities: ★★★★

A rural campground by a lake, Carthage Gap Campground has the little touches that make camping a pleasure, including friendly owners. The campground is well maintained, right down to such niceties as a clean, pleasantly decorated laundry room. Sites are level, with a choice of open or shaded. Located 10 miles west of Athens, the campground has 100 seasonal campers and 30 pull-through sites. The typical site width is 40 feet. No license or fee is required for campers to use the fishing lake. Many weekends feature campground-wide meals, such as a corn roast, bean soup supper, pancake breakfast, and ice-cream and dessert social. Security measures include one entrance/exit road, owners who live on site, and the presence of four local policemen as seasonal campers.

BASICS

Operated By: Floyd & Nina McDermott. **Open:** Apr. 15–Oct. 31. **Site Assignment:** Reservations w/ 1-night deposit; no refunds but will honor the deposit for a year. **Registration:** At campground office. **Fee:** $20–$25; cash, check. **Parking:** At site.

FACILITIES

Number of Multipurpose Sites: 135. **Hookups:** Electric (20, 30, 50 amps), water, sewer, Wi-Fi. **Each Site:** Picnic table, fire ring. **Dump Station:** Yes. **Laundry:** Yes. **Pay Phone:** Yes. **Restrooms and Showers:** Yes. **Fuel:** No. **Propane:** No. **Internal Roads:** Gravel, in good condition. **RV Service:** No. **Market:** 10 mi. east in Athens. **Restaurant:** 10 mi. east in Athens. **General Store:** No. **Vending:** Yes.

Swimming: No. **Playground:** Yes. **Other:** Swimming lake, fishing lake, basketball, volleyball, horseshoes, pavilion, hiking trails. **Activities:** Swimming, fishing, hiking, scheduled weekend activities. **Nearby Attractions:** Cave, golf, Ohio Univ., museums, historic homes, Fenton Glass Factory, antiques, arts & crafts. **Additional Information:** Athens Area Chamber of Commerce, (740) 594-2251.

RESTRICTIONS

Pets: On leash only. **Fires:** Fire ring only. **Alcoholic Beverages:** Allowed. **Vehicle Maximum Length:** 45 ft.

TO GET THERE

From the junction of Hwy. 7 and US 50, drive 3.5 mi. west on US 50, then 0.5 mi. north on CR 56. US 50 is wide and well maintained w/ broad shoulders. CR 56 is wide and well maintained w/ narrow shoulders. A steep, narrow, gravel hill leads into the campground.

DELAWARE MAP, B-2
Alum Creek State Park Campground

3615 South Old S.R., 43015. T: (740) 548-4631; www.alumcreek.com.

🚐 ★★★★   ▲ ★★★★

Beauty: ★★★★	Site Privacy: ★★★★
Spaciousness: ★★★★	Quiet: ★★★★
Security: ★★★★	Cleanliness: ★★★★
Insect Control: ★★	Facilities: ★★★

For beauty, it is hard to beat most state parks. At Alum Creek State Park Campground, the surroundings include mature forests of maple, oak, elm, and locust trees, along with a huge inland beach, lovely lake and pond, and a variety of hiking trails. Sites are mostly shaded and level with no pull-throughs. There are also no seasonal campers. RVs or tents have access to any site. The most popular areas are on G road because of its proximity to the beach, and the ends of B, G, L, and K roads because they are premium sites near the lake. Security includes a gatehouse, campground office, and regular patrols by campground officers.

BASICS

Operated By: State of Ohio. **Open:** All year. **Site Assignment:** First come, first served; no reservations. **Registration:** At campground office. **Fee:** $26–$34; cash, check, credit card. **Parking:** At site.

FACILITIES

Number of Multipurpose Sites: 289. **Hookups:** Electric (20, 30, 50 amps). **Each Site:** Picnic table, fire ring. **Dump Station:** Yes. **Laundry:** No. **Pay Phone:** Yes. **Restrooms and Showers:** Yes. **Fuel:** No. **Propane:** No. **Internal Roads:** Paved, in good condition. **RV Service:** No. **Market:** 6 mi. east in Delaware. **Restaurant:** 6 mi. east in Delaware. **General Store:** Yes. **Vending:** Yes. **Swimming:** No. **Playground:** Yes. **Other:** Swimming lake, beach, nature trails, fishing lake, amphitheater, pond, basketball, volleyball, horseshoes, boat dock, boat ramp, horse trails, sports field. **Activities:** Swimming, fishing, hiking, boating (rental boats available), scheduled activities. **Nearby Attractions:** Golf, Ohio State-house, Ohio State University, science museum, zoo, German Village, museums, historic homes, antiques, arts & crafts, tennis, baseball, horse racing. **Additional Information:** Greater Columbus CVB, (800) 800) 345-4386.

RESTRICTIONS

Pets: Leash only, pet camping area. **Fires:** Fire ring only. **Alcoholic Beverages:** Not allowed. **Vehicle Maximum Length:** 35 ft. **Other:** 14-day stay limit.

TO GET THERE

From the junction of I-71 and Hwy. 36/37, drive 1 mi. west on Hwy. 36/37. Road is wide and well maintained w/ broad shoulders.

DELAWARE MAP, B-2
Cross Creek Camping Resort

3190 South Old S.R., 43015. T: (740) 549-2267; www.alumcreek.com.

🚐 ★★★★ ⛺ ★★★★

Beauty: ★★★★	Site Privacy: ★★★★
Spaciousness: ★★★★	Quiet: ★★★★
Security: ★★★★	Cleanliness: ★★★★★
Insect Control: ★★★	Facilities: ★★★★

Ringed by woods, Cross Creek Camping Resort offers shaded or open spots on level sites. The campground is grassy with gravel parking spaces. Located 5 miles southeast of Delaware, the campground has 30 seasonal campers, 11 pull-through sites, and a typical site width of 35 feet. The facility is well maintained, with sparkling restrooms that have curtains on both the shower the dressing room. A whimsical touch is a fire hydrant painted like a dog. Security and safety measures include a five-mph speed limit, speed bumps, a traffic control gate, and a manager who lives on site and patrols the campground. Open year-round, Cross Creek Camping Resort is a popular winter stopover for campers because of its proximity to Columbus and because water hookups are available at the campground in the winter.

BASICS

Operated By: Steve Cross. **Open:** All year. **Site Assignment:** Reservations w/ 1-night deposit; refund w/ 7-day notice. **Registration:** At campground office. **Fee:** $29–$40. **Parking:** At site.

FACILITIES

Number of Tent-only Sites: 20. **Number of Multipurpose Sites:** 180. **Hookups:** Electric (30, 50 amps), water, sewer. **Each Site:** Picnic table, fire ring. **Dump Station:** Yes. **Laundry:** Yes. **Pay Phone:** Yes. **Restrooms and Showers:** Yes. **Fuel:** No. **Propane:** Yes. **Internal Roads:** Paved, in good condition. **RV Service:** No. **Market:** 5 mi. northwest in Delaware. **Restaurant:** 5 mi. northwest in Delaware. **General Store:** Yes. **Vending:** Yes. **Swimming:** Yes. **Playground:** Yes. **Other:** Pavilion, shuffleboard, basketball, tennis, horseshoes, clubhouse, game room, fishing pond, billiards, coin games, movies, volleyball, badminton. **Activities:** Swimming, fishing, hiking, scheduled activities. **Nearby Attractions:** Golf, Ohio Statehouse, Ohio State University, science museum, Columbus Zoo, German Village,

museums, historic homes, antiques, arts & crafts, tennis, baseball, horse racing. **Additional Information:** Greater Columbus CVB, (800) 345-4386.

RESTRICTIONS

Pets: On leash only. **Fires:** Fire ring only. **Alcoholic Beverages:** At sites only. **Vehicle Maximum Length:** No limit.

TO GET THERE

From the junction of I-71, US 36, and Hwy. 37, take Exit 131 and drive 3 mi. west on US 36/Hwy. 37, then 3 mi. south on Lackey Rd. Roads are wide and well maintained w/ broad shoulders.

EAST SPARTA MAP, B-3
Bear Creek Resort Ranch KOA

3232 Downing St. SW, 44626. T: (330) 484-3901; www.koa.com.

🚐 ★★★★ ⛺ ★★★★

Beauty: ★★★★	Site Privacy: ★★★★
Spaciousness: ★★★★	Quiet: ★★★★
Security: ★★★★	Cleanliness: ★★★★★
Insect Control: ★★	Facilities: ★★★★

A hilly campground with level sites, Bear Creek Resort Ranch KOA offers a Western flair. Horses and ponies are available, and the campground provides miles of wooded horse trails. Located 3 miles south of Canton, the campground has grassy sites with gravel parking spots, along with a choice of open or shaded sites. The campground has 12 seasonal campers, 42 pull-through sites, and a typical site width of 35 feet. The facility is very clean and well maintained, including such touches as a live ivy plant, curtains, and wallpaper border in the bathroom. The most popular sites for both tents and RVs are alongside the lake and in the woods. No generators or loud radios are permitted, and quiet times are between 11 p.m. and 8 a.m. Speed limit is ten mph—rather high for such a child-pleasing campground. Security includes owners who live on site and provide regular patrols.

BASICS

Operated By: Lee & Carol Soehnlen. **Open:** All year. **Site Assignment:** Reservations w/ 1-night deposit; refund w/ 1-day notice. **Registration:** At campground office. **Fee:** $26–$37; cash, credit card. **Parking:** At site.

FACILITIES

Number of RV-only Sites: 782. **Number of Tent-only Sites:** 100. **Hookups:** Electric (30, 50 amps), water, sewer. **Each Site:** Picnic table, fire ring. **Dump Station:** Yes. **Laundry:** Yes. **Pay Phone:** Yes. **Restrooms and Showers:** Yes. **Fuel:** No. **Propane:** Yes. **Internal Roads:** Paved/gravel, in good condition. **RV Service:** No. **Market:** 3 mi. north in Canton. **Restaurant:** 3 mi. north in Canton. **General Store:** Yes. **Vending:** Yes. **Swimming:** Yes. **Playground:** Yes. **Other:** Catch-&-release fishing pond, rental cabins, pavilion, mini-golf, activities field, basketball, volleyball, badminton, tetherball, horseshoes, game room, coin games, horseback riding trails. **Activities:** Swimming, fishing, horseback riding (rental horses available),

boating (rental paddleboat available), scheduled weekend activities. **Nearby Attractions:** Pro Football Hall of Fame, golf, Canton Classic Car Museum, antiques, arts & crafts, McKinley Museum of History, Science & Industry, McKinley National Memorial, historic homes, Amish community. **Additional Information:** Canton/Stark County CVB.

RESTRICTIONS

Pets: On leash only. **Fires:** Fire ring only. **Alcoholic Beverages:** At sites only. **Vehicle Maximum Length:** No limit.

TO GET THERE

From the junction of I-77 and Fohl Rd., take Exit 99, drive 3 mi. south on Sherman Church Rd., then 1 mi. east on Haut Rd. Roads are wide and well maintained w/ mostly broad shoulders.

GALENA MAP, B-2
Berkshire Lake Campground

1848 Alexander Rd., 43021. T: (740) 965-2321; www.berkshirelakecampground.com.

🚐 ★★★ ⛺ n/a

Beauty: ★★★	Site Privacy: ★★★
Spaciousness: ★★★	Quiet: ★★★★
Security: ★★★★	Cleanliness: ★★★
Insect Control: ★★	Facilities: ★★★

A tradition since 1966, Berkshire Lake Campground is still run by its original owner and now attracts the grandchildren of some old-time campers. The campground also has an action committee composed of veteran Berkshire campers to coordinate and oversee activities and help support campground improvements. Sites are mostly grassy and shaded, with 175 seasonal campers and eight pull-throughs. No tents are allowed. Laid out in a series of loops, the campground has a fishing-only lake (no swimming or boating). A ten-mph speed limit is enforced, as are quiet hours from midnight until 8 a.m. Security measures here include a gate, an owner who lives on site, and regular patrols of the campground.

BASICS

Operated By: Bill Davis. **Open:** All year. **Site Assignment:** Reservations w/ 1-night deposit; refund w/ 7-day notice. **Registration:** At campground office. **Fee:** $29; cash, check, credit card. **Parking:** At site.

FACILITIES

Number of RV-only Sites: 400. **Hookups:** Electric (30 amps), water, sewer. **Each Site:** Picnic table, fire ring. **Dump Station:** No. **Laundry:** Yes. **Pay Phone:** Yes. **Restrooms and Showers:** Yes. **Fuel:** No. **Propane:** Yes. **Internal Roads:** Gravel, in fair condition. **RV Service:** Yes. **Market:** 6 mi. northeast in Sunbury. **Restaurant:** 6 mi. northeast in Sunbury. **General Store:** Yes. **Vending:** No. **Swimming:** Yes. **Playground:** Yes. **Other:** Minigolf, basketball, horseshoes, volleyball, game room, meeting room, lake, sports field, coin games. **Activities:** Swimming, fishing, scheduled weekend activities. **Nearby Attractions:** Golf, Ohio Statehouse, Ohio State University, science museum, Columbus

Zoo, German Village, museums, historic homes, antiques, arts & crafts, tennis, baseball, horse racing. **Additional Information:** Greater Columbus CVB, (800) 345-4386.

RESTRICTIONS

Pets: On leash only. **Fires:** Fire ring only. **Alcoholic Beverages:** Not allowed. **Vehicle Maximum Length:** 40 ft. **Other:** No tents allowed.

TO GET THERE

From the junction of I-71 and Hwy. 36/37, drive 0.25 mi. east on Hwy. 36/37, then 3 mi. south on South Galena Rd. (CR 34), then 0.5 mi. southwest on Alexander. Bear left at the 5-way stop. Roads are wide and well maintained w/ broad shoulders, except for some narrow shoulders on South Galena Rd.

GENEVA-ON-THE-LAKE   MAP. A-3
Indian Creek Camping Resort

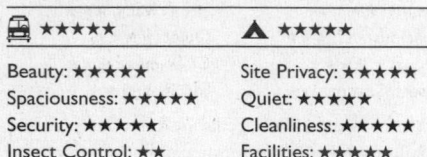

4710 Lake Rd. East, 44041. T: (440) 466-8191; www.indiancreekresort.com.

🚐 ★★★★★	⛺ ★★★★★
Beauty: ★★★★★	Site Privacy: ★★★★★
Spaciousness: ★★★★★	Quiet: ★★★★★
Security: ★★★★★	Cleanliness: ★★★★★
Insect Control: ★★	Facilities: ★★★★★

Make up a list of what the ideal campground would have. Then drive to Geneva-on-the-Lake; chances are that dream facility would be waiting at the Indian Creek Camping Resort. In addition to the beautiful nondenominational chapel (services every Sunday), there's also an "automatic external defibrillator" to save a life in the event of cardiac arrest. Then there are the two heated swimming pools—one for adults only and one for families. The tiled bathrooms are so clean they gleam and are dubbed "the best in Ohio." The grass is well manicured, and the folks are friendly. Sites are level and grassy, shaded or open, and with a typical site width of 45 feet. A full-service restaurant, Farone's, and the Step Above Lounge offer a good choice of food and drink. Security includes a traffic control gate and owners who live on site. Not surprisingly, about half the camping sites are taken by seasonal campers, which means it is a good idea to book a reservation.

BASICS

Operated By: The &rus family. **Open:** All year; limited facilities in winter. **Site Assignment:** Reservations w/ 1-night deposit; refund w/ 7-day notice. **Registration:** At campground office. **Fee:** $32–$42. **Parking:** At site.

FACILITIES

Number of RV-only Sites: 600. **Number of Tent-only Sites:** 30. **Hookups:** Electric (20, 30, 50 amps), water, sewer, phone, cable TV. **Each Site:** Picnic table, fire ring. **Dump Station:** Yes. **Laundry:** Yes. **Pay Phone:** Yes. **Restrooms and Showers:** Yes. **Fuel:** Yes. **Propane:** Yes. **Internal Roads:** Paved/gravel, in good condition. **RV Service:** No. **Market:** 4 mi. east in Geneva-On-The-Lake.

Restaurant: On site. **General Store:** Yes. **Vending:** Yes. **Swimming:** Yes. **Playground:** Yes. **Other:** Chapel, baseball, volleyball, shuffleboard, game room, horseshoes, pavilions, fishing lake, coin games, sports field, hiking trails, restaurant & lounge. **Activities:** Swimming, fishing, hiking, scheduled activities, local tours. **Nearby Attractions:** Lake Erie, boat races, roller skating, Lake Farmpark, golf, summer concerts, antiques, state parks, historic homes, scenic drives, covered bridges. **Additional Information:** Ashtabula County CVB, (800) 337-6746.

RESTRICTIONS

Pets: On leash only. **Fires:** Fire ring only. **Alcoholic Beverages:** Allowed. **Vehicle Maximum Length:** No limit.

TO GET THERE

From the junction of I-90 and Hwy. 45, take Exit 223 and drive 6 mi. north on Hwy. 45, then 4 mi. west on Hwy. 531. Roads are wide and well maintained w/ broad shoulders.

HILLSBORO   MAP, C-1
Rocky Fork State Park

9800 North Shore Dr., 45133.
T: (937) 393-4284;
www.dnr.state.oh.us/odnr/parks.

🚐 ★★★★	⛺ ★★★★
Beauty: ★★★★	Site Privacy: ★★★
Spaciousness: ★★★	Quiet: ★★★★
Security: ★★★★	Cleanliness: ★★★★
Insect Control: ★★	Facilities: ★★★★

At last, a state campground with full hookups. But you have to be fast to get one of those sites. Rocky Fork State Park has only 20 full hookups (sites 301–320), and folks are waiting in line for those precious spots. Located 4 miles east of Hillsboro, Rocky Fork State Park is a paradise for outdoor recreation enthusiasts. Unlimited horsepower boating allows for excellent skiing on the lake, which also provides catches of bass, muskellunge, and walleye. A scenic gorge, dolomite caves, and natural wetlands add to the beauty. Two large public beaches with changing booths and bathhouses are located on the north and south sides of the lake. A short hiking trail near the campground takes nature lovers to an observation station where excellent bird-watching can be enjoyed. Laid out in a series of loops, the grassy campground offers shaded and open sites with an average size of 12 by 35 feet. There are no pull-through sites. Park rangers provide security.

BASICS

Operated By: State of Ohio. **Open:** All year. **Site Assignment:** First come, first served; reservations accepted. **Registration:** At campground office. **Fee:** $19–$31; cash, check, credit card. **Parking:** At site.

FACILITIES

Number of RV-only Sites: 148. **Number of Tent-only Sites:** 82. **Hookups:** Electric (30 amps), water, sewer. **Each Site:** Picnic table, fire ring. **Dump Station:** Yes. **Laundry:** Yes. **Pay Phone:** Yes. **Restrooms and Showers:** Yes. **Fuel:** No. **Propane:** Yes. **Internal Roads:** Paved, in good con-

dition. **RV Service:** No. **Market:** 4 mi. west in Hillsboro. **Restaurant:** Restaurant on site. **General Store:** Yes. **Vending:** Yes. **Swimming:** No. **Playground:** Yes. **Other:** Rocky Fork Lake, swimming beach, boat launch, hiking trails, marinas, amphitheater, basketball, volleyball, horseshoes, mini-golf, boat dock. **Activities:** Swimming, fishing, boating (rental fishing boats & pontoons available), hiking, scheduled activities. **Nearby Attractions:** Nature sanctuary, Fort Hill Indian mounds, museums, Serpent Mound, golf, Kings Island amusement park. **Additional Information:** Highland County CVB, (937) 393-4883.

RESTRICTIONS

Pets: Leash only, In pet camping areas; $1 per night per pet, max. of 2 pets. **Fires:** Fire ring only. **Alcoholic Beverages:** Not allowed. **Vehicle Maximum Length:** 38 ft. **Other:** 14-day stay limit.

TO GET THERE

From Hillsboro, drive 3.5 mi. east on SR 124 to North Shore Dr., then 1 mi. northeast. Roads are wide and well maintained w/ broad shoulders.

JACKSON   MAP, C-2
Deerland Resort

974 Standpipe Rd., 45640. T: (740) 286-6422.

🚐 ★★★★	⛺ ★★★★
Beauty: ★★★★	Site Privacy: ★★★★
Spaciousness: ★★★★	Quiet: ★★★★
Security: ★★★★	Cleanliness: ★★★★
Insect Control: ★★★	Facilities: ★★★

Deerland Resort offers a country setting with rolling hills and a beautiful lake. But the resort lacks one popular recreation that campers often seek—there is no swimming. Located 2 miles south of Jackson, the campground is arranged in tiers overlooking the lake. The campground has 35 seasonal campsites, and all the sites are pull-throughs. Sites are open or shaded, with the best tent sites by the water and dam. A fee is charged for fishing. The resort has four pages of rules and regulations, including notice that children under the age of 18 must be at their sites during curfew from 11 p.m. to 8 a.m. unless accompanied by an adult. Curfew violators will be escorted back to their sites, a report will be filed with the resort manager, and second-time offenders will be required to leave Deerland Resort. A five-mph speed limit also is enforced. Security measures include a one-way road and traffic control gate.

BASICS

Operated By: Marge & Bill Parks. **Open:** Apr. 1–Nov. 1. **Site Assignment:** Reservations w/ 1-night deposit; refund w/ 7-day notice. **Registration:** At campground office. **Fee:** $24; cash, check, credit card. **Parking:** At site.

FACILITIES

Number of RV-only Sites: 79. **Number of Tent-only Sites:** 15. **Hookups:** Electric (30, 50 amps), water, sewer. **Each Site:** Picnic table, fire ring. **Dump Station:** Yes. **Laundry:** Yes. **Pay Phone:** Yes. **Restrooms and Showers:** Yes. **Fuel:** No. **Propane:** No. **Internal Roads:** Gravel, in fair condition. **RV Service:** No. **Market:** 2 mi. north in Jackson. **Restaurant:** 2 mi. north in Jackson. **General Store:** No. **Vending:** Yes. **Swimming:** No. **Playground:** Yes. **Other:** Fishing lake, rec room, coin games, mini-golf, basketball, shuffleboard, horseshoes, hiking trails, volleyball, rental paddleboats, rental cabins, banquet facilities. **Activities:** Fishing, hiking. **Nearby Attractions:** Noah's Ark Animal Farm, antiques, arts & crafts, gold, Bob Evans Original Farm, Splash Down Water Park, wildlife area. **Additional Information:** Jackson Area Chamber of Commerce, (740) 286-2722.

RESTRICTIONS

Pets: On leash only. **Fires:** Fire ring only. **Alcoholic Beverages:** Allowed. **Vehicle Maximum Length:** No limit.

TO GET THERE

From the junction of Hwy. 32 and US 35, drive 3 mi. southeast on US 35, then 1 mi. west on CR 55. Hwy. 32 is wide and well maintained w/ broad shoulders. CR 55 is wide and well maintained w/ narrow shoulders.

LATHAM   MAP, C-2
Long's Retreat Family Resort

50 Bell Hollow Rd., 45646. T: (937) 588-3725; www.longsretreat.com.

🚐 ★★★   ⛺ ★★★

Beauty: ★★★	Site Privacy: ★★★
Spaciousness: ★★★★	Quiet: ★★★★
Security: ★★★★	Cleanliness: ★★★
Insect Control: ★★	Facilities: ★★★

Long's Retreat Family Resort is built around a lake and offers a wide array of water activities and other recreation. Two giant 300 and 350 foot waterslides, a hydrotube slide, raindrop, diving boards, and sandy beach make the lake a popular place. Located 5 miles west of Latham, Ohio, Long's Retreat has open and shaded sites on rolling terrain. Most of the shade is from woods on the perimeter of the campground. Sites are level, with 300 seasonal campers, 100 pull-throughs, and a typical site width of 40 feet. The best RV sites are in area B because of the pine trees, proximity to facilities, and scenic views. Although those sites lack water hookups, many RV campers choose the benefits over that disadvantage. The best tent sites are in areas A or E because they are located on a peninsula on the lake where campers can fish almost from their campsite. Security includes an owner who lives on site and patrols by the local deputy sheriffs' department.

BASICS

Operated By: Eric Long. **Open:** Apr. 1–Nov. 1. **Site Assignment:** No reservations; first come, first served. **Registration:** At campground office. **Fee:** $18–$27; cabin, $70; cash, check, credit card. **Parking:** At site.

FACILITIES

Number of RV-only Sites: 350. **Number of Tent-only Sites:** 100. **Hookups:** Electric (30 amps), water, sewer. **Each Site:** Picnic table, fire ring. **Dump Station:** Yes. **Laundry:** Yes. **Pay Phone:** Yes. **Restrooms and Showers:** Yes. **Fuel:** No. **Propane:**

Yes. **Internal Roads:** Paved, in good condition. **RV Service:** No. **Market:** 3 mi. east in Latham. **Restaurant:** 3 mi. east in Latham. **General Store:** Yes. **Vending:** Yes. **Swimming:** Yes. **Playground:** Yes. **Other:** Swimming lake, sandy beach, giant waterslide, go-carts, mini-golf, arcade, rental cabins, basketball, fishing lake, go-cart track, mini-golf, tennis, game room, recreation field, badminton, hiking trails, volleyball. **Activities:** Swimming, fishing, hiking, boating (electric motors only, rental canoes, paddleboats available), scheduled weekend activities. **Nearby Attractions:** Fort Hill State Memorial & Nature Preserve, Indian mounds, museums, golf, Serpent Mound, Kings Island amusement park, Octagonal Schoolhouse, antiques. **Additional Information:** Highland County CVB, (937) 393-4883.

RESTRICTIONS

Pets: On leash only. **Fires:** Fire ring only. **Alcoholic Beverages:** Allowed. **Vehicle Maximum Length:** No limit.

TO GET THERE

From the junction of Hwy. 41 and Hwy. 124, drive 5.25 mi. east on Hwy. 124, then 0.1 mi. northwest on Bell Hollow Rd. Roads are wide and well maintained w/ broad shoulders.

LEAVITTSBURG   MAP, B-3
Pin-Oak Acre Campground

4063 Eagle Creek Rd., 44430.
T: (216) 898-8559 or (330) 898-8559.

🚐 ★★★   ⛺ ★★★

Beauty: ★★★	Site Privacy: ★★★
Spaciousness: ★★★	Quiet: ★★★
Security: ★★★	Cleanliness: ★★★
Insect Control: ★★★	Facilities: ★★★

A rural campground in a semi-wooded area, Pin-Oak Acres Family Camping offers level sites laid out in a series of loops. Located 5 miles east of Leavittsburg, the campground has 12 pull-through sites and a typical site width of 35 feet. The swimming lake is chemically treated, so it is almost like a swimming pool separate from the fishing lake. Sites are grassy, with a choice of open or shaded. The best RV sites are 69–78 in the rear of the campground, where it is quieter, has full hookups, and backs into the woods. Sites 1–17 also are favorites because they are on a creek. The primitive area has the best tent sites because it is more wooded and offers privacy. Security measures include one-way roads and owners who live on site and keep an eye on the campground.

BASICS

Operated By: Ray & Ele Price. **Open:** May 1–Oct. 15. **Site Assignment:** Reservations w/ 1-night deposit; no refunds. **Registration:** At campground office. **Fee:** RV, $17; tent, $16; cash. **Parking:** At site.

FACILITIES

Number of RV-only Sites: 81. **Number of Tent-only Sites:** 40. **Hookups:** Electric (30 amps), water, sewer. **Each Site:** Picnic table, fire ring. **Dump Station:** Yes. **Laundry:** Yes. **Pay Phone:** No. **Restrooms and Showers:** Yes. **Fuel:** No. **Propane:** No. **Internal Roads:** Gravel, in fair condition. **RV Service:** No. **Market:** 5 mi. east in Leav-

ittsburg. **Restaurant:** 5 mi. east in Leavittsburg. **General Store:** Yes. **Vending:** No. **Swimming:** No. **Playground:** Yes. **Other:** Swimming lake, fishing pond, horseshoes, pavilion, game room, coin games, basketball, volleyball, hiking trails, sports field, jogging area. **Activities:** Swimming, fishing, hiking, scheduled weekend activities. **Nearby Attractions:** Golf, covered bridge, Geauga Lake, coliseum, reservoir, Sea World, cheese factory, water mill, Hale Farm, Packard Music Hall, antiques. **Additional Information:** Youngstown CVB, (800) 447-8201.

RESTRICTIONS

Pets: On leash only. **Fires:** Fire ring only. **Alcoholic Beverages:** At sites only. **Vehicle Maximum Length:** 38 ft.

TO GET THERE

From the junction of Ohio Turnpike and Hwy. 5, take Exit 14/209, drive 0.2 mi. west on Hwy. 5, then 3.5 mi. north on Newton Falls–Braceville Rd., then 0.5 mi. east on Eagle Creek Rd. Roads are generally wide and well maintained but have narrow shoulders in spots.

LOUDONVILLE   MAP, B-2
Camp Toodik Family Campground, Cabins, and Canoe Livery

770 TR 462, 44842. T: (419) 994-3835; www.camptoodik.com.

🚐 ★★★★   ⛺ ★★★★

Beauty: ★★★★	Site Privacy: ★★★★
Spaciousness: ★★★★	Quiet: ★★★★
Security: ★★★★	Cleanliness: ★★★★
Insect Control: ★★★★	Facilities: ★★★★

Located in the foothills of the Appalachian Mountains, 4 miles north of Loudonville, Camp Toodik Family Campground, Cabins, and Canoe Livery offers beautiful, rolling, grassy terrain overlooking a river valley. Sites are level and mostly shaded, with three pull-through sites and a typical site width of 45 feet. The campground is convenient to the interstate and to the largest Amish settlement in the Midwest. A big plus at the campground is its convenient canoeing and kayaking. Campground personnel will take canoers or kayakers upstream for a quiet scenic float back to the campground. Campground restrooms are not only very clean but also have the added luxury touch of matted floors. For tenters, the campground offers great, shaded sites right on the river. Security and safety measures include a traffic control gate and owners who keep a close eye on the campground.

BASICS

Operated By: Britt & Nancy Young. **Open:** Apr. 1–Nov. 1. **Site Assignment:** Reservations w/ 1-night deposit; refund w/ 7-day notice. **Registration:** At campground office. **Fee:** $36–$44; cash, check, credit card. **Parking:** At site.

FACILITIES

Number of RV-only Sites: 172. **Number of Tent-only Sites:** 16. **Hookups:** Electric (20, 30, 50 amps), water, sewer, phone. **Each Site:** Picnic table, fire ring. **Dump Station:** Yes. **Laundry:** Yes. **Pay Phone:** Yes.

Restrooms and Showers: Yes. Fuel: No. Propane: Yes. Internal Roads: Gravel, in good condition. RV Service: No. Market: 4 mi. south in Loudonville. Restaurant: 4 mi. south in Loudonville. General Store: Yes. Vending: Yes. Swimming: Yes. Playground: Yes. Other: Rec hall, pavilion, coin games, river/pond fishing, mini-golf, basketball, shuffleboard, movies, badminton, sports field, horseshoes, hiking trails, volleyball, rental cabins, rental tent trailers. Activities: Swimming, hiking, fishing, canoeing, kayaking (rental canoes, kayaks available), scheduled activities. Nearby Attractions: Amish Country, Mid-Ohio Race Track, golf, Mohican Forest, plant tours, Malabar Farm State Park, Living Bible Museum, Richland Carousel Park, ski resorts, Ohio State Reformatory. Additional Information: Mansfield-Richland Area Chamber of Commerce, (419) 522-3211.

RESTRICTIONS

Pets: On leash only. Fires: Fire ring only. Alcoholic Beverages: Allowed. Vehicle Maximum Length: No limit.

TO GET THERE

From the junction of Hwy. 3 and Hwy. 39/60, drive 2.5 mi. southeast on Hwy. 39/60, then 0.75 mi. north on Township Rd. 462. Roads are wide and well maintained w/ broad shoulders.

MANTUA   MAP, A-3
Yogi Bear's Jellystone Park Camp-Resort

reserve america

3392 SR 82, 44255. T: (800) 344-YOGI; www.jellystoneohio.com.

🚐 ★★★★   ⛺ ★★★★

Beauty: ★★★	Site Privacy: ★★★★
Spaciousness: ★★★★	Quiet: ★★★★
Security: ★★★★★	Cleanliness: ★★★★★
Insect Control: ★★	Facilities: ★★★★

Pull into a Yogi Bear's Jellystone Park Camp-Resort and you know what to expect—clean facilities, good security, a family atmosphere, and plenty of activities. That's what the Yogi Bear 4 miles east of Aurora offers. The campground also has a great location—ten minutes from Sea World and Six Flags Ohio, ten minutes from the Ohio Turnpike, and a half hour from Cleveland. Situated on a 50-acre spring-fed lake, Yogi Bear's has 110 seasonal campers, an activities director, and a typical site width of 33 feet. Most popular RV sites are the 40 pull-throughs with full hookups. Although tents can be placed on any site, tent campers seem to prefer the rustic area with no hookups and more privacy. Laid out in a series of loops, the campground has mostly grassy, open sites, and trees are scarce. Security is tops, with an entrance gate manned 24 hours a day, along with regular patrols of the campground.

BASICS

Operated By: Yogi Bear's Jellystone Park Camp-Resorts. Open: May 1–Oct. 15. Site Assignment: Reservations w/ 1-night deposit; refunds w/ 7-day

notice. Registration: At campground office. Fee: $30–$52; cash, credit card. Parking: At site.

FACILITIES

Number of RV-only Sites: 310. Number of Tent-only Sites: 115. Hookups: Electric (30, 50 amps), water, sewer. Each Site: Picnic table, fire ring. Dump Station: Yes. Laundry: Yes. Pay Phone: Yes. Restrooms and Showers: Yes. Fuel: No. Propane: Yes. Internal Roads: Paved/gravel, in good condition. RV Service: No. Market: 4 mi. west in Aurora. Restaurant: 4 mi. west in Aurora. General Store: Yes. Vending: Yes. Swimming: Yes. Playground: Yes. Other: Lake, swimming beach, game room, snack bar, rental cottages & cabins, mini-golf, pavilion, coin games, wading pool, boat ramp, boat dock, basketball, shuffleboard, sports field, volleyball, hiking trails. Activities: Swimming, fishing, electric-motors-only boating (rental rowboats, paddleboats, canoes, kayaks available), hiking, scheduled activities. Nearby Attractions: Six Flags, golf, museums, antiques, historic homes, arts & crafts shops, outlet stores. Additional Information: Aurora Chamber of Commerce & CVB, (800) 648-6342.

RESTRICTIONS

Pets: On leash only. Fires: Fire ring only. Alcoholic Beverages: At sites only. Vehicle Maximum Length: 40 ft.

TO GET THERE

From the junction of Hwy. 306 and Hwy. 82, drive 4 mi. east on Hwy. 82. Roads are wide and well maintained w/ broad shoulders.

MARBLEHEAD   MAP, A-2
East Harbor State Park

1169 North Buck Rd., 43440. T: (419) 734-5857; www.eastharborstatepark.org.

🚐 ★★★   ⛺ ★★★★

Beauty: ★★★★	Site Privacy: ★★★
Spaciousness: ★★★	Quiet: ★★★★
Security: ★★★★	Cleanliness: ★★★
Insect Control: ★★	Facilities: ★★★

Situated on a peninsula stretching into the waters of Lake Erie, East Harbor State Park has the largest campground in the Ohio State Park system. Laid out in a series of loops, the campground offers level sites with a choice of open or shaded. Located 8 miles west of Port Clinton, Ohio, the campground is part of the 1,152-acre state park. A 1,500-foot sand beach is popular with swimmers. East Harbor lies on the fringe of Ohio's prairie marsh zone, home of more wildlife than any other type of habitat in the state. Hundreds of migrating songbirds rest here before winging north across the lake. The campground has 142 pull-through sites and welcomes big rigs. Lake Erie offers unlimited-horsepower boating opportunities, including a full-time boat mechanic, boat supplies, boat storage, and a restaurant. East Harbor's 7-mile hiking trail system leads through the many different habitats within the park. Park rangers provide security patrols and check on entering motorists.

BASICS

Operated By: State of Ohio. Open: All year. Site

Assignment: First come, first served; no reservations. Registration: At campground office. Fee: $19–$32; cash, check, credit card. Parking: At site.

FACILITIES

Number of RV-only Sites: 365. Number of Tent-only Sites: 205. Hookups: Electric (20, 30, 50 amps). Each Site: Picnic table, fire ring. Dump Station: Yes. Laundry: Yes. Pay Phone: Yes. Restrooms and Showers: Yes. Fuel: No. Propane: No. Internal Roads: Paved, in good condition. RV Service: No. Market: 8 mi. east in Port Clinton. Restaurant: 8 mi. east in Port Clinton. General Store: Yes. Vending: Yes. Swimming: No. Playground: Yes. Other: Swimming lake, fishing lake, pavilion, rec room, boat ramp, boat dock, sports field, hiking trails, volleyball, rental RVs, 2 rental cabins, nature center. Activities: Swimming, boating (rental rowboats available), hiking, fishing, scheduled activities. Nearby Attractions: Lake Erie, ferry, Put-in-Bay, Kelley's Island, lighthouse, winery, golf, Cedar Point Amusement Park, antiques, boating. Additional Information: Ottawa County Visitors Bureau, (800) 441-1271.

RESTRICTIONS

Pets: On leash only; 2 pet max. Fires: Fire ring only. Alcoholic Beverages: At site, inside unit. Vehicle Maximum Length: No limit. Other: 14-day stay limit during peak season.

TO GET THERE

From the junction of Hwy. 2 and Hwy. 269, drive 4 mi. north on Hwy. 269. Roads are wide and well maintained w/ broad shoulders.

MARIETTA   MAP, C-3
The Landings Family Campground

S.R. 7, Newport Pike Dr., 45773. T: (740) 373-6180.

🚐 ★★★   ⛺ ★★★

Beauty: ★★★	Site Privacy: ★★★
Spaciousness: ★★★	Quiet: ★★★★
Security: ★★★★	Cleanliness: ★★★
Insect Control: ★★	Facilities: ★★★

Don't even consider dropping by the Landings and finding an open campsite. Reservations are a must. With 103 seasonal campers, the campground has only five sites available for short-term visitors. And that number seems to dwindle with each passing year. Located 5 miles north of Marietta, the campground has over 1,200 feet of Ohio River frontage. Look at all the boat trailers and big boats, and you'll know what the main draw is for this campground. Campers by the river have a beautiful view, but campers back in the field are not so lucky. Sites are mostly open, but some shade is available. The speed limit is ten mph, and quiet time starts at 11 p.m. each night. Security includes a one-way road, an owner who lives on site, and regular patrols of the campgrounds.

BASICS

Operated By: David Cook. Open: Apr. 1–Nov. 1. Site Assignment: By reservation. Registration:

At campground office. **Fee:** $25; cash, check. **Parking:** At site.

FACILITIES

Number of RV-only Sites: 108. **Number of Tent-only Sites:** 75. **Hookups:** Electric (30 amps), water, sewer. **Each Site:** Picnic table, fire ring. **Dump Station:** No. **Laundry:** No. **Pay Phone:** Yes. **Restrooms and Showers:** Yes. **Fuel:** No. **Propane:** No. **Internal Roads:** Gravel, in good condition. **RV Service:** No. **Market:** 5 mi. south in Marietta. **Restaurant:** 5 mi. south in Marietta. **General Store:** No. **Vending:** No. **Swimming:** Yes. **Playground:** Yes. **Other:** Ohio River, boat ramp, horseshoes. **Activities:** Swimming, fishing, boating, waterskiing. **Nearby Attractions:** Showboat, Museum of the Northwest Territory, Ohio River museum, historic homes, Harmar Village, Mound Cemetery, trolley tours, stern-wheeler cruises, golf, antiques. **Additional Information:** Marietta/Washington County CVB, (800) 288-2577.

RESTRICTIONS

Pets: On leash only. **Fires:** Fire ring only. **Alcoholic Beverages:** Allowed. **Vehicle Maximum Length:** 40 ft.

TO GET THERE

From the junction of I-77 and SR 7, take Exit 1 and drive 3 mi. north on SR 7. Roads are wide and well maintained w/ broad shoulders.

MILLERSBURG — MAP, B-2
Scenic Hills RV Park

4483 TR 367, 44654. T: (330) 893-3258 (winter) or (330) 893-3607 (summer); www.scenichillsrvpark.com.

🚐 ★★★★	🏕 n/a
Beauty: ★★★	Site Privacy: ★★★★
Spaciousness: ★★★★	Quiet: ★★★★
Security: ★★★★	Cleanliness: ★★★★
Insect Control: ★★	Facilities: ★★★

Because there are so many nearby attractions here in the heart of Amish country, Scenic Hills RV Park offers little on-site recreation. Located 1 mile east of Berlin, the campground accepts full-hookup units only. No tents are allowed. The campground offers open sites on a grassy hilltop with sunrise and sunset views. Scenic Hills has 12 seasonal campers and 40 pull-through sites, with a typical site width of 40 feet. The campground has no restrooms. A craft shop and store are located on the grounds. Sites are laser leveled to assure easier parking for RVs and easy access for big rigs. Security and safety measures include a five-mph speed limit and owners who live nearby and keep a close eye on the campground.

BASICS

Operated By: Sam & Mary Hershberger. **Open:** Apr. 1–Nov. 1. **Site Assignment:** Reservations w/ 1-night deposit; refund w/ 7-day notice. **Registration:** At campground office. **Fee:** $22–$25; cash, check. **Parking:** At site.

FACILITIES

Number of RV-only Sites: 96. **Hookups:** Electric (20, 30, 50 amps), water, sewer, phone. **Each Site:**

Picnic table, fire ring. **Dump Station:** Yes. **Laundry:** No. **Pay Phone:** Yes. **Restrooms and Showers:** No. **Fuel:** No. **Propane:** No. **Internal Roads:** Gravel, in good condition. **RV Service:** No. **Market:** 1 mi. west in Berlin. **Restaurant:** 1 mi. west in Berlin. **General Store:** Yes. **Vending:** No. **Swimming:** No. **Playground:** No. **Other:** Sports field, horseshoes. **Activities:** None. **Nearby Attractions:** Amish country, Wendell August of Holmes County, arts & crafts, antiques, Behalt cyclorama, Rolling Ridge Ranch, Schrock's Amish Farm, scenic drives. **Additional Information:** Holmes County Chamber of Commerce & Tourism Bureau, (330) 674-3975.

RESTRICTIONS

Pets: On leash only. **Fires:** Fire ring only. **Alcoholic Beverages:** At sites only. **Vehicle Maximum Length:** No limit.

TO GET THERE

From the junction of US 62 and Hwy. 39, drive 1 mi. east on Hwy. 39, then 0.25 mi. south on TR 367. Roads are wide and well maintained w/ mostly broad shoulders.

MT. GILEAD — MAP, B-2
Mt. Gilead Campground

5961 S.R. 95, 43338. T: (419) 768-3428.

🚐 ★★★	🏕 ★★★
Beauty: ★★★	Site Privacy: ★★★
Spaciousness: ★★★	Quiet: ★★★
Security: ★★★★	Cleanliness: ★★★
Insect Control: ★★★	Facilities: ★★★

Located 3 miles west of Chesterville, Mt. Gilead Campground offers open or shaded sites, most of them grassy with gravel parking spots. Arranged in a series of loops, the campground has 40 seasonal campers, 154 pull-through sites, and a typical site width of 27 feet. No generators are permitted, and quiet hours are from 10 p.m. to 8 a.m. The best sites for tents are 21 and 141–147 because they are more level and located in the back of the campground with more green space and privacy. The best RV sites are 32–35 and 125–31 because they are bigger and closer to the facilities. Security measures include an entrance past the office, an owner who lives on site, and regular patrols of the campground.

BASICS

Operated By: Chris Hansen. **Open:** Apr. 1–Oct. 31. **Site Assignment:** First come, first served; no reservations. **Registration:** At campground office. **Fee:** $24–$27; cash, check, credit card. **Parking:** At site.

FACILITIES

Number of RV-only Sites: 150. **Number of Tent-only Sites:** 40. **Hookups:** Electric (30, 50 amps), water, sewer. **Each Site:** Picnic table, fire ring. **Dump Station:** Yes. **Laundry:** Yes. **Pay Phone:** Yes. **Restrooms and Showers:** Yes. **Fuel:** No. **Propane:** Yes. **Internal Roads:** Gravel, in fair condition. **RV Service:** No. **Market:** 3 mi. east in Chesterville. **Restaurant:** 0.5 mi. east toward Chesterville. **General Store:** Yes. **Vending:** No.

Swimming: Yes. **Playground:** Yes. **Other:** Fishing pond, game room, pavilion, horseshoes, volleyball, recreation field. **Activities:** Swimming, fishing, boating (rental paddleboats available), scheduled weekend activities. **Nearby Attractions:** Golf, flea markets, antiques, Living Bible Museum, carousel park, Amish village, state forest, covered bridge. **Additional Information:** Mansfield-Richland Area Chamber of Commerce, (419) 522-3211.

RESTRICTIONS

Pets: On leash only. **Fires:** Fire ring only. **Alcoholic Beverages:** Allowed. **Vehicle Maximum Length:** No limit.

TO GET THERE

From the junction of I-71 and US 95, take Exit 151 and drive 0.5 mi. west on US 95. Roads are wide and well maintained w/ broad shoulders.

PEEBLES — MAP, C-1
Mineral Springs Lake Resort

162 Bluegill Rd., 45660. T: (937) 587-3132.

🚐 ★★★	🏕 ★★★★
Beauty: ★★★★	Site Privacy: ★★★
Spaciousness: ★★★★	Quiet: ★★★
Security: ★★★★	Cleanliness: ★★★
Insect Control: ★★	Facilities: ★★★

A rural campground adjoining a pretty lake, Mineral Springs Lake Resort has natural beauty, but could fix up its entranceway. It's a shame one of the first things a visitor sees on entering is a clump of dumpsters and recycling bins. Located 2 miles southeast of Peebles, the campground has 240 seasonal campers, 12 pull-through sites, and a typical site width of 50 feet. The wooded campground offers mostly shaded sites on its rolling terrain. The best sites are by the lake. The speed limit is ten mph; rather high, especially because many golf carts are in use. Security measures include owners who live on site, surveillance cameras, and a gate. Rates are very reasonable for such a nice campground with a good array of activities.

BASICS

Operated By: Robin Waddell. **Open:** Apr. 1–Nov. 1. **Site Assignment:** By reservation. **Registration:** At campground office. **Fee:** $15–$18; cash, check, V, MC. **Parking:** At site.

FACILITIES

Number of RV-only Sites: 280. **Number of Tent-only Sites:** 100. **Hookups:** Electric (20, 30 amps), water, sewer. **Each Site:** Picnic table, fire ring. **Dump Station:** Yes. **Laundry:** Yes. **Pay Phone:** Yes. **Restrooms and Showers:** Yes. **Fuel:** No. **Propane:** Yes. **Internal Roads:** Paved/gravel, in good condition. **RV Service:** No. **Market:** 2 mi. northwest in Peebles. **Restaurant:** 2 mi. northwest in Peebles. **General Store:** Yes. **Vending:** Yes. **Swimming:** Yes. **Playground:** Yes. **Other:** Swimming lake, basketball, mini-golf, volleyball, crazy cars, surf bikes, mountain bikes, horseshoes, fishing lake, rec room, pavilion, coin games, boat ramp, boat dock, hiking trails. **Activities:** Swimming, fishing, hiking, boating (electric motors only; rental paddleboats, canoes, rowboats available). **Nearby Attractions:** Diving quarry, Serpent Mound,

Davis Memorial, Amish community, caves, *Tecumseh* outdoor drama, golf, historic homes, antiques, arts & crafts. **Additional Information:** Adams County Travel & Visitors Bureau, (877) 687-7446.

RESTRICTIONS

Pets: On leash only. **Fires:** Fire ring only. **Alcoholic Beverages:** At sites only. **Vehicle Maximum Length:** No limit.

TO GET THERE

From the junction of Hwy. 41 and Hwy. 32 at the south edge of town, drive 1.25 mi. east on Hwy. 32, then 2 mi. south on Steam Furnace Rd., then 2 mi. east on Mineral Springs Rd. Hwy. 32 is wide and well maintained w/ broad shoulders. Steam Furnace Rd. is winding w/ some narrow shoulders at points. Mineral Springs Rd. is generally well maintained w/ narrow shoulders.

PLEASANT PLAIN   MAP, C-1
Stonelick State Park

2895 Lake Dr., 45162. T: (513) 734-4323; www.dnr.state.oh.us/odnr/parks.

🚐 ★★★   ⛺ ★★★★

Beauty: ★★★★   Site Privacy: ★★★
Spaciousness: ★★★   Quiet: ★★★★
Security: ★★★★   Cleanliness: ★★★
Insect Control: ★★   Facilities: ★★★

Tucked away in the rolling highlands 6 miles southwest of Blanchester, Stonelick State Park was originally created in 1950 as a wildlife area for local sporting enthusiasts. Now the area is operated by the state and offers a variety of outdoor recreational activities centered around a 200-acre lake. The woodland campground setting offers mostly grassy, shady sites. The typical site size is 15 by 40 feet with no pull-throughs. Laid out in a series of loops, Stonelick offers six nonelectric sites for tent campers, although tents and RVs are permitted on any of the sites. Four Rent-A-Camp units consisting of a tent, dining canopy, cooler, cook stove, and other equipment can be rented during the summer months by reservation. The lake is well known for catches of bass, bluegill, crappie, and catfish. A valid Ohio hunting and/or fishing license is required. There is a laundry facility. Campground security is great, with a ranger-controlled access station and regular patrols.

BASICS

Operated By: State of Ohio. **Open:** All year. **Site Assignment:** First come, first served; no reservations. **Registration:** At campground office. **Fee:** $17–$23; cash, check, credit card. **Parking:** At site.

FACILITIES

Number of RV-only Sites: 108. **Number of Tent-only Sites:** 6. **Hookups:** Electric (50 amps). **Each Site:** Picnic table, fire ring. **Dump Station:** Yes. **Laundry:** Yes. **Pay Phone:** Yes. **Restrooms and Showers:** Yes. **Fuel:** No. **Propane:** Yes. **Internal Roads:** Paved, in good condition. **RV Service:** No. **Market:** 6 mi. northeast in Blanchester. **Restaurant:** 6 mi. northeast in Blanchester. **General Store:** No. **Vending:** Yes. **Swimming:** No. **Playground:** Yes. **Other:** Stonelick lake, beach, boat launch, amphitheater, hiking trail, rental camper units.

Activities: Swimming, fishing, boating (electric motors only), hiking, schedule activities. **Nearby Attractions:** Kings Island Amusement Park, *Blue Jacket* outdoor drama, Wilmington College, antiques, museums. **Additional Information:** Clinton County CVB, (877) 4-A-VISIT.

RESTRICTIONS

Pets: Leash only, pet camping area; $1 per night per pet, max. of 2 pets. **Fires:** Fire pit only. **Alcoholic Beverages:** Not allowed. **Vehicle Maximum Length:** 35 ft. **Other:** 14-day stay limit.

TO GET THERE

From the junction of Hwy. 28 and Hwy. 133, drive 6 mi. southwest on Hwy. 133, then 1.5 mi. south on Hwy. 727. Roads are wide and well maintained w/ good shoulders.

PORT CLINTON   MAP, A-2
Tall Timbers Campground Resort

340 Christy Chapel Rd., 43452. T: (419) 732-3938; www.camplakeerie.com.

🚐 ★★★   ⛺ ★★★

Beauty: ★★★   Site Privacy: ★★★
Spaciousness: ★★★   Quiet: ★★★
Security: ★★★★   Cleanliness: ★★★
Insect Control: ★★   Facilities: ★★★

Nestled in a woods near the shores of Lake Erie, Tall Timbers Campground Resort is in the heart of a popular recreation area and is the walleye fishing capital of the world. Not surprisingly, many of the campers who visit Tall Timbers come for all the area attractions. But the campground has a goodly number of recreation opportunities itself. Located in Port Clinton, the campground has 300 seasonal campers, five pull-through sites, and a typical site width of 30 feet. Laid out in a series of loops, the campground offers grassy, shaded, and open sites. The best RV sites are the pull-throughs; the best tent sites are 1–39, which offer water and electric hookups in an area by a pond. The primitive camping area is also a favorite with tenters because it is separated from RVs and has more grass and trees. Security and safety measures include a five-mph speed limit, one entrance/exit road, a manager who lives on site, and patrols of the campground.

BASICS

Operated By: Julie Young. **Open:** May 1–Oct. 31. **Site Assignment:** Reservations w/ 1-night deposit; refund w/ 7-day notice. **Registration:** At campground office. **Fee:** $22–$32; cash, check, V, MC. **Parking:** At site.

FACILITIES

Number of RV-only Sites: 400. **Number of Tent-only Sites:** 24. **Hookups:** Electric (30 amps), water. **Each Site:** Picnic table, fire ring. **Dump Station:** Yes. **Laundry:** Yes. **Pay Phone:** Yes. **Restrooms and Showers:** Yes. **Fuel:** No. **Propane:** No. **Internal Roads:** Gravel, in fair condition. **RV Service:** No. **Market:** 1 mi. east. **Restaurant:** 1 mi. east. **General Store:** Yes. **Vending:** Yes. **Swimming:** No. **Playground:** Yes. **Other:** Swimming pond, game room, fishing pond, fish-cleaning facility, sports field, volleyball, basketball, horseshoes, pavilion, activity

director. **Activities:** Swimming, fishing, weekend activities. **Nearby Attractions:** Lake Erie, ferry, Put-in-Bay, Kelley's Island, lighthouse, winery, golf, Cedar Point Amusement Park, antiques, boating, museums, historic homes. **Additional Information:** Ottawa County Visitors Bureau, (800) 441-1271.

RESTRICTIONS

Pets: On leash only. **Fires:** Fire ring only. **Alcoholic Beverages:** At sites only. **Vehicle Maximum Length:** 40 ft.

TO GET THERE

From the junction of Hwy. 2 and Hwy. 53, drive 1.25 mi. north on Hwy. 53, then 1.5 mi. west on Hwy. 163, then 0.25 mi. south on Christy Chapel Rd. Roads are wide and well maintained w/ generally broad shoulders.

PORTSMOUTH   MAP, D-2
Shawnee State Park

4404 SR 125, 45663-9003. T: (740) 858-4561; www.dnr.state.oh.us/odnr/parks.

🚐 ★★★★   ⛺ ★★★★

Beauty: ★★★★   Site Privacy: ★★★
Spaciousness: ★★★   Quiet: ★★★★
Security: ★★★★   Cleanliness: ★★★
Insect Control: ★★   Facilities: ★★★

Located in the Appalachian foothills near the banks of the Ohio River 15 miles east of Portsmouth, Shawnee State Park is nestled in the 63,000-acre Shawnee State Forest. Once the hunting grounds of the Shawnee Indians, the region is one of the most picturesque in the state, featuring erosion-carved valleys and wooded hills. The rugged beauty of the area has earned it the nickname "The Little Smokies." Shawnee State Forest is the largest of Ohio's 19 state forests and contains impressive stands of oak, hickory, sassafras, buckeye, black gum, pitch pine, and Virginia pine. It also includes a 42-mile backpack trail with primitive campsites, more than 70 miles of bridle trails, a horse campground, an 8,000-acre wilderness area, and five small fishing lakes. Laid out in a series of loops, the campground offers paved pads for RVs with back-in site sizes of 25 by 40 feet. Sites are a mix of shaded and open. A ranger station and regular campground patrols provide security.

BASICS

Operated By: State of Ohio. **Open:** All year. **Site Assignment:** By reservation or first come, first served. **Registration:** At campground office. **Fee:** $16–$21; cash, check, credit card. **Parking:** At site.

FACILITIES

Number of RV-only Sites: 104. **Number of Tent-only Sites:** 3. **Hookups:** Electric (20, 30, 50 amps). **Each Site:** Picnic table, fire ring. **Dump Station:** Yes. **Laundry:** Yes. **Pay Phone:** Yes. **Restrooms and Showers:** Yes. **Fuel:** No. **Propane:** No. **Internal Roads:** Paved, in good condition. **RV Service:** No. **Market:** 15 mi. east in Portsmouth. **Restaurant:** At lodge on site. **General Store:** Yes. **Vending:** Yes. **Swimming:** No. **Playground:** Yes. **Other:** Roosevelt Lake, Turkey Creek Lake, Bear Lake, swimming beach, pavilion, golf, horseback riding trails, hiking trails, horseshoes, volleyball, boat ramp, rental cottages, lodge, mini-golf, tennis, shuffleboard. **Activities:** Swimming, fishing, electric-motor boating (rental rowboats & canoes available), biking (rental bikes available), scheduled activities. **Nearby Attractions:** Serpent Mound, antiques, floodwall murals, Ohio River, museums, historic homes, raceway. **Additional Information:** Portsmouth Area CVB, (740) 353-1116.

RESTRICTIONS

Pets: On leash only, in pet camping area. 2 pets per site max. **Fires:** Fire ring only. **Alcoholic Beverages:** Not allowed. **Vehicle Maximum Length:** 35 ft. **Other:** 14-day stay limit.

TO GET THERE

From the junction of US 52 and OH 125, drive 6 mi. north on SR 125. Roads are wide and well maintained w/ usually good shoulders. SR 125 is very hilly and curvy.

SEVILLE   MAP, B-3
Maple Lakes Recreational Park

4275 Blake Rd., 44273. T: (330) 336-2251; www.maplelakes.com.

🚐 ★★★   ▲ ★★

Beauty: ★★★	Site Privacy: ★★★★
Spaciousness: ★★★★	Quiet: ★★★★
Security: ★★★★	Cleanliness: ★★★★
Insect Control: ★★	Facilities: ★★★

A grassy campground on hilly terrain, Maple Lakes Recreational Park offers both open and shaded spots. A steep hill leads into the campground. The speed limit is ten mph, but speed bumps slow it down even more. Arranged in a series of loops, the campground has 150 seasonal campers, ten pull-through sites, and a typical site width of 35 feet. Level campsites are grassy, with gravel parking spots. Be aware that pets must be kept on campsites; no dog-walking is allowed. Quiet hours are enforced between 11 p.m. and 8:30 a.m. With the woods surrounding it, autumn would be a peak time to view the changing foliage—but the campground closes October 1, just as the leaves are showing their colors. Security includes a gate, owners who live on site, and regular patrols of the campground.

BASICS

Operated By: Romeyn family. **Open:** Apr. 15–Oct. 1. **Site Assignment:** Reservations w/ 1-night deposit; refund w/ 7-day notice. **Registration:** At campground office. **Fee:** $28–$35; cash, check, credit card. **Parking:** At site.

FACILITIES

Number of Multipurpose Sites: 225. **Hookups:** Electric (30, 50 amps), water, sewer. **Each Site:** Picnic table, fire ring. **Dump Station:** Yes. **Laundry:** Yes. **Pay Phone:** Yes. **Restrooms and Showers:** Yes. **Fuel:** No. **Propane:** Yes. **Internal Roads:** Paved/gravel, in good condition. **RV Service:** No. **Market:** 3 mi. south in Seville. **Restaurant:** 3 mi. south in Seville. **General Store:** Yes. **Vending:** Yes. **Swimming:** Yes. **Playground:** Yes. **Other:** Game room, pavilion, 2 fishing lakes, badminton, coin games, horseshoes, volleyball, basketball, ball field. **Activi-**

ties: Swimming, fishing, scheduled weekend activities. **Nearby Attractions:** Amish country, golf, Pro Football Hall of Fame, Rock & Roll Hall of Fame, Sea World, Cleveland Zoo, antiques, arts & crafts, museums, historic homes. **Additional Information:** Medina County CVB, (800) 860-2943.

RESTRICTIONS

Pets: On leash only; pets cannot be walked in campground, have to be transported to pet area. **Fires:** Fire ring only. **Alcoholic Beverages:** At sites only. **Vehicle Maximum Length:** No limit. **Other:** No working transient caravans.

TO GET THERE

From the junction of I-76 and Hwy. 3, drive 1 mi. northeast on Hwy. 3, then 1 mi. east on CR 118 (Blake Rd.). Roads are wide and well maintained but have narrow shoulders in spots.

SHREVE   MAP, B-2, B-3
Whispering Hills Recreation

8248 SR 514, 44676.
T: (800) 992-2435 or (330) 567-2137;
www.whisperinghillsrvpark.com.

🚐 ★★★★   ▲ ★★★★

Beauty: ★★★	Site Privacy: ★★★
Spaciousness: ★★★	Quiet: ★★★★
Security: ★★★★	Cleanliness: ★★★★
Insect Control: ★★	Facilities: ★★★★

Located on rolling hills deep in the heart of Amish country, 3 miles south of Shreve, Whispering Hills Recreation is a destination campground. Most folks come here for vacations or brief getaways to enjoy the large array of recreational opportunities. Two big draws are the Olympic-sized swimming pool and the Ol' Smokehaus Restaurant (serving home-baked food, Amish baked goods, and Ruth's famous apple dumplings). The country campground has 85 seasonals, an average site size of 25 by 45, ten pull-throughs, and a tree on almost every site. Laid out in a series of loops, the campground is mostly grassy and quiet with natural tree buffers. The most popular RV sites are the six with pull-throughs and sewer hookups. A separate tent section allows for more privacy away from RVs. Security measures include owners who live on site, regular patrols, and random patrols from the local sheriff's department.

BASICS

Operated By: Ruth M Saurer. **Open:** Apr. 15–Oct. 15. **Site Assignment:** Reservations w/ 1-night deposit; refund (minus $5) w/ 48-hour notice. **Registration:** At campground office. **Fee:** $25; cabin, $115; cash, check, credit card. **Parking:** At site.

FACILITIES

Number of RV-only Sites: 300. **Number of Tent-only Sites:** 40. **Hookups:** Electric (30, 50 amps), water, sewer. **Each Site:** Picnic table, fire ring. **Dump Station:** Yes. **Laundry:** Yes. **Pay Phone:** Yes. **Restrooms and Showers:** Yes. **Fuel:** No. **Propane:** Yes. **Internal Roads:** Paved/gravel, in good condition. **RV Service:** No. **Market:** 3 mi. north in Shreve. **Restaurant:** On site. **General Store:** Yes. **Vending:** Yes. **Swimming:** Yes. **Play-**

ground: Yes. **Other:** Fishing lake, mini-golf, volleyball, hiking trails, basketball, rec room, pavilion, coin games, boat dock, sports field, RV rentals, cabin rentals. **Activities:** Swimming, fishing, boating (electric motors only), church services, free entertainment, scheduled weekend activities. **Nearby Attractions:** Golf, antiques, arts & crafts shops, nature preserve, railroad museum, Toy & Hobby Museum, wildlife area. **Additional Information:** Wayne County CVB (800) 362-6474.

RESTRICTIONS

Pets: On leash only. **Fires:** Fire ring only. **Alcoholic Beverages:** Allowed. **Vehicle Maximum Length:** No limit.

TO GET THERE

From the junction of US 30 and SR 3, drive 1.8 mi. southwest on SR 3 to SR 226, then 8.2 mi. south to SR 514, then 2 mi. south. The roads are generally in good condition w/ adequate shoulders.

VAN BUREN   MAP, B-1
Pleasant View Recreation

2611 Township Rd. 218, 45889. T: (419) 299-3897; www.pleasantviewcampground.com.

🚐 ★★★★   ▲ ★★★★

Beauty: ★★★	Site Privacy: ★★★★
Spaciousness: ★★★★	Quiet: ★★★★
Security: ★★★★	Cleanliness: ★★★★
Insect Control: ★★	Facilities: ★★★★

The name of this campground lets campers know what to expect—enough recreation possibilities to keep children and adults happy. A rural campground 1 mile off I-75 in Van Buren, Pleasant View Recreation offers both open and wooded sites with 40 pull-throughs. As often happens, seasonals have 230 of the campground sites, leaving 70 for overnight campers. Sites are level, with a typical site width of 32 feet. The speed limit is five mph with speed bumps. The best RV sites are in Campers Loop because they offer full hookups and are near the pond. Tent sites are in a separate area by the pond with more green space and privacy. Laid out in a series of loops, the campground is a bargain with rates running from $19 to $26 for a family of two adults, two children, and one vehicle. Security measures include a card-coded traffic gate, owners who live on site, and occasional campground patrols.

BASICS

Operated By: Dan & Kathy Gant. **Open:** All year. **Site Assignment:** Reservations w/ 1-night deposit; refunds w/ 7-day notice. **Registration:** At campground office. **Fee:** $19–$26; cash, check, AE, V, MC, D. **Parking:** At site.

FACILITIES

Number of RV-only Sites: 300. **Number of Tent-only Sites:** 45. **Hookups:** Electric (30, 50 amps), water, sewer. **Each Site:** Picnic table, fire ring. **Dump Station:** Yes. **Laundry:** Yes. **Pay Phone:** Yes. **Restrooms and Showers:** Yes. **Fuel:** No. **Propane:** Yes. **Internal Roads:** Paved/gravel, in good condition. **RV Service:** No. **Market:** 5 mi. northwest in North Baltimore. **Restaurant:** 5 mi. northwest in North

Baltimore. **General Store:** Yes. **Vending:** Yes. **Swimming:** Yes. **Playground:** Yes. **Other:** Fishing pond, adult card room, mini-golf, dance hall, game room, restaurant, horseshoes, baseball, sports field, volleyball, basketball, shuffleboard, coin games, tennis, badminton. **Activities:** Swimming, fishing, boating (rental paddleboats available), scheduled weekend activities. **Nearby Attractions:** Historic courthouse, golf, nature preserve, equestrian farm, motor sports park, Ghost Town, museums, Little Red Schoolhouse, planetarium, Riverside Train. **Additional Information:** Findlay CVB, (419) 423-3315.

RESTRICTIONS

Pets: On leash only. **Fires:** Fire ring only. **Alcoholic Beverages:** Allowed. **Vehicle Maximum Length:** No limit.

TO GET THERE

From the junction of I-75 and Hwy. 613, take Exit 164, drive 0.75 mi. east on Hwy. 613, then 0.25 mi. southeast on Township 218. Roads are wide and well maintained w/ broad shoulders.

WAPAKONETA   MAP, B-1
Wapakoneta/Lima South KOA

14719 Cemetery Rd., 45895. T: (419) 738-6016; www.koa.com.

🚐 ★★★★   ▲ ★★★★

Beauty: ★★★★	Site Privacy: ★★★★
Spaciousness: ★★★★	Quiet: ★★★
Security: ★★★★	Cleanliness: ★★★★
Insect Control: ★★★	Facilities: ★★★★

Wapakoneta/Lima East KOA offers easy interstate access, clean facilities, and comfortable amenities. Located close to I-75 1 mile east of Wapakoneta, the campground has to contend with some traffic noise. The campground has level grassy sites with gravel for parking. The typical site width is 27 feet, with a typical site length of 70 feet. There are 50 pull-through sites and no seasonal campers. The speed limit is eight mph, quiet hours are 10:30 p.m. to 8 a.m., and generators are not permitted at any time. The best RV sites are 1, 3, and 5 because they are bigger and have more grass. The best tent site is 44 because it has more trees and shade. Security includes owners who live on site, regular patrols, and a coded gate. Security gates are closed between 11 p.m. and 6 a.m.

BASICS

Operated By: John & Debbie Schuettler. **Open:** Feb. 14–Dec. 1. **Site Assignment:** Reservations w/ 1-night deposit; refund w/ 7-day notice. **Registration:** At campground office. **Fee:** $25–$40; cash, V, MC. **Parking:** At site.

FACILITIES

Number of RV-only Sites: 68. **Number of Tent-only Sites:** 6. **Hookups:** Electric (30, 50 amps), water, cable TV. **Each Site:** Picnic table, fire ring. **Dump Station:** Yes. **Laundry:** Yes. **Pay Phone:** Yes. **Restrooms and Showers:** Yes. **Fuel:** No. **Propane:** Yes. **Internal Roads:** Gravel, in good condition. **RV Service:** No. **Market:** 1 mi. west in Wapakoneta. **Restaurant:** 1 mi. west in Wapakoneta. **General Store:** Yes. **Vending:** Yes.

Swimming: Yes. **Playground:** Yes. **Other:** Club room, basketball, volleyball, horseshoes, pavilion, rental cabins, coin games, sports field, rental bikes. **Activities:** Swimming. **Nearby Attractions:** Neil Armstrong Air & Space Museum, Ohio Caverns, Piatt Castle, train displays, bicycle museum, antiques, US Air Force Museum, Indian Lake, golf. **Additional Information:** Wapakoneta Area Chamber of Commerce, (419) 738-2911.

RESTRICTIONS

Pets: On leash only. **Fires:** Fire ring only. **Alcoholic Beverages:** Allowed. **Vehicle Maximum Length:** No limit.

TO GET THERE

From I-75, take northbound Exit 110 or southbound Exit 111, drive east to first intersection, then 0.75 mi. north on Cemetery Rd., past membership resort. Roads are wide and well maintained w/ broad shoulders.

WAYNESVILLE   MAP, C-1
Caesar Creek State Park

8570 East SR 73, 45068-9719. T: (513) 897-3055; www.caesarcreekstatepark.com.

🚐 ★★★   ▲ ★★★

Beauty: ★★★★	Site Privacy: ★★★
Spaciousness: ★★★	Quiet: ★★★
Security: ★★★★	Cleanliness: ★★★
Insect Control: ★★	Facilities: ★★★

For beauty, natural amenities, naturalist programs, roads, and maintenance, it's usually hard to beat a state park. But for facilities like water hookups and laundries, state parks are often at the bottom of the scale. Caesar Creek State Park has all the pluses you would expect, as well as the minuses often found at a state-run park. The 2,830-acre Caesar Creek Lake was created in 1978 when Caesar's Creek, which empties into the Little Miami River, was dammed by the Army Corps of Engineers for flood control and as a water resource. Legend has it that the creek was named for a runaway slave called Cezar who camped on its banks and lived with a local Native American tribe. Popular for waterskiing, pleasure boating, swimming, and fishing, Caesar Creek Lake offers a huge beach and four boat ramps. A pioneer village, visitors center, and a wealth of nature-center programs are also big draws. Located 10 miles east of Waynesville, Caesar Creek State Park Campground offers sites with electricity that can be used by either tents or RVs. An equestrian camp with 25 sites is available for overnight trail rides. The typical site size is 12 by 35 feet. Guests have a choice of shaded or open sites, but no pull-throughs are available. Park rangers provide security patrols and check on entering motorists.

BASICS

Operated By: State of Ohio. **Open:** All year. **Site Assignment:** First come, first served; no reservations. **Registration:** At campground office. **Fee:** $25; cash, check, credit card. **Parking:** At site.

FACILITIES

Number of RV-only Sites: 287. **Hookups:** Electric (20, 30 amps). **Each Site:** Picnic table, fire ring.

Dump Station: Yes. **Laundry:** No. **Pay Phone:** Yes. **Restrooms and Showers:** Yes. **Fuel:** No. **Propane:** No. **Internal Roads:** Paved, in good condition. **RV Service:** No. **Market:** 10 mi. west in Waynesville. **Restaurant:** 10 mi. west in Waynesville. **General Store:** Yes. **Vending:** Yes. **Swimming:** No. **Playground:** Yes. **Other:** Caesar Creek Lake, swimming beach, boat ramp, pavilion, horseback riding trails, horseshoes, hiking trails, nature center, wildlife area, rental RV. **Activities:** Swimming, fishing, boating, hiking, scheduled activities. **Nearby Attractions:** Antiques, arts & crafts shops, skydiving, Kings Island amusement park, bike trails, pioneer village, golf, Quaker meeting house, *Blue Jacket* outdoor drama. **Additional Information:** Warren County CVB, (800) 433-1072.

RESTRICTIONS

Pets: Leash only, pet camping area. Max. of 2 pets. **Fires:** Fire ring only. **Alcoholic Beverages:** Not allowed. **Vehicle Maximum Length:** 35 ft. **Other:** 14-day stay limit.

TO GET THERE

From Waynesville, drive 8 mi. east on SR 73 to SR 380, then drive 3 mi. north to Center Rd., then 1 mi. west. Roads are wide and well maintained w/ broad shoulders.

WEST SALEM   MAP, B-2
Hidden Acres Campground

107 Township Rd. 810, No. 40, 44287. T: (419) 853-4687; www.hiddenacrescampground.net.

🚐 ★★★   ▲ ★★★

Beauty: ★★★★	Site Privacy: ★★★★
Spaciousness: ★★★★	Quiet: ★★★★
Security: ★★★	Cleanliness: ★★★★
Insect Control: ★★	Facilities: ★★★

Located 2.5 miles south of West Salem, Hidden Acres Campground offers level, grassy sites, mostly shaded by mature trees. Some open sites are available right on a lake. Laid out in a series of loops, the campground offers seasonal camping only. There are two pull-through sites, and a typical site width of 35 feet. Attractive touches include a gazebo, water fountain, and wooden fishing pier. The camp store offers fast food on weekends. They also serve special dishes such as chili or sauerkraut and kielbasa. A five-mph speed limit and quiet time from 11 p.m. to 9 a.m. are enforced. An unusual rule forbids perming or coloring of hair in the restrooms. An extra fee of $2 per pole is charged for fishing in the stocked lake, but there is a small pond where fishing is free. Hidden Acres is in back of a small mobile home park.

BASICS

Operated By: Jim & Ginger Kovacich; Jim & Sandy Whittlesey. **Open:** May 1–Oct. 15. **Site Assignment:** Reservations w/ 1-night deposit; refund w/ 7-day notice. **Registration:** At campground office. **Fee:** Seasonal camping only ($1,500). **Parking:** At site.

FACILITIES

Number of RV-only Sites: 130. **Hookups:** Electric (30, 50 amps), water, sewer. **Each Site:** Picnic table, fire ring. **Dump Station:** Yes. **Laundry:** No. **Pay Phone:** No. **Restrooms and Showers:** Yes. **Fuel:** No. **Propane:** No. **Internal Roads:** Paved/gravel, in good condition. **RV Service:** No. **Market:** 2.5 mi. north in West Salem. **Restaurant:** 1.5 mi. north in West Salem. **General Store:** Yes. **Vending:** No. **Swimming:** Yes. **Playground:** Yes. **Other:** Fishing lake, shuffleboard, basketball, game room, horseshoes, shelter house, sports field, volleyball. **Activities:** Fishing, swimming, boating (rental paddleboats available). **Additional Information:** Ashland Area Chamber of Commerce, (419) 281-4584.

RESTRICTIONS

Pets: Leash only. Proof of immunization required. **Fires:** Fire ring only. **Alcoholic Beverages:** At sites only. **Vehicle Maximum Length:** No limit. **Other:** No working caravans permitted; no tent camping; electric heaters are prohibited.

TO GET THERE

From the junction of Hwy. 301 and US 42, drive 3 mi. west on US 42, then 200 yards south on Township Rd 810. Roads are wide and well maintained w/ broad shoulders.

WEST SALEM   MAP, B-2
Town and Country Camp Resort

7555 Shilling Rd., 44287. T: (419) 853-4550; www.tccamp.com.

🚐 ★★★★   ▲ ★★★★

Beauty: ★★★★   Site Privacy: ★★★★
Spaciousness: ★★★★   Quiet: ★★★★
Security: ★★★★   Cleanliness: ★★★★
Insect Control: ★★   Facilities: ★★★★

Town and Country Camp Resort is only 2 miles south of West Salem, but it has a definite country feel. Sites are grassy with gravel parking spots, and campers have a choice of shaded or open sites. Several lakes and wooded areas add to the country atmosphere. Laid out in a series of loops, the campground has 120 seasonal campers and 12 pull-through sites. All sites have sewer connections, so there is no dump station. A five-mph speed limit is enforced, as is quiet time from 11 p.m. to 8 a.m. No license is required for fishing in the campground lakes, and there is no limit on bluegills. Bass must be at least 12 inches with a limit of four per day, and catfish must be returned to the lake. Security measures include owners who live on site, a security gate, and regular patrols of the campgrounds.

BASICS

Operated By: Don & Linda Castella. **Open:** Apr. 1–Oct. 31. **Site Assignment:** Reservations accepted w/o deposit except on holidays; holiday reservations w/ 1-night deposit; refunds w/ 7-day notice. **Registration:** At campground office. **Fee:** $25; cash, check; call ahead to confirm. **Parking:** At site.

FACILITIES

Number of RV-only Sites: 200. **Number of Tent-only Sites:** 25. **Hookups:** Electric (30 amps), water, sewer. **Each Site:** Picnic table, fire ring. **Dump Station:** No. **Laundry:** Yes. **Pay Phone:** Yes.

Restrooms and Showers: Yes. **Fuel:** No. **Propane:** Yes. **Internal Roads:** Gravel, in good condition. **RV Service:** No. **Market:** 2 mi. north in West Salem. **Restaurant:** 2 mi. north in West Salem. **General Store:** Yes, limited. **Vending:** Yes. **Swimming:** Yes. **Playground:** Yes. **Other:** Fishing lake, game room, pavilion, softball, horseshoes, basketball, volleyball. **Activities:** Swimming, fishing, scheduled activities. **Nearby Attractions:** State parks, antiques, golf, museums, historic homes, arts & crafts. **Additional Information:** Ashland Area Chamber of Commerce, (419) 281-4584.

RESTRICTIONS

Pets: On leash only. **Fires:** Fire ring only. **Alcoholic Beverages:** Must be kept in covered containers. **Vehicle Maximum Length:** 40 ft. **Other:** No working caravans are permitted.

TO GET THERE

From the junction of I-71 and SR 539, take Exit 198, drive 1 mi. northwest on SR 539 to Shilling Rd., drive 1 mi. north. SR 539 is a good road, well maintained w/ broad shoulders. The entry road is paved, but it's also narrow, hilly, and twisting, w/ a narrow squeeze past a farm silo.

WILMINGTON   MAP, C-1
Cowan Lake State Park

1750 Osborn Rd., 45177. T: (937) 382-1096; www.dnr.state.oh.us/odnr/parks.

🚐 ★★★   ▲ ★★★

Beauty: ★★★★   Site Privacy: ★★★
Spaciousness: ★★★   Quiet: ★★★★
Security: ★★★★   Cleanliness: ★★★
Insect Control: ★★   Facilities: ★★★

Located 5 miles west of Wilmington, Cowan Lake State Park has a 700-acre lake as a centerpiece. The lake is very popular for sailboats and pontoon boats. The lake has a ten-horsepower limit on motors. The Cowan Lake region was once a stronghold of the Miami and Shawnee Indians. Cowan Creek was named for the area's first surveyor, John Cowan. A dam was completed across Cowan Creek in 1950, and in 1968, Cowan Lake was dedicated as a state park. Campground sites are suitable for tents or RVs. Four sites are wheelchair accessible. Pet camping is offered on designated sites. Unlike many state campgrounds, Cowan Lake offers laundry facilities. Most sites are shaded by a beech and maple forest, and the average site size is 14 by 40 feet. There are no pull-through sites. Security is good, with park rangers who patrol and monitor motorists at a park gate.

BASICS

Operated By: State of Ohio. **Open:** All year. **Site Assignment:** First come, first served; no reservations. **Registration:** At campground office. **Fee:** $20; cash, check, credit card. **Parking:** At site.

FACILITIES

Number of RV-only Sites: 237. **Number of Tent-only Sites:** 18. **Hookups:** Electric (50 amps). **Each Site:** Picnic table, fire ring. **Dump Station:** Yes. **Laundry:** Yes. **Pay Phone:** Yes. **Restrooms and Showers:** Yes. **Fuel:** No. **Propane:** No. **Internal**

Roads: Paved, in good condition. **RV Service:** No. **Market:** 5 mi. east in Wilmington. **Restaurant:** 5 mi. east in Wilmington. **General Store:** Yes. **Vending:** Yes. **Swimming:** No. **Playground:** Yes. **Other:** Cowan Lake, beach, boat dock, boat ramp, hiking trails, pavilion, horseshoes, game room, mini-golf, mountain bike trail, rental cabins. **Activities:** Swimming, fishing, hiking, low-speed boating (rental canoes, motorboats available), scheduled activities. **Nearby Attractions:** Kings Island amusement park, *Blue Jacket* outdoor drama, antiques, covered bridge, pottery, pheasant farm, Wilmington College, rails-to-trails recreational trail. **Additional Information:** Clinton County CVB, (877) 4-A-VISIT.

RESTRICTIONS

Pets: On leash only; pet camping area. **Fires:** Fire ring only. **Alcoholic Beverages:** Not allowed. **Vehicle Maximum Length:** 35 ft. **Other:** 14-day stay limit.

TO GET THERE

From Wilmington, drive 3 mi. south on US 68 to Dalton Rd., then 1.5 mi. Roads are wide and well maintained w/ broad shoulders.

WILMINGTON   MAP, C-1
Thousand Trails—Wilmington

1786 SR 380, 45177. T: (937) 382-4230; www.1000trails.com.

🚐 ★★★★   ▲ ★★★★

Beauty: ★★★   Site Privacy: ★★★★
Spaciousness: ★★★★   Quiet: ★★★★
Security: ★★★★★   Cleanliness: ★★★★★
Insect Control: ★★   Facilities: ★★★★

Thousand Trails—Wilmington is part of a nationwide network of 57 campground resorts for members of a private camping club. Membership options with annual dues allow members to camp at every preserve in the system or choose only a favorite region. Nonmembers are allowed a get-acquainted visit. Located 7 miles west of Wilmington, the campground is on a preserve of gently rolling land surrounding a lake. The typical site width is 40 feet, and the campground has two pull-throughs. Sites are mostly shaded by mature oak, maple, and ash trees. Members have access to such extras as an iron and ironing board in the laundry and canoes and paddleboats on the small lake. The campground has 40 rally sites and 10 tent sites in a wooded area with water hookups. Three stocked ponds are for catch-and-release fishing only. Quiet time is enforced from 11 p.m. to 8 a.m., as is a five-mph speed limit. Security is excellent, with a gate that requires a code to get in, a manager on site, and regular patrols.

BASICS

Operated By: Thousand Trails Inc. **Open:** May 1–Oct. 31. **Site Assignment:** Reservations w/ 1-night deposit; refund w/ 24-hour notice. **Registration:** At campground office. **Fee:** $29; cash, check, credit card; call ahead to confirm rates. **Parking:** At site.

FACILITIES

Number of RV-only Sites: 164. **Number of Tent-only Sites:** 10. **Hookups:** Electric (30 amps), water,

---

sewer. **Each Site:** Picnic table, fire ring. **Dump Station:** Yes. **Laundry:** Yes. **Pay Phone:** Yes. **Restrooms and Showers:** Yes. **Fuel:** No. **Propane:** Yes. **Internal Roads:** Paved/gravel, in good condition. **RV Service:** No. **Market:** 10 mi. east in Wilmington. **Restaurant:** 7 mi. east in Wilmington. **General Store:** Yes. **Vending:** Yes. **Swimming:** No. **Playground:** Yes. **Other:** Adult lodge, basketball, campfire circle, family lodge, horseshoe, meeting room, mini-golf, shuffleboard, wad-

ing pool, whirlpool, tennis, volleyball, hiking trail, fishing pond, rental trailers. **Activities:** Swimming, fishing, hiking, electric-motor boating (free canoes, paddleboats available), scheduled weekend activities. **Nearby Attractions:** Kings Island amusement park, pottery, *Blue Jacket* outdoor drama, pheasant farm, Wilmington College, antiques, covered bridge, rails-to-trails recreational trail. **Additional Information:** Clinton County CVB, (877) 4-A-VISIT.

RESTRICTIONS

Pets: On leash only. **Fires:** Fire ring only. **Alcoholic Beverages:** Allowed. **Vehicle Maximum Length:** No limit. **Other:** 14-day stay limit.

TO GET THERE

From the junction of I-71 and Hwy. 73, take Exit 45, drive 0.25 mi. east on Hwy. 73, then 1.5 mi. south on Hwy. 380. Roads are wide and well maintained w/ broad shoulders.

Oklahoma

Oklahoma is a real slice of American pie. There's nobody more down-to-earth than a native Oklahoman working the land, having coffee with friends before a hard day's work, or going to church to start the week. Nobody's more hospitable. This is wave-at-your-neighbor-as-you-drive-past country, and strangers are greeted with the same friendly wave. Oklahoma's cowboy culture still lives on in festivals, museums, rodeos (such as the **Oklahoma State Prison Rodeo and Parade**), and in the rugged individualism that has long been a part of Okie character, but the diverse culture, rich history, and gorgeous landscape are what make Oklahoma so remarkable.

The panhandle of Oklahoma (from the New Mexico border almost to **Canton Lake**) does not offer much to travelers, but Interstate 35, which bisects the state, is where you'll find several of Oklahoma's visitor-friendly towns. **Tulsa** is a modern city steeped in a history soaked in the **Trail of Tears** and gushing oil. In **Bartlesville,** the **Woolaroc Museum and Wildlife Preserve** leaves quite an impression with its 3,500-acre spread, along with its petting zoo, **Native American Heritage Center,** and much more. Located on the **Grand Lake O' the Cherokees, Grove** is considered to be one of the state's best fishing spots. For those interested in Okie culture, Grove also hosts the fiddling/clogging-centered **American Heritage Music Festival** and **Har-Ber Village,** a reconstructed 19th-century village featuring more than 100 structures. In addition to being the home of the **University of Oklahoma, Norman** prides itself on preserving much of Oklahoma's rich and storied history. Oklahoma's cultural center, Norman is also home to 67 Native American tribes, the **Sam Noble Oklahoma Museum of Natural History,** and the **Fred Jones Jr. Museum of Art** (which permanently houses a fantastic collection of European paintings that includes works by Van Gogh, Renoir, and Monet). For a larger slice of American culture, you can still get your kicks on historic **Route 66,** the remnants of which run through both Tulsa and Oklahoma City.

Oklahoma City lies at the crossroads of I-35, I-40, and I-44, making it easily accessible for those traveling from neighboring states. It is indeed fitting that Oklahoma is home to the **National Cowboy Hall of Fame** and the **American Quarterhorse Show;** a promenade through the skywalks of downtown will provide a good view. Sights such as the **Air Space Museum,** the **Crystal Bridge** at **Myriad Gardens,** the **Oklahoma City Civic Center Music Hall** (spanning a whopping six blocks in the heart of downtown), and the touching **Oklahoma City National Memorial** are all sure to leave a lasting impression.

Campground Profiles

ARDMORE MAP, C-3
Ardmore/Marietta KOA

Rte. 1 Box 640, 73448.
T: (800) KOA-5893 or (580) 276-2800.

🚐 ★★★★   ⛺ ★★★★

Beauty: ★★★★
Site Privacy: ★★★★
Spaciousness: ★★★★
Quiet: ★★★
Security: ★★★★
Cleanliness: ★★★★★
Insect Control: ★★★★
Facilities: ★★★★

Built on a slope, this campground has leveled pull-throughs 84 by 25 feet in size. There is a distinct farm feeling on the campground, and it is surrounded on the south by a farm, on the west by trees (oak, crape myrtle, elm, maple), and the north by an open field with trees in the distance. Wildlife enthusiasts will like Ardmore/Marietta–coyotes, deer, armadillos, hawks, sparrows, and hummingbirds have all been spotted here. The most desirable sites are 15, 16, and 21–26, which all have shade trees. The other sites are in the open to a greater or lesser extent. Tenting is possible on the grassy field to the west of the RV sites, or—better yet—in the field to the north, where a handful of shade trees provide coverage. The restrooms and showers are extremely clean, although the floor is slightly peeling (but not dirty). The laundry room is equally clean and spacious, and very well decorated. This is a small but very nice campground. Tenters and RVers alike will enjoy a stay here.

BASICS

Operated By: Jerry Burns. **Open:** All year. **Site Assignment:** Upon registration; credit card required for reservation. **Registration:** At office. (Late arrivals use drop box in laundry.) **Fee:** RV, $23–$30; tent, $10–$18; kabin, $30–$40. **Parking:** At site.

FACILITIES

Number of RV-only Sites: 24. **Number of Tent-only Sites:** 6. **Hookups:** Electric (30, 50 amps), water, sewer. **Each Site:** Picnic table, grill. **Dump Station:** Yes. **Laundry:** Yes. **Pay Phone:** Yes. **Restrooms and Showers:** Yes. **Fuel:** No. **Propane:** Yes. **Internal Roads:** Gravel. **RV Service:** No. **Market:** 6 mi. south to Marietta. **Restaurant:** 6 mi. south to Marietta. **General Store:** Yes. **Vending:** No. **Swimming:** No. **Playground:** Yes. **Other:** Game room, 2 cabins. **Activities:** Volleyball, fishing, boating. **Nearby Attractions:** Arbuckle Mountains, Eliza Cruce Hall Doll Collection, Tucker Tower Nature Center, Charles B. Goddard Center for the Visual & Performing Arts. **Additional Information:** Ardmore Chamber of Commerce, (580) 223-7765.

RESTRICTIONS

Pets: On leash, cleaned up after. **Fires:** Grill only. **Alcoholic Beverages:** At sites. **Vehicle Maximum Length:** 90 ft.

TO GET THERE

From I-35, take Exit 21. Turn west onto Aswald Rd. and go 0.1 mi. Turn left at the sign onto the dirt entrance road.

BARTLESVILLE MAP, A-3
Riverside RV Resort

1211 SE Adams Blvd., 74003.
T: (888) 572-1241 or (918) 336-6431;
www.resortrv.com.

🚐 ★★★   ⛺ ★★★

Beauty: ★★★
Site Privacy: ★★★
Spaciousness: ★★
Quiet: ★★★★
Security: ★★★★
Cleanliness: ★★★
Insect Control: ★★★★
Facilities: ★★★

Located in a residential area, this campground features some attractive landscaping using flowers, bricks around some of the sites, and a fountain, but it also looks a little run-down. Sites 1–14 are in the northwest corner, along the entrance. These sites (especially 1–8) are closest to the pool. Sites 15–19, in the middle of the campground, are pull-throughs 65 by 21 feet, and 20–23, in the same area, are pull-throughs 60 by 21 feet. All of these sites but 21 are well shaded. Other 65-foot pull-throughs are 49–53 in the southeast corner. Sites 55–60, also in the southeast corner, are slightly shorter, at 60 feet. Any of these are a decent stay, depending on the length of site required for your vehicle. These sites are closest to the river, but are still up and off the bank. Tenting is allowed along the river bank. While shaded by pecan, cedar, and elm trees, these sites do not have abundant room for a tent—let alone recreating or relaxing at your site. The restrooms and showers, individual units located in the office building, are tidy and nicely decorated. Both the restrooms and the (small) laundry are clean. While adequate, this park is, as the name implies, better for RVs than tents—although it hardly lives up to the title "resort."

BASICS

Operated By: Dave & Joyce Butler. **Open:** All year. **Site Assignment:** Upon registration; verbal reservations OK. **Registration:** At office. (Late arrivals pay in morning.) **Fee:** RV (full), $24; tent, $8; check, no credit cards. **Parking:** At site.

FACILITIES

Number of RV-only Sites: 75. **Number of Tent-only Sites:** Undesignated sites. **Hookups:** Electric (20, 30, 50 amps), water, sewer, cable TV. **Each Site:** None. **Dump Station:** Yes. **Laundry:** Yes. **Pay Phone:** Yes. **Restrooms and Showers:** Yes. **Fuel:** No. **Propane:** Yes. **Internal Roads:** Gravel. **RV Service:** No. **Market:** Less than 0.5 mi. west. **Restaurant:** 1.5 mi. east. **General Store:** No. **Vending:** Yes. **Swimming:** Pool. **Playground:** No. **Other:** Data port, pavilion, river. **Activities:** Swimming, fishing. **Nearby Attractions:** Caney River, Woolaroc Ranch Museum. **Additional Information:** Bartlesville Area CVB, (800) 364-8708 or (918) 336-8708.

RESTRICTIONS

Pets: On leash, cleaned up after. **Fires:** Grill only. **Alcoholic Beverages:** Inside RV only. **Vehicle Maximum Length:** 70 ft.

TO GET THERE

From the junction of Hwy. 75 and Hwy. 60 west (Pawhuska/Ponca City exit), turn west onto Hwy. 60 and go 1.6 mi. to Quapaw Ave. Turn left onto Quapaw Ave. and take the first left into the campground.

BEAVER MAP, A-1
Beaver Dunes State Park

P.O. Box 1190, 73932. T: (580) 625-3373;
www.oklahomaparks.com.

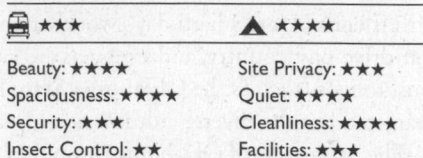

🚐 ★★★   ⛺ ★★★★

Beauty: ★★★★
Site Privacy: ★★★
Spaciousness: ★★★★
Quiet: ★★★★
Security: ★★★
Cleanliness: ★★★★
Insect Control: ★★
Facilities: ★★★

Just 1.5 miles north of town, this campground offers primitive sites and electrical hookups for campers who like to get close to nature. Native Oklahoma wildflowers and huckleberry bushes are scattered throughout the grounds, and blue jays and cardinals are permanent residents at Beaver Dunes. There are campsites right at the water's edge (although no swimming is permitted), as well as farther up on shore. (Sites are not numbered.) There are seven huge pull-throughs (85 feet long) to the north of the "comfort station" (restrooms and showers), which are the best bet for anything longer than 22 feet. There are, however, no shade trees in these sites. Following the one-way road, you come across three 27-foot back-ins that have covered picnic tables. One of these sites has water. Just to the southeast of the comfort station are four primitive sites: two are right on the lake, while the other two are on either side of the building. These are attractive sites, with nice tree coverage and good views of the lake and the bridge. However, they receive foot traffic to and from the restrooms, and cars drive past to reach other campsites. Perhaps the nicest campsite of all is the first one you see when you enter the campground. It is right on the water, has soft sand (on a bit of a slope), and some tree shade. The biggest drawback is that you must park above the site on the road, and walk down to the campsite, making RV parking at this site impossible. The "comfort station" is very spacious and clean, although the cement building itself seems a little old. This is a fine campground for those seeking to sleep out in nature, and has enough variety to satisfy pretty much any tastes.

BASICS

Operated By: Oklahoma State Parks. **Open:** All year. **Site Assignment:** First come, first served; no reservations. **Registration:** At office, or ranger will collect at site. **Fee:** Hookup, $19; primitive, $8; V, MC. **Parking:** At (or near) site.

FACILITIES

Number of RV-only Sites: 15. **Number of Tent-only Sites:** 10. **Hookups:** Electric (30 amps), water. **Each Site:** Picnic table, grill/pit. **Dump Station:** Yes. **Laundry:** No. **Pay Phone:** In office (collect or calling card only). **Restrooms and Showers:** Yes.

Fuel: No. **Propane:** No. **Internal Roads:** Paved. **RV Service:** No. **Market:** 1 mi. to Beaver. **Restaurant:** 1 mi. to Beaver. **General Store:** No. **Vending:** No. **Swimming:** No. **Playground:** Yes. **Other:** Picnic pavilion, wildlife. **Activities:** Hiking, ATV riding, volleyball, horseshoes, children's fishing. **Nearby Attractions:** Sand dunes, lake, ATV area. **Additional Information:** Beaver County Chamber of Commerce, (580) 625-4726.

RESTRICTIONS

Pets: On leash, cleaned up after. **Fires:** In grills; subject to bans. **Alcoholic Beverages:** Beer only. **Vehicle Maximum Length:** No limit. **Other:** No swimming, ATV regulations.

TO GET THERE

From the junction of Hwy. 64/270 and Hwy. 23, turn right onto Hwy. 23/270, and go 4.9 mi. south. Turn right at the sign into the campground, or left to get to the office.

CATOOSA — MAP, A-3, A-4
Tulsa Northeast KOA

19605 East Skelly Dr., 74015.
T: (800) 562-7657 or (918) 266-4227;
www.koakampgrounds.com/where/ok/36106.

🚐 ★★★★	⛺ ★★★★
Beauty: ★★★★	Site Privacy: ★★★★
Spaciousness: ★★★★	Quiet: ★★★
Security: ★★★★	Cleanliness: ★★★★★
Insect Control: ★★★★	Facilities: ★★★★

This campground offers open grassy sites in the front section and more shaded sites behind the office. All sites are pull-throughs. The front section has 75-foot sites that are roomier than most of the sites in the back (24 feet wide versus 18 feet wide). Northern-end sites (116, 130, 143, 153, 163, 177, 191, and 205) are closest to the entrance road and are therefore less desirable. End sites closer to the office (112 and 158 especially) receive more passing traffic from registering campers. Of the southern sites, the two rows (the 40s and 50s) directly behind the office are the widest and most suitable for rigs with slide-outs. Of the remaining sites, 10 and 16 in the eastern side are closest to a storage shed. Sites in the southwestern corner (77, 84, 91, 98, 104, 100) are farthest from the entrance and the office. Tent sites are directly behind the office, in a strip of grassy sites. The restrooms and showers are absolutely spotless and very comfortable. This campground makes a great home base for exploring Tulsa and its environs.

BASICS

Operated By: Private operator. **Open:** All year. **Site Assignment:** Upon registration; credit card required for reservation; 24-hour cancellation policy. **Registration:** At office. (Late arrivals use drop box.) **Fee:** RV, $24–$29; tent, $21–$25. **Parking:** At site.

FACILITIES

Number of RV-only Sites: 118. **Number of Tent-only Sites:** 9. **Hookups:** Electric (30, 50 amps), water, sewer. **Each Site:** Picnic table, grill. **Dump Station:** Yes. **Laundry:** Yes. **Pay Phone:** Yes.

Restrooms and Showers: Yes. **Fuel:** No. **Propane:** Yes. **Internal Roads:** Gravel. **RV Service:** No. **Market:** 3 blocks south. **Restaurant:** 0.25 mi. south. **General Store:** Yes. **Vending:** Yes. **Swimming:** Pool. **Playground:** Yes. **Other:** Cabins, pet walk, data port, rec room, video games, pavilion, meeting room. **Activities:** Swimming, volleyball, tours, softball/baseball, golf, fishing, boating, horse racing, Tulsa Run. **Nearby Attractions:** Trail of Tears, amusement parks, casinos, lakes, Gilcrease Museum, Tulsa Zoo, Big Splash Water Park, theatre, opera, dining. **Additional Information:** Tulsa CVB, (800) 558-3311 or (918) 585-1201.

RESTRICTIONS

Pets: On leash, cleaned up after. **Fires:** Grill only. **Alcoholic Beverages:** At sites. **Vehicle Maximum Length:** 75 ft.

TO GET THERE

From I-44 (Exit 240A: 193rd Ave.), turn north onto 193rd Ave. and go 0.15 mi. Turn right at the sign into the entrance. Follow the entrance road past the trucking companies. Turn right at the sign into the campground.

CLAYTON — MAP, C-4
Clayton Lake State Park

Rte. 1 Box 33-10, 74536. T: (918) 569-7981;
www.touroklahoma.com/pages/stateparks/
parks/cllspbig.html.

🚐 ★★★	⛺ ★★★★★
Beauty: ★★★★	Site Privacy: ★★★★
Spaciousness: ★★★	Quiet: ★★★★
Security: ★★★★	Cleanliness: ★★★
Insect Control: ★★★	Facilities: ★★

This state park is divided into two areas. Area 1 has a boat ramp and lake access, with RV sites to the north. RVers should take note that the road is steep and broken in places, and drivers should take it slowly. As you drive in, it can be a little confusing as to where the RV sites are (look for the sign that says "RV Area"), but note that the tent sites (to the southeast of the office) are all forested and have some degree of slope to them, whereas the RV sites are all on a level, open strip. These sites are all large back-ins with an open area to pull in, allowing a rig of any size to park here. There is only one (unnumbered) site that has a table, grill, and tree—the rest do not have these features. Area 2 is designated the "assigned camping" area. These are also large (75-foot) back-ins that any RV should be able to fit into. The first site is right at the entrance, and is therefore less desirable. Further from the water, but with excellent views, are sites E3 and E4. There is a small gated area away from the rest of the sites that has gravel sites and 50-foot back-ins. The sites in this area are all open but surrounded by forest. The restroom facilities are clean and modern, as are the showers. This park offers a nice getaway on a lake, with shaded spots that are fine for RVs and ideal for tents.

BASICS

Operated By: Oklahoma State Parks. **Open:** All year. **Site Assignment:** Upon registration; verbal

reservations OK. **Registration:** At office. (Late arrivals select site & pay in the morning.) **Fee:** Modern, $17; semi-modern, $14; primitive, $8. **Parking:** At site.

FACILITIES

Number of RV-only Sites: 29. **Number of Tent-only Sites:** 60. **Hookups:** Electric (30 amps), water. **Each Site:** Picnic table, grill. **Dump Station:** Yes. **Laundry:** No. **Pay Phone:** No. **Restrooms and Showers:** Yes. **Fuel:** No. **Propane:** No. **Internal Roads:** Paved. **RV Service:** No. **Market:** 5 mi. north. **Restaurant:** 2 mi. north. **General Store:** No. **Vending:** No. **Swimming:** Lake. **Playground:** Yes. **Other:** Covered pavilion, cabin rental. **Activities:** Swimming, boating, fishing, hiking, wildlife watching. **Nearby Attractions:** Talimena State Park, McGee Creek State Park. **Additional Information:** Choctaw County Chamber Of Commerce, (580) 326-7511.

RESTRICTIONS

Pets: On leash, cleaned up after. **Fires:** Grill only. **Alcoholic Beverages:** At sites. **Vehicle Maximum Length:** No limit.

TO GET THERE

From the junction of Hwy. 2 and Hwy. 271, turn south onto Hwy. 271 and go 4.4 mi. Turn right at the sign into the entrance. Area 1 is to the right, Area 2 lies straight ahead.

CLINTON — MAP, B-2
Wink's RV Park

1410 Neptune Rd., 73601. T: (580) 323-1664.

🚐 ★★★★	⛺ ★★★★
Beauty: ★★★★	Site Privacy: ★★★★
Spaciousness: ★★★★	Quiet: ★★★★
Security: ★★★★	Cleanliness: ★★★★★
Insect Control: ★★	Facilities: ★★★

This campground is divided into three tiers, providing a very different experience in the top tier than in the bottom two. The top tier contains all open back-ins averaging 40 by 18 feet. These sites are all level, but do not have shade, picnic tables, or grills. This makes for an unmistakably "urban" camping experience. However, the lower two tiers have beautiful campsites with huge shade trees and beautiful grass. These sites are all pull-throughs that average 35 feet in length, although there are much larger ones on the lower tier. The best sites are 11–13 and 33–39, as they are practically enveloped in shade trees and face a nice grassy area. Less nice is site 14, which seems clipped and looks out over junked autos in the neighboring yard. Sites 49 and 50 are the largest, as they are not delineated in size, but are rather spaces in a grassy field that could accommodate a rig of any size. These sites are separated from the others, as are sites 43–45, which offers more privacy. The restrooms and showers are spacious and clean, but have two flaws: the toilets are only separated by a curtain, and there is no space to hold clothes inside each individual shower. These are rather small faults, however, and the overall camping experience is excellent.

BASICS

Operated By: Winston & Ruthelma Hoffman.
Open: All year. **Site Assignment:** Upon registration; verbal reservations OK. **Registration:** At office. (Late arrivals use drop box.) **Fee:** RV, $18–$20; tent, $10. **Parking:** At site.

FACILITIES

Number of RV-only Sites: 65. **Hookups:** Electric (20, 30, 50 amps), water, sewer. **Each Site:** Picnic table. **Dump Station:** No (sewer at all sites). **Laundry:** Yes. **Pay Phone:** Yes. **Restrooms and Showers:** Yes. **Fuel:** No. **Propane:** No. **Internal Roads:** Gravel. **RV Service:** No. **Market:** 0.75 mi. north. **Restaurant:** 0.5 mi. north. **General Store:** No. **Vending:** No. **Swimming:** No. **Playground:** Yes. **Other:** Basketball net. **Activities:** Visiting museums, basketball. **Nearby Attractions:** Oklahoma Rte. 66 Museum. **Additional Information:** Clinton Chamber of Commerce, (800) 759-1397 or (580) 323-2222.

RESTRICTIONS

Pets: On leash, cleaned up after. **Fires:** Grill only. **Alcoholic Beverages:** At sites. **Vehicle Maximum Length:** No limit.

TO GET THERE

From the junction of I-40 (Exit 65A) and Historic Rte. 66, go 0.3 mi. south on Rte. 66. Turn right at the sign into the campground. The office is on the right.

COLBERT
Sherrard RV and KOA
MAP, C-3

411 Sherrard St., 74733.
T: (800) KOA-2485 or (580) 296-2485.

🚐 ★★★★   ⛺ ★★★★

Beauty: ★★★★	Site Privacy: ★★★★
Spaciousness: ★★★★	Quiet: ★★★
Security: ★★★★	Cleanliness: ★★★★
Insect Control: ★★★★	Facilities: ★★★★

Half RV sales and servicing, half campground, the Sherrard complex has much to offer the RV camper. The sites open to overnighters are on the west side of the park. (The sites to the north, 1–50 and 107–111, are reserved for monthly customers.) These sites are all 75-foot grassy pull-throughs arranged in rows (61–98) and two small groups on their own (53–56 and 101–106). Most every site is well shaded, although 64, 65, and 76 are not, and sites 101 and 104 have a single shade tree at the edge of their space. Sites 102, 103, 105, and 106 have several large shade trees each. The row numbered in the 80s has the most developed sites, with cement slabs, and the best sites in the park are on this row: 86–88. These three sites face a row of trees (that cover an RV storage area), and are farthest from the service building. Sites 66–68 are also very nice—they are closest to the attractive tenting area. The least desirable sites are 51–56, which are out in a field by the cabins and the park entrance. 54 and 56 are so close to the RVs for sale in the adjacent lot that you could put your hand out your window and touch them. Sites 51 and 52 are also less nice, being located on the parking lot

next to the office. The tenting area is just west of the pool in a very well-shaded area with good grass. The restrooms are clean and modern, but a touch "used" looking. This is a superb RV park that has much to offer the RVer, and is fine for the tent camper, too.

BASICS

Operated By: Charles Sherrard. **Open:** All year. **Site Assignment:** Upon registration; verbal reservations OK. **Registration:** At office. (Late arrivals use drop box.) **Fee:** RV, $22–$26; tent, $16–$18; kabin, $30–$35; call ahead to confirm. **Parking:** At site.

FACILITIES

Number of RV-only Sites: 48. **Number of Tent-only Sites:** 6. **Hookups:** Electric (30, 50 amps), water, sewer. **Each Site:** Picnic table, tree. **Dump Station:** Yes. **Laundry:** Yes. **Pay Phone:** Yes. **Restrooms and Showers:** Yes. **Fuel:** Yes. **Propane:** Yes. **Internal Roads:** Paved. **RV Service:** Yes. **Market:** 1 mi. to Colbert. **Restaurant:** 1 mi. to Colbert. **General Store:** Yes. **Vending:** No. **Swimming:** Pool. **Playground:** Yes. **Other:** TV lounge, pet walk area, rec room w/ pool table. **Activities:** Fishing, swimming, boating in area. **Nearby Attractions:** Denison Dam, boat shows, antique shops, Lake Texoma State Park. **Additional Information:** Durant Chamber of Commerce, (580) 924-0848.

RESTRICTIONS

Pets: On leash, cleaned up after. **Fires:** Grill only. **Alcoholic Beverages:** At sites. **Vehicle Maximum Length:** 75 ft. **Other:** Rule sheet on back of site map.

TO GET THERE

From the junction of Hwy. 75/69 and Hwy. 91, turn west onto Hwy. 91 and take the first right onto Sherrard Dr. Go 0.25 mi. and turn left at the sign into the entrance. Follow the road straight ahead to the office.

EL RENO
Best Western
MAP, B-2

2701 South Country Club Rd., 73036.
T: (800) 263-3844 or (405) 262-6490.

🚐 ★★★★   ⛺ n/a

Beauty: ★★★	Site Privacy: ★★★
Spaciousness: ★★★	Quiet: ★★★★
Security: ★★★★	Cleanliness: ★★★★★
Insect Control: ★★★★	Facilities: ★★★★

This RV park contains three rows of sites, the first two of which (sites 1–9 and 10–18) are 60-foot pull-throughs, and the final row of which contains 80-foot pull-throughs (19–23) and 40-foot pull-throughs (24–26). All sites are cement with a strip of grass and bushes in between them. Although mostly concrete, the park is quite attractive: There are two flowering bushes and a large rock at the end of each of the grassy strips. The park itself is bordered on the east and south by large bushes (although there is less attractive commercial development to the north and west). Although there is not a large amount of room between most sites (which average 18 feet wide), there are a few extra-wide

spaces that are 21 feet wide. The best sites are in the north/northeast corner (especially 9, 18, and 26, which have extra grassy space and a tree). Site 18 has the largest grassy section. The less desirable sites are 10 and (especially) 19, which are next to a commercial building. The laundry, restrooms, and showers are all clean and spacious, making this a very decent stop that only needs a little more room between sites to make for an even better stay.

BASICS

Operated By: Sadhna Kelly. **Open:** All year. **Site Assignment:** Upon registration; reservations can be made by credit card; cancel before 6 p.m. the day of arrival. **Registration:** At office (24 hours). **Fee:** RV, $25 plus tax; check, V, MC, AE, D, DC. **Parking:** At site.

FACILITIES

Number of RV-only Sites: 26. **Hookups:** Electric (30, 50 amps), water, sewer, cable TV. **Each Site:** Picnic table. **Dump Station:** No (sewer at all sites). **Laundry:** Yes. **Pay Phone:** Yes. **Restrooms and Showers:** Yes. **Fuel:** Next door. **Propane:** No. **Internal Roads:** Gravel. **RV Service:** No. **Market:** Less than 0.25 mi. **Restaurant:** Across the street. **General Store:** No. **Vending:** Yes. **Swimming:** Pool. **Playground:** Yes. **Other:** Data port. **Activities:** Fishing, boating, swimming, golf in area. **Nearby Attractions:** Downtown trolley, antique stores, Lake El Reno, golf course, Lucky Star Casino, Oklahoma City, Fort Reno. **Additional Information:** El Reno Chamber of Commerce, (405) 262-1188.

RESTRICTIONS

Pets: On leash, cleaned up after. **Fires:** Grill only. **Alcoholic Beverages:** At sites. **Vehicle Maximum Length:** No limit.

TO GET THERE

From I-40 (Exit 123): on the south side of the highway, turn left into the Best Western complex.

ENID
High Point RV Park
MAP, A-2

2700 North Van Buren, No. 93, 73703.
T: (580) 234-1726 or (580) 234-7380.

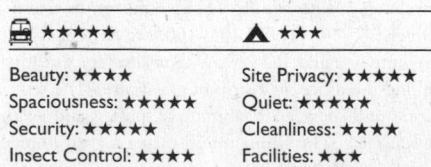

Beauty: ★★★★	Site Privacy: ★★★★★
Spaciousness: ★★★★★	Quiet: ★★★★★
Security: ★★★★★	Cleanliness: ★★★★
Insect Control: ★★★★	Facilities: ★★★

This RV park contains sites in three distinct locations. Closest to the office is the "Custer Circle"—a unique and really neat way of parking RVs: in a circle. Pull-through sites 73–92 form the inner circle, with 35–72 (all long-term sites) forming an outside ring. These pull-throughs are 105 by 45 feet—large enough for the largest rigs with slide-outs. In addition, all sites are separated by rows of hedges and have oak, sycamore, and cottonwood shade trees, making them both private and comfortable. These sites are by far the best in the entire park. The two other locations are to the west of the office, outside the main park entrance. On the south side are 18

102-foot back-ins that are enclosed by hedges. These sites are somewhat shaded, but many are occupied by long-term residents and mobile homes. The final area is to the northwest of the office. Laid out in two rather indistinct rows, these sites are shaded, gravel pull-throughs of varying lengths. Sites 2–6 are the largest at 105 feet, while 9–18 are 54 feet in length. Sites 17 and 18 are close to the road and share an oil pump, which makes these sites distinctly less desirable. Tenters can camp in an open grassy space in this last area. There is not much shade to protect tenters, and the grass is likewise rather sparse. This is much more of an RV-oriented park, and those who can "circle the wagons" will pass an extremely enjoyable stay here.

BASICS

Operated By: Robert Stewart. **Open:** All year. **Site Assignment:** Upon registration; verbal reservations OK. **Registration:** At office. (Late arrivals use drop box or pay in morning.) **Fee:** RV (full), $21; tent, $5; check, V, MC, AE, D, DC. **Parking:** At site.

FACILITIES

Number of RV-only Sites: 60. **Number of Tent-only Sites:** Undesignated sites. **Hookups:** Electric (30, 50 amps), water, sewer, instant phone. **Each Site:** None. **Dump Station:** Yes. **Laundry:** Yes. **Pay Phone:** Yes. **Restrooms and Showers:** Yes. **Fuel:** End of block. **Propane:** No. **Internal Roads:** Paved. **RV Service:** Call-in. **Market:** 0.25 mi. south. **Restaurant:** 0.25 mi. south. **General Store:** No. **Vending:** No. **Swimming:** No. **Playground:** No. **Other:** RV supplies, storm shelter, clubhouse. **Activities:** Visiting museums. **Nearby Attractions:** Museum of the Cherokee Strip, Railroad Museum of Oklahoma, Great Salt Plains State Park. **Additional Information:** Greater Enid Chamber of Commerce, (888) 229-2443 or (580) 237-2494.

RESTRICTIONS

Pets: On leash, cleaned up after. **Fires:** Grill only. **Alcoholic Beverages:** At sites. **Vehicle Maximum Length:** No limit.

TO GET THERE

From the junction of Hwy. 81 and Hwy. 60, go north on 81/60 2.2 mi. Turn left at the sign into the entrance.

GORE	MAP, B-4
Cookson Bend	

reserve america

Rte. 1 Box 259, 74435-9547. T: (918) 487-5252; www.reserveamerica.com.

🚐 ★★★★	⛺ ★★★★
Beauty: ★★★★	Site Privacy: ★★
Spaciousness: ★★	Quiet: ★★★
Security: ★★★	Cleanliness: ★★★★
Insect Control: ★★★	Facilities: ★★★

In Oklahoma's Green Country, Cookson Bend Campground on Lake Tenkiller is a recreational paradise. Tenkiller Ferry Lake, or more simply, "Lake Tenkiller," is a reservoir in eastern Oklahoma formed by the damming of the Illinois River. The earth-fill dam was constructed between 1947 and 1952 by the United States Army Corps of Engineers for purposes of flood control and hydroelectric power generation. The lake covers 12,900 acres in the Cookson Hills of Cherokee and Sequoyah counties, about 7 miles northeast of the town of Gore. Tenkiller is nestled in the foothills of the Ozark Mountains, surrounded with dogwood forests, hilly terrain, and beautiful foliage from spring until fall, when the changing autumn leaves draw many travelers around the lake and up scenic Highway 10. It also serves as one of the flyways of migratory animals, such as Canada geese, ducks, monarch butterflies, warblers, bald eagles, and many others. Camping, fishing, sightseeing, scuba diving, and picnicking are just a few of the activities enjoyed by visitors. They also have a beautiful view of 200 foot limestone bluffs across the water from the campground. There are 121 campsites, showers and toilets, swimming beaches, playground, picnic shelters, and boat ramps. There is a marina concession at the entrance to the park.

BASICS

Operated By: U.S. Army Corps of Engineers. **Open:** Jan. 1–Sept. 30. **Site Assignment:** Reservations must be made at least 2 days in advance. **Registration:** At office. **Fee:** Single, $10–$14; group, $25. **Parking:** At site.

FACILITIES

Number of Multipurpose Sites: 364. **Hookups:** Yes. **Dump Station:** Yes. **Laundry:** No. **Pay Phone:** Yes. **Restrooms and Showers:** Yes. **Fuel:** No. **Propane:** No. **Internal Roads:** Paved. **RV Service:** No. **Market:** No. **Restaurant:** No. **General Store:** No. **Vending:** No. **Swimming:** Yes. **Playground:** Yes. **Activities:** Fishing, sightseeing, scuba diving & picnicking.

RESTRICTIONS

Pets: Pets must be restrained or on a leash at all times while in developed recreation areas. **Fires:** In fire rings, stoves, grills, or fireplaces provided for that purpose. **Alcoholic Beverages:** Not allowed. **Vehicle Maximum Length:** Call ahead.

TO GET THERE

From Tahlequah, OK, go 17.5 mi. southeast on Hwy. 82, then right and go 2 mi. west on the paved access road.

GORE	MAP, B-4
Marval Family Camping Resort	

reserve america

Rte. 3 Box 60, P.O. Box 314M, 74435.
T: (918) 489-2295; www.marvalresort.com.

🚐 ★★★★	⛺ ★★★★★
Beauty: ★★★★	Site Privacy: ★★
Spaciousness: ★★★	Quiet: ★★★★
Security: ★★★★★	Cleanliness: ★★★★
Insect Control: ★★★★	Facilities: ★★★★

This campground is positively huge, with sites scattered from the river up to the entrance drive. Assuming availability, there is truly a site for any camper's tastes. (Note that aside from H, the lettered sites to the west and south of the pool are seasonal sites, and not for overnight use.) Sites 102–108 are 70-foot back-ins right along the riverbank, where a camper could put a canoe or small boat into the water, while 400–408 are back-ins close to the swimming access area. Across from these sites, 216–219 also offer proximity to the swimming beach. Sites 110–112, in the northeast corner, are 60-foot pull-throughs that are one row away from the water's edge. Fishermen will want to camp in sites 410–415, which are back-ins (as long as 75 feet) that run along the bank of the trout pond. Sites 207–215 are smaller back-ins (45 feet long), suitable for a pop-up. Some very nice, more developed, back-ins are 510–518, which have a concrete pad and wooden walkway on one side. These sites back up to a row of trees, beyond which is a huge open field. A large field in the southeast corner provides more than enough tenting space, although only one site (22) has a large shade tree. (Site 18 has several much smaller trees.) This field has excellent grass, and is surrounded by woods, lending it a nice, wild feel. The restrooms are individual unisex units that are clean and modern. The showers are also clean and cozy, if a little compact. This campground guarantees water fun for all ages, and should be a definite destination for families.

BASICS

Operated By: Val & Marc Marcum, Dan & Leia Nosalek, Lynn & Gary Cleek. **Open:** All year. **Site Assignment:** Most sites by reservation; credit card required; no holiday cancellations. **Registration:** At office. (No late arrivals. Gates locked at 10 p.m.) **Fee:** $22–30; varies widely by season & day of week. **Parking:** At site.

FACILITIES

Number of RV-only Sites: 128. **Number of Tent-only Sites:** 20. **Hookups:** Electric (30, 50 amps), water, sewer. **Each Site:** Picnic table. **Dump Station:** Yes. **Laundry:** Yes. **Pay Phone:** Yes. **Restrooms and Showers:** Yes. **Fuel:** No. **Propane:** Yes. **Internal Roads:** Gravel. **RV Service:** No. **Market:** 1.25 mi. south. **Restaurant:** 1 mi. south. **General Store:** Yes. **Vending:** Yes. **Swimming:** Pool, river. **Playground:** Yes. **Other:** Mini-golf, basketball, cabins, snack bar, trout fishing, horseback riding, events w/ activities director, recreation field. **Activities:** Volleyball, fishing, swimming. **Nearby Attractions:** Cherokee Courthouse. **Additional Information:** Gore Chamber, (918) 489-2534.

RESTRICTIONS

Pets: On leash, cleaned up after. **Fires:** Grill only. **Alcoholic Beverages:** At sites. **Vehicle Maximum Length:** No limit. **Other:** No ATVs.

TO GET THERE

From I-40 Exit 287, turn north onto Hwy. 100 and go 5.9 mi. Turn right onto Gore Landing Rd. and go 0.2 mi. Turn left onto Marval Ln. and go straight into the campground.

GORE   MAP, B-4
Pettit Bay

reserve america

Rte. 1 Box 259, 74435-9547. T: (918) 487-5252; www.reserveamerica.com.

🚐 ★★★★   ⛺ ★★★★

Beauty: ★★★   Site Privacy: ★★
Spaciousness: ★★   Quiet: ★
Security: ★   Cleanliness: ★★★★
Insect Control: ★★★   Facilities: ★★★

In Oklahoma's Green Country, Pettit Bay Campground on Lake Tenkiller is a recreational paradise. Tenkiller Ferry Lake, or more simply, "Lake Tenkiller," is a reservoir in eastern Oklahoma formed by the damming of the Illinois River. The earth-fill dam was constructed between 1947 and 1952 by the United States Army Corps of Engineers for purposes of flood control and hydroelectric power generation. The lake covers 12,900 acres in the Cookson Hills of Cherokee and Sequoyah counties, about 7 miles northeast of the town of Gore. Tenkiller is nestled in the foothills of the Ozark Mountains, surrounded with dogwood forests, hilly terrain, and beautiful foliage from spring until fall, when the changing autumn leaves draw many travelers around the lake and up scenic highway 10. It also serves as one of the flyways of migratory animals, such as Canada geese, ducks, monarch butterflies, warblers, bald eagles, and many others. Camping, fishing, sightseeing, scuba diving, and picnicking are just a few of the activities enjoyed by visitors. There are 93 campsites, showers and toilets, swimming beaches, playground, and wheelchair-accessible campsites and boat ramps. There is a marina concession in the middle of the park loops.

BASICS
Operated By: U.S. Army Corps of Engineers. **Open:** Jan. 1–Sept. 30. **Site Assignment:** Reservations must be made at least 2 days in advance. **Registration:** At office. **Fee:** Single, $10–$18. **Parking:** At site.

FACILITIES
Number of Multipurpose Sites: 225. **Hookups:** Yes. **Dump Station:** Yes. **Laundry:** No. **Pay Phone:** Yes. **Restrooms and Showers:** Yes. **Fuel:** No. **Propane:** No. **Internal Roads:** Paved. **RV Service:** No. **Market:** No. **Restaurant:** No. **General Store:** Yes. **Vending:** No. **Swimming:** Yes. **Playground:** Yes. **Activities:** Fishing, sightseeing, scuba diving & picnicking.

RESTRICTIONS
Pets: Pets must be restrained or on a leash at all times while in developed recreation areas. **Fires:** In fire rings, stoves, grills, or fireplaces provided for that purpose. **Alcoholic Beverages:** Not allowed. **Vehicle Maximum Length:** Call ahead.

TO GET THERE
From Tahlequah, OK: Go 8.5 mi. south on Hwy. 82, turn right on Indian Rd. and go 2 mi. south, then turn left and go 1 mi. southeast on the paved access road.

GROVE   MAP, A-4
Cedar Oaks RV Resort

1550 83rd St., 74344.
T: (800) 880-8884 or (918) 786-4303.

🚐 ★★★★★   ⛺ n/a

Beauty: ★★★★★   Site Privacy: ★★★★
Spaciousness: ★★★★   Quiet: ★★★★★
Security: ★★★★★   Cleanliness: ★★★★★
Insect Control: ★★★★   Facilities: ★★★★★

This RV park lives up to the standards implied by the word "resort." Sites are highly developed, averaging 30 feet wide, with nice grassy sections next to paved strips. The park is divided into two sections: the main park to the north and a smaller loop to the south. In the main section, sites 1–17 lie along the entrance road, and have nothing to recommend them (besides being in a nice park). Sites 18–31 back to the first 17 sites, and like them are 58-foot back-ins without any outstanding features. Sites 32–45 and 50–63 are 65-foot pull-throughs in the middle of the park that have decent views of the lake when the park is mostly empty. 46–49 and 74–76 are 51-foot back-ins located in a strip along the north edge. Site 76 is a good alternative to one of the pull-throughs, as it commands a very nice view of the lake. The most exquisite sites, however, are 64–73. These are 65-foot pull-throughs facing the lake. End site 73 has an enormous grassy section adjacent to it. The southern section of the park contains sites 77–110 in a large loop. These are all 45-foot back-ins on the outside of the loop. (The inside will contain some enormous 100-foot pull-throughs, but they are as-yet unfinished.) Sites 88–96 have the best views, while 80–86 are closest to the bathhouse. All facilities are sparkling clean, and the park has a security guard for peace of mind. Campers in this resort can count on a comfortable and secure stay.

BASICS
Operated By: The Coats Family. **Open:** All year. **Site Assignment:** Upon registration; verbal reservations highly recommended. **Registration:** At office. (Late arrivals use drop box.) **Fee:** $21; check, V, MC. **Parking:** At site.

FACILITIES
Number of RV-only Sites: 125. **Hookups:** Electric (30, 50 amps), water, sewer. **Each Site:** Picnic table, patio. **Dump Station:** Yes. **Laundry:** Yes. **Pay Phone:** Yes. **Restrooms and Showers:** Yes. **Fuel:** No. **Propane:** No. **Internal Roads:** Paved/gravel. **RV Service:** No. **Market:** 1.5 mi. over bridge. **Restaurant:** Less than 0.5 mi. southeast. **General Store:** Yes. **Vending:** No. **Swimming:** Lake. **Playground:** No. **Other:** Dock, boat ramps, private cove, meeting rooms (w/ kitchen), RV & boat storage, data port, pavilion. **Activities:** Boating, swimming, fishing, shuffleboard, horseshoes. **Nearby Attractions:** Har-Ber Village. **Additional Information:** Grove Area Chamber of Commerce, (918) 786-9079.

RESTRICTIONS
Pets: On leash, cleaned up after. **Fires:** Grill only. **Alcoholic Beverages:** At sites. **Vehicle Maximum Length:** No limit. **Other:** No tents.

TO GET THERE
From the junction of Hwy. 10 north and Hwy. 59 north, turn northwest onto Hwy. 59 and go 3.2 mi. Turn left at the sign into the entrance.

GUTHRIE   MAP, B-3
Pioneer RV Park

1601 Seward Rd., 73044. T: (405) 282-3557.

🚐 ★★★★   ⛺ ★★★

Beauty: ★★★★   Site Privacy: ★★★★
Spaciousness: ★★★★   Quiet: ★★★★
Security: ★★★★   Cleanliness: ★★★★
Insect Control: ★★★★   Facilities: ★★★

Laid out in strips, this campground offers grassy pull-throughs throughout the park and back-ins along the eastern edge. These back-ins (1–12) back to a chain-link fence, beyond which lie green agricultural fields. Sites 13–21 are 70-foot pull-throughs on the eastern side of the park, and 24–30 are 75-foot pull-throughs dead in the middle. Being an end site, 21 has a more generous amount of space and a shade tree, which make it one of the nicest sites in the park. To the west lie two rows of 70-foot pull-throughs, of which the southernmost strip (37–48) has slightly nicer sites due to their proximity to the tenting area and the view to the south. (The best views are from 30 and 36.) Site 32 has extremely limited space due to the landscaping and a fountain that encroaches on this space. Tenting is permitted on a strip along the southern edge of the campground. There is nice grass, but no real shade. RVers will be pleased with this campground, and tenters will enjoy a pleasant enough stay at this park.

BASICS
Operated By: Bill & Sue True. **Open:** All year. **Site Assignment:** Upon registration; reservations require credit card; cancellation requires 1-week notice. **Registration:** At office. (Late arrivals pay in morning.) **Fee:** RV, $17.50; tent, $10; check, V, MC. **Parking:** At site.

FACILITIES
Number of RV-only Sites: 72. **Number of Tent-only Sites:** 4. **Hookups:** Electric (30, 50 amps), water, sewer. **Each Site:** None. **Dump Station:** No (sewer at all sites). **Laundry:** Yes. **Pay Phone:** Yes. **Restrooms and Showers:** Yes. **Fuel:** No. **Propane:** Yes. **Internal Roads:** Gravel. **RV Service:** No. **Market:** 6 mi. north. **Restaurant:** 6 mi. north. **General Store:** Yes. **Vending:** Yes. **Swimming:** No. **Playground:** No. **Other:** Clubhouse. **Activities:** Tours to Oklahoma City, visiting museums. **Nearby Attractions:** Scottish Rite Temple, State Capital Publishing Museum, Oklahoma City. **Additional Information:** Guthrie CVB, (800) 299-1889 or (405) 282-1947.

RESTRICTIONS
Pets: On leash, cleaned up after. **Fires:** Grill only. **Alcoholic Beverages:** At sites. **Vehicle Maximum Length:** No limit.

TO GET THERE
From I-35 Exit 151, go 0.55 mi. Turn right at the sign into the campground.

GUYMON
MAP, C-2 INSET
Southwind RV Park

reserve america

3941 SW Hwy. 54, Rte. 3 Box 52-A, 73942.
T: (877) 861-8103 or (580) 338-7415.
www.reserveamerica.com

🚐 ★★★   ⛺ ★★

Beauty: ★★★	Site Privacy: ★★★★
Spaciousness: ★★★★	Quiet: ★★★
Security: ★★★★	Cleanliness: ★★★
Insect Control: ★★★★	Facilities: ★★★

This campground is arranged in rows of odd- and even-numbered pull-through sites. The odd-numbered sites in the row on the east side are 36–45 feet, while the even-numbered sites to the west are longer: 36–65 feet. The best sites are odd numbers 3–23, as they are longer, they face an agricultural field, they are located away from the mobile homes, and they have larger trees. The least desirable sites are the even-numbered sites 2–18, which are shorter pull-throughs next to the manager's mobile home and the office. This brings registration traffic right past these sites. There are mobile homes at the southwest end, and some in the campground itself (27, 29). There is only one site under tree coverage—the rest are out in the open and have no shade whatsoever. There is also scattered equipment and a shed in this area, making it less attractive. However, tent sites are well removed from the road, which makes them feel more private. The restroom and showers are modern and clean. RVers will enjoy this campground slightly more than tenters, who may want to check out one of the region's state parks.

BASICS
Operated By: Larry & Shari Remling. **Open:** All year. **Site Assignment:** Upon registration; verbal reservations OK, unless arriving after 6 p.m., which requires credit card; same-day cancellation before 6 p.m. for refund. **Registration:** At office. **Fee:** Inquire at office. Senior rates available. **Parking:** At site.

FACILITIES
Number of RV-only Sites: 40. **Number of Tent-only Sites:** 20. **Hookups:** Electric (30, 50 amps), water, sewer. **Each Site:** Some picnic tables. **Dump Station:** Yes (each site has full sewer hookup). **Laundry:** Yes. **Pay Phone:** Yes. **Restrooms and Showers:** Yes. **Fuel:** No. **Propane:** Cylinder exchange. **Internal Roads:** Gravel. **RV Service:** No. **Market:** 1 mi. outside Guymon. **Restaurant:** 1 mi. northeast. **General Store:** No. **Vending:** No. **Swimming:** No. **Playground:** Yes. **Other:** City water. **Activities:** Visiting museums, fishing, boating, swimming. **Nearby Attractions:** Large rodeo, museums, Optima Lake, Bowling alley, cineplex, Super Wal-Mart. **Additional Information:** Guymon Chamber of Commerce, (580) 338-3376.

RESTRICTIONS
Pets: On leash, cleaned up after. **Fires:** Grill only. **Alcoholic Beverages:** At sites. Under control. **Vehicle Maximum Length:** 65 ft. **Other:** No generators, additional charge for more than 2 people.

TO GET THERE
From the junction of Hwy. 3/136/412 and Hwy. 54, turn onto Hwy. 54 west and go 1.3 mi. southwest. (Keep your eyes peeled for the sign on the left-hand side.) Turn left at the sign onto the dirt road entrance. 54 west, 1 mi. out of Guymon.

HINTON
MAP, B-2
Red Rock Canyon State Park

P.O. Box 502, 73047.
T: (800) 654-8240 or (405) 542-6344;
www.touroklahoma.com.

🚐 ★★★★   ⛺ ★★★★★

Beauty: ★★★★★	Site Privacy: ★★★★
Spaciousness: ★★★★	Quiet: ★★★★★
Security: ★★★★	Cleanliness: ★★★
Insect Control: ★★★	Facilities: ★★★

Stunning views of red canyon walls and campsites smothered in shade trees: If that sounds unattractive to you, stay away from this campground. But everyone else should definitely make a stop here! This campground has sites divided into Areas 1–4. Area 1 has water and electric sites right up against the canyon walls. There are loads of trees, but some sites have only dirt and no grass. The section of the road leading to 5–7 is in disrepair, and may present a challenge. Sites 11–18 are 40- to 65-foot grassy back-ins, while 8 could fit a rig of any size. Some sites are not perfectly level. This area is also used for rappelling on the rocks, and therefore it sees a fair amount of day traffic. Area 2 offers group camping with 45-foot back-ins. These sites are more open, with shade trees around the perimeter. Area 3 has full hookups and open 50-foot back-ins in an area separated from the road. All sites have concrete slabs and grass, and some have shade trees. This is the easiest place for RVs to camp, as it involves the least amount of turns or technical driving. Area 4 is for overflow camping, but is used even when the other areas are not all full. These are the farthest sites in, and are less developed. These grassy, shaded sites are well off the road, but also have some degree of slope. Sites at the extreme south end (in the 50s and 60s) are in an open field with little shade. The restrooms are small but quite clean. This is a beautiful campground that will appeal to the whole family, whether in an RV or tents.

BASICS
Operated By: Oklahoma State Park. **Open:** All year. **Site Assignment:** First come, first served; no reservations. **Registration:** At office. Fees collected at sites. **Fee:** RV (full), $18; water/electric, $15; tent, $8. **Parking:** At site.

FACILITIES
Number of RV-only Sites: 52. **Number of Tent-only Sites:** 32. **Hookups:** Electric (30, 50 amps), water, sewer. **Each Site:** Picnic table, grill. **Dump Station:** Yes. **Laundry:** No. **Pay Phone:** Yes. **Restrooms and Showers:** Yes. **Fuel:** No. **Propane:** No. **Internal Roads:** Paved, gravel. **RV Service:** No. **Market:** 6 mi. in Hinton. **Restaurant:** 6 mi. in Hinton. **General Store:** No. **Vending:** No. **Swimming:** Pool. **Playground:** Yes. **Activities:** Swimming, rappelling, rock hounding, volleyball, hiking, horseback riding. **Nearby Attractions:** Ft. Cobb State Park, Crowder Lake State Park. **Additional Information:** Hinton Chamber of Commerce, (405) 542-6428.

RESTRICTIONS
Pets: On leash, cleaned up after. **Fires:** Grill only. **Alcoholic Beverages:** At sites. **Vehicle Maximum Length:** No limit. **Other:** 14-days stay limit, no amplified music.

TO GET THERE
From I-40, take Exit 101 and turn south onto Hwy. 2/281. Go 5.2 mi. then turn left at the sign into the entrance. The entrance road is steep and winding.

HODGEN
MAP, B-4
Big Cedar RV Park

0.3 mi. west of US 259 on OK 63, 74939.
T: (918) 651-3271; www.big-cedar.net.

🚐 ★★★★   ⛺ ★★★

Beauty: ★★★★	Site Privacy: ★★★★
Spaciousness: ★★★★	Quiet: ★★★★★
Security: ★★★★★	Cleanliness: ★★★★★
Insect Control: ★★★	Facilities: ★★★

This rural campground is surrounded by lush woods and forested hills to the north and east. It has a down-home, farmlike atmosphere and grassy pull-through sites laid out in rows. Sites are a lengthy 75 feet and a uniform 24 feet wide. The most desirable sites are the lowest in number (1–6), as these are farthest from the highway and closest to the "Bath Barn." Site 1 contains a tree, but is not itself shaded. Sites 12 and 13 share a small shed that impinges slightly on their space. The tenting area is an open field on the south and east sides of the RV sites. There is a very nice grass cover, which will appeal to tenters, and one large tree, but otherwise the tenting area is quite open. The laundry is spacious and clean and contains two small showers (normally not used). The facilities in the "Bath Barn" are self-contained units that include nicely decorated restrooms with a vanity and showers. All facilities are kept immaculate. Although this is a small campground, it is worthy as a destination, and its family-run atmosphere will make all visitors feel comfortable.

BASICS
Operated By: Darryl Medders. **Open:** All year. **Site Assignment:** First come, first served; verbal reservations OK. **Registration:** At office. (Late arrivals use drop box.) **Fee:** $20; check, V, MC. **Parking:** At site.

FACILITIES
Number of RV-only Sites: 21. **Number of Tent-only Sites:** Undesignated sites. **Hookups:** Electric (30, 50 amps), water, sewer. **Each Site:** Picnic table, fire rings. **Dump Station:** Yes. **Laundry:** Yes. **Pay Phone:** No. **Restrooms and Showers:** Yes. **Fuel:** No (0.3 mi.). **Propane:** No (0.3 mi.). **Internal Roads:** Gravel. **RV Service:** No. **Market:** 5 mi. in Muse. **Restaurant:** 5 mi. in Big Cedar. **General Store:** No. **Vending:** No. **Swimming:** No. **Playground:** No. **Activities:** Hiking, scenic drives, wildlife watching. **Nearby Attractions:** Winding Stair National Wildlife Reserve. **Additional Information:** Talihina Chamber of Commerce, (918) 567-3434.

RESTRICTIONS

Pets: On leash, cleaned up after. **Fires:** In grills & fire rings only. **Alcoholic Beverages:** At sites. **Vehicle Maximum Length:** No limit.

TO GET THERE

From the junction of Hwy. 63 and Hwy. 259, go 0.35 mi. west on Hwy. 63. Turn left at the sign into the entrance. The office is the green building on the left.

KINGFISHER   MAP, B-2
Sleepee Hollo RV Park

918 North Main, 73750. T: (405) 375-5010.

🚐 ★★★★   ▲ ★★★

Beauty: ★★★★	Site Privacy: ★★★★
Spaciousness: ★★★★	Quiet: ★★★
Security: ★★★★	Cleanliness: ★★★★
Insect Control: ★★★★	Facilities: ★★★

Farms surround this campground to the north, west, and south, giving it a rural feel. Sites are grassy and level pull-throughs, many of which are not numbered. Sites 1–7 are all super-long (105- to 120-foot) pull-throughs, all but one of which are well shaded. A row of unnumbered back-in sites to the south range in length from 45 feet (in the southeast corner) to 90 feet (in the southwest corner). One RV site just in front of the office is a shady, all-grass site that is quite attractive. The rest of the sites to the west and north are unnumbered sites on an open, grassy field. These are huge back-ins, ranging from 45 feet to 90 feet long. There is a potential to pull-through on some sites, if neighboring sites are vacant. Tenters have a huge, open space to the west in which to pitch a tent. The field is grassy, but has no shade trees. This is an attractive campground with lots of trees inside, and farms with cattle surround the perimeter. It makes a nice stop for any kind of camper, although is slightly better for RVs than tents.

BASICS

Operated By: Joe Farrell. **Open:** All year. **Site Assignment:** Upon registration; verbal reservations OK. **Registration:** At office. (Late arrivals select site & pay in the morning.) **Fee:** RV (50 amps), $19.50; RV (30 amps), $16.50; tent, $8. **Parking:** At site.

FACILITIES

Number of RV-only Sites: 29. **Number of Tent-only Sites:** Undesignated sites. **Hookups:** Electric (30, 50 amps), water, sewer. **Each Site:** None. **Dump Station:** Yes. **Laundry:** Yes. **Pay Phone:** Yes. **Restrooms and Showers:** Yes. **Fuel:** No. **Propane:** No. **Internal Roads:** Gravel. **RV Service:** No. **Market:** 2 mi. south. **Restaurant:** 2 mi. south. **General Store:** No. **Vending:** Yes. **Swimming:** No. **Playground:** No. **Other:** Basement for entertainment or storm shelter, pet walk area. **Activities:** Hiking, tours, biking. **Nearby Attractions:** Chisholm Trail Museum & Governor Seay Mansion, Oklahoma City. **Additional Information:** Kingfisher Chamber of Commerce, (405) 375-5176.

RESTRICTIONS

Pets: On leash, cleaned up after. **Fires:** Grill only. **Alcoholic Beverages:** At sites. **Vehicle Maximum Length:** No limit.

TO GET THERE

From the junction of Hwy. 33 and Hwy. 81, go 0.8 mi. north on Hwy. 81. Turn left at the sign into the entrance.

MUSKOGEE   MAP, B-4
Crossroads RV Park

P.O. Box 95-5, 74454. T: (918) 686-9104.

🚐 ★★★   ▲ ★★★

Beauty: ★★★	Site Privacy: ★★★
Spaciousness: ★★★★	Quiet: ★★★
Security: ★★★★	Cleanliness: ★★★★
Insect Control: ★★★★	Facilities: ★★★

As this RV park has numerous long-term residents, a sign indicates to all visitors that only sites 1–17 and B1–8 are for overnighters. Sites 1–17 are all large gravel sites in the north part of the park. Sites 1–10 are open-ended pull-throughs that can fit a rig of any size. End site 10 has a grassy space, which the other sites lack. In a row slightly east of the first strip, sites 11–17 are open-ended back-ins that can reasonably accommodate about 50–60 feet before encroaching on the (undefined) gravel drive. Sites B1-8 are in the southeast corner of the park. All of these sites are open-ended pull-throughs that can take RVs of almost any size (with the exception of B8, which is somewhat restricted in size due to its proximity to another site.) All other sites in the park are for long-term guests or mobile homes. This is a good overnight stay for RVers—moreso than for tenters—but lacks a certain something to make it as a destination.

BASICS

Operated By: Janie Burwell. **Open:** All year. **Site Assignment:** Upon registration; verbal reservations OK. **Registration:** At office. (Late arrivals use drop box.) **Fee:** RV (30 amps), $15; RV (50 amps), $16; tent, $8. **Parking:** At site.

FACILITIES

Number of RV-only Sites: 48. **Number of Tent-only Sites:** 5. **Hookups:** Electric (30, 50 amps), water, sewer. **Each Site:** Picnic table, grill. **Dump Station:** No. **Laundry:** Yes. **Pay Phone:** Yes. **Restrooms and Showers:** Yes. **Fuel:** No. **Propane:** Yes. **Internal Roads:** Gravel. **RV Service:** No. **Market:** 7 mi. to Muskogee. **Restaurant:** 6 mi. to Muskogee. **General Store:** No. **Vending:** Yes. **Swimming:** No. **Playground:** No. **Other:** Pavilion. **Activities:** Fishing, boating, swimming, hiking. **Nearby Attractions:** Ataloa Lodge Museum, Five Civilized Tribes Museum, Sequoya Bay State Park. **Additional Information:** Muskogee Convention & Tourism, (918) 684-6363.

RESTRICTIONS

Pets: On leash, cleaned up after. **Fires:** Grill only. **Alcoholic Beverages:** At sites. **Vehicle Maximum Length:** No limit.

TO GET THERE

From the junction of Hwy. 16/62 and Hwy. 69, go north on Hwy. 69 4.8 mi. (2 mi. north of the Arkansas River). At the junction with Hwy. 51B, turn right and go straight into the campground.

OOLOGAH   MAP, A-4
Spencer Creek

reserve america

P.O. Box 700, 74053-0700. T: (918) 341-3690; www.reserveamerica.com.

🚐 ★★★★   ▲ ★★★★

Beauty: ★★★	Site Privacy: ★★★
Spaciousness: ★★★	Quiet: ★★★★
Security: ★★★★	Cleanliness: ★★★★
Insect Control: ★★★	Facilities: ★★★★

Spencer Creek Campground is located on Oologah Lake. The lake provides a great getaway for fishing, boating, picnicking, camping, or just drifting and dreaming over the sky-blue waters. Plenty of wide stretches of water perfect for catching the wind make it one of the most popular lakes in the area for sailing. The forested hills around the lake provide excellent hunting opportunities. In 1974, the Army Corps of Engineers completed construction of the Oologah Dam and Lake Oologah, located in Rogers and Nowata counties, 30 miles northeast of Tulsa. As Tulsa's water demands were once again rapidly increasing, the City obtained rights for water from Lake Oologah, and construction began on a pipeline from the lake to the A. B. Jewell water treatment plant in 1976. The Lake Oologah watershed, an area of over 4,000 square miles that extends into Kansas, was the scene of intense oil and gas exploration and production starting in 1905, and production still continues at some wells. Oil and gas were produced from the Bartlesville Sand Formation, which is between 400 and 750 feet below the surface. On the Oklahoma side of the watershed alone, over 15,000 wells were drilled. Many of these were subsequently plugged, but many were abandoned without proper plugging. In addition, there are still many abandoned tanks and pumps, and some areas around the lake contain oil-contaminated soil. In 1999, the Environmental Protection Agency (EPA) and the Oklahoma Corporation Commission began a pilot project to locate and plug any remaining abandoned wells in the area around the lake. The goal is to restore the well sites as close as possible to their natural condition. Eleven public use areas are scattered around the lake and offer a variety of facilities making it easy to find something that's just right for you. The Campground offers 69 campsites.

BASICS

Operated By: U.S. Army Corps of Engineers. **Open:** Apr. 1–Sept. 30. **Site Assignment:** Reservations must be made at least 2 days in advance. **Registration:** At office. **Fee:** Single, $12–$16. **Parking:** At site.

FACILITIES

Number of Multipurpose Sites: 204. **Hookups:** Yes. **Dump Station:** Yes. **Laundry:** No. **Pay Phone:** Yes. **Restrooms and Showers:** Yes. **Fuel:** No. **Propane:** No. **Internal Roads:** Gravel. **RV Service:** No. **Market:** No. **Restaurant:** No. **General Store:** No. **Vending:** No. **Swimming:** Yes. **Playground:** Yes. **Activities:** Fishing, boating, picnicking.

RESTRICTIONS

Pets: Pets must be restrained or on a leash at all times while in developed recreation areas. **Fires:** In fire rings, stoves, grills, or fireplaces provided for that purpose. **Alcoholic Beverages:** Not allowed. **Vehicle Maximum Length:** Call ahead.

TO GET THERE

15 mi. from Oologah, OK, via county roads. Follow signs to campground entrance.

SALLISAW — Cowlington Point
MAP, B-4

reserve america

HC 61 Box 238, 74955-9445. T: (918) 775-4475; www.reserveamerica.com.

🚐 ★★★★ ⛺ ★★★★

Beauty: ★★★★	Site Privacy: ★★★
Spaciousness: ★★★	Quiet: ★★
Security: ★★	Cleanliness: ★★★★
Insect Control: ★★★	Facilities: ★★★

Cowlington Point Campground is located on Robert S. Kerr Lock and Dam and Reservoir. The lake area is beautiful any time of the year. It is especially scenic when flowering shrubs and leaf buds decorate the landscape with a soft glow in spring, or when the brilliant colors of fall start to unfold. For young and old alike, Kerr Lake has a variety of recreation, from swimming on the many beaches to camping and picnicking in one of the nine park areas. Camping areas are open year-round and include facilities such as boat-launching ramps, designated camp sites with full hookups, electric/water hookups, picnic areas, drinking water, shower facilities, and sanitary facilities. Robert S. Kerr Lake provides excellent opportunities for fishing and hunting. Principal species of fish in the lake include channel catfish, flathead catfish, white crappie, largemouth bass, striped bass, walleye, and various sunfish species. Whether by powerboat, sailboat or any type of craft, the broad expanse and depth of the water just above the dam and extending about 7 miles upstream will satisfy the demand for any type of pleasure craft. Cowlington Point offers 38 campsites, 32 with electric and water hookups. Other amenities include a trailer dump station, vault toilets, group picnic shelter, and a swimming beach. Kerr Reservoir is a 42,000-surface-acre lake located on the Oklahoma portion of the McClellan-Kerr Arkansas River Navigation System that offers extensive opportunities for outdoor recreation such as hunting, fishing, boating, camping, picnicking, and swimming.

BASICS

Operated By: U.S. Army Corps of Engineers. **Open:** May 1–Sept. 30. **Site Assignment:** Reservations must be made at least 3 days in advance. **Registration:** At office. **Fee:** Single, $15; group, $50. **Parking:** At site.

FACILITIES

Number of Multipurpose Sites: 94. **Hookups:** Yes. **Dump Station:** Yes. **Laundry:** No. **Pay Phone:** No. **Restrooms and Showers:** Yes. **Fuel:** No. **Propane:** No. **Internal Roads:** Paved. **RV Service:** No. **Market:** No. **Restaurant:** No. **General Store:** No. **Vending:** No. **Swimming:** Yes. **Playground:** No. **Other:** No Sat. reservation arrivals allowed on regular weekends. No Sat. or Sun. reservation arrivals allowed on holiday weekends. **Activities:** Hunting, fishing, boating, camping, picnicking, & swimming.

RESTRICTIONS

Pets: Pets must be restrained or on a leash at all times while in developed recreation areas. **Fires:** In fire rings, stoves, grills, or fireplaces provided for that purpose. **Alcoholic Beverages:** Not allowed. **Vehicle Maximum Length:** Call ahead.

TO GET THERE

Go 12 mi. south of Sallisaw, OK, on US 59, then 4 mi. west on paved county road following the signs to the campground.

SALLISAW — Lakeside RV Park
MAP, B-4

P.O. Box 1414, 74955. T: (918) 775-7522.

🚐 ★★★★ ⛺ n/a

Beauty: ★★★	Site Privacy: ★★★★★
Spaciousness: ★★★★★	Quiet: ★★★★
Security: ★★★★	Cleanliness: ★★★★★
Insect Control: ★★★★	Facilities: ★★★★

With woods to the north, east, and west, this campground has a definite rural feel, despite the numerous residences close to it. Sites are arranged in two rows of pull-throughs, with back-ins along the east and west sides. (Sites 21–28 to the west are reserved for long-term guests.) Back-ins 1–6 on the eastern edge of the campground are 60 by 45 feet. Site 6 is closest to the (covered) pool, whereas end sites 1 and 11 are farthest from the entrance and closest to the woods to the north, making these the nicest overnight spots. The eastern strip of pull-throughs boasts some incredibly long sites that range from 75 feet (13) to 90 feet (14) to 105 feet (15). End site 20 is slightly shorter, at 65 feet. The rec room is comfortable and tastefully furnished, and the restrooms (individual unisex units) would look great in anyone's home. One small drawback is that the coin-op shower runs for only four minutes per quarter. All facilities are clean and incredibly comfy, making this a very pleasant stay. (Note that there is an overt Christian theme to the park, with pamphlets, iconography, and other religious paraphernalia scattered throughout.)

BASICS

Operated By: Paula & Mike Mouzakis. **Open:** Mar.

15–Nov. 15. **Site Assignment:** Upon registration, but flexible; verbal reservations OK. **Registration:** At office. (Late arrivals use drop box.) **Fee:** RV (50 amps), $20; (30 amps), $18. **Parking:** At site.

FACILITIES

Number of RV-only Sites: 28. **Hookups:** Electric (30, 50 amps), water, sewer. **Each Site:** Picnic table. **Dump Station:** No (sewer at all sites). **Laundry:** Yes. **Pay Phone:** No. **Restrooms and Showers:** Yes. **Fuel:** No. **Propane:** Yes. **Internal Roads:** Gravel. **RV Service:** No. **Market:** 7 mi. to Sallisaw. **Restaurant:** 2 blocks. **General Store:** Across street. **Vending:** No. **Swimming:** Pool. **Playground:** No. **Other:** Rec room (w/ TV & chairs), pavilion. **Activities:** Board games. **Nearby Attractions:** Fourteen Flags Museum, Sequoyah's Home site. **Additional Information:** Sallisaw Chamber of Commerce, (918) 775-2558.

RESTRICTIONS

Pets: On leash, cleaned up after. **Fires:** Grill only. **Alcoholic Beverages:** At sites. **Vehicle Maximum Length:** No limit.

TO GET THERE

From I-40 Exit 308, turn south onto Hwy. 59 and go 7.2 mi. Turn left at the sign into the campground.

SAWYER — Sawyer RV Park
MAP, C-4

HC 66 Box 1430, 74756. T: (580) 326-0830.

🚐 ★★★★★ ⛺ ★★★★

Beauty: ★★★★★	Site Privacy: ★★★★
Spaciousness: ★★★★	Quiet: ★★★★★
Security: ★★★★★	Cleanliness: ★★★★★
Insect Control: ★★★★	Facilities: ★★★★

Surrounded by forest and pastureland, this campground has both a wilderness and an on-the-farm feel. The campground is very pretty (there are flowers and a small white fence that run along the entryway), and is located just 1 mile from the Hugo Lake Recreation Area. Sites are back-ins arranged on the outside of a loop. Sites 1–8 are 40-foot back-ins, while sites 14–17 can accommodate an RV of any size. Sites 10 and (especially) 11 have the best shade in the park and can likewise accommodate a big rig. Sites 1–4 have grassy patches but little shade. The restroom facility is a small individual restroom and shower in the laundry. All facilities are kept extremely clean. This is definitely one of the nicest parks in the region. Although small, it is a deserving destination for RV campers. Even campers who don't take advantage of the nearby Hugo Lake facilities will enjoy a stay at this park.

BASICS

Operated By: Rex Lyons. **Open:** All year. **Site Assignment:** Flexible, depending on availability; verbal reservations OK. **Registration:** At office. **Fee:** $14; check, no credit cards. **Parking:** At site.

FACILITIES

Number of RV-only Sites: 18. **Hookups:** Electric (30 amps), water, sewer, Wi-Fi. **Each Site:** Picnic table. **Dump Station:** No (sewer at all sites).

Laundry: Yes. **Pay Phone:** No. **Restrooms and Showers:** Yes. **Fuel:** No. **Propane:** No. **Internal Roads:** Gravel. **RV Service:** No. **Market:** 12 mi. to Hugo. **Restaurant:** 12 mi. to Hugo. **General Store:** No. **Vending:** No. **Swimming:** No (Lake). **Playground:** No. **Other:** Wildlife. **Activities:** Swimming, boating, fishing. **Nearby Attractions:** Hugo Lake, Raymond Gary State Park. **Additional Information:** Choctaw County Chamber of Commerce, (580) 326-7511.

RESTRICTIONS

Pets: On leash, cleaned up after. **Fires:** Grill only. **Alcoholic Beverages:** At site. **Vehicle Maximum Length:** No limit. **Other:** No refunds.

TO GET THERE

From the junction of Hwy. 70 and Hwy. 147, turn north onto Hwy. 147 and go 2.6 mi. Turn at the sign for Virgil Point Park.

SAWYER — MAP, C-4
Virgil Point

P.O. Box 99, 74756-0099. T: (580) 326-3345; www.reserveamerica.com.

🚐 ★★★★   ▲ ★★★★

Beauty: ★★★   Site Privacy: ★★
Spaciousness: ★★   Quiet: ★★★★★
Security: ★★★★★   Cleanliness: ★★★★
Insect Control: ★★★   Facilities: ★★★★

Virgil Point Campground is located on Hugo Lake on the Kiamichi River, about 7 miles east of Hugo, Oklahoma. Sportsmen will find a wide variety of fish, including largemouth and spotted bass, crappie, white bass, channel and flathead catfish, bluegill, sunfish, buffalo, carp, and drum. Skiers and speedboat enthusiasts can enjoy some 8,000 acres of open water in the lake. Boating lanes have been provided in the uncleared upper half of the lake for easy access by anglers. The Kiamichi River begins in eastern Le Flore County near the Arkansas border and flows about 165 miles in a south-southwest direction to the Red River on the Texas border. Generally the Kiamichi River is a flat, somewhat-slow river, but potential for Class I–II whitewater run at high water. Class II–III rapids on the extreme upper end near its headwaters. Access is very limited, as are commercial services, making this river more appropriate for the true adventure seeker. Be sure to bring everything you need when you visit the Kiamichi River. Recreational facilities including boat-launching ramps, group camping, picnic and camping areas, playgrounds, beaches, and bicycle and hiking trails at public-use areas around the lake.

BASICS

Operated By: U.S. Army Corps of Engineers. **Open:** Apr. 1–Sept. 30. **Site Assignment:** Reservations must be made at least 2 days in advance. **Registration:** At office. **Fee:** Single, $15. **Parking:** At site.

FACILITIES

Number of Multipurpose Sites: 128. **Hookups:** Yes. **Dump Station:** Yes. **Laundry:** No. **Pay Phone:** No. **Restrooms and Showers:** Yes. **Fuel:** No. **Propane:** No. **Internal Roads:** Paved. **RV Service:** No. **Market:** No. **Restaurant:** No. **General Store:** No. **Vending:** No. **Swimming:** No. **Playground:** Yes. **Activities:** Biking, boating, fishing, picnicking, hiking.

RESTRICTIONS

Pets: Pets must be restrained or on a leash at all times while in developed recreation areas. **Fires:** In fire rings, stoves, grills, or fireplaces provided for that purpose. **Alcoholic Beverages:** Not allowed. **Vehicle Maximum Length:** Call ahead.

TO GET THERE

From Hugo, OK: On Hwy. 70, go 10 mi. east to Hwy. 147, turn north, go 2 mi. north on Hwy. 147, turn left at Nell's.

SEMINOLE — MAP, B-3
Round-Up RV Park

Rte. 3 Box 285F, 74868. T: (405) 382-7957.

🚐 ★★★   ▲ n/a

Beauty: ★★★   Site Privacy: ★★★
Spaciousness: ★★★   Quiet: ★★★
Security: ★★★   Cleanliness: ★★★
Insect Control: ★★★★   Facilities: ★★★

Although this park is located in an urban setting, it has some features (such as flowering bushes and a wooden fence) that make it more attractive. In addition, each site has a shade tree, which makes a stay there more comfortable than it would otherwise be (especially in late summer). The restaurant parking lot (as well as the highway) lies to the west of the park, residences border it in the southeast and northeast, and a fishing pond (with a pretty pavilion) sits to the east. The RV sites, all pull-throughs, average 75 by 30 feet in size. End sites 1 and 14 are closest to the pond (1 is right next to the pavilion and its two grills), while end sites 13 and 27 are closest to the parking lot. The best area is in the middle of the south row (sites 19–22, more or less), which faces an open field and is away from both the entrance and the residences. The restrooms are air-conditioned, but rather small and basic. They also seem to suffer from some amount of neglect. Nevertheless, this park and its very nice restaurant make for quite a decent overnight stop.

BASICS

Operated By: Larry Kinslow. **Open:** All year. **Site Assignment:** First come, first served; no reservations. **Registration:** At restaurant. (Late arrivals use drop box.) **Fee:** RV, $14.10; check, V, MC, AE, D. **Parking:** At site.

FACILITIES

Number of RV-only Sites: 36. **Hookups:** Electric (50 amps), water, sewer. **Each Site:** Picnic table. **Dump Station:** Yes. **Laundry:** No. **Pay Phone:** Yes. **Restrooms and Showers:** Yes. **Fuel:** No.

Propane: No. **Internal Roads:** Gravel. **RV Service:** No. **Market:** 7 mi. in town. **Restaurant:** On site. **General Store:** No. **Vending:** No. **Swimming:** No. **Playground:** Yes. **Other:** Fishing pond (catch & release), dog walk, covered pavilion w/ 2 grills. **Activities:** Fishing, festivals. **Nearby Attractions:** Jasmine Moran Children's Museum, festivals. **Additional Information:** Seminole Chamber of Commerce, (405) 382-3640.

RESTRICTIONS

Pets: On leash, cleaned up after. **Fires:** Grill only. **Alcoholic Beverages:** At sites. **Vehicle Maximum Length:** No limit.

TO GET THERE

From I-40 (Exit 200): on the south side of the highway, go 0.2 mi. south on Hwy. 99 to the second commercial complex. Turn left at the sign for the restaurant into the entrance.

SPIRO — MAP, B-4
All-Season Inn/RV Park

Rte. 1 Box 267, 74959. T: (918) 962-2524.

🚐 ★★★   ▲ ★★★

Beauty: ★★★   Site Privacy: ★★★★
Spaciousness: ★★★   Quiet: ★★★★
Security: ★★★★   Cleanliness: ★★★
Insect Control: ★★★★   Facilities: ★★

This rural campground has grassy RV sites situated along a loop. Not all sites are numbered. Sites 2–7 are gravel pull-throughs without any shade. Sites 10 and 15 are 75-foot pull-throughs, while end site 12 is a 60-foot pull-through. Sites 21 and those to either side of 21 are 60-foot back-ins that back to a grassy field and then to woods. These are the nicest sites due to the grass and the natural surroundings. One site (possibly 16) in the southeast corner is exceptionally spacious. Tenting is possible in the field to the south of the RV sites. Tent sites have thick grass but no shade. The one restroom and one shower are acceptably clean.

BASICS

Operated By: Jack Jeffrey. **Open:** All year. **Site Assignment:** Upon registration; verbal reservations OK. **Registration:** At office. (Late arrivals use drop box.) **Fee:** Full, $20; weekly, $90; monthly, $255. **Parking:** At site.

FACILITIES

Number of RV-only Sites: 22. **Number of Tent-only Sites:** 0. **Hookups:** Electric (30 amps), water, sewer. **Each Site:** None. **Dump Station:** No (sewer at all sites). **Laundry:** Yes. **Pay Phone:** No. **Restrooms and Showers:** Yes. **Fuel:** No. **Propane:** No. **Internal Roads:** Gravel. **RV Service:** No. **Market:** Less than 1 mi. east. **Restaurant:** Less than 1 mi. east. **General Store:** No. **Vending:** Yes. **Swimming:** No. **Playground:** No. **Other:** Storm shelter, RV & boat storage. **Activities:** Fishing, boating, swimming, hiking. **Nearby Attractions:** Spiro Mounds Archaeological State Park, Robert S. Kerr Lake. **Additional Information:** Spiro Area Chamber of Commerce, (918) 962-3816.

RESTRICTIONS

Pets: On leash, cleaned up after. **Fires:** Grill only. **Alcoholic Beverages:** Not allowed. **Vehicle Maximum Length:** No limit.

TO GET THERE

From the junction of Main St. and Hwy. 9/271, turn west onto Hwy. 271 and go 1.2 mi. Turn right at the sign into the entrance.

SULPHUR   MAP, C-3
Buckhorn Campground

reserve america

1008 West 2nd, 73086. T: (580) 622-3165; www.reserveamerica.com.

🚐 ★★★★   ⛺ ★★★★

Beauty: ★★★★	Site Privacy: ★★★
Spaciousness: ★★★★	Quiet: ★★★
Security: ★★★★★	Cleanliness: ★★★★
Insect Control: ★★★	Facilities: ★★★★

Buckhorn National Park is located within Chickasaw National Recreation Area. The statement "Peaceful Valley of Rippling Waters" was used to describe this area's significance by early American Indian visitors, and these beautiful words can still be used today to describe Chickasaw National Recreation Area and its many resources. From prehistoric times to the present, access to the combination of cool water, mineral springs, cool breezes, shade, and wildlife has created at Chickasaw National Recreation Area an experience that sets it apart from the surrounding environment. The springs and streams of Chickasaw come from one of the most complex geological and hydrological features in the United States. These resources have been economically and environmentally significant throughout the history of the region, and are valuable for scientific research. Dating from the public works era of the 1930s, classic examples of Civilian Conservation Corps (CCC) architecture blend harmoniously with the natural environment. A trail system was designed and constructed during this period that meets the needs of the casual walker as well as the avid exerciser. The park holds within its boundaries a vast diversity of natural resources. These unique flora, fauna, waters, and geological formations have withstood the external pressures of man-made and natural changes. Chickasaw lies in a transition zone where the Eastern deciduous forest and the Western prairies meet. It has flora and fauna from both environments, and other flora and fauna specific to such transition areas. The view over Veterans Lake, especially beautiful at sunset, illustrates this transition. The park provides opportunities to experience a wide range of outdoor experiences—swimming, boating, fishing, hiking, wildlife viewing, hunting, camping, and picnicking—reminding us of the rural character in the history of the American people. It adds measurably to the quality of life for visitors and area residents. Chickasaw has been the setting for generations of traditional family activity that represents part of our American heritage. The park offers three different levels of water-based recreation: In the protected zone upstream from the nature center, visitors can enjoy the beauty of the natural springs and streams as a visual resource. Veteran's Lake offers a park-like atmosphere, where use is restricted to a slower pace and relatively quiet activities. At the Lake of the Arbuckles, visitors can engage in a full range of activities, including boating and fishing.

BASICS

Operated By: National Park Service. **Open:** May 12–Sept. 13. **Site Assignment:** Reservations must be made 7 days in advance. **Registration:** At registration office. **Fee:** Single, $10–$18. **Parking:** At park.

FACILITIES

Number of Multipurpose Sites: 238. **Hookups:** Yes. **Each Site:** Call ahead. **Dump Station:** Yes. **Laundry:** Less than 10 mi. **Pay Phone:** Yes. **Restrooms and Showers:** Yes. **Fuel:** No. **Propane:** No. **Internal Roads:** Paved. **RV Service:** No. **Market:** Local area. **Restaurant:** Local area. **General Store:** Local area. **Vending:** No. **Swimming:** Yes. **Playground:** No. **Other:** No ORVs, golf carts, or scooters permitted. All vehicles & drivers must be licensed. All water vessels require a Chickasaw National Recreation Area lake permit. **Activities:** Amphitheater, biking, bird-watching, boating, campfire programs, fishing, hiking, horseback riding, photography, sightseeing, waterskiing, wildlife viewing, windsurfing.

RESTRICTIONS

Pets: All pets must be leashed at all times are not permitted w/in the swimming or sunbathing areas. **Fires:** Allowed; Campfire Program. **Alcoholic Beverages:** Not allowed. **Vehicle Maximum Length:** Varies; call ahead.

TO GET THERE

From I-35, take Exit 55 and drive toward Davis, OK. Once in Davis, go east on Hwy. 7 to the Chickasaw National Recreation Area you desire. Watch for the Chickasaw National Recreation Area signs to direct you to your selected area: Buckhorn Campgrounds, Pavilion, and Picnic Area - Drive 8 mi. east of Davis to the only 4-way stop (junction Hwy. 7 and Hwy. 177) in the city of Sulphur. Turn south (right) 5 mi. on Hwy. 177. Turn west (right) at Buckhorn Rd. and drive 3 mi. west. Follow the directional signs. This loop is the southeast corner of Arbuckle Lake.

SULPHUR   MAP, C-3
The Point Campground

reserve america

1008 West 2nd, 73086. T: (580) 622-3165; www.reserveamerica.com.

🚐 ★★★★   ⛺ ★★★★

Beauty: ★★★★	Site Privacy: ★★★★
Spaciousness: ★★★★	Quiet: ★★★
Security: ★★★★★	Cleanliness: ★★★★
Insect Control: ★★★	Facilities: ★★★★

The Point Campground is located within Chickasaw National Recreation Area. The statement "Peaceful Valley of Rippling Waters" was used to describe this area's significance by early American Indian visitors, and these beautiful words can still be used today to describe Chickasaw National Recreation Area and its many resources. From prehistoric times to the present, access to the combination of cool water, mineral springs, cool breezes, shade, and wildlife has created at Chickasaw National Recreation Area an experience that sets it apart from the surrounding environment. The springs and streams of Chickasaw come from one of the most complex geological and hydrological features in the United States. These resources have been economically and environmentally significant throughout the history of the region, and are valuable for scientific research. Dating from the public works era of the 1930s, classic examples of Civilian Conservation Corps (CCC) architecture blend harmoniously with the natural environment. A trail system was designed and constructed during this period that meets the needs of the casual walker as well as the avid exerciser. The park holds within its boundaries a vast diversity of natural resources. These unique flora, fauna, waters, and geological formations have withstood the external pressures of man-made and natural changes. Chickasaw lies in a transition zone where the Eastern deciduous forest and the Western prairies meet. It has flora and fauna from both environments, and other flora and fauna specific to such transition areas. The view over Veterans Lake, especially beautiful at sunset, illustrates this transition. The park provides opportunities to experience a wide range of outdoor experiences— swimming, boating, fishing, hiking, observing nature, hunting, camping, and picnicking—reminding us of the rural character in the history of the American people. It adds measurably to the quality of life for visitors and area residents. Chickasaw has been the setting for generations of traditional family activity that represents part of our American heritage. The park offers three different levels of water-based recreation: In the protected zone upstream from the nature center, visitors can enjoy the beauty of the natural springs and streams as a visual resource. Veteran's Lake offers a park-like atmosphere, where use is restricted to a slower pace and relatively quiet activities. At the Lake of the Arbuckles, visitors can engage in a full range of activities, including boating and fishing.

BASICS

Operated By: National Park Service. **Open:** May 11–Sept. 12. **Site Assignment:** Reservations must be made at least 7 days in advance. **Registration:** At registration office. **Fee:** Single, $10–$16. **Parking:** At park.

FACILITIES

Number of Multipurpose Sites: 45. **Hookups:** Yes. **Each Site:** Call ahead. **Dump Station:** Yes. **Laundry:** Less than 10 mi. **Pay Phone:** Yes. **Restrooms and Showers:** Yes. **Fuel:** No. **Propane:** No. **Internal Roads:** Paved. **RV Service:** No. **Market:** W/in 10 mi. **Restaurant:** W/in 10 mi. **General Store:** W/in 10 mi. **Vending:** No. **Swimming:** Yes. **Playground:** No. **Other:** No

ORVs, golf carts, or scooters permitted. All water vessels require a Chickasaw National Recreation Area lake permit. State permits for hunting & fishing are required w/in Chickasaw National Recreation Area. All food must be kept in proper containers. **Activities:** Amphitheater, biking, bird-watching, boating, campfire programs, canoeing, fishing, hiking, horseback riding, hunting, photography, scuba diving, sightseeing, tubing, waterskiing, wildlife viewing, wind surfing.

RESTRICTIONS

Pets: Pets must be on a leash at all times. **Fires:** Allowed; Campfire Program. **Alcoholic Beverages:** Not allowed. **Vehicle Maximum Length:** Varies; call ahead.

TO GET THERE

From I-35, take Exit 55 and drive toward the city of Davis, OK. Once in Davis, go east on Hwy. 7 to the Chickasaw National Recreation Area you desire. Watch for the Chickasaw National Recreation Area signs to direct you to your selected area.

TAHLEQUAH — MAP, B-4
Diamondhead Resort

12081 Hwy. 10, 74464. T: (800) 722-2411 or (918) 456-4545; www.diamondresort.us.

🚐 ★★★	🏕 ★★★★
Beauty: ★★★★	Site Privacy: ★★★
Spaciousness: ★★★★	Quiet: ★★★★★
Security: ★★★★★	Cleanliness: ★★★
Insect Control: ★★★	Facilities: ★★★

All of the RV sites here are situated in a row in the northwest portion of the campground. These grounds are well maintained. Counting from the southwest by the gravel road, sites 1–10 and 12–16 are under large shade trees, which make them more attractive. Sites 11–22 could conceivably be pull-throughs, if the campground is relatively empty, but 1–10 back to trees and cannot be anything other than back-ins. However, since the field in which they sit is so large, these sites can take a rig of any size. There are loads of tenting sites, none of which are numbered. Since the campground is so natural and is surrounded by woods and the river, this is an ideal site for tenting. Restroom facilities are well maintained. Shower stalls are known as the cleanest on the river. Diamondhead Resort is situated on 43 acres along the beautiful Illinois River. Diamondhead also offers a motel and bunkhouses for lodging. Call ahead for reservations.

BASICS

Operated By: Kevin & Barbara Kelley. **Open:** Apr. 1–Oct. 1. **Site Assignment:** First come, first served; verbal reservations OK. **Registration:** At office, or w/ guard (nights & weekends). **Fee:** RV (electric), $15; tent, $10; V, MC, D. **Parking:** At site.

FACILITIES

Number of RV-only Sites: 22. **Number of Tent-only Sites:** Undesignated sites. **Hookups:** Electric (30 amps). **Each Site:** Picnic table, grill. **Dump Station:** Yes. **Laundry:** No. **Pay Phone:** No. **Restrooms and Showers:** Yes. **Fuel:** No.

Propane: No. **Internal Roads:** Gravel. **RV Service:** No. **Market:** 7 mi. to Talequah. **Restaurant:** 3 mi. toward Talequah. **General Store:** Yes. **Vending:** No. **Swimming:** River. **Playground:** No. **Other:** Canoe, raft, & kayak rentals. **Activities:** Canoeing, volleyball, basketball, game room. **Nearby Attractions:** Fishing, Elephant Rock hiking trail, horseback riding. **Additional Information:** Talequah Area Chamber of Commerce, (800) 456-4860 or (918) 456-3742.

RESTRICTIONS

Pets: On leash. **Fires:** In grills & rock pits. **Alcoholic Beverages:** At sites. **Vehicle Maximum Length:** No limit. **Other:** No glass or Styrofoam on or near river.

TO GET THERE

From the junction of Hwy. 51/62/82 and Hwy. 10 in town by Wal-Mart, go northeast on Hwy. 10/51/62/82 for 2.2 mi. Turn right onto Downing St. (3rd light) and go 1.9 mi. Turn left onto Scenic Hwy. 10 and go 5.3 mi. Turn right at the sign into the entrance. (Follow the gravel road to the back of the campground for electrical sites.)

TONKAWA — MAP, A-3
Woodland Camper Park

16600 West South Ave., 74653. T: (580) 628-2062.

🚐 ★★★	🏕 ★★★
Beauty: ★★★	Site Privacy: ★★★
Spaciousness: ★★★	Quiet: ★★★
Security: ★★★★	Cleanliness: ★★★
Insect Control: ★★★★	Facilities: ★★★

Just off the interstate, this campground is bordered by a gas station to the west and fields to the north and south. Mostly unnumbered, sites range from 75 feet (east row) to 95 feet (west row) long. They are all undeveloped grassy sites, averaging 40 feet wide. The least desirable sites are the end sites to the south, which are closest to the highway (especially the southeast end site, which also has no shade tree). The most desirable site, in the northeast corner, has a large shade tree, abuts a field, and is farthest from the highway. There is an enormous area where tenting is possible. The best tent site is in front of the house, under a large shade tree (unfortunately, closer to the road). The restrooms and showers are passable. This campground is mainly an overnighter, about equally decent for tenters and RVers.

BASICS

Operated By: Gary & Jo Wood. **Open:** All year. **Site Assignment:** Flexible, depending on availability; verbal reservations OK. **Registration:** At office. (Late arrivals use drop box.) **Fee:** RV (full), $15; tent, $10. **Parking:** At site.

FACILITIES

Number of RV-only Sites: 38. **Number of Tent-only Sites:** 4. **Hookups:** Electric (30 & 50 amps), water, sewer. **Each Site:** None. **Dump Station:** Yes. **Laundry:** No. **Pay Phone:** Across street (restaurant). **Restrooms and Showers:** Yes. **Fuel:** No. **Propane:** No. **Internal Roads:** Paved. **RV Service:** No. **Market:** 2 mi. east. **Restaurant:** Across the

street. **General Store:** Across street. **Vending:** No. **Swimming:** No. **Playground:** No. **Activities:** Boating, swimming, fishing. **Nearby Attractions:** Ponca City, Great Salt Plains State Park. **Additional Information:** Tonkawa Chamber of Commerce, (580) 628-2220.

RESTRICTIONS

Pets: On leash, cleaned up after. **Fires:** Grill only. **Alcoholic Beverages:** At sites. **Vehicle Maximum Length:** No limit.

TO GET THERE

From I-35 (Exit 214): On the west side of the highway, go 0.15 mi. west. Turn right at the sign into the entrance.

VALLIANT — MAP, C-4
Little River Park

reserve america

Rte. 1 Box 400, 74764-9615. T: (580) 876-3720; www.reserveamerica.com.

🚐 ★★★★	🏕 ★★★★
Beauty: ★★★	Site Privacy: ★★
Spaciousness: ★★	Quiet: ★★★★
Security: ★★★★	Cleanliness: ★★★★
Insect Control: ★★★	Facilities: ★★★★

Little River Park, located on the western shore of Pine Creek Lake in extreme southeast Oklahoma, is a popular camping area for those who like to enjoy the outdoors. Activities include camping, swimming, fishing, picnicking, hiking, and boating. Pine Creek Lake is located on the Little River, once part of the Choctaw Indian Nation. Fort Towson, a few miles southwest of the lake, was established in 1824, and it was here in 1865 that Cherokee General Stand Watie surrendered his troops, the last Confederate General to do so. The high ratio of shoreline to water area at Pine Creek Lake is conducive to good fish production. Principal species include crappie, white bass, largemouth bass, channel catfish, flathead catfish, and various sunfish. Most project lands are open for public hunting. There is a group camping shelter within the park, which has five electrical hookups. Additional amenities include hot showers, a dump station, playground, and boat launch.

BASICS

Operated By: U.S. Army Corps of Engineers. **Open:** Mar. 1–Nov. 30. **Site Assignment:** Reservations must be made at least 2 days in advance. **Registration:** At office. **Fee:** Single, $10–$18; group, $65. **Parking:** At site.

FACILITIES

Number of Multipurpose Sites: 206. **Hookups:** Yes. **Dump Station:** Yes. **Laundry:** No. **Pay Phone:** No. **Restrooms and Showers:** Yes. **Fuel:** No. **Propane:** No. **Internal Roads:** Paved. **RV Service:** No. **Market:** No. **Restaurant:** No. **General Store:** No. **Vending:** No. **Swimming:** Yes. **Playground:** Yes. **Activities:** Fishing, picnicking, hiking, & boating.

RESTRICTIONS

Pets: Pets must be restrained or on a leash at all times while in developed recreation areas. **Fires:** In fire rings, stoves, grills, or fireplaces provided for that purpose. **Alcoholic Beverages:** Not allowed. **Vehicle Maximum Length:** Call ahead.

TO GET THERE

From Broken Bow, OK: Take OK 3 south 23 mi. to park entrance. Turn south at sign and follow access road.

WAURIKA	MAP, C-2
Moneka Park	

1645 South 101st Ave., 73573. T: (580) 963-2111; www.lasr.net/lasr/oklahoma/waurika/body.html.

🚐 ★★★   ⛺ ★★★★

Beauty: ★★★★	Site Privacy: ★★★★
Spaciousness: ★★★★	Quiet: ★★★★★
Security: ★★★	Cleanliness: ★★★★
Insect Control: ★★	Facilities: ★★

Sites in this wilderness campground are situated around a loop. Depending on your preference, you can select a site on the outside of the loop (on the right side), nestled into the forest, or on the more open inside of the loop (left side). (Inside sites 12–23 at the south end are also totally forested.) Sites on the west side of the loop (1, 4, 6, and odd 7–17) have short footpaths to the creek. Sites 3 and 36–38 offer the best opportunity to recreate in the grassy field. Less desirable sites are 12 and 13, located at the intersection of two internal roads and therefore subject to road traffic. Sites 18–20 are apt to receive more passing foot traffic due to the proximity of the hiking trail between 18 and 19. Perhaps the only downside to this beautiful campground is that the restrooms are small (one non-flush toilet) and only naturally lit, but they are clean. This campground is a quiet and fun destination for RVers and tenters alike, as long as you can stand getting back to basics a little. Moneka Park is considered a Class A primitive campground.

BASICS

Operated By: Army Corps of Engineers. **Open:** Mar. 1–Oct. 31. **Site Assignment:** First come, first served; no reservations. **Registration:** At pay station. **Fee:** $8. **Parking:** At site.

FACILITIES

Number of RV-only Sites: 38. **Hookups:** None. **Each Site:** Picnic table, grill, wooden "prep table" by grill. **Dump Station:** No. **Laundry:** No. **Pay Phone:** No. **Restrooms and Showers:** Yes (No showers). **Fuel:** No. **Propane:** No. **Internal Roads:** Paved. **RV Service:** No. **Market:** 8 mi. to Waurika. **Restaurant:** 8 mi. to Waurika. **General Store:** No. **Vending:** No. **Swimming:** Lake. **Playground:** No. **Other:** Hiking trail. **Activities:** Hiking, swimming, boating, fishing. **Nearby Attractions:** Waurika Lake, Beaver Creek Trail. **Additional Information:** Waurika Chamber of Commerce, (580) 228-2081.

RESTRICTIONS

Pets: On leash, cleaned up after. **Fires:** Grill only. **Alcoholic Beverages:** At sites. **Vehicle Maximum Length:** No limit.

TO GET THERE

From the junction of Hwy. 70 and Hwy. 5, turn west onto Hwy. 5 and go 5.3 mi. Turn right at the wooden sign for Waurika Lake. Go 0.9 mi. (past the Project Office and Information Center), and veer left when the road starts along the lake. Go 0.8 mi. and turn left into the campground.

Oregon

Oregon is home to a variety of climates and ecosystems, not to mention the only state flag that boasts a backside pattern different from its front. Though much of the Interstate 5 corridor—the only through road on the West Coast that stretches from Mexico to Canada—has plenty of rain, big forests, and beautiful mountains, the **Cascade Range** divides the state into a temperate year-round wonderland on the west side and a forbidding desert on the east. On nearing the California border, the terrain relaxes into arid, rolling hills.

West of the Cascade Mountains are the I-5 cities of **Portland, Salem,** and **Eugene,** and the Highway 101 coastline. Portland resonates with cosmopolitan and blue-collar vibes, combining fine-arts venues, communities of foreign nationals, and funky things to do. Driving south down I-5, the next city is Salem, the surprisingly conservative capital of the state. The scenery along northern I-5—a mixture of forests, farms, and mountains—continues south past Eugene, home of the **University of Oregon** and one of the most liberal, earthy, scholarly concentrations of people of any city on the West Coast.

The forestlands surrounding the I-5 corridor between Portland and **Roseburg** (the rafting capital of Oregon) are indescribable. **Mount Hood** and the **Umpqua River Valley,** OR 38 to the coast from I-5, have must-see status for all travelers. If you head farther south and it happens to be the beginning of June, and your name also happens to be Betty, make your way to **Grant's Pass** in Josephine County to celebrate your day at the annual **Betty Picnic.**

For those with water on the mind, Highway 101 runs the length of the coast to California with cut-throughs to I-5 every 60 to 100 miles. Starting in **Astoria,** the Beaver State's coast offers huge surf breaking against high rock cliffs and gnarled rock formations off-shore. Rocky tidal pools at almost any beach hold all types of ecological wonders. During spring break and summer, the traffic jams on two-lane 101 can get hairy. Oregon state parks punctuate the whole drive, but if your time is limited, make sure to see **Oswald West.** Another point of interest, **Newport,** is brimming with activity—an aquarium, an oceanography satellite of OSU, an enormous fishing fleet, a brewery, and a wax museum are all merely suggestions of the cultural options available there. South of North Bend and the **Oregon Dunes,** tourist traffic drops off, although the blue-collar shipping, fishing, and logging villages that dot the coast are charming and well worth experiencing.

Driving east from Portland, I-84 follows the Columbia through the **Columbia River Gorge National Scenic Area.** Large rock formations, mountains, and, of course, the river make the drive appealing. Continuing past the gorge, the scenery changes into flat, high-altitude plains and rolling hills along the **Columbia and Snake rivers.** Eastern Oregon has very low population density and not many attractions; regardless, there's plenty of beautiful scenery to take in both in snowy winter and boiling summer weather.

The central part of the state has the second-largest tourism draw after the I-5 corridor (including the coast, the gorge, and Mount Hood). In the Bend-Sisters area, recreation attractions include skiing, rafting, horseback riding, and stream fishing.

Driving south from **Bend** on Highway 97, day trips abound. Recreation comes in one flavor: outdoors. Myriad lakes, national forests, and volcanoes sum up the attractions between **Bend** and **Klamath Falls.** For a truly unique experience, go for a night or two of camping at the country's deepest lake, **Crater Lake,** for breathtaking vistas and a chance to soak up a little history. If you're into spelunking, head down the road to visit the discovery place of the 9,000-year-old pair of sagebrush and bark shoes at **Fort Rock Cave.**

Campground Profiles

BEND   MAP, B-2
Crane Prairie—
Deschutes National Forest

reserve america

1230 NE 3rd Suite A262, 97701.
T: (541) 383-5300; www.reserveamerica.com.

🚐 ★★★★   ⛺ ★★★★

Beauty: ★★★★	Site Privacy: ★★★
Spaciousness: ★★★	Quiet: ★★★
Security: ★★★★	Cleanliness: ★★★★
Insect Control: ★★★★	Facilities: ★★

Crane Prairie campground is on Crane Prairie Reservoir, in the Deschutes National Forest, just off the scenic Cascade Lakes Highway. It is located 33 miles southwest of Bend and 20 miles from Sun River. Crane Prairie is a premier northwest trout fishery and an excellent largemouth bass fishery. Crane Prairie is intensely popular mainly because of the fishing opportunities it provides, but its success as a wildlife management area also attracts many people. A marvelous array of waterfowl flourishes here: sandhill cranes, Canadian geese, bald eagles, and osprey are just some of the large birds found in this area. The reservoir's scenic location and the fact that several other good fisheries are in close proximity also add to its popularity—various peaks of the Cascade Mountain Range rise above the pine tree–lined shore. The Deschutes and Ochoco national forests along with the Crooked River National Grassland encompass just over 2.5 million acres of central Oregon. These public lands extend about 100 miles along the east side of the Cascade Mountains crest and eastward into the Ochoco Mountains. They are rich in human and natural history and offer a multitude of diverse scenic and recreational opportunities. Alpine forests and lush meadows, sparkling lakes and scenic rivers, dense evergreen forests, and lava caves are contained within the spectacular snowcapped volcanic peaks of the Cascade Mountain Range to the west and high desert to the east. Newberry National Volcanic Monument offers an up-close look at volcanoes and is home to the endangered pumice grape fern.

BASICS

Operated By: U.S. Forest Service. **Open:** Apr. 23–Oct. 31. **Site Assignment:** Reservations must be made at least 5 days in advance. **Registration:** At office. **Fee:** Single, $10–$12; group, $80–$175. **Parking:** At park.

FACILITIES

Number of Multipurpose Sites: 178. **Hookups:** Yes. **Each Site:** Call ahead. **Dump Station:** No. **Laundry:** No. **Pay Phone:** No. **Restrooms and Showers:** Yes. **Fuel:** No. **Propane:** No. **Internal Roads:** Paved. **RV Service:** No. **Market:** Nearby. **Restaurant:** Nearby. **General Store:** Yes. **Vending:** No. **Swimming:** No. **Playground:** No. **Other:** All equipment must fit on the site pad. Vehicles park in the developed areas only. **Activities:**

Amphitheater, boating, campfire programs, fishing, hunting, interpretive programs, wildlife viewing.

RESTRICTIONS

Pets: Pets must be restrained or on a leash at all times while in developed recreation areas. **Fires:** In fire rings, stoves, grills, or fireplaces provided for that purpose. **Alcoholic Beverages:** Not allowed. **Vehicle Maximum Length:** Call ahead.

TO GET THERE

From Hwy. 58, turn east onto Crescent Rd. at the sign for Davis Lake and Wickiup Reservoir, midway between mile markers 72 and 73. In 3.3 mi., turn left on FS 46. Drive north 18 mi. and turn east on FS 42 at a sign for Twin Lakes and Crane Prairie.

BEND   MAP, B-2
Crown Villa RV Resort

60801 Brosterhous Rd., 97702.
T: (541) 388-1131 or (866) 500-5300;
www.crownvillarvresort.com.

🚐 ★★★★★   ⛺ ★

Beauty: ★★★★	Site Privacy: ★★
Spaciousness: ★★★★	Quiet: ★★★
Security: ★★	Cleanliness: ★★★★★
Insect Control: ★★	Facilities: ★★★★★

Crown Villa RV Park, off the Hwy. 97/20 Business Loop in Bend, provides a quiet, suburban setting for travelers. Not endowed with many in-house recreational activities, this park has more of an adult feel. The enormous, adjacent RV sites give the impression of camping on a golf course with ponderosa pines providing partial shade. The one common building, a clubhouse with a covered porch, is equipped with an array of propane grills. There's no privacy between sites, but site sizes make up for this. The best full-hookup sites within the grounds, designated 447–458 and 461–471, back up to a fairway-like grassy area; many other sites have similar backyards but these have the largest. On the other hand, sites 601–610 provide a contrast to the rest of the park, as they make up an area of open gravel with electric hookups only. The park also has several tent sites in different areas, also open but with grass surfaces. Both fair weather and winter weather recreation abound in Bend.

BASICS

Operated By: Crown Villa. **Open:** All year. **Site Assignment:** On arrival, by reservation; 24-hour cancellation, 14 days during peak season; no deposit; credit card. **Registration:** At office. **Fee:** $45–$55; credit card, personal check, cash. **Parking:** At site.

FACILITIES

Number of RV-only Sites: 106. **Hookups:** Electric (50 amps), water, sewer, cable TV. **Each Site:** Picnic table. **Dump Station:** No. **Laundry:** Yes. **Pay Phone:** Yes. **Restrooms and Showers:** Yes. **Fuel:** No. **Propane:** Yes. **Internal Roads:** Paved. **RV Service:** No. **Market:** 2 mi. west on 97. **Restaurant:** 2 mi. west on 97. **General Store:** No. **Vending:** Yes. **Swimming:** No. **Playground:** No. **Other:** Clubhouse w/ TV, kitchen, covered barbecue area w/

propane grills (noncommercial), horseshoes, volleyball, tennis, storage, hot tub, wireless Internet. **Activities:** Lounging. **Nearby Attractions:** City parks, Pilot Butte, Mt. Bachelor (Year-round skiing), Benham Falls, Newberry National Volcanic Monument, Oregon High Desert Museum, every type of outdoor recreation. **Additional Information:** Bend Chamber of Commerce, (541) 382-3221.

RESTRICTIONS

Pets: On leash only, no fighting breeds. **Fires:** No open fires. **Alcoholic Beverages:** At site. **Vehicle Maximum Length:** No limit. **Other:** Only newer (or well maintained) RVs allowed.

TO GET THERE

Driving south on Hwy. 97, turn left on Brosterhous Rd. (at traffic light near Hollywood Video), follow 0.8 mi. Brosterhous turns right (but is poorly marked) just after the Bend Trap Club on the left, continue to follow this road 0.9 mi., park entrance is on the right.

BEND   MAP, B-2
Sisters/Bend KOA

67667 Hwy. 20 West, 97701.
T: (541) 549-3021 or (800) 562-0363.

🚐 ★★★★   ⛺ ★★★

Beauty: ★★★★	Site Privacy: ★★
Spaciousness: ★★	Quiet: ★★★
Security: ★★	Cleanliness: ★★★★
Insect Control: ★★	Facilities: ★★★★

From the frontal appearance, Sisters/Bend KOA, located on Hwy. 20, doesn't look very attractive. But upon closer examination, one finds quality facilities. Within the grounds there is an eclectically themed nine-hole mini-golf course, a pool with a beautiful surrounding deck, and a movie room complete with the biggest of big-screen TVs and surround sound. The office/store also rents DVDs and videocassettes. In the camping area one finds many low juniper trees, adding a musty, pine fragrance to the air. Some areas have grass, but for the most part there is little cover. Sites are arranged in parallel rows. The full-hookup area consists of gravel surfaces; tent sites 17–19 and 5–8 have grass while 92–100 have dirt surfaces. Avoid tent sites 92–94 as they sit near a road; the general overflow area also sits near Hwy. 20. Sites afford little privacy or shade.

BASICS

Operated By: Sisters/Bend KOA. **Open:** Closed Jan.–Feb. **Site Assignment:** On arrival; reservation: required deposit is 1-night fee; refund less $5 service charge; 24-hour cancellation policy. **Registration:** At office, after-hours drop located out front of office. **Fee:** RV, $20–$40; tent, $20–$40; fee covers 2 people, extra adult, $4; children 5–17, $2; students 18–20, $3; extra vehicle, $1; V, MC, cash. **Parking:** At site.

FACILITIES

Number of RV-only Sites: 100. **Number of Tent-only Sites:** 20. **Hookups:** Electric (20, 30, 50 amps), water, sewer, cable TV. **Each Site:** Picnic table, fire ring (overflow section lacks these). **Dump Station:** Yes. **Laundry:** Yes. **Pay Phone:** Yes. **Restrooms and Showers:** Yes. **Fuel:** No. **Propane:** Yes. **Internal Roads:** Gravel. **RV Service:** No. **Market:** 4 mi. west in Sisters. **Restaurant:** 4 mi. west in Sisters. **General Store:** Yes. **Vending:** Yes. **Swimming:** Yes. **Playground:** Yes. **Other:** 9-hole mini-golf, Ping-Pong, volleyball, basketball, spa, movie room, fishing pond, movie/DVD rental, deli. **Activities:** Swimming, fishing, nightly movies. **Nearby Attractions:** Sisters Rodeo (first weekend June), Camp Sherman, fly-fishing, rafting, horseback riding, hiking, Deshutes National Forest, Bend. **Additional Information:** Sisters Area Chamber of Commerce, (541) 549-0251.

RESTRICTIONS

Pets: On leash only, not allowed on grass & some sections of park. Tie dogs to own RV only, must be attended. **Fires:** Fire pit only. **Alcoholic Beverages:** At site. **Vehicle Maximum Length:** No limit.

TO GET THERE

Located 3 mi. southeast of Sisters on Hwy. 20; westbound, entrance on left.

BONNEVILLE   MAP, A-2
Eagle Creek Campground

31520 SE Woodard Rd., 97060. T: (541) 308-1700.

🚐 ★★★	🏕 ★★★
Beauty: ★★★★	Site Privacy: ★★★★
Spaciousness: ★★★	Quiet: ★★★★
Security: ★★★	Cleanliness: ★★★★
Insect Control: ★★★	Facilities: ★★★

This campground sits just east of the Bonneville Dam. The campground can be easily missed by many Columbia Gorge travelers whose eyes are directed riverward to the massive plant that provides hydroelectric power for the metropolitan areas farther west. Despite its proximity to this hulking tribute to human engineering, Eagle Creek offers a woodsy setting amidst true fir, western red cedar, and hemlock, and provides access to some beautiful walks high above the river in the Mark O. Hatfield Wilderness. The nearby busy freeway quickly fades into oblivion as Eagle Creek Trail leaves the end of FSR 241 beside the campground and follows Eagle Creek for 13 miles to Wahtum Lake and the intersection with Pacific Crest National Scenic Trail. Along the way, the trail passes high cliffs along Eagle Creek and waterfalls too numerous to mention. Several other trails lead off very near the campground to other points within the Columbia Wilderness.

BASICS

Operated By: Mount Hood National Forest. **Open:** May–Oct. **Site Assignment:** First come, first served. **Registration:** Self-registration on site. **Fee:** $10. **Parking:** At site.

FACILITIES

Number of RV-only Sites: 20. **Hookups:** None. **Each Site:** Picnic table, fire ring & grill. **Dump Station:** No. **Laundry:** No. **Pay Phone:** No. **Restrooms and Showers:** Yes. **Fuel:** No. **Propane:** No. **Internal Roads:** Call ahead for

details. **RV Service:** No. **Market:** No. **Restaurant:** No. **General Store:** No. **Vending:** No. **Swimming:** No. **Playground:** No. **Activities:** Hiking. **Nearby Attractions:** Cascade Locks, Fort Dalles Museum, Crown Pointe Vista House & Observatory, Columbia Gorge Interpretive Center. **Additional Information:** Columbia River Gorge National Scenic Area, (541) 308-1700.

RESTRICTIONS

Pets: On leash only. **Fires:** Fire ring only. **Alcoholic Beverages:** Allowed. **Vehicle Maximum Length:** 22 ft.

TO GET THERE

From Portland, drive 41 mi. east on I-84 to the campground. It is 2 mi. past the town of Bonneville, just off the interstate.

BROOKINGS   MAP, C-1
Harris Beach

reserve america

1655 Hwy. 101 N, 97415. T: (541) 469-2021; www.reserveamerica.com.

🚐 ★★★★	🏕 ★★★★
Beauty: ★★★★★	Site Privacy: ★★★
Spaciousness: ★★★	Quiet: ★★★★★
Security: ★★★★	Cleanliness: ★★★★
Insect Control: ★★★★	Facilities: ★★★★

Harris Beach was named after the Scottish pioneer George Harris who settled here in the late 1880s to raise sheep and cattle. The park boasts the largest island off the Oregon coast. Bird Island (also called Goat Island) is a National Wildlife Sanctuary and breeding site for such rare birds as the tufted puffin. The park offers sandy beaches interspersed with eroded sea stacks. The park's beauty changes with the seasons. Many people are drawn to watch the powerful and dramatic winter storms; others seek the green and fragrant spring. Summer brings warm days and sunlit beaches while the fall brings clear cool days and often the best sunsets of the year. Wildlife viewing opportunities are abundant with gray whales on their winter and spring migrations, harbor seals, California sea lions, sea birds, and the rich marine gardens make the park a fascinating stop. 36 full hookup, 50 electrical, 63 tent (maximum site 50 feet, cable TV hookups in selected campsites); 6 yurts; hiker/biker camp.

BASICS

Operated By: Oregon State Parks. **Site Assignment:** Reservations can be made 9 months in advance. **Registration:** At office. **Fee:** Single, $13–$21; yurt, $29. **Parking:** At park.

FACILITIES

Number of Multipurpose Sites: 198. **Hookups:** Yes. **Dump Station:** Yes. **Laundry:** No. **Pay Phone:** Yes. **Restrooms and Showers:** Yes. **Fuel:** Less than 0.5 mi. **Propane:** Less than 0.5 mi. **Internal Roads:** Paved. **RV Service:** No. **Market:** No. **Restaurant:** Yes. **General Store:** Less than 0.5 mi. **Vending:** No. **Swimming:** Yes. **Playground:** Yes. **Activities:** Amphitheater, beachcombing, birdwatching, fishing, hiking, jogging/running, kite flying,

nature study, picnicking, scuba diving, sightseeing, snorkeling, surfing.

RESTRICTIONS

Pets: Pets must be confined by the owner, or on a leash not more than 6 feet long, kept under physical control at all times. You're responsible for removal of all waste and for keeping your pet quiet during campground quiet hours (10 p.m.–7 a.m.). **Fires:** In fire rings or fireplaces provided for such purposes & portions of the beach designated as permissible for fires. No fires shall be left unattended or be permitted to cause damage to park facilities or areas. **Alcoholic Beverages:** Possession or use of an alcoholic beverage by any person under 21 years of age is not allowed. **Other:** Discount programs may be offered. Fee adjustments will not be made after reservations have been confirmed using the Internet reservation service. A large campsite has at least a 12 ft. by 12 ft. tent pad area. Medium sites are at least 10 ft. x10 ft. Small sites are at least 8 ft. by 8 ft.

TO GET THERE

Harris Beach State Park is located on Hwy. 101 at the north end of Brookings city limits in Curry County on the Oregon south coast.

CAMP SHERMAN   MAP, B-2
Black Butte Resort
Motel and RV Park

25635 SW FR 1419, 97730.
T: (541) 595-6514 or (541) 822-3799;
www.blackbutterv.com.

🚐 ★★★★	🏕 ★★
Beauty: ★★★★	Site Privacy: ★
Spaciousness: ★★	Quiet: ★★★★
Security: ★	Cleanliness: ★★★★
Insect Control: ★★	Facilities: ★★★

Black Butte Resort, located west of Sisters off Hwy. 20, offers a serene setting within a resort community centered on fly-fishing and outdoor activities. The small campground consists of a grass field shaded by aspens, birch, and pine with a beautiful, unobstructed view of the butte providing the campground's name. Facilities are basic, but the campground's proximity to outdoor recreation and the cities of Sister and Bend increase its appeal. Sites are distributed along both sides of a loop road. The best of the gravel and dirt sites sit on the back perimeter, numbered 3–8, with lots of shade but no view of the butte. Nearby are a reservation-only five-star restaurant and a general store with a small selection of quality wines. No-hookup sites 23 and 24 A and B are less spacious back-ins, but have the best views of the nearby butte.

BASICS

Operated By: Hoodoo Recreation. **Open:** All year. **Site Assignment:** On arrival; reservation (1-night deposit; refund w/ 7-day notice). **Registration:** At office, after hours pay in morning. **Fee:** $28; extra person (age 6 or older), $3. **Parking:** At site.

FACILITIES

Number of RV-only Sites: 31. **Hookups:** Electric (30, 50 amps), water, sewer. **Each Site:** Picnic table. **Dump Station:** Yes. **Laundry:** Yes. **Pay Phone:** No. **Restrooms and Showers:** Yes. **Fuel:** No.

Propane: No. **Internal Roads:** Gravel. **RV Service:** No. **Market:** 0.1 mi. east (well-stocked convenience store). **Restaurant:** 0.1 mi. east (5-star, reservations only). **General Store:** No. **Vending:** No. **Swimming:** No. **Playground:** No. **Other:** Horseshoe pit, meeting room (w/ kitchen), book & game loans. **Activities:** Hiking, biking (trails across road from park). **Nearby Attractions:** Deshutes National Forest, hiking, fishing, boating, City of Sisters, City of Bend, horseback riding, Sisters Rodeo, Oregon Cascades Birding Trail, Blue Ribbon Fly Fishing on Metolius River. **Additional Information:** Sisters Area Chamber of Commerce, (541) 549-0251.

RESTRICTIONS

Pets: On leash only. **Fires:** Fire pit only. **Alcoholic Beverages:** At site. **Vehicle Maximum Length:** 40 ft. (call if over 40 for availability). **Other:** Laundry closed Sun. noon–4 p.m.

TO GET THERE

From Hwy. 20 westbound, turn right on Forest Service road marked Camp Sherman-Metolius River. This turn is located between mi. 91 and 92 about 15 minutes west of Sisters. Follow this road 2.5 mi.; when road forks take the left fork and drive 2.6 mi. on FR 1419. This road continues through a stop, goes right at the stop sign. The park entrance is on the right.

CANNON BEACH   MAP, A-1
Cannon Beach RV Resort

reserve america

345 Elk Creek Rd., P. O. Box 1037, 97110.
T: (503) 436-2231 or (800) 847-2231;
www.reserveamerica.com; www.cbrvresort.com.

🚐 ★★★★★   🏕 n/a

Beauty: ★★★★	Site Privacy: ★★★
Spaciousness: ★★★	Quiet: ★★★
Security: ★★★	Cleanliness: ★★★★
Insect Control: ★★	Facilities: ★★★★

Just off 101 on the west side of Cannon Beach sits the Cannon Beach RV Resort. This well-kept campground with plenty of trees provides a quiet escape from the bustle of the nearby resort town. The park has spacious, paved sites surrounded by grass and shaded by medium-sized pines, maples, and oaks. Quiet can be found in the back of the park in pull-through sites 84–89 and back-in sites 27–35 and 97–100. The campground has good views of the surrounding evergreen-dotted hills, and on rainy days, beautiful patches of clouds and mist drift serenely around the tops of these hills. The indoor hot tub is big enough to accommodate a family reunion, and the rec room has two pool tables. This campground has a unique advantage of easy access; a city shuttle stops at the entrance to pick up tourists every half hour, with stops throughout the Cannon Beach area. Best times to visit are just before or after the summer season.

BASICS

Operated By: RV Resort at Cannon Beach. **Open:** All year. **Site Assignment:** Reservation requires 1-night deposit; 72-hour cancellation policy.

Registration: At mini-mart, after hours, pay in morning. **Fee:** $38.52 (2 adults); V, MC, cash. **Parking:** At site.

FACILITIES

Number of RV-only Sites: 100. **Hookups:** Electric (30, 50 amps), water, sewer, cable TV, central data port. **Each Site:** Picnic table, fire pit. **Dump Station:** No. **Laundry:** Yes. **Pay Phone:** Yes. **Restrooms and Showers:** Yes. **Fuel:** Yes. **Propane:** Yes. **Internal Roads:** Paved. **RV Service:** No. **Market:** Across 101 in Cannon Beach. **Restaurant:** Across 101 in Cannon Beach. **General Store:** Yes. **Vending:** No. **Swimming:** Yes. **Playground:** Yes. **Other:** Reservable meeting room w/ TV, hot tub, basketball court, horseshoe pit, mini-storage, game room w/ 2 pool tables & 3 arcade games, free shuttle to Cannon Beach. **Activities:** Free hot dog roast Sat. in summer, Thanksgiving potluck. **Nearby Attractions:** Beaches, Haystack Rock, Tillimook Rock Lighthouse, Sandcastle Day. **Additional Information:** Cannon Beach Visitor's Information Center, (503) 436-2623.

RESTRICTIONS

Pets: On leash only. **Fires:** Fire pit only. **Alcoholic Beverages:** At site. **Vehicle Maximum Length:** 60 ft. **Other:** Max. 8 people per site.

TO GET THERE

From Hwy. 101, campground is across from 2nd Cannon Beach exit; turn southbound (left) onto Sunset Blvd. After 200 feet turn left into entrance.

CANNON BEACH   MAP, A-1
Saddle Mountain State Park

reserve america

P.O. Box 681, 97110. T: (503) 986-0707,
(800) 452-5687 or (800) 551-6949;
www.reserveamerica.com.

🚐 n/a   🏕 ★★

Beauty: ★★	Site Privacy: ★★★
Spaciousness: ★★	Quiet: ★★
Security: ★★	Cleanliness: ★
Insect Control: ★★★	Facilities: ★★★

Want to enjoy the beach, see the mountains, and not get trampled by the crowds? Saddle Mountain is the answer. You have the best of both worlds at Saddle Mountain because you'll be less than 15 miles from the nearest coastal attractions of Cannon Beach and Seaside, well away from the crowded Coast Highway corridor, and only a 2.6-mile hike from superb views atop the highest peak in northwestern Oregon. Add to that a campground (albeit primitive) that is for tent campers only and nearly 3,000 acres of forests, with meadows, and creeks that you'll share with a number of woodland critters and several rare and endangered plant species. Saddle Mountain was a haven for certain species of plant life during the Ice Age, and much of the flora that has evolved today high on the flanks of this 3,283-foot peak is not found anywhere else. Alpine wildflowers put on one of the best shows of colors in the region in early to mid-June.

BASICS

Operated By: Oregon State Parks & Recreation. **Open:** Mar. 1.–Oct.; depending on snow. **Site**

Assignment: First come, first served, no reservations. **Registration:** Self-registration on site. **Fee:** $5–$9; extra vehicle, $5. **Parking:** At site.

FACILITIES

Number of Tent-only Sites: 10. **Hookups:** None. **Each Site:** Picnic table, fire pit, piped water. **Dump Station:** No. **Laundry:** No. **Pay Phone:** No. **Restrooms and Showers:** Yes. **Fuel:** No. **Propane:** No. **Internal Roads:** Call ahead for details. **RV Service:** No. **Market:** No. **Restaurant:** No. **General Store:** No. **Vending:** No. **Swimming:** No. **Playground:** No. **Other:** Primitive camping. **Activities:** Hiking, picnicking. **Nearby Attractions:** Del Rey Beach, Hug Point, Arcadia Beach. **Additional Information:** Cannon Beach Visitor's Information Center, (503) 436-2623.

RESTRICTIONS

Pets: On leash only. **Fires:** Fire ring only. **Alcoholic Beverages:** Allowed. **Vehicle Maximum Length:** No limit. **Other:** No accommodations for RVs or trailers, but self-contained units are allowed in the parking lot, bring own firewood.

TO GET THERE

Turn north on Saddle Mountain Rd. off US 26 about 1.5 mi. east of Necanicum Junction. Drive 7 mi. to the campground.

CASCADE LOCKS   MAP, A-2
Ainsworth State Park Campground

reserve america

P.O. Box 100, 97019. T: (503) 695-2301,
(503) 695-2261 or (800) 551-6949;
www.reserveamerica.com.

🚐 ★★★   🏕 ★★★

Beauty: ★★★★	Site Privacy: ★★
Spaciousness: ★★	Quiet: ★
Security: ★★	Cleanliness: ★★★
Insect Control: ★★	Facilities: ★★★

Ainsworth State Park, in the Columbia River Scenic Area east of Portland off I-84, provides a scenic location on the Oregon side of the gorge. This beautiful wooded campground has paved, terraced pull-throughs and a row of paved back-ins under the shade of cottonwoods and out-of-place coastal pines. The more spacious terraced sites (A1–13) have tree-obscured views of surrounding cliffs. Facilities are limited in scope, and like all campgrounds in the gorge, train tracks run past the park to the north of the grounds. Still, Ainsworth is the quietest state park in the gorge. The few walk-in tent sites provide little privacy from other tenters, but are positioned away from the rest of the grounds. The loudest sites (B1–32), the paved back-ins, sit closest to the railroad tracks.

BASICS

Operated By: Oregon State Parks & Recreation. **Open:** Mar. 16–end of Oct. **Site Assignment:** First come, first served. **Registration:** At self-pay station. **Fee:** $10–$16; extra vehicle, $5; V, MC, check, cash. **Parking:** At site.

FACILITIES

Number of RV-only Sites: 44. **Number of Tent-only Sites:** 6. **Hookups:** Electric (20, 30 amps), water, sewer, cable TV. **Each Site:** Picnic table, fire ring. **Dump Station:** Yes. **Laundry:** No. **Pay Phone:** No. **Restrooms and Showers:** Yes. **Fuel:** No. **Propane:** No. **Internal Roads:** Paved. **RV Service:** No. **Market:** 10 mi. east in Cascade Locks. **Restaurant:** 10 mi. east in Cascade Locks. **General Store:** No. **Vending:** No. **Swimming:** No. **Playground:** Yes. **Other:** Small amphitheater, hiking trails, firewood available, waterfalls. **Activities:** Seasonal interpretive programs, hiking, picnicking, biking, wildlife viewing. **Nearby Attractions:** Bonneville Dam, Columbia Gorge Interpretive Center, Cascade Locks, hiking trails, Multnomah Falls. **Additional Information:** Portland Oregon Visitor's Assoc., 87-PORTLAND.

RESTRICTIONS

Pets: On leash only (max. length 6 ft.). **Fires:** Fire pit only. **Alcoholic Beverages:** At site. **Vehicle Maximum Length:** 60 ft. **Other:** No firewood collecting.

TO GET THERE

From I-84 Exit 35 turn right (south) off ramp, access road dead-ends after 0.2 mi.; turn left and drive 0.2 mi.; entrance to campground is on the left marked with a sign.

COOS BAY   MAP, B-1
Sunset Bay State Park

reserve america

89814 Cape Arago Hwy., 97420-9647.
T: (541) 888-4902; www.reserveamerica.com.

🚐 ★★★★   ⛺ ★★★★

Beauty: ★★★★	Site Privacy: ★★★
Spaciousness: ★★★	Quiet: ★★★
Security: ★★★★	Cleanliness: ★★★★
Insect Control: ★★★★	Facilities: ★★★★

Situated in one of the most scenic areas on the Oregon coast, Sunset Bay State Park features beautiful sandy beaches protected by towering sea cliffs. Only a short walk from the beach, the campground has sites for tent camping and RVs, as well as cozy and comfortable yurts. Day-use and picnic facilities are located along the bay to allow easy access for beachcombing, fishing, swimming, and boating. A network of hiking trails connects Sunset Bay with nearby Shore Acres and Cape Arago State Parks. Hiking these trails will give you a chance to experience pristine coastal forests, seasonal wildflowers, and spectacular ocean vistas from atop the rugged cliffs and headlands. From points along the trail, you'll be treated to views of Gregory Point and the Cape Arago lighthouse. A public golf course is located next to the park and the nearby fishing village of Charleston provides opportunities for crabbing, clamming, and fishing. In fact, there are plenty of secret treasures in the Sunset Bay area.

BASICS

Operated By: Oregon State Parks. **Open:** All year. **Site Assignment:** Reservations can be made 9 months in advance. **Registration:** At office. **Fee:** Single, $12–$20; meeting hall, $25; yurt, $27; group, $40–$63.40. **Parking:** At park.

FACILITIES

Number of Multipurpose Sites: 212. **Hookups:** Yes. **Dump Station:** Less than 3 mi. **Laundry:** No. **Pay Phone:** Yes. **Restrooms and Showers:** Yes. **Fuel:** Less than 3 mi. **Propane:** Less than 3 mi. **Internal Roads:** Paved. **RV Service:** No. **Market:** No. **Restaurant:** Less than 3 mi. **General Store:** Less than 3 mi. **Vending:** No. **Swimming:** Yes. **Playground:** No. **Activities:** Amphitheater, basketball, beachcombing, bird-watching, golfing, hiking, horseshoes, kayaking, kite flying, nature study, picnicking, scuba diving, sightseeing, volleyball.

RESTRICTIONS

Pets: Pets must be confined by the owner, or on a leash not more than 6 feet long, kept under physical control at all times. You're responsible for removal of all waste and for keeping your pet quiet during campground quiet hours (10 p.m.–7 a.m.). **Fires:** In fire rings or fireplaces provided for such purposes & portions of the beach designated as permissible for fires. No fires shall be left unattended or be permitted to cause damage to park facilities or areas. **Alcoholic Beverages:** Possession or use of an alcoholic beverage by any person under 21 years of age is not allowed. **Other:** Discount programs may be offered. Fee adjustments will not be made after reservations have been confirmed using the Internet reservation service. A large campsite has at least a 12 by 12–ft. tent-pad area. Medium sites are at least 10 by 10 ft. Small sites are at least 8 by 8 ft.

TO GET THERE

12 mi. southwest of Coos Bay. 3 mi. south of Charleston on Cape Arago Hwy.

DETROIT   MAP, B-2
Detroit Lake State Park

reserve america

P.O. Box 549, 97342. T: (503) 854-3346; www.reserveamerica.com.

🚐 ★★★★   ⛺ ★★★★

Beauty: ★★★	Site Privacy: ★★
Spaciousness: ★★	Quiet: ★★★★★
Security: ★★★★	Cleanliness: ★★★★
Insect Control: ★★★★	Facilities: ★★★★

Located in the Cascade Mountains, Detroit Lake State Park is the gateway to beautiful Detroit Lake. The 400-foot-deep lake was created in 1953 when the U.S. Army Corps of Engineers completed the Detroit Dam project. The lake is more than 9 miles long, with more than 32 miles of shoreline. This is the spot for all types of water sports: fishing, boating, swimming, waterskiing, and personal watercraft. The park offers a variety of campsites, modern restrooms with electricity and showers, boat ramps, boat moorage, and an accessible fishing dock. Detroit Lake is known for its fishing, boating of all types, waterskiing, jet skiing, scenery, and wildlife. The campground offers evening programs, children's crafts, and a junior ranger program. There are facilities for playing horseshoes or volleyball, basketball hoops in the C Loop playground area, and two designated swim areas. Firewood and the morning newspaper are available near the visitor center, which offers a free cup of coffee and an assortment of items for sale, including park souvenirs and apparel, games, educational books, and toys.

BASICS

Operated By: Oregon State Parks. **Open:** All year. **Site Assignment:** Reservations can be made 9 months in advance. **Registration:** At office. **Fee:** Single, $12–$20; boat moorage, $7. **Parking:** At park.

FACILITIES

Number of Multipurpose Sites: 504. **Hookups:** Yes. **Dump Station:** No. **Laundry:** No. **Pay Phone:** Yes. **Restrooms and Showers:** Yes. **Fuel:** Less than 3 mi. **Propane:** Less than 3 mi. **Internal Roads:** Paved. **RV Service:** No. **Market:** No. **Restaurant:** Less than 3 mi. **General Store:** Less than 3 mi. **Vending:** No. **Swimming:** Yes. **Playground:** No. **Activities:** Amphitheater, boating, canoeing, fishing, horseshoes, jet skiing, junior ranger program, sailing, scuba diving, waterskiing, volleyball, walking.

RESTRICTIONS

Pets: Pets must be confined by the owner, or on a leash not more than 6 feet long, kept under physical control at all times. You're responsible for removal of all waste and for keeping your pet quiet during campground quiet hours (10 p.m.–7 a.m.). **Fires:** In fire rings or fireplaces provided for such purposes & portions of the beach designated as permissible for fires. No fires shall be left unattended or be permitted to cause damage to park facilities or areas. **Alcoholic Beverages:** Possession or use of an alcoholic beverage by any person under 21 years of age is not allowed. **Other:** Discount programs may be offered. Fee adjustments will not be made after reservations have been confirmed using the Internet reservation service. A large campsite has at least a 12 by 12–ft. tent-pad area. Medium sites are at least 10 by 10 ft. Small sites are at least 8 by 8 ft.

TO GET THERE

Detroit Lake State Park is located just off Hwy. 22 at mile marker 48. It is 48 mi. east of Salem or 2 mi. west of Detroit.

DETROIT   MAP, B-2
Elk Lake Campground

HC 73 Box 320, 97360. T: (503) 854-3366.

🚐 ★★★★   ⛺ ★★★

Beauty: ★★★★★	Site Privacy: ★★★★
Spaciousness: ★★★★★	Quiet: ★★★★★
Security: ★★★	Cleanliness: ★★★★
Insect Control: ★★★	Facilities: ★★★

The word "foolhardy" may come to mind as you find yourself at the junction that leads to this gem of a spot in Willamette National Forest, about 10 miles above the small, historic burg of Detroit. The road is decidedly rough but not impassable. As long as your exhaust system and oil pan sit high and secure, you should be OK. Elk Lake's campsites are strung along the shore of the lake. Tall stands of Douglas fir and western hemlock share the land with white fir, birches, Oregon grape, ferns, and trillium to offer a prime collection of natural cover. This campground may be tough to get to, but once you're there, peaceful Elk Lake makes for a terrific base camp while you enjoy the recreational options. For anyone who brings a boat into this remote area, Elk Lake is a nice spot to take in lazy kayaking or canoeing.

BASICS

Operated By: Willamette National Forest. **Open:** June–Oct. **Site Assignment:** First come, first served; no reservations. **Registration:** Not necessary. **Fee:** None. **Parking:** At site, in parking lot, 4x4 recommended.

FACILITIES

Number of Tent-only Sites: 12. **Hookups:** None. **Each Site:** Picnic table, fire pit w/ grill. **Dump Station:** No. **Laundry:** No. **Pay Phone:** No. **Restrooms and Showers:** Vault toilets. **Fuel:** No. **Propane:** No. **Internal Roads:** Call ahead for details. **RV Service:** No. **Market:** No. **Restaurant:** No. **General Store:** No. **Vending:** No. **Swimming:** No. **Playground:** No. **Activities:** Fishing, hiking, nonmotorized boating. **Nearby Attractions:** Battle Ax Mountain, Mount Beachie. **Additional Information:** (503) 854-3366.

RESTRICTIONS

Pets: On leash only. **Fires:** Fire ring only. **Alcoholic Beverages:** Allowed. **Vehicle Maximum Length:** No trailers. **Other:** No low clearance RVs, no trash collection, fishing license required.

TO GET THERE

From Detroit, drive north on FS 46 4.5 mi. to FS 4697. Follow this 10 mi. to the campground. Stay to the left fork where FS 4697 and FS 4696 intersect at about 8 mi. The last 2 mi. are extremely rough.

DIAMOND LAKE — MAP, B-2
Diamond Lake Campground

2020 Toketee Ranger Station Rd., 97447.
T: (541) 498-2531 or (877) 444-6777;
www.reserveamerica.com.

🚐 ★★★ ⛺ ★★★★

Beauty: ★★★★★	Site Privacy: ★★★
Spaciousness: ★★★	Quiet: ★★★★
Security: ★★	Cleanliness: ★★★★
Insect Control: ★★	Facilities: ★

Diamond Lake Campground, located about ten minutes off Hwy. 230 on the shores of Diamond Lake, provides a particularly beautiful view of the summer sunset over the lake and mountains opposite the campground. This huge National Forest Campground covers more than 3 miles of shoreline, but only has about six showers per gender, although more claim to be in the works and the existing ones are free (a rarity in campgrounds on publicly owned lands). The campground is organized into several loops diverging from

a main access road that runs the span of the grounds. Sites have no hookups and can accept either a tent or RV. The best gravel-parking sites are on L loop with less site density, more shade, seclusion, and beautiful views. This is followed by K loop, which offers better than average space between sites. Loops M and G have the highest density with more open sites.

BASICS

Operated By: National Forest Service. **Open:** May 15–Oct. 31; weather permitting. **Site Assignment:** First come, first served; reservation (1-night deposit; 72-hour cancellation notice less $10 fee). **Registration:** At office/entrance gate; after hours see notice posted at window, pay in morning. **Fee:** Regular, $12; shoreline, $18; multiparty, $18; cash on arrival. **Parking:** At site, limited off site.

FACILITIES

Number of Multipurpose Sites: 238. **Hookups:** None. **Each Site:** Picnic table; fire ring. **Dump Station:** Yes. **Laundry:** No. **Pay Phone:** Yes. **Restrooms and Showers:** Yes. **Fuel:** No. **Propane:** No. **Internal Roads:** Paved. **RV Service:** No. **Market:** Small, nearby. **Restaurant:** Nearby, at a hotel. **General Store:** No. **Vending:** No. **Swimming:** No. **Playground:** No. **Other:** Paved bike trails, amphitheater, fish-cleaning stations, boat ramp. **Activities:** Hiking, fishing, boating, biking, interpretive programs on weekends. **Nearby Attractions:** Crater Lake National Park, Douglas County Museum, Umpqua Valley Wineries, Roseburg, rafting, fishing, biking, covered bridges. **Additional Information:** Douglas County Information, (541) 672-3311.

RESTRICTIONS

Pets: On leash only (max. length 6 ft.). **Fires:** Fire pit only. **Alcoholic Beverages:** At site. **Vehicle Maximum Length:** 45 ft. **Other:** Quiet hours 10 p.m.–6 a.m.

TO GET THERE

Located 80 mi. east of Roseburg on Hwy. 138, turn right onto Rd. 4795 (Diamond Lake Loop) at the north entrance to Diamond Lake Recreation Area. Proceed 2.5 mi. to the campground entrance. Diamond Lake may also be accessed via Hwy. 230 from Medford, or Hwy. 97 from Klamath Falls and Bend.

DIAMOND LAKE — MAP, B-2
Thielsen View Campground

Diamond Lake Loop Rd. 4795, 97731.
T: (541) 498-2531.

🚐 ★★★★ ⛺ ★★★★

Beauty: ★★★★★	Site Privacy: ★★★★
Spaciousness: ★★★★★	Quiet: ★★★★★
Security: ★★★★	Cleanliness: ★★★★★
Insect Control: ★★★	Facilities: ★★★

With two other campgrounds across scenic Diamond Lake that can accommodate several hundred campers between them, chances are you won't find yourself alone out in this remote territory. However, this spacious campground offers a relatively private stay. Diamond Lake is an immensely popular area, especially if you are trolling the lake's crystalline waters for trout. Great fishing notwithstanding, Diamond

Lake's popularity can be attributed to a number of other factors. For starters, it is one of the largest natural lakes in Oregon. Add to this its proximity to some spectacular mountain scenery, and follow that up with blissfully warm, dry summer weather. Last but not least, factor in the proximity of Crater Lake National Park to the south. The area is a fantastic natural playground that can turn the most resolute vacation planner into a miserable heap of indecision. The facilities here are limited, as is the norm in this national forest, but you won't need to spend a lot of time in the campground.

BASICS

Operated By: Umpqua National Forest. **Open:** May 15–Oct. **Site Assignment:** First come, first served, no reservation. **Registration:** Self-registration on site. **Fee:** $11; extra vehicle, $4. **Parking:** At site.

FACILITIES

Number of Multipurpose Sites: 59. **Hookups:** Water. **Each Site:** Picnic table, fire ring & grill. **Dump Station:** No. **Laundry:** No. **Pay Phone:** No. **Restrooms and Showers:** Vault toilets. **Fuel:** No. **Propane:** No. **Internal Roads:** Gravel. **RV Service:** No. **Market:** 3 mi. east. **Restaurant:** 3 mi. east. **General Store:** No. **Vending:** No. **Swimming:** No. **Playground:** No. **Activities:** Hiking, fishing, hunting, bird-watching, biking, canoeing, kayaking. **Nearby Attractions:** Crater Lake, North Umpqua River. **Additional Information:** Douglas County Information, (541) 672-3311; Diamond Lake Resort Lodge (800) 733-7593.

RESTRICTIONS

Pets: On leash only. **Fires:** Fire ring only. **Alcoholic Beverages:** Allowed. **Vehicle Maximum Length:** 35 ft. **Other:** 14-day stay limit.

TO GET THERE

From Roseburg and I-5, take SR 138 east/southeast to Clearwater (about 50 mi.), at Clearwater the road leaves the North Umpqua and parallels Clearwater River. At the intersection with FS 4795, turn right and go around the north end of Diamond Lake to find the campground.

FLORENCE — MAP, B-1
Carl G. Washburne Memorial State Park

reserve america

93111 Hwy. 101 North, 97439.
T: (541) 547-3416; www.reserveamerica.com.

🚐 ★★★★ ⛺ ★★★★

Beauty: ★★★★	Site Privacy: ★★★★
Spaciousness: ★★★★	Quiet: ★★★
Security: ★★★★	Cleanliness: ★★★★
Insect Control: ★★★★	Facilities: ★★★★

Washburne is located on the east side of Highway 101 with a buffer of native plants between spacious campsites and the highway. There are several trails of varying difficulty leading from the campsites to the beach, wildlife-viewing areas, and second-growth forests. A walking trail leads under the highway to a 5-mile sandy beach and a day-use area, where you'll find space to watch whales, hunt agates, beachcomb, and picnic. Another trail connects you to the Heceta Head Trail, which you can use to reach the historic Heceta Head lighthouse. The picturesque lighthouse is open daily for tours during the summer months and weekends during the off season October through March. Call year-round for group tours. In the campground at night, you can hear the pounding surf. There is a creek running through the campground, and elk have been known to wander through. Wild rhododendrons bloom in spring.

BASICS

Operated By: Oregon State Parks. **Open:** All year. **Site Assignment:** Reservations can be made 9 months in advance. **Registration:** At office. **Fee:** Yurt, $29. **Parking:** At park.

FACILITIES

Number of Multipurpose Sites: 86. **Hookups:** Yes. **Dump Station:** Yes. **Laundry:** No. **Pay Phone:** Yes. **Restrooms and Showers:** Yes. **Fuel:** No. **Propane:** No. **Internal Roads:** Paved. **RV Service:** No. **Market:** No. **Restaurant:** No. **General Store:** No. **Vending:** No. **Swimming:** Yes. **Playground:** No. **Activities:** Clam digging, fishing, gold panning, hiking, jogging/running, kayaking, kite flying, metal detecting, photography, picnicking, rock collecting, sightseeing, surfing, walking, whale-watching.

RESTRICTIONS

Pets: Pets must be confined by the owner, or on a leash not more than 6 feet long, kept under physical control at all times. You're responsible for removal of all waste and for keeping your pet quiet during campground quiet hours (10 p.m.–7 a.m.). **Fires:** In fire rings or fireplaces provided for such purposes & portions of the beach designated as permissible for fires. No fires shall be left unattended or be permitted to cause damage to park facilities or areas. **Alcoholic Beverages:** Possession or use of an alcoholic beverage by any person under 21 years of age is not allowed. **Other:** Discount programs may be offered. Fee adjustments will not be made after reservations have been confirmed using the Internet reservation service.

TO GET THERE

Carl G. Washburne Memorial State Park is on Hwy. 101, 14 mi. north of Florence, 11 mi. south of Yachats. The entrance to the overnight camp is located on the east side of Hwy. 101. Well signed.

FLORENCE   MAP, B-1
Jessie M. Honeyman Memorial State Park Campground

84505 Hwy. 101 South, 97439. T: (541) 997-3641, (800) 551-6949 or (800) 452-5687; www.reserveamerica.com.

  ★★★★   ▲ ★★★★★

Beauty: ★★★★★   Site Privacy: ★★★
Spaciousness: ★★★   Quiet: ★★★
Security: ★★   Cleanliness: ★★★★
Insect Control: ★★   Facilities: ★★★

Jessie M. Honeyman Memorial State Park Campground, located on Hwy. 101 a few minutes south of Florence, has a camping area as big as the name is long. The heavily forested park has many semiprivate sites. Unfortunately most full-hookup sites lack privacy. These make up the section open to ATVs in the winter (H loop). Further, avoid C loop with its proximity to the highway, and sites 283–299. The rest of the campground receives shade from tall cedars and firs, and gains privacy from the dense groves of huckleberry, salal, and rhododendron. As it is with most Oregon publicly owned camping property, the grounds have a very natural, woodland appearance. Tent sites and RV sites differ very little; both have paved parking and a flat side area of dirt and moss. The best time to visit is late spring when the rhododendron are in bloom all over the Florence area.

BASICS

Operated By: Oregon State Parks & Recreation. **Open:** All year; some seasonal areas. **Site Assignment:** First come, first served; reservation (1-night deposit plus nonrefundable fee; 48-hour cancellation policy). **Registration:** At entrance gate or self-pay station. **Fee:** $17–$22; extra vehicle, $5; V, MC, check, cash. **Parking:** At site.

FACILITIES

Number of RV-only Sites: 168. **Number of Tent-only Sites:** 187. **Hookups:** Electric (20, 30, 50 amps), water, sewer, cable TV. **Each Site:** Picnic table, fire ring. **Dump Station:** Yes. **Laundry:** No. **Pay Phone:** Yes. **Restrooms and Showers:** Yes. **Fuel:** No. **Propane:** No. **Internal Roads:** Paved. **RV Service:** No. **Market:** 5 mi. north in Florence. **Restaurant:** 5 mi. north in Florence. **General Store:** Yes. **Vending:** No. **Swimming:** No. **Playground:** Yes. **Other:** Kayak & paddleboat rentals, reservable meeting hall, reservable outdoor pavilion, boat ramp (day use), pedestrian dune access. **Activities:** Fishing, hiking, lake swimming, interpretive programs, boating, sand boarding, winter dune buggy & ATV access. **Nearby Attractions:** Sea Lion Caves, Oregon Dunes National Recreation Area, the covered bridges of Lane County, Haceta Head Lighthouse. **Additional Information:** Florence Chamber of Commerce, (541) 997-3128 or (800) 524-4864.

RESTRICTIONS

Pets: On leash only (max. length 6 ft.). **Fires:** Fire pit only. **Alcoholic Beverages:** At site only. **Vehicle Maximum Length:** 60 ft. **Other:** 14-day stay limit in winter, 10 days in summer.

TO GET THERE

Located 3 mi. south of Florence on Hwy. 101. Driving southbound, entrance is on right. Upon entering park, road forks; take left fork and pay attention to one-way signs; follow this road into the campground.

FORT KLAMATH   MAP, C-2
Crater Lake Resort
Fort Creek Campground

P.O. Box 457, 97626. T: (541) 381-2349; www.craterlakeresort.com.

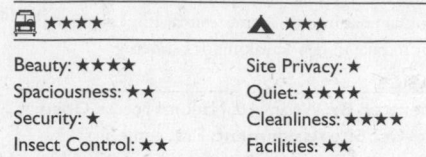

🚐 ★★★★   ▲ ★★★

Beauty: ★★★★   Site Privacy: ★
Spaciousness: ★★   Quiet: ★★★★
Security: ★   Cleanliness: ★★★★
Insect Control: ★★   Facilities: ★★

Crater Lake Resort, the closest private land campground to the south entrance of the national park, has a quaint, country feel. The park has few recreational opportunities on site due to its location, though it does have several canoes free to use for patrons wanting to explore the nearby creek. The best RV sites in the park sit on Fort Creek, numbered 12–23. The tenting area has no delineated sites, but can fit quite a few tents and has lots of grass and shade. The whole park has an open feel, with little sense of privacy. The worst sites sit on the edge of Hwy. 62 and are subject to infrequent but irritating road noise. In the summer, mosquitoes breed in nearby creeks and the weather is hot, so consider visiting during the late spring or early fall.

BASICS

Operated By: Crater Lake Resort. **Open:** May 1–Nov. 1. **Site Assignment:** On arrival; reservation w/ required 1-night deposit (cash, V, MC); refund w/ 4-day notice minus $10; less than 4 days, 1 night charged. **Registration:** At office, after hours ring bell outside office. **Fee:** $25; RV fee covers 2 people; extra person, $3; V, MC, cash, personal check. **Parking:** At site, limited off site.

FACILITIES

Number of RV-only Sites: 15. **Number of Tent-only Sites:** 10. **Hookups:** Electric (30, 50 amps), water, sewer. **Each Site:** Picnic table, fire ring. **Dump Station:** No. **Laundry:** No. **Pay Phone:** No. **Restrooms and Showers:** Yes. **Fuel:** No. **Propane:** No. **Internal Roads:** Gravel. **RV Service:** No. **Market:** 2 mi. northwest in Fort Klamath. **Restaurant:** 2 mi. northwest in Fort Klamath. **General Store:** No. **Vending:** No. **Swimming:** No. **Playground:** Yes. **Other:** Volleyball, horseshoes, canoes (free to guests), basketball, air hockey, Ping-Pong, foosball, meeting hall. **Activities:** Fishing, canoeing, cold swimming (in creek). **Nearby Attractions:** Crater Lake National Park, Williamson River, Collier Logging Museum, fish hatchery, Agency Lake. **Additional Information:** Klamath County Dept. of Tourism, (800) 445-6731.

RESTRICTIONS

Pets: On leash only; $3. **Fires:** Fire pit only. **Alcoholic Beverages:** At site. **Vehicle Maximum Length:** No limit.

TO GET THERE

Located a few mi. southeast of town on Hwy. 62, located at mile marker 92.

GOLD BEACH MAP, C-1
Illahe Campground

36977 Agnes Illahe Rd., 97444.
T: (541) 247-3600 or (800) 454-5687;
www.fs.fed.us/r6/siskiyou.

★★★★ ★★★★

Beauty: ★★★★ Site Privacy: ★★★★
Spaciousness: ★★★★ Quiet: ★★★
Security: ★★★★★ Cleanliness: ★★★★★
Insect Control: ★★★★ Facilities: ★★★

Just past the wilderness section of the Rogue River lies Illahe Campground. Nearby competitor campgrounds provide water access, and thus draw the greater crowds. But at Illahe, where a short, rough trail leads to a rugged shoreline, the relative inaccessibility of the river keeps the crowds away—that is, as long as you don't come from mid-June, when the jet boat racers take over the area, through the end of July. Campsites at Illahe have a thick buffer of vegetation that gives the sites a feeling of solitude. The area near the campground entrance is grassy and open, dotted with a few apple and plum trees. Campground hosts encourage guests to take the fruit when it ripens, because if the campers don't get it, the bears likely will. (Sensible campers will store food out of sight and out of reach of the critters.)

BASICS

Operated By: Gold Beach Ranger District, Siskiyou National Forest. **Open:** All year. **Site Assignment:** First come, first served, no reservations. **Registration:** Self-registration on site. **Fee:** $5. **Parking:** At site.

FACILITIES

Number of RV-only Sites: 14. **Number of Tent-only Sites:** 14. **Number of Multipurpose Sites:** 14. **Hookups:** None. **Each Site:** Picnic table, fire ring. **Dump Station:** No. **Laundry:** No. **Pay Phone:** No. **Restrooms and Showers:** Yes. **Fuel:** No. **Propane:** No. **Internal Roads:** Call ahead for conditions. **RV Service:** No. **Market:** No. **Restaurant:** No. **General Store:** No. **Vending:** No. **Swimming:** No. **Playground:** No. **Activities:** Hiking, boating, swimming. **Nearby Attractions:** Whitewater rafting on the Rogue River. **Additional Information:** Siskiyou National Forest, (541) 858-2200.

RESTRICTIONS

Pets: On leash only. **Fires:** Fire ring only. **Alcoholic Beverages:** Allowed. **Vehicle Maximum Length:** 22 ft.

TO GET THERE

From Gold Beach, turn east on Jerry's Flat Rd. north of town and on the south side of the Rogue River. Follow it as it turns into FSR 33 35 mi. At the junction after crossing the river, where Agness is left and Powers is straight, veer right on CR 375. Illahe Campground is 2 mi. on the right.

GOLD HILL MAP, C-1
Valley of the Rogue State Park

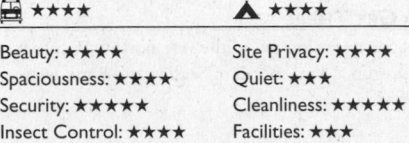

3792 N River Rd., 97525. T: (541) 582-3128;
www.reserveamerica.com.

★★★★ ★★★★

Beauty: ★★★ Site Privacy: ★★★
Spaciousness: ★★★ Quiet: ★★★★
Security: ★★★★ Cleanliness: ★★★★
Insect Control: ★★★★ Facilities: ★★★★

A pleasant green oasis awaits you in southern Oregon's Rogue Valley. Valley of the Rogue Park has both a day-use picnic area and an overnight campground along 3 miles of shoreline on the Rogue River. A meeting hall is available for groups. An easy, self-guided interpretive walking trail provides a relaxing 1.25-mile stroll along the river's edge. Camp and play along the river made famous by novelist and avid fisherman Zane Grey. The campground is also a great place to stay while taking in the local culture, history, and recreation opportunities in the area. You can take trips to Crater Lake National Park, the Oregon Caves National Monument, historic Jacksonville, Ashland's Shakespeare Festival, or the Britt Music Festival. The park is ideally located to give you all of this, plus friendly local shops, museums, and sights of interest. It is open all year and has Discovery Rates from October 1 through April 30.

BASICS

Operated By: Oregon State Parks. **Site Assignment:** Reservations can be made 9 months in advance. **Registration:** At office. **Fee:** Single, $12–$20; meeting hall, $25; yurt, $27; day use, $35; group, $61. **Parking:** At park.

FACILITIES

Number of Multipurpose Sites: 279. **Hookups:** Yes. **Dump Station:** Yes. **Laundry:** No. **Pay Phone:** Yes. **Restrooms and Showers:** Yes. **Fuel:** Less than 3 mi. **Propane:** Less than 3 mi. **Internal Roads:** Paved. **RV Service:** No. **Market:** No. **Restaurant:** Less than 3 mi. **General Store:** Less than 3 mi. **Vending:** No. **Swimming:** No. **Playground:** Yes. **Activities:** Amphitheater, berry picking, bird-watching, crawfishing, fishing, hiking, horseshoe, jogging/running, junior ranger program, kayaking, kite flying, nature study, photography, picnicking, sightseeing, skateboarding, skating, stargazing, volleyball.

RESTRICTIONS

Pets: Pets must be confined by the owner, or on a leash not more than 6 feet long, kept under physical control at all times. You're responsible for removal of all waste and for keeping your pet quiet during campground quiet hours (10 p.m.–7 a.m.). **Fires:** In fire rings or fireplaces provided for such purposes & portions of the beach designated as permissible for fires. No fires shall be left unattended or be permitted to cause damage to park facilities or areas. **Alcoholic Beverages:** Possession or use of an alcoholic beverage by any person under 21 years of age is not allowed. **Other:** Discount programs may be offered.

Fee adjustments will not be made after reservations have been confirmed using the Internet reservation service. A large campsite has at least a 12 by 12–ft. tent-pad area. Medium sites are at least 10 by10 ft. Small sites are at least 8 by 8 ft.

TO GET THERE

The Valley of the Rogue State Park is located off I-5, 12 mi. south of Grants Pass and 16 mi. north of Medford. Take Exit 45b, both north and south bound.

GRANT'S PASS MAP, C-1
Riverpark RV Resort

2956 Rogue River Hwy., 97527.
T: (541) 479-0046 or (800) 677-8857;
www.riverparkrvresort.com.

★★★★ n/a

Beauty: ★★★★ Site Privacy: ★
Spaciousness: ★★★ Quiet: ★★★
Security: ★★ Cleanliness: ★★★★
Insect Control: ★★ Facilities: ★★★

On the banks of the Rogue River just a couple of miles south of Downtown Grants Pass, travelers find an outdoor art museum, or is it an RV park? It's actually both; the owner/operator/avid sculptor of Riverpark RV Resort uses metal and wood to fill his campground with sculptures demonstrating both down-home crafty and contemporary artsy styles. The flat concrete sites shaded by tall mossy hardwoods have grass perimeters, and the grounds have some garden-like qualities including a large number of rose bushes in the public areas. Riverpark RVs 20 sites, numbered 5–24, are on the bank of a calm stretch of the Rogue, and of these numbers 5–12 sit farthest from a nearby road. On the negative side, all sites lack privacy. Avoid sites 25–29 and J–Q; these are located too close to the office, dump station, and entrance. Winters here stay mild; summer usually brings crowds and some hot days.

BASICS

Operated By: Riverpark RV Resort. **Open:** All year. **Site Assignment:** First come, first served; reservation (1-night deposit; 48-hour cancellation policy); credit card, check. **Registration:** At office, after hours follow instructions on office door. **Fee:** $25; fee covers 2 people; extra person, $3. **Parking:** At site.

FACILITIES

Number of RV-only Sites: 47. **Number of Tent-only Sites:** 47. **Number of Multipurpose Sites:** 47. **Hookups:** Electric (20, 30, 50 amps), water, cable TV. **Each Site:** Picnic table, trash can. **Dump Station:** Yes. **Laundry:** Yes. **Pay Phone:** No. **Restrooms and Showers:** Yes. **Fuel:** No. **Propane:** No. **Internal Roads:** Paved. **RV Service:** No. **Market:** 3 mi. north in Grant's Pass. **Restaurant:** 3 mi. north in Grant's Pass. **General Store:** No. **Vending:** No. **Swimming:** No. **Playground:** No. **Other:** Horseshoe pit, tennis court, sculptures. **Activities:** Swimming, fishing, tennis, horseshoes. **Nearby Attractions:** The Applegate Trail Interpretive Center, Hellgate Jetboat Excursions, rafting, fishing, golf, museums. **Additional Information:** Grants Pass Visitor Information, (800) 547-5927.

RESTRICTIONS

Pets: On leash only, limit 2 dogs. **Fires:** No open fires. **Alcoholic Beverages:** At site. **Vehicle Maximum Length:** No limit. **Other:** No vehicle washing.

TO GET THERE

From I-5 Exit 55, drive 1.8 mi. west on Hwy. 199, turn left and drive 0.2 mi. south on Parkdale Dr. Then turn left onto Rogue River Hwy. 99 and follow it 2 mi. to the entrance on the left.

GRESHAM   MAP, A-2
Oxbow Park

3010 SE Oxbow Pkwy., 97080.
T: (503) 797-1850;
www.metro-region.org (quicklink to oxbow park).

🚐 ★★★★   ⛺ ★★★★

Beauty: ★★★★★   Site Privacy: ★★★★
Spaciousness: ★★★★   Quiet: ★★★★
Security: ★★★★★   Cleanliness: ★★★★
Insect Control: ★★★★   Facilities: ★★★

Oxbow Park sets a prime example of what a metropolitan park can and should be. The grounds are a sprawling 1,000 acres of dense forests, grassy clearings, sandy riverbanks, and sheer canyon walls. Old-growth forest alone covers 200 acres. Native salmon spawn within a quarter mile of camping areas on Sandy River, known as the top-rated winter steelhead stream in Oregon. Wildlife abounds in the park (bear and elk have been known to visit occasionally), and a full-time naturalist employed year-round, is busiest in summer with a heavy schedule of public and private programs. 10 pull-through sites are offered. The first order of business once you get settled into your site is to explore the trails on foot. There are roughly 15 miles of trails that follow Sandy River and wind throughout the park. Even at the height of the summer season, you'll be amazed at how quickly you can find seclusion.

BASICS

Operated By: Metro Regional Parks. **Open:** All year. **Site Assignment:** First come, first served, no reservations. **Registration:** Daily fee collected each night; 1-time fee to enter park, $4. **Fee:** $15. **Parking:** At site.

FACILITIES

Number of Multipurpose Sites: 67. **Hookups:** None. **Each Site:** Picnic table, freestanding barbecue pit, lantern. **Dump Station:** No. **Laundry:** No. **Pay Phone:** Yes. **Restrooms and Showers:** Vault toilets. **Fuel:** No. **Propane:** No. **Internal Roads:** Call ahead for details. **RV Service:** No. **Market:** No. **Restaurant:** No. **General Store:** No. **Vending:** No. **Swimming:** No. **Playground:** Yes. **Other:** Equestrian area, group camps, interpretive programs. **Activities:** Hiking, horseback riding trails, fishing boating (nonmotorized watercraft only). **Nearby Attractions:** Crown Point Vista House. **Additional Information:** County info line, (503) 823-4000 or www.co.multnomah.or.us.

RESTRICTIONS

Pets: Not allowed. **Fires:** Fire ring only. **Alcoholic Beverages:** Not allowed. **Vehicle Maximum Length:** 35 ft. **Other:** No ATVs, guns or fireworks.

TO GET THERE

Take the Wood Village Exit 16 off I-84 in Gresham. Go south to Division St., turn left and continue to Oxbow Pkwy. From here follow the signs down to the park.

HAMMOND   MAP, A-1
Fort Stevens State Park

100 Peter Iredale Rd., 97121. T: (503) 861-1671; www.reserveamerica.com.

🚐 ★★★★   ⛺ ★★★★

Beauty: ★★★★   Site Privacy: ★★★
Spaciousness: ★★★   Quiet: ★★
Security: ★★★★   Cleanliness: ★★★★
Insect Control: ★★★★   Facilities: ★★★★

Fort Stevens was the primary military defense installation in the three-fort Harbor Defense System at the mouth of the Columbia River (Forts Canby and Columbia in Washington were the other two). The fort served for 84 years, beginning with the Civil War and closing at the end of World War II. Today, Fort Stevens has grown into a 3,700-acre park offering exploration of history, nature, and recreational opportunities. And you can help fund historic programs and restoration at the park! The Friends of Old Fort Stevens will run Wood on Wheels this summer, selling and delivering firewood right to your site. Check it out when you arrive. Camping, beachcombing, freshwater-lake swimming, trails, wildlife viewing, a historic shipwreck, and a historic military area make Fort Stevens a uniquely diversified park. A network of 9 miles of bicycle trails and 6 miles of hiking trails allow you to explore the park through spruce and hemlock forests, wetlands, dunes, and shore pine.

BASICS

Operated By: Oregon State Parks. **Open:** All year. **Site Assignment:** Reservations can be made 9 months in advance. **Registration:** At office. **Fee:** Single, $13–$22; yurt, $30; day use, $35. **Parking:** At park.

FACILITIES

Number of Multipurpose Sites: 1,126. **Hookups:** Yes. **Dump Station:** Yes. **Laundry:** No. **Pay Phone:** Yes. **Restrooms and Showers:** Yes. **Fuel:** No. **Propane:** Yes. **Internal Roads:** Paved. **RV Service:** No. **Market:** No. **Restaurant:** Less than 3 mi. **General Store:** Yes. **Vending:** No. **Swimming:** Yes. **Playground:** Yes. **Activities:** Hiking, horseshoe, jogging/running, junior ranger program, nature program, skating, walking.

RESTRICTIONS

Pets: Pets must be confined by the owner, or on a leash not more than 6 feet long, kept under physical control at all times. You're responsible for removal of all waste and for keeping your pet quiet during campground quiet hours (10 p.m.–7 a.m.). **Fires:** In fire rings or fireplaces provided for such purposes & portions of the beach designated as permissible for fires. No fires shall be left unattended or be permitted to cause damage to park facilities or areas. **Alcoholic Beverages:** Possession or use of an alcoholic

beverage by any person under 21 years of age is not allowed. **Other:** Discount programs may be offered. Fee adjustments will not be made after reservations have been confirmed using the Internet reservation service. A large campsite has at least a 12 by 12–ft. tent-pad area. Medium sites are at least 10 by 10 ft. Small sites are at least 8 by 8 ft.

TO GET THERE

Fort Stevens is located in the very northwest corner of Oregon, 14 mi. north of Seaside and 8 mi. west of Astoria.

HOOD RIVER   MAP, A-2
Memaloose State Park

P.O. Box 126, 97031. T: (541) 478-3008; www.reserveamerica.com.

🚐 ★★★★   ⛺ ★★★★

Beauty: ★★★★   Site Privacy: ★★★
Spaciousness: ★★★   Quiet: ★★★★
Security: ★★★★   Cleanliness: ★★★★
Insect Control: ★★★★   Facilities: ★★★★

The Chinook Indian tribes of the Columbia Gorge used to lay the bones of their dead on open pyres on Memaloose Island in the middle of the Columbia River near The Dalles. A granite monument visible from Memaloose State Park campground marks the resting place where a local pioneer named Victor Trevitt wished to chart his eternal course buried among honorable men. Today, Memaloose State Park is a virtual oasis of beauty in the hottest part of the Columbia River Gorge. Temperatures can top 110°F on a summer day, but Memaloose always manages to provide cool comfort, lush green grass, and shade thanks to the tall maples and willows that loom large in the park. The sound of pulsating sprinklers provides a melodic nighttime rhythm to the counterpoint of chirping crickets and lonesome train whistles. On summer nights, families select prime viewing spots on the cool grass and open meadows around the campground and observe the nightly celestial performances of shooting stars, wandering satellites, and faraway galaxies.

BASICS

Operated By: Oregon State Parks. **Open:** All year. **Site Assignment:** Reservations can be made 9 months in advance. **Registration:** At office. **Fee:** Single, $12–$20. **Parking:** At park.

FACILITIES

Number of Multipurpose Sites: 122. **Hookups:** Yes. **Dump Station:** Yes. **Laundry:** No. **Pay Phone:** Yes. **Restrooms and Showers:** Yes. **Fuel:** No. **Propane:** No. **Internal Roads:** Paved. **RV Service:** No. **Market:** No. **Restaurant:** Less than 20 mi. **General Store:** No. **Vending:** No. **Swimming:** Yes. **Playground:** No. **Activities:** Berry picking, educational programs, fishing, horseshoes, jogging/running, junior ranger program.

RESTRICTIONS

Pets: Pets must be confined by the owner, or on a leash not more than 6 feet long, kept under physical control at all times. You're responsible for removal of all waste and for keeping your pet quiet during campground quiet hours (10 p.m.–7 a.m.). **Fires:** In fire rings or fireplaces provided for such purposes & portions of the beach designated as permissible for fires. No fires shall be left unattended or be permitted to cause damage to park facilities or areas. **Alcoholic Beverages:** Possession or use of an alcoholic beverage by any person under 21 years of age is not allowed. **Other:** Discount programs may be offered. Fee adjustments will not be made after reservations have been confirmed using the Internet reservation service. A large campsite has at least a 12 by 12–ft. tent-pad area. Medium sites are at least 10 by 10 ft. Small sites are at least 8 by 8 ft.

TO GET THERE

If going east on I-84, turn off at Exit 76, the Rowena exit. Turn around and go 3 mi. west to Memaloose. Follow signs that say Memaloose Rest Area. If going west: No exit sign, but follow sign that says Memaloose Rest Area. When leaving the park, traveling west from park, just get on I-84 and go. If traveling east from park, go 3 mi. west to Mosier then turn around and get back on I-84.

HUNTINGTON MAP, B-4
Farewell Bend State Recreation Area

reserve america

23751 Old Hwy. 30, 97907. T: (541) 869-2365 or (800) 551-6949; www.reserveamerica.com.

🚐 ★★★★   ⛺ ★★

Beauty: ★★★★   Site Privacy: ★★★
Spaciousness: ★★   Quiet: ★★★
Security: ★   Cleanliness: ★★★
Insect Control: ★   Facilities: ★★★

Farewell Bend State Park is set on an irrigated, flat arm of the Snake River, and it makes a great stopover for whitewater rafters on their way to Idaho or Utah. The campground has two sections, A and B; both campgrounds have sites on the river. Sites A42–A52 (even numbers only) have shade and some privacy; section B has three premium sites on the river with gas grills and patios but without cover from the intense sun. The tenting area has 45 drive-in primitive sites with lots of shade, but no privacy or protection from occasional road noise. Remember that sites near the water receive, at times, copious amounts of wind, and that the high altitude summer sun here will burn skin very quickly. Winters in this part of Oregon are long and cold. Call before arrival to make sure the area has not flooded, as this is a recurring problem.

BASICS

Operated By: Oregon State Parks & Recreation. **Open:** All year; limited to 10 sites in winter. **Site Assignment:** On arrival; reservation required; deposit is 1 night plus nonrefundable reservation fee; refund w/ 48-hour notice. **Registration:** At self-pay station. **Fee:** $11–$17; extra vehicle, $5; V, MC, cash. **Parking:** At site.

FACILITIES

Number of RV-only Sites: 101. **Number of Tent-only Sites:** 40. **Hookups:** Electric (20, 30 amps),

water. **Each Site:** Picnic table, fire ring. **Dump Station:** Yes. **Laundry:** No. **Pay Phone:** Yes. **Restrooms and Showers:** Yes. **Fuel:** No. **Propane:** No. **Internal Roads:** Paved. **RV Service:** No. **Market:** 4 mi. in Huntington (north). **Restaurant:** 4 mi. in Huntington (north). **General Store:** No. **Vending:** No. **Swimming:** No. **Playground:** No. **Other:** Cabins, wagons, teepees available. **Activities:** Boating, fishing, relaxing, bird-watching, interpretive programs. **Nearby Attractions:** Snake River Reservoirs, water sports, Ontario. **Additional Information:** Ontario Chamber of Commerce, (541) 889-8012.

RESTRICTIONS

Pets: On leash only (max. length 6 ft.). **Fires:** Fire pit only. **Alcoholic Beverages:** At site. **Vehicle Maximum Length:** 50 ft.

TO GET THERE

From I-84 Exit 353, eastbound, turn right onto Hwy. 30. Drive 1 mi. to park entrance.

JOSEPH MAP, A-4
Wallowa Lake State Park

reserve america

72214 Marina Lane, 97846. T: (541) 432-4185; www.reserveamerica.com.

🚐 ★★★★   ⛺ ★★★★

Beauty: ★★★★★   Site Privacy: ★★★
Spaciousness: ★★★   Quiet: ★★★★
Security: ★★★★   Cleanliness: ★★★★
Insect Control: ★★★★   Facilities: ★★★★

If you're interested in a campground surrounded on three sides by 9,000-foot-tall tall snowcapped mountains and a large, clear lake, this is the area for you. The lake is a popular fishing and boating site. Around the Wallowa Lake area, you can enjoy hiking wilderness trails, horseback riding, bumper boats, canoeing, or mini-golf, or ride a tramway to the top of one of the mountains (a rise of 4,000 feet). Wildlife is abundant in the area. There are gift shops nearby and a thriving artist community which does world-class bronze castings. Tours are available through the foundries and the showroom displays (they'll keep you interested for hours). Wallowa Lake also serves as a gateway to visit Hells Canyon, the deepest gorge in North America. There are activities for everyone in the family. The campground offers 121 full-hookup sites, 89 tent sites (maximum 90 feet), one cabin, two yurts, and group tent sites (three areas, 25 people each). The day-use area and boat ramp open at 6 a.m. Most campsites close for the winter, but four sites stay open (with no water service), and the yurts are available all year.

BASICS

Operated By: Oregon State Parks. **Open:** All year. **Site Assignment:** Reservations can be made 9 months in advance. **Registration:** At office. **Fee:** Single, $13–$21; yurt, $29; boat moorage, $7; day use, $35.80; group, $42–$64; deluxe cabin, $58–$80. **Parking:** At park.

FACILITIES

Number of Multipurpose Sites: 263. **Hookups:** Yes. **Dump Station:** Yes. **Laundry:** No. **Pay Phone:**

Yes. **Restrooms and Showers:** Yes. **Fuel:** No. **Propane:** Less than 10 mi. **Internal Roads:** Paved. **RV Service:** No. **Market:** No. **Restaurant:** No. **General Store:** No. **Vending:** No. **Swimming:** Yes. **Playground:** Yes. **Activities:** Baseball, basketball, boating, canoeing, educational programs, fishing, picnicking, hiking, horseshoe, jet skiing, junior ranger program, kayaking, paddleboating, photography, sightseeing, snorkeling, volleyball.

RESTRICTIONS

Pets: Pets must be confined by the owner, or on a leash not more than 6 feet long, kept under physical control at all times. You're responsible for removal of all waste and for keeping your pet quiet during campground quiet hours (10 p.m.–7 a.m.). **Fires:** In fire rings or fireplaces provided for such purposes & portions of the beach designated as permissible for fires. No fires shall be left unattended or be permitted to cause damage to park facilities or areas. **Alcoholic Beverages:** Possession or use of an alcoholic beverage by any person under 21 years of age is not allowed. **Other:** Discount programs may be offered. Fee adjustments will not be made after reservations have been confirmed using the Internet reservation service. A large campsite has at least a 12 by 12–ft. tent-pad area. Medium sites are at least 10 by 10 ft. Small sites are at least 8 by 8 ft.

TO GET THERE

Wallowa Lake State Park is located 6 mi. south of Joseph, OR, on State 82.

JUNCTION CITY MAP, B-1
Richardson Park

25950 Richardson Pk. Rd, 97448. T: (541) 682-2000 or (541) 935-2005.

🚐 ★★★★   ⛺ ★★★

Beauty: ★★★   Site Privacy: ★★★
Spaciousness: ★★   Quiet: ★★★
Security: ★   Cleanliness: ★★★★
Insect Control: ★★   Facilities: ★★★

Richardson Park Campground, located in a quiet, rural county park 20 minutes west of Eugene and 8 miles off Hwy. 99, offers very private sites and nearby access to a wide array of water sports. The enormous and marina-plentiful Fern Ridge Reservoir creates the eastern boundary of the county park. The campground is separated into two sections by a main access road and organized into several loops within each section. There is an eclectic mix of sites here, some private and some not. The best sites, 12, 13, 15, and 17–24, have privacy created by a dense mix of lime-green, moss-encrusted pines, oaks, firs, and a thick bramble of secondary growth. Other sites stand totally open and adjacent. Those to avoid include 56–60 and 72–84. All paved sites have an area that will accommodate a tent, but there are no formal tent sites within the park. Winters mix mild and cold weather; summer brings better weather and is the best time to travel here.

BASICS

Operated By: Lane County Parks Division. **Open:** Apr. 15–Oct. 15. **Site Assignment:** First come, first served; reservations at (541) 935-2005; required deposit is 1-night's stay plus $10 nonrefundable fee; refund w/ 14-day notice). **Registration:** At office; after hours see camp host. **Fee:** $20; extra vehicle (more than 1 unit & 1 car), $5; cash, check, credit card. **Parking:** At site.

FACILITIES

Number of Multipurpose Sites: 88. **Hookups:** Electric (30, 50 amps), water. **Each Site:** Picnic table, fire ring. **Dump Station:** Yes. **Laundry:** No. **Pay Phone:** Yes. **Restrooms and Showers:** Yes. **Fuel:** No. **Propane:** No. **Internal Roads:** Paved. **RV Service:** No. **Market:** 5 mi. west in Venita. **Restaurant:** 5 mi. west in Venita. **General Store:** No. **Vending:** Yes. **Swimming:** No. **Playground:** Yes. **Other:** Small amphitheater, boat & Jet Ski rentals, boat launch, short hiking trails, horseshoe pits, lake. **Activities:** Swimming, fishing, boating, various planned activities during high volume. **Nearby Attractions:** Fern Ridge Reservoir, The Bridges of Lane County, wineries, hiking trails, whitewater rafting, art & cultural events. **Additional Information:** Convention & Visitors Assoc. of Lane County Oregon, (800) 547-5445.

RESTRICTIONS

Pets: On leash only (max. length 6 ft.). **Fires:** At site. **Alcoholic Beverages:** At site only. **Vehicle Maximum Length:** No limit. **Other:** Vehicles must be parked on paved surfaces; site max. 8 people; 2-week stay limit.

TO GET THERE

From I-5 Exit 194B, drive 3 mi. west on Hwy. 105/126 to West Eugene/Florence Exit for 99N/126W/6th Ave. Continue on 6th Ave. 5.2 mi., then turn left onto Clear Lake Rd. just after Beltline Hwy. underpass. Follow Clear Lake Rd. 5 mi. to the entrance on the right.

KLAMATH FALLS	MAP, C-2
Lake of the Woods Resort	

950 Harriman Rte., 97601.
T: (541) 949-8300 or (866) 201-4194;
www.lakeofthewoodsresort.com.

🚐 ★★★★	⛺ ★★★
Beauty: ★★★★	Site Privacy: ★
Spaciousness: ★★	Quiet: ★★★★★
Security: ★	Cleanliness: ★★★★
Insect Control: ★★	Facilities: ★★★★

Lake of the Woods Resort, a few minutes off Hwy. 140 and 40 miles north of Klamath Falls, provides a variety of outdoor recreational activities for all seasons. The campground area has open, flat sites on several islands, and a few sites on the perimeter. The best dirt tent sites, A–E, sit on the perimeter near the back of the campground while the best wood-chip-surfaced RV full hookups, 3–9, sit on one of the islands. Tent sites F–M and RV sites 10–20 have a more disorganized and crowded feel. The whole resort stays very shady with a large number of old firs and pines towering overhead. The campground and the common areas of the resort have a very spacious, open, woodland feel, which invites jackrabbits and beavers to visit occasionally. The marina rents a variety of boats including pontoon boats and even a sailboat. While the camp area has no scenic views, the common areas, beaches, and restaurant have beautiful, peaceful vistas of the trout and salmon-filled Lake of the Woods and its far, wooded shores. Any time of the year makes a good time to visit, as the grounds provide year-round recreation opportunities.

BASICS

Operated By: Doug & Becky Neuman. **Open:** All year. **Site Assignment:** 50% deposit upon reservation, full payment due 30 days prior to arrival; full advance payment required for holidays; cancellations accepted up to 30 days prior to arrival w/ $25 fee; cancellations w/ 30-day notice forfeit 1-night rental fee. **Registration:** At office. **Fee:** RV $32; extra vehicle, $5; pets, $5; V, MC, AE, D, cash. **Parking:** At site.

FACILITIES

Number of RV-only Sites: 27. **Hookups:** Electric (30 amps), water, sewer. **Each Site:** Picnic table, fire pit. **Dump Station:** Yes. **Laundry:** Yes. **Pay Phone:** Yes. **Restrooms and Showers:** Yes. **Fuel:** Yes. **Propane:** Yes. **Internal Roads:** Dirt w/ wood chips. **RV Service:** No. **Market:** In Klamath Falls. **Restaurant:** On site. **General Store:** Yes. **Vending:** No. **Swimming:** Yes. **Playground:** No. **Other:** Marina w/ supplies, horseshoes, amphitheater, restaurant & bar, beach, boat rentals (an assortment of powered & non), mountain bike rentals, moorage, movie rentals, VCR rentals, barbecue rentals, hiking & biking trails, lake swimming area, ice-skate rentals. **Activities:** Swimming, hiking, biking, fishing, boating, dining, occasional planned activities, cross-country skiing, snowshoeing, ice skating, snowmobiling. **Nearby Attractions:** City of Klamath Falls, Upper Klamath Lake, Crater Lake National Park, Arnold Palmer Golf Course. **Additional Information:** Klamath County Dept. of Tourism, (800) 445-6734.

RESTRICTIONS

Pets: On leash only. **Fires:** Fire pit only. **Alcoholic Beverages:** Not in public buildings. **Vehicle Maximum Length:** No limit. **Other:** No cutting of firewood.

TO GET THERE

Between mi. 37 and mi. 39 on Hwy. 140, turn (westbound-left) onto Dead Indian Memorial Dr. Follow 1 mi. and then turn right onto an unnamed road marked with "Resort" ODOT sign. This road dead ends into the resort.

LA GRANDE	MAP, A-4
Hot Lake RV Resort	

65182 Hot Lake Ln., 97850.
T: (541) 963-5253 or (800) 993-5253.

🚐 ★★★★	⛺ ★★
Beauty: ★★★★	Site Privacy: ★
Spaciousness: ★★★	Quiet: ★★★★
Security: ★	Cleanliness: ★★
Insect Control: ★★	Facilities: ★★

Hot Lake RV Resort, located in a peacefully scenic area, has some of the best views in eastern Oregon. The park sits in a very flat area in a valley. From the campground, guests have views of the surrounding grassy, golden brown, rolling hills, complete with a train visible miles away. Save the occasional, distant train noises, the campground is quiet; there being nothing around to generate noise. Gravel sites on the perimeters have the best views; these include sites 82–100 and 40–49. The totally unobscured views from these sites provide enchanting, big-sky sunsets and, at night, a stunning view of the heavens. With an organizational scheme of parallel rows, the RV section has some large pull-throughs, but the section lacks shade or privacy. The grassy tent area sits across a nearby stream, shaded by small, deciduous trees, but also lacks inter-site privacy. The pool area needs more upkeep than it receives. Visit right before or after summer for the best weather conditions, as summers here can be scorching.

BASICS

Operated By: Private Operator. **Open:** All year. **Site Assignment:** By reservation & first come, first served. **Registration:** At office; after hours drop by office. **Fee:** Full, $21; tent, $15; fee covers 2 people; children free; V, MC, cash. **Parking:** At site.

FACILITIES

Number of RV-only Sites: 100. **Number of Tent-only Sites:** Undesignated sites. **Hookups:** Electric (30, 50 amps), water, sewer. **Each Site:** None. **Dump Station:** No. **Laundry:** Yes. **Pay Phone:** Yes. **Restrooms and Showers:** Yes. **Fuel:** No. **Propane:** No. **Internal Roads:** Gravel. **RV Service:** No. **Market:** 5 mi. in La Grande. **Restaurant:** 5 mi. in La Grande. **General Store:** Yes (seasonal hours). **Vending:** No. **Swimming:** Yes. **Playground:** No. **Other:** Spa. **Activities:** Inquire at campground. **Nearby Attractions:** Golf, Anthony Lakes Mt. Resort & Recreation Area, Winom-Frazier Off Highway Vehicle Trail Complex, Spout Springs Ski Area. **Additional Information:** Union County Chamber of Commerce, (541) 963-8588.

RESTRICTIONS

Pets: On leash only. **Fires:** Not allowed. **Alcoholic Beverages:** At site. **Vehicle Maximum Length:** 90 ft. **Other:** No washing vehicles in park.

TO GET THERE

From I-84 Exit 265, drive 4.8 mi. east on Hwy. 203S. The campground is listed by a small ODOT sign. Pass the sign, turn right onto Hot Lake Ln. (gravel); drive 0.5 mi. to the campground.

LAKESIDE	MAP, B-1
William M. Tugman State Park	

reserve america

72549 Hwy. 101, 97449. T: (541) 759-3604;
www.reserveamerica.com.

🚐 ★★★★	⛺ ★★★★
Beauty: ★★★★	Site Privacy: ★★
Spaciousness: ★★	Quiet: ★★★★★
Security: ★★★★	Cleanliness: ★★★★
Insect Control: ★★★★	Facilities: ★★★★

Despite its close proximity to Highway 101, Tugman State Park is relatively unknown—a private hideaway on the wondrous south coast. Situated on Eel Lake near the community of Lakeside, Tugman offers 115 campsites with electric/water hookups tucked away in a mature stand of shore pines. The day-use area has a restroom and gazebo-style shelter surrounded by broad green lawns. There's plenty of space for large and small groups to enjoy themselves. The waters of Eel Lake are outstanding for fishing, swimming, canoeing, sailing, and boating. A trail around the south end of the lake allows hikers to get away from the developed area of the park and explore the lake's many inlets. Maybe you'll catch glimpses of osprey, crane, eagle, deer, and other forest creatures as you walk through forests of spruce, cedar, fir, and alder. The famous Oregon Dunes Recreation area is less than a mile away. Tugman is centrally located for visitors wishing to explore the Oregon coast from Reedsport to Coos Bay. Eel Lake is brimming with fishing opportunities. The brush-lined shore, steep drop-off, and underwater structure make it the perfect lake for a bass boat and bass fishing. The lake has a good population of largemouth bass (some running up to five pounds), and other fish species include crappie, rainbow trout (which are stocked), steelhead, and Coho salmon. All Coho, even those under 15 inches, must be released. There is a fully accessible fishing dock at the day-use area near the boat ramp. Trout and bass are often caught from the dock.

BASICS

Operated By: Oregon State Parks. **Open:** All year. **Site Assignment:** Reservations can be made 9 months in advance. **Registration:** At office. **Fee:** Single, $12–$16; yurt, $27; day use, $35.80. **Parking:** At park.

FACILITIES

Number of Multipurpose Sites: 226. **Hookups:** Yes. **Dump Station:** Yes. **Laundry:** No. **Pay Phone:** Yes. **Restrooms and Showers:** Yes. **Fuel:** Less than 0.5 mi. **Propane:** Less than 0.5 mi. **Internal Roads:** Paved. **RV Service:** No. **Market:** No. **Restaurant:** No. **General Store:** Less than 5 mi. **Vending:** Less than 0.5 mi. **Swimming:** Yes. **Playground:** No. **Activities:** Berry picking, boating, canoeing, junior ranger program, fishing, hiking, horseshoes, kayaking, photography, picnicking, sailing, whale-watching.

RESTRICTIONS

Pets: Pets must be confined by the owner, or on a leash not more than 6 feet long, kept under physical control at all times. You're responsible for removal of all waste and for keeping your pet quiet during campground quiet hours (10 p.m.–7 a.m.). **Fires:** In fire rings or fireplaces provided for such purposes & portions of the beach designated as permissible for fires. No fires shall be left unattended or be permitted to cause damage to park facilities or areas. **Alcoholic Beverages:** Possession or use of an alcoholic beverage by any person under 21 years of age is not allowed. **Other:** Discount programs may be offered. Fee adjustments will not be made after reservations have been confirmed using the Internet reservation service. A large campsite has at least a 12 by 12–ft. tent-pad area. Medium sites are at least 10 by10 ft. Small sites are at least 8 by 8 ft.

TO GET THERE

On US 101, 8 mi. south of Reedsport. On US 101, 17 mi. north of Coos Bay.

LA PINE   MAP, B-2
La Pine State Park

reserve america

15800 State Recreation Rd., 97739. T: (541) 536-2071; www.reserveamerica.com.

🚐 ★★★★   ⛺ ★★★★

Beauty: ★★★	Site Privacy: ★★★
Spaciousness: ★★★	Quiet: ★★★★
Security: ★★★★	Cleanliness: ★★★★
Insect Control: ★★★★	Facilities: ★★★★

If you want to immerse yourself in a subalpine pine forest where the air has that high-Cascades tang; to stay in a clean, quiet campground next to a twisting, cold river brimming with trout (and a nearby legendary fly-fishing spot) and surrounded by miles of waiting-to-be-explored wilderness; to sit smack in the middle of dozens of high-mountain lakes (in winter, near some of the best ski spots in the land); to see eagles or red-tailed hawks grabbing breakfast right in front of you; or, to just sit in a campsite pondering what you might do tomorrow, then La Pine State Park demands a visit. The park is also home to Oregon's largest ponderosa pine. Nicknamed "Big Red," the tree is 162 feet tall, 28.9 feet around, and may be in excess of 500 years old. The campground consists of 87 full-hookup and 50 electric sites, three yurts, and five log cabins. There are flush toilets and hot showers. Popular activities include fishing, hiking, biking, and wildlife viewing. Naturalist programs are usually provided weekends from June to Labor Day.

BASICS

Operated By: Oregon State Parks. **Open:** All year. **Site Assignment:** Reservations can be made 9 months in advance. **Registration:** At office. **Fee:** Single, $13–$17; meeting hall, $25; cabin, $38; deluxe cabin, $49–$70. **Parking:** At park.

FACILITIES

Number of Multipurpose Sites: 326. **Hookups:** Yes. **Dump Station:** Yes. **Laundry:** No. **Pay Phone:** Yes. **Restrooms and Showers:** Yes. **Fuel:** Less than 10 mi. **Propane:** Less than 10 mi. **Internal Roads:** Paved. **RV Service:** No. **Market:** No. **Restaurant:** Less than 10 mi. **General Store:** Less than 10 mi. **Vending:** No. **Swimming:** No. **Playground:** No. **Activities:** Amphitheater, biking, bird-watching, boating, canoeing, fishing, jogging/running, junior ranger program, kayaking, photography, picnicking, rafting, sightseeing, cross-country skiing, wildlife viewing.

RESTRICTIONS

Pets: Pets must be confined by the owner, or on a leash not more than 6 feet long, kept under physical control at all times. You're responsible for removal of all waste and for keeping your pet quiet during campground quiet hours (10 p.m.–7 a.m.). **Fires:** In fire rings or fireplaces provided for such purposes & portions of the beach designated as permissible for fires. No fires shall be left unattended or be permitted to cause damage to park facilities or areas. **Alcoholic Beverages:** Possession or use of an alcoholic beverage by any person under 21 years of age is not allowed. **Other:** Discount programs may be offered. Fee adjustments will not be made after reservations have been confirmed using the Internet reservation service. A large campsite has at least a 12 by 12–ft. tent-pad area. Medium sites are at least 10 by10 ft. Small sites are at least 8 by 8 ft.

TO GET THERE

From the south: Follow Hwy. 97 7 mi. north of Lapine. Turn left on State Recreation Rd. Continue 4.5 mi. to campground. From the north: Follow Hwy. 97 21 mi. south of Bend. Turn right on State Recreation Rd. Continue 4.5 mi. to campground.

LINCOLN CITY   MAP, A-1
Devils Lake State Park

reserve america

1452 NE 6th Dr., 97367. T: (541) 994-2002; www.reserveamerica.com.

🚐 ★★★★   ⛺ ★★★★

Beauty: ★★★	Site Privacy: ★★★
Spaciousness: ★★★	Quiet: ★★★★★
Security: ★★★★	Cleanliness: ★★★★
Insect Control: ★★★★	Facilities: ★★★

With downtown Lincoln City mere minutes away, you can glide quietly by canoe or kayak on the lake while you watch for coots, loons, ducks, cormorants, bald eagles, and grebes. As the only Oregon coast campground located in the midst of a city, the lake is a center of summertime activity. The park is nestled between the Pacific Ocean and the 678-acre Devils Lake. You'll find the campground on the west shore, and the East Devils Lake day-use area just down the road. The park features boat moorage slips and a fishing dock. The park features ten yurts. Yurts are domed tents with structural support, a plywood floor, lockable wooden door, lights, heating, and beds with mattresses. The park offers 32 full-hookup campsites and 55 tent sites (maximum site 62 feet); 10 yurts; hiker-biker camp. Boaters, waterskiers, swimmers, and jet skiers share the water. Kayak tours of the lake are scheduled in the summer (the park provides the kayak). In addition the park offers camping, picnicking and hiking, biking, yurt stays, nature programs, and outstanding waterfowl viewing.

BASICS

Operated By: Oregon State Parks. **Site Assignment:** Reservations can be made 9 months in advance. **Registration:** At office. **Fee:** Single, $13–$23; yurt, $29; boat moorage, $7. **Parking:** At park.

FACILITIES

Number of Multipurpose Sites: 209. **Hookups:** Yes. **Dump Station:** No. **Laundry:** No. **Pay Phone:** Yes. **Restrooms and Showers:** Yes. **Fuel:** No. **Propane:** No. **Internal Roads:** Paved. **RV Service:** No. **Market:** No. **Restaurant:** No. **General Store:** No. **Vending:** No. **Swimming:** No. **Playground:** No. **Activities:** Amphitheater, berry picking, biking, bird-watching, boating, canoeing, horseshoes, junior ranger program, nature program, waterskiing, stargazing.

RESTRICTIONS

Pets: Pets must be confined by the owner, or on a leash not more than 6 feet long, kept under physical control at all times. You're responsible for removal of all waste and for keeping your pet quiet during campground quiet hours (10 p.m.–7 a.m.). **Fires:** In fire rings or fireplaces provided for such purposes & portions of the beach designated as permissible for fires. No fires shall be left unattended or be permitted to cause damage to park facilities or areas. **Alcoholic Beverages:** Possession or use of an alcoholic beverage by any person under 21 years of age is not allowed. **Other:** Discount programs may be offered. Fee adjustments will not be made after reservations have been confirmed using the Internet reservation service. A large campsite has at least a 12 by 12–ft. tent-pad area. Medium sites are at least 10 by 10 ft. Small sites are at least 8 by 8 ft.

TO GET THERE

Devils Lake State Park is located in Lincoln City. From Hwy. 101 turn east onto NE 6th Dr. (at the stoplight). Park entrance is 500 feet.

LINCOLN CITY
Lincoln City KOA
MAP, A-1

5298 NE Park Ln., 97368. T: (541) 994-2961 or (800) 562-3316.

🚐 ★★★★   ▲ ★★★

Beauty: ★★★   Site Privacy: ★★
Spaciousness: ★★★   Quiet: ★★★★
Security: ★★   Cleanliness: ★★★★★
Insect Control: ★★   Facilities: ★★★

Lincoln City KOA Kampground, a few miles off 101 just north of Lincoln city, offers a quiet and serene retreat from surrounding beach culture. The grounds, shaded by pine and fir trees, and bordered on one side by a stream and all other sides by dense blackberry brambles, possess both terraced and field-set gravel pull-through and back-in sites. The terraced sites provide more of a feeling of spaciousness than the field sites. The best back-ins, 23–36 (some full hookup, some water/electric), and the best pull-throughs, 8–16, rise up the terraced hill to the entrance. None of the sites afford much privacy. Preferable tent sites, numbers 51–63, lie along the clear, gently flowing stream at the edge of the field. Many water/electric sites double as tent sites (be wary of sites where leaky motor homes have previously parked). Avoid the trailer city–like sites numbered 64–87. The playground here is large and well equipped, and the grounds are very quiet.

BASICS

Operated By: Lincoln City KOA. **Open:** All year. **Site Assignment:** First come, first served; reservation (required deposit is 1-night stay; refund w/ 48-hour notice). **Registration:** At office, after hours in drop box in front of office. **Fee:** $22–$32; extra person, $3; max. site occupancy is 6; V, MC, AE, D, cash. **Parking:** At site.

FACILITIES

Number of RV-only Sites: 56. **Number of Tent-only Sites:** 15. **Hookups:** Electric (20, 30 amps), water, sewer, cable TV. **Each Site:** Picnic table.

Dump Station: Yes. **Laundry:** Yes. **Pay Phone:** Yes. **Restrooms and Showers:** Yes. **Fuel:** No. **Propane:** Yes. **Internal Roads:** Gravel. **RV Service:** No. **Market:** 5 mi. west in Lincoln City. **Restaurant:** 5 mi. west in Lincoln City. **General Store:** Yes. **Vending:** Yes. **Swimming:** No. **Playground:** Yes. **Other:** Horseshoes, game room, volleyball, basketball, tetherball, RV supplies, on-site catering. **Activities:** Berry picking, ice-cream socials & other planned activities, wildlife viewing (elk), barbecues in summer. **Nearby Attractions:** Devil's Lake, beaches, Cascade Head Scenic Research Area, charter fishing, whale-watching, salmon river, Oregon Coast Aquarium, Tillamook Air Museum, Siletz River, golf, casino. **Additional Information:** Lincoln City Chamber of Commerce, (541) 994-3070.

RESTRICTIONS

Pets: On leash only. **Fires:** Fire pit only. **Alcoholic Beverages:** At site only. **Vehicle Maximum Length:** 60 ft. **Other:** No multiroom tents; no hanging tarps from trees; Don't drive through unoccupied sites; Quiet hours 10 p.m.–6 a.m.

TO GET THERE

Headed south on Hwy. 101: Just past Faith Baptist church, 1 mi. south of the junction of Hwy. 18 and US 101, turn left onto East Devil's Lake Rd. and follow 1 mi.; turn left on Park Ln. The entrance is on the right.

MANZANITA/
NEHALEM
Nehalem Bay State Park
MAP, A-1

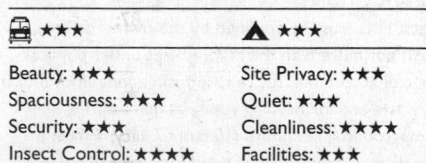

9500 Sandpiper Ln., 97131.
T: (503) 368-5154 or (800) 452-5687;
www.reserveamerica.com.

🚐 ★★★★   ▲ ★★★

Beauty: ★★★★   Site Privacy: ★★★
Spaciousness: ★★   Quiet: ★★★★
Security: ★★   Cleanliness: ★★★
Insect Control: ★★   Facilities: ★★★

Nehalem Bay State Park, positioned in between the tiny villages of Nehalem and Manzanita, makes up for its lack of commerce with access to natural beauty. Campers need hike only a few hundred feet over the dunes to find themselves on beautiful, narrow, driftwood-covered beaches of the great blue Pacific. The campground, divided into six loops, sits in a grove of short coastal pines that provide privacy for the sites. There are no official tent sites, save those reserved for coastal thru-hikers and bikers, but all of the campground sites have flat grassy areas to accommodate a tent. Sites vary significantly in width, and all have flat, paved areas for RVs. Avoid sites F41, F43, E34, E36, E40, E42, D36, D38, C38, C40, C47, B24, B34, B36, A25, and A27 as they are next to beach access trails (high traffic). Sacrificing some privacy, C43–46, B24–33, and A17–24 have the best views of the lovely, undeveloped surrounding coastal hills.

BASICS

Operated By: Oregon State Parks & Recreation. **Open:** All year. **Site Assignment:** First come, first served; reservation (required deposit is 1 night plus nonrefundable fee; refund w/ 3-day notice). **Registration:** At entrance gate or self-pay station. **Fee:** $8–$20; extra vehicle (more than 1 unit & 1 vehicle), $5; V, MC, cash. **Parking:** At site.

FACILITIES

Number of Multipurpose Sites: 265. **Hookups:** Electric (20, 30 amps), water. **Each Site:** Picnic table, fire ring. **Dump Station:** Yes. **Laundry:** No. **Pay Phone:** Yes. **Restrooms and Showers:** Yes. **Fuel:** No. **Propane:** No. **Internal Roads:** Paved. **RV Service:** No. **Market:** 5 mi. north in Manzanita. **Restaurant:** 5 mi. north in Manzanita. **General Store:** No. **Vending:** No. **Swimming:** Yes. **Playground:** Yes. **Other:** Amphitheater, horse camp, boat launch, beach, airstrip, nonmotorized traveler camp, bicycle trail, horse trail. **Activities:** Nightly interpretive programs, daytime Jr. Ranger programs, other various planned activities (all above listed are seasonal), fishing, hiking, kayaking. **Nearby Attractions:** Oswald West State Park, Nehalem Bay Winery, bike rentals. **Additional Information:** Nehalem Bay Area Chamber of Commerce, (503) 355-2335.

RESTRICTIONS

Pets: On leash only (max. length 6 ft.). **Fires:** Fire pit only. **Alcoholic Beverages:** At site only. **Vehicle Maximum Length:** Call park for details. **Other:** Quiet hours 10 p.m.–7 a.m.; stay away from driftwood on the beach (drowning hazard).

TO GET THERE

From Hwy. 101S, turn right at the Shell Station near Nehalem, drive 0.3 mi. to first stop, then turn right. Drive another 1.4 mi. to next stop and turn right into the park entrance. Drive 1 mi. and turn right at the wooden sign.

MCKENZIE BRIDGE
Trail Bridge Campground
MAP, B-2

57600 McKenzie Hwy., 97413. T: (541) 822-3381; www.fs.fed.us/r6/willamette.

🚐 ★★★   ▲ ★★★

Beauty: ★★★   Site Privacy: ★★★
Spaciousness: ★★★   Quiet: ★★★
Security: ★★★   Cleanliness: ★★★★
Insect Control: ★★★★   Facilities: ★★★

Think of Trail Bridge as the ultimate scenic drive, complete with campground. You can make it as short as 130 miles if your starting point is Redmond, or quite a bit longer if you are coming from points west and want to make more than a frenetic weekend of it. The drive takes you along one of Oregon's most prized trout streams, over two historic and scenic mountain passes, through a diverse assortment of picturesque landscapes ranging from alpine meadows to high desert grasslands, past many unusual geologic formations, across two of the state's largest national forests, and between two designated wildernesses. Trail Bridge Campground is located on Trail Bridge Reservoir, a small depository of McKenzie River headwaters and a good stopping point in the journey. Flowing pure and cold out of Clear Lake (a natural lava-dam lake just west of lava beds contained within Mount Jefferson Wilderness), the McKenzie River attracts both the drift boat community and vast numbers of rafters, kayakers, and canoeists who appreciate the McKenzie's gentle grade. The campground offers 26 multipurpose sites. Each site has a picnic table, a fire grill, and electricity, but there are no other hookups or special amenities. Restrooms and showers are adequate, without frills.

BASICS

Operated By: Willamette National Forest. **Open:** Apr.–Oct. **Site Assignment:** First come, first served. **Registration:** Self-registration. **Fee:** $6. **Parking:** At site.

FACILITIES

Number of Multipurpose Sites: 26. **Hookups:** None. **Each Site:** Picnic table, fire grill, electricity. **Dump Station:** No. **Laundry:** No. **Pay Phone:** No. **Restrooms and Showers:** Yes. **Fuel:** No. **Propane:** No. **Internal Roads:** Gravel. **RV Service:** No. **Market:** No. **Restaurant:** No. **General Store:** No. **Vending:** No. **Swimming:** Yes. **Playground:** No. **Activities:** Fishing, boating, hiking, picnicking. **Nearby Attractions:** Trout fishing. **Additional Information:** Willamette NF, (541) 822-3381.

RESTRICTIONS

Pets: On leash only. **Fires:** Fire ring only. **Alcoholic Beverages:** Allowed. **Vehicle Maximum Length:** 45 ft. **Other:** Must follow local fishing regulations.

TO GET THERE

Take SR 126 from Eugene or Redmond to McKenzie Bridge. Follow this road north until it becomes SR 26 in McKenzie Bridge. Continue driving to Trail Bridge Reservoir and campground.

MEACHAM MAP, A-4
Emigrant Springs State Park

reserve america

P.O. Box 85, 97859.
T: (541) 983-2277 or (800) 452-5687;
www.reserveamerica.com.

🚐 ★★★	🏕 ★★★
Beauty: ★★★★★	Site Privacy: ★★
Spaciousness: ★★	Quiet: ★★★★
Security: ★	Cleanliness: ★★★
Insect Control: ★★	Facilities: ★★★

Emigrant Springs State Park in eastern Oregon, makes a beautiful base for exploring the area or just taking a night off the interstate. Unlike many campgrounds in the region, this semi-arid, high altitude location has shade; sites sit underneath towering ponderosa pines and other evergreens. Although quiet, the area still has a close proximity to the interstate, making some sites louder than others. Sites B14–B5 and A18–A26 have the most protection from this noise. Sites have a mixture of gravel and paved surfaces, and all lack privacy. The park has an amphitheater and horse camp, but surrounding recreation outside the park is limited. Because of the higher altitude, the park has a milder climate than the surrounding desert, so a coat might be necessary when staying the night. And remember, eastern Oregon has cold weather nine months of the year.

BASICS

Operated By: Oregon State Parks & Recreation. **Open:** Apr.–Oct. 29. **Site Assignment:** First come, first served, reservation (required deposit is 1 night plus nonrefundable fee; refund w/ 48-hour notice). **Registration:** At self-pay station. **Fee:** Full, $16; tent, $14; extra vehicle, $5; V, MC, cash, check. **Parking:** At site.

FACILITIES

Number of RV-only Sites: 19. **Number of Tent-only Sites:** 33. **Hookups:** Electric (20, 30 amps), water, sewer. **Each Site:** Picnic table, fire ring. **Dump Station:** No. **Laundry:** No. **Pay Phone:** Yes. **Restrooms and Showers:** Yes. **Fuel:** No. **Propane:** No. **Internal Roads:** Paved. **RV Service:** No. **Market:** Pendleton, 26 mi. west. **Restaurant:** Pendleton, 26 mi. west. **General Store:** No. **Vending:** No. **Swimming:** No. **Playground:** No. **Other:** Amphitheater, horse camp, cabins available. **Activities:** Interpretive programs during summer, basketball, hiking. **Nearby Attractions:** Blue Mountain Crossing, Oregon Trail, Pendleton Woolen Mills. **Additional Information:** Pendleton Chamber of Commerce, (541) 276-7411.

RESTRICTIONS

Pets: On leash only (max. length 6 ft.). **Fires:** Fire pit only. **Alcoholic Beverages:** At site. **Vehicle Maximum Length:** 60 ft. **Other:** Bikes not permitted on hiking trails.

TO GET THERE

From I-84 Exit 234 (eastbound), drive straight toward Meacham, 0.8 mi, and turn left into the park.

MOUNT VERNON MAP, B-3
Clyde Holliday State Recreation Site

reserve america

P.O. Box 10, 97865. T: (541) 932-4453;
www.reserveamerica.com.

🚐 ★★★★	🏕 ★★★★
Beauty: ★★★	Site Privacy: ★★★★
Spaciousness: ★★★★	Quiet: ★★★★
Security: ★★★★	Cleanliness: ★★★★
Insect Control: ★★★★	Facilities: ★★★★

Think of Clyde Holliday State Recreation Site as an oasis. Its tall, willowy cottonwood trees provide shade and serenity. Clyde Holliday Campground offers 31 electrical sites with 1 pull-through, a hiker-biker camp, restrooms and showers, an outdoor amphitheater where a variety of interpretive programs take place in the summer, a large shaded picnic and day-use area, horseshoe pits, a dump station, and the John Day River running along the park. Each campsite is clothed with a variety of trees and other plants to give you that private, secluded feeling. The park borders the beautiful John Day River and is surrounded on all sides by some of Oregon's most pristine wilderness areas. You're as likely to have wildlife neighbors as human ones: the majestic Rocky Mountain elk and mule deer are frequent visitors. You can experience the thrill of seeing steelhead rush upriver to spawn. The park lies in the shadow of the Strawberry Mountain Range just a short drive away.

BASICS

Operated By: Oregon State Parks. **Open:** All year. **Site Assignment:** Reservations can be made 9 months in advance. **Registration:** At office. **Fee:** Single, $12–$17; tepee, $28. **Parking:** At park.

FACILITIES

Number of Multipurpose Sites: 10. **Hookups:** Yes. **Dump Station:** Yes. **Laundry:** No. **Pay Phone:** Yes. **Restrooms and Showers:** Yes. **Fuel:** No. **Propane:** Less than 10 mi. **Internal Roads:** Paved. **RV Service:** No. **Market:** No. **Restaurant:** No. **General Store:** No. **Vending:** No. **Swimming:** Yes. **Playground:** No. **Activities:** Amphitheater, bird-watching, educational programs, gold panning, horseshoe pitching, kayaking, nature program, picnicking, sightseeing, skating, stargazing, wildlife viewing.

RESTRICTIONS

Pets: Pets must be confined by the owner, or on a leash not more than 6 feet long, kept under physical control at all times. You're responsible for removal of all waste and for keeping your pet quiet during campground quiet hours (10 p.m.–7 a.m.). **Fires:** In fire rings or fireplaces provided for such purposes & portions of the beach designated as permissible for fires. No fires shall be left unattended or be permitted to cause damage to park facilities or areas. **Alcoholic Beverages:** Possession or use of an alcoholic beverage by any person under 21 years of age is not allowed. **Other:** Discount programs may be offered. Fee adjustments will not be made after reservations have been confirmed using the Internet reservation service.

TO GET THERE

Clyde Holliday State Park is located 1 mi. east of Mount Vernon, on US 26, on the right, and 7 mi. west of John Day on US 26 on the left.

MOUNT VERNON MAP, B-3
Unity Lake State Recreation Site

reserve america

P.O. Box 10, 97865. T: (541) 575-2773;
www.reserveamerica.com.

🚐 ★★★★	🏕 ★★★★
Beauty: ★★★	Site Privacy: ★★★★
Spaciousness: ★★★★	Quiet: ★★★
Security: ★★★★	Cleanliness: ★★★★
Insect Control: ★★★★	Facilities: ★★★★

The high desert surroundings of this park offer a unique experience to its guests. The fragrant smell of juniper lingers in the air and thrills the senses.

The cool grass of the park is a vibrant contrast to the sagebrush and cheat grass of the bordering lands. The Burnt River comes to rest behind the Unity Dam before continuing its path down the valley. Relax on the shores or enjoy water sports. There's a boat ramp to accommodate the waterskier as well as the angler. Peacefulness will engulf you at Unity Lake State Recreation Area whatever you choose to do. Two tepees offer unique camping experiences for Unity Lake visitors. The tepees have electricity, carpeting, and foam mattresses inside, and fire rings and picnic tables outside. The campground also provides 35 electrical campsites (21 at 30 amps, 14 at 50 amps; maximum site 40 feet; 5 pull-through sites). The day-use area is a large expanse of lawn and shade trees featuring restrooms, water, and picnic tables. You can swim or fish in the designated areas of Unity Reservoir.

BASICS

Operated By: Oregon State Parks. **Open:** All year. **Site Assignment:** Reservations can be made 9 months in advance. **Registration:** At office. **Fee:** Single, $13–$17; tepee,$29. **Parking:** At park.

FACILITIES

Number of Multipurpose Sites: 16. **Hookups:** Yes. **Dump Station:** Yes. **Laundry:** No. **Pay Phone:** Yes. **Restrooms and Showers:** Yes. **Fuel:** No. **Propane:** No. **Internal Roads:** Paved. **RV Service:** No. **Market:** No. **Restaurant:** No. **General Store:** No. **Vending:** No. **Swimming:** Yes. **Playground:** No. **Activities:** Bird-watching, boating, canoeing, educational programs, fishing, horseshoes, jet skiing, nature program, photography, picnicking, sailing, sightseeing, waterskiing, stargazing, wildlife viewing.

RESTRICTIONS

Pets: Pets must be confined by the owner, or on a leash not more than 6 feet long, kept under physical control at all times. You're responsible for removal of all waste and for keeping your pet quiet during campground quiet hours (10 p.m.–7 a.m.). **Fires:** In fire rings or fireplaces provided for such purposes & portions of the beach designated as permissible for fires. No fires shall be left unattended or be permitted to cause damage to park facilities or areas. **Alcoholic Beverages:** Possession or use of an alcoholic beverage by any person under 21 years of age is not allowed. **Other:** Discount programs may be offered. Fee adjustments will not be made after reservations have been confirmed using the Internet reservation service.

TO GET THERE

Located just off US 26, 53 mi. east of John Day, Oregon. Watch for park signs at the intersection of US 26 and Oregon Hwy. 245 just west of Unity, Oregon. Follow signs to park (about 3 mi. north).

NEHALEM   MAP, A-1
Nehalem Bay State Park

reserve america

P.O. Box 366, 97131. T: (503) 368-5154; www.reserveamerica.com.

🚐 ★★★★   ⛺ ★★★★

Beauty: ★★★★   Site Privacy: ★★★
Spaciousness: ★★★   Quiet: ★★★★★
Security: ★★★★   Cleanliness: ★★★★
Insect Control: ★★★★   Facilities: ★★★★

Imagine waking up to the song of the seagull, spending your afternoon on a kayak trip around Nehalem Bay, then taking a short walk over the dunes to the beach. There you'll sit with a blanket and watch the sun set over the ocean in the shadow of Neah-Kah-Nie Mountain. Finally, snuggle down for the night while the ocean waves sing you a lullaby. This is Nehalem Bay State Park. Many visitors find the serenity of Nehalem Bay State Park to be the most attractive feature. If you look closer you'll find a lot of ways to keep busy, though. Crabbing and fishing on Nehalem Bay are popular. For a breathtaking view of the bay, fitness and wildlife enthusiasts will enjoy the 1.75-mile bike trail that circles the park airplane landing strip. Along this route and in the campground itself, you're likely to see deer grazing, a herd of elk, or a coyote crossing the road. The park is also graced with a variety of birds. Fine dining and local boutiques in the neighboring communities of Manzanita and Nehalem offer a change of scenery from the park setting. Afternoon or moonlit walks on the beach and down to the end of the jetty enhance the serenity of this park.

BASICS

Operated By: Oregon State Parks. **Open:** All year. **Site Assignment:** Reservations can be made 9 months in advance. **Registration:** At office. **Fee:** Single, $16–$20; horse camp, $12–$16; meeting hall, $25; yurt, $27. **Parking:** At park.

FACILITIES

Number of Multipurpose Sites: 344. **Hookups:** Yes. **Dump Station:** Yes. **Laundry:** No. **Pay Phone:** Yes. **Restrooms and Showers:** Yes. **Fuel:** Less than 1 mi. **Propane:** Less than 1 mi. **Internal Roads:** Paved. **RV Service:** No. **Market:** No. **Restaurant:** Less than 1 mi. **General Store:** Less than 1 mi. **Vending:** No. **Swimming:** No. **Playground:** Yes. **Activities:** Amphitheater, berry picking, biking, bird-watching, hiking, horseback riding, jogging/running, junior ranger program, kite flying, photography, picnicking, sightseeing, skateboarding, stargazing.

RESTRICTIONS

Pets: Pets must be confined by the owner, or on a leash not more than 6 feet long, kept under physical control at all times. You're responsible for removal of all waste and for keeping your pet quiet during campground quiet hours (10 p.m.–7 a.m.). **Fires:** In fire rings or fireplaces provided for such purposes & portions of the beach designated as permissible for fires. No fires shall be left unattended or be permitted to cause damage to park facilities or areas. **Alcoholic**

Beverages: Possession or use of an alcoholic beverage by any person under 21 years of age is not allowed. **Other:** Discount programs may be offered. Fee adjustments will not be made after reservations have been confirmed using the Internet reservation service. A large campsite has at least a 12 by 12–ft. tent-pad area. Medium sites are at least 10 by10 ft. Small sites are at least 8 by 8 ft.

TO GET THERE

Turn off US 101 at the Shell station between Manzanita and Nehalem. Travel 1.5 mi. to the park. Follow signs to registration booth 0.5 mi. inside park entrance.

NETARTS   MAP, A-1
Cape Lookout State Park

reserve america

13000 Whiskey Creek Rd. West, 97141. T: (503) 842-4981, (503) 842-3182 or (800) 551-6949; www.reserveamerica.com.

🚐 ★★★   ⛺ ★★★★

Beauty: ★★★★★   Site Privacy: ★★★★
Spaciousness: ★★★   Quiet: ★★★★
Security: ★★★★   Cleanliness: ★★★★★
Insect Control: ★★★   Facilities: ★★★

Situated on one of the most scenic capes in the Northwest, Cape Lookout State Park is located just south of Netarts on the Three Capes Scenic Dr. that encompasses two other magnificent headlands (Cape Meares on the north and Cape Kiwanda on the south). These are also state parks but are limited to day-use activities. Collectively these three areas cover more than 2,500 acres of coastal rain forest, sheer cliffs, wide sandy beaches and dunes, narrow spits, rocky points and outcroppings, protected bays, and estuaries. To accommodate the sizable numbers of seashore enthusiasts, the well-maintained and efficiently designed Cape Lookout State Park offers a whopping 173 tent sites and 39 RV sites, many of which are accessible all year. In addition, it offers hikers and bikers a separate area not far from the central camping grounds. Group camps are also available, as well as a meeting hall.

BASICS

Operated By: Oregon State Parks & Recreation. **Open:** All year. **Site Assignment:** By reservation or first come, first served. **Registration:** Self-registration on site. **Fee:** $12–$20. **Parking:** At site.

FACILITIES

Number of RV-only Sites: 39. **Number of Tent-only Sites:** 173. **Hookups:** Electric (30 amps), water, sewer. **Each Site:** Picnic table, fire pit & grill, piped water, shade trees. **Dump Station:** Yes. **Laundry:** No. **Pay Phone:** Yes. **Restrooms and Showers:** Yes. **Fuel:** 6 mi. (in Netarts). **Propane:** 6 mi. (in Netarts). **Internal Roads:** Paved. **RV Service:** No. **Market:** 6 mi. in Netarts. **Restaurant:** 6 mi. in Netarts. **General Store:** 6 mi. in Netarts. **Vending:** No. **Swimming:** No. **Playground:** No. **Other:** 13 rental units, firewood. **Activities:** Beachcombing, hiking, walking, fishing, evening & historic programs.

Nearby Attractions: Tillamook Cheese Factory. **Additional Information:** Information: (503) 842-4981 or (503) 842-3182.

RESTRICTIONS

Pets: On leash only. **Fires:** Fire ring only. **Alcoholic Beverages:** Allowed. **Vehicle Maximum Length:** 60 ft.

TO GET THERE

From Tillamook, drive southwest on Netarts Hwy. and follow signs the entire way for Cape Lookout State Park; total distance from Tillamook is 10 mi.

NEWPORT — MAP, B-1
Pacific Shores Motorcoach Resort

6225 North Coast Hwy. 101, 97365.
T: (541) 265-3750 or (800) 333-1583;
www.pacificshoresrv.com.

🚐 ★★★★ | ⛺ n/a

Beauty: ★★★	Site Privacy: ★
Spaciousness: ★★★	Quiet: ★★
Security: ★★★★★	Cleanliness: ★★★★★
Insect Control: ★★	Facilities: ★★★★★

Pacific Shores Motorcoach Resort, on the northern edge of Newport and the coastal side of Hwy. 101, is a renovated, family-oriented beach resort. Many of the individual sites are privately owned but rented out when not occupied. The well-equipped facilities include a large indoor pool, several saunas, a hilly chip-and-putt six-hole golf area (with maintained grass) and a three-story-high viewing tower to watch whales playing off the coast. The park sits on cliffs above the beach and has beach access. The best (and also most expensive) sites, numbered 141, 161–168, 185, and 186, have a view of the Pacific and an outcropping to the south, finishing with a lighthouse. Additionally, sites 26–34 have a view slightly obscured by tall pines. Particular sites to avoid, located next to Hwy. 101, include 1–16, 237–252, and 76–93. The spacious, paved, grass-bordered, shadeless sites have wide access roads. Summer months make up the busiest and best time to visit.

BASICS

Operated By: Outdoor Resorts of America, Inc. **Open:** All year. **Site Assignment:** On arrival, reservation required; deposit is 1-night stay; credit card reservations refunded w/ notice before 1 p.m. the day before arrival; checks, cash, money order nonrefundable. **Registration:** At office, after hours at guardhouse. **Fee:** $35–$80; fee covers 4 people; extra person, $5; cash, check; V, MC. **Parking:** At site.

FACILITIES

Number of RV-only Sites: 211. **Hookups:** Electric (20, 30, 50 amps), water, sewer, cable TV. **Each Site:** Picnic table. **Dump Station:** No. **Laundry:** Yes. **Pay Phone:** Yes. **Restrooms and Showers:** Yes. **Fuel:** No. **Propane:** Yes. **Internal Roads:** Paved (wide). **RV Service:** No. **Market:** 2 mi. south in Newport. **Restaurant:** 2 mi. south in Newport. **General Store:** Yes. **Vending:** Yes. **Swimming:** Yes. **Playground:** Yes. **Other:** 2 hot tubs, 3 saunas, 6-hole chip & putt golf, arcade (w/ 2 pool tables), reservable large meeting room, enclosed viewing tower, deli, convenience store, gift shop. **Activities:**

Bingo, weekly dinners, occasional live entertainment, wine-&-cheese socials, saltwater swimming, fishing. **Nearby Attractions:** Yaquina Head Lighthouse, beaches, Oregon Coast Aquarium, Historic Bayfront, Ripley's Believe It or Not, Undersea Gardens, The Wax Works. **Additional Information:** Newport Chamber of Commerce, (800) 262-7844.

RESTRICTIONS

Pets: On leash only, no more than 2 per site. **Fires:** None. **Alcoholic Beverages:** At site. **Vehicle Maximum Length:** Min. vehicle length 25 ft.; no 5th wheels; motor coaches only; towed secondary vehicles OK.

TO GET THERE

From southbound on Hwy. 101, park is located on right-hand side just north of Newport City limits and 3 mi. north of Hwy. 101 junction with Hwy. 20.

NEWPORT — MAP, B-1
South Beach State Park

reserve america

5580 South Coast Hwy., 97366. T: (541) 867-4715; www.reserveamerica.com.

🚐 ★★★★ | ⛺ ★★★★

Beauty: ★★★	Site Privacy: ★★★
Spaciousness: ★★★	Quiet: ★★★
Security: ★★★★	Cleanliness: ★★★★
Insect Control: ★★★★	Facilities: ★★★★

At South Beach, miles of ocean beach and recreational offerings of Yaquina Bay enrich your camping experience. One of the most exciting services offered at South Beach is kayak tours. Those who register for the activity will launch from nearby Ona Beach (5 miles south) and spend two hours exploring the fascinating Beaver Creek area with a guide. Attractions nearby include the Yaquina Bay Lighthouse, marine life exhibits at the Hatfield Marine Science Center and the Oregon Coast Aquarium. These are just a few of the opportunities you will encounter when you visit and explore the central Oregon coast. Special features of the park include a campground, 22 yurts for overnight stays, a visitor center, and a gift shop. Yurts are domed tents with structural support, a plywood floor, lockable wooden door, lights, heating, and beds with mattresses. For sports enthusiasts, there is a volleyball and a basketball court. The campground offers 238 electrical campsites (maximum site 60 feet) and six primitive sites. The campground has showers. The park also provides 22 yurts, three group tent areas, and a hiker/biker camp. South Beach State Park and the surrounding areas offer a variety of recreational opportunities. Activities include fishing, crabbing, boating, windsurfing, hiking, picnicking, biking, beachcombing, camping, yurt stays, and viewing scenery. Adjacent to South Beach State Park, South Jetty offers horse access to the beach, fishing, clamming, surfing, scuba diving and (for the advanced) windsurfing when conditions permit.

BASICS

Operated By: Oregon State Parks. **Site Assignment:** Reservations can be made 9 months in

advance. **Registration:** At office. **Fee:** Single, $17–$22; yurt, $29; meeting hall, $35; group, $44–$65. **Parking:** At park.

FACILITIES

Number of Multipurpose Sites: 288. **Hookups:** Yes. **Dump Station:** Yes. **Laundry:** No. **Pay Phone:** Yes. **Restrooms and Showers:** Yes. **Fuel:** Less than 3 mi. **Propane:** No. **Internal Roads:** Paved. **RV Service:** No. **Market:** No. **Restaurant:** Less than 5 mi. **General Store:** Yes. **Vending:** No. **Swimming:** No. **Playground:** Yes. **Activities:** Amphitheater, biking, bird-watching, hiking, horseshoes, jogging/running, junior ranger program, nature program, sightseeing.

RESTRICTIONS

Pets: Pets must be confined by the owner, or on a leash not more than 6 feet long, kept under physical control at all times. You're responsible for removal of all waste and for keeping your pet quiet during campground quiet hours (10 p.m.–7 a.m.). **Fires:** In fire rings or fireplaces provided for such purposes & portions of the beach designated as permissible for fires. No fires shall be left unattended or be permitted to cause damage to park facilities or areas. **Alcoholic Beverages:** Possession or use of an alcoholic beverage by any person under 21 years of age is not allowed. **Other:** Discount programs may be offered. Fee adjustments will not be made after reservations have been confirmed using the Internet reservation service. A large campsite has at least a 12 by 12–ft. tent-pad area. Medium sites are at least 10 by10 ft. Small sites are at least 8 by 8 ft.

TO GET THERE

On Hwy. 101, 1 mi. south the Yaquina Bay Bridge in Newport, 15 mi. north of Waldport. Entrance to park is located on west side of Hwy. 101. Well signed.

ONTARIO — MAP, B-4
Lake Owyhee State Park

reserve america

23751 Old Hwy. 30, 97901.
T: (541) 339-2331 or (800) 551-6949;
www.reserveamerica.com.

🚐 ★★★ | ⛺ ★★

Beauty: ★★★★★	Site Privacy: ★
Spaciousness: ★★★	Quiet: ★★★★★
Security: ★	Cleanliness: ★★★
Insect Control: ★★	Facilities: ★

Lake Owyhee State Park, located in the absolute middle of nowhere in the desert, eastern-central part of the state, provides a scenic and quiet place to spend a few days. The park can only be accessed by small rigs and cars, the road is too narrow and treacherous for anything longer than 35 feet. Created by a dam, the artificial lake plays host to fishing and summer water sports and provides irrigation to nearby farmers. The campground's location, far from agrarian, sits in what was once a lush canyon. Downstream from the dam (on the way to the campground) the canyon still has such a look and feel.

The area before the dam provides some of the most interesting and beautiful scenery in the surrounding area. The state park has two campgrounds, one with water/electric hookups and one with no hookups. All sites have good views of the surrounding, arid, sage-covered red hills. The campground has little shade and no privacy; the summer sun here packs a punch. Also, the remote location means no services and lots of bugs. Visit during late spring or late summer for the best conditions. Do not attempt this trip in a large rig or during freezing weather; the road has steep, treacherous curves without guardrails.

BASICS

Operated By: Oregon State Parks & Recreation. **Open:** All year. **Site Assignment:** First come, first served. **Registration:** At self-pay station. **Fee:** Water/electric, $16; tent, $14; overflow or primitive, $8; extra vehicle, $5; V, MC (cash preferred as credit machine is unreliable). **Parking:** At site.

FACILITIES

Number of RV-only Sites: 80. **Number of Tent-only Sites:** 10. **Hookups:** Electric (20, 30, 50 amps), water. **Each Site:** Picnic table, fire ring. **Dump Station:** Yes. **Laundry:** No. **Pay Phone:** Yes. **Restrooms and Showers:** Yes. **Fuel:** Marina only (seasonal). **Propane:** No. **Internal Roads:** Paved, gravel. **RV Service:** No. **Market:** 30 mi. north. **Restaurant:** 30 mi. north. **General Store:** Yes (seasonal). **Vending:** No. **Swimming:** Yes. **Playground:** No. **Other:** Boat ramp. **Activities:** Boating, fishing, swimming, hiking, wildlife viewing, skiing. **Nearby Attractions:** Hiking, fishing, swimming, boating, wildlife viewing, dam museum.

RESTRICTIONS

Pets: On leash only (max. length 6 ft.). **Fires:** Fire pit only; small fires only, pay attention to wildfire conditions. **Alcoholic Beverages:** At site. **Vehicle Maximum Length:** 55 ft.

TO GET THERE

From Hwy. 201, turn west at Owyhee Junction onto Owyhee Ave. 5 mi., then turn south (left) onto Owyhee Dam Cutoff Rd. 22 mi. to the park. Warning: Parts of this road are steep and narrow with sharp corners, and with limited visibility. Please use caution.

PENDLETON　　　　MAP, A-3
Mountain View RV Park

1375 SE 3rd, 97801.
T: (541) 276-1041 or (866) 302-3311;
www.nwfamilyrvresorts.com.

🚐 ★★★★　　　　▲ ★

Beauty: ★★★★	Site Privacy: ★
Spaciousness: ★★★	Quiet: ★★
Security: ★★★★	Cleanliness: ★★★★
Insect Control: ★★	Facilities: ★★★

Mountain View RV Park in Pendleton has nice vistas and easy interstate access. Arranged in several parallel rows, the newer part has flat, paved, grass-bordered sites, both with and without views. Unfortunately none of the sites have any shade or privacy. The best RV sites sit on the perimeter, numbers 52–70, that have an open view of the golden, rolling hills and dry

flatlands to the south. The huge sky in this part of the countryside makes the scenery particularly impressive. The tenting section consists of a small grassy area with little shade and no inter-site privacy. The park has very limited in-house recreation, but makes a good base for exploring the area or for stopping overnight on the long trek through eastern Oregon. Winters here bring extremely cold temperatures and summers just the opposite; late spring and early fall provide the most comfortable climate.

BASICS

Operated By: Ron & Lottie Smith. **Open:** All year. **Site Assignment:** On arrival, reservation w/ credit card; refund w/ 24-hour notice. **Registration:** At office, after hours at drop or pay in morning. **Fee:** Premium, $29; full, $25; tent, $19.62; fee covers 2 people; extra person (age 6 or older), $2; V, MC, check, cash. **Parking:** At site, limited off site.

FACILITIES

Number of RV-only Sites: 100. **Number of Tent-only Sites:** 1. **Hookups:** Electric (20, 30, 50 amps), water, sewer, cable TV, Wi-Fi. **Each Site:** Picnic table. **Dump Station:** Yes. **Laundry:** Yes. **Pay Phone:** Yes. **Restrooms and Showers:** Yes. **Fuel:** No. **Propane:** Yes. **Internal Roads:** Paved. **RV Service:** No. **Market:** North in Pendleton. **Restaurant:** North in Pendleton. **General Store:** Yes. **Vending:** No. **Swimming:** No. **Playground:** Yes. **Other:** Meeting room (reservable), storage. **Activities:** Watching the sky. **Nearby Attractions:** All types of outdoor sports, casino gambling, Tamastslikt Cultural Institute (confederated tribes). **Additional Information:** Pendleton Chamber of Commerce, (541) 276-7411.

RESTRICTIONS

Pets: On leash only (max. quantity 2; max. weight 40 lbs. each). **Fires:** No open fires. **Alcoholic Beverages:** At site. **Vehicle Maximum Length:** No limit. **Other:** Max. 6 people per site.

TO GET THERE

From I-84 Exit 210 (eastbound turn right), turn south from the exit ramp and drive 1 block. Turn right on SE Nye and drive a short distance, turning right on SE 3rd St. This road dead-ends into the RV park after 0.2 mi.

PORT ORFORD　　　　MAP, C-1
Cape Blanco State Park

P.O. Box 1345, 97465.
T: (541) 332-6774 or (800) 551-6949;
www.reserveamerica.com.

🚐 ★★★　　　　▲ ★★★★

Beauty: ★★★★★	Site Privacy: ★★★
Spaciousness: ★★★★	Quiet: ★★★
Security: ★★★★	Cleanliness: ★★★★★
Insect Control: ★★★	Facilities: ★★★

This state park covers 1,895 acres of forested headlands and wildflower fields that flood the area with color in late spring and early summer. The lush vegetation of Cape Blanco is kept green by the year-round temperate marine climate that brings in half

of the total annual precipitation between December and February. This makes it an ideal place to enjoy during the off-season and to avoid at peak times. The summer tourist season along the Oregon coast—all 360 miles of it—is lovely weather-wise, and the scenery is consistently spectacular, but it is one of those experiences you could learn to hate. There is little relief from the crowds, campgrounds fill up quickly (including Cape Blanco), and the main north/south route (US 101) is one long, nearly unbroken procession of RVs and trailers.

BASICS

Operated By: Oregon State Parks & Recreation. **Open:** All year. **Site Assignment:** First come, first served; no reservations. **Registration:** At camp office. **Fee:** $12–$16. **Parking:** At site.

FACILITIES

Number of Multipurpose Sites: 53. **Hookups:** Electric. **Each Site:** Picnic table, fire grill. **Dump Station:** Yes. **Laundry:** No. **Pay Phone:** Yes. **Restrooms and Showers:** Yes. **Fuel:** No. **Propane:** No. **Internal Roads:** Call ahead for details. **RV Service:** Yes. **Market:** No. **Restaurant:** No. **General Store:** No. **Vending:** No. **Swimming:** No. **Playground:** No. **Other:** 4 reservable log cabins, horse camping, horse trails. **Activities:** Fishing, hiking, horseback riding. **Nearby Attractions:** Oregon Islands National Refuge, Dunes of Bandon, New River, Blacklock Point, Tower Rock, Oregon Coast Trail, lighthouse, Hughes House tours (Apr.–Sept.). **Additional Information:** Port Orford Chamber of Commerce, (541) 332-8055 or www.discoverportorford.com.

RESTRICTIONS

Pets: On leash only. **Fires:** Fire ring only. **Alcoholic Beverages:** Not allowed. **Vehicle Maximum Length:** 65 ft.

TO GET THERE

From Port Orford, drive north on US 101 to Cape Blanco Hwy., and then go 5 mi. west to the state park campground.

PORT ORFORD　　　　MAP, C-1
Historic Arizona Beach RV Park

36939 Arizona Ranch Rd., 97465.
T: (541) 332-6491; www.arizonabeachrv.com.

🚐 ★★★★　　　　▲ ★★★

Beauty: ★★★★★	Site Privacy: ★
Spaciousness: ★★★	Quiet: ★★★
Security: ★★★	Cleanliness: ★★★
Insect Control: ★★	Facilities: ★★

There are campgrounds in the Port Orford and Gold Beach area with nicer facilities and shadier sites than those found at Historic Arizona Beach RV Park, located on Hwy. 101 between the two cities. However, Arizona Beach is the only park in the area, and possibly on the Oregon coast, with beach back-ins. The grounds consist of two sections on either side of 101 with an underpass connecting them, and the east side backs up to steep wooded coastal hills. But on the west side sit 38 water/electric sites at sea level, five or so feet off a narrow, gray sand beach. The grass and dirt sites, numbered 112–165, have breathtaking views of the big, crashing Pacific surf and surrounding hills, and very easy beach access. The RV sites on either side lack privacy, except for beach-side tent sites numbered 6–10. The park, located right across the street from Prehistoric Gardens (plaster dinosaurs), is less crowded in late spring than summer, but summer has better weather.

BASICS

Operated By: Arizona Beach RV Park. **Open:** All year. **Site Assignment:** Reservable (required deposit is 1-night stay; refund w/ 30-day notice); first come, first served. **Registration:** At office, after hours see office window for varying directions. **Fee:** $16–$30; V, MC, check, cash. **Parking:** At site; ample off-site parking.

FACILITIES

Number of RV-only Sites: 125. **Number of Tent-only Sites:** 35. **Hookups:** Electric (20, 30 amps), water, sewer. **Each Site:** Picnic table, fire ring. **Dump Station:** Yes. **Laundry:** Yes. **Pay Phone:** Yes. **Restrooms and Showers:** Yes. **Fuel:** No. **Propane:** Yes. **Internal Roads:** Dirt & gravel. **RV Service:** No. **Market:** North or south 15 mi. in Bandon or Port Orford. **Restaurant:** North or south 15 mi. in Bandon or Port Orford. **General Store:** Yes. **Vending:** Yes. **Swimming:** No. **Playground:** Yes. **Other:** Large reservable rec room, basketball goal, chipping range, horseshoes, tide pools (on beach), beach, discount tickets to Prehistoric Gardens, crab nets, fishing equipment rentals. **Activities:** Fishing, crabbing, golfing, body boarding, surfing, planned activities, gold panning, berry picking, whale-watching (seasonal & inconsistent). **Nearby Attractions:** Prehistoric Gardens, Bandon Cheese Factory, golf, charter fishing, cranberry bogs. **Additional Information:** Bandon Chamber of Commerce, (541) 347-9616.

RESTRICTIONS

Pets: On leash only. **Fires:** Fire pit only, no beach fires. **Alcoholic Beverages:** At site. **Vehicle Maximum Length:** No limit. **Other:** No gathering, cutting of firewood; no mechanized vehicles on beach; quiet hours 10 p.m.–8 a.m.

TO GET THERE

Entrance marked by large sign on east side of Hwy. 101, 14 mi. north of Gold Beach, opposite from Prehistoric Gardens. If you can see a big green Tyrannosaurus Rex in your side view mirrors, you missed it.

PORTLAND   MAP, A-1
Mt. Hood Village

reserve america

65000 East Hwy. 26, 97067.
T: (503) 622-7665 or (800) 255-3069;
www.mhcrv.com.

🚐 ★★★★   ⛺ ★★

Beauty: ★★★   Site Privacy: ★
Spaciousness: ★★   Quiet: ★★★
Security: ★★★★★   Cleanliness: ★★★★
Insect Control: ★★   Facilities: ★★★★★

Mt. Hood Village, located on Hwy. 26 southeast of Portland, offers an amazing number of resort amenities close to the scenic National Forest Area. These facilities include, among others, a large indoor pool, tons of exercise equipment, resident massage therapists, and a very large lodge and outdoor pavilion for meetings of all sizes. The campground has several different sections offering different hookups, and these sections all have outdoorsy names. The best gravel, back-in, full-hookup sites can be found in Vine Maple Hollow, numbered 82–100; these adjacent sites, shaded by birch and pine, offer the most seclusion from the rest of the busy grounds. Conversely, the worst sites also sit in this section near a high-traffic area of the park, numbered 8–50. There exist some quality water/electric sites, numbers 38–70, in the section deemed Hemlock Meadows; these are perhaps the shadiest on the property. All sections within the park make an attempt at maintaining the wooded feel of the surrounding countryside. The grounds only have slim opportunities for tent camping, with the tent sites consisting of gravel and crushed shale.

BASICS

Operated By: Equity Lifestyle Properties. **Open:** All year. **Site Assignment:** On arrival; reservation (required deposit is 1-night fee; refund w/ 48-hour notice). **Registration:** At entrance gate, after hours use phone at gate-call attendant. **Fee:** Winter, $23–$32; summer, $41–$43; regular, $32–$36; V, MC, D, AE, personal check, cash. **Parking:** At site, some off site.

FACILITIES

Number of RV-only Sites: 352. **Number of Tent-only Sites:** 3. **Hookups:** Electric (20, 30, 50 amps), water, sewer, cable TV. **Each Site:** Picnic table, fire ring. **Dump Station:** Yes. **Laundry:** Yes. **Pay Phone:** Yes. **Restrooms and Showers:** Yes. **Fuel:** No. **Propane:** Yes. **Internal Roads:** Paved & gravel. **RV Service:** No. **Market:** 2 mi. east on 26. **Restaurant:** On site for breakfast, lunch. **General Store:** Yes. **Vending:** Yes. **Swimming:** Yes. **Playground:** Yes. **Other:** Game room (no video games, indoor pool, large indoor hot tub, saunas (1 per gender, small), cardio room, free weight room, fireside room (small meeting room), lodge (enormous meeting room), huge outdoor pavilion w/ tables & tents, basketball, volleyball. **Activities:** Weekend planned activities, swimming, ping-pong, pool, foosball, fishing, use of facilities, hiking, mountain biking. **Nearby Attractions:** Mt. Hood National Forest, Portland, winter sports. **Additional Information:** Mt. Hood Area Chamber of Commerce, (888) 622-4822.

RESTRICTIONS

Pets: On leash only. **Fires:** Fire pit only. **Alcoholic Beverages:** At site, not allowed inside common areas. **Vehicle Maximum Length:** No limit. **Other:** Washing vehicles allowed in site w/ biodegradable soap.

TO GET THERE

Take I-84 east to Exit 16 (Wood Village, Gresham, Mt. Hood). Drive south about 6 mi., then turn left (east) onto Burnside St. Burnside turns into Hwy. 26 east in about 1 mi. Take Hwy. 26 through the town of Sandy. About 15 mi. east of Sandy, the entrance will be on the right.

PORTLAND   MAP, A-1
Pheasant Ridge RV Park

reserve america

8275 SW Elligsen Rd., 97070. T: (503) 682-7829 or (800) 532-7829; www.pheasantridge.com.

🚐 ★★★   ⛺ ★★

Beauty: ★★★   Site Privacy: ★★
Spaciousness: ★★★   Quiet: ★★
Security: ★★   Cleanliness: ★★★★
Insect Control: ★★   Facilities: ★★★★

Pheasant Ridge RV Park, one-half hour south of Portland on I-5, provides a good place for people wanting to day-trip to surrounding areas. The terraced sites climb a hill to views of the surrounding developed hill country, providing a feeling of inter-site spaciousness. Young pines also scale the hill alongside the paved, grass-enclosed sites. The pines afford a sense of privacy but not much shade. Sites with the best view sit at the top of the grounds, numbered 86–90 and 104–109. 91 pull-through sites are available. Lucky and patient campers may spot deer at Pheasant Ridge. The campground was approved for its compliance with the Americans with Disabilities Act (although dumpsters are a long hike from most sites) and the indoor hot tub has a Hoyer lift for disabled access; the indoor pool does not. Several groups meet at the grounds in the rec room and open their doors to visitors, including a barbershop quartet on Tuesday nights, a men's Sunday morning prayer group, and a women's Wednesday morning craft and sewing circle.

BASICS

Operated By: Rick & Terri Dexheimer. **Open:** All year. **Site Assignment:** First come, first served; reservation (deposit 1-night stay); refund w/ 24-hour notice. **Registration:** At office, after hours ring bell. **Fee:** $32–$35; plus $1 per person; V, MC, check, cash. **Parking:** At site 1.

FACILITIES

Number of RV-only Sites: 130. **Hookups:** Electric (20, 30, 50 amps), water, sewer, cable TV, Wi-Fi. **Each Site:** None. **Dump Station:** No. **Laundry:** Yes. **Pay Phone:** Yes. **Restrooms and Showers:** Yes. **Fuel:** No. **Propane:** Yes. **Internal Roads:** Paved. **RV Service:** No. **Market:** North up I-5 3 mi. **Restaurant:** North up I-5 0.5 mi. **General Store:** Yes. **Vending:** Yes. **Swimming:** Yes. **Playground:** No. **Other:** Hoyer lift for hot tub, exercise equipment, horseshoe pit, hot tub. **Activities:** Barbecues & various planned activities. **Nearby Attractions:** End of the Oregon Trail Interpretive Center, wineries, Powell's Bookstore, Wilsonville Family Fun Center, outlet mall. **Additional Information:** Portland Oregon Visitor's Assoc., 87-PORTLAND.

RESTRICTIONS

Pets: On leash only, no larger than 40 lbs, no more than 2. **Fires:** No open flames. **Alcoholic Beverages:** At site. **Vehicle Maximum Length:** 45 ft. **Other:** No skateboards.

TO GET THERE

From I-5 Exit 286, drive 0.25 mi. east on Elligsen Rd.; entrance is on the left.

PRINEVILLE   MAP, B-2
Prineville Reservoir State Park

reserve america

19020 SE Parkland Dr., 97754. T: (541) 447-4363; www.reserveamerica.com.

🚐 ★★★★   🏕 ★★★★

Beauty: ★★★	Site Privacy: ★★★
Spaciousness: ★★★	Quiet: ★★★★
Security: ★★★★	Cleanliness: ★★★★
Insect Control: ★★★★	Facilities: ★★★★

Need a place to play? Where you can enjoy nature viewing at its finest? This is a place where those weary of hectic schedules and jangling telephones can find peace, a place where life can be pondered from a different and unique perspective. Most of all, a place carefully designed and maintained for people—for the mother and her baby out for a Sunday drive, for the father teaching his son how to fish, for the teenager who wants to get away for a bit, for the couple on a weekend camping trip, for the grandparents who just want to take it easy for a week. Mountain waters flow out of the Ochoco Mountain Range, joining together to form the Crooked River. This river, confined by its canyon and the Bowman Dam, forms Prineville Reservoir. The fishing can be good anytime at Prineville Reservoir. It supports rainbow and cutthroat trout, small and largemouth bass, catfish, crappie, and crayfish. The trout fishing experience is year-round; ice-fishing included in the dead of winter. Anywhere on the reservoir is suitable. Bass, catfish, and crappie are more suited toward warmer water temperatures, May through October. The upper reaches of the reservoir above Jasper Point and the Bear Creek tributary downstream from Prineville Reservoir State Park are known to produce fine fish. Fly-fishing opportunities are best along the Crooked River above Prineville Reservoir and downstream from Bowman Dam.

BASICS
Operated By: Oregon State Parks. **Open:** All year. **Site Assignment:** Reservations can be made 9 months in advance. **Registration:** At office. **Fee:** Single, $12–$20; cabin, $35; deluxe cabin, $45–$66; $7 boat moorage, $7. **Parking:** At park.

FACILITIES
Number of Multipurpose Sites: 131. **Hookups:** Yes. **Dump Station:** Less than 20 mi. **Laundry:** No. **Pay Phone:** Yes. **Restrooms and Showers:** Yes. **Fuel:** Less than 5 mi. **Propane:** Less than 3 mi. **Internal Roads:** Paved. **RV Service:** No. **Market:** No. **Restaurant:** Less than 5 mi. **General Store:** Less than 5 mi. **Vending:** No. **Swimming:** Yes. **Playground:** No. **Activities:** Amphitheater, biking, birdwatching, boating, canoeing, hiking, jogging/running, junior ranger program, nature program, photography, picnicking, stargazing, wildlife viewing.

RESTRICTIONS
Pets: Pets must be confined by the owner, or on a leash not more than 6 feet long, kept under physical control at all times. You're responsible for removal of all waste and for keeping your pet quiet during campground quiet hours (10 p.m.–7 a.m.). **Fires:** In fire rings or fireplaces provided for such purposes & portions of the beach designated as permissible for fires. No fires shall be left unattended or be permitted to cause damage to park facilities or areas. **Alcoholic Beverages:** Possession or use of an alcoholic beverage by any person under 21 years of age is not allowed. **Other:** Discount programs may be offered. Fee adjustments will not be made after reservations have been confirmed using the Internet reservation service. A large campsite has at least a 12 by 12–ft. tent-pad area. Medium sites are at least 10 by10 ft. Small sites are at least 8 by 8 ft.

TO GET THERE
From Portland (3.5 hours): Take Hwy. 26 east, over Mt. Hood, to Madras. Continue on Hwy. 26 to Prineville. At east end of Prineville, turn right on Combs Flat Rd. After approx. 1 mi., turn right on Juniper Canyon Rd. Proceed 15 mi. to park entrance which is SE Parkland Dr. From Salem (3.5 hours): Take Hwy. 22 over Santiam Pass, to Sisters, then take Hwy. 126 to Redmond. Continue on Hwy. 126 to Prineville. At east end of Prineville, turn right on Combs Flat Rd. After 1 mi., turn right on Juniper Canyon Rd. Proceed 15 mi. to park entrance, which is SE Parkland Dr.

PROSPECT   MAP, C-2
Natural Bridge Campground

47201 Hwy. 62, 97536. T: (541) 560-3623.

🚐 ★★★★   🏕 ★★★★

Beauty: ★★★★★	Site Privacy: ★★★★★
Spaciousness: ★★★	Quiet: ★★★★
Security: ★★★★	Cleanliness: ★★★★★
Insect Control: ★★★★	Facilities: ★★★

Natural Bridge is so named for the unique feature adjacent to it. It is at this point that the upper Rogue disappears from sight and runs underground for 200 feet. The campground sits virtually on top of water flowing beneath it. Natural Bridge is one of several campgrounds in the vicinity that is located on the banks of the Rogue or on small creeks that feed it. Given its proximity to Crater Lake, this area can be quite busy in the summertime, with the larger, more developed campsites filling up first. The surrounding Rogue River National Forest is characterized by dense forests of Douglas fir and sugar pine that soften the contours of the high plateau upon which the forests grow. This rugged land is full of thick vegetation, laced with more than 450 miles of trails within the national forest. Getting lost can happen easily. Make sure you have a good topographic or Forest Service map with you when you head out for lonely and distant spots.

BASICS
Operated By: Rogue River National Forest. **Open:** May–Oct. **Site Assignment:** First come, first served; no reservations. **Registration:** Not necessary. **Fee:** $6. **Parking:** At site.

FACILITIES
Number of Multipurpose Sites: 17. **Hookups:** None. **Each Site:** Picnic table, fire pit w/ grill. **Dump Station:** No. **Laundry:** No. **Pay Phone:** No. **Restrooms and Showers:** Vault toilets. **Fuel:** No. **Propane:** No. **Internal Roads:** Gravel. **RV Service:** No. **Market:** Union Creek, 5–6 mi. **Restaurant:** Union Creek, 5–6 mi. **General Store:** No. **Vending:** No. **Swimming:** No. **Playground:** No. **Activities:** Hiking, backpacking. **Nearby Attractions:** Rogue River. **Additional Information:** (541) 560-3623 May–early Nov.

RESTRICTIONS
Pets: On leash only. **Fires:** Fire ring only. **Alcoholic Beverages:** At site. **Vehicle Maximum Length:** 22 ft.

TO GET THERE
Travel northeast on SR 62 (about 32 mi. from Medford), from the Prospect turnoff. Continue north on SR 62 another 12 mi. or so to FS 300; turn left and the campground is 1 mi. in.

SALEM   MAP, A-1
Phoenix RV Park

4130 Silverton Rd. NE, 97305. T: (503) 581-2497 or (800) 237-2497.

🚐 ★★★★   🏕 n/a

Beauty: ★	Site Privacy: ★
Spaciousness: ★★★	Quiet: ★★
Security: ★★★	Cleanliness: ★★★★★
Insect Control: ★★	Facilities: ★★★

Phoenix RV Park, located just off I-5 on the northeast side of Salem, has the feel of a newly developed suburban community. The young campground occupies an L-shaped field of large paved sites surrounded by juvenile shrubs, small trees, and very well-maintained grass. The sites come minus shade or privacy, but the convenient location more than makes up for this. The newly furbished, spacious, indoor facilities include two large laundry rooms and a kitchen. One would be hard-pressed to find a campground with better access to metropolitan Salem. The grocery store and RV service on either side of the grounds, as well as nearby bus routes, only add to the park's convenient location. The campground is surrounded by privacy fencing and has night security. Sites 25-41 and 47-71 stay surprisingly quiet considering the urban location. The rec room has a Stairmaster, treadmill, two pinball games, and an assortment of jigsaw puzzles.

BASICS
Operated By: Phoenix RV Park. **Open:** All year. **Site Assignment:** First come, first served; reservation w/ credit card; refund w/ 48-hour notice. **Registration:** At office, after hours at drop box outside office. **Fee:** $29.80; fee covers 2 people; extra person (age 3 or older), $2. **Parking:** At site.

FACILITIES
Number of RV-only Sites: 107. **Hookups:** Electric (20, 30, 50 amps), water, sewer, cable TV. **Each Site:** Picnic table. **Dump Station:** No. **Laundry:** Yes. **Pay Phone:** Yes. **Restrooms and Showers:** Yes. **Fuel:** No. **Propane:** Yes. **Internal Roads:** Paved (wide). **RV Service:** No (next door). **Market:** Next door. **Restaurant:** 0.25 mi. east. **General Store:** Yes. **Vending:** Yes. **Swimming:** No. **Playground:** Yes. **Other:** Multipurpose room. **Activities:**

None. **Nearby Attractions:** State Capital, Silvercreek Falls, antique shops, Hallie Ford Museum of Art/Willamette University, Marion County Historical Society Museum. **Additional Information:** Salem Convention & Visitor's Assoc., (503) 581-4325 or (800) 874-7012.

RESTRICTIONS

Pets: On leash only (max. length 6 ft.), no fighting breeds; dogs over 25 lbs must be approved by management. **Fires:** No open fires or charcoal. **Alcoholic Beverages:** At site. **Vehicle Maximum Length:** No limit. **Other:** No motor or generator usage, no fireworks or lethal weapons, no parking anywhere other than registered sites, no clotheslines, no business operations legal or otherwise w/o approval of management.

TO GET THERE

From I-5 Exit 256, drive 0.25 mi. east on Market St., then turn left on Lancaster Dr. Follow 1.25 mi. then turn right onto Silverton Rd. Entrance is on the right after 1 block.

SISTERS   MAP, B-2
Perry South Campground— Deschutes National Forest

reserve america

P.O. Box 249, 97759. T: (541) 549-7700; www.reserveamerica.com.

🚐 ★★★★   ▲ ★★★★

Beauty: ★★★	Site Privacy: ★★★★
Spaciousness: ★★★★	Quiet: ★★★
Security: ★★★★	Cleanliness: ★★★★
Insect Control: ★★★★	Facilities: ★★

Situated at 2,000-foot elevation; 63 campsites, including 4 tent-only sites on the Metolius Arm of Lake Billy Chinook. Boating, swimming, fishing, and waterskiing in the lake. Lake Billy Chinook holds largemouth and smallmouth bass, rainbow, brown and bull trout, kokanee salmon, whitefish, and a handful of suckers, minnows, and dace. The most sought-after catch is the trophy bull trout, which has included the last three state records. Catch and release is encouraged for the trout. A fish-cleaning station is available near the day-use area. Deschutes and Ochoco national forests, where Perry South is located, along with the Crooked River National Grassland encompass more than 2.5 million acres of central Oregon. These public lands extend about 100 miles along the east side of the Cascade Mountains crest and eastward into the Ochoco Mountains. They are rich in human and natural history and radiate variety, offering a multitude of diverse scenic and recreation opportunities. Alpine forests and lush meadows, sparkling lakes and scenic rivers, dense evergreen forests, and lava caves are contained within the spectacular snowcapped volcanic peaks of the Cascade Mountain Range to the west and high desert to the east. Newberry National Volcanic Monument offers an up-close and personal look at volcanoes and is home to the endangered pumice grape fern.

BASICS

Operated By: U.S. Forest Service. **Open:** May 18–Sept. 7. **Site Assignment:** Reservations must be made at least 7 days in advance. **Registration:** At office. **Fee:** Single, $16. **Parking:** At park.

FACILITIES

Number of Multipurpose Sites: 60. **Hookups:** None. **Each Site:** Call ahead. **Dump Station:** No. **Laundry:** No. **Pay Phone:** No. **Restrooms and Showers:** Yes. **Fuel:** No. **Propane:** No. **Internal Roads:** Paved. **RV Service:** No. **Market:** No. **Restaurant:** No. **General Store:** No. **Vending:** No. **Swimming:** Yes. **Playground:** No. **Activities:** Biking, bird-watching, boating, canoeing, fishing, hiking, kayaking, photography, waterskiing, tubing, wildlife viewing, wind surfing.

RESTRICTIONS

Pets: Pets must be restrained or on a leash at all times while in developed recreation areas. **Fires:** In fire rings, stoves, grills, or fireplaces provided for that purpose. **Alcoholic Beverages:** Not allowed. **Vehicle Maximum Length:** Call ahead.

TO GET THERE

From Sisters, go about 6 mi. northwest on US 20, 21 mi. north on FR 11, 5 mi. east on FR 1170, then 3 mi. northwest on FR 64.

SISTERS   MAP, B-2
Riverside Campground

P.O. Box 249, 97759. T: (541) 549-7700.

🚐 ★★★   ▲ ★★★

Beauty: ★★★★	Site Privacy: ★★★
Spaciousness: ★★★★	Quiet: ★★★★
Security: ★★★	Cleanliness: ★★★
Insect Control: ★★★	Facilities: ★★★

Ah, the magical and mysterious Metolius. Welling up clear and bright from a tiny underground spring at the base of Black Butte, the river provides one of the finest trout habitats around before emptying into Lake Billy Chinook. The number of campgrounds on or near the Metolius is staggering, and are there primarily to serve the abundance of anglers. In addition to Riverside, there are Camp Sherman, Allingham, Smiling River, Pine Rest, Gorge, Allen Springs, Pioneer Ford, and Lower Bridge. Dominating the landscape in various stages of geologic splendor are the snowcapped peaks to the west. In order from north to south, they are Mount Jefferson, Mount Washington, North Sister, Middle Sister, South Sister, and last but not least even with its forlorn name, Broken Top. Highlights of a stay at Riverside Campground include short walks to Metolius Spring and Jack Creek Spring, the Metolius River Canyon near Camp Sherman, and the Wizard Falls Fish Hatchery.

BASICS

Operated By: Concessionaire. **Open:** May–Sept. **Site Assignment:** First come, first served, no reservations. **Registration:** Self-registration on site. **Fee:** $10. **Parking:** At access road, about 200–400 yards from the campground.

FACILITIES

Number of Tent-only Sites: 16. **Hookups:** None. **Each Site:** Picnic table, fire grill. **Dump Station:**

No. **Laundry:** No. **Pay Phone:** No. **Restrooms and Showers:** Vault toilets. **Fuel:** No. **Propane:** No. **Internal Roads:** Paved. **RV Service:** No. **Market:** 1–2 mi. **Restaurant:** 1–2 mi. **General Store:** No. **Vending:** No. **Swimming:** No. **Playground:** No. **Activities:** Fishing, biking, hiking. **Nearby Attractions:** Mountains, lakes. **Additional Information:** (541) 549-2111.

RESTRICTIONS

Pets: On leash only. **Fires:** Fire ring only. **Alcoholic Beverages:** Allowed. **Vehicle Maximum Length:** 21 ft. **Other:** 14-day stay limit.

TO GET THERE

Take SR 126/US 20 (Santiam Hwy.) north of Sisters to its intersection with FS 14 (Camp Sherman Rd.). Turn right, and follow FS 14 around the base of Black Butte to FS 900. The camp is less than 1 mi. north on this road.

ST. PAUL   MAP, A-1
Champoeg State Park

reserve america

7679 Champoeg Rd. NE, 97137. T: (503) 678-1251; www.reserveamerica.com.

🚐 ★★★★   ▲ ★★★★

Beauty: ★★★	Site Privacy: ★★★
Spaciousness: ★★★	Quiet: ★★★★
Security: ★★★★	Cleanliness: ★★★★
Insect Control: ★★★★	Facilities: ★★★★

Champoeg features a unique combination of history, nature, and recreation. This is the site where Oregon's first provisional government was formed by a historical vote in 1843. Situated on the south bank of the scenic Willamette River, Champoeg's acres of forest, fields, and wetlands recreate the landscape of a bygone era. Tour the park's visitor center, Newell House, and Pioneer Mothers Log Cabin museums to discover pioneer life at Champoeg. Take a guided walk to learn what happened to the bustling pioneer town of Champoeg, and how the Donald Manson Barn was built. An 1860s-style garden lies next to the visitor center. The park also includes the Historic Butteville Store founded in 1863. It is considered the oldest operating store in Oregon. The store is the last commercial vestige of the once thriving Willamette River community of Butteville. The Friends of Historic Champoeg operate the store Thursday–Sunday and holidays from 11 a.m.–5 p.m., Memorial Day weekend–Labor Day weekend.

BASICS

Operated By: Oregon State Parks. **Open:** All year. **Site Assignment:** Reservations can be made 9 months in advance. **Registration:** At office. **Fee:** Single, $12–$20; yurt, $27; cabin, $35; day use, $35; group, $41–$60; pavilion, $60. **Parking:** At park.

FACILITIES

Number of Multipurpose Sites: 214. **Hookups:** Yes. **Dump Station:** Yes. **Laundry:** No. **Pay Phone:** Yes. **Restrooms and Showers:** Yes. **Fuel:** No. **Propane:** No. **Internal Roads:** Paved. **RV Service:** No. **Market:** No. **Restaurant:** No. **General**

Store: No. **Vending:** No. **Swimming:** No. **Playground:** No. **Activities:** Amphitheater, berry picking, biking, bird-watching, boating, canoeing, fishing, hiking, jogging/running, junior ranger program, picnicking, sightseeing, skating, volleyball.

RESTRICTIONS

Pets: Pets must be confined by the owner, or on a leash not more than 6 feet long, kept under physical control at all times. You're responsible for removal of all waste and for keeping your pet quiet during campground quiet hours (10 p.m.–7 a.m.). **Fires:** In fire rings or fireplaces provided for such purposes & portions of the beach designated as permissible for fires. No fires shall be left unattended or be permitted to cause damage to park facilities or areas. **Alcoholic Beverages:** Possession or use of an alcoholic beverage by any person under 21 years of age is not allowed. **Other:** Discount programs may be offered. Fee adjustments will not be made after reservations have been confirmed using the Internet reservation service. A large campsite has at least a 12 by 12–ft. tent-pad area. Medium sites are at least 10 by10 ft. Small sites are at least 8 by 8 ft.

TO GET THERE

From I-5 north or south, take Exit 278 (Donald/Aurora). Follow state park signs 6 mi. west to park entrance. From Hwy. 99W (Newberg area), take Hwy. 219 south (toward St. Paul), 3 mi. to Champoeg Rd. Turn left on Champoeg Rd. and drive 3 mi. east to park entrance. From airport (PDX), Airport Way, take I-205 south (Portland). Drive 25 mi. south on I-205 to junction with I-5 south (Salem). Drive south on I-5, 10 mi. to Exit 278 (Donald/Aurora). Exit the freeway and follow the state park signs 6 mi. west to park entrance.

SUBLIMITY   MAP, A-1, B-1
Silver Falls State Park

reserve america

20024 Silver Falls Hwy. SE, 97385.
T: (503) 873-8681; www.reserveamerica.com.

🚐 ★★★★   ⛺ ★★★★

Beauty: ★★★★★	Site Privacy: ★★★
Spaciousness: ★★★	Quiet: ★★★
Security: ★★★★	Cleanliness: ★★★★
Insect Control: ★★★★	Facilities: ★★★★

Nestled in the lower elevation of Oregon's Cascade Mountains lies a temperate rain forest. The Canyon Trail and the falls descend to a forest floor covered with ferns, mosses, and wildflowers. You will also find stands of Douglas fir, hemlock, and cedar. While thousands visit the park every year, it is large enough for you to find quiet places to sit and watch for birds. The Canyon Trail is a nationally recognized trail system that leads hikers along the banks of the north and south forks of Silver Creek. It takes you to ten majestic waterfalls, ranging from the grand South Falls (177 feet) to the delicate Drake Falls (27 feet). Four of these falls have an amphitheater-like surrounding where you can walk behind the falls and feel the misty, crisp spray. The park has over 25 miles of trails for hiking (14 miles of horse trails) that are pet friendly. If you have any questions about which trails will accommodate pets, check with park staff, or refer to the Silver Falls State Park Trail Guide for more information on pet restrictions. At Silver Falls, you will find unique group camping areas like the Old and New Ranch buildings, Silver Creek Youth Camp, North Falls trailer and tent areas, RV, cabin and tent camping in the overnight campground. Additional cabin rentals and complete group accommodations can be found at the Silver Falls Conference Center (rates listed below are for the campground cabins, not the conference center cabins).

BASICS

Operated By: Oregon State Parks. **Site Assignment:** Reservations can be made 9 months in advance. **Registration:** At office. **Fee:** Single, $12–$20; horse camp, $12–$16; cabin, $35; horse camp/group area, $36–$48; group, $40–$61; meeting hall, $100. **Parking:** At park.

FACILITIES

Number of Multipurpose Sites: 245. **Hookups:** Yes. **Dump Station:** Yes. **Laundry:** No. **Pay Phone:** Yes. **Restrooms and Showers:** Yes. **Fuel:** No. **Propane:** No. **Internal Roads:** Paved. **RV Service:** No. **Market:** No. **Restaurant:** No. **General Store:** Yes. **Vending:** No. **Swimming:** Yes. **Playground:** Yes. **Activities:** Amphitheater, berry picking, biking, bird-watching, crawfishing, educational programs, picnicking, hiking, horseback riding, horseshoes, sightseeing, skateboarding, skating, cross-country skiing, sledding, stargazing.

RESTRICTIONS

Pets: Pets must be confined by the owner, or on a leash not more than 6 feet long, kept under physical control at all times. You're responsible for removal of all waste and for keeping your pet quiet during campground quiet hours (10 p.m.–7 a.m.). **Fires:** In fire rings or fireplaces provided for such purposes & portions of the beach designated as permissible for fires. No fires shall be left unattended or be permitted to cause damage to park facilities or areas. **Alcoholic Beverages:** Possession or use of an alcoholic beverage by any person under 21 years of age is not allowed. **Other:** Discount programs may be offered. Fee adjustments will not be made after reservations have been confirmed using the Internet reservation service. A large campsite has at least a 12 by 12–ft. tent-pad area. Medium sites are at least 10 by10 ft. Small sites are at least 8 by 8 ft.

TO GET THERE

From Salem: On Hwy. 22, known as N Santiam Hwy. Travel time 45 minutes. Take Hwy. 22 east from Salem to the Silver Falls State Park exit, 5 mi. east of Salem; follow Hwy. 214 20 mi. to the park. From Portland: On I-5. Travel time 75 minutes. Take I-5 south to the Woodburn exit (25 mi.). Take Hwy. 214 through Woodburn and follow signs on Hwy. 214 to Mt. Angel (7 mi.). Go through Mt. Angel on Hwy. 214 to Silverton (6 mi.). From Silverton follow the signs to Silver Falls State Park on Hwy. 214 (15 mi.). From Eugene: On I-5. Travel time 75 minutes. Take I-5 north to the Hwy. 22 exit. Go east to Hwy. 214 and follow signs to Silver Falls State Park. From Bend: On Hwy. 22. Travel time 3 hours. Take Hwy. 20 northwest from Bend to Hwy. 22 and follow north to Hwy. 214 exit. Follow signs to Silver Falls State Park. From Stayton-Sublimity: On Hwy. 214. Travel time 20 minutes. Take Hwy. 214 north. Follow signs to Silver Falls State Park.

TUALATIN   MAP, A-1
Roamers Rest RV Park

17585 SW Pacific Hwy., 97062.
T: (503) 692-6350 or (877) 4-RVPARK;
www.roamersrestrvpark.com.

🚐 ★★★★   ⛺ n/a

Beauty: ★★★	Site Privacy: ★
Spaciousness: ★★	Quiet: ★★★
Security: ★★	Cleanliness: ★★★★
Insect Control: ★★	Facilities: ★★★★

Southwest of Portland, in between the city and wine country on the Tualatin River, is Roamers Rest RV Park. The lower level of the park, a rectangular perimeter of sites with a central road, lies on a bank of the slow-moving murky green river. Lush green ferns, cedars, oak, and cottonwood climb a steep hill from the river sites to a small alternate section of the grounds. The latter section has thick growth on three sides; the former has 25 waterfront sites. Also on the grounds are some protected wetlands that consist of ponds surrounded by cattails. These house many different species of birds, making the park popular for avid bird-watchers. The best sites for bird-watching, numbered 34–29, sit across from one marshy pond. Portland public transit stops nearby, providing access to many parts of the city.

BASICS

Operated By: Roamer's Rest RV Park, L.L.C. **Open:** All year. **Site Assignment:** Reservation w/ credit card; refund w/ 24-hour notice. **Registration:** At office, after hours pay in morning. **Fee:** Full, $40; fee covers 2 people; extra person (age 5 or older), $2; V, MC, cash. **Parking:** At site, no parking on internal roads.

FACILITIES

Number of RV-only Sites: 93. **Hookups:** Electric (20, 30, 50 amps), water, sewer, cable TV, phone, Wi-Fi. **Each Site:** Pavement. **Dump Station:** No. **Laundry:** Yes. **Pay Phone:** Yes. **Restrooms and Showers:** Yes. **Fuel:** No. **Propane:** No. **Internal Roads:** Paved. **RV Service:** No. **Market:** North on Hwy. 99. **Restaurant:** North on Hwy. 99. **General Store:** No. **Vending:** Yes. **Swimming:** No. **Playground:** No. **Other:** Loaner books, protected wetlands. **Activities:** Bird-watching, fishing. **Nearby Attractions:** Portland Rose Gardens, Japanese Gardens, World Forestry Center Museum, Oregon Zoo, wineries. **Additional Information:** Portland Oregon Visitor's Assoc., 87-PORTLAND.

RESTRICTIONS

Pets: On leash only; restrictions depend on length of stay. **Fires:** No open fires. **Alcoholic Beverages:** At site. **Vehicle Maximum Length:** 40 ft. max. on 5th wheels, 42 ft. on motor homes. **Other:** No skates, skateboards, generators, or vehicle maintenance.

TO GET THERE

From I-5 Exit 292 A (junction with Hwy. 217), drive 2 mi. north on Hwy. 217 then 3.5 mi. southwest on

Hwy. 99W; entrance is on the right just past the Tualatin River.

WALDPORT — MAP, B-1
Beachside State Recreation Site

P.O. Box 693, 97394. T: (541) 563-3220; www.reserveamerica.com.

🚐 ★★★★　　🏕 ★★★★

Beauty: ★★★	Site Privacy: ★★★
Spaciousness: ★★★	Quiet: ★★★
Security: ★★★★	Cleanliness: ★★★★
Insect Control: ★★★★	Facilities: ★★★

Beachside State Recreation Site is a beautiful ocean-side campground with lots of trees and space between campsites. A few miles south of Waldport and north of Yachats on the central coast, this small, exquisite destination campground is right alongside miles of broad, sandy beach that make the park perfect for kite flying and watching. There are 32 electric sites (including two accessible to the disabled) and 42 tent sites that accommodate one vehicle per site. There are also two yurts that can be reserved as well as walk/bike-in campsites. Every site is mere seconds from the beach, which makes the park perfect for watching storms, sunsets, and whales. Recent erosion at the park has prompted changes to some trails and the start of an erosion-control program. Beachside is an excellent midpoint stop as you take a jaunt on the coast. Within 30 miles in either direction, you'll find visitor centers, tide pools, hiking and driving tours, three lighthouses, crabbing, clamming, fishing, aquarium, and science centers.

BASICS
Operated By: Oregon State Parks. **Open:** All year. **Site Assignment:** Reservations can be made 9 months in advance. **Registration:** At office. **Fee:** Single, $13–$21; yurt, $29. **Parking:** At park.

FACILITIES
Number of Multipurpose Sites: 208. **Hookups:** Yes. **Dump Station:** No. **Laundry:** No. **Pay Phone:** Yes. **Restrooms and Showers:** Yes. **Fuel:** No. **Propane:** No. **Internal Roads:** Paved. **RV Service:** No. **Market:** No. **Restaurant:** No. **General Store:** No. **Vending:** No. **Swimming:** No. **Playground:** No. **Activities:** Amphitheater, birdwatching, horseshoes, jogging/running, junior ranger program, kite flying, metal detecting, nature program, photography, picnicking, sightseeing, stargazing, volleyball, whale-watching.

RESTRICTIONS
Pets: Pets must be confined by the owner, or on a leash not more than 6 feet long, kept under physical control at all times. You're responsible for removal of all waste and for keeping your pet quiet during campground quiet hours (10 p.m.–7 a.m.). **Fires:** In fire rings or fireplaces provided for such purposes & portions of the beach designated as permissible for fires. No fires shall be left unattended or be permitted to cause damage to park facilities or areas. **Alcoholic Beverages:** Possession or use of an alcoholic

beverage by any person under 21 years of age is not allowed. **Other:** Discount programs may be offered. Fee adjustments will not be made after reservations have been confirmed using the Internet reservation service. A large campsite has at least a 12 by 12–ft. tent-pad area. Medium sites are at least 10 by 10 ft. Small sites are at least 8 by 8 ft.

TO GET THERE
Beachside State Recreation Site is 3 mi. south of Waldport and 5 mi. north of Yachats, located on the west side of Hwy. 101.

WARM SPRINGS — MAP, B-2
Kah Nee Ta Resort

P.O. Box 1240, 6823 Hwy. 8, 97761. T: (541) 553-1112 or (800) 554-4-SUN; www.kah-nee-ta.com.

🚐 ★★★★★　　🏕 n/a

Beauty: ★★★★	Site Privacy: ★
Spaciousness: ★★	Quiet: ★★★★
Security: ★★★★★	Cleanliness: ★★★★★
Insect Control: ★★	Facilities: ★★★★★

Ka-Nee-Ta resort, 20 minutes east of Warm Springs, is among the best destination parks in the Northwest. An astounding array of recreational activities operated under the resort's dominion, and shuttles every half hour to move visitors to and fro, provide plenty of incentive for an extended stay. Facilities include a top-notch health spa, an enormous pool, a waterslide, horse stables with trail rides, and a casino; the facilities are well maintained and frequently crowded. No tents are allowed on the property, but the RV section has 51 flat, paved, full-hookup spaces. The only slightly unattractive sites are even numbers 18–26 for their lack of surrounding grass. The rest have nice grassy areas, well manicured and creating an oasis-like feel in the middle of the high desert. Unfortunately there is little shade. Without an RV, lodging options include a hotel and concrete-floored tepees (your own bedding is required for the latter). Early summer provides the most opportune time to visit, August especially can reach temperatures up to and over 100 degrees Fahrenheit.

BASICS
Operated By: Confederated Tribes of Warm Springs. **Open:** All year. **Site Assignment:** On arrival; reservation (required deposit is 1-night stay; refund w/ 72-hour notice). **Registration:** At office (village gate); after hours at lodge front desk. **Fee:** Full, $39.52; tepee, $72.79; ($50 refundable deposit on tepees); fee covers 3 people plus 1 unit & 1 car; extra person (age 7 or older), $8; extra vehicle, $5; 2 night min. on weekends, 3 on holidays; V, MC, AE, D, check, cash. **Parking:** At site, limited off site.

FACILITIES
Number of RV-only Sites: 51. **Hookups:** Electric (30, 50 amps), water, sewer, cable TV. **Each Site:** Picnic table. **Dump Station:** Yes. **Laundry:** Yes. **Pay Phone:** Yes. **Restrooms and Showers:** Yes. **Fuel:** No. **Propane:** No. **Internal Roads:** Paved. **RV Service:** No. **Market:** 11 mi. west in Warm Springs. **Restaurant:** 1 mi. east at resort lodge. **General Store:** Yes, limited. **Vending:** Yes. **Swimming:** Yes.

Playground: Yes. **Other:** Arcade, mini-golf ($6 adults, $3 kids & seniors), basketball, picnic pavilion (small), huge pool, waterslide, 2 small spas, kiddie pool, golf course, horseback riding ($20/person), kayaking trips ($20/person), tennis, bike rentals, shuttles around resort. **Activities:** Hiking, biking, horseback riding, swimming, relaxing, kayaking, gambling. **Nearby Attractions:** Outside of the resort, not much save national forests & native cultural events & museum at Warm Springs.

RESTRICTIONS
Pets: On leash only (campground only). **Fires:** Pits only. **Alcoholic Beverages:** In areas where children are not present. **Vehicle Maximum Length:** 76 ft. **Other:** Be culturally sensitive; fires here can get out of hand very quickly; keep cigarette butts under control.

TO GET THERE
From Hwy. 26 west in Warm Springs, turn right on Hwy. 3 (marked with a big Kah-Nee-Tah sign, just after Texaco, westbound). Drive 10 mi. on Hwy. 3; at bottom of a hill with lots of switchbacks, turn right onto Hwy. 8 (marked with a large Kah-Nee-Tah sign). Drive 1.5 mi. to the entrance on the right. There is an alternate route about 15 minutes northwest of Warm Springs that ends up in the same place and is marked in a similar way.

WASCO — MAP, A-2
Deschutes River State Recreation Area

89600 Biggs-Rufus Hwy., 97065. T: (541) 739-2322; www.reserveamerica.com.

🚐 ★★★　　🏕 ★★★

Beauty: ★★★	Site Privacy: ★★★
Spaciousness: ★★★	Quiet: ★★★★★
Security: ★★★★	Cleanliness: ★★★★
Insect Control: ★★★★	Facilities: ★★★★

The Deschutes River State Recreation Area is a tree-shaded, overnight oasis for campers. The sparkle-laden, swift, green rush of the Deschutes converges with the Columbia here, and there's no better place for family outing activities like hiking, mountain biking, camping, rafting, world-class steelhead and trout fishing, and equestrian trail riding. Trail riding is permitted March through June. Reservations are required. Up to ten horses are permitted on the trail per day (read rest of trail rules), and to make your reservation, call (800) 452-5687. There is a $6 non-refundable reservation fee per phone call for this service; for example, if you use one call to make a reservation for a party of four horses, the reservation fee is still just $6. You can reserve one date per call. A mountain bike trail begins at the park entrance and follows the Deschutes River for 17 miles. Trailhead parking is located at the entrance. The trail itself is an old railroad bed; so it is very wide. The surface is dirt with some compacted gravel areas, and is not suited to street bicycles. Horses also travel on it from March 1 to June 30. Spring comes early in the Deschutes canyon, painting the walls of the canyon green for a few months each year, before heat begins to build in June, turning the vegetation a golden shade of brown. The canyon is sheltered and warmer than you might think; the first wildflowers break from winter's grip in late February. What a great escape from the rainy weather! The Atiyeh Deschutes River Trail at river level is a favorite jaunt for hikers on hot summer days. You just can't beat the cool river and the shade of white alder trees (and while you're resting, look for the hanging basket-type nests built by the orioles). The Deschutes, which is both a national and state scenic waterway, drops about a quarter mile in its final 100 miles as it twists through canyons 700 to 2,200 feet deep—great for days of fun whitewater rafting, kayaking, and inner-tubing.

BASICS

Operated By: Oregon State Parks. **Open:** All year. **Site Assignment:** Reservations can be made 9 months in advance. **Registration:** At office. **Fee:** Single, $12–$16; primitive, $5–$8; group, $40–$61. **Parking:** At park.

FACILITIES

Number of Multipurpose Sites: 135. **Hookups:** Yes. **Dump Station:** Less than 5 mi. **Laundry:** No. **Pay Phone:** Yes. **Restrooms and Showers:** Yes. **Fuel:** Less than 5 mi. **Propane:** Less than 5 mi. **Internal Roads:** Paved. **RV Service:** No. **Market:** No. **Restaurant:** Less than 5 mi. **General Store:** Less than 5 mi. **Vending:** No. **Swimming:** Yes. **Playground:** No. **Activities:** Biking, bird-watching, boating, canoeing, fishing, hiking, horseback riding, jogging/running, junior ranger program, kayaking, picnicking, rafting, whitewater rafting.

RESTRICTIONS

Pets: Pets must be confined by the owner, or on a leash not more than 6 feet long, kept under physical control at all times. You're responsible for removal of all waste and for keeping your pet quiet during campground quiet hours (10 p.m.–7 a.m.). **Fires:** In fire rings or fireplaces provided for such purposes & portions of the beach designated as permissible for fires. No fires shall be left unattended or be permitted to cause damage to park facilities or areas. **Alcoholic Beverages:** Possession or use of an alcoholic beverage by any person under 21 years of age is not allowed. **Other:** Discount programs may be offered. Fee adjustments will not be made after reservations have been confirmed using the Internet reservation service. A large campsite has at least a 12 by 12–ft. tent-pad area. Medium sites are at least 10 by10 ft. Small sites are at least 8 by 8 ft.

TO GET THERE

Traveling east: On I-84 travel 12 mi. east of The Dalles to the Deschutes State Recreation Area Exit 97/Biggs Rufus Hwy. Continue eastbound 4 mi.; cross the Deschutes River Bridge. The park is the first right after the bridge. Traveling west: On I-84 travel 34 mi. west of Arlington to Exit 104; turn left on Hwy. 97. Go 0.25 mi. and turn right on Biggs Rufus Hwy. Continue westbound 4.5 mi.; turn left into park before crossing the Deschutes River Bridge. Traveling south: On Hwy. 97 travel approx. 10 mi. from Goldendale, WA. Cross the Columbia River to Biggs Junction. Turn right on Biggs Rufus

Hwy. Continue westbound 4.5 mi. Turn left into park before crossing the Deschutes River Bridge. Traveling north: On Hwy. 97 from Bend travel to Biggs Junction, turn left on Biggs Rufus Hwy. Continue westbound 4.5 mi. Turn left into park before crossing the Deschutes River Bridge.

WESTFIR MAP, B-2
Black Canyon Campground— Willamette National Forest

reserve america

Black Canyon Campground, 97492. T: (541) 822-3799; www.reserveamerica.com.

🚐 ★★★★ ⛺ ★★★★

Beauty: ★★★★ Site Privacy: ★★★
Spaciousness: ★★★★ Quiet: ★★★★
Security: ★★★★ Cleanliness: ★★★★
Insect Control: ★★★★ Facilities: ★★★

Black Canyon is situated in a mixed conifer and broadleaf forest with many sites along the middle-fork of the Willamette River adjacent to Lookout Point Reservoir. Campsites are nestled amongst large, mature Douglas fir and cedar trees. This campground is engulfed with lush vegetation and old growth. Even on the hottest summer day, this site offers a little cooler temperature with the towering trees providing shade and a breeze blowing off the water. The scenic area suits many forms of recreation with a trailhead at the west end of the campground. There is also a 1-mile interpretive nature trail that winds through the campground. The Willamette National Forest stretches for 110 miles along the western slopes of the Cascade Range in western Oregon. It extends from the Mt. Jefferson area east of Salem to the Calapooya Mountains northeast of Roseburg. The Forest is 1,675,407 acres in size. The varied landscape of high mountains, narrow canyons, cascading streams, and wooded slopes offer excellent opportunities for visitors and make the forest valuable for many purposes.

BASICS

Operated By: U.S. Forest Service. **Open:** Apr. 21–Sept. 24. **Site Assignment:** Reservations must be made at least 7 days in advance. **Registration:** At office. **Fee:** Single, $14; double, $25–$65. **Parking:** At park.

FACILITIES

Number of Multipurpose Sites: 52. **Hookups:** Yes. **Each Site:** Call ahead. **Dump Station:** No. **Laundry:** No. **Pay Phone:** No. **Restrooms and Showers:** Yes. **Fuel:** No. **Propane:** No. **Internal Roads:** Paved. **RV Service:** No. **Market:** No. **Restaurant:** No. **General Store:** No. **Vending:** No. **Swimming:** Yes. **Playground:** No. **Activities:** Amphitheater, biking, bird-watching, canoeing, fishing, hiking, kayaking, photography, sightseeing, wildlife viewing.

RESTRICTIONS

Pets: Pets must be restrained or on a leash at all times while in developed recreation areas. **Fires:** In fire rings, stoves, grills, or fireplaces provided for that purpose. **Alcoholic Beverages:** Not allowed. **Vehicle Maximum Length:** Call ahead.

TO GET THERE

Traveling east on Hwy. 58 from Eugene through Lowell, Black Canyon is located directly off the main road before the city of West Fir.

WINCHESTER BAY MAP, B-1
Eel Creek Campground

reserve america

10101 Hwy. 101, 97449. T: (541) 759-2249; www.reserveamerica.com.

🚐 ★★★★ ⛺ ★★★★

Beauty: ★★★★★ Site Privacy: ★★★★★
Spaciousness: ★★★★ Quiet: ★★★★★
Security: ★★★★ Cleanliness: ★★★★
Insect Control: ★★★ Facilities: ★★★

Eel Creek is just one of many campgrounds that are clustered in the Florence/Reedsport/Coos Bay stretch of US 101. Heavy vegetation helps absorb traffic sounds and provides lovely secluded, sandy-bottomed sites. No sites are designated "tent-only," but tenters are free to choose from among the campgrounds all-purpose sites. Ocean breezes help keep insects to a minimum. Aside from its vegetation-lush private sites, Eel Creek's strongest selling point is the absence of off-road vehicle access to the dunes. If you want peace and quiet as part of your dunes experience, make sure you're not hiking in an area where they rent dune buggies. Eel Creek backs up against some of the largest dunes in the 46-mile-long protected beach. Always shifting, always changing, some dunes reach as high as 600 feet. Slog your way to the top of one of these monsters and look out over a most spectacular sight. Headquarters for Oregon Dunes National Recreation Area is right on US 101 at the junction of OR 38 in Reedsport. This is a well-stocked information bureau. The exhibits are worth a look, too.

BASICS

Operated By: Concessionaire NW Land Management. **Open:** May 20–Oct. 31. **Site Assignment:** First come, first served. **Registration:** Self-registration or camp host collects. **Fee:** $17; extra vehicle, $7. **Parking:** At site.

FACILITIES

Number of Multipurpose Sites: 53. **Hookups:** None. **Each Site:** Picnic table, fire grill. **Dump Station:** No. **Laundry:** No. **Pay Phone:** No. **Restrooms and Showers:** Yes. **Fuel:** No. **Propane:** No. **Internal Roads:** Call ahead for details. **RV Service:** No. **Market:** No. **Restaurant:** No. **General Store:** No. **Vending:** No. **Swimming:** No. **Playground:** No. **Activities:** Hiking, beach. **Nearby Attractions:** Dean Creek Elk Viewing Area. **Additional Information:** (541) 271-3611.

RESTRICTIONS

Pets: On leash only. **Fires:** Fire ring only. **Alcoholic Beverages:** Allowed. **Vehicle Maximum Length:** No limit.

TO GET THERE

From Reedsport, drive south on US 101 12 mi. The campground entrance is on the ocean side.

Pennsylvania

Pennsylvania has helped shape America's history since England's Charles II granted Quaker statesman William Penn leadership in the territory that became the second state. **Philadelphia,** the nation's first capital, is the birthplace of the **Declaration of Independence. Valley Forge** to the west and present-day Bucks County to the east are where George Washington crossed the **Delaware River.** On the south shore of **Presque Isle Bay** near Erie, Commodore Oliver Hazard Perry built his fleet, set sail, and defeated British troops in the Battle of Lake Erie in 1813. **Gettysburg,** the scene of perhaps the most infamous battle on U.S. soil, is rich with Civil War history.

A city that boasts the world's best cheesesteaks and grinders, Philadelphia blends colonial heritage with world-class museums, performing arts, and architecture. An ideal starting point for a visit to Philadelphia is the **Historic District,** which includes **Independence National Historic Park.** West of the Delaware River, the 45-acre park features **Independence Hall and Liberty Bell Pavilion,** among other historical buildings. The 8,700-acre **Fairmount Park** features the **Philadelphia Museum of Art, Philadelphia Zoo,** and 18th-century mansions authentically preserved and furnished. Northeast of Philadelphia in Bucks County, the **Washington Crossing Historic Park** is where George Washington and 200 soldiers crossed the Delaware River on Christmas night in 1776 and marched into **Trenton.** There, they surprised Hessian mercenaries and captured the city.

Northwest of Philadelphia, **Valley Forge National Historic Park** is the site of the Continental army's encampment from December 1777 to June 1778, when British troops occupied Philadelphia. **Washington Headquarters, Washington Memorial Chapel,** and the **Museum of the Valley Forge Historical Society** are among the attractions here.

Southwest of Philadelphia, the rolling countryside of the **Brandywine Valley** is adorned with charming villages, gardens, museums, chateau estates, and historic sites. Brandywine Valley straddles the Pennsylvania and Delaware border, so its attractions extend into the first state. The Pennsylvania side features **Brandywine Battlefield State Historic Park,** 1,050-acre **Longwood Gardens,** and the **Brandywine River Museum,** among other points of interest.

Located in the southeastern section of the state, **Pennsylvania Dutch** Country is home to an expansive population of **Amish, Mennonites,** and **Brethren.** The region has several small villages offering crafts, handmade furniture, and homemade delicacies. **Lancaster** is the heart of the Pennsylvania Dutch Country, and many of the area's best shops, museums, and restaurants are located there. Other destinations worth exploring include **Strasburg, Strasburg Railroad,** and the **Railroad Museum of Pennsylvania,** the **Reading** area, which is graced with the 2,400-acre **Hawk Mountain Sanctuary,** and the **Daniel Boone Homestead.**

About 55 miles southwest of Lancaster, Gettysburg is a quiet town with a load of history. **Gettysburg National Military Park,** which surrounds the town, is dotted with stores and homes much like it was during the Civil War. Must-see sites include **Cemetery Ridge,** the **Soldiers National Cemetery,** and the **National Tower,** which offers a battlefield view from 307 feet.

Also in south-central Pennsylvania, the state capital of **Harrisburg** is set on the shores of the **Susquehanna River.** East of Harrisburg, **Hershey** is renowned for **Hershey Park,** the 90-acre amusement park dedicated to that decadent confection, chocolate. In York, tour the **Harley-Davidson** plant and explore the **Rodney Gott Antique Motorcycle Museum.**

There was a time when **Pittsburgh** was a polluted city and the air was blackened by coal smoke. Pittsburgh still retains its iron- and steel-making heritage, but like Philadelphia, the city has undergone a renaissance. Situated at the **Three Rivers—the Ohio, Monongahela,** and **Allegheny**—the city offers much culture, architecture, and history. The **Andy Warhol Museum, Carnegie Science Center, Pittsburgh Children's Museum,** and **Pittsburgh Zoo** and **National Aviary** are interesting sites. Not far from Pittsburgh, the wooded and hilly **Laurel Highlands** features whitewater rafting on the **Youghiogheny River,** the 1,700-foot **Youghiogheny River Gorge** at **Ohiopyle State Park,** and two **Frank Lloyd Wright** architectural treasures in **Fallingwater** and **Kentuck Knob.**

Northern Pennsylvania is more natural and remote than the rest of the state. **Erie,** a port town located on the southern shore of Lake Erie, is home to **Presque Isle State Park,** the **Erie Maritime Museum,** and **Discovery Square.** The 797-square-mile **Allegheny National Forest,** the 301-foot-high **Kinzua Railroad Bridge,** and the town of **Scranton** are visitor favorites. Southeast of Scranton, the **Pocono Mountains** have 2,400 square miles of peaks, waterfalls, lakes, streams, and resort towns. A popular place for honeymooning couples, the Poconos are also a camper's haven—especially for those who like to fish, boat, swim, and hike.

Campground Profiles

ADAMSTOWN   MAP, D-5
Sill's Family Campground

1906 Bowmansville Rd., P.O. Box 566, 19501.
T: (717) 484-4806 or (800) 325-3002.

🚐 ★★★★   ⛺ ★★★

Beauty: ★★★	Site Privacy: ★★
Spaciousness: ★★	Quiet: ★★★★
Security: ★★★★	Cleanliness: ★★★
Insect Control: ★★★★	Facilities: ★★★

Located 15 miles northeast of Lancaster, in Pennsylvania Dutch Country, where well-kept farmhouses and barns dot the rolling terrain, Sill's Family Campground is a haven for campers seeking shelter from the sweltering sun. Many sites are shaded, and part of the park is wooded. There are 20 sites that accommodate pull-throughs and 25 that suit double slideouts. The location of Sill's is ideal for travelers interested in Pennsylvania Dutch Country attractions, but there are few activities other than swimming, badminton, horseshoes, volleyball, and softball. Shady Grove Campground, also in Adamstown, has a spring-fed lake, which offers campers more recreational opportunities. Both Sill's and Shady Grove are comfortable base camps when visiting Dutch Country attractions.

BASICS
Operated By: Russ South. **Open:** Apr. 1–Oct. 31. **Site Assignment:** Reservations recommended. **Registration:** At campground headquarters. **Fee:** $21.50 tent; $24 water & electricity; $25.50 full hookup (V, MC, D). **Parking:** At site.

FACILITIES
Number of RV-only Sites: 120. **Number of Tent-only Sites:** 20. **Hookups:** Electric (20, 30 amps), water, cable TV, Internet, sewer. **Each Site:** Picnic table, fire ring. **Dump Station:** Yes. **Laundry:** Yes. **Pay Phone:** Yes. **Restrooms and Showers:** Yes. **Fuel:** No. **Propane:** Yes. **Internal Roads:** Gravel & paved, in good condition. **RV Service:** No. **Market:** W/in 2 mi. **Restaurant:** W/in 2 mi. **General Store:** Yes. **Vending:** Yes. **Swimming:** Yes. **Playground:** Yes. **Other:** The campground has a traffic control gate. **Activities:** Game room, rec room, softball diamond, badminton, horseshoes, volleyball. **Nearby Attractions:** Pennsylvania Dutch Country, Lancaster County, antique markets, Maple Grove Racetrack, Reading outlet malls, Valley Forge. **Additional Information:** Pennsylvania Dutch CVB, (800) PA-DUTCH, www.padutchcountry.com.

RESTRICTIONS
Pets: On leash. **Fires:** At site. **Alcoholic Beverages:** At site. **Vehicle Maximum Length:** 45 ft.

TO GET THERE
Take Exit 21 (junction of I-76 and SR-272). Head north on SR-272 to Bowmansville Rd. Head east 0.5 mi. Campground is on the left.

BARNESVILLE   MAP, C-5
Locust Lake State Park

687 Tuscarora Park Rd., 18214.
T: (888) PA-PARKS or (570) 467-2404;
www.dcnr.state.pa.us/stateparks.

🚐 ★★★   ⛺ ★★★★

Beauty: ★★★★★	Site Privacy: ★★★★
Spaciousness: ★★★★	Quiet: ★★★★
Security: ★★★★	Cleanliness: ★★★★
Insect Control: ★★★★	Facilities: ★★★

Situated at the head of a steep, wooded valley, Locust Lake State Park is heavily forested. In fact, the only cleared area is the 52-acre lake. A bike trail and a number of hiking trails wind through the park. Known for its popular camping area, Locust Lake State Park is nestled on the side of Locust Mountain. The 282 campsites are divided into tent or trailer sides that encircle the lake. Tenting is permitted on the north side of the lake, and the trailer facilities are located on the south side of the lake. Boating, hiking, and fishing are favored activities at the 1,089-acre park. Because of its location in the Appalachian Mountain section of the Ridge and Valley Province, Locust Valley is positioned along the migration route used by many species of birds of prey, including red-shouldered hawks, red-tailed hawks, merlins, and osprey. Screech owls and great-horned owls are year-round residents.

BASICS
Operated By: State of Pennsylvania. **Open:** Apr.–Oct. **Site Assignment:** Reservations accepted. **Registration:** At campground office. **Fee:** $12–$19; V, MC. **Parking:** At designated spot.

FACILITIES
Number of RV-only Sites: 80. **Number of Tent-only Sites:** 59. **Hookups:** Electric (20, 30, 50 amps). **Each Site:** Fire ring, picnic table. **Dump Station:** Yes. **Laundry:** No. **Pay Phone:** Yes. **Restrooms and Showers:** Yes. **Fuel:** No. **Propane:** No. **Internal Roads:** Paved, in good condition. **RV Service:** No. **Market:** W/in 6 mi. **Restaurant:** W/in 6 mi. **General Store:** Yes. **Vending:** Yes. **Swimming:** Lake. **Playground:** Yes, 3. **Activities:** Boating, fishing, lake swimming, hiking, boat rentals. **Nearby Attractions:** Tuscarora State Park, Weiser State Forest. **Additional Information:** Schuylkill County Visitors Bureau, (800) 765-7282, www.schuykill.org.

RESTRICTIONS
Pets: Pets permitted at 25 sites only. **Fires:** At site. **Alcoholic Beverages:** No alcohol permitted. **Vehicle Maximum Length:** 40 ft.

TO GET THERE
From I-81, take Exit 37E and go 4 mi. west and south on SR 1006.

BEDFORD   MAP, D-3
Friendship Village Campground and RV Park

348 Friendship Village Rd., 15522.
T: (814) 623-1677 or (800) 992-3528;
www.bedfordcounty.net/camping/friendship.

🚐 ★★★★   ⛺ ★★★★

Beauty: ★★★★	Site Privacy: ★★★
Spaciousness: ★★★	Quiet: ★★★★
Security: ★★★★	Cleanliness: ★★★★★
Insect Control: ★★★★	Facilities: ★★★★★

In Bedford County, it seems like the covered bridges outnumber the stoplights. With this in mind, it's good that Friendship Village offers plenty of amenities and activities for families. Located midway between Pittsburgh and Harrisburg—not far from historic Bedford—Friendship Village has a full slate of planned activities, not counting the recreation menu that ranges from basketball and volleyball to mini-golf and fishing. Many sites are shaded or partially shaded. There is an ample number of pull-through sites, many of which are open. The best sites are along the trout-stocked stream. The tent sites are grassy and comfortable.

BASICS
Operated By: Ken & Darla Rhodes. **Open:** All year. **Site Assignment:** Reservations encouraged; first come, first served. **Registration:** At campground headquarters. **Fee:** $20–$30; V, MC, D. **Parking:** At site.

FACILITIES
Number of RV-only Sites: 200. **Number of Tent-only Sites:** 20. **Hookups:** Electric (20, 30, 50 amps), water, cable TV, phone. **Each Site:** Fire ring, picnic table. **Dump Station:** Yes. **Laundry:** Yes. **Pay Phone:** Yes. **Restrooms and Showers:** Yes. **Fuel:** No. **Propane:** Yes. **Internal Roads:** Gravel & paved, in good condition. **RV Service:** No. **Market:** W/in 1 mi. **Restaurant:** W/in 1 mi. **General Store:** Yes. **Vending:** Yes. **Swimming:** Yes. **Playground:** Yes. **Other:** Cabins available for rent. Friendship Village has a full slate of planned activities; check Web site for details. **Activities:** Rec hall, coin games, boating, canoeing, mini-golf, rowboat & paddleboat rentals, fishing, basketball, shuffleboard, sports field, horseshoes, volleyball. **Nearby Attractions:** Old Bedford Village, the Bison Corral, Fort Bedford Museum, Blue Knob Ski Resort, Shawnee Lake, Raystown Lake, Historic Bedford, covered bridges. **Additional Information:** Bedford County Visitors Bureau, (877) BC-GUIDE, www.bedfordcounty.net.

RESTRICTIONS
Pets: On leash only. **Fires:** At site. **Alcoholic Beverages:** At site. **Vehicle Maximum Length:** 60 ft. **Other:** No pets & no smoking permitted in cabins.

TO GET THERE
From I-76, take Exit 11 and head south 1 mi. on US 220, then west on Hwy. 30 to Friendship Village Rd. Campground is 0.25 mi.

BELLEFONTE MAP, C-3
Bellefonte/State College KOA

2481 Jacksonville Rd., 16823.
T: (814) 355-7912 or (800) 562-8127;
www.koa.com.

🚐 ★★★★ 　　　　⛺ ★★★★

Beauty: ★★★★	Site Privacy: ★★
Spaciousness: ★★	Quiet: ★★★
Security: ★★★★	Cleanliness: ★★★★
Insect Control: ★★★★	Facilities: ★★★★

With postcard-perfect mountain views and lots of amenities, Bellefonte/State College KOA is a comfortable place for your RV and tent. There are many grassy sites. Of the 100 RV sites, 18 accommodate pull-throughs and 26 accommodate slideouts. The campground is especially popular during the summer (considering all the outdoor activities nearby) and during college football season when the Penn State Nittany Lions play in Happy Valley. The free pancakes served Sunday 8–10 a.m. and 3:30–5 p.m. are a welcome bonus.

BASICS

Operated By: KOA. **Open:** Apr. 1–Nov. 20. **Site Assignment:** By reservation & first come, first served. **Registration:** At campground headquarters. **Fee:** RV, $25–$40; tent, $30–$36; V, MC, AE, D. **Parking:** At site.

FACILITIES

Number of RV-only Sites: 100. **Number of Tent-only Sites:** 35. **Hookups:** Electric (20, 30, 50 amps), water, cable TV, phone. **Each Site:** Fire ring, picnic table, lantern pole. **Dump Station:** Yes. **Laundry:** Yes. **Pay Phone:** Yes. **Restrooms and Showers:** Yes. **Fuel:** No. **Propane:** Yes. **Internal Roads:** Gravel, in good condition. **RV Service:** No. **Market:** W/in 5 mi. **Restaurant:** W/in 5 mi. **General Store:** Yes. **Vending:** Yes. **Swimming:** Yes. **Playground:** Yes. **Other:** 24-hour security. **Activities:** Swimming, rec hall, coin games, fishing, basketball, bike rentals, badminton, horseshoes, hiking trails, volleyball. **Nearby Attractions:** Historic Bellefonte, Penn State University, Belleville Amish Market, Knoebels Amusement Park, Johnstown Flood National Memorial, Ashland's Pioneer Tunnel Coal Mine, Allegheny Portage Railroad, Pennsylvania Military Museum, Penn's Cave, Woodward Cave, Happy Valley Friendly Farm. **Additional Information:** Victorian Bellefonte, www.bellefonte.com.

RESTRICTIONS

Pets: On leash only. **Fires:** At site in fire rings only. **Alcoholic Beverages:** At site only. **Vehicle Maximum Length:** No limit.

TO GET THERE

From I-80, take Exit 161 and go north 2 mi. on Hwy. 26. Entrance is on the left.

BOWMANSVILLE MAP, D-5
Oak Creek Campground

400 East Maplegrove Rd, P. O. Box 128, 17507.
T: (717) 445-6161 or (800) 446-8365;
www.oakcreekcamp.com.

🚐 ★★★★ 　　　　⛺ ★★★★

Beauty: ★★★★	Site Privacy: ★★★
Spaciousness: ★★★	Quiet: ★★★★
Security: ★★★★★	Cleanliness: ★★★★★
Insect Control: ★★★★	Facilities: ★★★★

In a region defined by natural beauty, with rolling green hills, towering trees, and rippling streams, Oak Creek Campground is a must-stay for campers who yearn for shady campsites and peaceful surroundings. Located outside of Bowmansville and covering 200 acres, the campground actually overlooks Oak Creek from a hillside densely packed with forest and nature trails. All RV sites are spacious and wooded. There are eight pull-through sites, 100 double slide-outs, and 152 full hookups. A cluster of sites along the pond and another cluster of sites at the northwest tip of the campground along Oak Creek are ideal. Near the center of the campground, there are sites on both sides of the creek, but these sites offer little privacy. With its creek, swimming pool, and colorful hiking trails, Oak Creek is a quiet and fun park to stay at while in Dutch Country. Oakley, the Amish cricket, is Oak Creek's unofficial mascot and can be heard and seen at the campground.

BASICS

Operated By: Dennis & Sue Cramer. **Open:** All year. **Site Assignment:** Reservations recommended. **Registration:** At campground office. **Fee:** Water/electric, $34–$37; sewer, $36–$39; V, MC, D. **Parking:** At site.

FACILITIES

Number of RV-only Sites: 307. **Number of Tent-only Sites:** 20. **Hookups:** Electric (30, 50 amps), water, cable TV. **Each Site:** Fire ring, picnic table. **Dump Station:** Yes. **Laundry:** Yes. **Pay Phone:** Yes. **Restrooms and Showers:** Yes. **Fuel:** No. **Propane:** Yes. **Internal Roads:** Gravel & paved, in good condition. **RV Service:** No. **Market:** W/in 6 mi. **Restaurant:** W/in 6 mi. **General Store:** Yes. **Vending:** Soft drinks. **Swimming:** Yes. **Playground:** 3 separate playgrounds. **Other:** Adult TV lounge, teen arcade. **Activities:** Rec hall, coin games, swimming, pond & stream fishing, shuffleboard, badminton, sports field, horseshoes, hiking trails, volleyball, basketball. **Nearby Attractions:** Pennsylvania Dutch Country, Rockvale Square Outlets, Hershey Park & Chocolate World, Strasburg Railroad, National Toy Train Museum, Dutch Wonderland Family Fun Park, The Amazing Maize Maze, Longwood Gardens, Gast Classic Motorcars Museum, Stoudt's Brewery. **Additional Information:** Pennsylvania Dutch CVB, (800) PA-DUTCH, www.padutchcountry.com.

RESTRICTIONS

Pets: On leash only. **Fires:** At site. **Alcoholic Beverages:** At site. **Vehicle Maximum Length:** 45 ft. **Other:** Check-in & check-out are both at 3 p.m.; early arrivals & late departures subject to half-day charge.

TO GET THERE

At SR 625 and Maple Grove Rd., go 1.5 mi. east on Maple Grove. Entrance to Oak Creek is at the end.

BOWMANSVILLE MAP, D-5
Sun Valley Campground

451 East Maple Grove Rd., P.O. Box 708, 17507.
T: (717) 445-6262 or (800) 700-3370;
www.sunvalleycamping.com.

🚐 ★★★★★ 　　　　⛺ ★★★★

Beauty: ★★★★	Site Privacy: ★★
Spaciousness: ★★★	Quiet: ★★★
Security: ★★★★	Cleanliness: ★★★★
Insect Control: ★★★★	Facilities: ★★★★★

Located near Oak Creek Campground outside of Bowmansville, Sun Valley Campground is a family haven where hayrides, pond fishing, and sand volleyball are among the activities offered. Overall, Sun Valley has fewer sites than Lake-In-Wood Camping Resort and Oak Creek Campground, but it does not take a back seat in cleanliness, beauty, and excitement. Sun Valley has a full-time activities director. The campground is semi-wooded with shaded and open sites—all level, some grass and some gravel. There are nine pull-through sites. Like its fellow Bowmansville campgrounds, Sun Valley is centrally located between Hershey (45 mi.), Gettysburg (50 mi.), Valley Forge (40 mi.), Philadelphia (50 mi.), Reading (15 mi.), and Lancaster (20 mi.).

BASICS

Operated By: Private operator. **Open:** Apr. 7–Oct. 29. **Site Assignment:** Reservations recommended; first come, first served. **Registration:** At campground office. **Fee:** RV, $28–$42; tent, $28; water, electricity, sewer & cable available; V, MC, D. **Parking:** At site.

FACILITIES

Number of RV-only Sites: 265. **Number of Tent-only Sites:** 21. **Hookups:** Electric (20, 30, 50 amps), water, cable TV, phone. **Each Site:** Fire ring, picnic table, lantern pole. **Dump Station:** Yes. **Laundry:** Yes. **Pay Phone:** Yes. **Restrooms and Showers:** Yes. **Fuel:** No. **Propane:** Yes. **Internal Roads:** Gravel & paved, in good condition. **RV Service:** No. **Market:** W/in 2 mi. **Restaurant:** W/in 2 mi. **General Store:** Yes. **Vending:** Yes. **Swimming:** Yes. **Playground:** Yes. **Other:** Full-time activities director on staff. Cabin, cottage & pop-up rentals available. **Activities:** Rec hall, coin games, swimming, pond fishing, basketball, badminton, sports field, hayrides, hiking trail, basketball, volleyball, horseshoes, petting zoo. **Nearby Attractions:** Pennsylvania Dutch Country, Dorney Park, Reading outlet malls, Gettysburg Battlefield, Valley Forge, Strasburg Railroad, golf courses, Sesame Place. **Additional Information:** Pennsylvania Dutch CVB, (800) PA-DUTCH, www.padutchcountry.com.

RESTRICTIONS

Pets: On leash only. **Fires:** At site. **Alcoholic Beverages:** At site. **Vehicle Maximum Length:** 35 ft.

TO GET THERE

From I-76, take Exit 22. Go south 1 mi. on Hwy. 10 to SR 23, west 7.4 mi. to SR 625, north 5.8 mi.

to E. Maple Grove Rd., and east 2 mi. to campground entrance on the left.

BRADFORD
Tracy Ridge—
Umpqua National Forest
MAP, A-2

reserve america

4001 West Washington St., 16701.
T: (814) 368-4158; www.reserveamerica.com.

🚐 ★★★★   ▲ ★★★★

Beauty: ★★★   Site Privacy: ★★★
Spaciousness: ★★★   Quiet: ★★★
Security: ★★★★   Cleanliness: ★★★★
Insect Control: ★★★★   Facilities: ★★

The Tracy Ridge campground is situated in a mature oak stand on top of a hill. Facilities include restrooms and a hand pump for water. Sites are spacious, with tent pads provided. Some sites are available on a first-come, first-served basis. Group sites are also available. Tracy Ridge campground is known for its trail system. The Tracy Ridge Trail begins on the flat ridgetop of the Tracy Ridge Recreation Area and travels downward to the shore of the Allegheny Reservoir. The area covers a large and unique area without roads within the Allegheny National Forest. Flora and fauna in the area includes oak, beech, hickory, hemlock, deer, grouse, and turkey. Hikers should be in good health, as the trail climbs steep slopes and rocky areas. When joining the Johnnycake Trail and the North Country National Scenic Trail, hikers on Tracy Ridge can enjoy a triangular 8.7-mile-long loop. In total, the Allegheny National Forest offers a network of more than 600 miles of trail. The forest contains Tionesta Natural and Scenic Area, boasting old growth forest, and the Heart's Content Scenic Area, an area of 300-year-old white pine.

BASICS

Operated By: U.S. Forest Service. **Open:** Apr. 15–Dec. 12. **Site Assignment:** Reservations must be made at least 4 days in advance. **Registration:** At office. **Fee:** Single, $10; group, $40–$75. **Parking:** Limited.

FACILITIES

Number of Multipurpose Sites: 284. **Hookups:** No. **Each Site:** Fire ring. **Dump Station:** Yes. **Laundry:** No. **Pay Phone:** No. **Restrooms and Showers:** Yes. **Fuel:** No. **Propane:** No. **Internal Roads:** Gravel. **RV Service:** No. **Market:** No. **Restaurant:** No. **General Store:** No. **Vending:** No. **Swimming:** No. **Playground:** No. **Activities:** Hiking.

RESTRICTIONS

Pets: Pets must be restrained or on a leash at all times while in developed recreation areas. **Fires:** In fire rings, stoves, grills, or fireplaces provided for that purpose. **Alcoholic Beverages:** Not allowed. **Vehicle Maximum Length:** Call ahead.

TO GET THERE

Take PA 321 north off PA 59, or south off PA 346.

BRADFORD
Twin Lakes—
Umpqua National Forest
MAP, A-2

reserve america

US Forest Service Dr., 16701. T: (814) 362-4613; www.reserveamerica.com.

🚐 ★★★★   ▲ ★★★★

Beauty: ★★★★   Site Privacy: ★★★★
Spaciousness: ★★★   Quiet: ★★★
Security: ★★★★   Cleanliness: ★★★★
Insect Control: ★★★★   Facilities: ★★★

Twin Lakes is a beautiful campground located on a peninsula between the Pamlico River and the Chocowinity Bay in a secluded mountain setting at 5,000 feet in elevation. The Twin Lakes area is a place of serenity and great beauty—the perfect spot to relax and be refreshed, shedding the noise and bustle of an active life. Situated at Big Twin Lake (a 14-acre lake with depth of 48 feet) is a shelter and six campsites, which include rustic log tables and fire rings. A pit toilet is also available. There is one campsite at Little Twin Lake, a 6-acre lake with a depth of 30 feet. A 1-mile loop trail, 1521, interconnects the lakes. Points of interest include alpine meadows abundant with wildflowers, scenic hiking trails, a cliff area overlooking the lakes, and grotto caves at the base of the cliffs. Twin Lakes is located within the Umpqua National Forest, which covers nearly 1 million acres along the western slopes of the Cascade Mountains in southwest Oregon. The forest encompasses a diverse area of rugged mountains to 9,200 feet in elevation, sparkling rivers and lakes, and deep canyons, producing a wealth of water resources, timber, wildlife, fish habitat, minerals, and outdoor recreation opportunities.

BASICS

Operated By: U.S. Forest Service. **Open:** Apr. 13–Dec. 10. **Site Assignment:** Reservations must be made at least 4 days in advance. **Registration:** At office. **Fee:** Single, $16–$21; double, $28. **Parking:** At park.

FACILITIES

Number of Multipurpose Sites: 332. **Hookups:** Yes. **Each Site:** Call ahead. **Dump Station:** Yes. **Laundry:** No. **Pay Phone:** No. **Restrooms and Showers:** Yes. **Fuel:** No. **Propane:** No. **Internal Roads:** Paved. **RV Service:** No. **Market:** No. **Restaurant:** No. **General Store:** No. **Vending:** No. **Swimming:** Yes. **Playground:** Yes. **Activities:** Fishing, hiking.

RESTRICTIONS

Pets: Pets must be restrained or on a leash at all times while in developed recreation areas. **Fires:** In fire rings, stoves, grills, or fireplaces provided for that purpose. **Alcoholic Beverages:** Not allowed. **Vehicle Maximum Length:** 50 ft. **Other:** Please do not bring firewood from home.

TO GET THERE

Located about 8 mi. south of Kane, PA. From PA 321 at large campground sign, turn onto FR 191. Follow FR 191 2 mi. to the campground. Railroad underpass on entrance road restricts vehicle height (check first).

BUTLER
Buttercup Woodlands
Campground
MAP, C-1

854 Evans City Rd., 16053. T: (724) 789-9340; www.buttercup.org.

🚐 ★★★★   ▲ ★★★★

Beauty: ★★★★   Site Privacy: ★★
Spaciousness: ★★★   Quiet: ★★★
Security: ★★★★   Cleanliness: ★★★★
Insect Control: ★★★   Facilities: ★★★★

Located about 30 miles northeast of Pittsburgh and 10 miles southeast of Moraine State Park and Lake Arthur, Butler's Buttercup Woodlands Campground features spacious grassy sites. Among the amenities are a library, playground, dance hall, and trolley rides. Buttercup's proximity to Moraine State Park is one of its top draws. Moraine State Park features 3,225-acre Lake Arthur, an outstanding warm-water fishery that is also ideal for sailing and boating. Visitors sometimes see osprey that were reintroduced to the park. Of special interest is the Frank Preston Conservation Area and a 7-mile paved bike trail that winds around the north shore of the lake. The gently rolling hills, lush forests, and sparkling waters disguise a land that has endured the effects of continental glaciers and massive mineral extraction.

BASICS

Operated By: Ed, Barb, & Christy Tanski. **Open:** May–Sept. **Site Assignment:** By reservation & first come, first served. **Registration:** At campground headquarters. **Fee:** RV, $27; tent, $16. **Parking:** At site.

FACILITIES

Number of RV-only Sites: 280. **Number of Tent-only Sites:** 20. **Hookups:** Electric (30, 50 amps), sewer, cable TV. **Each Site:** Fire ring, picnic table. **Dump Station:** No. **Laundry:** Yes. **Pay Phone:** Yes. **Restrooms and Showers:** Yes. **Fuel:** No. **Propane:** Yes. **Internal Roads:** Gravel & paved, in good condition. **RV Service:** No. **Market:** W/in 3 mi. **Restaurant:** W/in 3 mi. **General Store:** Yes. **Vending:** Yes. **Swimming:** Yes. **Playground:** Yes. **Other:** Cabins & RV available for rent. **Activities:** Rec room, trolley rides, coin games, swimming, basketball, sports field, badminton, horseshoes, volleyball, shuffleboard. **Nearby Attractions:** Pittsburgh, Moraine State Park, Lake Arthur, golf courses, Prime Outlets at Grove City, Butler County, Historic Zelienople. **Additional Information:** Greater Pittsburgh CVB, (800) 366-0093. www.visitpittsburgh.com; Butler County Tourist Promotion Agency, (888) 741-6772, www.butlercountychamber.com.

RESTRICTIONS

Pets: On leash only. **Fires:** Fire ring only. **Alcoholic Beverages:** At site. **Vehicle Maximum Length:** 65 ft. **Other:** No carpet permitted on grass.

TO GET THERE

From I-79, take Exit 27 and follow SR 528 1.5 mi. to SR 68. Go east on SR 68 and follow 8 mi. Campground is on the left.

COOKSBURG   MAP, B-2
Cook Forest State Park

P.O. Box 120, 16217.
T: (888) PA-PARKS or (814) 744-8407;
www.dcnr.state.pa.us/stateparks or
www.cookforest.com.

🚐 ★★★★   ▲ ★★★★

Beauty: ★★★★	Site Privacy: ★★★
Spaciousness: ★★★	Quiet: ★★★
Security: ★★★	Cleanliness: ★★★★
Insect Control: ★★★★	Facilities: ★★★

Cook Forest State Park encompasses 7,182 acres in
northwest Pennsylvania. Bordered by the picturesque
Clarion River, the park is most known for old-growth
white pine and hemlock forests. Classified as a
National Natural Landmark by the National Park
Service, Cook Forest State Park is often referred to as
the "Black Forest" of Pennsylvania. Ridge Camp, the
park's campground, is open year-round. On-site
hookups are not available and winter access is not
guaranteed. There are two cabin areas at Cook Forest.
The River Cabins are on a hillside overlooking the
Clarion River. These are large cabins with four rooms
and a fireplace. They will sleep either six or eight people. The Indian Cabins are smaller one-room structures that will accommodate four people. These
cabins are found along Tom's Run located behind the
park office. All cabins are rented with a minimum of
furniture, including beds, mattresses, a gas stove,
refrigerator, tables, and chairs. Occupants must provide their own bedding, cookware, and tableware.

BASICS

Operated By: State of Pennsylvania. **Open:** All year.
Site Assignment: By reservation & first come, first
served. **Registration:** At campground office. **Fee:**
$14–$17; V, MC. **Parking:** At designated spot.

FACILITIES

Number of Multipurpose Sites: 226. **Hookups:**
Electric (30, 50 amps). **Each Site:** Fire ring, picnic
table. **Dump Station:** Yes. **Laundry:** Yes. **Pay
Phone:** Yes. **Restrooms and Showers:** Yes. **Fuel:**
No. **Propane:** No. **Internal Roads:** Gravel & dirt,
in good condition. **RV Service:** No. **Market:** W/in
3 mi. **Restaurant:** W/in 3 mi. **General Store:** No.
Vending: Yes. **Playground:** Yes. **Activities:** Hiking,
river & stream fishing, swimming, planned activities
on weekends, sports field. **Nearby Attractions:**
Cook Forest Sawmill Center for the Arts, Eldred
World War II Museum, Allegheny River Islands
Wilderness, Historic Brookville Walking Tour, Raccoon Creek State Park, Punxsutawney. **Additional
Information:** Northwest Pennsylvania's Great Outdoors Visitors Bureau, (800) 348-9393,
www.pagreatoutdoors.com.

RESTRICTIONS

Pets: Allowed on sites 1–15. **Fires:** Fire ring only.
Alcoholic Beverages: No alcohol permitted. **Vehicle Maximum Length:** 45 ft.

TO GET THERE

From Clarion River Bridge in Cooksburg, go
1 mi. northwest on Hwy. 36 north. Entrance is on
the right.

COOKSBURG   MAP, B-2
Deer Meadow Campground

2761 Forest Rd., 16217.
T: (814) 927-8125 or (866) 4-DM-CAMP;
www.deermeadow.com.

🚐 ★★★★   ▲ ★★★★

Beauty: ★★★★	Site Privacy: ★
Spaciousness: ★★★	Quiet: ★★★
Security: ★★★★	Cleanliness: ★★★★
Insect Control: ★★★★	Facilities: ★★★★

Amid the majestic white pines and hemlocks of Cook
Forest State Park, Deer Meadow Campground is an
oasis for outdoor enthusiasts searching for a wealth of
activities and a clean and spacious campground to
enjoy them in. With 500 sites, Deer Meadow is the
largest campground in the Cook Forest area. The 65-
acre campground borders the 6,422-acre Cook Forest. A hiking trail even wanders from Deer Meadow
to other trails that lead deep into Cook Forest. Overall, there are 27 miles of hiking trails in Cook Forest.
Canoeing, tubing, fishing, and swimming are available in the Clarion River at the state park. Of course,
a full slate of activities is offered at Deer Meadow,
including a heated pool and mini-golf. Deer Meadow
has open and shaded sites, and many are wooded.
There are no pull-through sites, but there are 350
double slideout sites. Most sites are laid out in rows,
except for a cluster of sites on the eastern side, which
are situated in a circle.

BASICS

Operated By: Ed, Tracy, & Andy Betz. **Open:** May
1–Oct. 15. **Site Assignment:** By reservation & first
come, first served. **Registration:** At campground
office. **Fee:** Full hookup, $29; water/sewer/cable, $26;
no hookup, $22; V, MC. **Parking:** At site.

FACILITIES

Number of RV-only Sites: 500. **Number of
Tent-only Sites:** 72. **Hookups:** Electric (20, 30
amps), water, cable TV, phone. **Each Site:** Fire ring,
picnic table. **Dump Station:** Yes. **Laundry:** Yes.
Pay Phone: Yes. **Restrooms and Showers:**
Yes. **Fuel:** No. **Propane:** Yes. **Internal Roads:**
Gravel & paved, in good condition. **RV Service:** No.
Market: W/in 7 mi. **Restaurant:** W/in 7 mi.
General Store: Yes. **Vending:** Yes. **Swimming:**
Yes. **Playground:** Yes. **Other:** Church services,
hayrides. **Activities:** Rec hall, coin games, swimming,
mini-golf, shuffleboard, basketball, planned activities,
horseshoes, hiking trails, badminton, volleyball.
Nearby Attractions: Cook Forest State Park,
Leeper Flea Market, Sawmill Center for the
Arts, Clear Creek State Forest, Deer Ranch,
Kinzua Bridge State Park, antique shops.
Additional Information: Allegheny National
Forest Vacation Bureau, (814) 368-9370,
www.allegheny-vacation.com.

RESTRICTIONS

Pets: On leash only. **Fires:** At site. **Alcoholic Beverages:** Under control at campsite. **Vehicle Maximum Length:** 40 ft. **Other:** Reservations required
for Memorial Day & Labor Day.

TO GET THERE

At Hwy. 36 and Clarion River Bridge, go 0.1 mi.

northwest on Hwy. 36 and 3 mi. north on Forest
Rd. Deer Meadow; entrance is on left.

CROSS FORK   MAP, B-3
Ole Bull State Park

HCR 62 Box 9, 17729-9701.
T: (814) 435-5000 or (888) PA-PARKS;
www.dcnr.pa.us/stateparks.

🚐 ★★★★   ▲ ★★★★

Beauty: ★★★★	Site Privacy: ★★★★
Spaciousness: ★★★★	Quiet: ★★★★
Security: ★★★★	Cleanliness: ★★★★
Insect Control: ★★★★	Facilities: ★★★

Located in Galeton, Ole Bull State Park is referred
to as the Black Forest of Pennsylvania. Its dense tree
cover and mountainous terrain attract thousands of
campers who bask in the serenity of the forested
scenery along Kettle Creek. Camping is permitted
year-round. Two camping areas along Kettle Creek
provide sunny and shaded sites. There are 24 sites
with electric hookups in Area 2. Area 1 has two sites
with electric for people with disabilities. The 1.5-
story Ole Bull Cabin is available for rent year-
round. The cabin has a modern kitchen and bath
and sleeps ten people. The Beaver Dam Nature Trail
provides an introduction to the habitats along Kettle Creek. This flat, 0.75-mile trail starts at the concrete fordway. Go to the environmental education
and interpretation center for more information. The
sandy beach along Kettle Creek is open from
Memorial Day weekend to Labor Day unless posted
otherwise. Susquehannock State Forest surrounds
Ole Bull State Park and offers hiking on a variety of
trails.

BASICS

Operated By: State of Pennsylvania. **Open:** All
year. **Site Assignment:** By reservation & first come,
first served. **Registration:** At campground office.
Fee: $12–$19; V, MC. **Parking:** At site.

FACILITIES

Number of RV-only Sites: 81. **Hookups:** Electric
(20, 30, 50 amps). **Each Site:** Fire ring, picnic table.
Dump Station: Yes. **Laundry:** No. **Pay Phone:**
Yes. **Restrooms and Showers:** Restrooms, no
showers. **Fuel:** No. **Propane:** No. **Internal Roads:**
Gravel, in fair condition. **RV Service:** No. **Market:**
W/in 2 mi. **Restaurant:** W/in 2 mi. **General
Store:** No. **Vending:** No. **Playground:** Yes. **Activi-
ties:** River swimming, stream fishing, horseshoes,
hiking trails, planned activities, sports field. **Nearby
Attractions:** Susquehannock State Forest, Kettle
Creek State Park, Lyman Run State Park, Pennsylva-
nia Lumber Museum. **Additional Information:**
Potter Co. Visitors Assoc., (888) POTTER-2,
www.pottercountypa.org.

RESTRICTIONS

Pets: Not allowed. **Fires:** At site. **Alcoholic Beverages:** No alcohol permitted. **Vehicle Maximum
Length:** 36 ft.

TO GET THERE

From US 6, go 20 mi. south on Hwy. 144. Follow
signs.

DENVER MAP, D-5
Hickory Run Family Camping Resort

285 Greenville Rd., 17517. T: (717) 336-5564 or (800) 458-0612; www.pacampgrounds.com.

★★★★   ▲ ★★★★

Beauty: ★★★★★   Site Privacy: ★★★
Spaciousness: ★★★★   Quiet: ★★★★
Security: ★★★★   Cleanliness: ★★★★
Insect Control: ★★★★   Facilities: ★★★★

Located in the pristine countryside of northern Lancaster County, Hickory Run is only a short drive away from many local attractions. Sites are shaded and open. Our favorite sites are along Upper Lake View Dr., where campers have privacy and are still a short distance from the fishing lake and boating lake. Paddleboats and rowboats are available to rent on Hickory Run's 3-acre bass-stocked lake. Of course, the Amish way of life is alive and well in Lancaster County. You can also tour an operating farm, travel through scenic farm country on an authentic steam train or by horse and buggy, or spend the day with a knight in the 16th-century England at the Renaissance Faire. Enjoy German bands and great food at the Bavarian Beer Festival in nearby Adamstown, which is also the home of the 30,000-dealer Antique Row.

BASICS
Operated By: Private operator. **Open:** Apr. 1–Nov. 1. **Site Assignment:** By reservation & first come, first served. **Registration:** At campground office. **Fee:** $31–$36; V, MC. **Parking:** At site.

FACILITIES
Number of RV-only Sites: 170. **Number of Tent-only Sites:** 20. **Hookups:** Electric (20, 30 amps), water, sewer, phone; 90 full hookups. **Each Site:** Fire ring, picnic table. **Dump Station:** Yes. **Laundry:** Yes. **Pay Phone:** Yes. **Restrooms and Showers:** Yes. **Fuel:** No. **Propane:** Yes. **Internal Roads:** Gravel & paved, in good condition. **RV Service:** No. **Market:** 5 mi. in Denver. **Restaurant:** 5 mi. in Denver. **General Store:** Yes. **Vending:** Yes. **Swimming:** Yes. **Playground:** Yes. **Other:** RV & cabin rentals. **Activities:** Rec hall, pavilion, coin games, swimming, wading pool, rowboat & pedal boat rentals, canoeing, planned activities, tennis, sports field, volleyball, horseshoes, hiking trail, hayrides, mini-golf. **Nearby Attractions:** Amish Village, Amish Farm & House, Middle Creek Wildlife Preserve, Strasburg Railroad, Pennsylvania Dutch Country, Dorney Park, Green Dragon Farmer's Market, Eagle Falls Adventure Park, Kitchen Kettle Village, Living Waters Theatre, Choo-Choo Barn/Traintown USA, Longwood Gardens, National Toy Train Museum, Railroad Museum of Pennsylvania. **Additional Information:** Pennsylvania Dutch CVB, (800) PA-DUTCH, www.padutchcountry.com.

RESTRICTIONS
Pets: On leash only. **Fires:** Fire ring only. **Alcoholic Beverages:** At site. **Vehicle Maximum Length:** 45 ft. **Other:** Rates for standard site w/ electric & water increase to $33, Memorial Day–Labor Day.

TO GET THERE
From I-76, take Exit 21 and follow Hwy. 272 1.75 mi. south, then 2 mi. west on Church/Main St., then follow signs 2 mi. on paved road. Entrance to Hickory Run is on left.

DOVER MAP, D-4
Gettysburg Farm Campground/ Outdoor World

6200 Big Mount Rd., 17315. T: (717) 292-7191; www.campoutdoorworld.com.

★★★★   ▲ ★★★★

Beauty: ★★★★   Site Privacy: ★★★
Spaciousness: ★★★   Quiet: ★★★★
Security: ★★★★   Cleanliness: ★★★★
Insect Control: ★★★★   Facilities: ★★★★★

Few places have more history in the United States than Gettysburg, and Gettysburg Farm Campground is located adjacent to the Black Horse Tavern, a historical landmark used as an inn and hospital during the Civil War. Operated by Outdoor World, Gettysburg Farm Campground is actually a living farm, where guests can enjoy horse-drawn hayrides and pony rides, visit with farm animals at the petting zoo, and watch the planting and harvesting of crops. Though located on a farm, this campground is kept clean, and the facilities are well maintained. The country store is well stocked, and activities ranging from mini-golf, fishing, and canoeing to events in the recreation center and video arcade offer enough variety to keep children happily occupied. Gettysburg Farm has a mix of gravel and grassy sites, some shaded and others open. Twelve sites accommodate pull-throughs, and 174 handle double slideouts.

BASICS
Operated By: Outdoor World. **Open:** Apr. 15–Oct. 21. **Site Assignment:** First come, first served. **Registration:** At campground office. **Fee:** $36–$69; V, MC, AE, D. **Parking:** At site.

FACILITIES
Number of RV-only Sites: 241. **Number of Tent-only Sites:** 20. **Hookups:** Electric (20, 30, 50 amps), water, sewer; 174 full hookups. **Each Site:** Fire ring, grill, picnic table. **Dump Station:** Yes. **Laundry:** Yes. **Pay Phone:** Yes. **Restrooms and Showers:** Yes. **Fuel:** No. **Propane:** Yes. **Internal Roads:** Gravel & paved, in good condition. **RV Service:** No. **Market:** W/in 5 mi. **Restaurant:** W/in 5 mi. **General Store:** Yes. **Vending:** Yes. **Swimming:** Yes. **Playground:** Yes. **Other:** Living farm w/ pony rides & petting zoo. **Activities:** Swimming, wading pool, mini-golf, canoeing, basketball, volleyball, shuffleboard, horseshoes, fishing, video arcade, hayrides, rec center. **Nearby Attractions:** Gettysburg Battlefield Tours, National Civil War Wax Museum, Historic Downtown York, Harley-Davidson Museum, Lincoln Train Scenic Ride, Utz Potato Chip Factory, Magic Town, Land of Little Horses. **Additional Information:** Gettysburg CVB, (717) 334-6274, www.gettysburg.com.

RESTRICTIONS
Pets: On leash only. **Fires:** Fire ring only. **Alcoholic Beverages:** At site. **Vehicle Maximum Length:** 40 ft.

TO GET THERE
Take I-81 south to junction I-83. Take I-83 south to junction of Hwy. 30, Exit 22. Go west on Hwy. 30 to Big Mount Rd. Go 5 mi. Campground is on the left.

EAST STROUDSBURG MAP, B-6
Delaware Water Gap KOA

233 Hollow Rd., 18301. T: (570) 223-8000 or (800) 562-0375; www.koa.com.

★★★★   ▲ ★★★★

Beauty: ★★★   Site Privacy: ★★
Spaciousness: ★★★   Quiet: ★★★
Security: ★★★★   Cleanliness: ★★★★
Insect Control: ★★★   Facilities: ★★★★

Located near the Delaware River outside of East Stroudsburg, KOA—Delaware Water Gap offers clean and well spaced, open, and partially shaded sites. There are 50 pull-through sites. The campground has standard activities, such as basketball, horseshoes, badminton, and mini-golf, but its proximity to numerous Delaware Water Gap and Pocono Mountains attractions and events is what attracts many visitors. The Delaware Water Gap preserves 40 miles of the middle Delaware River and almost 70,000 acres of land along the river's New Jersey and Pennsylvania shores. At the south end of the park, the river cuts eastward through a scenic water gap in the Appalachian Mountains. Canoeing, camping, fishing, swimming, hiking; viewing wildlife, geologic features, and natural scenery—all this and more await visitors. The park includes historic Millbrook Village and several environmental education centers.

BASICS
Operated By: Carmen & Carla Prato. **Open:** Apr. 1–Oct. 31. **Site Assignment:** By reservation & first come, first served. **Registration:** At campground office. **Fee:** RV, $37; tent, $33–$37. **Parking:** At designated spot.

FACILITIES
Number of RV-only Sites: 164. **Number of Tent-only Sites:** 7. **Hookups:** Electric (20, 30, 50 amps), cable TV, phone. **Each Site:** Fire ring, picnic table. **Dump Station:** Yes. **Laundry:** Yes. **Pay Phone:** Yes. **Restrooms and Showers:** Yes. **Fuel:** No. **Propane:** Yes. **Internal Roads:** Gravel & paved, in good condition. **RV Service:** No. **Market:** W/in 6 mi. **Restaurant:** W/in 6 mi. **General Store:** Yes. **Vending:** Yes. **Swimming:** Yes. **Playground:** Yes. **Other:** Cabins available for rent. **Activities:** Rec room, coin games, mini-golf, sports field, basketball, volleyball, hiking trails, horseshoes, badminton, Ping-Pong. **Nearby Attractions:** Delaware River, Pocono Mountains, Bushkill Falls, Shawnee Place, Pocono International Raceway, golf courses, horseback riding. **Additional Information:** Pocono Mountains Vacation Bureau, (800) POCONOS, www.800poconos.org.

RESTRICTIONS
Pets: On leash only. **Fires:** At site. **Alcoholic Beverages:** At site. **Vehicle Maximum Length:** 55 ft.

TO GET THERE

From I-80, take Exit 52 and go 6 mi. north on US209 and 1 mi. east on Hollow Rd. Entrance is on left.

EAST STROUDSBURG MAP, B-6
Mountain Vista Campground

50 Taylor Dr., 18301. T: (570) 223-0111; www.mtnvistacampground.com.

🚐 ★★★★ 　　　 ⛺ ★★★★

Beauty: ★★★★	Site Privacy: ★★★★
Spaciousness: ★★★★	Quiet: ★★★★
Security: ★★★★	Cleanliness: ★★★★
Insect Control: ★★★★	Facilities: ★★★★

Expansive wooded sites dominate the landscape at Mountain Vista Campground, which is within 15 minutes of the Delaware Water Gap National Recreation Area. The view of the mountains from the campground's sundeck is breathtaking. Throughout the year, the campground hosts special events like the Chili Fest, Italian Fest, Irish Fest, Oktoberfest, and Luau. There are 12 pull-through sites and 65 spots for double slideouts. Mountain Vista is also near the Appalachian Trail, Delaware State Forest, and the Delaware River—a popular spot for canoeing, rafting, and tubing. Across the border in New Jersey (about a half-hour drive from Mountain Vista) is Waterloo Village, a National Registered Historic Site in Allamuchy Mountain State Park.

BASICS

Operated By: Vaughan family. **Open:** Apr. 15–Oct. 31. **Site Assignment:** Reservations accepted (1-night deposit to accompany reservation); walk-ins accepted. **Registration:** At campground headquarters. **Fee:** $29 $40.50; V, MC. **Parking:** At site.

FACILITIES

Number of RV-only Sites: 185. **Number of Tent-only Sites:** 15. **Hookups:** Electric (20, 30, 50 amps), water, phone, Internet. **Each Site:** Fire ring, grill. **Dump Station:** Yes. **Laundry:** Yes. **Pay Phone:** Yes. **Restrooms and Showers:** Yes. **Fuel:** No. **Propane:** No. **Internal Roads:** Gravel & paved, in good condition. **RV Service:** No. **Market:** W/in 3 mi. **Restaurant:** W/in 3 mi. **General Store:** Yes. **Vending:** Yes. **Swimming:** Yes. **Playground:** Yes. **Activities:** Rec hall, game room, swimming, boating, canoeing, float trips, pond fishing, basketball, shuffleboard, planned activities, tennis, badminton, sports field, horseshoes, hiking trails, volleyball, bocce. **Nearby Attractions:** Delaware Water Gap, Delaware River, Bushkill Falls, Appalachian Trail, Camelbeach & Alpine Slide, Memorytown USA, antique shops, factory outlets. **Additional Information:** Pocono Mountains Vacation Bureau, (800) POCONOS, www.800poconos.org.

RESTRICTIONS

Pets: On leash only. **Fires:** At site. **Alcoholic Beverages:** At site. **Vehicle Maximum Length:** No limit.

TO GET THERE

From I-80, take Exit 309 and go 0.1 mi. north on US 209, 2 mi. northwest on Hwy. 447, 3 mi. north on Business US 209, 1 mi. west on Craig's Meadow Rd., and 500 ft. south on paved road. Entrance is on the right.

EAST STROUDSBURG MAP, B-6
Pocono Vacation Park

Shafer School House Rd., 18360. T: (570) 424-2587; www.poconovacationpark.com.

🚐 ★★★★ 　　　 ⛺ ★★★★

Beauty: ★★★★★	Site Privacy: ★★★
Spaciousness: ★★★	Quiet: ★★★★★
Security: ★★★★	Cleanliness: ★★★★
Insect Control: ★★★★	Facilities: ★★★★

Located about 50 miles south of Scranton near the Delaware Water Gap, Pocono Vacation Park has 140 level pull-through sites. Weekly performances from professional entertainers, free chip-and-putt golf, and a comfortably sized swimming pool are among the activities. The park offers hayrides twice a week and bingo every Friday. With its proximity to the Delaware Water Gap and the Delaware River—and its perch in the Pocono Mountains—Pocono Vacation Park is central to numerous hiking, boating, and fishing spots. For a unique side trip, head to Scranton and visit the Houdini Museum. An expert on Harry Houdini hosts a two-hour tour, describing stories about the famous magician's life and career. Some of Houdini's secrets are revealed, followed by a demonstration and magic show.

BASICS

Operated By: Carl Willis. **Open:** All year. **Site Assignment:** Reservations recommended (stay 6 days & get 7th day free); walk-ins accepted. **Registration:** At campground office. **Fee:** $24.75–$29.50; V, MC. **Parking:** At designated spot.

FACILITIES

Number of RV-only Sites: 300. **Number of Tent-only Sites:** 10. **Hookups:** Electric (20, 30, 50 amps), water, cable TV, phone. **Each Site:** Fire ring, picnic table. **Dump Station:** Yes. **Laundry:** Yes. **Pay Phone:** Yes. **Restrooms and Showers:** Yes. **Fuel:** No. **Propane:** Yes. **Internal Roads:** Gravel, in good condition. **RV Service:** No. **Market:** W/in 6 mi. **Restaurant:** W/in 2 mi. **General Store:** Yes. **Vending:** Yes. **Swimming:** Yes. **Playground:** Yes. **Activities:** Rec hall, game room, swimming, wading pool, putting green, basketball, shuffleboard, planned activities on weekends, sports field, horseshoes, volleyball. **Nearby Attractions:** Delaware Water Gap, Delaware River, Bushkill Falls, Appalachian Trail, Camelbeach & Alpine Slide, Memorytown USA, antique shops, factory outlets. **Additional Information:** Pocono Mountains Vacation Bureau, (800) POCONOS, www.800poconos.org.

RESTRICTIONS

Pets: On leash only. **Fires:** At site. **Alcoholic Beverages:** At site. **Vehicle Maximum Length:** No limit.

TO GET THERE

From I-80, take Exit 48 and go 2 mi. south on Business US 209 and 0.5 mi. west on Shafer's School House Rd. Entrance is on the left.

ELIZABETHTOWN MAP, D-5
Rustic Meadows Camping and Golf Resort

1980 Turnpike Rd., 17022. T: (717) 367-7718 or (800) 562-4774; www.campwithrusty.com.

🚐 ★★★★ 　　　 ⛺ ★★★★

Beauty: ★★★★	Site Privacy: ★★★
Spaciousness: ★★★	Quiet: ★★★
Security: ★★★★	Cleanliness: ★★★★
Insect Control: ★★★★	Facilities: ★★★★

Located in southeastern Pennsylvania—central to Gettysburg, Harrisburg, Lancaster County, Hershey, and Philadelphia—Rustic Meadows Camping and Golf Resort offers spacious open and shaded sites amid rolling terrain. Hayrides, bonfires, and pond fishing are among the family-oriented activities. Linksters will like the three-par, nine-hole golf course. If the golfing experience humbles you, perhaps you can restore your pride at the mini-golf course. The Civil War sites at Gettysburg, historic Harrisburg, and even Philadelphia are a comfortable drive from Rustic Meadows. Among our favorite attractions is the Harley-Davidson Museum and Plant. The antique motorcycle museum features the history and heritage of America's top motorcycle manufacturer, and the plant tour shows the final assembly of the famous Harley-Davidson motorcycles. Of course, Chocolate World is equally interesting. Here, you can discover HersheyPark, the Hershey Museum, Hershey Gardens, and ZooAmerica North American Wildlife Park.

BASICS

Operated By: Karl & Linda Schmidt. **Open:** Mar. 31–Nov. 5. **Site Assignment:** By reservation & first come, first served. **Registration:** At campground office. **Fee:** Call ahead for rates; V, MC, D. **Parking:** At site.

FACILITIES

Number of RV-only Sites: 134. **Number of Tent-only Sites:** 14. **Hookups:** Electric (20, 30, 50 amps), water, phone. **Each Site:** Fire ring, picnic table. **Dump Station:** Yes. **Laundry:** Yes. **Pay Phone:** Yes. **Restrooms and Showers:** Yes. **Fuel:** No. **Propane:** Yes. **Internal Roads:** Gravel, in fair condition. **RV Service:** No. **Market:** W/in 5 mi. **Restaurant:** W/in 5 mi. **General Store:** Yes. **Vending:** Yes. **Swimming:** Yes. **Playground:** Yes. **Other:** Par 3 golf course. **Activities:** Golf, mini-golf, swimming, hayrides, pond fishing, coin games, basketball, sports field, badminton, horseshoes, hiking trails, volleyball, movies, planned activities. **Nearby Attractions:** Chocolate World, HersheyPark, Hershey Museum, Hershey Gardens, ZooAmerica North American Wildlife Park, Harrisburg, Pennsylvania Renaissance Faire, Harley-Davidson Museum & Plant Tour, Pennsylvania Dutch Country, Gettysburg. **Additional Information:** Pennsylvania Dutch CVB, (800) PA-DUTCH, www.padutchcountry.com.

RESTRICTIONS

Pets: On leash only. **Fires:** At site. **Alcoholic Beverages:** At site. **Vehicle Maximum Length:** No limit. **Other:** Early arrivals & late departures are subject to availability & additional charges.

TO GET THERE

From junction of Hwy. 283 and Hwy. 743, go 1.5 mi. south on Hwy. 743, 0.5 mi. southwest on Hwy. 241. and 2.5 mi. northwest on Turnpike Rd. Entrance is on left.

ELVERSON   MAP, D-5
French Creek State Park

843 Park Rd., 19520-9523.
T: (610) 582-9680 or (888) PA-PARKS;
www.dcnr.state.pa.us/stateparks.

🚐 ★★★   ▲ ★★★★

Beauty: ★★★★	Site Privacy: ★★★
Spaciousness: ★★★★	Quiet: ★★★★
Security: ★★★★	Cleanliness: ★★★
Insect Control: ★★★★	Facilities: ★★★

Set amid rolling farmland of southeast Pennsylvania, French Creek State Park is home to Hopewell Lake, Scotts Run Lake, dense forests, and almost 40 miles of hiking trails. Adjacent to the park lies Hopewell Furnace National Historic Site, where a cold-blast furnace is restored to its 1830s appearance. Towering oak, poplar, hickory, maple, and beech trees cover much of the park. Wetlands and pristine streams flowing through rich creek valleys offer additional habitats for plants and animals. Of the campground's 201 sites, 50 have electric hookups. These sites are shaded by mature trees and are central to bathroom and shower facilities. Though the campground itself does not have a swimming pool, there is a pool along the shores of Hopewell Lake (open between Memorial Day and Labor Day).

BASICS

Operated By: State of Pennsylvania. **Open:** All year. **Site Assignment:** Reservations recommended; walk-ins accepted. **Registration:** At campground office. **Fee:** $12–$19; V, MC. **Parking:** At site.

FACILITIES

Number of RV-only Sites: 201. **Number of Tent-only Sites:** 18. **Hookups:** Electric (30, 50 amps). **Each Site:** Fire ring, picnic table. **Dump Station:** Yes. **Laundry:** No. **Pay Phone:** Yes. **Restrooms and Showers:** Yes. **Fuel:** No. **Propane:** No. **Internal Roads:** Paved, in fair condition. **RV Service:** No. **Market:** W/in 7 mi. **Restaurant:** W/in 7 mi. **General Store:** No. **Vending:** No. **Swimming:** Yes. **Playground:** Yes. **Activities:** Boating, canoeing, boat rentals, lake fishing, planned activities on weekends, hiking trails. **Nearby Attractions:** Hopewell Furnace National Historic Site. **Additional Information:** Reading Berks Co. Visitors Bureau, (610) 375-4085.

RESTRICTIONS

Pets: Allowed at designated campsites. **Fires:** At fire rings only. **Alcoholic Beverages:** No alcohol permitted. **Vehicle Maximum Length:** 35 ft.

TO GET THERE

From Hwy. 23, go north on Hwy. 345. Entrance is on the right.

ENTRIKEN   MAP, C-3
Lake Raystown Resort and Lodge

100 Chipmunk Crossing Hwy. 994, 16638.
T: (814) 658-3500; www.raystownresort.com.

🚐 ★★★★   ▲ ★★★★

Beauty: ★★★★	Site Privacy: ★★★
Spaciousness: ★★★★	Quiet: ★★★★
Security: ★★★★★	Cleanliness: ★★★★
Insect Control: ★★★★	Facilities: ★★★★★

Located in central Pennsylvania between Harrisburg and Pittsburgh in Entriken, Lake Raystown Resort and Lodge is situated on Pennsylvania's largest inland lake, with 118 miles of scenic shoreline and thousands of acres of pristine woodlands and streams. With the vast menu of activities, many visitors never leave the lakeside campground. The *Proud Mary* Showboat offers cruises on Lake Raystown. Wild River Water park features Caddy's Revenge 19-hole mini-golf, two 380-foot-long twisting slides, two 70-foot-high speed slides, the White Water Innertube Ride, an in-ground heated swimming pool, and the Children's Splash and Play Pool. The campground has 210 double slideout sites and nine pull-through sites. We recommend the sites located on the water. Shaded by towering trees, these sites ooze tranquility. Primitive sites are available, as are platform tent rentals.

BASICS

Operated By: Samantha Ocelus. **Open:** Apr. 14–Oct. 31. **Site Assignment:** Reservations recommended. **Registration:** At campground headquarters. **Fee:** $30–$45; V, MC, AE. **Parking:** In designated spot.

FACILITIES

Number of RV-only Sites: 221. **Number of Tent-only Sites:** 47. **Hookups:** Electric (20, 30, 50 amps), water, cable TV. **Each Site:** Picnic table, fire ring. **Dump Station:** Yes. **Laundry:** Yes. **Pay Phone:** Yes. **Restrooms and Showers:** Yes. **Fuel:** Yes. **Propane:** No. **Internal Roads:** Gravel & paved, in good condition. **RV Service:** No. **Market:** W/in 7 mi. **Restaurant:** 2 on premises. **General Store:** Yes. **Vending:** Yes. **Swimming:** Yes. **Playground:** Yes. **Other:** Water park, marina, showboat, lodge, cabins, cottages, houseboats, meeting facilities. **Activities:** Wild River Water Park, boat rentals, canoeing, rec room, game room, lake fishing, mini-golf, planned activities, badminton, basketball, volleyball, horseshoes, hiking trails. **Nearby Attractions:** Lake Raystown, Penn's Cave, Lincoln Caverns. **Additional Information:** Laurel Highlands Visitors Bureau, (800) 925-7669, www.laurelhighlands.org.

RESTRICTIONS

Pets: On leash only. **Fires:** Fire ring only. **Alcoholic Beverages:** At site. **Vehicle Maximum Length:** No limit.

TO GET THERE

From Hwy. 26 and Hwy. 994, go 4 mi. east on Hwy. 994. Entrance is on right.

ERIE   MAP, A-1
Erie KOA

6645 West Rd., 16426.
T: (814) 476-7706 or (800) 562-7610;
www.eriekoa.com.

🚐 ★★★★   ▲ ★★★★

Beauty: ★★★★	Site Privacy: ★
Spaciousness: ★★	Quiet: ★★★
Security: ★★★★	Cleanliness: ★★★
Insect Control: ★★★★	Facilities: ★★★

With shaded sites for RVs and a mix of wooded and open sites for tents, Erie KOA is located outside of Erie and 9 miles from Presque Isle State Park. The camp store is well stocked and the grounds are clean and well kept. This campground is rated in the top 10 among all KOAs. Beyond the standard offerings—heated pool and kiddie pool, paddleboat rentals, lake fishing—there are not many activities. However, the campground is within a convenient distance to Presque Isle, Lake Erie beaches, and Erie itself. Presque Isle was named a top 20 fishing spot by *Field & Stream* and one of the nation's top 100 swimming holes by *Condé Nast Traveler*. Presque Isle has 7 miles of life-guarded sandy beaches and 21 miles of recreational and hiking trails.

BASICS

Operated By: KOA. **Open:** May 4–Oct. 1. **Site Assignment:** By reservation & first come, first served. **Registration:** At campground office. **Fee:** $31–$40; V, MC, AE, D. **Parking:** At site.

FACILITIES

Number of RV-only Sites: 100. **Number of Tent-only Sites:** 34. **Hookups:** Electric (15, 20, 30, 50 amps), water. **Each Site:** Fire ring, picnic table. **Dump Station:** Yes. **Laundry:** Yes. **Pay Phone:** Yes. **Restrooms and Showers:** Yes. **Fuel:** No. **Propane:** Yes. **Internal Roads:** Gravel & paved, in good condition. **RV Service:** No. **Market:** W/in 3 mi. **Restaurant:** W/in 3 mi. **General Store:** Yes. **Vending:** Yes. **Swimming:** Yes. **Playground:** Yes. **Other:** Cabins available for rent. **Activities:** Rec hall, game room, swimming, wading pool, pedal boat rentals, fishing, planned activities, volleyball, horseshoes. **Nearby Attractions:** Presque Isle State Park, Lake Erie beaches, Waldameer Park & Water World, Mazza Winery, Penn Shore Winery, Erie Zoo, minor league baseball, golf courses, Flagship Niagara, Erie Walking Tour, Girard-Lake City, Wooden Nickel Buffalo Farm, Oil Creek & Titusville Railroad/ Drakes Well Museum. **Additional Information:** Erie Area CVB, (800) 542-ERIE, www.tourerie.com.

RESTRICTIONS

Pets: On leash only. **Fires:** At site. **Alcoholic Beverages:** At site. **Vehicle Maximum Length:** No limit.

TO GET THERE

From I-90, take Exit 18 and go 1 mi. south on Hwy. 832 and 0.5 mi. east on West Rd. Entrance is on the right.

FORKSVILLE   MAP, B-5
World's End State Park

P.O. Box 62, 18616.
T: (570) 924-3287 or (888) PA-PARKS;
www.dcnr.state.pa.us/stateparks.

🚐 ★★★   ⛺ ★★★★

Beauty: ★★★★	Site Privacy: ★★★★
Spaciousness: ★★★★	Quiet: ★★★★★
Security: ★★★★	Cleanliness: ★★★
Insect Control: ★★★	Facilities: ★★★

Wild and rugged, World's End State Park is located in a narrow S-shaped valley of the Loyalsock Creek just south of Forksville in Sullivan County. Hiking on the Loyalsock Trail attracts many visitors to the park. The scenery is spectacular, especially the June mountain laurel and fall foliage. Canyon Vista, reached via Mineral Spring and Cold Run Roads, provides outstanding views. The campground is located along Hwy. 154, 1 mile east of the park office. The 19 rustic cabins there are available for rental year-round. Thirty-two campsites have electric hookups. Whitewater boaters may use the Loyalsock Creek at any time of the year, although the area by the swimming beach is closed during the summer. Due to rapid fluctuations in water level, kayakers should inquire about conditions before coming to the park with their 'yaks. The stream is not suitable for open canoes.

BASICS

Operated By: State of Pennsylvania. **Open:** All year. **Site Assignment:** By reservation & first come, first served. **Registration:** At campground office. **Fee:** Call ahead for cost information; V, MC, D, personal check. **Parking:** At designated spot.

FACILITIES

Number of Multipurpose Sites: 70. **Hookups:** Electric (30, 50 amps). **Each Site:** Fire ring, picnic table. **Dump Station:** Yes. **Laundry:** No. **Pay Phone:** Yes. **Restrooms and Showers:** Yes. **Fuel:** No. **Propane:** No. **Internal Roads:** Gravel, in good condition. **RV Service:** No. **Market:** W/in 4 mi. **Restaurant:** W/in 4 mi. **General Store:** No. **Vending:** Yes. **Playground:** No. **Activities:** River swimming, canoeing, stream fishing, planned activities, sports field, hiking trails, snowmobiling. **Nearby Attractions:** Wyoming State Forest, Endless Mountains, Pennsylvania Bow Hunters Festival. **Additional Information:** Endless Mountains Visitors Bureau, (800) 769-8999, www.endlessmountains.org.

RESTRICTIONS

Pets: Not allowed. **Fires:** At site. **Alcoholic Beverages:** No alcohol permitted. **Vehicle Maximum Length:** 40 ft.

TO GET THERE

From Forksville, go 2 mi. south on Hwy. 154. Entrance is on the right.

GARDNERS   MAP, D-4
Mountain Creek Campground

reserve america

349 Pine Grove Rd., 17324. T: (717) 486-7681; www.mtncreekcg.com.

🚐 ★★★★   ⛺ ★★★★

Beauty: ★★★★	Site Privacy: ★★★
Spaciousness: ★★★	Quiet: ★★★★
Security: ★★★★	Cleanliness: ★★★★
Insect Control: ★★★★	Facilities: ★★★★

Mountain Creek Campground is named for the stocked trout stream on the premises. When opening day of trout season comes in April, the campground gets busy with anglers participating in fishing contests or casting just for fun. The Appalachian Trail is located just a half mile away. Mountain Creek cuts through the middle of the campground, and sites on both sides directly bordering the creek offer spectacular views. All of the grassy sites are open or shaded. Hershey and Gettysburg are convenient to Mountain Creek, as are the lesser-known towns of Carlisle and York. York was actually the first capital of the United States, and the city has several 18th- and 19th-century buildings. Mountain Creek is an ideal base for the National Apple Harvest Festival, which is held during the first two weekends in October.

BASICS

Operated By: Private operator. **Open:** All year. **Site Assignment:** Reservations recommended, walk-ins accepted. **Registration:** At campground headquarters. **Fee:** $23–$33; V, MC, AE, D. **Parking:** At site.

FACILITIES

Number of RV-only Sites: 186. **Number of Tent-only Sites:** 14. **Hookups:** Electric (20, 30, 50 amps), water, phone. **Each Site:** Fire ring, picnic table. **Dump Station:** Yes. **Laundry:** Yes. **Pay Phone:** Yes. **Restrooms and Showers:** Yes. **Fuel:** No. **Propane:** Yes. **Internal Roads:** Gravel, in good condition. **RV Service:** No. **Market:** W/in 5 mi. **Restaurant:** W/in 5 mi. **General Store:** Yes. **Vending:** Yes. **Swimming:** Yes. **Playground:** Yes. **Other:** Spa, stocked trout stream. **Activities:** Rec hall, game room, swimming, wading pool, pond & stream fishing, basketball, planned activities on weekends, hiking trails, horseshoes, volleyball. **Nearby Attractions:** Gettysburg battlefields, Hershey, President Eishenhower's Farm, Omar Bradley Museum, Hessian Powder Museum, York, Pennsylvania State Museum in Harrisburg, Boiling Springs, walking tour of Carlisle, Huntsdale Fish Hatchery. **Additional Information:** Harrisburg-Hershey-Carlisle-Perry Co. Tourism CVB, (800) 995-0969, www.visithhc.com.

RESTRICTIONS

Pets: On leash only. **Fires:** At site. **Alcoholic Beverages:** No alcohol permitted. **Vehicle Maximum Length:** 45 ft.

TO GET THERE

From Hwy. 94, go 2 mi. south on Hwy. 34, 0.5 mi. west on Green Mt. Rd., and 1 mi. west on Pine Grove Rd. Entrance is on the right.

GETTYSBURG   MAP, D-4
Artillery Ridge Camping Resort

610 Taneytown Rd., 17325.
T: (717) 334-1288 or (866) 932-2674;
www.artilleryridge.com.

🚐 ★★★★   ⛺ ★★★★

Beauty: ★★★★	Site Privacy: ★★
Spaciousness: ★★★	Quiet: ★★★★
Security: ★★★★★	Cleanliness: ★★★★
Insect Control: ★★★★	Facilities: ★★★★

The closest campground to the Gettysburg Battlefield, Artillery Ridge Camping Resort is a haven for outdoor-minded Civil War enthusiasts. The campground has a mix of open and shaded grassy sites, 46 of which are pull-throughs. There is a large open area for tents, and the campground also has a few secluded tenting sites. Actively remembering Gettysburg's role in the Civil War is obviously the main purpose at Artillery Ridge. Battlefield tours (some on horseback) embark from the campground. Bringing Civil War history to life, the Gettysburg Battle Diorama Museum is truly one of the most unique and interesting attractions we have seen at any campground in Pennsylvania. The diorama features more than 750 square feet of model displays and about 20,000 hand-painted soldiers, horses, buildings, and other scenery on the battlefields and in Gettysburg itself. The diorama provides a bird's-eye view of the three days of battles with dramatic narration and impressive light and sound effects. The diorama is a learning tool for children and adults alike. If you savor Civil War history, you will especially enjoy Artillery Ridge.

BASICS

Operated By: Ray Sterner. **Open:** Apr. 1–Nov. 1. **Site Assignment:** Reservations recommended, call ahead to confirm; walk-ins accepted. **Registration:** At campground store. **Fee:** $29–$40.50; V, MC, D. **Parking:** At site.

FACILITIES

Number of RV-only Sites: 113. **Number of Tent-only Sites:** 42. **Hookups:** Electric (20, 30 amps), water, phone. **Each Site:** Fire ring, picnic table. **Dump Station:** Yes. **Laundry:** Yes. **Pay Phone:** Yes. **Restrooms and Showers:** Yes. **Fuel:** No. **Propane:** No. **Internal Roads:** Gravel, in good condition. **RV Service:** No. **Market:** W/in 5 mi. **Restaurant:** W/in 2 mi. **General Store:** Yes. **Vending:** Yes. **Swimming:** Yes. **Playground:** Yes. **Other:** Horse stalls available, camping w/ horses allowed. **Activities:** Rec room, swimming, pedal boat rentals, planned activities, horseback riding trails, horse rentals, sports field, badminton, hiking trails, horseshoes, volleyball, battlefield tours. **Nearby Attractions:** Gettysburg Civil War attractions. **Additional Information:** Gettysburg CVB, (717) 334-6274, www.gettysburg.com.

RESTRICTIONS

Pets: On leash only. **Fires:** At site. **Alcoholic Beverages:** At site. **Vehicle Maximum Length:** 40 ft.

TO GET THERE

From US 30, go 1.5 mi. south on Business US 15 and 1.25 mi. southeast on Hwy. 134. Campground entrance is on left.

GETTYSBURG   MAP, D-4
Drummer Boy Camping Resort

1300 Hanover Rd., 17325. T: (800) 293-2808;
www.drummerboycamping.com.

🚐 ★★★★★   ⛺ ★★★★

Beauty: ★★★★★   Site Privacy: ★★
Spaciousness: ★★★   Quiet: ★★★★
Security: ★★★★   Cleanliness: ★★★★
Insect Control: ★★★★   Facilities: ★★★★★

Drummer Boy Camping Resort is a full-service outdoor resort with 300 shaded and partially shaded sites located on 100 acres of beautiful woodlands 1 mile east of Gettysburg. Accommodations include spacious campsites for RVers and tenters, camping cabins, and housekeeping cottages. Of RV sites, 120 are full hookup (including 45 pull-throughs) and 115 sites offer water and electric; the remainder are primitive sites. There are four clean bathhouses and three dump stations. If you would like to camp along the fishing pond, three sites at the northwest side offer adequate space. Sites at the far eastern end border the hiking trails and offer the most privacy. Baltimore, Harper's Ferry, and Hershey are no more than an hour's drive away, and Washington, D.C. is about 1.5 hours away. Bus tours to Gettysburg battlefield and Washington, D.C., embark from the campground, and battlefield audio tapes are available. An activities director is on staff daily during summer and weekends during the spring and fall.

BASICS

Operated By: Ron Gilbert. **Open:** Apr. 1–Oct. 31. **Site Assignment:** By reservation & first come, first served. **Registration:** At campground office. **Fee:** $29–$47; V, MC, D. **Parking:** At designated spot.

FACILITIES

Number of RV-only Sites: 125. **Number of Tent-only Sites:** 50. **Number of Multipurpose Sites:** 165. **Hookups:** Electric (20, 30, 50 amps), water, sewer, cable TV, phone, 100 full hookups. **Each Site:** Fire ring, picnic table. **Dump Station:** Yes. **Laundry:** Yes. **Pay Phone:** Yes. **Restrooms and Showers:** Yes. **Fuel:** No. **Propane:** No. **Internal Roads:** Gravel & paved, in good condition. **RV Service:** No. **Market:** W/in 4 mi. **Restaurant:** W/in 4 mi. **General Store:** Yes. **Vending:** Yes. **Swimming:** Yes. **Playground:** Yes. **Other:** Tours of Gettysburg battlefield & Washington, D.C. **Activities:** Rec hall, game room, swimming, whirlpool, pond fishing, mini-golf, basketball, bike rentals, planned activities, movies, badminton, sports field, horseshoes, hiking trails, volleyball. **Nearby Attractions:** Gettysburg battlefield & Civil War sites, Washington, D.C., Baltimore, Amish Country, Harper's Ferry, Hershey, Battlefield Bus Tours from camp, Washington, D.C. Bus Tours from camp, Battlefield Auto Tape available. **Additional Information:** Gettysburg CVB, (717) 334-6274, www.gettysburg.com.

RESTRICTIONS

Pets: On leash only. **Fires:** Fire ring. **Alcoholic Beverages:** At site. **Vehicle Maximum Length:** 45 ft.

TO GET THERE

From US 15, go 100 yards east on Hwy. 116 and 0.1 mi. north on Rocky Grove Rd. Entrance is on the left.

GETTYSBURG   MAP, D-4
Gettysburg Campground

reserve america

2030 Fairfield Rd./Hwy. 116W, 17325.
T: (717) 334-3304 or (888) 879-2241;
www.gettysburgcampground.com.

🚐 ★★★★   ⛺ ★★★★

Beauty: ★★★★★   Site Privacy: ★★
Spaciousness: ★★   Quiet: ★★★
Security: ★★★★   Cleanliness: ★★★★
Insect Control: ★★★★   Facilities: ★★★★★

Located just 3 miles from the battlefield, Gettysburg Campground lies along tranquil Marsh Creek in the shadow of the South Mountains, where soldiers from both sides rested between battles. There are 240 level sites, both shaded and sunny, with 25 pull-throughs. Full-hookup sites on the campground's north side along Marsh Creek are our favorites. Some of the sites in the primitive tenting area on the northeast side border the creek. If you prefer camping along the banks, waterfront sites are located at the northern and western ends. There is also a cluster of full-hookup sites surrounding the activity centers. In downtown Gettysburg, a walking tour illustrates the impact the Battle of Gettysburg had on this small rural community during those fateful days of 1863, offering a sampling of Gettysburg's battle-related sites.

BASICS

Operated By: Joe, Lori, & Lorraine. **Open:** Apr. 7–Nov. 18. **Site Assignment:** Reservations recommended, walk-ins accepted. **Registration:** At office. **Fee:** $29.70–$38.70; V, MC. **Parking:** At site.

FACILITIES

Number of RV-only Sites: 230. **Number of Tent-only Sites:** 30. **Hookups:** Electric (20, 30, 50 amps), water, phone. **Each Site:** Fire ring, picnic table. **Dump Station:** Yes. **Laundry:** Yes. **Pay Phone:** Yes. **Restrooms and Showers:** Yes. **Fuel:** No. **Propane:** Yes. **Internal Roads:** Gravel & paved, in good condition. **RV Service:** Yes. **Market:** W/in 5 mi. **Restaurant:** W/in 5 mi. **General Store:** Yes. **Vending:** Yes. **Swimming:** Yes. **Playground:** Yes. **Other:** Ice-cream parlor, RV & cabin rentals. **Activities:** Rec hall, game room, swimming, stream fishing, shuffleboard, planned activities, basketball, movies, sports field, badminton, volleyball, mini-golf. **Nearby Attractions:** Gettysburg battlefields, Baltimore, Hershey, Washington, D.C., Lancaster County. **Additional Information:** Gettysburg CVB, (717) 334-6274, www.gettysburg.com.

RESTRICTIONS

Pets: On leash only. **Fires:** At site. **Alcoholic Beverages:** At site. **Vehicle Maximum Length:** No limit.

TO GET THERE

From Business US 15, go 3 mi. west on Hwy. 116. Entrance is on the left.

GETTYSBURG   MAP, D-4
Granite Hill Camping Resort and Adventure Golf

reserve america

3340 West Fairfield Rd., 17325.
T: (717) 642-8749 or (800) 642-TENT;
www.granitehillcampingresort.com.

🚐 ★★★★★   ⛺ ★★★★

Beauty: ★★★★   Site Privacy: ★★★
Spaciousness: ★★★   Quiet: ★★★★
Security: ★★★★   Cleanliness: ★★★★★
Insect Control: ★★★★   Facilities: ★★★★★

Located 6 miles from historic Gettysburg and home of the Gettysburg Bluegrass Festival, Granite Hill Campground offers 300 campsites spread over 150 acres, creating an uncrowded feeling even at the busiest time of the year. Granite Hill features many recreational options—including boat rentals, pond fishing, and lake fishing—but the highlight is its 18-hole Adventure Golf Course, which rivals the best mini-golf courses we have seen. Granite Hill has wooded sites, shaded sites with manicured grass, and a large, open, grassy overflow used when the regular campsites fill up, or when club rallies and special events require more space. Granite Hill offers a convenient pick-up service for guests purchasing Gettysburg Battlefield Tour tickets at the camp store. Package tickets are also available along with information on the many museums and attractions in the area. The campground offers a free shuttle to Gettysburg.

BASICS

Operated By: Private operator. **Open:** All year. **Site Assignment:** By reservation & first come, first served. **Registration:** At campground headquarters. **Fee:** $24–$36; V, MC. **Parking:** At designated spot.

FACILITIES

Number of RV-only Sites: 250. **Number of Tent-only Sites:** 100. **Hookups:** Electric (20, 30, 50 amps), water, sewer; 100 full hookups. **Each Site:** Fire ring, picnic table. **Dump Station:** Yes. **Laundry:** Yes. **Pay Phone:** Yes. **Restrooms and Showers:** Yes. **Fuel:** Yes. **Propane:** Yes. **Internal Roads:** Gravel & paved, in good condition. **RV Service:** No. **Market:** W/in 2 mi. **Restaurant:** W/in 2 mi. **General Store:** Yes. **Vending:** Yes. **Swimming:** Yes. **Playground:** Yes. **Other:** 3 dump stations, large general store. **Activities:** Rec hall, game room, swimming, wading pool, lake swimming, boat rentals, pond fishing, mini-golf, basketball, planned activities, shuffleboard, sports field, badminton, hiking trails, horseshoes, tennis, movies, volleyball. **Nearby Attractions:** Gettysburg battlefields, Civil War sites. **Additional Information:** Gettysburg CVB, (717) 334-6274, www.gettysburg.com.

RESTRICTIONS

Pets: On leash only. **Fires:** Fire ring. **Alcoholic Beverages:** At site. **Vehicle Maximum Length:** 50 ft.

TO GET THERE

From Business US 15, go 6 mi. west on Hwy. 116. Entrance is on the left.

GETTYSBURG   MAP, D-4
Round Top Campground

180 Knight Rd., 17325. T: (717) 334-9565;
www.roundtopcamp.com.

🚐 ★★★★   ⛺ ★★★★

Beauty: ★★★★   Site Privacy: ★★★
Spaciousness: ★★   Quiet: ★★★
Security: ★★★★   Cleanliness: ★★★★
Insect Control: ★★★★   Facilities: ★★★★★

Located 3 miles from the Gettysburg Battlefield Visitors Center and offering battlefield and Washington, D.C., tours from the park, Round Top Campground is remarkably clean and has spacious, semi-wooded open and shaded sites. We most like the sites on the east side of the campground. They offer privacy, and yet they are within a short walking distance of most of Round Top's activities, which include mini-golf, tennis, and shuffleboard. The cavernous recreation lodge overlooks the pool and can accommodate groups and special events.

BASICS

Operated By: Kenny & Judy Caudill, Steve & Wendy Dutterer. **Open:** May–Oct. **Site Assignment:** Reservations encouraged; walk-ins accepted. **Registration:** At campground office. **Fee:** $20–$40; V, MC, D. **Parking:** At site.

FACILITIES

Number of RV-only Sites: 206. **Number of Tent-only Sites:** 20. **Number of Multipurpose Sites:** 58. **Hookups:** Electric (20, 30, 50 amps), water, sewer; 202 full hookups. **Each Site:** Fire ring, picnic table. **Dump Station:** Yes. **Laundry:** Yes. **Pay Phone:** Yes. **Restrooms and Showers:** Yes. **Fuel:** No. **Propane:** Yes. **Internal Roads:** Paved, in good condition. **RV Service:** Adjacent to campground. **Market:** W/in 5 mi. **Restaurant:** W/in 1 mi. **General Store:** Yes. **Vending:** No. **Swimming:** Yes. **Playground:** Yes. **Other:** Park models & primitive cabins available for rent. **Activities:** Tennis, rec hall, game room, swimming, wading pool, mini-golf, basketball, shuffleboard, planned activities on weekends, sports field, badminton, horseshoes, volleyball. **Nearby Attractions:** Gettysburg battlefields & Civil War sites, 110-store outlet center 2 mi. away. **Additional Information:** Gettysburg CVB, (717) 334-6274, www.gettysburg.com.

RESTRICTIONS

Pets: On leash. **Fires:** At site. **Alcoholic Beverages:** At site. **Vehicle Maximum Length:** 40 ft. **Other:** Pets not permitted in buildings or pool area.

TO GET THERE

From US 15, go 0.1 mi. north on Hwy. 134 and 0.5 mi. west on Knight Rd. Entrance is on the left.

GREENTOWN   MAP, B-6
Promised Land State Park

R.R. 1, P.O. Box 96, 18426.
T: (570) 676-3428 or (888) PA-PARKS;
www.dcnr.state.pa.us/stateparks.

🚐 ★★★★   ⛺ ★★★★

Beauty: ★★★★★   Site Privacy: ★★★
Spaciousness: ★★★   Quiet: ★★★★
Security: ★★★★   Cleanliness: ★★★
Insect Control: ★★★   Facilities: ★★★★

Located amid the Pocono Mountains, Promised Land State Park is approximately 3,000 acres, 1,800 feet above sea level. The forest consists primarily of beech, oak, maple, and hemlock trees. Promised Land Lake is 422 acres and Lower Lake is 173 acres. All campgrounds are near swimming, boating, fishing, and hiking facilities. The Pines Campground is located at the northwestern end of Promised Land Lake, within walking distance of the day-use area and main beach. Pickerel Point Campground is located on a peninsula and provides patrons with the park's most primitive camping experience. Deerfield Campground is on a slight rise, near the old CCC (Civilian Conservation Corps) camp. Lower Lake Campground is found at the western edge of the Lower Lake and contains modern restrooms with showers. Nestled in hemlocks adjacent to Lower Lake, the Bear Wallow Cabin Colony contains 12 rustic rental cabins constructed by the CCC. These primitive cabins each have a fireplace, electricity, and an adjacent private bath.

BASICS

Operated By: State of Pennsylvania. **Open:** Apr. 13–Oct. 10. **Site Assignment:** By reservation & first come, first served. **Registration:** At campground office. **Fee:** $14–$19; V, MC, D, check. **Parking:** At designated spot.

FACILITIES

Number of RV-only Sites: 102. **Number of Tent-only Sites:** 385. **Hookups:** Electric (30, 50 amps). **Each Site:** Fire ring, picnic table. **Dump Station:** Yes. **Laundry:** Yes. **Pay Phone:** Yes. **Restrooms and Showers:** Yes. **Fuel:** No. **Propane:** No. **Internal Roads:** Gravel, in good condition. **RV Service:** No. **Market:** W/in 5 mi. **Restaurant:** W/in 5 mi. **General Store:** No. **Vending:** Yes. **Swimming:** Lake. **Playground:** Yes. **Activities:** Lake swimming, boating, canoeing, boat rentals, lake fishing, planned activities, hiking trails, volleyball, bicycling. **Nearby Attractions:** Delaware State Forest, Delaware Water Gap National Recreation Area, Lake Wallenpaupack. **Additional Information:** Pocono Mountains Vacation Bureau, (800) POCONOS, www.800poconos.org.

RESTRICTIONS

Pets: Allowed at designated campsites. **Fires:** At site. **Alcoholic Beverages:** No alcohol permitted. **Vehicle Maximum Length:** 40 ft.

TO GET THERE

From I-84, take Exit 7 and go 5 mi. south on Hwy. 390. Follow signs to campground.

HANOVER   MAP, D-4
Codorus State Park

2600 Smith Station Rd., 17331-9545.
T: (717) 637-2416;
www.dcnr.state.pa.us/stateparks.

🚐 ★★★★   ⛺ ★★★★

Beauty: ★★★★   Site Privacy: ★★★
Spaciousness: ★★★   Quiet: ★★★★
Security: ★★★★   Cleanliness: ★★★★
Insect Control: ★★★   Facilities: ★★★★

Codorus State Park, located 3 miles southeast of Hanover, boasts the 1,275-acre Lake Marburg—a hot spot for anglers, boaters, and swimmers with 26 miles of shoreline. The forests of Codorus stand in tall contrast to the surrounding farmlands. The 3,326-acre Codorus State Park is in the southwest corner of York County. The 198-site campground opens the second Friday in April and closes the third Sunday in October. Thirteen walk-in sites are available for tents only. Hot showers, flush toilets, and a sanitary dump station are available. Many campsites have electric hookups. Eight campsites with electricity can accommodate people with disabilities. A 27-hole disc golf course is located along Marina Rd. Score cards are at the first hole, which is next to the first parking lot on the right side of Marina Rd.

BASICS

Operated By: State of Pennsylvania. **Open:** Apr.–Oct. 19. **Site Assignment:** By reservation & first come, first served. **Registration:** At campground office. **Fee:** $12–$19; V, MC, AE, D, check. **Parking:** In designated area.

FACILITIES

Number of RV-only Sites: 185. **Number of Tent-only Sites:** 13. **Hookups:** Electric (30, 50 amps). **Each Site:** Fire ring, picnic table. **Dump Station:** Yes. **Laundry:** No. **Pay Phone:** Yes. **Restrooms and Showers:** Yes. **Fuel:** No. **Propane:** No. **Internal Roads:** Paved, in good condition. **RV Service:** No. **Market:** W/in 5 mi. **Restaurant:** W/in 5 mi. **General Store:** No. **Vending:** Yes. **Swimming:** Yes. **Playground:** No. **Other:** Lake Marburg. **Activities:** Pavilion, swimming, boating, boat rentals, lake fishing, hiking trails. **Nearby Attractions:** Factory tours (Frito-Lay, Crayola, Martin's Potato Chips, & Harley-Davidson, among others), factory outlet stores, factory-related museums. **Additional Information:** York County CVB, (888) 858-YORK, www.yorkpa.org.

RESTRICTIONS

Pets: Allowed; $2 extra per pet; at designated sites. **Fires:** At site. **Alcoholic Beverages:** No alcohol permitted. **Vehicle Maximum Length:** 50 ft. **Other:** 14-day stay limit Memorial Day–Labor Day.

TO GET THERE

From Hwy. 116, go 2 mi. east on Hwy. 216 and 0.5 mi. south on Dubb's Church Rd. Entrance is on the right.

HERSHEY
MAP, C-5
Hershey Highmeadow Campground

reserve america

P.O. Box 866, 1200 Matlack Rd., 17036.
T: (717) 534-8999 or (800) HERSHEY;
www.reserveamerica.com.

🚐 ★★★★   ⛺ ★★★★

Beauty: ★★★★   Site Privacy: ★★
Spaciousness: ★★   Quiet: ★★
Security: ★★★★★   Cleanliness: ★★★★★
Insect Control: ★★★★   Facilities: ★★★★★

Hershey bills itself as the sweetest place on Earth, and Hershey Highmeadow Campground is the lone campground within the sweetest city's limits. The campground has 300 open and shaded sites; the best are those away from the active freight railroad that borders the campground. Sites with no hookups along Swatara Creek are tranquil, as are pull-through sites bordered by pine trees off Matlack Rd. Hershey's attractions are plentiful, and they are not limited to the thrill rides of HersheyPark and the exotic animals of ZooAmerica and North American Wildlife Park. One of the attractions is Founder's Hall, where the story of Milton Hershey is detailed. Hershey was a beloved philanthropist. Of course, he is best known for founding the renowned chocolate company. A ride aboard the Hershey Trolley takes visitors to Hershey's Chocolate World, where you can learn the secrets of chocolate making, enjoy a free sample, and buy a five-pound chocolate bar in the gift shop.

BASICS
Operated By: Mark Panassow. **Open:** All year. **Site Assignment:** Reservations encouraged; first come, first served. **Registration:** At office. **Fee:** $24–$42; V, MC, AE, D. **Parking:** At designated spot.

FACILITIES
Number of RV-only Sites: 228. **Number of Tent-only Sites:** 72. **Hookups:** Electric (20, 30, 50 amps), water, cable TV, sewer. **Each Site:** Grill, picnic table. **Dump Station:** Yes. **Laundry:** Yes. **Pay Phone:** Yes. **Restrooms and Showers:** Yes. **Fuel:** No. **Propane:** Yes. **Internal Roads:** Gravel & paved, in good condition. **RV Service:** No. **Market:** W/in 1 mi. **Restaurant:** W/in 1 mi. **General Store:** Yes. **Vending:** Yes. **Swimming:** Yes. **Playground:** Yes. **Other:** Hershey tours. **Activities:** Rec room, 2 swimming pools, shuffleboard, game room, planned activities on weekends, volleyball, horseshoes. **Nearby Attractions:** Founder's Hall, Hershey Gardens, Hershey Museum of American Life, HersheyPark, Hershey's Chocolate World Visitors Center, Trolley Works, ZooAmerica & American Wildlife Park. **Additional Information:** Harrisburg-Hershey-Carlisle-Perry Co. Tourism CVB, (800) 995-0969, www.visithhc.com.

RESTRICTIONS
Pets: On leash only. **Fires:** At site. **Alcoholic Beverages:** At site. **Vehicle Maximum Length:** 60 ft.

TO GET THERE
From junction of US 422, US 322, and Hwy. 39, go 0.5 mi. northwest on Hwy. 39. Entrance is on the left.

HOWARD
MAP, B-3
Russell P. Letterman Campground

Bald Eagle State Park, 149 Main Park Rd., 16841-9607. T: (814) 625-2775 or (888) PA-PARKS; www.dcnr.state.pa.us.

🚐 ★★★   ⛺ ★★★

Beauty: ★★★★   Site Privacy: ★★★★
Spaciousness: ★★★★   Quiet: ★★★★
Security: ★★★   Cleanliness: ★★★
Insect Control: ★★★   Facilities: ★★★

The Russell P. Letterman Campground is located at Bald Eagle State Park, which is nestled amid rugged Bald Eagle Mountain and the Allegheny Plateau. The 1,730-acre Bald Eagle Lake features unlimited horsepower boating. The water is teeming with smallmouth and largemouth bass, blue gill, and crappie. Hiking and butterfly trails are teeming with colorful wildflowers and wildlife. Swimming is available at the sand beach. The Russell P. Letterman Campground has 101 sites within easy walking distance of the beach, marina, and other park facilities. It features paved camping spurs, showers, and a sanitary dump station. About half of the campsites have electrical hookups, and four sites can accommodate people with disabilities. A nearby primitive campground can accommodate both tents and RVs, with 35 sites for each. The wooded and shaded Skyline Drive Picnic Area has 115 picnic tables, one picnic pavilion, four public restrooms, two playfields, one volleyball court, and horseshoe pits.

BASICS
Operated By: State of Pennsylvania. **Open:** Second Friday in Apr.–end of deer season in December. **Site Assignment:** By reservation & first come, first served. **Registration:** At campground office. **Fee:** $12–$19. **Parking:** At site.

FACILITIES
Number of RV-only Sites: 101. **Number of Multipurpose Sites:** 99. **Hookups:** Electric (30, 50 amps). **Each Site:** Fire ring, picnic table. **Dump Station:** Yes. **Laundry:** Yes. **Pay Phone:** Yes. **Restrooms and Showers:** Yes. **Fuel:** No. **Propane:** No. **Internal Roads:** Paved, in good condition. **RV Service:** No. **Market:** W/in 10 mi. **Restaurant:** W/in 10 mi. **General Store:** Yes, small camp store. **Vending:** No. **Swimming:** Lake. **Playground:** Yes. **Activities:** Lake swimming, boating, canoeing, hiking trails, rowboat & canoe rentals, horseshoes, volleyball, fishing. **Nearby Attractions:** Curtin Mansion & Ironworks, the Pennsylvania Military Museum Woodward Caves, Penn's Cave, Pine Grove Mills Mountain & Centre Hall Mountain, Pennsylvania Fish & Boat Commission, Bald Eagle factory outlets, Penn State University. **Additional Information:** Centre Co. CVB–Penn State Country, (800) 385-5466, www.visitpennstate.org.

RESTRICTIONS
Pets: Not allowed. **Fires:** At site. **Alcoholic Beverages:** No alcohol permitted. **Vehicle Maximum Length:** 50 ft.

TO GET THERE
From I-80, take Exit 23 and go 9 mi. north on Hwy. 150. Entrance is on the right.

JIM THORPE
MAP, C-5
Jim Thorpe Camping Resort

129 Lentz Trail., P. O. Box 328, 18229.
T: (570) 325-2644; www.jimthorpecamping.com.

🚐 ★★★★   ⛺ ★★★★

Beauty: ★★★★   Site Privacy: ★★
Spaciousness: ★★★   Quiet: ★★★★
Security: ★★★★   Cleanliness: ★★★★
Insect Control: ★★★★   Facilities: ★★★★

Situated within the town limits of historic Jim Thorpe (formerly Mauch Chunk), Jim Thorpe Camping Resort is a 28-acre wooded campground that offers level, spacious, and wooded sites. The tent area is separate from the RV area. The campground is enlivened by blooming laurels in May and June and rhododendrons in July. A mountain stream borders the campground, and many miles of mountain bike trails wind through the facility. More than 15 miles of rail trails are available for hiking. Although the Switch Back Gravity Railroad has been gone as an operating entity for more than a half century, there are lots of places to experience the physical artifacts and memories in the region the railroad served between Jim Thorpe and Summit Hill. Downtown Jim Thorpe is an ideal starting point, and the campground arranges tours. Old Mauch Chunk Landing is located in the historic Central Railroad of New Jersey Station in downtown Jim Thorpe.

BASICS
Operated By: Harold Mauer. **Open:** Apr. 1–Dec. 15. **Site Assignment:** Reservations recommended; first come, first served. **Registration:** At campground office. **Fee:** $27–$38; V, MC. **Parking:** At site.

FACILITIES
Number of RV-only Sites: 200. **Number of Tent-only Sites:** 25. **Hookups:** Electric (20, 30 amps), water, sewer, cable TV, phone. **Each Site:** Fire ring, picnic table. **Dump Station:** Yes. **Laundry:** Yes. **Pay Phone:** Yes. **Restrooms and Showers:** Yes. **Fuel:** No. **Propane:** Yes. **Internal Roads:** Gravel, in good condition. **RV Service:** Minor repairs/service. **Market:** W/in 2 mi. **Restaurant:** W/in 2 mi. **General Store:** Yes. **Vending:** Yes. **Swimming:** Yes. **Playground:** Yes. **Other:** Trout nursery. **Activities:** Rec hall, game room, swimming, wading pool, stream fishing, shuffleboard, planned activities on weekends, volleyball, hiking trails, badminton, horseshoes. **Nearby Attractions:** Whitewater rafting, Historic Jim Thorpe, mountain bike trails & rentals, Mauch Chunk Lake, Beltzville State Park. **Additional Information:** Pocono Mountains Vacation Bureau, (800) POCONOS, www.800poconos.org.

RESTRICTIONS
Pets: On leash only. **Fires:** At fire ring only. **Alcoholic Beverages:** At site. **Vehicle Maximum Length:** 45 ft. **Other:** All campers must have & display car pass.

TO GET THERE

From Hwy. 903, go 0.25 mi. north on US 209 and 2.25 mi. west on Broadway. Entrance is on left.

KANE — MAP, B-2
Foote Rest Campground

3183 Hwy. 219, 16735. T: (814) 778-5336; users.penn.com/~cardinal.

🚐 ★★★★　　▲ ★★★★

Beauty: ★★★★★　　Site Privacy: ★★
Spaciousness: ★★　　Quiet: ★★★★
Security: ★★★★　　Cleanliness: ★★★★
Insect Control: ★★★★　　Facilities: ★★★★

Situated on 55 acres and featuring level, shaded sites—including several pull-throughs—Foote Rest Campground is a place that truly caters to families. Children are sure to like the duck pond, where tame rabbits also frolic. Fire-truck rides and hayrides are offered. Sites near the pond on Circle 3 and Circle 4 are highly recommended. Tent-only sites are wooded and open. Located in the Allegheny National Forest, Foote Rest is near Kinzua Bridge State Park. Kinzua Bridge itself is designated a National Engineering Landmark. An excursion train travels through the Allegheny National Forest and over the bridge. When this viaduct was built in 1881, it was the world's highest and longest railroad bridge, at 301 feet tall and 2,053 feet long. Foote Rest offers information on train excursions.

BASICS

Operated By: James & Beverly Tarbox, Bonnie Stake. **Open:** All year. **Site Assignment:** By reservation & first come, first served. **Registration:** At campground office. **Fee:** $26–$28; V, MC, D. **Parking:** At designated spot.

FACILITIES

Number of RV-only Sites: 162. **Number of Tent-only Sites:** 30. **Hookups:** Electric (20, 30 amps), water, sewer, cable TV, phone; 100 full hookups. **Each Site:** Fire ring, picnic table. **Dump Station:** Yes. **Laundry:** Yes. **Pay Phone:** No. **Restrooms and Showers:** Yes. **Fuel:** No. **Propane:** Yes. **Internal Roads:** Gravel & dirt, in good condition. **RV Service:** Yes. **Market:** W/in 4 mi. **Restaurant:** W/in 4 mi. **General Store:** Yes. **Vending:** Yes. **Playground:** Yes. **Other:** Allegheny National Forest Vacation Bureau & Visitors Center display on premises. **Activities:** Rec hall, game room, mini-golf, basketball, bike rentals, shuffleboard, planned activities on weekends, movies, sports field, hiking trails, horseshoes, volleyball. **Nearby Attractions:** Kinzua Bridge State Park, America's First Christmas Store, factory outlet stores, Kinzua Dam Fish Hatchery, Penn-Brad Oil Museum, Holgate Antique Toy Museum, Allegheny National Forest attractions. **Additional Information:** Allegheny National Forest Vacation Bureau, (814) 368-9370, www.allegheny-vacation.com.

RESTRICTIONS

Pets: On leash only. **Fires:** At site. **Alcoholic Beverages:** At site. **Vehicle Maximum Length:** 40 ft.

TO GET THERE

From Hwy. 321, go 7.5 mi. east on US 6 and 0.5 mi. north on US 219. Entrance is on the left.

KNOX — MAP, B-2
Wolf's Camping Resort

reserve america

308 Timberwolf Run, 16232. T: (814) 797-1103; www.wolfscampingresort.com or www.reserveamerica.com

🚐 ★★★★　　▲ ★★★★

Beauty: ★★★★★　　Site Privacy: ★
Spaciousness: ★★　　Quiet: ★★★
Security: ★★★★★　　Cleanliness: ★★★★
Insect Control: ★★★★　　Facilities: ★★★★★

Located in rural Clarion County, Wolf's Camping Resort provides all the amenities and activities RV and tent campers need. Sites are grassy—some are shaded—and there are 80 pull-throughs. Wolf's Den Restaurant and Mom's Snack Shack Restaurant are on the premises, as is an ice-cream parlor and a well-stocked general store. Wolf's even has a bed and breakfast in a 19th-century house that still has the original hardwood floors in the kitchen and entrance hall. The Allegheny National Forest is the main attraction near Wolf's, and an ideal way to see the natural beauty is on the Knox, Kane, and Kinzua Railroad, which covers 96 miles.

BASICS

Operated By: The Titley Family. **Open:** All year. **Site Assignment:** Reservations recommended; first come, first served. **Registration:** At camp headquarters. **Fee:** $22–$33; V, MC, D. **Parking:** At site.

FACILITIES

Number of RV-only Sites: 639. **Number of Tent-only Sites:** 23. **Hookups:** Electric (20, 30 amps), water, cable TV, phone. **Each Site:** Fire ring, picnic table. **Dump Station:** Yes. **Laundry:** Yes. **Pay Phone:** Yes. **Restrooms and Showers:** Yes. **Fuel:** No. **Propane:** Yes. **Internal Roads:** Gravel, in good condition. **RV Service:** No. **Market:** W/in 4 mi. **Restaurant:** On premises. **General Store:** Yes. **Vending:** Yes. **Swimming:** Yes. **Playground:** Yes. **Other:** Large pavilion, bed & breakfast, restaurant, ice-cream parlor. **Activities:** 9-hole golf course, boat rentals, large arcade, 300-yard driving range, mini-golf, lake fishing, rowboat & pedal boat rentals, canoeing, basketball, sports field, volleyball, horseshoes, movies, planned activities, shuffleboard, swimming. **Nearby Attractions:** Allegheny National Forest; Knox, Kane, & Kinzua Railroad; Oil Creek; Titusville Railroad. **Additional Information:** Allegheny National Forest Vacation Bureau, (814) 368-9370, www.allegheny-vacation.com.

RESTRICTIONS

Pets: On leash only. **Fires:** At site. **Alcoholic Beverages:** At site. **Vehicle Maximum Length:** 40 ft.

TO GET THERE

From I-80, take Exit 53 and follow Hwy. 338 0.1 mi. north. Entrance is on the right.

LANCASTER — MAP, D-5
Outdoor World—
Circle M Campground

2111 Millersville Rd., 17603. T: (717) 872-4651 or (800) 222-5557; www.campoutdoorworld.com.

🚐 ★★★★　　▲ ★★★★

Beauty: ★★★★　　Site Privacy: ★
Spaciousness: ★★　　Quiet: ★★★
Security: ★★★★★　　Cleanliness: ★★★★★
Insect Control: ★★★★　　Facilities: ★★★

In the heart of Pennsylvania Dutch Country, Circle M is one of Outdoor World's largest campgrounds. Amenities include two swimming pools, an indoor water park, a covered mini-golf course, and a nine-hole pitch-and-putt golf course. There are 25 pull-through sites. Amish-related attractions are plentiful in the area surrounding Circle M. The campground helps guests make arrangements for exploring the Amish farmlands in an air-conditioned bus via Amish Living Tours. Certified guides spin entertaining and informative stories about Amish life. Stops may include Amish farms, roadside stands, craft and quilt shops, and bakeries. Another must-see attraction is the Amish Farm and House, an 1805 stone farmhouse where guided house tours and self-guided farm tours are offered. The working farm includes barns, livestock, a blacksmith shop, and the Early Americana Museum.

BASICS

Operated By: Outdoor World. **Open:** All year. **Site Assignment:** Reservations encouraged. **Registration:** At campground office. **Fee:** $46–$62; V, MC, AE, D. **Parking:** At site.

FACILITIES

Number of RV-only Sites: 292. **Number of Tent-only Sites:** 30. **Hookups:** Electric (30, 50 amps), water, cable TV, phone. **Each Site:** Fire ring, picnic table. **Dump Station:** Yes. **Laundry:** Yes. **Pay Phone:** Yes. **Restrooms and Showers:** Yes. **Fuel:** No. **Propane:** Yes. **Internal Roads:** Gravel & paved, in good condition. **RV Service:** No. **Market:** W/in 3 mi. **Restaurant:** Yes. **General Store:** Yes. **Vending:** Yes. **Swimming:** Yes. **Playground:** Yes. **Other:** Indoor water park. **Activities:** Rec hall, 2 swimming pools (1 indoor), wading pool, whirlpool, canoeing, kayaking, river fishing, golf, mini-golf, basketball, shuffleboard, planned activities, movies, tennis, sports field, badminton, horseshoes, volleyball. **Nearby Attractions:** Hershey Chocolate World, Zoo America, Strasburg Railroad, Indian Echo Caverns, Amish Country Living Tours, Dutch Wonderland, American Music Theater, Dutch Apple Dinner Theater, Rainbow Dinner Theater, Sight & Sound Theater, Tanger Outlet Center, Rockvale Outlet Center, Roots Farmers Market. **Additional Information:** Pennsylvania Dutch CVB, (800) PA-DUTCH, www.padutchcountry.com.

RESTRICTIONS

Pets: On leash only. **Fires:** At site. **Alcoholic Beverages:** At site. **Vehicle Maximum Length:** 40 ft.

To Get There

From US 30, go 6 mi. east on Hwy. 741. Entrance is on the left.

LEBANON   MAP, C-5
Thousands Trails—Hershey

493 South Mt Pleasant Rd., 17042.
T: (800) 884-4451 or (717) 867-5515;
www.thousandtrails.com.

🚐 ★★★★   ⛺ ★★★★

Beauty: ★★★★   Site Privacy: ★★★
Spaciousness: ★★★   Quiet: ★★★★
Security: ★★★★★   Cleanliness: ★★★★
Insect Control: ★★★★   Facilities: ★★★★★

Situated on 200 acres of rolling farmland in the heart of Pennsylvania Dutch Country, Thousand Trails—Hershey is enclosed in a natural valley of grassy fields, sloping down to a small fishing lake. Located 6 miles from Hershey attractions like Hershey's Chocolate World and ZooAmerica, the campground is also near nature-oriented places such as Indian Echo Caverns, Stony Valley Wilderness Site, and Hawk Mountain. Dinosaur Rock and Middle Creek Wildlife Preserve are also worth a visit. At the campground, the adult lodge and family center brims with activity year-round. During warmer months, there are lots of outdoor activities, including canoeing, pond fishing, and enjoying the swimming pool and whirlpool. The campground features grassy open and shaded sites, including 20 pull-throughs.

BASICS

Operated By: Thousands Trails. **Open:** Mar.–Nov. **Site Assignment:** Reservations recommended. **Registration:** At campground office. **Fee:** $28; V, MC, AE, D; Membership campground. **Parking:** At designated spot.

FACILITIES

Number of RV-only Sites: 250. **Number of Tent-only Sites:** 92. **Hookups:** Electric (30, 50 amps), water, phone. **Each Site:** Fire ring, picnic table. **Dump Station:** Yes. **Laundry:** Yes. **Pay Phone:** Yes. **Restrooms and Showers:** Yes. **Fuel:** No. **Propane:** Yes. **Internal Roads:** Gravel & paved, in good condition. **RV Service:** No. **Market:** W/in 2 mi. **Restaurant:** W/in 2 mi. **General Store:** Yes. **Vending:** Yes. **Swimming:** Yes. **Playground:** Yes. **Other:** Adult lodge & family center. **Activities:** Rec hall, game room, swimming, wading pool, whirlpool, boat & canoe rentals, pond fishing, basketball, mini-golf, planned activities, shuffleboard, movies, volleyball, tennis, horseshoes. **Nearby Attractions:** Hershey attractions, Horseshoe Trail, Governor Dick & Dinosaur Rock Lookouts, Indian Echo Caverns, The Union Canal Tunnel, Susquehanna River, Stony Valley Wilderness Site in Cold Springs Township, Middle Creek Wildlife Preserve, Hawk Mountain, Gettysburg battlefields, Pennsylvania Grand Canyon. **Additional Information:** Harrisburg-Hershey-Carlisle-Perry Co. Tourism CVB, (800) 995-0969, www.visithhc.com.

RESTRICTIONS

Pets: On leash only. **Fires:** Fire ring only. **Alcoholic Beverages:** At site. **Vehicle Maximum Length:** 40 ft.

To Get There

From Hwy. 743, go 6.5 mi. east on US 322 and 1.25 mi. south on Mt. Pleasant road. Entrance is at the end.

LENHARTSVILLE   MAP, C-5
Robin Hill Camping Resort

149 Robin Hill Rd., 19534.
T: (610) 756-6117 or (800) 732-KAMP;
www.robinhillrvresort.com.

🚐 ★★★★   ⛺ ★★★★

Beauty: ★★★★★   Site Privacy: ★★
Spaciousness: ★★★★   Quiet: ★★★★
Security: ★★★★   Cleanliness: ★★★★
Insect Control: ★★★★   Facilities: ★★★★

Located in the foothills of the Blue Mountains and Pennsylvania Dutch Country, Robin Hill Camping Resort offers spacious, grassy sites, including 40 pull-throughs. We recommend the sites that offer water and electric and are located lakeside and near most of Robin Hill's activities. A bulk of the full-hookup sites are located on the campground's south end, away from the lake and activity centers. Robin Hill is surrounded by amusement parks, wineries, natural attractions, and, of course, Lancaster County's Amish-related sites. A unique attraction is the Ashland Pioneer Tunnel Coal Mine and Steam Train. Pioneer Tunnel ceased operation in 1931, then was re-timbered and reopened as a place where visitors experience a real anthracite-coal mine. The other featured attraction is a narrow-gauge steam train ride aboard the Lokie Henry Clay, which was used years ago to haul coal cars. Now it pulls passenger mine cars 3,000 feet along the side of Mahanoy Mountain.

BASICS

Operated By: Gary & Carolyn Krick. **Open:** May–Oct. **Site Assignment:** Reservations recommended; first come, first served. **Registration:** At campground office. **Fee:** $28–$38; V, MC, D. **Parking:** At designated spot.

FACILITIES

Number of RV-only Sites: 270. **Number of Tent-only Sites:** 10. **Hookups:** Electric (20, 30, 50 amps), cable TV, modem, water. **Each Site:** Fire ring, picnic table. **Dump Station:** Yes. **Laundry:** Yes. **Pay Phone:** Yes. **Restrooms and Showers:** Yes. **Fuel:** Yes. **Propane:** Yes. **Internal Roads:** Gravel & paved, in good condition. **RV Service:** Yes. **Market:** W/in 3 mi. **Restaurant:** W/in 3 mi. **General Store:** Yes. **Vending:** Yes. **Swimming:** Pool. **Playground:** Yes. **Other:** 50 cottage rental units available, winterized lodge available for group rentals. **Activities:** Rec hall, game room, boating, canoeing, pedal boat rentals, pond fishing, planned activities on weekends, basketball, volleyball, horseshoes. **Nearby Attractions:** Dorney Park & Wildwater Kingdom, Hawk Mountain Bird Sanctuary, Knoebel's Amusement Park, Ashland Pioneer Tunnel Coal Mine & Steam Train, Blue Marsh Lake, Crayola Factory, Pat Garrett Amphitheater. **Additional Information:** Lehigh Valley CVB, (800) 747-0561, www.lehighvalleypa.org.

RESTRICTIONS

Pets: On leash only. **Fires:** At site. **Alcoholic Beverages:** At site. **Vehicle Maximum Length:** 50 ft.

To Get There

From I-78, take Exit 11 and go 0.5 mi. south on Hwy. 143, 1.5 mi. east on Old US 22, and follow signs 1 mi. on paved road.

LIVERPOOL   MAP, C-4
Ferryboat Campsites

32 Ferry Lane, 17045.
T: (717) 444-3200 or (800) 759-8707;
www.ferryboatcampsites.com.

🚐 ★★★★   ⛺ ★★★★

Beauty: ★★★★★   Site Privacy: ★★
Spaciousness: ★★★   Quiet: ★★★★
Security: ★★★★   Cleanliness: ★★★★
Insect Control: ★★★★   Facilities: ★★★★

Ferryboat Campsites promises the finest bass fishing on the Susquehanna River. Of course, the bass will determine whether that promise is true, but the campground certainly has scenic sites along the river. Located in Liverpool near the historic Millersburg Ferry, Ferryboat Campsites features wooded sites, including 20 pull-throughs. The campground does not have a pool—nor does it need one with the river so close by. Tubing, canoeing, and kayaking are favorite activities of campground guests. A ride on the Millersburg Ferry is an event in itself. Crossing the river since the early 1800s, the ferry accommodates four vehicles and 50 passengers across the mile-wide Susquehanna. Hunter's Valley Winery is nearby, as is Harrisburg, which boasts a Civil War museum that is a must-see for history enthusiasts.

BASICS

Operated By: Private operator. **Open:** Apr. 15–Oct. 31. **Site Assignment:** By reservation & first come, first served. **Registration:** At campground store. **Fee:** $20–$36; V, MC. **Parking:** At site.

FACILITIES

Number of RV-only Sites: 285. **Number of Tent-only Sites:** 15. **Hookups:** Electric (20, 30 amps), water, cable TV, phone. **Each Site:** Fire ring, picnic table. **Dump Station:** Yes. **Laundry:** Yes. **Pay Phone:** Yes. **Restrooms and Showers:** Yes. **Fuel:** No. **Propane:** Yes. **Internal Roads:** Gravel & paved, in fair condition. **RV Service:** No. **Market:** W/in 5 mi. **Restaurant:** W/in 2 mi. **General Store:** Yes. **Vending:** Yes. **Swimming:** River (at your own risk). **Playground:** Yes. **Other:** Ferry boat, recreation on the Susquehanna River. **Activities:** Rec hall, game room, river swimming, river fishing, boating, canoeing, kayaking, canoe & kayak rentals, mini-golf, basketball, shuffleboard, planned activities on weekends, badminton, sports field, horseshoes, hiking trails, volleyball. **Nearby Attractions:** Millersburg Ferry, Hunter Valley Winery, Tobias Animal Haven, Knoebels Grove Amusement Park, Harrisburg State Capital, Selinsgrove Speedway, Golf Courses. City Island (Home of the Harrisburg Senators), Harrisburg Civil War Museum. **Additional Information:** Harrisburg-Hershey-Carlisle-Perry Co. Tourism CVB, (800) 995-0969, www.visithhc.com.

RESTRICTIONS

Pets: On leash only. **Fires:** At site. **Alcoholic Beverages:** At site. **Vehicle Maximum Length:** 40 ft.

TO GET THERE

From Hwy. 17, go 2 mi. south on US 11/15 and 0.25 mi. east on paved road. Entrance is on the right.

MANHEIM   MAP, D-5
Pinch Pond Family Campground

reserve america

3075 Pinch Rd., 17545.
T: (717) 665-7640 or (800) 659-7640;
www.pinchpond.com.

🚐 ★★★★   ▲ ★★★★

Beauty: ★★★★   Site Privacy: ★★
Spaciousness: ★★   Quiet: ★★★★
Security: ★★★★   Cleanliness: ★★★★
Insect Control: ★★★★   Facilities: ★★★★

Located in the Lancaster County town of Harrisburg inside Pennsylvania Dutch Country, Pinch Pond Family Campground features shaded sites, including 30 pull-throughs. The fishing pond is stocked with trout twice a year. An enclosed pavilion permits group gatherings rain or shine. Pinch Pond's location is convenient to attractions in Harrisburg, Hershey, and Lancaster County, including the Strasburg Railroad, which takes passengers on a restored locomotive through the rolling hills of Pennsylvania Dutch Country. Also nearby is the Railroad Museum of Pennsylvania, where visitors can sit in the engineer's seat of a powerful locomotive, inspect a 62-ton engine from underneath, and relax inside an early-19th-century replica passenger depot. The museum boasts a world-class collection of more than 100 historic locomotives and rail cars displayed both indoors and outdoors.

BASICS

Operated By: Jason Sheaffer. **Open:** All year. **Site Assignment:** Reservations recommended; first come, first served. **Registration:** At campground headquarters. **Fee:** $28–$36; cabin, $49–$52; cottage, $105; V, MC, D. **Parking:** At site.

FACILITIES

Number of RV-only Sites: 211. **Number of Tent-only Sites:** 25. **Hookups:** Electric (20, 30, 50 amps), water, cable TV, phone. **Each Site:** Fire ring, picnic table. **Dump Station:** Yes. **Laundry:** Yes. **Pay Phone:** Yes. **Restrooms and Showers:** Yes. **Fuel:** No. **Propane:** Yes. **Internal Roads:** Gravel & paved, in good condition. **RV Service:** Yes. **Market:** W/in 4 mi. **Restaurant:** W/in 4 mi. **General Store:** Yes. **Vending:** Yes. **Swimming:** Pool. **Playground:** Yes. **Other:** Enclosed pavilion. **Activities:** Rec hall, game room, pond fishing, basketball, shuffleboard, planned activities on weekends, badminton, sports field, horseshoes, volleyball. **Nearby Attractions:** Hershey, Pennsylvania Dutch Country, Harrisburg, Strasburg Railroad. **Additional Information:** Pennsylvania Dutch CVB, (800) PA-DUTCH, www.padutchcountry.com.

RESTRICTIONS

Pets: On leash only, under control. **Fires:** At site. **Alcoholic Beverages:** At site. **Vehicle Maximum Length:** No limit.

TO GET THERE

From I-76, take Exit 20 and go 1 mi. south on Hwy. 72., 0.5 mi. west on Cider Press Rd., and 1 mi. north on Pinch Rd. Entrance is on the right.

MANSFIELD   MAP, A-4
Bucktail Camping Resort

130 Bucktail Rd., 16933. T: (570) 662-2923;
www.bucktailcamping.com.

🚐 ★★★★   ▲ ★★★★

Beauty: ★★★★   Site Privacy: ★★★
Spaciousness: ★★★★   Quiet: ★★★★★
Security: ★★★★   Cleanliness: ★★★★
Insect Control: ★★★★   Facilities: ★★★★★

Bucktail Family Fun Park and Camping Resort rests in the mountains and valleys of Tioga County—otherwise known as Pennsylvania's Grand Canyon. With grassy open and shaded sites (including 12 pull-throughs), Bucktail is an attractive campground, but its amusement rides distinguish it from the typical family campground. A kiddie train winds through the grounds, and an antique carousel delights youngsters. RV and tents alike are welcome at the North Pole Rally Area at the park's northern tip. Sites that look out at the train near the batting cages and tower slide are convenient if you have children. An ideal way to marvel at canyon country is on horseback, and Tioga Trail Rides offers guided rides. Tioga Central Railroad has guided excursions through the countryside. Other family-friendly attractions near Bucktail include the Paddlewheel Riverboat Ride, Pennsylvania Lumber Museum, and Animaland Zoological Park.

BASICS

Operated By: Private operator. **Open:** Apr. 15–Oct. 31. **Site Assignment:** By reservation & first come, first served. **Registration:** At camp office. **Fee:** $35.75–$39.75; V, MC, AE, D. **Parking:** At site.

FACILITIES

Number of RV-only Sites: 190. **Number of Tent-only Sites:** 10. **Hookups:** Electric (20, 30 amps), water. **Each Site:** Fire ring, picnic table. **Dump Station:** Yes. **Laundry:** Yes. **Pay Phone:** Yes. **Restrooms and Showers:** Yes. **Fuel:** No. **Propane:** No. **Internal Roads:** Gravel & dirt, in fair condition. **RV Service:** No. **Market:** W/in 6 mi. **Restaurant:** W/in 6 mi. **General Store:** Yes. **Vending:** Yes. **Swimming:** Yes. **Playground:** Yes. **Other:** Kiddie train, antique carousel, other amusement rides. **Activities:** Rec hall, game room, mini-golf, basketball, planned activities on weekends, horseshoes, hiking trails, volleyball. **Nearby Attractions:** Tioga Trail Rides, Tioga Central Railroad, Pennsylvania Lumber Museum, Paddlewheel Riverboat Ride, Animaland Zoological Park. **Additional Information:** Tioga County Visitors Bureau, (888) TIOGA-28, www.visittiogapa.com.

RESTRICTIONS

Pets: On leash only. **Fires:** At site. **Alcoholic Beverages:** At site. **Vehicle Maximum Length:** 40 ft.

TO GET THERE

From US 15, go 0.5 mi. east on US 6, 1.5 mi. north on Lamb's Creek Rd., and 1 mi. west on Mann Creek Rd. Entrance is on the left.

MARSHALL'S CREEK   MAP, B-6
Otter Lake Camp Resort

P.O. Box 850, 18335.
T: (570) 223-0123 or (800) 345-1369;
www.otterlake.com.

🚐 ★★★★   ▲ ★★★★

Beauty: ★★★★★   Site Privacy: ★★★
Spaciousness: ★★★★   Quiet: ★★★★★
Security: ★★★★   Cleanliness: ★★★★
Insect Control: ★★★★   Facilities: ★★★★★

Surrounded by the Pocono Mountains and located 10 miles from the Delaware Water Gap, Otter Lake Camp Resort has shaded sites (including 25 pull-throughs) in a wooded lakeside setting. We recommend a cluster of sites that borders the lake at the campground's northwest end. If you prefer to camp away from the activity centers but near the lake, sites on the northeast side will satisfy you. Most of the recreational facilities are located near the park's entrance at the south end of the lake. The 60-acre and private Otter Lake is on the campground property, and miles of hiking and snowmobiling trails are adjacent to the campground. Ceramics classes are held four times a week, and children are treated to free fire-engine rides daily. Otter Lake and the resort are attractions themselves, but they are located near numerous Pocono Mountains and Delaware Water Gap sites. Called the "Niagara Falls of Pennsylvania," Bushkill Falls is truly one of the state's most picturesque natural wonders. Bushkill features eight waterfalls, accessible through an excellent network of hiking trails and bridges which afford fabulous views of the falls and the surrounding forest.

BASICS

Operated By: Private operator. **Open:** All year. **Site Assignment:** Reservations recommended; first come, first served. **Registration:** At campground headquarters. **Fee:** $40–$52; V, MC; water is shut off Nov.–Apr. **Parking:** At site.

FACILITIES

Number of RV-only Sites: 300. **Number of Tent-only Sites:** 20. **Hookups:** Electric (20, 30 amps), water, cable TV, phone. **Each Site:** Fire ring & picnic table. **Dump Station:** Yes. **Laundry:** Yes. **Pay Phone:** Yes. **Restrooms and Showers:** Yes. **Fuel:** No. **Propane:** Yes. **Internal Roads:** Paved, in good condition. **RV Service:** Yes, in nearby location. **Market:** W/in 7 mi. **Restaurant:** W/in 7 mi. **General Store:** Yes. **Vending:** Yes. **Swimming:** Pool (indoor & outdoor). **Playground:** Yes. **Other:** Snowmobile trails. **Activities:** Rec hall, game room, 2 swimming pools (indoor & outdoor), wading pool, lake swimming, sauna, whirlpool, boating, canoeing, boat rentals, lake fishing, basketball, planned activities, shuffleboard, basketball, tennis, sports field, horseshoes. **Nearby Attractions:** Bushkill Falls, Quiet Valley Living Historical Farm, golf, ice skating, skiing, horseback riding, Memorytown USA, Delaware Water Gap. **Additional**

Information: Pocono Mountains Vacation Bureau, (800) POCONOS, www.800poconos.org.

RESTRICTIONS

Pets: On leash only. **Fires:** At site. **Alcoholic Beverages:** At site. **Vehicle Maximum Length:** 40 ft.

TO GET THERE

From I-80, take Exit 309 and go 4 mi. north on US 209, 300 ft. northwest on Hwy. 402, and 7.5 mi. west on paved road. Entrance is on the left.

MEADVILLE   MAP, B-1
Brookdale Family Campground

25164 Hwy. 27, 16335.
T: (814) 789-3251 or (888) 789-9186;
www.brookdalecampground.com.

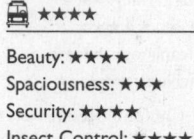

🚐 ★★★★   ⛺ ★★★★

Beauty: ★★★★	Site Privacy: ★★★
Spaciousness: ★★★★	Quiet: ★★★★
Security: ★★★★★	Cleanliness: ★★★★★
Insect Control: ★★★★	Facilities: ★★★★

Located on 62 acres 7 miles east of Meadville, Brookdale Family Campground has open and shaded sites that accommodate 26 pull-throughs and 119 double slideouts. The campground store is heavily stocked with items like groceries, RV supplies, fishing supplies, and cooking supplies, including mountain pie irons and Dutch ovens. Seven fishing ponds for catch and release fishing are scattered around the grounds of Brookdale, and no license is required. The campground is not far from the Crawford County Fairgrounds, which hosts one of the largest county fairs in Pennsylvania. Brookdale is also near two popular natural attractions, Pymatuning Lake and the Erie National Wildlife Refuge. Pymatuning has numerous boating, fishing, and hiking options. The Erie National Wildlife Refuge consists more than 8,700 acres of creeks, grasslands, wet meadows, and valleys teeming with birds, 47 species of mammals, 37 species of amphibians and reptiles, and several types of wildflowers.

BASICS

Operated By: Private operator. **Open:** Apr. 15–Oct. 31. **Site Assignment:** By reservation & first come, first served. **Registration:** At campground office. **Fee:** $24–$30; V, MC, AE, D. **Parking:** At designated spot.

FACILITIES

Number of RV-only Sites: 158. **Number of Tent-only Sites:** 20. **Hookups:** Electric (30, 50 amps), water, phone. **Each Site:** Fire ring, picnic table. **Dump Station:** Yes. **Laundry:** Yes. **Pay Phone:** Yes. **Restrooms and Showers:** Yes. **Fuel:** No. **Propane:** Yes. **Internal Roads:** Gravel, in good condition. **RV Service:** No. **Market:** W/in 5 mi. **Restaurant:** W/in 5 mi. **General Store:** Yes. **Vending:** Yes. **Swimming:** Yes. **Playground:** Yes. **Other:** Traffic control gate. **Activities:** Rec hall, game room, pedal boat rentals, pond fishing, basketball, planned activities on weekends, sports field, horseshoes, volleyball. **Nearby Attractions:** Erie National Wildlife Refuge, Crawford County Fairgrounds, Titusville & Oil Creek Railroad, Pymatuning Lake Spillway, rail trails in Titusville & Meadville,

Thurston Classic Hot Air Balloon Event. **Additional Information:** Crawford County CVB, (800) 332-2338, www.visitcrawford.org.

RESTRICTIONS

Pets: On leash only, under control. **Fires:** At site. **Alcoholic Beverages:** At site. **Vehicle Maximum Length:** No limit.

TO GET THERE

From Hwy. 77, go 5.5 mi. east on Hwy. 27. Entrance is on the left.

MIFFLINBURG   MAP, C-4
Hidden Valley Camping Resort

162 Hidden Valley Ln., 17844. T: (570) 966-1330; www.hiddenvalleycamping.com.

🚐 ★★★★   ⛺ ★★★★

Beauty: ★★★★	Site Privacy: ★
Spaciousness: ★★★	Quiet: ★★★
Security: ★★★★	Cleanliness: ★★★★
Insect Control: ★★★★	Facilities: ★★★★★

Located in central Pennsylvania's Buffalo Valley, Hidden Valley Camping Resort is a family-centered campground with 395 sites, including 40 pull-through sites. Wooded tent sites and primitive tent sites are also available. Full-hookup sites on Stallion Ledge along the lake are especially inviting. Sites off Hidden Valley Lane toward the entrance of the campground are most central to activities, including the petting farm and stables. Other nearby attractions include Penn's Cave, a water cavern and wildlife park explored by boat, and Hiawatha River Cruises, which board in nearby Williamsport and transport passengers on a paddleboat down the Susquehanna River.

BASICS

Operated By: Private operator. **Open:** Apr. 16–Oct. 17. **Site Assignment:** By reservation & first come, first served. **Registration:** At campground office. **Fee:** $25–$33; cabin, $43; V, MC, D. **Parking:** At site.

FACILITIES

Number of RV-only Sites: 378. **Number of Tent-only Sites:** 17. **Hookups:** Electric (20, 30, 50 amps), water, cable TV, phone. **Each Site:** Fire ring, picnic table. **Dump Station:** Yes. **Laundry:** Yes. **Pay Phone:** Yes. **Restrooms and Showers:** Yes. **Fuel:** No. **Propane:** Yes. **Internal Roads:** Gravel & paved, in good condition. **RV Service:** Yes. **Market:** W/in 5 mi. **Restaurant:** W/in 5 mi. **General Store:** Yes. **Vending:** Yes. **Swimming:** Pool. **Playground:** Yes. **Other:** Church services, gospel concerts. **Activities:** Rec room, game room, pedal boat rentals, mini-golf, lake fishing, basketball, shuffleboard, planned activities on weekends, sports field, badminton, horseshoes, hiking trails, volleyball, petting zoo. **Nearby Attractions:** Penn's Cave, Hiawatha River Cruises, Knoebel's Amusement Park, Clyde Peeling's Reptile Land, Pioneer Tunnel Coal Mine and Steam Train, Mifflinburg Buggy Museum, Slifer House Museum. **Additional Information:** Susquehanna Valley Visitors Bureau, (800) 525-7320, www.svvb.com.

RESTRICTIONS

Pets: On leash only, under control. **Fires:** At site. **Alcoholic Beverages:** At site. **Vehicle Maximum Length:** No limit.

TO GET THERE

From US 15, go 9 mi. west on Hwy. 192. Entrance is on the left.

MILL RUN   MAP, D-2
Yogi Bear's Jellystone Park Camp-Resort

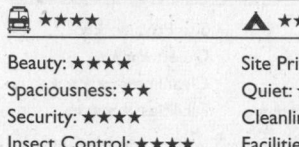

839 Mill Run Rd., P. O. Box 91, 15464.
T: (724) 455-2929 or (800) 439-9644;
www.jellystonemillrun.com.

🚐 ★★★★   ⛺ ★★★★

Beauty: ★★★★	Site Privacy: ★★
Spaciousness: ★★	Quiet: ★★★
Security: ★★★★	Cleanliness: ★★★★
Insect Control: ★★★★	Facilities: ★★★★

Snuggled in the Laurel Highlands, Yogi Bear's Jellystone Park Camp and Resort in Mill Run has shaded sites in a wooded setting, but only one pull-through site. Sites here offer little privacy, but the campground is located in a forested environment that offers lots of welcome shade in warmer months. Like most Yogi Bear campgrounds, Yogi and Boo Boo make occasional appearances, and the facility is located near numerous attractions. Children will love the two winding waterslides that cover 800 feet. The campground also offers train and wagon rides, and there is a mini-golf course on the grounds. A 7-mile mountain road in the Laurel Highlands connects Frank Lloyd Wright's extraordinary House on Kentuck Knob to his world-renowned house on the waterfall. Kentuck Knob is an example of residential design from the final decade of Wright's career. Its pristine condition, spectacular views, and woodland setting create a memorable experience. An impressive collection of contemporary sculpture and historic artifacts enhance that experience. At Fort Necessity National Battlefield, colonial troops commanded by then-22-year-old Colonel George Washington were defeated in this French and Indian War skirmish.

BASICS

Operated By: Private operator. **Open:** May 1–Oct. 31; cabin rental throughout winter. **Site Assignment:** Reservations recommended. **Registration:** At campground office. **Fee:** $31–$39; based on 2 people; V, MC. **Parking:** At site.

FACILITIES

Number of RV-only Sites: 114. **Number of Tent-only Sites:** 37. **Hookups:** Electric (20, 30 amps), water, sewer, cable TV; 100 full hookups. **Each Site:** Fire ring, picnic table. **Dump Station:** Yes. **Laundry:** Yes. **Pay Phone:** Yes. **Restrooms and Showers:** Yes. **Fuel:** No. **Propane:** Yes. **Internal Roads:** Gravel & paved, in good condition. **RV Service:** 30 mi. **Market:** W/in 2 mi. **Restaurant:** On premises. **General Store:** Yes. **Vending:** Yes. **Swimming:**

Pool. **Playground:** Yes. **Other:** Waterslides. **Activities:** Rec room, game room, pond fishing, mini-golf, planned activities, badminton, horseshoes, volleyball, train & wagon rides, carousel. **Nearby Attractions:** Golf courses, Ohiopyle Falls, Fort Necessity, Fort Ligonier, Caddie Shack Family Fun Center, Living Treasures Animal Park, antique shops, bike trails. **Additional Information:** Laurel Highlands Visitors Bureau, (800) 925-7669, www.laurelhighlands.org.

RESTRICTIONS

Pets: On leash only. $2 fee per pet. **Fires:** At site. **Alcoholic Beverages:** At site. **Vehicle Maximum Length:** 40 ft.

TO GET THERE

From Mill Run, go 0.25 mi. south on Hwy. 381. Entrance is on the right.

MILTON   MAP, B-4
Shangri-La on the Creek

670 Hidden Paradise Rd., 17847.
T: (570) 524-4561 or (800) 445-6660;
www.slcreek.com.

🚐 ★★★★   ▲ ★★★★

Beauty: ★★★★★   Site Privacy: ★★★
Spaciousness: ★★★   Quiet: ★★★★
Security: ★★★★   Cleanliness: ★★★★
Insect Control: ★★★★   Facilities: ★★★★

It seems that morning, noon, and night, Shangri-La on the Creek stirs with activity. Parents and children fish on Chillisquaque Creek, and art enthusiasts learn crafts in ceramics classes. Shangri-La's 52 creek-side sites and 115 additional wooded and semi-wooded sites are located at the foot of Montour Ridge along the Chillisquaque Creek. The row of water and electric sites along Chillisquaque Creek also border the recreation area for Frisbee golf, basketball, and badminton. A large recreation pavilion seats 200 for special events, and the Laundromat houses a tourist information center. Nearby, the Williamsport Trolley Tours take passengers past a series of lavish mansions on "Millionaire's Row" and the park where the first Little League Baseball game was played. The trolley debuted in Williamsport in 1865 and has operated ever since.

BASICS

Operated By: Bryant Management. **Open:** During season & select winter camping. **Site Assignment:** Reservations recommended; first come, first served. **Registration:** At campground office. **Fee:** $31–$43; V, MC. **Parking:** At site.

FACILITIES

Number of RV-only Sites: 167. **Number of Tent-only Sites:** 16. **Hookups:** Electric (20, 30, 50 amps), water, cable TV, phone. **Each Site:** Fire ring, picnic table. **Dump Station:** Yes. **Laundry:** Yes. **Pay Phone:** Yes. **Restrooms and Showers:** Yes. **Fuel:** No. **Propane:** Yes. **Internal Roads:** Gravel, in good condition. **RV Service:** Nearby. Will come to site. **Market:** W/in 7 mi. **Restaurant:** W/in 7 mi. **General Store:** Yes. **Vending:** Yes. **Swimming:** Pool. **Playground:** Yes. **Other:** Indoor & outdoor camping club areas. **Activities:** Rec hall, game room, swimming, wading pool, whirlpool, pond & stream fishing,

basketball, planned activities on weekends, hiking trails, volleyball, horseshoes. **Nearby Attractions:** Williamsport, Little League Museum, Reptileland, Hiawatha Paddle Wheeler, Knoebel's Grove Amusement Park, Woodward & Penn's Caves, museums, flea & farmer's markets, restaurants, Bucknell University. **Additional Information:** Susquehanna Valley Visitors Bureau (800) 525-7320, www.svvb.com.

RESTRICTIONS

Pets: On leash only. **Fires:** At site. **Alcoholic Beverages:** At site. **Vehicle Maximum Length:** No limit. **Other:** No beer kegs permitted.

TO GET THERE

From I-80, take Exit 31A and go 8 mi. south on Hwy. 147, 0.25 mi. northwest on Hwy. 405, and 0.75 mi. east on paved road. Entrance is at the end.

MILTON   MAP, B-4
Yogi Bear's Jellystone Park at Shangri-La

reserve america

670 Hidden Paradise Rd., 17847.
T: (570) 524-4561; www.reserveamerica.com
or www.slcreek.com.

🚐 ★★★★   ▲ ★★★★

Beauty: ★★★★   Site Privacy: ★★★★
Spaciousness: ★★★★   Quiet: ★★★★
Security: ★★★★   Cleanliness: ★★★★
Insect Control: ★★★★   Facilities: ★★★★

Whether you are an RV park enthusiast, enjoy the comfort of a cabin in the woods, or just like to tent-camp and sleep in the great outdoors, Jellystone Park's accommodations, amenities, and activities are top-notch. Amenities and activities include swimming, mini-golf, hay rides, tennis, volleyball, fishing, hiking, and appearances from Yogi Bear and friends.

BASICS

Operated By: State of Pennsylvania. **Open:** All year. **Site Assignment:** Reservations recommended. **Registration:** At ranger station. **Fee:** $31–$43. **Parking:** Limit 2 cars per site, overflow parking available.

FACILITIES

Hookups: Water, electric. **Each Site:** Picnic table, fire ring. **Dump Station:** Yes. **Laundry:** Yes. **Pay Phone:** No. **Restrooms and Showers:** Yes. **Fuel:** No. **Propane:** Yes. **Internal Roads:** Gravel. **RV Service:** 10 mi. **Market:** 5 mi. **Restaurant:** 3 mi. in Lewisburg. **General Store:** Camp store. **Vending:** Yes. **Swimming:** Pools. **Playground:** Yes. **Activities:** Themed weekends Apr.–Oct.; catch & release fishing pond, basketball, volleyball, horseshoes. **Nearby Attractions:** Knoebels Amusement park, Little League Museum, Flea Markets nearby. **Additional Information:** Susquehanna Visitors Bureau.

RESTRICTIONS

Pets: On leash only. **Fires:** Allowed. **Alcoholic Beverages:** At site only. **Vehicle Maximum Length:** 45 ft.

TO GET THERE

From I-80, take Exit 212S. Go 8 mi. south on Hwy. 147 to the junction of Hwy. 405; travel north 0.25 mi. to signs at bottom of hill. Go 0.75 mi. to campground. From US 15 at Lewisburg, take Hwy. 45 east to the junction of Hwy. 405; travel south (at bridge) 3 mi. to entrance sign on left. From junction of US 11 and US 15 at Sunbury, take US 11 north to Hwy. 147; go north to the junction of Hwy. 405. Go north 0.25 mi. to signs at bottom of hill. Go 0.75 mi. to campground.

MOUNT POCONO   MAP, B-6
Mount Pocono Campground

30 Edgewood Rd., P.O. Box 65, 18344.
T: (888) 55-POCONO or (570) 839-8950;
www.mtpoconocampground.com.

🚐 ★★★★   ▲ ★★★★

Beauty: ★★★★   Site Privacy: ★★★
Spaciousness: ★★★★   Quiet: ★★★★
Security: ★★★   Cleanliness: ★★★★
Insect Control: ★★★★   Facilities: ★★★★

Adjacent to Devil's Hole State Game Land and perched atop Mount Pocono, Mount Pocono Campground is the region's oldest private campground, founded by the Albert family. The semi-wooded campground has open and shaded sites, including 70 pull-throughs. From the mountaintop, sunrises and moonlit nights seem more spectacular. All of the Pocono Mountains attractions are downhill from the campground. At over 2,000 feet above sea level, the air is clean and piney. Though the campground is secluded, it is not far from restaurants and grocery stores in the town of Mount Pocono, located on the other side of the mountaintop. Horseback riding is an ideal way to see a part of the Pocono Mountains not visible by car. Near Mount Pocono, Carson's Riding Stable has more than 60 miles of trails geared for everyone from beginners to seasoned riders. Free instruction is offered for first-timers.

BASICS

Operated By: Scott & Debbie Roberts. **Open:** May 1–Oct. 31. **Site Assignment:** By reservation & first come, first served. **Registration:** At campground office. **Fee:** $20–$35. **Parking:** At designated spot.

FACILITIES

Number of RV-only Sites: 185. **Number of Tent-only Sites:** 15. **Hookups:** Electric (20, 30 amps), water, cable TV, phone. **Each Site:** Fire ring, picnic table. **Dump Station:** Yes. **Laundry:** No. **Pay Phone:** Yes. **Restrooms and Showers:** Yes. **Fuel:** No. **Propane:** Yes. **Internal Roads:** Gravel & paved, in good condition. **RV Service:** No. **Market:** W/in 1 mi. **Restaurant:** W/in 1 mi. **General Store:** Yes. **Vending:** Yes. **Swimming:** Yes. **Playground:** Yes. **Activities:** Rec hall, game room, swimming, wading pool, basketball, shuffleboard, planned activities on weekends, movies, sports field, badminton, hiking trails, horseshoes, hiking trails, volleyball. **Nearby Attractions:** Devil's Hole State Game Land, Pocono Mountains attractions. **Additional Information:**

Pocono Mountains Vacation Bureau, (800) POCONOS, www.800poconos.org.

RESTRICTIONS

Pets: On leash only. **Fires:** At site. **Alcoholic Beverages:** At site. **Vehicle Maximum Length:** 40 ft.

TO GET THERE

From Hwy. 611, go 0.75 mi. north on Hwy. 196 and 0.5 mi. east on Edgewood Rd. Entrance is at the end.

MT. BETHEL   MAP, C-6
Driftstone on the Delaware

2731 River Rd., 18343.
T: (570) 897-6859 or (888) 355-6859;
www.driftstone.com.

🚐 ★★★★   ⛺ ★★★★

Beauty: ★★★★	Site Privacy: ★★★
Spaciousness: ★★★	Quiet: ★★★★
Security: ★★★★★	Cleanliness: ★★★★
Insect Control: ★★★★	Facilities: ★★★★

Set along the Delaware River, 8 miles south of the Delaware Water Gap, Driftstone on the Delaware offers comfortable grassy sites, some of which are on the river. There are seven pull-through sites and 183 double slideout sites. Sites along the river are close to Driftstone Island, which can be reached with a short journey through the river. You can explore the Delaware River in a canoe, kayak, or raft during your stay at Driftstone; rentals are available to registered Driftstone campers or their paid visitors only. Driftstone also offers partial or whole-day rentals from its dock. From here, you can fish and explore several miles of the Delaware. Upstream paddling is required. Campground staff members will even transport you upstream if you prefer. Driftstone offers day trips of 4, 8, and 14 miles. All trips include short sections of Class One rapids. Trip prices include rental and transportation.

BASICS

Operated By: Earl Ackerman. **Open:** May 12–Sept. 17. **Site Assignment:** Reservations recommended (deposits must be received w/in 1 week of date reservation made), walk-ins accepted. **Registration:** At campground office. **Fee:** $31–$40; V, MC. **Parking:** At site.

FACILITIES

Number of RV-only Sites: 184. **Number of Tent-only Sites:** 6. **Hookups:** Electric (30 amps), water, phone. **Each Site:** Fire ring, picnic table. **Dump Station:** Yes. **Laundry:** Yes. **Pay Phone:** Yes. **Restrooms and Showers:** Yes. **Fuel:** No. **Propane:** Yes. **Internal Roads:** Gravel & paved, in good condition. **RV Service:** No. **Market:** W/in 12 mi. **Restaurant:** W/in 4 mi. **General Store:** Yes. **Vending:** Yes. **Swimming:** Pool. **Playground:** Yes. **Activities:** Rec hall, game room, swimming, wading pool, boating, canoeing, kayaking, canoe & kayak rentals, river fishing, basketball, planned activities, badminton, volleyball, horseshoes, sports field. **Nearby Attractions:** Delaware Water Gap, Shawnee Playhouse, Windrose Riding Center, Bushkill Park, Crayola Factory & Store, Crossings Factory Stores, Martin Guitar Company, National Canal Museum & Canal

Boat Rides, Nazareth Speedway. **Additional Information:** Pocono Mountains Vacation Bureau, (800) POCONOS, www.800poconos.org.

RESTRICTIONS

Pets: On leash attended only. 1 dog per campsite. **Fires:** At site. **Alcoholic Beverages:** At site. **Vehicle Maximum Length:** 45 ft. **Other:** No motorcycles or jet skis.

TO GET THERE

From Hwy. 611, go 3.75 mi. south on River Rd. Entrance is on the left.

NARVON   MAP, D-5
Lake-In-Wood Camping Resort

576 Yellow Hill Rd., 17555. T: (717) 445-5525;
www.lakeinwoodcampground.com.

🚐 ★★★★★   ⛺ ★★★★★

Beauty: ★★★★	Site Privacy: ★★★
Spaciousness: ★★★★	Quiet: ★★★★
Security: ★★★★	Cleanliness: ★★★★
Insect Control: ★★★★	Facilities: ★★★★★

Located near Bowmansville in Lancaster County, Lake-In-Wood is another campground nestled in the heart of Pennsylvania Dutch Country—and one of the best. In fact, with its cleanliness, natural splendor, and abundance of activities and amenities, Lake-In-Wood Camping Resort is one of the finest properties in the mid-Atlantic. Of Lake-In-Wood's 325 RV sites—some open, others shaded—36 handle pull-throughs and 200 accommodate double slideouts. Partial to staying near the water, we like the sites alongside the six-acre lake, where rowboats and pedal boats can be rented. For those people who do not own a tent or an RV but enjoy the camping experience, we like the novelty rental units at Lake-In-Wood. Chances are you haven't slept in a double-decker bus, a shipwreck, or a caboose. Also, though you've likely played mini-golf, perhaps you haven't tried chucker golf—a game more suited for those who cannot crush Tiger Woods–like drives. Chucker golf is played on a smaller course and is suited for beginners.

BASICS

Operated By: Klaas Bakker. **Open:** Apr. 1–Nov. 1. **Site Assignment:** By reservation & first come, first served. **Registration:** At office. **Fee:** Full hookup, $40; no hookup, $30; V, MC, D. **Parking:** At site.

FACILITIES

Number of RV-only Sites: 325. **Number of Tent-only Sites:** 18. **Hookups:** Electric (20, 30, 50 amps), water, cable TV, phone. **Each Site:** Picnic table, fire ring, lantern pole. **Dump Station:** Yes. **Laundry:** Yes. **Pay Phone:** Yes. **Restrooms and Showers:** Yes. **Fuel:** No. **Propane:** No. **Internal Roads:** Gravel & paved, in good condition. **RV Service:** No. **Market:** 4 mi. in Blue Ball. **Restaurant:** Yes. **General Store:** Yes. **Vending:** Yes. **Swimming:** Yes. **Playground:** Yes. **Other:** Fire-engine rides, church services, themed rental units, double-decker bus, shipwreck, tree house. **Activities:** Rec hall, coin games, swimming pool, wading pool, whirlpool, boating, canoeing, rowboat & paddleboat rentals, shuffleboard, badminton, horseshoes, sports field, hiking trails, fitness trail, volleyball, basketball,

mini-golf, chucker golf. **Nearby Attractions:** Pennsylvania Dutch Country, Pennsylvania Rail Museum, Landis Valley Museum, Valley Forge, Reading outlet malls, Onyx Cave, Crystal Cave, Gettysburg Battlefield, Pennsylvania Farm Museum, Longwood Gardens, Daniel Boone Homestead, Dorney Water Park. **Additional Information:** Pennsylvania Dutch CVB, (800) PA-DUTCH, www.padutchcountry.com; Valley Forge CVB, (888) VISITVF, www.valleyforge.org.

RESTRICTIONS

Pets: On leash only. **Fires:** Fire ring only. **Alcoholic Beverages:** Not allowed. **Vehicle Maximum Length:** 42 ft. **Other:** Check-in 3–9 p.m.; arrivals before noon will be charged a full night fee; arrivals noon–3 p.m. will be charged half-day fee.

TO GET THERE

From SR 23, go 4.5 mi. north on SR 625, 1 mi. northeast on Oaklyn Dr., and 1.5 mi. east on Yellow Hill Rd.

NEW CASTLE   MAP, C-6
Rose Point Park Campground

reserve america

RD 4 Box 410, 314 Rose Point Rd., 16101.
T: (724) 924-2415 or (800) 459-1561;
www.rosepointpark.com.

🚐 ★★★★   ⛺ ★★★★

Beauty: ★★★★	Site Privacy: ★
Spaciousness: ★★	Quiet: ★★★★
Security: ★★★★★	Cleanliness: ★★★★
Insect Control: ★★★★	Facilities: ★★★★

Located on Slippery Rock Creek near McConnell's Mill State Park and Moraine State Park near New Castle, Rose Point Park Campground has open and shaded grassy sites. There are seven pull-through sites and five double slideout sites. At McConnell's Mill State Park, you can tour the restored grist mill and covered bridges, or go hiking, rock climbing, and rappelling. Slippery Rock Gorge Trail is the longest trail in the park and extends from Hell's Hollow to Eckert Bridge. This 6-mile nonloop trail is designated as part of the North Country National Scenic Trail. Slippery Rock Creek is 49 miles long and full of slippery rocks; it's named for one exceptionally slick rock below the Armstrong Bridge.

BASICS

Operated By: Yeager family. **Open:** All year. **Site Assignment:** By reservation & first come, first served. **Registration:** At campground office (old white church). **Fee:** $20–$26; V, MC, AE, D. **Parking:** At designated spot.

FACILITIES

Number of RV-only Sites: 142. **Number of Tent-only Sites:** 10. **Hookups:** Electric (20, 30 amps), water, phone. **Each Site:** Fire ring, picnic table. **Dump Station:** Yes. **Laundry:** Yes. **Pay Phone:** Yes. **Restrooms and Showers:** Yes. **Fuel:** No. **Propane:** Yes. **Internal Roads:** Paved, in good condition. **RV Service:** Yes. **Market:** W/in 4 mi. **Restaurant:** W/in 4 mi. **General Store:** Yes. **Vending:** Yes. **Swimming:** Pool. **Playground:** Yes. **Activities:** Rec hall, game room, swimming, stream fishing, basketball, planned activities, sports field, hiking trails, horseshoes, volleyball. **Nearby Attractions:** Amish communities of New Wilmington & Volant, Grove City Outlet Shops, Harlansburg Station, Living Treasures Animal Park, McConnells Mill State Park, Moraine State Park & Lake Arthur. **Additional Information:** Pennsylvania Dutch CVB, (800) PA-DUTCH, www.padutchcountry.com.

RESTRICTIONS

Pets: On leash only. **Fires:** At site. **Alcoholic Beverages:** At site. **Vehicle Maximum Length:** 65 ft.

TO GET THERE

From I-79, take Exit 29 and go 3 mi. west on US 422 and 0.25 mi. north on Rose Point Rd. Entrance is on the right.

NEW COLUMBIA   MAP, B-4
Nittany Mountain Campground

2751 Millers Bottom Rd., 17856.
T: (570) 568-5541; www.fun-camping.com.

🚐 ★★★★   ⛺ ★★★★

Beauty: ★★★★★   Site Privacy: ★★
Spaciousness: ★★   Quiet: ★★★
Security: ★★★★   Cleanliness: ★★★★★
Insect Control: ★★★★   Facilities: ★★★★★

Located in the heart of Susquehanna Valley, Nittany Mountain Campground offers shaded and open campsites, including 20 pull-throughs. Nittany Mountain is set in wooded hills—not far from the highway, but far enough so that you hear birds singing, not automobiles. Nittany Mountain's petting zoo is a magnet that lures children to feed the goats and other farm animals. The 19-hole mini-golf course is another popular activity for children and parents alike. Every summer, the campground hosts a Sawmill Festival. Try log rolling, and then driving a golf ball on the fairway doesn't seem as hard. Nail driving (with a hammer) and crosscut sawing are among the events. For more entertainment, Knoebel's Amusement Park (free admission) in nearby Elysburg has 47 rides, including two wooden roller coasters, the Phoenix and the Twister.

BASICS

Operated By: Private operator. **Open:** All year. **Site Assignment:** Reservations recommended; first come, first served. **Registration:** At campground office. **Fee:** $26–$37; V, MC, D. **Parking:** At site.

FACILITIES

Number of RV-only Sites: 343. **Number of Tent-only Sites:** 7. **Hookups:** Electric (20, 30, 50 amps), water, cable TV, phone. **Each Site:** Fire ring, picnic table. **Dump Station:** Yes. **Laundry:** Yes. **Pay Phone:** Yes. **Restrooms and Showers:** Yes. **Fuel:** No. **Propane:** Yes. **Internal Roads:** Gravel & paved, in good condition. **RV Service:** No. **Market:** W/in 5 mi. **Restaurant:** W/in 5 mi. **General Store:** Yes. **Vending:** Yes. **Swimming:** Pool. **Playground:** Yes. **Other:** 19-hole mini-golf course. **Activities:** Rec hall, game room, swimming, wading pool, mini-golf, pond fishing, basketball, shuffleboard, planned activities, sports field, horseshoes, badminton, hiking trails, volleyball. **Nearby Attractions:** Knoebel's Amusement Park, Williamsport Trolleys, Pioneer Tunnel Coal

Mine & Steam Train. **Additional Information:** Susquehanna Valley Visitors Bureau, (800) 525-7320, www.svvb.com.

RESTRICTIONS

Pets: On leash only. **Fires:** At site. **Alcoholic Beverages:** At site. **Vehicle Maximum Length:** 40 ft.

TO GET THERE

From I-80, take Exit 210-A and go 0.25 mi. south on US 15, 4.25 mi. west on New Columbia Rd., and 0.25 mi. north on Millers Bottom Rd. Entrance is on the right.

NEW HOLLAND   MAP, D-5
Spring Gulch Resort Campground

reserve america ☼

475 Lynch Rd., 17557.
T: (717) 354-3100 or (866) 864-8524;
www.springgulch.com.

🚐 ★★★★   ⛺ ★★★★

Beauty: ★★★★   Site Privacy: ★
Spaciousness: ★★   Quiet: ★★★★
Security: ★★★★★   Cleanliness: ★★★★
Insect Control: ★★★★   Facilities: ★★★★★

Located in the Pennsylvania Dutch Country, Spring Gulch Resort Campground has 450 open and shaded sites amid forests and farmland in Lancaster County. With two heated pools, a stocked fishing lake, an 18-hole mini-golf course, and a dance barn, Spring Gulch boasts a wide assortment of activities. Just as guests of sister campground Mill Bridge have access to Spring Gulch amenities, Spring Gulch guests enjoy free admission to the historic Mill Bridge Village on the grounds of Mill Bridge Campground outside of Strasburg. Each May, the weekend-long Spring Gulch Folk Festival features music, campfire sing-a-longs, workshops, dancing, and crafts.

BASICS

Operated By: Private operator. **Open:** Mar.–Dec. **Site Assignment:** Reservations recommended; first come, first served. **Registration:** At campground office. **Fee:** $28–$52; V, MC, D. **Parking:** At designated spot.

FACILITIES

Number of RV-only Sites: 350. **Number of Tent-only Sites:** 100. **Hookups:** Electric (20, 30, 50 amps), water, cable TV, phone. **Each Site:** Fire ring, picnic table. **Dump Station:** Yes. **Laundry:** Yes. **Pay Phone:** Yes. **Restrooms and Showers:** Yes. **Fuel:** No. **Propane:** Yes. **Internal Roads:** Gravel & paved, in good condition. **RV Service:** No. **Market:** W/in 4 mi. **Restaurant:** W/in 4 mi. **General Store:** Yes. **Vending:** Yes. **Swimming:** Yes. **Playground:** Yes. **Other:** Dance barn, stocked fishing lake. **Activities:** Rec hall, game room, 2 swimming pools, lake swimming, whirlpool, mini-golf, basketball, shuffleboard, planned activities on weekends, movies, tennis, sports field, badminton, horseshoes, hiking trail, volleyball. **Nearby Attractions:** Mill Bridge Village, Pennsylvania Dutch Country, Hershey. **Additional Information:** Pennsylvania Dutch CVB, (800) PA-DUTCH, www.padutchcountry.com.

RESTRICTIONS

Pets: On leash only. **Fires:** At site. **Alcoholic Beverages:** At site. **Vehicle Maximum Length:** 55 ft.

TO GET THERE

From Hwy. 33, go 4 mi. south on Hwy. 897 and 50 yards east on Lynch Rd. Entrance is on the left.

NEWMANSTOWN   MAP, C-5
Shady Oaks Campground

40 Round Barn Rd., 17073.
T: (800) 807-3177 or (717) 949-3177.

🚐 ★★★★   ⛺ ★★★★

Beauty: ★★★★   Site Privacy: ★★★
Spaciousness: ★★★   Quiet: ★★★★
Security: ★★★★   Cleanliness: ★★★★
Insect Control: ★★★★   Facilities: ★★★★

Nestled in the woods of Newmanstown and located in the heart of Pennsylvania Dutch Country, Shady Oaks is surrounded by mountains and farmland. Shady Oaks is small compared to many campgrounds in Dutch Country, but it is clean, scenic, and quiet. Shady Oaks offers shaded and nonshaded sites, most in a wooded setting. Bath houses are clean and climate controlled, and the camp store is well stocked and sells hand-dipped ice cream. For groups, Shady Oaks has a safari circle with water and electric hookups. The best tent sites are at the campground's north end. Shady Oaks hosts Saturday night hayrides and Sunday morning church services. Two often-overlooked attractions in the vicinity are the Pennsylvania Farm Museum and the Arrowhead Springs Trout Hatchery.

BASICS

Operated By: McNally family. **Open:** Apr. 1–Nov. 1.; limited camping in winter. **Site Assignment:** By reservation & first come, first served. **Registration:** At campground office. **Fee:** $20–$28; V, MC, D. **Parking:** At site.

FACILITIES

Number of RV-only Sites: 66. **Number of Tent-only Sites:** 3. **Hookups:** Electric (20, 30 amps), water. **Each Site:** Fire ring, picnic table. **Dump Station:** Yes. **Laundry:** Yes. **Pay Phone:** Yes. **Restrooms and Showers:** Yes. **Fuel:** No. **Propane:** Yes. **Internal Roads:** Gravel, in good condition. **RV Service:** No. **Market:** W/in 4 mi. **Restaurant:** W/in 4 mi. **General Store:** Yes. **Vending:** Yes. **Swimming:** Pool. **Playground:** Yes. **Activities:** Rec hall, game room, swimming, basketball, sports field, horseshoes, volleyball, planned activities on weekends. **Nearby Attractions:** Arrowhead Springs Trout Hatchery, Middle Creek Wildlife Preserve, HersheyPark, Chocolate World, Crystal Cave, Indian Echo Caverns, Ephrata Cloisters, Reading factory outlets, Blue Marsh Lake & Recreation Area, Pennsylvania Farm Museum, Summer Resort w/ Lake in Mt. Gretna, Harrisburg. **Additional Information:** Pennsylvania Dutch CVB, (800) PA-DUTCH, www.padutchcountry.com.

RESTRICTIONS

Pets: On leash only. **Fires:** At site. **Alcoholic Beverages:** At site. **Vehicle Maximum Length:** 35 ft.

TO GET THERE

From west of Newmanstown limits, go 1 mi. southwest on paved road. Entrance is on the right.

NEWVILLE — MAP, D-4
Colonel Denning State Park

1599 Doubling Gap Rd., 17241.
T: (888) PA-PARKS or (717) 776-5272;
www.dcnr.state.pa.us/stateparks.

🚐 ★★★ ▲ ★★★★

Beauty: ★★★★
Spaciousness: ★★★★
Security: ★★★★
Insect Control: ★★★★

Site Privacy: ★★★★
Quiet: ★★★★
Cleanliness: ★★★★
Facilities: ★★★

Located 8 miles north of Newville, Colonel Denning State Park is nestled in a wooded area at the side of a mountain; it has a lake and well-marked hiking trails. The park has 273 acres of woodland and a 3.5-acre lake. The campground does not have showers. The mineral springs in Doubling Gap have drawn people to the area since the 1700s. Springs in the Doubling Gap area contain carbonate of soda and magnesia, glamber salt, epsom salt, carbonic acid, and bicarbonate of iron. With the advent of modern medicine, people began to learn that the bad-tasting waters were not as healing as their ancestors had thought, and the resort eventually closed in the 1920s. The main hotel still stands and is the focal point for a summer church camp.

BASICS

Operated By: State of Pennsylvania. **Open:** Apr.–Dec. **Site Assignment:** By reservation & first come, first served. **Registration:** At campground office. **Fee:** $12–$19; V, MC, personal check. **Parking:** At designated spot.

FACILITIES

Number of Multipurpose Sites: 52. **Hookups:** Electric (30, 50 amps). **Each Site:** Fire ring, picnic table. **Dump Station:** Yes. **Laundry:** W/in 5 mi. **Pay Phone:** Yes. **Restrooms and Showers:** No. **Fuel:** No. **Propane:** No. **Internal Roads:** Paved, in good condition. **RV Service:** No. **Market:** W/in 8 mi. **Restaurant:** W/in 8 mi. **General Store:** No. **Vending:** Yes. **Swimming:** Lake. **Playground:** Yes. **Activities:** Boating, lake swimming, ice skating rink, lake fishing, hiking trails, sports field. **Nearby Attractions:** Hemlocks Natural Area, Tuscarora State Park, Doubling Gap Sulphur Springs. **Additional Information:** Pennsylvania Capital Regions Vacation Bureau, (717) 249-4801, www.pacapitalregions.com.

RESTRICTIONS

Pets: Not allowed. **Fires:** At site. **Alcoholic Beverages:** No alcohol permitted. **Vehicle Maximum Length:** 35 ft.

TO GET THERE

From Newville, go 8 mi. north on Hwy. 233. Follow signs to campground.

NORTHUMBERLAND MAP, C-4, C-5
Splash Magic Campground

R.R. 1, Box 330, 17857.
T: (570) 473-8021 or (800) 496-4320;
www.riverandfun.com.

🚐 ★★★★ ▲ ★★★★

Beauty: ★★★★★
Spaciousness: ★★★
Security: ★★★★
Insect Control: ★★★★

Site Privacy: ★★★
Quiet: ★★★★
Cleanliness: ★★★★
Facilities: ★★★★

At Splash Magic Campground, there are 28 pull-through sites and 60 double slideouts. The sites along the lake at the south end and on the Susquehanna River at the north end are more serene and offer more privacy. At Splash Magic Campground, you can fish in Dolphin Cove, a stocked fishing lake where no license is required, or in the Susquehanna River. Rowboat, canoe, and kayak rentals are also available at the lake. You may prefer the 18-hole mini-golf course, complete with running fountain. The campground has a full menu of special events throughout the year.

BASICS

Operated By: Basil & Kathy Foster. **Open:** Apr. 21–Oct. 5. **Site Assignment:** By reservation & first come, first served. **Registration:** At campground office. **Fee:** $33–$46; V, MC, D. **Parking:** At designated spot.

FACILITIES

Number of RV-only Sites: 150. **Number of Tent-only Sites:** 30. **Hookups:** Electric (20, 30, 50 amps), water, cable TV, phone. **Each Site:** Fire ring, picnic table. **Dump Station:** Yes. **Laundry:** Yes. **Pay Phone:** Yes. **Restrooms and Showers:** Yes. **Fuel:** No. **Propane:** Yes. **Internal Roads:** Gravel & paved, in good condition. **RV Service:** W/in 10 mi. **Market:** W/in 2 mi. **Restaurant:** W/in 2 mi. **General Store:** Yes. **Vending:** Yes. **Swimming:** Pool. **Playground:** Yes. **Other:** Private fishing lake. **Activities:** Rec hall, game room, swimming, boating, canoeing, kayaking, boat rentals, lake & river fishing, mini-golf, basketball, bike rentals, planned activities, movies, sports field, badminton, horseshoes, volleyball. **Nearby Attractions:** Canoe Touring & whitewater instruction on the Susquehanna River, Clyde Peeling's Reptileland, Hiawatha Paddlewheeler Riverboat, Knoebels Amusement Park, Little League Museum & World Series, Penn's Cave, Pioneer Tunnel Coal Mine & Steam Train, T&D's Cats of the World. **Additional Information:** Susquehanna Valley Visitors Bureau, (800) 525-7320, www.svvb.com.

RESTRICTIONS

Pets: On leash only, under control. **Fires:** At site. **Alcoholic Beverages:** At site. **Vehicle Maximum Length:** 45 ft.

TO GET THERE

From Hwy. 147, go 2.5 mi. north on US 11 and 0.25 mi. southeast on gravel road. Entrance is at the end.

PARADISE — MAP, D-5
Mill Bridge Camp Resort

P.O. Box 7, 101 S. Ronks Rd., 17562.
T: (800) MIL-BRIG or (717) 687-8181;
www.millbridge.com.

🚐 ★★★★ ▲ ★★★★

Beauty: ★★★★
Spaciousness: ★★
Security: ★★★★
Insect Control: ★★★★

Site Privacy: ★★
Quiet: ★★★★
Cleanliness: ★★★★
Facilities: ★★★★

Adjacent to Mill Bridge Village (a recreated 18th-century Amish settlement), Mill Bridge Camp Resort boasts well-drained level sites, most of which are shaded and perched along Pequea Creek or amid a grove of walnut trees. Mill Bridge has 15 pull-through sites. Though Mill Bridge's amenities are not expansive (no pool), guests have free access to nearby New Holland's Spring Gulch Resort Campground, which has two heated pools, a fitness center, a dance barn, and lake swimming. Mill Bridge guests are also treated to a free Amish buggy ride and free admission to Mill Bridge Village. Of course, Mill Bridge's location is central to numerous other attractions in Pennsylvania Dutch Country, including the scenic Strasburg Railroad.

BASICS

Operated By: Mill Bridge Village. **Open:** All year. **Site Assignment:** By reservation & first come, first served. **Registration:** At campground store. **Fee:** $26–$38; V, MC, AE, D. **Parking:** At site.

FACILITIES

Number of RV-only Sites: 100. **Number of Tent-only Sites:** 25. **Hookups:** Electric (20, 30, 50 amps), water, sewer, cable TV; 50 full hookups. **Each Site:** Fire ring, picnic table. **Dump Station:** Yes. **Laundry:** Yes. **Pay Phone:** Yes. **Restrooms and Showers:** Yes. **Fuel:** No. **Propane:** No. **Internal Roads:** Gravel & paved, in good condition. **RV Service:** No. **Market:** W/in 2 mi. **Restaurant:** W/in 2 mi. **General Store:** Yes. **Vending:** Yes. **Swimming:** Yes. **Playground:** Yes. **Other:** Mill Bridge guests have free access to activities & amenities at Spring Gulch Resort Campground in nearby New Holland. **Activities:** Rec room, game room, boating, canoeing, stream fishing, basketball, planned activities, horseshoes, shuffleboard. **Nearby Attractions:** Mill Bridge Village, Pennsylvania Dutch Country, Strasburg Railroad. **Additional Information:** Pennsylvania Dutch CVB, (800) PA-DUTCH, www.padutchcountry.com.

RESTRICTIONS

Pets: On leash only. **Fires:** At site. **Alcoholic Beverages:** At site. **Vehicle Maximum Length:** 55 ft.

TO GET THERE

From Hwy. 62, go 3.5 mi. east on US 30 and 0.5 mi. south on Ronks Rd. Entrance is on the left.

PATTON   MAP, C-3
Prince Gallitzin State Park

966 Marina Rd., 16668-6317.
T: (888) PA-PARKS or (814) 674-1000;
www.dcnr.state.pa.us/stateparks.

🚐 ★★★★   ⛺ ★★★★

Beauty: ★★★★   Site Privacy: ★★★
Spaciousness: ★★★   Quiet: ★★★★
Security: ★★★★   Cleanliness: ★★★★
Insect Control: ★★★   Facilities: ★★★★

The 6,249-acre Prince Gallitzin State Park is located in the Allegheny Plateau Region of Pennsylvania. The major attractions of the park are the 1,600-acre Lake Glendale and the spacious campground. Consisting of 437 sites, the campground features a camp store with coin-operated laundry, guarded swimming beach, boat mooring area, showers, and flush toilets. Ten modern cabins are available for rent year-round. Cabins are furnished with a living area, kitchen/dining area, shower room, and two or three bedrooms. Two-bedroom cabins provide sleeping accommodations for six (one double bed and two bunks), while three-bedroom cabins sleep eight (one double bed and three bunks). Johnstown offers an interesting side trip for Prince Gallitzin campers. Especially interesting are the Johnstown Flood Museum and the Johnstown Flood Memorial, a somber tribute to those people who lost their lives in the infamous flood.

BASICS

Operated By: State of Pennsylvania. **Open:** Apr. 15–Dec. 15. **Site Assignment:** By reservation & first come, first served. **Registration:** At campground office. **Fee:** $12–$19; V, MC, D. **Parking:** At designated spot.

FACILITIES

Number of RV-only Sites: 85. **Number of Tent-only Sites:** 352. **Hookups:** Electric (30, 50 amps). **Each Site:** Fire ring, picnic table. **Dump Station:** Yes. **Laundry:** Yes. **Pay Phone:** Yes. **Restrooms and Showers:** Yes. **Fuel:** No. **Propane:** No. **Internal Roads:** Gravel, in good condition. **RV Service:** No. **Market:** W/in 6 mi. **Restaurant:** W/in 6 mi. **General Store:** Yes. **Vending:** Yes. **Swimming:** River. **Playground:** Yes. **Activities:** Canoeing, kayaking, fishing, river swimming, beach volleyball, basketball, badminton, croquet, tubing, mountain biking, soccer, football, softball. **Nearby Attractions:** Johnstown Flood Museum, Johnstown Flood Memorial, Fort Necessity Battlefield, Admiral Peary Monument, Allegheny Portage Railroad National Historic Site. **Additional Information:** Greater Johnstown/Cambria Co. CVB, (800) 237-8590, www.visitjohnstownpa.com.

RESTRICTIONS

Pets: Allowed at designated sites. **Fires:** Fire ring only. **Alcoholic Beverages:** No alcohol permitted. **Vehicle Maximum Length:** No limit.

TO GET THERE

From Hwy. 253, go 1.75 mi. south on Hwy. 53 and 3 mi. west on Marina Rd. Follow signs to campground.

PORTERSVILLE   MAP, C-1
Bear Run Campground

184 Badger Hill Rd., 16051.
T: (724) 368-3564 or (888) 737-2605;
www.bearruncampground.com.

🚐 ★★★★   ⛺ ★★★★

Beauty: ★★★★★   Site Privacy: ★★
Spaciousness: ★★★   Quiet: ★★★★
Security: ★★★★   Cleanliness: ★★★★
Insect Control: ★★★★   Facilities: ★★★★

Situated near Moraine State Park and Lake Arthur, Bear Run Campground consists of 60 acres of rolling hills dotted with open and shaded sites. The campground has eight pull-through sites, and 100 sites accommodate double slideouts. Moraine State Park features the 3,225-acre Lake Arthur, an outstanding warmwater fishery that is also great for sailing and boating. Visitors sometimes see osprey that were reintroduced to the park. Of special interest is the Frank Preston Conservation Area and a 7-mile paved bike trail that winds around the north shore of the lake. McConnell's Mill State Park is a five-minute drive from Bear Run. Slippery Rock Creek Gorge, a trout fisherman's paradise, is its main attraction. Bear Run is within 35 minutes of Pittsburgh and sites like Kennywood Amusement Park, Pittsburgh Zoo and Aquarium, and Carnegie museums. The Prime Outlets at Grove City are 20 minutes from Bear Run.

BASICS

Operated By: Wehr family. **Open:** Apr. 15–Oct. 31. **Site Assignment:** Reservations recommended (72-hour cancellation notice); first come, first served. **Registration:** At campground office. **Fee:** $25–$41; V, MC, D. **Parking:** At site.

FACILITIES

Number of RV-only Sites: 316. **Number of Tent-only Sites:** 60. **Hookups:** Electric (20, 30, 50 amps), water, sewer, phone, Internet; 187 full hookups. **Each Site:** Fire ring, picnic table. **Dump Station:** Yes. **Laundry:** Yes. **Pay Phone:** Yes. **Restrooms and Showers:** Yes. **Fuel:** No. **Propane:** Yes. **Internal Roads:** Gravel & paved, in good condition. **RV Service:** Nearby. **Market:** W/in 3 mi. **Restaurant:** W/in 3 mi. **General Store:** Yes. **Vending:** Yes. **Swimming:** Pool. **Playground:** Yes. **Activities:** Rec hall, game room, swimming, canoe rentals, lake fishing, planned activities on weekends, basketball, sports field, horseshoes, badminton, hiking trails, volleyball. **Nearby Attractions:** Moraine State Park, McConnelsville Mill State Park, Prime Outlets at Grove City, Living Treasures Animal Park. **Additional Information:** Butler County Tourist Promotion Agency, (888) 741-6772, www.butlercountychamber.com.

RESTRICTIONS

Pets: On leash only. **Fires:** At site. **Alcoholic Beverages:** At site. **Vehicle Maximum Length:** 35 ft.

TO GET THERE

From I-79, take Exit 28 and go 50 yards east on Hwy. 488 and 0.5 mi. north on Badger Hill Rd. Entrance is on the right.

QUAKERTOWN   MAP, C-6
Quakerwoods Campground

2225 Rosedale Rd., 18951.
T: (215) 536-1984 or (800) 235-2350;
www.quakerwoods.com.

🚐 ★★★★   ⛺ ★★★★

Beauty: ★★★★   Site Privacy: ★★★
Spaciousness: ★★★   Quiet: ★★★★
Security: ★★★★   Cleanliness: ★★★★
Insect Control: ★★★★   Facilities: ★★★★

Convenient to Allentown and Philadelphia, Quakerwoods Campground in Quakertown is a quiet place nestled in a wooded setting. There are three pull-throughs and 160 double slideout sites. The bathrooms here are especially clean. When we were here, the swimming pool and fishing pond were stirring with activity. Many families use Quakerwoods as a base for visiting Philadelphia, Dorney Park, and Sesame Place. However, when the grown-ups are weary from sightseeing, there is plenty for the children to do at the campground, such as basketball, volleyball, and shuffleboard. Quakerwoods offers discount tickets to Dorney Park and Sesame Place. Independence National Historic Park in Philadelphia—called the most historic square mile in America—commemorates more than 200 years of our nation's heritage. Here, you will find the Congress Hall, Independence Hall, the nation's first bank, and, of course, the Liberty Bell.

BASICS

Operated By: Tony Yu. **Open:** Apr. 1–Nov. 1. **Site Assignment:** By reservation & first come, first served. **Registration:** At campground office. **Fee:** $22–$35; V, MC, AE, D. **Parking:** At designated spot.

FACILITIES

Number of RV-only Sites: 170. **Number of Tent-only Sites:** 15. **Hookups:** Electric (20, 30, 50 amps), water, sewer, cable TV, phone, 100 full hookups. **Each Site:** Fire ring, picnic table. **Dump Station:** Yes. **Laundry:** Yes. **Pay Phone:** Yes. **Restrooms and Showers:** Yes. **Fuel:** No. **Propane:** Yes. **Internal Roads:** Gravel, in good condition. **RV Service:** Nearby. **Market:** W/in 5 mi. **Restaurant:** W/in 5 mi. **General Store:** Yes. **Vending:** Yes. **Swimming:** Pool. **Playground:** Yes. **Other:** Theme weekends. **Activities:** Rec hall, game room, swimming, wading pool, pond fishing, basketball, shuffleboard, planned activities on weekends, badminton, sports field, horseshoes, hiking trails, volleyball. **Nearby Attractions:** Allentown, Philadelphia, Dorney Park, Crayola Factory, Fairmount Park, Independence National Historic Park, Neshaminy Valley Music Theatre, Sesame Place, Philadelphia Zoo. **Additional Information:** Philadelphia CVB, (800) 537-7676, www.pcvb.org.

RESTRICTIONS

Pets: On leash only. **Fires:** At site. **Alcoholic Beverages:** At site. **Vehicle Maximum Length:** 50 ft.

TO GET THERE

From Hwy. 309, go 0.25 mi. southwest on Hwy. 663, 2.5 mi. north on Old Bethlehem Pk., and 0.5 mi. west on Rosedale Rd. Entrance is on the left.

QUARRYVILLE   MAP, D-5
Yogi Bear's Jellystone Park Camp-Resort

340 Blackburn Rd., 17566. T: (717) 786-3458;
www.jellystonepa.com.

🚐 ★★★★   ⛺ ★★★★

Beauty: ★★★★   Site Privacy: ★★★★
Spaciousness: ★★★★   Quiet: ★★★★
Security: ★★★★   Cleanliness: ★★★★
Insect Control: ★★★★   Facilities: ★★★★

Whether you are an RV park enthusiast, enjoy the comfort of a cabin in the woods, or just like to tent-camp and sleep in the great outdoors, Jellystone Park's accommodations, amenities, and activities are top-notch. Amenities and activities include swimming, mini-golf, hay rides, tennis, volleyball, fishing, hiking, and appearances from Yogi Bear and friends.

BASICS
Open: Apr. 6–Oct. 29. **Site Assignment:** Reservations recommended. **Registration:** At ranger station. **Fee:** $29–$60. **Parking:** Limit 2 cars per site, overflow parking available.

FACILITIES
Number of Multipurpose Sites: 160. **Hookups:** Electric (30 amps), water, 50 sites w/ sewer. **Each Site:** Picnic table, fire ring. **Dump Station:** Yes (3). **Laundry:** Yes. **Pay Phone:** Yes. **Restrooms and Showers:** Yes. **Fuel:** No. **Propane:** Yes. **Internal Roads:** Gravel. **RV Service:** 10 mi. north in Willow Street. **Market:** 5 mi. north in Quarryville. **Restaurant:** 5 mi. north in Quarryville. **General Store:** Camp store. **Vending:** Yes. **Swimming:** Pool. **Playground:** Yes. **Activities:** Hiking trails, fishing, lake swimming, organized summer activities, volleyball, lighted horseshoes, shuffleboard courts & basketball court.

RESTRICTIONS
Pets: On leash only. **Fires:** Allowed. **Alcoholic Beverages:** At site only. **Vehicle Maximum Length:** 50 ft. **Other:** 1-month stay limit; some permanent sites available.

TO GET THERE
From Lancaster , follow US 222S 3 mi. south of Quarryville. Turn left onto Blackburn Rd. Camp entrance is 1.5 mi. on left.

ROBESONIA   MAP, C-5
Eagles Peak RV Park and Campground

397 Eagles Peak Rd., 19551.
T: (610) 589-4800 or (800) 336-0889;
www.abeaglespeak.com.

🚐 ★★★★★   ⛺ ★★★★

Beauty: ★★★★★   Site Privacy: ★★
Spaciousness: ★★★   Quiet: ★★★★
Security: ★★★★★   Cleanliness: ★★★★★
Insect Control: ★★★★   Facilities: ★★★★★

Central to Lancaster, Reading, and Hershey, Eagles Peak RV Park and Campground is situated on 77 acres arranged in secluded tent areas and full-hookup sites. All sites are either in meadows or wooded with a mountainside view. Sites along Mallard Ln. at the north tip of Eagles Peak (near Peak Pond) offer the most privacy. Sites in the center of the campground are closest to most of the activities. Favorite offerings include barbecue dinners and the swim-up snack bar at the swimming pool. Eagles Peak's pool has built-in benches and water volleyball, among other features. There is even a separate pool open to adults only. In nearby Amish country, you can find old-time farmer's markets and Amish-operated stores where gas lamps are used for lighting. The attractions in Hershey and Pennsylvania Dutch Country are a short drive away, as is Blue Marsh Lake, where fishing and boating are king.

BASICS
Operated By: Adventure Bound Camping Resorts. **Open:** Mar. 31–Oct. 31. **Site Assignment:** Reservations accepted (no refund or credit given w/ cancellation on less than 1-week notice); first come, first served. **Registration:** At campground. **Fee:** $26–$44; V, MC, D. **Parking:** At designated spot.

FACILITIES
Number of RV-only Sites: 320. **Number of Tent-only Sites:** 30. **Hookups:** Electric (20, 30, 50 amps), water, cable TV, phone. **Each Site:** Fire ring, picnic table. **Dump Station:** Yes. **Laundry:** Yes. **Pay Phone:** Yes. **Restrooms and Showers:** Yes. **Fuel:** No. **Propane:** Yes. **Internal Roads:** Gravel & paved, in good condition. **RV Service:** No. **Market:** W/in 5 mi. **Restaurant:** W/in 5 mi. **General Store:** Yes. **Vending:** Yes. **Swimming:** Pool. **Playground:** Yes. **Other:** Separate adult pool. **Activities:** Rec hall, game room, swimming, wading pool, whirlpool, boating, canoeing, pond fishing, mini-golf, basketball, shuffleboard, planned activities, movies, tennis, badminton, sports field, horseshoes, volleyball. **Nearby Attractions:** HersheyPark, Hershey Chocolate World, Dutch Wonderland, Crystal Cave, Mount Hope Estate & Winery, Lancaster County Amish attractions, Blue Marsh Lake, Daniel Boone Homestead, Reading outlets. **Additional Information:** Pennsylvania Dutch CVB, (800) PA-DUTCH, www.padutchcountry.com.

RESTRICTIONS
Pets: On leash only. **Fires:** At site. **Alcoholic Beverages:** At site. **Vehicle Maximum Length:** 50 ft.

TO GET THERE
From west of Robesonia, go 4 mi. west on US 422, 3 mi. south on Hwy. 419, 1.5 mi. east on Sheridan Rd., and 0.5 mi. north on Eagles Peak Rd. Entrance is on the right.

ROCKWOOD   MAP, D-2
Scottyland Camping Resort

1618 Barron Church Rd., 15557.
T: (814) 926-3200 or (800) 242-CAMP;
www.scottylandrvresort.com.

🚐 ★★★★   ⛺ ★★★★

Beauty: ★★★★   Site Privacy: ★★★
Spaciousness: ★★★   Quiet: ★★★
Security: ★★★★   Cleanliness: ★★★★★
Insect Control: ★★★★   Facilities: ★★★★★

Scottyland Camping Resort is located in the mountainous Laurel Highlands region and situated on 311 acres. Primitive sites are located adjacent to the Laurel Hill Creek. Sites that surround the fishing lake are especially attractive, as are the sites that border the pine grove at the campground's northeast end; they offer privacy and solitude. Scottyland has an RV sales and service center with a mechanic on duty, and a snack bar with daily specials and delivery to your campsite. What is most impressive about Scottyland is the 2,000-square-foot indoor Playport designed for children 3–12. The Playport offers slides, ball pits, ropes, ladders, trolley, and tubes. Nearby is an indoor mini-golf course and skating rink. For seniors, the campground offers complimentary help with site hookup, propane, and lighting the water heater and furnace.

BASICS
Operated By: Gary Pirschl. **Open:** All year. **Site Assignment:** By reservation & first come, first served. **Registration:** At campground office. **Fee:** $21–$25; V, MC, D. **Parking:** At designated spot.

FACILITIES
Number of RV-only Sites: 610. **Number of Tent-only Sites:** 100. **Hookups:** Electric (20, 30 amps), water, cable TV, phone. **Each Site:** Fire ring, picnic table. **Dump Station:** Yes. **Laundry:** Yes. **Pay Phone:** Yes. **Restrooms and Showers:** Yes. **Fuel:** Yes. **Propane:** Yes. **Internal Roads:** Paved, in good condition. **RV Service:** Yes. **Market:** W/in 10 mi. **Restaurant:** W/in 10 mi. **General Store:** Yes. **Vending:** Yes. **Swimming:** Yes. **Playground:** Yes. **Other:** Indoor mini-golf course & skating rink, Scottyland RV Sales & Service Center. **Activities:** Rec hall, game room, swimming, wading pool, lake & stream fishing, mini-golf, basketball, shuffleboard, planned activities on weekends, movies, tennis, badminton, sports field, horseshoes, hiking trails, volleyball. **Nearby Attractions:** Laurel Caverns, Seven Springs Mountain Resort, Ft. Ligonier, Idlewood Amusement Park, Ohiopyle State Park. **Additional Information:** Laurel Highlands Visitors Bureau, (800) 925-7669, www.laurelhighlands.org.

RESTRICTIONS
Pets: On leash only. **Fires:** At site. **Alcoholic Beverages:** At site. **Vehicle Maximum Length:** No limit.

TO GET THERE
From I-76, take Exit 10 and go 0.5 mi. south on Hwy. 601, 10 mi. south on Hwy. 281, and 1 mi. west on Hwy. 653. Entrance is on the right.

SHARTLESVILLE MAP, C-5
Appalachian Campsites

60 Motel Dr., P.O. Box 289, 19554.
T: (610) 488-6319 or (800) 424-5746;
www.appalachianrvresort.com.

🚐 ★★★★   ⛺ ★★★★

Beauty: ★★★★★   Site Privacy: ★★
Spaciousness: ★★★   Quiet: ★★★★
Security: ★★★★★   Cleanliness: ★★★★
Insect Control: ★★★★   Facilities: ★★★★★

Set in the foothills of the Blue Mountains in Dutch Country's northern Berks County, Appalachian Campsites has 375 wooded and open sites on 87 acres. There are 50 pull-through sites and 25 double slideout sites. Full-hookup sites on the south end of the campground are near the fishing pond and a short walk away from the frog pond. Sausage and biscuits are just one of the tasty menu items at Johnny Appleseed Hall, the on-premises restaurant where breakfast is served daily (dinner on weekends). Meals are also served during annual events such as Easter dinner, autumn harvest feast, and New Year's Eve. Appalachian Campsites also has cabins, cottages, and tepees for rent.

BASICS
Operated By: Jim & Sylvia Cox. **Open:** All year. **Site Assignment:** Reservations accepted (deposit must be made by credit card or check w/in 5 days to hold reservation), first come, first served. **Registration:** At campground office. **Fee:** Camping season, $27–$40; holidays, $35–43; V, MC, D. **Parking:** At site.

FACILITIES
Number of Multipurpose Sites: 375. **Hookups:** Electric (20, 30, 50 amps), water, cable TV, phone. **Each Site:** Fire ring, picnic table. **Dump Station:** Yes. **Laundry:** Yes. **Pay Phone:** Yes. **Restrooms and Showers:** Yes. **Fuel:** Yes. **Propane:** Yes. **Internal Roads:** Gravel & paved, in good condition. **RV Service:** No. **Market:** W/in 7 mi. **Restaurant:** Yes. **General Store:** Yes. **Vending:** Yes. **Swimming:** Yes. **Playground:** Yes. **Other:** 6,500 square-ft. activities center & mini-golf course. **Activities:** Rec hall, game room, swimming, wading pool, pond fishing, mini-golf, basketball, planned activities on weekends, sports field, horseshoes, hiking trails, volleyball. **Nearby Attractions:** HersheyPark & Chocolate World, Dorney Park & Wildwater Kingdom, Shartlesville antique shops, Hawk Mountain, Crystal Cave, Pat Garrett Amphitheatre. **Additional Information:** Pennsylvania Dutch CVB, (800) PA-DUTCH, www.padutchcountry.com.

RESTRICTIONS
Pets: On leash only. **Fires:** At site. **Alcoholic Beverages:** At site. **Vehicle Maximum Length:** 40 ft.

TO GET THERE
From I-78, take Exit 8 and go 0.1 mi. west on N. Service Rd. Entrance is on the right.

SHARTLESVILLE MAP, C-5
Mountain Springs Camping Resort

P.O. Box 365, 3450 Mountain Rd., 19554.
T: (610) 488-6859;
www.mountainspringscampground.com.

🚐 ★★★★   ⛺ ★★★★

Beauty: ★★★★   Site Privacy: ★★★
Spaciousness: ★★★   Quiet: ★★★★
Security: ★★★★   Cleanliness: ★★★★
Insect Control: ★★★★   Facilities: ★★★★★

Located in Pennsylvania Dutch Country near Shartlesville, Mountain Springs Camping Resort is like many of the clean and amenity-rich campgrounds central to Lancaster County and Hershey attractions. It has fishing lakes, boating, and swimming pools. What separates Mountain Springs from the other campgrounds in the region is its arena, which hosts professional and amateur rodeos, demolition derbies, horse sales, monster truck shows, and authentic Native American pow-wows. Mountain Springs also hosts bingo games and dances that aren't of the Native American variety. The campground itself has wooded and open sites on rolling hills. There are 15 pull-throughs and 50 double slideout sites. The row of water and electric sites near the cabins are convenient to the large fishing lake, while the full-hookup sites on the south end of the campground of close to most of the activities (including the arena).

BASICS
Operated By: Theresa Miller. **Open:** Apr. 1–Oct. 1. **Site Assignment:** Reservations accepted (deposit due 7 days from reservation date); first come, first served. **Registration:** At campground office. **Fee:** $27 $35; V, MC. **Parking:** At designated spot.

FACILITIES
Number of RV-only Sites: 300. **Number of Tent-only Sites:** 25. **Hookups:** Electric (20, 30, 50 amps), water. **Each Site:** Fire ring, picnic table. **Dump Station:** Yes. **Laundry:** Yes. **Pay Phone:** Yes. **Restrooms and Showers:** Yes. **Fuel:** No. **Propane:** Yes. **Internal Roads:** Gravel & paved, in good condition. **RV Service:** No. **Market:** W/in 3 mi. **Restaurant:** W/in 3 mi. **General Store:** Yes. **Vending:** Yes. **Swimming:** Pool. **Playground:** Yes. **Other:** Arena for rodeos, demolition derbies, & other events. **Activities:** Rec hall, game room, swimming, wading pool, canoeing, pond fishing, basketball, shuffleboard, planned activities on weekends, movies, badminton, sports field, horseshoes, hiking trails, volleyball, the game of quoits. **Nearby Attractions:** Shartlesville antique shops, Pennsylvania Dutch Country attractions, Hershey attractions. **Additional Information:** Pennsylvania Dutch CVB, (800) PA-DUTCH, www.padutchcountry.com.

RESTRICTIONS
Pets: On leash only. **Fires:** At site. **Alcoholic Beverages:** At site. **Vehicle Maximum Length:** No limit.

TO GET THERE
From I-78, take Exit 23 and go 1 mi. north on Mountain Rd. Entrance is on the left.

SOMERSET MAP, D-2
Laurel Hill State Park

1454 Laurel Hill Park Rd., 15501.
T: (814) 445-7725 or (888) PA-PARKS;
www.dcnr.state.pa.us/stateparks.

🚐 ★★★★   ⛺ ★★★★

Beauty: ★★★★   Site Privacy: ★★
Spaciousness: ★★★   Quiet: ★★★★
Security: ★★★★   Cleanliness: ★★★
Insect Control: ★★★   Facilities: ★★★★

Laurel Hill State Park is home to 63-acre Laurel Hill Lake. The park consists of 3,935 acres of mountainous terrain in Somerset County. Of the 264 sites at the campground, 169 have electric hookups. There is also one walled tent available for rent. This tent sleeps six people in bunk beds and offers electricity and a refrigerator. The campground has flush toilets and hot showers. Laurel Hill has a 12-mile trail system which leads past the remains of a logging railroad. Hikers commonly see wooden crossties and rusty rail spikes along the Tramroad Trail. This railroad hauled logs from the mountains to a sawmill located at Humbert, near Confluence. A lush stand of old-growth timber may be seen along the popular Hemlock Trail. The 10-mile snowmobile trail system in the park connects with a longer trail system at Forbes State Forest, which is open for registered snowmobiles after the end of antlerless deer season in late December. During warmer and sunnier months, a 1,200-foot-long sandy beach is open from late-May to mid-September.

BASICS
Operated By: State of Pennsylvania. **Open:** Camping, Apr. 15–Oct. 19; park open all year. **Site Assignment:** By reservation & first come, first served. **Registration:** At campground office. **Fee:** $12–$19. (V, MC). **Parking:** At designated spot.

FACILITIES
Number of RV-only Sites: 162. **Number of Tent-only Sites:** 70. **Hookups:** Electric (20, 30, 50 amps), water. **Each Site:** Fire ring, picnic table. **Dump Station:** Yes. **Laundry:** Yes, coin-operated. **Pay Phone:** Yes. **Restrooms and Showers:** Yes. **Fuel:** No. **Propane:** No. **Internal Roads:** Paved, in good condition. **RV Service:** No. **Market:** W/in 12 mi. **Restaurant:** W/in 3 mi. **General Store:** No. **Vending:** Yes. **Swimming:** Lake. **Playground:** Yes. **Activities:** Lake swimming & fishing, boating, canoeing, boat rentals, stream fishing, planned activities, hiking trails. **Nearby Attractions:** Covered bridges at Barronville & Kings Bridge, Kooser State Park, Laurel Ridge State Park, Ohiopyle State Park, Frank Lloyd Wright's Falling Water house, Mt. Davis. **Additional Information:** Laurel Highlands Visitors Bureau, (800) 925-7669, www.laurelhighlands.org.

RESTRICTIONS
Pets: Not allowed. **Fires:** At site. **Alcoholic Beverages:** No alcohol permitted. **Vehicle Maximum Length:** 40 ft.

TO GET THERE
From I-70/I-76, take Exit 10, go 10 mi. west on Hwy. 31, and follow signs 2 mi. south. Entrance is on the right.

SOMERSET   MAP, D-2
Pioneer Park Campground

reserve america

273 Trent Rd., 15501. T: (814) 445-6348;
www.pioneerparkcampground.com.

🚐 ★★★★   ⛺ ★★★★

Beauty: ★★★★★   Site Privacy: ★★★
Spaciousness: ★★★   Quiet: ★★★★
Security: ★★★★   Cleanliness: ★★★★★
Insect Control: ★★★★   Facilities: ★★★★

Located at the foot of the Laurel Ridge Mountains, Pioneer Park Campground features well-manicured, grassy, open, and shaded sites with spectacular mountain views. Pioneer Park's main draw is its 50 acres of spring-fed lakes. Three of the lakes are stocked with trout two times a week. The other lake is for pedal boating and children's fishing. Pioneer Park also has pedal boat races as well as some treasure hunts. Sites at the northeast end of campground are closest to the largest fishing lake. Sites at the southeast border a small lake. There are 200 full hookups and 18 level pull-through sites. Close to Seven Springs Mountain Resort and Ft. Ligonier, Pioneer Park is also near Laurel Caverns, which has 3 miles of underground caves open for exploration year-round.

BASICS
Operated By: Frank Sujanksi. **Open:** Mar. 25–Oct. 29. **Site Assignment:** Reservations recommended; first come, first served. **Registration:** At campground office. **Fee:** $21–$32; V, MC. **Parking:** At designated spot.

FACILITIES
Number of RV-only Sites: 200. **Number of Tent-only Sites:** 145. **Hookups:** Electric (20, 30, 50 amps), cable TV, phone. **Each Site:** Fire ring, picnic table. **Dump Station:** Yes. **Laundry:** Yes. **Pay Phone:** Yes. **Restrooms and Showers:** Yes. **Fuel:** No. **Propane:** Yes. **Internal Roads:** Gravel & paved, in good condition. **RV Service:** No. **Market:** W/in 10 mi. **Restaurant:** W/in 2 mi. **General Store:** Yes. **Vending:** Yes. **Swimming:** Pool. **Playground:** Yes. **Other:** 50 acres of stocked fishing lakes. **Activities:** Lake fishing, rec hall, game room, wading pool, pedal boat rentals, mini-golf, basketball, shuffleboard, planned activities on weekends, tennis, sports field, horseshoes, hiking trails, volleyball. **Nearby Attractions:** Laurel Caverns, Seven Springs Mountain Resort, Ft. Ligonier, Idlewood Amusement Park. **Additional Information:** Laurel Highlands Visitors Bureau, (800) 925-7669, www.laurelhighlands.org.

RESTRICTIONS
Pets: On leash only. **Fires:** At site. **Alcoholic Beverages:** At site, under control. **Vehicle Maximum Length:** 40 ft.

TO GET THERE
From I-76, take Exit 10 and go 0.5 mi. south on Hwy. 601, 7 mi. west on Hwy. 31, and 0.25 mi. south on Trent Rd. Entrance is on the right.

ST. PETERS   MAP, D-5
Warwick Woods Family Camping Resort

P.O. Box 280, 19470. T: (610) 286-9655; www.warwickwoods.com.

🚐 ★★★★   ⛺ ★★★★

Beauty: ★★★★   Site Privacy: ★★★
Spaciousness: ★★★★   Quiet: ★★★★★
Security: ★★★★   Cleanliness: ★★★★★
Insect Control: ★★★★   Facilities: ★★★★

Located in Chester County, Warwick Woods Family Camping Resort offers 226 large, secluded sites on 100 acres. Warwick Woods has everything from primitive sites to expansive sites with full hookups. All sites are wooded, and most have foliage between them for added privacy. The renowned Horseshoe Trail meanders through the campground and can be hiked to various nearby and distant destinations. An acre in size, the campground's fishing pond is stocked with bass, trout, catfish, and bluegill. Though you likely know about the attractions in Hershey, Philadelphia, and Pennsylvania Dutch Country, you may not know about the hidden gem of small-town Kennett Square. Situated in the Brandywine Valley in southern Chester County, about 3 miles west of Longwood Gardens, Kennett Square is the "Mushroom Capital of the World" as well as the smallest town in America with a symphony orchestra.

BASICS
Operated By: The Daly family. **Open:** Mar. 30–Nov. 4. **Site Assignment:** By reservation & first come, first served. **Registration:** At campground office. **Fee:** $32–$38; V, MC. **Parking:** At designated spot.

FACILITIES
Number of RV-only Sites: 195. **Number of Tent-only Sites:** 30. **Hookups:** Electric (20, 30 amps), water, phone. **Each Site:** Fire ring, picnic table. **Dump Station:** Yes. **Laundry:** Yes. **Pay Phone:** Yes. **Restrooms and Showers:** Yes. **Fuel:** No. **Propane:** Yes. **Internal Roads:** Gravel & paved, in good condition. **RV Service:** No. **Market:** W/in 6 mi. **Restaurant:** W/in 6 mi. **General Store:** Yes. **Vending:** Yes. **Swimming:** Yes. **Playground:** Yes. **Other:** Live music & entertainment. **Activities:** Lake fishing, volleyball, basketball horseshoes, shuffleboard, 2 playgrounds, hiking trails, planned activities. **Nearby Attractions:** Sesame Place, Philadelphia, Pennsylvania Dutch Country, Valley Forge, Reading outlets, Hopewell Village, Hershey, Longwood Gardens. **Additional Information:** Chester Co. CVB, (800) 228-9933, www.brandywinevalley.com.

RESTRICTIONS
Pets: On leash only, under control. **Fires:** At site. **Alcoholic Beverages:** At site. **Vehicle Maximum Length:** 40 ft.

TO GET THERE
From I-76, take Exit 22 and go 1 mi. south on Hwy. 10, 7.5 mi. east on Hwy. 23, and 0.5 mi. north on Trythall Rd. Entrance is on the left.

UPPER BLACK EDDY   MAP, C-6
Colonial Woods Family Camping Resort

545 Lonely Cottage Dr., 18972. T: (610) 847-5808 or (800) 887-2267; www.colonialwoods.com.

🚐 ★★★★   ⛺ ★★★★

Beauty: ★★★★   Site Privacy: ★★★
Spaciousness: ★★★   Quiet: ★★★
Security: ★★★★   Cleanliness: ★★★★
Insect Control: ★★★★   Facilities: ★★★★★

Rich with 18th-century history, Bucks County is called the cradle of American heritage, and Colonial Woods Family Camping Resort is in the heart of that heritage. Situated in a wooded and rolling setting, Colonial Woods offers secluded sites beneath towering timber. There are ten pull-through sites and 175 double slideouts. Most of the water, electric, and cable sites are at the north end of the campground—close to the pond, the lakes, and most of the activities. Of course, Colonial Woods is a cozy place, so everything is a short walk away. The climate-controlled lodge is especially inviting in cold weather, when the fireplace crackles inside. Mini-golf and fishing in the pond are among the activities. Nearby, the Delaware River is ideal for tubing, boating, and swimming. Philadelphia and its wealth of attractions are less than 30 minutes away.

BASICS
Operated By: David & Lynn Harbert. **Open:** Apr. 15–Nov. 1. **Site Assignment:** Reservations accepted ($100 deposit required, no refunds w/in 14 days of reservation); first come, first served. **Registration:** At campground office. **Fee:** $30–$37; V, MC, AE, D. **Parking:** At site.

FACILITIES
Number of RV-only Sites: 208. **Number of Tent-only Sites:** 30. **Hookups:** Electric (20, 30 amps), water, cable TV, phone. **Each Site:** Fire ring, picnic table. **Dump Station:** Yes. **Laundry:** Yes. **Pay Phone:** Yes. **Restrooms and Showers:** Yes. **Fuel:** No. **Propane:** Yes. **Internal Roads:** Gravel & paved, in good condition. **RV Service:** Yes. **Market:** W/in 5 mi. **Restaurant:** W/in 5 mi. **General Store:** Yes. **Vending:** Yes. **Swimming:** Pool. **Playground:** Yes. **Activities:** Rec hall, game room, swimming, wading pool, whirlpool, boating, canoeing, pond fishing, basketball, mini-golf, planned activities, movies, tennis, badminton, sports field, horseshoes, volleyball. **Nearby Attractions:** Philadelphia, Crayola Factory, Land of Make Believe, Lake Nockamixon State Park, Washington Crossing, Bowman's Tower, Valley Forge, Delaware River tubing, Buckingham Valley Vineyard & Winery. **Additional Information:** Bucks Co. Conference Visitors Bureau, (800) 836-BUCKS, www.buckscountycvb.org.

RESTRICTIONS
Pets: On leash only. **Fires:** At site. **Alcoholic Beverages:** At site. **Vehicle Maximum Length:** 40 ft.

TO GET THERE
From Hwy. 412, go 2 mi. north on Hwy. 611, 1.5 mi. east on Marienstein Rd., and 0.75 mi. north on Lonely Cottage Rd. Entrance is on the right.

WAPWALLOPEN MAP, B-5
Moyer's Grove Campground and Country RV

R.R. 2 Box 95, 18660.
T: (800) 722-1912 or (570) 379-3375;
www.moyercgrv.com.

🚐 ★★★★   ▲ ★★★★

Beauty: ★★★★   Site Privacy: ★★★
Spaciousness: ★★★   Quiet: ★★★
Security: ★★★★   Cleanliness: ★★★★
Insect Control: ★★★★   Facilities: ★★★★

Located in northeastern Pennsylvania about 20 miles southwest of Wilkes-Barre, Moyer's Grove Campground and Country RV is clean and boasts friendly customer service. Many of the 150 sites are perched alongside a babbling brook, which provides a perfect harmony for a good night's sleep—at least when it's warm enough to leave your RV's windows open. The campground has two ponds, one for fishing and the other for boating. Pedal boats and canoes are available for rent, as are kayaks. For beginners, the calm waters of the Moyer's Grove pond is ideal for learning kayaking techniques before venturing to the more challenging Lackawanna River. Moyer's Grove has an on-premises RV sales and service facility. Among the more interesting attractions near Moyer's Grove are the Lackawanna Coal Mine Tour and Museum, Eckley Miner's Village, Electric City Trolley Station and Museum, and the Houdini Museum.

BASICS
Operated By: Todd, Janet, & Jen Lightner. **Open:** All year. **Site Assignment:** By reservation & first come, first served. **Registration:** At campground headquarters. **Fee:** $27–$30; V, MC, D. **Parking:** At site.

FACILITIES
Number of RV-only Sites: 150. **Hookups:** Electric (20, 30, 50 amps), water, phone. **Each Site:** Fire ring, picnic table. **Dump Station:** Yes. **Laundry:** Yes. **Pay Phone:** Yes. **Restrooms and Showers:** Yes. **Fuel:** No. **Propane:** Yes. **Internal Roads:** Gravel, in good condition. **RV Service:** Yes. **Market:** W/in 5 mi. **Restaurant:** W/in 5 mi. **General Store:** Yes. **Vending:** Yes. **Playground:** Yes. **Other:** Kayak rentals. **Activities:** Rec room, game room, swimming, pond & stream fishing, mini-golf, basketball, shuffleboard, planned activities, volleyball. **Nearby Attractions:** Knoebel's Grove Amusement Park, Steamtown National Historic Site, Electric City Trolley Station & Museum, Claws & Paws Wild Animal Park, Lackawanna Coal Mine Tour & Museum, Bushkill Falls, Pocono Indian Museum, Scranton, Wilkes-Barre, Eckley Miner's Village, Houdini Museum. **Additional Information:** Luzerne Co. Tourist Promotion Agency, (888) 905-2872, www.tournepa.com.

RESTRICTIONS
Pets: On leash only. **Fires:** At site. **Alcoholic Beverages:** At site. **Vehicle Maximum Length:** No limit. **Other:** No pets or smoking permitted in rental cabins or trailers.

TO GET THERE
From I-80, go 3.75 mi. northeast on Hwy. 239 and follow signs 3.5 mi. on paved roads. Entrance is on the right.

WATERVILLE MAP, B-4
Little Pine State Park

4205 Little Pine Creek Rd., 17776.
T: (570) 753-6000 or (888) PA-PARKS;
www.dcnr.state.pa.us/stateparks.

🚐 ★★★   ▲ ★★★★

Beauty: ★★★★   Site Privacy: ★★★
Spaciousness: ★★★★   Quiet: ★★★★
Security: ★★★★   Cleanliness: ★★★
Insect Control: ★★★   Facilities: ★★★★

Set in postcard-perfect Tiadaghton State Forest in the Appalachian Mountains, the 2,158-acre Little Pine State Park is located in Lycoming County, 4 miles north of Hwy. 44 at Waterville and 8 miles south of Hwy. 287 at English Center. The campground has open and shaded sites along a stream. A special attraction of the park is the trail system. Spikebuck Hollow Trail, with its picturesque vistas, outcroppings of rock, and varieties of trees and plants, is an enjoyable challenge. For parents with small children, the 0.8-mile-long Carsontown Trail is ideal. The walk is easy, a variety of wildflowers bloom, and deer are frequently seen. At 2.7 miles long, Panther Run Trail is Little Pine's most scenic hike, but it is intended for the most seasoned and conditioned hikers. Excellent views, rock formations, and a flagstone quarry can be seen along the trail.

BASICS
Operated By: State of Pennsylvania. **Open:** Apr. 1 to start of deer-hunting season. **Site Assignment:** By reservation & first come, first served. **Registration:** At campground office. **Fee:** $12–$19; V, MC, D. **Parking:** At designated spot.

FACILITIES
Number of RV-only Sites: 98. **Number of Tent-only Sites:** 6. **Hookups:** Electric (20, 30, 50 amps), water. **Each Site:** Fire ring, picnic table. **Dump Station:** Yes. **Laundry:** No. **Pay Phone:** Yes. **Restrooms and Showers:** Restrooms. **Fuel:** No. **Propane:** Yes. **Internal Roads:** Paved, in good condition. **RV Service:** Yes. **Market:** W/in 7 mi. **Restaurant:** W/in 7 mi. **General Store:** No. **Vending:** Yes. **Swimming:** Lake. **Playground:** 2. **Activities:** Lake swimming, boating, boat rentals, lake & stream fishing, horseshoes, hiking trails, volleyball. **Nearby Attractions:** Upper Pine Bottom State Park. **Additional Information:** Lycoming County Visitors Bureau, (800) 358-9900, www.williamsport.org.

RESTRICTIONS
Pets: Not allowed. **Fires:** At site. **Alcoholic Beverages:** No alcohol permitted. **Vehicle Maximum Length:** 36 ft.

TO GET THERE
From Hwy. 44, go 4 mi. north on 4001. Follow signs to campground.

WAYMART MAP, B-6
Keen Lake Camping and Cottage Resort

155 Keen Lake Rd., 18472.
T: (800) 443-0412 or (570) 488-5522;
www.keenlake.com.

🚐 ★★★★★   ▲ ★★★★

Beauty: ★★★★   Site Privacy: ★★★
Spaciousness: ★★★   Quiet: ★★★★★
Security: ★★★★   Cleanliness: ★★★★
Insect Control: ★★★★   Facilities: ★★★★★

Perched on a high plateau in the Pocono Mountains, Keen Lake Camping and Cottage Resort has more than 300 sites on 90 acres, but the sites are by no means crowded. The open and shaded sites are well maintained. Campsites are nestled along a rail system's former tracks in a cluster known as Gravity Lane, named in honor of this railroad. Keen Lake has been a part of the Keen family since 1814 when the family purchased land on what was then the Elk Forest tract. Sixth-generation members are active in the family business, and the customer service here is friendly. Other buildings of historical significance located on the resort grounds include the Island cottage located on Hermit Island, the School House cottage, and the Pre–Civil War Barn cottage. Keen Lake has a 50-foot hill slide, a scenic waterfall, train rides, and activities ranging from fishing and boating to bocce ball and arts and crafts.

BASICS
Operated By: Keen family. **Open:** May 1–Oct. 1. **Site Assignment:** Reservations recommended (2-night min. except major holidays); first come, first served. **Registration:** At campground headquarters. **Fee:** $30–$41; V, MC. **Parking:** At designated spot.

FACILITIES
Number of RV-only Sites: 300. **Number of Tent-only Sites:** 75. **Hookups:** Electric (20, 30 amps), water, cable TV, sewer. **Each Site:** Fire ring, picnic table. **Dump Station:** Yes. **Laundry:** Yes. **Pay Phone:** Yes. **Restrooms and Showers:** Yes. **Fuel:** No. **Propane:** No. **Internal Roads:** Gravel & paved, in good condition. **RV Service:** Yes. **Market:** W/in 5 mi. **Restaurant:** W/in 4 mi. **General Store:** Yes. **Vending:** Yes. **Swimming:** Pool, lake. **Playground:** Yes. **Other:** 90-acre spring-fed lake. **Activities:** Rec hall, game room, lake swimming, boating, canoeing, boat & kayak rentals, lake & stream fishing, basketball, shuffleboard, movies, badminton, sports field, horseshoes, volleyball, hiking trails. **Nearby Attractions:** Horseback riding, Zane Grey Museum, Claws & Paws Wild Animal Park, Steamtown National Historic Site, Houdini Museum, Montague Mt. Amphitheatre, Mt. Laurel Performing Center for the Arts. **Additional Information:** Pocono Mountains Vacation Bureau, (800) POCONOS, www.800poconos.org.

RESTRICTIONS
Pets: On leash only. **Fires:** At site. **Alcoholic Beverages:** At site. **Vehicle Maximum Length:** 38 ft. (limited).

TO GET THERE
From Hwy. 296, go 1.5 mi. east on US 6. Entrance is on the right.

Rhode Island

Even as the country's smallest state, Rhode Island more than compensates for its lack of relative square miles by establishing itself in the travel sector as one of the premier destinations on the Northeast coast. It will come as no surprise, then, that Rhode Island's second largest industry is tourism (next to health services). With more than 400 miles of coastline, which includes 100 public and private beaches, 17 state parks, four wineries, and its fair share of wonderful curiosities, Little Rhody can easily satisfy even the most skeptical camper.

Founded as the 13th state to the union May 29, 1790, Rhode Island quickly realized its role in the turbulent, formative years of the country. Realizing that it could not permit its size to be indicative of its significance in the New World, Rhode Island became the first state to enact a law in opposition to slavery in 1652. The **"Birthplace of the American Industry"** is **Pawtucket** at **Old Slater Mill,** where cotton yarn was first produced, introducing the Industrial Revolution to the country. With the founding of the American jewelry industry, **Providence** made a name for itself in New England as a prime force in the new industrial age.

Visitors to the Ocean State with an uncontrollable urge to be in, on, or around water will have no complaints. There are more than 100 boating events every year in **Narragansett Bay** and the surrounding sounds, including regattas, tours, and races. Don't hesitate to drop a line or two either, as the fishing here is outstanding. Canoers and kayakers will find no difficulty in locating a spot to drop in for a paddle. For those looking for a clean break in any number of conditions, Rhode Island is unlikely yet astounding as a windsurfing and surfing destination. Needless to say, camping here at the beach is a very affordable and convenient way to make the most of your visit.

Rhode Island has a national reputation for its mansions, and the city of **Newport** has long been a tourist attraction. It has numerous museums, excellent restaurants, and nearby state park land. Newport is also home to America's oldest tavern, the **White Horse Tavern,** founded in 1673. Before you leave, fans that love a racket should make their way to the **International Tennis Hall of Fame** at the **Newport Casino.**

Those looking for a more cosmopolitan city will do well in Providence. Although it's not New York or Boston, Providence combines small-town appeal with many of the amenities of its bigger cousins. The city also has a park downtown that's the center of activity in the summer, with concerts and other forms of entertainment.

While you're on the road, it might make sense to stop off and explore the state's four vintners. In **Little Compton,** visit **Sakonnet Vineyards** and **Winery; Diamond Hill Vineyards** is located in **Cumberland; Middletown** is host to **Newport Vineyards** and **Winery;** and rounding out the tour is **Greenvale Vineyards** in **Portsmouth.**

Along the way, travelers through Rhode Island with a penchant for and appreciation of the peculiar will have countless opportunities to come into contact with the fascinating.

After state founder Roger Williams died, he was buried at his farm in Providence. Historians conducting an exhumation of his grave site found, instead of Williams, a root shaped like a person. Apparently, the apple tree growing above his burial site had entered the coffin and devoured him. You might get a glimpse of it at the **John Brown House.**

No matter where you are in the state, don't be surprised if you catch a glimpse of what appears to be a life-sized **Mr. Potato Head.** Because it is. In fact, the spud buddy was declared Rhode Island's **Family Travel Ambassador** in 2000. There were 47 different Mr. Potato Heads commissioned for display throughout the state, ranging from one shaped like a light bulb to one molded as if from sand.

Other things to look out for on your journey include **Nibbles Woodaway,** the world's largest bug in Providence; the **Point Judith Corrosion Test Site** in **Narragansett,** where you can witness the effects of weathering by the sea and elements against different exposed materials; and a mysterious stone tower thought by many locals to be built by Vikings and perhaps the oldest structure in the country.

Campground Profiles

CHARLESTOWN   MAP, C-2
Charlestown Breachway Camping Area

Burlingame State Park, 1 Burlingame State Park Rd., 02813. T: (401) 364-7000; www.riparks.com.

🚐 ★★★★   ▲ n/a

Beauty: ★★★★	Site Privacy: ★
Spaciousness: ★★★	Quiet: ★★
Security: ★★	Cleanliness: ★★★
Insect Control: ★★	Facilities: ★★

Location, location, location. That's what it's all about here. True, the "camping area" here is nothing more than a parking lot, but who cares when you've got access to the Atlantic Ocean and panoramic views of Block Island Sound? Located on the east side of "the Breachway" is a camping area for self-contained RVs, a state beach, some of the best saltwater fishing in South County, a saltwater beach, and a panoramic view of Block Island Sound. Did we mention this is a prime spot for saltwater fishing? If you'd rather not fish from the shore or jetty, you can launch your boat here. A pathway leads to the beach, a picture-perfect crescent of tawny sand. The 75 RV sites, designated for self-contained units only, are marked with a rock painted with a number; higher numbers face the water. Good luck, though; this place is first come, first served, and scores of local folk have been coming year after year. The maximum stay during high season is one week, with a four-day break before returning.

BASICS

Operated By: Rhode Island Dept. of Environmental Management. **Open:** Apr. 15–Oct. 31. **Site Assignment:** First come, first served. **Registration:** At gate. **Fee:** Rhode Island residents, $14; nonresidents, $20. **Parking:** At site.

FACILITIES

Number of RV-only Sites: 1. **Number of Tent-only Sites:** 75. **Dump Station:** No (at Burlingame State Park). **Laundry:** No. **Pay Phone:** Yes. **Restrooms and Showers:** Restroom, no shower. **Fuel:** No. **Propane:** No. **Internal Roads:** Gravel. **RV Service:** No. **Market:** 10 mi. **Restaurant:** 10 mi. **General Store:** No. **Vending:** No. **Swimming:** Ocean. **Playground:** No. **Other:** Boat ramp. **Activities:** Ocean swimming, boating, kayaking, clamming, saltwater fishing (license required for nonresidents). **Nearby Attractions:** Foxwoods Casino. **Additional Information:** South County Tourism Council, (401) 789-4422 or (800) 548-4662; www.southcountyri.com.

RESTRICTIONS

Pets: Not allowed. **Fires:** Not allowed. **Alcoholic Beverages:** Not allowed. **Vehicle Maximum Length:** 40 ft. (plus a few sites available for 45 ft.). **Other:** After June 21, stay policy is 7 days in, 4 days out. Daily parking May 1–Sept. 30.

TO GET THERE

Take I-95 to Hwy. 4 south to Hwy. 1 south, to Charlestown Breachway exit. Follow signs.

EXETER   MAP, B-2
Peeper Pond Campground

159 Liberty Church Rd., 02822. T: (401) 294-5540; www.peeperpond.com.

🚐 ★★★   ▲ ★★★★

Beauty: ★★★	Site Privacy: ★★★
Spaciousness: ★★★★	Quiet: ★★★★
Security: ★★★	Cleanliness: ★★★
Insect Control: ★★★	Facilities: ★★

This rustic campground bills itself as the "alternative camping experience." Meaning? "No bells and whistles," as owner Phil Quish puts it. There are no campground bingo parties or sing-alongs here, just quiet, adult-oriented camping on 70 wooded acres. A nod to modernity: they do have a data port, so you can check your e-mail while you rough it. Stone walls remind one of old New England, and the scenic pond attracts otters, beavers, herons, Canada geese and, of course, peepers. City folk may find it difficult to sleep pondside; as Quish puts it, "The peepers' peeping can be deafening." The mix includes about one-third seasonal campers, the rest extended stay and transients. Tent sites include some primitive spots, restricted to parties of two adults only. We like the sites with tent decks (platforms that keep your tent off the ground). Site 1-A, a tent site, is private and faces the pond, and site 18 is a pretty pull-through accented with a stone wall. Site 27 is another lovely spot, set amid the pines. Noisy frogs aside, Peeper Pond is a serene base camp for exploring coastal Rhode Island.

BASICS

Operated By: Geraldine & Philip Quish. **Open:** May 1–Sept. 30. **Site Assignment:** Reservations required July & Aug. weekends; 1-night deposit to hold site; 7-day cancellation policy; 2-night min. July & Aug.; 3-night min. on holidays. **Registration:** At office. **Fee:** Trailer, $26; tent, $22; additional adult, $5; additional child, $3. **Parking:** At site; 1 car per site.

FACILITIES

Number of RV-only Sites: 6. **Number of Tent-only Sites:** 29. **Hookups:** Electric (20, 30 amps), water. **Each Site:** Picnic table, fire ring. **Dump Station:** Yes. **Laundry:** No. **Pay Phone:** Yes. **Restrooms and Showers:** Yes. **Fuel:** No. **Propane:** No. **Internal Roads:** Gravel. **RV Service:** No. **Market:** 4 mi. south. **Restaurant:** 2 mi. south on Hwy. 2. **General Store:** Yes. **Vending:** No. **Swimming:** No. **Playground:** No. **Other:** MC, V accepted. **Activities:** Badminton, horseshoes, volleyball. **Nearby Attractions:** Arcadia Management Area, Wickford Village (quaint New England town), Barber's Pond fishing area, Newport, Jamestown, Block Island, University of RI. **Additional Information:** South County Tourism Council, (401) 789-4422 or (800) 548-4662; www.southcountyri.com.

RESTRICTIONS

Pets: 1 per site. Must be leashed, quiet, cleaned up after. Must be under control. Allowed at owner's discretion. Some dogs restricted. **Fires:** In fire rings only; 6 p.m.–midnight. **Alcoholic Beverages:** W/in reason. **Vehicle Maximum Length:** 32–34 ft.

TO GET THERE

From I-95 south, take Exit 9. Travel south on Hwy. 4 to Exit 5B; go north on Hwy. 103, then south (left) on Hwy. 2. From Providence/Boston, the campground is located off Hwy. 2 between Hwy. 102 and Hwy. 138. Follow blue-and-white camping signs on Hwy. 2 to Mail Rd., then 1.5 mi. to Liberty Church Rd., and 0.8 mi. to campground. From I-95 north, take Exit 3A. Travel east on Hwy. 138, then go north (left) on Hwy. 2.

FOSTER   MAP, B-1
Ginny-B Campground

46 Johnson Rd., 02825.
T: (401) 397-9477 or (401) 397-7982;
www.ginny-b.com.

🚐 ★★★   ▲ ★★★

Beauty: ★★★	Site Privacy: ★★★
Spaciousness: ★★★	Quiet: ★★★
Security: ★★★	Cleanliness: ★★★
Insect Control: ★★★	Facilities: ★★★

This modest rural campground sits adjacent to the local country club golf course and offers a quiet place to call home for the night or longer. The property has a nice three-acre pond and swimming beach, a favorite spot for traveling families. There's also a tiny stream that runs through the campground, but it's small and often shallow and mucky. There are sites along the stream, but you might do better in the open sites, where there is more sunshine and fewer bugs. Sites 20–210 are nice, level wooded sites for those who prefer a bit more privacy. Some of the shower and toilet buildings are old and rusty but clean.

BASICS

Operated By: Virginia Bassett. **Open:** May 1–Sept. 30. **Site Assignment:** Reservations accepted. **Registration:** At office. **Fee:** Water/electric (midweek), $27; water/electric (Fri./Sat.), $28; weekly, $164. **Parking:** At site.

FACILITIES

Number of Multipurpose Sites: 200. **Hookups:** Electric (15, 20, 30, 50 amps), water, sewer. **Each Site:** Picnic table, fire ring. **Dump Station:** Yes. **Laundry:** Yes. **Pay Phone:** Yes. **Restrooms and Showers:** Yes. **Fuel:** No. **Propane:** Yes. **Internal Roads:** Paved, gravel (good). **RV Service:** No. **Market:** Foster, 5 mi. **Restaurant:** Foster, 5 mi. **General Store:** Yes. **Vending:** No. **Swimming:** Pond, river through middle of campground. **Playground:** Yes. **Other:** 2 rec halls, sports fields, pond, river frontage, safari field, adjacent to public golf course. **Activities:** Swimming, softball, horseshoes, basketball, volleyball, Sat. night dances, fishing, playground. **Nearby Attractions:** Farms, antiques shops, biking, hiking, Providence. **Additional Information:** Providence Warwick CVB, One West Exchange St., Providence, RI 02903; (800) 233-1636 or (401) 274-1636; www.providencecvb.com.

RESTRICTIONS

Pets: On leash only. **Fires:** Fire pits, grills only. **Alcoholic Beverages:** At site.

TO GET THERE

From Hwy. 6 on the Rhode Island–Connecticut state line, turn onto Cucumber Hill Rd., then travel 3.5 mi. to Harrington Rd. Turn left and drive 0.5 mi. to the campground.

GLOCESTER   MAP, A-1
George Washington Management Area

2185 Putnam Pike, 02814. T: (401) 568-2013.

🚐 ★★★   ▲ ★★★★★

Beauty: ★★★★★   Site Privacy: ★★★★
Spaciousness: ★★★★★   Quiet: ★★★★
Security: ★★★   Cleanliness: ★★★★
Insect Control: ★★★   Facilities: ★★

This back-to-basics, state-owned campground is part of the 3,489-acre wildlife management area and is perfect for campers looking for simple outdoor pursuits. There are two large ponds with a beach area, swimming, and lifeguard on duty. There are also miles of hiking trails accessible from the campground, meandering through woodlands, fields, and along ponds and streams. Campsites are set in the woods, with plenty of elbow room and privacy. Sites 15 and 16 are favorites, tucked under the trees with a pretty view of the lake. The nearby Bowdish Reservoir is a popular daytime excursion, where summer crowds congregate to swim, waterski, and powerboat.

BASICS

Operated By: State of Rhode Island. **Open:** Apr. 11–mid-Oct. **Site Assignment:** First come, first served; no credit cards. **Registration:** At office. **Fee:** Rhode Island residents, $8; nonresidents, $12; shelter, $20. **Parking:** At site.

FACILITIES

Number of RV-only Sites: 45. **Number of Multipurpose Sites:** 45. **Each Site:** Picnic table, fire ring. **Dump Station:** No. **Laundry:** No. **Pay Phone:** Yes. **Restrooms and Showers:** Outhouses, no showers. **Fuel:** No. **Propane:** No. **Internal Roads:** Gravel, dirt (good). **RV Service:** No. **Market:** Chepachet, 6 mi. **Restaurant:** Chepachet, 2 mi. **General Store:** No. **Vending:** No. **Swimming:** Freshwater swimming, public beach. **Playground:** No. **Other:** Lake frontage, beach, hiking trails, boat launch, grill, waterfront, campground. **Activities:** Swimming, biking, hiking, boating, fishing, canoeing, horseshoe pits, hunting, kayaking. **Nearby Attractions:** Farms, hiking, biking, boating, fishing, Blackstone Valley, Northern Rhode Island, Glocester Motor Inn, Freeman Farm. **Additional Information:** Blackstone River Valley Tourism Council, 175 Main St., Pawtucket, RI 02860; (800) 454-BVTC or (401) 724-2200; www.tourblackstone.com.

RESTRICTIONS

Pets: No pets. **Fires:** Fire pits, grills only. **Alcoholic Beverages:** Not allowed.

TO GET THERE

Campground is off Hwy. 44, about 10 mi. west of Chepachet near Connecticut border. Hwy. 44, 2 mi. east of Connecticut state line, 5.4 mi. west of the junction of Hwy. 44.

HOPE VALLEY   MAP, C-1
Whispering Pines Family Campground

P.O. Box 435, 41 Saw Mill Rd., 02832.
T: (401) 539-7011;
www.whisperingpinescamping.com.

🚐 ★★★★   ▲ ★★

Beauty: ★★★★   Site Privacy: ★★
Spaciousness: ★★★   Quiet: ★★★
Security: ★★   Cleanliness: ★★
Insect Control: ★★★   Facilities: ★★★

Located near the southwestern corner of Rhode Island, Whispering Pines is a dice toss from I-95 and Connecticut's Foxwoods Casino. Yes, we know, they all say they're close to Foxwoods, but this campground really means it! There's nothing glitzy about this place, though. It's heavily wooded, as the name implies, and rocky and hilly. It looks more like a state park property than a private campground, but there are all the frills of the latter, including mini-golf, a tennis court, a rec center, and even boat and bike rentals. There's also a swimming pond. Although the tall pines don't provide much buffer between campsites, site G-14 offers a bit of privacy. Sites W16–19 are also pretty and secluded. A nice touch here, and something we don't see often enough at private campgrounds: recycling bins. There's so much to do here, you may not even make it to the casino.

BASICS

Operated By: Private operator. **Open:** Mid-Apr.–mid-Oct. **Site Assignment:** May reserve online; $75 deposit required for each week of reservation; payment in full due for reservations of 3 days or less; 14-day cancellation policy; $10 fee. **Registration:** At office. **Fee:** Hookup, $36; no hookup, $32; hookup (Fri./Sat.), $44; no hookup (Fri./Sat.), $35; V, MC, AE. **Parking:** At site.

FACILITIES

Number of Tent-only Sites: 180. **Hookups:** Electric, water, sewer. **Each Site:** Picnic table, fire ring. **Dump Station:** Yes. **Laundry:** Yes. **Pay Phone:** Yes. **Restrooms and Showers:** Yes. **Fuel:** No. **Propane:** Yes. **Internal Roads:** Paved, gravel. **RV Service:** No. **Market:** 5 mi. east. **Restaurant:** 5 mi. east. **General Store:** Yes. **Vending:** Yes. **Swimming:** Pool. **Playground:** Yes. **Other:** Sports field, mini-golf, swimming pond, rec room, tennis courts. **Activities:** Biking (rentals available), boating (free use of pedal boats, rowing skiffs, & canoes), volleyball, shuffleboard, tennis, planned activities. **Nearby Attractions:** Foxwoods Casino, 20 minutes from Rhode Island's beaches, Mohegan Sun Casino. **Additional Information:** South County Tourism Council, (401) 789-4422 or (800) 548-4662; www.southcountyri.com.

RESTRICTIONS

Pets: Must be leashed, quiet, cleaned up after. Must not be left unattended. Keep pets off beach. **Fires:** In fire rings only, out after midnight. **Alcoholic Beverages:** At sites only.

TO GET THERE

From I-95, take Exit 3B (Hwy. 138); go 3.5 mi. west on Hwy. 138 to Saw Mill Rd.

JAMESTOWN   MAP, C-2
Fort Getty Recreation Area

P.O. Box 377, 02835. T: (401) 423-7211.

🚐 ★★★★★   ▲ ★★★★★

Beauty: ★★★★★   Site Privacy: ★★★
Spaciousness: ★★★★   Quiet: ★★★
Security: ★★★   Cleanliness: ★★★
Insect Control: ★★★   Facilities: ★★★

You won't find prettier views or a better location than this oceanfront park overlooking Narragansett Bay. Perched on a promontory near the southern tip of Jamestown Island, this campground is a premier property, popular with campers and day-use visitors. It occupies a former fort site; there are bunkers remaining from when Fort Getty was an ammunition depot during World War II. History buffs find it interesting, and kids like to explore the bunkers. Sites are set in an open, grassy field with views of the islands in Narragansett Bay and open ocean beyond. The park is also a great place to view the Dutch Island Lighthouse. A short walk from the campground leads to a nice beach and pavilion. Nearby is a boat ramp and fishing dock. On the opposite side of the campground, a short walk away, are nature trails leading through salt marshes and fields.

BASICS

Operated By: Jamestown township. **Open:** May 19–Oct. 3. **Site Assignment:** Reservations essential (a month in advance). **Registration:** At gate house. **Fee:** Tent, $20; parking, $15. **Parking:** At site.

FACILITIES

Number of RV-only Sites: 100. **Number of Tent-only Sites:** 25. **Number of Multipurpose Sites:** 103. **Hookups:** Electric (30 amps), water. **Each Site:** Fire ring. **Dump Station:** Yes. **Laundry:** No. **Pay Phone:** Yes. **Restrooms and Showers:** Yes. **Fuel:** No. **Propane:** No. **Internal Roads:** Paved (good). **RV Service:** No. **Market:** Jamestown, 2 mi. **Restaurant:** Jamestown, 2 mi. **General Store:** No. **Vending:** No. **Swimming:** Ocean beach. **Playground:** No. **Other:** Beach, ocean frontage, boat ramp, fishing dock, pavilion, trails. **Activities:** Swimming, boating, fishing, hiking, horseshoes. **Nearby Attractions:** Jamestown, Newport. **Additional Information:** Newport Visitor Information Center, 23 America's Cup Ave., Newport, RI 02840; (401) 845-9123 or (800) 976-5122; www.gonewport.com.

RESTRICTIONS

Pets: On leash only. **Fires:** Fire pits, grills only. **Alcoholic Beverages:** At site. **Vehicle Maximum Length:** 45 ft.

TO GET THERE

From Jamestown, take North Main St. to the south (toward Beavertail State Park). This road will cross Narragansett Rd. and turn into Southwest Ave. Follow Southwest Ave. to Beavertail Rd. The campground entrance is on the right. From Newport, follow Hwy. 138 west over Newport Bridge. Take the Jamestown exit. Bear right at the yield sign and continue until stop sign. Turn left onto Conanicus Ave. and go straight at the intersection. Follow road approx. 0.5 mi.; take a right onto Hamilton Ave. Go straight at stop sign and follow road out past

Mackarel Cove Beach. Take first right onto Fort Getty Rd.

NARRAGANSETT   MAP, C-2
Fishermen's Memorial State Park

Hwy. 108, 1011 Point Judith Rd., 02882.
T: (401) 789-8374; www.riparks.com.

🚐 ★★★★   ▲ ★★★★

Beauty: ★★★★   Site Privacy: ★★★
Spaciousness: ★★★   Quiet: ★★
Security: ★★★   Cleanliness: ★★★
Insect Control: ★★   Facilities: ★★★

Set on a salt pond overlooking Rhode Island Sound, this popular park is a former ammunition storage facility. That fact won't be terribly obvious to most campers, who are drawn to sweeping views of salt marsh and—beyond the state park—nearby ocean beaches. Sites are laid down in four grid-like pods, with the most desirable spots being numbers 70–75, which are fringed with sea oats and overlook the water. Site widths vary and include some good-sized pull-throughs. Among the grassy, open tent sites, 121, 125, and 126 offer the most privacy. Despite the crowds, this park is well maintained. The park draws lots of families, who stick around for the on-site farmer's market on summer Sundays. If you visit in high season (Memorial Day through Labor Day), plan to stay awhile—they've got a five-night minimum here. Happily, sites can be reserved in advance, starting in January, with sign-up forms available on the Internet.

BASICS

Operated By: Rhode Island Division of Parks & Recreation. **Open:** Apr. 15–Oct. 31. Winter camping, Nov. 1–14. **Site Assignment:** Reserve in advance online; reservations open Jan. 14; unreserved sites are first come, first served. **Registration:** At office. Opens 6 a.m.; sites sold at 8:30 a.m. **Fee:** Rhode Island residents, $14–$20; nonresidents, $20–$35. **Parking:** Residents, $2; nonresidents, $3 per car.

FACILITIES

Number of RV-only Sites: 34. **Number of Tent-only Sites:** 150. **Hookups:** Electric (30 amps), water, sewer. **Each Site:** Picnic table, fire ring. **Dump Station:** Yes. **Laundry:** No. **Pay Phone:** No. **Restrooms and Showers:** Yes. **Fuel:** No. **Propane:** No. **Internal Roads:** Paved. **RV Service:** No. **Market:** 1 mi. each direction. **Restaurant:** 1 mi. south. **General Store:** No. **Vending:** No. **Swimming:** No. **Playground:** Yes. **Other:** Tennis courts, basketball court, horseshoe pit. **Activities:** Tennis, basketball, horseshoes, farmer's market on site. **Nearby Attractions:** Ocean beaches, Sea Watch, Iggy's Doughboys & Chowder House. **Additional Information:** South County Tourism Council, (401) 789-4422 or (800) 548-4662; www.southcountyri.com.

RESTRICTIONS

Pets: Not allowed. **Fires:** In fire rings only. **Alcoholic Beverages:** Not allowed. **Other:** 5-night min. stay, Memorial Day–Labor Day.

TO GET THERE

From the junction of US 1 and Hwy. 108, go south 3.5 mi. on Hwy. 108. Take I-95 south, to Hwy. 4

south, to US 1 south, to Hwy. 108 south; 4 mi. along Hwy. 108 on right.

PASCOAG   MAP, A-1
Buck Hill Family Campground

464 Wakefield Pond Rd., 02859. T: (401) 568-0456.

🚐 ★★★★   ▲ ★★★★

Beauty: ★★★★   Site Privacy: ★★★★
Spaciousness: ★★★★   Quiet: ★★★★
Security: ★★★   Cleanliness: ★★★
Insect Control: ★★★   Facilities: ★★★

This off-the-beaten-path campground on the Massachusetts, Connecticut, and Rhode Island borders is an outdoor lover's paradise. The campground rests on the shores of 80-acre Wakefield Pond, with thousands of acres of wildlife preserve at its doorstep. There's a fine beach area (lifeguard on duty), boat rentals (paddleboats and canoes), archery and rifle ranges, and miles of hiking trails. Sites are extra spacious, and many are on the lake or have water views. Sites 35 and 36 are favorites, sitting on a tiny bluff overlooking the water, with lots of woods and privacy surrounding them. But you can't go wrong with any site. If you're looking for simple outdoor pursuits, lots of space, and plenty of peace and quiet, you'll find it here.

BASICS

Operated By: Rhode Island Boy Scouts. **Open:** May 1–Sept. 30. **Site Assignment:** Reservations essential; 50% deposit; 2-week cancellation policy; no credit cards. **Registration:** At office. **Fee:** Waterfront, $25; water view, $23; wooded, $21; tent, $15. **Parking:** At site.

FACILITIES

Number of RV-only Sites: 58. **Number of Tent-only Sites:** 41. **Number of Multipurpose Sites:** 52. **Hookups:** Electric (30 amps), water. **Each Site:** Picnic table, fire ring. **Dump Station:** Yes. **Laundry:** Yes. **Pay Phone:** Yes. **Restrooms and Showers:** Yes. **Fuel:** No. **Propane:** No. **Internal Roads:** Gravel, dirt (good). **RV Service:** No. **Market:** Pascoag, 6 mi. **Restaurant:** Pascoag, 6 mi. **General Store:** Yes. **Vending:** Yes. **Swimming:** Lake. **Playground:** Yes. **Other:** Lake frontage, beach, hiking trails, rec hall, rifle & archery ranges, boat rentals, game room. **Activities:** Swimming, fishing, boating, archery, skeet shooting, hiking, soccer, basketball, volleyball, baseball, rowing, hunting. **Nearby Attractions:** Farms, hiking, biking, fishing, boating, Blackstone Valley. **Additional Information:** Blackstone River Valley Tourism Council, 175 Main St., Pawtucket, RI 02860; (800) 454-BVTC or (401) 724-2200; www.tourblackstone.com.

RESTRICTIONS

Pets: On leash only. **Fires:** Fire pits, grills only (fireplaces provided). **Alcoholic Beverages:** At site.

TO GET THERE

From Pascoag, take Hwy. 100 north to Buck Hill Rd., then turn left on Wakefield Rd.

PORTSMOUTH   MAP, B-3
Melville Ponds Campground

181 Bradford Ave., 02871-6306. T: (401) 682-2424.

🚐 ★★★   ▲ ★★★

Beauty: ★★★   Site Privacy: ★★★
Spaciousness: ★★★   Quiet: ★★★
Security: ★★★   Cleanliness: ★★★
Insect Control: ★★★   Facilities: ★★

This modest, no-frills campground on Aquidneck Island in Portsmouth is town-owned and popular with traveling tourists and base campers. You can't beat the location—minutes from Newport attractions and some of Rhode Island's best beaches. During the day, the campground is usually quiet; campers head out to explore the area. Newport is the number one destination, but Cape Cod, Massachusetts, and Mystic Seaport, Connecticut, are both only about an hour's drive away. If you don't want to go far, the campground offers free passes to the town beach, a pretty cove, perfect for relaxing, swimming, and sunbathing. Shaded and open sites are available, half are reserved for tents and small pop-ups, but big rigs are welcome, too.

BASICS

Operated By: Town of Portsmouth. **Open:** Apr.–Oct. **Site Assignment:** Reservations suggested for holidays & festival weekends; 50% deposit; no refunds; no credit cards. **Registration:** At office. **Fee:** Full hookup, $35; tent, $22. **Parking:** At site.

FACILITIES

Number of RV-only Sites: 68. **Number of Tent-only Sites:** 60. **Number of Multipurpose Sites:** 33. **Hookups:** Electric (30 amps), water, sewer. **Each Site:** Picnic table, fire ring. **Dump Station:** Yes. **Laundry:** No. **Pay Phone:** Yes. **Restrooms and Showers:** Yes. **Fuel:** No. **Propane:** Yes. **Internal Roads:** Dirt, gravel (good). **RV Service:** No. **Market:** Portsmouth, 1 mi. **Restaurant:** Portsmouth, 1 mi. **General Store:** No. **Vending:** Yes. **Swimming:** No. **Playground:** Yes. **Other:** Free passes to local beach. **Activities:** Picnics, fishing. **Nearby Attractions:** Newport, beaches. **Additional Information:** Newport Visitor Information Center, 23 America's Cup Ave., Newport, RI 02840; (401) 845-9123 or (800) 976-5122; www.gonewport.com.

RESTRICTIONS

Pets: On leash only. **Fires:** Fire pits, grills only. **Alcoholic Beverages:** At site.

TO GET THERE

From Hwy. 114 in Portsmouth, take Stringham Rd., then turn right on Sullivan Rd. From the intersection of Hwy. 114 and Hwy. 138 go north 4.7 miles on Hwy. 114. From intersection of Hwy. 24 and Hwy. 114 go 1.7 mi. south on Hwy. 114 then 0.5 mi. west on Stringham Rd. The campground entrance is 0.5 mi. north on Sullivan Rd.

WEST GLOCESTER   MAP, A-1
Bowdish Lake Campground

P.O. Box 25, 02814. T: (401) 568-8890;
www.bowdishlake.com.

🚐 ★★★★   ⛺ ★★★★

Beauty: ★★★★   Site Privacy: ★★★★
Spaciousness: ★★★★   Quiet: ★★★★
Security: ★★★★   Cleanliness: ★★★★
Insect Control: ★★★   Facilities: ★★★★★

This campground in the northwest corner of Rhode Island, near the Connecticut and Massachusetts borders, blends outdoor scenery and pursuits with convenience and modern amenities. The property is large, spread across woods and fields, and with the George Washington Management Area next door, campers have acres of woods to roam and miles of trails to hike. The campground boasts two waterholes: a 300-acre lake with a half mile of frontage and a beautiful sandy beach and a 30-acre pond that is great for fishing. There are boat rentals and a boat launch at the campground. They also offer karaoke contests, live music, magicians, pony rides, and chainsaw wood-carving demonstrations. Alas, there is a good amount of seasonals at this campground, but more than 100 sites are available to transient campers. All sites are of decent size and feature stone fire pits and varied views.

BASICS
Operated By: Anna Tillinghast. **Open:** May–Oct. **Site Assignment:** Reservations accepted; 2-night min. weekends; 3-night min. holidays; 1-night deposit; no cash refunds, credit for future camping will be given for all reasonable cancellations made in writing before camping date; no credit cards. **Registration:** At office. **Fee:** Waterfront, $40; water area, $35; wooded, $30; field, $25. **Parking:** At site.

FACILITIES
Number of Multipurpose Sites: 400. **Hookups:** Electric (20, 30, 50 amps), water. **Each Site:** Picnic table, fire ring. **Dump Station:** Yes. **Laundry:** No. **Pay Phone:** Yes. **Restrooms and Showers:** Yes. **Fuel:** No. **Propane:** No. **Internal Roads:** Gravel, dirt (fair). **RV Service:** Yes. **Market:** Chepachet, 4 mi. **Restaurant:** Snack bar on site. **General Store:** Yes. **Vending:** Yes. **Swimming:** Lake. **Playground:** Yes. **Other:** Lake frontage, beach, boat rentals, tennis court, safari field, craft house, 2 rec halls, hiking trails. **Activities:** Swimming, hiking, boating, horseshoes, volleyball, planned activities. **Nearby Attractions:** Farms, hiking, biking, swimming, boating, fishing, Blackstone Valley, Providence, RISD Museum, Roger Williams Zoo. **Additional Information:** Blackstone River Valley Tourism Council, 175 Main St., Pawtucket, RI 02860, (800) 454-BVTC or (401) 724-2200; www.tourblackstone.com.

RESTRICTIONS
Pets: On leash only. Some breeds prohibited. $10/day charge. **Fires:** Fire pits, grills only. **Alcoholic Beverages:** At site.

TO GET THERE
Campground is located off Hwy. 44, about 10 mi. west of Chepachet. From junction of I-395 and Hwy. 44 E, travel 6 mi. on Hwy. 44.

WEST GREENWICH   MAP, B-1
Oak Embers

219 Escoheag Rd., 02817. T: (401) 397-4042;
www.oakembers.com.

🚐 ★★★   ⛺ ★★★

Beauty: ★★★   Site Privacy: ★★★
Spaciousness: ★★★★   Quiet: ★★★★
Security: ★★★★   Cleanliness: ★★★★
Insect Control: ★★★   Facilities: ★★★

This rural campground in western Rhode Island, next to the Connecticut border, looks and feels like an old-time summer camp. Remember days spent swimming and hiking, tossing a horseshoe or riding a horse, and ghost stories around the campfire? You can relive those days at this campground. Oak Embers combines old-fashioned fun with modern amenities. The campground is nestled in the woods, with decent-size sites set in loops and a separate tent area. Don't forget to bring your hiking boots. Nearby is Rhode Island's largest preserve. The 13,817-acre Arcadia Wildlife Management Area offers an extensive system of trails—more than 30 miles—through woodlands, freshwater wetlands, and along scenic rivers and ponds. Oak Embers pool and hot showers will look mighty good when you return.

BASICS
Operated By: Jack & Fran Smith. **Open:** May–Sept. **Site Assignment:** Reservations suggested; 1-night deposit; 1-week cancellation policy; no credit cards. **Registration:** At office. **Fee:** Water/electric, $30; no hookup, $28; A/C & heaters, $2. **Parking:** At site.

FACILITIES
Number of RV-only Sites: 23. **Number of Multipurpose Sites:** 37. **Hookups:** Electric (30 amps), water. **Each Site:** Picnic table, fire ring. **Dump Station:** Yes. **Laundry:** Yes. **Pay Phone:** Yes. **Restrooms and Showers:** Yes. **Fuel:** No. **Propane:** No. **Internal Roads:** Gravel, some pavement (good). **RV Service:** No. **Market:** Voluntown, 5 mi. **Restaurant:** Voluntown, 5 mi. **General Store:** Yes. **Vending:** Yes. **Swimming:** Pool. **Playground:** Yes. **Other:** Rec room, sports fields, trails, Internet available. **Activities:** Swimming, horseback riding, volleyball, softball, horseshoes, badminton, hiking. **Nearby Attractions:** Swimming, hiking, biking, fishing, boating, Foxwoods & Mohegan Sun casinos, South County beaches. **Additional Information:** Contact the South County Tourism Council, 4808 Tower Hill Rd., Wakefield, (800) 548-4662 or (401) 789-4422; or the East Greenwich Chamber of Commerce, 591 Main St., East Greenwich, RI 02818, (401) 885-0020; www.eastgreenwichchamber.com.

RESTRICTIONS
Pets: On leash only. Some breeds prohibited. **Fires:** Fire pits, grills only. **Alcoholic Beverages:** At site. **Vehicle Maximum Length:** 40 ft.

TO GET THERE
From I-95, take Exit 5A. Follow Hwy. 5 to Hwy. 3. Continue on Hwy. 3 to Hwy. 165; turn right and continue to Escoheag Rd.; turn right to campground.

WEST KINGSTON   MAP, C-2
Wawaloam Campground

510 Gardiner Rd., 02892. T: (401) 294-3039;
www.wawaloam.com.

🚐 ★★★★   ⛺ ★

Beauty: ★★★   Site Privacy: ★★
Spaciousness: ★★★   Quiet: ★★★
Security: ★★★★   Cleanliness: ★★★★
Insect Control: ★★★   Facilities: ★★★★

A sure sign this RV campground caters to families: a swimming pool with a serpentine waterslide. It's little wonder that weekend stays are booked a year in advance—few active families can resist a park that offers a fishing pond, mini-golf, and sports fields to play catch and kick around a soccer ball. Not to mention the planned activities and playground area. Of the 300 RV sites, about 200 are seasonal, which adds to the neighborhood feel of the place. Tent sites are open and grassy, set around the playground and pool area (near the restrooms), whereas RV sites are laid out on streets that run behind the public areas. Squirrel Street and Mohawk are fairly peaceful and wooded, especially sites 47 and 52, with views of the waterslide. Site 83, located on a corner, offers a good degree of privacy. You'll never mistake this place for a secluded woodland getaway, but it offers plenty of fun.

BASICS
Operated By: Jim & Maureen Smith. **Open:** Apr. 28–Oct. 29. **Site Assignment:** Reservations required in summer, especially weekends; deposit of 1-night's stay required w/in 2 weeks. **Registration:** At office. **Fee:** Water/electric, $36; weekly, $75; V, MC, D, AE. **Parking:** At site & visitor's lot.

FACILITIES
Number of RV-only Sites: 20. **Number of Tent-only Sites:** 280. **Number of Multipurpose Sites:** 20. **Hookups:** Electric, water, sewer. **Each Site:** Picnic table, fire ring. **Dump Station:** Yes. **Laundry:** Yes. **Pay Phone:** Yes. **Restrooms and Showers:** Yes, fee. **Fuel:** Yes. **Propane:** Yes. **Internal Roads:** Paved, gravel. **RV Service:** No. **Market:** 3 mi. east. **Restaurant:** Snack bar on site. **General Store:** Yes. **Vending:** Yes. **Swimming:** Pool w/ waterslide. **Playground:** Yes. **Other:** Sports field, basketball court, mini-golf, rec halls. **Activities:** Basketball, mini-golf, horseshoes, planned activities, fishing, Fri. night dinner & Sun. morning breakfast. **Nearby Attractions:** Ocean beaches, restaurants, Newport, Mystic Seaport & Aquarium, Block Island, Foxwoods Casino. **Additional Information:** South County Tourism Council, (401) 789-4422 or (800) 548-4662; www.southcountyri.com.

RESTRICTIONS
Pets: Must be leashed, quiet, cleaned up after. Must not be left unattended. **Fires:** In fire rings only. **Alcoholic Beverages:** At sites only. **Vehicle Maximum Length:** 35 ft. box length (hitch not included).

TO GET THERE
From I-95, take Exit 5A; bear right on Hwy. 3. Take first left onto Hwy. 102 south; go 1.5 mi. to Town Hall Rd. (school), bear right. Gardiner Rd. is first left after old Town Hall. Go 1.5 mi. on Gardiner to campground.

South Carolina

South Carolina really packs it in. Visitors encounter a small state rich in history, the arts, and outdoor beauty. Three geographical regions offer diversity not found in many larger states. The coastal **Low Country** is known for its gorgeous live oak and marshes, complete with blue herons and other birds. The rolling **Piedmont** offers hunting and freshwater recreation. The **Highlands** lie in the foothills of the Blue Ridge Mountains and reach elevations over 3,500 feet.

South Carolina's many native peoples include the Catawba, known for their pottery, which has been produced by the same techniques for almost 1,000 years. The Catawba, which means "people of the river," are indigenous to the banks of what is now known as the **Catawba River.** Their territory extended to **Broad River,** which was their boundary with the Cherokee. Their population rapidly declined as a result of consistent warfare and disease. Although there are no longer any full-blooded Catawba natives, about 2,200 descendents occupy a 640-acre reservation located in the vicinity of **Rock Hill.**

European settlers found the South Carolina Low Country perfect for rice cultivation, which began in the 1680s. Rice remained essential even as cotton production became more profitable after the invention of the cotton gin in 1793. Rice, cotton, and slave labor brought vast fortunes to antebellum South Carolina. Many historic homes and plantations still stand today and are open for touring. Charleston's historic district is the site of urban antebellum buildings as well as the **Dock Street Theater,** the oldest theater building in America. Notable plantations include Middleton Place, where Southern strategists gathered in the American Revolution, and **Magnolia Plantation,** home of the nation's oldest landscaped garden. The Low Country covers about two-thirds of South Carolina, from the Atlantic Ocean extending west. The land rises gradually from the southeast to the northwest.

The Fall Line, where the upland rivers "fall" to the Low Country is the border between the Low Country and the Piedmont region. The Piedmont region is marked by higher elevations, ranging from 400 to 1,200 feet above sea level. The rolling hills here begin moderately in the east and gradually become more intense moving westward.

The Highlands region covers the northwestern corner of South Carolina. This region is part of the **Blue Ridge Mountain** chain, which extends from Pennsylvania all the way to Georgia. The portion located in South Carolina is lower and less rugged than those to the north, rarely exceeding 3,000 feet.

The Civil War began on April 12, 1861, when Confederates attacked **Fort Sumter** at **Charleston Harbor.** After this battle, South Carolina saw relatively little fighting, though roughly 13,000 South Carolinians died in the Civil War. In 1864, Charleston was the launch site for the *H. L. Hunley,* a prototypical submarine that successfully torpedoed and sank the **USS** *Housatonic.* A replica of the *Hunley* is on display at the **South Carolina State Museum** in Columbia. The aftermath of the Civil War was devastating to South Carolina. The state lost almost one-fifth of its white male population, and the economy received a crippling blow when Gen. William T. Sherman marched his troops through the state, burning plantations and much of the city of Columbia.

South Carolina's economy still depends on agriculture (especially soy, tobacco, peaches, and livestock), but textiles, tourism, and numerous other industries also flourish. Tourists and locals support performing arts in South Carolina. Fine performing arts are appreciated in the state's refurbished opera houses (in **Newberry, Abbeville, and Sumter**) and larger venues in Charleston and **Greenville.** For casual entertainment, **Myrtle Beach** stages numerous production shows.

Golfers from all over the world pilgrimage to **Hilton Head Island,** site of the **Worldcom Classic**—the **Heritage of Golf** (formerly the Heritage Classic). Of the 36 courses in the Hilton Head area, **Harbor Town** is instantly recognizable with its red-and-white-striped lighthouse, visible from many holes. Myrtle Beach and the **Grand Strand** now contain more than 100 courses, some excellent and others inexpensive. There are few areas in the world that offer so many golfing choices.

Campground Profiles

ANDERSON   MAP, A-1
Springfield Campground

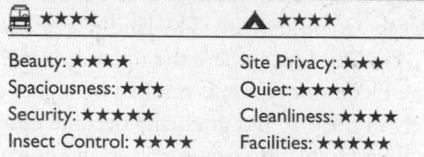

Hartwell Lake, Providence Church Rd., 29625.
T: (888) 893-0678 or (877) 444-6777;
www.reserveamerica.com.

🚐 ★★★★   ⛺ ★★★★

Beauty: ★★★★★   Site Privacy: ★★★★
Spaciousness: ★★★★★   Quiet: ★★★★
Security: ★★★★★   Cleanliness: ★★★★
Insect Control: ★★★   Facilities: ★★★

Springfield Campground at Hartwell Lake boasts some of the most beautiful campsites we've seen. Along the shoreline, most sites have gorgeous water views. Sites 67–79 are especially stunning—huge and private with fabulous views. Sites 32–36 are less private, but have even better views. Sites 25, 26, 47, and 48 are good for families as they are roomy and close to the playground. Sites have gravel parking in pull-throughs and back-ins. There are plenty of shady trees, although site privacy varies. One of three reservoirs on the Savannah River, 56,000-acre Lake Hartwell is stocked with crappie, stripers, catfish, and largemouth and hybrid bass. There are a number of other recreation areas within 10 miles of the park. Security is outstanding at this rural campground. The gate is guarded by day and locked by night. Avoid Lake Hartwell on holiday weekends and during summer heat.

BASICS
Operated By: U.S. Army Corps of Engineers. **Open:** Apr. 1–Sept. 30. **Site Assignment:** First come, first served; reservations accepted through National Recreation Reservation Service (NRRS) at (877) 444-6777; reservations can be made up to 240 days in advance, full payment required upon making reservation; credit card preferred (V, MC, D, AE), or pay by money order if at least 21 days in advance of arrival; $10 fee for cancellation or change of site or dates; cancellation w/in 3 days of arrival charged 1 night, no-show charged $20 plus 1 night. **Registration:** At gate house. **Fee:** Peak season, $18; off-season, $16; 10 people max.; includes 1 wheeled camping unit or tents that fit on impact pad. **Parking:** 3 vehicles per site.

FACILITIES
Number of Multipurpose Sites: 79. **Hookups:** Electric (50 amps), water. **Each Site:** Picnic table, fire ring or grill, lantern post. **Dump Station:** Yes. **Laundry:** No. **Pay Phone:** Yes. **Restrooms and Showers:** Yes. **Fuel:** No. **Propane:** No. **Internal Roads:** Paved. **RV Service:** 30 mi. north in Greenville. **Market:** 7 mi. east in Anderson. **Restaurant:** 4 mi. east in Anderson. **General Store:** 1 mi. east in Anderson. **Vending:** No. **Swimming:** Lake swimming, beach. **Playground:** Yes. **Other:** Boat ramp (w/ security light), courtesy dock, picnic area. **Activities:** Swimming beaches, fishing, swim access from most campsites. **Nearby Attractions:** Historic Pendleton,

Clemson University, Anderson Flea Market, Anderson County Museum, Arts Center. **Additional Information:** Anderson Chamber of Commerce, (864) 226-3454, www.andersonsc.com.

RESTRICTIONS
Pets: On leash only. **Fires:** Campsites only. **Alcoholic Beverages:** Not allowed. **Vehicle Maximum Length:** No limit. **Other:** 14-day stay limit during any 30 consecutive-day period.

TO GET THERE
From I-85, take Exit 11 onto Hwy. 24 east. Drive 4 mi. to Hwy. 187S. Turn right onto Hwy. 187 and drive south 5 mi. Turn right on Providence Church Rd. Follow Providence Church Rd. to the campground.

BISHOPVILLE   MAP, A-3, B-3
Lee State Natural Area

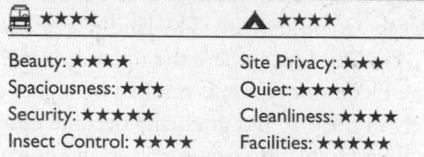

487 Loop Rd., 29010. T: (803) 428-5307;
www.reserveamerica.com.

🚐 ★★★★   ⛺ ★★★★

Beauty: ★★   Site Privacy: ★★★
Spaciousness: ★★★   Quiet: ★★★★
Security: ★★★★   Cleanliness: ★★★
Insect Control: ★★★   Facilities: ★★★★

Lee State Park, built in the 1930s by the Civilian Conservation Corps, is a gateway to the state scenic Lynches River. Other natural features in the park include a vast hardwood floodplain forest, numerous artesian springs, and sandhills habitat. A variety of plants and animals are found throughout the park. The campground has 25 campsites. Each site is rented on a first-come, first-served basis, except for two sites that may be reserved exclusively for the handicapped. Each site is packed soil, has individual water and electrical hookups and a picnic table. The campground has heated restroom facilities with hot showers. Some sites accommodate RVs up to 36 feet, others up to 30 feet. Nine sites are pull-through. There are dump stations for RVs. Camping clubs are allowed to reserve 10–15 sites. There is a primitive camping area for organized groups. This area includes central water and a privy. The capacity is 100 people. There are also two picnic shelters, available on a first-come, first-served basis. The park offers a short nature trail, equestrian stables, and a 12-mile nature trail. Enjoy fishing in Lynches River for bream, catfish, and bass.

BASICS
Operated By: South Carolina State Parks. **Open:** All year. **Site Assignment:** Reservations can be made 11 months in advance. **Registration:** At office. **Fee:** Single, $9–$14; picnic shelters, $25–$32; group, $135–$169. **Parking:** At site.

FACILITIES
Number of Multipurpose Sites: 56. **Hookups:** Yes. **Each Site:** Fire ring. **Dump Station:** Yes.

Laundry: No. **Pay Phone:** Yes. **Restrooms and Showers:** Yes. **Fuel:** Less than 5 mi. **Propane:** No. **Internal Roads:** Paved. **RV Service:** Less than 20 mi. **Market:** Less than 5 mi. **Restaurant:** Less than 5 mi. **General Store:** Less than 5 mi. **Vending:** No. **Swimming:** Yes. **Playground:** No. **Activities:** Bird-watching, canoeing, fishing, hiking, kayaking, nature study, photography, picnicking, walking, wildlife viewing.

RESTRICTIONS
Pets: On a leash or other physical restraint at all times. **Fires:** In designated fireplaces. **Alcoholic Beverages:** Not allowed. **Vehicle Maximum Length:** 36 ft.

TO GET THERE
Lee State Natural Area is located 7 mi. east of Bishopville. From I-20, take Exit 123 (Lee State Park Rd.). Go 1 mi. N. and turn left into the park entrance.

BLACKSBURG   MAP, A-2
Kings Mountain State Park

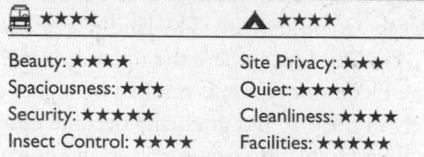

1277 Park Rd., 29702. T: (803) 222-3209;
www.reserveamerica.com.

🚐 ★★★★   ⛺ ★★★★

Beauty: ★★★★   Site Privacy: ★★★
Spaciousness: ★★★   Quiet: ★★★★
Security: ★★★★★   Cleanliness: ★★★★
Insect Control: ★★★★   Facilities: ★★★★★

Bordering King's Mountain National Military Park Revolutionary War battle sight, this park is home to the Living History Farm. This park also offers impressive outdoor activities. Situated in a gorgeous stand of white and red oak and hickory, the hilly campground includes both back-in and pull-through sites. Want a level site? Try 1, 4, 6, 8, 39, or 47 (all back-ins). If you're attached to a pull-through, you may have to deal with sloped parking. All sites are comfortably spaced with some plant growth to provide privacy between sites. Parking is on dirt or gravel. Security is excellent at rural King's Mountain; the park gates are closed at all times and campers are given a combination to open them. The campground was extremely quiet when we visited. In fact, King's Mountain only fills to capacity on holiday weekends, making it an excellent destination on other summer weekends.

BASICS
Operated By: South Carolina State Parks. **Open:** All year. **Site Assignment:** Camping reservations accepted online or by phone (866) 345-PARK; 2-night min. **Registration:** Camp store, ranger makes rounds off-season. **Fee:** Water/electric, $16–$18; tent, $12–$13; South Carolina seniors & disabled, discounted rate. **Parking:** At sites except tent sites.

FACILITIES
Number of Tent-only Sites: 10. **Number of**

Multipurpose Sites: 116. **Hookups:** Electric (20, 30 amps), water. **Each Site:** Picnic table. **Dump Station:** Yes. **Laundry:** Yes (in-season). **Pay Phone:** Yes. **Restrooms and Showers:** Yes. **Fuel:** No. **Propane:** No. **Internal Roads:** Main park roads paved, campground roads gravel. **RV Service:** 8 mi. northwest in Kings Mountain. **Market:** 8 mi. northwest in Kings Mountain. **Restaurant:** 5 mi. **General Store:** 10 mi. southeast in Clover, Ace Hardware, or Wal-Mart 16 mi. southeast in York. **Vending:** Yes. **Swimming:** No. **Playground:** No. **Other:** Living history farm (barn, cotton gin, blacksmith/carpenter shop, gardens, livestock), park store, picnic shelters. **Activities:** Hiking & equestrian trails, equestrian camping, fishing, fishing boat, paddleboat & canoe rentals, mini-golf. **Nearby Attractions:** Kings Mountain National Military Park, Anne Springs Close Greenway nature preserve, Historic Brattonsville, Fort Mill Confederate Park, 30 miles from Charlotte, North Carolina. **Additional Information:** Clover Chamber of Commerce, (803) 222-3312.

RESTRICTIONS

Pets: Leash (6 ft. max.). **Fires:** Allowed. **Alcoholic Beverages:** Not allowed. **Vehicle Maximum Length:** 40 ft.

TO GET THERE

From I-85 (NC Exit 2), drive east on SC 216. SC 216 turns into Park Rd. and goes through Kings Mountain National Military Park. Headquarters is on the right approx. 9 mi. from I-85.

BLACKVILLE   MAP, B-2
Barnwell State Park

reserve america

223 State Park Rd., 29817. T: (803) 284-2212; www.reserveamerica.com.

🚐 ★★★★   ⛺ ★★★★

Beauty: ★★★	Site Privacy: ★★
Spaciousness: ★★	Quiet: ★★★
Security: ★★★★	Cleanliness: ★★★
Insect Control: ★★★	Facilities: ★★★

Acquired in 1937, Barnwell State Park is a 307-acre park situated along the coastal plain in Barnwell County. Known for its lake fishing and large meeting facility, Barnwell features five vacation cabins, a 25-site camping area, and a nature trail. The two park lakes provide day-visitors and overnight guests the opportunity to appreciate the natural features while enjoying the recreational opportunities on the park. The park was originally constructed by the Civilian Conservation Corps, a public works program set up in the 1930s by President Franklin D. Roosevelt's New Deal. Examples of its work can be seen at the spillway, picnic shelters, and the lower lake. Each of the 25 campsites available at Barnwell State Park is packed gravel and includes individual water and electrical hookups. Two of the campsites may be reserved exclusively for the handicapped. The campground is convenient to restrooms with hot showers. Four sites accommodate RVs up to 36 feet, others up to 28 feet. A dump station is available for

RVs. Camping clubs may reserve up to 20 sites. The primitive group camping area is ideal for organized groups up to 50 people. The area includes picnic tables, fire ring, and nearby restroom. Cabins are completely furnished, heated, air-conditioned, and supplied with linens, basic cooking and eating utensils, coffee maker, and a television. The cabins are located 100 yards from the upper lake and 300 yards from the lower lake. Pets are not permitted in the cabins or cabin area. Four picnic shelters are available for family or other group gatherings.

BASICS

Operated By: South Carolina State Parks. **Open:** All year. **Site Assignment:** Reservations can be made 11 months in advance. **Registration:** At office. **Fee:** Single, $10–$13; picnic shelter, $25–$32; cabin, $39–$360; community building, $200–$250. **Parking:** At site.

FACILITIES

Number of Multipurpose Sites: 38. **Hookups:** Yes. **Each Site:** Fire ring. **Dump Station:** Yes. **Laundry:** Less than 5 mi. **Pay Phone:** Less than 5 mi. **Restrooms and Showers:** Yes. **Fuel:** Less than 5 mi. **Propane:** No. **Internal Roads:** Paved. **RV Service:** No. **Market:** Less than 5 mi. **Restaurant:** Less than 5 mi. **General Store:** Less than 5 mi. **Vending:** No. **Swimming:** Yes. **Playground:** No. **Activities:** Biking, bird-watching, fishing, hiking, paddleboating, photography, picnicking, stargazing.

RESTRICTIONS

Pets: On a leash or other physical restraint at all times. **Fires:** In designated fireplaces. **Alcoholic Beverages:** Not allowed. **Vehicle Maximum Length:** 36 ft.

TO GET THERE

Barnwell State Park is located 7 mi. northeast of Barnwell and 3 mi. southwest of Blackville on SC 3. From I-20, take Exit 18 or Exit 22 to Aiken. From Aiken take Hwy. 78 east to Blackville. Turn right onto SC 3 and travel 2 mi. Park is on the right.

CALHOUN FALLS   MAP, B-1
Calhoun Falls State Park

reserve america

46 Maintenance Shop Rd., 29628. T: (864) 447-8267; www.reserveamerica.com.

🚐 ★★★★★   ⛺ ★★★★★

Beauty: ★★★★★	Site Privacy: ★★★★★
Spaciousness: ★★★★★	Quiet: ★★★★★
Security: ★★★★	Cleanliness: ★★★★★
Insect Control: ★★★★	Facilities: ★★★★

Calhoun Falls SRA was developed jointly by the U.S. Army Corps of Engineers and South Carolina State Parks. The collaboration is a boon to campers, with recreation typical of state parks and large, gorgeous campsites typical of Corps campgrounds. For anglers, Lake Russell is home to a variety of bass, bluegill, crappie, and catfish. For the children there are six playgrounds. The campground features extremely spacious sites with paved parking. Each

site has a sandy picnic and tent area. Sites are afforded shade and privacy by thick, lovely woods. Campsites with hookups are found in two areas and tent-only sites in a third. Of the lakefront sites, back-ins are often more attractive than pull-throughs. Security is fair at Calhoun Falls; although the park is extremely rural and gates are locked at night, the gates are not always attended during the day. Avoid visiting on busy summer weekends.

BASICS

Operated By: South Carolina State Parks. **Open:** All year. **Site Assignment:** Camping reservations accepted online or by phone (866) 345-PARK; 2-night min. **Registration:** At camp store, rangers collect after hours. **Fee:** Water/electric, $19–$21; tent, $14–$15. **Parking:** Site plus overflow parking.

FACILITIES

Number of Tent-only Sites: 14. **Number of Multipurpose Sites:** 86. **Hookups:** Electric (20, 30 amps), water. **Each Site:** Picnic table, grill, fire ring, lantern holder. **Dump Station:** Yes. **Laundry:** Yes. **Pay Phone:** Yes. **Restrooms and Showers:** Yes. **Fuel:** No. **Propane:** At marina. **Internal Roads:** Paved. **RV Service:** 30 mi. north in Anderson. **Market:** 2 mi. south in Calhoun Falls. **Restaurant:** 2 mi. south in Calhoun Falls. **General Store:** Camp store. **Vending:** Beverages. **Swimming:** Lake (at own risk). **Playground:** Yes. **Other:** Boat ramp. **Activities:** Fishing, skiing, boating, nonmotorized boat rentals, swimming when lifeguard on duty, walking trail, basketball, tennis. **Nearby Attractions:** Sumter National Forest, Lake Russell Dam (Information Center in Georgia), Abbeville Historic District, walking tours. **Additional Information:** Abbeville Chamber of Commerce, (864) 459-4600.

RESTRICTIONS

Pets: On leash only. Leash not longer than 6 feet. **Fires:** At sites, rings only. **Alcoholic Beverages:** In sites, out of view. **Vehicle Maximum Length:** Varies. **Other:** 14-day stay limit.

TO GET THERE

From Calhoun Falls, at the intersection of SC 81 and SC 72, take SC 81 north 1 mi. The park entrance is on the left.

CANADYS   MAP, C-3
Colleton State Park

reserve america

147 Wayside Lane, 29433. T: (843) 538-8206; www.reserveamerica.com.

🚐 ★★★★   ⛺ ★★★★

Beauty: ★★★	Site Privacy: ★★★
Spaciousness: ★★★	Quiet: ★★★★
Security: ★★★★	Cleanliness: ★★★
Insect Control: ★★★	Facilities: ★★★★

This 35-acre park was originally built as a wayside park in the 1930s by the Civilian Conservation Corps. Campers, anglers, canoeists, and other outdoor enthusiasts enjoy the peaceful and relaxing black waters of the Edisto River. Only five minutes from I-95, this park is a popular stopover for interstate travelers. Colleton State Park is on a portion of the river that has been designated as an official canoe and kayak trail which carries paddlers into a rare, natural world of wildlife and scenic beauty. The canoe trail between Colleton and Givhans Ferry is 23 miles by river—seven to nine hours, depending on current and paddling skills. The camping area offers 25 campsites on the Edisto River. Each campsite is rented on a first-come, first-served basis, except for two sites that may be reserved exclusively for the handicapped. Enjoy fishing in the Edisto River for bream, redbreast, catfish. River access for private boats is 0.25 miles from the park. Picnic shelters are available on a first-come, first-served basis.

BASICS

Operated By: South Carolina Dept. of Parks, Recreation & Tourism. **Open:** All year. **Site Assignment:** Reservations can be made up to 16 weeks in advance. **Registration:** At office. **Fee:** Single, $10–$13; day-use picnic shelter, $25–$32. **Parking:** 2 vehicles per site.

FACILITIES

Number of Multipurpose Sites: 28. **Hookups:** Yes. **Dump Station:** Yes. **Laundry:** Less than 20 mi. **Pay Phone:** Yes. **Restrooms and Showers:** Yes. **Fuel:** Less than 5 mi. **Propane:** Less than 1 mi. **Internal Roads:** Paved. **RV Service:** Yes. **Market:** Less than 20 mi. **Restaurant:** Less than 5 mi. **General Store:** Less than 1 mi. **Vending:** No. **Swimming:** Yes. **Playground:** Yes. **Activities:** Baseball, bird-watching, fishing, hiking, picnicking, stargazing, volleyball, wildflower viewing. **Nearby Attractions:** Boating, canoeing, kayaking, fruit picking, scenic driving routes.

RESTRICTIONS

Pets: All pets must remain on leash. **Alcoholic Beverages:** Not allowed. **Vehicle Maximum Length:** 40 ft. **Other:** Quiet hours are 10 p.m.–7 a.m.

TO GET THERE

Colleton State Park is located off I-95, Exit 68. Head east toward Canadys on Hwy. 61. Go 3 mi. to Hwy. 15. Take Hwy. 15N. (left) 0.5 mi. The park is on the left.

CHERAW
Cheraw State Park   MAP, A-3

reserve america

100 State Park Rd., 29520. T: (843) 537-9656; www.reserveamerica.com.

🚐 ★★★   ⛺ ★★★

Beauty: ★★★   Site Privacy: ★★★
Spaciousness: ★★★   Quiet: ★★★★
Security: ★★★★   Cleanliness: ★★★
Insect Control: ★★★   Facilities: ★★★★

South Carolina's first state park property was originally built in the 1930s by the Civilian Conservation Corps. Cheraw State Park is located in the Sandhills region. The park's 360-acre lake offers fishing and

various recreational opportunities in a beautiful setting. Towering cypress trees at the upper end of the lake are among the park's best kept secrets. Cabins and lakefront campsites are available for overnight guests. A championship 18-hole golf course with a full-service pro shop is the park's newest addition. Eight one-bedroom/one-bath cabins accommodate four people each. Contact the park for reservations, and specifics on cabins. The campground has 17 campsites that are rented on a first-come, first-served basis, except for one site that may be reserved exclusively for the handicapped. Each site has individual water and electrical hookups, fire ring, and picnic table. There are two group camp sites. The park's newest addition is an 18-hole championship golf course and pro shop. The park's equestrian trails connect to Sandhills State Forest equestrian trails. Other park amenities include: walking and nature trails, fishing, equestrian facilities, picnic shelters, and playground equipment. Cheraw State Park offers numerous outdoor recreation activities. The main activities are camping, picnicking, fishing, boating, hiking, horseback riding and golfing. Seasonal lake swimming and paddleboat rentals are offered upon availability of lifeguards. The park also protects habitats for the threatened Red Cockaded woodpecker.

BASICS

Operated By: South Carolina Dept. of Parks, Recreation & Tourism. **Open:** All year. **Site Assignment:** Reservations can be made up to 16 weeks in advance. **Registration:** At office. **Fee:** Single, $6–$15; group, $135–$280; cabin, $52–$164; day-use community building, $180–$225; picnic shelter, $25–$32. **Parking:** 2 vehicles per site.

FACILITIES

Number of Multipurpose Sites: 46. **Hookups:** Yes. **Dump Station:** Yes. **Laundry:** Less than 5 mi. **Pay Phone:** Yes. **Restrooms and Showers:** Yes. **Fuel:** Less than 5 mi. **Propane:** Less than 5 mi. **Internal Roads:** Paved. **RV Service:** Yes. **Market:** Less than 5 mi. **Restaurant:** Less than 5 mi. **General Store:** Yes. **Vending:** Yes. **Swimming:** Yes. **Playground:** Yes. **Activities:** Bird-watching, boating, equestrian camping, canoeing, fishing, golfing, hiking, horseback riding, picnicking, kayaking, paddleboating, volleyball, wildlife/wildflowers. **Nearby Attractions:** Biking, field sports, tennis, waterskiing, jet skiing. **Additional Information:** Please contact the park to reserve ADA (disabled access) standard full-service sites. "Stay Play" golf specials are available for Cheraw.

RESTRICTIONS

Pets: On a leash not to exceed 6 feet. **Fires:** Fire rings are furnished for campfires. **Vehicle Maximum Length:** 45 ft.

TO GET THERE

Cheraw State Park is located 4 mi. south of the town of Cheraw on Hwy. 52. Turn right off Hwy. 52 at the main park entrance for the golf course, cabins, picnic area, shelters, community/recreation building, boat rentals, and park office. For the campground, boat landing, horse area, and group camps, continue on Hwy. 52 to the next park entrance road located on the right.

CHESTER
Chester State Park   MAP, A-2

reserve america

759 State Park Dr., 29706. T: (803) 385-2680; www.reserveamerica.com.

🚐 ★★★★   ⛺ ★★★★

Beauty: ★★★   Site Privacy: ★★★
Spaciousness: ★★★   Quiet: ★★★★
Security: ★★★★   Cleanliness: ★★★
Insect Control: ★★★   Facilities: ★★★★

Chester State Park rests in the quiet hills of the South Carolina Piedmont and for generations has offered retreat and recreation to the surrounding communities. The park's 523 acres include a 160-acre lake, itself surrounded by a 2-mile nature trail through the pine forest. Jon boat rentals are popular in the warmer months, and the park also offers picnicking, camping, archery, and a place to simply enjoy the serenity of the placid setting. The Civilian Conservation Corps built the park, and its work can still be seen and enjoyed today. The community building is heavily used year-round, adding to the secluded park's value as a place to both gather and get away. Each site is packed soil and has individual water and electrical hookups. Some sites accommodate RVs up to 33 feet, others up to 28 feet, while five sites are pull-through. The campground is convenient to restrooms with hot showers.

BASICS

Operated By: South Carolina State Parks. **Open:** All year. **Site Assignment:** Reservations can be made 11 months in advance. **Registration:** At office. **Fee:** Single, $10–$13; picnic shelter, $25–$32; community building, $160–$200. **Parking:** At site.

FACILITIES

Number of Multipurpose Sites: 35. **Hookups:** Yes. **Each Site:** Fire ring. **Dump Station:** Yes. **Laundry:** Less than 5 mi. **Pay Phone:** Yes. **Restrooms and Showers:** Yes. **Fuel:** Less than 5 mi. **Propane:** No. **Internal Roads:** Paved. **RV Service:** No. **Market:** Less than 5 mi. **Restaurant:** Less than 5 mi. **General Store:** Less than 5 mi. **Vending:** Yes. **Swimming:** No. **Playground:** Yes. **Activities:** Archery, biking, bird-watching, boating, canoeing, fishing, hiking, jogging/running, kayaking, paddleboating, photography, walking, wildlife viewing.

RESTRICTIONS

Pets: On a leash or other physical restraint at all times. **Fires:** In designated fireplaces. **Alcoholic Beverages:** Not allowed. **Vehicle Maximum Length:** 33 ft.

TO GET THERE

Located 2 mi. west of the town of Chester on Hwy. 72 going toward the town of Whitmire.

CLEVELAND   MAP, A-1
Jones Gap State Park

reserve america

8155 Geer Hwy., 29635. T: (843) 546-9361; www.reserveamerica.com.

🚐   ▲ ★★★★

Beauty: ★★★★   Site Privacy: ★★★★
Spaciousness: ★★★★   Quiet: ★★★★
Security: ★★★★   Cleanliness: ★★★
Insect Control: ★★★   Facilities: ★★★

Caesars Head and Jones Gap State Parks comprise the Mountain Bridge Wilderness Area. Primary recreational opportunity is hiking, with 50 miles of hiking trails between the two parks. The highest waterfall in South Carolina, Raven Cliff Falls (400 ft.) can be found here as well as the Middle Saluda River, designated the state's first scenic river. Many scenic overlooks are also within the park. Trails range from easy to very strenuous. Trailside camping in one of South Carolina's most pristine wilderness areas in the Upcountry can be enjoyed at this 3,346-acre park. In addition, the park is an access point to the Foothills Hiking Trail. More than 400 species of flora including rare and endangered plants and state record trees, are also found here. The park's Environmental Education Center offers nature exhibits and a lab area. Portions of the old Cleveland Fish Hatchery have been restored and are stocked with trout for observation only. The park offers 52 miles of easy to strenuous hiking trails in the Mountain Bridge Wilderness Area. Trailside camping is allowed at 23 designated trail sites, with a permit. Enjoy fishing in the Middle Saluda and Matthews Creek for brook, spotted, and rainbow trout.

BASICS
Operated By: South Carolina State Parks. **Open:** All year. **Site Assignment:** Reservations can be made 11 months in advance. **Registration:** At office. **Fee:** Single, $4–$20. **Parking:** At site.

FACILITIES
Number of Multipurpose Sites: 14. **Hookups:** None. **Each Site:** Fire ring. **Dump Station:** No. **Laundry:** No. **Pay Phone:** Yes. **Restrooms and Showers:** Yes. **Fuel:** No. **Propane:** No. **Internal Roads:** Paved. **RV Service:** No. **Market:** No. **Restaurant:** No. **General Store:** No. **Vending:** No. **Swimming:** No. **Playground:** No. **Other:** No cutting of standing trees for firewood. **Activities:** Hiking.

RESTRICTIONS
Pets: On a leash or other physical restraint at all times. **Fires:** In designated fireplaces. **Alcoholic Beverages:** Not allowed.

TO GET THERE
Jones Gap is 25 mi. northwest of Greenville off US 276 and 11 mi. northwest of Marietta. From Greenville take Hwy. 276 through Travelers Rest, Marietta, and Cleveland. Approx. 2 mi. north of Cleveland turn right at park sign onto River Falls Rd. Stay on River Falls Rd. until the name changes to Jones Gap Rd. The park is 6 mi. off Hwy. 276.

Caesars Head is located on Hwy. 276 just 2 mi. from the North Carolina state line. Scenic Hwy. 11 can be used to access the park from I-85 north or south. Allow approx. 1 hour to drive from Greenville.

CLEVELAND   MAP, A-1
Caesars Head State Park

reserve america

8155 Geer Hwy., 29635. T: (864) 836-6115; www.reserveamerica.com.

🚐   ▲ ★★★★

Beauty: ★★★★   Site Privacy: ★★★★
Spaciousness: ★★★★   Quiet: ★★★★
Security: ★★★★   Cleanliness: ★★★
Insect Control: ★★★   Facilities: ★★

Caesars Head and Jones Gap State Parks comprise the Mountain Bridge Wilderness Area. Primary recreational opportunity is hiking, with 50 miles of hiking trails between the two parks. The highest waterfall in South Carolina, Raven Cliff Falls (400 ft. high) can be found here as well as the Middle Saluda River, designated the state's first scenic river. Many scenic overlooks are also within the park. Trails range from easy to very strenuous. Trailside camping in one of South Carolina's most pristine wilderness areas in the Upcountry can be enjoyed at this 3,346-acre park. In addition, the park is an access point to the Foothills Hiking Trail. More than 400 species of flora including rare and endangered plants and state record trees, are also found here. The park's Environmental Education Center offers nature exhibits and a lab area. Portions of the old Cleveland Fish Hatchery have been restored and are stocked with trout for observation only. The park offers 52 miles of easy to strenuous hiking trails in the Mountain Bridge Wilderness Area. Trailside camping is allowed at 23 designated trail sites, with a permit. Enjoy fishing in the Middle Saluda and Matthews Creek for brook, spotted and rainbow trout.

BASICS
Operated By: South Carolina State Parks. **Open:** All year. **Site Assignment:** Reservations can be made 11 months in advance. **Registration:** At office. **Fee:** Single, $4–$14. **Parking:** At site.

FACILITIES
Number of Multipurpose Sites: 12. **Hookups:** None. **Each Site:** Fire ring. **Dump Station:** No. **Laundry:** No. **Pay Phone:** Yes. **Restrooms and Showers:** Yes. **Fuel:** No. **Propane:** No. **Internal Roads:** Paved. **RV Service:** No. **Market:** No. **Restaurant:** No. **General Store:** No. **Vending:** No. **Swimming:** No. **Playground:** No. **Other:** No cutting of standing trees for firewood. **Activities:** Hiking, fishing.

RESTRICTIONS
Pets: On a leash or other physical restraint at all times. **Fires:** In designated fireplaces. **Alcoholic Beverages:** Not allowed.

TO GET THERE
Jones Gap is 25 mi. northwest of Greenville off US

276 and 11 mi. northwest of Marietta. Driving Directions: From Greenville take Hwy. 276 through Travelers Rest, Marietta, and Cleveland. Approx. 2 mi. north of Cleveland turn right at park sign onto River Falls Rd. Stay on River Falls Rd. until the name changes to Jones Gap Rd. The park is 6 mi. off Hwy. 276. Caesars Head is located on Hwy. 276 just 2 mi. from the North Carolina state line. Scenic Hwy. 11 can be used to access the park from I-85 north or south. Allow approx. 1 hour to drive from Greenville.

COLUMBIA   MAP, B-2
Sesquicentennial State Park

reserve america

9564 Two Notch Rd., 29223. T: (803) 788-2706; www.reserveamerica.com.

🚐 ★★★★   ▲ ★★★★

Beauty: ★★★★   Site Privacy: ★★★
Spaciousness: ★★★★   Quiet: ★★★★★
Security: ★★★★★   Cleanliness: ★★★★
Insect Control: ★★★   Facilities: ★★★★

This 1,419-acre urban green space includes a 30-acre lake stocked with bass and bream. The log house was built in 1756 in Richland County and moved to Sesquicentennial in 1961. The park's location is excellent if you like to shop and enjoy eating out. The campground consists of two loops, nicely shaded by a gorgeous stand of loblolly and longleaf pine. Campsites are large and most have back-in parking. However, we recommend the larger and more private pull-through sites. Parking is on a mixture of sand, gravel, grass, and pine straw. The campground was quiet when we visited on Labor Day weekend. It's often empty in the fall, so it's a great place to stay for University of South Carolina football games or on a holiday weekend.

BASICS
Operated By: South Carolina State Parks. **Open:** All year. **Site Assignment:** Camping reservations accepted online or by phone (866) 345-PARK; 2-night min. **Registration:** Set-up first, then register at office. Ranger makes rounds. **Fee:** Water/electric, $16–$18. **Parking:** Sites only.

FACILITIES
Number of Multipurpose Sites: 87. **Hookups:** Electric (30 amps), water. **Each Site:** Picnic table. **Dump Station:** Yes. **Laundry:** No. **Pay Phone:** Yes. **Restrooms and Showers:** Yes. **Fuel:** No. **Propane:** No. **Internal Roads:** Paved & dirt. **RV Service:** 20 mi. northeast in Elgin. **Market:** 1 mi. **Restaurant:** 0.25 mi. **General Store:** 1 mi. **Vending:** No. **Swimming:** No. **Playground:** Yes. **Other:** 1756 log house, picnic shelters, meeting facilities, nature center. **Activities:** Nature programs, nature trail, bicycle trail, fishing, exercise course, (nonmotor) boat rentals, swimming, & paddleboat rentals when lifeguard is present. **Nearby Attractions:** Columbia historic homes, South Carolina Confederate Relic Room & Museum, Fort Jackson Museum, South Carolina State Museum. **Additional Information:**

Columbia Metropolitan CVB, (803) 254-0479 or (800) 264-4884.

RESTRICTIONS

Pets: On leash only. Permit required for each dog. 2-acre dog park available. **Fires:** At sites only. **Alcoholic Beverages:** Not allowed. **Vehicle Maximum Length:** Varies (up to 40 ft.). **Other:** 14-day stay limit.

TO GET THERE

From I-77, take Exit US 1 (Two Notch Rd.) northeast 2 mi. Park entrance is on right.

DILLON — MAP, A-4
Little Pee Dee State Park

1298 State Park Rd., 29536. T: (843) 774-8872; www.reserveamerica.com.

🚐 ★★★★   ⛺ ★★★★

Beauty: ★★★	Site Privacy: ★★★
Spaciousness: ★★★	Quiet: ★★★★
Security: ★★★★	Cleanliness: ★★★
Insect Control: ★★★	Facilities: ★★★★

Quiet camping in an unspoiled setting is popular at this park, which features a small river swamp and part of the scenic Little Pee Dee River. This sandhills area has a variety of trees, plant life, and a nature trail that leads to a beaver pond. A tract recently acquired by the Heritage Trust features a Carolina bay. The park campground has 50 sites, 32 of which have hookups and can accommodate RVs up to 40 feet. Eighteen sites are tent sites with central water. Two sites may be reserved exclusively for the handicapped. The campground has heated restroom facilities with hot showers. The Beaver Pond nature trail is an easy 1.25-mile loop. Enjoy fishing in the Little Pee Dee River. Three picnic areas are available on a first-come, first-served basis, however, the large shelter may be reserved for a fee. Diverse ecosystems, from the flood plain along the river's edge to the dry sandy areas, provide habitat for a variety of flora and fauna. The park's 54-acre Lake Norton offers anglers the opportunity to try their luck for bream, bass, and catfish.

BASICS

Operated By: South Carolina State Parks. **Open:** All year. **Site Assignment:** Reservations can be made 11 months in advance. **Registration:** At office. **Fee:** Single, $8–$13; picnic shelter, $25–$32. **Parking:** At site.

FACILITIES

Number of Multipurpose Sites: 54. **Hookups:** None. **Each Site:** Fire ring. **Dump Station:** Yes. **Laundry:** No. **Pay Phone:** No. **Restrooms and Showers:** Yes. **Fuel:** No. **Propane:** No. **Internal Roads:** Paved. **RV Service:** No. **Market:** No. **Restaurant:** No. **General Store:** No. **Vending:** No. **Swimming:** Yes. **Playground:** Yes. **Activities:** Baseball, bird-watching, canoeing, fishing, hiking, kayaking, paddleboating, picnicking, walking, wildlife viewing.

RESTRICTIONS

Pets: On a leash or other physical restraint at all times. **Fires:** In designated fireplaces. **Alcoholic Beverages:** Not allowed.

TO GET THERE

From I-95 take Exit 193 on Hwy. 9 to Hwy. 57. Follow Hwy. 57 to state park road, then take a left and go 2 mi. to the park entrance on the right.

EUTAWVILLE — MAP, B-3
Rocks Pond Campground and Marina

108 Campground Rd., 29048. T: (803) 492-7711 or (800) 982-0271; www.rockspondcampground.net.

🚐 ★★★★   ⛺ ★★

Beauty: ★★★	Site Privacy: ★★
Spaciousness: ★★★	Quiet: ★★
Security: ★★★★★	Cleanliness: ★★★★
Insect Control: ★★★★	Facilities: ★★★★

With more than 250 tightly spaced campsites, Rocks Pond has created urban crowding in rural Eutawville. And folks seem to love it, ostensibly because of extensive amenities and recreation, including live bands on the weekends and a children's fishing pond. Avoid this joint on summer weekends and holidays when the crowds are sure to be unbearable. Sites are laid out in a series of monotonous grids except for waterfront sites (numbers 109–127 and 249–268). With boat dockage, sites 128–132 are nearly impossible to obtain. Call well in advance if you'd like one of these. None of the sites are knockout beautiful—choose your site based on location. Most are treeless pull-throughs. Parking is on packed clay or grass. All are level and none have any privacy. Security is excellent—the front entrance is guarded.

BASICS

Operated By: Rutledge Connor. **Open:** All year. **Site Assignment:** Site assigned at registration.; reservations accepted for 3-night min., $20 deposit; 7-day cancellation notice for refund less $5 fee. **Registration:** At office, late-comers register next morning. **Fee:** $30–$35; based on location relative to water; fees include 4 people; $5 per extra person up to 6 total. **Parking:** Site plus overflow parking.

FACILITIES

Number of RV-only Sites: 226. **Number of Tent-only Sites:** 30. **Hookups:** Electric (20, 30, 50 amps), water, sewer; 256 sites w/ full hookup. **Each Site:** Picnic table. **Dump Station:** Yes. **Laundry:** Yes. **Pay Phone:** Yes. **Restrooms and Showers:** Yes. **Fuel:** Yes. **Propane:** Yes. **Internal Roads:** Paved & gravel. **RV Service:** On call service available. **Market:** 6 mi. in Eutawville. **Restaurant:** 6 mi. in Eutawville, snack bar in-season. **General Store:** Camp store. **Vending:** Beverages. **Swimming:** Lake (no lifeguard). **Playground:** Yes. **Other:** Marina, rec hall, gazebos, meeting rooms, fire rings on request. **Activities:** Boating (rentals available), lake swimming, mini-golf, driving range, skeet range, archery, unique soccer sports, bicycle rentals, fishing guide

service (call for rates), Sat. night dances in-season. **Nearby Attractions:** Four golf courses w/in 25 miles, Lake Marion, Santee community, Palmetto trailhead, 1 hour from Charleston & Columbia. **Additional Information:** Santee Cooper Country Promotions (803) 854-2131.

RESTRICTIONS

Pets: Leash, clean-up enforced. **Fires:** Fire ring only (available on request). **Alcoholic Beverages:** Discouraged. **Vehicle Maximum Length:** No limit.

TO GET THERE

From I-95, take Exit 98. Drive east on Hwy. 6 9 mi. to Eutawville. At the stop sign, go left following Hwy. 6. Look for the Rocks Pond sign and turn left on Rocks Pond Rd., then right at the dead end. The campground is 18 mi. from I-95.

FAIR PLAY — MAP, A-1
Lake Hartwell State Recreation Area

19138-A Hwy. 11 S, 29643. T: (864) 972-3352; www.reserveamerica.com.

🚐 ★★★★   ⛺ ★★★★

Beauty: ★★★★★	Site Privacy: ★★★★
Spaciousness: ★★★★★	Quiet: ★★★
Security: ★★★★	Cleanliness: ★★★★
Insect Control: ★★★	Facilities: ★★★

This popular park is located 1 mile from I-85 on 56,000-acre Lake Hartwell. Activities include fishing for crappie, bream, catfish, stripers, largemouth, and hybrid bass. There are few land activities at this 680-acre park. Adrenaline lovers should consider a trip down the nearby Chattooga Wild and Scenic River. The campground is laid out in three main loops on two lake peninsulas, with many sites enjoying water views. Site size varies from ample to huge, with shady trees in most areas. Reservable sites, 69–108, are densely wooded. We recommend number 92, which is incredibly secluded (great honeymoon suite!). In the nonreservable sites, 6 and 17 are both large and private with lovely views. All parking is paved. There are both pull-through and back-in sites. Security is not great here; the park is only 1 mile from the interstate and has no gates. Visit on weekdays or in spring or fall for maximum peace and quiet.

BASICS

Operated By: South Carolina State Parks. **Open:** All year. **Site Assignment:** Camping reservations accepted online or by phone (866) 345-PARK; 2-night min. **Registration:** At store, late-comers register next morning. **Fee:** Water/electric, $16–$18; tent, $12–$13; plus visitor's fee; cash, personal check, V, MC, D. **Parking:** At sites except walk-in, overflow parking available.

FACILITIES

Number of Tent-only Sites: 13. **Number of Multipurpose Sites:** 117. **Hookups:** Electric (30 amps), water. **Each Site:** Picnic table, fire ring.

Dump Station: Yes. **Laundry:** Yes. **Pay Phone:** Yes. **Restrooms and Showers:** Yes. **Fuel:** No. **Propane:** No. **Internal Roads:** Paved. **RV Service:** 13 mi. north toward Seneca. **Market:** 8 mi. south in Lavonia, GA. **Restaurant:** 1.5 mi. **General Store:** 17 mi. north in Seneca. **Vending:** Beverages. **Swimming:** No. **Playground:** Yes. **Other:** Boat ramp, picnic shelter, park store. **Activities:** Nature trail, fishing, boating, lake swimming. **Nearby Attractions:** Anderson Historic District, Chattooga National Wild & Scenic River, Cherokee Foothills Scenic Hwy. (11), Sumter National Forest, Walhalla National Fish Hatchery, Issaqueena Falls, Clemson University. **Additional Information:** Anderson Chamber of Commerce, (864) 226-3454.

RESTRICTIONS

Pets: On leash, clean-up enforced. **Fires:** Allowed. **Alcoholic Beverages:** Not allowed. **Vehicle Maximum Length:** 45 ft. **Other:** No firearms or fire works.

TO GET THERE

From I-85, take Exit 1 onto South Carolina Hwy. 11. Drive about 0.25 mi. to the top of the hill. The park is on the left.

HAMPTON   MAP, C-2
Lake Warren State Park

reserve america

1079 Lake Warren Rd. , 29924. T: (803) 943-5051; www.reserveamerica.com.

🚐   ⛺ ★★★★

Beauty: ★★★	Site Privacy: ★★★★
Spaciousness: ★★★★	Quiet: ★★★★
Security: ★★★★	Cleanliness: ★★★
Insect Control: ★★★	Facilities: ★★★★

Lake Warren State Park picnic facilities, a 200-acre lake and a community building are prominent features of this South Carolina state park. This 440-acre park has large tracts of wetlands and woodlands that support a wide range of plant species and wildlife habitats. The park's flat terrain features a flood plain forest with a variety of large trees, including four species of pines. In addition to Lake Warren, the park also includes a three-acre park lake. The lakes offer fishing for largemouth bass, brim, redbreast, crappie and catfish. Yemassee Nature Trail a short, 0.3-mile nature trail. There are three boat ramps. Boats are limited to 10 horse power motors. In addition a floating dock provides boaters access to the park. Primitive group camping area is available for organized groups up to 100 people. The area includes picnic tables, central water and nearby restroom. There are several picnic areas, and a community building overlooks the lake.

BASICS

Operated By: South Carolina State Parks. **Open:** All year. **Site Assignment:** Reservations can be made 11 months in advance. **Registration:** At office. **Fee:** Single, $10–$12.50; community building, $180–$225. **Parking:** At site.

FACILITIES

Number of Multipurpose Sites: 5. **Hookups:** None. **Each Site:** Fire ring. **Dump Station:** No. **Laundry:** Less than 10 mi. **Restrooms and Showers:** Yes. **Fuel:** Less than 10 mi. **Propane:** No. **Internal Roads:** Paved. **RV Service:** Greater than 20 mi. **Market:** Less than 10 mi. **Restaurant:** Less than 10 mi. **General Store:** Less than 5 mi. **Vending:** No. **Swimming:** Yes. **Playground:** Yes. **Activities:** Amphitheater, baseball, bird-watching, fishing, hiking, nature study, picnicking, volleyball, walking, wildlife viewing.

RESTRICTIONS

Pets: On a leash or other physical restraint at all times. **Fires:** In designated fireplaces. **Alcoholic Beverages:** Not allowed.

TO GET THERE

Lake Warren State Park is located 5 mi. west of Hampton between SC 363 and US 601 on secondary road 501 (Lake Warren Rd.). Travel on US 601 S. from the town of Hampton 5 mi., then turn right onto Lake Warren Rd. at the sign for Lake Warren State Park. Travel 1 mi. to arrive at the park's gate on the left side of the road.

HUNTING ISLAND   MAP, C-3
Hunting Island State Park

2555 Sea Island Pkwy., 29920.
T: (843) 838-2011 or (866) 345-PARK; www.southcarolinaparks.com.

🚐 ★★★★   ⛺ ★★★★

Beauty: ★★★★★	Site Privacy: ★★★
Spaciousness: ★★★	Quiet: ★★★
Security: ★★★★	Cleanliness: ★★★★
Insect Control: ★★★★	Facilities: ★★★★

The atmosphere here is deliciously mellow. The children seem more laid-back than at other campgrounds. It could be the gorgeous shade provided by mature pine, palm, and palmetto or the sound of the ocean. Relax in a hammock. Get yourself off the hammock to tour the Hunting Island Lighthouse, in use from 1875 until 1933. Two of the four main loops contain sites near the beach. Site size varies, as does privacy. If you're seeking ample space and privacy, head for sites 166–173 in the back of the campground (farthest from the beach). For the nicest beachfront sites, head for 49–55, 71, and 73. All of these have pretty views of beach dunes. Most parking is back-in on packed sand and pine straw. Mosquitoes and "no-see-ums" are a nuisance, so bring insect repellent. This park is extremely popular—prepare for crowds April through October, or try visiting during the week. Security is good, with gates locked at night.

BASICS

Operated By: South Carolina State Parks. **Open:** All year. **Site Assignment:** Camping reservations accepted online or by phone (866) 345-PARK; 2-night min. **Registration:** At store, late-comers register next morning. **Fee:** Water/electric, $23–$25; tent, $17–$19. **Parking:** Limit 2 vehicles per site, overflow parking available.

FACILITIES

Number of Tent-only Sites: 10. **Number of Multipurpose Sites:** 200. **Hookups:** Electric (30 amps), water. **Each Site:** Picnic table, fire ring. **Dump Station:** Yes. **Laundry:** No. **Pay Phone:** Yes. **Restrooms and Showers:** Yes. **Fuel:** No. **Propane:** No. **Internal Roads:** Paved, packed soil at sites. **RV Service:** 16 mi. west in Beaufort. **Market:** 12 mi. west on Lady's Island. **Restaurant:** 12 mi. west on Lady's Island. **General Store:** Park store. **Vending:** Yes. **Swimming:** Ocean (no lifeguard). **Playground:** No. **Other:** Boat ramp, visitor's center, lighthouse, beach shop, picnic shelters. **Activities:** Lighthouse tours, hiking & bicycling trail, boardwalk, fishing pier, crabbing, boating, swimming, nature programs, bird-watching. **Nearby Attractions:** Historic Beaufort, boat tours, gardens, walking tours, horse-drawn carriage tours, Port Royal. **Additional Information:** Greater Beaufort Chamber of Commerce, & Visitors Center, (843) 524-3163, www.beaufortsc.org.

RESTRICTIONS

Pets: On leash only, leash no longer than 6 ft.; not allowed in cabins or cabin areas. **Fires:** Fire ring only. **Alcoholic Beverages:** Not allowed. **Vehicle Maximum Length:** 40 ft. **Other:** 2-week stay limit.

TO GET THERE

From I-95, take Hwy. 21 east toward Beaufort. Drive 42 mi. Hwy. 21 ends at the park.

LANCASTER   MAP, A-2, A-3
Andrew Jackson State Park

reserve america

196 Andrew Jackson Park Rd., 29720.
T: (803) 285-3344; www.reserveamerica.com.

🚐 ★★★★   ⛺ ★★★★

Beauty: ★★	Site Privacy: ★★
Spaciousness: ★★	Quiet: ★★★★
Security: ★★★★	Cleanliness: ★★★
Insect Control: ★★★	Facilities: ★★★★

This 360-acre park was created as a memorial to the seventh President of the United States. Andrew Jackson spent his earlier years in this rugged pioneer area known as the Waxhaws. A museum displays historic tools, textiles, and household furnishings typical of the Jacksonian era. Other features on the park are a sculpture of young Jackson by Anna Hyatt Huntington and a replica of an 18th-century one-room schoolhouse. The park also includes an 18-acre lake, two nature trails, an amphitheater, and a meeting house. The two nature trails provide moderate 1-mile loops. The park lake provides fishing for catfish, bass, and bluegill. Boats can be rented for a reasonable fee but private boats are not allowed in the park lake. There are two picnic shelters available free on a first-come, first-served basis or reserved for a fee. The recreation activities at this park include camping, fishing, picnicking, hiking, and touring the museum.

BASICS

Operated By: South Carolina Dept. of Parks, Recreation & Tourism. **Open:** All year. **Site Assignment:**

Reservations can be made up to 16 weeks in advance. **Registration:** At office. **Fee:** Single, $10–$13; day-use amphitheater, $90–$112; day-use community building, $120–$150; picnic shelter, $25–$32. **Parking:** 2 vehicles per site.

FACILITIES

Number of Multipurpose Sites: 30. **Hookups:** Yes. **Dump Station:** Yes. **Laundry:** Less than 10 mi. **Pay Phone:** Yes. **Restrooms and Showers:** Yes. **Fuel:** Less than 5 mi. **Propane:** No. **Internal Roads:** Paved. **RV Service:** Yes. **Market:** Less than 10 mi. **Restaurant:** Less than 10 mi. **General Store:** Yes. **Vending:** Yes. **Swimming:** Yes. **Playground:** Yes. **Other:** Boats are available for rental but private boats are not allowed in the park lake. **Activities:** Amphitheater, fishing, hiking, horseshoes, paddleboating, picnicking, boating, swimming. **Nearby Attractions:** Tennis, horseback riding, canoeing, hunting, kayaking. **Additional Information:** Check-in time is 2–9 p.m. (DST), 2–6 p.m. (EST). Check-out time is noon. Campers arriving after hours should notify park staff for gate requirements. No one under age 18 may register or reserve a campsite.

RESTRICTIONS

Pets: Pets must remain leashed at all times. **Alcoholic Beverages:** Not allowed. **Vehicle Maximum Length:** 38 ft.

TO GET THERE

Andrew Jackson State Park is located 9 mi. north of Lancaster, SC on US 521. It can be reached from I-77 by taking Exit 77, traveling 12 mi. on SC 5. Or it can be reached from I-485 by taking the Johnston Rd. exit and traveling 18 mi. south on US 521.

McCORMICK MAP, B-1
Baker Creek State Park

reserve america

863 Baker Creek Rd., 29835. T: (864) 443-2457; www.reserveamerica.com.

🚐 ★★★★	⛺ ★★★★
Beauty: ★★★★★	Site Privacy: ★★★★
Spaciousness: ★★★★	Quiet: ★★★
Security: ★★★★	Cleanliness: ★★★★
Insect Control: ★★★	Facilities: ★★★

Baker Creek includes 1,300 gorgeous acres of rolling forest. J. Strom Thurmond Reservoir consists of 70,000 acres stocked with crappie, catfish, bream, striper, and several bass species. Despite its rural locale, this popular park should be avoided on summer weekends and holidays. Shaded by a gorgeous stand of loblolly pine trees, campsites at Baker Creek are more spacious than average. Most offer back-in parking. Foliage provides a bit of privacy between sites. Eight sites offer pull-through parking; none are lakefront. Parking is on dirt, gravel, or pine straw. The campgrounds contain two loops forming semi-circles with lake views at many sites. In campground No. 1, the nicest sites are 32–34, 37, 38, 40, 41, and 43. In campground No. 2, the nicer sites, 86–90, are on a small peninsula. Baker Creek locks its gates at night, but the front gate is not attended during the day.

BASICS

Operated By: South Carolina State Parks. **Open:** All year. **Site Assignment:** Camping reservations accepted online or by phone (866) 345-PARK; 2-night min. **Registration:** At campsites. **Fee:** Water/electric, $15–$17; tent, $10–$13; plus park admission fee. **Parking:** At sites only.

FACILITIES

Number of Multipurpose Sites: 100. **Hookups:** Electric (20, 30 amps), water. **Each Site:** Picnic table, some sites w/ grill. **Dump Station:** Yes. **Laundry:** No. **Pay Phone:** Yes. **Restrooms and Showers:** Yes. **Fuel:** No. **Propane:** No. **Internal Roads:** Gravel, main roads paved. **RV Service:** 30 mi. north in Greenwood. **Market:** 4 mi. east in McCormick. **Restaurant:** 4 mi. east in McCormick. **General Store:** 4 mi. east in McCormick. **Vending:** Beverages. **Swimming:** No. **Playground:** Yes. **Other:** Boat ramps, picnic shelters, pavilion rental. **Activities:** walking & hiking trails, fishing, basketball, volleyball, horseshoes, mountain bike trails. **Nearby Attractions:** Historic McCormick County, Revolutionary War sites, Steven's Creek Heritage Preserve. **Additional Information:** McCormick Chamber of Commerce, (864) 465-2835.

RESTRICTIONS

Pets: On leash only. **Fires:** Ground fires only. **Alcoholic Beverages:** Not allowed. **Vehicle Maximum Length:** 40 ft.

TO GET THERE

From I-20, take Georgia Exit 200 (River Watch Pkwy.). Drive west approx. 2 mi. and turn right onto Hwy. 28 (Furys Ferry Rd.). Drive north on Hwy. 28 to McCormick and turn left onto US 378. Drive west on US 378 4 mi., then turn right at the park sign. The park is 1 mi. ahead on the left.

MODOC MAP, B-1, B-2
Modoc Campground

reserve america

296 Modoc Camp Rd., Rte. 1 Box 2-D, 29838. T: (864) 333-2272; www.reserveamerica.com.

🚐 ★★★★★	⛺ ★★★★★
Beauty: ★★★★★	Site Privacy: ★★★★★
Spaciousness: ★★★★★	Quiet: ★★★★★
Security: ★★★★★	Cleanliness: ★★★★
Insect Control: ★★★★	Facilities: ★★★

Modoc campground on J. Strom Thurmond Lake is one of the most beautiful campgrounds in the Southeast. Sites are incredibly spacious with a large sandy picnic and tent area. Sites are shaded and secluded by lovely loblolly and shortleaf pine and other tree species. All sites have gravel parking. Back-in sites are nice, but many of the pull-throughs are huge. The campground contains four main spurs on two peninsulas. Sites 4–10 are gorgeous, with views of a small inlet. Site 11 is one of the most beautiful we've seen anywhere—unfortunately, it has no hookups. Fisher-folk will find smallmouth, striped, and hybrid bass. Few day-use facilities at the campground keep it blissfully quiet most of the

time. Only 40 minutes from Augusta, Modoc's location is extremely rural. Security is excellent as the campground is gated and guarded. Visit Modoc anytime except holiday weekends. It rarely fills to capacity.

BASICS

Operated By: U.S. Army Corps of Engineers. **Open:** Apr. 1–Oct. 30. **Site Assignment:** First come, first served; reservations accepted through National Recreation Reservation Service (NRRS) at (877) 444-6777; reservations can be made up to 240 days in advance, full payment required upon making reservation; credit card preferred (V, MC, D, AE), or pay by money order if at least 21 days in advance of arrival; $10 fee for cancellation or change of site or dates; cancellation w/in 3 days of arrival charged 1 night, no-show charged $20 plus 1 night. **Registration:** At gatehouse, gates locked at 10 p.m. **Fee:** $18; for up to 12 people. **Parking:** At sites, 4-vehicle limit, $3 per extra vehicle, overflow parking available.

FACILITIES

Number of Multipurpose Sites: 49. **Hookups:** Electric (50 amps), water. **Each Site:** Picnic table, grill, fire ring, utility table, lantern holder. **Dump Station:** Yes. **Laundry:** Yes. **Pay Phone:** Yes. **Restrooms and Showers:** Yes. **Fuel:** No. **Propane:** No. **Internal Roads:** Most Paved. **RV Service:** 20 mi. south in Augusta. **Market:** 20 mi. south in Augusta. **Restaurant:** 15 mi. north in McCormick. **General Store:** 1 mi. in Modoc. **Vending:** No. **Swimming:** No. **Playground:** Yes. **Other:** Boat ramp, picnic shelter. **Activities:** Hiking trail, beach, swimming, boating, fishing. **Nearby Attractions:** Thurmond Visitor Information Center & Dam; Golf & Gardens in Augusta, Woodrow Wilson's childhood home, Lucy Craft Laney Museum of Black History. **Additional Information:** Aug.a Metropolitan CVB, (800) 726-0243.

RESTRICTIONS

Pets: On leash; not allowed in swimming area. **Fires:** Grill or rings in sites only. Never unattended. **Alcoholic Beverages:** Not allowed. **Vehicle Maximum Length:** 50 ft. **Other:** 14-day stay limit in 30-day period.

TO GET THERE

From I-20, take Georgia Exit 200 (River Watch Pkwy.), then drive west 2 mi. to Furys Ferry Rd. (Hwy. 28 west). Turn right and drive north 13 mi. to Clarks Hill. Continue northwest on Hwy. 221 4 mi. The campground entrance is on the left.

MOUNTAIN REST MAP, A-1
Oconee State Park

624 State Park Rd., 29664. T: (864) 638-5353; www.reserveamerica.com.

🚐 ★★★★	⛺ ★★★★
Beauty: ★★★★★	Site Privacy: ★★★★
Spaciousness: ★★★★	Quiet: ★★★★★
Security: ★★★★	Cleanliness: ★★★★
Insect Control: ★★★★	Facilities: ★★★★

Oconee State Park offers large, gorgeous sites in one of the most beautifully forested campgrounds we've seen. Various oak and pine species provide shade and some privacy. A few sites have paved parking, and the rest are gravel. There are pull-through and back-in campsites. Our favorite sites are 30, 31, 32, 34, and 36—totally fabulous wooded sites with pull-through, gravel parking and lovely views of the small lake. Other recommendations are 66 and 78. Unfortunately, the bathhouses were grimy during our visit. This remote, peaceful park is cherished by nature lovers. Seeking adventure? Raft the nearby Chattooga National Wild and Scenic River. In season, the gate is attended during the day and locked at night, making security good. This off-the-beaten-path park is a good destination on all but the busiest summer weekends. With an elevation of 1,700 feet, the park is usually a few degrees cooler than the South Carolina Piedmont region.

BASICS

Operated By: South Carolina State Parks. **Open:** All year. **Site Assignment:** Camping reservations accepted online or by phone (866) 345-PARK; 2-night min. **Registration:** At trading post, park office off-season. **Fee:** Water/electric, $16–$18; tent, $12–$13. **Parking:** At sites except tent sites (walk-in).

FACILITIES

Number of Tent-only Sites: 15. **Number of Multipurpose Sites:** 125. **Hookups:** Electric (30 amps), water. **Each Site:** Picnic table; walk-in sites have picnic table, grill, fire ring, lantern stand & tent pad. **Dump Station:** Yes. **Laundry:** Yes. **Pay Phone:** Yes. **Restrooms and Showers:** Yes. **Fuel:** No. **Propane:** No. **Internal Roads:** Gravel or paved. **RV Service:** 30 mi. south in Clemson. **Market:** 15 mi. south in West Union. **Restaurant:** 4 mi. west in Mountain Rest. **General Store:** 4 mi. west in Mountain Rest, Wal-Mart & K-mart 22 mi. south in Seneca. **Vending:** Beverages. **Swimming:** No. **Playground:** Yes. **Other:** Civilian Conservation Corps Museum, park store in-season, picnic shelters, multi-purpose recreation building, meeting room. **Activities:** Fishing, boating, canoe & fishing boat rentals (check w/ park about bringing your own boat), swimming & paddleboat rentals when lifeguard is present, nature trails, mini-golf, archery range. **Nearby Attractions:** Chattooga National Wildlife & Scenic River, Oconee Station state Historic Site, Cherry Hill National Forest, Devil's Fork State Park, Foothills Trail, Stumphouse Tunnel, golf courses. **Additional Information:** Greater Walhalla Area Chamber of Commerce, (864) 638-2727.

RESTRICTIONS

Pets: 6-ft. leash only. Pets not allowed in cabins or cabin areas. **Fires:** In designated areas only. **Alcoholic Beverages:** Not allowed. **Vehicle Maximum Length:** 35 ft.

TO GET THERE

From I-85, take Exit 1 and drive 23 mi. north on Hwy. 11. At Hwy. 28, turn left and head west 10 mi. At the fork at Hwy. 107, bear right and drive 2 mi. The park is on the right.

MURRELLS INLET   MAP, B-4
Huntington Beach State Park

16148 Ocean Hwy., 29576. T: (843) 237-4440; www.southcarolinaparks.com.

🚐 ★★★★		⛺ ★★★★
Beauty: ★★★★		Site Privacy: ★★★★
Spaciousness: ★★★★		Quiet: ★★★
Security: ★★★★★		Cleanliness: ★★★★
Insect Control: ★★★		Facilities: ★★★

Though Huntington Beach is more remote than Myrtle Beach State Park, it's almost as popular, with numerous activities and a pristine beach. Wildlife enthusiasts may see American alligators or loggerhead sea turtles. Bird lovers can spot many species of waterfowl, wading birds, or raptors (including bald eagles). Interpretive programs enrich the experience of low-country ecosystems. Also here is "Atalaya," the 1931 Mediterranean Moorish-style home of the Huntington family. Per Murphy's Law, the nicest campsites are the farthest from the beach. Sites 134–186 are closest to the beach and the least attractive. Walk farther to the beach and choose sites 104–130. These are larger, more private and shadier than the rest of the campground, and their bath house is clean and modern. Sites have gravel parking and most are back-in. Size varies. Gated and guarded, security at Huntington Beach is excellent. Avoid this park on summer weekends, when its popularity becomes its downfall.

BASICS

Operated By: South Carolina State Parks. **Open:** All year. **Site Assignment:** Camping reservations accepted online or by phone (866) 345-PARK; 2-night min. **Registration:** At camp store, ranger on duty 24 hours. **Fee:** Water/electric/sewer, $23–$25; tent, $17–$19. **Parking:** Site plus overflow parking.

FACILITIES

Number of RV-only Sites: 133. **Number of Tent-only Sites:** 6. **Hookups:** Electric (20, 30 amps), water, sewer; 24 sites w/ full hookup; 133 sites w/ water & electric. **Each Site:** Picnic table, fire ring. **Dump Station:** Yes. **Laundry:** No. **Pay Phone:** Yes. **Restrooms and Showers:** Yes. **Fuel:** No. **Propane:** No. **Internal Roads:** Gravel in campground, park is paved. **RV Service:** 25 mi. north in Conway. **Market:** Grocery 3 mi. north or south in Murrells Inlet, Wal-Mart 10 mi. north in Surfside. **Restaurant:** 3 mi. north or south in Murrells Inlet. **General Store:** Camp store. **Vending:** No. **Swimming:** No. **Playground:** No. **Other:** Recreation room, picnic shelters. **Activities:** Beach, swimming, fishing, kayaking, canoeing, hiking trails, coastal exploration program, Atalaya Castle. **Nearby Attractions:** Water Park, Myrtle Beach, Hampton Plantation State Historic Site, Brookgreen Gardens, Pawley's Island. **Additional Information:** Myrtle Beach Area Chamber of Commerce, (843) 626-7444.

RESTRICTIONS

Pets: On leash only. **Fires:** Fire ring only. **Alcoholic Beverages:** Not allowed. **Vehicle Maximum Length:** 50 ft. **Other:** 2-week stay limit.

TO GET THERE

From Georgetown, take Hwy. 17 north 20 mi. The park entrance is on the right. From Myrtle Beach, take Hwy. 17 south 15 mi. The park entrance is on the left.

MYRTLE BEACH   MAP, B-4
Lakewood Camping Resort

5901 South Kings Hwy., 29575. T: (877) 525-3966; www.lakewoodcampground.com.

🚐 ★★★★		⛺ ★★★
Beauty: ★★★★		Site Privacy: ★★
Spaciousness: ★★★		Quiet: ★★★
Security: ★★★★★		Cleanliness: ★★★★
Insect Control: ★★★		Facilities: ★★★★★

Gigantic Lakewood is similar to its Myrtle Beach competitors in that it has scads of identical campsites. Tidy and nicely landscaped, Lakewood was awarded National Association of RV Parks and Campgrounds "National RV Park of the Year 2000–2001." Extensive amenities cater to all ages. Choose open sites in the northeastern corner of the park or shadier sites in blocks 1, 2, and 3 south. A variety of trees, including oaks, pines, dogwood, pecan, and cedar provide shade. Parking is on grass, packed sand, or dirt. Laid out in rows with mostly back-in parking, sites are small and there is little privacy. For a quaint view, try sites 2801–2867, which line the small lakes. Families should request sites near the playground. There are restaurants and tourist attractions nearby. Excellent security includes a gated entrance and 24-hour security patrols. Avoid Myrtle Beach during spring break and summer holidays. For quiet, visit in March or October.

BASICS

Operated By: Lakewood Camping Resort, Inc. **Open:** All year. **Site Assignment:** First come, first served, guests may request sites; reservations accepted 48 hours to 1 year in advance w/ deposit, checks accepted well in advance; in-season oceanfront 7-night min., other sites 4-night min.; 48-hour notice required for refund. **Registration:** At gatehouse, express check-in also available; inquire when making reservations. **Fee:** $25–$60; prices for 5 people; cash, personal check, V, MC, D. **Parking:** 2 vehicles per site (charge for extras in-season).

FACILITIES

Number of Multipurpose Sites: 1200. **Hookups:** Electric (20, 30, 50 amps), water, sewer, cable TV; 1,400 sites w/ hookups, Wi-Fi. **Each Site:** Picnic table. **Dump Station:** Yes. **Laundry:** Yes. **Pay Phone:** Yes. **Restrooms and Showers:** Yes. **Fuel:** No. **Propane:** Yes. **Internal Roads:** Paved. **RV Service:** 1 mi. south in Myrtle Beach. **Market:** Camp store (Trading Post). **Restaurant:** 0.25 mi. in Myrtle Beach. **General Store:** Camp store, Wal-Mart 2 mi. south in Myrtle Beach. **Vending:** Yes. **Swimming:** 1 indoor, 1 outdoor pool. Seasonal lifeguard. **Playground:** Yes. **Other:** Hot tub, RV storage, freshwater fishing, golf-cart rentals, convention services, nondenominational ministry, snack bar. **Activities:** Mini-golf, arcade, pedal boat, kayak, & bicycle rentals, shuffleboard, basketball, horseshoes, volleyball, amphitheater, live entertainment. **Nearby Attractions:** Myrtle Beach historic tours & gardens, Grand Strand, Barefoot Landing, House of Blues, Alabama Theater, Dixie Stampede, Intracoastal Waterway. **Additional Information:** Myrtle Beach Area Chamber of Commerce, (843) 626-7444.

RESTRICTIONS

Pets: On leash (6 ft. max.). **Fires:** Allowed. **Alcoholic Beverages:** Not allowed. **Vehicle Maximum Length:** No limit.

TO GET THERE

From the intersection of Hwy. 501 and Hwy. 17, drive south on 17 approx. 5 mi. The entrance is on the left.

MYRTLE BEACH   MAP, B-4
Myrtle Beach State Park

4401 South Kings Hwy., 29575. T: (843) 238-5325; www.reserveamerica.com.

🚐 ★★★★   ⛺ ★★★★

Beauty: ★★★★	Site Privacy: ★★★★
Spaciousness: ★★★★	Quiet: ★★★
Security: ★★★★★	Cleanliness: ★★★
Insect Control: ★★★	Facilities: ★★★

Myrtle Beach State Park maintains a massive campground with large shady sites laid out in a series of semi-circles. Sweet gum, hickory, longleaf pine, and various oak species provide plenty of shade and varying amounts of privacy. Parking is on packed coquina and pine straw. A few sites offer pull-through parking. For privacy and quiet, try Circle 6 (numbers 293–336). Want to be closer to the beach? Try 166–172; these quiet sites are on a dead-end road. With plenty of recreation, Myrtle Beach State Park is popular with locals and tourists. This makes for unbearable crowds on holiday and summer weekends. We urge you to visit in the off-season, preferably autumn, to avoid spring-break crowds. This urban park is convenient to restaurants, world-class golf, and other tourist attractions. Security is excellent; the front gate is attended at all times and locked at night.

BASICS

Operated By: South Carolina State Parks. **Open:** All year. **Site Assignment:** Camping reservations accepted online or by phone (866) 345-PARK; 2-night min. **Registration:** At trading post. **Fee:** Water/electric, $23–$25; tent, $17–$19; cash, personal check, V, MC. **Parking:** At sites.

FACILITIES

Number of Tent-only Sites: 45. **Number of Multipurpose Sites:** 302. **Hookups:** Electric (50 amps), water; 300 sites w/ hookups. **Each Site:** Picnic table. **Dump Station:** Yes. **Laundry:** Yes. **Pay Phone:** Yes. **Restrooms and Showers:** Yes. **Fuel:** No. **Propane:** No. **Internal Roads:** Park paved, campground packed coquina. **RV Service:** 0.25 mi. **Market:** 0.25 mi. **Restaurant:** 0.5 mi. **General Store:** 10 mi. south in Surfside (Wal-Mart). **Vending:** Yes. **Swimming:** No. **Playground:** Yes. **Other:**

Fishing pier, boardwalks to beach, snack bar, gift shop, picnic shelters, amphitheater, activity center. **Activities:** Nature center, nature trail, fishing. **Nearby Attractions:** Myrtle Beach historic tours & gardens, Grand Strand, Barefoot Landing, House of Blues, Alabama Theater, Dixie Stampede, Intracoastal Waterway. **Additional Information:** Myrtle Beach Area Chamber of Commerce, (843) 626-7444.

RESTRICTIONS

Pets: On leash only. Pets not allowed in apartments, cabins, or cabin areas. **Fires:** Allowed. **Alcoholic Beverages:** Not allowed. **Vehicle Maximum Length:** 50 ft.

TO GET THERE

From the junction of Hwy. 501 and Hwy. 17, go south 5 mi. The park is on the left.

MYRTLE BEACH   MAP, B-4
Myrtle Beach Travel Park

10108 Kings Rd., 29572. T: (800) 255-3568; www.myrtlebeachtravelpark.com.

🚐 ★★★★   ⛺ ★★★★

Beauty: ★★★★	Site Privacy: ★★
Spaciousness: ★★★	Quiet: ★★
Security: ★★★★★	Cleanliness: ★★★★
Insect Control: ★★★	Facilities: ★★★★★

This park and its competitors offer frighteningly similar campsites. Resolution between parks is found in activities and amenities offered. This one offers a 17-acre freshwater fishing lake. Most nightly and weekly sites lie between the lake and the ocean. Oceanside sites form 25 identical rows of pull-throughs and three identical rows of back-ins. Each treeless site has a covered picnic table. Sites are small, and there is no privacy. Parking is on patchy grass and sand. Nicer sites enjoy views of dunes and sea grasses. The shady, nicely landscaped back-in sites on the other side of the lake are the prettiest. Sites 700–709 and 576–588 are delightful, with pleasant views of the fishing lake.

BASICS

Operated By: Myrtle Beach Travel Park. **Open:** All year. **Site Assignment:** Reservations recommended, w/ $50 deposit, 14 days in advance, 7-night min. June 6–Aug. 15, 3-night min. off-season min.; 7-day cancellation notice required for refund. **Registration:** At office. **Fee:** $28–$52; for 4 people, $4 per extra person up to 8 total; prices vary seasonally; cash, personal check, V, MC, AE. **Parking:** 1 vehicle per site, $2/day per extra vehicle.

FACILITIES

Number of Tent-only Sites: 7. **Number of Multipurpose Sites:** 750. **Hookups:** Electric (30, 50 amps), water, sewer, cable TV. **Each Site:** Picnic table. **Dump Station:** Yes. **Laundry:** Yes. **Pay Phone:** Yes. **Restrooms and Showers:** Yes. **Fuel:** No. **Propane:** Yes. **Internal Roads:** Most paved, some coquina or gravel. **RV Service:** On call for onsite. **Market:** 2 mi. in Myrtle Beach. **Restaurant:** On site. **General Store:** On site. **Vending:** Yes. **Swimming:** 1 indoor, 1 outdoor pool. Limited ocean swimming. Seasonal lifeguard. **Playground:** Yes. **Other:** Pavilion, rec room, chapel, RV storage.

Activities: Freshwater lake, beachfront, arcade, paddleboat rental, activities director. **Nearby Attractions:** Myrtle Beach historic plantations, tours, Intracoastal Waterway, amusement parks, Grand Strand, Brookgreen Gardens. **Additional Information:** Myrtle Beach Area Chamber of Commerce, (843) 626-7444.

RESTRICTIONS

Pets: On leash only. No pets in ocean villas or rental travel trailers. **Fires:** Allowed. **Alcoholic Beverages:** At site only. **Vehicle Maximum Length:** No limit. **Other:** No fireworks.

TO GET THERE

From the intersection of US 501 and US 17, drive north on US 17 approx. 10 mi. to Kings Rd. Turn right, and the entrance is on the left.

MYRTLE BEACH   MAP, B-4
Ocean Lakes Family Campground

6001 South Kings Hwy., 29575. T: (877) 510-1413 or (843) 238-5636; www.oceanlakes.com.

🚐 ★★★★   ⛺ ★★★

Beauty: ★★★★	Site Privacy: ★★
Spaciousness: ★★★	Quiet: ★★
Security: ★★★★★	Cleanliness: ★★★★
Insect Control: ★★★	Facilities: ★★★★★

Like its competitor (Lakewood Camping Resort), Ocean Lakes has received the "National RV Park of the Year Award" from the National Association of RV Parks and Campgrounds. Campsites are pull-throughs and parking is on grass. Sites are small. Most are completely treeless, so there is no privacy between sites. Short-term sites are laid out in tidy rows on the northeast corner of the park. If you're traveling with children, we recommend a site in the HH area, which is between the pool and the beach. Otherwise choose your site according to proximity to the beach. Ocean Lakes is convenient to all Myrtle Beach attractions, restaurants, and shopping. Security is excellent at this urban resort, which is gated and has 24-hour security patrols. Visits during spring break and summer holidays should be avoided completely. If you would like a little peace and quiet visit in March or October.

BASICS

Operated By: Jackson Family. **Open:** All year. **Site Assignment:** Reservations recommended spring, summer, & fall (by site number), 4-night min. June 15–Aug. 15, $50 deposit; 7-day cancellation notice for refund, $10 cancellation fee. **Registration:** Main gate staffed 24 hours, express check-in available—inquire when making reservations. **Fee:** $24.50–$59. **Parking:** 2 cars per site, overflow parking available, $3 per extra car.

FACILITIES

Number of Multipurpose Sites: 893. **Hookups:** Electric (20, 30, 50 amps), water, sewer, cable TV, modem-friendly phone line (free local calls); all sites are pull-throughs w/ full hookups, Wi-Fi. **Each Site:** Picnic table. **Dump Station:** No. **Laundry:** Yes. **Pay Phone:** Yes. **Restrooms and Showers:** Yes. **Fuel:** No. **Propane:** Yes. **Internal Roads:** Paved. **RV**

Service: On site. **Market:** Across street from entrance. **Restaurant:** Across street from entrance. **General Store:** Snack bar. **Vending:** Yes. **Swimming:** 3 kiddie pools, 1 Olympic-size outdoor pool, 1 all-season indoor pool; lifeguard in season. **Playground:** Yes. **Other:** Sailboat launch, snack bars, awning sales, golf cart, & automobile rental. **Activities:** Recreation center (full-time staff, year-round), marine life nature center, observation deck, arcade, bank fishing, freshwater lake fishing, mini-golf, golf car & bicycle rentals, basketball, volleyball, shuffleboard, horseshoes, bocce ball. **Nearby Attractions:** Myrtle Beach historic tours & gardens, Grand Strand, Barefoot Landing, House of Blues, Alabama Theater, Dixie Stampede, Intracoastal Waterway, NASCAR speed track. **Additional Information:** Myrtle Beach Area Chamber of Commerce, (800) 356-3016.

RESTRICTIONS

Pets: On leash, enforced cleanup, some breeds not allowed (inquire). **Fires:** Allowed (not encouraged). **Alcoholic Beverages:** At site only. **Vehicle Maximum Length:** 45 ft. **Other:** No motorcycles.

TO GET THERE

From US 501, take Hwy. 544 south until it ends at the coast at Ocean Lakes. The park is 1 mi. north of Surfside Beach and 3 mi. south of downtown Myrtle Beach on South Kings Hwy. (17).

NINETY-SIX   MAP, B-2
Lake Greenwood State Recreation Area

reserve america

302 State Park Rd., 29666. T: (864) 543-3535; www.reserveamerica.com.

🚐 ★★★★   ⛺ ★★★★

Beauty: ★★★★★	Site Privacy: ★★★
Spaciousness: ★★★★	Quiet: ★★★
Security: ★★★★★	Cleanliness: ★★★★
Insect Control: ★★★★	Facilities: ★★★

The lovely campground at Lake Greenwood occupies gently rolling hills with pine straw ground cover. With shadier, prettier sites, campground No. 1 is preferable to campground No. 2. Sites are mostly back-ins with a few pull-throughs. Many have views of Lake Greenwood. Sites are spacious and all parking is paved. Though many sites are shaded by trees, privacy is poor as there is little foliage between sites. Lake Greenwood is stocked with bass, crappie, bream, perch, catfish, and stripers. Visit nearby Greenwood Museum, two-time recipient of "South Carolina Tourist Attraction of the Year" award, or the Ninety-Six National Historical site, which includes ruins of a British Fort used in the American Revolution. Security is excellent at this rural, gated, and guarded state park. This park is extremely popular and should be studiously avoided on summer holidays and weekends. Visit midweek, in spring or fall.

BASICS

Operated By: South Carolina State Parks. **Open:** All year. **Site Assignment:** Camping reservations accepted online or by phone (866) 345-PARK; 2-night min. **Registration:** At Drummond Center. Rangers make rounds, late-comers can register the next morning. **Fee:** Water/electric, $16–$18; tent, $12–$13. **Parking:** 2 vehicles per site, overflow parking available.

FACILITIES

Number of Tent-only Sites: 5. **Number of Multipurpose Sites:** 125. **Hookups:** Electric (50 amps), water; 125 sites w/ hookups. **Each Site:** Picnic table, fire pit. **Dump Station:** Yes. **Laundry:** No. **Pay Phone:** Yes. **Restrooms and Showers:** Yes. **Fuel:** No. **Propane:** No. **Internal Roads:** Paved. **RV Service:** On call. **Market:** 5 mi. west in Ninety-Six. **Restaurant:** 5 mi. west toward Greenwood. **General Store:** 1 mi. (also seasonal park store/tackle shop). **Vending:** No. **Swimming:** Lake (no lifeguard). **Playground:** No. **Other:** Boat ramps, picnic shelters, recreation building, barbecue shelter. **Activities:** Nature trails, fishing wall, boating, swimming, water sports. **Nearby Attractions:** Ninety-Six historic sites, historic Abbeville, Festival of Flowers. **Additional Information:** Greenwood Chamber of Commerce, (864) 223-8431.

RESTRICTIONS

Pets: On leash only. **Fires:** Allowed. **Alcoholic Beverages:** Not allowed. **Vehicle Maximum Length:** 45 ft. **Other:** 14-day stay limit; swim at your own risk.

TO GET THERE

From I-26, take Exit 74 and go west on SC 34 20 mi. Turn right on SC 702 and go north 1 mi. The park is on the right.

PICKENS   MAP, A-1
Table Rock State Park

reserve america

158 East Ellison Ln., 29671. T: (864) 878-9813; www.reserveamerica.com.

🚐 ★★★★   ⛺ ★★★★

Beauty: ★★★★	Site Privacy: ★★★
Spaciousness: ★★★	Quiet: ★★★★
Security: ★★★★	Cleanliness: ★★★★
Insect Control: ★★	Facilities: ★★★★

Nature lovers enjoy Table Rock and nearby Mountain Bridge Wilderness Area, which includes Caesar's Head State Park and Jones Gap State Park. Caesar's Head boasts dramatic granite cliffs while Jones Gap offers cool valley trails along the Middle Saluda River. A flat granite mountain serves as Table Rock's centerpiece and namesake. The campground includes two loops with mostly back-in parking. Beauty and privacy vary. The nicest section includes sites 25–40 and is heavily wooded. The park does not recommend this area for RVs. But parking spaces are level. If you have a small camper, give them a try. Sites are large, but there is little space between them. All parking is on gravel. Remote and gated, this park has excellent security. Elevations in this area range from 2,000 to 3,500 feet, so summer weather is mild. Visit in spring for solitude or in autumn for beautiful colors.

BASICS

Operated By: South Carolina State Parks. **Open:** All year. **Site Assignment:** Camping reservations accepted online or by phone (866) 345-PARK; 2-night min. **Registration:** At camp store or park office. **Fee:** Water/electric, $16–$18; tent, $6–$8; cash, personal check, V, MC. **Parking:** At site, 2 vehicles max.

FACILITIES

Number of Multipurpose Sites: 100. **Hookups:** Electric (20, 30 amps), water. **Each Site:** Grill, picnic table, fire ring. **Dump Station:** Yes. **Laundry:** Yes. **Pay Phone:** Yes. **Restrooms and Showers:** Yes. **Fuel:** No. **Propane:** No. **Internal Roads:** Paved. **RV Service:** 40 mi. west in Greenville. **Market:** 10 mi. south in Pickens. **Restaurant:** On site. **General Store:** 1 mi. **Vending:** No. **Swimming:** Yes. **Playground:** No. **Other:** Boat ramp, fishing pier, park store, meeting facilities, rec center. **Activities:** Minigolf, paddleboat, canoe & kayak rentals, nature center, year-round nature programs, hiking trails, fishing, swimming. **Nearby Attractions:** World of Energy at Lake Keowee, Issaqueena & Whitewater Falls, Foothills Trail, Sassafras Mountain. **Additional Information:** Cherokee Foothills Visitors Center/Table Rock State Park Headquarters (864) 878-9813, Pickens Chamber of Commerce (864) 878-3258.

RESTRICTIONS

Pets: On leash only. **Fires:** Allowed. **Alcoholic Beverages:** Not allowed. **Vehicle Maximum Length:** 36 ft.

TO GET THERE

From Pickens, take Hwy. 178 north 9 mi. Turn right and drive east on Hwy. 11 5 mi. The park is on the left.

PLUM BRANCH   MAP, B-1, B-2
Hamilton Branch State Recreation Area

reserve america

111 Campground Rd., 29845. T: (864) 333-2223; www.reserveamerica.com.

🚐 ★★★★   ⛺ ★★★★

Beauty: ★★★★★	Site Privacy: ★★★★
Spaciousness: ★★★★★	Quiet: ★★★★
Security: ★★★	Cleanliness: ★★★★
Insect Control: ★★★	Facilities: ★★★

Hamilton Branch is gorgeous. Flatter than others along the Savannah River, this campground features large sites. Loblolly pine and other species provide shade, though there is not much foliage surrounding the sites. With most sites on the waterfront, choosing the prettiest is tough. We recommend 36–54 and 71–78 for privacy and the nicest views. Most sites are laid out in pairs. Parking is on gravel or packed soil. Ten sites offer pull-through parking. Dock your boat at your campsite when lake levels permit. J. Strom Thurmond is one of the largest lakes in the southeast and is known for bream, crappie, striper, various bass, and catfish. Hamilton Branch doesn't offer many day-use activities, so explore outside the park. Remote, with gates locked at night, security is good at Hamilton Branch. This popular campground is likely to fill up on summer weekends. Plan a visit in the spring or during the week.

BASICS

Operated By: South Carolina State Parks. **Open:** All year. **Site Assignment:** Camping reservations accepted online or by phone (866) 345-PARK; 2-night min. **Registration:** In-season at office, off-season at sites. **Fee:** Water/electric, $15–$17. **Parking:** At site.

FACILITIES

Number of Tent-only Sites: 40. **Number of Multipurpose Sites:** 140. **Hookups:** Electric (20, 30 amps), water; 34 sites w/ 20 amps; 114 w/ 30 amps. **Each Site:** Picnic table, tent pad, fire ring (some sites), grill (some sites). **Dump Station:** Yes. **Laundry:** No. **Pay Phone:** Yes. **Restrooms and Showers:** Yes. **Fuel:** No. **Propane:** No. **Internal Roads:** Paved (most). **RV Service:** 30 mi. south in Augusta. **Market:** 12 mi. north in McCormick. **Restaurant:** 12 mi. north in McCormick. **General Store:** 2 mi. outside park, Wal-Mart 30 mi. south in Augusta. **Vending:** Beverages. **Swimming:** No. **Playground:** Yes. **Other:** Boat ramps, picnic shelters. **Activities:** Fishing on J. Strom Thurmond Lake, water sports. **Nearby Attractions:** Historic McCormick, Antebellum homes & museums in Edgefield, Parkseed Company & Gardens in Greenwood, 30 mi. to Augusta. **Additional Information:** McCormick Chamber of Commerce, (864) 465-2835, Augusta Chamber of Commerce, (706) 821-1300.

RESTRICTIONS

Pets: Leash (6 ft. max.). **Fires:** Allowed. **Alcoholic Beverages:** Not allowed. **Vehicle Maximum Length:** 40 ft.

TO GET THERE

From I-20, take Georgia Exit 200 (River Watch Pkwy.), then drive west 2 mi. to Furys Ferry Rd. (Hwy. 28 west). Turn right and drive north 13 mi. to Clarks Hill. Continue north on Hwy. 28 12 more mi. The park entrance is on the left.

PROSPERITY
Dreher Island State Recreation Area

MAP, B-2

reserve america

3677 State Park Rd., 29127. T: (803) 364-4152; www.reserveamerica.com.

🚐 ★★★★	🏕 ★★★★
Beauty: ★★★★	Site Privacy: ★★★
Spaciousness: ★★★	Quiet: ★★★★
Security: ★★★★★	Cleanliness: ★★★★
Insect Control: ★★★★	Facilities: ★★★

Recreation includes fishing and boating on Lake Murray. Fisher-folk hook catfish, bream, crappie, yellow perch, and largemouth and striped bass. Day-use facilities at this 348-acre park are not extensive, but the campgrounds are lovely. Of the two camping loops, B is nicer. On loop B, we recommend the

lakefront sites, which are large and secluded with pretty views. At both loops, site size and privacy vary, but none are small. Gorgeous trees include a variety of oak species, which provide plenty of shade at most sites. All parking is paved. There are a few pull-through sites and plenty of back-in sites. Located in a rural but touristy area, security is good. Gates are attended during the day and locked at night. Close to Columbia, Dreher Island stays full on summer weekends and holidays. We recommend a weekday, spring, or fall visit.

BASICS

Operated By: South Carolina State Parks. **Open:** All year. **Site Assignment:** Camping reservations accepted online or by phone (866) 345-PARK; 2-night min. **Registration:** At visitor center, late arrivals may camp in area outside gate. **Fee:** Water/electric, $18–$20; tent, $18–$20; plus admission fee. **Parking:** Limit 2 vehicles, overflow parking available.

FACILITIES

Number of Tent-only Sites: 15. **Number of Multipurpose Sites:** 97. **Hookups:** Electric (30 amps), water. **Each Site:** Picnic table, fire ring, water, electric. **Dump Station:** Yes. **Laundry:** No. **Pay Phone:** Yes. **Restrooms and Showers:** Yes. **Fuel:** Yes (automobile & boat). **Propane:** No. **Internal Roads:** Paved. **RV Service:** 30 mi. east in Columbia. **Market:** 10 mi. north in Chapin. **Restaurant:** 10 mi. north in Chapin. **General Store:** Camp store. **Vending:** No. **Swimming:** No. **Playground:** Yes. **Other:** Boat ramps, tackle shop, picnic shelters, screened meeting shelter. **Activities:** Fishing, pontoon boat rentals available, walking trails, bike trail. **Nearby Attractions:** Columbia historic homes, South Carolina Confederate Relic Room & Museum, Fort Jackson Museum, South Carolina State Museum. **Additional Information:** Capital City Lake Murray Country Visitor Information, (803) 781-5940.

RESTRICTIONS

Pets: On leash only. Leash no longer than 6 feet. No pets in villas/villa areas. **Fires:** Fire ring in sites only. **Alcoholic Beverages:** Not allowed. **Vehicle Maximum Length:** 45 ft. **Other:** 14-day stay limit.

TO GET THERE

From I-26, take Exit 91 at Chapin and drive west 12 mi. to Hwy. 76. At Hwy. 76, turn right and look for St. Peters Church Rd. on the left. Turn left and continue until Dreher Island Rd. Turn left and look for State Park Rd. Turn left again. The park is about 22 mi. from I-26.

RIDGEVILLE
Givhans Ferry State Park

MAP, C-3

reserve america

746 Givhans Ferry Rd., 29472. T: (843) 873-0692; www.reserveamerica.com.

🚐 ★★★★	🏕 ★★★★
Beauty: ★★★	Site Privacy: ★★★
Spaciousness: ★★★	Quiet: ★★★★
Security: ★★★★	Cleanliness: ★★★
Insect Control: ★★★	Facilities: ★★★★

This area was originally a ferry crossing in the 18th and 19th centuries, then later developed by the Civilian Conservation Corps in the 1930s. Today visitors enjoy camping, staying in a cabin on a high bluff overlooking the Edisto, and great fishing among the Spanish moss-draped oaks. Canoeists enjoy paddling to this 988-acre park from Colleton State Park. A stretch of the Edisto River in this area has been designated the Edisto River Canoe and Kayak Trail, a blackwater river course which carries paddlers into a fascinating world of wildlife and scenic beauty. The canoe trail between Colleton and Givhans Ferry is 23 miles by river and 15 miles by highway. The trip takes seven to nine hours, depending on current. The park has a 1.5-mile nature trail. Enjoy fishing in the Edisto River for flathead, catfish, red breast, channel catfish, largemouth bass, striped bass, shellcrackers, blue catfish, eels. Visitors can choose a cabin, or camping for their overnight accommodations. The campground has 25 sites and can accommodate RVs. Each site is rented on a first-come, first-served basis, except for two sites that may be reserved exclusively for the handicapped. The park has four two-bedroom/one-bath cabins which accommodate six people. Also available are a boat ramp, picnic shelters, and a meeting building. Visitors to Givhans Ferry State Park enjoy camping, picnicking, canoeing, kayaking, fishing, hiking, and staying in the rented cabins.

BASICS

Operated By: South Carolina Dept. of Parks, Recreation & Tourism. **Open:** All year. **Site Assignment:** Reservations can be made up to 16 weeks in advance. **Registration:** At office. **Fee:** Single, $10–$13; cabin, $39–$120; day-use community building, $140–$175; picnic shelter, $25–$32. **Parking:** 2 vehicles per site.

FACILITIES

Number of Multipurpose Sites: 34. **Hookups:** Yes. **Dump Station:** Yes. **Laundry:** Less than 10 mi. **Pay Phone:** Yes. **Restrooms and Showers:** Yes. **Fuel:** Less than 5 mi. **Propane:** Less than 5 mi. **Internal Roads:** Paved. **RV Service:** Yes. **Market:** Less than 20 mi. **Restaurant:** Less than 10 mi. **General Store:** No. **Vending:** No. **Swimming:** Yes. **Playground:** No. **Activities:** Bird-watching, hiking, photography, picnicking, stargazing, volleyball, swimming, wildlife/wildflower, canoeing, fishing, kayaking, scuba diving. **Nearby Attractions:** Nature study, tennis, boating, waterskiing, golf, horseback riding, scenic driving routes. **Additional Information:** Check-out time is noon for all campers. Quiet hours are 10 p.m.–7 a.m. Person must be 18 years old to rent or reserve a campsite. Max. campsite occupancy is 6 persons. Please contact the park to reserve ADA (disabled access).

RESTRICTIONS

Pets: Pets must remain on a leash no longer than 6 feet in length. **Vehicle Maximum Length:** 50 ft.

TO GET THERE

From I-95, take Exit 68 onto SC 61 east. Go 3 mi. to stop sign at US 15. Continue on Hwy. 61 approx. 14 mi. Givhans Ferry Rd. will be the 1st left after crossing the Edisto River. Givhans Ferry State Park is situated less than 1 mi. on left.

SANTEE · MAP, B-3
Santee State Park

reserve america

251 State Park Rd., 29142. T: (803) 854-2408; www.reserveamerica.com.

🚐 ★★★★   ⛺ ★★★★

Beauty: ★★★★★   Site Privacy: ★★★
Spaciousness: ★★★   Quiet: ★★★
Security: ★★   Cleanliness: ★★★★
Insect Control: ★★★★   Facilities: ★★★★

On Lake Marion, Santee is popular with anglers. Cypress trees and other tree stumps on the lake create a rich habitat for fish. The lake is known for its striped bass, an ocean bass which was trapped during dam construction and has since adapted to fresh water. Two delightful campgrounds offer lakefront sites. Small, quiet "Cypress View" features shady pull-through and back-in sites. "Lakeshore" features rows of mainly back-in sites. Close to the water and shaded by hickory and oak laden with Spanish moss, sites 94, 96, and 98 are especially beautiful. Site size is ample, but there is little privacy between sites. Parking is on sand, dirt, and pine straw. Despite the park's laid-back atmosphere, it's only 2 miles from I-95. Security is not adequate here. Gates are not attended or locked at night. This extremely popular campground stays busy. We recommend midweek or off-season touring.

BASICS
Operated By: South Carolina State Parks. **Open:** All year. **Site Assignment:** Camping reservations accepted online or by phone (866) 345-PARK; 2-night min. **Registration:** At visitor center, after-hours registration available. **Fee:** $16–$18; cash, personal check, V, MC. **Parking:** 2 vehicles per site, overflow parking available.

FACILITIES
Number of Multipurpose Sites: 163. **Hookups:** Electric (20, 30 amps), water. **Each Site:** Picnic table. **Dump Station:** Yes. **Laundry:** Yes. **Pay Phone:** Yes. **Restrooms and Showers:** Yes. **Fuel:** No. **Propane:** No. **Internal Roads:** Gravel. **RV Service:** On call. **Market:** 4 mi. south in Santee. **Restaurant:** 4 mi. south in Santee. **General Store:** Camp store. **Vending:** Beverages. **Swimming:** No. **Playground:** Yes, in day-use area. **Other:** Visitor's center, boat ramps, picnic shelters, meeting building, 30 rental cabins. **Activities:** Nature & bicycle trails, fishing pier, seasonal swimming & paddleboat rentals when lifeguard on duty, tennis, nature boat tours. **Nearby Attractions:** Palmetto Trailhead, 3 golf courses, Lake Marion, Santee community, Lonestar Mercantile historic village & restaurant, 1 hour from Charleston & Columbia. **Additional Information:** Santee Cooper Country, (803) 854-2152, ext. 5, www.santeetourism.com.

RESTRICTIONS
Pets: On leash only; not allowed in cabins or cabin area. **Fires:** Allowed. **Alcoholic Beverages:** Not allowed. **Vehicle Maximum Length:** 45 ft. **Other:** 14-day stay limit.

TO GET THERE
From I-95, take Exit 98 at Santee. Drive northwest on Hwy. 6 about 1 mi. Turn right onto State Park Rd. The campground is 2 mi. ahead.

SPARTANBURG · MAP, A-2
Croft State Natural Area

reserve america

450 Croft State Park Rd., 29302.
T: (864) 585-1283; www.reserveamerica.com.

🚐 ★★★★   ⛺ ★★★★

Beauty: ★★★   Site Privacy: ★★★
Spaciousness: ★★★   Quiet: ★★★★
Security: ★★★★   Cleanliness: ★★★
Insect Control: ★★★   Facilities: ★★★★

Once part of a World War II Army training camp, Croft today is a popular park for area residents as well as out-of-state visitors. The adventurous park visitor may visit several cemeteries from early settlers, or numerous remnant Army structures. Its rolling terrain of 7,054 acres includes a wide variety of facilities. The park has 21.5 miles of equestrian trails, a stable and show ring. Horse shows are held regularly by a local equestrian club. There is a moderate 2-mile hiking trail. The sheer size of the park provides an extremely large variety of habitats for deer, wild turkey, and many other species. The park includes 50 campsites that are available on a first-come, first-served basis, except for two sites that may be reserved exclusively for the handicapped. Each site is packed gravel and has individual water and electrical hookups and a picnic table. The campground has heated restroom facilities with hot showers. There is a dump station for RVs. Five sites accommodate RVs up to 40 feet, others up to 30 feet. Day-use facilities include a park store, hiking trail, equestrian trails, stables, and show ring. Enjoy fishing for bass, bream, crappie and catfish. Private boats are restricted to trolling motors only. Also available are picnic shelters, playground equipment, a swimming pool, and seasonal tennis courts.

BASICS
Operated By: South Carolina State Parks. **Open:** All year. **Site Assignment:** Reservations can be made 11 months in advance. **Registration:** At office. **Fee:** Single, $10–$13; horse stall, $6–$7.50; picnic shelter, $25–$32. **Parking:** At site.

FACILITIES
Number of Multipurpose Sites: 117. **Hookups:** Yes. **Each Site:** Fire ring. **Dump Station:** Yes. **Laundry:** Less than 5 mi. **Pay Phone:** Yes. **Restrooms and Showers:** Yes. **Fuel:** Less than 5 mi. **Propane:** No. **Internal Roads:** Paved. **RV Service:** No. **Market:** Less than 10 mi. **Restaurant:** Less than 10 mi. **General Store:** Less than 5 mi. **Vending:** Yes. **Swimming:** No. **Playground:** Yes. **Other:** Use of metal detectors is prohibited. **Activities:** Biking, bird-watching, boating, canoeing, fishing, hiking, horseback riding, kayaking, nature study, photography, picnicking, tennis, walking, wildflower viewing, wildlife viewing.

RESTRICTIONS
Pets: On a leash or other physical restraint at all times. **Fires:** In designated fireplaces. **Alcoholic Beverages:** Not allowed. **Vehicle Maximum Length:** 40 ft.

TO GET THERE
Croft is located 5 mi. southeast of Spartanburg off SC 56 on Dairy Ridge Rd. From I-26, take Exit 22, go east on Hwy. 296. approx. 1 mi.; turn onto Hwy. 295 until it intersects with Hwy. 56. Turn right onto Hwy. 56, then take a left at Dairy Ridge Rd. and follow signs.

SUNSET · MAP, A-1
Keowee-Toxaway State Natural Area

reserve america

108 Residence Dr., 29685. T: (864) 868-2605; www.reserveamerica.com.

🚐 ★★★★   ⛺ ★★★★

Beauty: ★★★   Site Privacy: ★★★
Spaciousness: ★★★   Quiet: ★★★★
Security: ★★★★   Cleanliness: ★★★
Insect Control: ★★★   Facilities: ★★★

This 1,000-acre South Carolina state park features outstanding rock outcroppings and views of the Foothills and Blue Ridge mountains. Rhododendron, mountain laurel, and other mountain vegetation can be found along the streams in the park. A museum tells the story of the Cherokee Native Americans who once roamed this area and their relationship with the European settlers of South Carolina. A large rental cabin in a wooded area features an upper deck porch overlooking Lake Keowee and a private floating courtesy dock. The campground offers 24 campsites. All sites are rented on a first-come, first-served basis, except for two paved sites that may be reserved exclusively for the handicapped. The campground has a heated restroom facility with hot showers. There are no waterfront sites. Ten sites are paved, with individual water and electrical hookups, a grill, a fire ring and picnic table, and can accommodate RVs up to 40 feet. There is a dump station for RVs. Fourteen sites offer tent pads with central water, a fire ring, and a picnic table. One tent per pad is permitted. The park offers a short interpretive trail and two other moderate to strenuous hiking trails. Enjoy fishing in nearby Lake Keowee for bass, bream, crappie, catfish, carp. Boat access to Lake Keowee is 5 miles from the park. The park also offers picnic shelters and a former chapel that serves as a meeting facility for up to 100 people.

BASICS
Operated By: South Carolina State Parks. **Open:** All year. **Site Assignment:** Reservations can be made 11 months in advance. **Registration:** At office. **Fee:** Single, $6–$13; picnic shelter, $25–$32; cabin, $92–$863. **Parking:** At site.

FACILITIES
Number of Multipurpose Sites: 34. **Hookups:** Yes. **Each Site:** Fire ring. **Dump Station:** Yes.

Reserve your campsite online at www.ReserveAmerica.com

Laundry: No. **Pay Phone:** No. **Restrooms and Showers:** Yes. **Fuel:** Less than 5 mi. **Propane:** No. **Internal Roads:** Paved. **RV Service:** No. **Market:** No. **Restaurant:** No. **General Store:** Yes. **Vending:** No. **Swimming:** No. **Playground:** No. **Activities:** Bird-watching, hiking, nature study, picnicking, kayaking, wildlife viewing.

RESTRICTIONS

Pets: On a leash no longer than 6 feet or under physical restraint at all times; not permitted in the cabin or cabin area. **Fires:** In designated fireplaces. **Alcoholic Beverages:** Prohibited. **Vehicle Maximum Length:** 40 ft.

TO GET THERE

Keowee-Toxaway is located 12 mi. northwest of Pickens at the intersection of SC 133 and SC 11 at Lake Keowee. The park is 12 mi. northwest of Pickens at the intersection of SC 11 and SC 133.

UNION   MAP, A-2
Sadlers Creek State Recreation Area

reserve america

2647 Sardis Rd., 29379. T: (864) 427-5966; www.reserveamerica.com.

🚐 ★★★★   ⛺ ★★★★

Beauty: ★★★	Site Privacy: ★★★
Spaciousness: ★★	Quiet: ★★★★
Security: ★★★★	Cleanliness: ★★★
Insect Control: ★★★	Facilities: ★★★★

Popular with fishermen, boaters, day-users, and campers, the 395-acre park is on a peninsula providing access to Lake Hartwell. Nearby residents and travelers enjoy its peaceful surroundings and convenient location. Opportunities at the park abound for viewing deer, wild turkey, and other wildlife. Lake Hartwell, with its 56,000 acres of water, provides numerous opportunities for water activities. The campground offers both RV sites and tent sites. Each site is rented on a first-come, first-served basis, except for two sites that may be reserved exclusively for the handicapped. The campground has restroom facilities with hot showers. Two are heated for the winter. Thirty-seven RV sites are packed gravel with individual water and electrical hookups. Some sites accommodate RVs up to 40 feet, others up to 30 feet. Most sites are waterfront. Three sites are pull-through. There is a dump station for RVs. The tent sites are packed sand and have central water available. There is a primitive camping area for organized groups. The area includes picnic tables, central water, and fire rings. It has a capacity of 75 people. Three picnic shelters are available free on a first-come, first-served basis or can be reserved for a fee. Enjoy fishing in Lake Hartwell for several species of bass, bream, crappie, and trout. The park has a boat ramp. Pine Grove trail is an easy half mile one-way hiking trail.

BASICS

Operated By: South Carolina State Parks. **Open:** All year. **Site Assignment:** Reservations can be made 11 months in advance. **Registration:** At

office. **Fee:** Single, $9–$17; picnic shelter, $25–$32; pavilion, $90–$112; recreation building, $100–$125. **Parking:** At site.

FACILITIES

Number of Multipurpose Sites: 71. **Hookups:** Yes. **Each Site:** Fire ring. **Dump Station:** Yes. **Laundry:** Less than 10 mi. **Pay Phone:** Yes. **Restrooms and Showers:** Yes. **Fuel:** Less than 5 mi. **Propane:** No. **Internal Roads:** Paved. **RV Service:** No. **Market:** Less than 10 mi. **Restaurant:** Less than 10 mi. **General Store:** Less than 10 mi. **Vending:** No. **Swimming:** No. **Playground:** Yes. **Activities:** Baseball, biking, fishing, hiking, horseshoe, jogging/running, picnicking, volleyball, walking, wildflower viewing, wildlife viewing.

RESTRICTIONS

Pets: On a leash or other physical restraint at all times. **Fires:** In designated fireplaces. **Alcoholic Beverages:** Not allowed. **Vehicle Maximum Length:** 40 ft.

TO GET THERE

Sadlers Creek is located 12 mi. southwest of Anderson off SC 187 and 14 mi. from I-85 (Exit 14). From I-85, take Exit 14 to SC 187 S. 14 mi. Turn right onto Sadlers Creek Rd. Park is 1.1 mi. off SC 187.

WEDGEFIELD   MAP, B-3
Poinsett State Park

reserve america

6660 Poinsett Park Rd., 29168. T: (803) 494-8177; www.reserveamerica.com.

🚐 ★★★   ⛺ ★★★★

Beauty: ★★★★	Site Privacy: ★★★
Spaciousness: ★★★	Quiet: ★★★★
Security: ★★★★	Cleanliness: ★★★
Insect Control: ★★★	Facilities: ★★★★

Poinsett State Park is located in an outlying area of the Sandhills, yet is still within the coastal plain. The park's terrain allows for an amazing diversity of plant and animal life. Plant communities represented within the park include sandhills, swamps, mountain bluffs, and pine-hardwood. Mountain laurel and galax grow on steep facing hillsides, while Spanish moss–draped cypress and tupelo trees rise from the swamp. This 1,000-acre park, with its abundant resources, nature center, and full-time naturalist, is an excellent laboratory for outdoor education. The campground offers 50 campsites. Each campsite is rented on a first come, first served basis, except for two sites that may be reserved exclusively for the handicapped. Each site is packed soil and has individual water and electrical hookups, and a picnic table. The campground has heated restroom facilities with hot showers. Some sites accommodate RVs up to 40 feet, other sites up to 20 feet. Two sites are pull-through. There is a dump station for RVs. Camping clubs are allowed to reserve 10 to 25 sites. There is a primitive-camping area for organized groups. The area includes water and a toilet. The capacity at the group site is 200 people. There are four cabins available for rental. There is an equestrian

campground. Five picnic shelters are available and can be reserved for a fee. The nature center includes displays on native Sumter County animals, plants, and history. There are several hiking trails, an equestrian trail, and a bike trail. Enjoy fishing in the park's ten-acre lake for bass, bream, and catfish. Fishing boats can be rented but no private boats are permitted. Seasonal lake swimming and rental pedal boats are offered upon availability of lifeguards.

BASICS

Operated By: South Carolina State Parks. **Open:** All year. **Site Assignment:** Reservations can be made 11 months in advance. **Registration:** At office. **Fee:** Single, $6–$13; picnic shelter, $25–$32; cabin, $36–$586. **Parking:** At site.

FACILITIES

Number of Multipurpose Sites: 77. **Hookups:** Yes. **Each Site:** Fire ring. **Dump Station:** Yes. **Laundry:** Less than 20 mi. **Pay Phone:** Yes. **Restrooms and Showers:** Yes. **Fuel:** Less than 10 mi. **Propane:** No. **Internal Roads:** Paved. **RV Service:** No. **Market:** Less than 20 mi. **Restaurant:** Less than 20 mi. **General Store:** Less than 10 mi. **Vending:** No. **Swimming:** Yes. **Playground:** No. **Activities:** Biking, bird-watching, fishing, hiking, horseback riding, jogging/running, paddleboating, picnicking, volleyball, walking, wildflower viewing, wildlife viewing.

RESTRICTIONS

Pets: On a leash or other physical restraint at all times. **Fires:** In designated fireplaces. **Alcoholic Beverages:** Prohibited. **Vehicle Maximum Length:** 40 ft.

TO GET THERE

Poinsett State Park is located off SC 261, 18 mi. southwest of Sumter near the town of Wedgefield.

WINDSOR   MAP, B-2
Aiken State Natural Area

1145 State Park Rd., 29856. T: (803) 649-2857; www.reserveamerica.com.

🚐 ★★★★   ⛺ ★★★★

Beauty: ★★★	Site Privacy: ★★★
Spaciousness: ★★★	Quiet: ★★★★
Security: ★★★★	Cleanliness: ★★★
Insect Control: ★★★	Facilities: ★★★★

Four spring-fed lakes and the meandering South Edisto River make Aiken State Park popular with both fishermen and campers. This area is a combination of a river swamp and dry sand hills; the latter provides evidence of an era when the sea reached this far inland. Built in the 1930s by the Civilian Conservation Corps, this 1,067-acre park has a variety of animal and plant life, making it an excellent location for nature study. The park offers 25 campsites and sites that can accommodate RVs up to 35 feet. Each campsite is rented on a first-come, first-served basis, except for two sites that may be reserved exclusively for the handicapped. Camping clubs are allowed to reserve a maximum of ten sites. Each site is packed sand and has individual water and electrical hookups, a fire ring, and a picnic table. The campground has a heated restroom facility with hot showers. There is a dump station for RVs. There is a 3-mile nature trail that provides an easy hike. The Edisto River has a 2-mile canoe trail with canoes rentals available. Fishing is available for bream, bass, and catfish, in one of the three park lakes or the Edisto River. A South Carolina fishing license is required. Fishing boats (nonmotorized) can be rented at the park for a reasonable price. Private boats are not allowed on the park lake. Picnic shelters are available free on a first-come, first-served basis, or reserved for a fee.

BASICS

Operated By: South Carolina State Parks. **Open:** All year. **Site Assignment:** Reservations can be made 11 months in advance. **Registration:** At office. **Fee:** Single, $10–13; picnic shelter, $25–$32. **Parking:** At site.

FACILITIES

Number of Multipurpose Sites: 36. **Hookups:** Yes. **Each Site:** Fire ring. **Dump Station:** Yes. **Laundry:** Less than 10 mi. **Pay Phone:** No. **Restrooms and Showers:** Yes. **Fuel:** No. **Propane:** No. **Internal Roads:** Paved. **RV Service:** No. **Market:** Less than 20 mi. **Restaurant:** Less 20 mi. **General Store:** Less than 10 mi. **Vending:** Yes. **Swimming:** Yes. **Playground:** Yes. **Activities:** Baseball, biking, bird-watching, canoeing, fishing, hiking, jogging/running, kayaking, paddleboating, photography, walking, wildlife viewing.

RESTRICTIONS

Pets: On a leash or other physical restraint at all times. **Fires:** In designated fireplaces. **Alcoholic Beverages:** Not allowed. **Vehicle Maximum Length:** 35 ft.

TO GET THERE

Aiken State Natural Area is 16 mi. east of Aiken off US 78 or off Hwy. 302 from Columbia. From Hwy. 302, turn onto Mackney Scott Rd. and follow signs.

WINNSBORO   MAP, A-2
Lake Wateree State Recreation Area

reserve america

881 State Park Rd., 29180.
T: (803) 482-6401 or (803) 482-6651;
www.reserveamerica.com.

🚐 ★★★★   ⛺ ★★★★

Beauty: ★★★★★	Site Privacy: ★★★★★
Spaciousness: ★★★★	Quiet: ★★★★★
Security: ★★★★★	Cleanliness: ★★★★
Insect Control: ★★★★	Facilities: ★★★

This small state park is situated on 13,700-acre Lake Wateree, one of South Carolina's oldest and best-loved fishing lakes. Waterfowl at Lake Wateree include egrets, blue heron, mallards, and wood ducks. Here, recreation revolves around boating and fishing—there isn't even a swimming beach. But, the lake and the campground are breathtakingly gorgeous. The campground consists of one loop of paved sites. Of these, five offer pull-through parking and the remainder offer back-in parking. Site size varies from average to huge. Tree cover, consisting mainly of pine, is lovely and includes plenty of foliage to provide privacy between sites. Lakefront sites (odd numbers 11–27) and heavily wooded sites in the 50s and 60s are all gorgeous. Security is excellent at this rural state park, as gates are locked at night. For maximum peace and quiet, visit this very pretty little park on weekdays or in the spring or fall.

BASICS

Operated By: South Carolina State Parks. **Open:** All year except Christmas. **Site Assignment:** Camping reservations accepted online or by phone (866) 345-PARK; 2-night min. **Registration:** At park store, late-comers must have combination to open gate. **Fee:** Water/electric, $16–$18. **Parking:** All wheels on pavement, overflow parking available.

FACILITIES

Number of Multipurpose Sites: 72. **Hookups:** Electric (20, 30 amps); water; 72 sites w/ hookups. **Each Site:** Picnic table, fire ring. **Dump Station:** Yes. **Laundry:** No. **Pay Phone:** Yes. **Restrooms and Showers:** Yes. **Fuel:** No. **Propane:** No. **Internal Roads:** Paved (excellent condition). **RV Service:** 40 mi. south in Columbia. **Market:** 15 mi. west in Winnsboro. **Restaurant:** 7 mi. west in Winnsboro. **General Store:** Park store. **Vending:** Beverages. **Swimming:** No. **Playground:** Yes. **Other:** Boat ramp, fueling dock, tackle shop, picnic area. **Activities:** Nature trail, fishing, boating, swimming area. **Nearby Attractions:** Ridgeway historic village, Columbia historic homes, South Carolina Confederate Relic Room & Museum, Fort Jackson Museum, South Carolina State Museum. **Additional Information:** Columbia Metropolitan CVB, (800) 264-4884 or (803) 254-0479.

RESTRICTIONS

Pets: On leash only. **Fires:** Fire ring only. **Alcoholic Beverages:** Not allowed. **Vehicle Maximum Length:** 40 ft. **Other:** 14-day stay limit.

TO GET THERE

From I-77, take Exit 41 and drive east on SC 20 5 mi. to Hwy. 21. Turn left (north) and drive 2 mi. to the first paved road. Turn right on River Rd. and drive 5–7 mi. The park is on the left.

South Dakota

Located in the north-central part of the United States, South Dakota is generally considered part of the Midwest. The east part of the state, with its flat or rolling soils, resembles the landscape of other states in the Midwest, and the western section unfurls out onto the **Great Plains.**

South Dakota is filled to the brim with campgrounds that take advantage of its magnificent scenery, rich natural resources, and varied wildlife. The state's largest cities are **Sioux Falls; Rapid City,** which serves as the center of the state's resort area; and **Pierre,** the state capital, where city and country collide. The **Missouri River** divides the state into two major regions. The other major river is **Big Sioux River.** South Dakota is covered with countless other rivers and lakes, providing limitless opportunities to enjoy fishing, boating, and waterskiing.

Although the bulk of South Dakota's population makes its home in the east, the crown jewels of the state are clearly in the southwestern part, though beautiful spots exist throughout. The **Badlands** and **Black Hills** typically take the cake for drawing the most tourists, although it's hard to say whether or not the **International Vinegar Museum** in the Day County town of **Roslyn** can be considered a contender. The Black Hills is a region of deeply eroded gullies of colorful, mesmerizing shapes. Within this expanse of land are five national parks, waterfalls, abundant wildlife, acclaimed recreational trails, and trout fishing. Bison, elk, pronghorn, mule deer, prairie dogs, coyotes, and wild horses still roam free here, so perhaps that's why the producers of the award-winning film *Dances With Wolves* chose the 40th state as its prime shooting location. The **Black Hills Caverns** and **Black Hill Maze** offer countless hours of fun for families. In the southwest corner of the state, **Badlands National Park** is a 244,000-acre park of spires, pinnacles, buttes, and gorges. This breathtakingly spectacular marvel of the earth was created by millions of years of erosion.

Other intriguing places include **Mount Rushmore National Memorial,** which has the famous stone-carved faces of former U.S. presidents George Washington, Abraham Lincoln, Thomas Jefferson, and Teddy Roosevelt; the **Petrified Wood Park** in the Perkins County town of Lemmon; **Jewel Cave National Monument,** recognized as the third-longest cave in the world; **Wind Cave National Park,** one of the oldest caves in the world; and **Dell Rapids,** known for its beautiful scenery. One can also spend time at **Buffalo Gap** or **Grand River National Grasslands,** regions set aside to protect the state's complex ecosystem. Even though its outside murals are the only part of it constructed of corn (an annual process), the **Corn Palace,** also known as the **World's Largest Birdfeeder,** is a unique building. The Palace, located in Mitchell, celebrates the state's rich agriculture. Perhaps a proportional homage paid to the Corn Palace is made by the **World's Largest Pheasant,** standing some 20 feet tall and 40 feet wide, located in the county seat of Beadle, Huron. At one time, the state laid claim to being the home of **Sue,** the world-famous *T. rex* fossil. That is, until she was purchased by and carted off to the Field Museum of Natural History in Chicago for a cool $8.4 million because she was discovered on federal land.

The state's national forests, national parks, and state parks all have facilities for camping, fishing, picnicking, and hunting. The Midwest Plains weather is definitely a matter of extremes—cold, long winters and hot summers—so be prepared and don't let a little sweat get in the way of really discovering the quirks and pleasures South Dakota has to offer.

Campground Profiles

BROOKINGS MAP, B-4
Oakwood Lakes State Park

46109 202nd St., 57220. T: (605) 627-5441;
www.sdgfp.info/parks/index.htm.

🚐 ★★★★   ⛺ ★★★★

Beauty: ★★★★	Site Privacy: ★★★★
Spaciousness: ★★★★	Quiet: ★★★★
Security: ★★★★	Cleanliness: ★★★★
Insect Control: ★★★	Facilities: ★★

Located where Native Americans once gathered for summer camp, Oakwood Lakes State Park presents a small piece of early American history in a beautiful scenic setting. Level, asphalted camping pads under a canopy of trees make for a relaxing getaway. Within a stone's throw away are eight glacial lakes that are excellent for all water sports. In addition, there are miles of hiking trails, three Native American burial grounds, and the restored cabin of the first settler in the area, Samuel Mortimer. The campground is set in a figure-eight configuration, with most sites being back-ins. There are a limited number of pull-through sites. There is also a horse camp for those wishing to travel with their horses. Summer days average in the 80s, with nights cooling to the 50s. June is an excellent time to visit, before the bugs hatch. There is an employee in residence in addition to a camp host, offering the best of security.

BASICS
Operated By: South Dakota Game, Fish, & Parks Dept. **Open:** All year; water turned off in winter. **Site Assignment:** By reservation (800) 710-CAMP. **Registration:** At entrance booth. **Fee:** Electric, $14; no electric, $10. **Parking:** At site.

FACILITIES
Number of Tent-only Sites: 4. **Number of Multipurpose Sites:** 68. **Hookups:** Electric (30, 50 amps). **Each Site:** Picnic table, grated fire pit. **Dump Station:** Yes. **Laundry:** No. **Pay Phone:** Yes. **Restrooms and Showers:** Yes. **Fuel:** No. **Propane:** No. **Internal Roads:** Paved. **RV Service:** 17 mi. southeast in Brookings. **Market:** In Brookings. **Restaurant:** In Brookings. **General Store:** No. **Vending:** No. **Swimming:** Lakefront swimming beach (no lifeguard). **Playground:** Yes. **Other:** Boat ramp, picnic shelters w/ grills, amphitheater, 3 cabins, 2 group camp areas, hiking trail, interpretive shelter, visitor center, canoe rentals. **Activities:** Water & snow skiing, boating, swimming, interpretive programs, hiking, fishing (walleye, northerns, bass), volleyball, weekly park programs, hay rides, junior naturalist program, Sun. worship services. **Nearby Attractions:** State Agricultural Heritage Museum, McCrory Gardens. **Additional Information:** South Dakota State Parks, (605) 773-3391 or Brookings Chamber of Commerce, (605) 692-6125.

RESTRICTIONS
Pets: On leash. **Fires:** Fire pit only; fires may be restricted due to weather conditions. **Alcoholic Beverages:** Allowed. **Vehicle Maximum Length:** No limit. **Other:** 14-day stay limit.

TO GET THERE
From I-29 7 mi. north of Brookings, take Exit 140. Go west on Hwy. 30 (this will turn into CR 6) about 10 mi.; you will see a large sign for Oakwood Lake State Park. Turn north and follow signs to the campground.

CUSTER MAP, B-1
Custer Mountain Cabins and Campground

P.O. Box 472, 57730.
T: (800) 239-5505 or (605) 673-5440;
www.custermountain.com.

🚐 ★★★   ⛺ ★★★★

Beauty: ★★★★★	Site Privacy: ★★★
Spaciousness: ★★★	Quiet: ★★★★★
Security: ★★★★	Cleanliness: ★★★★
Insect Control: ★★★	Facilities: ★★

Custer Mountain Cabins and Campground is an exquisite private facility. It offers deluxe modern cabins and a charming campground nestled deep in the Black Hills, 2 miles east of Custer. The Black Hills offer breathtaking scenic drives, wonderful wildlife, Custer State Park, and Mt. Rushmore. The campground is situated on 50 acres of pristine land encircled by stands of black hill spruces. The RV area is located in a loop near the front of the grounds, and it has both pull-through and back-in sites. Each site has a gravel camping pad, but expect to have to level it out. Large tent sites can be found among the trees, giving tent campers more seclusion and privacy. The air is crisp in the morning, and summer days are pleasant. Visitors can experience a vast array of recreational and historic activities. Inviting hosts are available to assist you with all your vacation needs.

BASICS
Operated By: Paul Nordstrom. **Open:** All year; water turned off in winter. **Site Assignment:** By reservations; deposit required for cabins only; first come, first served sites available. **Registration:** At general store. **Fee:** RV, $30.75; tent, $22.50; partial hookup, $27. **Parking:** At site.

FACILITIES
Number of RV-only Sites: 26. **Number of Tent-only Sites:** 40. **Hookups:** Electric (30, 50 amps), water, sewer, cable TV. **Each Site:** Picnic table, fire pit. **Dump Station:** Sewer at each site. **Laundry:** Yes. **Pay Phone:** No. **Restrooms and Showers:** Yes. **Fuel:** 2 mi. in Custer. **Propane:** 2 mi. in Custer. **Internal Roads:** Gravel, w/ some bumps. **RV Service:** In Rapid City. **Market:** 2 mi. in Custer. **Restaurant:** 2 mi. in Custer or in Custer State Park. **General Store:** Yes. **Vending:** General store. **Swimming:** No. **Playground:** Yes. **Other:** Very nice cabins & summer vacation homes. **Activities:** Large open recreation field, hiking, biking. **Nearby Attractions:** Custer State Park, Flinstone Village, Mt. Rushmore, Crazy Horse Monument. Most attractions w/in 1-hour drive. **Additional Information:** Custer Chamber of Commerce, (605) 673-2244.

RESTRICTIONS
Pets: Must be on leash. In campsites only, not in cabins. **Fires:** In designated fire pits or grills only; fires may be restricted due to weather conditions; please ask management before starting any open fires. **Alcoholic Beverages:** Allowed but not sold. **Vehicle Maximum Length:** No limit.

TO GET THERE
The campground is 1.5 mi. east of Custer on Hwy. 16A.

CUSTER MAP, B-1
Custer State Park

13329 US 16A, 57730.
T: (605) 255-4515 or (800) 710-2267;
www.custerstatepark.info.

🚐 ★★★   ⛺ ★★★★

Beauty: ★★★★	Site Privacy: ★★★
Spaciousness: ★★★	Quiet: ★★★★
Security: ★★★★	Cleanliness: ★★★
Insect Control: ★★★	Facilities: ★★

Custer State Park is a 73,000-acre resort in the heart of the Black Hills. Created in 1913 as a game reserve, this magnificent park has become world-renowned as a showcase of the area's natural resources and wildlife. The park was named after George A. Custer, who was enthralled by the region's uncommon natural beauty. The park has eight campgrounds, including a horse camp where your equine friend is more than welcome. The majority of the campgrounds have level asphalt camping pads, potable water, laundry, evening programs, fishing, and nearby swimming. Most of the campgrounds are arranged in loops, many with sites overlooking streams, mountains, or forests. The state park works in conjunction with Custer State Park Resort Co. to offer restaurant service, group events, jeep tours, and other additional activities. There are hiking and biking trails throughout the park, as well as excellent trout fishing. The weather is typical of the area, experiencing warm summer days and cooling in the evening. The park has very tight security, and all vehicles are required to have a park license obtainable at any entrance gate.

BASICS
Operated By: South Dakota Game, Fish, & Parks Dept. **Open:** All year, limited campgrounds in winter. **Site Assignment:** By reservation (800) 710-2267, starting Jan. 2 each year. **Registration:** At the information station, located at each campground entrance. **Fee:** $13–$18; depending on choice of Custer campground, plus a gate fee. **Parking:** At site.

FACILITIES
Number of Multipurpose Sites: 354. **Hookups:** None. **Each Site:** Picnic table, grated fire pit. **Dump Station:** Yes, located just east of the Game Lodge Resort in the maintenance complex. **Laundry:** Yes, located in Blue Bell, Game Lodge, Grace Coolidge, & Sylvan Lake. **Pay Phone:** Yes, in service area & most camping areas. **Restrooms and Showers:** Yes. **Fuel:** Yes, located near Blue Bell,

Grace Lodge, Grace Coolidge. **Propane:** Only in Custer. **Internal Roads:** Most roads are paved. **RV Service:** In Custer. **Market:** Sylvan Lake General Store & Coolidge Inn & Blue Bell Store are w/in the park. **Restaurant:** 6 places to eat w/in the park. **General Store:** 4 general stores: Coolidge, Sylvan Lake, Blue Bell, & Legion Lake. **Vending:** Soft drinks. **Swimming:** 5 park beaches available: Center, Legion, Stockade, & Sylvan Lakes & the Game Lodge Pond. Life jackets are advised. Jumping from cliffs & rocks strictly prohibited. No lifeguards. **Playground:** At Gamelodge, Stockade & near Blue Bell. **Other:** Cabins, Peter Norbeck Visitor Center, Wildlife Station Visitor Center, Black Hills Play House, 3 chapels, several restaurants, Sylvan Auditorium, mountain bike rentals, boat rentals, art gallery. **Activities:** Horseback riding, fishing (trout, perch, crappie, bullhead, walleye, bass), boating, 5 swimming beaches, family evening programs, guided nature walks, gold panning, junior naturalist programs, interpretive trails, special events, scenic drives, Buffalo. **Nearby Attractions:** Mt. Rushmore, scenic drives, Crazy Horse Memorial, natural hot springs, rodeos, shopping, museums, caves. **Additional Information:** Custer Chamber of Commerce; (605) 673-2244; for tickets to the Black Hills Playhouse, (605) 255-4141 or www.blackhillsplayhouse.com.

RESTRICTIONS

Pets: On leash only. Not allowed on beaches. **Fires:** Fire pit only; fires may be restricted due to weather conditions. **Alcoholic Beverages:** Allowed. No glass containers on beaches. **Vehicle Maximum Length:** Check specific campground measurements. **Other:** 14-day stay limit.

TO GET THERE

There are 7 entrances into this park. It is 22.3 mi. from Rapid City following Hwy. 16A south, 10.2 mi. from Hermosa following Hwy. 36 west, or you may take the scenic Needles Hwy. Campgrounds are scattered throughout the park.

FT. PIERRE   MAP, B-3
Oahe Downstream Recreation Area

20439 Marina Loop Rd., 57532.
T: (605) 223-7722 or (800) 710-2267;
www.sdgfp.info/parks/regions/oahesharpe/
oahedownstream.htm.

🚐 ★★★★   ⛺ ★★★★★

Beauty: ★★★★	Site Privacy: ★★★★
Spaciousness: ★★★★	Quiet: ★★★★
Security: ★★★★★	Cleanliness: ★★★★
Insect Control: ★★	Facilities: ★★

Downstream is a huge park located about 10 miles outside of Ft. Pierre on the Oahe Dam, encompassing both the Missouri River and Lake Oahe. The U.S. Corps of Engineers Downstream Recreation Area is broken into three campgrounds with more than 300 sites between them. Each site has a paved camping pad and is under a forest of mature cottonwoods and willows. There are large common areas in each campground, complete with playgrounds and comfort stations with hot showers. The campgrounds are in loops and have both pull-through and back-in sites. There is a full-service marina on the property, as well as a restaurant, convenience store, and bait shop. Each campground has a camp host, and there is a staffed entrance booth for your protection. There are four distinct seasons in Ft. Pierre, with temperatures on summer days averaging in the mid-80s. Bring insect repellent if visiting in the late summer; otherwise, the deer flies will eat you for lunch.

BASICS

Operated By: South Dakota Game, Fish, & Parks Dept. **Open:** May–Sept. 30. **Site Assignment:** By reservations, all fees payable at that time; call (800) 710-2267 or visit www.campsd.com to make reservations. **Registration:** Self-registration or at the guard shack. **Fee:** $14. **Parking:** At site.

FACILITIES

Number of Multipurpose Sites: 205. **Hookups:** Electric (30, 50 amps), water (not on every site). **Each Site:** Picnic table, grated fire pit. **Dump Station:** Yes. **Laundry:** No. **Pay Phone:** Yes. **Restrooms and Showers:** Yes. **Fuel:** No. **Propane:** No. **Internal Roads:** Paved. **RV Service:** In Pierre. **Market:** In Pierre. **Restaurant:** Yes. **General Store:** Yes. **Vending:** No. **Swimming:** No, but there is a huge swimming beach on the Missouri River. **Playground:** Several. **Other:** Picnic area, Oahe Marina, archery range, rifle range, Oahe Chapel, visitors center. **Activities:** Swimming, archery, nature trails, boating, jet skiing, waterskiing, biking, fishing. **Nearby Attractions:** Fort Pierre, South Dakota Discovery Center & Aquarium, State Capitol, Capitol Grounds Arboretum Trail, South Dakota Cultural Heritage Center. **Additional Information:** Pierre Chamber of Commerce, (605) 224-7361 or (800) 962-2034.

RESTRICTIONS

Pets: Allowed. **Fires:** Fire pit only; fires may be restricted due to weather conditions; please ask management before starting any open fires. **Alcoholic Beverages:** Allowed. **Vehicle Maximum Length:** No limit.

TO GET THERE

From Fort Pierre take Hwy. 83N to just before the river; take a left on Hwy. 14. Go about 1 mi. and take a right on 1806. The campground is about 5 mi. on the right. There are signs all the way from Fort Pierre.

GARRETSON   MAP, B-4
Palisades State Park

25495 485th Ave., 57030.
T: (605) 594-3824 or (800) 710-2267;
www.sdgfp.info/parks/regions/heartland/
palisades.htm.

🚐 ★★★★   ⛺ ★★★★★

Beauty: ★★★★★	Site Privacy: ★★★★
Spaciousness: ★★★★	Quiet: ★★★★
Security: ★★★★	Cleanliness: ★★★★
Insect Control: ★★	Facilities: ★★★

Palisades State Park is nestled in a unique landscape of quartzite spires cut by Split Rock Creek. It has become famous for its geological wonders and legends of the infamous Jesse James eluding a posse through Devils Gulch. Palisade State Park is located near Garretson, which has a history as unique as the land. The campground is a large loop, with both back-in and pull-through sites. The sites are spaced for optimal privacy, each with a paved parking pad and a spectacular view. The campground is well shaded with a variety of foliage. Many of the sites overlook Split Rock Creek and the magnificent quartzite spires. Palisade State Park is known for its rock climbing, and many climbers practice their scaling and rappelling. Like most of South Dakota summers, temperatures here average in the 80s, and it tends to be dry. Palisades State Park has around-the-clock security with a manager in residence.

BASICS

Operated By: South Dakota Game, Fish, & Parks Dept. **Open:** All year; water may be turned off in winter. **Site Assignment:** By reservation (800) 710-2267. **Registration:** At park entrance gate. **Fee:** Electric, $14; no hookup, $10. **Parking:** At site.

FACILITIES

Number of Tent-only Sites: 13. **Number of Multipurpose Sites:** 35. **Hookups:** Electric (20, 30 amps). **Each Site:** Picnic table, grated fire pit. **Dump Station:** In Garretson (2 mi.). **Laundry:** No. **Pay Phone:** Yes. **Restrooms and Showers:** Yes. **Fuel:** No. **Propane:** No. **Internal Roads:** Paved. **RV Service:** 15 mi. southwest in Sioux Falls. **Market:** Garretson or Sioux Falls. **Restaurant:** Garretson or Sioux Falls. **General Store:** No. **Vending:** No. **Swimming:** Creek. **Playground:** Yes. **Other:** Picnic area, cabins, amphitheater, 3 trails, pavilions, 1.2 billion-year-old Sioux quartzite spires, 1908 historic bridge. **Activities:** Guided hikes, summer weekend recreation programs, junior naturalist program & ECHOES program, repelling & rock climbing, fishing, sand volleyball, horseshoes. **Nearby Attractions:** Golf, Sioux Falls, Devil's Gulch, Great Plains Zoo, Jesse James River Runs (pontoon rides). **Additional Information:** Garretson Chamber of Commerce, (605) 594-6721.

RESTRICTIONS

Pets: On leash only. **Fires:** Fire pit only; fires may be restricted due to weather conditions; please ask management before starting any open fires. **Alcoholic Beverages:** Allowed. **Vehicle Maximum Length:** No limit. **Other:** 14-day stay limit; limit of 6 people per camping site.

TO GET THERE

From I-90 take Exit 406, go north on Hwy. 11 8.5 mi. then turn right and follow the signs into the park.

GETTYSBURG MAP, A-3
West Whitlock Recreation Area

16157A West Whitlock Rd., 57442.
T: (605) 765-9410 or (800) 710-2267;
www.sdgfp.info/parks/regions/oahesharpe/
westwhitlock.htm.

🚐 ★★★ ⛺ ★★★

Beauty: ★★★ Site Privacy: ★★★
Spaciousness: ★★★ Quiet: ★★★★
Security: ★★★★ Cleanliness: ★★★
Insect Control: ★★★ Facilities: ★★

Twenty-two miles west of Gettysburg in South Dakota's Great Lake Region, West Whitlock Recreation Area is situated on the Lake Oahe Reservoir. First explored by Lewis and Clark, this area is a small, hidden treasure and a sportsman's sanctuary. The park offers a variety of coordinated interpretive and educational programs. Lake Oahe Reservoir has more than 2,000 acres of shoreline, making it ideal for boating, jet skiing, fishing, or diving. Anglers can find walleye, northern pike, chinook salmon, and bass. There is also a large variety of hunting game including pheasant, grouse, deer, and antelope. The campground is one large loop with back-in, level parking pads. Mature trees are found throughout the campground area, providing shade and adding ambiance. The weather is warm during the summer and cold in the winter. The late spring is a great time to visit before the insects come to life.

BASICS

Operated By: South Dakota Game, Fish, & Parks Dept. **Open:** All year; water turned off in winter. **Site Assignment:** Reservations, Memorial Day–Labor Day at (800) 710-2267. **Registration:** At entrance booth. **Fee:** $8–$14; plus entrance fee. **Parking:** At site.

FACILITIES

Number of Multipurpose Sites: 103. **Hookups:** Electric (20, 30 amps). **Each Site:** Picnic table, grated fire pit. **Dump Station:** Yes. **Laundry:** No. **Pay Phone:** At dock. **Restrooms and Showers:** Yes (seasonal). **Fuel:** Next door. **Propane:** Next door. **Internal Roads:** Paved. **RV Service:** 22 mi. in Gettysburg. **Market:** In Gettysburg. **Restaurant:** Next door or in Gettysburg. **General Store:** Near entrance, outside the park, Apr.–Oct. **Vending:** Yes. **Swimming:** No, but there is a swimming beach on Lake Oahe. **Playground:** Yes. **Other:** Cabins, fish-cleaning station, cross-country ski trail, boat ramp, beach, picnic area, pavilion, interpretive center, Arikara Lodge replica. **Activities:** Cross-country skiing, boating, swimming, interpretive programs during season, hiking, fishing (walleye, northerns, bass), biking. **Nearby Attractions:** Whitlock salmon spawning & imprinting station; state capitol, bi-annual Civil War festival. **Additional Information:** Gettysburg Chamber of Commerce, (605) 765-9309.

RESTRICTIONS

Pets: On leash. **Fires:** Fire pit only; fires may be restricted due to weather conditions; please ask management before starting any open fires. **Alcoholic Beverages:** Allowed. **Vehicle Maximum Length:** No limit. **Other:** 14-day stay limit.

TO GET THERE

From Gettysburg on US 212, go 18 mi. (stay on 212; do not get on 83), then take 1804N (right). Travel 4 mi. until the pavement ends. Turn left and follow road into the park. Watch for signs.

HILL CITY MAP, B-1
Horse Thief Campground and RV Resort

Box 307, 57745.
T: (605) 574-2668 or (800) 657-5802;
www.horsethief.com.

🚐 ★★★★ ⛺ ★★★★

Beauty: ★★★★ Site Privacy: ★★★
Spaciousness: ★★★ Quiet: ★★★
Security: ★★★★ Cleanliness: ★★★
Insect Control: ★★★ Facilities: ★★★

Deep in the groves of the Black Hills is a beautiful, 50-acre camping heaven, nestled in mountains, pines, streams, and ponds. Horse Thief Campground and Resort is a secluded family getaway conveniently located near Custer State Park, Mt. Rushmore, and the Scenic Needles Highway. The campground is a full-service facility, with both pull-through and back-in sites, a lodge, and a pool with a breathtaking view. The campground consists of an RV area where you may choose open or wooded campsites. The tent-camper's section is spectacular, with wooded campsites and a huge common area. In addition to superb camping, Horse Thief is also a horse camp—meaning there are accommodations available for equine family members. However, advance reservations must be made if traveling with your horse. The temperatures in the area average in the mid-80s for the summer and 30s in the winter. There is an entrance gate and excellent security.

BASICS

Operated By: Steve & Sandy Ferrin. **Open:** May–Oct. **Site Assignment:** By reservation held on a credit card. **Registration:** At general store. **Fee:** RV, $28–$35; tent, $18; for 2 people; extra person over 11, $3. **Parking:** At site.

FACILITIES

Number of RV-only Sites: 63. **Number of Tent-only Sites:** 43. **Hookups:** Electric (30 amps), water, sewer, phone, TV sites, Wi-Fi. **Each Site:** Picnic table, fire pit. **Dump Station:** Yes. **Laundry:** Yes. **Pay Phone:** Yes. **Restrooms and Showers:** Yes. **Fuel:** No. **Propane:** No. **Internal Roads:** Gravel w/ some bumps & parts that are not level. **RV Service:** No. **Market:** Hill City, 5 mi. **Restaurant:** Hill City, 5 mi. **General Store:** Yes. **Vending:** Soda. **Swimming:** Yes. **Playground:** Yes. **Other:** Huge central fire ring, fax & copy service, heated pool, cabin rentals. **Activities:** Hiking, fishing, biking, volleyball, basketball, horseshoes. **Nearby Attractions:** Mt. Rushmore, Custer State Park, Crazy Horse, museums, hot springs, Harney Peak. **Additional Information:** South Dakota Tourism, (605) 773-3301 or (800) 732-5682.

RESTRICTIONS

Pets: Dogs on a short leash only; horses allowed; must show a valid health certificate for all animals; horses must have proof of current negative Coggins test. **Fires:** In approved fire pits only; fires may be restricted due to weather conditions. **Alcoholic Beverages:** Allowed. **Vehicle Maximum Length:** No limit.

TO GET THERE

From the south side of Hill City, go 3 mi. south on US 16/385; turn left on Hwy. 87. Go 2 mi. and the campground is on the right.

HILL CITY MAP, B-1
Rafter J. Bar Ranch Campground

P.O. Box 128, 57745.
T: (605) 574-2527 or (888) 723-8375;
www.rafterj.com.

🚐 ★★★★ ⛺ ★★★★

Beauty: ★★★★★ Site Privacy: ★★★
Spaciousness: ★★★ Quiet: ★★★★
Security: ★★★★ Cleanliness: ★★★
Insect Control: ★★★ Facilities: ★★★

Located in the Black Hills, Rafter J. Bar Ranch is a huge full-service camping facility. It is divided into five camping areas, each under a canopy of large ponderosa pines. The camping areas each share beautiful commons, bike trails, hiking trails, and open meadows. The camping areas are large loops; three have their own restrooms, showers, and laundry. Campsites, however, are not well spaced, nor are they any larger than most campground sites despite the enormous acreage of the property. The ranch offers lots of amenities, including fuel, fishing licenses, horseback riding, bike rentals, and an information center. In addition to being inclusive, it is in very close proximity to Mt. Rushmore, the Crazy Horse monument, and Custer State Park. Summer temperatures average in the mid 80s, with evenings dropping into the 60s. The ranch has staff on duty around the clock and several host families to assist with any need that may arise.

BASICS

Operated By: Todd George. **Open:** May 1–Oct. 1. **Site Assignment:** By reservation held on a credit card. **Registration:** At camp office. **Fee:** RV, $35–$41; tent, $27; for 2 people. **Parking:** At site.

FACILITIES

Number of RV-only Sites: 160. **Number of Tent-only Sites:** 17. **Hookups:** Electric (30, 50 amps), water, sewer, satellite TV (limited numbers), Wi-Fi. **Each Site:** Picnic table, grated fire pit. **Dump Station:** Yes. **Laundry:** Yes. **Pay Phone:** Yes. **Restrooms and Showers:** Yes. **Fuel:** Yes. **Propane:** Yes. **Internal Roads:** Combination of paved & gravel. **RV Service:** No. **Market:** In Hill City, 3 mi. **Restaurant:** Snack bar on property, or there are restaurants all over the Black Hills. **General Store:** Yes. **Vending:** No. **Swimming:** Yes, & hot tub. **Playground:** Yes. **Other:** Wireless Internet in information room. Cabin rentals available. **Activities:** Trail rides, swimming, hot tub, fishing, hiking, bike rental, arcade. **Nearby Attractions:** Mt. Rushmore, Custer State Park, Needles Dr., Iron Mountain Rd., Borglum Story Museum, Crazy Horse. **Additional Information:** Hill City Chamber of Commerce, (605) 574-2368 or (800) 888-1798.

RESTRICTIONS

Pets: On leash, quiet, cleaned up after. **Fires:** Fire pits or grills only; fires may be restricted due to weather conditions; please ask management before starting any open fires. **Alcoholic Beverages:** Allowed. **Vehicle Maximum Length:** No limit. **Other:** 14-day stay limit; 1 family unit per site; no pets or smoking in cabins. Good Sam Club.

TO GET THERE

The campground is located on Sylvan Lake–Needles Rd. (SD Hwy. 16) between the towns of Custer and Hill City.

INTERIOR   MAP, B-2
Badlands/White River KOA

20720 South Dakota Hwy. 44, 57750.
T: (605) 433-5337 or (800) 562-3897;
www.koa.com/where/sd/41111/.

🚐 ★★★★   ⛺ ★★★

Beauty: ★★★   Site Privacy: ★★★
Spaciousness: ★★★   Quiet: ★★★★
Security: ★★★★   Cleanliness: ★★★★
Insect Control: ★★★   Facilities: ★★★

Only a few miles from the Badlands National Park in the small community of Interior is the manicured landscape of the Badlands KOA. As with most KOAs, this is a full-service campground, with some of the only shade trees in the area. Due to the hard work of the owners and ongoing irrigation, the Badland KOA offers green grass and shade. There is a nice pool, mini-golf, and a courtesy phone. The campground is laid out in a series of rows and loops, with the majority of the sites being pull-through. The owners' private residence is in the middle of the property. In addition, several tent sites have electric and water hookups in what KOA refers to as a tent village. Please make note that this campground is in a very small community, and the nearest services are 32 miles away in Wall.

BASICS

Operated By: Joe & Mary Lusk. **Open:** Apr. 15–Sept. 30. **Site Assignment:** By reservation held on a credit card. **Registration:** At general store. **Fee:** RV, $24–$32; tent, $19–$23; for 2 people; extra child, $2.50; extra adult, $3.50; age 5 & under free. Fees are 10% less in Apr. **Parking:** At site.

FACILITIES

Number of RV-only Sites: 78. **Number of Tent-only Sites:** 54. **Hookups:** Electric (20, 30, 50 amps), water, sewer, cable TV, Wi-Fi. **Each Site:** Picnic table, fire pit. **Dump Station:** Yes. **Laundry:** Yes. **Pay Phone:** Courtesy phone. **Restrooms and Showers:** Yes. **Fuel:** No. **Propane:** Yes. **Internal Roads:** Gravel. **RV Service:** 32 mi. Northwest in Wall, SD. **Market:** 32 mi. northwest in Wall, SD, & small market in Interior (4 mi.). **Restaurant:** In Interior; pancake breakfast & Indian tacos served during summer season at the campground. **General Store:** Yes. **Vending:** Soft drinks. **Swimming:** Yes. **Playground:** Yes. **Other:** Internet kiosk, Wi-Fi, 10 cabins. **Activities:** Fishing, hiking, horseshoes, basketball, mini-golf, volleyball, fun-cycle rentals. **Nearby Attractions:** Badlands National Park, Pine Ridge

Indian Reservation, fossil digging. **Additional Information:** South Dakota Tourism, (605) 773-3301.

RESTRICTIONS

Pets: On leash. Off-leash "pet park" available. **Fires:** Fire pits or grills only; fires may be restricted due to weather conditions; please ask management before starting any open fires. **Alcoholic Beverages:** Allowed. **Vehicle Maximum Length:** 72 ft.

TO GET THERE

From I-90 take Exit 131, take SD 240/Badland Loop into the Badlands National Park, then take SD 377, which will become SD 44. The campground is approx. 6 mi. south of the Badlands National Park's south gate on Hwy. 44. It is approx. 14 mi. from I-90.

SIOUX FALLS   MAP, B-4
Yogi Bear's Jellystone Park

reserve america

26014 478th Ave., 57005.
T: (605) 332-2233 or (800) 638-9043;
www.jellystonesiouxfalls.com.

🚐 ★★★   ⛺ ★★★

Beauty: ★★★   Site Privacy: ★★★
Spaciousness: ★★★   Quiet: ★★★
Security: ★★★★   Cleanliness: ★★★★
Insect Control: ★★★   Facilities: ★★★

Directly off I-90, only 5 miles east of Sioux City, Yogi Bear's Jellystone Campground is a full-service, modern facility offering a multitude of amenities and activities for the entire family. The campground is conveniently located for travelers wishing to enjoy the Sioux Falls area and neighboring state parks. The campground offers all modern hookups, including cable, phone, and Wi-Fi. There are two main sections to the campground, and roads are laid out in rows. There is a tree between most sites. Most sites are pull-throughs, and there is little interference for those who wish to receive satellite TV. The campground is open year-round; however, there are limited hookups in the winter. The weather in this part of the state goes from one extreme to the other—very warm and dry in summer, and ice-cold in winter. The owners are on site during the busy season, and security is good.

BASICS

Operated By: The Aljets. **Open:** All year; water turned off in winter. **Site Assignment:** By reservation, (800) 638-9043; 2-day cancellation policy minus $5; 7-day cancellation policy for holidays. V, MC, D, personal checks accepted. **Registration:** At general store. **Fee:** RV, $29–$31; tent, $22; for 2 people; extra person, $2; kids age 4 & under stay free. **Parking:** At site.

FACILITIES

Number of RV-only Sites: 112. **Number of Tent-only Sites:** 33. **Hookups:** Electric (20, 30, 50 amps), water, sewer, cable TV, phone, Wi-Fi. **Each Site:** Picnic table, grated fire pit. **Dump Station:** Yes. **Laundry:** Yes. **Pay Phone:** Yes. **Restrooms and Showers:** Yes. **Fuel:** No, just down the street.

Propane: Yes. **Internal Roads:** Gravel. **RV Service:** In Sioux Falls, 3 mi. **Market:** In Sioux Falls, 3 mi. **Restaurant:** Snack bar on site or restaurants in town. **General Store:** Yes. **Vending:** No. **Swimming:** Yes, & hot tub. **Playground:** Yes. **Other:** Cabins (10), hot tub, indoor theater, pavilion, arcade game room, nightly visits by Yogi, picnic area, Wi-Fi. **Activities:** Swimming, 19-hole mini-golf, volleyball, pedal bikes, planned activities in the summer, summer Sun. morning pancake breakfast. **Nearby Attractions:** Thunder Road Family Fun Park, Great Plains Zoo & Delbridge Museum, USS *South Dakota* Battleship Memorial, Falls Park. **Additional Information:** Sioux Falls, (800) 593-2228.

RESTRICTIONS

Pets: On leash. **Fires:** Fire pit only; fires may be restricted due to weather conditions; please ask management before starting any open fires. **Alcoholic Beverages:** Allowed. **Vehicle Maximum Length:** No limit.

TO GET THERE

From I-90 at Exit 402, go 0.25 mi. north on City Rd. 121; the park is located on the right.

WATERTOWN   MAP, B-4
Stokes-Thomas Lake City Park

90 South Lake Dr., 57201. T: (605) 882-6264.

🚐 ★★★★★   ⛺ ★★★★★

Beauty: ★★★★   Site Privacy: ★★★★
Spaciousness: ★★★★   Quiet: ★★★★
Security: ★★★★   Cleanliness: ★★★★
Insect Control: ★★   Facilities: ★★★

Stokes-Thomas Lake City Park is one of South Dakota's wonderful city parks. It reflects the pride South Dakota places on its towns and offers the local population, as well as travelers, a beautiful place for recreation. Stokes-Thomas is located on Lake Kampeska, about 5 miles out of Watertown. Watertown is known for its rich grain fields and grasslands. The park is kept in pristine condition, with lush green grass and 42 paved camping pads, all under an awning of large, mature oak trees. The park offers full-hookup sites with all the amenities. Stokes-Thomas Lake City Park has a large boat ramp, a swimming beach, and three picnic shelters. This park is a fantastic weekend getaway. The weather is pleasant for water sports in the summer, and there is a manager in residence.

BASICS

Operated By: Watertown Parks, Recreation & Forestry Dept., Kelly Stavig, Manager. **Open:** May–Sept. 30. **Site Assignment:** First come, first served. **Registration:** In park office. **Fee:** $16.50; call ahead for information. **Parking:** At site.

FACILITIES

Number of Multipurpose Sites: 43. **Hookups:** Electric (20, 30 amps), water, sewer. **Each Site:** Picnic table, fire pit. **Dump Station:** Yes. **Laundry:** No. **Pay Phone:** No. **Restrooms and Showers:** Yes. **Fuel:** No. **Propane:** No. **Internal Roads:** Paved. **RV Service:** In Watertown. **Market:** In Watertown. **Restaurant:** In Watertown. **General Store:** No. **Vending:** Yes. **Swimming:** No, but there is a roped-off swimming beach on Lake Kampeska. **Playground:** Yes. **Other:** Boat launch, 3 picnic shelters, park manager's home/office. **Activities:** Boating, swimming, fishing, softball field, sand volleyball, horseshoes, basketball. **Nearby Attractions:** Golf, Thunder Road Family Fun Park, Bramble Park Zoo & Discovery Center, Watertown Family Aquatic Center. **Additional Information:** Watertown Area Chamber of Commerce, (800) 658-4505, or www.watertownsd.com.

RESTRICTIONS

Pets: On leash. **Fires:** Fire pit only; fires may be restricted due to weather conditions; please ask management before starting any open fires. **Alcoholic Beverages:** Allowed. **Vehicle Maximum Length:** No limit.

TO GET THERE

From the junction of US 212 and Hwy. 20 in Watertown, go 3 mi. northwest on Hwy. 20 to South Lake Drive.

YANKTON   MAP, C-4
Lewis and Clark Recreation Area, Resort, and Marina

43349 SD Hwy. 52, 57078.
T: (605) 668-2985 or (800) 710-2267;
www.sdgfp.info/parks/regions/lewisclark/
lewisclark.htm.

🚐 ★★★   ⛺ ★★★

Beauty: ★★★		Site Privacy: ★★★
Spaciousness: ★★★		Quiet: ★★★★
Security: ★★★★		Cleanliness: ★★★
Insect Control: ★★★		Facilities: ★★

Located in one of South Dakota's most popular recreation areas, the campground at Lewis and Clark Recreation Area is a full-service modern resort facility. It's located on the Missouri River, 5 miles from Yankton, just north of the South Dakota/Nebraska border. Lewis and Clark Resort is broken into three areas. There's a campground consisting of 392 level, paved camping sites in several loop configurations, with grass common areas and plenty of trees for shade. You'll also find a concession area equipped with a marina, lodging, dining, and a theater. Lastly, Gravins Point is the horse camp and day-use section of the park. The park offers many organized activities for all ages, and it rents anything from RVs to bikes. So, pack your insect repellent and sunscreen, and whether you enjoy horseback riding or jet skiing down the Missouri River, Lewis and Clark Recreation Area can provide it all. During the warmer summer months, insects can be a problem. Security is excellent.

BASICS

Operated By: South Dakota Game, Fish, & Parks Dept. **Open:** All year; water turned off in winter. **Site Assignment:** By reservation, (800) 710-2267 or at campsd.com; 82 sites are first come, first served. **Registration:** At entrance booth. **Fee:** $10–$16; per camping unit plus entrance fee. **Parking:** At site.

FACILITIES

Number of Multipurpose Sites: 392. **Hookups:** Electric (20, 30, 50 amps); water available but not at each site. **Each Site:** Picnic table, grated fire pit. **Dump Station:** Yes. **Laundry:** No. **Pay Phone:** Yes. **Restrooms and Showers:** Yes. **Fuel:** No. **Propane:** No. **Internal Roads:** Paved. **RV Service:** In Yankton. **Market:** In Yankton. **Restaurant:** Marina Grille. **General Store:** Yes, at the Marina. **Vending:** Yes. **Swimming:** There is a pool at the Lewis &

Clark Resort Hotel for guests, & there are 3 riverfront beaches available for swimming. **Playground:** Yes. **Other:** Lewis & Clark Resort Hotel, Marina Grille Restaurant, marina, cabins, Horse Trail Camp, several boat ramps, convenience store, bicycle rental, boat rental, showers at the beach, picnic shelters w/ grills, amphitheater. **Activities:** Waterskiing, boating, swimming, interpretive programming, hiking, fishing (walleye, northerns, bass), 6 mi. of bike trails, 4 mi. of equestrian trails, fishing guide service, volleyball, archery, weekly park programs. **Nearby Attractions:** Gavens Point Dam & Visitor's Center, historic homes, Dakota Territorial Museum, National Fish Hatchery & Aquarium, Territorial Capitol, golf courses. **Additional Information:** South Dakota State Parks, 523 E. Capitol, Pierre, SD 57501, (605) 773-3391, or Yankton Chamber of Commerce, (605) 665-3636.

RESTRICTIONS

Pets: On leash. **Fires:** Restricted to fire grates. **Alcoholic Beverages:** Allowed. **Vehicle Maximum Length:** No limit. **Other:** 14-day stay limit.

TO GET THERE

The park is located 6 mi. west of Yankton, directly off SD 52.

Tennessee

Tennessee was inhabited by Chickasaw, Cherokee, and other Native Americans when Hernando de Soto explored the shore near Memphis in 1541. From that time on, the Spanish maintained a landing site at present-day Memphis. The Spanish brought diseases that killed many Native Americans. As their populations decreased, tribes formed nations. The Cherokee Nation had a particularly strong impact on the culture and history of Tennessee.

In 1682, the French built a temporary post near Memphis under the direction of Rene-Robert Cavalier, Sieur de La Salle. After traveling to the Gulf of Mexico, La Salle claimed all of the land drained by the Mississippi for France. When Britain won the French and Indian War in 1763, it gained control of all territories between the Atlantic Ocean and the Mississippi River.

In spite of a royal proclamation banning white settlement west of the Appalachians, North Carolinians began to settle in Tennessee in the 1760s. These settlers fought against the British in the American Revolution. Though Tennessee has no official nickname, it's often referred to as the Volunteer State to commemorate the valor of native soldiers in wars dating back to the American Revolution.

In the 1770s Daniel Boone blazed the famous **Wilderness Road Trail** through **Cumberland Gap** to the **Kentucky River.** Under the leadership of William Blount, John Sevier, and Andrew Jackson, Tennessee attained statehood in 1796.

The young state experienced growth in three distinct economic and cultural regions. The western portion of the state produced cotton. Due to its strong cultural and economic ties to the Deep South, western Tennessee was loyal to the Confederacy during the Civil War. Central Tennessee saw diversified commercial farming and also tended to side with the rebels in the Civil War. Hilly eastern Tennessee was home to small subsistence farms. These independent farmers remained loyal to the Union and tried to form their own state to avoid secession.

Tennesseans still divide their state into three main regions. Today, the flat western region, with its fertile soil, is the most heavily farmed. Though Tennessee is filled with beautiful country, it's hard to deny the glitzy (and often cheesy) allure of many of its big cities. Home of world-famous **Sun Studios** and **Stax Studios** (now the **Stax Museum of American Soul Music**) among others, **Memphis** is widely considered to be the birthplace of rock and roll and arguably the birthplace of the blues. **Beal Street** is home to many of Memphis's music venues and museums. Of course, no trip to Memphis would be complete without a visit to **Graceland**—Elvis's legendarily garish home and resting place. Casual fans and sightseers might make do with a drive by, but curious travelers (and fanatical devotees) will want to bring along plenty of cash for the tours and gift shop. Memphis is also home to some of the greatest moments of the civil rights movement. Civic-minded travelers will find a visit to the **National Civil Rights Museum** to be quite a moving experience.

The rolling hills of central Tennessee have an extremely diversified economy, with livestock, including the majestic Tennessee walking horse, the most important farm product. The region is also known for automobile and parts manufacturing. In **Nashville,** the **Grand Ole Opry** has been around since 1925. Much of Tennessee's Civil War history and river life is preserved in this part of the state. **The Tennessee River Folk Life Museum** hearkens back to a time when these mighty ships accounted for much of Tennessee's business and pleasure. Civil War buffs will want to spend some time at **Fort Donelson National Battlefield and Cemetery.**

Hilly-to-mountainous eastern Tennessee is now dependent on manufacturing and tourism. The area is home to the **Cherokee National Forest** and the western half of the **Great Smoky Mountains National Park,** an environmentally important region. Botanists estimate that there are more species of plants in Great Smoky Mountains National Park than in all of Europe. An engineering marvel, **Chattanooga**—much like Louisville, Kentucky—is an amazing synthesis of urban smarts and natural splendor. Located on the **Tennessee River,** much of Chattanooga's urban renewal is built around the **Tennessee Aquarium,** a stunning facility that will delight travelers of all ages. Running through the Cherokee National Forest, the **Ocoee River** is easily one of Tennessee's most popular tourist attractions. The Ocoee has more than 20 continuous rapids and many gentle spots for play. The rapids are diverse enough that both novice and experienced rafters can spend an enjoyable afternoon on the river. Of course, guided trips are available.

Campground Profiles

ASHLAND CITY — MAP, A-3
Cheatham Lake Lock A Campground

1797 Cheatham Dam Rd., 37015.
T: (615) 792-3715 or (877) 444-6777;
www.reserveusa.com.

🚐 ★★★★   ⛺ ★★★★

Beauty: ★★★★★	Site Privacy: ★★★
Spaciousness: ★★★★★	Quiet: ★★★★
Security: ★★★★★	Cleanliness: ★★★★★
Insect Control: ★★★★	Facilities: ★★★

Located on Cheatham Lake, a development intended to improve navigation on the Cumberland River, Lock A campground is popular with anglers. Catches include crappie, catfish, sauger, bream, and largemouth, striped, and white bass. Neighboring Cheatham State Wildlife Management Area provides hunting opportunities. The campground consists of two RV areas and one tent area. RV parking is paved, back-in style. RV sites are extremely large, while tent sites are a bit smaller. There are some pretty shade trees, but little foliage between sites; privacy is at a minimum while views of Cheatham Lake are optimized. For the loveliest views, head to sites 24–29. Security is excellent at this remote campground; the staff is extremely vigilant and the gates are locked at night. Central Tennessee is very hot and humid in late summer—visit in spring or fall for the nicest weather.

BASICS

Operated By: U.S. Army Corps of Engineers. **Open:** May 1–Oct. 30. **Site Assignment:** Some first come, first served; most sites available for reservation through the National Recreation Reservation Service (NRRS) at (877) 444-6777 or www.reserveusa.com; reservations can be made up to 240 days in advance, full payment required upon reservation; credit card preferred (V, MC, D, AE), or pay by money order if at least 21 days in advance of arrival; $10 fee for cancellation, or change of site or dates; cancellation w/in 3 days of arrival charged 1 night, no-show charged $20 plus 1 night; holidays 3-night min., weekends 2-night. **Registration:** At entrance station, gates close at 10 p.m. **Fee:** Waterfront, $23; nonwaterfront/tent, $19; cash, personal check, V, D, MC, AE. **Parking:** At site, on impact area, in parking lot.

FACILITIES

Number of Tent-only Sites: 8. **Number of Multipurpose Sites:** 45. **Hookups:** Electric (30 amps), water. **Each Site:** Picnic table, grill, fire ring, lantern pole. **Dump Station:** Yes. **Laundry:** Yes. **Pay Phone:** No. **Restrooms and Showers:** Yes. **Fuel:** No. **Propane:** No. **Internal Roads:** Paved. **RV Service:** 20 mi. in Nashville. **Market:** 11 mi. in Ashland City. **Restaurant:** 11 mi. in Ashland City. **General Store:** 11 mi. in Ashland City. **Vending:** No. **Swimming:** Yes. **Playground:** Yes. **Other:** Boat launch, fish-cleaning station, amphitheater. **Activities:** Beach swimming, hiking trails, ball field, fishing, water sports, volleyball, basketball, picnic shelter, courtesy dock.

Nearby Attractions: Nashville, Country Music Hall of Fame, The Parthenon, Belle Meade Plantation, Grand Ole Opry, Opryland Hotel, Hermitage Andrew Jackson Home. **Additional Information:** Nashville Tourism Information, (615) 259-4700.

RESTRICTIONS

Pets: Leash only, not allowed on beach. **Fires:** Fire rings, grills only. **Alcoholic Beverages:** Allowed, at sites only. **Vehicle Maximum Length:** 40 ft. **Other:** 14-day stay limit.

TO GET THERE

From Nashville, take US 12 west 15 mi. to Ashland City. Continue on 12 another 8 mi. to Cheap Hill. Turn left (southwest) on Cheatham Dam Rd. and drive 4 mi. Turn left into the campground.

BENTON — MAP, B-6
Chilhowee Campground

Cherokee National Forest,
Rte. 1 Box 348-D, 37307. T: (423) 338-5201;
www.southernregion.fs.fed.us/cherokee.

🚐 ★★★★   ⛺ ★★★★★

Beauty: ★★★★★	Site Privacy: ★★★★
Spaciousness: ★★★★★	Quiet: ★★★★★
Security: ★★★★★	Cleanliness: ★★★★
Insect Control: ★★★	Facilities: ★★★

Expansive Cherokee National Forest is divided by Great Smoky Mountains National Park and encompasses 620,000 acres of natural and recreation areas. The park includes much of the southern Appalachian Mountains that were razed by poor farming and timbering techniques in the late 19th century. In 1911, Congress passed the Weeks Act, establishing National Forests, and Cherokee became one of the first tracts of national forest land. Today, it supports thousands of species of flora and fauna. Breathtaking Chilhowee Campground offers both back-in and pull-through sites on a pristine mountainside. Parking is on pea gravel. Many sites also offer soft pea gravel tent pads. Sites are shaded by a variety of hardwoods, and privacy is provided by foliage between sites. Though site size varies, all are spacious. For space and privacy, we recommend loops A, B, and F. Restrooms vary; some loops have too few toilets. Families should head for the extremely nice restrooms at loops A and B. Security at Chilhowee is excellent. It's extremely remote and gated. Visit any time except summer holidays.

BASICS

Operated By: U.S. Forest Service. **Open:** Apr.–Oct. **Site Assignment:** First come, first served; no reservations. **Registration:** Self-pay fee station. **Fee:** RV, $15–$18; tent, $12; 5 people maximum.; cash, personal check. **Parking:** At site (2 cars), day-use parking lot $3 per day.

FACILITIES

Number of Tent-only Sites: 58. **Number of Multipurpose Sites:** 80. **Hookups:** Electric (20, 30 amps); loops A & B only. **Each Site:** Picnic table, fire ring, grill, lantern pole, tent pad. **Dump Station:** Yes.

Laundry: No. **Pay Phone:** No. **Restrooms and Showers:** Yes. **Fuel:** No. **Propane:** No. **Internal Roads:** Paved. **RV Service:** 25 mi. in Cleveland. **Market:** 12 mi. in Benton. **Restaurant:** 10 mi. on Hwy. 64 West. **General Store:** 12 mi. down Hwy. 64. **Vending:** No. **Swimming:** Yes. **Playground:** No. **Other:** Group picnic area. **Activities:** 7-acre private lake w/ swimming beach, boating (electric trolling motors only), fishing, hiking & mountain-biking trails. **Nearby Attractions:** Benton Falls, kayaking & rafting on the Ocoee & Hiwassee Rivers, Ocoee Whitewater center, Cherohala Skyway National Scenic Byway, Nancy Ward Grave Site, antique shopping. **Additional Information:** Polk county/Copper Basin Chamber of Commerce, (423) 338-5040; Tennessee Overhill Heritage Tourism Assoc., (423) 263-7232.

RESTRICTIONS

Pets: On leash only. **Fires:** Grill, fire ring only. **Alcoholic Beverages:** Not allowed. **Vehicle Maximum Length:** 50 ft. (sites vary).

TO GET THERE

From I-75, take Exit 20 (Cleveland) and go east on the bypass. Drive 5 mi. and take the US 64 (Ocoee) Exit. Drive 14 mi. east on 64 to FR 77. Turn left and drive 7 mi. to the campground.

BUCHANAN — MAP, A-2
Paris Landing State Resort Park

16055 Hwy. 79-N., 38222.
T: (731) 641-4465 or (800) 250-8614;
www.tnstateparks.com.

🚐 ★★★★   ⛺ ★★★★

Beauty: ★★★★	Site Privacy: ★★★
Spaciousness: ★★★	Quiet: ★★★
Security: ★★★	Cleanliness: ★★★★
Insect Control: ★★★★	Facilities: ★★★★★

Paris Landing offers outstanding recreational amenities, including an 18-hole golf course which has consistently earned four stars from *Golf Digest* magazine. On Kentucky Lake, the marina offers 200 rental slips plus other amenities. In the summer, the amphitheater hosts various live performances. The campground is laid out in four loops among various tree species, including hickory, white, and red oak. Most sites are nicely shaded although there is little privacy. Sites with hookups feature paved, back-in parking. Each site has a gravel patio area and sites are midsized. For space and privacy, we like sites 21–39 in the back of the campground. There are no gates at Paris Landing, but the park is fairly remote, making security OK. This area sees cold winters and hot summers. Try to visit in late spring or fall.

BASICS

Operated By: Tennessee State Parks. **Open:** All year. **Site Assignment:** First come, first served; no reservations. **Registration:** At site, host or ranger makes rounds. **Fee:** Water/electric, $14–$17; tent, $7; prices for 2 people; each additional person, $.50; under age 7, free; seniors & disabled, discounts available; cash, personal check. **Parking:** At sites.

FACILITIES

Number of Tent-only Sites: 17. **Number of Multipurpose Sites:** 43. **Hookups:** Electric (30 amps), water. **Each Site:** Picnic table, grill. **Dump Station:** Yes. **Laundry:** Yes (closed in winter). **Pay Phone:** Yes. **Restrooms and Showers:** Yes (closed in winter). **Fuel:** No (boat fuel available at marina). **Propane:** No. **Internal Roads:** Paved. **RV Service:** 22 mi. northwest in Murray. **Market:** 18 mi. southwest in Paris. **Restaurant:** Park restaurant, also w/in 0.25 mi. **General Store:** 1 mi. hardware, 18 mi. southwest in Paris (Wal-Mart). **Vending:** Yes. **Swimming:** Yes. **Playground:** Yes. **Other:** Marina, rental slips, boat launch, picnic grounds w/ pavilions, amphitheater. **Activities:** 18-hole golf course, driving range, practice greens, club & cart rentals, archery range, fishing, water sports, swimming beach, hiking trails, tennis, basketball. **Nearby Attractions:** Natchez Trace, Nathan Bedford Forrest, New Johnsonville, Port Royal & Dunbar Cave State Parks, Fort Donelson National Military Park, Land Between the Lakes National Recreation Area w/ more than 100 mi. of mountain-biking trails. **Additional Information:** Paris/Henry County Chamber of Commerce, (731) 642-3431.

RESTRICTIONS

Pets: On leash only. **Fires:** Allowed. **Alcoholic Beverages:** Not allowed. **Vehicle Maximum Length:** 40 ft. (sites vary). **Other:** 14-day stay limit May 1–Aug. 31. No gray water.

TO GET THERE

From Memphis, take US 79 east approx. 130 mi. The park is on the left (north) before the bridge across the Tennessee River. From I-24, take Exit 4 (40 mi. northwest of Nashville) and drive west on Hwy. 79 approx. 45 mi. The park entrance is the first right after the bridge. The campground is on the left inside the park.

BURNS   MAP, A-3
Montgomery Bell State Park

1020 Jackson Hill Rd., 37029. T: (615) 797-9052; www.tnstateparks.com.

🚐 ★★★★	▲ ★★★★
Beauty: ★★★★★	Site Privacy: ★★★
Spaciousness: ★★★	Quiet: ★★★★
Security: ★★★★	Cleanliness: ★★★★
Insect Control: ★★★★	Facilities: ★★★★★

Montgomery Bell maintains excellent facilities, including an indoor pool (open all year) and an 18-hole golf course, which *Golf Digest* magazine has rated as one of the top 100 public courses in the United States. Other interesting sites include an 1810 Presbyterian church and reconstructed minister's home. An ancillary facility, Narrows of the Harpeth State Park, offers canoe access to the Harpeth River. The campground contains small, picturesque sites shaded by a variety of hardwoods, including cedar. There is little undergrowth to provide privacy between sites. Some parking spaces are gravel, while others are paved. Most sites offer back-in parking, with the exception of two pull-throughs reserved for disabled use. The nicest sites line Four Mile Creek,

along the back of the campground. Security is fair at this rural park. A ranger is on duty at all times. Don't visit on summer weekends, when the park fills to capacity. Also avoid hot, humid July and August.

BASICS

Operated By: Tennessee State Parks. **Open:** All year. **Site Assignment:** First come, first served; no reservations. **Registration:** Attendant or at site. **Fee:** Water/electric, $18.25; tent, $12.25; prices for 2 people; each additional person, $.50; senior discounts; cash, personal check. Price includes access fee. **Parking:** At site.

FACILITIES

Number of Tent-only Sites: 27. **Number of Multipurpose Sites:** 89. **Hookups:** Electric (20, 30, 50 amps), water. **Each Site:** Picnic table, ground grill, & trash can. **Dump Station:** Yes. **Laundry:** No. **Pay Phone:** Yes. **Restrooms and Showers:** Yes. **Fuel:** No. **Propane:** No. **Internal Roads:** Paved. **RV Service:** 35 mi. in Nashville. **Market:** W/in 5 mi. **Restaurant:** Park Restaurant (may close in winter), 6 mi. in Dickson. **General Store:** No. **Vending:** Seasonal. **Swimming:** No. **Playground:** Yes. **Other:** Boat ramp (electric trolling motors only), conference center, picnic areas & pavilions. **Activities:** Lake swimming, fishing boat & canoe rentals (summer), 18-hole golf course, hiking trails, overnight back-country camping w/ permit, bicycling (on park roads), tennis, basketball, croquet, shuffleboard, volleyball, ball fields, mountain bike trail. **Nearby Attractions:** Historic Franklin, Harpeth River, Country Music Hall of Fame, Grand Ole Opry, Opryland Hotel, The Parthenon, Hermitage Andrew Jackson Home, Belle Meade Plantation, Vanderbilt University, downtown Dixon Renaissance Center. **Additional Information:** Dixon Chamber of Commerce, (615) 446-2349.

RESTRICTIONS

Pets: On leash at all times, never left unattended. **Fires:** In ground grills only. **Alcoholic Beverages:** Not allowed. **Vehicle Maximum Length:** 35–40 ft. (sites vary). **Other:** 14-day stay limit, no skateboards or rollerblades; under 13 years of age helmet required on bicycle.

TO GET THERE

From Nashville, take I-40 west 20 mi. to Exit 182. Drive 8 mi. northwest on TN 96 and turn right on TN 70. Drive 5 mi. to the park entrance on the right. From the west, take I-40 Exit 172. Drive north on TN 46 approx. 2 mi. until it intersects TN 70.

CARYVILLE   MAP, A-6
Cove Lake State Park

110 Cove Lake Ln., 37714. T: (423) 566-9701.

🚐 ★★★	▲ ★★★
Beauty: ★★★	Site Privacy: ★★★
Spaciousness: ★★★	Quiet: ★★★
Security: ★★★	Cleanliness: ★★★
Insect Control: ★★★	Facilities: ★★★★

Cove Lake offers nice facilities, including an Olympic-sized swimming pool and separate kiddie pool. Supporting bass, bluegill, and other species, 210-acre Cove Lake is available for bank or row-boat fishing.

The campground includes some pretty lakefront sites. Unfortunately, these sites have sloped parking spaces and are best for tent campers. Sites are on the small side to average, with little privacy. What's more, this campground is extremely popular. We felt claustrophobic. Sites have gravel, back-in parking. Tree cover ranges from totally shady to totally open. For RVs we recommend the large sites 23, 25, 54, 56, 57, and 59. Security is fine here, with 24-hour patrols. Cold weather aficionados should visit in the winter when hundreds of Canada geese make Cove Lake their home. Others should visit in spring or fall to avoid the folks that flock here in the summer.

BASICS

Operated By: Tennessee State Parks. **Open:** All year. **Site Assignment:** First come, first served; no reservations. **Registration:** At campground office. **Fee:** $14.25–$17.25; cash, personal check; access fee per person, $.50. **Parking:** 2 vehicles per site, plus additional parking lot.

FACILITIES

Number of Tent-only Sites: 4. **Number of Multipurpose Sites:** 100. **Hookups:** Electric (30 amps), water (except in the winter). **Each Site:** Picnic table, grill. **Dump Station:** Yes. **Laundry:** No. **Pay Phone:** Yes. **Restrooms and Showers:** Yes. **Fuel:** No. **Propane:** No. **Internal Roads:** Paved. **RV Service:** 40 mi. south in Knoxville. **Market:** Less than 1 mi. **Restaurant:** At park. **General Store:** Less than 1 mi. **Vending:** Yes. **Swimming:** Yes. **Playground:** Yes. **Other:** Softball field, basketball half-court, tennis courts, paved walking & bicycling trail, indoor pavilion w/ kitchen, picnic tables & pavilions, pool concession stand, pool bathhouse. **Activities:** Ranger programs, bank fishing, volleyball, tennis, basketball, softball, horseshoes, row boat & paddle-boat rental, badminton, shuffleboard, Ping-Pong. **Nearby Attractions:** Smoky Mountains, Pigeon Forge, Dollywood, Cumberland Gap National Park. **Additional Information:** Campbell County Chamber of Commerce, (423) 566-0329.

RESTRICTIONS

Pets: On leash only. **Fires:** At sites only. **Alcoholic Beverages:** Not allowed. **Vehicle Maximum Length:** No limit. **Other:** No guns allowed on property.

TO GET THERE

From I-75 take Exit 132, travel east on 25W, go through the traffic light, and the next left is the park's entrance.

COSBY   MAP, B-7
Cosby Campground

Great Smoky Mountains National Park, Hwy. 32, 37738. T: (865) 436-1200; www.nps.gov/grsm.

🚐 ★★★★	▲ ★★★★★
Beauty: ★★★★★	Site Privacy: ★★★★
Spaciousness: ★★★★	Quiet: ★★★★
Security: ★★★★	Cleanliness: ★★★
Insect Control: ★★★★	Facilities: ★★★★

Faithful fans laud Cosby as the best-kept secret in Great Smoky Mountains National Park. Cosby is rarely crowded, which makes it a fine destination for a summer weekend. The cool mountain air is always refreshing in late summer. Many of the hiking trails emanating from Cosby lead to picturesque waterfalls. The town of Cosby is rich in local lore—it was once considered the "moonshine capitol of the world." This gorgeous campground is designed primarily for tent campers, although many sites accommodate RVs. Site size ranges from large to huge. Sites are found in two sections built into a terraced mountainside. Thick woods shade the sites and provide some privacy between sites. Parking is back-in-style, on gravel. Sites at the end of the loops are often more private. Security is fine at Cosby; there are no gates, but the campground is very remote.

BASICS

Operated By: National Park Service. **Open:** Mar. 10–Oct. 31. **Site Assignment:** First come, first served; no reservations. **Registration:** Self-register. **Fee:** $14; 6 people max. per site; 2 tents or 1 RV/ 1 tent; cash. **Parking:** At site (2 vehicles).

FACILITIES

Number of RV-only Sites: 157. **Hookups:** None. **Each Site:** Picnic table, fire ring, grill, tent pad. **Dump Station:** Yes. **Laundry:** No. **Pay Phone:** Yes. **Restrooms and Showers:** Restrooms, no showers. **Fuel:** No. **Propane:** No. **Internal Roads:** Paved. **RV Service:** 20 mi. in Newport. **Market:** 20 mi. in Newport. **Restaurant:** 3 mi. in Cosby. **General Store:** 20 mi. in Newport. **Vending:** No. **Swimming:** No. **Playground:** No. **Other:** Amphitheater, picnic area, horse trail, interpretive trail. **Activities:** Hiking, fishing, horseback riding, canoeing, backcountry hiking, ranger programs (seasonal). **Nearby Attractions:** Golf courses, Cades Cove, Pigeon Forge, Dollywood, Gatlinburg, whitewater rafting, Cherokee Indian Reservation. **Additional Information:** Gatlinburg Dept. of Tourism, (800) 343-1475; Park Information, (865) 436-1200.

RESTRICTIONS

Pets: 6-ft. leash only. **Fires:** Fire ring only. **Alcoholic Beverages:** Allowed. **Vehicle Maximum Length:** 25 ft.

TO GET THERE

From US 321 at Cosby, drive south 2 mi. and stay southeast on TN 32 another 2 mi. Stay right and continue approx. 3 mi. to the campground.

COUNCE   MAP, C-2
TVA Pickwick Dam Campground

Park Rd., 38326. T: (256) 386-2228; www.tva.gov.

🚐 ★★★★   ⛺ ★★★★

Beauty: ★★★★★	Site Privacy: ★★★
Spaciousness: ★★★★	Quiet: ★★★★
Security: ★★★	Cleanliness: ★★★★
Insect Control: ★★★★	Facilities: ★★

When we compare it to the campground at neighboring Pickwick Landing State Park, we prefer the campground at Pickwick Dam because it's enveloped in a gorgeous stand of southern pine. Although the campground is situated parallel to the Tennessee River, sites don't have water views. We recommend the quiet sites in the back of the campground, next to a lovely forest. The campground is completely flat and offers back-in parking on dilapidated gravel. Sites are larger than average. Without undergrowth, there are few privacy barriers between sites. The TVA provides little recreation, but Pickwick Landing State Park offers excellent amenities, including an 18-hole golf course and a restaurant. Pickwick Landing also provides access to mammoth Pickwick Lake and excellent fishing amenities. Anglers catch bass, bream, catfish, crappie, and sauger. The TVA campground is popular. Avoid visiting on summer weekends. Security is marginal; there is no fence around the campground, but it's in a fairly remote area.

BASICS

Operated By: Tennessee Valley Authority. **Open:** All year. **Site Assignment:** First come, first served; no reservations. **Registration:** Self-registration honor system. **Fee:** Hookup, $16; tent, $12; prices for 10 people max.; 1 RV; Golden Age & Golden Access discounts honored. **Parking:** At sites (3 vehicles).

FACILITIES

Number of Multipurpose Sites: 88. **Hookups:** 66 w/ electric (50 amps), water. **Each Site:** Picnic table, grill, lantern pole, some fire rings. **Dump Station:** Yes. **Laundry:** No. **Pay Phone:** No. **Restrooms and Showers:** Yes. **Fuel:** No. **Propane:** No. **Internal Roads:** Paved. **RV Service:** 30 mi. in Burnsville, MS. **Market:** 5 mi. in Counce. **Restaurant:** 2 mi. in Pickwick Landing State Park. **General Store:** Hardware 3 mi. in Counce. **Vending:** No. **Swimming:** No. **Playground:** No. **Activities:** Volleyball, horseshoes, fishing, waterfront walking & biking; water too swift for water sports at campground, 200 yards to activities at Pickwick Landing State Park above the dam. **Nearby Attractions:** Pickwick Landing State Park, Big Hill Pond State Natural Area, Shiloh National Military Park, Corinth National Cemetery & historic district, Tennessee River Museum, historic Savannah, historic Saltillo. **Additional Information:** Savannah/Hardin County CVB, (731) 925-2364.

RESTRICTIONS

Pets: 6-ft. leash max. **Fires:** Allowed. **Alcoholic Beverages:** Not allowed. **Vehicle Maximum Length:** No limit.

TO GET THERE

From Jackson, drive approx. 40 mi. south on US 45. Drive 21 mi. east on US 64 to Savannah, then 10 mi. south on TN 128. Turn right at the campground (200 yards before reaching the dam).

CROSSVILLE   MAP, B-5
Bean Pot Campground

23 Bean Pot Campground Loop, 38571.
T: (931) 484-7671;
www.beanpotcampground.com.

🚐 ★★★   ⛺ ★★★

Beauty: ★★★★	Site Privacy: ★★★
Spaciousness: ★★★	Quiet: ★★★★
Security: ★★★	Cleanliness: ★★★★
Insect Control: ★★★	Facilities: ★★★

This pleasant campground offers comfortably spaced sites and decent amenities. Bean Pot is convenient to I-40 and Crossville restaurants and shopping. The historic town of Rugby is nearby. Or trek to one of the area's popular waterfalls. Campsites are laid out in five rows of pull-throughs (full hookups), plus one row of back-in sites (water only). Sites are all the same size. Some are more level or shadier than others. All sites have gravel parking and concrete patios. The nicest sites, 5–8 and 14–18, are shady pull-throughs in the back of the park. However, families may prefer sites closer to the pool and game room in the front of the park. Security is fair. There are no gates, but the campground is not visible from the main road. Make advance reservations if you want to visit on the weekend of the world's largest yard sale (mid-August), when Crossville is very congested.

BASICS

Operated By: Jim and Ghislaine Gallagher. **Open:** All year. **Site Assignment:** First come, first served; reservations recommended w/ 1-night deposit; cancellation by noon of arrival date for refund. **Registration:** At office, after-hours registration also. **Fee:** Full hookup, $22; water/electric, $19; tent, $16; prices for 2 people; each additional person, $2; children 5 years or younger, free; cash, personal check, V, MC. **Parking:** At site (2 cars), in parking lot.

FACILITIES

Number of RV-only Sites: 51. **Number of Tent-only Sites:** 10. **Number of Multipurpose Sites:** 10. **Hookups:** Electric (20, 30, 50 amps), water, sewer, cable TV. **Each Site:** Picnic table, some grills, some fire rings. **Dump Station:** Yes. **Laundry:** Yes. **Pay Phone:** Yes. **Restrooms and Showers:** Yes. **Fuel:** No. **Propane:** Yes. **Internal Roads:** Gravel & paved. **RV Service:** 6 mi. in Crossville. **Market:** 6 mi. in Crossville. **Restaurant:** 1.5 mi. in Crossville. **General Store:** Yes, limited stock. **Vending:** Yes. **Swimming:** Yes. **Playground:** Yes. **Other:** Clubhouse, RV storage. **Activities:** Nature trail, putting green, horseshoes, basketball, activity field. **Nearby Attractions:** Golf ("Golf Capital of Tennessee"), antique shopping, Historic Oak Ridge, Ozone, Fall Creek & Burgess Falls, Muddy Pond Mennonite Community, wineries. **Additional Information:** Crossville Chamber of Commerce, (931) 484-8444.

RESTRICTIONS

Pets: On leash only. **Fires:** In designated areas only. **Alcoholic Beverages:** Allowed at sites only. **Vehicle Maximum Length:** No limit.

TO GET THERE

From I-40, take Exit 322. Drive north 1.5 mi. on Peavine Rd./TN 101. Turn right on Bean Pot Campground Rd. The campground is 0.25 mi. ahead on the left.

CROSSVILLE   MAP, B-5
Cumberland Mountain State Park

24 Office Dr., 38555.
T: (931) 484-6138 or (800) 250-8618;
www.tnstateparks.com.

🚐 ★★★★   ⛺ ★★★★

Beauty: ★★★★   Site Privacy: ★★★
Spaciousness: ★★★★   Quiet: ★★★★
Security: ★★★★★   Cleanliness: ★★★★
Insect Control: ★★★★   Facilities: ★★★★★

Cumberland Mountain is home to the largest masonry structure built by the Civilian Conservation Corps, a lovely dam and bridge made of indigenous Crab Orchard stone (a type of sandstone). The park's restaurant offers picturesque lake views. On site, Bear Trace golf course was designed by Jack Nicklaus. Shore fishing on the small lake yields catfish, bass, brim, and bluegill. Unfortunately, the campground is not the most attractive area of the park. It's laid out in a series of loops with some extremely spacious sites. Other sites are average sized. Most sites are nicely shaded, although there is little foliage to provide privacy between sites. Parking is paved, back-in style. For privacy, try sites 11, 30, or 31. The park is in the small town of Crossville. Nonetheless, security is excellent; gates close at night and rangers patrol until midnight. Visit in the spring, early summer, or fall to avoid heat and humidity.

BASICS
Operated By: Tennessee State Parks. **Open:** Area 1, all year; other areas, Apr. 1–Nov. 1. **Site Assignment:** First come, first served; no reservations. **Registration:** At camp store, ranger makes rounds at night. **Fee:** $17.25; for 2 people; each additional person (ages 7 and up), $.50; senior/disabled discounts available; cash, personal check, V, MC, D, AE. **Parking:** At site (2 vehicles).

FACILITIES
Number of Multipurpose Sites: 145. **Hookups:** Electric (30 amps), water, sewer. **Each Site:** Picnic table, grill, some sites w/ lantern pole, fire ring & small gravel pad. **Dump Station:** Yes. **Laundry:** No. **Pay Phone:** Yes. **Restrooms and Showers:** Yes. **Fuel:** No. **Propane:** No. **Internal Roads:** Paved. **RV Service:** 4 mi. in Crossville. **Market:** 4 mi. in Crossville. **Restaurant:** Park restaurant (seasonal), several restaurants w/in 5 mi. **General Store:** Camp store, 4 mi. in Crossville. **Vending:** Yes. **Swimming:** Yes. **Playground:** Yes. **Other:** Boat house, recreation lodge available for rent, picnic area. **Activities:** 18-hole golf course, ball field, tennis, volleyball, rowboat, paddleboat, & canoe rentals (no private boats), hiking & nature trails, basketball, horseshoes, summer naturalist programs. **Nearby Attractions:** Cumberland Homestead Tower Center & Museum, Crossville ("Golf Capitol of Tennessee"), Palace Theater, Chestnut Hill, Highland Manor & Stonehaus Wineries, Bledsoe & Mount Roosevelt State Forests. **Additional Information:** Crossville Chamber of Commerce, (931) 484-8444.

RESTRICTIONS
Pets: On leash & kept quiet. **Fires:** Fire ring only. **Alcoholic Beverages:** Not allowed. **Vehicle Maximum Length:** No limit. **Other:** 14-day stay limit (except designated sites), quiet enforced.

TO GET THERE
From I-40 (70 mi. west of Knoxville and 100 mi. east of Nashville), take Exit 317 at Crossville. Drive south 8 mi. on US 127. The park entrance is on the right (west).

DOVER   MAP, A-3
Piney Campground

Land Between the Lakes, 100 Van Morgan Dr., 42211. T: (931) 232-5331; www.lbl.org.

🚐 ★★★★   ⛺ ★★★★

Beauty: ★★★★★   Site Privacy: ★★★
Spaciousness: ★★★★   Quiet: ★★★
Security: ★★★★★   Cleanliness: ★★★★★
Insect Control: ★★★★   Facilities: ★★★★★

Land Between the Lakes, administered by the U.S. Department of Agriculture, offers interesting activities, including hundreds of miles of hiking, canoeing, and mountain-biking trails. Other unique facilities include the planetarium and observatory (call for schedule), a 19th-century farm, and an elk and bison prairie. There are three multipurpose campgrounds. Piney, located at the south end of the recreation area, offers eight camping loops. Though most sites are larger than average, size varies. Lovely trees, including loblolly and shortleaf pine, shade the campgrounds. There is little foliage between sites. Most sites offer pea gravel, back-in parking. At Black Oak Loop, sites 14, 23–26, 30, and 32 are fabulous, with gorgeous views of Kentucky Lake. Tent campers should head for waterfront sites on the nearly deserted Virginia and Sweet gum loops (nonelectric). Extremely remote and gated, Piney is very safe. Avoid this area on summer weekends and holidays. For solitude, plan a late spring or early fall visit.

BASICS
Operated By: U.S.D.A. Forest Service. **Open:** Mar. 1–Nov. 30. **Site Assignment:** First come, first served; no reservations. **Registration:** At gatehouse, campground entrance. **Fee:** Full hookup, $20; water/electric, $16; tent, $12; prices for 8 people; Golden Age & Golden Access discounts available; cash, personal check, V, MC, D, AE. **Parking:** At site (2 vehicles plus camping unit, $3 per additional vehicle).

FACILITIES
Number of RV-only Sites: 44. **Number of Tent-only Sites:** 59. **Hookups:** Electric (20, 30 amps), water. **Each Site:** Picnic table, fire ring, tent pad, lantern pole in primitive area. **Dump Station:** Yes. **Laundry:** Yes. **Pay Phone:** Yes, calling card required. **Restrooms and Showers:** Yes. **Fuel:** No. **Propane:** No. **Internal Roads:** Asphalt/gravel. **RV Service:** 25 mi. in Dover. **Market:** 8 mi. in Dover. **Restaurant:** 4 mi. in Dover. **General Store:** Camp store, limited stock. Also 8 mi. in Dover. **Vending:** Yes. **Swimming:** No. **Playground:** Yes. **Other:** Elk & Bison prairie, visitor center, planetarium, The Homeplace–1850, nature center, campfire theater, boat ramps, fishing pier. **Activities:** Swimming beach, fishing, archery range, ball field, bicycle trails, mountain biking trails, equestrian trails, canoeing, hiking trails, softball, volleyball, basketball, summer recreation programs, nondenominational services Apr.–Oct. **Nearby Attractions:** Kentucky Lake, Fort Donelson National Battlefield, Paris Landing State Resort Park, Cross Creek Wildlife Refuge. **Additional Information:** Clarksville Chamber of Commerce, (931) 647-2331; Stewart County Chamber of Commerce, (931) 232-8290; Land Between the Lakes Information, (800) LBL-7077.

RESTRICTIONS
Pets: On leash only. **Fires:** Fire ring only. **Alcoholic Beverages:** Allowed, sites only. **Vehicle Maximum Length:** No limit. **Other:** 21-day stay limit.

TO GET THERE
From I-24, take TN Exit 4. Drive west on Hwy. 79 26 mi. Go through the town of Dover and drive west 8 more mi. Turn right onto CR 100 and drive north 4 mi. (When you enter Land between the Lakes, CR 100 turns into The Trace.) Turn left onto Fort Henry Rd. The campground is 8 mi. ahead. From the north, take I-24 to KY Exit 31. Drive south on The Trace 35 mi. to Fort Henry Rd. Turn right and drive west 8 mi. to Piney Campground.

EVA   MAP, A-3
Nathan Bedford Forrest State Park

1825 Pilot Knob Rd., 38333. T: (731) 584-6356; www.tnstateparks.com.

🚐 ★★★★   ⛺ ★★★★

Beauty: ★★★★   Site Privacy: ★★★
Spaciousness: ★★★★   Quiet: ★★★★
Security: ★★★   Cleanliness: ★★★★
Insect Control: ★★   Facilities: ★★★★

Located at the southern end of Kentucky Lake, attractive Nathan Bedford Forrest State Park offers limited recreation. Recreation within the park includes a 10-mile hiking trail. Off property, there are marinas and public boat ramps, which provide access to Kentucky Lake, known for its sauger, crappie, bream, catfish, and various bass populations. The Happy Hollow camping loop includes various sized sites under a shady cover of white and red oak, maple, cedar, sycamore, sweetgum, and hackberry. However, there is little foliage between sites to provide privacy. Parking is paved, back-in style. The nicest sites, 1, 3, 5, 23, 24, and 31–35, abut the woods in the back of the campground. There are no gates at Nathan Bedford Forrest. However, the park is extremely remote, making security fair. Avoid this part of Tennessee in late summer, when the weather tends to extremes of heat and humidity.

BASICS
Operated By: Tennessee State Parks. **Open:** All year. **Site Assignment:** First come, first served; no reservations. **Registration:** Park office staff or ranger makes rounds. **Fee:** RV, $17.25; developed tent, $14.25; primitive, $10; prices for 2 people, each additional person, $.50; senior & disabled discounts available; cash, personal check. **Parking:** At sites in designated areas only.

FACILITIES

Number of Tent-only Sites: 13. **Number of Multipurpose Sites:** 38. **Hookups:** Electric (20, 30, 50 amps), water. **Each Site:** Picnic table, grill, concrete pad. **Dump Station:** Yes, $3–5 fee. **Laundry:** No. **Pay Phone:** Yes. **Restrooms and Showers:** Yes. **Fuel:** No. **Propane:** No. **Internal Roads:** Paved. **RV Service:** Local service. **Market:** 3 mi. in Eva. **Restaurant:** 8 mi. in Camden. **General Store:** 8 mi. in Camden. **Vending:** Beverages. **Swimming:** No. **Playground:** Yes. **Other:** Boat launch, folk-life museum, picnic areas, & pavilions. **Activities:** Beach swimming in designated areas, fishing, skiing, hiking trails, backpacking, softball, horseshoes, volleyball, ball field, planned programs, managed hunts. **Nearby Attractions:** Paris Landing & Natchez Trace State Parks, Fort Donelson National Historic Site, Lorretta Lynn's Dude Ranch. **Additional Information:** Camden Chamber of Commerce, (731) 584-8395.

RESTRICTIONS

Pets: On leash only. **Fires:** Allowed (subject to burn ban). **Alcoholic Beverages:** Not allowed. **Vehicle Maximum Length:** 30 ft. **Other:** No firearms.

TO GET THERE

From Nashville, drive west on I-40 and take Exit 126. Drive north approx. 15 mi. on US 641 straight through the bypass. Continue 2 mi. and turn right onto Main St. Drive through town to Court Square and turn right on Local Hwy. 191. This dead-ends in 9 mi. at the park.

GATLINBURG   MAP, B-7
Elkmont Campground

Great Smoky Mountains National Park, 1 mile south off Little River Rd., 37738.
T: (865) 436-1200; www.nps.gov.

★★★★★   ★★★★

Beauty: ★★★★★	Site Privacy: ★★★
Spaciousness: ★★★★	Quiet: ★★★
Security: ★★	Cleanliness: ★★★★
Insect Control: ★★★★	Facilities: ★★★★

Of the Great Smoky Mountains National Park campgrounds, Elkmont is the closest to the tourist attractions at Gatlinburg and Pigeon Forge and the park's Sugarland visitor's center. This campground stays busy all summer, and should be completely avoided on summer holidays. We recommend Elkmont in the spring, when crowds are minimal and wildflowers are blooming. The campground is laid out in a series of loops that are sandwiched together. Though site size is above average, the campground is often so packed with people that you may feel cramped. Shade is provided by a variety of trees, with a little foliage to provide privacy between sites. Sites offer back-in, gravel parking. For peace and quiet, we prefer sections G, H, K, L, M, and N. Security is poor at Elkmont; there are no gates. Safeguard your valuables. Also, mosquitoes can be a nuisance in late summer—bring insect repellent.

BASICS

Operated By: National Park Service. **Open:** Mid-Mar.–Nov. **Site Assignment:** First come, first served; reservations accepted for May 15–Oct. 31 up to 6 months in advance, w/ full deposit; $13.25 cancellation fee w/ 24-hour notice, otherwise 1 night plus fee charged; reservations made by calling (800) 365-CAMP or at reservations.nps.gov (personal check, money order, V, D, MC). **Registration:** Self-registration. **Fee:** $14–$20; for 6 people max. per site; 2 tents or 1 tent/1 RV; Golden Age & Golden Access discounts available; cash only during self-registration off-season. **Parking:** At site (2 vehicles).

FACILITIES

Number of Tent-only Sites: 5. **Number of Multipurpose Sites:** 220. **Hookups:** None. **Each Site:** Picnic table, fire ring, grill, gravel tent pad. **Dump Station:** Yes. **Laundry:** No. **Pay Phone:** Yes. **Restrooms and Showers:** Restrooms, no showers. **Fuel:** No. **Propane:** No. **Internal Roads:** Paved. **RV Service:** 10 mi. in Gatlinburg. **Market:** 10 mi. in Gatlinburg. **Restaurant:** 10 mi. in Gatlinburg. **General Store:** 10 mi. in Gatlinburg. **Vending:** No. **Swimming:** No. **Playground:** No. **Other:** Amphitheater, picnic areas, horse trails, interpretive trails. **Activities:** Hiking, fishing, horseback riding, canoeing, backcountry hiking, ranger programs (seasonal). **Nearby Attractions:** Golf courses, Cades Cove, Pigeon Forge, Dollywood, Gatlinburg, whitewater rafting, Cherokee Indian Reservation. **Additional Information:** Pigeon Forge Visitor information, (865) 453-5700; Park Information, (865) 436-1200.

RESTRICTIONS

Pets: 6-ft. leash only. **Fires:** Fire ring only. **Alcoholic Beverages:** Allowed. **Vehicle Maximum Length:** 32 ft.

TO GET THERE

From Gatlinburg, drive approx. 6 mi. southwest on Little River Rd. Elkmont Campground is 1 mi. south (left) off Little River Rd.

GATLINBURG   MAP, B-7
Outdoor Resorts of America

4229 Pkwy. East, 37738.
T: (865) 436-5861 or (800) 677-5861;
www.gocampingamerica.com.

★★★★★   n/a

Beauty: ★★★★★	Site Privacy: ★★★
Spaciousness: ★★★★	Quiet: ★★★★★
Security: ★★★★★	Cleanliness: ★★★★★
Insect Control: ★★★★	Facilities: ★★★★

One of the prettiest campgrounds in Gatlinburg, Outdoor Resorts offers extremely well-kept recreational facilities. Children enjoy the playground, pool, and mini-golf. Adults appreciate the carefully manicured landscaping, which includes shady weeping willow trees. The campground has two areas separated by the main road. Two creeks flow through the park, lulling campers with their soft bubbling sound. The park would be very quiet in any event—most of the spots are occupied by long-term rentals. RV sites are large, with shrubs and trees providing privacy between many. All parking is paved, back-in style. Each site has a bit of grass and a concrete patio. Ask for a creek-side site. Security is excellent; the gate is locked 24 hours a day. Gatlinburg is extremely pleasant in late summer due to its high elevation.

Visit on weekdays for fall "leaf peeping"—weekend crowds are unbearable.

BASICS

Operated By: Outdoor Resorts. **Open:** All year. **Site Assignment:** Pick your site; reserve from Jan. 1; $35 deposit holds reservation (pay by check or credit card); cancel 3 days in advance for full refund. **Registration:** At camp office. **Fee:** Waterfront, $35; interior, $30; fees include 4 people; cash, check, MC, V. **Parking:** At sites.

FACILITIES

Number of RV-only Sites: 376. **Hookups:** Electric (20, 30, 50 amps), water, sewer, cable TV. **Each Site:** Picnic table, fire ring (most), concrete pad. **Dump Station:** Yes. **Laundry:** Yes. **Pay Phone:** Yes. **Restrooms and Showers:** Yes. **Fuel:** No. **Propane:** Yes. **Internal Roads:** Paved. **RV Service:** Yes. **Market:** 7 mi. west in Gatlinburg. **Restaurant:** On site, in season. **General Store:** Yes. **Vending:** Beverages. **Swimming:** Yes. **Playground:** Yes. **Other:** Game room & lodge. **Activities:** Fishing lake, trout streams, tennis, shuffleboard, mini-golf, horseshoes, volleyball, church service in-season. **Nearby Attractions:** Gatlinburg attractions, Pigeon Forge attractions, Dollywood, Great Smoky Mountains National Park. **Additional Information:** Pigeon Forge Dept. of Tourism, (800) 251-9100.

RESTRICTIONS

Pets: On leash only. **Fires:** Fire ring only. **Alcoholic Beverages:** Not allowed. **Vehicle Maximum Length:** 40 ft.

TO GET THERE

From I-40, take Exit 440 (Hwy. 321S). Go south 7 mi. and turn right before the post office. The entrance is 6.5 mi. ahead on the right.

GATLINBURG   MAP, B-7
Twin Creek RV Resort

1202 East Pkwy., 37738.
T: (865) 436-7081 or (800) 252-8077;
www.twincreekrvresort.com.

★★★★   n/a

Beauty: ★★★★	Site Privacy: ★★★
Spaciousness: ★★★	Quiet: ★★★
Security: ★★★	Cleanliness: ★★★★★
Insect Control: ★★★★	Facilities: ★★★

Though it's only 2 miles from downtown Gatlinburg, Twin Creek feels secluded. Built in a picturesque valley, the campground is nicely landscaped and extremely tidy. The pool, whirlpool, and other facilities are in good condition. Beautiful trees shade the campground. Site size is average, and there is little privacy. All parking is paved. Some sites offer parallel parking while others offer back-in. Each site has a wooden patio. The prettiest sites, 54–56, are along the creek. Gatlinburg roads become very congested on busy weekends, especially in the fall. We recommend weekday visits. If you visit on a weekend, take advantage of the trolley, which stops inside the park and can take you all the way to outlet malls in Pigeon Forge. With no gates, security is fair.

BASICS

Operated By: Twin Creek RV Resort. **Open:** Apr.–Nov. **Site Assignment:** Sites assigned; reservations recommended, deposit policy varies. **Registration:** At office, night arrival w/ reservation preferred. **Fee:** Peak season, $38–$40; prices vary; AAA, AARP, FMCA, Good Sam discounts available; cash, V, MC. **Parking:** At site (1 car, charge may apply for additional vehicles).

FACILITIES

Number of RV-only Sites: 75. **Hookups:** Electric (30, 50 amps), water, sewer, cable TV. **Each Site:** Picnic table, fire ring, grill. **Dump Station:** No. **Laundry:** Yes. **Pay Phone:** Yes. **Restrooms and Showers:** Yes. **Fuel:** No. **Propane:** No. **Internal Roads:** Paved. **RV Service:** Yes. **Market:** Across the street. **Restaurant:** 1 block. **General Store:** Camp store, hardware 0.25 mi. **Vending:** Beverages. **Swimming:** Yes (also whirlpool & wading pool). **Playground:** Yes. **Other:** Arcade, boutique, trolley service to Gatlinburg & Pigeon Forge. **Activities:** Jacuzzi, children's pool, Sun. worship service. **Nearby Attractions:** Trolley to Pigeon Forge, Dollywood, Gatlinburg attractions, water park, Dixie Stampede, Elvis Museum, Kids Country, helicopter tours, whitewater rafting, Cherokee Indian Reservation. **Additional Information:** Pigeon Forge Visitor information, (865) 453-5700.

RESTRICTIONS

Pets: On leash only. Call ahead about pet restrictions. **Fires:** Fire ring only. **Alcoholic Beverages:** Allowed, at sites only. **Vehicle Maximum Length:** 45 ft. (sites vary). **Other:** No motorcycles.

TO GET THERE

From Knoxville, Take I-40 east to Exit 407 and drive approx. 20 mi. south on US 441. Turn left on US 321 at light No. 3 and the campground is 2 mi. on the right. From Asheville, take I-40 west to Exit 440 and turn south on Hwy. 321. The campground is approx. 25 mi. on the left.

GATLINBURG   MAP, B-7
Yogi Bear's Jellystone Park

P.O. Box 282, 37738.
T: (423) 487-5534 or (800) 210-2119;
www.greatsmokyjellystone.com.

🚐 ★★★★   ⛺ ★★★★

Beauty: ★★★★	Site Privacy: ★★★★
Spaciousness: ★★★	Quiet: ★★★
Security: ★★★★	Cleanliness: ★★★
Insect Control: ★★★★	Facilities: ★★★★★

Seasoned camping families know that Yogi Bear campgrounds offer excellent children's recreation. This park is no exception. Facilities are well maintained and activities are well planned. There are separate tent and RV camping areas. RV site size varies, but none are huge. Parking is on gravel. There are back-in and pull-through sites. Most are shady, and the nicest are along the bubbling creek. Creek-side sites 59–61 are small, but extremely pretty, while creek-side sites 41–50 are more spacious, but not as attractive. The largest site (77, a pull-through) is not creek-side. Tent sites are pretty and slightly secluded

from the RV sites. There are no gates at this small-town campground, but employees are vigilant (we were questioned twice while on property). Security is good. Visit Gatlinburg in August to enjoy the cool mountain air. Avoid fall weekends, when leaf peepers cause legendary traffic jams in small mountain towns.

BASICS

Operated By: Tim Gordon. **Open:** Mar. 31–Oct. 29. **Site Assignment:** Usually assigned at check-in; reserve 1 year in advance; $50 deposit, refund w/ 7-day notice for cancellation (less $5 fee). **Registration:** At camp office. **Fee:** RV, $34; tent, $26; 2 people, $31; AAA, Good Sam, Club Yogi discount. **Parking:** In sites, except some walk-in tent sites.

FACILITIES

Number of RV-only Sites: 63. **Number of Tent-only Sites:** 21. **Hookups:** Electric, water, sewer, cable TV. **Each Site:** Picnic table, fire ring, gravel. **Dump Station:** Yes. **Laundry:** Yes. **Pay Phone:** Yes. **Restrooms and Showers:** Yes. **Fuel:** No. **Propane:** No. **Internal Roads:** Gravel. **RV Service:** 30 mi. west in Sevierville. **Market:** 14 mi. east in Newport. **Restaurant:** 1 mi. west in Cosby. **General Store:** In campground. **Vending:** Yes. **Swimming:** Yes. **Playground:** Yes. **Other:** Movie theater, pavilion. **Activities:** Children's Day Camp (in season), mini-golf, game room, swimming, fishing, hiking, basketball, horseshoes, bingo, live entertainment, wagon rides, church services (in-season). **Nearby Attractions:** Great Smoky Mountains National Park, Pigeon Forge, whitewater rafting, outlet shopping, Dollywood, museums, caverns. **Additional Information:** Gatlinburg Dept. of Tourism, (800) 343-1475.

RESTRICTIONS

Pets: Not in tent area; some breeds restricted. **Fires:** Fire ring only. **Alcoholic Beverages:** In sites only. **Vehicle Maximum Length:** 40 ft. **Other:** max. 6 people per site.

TO GET THERE

From I-40, take Exit 435. Turn right onto Hwy. 321 and go southeast approx. 15 mi. Follow Yogi signs, right at 6 mi., left at 0.25 mi., right at 7 mi., then 2.5 mi. The entrance is on the left.

HARRISON   MAP, B-5
Harrison Bay State Park

8411 Harrison Bay Rd., 37341. T: (423) 344-2272; www.tnstateparks.com.

🚐 ★★★★★   ⛺ ★★★★★

Beauty: ★★★★★	Site Privacy: ★★★★
Spaciousness: ★★★★★	Quiet: ★★★★
Security: ★★★★	Cleanliness: ★★★★
Insect Control: ★★★★	Facilities: ★★★★★

Attractive Harrison Bay, situated on Chickamauga Lake, offers some of the finest fishing facilities in the state. The Lake supports largemouth bass, crappie, bream, striped bass, and catfish. Other recreation amenities include a swimming pool and separate children's pool. There are four camping areas. We recommend areas A and C, which offer lakefront camping. Although the waterfront sites are gorgeous,

they tend to be smaller than inland sites. Luckily, all sites are spacious, but some are huge. The campgrounds are shaded by various tree species, including white oak, maple, hickory, and pine. Privacy varies from site to site. Parking is on gravel and usually back-in style. Area B contains some pull-through sites. Security is excellent at this rural park. Gates close at 10 p.m., and there is a night watchman. Visit in spring or fall for the nicest weather. Avoid the park on holiday weekends.

BASICS

Operated By: Tennessee State Parks. **Open:** All year. **Site Assignment:** First come, first served; no reservations. **Registration:** In-season, at camp store; park personnel make rounds. **Fee:** RV, $10.25–$19.25; tent, $6.50; prices for 2 people; each additional person, $.50; cash, personal check; credit card accepted at camp store, summer only. **Parking:** At site (2 cars), in parking lot.

FACILITIES

Number of RV-only Sites: 128. **Number of Tent-only Sites:** 28. **Number of Multipurpose Sites:** 135. **Hookups:** Electric (30 amps), water. **Each Site:** Picnic table, fire ring. **Dump Station:** Yes. **Laundry:** No. **Pay Phone:** Yes. **Restrooms and Showers:** Yes. **Fuel:** No (boat fuel at marina). **Propane:** No. **Internal Roads:** Paved. **RV Service:** 3 mi. south on Hwy. 58. **Market:** 3 mi. north on Hwy. 58. **Restaurant:** Park restaurant (seasonal), 3 mi. on Hwy. 58. **General Store:** Camp store (seasonal), 6 mi. in Chattanooga. **Vending:** Yes. **Swimming:** Yes. **Playground:** Yes. **Other:** Recreation hall, marina (w/ boat fuel), boat launch, boat slips, children's pool, picnic area & shelters. **Activities:** Golf, fishing, boat rentals, hiking & bicycle trails, nature trail, ball field, badminton, tennis, volleyball, horseshoes, summer programs & entertainment. **Nearby Attractions:** Chattanooga Choo-Choo, Railroad Museum, Tennessee Aquarium, Lookout Mountain, Ruby Falls, Rock City, Incline Railway, Booker T. Washington State Park, Walnut St. Bridge, Chickamauga Battlefield. **Additional Information:** Chattanooga Area CVB, (800) 322-3344 or (423) 756-8687, www.chattanoogafun.com.

RESTRICTIONS

Pets: On leash only. **Fires:** Fire ring only. **Alcoholic Beverages:** Not allowed. **Vehicle Maximum Length:** 32 ft. **Other:** 14-day stay limit, firearms, & metal detectors prohibited.

TO GET THERE

From Chattanooga, take Exit 4 off I-75 onto TN 153. Drive north on TN 153 to the sixth exit and turn north onto TN 58. Drive 12 mi. to Harrison Bay Rd. and turn left. The park entrance is 1 mi. ahead on the left.

HENDERSON   MAP, B-2
Chickasaw State Park

20 Cabin Ln., 38340.
T: (731) 989-5141 or (800) 458-1752;
www.tnstateparks.com.

🚐 ★★★★   ⛺ ★★★★

Beauty: ★★★★★   Site Privacy: ★★★★
Spaciousness: ★★★★   Quiet: ★★★★
Security: ★★★   Cleanliness: ★★★★
Insect Control: ★★★★   Facilities: ★★★★★

Shady tall pines and hardwoods grace the campgrounds at Chickasaw. There are separate campgrounds for RVs, tents, and equestrian use. The RV campground consists of two loops, each with its own bathhouse. Sites are above average in size. All parking is paved and there are pull-through and back-in sites. Foliage between some sites provides seclusion. Our favorite RV sites are the 30s and number 40, which is absolutely gorgeous. The small tent campground is nicely wooded with views of picturesque Lake Placid. With only six sites, the ratio of toilets to campsites is unusually high. Lake Placid is stocked with bass and bluegill (no personally owned boats allowed). Adjoining the state park, Chickasaw State Forest contains 50 miles of roads and multiuse trails. There are no gates, but the park is off the beaten path—security is fair. Visit any time except summer holidays and hot late summer.

BASICS

Operated By: Tennessee State Parks. **Open:** All year. **Site Assignment:** First come, first served; no reservations. **Registration:** At sites, ranger makes rounds. **Fee:** RV/Wrangler, $17.25; tent, $11.25; for 2 people; each additional person, $.50; Golden Access senior discounts; cash, personal check, V, MC, D, AE, DC, CB. **Parking:** At sites, in parking lot.

FACILITIES

Number of Tent-only Sites: 29. **Number of Multipurpose Sites:** 52. **Hookups:** Electric (20, 30 amps), water. **Each Site:** Picnic table, grill. **Dump Station:** Yes. **Laundry:** No. **Pay Phone:** Yes. **Restrooms and Showers:** Yes. **Fuel:** No. **Propane:** No. **Internal Roads:** Paved. **RV Service:** 25 mi. in Jackson. **Market:** 3 mi. on Hwy. 100. **Restaurant:** Park restaurant, also 8 mi. in Henderson. **General Store:** No. **Vending:** Beverages. **Swimming:** No. **Playground:** Yes. **Other:** Stables, 18-hole golf course, boat dock (electric motors only), picnic shelters, group lodge. **Activities:** Nature trail, equestrian trails, beach, swimming (when lifeguard on duty), fishing, rowboat & paddleboat rentals, archery range, tennis, basketball, volleyball, ball field, summertime organized activities. **Nearby Attractions:** Shiloh Military Park, Pinson Mounds State Park, Casey Jones Museum, Parker's Crossroads & Britton Lane Civil War Battlefields. **Additional Information:** Jackson Chamber of Commerce, (731) 423-2200.

RESTRICTIONS

Pets: On leash only. **Fires:** In designated areas, grills only. **Alcoholic Beverages:** Not allowed. **Vehicle Maximum Length:** Sites vary. **Other:** 2-week stay limit, no firearms.

TO GET THERE

From US 45 (17 mi. south of Jackson), drive west 8 mi. on TN 100. The park is on the left. From Memphis, drive 80 mi. east on US 64, which becomes TN 100.

HILHAM   MAP, A-5
Standing Stone State Park

1674 Standing Stone Park Hwy., 38568.
T: (931) 823-6347; www.tnstateparks.com.

🚐 ★★★★   ⛺ ★★★★

Beauty: ★★★★   Site Privacy: ★★★★
Spaciousness: ★★★★   Quiet: ★★★★★
Security: ★★★★   Cleanliness: ★★★★
Insect Control: ★★★★   Facilities: ★★★★

Located on the Cumberland Plateau, Standing Stone offers sites with gravel, back-in parking. Though most sites are ample, size varies. However, this park is extremely remote and rarely crowded, so you're likely to have plenty of elbow-room. Most sites have some greenery to provide seclusion, and all are nicely shaded by various hardwood species. The largest sites include 1, 24, and 28. Standing Stone maintains nice facilities including an archery range and 10 miles of hiking trails. They also host special events such as the Roley Hole Marble Tournament. On property, 69-acre Standing Stone Lake is stocked with bass and bluegill. Nearby, giant Dale Hollow Lake offers some of the best fishing in Tennessee and Kentucky. There are no gates at Standing Stone, making security fair. This pretty park is an excellent destination on summer weekends, though holidays should be avoided.

BASICS

Operated By: Tennessee State Parks Dept. of Environment and Conservation. **Open:** All year. **Site Assignment:** First come, first served; no reservations. **Registration:** At office, or campground host will make rounds; night arrival register next morning. **Fee:** RV, $17.25; tent, $14.25; prices for 2 people; each additional person, $.50; Golden Age & Golden Access discounts available; cash, personal check, V, MC, D, AE. **Parking:** At site (2 cars).

FACILITIES

Number of Multipurpose Sites: 36. **Hookups:** Electric (30 amps), water. **Each Site:** Picnic table, grill, fire ring. **Dump Station:** Yes. **Laundry:** Yes. **Pay Phone:** Yes (in park). **Restrooms and Showers:** Yes (closed in winter). **Fuel:** No. **Propane:** No. **Internal Roads:** Paved. **RV Service:** 21 mi. in Cookeville. **Market:** 8 mi. on Hwy. 52. **Restaurant:** 12 mi. in Livingston. **General Store:** 12 mi. in Livingston hardware or 21 mi. in Cookeville (Wal-Mart). **Vending:** Beverages. **Swimming:** Yes (seasonal). **Playground:** Yes (2). **Other:** Picnic areas & pavilions, meeting room, rec center w/ Ping-Pong. **Activities:** John boat rentals (bring your own trolling motor—electric motors only), bank fishing, hiking trails, basketball, softball field, volleyball, horseshoes, tennis, archery range, Roley Hole Marble tournament in Sept. **Nearby Attractions:** Dale Hollow Lake, Cordell Hull Birthplace Museum & State Park, Big South Fork National River & Recreation Area, Sgt. Alvin C. York State Historic Site. **Additional Information:** Livingston/Overton County Chamber of Commerce, (931) 823-6421.

RESTRICTIONS

Pets: On leash only. **Fires:** Grill, fire rings only. **Alcoholic Beverages:** Not allowed. **Vehicle Maximum Length:** 30 ft. (sites vary). **Other:** 14-day stay limit.

TO GET THERE

From I-40, take Exit 288 at Cookeville and drive north approx. 10 mi. on TN 111. Take the bypass to TN 52 north and drive 12 mi. to the park entrance on the left. This is Hwy. 136, and the campground is 1 mi. from TN 52. (This is the only access for RVs, due to a 1-lane bridge on Hwy. 136 north of the park.)

HURRICANE MILLS   MAP, A-3
Loretta Lynn Dude Ranch

I-40 west, Exit 143, 37078. T: (931) 296-7700; www.lorettalynn.com.

🚐 ★★★★   ⛺ ★★★★

Beauty: ★★★★   Site Privacy: ★★★
Spaciousness: ★★★   Quiet: ★★★
Security: ★★★   Cleanliness: ★★★★
Insect Control: ★★★   Facilities: ★★★★

Ms. Lynn's ranch and grounds are enchanting. On property, you'll find her massive, beautifully landscaped neoclassical mansion complete with Doric columns. The restored gristmill across the river provides idyllic photo opportunities. Inside the gristmill is a museum housing the star's memorabilia and costumes. In season, there are festivals and special events on the grounds (call for schedule). Various outdoor activities are available nearby. The massive campground features some extremely attractive sites, and some downright disappointing sites. Luckily, the less attractive sites are used only on the busiest weekends. In order to choose a pretty site, we recommend arriving a day early if you're visiting on a special event weekend. The nicer portion of the campground has a picturesque creek flowing through the middle and features average-sized sites shaded by a variety of hardwoods. Parking is on gravel, and there are both back-in and pull-through sites. Loretta Lynn's Ranch is extremely remote, making gates unnecessary. Security is fine.

BASICS

Operated By: Loretta Lynn Ranch, Inc. **Open:** Apr.–Oct. **Site Assignment:** First come, first served; reservations accepted w/ 1-night deposit; 72-hour cancellation notice. **Registration:** At main office, night arrival register next morning. **Fee:** Full hookup, $22; water/electric, $19; tent, $17; for 2 people; each additional person, $5; seniors, 10% discount; cash, personal check, V, MC, D. **Parking:** At sites (2 max.), in parking lot.

FACILITIES

Number of RV-only Sites: 200. **Number of Tent-only Sites:** 100. **Hookups:** Electric (30, 50 amps), water, sewer. **Each Site:** Some sites w/ picnic table, grill, fire ring. **Dump Station:** Yes. **Laundry:** Yes. **Pay Phone:** Yes. **Restrooms and Showers:** Yes. **Fuel:** No. **Propane:** No. **Internal Roads:** Paved & gravel. **RV Service:** 45 mi. in Dixon. **Market:** 7.5 mi. in Waverly. **Restaurant:** Snack bar on-site or 7 mi. in Waverly. **General Store:** Camp store, 7 mi. in Waverly. **Vending:** Yes. **Swimming:** Yes (seasonal). **Playground:** Yes. **Other:** Recreation Hall. **Activities:** Loretta Lynn Home Tour, Western town, Loretta Lynn Museum, fishing, canoeing (seasonal), mountain biking & hiking trails, campfire entertainment (seasonal), hayrides (occasional), horseshoes, softball, volleyball. **Nearby Attractions:** Humphreys County Museum & Civil War Fort, Blue Creek Nature Center, Johnsonville State Historic Park, Tennessee National Wildlife Refuge, Duck River, Nathan Bedford Forrest State Park, 65 mi. to Nashville. **Additional Information:** Waverly Chamber of Commerce, (931) 296-4865.

RESTRICTIONS

Pets: On leash only. **Fires:** Fire ring only (weather permitting). **Alcoholic Beverages:** Allowed. **Vehicle Maximum Length:** 60 ft. (sites vary). **Other:** No ATVs.

TO GET THERE

From I-40, take Exit 143 and drive north 8 mi. on Loretta Lynn Pkwy. The entrance is on the left.

JAMESTOWN   MAP, A-6
Pickett C.C.C. Memorial Park

4605 Pickett Park Hwy., 38556-4141.
T: (931) 879-5821; www.tnstateparks.com.

🚐 ★★★★   ⛺ ★★★★

Beauty: ★★★★	Site Privacy: ★★★
Spaciousness: ★★★★	Quiet: ★★★★★
Security: ★★★★	Cleanliness: ★★★
Insect Control: ★★★★	Facilities: ★★★★

Pickett State Park is adjacent to Daniel Boone National Forest and Big South Fork National River and Recreation Area. The park is known for its surreal rock formations, caves, and natural bridges as well as its botanical diversity. Some scientists believe that Pickett supports the second most diverse flora in the United States (Great Smoky Mountains National Park has the most diverse plant life in the United States). The campgrounds at Pickett are reasonably attractive, with some open sites and others shaded by white pine trees. Sites are small, but they are spaced far apart, giving campers the feeling of spaciousness. Sites have paved, back-in parking. For space and privacy, we like tent sites 20–30. RVs should head for site 1. Pickett is patrolled by rangers at night and has no gates. Nonetheless, the park's isolation makes it fairly safe. Visit Pickett State Park any time except for summer holidays—it's rarely crowded.

BASICS

Operated By: Tennessee State Parks. **Open:** All year. **Site Assignment:** First come, first served; no reservations. **Registration:** Campground host makes rounds (check-in at office in winter). **Fee:** $11.25; for 2 people; each additional person, $.50; senior & disabled discounts available; cash, personal check, V, MC, D, AE. **Parking:** At sites.

FACILITIES

Number of Multipurpose Sites: 40. **Hookups:** Electric (20 amps), water. **Each Site:** Picnic table, grill, fire ring. **Dump Station:** Yes. **Laundry:** Yes. **Pay Phone:** Yes. **Restrooms and Showers:** Yes. **Fuel:** No. **Propane:** No. **Internal Roads:** Paved. **RV Service:** 60 mi. in Cookeville. **Market:** 13 mi. in Jamestown. **Restaurant:** 13 mi. in Jamestown. **General Store:** 13 mi. in Jamestown. **Vending:** Beverages. **Swimming:** No. **Playground:** Yes. **Other:**

Picnic areas & shelters, nature center, boat dock. **Activities:** Lake swimming, boating, fishing (boat rentals available), tennis, hiking trail, seasonal interpretive programs, seasonal hunts. **Nearby Attractions:** Big South Fork National River & Recreation Area, Rugby, Cordell Hull Birthplace, Alvin C. York Grist Mill. **Additional Information:** Jamestown Chamber of Commerce, (931) 879-9948. Park office (931) 260-0018.

RESTRICTIONS

Pets: On leash only. **Fires:** Fire ring only. **Alcoholic Beverages:** Not allowed. **Vehicle Maximum Length:** 25 ft. (sites vary). **Other:** 14-day stay limit.

TO GET THERE

From I-40 Exit 317 (Crossville), drive north 35 mi. on US 127. Turn north onto local Hwy. 154 and drive another 13 mi. The park entrance is on the left.

KINGSPORT   MAP, A-8
Warrior's Path State Park

Hemlock Rd., P.O. Box 5026, 37663.
T: (423) 239-8531; www.tnstateparks.com.

🚐 ★★★★   ⛺ ★★★★

Beauty: ★★★★	Site Privacy: ★★★
Spaciousness: ★★★★	Quiet: ★★★
Security: ★★★	Cleanliness: ★★★
Insect Control: ★★	Facilities: ★★★★★

Situated on the Patrick Henry Reservoir on the Holsten River, Warrior's Path offers great recreation facilities, including an 18-hole golf course and extensive boating and fishing amenities. Fish caught in the reservoir include catfish, crappie, bass, bream, and trout. The Olympic-sized pool is next to the campground. The campground consists of one large loop and one small one. Sites are large, though size varies greatly. Although some sites are open, most are shaded by sugar maple, persimmon, tulip poplars, and various oaks. There are no natural privacy barriers. All sites have paved, back-in parking. We like sites 75–79 for pretty views of the reservoir. Others are too densely wooded to afford views of the water. Warrior's Path is popular with locals, and there are no gates, which makes security fair. Insects can be a problem here when it's warm and humid. Avoid popular Warrior's Path on summer weekends.

BASICS

Operated By: Tennessee State Parks. **Open:** All year. **Site Assignment:** First come, first served; no reservations. **Registration:** At camper check-in station or park office, night arrival register the next day. **Fee:** Water/electric, $17.25; overflow area, $11.25; for 2 people; each additional person, $.50; seniors, 25% discount; disabled, 50% discount; cash, personal check, traveler's check, no credit cards. **Parking:** At sites, in parking lot.

FACILITIES

Number of Multipurpose Sites: 135. **Hookups:** Electric (20, 30, 50 amps), water. **Each Site:** Picnic table, grill, fire ring. **Dump Station:** Yes. **Laundry:** No. **Pay Phone:** Yes. **Restrooms and Showers:** Yes. **Fuel:** No. **Propane:** No. **Internal Roads:** Paved. **RV Service:** 5 mi. in Kingsport. **Market:** 1 mi. in Kingsport. **Restaurant:** Snack bars seasonal, 1 mi.

in Kingsport. **General Store:** 1.5 mi. to Wal-Mart. **Vending:** Beverages. **Swimming:** Yes (seasonal). **Playground:** Yes. **Other:** Recreation building w/ table tennis & pool tables, boat ramps, marina, riding stables, picnic area, amphitheater. **Activities:** 18-hole golf course, fishing, boating (boat rentals available, paddle boats seasonal), horseback riding (seasonal), hiking trails, mountain-bike trails, disc-golf, tennis, basketball, volleyball, horseshoes, soccer field. **Nearby Attractions:** Bays Mountain Nature Center, Allandale Mansion, Appalachian Caverns, The Netherland Inn, Steels Creek Park & Nature Center. **Additional Information:** Kingsport Chamber of Commerce, (423) 392-8820.

RESTRICTIONS

Pets: On leash only. **Fires:** Fire ring only. **Alcoholic Beverages:** Not allowed. **Vehicle Maximum Length:** 40 ft. (sites vary). **Other:** 2-week stay limit, no firearms.

TO GET THERE

From I-81, take Exit 59 and turn north on SR 36/Fort Henry Dr. Drive 5 mi. and turn right at the fifth traffic light onto Hemlock Rd. Drive 1.5 mi. to the park entrance on the right.

LAWRENCEBURG   MAP, B-3
David Crockett State Park

P.O. Box 398, 38464-0398. T: (931) 762-9408;
www.tnstateparks.com.

🚐 ★★★★   ⛺ ★★★★

Beauty: ★★★★★	Site Privacy: ★★★★
Spaciousness: ★★★★	Quiet: ★★★★
Security: ★★★★★	Cleanliness: ★★★★
Insect Control: ★★★★	Facilities: ★★★★

Of the two campgrounds at David Crockett, Campground No. 2 is the prettiest. Flat and shady, with comfortably spaced sites, No. 2 has lovely trees. A little greenery provides barriers between some sites. All sites in No. 2 have back-in parking. The most private sites in No. 2 are 99–101. Campground No. 1 is more open and includes attractive sites along a creek (15–32). Sites 1, 2, and 3 in Campground No. 1 are the only pull-throughs. Some sites have paved parking while others have gravel. Facilities at David Crockett are very nice and include an Olympic-size swimming pool and a 40-acre fishing lake (no personally owned boats allowed; rentals available). There's a large Amish community in this area, with farm tours available. The James D. Vaughan Museum, memorializing the "Father of Southern Gospel," is also nearby. Security is excellent at remote David Crockett, with gates locked at night. Avoid the park on summer weekends. For the nicest weather, visit in spring or fall.

BASICS

Operated By: Tennessee State Parks. **Open:** All year. **Site Assignment:** First come, first served; no reservations. **Registration:** At office, ranger makes rounds after hours. **Fee:** RV, $17.25; tent, $14.25; for 2 people; each additional person, $.50; senior discount available; cash, personal check, V, MC, D, AE. **Parking:** At site.

FACILITIES

Number of Tent-only Sites: 7. **Number of Multi-purpose Sites:** 107. **Hookups:** Electric (30 amps), water; adaptors available. **Each Site:** Picnic table, grill, fire ring. **Dump Station:** Yes. **Laundry:** No, 2 blocks. **Pay Phone:** Yes. **Restrooms and Showers:** Yes. **Fuel:** No. **Propane:** No. **Internal Roads:** Paved. **RV Service:** 2 mi. east on Hwy. 64. **Market:** 2 mi. north on Hwy. 43. **Restaurant:** Park restaurant. **General Store:** 3 mi. on Hwy. 43. **Vending:** Beverages. **Swimming:** Yes. **Playground:** Yes. **Other:** Boat launch, interpretive center, wading pool, pool concessions, pool bathhouse, Internet access. **Activities:** Fishing, paddle-boat rentals (seasonal), fishing-boat rentals, archery range, hiking & biking trails, tennis, softball, volleyball. **Nearby Attractions:** Historic Downtown Lawrenceburg, Amish Country farm & wagon tours, James D. Vaughan Museum ("The Birthplace of Southern Gospel Music"), Coca Cola Palace, Laurel Hill Lake, Scenic Buffalo River. **Additional Information:** Lawrenceburg Chamber of Commerce, (931) 762-4911.

RESTRICTIONS

Pets: On leash only. **Fires:** In grills & Campground No. 1 only. **Alcoholic Beverages:** Not allowed. **Vehicle Maximum Length:** 40 ft. **Other:** 14-day stay limit, fireworks prohibited.

TO GET THERE

From I-65, take Exit 14 onto US 64. Drive 30 mi. west to Lawrenceburg. The park is on the right (north) of Hwy. 64, 0.5 mi. west of Lawrenceburg.

LEBANON   MAP, A-4
Cedars of Lebanon State Park

328 Cedar Forest Rd., 37090. T: (615) 443-2769; www.tnstateparks.com

🚐 ★★★★   ⛺ ★★★★

Beauty: ★★★★   Site Privacy: ★★★
Spaciousness: ★★★★   Quiet: ★★★★
Security: ★★★★   Cleanliness: ★★★★
Insect Control: ★★★★ Facilities: ★★★★

Named after Biblical references to dense cedar woods in ancient Lebanon, this park maintains nice facilities even though its entrance looks dumpy. There are 8 miles of hiking trails, 6 miles of equestrian trails, and an Olympic-size pool. The park is on flat land without a major body of water; the draw here is the forest. Campgrounds 2 and 3 are the shadiest and prettiest, situated in mature tree stands consisting of about 50% cedar. Sites are large, but there is no greenery between them. There are both back-in and pull-through sites with paved parking. In campground No. 2, we liked site 18. Campground No. 3 contains the largest sites (13–15 were our favorites). There are no gates at this small town park, making security fair. A ranger is on duty at all times. Visit in spring, early summer, or fall. Avoid holiday weekends.

BASICS

Operated By: Tennessee State Parks. **Open:** All year. **Site Assignment:** First come, first served; no reservations. **Registration:** At office or camp store, host will check-in late-comers. **Fee:** RV, $17.25; tent,

$14.25; for 2 people; each additional person, $.50; senior discount available; cash, personal check, V, MC, AE, D; $3 entrance fee per vehicle. **Parking:** At site.

FACILITIES

Number of Tent-only Sites: 30. **Number of Multipurpose Sites:** 87. **Hookups:** Electric (20, 30, 50 amps), water; 1 wheelchair-accessible site w/ sewer. **Each Site:** Picnic table, grill, fire ring, some lantern poles. **Dump Station:** Yes. **Laundry:** Yes. **Pay Phone:** Yes. **Restrooms and Showers:** Yes. **Fuel:** No. **Propane:** No. **Internal Roads:** Paved. **RV Service:** 10 mi. in Lebanon. **Market:** In Lebanon. **Restaurant:** 7 mi. in Lebanon. **General Store:** Camp store (seasonal), 8 mi. in Lebanon. **Vending:** Beverages. **Swimming:** Yes (seasonal). **Playground:** Yes. **Other:** Recreation lodge, assembly hall, nature center, picnic area & shelters, riding stables. **Activities:** Hiking trails, equestrian trails, disc-golf course, ball field, basketball, volleyball, tennis, horseshoes, organized activities in season. **Nearby Attractions:** Lebanon "Antique Capital of the South," Country Music Hall of Fame, Grand Ole Opry, Opryland Hotel, The Parthenon, Hermitage Andrew Jackson Home, Belle Meade Plantation, Vanderbilt University. **Additional Information:** Nashville Tourism information, (615) 259-4700.

RESTRICTIONS

Pets: On leash only. **Fires:** Fire ring only. **Alcoholic Beverages:** Not allowed. **Vehicle Maximum Length:** No limit. **Other:** 14-day stay limit.

TO GET THERE

From I-40, take Exit 238 and drive south 6 mi. on US 231. Turn left (east) on Cedar FR and drive into the park. Drive 1 mi. and turn right on WPA Rd. Drive 0.5 mi. to the campground entrance.

MANCHESTER   MAP, B-4, B-5
Old Stone Fort State Archaeological Area

732 Stone Fort Dr., 37355. T: (931) 723-5073 or (931) 723-5037; www.tnstateparks.com

🚐 ★★★★   ⛺ ★★★★

Beauty: ★★★★   Site Privacy: ★★★★★
Spaciousness: ★★★★★   Quiet: ★★★★
Security: ★★★   Cleanliness: ★★★★
Insect Control: ★★★★ Facilities: ★★★★

This park's namesake is a 2,000-year-old Native American ceremonial site nestled into two forks of the Duck River. The Old Stone Fort consists of 50 acres of flat land enclosed by mounds, walls, and river cliffs, and was actively used for 500 years. The park maintains hiking trails for exploring the ceremonial site and area waterfalls. The campground consists of three loops near the Duck River (no water views). Campsites are commodious and very private due to nice greenery between them. Sites are heavily wooded, with various oak species and other hardwoods. All sites feature paved, back-in parking. The sites in the back of the campground (on the third circle) are the most spacious and private. Old Stone Fort is on the outskirts of Manchester. Gates are

locked at night, making security good. Old Stone Fort is rarely crowded, so it's a good destination for a summer weekend.

BASICS

Operated By: Tennessee State Parks. **Open:** All year. **Site Assignment:** First come, first served; no reservations. **Registration:** Ranger makes rounds. **Fee:** RV, $18; tent, $15; for 2 people; each additional person, $.50; senior & disabled discounts available; cash, check. **Parking:** At sites.

FACILITIES

Number of Multipurpose Sites: 51. **Hookups:** Electric (20 amps), water. **Each Site:** Picnic table, grill, paved pads, most have fire rings. **Dump Station:** Yes. **Laundry:** No. **Pay Phone:** Yes. **Restrooms and Showers:** Yes. Shower is seasonal. **Fuel:** No. **Propane:** No. **Internal Roads:** Paved. **RV Service:** 1 mi. **Market:** 3 mi. in Manchester. **Restaurant:** W/in 2 mi. **General Store:** 0.25 mi. south. **Vending:** Beverages. **Swimming:** No. **Playground:** Yes. **Other:** Picnic areas, museum & visitor center, boat ramp. **Activities:** 9-hole golf course, pro shop (cart & club rentals), nature trails, hiking, fishing (electric trolling motors only), summer organized programs. **Nearby Attractions:** Jack Daniels Distillery, Cumberland Caverns Park, Foothills Craft Shop, Tims Ford Lake, 18-hole golf, Manchester Arts Center. **Additional Information:** Manchester Chamber of Commerce, (931) 728-7635.

RESTRICTIONS

Pets: On leash only. **Fires:** Fire ring only. **Alcoholic Beverages:** Not allowed. **Vehicle Maximum Length:** No limit. **Other:** 14-day stay limit.

TO GET THERE

From I-24 (approx. 60 mi. south of Nashville) take Exit 110 and turn southwest on TN 53. Drive 1 mi and turn right (north) on US 41. The park is 0.5 mi. on the left.

MILLINGTON   MAP, B-1
Meeman-Shelby Forest State Park

910 Riddier Rd., 38053. T: (901) 876-5215; www.tnstateparks.com

🚐 ★★★★   ⛺ ★★★★

Beauty: ★★★★   Site Privacy: ★★★★
Spaciousness: ★★★   Quiet: ★★★★
Security: ★★★★   Cleanliness: ★★★★
Insect Control: ★★★   Facilities: ★★★★

Meeman-Shelby is bordered on the west by the Chickasaw Bluffs lining the Mississippi River. The park offers lovely wooded campsites, 20 miles of hiking and bridle paths, and an Olympic-size swimming pool. Boat ramps provide access to the Mississippi and 125-acre Poplar Tree Lake, home to bream, catfish, and largemouth bass. The park is about 15 miles from Memphis, so it's a fine place to stay if you're touring the river town. The flat campground is situated in a delightful stand of shady hardwoods, including sweetgum and poplar. In most cases, foliage provides a privacy barrier between sites. Campsites are mid-sized, with paved, back-in parking. For privacy and shade, we like sites 10 and 30. Sites 33–49, which lead out of the campground, are also spacious. Rural Meeman-Shelby closes its gates at night, making security good. Western Tennessee is extremely hot and humid in late summer and should be avoided. Also avoid holiday weekends.

BASICS

Operated By: Tennessee State Parks Dept. of Environment and Conservation. **Open:** All year. **Site Assignment:** First come, first served; 5 sites available for reservation w/ $5 nonrefundable deposit. **Registration:** At visitor center, night arrival register next morning. **Fee:** $14–16. **Parking:** At site (2 cars), in parking lot.

FACILITIES

Number of Multipurpose Sites: 49. **Hookups:** Electric (15, 20, 30 amps), water. **Each Site:** Picnic table, grill, most sites have fire ring. **Dump Station:** Yes. **Laundry:** No. **Pay Phone:** Yes. **Restrooms and Showers:** Yes. **Fuel:** No. **Propane:** No. **Internal Roads:** Paved. **RV Service:** 25 mi. south of Memphis. **Market:** 0.75 mi. **Restaurant:** 9 mi. in Millington. **General Store:** No. **Vending:** Yes. **Swimming:** Pool (seasonal). **Playground:** Yes. **Other:** Boat launches (electric motor only), boat dock, fishing pier, visitor center, nature center, recreation lodge, picnic shelters. **Activities:** 2 fishing lakes, fishing-boat rentals (seasonal), hiking trails, bicycle trail, disc-golf, horse rentals, bridle paths, volleyball, badminton, horseshoes, softball, managed hunts. **Nearby Attractions:** Graceland, Beale St., Mud Island, Alex Haley House Museum, National Civil Rights Museum, Peabody Hotel. **Additional Information:** Memphis CVB, (901) 543-5333.

RESTRICTIONS

Pets: On leash only. **Fires:** Grill, fire rings only. **Alcoholic Beverages:** Not allowed. **Vehicle Maximum Length:** 45 ft. (sites vary). **Other:** 14-day stay limit, quiet enforced.

TO GET THERE

From I-240, take US 51 north 3 mi. to TN 388/ North Watkins. Drive north 8 mi. and turn left on Benjestown Rd. Drive 1 mi. to the 4-way stop and turn right. The park entrance is 0.75 mi. on the left. (US 55 is accessible from the west from I-40 and I-55 as well.)

NASHVILLE   MAP, A-4
Nashville KOA

2626 Music Valley Dr., 37214. T: (615) 889-0282; www.koa.com.

🚐 ★★★★	🏕 ★★
Beauty: ★★★★	Site Privacy: ★★
Spaciousness: ★★★	Quiet: ★★★★
Security: ★★	Cleanliness: ★★★★
Insect Control: ★★★★	Facilities: ★★★★

Nashville KOA campground is fairly attractive and convenient to area attractions, restaurants, and shopping. In the campground, there's a kiddie pool, a playground, and plenty of room for children to run around. Without gates, security at this suburban campground is iffy. Take care of your valuables. Nashville can become unbearably hot and humid in

late summer. Visit in spring or fall for optimal weather. Sites are laid out in rows of mostly pull-throughs. All sites are the same passable size and there is no greenery to provide privacy. In other respects, sites vary. Many sites are nicely shaded by mature poplars and other hardwoods. Some sites are completely open. Most parking is paved, though some is gravel. For shade and quiet, head for 50-amp sites Z–Z27, along the back perimeter of the park. Most tent sites are very small and located near the noisy road.

BASICS

Operated By: Kampgrounds of America. **Open:** All year. **Site Assignment:** First come, first served; reservations accepted w/ 1-night deposit; 48-hour cancellation notice. **Registration:** At store/main building, night registration also. **Fee:** Full hookup, $39.95; water/electric, $35.95; tent, $26.95; for 2 people; each additional adult, $6; each additional child, $2; 6 people max.; KOA discount, 10%; cash, V, MC, D. **Parking:** At site (1 car), in parking lot.

FACILITIES

Number of RV-only Sites: 240. **Number of Tent-only Sites:** 60. **Number of Multipurpose Sites:** 100. **Hookups:** Electric (30, 50 amps), water, 240 sites w/ sewer. **Each Site:** Picnic table. **Dump Station:** Yes. **Laundry:** Yes. **Pay Phone:** Yes. **Restrooms and Showers:** Yes. **Fuel:** No. **Propane:** Yes. **Internal Roads:** Paved. **RV Service:** Next door. **Market:** 6 mi. in Nashville. **Restaurant:** At entrance. **General Store:** Convenience store w/ camp supplies on site, K-Mart 6 mi. in Nashville. **Vending:** No. **Swimming:** Yes. **Playground:** Yes. **Other:** Game room, pool tables, outdoor theater, music barn. **Activities:** Basketball, horseshoes, mini-golf, bicycle rental. **Nearby Attractions:** Country Music Hall of Fame, Grand Ole Opry, Opryland Hotel, The Parthenon, Hermitage Andrew Jackson Home, Belle Meade Plantation, Vanderbilt University. **Additional Information:** Nashville Tourism information, (615) 259-4700.

RESTRICTIONS

Pets: On leash only. **Fires:** Not allowed. **Alcoholic Beverages:** Allowed. **Vehicle Maximum Length:** No limit. **Other:** Quiet hours enforced, no generators.

TO GET THERE

Interstates 40, 24, and 65 all intersect with Briley Pkwy. in Nashville. From Briley Pkwy., take Exit 12 and drive north (the only option) 2 mi. on Music Valley Dr. The campground is on the left.

NASHVILLE   MAP, A-4
Nashville Yogi Bear's
Jellystone Park

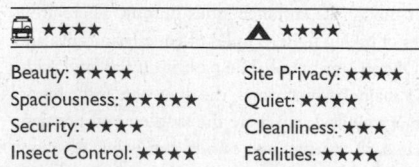

2572 Music Valley Dr., 37214. T: (615) 889-4225 or (800) 547-0449; www.nashvillejellystone.com, www.reserveamerica.com.

🚐 ★★★★	🏕 ★★★★

Beauty: ★★★★	Site Privacy: ★★★★
Spaciousness: ★★★★	Quiet: ★★★★
Security: ★★★★	Cleanliness: ★★★★
Insect Control: ★★★★	Facilities: ★★★★

Whether you are an RV park enthusiast, enjoy the comfort of a cabin in the woods, or just like to tent-camp and sleep in the great outdoors, Jellystone Park's accommodations are top-notch. Amenities and activities include swimming, mini-golf, hayrides, tennis, volleyball, fishing, hiking, and appearances from Yogi Bear and friends.

BASICS

Open: All year. **Site Assignment:** Reservations recommended. **Registration:** At ranger station and late-night registration kiosk. **Parking:** Limit 1 car per site; overflow parking available.

FACILITIES

Number of RV-only Sites: 235. **Number of Tent-only Sites:** 30. **Hookups:** Electric (30, 50 amps), water, sewer. **Each Site:** Picnic table (most), tent sites have grill, picnic table. **Dump Station:** Yes. **Laundry:** Yes. **Pay Phone:** Yes. **Restrooms and Showers:** Yes. **Fuel:** No. **Propane:** Yes. **Internal Roads:** Pea gravel, paved. **RV Service:** Less than 1 mi. **Market:** Camp store available; chain grocery store, 5 mi. **Restaurant:** Several w/in 1 mi. **General Store:** Camp store. **Vending:** Yes. **Swimming:** Pool (in season). **Playground:** Yes (2). **Activities:** Planned summer activities; volleyball, shuffleboard; basketball, horseshoe pits, covered pavilion; activity room, game room. **Nearby Attractions:** Opry Mills Outlet Mall; Grand Ole Opry; General Jackson Showboat, Tours available through Grayline Tours.

RESTRICTIONS

Pets: On leash; breed restrictions. **Fires:** Allowed. **Alcoholic Beverages:** At site only. **Vehicle Maximum Length:** 60 ft. total length.

ONEIDA   MAP, A-6
Brandy Creek Campground

Big South Fork National River and Recreation Area, 4563 Leatherwood Rd., 37841. T: (931) 879-4869 or (800) 365-CAMP; www.nps.gov.

🚐 ★★★★	🏕 ★★★★
Beauty: ★★★★	Site Privacy: ★★★★
Spaciousness: ★★★★★	Quiet: ★★★★
Security: ★★★★	Cleanliness: ★★★
Insect Control: ★★★★	Facilities: ★★★★

Straddling the Kentucky-Tennessee border, Big South Fork NRA is far less crowded than nearby Great Smoky Mountains National Park and offers outstanding outdoor recreation. It's known for excellent paddling, with mellow flat water and class I–IV white water. Big South Fork also has 150 miles of hiking trails. Nearby Cumberland Falls is one the most beautiful sights in the United States. The campground at Bandy Creek offers attractive and extremely spacious sites. Though most sites are shady, privacy varies greatly, with some very secluded sites and others sandwiched together. There are both back-in and pull-through sites. All have gravel parking. Gorgeous Loop A is for tent campers only. The rest are multipurpose. For seclusion, we like sites 16–19 on loop D. Avoid Big South Fork on holiday weekends and fall leaf-peeping weekends. Otherwise, the campground is rarely full. Security is fine at this extremely remote campground.

Basics

Operated By: National Park Service. **Open:** All year; some areas seasonal. **Site Assignment:** First come, first served; reservations accepted Apr.–Oct. up to 5 months in advance; full deposit, $13.85 cancellation fee w/ 2-day notice or more; same-day cancellation, 1 night charged plus fee. **Registration:** At kiosk, after hours register next morning. **Fee:** Water/electric, $17–$20; tent, $15; for 6 people; Golden Age & Golden Access discounts available; cash, personal check, V, MC, D. **Parking:** At site (2 cars), in parking lot.

Facilities

Number of Tent-only Sites: 50. **Number of Multipurpose Sites:** 100. **Hookups:** Electric (20, 30 amps), water. **Each Site:** Picnic table, fire ring w/ grill, lantern pole, tent pad. **Dump Station:** Yes. **Laundry:** No. **Pay Phone:** Yes. **Restrooms and Showers:** Yes. **Fuel:** No. **Propane:** No. **Internal Roads:** Paved. **RV Service:** 80 mi. in Knoxville. **Market:** 12 mi. in Oneida. **Restaurant:** 12 mi. in Oneida. **General Store:** 12 mi. in Oneida. **Vending:** Yes. **Swimming:** Yes (Memorial Day–Labor Day). **Playground:** Yes. **Other:** Visitor center, stables, picnic area, covered pavilion, Big South Fork Scenic Railway, Blue Heron Outdoor Historical Museum. **Activities:** Hiking & biking trails, horseback riding, fishing, hunting, rafting, canoeing, kayaking, volleyball. **Nearby Attractions:** Highland Manor Winery, Historic Rugby restored Victorian village, Alvin York's Farm & Grist Mill, Cordell Hull Birthplace, Indian Mountain State Park, Pickett State Rustic Park, 80 mi. to Knoxville. **Additional Information:** Oneida Chamber of Commerce, (423) 569-6900; Jamestown Chamber of Commerce, (931) 879-9948.

Restrictions

Pets: On leash only. **Fires:** Fire ring only. **Alcoholic Beverages:** Allowed, at sites only. **Vehicle Maximum Length:** 45 ft. (sites vary). **Other:** 13% grade entering campground, 14-day stay limit, quiet hours enforced.

To Get There

From I-75, take Exit 141 (145 from the north) and drive 20 mi. west on TN 63. At US 27, turn right and drive 7 mi. north to Oneida. At the first traffic light, turn left onto local Hwy. 297 and drive 15 mi. to the campground on the right.

PIKEVILLE — MAP, B-5
Fall Creek Falls State Park

Hwy. 3 , P.O. Box 300, 37367-9803.
T: (423) 881-5298 or (800) 250-8611;
www.tnstateparks.com.

RV ★★★★★ Tent ★★★★★

Beauty: ★★★★★	Site Privacy: ★★★★★
Spaciousness: ★★★★★	Quiet: ★★★★★
Security: ★★★★	Cleanliness: ★★★★
Insect Control: ★★★★	Facilities: ★★★★★

This gorgeous park's namesake is the highest waterfall east of the Rocky Mountains. A moderate hike (less than 2 miles) leads to an area that overlooks the 256-foot waterfall. A short but difficult hike leads to the shady pool at the bottom of the waterfall. In the park are many miles of hiking, walking, road-biking, and mountain-biking trails leading to other beautiful waterfalls and gorges. The campgrounds at Fall Creek Falls are also fabulous, especially the reservation-only area, which is deliciously shaded by an indigenous oak-hickory forest. Though sites are spacious and secluded, the campground often feels crowded because it's so large and popular. Most sites offer gravel, back-in parking. A few sites in areas D and E have pull-through parking. Call ahead and obtain a reservation-only site. Security is decent at this very rural park; without gates, rangers patrol nightly. Plan to visit on weekdays, in spring, or in autumn.

Basics

Operated By: Tennessee State Parks. **Open:** All year. **Site Assignment:** 117 sites first come, first served (plus 10 walk-in sites); 109 sites available for reservation; deposit 2 nights plus $10 fee; 1-week cancellation notice for refund less $10 fee. **Registration:** At camper check-in station or headquarters, night arrivals register next day or ranger makes rounds. **Fee:** Full hookup, $20.50; water/electric, $18.50; walk-in, $10; for 2 people; each additional person, $.50; Golden Access, 50% discount; TN seniors, 25% discount; out-of-state seniors, $1.50 discount; cash, personal check, V, MC, D, AE. **Parking:** At sites, in parking lot.

Facilities

Number of Tent-only Sites: 10. **Number of Multipurpose Sites:** 226. **Hookups:** Electric (30, 50 amps), water, sewer. **Each Site:** Picnic table, grill, fire ring. **Dump Station:** Yes. **Laundry:** Yes. **Pay Phone:** Yes. **Restrooms and Showers:** Yes. **Fuel:** No. **Propane:** Yes (exchange). **Internal Roads:** Paved. **RV Service:** 60 mi. south in Chattanooga. **Market:** 17 mi. east in Pikeville. **Restaurant:** On site. **General Store:** Camp store, 17 mi. east in Pikeville. **Vending:** Yes. **Swimming:** Pool (seasonal). **Playground:** Yes. **Other:** Nature center, rec hall & arcade, picnic shelters. **Activities:** 18-hole golf course, horseback riding (seasonal), hiking trails, mountain-bike trails (seasonal mountain-bike rental), lake fishing, paddle boat & canoe rentals, basketball, softball, tennis, volleyball, horseshoes, shuffleboard, Ping-Pong. **Nearby Attractions:** Pikeville Historic District, Pumpkin Festival, Cumberland Caverns, Ocoee River rafting, 60 mi. to Chattanooga. **Additional Information:** Van Buren County Chamber of Commerce, (931) 946-7033.

Restrictions

Pets: On leash only. **Fires:** Fire ring only. **Alcoholic Beverages:** Not allowed. **Vehicle Maximum Length:** 48 ft. **Other:** 2-week stay limit, except Area D.

To Get There

From Chattanooga, take US 27 north 15 mi. Just past Soddy-Daisy, turn left onto TN 111. Drive northwest approx. 40 mi. and turn right onto TN 284. Drive east 8 mi. to the campground. From I-40, take Exit 287 and drive south 30 mi. on TN 111. Turn left on TN 284.

ROCK ISLAND — MAP, B-5
Rock Island State Park

82 Beach Rd., 38581.
T: (931) 686-2471 or (800) 713-6065;
www.tnstateparks.com.

RV ★★★★ Tent ★★★★

Beauty: ★★★★	Site Privacy: ★★★★★
Spaciousness: ★★★★	Quiet: ★★★★★
Security: ★★★★	Cleanliness: ★★★★
Insect Control: ★★★★	Facilities: ★★★★

This park's centerpiece is the Twin Falls of the Caney Fork River, a dramatic limestone gorge decked out with waterfalls. East of the park is TVA Great Falls Dam and hydroelectric plant. The Blue Hole, one of the best fishing spots in the state of Tennessee, is accessible from the park's boat launch. Nearby, Big Bone Cave offers tours by reservation. The attractive campgrounds at Rock Island include a multipurpose area and a tent-only area. Sites with hookups feature paved, back-in parking spaces. Sites and parking spaces vary greatly in size, though most are ample. The campground is nicely treed, with Virginia pine, tulip poplar, beech, and ample foliage to provide privacy between sites. The nicest sites are 21–23, 41, 43, 45, 47, 48, and 50. Though rangers close the gates nightly, they're not always locked. Rock Island is extremely remote, making security fair. Visit in spring, when heavy rains feed the waterfalls. Avoid holiday weekends.

Basics

Operated By: Tennessee State Parks. **Open:** All year; closed Monday and Tuesday. **Site Assignment:** First come, first served; reservations available w/ non-refundable deposit of 1-night fee plus $5. **Registration:** At park office, night arrival register next day. **Fee:** 2 people, $16.25; tent, $14.25; each additional person, $.50, up to 9 max; TN seniors, 25% discount, out-of-state seniors, 10%; cash, personal check, V, MC, D, AE. **Parking:** At sites, in parking lots.

Facilities

Number of Multipurpose Sites: 60. **Hookups:** Electric (30 amps), water. **Each Site:** Picnic table, grill. **Dump Station:** Yes. **Laundry:** Yes. **Pay Phone:** Yes. **Restrooms and Showers:** Yes. **Fuel:** No. **Propane:** No. **Internal Roads:** Paved. **RV Service:** 32 mi. in Cookeville. **Market:** Less than 2 mi. **Restaurant:** Less than 2 mi. **General Store:** Less than 2 mi. **Vending:** Yes. **Swimming:** No. **Playground:** Yes. **Other:** Boat launch, picnic areas & pavilions. **Activities:** Beach swimming, boating, fishing, water sports, hiking trails, mountain biking, horseshoes, tennis, volleyball, basketball, multiuse fields, interpretive programs, summertime organized activities. **Nearby Attractions:** Cumberland Caverns Park, Virgin Falls Pocket Wilderness, Burgess Falls State Natural Area, Edgar Evins State Park, Fall Creek Falls State Park. **Additional Information:** McMinnville Chamber of Commerce, (931) 473-6611.

Reserve your campsite online at www.ReserveAmerica.com

RESTRICTIONS

Pets: On leash only. Fires: Allowed. Alcoholic Beverages: Not allowed. Vehicle Maximum Length: No limit. Other: 2-week stay limit.

TO GET THERE

From I-24, take the Cookeville exit onto TN 111S. Drive south approx. 30 mi. and turn north on TN 136. Drive 2 mi. and turn left onto TN 287. Drive 2 mi. to the park entrance on the right. From I-40, take the Manchester exit and drive northeast on TN 55/70 approx. 35 mi. to TN. 136.

SILVER POINT   MAP, A-5
Edgar Evins State Park

1630 Edgar Evins State Park Rd., 38582-7917. T: (800) 250-8619 or (931) 858-2446; www.tnstateparks.com.

🚐 ★★★	🏕 ★★★
Beauty: ★★★★	Site Privacy: ★★★★
Spaciousness: ★★	Quiet: ★★★
Security: ★★★	Cleanliness: ★★★★
Insect Control: ★★★	Facilities: ★★★★

The lovely campground at Edgar Evins offers unique sites, which are built into a terraced hillside and have views of Center Hill Reservoir. Campsites consist of large wooden decks, which accommodate 36-foot campers, depending on availability. Fire rings are beside the camping deck. Although the decks confine your living space to a small area, sites are nicely spaced and buffered by foliage, so you'll have ample privacy. Most sites are plenty shady. Waterfront sites, 43–60, are worth the extra fees—views from these sites are gorgeous. Activities and facilities at Edgar Evins revolve around fishing and boating in the reservoir. Catches include largemouth bass, smallmouth bass, and walleye. The marina is open all year. Security is fair at this rural park; there are no gates, but the park is off the beaten path. This campground only fills on holiday weekends, so it's a good destination for early summer weekends.

BASICS

Operated By: Tennessee State Parks. Open: All year. Site Assignment: First come, first served; no reservations. Registration: Campground host makes rounds. Fee: $18; up to 4 people; each additional person, $.50; senior & disabled discounts available; cash, personal check, traveler's check. Parking: At site (2 vehicles).

FACILITIES

Number of Multipurpose Sites: 60. Hookups: Electric (30, 50 amps), water. Each Site: Picnic table, grill, fire ring. Dump Station: Yes. Laundry: Yes. Pay Phone: Yes. Restrooms and Showers: Yes. Fuel: No. Propane: No. Internal Roads: Paved. RV Service: 60 mi. in Nashville. Market: 20 mi. in Cookeville. Restaurant: Park restaurant at marina (seasonal), 7 mi. in Silver Point. General Store: Limited stock available at marina. Vending: Beverages. Swimming: No. Playground: Yes. Other: Marina w/ rental slips, boat ramps, visitor center, picnic areas & shelters. Activities: Nature trails, fishing, boating, lake swimming, horseshoes, badminton, hiking.

Nearby Attractions: Burgess Falls State Natural Area, Rock Island State Rustic Park, Cumberland Caverns Park, Cedars of Lebanon, 60 miles to Nashville. Additional Information: Smithville Chamber of Commerce, (615) 597-4163; Nashville Tourism Info, (615) 259-4700.

RESTRICTIONS

Pets: On leash only (no pit bulls). Pet policy strictly enforced. Fires: Fire ring only (subject to burn ban). Alcoholic Beverages: Not allowed. Vehicle Maximum Length: 38 ft. (sites vary). Other: 14-day stay limit, quiet hours enforced, no gray water dumping.

TO GET THERE

From I-40, take Exit 268 and drive south 4.5 mi. on TN 96. At the stop sign, the park entrance is straight ahead.

TELLICO PLAINS   MAP, B-6
Indian Boundary Campground

reserve america™

Cherokee National Forest, 250 Ranger Station Rd., 37385. T: (423) 253-2520 or (877) 444-6777; www.reserveamerica.com.

🚐 ★★★★	🏕 ★★★★★
Beauty: ★★★★★	Site Privacy: ★★★★★
Spaciousness: ★★★★★	Quiet: ★★★★
Security: ★★★★★	Cleanliness: ★★★★
Insect Control: ★★★★	Facilities: ★★★

Located in Cherokee National Forest, Indian Boundary is an excellent choice for those who savor solitude. The campground is gorgeous and the sites are huge—possibly the largest in the state. Most sites are shaded by thick woods, and afforded privacy by lush foliage. If you prefer a more open site, they're also available. Parking is back-in style, on pea gravel. The nicest sites, 17–20, feature views of the 70-acre lake. Recreation includes driving along the Cherohola Skyway National Scenic Highway, which stretches from Tellico Plains, Tennessee to Robbinsville, North Carolina. Outdoor recreation abounds: world class whitewater on a number of rivers; 650 miles of trails designated for various uses, including portions of the Appalachian Trail and the John Muir National Recreation Trail; and fishing on the charming Hiwassee River. Security is excellent at remote, gated Indian Boundary campground. Avoid visiting on holiday and autumn weekends.

BASICS

Operated By: U.S. Forest Service. Open: Apr.–Nov. Site Assignment: 20 sites available first come, first served; reservations accepted through National Recreation Reservation Service (NRRS) at (877) 444-6777 or www.reserveusa.com; reservations can be made up to 240 days in advance, full payment required upon reservation; credit card preferred (V, MC, D, AE), or pay by money order if at least 21 days in advance; $10 cancellation fee, cancellation w/in 3 days of arrival charged 1 night, no-show charged $20 plus 1 night. Registration: Self-service

fee station. Fee: B & C loops, $20; A & D loops, $10; fees include 5 people, 1 sleeping unit; Golden Age & Golden Access discounts available; cash, personal check. Parking: At site, 2 vehicles maximum.

FACILITIES

Number of Multipurpose Sites: 92. Hookups: Electric (20, 30 amps). Each Site: Picnic table, grill, lantern pole, tent pad. Dump Station: Yes. Laundry: No. Pay Phone: No. Restrooms and Showers: Yes. Fuel: No. Propane: No. Internal Roads: Paved. RV Service: Athens or Maryville. Market: 17 mi. in Tellico Plains. Restaurant: 17 mi. in Tellico Plains. General Store: Camp store, also 17 mi. in Tellico Plains or 30 mi. in Madisonville. Vending: Beverages. Swimming: Yes. Playground: No. Other: Boat ramp. Activities: Lake sports, swimming, boating (electric trolling motor only), canoe rentals, fishing, hiking, bicycling. Nearby Attractions: Bald River Falls, Cherohala Scenic Skyway National Scenic Byway, Fort Loudon State Historic Area, Sequoyah Birthplace Museum, The Lost Sea, Orr Mountain Winery, Coker Creek Village. Additional Information: Madisonville Chamber of Commerce, (423) 442-4588.

RESTRICTIONS

Pets: On leash only. Fires: Fire ring only. Alcoholic Beverages: Allowed, at sites only. Vehicle Maximum Length: 25 ft. (sites vary). Other: 14-day stay limit, must stay first night, must not leave site unattended for more than 24 hours. No gas-powered motors on lake.

TO GET THERE

From I-75 at Sweetwater, take Exit 60 onto TN 68. Drive 30 mi. southeast on TN 68 to Tellico Plains. Take TN 165 east 17 mi. to the Indian Boundary Campground sign at FS 345. Turn left and drive 2 mi. on FS 345 to the stop sign. Turn right and the campground entrance is 0.25 mi. on the right.

TIPTONVILLE   MAP, A-1
South Campground

Reelfoot Lake State Park, P.O. Box 2345, 38079. T: (731) 253-7756 or (800) 250-8617; www.tnstateparks.com.

🚐 ★★★★	🏕 ★★★★
Beauty: ★★★★★	Site Privacy: ★★★
Spaciousness: ★★★★	Quiet: ★★★
Security: ★★★	Cleanliness: ★★★★★
Insect Control: ★★	Facilities: ★★★★

Reelfoot Lake State Park is extremely remote, but it's worth the drive. This beautiful campground features cypress trees along the water and shady hardwoods in the rest of the campground. Sites are mid-sized, but feel a little cramped because the campground is often full. Most sites offer paved parking, though a few in the back have gravel parking. Five sites include pull-through parking and the rest offer back-in parking. With little undergrowth, sites are not very private. The nicest sites, 1–21, are right on the water. The most productive natural fish hatchery in the United States, Reelfoot Lake supports more than 50 fish species. There are no limits on crappie or bluegill. A large population of bald eagles winter on Reelfoot Lake. Naturalists conduct boat tours for viewing the dignified birds. This is one of the most popular parks in Tennessee, and should be avoided on summer weekends and holidays. Instead, visit in the winter or spring (when aquatic flowers bloom). Security is fine.

BASICS

Operated By: Tennessee State Parks. **Open:** All year; closed Monday and Tuesday. **Site Assignment:** First come, first served; no reservations. **Registration:** At entrance station. **Fee:** RV lakefront, $19; RV off lake, $17; tent lakefront, $16; tent off lake, $14; for 2 people, each additional person, $.50; senior & disabled discounts; cash, personal check. **Parking:** At site.

FACILITIES

Number of Tent-only Sites: 20. **Number of Multipurpose Sites:** 86. **Hookups:** Electric (30, 50 amps), water. **Each Site:** Picnic table, grill, some fire rings. **Dump Station:** Yes. **Laundry:** Yes. **Pay Phone:** Yes. **Restrooms and Showers:** Yes. **Fuel:** No. **Propane:** No. **Internal Roads:** Paved. **RV Service:** 50 mi. in Mayfield. **Market:** 5 mi. in Tiptonville. **Restaurant:** Park restaurant, several w/in 5 mi. **General Store:** 5 mi. in Tiptonville, Wal-Mart 20 mi. in Union City. **Vending:** Yes. **Swimming:** Yes (& wading pool). **Playground:** Yes. **Other:** Boat dock, fish-cleaning station, boat launches, picnic areas & pavilions, visitor center & auditorium. **Activities:** Fishing, boating (boat rentals available), seasonal cruise boats, swimming beach, tennis, horseshoes, Ping-Pong, badminton, basketball, nature trails, year-round nature programs. **Nearby Attractions:** Mississippi River, Reelfoot National Wildlife Refuge & Visitor Center, Big Cypress Tree State Natural Area, golf in Union City, Dixie Gunworks Museum, Casino Aztar. **Additional Information:** Reelfoot Lake Tourism Council, (731) 253-2007, www.reelfoottourism.com.

RESTRICTIONS

Pets: On leash only; fee $10 first night, $5 each additional night. **Fires:** Allowed. **Alcoholic Beverages:** Not allowed. **Vehicle Maximum Length:** No limit.

TO GET THERE

From Union City (the junction of US 51 with US 45), drive west 15 mi. on TN 22. The park is on the right.

TOWNSEND   MAP, B-7
Cades Cove Campground

Great Smoky Mountains National Park, Laurel Creek Rd., 37738. T: (865) 436-1200; www.nps.gov/grsm.

🚐 ★★★★   ⛺ ★★★★

Beauty: ★★★★   Site Privacy: ★★★
Spaciousness: ★★★★   Quiet: ★★★
Security: ★★   Cleanliness: ★★★★
Insect Control: ★★★   Facilities: ★★★★

Cades Cove, the flattest campground in the national park, offers the best RV maneuverability. Located in a mountain valley, this area was once heavily settled and farmed, and evidence of previous human habitation

is abundant on area walks and drives. There are plenty of activities at Cades Cove, including bicycle rental and fishing in lovely mountain creeks. Cades Cove is the most popular campground in the national park. Bears are drawn here, so protect your food. With high attendance and no security precautions, you should also protect your valuables. Since the campground stays full all summer, you won't enjoy the solitude offered at Cosby. Circumvent this problem by visiting mid-week in the spring, when wildflowers bloom. The campground is laid out in rows of back-in sites with gravel parking. Pine and various oak species provide shade. Campsites are large, but not very private.

BASICS

Operated By: National Park Service. **Open:** All year. **Site Assignment:** First come, first served; reservations accepted for May 15–Oct. 31 up to 5 months in advance, w/ full deposit; $13.25 cancellation fee w/ 24-hour notice, otherwise 1 night plus fee charged; reservations made by calling (800) 365-CAMP or at reservations.nps.gov (personal check, money order, V, D, MC). **Registration:** Self-registration. **Fee:** $14–$17; 6 people max. per site; 2 tents or 1 tent/1 RV; Golden Age & Golden Access discount available; cash only during self-registration off-season. **Parking:** At site (2 vehicles).

FACILITIES

Number of Tent-only Sites: 22. **Number of Multipurpose Sites:** 139. **Hookups:** None. **Each Site:** Picnic table, fire ring, grill, pea gravel tent pad. **Dump Station:** Yes. **Laundry:** No. **Pay Phone:** Yes. **Restrooms and Showers:** Yes. **Fuel:** No. **Propane:** No. **Internal Roads:** Paved. **RV Service:** 23 mi. in Maryville. **Market:** 8 mi. in Townsend. **Restaurant:** 8 mi. in Townsend. **General Store:** 23 mi. in Maryville. **Vending:** Yes. **Swimming:** No. **Playground:** No. **Other:** Amphitheater, picnic area, horse trail, interpretive trail. **Activities:** Hiking, fishing, horseback riding, canoeing, backcountry hiking, ranger programs (seasonal). **Nearby Attractions:** Golf courses, Cades Cove, Pigeon Forge, Dollywood, Gatlinburg, whitewater rafting, Cherokee Indian Reservation. **Additional Information:** Pigeon Forge Visitor information, (865) 453-5700; Park Information, (865) 436-1200.

RESTRICTIONS

Pets: 6-ft. leash only. **Fires:** Fire ring only. **Alcoholic Beverages:** Allowed. **Vehicle Maximum Length:** 35 ft. **Other:** Be aware of bear precautions.

TO GET THERE

From US 321 on the east side of Townsend, turn south on TN 73. Drive 2 mi. and turn right on Laurel Creek Rd. Continue approx. 5 mi. to the campground on the right.

TOWNSEND   MAP, B-7
Lazy Daze Campground

8429 Scenic Tennessee Hwy. 73, 37882. T: (865) 448-6061; www.lazydazecampground.com.

🚐 ★★★   ⛺ ★★★

Beauty: ★★★★   Site Privacy: ★★★
Spaciousness: ★★★   Quiet: ★★★
Security: ★★★   Cleanliness: ★★★
Insect Control: ★★★   Facilities: ★★★★

Conveniently located within 1 mile of the Townsend entrance to Great Smoky Mountains National Park, Lazy Daze offers small, clean sites with plenty of shade provided by sweet gum and tulip poplar. The rectangular campground offers three types of sites: those with gravel parking only, sites with gravel parking and a concrete patio, and riverside sites. Sites on the Little River are well worth the extra fees—each site has gravel parking, a concrete patio, and a charming view. All sites offer back-in parking and little privacy. Visitors can take inner tubes down the Little River, with access from the campground, or take a bike ride along Hwy. 73 (also known as Foothills Parkway). Townsend is an excellent home base for outdoor exploration on summer and fall weekends when the Gatlinburg area becomes unbearably crowded. Nonetheless, reservations are recommended. Holiday visits are not recommended.

BASICS

Operated By: Troy and Judy Proffitt and Kathy and Jimmy Frye. **Open:** All year. **Site Assignment:** First come, first served; reservations accepted w/ 1-night deposit; 10-day notice required for refund. **Registration:** At camp store. **Fee:** $25–$30; 2 adults & 2 children; $2 a person; Good Sam, Family Campers, senior & group discounts available; cash, personal check, V, MC, D. **Parking:** At site (1 vehicle), plus limited overflow.

FACILITIES

Number of RV-only Sites: 63. **Number of Multipurpose Sites:** 10. **Hookups:** Electric (20, 30 amps), water, sewer, cable TV. **Each Site:** Picnic table, fire ring, concrete pads at some RV sites. **Dump Station:** Yes. **Laundry:** Yes. **Pay Phone:** Yes. **Restrooms and Showers:** Yes. **Fuel:** No. **Propane:** Yes. **Internal Roads:** Gravel. **RV Service:** 35 mi. in Chilhowee. **Market:** 0.5 mi. **Restaurant:** Yes. **General Store:** Camp store, hardware 3.5 mi. in Townsend, Wal-Mart 30 mi. **Vending:** No. **Swimming:** Yes. **Playground:** Yes. **Other:** Pavilion, game room, souvenir shop, cabins. **Activities:** River access, tubing, swimming, fishing (fishing supplies at camp store), shuffleboard, badminton, volleyball, horseshoes, basketball. **Nearby Attractions:** Golf courses, Cades Cove, Pigeon Forge, Dollywood, Gatlinburg, whitewater rafting, Cherokee Indian Reservation. **Additional Information:** Pigeon Forge Visitor information, (865) 453-5700.

RESTRICTIONS

Pets: On leash only. **Fires:** Fire ring only. **Alcoholic Beverages:** Allowed, in site only. **Vehicle Maximum Length:** 40 ft. **Other:** No diving in the pool, family-oriented campground, quiet enforced.

TO GET THERE

Driving north on US 321 into Townsend, continue straight at the traffic light. This becomes TN 73 and the campground is 1 mi. on left.

TOWNSEND   MAP, B-7
Little River Village

8533 TN 73, 37882.
T: (865) 448-2241 or (800) 261-6370;
www.littlerivervillage.com.

★★★★   ▲ ★★★★

Beauty: ★★★★   Site Privacy: ★★★
Spaciousness: ★★★   Quiet: ★★★
Security: ★★★   Cleanliness: ★★★★
Insect Control: ★★★★   Facilities: ★★★★

Convenient for entering Great Smoky Mountains National Park at Cades Cove, Little River Village offers nice facilities in a reasonably attractive campground. The playground is excellent for small children, while older children enjoy swimming and tubing in the Little River. The campground contains both back-in and pull-through sites, as well as an unusually large number of tent sites. Site size varies greatly, but most are long, narrow, and sandwiched together. Most are shady, but few enjoy any privacy. Parking is on gravel. Sites along the river are the prettiest. Pop-ups and small rigs should ask for sites 77–84. Tent campers should ask for 121–126. Big rigs should ask for sites 11–15. Security is fair—there are no gates, but the location is extremely rural. Visit in late summer to enjoy the cool mountain air. Visit on weekdays in the fall, when leaf peepers descend in droves.

BASICS

Operated By: Chipperfield Family. **Open:** All year. **Site Assignment:** Assigned by number, drop-ins choose; reserve up to 1 year in advance w/ credit card, $25 deposit; partial refund if you cancel 7 days ahead. **Registration:** At camp office. **Fee:** Off river: full hookup, $28; water/electricity, $26; primitive tent, $20. On river: full hookup, $33; water/electricity, $31; primitive tent, $25; each extra person over 5, $4. **Parking:** Yes.

FACILITIES

Number of RV-only Sites: 67. **Number of Tent-only Sites:** 27. **Number of Multipurpose Sites:** 27. **Hookups:** Electric (50 amps), water, sewer, cable TV. **Each Site:** Picnic table, fire ring, lantern post, full hookup sites have paved patio. **Dump Station:** Yes. **Laundry:** Yes. **Pay Phone:** Yes. **Restrooms and Showers:** Yes. **Fuel:** Yes. **Propane:** Yes. **Internal Roads:** Paved & gravel. **RV Service:** 22 mi. west in Maryville. **Market:** On property or 3 mi. west in Townsend. **Restaurant:** Fast food on property, 2 mi. to more restaurants. **General Store:** Yes. **Vending:** Yes. **Swimming:** Yes. **Playground:** Yes. **Other:** Pavilion. **Activities:** Fishing, swimming, tubing (rentals), walking & bicycle trail, arcade, pool table, horseshoes, volleyball, basketball. **Nearby Attractions:** Great Smoky Mountains National Park, Pigeon Forge, Gatlinburg, Cades Cove pioneer area. **Additional Information:** Townsend Visitors Center, (865) 448-6134; Pigeon Forge Dept. of Tourism, (800) 251-9100.

RESTRICTIONS

Pets: On leash only. **Fires:** Fire ring only. **Alcoholic Beverages:** At sites only. **Vehicle Maximum Length:** 40 ft. **Other:** Max. 6 people, 2 tents.

TO GET THERE

From I-40, take Exit 386 and go south on Hwy. 129 to Maryville. After the Maryville Hospital, bear left onto 321N and drive 18 mi. into Townsend. In Townsend, go through the stoplight. The campground is 1 mi. ahead on the left.

TOWNSEND   MAP, B-7
Tremont Hills Campground

Hwy. 73, P.O. Box 5, 37882. T: (865) 448-6363;
www.tremontcamp.com.

★★★★   ▲ ★★★★

Beauty: ★★★★   Site Privacy: ★★★★
Spaciousness: ★★★★   Quiet: ★★★
Security: ★★★   Cleanliness: ★★★★
Insect Control: ★★★★   Facilities: ★★★

This pretty campground offers unusually large sites and is convenient to the Cades Cove entrance to Great Smoky Mountains National Park. In addition to the usual amenities, Tremont Hills offers river inner tubing. The campground consists of three areas. The tent-only and RV-only sections are adjacent to the Little River. While the riverside sites have the prettiest views, they are also the noisiest—Highway 73 follows the river on the park's boundary. All sites have gravel, back-in parking. Tremont Hills is nicely shaded and there is some foliage to provide privacy between sites. Like other Smoky Mountain tourist towns, Townsend becomes unbearably crowded on fall weekends. If you can't resist seeing the autumn leaves, visit on a weekday. Security is passable. There are no gates, but Townsend is a safe little town.

BASICS

Operated By: Rob and Sherry Hill. **Open:** Mar.–Nov.; cabins and self-contained rigs remain open in winter. **Site Assignment:** First come, first served; specific sites can be guaranteed w/ 6 days or more; nonrefundable deposit, varies w/ length of stay. **Registration:** At camp store; after hours, register next day. **Fee:** Full hookup waterfront, $34; full hookup off water, $30; water/electric, $25; tent waterfront, $23; tent off-water, $20; prices for 2 people; each additional person, $3; FMCA discount available; cash, TN check, V, MC, D. **Parking:** At site (1 car plus camping unit), in parking lot.

FACILITIES

Number of RV-only Sites: 50. **Number of Tent-only Sites:** 35. **Number of Multipurpose Sites:** 21. **Hookups:** Electric (30 amps), water, sewer, cable TV. **Each Site:** Picnic table, fire ring. **Dump Station:** Yes. **Laundry:** Yes. **Pay Phone:** Yes. **Restrooms and Showers:** Yes. **Fuel:** No. **Propane:** No. **Internal Roads:** Paved & gravel. **RV Service:** Available. **Market:** 3 mi. in Townsend. **Restaurant:** 3 mi. in Townsend. **General Store:** Camp store. **Vending:** Beverages. **Swimming:** Yes. **Playground:** Yes. **Other:** Pavilion, game room. **Activities:** Fishing, river tubing, basketball, summer day-camp for children. **Nearby Attractions:** Golf courses, Cades Cove, Great Smoky Mountains National Park, Pigeon Forge, Dollywood, Gatlinburg, whitewater rafting, Cherokee Indian Reservation.

Additional Information: Pigeon Forge Visitor Information, (865) 453-5700.

RESTRICTIONS

Pets: On leash only. **Fires:** Fire ring only. **Alcoholic Beverages:** Allowed, at sites only. **Vehicle Maximum Length:** 40 ft. (sites vary). **Other:** No parking on the grass, visitors must be registered.

TO GET THERE

From I-40, take Exit 407 and drive 13 mi. south on US 441. At Pine Grove, turn southwest on US 321/Scenic Hwy. 73 and drive 16 mi. to Townsend. The campground is on the right.

UNICOI   MAP, A-8
Little Oak Campground

Cherokee National Forest, P.O. Box 400, 37692.
T: (423) 735-1500.

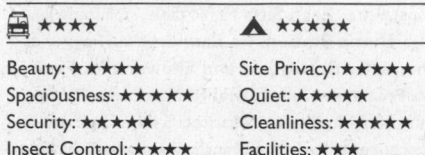

★★★★   ▲ ★★★★★

Beauty: ★★★★★   Site Privacy: ★★★★★
Spaciousness: ★★★★★   Quiet: ★★★★★
Security: ★★★★★   Cleanliness: ★★★★★
Insect Control: ★★★★   Facilities: ★★★

With few recreational amenities, the draw at this beautiful campground is the solitude. The campground is laid out on four narrow peninsulas, so almost every site has a view of South Holsten Lake. Sites are large and amply shaded by various oak species, poplar, white pine, and hemlock. Greenery provides privacy between sites. Sites have gravel, back-in parking. Although all sites here are nice, the loveliest views are found on Big Oak Loop. Huge Cherokee National Forest includes hundreds of miles of hiking, mountain biking, and equestrian trails, including the Appalachian Trail, only a few miles from the campground. A popular hike from the campground leads to the Holsten Mountain Fire tower. Security is excellent at Little Oak; the campground is extremely remote. When we visited on a May weekend, the campground was nearly deserted. This is an excellent choice for any summer weekend except for holidays.

BASICS

Operated By: U.S.D.A. Forest Service. **Open:** Mid-Apr.–mid-Oct. **Site Assignment:** First come, first served; no reservations. **Registration:** Self-registration at fee box. **Fee:** $6; limit 5 people per site. **Parking:** At site.

FACILITIES

Number of Multipurpose Sites: 72. **Hookups:** None; water available. **Each Site:** Picnic table, fire ring, lantern pole. **Dump Station:** No. **Laundry:** No. **Pay Phone:** Yes. **Restrooms and Showers:** No shower, vault toilets. **Fuel:** No. **Propane:** No. **Internal Roads:** Gravel. **RV Service:** 22 mi. north in Bristol. **Market:** 22 mi. north in Bristol. **Restaurant:** 22 mi. north in Bristol. **General Store:** 22 mi. north in Bristol. **Vending:** No. **Swimming:** No. **Playground:** No. **Other:** Boat ramp, amphitheater, interpretive trails. **Activities:** Hiking, boating, fishing. **Nearby Attractions:** Bristol Caverns, Bristol Motor Speedway. **Additional Information:** Bristol CVB, (423) 989-4850.

RESTRICTIONS

Pets: On leash only. **Fires:** Fire ring only. **Alcoholic Beverages:** Not allowed. **Vehicle Maximum Length:** 30 ft.

TO GET THERE

From Bristol drive south on US 421 12 mi. Turn right onto Camp Tom Howard Rd. After 0.5 mi., the road becomes gravel FR 87. Continue on 87 6 mi. and then turn right onto FR 87G. The campground is 1.5 mi. ahead.

WILDERSVILLE   MAP, B-2
Pin Oak Campground

Natchez Trace State Resort Park, 24845 Natchez Trace Rd., 38388. T: (731) 968-3742 or (800) 250-8616 (Pin Oak Lodge); www.tnstateparks.com.

🚐 ★★★★   ⛺ ★★★

Beauty: ★★★★	Site Privacy: ★★★
Spaciousness: ★★★★	Quiet: ★★★★
Security: ★★★	Cleanliness: ★★★★
Insect Control: ★★★★	Facilities: ★★★★★

Natchez Trace offers top-notch recreational facilities built into rolling hills and woodlands including white oak, pin oak, loblolly pine, and other species. Unique facilities include four small lakes and 250 miles of equestrian trails. The park is also the proud home of the third largest pecan tree in North America. Tidy Pin Oak Campground consists of three loops, each with views of Pin Oak Lake. Landscaping consists of meticulous grass patches and a few young hardwoods planted throughout. There is no shade or privacy. However, the campground's openness makes views of Pin Oak Lake all the more stunning. All sites are larger than average and have gravel parking. Most sites are back-in, although one loop has long narrow pull-throughs. We recommend any of the waterfront sites. Security at Pin Oak is mediocre. There are no gates, but the campground is extremely remote. Avoid western Tennessee in hot, humid late summer.

BASICS

Operated By: Tennessee State Parks. **Open:** All year. **Site Assignment:** First come, first served; no reservations. **Registration:** Attendant makes rounds, self-register at night. **Fee:** Waterfront, $19.25; off water, $17.25; for 2 people, each additional person, $.50; senior & disabled discounts available; cash, personal check. **Parking:** At site (2 vehicles).

FACILITIES

Number of Multipurpose Sites: 74. **Hookups:** Electric (50 amps), water, sewer. **Each Site:** Picnic table, grill, fire ring w/ grill, lantern pole, gravel pad. **Dump Station:** No. **Laundry:** Yes. **Pay Phone:** Yes. **Restrooms and Showers:** Yes. **Fuel:** Yes. **Propane:** No. **Internal Roads:** Paved. **RV Service:** 100 mi. in Nashville. **Market:** 10 mi. in Lexington. **Restaurant:** Park restaurant (seasonal), 10 mi. in Lexington. **General Store:** Park store, hardware 7 mi., Wal-Mart 10 mi. in Lexington. **Vending:** Yes. **Swimming:** Lake (no lifeguard). **Playground:** Yes. **Other:** Picnic shelter, boat dock, camping cabins, horse rentals, firing range, ball field, paddle-boat rentals, archery range. **Activities:** Swimming beach, fishing, hunting, hiking trails (including overnight backpacking w/ permit), roads for motorcycles & off-road vehicles, equestrian trails & summer naturalist. **Nearby Attractions:** Nathan Bedford Forrest State Historic Area, Mousetail Landing State Rustic park, Tennessee national Wildlife Refuge, Tennessee River, Hurricane Mills Loretta Lynn Dude Ranch. **Additional Information:** Lexington Chamber of Commerce, (731) 968-2126.

RESTRICTIONS

Pets: On leash only. **Fires:** Fire ring only. **Alcoholic Beverages:** Not allowed. **Vehicle Maximum Length:** No limit. **Other:** 14-day stay limit, quiet enforced, no parking on the grass.

TO GET THERE

From I-40 Exit 116, drive 10 mi. south on local Hwy. 114 to Pin Oak Lodge Rd. Turn left to get to the campground.

WINCHESTER   MAP, B-4
Tims Ford State Park

570 Tims Ford Dr., 37398. T: (931) 962-1183; www.tnstateparks.com.

🚐 ★★★★   ⛺ ★★★

Beauty: ★★★	Site Privacy: ★★★★
Spaciousness: ★★★	Quiet: ★★★★
Security: ★★★	Cleanliness: ★★★
Insect Control: ★★★	Facilities: ★★★★★

Tims Ford State Park has a passably attractive campground, with sites nicely shaded by red and white oak, maple, and hickory. Most sites also have a little greenery providing privacy between them. Site size varies—some are among the smallest in the Tennessee State Parks system. Others are livable. A few sites, including 34 and 35, have views of the lake. Many of the sites have very small parking pads. Sites feature paved, back-in parking. 10,700-acre Tims Ford Lake is known for excellent bass fishing, and the park provides ample fishing facilities. In addition to a large swimming pool, the park maintains a diving pool and a children's pool. The 18-hole bentgrass golf course was designed by Jack Nicklaus. There are also paved multiuse trails available for exploring the rolling countryside. This park is extremely remote and has no gates, so security is fair. It's extremely popular with families and should be avoided on summer weekends.

BASICS

Operated By: Tennessee State Parks. **Open:** All year. **Site Assignment:** First come, first served; no reservations. **Registration:** Attendant makes rounds in-season (winter check-in at visitor center). **Fee:** RV, $14.70–$17.85; each additional person (up to 10 max.), $.50; senior & disabled discounts available; cash, personal check, V, MC, D, AE. **Parking:** At sites, in overflow lot (not on grass).

FACILITIES

Number of Multipurpose Sites: 52. **Hookups:** Electric (20, 30 amps), water. **Each Site:** Picnic table, grill, fire pit, tent pad. **Dump Station:** Yes. **Laundry:** Yes. **Pay Phone:** Yes. **Restrooms and Showers:** Yes. **Fuel:** No. **Propane:** No. **Internal Roads:** Paved. **RV Service:** 12 mi. in Winchester. **Market:** 5 mi. **Restaurant:** Park restaurant (seasonal), 12 mi. in Winchester. **General Store:** 12 mi. in Winchester. **Vending:** Beverages. **Swimming:** Pool (Memorial Day–mid-Aug.). **Playground:** Yes. **Other:** Picnic areas & shelters, marina w/ snack bar, bait shop & fish-cleaning station, boat dock & launch, recreation complex, visitor center. **Activities:** 18-hole golf course, bicycle trails, hiking, fishing (boat rentals), badminton, table tennis, basketball, summer interpretive programs. **Nearby Attractions:** Jack Daniels Distillery, Old Stone Fort State Archaeological Area, Falls Mill, Railroad Museum, Franklin State Forest, South Cumberland State Recreation Area, University of the South. **Additional Information:** Winchester Chamber of Commerce, (931) 967-6788.

RESTRICTIONS

Pets: On leash only. **Fires:** Fire pits grills only. **Alcoholic Beverages:** Not allowed. **Vehicle Maximum Length:** Sites vary. **Other:** 14-day stay limit, no parking on the grass.

TO GET THERE

From I-24 Exit 111, turn southwest on TN 55. Drive approx. 15 mi. into Tullahoma to the second traffic light (US 41A). Drive straight onto TN 130. Continue south on TN 130 0.75 mi. to Westside Dr. and turn left onto 130 and Westside Dr. Drive 3.5 mi. to the Awalt Rd. fork on the left. Drive 5.5 mi. on Awalt and turn left at Mansford Rd. Drive 1.6 mi. to the park entrance on the right.

Texas

Texans are proud of their state's size, natural beauty, colorful history, and rich culture, which make the 28th state's bounty of treasures all the more appealing to those in search of the immense as well as some rest and relaxation.

Texans divide their state into seven geographic and cultural regions. Big Bend country begins at **El Paso** and is bordered by New Mexico to the north and the **Rio Grande River** on the south. Big Bend country is home to two breathtaking national parks, Guadalupe Mountains and Big Bend.

The panhandle plains includes **Amarillo, Lubbock, Wichita Falls,** and **Abilene. Amarillo** is the gateway to the nation's second largest canyon, **Palo Duro,** and home to the famous Cadillac Ranch, where ten cars stand in the ground nose-first facing west. Lubbock, Wichita Falls, and Abilene experienced massive growth in the 1880s, when railroad expansion fueled the cattle industry.

The prairies and lakes region is bordered on the north by Oklahoma, stretches south to the Gulf Coast region, and includes the **Dallas–Fort Worth Metroplex.** Lake recreation, urban tourist attractions, and business draw millions to this area annually.

The eastern piney woods region borders Arkansas and Louisiana and stretches from **Texarkana** to north of **Houston.** In the heart of the rolling hills of the piney woods, tranquil **Angelina National Forest** surrounds massive **Sam Rayburn Reservoir.**

Texas's Gulf Coast region stretches from industrial **Beaumont** to the important agricultural area near **Brownsville.** In the 1970s the coast was transformed by OPEC's embargo on oil exported to the United States, which caused Texas oil prices to skyrocket and stimulated industrial growth.

The south Texas plains stretch from **San Antonio** to **McAllen** and are bordered on the southwest by the Rio Grande River. Greatly influenced by Mexican culture, this region has been the focus of numerous territory disputes, wars, and skirmishes. In the famous 1835 battle of the **Alamo,** Texas revolutionary forces were defeated by the Mexican army.

The hill country is anchored by Austin on its eastern border and includes the charming tourist towns of **Fredericksburg** and **Kerrville.** The **Lyndon B. Johnson National Historic Park,** near **Stonewall,** includes the former president's boyhood home, grave, and family ranch.

The Lone Star State can be overwhelming in its relentless abundance of things to do and places to visit. You can find a trunkful of popular and not-so-popular points of interest that make Texas a unique destination for those cruising the highways of America.

Austin attractions: Lyndon B. Johnson Library and Museum, Lady Bird Johnson Wildflower Center, Cathedral of Junk on the city's south side, State Capitol Complex, the University of Texas. **Corpus Christi attractions:** Texas State Aquarium, Padre Island National Seashore, USS *Lexington* Museum on the Bay. **Dallas–Forth Worth attractions:** the Dallas Cowboys, Dallas Zoo, Fair Park, Six Flags over Texas, Billy Bob's Texas, the world's largest honky-tonk, Fort Worth Museum of Science and History, Fort Worth Zoo, Texas Motor Speedway. **El Paso attractions:** Juarez tours, Fort Bliss, U.S. Border Patrol Museum, old missions. **Houston attractions:** Astrodome, downtown Houston theater district, museum district (includes 14 museums, galleries, and gardens), Six Flags AstroWorld/WaterWorld, Space Center Houston. Twenty-five miles west of Houston in Katy is a replica of China's Forbidden Gardens, an awesome scale-model site to behold complete with the first emperor's 6000-strong terra-cotta army. **San Antonio attractions:** the Alamo, Military Bases Complex, Buckhorn Hall of Horns, missions of San Antonio, San Antonio Zoo, world's largest boots, Sea World of Texas, Six Flags Fiesta Texas, and of course, Barney Smith's world-famous Toilet Seat Museum.

Campground Profiles

ALAMO
Alamo Palms

MAP, D-4

reserve america

1341 Business Hwy. 83, 78516.
T: (956) 787-7571 or (800) 780-7571;
www.alamopalms.com.

🚐 ★★★   ⛺ n/a

Beauty: ★★★   Site Privacy: ★★
Spaciousness: ★★   Quiet: ★★★★
Security: ★★★★   Cleanliness: ★★★★
Insect Control: ★★★★ Facilities: ★★★★

Alamo Palms is a misnomer. Incredibly, the park's brochure also boasts about its trees. Alas, the campground is almost completely treeless. But Alamo Palms does offer top-notch amenities and recreation, including 20 shuffleboard courts, eight billiard tables, and weekly ballroom dances. Alamo Palms is a community-oriented adult-only park. The campground consists of row after row of nearly identical sites. So choose your site based on location; sites in the 200s, 300s, and 400s are close to the pool and clubhouse. All RV sites are small and nondescript, with paved back-in parking. Suburban Alamo Palms is convenient to shopping and restaurants. Drive to the beach or to Mexico in about an hour. Fenced and gated at night, security is good. Don't visit south Texas in the heat of summer. Make reservations well in advance in winter.

BASICS
Operated By: Hynes Group. **Open:** All year. **Site Assignment:** Reservations for 3 months or more, $250 deposit; call (800) 780-7571. **Registration:** At office. **Fee:** $25–$45; for 2 people; each additional person, $2. **Parking:** At site.

FACILITIES
Number of RV-only Sites: 351. **Hookups:** Electric (30, 50 amps), water, sewer, cable TV, data port, Wi-Fi. **Dump Station:** No. **Laundry:** Yes. **Pay Phone:** Yes. **Restrooms and Showers:** Yes. **Fuel:** No. **Propane:** No. **Internal Roads:** Paved. **RV Service:** Across street. **Market:** 1 mi. **Restaurant:** 0.5 mi. **General Store:** 0.5 mi. **Vending:** Yes. **Swimming:** Pool (no lifeguard). **Playground:** No. **Other:** Spa, tennis courts, exercise facilities, pool room, game room, ballroom, storage facilities. **Activities:** Shuffleboard, dancing, crafts, table tennis. **Nearby Attractions:** Sabal Palm Audubon Center & Sanctuary, Gladys Porter Zoo, Brownsville Battlefields, CAF/ Confederate Air Force Rio Grande Valley Wing, Historic Brownsville Museum. **Additional Information:** Alamo Chamber of Commerce, (956) 787-2117; Rio Grande Valley Chamber of Commerce, (956) 968-3141.

RESTRICTIONS
Pets: On leash. **Fires:** In grill. **Alcoholic Beverages:** Allowed. **Vehicle Maximum Length:** 40 ft.

TO GET THERE
Travel south on US 281 (south of San Antonio), take the Cesar-Chavez Rd. Exit. Turn left on Business 83E.

ALBANY
Fort Griffin State Park and State Historic Site

MAP, A-3

reserve america

1701 North US 283, 76430. T: (325) 762-3592;
www.reserveamerica.com.

🚐 ★★★   ⛺ ★★★★

Beauty: ★★★★   Site Privacy: ★★★
Spaciousness: ★★★   Quiet: ★★★★★
Security: ★★★★   Cleanliness: ★★★★
Insect Control: ★★★   Facilities: ★★★★

Fort Griffin State Park and Historic Site is 506.2 acres, with 1500 feet of river area north of Albany in Shackelford County. The state was deeded the land by Shackelford County in 1935. The Civilian Conservation Corps (CCC) built many of the park's facilities before the park opened to the public in 1938. Within the park, partially restored ruins of Old Fort Griffin are on a bluff overlooking the town site of Fort Griffin and the Clear Fork of the Brazos River Valley. The ruins include a hand dug well, a mess hall, a ghost building, barracks, a library, a rock chimney, a store, an administration building, a cistern, a hospital, a powder magazine, the foundation of the officers' quarters, the first sergeant's quarters, a restored bakery, and replicas of enlisted men's huts. A portion of the official Texas Longhorn herd resides in the park. The park offers camping, hiking, fishing, picnicking, living history, historical reenactments, and nature study. Fort Griffin once held command of the southern plains, saw the end of both the great herds of buffalo and those who hunted them, and was home to a rugged group of men. The fort was constructed in 1867 and deactivated in 1881.

BASICS
Operated By: Texas Parks and Wildlife. **Open:** All year. **Site Assignment:** Reservations can be made 11 months in advance. **Registration:** At office. **Fee:** Single, $12–$15; primitive, $10; shelter, $27. **Parking:** 2 vehicles per site; extra parking available for fee.

FACILITIES
Number of Multipurpose Sites: 171. **Hookups:** Yes. **Dump Station:** Yes. **Laundry:** No. **Pay Phone:** Yes. **Restrooms and Showers:** Yes. **Fuel:** No. **Propane:** No. **Internal Roads:** Paved. **RV Service:** No. **Market:** No. **Restaurant:** No. **General Store:** Yes. **Vending:** No. **Swimming:** No. **Playground:** Yes. **Other:** Park does not have a gate. **Activities:** Amphitheater, biking, boating, canoeing, fishing, picnicking, stargazing, wildlife viewing.

RESTRICTIONS
Pets: On a 6-ft. leash, never unattended, under control at all times, cleaned up after. **Fires:** Fires may be built only in campsite grills, fire rings, or fireplaces. Some sites allow only containerized fuel fires. When warranted, fire bans are implemented by county judges and/or county commissioners courts. Inquire when making reservations. **Alcoholic Beverages:** It is an offense to consume or display an open container of an alcoholic beverage in a public place or sell alcoholic beverages w/in a state park.

TO GET THERE
From Ft. Worth: Take Hwy. 180 west to Albany. From Albany, take Hwy. 283 north 15 mi. The park is on the left. From Abilene: Take I-20 east to Baird. Take Hwy. 283 north through Albany 15 mi. The park is on the left.

ALEDO
Cowtown RV Park

MAP, A-4

reserve america

7000 I-20 East, 76008. T: (817) 441-7878;
www.cowtownrvpark.com.

🚐 ★★★   ⛺ n/a

Beauty: ★★★   Site Privacy: ★★★
Spaciousness: ★★★   Quiet: ★★★
Security: ★★   Cleanliness: ★★★★
Insect Control: ★★★   Facilities: ★★★

Approximately 20 miles west of downtown Fort Worth, plain-looking Cowtown provides convenient and tidy campsites. "Cowtown" is an old nickname for Fort Worth and not descriptive of this area. A bustling suburb with plenty of restaurants and shops, Aledo is no cowtown. Arranged in two long, straight rows of pull-throughs and two smaller sections containing back-in sites, all sites are narrow and basically unattractive. Each site contains a paved parking pad, a grassy area, and a sapling. The young trees break the visual monotony but provide no shade or privacy. For couples, we recommend sites in the 90s and 100s—farthest from the interstate, these are likely the quietest. Families should look for a site in the front, near the pool and playground. Close to I-20, with no gates and no security guard, security at Cowtown is poor. For the nicest weather, visit northeastern Texas in spring or fall.

BASICS
Operated By: The Beadels. **Open:** All year. **Site Assignment:** For reservations, call (800) 781-4678; credit card holds site, no-show charged 1 night. **Registration:** At office. **Fee:** $29.95; for 2 people; each extra person over age 11, $1. **Parking:** At site.

FACILITIES
Number of Multipurpose Sites: 104. **Hookups:** Electric (30, 50 amps), water, sewer. **Each Site:** Some picnic tables, some grills. **Dump Station:** Yes. **Laundry:** Yes. **Pay Phone:** Yes. **Restrooms and Showers:** Yes. **Fuel:** No. **Propane:** Yes. **Internal Roads:** Some paved, some gravel. **RV Service:** 7 mi. east in Fort Worth. **Market:** 2 mi. in Willow Park. **Restaurant:** 2 mi. in Willow Park. **General Store:** At park. **Vending:** Yes. **Swimming:** Pool. **Playground:** Yes. **Other:** Rally room, mail service, fax service, car rental. **Activities:** Volleyball, horseshoes, planned activities. **Nearby Attractions:** Trinity Meadows Race Track, Texas Opry, Six Flags Over

Texas, Fort Worth Cowtown Coliseum, Fort Worth Sundance Square, Fort Worth Zoo, Fort Worth Museum of Science & History. **Additional Information:** Fort Worth CVB, (800) 433-5747.

RESTRICTIONS

Pets: On leash & not allowed in playground or pool area. **Fires:** Grill only. **Alcoholic Beverages:** Not allowed inside buildings. **Vehicle Maximum Length:** 45 ft. **Other:** Speed limit 7 mph. Tent campers may rent a site for the RV price.

TO GET THERE

From Fort Worth head west on I-30. Pass the junction of I-30 and I-20 and continue west on I-20 to Exit 418 (Ranch House Rd.). Campground is 1 mi. east on South Access Rd.

ARLINGTON   MAP, A-4
Treetops RV Village

1901 West Arbrook Blvd., 76015.
T: (817) 467-7943 or (800) 747-0787;
www.flash.net/~tweetops/treetop.html.

🚐 ★★★   ⛺ n/a

Beauty: ★★★★	Site Privacy: ★★★★
Spaciousness: ★★★	Quiet: ★★★
Security: ★★★	Cleanliness: ★★★★
Insect Control: ★★★	Facilities: ★★★

Convenient and attractive, Treetops is located in a thriving suburb about halfway between Dallas and Fort Worth. Spend your days off property; area shopping, dining, and tourist attractions are plentiful, while amenities at the campground are not. Sites include both back-ins and pull-throughs, and they are laid out on a winding road. Site size varies, but most are small and crowded. Even so, sites feel private thanks to 2001 shady oak trees and landscaped shrubbery between many sites. Each site contains a gravel RV parking space and a grassy area. Sites 338–361 are the farthest from busy roads and likely to be the quietest. We also recommend any of the sites along the small creek that runs through the park. There are no gates at this park, making security marginal. This park stays busy, so we recommend year-round advance reservations.

BASICS

Operated By: Privately owned. **Open:** All year. **Site Assignment:** Reservations accepted, credit card holds site, 24-hour cancellation notice required. **Registration:** At office. **Fee:** $28; for 2 people; each additional person over age 6, $3; MC, V, D. **Parking:** Gravel.

FACILITIES

Number of RV-only Sites: 160. **Hookups:** Electric (30, 50 amps), water, sewer, cable TV, Wi-Fi. **Each Site:** Picnic table, cement patio. **Dump Station:** Yes. **Laundry:** Yes. **Pay Phone:** Yes. **Restrooms and Showers:** Yes. **Fuel:** No. **Propane:** Yes. **Internal Roads:** Paved. **RV Service:** 15 mi. west in Fort Worth. **Market:** 0.25 mi. **Restaurant:** 0.25 mi. **General Store:** 0.25 mi. **Vending:** No. **Swimming:** Seasonal pool (no lifeguard). **Playground:** No. **Other:** Dog walking area, data port, mailboxes, newspaper vending, pavilion. **Activities:** Swimming. **Nearby Attractions:** Six Flags, Hurricane Harbor,

Fort Worth Stockyards, Texas Motor Speedway, Texas Rangers Baseball, Lone Star Park, DFW International Airport, Dallas Mavericks, Mesquite Rodeo, Dallas Cowboys, convention centers, numerous retail shops. **Additional Information:** Fort Worth CVB, (800) 433-5747; Dallas CVB, (800) 232-5527.

RESTRICTIONS

Pets: Small pets only, must be on leash. **Fires:** Not allowed; bring your own grill. **Alcoholic Beverages:** Allowed. **Vehicle Maximum Length:** 45 ft. **Other:** No pop-ups or tents allowed.

TO GET THERE

From I-20, take Exit 449 (Cooper St.). Go north 0.5 mi. and turn left (west) onto Arbrook Blvd., park is on the right, 0.25 mi.

ATLANTA   MAP, A-5
Atlanta State Park

reserve america

927 Park Rd. 42, 75551.
T: (903) 796-6476 or (512) 389-8900;
www.reserveamerica.com.

🚐 ★★★★   ⛺ ★★★★★

Beauty: ★★★★	Site Privacy: ★★★★
Spaciousness: ★★★★	Quiet: ★★★★★
Security: ★★★★	Cleanliness: ★★★★
Insect Control: ★★	Facilities: ★★★

This state park offers two of the things that all RVers love in a campsite: full hookups and pull-throughs. (Of the nearly 60 sites in the park, about half are 110-foot pull-throughs, and nearly a third have full hookups.) While this park does not offer any sites right on the water's edge, sites 15–17 in the Knights Bluff area have decent lake views. (16 and 17 are pull-throughs.) Sites 4 and 5 are the most secluded, being 40-foot back-ins at the end of a roundabout. Sites 1 and 8 are closest to the entrance to this area and are therefore less desirable. Sites 16–23 are pull-throughs but are all quite open to the sun. The Wilkins Creek camping area offers forested pull-throughs away from the water's edge. Even-numbered sites 32–36 are particularly well shaded. Site 65 is the only back-in in the area and seems out of place: it looks like an outdated hookup that may not be in use. Like Knights Bluff, white Oak Ridge offers views of the lake (especially sites 51–54) but no sites on the water's edge. These sites are slightly smaller back-ins (35 feet) than in Knights Bluff, and all are pretty well shaded. These sites, unlike the others, have a dirt floor instead of grass. Sites 52 and 53, at the end of a roundabout, are the most secluded. The restrooms in this park are clean and have flush toilets, and each camping area has hot-water showers. This is a worthwhile destination for a family outing or a loner's getaway. There is something to suit just about anyone who doesn't mind getting out and about.

BASICS

Operated By: Texas Parks and Wildlife. **Open:** All year. **Site Assignment:** First come, first served; credit card required to make a reservation; reserva-

tion fee, $3; cancellation fee, $5. **Registration:** At office. (Late arrivals use drop box at entrance.) **Fee:** RV (full), $14; water/electric, $12; tent/primitive, $10; plus $1/person entrance fee; V, MC, D accepted in the office or for reservation. **Parking:** At site.

FACILITIES

Number of RV-only Sites: 61. **Number of Tent-only Sites:** 5. **Hookups:** Electric (20, 30, 50 amps), water, sewer. **Each Site:** Picnic table, grill, fire pit, lantern post, tent pad, water. **Dump Station:** Yes. **Laundry:** No. **Pay Phone:** No. **Restrooms and Showers:** Yes. **Fuel:** No. **Propane:** No. **Internal Roads:** Paved. **RV Service:** No. **Market:** 10 mi. to Queen's City. **Restaurant:** 10 mi. to Queen's City. **General Store:** Gift shop. **Vending:** Yes. **Swimming:** Lake (no lifeguard). **Playground:** Yes. **Other:** Amphitheater, group picnic area, fish-cleaning station. **Activities:** Swimming, boating, fishing, hiking, mountain biking. **Nearby Attractions:** Lake Wright Patman, Caddo Lake State Park, Starr Family State Historical Park. **Additional Information:** Park Office: (903) 796-6476.

RESTRICTIONS

Pets: On 6-ft. leash, cleaned up after. **Fires:** Grill only. **Alcoholic Beverages:** Not allowed. **Vehicle Maximum Length:** No limit. **Other:** Each visitor must pay $2 entrance fee per day.

TO GET THERE

From Texarkana, drive 20 mi. on Hwy. 59 S. to FM 96. Turn west onto FM 96 and go 7.2 mi. Turn right onto FM 1154 and go 1.6 mi. to Park Rd. 42, which leads to the park entrance.

AUSTIN   MAP, B-4
Austin Lone Star RV Resort

7009 South IH-35, 78744.
T: (800) 284-0206 or (512) 444-6322;
www.austinlonestar.com.

🚐 ★★★★   ⛺ ★★

Beauty: ★★★★	Site Privacy: ★★★★
Spaciousness: ★★★★	Quiet: ★★★
Security: ★★★	Cleanliness: ★★★★
Insect Control: ★★★★	Facilities: ★★★★

With convenient interstate access and a variety of nearby restaurants and shopping, Austin Lone Star is an excellent choice if you're touring the capital city. Sites at this pretty park are fairly spacious, with gravel parking and grassy plots at each site. Laid out in a series of tidy rows, sites include both back-ins and pull-throughs. Most sites have shade from ash, elm, and oak trees. The shadiest sites include 105–138, which are bordered by trees to the south. Eight log cabins and four deluxe cottages are available. Families should go for sites near the neat playground and recreation area at the front of the park. The restrooms are outstanding—clean, spacious, and private. Unfortunately, the small, unattractive tent sites are not recommended. Visit Austin in spring or fall for the nicest weather. Luckily, insects are rarely a concern—Austin's famous bat community feeds on mosquitoes. With controlled access gates, security is good at this urban campground.

BASICS

Operated By: The Rowleys. **Open:** All year. **Site Assignment:** Reservations accepted, credit card holds site, 24-hour cancellation notice required, (800) 284-0206. **Registration:** At office. **Fee:** RV/Tent, $26–45. **Parking:** At site.

FACILITIES

Number of RV-only Sites: 159. **Number of Tent-only Sites:** 4. **Hookups:** Electric (30, 50 amps), water, sewer, phone, cable TV, Wi-Fi. **Each Site:** Picnic table, barbecue pit. **Dump Station:** Yes. **Laundry:** Yes. **Pay Phone:** Yes. **Restrooms and Showers:** Yes. **Fuel:** No. **Propane:** Yes. **Internal Roads:** Paved. **RV Service:** 0.5 mi. **Market:** 0.5 mi. **Restaurant:** In park. **General Store:** In park. **Vending:** Yes. **Swimming:** Pool. **Playground:** Yes. **Other:** Hot tub, heated pool, mini-mart, gift shop, lodge, ATM, wireless high-speed Internet access (Wi-Fi). **Activities:** Tours, organized activities, pool tables, horseshoes, volleyball, basketball, free pancake breakfast, ice-cream socials, Sat. night steak dinners. **Nearby Attractions:** Texas state capitol, National Wildflower Center, Zilker Park, Pioneer Farm, Slaughter-Leftwich Winery, Mexican Free-Tailed Bat Colony, Barton Creek Greenbelt Preserve, Texas State History Museum, 6th St. Music Arena. **Additional Information:** Austin CVB, (800) 926-2282.

RESTRICTIONS

Pets: On 6-ft. max. leash at all times. Some breeds not allowed. **Fires:** In barbecue pits only. **Alcoholic Beverages:** Allowed. **Vehicle Maximum Length:** No limit. **Other:** 5 mph speed limit; no bicycle riding after dark; high water pressure, suggest use of water pressure regulator; 3-day tent limit.

TO GET THERE

If heading north on I-35, take Exit 228 and it is 1 block on the right side. If heading south on I-35, take Exit 227, make a U-turn to the left, go back under the interstate onto the service road heading north. Park is 1.5 mi. ahead on the right.

BASTROP   MAP, B-4
Bastrop State Park

reserve america

130 Hwy. 21 E, P.O. Box 518, 78602-0518.
T: (512) 321-2101; www.reserveamerica.com.

🚐 ★★★★   ⛺ ★★★★

Beauty: ★★★★★		Site Privacy: ★★★★
Spaciousness: ★★★★		Quiet: ★★★★
Security: ★★★		Cleanliness: ★★★★
Insect Control: ★★★		Facilities: ★★★★★

Part of a recreation complex including Lake Bastrop, Buescher State Park, and Lake Somerville State Park, the area is home to the Lost Pines, a stand of isolated loblolly pines. Fauna includes the endangered Houston toad (mating and male trilling peak in February and March). The park's amenities are excellent. Though campsites at Buescher are more private and spacious than campsites here, there are fewer insects at drier Bastrop. The Piney Hill area offers RV sites with full hookups and gravel pull-throughs (we fancied sites 1, 23, 24, and 25). The Copperas Creek area includes multiuse sites with water and electric hookups and gravel back-in parking. Tent campers should rough it at serene Creekside campground. All sites are spacious, with lovely tree cover. There is no gate, but Bastrop's rural setting makes it reasonably safe. Visit during the week. Only 32 miles from Austin, the park stays busy weekends March through November.

BASICS

Operated By: Texas Parks and Wildlife. **Open:** All year. **Site Assignment:** Reservations (512) 389-8900; reservations must be made at least 48 hours in advance; deposit (1-night fee) required to hold reservation; cancellations more than 2 days prior to reservation result in $5 fee, cancellations w/in 2 days of reservation result in loss of deposit. **Registration:** At headquarters. **Fee:** Water/electric/sewer, $17; water/electric, $15; water, $12; primitive tent, $10; per person per day charge (over age 13), $4; cash, check, D, V, MC. **Parking:** At most sites.

FACILITIES

Number of RV-only Sites: 54. **Number of Tent-only Sites:** 73. **Hookups:** Electric (30, 50 amps), water, sewer. **Each Site:** Picnic table, fire ring, grill. **Dump Station:** Yes. **Laundry:** No. **Pay Phone:** No. **Restrooms and Showers:** Yes. **Fuel:** No. **Propane:** No. **Internal Roads:** Paved. **RV Service:** 8 mi., west of Bastrop. **Market:** 1 mi. east in Bastrop. **Restaurant:** 1 mi. east in Bastrop. **General Store:** Wal-Mart, 1 mi. east in Bastrop. **Vending:** Beverages. **Swimming:** Seasonal pool (no lifeguard). **Playground:** Yes. **Other:** 18-hole golf course (6,152 yards, Bermuda greens, electric & pull carts for rent), picnic area, cabins, lodges, group barracks, group dining hall, outdoor sports area, gift shop. **Activities:** Golfing, hiking, backpacking, fishing, canoeing, swimming, road cycling, & guided tours. **Nearby Attractions:** Lake Bastrop, Buescher State Park, Lake Somerville State Park & Trailway, Austin (32 mi. west). **Additional Information:** Austin CVB, (800) 926-2282; Smithville Chamber of Commerce, (512) 237-2313; Bastrop Chamber of Commerce, (512) 321-2419.

RESTRICTIONS

Pets: On leash only. **Fires:** Fire ring only. **Alcoholic Beverages:** Not allowed. **Vehicle Maximum Length:** 50 ft.

TO GET THERE

From Bastrop, drive east on TX 21 1 mi. Park entrance is on the right. The park is also accessible from Buescher State Park and Hwy. 71.

BIG BEND   MAP. C-2
NATIONAL PARK
Chisos Basin Campground

reserve america

P.O. Box 129, 79834. T: (432) 477-1121; www.reserveamerica.com.

🚐 ★★★★   ⛺ ★★★★

Beauty: ★★★★		Site Privacy: ★★★
Spaciousness: ★★★★		Quiet: ★★★★
Security: ★★★★★		Cleanliness: ★★★★
Insect Control: ★★★		Facilities: ★★★

The Chisos Basin Campground is rugged and hilly. The sites are small and most are not suited to RVs or Trailers. The road to the basin is steep and curvy. The road into the campground is a 15% grade. All sites are within 5 to 200 feet of comfort station. Chisos Basin Campground (elev. 5,400 feet) is located within Big Bend National Park, which encompasses more than 1,100 square miles of rugged mountains, painted desert badlands, and towering river canyons. Big Bend National Park is one of the largest and least visited parks in the entire system. The park and region are named after the great northeast turn of the Rio Grande that forms the distinctive boot heel found at lower left on a Texas map. An area at the very tip of the curve, containing the most striking examples of naked geology found in Texas and an abundant diversity of Chihuahuan Desert flora and fauna, was dedicated as a national park in 1944. Since then, Big Bend Ranch State Park has been opened right next door, and along with two protected natural areas in Mexico, Big Bend National Park and the adjacent public lands offer over 2 million acres of outstanding wilderness scenery and wildlife habitat. Big Bend National Park contains over 85 miles of surfaced road, with many interpretive pullouts, historic sites, and short walks available to visitors without leaving the pavement. There are 200 miles of hiking trails and 115 miles of backcountry dirt road. Trails and back roads run the gamut from short and easy, including wheelchair accessible, to long and difficult even for the fit and well equipped.

BASICS

Operated By: National Park Service. **Open:** All year. **Site Assignment:** Reservations must be made 4 days in advance; additional sites first come, first served. **Registration:** At registration office. **Fee:** Single, $14; group, $33. **Parking:** Basin Area (0.5 mile).

FACILITIES

Number of Multipurpose Sites: 118. **Hookups:** None. **Each Site:** Call ahead. **Dump Station:** Yes. **Laundry:** No. **Pay Phone:** Yes. **Restrooms and Showers:** Yes. **Fuel:** No. **Propane:** No. **Internal Roads:** Paved. **RV Service:** No. **Market:** No. **Restaurant:** No. **General Store:** No. **Vending:** No. **Swimming:** Yes. **Playground:** No. **Activities:** Biking, bird-watching, hiking, photography, sightseeing, wildlife viewing.

RESTRICTIONS

Pets: On leash at all times, never unattended. Not allowed on trails or in the backcountry. **Fires:** Allowed; campfire program. **Alcoholic Beverages:** Not allowed. **Vehicle Maximum Length:** Trailers longer than 20 ft. or RVs longer than 24 ft. are not recommended due to sharp switchbacks on the main road leading to the campsite. **Other:** Generator users must observe quiet time. No generator use between 8 p.m. & 8 a.m. No wood or ground fires. Bear-proof storage containers at each campsite. Do not feed wildlife, including birds. Washing of vehicles is prohibited. Do not connect hoses to spigots.

TO GET THERE

From I-10, take Hwy. 385 south to Fort Stockton and then on to Marathon. From Marathon it is 40 mi. south on Hwy. 385 to the north entrance to Big Bend National Park. Drive 26 mi. to park headquarters at Panther Junction. To reach Rio Grande Village, turn left and travel 20 mi. To reach Chisos Basin Campground, turn right 3 mi. then turn left at the Basin sign and go 7 mi.

BIG BEND NATIONAL PARK
Rio Grande Village Campground

MAP. C-2

reserve america

P.O. Box 129, 79834. T: (432) 477-1121; www.reserveamerica.com.

🚐 ★★★★   ⛺ ★★★★

Beauty: ★★★★   Site Privacy: ★★★★
Spaciousness: ★★★★   Quiet: ★★★
Security: ★★★★★   Cleanliness: ★★★★
Insect Control: ★★★   Facilities: ★★★★

Rio Grande Village Visitor Center is open seasonally (November to April) and offers information, exhibits, book sales, and a mini-theater for viewing Big Bend videos. Backcountry and river use permits are available. The Rio Grande Village store is open daily and offers groceries, gas, a Laundromat, and coin-operated showers. Rio Grande Village has the only public showers in the park. The Rio Grande Village campground (elev. 1850 feet) is located near the river and has 100 sites. The sites are first come, first served and are suitable for both tents and RVs. Encompassing more than 1,100 square miles of rugged mountains, painted desert badlands, and towering river canyons, Big Bend National Park is one of the largest and least visited parks in the entire system. The park and region are so named after the great northeast turn of the Rio Grande that forms the distinctive boot heel found at lower left on a Texas map. An area at the very tip of the curve, containing the most striking examples of naked geology in Texas and an abundant diversity of Chihuahuan Desert flora and fauna, was dedicated as a national park in 1944. Since then, Big Bend Ranch State Park has been opened right next door, and along with two protected natural areas in Mexico, Big Bend National Park and the adjacent public lands offers over 2 million acres of outstanding wilderness scenery and wildlife habitat. Big Bend National Park contains over 85 miles of surfaced road, with many interpretive pullouts, historic sites, and short walks available to visitors without leaving the pavement. There are 200 miles of hiking trails and 115 miles of backcountry dirt road. Trails and back roads run the gamut from short and easy, including wheelchair accessible, to long and difficult even for the fit and well equipped.

BASICS

Operated By: National Park Service. **Open:** All year. **Site Assignment:** Reservations must be made 4 days in advance. **Registration:** At registration office. **Fee:** Single, $14; group, $33. **Parking:** At site.

FACILITIES

Number of Multipurpose Sites: 180. **Hookups:** None. **Each Site:** Grill, picnic table, site pad (most). **Dump Station:** Less than 0.25 mi. **Laundry:** Less than 1 mi. **Pay Phone:** Less than 1 mi. **Restrooms and Showers:** Yes. **Fuel:** No. **Propane:** No. **Internal Roads:** Paved. **RV Service:** No. **Market:** Yes. **Restaurant:** Yes. **General Store:** Yes. **Vending:** No. **Swimming:** No. **Playground:** No. **Activities:** Biking, bird-watching, canoeing, fishing, hiking, horseback riding, photography, rafting, sightseeing, tubing (no rentals).

RESTRICTIONS

Pets: On a leash at all times. **Fires:** Allowed; campfire program. **Alcoholic Beverages:** Not allowed. **Vehicle Maximum Length:** Varies; call ahead. **Other:** Do not place food boxes on ground at any time. Do not feed wildlife. Motorboats permitted on river w/ restrictions. Tents must be set up on pad if located in grassy area due to flooding.

TO GET THERE

From I-10, take Hwy. 385 south to Fort Stockton and then on to Marathon. From Marathon it is 40 mi. south on Hwy. 385 to the north entrance of Big Bend National Park. Drive 26 mi. to park headquarters at Panther Junction. To reach Rio Grande Village, turn left and travel 20 mi. To reach Chisos Basin Campground turn right and go 3 mi., then turn left and go 7 mi.

BLANCO
Blanco State Park

MAP, B-4

reserve america

P.O. Box 493, 78606. T: (830) 833-4333; www.reserveamerica.com.

🚐 ★★★   ⛺ ★★★

Beauty: ★★★   Site Privacy: ★★★
Spaciousness: ★★★   Quiet: ★★★
Security: ★   Cleanliness: ★★★
Insect Control: ★★★   Facilities: ★★★

At 104 acres, Blanco is neither large nor pretty. It feels like a city park, although original facilities were built by the Civilian Conservation Corps in the 1930s. Fishing along the Blanco River is the most popular activity. Catches include rainbow trout, perch, catfish, and bass. The campground consists of two small loops. Site size is adequate. Sites 1–10 have full hookups and are slightly smaller than sites 11–30. Most sites have paved, back-in parking (site 16 is the only pull-through). There are a few shady sites, but most are open to neighbors and the elements. Families should try for sites 27 or 31, near the playground. Otherwise, there is little difference between sites. There is no gate at Blanco, making security marginal. Visit in late spring, summer, or fall, avoiding holiday weekends.

BASICS

Operated By: Texas Parks and Wildlife. **Open:** All year. **Site Assignment:** Reservations (512) 389-8900, reservations must be made at least 48 hours in advance, deposit required (equivalent to 1 night's fee)

to hold reservation; cancellations more than 2 days prior to reservation result in $5 fee; cancellations w/in 2 days of reservation result in loss of deposit. **Registration:** At headquarters. **Fee:** Water/electric/sewer, $18; water/electric, $15; charge per person per day (over 13), $3; cash, check, D, V, MC. **Parking:** At site.

FACILITIES

Number of RV-only Sites: 29. **Hookups:** Electric (30, 50 amps), water, sewer. **Each Site:** Picnic table, fire ring. **Dump Station:** Yes. **Laundry:** No. **Pay Phone:** No. **Restrooms and Showers:** Yes. **Fuel:** No. **Propane:** No. **Internal Roads:** Paved. **RV Service:** 20 mi. south in Spring Branch. **Market:** 1 mi. south. **Restaurant:** 200 yards from park. **General Store:** 0.5 mi. **Vending:** Yes. **Swimming:** Lake. **Playground:** Yes. **Other:** Gift shop, group day-use facilities, screened shelters. **Activities:** Swimming in Blanco River, picnicking, hiking, boating (electric motors only), fishing. **Nearby Attractions:** Nearby attraction include Lyndon B. Johnson State Historical Park & LBJ Ranch, Pedernales Falls & Guadalupe River state parks, Canyon Lake, Cascade Caverns, Natural Bridge Caverns, Aquarena Springs. **Additional Information:** Blanco Chamber of Commerce, (830) 833-5101; www.texashillcountryinfo.com.

RESTRICTIONS

Pets: On leash only. **Fires:** Fire ring only. **Alcoholic Beverages:** Not allowed. **Vehicle Maximum Length:** 50 ft. **Other:** Max. 8 people per campsite; quiet time 10 p.m.–6 a.m.; 14-day stay limit; swim at your own risk; gathering of firewood prohibited.

TO GET THERE

From Austin, drive west on US 290 42 mi. Turn left on US 281, and go south 10 mi. Go through Blanco, then turn right onto Park Rd. 23. The park entrance is within 200 yards. From San Antonio, drive north on US 281. Cross TX 46 and continue until reaching Blanco (about 30 mi.). Cross the Blanco River and then take the first left, onto Park Rd. 23. The park entrance is within 200 yards.

BOERNE
Alamo Fiesta RV Resort

MAP, C-4

reserve america

33000 IH-10 West, 78006. T: (830) 249-4700 or (800) 321-CAMP; www.alamofiestarv.com.

🚐 ★★★   ⛺ ★★★

Beauty: ★★★   Site Privacy: ★★★
Spaciousness: ★★★★   Quiet: ★★★★
Security: ★★★   Cleanliness: ★★★
Insect Control: ★★★★   Facilities: ★★★★

Alamo Fiesta is a good camping option if you would like to tour the hill country and San Antonio without switching campgrounds. Bandera, Kerrville, and Fredericksburg are within 40 miles of Boerne. Downtown San Antonio is a little closer and Six Flags Fiesta Texas is 12 miles away. The campground consists mainly of rows of pull-throughs with back-in sites along the perimeter of the park. Sites are on the large side of average, and most have no shade. There is a bit of well-intentioned (but poorly maintained) landscaping. Each site has a grassy plot, which often bleeds haphazardly into the gravel parking spaces. Near the playground, sites 1–5 and 128–133 are good choices for families. For tranquility, obtain a back-in site in the back of the park (70–94). With no gates, this small town/suburban park has marginal security. Visit Texas Hill Country on weekdays for breezy touring.

BASICS

Operated By: Robert and Doug Hurley. **Open:** All year. **Site Assignment:** Reservations held w/credit card; call (800) 321-CAMP; all credit cards, checks, cash accepted. **Registration:** At office. **Fee:** RV (2 people), $33; pop-ups/vans, $27; each extra person over age 6, $3. **Parking:** At site.

FACILITIES

Number of RV-only Sites: 221. **Hookups:** Electric (30, 50 amps), water, sewer, cable TV, data port. **Each Site:** Picnic table. **Dump Station:** Yes. **Laundry:** Yes. **Pay Phone:** Yes. **Restrooms and Showers:** Yes. **Fuel:** No. **Propane:** Yes. **Internal Roads:** Paved. **RV Service:** 1.5 mi. southeast in Boerne. **Market:** 1 mi. southeast in Boerne. **Restaurant:** 1 mi. southeast in Boerne. **General Store:** Yes, limited stock. **Vending:** No. **Swimming:** Pool. **Playground:** Yes. **Other:** Basketball courts, banquet rooms, soccer field, tennis court, horseshoe pit, pavilion. **Activities:** Horseshoes, washer pitching. **Nearby Attractions:** King House Museum, The Alamo, Six Flags Fiesta Texas, historic missions, SeaWorld, Riverwalk, Cowboy Artists of America Museum. **Additional Information:** San Antonio CVB, (800) 447-3372; Boerne Chamber of Commerce, (888) 842-8080.

RESTRICTIONS

Pets: On leash. **Fires:** Not allowed. **Alcoholic Beverages:** Allowed. **Vehicle Maximum Length:** 75 ft.

TO GET THERE

From San Antonio go west on I-10, take Exit 543. Go 1 mi. to the entrance.

BROWNSVILLE   MAP, D-4
River Bend Resort

Hwy. 8 , P.O. Box 649, 78520. T: (956) 548-0191.

🚐 ★★★★	⛺ n/a
Beauty: ★★★★★	Site Privacy: ★★★
Spaciousness: ★★★★	Quiet: ★★★★
Security: ★★★★	Cleanliness: ★★★★★
Insect Control: ★★★★★	Facilities: ★★★★★

Seniors-only River Bend is among the most attractive parks in south Texas. The park's facilities are outstanding considering how few sites it offers. The swimming pool and clubhouse overlook a pretty bend in the Rio Grande River, and the golf course features many holes with nice river views. The campground consists of back-in sites laid out along two main roads. Sites are spacious and incredibly tidy.

Landscaping at each site adds to the manicured look of the park, but provides no shade or privacy—there are no trees. All parking is paved. The nicest sites overlook the golf course. Brownsville is convenient to attractions, restaurants, and shopping galore. Gates lock at night, making security at this suburban park fair. Make reservations months in advance for winter visits. Avoid south Texas in the summer.

BASICS

Operated By: John Alberg. **Open:** All year. **Site Assignment:** Reservations are required & are taken Mon.–Fri., 9 a.m.-noon. **Registration:** At office. **Fee:** $21; for 2 people; each additional person, $2.50; A/C charge per day per unit, $2; charge per day for more than 30-amp usage, $4. **Parking:** At site.

FACILITIES

Number of RV-only Sites: 30. **Hookups:** Electric (30, 50 amps), water, sewer, cable TV. **Dump Station:** No. **Laundry:** Yes. **Pay Phone:** Yes. **Restrooms and Showers:** Yes. **Fuel:** No. **Propane:** No, daily service comes to the park, Mon.–Sat. **Internal Roads:** Paved. **RV Service:** 60 mi. northwest in McAllen. **Market:** 5 mi. east in Brownsville. **Restaurant:** 5 mi. east in Brownsville. **General Store:** 4 mi. east in Brownsville. **Vending:** Beverages. **Swimming:** Pool. **Playground:** No. **Other:** 18-hole golf course, tennis courts, rec hall, dance hall. **Activities:** Horseshoes, shuffleboard, swimming, arts & crafts, golf. **Nearby Attractions:** Gladys Porter Zoo, CAF/Confederate Air Force Rio Grande Valley Wing, South Padre Island, Boca Chica Beach. **Additional Information:** Brownsville Chamber of Commerce, (956) 542-4341.

RESTRICTIONS

Pets: On leash only. **Fires:** In grills only, bring your own. **Alcoholic Beverages:** Allowed. **Vehicle Maximum Length:** 40 ft.

TO GET THERE

From Hwy. US 77/83, exit at local Hwy. 802. Go west 2 mi. to US 281. Turn right on Hwy. 281 and go west 3 mi. Entrance is on the left.

BROWNWOOD   MAP, B-3
Lake Brownwood State Park

reserve america

200 State Park Rd. 15, P.O. Box 160, 76801. T: (325) 784-5223 or (800) 792-1112; www.reserveamerica.com.

🚐 ★★★★	⛺ ★★★★
Beauty: ★★★★	Site Privacy: ★★★
Spaciousness: ★★★★	Quiet: ★★★★
Security: ★★★★	Cleanliness: ★★★★
Insect Control: ★★	Facilities: ★★★★

Fishermen enjoy Lake Brownwood, an 8,000-acre reservoir supporting crappie, perch, catfish, and bass. There are extensive fishing and boating facilities. Landlubbers explore the shoreline, especially when adorned with spring wildflowers. There are

four types of sites in three campgrounds. Those seeking peace, quiet, and full hookups should obtain a site at the Council Bluff loop. Tent campers should ask for sites 60–67—with water and electric hookups, these are the only heavily wooded sites. Boaters prefer lake level sites at Willow Point, with water and electric hookups. All sites are relatively spacious, with back-in gravel parking and at least a little shade. The park's extremely rural location makes it fairly safe even though there is no locked gate at night. The Panhandle Plains are cold in the winter and hot in the summer. Visit in spring or fall. Avoid summer weekends, when this state park more closely resembles a theme park.

BASICS

Operated By: Texas Parks and Wildlife. **Open:** All year. **Site Assignment:** Reservations (512) 389-8900; reservations must be made at least 48 hours in advance, deposit required (equivalent to 1-night fee) to hold reservation; cancellations more than 2 days prior to reservation result in $5 fee; cancellations w/in 2 days of reservation result in loss of deposit. **Registration:** At headquarters. **Fee:** Depending on hookup, $12–$25; per person per day (13 and over), $3; third vehicle at a campsite, $5; cash, check, D, V, MC. **Parking:** At site.

FACILITIES

Number of RV-only Sites: 66. **Number of Tent-only Sites:** 21. **Hookups:** Electric (20, 30, 50 amps), water, sewer. **Each Site:** Picnic table, grill. **Dump Station:** Yes. **Laundry:** No. **Pay Phone:** No. **Restrooms and Showers:** Yes. **Fuel:** No. **Propane:** No. **Internal Roads:** Paved. **RV Service:** Inquire at campground. **Market:** 8 mi. southwest toward Brownwood. **Restaurant:** 8 mi. southwest toward Brownwood. **General Store:** Wal-Mart 20 mi. in Brownwood. **Vending:** Beverages. **Swimming:** Lake. **Playground:** No. **Other:** Volleyball court, basketball court, softball field, park store, boat launches, floating boat dock w/boat slip & courtesy fuel dock, cabins, screened shelters, group camping, dining, & lodge facilities. **Activities:** Picnicking, hiking, boating (motors, water skis, & Jet skis all allowed), fishing, swimming, bird-watching. **Nearby Attractions:** Howard Payne College, Douglas McArthur Academy of Freedom, Camp Bowie Memorial Park, Coleman City Park, Camp Colorado Museum Replica. **Additional Information:** Brownwood Chamber of Commerce, (915) 646-9535.

RESTRICTIONS

Pets: Leash only, not allowed in buildings. Special pet restrictions. **Fires:** In grills, fire rings only. **Alcoholic Beverages:** Not allowed. **Vehicle Maximum Length:** 65 ft. (all sites are back-in). **Other:** Max. 8 people per campsite, quiet time 10 p.m.–6 a.m., 14-day stay limit, gathering of firewood prohibited, number of vehicles per campsite is restricted (call for details), swim at your own risk.

TO GET THERE

From Brownwood, go northwest on TX 279 16 mi. Turn right on Park Rd. 15 and follow it 6 mi. to the park entrance.

BURNET   MAP, B-4
Inks Lake State Park

reserve america

3630 Park Rd. 4 West, 78611. T: (512) 793-2223; www.reserveamerica.com.

🚐 ★★★★   ⛺ ★★★★

Beauty: ★★★★	Site Privacy: ★★★
Spaciousness: ★★★	Quiet: ★★★
Security: ★★★★	Cleanliness: ★★★★
Insect Control: ★★★★	Facilities: ★★★★

Pink granite hills and cedar-and-oak woodlands provide the backdrop for a variety of recreation at Inks Lake, including a nine-hole golf course. Inks Lake supports bass, crappie, and catfish, while the land supports turkey quail and many other species. The area is famous for its spring wildflowers. Campgrounds are partially shaded, with mid-sized sites and paved back-in parking. Tent sites include paved tent pads. Tent campers looking for ample space and lake views should ask for 311, 314, 317, 333, or 346. RV campers should ask for 43, 48, 65, 67, 92, 279, or 287. Families should consider a site adjacent to one of the six playgrounds or the swimming beach. Spring and early summer are ideal times to visit, since late summer is very hot and autumn can be rainy. There is no gate at Inks Lake, but its remote location makes it fairly safe.

BASICS
Operated By: Texas Parks and Wildlife. **Open:** All year; park closed during hunting season; call park for details. **Site Assignment:** Reservations (512) 389-8900; reservations must be made at least 48 hours in advance; deposit (equivalent to 1-night fee) required to hold reservation; cancellations more than 2 days prior to reservation result in $5 fee; cancellations w/in 2 days of reservation result in loss of deposit. **Registration:** At headquarters. **Fee:** Water/electric, $18; water, $12; primitive tent, $8; daily charge per person (13 and over), $5; over 2 vehicles per site, $5; cash, check, V, MC, D. **Parking:** At most sites.

FACILITIES
Number of RV-only Sites: 137. **Number of Tent-only Sites:** 50. **Hookups:** Electric (20, 30, 50 amps), water. **Each Site:** Picnic table, lantern hanger, fire pit/grill combination. **Dump Station:** Yes. **Laundry:** No. **Pay Phone:** Yes. **Restrooms and Showers:** Yes. **Fuel:** No. **Propane:** No. **Internal Roads:** Paved. **RV Service:** 21 mi. south in Marble Falls. **Market:** 12 mi. east in Burnet. **Restaurant:** 5 mi. **General Store:** In park, hardware 12 mi. in Burnet, Wal-Mart 21 mi. in Marlboro Falls. **Vending:** Yes. **Swimming:** Yes. **Playground:** Yes. **Other:** 9-hole golf course, picnic area, amphitheater, fishing piers, boat ramp, mini-cabins, screened shelters, park store. **Activities:** Hiking, backpacking, golf (cart & club rental available), lake swimming, fishing, waterskiing, scuba diving, guided tours at specific times, boating (canoe, paddle boat, & surf bike rentals available at park store). **Nearby Attractions:** Lyndon B. Johnson Ranch & State Historical Parks, Vanishing Texas river cruise, Lake Buchanan & Buchanon Dam, towns of Burnet, Fredericksburg, & Johnson City, numerous Hill Country lakes & state parks. **Additional Information:** Inks Lake & Lake Buchanon Chamber of Commerce, (512) 793-2803; Burnet Chamber of Commerce, (512) 756-4297.

RESTRICTIONS
Pets: On leash, attended. **Fires:** Restrictions vary; call park. **Alcoholic Beverages:** Not allowed. **Vehicle Maximum Length:** 40 ft. **Other:** Follow boat launch protocol; swim at your own risk.

TO GET THERE
From Burnet, drive west on TX 29 9 mi. Turn left on Park Rd. 4 and drive south 3 mi. to the park headquarters.

CADDO   MAP, A-4
Possum Kingdom State Park

reserve america

P.O. Box 70, 76429.
T: (940) 549-1803 or (800) 792-1112; www.reserveamerica.com.

🚐 ★★★   ⛺ ★★★

Beauty: ★★★	Site Privacy: ★★★
Spaciousness: ★★★	Quiet: ★★★
Security: ★★★★★	Cleanliness: ★★★
Insect Control: ★★	Facilities: ★★★★

The 20,000-acre Lake Possum Kingdom offers exceptionally clear water, attracting snorkelers and scuba divers. The lake supports crappie, perch, and various bass and catfish species. The park offers extensive fishing facilities. Five campgrounds are situated along the lakeshore. Walk-in campsites have no potties and fire-rings only. Happy with water only? Try sites 79–85 and 100, 104, 105, and 113 in the Chaparral Trail area. With full hookups and proximity to the playground and beach, the Spanish Oaks area is good for RV campers with children. Tent campers enjoy the Lakeview area, which offers water and electric hookups. Sites 22–26 have nice views. Most sites are partially shaded, with paved back-in parking. Site size varies immensely—arrive early for your choice of sites. Security is excellent due to extreme remoteness. Low year-round humidity and pleasant swimming make this park bearable (and crowded) in late summer. Visit any time except busy summer weekends.

BASICS
Operated By: Texas Parks and Wildlife. **Open:** All year. **Site Assignment:** Reservations (512) 389-8900; reservations must be made at least 48 hours in advance; deposit (equivalent to 1-night fee) required to hold reservation; cancellations more than 2 days prior to reservation result in $5 fee; cancellations w/in 2 days of reservation result in loss of deposit. **Registration:** At headquarters. **Fee:** $7–$20; daily charge per person (13 and older), $4; cash, check, V, MC, D. **Parking:** At most sites.

FACILITIES
Number of RV-only Sites: 60. **Number of Tent-only Sites:** 75. **Hookups:** Electric (30 amps), water. **Each Site:** Picnic table, either fire ring or grill.
Dump Station: Yes. **Laundry:** No. **Pay Phone:** No. **Restrooms and Showers:** Yes. **Fuel:** Yes. **Propane:** No. **Internal Roads:** Paved. **RV Service:** 50 mi. east in Mineral Wells. **Market:** Marina store in park. **Restaurant:** Restaurant: 18 mi. north on Possum Kingdom Lake. **General Store:** Marina store in park, 32 mi. to Wal-Mart in Breckinridge or Graham. **Vending:** No. **Swimming:** Yes. **Playground:** Yes. **Other:** Concrete boat ramp w/ courtesy dock, gas dock, covered slip rental, marina store (hours vary w/ season), fishing pier, fish-cleaning facility. **Activities:** Boating (motorized & nonmotorized boat rentals available), jet skiing (rentals available), fishing, waterskiing, swimming, hiking, biking. **Nearby Attractions:** Fort Griffin & Fort Richardson, Lake Mineral Wells, Lake Arrowhead State Park. **Additional Information:** Possum Kingdom Chamber of Commerce, (888) 779-8330.

RESTRICTIONS
Pets: Leash only, attended. Not allowed in buildings. **Fires:** In grills, fire rings only. **Alcoholic Beverages:** Not allowed. **Vehicle Maximum Length:** 40 ft. **Other:** Max. 8 people per campsite; quiet time 10 p.m.–6 a.m.; 14-day stay limit; swim at your own risk; follow boat-launch protocol; gathering of firewood prohibited.

TO GET THERE
From I-20, take Exit 414. Go west on US 180, through the towns of Weatherford and Palo Pinto. Continue west on 180 25 mi. past Palo Pinto, until you reach a blinking light. Then turn right onto Park Rd. 33. Go north on Park Rd. 33 17 mi. Road ends at park entrance.

CADDO   MAP, A-4
Possum Kingdom State Park

reserve america

P.O. Box 70, 76429. T: (940) 549-1803; www.reserveamerica.com.

🚐 ★★★★   ⛺ ★★★★

Beauty: ★★★★★	Site Privacy: ★★★★
Spaciousness: ★★★★	Quiet: ★★★★★
Security: ★★★★	Cleanliness: ★★★★
Insect Control: ★★★	Facilities: ★★★★

Possum Kingdom State Park, west of Mineral Wells in Palo Pinto County, is 1528.7 acres adjacent to Lake Possum Kingdom. Some of the rock facilities at the park were constructed by the Civilian Conservation Corps (CCC) in the early 1940s. The area was acquired by deed from the Brazos River Authority in 1940 and was opened to the public in 1950. This park is located in the rugged canyon country of the Palo Pinto Mountains and Brazos River Valley, and is adjacent to Lake Possum Kingdom, 20,000 acres of the clearest, bluest water in the southwest. Numerous white-tailed deer make their home in the park. The Possum Kingdom Longhorns are on sabbatical roaming the rolling plains and woodlands of San Angelo State Park while their home range is being rested and restored for their return in a few years. This park has six cabins that accommodate four people each, and one that accommodates eight people; campsites with water and electricity (premium campsites are available); campsites with water; walk-in primitive campsites (50–100 yards, fire ring only); a trailer dump station; picnic tables; a fishing pier; restrooms with showers; a fish-cleaning facility; a concrete boat ramp with a courtesy dock; playgrounds; and 2 miles of hiking/nature trails.

BASICS

Operated By: Texas Parks and Wildlife. **Open:** All year. **Site Assignment:** Reservations can be made 11 months in advance. **Registration:** At office. **Fee:** Single, $12–$20; primitive, $7; cabin, $75–$135. **Parking:** Limit of 2 vehicles per site; extra parking available for a fee.

FACILITIES

Number of Multipurpose Sites: 237. **Hookups:** Yes. **Dump Station:** Yes. **Laundry:** No. **Pay Phone:** Yes. **Restrooms and Showers:** Yes. **Fuel:** No. **Propane:** No. **Internal Roads:** Paved. **RV Service:** No. **Market:** No. **Restaurant:** No. **General Store:** Yes. **Vending:** No. **Swimming:** Yes. **Playground:** Yes. **Other:** Water at Possum Kingdom is nonpotable due to a high salt content; bring own water for consumption. Nonpotable water available at restrooms, showers, & campsites. Gate open 24 hours. **Activities:** Biking, boating, canoeing, fishing, hiking, waterskiing.

RESTRICTIONS

Pets: On a 6-ft. leash, never unattended, under control at all times, cleaned up after. **Fires:** Fires may be built only in campsite grills, fire rings, or fireplaces. Some sites allow only containerized fuel fires. When warranted, fire bans are implemented by county judges and/or county commissioners courts. Inquire when making reservations. **Alcoholic Beverages:** It is an offense to consume or display an open container of an alcoholic beverage in a public place or sell alcoholic beverages w/in a state park.

TO GET THERE

From Fort Worth: Take I-20 west to Weatherford. Exit on US 180. Stay on US 180 to Caddo. Turn north on Park Road 33 and to 17 mi. to park.

CALLIHAM · MAP, C-4
Choke Canyon State Park
Calliham Unit

reserve america

P.O. Box 2, 78007. T: (361) 786-3868; www.reserveamerica.com.

🚐 ★★★★   ⛺ ★★★★

Beauty: ★★★	Site Privacy: ★★★★
Spaciousness: ★★★★	Quiet: ★★★★
Security: ★★★★★	Cleanliness: ★★★★
Insect Control: ★	Facilities: ★★★★★

Many Mexican bird species grace Choke Canyon Reservoir, which forms the northern border of their natural range. Birding is augmented with feeders and trails. Of the two park units, Calliham hosts more birds and is more densely wooded. The reservoir supports various bass, catfish, and sunfish species, as well as crappie, bluegill, carp, and gar. The park provides excellent facilities for anglers. The campgrounds aren't gorgeous, but they are tidy and functional. Sites are large, with gravel and back-in parking. Most have partial shade. For water views, head for RV sites 115–131 at Calliham. RV sites 106–108 are the most shady and private. For tents, we prefer sites 200–218, which are situated on a 75-acre lake at Calliham. Security is excellent; the park is extremely remote with locked gates at night. For the best weather, visit in spring or fall. Crowds are only a problem on holiday weekends.

BASICS

Operated By: Texas Parks and Wildlife. **Open:** All year. **Site Assignment:** Reservations (512) 389-8900; reservations must be made at least 48 hours in advance; deposit (equivalent to 1-night fee) required to hold reservation; cancellations more than 2 days prior to reservation result in $5 fee; cancellations w/in 2 days of reservation result in loss of deposit. **Registration:** At headquarters. **Fee:** Water/electric, $16; water, $11; daily charge per person (13 and over), $3; cash, check, V, MC, D. **Parking:** At most sites.

FACILITIES

Number of RV-only Sites: 40. **Number of Tent-only Sites:** 19. **Hookups:** Electric (30, 50 amps), water. **Each Site:** Picnic table, lantern post, fire ring, shade covers at Calliham Unit. **Dump Station:** Yes. **Laundry:** No. **Pay Phone:** Yes. **Restrooms and Showers:** Yes. **Fuel:** 0.25 mi. outside park. **Propane:** 12 mi. east in Three Rivers. **Internal Roads:** Paved. **RV Service:** 75 mi. southeast in Corpus Christi. **Market:** 12 mi. east in Three Rivers. **Restaurant:** 3.5 mi. east of park. **General Store:** 8 mi. at office. **Vending:** Beverages. **Playground:** Yes. **Other:** Calliham Unit: screened shelters for rent, picnic area, group picnic area, group dining hall, group rec hall, amphitheater, sports complex (including gym & stage), swimming pool bathhouse, shuffleboard, tennis, volleyball & basketball courts, wildlife. **Activities:** Picnicking, boating, fishing, hiking, backpacking, birding, lake beach & pool swimming, various team sports, educational & interpretive programs. **Nearby Attractions:** Lake Corpus Christi State Park, Lipantitlan State Historical Park, San Antonio (about 80 mi.), Corpus Christi (about 70 mi.). **Additional Information:** Three Rivers Chamber of Commerce, (361) 786-2528; San Antonio CVB, (800) 447-3372; Corpus Christi Area CVB, (800) 678-6232.

RESTRICTIONS

Pets: On leash only. **Fires:** Fire ring only. **Alcoholic Beverages:** Not allowed. **Vehicle Maximum Length:** 50 ft.

TO GET THERE

To reach the South Shore Unit from Three Rivers, drive west on TX 72 3.5 mi. To reach the Calliham Unit from Three Rivers, drive west on TX 72 12 mi.

CANYON · MAP, D-1
Palo Duro Canyon State Park

reserve america

R.R. 2 Box 285, 11450 Park Rd. 5, 79015-9628. T: (806) 488-2227; www.reserveamerica.com.

🚐 ★★★★   ⛺ ★★★★

Beauty: ★★★★	Site Privacy: ★★★
Spaciousness: ★★★	Quiet: ★★★
Security: ★★★★★	Cleanliness: ★★★★
Insect Control: ★★★	Facilities: ★★★★

At 800 feet deep, 120 miles long, and 0.5 to 20 miles wide, Palo Duro is the second-largest canyon in the United States. Exposed rock includes white gypsum, red claystone, and gray, yellow, and lavender mudstone. The park's mascot is The Lighthouse, a 300-foot rock spire. Hardwoods throughout the canyon include juniper and mesquite. The canyon rim supports a short grass prairie. Campsites vary in privacy and spaciousness, with some 60 feet from neighbors and others stacked together. Low trees and brush provide no shade. Parking is paved. RV campers enjoy pull-throughs at the Hackberry area (30-amp service). Need 50-amp service? Try the Sagebrush area (sites 137 and 139 are pull-throughs). The Mesquite area has gorgeous views of red rock formations. Security is excellent—the park is in a remote area and locks its gate at night. If you're not seeing *Texas*, the musical, visit in spring or fall. Otherwise, visit during the week.

BASICS

Operated By: Texas Parks and Wildlife. **Open:** All year. **Site Assignment:** Reservations (512) 389-8900; reservations must be made at least 48 hours in advance; deposit (equivalent to 1-night fee) required to hold reservation; cancellations more than 2 days prior to reservation result in $5 fee; cancellations w/in 2 days of reservation result in loss of deposit. **Registration:** At headquarters. **Fee:** Water/electric, $20; primitive camping, $12; daily charge per person (13 and over), $4; check, V, MC, D. **Parking:** At site.

FACILITIES

Number of RV-only Sites: 79. **Number of Tent-only Sites:** 22. **Hookups:** Electric (30, 50 amps), water. **Each Site:** Picnic table, grill, some have shade shelters. **Dump Station:** Yes. **Laundry:** No. **Pay Phone:** Yes. **Restrooms and Showers:** Yes. **Fuel:** No. **Propane:** No. **Internal Roads:** Paved. **RV Service:** 30 mi. north in Amarillo. **Market:** In park, closed in winter. **Restaurant:** In park. **General Store:** In park, or Wal-Mart 13 mi. west in Canyon. **Vending:** Yes. **Swimming:** No. **Playground:** Yes. **Other:** Equestrian area, interpretive center, gift shop, park store, picnic area, amphitheatre, historical markers, equestrian camping area, separate trails for hiking, mountain biking, & equestrian use. **Activities:** Guided tours, hiking, horseback riding, mountain biking, bird-watching, scenic drives, *Texas* musical drama nightly during the summer (no Wed. performances). **Nearby Attractions:** Cowboy Morning at Figure 3 Ranch, Panhandle Plains Museum, Storyland Zoo for Children, Nielson Memorial Museum, Alibates Flint

Quarries National Monument, Lake Meredith National Recreation Area, Amarillo. **Additional Information:** Amarillo CVB, (800) 692-1338; *Texas box office,* (806) 655-2181.

RESTRICTIONS

Pets: On leash only, attended. Not allowed in buildings. **Fires:** Contact park. **Alcoholic Beverages:** Not allowed. **Vehicle Maximum Length:** 60 ft. **Other:** Be aware of flash flood precautions & rough terrain.

TO GET THERE

From I-27, take Exit 106, TX 217. Go east on TX 217 8 mi.

CEDAR HILL   MAP, A-4
Cedar Hill State Park

reserve america

1570 FM 1382, 75104. T: (972) 291-3900; www.reserveamerica.com.

🚐 ★★★   ⛺ ★★★★

Beauty: ★★★★★	Site Privacy: ★★★
Spaciousness: ★★★	Quiet: ★★★
Security: ★★★★	Cleanliness: ★★★★
Insect Control: ★★★	Facilities: ★★★★

In 1854, John Anderson Penn settled in the rugged cedar-covered hills of southwest Dallas County—an area known as the Cedar Mountains. Today, remnants of the original Penn Farm survive intact in the confines of Cedar Hill State Park. Cedar Hill State Park is a 1,826 acre urban nature preserve located on the 7,500-acre Joe Pool Reservoir. The park's proximity to major metropolitan cities makes it an ideal destination for families who want to enjoy the great outdoors without spending precious time driving. The ruggedness and scenic beauty of the area combined with over 100 miles of shoreline and the water-based recreation on Joe Pool is a major attraction. The Metroplex skyline reflecting on Joe Pool at night adds to the relaxing wilderness atmosphere. The park was acquired in 1982 and was opened in 1991. Penn Farm Agricultural History Center pays tribute to the disappearing Texas family farm and affords a glimpse into agrarian history as farm machinery took the place of the horse and mule almost a century ago. The Farm is open seven days a week to self-guided tours. There are reconstructed and historic buildings from the mid-1800s through the mid-1900s. The Penn Farm has a very relaxing atmosphere and is perfect for family walks. Self-guided and guided tours are available.

BASICS

Operated By: Texas Parks and Wildlife. **Open:** All year. **Site Assignment:** Reservations can be made 11 months in advance. **Registration:** At office. **Fee:** Single, $20; group pavilion, $65–$85. **Parking:** Limit of 2 vehicles per site; extra parking available for a fee.

FACILITIES

Number of Multipurpose Sites: 712. **Hookups:** Yes. **Dump Station:** Yes. **Laundry:** No. **Pay Phone:** Yes. **Restrooms and Showers:** Yes. **Fuel:**

No. **Propane:** No. **Internal Roads:** Paved. **RV Service:** No. **Market:** No. **Restaurant:** No. **General Store:** Yes. **Vending:** No. **Swimming:** Yes. **Playground:** Yes. **Other:** If you arrive later than 10 p.m., you must call the office by 5 p.m. on the day of arrival to obtain gate code. **Activities:** Biking, boating, fishing, paddleboats, picnicking, hiking, water-skiing, wildlife viewing.

RESTRICTIONS

Pets: On a 6-ft. leash, never unattended, under control at all times, cleaned up after. **Fires:** Fires may be built only in campsite grills, fire rings, or fireplaces. Some sites allow only containerized fuel fires. When warranted, fire bans are implemented by county judges and/or county commissioners courts. Inquire when making reservations. **Alcoholic Beverages:** It is an offense to consume or display an open container of an alcoholic beverage in a public place or sell alcoholic beverages w/in a state park.

TO GET THERE

From Dallas take I-20 west to FM 1382 exit. Park is located 4.5 mi. south on FM 1382. From Austin and Waco take I-35W (Ft Worth) and exit on Hwy. 67N at Alvarado. Travel approx. 25 mi. to Cedar Hill. Take the FM 1382 exit. The park is located 2 mi. west on FM 1382.

COLDSPRING   MAP, B-5
Double Lake Recreation Area—
Sam Houston National Forest

reserve america

301 FM 2025, 77331. T: (936) 653-3448; www.reserveamerica.com.

🚐 ★★★★   ⛺ ★★★★

Beauty: ★★★	Site Privacy: ★★★
Spaciousness: ★★★	Quiet: ★★★
Security: ★★★★	Cleanliness: ★★★★
Insect Control: ★★★★	Facilities: ★★★

Built in 1937 by the Civilian Conservation Corps, Double Lake offers a little of everything including camping, fishing, picnicking, hiking, or just getting back in touch with nature. The Double Lake Recreation Area is open to day-use and camping year-round, and is a popular destination all four seasons. Campers have ample places to park their gear with 65 family sites (some with electric and sewer hookups) and nine group sites. Thirty-seven camp-sites are accessible for persons with disabilities. Double Lake Recreation Area, 50 miles north of Houston, is located within the Sam Houston National Forest and is one of four National Forests in Texas. The forest contains 163,037 acres between Huntsville, Conroe, Cleveland, and Richards, Texas. With land in Montgomery, Walker, and San Jacinto counties, the Sam Houston National Forest is inter-mingled with privately owned timberlands and small farms. The three counties that contain the Sam Houston National Forest have yielded evidence of human occupation dating back 12,000 years. More recently, the basins of the San Jacinto and Trinity

---

rivers were home to Atakapan-speaking groups known as the Bidai, Patiri, Deadose, and Akokisa. Primarily hunters and gatherers, some from these groups may have practiced some form of agriculture. Disease and pressure from European settlers led to their eventual extinction in the early 1800s. Evidence of occupations from as early as 7,000 years ago to the 20th century has been documented by a number of archaeological sites within the national forest. The remains of our heritage, both prehistoric and historic, are a nonrenewable resource protected by federal and state regulations. Please remember not to disturb any sites, cemeteries, or structures. If you discover any artifacts during your visit to the national forest, please leave them in place and contact the Sam Houston Ranger District Office.

BASICS

Operated By: U.S. Forest Service. **Open:** All year. **Site Assignment:** Reservations must be made at least 2 days in advance. **Registration:** At office. **Fee:** Single, $15–$25; double, $40–$50. **Parking:** At park.

FACILITIES

Number of Multipurpose Sites: 140. **Hookups:** Yes. **Each Site:** Picnic table, level pad, lantern holder, fire ring/grill. **Dump Station:** 2 mi. **Laundry:** No. **Pay Phone:** No. **Restrooms and Showers:** Yes. **Fuel:** No. **Propane:** No. **Internal Roads:** Paved. **RV Service:** No. **Market:** No. **Restaurant:** No. **General Store:** Yes. **Vending:** No. **Swimming:** Yes. **Playground:** No. **Other:** No access 10 p.m.–6 a.m. for new campers. **Activities:** Biking, canoeing, hiking, interpretive programs.

RESTRICTIONS

Pets: Restrained or on a leash at all times while in developed recreation areas. **Fires:** In fire rings, stoves, grills, or fireplaces provided for that purpose. **Alcoholic Beverages:** Not allowed. **Vehicle Maximum Length:** Call ahead.

TO GET THERE

From New Waverly, TX, go 22 mi. east on Hwy. 150 to FM 2025, then south 0.25 mi. to campground.

COLORADO CITY   MAP, A-3
Lake Colorado City State Park

reserve america

4582 FM 2836, 79512. T: (325) 728-3931; www.reserveamerica.com.

🚐 ★★★★   ⛺ ★★★★

Beauty: ★★★	Site Privacy: ★★★
Spaciousness: ★★★	Quiet: ★★★
Security: ★★★★	Cleanliness: ★★★★
Insect Control: ★★★	Facilities: ★★★★

Lake Colorado City State Park is a 500-acre park, leased for 99 years from a utility company in Mitchell County, southwest of Colorado City. It was acquired in 1971 and was opened in 1972. Lake Colorado City was built in 1949 on Morgan Creek, a tributary of the Colorado River, by Texas Electric Service

Company to provide cooling water for the power plant, a water supply for Colorado City, and recreation. Morgan Creek Power Plant is the largest modern steam electric station in West Texas. Activities include picnicking, camping, fishing, and lake swimming (unsupervised). Containing more than 5 miles of shoreline, the 500 acres of park land afford numerous outdoor activities for lake swimmers, fisherman, skiers, jet-skiers, campers, hikers, and naturalists. Park visitors of all ages enjoy seeing part of the Texas Longhorn herd. Some of the wildlife that can be observed and photographed includes white-tailed deer, mallard duck, raccoon, armadillo, and squirrel. Popular fish are crappie, perch, catfish, bass, and red drum.

BASICS

Operated By: Texas Parks and Wildlife. **Open:** All year. **Site Assignment:** Reservations can be made 11 months in advance. **Registration:** At office. **Fee:** Single, $12–$20; pavilion, $35; cabin, $50; group hall, $100. **Parking:** Limit of 2 vehicles per site; extra parking available for a fee.

FACILITIES

Number of Multipurpose Sites: 228. **Hookups:** Yes. **Dump Station:** Yes. **Laundry:** No. **Pay Phone:** Yes. **Restrooms and Showers:** Yes. **Fuel:** No. **Propane:** No. **Internal Roads:** Paved. **RV Service:** No. **Market:** No. **Restaurant:** No. **General Store:** Yes. **Vending:** No. **Swimming:** Yes. **Playground:** Yes. **Other:** Gate is open 8 a.m.–10 p.m. If you will be a late arrival, you must call the park prior to 5 p.m. on arrival date for late arrival instructions. **Activities:** Biking, fishing, nature study, picnicking, waterskiing, wildlife viewing.

RESTRICTIONS

Pets: On a 6-ft. leash, never unattended, under control at all times, cleaned up after. **Fires:** Fires may be built only in campsite grills, fire rings, or fireplaces. Some sites allow only containerized fuel fires. When warranted, fire bans are implemented by county judges and/or county commissioners courts. Inquire when making reservations. **Alcoholic Beverages:** It is an offense to consume or display an open container of an alcoholic beverage in a public place or sell alcoholic beverages w/in a state park.

TO GET THERE

From Abilene: Take I-20 west through Colorado City 6 mi. Take Exit 210 on FM 2836. Take FM 2836 6 mi. south to the Park entrance. From Midland: Take I-20 east through Westbrook to FM 2836. Take FM 2836 south 6 mi. to the park entrance.

COMSTOCK   MAP, C-3
Seminole Canyon State Park and Historical Site

P. O. Box 820, Hwy. 90 West, Park Rd. 67, 78837. T: (432) 292-4464 or (800) 792-1112; www.reserveamerica.com.

 ★★★★★    ★★★★★

Beauty: ★★★★★   Site Privacy: ★★★★
Spaciousness: ★★★★   Quiet: ★★★★★
Security: ★★★★★   Cleanliness: ★★★★★
Insect Control: ★★★   Facilities: ★★★★

Deep canyons, big skies, and rocky terrain create a stunning landscape. Awesome vistas at Seminole Canyon belie the region's harshness (annual rainfall is 12 to 14 inches). Almost everything in this environment bites, stings, or scratches. Nonetheless, human habitation dates back thousands of years. Prehistoric pictographs endure in rock shelters (viewed by guided tour only). Diverse wildlife includes many bird species unique to Mexican borderlands. The multiuse campground contains few sites—forget about choosing your own. Sites are spacious with enough short scrubby brush between them to provide a little privacy. There is no shade here, so plan accordingly. Most sites have a stunning view. Parking is back-in and paved. Security is excellent at Seminole Canyon due to its extreme remoteness. Plan to visit in the fall, as this park experiences heavy traffic in the spring and intense heat in the summer.

BASICS

Operated By: Texas Parks and Wildlife. **Open:** All year. **Site Assignment:** Reservations (512) 389-8900; reservations must be made at least 48 hours in advance; deposit (equivalent to 1-night fee) required to hold reservation; cancellations more than 2 days prior to reservation result in $5 fee; cancellations w/in 2 days of reservation result in loss of deposit. **Registration:** At headquarters. **Fee:** Electric, $14; water, $10; daily charge per person (13 and over), $3; check, V, MC, D. **Parking:** At site.

FACILITIES

Number of RV-only Sites: 23. **Number of Tent-only Sites:** 8. **Hookups:** Electric (30 amps), water. **Each Site:** Picnic table, shade shelter, tent pad, fire ring or grill. **Dump Station:** Yes. **Laundry:** No. **Pay Phone:** Yes. **Restrooms and Showers:** Yes. **Fuel:** No. **Propane:** No. **Internal Roads:** Paved. **RV Service:** 42 mi. east in Del Rio. **Market:** 9 mi. east in Comstock. **Restaurant:** 9 mi. east in Comstock. **General Store:** 42 mi. east in Del Rio. **Vending:** Snacks at park headquarters 8 a.m.–5 p.m. **Swimming:** No. **Playground:** No. **Other:** Interpretive center, picnic area, gift shop. **Activities:** Guided tours of Seminole Canyon, hiking, mountain biking, historical study, nature interpretation. **Nearby Attractions:** Judge Roy Bean Visitor Center in Langtry, Lake Amistad National Recreation Area (about 35 mi.), Whitehead Memorial Museum & The Old Perry Store in Del Rio (about 42 mi.). **Additional Information:** Del Rio Chamber of Commerce, (830) 775-3551; Judge Roy Bean Visitor Center, (830) 291-3340.

RESTRICTIONS

Pets: On leash only. **Fires:** In designated areas only. **Alcoholic Beverages:** Not allowed in public. **Vehicle Maximum Length:** 45 ft. **Other:** Canyons are closed to the public except for guided tours; max. 8 people per campsite; quiet time 10 p.m.–6 a.m.; 14-day stay limit; gathering of firewood prohibited.

TO GET THERE

From Del Rio drive west on US 90 40 mi. The park entrance is 9 mi. past the town of Comstock, just east of the Pecos River Bridge.

CONCAN   MAP, C-3
Garner State Park

HCR 70, P.O. Box 599, 78838. T: (830) 232-6132; www.reserveamerica.com.

★★★★   ★★★★★

Beauty: ★★★★★   Site Privacy: ★★★★
Spaciousness: ★★★★   Quiet: ★★★★
Security: ★★★★   Cleanliness: ★★★★
Insect Control: ★★★★   Facilities: ★★★★★

Garner's campgrounds are the most popular in the state. It's no wonder—the campgrounds are in a valley surrounded by beautiful rolling hills adorned with crooked Spanish and lacey oak. Garner offers unique recreation including jukebox dances and inner tubing the rapids of the Frio River. In season, the Friends of Garner State Park present the Cowboy Sunset Serenade, celebrating American cowboys through poetry and song. Of five camping areas, three have hookups. We prefer Live Oak area, which is quieter than Oakmont and Shady Meadows. It's also the best for families, with a playground next to the washhouse. Sites are spacious, with paved, back-in parking (pull-throughs available at other camp areas). Most are shady. We recommend even-numbered sites 334–358, which are a stone's throw from the Frio River. Security is very good at this remote park. Campgrounds are crowded spring, summer, and fall—make advance reservations.

BASICS

Operated By: Texas Parks and Wildlife. **Open:** All year; park closes for hunting season; contact park for details. **Site Assignment:** Reservations (512) 389-8900; reservations must be made at least 48 hours in advance; deposit (equivalent to 1-night fee) required to hold reservation; cancellations more than 2 days prior to reservation result in $5 fee; cancellations w/in 2 days of reservation result in loss of deposit. **Registration:** At headquarters. **Fee:** Water/electric, $15–$20; water, $10–$15; daily charge per person (13 and older), $4; cash, check, V, MC, D. **Parking:** At site, fee charged for more than 2 vehicles.

FACILITIES

Number of RV-only Sites: 161. **Number of Tent-only Sites:** 206. **Hookups:** Electric (30 amps), water. **Each Site:** Picnic table, grill, fire ring, tent pad, some w/lantern hooks & shade shelters. **Dump Station:** Yes. **Laundry:** Yes. **Pay Phone:** No. **Restrooms and Showers:** Yes. **Fuel:** 9 mi. north in Leakey. **Propane:** 9 mi. north in Leakey. **Internal Roads:** Paved. **RV Service:** 100 mi. west in Del Rio. **Market:** In park. **Restaurant:** 9 mi. north in Leakey. **General Store:** 9 mi. north in Leakey. **Vending:** Beverages. **Swimming:** Yes. **Playground:** No. **Other:** Screened shelters, overflow camping area, picnic shelter w/kitchen, dining hall, picnic sites, group camp area w/screened shelters, surfaced road area for bike riding & day hiking, unpaved hiking trails, gift shop, snack bar, mini-golf course, paddle boat. **Activities:** River swimming, tubing, boating, hiking, walking, bicycling, mini-golf, picnicking, fishing, & jukebox dancing nightly in the summer. **Nearby Attractions:** Hill Country, Lost Maples, & Devil's Sinkhole natural areas; Kickapoo Cavern State Park; John Nance "Cactus Jack" Garner Museum in Uvalde; historic Mission Nuestra Senora de la Candelaria del Canon; Camp Sabinal; Fort Inge. **Additional Information:** Frio Canyon Chamber of Commerce, (830) 232-5222; Uvalde Chamber of Commerce, (830) 278-3361.

RESTRICTIONS

Pets: On leash only; not allowed in buildings. **Fires:** Fire ring only. **Alcoholic Beverages:** Not allowed. **Vehicle Maximum Length:** 30 ft. parking pads. **Other:** Read safety warnings. No gathering firewood.

TO GET THERE

From San Antonio take US 90 west to Sabinal. At Sabinal turn right onto US 127 and follow it 30 mi. Turn right onto US 83 and go 8 mi. to FM 1050. Go 0.2 mi. and turn right onto Park Rd. 29.

COOPER   MAP, A-5
Cooper Lake State Park (Doctor's Creek Unit)

reserve america

1664 FR 1529 South, 75432. T: (903) 395-3100; www.reserveamerica.com.

🚐 ★★★★	⛺ ★★★★★
Beauty: ★★★★	Site Privacy: ★★★★
Spaciousness: ★★★★	Quiet: ★★★★★
Security: ★★★★	Cleanliness: ★★★★
Insect Control: ★★	Facilities: ★★★

Sites in this wilderness park are mostly grassy and forested, and they include 55-foot back-ins and 120-foot pull-throughs. Sites 1 and 42 at the entrance are well shaded but rather close to the internal road. Site 4 is similarly close to the intersection of two internal roads, and it may not suit many campers due to the higher volume of passing traffic (which, admittedly, is still rather limited). Site 8 is reserved for the park host, and the sites on either side seem to be popular with campers either seeking the added security or the added companionship. Sites 12 and 13 are both back-ins on a concrete slab and are very open to the sun. The best sites, depending on taste, are either 15–17 (although 17 is next to a parking area); 22 and 23, which back to the edge of the lake; or 22 (especially if 23 is unoccupied), which is well shaded, by the water, and somewhat secluded. The restrooms are quite clean, well lit, and spacious, with modern facilities. And as for activities in the park, there is plenty to do for anyone in the family. This is a typical high-quality Texas state park, with water activities, sports, and hiking available. A definite destination for a family holiday.

BASICS

Operated By: Texas Parks and Wildlife. **Open:** All year. **Site Assignment:** First come, first served;

---

overnight camping Fri. & Sat. only; 48-hour cancellation policy. **Registration:** At office. (Late arrivals use drop box at entrance.) **Fee:** Water/electric, $12; water, $8; plus $2 entrance fee; V, MC, D accepted in the office or for reservation. **Parking:** At site.

FACILITIES

Number of Multipurpose Sites: 42. **Hookups:** Electric (30 amps), water. **Each Site:** Picnic table, grill, fire pit, lantern post. **Dump Station:** Yes. **Laundry:** No. **Pay Phone:** Courtesy. **Restrooms and Showers:** Yes. **Fuel:** No. **Propane:** No. **Internal Roads:** Paved. **RV Service:** No. **Market:** 3 mi. to Cooper. **Restaurant:** 3 mi. to Cooper. **General Store:** Yes. **Vending:** Yes. **Swimming:** Lake. **Playground:** Yes. **Other:** 6 shelters, 1 cottage, amphitheater, boat ramp, fish-cleaning table. **Activities:** Swimming, boating, fishing, hiking, mountain biking, volleyball, waterskiing, bird-watching. **Nearby Attractions:** Sam Bell Maxey House State Historical Park, Bonham State Park, Lake Bob Sandlin State Park. **Additional Information:** (512) 389-8900.

RESTRICTIONS

Pets: On 6-ft. leash, attended, cleaned up after. **Fires:** Grill only. **Alcoholic Beverages:** Not allowed. **Vehicle Maximum Length:** No limit. **Other:** All visitors must pay $2 entrance fee per day. No gathering wood.

TO GET THERE

From Business Hwy. 24 and Hwy. 154 (First and Dallas in the town square), go 1.3 mi. east on Hwy. 154 (Dallas), then turn south onto FM 1529 and go 1.6 mi. Turn right at the sign into the entrance.

CORPUS CHRISTI   MAP, D-4
Colonia del Rey RV Park

1717 Waldron Rd., 78418. T: (361) 937-2435; www.gocampingamerica.com.

🚐 ★★★	⛺ n/a
Beauty: ★★★★	Site Privacy: ★★★
Spaciousness: ★★★	Quiet: ★★★
Security: ★★★	Cleanliness: ★★★
Insect Control: ★★	Facilities: ★★★

This suburban park is convenient to cosmopolitan Corpus Christi attractions, Corpus Christi Naval Air Station, and gorgeous beaches at Padre Island National Seashore and Mustang Island. Most of the sites at this nice-looking campground are laid out in tidy rows of pull-throughs. Sites are decent-sized and partially shaded by palm and other tree species. Parking is on grass. The most attractive sites are in section 32. Families should head for sites 16–23, large sites near the pool and playground. The quietest sites are those in section 60. With no gates and no fence around the property, security is poor at Colonia Del Rey. Although the city regularly sprays, insects can be unbearable in this area. Prepare yourself with bug spray, and avoid southern Texas in late summer.

BASICS

Operated By: The Simms. **Open:** All year. **Site Assignment:** Advance reservations are accepted, credit card holds site for daily or weekly camping; 24-hour cancellation notice; sites are usually

---

assigned by the campground; cancellations made w/in 1 day of arrival subject to a penalty equal to 1-night fee. **Registration:** At office. **Fee:** $28–$37. **Parking:** At site.

FACILITIES

Number of RV-only Sites: 210. **Hookups:** Electric (30, 50 amps), water, sewer, cable TV, phone, data port. **Each Site:** Picnic table. **Dump Station:** Yes. **Laundry:** Yes. **Pay Phone:** Yes. **Restrooms and Showers:** Yes. **Fuel:** No. **Propane:** Yes. **Internal Roads:** Paved. **RV Service:** Colonia del Rey RV Sales, (361) 937-5703. **Market:** 0.5 mi. north. **Restaurant:** 0.5 mi. north. **General Store:** 0.5 mi. north Wal-Mart. **Vending:** Beverages. **Swimming:** Pool. **Playground:** Yes. **Other:** Rec hall, hot tub. **Activities:** Planned activities, Mexico tours, swimming. **Nearby Attractions:** USS *Lexington*, Texas State Aquarium, The Columbus Ships, Greyhound Racetrack, Padre Island National Seashore. **Additional Information:** Corpus Christi Area CVB, (800) 678-6232; Padre Island National Seashore, (361) 949-8068.

RESTRICTIONS

Pets: On leash only. **Fires:** No ground fires. **Alcoholic Beverages:** Allowed. **Vehicle Maximum Length:** 45 ft.

TO GET THERE

From I-358, exit at Waldron Rd. Go south 0.5 mi. Entrance is on the left.

DAINGERFIELD   MAP, A-5
Daingerfield State Park

reserve america

455 Park Rd. 17, 75638. T: (903) 645-2921 or (800) 792-1112; www.reserveamerica.com.

🚐 ★★★★★	⛺ ★★★★★
Beauty: ★★★★★	Site Privacy: ★★★★★
Spaciousness: ★★★★★	Quiet: ★★★★★
Security: ★★★★	Cleanliness: ★★★★
Insect Control: ★★	Facilities: ★★★

This state park has three smallish camping areas (approximately ten units each), which can all take RVs, but one of which (Big Pine) is off-limits for tents. This is just as well, since these are huge (120-foot) pull-throughs that overlook the water (1–5) or back to the water (6–10) and make the trip worthwhile for an RVer. The space is very generous, as is typical in Texas state parks, and any rig that can drive on the highway can fit into these sites. The restroom in the camping area also leaves nothing to be desired: it is big and clean and has flush toilets and hot showers. The Dogwood camping area provides shaded electrical sites in a loop near the water. Site 17 is particularly close, while 18 and 19 have nice views of the lake. The Mountain View area is also in a loop, and offers secluded 40-foot back-ins away from the water (but with nary a mountain in view!). The best sites for someone wanting to get away from it all are 31, 33, and 34, which are on the farthest edge of a dead-end roundabout. Families, couples, and anyone with a love of the outdoors should find their way to Daingerfield State Park, which offers activities galore in a beautiful wilderness setting.

BASICS

Operated By: Texas Parks and Wildlife. **Open:** All year. **Site Assignment:** Reservations, call (512) 389-8900 48 hrs. in advance; refund (minus $5) w/ 48-hr. notice; less than 48 hrs., lose 1-night deposit. **Registration:** At office. (Late arrivals use drop box at entrance.) **Fee:** RV (full), $18; water/electric, $12; plus $2 entrance fee; V, MC, D accepted in the office or for reservation. **Parking:** At site.

FACILITIES

Number of Multipurpose Sites: 40. **Hookups:** Electric (30 amps), water, sewer. **Each Site:** Picnic table, grill, fire pit, lantern post. **Dump Station:** Yes. **Laundry:** No. **Pay Phone:** No. **Restrooms and Showers:** Yes. **Fuel:** No. **Propane:** No. **Internal Roads:** Paved. **RV Service:** No. **Market:** 3 mi. to Daingerfield. **Restaurant:** 3 mi. to Daingerfield. **General Store:** Gift shop. **Vending:** Yes. **Swimming:** Lake. **Playground:** Yes. **Other:** Lodge, amphitheater, boat ramp, fish-cleaning station. **Activities:** Swimming, boating, fishing, hiking, mountain biking. **Nearby Attractions:** Lake Bob Sandlin, Starr Mansion Historical State Park, Caddo Lake State Park, Atlanta State Park.

RESTRICTIONS

Pets: On 6-ft. leash, cleaned up after. **Fires:** Grill only. **Alcoholic Beverages:** Not allowed. **Vehicle Maximum Length:** No limit (sites vary). **Other:** All visitors must pay $2 entrance fee per day.

TO GET THERE

From the junction of Hwy. 259 and Hwy. 49, go 2.4 mi. east on Hwy. 49. Turn right at the sign onto a paved road (the sign bearing the street name and number—Park Rd. 17—is not visible from Hwy. 49) and follow it to the entrance of the park.

DALLAS/FORT WORTH   MAP, A-4
Trader's Village Grand Prairie RV Park

2602 Mayfield Rd., 75052.
T: (972) 647-2331 or (972) 647-8205;
www.tradersvillage.com/en/grandprairie/rv.

🚐 ★★★   ⛺ ★

Beauty: ★★★	Site Privacy: ★★
Spaciousness: ★★★	Quiet: ★★★
Security: ★★★	Cleanliness: ★★★
Insect Control: ★★★★	Facilities: ★★★

Trader's Village Flea Market covers 100 acres and accommodates 1,800 dealers. Open Sat. and Sun. all year, the flea market also offers food stands and children's rides and games. Call ahead for special event information. The campground is bland and completely flat. A few trees make the park aesthetically bearable but provide little shade. Most sites offer pull-through parking. Those on the perimeter of the campground offer back-in parking. Parking is paved,

and each site has a little patch of grass. Sites in the 40s, 50s, 60s, 70s, 80s, and 90s have the most mature trees. However, families should go for sites in the 200s, the closest to the pool and rec hall. We don't recommend this suburban campground unless you're buying or selling at Trader's Village. Security is fair—gates are never locked but the campground is patrolled by armed guards. Make advance reservations at Christmastime.

BASICS

Operated By: Traders Village. **Open:** All year. **Site Assignment:** Advance reservations recommended, credit card holds site; 1-day cancellation notice; call 8:30 a.m.–8 p.m. V, MC, AE, D, personal check, cash; sites held until 6 p.m. unless previous arrangements are made. **Registration:** At office. **Fee:** RV, $24.95–$30.95; tent, $23. **Parking:** At site.

FACILITIES

Number of RV-only Sites: 212. **Hookups:** Electric (50 amps), water, sewer. **Each Site:** Picnic table, barbecue pit. **Dump Station:** Yes. **Laundry:** Yes. **Pay Phone:** Yes. **Restrooms and Showers:** Yes. **Fuel:** Yes, no diesel. **Propane:** Yes. **Internal Roads:** Paved. **RV Service:** 20 mi. in Dallas. **Market:** In park. **Restaurant:** 0.25 mi. **General Store:** Yes. **Vending:** Yes. **Swimming:** Pool. **Playground:** Yes. **Other:** Rec hall, mini-mart, hair salon, ATM machine on-site, modem friendly. **Activities:** Shopping on weekends, festivals, tours available. **Nearby Attractions:** Six Flags, Hurricane Harbor, Fort Worth Stockyards, Texas Motor Speedway, Texas Rangers Baseball, Lone Star Park, DFW International Airport, Dallas Mavericks, Mesquite Rodeo, Dallas Cowboys, convention centers, numerous retail shops. **Additional Information:** Fort Worth CVB, (800) 433-5747; Dallas CVB, (800) 232-5527.

RESTRICTIONS

Pets: 2 pets per site, on leash only, never unattended. **Fires:** Not allowed. **Alcoholic Beverages:** Allowed. **Vehicle Maximum Length:** 45 ft. **Other:** Speed limit of 10 mph strictly enforced.

TO GET THERE

From I-20, take the Great Southwest Pkwy. exit. Go north on Great Southwest Pkwy. 0.25 mi. to Mayfield Rd. Take a left on Mayfield Rd. Entrance is 300 yards on the right.

DEL RIO   MAP, C-3
Devils River State Natural Area

reserve america

HCR 1 Box 513, 78840. T: (830) 395-2133;
www.reserveamerica.com.

🚐   ⛺ ★★★★

Beauty: ★★★★	Site Privacy: ★★★★★
Spaciousness: ★★★★	Quiet: ★★★★★
Security: ★★★★	Cleanliness: ★★★★
Insect Control: ★★★	Facilities: ★★

Devils River State Natural Area, in Val Verde County north of Del Rio, was officially acquired in May

1988. The area's acreage is approximately 19,988.6, with 447.73 held in a trust. The site possesses good biological diversity, and the scenic river corridor offers a rugged river experience. The archeological significance appears substantial and preserves sites similar to those lost when Lake Amistad was impounded. Archeological evidence suggests that cultural influences from the west and east met at Devils River. The park's large size and remoteness support day hiking, primitive camping, nature study, mountain biking, and canyon tours. Access to the river (1.5 miles) is by hiking, biking, or park tour only; no vehicle access permitted. The park is a put-in point (no take-out) for canoes and kayaks. Nearest take-out point is about 10 miles downriver from the Park and only outfitters are allowed to take boats out on these private lands. Lake Amistad is about 32 miles downriver from the Park, and there is no cost to take boat out there.

BASICS

Operated By: Texas Parks and Wildlife. **Open:** All year. **Site Assignment:** Reservations can be made 11 months in advance. **Registration:** At office. **Fee:** Primitive, $6; group barracks, $20; group dining hall, $65. **Parking:** Limit of 2 vehicles per site; extra parking available for a fee.

FACILITIES

Number of Multipurpose Sites: 30. **Hookups:** Yes. **Dump Station:** No. **Laundry:** No. **Pay Phone:** No. **Restrooms and Showers:** Yes. **Fuel:** No. **Propane:** No. **Internal Roads:** Paved. **RV Service:** No. **Market:** No. **Restaurant:** No. **General Store:** No. **Vending:** No. **Swimming:** No. **Playground:** No. **Other:** Catch & release fishing only. No live bait is permitted. No boats or motorized watercraft are allowed, only canoes or kayaks are allowed in the water. This is a flash flood area; exercise caution. The nearest hospital is 70 mi. away. **Activities:** Biking, bird-watching, canoeing, wildlife viewing.

RESTRICTIONS

Pets: Not allowed at this park. **Fires:** Only containerized fuel fires allowed. **Alcoholic Beverages:** It is an offense to consume or display an open container of an alcoholic beverage in a public place or sell alcoholic beverages w/in a state park.

TO GET THERE

From Del Rio: yake Hwy. 277 north to Loma Alta then 3.5 mi. north to Dolan Creek Rd. Turn left and go 22 mi. to park headquarters. From San Antonio: Take I-10 east to Junction. Take Hwy. 377 south to intersection with Hwy. 277. Turn right on Hwy. 277 to 3.5 mi. north of Loma Alta. Turn left on Dolan Creek Rd. Go 22 mi. to park headquarters.

DENISON   MAP, A-4
Eisenhower State Park

reserve america™

50 Park Rd. 20, 75020-4878.
T: (903) 465-1956 or (800) 792-1112;
www.reserveamerica.com.

🚐 ★★★★   ⛺ ★★★★

Beauty: ★★★★	Site Privacy: ★★★
Spaciousness: ★★★★	Quiet: ★★★★★
Security: ★★★★	Cleanliness: ★★★★
Insect Control: ★★	Facilities: ★★★

This park is divided into five camping areas, along with a screened lean-to area. Armadillo Hill has 45-foot grassy back-ins. The sites are very open but are surrounded by forest. Sites 4 and 5 are very close to the playground, which some campers may not prefer. Sites 16–22 have a partial view of the water, but all sites are some distance from the water's edge. The restrooms are clean and modern and have flush toilets, but there is no shower. Bois d'Arc Ridge has all 110-foot pull-throughs, making it the best bet for larger rigs or anyone who doesn't want to spend time parking. These grassy sites are forested, offering good shade, but are also away from the water. The Cedar Hollow Group Trailer area consists of 110-foot pull-throughs on the blacktop, with no shade and no direct access to the water—not the prettiest camping area. Fossil Ridge, however, is much nicer, with grassy, forested sites that overlook the water (especially 152–155). The Elm Point area is similarly close to the water, with 40-foot back-ins but no shade. It would be difficult not to find a campsite to your liking in this state park, but as the office staff agree, don't come in the dead heat of August!

BASICS
Operated By: Texas Parks and Wildlife. **Open:** All year. **Site Assignment:** Reservations, call (512) 389-8900 48 hrs. in advance; refund (minus $5) w/ 48-hour notice; less than 48 hours, lose 1-night deposit. **Registration:** At office. (Late arrivals use drop box at entrance.) **Fee:** RV (full), $17; water/electric, $15; water, $12–$14; plus $2 entrance fee per person; V, MC, D accepted in the office or for reservation. **Parking:** At site.

FACILITIES
Number of RV-only Sites: 95. **Number of Tent-only Sites:** 47. **Hookups:** Electric (30 amps), water, sewer. **Each Site:** Fire ring. **Dump Station:** Yes. **Laundry:** No. **Pay Phone:** No. **Restrooms and Showers:** Yes. **Fuel:** No. **Propane:** No. **Internal Roads:** Paved. **RV Service:** No. **Market:** 8 mi. south (Exit 69). **Restaurant:** 3 mi. across lake. **General Store:** Yes (marina). **Vending:** Yes. **Swimming:** Lake. **Playground:** Yes (3). **Other:** Rec hall, pavilion, fish-cleaning station, lighted fishing pier. **Activities:** Swimming, boating, fishing, hiking, mountain biking. **Nearby Attractions:** Eisenhower Birthplace Historical State Park, Bonham State Park, Lake Texoma, Hagerman National Wildlife Refuge. **Additional Information:** Eisenhower State Park Office, (903) 465-1956.

RESTRICTIONS
Pets: On 6-ft. leash, cleaned up after. **Fires:** Grill only. **Alcoholic Beverages:** Not allowed. **Vehicle Maximum Length:** No limit. **Other:** All visitors must pay $3 entrance fee per day.

TO GET THERE
Take US 75 out of Dallas; take Exit 72 to TX 91 north to Denison Dam to FM 1310W. Traveling 1.8 mi. to Park Road 20 entrance.

DONNA   MAP, D-4
Victoria Palms Resort

reserve america™

602 North Victoria Rd., 78537.
T: (956) 464-7801 or (800) 551-5303;
www.victoriapalms.com.

🚐 ★★★   ⛺ n/a

Beauty: ★★★★	Site Privacy: ★★★
Spaciousness: ★★★★	Quiet: ★★★★
Security: ★★★★	Cleanliness: ★★★★
Insect Control: ★★★★	Facilities: ★★★★

This retirement resort in suburban Donna offers extensive and well-maintained recreational facilities. Scheduled classes and entertainment (in-season) help this large complex retain a community atmosphere. It also offers easy access to shopping and restaurants and extremely tidy sites. The spacious sites are laid out in rows, and most feature back-in parking. All parking is paved. Newer sites are completely open, with no shade and no privacy. We recommend the older sites, which enjoy a bit of shade and privacy. Each of the older sites contains one lovely mature palm tree and one mature grapefruit tree. Guests are encouraged to pick their own grapefruits. In all other respects, the sites are exactly alike. This gated and fenced property offers good security. Avoid the Lower Rio Grande Valley in the summer, and be sure to make advance reservations in the winter.

BASICS
Operated By: Stephen Hynes. **Open:** All year. **Site Assignment:** Reservations for 3–4 month min. w/ $250 deposit; $25 cancellation fee w/ notice by Oct. 15, call (800) 551-5303. **Registration:** At office. **Fee:** $25–$45. **Parking:** At site.

FACILITIES
Number of RV-only Sites: 760. **Hookups:** Electric (50 amps), water, sewer, cable TV, data port, Wi-Fi, telephone. **Each Site:** 1 palm tree, 1 grapefruit tree, concrete parking slot, concrete patio. **Dump Station:** No. **Laundry:** Yes. **Pay Phone:** Internet phones. **Restrooms and Showers:** Yes. **Fuel:** No. **Propane:** Truck. **Internal Roads:** Paved. **RV Service:** 5 mi. south in Donna. **Market:** 5 mi. south in Donna. **Restaurant:** On site, open in the winter only. **General Store:** 5 mi. southwest in Weslaco. **Vending:** Yes. **Swimming:** Pool. **Playground:** No. **Other:** Tennis courts, mail room, card rooms, library, ballroom, beauty & barber shop, rec center, lounge, sewing room, billiard room, exercise facilities, computer club, poolside bar. **Activities:** Fishing, hunting, arts & crafts, dancing, shuffleboard, horseshoes, golf.

Nearby Attractions: Sabal Palm Audubon Center & Sanctuary, Gladys Porter Zoo, Brownsville Battlefields, Confederate Air Force Rio Grande Valley Wing, Historic Brownsville Museum. **Additional Information:** Donna Chamber of Commerce, (956) 464-3272; Rio Grande Valley Chamber of Commerce, (956) 968-3141.

RESTRICTIONS
Pets: On leash only. **Fires:** Only in your own grill. **Alcoholic Beverages:** Allowed. **Vehicle Maximum Length:** 60 ft. **Other:** No tents.

TO GET THERE
From US 83, exit at Victoria Rd. and go south 0.25 mi., entrance on the left.

EL PASO   MAP, B-1
Mission RV Park

1420 RV Dr., 79928.
T: (800) 447-3795 or (915) 859-1133;
www.missionrvparklp.com.

🚐 ★★★★   ⛺ ★★★

Beauty: ★★★	Site Privacy: ★★★★
Spaciousness: ★★★	Quiet: ★★★★
Security: ★★★★★	Cleanliness: ★★★★★
Insect Control: ★★★★	Facilities: ★★★★★

This huge RV park is laid out like a V, with the 2 branches off-limits to pets. While most areas border nothing much to look at (there is a mobile home along the "E" strip to the south/southwest and a residential area to the northeast), there is a fairly nice view of the mountains from sites E69–97, only slightly spoiled by a commercial area in the foreground. Most of the perimeter of the park is fenced off with barbed wire; in the rest of the areas, a stone or chain link fence provides security. Pull-throughs are a good 70 feet long and 21 feet wide; back-ins are equally wide and vary up to 45 feet long. While most sites are open to the sun without any tree cover, end sites do get the benefit of trees and other vegetation and are therefore the best sites. Back-ins D49–97 also have a tree and are therefore a good choice for those willing to forego a pull-through. The recreation areas are fenced off and well maintained. Likewise, the laundry facilities are huge, modern, and clean, with plenty of space and even an ironing board. Restrooms and showers are clean and modern. This campground is clean, safe, and delightful, lacking only in shade trees to be an unbeatable destination.

BASICS
Operated By: Phylis Bracewelle. **Open:** All year. **Site Assignment:** Upon registration (flexible). **Registration:** At office. (Late arrivals register w/security in guard box at gate.) **Fee:** $28.50. **Parking:** At site.

FACILITIES
Number of RV-only Sites: 188. **Number of Tent-only Sites:** 2. **Hookups:** Electric (30, 50 amps), water, sewer. **Each Site:** Overturned cable spool for a table. **Dump Station:** Yes. **Laundry:** Yes. **Pay Phone:** Yes. **Restrooms and Showers:** Yes. **Fuel:** No. **Propane:** Yes (Mon. only). **Internal Roads:** Dirt. **RV Service:** Yes. **Market:** 4 mi. north or south. **Restaurant:** 2 mi. west. **General Store:** Yes. **Vending:** Yes. **Swimming:** Pool (indoor). **Playground:**

Yes. **Other:** Jacuzzi, wash/wax RV service, dog walk, RV storage, sell utility trailers. **Activities:** Basketball, tennis, horseshoes, Mexico tours. **Nearby Attractions:** Mexico. **Additional Information:** El Paso Chamber of Commerce, (915) 534-0500.

RESTRICTIONS

Pets: On leash, cleaned up after, restricted from half of park. **Fires:** Grill only. **Alcoholic Beverages:** At sites. **Vehicle Maximum Length:** 75 ft. **Other:** No motorcycles (Rule sheet provided along w/ campground map).

TO GET THERE

From I-10, take Exit 34 east onto the north loop of Americas Ave. and drive 1.8 mi. As soon as possible, get into the far left lane and take the turnaround under the overpass. Drive 1.6 mi. on Joe Battle Blvd. (straight through past the Van Buren exit). Turn right onto Rojas and drive 0.2 mi. Turn right onto RV Dr., then go another 0.2 mi. and turn left at the sign into the campground entrance. Pull in as far as possible past the office on the right to allow others to enter.

FAIRFIELD · MAP, B-5
Fairfield Lake State Park

reserve america

123 State Park Rd. 64, 75840. T: (903) 389-4514; www.reserveamerica.com.

🚐 ★★★★   ▲ ★★★★

Beauty: ★★★★	Site Privacy: ★★★
Spaciousness: ★★★	Quiet: ★★★★★
Security: ★★★★	Cleanliness: ★★★★
Insect Control: ★★★	Facilities: ★★★★

Fairfield Lake State Park is 1,460 acres northeast of the City of Fairfield in Freestone County. The park was acquired in 1971 and 1972 by lease from Texas Utilities and was opened to the public in 1976. The history of the area around Fairfield Lake State Park resembles that of much of rural eastern Texas. Long occupied by Native Americans who exploited its waterways, the land was first broken in the mid-19th century and planted in cotton and corn by Anglo farmers and, about a third of the time, their African-American slaves. Following the Civil War, the crop-lien system took root. Blacks and whites alike worked in the service of the cotton crop until after World War II, when changes in American agriculture and increased employment opportunities away from the farm brought an end to the era of widespread cotton farming. Since that time, cattle ranching has prevailed throughout the region. The human population of the Brown Creek area, never large, is now widely scattered over the region. In this sparsely populated area, Texas Utilities built its dam, creating Fairfield Lake as a cooling system for its power plant.

BASICS

Operated By: Texas Parks and Wildlife. **Open:** All year. **Site Assignment:** Reservations can be made 11 months in advance. **Registration:** At office. **Fee:** Single, $12–$18; group, $75. **Parking:** Limit of 2 vehicles per site; extra parking available for a fee.

FACILITIES

Number of Multipurpose Sites: 270. **Hookups:** Yes. **Dump Station:** Yes. **Laundry:** No. **Pay Phone:** Yes. **Restrooms and Showers:** Yes. **Fuel:** No. **Propane:** No. **Internal Roads:** Paved. **RV Service:** No. **Market:** No. **Restaurant:** No. **General Store:** Yes. **Vending:** No. **Swimming:** Yes. **Playground:** Yes. **Other:** Check hunt dates. Park gate only locks during park hunts, otherwise open 24 hours. **Activities:** Amphitheater, biking, bird-watching, boating, canoeing, fishing, water & jet skiing.

RESTRICTIONS

Pets: On a 6-ft. leash, never unattended, under control at all times, cleaned up after. **Fires:** Fires may be built only in campsite grills, fire rings, or fireplaces. Some sites allow only containerized fuel fires. When warranted, fire bans are implemented by county judges and/or county commissioners courts. Inquire when making reservations. **Alcoholic Beverages:** It is an offense to consume or display an open container of an alcoholic beverage in a public place or sell alcoholic beverages w/in a state park.

TO GET THERE

From Houston: Take I-45N to Fairfield. Take Hwy. 84E to FM 488. Go north on FM 488 to FM 2570. Go east to the park entrance. From Dallas: Take I-45 south to Fairfield. Take Hwy. 84E to FM 488. Go north on FM 488 to FM 2570. Go east to the park entrance.

FALCON HEIGHTS · MAP, D-3, D-4
Falcon State Park

reserve america

P.O. Box 2, 78545. T: (956) 848-5327; www.reserveamerica.com.

🚐 ★★★★   ▲ ★★★★

Beauty: ★★★★	Site Privacy: ★★★
Spaciousness: ★★★	Quiet: ★★★★
Security: ★★★★	Cleanliness: ★★★★
Insect Control: ★★★	Facilities: ★★★★

Falcon State Park is 572.6 (144 developed) acres located north of Roma at the southern end of the 98,960-surface-acre International Falcon Reservoir in Starr and Zapata Counties. The park was leased from the International Boundary and Water Commission in 1949 and was opened to the public in 1965. Falcon Dam was dedicated by Mexican President Adolfo Ruiz Cortines and President Dwight D. Eisenhower in October 1953. The waters of the Rio Grande River have formed a beautiful 60-mile-long lake behind the dam. This dam was built for conservation, irrigation, power, flood control, and recreational purposes. Gently rolling hills are covered by mesquite, huisache, wild olive, ebony, and cactus native grasses. Falcon Lake is a big fishing paradise, especially for those seeking black and white bass, catfish, and stripers. The area is very popular with bird-watchers; varied and interesting bird life consists of common resident birds, which range throughout the American Southwest, and many of the tropical species for which this is the northwestern most out-post. Also, there are uncommon varieties such as the small green kingfisher and the varied bunting.

BASICS

Operated By: Texas Parks and Wildlife. **Open:** All year. **Site Assignment:** Reservations can be made 11 months in advance. **Registration:** At office. **Fee:** Single, $12–$14; shelter, $18–$30; group hall, $120. **Parking:** Limit of 2 vehicles per site; extra parking available for a fee.

FACILITIES

Number of Multipurpose Sites: 130. **Hookups:** Yes. **Dump Station:** Yes. **Laundry:** No. **Pay Phone:** Yes. **Restrooms and Showers:** Yes. **Fuel:** No. **Propane:** No. **Internal Roads:** Paved. **RV Service:** No. **Market:** No. **Restaurant:** No. **General Store:** Yes. **Vending:** No. **Swimming:** Yes. **Playground:** Yes. **Other:** Gate is open 6 a.m.–10 p.m. If you will be a late arrival, you must call the park prior to 5 p.m. on arrival date for late arrival instructions. **Activities:** Boating, fishing, waterskiing.

RESTRICTIONS

Pets: On a 6-ft. leash, never unattended, under control at all times, cleaned up after. **Fires:** Fires may be built only in campsite grills, fire rings, or fireplaces. Some sites allow only containerized fuel fires. When warranted, fire bans are implemented by county judges and/or county commissioners courts. Inquire when making reservations. **Alcoholic Beverages:** It is an offense to consume or display an open container of an alcoholic beverage in a public place or sell alcoholic beverages w/in a state park.

TO GET THERE

From Laredo, take Hwy. 83 south to Falcon. From Falcon Heights, take Park Road 46 to park headquarters. From Corpus Christi, take Hwy. 44 west through Alice 10 mi. Turn south on SH 359 to Zapata. Turn south on Hwy. 83 to Falcon. From Falcon Heights, take Park Road 46 to park headquarters. The park is 30 mi. south of Zapata and 14 mi. west of Roma.

GALVESTON · MAP, C-5
Galveston Island State Park

14901 FM 3005, P.O. Box 156A, 77554.
T: (409) 737-1222; www.reserveamerica.com.

🚐 ★★★   ▲ ★★

Beauty: ★★★	Site Privacy: ★
Spaciousness: ★★	Quiet: ★★★
Security: ★★★	Cleanliness: ★★★
Insect Control: ★	Facilities: ★★★★

Campsites are cookie-cutter dull and extremely close to one another. The draw is the pristine beach (mere yards from campsites) and its wildlife. Over 300 species of birds have been recorded here. Observation blinds and platforms enrich the bird-watching experience. Anglers appreciate the choice of ocean or freshwater intermittently stocked with bass, catfish, perch, and rainbow trout. Each Lilliputian campsite has paved back-in parking and absolutely no shade or privacy. There is also a group camping area. Mosquitoes and heat can be brutal here. We recommend insect repellent and a golf-style umbrella for each member of the family. Visit during the week to avoid crowds. Go during late spring, summer, or fall if you plan to sun and swim. We visited in December, and the weather was pleasant for beach walks. This suburban park is situated on a major roadway—valuables should be protected, though gates are locked at night.

BASICS

Operated By: Texas Parks and Wildlife. **Open:** All year. **Site Assignment:** Reservations (512) 389-8900; reservations must be made at least 48 hrs. in advance; deposit required (equivalent to 1-night fee) to hold reservation; cancellations more than 2 days prior to reservation result in $5 fee; cancellations w/in 2 days of reservation result in loss of deposit. **Registration:** At headquarters. **Fee:** Premium, $25; standard, $15; daily charge per person (13 and over), $5; fee required for more than 2 vehicles. **Parking:** At site.

FACILITIES

Number of RV-only Sites: 120. **Hookups:** Electric (30, 50 amps), water. **Each Site:** Picnic table, grill, fire ring (most sites). **Dump Station:** Yes. **Laundry:** No. **Pay Phone:** Yes. **Restrooms and Showers:** Yes. **Fuel:** No. **Propane:** No. **Internal Roads:** Paved. **RV Service:** 25 mi. west in La Marque. **Market:** 2 mi. east in Galveston. **Restaurant:** 1 mi. east in Galveston. **General Store:** Wal-Mart 10 mi. east in Galveston. **Vending:** Beverages. **Swimming:** Beach. **Playground:** No. **Other:** Bathhouse on the beach, outdoor showers, interpretive center, gift shop, screened shelters, fish-cleaning shelter. **Activities:** Picnicking, fishing, bird-watching, hiking, walking, mountain biking, swimming (at your own risk). **Nearby Attractions:** Moody Gardens, numerous historical homes in Galveston, the Railroad Museum, the Strand Historical District, Tall Ship Elissa (an 1877 sailing vessel), the Seaport Museum, Ocean Star Offshore Drilling Rig & Museum, attractions in Houston & San Jacinto. **Additional Information:** Galveston Chamber of Commerce, (409) 763-5326.

RESTRICTIONS

Pets: On leash only. **Fires:** In grills, fire rings only. **Alcoholic Beverages:** Not allowed. **Vehicle Maximum Length:** 40 ft. **Other:** Max. 8 people per campsite; quiet time 10 p.m.–6 a.m.; 14-day stay limit; swim at your own risk; no glass on beach; beware of poisonous snakes, jellyfish, & undercurrents.

TO GET THERE

From I-45, drive south on 61st St. to Seawall Blvd. Turn right on Seawall Blvd., and then right on Seawall (FM 3005). Follow FM 3005 10 mi. Park entrance is on the left.

GOLIAD   MAP, C-4
Goliad State Park

108 Park Rd. 6, 77963-3206. T: (361) 645-3405; www.reserveamerica.com.

🚐 ★★★★　　🏕 ★★★★

Beauty: ★★★★　　Site Privacy: ★★★★
Spaciousness: ★★★★　　Quiet: ★★★★★
Security: ★★★★　　Cleanliness: ★★★★
Insect Control: ★★★　　Facilities: ★★★★

A wonderful opportunity to experience a blending of natural and cultural resources awaits visitors to Goliad State Park. Situated within three ecological zones and located on the San Antonio River, the park offers a variety of flora and fauna blending with tangible remains of Texas history and culture. The park serves as a hub for visiting the Mission Espíritu Santo State Historic Site (located in the park), the Presidio La Bahía, the Ignacio Zaragoza Birthplace State Historic Site, Fannin Battleground State Historic Site, the Goliad Historic District, and Mission Rosario State Historic Site. Surrounding ranches and oil fields remind visitors of the role the area played in the unfolding of Texas' history and economy. The park offers outstanding recreational activities and facilities. At Goliad State Park, tour the beautiful reconstructed Franciscan Mission Espíritu Santo—home of the largest ranching operation in Texas in the 18th century. Enjoy the serenity of this Spanish colonial church and view exhibits that explore the history and daily life of the missionaries and Indian converts—including some of the original artifacts they used.

BASICS

Operated By: Texas Parks and Wildlife. **Open:** All year. **Site Assignment:** Reservations can be made 11 months in advance. **Registration:** At office. **Fee:** Single, $8–$15; group shelter, $21; group hall, $65. **Parking:** Limit of 2 vehicles per site; extra parking available for a fee.

FACILITIES

Number of Multipurpose Sites: 108. **Hookups:** Yes. **Dump Station:** Yes. **Laundry:** No. **Pay Phone:** Yes. **Restrooms and Showers:** Yes. **Fuel:** No. **Propane:** No. **Internal Roads:** Paved. **RV Service:** No. **Market:** 1 mi. **Restaurant:** No. **General Store:** Yes. **Vending:** No. **Swimming:** Yes. **Playground:** Yes. **Other:** Gate to the park opens at 7 a.m. & locks at 10 p.m. Call the park before 5 p.m. for late arrival notification & gate combination on your arrival date. The swimming pool located across the street from the park is open Memorial Day–Labor Day 2–7 p.m. except Wed. for maintenance. **Activities:** Biking, canoeing, fishing, museum & exhibits, picnicking, hiking.

RESTRICTIONS

Pets: On a 6-ft. leash, never unattended, under control at all times, cleaned up after. **Fires:** Fires may be built only in campsite grills, fire rings, or fireplaces. Some sites allow only containerized fuel fires. When warranted, fire bans are implemented by county judges and/or county commissioners courts. Inquire when making reservations. **Alcoholic Beverages:** It is an offense to consume or display an open container of an alcoholic beverage in a public place or sell alcoholic beverages w/in a state park.

TO GET THERE

From Austin, take Hwy. 183S to Goliad. From Houston, take Hwy. 59S to Goliad. Take a right on Hwy. 77A/183 and travel 1 mi. south. From Corpus Christi, take I-37 to Hwy. 77. Take a right on Hwy. 77 to Refugio. Tale a left on Hwy. 77A/183N to Goliad State Park. From San Antonio, take Hwy. 181 to Kenedy. Take a left on FM 72 then right on FM 239. Take a left on Hwy. 59 to Hwy. 77A/183. Turn right on 77A/183 and go 1 mi. south to Goliad State Park. From Laredo, take Hwy. 59N to Goliad. Turn right on Hwy. 77A/183 and go 1 mi. to Goliad State Park.

GRAPELAND   MAP, B-5
Mission Tejas State Park

Rte. 2 Box 108, 75844. T: (936) 687-2394; www.reserveamerica.com.

🚐 ★★★★　　🏕 ★★★★

Beauty: ★★★　　Site Privacy: ★★★
Spaciousness: ★★★　　Quiet: ★★★★
Security: ★★★★　　Cleanliness: ★★★★
Insect Control: ★★★　　Facilities: ★★★★

Mission Tejas State Park is a 363.5-acre park in Houston County, 22 miles northeast of Crockett. The park was acquired in 1957 by Legislative Act from the Texas Forest Service, at which time it was opened to the public. The park was built in 1934 by Co. 888 of Civilian Conservation Corps (CCC) as a commemorative representation of Mission San Francisco de los Tejas, the first Spanish mission in the province of Texas, which was established in 1690. Also in the park is the restored Rice Family Log Home, built in 1828 and restored in 1974. The home, which Joseph Redmund Rice, Sr. constructed between 1828 and 1838, is one of the oldest structures in the area. The home served as a stopover for immigrants, adventurers, and local residents traveling the Old San Antonio Road across pioneer Texas. Activities include camping, picnicking, hiking, and fishing. A pond located near the picnic area offers an excellent opportunity to explore aquatic life and fish. Hiking and nature trails provide access to the natural beauty of the east Texas Pineywoods. The dogwood are beautiful the last week or so of March, usually around the 25th. Facilities include commemorative representation of Mission San Francisco de los Tejas; the restored Rice Family Log Home; picnic sites; campsites with water; campsites with water and electricity; campsites with water, electricity, and sewer; group picnic areas; a group picnic pavilion; restrooms with and without showers; a group camping area; an amphitheater; a trailer dump station; 3.5 miles of hiking trails; a playground; and a nature pond (approximately 1 acre in size).

BASICS

Operated By: Texas Parks and Wildlife. **Open:** All year. **Site Assignment:** Reservations can be made up to 16 weeks in advance. **Registration:** At office. **Fee:** Single, $8–$12; picnic, $25; youth area, $25. **Parking:** 2 vehicles per site.

FACILITIES

Number of Multipurpose Sites: 29. **Hookups:** Yes. **Dump Station:** Yes. **Laundry:** No. **Pay Phone:** Yes. **Restrooms and Showers:** Yes. **Fuel:** No. **Propane:** No. **Internal Roads:** Paved. **RV Service:**

Yes. **Market:** More than 10 mi. **Restaurant:** No. **General Store:** No. **Vending:** No. **Swimming:** No. **Playground:** Yes. **Activities:** Biking, fishing, nature study, picnicking, hiking. **Nearby Attractions:** Swimming.

RESTRICTIONS

Pets: On a 6-ft. leash, never unattended, under control at all times, cleaned up after. **Fires:** Fires may be built only in campsite grills, fire rings, or fireplaces. Some sites allow only containerized fuel fires. When warranted, fire bans are implemented by county judges and/or county commissioners courts. Inquire when making reservations. **Alcoholic Beverages:** It is an offense to consume or display an open container of an alcoholic beverage in a public place or sell alcoholic beverages w/in a state park. **Vehicle Maximum Length:** 30 ft.

TO GET THERE

From Houston, take I-45 north to Huntsville, then Hwy. 19 north to Crockett, then Hwy. 21 east 21 mi. to the park. Or take Hwy. 59 to Lufkin, then 69 north to Alto, then Hwy. 21 west 12 mi. to park. From Dallas, take I-45 south to Centerville, then Hwy. 7 east to Crockett, then Hwy. 21 east 21 mi. to the park. Or take Hwy. 175 south to Jacksonville, then Hwy. 69 south to Alto, then Hwy. 21 west 12 mi. to the park.

HOUSTON   MAP, C-5
Houston Leisure RV Resort

1601 South Main St., 77562.
T: (281) 426-3576 or (800) 982-8285;
www.gocampingamerica.com.

🚐 ★★★   ⛺ ★★★

Beauty: ★★★   Site Privacy: ★★★
Spaciousness: ★★★   Quiet: ★★★
Security: ★★★   Cleanliness: ★★★★
Insect Control: ★★   Facilities: ★★★

Located in suburban Highlands, Houston Leisure is approximately 19 miles east of downtown Houston. There are restaurants and shopping within minutes of the park, and attractions such as Space Center Houston and the Battleship Texas are easily accessible. The campground is attractive and consists of nine rows of long narrow pull-throughs and five rows of back-ins. Parking spaces were paved in the past, but they now more closely resemble gravel. Site size is average, and site privacy is poor. Many of the sites have a shady tree or two while a few others are completely open. Security is fair—the office is attended until 11 p.m., but there are no gates. Avoid Houston in the heat of the summer.

BASICS

Operated By: Richard McBroom. **Open:** All year. **Site Assignment:** Sites assigned; credit card holds reservation, no-show charged 1 night. **Registration:** At office in store, night host & self-registration. **Fee:** RV, $29–$32; tent, $18 (3 nights max.); for 2 people; each additional person, $2; cash, check, V, MC, D, AE. **Parking:** At site, in parking lot.

FACILITIES

Number of RV-only Sites: 205. **Number of Tent-only Sites:** 5. **Hookups:** Electric (30, 50, 100 amps),

water, sewer, cable TV. **Each Site:** Picnic table, asphalt pad. **Dump Station:** Yes. **Laundry:** Yes. **Pay Phone:** Yes. **Restrooms and Showers:** Yes. **Fuel:** No. **Propane:** Yes. **Internal Roads:** Paved. **RV Service:** 5 mi. in Channel View. **Market:** 1 mi. north. **Restaurant:** W/in 1 mi. **General Store:** Park store, groceries and RV supplies. **Vending:** No. **Swimming:** Pool. **Playground:** Yes. **Other:** Pavilion, exercise room. **Activities:** Basketball, tennis, horseshoes, shuffleboard. **Nearby Attractions:** Space Center Houston, Battleship Texas, Moody Gardens aquarium, rainforest & discovery pyramids, San Jacinto Monument & Battleground, Arm & Bayou Nature Center, Traders Village outdoor market, Lone Star Flight Museum in Galveston. **Additional Information:** Greater Houston CVB, (800) 4-HOUSTON.

RESTRICTIONS

Pets: 6-ft. leash max. **Fires:** Not allowed, bring your own grill. **Alcoholic Beverages:** Allowed. **Vehicle Maximum Length:** 45 ft. (sites vary). **Other:** Quiet hours enforced.

TO GET THERE

From Houston, take I-10 east to Exit 787/Crosby-Lynchburg Rd. Drive north 0.5 mi. on South Main St. and the resort is on the right.

HUNTSVILLE   MAP, B-5
Huntsville State Park

reserve america

P.O. Box 508, 77342-0508.
T: (936) 295-5644 or (800) 792-1112;
www.reserveamerica.com.

🚐 ★★★★   ⛺ ★★★★

Beauty: ★★★★   Site Privacy: ★★★
Spaciousness: ★★★   Quiet: ★★★
Security: ★★★★   Cleanliness: ★★★
Insect Control: ★★★   Facilities: ★★★★

Because of its proximity to Houston and its rural feel, Huntsville State Park is one of the most popular state parks in Texas, with campgrounds booking to capacity months in advance. The 210-acre Lake Raven is stocked with crappie, perch, catfish, and bass. The gently sloping terrain is complemented by plenty of open space and three playgrounds. Huntsville is a great place for children to expend their seemingly limitless energy. Loblolly and short-leaf pines, trees typical of the Texas Pineywoods region, provide excellent shade cover. Campsites are spacious, with paved parking and some pull-throughs large enough to handle 56-foot RVs. The most private sites, 174 and 175, are quickly taken year-round. When planning your visit, avoid hot, humid August and rainy September. Gates are locked at 10 p.m., making security good.

BASICS

Operated By: Texas Parks and Wildlife. **Open:** All year. **Site Assignment:** Reservations (512) 389-8900; reservations must be made at least 48 hrs. in advance; deposit required (equivalent to 1-night fee) to hold reservation; cancellations more than 2 days prior to reservation result in $5 fee; cancellations

w/in 2 days of reservation result in loss of deposit. **Registration:** At headquarters. **Fee:** RV (water/electric), $16; tent, $12; daily charge per person (13 and over), $4; cash, check, V, MC, D. **Parking:** At site.

FACILITIES

Number of RV-only Sites: 62. **Number of Tent-only Sites:** 125. **Hookups:** Electric (20 amps), water. **Each Site:** Picnic table, grill, fire ring, lantern post. **Dump Station:** Yes. **Laundry:** No. **Pay Phone:** Yes. **Restrooms and Showers:** Yes. **Fuel:** No. **Propane:** No. **Internal Roads:** Paved. **RV Service:** 10 mi. south in New Waverly. **Market:** 5 mi. north in Huntsville. **Restaurant:** 5 mi. north in Huntsville. **General Store:** 5 mi. north in Huntsville. **Vending:** Beverages; concession stand open May–Sept. **Swimming:** Yes. **Playground:** Yes. **Other:** Sandy beach on lake, interpretive center, gift shop, group picnic shelter (capacity 75 people), group lodge (capacity 150 people). **Activities:** Picnicking, swimming, boating (rental of canoes, paddle boats, & flat-bottomed boats in season), fishing, hiking, biking, horseback riding, miniature golf. **Nearby Attractions:** General Sam Houston's Old Homestead, Sam Houston Memorial Museum, Sam Houston Visitor Center & Statue, The Walls Unit (the first Texas prison), the Prison Museum, Historic Huntsville (one of Texas' oldest towns). **Additional Information:** Horseback riding at Lake Raven Stables, (936) 295-1985; Huntsville Chamber of Commerce, (936) 295-8113.

RESTRICTIONS

Pets: On leash only. **Fires:** In grills, fire rings only. **Alcoholic Beverages:** Not allowed. **Vehicle Maximum Length:** 56 ft. **Other:** Max. 8 people per campsite; quiet time 10 p.m.–6 a.m.; 14-day stay limit; gathering of firewood prohibited.

TO GET THERE

From Exit 109 on I-45, drive 6 mi. southwest on Park Rd. 40.

JACKSBORO   MAP, A-4
Fort Richardson State Park

reserve america

228 Park Rd. 61, 76458. T: (940) 567-3506;
www.reserveamerica.com.

🚐 ★★★★   ⛺ ★★★★

Beauty: ★★★★   Site Privacy: ★★★
Spaciousness: ★★★   Quiet: ★★★★★
Security: ★★★★   Cleanliness: ★★★★
Insect Control: ★★★   Facilities: ★★★★

Fort Richardson State Park, located northwest of Fort Worth in Jack County, contains more than 450 acres. Fort site structures include seven of the original buildings that have been restored: the post hospital; the officers' quarters; a powder magazine; a morgue; a commissary; a guardhouse; and a bakery, which baked 600 loaves per day. There are also two replicas: officers' and enlisted men's barracks. The officers' barracks houses the interpretive center. Activities include historical study, picnicking, camping, fishing, hiking, day-use equestrian, nature study, wading in the creek (seasonal), and swimming (accessible via Lost Creek Reservoir State Trailway or by road). Guided historical tours are held at 10 a.m. on Saturday and Sunday and by appointment; tour fees apply. Special events held throughout the year include military reenactments, baarbecue cook-off, a trout fishing tournament, and living history presentations. Facilities include screened shelters; campsites with water and electricity; hike-in primitive sites; picnic sites; a lighted group picnic pavilion; restrooms with and without showers; volleyball court; horseshoe pits; a trailer dump station; Prickly Pear Trail for hiking in the open prairie land for 2 miles; a nature walk, which follows Lost Creek for 0.25 miles; the Lost Creek Reservoir 10-mile hike, bike, and equestrian trail; swimming beach on Lost Creek Reservoir; and a Texas State Park Store. Fishing is allowed in the eight-acre Quarry Lake located by park headquarters.

BASICS

Operated By: Texas Parks and Wildlife. **Open:** All year. **Site Assignment:** Reservations can be made up to 16 weeks in advance. **Registration:** At office. **Fee:** Single, $16–$18; primitive, $5; shelter, $22–$24; picnic pavilion, $50. **Parking:** 2 vehicle per site.

FACILITIES

Number of Multipurpose Sites: 134. **Hookups:** Yes. **Dump Station:** Yes. **Laundry:** No. **Pay Phone:** Yes. **Restrooms and Showers:** Yes. **Fuel:** No. **Propane:** No. **Internal Roads:** Paved. **RV Service:** Yes. **Market:** No. **Restaurant:** No. **General Store:** Yes. **Vending:** Yes. **Swimming:** Yes. **Playground:** Yes. **Activities:** Biking, fishing, horseshoe pits, hiking, horseback riding, picnicking, swimming, volleyball.

RESTRICTIONS

Pets: On a 6-ft. leash, never unattended, under control at all times, cleaned up after. **Fires:** Fires may be built only in campsite grills, fire rings, or fireplaces. Some sites allow only containerized fuel fires. When warranted, fire bans are implemented by county judges and/or county commissioners courts. Inquire when making reservations. **Alcoholic Beverages:** It is an offense to consume or display an open container of an alcoholic beverage in a public place or sell alcoholic beverages w/in a state park. **Vehicle Maximum Length:** 80 ft.

TO GET THERE

From Ft. Worth: Take 199N into Jacksboro. Park will be on left, 0.5 mi. past Village Kitchen, a 24-hour cafe. From Denton: Take 380W into Jacksboro. Park will be on left, 0.5 mi. past Village Kitchen, a 24-hour cafe. From Mineral Wells: Take 281N into Jacksboro. Park will be on left, 0.5 mi. past Village Kitchen, a 24-hour cafe. From Wichita Falls: Take 281S in Jacksboro. Park will be on right, 0.5 mi. past Court House square.

JASPER	MAP, B-5
Martin Dies, Jr. State Park	

reserve america

Rte. 4 Box 274, 75951-9419. T: (409) 384-5231; www.reserveamerica.com.

🚐 ★★★   ⛺ ★★★★

Beauty: ★★★★	Site Privacy: ★★★★
Spaciousness: ★★★★	Quiet: ★★★★★
Security: ★★★★	Cleanliness: ★★★★
Insect Control: ★★★	Facilities: ★★★★

Martin Dies, Jr. State Park, until 1965 known as the Dam B State Park, is a 705-acre recreational area in Jasper and Tyler Counties between Woodville and Jasper on B. A. Steinhagen Reservoir (15,000 acres). Located at the edge of the Big Thicket National Preserve, the park is in the heavily forested area known as the East Texas Pineywoods. The park has numerous creeks, known as sloughs, and cypress, willow, beech, magnolia, and sweet bay are common. Each fall the golden hues of beeches are brilliant against the reds of blackgums and oaks, mixed among the evergreen pines. Hiking trails provide excellent opportunities to view wildlife, including woodland warblers, woodpeckers, bluebirds, herons, wood ducks, cranes, and alligators, as the park is adjacent to Angelina-Neches-Dam B Wildlife Management Area.

BASICS

Operated By: Texas Parks and Wildlife. **Open:** All year. **Site Assignment:** Reservations can be made 11 months in advance. **Registration:** At office. **Fee:** Single, $8–$15; group shelter, $18–$20; cabin, $45; group hall, $100. **Parking:** Limit of 2 vehicles per site; extra parking available for a fee.

FACILITIES

Number of Multipurpose Sites: 446. **Hookups:** Yes. **Dump Station:** Yes. **Laundry:** No. **Pay Phone:** Yes. **Restrooms and Showers:** Yes. **Fuel:** W/in 0.25 mi. **Propane:** No. **Internal Roads:** Paved. **RV Service:** No. **Market:** No. **Restaurant:** No. **General Store:** Yes. **Vending:** No. **Swimming:** Yes. **Playground:** No. **Other:** This park does not have a gate. **Activities:** Amphitheater, birdwatching, boating, canoeing, fishing, nature study, hiking, waterskiing, wildlife viewing.

RESTRICTIONS

Pets: On a 6-ft. leash, never unattended, under control at all times, cleaned up after. **Fires:** Fires may be built only in campsite grills, fire rings, or fireplaces. Some sites allow only containerized fuel fires. When warranted, fire bans are implemented by county judges and/or county commissioners courts. Inquire when making reservations. **Alcoholic Beverages:** It is an offense to consume or display an open container of an alcoholic beverage in a public place or sell alcoholic beverages w/in a state park.

TO GET THERE

From Houston: Take US 59N to Livingston. Right (east) on US 190 to Woodville. Continue on US 190 another 17 mi., follow signs to park. From Dallas: Take US 175 to Jacksonville. Right (south) on Hwy. 69 to Woodville. Left (east) on US 190, go 17 mi., follow signs to park.

JASPER	MAP, B-5
Rayburn Park	

reserve america

Rte. 3 Box 486, 75951-9598. T: (409) 384-5716; www.reserveamerica.com.

🚐 ★★★★   ⛺ ★★★★

Beauty: ★★★★	Site Privacy: ★★
Spaciousness: ★★	Quiet: ★★★★
Security: ★★★★	Cleanliness: ★★★★
Insect Control: ★★★	Facilities: ★★★

Rayburn Park is a developed park located on the north shoreline of Sam Rayburn Reservoir, 70 miles north of Beaumont. The reservoir is fed by the Angelina River, the major tributary of the Neches River. With a capacity of 3,997,600 acre-feet, the reservoir is the largest lake wholly located within the state of Texas. The main purposes of the reservoir are flood control, hydroelectric power generation, and conservation of water. Sam Rayburn Reservoir is located in the Piney Woods of southeast Texas, approximately 18 miles north of Jasper, Texas. The park features 75 campsites with varying connections (16 with 30 amp electric & water, 8 with 50 amp electric & water, and 51 without electric or water connections). Additional amenities include day-use sites, a boat launch, playground, hot showers, and a dump station.

BASICS

Operated By: U.S. Army Corps of Engineers. **Open:** All year. **Site Assignment:** Call for details. **Registration:** At office. **Fee:** Single, $11–$18; group, $20. **Parking:** At site.

FACILITIES

Number of Multipurpose Sites: 138. **Hookups:** Yes. **Dump Station:** Yes. **Laundry:** No. **Pay Phone:** No. **Restrooms and Showers:** Yes. **Fuel:** No. **Propane:** No. **Internal Roads:** Paved. **RV Service:** No. **Market:** No. **Restaurant:** No. **General Store:** No. **Vending:** No. **Swimming:** No. **Playground:** Yes. **Activities:** Boating.

RESTRICTIONS

Pets: Restrained or on a leash at all times while in developed recreation areas. **Fires:** W/in campgrounds and other recreation areas, fires may only be built in fire rings, stoves, grills, or fireplaces provided for that purpose. **Alcoholic Beverages:** Not allowed. **Vehicle Maximum Length:** Call ahead.

TO GET THERE

From Pineland, TX, take FM 83 west 10 mi., then go south on FM 705 11 mi. to FM 3127, then west 1.5 mi. and make a left into the park entrance.

JOHNSON CITY · MAP, B-4
Pedernales Falls State Park

reserve america

2585 Park Rd. 6026, 78636.
T: (830) 868-7304 or (800) 792-1112;
www.reserveamerica.com.

🚐 ★★★★★ · ⛺ ★★★★★

Beauty: ★★★★★
Spaciousness: ★★★★★
Security: ★★★
Insect Control: ★★★
Site Privacy: ★★★★★
Quiet: ★★★★★
Cleanliness: ★★★★★
Facilities: ★★★★

Striking limestone falls resulted from 300 million years of geological change. Hikers appreciate 20 miles of trails in this park. Ash and cypress trees are found along the river, while the drier woodlands support oak and juniper stands. Hill Country fauna includes the elusive golden-cheeked warbler. Multi-purpose campsites with paved back-in parking are situated in one area. Spacious and heavily wooded, with dense foliage between each site, these are some of the most beautiful campsites in the state. The park also maintains a sponsored youth camping area. Atop the river bluffs is a hike-in primitive tent camping area with nearby water and chemical toilets. Although there are no locked gates, security is good here because of the park's remote location (9 miles from Johnson City). August and September are wet and hot, and winter can be very cold here. Plan to visit in spring, early summer, or fall.

BASICS
Operated By: Texas Parks and Wildlife. **Open:** All year. **Site Assignment:** Reservations (512) 389-8900, reservations must be made at least 48 hrs. in advance; deposit required (equivalent to 1-night fee) to hold reservation; cancellations more than 2 days prior to reservation result in $5 fee; cancellations w/in 2 days of reservation result in loss of deposit. **Registration:** At headquarters. **Fee:** Water/electric, $20; primitive tent, $10; daily charge per person (13 and older), $3; cash, check, V, MC, D. **Parking:** At most sites.

FACILITIES
Number of RV-only Sites: 69. **Hookups:** Electric (20, 30 amps), water. **Each Site:** Picnic table, fire ring, flat tent pad. **Dump Station:** Yes. **Laundry:** No. **Pay Phone:** No. **Restrooms and Showers:** Yes. **Fuel:** No. **Propane:** No. **Internal Roads:** Paved. **RV Service:** 34 mi. north in Marble Falls. **Market:** 10 mi. west in Johnson City. **Restaurant:** 10 mi. west in Johnson City. **General Store:** 10 mi. west in Johnson City. **Vending:** Beverages. **Swimming:** River. **Playground:** No. **Other:** Horse corral (day use only), covered bird viewing station, amphitheater, sponsored youth group area, gift shop. **Activities:** Picnicking, hiking, river swimming, tubing, wading, mountain biking, fishing, bird-watching, horseback riding. **Nearby Attractions:** Lyndon B. Johnson National & State Historic Parks (Johnson City), Admiral Nimitz Museum & Historical Center (Fredericksburg), numerous state parks & natural areas,

numerous wineries, Austin attractions. **Additional Information:** Fredericksburg CVB, (830) 997-6523; Austin CVB, (800) 926-2282.

RESTRICTIONS
Pets: On leash only. **Fires:** In grills, fire rings only. **Alcoholic Beverages:** Not allowed. **Vehicle Maximum Length:** 45 ft. **Other:** Max. 8 people per campsite, quiet time 10 p.m.–6 a.m., 14-day stay limit, gathering of firewood prohibited, swim at your own risk, no pets or open fires allowed in primitive camping area.

TO GET THERE
From Austin, drive west on US 290 32 mi., then turn right on FM 3232. Drive north on FM 3232 6 mi. to the park entrance. From Johnson City drive east on FM 2766 9 mi. to the park entrance.

KARNACK · MAP, A-5
Caddo Lake State Park

reserve america

245 Park Rd. 2, 75661.
T: (903) 679-3351 or (800) 792-1112;
www.reserveamerica.com.

🚐 ★★★★★ · ⛺ ★★★★★

Beauty: ★★★★★
Spaciousness: ★★★★
Security: ★★★★
Insect Control: ★★
Site Privacy: ★★★★
Quiet: ★★★★★
Cleanliness: ★★★
Facilities: ★★★

Visitors to this state park who come in RVs should take note that the entrance road is quite steep in some areas, but visitors delight in the humongous pull-throughs with full hookups once they've negotiated their way in. The road is also a little more complicated because of several one-way streets, making it necessary to drive first to the day-use area (near Big Cypress Bayou), then cutting across to the left to the camping areas. The first camping area you come across is Mill Pond, which is off-limits to RVs. These are 40-foot sites that are very close to the water's edge (61–65 are right on the water), which can make them buggy. The most remote site is 60, at the end of the roundabout. The next camping area is Squirrel Haven, which merges into Armadillo Run. These two areas consist of 40-foot forested and grassy sites. Sites 37–45 are located across from a row of screened shelters. The best sites are 29 and 30, at the end of a roundabout. The last camping area, Woodpecker Hollow, is designed with the big rig in mind. These are 120-foot pull-through sites with full hookups. All sites are forested and grassy, and the best two are next to the camp host (21 and 23) at the end of the roundabout. These are probably the safest, most comfortable sites in the park. Anyone with an interest in nature or living in the wild should come to Caddo Lake State Park for a camping holiday. Boat rentals are available and make for a fun afternoon—especially if you catch sight of one of the lake's native alligators! Like other parks this far South, however, July and August are unbearably hot, and September and October are very busy.

BASICS
Operated By: Texas Parks and Wildlife. **Open:** All year. **Site Assignment:** Reservations, call (512) 389-8900 48 hrs. in advance; refund (minus $5) w/ 48-hr. notice; less than 48 hrs., lose 1-night deposit. **Registration:** At office. (Late arrivals use drop box at entrance.) **Fee:** RV (full), $18; water, $8; plus $2 entrance fee per person; V, MC, D accepted in the office or for reservation. **Parking:** At site.

FACILITIES
Number of RV-only Sites: 26. **Number of Tent-only Sites:** 20. **Hookups:** Electric (30 amps), water, sewer. **Each Site:** Picnic table, grill, fire pit. **Dump Station:** Yes. **Laundry:** No. **Pay Phone:** No. **Restrooms and Showers:** Yes. **Fuel:** No. **Propane:** No. **Internal Roads:** Paved. **RV Service:** No. **Market:** 13 mi. to Marshall. **Restaurant:** 2 w/in 1 mi. **General Store:** Park store, adjacent convenience store. **Vending:** No. **Swimming:** Lake. **Playground:** Yes. **Other:** Canoe/boat rentals & tours, interpretive center, rec hall, cabins, amphitheater, fishing pier, cabins. **Activities:** Swimming, boating, fishing, hiking, mountain biking, wildlife viewing. **Nearby Attractions:** Starr Family State Historical Park. **Additional Information:** Marshall Chamber of Commerce, (903) 935-7868; Caddo Lake Office State Park Office, (903) 679-3351.

RESTRICTIONS
Pets: On 6-ft. leash, cleaned up after. **Fires:** Grill only. **Alcoholic Beverages:** Not allowed. **Vehicle Maximum Length:** No limit. **Other:** All visitors must pay $2 entrance fee per day.

TO GET THERE
From the junction of Hwy. 43/134 and FM 2198, go 0.5 mi. east on FM 2198. Turn left onto Park Rd. 2 and follow it to the park entrance.

KERRVILLE · MAP, C-3
Guadalupe River RV Resort

2605 Junction Hwy. 27, 78028.
T: (830) 367-5676 or (800) 582-1916;
www.guadaluperiverrvresort.com.

🚐 ★★★ · ⛺ n/a

Beauty: ★★★★
Spaciousness: ★★★★
Security: ★★★
Insect Control: ★★★★
Site Privacy: ★★★
Quiet: ★★★★
Cleanliness: ★★★★
Facilities: ★★★★

This resort offers excellent amenities, including separate adult and family swimming pools. Charming Kerrville is known as a cultural hub. With fantastic weather, Kerrville is also known as a gateway to great outdoor recreation. Lost Maples State Natural Area and Kerrville-Schreiner State Park are both nearby. Many sites at Guadalupe River are extremely attractive, while others are unappealing. Stay away from the dull, noisy sites near Hwy. 27. Instead, try to score a riverfront site (1–10 or 50–61) and enjoy the gorgeous view of the gently sloping riverbank. Riverside sites have back-in parking, but most other sites are pull-throughs. All sites are spacious, with a large patch of grass at each. Many are shady, though few are very private. All parking is paved. Security is passable; there are no gates, but the park is very remote. Visit popular Kerrville during the week.

BASICS

Operated By: Don Temple. **Open:** All year. **Site Assignment:** Credit card required to hold reservation, call (800) 582-1916; 48-hour cancellation policy. **Registration:** At office. **Fee:** $29.95–$35.95; for 2 people; phone hookup, $2; each extra person (6 and over), $5; each kilowatt hour of electricity, $.09; cash, personal check only. **Parking:** On paved area per site.

FACILITIES

Number of RV-only Sites: 202. **Hookups:** Electric (30, 50 amps), water, sewer, phone, cable TV, Wi-Fi. **Each Site:** Picnic table, barbecue pit. **Dump Station:** Yes. **Laundry:** Yes. **Pay Phone:** Yes. **Restrooms and Showers:** Yes. **Fuel:** Once per week, otherwise, 1 mi. **Propane:** Once per week, otherwise, 1 mi. **Internal Roads:** Paved. **RV Service:** 0.25 mi. **Market:** 0.5 mi. **Restaurant:** 1 mi. **General Store:** At park. **Vending:** Yes. **Swimming:** Pool. **Playground:** Yes. **Other:** 2 group facilities, pavilion w/ barbecue pit, fireplace & dance floor, health spa, Jacuzzi, steam room, sauna, game room, clubhouse, adult-only area. **Activities:** Fishing, walking, boating, horseshoes, tetherball, Ping-Pong, shuffleboard, volleyball, basketball, organized activities. **Nearby Attractions:** Hill County Arts Foundation, Point Theater, Stonehenge II, Scott Schreiner Municipal Golf Course, H.E.B. Municipal Tennis Center, Texas Arts & Crafts Fair, Cowboy Artists of America Museum. **Additional Information:** Kerrville CVB, (800) 221-7958.

RESTRICTIONS

Pets: On 10-ft. max. leash at all times, even in river. **Fires:** Fire pit only. **Alcoholic Beverages:** Allowed. **Vehicle Maximum Length:** 55 ft. **Other:** No tent camping allowed.

TO GET THERE

From San Antonio, take I-10 west toward El Paso and take Exit 505. Drive about 2 mi. south on FM 783. Take a right onto Hwy. 27 heading west, and the campground will be 2.5 mi. on the left.

LUMBERTON   MAP, B-5
Village Creek State Park

P.O. Box 8565, 77657. T: (409) 755-7322; www.tpwd.state.tx.us.

🚐 ★★★★   ⛺ ★★★★

Beauty: ★★★★	Site Privacy: ★★★★
Spaciousness: ★★★★	Quiet: ★★★★★
Security: ★★★★★	Cleanliness: ★★★★
Insect Control: ★★★	Facilities: ★★★★

Village Creek is a wooded retreat surrounded by suburbia. The flat-water creek, a favorite amongst anglers and paddle-sports enthusiasts, winds southeasterly and eventually joins the Neches River. Abundant rainfall supports cypress swamps, water tupelo, and river birch. Birders spot egrets and herons. The campground includes long and narrow yet attractive sites. Site size and privacy vary—some are incredibly huge and secluded, others ho-hum. There are no creek-side RV sites due to flooding. However, tent-campers may choose walk-in sites along Village Creek. All sites are nicely wooded and shady. At the RV area, all sites are back-ins with paved parking. Sites 1 and 3 are very secluded. Security is good—the park is gated at night. Although native bats dine on mosquitoes, insects flourish after heavy rains in the warmer months. Call before you visit Village Creek to check on water levels. Make advance reservations at this extremely popular park.

BASICS

Operated By: Texas Parks and Wildlife. **Open:** All year. **Site Assignment:** Reservations (512) 389-8900; reservations must be made at least 48 hrs. in advance; deposit required (equivalent to 1-night fee) to hold reservation; cancellations more than 2 days prior to reservation result in $5 fee; cancellations w/in 2 days of reservation result in loss of deposit. **Registration:** At office, after hours register next morning (gate locks at 10 p.m.). **Fee:** Developed (water/electric), $15; primitive, $7; plus entrance fee (each person 13 and older), $2; up to 8 people maximum; cash, check, V, MC, D. **Parking:** At site (2 cars), in parking lot about 75 yards from walk-in sites.

FACILITIES

Number of RV-only Sites: 25. **Number of Tent-only Sites:** 16. **Hookups:** Electric (20, 30 amps), water. **Each Site:** Picnic table, fire ring, lantern pole. **Dump Station:** Yes. **Laundry:** No. **Pay Phone:** Yes. **Restrooms and Showers:** Yes. **Fuel:** No. **Propane:** No. **Internal Roads:** Paved (gravel road to walk-in sites). **RV Service:** 2 mi. in Lumberton. **Market:** 1 mi. in Lumberton. **Restaurant:** 2 mi. in Lumberton. **General Store:** Park store, hardware, & Wal-Mart 3 mi. in Lumberton. **Vending:** Beverages. **Swimming:** Yes. **Playground:** Yes. **Other:** Picnic area, pavilion, rec hall, meeting room. **Activities:** Swimming at sandbar (1 mi. hike), fishing (local canoe rentals & fishing supplies), hiking, mountain biking, bird-watching, year-round nature study programs. **Nearby Attractions:** Sea Rim & Martin Dies Jr. State Parks, Big Thicket National Preserve, Cattail Marsh, Pleasure Island, Sabine Pass Battlefield, Beaumont museums, 80 mi. to Houston. **Additional Information:** Beaumont CVB, (409) 880-3749, www.beaumontcvb.com.

RESTRICTIONS

Pets: 6-ft. leash max. **Fires:** Fire ring (except under fire ban). **Alcoholic Beverages:** Not allowed. **Vehicle Maximum Length:** 55 ft. (sites vary). **Other:** No gathering firewood, no dumping gray water.

TO GET THERE

From Beaumont, drive north approx. 9 mi. on US 69/96 and take the Mitchell Rd. exit. Drive almost 0.5 mi. on the access road and turn right (east) onto Mitchell Rd. Immediately turn left (north) onto FM 3513/Village Creek Pkwy. Drive approx. 2 mi. and turn right (east) onto Alma Dr. Cross the railroad tracks, veer to the left and go 0.5 mi. to the park entrance.

MATHIS   MAP, C-4
Lake Corpus Christi State Park

reserve america

P.O. Box 1167, 78368. T: (361) 547-2635; www.reserveamerica.com.

🚐 ★★★★   ⛺ ★★★★

Beauty: ★★★★	Site Privacy: ★★★★
Spaciousness: ★★★★	Quiet: ★★★★
Security: ★★★★	Cleanliness: ★★★★
Insect Control: ★★★★	Facilities: ★★★

Anglers fish for catfish, bass, sunfish, and crappie in 21,000-acre Lake Corpus Christi. Adjacent Lake Corpus Christi State Park is instrumental in conserving the mesquite grassland ecosystem. Despite the park's gorgeous setting, there are no walking trails. There are four main camping loops: two contain full hookups and pull-through parking while the other two contain no hookups and back-in parking. For RVs, sites 1–23 are larger and more private than sites 24–48. There are no lakefront RV sites. Tent campers (or RVs foregoing hookups) should head for waterfront sites, including 57–66 and 91–99. All sites are spacious, with shade and privacy provided by mesquite trees and other brushy flora. Parking is paved and each site has a large patch of grass. Security is good at this remote park. Gates lock at night, and peace officers live on property. Convenient to Corpus Christi, the park stays busy from February to August. Visit in autumn for tranquility.

BASICS

Operated By: Texas Parks and Wildlife. **Open:** All year. **Site Assignment:** Reservations (512) 389-8900; 1-night fee required to hold reservation; 48-hour cancellation policy plus $5 fee; less than 48-hour notice will result in loss of deposit. **Fee:** Full hookup, $18; water/electric, $16; primitive tent, $10; fee for each person (13 and over), $4. **Parking:** At site; additional fee for more than 2 vehicles, $4.

FACILITIES

Number of RV-only Sites: 48. **Number of Tent-only Sites:** 60. **Hookups:** Electric (50 amps), water, sewer. **Each Site:** Picnic table (some covered), either barbecue pit or fire ring & grill. **Dump Station:** Yes. **Laundry:** No. **Pay Phone:** Yes. **Restrooms and Showers:** Yes. **Fuel:** No. **Propane:** No. **Internal Roads:** Paved. **RV Service:** 30 mi. southeast in Odem. **Market:** 3 mi. east in Mathis. **Restaurant:** 3 mi. east in Mathis. **General Store:** 3 mi. east in Mathis. **Vending:** Beverages. **Swimming:** Yes. **Playground:** No. **Other:** Screened shelters, gift shop, picnic area, picnic pavilion, boat ramp, fishing pier, fish-cleaning facility, scenic overlook. **Activities:** Lake swimming (at your own risk), fishing, boating, nature study. **Nearby Attractions:** Choke Canyon, Goose Island, & Mustang Island State parks; Fulton Mansion & Goliad State Historical parks; Padre Island National Seashore; Aransas Wildlife Refuge; Corpus Christi attractions. **Additional Information:** Corpus Christi Area CVB, (800) 678-6232.

RESTRICTIONS

Pets: Leash only, attended, not in buildings. **Fires:** Fire rings, barbecue pits only. **Alcoholic Beverages:** Not allowed. **Vehicle Maximum Length:** 40 ft. **Other:** No lifeguards; no gathering firewood.

TO GET THERE

From I-37, take Exit 34 and drive southwest on TX 359 4 mi. Turn right onto Park Road 25. The park entrance is on the left.

MERIDIAN   MAP, B-4
Meridian State Park

reserve america

173 Park Rd., No. 7, 76665. T: (254) 435-2536; www.reserveamerica.com.

🚐 ★★★★   ⛺ ★★★★★

Beauty: ★★★★★	Site Privacy: ★★★★
Spaciousness: ★★★★	Quiet: ★★★★★
Security: ★★★★	Cleanliness: ★★★★
Insect Control: ★★★	Facilities: ★★★★

Heavily wooded with ash, juniper, oak, and other species, Meridian offers extremely attractive campgrounds. Sites are large and shady, with paved back-in and pull-through parking. Site privacy varies, with dense greenery between some and others open to neighbors. RVs should head for one of the pull-throughs with full hookups. Tent campers should head for one of the pretty lakefront sites (no hookups). Meridian's rolling woods support myriad wildlife, including golden cheeked warblers in the spring. The 72-acre lake supports bream, crappie, catfish, bass, and rainbow trout (winter only). Security is good at this extremely rural park which locks its gates at night. Visit Meridian in the spring, early summer, or fall for the nicest weather. Avoid this park on summer weekends, when the small campgrounds are likely to be crowded.

BASICS

Operated By: Texas Parks and Wildlife. **Open:** All year. **Site Assignment:** Reservations (512) 389-8900; reservations must be made at least 48 hrs. in advance; deposit required (equivalent to 1-night fee) to hold reservation; cancellations more than 2 days prior to reservation result in $5 fee; cancellations w/in 2 days of reservation result in loss of deposit. **Registration:** At park headquarters, after hours self-registration (gate locks at 10 p.m.). **Fee:** Pull-through (water/electric/sewer), $20; back-in (water/electric), $17; entrance fee per person (13 and older), $5; cash, personal check, V, MC, D. **Parking:** At site (2 cars). Fee charged for additional vehicles, $3.

FACILITIES

Number of RV-only Sites: 15. **Number of Tent-only Sites:** 14. **Hookups:** Electric (30 amps), water, sewer. **Each Site:** Picnic table, fire ring. **Dump Station:** Yes. **Laundry:** No. **Pay Phone:** No. **Restrooms and Showers:** Yes. **Fuel:** No. **Propane:** No. **Internal Roads:** Paved. **RV Service:** 45 mi. in Waco. **Market:** Grocery 2 mi. in Meridian. **Restaurant:** 2 mi. in Meridian. **General Store:** Yes.

Vending: Beverages. **Swimming:** Yes. **Playground:** Yes. **Other:** Screened shelters, picnic area, boat ramp, boat dock, group dining hall, gift shop. **Activities:** Lake swimming, boating (no-wake lake), pedal boat rentals (summertime), fishing, bird-watching, hiking, bicycling. **Nearby Attractions:** Meridian golf, Bosque County Courthouse, Norse historic Norwegian settlement, Dinosaur Valley, Lake Whitney & Cleburne State Parks, Fossil Rim, Waco historic homes, Homestead Heritage Traditional Crafts Village, Texas Sports Hall of Fame. **Additional Information:** Meridian Chamber of Commerce, (254) 435-2966; Waco CVB, (800) 321-9226.

RESTRICTIONS

Pets: 6-ft. max leash. Pets not allowed in shelters or buildings. **Fires:** Fire ring only. **Alcoholic Beverages:** Not allowed. **Vehicle Maximum Length:** 40 ft. (back-in sites 20 ft.). **Other:** No-wake lake.

TO GET THERE

From Waco, take TX 6 northwest approx. 45 mi. to Meridian and turn left (southwest) on TX 22. Drive 2.5 mi. and turn right on Park Rd. 7, directly into the park.

MEXIA   MAP, B-4
Fort Parker State Park

reserve america

194 Park Rd. 28, 76667. T: (254) 562-5751; www.reserveamerica.com.

🚐 ★★★★   ⛺ ★★★★

Beauty: ★★★★★	Site Privacy: ★★★
Spaciousness: ★★★★	Quiet: ★★★★★
Security: ★★★	Cleanliness: ★★★★
Insect Control: ★★★	Facilities: ★★★★

Most campsites here offer stunning views of the sunset over 700-acre Fort Parker Lake. The lake supports crappie, bass, catfish, and trout (in season). Guided boat tours of the lake are available (call for schedule). The RV campground consists of one area alongside the lake. There are back-in and pull-through sites with paved parking. Some sites could cause mild claustrophobia, while others are amply sized. Most are nicely shaded, but none are very private. Arrive early and angle for a lakefront site, the prettiest of which is number 18—a gorgeous pull-through. The primitive tent-camping area is nicely wooded. Visit popular Fort Parker on weekdays between March and June when wildflowers are blooming and crowds are at a minimum. Security is fair at this small-town park; there are no gates.

BASICS

Operated By: Texas Parks and Wildlife. **Open:** All year. **Site Assignment:** Reservations (512) 389-8900; reservations must be made at least 48 hrs. in advance; deposit required (equivalent to 1-night fee) to hold reservation; cancellations more than 2 days prior to reservation result in $5 fee; cancellations w/in 2 days of reservation result in loss of deposit. **Registration:** At park headquarters, after hours register next morning. **Fee:** Water/electric, $15; developed, $10; primitive, $7; plus entry fee $2 per

adult; cash, check, V, MC, D. **Parking:** At site, in parking lot.

FACILITIES

Number of RV-only Sites: 25. **Number of Tent-only Sites:** 13. **Hookups:** Electric (30 amps), water. **Each Site:** Picnic table, fire ring grill combination, lantern pole. **Dump Station:** Yes. **Laundry:** No. **Pay Phone:** No. **Restrooms and Showers:** Yes. **Fuel:** No. **Propane:** No. **Internal Roads:** Paved. **RV Service:** 40 mi. in Waco. **Market:** 5 mi. in Groesbeck. **Restaurant:** 5 mi. in Groesbeck. **General Store:** No. **Vending:** Beverages. **Swimming:** Lake. **Playground:** Yes. **Other:** Activity center, screened shelters, picnic area & shelter, boat ramp, fish-cleaning station. **Activities:** Lake swimming, fishing, canoe & paddle-boat rentals, Cynthia Ann boat tours, hiking, biking trails, mountain biking. **Nearby Attractions:** Confederate Reunion Grounds, Old Fort Parker Historic Site, Waco historic homes, Homestead Heritage Traditional Crafts Village, Texas Sports Hall of Fame. **Additional Information:** Waco CVB, (800) 321-9226.

RESTRICTIONS

Pets: On leash only, attended. **Fires:** Fire ring only (except under fire ban). **Alcoholic Beverages:** Not allowed. **Vehicle Maximum Length:** No limit (sites vary). **Other:** Texas State Park regulations apply.

TO GET THERE

From US 84 in Mexia, turn south on TX 14. Drive 7 mi. to the park entrance on the right. The campground is 1 mi. inside the park. (Park Rd. 28).

MINERAL WELLS   MAP, A-4
Lake Mineral Wells State Park and Trailway

reserve america

100 Park Rd. 71, 76067.
T: (940) 328-1171 or (800) 792-1112; www.reserveamerica.com.

🚐 ★★★★★   ⛺ ★★★★★

Beauty: ★★★★★	Site Privacy: ★★★★★
Spaciousness: ★★★★★	Quiet: ★★★★★
Security: ★★★	Cleanliness: ★★★★
Insect Control: ★★★	Facilities: ★★★★

The only major rock climbing and rappelling region in north Texas, Mineral Wells offers 85 climbs (difficulty ranges from 5.5 to 5.11d). Nearby, the State Trailway is a 20-mile rail to trail conversion open to pedestrians, cyclists, and equestrians. The lake supports bass, catfish, crappie, and perch. Three campgrounds are lakeside: The Post Oak tent-only area contains 11 gorgeous sites under a romantic post oak canopy. The Plateau area offers water and electric sites (ask for 59, 60, and 64–66 for the best lake views). The Live Oak area contains water-only sites (ask for 31–34 for the nicest lake views). Sites are spacious and situated on loops with back-in gravel parking. The entrance is within Mineral Wells city limits, so protect your valuables (gates lock at night).

April and May are the wettest months. Winters can be very cold and summers very hot. Visit in March, June (on weekdays), September, or October.

BASICS

Operated By: Texas Parks and Wildlife. **Open:** All year; park closes for hunting season; call park for details. **Site Assignment:** Reservations (512) 389-8900; reservations must be made at least 48 hrs. in advance; deposit required (equivalent to 1-night fee) to hold reservation; cancellations more than 2 days prior to reservation result in $5 fee; cancellations w/in 2 days of reservation result in loss of deposit. **Registration:** At headquarters. **Fee:** Water/electric, $18–$20; water, $12; daily charge per person (13 and older), $5. **Parking:** At most sites (2 max). Additional fee charged for extra vehicles, $3.

FACILITIES

Number of RV-only Sites: 64. Number of Tent-only Sites: 51. **Hookups:** Electric (30, 50 amps), water. **Each Site:** Picnic table, fire ring, grill. **Dump Station:** Yes. **Laundry:** No. **Pay Phone:** Yes. **Restrooms and Showers:** Yes. **Fuel:** No. **Propane:** No. **Internal Roads:** Paved. **RV Service:** 0.5 mi. west of park. **Market:** 3 mi. west in Mineral Wells. **Restaurant:** 3 mi. west in Mineral Wells. **General Store:** Yes. **Vending:** Park concession open daily Mar.–Dec. **Swimming:** Yes. **Playground:** No. **Other:** Picnic sites, equestrian camp-sites, screened shelters, seasonal park store, boat ramp, fishing piers, screened shelters. **Activities:** Swimming, fishing, boating (row boat, canoe, & paddle-boat rental available), rock climbing, rappelling, mountain biking, equestrian camping, horseback riding, hiking. **Nearby Attractions:** Fort Richardson State Historical Park, Lost Creek Reservoir State Trailway, Possum Kingdom State Park, Cleburne State Park, Dinosaur Valley State Park, Clark Gardens, The Brazos River, Possum Kingdom Lake. **Additional Information:** Mineral Wells Area Chamber of Commerce, (800) 252-MWTX.

RESTRICTIONS

Pets: Leash only, attended, not in buildings. **Fires:** In grills, fire rings only. **Alcoholic Beverages:** Not allowed. **Vehicle Maximum Length:** 60 ft. **Other:** Max. 8 people per campsite; quiet time 10 p.m.–6 a.m.; 14-day stay limit; gathering of firewood prohibited; climbers & rappelers must check in at headquarters, no skiing, jet skiing, or tubing permitted. Rock climbers must bring their own equipment.

TO GET THERE

From Mineral Wells, drive east on US 180 4 mi. From Weatherford, drive west on US 180 14 mi.

MISSION   MAP, D-4
Bentsen-Rio Grande Valley State Park

P.O. Box 988, 2800 S. Bentsen Palm Dr., 78572. T: (956) 585-1107 or (800) 792-1112; www.reserveamerica.com.

🚐 ★★★★   ▲ ★★★★

Beauty: ★★★★★   Site Privacy: ★★★
Spaciousness: ★★★   Quiet: ★★★★
Security: ★★★   Cleanliness: ★★★★
Insect Control: ★   Facilities: ★★★★

Year-round warmth makes for delightful winter or early spring retreats at this campground. Situated on a resaca—a former Rio Grande River channel (now still-water)—the lush flora and varied fauna of the park are typical of the Mexican subtropics. Fish for bass and catfish in the resaca. The surrounding brushlands form natural habitats for exotic cats such as ocelot and jaguarundi. Exotic birds include paraque, groove-billed ani, black-bellied whistling duck, and scores more. The lovely campsites are large, usually shady, and flat. Tent sites offer paved back-in parking and water at each site. Tent campers will find the prettiest sites lining the resaca (110–139). Searching for exotic birds and full hookups? Try sites 3–36. RV sites offer fewer trees and paved pull-through parking. In spite of its quiet feel, this suburban park is about 3 miles from afternoon traffic jams. Watch your valuables even though the gates lock at 10 p.m.

BASICS

Operated By: Texas Parks and Wildlife. **Open:** All year. **Site Assignment:** Reservations (512) 389-8900; reservations must be made at least 48 hrs. in advance; deposit required (equivalent to 1-night fee) to hold reservation; cancellations more than 2 days prior to reservation result in $5 fee; cancellations w/in 2 days of reservation result in loss of deposit. **Registration:** At headquarters. **Fee:** Primitive camping, $18; daily charge per person (18 and older), $5; cash, check, V, MC, D. **Parking:** At site.

FACILITIES

Number of Sites: 100. **Hookups:** Only primitive sites available. **Dump Station:** No. **Laundry:** No. **Pay Phone:** Yes. **Restrooms and Showers:** Yes. **Fuel:** No. **Propane:** No. **Internal Roads:** Paved. **RV Service:** 5 mi. north in Mission. **Market:** 3 mi. north in Palmview. **Restaurant:** 3 mi. north in Palmview. **General Store:** On site. **Vending:** No. **Swimming:** No. **Playground:** No. **Other:** Bicycle rental, volleyball court, shuffleboard, fish-cleaning table, bird observation blinds, birding information center Dec.–Mar., World Birding Center. **Activities:** Hiking, picnicking, bird-watching, boating, bicycling, & fishing. **Nearby Attractions:** Falcon State Park, Santa Ana National Wildlife Refuge, Sabal Palm Sanctuary, Mexico attractions. **Additional Information:** Mission Chamber of Commerce, (956) 585-2727; Rio Grande Valley Chamber of Commerce, (956) 968-3141; McAllen CVB, (956) 682-2871.

RESTRICTIONS

Pets: On leash only. **Fires:** In grills, fire rings only. **Alcoholic Beverages:** Not allowed. **Other:** Max. 8 people per campsite, quiet time 10 p.m.–6 a.m., 14-day stay limit, gathering of firewood prohibited.

TO GET THERE

From McAllen, go west on I-83. Exit at Bentsen Palm Drive, turn left, and drive south. After crossing Business 83, Bentsen Palm Drive becomes FM 2062. The park entrance is about 3 mi. from I-83.

MISSION   MAP, D-4
Chimney Park RV Resort

4224 South Conway, 78572-1568. T: (956) 585-5061; www.chimneyparkresort.com.

🚐 ★★★   ▲ n/a

Beauty: ★★★   Site Privacy: ★★★
Spaciousness: ★★★   Quiet: ★★★
Security: ★★★★   Cleanliness: ★★★
Insect Control: ★★★   Facilities: ★★★

Another seniors-only park in south Texas, Chimney Park is sandwiched between a levee and the Rio Grande River. However, the river view is deadened by the concrete sea wall that runs the length of the park. The park's namesake is a 1907 steam-powered water-pump chimney. Campsites are generally plain and small—we imagine you'll get to know your neighbors. With little shade or privacy, each site has paved back-in parking, a grassy area, and a concrete patio. Permanent park models occupy all of the riverfront sites. The nicest available sites, including 16–20, 150–154, and 261–268, have trees nearby. Fenced and guarded, security is excellent at suburban Chimney Park. Within a mile, there are restaurants and shops galore. Stay away from South Texas in the summer, and make advance reservations in the winter.

BASICS

Operated By: Earl and Sharon Page. **Open:** All year. **Site Assignment:** Reservations accepted, payable w/ personal check or cash. **Registration:** At office. **Fee:** $20–$30 for 2 people; per night charge each extra person, $2. **Parking:** On site.

FACILITIES

Number of RV-only Sites: 276. **Hookups:** Electric, water, sewer, phone, data port, Wi-Fi. **Each Site:** Fire ring. **Dump Station:** No. **Laundry:** Yes. **Pay Phone:** No. **Restrooms and Showers:** Yes. **Fuel:** No. **Propane:** Yes. **Internal Roads:** Paved. **RV Service:** 0.5 mi. **Market:** 0.5 mi. **Restaurant:** 0.25 mi. **General Store:** 0.5 mi. **Vending:** Yes. **Swimming:** Pool. **Playground:** No. **Other:** Boat ramp, boat dock, floating dock, fishing dock, Jacuzzi, game room. **Activities:** Horseshoes, shuffleboard, fishing, boating, billiards, variety shows, card games, dances, bingo, ice-cream socials. **Nearby Attractions:** Azalduas Dam, Banworth Park, Mission Nature Park. **Additional Information:** Mission Chamber of Commerce, (956) 585-2727.

RESTRICTIONS

Pets: On leash. **Fires:** Grill only. **Alcoholic Beverages:** Allowed. **Vehicle Maximum Length:** 38 ft. **Other:** Campers must be 55 & older.

TO GET THERE

Exit Expressway 83 in Mission, go south on South Conway Rd., FM1016, about 2 mi., look for the sign for Chimney Park RV Resort on your right.

MONAHANS   MAP, B-2
Monahans Sandhills State Park

reserve america

P.O. Box 1738, 79756. T: (432) 943-2092;
www.reserveamerica.com.

🚐 ★★★   ⛺ ★★★

Beauty: ★★★★   Site Privacy: ★★★
Spaciousness: ★★★   Quiet: ★★★
Security: ★★   Cleanliness: ★★★★
Insect Control: ★★★   Facilities: ★★★

At the end of a vast dune field which continues 200 miles northeast into New Mexico, the park contains active dunes that move and change seasonally because they're not anchored by vegetation. Try dusk or dawn wildlife viewing at the ponds. Look for coyote, bobcat, porcupine, and others. The unique shinoak tree is mature at under four feet tall. The campgrounds are odd. Sites nestle into the dunes in pairs, with each pair sharing a shade shelter. Each site has its own picnic table. While you are nose-to-nose with your shelter-mate, dunes and ample space provide privacy between pairs of sites. Some sites offer paved pull-through parking. All others have paved back-in parking. You will be assigned a site. There are no gates, and we easily entered the park after dark. Be cautious with your valuables—the entrance is yards from the freeway exit. Visit Monahans any time but late summer.

BASICS
Operated By: Texas Parks and Wildlife. **Open:** All year. **Site Assignment:** Reservations (512) 389-8900; reservations must be made at least 48 hrs. in advance; deposit required (equivalent to 1-night fee) to hold reservation; cancellations more than 2 days prior to reservation result in $5 fee; cancellations w/in 2 days of reservation result in loss of deposit. **Registration:** At headquarters. **Fee:** Water/electric, $13; daily charge per person (13 and older), $2; cash, check, V, MC, D. **Parking:** At site.

FACILITIES
Number of RV-only Sites: 26. **Hookups:** Electric (20, 30, 50 amps), water. **Each Site:** Grill, picnic table. **Dump Station:** Yes. **Laundry:** No. **Pay Phone:** Yes. **Restrooms and Showers:** Yes. **Fuel:** 5 mi. west in Monahans. **Propane:** 5 mi. west in Monahans. **Internal Roads:** Paved. **RV Service:** 30 mi. east in Odessa. **Market:** 5 mi. west in Monahans. **Restaurant:** 5 mi. west in Monahans. **General Store:** Gift shop. **Vending:** Yes. **Swimming:** No. **Playground:** No. **Other:** Interpretive center, equestrian day-use area, group dining hall, one working oil well, picnic area, sand toboggan & disc rental. **Activities:** Hiking, picnicking, sand surfing, bird-watching at interpretive center. **Nearby Attractions:** Million Barrel Museum, Balmorhea State Park, Odessa Meteor Crater. **Additional Information:** Odessa Chamber of Commerce, (915) 332-9111; Monahans Chamber of Commerce, (915) 943-2187.

RESTRICTIONS
Pets: On leash only, attended, not in buildings. **Fires:** Grill only. **Alcoholic Beverages:** Not allowed.

Vehicle Maximum Length: 40 ft. **Other:** No four-wheelers or motorcycles allowed.

TO GET THERE
From I-20, take Exit 86 to Park Rd. 41. The park entrance is visible from the interstate.

MOODY   MAP, B-4
Mother Neff State Park

reserve america

1680 Texas Hwy. 236, 76557. T: (254) 853-2389;
www.reserveamerica.com.

🚐 ★★★★   ⛺ ★★★★

Beauty: ★★★   Site Privacy: ★★★★
Spaciousness: ★★★★   Quiet: ★★★★★
Security: ★★★★   Cleanliness: ★★★★
Insect Control: ★★★   Facilities: ★★

Mother Neff State Park is the first official state park in Texas. It is named for Mrs. Isabella Eleanor (Mother) Neff who in 1916 donated six acres of land along the Leon River, which became the first park site. Her son was Pat M. Neff, who served as Governor of Texas from 1921 to 1925. After the death of his mother in 1921, Governor Neff created the Mother Neff Memorial Park which later became the nucleus of the Texas State Park System. The park, located west of Moody, now contains 259 acres in Coryell County. The additional land was deeded to the state in 1934 by private owners; Governor Neff deeded 250 acres and Mr. Frank Smith deeded 3 acres. The park was opened to the public in 1937. In the 1930s, the Civilian Conservation Corps (CCC) restored the park to its historical setting. An excavation in 1935 unearthed three Native American graves and many artifacts. During prehistoric times this area was occupied by several groups of Native Americans, including some groups probably related to the Tonkawas. Heavily wooded, the park is ideal for camping, hiking, picnicking, and fishing. Facilities include campsites with water and electricity; campsites with water nearby; primitive campsites; a group primitive area; picnic sites; a group (wooden) picnic pavilion and a group (rock) picnic pavilion that are often used for reunions, church group gatherings, and weddings; a heated and air-conditioned recreation hall with kitchen facilities; restrooms with and without showers; a playground; and an outdoor sports area.

BASICS
Operated By: Texas Parks and Wildlife. **Open:** All year. **Site Assignment:** Reservations can be made up to 16 weeks in advance. **Registration:** At office. **Fee:** Single, $10–$15; primitive, $5; picnic pavilion, $30–$50; group hall, $75. **Parking:** 2 vehicles per site.

FACILITIES
Number of Multipurpose Sites: 52. **Hookups:** None. **Dump Station:** No. **Laundry:** No. **Pay Phone:** Yes. **Restrooms and Showers:** Yes. **Fuel:** No. **Propane:** No. **Internal Roads:** Paved. **RV Service:** No. **Market:** No. **Restaurant:** No. **General Store:** No. **Vending:** No. **Swimming:** No. **Play-**ground: No. **Activities:** Canoeing, fishing, group sports, picnicking, trailer rides. **Nearby Attractions:** Hiking, swimming.

RESTRICTIONS
Pets: On a 6-ft. leash, never unattended, under control at all times, cleaned up after. **Fires:** Fires may be built only in campsite grills, fire rings, or fireplaces. Some sites allow only containerized fuel fires. When warranted, fire bans are implemented by county judges and/or county commissioners courts. Inquire when making reservations. **Alcoholic Beverages:** It is an offense to consume or display an open container of an alcoholic beverage in a public place or sell alcoholic beverages w/in a state park. **Vehicle Maximum Length:** 30 ft.

TO GET THERE
From Dallas or Fort Worth: Take I-35S to Waco. Continue south 17 mi. to Hwy. 107. Take 107W 15 mi. to SH 236. Travel south on SH 236 2 mi. to the park. From Austin: Take I-35N to approx. 16 mi. north of Temple. Take Hwy. 107W 15 mi. to SH 236. Travel south on SH 236 2 mi. to the park.

NEEDVILLE   MAP, C-5
Brazos Bend State Park

reserve america

21901 FM 762, 77461. T: (979) 553-5101;
www.reserveamerica.com.

🚐 ★★★★   ⛺ ★★★★

Beauty: ★★★★   Site Privacy: ★★★
Spaciousness: ★★★★   Quiet: ★★★
Security: ★★★★   Cleanliness: ★★★★
Insect Control: ★   Facilities: ★★★★

A nature-lover's paradise, Brazos Bend contains fascinating ecosystems, including river floodplains, upland coastal prairies, freshwater marshes, oxbow lakes, the Brazos River, and creeks. Wildlife spotted from the observation tower and viewing platforms includes feral hogs and 270 bird species. The 0.5-mile paved Creekfield Lake Nature Trail is wheelchair-accessible and includes tactile interpretive panels and audio tours. On property, George Observatory offers public stargazing—call for schedule. Attractive campgrounds consist of two loops of back-in sites with gravel parking. Large campsites are shaded by black willow, sycamore, and cottonwood trees. There is little privacy. Many sites in both sections are situated along Big Creek. Pretty creek side sites include 101, 214, and 215. For privacy, we recommend site 105. Grassy tent pads are found at each site. Security is good at this rural park. Popular with Houston city slickers, Brazos Bend stays busy on all but the most inclement weekends. Visit on weekdays.

BASICS
Operated By: Texas Parks and Wildlife. **Open:** All year; park closes for hunting season; call park for details. **Site Assignment:** Reservations (512) 389-8900; reservations must be made at least 48 hrs. in advance; deposit required (equivalent to 1-night fee) to hold reservation; cancellations more than 2 days

prior to reservation result in $5 fee; cancellations w/in 2 days of reservation result in loss of deposit. **Registration:** At headquarters. **Fee:** Electric/water, $16; primitive, $12; daily entrance fee (13 and older), $4; cash, check, V, MC, D. **Parking:** At site.

FACILITIES

Number of RV-only Sites: 77. **Number of Tent-only Sites:** 20. **Hookups:** Electric (30 amps), water. **Each Site:** Picnic table, fire ring, grill. **Dump Station:** Yes. **Laundry:** Yes. **Pay Phone:** Yes. **Restrooms and Showers:** Yes. **Fuel:** No. **Propane:** No. **Internal Roads:** Paved. **RV Service:** 30 mi. northeast in Sugarland. **Market:** Convenience store 1 mi. south in community of Woodrow, full market 18 mi. northwest in Needville. **Restaurant:** Deli 1 mi. south in community of Woodrow, full-service 18 mi. northwest in Needville. **General Store:** Wal-Mart, 18 mi. south in West Columbia. **Vending:** Beverages. **Swimming:** No. **Playground:** Yes. **Other:** George Observatory (call for hours), interpretive center, group dining hall, group picnic pavilions, picnic areas, screened shelters, amphitheater, gift shop, fishing piers, fish-cleaning area, wheelchair-accessible nature trail. **Activities:** Picnicking, hiking, bicycling, mountain biking, boating, fishing, interpretive tours & educational programs, stargazing (special parties & programs). **Nearby Attractions:** San Jacinto Battleground Historical Complex including the San Jacinto Monument & Battleship Texas, Galveston Island State Park, George Ranch, Houston. **Additional Information:** Houston CVB, (800) 4-HOUSTON; Fort Bend CVB, (281) 491-0800.

RESTRICTIONS

Pets: On leash only, cleaned up after. **Fires:** Fire ring only. **Alcoholic Beverages:** Not allowed. **Vehicle Maximum Length:** 45 ft. **Other:** Special alligator precautions, check w/ park for current restrictions: do not feed or molest the alligators, no swimming or wading, keep pets & children away from alligators, stay at least 30 ft. away from alligators.

TO GET THERE

From Houston, follow TX 288 to Rosharon. At Rosharon, turn left on FM 1462 and travel west roughly 20 mi. Park entrance on right.

NEW CANEY   MAP, B-5
Lake Houston State Park

reserve america

22031 Baptist Encampment Rd., 77357-7731. T: (281) 354-6881; www.reserveamerica.com.

🚐 ★★★★	▲ ★★★★
Beauty: ★★★	Site Privacy: ★★★★
Spaciousness: ★★★★	Quiet: ★★★★
Security: ★★★★	Cleanliness: ★★★★
Insect Control: ★★★	Facilities: ★★

Facilities include walk-in campsites with a lantern post, a picnic table, a fire ring, and a grill; water is centrally located. There are two areas of eight campsites (Camp Oakwood and Ironwood) that share a picnic pavilion (capacity 25), but Camp Magnolia

area does not. A shower building with restrooms is hiking distance from these campsites. A Sponsored Youth Group Area has 6 walk-in campsites. Each has a fire ring, tent pad, picnic table, and lantern hook. This area is alongside Peach Creek; parking in the area. Not restricted to nonprofit youth groups; any supervised group may use it. There are restrooms and showers nearby and a covered area to wash your hands. There is a 12-mile hike/bike trail and 8 miles of equestrian trails where a maximum of 20 riders per day are allowed. Reservations must be made in advance by calling the park and may be made up to two weeks ahead of your visit. There is a group dining hall with a kitchen (Pine Grove Dining Hall/Day Lodge), which can accommodate up to 100. Lazy Creek Cottage Lodge sleeps up to 26 persons and has a full-sized kitchen, 26 bunk beds, a fireplace, air-conditioning, gas heat, showers and restrooms. Forest Cottage (Lodge) meets ADA requirements, accommodates 12, and has ceiling fans, air-conditioning, gas heater, fireplace, and screened windows with a cathedral ceiling. The kitchen has stove, refrigerator, counter, storage space; no cooking utensils. There is a large bath with showers and a changing area; bunk beds in the main area, private bedroom with two twin beds; no linens; and a half bath. The dining/activity area has tables and seating; there is a large outdoor patio overlooking woods with a large grill and a seating area around the large fire ring; ADA accessible. Activities include camping, nature study, bird-watching, hiking, biking, and horseback riding (the park does not furnish horses).

BASICS

Operated By: Texas Parks and Wildlife. **Open:** All year. **Site Assignment:** Reservations can be made up to 16 weeks in advance. **Registration:** At office. **Fee:** Single, $7; youth area, $40; dining hall, $100; lodge, $125–$160. **Parking:** 2 vehicles per site w/ water; primitive sites are a 2-mi. hike into the park.

FACILITIES

Number of Multipurpose Sites: 58. **Hookups:** None. **Dump Station:** No. **Laundry:** No. **Pay Phone:** No. **Restrooms and Showers:** Yes. **Fuel:** No. **Propane:** No. **Internal Roads:** Paved. **RV Service:** No. **Market:** No. **Restaurant:** Yes. **General Store:** No. **Vending:** No. **Swimming:** No. **Playground:** No. **Activities:** Backpacking, biking, bird-watching, fishing, hiking, horseback riding. **Nearby Attractions:** Canoeing.

RESTRICTIONS

Pets: On a 6-ft. leash, never unattended, under control at all times, cleaned up after. **Fires:** Fires may be built only in campsite grills, fire rings, or fireplaces. Some sites allow only containerized fuel fires. When warranted, fire bans are implemented by county judges and/or county commissioners courts. Inquire when making reservations. **Alcoholic Beverages:** It is an offense to consume or display an open container of an alcoholic beverage in a public place or sell alcoholic beverages w/in a state park. **Vehicle Maximum Length:** 25 ft.

TO GET THERE

From Houston: Take US 59N to New Caney. Turn right on FM 1485. Go east 2 mi. and turn right on Baptist Encampment Rd. Go 1.5 mi. to park entrance.

PADRE ISLAND   MAP, D-4
Malaquite Beach Campground

Padre Island National Seashore, P.O. Box 181300, 78480-1300. T: (361) 949-8068; www.nps.gov.

🚐 ★★★★	▲ ★★★★
Beauty: ★★★★	Site Privacy: ★★
Spaciousness: ★★★	Quiet: ★★★
Security: ★★★★	Cleanliness: ★★★★
Insect Control: ★	Facilities: ★★★★

At 70 miles long, Padre Island National Seashore is one of the largest pieces of undeveloped shoreline in the United States. The island is rich in folklore concerning buried pirate's treasure. It's also rich in natural beauty and wildlife, including graceful waterfowl such as herons. Much of the island is accessible only by foot or four-wheel drive. Attractive Malaquite Campground is 100 feet from the beach, nestled into graceful dunes. There is no vegetation other than dune grasses. Sites have parallel paved parking and are completely open to each other. All sites are small, and there is no shade. If your RV doesn't have an awning, bring large umbrellas. Sites are all the same, so choose your site based on location. Mosquitoes thrive at Padre Island, so come prepared. Security is good—although there are no gates, the campground is extremely remote. Rarely crowded, Malaquite is an excellent destination in late spring, early summer, and autumn.

BASICS

Operated By: National Park Service. **Open:** All year. **Site Assignment:** No reservations; first come, first served. **Registration:** At visitor center. **Fee:** $8; plus day-use fees of $10 per car or $5 per cyclist/pedestrian each week. **Parking:** At site.

FACILITIES

Number of RV-only Sites: 42. **Number of Tent-only Sites:** 8. **Hookups:** None. **Each Site:** Picnic table. **Dump Station:** Yes. **Laundry:** No. **Pay Phone:** No. **Restrooms and Showers:** Yes. **Fuel:** No. **Propane:** No. **Internal Roads:** Paved except for beach driving. **RV Service:** 18 mi. north in Corpus Christi. **Market:** 15 mi. in Corpus Christi. **Restaurant:** 10 mi. north in Corpus Christi. **General Store:** In park, 25 mi. in Corpus Christi. **Vending:** No. **Swimming:** No. **Playground:** No. **Other:** Visitor center, scenic drive, observation deck, bathhouses. **Activities:** Wind surfing, picnicking, four-wheel-driving, hiking, bird-watching, beachcombing, swimming, surfing, boating, volunteering, waterskiing, fishing, guided tours. **Nearby Attractions:** Texas State Aquarium, USS *Lexington*, Ships of Christopher Columbus, convention center, Corpus Christi Museum of Science and History. **Additional Information:** Corpus Christi Area CVB, (800) 678-6232.

RESTRICTIONS

Pets: On leash only. **Fires:** Contained fires only. **Alcoholic Beverages:** Allowed. **Vehicle Maximum Length:** No limit.

TO GET THERE

From Corpus Christi, take US 358 to Park Road 22. Drive approx. 20 mi. and follow the signs to camping areas.

PITTSBURG   MAP, A-5
Lake Bob Sandlin State Park

reserve america

341 State Park Rd. 2117, 75686.
T: (903) 572-5531; www.reserveamerica.com.

🚐 ★★★★   ⛺ ★★★★

Beauty: ★★★	Site Privacy: ★★★
Spaciousness: ★★★	Quiet: ★★★
Security: ★★★★	Cleanliness: ★★★★
Insect Control: ★★★	Facilities: ★★★★

Lake Bob Sandlin State Park is a 639.8-acre park located on the heavily wooded shoreline on the north side of the 9400-acre Lake Bob Sandlin, located southeast of Mount Pleasant in Titus County. It was acquired in 1979 and was opened 1987. There is evidence of prehistoric Caddoan people, which occupied East Texas from 200 B.C. to 1700. The French and Spanish periodically occupied the area, establishing relations with the Caddo. Choctaw, Cherokee, and Kickapoo moved into East Texas in the late 18th to early 19th century. By 1841, Fort Sherman, a wooden stockade whose site is believed to be in or near the park, was established. The Fort Sherman cemetery is located in the park. Since 1860, the land has been used for farming and ranching. Varieties of oak, hickory, pine, dogwood, redbud, and maple produce spectacular fall color. Facilities include restrooms with showers; premium lakeside campsites with water and electricity; two primitive camping areas; campsites (back-in) with water and electricity; screen shelters; Limited use cabins (air-conditioning and heating, bunk beds with mattresses, no linens, no inside plumbing); a group picnic pavilion with 6 or 8 tables, water and electricity; a large barbecue grill, and restrooms; 5 miles of hiking and mountain biking trails with 8 footbridges; a playground; a lighted fishing pier; a fish-cleaning facility; a two-lane boat ramp; and a Texas State Park Store. Popular fish include largemouth bass, catfish, and crappie.

BASICS
Operated By: Texas Parks and Wildlife. **Open:** All year. **Site Assignment:** Reservations can be made 11 months in advance. **Registration:** At office. **Fee:** Single, $12–$16; primitive, $6; group shelter, $20; group pavilion, $30; cottage, $35. **Parking:** Limit of 2 vehicles per site; extra parking available for a fee.

FACILITIES
Number of Multipurpose Sites: 206. **Hookups:** Yes. **Dump Station:** Yes. **Laundry:** No. **Pay Phone:** Yes. **Restrooms and Showers:** Yes. **Fuel:** No. **Propane:** No. **Internal Roads:** Paved. **RV Service:** No. **Market:** No. **Restaurant:** 1 mi. **General Store:** Yes. **Vending:** No. **Swimming:** Yes. **Playground:** Yes. **Other:** Check hunt dates. Park does not have a gate. **Activities:** Backpacking, birdwatching, boating, canoeing, fishing, picnicking, waterskiing, wildlife viewing.

RESTRICTIONS
Pets: On a 6-ft. leash, never unattended, under control at all times, cleaned up after. **Fires:** Fires may be built only in campsite grills, fire rings, or fireplaces. Some sites allow only containerized fuel fires. When warranted, fire bans are implemented by county judges and/or county commissioners courts. Inquire when making reservations. **Alcoholic Beverages:** It is an offense to consume or display an open container of an alcoholic beverage in a public place or sell alcoholic beverages w/in a state park.

TO GET THERE
From Dallas: Take I-30 east to Mt. Vernon. Exit on Hwy. 37S, and go 0.8 mi. Turn left on Hwy. 21, go 10 mi. Park will be on the left side of the road. From Texarkana: Take I-30 west to Mt. Pleasant. Take the 3rd exit, Ferguson Rd./Hwy. 271S. Go south to Hwy. 127, turn right, and continue to Hwy. 21. Turn south in about a mi. Park will be on left.

PORT ARANSAS   MAP, D-4
Mustang Island State Park

reserve america

P.O. Box 326, 78373. T: (361) 749-5246; www.reserveamerica.com.

🚐 ★★★   ⛺ ★★★★★

Beauty: ★★★	Site Privacy: ★
Spaciousness: ★★	Quiet: ★★★
Security: ★★★	Cleanliness: ★★★★
Insect Control: ★★★	Facilities: ★★

Tent campers are in luck at Mustang Island—gorgeous beachfront tent sites include a picnic table and shade shelter at each site (call ahead regarding beach conditions). RV sites are disappointing. The RV campground is a sea of unnecessary pavement. Sites are small, extremely close together, and offer no shade or privacy. All sites are back-in, and there is no vegetation in the campground. It doesn't matter which site you choose. The beach and birding are the draws here. The park provides nice, not extensive, beach facilities and no special birding facilities. Though the park feels rural, restaurants are 10 minutes away. The mosquitoes can be oppressive here, so come prepared with insect repellent. Mustang Island is busiest in the spring and summer. For tranquility, visit in the fall. Security is good; the front gates are locked at night, and the campground is a long walk from Hwy. 361.

BASICS
Operated By: Texas Parks and Wildlife. **Open:** All year. **Site Assignment:** Reservations (512) 389-8900; reservations must be made at least 48 hrs. in advance; deposit required (equivalent to 1-night fee) to hold reservation; cancellations more than 2 days prior to reservation result in $5 fee; cancellations w/in 2 days of reservation result in loss of deposit. **Registration:** At park headquarters, after hours register next morning. **Fee:** Developed, $15; primitive, $8; plus $4 entrance fee per person over 13 years; cash, check, V, MC, D. **Parking:** At site (2 cars), on beach for primitive camping.

FACILITIES
Number of RV-only Sites: 26. **Number of Tent-only Sites:** 300. **Hookups:** Electric (50 amps), water. **Each Site:** Covered shelter, barbecue pit. **Dump Station:** Yes. **Laundry:** no. **Pay Phone:** Yes. **Restrooms and Showers:** Yes. **Fuel:** No. **Propane:** No. **Internal Roads:** Paved. **RV Service:** 15 mi. in Corpus Christi. **Market:** 10 mi. in Corpus Christi. **Restaurant:** 5 mi. in Corpus Christi. **General Store:** Yes. **Vending:** Yes. **Swimming:** Yes. **Playground:** No. **Other:** Shaded shelters. **Activities:** Fishing, swimming, surfing, beach combing, birdwatching. **Nearby Attractions:** USS *Lexington,* Texas State Aquarium, Ships of Christopher Columbus, Greyhound Racetrack, Padre Island National Seashore, University of Texas Marine Science Center, Port Aransas Birding Center. **Additional Information:** Port Aransas Chamber of Commerce, (361) 749-5919; Corpus Christi Area CVB, (800) 678-6232.

RESTRICTIONS
Pets: On leash only, attended. **Fires:** On the beach only (or grill). **Alcoholic Beverages:** Not allowed. **Vehicle Maximum Length:** 45 ft. **Other:** No lifeguards, water sports at your own risk; call park to determine beach camping conditions.

TO GET THERE
From Corpus Christi, take TX 358 southeast to Padre Island. Cross the causeway and drive 1 mi. to the traffic light. Turn left on TX 361 and drive 5 mi. to the park.

PORT ARANSAS   MAP, D-4
Pioneer RV Resort

120 Gulfwind Dr., 78373.
T: (361) 749-6248 or (888) 480-3246.

🚐 ★★★   ⛺ n/a

Beauty: ★★★★	Site Privacy: ★★★
Spaciousness: ★★★	Quiet: ★★★★
Security: ★★★	Cleanliness: ★★★★
Insect Control: ★★★★	Facilities: ★★★★

Port Aransas on Mustang Island is known for its excellent birding, with boardwalks and raised observation towers at both the Port Aransas Birding Center and the Port Aransas Wetlands Park. Excellent deep-sea fishing and lovely beaches appeal to families and retirees. Pioneer's campground is attractive and tidy, with both back-in and pull-through spaces. The L-shaped campground hugs a pretty pond that attracts many birds. Sites are situated in long rows and feature paved parking. There are no trees, but each site has a grassy area. Most sites are of average size. We recommend the premium sites (the 300s), which are larger, quieter, and closer to the beach. Security is fair at Pioneer—there are no gates, but the park's serene location gives no cause for concern. Insects are not as problematic here as at nearby Mustang Island State Park. For solitude, visit Port Aransas in the fall.

BASICS
Operated By: Ralph Fels. **Open:** All year. **Site Assignment:** For reservations, call (888) 480-3246; credit card holds reservation; monthly reservations require 1-month deposit; you may request a certain area, but not a certain site; V, MC, D, personal check, cash; refund w/ 1-day notice as long as

before scheduled check-in. **Registration:** At office. **Fee:** $28.95–33.95; for 2 people; each additional adult, $3. **Parking:** On site.

FACILITIES

Number of RV-only Sites: 361. **Hookups:** Electric (20, 30, 50 amps), water, sewer, phone, cable TV, Wi-Fi. **Each Site:** Concrete patio, picnic table. **Dump Station:** Yes. **Laundry:** Yes. **Pay Phone:** Yes. **Restrooms and Showers:** Yes. **Fuel:** No. **Propane:** Yes. **Internal Roads:** Concrete. **RV Service:** 30 mi. in Corpus Christi. **Market:** 3.5 mi. north in Port Aransas. **Restaurant:** 3.5 mi. north in Port Aransas. **General Store:** On site. **Vending:** Beverages, ice, beer. **Swimming:** Pool. **Playground:** Yes. **Other:** Spa, rec hall, fish-cleaning facility, trolley service. **Activities:** Birding areas, arts & crafts, deep sea fishing trips, aerobics, dancing, golf, ladies lunches, cribbage, washers, dominoes, bridge, bunko, pool, horseshoes, shuffleboard, quilting. **Nearby Attractions:** Texas State Aquarium, The USS *Lexington*, Corpus Christi Greyhound Racetrack, University of Texas Marine Science Center, Port Aransas Birding Center. **Additional Information:** Port Aransas Chamber of Commerce, (361) 749-5919; Corpus Christi Area CVB, (800) 678-6232.

RESTRICTIONS

Pets: On leash only; must be approved if over 50 lbs.; absolutely no pit bulls, Dobermans, rottweilers, chows, or wolf hybrids allowed. **Fires:** Grill only. **Alcoholic Beverages:** Allowed. **Vehicle Maximum Length:** 60 ft.

TO GET THERE

From Corpus Christi, take TX 358 which becomes Park Rd. 22. After you cross the JFK Causeway, take a left at the next traffic light (Hwy. 361) and the park will be 15 mi. on the right.

PORT ISABEL   MAP, D-4
Long Island Village

950 South Garcia St., P.O. Box 695, 78578. T: (956) 943-6449 or (800) 292-7261; www.longislandvillage.com.

🚐 ★★★★   ⛺ n/a

Beauty: ★★★★	Site Privacy: ★★★
Spaciousness: ★★★★	Quiet: ★★★★
Security: ★★★★★	Cleanliness: ★★★★★
Insect Control: ★★★★	Facilities: ★★★★★

Ultra-tidy Long Island Village welcomes families and retirees and maintains extensive facilities, including an 18-hole golf course. Located on Long Island, south of Port Isabel, the park is convenient to South Padre Island and restaurants and shopping. Though sites are small and crowded, the campground is laid out in a series of rows dissected by picturesque canals. Waterfront sites often have private docks. The sites are extremely clean with paved, back-in parking. There are few trees. Landscaping enhances the park's beauty, though it provides no shade or privacy. Since Long Island is so large, families should look for a site near the pool. Couples should ask for a quiet site in the back. Security is excellent; the complex is gated and surrounded by water. Popular with families in the spring and summer and with snow birds in the winter, it's best to visit Long Island in the fall.

BASICS

Operated By: Outdoor Owners Assoc. of Long Island Texas. **Open:** All year. **Site Assignment:** Lots assigned; credit card holds lot, 48-hour cancellation notice required or 1-night fee charged; reservations require a deposit of 1-night stay. **Registration:** At office, register w/security at night. **Fee:** $46–$52; for 3 people; each additional person, $2; 8 people max.; cash, personal Check, V, MC, AE, D. **Parking:** At site only.

FACILITIES

Number of RV-only Sites: 200. **Hookups:** Electric (50 amps), water, sewer, cable TV. **Each Site:** Concrete pad, picnic table. **Dump Station:** No. **Laundry:** Yes. **Pay Phone:** Yes. **Restrooms and Showers:** Yes. **Fuel:** No. **Propane:** Service. **Internal Roads:** Paved. **RV Service:** 0.5 mi. in Port Isabel. **Market:** 0.5 mi. in Port Isabel. **Restaurant:** On site (seasonal), also w/in one block of resort. **General Store:** W/in 2 blocks. **Vending:** Yes. **Swimming:** Pool (indoor & outdoor). **Playground:** No. **Other:** Rec hall, exercise room, sauna, library, ballroom, billiard room. **Activities:** 18-hole par 3 golf course, mini-golf, tennis, shuffleboard, volleyball, basketball, horseshoes, arts & crafts. **Nearby Attractions:** Padre Island National Seashore, Port Isabel Lighthouse & Boca Chica State Parks, dolphin watching, charter fishing, Rio Grande, South Padre Island. **Additional Information:** Port Isabel Chamber of Commerce, (800) 527-6102; South Padre Island CVB, (800) SO-PADRE.

RESTRICTIONS

Pets: On leash only, 2 pet limit. **Fires:** Not allowed, bring your own grill. **Alcoholic Beverages:** Allowed. **Vehicle Maximum Length:** 60 ft. **Other:** No pop-ups, vans, or tents, no fish-cleaning on picnic tables.

TO GET THERE

From US 77/83, take TX 100 east approx. 25 mi. Just before the causeway, turn right on Garcia St. and follow it 0.5 mi. to the Resort at the end.

POWEDERLY   MAP, A-5
Sanders Cove Campground

reserve america

P.O. Box 129, 75473-0129. T: (903) 732-3020; www.reserveamerica.com.

🚐 ★★★★   ⛺ ★★★★

Beauty: ★★★	Site Privacy: ★★
Spaciousness: ★★	Quiet: ★★★★★
Security: ★★★★★	Cleanliness: ★★★★
Insect Control: ★★★	Facilities: ★★★★

Sanders Cove Campground is located at Pat Mayse Lake on the Red River Basin in Lamar County, Texas. Easy access to developed park areas has made the lake a mecca for families who enjoy camping, picnicking, swimming, boating, fishing and other outdoor recreation. The lake provides excellent opportunities for fishing and hunting. Sport fish species in the lake include largemouth bass, white crappie, sunfish, striped bass, channel and flathead catfish, and other common fish species. These lands are managed for upland game and white tail deer and are open to the public as a public hunting area. The game species present include deer, fox squirrel, gray squirrel, bobwhite quail, morning dove, cottontail rabbit, raccoon, and fox. Fur bearers such as opossum, beaver, mink, skunk, and nutria are present as well. The lake provides resting and feeding habitat for migratory waterfowl. A few miles north of the project area are the famed Red River Bottoms, where waterfowl congregate in great numbers.

BASICS

Operated By: U.S. Army Corps of Engineers. **Open:** All year. **Site Assignment:** Reservations must be made at least 2 days in advance. **Registration:** At office. **Fee:** Single, $10–$15. **Parking:** At site.

FACILITIES

Number of Multipurpose Sites: 204. **Hookups:** Yes. **Dump Station:** Yes. **Laundry:** No. **Pay Phone:** Yes. **Restrooms and Showers:** Yes. **Fuel:** No. **Propane:** No. **Internal Roads:** Gravel. **RV Service:** No. **Market:** No. **Restaurant:** No. **General Store:** No. **Vending:** No. **Swimming:** Yes. **Playground:** No. **Other:** This area was a military artillery range in the 1940s. Visitors should not touch or molest remaining ordnance. **Activities:** Picnicking, swimming, boating, fishing.

RESTRICTIONS

Pets: Restrained or on a leash at all times while in developed recreation areas. **Fires:** W/in campgrounds and other recreation areas, fires may only be built in fire rings, stoves, grills, or fireplaces provided for that purpose. **Alcoholic Beverages:** Not allowed. **Vehicle Maximum Length:** Call ahead.

TO GET THERE

From Paris, TX: Take Hwy. 271 N 12 mi to FM 906 W and follow 1 mi to CR 35920. Turn left into the park following signs.

QUANAH   MAP, A-3
Copper Breaks State Park

reserve america

777 Park Rd. 62, 79252-7679. T: (940) 839-4331; www.reserveamerica.com.

🚐 ★★★★   ⛺ ★★★★

Beauty: ★★★★	Site Privacy: ★★★★
Spaciousness: ★★★★	Quiet: ★★★★
Security: ★★★★	Cleanliness: ★★★★
Insect Control: ★★★	Facilities: ★★★★

Taking its name from the copper deposits found in the area, this park boasts striking rock formations with alternating layers of gypsum, red clays, and shales. Recreation revolves around the 60-acre lake, which is stocked with rainbow trout in the winter. Lake Copper Breaks also hosts many migratory waterfowl, including great blue heron. Part of the Texas state longhorn herd lives at Copper Breaks. Comanche campground (water/electric) is not as pretty as Kiowa (no hookups). Both offer spacious, paved, back-in sites. Kiowa includes sites shaded by tall trees and secluded by foliage between many sites. Families might appreciate Kiowa's proximity to the swimming beach. Comanche's sites are cookie-cutter boring and have no shade and little privacy. Security is good at this rural park. North Texas experiences cold winters and hot summers; visit in spring, early summer, or fall.

BASICS

Operated By: Texas Parks and Wildlife. **Open:** All year. **Site Assignment:** Reservations available, not by site but by campground; cancellation fee, $5. **Registration:** At headquarters, after hours use honor boxes. **Fee:** Water/electric, $20; water, $10; primitive tent, $7; entrance fee per person (13 and older), $2. **Parking:** At site.

FACILITIES

Number of RV-only Sites: 25. **Number of Tent-only Sites:** 27. **Hookups:** Electric (50 amps), water. **Each Site:** Fire ring, grill, picnic table. **Dump Station:** Yes. **Laundry:** No. **Pay Phone:** Yes. **Restrooms and Showers:** Yes. **Fuel:** No. **Propane:** No. **Internal Roads:** Paved. **RV Service:** 63 mi. northeast in Altus, OK. **Market:** 13 mi. north in Quanah. **Restaurant:** 8 mi. south in Crowell or in Quanah. **General Store:** Yes. **Vending:** No. **Swimming:** Yes. **Playground:** Yes. **Other:** Visitor center, meeting room, picnic area, picnic pavilion, swimming beach, boat ramp, boat dock, fishing pier, amphitheater, scenic overlook, group camp, equestrian camping. **Activities:** Hiking, backpacking, equestrian trails, swimming, boating, fishing, paddleboat rental (in-season), horseshoes, basketball, volleyball, mountain biking. **Nearby Attractions:** Hardeman County Historical Museum, Medicine Mound (on private property), Firehall Museum in Crowell, Lake Pauline, Greenbelt Reservoir. **Additional Information:** (800) 792-1112.

RESTRICTIONS

Pets: Leash only, attended. **Fires:** Fire ring only. **Alcoholic Beverages:** Not allowed. **Vehicle Maximum Length:** 50 ft. **Other:** No gathering wood.

TO GET THERE

From Quanah, drive south on TX 6 25 mi. Park Rd. 62 entrance is on right.

QUITAQUE — MAP, A-3
Caprock Canyons State Park and Trailway

reserve america

P.O. Box 204, 79255. T: (806) 455-1492; www.reserveamerica.com.

🚐 ★★★★★   ⛺ ★★★★★

Beauty: ★★★★★   Site Privacy: ★★★★
Spaciousness: ★★★★★   Quiet: ★★★★★
Security: ★★★★   Cleanliness: ★★★★★
Insect Control: ★★★   Facilities: ★★★★

This gorgeous state park is adjacent to 64-mile Caprock Canyon Trailway, a multiuse rail-to-trail conversion completed in 1993. Catering to expert hikers and mountain bikers, 25 miles of extremely rugged trails are found inside the park. Wildlife includes African aoudad sheep, a herd of pronghorn antelope, and the largest herd of buffalo in the state park system. Pretty Honea Flat campground features sites with paved back-in RV parking. Site size varies. Cottonwood trees and foliage provide shade and privacy at some sites, while others are more open. Families should go for sites 15 and 17 (near the playground and potties). Those seeking privacy should try to score site 23. The tent-only campgrounds are also very attractive. Visit Caprock on weekdays in spring, summer, or fall. Call ahead to avoid special event weekends. Security is good-there are no gates, but the park is extremely remote.

BASICS

Operated By: Texas Parks and Wildlife. **Open:** All year; park closes for hunting season; call park for details. **Site Assignment:** Reservations (512) 389-8900; reservations must be made at least 48 hrs. in advance; deposit required (equivalent to 1-night fee) to hold reservation; cancellations more than 2 days prior to reservation result in $5 fee; cancellations w/in 2 days of reservation result in loss of deposit. **Registration:** At park headquarters, after hours self-registration. **Fee:** RV, $15–$20; tent, $8–$12; plus $3 entrance fee per person (13 and older); cash, check, V, MC, D. **Parking:** At site (2 cars, $2 per additional vehicle).

FACILITIES

Number of RV-only Sites: 35. **Number of Tent-only Sites:** 89. **Hookups:** Electric (30, 50 amps), water. **Each Site:** Picnic table, fire ring, lantern pole. **Dump Station:** Yes. **Laundry:** No. **Pay Phone:** Yes. **Restrooms and Showers:** Yes, showers close during water shortages (call park). **Fuel:** No. **Propane:** No. **Internal Roads:** Paved. **RV Service:** Inquire at campground. **Market:** 3 mi. in Quitaque. **Restaurant:** 3 mi. in Quitaque. **General Store:** Texas park store. **Vending:** Beverages. **Swimming:** Lake. **Playground:** Yes. **Other:** Interpretive exhibits, gravel equestrian loop, amphitheater, backpacking trails, picnic pavilion, fishing pier boat ramp. **Activities:** Hiking, horseback riding, seasonal horse rentals, mountain biking, boating, fishing, lake swimming, scenic drive, guided tours. **Nearby Attractions:** Turkey, Panhandle-Plains Historical Museum & West Texas State University in Canyon, Palo Duro Canyon & Copper Breaks State Parks, Lake Mackenzie, Ranching Heritage Center, 2 hours from Amarillo & Lubbock. **Additional Information:** Turkey City Hall, (806) 423-1033; Amarillo CVB, (800) 692-1338; Lubbock CVB, (800) 692-4035.

RESTRICTIONS

Pets: On leash only, not in buildings. **Fires:** Not allowed when fire ban in effect. **Alcoholic Beverages:** Not allowed. **Vehicle Maximum Length:** No limit. **Other:** Take personal water supply on trails; check w/ park for current restrictions.

TO GET THERE

From I-27, take Exit 74 and head east on TX 86 approx. 45 mi. to Quitaque. Turn north on FM 1065 and drive 3 mi. to the park.

RUSK — MAP, B-5
Rusk Palestine State Park

reserve america

RR 4 Box 431, 75785. T: (903) 683-5126; www.reserveamerica.com.

🚐 ★★★★   ⛺ ★★★★

Beauty: ★★★★   Site Privacy: ★★★★
Spaciousness: ★★★★   Quiet: ★★★
Security: ★★★★   Cleanliness: ★★★★
Insect Control: ★★★★   Facilities: ★★★★

Rusk and Palestine recreation areas are connected by the 25-mile Texas State Railroad. The park maintains four steam engines and four antique diesel engines and offers four-hour, 50-mile round trip excursions between Rusk and Palestine (depart at either terminus). Children especially enjoy visiting the engineer and touring the steam engine cab. After the trains, explore the lake and woods. We prefer the RV campground at Rusk, which is nicer than Palestine, with tall pine trees providing shade at most sites. Pull-through sites offer full hookups and paved parking. Sites are comfortably spaced, but not huge. Sites 7–12, situated away from Hwy. 84, are the quietest. Families enjoy sites 17 and 19, which are adjacent to the playground. Site 14, the only back-in, is the most secluded. Avoid Rusk/Palestine on summer weekends. Opt for weekday and off-season visits. Security is good at this rural recreation area. Gates lock at 10 p.m.

BASICS

Operated By: Texas Parks and Wildlife Dept. **Open:** All year. **Site Assignment:** Reservations (512) 389-8900; reservations must be made at least 48 hrs. in advance; deposit required (equivalent to 1-night fee) to hold reservation; cancellations more than 2 days prior to reservation result in $5 fee; cancellations w/in 2 days of reservation result in loss of deposit. **Registration:** At park office, after hours register next morning. **Fee:** $11–$15; plus entry fee, $2 per adult; cash, check, V, MC, D. **Parking:** At site (2 cars), in parking lot.

FACILITIES

Number of RV-only Sites: 71. **Hookups:** Electric (30, 50 amps), water, sewer. **Each Site:** Picnic table, grill, fire ring. **Dump Station:** Yes. **Laundry:** No. **Pay Phone:** No. **Restrooms and Showers:** Yes. **Fuel:** No. **Propane:** No. **Internal Roads:** Paved. **RV Service:** 30 mi. in Nacogdoches. **Market:** 4 mi. in Rusk. **Restaurant:** 5 mi. in Rusk. **General Store:** Yes. **Vending:** Beverages. **Swimming:** Yes (lake). **Playground:** Yes. **Other:** Picnic areas & pavilions, gift shop & food at train depots, group dining hall, fishing jetty, tennis courts, fishing pier. **Activities:** Steam engine tours (weekends Mar.-Nov.), lake swimming, fishing, pedal boat & canoe rentals, nature trails, biking, volleyball, horseshoes, basketball. **Nearby Attractions:** Mission Tejas & Caddoan Mounds State Historical Parks, Tyler & Fairfield State Parks, Museum of East Texas, NASA Scientific Balloon Base. **Additional Information:** Palestine CVB, (800) 659-3484.

RESTRICTIONS

Pets: On leash only, attended, not allowed in buildings. **Fires:** Fire ring (except under fire ban). **Alcoholic Beverages:** Not allowed. **Vehicle Maximum Length:** 40 ft. (sites vary). **Other:** Checkout 2 p.m., daytime visitors must exit park by 10 p.m.

TO GET THERE

From US 84, about 3 mi. west of downtown Rusk, turn south onto Park Rd. 76 and drive 0.25 mi. to the park.

SABINE PASS   MAP, C-5
Sea Rim State Park

reserve america

10 miles West of Sabine Pass off Hwy. 87, P. O. Box 356, 77655. T: (409) 971-2559; www.reserveamerica.com.

🚐 ★★★	⛺ ★★★★
Beauty: ★★★	Site Privacy: ★
Spaciousness: ★★	Quiet: ★★★
Security: ★★★	Cleanliness: ★★
Insect Control: ★	Facilities: ★★★

Spend little time in the uninspired campgrounds. Rather, enjoy the often deserted beach or explore the Sea Rim marshlands via canoe, kayak, or boardwalk. This biologically important area includes marsh grasses that inhabit a tidal zone, and it's a winter home for numerous bird species. RV sites are small and crowded. The entire campground is paved, with no trees or shrubs. Bring your own shade and live without privacy. All sites are unattractive, so pick one near the beach. Tent campers fare better—sites are more spacious and attractive, but offer little privacy. For sheer beauty, the best option for tent campers is primitive camping on the beach. September is the wettest month at Sea Rim. Visit in late spring or early summer before the heat becomes unbearable. Security is good at this very rural park. We cannot overstate the terror caused by Sea Rim mosquitoes. Prepare to battle these beasts.

BASICS

Operated By: Texas Parks and Wildlife. **Open:** All year. **Site Assignment:** Reservations (512) 389-8900; reservations must be made at least 48 hrs. in advance; deposit required (equivalent to 1-night fee) to hold reservation; cancellations more than 2 days prior to reservation result in $5 fee; cancellations w/in 2 days of reservation result in loss of deposit. **Registration:** At headquarters. **Fee:** RV, $11; tent, $8; primitive tent (on beach), $6; daily fee per person (13 and older), $2; cash, check, D, V, MC. **Parking:** At site.

FACILITIES

Number of RV-only Sites: 20. **Number of Tent-only Sites:** 10. **Hookups:** Electric (30 amps), water. **Each Site:** Picnic table, grill, tent-only sites also have lantern hook & tent pad. **Dump Station:** Yes. **Laundry:** No. **Pay Phone:** No. **Restrooms and Showers:** Yes. **Fuel:** No. **Propane:** No. **Internal Roads:** Paved. **RV Service:** 25 mi. northeast in Port Arthur. **Market:** 10 mi. east in Sabine Pass. **Restaurant:** 10

mi. east in Sabine Pass. **General Store:** Wal-Mart 20 mi. northeast in Port Arthur. **Vending:** No. **Swimming:** Beach. **Playground:** No. **Other:** Sandy swimming beach, picnic area, gift shop, visitor center, observation deck, observation blinds for bird-watching, air boat tours (by reservation only). **Activities:** Hiking, walking, bicycling, bird-watching, beach combing, boating (canoe & kayak rentals available), beach swimming, fishing, seasonal waterfowl hunting. **Nearby Attractions:** Sabine Pass Battleground State Historical Park, festivals & historic homes in Port Arthur & surrounding towns. **Additional Information:** Port Arthur CVB, (800) 235-7822.

RESTRICTIONS

Pets: On leash only. **Fires:** Ground fires allowed on beach or in fire rings. **Alcoholic Beverages:** Not allowed. **Vehicle Maximum Length:** 40 ft. **Other:** Swim at your own risk; don't approach, annoy, or feed the alligators.

TO GET THERE

From I-10, take Exit 829 at Winnie and drive 28 mi. east on TX 73. Turn south on TX 82 and drive 10 mi. to the traffic light in Sabine Pass at TX 87. Turn right and drive 10 mi. into the park.

SAN ANGELO   MAP, B-3
San Angelo State Park

reserve america

3900-2 Mercedes, 76901. T: (325) 949-4757 or (325) 949-8935; www.reserveamerica.com.

🚐 ★★★	⛺ ★★★
Beauty: ★★★	Site Privacy: ★★★
Spaciousness: ★★★★	Quiet: ★★★★
Security: ★★★	Cleanliness: ★★★★
Insect Control: ★★★	Facilities: ★★★

Three campgrounds are situated along the North Concho River, and four are adjacent to O.C. Fisher Lake. Sites are spacious, if lackluster. RV campers looking for elbow room should ask for pull-through sites 1–11 (Red Arroyo area). Tent campers looking for lake views should head for sites 13–16 (Red Arroyo area). Many sites have partial lake views since there are few trees. Gravel parking is the norm. Ecologically diverse, this park is home to roughly 350 species of birds. The Concho River is named after indigenous freshwater mussels that produce iridescent pink or purple "Concho pearls." Also of interest are dinosaur tracks and Native American petroglyphs (access via reserved group tours). Suburban (fewer than 3 miles from San Angelo), but with locked gates at night, security is decent. The weather at this park can be extreme, so try to visit in spring, early summer, or fall.

BASICS

Operated By: Texas Parks and Wildlife. **Open:** All year. **Site Assignment:** Reservations (512) 389-8900; reservations must be made at least 48 hrs. in advance; deposit required (equivalent to 1-night fee) to hold reservation; cancellations more than 2 days prior to reservation result in $5 fee; cancellations w/in 2 days of reservation result in loss of deposit. **Registration:** At headquarters. **Fee:** Water/electric,

$18; primitive, $8; daily fee per person (13 and older), $2; cash, check, V, MC, D. **Parking:** At site.

FACILITIES

Number of RV-only Sites: 184. **Number of Tent-only Sites:** 93. **Hookups:** Electric (50 amps), water. **Each Site:** Picnic table, fire ring, grill. **Dump Station:** Yes. **Laundry:** No. **Pay Phone:** No. **Restrooms and Showers:** Yes. **Fuel:** No. **Propane:** No. **Internal Roads:** Paved. **RV Service:** 3 mi. southeast in San Angelo. **Market:** Super Wal-Mart 3 mi. southeast in San Angelo. **Restaurant:** 3 mi. southeast in San Angelo. **General Store:** Super Wal-Mart, 3 mi. southeast in San Angelo. **Vending:** Beverages. **Swimming:** No. **Playground:** Yes. **Other:** High & low level boat ramps, courtesy docks, fishing platform, log shelters, group camping & picnic areas, equestrian camping. **Activities:** Picnicking, hiking, mountain biking, horseback riding, swimming, boating, birding, group tours upon request. **Nearby Attractions:** Fort Concho, Concho Ave. shopping district, Concho River Walk, Miss Hattie's Museum. **Additional Information:** San Angelo CVB, (800) 375-1206.

RESTRICTIONS

Pets: Must be kept on leash at all times. **Fires:** Fire rings, grills only. **Alcoholic Beverages:** Not allowed. **Vehicle Maximum Length:** 60 ft. **Other:** Max. 8 people per campsite, quiet time 10 p.m.–6 a.m., gathering of firewood prohibited.

TO GET THERE

To reach the south shore park entrance from San Angelo, take US 67 south about 2 mi. and then turn right on FM 853. To reach the north shore park entrance from San Angelo, go north on US 87 about 2 mi., and then turn left on FM 2288.

SAN ANTONIO   MAP, C-4
Admiralty RV Resort

1485 North Ellison Dr., 78251. T: (210) 647-7878 or (800) 999-7872; www.admiraltyrvresort.com.

🚐 ★★★	⛺ n/a
Beauty: ★★★★	Site Privacy: ★★★
Spaciousness: ★★★	Quiet: ★★★
Security: ★★★	Cleanliness: ★★★★★
Insect Control: ★★★★★	Facilities: ★★★★

This gleefully tidy park is convenient to SeaWorld, restaurants, and shopping. Six Flags Fiesta Texas, the Alamo, and the River Walk are within 30 miles. Spending the day at the park? Facilities are well maintained. The nicely landscaped campground is laid in rows of pull-throughs, with back-ins along the perimeter of the park. Sites are small, with little privacy. Some sites enjoy shady trees, but many are open. RV parking is paved, though some internal roads are gravel. Families should head for sites 1–10, 101–110, or 201–210, the closest to the playground. Couples looking for a little solitude should go for sites in the 600s. Security is fair at this suburban campground—there are no gates, but a guard patrols the property at night. The brochures claim that San Antonio has mild weather all year, but it sometimes gets chilly in the winter; visit in spring or fall.

BASICS

Operated By: Mary and Rick Pearce. **Open:** All year; park closes for hunting season; call for details. **Site Assignment:** Reservations accepted all year, (800) 999-7872; credit card required for reservation; no-show charged 1 night; deposit & refund policies vary for weekly & monthly stays; call campground for more details. **Registration:** At office. **Fee:** $32–$45; for 2 people; each additional person (up to 8 max.), $3. **Parking:** At site.

FACILITIES

Number of RV-only Sites: 240. **Hookups:** Electric (30, 50 amps), water, sewer, cable TV, Wi-Fi. **Each Site:** Picnic table, concrete pads, some grills. **Dump Station:** No. **Laundry:** Yes. **Pay Phone:** Yes. **Restrooms and Showers:** Yes. **Fuel:** No. **Propane:** No (weekly salesman). **Internal Roads:** Paved. **RV Service:** 2 mi. west. **Market:** 2 mi. east in San Antonio. **Restaurant:** 7 mi. east in San Antonio. **General Store:** Yes. **Vending:** Yes. **Swimming:** Pool. **Playground:** Yes. **Other:** Game room, exercise room, adult Jacuzzi, clubhouse, RV supplies. **Activities:** Basketball, water aerobics, volleyball, year-round schedule of activities including bingo, crafts, dances, ice-cream socials. **Nearby Attractions:** The Alamo, Botanical Gardens, San Antonio Zoo & Aquarium, Sea World, Mexican-American Cultural Center, Riverwalk, McNay Art Museum, Market Square, IMAX Theater, Institute of Texan Cultures. **Additional Information:** San Antonio CVB, (800) 447-3372.

RESTRICTIONS

Pets: On 6-ft. max. leash at all times. **Fires:** Only in barbecue grills. **Alcoholic Beverages:** Allowed. **Vehicle Maximum Length:** 60 ft. **Other:** Check w/ park for current restrictions.

TO GET THERE

From I-410 (loop), take Exit 9A and drive northwest 2 mi. on TX 151. Turn left on Potranco Rd. and drive 2 mi. to North Ellison Rd. Turn right and the resort is 1 mi. on the left.

SAN BENITO   MAP, D-4
Fun n Sun Resort

reserve america

1400 Zillock Rd., 78586-9730. T: (956) 399-5129; www.mhcrv.com.

🚐 ★★★   ▲ n/a

Beauty: ★★★	Site Privacy: ★★★
Spaciousness: ★★★	Quiet: ★★★
Security: ★★★★	Cleanliness: ★★★★
Insect Control: ★	Facilities: ★★★★

Open to seniors only, Fun n Sun offers activities galore and keeps its extensive facilities in good shape. South Padre Island, Brownsville, and Mexico are easy to reach, as well as a plethora of restaurants and shopping. Though Fun n Sun only accepts reservations for one month or longer, there are eight overnight sites near the front gate. Sites are small and have little privacy. Some are shaded by trees. All have paved, back-in parking. Each site has a little grassy area. Ask for

---

sites 5–8, which are away from Zillock Rd. and quieter. Security is good. The gate is attended 24 hours. Don't visit south Texas in the summer, and be prepared for major crowds in the winter.

BASICS

Operated By: Equity Lifestyle Properties. **Open:** All year. **Site Assignment:** Reservations for 1 month or more, $200 deposit, call (800) 399-5127; V, MC, checks, cash. **Registration:** At office, Mon.–Fri., 8 a.m.–5 p.m.; at security building after hours. **Fee:** $25–$27. **Parking:** At site.

FACILITIES

Number of RV-only Sites: 1408. **Hookups:** Electric (30, 50 amps), water, sewer, cable TV. **Each Site:** None. **Dump Station:** No. **Laundry:** Yes. **Pay Phone:** Yes. **Restrooms and Showers:** Yes. **Fuel:** No. **Propane:** Yes. **Internal Roads:** Paved. **RV Service:** 15 mi. **Market:** 1 mi. **Restaurant:** 2 mi. **General Store:** 3 mi. **Vending:** Yes. **Swimming:** Pool. **Playground:** No. **Other:** Barber & beauty shops, billiards, exercise facility, post office, chapel, woodworking shop, music room, meeting rooms, rec hall, dance hall, sewing room, library, lapidary shop, tennis courts, hot tub, silver smithing shop. **Activities:** Dancing, pool, shuffleboard, horseshoes, bocce ball, birding. **Nearby Attractions:** South Padre Island Beaches, Gladys Porter Zoo, Mexico. **Additional Information:** San Benito Chamber of Commerce, (956) 399-5321.

RESTRICTIONS

Pets: On leash only. **Fires:** Grill only. **Alcoholic Beverages:** Allowed. **Vehicle Maximum Length:** 40 ft. **Other:** All rates are based on occupancy of 2 people per unit. 1 person must be at least 55 years old & the other person at least 40 years old.

TO GET THERE

From US 77/83, take the Paso Real/Hwy. 509 exit. Stay on the frontage road 0.25 mi. past Paso Real and turn right on Zillock Rd. The campground is 0.25 mi.

SMITHVILLE   MAP, C-4
Buescher State Park

reserve america

P.O. Box 75, 78957-0075. T: (512) 237-2241; www.reserveamerica.com.

🚐 ★★★★★   ▲ ★★★★★

Beauty: ★★★★★	Site Privacy: ★★★★★
Spaciousness: ★★★★★	Quiet: ★★★★★
Security: ★★★★	Cleanliness: ★★★★
Insect Control: ★	Facilities: ★★★★★

Part of a complex of state parks, Buescher connects to Bastrop State Park with a 13-mile paved, winding, hilly road that's appreciated by experienced cyclists. Unlike Bastrop, Buescher's facilities surround a small lake (approximately 25 acres) supporting catfish, bass, crappie, perch, and seasonal rainbow trout. The Lost Pines of Texas are prominent on the road from Bastrop. Post and live oak steal the show at Buescher. We prefer sites at Buescher over Bastrop because of

---

their gorgeous foliage between sites. But mosquitoes are far worse here—stay at drier Bastrop if it's been raining. Three campgrounds dot the small lake. RV campers find paved, back-in sites at Cozy Circle. With shady oak trees and paved back-in parking, we prefer the multiuse sites at Oak Haven. All sites are spacious. Rural location and locked nighttime gates make security excellent. Plan to visit on weekdays to avoid the mob. Park closes for hunting seasons. Call park for details.

BASICS

Operated By: Texas Parks and Wildlife. **Open:** All year. **Site Assignment:** Reservations (512) 389-8900; reservations must be made at least 48 hrs. in advance; deposit required (equivalent to 1-night fee) to hold reservation; cancellations more than 2 days prior to reservation result in $5 fee; cancellations w/in 2 days of reservation result in loss of deposit. **Registration:** At headquarters. **Fee:** Water/electric, $15; water, $12; daily charge per person (13 and older), $4; cash, check, V, MC, D. **Parking:** At most sites.

FACILITIES

Number of RV-only Sites: 32. **Number of Tent-only Sites:** 25. **Hookups:** Electric (30 amps), water; some tent sites w/ only water. **Each Site:** Picnic table, grill, fire ring. **Dump Station:** Yes. **Laundry:** No. **Pay Phone:** No. **Restrooms and Showers:** Yes. **Fuel:** No. **Propane:** No. **Internal Roads:** Paved. **RV Service:** 45 mi. west in Austin. **Market:** 1 mi. southwest in Smithville. **Restaurant:** 1 mi. southwest in Smithville. **General Store:** Park store at headquarters. **Vending:** Beverages. **Swimming:** No. **Playground:** Yes. **Other:** Picnic area, group picnic pavilion, rec hall, gift shop, screened shelters. **Activities:** Hiking, boating, fishing, road biking. **Nearby Attractions:** Lake Bastrop, Bastrop State Park, Lake Somerville State Park & Trailway, towns of Smithville & Bastrop, Texas state capitol Austin. **Additional Information:** Austin CVB, (800) 926-2282; Smithville Chamber, (512) 237-2313; Bastrop Chamber, (512) 321-2419.

RESTRICTIONS

Pets: On leash only, not allowed in buildings. **Fires:** Fire ring only. **Alcoholic Beverages:** Not allowed. **Vehicle Maximum Length:** Call park for details. **Other:** No gathering firewood.

TO GET THERE

From Smithville, go northwest on TX 71 2 mi. Turn right on FM 153 and go north 0.5 mi. to Park Rd. 1.

SNYDER   MAP, A-3
Wagon Wheel Guest Ranch

5996 CR 2128, 79549. T: (325) 573-2348.

🚐 ★★★★   ▲ ★★★★

Beauty: ★★★★	Site Privacy: ★★★
Spaciousness: ★★★★	Quiet: ★★★★
Security: ★★★	Cleanliness: ★★★★
Insect Control: ★★★★	Facilities: ★★★★★

Wagon Wheel is an excellent destination for families with energetic children. In addition to planned recreation, kids love to run around and explore the ranch. If your group is big enough (10 or more people), you can schedule a chuck wagon meal. The campground includes older and newer sections, though sites at both are basically the same. Both offer pull-throughs with gravel parking and a patchy grass and dirt area. Sites are large, some a long as 90 feet. With few trees and scrubby foliage, there is little shade or privacy at the campground. Families should pick a site close to the bathrooms. Tent campers should head for the more picturesque area near the pond (no hookups). Extremely remote, security is not a problem at Wagon Wheel. The panhandle plains sometimes experience extreme weather and should be avoided during winter and late summer.

BASICS

Operated By: Billy Ray and Pam Browning. **Open:** All year. **Site Assignment:** Reservations recommended, credit card deposit, 1-week cancellation notice required. **Registration:** At office. **Fee:** RV, $18.50; tent, $10. **Parking:** At site.

FACILITIES

Number of RV-only Sites: 25. **Number of Tent-only Sites:** 40. **Hookups:** Electric (30, 50 amps), water, sewer. **Each Site:** Picnic table, fire ring. **Dump Station:** Yes. **Laundry:** Yes. **Pay Phone:** No. **Restrooms and Showers:** Yes, in ranch house rooms, guest barn. **Fuel:** No. **Propane:** No. **Internal Roads:** Gravel. **RV Service:** 8 mi. east in Snyder. **Market:** 8 mi. east in Snyder. **Restaurant:** 2 mi. in Snyder. **General Store:** 8 mi. east in Snyder. **Vending:** Beverages. **Swimming:** Pool. **Playground:** Yes. **Other:** Ranch house, guest house, guest barn, paddleboats, ATV trails, game room, party barn. **Activities:** Washer pitching, horseshoes, softball, fishing, basketball, hiking, skeet shooting, quail & dove hunting. **Nearby Attractions:** Buffalo Gap Historic Village, Scurry County Museum, Abilene Zoo, Grace Museum, Dyess Air Force Base. **Additional Information:** Snyder Chamber of Commerce, (915) 573-3558; City of Snyder (915) 573-4957.

RESTRICTIONS

Pets: On leash only. **Fires:** Fire ring only. **Alcoholic Beverages:** Allowed. **Vehicle Maximum Length:** No limit.

TO GET THERE

From Lubbock, take the Post Exit (US 84) off of Loop 289. Continue southeast toward Snyder. 37 mi. past the town of Post, turn left on CR 2128. Go 3 mi. to ranch; entrance on the left.

SOMERVILLE   MAP, B-4
Lake Somerville State Park and Trailway

reserve america

Rte. 1 Box 499, 14222 Park Rd. 57, 77879-9713. T: (979) 535-7763; www.reserveamerica.com.

🚐 ★★★★★	🏕 ★★★★★
Beauty: ★★★★★	Site Privacy: ★★★★★
Spaciousness: ★★★★★	Quiet: ★★★★★
Security: ★★★★	Cleanliness: ★★★★★
Insect Control: ★	Facilities: ★★★

Comprising over 8,700 acres, gorgeous Lake Somerville consists of three units: Nails Creek, Birch Creek, and the Somerville Wildlife Management Area (a public hunting area). Nails Creek and Birch Creek are connected by a 13-mile multiuse trail known for its spring wildflowers. Both Nails Creek and Birch Creek have lovely campgrounds with spacious sites. Exceptional privacy is provided by dense trees, including post oak, hickory, blackjack oak, and others. Each site has paved back-in parking and a large grassy area. Birch Creek is popular with college students. Families and couples prefer quieter Nails Creek. At Nails Creek, there are gorgeous lakefront sites in the Cedar Creek Loop. At Birch Creek, the prettiest views are at the Cedar Elm camping area (no hookups). Security is fair—there are no gates, but both campgrounds are extremely remote. Mosquitoes proliferate when it's rainy, so come prepared. For optimal weather, visit in spring or fall.

BASICS

Operated By: Texas Parks and Wildlife. **Open:** All year; closed for specific hunting dates; call park for details. **Site Assignment:** Reservations (512) 389-8900; reservations must be made at least 48 hrs. in advance; deposit required (equivalent to 1-night fee) to hold reservation; cancellations more than 2 days prior to reservation result in $5 fee; cancellations w/in 2 days of reservation result in loss of deposit. **Registration:** At headquarters. **Fee:** Water/electric, $15; water, $10; primitive, $6; daily fee per person (13 and older), $3. **Parking:** At site.

FACILITIES

Number of RV-only Sites: 100. **Number of Tent-only Sites:** 55. **Hookups:** Electric (30, 50 amps), water. **Each Site:** Picnic table, fire ring, lantern post, tent pad. **Dump Station:** Yes. **Laundry:** No. **Pay Phone:** No. **Restrooms and Showers:** Yes. **Fuel:** No. **Propane:** No. **Internal Roads:** Paved. **RV Service:** 20 mi. west in Giddings. **Market:** Adjacent to park entrance. **Restaurant:** 3 mi. west of park. **General Store:** Gift shop. **Vending:** No. **Swimming:** Yes. **Playground:** No. **Other:** Birch Creek Unit: equestrian camping, group picnic pavilions, group camping, group dining hall, fish-cleaning shelter, boat ramps, boat dock, volleyball courts, gift shop. Nails Creek Unit: group picnic area, equestrian camping, fish-cleaning shelter. **Activities:** Picnicking, boating, fishing, swimming, hiking, backpacking, bicycling, mountain biking, horseback riding, volleyball, group tours available. **Nearby Attractions:** Bluebell Creamery, Presidential Corridor between Austin & College Station, Bastrop & Buescher State Parks, Stephen F. Austin & Washington-on-the-Brazos State Historical Parks, Austin (about 85 mi.), College Station (about 60 mi.). **Additional Information:** Austin CVB, (800) 926-2282; Bryan-College Station CVB, (800) 777-8292.

RESTRICTIONS

Pets: On leash only, attended, not in buildings. **Fires:** Fire ring only. **Alcoholic Beverages:** Not allowed. **Vehicle Maximum Length:** 40 ft.

TO GET THERE

To access Birch Creek Unit from Somerville, drive north on TX 36 4 mi. to the town of Lyons. Then drive west on TX 60 8 mi. and turn left onto Park Rd. 57. To get to Nails Creek Unit from Giddings,

head east on TX 290 6 mi. Turn left on FM 180 and follow it 15 mi.

SPRING BRANCH   MAP, C-4
Guadalupe River State Park

reserve america

3350 Park Rd. 31, 78070. T: (830) 438-2656 or (800) 792-1112; www.reserveamerica.com.

🚐 ★★★★★	🏕 ★★★★★
Beauty: ★★★★★	Site Privacy: ★★★★
Spaciousness: ★★★★★	Quiet: ★★★★★
Security: ★★★★★	Cleanliness: ★★★★
Insect Control: ★	Facilities: ★★★

Three campgrounds nestle into a bend in the Guadalupe River. For tent campers only, Cedar Sage Camping area has water at each site and paved back-in parking spaces. Sites 33–37 are the roomiest, and families with children should ask for sites 24 or 26, which flank the playground. Turkey Sink camping area contains spacious sites with paved back-in parking for RVs. The Guadalupe is lined with bald cypress and limestone bluffs. A variety of hardwoods provide shade and privacy for campers. Bird-atchers look for golden-cheeked warblers who nest in the park's virgin ash juniper woodlands. Adjacent Honey Creek State Natural Area is home to live-oak grassland, a vanishing Central Texas ecosystem (access by guided tour only). Security is excellent here, with gates that lock at 10 p.m. Only 30 miles from San Antonio, this park is an excellent, quick getaway for city folk. Plan a visit during mild spring or autumn.

BASICS

Operated By: Texas Parks and Wildlife. **Open:** All year; park closes for specific hunting dates; call park for details. **Site Assignment:** Reservations (512) 389-8900; reservations must be made at least 48 hrs. in advance; deposit required (equivalent to 1-night fee) to hold reservation; cancellations more than 2 days prior to reservation result in $5 fee; cancellations w/in 2 days of reservation result in loss of deposit. **Registration:** At headquarters. **Fee:** Full hookup, $19; water/electric, $18; water, $14; primitive, $12; daily fee per person (13 and older), $6; excess vehicle charge, $4; cash, check, D, V, MC. **Parking:** At most sites. If more than 2 vehicles, fee of $4 per vehicle applies.

FACILITIES

Number of RV-only Sites: 44. **Number of Tent-only Sites:** 46. **Hookups:** Electric (30 amps), water. **Each Site:** Picnic table, fire ring, 16-ft. by 16-ft. tent pad. **Dump Station:** Yes. **Laundry:** No. **Pay Phone:** Yes. **Restrooms and Showers:** Yes. **Fuel:** No. **Propane:** No. **Internal Roads:** Paved. **RV Service:** 13 mi. west in Boerne. **Market:** 7 mi. east in Bulverde. **Restaurant:** 7 mi. east in Bulverde. **General Store:** 3 mi. west in Bergheim. **Vending:** Beverages. **Swimming:** Yes. **Playground:** Yes. **Other:** Interpretive Center, gift shop, amphitheater. **Activities:** Canoeing, tubing, fishing, swimming, picnicking, hiking. **Nearby Attractions:** Honey Creek State Natural Area, Blanco State Park, San Antonio, Boerne, New Braunfels, & San Marcos attractions.

Additional Information: San Antonio CVB, (210) 270-8700; Boerne CVB, (800) 842-8080; New Braunfels CVB, (800) 572-2626; San Marcos CVB, (888) 200-5620.

RESTRICTIONS

Pets: Leash only, not allowed in buildings. **Fires:** Fire ring only. **Alcoholic Beverages:** Not allowed. **Vehicle Maximum Length:** 50 ft. **Other:** Max. 8 people per campsite, quiet time 10 p.m.–6 a.m., 14-day stay limit, gathering of firewood prohibited.

TO GET THERE

From I-10 (Boerne), drive east on TX 46 13 mi., and then turn left on Park Rd. 31. From San Antonio, drive north on US 281, and then turn left on TX 46. Drive west on TX 46 8 mi., and then turn right on Park Rd. 31. The park entrance is at the north end of Park Rd. 31.

SULPHER SPRINGS   MAP, A-5
Cooper Lake State Park
(South Sulpher Unit)

Hwy. 3 , P.O. Box 741, 75482. T: (512) 389-8900, (903) 945-5256 or (800) 792-1112; www.reserveamerica.com.

🚐 ★★★★   ⛺ ★★★★★

Beauty: ★★★★	Site Privacy: ★★★★
Spaciousness: ★★★★	Quiet: ★★★★★
Security: ★★★★	Cleanliness: ★★★
Insect Control: ★★★	Facilities: ★★★

This state park is divided up into four camping areas, several day-use areas, and a screened shelter and cabin area on the water's edge. RV campers will be mostly concerned with the Bright Star and Deer Haven camping areas, unless they wish to bring a horse to the Buggy Whip equestrian area. All sites are grassy and forested, although often the trees that encircle the sites do not shade them. The Bright Star area is laid out in a loop, with sites on the inside being more open to the sun. (A shaded picnic table at these sites helps reduce exposure.) Site 2 is well shaded, but close to a dumpster. Also very well shaded are 12–15 (which back to the lake) and 19. Of these, 14 and 15 are 110-foot pull-throughs. Nominally part of the Deer Haven area, sites 47–58 and 78–87 are located along the internal road, and are for this reason less desirable than those closer to the water and off the beaten path. Even-numbered sites 62–66, which back to the water, are the best sites in this area for their superior shade. The Oak Grove area provides walk-in tenting sites on a dirt (not grass) floor. The best sites are 92 and 94–101, which are right on the water; the least desirable is 88, right by the entrance to Oak Grove. For those campers with horses, Buggy Whip offers back-in sites as spokes around a looped road. Each site has a trailhead that leads to horse trails. More than nearly any other campground, this park offers a huge selection of activities, and everyone should enjoy their stay enough to return year after year.

BASICS

Operated By: Texas Parks and Wildlife. **Open:** All year. **Site Assignment:** Reservations call (512) 389-8900, ReserveAmerica; refund (minus $5) w/ 48-hr. notice; less than 48 hrs., lose 1-night deposit. **Registration:** At office. (Late arrivals use drop box at entrance.) **Fee:** Water/electric, $12; water, $8, plus $3 entrance fee per person; V, MC, D accepted in the office or for reservation. **Parking:** At site, additional parking for walk-ins.

FACILITIES

Number of RV-only Sites: 102. **Number of Tent-only Sites:** 15. **Hookups:** Electric (30 amps), water. **Each Site:** Picnic table, grill, fire pit, lantern post. **Dump Station:** Yes. **Laundry:** No. **Pay Phone:** Courtesy phone. **Restrooms and Showers:** Yes. **Fuel:** No. **Propane:** No. **Internal Roads:** Paved. **RV Service:** No. **Market:** 12 mi. to Sulpher Springs. **Restaurant:** 12 mi. to Sulpher Springs. **General Store:** No. **Vending:** Yes. **Swimming:** Lake. **Playground:** Yes. **Other:** Boat ramp, fish-cleaning station, pavilion, cabins, shelters, firewood. **Activities:** Swimming, boating, fishing, hiking, mountain biking. **Nearby Attractions:** Sam Bell Maxey Historical State Park, Bonham State Park, Lake Bob Sandlin State Park. **Additional Information:** South Sulpher Unit Office: (903) 945-5256.

RESTRICTIONS

Pets: On 6-ft. leash, cleaned up after. **Fires:** Grill only. **Alcoholic Beverages:** Not allowed. **Vehicle Maximum Length:** No limit. **Other:** All visitors must pay $3 entrance fee per day.

TO GET THERE

From the junction of Hwy. 19/154 and Hwy. 71, go 4.25 mi. west on Hwy. 71. Turn north onto FM 3505 and go 1.5 mi. to the entrance.

THREE RIVERS   MAP, C-4
Choke Canyon State Park—
South Shore

P.O Box 1548, 78071. T: (361) 786-3538; www.reserveamerica.com.

🚐 ★★★★   ⛺ ★★★★

Beauty: ★★★★	Site Privacy: ★★★
Spaciousness: ★★★	Quiet: ★★★★
Security: ★★★★	Cleanliness: ★★★★
Insect Control: ★★★	Facilities: ★★★★

Choke Canyon State Park consists of two units, South Shore and Calliham. It is located on 26,000-acre Choke Canyon Reservoir, a water supply for Corpus Christi. From scant evidence available, we know that Paleo Indians crossed the Frio River Valley more than 10,000 years ago following game such as bison and mammoth. After the disappearance of large game more than 8,000 years ago, nomadic hunters and gatherers associated with the archaic culture camped near the river making tools, building fires, and gathering and processing food. Numerous archaic sites in the Choke Canyon area have been recorded. The South Shore Unit has a day-use only park (6 a.m.-10 p.m.) and offers boating, fishing, picnicking, wildlife viewing, and birding. As part of a joint project of the Bureau of Reclamation and the American Birding Association, Choke Canyon Reservoir has been recognized as a place of special importance for birds and bird-watchers. Large numbers and varieties of birds are attracted to the water and to the adjacent upland habitats. Also, many typically Mexican species of birds approach the northern limits of their range here, making this one of Texas' finest places to watch birds. Facilities include restrooms; shaded picnic sites on the lake; a 6-lane boat ramp and an auxiliary 2-lane boat ramp; lighted fish-cleaning tables; and a lake overlook. The reservoir and surrounding terrain are characterized by eroded, gently rolling brush land crossed by silted stream valleys. Both Calliham and South Shore have a wide variety of wildlife that inhabits dense thickets of mesquite and blackbush acacia. Choke Canyon is the westernmost common occurrence of the American alligator. Rio Grande turkey, whitetail deer, javelina, coyote, opossum, fox squirrel, raccoon, and various skunks are among the most common animals. The crested caracara (Mexican eagle) can also be seen in the area. The following fish are in the reservoir: largemouth bass, white bass, striped bass, white crappie, bluegill, longear sunfish, green sunfish, flathead, channel and blue catfish, carp, freshwater drum, and gar.

BASICS

Operated By: Texas Parks and Wildlife. **Open:** All year. **Site Assignment:** Reservations can be made up to 16 weeks in advance. **Registration:** At office. **Fee:** Single, $12. **Parking:** 2 vehicles per site.

FACILITIES

Number of Multipurpose Sites: 40. **Hookups:** Yes. **Dump Station:** Yes. **Laundry:** No. **Pay Phone:** Yes. **Restrooms and Showers:** Yes. **Fuel:** No. **Propane:** No. **Internal Roads:** Paved. **RV Service:** Yes. **Market:** More than 5 mi. **Restaurant:** No. **General Store:** Yes. **Vending:** Yes. **Swimming:** Yes. **Playground:** Yes. **Activities:** Biking, boating, canoeing, horseback riding, fishing, baseball, volleyball, picnicking, hunting, swimming, hiking, waterskiing.

RESTRICTIONS

Pets: On a 6-ft. leash, never unattended, under control at all times, cleaned up after. **Fires:** Fires may be built only in campsite grills, fire rings, or fireplaces. Some sites allow only containerized fuel fires. When warranted, fire bans are implemented by county judges and/or county commissioners courts. Inquire when making reservations. **Alcoholic Beverages:** It is an offense to consume or display an open container of an alcoholic beverage in a public place or sell alcoholic beverages w/in a state park. **Vehicle Maximum Length:** 50 ft.

TO GET THERE

From San Antonio, take I-37S to Hwy. 281S at Exit 72. Go 3 mi. to Three Rivers, then west on Hwy. 72. It is 4 mi. to park entrance on right. From Corpus Christi, take I-37N to Exit 69 and turn left on Hwy. 72W. Go 3 mi. to red light. Turn left on Hwy. 281S and go to 2nd red light. Turn right on Hwy. 72W and travel 4 mi. Turn right to headquarters.

From Houston, take Hwy. 59S to George West then turn right on Hwy. 281N. Go 10 mi. to Three Rivers. Turn left at red light, Hwy. 72W. Go 4 mi. west then turn right to headquarters.

TUSCOLA
Abilene State Park

MAP, B-3

reserve america

150 Park Rd 32, 79562. T: (325) 572-3204; www.reserveamerica.com.

🚐 ★★★★   ⛺ ★★★★

Beauty: ★★★★	Site Privacy: ★★★★
Spaciousness: ★★★★	Quiet: ★★★★★
Security: ★★★★	Cleanliness: ★★★★
Insect Control: ★★★	Facilities: ★★★★

Abilene State Park, southwest of Abilene, in Taylor County, is among a low range of hills called the Callahan Divide in the extreme western portion of North Central Texas. Acquired in 1933 by deed from the City of Abilene, the park's total acreage is 529.4. Original park construction was done by the Civilian Conservation Corps (CCC) in the early 1930s. A portion of the official Texas longhorn herd and one buffalo are located on site. Comanches frequented what is now the park, using the groves of native pecan trees as campgrounds, much like the present park's picnic area. Abilene is in a semi-arid region of short prairie grass, brushland, and wooded stream valleys of mesquite, juniper, cedar, native pecan, elm, live oaks, hackberry, Texas red oak, red bud, and various other plants, and wildflowers. Wildlife observation and photography include white-tailed deer, raccoon, armadillo, fox, squirrel, cottontail rabbit, and a large variety of birds including Mississippi kite, roadrunner, cardinal, hummingbird, mockingbird, and many others. Popular fish include bass, crappie, catfish, and perch.

BASICS

Operated By: Texas Parks and Wildlife. **Open:** All year. **Site Assignment:** Reservations can be made 11 months in advance. **Registration:** At office. **Fee:** Single, $5–$18; group trailer, $5–$10; shelter, $8–$40; group hall, $80. **Parking:** Limit of 2 vehicles per site; extra parking available for a fee.

FACILITIES

Number of Multipurpose Sites: 154. **Hookups:** Yes. **Dump Station:** Yes. **Laundry:** No. **Pay Phone:** Yes. **Restrooms and Showers:** Yes. **Fuel:** No. **Propane:** No. **Internal Roads:** Paved. **RV Service:** No. **Market:** No. **Restaurant:** No. **General Store:** Yes. **Vending:** No. **Swimming:** Yes. **Playground:** Yes. **Other:** Check hunt dates. Park does not have a gate. Swimming pool is only open Thurs.–Sun. (Memorial Day–Labor Day) 11 a.m.– 7 p.m. Pool is available for private parties; contact park office. **Activities:** Baseball, basketball, biking, bird-watching, fishing, horseshoes, volleyball, hiking.

RESTRICTIONS

Pets: On a 6-ft. leash, never unattended, under control at all times, cleaned up after. **Fires:** Fires may be built only in campsite grills, fire rings, or fireplaces.

Some sites allow only containerized fuel fires. When warranted, fire bans are implemented by county judges and/or county commissioners courts. Inquire when making reservations. **Alcoholic Beverages:** It is an offense to consume or display an open container of an alcoholic beverage in a public place or sell alcoholic beverages w/in a state park.

TO GET THERE

From Abilene: Take FM 89 southwest 16 mi. through Buffalo Gap. The park is 5 mi. southwest of Buffalo Gap. From Dallas/Ft. Worth: Take I-20 west to Abilene. Take FM 89 southwest 16 mi. through Buffalo Gap. The park is 5 mi. southwest of Buffalo Gap.

VALLEY VIEW
Ray Roberts State Park
(Johnson Branch Unit)

MAP, A-4

reserve america

100 PW 4153, 76272.
T: (512) 389-8900, (970) 637-2294 or (800) 792-1112; www.reserveamerica.com.

🚐 ★★★★   ⛺ ★★★★

Beauty: ★★★★	Site Privacy: ★★★★
Spaciousness: ★★★★	Quiet: ★★★★★
Security: ★★★★	Cleanliness: ★★★★★
Insect Control: ★★★	Facilities: ★★★

This park is divided into four camping areas. The Dogwood Canyon area is the first campground inside the entrance. It is farthest from the water, and also the most primitive, suitable for tents but not RVs. (Sites are walk-ins.) The restrooms have nonflush toilets. Oak Point is likewise a walk-in area suitable for tenting. Sites are open and grassy with great views of the lake. There is a small flush toilet but no showers. The Juniper Cove area is the very antithesis of Dogwood Canyon—some of its sites are right up by the water's edge (7–14), and the restrooms are very clean and modern, with flush toilets and hot showers. These sites are 40-foot back-ins separated from the water by a row of wild bushes (except for 11–13, which are right on the water). Much less natural (and bordering on the ugly) are sites 1–6, 25, and 36–39, which are very open sites located on the blacktop. (Sites 5, 6, 36, 37 are pull-throughs.) While these may appeal to certain campers, they definitely miss the point of coming to such a beautiful lake. In the Walnut area, most sites are open to the sun, but sites 57 and 73 have exceptional shade. Sites 45, 49–52, and 55 have views of the water, while 41–44 and 87–89 are open blacktop sites like those described above. The restrooms are clean and modern, like those in Juniper Cove. This campground is a delightful destination for anyone who enjoys water activities or just going wild for a while.

BASICS

Operated By: Texas Parks and Wildlife. **Open:** All year. **Site Assignment:** Reservations call (512) 389-8900, ReserveAmerica; refund (minus $5) w/ 48-hr. notice; less than 48 hrs., lose 1-night deposit. **Registration:** At office. (Late arrivals use drop box at entrance.) **Fee:** Water/electric, $20; water (walk-in), $12; primitive (walk-in), $6; plus $5 entrance fee; V,

MC, D accepted in the office or for reservation. **Parking:** At site.

FACILITIES

Number of RV-only Sites: 104. **Number of Tent-only Sites:** 83. **Hookups:** Electric (30 amps), water. **Each Site:** Picnic table, grill, fire pit, lantern post. **Dump Station:** Yes. **Laundry:** No. **Pay Phone:** Yes. **Restrooms and Showers:** Yes. **Fuel:** No. **Propane:** No. **Internal Roads:** Paved. **RV Service:** No. **Market:** 7 mi. to Valley View. **Restaurant:** 7 mi. to Valley View. **General Store:** Yes. **Vending:** Yes. **Swimming:** Lake. **Playground:** Yes. **Other:** Pavilion, fish-cleaning station, boat ramp. **Activities:** Swimming, boating, fishing, hiking, mountain biking. **Nearby Attractions:** Eisenhower State Park, Tioga, Frank Buck Zoo, Morton Museum. **Additional Information:** Johnson Branch Unit Office: (940) 637-2294.

RESTRICTIONS

Pets: On 6-ft. leash, cleaned up after. **Fires:** Grill only. **Alcoholic Beverages:** Not allowed. **Vehicle Maximum Length:** No limit. **Other:** All visitors must pay $5 entrance fee per day. max. 8 people per site.

TO GET THERE

From I-35, take Exit 483 and go 6.5 mi. east on FM 3002. Turn right at the sign into the entrance.

VANDERPOOL
Lost Maples State Natural Area

MAP, C-3

reserve america

37221 FM 187, 78885. T: (830) 966-3413; www.reserveamerica.com.

🚐 ★★★★   ⛺ ★★★★

Beauty: ★★★★★	Site Privacy: ★★★
Spaciousness: ★★★★	Quiet: ★★★★
Security: ★★★★★	Cleanliness: ★★★★★
Insect Control: ★★	Facilities: ★★★

Famed for its isolated stand of Uvalde bigtooth maples, this natural area is popular with autumn leaf-peepers. However, the trees include other showy species such as sumac and complement the area's striking granite outcroppings year-round. Built in a valley, the small campground offers exceptionally lovely views. The campsites are contained in one area and offer paved, back-in parking. Sites are decent-sized, with a little shade at most. Those without many trees benefit from the shaded picnic table found at each site. Few sites are very private. The most secluded are 17 and 18—we recommend these for tent campers and small RVs. Security at Lost Maples is fine. The park is so remote that gates are unnecessary. If you must visit in the fall, plan your trip for a weekday and make advance reservations. Ticks can proliferate here, so examine your hair and clothes regularly.

BASICS

Operated By: Texas Parks and Wildlife. **Open:** All year. **Site Assignment:** Reservations call (512) 389-8900, ReserveAmerica; refund (minus $5) w/ 48-hr. notice; less than 48 hrs., lose 1-night deposit. **Registration:** At headquarters. **Fee:** Water/electric, $15; per person day-use fee during Oct. and Nov., $6; rest of year, $5. **Parking:** At site except primitive.

FACILITIES

Number of RV-only Sites: 30. **Number of Multipurpose Sites:** 30. **Hookups:** Electric, water. **Each Site:** Shaded picnic table, fire ring. **Dump Station:** Yes. **Laundry:** No. **Pay Phone:** Yes. **Restrooms and Showers:** Yes. **Fuel:** No. **Propane:** No. **Internal Roads:** Paved. **RV Service:** 48 mi. northeast in Kerrville. **Market:** 4 mi. south in Vanderpool. **Restaurant:** 15 mi. south in Utopia. **General Store:** 15 mi. south in Utopia. **Vending:** No. **Swimming:** River. **Playground:** No. **Other:** Picnic sites, scenic drive, gift shop. **Activities:** Hiking, nature trail. **Nearby Attractions:** Garner & Kerrville-Schreiner State Parks, Hill Country State Natural Area, Frontier Times Museum, rodeos in Bandera. **Additional Information:** Bandera CVB, (800) 364-3833.

RESTRICTIONS

Pets: On leash only. **Fires:** Fire ring only. **Alcoholic Beverages:** Not allowed. **Vehicle Maximum Length:** 50 ft. **Other:** Campfires not allowed in primitive sites; max. 8 people per site.

TO GET THERE

From Vanderpool, drive 5 mi. north on Ranch Rd. 187. The park is on the left.

WALLER   MAP, C-5
Lonestar Yogi Bear's Jellystone Park

reserve america

34843 Betka Rd., 77484.
T: (800) 347-5106 or (979) 826-4111;
www.lonestarcamping.com.

🚐 ★★★★   ⛺ ★★★★

Beauty: ★★★★	Site Privacy: ★★★
Spaciousness: ★★	Quiet: ★★
Security: ★★★★	Cleanliness: ★★★
Insect Control: ★★★	Facilities: ★★★★

Lonestar Yogi Bear's Jellystone Park is open year-round with both pull-through and back-in sites (both grassy and gravel) plus 4 bare-bones cabins and 12 full-service cabins. This family-oriented campground features a water park with splash pool and family pool—the only one in the area. Amenities and activities also include sports courts, a stocked fishing lake, mini-golf, hay rides, tennis, volleyball, hiking, and appearances from Yogi Bear™ and friends.

BASICS

Operated By: Bryant Friendswood Management. **Open:** All year. **Site Assignment:** By reservation. **Registration:** At store. **Fee:** FHU: base, $30; plus $5 per person; WE: base, $27; plus $5 per person. **Parking:** Limit 2 cars per site; overflow parking available.

FACILITIES

Number of RV-only Sites: 123. **Hookups:** Electric (30, 50 amps). **Each Site:** Picnic table, fire ring. **Dump Station:** Yes. **Laundry:** 2. **Pay Phone:** Yes. **Restrooms and Showers:** Yes; several. **Fuel:** No.

Propane: Yes. **Internal Roads:** Partially paved. **RV Service:** 30 mi. south; private individual will service at campground. **Market:** 5 mi. east; 7 mi. west. **Restaurant:** Several w/in 10 mi. **General Store:** Yes. **Vending:** Yes. **Swimming:** Water park, splash pool, family pool. **Playground:** Yes. **Activities:** Mini-golf, shuffle board, horseshoes, basketball, volleyball, tennis, tether ball, petting zoo, outdoor theater, arts & crafts. **Nearby Attractions:** Washington on the Brazos, Monastery of St. Clare Miniature Horse Farm, Blue Bell Creameries, winery. **Additional Information:** Waller Chamber of Commerce.

RESTRICTIONS

Pets: Limit 2, leashed, cleaned up after. Not allowed in or out of the cabins. **Fires:** Fire rings. **Alcoholic Beverages:** At site only. **Vehicle Maximum Length:** 50 ft. **Other:** Monthly sites available.

TO GET THERE

Located 35 mi. northwest of Houston 610 Loop. From US 290, between Hempstead & Waller, take the Prairie View exit (FM 1098) south, go 4.5 mi. From I-10, exit at Brookshire on FM 359, then north 18 mi. on FM 362 to Betka Rd., left 2 mi.

WHITNEY   MAP, B-4
Lake Whitney State Park

reserve america

P.O. Box 1175, 76692. T: (254) 694-3793;
www.reserveamerica.com.

🚐 ★★★   ⛺ ★★★

Beauty: ★★	Site Privacy: ★★★
Spaciousness: ★★★	Quiet: ★★★
Security: ★★★	Cleanliness: ★★★
Insect Control: ★★★★	Facilities: ★★★

If you don't mind the crowds, visit in the spring, when over 40 species of wildflowers bloom. The rest of the year, this is one of the least attractive state parks in Texas. The park is in a rural area, but the town of Whitney is visible from the campgrounds. Even so, the park stays busy March through October due to its unique offerings, including an airstrip. There are three types of campsites in a number of separate areas. No sites with full hookups have water views. We recommend the water/electric areas, which contain a number of waterfront sites. Sites are spacious and parking is paved. There are both back-in and pull-through sites. Waterfront pull-throughs 124–130 are the nicest. With very few trees in the campground, snag a site with a shade shelter. Tent campers have no trouble finding a waterfront site. Security is good, with locked gates at night.

BASICS

Operated By: Texas Parks and Wildlife. **Open:** All year. **Site Assignment:** Reservations (512) 389-8900; reservations must be made at least 48 hrs. in advance; deposit required (equivalent to 1-night fee) to hold reservation; cancellations more than 2 days prior to reservation result in $5 fee; cancellations w/in 2 days of reservation result in loss of deposit. **Registration:** At headquarters. **Fee:** Full hookup/shade shelter, $23; full hookup, $15;

water/electric, $14; water, $9; daily fee per person (13 and older), $3; cash, check, D, V, MC. **Parking:** At site.

FACILITIES

Number of RV-only Sites: 87. **Number of Tent-only Sites:** 71. **Hookups:** Electric (30 amps), water, sewer. **Each Site:** Fire ring, stand-up grill, some picnic tables & shade shelters. **Dump Station:** Yes. **Laundry:** No. **Pay Phone:** No. **Restrooms and Showers:** Yes. **Fuel:** No. **Propane:** No. **Internal Roads:** Paved. **RV Service:** 30 mi. north in Cleburne. **Market:** 4 mi. east in Whitney. **Restaurant:** 4 mi. east in Whitney. **General Store:** 4 mi. east in Whitney. **Vending:** Beverages, ice, wood. **Swimming:** Allowed in lake w/in buoyed area. **Playground:** Yes. **Other:** Airstrip, 21 screened shelters. **Activities:** Hiking, picnicking, boating, fishing, swimming, scuba diving, waterskiing, nature study, birding, & limited mountain biking. **Nearby Attractions:** Cleburne, Meridian, Dinosaur Valley, & Mother Neff State Parks; The Confederate Museum; Texas Ranger Hall of Fame; Fossil Rim Exotic Wildlife Ranch. **Additional Information:** Lake Whitney Chamber of Commerce, (254) 694-2540.

RESTRICTIONS

Pets: Must be on leash at all times, must have proof of current shots, not allowed in swimming area. **Fires:** Fire ring only. **Alcoholic Beverages:** Not allowed. **Vehicle Maximum Length:** 100 ft. **Other:** Max. of 8 people per campsite.

TO GET THERE

From I-35, take the Hillsboro exit. In Hillsboro take TX 22 west approx. 15 mi. to Whitney. At the first traffic light, turn right on TX 933 and drive 0.5 mi. to FM 1244. Turn left and the park is 3 mi. in.

WICHITA FALLS   MAP, A-4
Lake Arrowhead State Park

reserve america

229 Park Rd. 63, 76310. T: (940) 528-2211;
www.reserveamerica.com.

🚐 ★★★★   ⛺ ★★★★

Beauty: ★★★★	Site Privacy: ★★★★★
Spaciousness: ★★★★★	Quiet: ★★★★
Security: ★★★★	Cleanliness: ★★★★
Insect Control: ★★★	Facilities: ★★★★

Lake Arrowhead State Park consists of 524 acres in Clay County, 14 miles southeast of Wichita Falls. The area was acquired in 1970 from the City of Wichita Falls under the State Parks Bond Program and was opened the same year. Lake Arrowhead itself is a reservoir on the Little Wichita River and covers approximately 16,200 surface acres, with 106 miles of shoreline. Built primarily as a water supply by the City of Wichita Falls, the lake is also a major recreational site for the North Central Plains. The land surrounding the lake is generally semiarid, gently rolling prairie, much of which has been covered by mesquite in recent decades. Lake Arrowhead State Park is home to a Black-tailed Prairie Dog "town", Waterfowl and wading birds are common park visitors and residents.

Popular fish include crappie, perch, catfish, and bass. The park offers fishing and is a participant in the Loan A Tackle Program (the park lends out fishing tackle to its visitors); lake swimming on unsupervised beach; waterskiing; disc golf; picnicking; camping; nature study; hiking; horseback riding, boating.

BASICS

Operated By: Texas Parks and Wildlife. **Open:** All year. **Site Assignment:** Reservations can be made 11 months in advance. **Registration:** At office. **Fee:** Single, $10–$20; primitive, $7; single equestrian, $20; group pavilion, $25; group hall, $80. **Parking:** Limit of 2 vehicles per site; extra parking available for a fee.

FACILITIES

Number of Multipurpose Sites: 151. **Hookups:** Yes. **Dump Station:** Yes. **Laundry:** No. **Pay Phone:** Yes. **Restrooms and Showers:** Yes. **Fuel:** No. **Propane:** No. **Internal Roads:** Paved. **RV Service:** No. **Market:** No. **Restaurant:** No. **General Store:** Yes. **Vending:** No. **Swimming:** Yes. **Playground:** Yes. **Other:** This park does not have any gates. **Activities:** Boating, fishing, golfing, horseback riding, hiking, waterskiing, wildlife viewing.

RESTRICTIONS

Pets: On a 6-ft. leash, never unattended, under control at all times, cleaned up after. **Fires:** Fires may be built only in campsite grills, fire rings, or fireplaces. Some sites allow only containerized fuel fires. When warranted, fire bans are implemented by county judges and/or county commissioners courts. Inquire when making reservations. **Alcoholic Beverages:** It is an offense to consume or display an open container of an alcoholic beverage in a public place or sell alcoholic beverages w/in a state park.

TO GET THERE

From Wichita Falls: Take US 281S 5 mi. Turn east on FM 1954, go 8 mi. to park. From Dallas/Ft. Worth Metroplex: Take US 287N to Jolly, Texas. Exit on FM 2393. Follow signs 10 mi. to FM 1954. Turn east on FM 1954. Go 3 mi. to the park.

WOODVILLE MAP, B-5
Sandy Creek Park

reserve america

890 FM 92, 75979-9509. T: (409) 429-3491; www.reserveamerica.com.

🚐 ★★★★ ⛺ ★★★★

Beauty: ★★★	Site Privacy: ★★
Spaciousness: ★★	Quiet: ★★★★
Security: ★★★	Cleanliness: ★★★★
Insect Control: ★★★★	Facilities: ★★★★

Sandy Creek Park is located on the southeast side of B. A. Steinhagen Lake, between the towns of Woodville and Jasper in southeast Texas. The area provides the ideal setting to fish, camp, boat, or just get away from it all. The Neches River flows for 416 miles through east Texas to its mouth on Sabine Lake near the Rainbow Bridge. Two major reservoirs, Lake

Palestine and Lake B. A. Steinhagen, are located on the Neches. Several cities are located along the Neches River Basin, including Tyler, Lufkin, Silsbee, Beaumont, Vidor, Port Neches, Nederland, Groves, and Port Arthur. From Lake B.A. Steinhagen down to Beaumont, the Neches River flows through the 97,000-acre Big Thicket National Preserve. This important ecosphere preserves the area where several eco-systems converge—an event that harkens back to the last ice age. The Big Thicket Visitor Center is off U.S. Highway 69 several miles north of Kountze. The Lower Neches Valley Authority is the river authority which oversees the Neches River in Tyler County, Hardin County, Liberty County, Chambers County, and Jefferson County. Sandy Creek Park is an overnight campground that offers 72 campsites, 66 sites with water and electric hookups. Other facilities include a volleyball court and fishing docks.

BASICS

Operated By: U.S. Army Corps of Engineers. **Open:** All year. **Site Assignment:** First come, first served; no reservations. **Registration:** At office. **Fee:** Single, $10–$25. **Parking:** At site and at fee lot.

FACILITIES

Number of Multipurpose Sites: 212. **Hookups:** Yes. **Dump Station:** Yes. **Laundry:** No. **Pay Phone:** Yes. **Restrooms and Showers:** Yes. **Fuel:** No. **Propane:** No. **Internal Roads:** Paved. **RV Service:** No. **Market:** No. **Restaurant:** No. **General Store:** No. **Vending:** No. **Swimming:** Yes. **Playground:** No. **Other:** No ATVs or ORVs allowed. **Activities:** Boating, fishing, hunting.

RESTRICTIONS

Pets: Restrained or on a leash at all times while in developed recreation areas. **Fires:** W/in campgrounds and other recreation areas, fires may only be built in fire rings, stoves, grills, or fireplaces provided for that purpose. **Alcoholic Beverages:** Not allowed. **Vehicle Maximum Length:** Call ahead.

TO GET THERE

From Jasper, TX, go west on US 190 10 mi. to FM 777. Turn south on FM 777 and travel 2 mi. to CR 155. Turn west on CR 155 and travel 2.5 mi. Park signs will lead to the campground entrance. Follow signs into the campground.

ZAVALLA MAP, B-5
Boykin Springs and Sandy Creek Recreation Areas

Angelina National Forest, 111 Walnut Ridge Rd., 75980. T: (936) 897-1068; www.southernregion.fs.fed.us/texas.

🚐 ★★★★★ ⛺ ★★★★★

Beauty: ★★★★★	Site Privacy: ★★★★★
Spaciousness: ★★★★★	Quiet: ★★★★★
Security: ★★★★	Cleanliness: ★★★★
Insect Control: ★★★	Facilities: ★★★★

About 150,000 acres of national forest flank the Sam Reyburn Reservoir, with incredibly inexpensive

camping areas. Boykin Springs, near man-made Boykin Lake, is the largest. Sandy Creek, a smaller camping area, contains sites with water views. The untidy campground host sites were disappointing. Sites at both campgrounds are beautiful and fairly similar, though Boykin's are often more private. The woods are lovely and provide shade at both campgrounds. Most sites are back-ins with gravel parking. Site size varies at both. At Sandy Creek, try to score site 10 (private and heavily wooded, with a lake view). At Boykin, head for sites 12, 14, and 15, bordering picturesque Boykin Creek. Security is good at Angelina National Forest owing to campground remoteness. Boykin Springs stays busy on spring and summer weekends—visit in autumn or during the week. Sandy Creek is less popular and may be visited on all but the busiest holiday weekends.

BASICS

Operated By: U.S. Forest Service. **Open:** All year. **Site Assignment:** First come, first served; no reservations. **Registration:** Pay station, self-registration. **Fee:** $6 for 7 people; cash, check. **Parking:** At site (2 vehicles).

FACILITIES

Number of Multipurpose Sites: 56. **Hookups:** None (water available). **Each Site:** Picnic table, fire ring &/or grill, tent pad. **Dump Station:** Yes (at Caney Creek). **Laundry:** No. **Pay Phone:** No. **Restrooms and Showers:** Yes (cold shower only at Sandy Creek). **Fuel:** No. **Propane:** No. **Internal Roads:** Paved. **RV Service:** 20 mi. in Jasper. **Market:** 20 mi. in Jasper. **Restaurant:** 20 mi. in Jasper. **General Store:** 20 mi. in Jasper. **Vending:** No. **Swimming:** No. **Playground:** No. **Other:** Sheltered picnic areas, boat launches. **Activities:** Fishing, hunting, swimming beaches (no lifeguard), horse trails, hiking, backpacking, mountain biking, canoeing, kayaking, bird-watching. **Nearby Attractions:** Jasper "Bass Fishing Capitol of the World," Museum of East Texas, Texas Forestry Museum, Millards Crossing historic Nacogdoches, antiques & flea markets, Sabine National Forest, Martin Dies Jr. State Park. **Additional Information:** Lufkin/Angelina County Chamber of Commerce, (936) 634-6644.

RESTRICTIONS

Pets: On leash only, must be kept quiet, not allowed on beaches. **Fires:** Fire rings, grills only. **Alcoholic Beverages:** Allowe at sites. **Vehicle Maximum Length:** 24 ft. (sites vary). **Other:** No generators 10 p.m.–7 a.m.

TO GET THERE

From Zavalla, drive east on TX 63. To get to Boykin Springs, drive 11 mi. and turn right (south) on FS 313. Drive 2.5 mi. To get to Sandy Creek, drive 17.5 mi. and turn left (north) on FS 333. Drive 3 mi.

Utah

Campers and RVers familiar with the Beehive State (named by Mormon settlers who held the symbolism of the hardworking, entrepreneurial insect in high regard) know that for unequivocal landscapes and poetic horizons, Utah comes as close to terrestrial heaven as it gets. Unforgiving, it is a land of high deserts, sagebrush, staggering mountains, mesas, canyons, weathered red-orange Navajo sandstone formations, and ancient Native American rock art and ruins. Outdoor enthusiasts thrill at its world famous national parks, the lesser-known but no less magnificent state parks, its Olympic ski slopes, river rafting, and enough lakes and reservoirs to make boating and fishing an exclusive part of the happily removed-from-civilization experience.

Southeast Utah is one of the more popular destinations, being home to **Monument Valley, Natural Bridges,** and **Hovenweep National Monuments,** as well as **Arches and Canyonlands National Parks. The Halls Crossing** and **Bullfrog Marina** portions of **Lake Powell** and the **Colorado, San Juan,** and **Green Rivers** make for premier river rafting and kayaking. Mountain biking, ATVing, backpacking, and four-wheel-drive and jeep explorations are the most efficient ways of making roads beyond the campground. Better views of the desert washes, slickrock benches, canyons, flattop mesas, dashing buttes, eroded spires, hoodoos, entrenched meanders, and precariously balanced rocks are hard to find.

It suffices to say that campgrounds barely scratch the surface of **Grand Staircase–Escalante National Monument's** 1.7 million acres. But make adequate preparations and take the usual sensible precautions in typically unpredictable terrain, because this is a land of summer flash floods, rattlesnakes, and long distances between gas stations and fresh water.

Zion and **Bryce Canyon National Parks** in southwestern Utah are among the most popular and frequented national parks in the United States, though the red sandstone monoliths and pioneer fruit orchards of **Capitol Reef** by no means pale in comparison. Don't overlook the elusively spectacular scenery of lesser-known areas, like **Cedar Breaks National Monument,** which is akin to a more compact, higher-elevation version of Bryce Canyon's multiprismatic sandstone amphitheaters. Similarly, the more obscure **Kodachrome Basin, Coral Pink Sand Dunes,** and **Goblin Valley State Parks** explode with their own unique brands of visual intensity and are among the many geologically awe-inspiring Utah state park camping experiences.

Utah's plentiful lakes and reservoirs are popular with the locals for boating and fishing, and it's safe to say that you could easily walk across water from boat to boat during the hectic summer and holiday weekends. Keeping relaxation and communing with nature in mind, weekdays and before Memorial Day and after Labor Day it is often possible to find a decent sprig of solitude. Near **Salt Lake City** are many campground escapes off the beaten path, including **Antelope Island State Park,** which sits in the middle of the **Great Salt Lake,** and **Wasatch Mountain State Park,** the 45th state's most developed state park and home to one of the most lauded 27-hole golf courses in Utah.

Utah is famed for its powder and is the stomping ground of serious skiers and snowboarders alike. Mostly located in the northern part of the state, the ski resorts accommodate both persuasions of downhill recreationist. Some of the more popular and revered are **Snowbird, Powder Mountain, Sundance,** and **Brighton,** although **Elk Meadows** and **Brian Head** to the south should not be left out.

Equally as mesmerizing as its natural wonders, Utah is host to numerous cultural anomalies and off-road curiosities that lend visitors yet another glimpse into its fascinating charm. Metaphor: the **Tree of Utah** can be found just off Highway 80 in **Wendover,** sprouting 90 feet out of the **Bonneville Salt Flats.** There's the ever-popular **Four Corners,** deemed by Roadside America as perhaps the country's "most arbitrary photo opportunity." Other, less obvious jaunts might be to **Moab** to the late **Albert Christensen's Hole 'n' the Rock,** a hand-carved complex of rooms crammed with the unimaginable; to Huntsville to witness the stuffed head of the world's largest dog; or, for those age 50 and over with a good exercise regimen, the **Hunstman Senior Olympics** in **St. George** take place every October.

Call ahead to the parks to make reservations where available, or plan to arrive early in realistic anticipation of the dedicated throngs who traditionally flock here. If you luck out and find it difficult to secure a naturally pristine location to camp, there are many excellent commercial campgrounds with all the modern-day amenities just outside the park boundaries.

Campground Profiles

ANTIMONY MAP, C-2
Otter Creek State Park

reserve america

Box 43, 84712-0043. T: (435) 624-3268;
www.reserveamerica.com.

🚐 ★★★★   ⛺ n/a

Beauty: ★★★★   Site Privacy: ★★★★
Spaciousness: ★★★★   Quiet: ★★★★
Security: ★★★★   Cleanliness: ★★★★
Insect Control: ★★★   Facilities: ★★★★

In the fall of 1897, construction began on one of the oldest dam projects in Utah, creating what is now Otter Creek Reservoir. Once the 40-foot-high dam was complete, state engineers described it as "one of the best and more secure earth reservoir dams in the country." The original dam structure held up very well over many years, although some recent improvements have been made by the state. Otter Creek State Park is a perfect destination for ATVers, boaters, and birders. Year-round fishing and boating on the 3,120-acre reservoir are the park's featured activities along with convenient access to three ATV trails, including the popular Paiute ATV Trail. During the spring and fall, many types of birds pass through Otter Creek on their journey along the Pacific Migratory Bird Flyway. The park is a quiet, out-of-the-way respite located in south central Utah. The campground is located on the eastern shore of the reservoir.

BASICS
Operated By: Utah State Parks. **Open:** All year.
Site Assignment: Reservations can be made up to 16 weeks in advance. **Registration:** At office. **Fee:** Single, $15. **Parking:** 1 vehicle per site; additional vehicle fee, half of nightly camping fee w/ the exception of $8 camp sites (fee is $8).

FACILITIES
Number of RV-only Sites: 31. **Hookups:** None.
Dump Station: Yes. **Laundry:** No. **Pay Phone:** No.
Restrooms and Showers: Yes. **Fuel:** No. **Propane:** No. **Internal Roads:** Paved. **RV Service:** Yes. **Market:** No. **Restaurant:** No. **General Store:** No.
Vending: No. **Swimming:** Yes. **Playground:** No.
Activities: Boating, kayaking, canoeing, sailing, fishing, ice fishing, picnicking, swimming, hiking, wildlife, birdwatching. **Nearby Attractions:** ORV area.

RESTRICTIONS
Pets: On a 6-ft. leash, never unattended, cleaned up after. Not allowed in buildings, on beaches, in lakes or reservoirs. **Fires:** Fires may only be built in fire rings, stoves, grills, or fireplaces provided for that purpose. Be sure your fire is completely extinguished before leaving. Do not leave your fire unattended. Obey any restrictions on fires. **Alcoholic Beverages:** Allowed w/in state parks, except for visitor centers, museums, & administrative offices. **Vehicle Maximum Length:** 60 ft.

TO GET THERE
Travel east 11 mi. on UT 62 from the junction of US 89 and UT 62. Where UT 62 turns north, continue east 0.5 mi. on UT 22.

ARCHES NATIONAL PARK MAP, C-3
Devil's Garden Campground

reserve america

P. O. Box 907, 5 miles north of Moab, 84532-0907.
T: (435) 719-2299 or (877) 444-6777;
www.reserveamerica.com.

🚐 ★★★★   ⛺ ★★★★★

Beauty: ★★★★★   Site Privacy: ★★★★★
Spaciousness: ★★★★   Quiet: ★★★★
Security: ★★★★   Cleanliness: ★★★★★
Insect Control: ★★★   Facilities: ★★

Arches National Park, where disabled Civil War veteran John Wesley Wolfe and son Fred once lived a solitary log-cabin life grazing cattle and sheep, now gets a million visitors a year. But Devil's Garden is like paradise to self-sufficient campers eschewing the showers, shops, and amenities of Moab to show up early in the morning and snag a campsite among the sandstone fins and balanced rocks. Parking spaces become maddeningly scarce on busy holiday weekends, but campground denizens have solar powered restrooms and their own trailheads to Broken Arch and Sand Dune Arch. Many campsites have 50-foot-long pads, though most are 12-foot-wide back-ins (some 25-foot-long sites are 20-feet wide) tucked in amongst Navajo sandstone formations and flanked with junipers, pines, and desert scrub. This is as close as it gets outside the backcountry to having a private vista of this 2,000-arch park.

BASICS
Operated By: National Park Service. **Open:** All year. **Site Assignment:** First come, first served; group site reservations. **Registration:** At self-pay fee station. **Fee:** $10–$15; cash, check. **Parking:** At site.

FACILITIES
Number of RV-only Sites: 54. **Hookups:** None.
Each Site: Table, grill. **Dump Station:** No. **Laundry:** No. **Pay Phone:** No. **Restrooms and Showers:** No showers. **Fuel:** No. **Propane:** No. **Internal Roads:** Paved, good. **RV Service:** No. **Market:** Moab, 23 mi. **Restaurant:** Moab, 23 mi. **General Store:** No. **Vending:** No. **Swimming:** No. **Playground:** No. **Other:** Amphitheater, 1 wheelchair-accessible site. **Activities:** Hiking; evening ranger programs; hunting season mid-Mar.–Oct. **Nearby Attractions:** Canyonlands, Moab, Dead Horse State Park. **Additional Information:** Canyonlands Natural History Assoc., (435) 259-6003, www.cnha.org; Grand County Travel Council, (800) 635-MOAB.

RESTRICTIONS
Pets: On 6-ft. leash, under owner's control, not allowed on hiking trails. **Fires:** Allowed (in grills only, no collecting firewood). **Alcoholic Beverages:** Allowed. **Vehicle Maximum Length:** 50 ft. **Other:** 7-day stay limit; no feeding wildlife.

TO GET THERE
From Moab go 5 mi. north on US 191, then follow park entrance road 18 mi. north.

BEAR LAKE STATE PARK MAP, A-2
Rendezvous Beach

Hwy. 30, 84028.
T: (435) 946-3343 or (800) 322-3770;
www.stateparks.utah.gov.

🚐 ★★★★★   ⛺ ★★★★

Beauty: ★★★★   Site Privacy: ★★★★
Spaciousness: ★★★★   Quiet: ★★★★
Security: ★★★★   Cleanliness: ★★★★
Insect Control: ★★★   Facilities: ★★★

A 28,000 year old earthquake-created freshwater lake with warm summer waters (60–70° F June–July) and 120 miles of groomed snowmobile trails in winter, Bear Lake is ringed with camping sites (mostly primitive) on both the Utah and Idaho sides. But Rendezvous Beach contains the best collection of developed campgrounds. Odd-numbered Willow Campground tent sites are beachfront (except 29), and even-numbered sites are in deep vegetation on the opposite side of what is essentially a paved vehicle parking lot. Cottonwood Campground tent sites 5–42 are beachfront. Birch Campground has 60 50-amp sites, with 16, 18, 27, 28, 30, 38, 39, 48, 49, and 51 being the beachfront best. At Big Creek, an older (20, 30 amp) RV campground, sites 15–33 and 35–38 are beachfront. RV sites are quieter than tent sites, which get group party action on weekends and holidays, when those without reservations get shunted to more primitive and rockier East Side beaches (only South Eden has drinking water: 14 reservable sites.)

BASICS
Operated By: Utah State Parks. **Open:** All year; no sewer after November; electricity on in winter. **Site Assignment:** First come, first served; reservations recommended Memorial Day–Labor Day. **Registration:** At entrance kiosk (rangers collect fees in winter). **Fee:** Hookup, $21; no hookup, $15; reservation fee, $7. **Parking:** At site.

FACILITIES
Number of RV-only Sites: 106. **Number of Tent-only Sites:** 67. **Hookups:** Electric (20, 30, 50 amps), water, sewer. **Each Site:** Table, fire ring. **Dump Station:** Yes. **Laundry:** No. **Pay Phone:** Yes.
Restrooms and Showers: Yes. **Fuel:** For boats only.
Propane: No. **Internal Roads:** Paved, excellent. **RV Service:** No. **Market:** Garden City, 8 mi. **Restaurant:** Garden City, 6 mi. **General Store:** Basic concessions sold. **Vending:** Yes. **Swimming:** Yes. **Playground:** No. **Other:** Birch sites have sheltered table on cement pad, marina, boat & slip rentals.
Activities: ATV (surrounding national forest), fishing, boating, water sports, winter sports. **Nearby Attractions:** Logan, Ogden. **Additional Information:** Bear Lake Regional Commission (208) 945-2333.

RESTRICTIONS
Pets: On leash under owner's control, not allowed on beach. **Fires:** Allowed, in fire rings only. **Alcoholic Beverages:** Allowed. **Vehicle Maximum Length:** 36 ft. **Other:** Gates closed 10 p.m.–6 a.m. in summer.

TO GET THERE

From Laketown, go 2 mi. north on UT 30.

BEAVER   MAP, C-1
Minersville State Park

P.O. Box 1531, 84713. T: (435) 438-5472;
www.nr.utah.gov.

🚐 ★★★★   ⛺ ★★★★★

Beauty: ★★★★   Site Privacy: ★★★
Spaciousness: ★★★   Quiet: ★★★★★
Security: ★★★★   Cleanliness: ★★★★
Insect Control: ★★★★   Facilities: ★★

Known for trophy rainbow and cutthroat trout that
fatten up on crayfish and shrimp, Minersville is also
popular for its hookups. But the lake, which holds
water for downstream irrigation and freezes in cold
weather, has a limit of one 20-inch trout that must be
caught using only artificial lures and flies. Bicyclists
from around the world brave strong winds to stop at
this jewel in the sagebrush desert for the gravel campsites backed by grass strips. Tent pad users can tap
into the 20-amp outlets (30-amp outlets are kept for
RVs). Rock hounds hunt top-grade obsidian, chal-
cedony, and agates in the surrounding region. Bird-
watchers flock for waterfowl like white-faced ibis,
great blue herons, white pelicans, western grebes, and
double-crested cormorants. Cottonwood, willow,
elm, mulberry, and Russian olive trees provide shade.
There are also three narrow (12 feet) wheelchair-
accessible sites and a large gravel overflow area.

BASICS

Operated By: Utah State Parks. **Open:** All year, full
services; Apr.–Nov., depending on weather. **Site
Assignment:** First come, first served. **Registration:**
At self-pay fee station. **Fee:** $13. **Parking:** At site.

FACILITIES

Number of RV-only Sites: 29. **Number of Tent-
only Sites:** 18. **Hookups:** Electric (20, 30 amps),
water. **Each Site:** Sheltered table, grill. **Dump Sta-
tion:** Yes. **Laundry:** No. **Pay Phone:** Yes.
Restrooms and Showers: Yes. **Fuel:** No.
Propane: No. **Internal Roads:** Gravel, good. **RV
Service:** No. **Market:** Beaver, 12 mi. **Restaurant:**
Beaver, 12 mi. **General Store:** No. **Vending:** No.
Swimming: Lake (at own risk). **Playground:** No.
Other: Boat ramp, horseshoes, volleyball, air com-
pressor, 3 wheelchair-accessible sites. **Activities:**
Boating, water sports, fishing, biking, bird-watching,
rock hounding, golf. **Nearby Attractions:** Fishlake
National Forest. **Additional Information:** Beaver
County Travel Council, (435) 438-2975.

RESTRICTIONS

Pets: On leash (keep out of grass). **Fires:** Allowed
(in grills only, firewood available). **Alcoholic Beverages:** Allowed. **Vehicle Maximum Length:** 30 ft.
Other: No boats inside campground, Jan. 1–May 28
no fishing (certain years).

TO GET THERE

From Beaver go 12 mi. southwest on UT 21.

BEAVER   MAP, C-1
United Beaver Camperland

1603 S. Campground Rd., 84713.
T: (435) 438-2808 or (877) 438-2808;
www.unitedbeavercamperland.com/index.html.

🚐 ★★★★   ⛺ ★★★

Beauty: ★★★★   Site Privacy: ★★★
Spaciousness: ★★★★   Quiet: ★★★★
Security: ★★★★   Cleanliness: ★★★★
Insect Control: ★★★★   Facilities: ★★★★

Situated at the gateway to Fishlake National Forest,
which has a number of small high-elevation (5,900
to 9,300 feet) summer campgrounds, United Beaver
is top-notch, one of the few area campgrounds open
year-round with long level pull-through sites and
hookups. United Beaver is also a good stopping place
on the way to Great Basin National Park in Nevada,
Salt Lake City, and southern destinations like the
Grand Canyon and Las Vegas. Beaver is a relaxed and
friendly travel stop. There are grass strips between
RV sites at this campground conveniently located
near a highway exit at the south end of town. United
Beaver is relatively quiet, with the wind blowing in
the trees and chirping birds being louder than the
highway. All in all, United Beaver is a friendly place
where people are on a first-name basis and helpful-
ness prevails.

BASICS

Operated By: Betty Massey, Betty Burns, Betty
Miller, and Mary Friedman. **Open:** All year. **Site
Assignment:** Reservations requested, otherwise,
first come, first served. **Registration:** At office.
Fee: RV, $24.95; tent, $18; overnight, $19. **Parking:**
At site.

FACILITIES

Number of RV-only Sites: 85. **Number of Tent-
only Sites:** 30. **Hookups:** Electric (20, 30, 50 amps),
water, sewer. **Each Site:** Table, grill. **Dump Station:**
Yes. **Laundry:** Yes. **Pay Phone:** Yes. **Restrooms
and Showers:** Yes. **Fuel:** No. **Propane:** Yes. **Internal Roads:** Gravel, good. **RV Service:** No. **Market:**
Beaver, 1 mi. **Restaurant:** Beaver, across road. **General Store:** Yes. **Vending:** Yes. **Swimming:** Pool.
Playground: Yes. **Other:** Game room, dog run,
horseshoes, Dutch-oven pit in tent area. **Activities:**
Golf, horseshoes, volleyball, fishing, boating, hunting,
skiing, winter sports. **Nearby Attractions:** Cedar
Breaks, Bryce, Paiute ATV Trail. **Additional Information:** Cedar City Ranger District, (435) 865-
3200; Beaver County Travel Council, (435) 438-2975,
(800) 280-2975.

RESTRICTIONS

Pets: On leash. **Fires:** Allowed; no open fires. **Alcoholic Beverages:** Allowed. **Vehicle Maximum
Length:** No limit. **Other:** No parking or carpets on
grass.

TO GET THERE

From US I-15 get off at Exit 109.

BLANDING   MAP, D-3
Devils Canyon Campground

reserve america

Monticello Ranger District, 496 East Central,
84535. T: (435) 587-2041 or (877) 446-6777;
www.reserveamerica.com.

🚐 ★★   ⛺ ★★★★★

Beauty: ★★★★★   Site Privacy: ★★★★★
Spaciousness: ★★★   Quiet: ★★★★
Security: ★★★★   Cleanliness: ★★★★★
Insect Control: ★★★   Facilities: ★

Located in the Manti-Lasal National Forest, Devils
Canyon is a U.S. Forest Service campground operated under permit by a private concessionaire,
United Land Management (P.O. Box 970099,
Orem, UT 84097). Reservations are usually not necessary but may be a good idea during peak seasons,
particularly when special events come to the area and
all the campgrounds in Moab, Green River, and the
surrounding environs book full. If hookups and all
the amenities are a prerequisite, the numerous commercial roadside RV campgrounds between Mexican
Hat and Green River are a better choice. But if the
feeling of camping in the forest is paramount, then
Devils Canyon offers self-sufficient campers a good
location for exploring Hovenweep, Natural Bridges,
the Needles District of Canyonlands, and even
Arches. Sites 9 and 10 are best for big RVs. For the
most seclusion and privacy among the tall junipers
and ponderosa pines choose sites 1–7.

BASICS

Operated By: United Land Management. **Open:**
Apr. 1–Nov. 1. **Site Assignment:** First come, first
served. **Registration:** At self-pay fee station. **Fee:**
$10; cash, check; call ahead to confirm prices. **Park-
ing:** At site.

FACILITIES

Number of RV-only Sites: 33. **Hookups:** None.
Each Site: Table, fire pit. **Dump Station:** No.
Laundry: No. **Pay Phone:** No. **Restrooms and
Showers:** No showers, pit toilets. **Fuel:** No.
Propane: No. **Internal Roads:** Paved, rutted. **RV
Service:** No. **Market:** Blanding, 10 mi. **Restaurant:**
Blanding, 10 mi. **General Store:** No. **Vending:** No.
Swimming: No. **Playground:** No. **Activities:** Hik-
ing trails. **Nearby Attractions:** Natural Bridges and
Arches, Hovenweep, Canyonlands. **Additional
Information:** San Juan County Visitor Services,
(435) 587-3235, (800) 574-4386.

RESTRICTIONS

Pets: On leash. **Fires:** Allowed, but restrictions
sometimes in place. **Alcoholic Beverages:**
Allowed. **Vehicle Maximum Length:** No limit.
Other: Protect food from bears, no fireworks.

TO GET THERE

From Blanding go 9.5 mi. northeast on US 191.

BLUFF — MAP, D-3
Cadillac Ranch RV Park

Hwy. 191, P. O. Box 157, 84512.
T: (435) 672-2262 or (800) 538-6195;
www.bluffutah.org/cadillacranch.

🚐 ★★★★   ⛺ ★★★

Beauty: ★★★★   Site Privacy: ★★★★
Spaciousness: ★★★★   Quiet: ★★★★
Security: ★★★★★   Cleanliness: ★★★★★
Insect Control: ★★★★   Facilities: ★★★★

A good overnight stopping place south of Moab and
north of Monument Valley and Kayenta, AZ, Bluff
and Cadillac Ranch also make a good base for
exploring this part of southeastern Utah. Cadillac
Ranch is a homey little campground with 30-foot-
wide RV spaces where deer and wild turkey wander
in and out on their own schedules. The atmosphere
is friendly, and TV antennas pick up six channels. In
the evening people sit and talk while having a drink
on the office veranda overlooking the pond. The
pond is available for free fishing (bass, bluegill, catfish, trout) and paddle boating, or just watching
aquatic waterfowl like ducks, geese, ibis, cranes, and
blue herons. The tent sites are especially attractive,
being on the opposite side of the pond from the
RVs, though sometimes Europeans pack their tents
tightly on the lawns around the office when the official tent sites are all taken.

BASICS
Operated By: Rayma Percell. **Open:** All year. **Site
Assignment:** First come, first served and by reser-
vations. **Registration:** At office. **Fee:** $16; 50 amp,
$18; V, MC. **Parking:** At site.

FACILITIES
Number of RV-only Sites: 17. **Number of Tent-
only Sites:** 10. **Hookups:** Electric (30, 50 amps),
water, sewer, phone (modem). **Each Site:** Table,
some have grill. **Dump Station:** No. **Laundry:** No.
Pay Phone: Yes. **Restrooms and Showers:** Yes.
Fuel: No. **Propane:** No. **Internal Roads:** Gravel,
good. **RV Service:** No. **Market:** Bluff, less than 1 mi.
Restaurant: Bluff, less than 1 mi. **General Store:**
No. **Vending:** No. **Swimming:** No. **Playground:**
No. **Other:** Paddleboats. **Activities:** Horseback rid-
ing, horseshoes, volleyball, pond fishing, hiking.
Nearby Attractions: Valley of the Gods, Monu-
ment Valley, Natural Bridges, Hovenweep, Lake Pow-
ell. **Additional Information:** San Juan County
Visitor Services, (435) 587-3235, (800) 574-4386.

RESTRICTIONS
Pets: On leash under owner's control. **Fires:**
Allowed (firewood supplied gratis). **Alcoholic Beverages:** Allowed. **Vehicle Maximum Length:** 65
ft. **Other:** Don't let children throw or roll rocks.

TO GET THERE
On east end of US 191 in town.

BRYCE CANYON — MAP, D-2
Bryce Canyon North

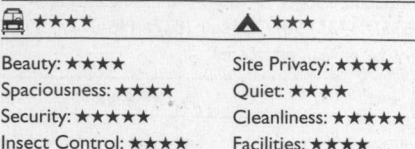

P.O. Box 64020, 84764. T: (435) 834-5322;
www.reserveamerica.com.

🚐 ★★★   ⛺ ★★★★★

Beauty: ★★★★   Site Privacy: ★★★★
Spaciousness: ★★★★   Quiet: ★★★
Security: ★★★★★   Cleanliness: ★★★★
Insect Control: ★★★   Facilities: ★★★★

North Campground is in a ponderosa pine forest
with pink cliffs and hoodoos at 8,000 feet elevation,
where winter comes early and spring late. The primitive feel is reinforced by placement of facilities like
showers a short walk outside the campground.
Campsites are spread out on a tiered hillside in four
loops, all of which fill up on summer weekends.
Loop A is lowest, and Loop D is highest in elevation
and most private. Loops A and B nearest the
entrance allow only vehicles 20 feet and longer, and
they hum with the noise of generators from 8 a.m. to
8 p.m. Loop C bans generators. Loop D bans generators and vehicles over 20 feet, making it a haven for
tent campers. The site is windy, but the cool breezes
are welcomed in summer. Though the tendency is to
seek shady sites, summer tent campers should opt for
sunny sites so tents can dry off from thunderstorms.

BASICS
Operated By: National Park Service. **Open:** All
year. **Site Assignment:** Reservations must be made
2 days in advance; reservable season May 14–Sept.
30. **Registration:** At registration office. **Fee:** Single,
$10. **Parking:** At park and on-site pad.

FACILITIES
Number of Multipurpose Sites: 128. **Hookups:**
None. **Each Site:** Call ahead. **Dump Station:** Yes.
Laundry: Yes. **Pay Phone:** Yes. **Restrooms and
Showers:** Yes. **Fuel:** No. **Propane:** No. **Internal
Roads:** Paved. **RV Service:** No. **Market:** No.
Restaurant: Yes. **General Store:** Yes. **Vending:**
No. **Swimming:** No. **Playground:** No. **Other:** No
ATVs or OTVs. **Activities:** Amphitheater, bird-
watching, horseback riding, sightseeing. **Nearby
Attractions:** Kodachrome Basin, Red Canyon.
Additional Information: National Park Service,
www.nps.gov/brca.

RESTRICTIONS
Pets: On a leash at all times. **Fires:** Allowed; camp-
fire program. **Alcoholic Beverages:** Not allowed.
Vehicle Maximum Length: Varies; call ahead.

TO GET THERE
From intersection of UT 89 and UT 12, follow UT
12 east to UT 63. Turn right on UT 63 and watch
for signs indicating entrance to Bryce Canyon
National Park. After passing through park entrance
station take first left into North Campground.

BRYCE CANYON — MAP, D-2
Bryce Canyon Pines

Bryce Canyon National Park, Mile Marker 10, UT
12, 84764. T: (435) 834-5441 or (800) 892-7923;
www.brycecanyonpines.com.

🚐 ★★★★   ⛺ ★★★★

Beauty: ★★★★   Site Privacy: ★★★★
Spaciousness: ★★★★   Quiet: ★★★★
Security: ★★★★   Cleanliness: ★★★★
Insect Control: ★★★★   Facilities: ★★★★

A convenient campground for excursions into Bryce
National Park (just 6 miles away) and Red Canyon,
Bryce Canyon Pines has ample amenities and is
nicely set back from the highway. The campground
itself is intimate, like being in a small pine forest
bisected by gravel roads. Little patches of meadow
between campsites add to the rustic feel. Occasional
power outages from the area's high winds are a nuisance that comes with the territory. A heated pool (at
the motel, but available to campers), a restaurant, gas
pumps (fill up when the power grid is working,
because they are electronic) and a well-stocked store
with a pool table add up to ample comforts without
the crush of the crowds and tour buses at the nearby
national park. In short, being outside of Bryce and
away from the summer crowds is a good reason to
put down here for the night.

BASICS
Operated By: Kenny and Randy Miller. **Open:** Apr.
1–Oct. 31. **Site Assignment:** First come, first
served; reservations accepted. **Registration:** At
store. **Fee:** RV, $24; tent, $16; V, MC, AE, D. **Parking:**
At site.

FACILITIES
Number of RV-only Sites: 24. **Number of Tent-
only Sites:** 15. **Hookups:** Electric (30 amps), water,
sewer; 24 sites w/ full hookups. **Each Site:** Table, fire
pit. **Dump Station:** Yes. **Laundry:** Yes. **Pay Phone:**
Yes. **Restrooms and Showers:** Yes. **Fuel:** Yes.
Propane: No. **Internal Roads:** Gravel, good condi-
tion. **RV Service:** No. **Market:** Part of country
store. **Restaurant:** At motel. **General Store:** Yes.
Vending: Yes. **Swimming:** Heated pool in motel.
Playground: No. **Other:** Portable grills on request.
Activities: Horseback riding, horseshoes, game
room (TV, pool table). **Nearby Attractions:** Red
Canyon, Bryce Canyon. **Additional Information:**
Bryce Canyon National Park, (435) 834-5322.

RESTRICTIONS
Pets: Small pets on leash. **Fires:** Allowed (firewood
sold). **Alcoholic Beverages:** Allowed. **Vehicle
Maximum Length:** No limit. **Other:** 11 a.m.
checkout.

TO GET THERE
Go 4 mi. west on UT 12 from the UT 63 junction.

BRYCE CANYON   MAP, D-2
Ruby's RV Park and Campground

Bryce Canyon National Park,
1280 South State, Hwy. 63, 84764.
T: (435) 834-5301 or (866) 866-6616;
www.rubysinn.com.

🚐 ★★★★★   ⛺ ★★★★★

Beauty: ★★★★   Site Privacy: ★★★★
Spaciousness: ★★★★★   Quiet: ★★★★
Security: ★★★★   Cleanliness: ★★★★
Insect Control: ★★★   Facilities: ★★★★★

Just a mile north of the Park entrance, Ruby's is part of a tourist complex that includes an excellent buffet (good value; friendly staff) packed with tour buses at peak hours. The Ruby family first settled on a ranch here in 1916, seven years before Bryce became a national monument, and has been doing an excellent job in tourism ever since, now handling 1.7 million visits per year. Full hookup sites are closest to the highway, just behind the RV-park office. Electric and water sites are hidden from the tourist hordes at a lower elevation in a more rustic world of their own, with many pine trees and little depressions between sites containing bits of meadow greenery. Many of these back sites share water views with the large expanse of meadow (no designated sites) reserved for tents. Though Bryce seems hectic, with long lines of cars looking for parking in summer, Ruby's is as good as commercial camping gets.

BASICS
Operated By: The Ruby family, Shauna and Blaine. **Open:** Apr. 1–Oct. 31. **Site Assignment:** First come, first served; reservations recommended. **Registration:** At office. **Fee:** RV, $26–$29; tent, $18; V, MC, AF, D, DC. **Parking:** At site.

FACILITIES
Number of RV-only Sites: 118. **Number of Tent-only Sites:** 100. **Hookups:** Electric (20, 30, 50 amps), water, sewer. **Each Site:** Table. **Dump Station:** Yes. **Laundry:** Yes. **Pay Phone:** Yes. **Restrooms and Showers:** Yes. **Fuel:** Yes. **Propane:** Yes. **Internal Roads:** Gravel, good condition. **RV Service:** Yes. **Market:** Yes. **Restaurant:** Yes. **General Store:** Yes. **Vending:** Yes. **Swimming:** Pool. **Playground:** No. **Other:** ATM machine, business center, bus wash, car rentals, film processing, tram stop. **Activities:** Helicopter & horseback rides, mountain biking, petting farm, gold panning, rodeo, country music dinners, cross-country skiing. **Nearby Attractions:** Bryce Canyon National Park. **Additional Information:** Bryce Canyon National Park, (435) 834-5322.

RESTRICTIONS
Pets: On leash at all times. **Fires:** Allowed (charcoal). **Alcoholic Beverages:** Allowed. **Vehicle Maximum Length:** No limit. **Other:** Noon check-out time.

TO GET THERE
On UT 63, 1 mi. north of park entrance.

BRYCE CANYON   MAP, D-2
Sunset Campground

reserve america

Bryce Canyon National Park, Scenic Dr., 84764.
T: (435) 834-5322/4801;
www.reserveamerica.com.

🚐 ★★★★   ⛺ ★★★★★

Beauty: ★★★★   Site Privacy: ★★★★
Spaciousness: ★★★★   Quiet: ★★★★
Security: ★★★★   Cleanliness: ★★★★
Insect Control: ★★★   Facilities: ★★

Sunset is usually the last park campground opening in the spring, after the snowfall has melted and camper demand has filled up North Campground's loops. Sunset has an isolated ponderosa pine forest feel, being farthest from Visitor Center crowds and a mile from amenities such as showers. No tents are allowed on loop A, whose widely dispersed sites are set aside for RVs and their noisy generators. The smaller and more intimate Loops B and C accommodate tents and ban generators and vehicles over 20 feet. Wheelchair accessibility, including at the group site, is another plus. Mule deer grazing under the shade of ponderosa pines are a common sight. Overall, Sunset is worthwhile because it puts some distance between campers and the park crowds, though the tradeoff is hiking, driving, or riding the park shuttles to showers and other facilities.

BASICS
Operated By: National Park Service. **Open:** Spring–fall; exact dates depend on weather. **Site Assignment:** First come, first served; group site requires reservation. **Registration:** At self pay entrance fee station. **Fee:** $10. **Parking:** At site.

FACILITIES
Number of Multipurpose Sites: 101. **Hookups:** None. **Each Site:** Table, fire ring. **Dump Station:** Yes. **Laundry:** No. **Pay Phone:** Yes. **Restrooms and Showers:** Yes (showers 1 mi.). **Fuel:** No. **Propane:** No. **Internal Roads:** Paved, weathered. **RV Service:** No. **Market:** At Ruby's, 2 mi. north. **Restaurant:** At lodge, 1 mi. north. **General Store:** 1 mi. **Vending:** No. **Swimming:** No. **Playground:** No. **Activities:** Horseback riding, ranger interpretative programs, hiking. **Nearby Attractions:** Kodachrome Basin, Red Canyon, Escalante, Cedar Breaks. **Additional Information:** National Park Service, www.nps.gov/brca or Bryce Canyon National Park, (435) 834-5322.

RESTRICTIONS
Pets: On leash under owner's control; not allowed on trails. **Fires:** Allowed in grills only. **Alcoholic Beverages:** Allowed. **Vehicle Maximum Length:** No limit. **Other:** 14-day stay limit; no firewood gathering; don't feed squirrels or chipmunks.

TO GET THERE
From visitor center, go 2 mi. south on Hwy. 63.

CANNONVILLE   MAP, D-2
Cannonville/Bryce Valley KOA

P.O. Box 50, Hwy. 12, 84718.
T: (435) 679-8988 or (888) 562-4710;
www.brycecanyonkoa.com.

🚐 ★★★★★   ⛺ ★★★★★

Beauty: ★★★★   Site Privacy: ★★★★
Spaciousness: ★★★★   Quiet: ★★★★
Security: ★★★★   Cleanliness: ★★★★
Insect Control: ★★★   Facilities: ★★★★

One of the more attractive campgrounds, public or private, this KOA has integrated an old apple orchard into its front RV sites. There is a separate tent-site loop, but a dirt road leading behind the hills has even more isolated campsites that are real wilderness with good sand pads for tents. These sites are invisible from the highway and nestled among scenic red sandstone badlands, with native high-desert pinyon pine, juniper, and desert scrub. Cannonville is a town of 131 people, so campground vistas facing away from the main highway tend to be mostly banded sandstone hills and pastoral irrigated ranches, though a gas station, restaurant, and motel are only a block away. All in all, not a bad base from which to explore Bryce Canyon National Park and Kodachrome Basin State Park.

BASICS
Operated By: John Holland. **Open:** Mar. 15–Nov. 15. **Site Assignment:** First come, first served; reservations accepted. **Registration:** At office. **Fee:** RV, $25–$32; tent, $22. **Parking:** At site.

FACILITIES
Number of RV-only Sites: 60. **Number of Tent-only Sites:** 20. **Hookups:** Electric (30, 50 amps), water, sewer. **Each Site:** Table, fire ring. **Dump Station:** Yes. **Laundry:** Yes. **Pay Phone:** Yes. **Restrooms and Showers:** Yes. **Fuel:** No. **Propane:** Yes. **Internal Roads:** Gravel, good. **RV Service:** No. **Market:** In Cannonville. **Restaurant:** In Cannonville. **General Store:** Yes. **Vending:** Yes. **Swimming:** Heated outdoor pool (May 1–Oct. 1). **Playground:** Yes. **Other:** Covered pavilion w/ kitchen, some grills, game room, data ports. **Activities:** Biking, horseback riding, fishing, rock hounding, hiking. **Nearby Attractions:** Bryce, Kodachrome Basin, Boulder Mountain lakes, Grand Staircase Escalante National Monument. **Additional Information:** Cannonville Visitor Center (435) 679-8981.

RESTRICTIONS
Pets: On leash under owner's control at all times. **Fires:** Allowed (firewood sold). **Alcoholic Beverages:** At site only. **Vehicle Maximum Length:** 60 ft. **Other:** No digging holes, disturbing ground cover, chopping vegetation, or placing doormats on grass; no firearms or fireworks; 11 a.m. checkout.

TO GET THERE
15 mi. east of Bryce at junction of UT 12 and Red Rock Rd. in Cannonville.

CANNONVILLE   MAP, D-2
Kodachrome Basin State Park

P.O. Box 180069, 84718.
T: (435) 679-8562 or (800) 322-3770 (group only); www.reserveamerica.com.

🚐 ★★★★   ⛺ ★★★★★

Beauty: ★★★★★   Site Privacy: ★★★★
Spaciousness: ★★★★   Quiet: ★★★★
Security: ★★★★   Cleanliness: ★★★★
Insect Control: ★★★★   Facilities: ★★★

Named after the film, Kodachrome Basin State Park is noted for its colorful sandstone spires resembling huge chimneys. The campground is surrounded by colorful banded sandstone hills, sand pipes, and hoodoos. Big gnarly barked junipers add privacy to the sites. There is even a wheelchair-accessible site with a raised wood tent platform with ramps. The general store, which also rents cabins, is a bit eccentric and liable to close on a whim on a busy Saturday. This is one of the few places where you are encouraged to feed an animal, namely the chukars, an introduced bird that resembles a partridge and needs help making it through the harsh winters. Dirt roads and trails lead to rock formations, coves, and colorful geyser remnants (e.g. chimneys) where the play of light changes the colors through a moody array of whites, grays, reds, and oranges. Add in the proximity to Bryce and Escalante, and this makes a fine stopping place.

BASICS

Operated By: Utah State Parks. **Open:** All year. **Site Assignment:** First come, first served; reservations for 4 group sites. **Registration:** At self-pay fee station. **Fee:** Camping, $15; per vehicle fee, $5–$9. **Parking:** At site.

FACILITIES

Number of RV-only Sites: 27. **Hookups:** None. **Each Site:** Table, grill on cement pad. **Dump Station:** Yes. **Laundry:** No. **Pay Phone:** Yes. **Restrooms and Showers:** Yes. **Fuel:** No. **Propane:** No. **Internal Roads:** Pavement, excellent condition. **RV Service:** No. **Market:** 14 mi. in Tropic. **Restaurant:** 9 mi. in Cannonville. **General Store:** Yes. **Vending:** Yes. **Swimming:** No. **Playground:** No. **Other:** Wheelchair-accessible site. **Activities:** Horseback riding, mountain biking, picnicking. **Nearby Attractions:** Bryce, Escalante, Cottonwood Canyon, Grosvenor Arch. **Additional Information:** Escalante Interagency Office, (435) 826-5499.

RESTRICTIONS

Pets: On leash under owner's control at all times. **Fires:** Allowed. **Alcoholic Beverages:** Allowed. **Vehicle Maximum Length:** 30 ft. **Other:** 14-day stay limit; no guns, bows, slingshots, or fireworks, no firewood collecting; ATVs must remain on trailers while in park; no climbing on rocks.

TO GET THERE

From junction of UT 12 in Cannonville, go 9 mi. southeast on Cottonwood Canyon Rd.

CANYONLANDS   MAP. C-3
NATIONAL PARK
Squaw Flat Campground

Needles District, Hwy. 211, 84532.
T: (435) 719-2313 or (319) 259-7164; www.nps.gov/cany/camp.html.

🚐 ★★★★   ⛺ ★★★★★

Beauty: ★★★★★   Site Privacy: ★★★★★
Spaciousness: ★★★★★   Quiet: ★★★★★
Security: ★★★★★   Cleanliness: ★★★★★
Insect Control: ★★★   Facilities: ★★

Make sure the gas tank is full and that you have enough water and firewood for the duration before turning onto UT 211 en route to the Needles District of Canyonlands National Park. There is a small private campground catering to RVs (no hookups; $15) with gas, propane, showers, and a store with haphazard hours just outside the park boundary at Needles Outpost (call (435) 979-4007), but Squaw Flat Campground demands self-sufficiency. In return, Squaw Flat offers relatively large sites, each tucked into its own little sandstone rock formation and far from its neighbor. Walk-in tent sites nestled among the orange sandstone rocks provide an even more primitive slot canyon feel. High-clearance four-wheel-drive vehicles and technical driving skills are needed to visit the major geologic features; even mountain bikes quit moving in the deep sandy washes. Peak season (March–May and mid-September–October), campsites are all snagged by 10 a.m. Water is available year-round at Squaw Flat Campground. Flush toilets and portable toilets are available.

BASICS

Operated By: National Park Service. **Open:** All year. **Site Assignment:** For groups of 11 or more, reservations are recommended; otherwise, first come, first served; check at visitor center for availability of sites. **Registration:** At self-pay fee station. **Fee:** $15; cash, check. **Parking:** At site.

FACILITIES

Number of Multipurpose Sites: 26. **Hookups:** None. **Each Site:** Table, fire ring. **Dump Station:** No. **Laundry:** No. **Pay Phone:** Yes. **Restrooms and Showers:** No showers. **Fuel:** No. **Propane:** No. **Internal Roads:** Paved. **RV Service:** No. **Market:** Monticello, 55 mi. **Restaurant:** Monticello, 55 mi. **General Store:** No. **Vending:** No. **Swimming:** No. **Playground:** No. **Other:** Visitor center, campfire circle. **Activities:** Four-wheel driving, mountain biking, hiking, interpretive programs. **Nearby Attractions:** Newspaper Rock, Canyon Rims Recreation Area, Chesler Park. **Additional Information:** Canyonlands Natural History Assoc., (435) 259-6003, www.cnha.org.

RESTRICTIONS

Pets: On leash & attended at all times (not allowed on hiking trails or 4WD roads, even in a vehicle). **Fires:** Allowed only in metal fire rings; no wood gathering. **Alcoholic Beverages:** Allowed. **Vehicle Maximum Length:** 28 ft. **Other:** No ATVs; 2 vehicles & 10 people per site, 10 a.m. checkout, 14-day stay limit.

TO GET THERE

From US 191 14 mi. north of Monticello go 34 mi. west on UT 211.

CEDAR CITY   MAP, D-1
Cedar Canyon Campground

reserve america

82 North 100 East, Suite 101, 84721.
T: (435) 865-3700 or (877) 444-6777; www.reserveamerica.com.

🚐 ★★   ⛺ ★★★★

Beauty: ★★★★★   Site Privacy: ★★★★★
Spaciousness: ★★★   Quiet: ★★★★
Security: ★★★★   Cleanliness: ★★★★
Insect Control: ★★★   Facilities: ★★

Perched at 8,100-feet elevation on UT 14, Cedar Canyon offers self-sufficient campers the best of both worlds: Cedar City's Tony Award–winning Shakespeare festival and the orange-and-white spires and columns of higher elevation Cedar Breaks National Monument. Cedar Canyon Campground is situated in a beautiful forest of spruce, fir, and aspen. Rocky, tree-lined Crow Creek separates the campground from the highway. Run by National Forest Service concessionaire AuDi, sites 4, 6, 7, and 17 can be reserved. For closest creek proximity select sites 2, 4, 6–8, 12, 14, or 16; site 12, one of three double sites, accommodates up to 16 people. The campground creek is not fishable, but there is a kid's fishing pond nearby at Iron County's Wood Ranch. Though water (piped in from a nearby spring) and sanitation services are shut down after Labor Day to avoid freezing, the campground can still be used.

BASICS

Operated By: AuDi, Inc. **Open:** June 15–Sept. 6. **Site Assignment:** First come, first served; group & some individual sites can be reserved. **Registration:** At self-pay fee station. **Fee:** Double, $20; single, $10; cash, check. Group sites (up to 40 people), $40 per night. **Parking:** At site.

FACILITIES

Number of RV-only Sites: 19. **Number of Multipurpose Sites:** 19. **Hookups:** None. **Each Site:** Table, fire ring. **Dump Station:** Yes. **Laundry:** No. **Pay Phone:** No. **Restrooms and Showers:** No showers. Vault toilets. **Fuel:** No. **Propane:** No. **Internal Roads:** Paved, excellent. **RV Service:** No. **Market:** Cedar City, 14 mi. **Restaurant:** Cedar City, 14 mi. **General Store:** No. **Vending:** No. **Swimming:** No. **Playground:** No. **Activities:** Biking, horseback riding, fishing, hiking. **Nearby Attractions:** Cedar Breaks National Monument, Virgin River Rim Trail, Brian Head, Zion. **Additional Information:** Iron County Tourism, (800) 354-4849.

RESTRICTIONS

Pets: On leash & always attended. **Fires:** Allowed in fire rings & stoves only. **Alcoholic Beverages:** Allowed. **Vehicle Maximum Length:** 24 ft. **Other:** 14-day stay limit; lock food away from bears.

To Get There
From Cedar City go 14 mi. east on UT 14.

CEDAR CITY   MAP, D-1
Duck Creek Campground

reserve america

P.O. Box 627, 1789 Wedgewood, 84720.
T: (435) 865-3200 or (877) 444-6777;
www.reserveamerica.com.

🚐 ★★★★   ▲ ★★★★

Beauty: ★★★★   Site Privacy: ★★★★
Spaciousness: ★★★★   Quiet: ★★★★
Security: ★★★★   Cleanliness: ★★★★
Insect Control: ★★   Facilities: ★★★

A large duck pond at 8,600-feet elevation and camp-sites heavily forested with tall aspens and spruce make Duck Creek's five loops an attractive, reserv-able alternative to driving gravel roads to reach the smaller 9,200-foot-elevation Te-Ah and Navajo Lake Campgrounds (see Appendix). National Forest Ser-vice concessionaire AuDi keeps Duck Creek in top shape, and added amenities like electric hookups are not too far-fetched a possibility in coming seasons. At Loop A, which is nearest the highway and has a very large picnic area, sites 4–13, 15, 17–20, and 24–37 are reservable. At smaller and more intimate Loop B, sites 38–40, 42, 43, and 46–48 can be reserved. Loops C, D and E are most primitive in feel, and only the Roundup and Wagon Train group areas can be reserved in these loops. Nearby Duck Creek Village provides many of the amenities miss-ing at the campground.

BASICS
Operated By: AuDi, Inc. **Open:** Apr. 15–Sept. 6. **Site Assignment:** First come, first served. **Regis-tration:** At self-pay entrance fee station. **Fee:** Dou-ble, $18; single, $10; cash, check. **Parking:** At site.

FACILITIES
Number of RV-only Sites: 96. **Hookups:** None. **Each Site:** Table, fire ring. **Dump Station:** Yes. **Laundry:** No. **Pay Phone:** Yes. **Restrooms and Showers:** No showers. **Fuel:** No. **Propane:** No. **Internal Roads:** Gravel, good. **RV Service:** No. **Market:** Cedar City, 30 mi. **Restaurant:** Duck Creek Village, 2 mi. **General Store:** No. **Vending:** No. **Swimming:** No. **Playground:** No. **Other:** Amphitheater, picnic area, boat ramp. **Activities:** Boating, fishing, horseback riding. **Nearby Attrac-tions:** Cedar Breaks, Navajo Lake, Brian Head, Bryce, Zion. **Additional Information:** Iron County Tourism, (800) 354-4849.

RESTRICTIONS
Pets: On leash. **Fires:** Allowed (firewood sold). **Alcoholic Beverages:** Allowed. **Vehicle Maxi-mum Length:** 45 ft. **Other:** No fireworks.

TO GET THERE
From Cedar City go 30 mi. east on UT 14.

DUCHESNE   MAP, B-3
Starvation Group Area

reserve america

Box 584, 84021-0584. T: (435) 738-2326;
www.reserveamerica.com.

🚐 ★★★★   ▲ ★★★★

Beauty: ★★★   Site Privacy: ★★★
Spaciousness: ★★★   Quiet: ★★★★
Security: ★★★★   Cleanliness: ★★★★
Insect Control: ★★★   Facilities: ★★★★

The sprawling waters of Starvation Reservoir provide for fishing and boating in a stark desert landscape. Located 4 miles northwest of Duchesne on Highway 40, the campground is popular with anglers, boaters, and those using Starvation as a base camp for nearby off-highway vehicle riding. Primitive camping is allowed at designated areas around the reservoir. In the late 1800s and early 1900s, cattlemen and home-steaders tried to make a go of it along the banks of the Strawberry River in the area now occupied by the reservoir and dam. Their story is one of hardship, perseverance, and facing near starvation in a very hostile and harsh environment. Winters were hard, long and extremely cold. Their cattle and livestock often froze during these winter months, and the short growing season was hindered by flooding, hail-storms, early frosts, and other calamities. They nick-named the area Starvation and it was from this reference that the highway bridge, reservoir, dam, and state park received their names.

BASICS
Operated By: Utah State Parks. **Open:** May 20–Sept. 20. **Site Assignment:** Group reservations are accepted up to 11 months in advance of park depar-ture date. **Registration:** At office. **Fee:** Group, $75–$78. **Parking:** At site.

FACILITIES
Hookups: None. **Dump Station:** Yes. **Laundry:** No. **Pay Phone:** No. **Restrooms and Showers:** Yes. **Fuel:** No. **Propane:** No. **Internal Roads:** Paved. **RV Service:** Yes. **Market:** No. **Restaurant:** No. **General Store:** No. **Vending:** No. **Swim-ming:** Yes. **Playground:** No. **Activities:** Boating, kayaking, canoeing, sailing, fishing, ice fishing, picnick-ing, swimming, wildlife.

RESTRICTIONS
Pets: On a 6-ft. leash, never unattended, cleaned up after. Not allowed in buildings, on beaches, in lakes or reservoirs. **Fires:** In fire rings, stoves, grills, or fire-places provided for that purpose. Be sure your fire is completely extinguished before leaving. Do not leave your fire unattended. **Alcoholic Beverages:** Allowed w/in state parks, except for visitor centers, museums, & administrative offices. **Vehicle Maxi-mum Length:** Call ahead.

TO GET THERE
Starvation State Park is located 4 mi. northwest of Duchesne on Hwy. 40.

ESCALANTE   MAP, D-2
Broken Bow RV Camp

495 West Main St., P.O. Box 505, 84726.
T: (888) 241-8785 or (435) 826-4959;
www.go-utah.com/broken-bow-campground.

🚐 ★★★★   ▲ ★★★

Beauty: ★★★   Site Privacy: ★★★
Spaciousness: ★★★   Quiet: ★★★
Security: ★★★★   Cleanliness: ★★★★
Insect Control: ★★★★   Facilities: ★★★

This small family operation on Escalante's Main Street is easy to miss, being fronted by a hand painted wooden sign of Broken Bow Arch (the owner's favorite place). The Moqui Motel and Nature Sounds Drum Factory are just across the street. Though a bit hidden, the RV park is well maintained. A pine building has pine toilet stalls, showers, and a laundry room. A large sloping grassy strip along a fence is set aside for tents, and there is a group or extended tent area. Between the tent areas are two gravel rows of RV sites, with small grassy strips between the sites. Nothing fancy here, but the popular Cowboy Blues restaurant and the whole town are within a few block radius, making this a convenient stopping place.

BASICS
Operated By: Catherine Barney. **Open:** All year. **Site Assignment:** Reservations accepted; other-wise, first come, first served. **Registration:** At office trailer. **Fee:** RV, $18–$29; tent, $12. **Parking:** At site.

FACILITIES
Number of RV-only Sites: 29. **Number of Tent-only Sites:** 40. **Hookups:** Electric (30, 50 amps), water, sewer. **Each Site:** Table, grill. **Dump Station:** Yes. **Laundry:** Yes. **Pay Phone:** Yes. **Restrooms and Showers:** Yes. **Fuel:** No. **Propane:** No. **Inter-nal Roads:** Gravel, good. **RV Service:** No. **Market:** Escalante, 4 blocks distant. **Restaurant:** Escalante, across the street. **General Store:** No. **Vending:** No. **Swimming:** No. **Playground:** No. **Other:** Modem access, rock shop. **Activities:** Fishing, water sports, horseback riding. **Nearby Attractions:** Grand Staircase-Escalante National Monument, Anasazi Indian Village State Park, Boulder Mountain lakes, Bryce. **Additional Information:** Escalante Interagency Office, (435) 826-5499.

RESTRICTIONS
Pets: Allowed; must be leashed at all times. **Fires:** Allowed only in fire pits. **Alcoholic Beverages:** Allowed. **Vehicle Maximum Length:** 49 ft.

TO GET THERE
At the corner of Main & 500 W St. in Escalante, where UT 12 becomes Main St.

ESCALANTE
Escalante Group Area

MAP, D-2

reserve america

Box 350, 84726-0350. T: (435) 826-4466;
www.reserveamerica.com.

🚐 ★★★★　　　⛺ ★★★★

Beauty: ★★★★★　　Site Privacy: ★★★
Spaciousness: ★★★　Quiet: ★★★★
Security: ★★★★　　Cleanliness: ★★★★
Insect Control: ★★★　Facilities: ★★★★

Escalante State Park features colorful deposits of mineralized wood and dinosaur bones 'Escalante State Park' is really kind of a misnomer. 'Escalante' is the name of a Mexican Catholic friar who in 1776 helped lead a group of Mexican Spaniards north from Santa Fe in an attempt to find passage to San Bernardino. The group never even got close to California—they were turned back by deep September snows while in west-central Utah—but they did become the first verifiable expedition of non-Indians to visit Utah. So, Escalante never made it to Escalante, the town or the state park. What most people call this park is Escalante Petrified Forest State Park. The nearby 130-acre Wide Hollow Reservoir provides water recreation and fishing. Off-highway vehicle riding areas are also nearby. The park is an ideal base for trips within the area, including Grand Staircase Escalante National Monument. The small, quiet campground rests at the shores of the reservoir.

BASICS
Operated By: Utah State Parks. **Open:** All year; group day-use only. **Site Assignment:** Group reservations are accepted up to 11 months in advance of park departure date. **Registration:** At office. **Fee:** Group, $50–$52. **Parking:** At site.

FACILITIES
Hookups: None. **Dump Station:** Yes. **Laundry:** No. **Pay Phone:** No. **Restrooms and Showers:** Yes. **Fuel:** No. **Propane:** No. **Internal Roads:** Paved. **RV Service:** Yes. **Market:** No. **Restaurant:** No. **General Store:** No. **Vending:** No. **Swimming:** Yes. **Playground:** No. **Other:** It is illegal to gather firewood or remove petrified wood; please bring your own firewood. **Activities:** Boating, bird-watching, canoeing, kayaking, hiking, interpretive/nature programs, picnicking, scenic views, swimming, wildlife. **Nearby Attractions:** Grand Staircase Escalante National Monument, Wide Hollow Reservoir.

RESTRICTIONS
Pets: On a 6-ft. leash, never unattended, cleaned up after. Not allowed in buildings, on beaches, in lakes or reservoirs. **Fires:** In fire rings, stoves, grills, or fireplaces provided for that purpose. Be sure your fire is completely extinguished before leaving. Do not leave your fire unattended. **Alcoholic Beverages:** Allowed w/in state parks, except for visitor centers, museums, & administrative offices. **Vehicle Maximum Length:** 27 ft.

TO GET THERE
Located 1.5 mi. west of Escalante off Hwy. 12.

ESCALANTE
Escalante State Park

MAP, D-2

reserve america

710 North Reservoir Rd., 84726.
T: (435) 826-4466 or (800) 322-3770;
www.reserveamerica.com.

🚐 ★★　　　⛺ ★★★★★

Beauty: ★★★★★　　Site Privacy: ★★★★★
Spaciousness: ★★★　Quiet: ★★★★
Security: ★★★★　　Cleanliness: ★★★★
Insect Control: ★★　　Facilities: ★★★

Escalante State Park stretches along the shoreline of Wide Hollow Reservoir, which supplies Escalante with its irrigation water. The Aquarius Plateau and views of red rocks add to the rugged charm of the campground, which is a short distance back from the water and slightly buffered from day users. Aside from water activities like boating and fishing for bluegill and rainbow trout, there is a popular 1-mile petrified-forest trail and an array of aquatic birds ranging from loons and cormorants to spotted sandpipers and marbled godwits. The mixture of flat dirt and grassy sites, some with junipers and shade canopies and others under tall cottonwood trees, works best for tents and small vehicles. Gnats and deer flies are an occasional nuisance, but the area is still very popular with day users. All in all, a pleasant place to spend the day or even have a picnic lunch if just passing through.

BASICS
Operated By: Utah State Parks. **Open:** All year. **Site Assignment:** First come, first served; reservations (1 night only; up to 16 weeks in advance of checkout date for individuals; 11 months for group site). **Registration:** At visitor center (if open); otherwise self-pay fee station. **Fee:** $12; day-use fee, $4. **Parking:** At site.

FACILITIES
Number of Multipurpose Sites: 22. **Hookups:** None. **Each Site:** Table, bench, grill on cement pad. **Dump Station:** Yes. **Laundry:** No. **Pay Phone:** Yes. **Restrooms and Showers:** Yes. **Fuel:** No. **Propane:** No. **Internal Roads:** Paved, excellent. **RV Service:** No. **Market:** Escalante, 2 mi. **Restaurant:** Escalante, 2 mi. **General Store:** No. **Vending:** Yes. **Swimming:** Lake. **Playground:** No. **Other:** Boat ramp, canoe rentals, shade canopies at some sites. **Activities:** Boating, waterskiing, lake fishing, aquatic bird-watching, petrified forest, biking. **Nearby Attractions:** Grand Staircase-Escalante National Monument, Anasazi Indian Village State Park, Boulder Mountain lakes & forest, Calf Creek, Bryce. **Additional Information:** Escalante Interagency Office, (435) 826-5499.

RESTRICTIONS
Pets: On leash. **Fires:** Allowed (firewood sold). **Alcoholic Beverages:** Allowed. **Vehicle Maximum Length:** 50 ft. **Other:** 14-day stay limit.

TO GET THERE
1 mi. west of Escalante on UT 12, then 1 mi. north on Wide Hollow Rd.

FILLMORE
Fillmore KOA

MAP, C-2

410 West 900 South, 84631.
T: (435) 743-4420 or (800) 562-1516;
www.koa.com.

🚐 ★★★★　　　⛺ ★★★★

Beauty: ★★★★★　　Site Privacy: ★★★★
Spaciousness: ★★★★　Quiet: ★★★★
Security: ★★★★　　Cleanliness: ★★★★★
Insect Control: ★★★　Facilities: ★★★★

Named after Millard Fillmore, a U.S. President friendly to persecuted Mormons, and briefly Utah's state capital in the 1850s, Fillmore is now the sleepy anchor for surrounding alfalfa and cattle ranches. It is easy to whiz by the I-15 Fillmore Exit without stopping at the Territorial Statehouse State Park Museum or the Fillmore KOA, a grassy poplar-shaded little gem of a campground in a windy area away from the highway. The office and general store are inside a log cabin, and the pool looks like stone (actually Gunite and white paint). Geology buffs should consult the host, a survivor of Mt. St. Helen's who can wax on about the geothermal ice caves, lava flows to the west, and differences in age and type between Utah and Pacific Northwest volcanoes.

BASICS
Operated By: Ann and Dick Flones. **Open:** Mar. 1–Dec. 8. **Site Assignment:** First come, first served. **Registration:** At office. **Fee:** RV, $20–$26; tent, $18–$20; V, MC, AE, D. **Parking:** At site.

FACILITIES
Number of RV-only Sites: 49. **Number of Tent-only Sites:** 7. **Hookups:** Electric (20, 30, 50 amps), water, sewer. **Each Site:** Table. **Dump Station:** Yes. **Laundry:** Yes. **Pay Phone:** Yes. **Restrooms and Showers:** Yes. **Fuel:** No. **Propane:** Yes. **Internal Roads:** Gravel, good. **RV Service:** No. **Market:** Fillmore, 1 mi. **Restaurant:** Fillmore, 1 mi. **General Store:** Yes. **Vending:** Yes. **Swimming:** Pool. **Playground:** Yes (also volleyball, tetherball, game room). **Other:** Tent sites have grass pads, electric, water, sheltered tables, grills, fire rings; 5 cabins. **Activities:** Fishing, boating, hunting, golf, rock hounding. **Nearby Attractions:** Paiute ATV Trail, Cove Fort. **Additional Information:** Fillmore Area Chamber of Commerce, (435) 743-6121.

RESTRICTIONS
Pets: On leash. **Fires:** Allowed. **Alcoholic Beverages:** Allowed. **Vehicle Maximum Length:** 85 ft.

TO GET THERE
From US I-15 Exit163 go 0.25 mi. north on business loop and 0.5 mi. east on 900S.

GARDEN CITY   MAP, A-2
Bear Lake Group Areas

reserve america

P.O. Box 184, 84028-0184. T: (435) 946-3343;
www.reserveamerica.com.

🚐 ★★★★   ⛺ ★★★★

Beauty: ★★★★★	Site Privacy: ★★★
Spaciousness: ★★★	Quiet: ★★★★
Security: ★★★★	Cleanliness: ★★★★
Insect Control: ★★★	Facilities: ★★★★

The Caribbean-blue waters of Bear Lake are nestled high in the Rocky Mountains at the Utah-Idaho border. Waterskiing, swimming, scuba diving, and sailing are favorite activities. Anglers enjoy fishing for cutthroat, mackinaw, and whitefish. Winter draws snowmobilers, ice anglers, and eagle watchers. Three state-owned facilities provide boating access and camping and day-use opportunities. Bear Lake Marina on the western shore offers a group day-use pavilion and boat slip rentals. Bear Lake Rendezvous Beach is located on the south shore near Laketown on State Route 30. The Beach includes Willow group-use area, and the Cottonwood, Birch, and Big Creek campgrounds. All campgrounds provide modern restrooms and hot showers, and many sites offer utility hookups. A wide, sandy beach is popular with groups. A local concessionaire provides small boat rentals. Bear Lake Eastside provides six primitive campgrounds and two boat ramps. Activities include scuba diving, boating, and fishing. Drinking water is available nearby at the South Eden Campground.

BASICS
Operated By: Utah State Parks. **Open:** May 1–Sept. 30. **Site Assignment:** Group reservations are accepted up to 11 months in advance of park departure date. **Registration:** At office. **Fee:** Group, $75–$78; day use, $50. **Parking:** Willow: max. 20 vehicles; South Eden: max. 8 vehicles; Bear Lake day use: max. 15 vehicles.

FACILITIES
Number of Multipurpose Sites: 7. **Hookups:** Yes. **Dump Station:** Yes. **Laundry:** No. **Pay Phone:** No. **Restrooms and Showers:** Yes. **Fuel:** No. **Propane:** No. **Internal Roads:** Paved. **RV Service:** Yes. **Market:** No. **Restaurant:** No. **General Store:** No. **Vending:** Yes. **Swimming:** Yes. **Playground:** No. **Other:** South Eden offers primitive group camping facilities & 2-2 lane concrete boat launching ramps. **Activities:** Boating, kayaking, canoeing, sailing, fishing, ice fishing, picnicking, swimming, visitor center, wildlife, covered pavilion (Willow 1, 20 ft. by 40 ft.)). **Nearby Attractions:** ORV area.

RESTRICTIONS
Pets: On a 6-ft. leash, never unattended, cleaned up after. Not allowed in buildings, on beaches, in lakes or reservoirs. **Fires:** In fire rings, stoves, grills, or fireplaces provided for that purpose. Be sure your fire is completely extinguished before leaving. Do not leave your fire unattended. **Alcoholic Beverages:** Allowed w/in state parks, except for visitor centers, museums, & administrative offices. **Vehicle Maximum Length:** Call ahead.

TO GET THERE
Marina: Through Logan, UT, take I-15 north to US 89-91 north to Logan. Stay on US 89 to Garden City. Turn left on US 89 at 1.5 mi. north of Garden City. Through Evanston, WY, take WY 89/UT 16 north to Sage Creek Junction. Turn left on UT 30 and continue 1.5 mi. past Garden City on US 89. Rendezvous Beach: From Salt Lake City, take I-15 north to US 89/91 north to Logan. Stay on US 89 to Garden City. Turn right on UT 30 heading south and proceed 10 mi. From Evanston, take WY 89/UT 16 north to Sage Creek Junction. Turn left on UT 30 heading west and proceed 12 mi. Bear Lake Eastside is 10 mi. north of Laketown.

GLENDALE   MAP, D-1
Glendale KOA

P.O. Box 189, US 89, 84729.
T: (435) 648-2490 or (800) 562-8635;
www.koa.com.

🚐 ★★★   ⛺ ★★★

Beauty: ★★★★	Site Privacy: ★★★★
Spaciousness: ★★★★	Quiet: ★★★
Security: ★★★★	Cleanliness: ★★★★
Insect Control: ★★★★	Facilities: ★★★★

Though alongside a grade in US 89 with tour-bus and truck engine noise, the strategic location merits careful consideration, as it is only 25 miles to Coral Pink Sand Dunes State Park, 30 miles to Zion, 35 miles to Cedar Breaks, and 45 miles to Bryce. A horse pasture and spring-fed pond border one side, and Bryce-like orange sandstone spires on the surrounding hills add a park-like ambience. The grassy sites and gravel roads of Bryce/Zion KOA add to the impression of pastoral tranquility. Buffalo Bistro next door, almost an east Zion institution before relocating here, is known area-wide for its buffalo burgers, fruit cobblers, and rabbit-rattlesnake sausage served with spicy mustard. The group tent sites, dog walk, car wash, and horse and hiking trails are added bonuses. Though there are some poplar trees, not every site has shade. Nevertheless, overall this is a superior stopping place.

BASICS
Operated By: Ellen Lamb. **Open:** May 1–Sept. 30. **Site Assignment:** First come, first served and by reservation. **Registration:** At office. **Fee:** RV, $24–$26; tent, $20; V, MC, AE, D. **Parking:** At site.

FACILITIES
Number of RV-only Sites: 62. **Number of Tent-only Sites:** 20. **Hookups:** Electric (20, 30 amps), water, sewer. **Each Site:** Table, grill. **Dump Station:** Yes. **Laundry:** Yes. **Pay Phone:** Yes. **Restrooms and Showers:** Yes. **Fuel:** No. **Propane:** No. **Internal Roads:** Gravel, good condition. **RV Service:** No. **Market:** 5 mi. south in Glendale. **Restaurant:** Adjacent Buffalo Bistro. **General Store:** Yes. **Vending:** Yes. **Swimming:** Pool. **Playground:** Yes. **Other:** Modem connection. **Activities:** Fishing, horseback riding, golf, rock hounding. **Nearby Attractions:** Bryce, Zion, Cedar Breaks, Escalante. **Additional Information:** Kane County Office of Tourism, 78 S. 100 East, Kanab, UT 84741; (435) 644-5033; (800) 733-5263; kanetrav@kaneutah.com, www.kaneutah.com.

RESTRICTIONS
Pets: On leash under owner's control. **Fires:** Allowed (firewood sold). **Alcoholic Beverages:** Allowed. **Vehicle Maximum Length:** 75 ft.

TO GET THERE
5 mi. north of Glendale on US 89.

GREEN RIVER   MAP, C-3
Goblin Valley Group Area

reserve america

Box 637, 84525-0637. T: (435) 564-3633;
www.reserveamerica.com.

🚐 ★★★★   ⛺ ★★★★

Beauty: ★★★★	Site Privacy: ★★★
Spaciousness: ★★★	Quiet: ★★★★
Security: ★★★★	Cleanliness: ★★★★
Insect Control: ★★★	Facilities: ★★★

Scores of intricately eroded creatures greet visitors to Goblin Valley. Hike among miles and miles of rock formations. Off-highway vehicle enthusiasts will find hundreds of miles of dirt roads to explore in areas surrounding the park. Goblin Valley is a great base camp to explore and hike in the adjacent San Rafael Swell. This remote but very popular campground offers great access to area recreation. Spring and fall are the best times to visit, due to intense heat during summer months (June through August). Goblin Valley State Park is a showcase of geologic history. Exposed cliffs reveal parallel layers of rock bared by erosion. Because of the uneven hardness of sandstone, some patches resist erosion much better than others. The softer material is removed by wind and water, leaving thousands of unique, geologic goblins. Water erosion and the smoothing action of windblown dust work together to shape the goblins. Bedrock is exposed because of the thin soil and lack of vegetation. When rain does fall, there are few plant roots and little soil to capture and hold the water, which quickly disappears in muddy streams without penetrating the bedrock.

BASICS
Operated By: Utah State Parks. **Open:** Mar. 1–Nov. 30. **Site Assignment:** Group reservations are accepted up to 11 months in advance of park departure date. **Registration:** At office. **Fee:** Group, $75–$78. **Parking:** At site.

FACILITIES
Hookups: None. **Dump Station:** Yes. **Laundry:** No. **Pay Phone:** No. **Restrooms and Showers:** Yes. **Fuel:** No. **Propane:** No. **Internal Roads:** Paved. **RV Service:** Yes. **Market:** No. **Restaurant:** No. **General Store:** No. **Vending:** No. **Swimming:** No. **Playground:** No. **Activities:** Biking, picnicking, hiking, wildlife, visitor center.

RESTRICTIONS
Pets: On a 6-ft. leash, never unattended, cleaned up after. Not allowed in buildings, on beaches, in lakes or reservoirs. **Fires:** In fire rings, stoves, grills, or fireplaces provided for that purpose. Be sure your fire is completely extinguished before leaving. Do not leave your fire unattended. **Alcoholic Beverages:**

Allowed w/in state parks, except for visitor centers, museums, & administrative offices. **Vehicle Maximum Length:** 50 ft.

TO GET THERE

Located 48 mi. southwest of Green River, UT, via UT24.

GREEN RIVER   MAP, C-3
Green River Group Areas

reserve america

Box 637, 84525-0637. T: (435) 564-3633; www.reserveamerica.com.

🚐 ★★★★   ⛺ ★★★★

Beauty: ★★★★   Site Privacy: ★★★
Spaciousness: ★★★   Quiet: ★★★★
Security: ★★★★   Cleanliness: ★★★★
Insect Control: ★★★   Facilities: ★★★★

The Green River originates in Wyoming, where it flows 291 miles before entering the state of Utah. It runs for 42 miles in Colorado, and once journeying into Utah, runs another 397 miles. Eventually the Green connects with the Colorado River, where it empties into Lake Powell. The Green River is a favorite among many river runners. Labyrinth, Stillwater, and Cataract Canyons offer experiences from flat water to serious whitewater. Permits are required for most stretches of the Green and are available from the Bureau of Land Management and the National Park Service. Green River State Park is the put-in point for the 186-mile float through Labyrinth and Stillwater Canyons. This section of the river is rated for beginners and intermediate boaters. This trip takes you through beautiful desert scenery and is enjoyable to all. Green River State Park is also home to a challenging nine-hole golf course, campground with tall, shady cottonwood trees, and numerous species of birds. If fishing is your activity of choice, the Green has catfish, carp, and four unique native fish that are threatened with extinction and protected—Colorado Squawfish, razorback sucker, humpback chub, and bony tail chub. Anglers should release any of the unique fish.

BASICS

Operated By: Utah State Parks. **Open:** Mar. 1– Nov. 1. **Site Assignment:** Group reservations are accepted up to 11 months in advance of park departure date. **Registration:** At office. **Fee:** Group, $45–$48. **Parking:** 6 vehicles per site.

FACILITIES

Hookups: None. **Dump Station:** Yes. **Laundry:** No. **Pay Phone:** No. **Restrooms and Showers:** Yes. **Fuel:** No. **Propane:** No. **Internal Roads:** Paved. **RV Service:** Yes. **Market:** No. **Restaurant:** No. **General Store:** No. **Vending:** Yes. **Swimming:** Yes. **Playground:** No. **Other:** Overnight group area 1 is located on the west side of the 9-hole golf course & close to the river. **Activities:** Canoeing, kayaking, boating, fishing, golfing, hiking, scenic views, wildlife, picnicking.

RESTRICTIONS

Pets: On a 6-ft. leash, never unattended, cleaned up after. Not allowed in buildings, on beaches, in lakes or reservoirs. **Fires:** In fire rings, stoves, grills, or fireplaces provided for that purpose. Be sure your fire is completely extinguished before leaving. Do not leave your fire unattended. **Alcoholic Beverages:** Allowed w/in state parks, except for visitor centers, museums, & administrative offices. **Vehicle Maximum Length:** 50 ft.

TO GET THERE

Located within the city limits of Green River, UT, just off I-70.

GREEN RIVER   MAP, C-3
Green River State Park

reserve america

P.O. Box 637, 84525.
T: (435) 564-3633 or (800) 322-3770; www.reserveamerica.com.

🚐 ★★★★   ⛺ ★★★★★

Beauty: ★★★★   Site Privacy: ★★★★★
Spaciousness: ★★★★★   Quiet: ★★★★
Security: ★★★★★   Cleanliness: ★★★★★
Insect Control: ★★   Facilities: ★★★

Muskrats, beavers, ibises, egrets, and herons share Green River State Park with golfers, campers, picnickers, boaters, rafters, and river runners. This well-run park is near the center of town, the river museum, and restaurants, but it feels away from it all, except for the pesky summer gnats (bird food) and the train that rumbles by the river. Large pull-through sites can handle the biggest rigs and are shaded by cottonwoods, willows, and Russian olive trees full of chirping birds. During summer the grass is watered at 10 a.m. and everything needs to be sealed up or put away to avoid a soaking. Tents need to be moved at least every other day anyway to avoid killing the grass. Though hookups are lacking, this is the premier campground in Green River, and it is less than an hour from Arches.

BASICS

Operated By: Utah State Parks. **Open:** Closed Dec., Jan., & Feb. **Site Assignment:** First come, first served; all but 10 sites can be reserved (3–110 days in advance). **Registration:** At entrance kiosk. **Fee:** $14 per vehicle. **Parking:** At site.

FACILITIES

Number of Multipurpose Sites: 42. **Hookups:** None. **Each Site:** Table on cement pad, grill or fire pit. **Dump Station:** Yes. **Laundry:** No. **Pay Phone:** Yes. **Restrooms and Showers:** Yes. **Fuel:** No. **Propane:** No. **Internal Roads:** Paved, some ruts. **RV Service:** No. **Market:** In Green River. **Restaurant:** In Green River. **General Store:** No. **Vending:** Yes. **Swimming:** No. **Playground:** No. **Other:** 9-hole golf course, boat ramp & dock, vehicle storage, amphitheater, wheelchair-accessible restroom. **Activities:** River float trips, Memorial Day Friendship Cruise to Moab, Sept. Melon Days, boating, fishing. **Nearby Attractions:** John Wesley Powell River

History Museum, Canyonlands, Dead Horse State Park, Goblin Valley State Park, Arches, Moab, biking trails, hiking trails. **Additional Information:** Emery County Travel Bureau, (888) 564-3600, www.emerycounty.com.

RESTRICTIONS

Pets: On leash under owner's control. **Fires:** Allowed. **Alcoholic Beverages:** Allowed at site, but not to the point of public intoxication. **Vehicle Maximum Length:** 45 ft. **Other:** 14-day stay limit, tents must be moved every other day.

TO GET THERE

From US I-70 Exit 162, go west on Main St., turn south on Green River Blvd.

GREEN RIVER   MAP, C-3
Shady Acres RV Park and Campground

350 Main St., P.O. Box 598, 84525.
T: (800) 537-8674 or (435) 564-8290; www.shadyacresrv.com.

🚐 ★★★★★   ⛺ ★★★★

Beauty: ★★★★   Site Privacy: ★★★★
Spaciousness: ★★★★★   Quiet: ★★★★
Security: ★★★★   Cleanliness: ★★★★
Insect Control: ★★   Facilities: ★★★★★

On the opposite side of the muddy brown Green River from United Campground and a block across the street from the truck scales and the 24-hour West Winds Restaurant (hearty trucker meals), Shady Acres shields itself from Main Street with cottonwood trees. But everything is here, including groceries, free cable TV, and a gas station that has an RV Wash and a submarine sandwich franchise. The paved campsites are well back from Main Street, and the cottonwood trees blowing in the wind make more noise than the steady parade of slow trucks exiting I-70. The basketball and volleyball courts among the swings and horseshoes add a touch of resort ambience. This well-run family operation has almost zero tolerance for offensive language, and the county sheriff takes care of intoxicated trouble-makers. With the Powell River History Museum down the street and the state park nearby, the range of amenities here may tip the scales for some.

BASICS

Operated By: Private family. **Open:** All year. **Site Assignment:** First come, first served; reservations recommended for long holiday weekends. **Registration:** At office. **Fee:** RV, $27–$35; tent, $20; V, MC, AE, D. **Parking:** At site.

FACILITIES

Number of RV-only Sites: 97. **Number of Tent-only Sites:** 14. **Hookups:** Electric (50 amps), water, sewer, cable TV, Wi-Fi. **Each Site:** Table, grill. **Dump Station:** Yes. **Laundry:** Yes. **Pay Phone:** Yes. **Restrooms and Showers:** Yes. **Fuel:** Yes. **Propane:** No. **Internal Roads:** Asphalt. **RV Service:** No. **Market:** On premises. **Restaurant:** On premises. **General Store:** Yes. **Vending:** Yes. **Swimming:** No. **Playground:** Yes, 3 playgrounds. **Other:** Dog walk, wheelchair-accessible sites, Internet connection in office, car/RV wash. **Activities:** Golf. **Nearby Attractions:** Crystal Geyser, Black Dragon Pictograph, Goblin Valley, Arches, Canyonlands. **Additional Information:** Emery County Travel Bureau, (888) 564-3600, www.emerycounty.com.

RESTRICTIONS

Pets: On leash. **Fires:** Allowed. **Alcoholic Beverages:** Intoxication is not tolerated. **Vehicle Maximum Length:** 100 ft. **Other:** No foul language; no changing oil, washing vehicles, or mechanical repairs in park.

TO GET THERE

From US I-70, exit Green River at Main St., go to 350 E. Main St.

GREEN RIVER   MAP, C-3
United Campground

910 East Main St., P.O. Box 261, 84525.
T: (435) 564-8195.

🚐 ★★★★   ⛺ ★★★★

Beauty: ★★★★   Site Privacy: ★★★★
Spaciousness: ★★★★★   Quiet: ★★★
Security: ★★★★★   Cleanliness: ★★★★★
Insect Control: ★★   Facilities: ★★★★

One of the better I-70 halfway stops between Las Vegas and Denver, United is also a good overflow site for Moab, Arches, and Canyonlands (within 45 miles) on holidays like Easter. Tucked well back from Main Street behind the Motel 6 and adjacent to an alfalfa field, the campground is a collection of large grassy sites shaded by tall trees and bisected by a gravel roadway and parking. The Tamarisk Restaurant at the Best Western next door is one of Green River's best, with seating overlooking the river bridge and colonies of swifts swooping down to catch insects (bug repellent is a good summer precaution). Across the street is the John Wesley Powell River History Museum building, which also houses a gallery and visitor center. Overall, the location is very convenient for parking and walking once settled in, and it's a good base for exploring the surrounding area.

BASICS

Operated By: Charles and Linda Burrage. **Open:** All year (limited after November). **Site Assignment:** First come, first served; reservations recommended holiday weekends. **Registration:** At office. **Fee:** RV, $39; tent, $22; V, MC, AE, D. **Parking:** At site.

FACILITIES

Number of RV-only Sites: 65. **Number of Tent-only Sites:** 15. **Hookups:** Electric (20, 30, 50 amps), water, sewer, cable TV. **Each Site:** Table. **Dump Station:** Yes. **Laundry:** Yes. **Pay Phone:** Yes. **Restrooms and Showers:** Yes. **Fuel:** No. **Propane:** Yes. **Internal Roads:** Gravel, excellent. **RV Service:** No. **Market:** 2 blocks. **Restaurant:** Next door. **General Store:** Yes. **Vending:** No. **Swimming:** Pool. **Playground:** Yes. **Other:** Portable grill on request, modem hookup in office. **Activities:** Boating, river rafting, swimming. **Nearby Attractions:** Arches, Canyonlands, Capitol Reef, Goblin Valley State Park, Museum across street. **Additional Information:** Emery County Travel Bureau, (888) 564-3600, www.emerycounty.com.

RESTRICTIONS

Pets: On leash under owner's control. **Fires:** Allowed. **Alcoholic Beverages:** Allowed. **Vehicle Maximum Length:** No limit. **Other:** 11 a.m. checkout.

TO GET THERE

Exit I-70 at Main St. in Green River, enter via driveway between Motel 6 and Best Western.

HANKSVILLE   MAP, C-3
Goblin Valley State Park

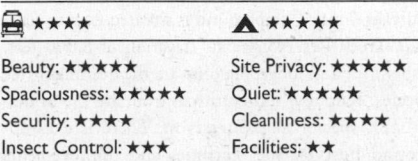

P.O. Box 637, 84525.
T: (435) 564-3633 or (800) 322-3770;
www.reserveamerica.com.

🚐 ★★★★   ⛺ ★★★★★

Beauty: ★★★★★   Site Privacy: ★★★★★
Spaciousness: ★★★★★   Quiet: ★★★★★
Security: ★★★★   Cleanliness: ★★★★
Insect Control: ★★★   Facilities: ★★

The intriguing chocolate-colored goblins giving this park its name result from uneven wind and rain erosion of sandstone layers of varying hardness in this remote area once frequented by uranium miners and ancient Native Americans. The San Rafael Reef, which has steep canyons hidden inside its sawtooth swells, is also part of the Jurassic and Triassic sandstone and siltstone scenery left behind by an ancient sea in what is now the Green River Desert. The campground itself is a half loop backed by orange-and-white sandstone walls with hoodoos, spires, and a hilltop oil well pumping away next to solar panels. The restroom and hot showers are also powered by solar arrays. There is little shade from the midday sun. On hot summer days, the sandstone walls surrounding the spacious campground sites radiate extra heat. But the goblins, reefs, badlands, balanced rocks, spires, and hoodoos make a colorful geologic adventure for self-sufficient campers.

BASICS

Operated By: Utah State Parks. **Open:** All year. **Site Assignment:** First come, first served; 14 sites can be reserved (up to 16 weeks in advance of checkout date for individuals; up to 11 months in advance for group site). **Registration:** At self-pay entrance fee station. **Fee:** $14; per vehicle. **Parking:** At site.

FACILITIES

Number of RV-only Sites: 13. **Number of Tent-only Sites:** 11. **Number of Multipurpose Sites:** 24. **Hookups:** Water. **Each Site:** Table, grill. **Dump Station:** Yes. **Laundry:** No. **Pay Phone:** No. **Restrooms and Showers:** Yes. **Fuel:** No. **Propane:** No. **Internal Roads:** Paved, good condition. **RV Service:** No. **Market:** Hanksville, 32 mi.; Green River, 35 mi. **Restaurant:** Hanksville, 32 mi.; Green River, 35 mi. **General Store:** No. **Vending:** Soft-drink machine. **Swimming:** No. **Playground:** No. **Other:** Covered picnic pavilion at observation point, wheelchair-accessible restroom. **Activities:** Geologic exploration, hiking. **Nearby Attractions:**

Capitol Reef, Canyonlands. **Additional Information:** Emery County Travel Bureau, (888) 564-3600, www.emerycounty.com.

RESTRICTIONS

Pets: On leash under owner's control cleaned up after. **Fires:** Not allowed. **Alcoholic Beverages:** Allowed. **Vehicle Maximum Length:** 30 ft. **Other:** No ground fires; 14-day stay limit.

TO GET THERE

Go 20 mi. north from Hanksville on UT 24, at mile marker 137 turn west onto Temple Mountain Rd. 5 mi., then at intersection go 7 mi. south on graded dirt county road.

HANKSVILLE   MAP, C-3
Red Rock Restaurant and
Campground

East 100 North (Hwy. 24), P.O. Box 55, 84734.
T: (435) 542-3235; www.redrockcampground.net.

🚐 ★★★★   ⛺ ★★★

Beauty: ★★★   Site Privacy: ★★
Spaciousness: ★★   Quiet: ★★★★
Security: ★★★★   Cleanliness: ★★★★
Insect Control: ★★★★   Facilities: ★★★★

With gas stations, RV repair, a post office, and other amenities within blocks, this friendly restaurant with a well-maintained campground in back makes a good stopping point en route to Capitol Reef, Bullfrog Marina on Lake Powell, or Canyonlands. The restaurant has everything from steaks to beer and wine, which is handy, as there are no grills. Just behind the restaurant is a grassy area for tent camping that will suffice for a night. Three gravel rows for RVs extend farther back, with a small tree between each site and a fence separating the property from an irrigated field at the rear. Though more an overnight stop, the location does lend itself to day trips to Goblin Valley State Park, Capitol Reef, and an adventurous dirt-road excursion (not to be attempted when rain threatens) heading north to Green River via the San Rafael Desert.

BASICS

Operated By: Elliot and Layne Arnoldson. **Open:** Mar. 15–Nov. 1. **Site Assignment:** First come, first served; reservations accepted. **Registration:** At restaurant. **Fee:** RV, $18; tent, $12; V, MC, D. **Parking:** At site.

FACILITIES

Number of RV-only Sites: 60. **Number of Tent-only Sites:** 60. **Hookups:** Electric (30, 50 amps), water, sewer. **Each Site:** Most sites have table. **Dump Station:** Yes. **Laundry:** Yes. **Pay Phone:** Yes. **Restrooms and Showers:** Yes. **Fuel:** No. **Propane:** No. **Internal Roads:** Gravel, good condition. **RV Service:** No. **Market:** 1.5 blocks. **Restaurant:** On site. **General Store:** No. **Vending:** Yes. **Swimming:** No. **Playground:** No. **Activities:** Geologic exploration. **Nearby Attractions:** Goblin Valley State Park, Capitol Reef, Canyonlands, Hite Marina, Natural Bridges. **Additional Information:** Emery County Travel Bureau, (888) 564-3600, www.emerycounty.com.

RESTRICTIONS

Pets: On leash. **Fires:** No wood fires, charcoal only. **Alcoholic Beverages:** Allowed. **Vehicle Maximum Length:** Unlimited in circle area.

TO GET THERE

Go 200 ft. west on Hwy. 24 from junction of UT Hwys. 24 & 95.

HATCH   MAP, D-1
Riverside Motel and RV Park

594 Hwy. 89 Box 521, 84735.
T: (435) 735-4223 or (800) 824-5651;
www.riversideresort-utah.com.

★★★   ★★★

Beauty: ★★★★   Site Privacy: ★★★★
Spaciousness: ★★★★   Quiet: ★★★★
Security: ★★★★   Cleanliness: ★★★★
Insect Control: ★★★   Facilities: ★★★★

Strategically situated on the banks of the Sevier River just south of the Bryce Junction (where UT 12 intersects US 89), Riverside is a magnet for tour buses. The campground is isolated in a small valley behind an office/gift shop, motel, and restaurant and is bordered by the river on two sides. Tent sites are along the river, separated from the RVs by a large grass playing field that doubles as a tour bus group tent site. International groups, ranging from musicians to teens, like the river and distant Red Canyon mountain backdrops as well as the group pavilion. But the campground quiets down after 10 p.m., and an occasional truck and the raging wind are about the extent of the noise most nights. The 18-foot wide pull-through sites, network TV reception, and convenient location make this a good RV stop.

BASICS

Operated By: Cordell and Julie Peters/Brent and Kathy Parkinson. **Open:** Mar. 1–Nov. 1. **Site Assignment:** First come, first served; reservations accepted. **Registration:** At office in store. **Fee:** RV, $26; tent, $15; V, MC. RV rate in off-season is free. **Parking:** At site.

FACILITIES

Number of RV-only Sites: 65. **Number of Tent-only Sites:** Undesignated sites. **Hookups:** Electric (20, 30, 50 amps), water, sewer. **Each Site:** Table, grill. **Dump Station:** Yes. **Laundry:** Yes. **Pay Phone:** Yes. **Restrooms and Showers:** Yes. **Fuel:** No. **Propane:** Yes. **Internal Roads:** Gravel, good. **RV Service:** No. **Market:** Panguitch, 8 mi. **Restaurant:** On site. **General Store:** Yes. **Vending:** Yes. **Swimming:** River. **Playground:** Yes. **Other:** Horseshoe pit, basketball court, motel, game room, volleyball court. **Activities:** Fishing, swimming, Ping-Pong. **Nearby Attractions:** Panguitch Lake, Red Canyon, Cedar Breaks, Bryce, Zion. **Additional Information:** Garfield County Travel Council, (800) 444-6689; Bryce Canyon National Park Headquarters, (435) 834-5322.

RESTRICTIONS

Pets: On leash under owner's control. **Fires:** Allowed. **Alcoholic Beverages:** Allowed. **Vehicle Maximum Length:** Over 45 ft.

TO GET THERE

From junction w/ UT 12, go 2 mi. south on US 89.

HEBER CITY   MAP, B-2
Currant Creek—
Uinta National Forest

reserve america

2460 South Hwy. 40, 84032. T: (435) 654-0470;
www.reserveamerica.com.

★★★   ★★★★

Beauty: ★★★★   Site Privacy: ★★★
Spaciousness: ★★★   Quiet: ★★★
Security: ★★★★   Cleanliness: ★★★★
Insect Control: ★★★★   Facilities: ★★

Currant Creek Campground is situated next to Currant Creek Reservoir at an elevation of 8,000 feet. Aspen, fir, and lodgepole pine are the dominant tree species. Rainbow and cutthroat trout are the principal fish species in the reservoir. There is a campground host on site. Facilities and improvements include paved roads and parking spurs, flush toilets, dump station, boat ramp, wheelchair-accessible fishing pier and playground. Popular activities include hiking, fishing and boating. Currant Creek Campground is located in Uinta National Forest and offers an inspiring view and the promise of mountain recreation to the residents of cities below. American Fork Canyon and Provo Canyon located in the Uinta National Forest have an autumn mix of aspen and pine. Between the two canyons lies the 10,750 acre Timpanogos Wilderness. One paved drive full of rugged mountain beauty and many stunning overlooks of surrounding valleys can be found in the Uinta National Forest. In autumn, the brilliant display of colors found on this drive in Uinta National Forest is hard to match anywhere in the nation.

BASICS

Operated By: U.S. Forest Service. **Open:** May 25–Oct 31. **Site Assignment:** Reservations must be made at least 5 days in advance. **Registration:** At office. **Fee:** Single, $12–$14; group, $55–$88. **Parking:** At park.

FACILITIES

Number of Multipurpose Sites: 117. **Hookups:** None. **Each Site:** Call ahead. **Dump Station:** Yes. **Laundry:** No. **Pay Phone:** No. **Restrooms and Showers:** Yes. **Fuel:** No. **Propane:** No. **Internal Roads:** Paved. **RV Service:** No. **Market:** No. **Restaurant:** No. **General Store:** No. **Vending:** No. **Swimming:** No. **Playground:** Yes. **Other:** No discharge of firearms or fireworks. **Activities:** Hiking, fishing, boating.

RESTRICTIONS

Pets: Pets must be restrained or on a leash at all times while in developed recreation areas. **Fires:** In fire rings, stoves, grills, or fireplaces provided for that purpose. **Alcoholic Beverages:** Not allowed. **Vehicle Maximum Length:** 40 ft.

TO GET THERE

From Heber City go 45 mi. on US 40 to Currant Creek Junction then 17 mi. north on FS 083.

HEBER CITY   MAP, B-2
Renegade—Uinta National Forest

reserve america

2461 South Hwy. 40, 84032. T: (435) 654-0470;
www.reserveamerica.com.

★★★★   ★★★★

Beauty: ★★★★   Site Privacy: ★★★
Spaciousness: ★★★   Quiet: ★★★
Security: ★★★★   Cleanliness: ★★★★
Insect Control: ★★★★   Facilities: ★★

Renegade Campground is located in the Uinta Forest, 23 miles souheast of Heber. The elevation is 7,700 feet. The campground is located on Strawberry Reservoir amidst rolling sage brush hills and valleys. Anglers will appreciate the abundant rainbow trout, cutthroat trout, and kokanee salmon. American Fork Canyon and Provo Canyon located in the Uinta National Forest have an autumn mix of aspen and pine. Between the two canyons lies the 10,750-acre Timpanogos Wilderness. One paved drive full of rugged mountain beauty and many stunning overlooks of surrounding valleys can be found in the Uinta National Forest. In autumn, the brilliant display of colors found on this drive is hard to match anywhere in the nation.

BASICS

Operated By: U.S. Forest Service. **Open:** May 12–Oct 31. **Site Assignment:** Reservations must be made at least 5 days in advance. **Registration:** At office. **Fee:** Single, $10; group, $130. **Parking:** At park.

FACILITIES

Number of Multipurpose Sites: 128. **Hookups:** None. **Each Site:** Fire ring, picnic table, grill. **Dump Station:** No. **Laundry:** No. **Pay Phone:** Nearby. **Restrooms and Showers:** Yes. **Fuel:** No. **Propane:** No. **Internal Roads:** Paved. **RV Service:** No. **Market:** Nearby. **Restaurant:** Nearby. **General Store:** Nearby. **Vending:** No. **Swimming:** No. **Playground:** No. **Activities:** Boating, canoeing, fishing, jet skiing, waterskiing, wildlife viewing.

RESTRICTIONS

Pets: Restrained or on a leash at all times while in developed recreation areas. **Fires:** In fire rings, stoves, grills, or fireplaces provided for that purpose. **Alcoholic Beverages:** Not allowed. **Vehicle Maximum Length:** 40 ft.

TO GET THERE

From Heber City, take US 40 east 21.7 mi. to Strawberry.

HEBER CITY — MAP, B-2
Soldier Creek— Uinta National Forest

reserve america

2460 South US 40, 84032. T: (801) 226-3564; www.reserveamerica.com.

🚐 ★★★★   ▲ ★★★★

Beauty: ★★★★   Site Privacy: ★★★★
Spaciousness: ★★★★   Quiet: ★★★
Security: ★★★★   Cleanliness: ★★★★
Insect Control: ★★★★   Facilities: ★★★★

Located adjacent to Strawberry Reservoir with restrooms, dump station and boat ramps provided. Roads are paved. Each site has picnic table and fire ring. Elevation is 7,200 feet. There are panoramic views of Strawberry Reservoir and valley. Camping spurs are between 50–75 feet apart. Water and flush toilets are provided. Marina and store are close. Popular activities include trout fishing, boating, waterskiing, hiking, biking and interpretive programs. There is horseback riding outside the campground. Campground loops are adjacent to marina and boat launch. Boat rentals, slip rentals, fuel, groceries and supplies are available. Soldier Creek is located in Uinta National Forest and offers an inspiring view and the promise of mountain recreation to the residents of cities below. American Fork Canyon and Provo Canyon located in the Uinta National Forest have an autumn mix of aspen and pine. Between the two canyons lies the 10,750 acre Timpanogos Wilderness. One paved drive full of rugged mountain beauty and many stunning overlooks of surrounding valleys can be found in the Uinta National Forest. In autumn, the brilliant display of colors found on this drive in Uinta National Forest is hard to match anywhere in the nation.

BASICS
Operated By: U.S. Forest Service. **Open:** May 25–Oct 31. **Site Assignment:** Reservations must be made at least 5 days in advance. **Registration:** At office. **Fee:** Single, $12–$14; double, $24–$28; group, $225. **Parking:** Limited.

FACILITIES
Number of Multipurpose Sites: 141. **Hookups:** None. **Each Site:** Picnic table, fire ring. **Dump Station:** Yes. **Laundry:** No. **Pay Phone:** No. **Restrooms and Showers:** Yes. **Fuel:** Yes. **Propane:** Yes. **Internal Roads:** Paved. **RV Service:** No. **Market:** No. **Restaurant:** No. **General Store:** No. **Vending:** No. **Swimming:** No. **Playground:** No. **Activities:** Fishing, boating, waterskiing, hiking, biking, and interpretive programs.

RESTRICTIONS
Pets: Restrained or on a leash at all times while in developed recreation areas. **Fires:** In fire rings, stoves, grills, or fireplaces provided for that purpose. **Alcoholic Beverages:** Not allowed. **Vehicle Maximum Length:** Call ahead.

TO GET THERE
Take Hwy. 40 eastbound from Heber City 37 mi. to Soldier Creek exit, then 2 mi. south to Soldier Creek Campground.

HEBER CITY — MAP, B-2
Strawberry Bay— Uinta National Forest

reserve america

2461 South US 40, 84032. T: (435) 654-0470; www.reserveamerica.com.

🚐 ★★★★   ▲ ★★★★

Beauty: ★★★★   Site Privacy: ★★★
Spaciousness: ★★★   Quiet: ★★★
Security: ★★★★   Cleanliness: ★★★★
Insect Control: ★★★★   Facilities: ★★

Strawberry Campground is located adjacent to Strawberry Reservoir at an elevation of 7,200 feet. The campground is in a setting of rolling hills covered with sagebrush. The Strawberry Bay and Soldier Creek Recreation complexes are full-service developments which contain numerous campground loops, sanitary dump stations, day-use areas, group pavilions, and marina stores. In addition, the Strawberry Bay Recreation Area contains a restaurant and a full-service lodge. Strawberry Reservoir contains four major fishing areas including the Strawberry Basin, Meadows Basin (sometimes referred to Indian Creek Bay), the Narrows, and Soldier Creek Basin. The Strawberry Basin encompasses the old 8,400-acre Strawberry Reservoir which was contained by the original Strawberry Dam and Indian Creek Dike. Strawberry Campground is located in Uinta National Forest and offers an inspiring view and the promise of mountain recreation to the residents of cities below. American Fork Canyon and Provo Canyon located in the Uinta National Forest have an autumn mix of aspen and pine. Between the two canyons lies the 10,750-acre Timpanogos Wilderness. One paved drive full of rugged mountain beauty and many stunning overlooks of surrounding valleys can be found in the Uinta National Forest. In autumn, the brilliant display of colors found on this drive in Uinta National Forest is hard to match anywhere in the nation.

BASICS
Operated By: U.S. Forest Service. **Open:** May 12–Oct 31. **Site Assignment:** Reservations must be made at least 5 days in advance. **Registration:** At office. **Fee:** Single, $12–$24; double, $28; group, $135–$225. **Parking:** At park.

FACILITIES
Number of Multipurpose Sites: 226. **Hookups:** None. **Each Site:** Call ahead. **Dump Station:** No. **Laundry:** No. **Pay Phone:** Yes. **Restrooms and Showers:** Yes. **Fuel:** No. **Propane:** No. **Internal Roads:** Paved. **RV Service:** No. **Market:** No. **Restaurant:** No. **General Store:** No. **Vending:** No. **Swimming:** No. **Playground:** No. **Other:** No ATVs or ORVs in campground. **Activities:** Boating, canoeing, waterskiing, hiking, biking, horseback riding, fishing.

RESTRICTIONS
Pets: Restrained or on a leash at all times while in developed recreation areas. **Fires:** In fire rings, stoves, grills, or fireplaces provided for that purpose. **Alcoholic Beverages:** Not allowed. **Vehicle Maximum Length:** Any size.

TO GET THERE
From Heber City, take US 40 east 21.7 mi. to Strawberry.

HUNTINGTON — MAP, C-2
Scofield Group Area

reserve america

Box 1343, 84528-1343. T: (435) 448-9449; www.reserveamerica.com.

🚐 ★★★★   ▲ ★★★★

Beauty: ★★★   Site Privacy: ★★★
Spaciousness: ★★★   Quiet: ★★★★
Security: ★★★★   Cleanliness: ★★★★
Insect Control: ★★★   Facilities: ★★★★

Scofield State Park is situated 7,600 feet above sea level in the Manti-LaSal Mountains of the Wasatch Plateau. The 2,800-acre lake offers excellent boating and year-round fishing. During winter months, the area serves as a base for snowmobile and cross-country skiing in the spectacular mountains surrounding the park. Three state-owned facilities are available. Mountain View, located 6 miles north of the town of Scofield, offers a 34-unit campground, modern restrooms, hot showers, fish-cleaning and sanitary disposal stations, group use areas, and boat launch ramp. Madsen Bay, located on the north end of the reservoir, is a popular area for groups and family reunions. Settlers came to Pleasant Valley in the 1870s because of large tracts of grazing land. Scofield was named after General Charles W. Scofield, a timber contractor who became president of the state's first coal mining company. Mining peaked in the early 1920s when Scofield had 12 stores, 13 saloons, four large hotels, a post office, and a population of more than 6,000 residents. Today, less than 100 reside in the town.

BASICS
Operated By: Utah State Parks. **Open:** May 15–Sept. 15. **Site Assignment:** Group reservations are accepted up to 11 months in advance of park departure date. **Registration:** At office. **Fee:** Mountain view group, $75–$78; lakeside group, $50–$52.

FACILITIES
Number of Multipurpose Sites: 61. **Hookups:** None. **Dump Station:** Yes. **Laundry:** No. **Pay Phone:** Yes. **Restrooms and Showers:** Yes. **Fuel:** No. **Propane:** No. **Internal Roads:** Paved. **RV Service:** Yes. **Market:** No. **Restaurant:** No. **General Store:** No. **Vending:** No. **Swimming:** Yes. **Playground:** No. **Activities:** Bird-watching, boating, canoeing, kayaking, fishing, picnicking, scenic views, sports activities, wildlife.

RESTRICTIONS

Pets: On a 6-ft. leash, never unattended, cleaned up after. Not allowed in buildings, on beaches, in lakes or reservoirs. **Fires:** In fire rings, stoves, grills, or fireplaces provided for that purpose. Be sure your fire is completely extinguished before leaving. Do not leave your fire unattended. **Alcoholic Beverages:** Allowed w/in state parks, except for visitor centers, museums, & administrative offices. **Vehicle Maximum Length:** 40 ft.

TO GET THERE

From Salt Lake, take I-15 south to the Price/Manti Exit. Go east on UT 6 approx. 6 mi. from Soldier Summit. Turn right at the railroad crossing on UT 96. It is then 10 mi. to the park.

HURRICANE   MAP, D-1
Sand Hollow State Park

reserve america

4405 West 3600 South, 84737. T: (435) 680-0715; www.reserveamerica.com.

🚐 ★★★★   ⛺ ★★★★

Beauty: ★★★★   Site Privacy: ★★★
Spaciousness: ★★★   Quiet: ★★★★
Security: ★★★★   Cleanliness: ★★★★
Insect Control: ★★★   Facilities: ★★★★

The sprawling 20,000-acre park, which rests mostly on USDI Bureau of Land Management (BLM) land, rivals Utah's two largest state parks—Wasatch Mountain and Antelope Island. Sand Hollow already one of the most visited destinations in the Utah State Park system, with recreation opportunities for nearly every user from boaters to bikers, and OHV riders to equestrians. A favorite destination for local off-highway vehicle (OHV) enthusiasts, Sand Mountain provides 15,000 acres of perfectly sculpted dunes. The red sand is an incredible backdrop for Sand Hollow reservoir. At nearly twice the size of nearby Quail Creek Reservoir, Sand Hollow offers boating and other water recreation in a spectacular setting. Sand Hollow is located approximately 15 miles east of St. George, and 7 miles east of the I-15 Hurricane exit.

BASICS

Operated By: Utah State Parks. **Open:** All year. **Site Assignment:** Reservations can be made up to 16 weeks in advance. **Registration:** At office. **Fee:** Single, $21. **Parking:** 1 vehicle per site; additional vehicle fee, half of nightly camping fee w/ the exception of $8 camp sites (fee is $8).

FACILITIES

Number of Multipurpose Sites: 40. **Hookups:** Yes. **Dump Station:** Yes. **Laundry:** No. **Pay Phone:** No. **Restrooms and Showers:** Yes. **Fuel:** No. **Propane:** No. **Internal Roads:** Paved. **RV Service:** Yes. **Market:** No. **Restaurant:** No. **General Store:** No. **Vending:** No. **Swimming:** Yes. **Playground:** No. **Activities:** Boating, kayaking, canoeing, sailing, fishing, horseback riding, ATV riding, picnicking, swimming, hiking, visitor center, wildlife. **Nearby Attractions:** ORV area.

RESTRICTIONS

Pets: On a 6-ft. leash, never unattended, cleaned up after. Not allowed in buildings, on beaches, in lakes or reservoirs. **Fires:** In fire rings, stoves, grills, or fireplaces provided for that purpose. Be sure your fire is completely extinguished before leaving. Do not leave your fire unattended. **Alcoholic Beverages:** Allowed w/in state parks, except for visitor centers, museums, & administrative offices. **Vehicle Maximum Length:** 40 ft.

TO GET THERE

From I-15 take the Hurricane Exit 16. Travel 4 mi. to Turf Sod Rd. and turn right. Go 1 mi. and turn left onto the main park access road and follow to the park.

HURRICANE   MAP, D-1
Zion's Gate RV Resort

150 North 3700 West, 84737.
T: (435) 635-2320 or (800) 447-2239;
www.zionsgaterv.com.

🚐 ★★★★   ⛺ ★★

Beauty: ★★★★   Site Privacy: ★★★★
Spaciousness: ★★★★   Quiet: ★★★★
Security: ★★★★   Cleanliness: ★★★★
Insect Control: ★★★   Facilities: ★★★★

Hurricane is located between St. George and Zion National Park and makes a good shopping place for those wanting to purchase food, hardware, and other supplies. There are many fine campground options between St. George and Zion, but Zion's Gate boasts a convenient roadside location, wide spaces for slide-outs, and amenities like bowling and billiards. Tent campers have a grassy area near the playground and tennis courts with mulberries and other trees to provide shade. The shadiest part of the tent area has four spaces right up against the tennis courts. Canyons RV Resort and Willowind RV Park (see Appendix) are grassier, smaller, and farther back from the road. Nearby Quail Creek State Park is probably the better place for a boating weekend. If Zion National Park is the destination, then Zion River Resort in Virgin, Zion Canyon Campground in Springdale, and the two National Park Service campgrounds should be considered.

BASICS

Operated By: Private operator. **Open:** All year. **Site Assignment:** First come, first served; reservations accepted. **Registration:** At office. **Fee:** RV, $24; tent, $15; V, MC, AE, D. **Parking:** At site.

FACILITIES

Number of RV-only Sites: 187. **Number of Tent-only Sites:** Undesignated sites. **Hookups:** Electric (30, 50 amps), water, sewer. **Each Site:** Table. **Dump Station:** Yes. **Laundry:** Yes. **Pay Phone:** Yes. **Restrooms and Showers:** Yes. **Fuel:** No. **Propane:** No. **Internal Roads:** Paved, good. **RV Service:** No. **Market:** Hurricane, 3.5 mi. **Restaurant:** Hurricane, 3.5 mi. **General Store:** No. **Vending:** Yes. **Swimming:** Indoor pool & Jacuzzi. **Playground:** Yes. **Other:** Bowling, billiards, tennis, some grills. **Activities:** Horseshoes, shuffleboard, boating, fishing, golf. **Nearby Attractions:**

Quail Creek SP, Zion. **Additional Information:** Washington County Travel Bureau, (435) 634-5747, (800) 869-6635.

RESTRICTIONS

Pets: On leash under owner's control. **Fires:** Allowed. **Alcoholic Beverages:** Allowed. **Vehicle Maximum Length:** 60 ft. **Other:** Children under 18 must be under parental supervision.

TO GET THERE

From US I-15 8 mi. north of St. George go east 5 mi. on UT 9.

HYRUM   MAP, A-2
Hyrum Group Area

reserve america

405 West 300 South, 84319-1547.
T: (435) 254-6866; www.reserveamerica.com.

🚐 ★★★★   ⛺ ★★★★

Beauty: ★★★   Site Privacy: ★★★
Spaciousness: ★★★   Quiet: ★★★★
Security: ★★★★   Cleanliness: ★★★★
Insect Control: ★★★   Facilities: ★★★

Tucked into beautiful Cache Valley, Hyrum State Park invites boating, year-round fishing, waterskiing, camping and swimming. The park is a favorite with locals. Attractions less than 15 minutes from the park include Utah State University, Logan Mormon Temple, scenic mountains and year-round blue ribbon fishing streams. Hardware Ranch, a winter feed elk ranch, is 16 miles from the park up beautiful Blacksmith Fork Canyon. The campground rests at the north end of the reservoir. Mormon settlers founded the area of Hyrum, which is named after the brother of the founder of the Mormon Church. Before the dam was built in 1939, Mormon settlers had to dig a 9-mile canal from the Little Bear River for farm irrigation in Hyrum. Years before the Mormon settlers arrived in the valley, General William H. Ashley stopped near what is now the edge of Hyrum Reservoir and cached $150,000 worth of furs, mostly beaver, in the winter of 1825–26. They were stored in a cave dug in a clay bank until they were retrieved the following summer. This history resulted in the French-Canadian name of Cache Valley and Cache County.

BASICS

Operated By: Utah State Parks. **Open:** May 1– Sept. 30. **Site Assignment:** Group reservations are accepted up to 11 months in advance of park departure date. **Registration:** At office. **Fee:** Group, $150–$153. **Parking:** At site.

FACILITIES

Hookups: None. **Dump Station:** No. **Laundry:** No. **Pay Phone:** No. **Restrooms and Showers:** Yes. **Fuel:** No. **Propane:** No. **Internal Roads:** Paved. **RV Service:** Yes. **Market:** No. **Restaurant:** No. **General Store:** No. **Vending:** No. **Swimming:** Yes. **Playground:** No. **Activities:** Boating, fishing, ice fishing, sports activities, swimming.

RESTRICTIONS

Pets: On a 6-ft. leash, never unattended, cleaned up after. Not allowed in buildings, on beaches, in lakes or reservoirs. **Fires:** In fire rings, stoves, grills, or fireplaces provided for that purpose. Be sure your fire is completely extinguished before leaving. Do not leave your fire unattended. **Alcoholic Beverages:** Allowed w/in state parks, except for visitor centers, museums, & administrative offices. **Vehicle Maximum Length:** 100 ft.

TO GET THERE

From Salt Lake City, turn onto Hwy. 89 at the Brigham City exit, travel 25 mi. to Cache Valley, then turn onto Hwy. 101. Go 3 mi. and turn south on 400W in Hyrum and follow the signs to the park.

IVINS   MAP, D-1
Snow Canyon State Park

reserve america

1002 Snow Canyon Dr., 84738.
T: (435) 628-2255 or (800) 322-3770;
www.reserveamerica.com.

🚐 ★★★★   ▲ ★★★★

Beauty: ★★★★★   Site Privacy: ★★★★
Spaciousness: ★★★★   Quiet: ★★★★★
Security: ★★★★   Cleanliness: ★★★★
Insect Control: ★★   Facilities: ★★★

Located west of Leeds among 170-million-year-old eroding red-orange sandstone mountains and white hills in the Red Cliffs Desert Reserve, Snow Canyon was chanced upon by cowboys searching for lost cattle and named after early pioneers Erastus and Lorenzo Snow. Also popular for day trips, as picnic areas as well as 25 campsites in the two loops are reservable, Snow Canyon's geologic riches include recent lava flows, deep caves, steep canyons, soft red and petrified sand dunes, and Anasazi petroglyphs. Wildlife ranges from ringtail cats to giant desert hairy scorpions (shake boots upside down in the morning before wearing). The paved sites (1–14, 3–8, and 11–14 reservable) with electric hookups at the front of the campground have sheltered tables, but their 15-foot width is too narrow for big rigs with sliders and tip-outs. A smattering of trees and desert scrub separates the other more primitive campsites.

BASICS

Operated By: Utah State Parks. **Open:** All year. **Site Assignment:** First come, first served; some sites can be reserved (120 days in advance). **Registration:** At self-pay fee station. **Fee:** $12–$14; cash, check. **Parking:** At site.

FACILITIES

Number of RV-only Sites: 35. **Hookups:** Electric (30 amps), water. **Each Site:** Table, grill. **Dump Station:** Yes. **Laundry:** No. **Pay Phone:** Yes. **Restrooms and Showers:** Yes. **Fuel:** No. **Propane:** No. **Internal Roads:** Paved, excellent. **RV Service:** No. **Market:** St. George, 10 mi. **Restaurant:** St. George, 10 mi. **General Store:** No. **Vending:** Yes. **Swimming:** No. **Playground:** No. **Other:** Picnic area, basketball court in group

area, cactus/native-plant garden. **Activities:** Biking, horseback riding, hiking, wildlife watching. **Nearby Attractions:** Zion National Park. **Additional Information:** Washington County CVB, (435) 634-5747 or (800) 869-6635.

RESTRICTIONS

Pets: On leash (not allowed on trail). **Fires:** In grills only (firewood available); no fires June 1–Sept. 15. **Alcoholic Beverages:** Allowed. **Vehicle Maximum Length:** No limit. **Other:** No climbing on rocks behind campground.

TO GET THERE

From St. George go 10 mi. north on UT 18.

KANAB   MAP, D-1
Coral Pink Group Areas

reserve america

Box 95, 84741-0095. T: (435) 648-2800;
www.reserveamerica.com.

🚐 ★★★★   ▲ ★★★★

Beauty: ★★★★★   Site Privacy: ★★★
Spaciousness: ★★★   Quiet: ★★★★
Security: ★★★★   Cleanliness: ★★★★
Insect Control: ★★★   Facilities: ★★★★

Located near Kanab lies the wide-sweeping expanse of Coral Pink Sand Dunes State Park. Contrasted by blue skies, juniper and piñon pines, and steep red cliffs, the park is a wonderful place for camping, riding off-highway vehicles, taking photographs or just relaxing and playing in the sand. It serves as an excellent base camp for exploring Utah's extraordinary scenery. Within a short drive are Cedar Breaks National Monument, Kodachrome Basin State Park, Lake Powell, Zion, Bryce Canyon, and Grand Canyon National Parks. The campground rests in a beautiful desert environment filled with juniper trees and the coral pink sands. The geology of the sand dunes is an intriguing subject. The sand comes from Navajo sandstone from the geologic period call Middle Jurassic. The same iron oxides and minerals that give us spectacular red rock country are responsible for this landscape of pink sand. Coral Pink Sand Dunes support a diverse population of insects, including the Coral Pink tiger beetle that is found only here. Melting snow often creates small ponds on the dunes that support amphibians such as salamanders and toads.

BASICS

Operated By: Utah State Parks. **Open:** All year; group day use only. **Site Assignment:** Reservations can be made up to 16 weeks in advance. **Registration:** At office. **Fee:** Group, $75–$78. **Parking:** Maximum 5 vehicles per site.

FACILITIES

Hookups: None. **Dump Station:** Yes. **Laundry:** No. **Pay Phone:** No. **Restrooms and Showers:** Yes. **Fuel:** No. **Propane:** No. **Internal Roads:** Paved. **RV Service:** Yes. **Market:** No. **Restaurant:** No. **General Store:** Yes. **Vending:** No. **Swimming:** No. **Playground:** No. **Activities:** Hiking, interpretive/nature programs, ORV area, photography, visitor center, wildlife. **Nearby Attractions:**

Cedar Breaks National Monument, Kodachrome Basin State Park, Lake Powell, Zion, Bryce Canyon and Grand Canyon National Parks.

RESTRICTIONS

Pets: On a 6-ft. leash, never unattended, cleaned up after. Not allowed in buildings, on beaches, in lakes or reservoirs. **Fires:** In fire rings, stoves, grills, or fireplaces provided for that purpose. Be sure your fire is completely extinguished before leaving. Do not leave your fire unattended. **Alcoholic Beverages:** Allowed w/in state parks, except for visitor centers, museums, & administrative offices. **Vehicle Maximum Length:** 100 ft.

TO GET THERE

Travel south on I-15 to Nephi, In Nephi take Hwy. 28 to Salina, at Salina take I-70 past Richfield to the East Zion/Bryce Canyon Exit. Take Hwy. 89 south to Mt. Carmel Junction, approx. 5 mi. past Mt. Carmel Junction still on 89, take the Coral Pink Sand Dunes Exit, and drive 12 mi. west to the park entrance.

KANAB   MAP, D-1
Coral Pink Sand Dunes
State Park

reserve america

12500 Sand Dunes Rd., P. O. Box 95, 84741.
T: (435) 648-2800 or (800) 322-3770;
www.reserveamerica.com.

🚐 ★★★★   ▲ ★★★★

Beauty: ★★★★★   Site Privacy: ★★★★★
Spaciousness: ★★★★★   Quiet: ★★★★
Security: ★★★★★   Cleanliness: ★★★★
Insect Control: ★★★   Facilities: ★★

Beautiful orange-sand dunes dotted with ponderosa pine trees and six-foot-tall dune grasses support both off-highway vehicle activity and scientific study areas with the unique Coral Pink Sand Dunes tiger beetle and Welsh milkweed. Coral Pink Sand Dunes State Park is also very popular with student groups, who come to learn about dune life from wood walkways protecting the dunes. Campsites are especially spacious, with parking loops accommodating extra long vehicles (e.g. 75–148 feet) or multiple smaller vehicles. Tall junipers growing out of the orange sand screen campsites from each other, and bicyclists pedal the paved roads. At 6,000 feet elevation, the park gets snow for winter activities. Hiking trails offer views of Zion, the Grand Canyon's North Rim, and ancient Native American pictographs. Reservations are advised at this popular park, and can be made 11 months in advance by groups or up to 16 weeks in advance of checkout date (a minimum of three days in advance of arrival) by individuals.

BASICS

Operated By: Utah State Parks. **Open:** All year. **Site Assignment:** First come, first served; group reservations; specific sites can be reserved 2 weeks at a time. **Registration:** At entrance kiosk. **Fee:** Camping, $15; plus per vehicle charge, $5; V, MC, Utah check. **Parking:** Loops at site.

FACILITIES

Number of Multipurpose Sites: 22. **Hookups:** Electric (30 amps), water. **Each Site:** Table, grill. **Dump Station:** Yes. **Laundry:** No. **Pay Phone:** Yes. **Restrooms and Showers:** Yes. **Fuel:** No. **Propane:** No. **Internal Roads:** Paved, good condition. **RV Service:** No. **Market:** 22 mi. northwest in Kanab. **Restaurant:** 22 mi. northwest in Kanab. **General Store:** No. **Vending:** Yes. **Swimming:** No. **Playground:** No. **Other:** ADA accessible wood walkways over sand dunes, off-highway access to dunes. **Activities:** Off-highway vehicle riding, biking, snow mobiling, snow tubing, hiking. **Nearby Attractions:** Pipe Springs National Monument, Kanab, Escalante Staircase National Monument, Zion, Grand Canyon North Rim. **Additional Information:** Kane County Office of Tourism, 78 S. 100 East, Kanab, UT 84741; (435) 644-5033; (800) 733-5263; kanetrav@kaneutah.com, www.kaneutah.com.

RESTRICTIONS

Pets: On leash, never unattended. **Fires:** In fire pits only (firewood sold). **Alcoholic Beverages:** Allowed. **Vehicle Maximum Length:** 32 ft. **Other:** 14-day stay limit, no wood gathering, no fireworks.

TO GET THERE

Go 13 mi. north from Kanab on US 89, then southwest on Hancock Rd. to Sand Dunes Rd. 11 mi.

LAKE POWELL   MAP, D-3
Bullfrog Resort and Marina Campground/RV Park

P.O. Box 56909, 84533.
T: (435) 684-7000 or (435) 684-3000; www.visitlakepowell.com.

🚐 ★★★★   ▲ ★★★★

Beauty: ★★★★★   Site Privacy: ★★★★
Spaciousness: ★★★★   Quiet: ★★★★
Security: ★★★★   Cleanliness: ★★★★
Insect Control: ★★   Facilities: ★★★★★

Bullfrog Resort and Marina in Glen Canyon National Recreation Area includes the Painted Hills RV Park and Bullfrog Campground. Both are operated by Aramark Parks and Resorts, an authorized National Park Service concessionaire. The year-round RV Park has full hookups and is attractively nestled among tall conifers and low yellowish sandstone hills. The RV Park does not allow tents. Tent camping is allowed only at the seasonal campground, which is also open to RV vehicles; sites 1–21 on Loop A have the best lake views. Tent campers must go to the village store and shell out additional money ($2) to take a shower, whereas the RV Park has showers. But it is the boating, fishing, and water sports, not campground amenities, that is the attraction here. Indeed, many locals skip the two pricey campgrounds in favor of primitive camping on the beaches (no designated sites) lining the shores of Lake Powell.

BASICS

Operated By: Aramark Parks and Resorts. **Open:** RVs, all year; tents, Mar.–Oct. only. **Site Assign-**

ment: First come, first served; reservations. **Registration:** At self-pay fee station (Campground); Lodge (RV Park). **Fee:** $27.25; cash only; US currency, no checks. **Parking:** At site.

FACILITIES

Number of RV-only Sites: 32. **Hookups:** Electric (20, 30 amps), water, sewer; 32 sites w/ full hookups. **Each Site:** Table, grill. **Dump Station:** Yes. **Laundry:** Yes. **Pay Phone:** No. **Restrooms and Showers:** Yes (coin-op). **Fuel:** Yes. **Propane:** Yes. **Internal Roads:** Paved & gravel, good. **RV Service:** No. **Market:** Blanding, 84 mi. **Restaurant:** Bullfrog Marina. **General Store:** Yes. **Vending:** Yes. **Swimming:** Lake. **Playground:** No. **Other:** Ferry, boat rental, motel. **Activities:** Boating, fishing, water sports. **Nearby Attractions:** Natural Bridges. **Additional Information:** National Park Service, (435) 684-7400; Lake Powell Ferry, (435) 684-3000; Glen Canyon Natural History Assoc., www.pagelakepowell.org.

RESTRICTIONS

Pets: On leash & under control at all times. **Fires:** In grills only, no ground fires. **Alcoholic Beverages:** Allowed. **Vehicle Maximum Length:** No limit. **Other:** No fireworks or loaded firearms.

TO GET THERE

From junction of UT 95 & UT 276 south of Hanksville, go 46 mi. south on UT 276.

LAKE POWELL   MAP, D-3
Halls Crossing RV Park/ Campground

Hwy. 276, P.O. Box 5101, 84533.
T: (435) 684-2261; www.visitlakepowell.com.

🚐 ★★★   ▲ ★★★

Beauty: ★★★★   Site Privacy: ★★★★
Spaciousness: ★★★   Quiet: ★★★★
Security: ★★★★   Cleanliness: ★★★★
Insect Control: ★★   Facilities: ★★★★

A National Park Service concessionaire, Aramark Parks and Resorts, operates two camping areas on the Halls Crossing side of Lake Powell in the Glen Canyon National Recreation Area. Halls Crossing is most easily reached by highway from Blanding to the east, though a ferry (hours vary seasonally and are limited, ending well before nightfall) links Halls Crossing with Bullfrog Marina to the north. The gravel RV park sites are attractively nestled in an oasis of trees providing shade and a buffer from the surrounding high-desert sagebrush and scrub. Tents are not allowed in Halls Crossing RV Park, which has full hookups. But Halls Crossing Campground, which lacks hookups, is open to both tents and self-sufficient RVs and trailers. The campground has trees shading the tents from the hot summer sun and good lake views looking down from an elevation across sagebrush-studded orange sands.

BASICS

Operated By: Aramark Parks and Resorts. **Open:** All year. **Site Assignment:** First come, first served; reservations. **Registration:** At self-pay fee station.

Fee: $27; cash only; US currency, no checks. **Parking:** At site.

FACILITIES

Number of RV-only Sites: 32. **Hookups:** Electric (20, 30 amps), water, sewer. **Each Site:** Table, grill. **Dump Station:** Yes. **Laundry:** Yes. **Pay Phone:** Yes. **Restrooms and Showers:** Yes. **Fuel:** No. **Propane:** Yes. **Internal Roads:** Paved, good. **RV Service:** No. **Market:** Blanding, 84 mi. **Restaurant:** Bullfrog Marina. **General Store:** Yes. **Vending:** Yes. **Swimming:** Lake. **Playground:** No. **Other:** Ferry, boat rental. **Activities:** Boating, fishing, water sports, swimming. **Nearby Attractions:** Natural Bridges. **Additional Information:** National Park Service, (435) 684-7400; Lake Powell Ferry, (435) 684-3000; Glen Canyon Natural History Assoc., www.pagelakepowell.org.

RESTRICTIONS

Pets: On leash (not allowed at marina or archaeological sites). **Fires:** In grills only, no ground fires. **Alcoholic Beverages:** Allowed (but not when driving a boat). **Vehicle Maximum Length:** No limit. **Other:** No fireworks or loaded firearms.

TO GET THERE

From junction of UT 95 & UT 276 west of Blanding, go 42 mi. west on UT 276.

LEEDS   MAP, D-1
Zion West RV Park

175 South Valley Rd., P.O. Box 460721, 84746.
T: (435) 879-2854.

🚐 ★★★★   ▲ ★★★★

Beauty: ★★★★   Site Privacy: ★★★★
Spaciousness: ★★★★   Quiet: ★★★★
Security: ★★★★   Cleanliness: ★★★★
Insect Control: ★★★★   Facilities: ★★★★

Carved out of an alfalfa field belonging to the farmer next door, the trees at Zion West still do not provide as much shade as is found at the Leeds RV Park and Motel next door. At 3,200 feet there is rarely snow, but Brian Head ski area is about an hour away, making this such a popular destination that the RV park is booked full from October to May. Indeed, many snowbirds book their October reservations when leaving in May. Tent campers have a large grassy area with tables without designated sites, as well as another area when more space is needed. Leeds RV parks make a good alternative to the roadside RV parks in nearby St. George, as they are farther back from the road. But the tradeoff for additional quietness is being farther from the urban amenities of St. George.

BASICS

Operated By: Jim and Gloria Parnell. **Open:** All year. **Site Assignment:** First come, first served; reservations advised Oct.–May. **Registration:** At office. **Fee:** RV, $26; tent, $16; cash, check. **Parking:** At site.

FACILITIES

Number of RV-only Sites: 30. **Number of Tent-only Sites:** 15. **Hookups:** Electric (30, 50 amps), water, sewer. **Each Site:** Table. **Dump Station:** Yes. **Laundry:** Yes. **Pay Phone:** No. **Restrooms and**

Showers: Yes. **Fuel:** No. **Propane:** No. **Internal Roads:** Paved, good. **RV Service:** No. **Market:** Leeds, 0.5 mi. **Restaurant:** Leeds, 0.5 mi. **General Store:** No. **Vending:** No. **Swimming:** No. **Playground:** No. **Other:** Dog walk. **Activities:** Rock climbing, biking, golf, horseback riding. **Nearby Attractions:** Zion, Quail Creek, Cedar Breaks, Brian Head. **Additional Information:** Washington County Travel Bureau, (435) 634-5747, (800) 869-6635.

RESTRICTIONS

Pets: On leash (noisy pets not tolerated). **Fires:** Not allowed. **Alcoholic Beverages:** At sites only. **Vehicle Maximum Length:** 45 ft.

TO GET THERE

From St. George take US I-15 11 mi. north to Exit 22, then go 0.5 mi. north on frontage road and south a block on Mulberry Lane.

LEVAN   MAP, B-2
Oasis Campground

Yuba State Park, P.O. Box 159, 84639.
T: (435) 758-2611 or (800) 322-3770;
www.stateparks.utah.gov/park/index.php?id=ylsp.

🚐 ★★★★   ⛺ ★★★★★

Beauty: ★★★★★	Site Privacy: ★★★★
Spaciousness: ★★★★★	Quiet: ★★★★
Security: ★★★★	Cleanliness: ★★★★
Insect Control: ★★★	Facilities: ★★★

Warm (70–75° F) summer waters keep the small Oasis Campground fronting the rock-strewn sandy shores of Yuba Reservoir full most weekends and holidays during the school-vacation season. But on weekdays after the holiday crunch it is not unusual for a lone boater or two to have the whole 22-mile long, 80-foot deep lake as a private playground. Bait machines near the fish-cleaning area dispense night crawlers and leeches to tempt walleye, northern pike, channel catfish, and yellow perch. Half the campground sites are over 60 feet long and the landscaping of green grass, sagebrush, cottonwood, and other trees makes this a real oasis from the seemingly distant (5 miles) interstate highway. On the opposite side of the lake, Eagle View Campground's primitive boat-access-only sites (1, 2, 3, 5, 7, 13, and 17) alongside a sandy day-use beach can be reserved with boat docks (sites 3 and 7 are wheelchair-accessible).

BASICS

Operated By: Utah State Parks. **Open:** All year. **Site Assignment:** First come, first served; reservations recommended weekends, holidays. **Registration:** At entrance kiosk. **Fee:** $14; Eagle View Campground, $8; cash, check. **Parking:** At site.

FACILITIES

Number of RV-only Sites: 26. **Hookups:** None. **Each Site:** Table on cement pad, grill, fire ring. **Dump Station:** Yes. **Laundry:** No. **Pay Phone:** Yes. **Restrooms and Showers:** Yes. **Fuel:** No. **Propane:** No. **Internal Roads:** Paved, excellent. **RV Service:** No. **Market:** Nephi, 25 mi. **Restaurant:** Nephi, 25 mi. **General Store:** No. **Vending:** Yes. **Swimming:** Lake. **Playground:** No. **Other:** Boat ramp, beaches. **Activities:** Fishing, water sports, swimming. **Nearby Attractions:** Mormon

Temple (Manti), Territorial Statehouse (Fillmore). **Additional Information:** Nephi/Juab County Chamber of Commerce, (435) 623-2411.

RESTRICTIONS

Pets: On leash under owner's control. **Fires:** Allowed. **Alcoholic Beverages:** Allowed. **Vehicle Maximum Length:** 45 ft. **Other:** Turn in tagged walleyes for research use.

TO GET THERE

From US I-15 Exit 202 near Mills, go 5 mi. south on reservoir perimeter road.

MIDWAY   MAP, B-2
Wasatch Mountain State Park

reserve america ☼

1281 Warm Spring Rd., P. O. Box 10, 84049.
T: (435) 654-1791 or (800) 322-3770;
www.reserveamerica.com.

🚐 ★★★★★   ⛺ ★★★★★

Beauty: ★★★★★	Site Privacy: ★★★★★
Spaciousness: ★★★★★	Quiet: ★★★★
Security: ★★★★	Cleanliness: ★★★★
Insect Control: ★★★	Facilities: ★★★

Three different campgrounds with 27 holes of golf and secluded oak thickets within an hour of Salt Lake City make Wasatch Mountain so desirable that anyone without a weekend reservation is usually turned away. Park City's Olympic ski lifts and the Olympic biathlon park at Soldier Hollow are nearby, as are state parks at Jordenelle, and Deer Creek Reservoirs for water recreation. Two Wasatch Mountain campgrounds have hookups, and one loop is set aside for tents. Mahogany Campground is popular for its pull-through sites (1, 3, 5, 21, 23, 25, 27); sites 15–26 have great views across Heber Valley. Cottonwood Campground RV sites 36–47 are coveted for their tall cottonwood trees providing shade all day. Tent camping is restricted to Oak Hollow Campground's 40 sites, many enclosed in oak canopies. Children can use the playground and fish in a pond near the visitor center, which has a display explaining the hot springs underlying the area.

BASICS

Operated By: Utah State Parks. **Open:** Early Apr.–until snow closes area; no reservations taken after Oct. 15. **Site Assignment:** Reservations are necessary weekends Memorial Day–Labor Day. **Registration:** At office. **Fee:** $17–$20; site reservation fee, $6.25; V, MC. **Parking:** At site.

FACILITIES

Number of RV-only Sites: 109. **Number of Multipurpose Sites:** 30. **Hookups:** Electric (20, 30, 50 amps), water, sewer. **Each Site:** Table, grill or fire ring. **Dump Station:** Yes. **Laundry:** No. **Pay Phone:** Yes. **Restrooms and Showers:** Yes. **Fuel:** No. **Propane:** No. **Internal Roads:** Paved, cracks patched. **RV Service:** No. **Market:** Midway, 6 or 7 mi. **Restaurant:** Midway, 0.5 mi. **General Store:** No. **Vending:** No. **Swimming:** No. **Playground:** Yes (at Visitor Center). **Other:** 27 holes of golf, ice for sale, pavilions, amphitheater. **Activities:** Golf,

horseback riding, fishing, boating. **Nearby Attractions:** Park City, Soldier Hollow, Timpanogos Cave National Monument, historic railway, reservoirs. **Additional Information:** Heber Valley Chamber of Commerce, (435) 654-3666, www.hebervalleycc.org.

RESTRICTIONS

Pets: On leash under owner's control. **Fires:** In grill or fire pit only (firewood sold); no fires when extreme summer danger. **Alcoholic Beverages:** Allowed. **Vehicle Maximum Length:** 75 ft. **Other:** Gate locked 10 p.m.–8 a.m.; no fireworks.

TO GET THERE

From junction of UT 113 and Main St. in Midway, go 6 mi. north on Pine Canyon Rd.

MOAB   MAP, C-3
Canyonlands Campground

555 South Main St., 84532.
T: (435) 259-6848 or (800) 522-6848;
www.canyonlandsrv.com.

🚐 ★★★★   ⛺ ★★★★

Beauty: ★★★	Site Privacy: ★★★
Spaciousness: ★★★	Quiet: ★★★
Security: ★★★★★	Cleanliness: ★★★★★
Insect Control: ★★★	Facilities: ★★★★★

In the center of Moab, within walking distance of bakeries with cappuccino, microbreweries, galleries, and shops, Canyonlands has tall cottonwood trees and level shaded pull-through spaces with cement pads. RV spaces in rows 5–8 can also be used for tents, and there are also two separate dirt areas for tents. The best tent sites in row G have sheltered tables. A footbridge across Pack Creek leads to 15 more secluded walk-in tent sites sharing a common sheltered eating area. Though in the center of town, Canyonlands is surprisingly quiet late at night, with less truck noise than the KOA outside of town, because speeds slow to 25 miles per hour downtown and there is no need for truckers to use noisy engine brakes. Thus, Moab's oldest campground remains very popular, and reservations are a must on holiday weekends and from June on, when Canyonlands fills up every night.

BASICS

Operated By: Paul and Aggie Evans. **Open:** All year. **Site Assignment:** First come, first served; reservations recommended peak times. **Registration:** At office. **Fee:** $19–$30; V, MC, AE, D. **Parking:** At site; separate parking for walk-in tent sites.

FACILITIES

Number of RV-only Sites: 105. **Number of Tent-only Sites:** 28. **Hookups:** Electric (30, 50 amps), water, sewer, cable TV, phone (modem). **Each Site:** Table, grill. **Dump Station:** Yes. **Laundry:** Yes. **Pay Phone:** Yes. **Restrooms and Showers:** Yes. **Fuel:** Yes. **Propane:** No. **Internal Roads:** Gravel, good. **RV Service:** No. **Market:** Moab, 1 block. **Restaurant:** Moab, less than 1 block. **General Store:** Yes. **Vending:** Yes. **Swimming:** Pool. **Playground:** No. **Other:** Pavilion, pet walk, horseshoes, cabins. **Activities:** Biking, boating, rafting, fishing, golf, jeep touring. **Nearby Attractions:** Arches, Canyonlands. **Additional Information:** Grand County Travel Council, (800) 635-MOAB.

RESTRICTIONS

Pets: On leash, not left unattended. **Fires:** Allowed. **Alcoholic Beverages:** Allowed. **Vehicle Maximum Length:** 45 ft. **Other:** No hammocks.

TO GET THERE

From Main (US 191) & Center streets in downtown Moab, take Main St. 5 blocks south to service station and take the campground entrance.

MOAB   MAP, C-3
Dead Horse Point Group Area

reserve america

P.O. Box 609, 84532-0609. T: (435) 259-2614; www.reserveamerica.com.

🚐 ★★★★   ⛺ ★★★★

Beauty: ★★★★★	Site Privacy: ★★★★
Spaciousness: ★★★★	Quiet: ★★★★
Security: ★★★★	Cleanliness: ★★★★
Insect Control: ★★★	Facilities: ★★★★

Towering 2,000 feet directly above the Colorado River, Dead Horse Point State Park provides a breathtaking panorama of the sculptured pinnacles and buttes of Canyonlands National Park. A visitor center offers information on the history, geology, and biology of the area. The small and remote but very popular campground rests in a beautiful red rock desert environment. There are no showers available and the closest town of Moab is 25 miles away. According to one legend, around the turn of the century the point was used as a corral for wild mustangs roaming the mesa top. Cowboys rounded up these horses, herded them across the narrow neck of land and onto the point. The neck, which is only 30 yards wide, was then fenced off with branches and brush. This created a natural corral surrounded by precipitous cliffs straight down on all sides, affording no escape. Cowboys then chose the horses they wanted and let the culls or broomtails go free. One time, for some unknown reason, horses were left corralled on the waterless point where they died of thirst within view of the Colorado River, 2,000 feet below.

BASICS

Operated By: Utah State Parks. **Open:** Mar. 1–Oct. 31. **Site Assignment:** Group reservations are accepted up to 11 months in advance of park departure date. **Registration:** At office. **Fee:** Group, $36–$39. **Parking:** At site.

FACILITIES

Hookups: Yes. **Dump Station:** Yes. **Laundry:** No. **Pay Phone:** No. **Restrooms and Showers:** Yes. **Fuel:** No. **Propane:** No. **Internal Roads:** Paved. **RV Service:** Yes. **Market:** No. **Restaurant:** No. **General Store:** No. **Vending:** No. **Swimming:** No. **Playground:** No. **Activities:** Biking, picnicking, hiking, wildlife.

RESTRICTIONS

Pets: On a 6-ft. leash, never unattended, cleaned up after. Not allowed in buildings, on beaches, in lakes or reservoirs. **Fires:** In fire rings, stoves, grills, or fireplaces provided for that purpose. Be sure your fire is

---

completely extinguished before leaving. Do not leave your fire unattended. **Alcoholic Beverages:** Allowed w/in state parks, except for visitor centers, museums, & administrative offices. **Vehicle Maximum Length:** 45 ft.

TO GET THERE

Dead Horse Point is on UT 313, 18 mi. off Hwy. 191 near Moab.

MOAB   MAP, C-3
Dead Horse Point State Park

reserve america

S.R. 313, P.O. Box 609, 84532.
T: (435) 259-2614 or (800) 322-3770;
www.reserveamerica.com.

🚐 ★★★★   ⛺ ★★★★

Beauty: ★★★★★	Site Privacy: ★★★★
Spaciousness: ★★★★★	Quiet: ★★★★
Security: ★★★★★	Cleanliness: ★★★★★
Insect Control: ★★★	Facilities: ★★

Named after a wild mustang corral where horses died of thirst, Dead Horse Point Overlook offers a marvelous view (80 to 100 miles most clear days) across deep sandstone mesas and a gooseneck in the Colorado River where the silence is so complete that a lone motorized raft can be clearly heard far below. Water is scarce on this high plateau, as it has to be trucked in from Moab, so bring your own or buy it by the gallon (limited) from the visitor center. The campground loop has tall pinyon pines and Utah junipers separating spacious orange-sand sites, the smallest accommodating a 40-foot rig. If the crowds in Arches and Moab get too much, this is a good place to come for quiet, though noises can really travel through the campground. At the very least, this is a scenic stop en route to Canyonlands Island in the Sky District.

BASICS

Operated By: Utah State Parks. **Open:** All year. **Site Assignment:** First come, first served; reservations accepted (required for group site). **Registration:** At park entrance. **Fee:** $14. **Parking:** At site.

FACILITIES

Number of RV-only Sites: 21. **Number of Multipurpose Sites:** 21. **Hookups:** Electric (20 amps), water. **Each Site:** Sheltered table, charcoal grill, sand tent pad. **Dump Station:** Yes. **Laundry:** No. **Pay Phone:** Yes. **Restrooms and Showers:** No showers. **Fuel:** No. **Propane:** No. **Internal Roads:** Paved, good condition. **RV Service:** No. **Market:** Moab, 32 mi. **Restaurant:** Moab, 32 mi. **General Store:** No. **Vending:** Yes. **Swimming:** No. **Playground:** No. **Other:** One wheelchair-accessible site. **Activities:** Evening ranger programs in amphitheater (May–Sept.), hiking. **Nearby Attractions:** Canyonlands, Arches, Moab. **Additional Information:** Canyonlands Natural History Assoc., (435) 259-6003, www.cnha.org; Grand County Travel Council, (800) 635-MOAB.

RESTRICTIONS

Pets: On 6-ft. leash under owner's control. **Fires:** Charcoal only in grills; no ground or wood fires.

Alcoholic Beverages: Allowed. **Vehicle Maximum Length:** No limit. **Other:** 8 people & 2 vehicles per site; no firearms; no fireworks; do not harass the wildlife.

TO GET THERE

Go 11 mi. northwest from Moab on US 191, then 23 mi. southwest on UT 313.

MOAB   MAP, C-3
Devils Garden Campground

reserve america

Arches National Park, P.O. Box 907, 84532-0907.
T: (435) 719-2299; www.reserveamerica.com.

🚐 ★★★★   ⛺ ★★★★

Beauty: ★★★★	Site Privacy: ★★★
Spaciousness: ★★★★	Quiet: ★★★
Security: ★★★★★	Cleanliness: ★★★★
Insect Control: ★★★	Facilities: ★

Devils Garden Campground is the only campground located within Arches National Park and it preserves over two thousand natural sandstone arches, including the world-famous Delicate Arch, in addition to a variety of unique geological resources and formations. In some areas, faulting has exposed millions of years of geologic history. The extraordinary features of the park, including balanced rocks, fins, and pinnacles, are highlighted by a striking environment of contrasting colors, landforms, and textures. Rocks have attracted visitors to Arches National Park for thousands of years. However, sightseeing has not been the main activity for very long. Hunter-gatherers migrated into the area about 10,000 years ago at the end of the Ice Age. As they explored Courthouse Wash and other areas in what is now Arches, they found pockets of rock perfect for making stone tools. The forces of nature have acted in concert to create the landscape of Arches, which contains the greatest density of natural arches in the world. Throughout the park, rock layers reveal millions of years of deposition, erosion, and other geologic events. These layers continue to shape life in Arches today, as their erosion influences elemental features like soil chemistry and where water flows when it rains.

BASICS

Operated By: National Park Service. **Open:** All year. **Site Assignment:** Reservable season is Mar. 1–Oct. 31. **Registration:** At registration office. **Fee:** Single, $15; group, $36. **Parking:** At site.

FACILITIES

Number of Multipurpose Sites: 116. **Hookups:** None. **Each Site:** Picnic table, fire ring. **Dump Station:** No. **Laundry:** No. **Pay Phone:** No. **Restrooms and Showers:** Yes. **Fuel:** No. **Propane:** No. **Internal Roads:** Paved. **RV Service:** No. **Market:** No. **Restaurant:** No. **General Store:** No. **Vending:** No. **Swimming:** No. **Playground:** No. **Other:** All food must be kept in hard-sided containers. **Activities:** Amphitheater, biking, birdwatching, climbing, campfire programs, hiking, photography, sightseeing.

RESTRICTIONS

Pets: On a leash at all times. **Fires:** Allowed; campfire program. **Alcoholic Beverages:** Not allowed. **Vehicle Maximum Length:** Varies; call ahead.

TO GET THERE

From I-70 take Exit 182. Go south 26 mi. to Arches National Park entrance. Proceed 18 mi. to Devils Garden Campground. From Moab, take Hwy. 191 north 4.5 mi. and enter Arches National Park. Proceed 18 mi. to Devils Garden Campground.

MOAB
Moab KOA

MAP, C-3

3225 South Hwy. 191, 84532.
T: (435) 259-6682 or (800) 562-0372;
www.moabkoa.com.

🚐 ★★★★   ⛺ ★★★

Beauty: ★★★	Site Privacy: ★★★
Spaciousness: ★★★	Quiet: ★★★
Security: ★★★★★	Cleanliness: ★★★★★
Insect Control: ★★★★	Facilities: ★★★★★

Surrounded by farms, mountains, and sagebrush-covered desert land, the Moab KOA has what appears to be an idyllic location. The gravel sites and abundance of trees reinforce the rural feel of the open countryside and surrounding mountains. There are two playgrounds, mini-golf, a pool, and more than enough amenities to make this a worthwhile base for exploring the territory both north and south of Moab. Besides, all the shops, galleries, restaurants, and microbreweries of Moab are only 4 miles down the road. The only drawback for those who are light sleepers is that the campground is situated alongside a steep highway grade where truckers use their noisy engine brakes late at night. But other than that, it is hard to find fault with this clean, well-maintained campground and its hard-working and helpful hosts.

BASICS

Operated By: Bob and Lila Ott. **Open:** Mar.–Oct. **Site Assignment:** First come, first served; reservations accepted. **Registration:** At office. **Fee:** $21–$32; V, MC, AE, D. **Parking:** At site.

FACILITIES

Number of RV-only Sites: 73. **Number of Tent-only Sites:** 52. **Hookups:** Electric (30, 50 amps), water, sewer, cable TV, Internet. **Each Site:** Table, grill. **Dump Station:** Yes. **Laundry:** Yes. **Pay Phone:** Yes. **Restrooms and Showers:** Yes. **Fuel:** No. **Propane:** Yes. **Internal Roads:** Gravel, good. **RV Service:** No. **Market:** Moab, 4 mi. **Restaurant:** Moab, 4 mi. **General Store:** Yes. **Vending:** Yes. **Swimming:** Pool. **Playground:** Yes. **Other:** Game room, mini-golf, dog walk, cabins, bike rentals. **Activities:** Boating, rafting, arranged horseback riding, golf, rock climbing, biking, arranged jeep touring, horseshoes. **Nearby Attractions:** Arches, Canyonlands, Newspaper Rock, Deadhorse State Park. **Additional Information:** Grand County Travel Council, (800) 635-MOAB.

RESTRICTIONS

Pets: On leash & attended by owner at all times (not allowed in playground or store area). **Fires:** Only charcoal fires in grills allowed. **Alcoholic Bev-**

erages: Allowed at site only. **Vehicle Maximum Length:** 70 ft. **Other:** No wasting water or running generators; children must be supervised.

TO GET THERE

From Moab go 4 mi. south on US 191.

MOAB
Moab Rim Campark and Cabins

MAP, C-3

1900 South Hwy. 191, 84532.
T: (435) 259-5002 or (888) 599-6622;
www.moab-utah.com/moabrim/campark.html.

🚐 ★★★   ⛺ ★★

Beauty: ★★★★	Site Privacy: ★★★
Spaciousness: ★★★	Quiet: ★★★
Security: ★★★★	Cleanliness: ★★★★★
Insect Control: ★★★★	Facilities: ★★★

Fronted by vineyards that provide a bit of a highway noise buffer and remind us of the wine industry here, Moab Rim is attractively situated part way up a hillside across the street from the Crazy Horse Saloon. Only ten RV sites have full hookups, while nine have electric and water. Moab Rim is one of the few commercial campgrounds with more tent sites than RV sites. Fire pits are located at designated locations rather than at every site, in expectation than many travelers will partake of Moab's many restaurants and microbreweries instead of cooking for themselves after a hard day of hiking or sightseeing. In any case, the fire pit areas are excellent locations for sitting in the evening, as they offer superb vistas of Moab and the surrounding mountains. All in all, a good stop for those preferring a small, intimate, almost boutique type of campground.

BASICS

Operated By: Jim and Sue Farrell. **Open:** Mar.–Nov. **Site Assignment:** First come, first served; reservations recommended on weekends. **Registration:** At office. **Fee:** RV, $24; tent, $16; V, MC. **Parking:** At site.

FACILITIES

Number of RV-only Sites: 22. **Number of Tent-only Sites:** 30. **Hookups:** Electric (30, 50 amps), water, sewer, cable TV. **Each Site:** Table, grill. **Dump Station:** Yes. **Laundry:** No. **Pay Phone:** No. **Restrooms and Showers:** Yes. **Fuel:** No. **Propane:** No. **Internal Roads:** Gravel, good. **RV Service:** No. **Market:** Moab, 2 mi. **Restaurant:** Moab, 2 mi. **General Store:** Yes. **Vending:** Yes. **Swimming:** No. **Playground:** Yes. **Other:** Cabins, fire pits at designated locations, rinse sink room for dishwashing. **Activities:** Boating, rafting, horseback riding, golf, biking, hiking. **Nearby Attractions:** Arches, Canyonlands, Newspaper Rock. **Additional Information:** Grand County Travel Council, (800) 635-MOAB.

RESTRICTIONS

Pets: On leash under owner's control. **Fires:** Allowed. **Alcoholic Beverages:** Allowed. **Vehicle Maximum Length:** 50 ft.

TO GET THERE

From downtown Moab, go 2 mi. south on US 191.

MOAB
Portal RV Park

MAP, C-3

1261 North Hwy. 191, 84532.
T: (435) 259-6108 or (800) 574-2028;
www.portalrvpark.com.

🚐 ★★★★   ⛺ ★★★★

Beauty: ★★★★	Site Privacy: ★★★
Spaciousness: ★★★★	Quiet: ★★★★
Security: ★★★★	Cleanliness: ★★★★★
Insect Control: ★★★★	Facilities: ★★★★

Just south of the Colorado River Bridge and the bend in US 191 north of Moab, Portal is positioned behind a pasture well back from the main highway, which means less noise than at the roadside Spanish Trail RV Park next door. Portal has fishing ponds, optional hookups to a private well with mountain spring water, trails to view birds and wildlife, horses and geese next door, and good La Sal Mountain views. Tent campers will like the grassy sheltered sites, and two group areas hold 25 tents each. Thus, Portal makes an excellent base for exploring Canyonlands and Arches National Parks and Moab. The small friendly campground is usually booked full during peak season (March–May) and holidays, when reservations are always recommended.

BASICS

Operated By: Kent and Ann Oldham. **Open:** All year. **Site Assignment:** First come, first served; reservations recommended. **Registration:** At self-pay entrance fee station; in office during winter. **Fee:** $16–$27; V, MC. **Parking:** At site.

FACILITIES

Number of RV-only Sites: 36. **Number of Tent-only Sites:** 10. **Hookups:** Electric (20, 30, 50 amps), water, sewer, cable TV, phone (modem). **Each Site:** Table, grill. **Dump Station:** Yes. **Laundry:** Yes. **Pay Phone:** Yes. **Restrooms and Showers:** Yes. **Fuel:** No. **Propane:** No. **Internal Roads:** Paved. **RV Service:** No. **Market:** Moab, 2 mi. **Restaurant:** 0.25 mi. on Hwy 191. **General Store:** Yes. **Vending:** Yes. **Swimming:** Pond (spring water). **Playground:** No. **Other:** Pavilion, picnic areas, dog walk, fishing ponds, cabins. **Activities:** Horseback riding, biking, boating, rafting, golf. **Nearby Attractions:** Arches, Canyonlands. **Additional Information:** Canyonlands Natural History Assoc., (435) 259-6003, www.cnha.org; Grand County Travel Council, (800) 635-MOAB.

RESTRICTIONS

Pets: On leash under owner's control. **Fires:** Allowed only in tent site fire rings, no fires at RV sites. **Alcoholic Beverages:** Allowed (must be confined to site; no rowdiness or drunkenness). **Vehicle Maximum Length:** No limit. **Other:** No firearms or fireworks, no dirt bike or ATV riding.

TO GET THERE

Go 2 mi. north of Moab on US 191.

MONUMENT VALLEY MAP, D-3
Goulding's Monument Valley Campground

1000 Main St., P.O. Box 360001, 84536.
T: (435) 727-3235 or (435) 727-3225;
www.gouldings.com.

🚐 ★★★★ ⛺ ★★★★

Beauty: ★★★★ | Site Privacy: ★★
Spaciousness: ★★★ | Quiet: ★★★★
Security: ★★★★★ | Cleanliness: ★★★★
Insect Control: ★★★★ | Facilities: ★★★★★

Long the premier establishment in Monument Valley and headquarters for filmmakers such as John Ford, whose film *Stagecoach* with John Wayne turned the area into a popular movie and TV commercial locale, Goulding's has successfully extended its quality franchise from trading post to lodge to campground. With an indoor swimming pool and nearby gas station, grocery store, restaurant, and air strip, Goulding's red-dirt campground is a compact oasis surrounded by imposing red rock sandstone formations. The only real activity here, besides touring Goulding's Trading Post Museum, watching a multimedia presentation, and visiting the tribal visitor center, is touring Monument Valley itself. While private vehicles are allowed down some of the dirt roads, half and full-day (and longer) jeep and horseback riding tours are a popular alternative. There are obligatory stops at Navajo hogans to watch women weave, photograph Navajos (a gratuity is expected) in their finery on horseback, and view the area's geology and petroglyphs.

BASICS
Operated By: Goulding's Lodge and Trading Post. **Open:** All year. **Site Assignment:** By reservation; otherwise, first come, first served. **Registration:** At office in campground store. **Fee:** RV, $36; tent, $22; V, MC, AE, D, DC. **Parking:** At site.

FACILITIES
Number of RV-only Sites: 66. **Number of Tent-only Sites:** 45. **Hookups:** Electric (20, 30, 50 amps), water, sewer, cable TV, phone (modem). **Each Site:** Table, grill. **Dump Station:** Yes. **Laundry:** Yes. **Pay Phone:** Yes. **Restrooms and Showers:** Yes. **Fuel:** Yes. **Propane:** Yes. **Internal Roads:** Paved, good. **RV Service:** No. **Market:** On site. **Restaurant:** On site. **General Store:** Yes. **Vending:** Yes. **Swimming:** Indoor pool. **Playground:** Yes. **Other:** Free shuttle to lodge, air strip. **Activities:** Navajo Tribal Park tours, horseback riding, Earth Spirit show. **Nearby Attractions:** Navajo Tribal Park. **Additional Information:** Monument Valley Visitors Center, (435) 727-3287; Black's Hiking & Jeep Tours, (435) 739-4226, (800) 749-4226.

RESTRICTIONS
Pets: On leash at all times (not allowed in restrooms, store, laundry, or undeveloped areas). **Fires:** Allowed. **Alcoholic Beverages:** Allowed. **Vehicle Maximum Length:** No limit. **Other:** Do unto others as you would have them do unto you.

TO GET THERE
From US 163 0.5 mi. north of UT–AZ border, go 2.5 mi. west on Monument Valley Rd.

MONUMENT VALLEY MAP, D-3
Mitten View Campground

P.O. Box 360289, 84536.
T: (435) 727-5870 or (435) 727-3353.

🚐 ★★★★ ⛺ ★★★★★

Beauty: ★★★★★ | Site Privacy: ★★★★
Spaciousness: ★★★★ | Quiet: ★★★★
Security: ★★★★ | Cleanliness: ★★★★
Insect Control: ★★★★ | Facilities: ★★★

Surrounded by sandstone mesas and a panorama of red plateaus, buttes, pinnacles, and talus piles, Mitten View Campground is one of the best places to wake up to the morning light and watch the sunrise turn the sagebrush-studded land into a palette of reds, browns, and oranges. Mitten View is adjacent to the Monument Valley Visitors Center, where payment is made to drive the 17 miles of dirt road open to the public. The road is rough, and many visitor's opt for a guided tour by jeep to save the wear and tear on their vehicles and learn from the Navajo guides. Fortunately the campground has sheltered tables, as the few short junipers and desert scrub provide little shade. Indeed, tents can become virtual hothouses in hot weather. But the small tent sites ringing the perimeter have better views of the 30,000-acre Monument Valley than the larger interior pull-through sites.

BASICS
Operated By: Navajo Parks and Recreation Bureau. **Open:** All year. **Site Assignment:** First come, first served; reservations advised May–Sept. **Registration:** At self-pay fee station. **Fee:** $10; cash, check. **Parking:** At site.

FACILITIES
Number of RV-only Sites: 55. **Number of Tent-only Sites:** 45. **Hookups:** None; water available but limited. **Each Site:** Sheltered table, grill. **Dump Station:** Yes. **Laundry:** Yes. **Pay Phone:** No. **Restrooms and Showers:** Yes. **Fuel:** No. **Propane:** No. **Internal Roads:** Gravel, good. **RV Service:** No. **Market:** Goulding's, 4 mi. **Restaurant:** Goulding's, 4 mi. **General Store:** No. **Vending:** No. **Swimming:** No. **Playground:** No. **Other:** Visitor center nearby. **Activities:** Monument Valley tours, horseback riding. **Nearby Attractions:** Goulding's Trading Post. **Additional Information:** Monument Valley Visitors Center, (435) 727-3287; Black's Hiking & Jeep Tours, (435) 739-4226, (800) 749-4226.

RESTRICTIONS
Pets: On leash. **Fires:** In grill only. **Alcoholic Beverages:** Prohibited on tribal lands. **Vehicle Maximum Length:** 36 ft. **Other:** No rock climbing.

TO GET THERE
Follow US 163 to Monument Valley Visitors Center.

MORGAN MAP, A-2
East Canyon State Park

reserve america

5535 South Hwy. 66, 84050-9694.
T: (801) 829-6866; www.reserveamerica.com.

🚐 ★★★★ ⛺ ★★★★

Beauty: ★★★★ | Site Privacy: ★★★★
Spaciousness: ★★★★ | Quiet: ★★★★
Security: ★★★★ | Cleanliness: ★★★★
Insect Control: ★★★ | Facilities: ★★★★

East Canyon State Park and Reservoir is nestled in the mountains northeast of Salt Lake City on State Routes 65 and 66. Although popular with water recreationists, East Canyon is also an attraction for history buffs. Nearby trails mark the steps of the Donner Party and the first Mormon settlers. The Donner Party was a group of farmers from Iowa and Illinois going west to find fertile land for their crops. On their way to California, they passed through East Canyon in 1846, the first wagon train to pass through this way. Many obstacles, including high brush and rocky obstacles, slowed them down a great deal. Not realizing the harsh conditions they would encounter while on their trek, only 47 of the original 87 reached their destination. One year after the Donner Party passed through East Canyon, Mormon pioneers followed that same trail; however, this time was much easier due to the trail work the Donner party had accomplished. The main campground is located at the northern end of reservoir. The boat launch ramp is located near the campground. Campfire programs are held each weekend from Memorial Day through Labor Day. A large primitive campground is located at the southern end of the reservoir with plenty of room for overflow campers. A concessionaire provides boat rentals and refreshments.

BASICS
Operated By: Utah State Parks. **Open:** Apr. 14–Oct. 15. **Site Assignment:** Reservations can be made up to 16 weeks in advance. **Registration:** At office. **Fee:** Single, $18–$21; double, $36–$42. **Parking:** 2 vehicles per campsite.

FACILITIES
Number of Multipurpose Sites: 29. **Hookups:** Yes. **Dump Station:** No. **Laundry:** No. **Pay Phone:** No. **Restrooms and Showers:** Yes. **Fuel:** Yes. **Propane:** No. **Internal Roads:** Paved. **RV Service:** Yes. **Market:** No. **Restaurant:** No. **General Store:** No. **Vending:** Yes. **Swimming:** Yes. **Playground:** No. **Activities:** Boating, canoeing, kayaking, fishing, picnicking, wildlife.

RESTRICTIONS
Pets: On a 6-ft. leash, never unattended, cleaned up after. Not allowed in buildings, on beaches, in lakes or reservoirs. **Fires:** In fire rings, stoves, grills, or fireplaces provided for that purpose. Be sure your fire is completely extinguished before leaving. Do not leave your fire unattended. **Alcoholic Beverages:** Allowed w/in state parks, except for visitor centers, museums, & administrative offices. **Vehicle Maximum Length:** 42 ft.

TO GET THERE

From Salt Lake City, take I-80 east 6 mi. Take the Emigration/East Canyon exit, then go 21 mi. northeast on UT 65, then 1 mi. west on UT 66 (north end of reservoir). From Ogden, go 17 mi. east on I-84 to the Morgan Exit 103, then south on UT 66, 14 mi. southeast on UT 66 1 mi. past the dam) to the entrance.

ORDERVILLE — MAP, D-1
Mukuntuweep RV Park and Campground

Zion National Park, 12120 West Hwy. 9, 84758.
T: (435) 648-3011; www.xpressweb.com/zionpark.

🚐 ★★★　　🔺 ★★★

Beauty: ★★★★	Site Privacy: ★★★★
Spaciousness: ★★★★	Quiet: ★★★★
Security: ★★★★	Cleanliness: ★★★★
Insect Control: ★★★★	Facilities: ★★★★

Mukuntuweep, the Paiute word for sacred cliffs, was the pre-Mormon name for the Zion National Park area. Mukuntuweep RV Park and Campground actually borders the park's eastern boundary, and the majestic rock-cliffs characteristic of Zion provide a scenic backdrop. Besides being the closest RV park to Zion, Mukuntuweep is somewhat of a refuge from the national park campground hustle and bustle, though it is right off the state highway. A gravel loop with 5 pull-through sites (up to 40-feet wide) circles like a wagon train around an inner cluster of RV sites near the entrance. Cottonwoods in the RV area provide noticeable shade. Tenters have two gravel roads to choose from, are out of sight of the RVs, and have grass and junipers that add a more rugged wilderness feel. With ample amenities and diligent, onsite management, Mukuntuweep makes a good base for exploring Zion National Park.

BASICS

Operated By: Frank Baca. **Open:** All year. **Site Assignment:** First come, first served; reservations available. **Registration:** At office. **Fee:** RV, $22; tent, $15. **Parking:** At site.

FACILITIES

Number of RV-only Sites: 30. **Number of Tent-only Sites:** 110. **Hookups:** Electric (20, 30 amps), water, sewer. **Each Site:** Table, grill. **Dump Station:** Yes. **Laundry:** Yes. **Pay Phone:** Yes. **Restrooms and Showers:** Yes. **Fuel:** Yes. **Propane:** No. **Internal Roads:** Gravel, good. **RV Service:** No (limited repairs). **Market:** Yes. **Restaurant:** Yes. **General Store:** Yes. **Vending:** Yes. **Swimming:** No. **Playground:** No. **Other:** Mountain bike rentals, horseback riding, video arcade w/ pool table, wheelchair accessible. **Activities:** Stream fishing, golf. **Nearby Attractions:** Zion, Bryce. **Additional Information:** Kane County Office of Tourism, 78 S. 100 East, Kanab, UT 84741; (435) 644-5033; (800) 733-5263; kanetrav@kaneutah.com, www.kaneutah.com.

RESTRICTIONS

Pets: On leash, cleaned up after, kept out of buildings. **Fires:** Allowed (firewood sold). **Alcoholic**

Beverages: Allowed. **Vehicle Maximum Length:** 70 ft. **Other:** 11 a.m. checkout.

TO GET THERE

On UT 9, go 0.25 mi. east from east entrance to Zion National Park; or from junction of UT 9 and US 89 at Mt. Carmel Junction, go 13 mi. west.

PANGUITCH — MAP, D-2
Panguitch Big Fish KOA

555 South Main St., P.O. Box 384, 84759.
T: (435) 676-2225 or (800) 562-1625;
www.koakampgrounds.com.

🚐 ★★★★　　🔺 ★★★★

Beauty: ★★★★	Site Privacy: ★★★★
Spaciousness: ★★★★	Quiet: ★★★★
Security: ★★★★★	Cleanliness: ★★★★
Insect Control: ★★★	Facilities: ★★★★

A very well-maintained campground with plenty of shade trees and grass, Panguitch Big Fish KOA feels very rural, with distant mountains and neighboring pastures where horse and sheep graze only five blocks from town. The tent sites are grassy, and the afternoon breeze is welcome in the summer. Over half the clientele is European, drawn to this location because it is quiet and off the main drag, as well as near town and equidistant between important park destinations. To the west, Panguitch Lake and Cedar Breaks are less than an hour away. To the east, Bryce Canyon and Kodachrome Basin are similarly near, making this a good central location for area exploration, though not as wilderness in feel as the Red Canyon or Cannonville KOA campgrounds. Overall, this is a safe choice, reliable and well run, with ample activities (e.g. video games, pool, badminton net) for kids.

BASICS

Operated By: Gregg and Jo Green. **Open:** Apr. 15–Oct. 15. **Site Assignment:** First come, first served; reservations accepted. **Registration:** At office. **Fee:** RV, $27–$35; tent, $20–$28; V, MC, AE, D. **Parking:** At site.

FACILITIES

Number of RV-only Sites: 45. **Number of Tent-only Sites:** 30. **Hookups:** Electric (50 amps), water, sewer. **Each Site:** Table, grill. **Dump Station:** Yes. **Laundry:** Yes. **Pay Phone:** Yes. **Restrooms and Showers:** Yes. **Fuel:** No. **Propane:** Yes. **Internal Roads:** Gravel, good condition. **RV Service:** No. **Market:** In Panguitch, 5 blocks north. **Restaurant:** In Panguitch. **General Store:** Yes. **Vending:** No. **Swimming:** Pool. **Playground:** Yes. **Other:** Game room, Internet access, pet walk. **Activities:** Wildlife museum in town, fishing, hiking, horseback riding. **Nearby Attractions:** Panguitch Lake, Cedar Breaks, Red Canyon, Bryce. **Additional Information:** Garfield County Travel Council, (800) 444-6689.

RESTRICTIONS

Pets: On leash under owner's control. **Fires:** In grill only (firewood sold). **Alcoholic Beverages:** Allowed. **Vehicle Maximum Length:** 63 ft. **Other:** No running of generators, 11 am checkout.

TO GET THERE

From US 89 in Panguitch at intersection of Main and Center streets, go 5 blocks south on Main St.

PANGUITCH — MAP, D-2
Red Canyon RV Park

3279 Hwy. 12, P.O. Box 717, 84759.
T: (435) 676-2690 or (435) 676-2243;
www.redcanyon.net.

🚐 ★★★　　🔺 ★★

Beauty: ★★★	Site Privacy: ★★★
Spaciousness: ★★★★	Quiet: ★★★
Security: ★★★★	Cleanliness: ★★★★
Insect Control: ★★★	Facilities: ★★★

Red Canyon RV Park (not to be confused with the U.S. Forest Service Red Canyon Campground) is on a relatively isolated stretch of UT 12, just 16 miles from Bryce and 7 miles from Panguitch. The compact, well-run RV park, whose clientele is mostly seniors, has a few large pull-through sites among two short rows of RV sites. The grassy tent area is almost close enough to the highway to double as a roadside shoulder. But this is a good base camp to park the RV while biking area trails or taking a jeep or four-wheel-drive vehicle into Red Canyon. Coyote, elk, deer, cottontail, and jackrabbits visit the RV park, and red-headed woodpeckers peck away at the trees, adding a sense of wilderness to what would otherwise be a roadside stop. All in all, not a bad alternative for Red Canyon explorers and national park visitors when the campgrounds closer to Bryce fill up.

BASICS

Operated By: Arthur and Wenda Mae Tebbs. **Open:** Apr. 1–Oct. 31; weather permitting. **Site Assignment:** By reservations and first come, first served. **Registration:** At office. **Fee:** RV, $24; tent, $11; number of full hookups: 40; V, MC, D. **Parking:** At site.

FACILITIES

Number of RV-only Sites: 30. **Number of Tent-only Sites:** Undesignated sites. **Hookups:** Electric (20, 30, 50 amps), water, sewer. **Each Site:** Table, shade canopy, grill. **Dump Station:** Yes. **Laundry:** No. **Pay Phone:** Yes. **Restrooms and Showers:** Yes. **Fuel:** Yes. **Propane:** No. **Internal Roads:** Gravel, excellent. **RV Service:** No. **Market:** 7 mi. northwest in Panguitch. **Restaurant:** 7 mi. northwest in Panguitch. **General Store:** Yes. **Vending:** Yes. **Swimming:** No. **Playground:** No. **Other:** Native American crafts store, rock shop, dog walk area. **Activities:** Jeep tours, bike trails. **Nearby Attractions:** Bryce, Lake Panguitch, Red Canyon. **Additional Information:** Powell Ranger District, (435) 676-8815.

RESTRICTIONS

Pets: On leash under owner's control. **Fires:** Allowed. **Alcoholic Beverages:** Allowed. **Vehicle Maximum Length:** No limit.

TO GET THERE

Go 16 mi. west on UT 12 from Bryce Canyon; or 1 mi. east on Hwy. 12 from the junction w/ US 89.

PANGUITCH LAKE   MAP, D-2
Bear Paw Lakeview Resort

905 South Hwy. 143, 84759.
T: (435) 676-2650 or (888) 553-8439;
www.bearpawfishingresort.com.

🚐 ★★★   ⛺ n/a

Beauty: ★★★★   Site Privacy: ★★★★
Spaciousness: ★★★   Quiet: ★★★★
Security: ★★★★   Cleanliness: ★★★★
Insect Control: ★★   Facilities: ★★★

Located in Dixie National Forest near an area of massive lava flows, Bear Paw Lakeview Resort is a mixture of cabins and RV sites on a hillside dotted with pine trees and sage. A rustic pine wood general store and small cafe anchor the steeply sloping hillside. A 40-foot walk crossing UT 143 leads to Panguitch Lake's rainbow, cutthroat, brook, and brown trout (worms, tackle, and fishing licenses for sale at the general store). Ironically, the Resort's small roadside cafe serves up almost everything but lake trout, claiming Utah state law allows restaurants to serve only USDA-inspected trout from fish farms. Kids and pets do well here, but space is limited and reservations are recommended. Indeed, the 32 RV sites up the road at Rustic Lodge and RV Park, which is under the same ownership, are booked up year after year in advance by the same people, many of whom have even built their own private fenced-in decks.

BASICS

Operated By: Laura and Glenn Adams. **Open:** First week in May–Oct. 31. **Site Assignment:** First come, first served; reservations (1 night; refundable 1 week prior to arrival). **Registration:** At store. **Fee:** $21; V, MC, AE, D. **Parking:** At site.

FACILITIES

Number of RV-only Sites: 17. **Hookups:** Electric (20, 30 amps), water, sewer. **Each Site:** Table, fire ring. **Dump Station:** Yes. **Laundry:** Yes. **Pay Phone:** Yes. **Restrooms and Showers:** Yes. **Fuel:** No. **Propane:** No. **Internal Roads:** Graded gravel, on slope. **RV Service:** No. **Market:** 15 mi. in Panguitch. **Restaurant:** Resort cafe serves 3 meals a day. **General Store:** Yes. **Vending:** Yes. **Swimming:** Lake. **Playground:** Yes. **Other:** Boat launch, horseriding, boat slip, boat & mountain-bike rentals. **Activities:** Trout fishing in lake & creeks. **Nearby Attractions:** Cedar Breaks, Bryce, Brian Head Ski Resort. **Additional Information:** Dixie National Forest, (435) 865-3200, www.fs.fed.us/dxnf.

RESTRICTIONS

Pets: On leash under owner's control. **Fires:** Allowed. **Alcoholic Beverages:** Allowed. **Vehicle Maximum Length:** No limit.

TO GET THERE

17 mi. west of Panguitch or 12 mi. east of Cedar Breaks on UT 143.

PANGUITCH LAKE   MAP, D-2
White Bridge Campground

reserve america

P.O. Box 80, 84759.
T: (877) 444-6777 or (435) 865-3200;
www.reserveamerica.com.

🚐 ★★★   ⛺ ★★★★

Beauty: ★★★★★   Site Privacy: ★★★★
Spaciousness: ★★★★   Quiet: ★★★★★
Security: ★★★★   Cleanliness: ★★★★
Insect Control: ★★   Facilities: ★

At 7,900-feet elevation, this Dixie National Forest campground nestled among hillsides covered with gray-green desert scrub opens and closes based on local snowfall dates. Campsites are widely dispersed on alternating sides of a good gravel road. Panguitch Creek flows through White Bridge, adding a bucolic burbling backdrop. However, for the entomophobic, Utah's lake and creek ecosystems may be too much nature. Periodic hatches of mayflies and other flying insects signify a healthy ecosystem (and are not sprayed in the National Forest) and fatten the trout, lizards, birds, and other wildlife for the tough winter ahead. (They were also a high-protein food source gathered by ancient Native Americans.) The only warm-weather alternative for those who would rather appreciate the landscape without any nuisance or DEET (insect repellent) is to stick to drier desert areas. Seasoned campers already accustomed to watching out for the region's legendary rattlers and scorpions will find Utah's lake and creek campgrounds a pleasant base for boating, trout fishing, horseback riding, and exploring nearby national parks.

BASICS

Operated By: AuDi Campground Services (U.S. Forest Service concessionaire). **Open:** May–first snow (Sept. or Oct.). **Site Assignment:** First come, first served; 11 sites can be reserved. **Registration:** At self-pay fee station at entrance. **Fee:** $11. **Parking:** At site.

FACILITIES

Number of RV-only Sites: 24. **Number of Tent-only Sites:** 5. **Hookups:** None. **Each Site:** Table, grill. **Dump Station:** Yes. **Laundry:** Yes. **Pay Phone:** No. **Restrooms and Showers:** No showers. **Fuel:** No. **Propane:** No. **Internal Roads:** Gravel, good condition. **RV Service:** No. **Market:** 10 mi. northeast in Panguitch. **Restaurant:** 4 mi. west at Panguitch Lake. **General Store:** No. **Vending:** No. **Swimming:** Lake. **Playground:** No. **Activities:** Fishing, biking, hiking, boating. **Nearby Attractions:** Panguitch Lake, Cedar Breaks, Bryce. **Additional Information:** Dixie National Forest, (435) 865-3200, www.fs.fed.us/dxnf.

RESTRICTIONS

Pets: On leash. **Fires:** Allowed. **Alcoholic Beverages:** Allowed. **Vehicle Maximum Length:** 32 ft. **Other:** No fireworks or firearms, noon checkout, 14-day stay limit.

TO GET THERE

Go 10 mi. southwest of Panguitch on UT 143 or 4 mi. east from Panguitch Lake.

PROVO   MAP, B-2
Utah Lake State Park

reserve america

4400 West Center St., 84601-9715.
T: (801) 375-0731; www.reserveamerica.com.

🚐 ★★★★   ⛺ ★★★★

Beauty: ★★★   Site Privacy: ★★★
Spaciousness: ★★★   Quiet: ★★★★
Security: ★★★★   Cleanliness: ★★★★
Insect Control: ★★★   Facilities: ★★★★

Utah Lake is unique in that it is one of the largest freshwater lakes in the West and yet it lies in an arid area that receives only about 15 inches of rainfall a year. The mouth of the Provo River, where it empties into Utah Lake, was undoubtedly a very popular camping place for the early inhabitants of Utah Valley. In fall 1776, the Dominguez–Escalante party traversed Spanish Fork Canyon and on September 21, they climbed a small hill near its mouth and looked down upon the large lake situated in a vast valley. One member of that party, Bernardo Y. Pacheco, reported to his king, "This place is the most pleasant, beautiful and fertile in all New Spain." From the time of Escalante's exploration until the early part of the 19th century, no accurate records revealing further travel to Utah Lake are available. A thriving market for furs brought another breed of men into Utah Valley; the mountain men. Some who visited near the lake were Peter Skeen Ogden, Osborne Russell, Daniel T. Potts, Jim Bridger, and Jedediah Strong Smith. Smith, in a letter written in 1827, became one of the first men to mention Utah as the name of the lake. In 1844 and 1845, John C. Fremont visited the lake. Local leaders, especially boaters, had been interested in construction of a facility on the lake that would permit them to launch boats year round. In 1933, an application requesting the help of the Civilian Conservation Corps was made and a marina was completed within a few years. Upon completion, Provo City began constructing shoreline picnic and camp facilities.

BASICS

Operated By: Utah State Parks. **Open:** Mar. 24–Oct. 29. **Site Assignment:** Reservations can be made up to 16 weeks in advance. **Registration:** At office. **Fee:** Single, $18; double, $36. **Parking:** 1 vehicle per site; 2 on double sites; additional vehicle fee, half of camping fee each night w/ the exception of $8 camp sites ($8 fee).

FACILITIES

Number of Multipurpose Sites: 45. **Hookups:** Yes. **Dump Station:** Yes. **Laundry:** No. **Pay Phone:** No. **Restrooms and Showers:** Yes. **Fuel:** No. **Propane:** No. **Internal Roads:** Paved. **RV Service:** Yes. **Market:** No. **Restaurant:** No. **General Store:** No. **Vending:** Yes. **Swimming:** Yes. **Playground:**

No. **Other:** Lawn area will accommodate one 16-ft. by 16-ft. tent. **Activities:** Boating, kayaking, canoeing, sailing, fishing, ice fishing, picnicking, swimming, visitor center, wildlife. **Nearby Attractions:** ORV area.

RESTRICTIONS

Pets: On a 6-ft. leash, never unattended, cleaned up after. Not allowed in buildings, on beaches, in lakes or reservoirs. **Fires:** In fire rings, stoves, grills, or fireplaces provided for that purpose. Be sure your fire is completely extinguished before leaving. Do not leave your fire unattended. **Alcoholic Beverages:** Allowed w/in state parks, except for visitor centers, museums, & administrative offices. **Vehicle Maximum Length:** 42 ft.

TO GET THERE

From Salt Lake City: travel south on I-15 to Provo Center St., Exit 268B. Travel west on Center St. 2 mi. to the park.

RED CANYON   MAP, B-3
Red Canyon Campground

reserve america

Hwy. 12, 84759.
T: (435) 676-8815 or (435) 676-9300; www.reserveamerica.com.

🚐 ★★★★   ⛺ ★★★★★

Beauty: ★★★★★   Site Privacy: ★★★★★
Spaciousness: ★★★★★   Quiet: ★★★★
Security: ★★★★   Cleanliness: ★★★★
Insect Control: ★★★   Facilities: ★★

This National Forest Service campground, nestled among tall pines and breathtaking red-spired sandstone hills within 10 miles of Bryce, is run by a Mom and Pop concessionaire, High Country Recreation, which has been among the region's best over the past two decades. Red Canyon Campground is just a few thousand yards east of the Dixie National Forest Visitor Center, which has soda machines, a pay phone, and the short Pink Ledges Nature Walk trailhead. Campsites, some big enough for three to four vehicles, are on alternating sides of the road on uphill and downhill loops, with lots of sage, junipers, and pine trees offering an extra measure of privacy. Unlike Kings Creek (see Appendix), which opens later in the season and gets people coming in for a week with four-wheel-drive vehicles, Red Canyon tends to be an overnight stop, though there are good trails from which a horse can be ridden into Bryce.

BASICS

Operated By: High Country Recreation. **Open:** Apr. 15-Oct. 25; weather permitting. **Site Assignment:** First come, first served. **Registration:** At self-pay entrance fee station. **Fee:** $11. **Parking:** At site.

FACILITIES

Number of Multipurpose Sites: 37. **Hookups:** None. **Each Site:** Table, grill. **Dump Station:** Yes. **Laundry:** No. **Pay Phone:** No. **Restrooms and Showers:** Yes. **Fuel:** No. **Propane:** No. **Internal Roads:** Gravel, excellent condition. **RV Service:** No. **Market:** Mile marker 10 on Hwy. 12 at Bryce

Canyon Pines. **Restaurant:** mi. marker 10 on Hwy. 12 at Bryce Canyon Pines. **General Store:** No. **Vending:** Yes. **Swimming:** No. **Playground:** Yes. **Other:** Asphalt bike trail. **Activities:** Horseback riding, volleyball, horseshoe pit, hiking, biking. **Nearby Attractions:** Red Canyon, Bryce, Kodachrome Basin, Escalante. **Additional Information:** Powell Ranger District, (435) 676-8815.

RESTRICTIONS

Pets: On leash under owner's control. **Fires:** Allowed in fire rings or grills; seasonal fire restrictions. **Alcoholic Beverages:** Allowed. **Vehicle Maximum Length:** 45 ft. **Other:** 14-day stay limit.

TO GET THERE

From junction of US 89 & UT 12, go 10 mi. east on Hwy. 12.

ROOSEVELT   MAP, B-3
Moon Lake Campground—
Uinta National Forest

reserve america

P.O. Box 127, 84006. T: (435) 722-5018; www.reserveamerica.com.

🚐 ★★★★   ⛺ ★★★★

Beauty: ★★★   Site Privacy: ★★★
Spaciousness: ★★★★   Quiet: ★★★
Security: ★★★★   Cleanliness: ★★★★
Insect Control: ★★★★   Facilities: ★★

Moon Lake Campground is located in lodgepole pine trees, adjacent to Moon Lake Reservoir. Moon Lake has a 55-unit campground, two group-use areas that can be reserved, and a resort run by a private concessionaire. Moon Lake is the trailhead to the Brown Duck and Upper Lake Fork areas. Moon Lake's blue water and sandy beach are in a most scenic area. Boating, fishing and hunting (in season) are allowed. Moon Lake is located in Uinta National Forest and offers an inspiring view and the promise of mountain recreation to the residents of cities below. American Fork Canyon and Provo Canyon located in the Uinta National Forest have an autumn mix of aspen and pine. Between the two canyons lies the 10,750 acre Timpanogos Wilderness. One paved drive full of rugged mountain beauty and many stunning overlooks of surrounding valleys can be found in the Uinta National Forest. In autumn, the brilliant display of colors found on this drive in Uinta National Forest is hard to match anywhere in the nation.

BASICS

Operated By: U.S. Forest Service. **Open:** May 27-Sept. 6. **Site Assignment:** Reservations must be made at least 5 days in advance. **Registration:** At office. **Fee:** Single, $10. **Parking:** At park.

FACILITIES

Number of Multipurpose Sites: 136. **Hookups:** None. **Each Site:** Fire ring, grill, picnic table. **Dump Station:** No. **Laundry:** No. **Pay Phone:** No. **Restrooms and Showers:** Yes. **Fuel:** No. **Propane:** No. **Internal Roads:** Paved. **RV Service:**

No. **Market:** No. **Restaurant:** No. **General Store:** No. **Vending:** No. **Swimming:** Yes. **Playground:** No. **Activities:** Bird-watching, biking, boating, canoeing, fishing, hiking, horseback riding, photography, sightseeing, wildlife viewing.

RESTRICTIONS

Pets: Restrained or on a leash at all times while in developed recreation areas. **Fires:** In fire rings, stoves, grills, or fireplaces provided for that purpose. **Alcoholic Beverages:** Not allowed. **Vehicle Maximum Length:** Call ahead.

TO GET THERE

On Hwy. 40 from Duchesne City, go north to Mountain Home via UT 87. Travel on CR to FS 131 (about 36 mi. from Duchesne City).

SALINA   MAP, C-2
Butch Cassidy Campground

1100 South State St., 84654.
T: (435) 529-7400 or (800) 551-6842.

🚐 ★★★   ⛺ ★★

Beauty: ★★★★   Site Privacy: ★★★★
Spaciousness: ★★★★   Quiet: ★★★
Security: ★★★★   Cleanliness: ★★★★
Insect Control: ★★★   Facilities: ★★★★

A rural crossroads for coal, salt, and gypsum (wallboard) mining traffic, Salina is a rustic overnight stop on the long trek across Utah on I-70. Tent camping is on the grass under trees alongside the highway or in quieter back-in RV sites. The RV sites, including 26 pull-throughs, are elevated on a hillside with less highway noise. Mobile homes are on a terrace above the RVs. Trees and grass provide pleasant visuals, but the real attraction is Mom's Cafe at the corner of Main and State streets (US 89). Mom sits at a desk under a clock above the salad bar surveying the restaurant, and prides herself on some remarkably good road food. For breakfast try the Mad House Cafe on Main Street, where ceramics and children's art decorate the walls, and portions are large enough for a hungry trucker and a famished farmer to split (or just order blueberry pancakes at a buck apiece).

BASICS

Operated By: Lee, Danielle and Mich Crysel. **Open:** All year. **Site Assignment:** First come, first served; reservations accepted. **Registration:** At office. **Fee:** RV, $15-$20; tent, $12; V, MC. **Parking:** At site.

FACILITIES

Number of RV-only Sites: 70. **Number of Tent-only Sites:** 50. **Hookups:** Electric (20, 30, 50 amps), water, sewer. **Each Site:** Table. **Dump Station:** Yes. **Laundry:** Yes. **Pay Phone:** Yes. **Restrooms and Showers:** Yes. **Fuel:** No. **Propane:** No. **Internal Roads:** Gravel, good. **RV Service:** No. **Market:** Salina, 1 mi. **Restaurant:** Across the street. **General Store:** Yes. **Vending:** Yes. **Swimming:** Pool. **Playground:** Yes. **Other:** Tent & back-in sites have grills. **Activities:** ATVs, fishing, boating, swimming. **Nearby Attractions:** Fish Lake. **Additional Information:** Fish Lake National Forest, (435) 896-9233.

RESTRICTIONS

Pets: On leash at all times. **Fires:** In designated fire pits or grills. **Alcoholic Beverages:** Allowed. **Vehicle Maximum Length:** 60 ft. **Other:** No fireworks, no clothes lines.

TO GET THERE

From US I-70 Exit 54, go north 0.5 mi. on State St. (US 89).

SPRINGDALE   MAP, D-1
South and Watchman Campgrounds

Zion National Park, UT. 9, 84767.
T: (435) 772-3256;
www.nps.gov/zion/campgrounds.htm.

🚐 ★★★★   ⛺ ★★★★★

Beauty: ★★★★★	Site Privacy: ★★★★
Spaciousness: ★★★★	Quiet: ★★★★
Security: ★★★★★	Cleanliness: ★★★★
Insect Control: ★★★★	Facilities: ★★★

Two Zion National Park campgrounds, South and Watchman, can handle RVs. But only Watchman Campground's Loop A and B have electric hookups (73 are 30 amp, 2 are 50 amp); Loop B has five 40-foot sites, but most are 35–36 feet. Tunnels on roads leading into the park will not accommodate vehicles over 50 feet long, and big rigs need special escort vehicles ($10). South Campground's two loops have a 24-foot length limit and tight turns difficult for large wider-bodied RVs. Watchman Loops C and D are for tent camping. Loop D's 36 sites are most coveted, being right up against scenic Mount Watchman. South Campground has three wheelchair-accessible sites (103, 114, 115) and 69 tent-only sites, including seven walk-in sites along the river. Watchman fills via reservation many days from Easter to Halloween, while South fills by 2:30 p.m. on a first-come-first-served basis.

BASICS

Operated By: National Park Service. **Open:** Watchman, all year; South, Mar.–Nov 1. **Site Assignment:** First come, first served (South); reservations (Watchman; Easter-Halloween). **Registration:** At entry kiosk; self-pay fee station. **Fee:** $16–$20; cash, check. **Parking:** At site; parking area for the seven walk-in sites at South Campground.

FACILITIES

Number of RV-only Sites: 180. **Number of Tent-only Sites:** 7. **Hookups:** Watchman: electric. **Each Site:** Table, fire pit. **Dump Station:** Yes. **Laundry:** No. **Pay Phone:** Yes. **Restrooms and Showers:** No showers. **Fuel:** No. **Propane:** No. **Internal Roads:** Paved, some bumps. **RV Service:** No. **Market:** Springdale, 1 mi. **Restaurant:** Springdale, 1 mi. **General Store:** No. **Vending:** No. **Swimming:** No. **Playground:** No. **Other:** Visitor center, amphitheater, several wheelchair-accessible sites at both campgrounds. **Activities:** Fishing, ranger programs, hiking, shuttle service to Zion Canyon. **Nearby Attractions:** Bryce Canyon. **Additional Information:** Washington County Travel Bureau, (435) 634-5747 or (800) 869-6635.

RESTRICTIONS

Pets: On leash. **Fires:** in fire pit only, no wood gathering; fire restrictions may be in effect, check first w/ ranger. **Alcoholic Beverages:** Allowed (at site only; zero tolerance for drinking & driving & marijuana). **Vehicle Maximum Length:** 40 ft.

TO GET THERE

Go 0.5 mi. north of Springdale on UT 14 to Zion National Park entrance.

SPRINGDALE   MAP, D-1
Zion Canyon Campground

479 Zion Park Blvd., P.O. Box 99, 84767.
T: (435) 772-3237;
www.zioncanyoncampground.com.

🚐 ★★★★   ⛺ ★★★★

Beauty: ★★★★	Site Privacy: ★★★★
Spaciousness: ★★★★	Quiet: ★★★★
Security: ★★★★	Cleanliness: ★★★★
Insect Control: ★★★	Facilities: ★★★★

The Zion National Park shuttle bus stops in front and the Virgin River is the back border of Zion Canyon Campground, a bustling little village run by the same family for the past three decades. A popular pizza restaurant next door to the office and store has outdoor tables bordering UT 14 and the campground's front entrance. The showers here are very popular with campers staying at the two campgrounds inside Zion National Park. Indeed, Zion Canyon is held in such high regard that National Park overflow is sent here. While not as rustic as the National Park campgrounds, the views of Zion's sandstone mountains are still good. The campground also has plenty of trees and a pond. RV sites B20 and B21 are open-ended and can accommodate any RV currently on the road. There are also numerous grassy sites with dirt perimeters close to the river.

BASICS

Operated By: Dave and Stew Ferber. **Open:** All year. **Site Assignment:** Varies by type of vehicle; first come, first served. **Registration:** At office. **Fee:** $22–$27; V, MC, AE. **Parking:** At site.

FACILITIES

Number of RV-only Sites: 120. **Number of Tent-only Sites:** 100. **Hookups:** Electric (30, 50 amps), water, sewer, cable TV. **Each Site:** Table, grill. **Dump Station:** Yes. **Laundry:** Yes. **Pay Phone:** Yes. **Restrooms and Showers:** Yes. **Fuel:** No. **Propane:** No. **Internal Roads:** Gravel, good. **RV Service:** No. **Market:** Springdale, 1 mi. **Restaurant:** On premises. **General Store:** Yes. **Vending:** Yes. **Swimming:** Pool, river. **Playground:** Yes. **Other:** Game room, pavilion. **Activities:** Biking, horseback riding. **Nearby Attractions:** Zion National Park. **Additional Information:** Washington County Travel Bureau, (435) 634-5747, (800) 869-6635.

RESTRICTIONS

Pets: On leash (in RV area; no pets in tent area). **Fires:** Allowed. **Alcoholic Beverages:** Allowed. **Vehicle Maximum Length:** No limit.

TO GET THERE

Go 0.5 mi. south of Zion National Park south entrance on UT 9.

ST. GEORGE   MAP, D-1
Quail Creek State Park

reserve america

P.O. Box 1943, 84770.
T: (435) 879-2378 or (800) 322-3770;
www.reserveamerica.com.

🚐 ★★★★   ⛺ ★★★★

Beauty: ★★★★	Site Privacy: ★★★★
Spaciousness: ★★★★	Quiet: ★★★★
Security: ★★★★	Cleanliness: ★★★★
Insect Control: ★★	Facilities: ★★

Hundred-foot-deep warm blue waters and a red sandstone cliff backdrop only 15 miles northeast of St. George make 3,300-foot-elevation Quail Creek Reservoir one of Utah's most popular summer water playgrounds. The 600 acre reservoir was created in 1990 by damming Quail Creek for hydroelectric power below the lower slopes of the Pine Mountains and filling the basin behind the 202-foot-tall dam with Virgin River water. Most of the namesake quail have been hunted out of the area. But the small hillside campground and its large curving pull-through and flat tent sites command good views across waters crowded with boaters and water skiers. Sheltered picnic tables overlooking the reservoir also make this a popular day-trip party destination. Though a jaunt to Hurricane is needed for amenities, a campsite here can also be a base for exploring the Red Cliffs and Silver Reef near Leeds as well as Zion National Park.

BASICS

Operated By: Utah State Parks. **Open:** All year. **Site Assignment:** First come, first served; reservations advised peak times. **Registration:** At entrance kiosk. **Fee:** $11; cash, check. **Parking:** At site.

FACILITIES

Number of RV-only Sites: 23. **Hookups:** None. **Each Site:** Sheltered table on cement pad, grill. **Dump Station:** No. **Laundry:** Yes. **Pay Phone:** No. **Restrooms and Showers:** No showers. **Fuel:** No. **Propane:** No. **Internal Roads:** Paved, good. **RV Service:** No. **Market:** 3 mi. **Restaurant:** 3 mi. **General Store:** No. **Vending:** No. **Swimming:** Lake. **Playground:** No. **Other:** Boat launch, fish-cleaning station, 3 wheelchair-accessible sites. **Activities:** Boating, fishing, swimming, picnicking. **Nearby Attractions:** Zion National Park. **Additional Information:** Washington County CVB, (435) 634-5747 or (800) 869-6635.

RESTRICTIONS

Pets: On leash under owner's control. **Fires:** Allowed. **Alcoholic Beverages:** Allowed. **Vehicle Maximum Length:** 35 ft. **Other:** 3-day stay limit w/o reservations.

TO GET THERE

From St. George go north on I-15 to Exit 16, and then 3 mi. east on UT 9.

STERLING   MAP, C-2
Palisade State Park

reserve america

2200 Palisade Rd., P.O. Box 650070, 84655.
T: (435) 835-7275 or (800) 322-3770;
www.reserveamerica.com.

🚐 ★★★★   ⛺ ★★★★

Beauty: ★★★★   Site Privacy: ★★★★
Spaciousness: ★★★★   Quiet: ★★★★
Security: ★★★★   Cleanliness: ★★★★
Insect Control: ★★   Facilities: ★★★★

Started in the 1860s by rancher Daniel Funk, who built the original reservoir (Funk's Lake) and a dance pavilion at what became a popular resort in the horse-and-buggy days, Palisade State Park now boasts a golf course with a clubhouse and PGA pro a short walk from the North Campground, which has the largest pull-through sites. The South Campground, farthest from the golf course and nearest the sandy beach, has a group pavilion and tent area. Eleven double sites are spread out among the South, North, and East Campgrounds. Developers are trying to sell homes and commercial spaces on the 2 miles of Palisades Road leading into the park. But for now this remains a sleepy backwater campground (use peaks on summer weekends) with lake-view campsites (50–53 are best), nonmotorized boating, cutthroat and rainbow trout, and ice fishing and ice skating during the winter.

BASICS
Operated By: Utah State Parks. **Open:** All year. **Site Assignment:** First come, first served; reservations for individuals (120 days in advance) & groups (1 year in advance). **Registration:** Entry kiosk (sporadically open) or self-pay fee station. **Fee:** $15; V, MC if entry kiosk open; otherwise cash, check. **Parking:** At site.

FACILITIES
Number of RV-only Sites: 10. **Number of Multipurpose Sites:** 43. **Hookups:** None. **Each Site:** Table, grill. **Dump Station:** Yes. **Laundry:** No. **Pay Phone:** Yes. **Restrooms and Showers:** Yes. **Fuel:** No. **Propane:** No. **Internal Roads:** Paved, excellent. **RV Service:** No. **Market:** Manti, 7 mi. **Restaurant:** Manti, 7 mi. **General Store:** Yes. **Vending:** Yes. **Swimming:** Lake (swimmer's itch, schistosomiasis warning). **Playground:** No. **Other:** Boat ramp, canoe & paddleboat rental, golf course (18-hole, par 72) & clubhouse w/ pro, amphitheater, extensive picnic areas. **Activities:** Golf, fishing, nonmotorized boating, winter sports, swimming. **Nearby Attractions:** Manti Temple, national forest. **Additional Information:** Sanpete County Heritage Council, (435) 283-4321, (800) 281-4346, www.sanpete.com.

RESTRICTIONS
Pets: On leash under owner's control (kept off beach & out of water). **Fires:** In grills or metal containers 6 inches off ground. **Alcoholic Beverages:** Allowed if not mixed w/ boating. **Vehicle Maximum Length:** 45 ft. **Other:** No diving from rocks; no hanging or tying things to trees; personal flotation devices must be worn on boats; firearms must be unloaded & locked away.

TO GET THERE
Go 6 mi. south of Manti on US 89 and 2 mi. east on Palisades Rd.

SYRACUSE   MAP, A-2
Antelope Island State Park

reserve america

4528 West 1700 South, 84075.
T: (801) 773-2941 or (800) 322-3770;
www.reserveamerica.com.

🚐 ★★★★   ⛺ ★★★★

Beauty: ★★★★★   Site Privacy: ★★★★★
Spaciousness: ★★★★   Quiet: ★★★★★
Security: ★★★★★   Cleanliness: ★★★★
Insect Control: ★★★   Facilities: ★★★

An 8-mile-long two-lane causeway with swooping birds diving down and scaring drivers crosses the Great Salt Lake on the drive from the Antelope Island entrance kiosk to Bridger Bay Campground. Though the area is a popular day-use park with many migratory waterfowl and secluded turnouts and beaches for picnics, campers must bring their own water (or use the visitor center faucets and soft drink vending machines). Wildlife, including introduced bison and re-introduced antelope, have it better, as this largest of the 10 Great Salt Lake islands has 40 springs. The primitive campsites are widely dispersed and attractively situated among the rocky grasslands and sagebrush coming down from the hills overlooking the lake. Campsites are booked up well in advance for weekends, particularly prime vacation holidays, and visitors without reservations are frequently turned away. The sites are long and narrow; very wide or long vehicles should call the park before coming.

BASICS
Operated By: Utah State Parks. **Open:** All year. **Site Assignment:** First come, first served; reservations (120 days in advance for individuals, 1 year for groups) an absolute necessity holidays, weekends. **Registration:** At entrance kiosk. **Fee:** $12; reservation fee, $7; cash, check. **Parking:** At site.

FACILITIES
Number of RV-only Sites: 26. **Hookups:** None. **Each Site:** Table, fire ring w/ grill. **Dump Station:** Yes. **Laundry:** No. **Pay Phone:** No. **Restrooms and Showers:** Yes. **Fuel:** No. **Propane:** No. **Internal Roads:** Gravel, good. **RV Service:** No. **Market:** Syracuse, 12 mi. **Restaurant:** Buffalo Point, 2 mi. (limited hours; outdoor tables). **General Store:** No. **Vending:** Yes. **Swimming:** Lake. **Playground:** No. **Other:** Visitor center, gift shop, marina, horse concessions, ranger programs, boat launch. **Activities:** Biking, horseback riding, bird-watching, hiking, skiing. **Nearby Attractions:** Farmington Bay Waterfowl Management Area, boating. **Additional Information:** Davis County Tourism, (801) 451-3286, www.co.davis.ut.us/discoverdavis; Farmington Bay Waterfowl Area, (801) 451-7386.

RESTRICTIONS
Pets: On leash (not allowed on beach). **Fires:** Charcoal in fire rings or gas stoves when fire danger is low. Absolutely no fires when grasslands are dry in summer. **Alcoholic Beverages:** Allowed. **Vehicle Maximum Length:** No limit. **Other:** Horses not allowed in campground.

TO GET THERE
From I-15 Exit 335 18 mi. north of Salt Lake City, go 14 mi. west on UT 127.

TORREY   MAP, C-2
Fruita Campground

HC 70 Box 15, 84775. T: (435) 425-3791;
www.nps.gov/care/camp.htm.

🚐 ★★★★   ⛺ ★★★★

Beauty: ★★★★   Site Privacy: ★★★★
Spaciousness: ★★★   Quiet: ★★★★
Security: ★★★★   Cleanliness: ★★★★
Insect Control: ★★   Facilities: ★★

Fruita Campground is named for the surrounding historic orchards, where cherries, peaches, and other fruit can be picked in season. As the only developed campground within Capitol Reef National Park, campsites in Fruita are coveted and the campground often fills by early afternoon. Fruita is laid out alongside the Fremont River (so be prepared with bug repellent during warm months) and is noted for its many large shade trees and grassy tent sites. The three loops resemble a dense little village, with Loop C having the largest RV sites. Tent campers wanting a more primitive camping experience (no water provided) in the park may wish to head to the campgrounds at Cedar Mesa (5 no-fee tent sites; but navigating the dirt road is not advised during wet weather) or Cathedral Valley (6 no-fee sites; road conditions also a wet-weather concern). For hookups and amenities, head to Torrey.

BASICS
Operated By: National Park Service. **Open:** All year. **Site Assignment:** First come, first served; reservations for group site. **Registration:** At self-pay entrance fee station. **Fee:** $10; half price for Golden Age or Golden Access; cash, check only. **Parking:** At site.

FACILITIES
Number of RV-only Sites: 64. **Number of Tent-only Sites:** 6. **Hookups:** None. **Each Site:** Table, grill. **Dump Station:** Yes. **Laundry:** No. **Pay Phone:** Yes. **Restrooms and Showers:** No showers. **Fuel:** No. **Propane:** No. **Internal Roads:** Paved, good condition. **RV Service:** No. **Market:** In Torrey, 11 mi. west. **Restaurant:** In Torrey, 11 mi. west. **General Store:** No. **Vending:** No. **Swimming:** No. **Playground:** No. **Nearby Attractions:** Capitol Reef, Escalante, Goblin Valley State Park. **Additional Information:** Capitol Reef Country, (800) 858-7951, (435) 425-3365, www.capitolreef.org; Wayne County Travel Council, (800) 858-7159.

RESTRICTIONS
Pets: On leash under owner's control. **Fires:** Allowed. **Alcoholic Beverages:** Allowed if over 21

years old. **Vehicle Maximum Length:** 30 ft.
Other: Do not feed or approach wildlife; 14-day stay limit Apr. 1–Nov. 30, 30-day limit Dec. 1–Mar. 31.

TO GET THERE

11 mi. east of Torrey on UT 24, then 1 mi. south on scenic road past visitor center.

TORREY — MAP, C-2
Thousand Lakes RV Park

1050 W Hwy. 24, P.O. Box 750070, 84775.
T: (800) 355-8995 or (435) 425-3500;
www.thousandlakesrvpark.com.

🚐 ★★★★   ⛺ ★★★★

Beauty: ★★★★★	Site Privacy: ★★★★
Spaciousness: ★★★★	Quiet: ★★★★
Security: ★★★★	Cleanliness: ★★★★★
Insect Control: ★★★★	Facilities: ★★★★

Tall cottonwood trees and grass between the gravel sites lend a pleasant pastoral feel to Thousand Lakes RV Park, which boasts an exceptionally good gift shop and is within a mile of such Torrey institutions as Cafe Diablo, the Capitol Reef Inn and Cafe, and Robber's Roost Books and Beverages. Weeknights from May to early October, Thousand Lakes serves up a western cookout complete with Dutch oven potatoes, cowboy beans, buttermilk scones, and entrees ranging from ribeye steak to vegetarian. With everything from horseshoes, a playground for the kids, a dog walk, and nearby espressos, guests sometimes forget that they came here for the national park and the incomparable sunrise and sunset light on the chiseled sandstone cliffs that define Capitol Reef. The combination of hookups and nearby restaurants and amenities brings a fair amount of repeat business and makes this a pleasant base camp for commuting to Capitol Reef National Park.

BASICS

Operated By: John and Vally Reilly. **Open:** Mar. 25–Oct. 25. **Site Assignment:** First come, first served; reservations accepted. **Registration:** At office. **Fee:** RV, $18.50–$19.50; tent, $13.50; V, MC, AE. **Parking:** At site.

FACILITIES

Number of RV-only Sites: 58. **Number of Tent-only Sites:** 9. **Hookups:** Electric (30, 50 amps), water, sewer. **Each Site:** Table, grill. **Dump Station:** Yes. **Laundry:** Yes. **Pay Phone:** Yes. **Restrooms and Showers:** Yes. **Fuel:** No. **Propane:** No. **Internal Roads:** Gravel, good condition. **RV Service:** Next door. **Market:** In Torrey, 1 mi. east. **Restaurant:** On site. **General Store:** Yes. **Vending:** No. **Swimming:** Heated pool. **Playground:** Yes. **Other:** Modem hookup in store, 4WD rentals, hair care, pavilion. **Activities:** Western cookouts, horseshoes. **Nearby Attractions:** Capitol Reef, Boulder Mountain lakes, Escalante. **Additional Information:** Capitol Reef Country, (800) 858-7951, (435) 425-3365, www.capitolreef.org; Wayne County Travel Council, (800) 858-7159.

RESTRICTIONS

Pets: On leash under owner's control. **Fires:** In fire pit. **Alcoholic Beverages:** Allowed. **Vehicle Maximum Length:** 65 ft.

TO GET THERE

On UT 24, 2 mi. west of junction w/ UT 12.

TORREY — MAP, C-2
Wonderland RV Park

Hwy. 12 and Hwy. 24, 84775.
T: (435) 425-3344 or (877) 854-0184;
www.capitolreefwonderland.com.

🚐 ★★★★   ⛺ ★★★★

Beauty: ★★★★	Site Privacy: ★★★★
Spaciousness: ★★★★	Quiet: ★★★★
Security: ★★★★	Cleanliness: ★★★★★
Insect Control: ★★★★	Facilities: ★★★★

Though situated at a key highway junction with a chain motel and two gas stations with mini-marts, Wonderland RV Park looks out on a scenic vista of pasture and high desert that merges into the distant mountains. Tent sites are along a grassy strip protected by a windbreak fence. The highway gets little truck traffic, though the coyotes can howl up a storm. Almost all the amenities are here or very nearby, including use of the motel pool and restaurant, which are atop an adjacent hill. This family-run enterprise, which includes the gas station, mini-mart, and motel, also has Malfunction Junction for arranging 4WD and fishing tours with guides who have exclusive access to 25 miles of streams on the Fremont River and Boulder Creek. All in all, it's well situated for exploring Torrey and Capitol Reef and even the Boulder Mountains or Escalante.

BASICS

Operated By: Raymond and Diane Potter. **Open:** Mar.–Nov. or until first freeze. **Site Assignment:** First come, first served; reservations advised after June 1. **Registration:** At office or in Texaco mini-mart. **Fee:** RV, $20; tent, $14; V, MC, AE, D, DC. **Parking:** At site.

FACILITIES

Number of RV-only Sites: 39. **Number of Tent-only Sites:** 20. **Hookups:** Electric (20, 30, 50 amps), water, sewer, cable TV. **Each Site:** Table; portable fire pits available. **Dump Station:** Yes. **Laundry:** Yes. **Pay Phone:** Yes. **Restrooms and Showers:** Yes. **Fuel:** Yes. **Propane:** Yes. **Internal Roads:** Gravel, good. **RV Service:** No. **Market:** Texaco mini-mart. **Restaurant:** On site and nearby. **General Store:** Yes. **Vending:** Yes. **Swimming:** At Wonderland Inn (motel) pool. **Playground:** No. **Other:** 13 sites have phone (modem) hookup, RV/car wash. **Activities:** 4WD & fishing tours. **Nearby Attractions:** Capitol Reef, Boulder Mountains, Escalante. **Additional Information:** Capitol Reef Country, (800) 858-7951, (435) 425-3365, www.capitolreef.org; Wayne County Travel Council, (800) 858-7159.

RESTRICTIONS

Pets: On leash. **Fires:** In fire pit only. **Alcoholic Beverages:** Allowed. **Vehicle Maximum Length:** 72 ft.

TO GET THERE

At the junction of Utah 12 & UT 24, enter across the street from Texaco station.

VERNAL — MAP, B-3
Red Fleet State Park

reserve america

8750 North Hwy. 191, 84078-7801.
T: (435) 789-4432; www.reserveamerica.com.

🚐 ★★★★   ⛺ ★★★★

Beauty: ★★★	Site Privacy: ★★★
Spaciousness: ★★★	Quiet: ★★★★
Security: ★★★★	Cleanliness: ★★★★
Insect Control: ★★★	Facilities: ★★★★

Nestled among scenic red slick-rock formations, Red Fleet Reservoir offers excellent boating and year-round fishing. This picturesque state park is located 10 miles north of Vernal just off Highway 191. It's a great base for exploring nearby Dinosaur National Monument, Utah Field House of Natural History Museum, and Flaming Gorge National Recreation Area. Dinosaurs inhabited the land in and around present day Vernal. Red Fleet State Park is home of numerous dinosaur tracks. These tracks are believed to be more than 200 million years old. Paleontologists can tell from these tracks preserved in Navajo sandstone that the dinosaurs were three-toed (tridactyl) and walked on two legs (bipedal). The tracks range from three to 17 inches. A second site of about 40 dinosaur tracks of four to five inches, in the more recent Carmel Formation, has been found in the area, however, the species has not yet been identified. The tracks can be reached by hiking a 1.25-mile trail that is somewhat strenuous because of its several uphill and downhill sections. The best viewing times of the tracks are early morning or late afternoon. The tracks are somewhat difficult to see when the sun is directly overhead.

BASICS

Operated By: Utah State Parks. **Open:** Apr. 15–Oct. 16. **Site Assignment:** Reservations can be made up to 16 weeks in advance. **Registration:** At office. **Fee:** Single, $12–$18. **Parking:** 1 vehicle per site; additional vehicle fee, half of nightly camping fee w/ the exception of $8 camp sites (fee is $8).

FACILITIES

Number of Multipurpose Sites: 25. **Hookups:** None. **Dump Station:** Yes. **Laundry:** No. **Pay Phone:** No. **Restrooms and Showers:** Yes. **Fuel:** No. **Propane:** No. **Internal Roads:** Paved. **RV Service:** Yes. **Market:** No. **Restaurant:** No. **General Store:** No. **Vending:** No. **Swimming:** Yes. **Playground:** No. **Other:** Vehicle length refers to the length of the trailer that will fit in the site allowing additional space for a tow vehicle. **Activities:** Boating, kayaking, canoeing, sailing, fishing, ice fishing, picnicking, swimming, hiking, wildlife. **Nearby Attractions:** ORV area.

RESTRICTIONS

Pets: On a 6-ft. leash, never unattended, cleaned up after. Not allowed in buildings, on beaches, in lakes or reservoirs. **Fires:** In fire rings, stoves, grills, or fireplaces provided for that purpose. Be sure your fire is completely extinguished before leaving. Do not leave your fire unattended. **Alcoholic Beverages:**

Allowed w/in state parks, except for visitor centers, museums, & administrative offices. **Vehicle Maximum Length:** 30 ft.

TO GET THERE

Take I-80 east to UT 40 to Heber. Travel through Heber on this road past Duchesne and Roosevelt and on into Vernal. In Vernal, travel on UT 40 (Main St.), to Vernal Ave. (UT 191). Turn left at Vernal Ave. The park is located 13 mi. north of Vernal off UT 191.

VERNAL   MAP, B-3
Steinaker Group Areas

4335 North Hwy. 191, 84078-7800.
T: (435) 789-4432; www.reserveamerica.com.

🚐 ★★★★   ▲ ★★★★

Beauty: ★★★★	Site Privacy: ★★★
Spaciousness: ★★★	Quiet: ★★★★
Security: ★★★★	Cleanliness: ★★★★
Insect Control: ★★★	Facilities: ★★★

Sandy beaches, swimming, boating, and waterskiing top the list of activities at Steinaker. Anglers enjoy fishing year-round for rainbow trout and largemouth bass. Located in the heart of Dinosaurland, the park is 7 miles north of Vernal, just off Utah 191 in northeastern Utah. Off-highway vehicle riding areas are nearby. In addition to its obvious attractions for water recreation, Steinaker State Park is located in a region well known to geologists, historians, and collectors of artifacts. Fossilized relics once found in ancient seas such as oysters, clams, and other shellfish are found here. Steinaker's convenient location makes it a popular base for exploring the many attractions of Dinosaurland in northeast Utah or the Flaming Gorge National Recreation Area to the north. Steinaker Reservoir is an unusual water storage facility. A canal from a diversion dam on Ashley Creek several miles to the west supplies the reservoir. One of the first units to be constructed in the vast Central Utah Project, Steinaker Reservoir stores runoff water from Ashley Creek to provide irrigation water to the Ashley Valley. The area is named for General William H. Ashley, famous for his leadership in the fur trade in the West in the 1820s and 1830s.

BASICS

Operated By: Utah State Parks. **Open:** Apr. 15–Oct. 15. **Site Assignment:** Group reservations are accepted up to 11 months in advance. **Registration:** At office. **Fee:** Group, $75; day use, $50. **Parking:** At site.

FACILITIES

Hookups: None. **Dump Station:** Yes. **Laundry:** No. **Pay Phone:** No. **Restrooms and Showers:** Yes. **Fuel:** No. **Propane:** No. **Internal Roads:** Paved. **RV Service:** Yes. **Market:** No. **Restaurant:** No. **General Store:** No. **Vending:** No. **Swimming:** Yes. **Playground:** No. **Activities:** Boating, fishing, hiking, picnicking, scenic views, sports activities, swimming.

RESTRICTIONS

Pets: On a 6-ft. leash, never unattended, cleaned up after. Not allowed in buildings, on beaches, in lakes or reservoirs. **Fires:** In fire rings, stoves, grills, or fireplaces provided for that purpose. Be sure your fire is completely extinguished before leaving. Do not leave your fire unattended. **Alcoholic Beverages:** Allowed w/in state parks, except for visitor centers, museums, & administrative offices. **Vehicle Maximum Length:** 40 ft.

TO GET THERE

Take I-80 east to US 40 to Heber City. Travel through Heber on this road through Duchesne and Roosevelt and into Vernal. From Vernal, travel on US 40 (Main St.) to Vernal Ave. (Hwy. 191). Turn left and follow 7 mi. to the park.

VERNAL   MAP, B-3
Steinaker State Park

reserve america

4335 North Hwy. 191, 84078-7800.
T: (435) 789-4432; www.reserveamerica.com.

🚐 ★★★★   ▲ ★★★★

Beauty: ★★★★	Site Privacy: ★★★
Spaciousness: ★★★	Quiet: ★★★★
Security: ★★★★	Cleanliness: ★★★★
Insect Control: ★★★	Facilities: ★★★

Sandy beaches, swimming, boating, and waterskiing top the list of activities at Steinaker. Anglers enjoy fishing year-round for rainbow trout and large-mouth bass. Located in the heart of Dinosaurland, the park is 7 miles north of Vernal, just off Utah 191 in northeastern Utah. ORV riding areas are nearby. In addition to its obvious attractions for water recreation, Steinaker State Park is located in a region well known to geologists, historians and collectors of artifacts. Fossilized relics once found in ancient seas such as oysters, clams, and other shellfish are found here. Steinaker's convenient location makes it a popular base for exploring the many attractions of Dinosaurland in northeast Utah or the Flaming Gorge National Recreation Area to the north. Steinaker Reservoir is an unusual water storage facility. A canal from a diversion dam on Ashley Creek several miles to the west supplies the reservoir. One of the first units to be constructed in the vast Central Utah Project, Steinaker Reservoir stores runoff water from Ashley Creek to provide irrigation water to the Ashley Valley. The area is named for General William H. Ashley, famous for his leadership in the fur trade in the West in the 1820s and 1830s.

BASICS

Operated By: Utah State Parks. **Open:** Apr. 15–Oct. 16. **Site Assignment:** Reservations can be made up to 16 weeks in advance. **Registration:** At office. **Fee:** Single, $12; double, $24. **Parking:** 1 vehicle per site; additional vehicle fee, half of nightly camping fee w/ the exception of $8 camp sites (fee is $8).

FACILITIES

Number of Multipurpose Sites: 25. **Hookups:**

None. **Dump Station:** Yes. **Laundry:** No. **Pay Phone:** No. **Restrooms and Showers:** No. **Fuel:** No. **Propane:** No. **Internal Roads:** Paved. **RV Service:** Yes. **Market:** No. **Restaurant:** No. **General Store:** No. **Vending:** No. **Swimming:** Yes. **Playground:** No. **Other:** Must bring your own firewood. **Activities:** Boating, kayaking, canoeing, sailing, fishing, ice fishing, picnicking, swimming, wildlife. **Nearby Attractions:** ORV area.

RESTRICTIONS

Pets: On a 6-ft. leash, never unattended, cleaned up after. Not allowed in buildings, on beaches, in lakes or reservoirs. **Fires:** In fire rings, stoves, grills, or fireplaces provided for that purpose. Be sure your fire is completely extinguished before leaving. Do not leave your fire unattended. **Alcoholic Beverages:** Allowed w/in state parks, except for visitor centers, museums, & administrative offices. **Vehicle Maximum Length:** 35 ft.

TO GET THERE

Take I-80 east to US 40 to Heber City. Travel through Heber on this road through Duchesne and Roosevelt and into Vernal. From Vernal, travel on US 40 (Main St.), to Vernal Ave. (Hwy. 191). Turn left and follow 7 mi. to the park.

VIRGIN   MAP, D-1
Zion River Resort RV Park and Campground

reserve america

730 East Hwy. 9, P.O. Box 790219, 84779.
T: (435) 635-8594 or (888) 822-8594;
www.zionriverresort.com

🚐 ★★★★   ▲ ★★★

Beauty: ★★★★	Site Privacy: ★★★★
Spaciousness: ★★★★	Quiet: ★★★
Security: ★★★★	Cleanliness: ★★★★★
Insect Control: ★★★	Facilities: ★★★★

With spacious pull-through sites able to handle double sliders, Zion River Resort is the place for big rigs. Even though winter night temperatures drop a few degrees below freezing, snowbirds flock here from November to March for the Zion mountain views through the surrounding trees. A well-stocked office store adds convenience, and there are enough amenities, including coin-operated video games, a pool table, and big-screen TV, to keep children occupied. Tent sites 123–131 are alongside the Virgin River, while sites 118–122 are roadside. The RV sites closest to the cottonwood tree–lined Virgin River Walk are back-ins numbered 48–73 and 88–99. Budget campers will probably want to go elsewhere, as the fine facilities do not come cheap. Others will prefer camping inside Zion National Park itself, sacrificing amenities for a forested setting and closeness to park sites. Only Zion Canyon Campground in Springdale, just outside the Zion National Park entrance, offers comparable amenities.

BASICS

Operated By: Robert, Todd, and Ron Smith. **Open:** All year. **Site Assignment:** First come, first served;

reservations accepted. **Registration:** At office. **Fee:** RV, $39–$47; tent, $32; V, MC, AE, D. **Parking:** At site.

FACILITIES

Number of RV-only Sites: 110. **Number of Tent-only Sites:** 9. **Hookups:** Electric (30, 50 amps), water, sewer, phone (modem). **Each Site:** Table, grill. **Dump Station:** No. **Laundry:** Yes. **Pay Phone:** Yes. **Restrooms and Showers:** Yes. **Fuel:** No. **Propane:** Yes. **Internal Roads:** Paved, excellent. **RV Service:** No. **Market:** 6 mi. **Restaurant:** 6 mi. **General Store:** Yes. **Vending:** No. **Swimming:** Pool. **Playground:** Yes. **Other:** Cabins, teepees, whirlpool, volleyball, badminton, pet exercise area, theater. **Activities:** Biking, horseback riding, golf, river tubing, ATV rides, rock climbing. **Nearby Attractions:** Zion National Park. **Additional Information:** Washington County Travel Bureau, (435) 634-5747, (800) 869-6635.

RESTRICTIONS

Pets: On leash (not allowed w/ tents). **Fires:** Charcoal or wood, in fire rings only. **Alcoholic Beverages:** Allowed. **Vehicle Maximum Length:** 72 ft. **Other:** No firearms, fireworks, or RV storage.

TO GET THERE

From US I-15 8 mi. north of St. George go east 18 mi. on UT 9.

WILLARD
Willard Bay State Park

MAP, A-2

reserve america

900 West 650 North Box A, 84340.
T: (435) 734-9494 or (800) 322-3770;
www.reserveamerica.com.

🚐 ★★★★	⛺ ★★★★
Beauty: ★★★★	Site Privacy: ★★★★
Spaciousness: ★★★★	Quiet: ★★★
Security: ★★★★	Cleanliness: ★★★★
Insect Control: ★★★★	Facilities: ★★★

About 12 miles north of Ogden and 35 miles north of Salt Lake City, Willard Bay has a more primitive tree-shaded grassy South Marina camping area favored by fishermen in the South Recreation Area (US I-15 Exit 354) and two more developed campgrounds 5 miles north in the North Recreation Area (US I-15 Exit 360). In the North, Cottonwood Campground has hookups, gray soil, and cottonwood trees for shade; sites 1–3, 10, 17, and 19–23 get the most highway noise. Willow Creek Campground lacks hookups but has a creek running through the campground, a pond, and sites tucked away in deep arbors of vegetation resembling coastal rainforest more than the arid grasslands and sage surrounding this Great Salt Lake floodplain. Willow Creek sites 10–35 have the best water views; sites 3–9 are nearest the pond. The bird refuge is a big attraction, and traffic picks up in January when the bald eagles start arriving.

BASICS

Operated By: Utah State Parks. **Open:** All year. **Site Assignment:** First come, first served; reservations recommended for weekends & holidays, can be made 120 days in advance. **Registration:** At entrance kiosk. **Fee:** $14–$20; cash, check. **Parking:** At site.

FACILITIES

Number of RV-only Sites: 101. **Hookups:** Electric (30 amps), water, sewer (Cotton Campground only). **Each Site:** Table, grill or fire ring. **Dump Station:** Yes. **Laundry:** No. **Pay Phone:** No. **Restrooms and Showers:** Yes. **Fuel:** No. **Propane:** No. **Internal Roads:** Paved, excellent. **RV Service:** No. **Market:** Ogden, 12 mi. **Restaurant:** Willard, 1 mi. **General Store:** No. **Vending:** No. **Swimming:** Beach. **Playground:** No. **Other:** 3 boat launch ramps. **Activities:** Fishing, bird-watching, boating. **Nearby Attractions:** Great Salt Lake. **Additional Information:** Golden Spike Empire, (801) 627-8288, www.ogdencvb.org.

RESTRICTIONS

Pets: On leash under owner's control (not allowed in public buildings). **Fires:** In fire pits & grills. **Alcoholic Beverages:** Allowed (if over 21 years). **Vehicle Maximum Length:** 53 ft. **Other:** ORVs & firearms prohibited; 14-day stay limit.

TO GET THERE

From US I-15 follow signs from Exit 360 into north campgrounds; take Exit 354 for more primitive south campground.

Vermont

Since its modern discovery by Samuel de Champlain in 1609, not much has changed with regard to the natural beauty, awe-inspiring expansiveness, and fierce independence that makes Les Verts Monts, or Vermont, the true outdoorsperson's destination. When folks think of Vermont, they think of the outdoors.

It's difficult not to picture any part of the state without seeing trees, undeveloped space, mountains, and water. That reputation is deserved, as the 14th state has enormous amounts of unpopulated terrain. There are forests, mountains, lakes, and a seemingly endless amount of land, making this one of the most impressive states in the nation for roughing it.

Camping in Vermont is fairly popular with residents and visitors alike, and most campers in the state go out of their way to brush up with nature. Though there are some super-developed commercial campgrounds, as with any state that hosts traveling enthusiasts, most suggest outdoor activities as the prime appeal. Even at the big RV parks with pools, rec halls, and other amenities, it's very rare that excellent hiking and natural places to swim aren't nearby.

The Green Mountain State also has a large number of state-run campgrounds, most of which—no surprise to the rugged outdoorsperson—are bare-bones facilities. For the most part, they accommodate RVs but offer no hookups and minimal amenities. What these sites lack in contemporary amenities they more than make for with ample offerings of nature at its best. The state has secured and maintained an enormous amount of public land, all of which remains undeveloped and will more than likely stay that way, as Vermont takes its nature seriously.

The bustling metropolis in Vermont is a myth. Even the "big" cities in the state are relatively small, and Boston is a sizable trek away. Vermont, as with any state unfazed by the gamble of urban sprawl, does have lots of little towns that have retained their folksy charm and interesting local residents for generations. The state is also so large that many areas don't get a lot of tourists, making them ideal spots to visit if you're looking to stay off the beaten path.

Even in many of its larger towns, Vermont does have an astounding amount of antiques and curiosity shops. Small cities like historic **Brattleboro** offer more than enough for a day's worth of browsing by even the most finicky of secondhand shoppers, and many have regional theaters or small concert venues to complement the cities' daily diversions.

In the winter months, Vermont is home to some of the best snow-oriented activities in the country, namely skiing. There are campgrounds affiliated with or near to some of the state's 16 skiable mountains, though you'd have to be pretty hearty to camp in a tent during the dead of winter. Snowshoeing fanatics, snowboarding hobbiests, and cross-country trainers will all be wowed by the state's diverse and accommodating topography.

Vermont is not slack either in the wonderful oddities department. Those interested in the back roads and all things unique to the state will be impressed. For example, a day trip to **Knight's Spider Web Farm** in **Williamston** would not be out of the question. In Barre, the world's largest quarry yawns its gigantic jaw out of the earth at **Rock of Ages.** Young hikers who just can't seem to part with their well-worn trail shoes might be inclined to enter Montpelier's **International Rotten Sneaker Contest** held every March. Because most everybody has a sweet tooth for ice cream now and again, **Ben and Jerry's Flavor Graveyard** in Waterbury is a bizarre and serious memorial to the tastes once offered by the New England–based confectioner but that now rest in peace—the flavors left only to the imagination. In a nutshell, Vermont offers an array of individualistic charm and traditional camping with almost endless sites to choose from. Simply hiking all the trails in the state would take years, and canoeing all the rivers, climbing all the mountains, and fishing every lake would take a lifetime. Perhaps that's why many extreme outdoors enthusiasts now call Vermont their home.

Campground Profiles

ADDISON D.A.R.
MAP, B-1

6750 Hwy. 17W, 05491.
T: (802) 759-2354 or (888) 409-7579;
www.vtstateparks.com.

🚐 ★★★   ⛺ ★★★★

Beauty: ★★★★   Site Privacy: ★★★
Spaciousness: ★★★★   Quiet: ★★★
Security: ★★★   Cleanliness: ★★★★
Insect Control: ★★★   Facilities: ★★

If you're looking for a no-frills, economical base to explore the southern end of Lake Champlain, check into this state park. The 95-acre parcel of land, once open farmland and meadow, was donated by the Daughters of the American Revolution in 1955. (The DAR operates the museum located next to the park.) The campground features open, expansive fields. Campers have impressive views of the lake and the Adirondacks in the distance. Most sites are set in the open, though a few are situated in a stand of hickory trees, if you prefer the shade. A stone pavilion and picnic area sit on a bluff overlooking the lake; this is a popular place to hang out, have dinner, and relax. Be sure to check out the old building foundations next to the picnic area. These are remnants of the first English settlers in the area in 1765. Note: If you'd like a few more facilities, Button Bay State Park in Vergennes has boat rentals and nature trails. The nearby privately owned Ten Acres campground has a pool, trailer rentals, laundry, and planned activities.

BASICS
Operated By: State of Vermont. **Open:** Late May–Labor Day. **Site Assignment:** Reservations may be made up to 11 months in advance; 2-night min. required; reservations accepted at (888) 409-7579; contact park directly only for reservations w/in 10 days of stay; no refunds for 2-night min. **Registration:** At office. **Fee:** $14; lean-tos, $21; V, MC. **Parking:** At site.

FACILITIES
Number of Multipurpose Sites: 70 (24 lean-tos). **Each Site:** Picnic table, fire ring. **Dump Station:** Yes. **Laundry:** No. **Pay Phone:** No. **Restrooms and Showers:** Yes (coin-op). **Fuel:** No. **Propane:** No. **Internal Roads:** Gravel (good). **RV Service:** No. **Market:** Vergennes, 13 mi. **Restaurant:** Vergennes, 13 mi. **General Store:** No. **Vending:** No. **Swimming:** No. **Playground:** No. **Other:** Picnic area, pavilion. **Nearby Attractions:** Boating, swimming, fishing, hiking, biking, Lake Champlain, Middlebury, Vergennes. **Additional Information:** Addison County, Vermont Chamber of Commerce, 2 Court St., Middlebury, VT 05753; (802) 388-7951. Lake Champlain Regional Chamber of Commerce, 60 Main Street, Suite 100, Burlington, VT 05401; (802) 863-3489 or (877) 686-5253; www.vermont.org.

RESTRICTIONS
Pets: On leash only. **Fires:** Fire pits, grills only. **Alcoholic Beverages:** At site.

TO GET THERE
From Vergennes, follow Hwy. 22A southwest 6 mi., then take Hwy. 17 southwest 7 mi.

ADDISON
Ten Acres Campground and RV Park
MAP, B-1

9 Ten Acre Dr., 05491. T: (802) 759-2662;
www.10acrescampground.com.

🚐 ★★★   ⛺ ★★★

Beauty: ★★★   Site Privacy: ★★★
Spaciousness: ★★★   Quiet: ★★★
Security: ★★★   Cleanliness: ★★★
Insect Control: ★★★   Facilities: ★★★

You'll find lots of seasonals at this campground, mostly anglers, with boats and gear in tow, who come to fish Lake Champlain. But on summer weekends, the campground fills with vacationing families, too, clamoring to be near the lake. The campground boasts 650 feet of Lake Champlain frontage, a rocky piece of shoreline on the southern tip. It's pretty to look at; unfortunately, there's no swimming access or beach area. There are docks and boat lifts for campers who bring their own watercraft. Kids have a small fishing pond to practice casting, catching, and releasing small fry. There's also a pool, recreation room, and sports equipment. Sites are ordinary, set in rows, with little privacy. Tenters have it better; they're located in a separate area next to a small creek.

BASICS
Operated By: Leanne Silber. **Open:** May–Oct. 15. **Site Assignment:** Reservations accepted; no deposit required. **Registration:** At office. **Fee:** Full hookup, $28; lean-to, $27; water/electric, $25; no hookup, $22; V, MC. **Parking:** At site.

FACILITIES
Number of RV-only Sites: 7. **Number of Tent-only Sites:** 84. **Number of Multipurpose Sites:** 8. **Hookups:** Electric (30 amps), water, sewer. **Each Site:** Picnic table, fire ring. **Dump Station:** Yes. **Laundry:** Yes. **Pay Phone:** No. **Restrooms and Showers:** Yes. **Fuel:** No. **Propane:** Yes. **Internal Roads:** Gravel (good). **RV Service:** Motor home refills. **Market:** Addison, 3 mi. **Restaurant:** Addison, 1 mi. **General Store:** Yes. **Vending:** No. **Swimming:** Pool. **Playground:** Yes. **Other:** Kiddie fishing pond, docks, boat lifts, trailer rentals. **Activities:** Swimming, fishing, shuffleboard, horseshoes, planned events. **Nearby Attractions:** Swimming, fishing, boating, hiking, biking, Lake Champlain, Vergennes, Middlebury. **Additional Information:** Addison County, Vermont Chamber of Commerce, 2 Court St., Middlebury, VT 05753; (802) 388-7951. Lake Champlain Regional Chamber of Commerce, 60 Main St., Suite 100, Burlington, VT 05401; (802) 863-3489 or (877) 686-5253; www.vermont.org.

RESTRICTIONS
Pets: On leash only. **Fires:** Fire pits, grills only. **Alcoholic Beverages:** At site. **Vehicle Maximum Length:** 40 ft.

TO GET THERE
Campground is located on Hwy. 125 in Addison, 1 mi. south of the bridge to New York & 15 mi. west of Middlebury.

ALBURG
Alburg RV Resort
MAP, A-1

P.O. Box 50, Blue Rock Rd., 05440-0050.
T: (802) 796-3733;
www.campvermont.com/html/cgs/
north/alburgrv.htm.

🚐 ★★★★   ⛺ ★

Beauty: ★★★★   Site Privacy: ★★★
Spaciousness: ★★★★   Quiet: ★★★
Security: ★★★   Cleanliness: ★★★
Insect Control: ★★★★   Facilities: ★★★★

Set on the shores of Lake Champlain, this park offers grassy sites laid out in a grid and nicely shaded with mature trees. If that sounds inviting, it is—especially the sandy beach that beckons sun-seekers and windsurfers. The city sights of Montreal are just 55 miles away. The park caters to Canadians, and you'll hear lots of Quebecois speech as you mingle around the pool (with a diving board) or hang out at the inviting rec hall (with a fireplace and pool table). If it seems as though everyone knows each other, you might be right; this park has a large number of guests who stay for the season. However, transient sites are sprinkled among them, and this well-maintained park is pleasant enough that it's worth seeking them out. Hint: Reserve early.

BASICS
Operated By: ATTP Co. **Open:** May 1–Oct. 1. **Site Assignment:** Early reservations required; 1-night deposit required; deposit refunded w/ 7-day notice. **Registration:** At office. **Fee:** $28–$30. **Parking:** At site.

FACILITIES
Number of Multipurpose Sites: 177. **Hookups:** Electric (20, 30, 50 amp), water, sewer. **Each Site:** Picnic table, fire ring. **Dump Station:** Yes. **Laundry:** Yes. **Pay Phone:** Yes. **Restrooms and Showers:** Yes, fee. **Fuel:** No. **Propane:** Yes. **Internal Roads:** Gravel. **RV Service:** No. **Market:** 11 mi. east, in Swanton. **Restaurant:** 8 mi. west, in Rouses Pt., NY. **General Store:** Yes. **Vending:** Yes. **Swimming:** Lake, pool. **Playground:** Yes. **Other:** Ball field, rec hall, shuffleboard, pool table, petanque court, sandy beach, pool, boat ramp. **Activities:** Swimming (lake & pool), boating, canoeing, waterskiing, windsurfing, fishing, softball, volleyball, basketball. **Nearby Attractions:** St. Anne's Shrine, Isle LaMotte. **Additional Information:** Lake Champlain Islands Chamber of Commerce; (802) 372-8400; www.champlainislands.com.

RESTRICTIONS
Pets: On leash only; must be quiet cleaned up after. **Fires:** In fire rings only. **Alcoholic Beverages:** At site. **Vehicle Maximum Length:** 45 ft. **Other:** No visitors allowed Sat., Sun., & holidays except for seasonal rentals.

TO GET THERE
From junction of US 2 and VT 78, go 2 mi. east on Hwy. 78, then 0.5 mi. south on Blue Rock Rd.

ANDOVER   MAP, C-2
Horseshoe Acres

1978 Weston Andover Rd., 05143.
T: (802) 875-2960.

🚐 ★★★   ▲ ★★★

Beauty: ★★★   Site Privacy: ★★★
Spaciousness: ★★★   Quiet: ★★★
Security: ★★★   Cleanliness: ★★★
Insect Control: ★★★   Facilities: ★★★

You'll find lots of seasonal RV sites at this bustling campground, but it's large enough (175 sites) to accommodate weekend and overnight visitors, too. There's usually lots going on here, from dances and potluck dinner get-togethers to group safari gatherings. Families tend to congregate around the swimming pool or head to the game room. A leisurely paddleboat ride on the pond is a nice way to start or end the day. Campsites are on the smallish side, with choice of shaded or open areas. There are more than 70 pull-through sites that are popular with campers with large RVs.

BASICS
Operated By: Gary and Lyn Hale. **Open:** Apr. 15–Dec. 1. **Site Assignment:** Reservations suggested at least 1 week in advance; 1-night deposit; 2-week cancellation policy. **Registration:** At office. **Fee:** $26–$30; V, MC, D. **Parking:** At site.

FACILITIES
Number of Tent-only Sites: 25. **Number of Multipurpose Sites:** 150. **Hookups:** Electric (30 amps), water, sewer, cable TV. **Each Site:** Picnic table, fire ring. **Dump Station:** Yes. **Laundry:** Yes. **Pay Phone:** Yes. **Restrooms and Showers:** Yes. **Fuel:** No. **Propane:** Yes. **Internal Roads:** Gravel (good). **RV Service:** No. **Market:** Springfield, 19 mi. **Restaurant:** Springfield, 19 mi. **General Store:** Yes. **Vending:** No. **Swimming:** Pool, pond. **Playground:** Yes. **Other:** Game room, arcade, safari field, dance hall, mini-golf, paddleboat rentals, trailer rentals. **Activities:** Swimming, boating, shuffleboard, badminton, volleyball. **Nearby Attractions:** Farms, antiques shops, hiking, biking, swimming, boating, Woodstock. **Additional Information:** Woodstock Area Chamber of Commerce, P.O. Box 486, 4 Central St., Woodstock, VT 05091; (802) 457-3555; www.woodstockvt.com.

RESTRICTIONS
Pets: On leash only. **Fires:** In fire pits & grills only. **Alcoholic Beverages:** At site.

TO GET THERE
Take I-91 Exit 6, then go north on Hwy. 103 to Chester. Follow Hwy. 11 west 4 mi., then go north on Andover-Weston Rd. 4 mi. to the campground.

ARLINGTON   MAP, D-1
Camping on the Battenkill

RD 2 Box 3310, Hwy. 7A, 05250.
T: (802) 375-6663 or (800) 830-6663;
www.campvermont.com/battenkill.

🚐 ★★★   ▲ ★★★★

Beauty: ★★★★   Site Privacy: ★★★★
Spaciousness: ★★★   Quiet: ★★★
Security: ★★★   Cleanliness: ★★★
Insect Control: ★★★   Facilities: ★★

The renowned Battenkill River draws anglers from around the country for some of the best trout fishing in the East. As you'd expect, this riverfront campground (yes, on the Battenkill!) is especially popular in the spring and fall when the fish are feeding. Come summer, there's swimming and tubing the river and die-hard angling. The campground boasts a pretty little swimming hole on the river, with smooth rocks and cold mountain waters. The campsites are woodsy and spacious, most with fine views of the surrounding mountains. Sites 13 and 14 are near the swimming beach and popular with families. You won't find many frills here (no game rooms, swimming pools, and such); nature takes front seat. That's exactly what makes this campground so appealing to some.

BASICS
Operated By: Pratt family. **Open:** Mid-Apr.–mid-Oct. **Site Assignment:** Reservations suggested; weekly rentals required July & Aug. for riverfront sites; $25 nonrefundable deposit; $50 nonrefundable deposit on holiday weekends. **Registration:** At office. **Fee:** $20–$28. **Parking:** At site.

FACILITIES
Number of RV-only Sites: 9. **Number of Tent-only Sites:** 11. **Number of Multipurpose Sites:** 80. **Hookups:** Electric (30, 50 amps), water, sewer, cable TV. **Each Site:** Picnic table, fire ring, trash can. **Dump Station:** Yes. **Laundry:** No. **Pay Phone:** Yes. **Restrooms and Showers:** Yes. **Fuel:** No. **Propane:** Yes. **Internal Roads:** Gravel, dirt (fair). **RV Service:** No. **Market:** Arlington, 0.75 mi. **Restaurant:** Arlington, 0.75 mi. **General Store:** Yes. **Vending:** No. **Swimming:** River. **Playground:** Yes. **Other:** Sports field, small beach. **Activities:** Swimming, fishing, river tubing. **Nearby Attractions:** Farms, antiques shops, swimming, fishing, boating, hiking, Arlington Village, Manchester, Bennington. **Additional Information:** Manchester the Mountains Chamber of Commerce, 5046 Main St. Suite 1, Manchester Center, VT 05255-3451; (802) 362-2100 or (800) 362-4144; www.manchestervermont.net. Bennington Area Chamber of Commerce, 100 Veterans Memorial Dr., Bennington, VT.

RESTRICTIONS
Pets: On leash only. **Fires:** In fire pits & grills only. **Alcoholic Beverages:** At site. **Vehicle Maximum Length:** 40 ft. **Other:** No motorcycles.

TO GET THERE
Campground is on historic Hwy. 7A, 0.5 mi. north of Arlington Village.

ASCUTNEY   MAP, C-2
Getaway Mountain Campground

P.O. Box 372, 05030. T: (802) 674-2812;
www.campvermont.com.

🚐 ★★★   ▲ ★★★

Beauty: ★★★   Site Privacy: ★★★
Spaciousness: ★★★   Quiet: ★★★
Security: ★★★   Cleanliness: ★★★★
Insect Control: ★★★   Facilities: ★★★

This quaint little campground with its own berry farm is a nice oasis for campers looking for a bit of peace and quiet. A row of open sites, including some seasonals, line the entrance road. Travel up the hill and you'll find a cluster of shaded, woodsy sites with a fair amount of privacy and space. Small trailers and RVs are the norm here (and usually fill the campground on summer and fall weekends) but there are tent-only sites set apart from the others. Campers spend lazy days picking berries at the farm or lounging near the pool area. Nearby, there's hiking at Mt. Ascutney and Wilgus State Park trails and boating on the Connecticut River.

BASICS
Operated By: Ellen, Dave Fraczek, and Jason Haber. **Open:** May–Oct. **Site Assignment:** Reservations accepted; 1-night deposit, 2-week cancellation policy unless site is re-rented. **Registration:** At office. **Fee:** $24; V, MC. **Parking:** At site.

FACILITIES
Number of RV-only Sites: 10. **Number of Tent-only Sites:** 55. **Hookups:** Electric (20, 30 amps), water, sewer. **Each Site:** Picnic table, fire ring. **Dump Station:** Yes. **Laundry:** Yes. **Pay Phone:** Yes. **Restrooms and Showers:** Yes. **Fuel:** No. **Propane:** Yes. **Internal Roads:** Gravel (good). **RV Service:** No. **Market:** Ascutney, 3 mi. **Restaurant:** Snack bar on site. **General Store:** Yes. **Vending:** No. **Swimming:** Pool. **Playground:** Yes. **Other:** Rec room, pick-your-own berry farm, hot tub rental. **Activities:** Swimming, berry picking, bonfires, hayrides. **Nearby Attractions:** Farms, antiques shops, hiking, biking, swimming, boating, fishing, Ascutney. **Additional Information:** Mount Ascutney Region, Chamber of Commerce, P.O. Box 5, Windsor, VT 05089; (802) 674-5910.

RESTRICTIONS
Pets: On leash only. **Fires:** In fire pits & grills only. **Alcoholic Beverages:** At site.

TO GET THERE
Take I-91 Exit 8, then follow Hwy. 5S 5 mi. to the campground.

ASCUTNEY   MAP, C-2
Running Bear Camping Area

6248 Hwy. 5, P.O. Box 378, 05030.
T: (802) 674-6417;
www.runningbearvermont.com.

🚐 ★★★   ⛺ ★★★

Beauty: ★★★   Site Privacy: ★★★
Spaciousness: ★★   Quiet: ★★★
Security: ★★★   Cleanliness: ★★★
Insect Control: ★★★   Facilities: ★★★

Yes, there are the expected wood-carved lawn bears dotting the landscape (including cute bear signs numbering each site) and a fair amount of seasonal campers who've decorated their own space. But you'll also find some woodsy sites tucked in the pines, a convenient location, and enough amenities (like a heated pool, and recreation room) to keep you comfortable. (Those who want a more rustic, back-to-nature experience should check into the area's state park campgrounds, including Ascutney State Park and Wilgus State Park.) The sites are a bit crowded for our taste. Tent sites C, D, E, and F, tucked in the pines, are the best. Avoid sites 11–14, which back up to a chain-link fence and receive a bit of highway noise. If you enjoy outdoor winter pursuits, like skiing, ice fishing, and snowmobiling, take note: This campground is open all year. In summer and fall, there's hiking at nearby Wilgus and Ascutney State Parks and canoeing on the Connecticut River.

BASICS

Operated By: Ross and Buffy Girard. **Open:** All year. **Site Assignment:** Reservations suggested; 7-day cancellation policy; 2-night min. on holidays, paid in advance, no refunds. **Registration:** At office. **Fee:** $25–$31; V, MC. **Parking:** At site.

FACILITIES

Number of RV-only Sites: 20. **Number of Tent-only Sites:** 45. **Number of Multipurpose Sites:** 22. **Hookups:** Electric (20, 30 amps), water, sewer, cable TV. **Each Site:** Picnic table, fire ring. **Dump Station:** Yes. **Laundry:** Yes. **Pay Phone:** Yes. **Restrooms and Showers:** Yes. **Fuel:** No. **Propane:** Yes. **Internal Roads:** Gravel (good). **RV Service:** No. **Market:** Windsor, 3 mi. **Restaurant:** Windsor, 3 mi. **General Store:** Yes. **Vending:** No. **Swimming:** Pool. **Playground:** Yes. **Other:** Rec hall, safari field, sports field. **Activities:** Swimming, horseshoes, badminton, basketball, baseball, hay rides. **Nearby Attractions:** Farms, hiking, biking, swimming, boating, fishing, skiing, snowmobiling, Mt. Ascutney. **Additional Information:** Mount Ascutney Region, Chamber of Commerce, P.O. Box 5, Windsor, VT 05089; (802) 674-5910.

RESTRICTIONS

Pets: On leash only. **Fires:** In fire pits & grills only. **Alcoholic Beverages:** At site.

TO GET THERE

Take I-91 Exit 8 to Hwy. 5N. Campground is 1 mi. on the left.

ASCUTNEY   MAP, C-2
Wilgus State Park

P.O. Box 196, 05030.
T: (802) 674-5422 or (888) 409-7579;
www.vtstateparks.com.

🚐 ★★★   ⛺ ★★★★

Beauty: ★★★★   Site Privacy: ★★★★
Spaciousness: ★★★★   Quiet: ★★★
Security: ★★★   Cleanliness: ★★★★
Insect Control: ★★★   Facilities: ★★

If you like the sound of running water, you'll like the rustic sites at this small state campground on the banks of the Connecticut River in south-central Vermont. The campground is popular with anglers and canoeists (canoe-camping groups often congregate in the group camping and picnic area) who enjoy the direct river access. We like the large stone fireplace in the open-sided lodge area, reminiscent of national park venues. The campground, built by the CCC in the 1930s, has spacious sites overlooking or on the banks of the river, nature trails, and coin-op hot showers. Pretty, quiet (except for an occasional rowdy group), and clean.

BASICS

Operated By: State of Vermont. **Open:** May 26–Oct. 9. **Site Assignment:** Reservations may be made up to 11 months in advance; 2-night min. required; reservations accepted at (888) 409-7579; contact park directly only for reservations w/in 10 days of stay; no refunds for 2-night min. **Registration:** At office. **Fee:** $14–$23; V, MC. **Parking:** At site.

FACILITIES

Number of Multipurpose Sites: 19 (6 lean-tos). **Each Site:** Picnic table, fire ring. **Dump Station:** Yes. **Laundry:** No. **Pay Phone:** Yes. **Restrooms and Showers:** Yes (coin-op). **Fuel:** No. **Propane:** No. **Internal Roads:** Gravel, dirt (good). **RV Service:** No. **Market:** Ascutney, 3 mi. **Restaurant:** Ascutney, 3 mi. **General Store:** No. **Vending:** Yes. **Swimming:** River. **Playground:** Yes. **Other:** Canoe & rowboat rentals, picnic area, nature trails. **Activities:** Swimming, boating, fishing, hiking, volleyball. **Nearby Attractions:** Farms, antiques shops, hiking, biking, boating, fishing, Mt. Ascutney. **Additional Information:** Mount Ascutney Region, Chamber of Commerce, P.O. Box 5, Windsor, VT 05089; (802) 674-5910.

RESTRICTIONS

Pets: On leash only. **Fires:** In fire pits & grills only. **Alcoholic Beverages:** At site. **Other:** No generators allowed.

TO GET THERE

Take I-91 Exit 8; the campground is 1.5 mi. south on Hwy. 5.

BARTON   MAP, A-2
Belview Campground

Hwy. 16E, P.O. Box 222, 05822. T: (802) 525-3242;
www.belviewcampground.com.

🚐 ★★★★   ⛺ ★

Beauty: ★★★   Site Privacy: ★★
Spaciousness: ★★★★   Quiet: ★★★★
Security: ★★★   Cleanliness: ★★★
Insect Control: ★★   Facilities: ★★★

Located in Vermont's beautiful Northeast Kingdom, this campground has a homey feel. The wreaths in the restrooms are one clue that the owners treat the place like their own home. "We used to get lots of families, but the kids grew up!" says owner Joyce Morse, noting that lots of grandkids show up on weekends. Still, Belview Campground tends to be a quiet getaway, with the benefit of close proximity to Crystal Lake (a five-minute walk) and access to a swimming beach. Sites are set in semi-circles, with the most desirable spots being site 31, with full hookups located near the pathway to the public beach, and 27, where, if you're tenting, you can hear the nearby brook as you drift off to sleep. There's plenty of water around here, including May Pond (fine for nonmotorized boating), three lakes, and several rivers. There's also plenty of golf in the area and wonderful mountain biking, thanks to the Kingdom Trails system.

BASICS

Operated By: Bob and Joyce Morse. **Open:** Mid-May–mid-Oct. **Site Assignment:** Reservations recommended; reserve as soon as you know and 50% of total w/in 1 week. **Registration:** At office. **Fee:** $18–$26; checks, no credit cards. **Parking:** At site.

FACILITIES

Number of RV-only Sites: 2. **Number of Multipurpose Sites:** 50. **Hookups:** Electric, water, sewer, some cable TV. **Each Site:** Picnic table, fire ring. **Dump Station:** Yes. **Laundry:** No. **Pay Phone:** No. **Restrooms and Showers:** Yes, fee. **Fuel:** No. **Propane:** No. **Internal Roads:** Gravel. **RV Service:** No. **Market:** 0.5 mi. west, in village. **Restaurant:** 0.5 mi. west, in village. **General Store:** No. **Vending:** No. **Swimming:** Lake (5-min. walk). **Playground:** No. **Other:** Playing field. **Activities:** Potluck dinners, lake swimming & boating/boat rentals (nearby). **Nearby Attractions:** Crystal Lake State Park, 4 18-hole golf courses, Kingdom Trails mountain biking, hiking, country stores. **Additional Information:** Northeast Kingdom Travel & Tourism Assoc.; (800) 884-8001; www.travelthekingdom.com.

RESTRICTIONS

Pets: Allowed. **Fires:** In fire rings only. **Alcoholic Beverages:** At site. **Vehicle Maximum Length:** 40 ft.

TO GET THERE

From I-91, take Exit 25. Heading east, go 1 mi. into the village, bear right on Hwy. 5S 0.5 mi., then turn left over railroad tracks onto Hwy. 16E. Campground is 0.5 mi. on right just before the road heads uphill.

BETHEL   MAP, C-2
Silver Lake State Park

P.O. Box 67, 214 North Rd., 05031.
T: (802) 234-9451 (summer) or (888) 409-7579;
www.vtstateparks.com.

🚐 ★★★   ⛺ ★★★

Beauty: ★★★★	Site Privacy: ★★★★
Spaciousness: ★★★★	Quiet: ★★★★
Security: ★★★	Cleanliness: ★★★★
Insect Control: ★★★	Facilities: ★★★

This low-key, pleasant state campground is popular with summer day visitors and water-loving campers. Pretty Silver Lake, ringed with trees, is a great place to paddle a canoe or rowboat. You'll find boat rentals at the grassy, open picnic area, as well as a nice swimming area and beach that are perfect spots to cool off on hot summer days. The lake is also known for good fishing. The campground boasts 1,200 feet of shore frontage, but sites are tucked off the shoreline and into the woods. There are three campsite loops, all offering woodsy, shaded sites with lots of elbow room and privacy.

BASICS

Operated By: Vermont Agency of Natural Resources, Dept. of Forests, Parks and Recreation. **Open:** May 26–Sept. 4. **Site Assignment:** Reservations may be made up to 11 months in advance; 2-night min. required; reservations accepted at (888) 409-7579; contact park directly only for reservations w/in 10 days of stay; no refunds for the 2-night min. **Registration:** At office. **Fee:** $16; lean-to, $23; V, MC. **Parking:** At site.

FACILITIES

Number of Multipurpose Sites: 40 (7 lean-tos). **Each Site:** Picnic table, fire ring. **Dump Station:** Yes. **Laundry:** No. **Pay Phone:** Yes. **Restrooms and Showers:** Yes (coin-op). **Fuel:** No. **Propane:** No. **Internal Roads:** Gravel, paved (good). **RV Service:** No. **Market:** Barnard, 1 mi. **Restaurant:** Snack bar on site. **General Store:** Yes. **Vending:** No. **Swimming:** Lake. **Playground:** Yes. **Other:** Picnic area, beach, boat rentals, volleyball, nature center. **Activities:** Swimming, boating, fishing (VT license needed), lake swimming, campfire programs. **Nearby Attractions:** Antiques shops, hiking, biking, boating, fishing, swimming, Woodstock, Marsh-Billings National Park, Vermont Institute of Natural Science Raptor Center, Billings Farm & Museum, Rock of Ages granite quarry, Quechee Gorge. **Additional Information:** Woodstock Area Chamber of Commerce, 18 Central St., P.O. Box 486-4, Woodstock, VT 05091; (802) 457-3555; www.woodstockvt.com.

RESTRICTIONS

Pets: On leash only, cleaned up after, in camping area only. Proof of current rabies vaccination required. **Fires:** In fire pits & grills, at site only. **Alcoholic Beverages:** At site; intoxication not permitted. No containers larger than 1 gallon permitted. **Vehicle Maximum Length:** 34 ft.

TO GET THERE

In Barnard Village, turn onto North Rd. from VT 12. Park is 0.25 mi. on right.

BRANDON   MAP, C-1
Smokerise Family Campground

2145 Grove St., 05733. T: (802) 247-6984.

🚐 ★★★   ⛺ ★★

Beauty: ★★★	Site Privacy: ★★★
Spaciousness: ★★★	Quiet: ★★★
Security: ★★★	Cleanliness: ★★★
Insect Control: ★★★	Facilities: ★★★

This small, basic campground, smack in the middle between Middlebury and Rutland, is a convenient location for those exploring central Vermont. On-site facilities are sparse, but there is a pool and plenty of fields and sports equipment for traveling families. Most campers use this property as an overnight or weekend base. Large fields help the campground seem more open and spacious, though the sites are average to small in size. Large-rig campers prefer the open sites near the road, with full hookups. Not much privacy, but the sites are level and easy to drive in and out of. There's a choice of shaded sites, too; we like sites 22, 24, and 25 for their added privacy. A clean, quite adequate place to call home on the road.

BASICS

Operated By: Mel and Bea Cousino. **Open:** Mid-May–mid-Oct. **Site Assignment:** Reservations accepted; no deposit required. **Registration:** At office. **Fee:** Full hookup, $25; water/electric, $20; no hookup, $15; No credit cards. **Parking:** At site.

FACILITIES

Number of RV-only Sites: Undesignated sites. **Number of Tent-only Sites:** 23. **Number of Multipurpose Sites:** 36. **Hookups:** Electric (20, 30 amps), water, sewer. **Each Site:** Picnic table, fire ring. **Dump Station:** Yes. **Laundry:** Yes. **Pay Phone:** Yes. **Restrooms and Showers:** Yes. **Fuel:** No. **Propane:** Yes. **Internal Roads:** Gravel (good). **RV Service:** No. **Market:** Middlebury, 12 mi. **Restaurant:** On-site. **General Store:** Yes. **Vending:** No. **Swimming:** Pool. **Playground:** Yes. **Other:** Sports fields. **Activities:** Swimming, volleyball, basketball, shuffleboard, horseshoes, badminton, tetherball. **Nearby Attractions:** Farms, antiques shops, biking, hiking, boating, fishing, Rutland, Middlebury. **Additional Information:** Brandon Area Chamber of Commerce, Brandon Information Center, Hwy. 7, P.O. Box 267, Brandon, VT 05733; (802) 247-6401. Rutland Region Chamber of Commerce, 256 North Main St., Rutland, VT 05701; (802)773-2747; www.rutlandvermont.com.

RESTRICTIONS

Pets: On leash only. **Fires:** In fire pits & grills only. **Alcoholic Beverages:** At site.

TO GET THERE

Campground is located on Hwy. 7, 17 mi. north of Rutland and 12 mi. south of Middlebury.

BRATTLEBORO   MAP, D-2
Fort Dummer State Park

517 Old Guilford Rd., 05301.
T: (802) 254-2610 (summer) or (800) 299-3071; www.vtstateparks.com.

🚐 ★★★   ⛺ ★★★★

Beauty: ★★★	Site Privacy: ★★★★
Spaciousness: ★★★★	Quiet: ★★★★
Security: ★★★	Cleanliness: ★★★
Insect Control: ★★★	Facilities: ★★

Looking for a quiet, private spot to get away from it all? This woodsy state campground is located just minutes from downtown Brattleboro, but worlds away. Nestled in the southern foothills of the Green Mountains, this campground is perfect for anyone who wants lots of space and back-to-nature surroundings. Sites are large, ringed with trees for added privacy, and set in three loops cut out of the forest. The park was named after Fort Dummer, the first white settlement in Vermont, and overlooks the fort site. There are two small hiking trails at the campground but, alas, no water hole for swimming. You'll have to head to the nearby Townshend Dam and Reservoir for that.

BASICS

Operated By: State of Vermont. **Open:** Apr. 16–Oct. 30. **Site Assignment:** Reservations may be made up to 11 months in advance; 2-night min. required; reservations accepted at (888) 409-7579; contact park directly only for reservations w/in 10 days of stay; no refunds for the 2-night min. **Registration:** At office. **Fee:** No hookup, $14; lean-tos, $21; V, MC. **Parking:** At site.

FACILITIES

Number of Multipurpose Sites: 51 (10 lean-tos). **Each Site:** Picnic table, fire ring. **Dump Station:** Yes. **Laundry:** No. **Pay Phone:** No. **Restrooms and Showers:** Yes. **Fuel:** No. **Propane:** No. **Internal Roads:** Gravel, dirt (good). **RV Service:** No. **Market:** Brattleboro, 2 mi. **Restaurant:** Brattleboro, 2 mi. **General Store:** Brattleboro, 2 mi. **Vending:** Yes. **Swimming:** No. **Playground:** No. **Other:** Fort site, hiking trails. **Activities:** Hiking, biking. **Nearby Attractions:** Farms, antiques shops, swimming, boating, hiking, biking, fishing, Brattleboro, Mt. Snow. **Additional Information:** Brattleboro Area Chamber of Commerce, 180 Main St., Brattleboro, VT 05301; (802) 254-4565; www.brattleborochamber.org.

RESTRICTIONS

Pets: On leash only. **Fires:** In fire pits & grills only. **Alcoholic Beverages:** At site.

TO GET THERE

Take I-91, Exit 1, follow signs to state park.

DANVILLE   MAP, B-2, B-3
Sugar Ridge RV Village and Campground

24 Old Stage Coach Rd., Hwy. 2, 05828.
T: (802) 684-2550; www.sugarridgervpark.com.

🚐 ★★★★   ⛺ ★★★★

Beauty: ★★★	Site Privacy: ★★★
Spaciousness: ★★★	Quiet: ★★
Security: ★★★★	Cleanliness: ★★★
Insect Control: ★★★	Facilities: ★★★★

If you like your campgrounds with all the trimmings, this place will definitely appeal to you. The first thing you'll notice as you drive in is the 18-hole mini-golf course right out in front. Then there's the camp store and office, built of logs harvested here—big and multileveled, with little departments set up for fixing s'mores, camp furniture, and the like. Everything here is shiny and modern, created with family fun in mind, from the Belgian-drawn wagon rides to swimming lessons, tennis courts, and hiking trails. Sugar Ridge seems more resort than campground. Yes, it's a lively scene, but happily they've sent the no-hookup (tenting) sites at the far southern edge of the property, abutting woods and hiking trails (mini-golf and Hwy. 2 are at the other end) and somewhat protected from the bustle. Among the full-hookup sites, ST11–ST33 (odd numbers), are most popular and near the pools, tennis, courts and rec hall, but we'd go for H102, 104, 106, or 108, nudging the tent sites and lightly trafficked, for the sake of privacy.

BASICS

Operated By: Kirk Fenoss. **Open:** May–Oct. **Site Assignment:** Reservations recommended. **Registration:** At office. **Fee:** $30–$37.50; V, MC, D. **Parking:** At site.

FACILITIES

Number of Multipurpose Sites: 150. **Hookups:** Electric (30, 50 amps), water, sewer, cable TV, phone, modem. **Each Site:** Picnic table, fire ring. **Dump Station:** Yes. **Laundry:** Yes. **Pay Phone:** Yes. **Restrooms and Showers:** Yes. **Fuel:** No. **Propane:** Yes. **Internal Roads:** Paved. **RV Service:** No. **Market:** 4.5 mi. east, St. Johnsbury. **Restaurant:** 1 mi. west, Danville. **General Store:** Yes. **Vending:** Yes. **Swimming:** 2 pools. **Playground:** Yes. **Other:** 18-hole mini-golf, tennis, basketball, volleyball, arcade. **Activities:** Horse-drawn wagon rides, swimming, mini-golf, hiking (trails), biking, sand volleyball, pond fishing, planned activities. **Nearby Attractions:** Maple Grove Farms, Fairbanks Museum. **Additional Information:** Northeast Kingdom Chamber of Commerce; (802) 748-3678 or (800) 639-6379.

RESTRICTIONS

Pets: On leash only; must be quiet & cleaned up after. Must not be left unattended. **Fires:** In fire rings only. **Alcoholic Beverages:** At site.

TO GET THERE

Take I-91 to Exit 21, then go 4 mi. west on Hwy. 2 in Danville.

DERBY   MAP, A-2
Char-Bo Campground

P.O. Box 602 347 Hayward Rd., 05829.
T: (802) 766-8807;
www.char-bo-campground.com.

🚐 ★★★★	🔺 ★★
Beauty: ★★★	Site Privacy: ★★
Spaciousness: ★★★	Quiet: ★★★★
Security: ★★★	Cleanliness: ★★
Insect Control: ★★★	Facilities: ★★

Located in Vermont's lake-dotted north country, not far from Newport and the Canadian border, Char-Bo Campground overlooks Salem Lake. Campers can access Little Salem Pond and try their luck at fishing for salmon, walleye, or perch. Set up on a hill, a good distance from the road, the campground offers a pastoral setting. You'll take best advantage of the views on sites A through F here, RVs are perched on a hill, with

panoramas of rolling farmland. Site 29 has the best water views. It's peaceful and quiet, but don't count on a lot of privacy here; sites are separated by tall trees or a split-rail fence. Owner Lyinda Ladd says they get a lot of repeat business here, after six seasons of operation—mostly families and folks who want to take advantage of the great outdoors in northern Vermont.

BASICS

Operated By: William and Lyinda Ladd. **Open:** May–mid-Oct.; weather permitting. **Site Assignment:** Reservations suggested; registration opens in Jan.; use a credit card to hold reservation; 48-hr. cancellation policy; $3 charge; reservations are not a must. **Registration:** At office. **Fee:** $23–$29; V, MC. **Parking:** At site.

FACILITIES

Number of Multipurpose Sites: 53. **Hookups:** Electric (30 amps), water, sewer. **Each Site:** Picnic table, fire ring. **Dump Station:** Yes. **Laundry:** Yes. **Pay Phone:** Yes. **Restrooms and Showers:** Yes, fee. **Fuel:** No. **Propane:** Yes. **Internal Roads:** Gravel. **RV Service:** No. **Market:** 3 mi. west, Derby. **Restaurant:** 3 mi. west, Derby. **General Store:** Yes. **Vending:** No. **Swimming:** Pool. **Playground:** Yes. **Other:** Game room, boat rentals (paddleboats, rowboats, canoes), 9-hole pitch & putt. **Activities:** Swimming, boating, fishing (nearby, need VT license). **Nearby Attractions:** Little Salem Pond access area. **Additional Information:** Vermont's North Country Chamber of Commerce; (802) 334-8478 or (802) 334-9990; www.vtnorthcountry.com.

RESTRICTIONS

Pets: On leash only; must be quiet & cleaned up after. Must not be left unattended. **Fires:** In fire rings only. **Alcoholic Beverages:** At site. **Other:** 2-night min. on weekends; 3-night min. on holidays.

TO GET THERE

Take Exit 28 off I-91; go 3 mi. east of Derby Center on Hwy. 105. Turn left on Hayward Rd.

DORSET   MAP, C-1
Dorset RV Park

1567 Hwy. 30, 05251. T: (802) 867-5754;
www.dorsetrvpark.com.

🚐 ★★★	🔺 ★★★
Beauty: ★★★	Site Privacy: ★★★
Spaciousness: ★★★	Quiet: ★★★
Security: ★★★	Cleanliness: ★★★
Insect Control: ★★★	Facilities: ★★

Tim and Mary Baker have owned this small, clean, basic, no-frills campground since 1988 and attract a loyal clientele. If you're looking for lots of action, you won't find it here. But it's a fine base for exploring the area and a relaxing place to come home to. Hookup sites are set in rows with decent space, though not much privacy. The pull-through sites are most popular, especially with the transient crowd. There is a separate wooded tent area and nine walk-in sites. This campground fills up fast during the popular fall foliage season.

BASICS

Operated By: The Baker-Haskins Family. **Open:** May–Oct. **Site Assignment:** Reservations sug-

gested; 1-night deposit; 1-week cancellation policy. **Registration:** At office. **Fee:** $19–$26; V, MC. **Parking:** At site. Separate tent area parking for walk-in tent sites.

FACILITIES

Number of RV-only Sites: 13. **Number of Tent-only Sites:** 13. **Number of Multipurpose Sites:** 14. **Hookups:** Electric (30, 50 amps), water, sewer. **Each Site:** Picnic table, fire ring. **Dump Station:** Yes. **Laundry:** Yes. **Pay Phone:** Yes. **Restrooms and Showers:** Yes. **Fuel:** No. **Propane:** No. **Internal Roads:** Gravel (good). **RV Service:** No. **Market:** Manchester, 4 mi. **Restaurant:** Manchester, 4 mi. **General Store:** Yes. **Vending:** Yes. **Swimming:** No. **Playground:** Yes. **Other:** Rec center. **Activities:** Horseshoes, volleyball, shuffleboard. **Nearby Attractions:** Farms, antiques shops, hiking, biking, boating, fishing, Manchester. **Additional Information:** Manchester the Mountains Chamber of Commerce, 5046 Main St. Suite 1, Manchester Center, VT 05255-3451; (802) 362-2100 or (800) 362-4144; www.manchestervermont.net.

RESTRICTIONS

Pets: On leash only. **Fires:** In fire pits & grills only. **Alcoholic Beverages:** At site.

TO GET THERE

Campground is located on Hwy. 30, 4 mi. north of Manchester.

DUMMERSTON   MAP, D-2
Hidden Acres Camping Resort

792 Hwy. 5, 05301.
T: (802) 254-2098 or (866) 411-CAMP; www.hidden-acresvt.net.

🚐 ★★★	🔺 ★★★★
Beauty: ★★★	Site Privacy: ★★★★
Spaciousness: ★★★★	Quiet: ★★★★
Security: ★★★	Cleanliness: ★★★★
Insect Control: ★★★	Facilities: ★★★

This super-friendly campground just north of Brattleboro is a hit with traveling families. The kids will love the mini-golf course, which is a step above most campground putt-putts. There's a decent swimming pool, and planned activities, like hay rides and ice-cream socials, keep the kids busy. There's also a spider web of woodsy hiking trails traversing the campground property. Head to the back of the campground where you'll find an open, sunny meadow and recreation field ringed with campsites. Rolling mountains in the background add to the scenic appeal. We like tent site 14, tucked at the end of a cul de sac, offering additional space and privacy. Site numbers G2–G9 are extra spacious, set back against the woods and near the hiking trails. There's a nice KOA campground up the street (see listing) that caters to RVs, but families and tenters might prefer this quaint, more natural setting.

BASICS

Operated By: Karen and David Hackney. **Open:** May 15–Nov. 15. **Site Assignment:** Reservations recommended; 1-night deposit. **Registration:** At office. **Fee:** Full hookup, $40; water/electric, $36; no hookup, $28. **Parking:** At site.

FACILITIES

Number of RV-only Sites: 12. **Number of Tent-only Sites:** 9. **Number of Multipurpose Sites:** 40. **Hookups:** Electric (30, 50 amps), water, sewer. **Each Site:** Picnic table, fire ring. **Dump Station:** Yes. **Laundry:** Yes. **Pay Phone:** Yes. **Restrooms and Showers:** Yes. **Fuel:** No. **Propane:** Yes. **Internal Roads:** Dirt, gravel (fair). **RV Service:** Emergency only. **Market:** Brattleboro, 4 mi. **Restaurant:** ice-cream shop on site; Brattleboro, 4 mi. **General Store:** Yes. **Vending:** Yes. **Swimming:** Pool. **Playground:** Yes. **Other:** Rec field, safari field, mini-golf, game room. **Activities:** Swimming, horseshoes, shuffleboard, volleyball, hiking, planned activities. **Nearby Attractions:** Boating and fishing on Connecticut River, hiking, biking, antiques shops, farms, Brattleboro. **Additional Information:** Brattleboro Area Chamber of Commerce, 180 Main St., Brattleboro, VT 05301; (802) 254-4565; www.brattleborochamber.org.

RESTRICTIONS

Pets: On leash only. **Fires:** In fire pits & grills only. **Alcoholic Beverages:** At site.

TO GET THERE

Take I-91 Exit 3 or 4; turn left on Hwy. 5N. Campground is 2.5 mi. north of Exit 3.

EAST DORSET   MAP, C-1
Emerald Lake State Park

374 Emerald Lake Ln., 05253-9788.
T: (802) 362-1655 (summer) or (888) 409-7579; www.vtstateparks.com.

★★★   ★★★★

Beauty: ★★★★	Site Privacy: ★★★★
Spaciousness: ★★★★	Quiet: ★★★★
Security: ★★★	Cleanliness: ★★★
Insect Control: ★★★	Facilities: ★★

Just minutes from the oh-so-manicured and upscale Manchester Village and the bustling factory outlet shops (and $200+ rooms) is this rustic, back-to-nature getaway. Set on 430 acres on the side of Dorset Mountain, the woodsy park includes mountain vistas, walking trails, and access to pretty Emerald Lake beach and picnic area. Canoeing on the lake and swimming in its cool, mountain-fed waters are popular daytime activities. The nearby Green Mountain National Forest has additional hiking trails. Sites are well spaced, each tucked into the trees for privacy. There are limited facilities and coin-op showers, but you can't beat the views—or the price.

BASICS

Operated By: State of Vermont. **Open:** Mid-May–Oct. 15. **Site Assignment:** Reservations may be made up to 11 months in advance; 2-night min. required; reservations accepted at (888) 409-7579; contact park directly only for reservations w/in 10 days of stay; no refunds for the 2-night min. **Registration:** At office. **Fee:** $16–$25; V, MC. **Parking:** At site.

FACILITIES

Number of Multipurpose Sites: 105 (36 lean-tos). **Each Site:** Picnic table, fire ring. **Dump Station:** Yes. **Laundry:** No. **Pay Phone:** Yes.

Restrooms and Showers: Yes (coin-op). **Fuel:** No. **Propane:** No. **Internal Roads:** Gravel, dirt (good). **RV Service:** No. **Market:** Manchester, 9 mi. **Restaurant:** Snack bar on site. **General Store:** No. **Vending:** Yes. **Swimming:** Lake. **Playground:** No. **Other:** Picnic area, pavilion, boat rentals, hiking trails. **Activities:** Hiking, swimming, boating, fishing. **Nearby Attractions:** Farms, antiques shops, hiking, biking, swimming, boating, fishing, Manchester. **Additional Information:** Manchester the Mountains Chamber of Commerce, 5046 Main St. Suite 1, Manchester Center, VT 05255-3451; (802) 362-2100 or (800) 362-4144; www.manchestervermont.net.

RESTRICTIONS

Pets: On leash only. **Fires:** In fire pits & grills only. **Alcoholic Beverages:** At site.

TO GET THERE

Campground is located on Hwy. 7, 9 mi. north of Manchester.

FAIR HAVEN   MAP, C-1
Bomoseen State Park

22 Cedar Mountain Rd., 05743.
T: (802) 265-4242 or (888) 409-7579; www.vtstateparks.com.

★★★   ★★★★

Beauty: ★★★★	Site Privacy: ★★★★
Spaciousness: ★★★★	Quiet: ★★★
Security: ★★★	Cleanliness: ★★★
Insect Control: ★★★	Facilities: ★★★

This large preserve in the Taconic Mountain range sits on the western shore of Lake Bomoseen and draws outdoor lovers, anglers, and boaters. Stop by the ranger station to pick up a self-guided Slate History Trail map of the campground. This was once a major slate-producing region, and several quarry holes, rubble piles, slate buildings, and foundations can still be found throughout the campground. When you're done with the history lesson, head to the shoreline, where you'll find a small beach and swimming area, boat rentals, and a snack bar. Campers can also take to the woods; there are several hiking trails in the park, including one that takes you to adjacent Half Moon State Park. Nearby Glen Lake is also a popular day excursion. Campsites are set in two major loops, in both shaded and grassy open areas. There are a handful of sites on the shoreline, but you'll have to reserve these weeks in advance or plan a midweek, off-season getaway.

BASICS

Operated By: State of Vermont. **Open:** Mid-May–Oct. 15. **Site Assignment:** Reservations may be made up to 11 months in advance; 2-night min. required; reservations accepted at (888) 409-7579; contact park directly only for reservations w/in 10 days of stay; no refunds for the 2-night min. **Registration:** At office. **Fee:** $16–$25; V, MC. **Parking:** At site.

FACILITIES

Number of Multipurpose Sites: 66 (10 lean-tos). **Each Site:** Picnic table, fire ring. **Dump Station:** Yes. **Laundry:** No. **Pay Phone:** No. **Restrooms and Showers:** Yes (coin-op). **Fuel:**

No. **Propane:** No. **Internal Roads:** Gravel, dirt (good). **RV Service:** No. **Market:** Hydeville, 4 mi. **Restaurant:** Snack bar on site. **General Store:** No. **Vending:** No. **Swimming:** Lake. **Playground:** No. **Other:** Beach, pavilion, picnic area, boat rentals. **Activities:** Swimming, boating, fishing, hiking. **Nearby Attractions:** Farms, antiques shops, swimming, boating, fishing, hiking, biking, Middlebury. **Additional Information:** Addison County, Vermont Chamber of Commerce, 2 Court St., Middlebury, VT 05753; (802) 388-7951.

RESTRICTIONS

Pets: On leash only. **Fires:** In fire pits & grills only. **Alcoholic Beverages:** At site.

TO GET THERE

From Hydeville, go 4 mi. north on West Shore Rd.

FAIRFAX   MAP, A-1
Maple Grove Campground

1627 Main St., 05454. T: (802) 849-6439; www.campvermont.com.

★★★★   ★★

Beauty: ★★★	Site Privacy: ★★★
Spaciousness: ★★★	Quiet: ★★★★
Security: ★★★	Cleanliness: ★★★★
Insect Control: ★★★	Facilities: ★★★★

Neat as a pin, this quiet campground is a terrific base for fall foliage tours. Lake Champlain is west of the campground; Smuggler's Notch, with its jaw-dropping hairpin turns along Hwy. 108, is 20 miles to the southeast. Aside from a few planned events, like potluck suppers and strawberry socials, there's not much in the way of activities offered here, more proof that visitors tend to explore the area using Maple Grove campground as a peaceful, adult-friendly base camp. Sites are set in a big loop, with plenty of shade and some good pull-throughs in 8–11. Sites 24 and 25 are set against the woods and are quite pretty. The owners are experienced in this business; they operated Homestead Campground for 16 years before running this place. Their caring touch shows in some details here, like the pristine laundry room with a lending library.

BASICS

Operated By: Joe and Sue Monty. **Open:** May 1–Oct. 12. **Site Assignment:** Reserve 4–6 months in advance; 1-night deposit required. **Registration:** At office. **Fee:** $19–$24; V, MC. **Parking:** At site.

FACILITIES

Number of Multipurpose Sites: 26. **Hookups:** Electric, water, sewer, modem. **Each Site:** Picnic table, fire ring. **Dump Station:** Yes. **Laundry:** Yes. **Pay Phone:** No. **Restrooms and Showers:** Yes, fee. **Fuel:** No. **Propane:** No. **Internal Roads:** Gravel. **RV Service:** No. **Market:** 1.5 mi. south. **Restaurant:** 1.5 mi. south. **General Store:** Yes. **Vending:** No. **Swimming:** No. **Playground:** Yes (swing set). **Activities:** Planned activities. **Nearby Attractions:** Burlington shopping & restaurants, Shelburne Museum, Smuggler's Notch. **Additional Information:** St. Albans Area Chamber of Commerce; (802) 524-2444; www.stalbanschamber.com.

RESTRICTIONS

Pets: On leash only; must be cleaned up after & under control. **Fires:** In fire rings only. **Alcoholic Beverages:** At site. **Vehicle Maximum Length:** 40 ft.

TO GET THERE

Take Exit 18 off I-89. Go 0.1 mi. south on VT 7 and east on VT 104-A 5 mi. At stop sign, go north on VT 104 1 mi. Entrance is on right.

GAYSVILLE — MAP, C-2
White River Valley Campground

P.O. Box 106, Hwy. 107, 05746. T: (802) 234-9115; www.whiterivervalleycamping.com.

🚐 ★★★   ⛺ ★★★★

Beauty: ★★★★	Site Privacy: ★★★★
Spaciousness: ★★★	Quiet: ★★★
Security: ★★★	Cleanliness: ★★★
Insect Control: ★★★	Facilities: ★★★

Attention, all river rats! This very rustic campground is located on the rocky shores of the White River. Just outside the entrance of the place is a swimming hole underneath an old bridge, known as the Ledges. Also adjacent to the campground are several old logging roads that wind through the mountains. Everybody rents an inner tube and floats the White (they offer tube rentals here, at the trading post). If you're not into this stuff, don't bother coming. It's an outdoorsy, family fun kind of place. Sites R20–R22 (the best) are big and flat, and campers can sleep to the sounds of the rushing river. Site R26, also on the river, is very nice as well. Big rigs get comfortable at M sites. The campground's facilities are basic, but there are nice touches, like a full-length mirror in the ladies' room. And what's not to love about a campground with a whirlpool tub? You won't find a better place to play, river rat.

BASICS

Operated By: Drew and Rebecca Smith. **Open:** May–Oct. 15. **Site Assignment:** Reservations suggested; $20 deposit. **Registration:** At office. **Fee:** $24–$33; V, MC, D. **Parking:** At site.

FACILITIES

Number of RV-only Sites: 51. **Number of Tent-only Sites:** 19. **Number of Multipurpose Sites:** 102. **Hookups:** Electric (15, 30 amps), water, sewer. **Each Site:** Picnic table, fire ring. **Dump Station:** No. **Laundry:** Yes. **Pay Phone:** Yes. **Restrooms and Showers:** Yes. **Fuel:** No. **Propane:** No. **Internal Roads:** Gravel, dirt (good). **RV Service:** No. **Market:** Royalton, 5 mi. **Restaurant:** Royalton, 5 mi. **General Store:** Yes. **Vending:** No. **Swimming:** River. **Playground:** No. **Other:** Spa, game room, tube rentals, microwave. **Activities:** Swimming, tubing, fishing, basketball, volleyball, horseshoes, badminton, shuffleboard, special events. **Nearby Attractions:** Biking, hiking, swimming, boating, fishing, White River Junction, Rutland, Woodstock. **Additional Information:** Upper Valley Chamber of Commerce, P.O. Box 697, White River Junction, VT 05001; (802) 295-6200; www.uppervalleychamber.com. Woodstock Area Chamber of Commerce, 18 Central St., P.O. Box 486-4, Woodstock, VT 05091; (802) 457-3555.

RESTRICTIONS

Pets: On leash only. $1 daily pet fee. **Fires:** In fire pits & grills only. **Alcoholic Beverages:** At site.

TO GET THERE

From I-89 Exit 3, take Hwy. 107 west 8.5 mi.

GRAND ISLE — MAP, A-1
Grand Isle State Park

36 East Shore Rd. S., 05458. T: (802) 372-4300 (summer) or (888) 409-7579; www.vtstateparks.com.

🚐 ★★★★   ⛺ ★★★★

Beauty: ★★★★	Site Privacy: ★★★
Spaciousness: ★★★	Quiet: ★★★
Security: ★★★	Cleanliness: ★★★
Insect Control: ★★★	Facilities: ★★★

Grand Isle, Vermont's second-largest state park, is also its most-visited recreation hot spot. And why not? Set on South Hero Island (also known as Grand Isle) on Lake Champlain, the campground boasts 4,000 feet of shoreline. The sparkling blue water contrasts nicely with the rolling green slopes of Vermont's Green Mountains. Pretty sweet, eh? If you're a tent camper, you can usually luck into a spot here on the spur of the moment. To get a lean-to set right on the beach with views too pretty to imagine—well, that takes some planning. Reserve one of these in advance—like, right this minute—if the idea of waking up to gorgeous vistas appeals to you. RVers have fewer options, although about 50 percent of the sites here are large enough to accommodate self-contained units. Overall, the peachiest sites, view-wise, are 1–8 and 101–112. No matter which site you snag, you'll be eager to explore the lake, in a rental boat or kayak (available here), or by taking a dip in the tingly waters of Lake Champlain. Easy access to Burlington and Montreal (we'd take the car) are a bonus.

BASICS

Operated By: Vermont Agency of Natural Resources, Dept. of Forests, Parks and Recreation. **Open:** Mid-May–mid-Oct. **Site Assignment:** Can reserve up to 11 months in advance by calling (888) 409-7579; 2-night min.; 1-night OK for walk-ins; $10 cancellation fee. **Registration:** At office. **Fee:** $16–$25; V, MC. **Parking:** At site.

FACILITIES

Number of RV-only Sites: 36 (lean-tos). **Number of Multipurpose Sites:** 120. **Hookups:** None. **Each Site:** Picnic table, fire ring. **Dump Station:** Yes. **Laundry:** No. **Pay Phone:** Yes. **Restrooms and Showers:** Yes, fee. **Fuel:** No. **Propane:** No. **Internal Roads:** Gravel. **RV Service:** No. **Market:** 2 mi. north. **Restaurant:** 2 mi. north. **General Store:** No. **Vending:** No. **Swimming:** Lake. **Playground:** Yes. **Other:** Boat ramp, nature center. **Activities:** Lake swimming, boating, volleyball, horseshoes, nature trail. **Nearby Attractions:** Hermann's Royal Lippizans, St. Anne's Shrine. **Additional Information:** Lake Champlain Islands Chamber of Commerce; (802) 372-8400; www.champlainislands.com.

RESTRICTIONS

Pets: On leash only; must be quiet & cleaned up after. Proof of current rabies vaccination required. **Fires:** At site only. **Alcoholic Beverages:** At site. **Vehicle Maximum Length:** 35 ft.

TO GET THERE

Take Exit 17 off I-89 to Champlain Islands, then VT 2 12 mi. to park entrance (on left).

GROTON — MAP, B-2
Big Deer State Park

Stillwater State Park, 126 Boulder Beach Rd., 05046. T: (802) 584-3822 (summer only) or (888) 409-7579; www.vtstateparks.com.

🚐 ★★★   ⛺ ★★★

Beauty: ★★★	Site Privacy: ★★★★
Spaciousness: ★★★	Quiet: ★★★★
Security: ★★★	Cleanliness: ★★★
Insect Control: ★★★	Facilities: ★★★

Originally built as an overflow area for Stillwater State Park (see listing), Big Deer Campground has plenty to recommend it. Sites are fairly private and level (more so than at Stillwater), and campers have access to popular Boulder Beach on 423-acre Lake Groton (alas, no lake frontage at Big Deer, however). Set in a loop, sites are generally grassy, with a good barrier between them. Site 25 is especially private. With fewer sites, Big Deer is generally quieter on busy weekends and often populated with families who visit Groton Nature Center (nearby) and hike Little Deer Trail or climb to the summit of Little Deer (1,760 feet) or Big Deer mountains (1,992 feet). (Note: both of these trails have some steep sections.) With more than 20 miles of trails crisscrossing Groton State Forest, you'll find lots of opportunity to get off the beaten track and find some solitude, even on a midsummer weekend. A casual walk in the woods is rewarding here. You might catch a glimpse of some local residents here, like turkey vultures, rabbits, wild turkeys, and perhaps—if you're really lucky—a moose.

BASICS

Operated By: Vermont Agency of Natural Resources, Dept. of Forests, Parks and Recreation. **Open:** Mid-May–Labor Day. **Site Assignment:** 2-night min. required for reservations. **Registration:** At office. **Fee:** $16–$23; V, MC. **Parking:** At site.

FACILITIES

Number of RV-only Sites: 5 (lean-tos). **Number of Multipurpose Sites:** 23. **Each Site:** Picnic table, fire ring. **Dump Station:** At Stillwater State Park (also in Groton State Forest). **Laundry:** No. **Pay Phone:** Yes. **Restrooms and Showers:** Yes, fee. **Fuel:** No. **Propane:** No. **Internal Roads:** Paved, gravel. **RV Service:** No. **Market:** General store nearby (on park road). **Restaurant:** 30 mi. northwest, St. Johnsbury. **General Store:** No. **Vending:** No. **Swimming:** Nearby, at Boulder Beach. **Playground:** No. **Activities:** Hiking, lake swimming. **Nearby Attractions:** Cabot Creamery, Rock of Ages granite quarry, Vermont State Capitol (Montpelier). **Additional Information:** Central

Vermont Chamber of Commerce; (802) 229-5711; www.central-vt.com.

RESTRICTIONS

Pets: On leash only; must be quiet & cleaned up after. Must have proof of current rabies vaccination. **Fires:** In fire rings only. **Alcoholic Beverages:** At site. **Vehicle Maximum Length:** 30 ft.

TO GET THERE

Take I-91N to US 302. Head 12 mi. west on US 302, then 6 mi. north on VT 232. From there, head 1 mi. east on Boulder Beach Rd.

GROTON   MAP, B-2
Stillwater State Park

126 Boulder Beach Rd., 05046.
T: (802) 584-3822 (summer) or (888) 409-7579; www.vtstateparks.com.

🚐 ★★★★   ⛺ ★★★★

Beauty: ★★★★	Site Privacy: ★★★
Spaciousness: ★★★★	Quiet: ★★★
Security: ★★★	Cleanliness: ★★★
Insect Control: ★★★	Facilities: ★★★

One of four public campgrounds in 26,000-acre Groton State Forest, Stillwater State Park is plenty scenic. Located just half an hour from St. Johnsbury, this camping area offers a taste of the wilderness and lots of options for outdoor fun. Campsites—wonderfully roomy—are clustered on the shores of 423-acre Lake Groton. Although there are no hookups for RVs, trailer sites are as big as 55 by 40 feet. (Grab site 22 if you can; it's roomy, nice, and not far from the lake.) Beware: Some sites are uneven and a bit bumpy, thanks to the abundant boulders lurking underground. These same mega-rocks work nicely as furniture if you're tenting, though. Of course, everybody wants to be on the lake. Most desirable sites include 14 (very open, with views of the lake) and the cluster that includes sites 53–55, closest to the camper's swim area. The Hemlock and Tamarack lean-tos boast fabulous locations. Beware site 4—although it's close to the beach (and looks good on paper), it's really lumpy. If there's nothing left on the lake, opt for site 43—at least you've got a nice boulder formation and plenty of privacy. A footbridge and pathway leads to the beach. There's plenty to do here. Bring your own boat or rent one, take a short drive to Boulder Beach (bigger than the campground beach and open to campers and the public for day use), or take one of the numerous hiking trails and explore Groton State Forest. Hike to Peacham Bog, one of the largest natural bogs in Vermont, or take one of several trails off the Osmore Pond hiking loop (the campground office has trail maps for Groton State Forest.)

BASICS

Operated By: Vermont Agency of Natural Resources, Dept. of Forests, Parks and Recreation. **Open:** Mid-May–mid-Oct. **Site Assignment:** Reserve up to 11 months in advance by calling (888) 409-7549; 2-night min. required for reservations. **Registration:** At office. **Fee:** $16–$23; V, MC. **Parking:** At site.

FACILITIES

Number of RV-only Sites: 19 (lean-tos). **Number of Multipurpose Sites:** 60. **Each Site:** Picnic table, fire ring. **Dump Station:** Yes. **Laundry:** No. **Pay Phone:** Yes. **Restrooms and Showers:** Yes, fee. **Fuel:** No. **Propane:** No. **Internal Roads:** Paved, gravel. **RV Service:** No. **Market:** 5 mi. south, Groton, or 30 mi. southwest, St. Johnsbury. **Restaurant:** 5 mi. south or 30 mi. southwest. **General Store:** No. **Vending:** Yes. **Swimming:** Lake. **Playground:** Yes. **Other:** Boat launch, boat rentals. **Activities:** Horseshoes, swimming, boating, hiking. **Nearby Attractions:** Cabot Creamery, Rock of Ages granite quarry, Vermont State Capitol (Montpelier). **Additional Information:** Central Vermont Chamber of Commerce; (802) 229-5711; www.central-vt.com.

RESTRICTIONS

Pets: On leash only; must be quiet & cleaned up after. Must have proof of current rabies vaccination. **Fires:** In fire rings only. **Alcoholic Beverages:** At site.

TO GET THERE

Take I-91 north to US 302; follow US 302 west 12 mi., then 6 mi. north on VT 232. Go 0.5 mi. east on Boulder Beach Rd. to campground.

GUILDHALL   MAP, B-2
Maidstone State Park

Hwy. 1, P.O. Box 388, 05905.
T: (802) 676-3930 (summer) or (888) 409-7579; www.vtstateparks.com.

🚐 ★★★   ⛺ ★★★★

Beauty: ★★★★	Site Privacy: ★★★★
Spaciousness: ★★★	Quiet: ★★★★
Security: ★★★★	Cleanliness: ★★★
Insect Control: ★★	Facilities: ★★★

As Vermont state parks go, there's nothing as remote as this one. Once you finally find Maidstone State Park, way up at the state's undeveloped northeastern edge, you still have 5 miles to go on a dirt road into the campground. What a beauty, though! Maidstone Lake is one of the cleanest and clearest in the state, and so unused, it is said to be loaded with 25-pound lake trout, rainbow trout, and brook trout. (Well, perhaps those rangers do exaggerate a bit.) Moose sightings are fairly common up here as well. Plan to be awakened in the morning by the haunting call of Maidstone's pair of common loons. There are hiking trails around the property (you may not see another soul as you ramble) and wonderful nooks and crannies to explore by boat. Campsites are just as you'd picture them—woodsy, private, and lovely. If you're yearning for a real wilderness escape, you won't do better.

BASICS

Operated By: Vermont Agency of Natural Resources, Dept. of Forests, Parks and Recreation. **Open:** Mid-May–Labor Day. **Site Assignment:** Reserve up to 11 months in advance by calling (888) 406-7579; 2-night min. required for reservations. **Registration:** At contact station. **Fee:** $16–$25; V, MC. **Parking:** At site.

FACILITIES

Number of RV-only Sites: 37 (lean-tos). **Number of Multipurpose Sites:** 45 tent/trailer sites. **Each Site:** Picnic table, fireplace. **Dump Station:** Yes. **Laundry:** No. **Pay Phone:** Yes. **Restrooms and Showers:** Yes, fee. **Fuel:** No. **Propane:** No. **Internal Roads:** Paved, gravel. **RV Service:** No. **Market:** 20 mi. northwest. **Restaurant:** 20 mi. northwest. **General Store:** No. **Vending:** No. **Swimming:** Lake (limited). **Playground:** Yes. **Other:** Boat rentals, tubing. **Activities:** Boating, tubing, hiking, fishing lake swimming. **Additional Information:** Lyndon Area Chamber of Commerce; (802) 626-6498 or (802) 626-9770; www.lyndonvermont.com.

RESTRICTIONS

Pets: On leash only; must be quiet & cleaned up after. Must not be left unattended. Proof of current rabies vaccination required. **Fires:** In fireplaces only. **Alcoholic Beverages:** At site. **Vehicle Maximum Length:** 30 ft.

TO GET THERE

Head 11 mi. north on VT 102 from US 2, then 5 mi. southwest on State Forest Hwy.

HUBBARDTON   MAP, B-2
Half Moon Pond State Park

1621 Black Pond Rd., 05743.
T: (802) 273-2848 or (888) 409-7579; www.vtstateparks.com.

🚐 ★★★★   ⛺ ★★★★

Beauty: ★★★★★	Site Privacy: ★★★★★
Spaciousness: ★★★★	Quiet: ★★★★
Security: ★★★★	Cleanliness: ★★★★★
Insect Control: ★★★	Facilities: ★★

If you're yearning for peace and quiet and enjoy a remote, rustic location, this state park campground is for you. The park, surrounded by dense forest, is located within the 3,576-acre Bomoseen State Park and offers a secluded, back-to-nature camping experience. Campsites are nestled in deep woods (bring the bug spray!) or along pretty Half Moon Pond. There's a small swimming area, but most campers choose to paddle or fish the pond (there are boat rentals available on site) or to walk the network of hiking trails. The web of trails connects ponds, marshlands, and abandoned quarry sites; trails range in length from 0.3 to 4.5 miles. As expected, waterfront campsites go first, but the in-the-woods sites are very private.

BASICS

Operated By: State of Vermont. **Open:** Mid-May–Oct. 15. **Site Assignment:** Reservations may be made up to 11 months in advance; 2-night min. required; reservations accepted at (888) 409-7579; contact park directly only for reservations w/in 10 days of stay; no refunds for the 2-night min. **Registration:** At office. **Fee:** $16–$25; V, MC. **Parking:** At site.

FACILITIES

Number of Multipurpose Sites: 59 (10 lean-tos). **Each Site:** Picnic table, fire ring. **Dump Station:** Yes. **Laundry:** No. **Pay Phone:** No. **Restrooms and Showers:** Yes (coin-op). **Fuel:** No. **Propane:** No. **Internal Roads:** Gravel, dirt (good). **RV Service:**

No. **Market:** Fair Haven, 10 mi. **Restaurant:** Fair Haven, 10 mi. **General Store:** No. **Vending:** No. **Swimming:** Pond. **Playground:** Yes. **Other:** Boat rentals. **Activities:** Swimming, boating, fishing, hiking. **Nearby Attractions:** Farms, antiques shops, hiking, biking, fishing, boating, swimming, Rutland. **Additional Information:** Rutland Region Chamber of Commerce, 256 North Main St., Rutland, VT 05701; (802) 773-2747; www.rutlandvermont.com.

RESTRICTIONS

Pets: On leash only. **Fires:** In fire pits & grills only. **Alcoholic Beverages:** At site.

TO GET THERE

The campground is located halfway between Fair Haven and Rutland. Follow Hwy. 4 to Exit 4. Go north on Hwy. 30 6.5 mi., then left on Hortonia Rd. 2 mi. Take a left on Black Pond Rd.; go 2 mi. to the campground.

ISLAND POND
Lakeside Camping
MAP, A-3

1348 Hwy. 105, 05846.
T: (802) 723-6649 or (802) 723-6331; www.lakesidecamping.com.

🚐 ★★★★   ▲ ★

Beauty: ★★★★	Site Privacy: ★★
Spaciousness: ★	Quiet: ★★★
Security: ★★★	Cleanliness: ★★★★
Insect Control: ★★★	Facilities: ★★★

Campground owner Maurice Barnes's parents started the business nearly 40 years ago, and the personal touch is evident. Barnes himself was whipping up a huge pot of chili when we visited, part of an impromptu potluck supper. "We're pretty laid-back," Barnes says. "We're not commercial. We don't offer a lot of activities for kids." But when you're located smack on the lakeshore of Island Pond, what else do you need but some sunshine and maybe a boat? Bring you own, or rent a pedal boat, rowboat, or canoe, and get out on the water to look for loons. There's also a 1,500-foot beach, and the close proximity of Hwy. 114, a.k.a. Moose Valley, where Barnes can show you the most likely places to spot Bullwinkle's kin in these parts. (He's printed up self-guided moose-watching maps.) You might also consider a walk around the lake (6 miles) or perhaps a hike up Bluff Mountain. They've packed a lot of campsites around this scoop of shoreline; most are grassy, with back-in sites hugging the shore. These spots are great, but take note: the railroad runs right behind them! Pull-through sites for big rigs are located a bit inland, numbered from 48–63 or so. Sites 44–47A are isolated a bit and really pretty. There's not much privacy here, as sites are set pretty much side by side, so this is a better choice for the RV set than for tenters (for the latter, nearby Brighton State Park is wonderful and also set on Island Pond). But you will find plenty of shade and—if you can read a map—maybe a moose or two.

BASICS

Operated By: Maurice Barnes. **Open:** Mid-May–mid-Sept. **Site Assignment:** Reservations required, up to 1 year in advance; $25 deposit; 3-night min. on holidays. **Registration:** At office. **Fee:** $28–$32; checks, no credit cards. **Parking:** At site.

FACILITIES

Number of RV-only Sites: 5. **Number of Tent-only Sites:** 200. **Hookups:** Electric (30, 50 amps), water, sewer. **Each Site:** Picnic table, fireplace. **Dump Station:** Yes. **Laundry:** Yes. **Pay Phone:** No. **Restrooms and Showers:** Yes, fee. **Fuel:** No. **Propane:** Yes. **Internal Roads:** Gravel (fair). **RV Service:** No. **Market:** 1 mi. west. **Restaurant:** 1 mi. west. **General Store:** Yes. **Vending:** No. **Swimming:** Lake. **Playground:** Yes. **Other:** Boat rentals. **Activities:** Swimming, boating. **Nearby Attractions:** Rtes. 105, 102, & 114 for moose watching, Bluff Mountain hiking trail, Maple Grove Museum, Fairbanks Museum, St. Johnsbury Athenaeum, Kingdom Trails (mountain biking). **Additional Information:** Island Pond Chamber of Commerce; (802) 723-6300; www.islandpond.com.

RESTRICTIONS

Pets: On leash only at campsite. Must be cleaned up after. **Fires:** At site only. **Alcoholic Beverages:** Not allowed. **Vehicle Maximum Length:** 40 ft. **Other:** No bicycles, mini-bikes, or motorcycles permitted.

TO GET THERE

Take I-91 to Exit 23. Take a right onto VT 5 to Hwy. 114N. Follow Hwy. 114N through Island Pond to Hwy. 105E. Follow 2 mi. to campground on right.

JAMAICA
Jamaica State Park
MAP, D-2

P.O. Box 45, 05343.
T: (802) 874-4600 (summer) or (888) 409-7579; www.vtstateparks.com.

🚐 ★★★   ▲ ★★★★

Beauty: ★★★★	Site Privacy: ★★★★
Spaciousness: ★★★★	Quiet: ★★★★
Security: ★★★	Cleanliness: ★★★
Insect Control: ★★★	Facilities: ★★★

Twice a year, early spring and fall, this park crawls with hordes of kayakers who come from all over New England and beyond to run the wild West River during the scheduled dam release. At any other time, the state park campground is relatively peaceful and quiet and a great place for outdoor pursuits. The campground sits on the banks of the rambling West River, with lots of places for fishing, tubing, and swimming. There are three hiking trails that meander the campground's 756 acres. Don't miss the trail that leads to 125-foot Hamilton Falls, a pretty cascade of falling water that dumps into three deep, clear pools. Campsites are set in the woods with nice privacy and plenty of elbow room.

BASICS

Operated By: State of Vermont. **Open:** Last Friday in Apr.–Oct. 15. **Site Assignment:** Reservations may be made up to 11 months in advance; 2-night min. required; reservations accepted at (888) 409-7579; contact park directly only for reservations w/in 10 days of stay; no refunds for the 2-night min. **Registration:** At office. **Fee:** No hookup, $16; lean-to, $23; V, MC. **Parking:** At site.

FACILITIES

Number of Multipurpose Sites: 43 (18 lean-tos). **Each Site:** Picnic table, fire ring. **Dump Station:** Yes. **Laundry:** No. **Pay Phone:** No. **Restrooms and Showers:** Yes. **Fuel:** No. **Propane:** No. **Internal Roads:** Gravel, dirt (good). **RV Service:** No. **Market:** Jamaica, 1 mi. **Restaurant:** Jamaica, 1 mi. **General Store:** No. **Vending:** Yes. **Swimming:** River. **Playground:** No. **Other:** Nature center, hiking trails, nature programs. **Activities:** Hiking, biking, boating, swimming. **Nearby Attractions:** Farms, antiques shops, hiking, biking, boating, fishing, swimming, Brattleboro, Mt. Snow. **Additional Information:** Brattleboro Area Chamber of Commerce, 180 Main St., Brattleboro, VT 05301; (802) 254-4565; www.brattleborochamber.org.

RESTRICTIONS

Pets: On leash only. **Fires:** In fire pits & grills only. **Alcoholic Beverages:** At site.

TO GET THERE

Campground is just off Hwy. 30 in Jamaica.

LAKE BOMOSEEN
Lake Bomoseen Campground
MAP, A-3

Hwy. 30, 05732.
T: (802) 273-2061; www.lakebomoseen.com.

🚐 ★★★★★   ▲ ★★★★

Beauty: ★★★★	Site Privacy: ★★★
Spaciousness: ★★★	Quiet: ★★★
Security: ★★★★	Cleanliness: ★★★★
Insect Control: ★★★	Facilities: ★★★★★

This camping resort, located on Vermont's largest lake, is a bustling locale with lots of activities and family-friendly features. Lake Bomoseen is the big draw for most campers. Alas, there are no campsites on the shoreline but you'll find two docks, a boat launch, and boat rentals. There's a full-service marina and RV sales office at the campground, too. Fishing is popular, with anglers netting pike, pickerel, bass, trout, and perch. It's not uncommon to see fish frying in pans around dinnertime. Families congregate at the large-size pool area, complete with waterslides and whirlpool. Mini-golf, arcade games, movies, and sports keep kids busy, too. While the kids are catching a flick at the small, on-site movie theater, Mom and Dad can relax in the adults-only recreation hall or sit on the banks of the lake and watch the sun set. Moonlight canoe paddle, anyone?

BASICS

Operated By: Dan and Estelle Adams. **Open:** May–mid-Oct. **Site Assignment:** Reservations suggested; no refunds; 3-night min.; prepaid for holiday weekends. **Registration:** At office. **Fee:** Water/electric (50 amp) pull-through, $39; water/electric (30 amp), $36; no hookup, $27; D, V, MC. **Parking:** At site.

FACILITIES

Number of Tent-only Sites: 44. **Number of Multipurpose Sites:** 56. **Hookups:** Electric (30, 50 amps), water, sewer, cable TV. **Each Site:** Picnic table, fire ring. **Dump Station:** Yes. **Laundry:** Yes. **Pay Phone:** Yes. **Restrooms and Showers:** Yes. **Fuel:** No. **Propane:** Yes. **Internal Roads:** Gravel (good). **RV Service:** Yes. **Market:** Rutland, 12 mi. **Restaurant:** Rutland, 12 mi. **General Store:** Yes. **Vending:** No. **Swimming:** Pool, lake. **Playground:** Yes. **Other:** Arcade & game room, mini-golf, adult rec room, sports courts, movie theater, boat ramp, dock, boat rentals, safari area, cabin & trailer rentals. **Activities:** Swimming, boating, fishing, horseshoes, basketball. **Nearby Attractions:** Farms, antiques shops, biking, hiking, boating, fishing, swimming, Rutland, Middlebury. **Additional Information:** Rutland Region Chamber of Commerce, 256 North Main St., Rutland, VT 05701 (802)773-2747; www.rutlandvermont.com. Addison County, Vermont Chamber of Commerce, 2 Court St., Middlebury, VT 05753; (802) 388-7951.

RESTRICTIONS

Pets: On leash only ($1 per pet, per day). Not allowed in the rental units. **Fires:** In fire pits & grills only. **Alcoholic Beverages:** At site.

TO GET THERE

Campground is located halfway between Middlebury and Rutland on Hwy. 30.

LAKE ELMORE   MAP, A-2
Elmore State Park

856 VT 12, 05657. T: (802) 888-2982 (summer only) or (888) 409-7579; www.vtstateparks.com.

🚐 ★★★★	▲ ★★★★
Beauty: ★★★★	Site Privacy: ★★★
Spaciousness: ★★★	Quiet: ★★★
Security: ★★★★	Cleanliness: ★★★
Insect Control: ★★★	Facilities: ★★★

Talk about an embarrassment of riches! At Lake Elmore State Park (with sites big enough for large rigs), campers can enjoy great hiking, paddling, fishing, and swimming, amid the self-proclaimed "Beauty Spot of Vermont," the town of Lake Elmore. Located not far from Stowe, in the southeastern part of Lamoille County, the park is set on a sandy-bottomed, 219-acre lake, flanked by mountains and hills. To really appreciate this place, it's a good idea to take the two-hour hike to the summit of Elmore Mountain (2,608 feet). Once you reach the top, climb about 55 feet more on one of Vermont's last remaining fire towers and take in a breathtaking, nearly panoramic view of the Hogback Range. Hike down the mountain and cool off in the lake; there's a buoyed-off swimming area and a good-sized sandy beach. They'll also rent you a canoe or pedal boat so you can explore the lake's nooks and crannies. The camping area is set apart from the beach and picnic areas, with sites set in two loops, some shaded, some open and grassy. You really can't go wrong here; all sites are equally pleasant. Check out the snack bar (believe it or not), set in a beautiful building erected by the Civilian Conservations Corps in 1936. Today, the Vermont Youth Conservation Corps staffs the park with young people aged 17–24 who live and work in the park under a team of adult managers.

BASICS

Operated By: Vermont Agency of Natural Resources, Dept. of Forests, Parks and Recreation. **Open:** Late May–mid-Oct. **Site Assignment:**

Reservations may be made up to 11 months in advance; 2-night min. required; reservations accepted at (888) 409-7579; contact park directly only for reservations w/in 10 days of stay; no refunds for the 2-night min. **Registration:** At office. **Fee:** $16–$23; V, MC. **Parking:** At site.

FACILITIES

Number of RV-only Sites: 15 (lean-tos). **Number of Multipurpose Sites:** 45. **Hookups:** None. **Each Site:** Picnic table, fireplace. **Dump Station:** Yes. **Laundry:** No. **Pay Phone:** Yes. **Restrooms and Showers:** Yes, fee. **Fuel:** No. **Propane:** No. **Internal Roads:** Gravel. **RV Service:** No. **Market:** 7 mi. northwest. **Restaurant:** 7 mi. northwest. **General Store:** No. **Vending:** Yes. **Swimming:** Lake. **Playground:** Yes. **Other:** Boat ramp. **Activities:** Boating, lake swimming, hiking Elmore Mountain. **Nearby Attractions:** Stowe shopping & dining, Mt. Mansfield, Stowe Alpine Slide, gondola & toll road, Stowe rec path, Moss Glen Falls, Smuggler's Notch. **Additional Information:** Stowe Area Assoc.; (802) 253-7321 or (877) 603-8693; www.gotstowe.com.

RESTRICTIONS

Pets: On leash only; must be quiet & cleaned up after. Restricted to certain areas. Proof of current rabies vaccination required. **Fires:** In fireplaces only. **Alcoholic Beverages:** At site.

TO GET THERE

The campground is located 5 mi. south of Morrisville on VT 12.

LEICESTER   MAP, B-2
Country Village Campground

40 Hwy. 7, 05733. T: (802) 247-3333.

🚐 ★★★	▲ ★★★
Beauty: ★★★	Site Privacy: ★★★★
Spaciousness: ★★★★	Quiet: ★★★
Security: ★★★★★	Cleanliness: ★★★★
Insect Control: ★★★	Facilities: ★★

This modest, clean, and friendly campground boasts super-sized, woodsy sites with plenty of privacy. The sites are scattered in pine-scented woods with an open meadow and field in front of them for sunshine and light. Seasonals, about 20 of them, are located in a separate area, so the campground retains a more back-to-nature atmosphere. Most campers explore the area, browse antiques shops, or spend the day at nearby Lake Dunmore. On site, there's a solar heated pool and mini-golf, popular with the young crowd. Favorite site: 22, though sites 20–30 and 9–16 are nice, too.

BASICS

Operated By: Joe and Barb Ceccoli. **Open:** Mid-May–mid-Oct. **Site Assignment:** Reservations suggested; 1-night deposit; 2-night deposit on holiday weekends; 10-day cancellation policy plus handling fee. **Registration:** At office. **Fee:** $14–$20; no credit cards. **Parking:** At site.

FACILITIES

Number of RV-only Sites: 5. **Number of Multipurpose Sites:** 36. **Hookups:** Electric (20, 30 amps), water. **Each Site:** Picnic table, fire ring,

water. **Dump Station:** Yes. **Laundry:** No. **Pay Phone:** No. **Restrooms and Showers:** Yes (coin-op). **Fuel:** No. **Propane:** No. **Internal Roads:** Gravel (good). **RV Service:** No. **Market:** Brandon, 3 mi. **Restaurant:** Brandon, 3 mi. **General Store:** Yes. **Vending:** Yes. **Swimming:** Pool. **Playground:** Yes. **Other:** Mini-golf, rec area. **Activities:** Swimming, shuffleboard, horseshoes, volleyball. **Nearby Attractions:** Farms, antiques shops, hiking, biking, swimming, boating, fishing, Lake Dunmore, Middlebury. **Additional Information:** Brandon Area Chamber of Commerce, Brandon Information Center, Hwy. 7, P.O. Box 267, Brandon, VT 05733; (802) 247-6401; www.brandon.org.

RESTRICTIONS

Pets: On leash only. **Fires:** In fire pits & grills only. **Alcoholic Beverages:** At site.

TO GET THERE

Campground is located 3 mi. north of Brandon on Hwy. 7.

NEW HAVEN   MAP, XX-00
Rivers Bend Campground

1000 Dog Team Rd., P.O. Box 110, 05472. T: (802) 388-9092; www.riversbendcampground.com.

🚐 ★★★	▲ ★★★
Beauty: ★★★★	Site Privacy: ★★★
Spaciousness: ★★★	Quiet: ★★★★
Security: ★★★	Cleanliness: ★★★★
Insect Control: ★★★	Facilities: ★★★

A river runs through it. The New Haven River and Otter Creek converge at this campground with 1,000 feet of prime river frontage. The campground is popular with anglers who can fish—most often successfully—from the banks or canoes. Canoe and kayak rentals are available at the campground, or bring your own and launch from your site or the campground beach. There are several sites on the river; we especially like sites 40–42 on a small point at the bend in the river. There are also large sites that can accommodate more than one RV or tent. The campground is a relaxing place to hang out, dangle your feet in the river, read a book at the beach, or paddle the river. It's also conveniently located in mid-Vermont, with the pretty college town of Middlebury up the road, the Green Mountains to the east, and Lake Champlain to the west.

BASICS

Operated By: Tom Crilly and Michelle Cornet. **Open:** May–Oct. 15. **Site Assignment:** Reservation requires 50% deposit. **Registration:** At office. **Fee:** $27.50–$30. **Parking:** At site.

FACILITIES

Number of RV-only Sites: Undesignated sites. **Number of Multipurpose Sites:** 67. **Hookups:** Electric (20 & 30 amps), water. **Each Site:** Picnic table, fire ring. **Dump Station:** No. **Laundry:** Yes. **Pay Phone:** Yes. **Restrooms and Showers:** Yes. **Fuel:** No. **Propane:** Yes. **Internal Roads:** Gravel, dirt (good). **RV Service:** No. **Market:** Middlebury, 4 mi. **Restaurant:** Middlebury, 4 mi. **General Store:** Yes. **Vending:** No. **Swimming:** River. **Playground:**

Yes. **Other:** Beach, canoe & kayak rentals, pavilion, RV rentals, safari area, nature trails. **Activities:** Swimming, fishing, boating, hiking. **Nearby Attractions:** Antiques shops, art galleries, biking, hiking, boating, fishing, swimming, Middlebury. **Additional Information:** Addison County, Vermont Chamber of Commerce, 2 Court St., Middlebury, VT 05753; (802) 388-7951.

RESTRICTIONS

Pets: On leash only. Must present valid rabies certification on check-in. **Fires:** In fire pits & grills only. **Alcoholic Beverages:** At site.

TO GET THERE

From Middlebury, take Hwy. 7N 3 mi.; turn left on Dog Team Rd. Campground is 1 mi.

NEWFANE   MAP, D-2
Kenolie Village Campground

16 Kenolie Campground Rd., 05345.
T: (802) 365-7671; www.kenolievillage.com.

🚐 ★★★   ⛺ ★★★

Beauty: ★★★	Site Privacy: ★★★
Spaciousness: ★★★	Quiet: ★★★★
Security: ★★★	Cleanliness: ★★★
Insect Control: ★★★	Facilities: ★★

This off-the-beaten-path campground will appeal to those who want a rustic, relaxed camping experience. It's a pretty ride to the campground, along a bubbling river and rolling farmlands and horse fields. Surrounding mountains frame the backdrop of the campground, and the West River is a short walk away, where you'll find a classic rocky beach area and a great swimming hole. There are some seasonals lined on both sides of the property, backing up to the woods. But you'll also find plenty of transient sites to rent. We like the wooded sites resting on a small knoll with views of the surrounding mountains. There's not much in the way of on-site activities, but you'll find plenty of nearby outdoor pursuits, like biking, hiking, fishing, boating, tubing, and more.

BASICS

Operated By: Ken and Stella Dowley. **Open:** Apr. 21–Oct. 16. **Site Assignment:** Reservations suggested; 1-night deposit; 2-week cancellation policy. **Registration:** At office. **Fee:** Trailer (50 amp), $19.75; trailer (30 amp), $18.75; no hookup, $15.75; V, MC, D. **Parking:** At site.

FACILITIES

Number of RV-only Sites: 9. **Number of Multipurpose Sites:** 150. **Hookups:** Electric (30, 50 amps), water. **Each Site:** Picnic table, fire ring. **Dump Station:** No. **Laundry:** Yes. **Pay Phone:** Yes. **Restrooms and Showers:** Yes (coin-op). **Fuel:** No. **Propane:** No. **Internal Roads:** Gravel (good). **RV Service:** No. **Market:** Brattleboro, 12 mi. **Restaurant:** Brattleboro, 12 mi. **General Store:** Yes. **Vending:** No. **Swimming:** Nearby river. **Playground:** Yes. **Other:** Game room. **Activities:** Horseshoes, shuffleboard, planned weekend activities. **Nearby Attractions:** Farms, antiques shops, swimming, hiking, biking, fishing, boating, Brattleboro. **Additional Information:** Brattleboro Area Chamber of Commerce, 180 Main St., Brattleboro, VT 05301; (802) 254-4565; www.brattleborochamber.org.

RESTRICTIONS

Pets: On leash only. **Fires:** In fire pits & grills only. **Alcoholic Beverages:** At site.

TO GET THERE

Take I-91, Exit 2; follow Hwy. 30N 14 mi. to Radway Rd. Go east 1 mi. to River Rd. South; campground is 1 mi. on the right.

NORTH HERO   MAP, A-1
North Hero State Park

3803 Lakeview Dr., 05474.
T: (802) 372-8727 (summer) or (888) 409-7579; www.vtstateparks.com.

🚐 ★★★   ⛺ ★★★★

Beauty: ★★★	Site Privacy: ★★★★
Spaciousness: ★★★★	Quiet: ★★★★
Security: ★★★	Cleanliness: ★★★
Insect Control: ★★★	Facilities: ★★★

Here's a hot tip if you're the spontaneous type: It's often possible to camp on the Lake Champlain Islands, even on July 4 weekend, without a reservation, if you make your way to this hidden gem of a campground! Other state parks in this string, Grand Isle and South Hero, fill up first, and then campers come here, a ranger told us conspiratorially. This one, North Hero, is set on the northern tip of Champlain's North Hero Island. It's true, this campground doesn't have water views of Lake Champlain, nor are the campsites directly accessible to the water—you have to walk a sandy trail or drive to the beach. But North Hero State Park is surrounded by woodlands, with plenty of wildlife (mostly whitetail deer and waterfowl), and its grassy, woodsy sites offer plenty of privacy. Campsites have long entrances, and there really isn't a bad spot among them. Set in three loops, the camping areas are linked by trails to the beach. Loop 3 is closest to the camper's beach—a rock-strewn crescent of sand—and the boat launch. Watch where you walk on the beach; there's a roped-off nesting area for endangered spiny soft-shell turtles.

BASICS

Operated By: Vermont Agency of Natural Resources, Dept. of Forests, Parks and Recreation. **Open:** Mid-May–Labor Day. **Site Assignment:** Reservations usually not needed but accepted for a 2-night min. stay. **Registration:** At contact station. **Fee:** $14–$21; V, MC. **Parking:** At site.

FACILITIES

Number of RV-only Sites: 18 (lean-tos). **Number of Multipurpose Sites:** 99. **Each Site:** Picnic table, fire ring. **Dump Station:** Yes. **Laundry:** No. **Pay Phone:** Yes. **Restrooms and Showers:** Yes, fee. **Fuel:** No. **Propane:** No. **Internal Roads:** Paved, gravel. **RV Service:** No. **Market:** 7 mi. **Restaurant:** 7 mi. **General Store:** No. **Vending:** No. **Swimming:** Lake. **Playground:** Yes. **Other:** Boat ramp, boat rentals (canoes, rowboats, kayaks). **Activities:** Swimming, fishing, boating. **Nearby Attractions:** Hermann's Royal Lippizan Stallions, St. Anne's Shrine, Burlington shopping & restaurants. **Additional Information:** Lake Champlain Islands Chamber of Commerce; (802) 372-8400; www.champlainislands.com.

RESTRICTIONS

Pets: On leash only; must be quiet & cleaned up after; proof of current rabies vaccination required. **Fires:** In fire rings only. **Alcoholic Beverages:** At site. **Vehicle Maximum Length:** 35 ft.

TO GET THERE

Follow US 2 north 3 mi. beyond North Hero Village, then bear right at intersection onto Lakeview Rd. Follow 4 mi. to park entrance. From Alburg: Go 6 mi. southwest on US 2, then 3 mi. northeast on Town Rd.

PERU   MAP, C-2
Hapgood Pond Campground

Manchester Ranger District,
RR 1. 2538 Depot Rd., 05255.
T: (802) 362-2307 or (877) 444-6777; www.fs.fed.us/r9/gmfl.

🚐 ★★★   ⛺ ★★★★

Beauty: ★★★	Site Privacy: ★★★
Spaciousness: ★★★	Quiet: ★★★★
Security: ★★★	Cleanliness: ★★★★
Insect Control: ★★	Facilities: ★★

This rustic campground, built by the Civilian Conservation Corps between 1936 and 1938, is one of the busiest of the Green Mountain National Forest campgrounds. But that's not saying much. You'll find plenty of peace and quiet here and lots of woods and fields to roam. Bring your fishing poles; the pond is well stocked with trout. (It's not uncommon to see fresh trout grilling on coals around dinnertime.) There's also a nice sandy beach and bathhouse that are popular with local day visitors. Canoes and small boats are allowed on the pond, too. Birders and nature lovers will want to walk the short, 0.8-mile trail that skirts around the north edge of the pond. Campsites are spacious and private, set in a circle and tucked in the woods. There are four walk-in sites, numbers 17–20, that offer even more seclusion. Trailers and RVs can be accommodated at most sites, but larger RVs should use caution because most sites have a small turning radius to get in and out.

BASICS

Operated By: U.S. Forest Service. **Open:** Memorial Day–Labor Day. **Site Assignment:** First come, first served; no reservations. **Registration:** At fee station, near campground entrance. **Fee:** $13. **Parking:** At site. 4 walk-in sites.

FACILITIES

Number of RV-only Sites: 7. **Number of Multipurpose Sites:** 21. **Each Site:** Picnic table, grill. **Dump Station:** No. **Laundry:** No. **Pay Phone:** No. **Restrooms and Showers:** No flush vault toilets; no showers. **Fuel:** No. **Propane:** No. **Internal Roads:** Gravel, dirt (fair). **RV Service:** No. **Market:** Weston, 5 mi. **Restaurant:** Peru, 2 mi. **General Store:** No. **Vending:** No. **Swimming:** Lake. **Playground:** No. **Other:** Beach (lifeguard on duty during summer months), pavilion, fishing pier, nature trail. **Activities:** Fishing, boating, hiking, swimming. **Nearby Attractions:** Farms, antiques shops, hiking, biking, boating, fishing, swimming, Manchester. **Additional Information:** Manchester the Mountains Chamber of Commerce, 5046 Main St. Suite 1,

Manchester Center, VT 05255-3451; (802) 362-2100 or (800) 362-4144; www.manchestervermont.net.

RESTRICTIONS

Pets: On leash only. **Fires:** In fire pits & grills only. **Alcoholic Beverages:** At site.

TO GET THERE

The campground is located about 6 mi. east of Manchester. Take Hwy. 11, go left into Peru. Turn north on Hapgood Pond Rd.; campground is 2 mi. up the road.

PLYMOUTH   MAP, C-2
Coolidge State Park

855 Coolidge State Park Rd., 05056.
T: (802) 672-3612 or (888) 409-7579;
www.vtstateparks.com.

🚐 ★★★   ▲ ★★★★

Beauty: ★★★	Site Privacy: ★★★★
Spaciousness: ★★★★	Quiet: ★★★★
Security: ★★★	Cleanliness: ★★★
Insect Control: ★★★	Facilities: ★★

Sometimes, all you really need is a quiet place to lay down your head, away from the crowds, the traffic, and the commotion. This is it. The 500-acre state park campground sits at the eastern edge of the larger Coolidge State Forest and is a rustic, woodsy retreat for campers in the south-central section of Vermont. The campground appeals mostly to tenters and pop-up campers. Though there's no limit to vehicle size, larger rigs will need to use caution in the tight turning quarters. The dense woods are criss-crossed with an extensive network of trails leading to brooks, streams, ponds, meadows, and vistas. Lots of day hikes are possible from the campground. Camp-sites are of good size and private, set in two loops in the woods. Several brooks flow through the property, and if the crickets aren't too loud, you'll be able to here the gurgling water as you nod off to sleep.

BASICS

Operated By: State of Vermont. **Open:** Mid-May–Oct. 15. **Site Assignment:** Reservations may be made up to 11 months in advance; 2-night min. required; reservations accepted at (888) 409-7579; contact park directly only for reservations w/in 10 days of stay; no refunds for the 2-night min. **Registration:** At office. **Fee:** $14–$23; V, MC. **Parking:** At site.

FACILITIES

Number of Multipurpose Sites: 25 (35 lean-tos). **Each Site:** Picnic table, fire ring. **Dump Station:** Yes. **Laundry:** No. **Pay Phone:** No. **Restrooms and Showers:** Yes (coin-op). **Fuel:** No. **Propane:** No. **Internal Roads:** Gravel, dirt (fair). **RV Service:** No. **Market:** Plymouth, 2 mi. **Restaurant:** Ply-mouth, 2 mi. **General Store:** No. **Vending:** No. **Swimming:** Nearby. **Playground:** No. **Other:** Pic-nic area, pavilion. **Activities:** Hiking, biking. **Nearby Attractions:** Swimming, hiking, biking, fishing, boat-ing, White River, Woodstock, Killington mountain resort. **Additional Information:** Woodstock Area Chamber of Commerce, 18 Central St., P.O. Box 486-4, Woodstock, VT 05091; (802) 457-3555; www.woodstockvt.com. Killington/Pico Area

Chamber of Commerce, P.O. Box 114, Killington, VT 05751; (802) 773-4181.

RESTRICTIONS

Pets: On leash only. **Fires:** At site only. **Alcoholic Beverages:** At site.

TO GET THERE

In Plymouth, from junction of Hwy. 100 and Hwy. 100A, follow Hwy. 100A 2 mi.

POULTNEY   MAP, C-1
Lake St. Catherine State Park

3034 Hwy. 30, 05764.
T: (802) 287-9158 or (888) 409-7579;
www.vtstateparks.com.

🚐 ★★★★   ▲ ★★★★

Beauty: ★★★★	Site Privacy: ★★★★
Spaciousness: ★★★★	Quiet: ★★★
Security: ★★★	Cleanliness: ★★★
Insect Control: ★★★	Facilities: ★★★

This popular day-use park and state campground is one of the most developed in the park system, with picnic areas, a playground, and beach. There are even flush toilets! (Showers are hot but coin-operated.) The scenic lake, surrounded by woods, is perfect for boating, fishing, and swimming on hot summer days. The campground is set apart from the day-use area and features three main loops of sites. Like most state campgrounds, sites are spacious and private. Site 35 is one of the most secluded, tucked back into a pine grove. If you're with a small group, check into sites 38 and 39, adjacent to a large, open grassy area. Site 47 is particularly large. Be sure to make reserva-tions early, because this park often fills quickly, espe-cially on summer and fall weekends.

BASICS

Operated By: State of Vermont. **Open:** Mid-May–Oct. 15. **Site Assignment:** Reservations may be made up to 11 months in advance; 2-night min. required; reservations accepted at (888) 409-7579; contact park directly only for reservations w/in 10 days of stay; no refunds for the 2-night min. **Registration:** At office. **Fee:** $16; lean-to, $23; V, MC. **Parking:** At site.

FACILITIES

Number of Multipurpose Sites: 50 (11 lean-tos). **Each Site:** Picnic table, fire ring. **Dump Station:** Yes. **Laundry:** No. **Pay Phone:** Yes. **Restrooms and Showers:** Yes (coin-op). **Fuel:** No. **Propane:** No. **Internal Roads:** Gravel (good). **RV Service:** No. **Market:** Poultney, 3 mi. **Restaurant:** Snack bar on site. **General Store:** No. **Vending:** No. **Swim-ming:** Lake. **Playground:** Yes. **Other:** Boat rentals, picnic area, beach. **Activities:** Swimming, boating, fishing. **Nearby Attractions:** Farms, antiques shops, hiking, biking, boating, fishing, swimming, Man-chester, Bennington. **Additional Information:** Manchester the Mountains Chamber of Commerce, 5046 Main St. Suite 1, Manchester Center, VT 05255-3451; (802) 362-2100 or (800) 362-4144; www.manchestervermont.net. Bennington Area Chamber of Commerce, 100 Veterans Memorial Dr., Bennington, VT.

RESTRICTIONS

Pets: On leash only. **Fires:** In fire pits & grills only. **Alcoholic Beverages:** At site.

TO GET THERE

From Poultney, go 3 mi. south on Hwy. 30.

SALISBURY   MAP, B-1
Branbury State Park

3570 Lake Dunmore, Hwy. 53, 05733.
T: (802) 247-5925 (summer) or (888) 409-7579;
www.vtstateparks.com.

🚐 ★★★   ▲ ★★★

Beauty: ★★★	Site Privacy: ★★★★
Spaciousness: ★★★★	Quiet: ★★★
Security: ★★★	Cleanliness: ★★★★
Insect Control: ★★★	Facilities: ★★★

This state park campground on pretty Lake Dun-more is great for outdoor enthusiasts who like to hike, swim, boat (bring your own), or simply relax in the woods. The 69-acre property sits on the eastern shore of the lake at the base of Mt. Moosalamoo, with the Green Mountains to the east. Campers have a net-work of fine hiking trails at their doorstep, leading to mountain vistas, lakes, streams, cascades, and water-falls. There's also a short interpretive nature trail. When you're done hiking, cool down with a swim in the lake. There's a nice 1,000-foot sandy beach at one end of the campground. The highway divides the property. Some sites are located in the woods on one side of Hwy. 53. The rest are on the other side of the highway, in an open grassy area near the beach.

BASICS

Operated By: State of Vermont. **Open:** Mid-May–Oct. 15. **Site Assignment:** Reservations may be made up to 11 months in advance; 2-night min. required; reservations accepted at (888) 409-7579; contact park directly only for reservations w/in 10 days of stay; no refunds for the 2-night min. **Regis-tration:** At office. **Fee:** $16; lean-to, $23; V, MC. **Parking:** At site.

FACILITIES

Number of Multipurpose Sites: 39 (6 lean-tos). **Each Site:** Picnic table, fire ring. **Dump Station:** Yes. **Laundry:** No. **Pay Phone:** No. **Restrooms and Showers:** Yes (coin-op). **Fuel:** No. **Propane:** No. **Internal Roads:** Gravel, dirt (good). **RV Ser-vice:** No. **Market:** Middlebury, 11 mi. **Restaurant:** Middlebury, 11 mi. **General Store:** No. **Vending:** No. **Swimming:** Lake. **Playground:** No. **Other:** Beach, hiking trails. **Activities:** Swimming, hiking, fishing. **Nearby Attractions:** Farms, antiques shops, hiking, biking, swimming, boating, fishing, Middlebury. **Additional Information:** Addison County, Ver-mont Chamber of Commerce, 2 Court St., Middle-bury, VT 05753; (802) 388-7951.

RESTRICTIONS

Pets: On leash only. **Fires:** In fire pits & grills only. **Alcoholic Beverages:** At site.

TO GET THERE

From Middlebury, go south 7 mi. on Hwy. 7, then 4 mi. south on Hwy. 53.

SALISBURY MAP, B-1
Lake Dunmore Kampersville Campground

P.O. Box 56, Hwy. 53, 05769.
T: (802) 352-4501 or (877) 250-2568;
www.kampersville.com.

🚐 ★★★★   ⛺ ★★★

Beauty: ★★★   Site Privacy: ★★★
Spaciousness: ★★★   Quiet: ★★★
Security: ★★★   Cleanliness: ★★★★
Insect Control: ★★★   Facilities: ★★★★★

There's never a dull moment at this bustling, activity-based campground located on the shores of pretty Lake Dunmore. Local families and Vermont's summer tourists clamor to this mini-resort, with enough goings-on to keep everyone hopping. The soft, sandy beach is a great place to hang out; if you're yearning to get out on the lake, there are boat rentals on site. Lake water too cold for your liking? No problem. Head to one of the two pools (there's a separate kiddie pool, too), a popular gathering spot for families. Sports fields, mini-golf, hay rides, arts and crafts. the fun never stops. You can even try your hand at disc golf. This is a destination campground; most campers stick around to enjoy the lake and on-site facilities. But the quaint college town of Middlebury (with cafes and art galleries) is minutes away; Burlington, with museums, restaurants, theater, and more, is less than an hour away. You don't have much choice in campsites; they're all pretty much the same: set in rows, close together, with little privacy. Families who like to be close to the action may like sites 171–182, clustered around the pool and playground area.

BASICS
Operated By: Jean Wilnowski. **Open:** All year. **Site Assignment:** Reservations suggested, nonrefundable $30 deposit required. **Registration:** At office. **Fee:** Electric/water/sewer, $38; electric/water, $33; no hookup, $22; V, MC. **Parking:** At site.

FACILITIES
Number of Tent-only Sites: 134. **Number of Multipurpose Sites:** 76. **Hookups:** Electric, water, sewer, cable TV. **Each Site:** Picnic table, fire ring. **Dump Station:** Yes. **Laundry:** Yes. **Pay Phone:** Yes. **Restrooms and Showers:** Yes. **Fuel:** No. **Propane:** Yes. **Internal Roads:** Paved, gravel (good). **RV Service:** No. **Market:** Salisbury, 3 mi. **Restaurant:** Snack bar, restaurant, deli, pizza parlor on site. **General Store:** Yes. **Vending:** No. **Swimming:** 2 pools, lake. **Playground:** Yes. **Other:** Rec hall, arcade, mini-golf, beach, dock, boat rentals, sports fields, cottage rentals, lodge. **Activities:** Swimming, boating, shuffleboard, horseshoes, basketball, volleyball, disc golf, planned activities. **Nearby Attractions:** Antiques shops, art galleries, hiking, biking, boating, fishing, swimming, Shelburne, Burlington. **Additional Information:** Lake Champlain Regional Chamber of Commerce, 60 Main St., Suite 100, Burlington, VT 05401; (802) 863-3489 or (877) 686-5253; www.vermont.org.

RESTRICTIONS
Pets: On leash only. Up-to-date vaccination records must be presented at check-in. **Fires:** In fire pits & grills only. **Alcoholic Beverages:** At site.

TO GET THERE
From Salisbury, Hwy. 7, take Hwy. 53 south 1.5 mi.

SALISBURY MAP, B-1
Waterhouses Campground and Marina

937 West Shore Rd., 05769. T: (802) 352-4433;
www.waterhouses.com.

🚐 ★★★   ⛺ ★★★

Beauty: ★★★★   Site Privacy: ★★★
Spaciousness: ★★★★   Quiet: ★★★
Security: ★★★   Cleanliness: ★★★
Insect Control: ★★★   Facilities: ★★★

Lucky for Vermont travelers, this old-fashioned lakefront campground that was once a summer home for seasonal campers is now a transient site. Come for a night, come for a weekend, come for a week! Located on the shores of pristine Lake Dunmore, across from Mt. Moosalamoo, this campground is a lovely place to relax and enjoy outdoor pursuits. The lake is the big draw, and the on-site, full-service marina rents several types of watercraft. There's also a nice beach and picnic table at the marina. Campers have a choice of nicely spaced, grassy sites in open fields, woods, or on the riverfront. This campground has bright, glistening bathrooms and an updated general store. There are woods and fields to roam surrounding the campsites. Don't miss the short hike up Sunset Hill for expansive views of Lake Champlain Valley to the west and Lake Dunmore and the Green Mountains to the east.

BASICS
Operated By: Dunmore Group. **Open:** May 15–Oct. 15. **Site Assignment:** First come, first served; 2-night min. required for reservations; 1-night, nonrefundable deposit. **Registration:** At office. **Fee:** Water/electric, $29; additional charge for holidays, $5; V, MC. **Parking:** At site.

FACILITIES
Number of RV-only Sites: 3. **Number of Multipurpose Sites:** 68. **Hookups:** Electric (30 amps), water. **Each Site:** Picnic table, fire ring. **Dump Station:** Yes. **Laundry:** No. **Pay Phone:** Yes. **Restrooms and Showers:** Yes. **Fuel:** No. **Propane:** Yes. **Internal Roads:** Gravel (good). **RV Service:** No. **Market:** Salisbury, 0.5 mi. **Restaurant:** Salisbury, 0.5 mi. **General Store:** Yes. **Vending:** No. **Swimming:** Beach. **Playground:** No. **Other:** Full-service marina, boat rentals, picnic area, sports fields, mini-golf, yurt rentals. **Activities:** Swimming, boating, fishing, volleyball, baseball, hiking, mountain biking. **Nearby Attractions:** Antiques shops, hiking, biking, swimming, boating, fishing. **Additional Information:** Addison County, Vermont Chamber of Commerce, 2 Court St., Middlebury, VT 05753; (802) 388-7951.

RESTRICTIONS
Pets: On leash only. **Fires:** In fire pits & grills only. **Alcoholic Beverages:** At site. **Vehicle Maximum Length:** 35 ft.

TO GET THERE
From Salisbury, Hwy. 7S, take Hwy. 53, go 1 mi.

SOUTH HERO MAP, A-1
Camp Skyland

398 South St., 05486. T: (802) 372-4200;
www.campvermont.com.

🚐 ★★★★★   ⛺ ★★★★

Beauty: ★★★★★   Site Privacy: ★★
Spaciousness: ★★★★   Quiet: ★★★★
Security: ★★★   Cleanliness: ★★★★
Insect Control: ★★★★   Facilities: ★★★

"To get a cabin or one of their seasonal sites, somebody has to die," a Camp Skyland regular (age 76, a visitor for 18 years and counting) told us. This place is so desirable that folks don't let it go unless, well, you know. "It's a little piece of heaven!" the gent told us, though he didn't need to. Camp Skyland occupies an amazing spot on the southern tip of South Hero Island. It claims its own peninsula where Mallets Bay meets Lake Champlain. Sites are set on a grassy bluff overlooking the water, a very peachy place to watch sailboats cut through the prevailing southerlies. Virtually everybody gets a view. The grounds are beautifully manicured, and small personal touches win you over, like the games, toys, and magazines available at the lending library. It does get windy here, which is fine if you're in your own unit, not so good for tenting—but then, they've got a row of sweet little cabins for rent. Sign up now if you want one in, say, your lifetime! There's a small beach area, with dock, playground, and sports equipment, along with rental boats for coastal exploring. This is also a great place for windsurfing (bring your own boat). Take a peek at the original dining hall from this former summer camp, built in 1927 with a wonderful beamed ceiling. Camp Skyland truly is breathtaking, and it really raises the bar for campgrounds on the Lake Champlain islands.

BASICS
Operated By: Arnold family. **Open:** Memorial Day–Sept. 15. **Site Assignment:** Advance reservations required; $15 deposit (nonrefundable). **Registration:** At office. **Fee:** $24; cabin, $350; checks, no credit cards. **Parking:** At site.

FACILITIES
Number of RV-only Sites: 11. **Number of Multipurpose Sites:** 22. **Hookups:** Electric, water, sewer. **Each Site:** Picnic table, fire ring. **Dump Station:** No. **Laundry:** Yes. **Pay Phone:** No. **Restrooms and Showers:** Yes. **Fuel:** No. **Propane:** No. **Internal Roads:** Gravel. **RV Service:** No. **Market:** 10 mi. north. **Restaurant:** 10 mi. north. **General Store:** Yes. **Vending:** Yes. **Swimming:** Lake. **Playground:** Yes (swing set). **Other:** Rec hall, game room, rowboat & canoe rentals, boat ramp (for lightweight boats), lending library. **Activities:** Swimming, boating, fishing, windsurfing, table tennis, horseshoes. **Nearby Attractions:** Burlington shopping & restaurants, Shelburne Museum, Grand Isle Log Cabin. **Additional Information:** Lake Champlain Islands Chamber of Commerce; (802) 372-8400; www.champlainislands.com.

RESTRICTIONS
Pets: On leash only; must be quiet & cleaned up after. Must not be left unattended. **Fires:** In fire rings

only. **Alcoholic Beverages:** At site. **Vehicle Maximum Length:** 26 ft.

TO GET THERE

Located at southernmost tip of South Hero Island, 10 mi. off Exit 17 on I-89; 3.5 mi. off US 2 at the end of South St.

ST. ALBANS MAP, A-1
Burton Island State Park

P.O. Box 123, 05481. T: (802) 524-6353 or (802) 252-2363; www.vtstateparks.com.

🚐 n/a ⛺ ★★★★

Beauty: ★★★★	Site Privacy: ★★★
Spaciousness: ★★★★	Quiet: ★★★★
Security: ★★★★	Cleanliness: ★★★
Insect Control: ★★★	Facilities: ★★★

Eighteenth-century maps called Burton Island the Isle of White. Later, it was owned by one Sidney Burton, who leased it to tenant farmers who grazed cows, pigs, sheep, and chickens. Today, as you hike around the 253-acre island, you might notice the odd stone pile or rusted farm implement. More likely, though, your eyes will be riveted to the surrounding, intensely blue waters of Lake Champlain. This wonderfully rustic property—available overnight to tenters only—sits off the southwestern tip of St. Albans Point in Vermont's inland sea. No vehicles are allowed here, except park service equipment, meaning you either come over by private pleasure boat and take a slip at the marina, or grab a mooring, or you come by ferry, carrying your camping gear. The walk to the farthest site isn't far, and you can use a cart if you like. Then rent a boat (you can't bring one on the ferry, alas), wander around the island, watch the sun set in front of your campfire, and enjoy an unforgettable camping experience.

BASICS

Operated By: Vermont Agency of Natural Resources/Vermont Dept. of Forests, Parks and Recreation. **Open:** Late May–Labor Day. **Site Assignment:** Reservations open the 15th of every month; campers may reserve up to 11 months in advance by calling (888) 409-7549; for reservations w/in 10 days of arrival, call campground directly; 4-night min. for reservations. **Registration:** At office. **Fee:** $16–$23; V, MC. Passenger ferry service via Island Runner, $3 per person, one-way. **Parking:** No cars; arrive via ferry or own boat.

FACILITIES

Number of Tent-only Sites: 17 (26 lean-tos). **Each Site:** Picnic table, fireplace. **Dump Station:** No. **Laundry:** No. **Pay Phone:** Yes. **Restrooms and Showers:** Yes. **Fuel:** Yes, for boats. **Propane:** No. **Internal Roads:** Gravel. **RV Service:** No. **Market:** On the mainland, in St. Albans. **Restaurant:** Limited food service at park store. **General Store:** Yes. **Vending:** Yes. **Swimming:** Lake. **Playground:** No. **Other:** Nature center/museum, marina. **Activities:** Boating, canoeing (rowboat and canoe rentals available), lake swimming, picnicking, hiking (4 miles of trails). **Nearby Attractions:** Lake Champlain islands. **Additional Information:** Lake

Champlain Islands Chamber of Commerce; (802) 372-8400; www.champlainislands.com.

RESTRICTIONS

Pets: On leash only & cleaned up after. Allowed in designated areas only. Proof of current rabies vaccination required. **Fires:** In fire ring only. **Alcoholic Beverages:** OK if consumed responsibly. No containers larger than 1 gallon.

TO GET THERE

From St. Albans, take VT 36W (Lake St.) 3 mi., bearing sharply right at St. Albans Bay. Go 1 mi. and turn left after crossing a bridge onto Hathaway Point Rd. Go 3 mi. to the end and park at Kill Kare State Park. Burton Island ferry, the Island Runner, runs between Kill Kare and Burton Island 5 times per day in season. No canoes or kayaks transported via ferry.

ST. JOHNSBURY MAP, B-3
Moose River Campground

2870 Portland St., 05819. T: (802) 748-4334; www.mooserivercampground.com.

🚐 ★★★★ ⛺ ★★

Beauty: ★★	Site Privacy: ★★★
Spaciousness: ★★	Quiet: ★★
Security: ★★★	Cleanliness: ★★★
Insect Control: ★★★	Facilities: ★★★

Set in Vermont's Northeast Kingdom, just over the New Hampshire border, Moose River is an interesting alternative to the scene at nearby Sugar Ridge (see listing). There isn't much in the way of amenities, except a natural one: the Moose River, where it's fine to cast a line (provided you've picked up a Vermont fishing license along the way). On any given weekend, there's a pig roast or a chili cook-off or a bean hole supper going on, often highlighted with a performance by a country music artist. The campground is grassy and fairly open, with sites set in a loop. There's some shade, but not much buffer between sites. At this campground, however, socializing has a higher priority than privacy—once you've done the limbo or competed in a watermelon-eating contest with a fellow camper, you've pretty much gotten acquainted! Tip: This area is great for leaf-peeping as seven towns here offer fall foliage festivals in late September.

BASICS

Operated By: Mary and Gary Lunderville. **Open:** Mid-May–mid-Oct. **Site Assignment:** Reservations recommended; reserve any time after Jan. 1; for cancellations w/in 14 days of stay, $15 charge.; charge for cancellations during holiday periods or special events; charge of 1-night fee for no-shows and same-day cancellations. **Registration:** At office. **Fee:** $20–$30; V, MC. **Parking:** At site.

FACILITIES

Number of RV-only Sites: 5. **Number of Tent-only Sites:** 3. **Number of Multipurpose Sites:** 50. **Hookups:** Electric (30, 50 amps), water, cable, sewer, Wi-Fi. **Each Site:** Picnic table, fire ring. **Dump Station:** No. **Laundry:** Yes. **Pay Phone:** Yes. **Restrooms and Showers:** Yes, fee. **Fuel:** No.

Propane: Yes. **Internal Roads:** Gravel. **RV Service:** No. **Market:** 3 mi. west, St. Johnsbury. **Restaurant:** 3 mi. west. **General Store:** Yes (across the street) and full-service store in the campground. **Vending:** No. **Swimming:** No. **Playground:** No. **Other:** Rec hall. **Activities:** Planned activities. **Nearby Attractions:** Maple Grove Farms (syrup, candy factory), Fairbanks Museum of Natural Science. **Additional Information:** Northeast Kingdom Chamber of Commerce; (802) 748-3678 or (800) 639-6379; www.nekchamber.com.

RESTRICTIONS

Pets: On leash only; must be quiet & cleaned up after. Must not be left unattended. **Fires:** In fire ring only. **Alcoholic Beverages:** W/ discretion. **Vehicle Maximum Length:** 110 ft.

TO GET THERE

Take Exit 19 off I-91, onto I-93, then Exit 1 onto VT 18. Head north to junction of VT 18 and US 2.

STOWE MAP, B-2
Gold Brook Campground

P.O. Box 1028, VT 100, 05672. T: (802) 253-7683; www.campvermont.com/html/cgs/north/goldbrook.htm.

🚐 ★★★★ ⛺ ★★★

Beauty: ★★★★	Site Privacy: ★★★
Spaciousness: ★★★★	Quiet: ★★★★
Security: ★★★	Cleanliness: ★★★
Insect Control: ★★	Facilities: ★★★

Located right alongside VT 100 en route to Stowe Village, this grassy campground is set alongside Gold Brook. The backdrop of velvety green mountains tells you you're in Vermont and you've picked a really swell spot! The shops and restaurants of Stowe are but a short drive away, and you can choose from among numerous hikes in the area. Stop at the Green Mountain Club headquarters in Waterbury (you'll drive right past it) to pick up guidebooks and trail maps. You can even take on Mt. Mansfield, Vermont's highest peak, or take the easy route and ride up the gondola. There's good fishing to be had at the campsite; pick a riverfront site, say, 35–43 or so, and you can cast your line from a lawn chair if you choose. Tent sites line the riverbank and boast plenty of shade; RVs are set in an open, grassy field. This area is rich with outdoor fun, summer, fall, and winter (skip mud season)—so Gold Brook caters to the ski and snowmobile set when the snow flies. This is the area's best bet for the RV crowd. Tent campers who like things more rustic and private will be happier at Smuggler's Notch State Park (see listing), a few miles up the road.

BASICS

Operated By: John, Kay, and Mary Nichols. **Open:** All year. **Site Assignment:** Reservations recommended; deposit of 1-night stay required. **Registration:** At office. **Fee:** $22–$34. **Parking:** At site.

FACILITIES

Number of Multipurpose Sites: 79. **Hookups:** Electric (30, 50 amps), water, cable, phone. **Each Site:** Picnic table, fire ring. **Dump Station:** Yes. **Laundry:** Yes. **Pay Phone:** Yes. **Restrooms and**

Showers: Yes. Fuel: No. Propane: Yes. Internal Roads: Paved, gravel. RV Service: No. Market: 2 mi. north. Restaurant: 2 mi. north. General Store: Yes. Vending: Yes. Swimming: Pool. Playground: Yes. Other: Rec hall, softball diamond. Activities: Swimming, fishing volleyball, softball, hiking (nearby). Nearby Attractions: Ben & Jerry's Ice Cream Factory, Cold Hollow Cider Mill, Stowe Recreation Path, Smuggler's Notch, Bingham Falls, Mt. Mansfield. Additional Information: Stowe Area Assoc.; (802) 253-7321 or (877) 603-8693; www.gostowe.com.

RESTRICTIONS

Pets: On leash only; must be quiet & cleaned up after. Must not be left unattended. Fires: In fire rings only. Alcoholic Beverages: At site. Vehicle Maximum Length: 40 ft.

TO GET THERE

Take Exit 10 off I-89; follow VT 100 7.5 mi. north. Campground is on the left, beside Nichols Lodge.

STOWE — MAP, B-2
Smuggler's Notch State Park

6443 Mountain Rd., 05672.
T: (802) 253-4014 or (888) 409-7579;
www.vtstateparks.com.

🚐 ★★★★   ⛺ ★★★★★

Beauty: ★★★★★   Site Privacy: ★★★★★
Spaciousness: ★★★★   Quiet: ★★★★
Security: ★★★   Cleanliness: ★★★★
Insect Control: ★★★   Facilities: ★★★★

How often does a state park move to new digs? This one did, relocating in 2003, with more campsites and more breathing room around them. Another benefit of the move was energy-efficient restrooms, and (get this) they don't charge for showers. Campsites are set in a loop and offer tons of privacy. The camping area is framed by forest land and the Green Mountains; you might get a glimpse of Camel's Hump on a clear day. Site 1 is great. Some tent sites are walk-ins; you walk maybe 100 yards up a driveway to your own private hideaway (well, once you erect that tent!). The lean-to named Birch has awesome views. The campground also has historic structures built by the Civilian Conservation Corps; these have been relocated here and restored. The access trail to Bingham Falls is a quick walk from the campground. Another cool thing about Smuggler's Notch park is simply getting here—coming from the south, you'll drive through the famous Smuggler's Notch, a narrow road of hairpin turns lined with 1,000-foot cliffs on either side. The notch was once used for illegal trade with Canada, and fugitive slaves used it as an escape route to the North. Liquor was smuggled through the notch during Prohibition. All of this, we think, simply adds to the allure of one of Vermont's most private and beautiful camping areas.

BASICS

Operated By: Vermont Agency of Natural Resources, Dept. of Forests, Parks and Recreation. Open: Mid-May–mid-Oct. Site Assignment: Reservations suggested; call (888) 409-7579; 2-night min. required. Registration: At contact station. Fee: $14–$21; V, MC. Parking: At site.

FACILITIES

Number of RV-only Sites: 14 (lean-tos). Number of Multipurpose Sites: 20 tent/trailer sites. Hookups: None. Each Site: Picnic table, fire ring or fireplace. Dump Station: Yes. Laundry: No. Pay Phone: Yes. Restrooms and Showers: Yes. Fuel: No. Propane: No. Internal Roads: Paved. RV Service: No. Market: 7 mi. south, Stowe. Restaurant: 5 mi. south. General Store: No. Vending: No. Swimming: No. Playground: No. Activities: Hiking, wildlife viewing. Nearby Attractions: Ben & Jerry's Ice Cream Factory, Cold Hollow Cider Mill, Stowe Recreation Path, Bingham Falls, Mt. Mansfield. Additional Information: Stowe Area Assoc.; (802) 253-7321 or (877) 603-8693; www.gostowe.com.

RESTRICTIONS

Pets: On leash only; must be quiet & cleaned up after. Must not be left unattended. Proof of current rabies vaccination required. Fires: In fire rings or fireplaces only. Alcoholic Beverages: At site. Vehicle Maximum Length: 26 ft.

TO GET THERE

Take Exit 10 off I-89 to VT 100 (toward Stowe); in village, take Hwy. 108N about 5 mi. Campground is on the left.

THETFORD — MAP, C-2
Thetford Hill State Park

P.O. Box 132, 05074.
T: (802) 785-2266 or (800) 299-3071;
www.vtstateparks.com.

🚐 ★★★   ⛺ ★★★★

Beauty: ★★★★   Site Privacy: ★★★★
Spaciousness: ★★★★   Quiet: ★★★★
Security: ★★★   Cleanliness: ★★★★
Insect Control: ★★   Facilities: ★★★

"There's really not much here!" says one park ranger at Thetford Hill State Park. Not much, unless you consider the beautiful views of hills and valleys that greet you just before the park's entrance or the awesome overlook from what used to be called Sunset Hill, inside the park. Located a bit north of White River Junction, nudging the New Hampshire border, Thetford Hill is all about communing with nature and great hiking. An award-winning system of cross-country ski trails, developed by neighbor Thetford Academy, makes excellent hiking paths in the summer. Some campers discover the place almost by accident, when dropping their kids off at nearby summer camps. This park was developed by the Civilian Conservation Corps in the 1930s, and the camping area was added in 1964 or so. Some sites are gravel, some are grassy, and all are fairly level. An overflow area can handle the big rigs. It's very quiet and peaceful here, except perhaps at sunset, when everyone heads one-half mile up Sunset Hill to ooh and ahh at Mother Nature's display from a lofty vantage point. There's swimming about 10 miles north at Lake Fairlee.

BASICS

Operated By: Vermont Agency of Natural Resources, Dept. of Forests, Parks and Recreation.

Open: May 26–Sept. 4. Site Assignment: Reservations recommended; 2-night min. required; midweek it is usually possible to find a site. Registration: At contact station. Fee: $14–$21; V, MC. Parking: At site.

FACILITIES

Number of RV-only Sites: 2 (lean-tos). Number of Multipurpose Sites: 14 tent/trailer sites. Each Site: Picnic table, fire ring. Dump Station: Yes. Laundry: No. Pay Phone: No. Restrooms and Showers: Yes, fee. Fuel: No. Propane: No. Internal Roads: Gravel. RV Service: No. Market: 10 mi. south. Restaurant: 5 mi. east. General Store: No. Vending: No. Swimming: No. Playground: Yes (swing set). Activities: Hiking, picnicking. Nearby Attractions: Quechee Gorge, Billings Farm Museum, Montshire Museum, Simon Pearce Glass-Blowing Studio. Additional Information: Upper Valley Bi-State Regional Chamber of Commerce; (302) 295-6200; www.uppervalleychamber.com.

RESTRICTIONS

Pets: On leash only; must be quiet & cleaned up after. Must not be left unattended. Proof of current rabies vaccination required. Fires: In fire rings only. Alcoholic Beverages: At site.

TO GET THERE

The campground is located just off Exit 14 on I-91, 1 mi. south of Thetford Hill on the road to Union Village.

TOWNSHEND — MAP, D-2
Camperama Campground

P.O. Box 282, 192 Depot Rd., 05353.
T: (802) 365-4315 or (800) 63-CAMPS;
www.gocampingamerica.com.

🚐 ★★★★   ⛺ ★★★

Beauty: ★★★   Site Privacy: ★★★
Spaciousness: ★★★   Quiet: ★★★
Security: ★★★   Cleanliness: ★★★
Insect Control: ★★★   Facilities: ★★★

If you're looking to stay put for a while, check into this top-notch campground in southern Vermont. This campground caters to seasonal and transient guests. It's a large campground, with more than 200 mostly shaded sites, including several on the West River. If you prefer sunny sites, there's also a row of level, easy pull in and out, open sites near the front of the property. Many campers spend the day relaxing around the campground, swimming in the pool, or dangling their feet in the cool waters of the West River. Tubing the river is also popular. Planned activities, like potluck dinners and picnics, are held on busy summer weekends. The surrounding countryside, with rolling hills, farmlands, mountains, and streams, is picturesque, especially during fall foliage season.

BASICS

Operated By: Annamae Ray. Open: May 15–Oct. 15. Site Assignment: Reservations suggested; 1-night deposit; 3-night cancellation policy. Registration: At office. Fee: $21–$25; V, MC. Parking: At site.

FACILITIES

Number of Multipurpose Sites: 219. **Hookups:** Electric (20, 30 amps), water, sewer, cable TV. **Each Site:** Picnic table, fire ring. **Dump Station:** Yes. **Laundry:** Yes. **Pay Phone:** Yes. **Restrooms and Showers:** Yes. **Fuel:** No. **Propane:** Yes. **Internal Roads:** Gravel (good). **RV Service:** No. **Market:** Townshend, 2 mi. **Restaurant:** Jamaica, 6 mi. **General Store:** Yes. **Vending:** Yes. **Swimming:** Pool, river. **Playground:** Yes. **Other:** Hayrides, planned events. **Activities:** Volleyball, basketball, shuffleboard, horseshoes, swimming, tubing. **Nearby Attractions:** Farms, antiques shops, swimming, hiking, biking, boating, fishing, Manchester, Bennington. **Additional Information:** Manchester the Mountains Chamber of Commerce, 5046 Main St. Suite 1, Manchester Center, VT 05255-3451; (802) 362-2100 or (800) 362-4144; www.manchestervermont.net. Bennington Area Chamber of Commerce, 100 Veterans Memorial Dr., Bennington, VT.

RESTRICTIONS

Pets: On leash only. **Fires:** In fire pits & grills only. **Alcoholic Beverages:** At site.

TO GET THERE

From I-91, take Exit 2; follow Hwy. 30 west toward Manchester. Take left on Depot Rd. (about 17 mi. west of Brattleboro).

VERGENNES   MAP, B-1
Button Bay State Park

5 Button Bay, 05491.
T: (802) 475-2377 or (888) 409-7579;
www.vtstateparks.com.

🚐 ★★★   ⛺ ★★★

Beauty: ★★★★   Site Privacy: ★★★
Spaciousness: ★★★   Quiet: ★★★
Security: ★★★   Cleanliness: ★★★★
Insect Control: ★★★   Facilities: ★★★

Expansive views of Lake Champlain and the Adirondacks to the west are the main attractions of this state park. The campground features two loops of open, grassy sites that sit on a bluff overlooking the lake. It's a bit of a communal atmosphere, all sites clustered in the field, but the views are impressive and access to the lake a prime benefit. Check out the nature center and trail that are on site, then rent a boat (boat rentals available at the campground) to explore the 130-mile-long Lake Champlain. You could spend days on the lake, or do what some campers choose: Head to bustling Burlington or Shelburne museums for daytime excursions. It's the best of two worlds.

BASICS

Operated By: State of Vermont. **Open:** Mid-May–Oct. 15. **Site Assignment:** Reservations may be made up to 11 months in advance; 2-night min.; reservations accepted at (888) 409-7579; contact park directly only for reservations w/in 10 days of stay; no refunds for 2-night minimum. **Registration:** At office. **Fee:** $16; lean-to, $23; V, MC. **Parking:** At site.

FACILITIES

Number of Multipurpose Sites: 73 (13 lean-tos).

Each Site: Picnic table, fire ring. **Dump Station:** No. **Laundry:** No. **Pay Phone:** Yes. **Restrooms and Showers:** Yes (coin-op). **Fuel:** No. **Propane:** No. **Internal Roads:** Gravel (good). **RV Service:** No. **Market:** Shelburne, 10 mi. **Restaurant:** Shelburne, 10 mi. **General Store:** No. **Vending:** No. **Swimming:** Lake. **Playground:** Yes. **Other:** Nature center, nature trail, boat rentals, pavilion, picnic area. **Activities:** Swimming, boating, fishing, hiking. **Nearby Attractions:** Shelburne, Burlington. **Additional Information:** Lake Champlain Regional Chamber of Commerce, 60 Main St., Suite 100, Burlington, VT 05401; (802) 863-3489 or (877) 686-5253; www.vermont.org.

RESTRICTIONS

Pets: On leash only. **Fires:** In fire pits & grills only. **Alcoholic Beverages:** At site.

TO GET THERE

From Vergennes, go 0.5 mi. south on Hwy. 22A, then west on Panton Rd. about 6.5 mi. to the campground.

WEST BARNET   MAP, B-2
Harvey's Lake Cabins and Campground

190 Campers Lane, 05821. T: (802) 633-2213;
www.harveyslakecabins.com.

🚐 ★★★   ⛺ ★★★

Beauty: ★★★★   Site Privacy: ★★★★
Spaciousness: ★★★   Quiet: ★★★★
Security: ★★★★   Cleanliness: ★★★★
Insect Control: ★★★   Facilities: ★★★

Harvey's Lake is the spot where a young Jacques Cousteau took his first dive at the age of 10 in 1920. This off-the-beaten-path property offers 800 feet of frontage on the lake in a pleasant, woodsy setting. Once you see the lakefront cabins, you'll realize they're the main draw here, but campers have it pretty good, too. Sites 14 and 20, on the lake, are terrific. Near the swimming area, where the cabins are set, is prime territory. Tent sites are clustered in a loop near the main house, restrooms, and rec hall. The quiet, rural setting—this is general store, white-steepled church country—will appeal to those looking to get away from it all. Of course, the 150-foot-deep lake is a big draw. The campground offers rental canoes, pedal boats, and rowboats so campers can explore.

BASICS

Operated By: Marybeth Vereline. **Open:** May 15–Oct. 15. **Site Assignment:** 50% deposit due ahead of time. **Registration:** At office. **Fee:** $19–$29; $90–$120; V, MC. **Parking:** At site.

FACILITIES

Number of RV-only Sites: 8. **Number of Tent-only Sites:** 14. **Number of Multipurpose Sites:** 31. **Hookups:** Electric (15, 20, 30 amps), water, sewer. **Each Site:** Picnic table, fireplace. **Dump Station:** Yes. **Laundry:** Yes. **Pay Phone:** Yes. **Restrooms and Showers:** Yes. **Fuel:** No. **Propane:** No. **Internal Roads:** Paved, gravel. **RV Service:** No. **Market:** 9 mi. north. **Restaurant:**

9 mi. north. **General Store:** No. **Vending:** Yes. **Swimming:** Lake. **Playground:** Yes. **Other:** Rec hall. **Activities:** Canoeing, boat (rentals available), swimming, table tennis, billiards. **Nearby Attractions:** Fairbanks Museum, Maple Grove Farm. **Additional Information:** Northeast Kingdom Chamber of Commerce; (802) 748-3678 or (800) 639-6379; www.nekchamber.com.

RESTRICTIONS

Pets: On leash only; must be quiet & cleaned up after. Must not be left unattended. **Fires:** In fireplaces only. **Alcoholic Beverages:** At site. **Vehicle Maximum Length:** 35 ft.

TO GET THERE

Take I-91 south to Exit 18, turn right onto Barnet-West Barnet Rd. Stay on paved road 5 mi. into the small village of West Barnet. As you approach the village, a campground sign and Paula's Place, (a general store on your left) is your signal to slow down for the upcoming sharp left hand turn over a little bridge next to the white church. Go over the bridge and immediately in front of you will be an orange dead-end sign, a campground sign, and a Campers Lane sign.

WESTFIELD   MAP, A-2
Mill Brook Campground

P.O. Box 133, 05874. T: (802) 744-6673.

🚐 ★★★   ⛺ ★★★

Beauty: ★★★   Site Privacy: ★★★★
Spaciousness: ★★★★   Quiet: ★★★★
Security: ★★★   Cleanliness: ★★★
Insect Control: ★★★   Facilities: ★★

Located in northern Vermont, not far from Newport, this small, homey campground gets a lot of repeat business. Bicycle groups are frequent guests here, as are mature travelers seeking a peaceful outdoor escape. Says owner Marjorie Paxman, "Lots of elderly people come through—they like it because it's quiet." It's pretty, too. Some of the grassy campsites are set along Mill Brook, over a bridge. The nicest sites are shaded and back up into the woods. You'll find tents set up amid the trees, with a real state park ambience, and RVs are lined up along the brook. Tent site 5 is a gem. The best tent site, though, is 18, atop a bluff and overlooking two small waterfalls. (Some of these would be pretty soggy in the rain, though.) The facilities are fairly basic, especially the restrooms, but they're kept clean. Mill Brook is a pleasant base for Jay Peak hiking and north country bicycle tours.

BASICS

Operated By: Paxman family. **Open:** Mid-May–mid-Sept. **Site Assignment:** Reservations recommended; $10 deposit required. **Registration:** At office. **Fee:** $17.50–$20.50; checks, no credit cards. **Parking:** At site.

FACILITIES

Number of RV-only Sites: 6. **Number of Tent-only Sites:** 24. **Hookups:** Electric (20, 30 amps), water, sewer. **Each Site:** Picnic table, fireplace. **Dump Station:** Yes. **Laundry:** No. **Pay Phone:**

Yes. **Restrooms and Showers:** Yes. **Fuel:** No. **Propane:** No. **Internal Roads:** Paved, gravel. **RV Service:** No. **Market:** Next door. **Restaurant:** In town. **General Store:** No. **Vending:** No. **Swimming:** No. **Playground:** Yes. **Activities:** Volleyball, horseshoes. **Nearby Attractions:** Jay Peak (hiking), golf, lakes, fishing. **Additional Information:** Jay Peak Area Assoc.; (802) 988-2259 or (800) 882-7460; www.jaypeakvermont.com.

RESTRICTIONS

Pets: On leash only; must be quiet & cleaned up after. Must not be left unattended. **Fires:** In fireplaces only. **Alcoholic Beverages:** At site.

TO GET THERE

Take Exit 26 off I-91, then VT 5 to VT 100 (Westfield Village).

WESTMORE   MAP, A-3
White Caps Campground

5659 VT 5A, 05860. T: (802) 467-3345; www.whitecapscampground.com.

🚐 ★★★★   ▲ ★★

Beauty: ★★★★
Site Privacy: ★★
Spaciousness: ★★★
Quiet: ★★
Security: ★★
Cleanliness: ★★★
Insect Control: ★★★
Facilities: ★★★

If your idea of a great campground includes proximity to fishing, boating, and hiking, look no farther. White Caps is set on the south end of Lake Willoughby, a 5-mile-long glacial lake in the northeast corner of Vermont. A world-record-setting lake trout was pulled from these waters through the ice, we're told. The campground is located right across the street from the lake and the state beach. Paddlers and divers find this campground a handy base. Planned activities, like pig roasts, keep things hopping come evening. A friendship garden has been planted by seasonal campers. Tent sites are gravel, with the best of the bunch being T5 and T6, both shady and set back from the road. Busy VT 5A is right out front, though, and the traffic goes past steadily all day. That won't bother the RV crowd.

BASICS

Operated By: Hosts Don, Vi, J.C., and Diane. **Open:** Mid-May–mid-Oct. **Site Assignment:** Reservations recommended; 50% of fee due 10 days in advance; 3-night min. required for holidays; stay 7 nights, pay for 6. **Registration:** At office. **Fee:** $18–$28; V, MC. **Parking:** At site.

FACILITIES

Number of Multipurpose Sites: 52. **Hookups:** Electric (20, 30 amps), water, sewer. **Each Site:** Picnic table, fire ring. **Dump Station:** No. **Laundry:** Yes. **Pay Phone:** No. **Restrooms and Showers:** Yes (wheelchair-accessible). **Fuel:** No. **Propane:** No. **Internal Roads:** Gravel, sand. **RV Service:** No. **Market:** 6 mi. west. **Restaurant:** 6 mi. west. **General Store:** Yes (fully stocked). **Vending:** No. **Swimming:** State beach (across the street). **Playground:** Yes. **Other:** Kayak & canoe rentals. **Activities:** Hiking (Mt. Pisgah & Mt. Hor), swimming, boating, diving. **Nearby Attractions:** Hiking & bike trails, golf, Old Stone Museum, antiques shops, Fair-

banks Museum. **Additional Information:** Barton Area Chamber of Commerce; (802) 525-243; www.bartonareachamber.com.

RESTRICTIONS

Pets: On leash only; must be quiet & cleaned up after. Must not be left unattended. **Fires:** In fire rings only. **Alcoholic Beverages:** At site. **Vehicle Maximum Length:** 45 ft.

TO GET THERE

Take Exit 23 off I-91, then VT 5 north to West Burke. Take VT 5A 6 mi. to campground.

WHITE RIVER JUNCTION   MAP. C-2
Pine Valley RV Resort

3700 Woodstock Rd., 05001. T: (802) 296-6711 or (802) 295-6076.

🚐 ★★★   ▲ n/a

Beauty: ★★★★
Site Privacy: ★★★
Spaciousness: ★★
Quiet: ★★★
Security: ★★★
Cleanliness: ★★★★
Insect Control: ★★★
Facilities: ★★★★

There's plenty to see and do in the Quechee Gorge area of east-central Vermont, and this campground makes an appealing base for RVers. Campsites are set in a grid, with the front entrance dominated by a scenic pond surrounded by mature trees. Site 14A (water and electric), a corner spot, is especially spacious and private. Site 50, in the group farthest from the road, is the shadiest among the full-hookup sites. Although there's no swimming in the pond, you can paddle around a bit in one of their rental canoes or pedal boats. This campground boasts some nice small touches, like umbrellas around the swimming pool and plastic chairs near the showers for stowing stuff. There's no tenting here, but tenters are well served by nearby Quechee Gorge State Park (see listing).

BASICS

Operated By: Margie and Wayne Parker. **Open:** May 1–late Oct. 20. **Site Assignment:** Reservations recommended for holiday weekends; 25% deposit required; deposit will be refunded (less $5 fee) w/ 7-day notice. **Registration:** At office. **Fee:** $28–$33; V, MC, D. **Parking:** At site.

FACILITIES

Number of Multipurpose Sites: 90. **Hookups:** Electric (20, 30, 50 amps), water, cable, phone, modem. **Each Site:** Picnic table, fire ring. **Dump Station:** Yes. **Laundry:** Yes. **Pay Phone:** Yes. **Restrooms and Showers:** Yes. **Fuel:** No. **Propane:** Yes. **Internal Roads:** Gravel. **RV Service:** No. **Market:** 7 mi. east. **Restaurant:** 2 mi. west. **General Store:** Yes. **Vending:** No. **Swimming:** Pool. **Playground:** Yes. **Other:** Rec hall. **Activities:** Canoeing, boating, basketball. **Nearby Attractions:** Billings Farm Museum, Montshire Museum, Quechee Gorge, Quechee Gorge Village (antiques), Simon Pearce Glass-Blowing Studio, Coolidge Homestead, Vermont Institute of Natural Science. **Additional Information:** Upper Valley Bi-State Regional Chamber of Commerce; (802) 295-6200; www.uppervalleychamber.com.

RESTRICTIONS

Pets: On leash only; must be quiet & cleaned up after. Must not be left unattended. **Fires:** In fire rings only. **Alcoholic Beverages:** W/ discretion.

TO GET THERE

From junction of I-89, Exit 1 and US 4, go 0.9 mi. west on US 4. Go left 0.1 mi., turn left.

WHITE RIVER JUNCTION   MAP. C-2
Quechee Gorge State Park

764 Dewey Mills Rd., 05001. T: (802) 295-2990 or (888) 409-7579; www.vtstateparks.com.

🚐 ★★★★   ▲ ★★★★

Beauty: ★★★★
Site Privacy: ★★★★
Spaciousness: ★★★★
Quiet: ★★★
Security: ★★★
Cleanliness: ★★★★
Insect Control: ★★★
Facilities: ★★

The spectacular 200-foot-deep Quechee Gorge, dubbed the Grand Canyon of the East, is one of Vermont's top natural attractions, drawing thousands of visitors each year. Check into this state park campground and you'll be perched above the gorge, with quick walking access to gorge vistas and waterfalls. The 611-acre park, leased from the US Army Corps of Engineers, was a former mill and dam site. Today, there are still remnants of the mill town in the park. (Pick up an information sheet and guide at the park information center.) Campsites are extra-big and can accommodate large RVs. Hiking trails to the gorge leave from the campground. The campground is also a great base for exploring central Vermont, including the picturesque Woodstock and Killington areas.

BASICS

Operated By: State of Vermont/U.S. Army Corps of Engineers. **Open:** Mid-May–Oct. 15. **Site Assignment:** Reservations may be made up to 11 months in advance; 2-night min.; reservations accepted at (888) 409-7579; contact park directly only for reservations w/in 10 days of stay; no refunds for 2-night minimum. **Registration:** At office. **Fee:** $14–$23; V, MC. **Parking:** At site and visitor parking area.

FACILITIES

Number of Multipurpose Sites: 47 (7 lean-tos). **Each Site:** Picnic table, fire ring. **Dump Station:** Yes. **Laundry:** No. **Pay Phone:** No. **Restrooms and Showers:** Yes (fee). **Fuel:** No. **Propane:** No. **Internal Roads:** Paved/gravel. **RV Service:** No. **Market:** 1 mi. east. **Restaurant:** 0.5 mi. east. **General Store:** No. **Vending:** No. **Swimming:** No. **Playground:** Yes. **Other:** Picnic area, play fields, hiking trails. **Activities:** Hiking. **Nearby Attractions:** Quechee Gorge, hiking, biking, swimming, boating, fishing, Woodstock, Billings Farm Museum, Montshire Museum, Quechee Gorge Village (antiques), Simon Pearce Glass-Blowing Studio, Coolidge Homestead, Vermont Institute of Natural Science. **Additional Information:** Woodstock Area Chamber of Commerce, 18 Central St., P.O. Box 486-4, Woodstock, VT 05091; (802) 457-3555; www.woodstockvt.com.

RESTRICTIONS

Pets: On leash only, must be quiet & cleaned up after. Must not be left unattended. Proof of current rabies vaccination required. No puppies less than 6 months old. **Fires:** In grills & fireplaces only. **Alcoholic Beverages:** No kegs, no containers larger than 1 gallon.

TO GET THERE

From junction of I-89, Exit 1 and US 4, go 3 mi. west on US 4.

WILMINGTON   MAP, D-2
Molly Stark State Park

705 Hwy. 9, 05363.
T: (802) 464-5460 or (800) 299-3071;
www.vtstateparks.com.

🚐 ★★★   ▲ ★★★★

Beauty: ★★★★   Site Privacy: ★★★★
Spaciousness: ★★★★   Quiet: ★★★★
Security: ★★★   Cleanliness: ★★★★
Insect Control: ★★★   Facilities: ★★

This small, rustic state campground, named for the famous wife of General John Stark of the American Revolution, is popular with tenters and small trailer campers who don't require a lot of on-site amenities. It's smaller than other state and private campgrounds located on Hwy. 9, the popular and scenic byway that slices through southern Vermont. It also lacks the water frontage that others have. But it offers peace and quiet and some great mountain views. Bring your hiking boots; the campground is nestled at the base of Mt. Olga, with a trail to the summit. A fire tower at the top of the mountain offers spectacular, sweeping vistas. The hike is especially popular during fall foliage season. The campground is typically quiet; most campers take off for the day for hiking, biking, and canoeing. Spacious campsites and 11 lean-to sites are located along two loops tucked in the woods or in open grassy areas. A restroom with showers is located in each loop.

BASICS

Operated By: State of Vermont. **Open:** May 26–Oct. 9. **Site Assignment:** Reservations may be made up to 11 months in advance; 2-night min.; reservations accepted at (888) 409-7579; contact park directly only for reservations w/in 10 days of stay; no refunds for 2-night minimum. **Registration:** At office. **Fee:** Tent/trailer, $14; lean-to, $21; V, MC. **Parking:** At site.

FACILITIES

Number of RV-only Sites: 11. **Number of Multipurpose Sites:** 23. **Each Site:** Picnic table, fire ring. **Dump Station:** Yes. **Laundry:** No. **Pay Phone:** No. **Restrooms and Showers:** Yes. **Fuel:** No. **Propane:** No. **Internal Roads:** Gravel (good). **RV Service:** No. **Market:** Wilmington, 1 mi. **Restaurant:** Wilmington, 1 mi. **General Store:** No. **Vending:** No. **Swimming:** No. **Playground:** Yes. **Other:** Hiking trails, pavilion. **Activities:** Hiking, biking, horseshoes, volleyball. **Nearby Attractions:** Farms, antiques shops, Mt. Snow, Bennington Museum. **Additional Information:** Wilmington-Mount Snow-Haystack Region Chamber of Com-

merce, East Main St., Wilmington, VT 05363; (877) 887-6884; www.visitvermont.com.

RESTRICTIONS

Pets: Permitted at camping site; Not allowed in day-use areas. Must present valid rabies certificate or town dog license at check-in. **Fires:** In fire rings & grills only. **Alcoholic Beverages:** At site.

TO GET THERE

Take Hwy. 9 to park entrance.

WINDSOR   MAP, C-2
Ascutney State Park

1826 Back Mountain Rd., 05089.
T: (802) 674-2060 or (802) 885-8891;
www.vtstateparks.com.

🚐 ★★★★   ▲ ★★★★★

Beauty: ★★★★★   Site Privacy: ★★★★
Spaciousness: ★★★★   Quiet: ★★★
Security: ★★★   Cleanliness: ★★★
Insect Control: ★★★   Facilities: ★★★

On clear days, the skies around this pretty state campground are often filled with bright-colored hang gliders. The campground boasts two hang-gliding launch sites and spectacular mountain views. Located at the base of Ascutney Mountain, the property includes four hiking trails and a summit fire tower. You can drive the mountain road, a steep path through the woods to 2,800 feet, then walk the 0.8 miles to the summit. Don't miss it; the sweeping views of the Green Mountains, White Mountains, and Connecticut River Valley are jaw-dropping. The campground, developed by the CCC, features a stone shelter, picnic area, and two loops of woodsy sites. There are no hookups, but RVs can be accommodated. Like most Vermont state parks, the sites are large, surrounded by woods for added privacy.

BASICS

Operated By: State of Vermont. **Open:** Mid-May–Oct. 15. **Site Assignment:** Reservations may be made up to 11 months in advance; 2-night min.; reservations accepted at (888) 409-7579; contact park directly only for reservations w/in 10 days of stay; no refunds for 2-night minimum. **Registration:** At office. **Fee:** $14; lean-tos, $21; V, MC. **Parking:** At site.

FACILITIES

Number of Multipurpose Sites: 39 (10 lean-tos). **Each Site:** Picnic table, fire ring. **Dump Station:** Yes. **Laundry:** No. **Pay Phone:** No. **Restrooms and Showers:** Yes (coin-op). **Fuel:** No. **Propane:** No. **Internal Roads:** Gravel, dirt (good). **RV Service:** No. **Market:** Windsor, 2 mi. **Restaurant:** Windsor, 2 mi. **General Store:** No. **Vending:** No. **Swimming:** No. **Playground:** No. **Other:** Picnic area, hang-gliding launch sites, trails, fire tower. **Activities:** Hiking, biking, hang gliding. **Nearby Attractions:** Farms, antiques shops, hiking, biking, boating, fishing, Ascutney. **Additional Information:** Mount Ascutney Region, Chamber of Commerce, P.O. Box 5, Windsor, VT 05089; (802) 674-5910.

RESTRICTIONS

Pets: On leash only. **Fires:** At site only. **Alcoholic Beverages:** At site.

TO GET THERE

Take I-91 Exit 8 to Hwy. 131 east. At stoplight, turn left on Hwy. 5 1.2 mi., then bear left on Hwy. 44A. Campground is 1 mi.

WOODFORD   MAP, D-1
Greenwood Lodge and Campsites

P.O. Box 246, 05201. T: (802) 442-2547;
www.campvermont.com/greenwood.

🚐 ★★★   ▲ ★★★★

Beauty: ★★★★   Site Privacy: ★★★
Spaciousness: ★★★★   Quiet: ★★★★
Security: ★★★   Cleanliness: ★★★
Insect Control: ★★★   Facilities: ★★★★

Swimming, boating, canoeing, fishing, hiking. It's all at your doorstep at this pretty oasis in southern Vermont. The 120-acre campground sits at the base of Prospect Ski Mountain and is a magnet for outdoor lovers and sports enthusiasts. There are three ponds on the property; two of them are small and boggy, but the third is large enough for swimming and boating. Campsites are tucked in the woods, along rolling fields, with plenty of mountain views. Large RV campers may prefer the more open field areas with easy in and out level sites. The campground is also home to hostel lodging, so expect small groups of young outdoorsy types camping out in the two dorms and two private bedrooms located in the lodge. Many campers head for the nearby Appalachian Trail or Somerset and Harriman Reservoirs for day trips.

BASICS

Operated By: Ed, Ann, and Chris Shea. **Open:** Mid-May–late Oct. **Site Assignment:** Reservations recommended; 1-night deposit. **Registration:** At office. **Fee:** $21–$26; V, MC. **Parking:** At site.

FACILITIES

Number of Multipurpose Sites: 20. **Hookups:** Electric (20, 30, 50 amps), water. **Each Site:** Picnic table, fire ring. **Dump Station:** Yes. **Laundry:** Yes. **Pay Phone:** Yes. **Restrooms and Showers:** Yes. **Fuel:** No. **Propane:** Yes. **Internal Roads:** Gravel (good). **RV Service:** No. **Market:** Bennington, 8 mi. **Restaurant:** Bennington, 8 mi. **General Store:** Yes. **Vending:** Yes. **Swimming:** Pond. **Playground:** Yes. **Other:** Three ponds, rec room, common room, hostel lodging, dishwashing sink, microwave, hiking trails. **Activities:** Boating, hiking, biking, horseshoes, basketball, volleyball, swimming. **Nearby Attractions:** Farms, antiques shops, hiking, biking, fishing, boating, Bennington, Mt. Snow. **Additional Information:** Bennington Area Chamber of Commerce, 100 Veterans Memorial Dr., Bennington, VT 05201; (802) 447-3311; www.bennington.com/chamber.

RESTRICTIONS

Pets: On leash only. **Fires:** In fire rings & grills only. **Alcoholic Beverages:** At site.

TO GET THERE

Campground entrance is at Prospect Ski Mountain, off Hwy. 9, 8 mi. east of Bennington.

WOODFORD
Woodford State Park

MAP, D-1

142 State Park Rd., 05201.
T: (802) 447-7169 or (888) 409-7579;
www.vtstateparks.com.

🚐 ★★★★   ▲ ★★★★★

Beauty: ★★★★★   Site Privacy: ★★★★★
Spaciousness: ★★★★★   Quiet: ★★★★
Security: ★★★   Cleanliness: ★★★
Insect Control: ★★★   Facilities: ★★★

This premier state park and campground is a delight for outdoor enthusiasts. The campground is located on a mountain plateau and is one of Vermont's highest parks in elevation at 2,400 feet. The nearly 400-acre property surrounds the Adams Reservoir, where there's a small beach area and canoe and boat rentals available. The campground borders the pristine George Aiken Wilderness Area in the Green Mountain National Forest, which adds to its natural wilderness setting. An easy and pleasant 2.7-mile hiking trail leaves the campground and circles the reservoir. Two clusters of campsites are available; most sites are tucked into the woods for added privacy and ambience. Campers can walk or drive to the picnic and beach areas.

BASICS

Operated By: State of Vermont. **Open:** Mid-May–Oct. 15. **Site Assignment:** Reservations may be made up to 11 months in advance; 2-night min.; reservations accepted at (888) 409-7579; contact park directly only for reservations w/in 10 days of stay; no refunds for 2-night minimum. **Registration:** At office. **Fee:** Tent/trailers, $16; lean-to, $23; V, MC. **Parking:** At site.

FACILITIES

Number of Multipurpose Sites: 103 (20 lean-tos). **Each Site:** Picnic table, fire ring. **Dump Station:** Yes. **Laundry:** No. **Pay Phone:** No. **Restrooms and Showers:** Yes. **Fuel:** No. **Propane:** No. **Internal Roads:** Gravel, dirt (good).

RV Service: No. **Market:** Bennington, 11 mi. **Restaurant:** Bennington, 11 mi. **General Store:** No. **Vending:** No. **Swimming:** Lake. **Playground:** No. **Other:** Beach, boat rentals, picnic area, nature trails. **Activities:** Swimming, boating, hiking. **Nearby Attractions:** Farms, antiques shops, hiking, biking, fishing, boating, Bennington, Brattleboro. **Additional Information:** Brattleboro Area Chamber of Commerce, 180 Main St., Brattleboro, VT 05301; (802) 254-4565; www.brattleborochamber.org. Bennington Area Chamber of Commerce, 100 Veterans Memorial Dr., Bennington, VT 05201; (802) 447-3311; www.bennington.com/cha.

RESTRICTIONS

Pets: Permitted at camping site; Not allowed in day-use areas. Must present valid rabies certificate or town dog license at check-in. **Fires:** In fire pits & grills only. **Alcoholic Beverages:** At site.

TO GET THERE

Campground is located off Hwy. 9, 11 mi. east of Bennington.

Virginia

Like neighboring Delaware and Maryland, Virginia is blessed with diverse terrain and a multitude of well-preserved historical attractions. Outdoor enthusiasts and history buffs alike will fawn over the charm oozing from the Old Dominion State.

The historic triangle in southeastern Virginia consists of three towns—Williamsburg, Jamestown, and Yorktown—linked by the 23-mile Colonial Parkway. Williamsburg has amusement parks **Busch Gardens** and **Water Country USA,** but **Colonial Williamsburg** is what preserves the city's eighteenth-century heritage. Colonial Williamsburg is a 173-acre reproduction of America's colonial capital—a historical theme park with about 600 restored or rebuilt structures occupied by townspeople in period dress. East of Williamsburg lies the **Jamestown Settlement,** a living museum with costumed interpreters staffing buildings and ships. Your history lesson is not complete without venturing to **Yorktown,** where American and French troops under George Washington's command defeated Lord Cornwallis and his British forces in 1781.

Washington, D.C. certainly has enough attractions to keep you occupied for days, as does northern Virginia. Arlington is an ideal starting point. Here, you can explore **Arlington National Cemetery.** Other touring options include the **Newseum,** a 72,000-square-foot interactive facility dedicated to the history of the news; and the **Pentagon,** America's military think tank.

In Fairfax County, George Washington's **Mount Vernon** homestead sees more than 100,000 tourists each year. Washington's tomb is located here, as well as a small museum. South of Fairfax County, Fredericksburg is a well-preserved colonial town rich in American Revolution and Civil War heritage. The **Fredericksburg and Spotsylvania National Military Park** consists of sites related to four Civil War battles. Visitors centers in Chancellorsville and Fredericksburg, **Fredericksburg National Cemetery,** the **Stonewall Jackson Shrine,** and the four battlefields are points of interest. Nearby, the **Quantico Marine Corps Base and Marine Corps Air-Ground Museum** offer an overview of marines history.

Richmond is easily one of America's most culturally and historically rich state capitals. The **State Capitol, Edgar Allan Poe Museum,** and **Richmond National Battlefield Park** are favorite attractions, as are the **Museum of the Confederacy** and the **White House of the Confederacy.** Presidents James Monroe and James Tyler, Confederate president Jefferson Davis, and more than 18,000 Confederate soldiers are among those buried at Richmond's **Hollywood Cemetery.** For modern excitement north of Richmond, **Paramount's Kings Dominion** has more than 100 rides, shows, and a water park.

Central and southern Virginia is primarily rural and adorned with pastoral farms and pleasant small towns. Perhaps the most famous estate in the tenth state is Monticello in Charlottesville. Situated on a mountaintop, it was designed and occupied by Thomas Jefferson, who started construction in 1771 and finished in 1809. Some historians believe that the Berkeley Plantation in Charles City is where the first Thanksgiving was celebrated in 1619. Attractions in Petersburg include the Pamplin Park Civil War Site and the 2,700-acre Petersburg National Battlefield Park. Union victories and Confederate failures in Petersburg led to Gen. Robert E. Lee's surrender to Gen. Ulysses S. Grant at the present-day Appomattox Court House National Historic Park in the village of Appomattox.

In southeast Virginia, Newport News, Norfolk, Hampton, and Virginia Beach are popular destinations in the tidewater peninsula. Newport News's crown jewel is the Mariners Museum, which boasts a collection of more than 35,000 nautical artifacts. In Norfolk, guided bus tours are given at the Norfolk Naval Base. The Virginia Air and Space Center in Hampton is a museum and the official visitor center for nearby NASA Langley Research Center, where guests can observe NASA engineers at work. With a three-mile boardwalk and 28 miles of beach along the Atlantic Ocean and Chesapeake Bay, Virginia Beach is the state's finest resort area. First Landing State Park at Cape Henry has more than 2,700 acres of sand dunes, lagoons, and cypress trees.

Named one of the seven engineering wonders of the modern world, the Chesapeake Bay Bridge and Tunnel carries passengers from mainland Virginia to the quaint eastern shore, known locally as Delmarva for the land it shares with Maryland and Delaware. Here are several islands and villages, such as the colonial-era Accomac and Onancock. Near the Maryland border, Assateague Island includes the Chincoteague National Wildlife Refuge and the Assateague Island National Seashore.

Back on the mainland, Shenandoah National Park is the highlight of western Virginia. The park is 80 miles long and features deep canyons, dense forests, and majestic peaks. There are more than 200 species of birds here, as well as deer, bears, foxes, and bobcats. Campgrounds, hiking trails, and bridle trails are plentiful. The 105-mile-long Skyline Drive, known for its spectacular display of colors in autumn, covers the entire length of Shenandoah National Park, starting at Front Royal to the north and connecting with the Blue Ridge Parkway to the south, with numerous overlooks along the way.

Campground Profiles

ABINGDON   MAP, A-1
Riverside Campground

18496 North Fork River Rd., 24210.
T: (276) 628-5333.

🚐 ★★★★   🏕 ★★★★

Beauty: ★★★★   Site Privacy: ★★
Spaciousness: ★★★   Quiet: ★★★★
Security: ★★★★★   Cleanliness: ★★★★
Insect Control: ★★★★   Facilities: ★★★★

Nestled in the Appalachian Mountains of southwest Virginia, Riverside Campground is located near historic Abingdon along the north fork of the Holston River. Riverside has 133 level grassy and semi-wooded sites. These sites are clean and well kept, but most offer little privacy. For families, the campground has a swimming pool, a children's pool, and a sand volleyball court. Bass fishing in the Holston River is lively, as is Abingdon itself. Nearby, the Virginia Creeper Trail is a 34.3-mile-long multiuse trail extending from Abingdon to the Virginia–North Carolina line. Walkers, bicyclers, and horses are welcome on the trail (but not motorized vehicles). The Virginia Creeper Trail started as a Native American footpath. Later, pioneers like Daniel Boone used the trail, which is named for the early steam locomotives that struggled slowly up the railroad's steep grades. The Virginia Creeper engine is now showcased at the Abingdon Trailhead.

BASICS
Operated By: Steve Loggans. **Open:** Apr. 1–Dec. 1. **Site Assignment:** Reservations and walk-ins accepted. **Registration:** At campground office. **Fee:** $22–$28; V, MC. **Parking:** At designated spot.

FACILITIES
Number of RV-only Sites: 131. **Number of Tent-only Sites:** 30. **Hookups:** Electric (20, 30 amps), water, phone. **Each Site:** Fire ring, picnic table. **Dump Station:** Yes. **Laundry:** Yes. **Pay Phone:** Yes. **Restrooms and Showers:** Yes. **Fuel:** No. **Propane:** Yes. **Internal Roads:** Gravel, in good condition. **RV Service:** Nearby. **Market:** W/in 5 mi. **Restaurant:** W/in 5 mi. **General Store:** Yes. **Vending:** Yes. **Swimming:** Pool. **Playground:** Yes. **Other:** Children's pool. **Activities:** Rec hall, game room, swimming, wading pool, river swimming, stream fishing, basketball, horseshoes, volleyball, planned activities on weekends. **Nearby Attractions:** Historic Abingdon, Virginia Creeper National Recreation Trail, White's Mill, Mt. Rogers National Recreation Area, Appalachian Trail, Barter Theater. **Additional Information:** Abingdon CVB, (800) 435-3440, www.abingdon.com.

RESTRICTIONS
Pets: On leash only. **Fires:** At site. **Alcoholic Beverages:** At site. **Vehicle Maximum Length:** No limit.

TO GET THERE
From I-81, take Exit 14 and go 0.5 mi. west on Hwy. 140N, 1 mi. east on Hwy. 11, 7 mi. north on US 19, and 2 mi. east on Hwy. 611. Entrance is on the right.

APPOMATTOX   MAP, C-2
Holliday Lake State Park

reserve america

Rte. 2 Box 622, 24522.
T: (434) 248-6308 or (800) 933-PARK;
www.reserveamerica.com.

🚐 ★★★★   🏕 ★★★★

Beauty: ★★★★   Site Privacy: ★★★
Spaciousness: ★★★   Quiet: ★★★
Security: ★★★   Cleanliness: ★★★★
Insect Control: ★★★   Facilities: ★★★★

Twelve miles from the Appomattox Court House National Historic Park, Holliday Lake State Park boasts a 150-acre lake stocked with bass, northern pike, crappie, sunfish, and channel catfish. It also has a 30-site campground connected to the lake by the Saunders Creek Trail. The mostly open sites are level and spacious. Swimming and boating are popular activities at Holliday Lake, and boat rentals are available. The 12-mile Carter Taylor loop trail starts across from the campground, which is near the 19,710-acre Appomattox-Buckingham State Forest. Gen. Robert E. Lee's weary and battered army passed within 1.5 miles of the present park site on its way to the Civil War's final battles. Appomattox National Court House Historic Park consists of 1,700 acres of rolling hills. The reconstructed court house serves as the park's visitor center and is located on US 24 2 miles northeast of town.

BASICS
Operated By: State of Virginia. **Open:** Mar.–Dec. **Site Assignment:** Reservations accepted (no refund w/in 1 week of reserved date); walk-ins accepted. **Registration:** At campground office. **Fee:** $15–$20; V, MC. **Parking:** At site only.

FACILITIES
Number of RV-only Sites: 13. **Number of Tent-only Sites:** 17. **Hookups:** Electric (30 amps), water. **Each Site:** Grill, lantern pole. **Dump Station:** Yes. **Laundry:** No. **Pay Phone:** Yes. **Restrooms and Showers:** Yes. **Fuel:** No. **Propane:** No. **Internal Roads:** Gravel, in good condition. **RV Service:** No. **Market:** W/in 12 mi. **Restaurant:** W/in 10 mi. **General Store:** No. **Vending:** Yes. **Swimming:** Yes. **Playground:** Yes. **Other:** Visitor center, picnic shelters, boat ramp, firewood available. **Activities:** Lake swimming, boating, hiking trails, lake fishing, boat rentals, volleyball, biking. **Nearby Attractions:** Appomattox Courthouse National Historic Park, Booker T. Washington Monument, Monticello, Richmond, Edgar Allan Poe Museum, Museum and White House of the Confederacy. **Additional Information:** Richmond CVB, (800) 370-9004, www.richmondva.org.

RESTRICTIONS
Pets: Must be on leash attended. **Fires:** In fire grills only. **Alcoholic Beverages:** No alcohol permitted. **Vehicle Maximum Length:** 30 ft. **Other:** 14-day stay limit in 30-day period; no gas-powered boats.

TO GET THERE
From Appomattox, go 9 mi. east on Hwy. 24 and 6 mi. southeast on Hwy. 626/692. Follow signs to park entrance.

ASHLAND   MAP, B-3
Americamps Richmond North

11322 Air Park Rd., 23005. T: (800) 628-2802;
www.americamps.com.

🚐 ★★★★   🏕 ★★★★

Beauty: ★★★★   Site Privacy: ★
Spaciousness: ★★   Quiet: ★★
Security: ★★★★   Cleanliness: ★★★★
Insect Control: ★★★★   Facilities: ★★★★

Located 8 miles north of Richmond on I-95, Americamps Richmond North—a Best Holiday Trav-L-Park—bills itself as the closest full-service campground to Richmond. The campground has 146 well-maintained sites, including 98 full hookups and 32 pull-throughs. Americamps has a 400-seat pavilion for special events and amenities like a swimming pool, a game room, a playground, and a volleyball court. Though there is nothing spectacular about this campground, its proximity to I-95 makes it ideal for overnight stays during a long journey down the interstate. Of course, it's also a central base for attractions in Richmond, like the Richmond battlefield site, the Edgar Allan Poe Museum, Paramount's Kings Dominion, and the White House of the Confederacy, where Gen. Robert E. Lee's surrender sword is among the exhibits.

BASICS
Operated By: Americamps. **Open:** All year. **Site Assignment:** Reservations recommended, walk-ins accepted. **Registration:** At campground store. **Fee:** $21–$50; V, MC, AE, D. **Parking:** At site.

FACILITIES
Number of RV-only Sites: 136. **Number of Tent-only Sites:** 10. **Hookups:** Electric (20, 30, 50 amps), water, phone (w/ extended stay). **Each Site:** Picnic table. **Dump Station:** Yes. **Laundry:** Yes. **Pay Phone:** Yes. **Restrooms and Showers:** Yes. **Fuel:** No. **Propane:** Yes. **Internal Roads:** Gravel & paved, in good condition. **RV Service:** No. **Market:** W/in 2 mi. **Restaurant:** W/in 2 mi. **General Store:** Yes. **Vending:** Yes. **Swimming:** Pool. **Playground:** Yes. **Other:** 400-seat pavilion. **Activities:** Rec area, game room, swimming, basketball, badminton, horseshoes, volleyball. **Nearby Attractions:** Kings Dominion, Edgar Allan Poe Museum, White House of the Confederacy, Virginia State Capitol, Virginia State Fairgrounds, Virginia Museum of Fine Arts, Richmond National Battlefield Park, Richmond International Raceway. **Additional Information:** Richmond CVB, (800) 370-9004, www.richmondva.org.

RESTRICTIONS
Pets: On leash only. **Fires:** Must be contained. No ground fires. **Alcoholic Beverages:** At site. **Vehicle Maximum Length:** No limit.

TO GET THERE

From I-95, take Exit 89 and go 0.1 mi. east on Hwy. 802 and 1 mi. south on Air Park Rd. Entrance is on the left.

BEDFORD   MAP, C-1, C-2
Peaks of Otter Campground

Blue Ridge Pkwy.—Hwy. 2, P.O. Box 163, 24523. T: (540) 586-4357.

🚐 ★★★   ▲ ★★★★

Beauty: ★★★★	Site Privacy: ★★★
Spaciousness: ★★★	Quiet: ★★★★
Security: ★★★	Cleanliness: ★★★★
Insect Control: ★★★	Facilities: ★★★

Located near milepost 86 of the 470-mile-long Blue Ridge Parkway, Peaks of Otter Campground is across the road from Peaks of Otter Lodge and Abbott Lake. The campground is nestled in the woods on the flanks of Sharp Top Mountain, which rises to 3,875 feet. There are 46 RV sites, but no electric or water hookups. A 1.5-mile trail leads to the top of Sharp Top; if you don't want to hike, bus rides to the top are available near the visitors center. You can also climb to the summit of 4,001-foot-high Flat Top Mountain via a 4.4-mile-long trail. At the Peaks of Otter Visitors Center at milepost 86 of the Blue Ridge Parkway, you can see a living history demonstration on weekends at the Johnson Farm, a homestead dating back to the 1800s.

BASICS

Operated By: National Park Service. **Open:** May 1–Oct. 31. **Site Assignment:** First come, first served. **Registration:** At campground store. **Fee:** $16; cash only. **Parking:** At site.

FACILITIES

Number of Tent-only Sites: 92. **Number of Multipurpose Sites:** 52. **Hookups:** None. **Each Site:** Grill, picnic table, & lantern pole. **Dump Station:** Yes. **Laundry:** No. **Pay Phone:** Yes. **Restrooms and Showers:** Restrooms only, no showers. **Fuel:** No. **Propane:** No. **Internal Roads:** Paved, in good condition. **RV Service:** No. **Market:** W/in 10 mi. **Restaurant:** W/in 10 mi. **General Store:** Yes. **Vending:** Yes. **Playground:** No. **Other:** Peaks of Otter Lodge, Abbott Lake. **Activities:** Hiking trails, fishing. **Nearby Attractions:** Blue Ridge Parkway, Appalachian Trail, Booker T. Washington National Monument, Natural Bridge of Virginia. **Additional Information:** Roanoke Valley CVB, (800) 635-5535, www.visitroanokeva.com.

RESTRICTIONS

Pets: On leash only. **Fires:** At site. **Alcoholic Beverages:** At site. **Vehicle Maximum Length:** 30 ft. **Other:** Quiet hours 10 p.m.–6 a.m.

TO GET THERE

Take the Blue Ridge Pkwy. to milepost 86 and go 0.25 mi. south on Hwy. 43 to campground entrance.

BENTONVILLE   MAP, A-2
Shenandoah River State Park

reserve america

350 Daughter of Stars Dr., 22610. T: (540) 622-6840; www.reserveamerica.com.

🚐   ▲ ★★★★

Beauty: ★★★	Site Privacy: ★★★★★
Spaciousness: ★★★★★	Quiet: ★★★★
Security: ★★★★	Cleanliness: ★★★★
Insect Control: ★★★	Facilities: ★

One of Virginia's newest parks and still in the development stage, it promises to be a favorite for both the instate and out-of-state visitor. This park is beautifully situated in northwest Virginia. Massanutten Mountain is visible to the west and the Shenandoah National Park is visible to the east. Presently, there are picnic shelters, shore fishing, and primitive individual and group campsites. No swimming or hunting is permitted. The park has 1,604 acres with 5.6 miles of river frontage along the beautiful Shenandoah River. The park is the site of the first Virginia Youth Conservation Corps where young men and women volunteer a few weeks each summer to restore park roads, build and maintain trails, evaluate river conditions, and more. The park provides a small boat launch 3.2 miles downstream from the Bentonville access area. Fishing is especially popular. Many anglers enjoy wading out into the river for an opportunity to catch large and smallmouth bass and bluegill. Hiking, biking, and bridle paths are now open. A horse concession has a stable full of young calm animals waiting to be ridden through the woods and open fields. You tell them your riding experience and they'll pick out the perfect horse for an enjoyable park excursion.

BASICS

Operated By: Virginia State Parks. **Open:** All year. **Site Assignment:** Reservations can be made 11 months in advance. **Registration:** At office. **Fee:** Single, $19; picnic shelter, $45–$50. **Parking:** At site.

FACILITIES

Number of Multipurpose Sites: 41. **Hookups:** None. **Each Site:** Picnic table, fire ring. **Dump Station:** No. **Laundry:** No. **Pay Phone:** No. **Restrooms and Showers:** Yes. **Fuel:** No. **Propane:** No. **Internal Roads:** Paved. **RV Service:** No. **Market:** No. **Restaurant:** No. **General Store:** No. **Vending:** No. **Swimming:** No. **Playground:** No. **Other:** This park is a Trash Free Facility—refuse must be removed by park visitor. A central refuse collection area is at the Three Bends Overlook. **Activities:** Boating, fishing, hiking, horseback riding, picnicking.

RESTRICTIONS

Fires: In designated fireplaces.

TO GET THERE

The park is in Warren County, 8 mi. south of Front Royal and 15 mi. north of Luray, just off US 340 in Bentonville. From northern VA, take Hwy. 66W to Linden exit. At light, turn right on Hwy. 55W to Front Royal, then left on US 340S 8 mi. From I-81, take the Front Royal exit to US 340S to Ben-

---

tonville. Look for park signs along the way. Turn right on Daughter of Stars Dr. Contact station is located at the top of the hill.

BLUEFIELD   MAP, A-2
Richwood Golf Club and Campground

Rte. 2 Box 109, 24605. T: (276) 322-4575; www.richwood-golfandcamp.com.

🚐 ★★★★   ▲ ★★★★

Beauty: ★★★	Site Privacy: ★★
Spaciousness: ★★	Quiet: ★★★
Security: ★★★★	Cleanliness: ★★★★
Insect Control: ★★★★	Facilities: ★★★

Located in the Appalachian Mountains and straddling the borders of Virginia and West Virginia, Bluefield is the home of Richwood Golf Club and Campground. Founded in 1968, Richwood offers 18 sites that accommodate pull-throughs. The campground has a game room and hiking trails, but the main draw here is the adjacent 9-hole, par 35 golf course situated on 52 acres of former farmland. Even if you don't drive the ball onto the fairway, you have a beautiful view of the mountains to minimize your anger. Mayflower Seafood Restaurant is on Richwood's premises. Pipestem State Park is a short drive from Richwood. In Bluefield, the border of Virginia and West Virginia is defined by East River Mountain, which peaks at 3,400 ft.—a breathtaking site from Richwood and anywhere in Bluefield.

BASICS

Operated By: Private operator. **Open:** All year. **Site Assignment:** Reservations and walk-ins accepted. **Registration:** At campground office. **Fee:** RV, $15–$18; tent, $6; V, MC, D. **Parking:** At designated spot.

FACILITIES

Number of RV-only Sites: 39. **Number of Tent-only Sites:** 5. **Hookups:** Electric (15, 30, 50 amps), water, sewer, phone. **Each Site:** Picnic table. **Dump Station:** Yes. **Laundry:** Yes. **Pay Phone:** Yes. **Restrooms and Showers:** Yes. **Fuel:** No. **Propane:** No. **Internal Roads:** Paved, in good condition. **RV Service:** No. **Market:** W/in 3 mi. **Restaurant:** On premises. **General Store:** Yes. **Vending:** Yes. **Playground:** No. **Other:** 9-hole golf course. **Activities:** Golf, putting green, hiking trails, game room. **Nearby Attractions:** Pipestem State Park, minor league baseball, Bluefield, Princeton. **Additional Information:** Mercer County CVB, (800) 221-3206, www.mccvb.com.

RESTRICTIONS

Pets: On leash only. **Fires:** At site. **Alcoholic Beverages:** At site. **Vehicle Maximum Length:** No limit.

TO GET THERE

From I-77, go 2 mi. north on US 52, 7 mi. west on US 460, and 0.25 mi. north on Hockman Pike. Entrance is on the left.

Reserve your campsite online at www.ReserveAmerica.com

BOWLING GREEN   MAP, B-3
Hidden Acres KOA

17391 Richmonds Turnpike, 22514.
T: (800) 562-2482 or (804) 633-7592;
www.koa.com.

🚐 ★★★★   ▲ ★★★★

Beauty: ★★★	Site Privacy: ★★★
Spaciousness: ★★★	Quiet: ★★★★
Security: ★★★	Cleanliness: ★★★★
Insect Control: ★★★★	Facilities: ★★★★

Located near Bowling Green in northeast Virginia, Hidden Acres KOA has 120 open and wooded sites in a setting near the roller coasters and thrill rides of Paramount's King's Dominion. Children have several options for entertainment, including the Krazy Kritter Park and Kids Water Works. Paddle boats are available for rent, and Hidden Acres has a stocked fishing pond. Fredericksburg, which was George Washington's hometown, is a short drive from Hidden Acres. The area has four Civil War battlefields at Fredericksburg and Spotsylvania Military Park, a historic district, and several antique shops. Richmond is an ideal day trip for Hidden Acres campers. In addition to King's Dominion, the city has several attractions, including the White House of the Confederacy. For campers who can't get enough thrills, Hidden Acres offers special packages in conjunction with King's Dominion.

BASICS
Operated By: Beverages Enterprises Inc. **Open:** All year. **Site Assignment:** Reservations and walk-ins accepted. **Registration:** At campground office. **Fee:** $25–$39; cabin, $42–$50; V, MC, AE, D. **Parking:** At site.

FACILITIES
Number of RV-only Sites: 100. **Number of Tent-only Sites:** 26. **Hookups:** Electric (20, 30 amps), water. **Each Site:** Fire ring, picnic table. **Dump Station:** Yes. **Laundry:** Yes. **Pay Phone:** Yes. **Restrooms and Showers:** Yes. **Fuel:** No. **Propane:** Yes. **Internal Roads:** Gravel, in good condition. **RV Service:** No. **Market:** W/in 3 mi. **Restaurant:** W/in 2 mi. **General Store:** Yes. **Vending:** Yes. **Swimming:** Pool. **Playground:** Yes. **Other:** Krazy Kritter Park, cabins. **Activities:** Rec hall, game room, swimming, boat rentals, pond fishing, mini-golf, shuffleboard, planned activities on weekends, badminton, sports field, hiking trails, volleyball, horseshoes. **Nearby Attractions:** Paramount's Kings Dominion, General Lee's Stratford Hall, Fredericksburg battlefields, Richmond, Port Royal, Monticello. **Additional Information:** Richmond CVB, (800) 370-9004, www.richmondva.org.

RESTRICTIONS
Pets: On leash only. **Fires:** At site. **Alcoholic Beverages:** At site. **Vehicle Maximum Length:** No limit.

TO GET THERE
From I-95, take Exit 104 and go 11 mi. northeast on SR 207 and 2 mi. south on SR 2/US 301. Entrance is on the left.

BRACEY   MAP, C-2
Americamps Lake Gaston

409 Americamps Dr., 23919. T: (434) 636-2668; www.americampslakegaston.com.

🚐 ★★★★   ▲ ★★★★

Beauty: ★★★★	Site Privacy: ★★★
Spaciousness: ★★★	Quiet: ★★★
Security: ★★★★★	Cleanliness: ★★★★
Insect Control: ★★★★	Facilities: ★★★★

The area around Bracey, where Americamps Lake Gaston is located, is near acres and acres of water. To the west lies John H. Kerr Reservoir, and Lake Gaston is even closer. Lake Gaston is 35 miles long and features 350 miles of scenic shoreline wandering from Virginia into North Carolina. Fishing, boating, swimming, and hiking are among the activities here. Anglers will find Lake Gaston fishing excellent year-round for bass, northern pike, rock, crappie, walleye, and catfish. Set in the woods on the lake's north shore, Americamps—Lake Gaston is a 140-acre complex with 245 shaded sites, including 20 pull-throughs. A dip in the 200,000-gallon swimming pool is refreshing during the hot summer; there is also a children's pool. An 18-hole mini-golf course, a recreational pavilion with indoor games and pool tables, and a dance and barbecue pavilion are other popular facilities.

BASICS
Operated By: Jack and Barbara Stewart. **Open:** All year. **Site Assignment:** Reservations and walk-ins accepted. **Registration:** At campground office. **Fee:** $24–$26; V, MC. **Parking:** At designated spot.

FACILITIES
Number of RV-only Sites: 275. **Number of Tent-only Sites:** 15. **Hookups:** Electric (20, 30 amps), water. **Each Site:** Fire ring, picnic table. **Dump Station:** Yes. **Laundry:** Yes. **Pay Phone:** Yes. **Restrooms and Showers:** Yes. **Fuel:** No. **Propane:** Yes. **Internal Roads:** Gravel & paved, in good condition. **RV Service:** No. **Market:** W/in 5 mi. **Restaurant:** W/in 5 mi. **General Store:** Yes. **Vending:** Yes. **Swimming:** Yes. **Playground:** Yes. **Other:** Lake Gaston. **Activities:** Rec hall, game room, swimming, wading pool, boating, canoeing, kayaking, lake fishing, mini-golf, basketball, planned activities on weekends, sports field, horseshoes, volleyball. **Nearby Attractions:** Appomattox Court House National Historic Park, Booker T. Washington National Monument, John H. Kerr Reservoir. **Additional Information:** Virginia Tourism Corp., (800) 371-8164, www.virginia.org.

RESTRICTIONS
Pets: On leash only. **Fires:** At site. **Alcoholic Beverages:** At site. **Vehicle Maximum Length:** No limit.

TO GET THERE
From I-85, take Exit 4 and go 5 mi. east on Hwy. 903. Entrance is on the right.

BREAKS   MAP, A-1
Breaks Interstate Park

Hwy. 80, P. O. Box 100, 24607. T: (276) 865-4413; www.breakspark.com.

🚐 ★★★★   ▲ ★★★★

Beauty: ★★★★★	Site Privacy: ★★★★
Spaciousness: ★★★	Quiet: ★★★
Security: ★★★★	Cleanliness: ★★★★
Insect Control: ★★★★★	Facilities: ★★★★

Administered jointly by the states of Kentucky and Virginia, Breaks Interstate contains the largest canyon east of the Mississippi. The canyon was formed by the Russell Fork River over a period of 250 million years. Today, the Russell Fork is frequented by whitewater rafters and stocked with trout. Anglers can also head for 12-acre Laurel Lake, which is stocked with bass and bluegill. Equestrian trails meander through the wooded uplands. Twelve miles of hiking trails include a demanding path to the river. The lovely campground features small, but picturesque sites situated on a heavily wooded mountainside. Parking is on gravel, and there are both back-in and pull-through sites, with a little bit of greenery between them. Loop B offers more spacious, yet less private sites than Loop A. Our favorite sites in Loop A are 56, 60, and 61. On Loop B, we like site 34. Section C is our absolute favorite, containing some large pull-through sites on top of the mountain. Security is fine at this remote park. Treat yourself—visit in June when the rhododendrons are in bloom.

BASICS
Operated By: VA and KY state parks. **Open:** Apr.–Oct. **Site Assignment:** First come, first served. **Registration:** At office. **Fee:** $9–$15. **Parking:** On site.

FACILITIES
Number of RV-only Sites: 122. **Hookups:** Electric (50 amps), water, sewer. **Each Site:** Picnic tables, grill. **Dump Station:** Yes. **Laundry:** Yes. **Pay Phone:** Yes. **Restrooms and Showers:** Yes. **Fuel:** No. **Propane:** No. **Internal Roads:** Paved. **RV Service:** Yes. **Market:** Yes. **Restaurant:** Yes. **General Store:** Yes. **Vending:** Yes. **Swimming:** Yes. **Playground:** Yes. **Other:** Horseback riding stable. **Activities:** Boating, fishing, mountain biking, hiking. **Nearby Attractions:** Red River Gorge. **Additional Information:** (800) 982-5122.

RESTRICTIONS
Pets: On leash. **Fires:** Only in designated areas. **Alcoholic Beverages:** Not allowed. **Vehicle Maximum Length:** 40 ft.

TO GET THERE
I-64E to Exit 98 onto Bert T. Combs Mountain Pkwy. East. Turn right onto US 460. Stay straight onto KY 114. Take US 23S to US 199S. Take the US 460/KY 80 ramp. Stay straight to go onto US 460. Turn right onto KY 80E that goes by the park.

BROADWAY
Harrisonburg/New Market KOA

MAP, B-2

12480 Mountain Valley Rd., 22815.
T: (540) 896-8929 or (800) KOA-5406;
www.koa.com.

🚐 ★★★★   ⛺ ★★★★

Beauty: ★★★★   Site Privacy: ★★★
Spaciousness: ★★★   Quiet: ★★★★
Security: ★★★★   Cleanliness: ★★★★
Insect Control: ★★★★   Facilities: ★★★★

Nestled at the base of the Massanutten Mountains in the Shenandoah Valley, Harrisonburg/New Market KOA offers spacious, wooded sites, including 17 pull-throughs. For recreation, there's a swimming pool and a fishing pond. Hiking trails lead from the campground to Jefferson National Forest. New Market is the site of New Market Battlefield State Historical Park, where on May 15, 1864, cadets from nearby Virginia Military Institute were ordered to join the Confederate attack on Union troops. The cadets, who were no older than 20, helped achieve a Confederate victory. The New Market Battlefield Military Museum is located on the actual battlefield and showcases more than 2,000 artifacts of American soldiers, from the Revolutionary War to Desert Storm. In Harrisonburg, Grand Caverns Regional Park has expansive underground chambers used by Union and Confederate troops during the Civil War. The campground is also near Endless Caverns, Luray Caverns, and Shenandoah Caverns.

BASICS

Operated By: Roy and Mary Kircher. **Open:** All year. **Site Assignment:** Reservations recommended, walk-ins accepted. **Registration:** At campground office. **Fee:** $24–$35; V, MC. **Parking:** At site only.

FACILITIES

Number of RV-only Sites: 52. **Number of Tent-only Sites:** 28. **Hookups:** Electric (20, 30, 50 amps), water, phone. **Each Site:** Fire ring, picnic table. **Dump Station:** Yes. **Laundry:** Yes. **Pay Phone:** Yes. **Restrooms and Showers:** Yes. **Fuel:** No. **Propane:** Yes. **Internal Roads:** Paved, in fair condition. **RV Service:** No. **Market:** W/in 5 mi. **Restaurant:** W/in 5 mi. **General Store:** Yes. **Vending:** Yes. **Swimming:** Yes. **Playground:** Yes. **Activities:** Swimming, pond fishing, game room, rec hall, basketball, movies, badminton, horseshoes, hiking trails, volleyball. **Nearby Attractions:** Shenandoah National Park, Skyline Drive, Blue Ridge Parkway, New Market Battlefield State Historical Park, New Market Battlefield Military Museum, Endless Caverns, Shenandoah Caverns, Luray Caverns. **Additional Information:** Shenandoah Valley Travel Assoc., (540) 740-3132, www.svta.org.

RESTRICTIONS

Pets: On leash only. No pets in cabins. **Fires:** At site only. **Alcoholic Beverages:** At site only. **Vehicle Maximum Length:** No limit.

TO GET THERE

From I-81, take Exit 257 and go 0.1 mi. north on US 11 and 3 mi. east on Hwy. 608. Entrance is at the end.

BUCHANAN
Middle Creek Campground

MAP, C-1

1164 Middle Creek Rd., 24066.
T: (540) 254-2176 or (540) 254-2550;
www.middlecreekcampground.com.

🚐 ★★★★   ⛺ ★★★★

Beauty: ★★★★   Site Privacy: ★★★
Spaciousness: ★★★   Quiet: ★★★★
Security: ★★★   Cleanliness: ★★★★
Insect Control: ★★★★   Facilities: ★★★★

Middle Creek Campground near Buchanan in western Virginia has a swimming pool and a 100-foot double-flume waterslide, a mini-golf course, a stocked fishing pond, and paddle-boat rentals. The sites are semi-wooded, and there are 12 pull-throughs. Nearby is the Appalachian Trail, located in the George Washington and Jefferson National Forests, where hiking and backpacking are king. Dixie Caverns is a short drive from the campground. The caverns tour travels up into the mountain to see the cathedral room before venturing underground to marvel at the famous wedding bell and other breathtaking formations. Of course, don't forget to visit the pottery shop before leaving.

BASICS

Operated By: Susan Martin. **Open:** All year. **Site Assignment:** Reservations and walk-ins accepted. **Registration:** At campground office. **Fee:** $18–$30; V, MC. **Parking:** At site.

FACILITIES

Number of RV-only Sites: 120. **Number of Tent-only Sites:** 18. **Hookups:** Electric (20, 30 amps), water, phone. **Each Site:** Fire ring, picnic table. **Dump Station:** Yes. **Laundry:** Yes. **Pay Phone:** Yes. **Restrooms and Showers:** Yes. **Fuel:** No. **Propane:** Yes. **Internal Roads:** Gravel & paved, in good condition. **RV Service:** No. **Market:** W/in 10 mi. **Restaurant:** W/in 10 mi. **General Store:** Yes. **Vending:** Yes. **Swimming:** Yes. **Playground:** Yes. **Other:** 100-foot double-flume waterslide. **Activities:** Swimming, rec hall, game room, pond swimming, boat rentals, pond and stream fishing, mini-golf, basketball, planned activities, movies, badminton, horseshoes, volleyball. **Nearby Attractions:** Appalachian Trail, Blue Ridge Parkway, Lee Chapel and Museum, Stonewall Jackson Home, James River, Natural Bridge of Virginia. **Additional Information:** Roanoke Valley CVB, (800) 635-5535, www.visitroanokeva.com.

RESTRICTIONS

Pets: On leash only. **Fires:** At site. **Alcoholic Beverages:** At site. **Vehicle Maximum Length:** 48 ft.

TO GET THERE

From I-81, take Exit 168 at Arcadia. Heading north, turn right at the stop sign. Heading south, take a left at the stop sign. Go 5.3 mi. and turn right on Middle Creek Rd. Drive 1 mi. down the road until you reach the campground.

CAPE CHARLES
Kiptopeke State Park

MAP, C-4

3540 Kiptopeke Dr., 23310. T: (757) 331-2267;
www.reserveamerica.com.

🚐 ★★★★   ⛺ ★★★★

Beauty: ★★★★   Site Privacy: ★★
Spaciousness: ★★   Quiet: ★★★★
Security: ★★★★   Cleanliness: ★★★★
Insect Control: ★★★   Facilities: ★★★★

Located on the eastern shore of Virginia, this park offers recreational access to the Chesapeake Bay and the chance to explore a unique coastal habitat featuring a major flyway for migratory birds. Since 1963, Kiptopeke has been the site of bird population studies. Sponsored by the Coastal Virginia Wildlife Observatory, formerly known as KESTRSAL, and licensed by the U.S. Fish and Wildlife Service, volunteers capture, examine, weigh, band, and release resident and migratory birds in September and October of each year. In the raptor research area, hawks, kestrels, osprey, and other birds of prey are observed and banded from September through November. Kiptopeke's hawk observatory is among the top 15 nationwide. The park features a fishing pier, boat launch, beach, and guarded swimming area during the summer, Memorial Day to Labor Day. There is a yurt as well as camping lodges available to reserve. The yurt, which is a cross between a tent and a cabin and is the only one of its kind in the Virginia park system, has a spectacular view of Chesapeake Bay from its large wooden deck.

BASICS

Operated By: Virginia State Parks. **Open:** Mar. 1–1st Mon. in Dec. **Site Assignment:** Reservations can be made 11 months in advance. **Registration:** At office. **Fee:** Single, $23–$33; lodge, $237–$353. **Parking:** 1 vehicle per campsite; additional vehicles park in overflow and will be charged a parking fee.

FACILITIES

Number of Multipurpose Sites: 109. **Hookups:** Yes. **Dump Station:** Yes. **Laundry:** Yes. **Pay Phone:** No. **Restrooms and Showers:** Yes. **Fuel:** No. **Propane:** No. **Internal Roads:** Paved. **RV Service:** Yes. **Market:** No. **Restaurant:** No. **General Store:** Yes. **Vending:** No. **Swimming:** Yes. **Playground:** Yes. **Other:** Boat launch fee, $4–$8; fishing pier fee, $1–$3 or 10 visits for $20. **Activities:** Biking, boating, saltwater fishing, hiking, swimming.

RESTRICTIONS

Pets: Allowed in all Virginia State Parks, except on public beaches & in public facilities (bathhouses, visitor centers, park offices, restaurants, etc.). Confined or kept on a 6-ft. leash. **Fires:** Fire ban in effect during certain times of the year. **Alcoholic Beverages:** Not allowed in public. **Vehicle Maximum Length:** 40 ft.

TO GET THERE

Kiptopeke is 3 mi. from the northern terminus of the Chesapeake Bay Bridge Tunnel, which has a substantial toll charge each way, on Hwy. 13. Turn west on Hwy. 704; the park entrance is within 0.5 mi.

CENTREVILLE   MAP, A-3
Bull Run Regional Park

7700 Bull Run Dr., 20121. T: (703) 631-0550;
www.nvpra.org.

🚐 ★★★★   ⛺ ★★★★

Beauty: ★★★   Site Privacy: ★★
Spaciousness: ★★★   Quiet: ★★★
Security: ★★★★   Cleanliness: ★★★★
Insect Control: ★★★★   Facilities: ★★★★

Bull Run Regional Park is located 27 miles west of
Washington, D.C., but it is better known for its
proximity to nearby Manassas National Battlefield
Park, where two Civil War battles were fought. The
heavily wooded campground, situated in the middle
of the 1,500-acre park, offers spacious and level sites.
Thirty miles of hiking trails and 20 miles of horseback-riding trails adorn the 4,500 acres of nearby
Manassas Battlefield. Civil War enthusiasts will treasure the mile-long, self-guided walking tour of the
First Manassas Battlefield. Signs and audio messages
describe the scenes of this battle between Confederate and Union troops on July 21, 1861. Confederate
forces prevailed, and Gen. Thomas J. Jackson earned
the nickname "Stonewall." The town of Manassas is
a worthwhile stop. Its visitor center is located in a
refurbished train depot, where tours of Old Town
Manassas begin.

BASICS
Operated By: Northern Virginia Regional Park
Authority. **Open:** Mar. 6–Nov. 18. **Site Assignment:**
First come, first served. **Registration:** At camp-
ground office. **Fee:** $13–$16; $7 entry fee for first 9
people; V, MC. **Parking:** At site.

FACILITIES
Number of RV-only Sites: 100. **Number of Tent-
only Sites:** 50. **Hookups:** Electric (15, 20, 30 amps).
Each Site: Fire ring, picnic table. **Dump Station:**
Yes. **Laundry:** Yes. **Pay Phone:** Yes. **Restrooms
and Showers:** Yes. **Fuel:** No. **Propane:** No. **Inter-
nal Roads:** Paved, in good condition. **RV Service:**
No. **Market:** W/in 3 mi. **Restaurant:** W/in 3 mi.
General Store: Yes. **Vending:** Yes. **Swimming:** Yes.
Playground: Yes. **Activities:** Swimming, wading
pool, stream fishing, mini-golf, horseback riding, hiking
trails, sports field, volleyball, disc golf, soccer. **Nearby
Attractions:** Manassas National Battlefield Park,
Washington, D.C. **Additional Information:** Prince
William Co. Conference Visitors Bureau, (703) 792-
4254, www.visitpwc.com.

RESTRICTIONS
Pets: On leash only. **Fires:** At site. **Alcoholic Bev-
erages:** No alcohol permitted. **Vehicle Maximum
Length:** 45 ft. **Other:** 7-day stay limit.

TO GET THERE
From I-66, take Centreville exit and go 3 mi. west
on US 29. Entrance is on the left.

CHARLOTTESVILLE   MAP, B-2
Charlottesville KOA

3825 Red Hill Rd., 22903.
T: (800) KOA-1743 or (434) 296-9881;
www.koa.com.

🚐 ★★★★   ⛺ ★★★★

Beauty: ★★★   Site Privacy: ★★
Spaciousness: ★★   Quiet: ★★★★
Security: ★★★★   Cleanliness: ★★★★
Insect Control: ★★★★   Facilities: ★★★

Charlottesville KOA is near Monticello, the home of
Thomas Jefferson; Montpelier, the home of James
and Dolly Madison; and Ash Lawn, the home of
James Monroe. Those sites are interesting, but
equally intriguing is Walton's Mountain Museum,
the former home of John Walton. Yes, there actually
is a Walton's Mountain. Charlottesville KOA offers
71 wooded sites, including 18 pull-throughs. There
is a swimming pool and a fishing lake. James River is
a short drive away; fishing, tubing, and canoeing are
among the activities there. This campground is ideal
for families looking for a base as they explore the area
attractions. Luray Caverns, open since 1878, offers
one-hour guided tours. Should you prefer to remain
in your car, the Skyline Drive meanders along the
crest of the Blue Ridge Mountains, wanders through
Shenandoah National Park, and continues on the
Blue Ridge Parkway. If you're not tired of presidential house museums, Woodrow Wilson's one-time
home is 40 miles from the campground in Staunton.

BASICS
Operated By: KOA. **Open:** Mar. 1–Oct. 31. **Site
Assignment:** Reservations and walk-ins accepted.
Registration: At campground office. **Fee:** $23–$33;
V, MC, D. **Parking:** At designated spot.

FACILITIES
Number of RV-only Sites: 57. **Number of Tent-
only Sites:** 14. **Hookups:** Electric (20, 30 amps),
water. **Each Site:** Fire ring, picnic table. **Dump Station:** Yes. **Laundry:** Yes. **Pay Phone:** Yes.
Restrooms and Showers: Yes. **Fuel:** No.
Propane: Yes. **Internal Roads:** Gravel, in good condition. **RV Service:** No. **Market:** W/in 6 mi.
Restaurant: W/in 6 mi. **General Store:** Yes. **Vending:** Yes. **Swimming:** Yes. **Playground:** Yes. **Other:**
Fishing lake. **Activities:** Rec hall, game room, swimming, pond fishing, basketball, horseshoes, volleyball,
hiking trails, planned activities on weekends. **Nearby
Attractions:** Monticello, Montpelier, Ash Lawn, Walton's Mountain Museum, James River, Luray Caverns.
Additional Information: Virginia Tourism Corp.,
(800) 371-8164, www.virginia.org.

RESTRICTIONS
Pets: On leash only. **Fires:** At site. **Alcoholic Beverages:** At site. **Vehicle Maximum Length:** 40 ft.

TO GET THERE
From I-64, take Exit 118A and go 6 mi. south on
US 29 and 4 mi. southeast on CR 708. Entrance is
on the left.

CHARLOTTESVILLE   MAP, B-2
Misty Mountain Camp Resort

56 Misty Mountain Rd., 22943. T: (888) 647-8900;
www.mistycamp.com.

🚐 ★★★★   ⛺ ★★★★

Beauty: ★★★★   Site Privacy: ★★★
Spaciousness: ★★★   Quiet: ★★★★
Security: ★★★★   Cleanliness: ★★★★
Insect Control: ★★★★   Facilities: ★★★★

Nestled on the mountain for which it is named,
Misty Mountain Camp Resort is a 50-acre park near
Charlottesville. There are wooded and creek side
sites, and 29 pull-throughs. A recreational building
has banquet tables and chairs to accommodate
groups. Hiking trails are scattered throughout the
campground, and scenic vistas are plentiful. If you're
hungry, you can have a pizza delivered right to your
campsite. Like Charlottesville KOA, Misty Mountain is located within a half-hour drive of Washington, D.C., and near the presidential homes of
Thomas Jefferson, James Madison, James Monroe,
and Woodrow Wilson. At Walton's Mountain
Museum in nearby Schuyler, the set of *The Waltons*
television show is showcased. Though KOA and
Misty Mountain offer similar recreational opportunities, Misty Mountain's facilities are cleaner, and the
mountain aura is peaceful, especially at sunrise.

BASICS
Operated By: Mike Mellom. **Open:** All year.
Site Assignment: Reservations accepted (cancellation must be 7 days from reservation date for
refund), walk-ins accepted. **Registration:** At campground office. **Fee:** $21–$30; V, MC. **Parking:** At
designated spot.

FACILITIES
Number of RV-only Sites: 79. **Number of Tent-
only Sites:** 16. **Hookups:** Electric (15, 20, 30, 50
amps), water. **Each Site:** Fire ring, picnic table.
Dump Station: Yes. **Laundry:** Yes. **Pay Phone:** Yes.
Restrooms and Showers: Yes. **Fuel:** No.
Propane: Yes. **Internal Roads:** Gravel, in good con-
dition. **RV Service:** No. **Market:** W/in 2 mi.
Restaurant: On premises. **General Store:** Yes.
Vending: Yes. **Swimming:** Yes. **Playground:** Yes.
Activities: Rec hall, game room, wagon rides, swim-
ming, stream fishing, planned activities, badminton,
sports field, horseshoes, hiking trails, volleyball.
Nearby Attractions: Monticello, Montpelier, Ash
Lawn, Walton's Mountain Museum, James River, Luray
Caverns. **Additional Information:** Virginia Tourism
Corp., (800) 371-8164, www.virginia.org.

RESTRICTIONS
Pets: On leash only. **Fires:** At site. **Alcoholic Bev-
erages:** At site. **Vehicle Maximum Length:** 65 ft.
Other: Pets not allowed in play areas.

TO GET THERE
From I-64, take Exit 107 and go 1 mi. west on US
250. Entrance is on the left.

CHERITON   MAP, C-4
Cherrystone Family Camping and RV Resort

P.O. Box 545, 23316. T: (757) 331-3063;
www.cherrystoneva.com.

🚐 ★★★★★   ⛺ ★★★★★

Beauty: ★★★★   Site Privacy: ★★
Spaciousness: ★★★   Quiet: ★★★
Security: ★★★★   Cleanliness: ★★★★★
Insect Control: ★★★★   Facilities: ★★★★★

It would be hard to logically argue that Cherrystone Family Camping and RV Resort is not the overall finest campground in Virginia. Located on Chesapeake Bay, Cherrystone has 110 pull-through sites, bayview sites located near fishing piers, an adults-only swimming pool, and a paddleboat lake. The campground's eastern side is composed of several clusters of sites that offer little privacy. You can easily and happily spend your entire vacation without leaving Cherrystone's 300-acre grounds. With Cherrystone's location, ocean swimming, boating, and fishing are big draws. The property is bordered on three sides by Kings Creek, Cherrystone Creek, and Chesapeake Bay. These waters are teeming with oysters, clams, crabs, and fish such as flounder, trout, croaker, and spot. *Miss Jennifer* charter fishing boat departs from the Cherrystone dock Memorial Day–Labor Day. The campground has four swimming pools (including one solely for adults) and a beach-entry family pool. An 18-hole mini-golf course, several playgrounds, volleyball and basketball courts, and a game room are also on the grounds. Cherrystone has a restaurant, snack bar, and a farm stand that carries fresh local vegetables, fruit, and seafood.

BASICS

Operated By: Ed and Mary Davidson. **Open:** All year. **Site Assignment:** Reservations accepted (deposit required w/in 10 days of making reservation), walk-ins accepted. **Registration:** At campground headquarters. **Fee:** $17–$47; V, MC, AE. **Parking:** At designated spot.

FACILITIES

Number of RV-only Sites: 450. **Number of Tent-only Sites:** 200. **Hookups:** Electric (20, 30, 50 amps), water, phone. **Each Site:** Fire ring, grill. **Dump Station:** Yes. **Laundry:** Yes. **Pay Phone:** Yes. **Restrooms and Showers:** Yes. **Fuel:** No. **Propane:** Yes. **Internal Roads:** Gravel & paved, in good condition. **RV Service:** No. **Market:** W/in 3 mi. **Restaurant:** W/in 2 mi. **General Store:** Yes. **Vending:** Yes. **Swimming:** Yes. **Playground:** Yes. **Other:** 4 pools & 4 fishing piers on Chesapeake Bay waterfront. **Activities:** Swimming at four pools and wading pool, ocean swimming, boating, canoeing, kayaking, rec hall, game room, ocean and pond fishing, mini-golf, basketball, bike rentals, shuffleboard, planned activities, movies, tennis, sports field, horseshoes. **Nearby Attractions:** Chesapeake Bay, Virginia Beach, Norfolk, Williamsburg. **Additional Information:** Virginia Tourism Corp., (800) 371-8164, www.virginia.org.

RESTRICTIONS

Pets: On leash only. **Fires:** At site. **Alcoholic Beverages:** At site. **Vehicle Maximum Length:** 60 ft.

Other: No refunds for early departures.

TO GET THERE

From US 13 Bypass, go 1.5 mi. west on Townsfield Dr. Entrance is at the end.

CHESTERFIELD   MAP, C-3
Pocahontas State Park

reserve america

10301 State Park Rd., 23832-6355.
T: (804) 796-4255; www.reserveamerica.com.

🚐 ★★★★   ⛺ ★★★★

Beauty: ★★★★   Site Privacy: ★★
Spaciousness: ★★   Quiet: ★★★★
Security: ★★★★   Cleanliness: ★★★★
Insect Control: ★★★   Facilities: ★★★

Just 20 miles from downtown Richmond, the capital of Virginia, Pocahontas State Park is one of the more popular parks in the state park system. Swift Creek forms the nucleus of the park, which is centered in a wildlife management area. Hiking, biking, and horseback riding are popular activities. The park's olympic-sized swimming pool is a welcome relief from the summer heat. Other facilities at the park include a Civil Conservation Corps Museum, an amphitheater featuring events from the Richmond Symphony to a Civil War Day, and the Heritage Center, which is a modern conference-center facility that is available for banquets, receptions, and group meetings and accommodates groups up to 200. The park also offers group bunkhouses which are rustic and contain only beds. These bunkhouses (group cabins) accommodate from 28 to 112 people and may include dining-hall facilities depending on the group's needs.

BASICS

Operated By: Virginia State Parks. **Open:** Mar. 1–1st Mon. in Dec. **Site Assignment:** Reservations can be made 11 months in advance. **Registration:** At office. **Fee:** Single, $20; picnic shelter, $30–$45. **Parking:** 1 vehicle plus the camping unit are allowed at the campsite; additional parking is available and a parking fee will be charged.

FACILITIES

Number of Multipurpose Sites: 133. **Hookups:** Yes. **Dump Station:** No. **Laundry:** No. **Pay Phone:** No. **Restrooms and Showers:** No. **Fuel:** No. **Propane:** No. **Internal Roads:** Paved. **RV Service:** Yes. **Market:** No. **Restaurant:** No. **General Store:** No. **Vending:** No. **Swimming:** Yes. **Playground:** Yes. **Activities:** Biking, boating, horseback riding, freshwater fishing, hiking, swimming.

RESTRICTIONS

Pets: Allowed in all Virginia State Parks, except on public beaches & in public facilities (bathhouses, visitor centers, park offices, restaurants, etc.). Confined or kept on a 6-ft. leash. **Fires:** Fire ban in effect during certain times of the year. **Alcoholic Beverages:** Not allowed in public. **Vehicle Maximum Length:** 40 ft.

TO GET THERE

In Chesterfield County, about 20 mi. from Richmond. From I-95, take Exit 61 and go west on

Hwy. 10 to Hwy. 655 which is Beach Rd.; or take Exit 67, go north on Hwy. 150 to Hwy. 10; go east to Beach Rd. The park is 4 mi. on right; or take Hwy. 288 from I-95 to Hwy. 10E and go 1 mi. to Beach Rd. Follow park signs from there.

CHINCOTEAGUE   MAP, B-4
Maddox Family Campground

6742 Maddox Blvd., P.O. Box 82, 23336.
T: (757) 336-3111;
www.chincoteague.net/i-maddox.

🚐 ★★★★   ⛺ ★★★★

Beauty: ★★★★   Site Privacy: ★★
Spaciousness: ★★   Quiet: ★★★
Security: ★★★★   Cleanliness: ★★★★
Insect Control: ★★★★   Facilities: ★★★★

The closest campground to Assateague Island National Seashore, Chincoteague Island's Maddox Family Campground has more than 550 open and shaded sites, including 68 pull-throughs. Wooded sites are inviting to RVers and tenters alike. The campground has a swimming pool and a playground, and the facilities are clean. Yet, many campers stay here for what the park is near, not for what it is has on the grounds. The national seashore and the national wildlife refuge are the magnets for outdoor enthusiasts. Two herds of wild horses make their home on Assateague Island, separated by a fence at the Maryland-Virginia line, and they are often seen wandering the beaches, roadways, trails, and campgrounds on the island. These small and shaggy horses have adapted to their environment over the years by eating dune and marsh grasses and drinking fresh water from ponds.

BASICS

Operated By: Private operator. **Open:** Mar. 1–Nov. 30. **Site Assignment:** Reservations and walk-ins accepted. **Registration:** At campground office. **Fee:** $27–$35; V, MC, D. **Parking:** At site.

FACILITIES

Number of RV-only Sites: 341. **Number of Tent-only Sites:** 250. **Hookups:** Electric (20, 30 amps), water. **Each Site:** Fire ring, picnic table. **Dump Station:** Yes. **Laundry:** Yes. **Pay Phone:** Yes. **Restrooms and Showers:** Yes. **Fuel:** No. **Propane:** Yes. **Internal Roads:** Gravel, in good condition. **RV Service:** No. **Market:** W/in 1 mi. **Restaurant:** W/in 1 mi. **General Store:** Yes. **Vending:** Yes. **Swimming:** Yes. **Playground:** Yes. **Other:** Duck pond, bird-watching sites. **Activities:** Bird-watching, crabbing, rec hall, game room, mini-golf, shuffleboard. **Nearby Attractions:** Assateague National Seashore, Chincoteague Wildlife Refuge. **Additional Information:** Eastern Shore of Virginia Tourism Commission, (757) 787-2460, www.esva.net/~esvatourism.

RESTRICTIONS

Pets: On leash only. **Fires:** At site. **Alcoholic Beverages:** At site. **Vehicle Maximum Length:** No limit.

TO GET THERE

From SR 175, go 0.5 mi. on Main St. to Maddox Blvd. and 1 mi. to campground.

CHINCOTEAGUE   MAP, B-4
Tom's Cove Park

8128 Beebe Rd., 23336. T: (757) 336-6498;
www.tomscovepark.com.

🚐 ★★★★   ⛺ ★★★★

Beauty: ★★★★   Site Privacy: ★
Spaciousness: ★★   Quiet: ★★★
Security: ★★★★   Cleanliness: ★★★★
Insect Control: ★★★★   Facilities: ★★★★★

Situated on the waterfront on Chincoteague Island—one of the largest migratory bird sanctuaries on the east coast—Tom's Cove Park is a short drive away from Assateague Island National Seashore and Chincoteague National Wildlife Refuge. Ocean fishing, crabbing, boating, and swimming are just a sampling of the activities offered at the 88-acre campground, home to 920 open and wooded sites. These sites are well maintained, but they offer little privacy and can feel crowded, especially on summer weekends. The marina has a double-wide boat ramp. The campground hosts live entertainment on Saturday nights during the summer in the air-conditioned pavilion. Chincoteague Island, Virginia's only resort island, is a destination in itself. World-famous for its oyster beds and clam shoals, Chincoteague is the gateway to Assateague Island National Seashore, home to a unique breed of wild ponies. Chincoteague Island is also the home of many outstanding craftsmen and artists who produce some of the world's finest hand-carved duck decoys and reproductions of soaring wildfowl.

BASICS

Operated By: Private operator. **Open:** Mar. 1–Nov. 30. **Site Assignment:** Reservations accepted (guarantees water and electric site only), walk-ins accepted. **Registration:** At campground office. **Fee:** $27–$37; V, MC. **Parking:** At designated spot.

FACILITIES

Number of RV-only Sites: 865. **Number of Tent-only Sites:** 55. **Hookups:** Electric (20, 30 amps), water, cable TV, phone. **Each Site:** Picnic table. **Dump Station:** Yes. **Laundry:** Yes. **Pay Phone:** Yes. **Restrooms and Showers:** Yes. **Fuel:** No. **Propane:** Yes. **Internal Roads:** Gravel & paved, in good condition. **RV Service:** No. **Market:** W/in 3 mi. **Restaurant:** W/in 3 mi. **General Store:** Yes. **Vending:** Yes. **Swimming:** Yes. **Playground:** Yes. **Other:** 3 fishing & crabbing piers on Chincoteague Island. **Activities:** Ocean fishing, swimming, boating, canoeing, kayaking, bike rentals, sports field, horseshoes, rec hall, game room, crabbing. **Nearby Attractions:** Assateague National Seashore, Chincoteague Wildlife Refuge. **Additional Information:** Eastern Shore of Virginia Tourism Commission, (757) 787-2460, www.esva.net/~esvatourism.

RESTRICTIONS

Pets: On leash only. **Fires:** At site. **Alcoholic Beverages:** At site. **Vehicle Maximum Length:** No limit.

TO GET THERE

From US 13, go 11 mi. east on SR 175, 1.25 mi. south on Main St., and 0.5 mi. east on Beebe Rd. Entrance is at the end.

CLARKSVILLE   MAP, C-2
Occoneechee State Park

reserve america

1192 Occoneechee Park Rd., 23927.
T: (434) 374-2210 or (800) 933-PARK;
www.reserveamerica.com.

🚐 ★★★   ⛺ ★★★★

Beauty: ★★★★   Site Privacy: ★★★
Spaciousness: ★★★   Quiet: ★★★★
Security: ★★★★   Cleanliness: ★★★★
Insect Control: ★★★★   Facilities: ★★★

Though it's officially named the John H. Kerr Reservoir, most people know it as Buggs Island Lake. Regardless of what it's called, the 48,000-acre body of water is the main attraction at Occoneechee State Park, located in southern Virginia near the North Carolina border. The campground has 88 sites, many shaded and some with a lake view. There are several hiking trails near the campground, including the Old Plantation Interpretive Trail (which wanders past the one-time site of a 3,105-acre plantation) and the Warriors Path Nature Trail. Swimming is not permitted from the shoreline because of hazardous drop-offs and heavy boating traffic. Buggs Island Lake and connecting Lake Gaston are famous for the number and size of fish found there. Striped and largemouth bass, bluegill, crappie, and perch are plentiful. Fishing boats with motors, canoes, paddleboats, seven-speed off-road bikes, and one- and two-person kayaks are available for rent.

BASICS

Operated By: State of Virginia. **Open:** Mar.–Dec. **Site Assignment:** First come, first served. **Registration:** At visitor center. **Fee:** $19–$24; V, MC. **Parking:** At site.

FACILITIES

Number of RV-only Sites: 39. **Number of Tent-only Sites:** 49. **Hookups:** Electric (15 amps). **Each Site:** Grill, picnic table, & lantern pole. **Dump Station:** Yes. **Laundry:** No. **Pay Phone:** Yes. **Restrooms and Showers:** Yes. **Fuel:** No. **Propane:** No. **Internal Roads:** Paved, in good condition. **RV Service:** No. **Market:** W/in 1 mi. **Restaurant:** W/in 1 mi. **General Store:** No. **Vending:** Yes. **Swimming:** No. **Playground:** No. **Other:** Visitor center, gift shop. **Activities:** Fishing, boating, hiking trails, boat rentals. **Nearby Attractions:** Prestwood Plantation, John H. Kerr Dam. **Additional Information:** Virginia Tourism Corp., (800) 371-8164, www.virginia.org.

RESTRICTIONS

Pets: On leash only. **Fires:** At site. **Alcoholic Beverages:** No alcohol permitted. **Vehicle Maximum Length:** 30 ft. **Other:** Max. 14-day stay every 30 days.

TO GET THERE

From Clarksville, go 1 mi. east on US 58. Follow signs to park.

COVINGTON   MAP, B-1
Morris Hill Campground

reserve america

810-A Madison Ave., 24426. T: (540) 962-2214;
www.reserveamerica.com.

🚐 ★★★   ⛺ ★★★★

Beauty: ★★★★   Site Privacy: ★★★
Spaciousness: ★★★   Quiet: ★★★★
Security: ★★★★   Cleanliness: ★★★★
Insect Control: ★★★★   Facilities: ★★★

Sometimes, when you hit the open road in your RV, amenities like mini-golf courses, swimming pools, rec halls—even electric hookups—can be sacrificed for solitude and serenity. This is why campers come to Morris Hill Campground near Covington in western Virginia. You'll find restrooms and showers here, but that's about it. No phone and no hookups. You'll also find 2,500-acre Lake Moomaw, which is surrounded at the north by the 13,428-acre Gathright Wildlife Management Area. Formed by the construction of the Gathright Dam in 1981, Lake Moomaw is 12 miles long. Largemouth bass, crappie, bluegill, and channel catfish are among the fish that swim in the lake's waters. There is a beach at Coles Point Recreation Area. Morris Hill actually sits on a hilltop amid tall hardwoods. Though it's steep and strenuous, the 5.3-mile Oliver Mountain Trail provides stunning mountain views and a peek at Lake Moomaw.

BASICS

Operated By: U.S. Forest Service. **Open:** Apr. 30–Nov. 1. **Site Assignment:** Reservations and walk-ins accepted. **Registration:** Self-registration on site. **Fee:** $10; V, MC. **Parking:** At site spur.

FACILITIES

Number of RV-only Sites: 53. **Number of Tent-only Sites:** 2. **Hookups:** None. **Each Site:** Fire ring, picnic table. **Dump Station:** Yes. **Laundry:** No. **Pay Phone:** No. **Restrooms and Showers:** Yes. **Fuel:** No. **Propane:** No. **Internal Roads:** Paved, in good condition. **RV Service:** No. **Market:** W/in 12 mi. **Restaurant:** W/in 10 mi. **General Store:** No. **Vending:** No. **Swimming:** Yes. **Playground:** Yes. **Other:** Lake Moomaw. **Activities:** Lake fishing and swimming, boating, canoeing, hiking. **Nearby Attractions:** George Washington National Forest, the Homestead, Warm Springs Baths, Lexington, Virginia Military Institute, Lee Chapel, Stonewall Jackson House, Roanoke. **Additional Information:** Virginia Tourism Corp., (800) 371-8164, www.virginia.org.

RESTRICTIONS

Pets: On leash only. **Fires:** At site. **Alcoholic Beverages:** At site. **Vehicle Maximum Length:** 22 ft. **Other:** Quiet time 10 pm.–6 a.m.

TO GET THERE

From US 220, go 6 mi. north on Hwy. 687, 3 mi. west on Hwy. 641, and 5 mi. north on Hwy. 666. Follow signs to campground.

CULPEPER   MAP, B-3
Cedar Mountain Campground

20114 Camp Rd., 22701.
T: (540) 547-3374 or (800) 234-0968.

🚐 ★★★★   ⛺ ★★★★

Beauty: ★★★★	Site Privacy: ★★
Spaciousness: ★★★	Quiet: ★★★★
Security: ★★★★	Cleanliness: ★★★★
Insect Control: ★★★★	Facilities: ★★★★

Located in a forested setting east of Shenandoah National Park and southwest of Washington, D.C., Cedar Mountain Campground is near eight historic battlefields. This is a perfect base for outdoor enthusiasts who are also Civil War buffs. The 16-acre campground has room for eight pull-throughs. RVers and tenters have their choice of wooded sites that are especially cool and comfortable on sizzling summer days. Outdoor enthusiasts will like the nature walk and the fishing pond. The spacious pavilion has a fireplace and barbecue pits. Four bloody battles were fought on the soil of the Fredericksburg and Spotsylvania Military Park, about 25 miles southeast of Cedar Mountain. About 40 miles northeast of Cedar Mountain lies the Manassas National Battlefield Park, where the first and second Battles of Bull Run happened. Of course, Virginia has its share of Revolutionary War heritage too. Ferry Farm, George Washington's boyhood home, graces the banks of the Rappahannock River.

BASICS
Operated By: Private operator. **Open:** All year. **Site Assignment:** Reservations and walk-ins accepted. **Registration:** At campground office. **Fee:** $15–$18; V, MC. **Parking:** At designated spot.

FACILITIES
Number of RV-only Sites: 41. **Number of Tent-only Sites:** 20. **Hookups:** Electric (30 amps), water. **Each Site:** Fire ring, picnic table. **Dump Station:** Yes. **Laundry:** No. **Pay Phone:** Yes. **Restrooms and Showers:** Yes. **Fuel:** No. **Propane:** Yes. **Internal Roads:** Gravel, in good condition. **RV Service:** No. **Market:** W/in 5 mi. **Restaurant:** W/in 5 mi. **General Store:** Yes. **Vending:** Yes. **Swimming:** Yes. **Playground:** Yes. **Other:** Cable slides. **Activities:** Pond fishing, game room, rec hall, mini-golf, basketball, shuffleboard, badminton, sports field, horseshoes, volleyball. **Nearby Attractions:** Museum of Culpeper History, Fredericksburg and Spotsylvania battlefields, Manassas battlefields, Washington, D.C., Shenandoah National Park. **Additional Information:** Virginia Tourism Corp., (800) 371-8164, www.virginia.org.

RESTRICTIONS
Pets: On leash only. **Fires:** At site. **Alcoholic Beverages:** At site. **Vehicle Maximum Length:** 40 ft.

TO GET THERE
From Business US 29, go 3 mi. south on US 29 and 2.25 mi. east and south on CR 603/657/645/752. Follow signs. Entrance is on the right.

CUMBERLAND   MAP, C-2, C-3
Bear Creek Lake State Park

reserve america

929 Oak Hill Rd., 23040. T: (804) 492-4410; www.reserveamerica.com.

🚐 ★★★   ⛺ ★★★

Beauty: ★★★★	Site Privacy: ★★★
Spaciousness: ★★★	Quiet: ★★★
Security: ★★★★	Cleanliness: ★★★★
Insect Control: ★★★★	Facilities: ★★★

Situated amid the towering sweet gum, oak, and tulip poplar trees of Cumberland State Forest in central Virginia, Bear Creek Lake State Park typically does not draw large crowds—all the better for campers looking for rest and relaxation. The camping area has 53 shaded sites and is actually divided in three sections. Campground A, the only campground by the lake, has 13 tent sites with no electric or water hookups and nine sites with hookups for vehicles up to 20 ft. Campground B offers 14 sites with water and electric hookups for RVs up to 20 ft. and six sites with hookups to handle vehicles up to 35 ft. Campground C, open from Memorial Day–Labor Day, has 11 tent sites with no electric or water hookups. A campground host is available at most times in campsite A-25, adjacent to the picnic shelter. The park is surrounded by the 16,000-acre Cumberland State Forest, which is teeming with fishing and swimming areas and hiking trails.

BASICS
Operated By: State of Virginia. **Open:** Mar.–Dec. **Site Assignment:** Reservations and walk-ins accepted. **Registration:** At campground office. **Fee:** $15–$21; V, MC. **Parking:** At site.

FACILITIES
Number of RV-only Sites: 29. **Number of Tent-only Sites:** 24. **Hookups:** Electric (20, 30 amps). **Each Site:** Grill, picnic table. **Dump Station:** Yes. **Laundry:** No. **Pay Phone:** Yes. **Restrooms and Showers:** Yes. **Fuel:** No. **Propane:** No. **Internal Roads:** Paved, in good condition. **RV Service:** No. **Market:** W/in 7 mi. **Restaurant:** W/in 7 mi. **General Store:** No. **Vending:** No. **Swimming:** Yes. **Playground:** No. **Other:** Small market outside the park sells a limited number of groceries. **Activities:** Lake swimming and fishing, hiking trails, boating, boat rentals, canoeing. **Nearby Attractions:** Lee's Retreat Driving Tour, Farmville, Appomattox Court House National Historic Park, Richmond. **Additional Information:** Virginia Tourism Corp., (800) 371-8164, www.virginia.org.

RESTRICTIONS
Pets: On leash only. **Fires:** At site. **Alcoholic Beverages:** No alcohol permitted. **Vehicle Maximum Length:** 30 ft. **Other:** 14-day stay limit in 30-day period.

TO GET THERE
From Cumberland, go 0.5 mi. east on US 60 and 4.5 mi. west on Hwy. 622/629. Follow signs to park.

DELAPLANE   MAP, A-3
Sky Meadows State Park

reserve america

11012 Edmonds Lane, 20144-1710. T: (540) 592-3556; www.reserveamerica.com.

🚐   ⛺ ★★★★

Beauty: ★★★	Site Privacy: ★★★
Spaciousness: ★★★	Quiet: ★★★★
Security: ★★★★	Cleanliness: ★★★★
Insect Control: ★★★	Facilities: ★

The land for this park was donated in 1975 by Paul Mellon of Upperville to the Commonwealth of Virginia. It consisted of 1,132 acres. The name Sky Meadows came from former owner Sir Robert Hadow, who named the property Skye Farm after an island in Scotland. In 1988 Mellon donated another 486 acres. This area has been developed into an equestrian staging and bridle trail area. Just an hour's drive from Washington, D.C., Sky Meadows State Park in Clarke and Fauquier counties offers a peaceful getaway on the eastern side of the Blue Ridge Mountains. Rich in history, the park has rolling pastures, woodlands, and scenic vistas and provides a look into a bygone era. The park also has access to the Appalachian Trail and a primitive hike-in campground, as well as picnicking, hiking and riding trails, interpretive programs, and a visitor center in the historic Mount Bleak House.

BASICS
Operated By: Virginia State Parks. **Open:** All year. **Site Assignment:** Reservations can be made 11 months in advance. **Registration:** At office. **Fee:** Single, $12–$27. **Parking:** At site.

FACILITIES
Number of Multipurpose Sites: 11. **Hookups:** None. **Each Site:** Fire ring, tent pad, picnic table. **Dump Station:** No. **Laundry:** No. **Pay Phone:** No. **Restrooms and Showers:** Yes. **Fuel:** No. **Propane:** No. **Internal Roads:** Paved. **RV Service:** No. **Market:** No. **Restaurant:** No. **General Store:** No. **Vending:** No. **Swimming:** No. **Playground:** No. **Other:** Hike-in campground. No vehicles allowed. The park closes at dusk so campers must arrive before dusk. **Activities:** Fishing, hiking, picnicking.

RESTRICTIONS
Fires: In designated fireplaces.

TO GET THERE
The park is less than 2 mi. south of Paris, VA, via US 50 to Hwy. 17S; or 7 mi. north of I-66, Exit 23 on Hwy. 17N. The park entrance is on VA 710.

DOSWELL MAP, B-3
Paramount's Kings Dominion Campground

10061 Kings Dominion Blvd., 23047.
T: (800) 922-6710 or (804) 876-5355;
www.kingsdominion.com.

🚐 ★★★★   ⛺ ★★★★

Beauty: ★★★★   Site Privacy: ★
Spaciousness: ★★   Quiet: ★★
Security: ★★★★   Cleanliness: ★★★★
Insect Control: ★★★★   Facilities: ★★★★

Located 20 miles north of Richmond, Paramount's Kings Dominion Amusement Park has its shows, more tranquil family-oriented rides, and water park area, but we think that nothing compares to the assortment of thrill rides that await here. After an exhaustive day of exploring the amusement park, Paramount's Kings Dominion Campground is just a half-mile from the park's entrance. The semi-wooded campground has 37 pull-throughs and a primitive tent camping area. The facilities are well maintained, and when campers are not frolicking in the amusement park, they can swim in the campground's pool or play mini-golf. Of course, the main reason for camping here is to have a place to rest between visits to Kings Dominion. After a long day in the park, you'll appreciate the free shuttle service back to the campground even more than when you arrived at the park that morning.

BASICS
Operated By: Paramount. **Open:** All year. **Site Assignment:** Reservations and walk-ins accepted. **Registration:** At campground headquarters. **Fee:** $20–$30; V, MC, AE, D. **Parking:** At designated spot.

FACILITIES
Number of RV-only Sites: 190. **Number of Tent-only Sites:** 40. **Hookups:** Electric (20, 30, 50 amps), water. **Each Site:** Picnic table. **Dump Station:** Yes. **Laundry:** Yes. **Pay Phone:** Yes. **Restrooms and Showers:** Yes. **Fuel:** No. **Propane:** Yes. **Internal Roads:** Gravel & paved, in good condition. **RV Service:** No. **Market:** W/in 2 mi. **Restaurant:** W/in 2 mi. **General Store:** Yes. **Vending:** Yes. **Swimming:** Yes. **Playground:** Yes. **Other:** Paramount's Kings Dominion Amusement Park is 1 mi. from campground entrance. Shuttles available. Cabin rentals are available. **Activities:** Rec hall, swimming, mini-golf, horseshoes, volleyball. **Nearby Attractions:** Paramount's Kings Dominion Amusement Park, Richmond, White House of the Confederacy, Fredericksburg and Spotsylvania battlefields. **Additional Information:** Richmond CVB, (888) RICHMOND, www.richmondva.org.

RESTRICTIONS
Pets: On leash only. **Fires:** At site. **Alcoholic Beverages:** At site. **Vehicle Maximum Length:** No limit.

TO GET THERE
From I-95, take Exit 98 and go 0.5 mi. on Hwy. 30. Entrance is on the right.

DUBLIN MAP, C-1
Claytor Lake State Park

reserve america

6620 Ben Bolen Dr., 24084-5643.
T: (540) 643-2500; www.reserveamerica.com.

🚐 ★★★★   ⛺ ★★★★

Beauty: ★★★   Site Privacy: ★★★
Spaciousness: ★★★   Quiet: ★★★★
Security: ★★★★   Cleanliness: ★★★★
Insect Control: ★★★   Facilities: ★★★★

Located on the 4,500 acre, 21-mile-long Claytor Lake (from which the park was named) in the New River Valley of southwestern Virginia, Claytor Lake State Park offers a wide variety of activities for water and land enthusiasts. Easily accessible from I-81, the park features the only full-service marina in the state park system. In addition, there are miles of hiking trails, swimming, camping facilities, cabins, and a visitor center. The visitor center is located in the historic Howe House. The lake and the park are named after Graham Claytor (1886–1971), who was vice president of Appalachian Power and supervised construction of the dam (motorboats permitted). Bass, catfish, Muskie, walleye, and striped bass are among the popular sport fish found in the lake. A private concessionaire rents all types of boats, conducts interpretive lake tours, and has water sports packages available at the park. Each year in November, the lake is drawn down approximately five feet for maintenance. During this period, usually two weeks, it may be impossible to launch boats from the Claytor Lake boat launch, and fishing from the shore is difficult. There is a public boat launch just outside the park from which guests may be able to launch unless they have particularly large boats. The lake level will return to normal over time depending on rain.

BASICS
Operated By: Virginia State Parks. **Open:** All year. **Site Assignment:** Reservations can be made 11 months in advance. **Registration:** At office. **Fee:** Single, $19–$24; cabin, $79–$353. **Parking:** At site.

FACILITIES
Number of Multipurpose Sites: 161. **Hookups:** Electric (30 amps). **Each Site:** Fire ring. **Dump Station:** Yes. **Laundry:** No. **Pay Phone:** No. **Restrooms and Showers:** Yes. **Fuel:** No. **Propane:** No. **Internal Roads:** Paved. **RV Service:** No. **Market:** No. **Restaurant:** No. **General Store:** Yes. **Vending:** Yes. **Swimming:** Yes. **Playground:** Yes. **Activities:** Beach, boating, environmental center, fishing, hiking, picnicking.

RESTRICTIONS
Fires: In designated fireplaces. **Vehicle Maximum Length:** 35 ft.

TO GET THERE
From I-81, take Exit 101 (Claytor Lake) to VA 660. VA 660 ends at the park entrance.

DUFFIELD MAP, A-1
Natural Tunnel State Park

reserve america

Rte. 3, Box 250, 24244-9361. T: (276) 940-2674;
www.reserveamerica.com.

🚐 ★★★   ⛺ ★★★★

Beauty: ★★★★   Site Privacy: ★★★
Spaciousness: ★★★   Quiet: ★★★★
Security: ★★★★   Cleanliness: ★★★★
Insect Control: ★★★   Facilities: ★★★★

The Commonwealth of Virginia acquired the tunnel and 100 surrounding acres in 1967 from the Natural Tunnel Chasm and Caverns Corp. to establish Natural Tunnel State Park. Approximately 750 additional acres were later acquired and the park opened in 1971. Natural Tunnel, called the Eighth Wonder of the World by William Jennings Bryan, has been attracting sightseers to the mountains of southwestern Virginia for more than 100 years. Today it is the focal point of Natural Tunnel State Park, a park which offers visitors not only spectacular sights but also swimming, camping, picnicking, hiking, a visitor center, an amphitheater, and interpretive programs. The Cove Ridge Center offers conference center facilities, both overnight and meeting space. The creation of Natural Tunnel began more than a million years ago in the early glacial period when groundwater bearing carbonic acid percolated through crevices and slowly dissolved surrounding limestone and dolomite bedrock. Then, what is now Stock Creek was probably diverted underground to continue carving the tunnel slowly over many centuries. The walls of the tunnel show evidence of prehistoric life, and many fossils can be found in the creek bed and on tunnel walls.

BASICS
Operated By: Virginia State Parks. **Open:** All year. **Site Assignment:** Reservations can be made 11 months in advance. **Registration:** At office. **Fee:** Single, $15–$21. **Parking:** At site.

FACILITIES
Number of Multipurpose Sites: 41. **Hookups:** Electric (30 amps). **Each Site:** Lantern post, table, grill, fire ring, tent pad. **Dump Station:** No. **Laundry:** No. **Pay Phone:** No. **Restrooms and Showers:** Yes. **Fuel:** No. **Propane:** No. **Internal Roads:** Paved. **RV Service:** No. **Market:** Yes. **Restaurant:** No. **General Store:** Yes. **Vending:** Yes. **Swimming:** Yes. **Playground:** Yes. **Activities:** Environmental center, fishing, hiking, picnicking.

RESTRICTIONS
Fires: In designated fireplaces. **Vehicle Maximum Length:** 38 ft.

TO GET THERE
Natural Tunnel State Park is in Scott County, approx. 13 mi. north of Gate City and 20 mi. north of Kingsport, TN. To get there, from I-81, take US 23 north to Gate City (approx. 20 mi.). Take VA 871 and go 1 mi. east to park entrance.

EDINBURG — MAP, A-2
Creekside Campground

108 Palmyra Rd., P.O. Box 277, 22824-0277.
T: (540) 984-4299 or (540) 984-8471;
www.fulltiming-america.com/creekside.

🚐 ★★★★   ⛺ ★★★★

Beauty: ★★★★   Site Privacy: ★★★
Spaciousness: ★★★   Quiet: ★★★★
Security: ★★★★   Cleanliness: ★★★★
Insect Control: ★★★★ Facilities: ★★★

Creekside Campground, near Edinburgh, is an immaculately landscaped, cozy place with shaded sites situated along Stoney Creek in the Shenandoah Valley. Fishermen cast their lines at Stoney Creek and in the nearby Shenandoah River's north fork. At night, the trees at Creekside are illuminated with white lights, casting a cheerful glow on the campground. Creekside has few activities—just fishing and horseshoes—but an assortment of outdoor recreation is available at Shenandoah National Park and the George Washington National Forest. The Skyline Drive is a pleasant nearby day trip. The 105-mile highway winds from Front Royal through the Blue Ridge Mountains and the Shenandoah National Park to Waynesboro, where it stretches south on the Blue Ridge Parkway.

BASICS

Operated By: Private operator. **Open:** All year. **Site Assignment:** Reservations recommended, walk-ins accepted. **Registration:** At campground office. **Fee:** $20–27;V, MC. **Parking:** At site.

FACILITIES

Number of RV-only Sites: 26. **Number of Tent-only Sites:** 7. **Hookups:** Electric (20, 30, 50 amps), cable TV, phone. **Each Site:** Fire ring, picnic table. **Dump Station:** Yes. **Laundry:** Nearby. **Pay Phone:** Yes. **Restrooms and Showers:** Yes. **Fuel:** No. **Propane:** No. **Internal Roads:** Gravel, in good condition. **RV Service:** No. **Market:** W/in 1 mi. **Restaurant:** W/in 1 mi. **General Store:** No. **Vending:** Yes. **Swimming:** No. **Playground:** No. **Other:** Stoney Creek. **Activities:** Fishing, horseshoes. **Nearby Attractions:** Luray Caverns, George Washington National Forest, Shenandoah National Park, Edinburg, Shenandoah Vineyards. **Additional Information:** Virginia Tourism Corp., (800) 847-4882, www.virginia.org.

RESTRICTIONS

Pets: On leash only. **Fires:** At site. **Alcoholic Beverages:** At site. **Vehicle Maximum Length:** No limit.

TO GET THERE

From I-81, take Exit 279 and go 1 mi. east on Hwy. 675, 0.75 mi. south on US 11, 0.5 mi. east on Palmyra Church Rd., and 0.25 mi. northeast on Palmyra Rd. Entrance is on the left.

EMPORIA — MAP, C-3
Yogi Bear's Jellystone Park Camp-Resort

2940 Sussex Dr., 23847.
T: (800) 545-4248 or (434) 634-3115;
www.jellystone.com.

🚐 ★★★★   ⛺ ★★★★

Beauty: ★★★★   Site Privacy: ★★★
Spaciousness: ★★★   Quiet: ★★★★
Security: ★★★★   Cleanliness: ★★★★
Insect Control: ★★★★ Facilities: ★★★★

Located a mile off Interstate 95 in Emporia, Yogi Bear's Jellystone Park Camp-Resort is a clean campground with a generously sized swimming pool and a 15-acre fishing lake. There are 83 shaded and grassy sites, including 57 pull-throughs. Because of its location—the campground is about an 1.5-hour drive from Norfolk and Newport News to the west and a 45-minute drive from Lake Gaston to the west—Emporia is mostly an overnight stop for campers on the way to destinations in Florida and South Carolina. The Emporia area is home to the Virginia Pork Festival every June and the Virginia Peanut Festival every September. If you choose the campground in Emporia as your base, Newport News and Norfolk are ideal day trips. Lake Gaston and John H. Kerr Reservoir to the west offer extensive boating and fishing opportunities.

BASICS

Operated By: Yogi Bear's Jellystone Park. **Open:** All year. **Site Assignment:** Reservations and walk-ins accepted. **Registration:** At campground office. **Fee:** $28–$33;V, MC, D. **Parking:** At designated spot.

FACILITIES

Number of RV-only Sites: 83. **Number of Tent-only Sites:** 10. **Hookups:** Electric (20, 30, 50 amps), water, phone. **Each Site:** Fire ring, picnic table. **Dump Station:** Yes. **Laundry:** Yes. **Pay Phone:** Yes. **Restrooms and Showers:** Yes. **Fuel:** No. **Propane:** Yes. **Internal Roads:** Gravel, in good condition. **RV Service:** No. **Market:** W/in 1 mi. **Restaurant:** W/in 1 mi. **General Store:** Yes. **Vending:** Yes. **Swimming:** Yes. **Playground:** Yes. **Activities:** Game room, rec hall, swimming, basketball, planned activities, movies, badminton, horseshoes, volleyball. **Nearby Attractions:** Historic Jamestown Settlement, Newport News, Norfolk, Nauticus: The National Maritime Center, Virginia Air and Space Museum. **Additional Information:** Virginia Tourism Corp., (800) 371-8164, www.virginia.org.

RESTRICTIONS

Pets: On leash only. **Fires:** At site. **Alcoholic Beverages:** At site. **Vehicle Maximum Length:** No limit.

TO GET THERE

From I-95, take Exit 17 and go 1 mi. south on US 301. Entrance is on the right.

FAIRFAX — MAP, A-3
Burke Lake Park

7315 Ox Rd., 22039. T: (703) 323-6601;
www.co.fairfax.va.us.

🚐 ★★★★   ⛺ ★★★★

Beauty: ★★★★   Site Privacy: ★★
Spaciousness: ★★   Quiet: ★★★
Security: ★★★★   Cleanliness: ★★★★
Insect Control: ★★★★ Facilities: ★★★★

Relaxing in a boat somewhere on serene Burke Lake, it's hard to believe the concrete jungle and snarled traffic of Washington, D.C., are a short Metro Rail ride away. Fairfax County Park Authority officials promote Burke Lake Park—and its sister recreational area Lake Fairfax Park—as metropolitan D.C.'s country side. This time, the bureaucrats are not blowing smoke. Burke Lake Park consists of 888 acres, and its centerpiece is the 218-acre Burke Lake, where boating and fishing are encouraged, but swimming is not allowed. Burke Lake Park has 163 shaded sites, including six pull-throughs. The park is ideal for families; there's a miniature train and carousel for children and lots of hiking trails. If you want to catch the Metro Rail for a journey to Washington, D.C., the closest stop from Burke Lake Park is the Springfield/Franconia station, which is about 8 miles away.

BASICS

Operated By: Fairfax County Park Authority. **Open:** Mar. 1–Dec. 1. **Site Assignment:** First come, first served; no reservations. **Registration:** At campground headquarters. **Fee:** $14;V, MC. **Parking:** At designated spot.

FACILITIES

Number of RV-only Sites: 103. **Number of Tent-only Sites:** 60. **Hookups:** None. **Each Site:** Grill, picnic table. **Dump Station:** Yes. **Laundry:** Yes. **Pay Phone:** Yes. **Restrooms and Showers:** Yes. **Fuel:** No. **Propane:** No. **Internal Roads:** Gravel, in good condition. **RV Service:** No. **Market:** W/in 2 mi. **Restaurant:** W/in 1 mi. **General Store:** Yes. **Vending:** Yes. **Swimming:** No. **Playground:** Yes. **Other:** Burke Lake. **Activities:** Boating, canoeing, rowboat rentals, lake fishing, golf, driving range, putting green, hiking trails, volleyball. **Nearby Attractions:** Washington, D.C. **Additional Information:** Washington, D.C., CVB, (202) 789-7000, www.washington.org.

RESTRICTIONS

Pets: On leash only. **Fires:** At site. **Alcoholic Beverages:** At site. **Vehicle Maximum Length:** 25 ft. **Other:** No swimming permitted in lake.

TO GET THERE

From Fairfax, go 9 mi. south on Hwy. 123 and 1.5 mi. on park road. Entrance is on the left.

FANCY GAP　　　　MAP, C-1
Fox Trail Family Campground

P.O. Box 233, 24328. T: (276) 728-7776;
www.foxtrailcg.com.

🚐 ★★★★	⛺ n/a
Beauty: ★★★★	Site Privacy: ★
Spaciousness: ★★	Quiet: ★★★★
Security: ★★★★	Cleanliness: ★★★★
Insect Control: ★★★★	Facilities: ★★★★

Known for stunning natural splendor, the Blue Ridge Mountains are also known as a region where bluegrass music is king. Located atop Fancy Gap Mountain near the town of Fancy Gap, Fox Trail Family Campground is near several bluegrass music events, such as the annual Old Time Fiddlers Convention in Galax. This event is regarded as the oldest and largest gathering of bluegrass music enthusiasts in the world. Many campers use Fox Trail as an overnight stopping point on their way to Myrtle Beach and Florida. Fox Trail has large, wooded sites. There's a fishing pond, hiking trails, and a nearby mountain overlook. The campground is about 10 miles from the North Carolina border, a short drive from Mayberry Days, the Autumn Leaves Festival, and Mayberry USA in Mt. Airy. Sites on the campground's north tip are the most secluded, and sites near the entrance provide a view of the pond.

BASICS

Operated By: Mark and Cheryl Manning. **Open:** All year. **Site Assignment:** Reservations accepted (14-day cancellation notice required for refund), walk-ins accepted. **Registration:** At campground office. **Fee:** $16.50–$24.50; V, MC. **Parking:** At site.

FACILITIES

Number of RV-only Sites: 96. **Hookups:** Electric (20, 30, 50 amps), water, sewer. **Each Site:** Fire ring, picnic table. **Dump Station:** Yes. **Laundry:** Yes. **Pay Phone:** Yes. **Restrooms and Showers:** Yes. **Fuel:** No. **Propane:** Yes. **Internal Roads:** Gravel & paved, in good condition. **RV Service:** No. **Market:** W/in 2 mi. **Restaurant:** W/in 3 mi. **General Store:** Yes. **Vending:** Yes. **Playground:** Yes. **Other:** Fishing pond. **Activities:** Rec hall, game room, pond fishing, horseshoes, Wi-Fi. **Nearby Attractions:** Blue Ridge Parkway, Mayberry USA, Wytheville, Historic Crab Orchard Museum and Pioneer Park. **Additional Information:** Virginia Tourism Corp., (800) 371-8164, www.virginia.org.

RESTRICTIONS

Pets: On leash only. **Fires:** At site. **Alcoholic Beverages:** At site. **Vehicle Maximum Length:** No limit.

TO GET THERE

From I-77, take Exit 8 and go 1 mi. east on Hwy. 148, 1 mi. south on US 52 to junction with Blue Ridge Pkwy. Follow blue camping signs.

FOSTER FALLS　　　　MAP, A-2
New River Trail State Park

reserve america

176 Orphanage Dr., 24360. T: (276) 699-6778;
www.reserveamerica.com.

🚐	⛺ ★★★★
Beauty: ★★★	Site Privacy: ★★
Spaciousness: ★★	Quiet: ★★★★
Security: ★★★★	Cleanliness: ★★★★
Insect Control: ★★★	Facilities: ★

Named a Millennium Legacy Trail by the White House, New River Trail State Park parallels 39 miles of the New River, the second oldest river in the world and one of the few flowing north. New River Trail is a 57-mile-long state park that follows an abandoned railroad right-of-way. The park meanders through Grayson, Carroll, Wythe, and Pulaski counties in southwestern Virginia. This park is part of the Rails-to-Trails Program as it was donated to the state by Norfolk Southern Railroad when the railroad discontinued the line and removed the tracks. This park also serves as a link to numerous other outdoor recreational areas, including a town park in Fries, Mt. Rogers National Recreational Area, four Department of Game and Inland Fisheries boat launches, and Shot Tower Historical State Park. New River Trail is just minutes from Claytor Lake State Park and Grayson Highlands State Park. A link to the Virginia Creeper Trail has been recently opened. The multi-use trail is a favorite for hiking, biking, and horseback riding. It features two tunnels (135 and 193 feet long); three major bridges (Hiwasee, 951 feet; Ivanhoe, 670 feet; Fries Junction, 1,089 feet), as well as nearly 30 smaller bridges and trestles. New River Trail State Park offers five unique campgrounds (Cliffview, Millrace, Baker Island, Double Shoals, and the New River Forest Service Campground) in different locations with different types of sites.

BASICS

Operated By: Virginia State Parks. **Open:** All year. **Site Assignment:** Reservations can be made 11 months in advance. **Registration:** At office. **Fee:** Single, $11–$14. **Parking:** At site.

FACILITIES

Number of Multipurpose Sites: 47. **Hookups:** None. **Dump Station:** No. **Laundry:** No. **Pay Phone:** No. **Restrooms and Showers:** Yes. **Fuel:** No. **Propane:** No. **Internal Roads:** Paved. **RV Service:** No. **Market:** No. **Restaurant:** No. **General Store:** No. **Vending:** No. **Swimming:** No. **Playground:** No. **Other:** Confirmation letters must be placed on the dashboard of vehicle. **Activities:** Biking, fishing, hiking, horse camping, picnicking.

RESTRICTIONS

Fires: In designated fireplaces.

TO GET THERE

To New River Trail administrative offices in Foster Falls: From I-77, take Exit 24, go east on Route 69 to Route 52, go north to Route 608, go east and follow signs. Parking fee required.

FREDERICKSBURG　　　　MAP, B-3
Fredericksburg/ Washington, D.C., South KOA

7400 Brookside Ln., 22408.
T: (800) 562-1889 or (540) 898-7252;
www.fredericksburgkoa.com.

🚐 ★★★★	⛺ ★★★★
Beauty: ★★★★	Site Privacy: ★★★
Spaciousness: ★★★	Quiet: ★★★★
Security: ★★★★	Cleanliness: ★★★★
Insect Control: ★★★★	Facilities: ★★★★

If you prefer KOA campgrounds, Fredericksburg/ Washington, D.C., KOA is the closest KOA facility to the District of Columbia and all of its attractions. There are 100-plus semi-wooded sites, including 49 level and shaded pull-throughs. The birthplace of George Washington, Fredericksburg is a treasure chest of history. The town has a 40-block historic district with trolley and carriage tours. The Fredericksburg and Spotsylvania National Military Park tells the story of the Civil War battles of Fredericksburg, Chancellorsville, Wilderness, and Spotsylvania Court House. The Manassas National Battlefield Park is a short drive away. If you do choose to visit Washington, D.C., the campground offers a free shuttle to the VRE Train on weekdays. This will transport you downtown, where several guided tour options await.

BASICS

Operated By: KOA. **Open:** All year. **Site Assignment:** Reservations recommended, walk-ins accepted. **Registration:** At campground office. **Fee:** $25–$44; V, MC, D. **Parking:** At designated spot.

FACILITIES

Number of RV-only Sites: 75. **Number of Tent-only Sites:** 25. **Hookups:** Electric (20, 30, 50 amps), water, cable TV, phone. **Each Site:** Grill, picnic table. **Dump Station:** Yes. **Laundry:** Yes. **Pay Phone:** Yes. **Restrooms and Showers:** Yes. **Fuel:** No. **Propane:** Yes. **Internal Roads:** Paved, in good condition. **RV Service:** No. **Market:** W/in 4 mi. **Restaurant:** W/in 4 mi. **General Store:** Yes. **Vending:** Yes. **Swimming:** Pool. **Playground:** Yes. **Other:** Car rental service available. **Activities:** Game room, swimming, paddleboat rentals, pond fishing, bike rentals, sports field, horseshoes, hiking trails, volleyball. **Nearby Attractions:** Historic Fredericksburg, Washington, D.C., Paramount's Kings Dominion, Mt. Vernon, golf courses, Lake Anna, Fredericksburg and Spotsylvania Military Park, Manassas National Battlefield Park. **Additional Information:** Virginia Tourism Corp., (800) 371-8164, www.virginia.org.

RESTRICTIONS

Pets: On leash only. **Fires:** At site. **Alcoholic Beverages:** At site. **Vehicle Maximum Length:** No limit.

TO GET THERE

From I-95, take Exit 118 and go 4 mi. north on US 1 and 2.5 mi. east on Hwy. 607. Entrance is on the right.

FRONT ROYAL   MAP, A-2
Front Royal/
Washington, D.C., West KOA

P.O. Box 274, 22630.
T: (800) 562-9114 or (540) 635-2741;
www.koa.com.

🚐 ★★★★   ⛺ ★★★★

Beauty: ★★★★   Site Privacy: ★★
Spaciousness: ★★★   Quiet: ★★★
Security: ★★★★   Cleanliness: ★★★★
Insect Control: ★★★★   Facilities: ★★★★

Located at the north end of Skyline Drive, Front Royal/Washington, D.C., West KOA is the type of campground both parents and their children can enjoy. There's a swimming pool, a whirlpool, a sauna, and a thrilling waterslide. Perched on a hilltop, the campground has more than 150 open and wooded sites, including 47 pull-throughs. From Front Royal, the 105-mile-long Skyline Drive follows the crest of the Blue Ridge Mountains through Shenandoah National Park, and it continues to the Blue Ridge Parkway. Tubing, canoeing, and fishing in the Shenandoah River and hiking through Shenandoah National Park are among the activities that KOA campers partake in. Spelunkers can explore Luray Caverns and Skyline Caverns. In conjunction with its proximity to Washington, D.C., (about 50 miles west), KOA can arrange tours for campers.

BASICS
Operated By: KOA. **Open:** Mar. 15–Nov. 1. **Site Assignment:** Reservations and walk-ins accepted. **Registration:** At campground office. **Fee:** $27–$35; V, MC, D. **Parking:** At site.

FACILITIES
Number of RV-only Sites: 110. **Number of Tent-only Sites:** 40. **Hookups:** Electric (20, 30 amps), water, phone. **Each Site:** Fire rings, picnic table. **Dump Station:** Yes. **Laundry:** Yes. **Pay Phone:** Yes. **Restrooms and Showers:** Yes. **Fuel:** No. **Propane:** Yes. **Internal Roads:** Gravel & paved, in good condition. **RV Service:** No. **Market:** W/in 2 mi. **Restaurant:** W/in 2 mi. **General Store:** Yes. **Vending:** Yes. **Swimming:** Yes. **Playground:** Yes. **Other:** Waterslide. **Activities:** Swimming, game room, rec hall, whirlpool, pond fishing, mini-golf, basketball, planned activities on weekends, horseshoes, volleyball. **Nearby Attractions:** Skyline Drive, Shenandoah River, Skyline Caverns, Luray Caverns, Shenandoah National Park, Washington, D.C. **Additional Information:** Shenandoah Valley Travel Assoc., (540) 740-3132, www.svta.org.

RESTRICTIONS
Pets: On leash only. **Fires:** At site. **Alcoholic Beverages:** At site. **Vehicle Maximum Length:** No limit.

TO GET THERE
From Hwy. 55, go 2.5 mi. south on US 340 and 1 mi. southeast to entrance on the left.

GLADSTONE   MAP, C-2
James River State Park

Rte. 1, Box 787, 24553. T: (434) 933-4355; www.reserveamerica.com.

🚐 ★★★   ⛺ ★★★★

Beauty: ★★★★   Site Privacy: ★★★
Spaciousness: ★★★   Quiet: ★★★★
Security: ★★★★   Cleanliness: ★★★★
Insect Control: ★★★   Facilities: ★★

James River State Park is one of the state's newest parks. It offers access to 20 miles of hiking, biking, and horseback-riding trails. There are restrooms in major day-use areas. No water is available in the campgrounds. The primitive aspect of the camping must be considered. If you like to fish, like a more primitive and less crowded setting, like to canoe, or like river activities, make note of this camping opportunity. While it's not for those who bring hair dryers and fans, if you don't mind roughing it, you'll love the park. Important! Because the park was still under development at press time, staff is limited. There are, however, very good signs to direct customers to the Branch Pond sites or canoe landing sites. Take the first right to reach Branch Pond sites; take the first left, farther down, for canoe landing sites.

BASICS
Operated By: Virginia State Parks. **Open:** All year. **Site Assignment:** Reservations can be made 11 months in advance. **Registration:** At office. **Fee:** Single, $11; horse stall/site, $7–$83; picnic shelter, $45. **Parking:** At site.

FACILITIES
Number of Multipurpose Sites: 118. **Hookups:** None. **Each Site:** Picnic table, fire ring. **Dump Station:** Yes. **Laundry:** No. **Pay Phone:** No. **Restrooms and Showers:** Yes. **Fuel:** No. **Propane:** No. **Internal Roads:** Paved. **RV Service:** No. **Market:** No. **Restaurant:** No. **General Store:** No. **Vending:** No. **Swimming:** No. **Playground:** No. **Other:** Walk-ins are highly discouraged. **Activities:** Biking, boating, fishing, hiking, horseback riding, picnicking.

RESTRICTIONS
Fires: In designated fireplaces. **Vehicle Maximum Length:** 30 ft.

TO GET THERE
In Buckingham County. From US 60 west, turn right onto Hwy. 605 at the James River Bridge. Travel 7 mi., then turn left onto Hwy. 606.

GLADYS   MAP, C-2
Thousand Trails—Lynchburg

405 Mollies Creek Rd., 24554.
T: (800) 615-4878 or (804) 332-6672;
www.thousandtrails.com.

🚐 ★★★★   ⛺ ★★★★

Beauty: ★★★★   Site Privacy: ★★
Spaciousness: ★★   Quiet: ★★★★
Security: ★★★★   Cleanliness: ★★★★
Insect Control: ★★★★   Facilities: ★★★★

Situated on Big Lake Grandview, Thousand Trails—Lynchburg is a water lover's delight. Campers can swim from the beach, fish, or rent rowboats, canoes, and kayaks. The campground also has a swimming pool, a whirlpool, an adult lodge, and a mini-golf course. The park has 191 full hookups, but there are no overflow sites. There are several interesting attractions in nearby Lynchburg, including Fort Early, the Maier Museum of Art, the Point of Honor, and the Pest House Medical Museum. Lynchburg has several 19th century residential districts. In fact, five hills of the City of Seven Hills are listed on the National Register of Historic Districts. Appomattox Court House National Historical Park is located about 20 miles east of Lynchburg and Thousand Trails. The 1,743-acre park includes the village of Appomattox, which is restored to look much like it did when Gen. Robert E. Lee surrendered to Gen. Ulysses S. Grant on April 9, 1865, bringing an end to the Civil War.

BASICS
Operated By: Thousand Trails. **Open:** May 1–Oct. 31. **Site Assignment:** Reservations accepted (online and phone), walk-ins accepted. **Registration:** At campground headquarters. **Fee:** $20; V, MC, AE, D. **Parking:** At site.

FACILITIES
Number of RV-only Sites: 232. **Number of Tent-only Sites:** 12. **Hookups:** Electric (30 amps), water, phone. **Each Site:** Grill, picnic table. **Dump Station:** Yes. **Laundry:** Yes. **Pay Phone:** Yes. **Restrooms and Showers:** Yes. **Fuel:** No. **Propane:** Yes. **Internal Roads:** Gravel & paved, in good condition. **RV Service:** No. **Market:** W/in 7 mi. **Restaurant:** W/in 7 mi. **General Store:** Yes. **Vending:** Yes. **Swimming:** Yes. **Playground:** Yes. **Other:** Big Lake Grandview. **Activities:** Game room, rec hall, lake swimming, badminton, horseshoes, volleyball, wading pool, whirlpool, boating, canoeing, kayaking, boat rentals, lake fishing, mini-golf, basketball, shuffleboard, planned activities on weekends, tennis, sports field. **Nearby Attractions:** Appomattox Court House National Historic Park, Lynchburg, Blackwater Creek Natural Area, Jefferson's Polar Forest, Old Court House Museum, Pest House Medical Museum, Point of Honor. **Additional Information:** Virginia Tourism Corp., (800) 371-8164, www.virginia.org.

RESTRICTIONS
Pets: On leash only. **Fires:** At site. **Alcoholic Beverages:** At site. **Vehicle Maximum Length:** No limit.

TO GET THERE
From US 501, go 0.75 mi. east on Hwy. 24, 5.5 mi. south on CR 515, and 0.5 mi. southwest on CR 650. Entrance is on the right.

GLOUCESTER MAP, C-4
Thousand Trails—Chesapeake Bay

12014 Trails Ln., 23061. T: (800) 693-6901; www.thousandtrails.com.

🚐 ★★★★   ⛺ ★★★★

Beauty: ★★★★★   Site Privacy: ★★
Spaciousness: ★★★   Quiet: ★★★
Security: ★★★★   Cleanliness: ★★★★
Insect Control: ★★★★   Facilities: ★★★★★

Situated on the Piankatank River a short drive from Chesapeake Bay, Thousand Trails—Chesapeake Bay certainly doesn't have a shortage of activities and amenities. A 280-acre preserve adorned with pine, oak, and dogwood forests, the campground has two piers for fishing, boating, and waterskiing; an adult lodge and a family center; indoor and outdoor swimming pools; and canoe and pedal-boat rentals. RV camping is especially convenient with 355 full hookups. There are too many attractions and destinations near the campground to fit in one vacation, unless that vacation is a month long. Many campers head for Chesapeake Bay or the heritage attractions at Colonial Williamsburg and Yorktown. Busch Gardens and Water Country USA are in Williamsburg; Yorktown was the site of British General Cornwallis's surrender to Gen. George Washington. The Yorktown Victory Center is a must-see for any history enthusiast.

BASICS
Operated By: Thousand Trails. **Open:** All year. **Site Assignment:** Reservations and walk-ins accepted. **Registration:** At campground headquarters. **Fee:** $20; V, MC, AE, D. **Parking:** At designated area.

FACILITIES
Number of RV-only Sites: 373. **Number of Tent-only Sites:** 21. **Hookups:** Electric (30, 50 amps), water, phone. **Each Site:** Fire ring, picnic table. **Dump Station:** Yes. **Laundry:** Yes. **Pay Phone:** Yes. **Restrooms and Showers:** Yes. **Fuel:** No. **Propane:** Yes. **Internal Roads:** Gravel & paved, in good condition. **RV Service:** No. **Market:** W/in 6 mi. **Restaurant:** On premises. **General Store:** Yes. **Vending:** Yes. **Swimming:** Yes. **Playground:** Yes. **Other:** Adult lodge, family center, indoor spa. **Activities:** Swimming, rec hall, game room, whirlpool, boating, canoeing, kayaking, boat rentals, ocean fishing, river fishing, pond fishing, mini-golf, basketball, bike rentals, shuffleboard, planned weekend activities, tennis, sports field, horseshoes. **Nearby Attractions:** Chesapeake Bay, Colonial Williamsburg, Historic Jamestown Settlement, Fredericksburg, Williamsburg Pottery, Yorktown, Busch Gardens, Water Country USA, Paramount's Kings Dominion. **Additional Information:** Williamsburg Area CVB, (757) 253-0192, www.visitwilliamsburg.com.

RESTRICTIONS
Pets: On leash only. **Fires:** At site. **Alcoholic Beverages:** At site. **Vehicle Maximum Length:** No limit.

TO GET THERE
From US 17, go 5.5 mi. east on Hwy. 198 and 0.5 mi. north on Dutton Rd. Entrance is on the left.

GREEN BAY MAP, C-2
Cedar Crest at Twin Lakes State Park

reserve america™

22 Cedar Crest Rd., 23942-9544. T: (434) 767-2398; www.reserveamerica.com.

🚐 ★★★   ⛺ ★★★★

Beauty: ★★★★   Site Privacy: ★★★
Spaciousness: ★★★   Quiet: ★★★★
Security: ★★★★   Cleanliness: ★★★★
Insect Control: ★★★   Facilities: ★★★★

Twin Lakes State Park, centrally located in Virginia's Piedmont region, provides visitors from all over the Commonwealth with a variety of lakefront activities in a secluded setting. Swimming, camping, fishing, biking, canoeing and hiking are popular activities. Recently renovated facilities are available for group meetings, family reunions, and company picnics. The Cedar Crest Conference Center offers group camping sites which are site specific, require a three site minimum, and do not have water and electric hookups. Seven cabins and the Mistletoe Lodge are also available for rental through the reservation center only. These sites are reserved through the center for the following month after the 15th. Prior to that time the sites are available as part of conference packages and can be reserved directly through the conference center. Seven two-bedroom cabins and a small lodge are available. Cabins 1 through 6 (CT2B) have a set of bunk beds and a single bed in each bedroom; bathrooms are wheelchair-accessible. All have a view of the lake. Cabin 7 has a double bed in one room and two singles in the other and sleeps a maximum of four people (no rental beds available). Mistletoe Lodge has four bedrooms with two single beds in each (sleeps 6); great room (suitable for meetings); kitchen with pantry common bathroom; deck; patio tables to seat eight; heating and air-conditioning; and carpet. Adjacent to the lodge is a large deck with lounge furniture and charcoal grill. The lodge has a TV and VCR. Audiovisual equipment and a dry-erase board are available for meetings at the lodge.

BASICS
Operated By: Virginia State Parks. **Open:** Mar. 1–1st Mon. in Dec. **Site Assignment:** Reservations can be made 11 months in advance. **Registration:** At office. **Fee:** Single, $21; group, $200; cabin, $71–$119; lodge, $106–$159. **Parking:** 2 vehicles allowed per cabin.

FACILITIES
Number of Multipurpose Sites: 46. **Hookups:** Yes. **Dump Station:** Yes. **Laundry:** No. **Pay Phone:** No. **Restrooms and Showers:** Yes. **Fuel:** No. **Propane:** No. **Internal Roads:** Paved. **RV Service:** Yes. **Market:** No. **Restaurant:** No. **General Store:** Yes. **Vending:** No. **Swimming:** Yes. **Playground:** Yes. **Activities:** Biking, boating, bridle trails, freshwater fishing, hiking.

RESTRICTIONS
Pets: Allowed in all Virginia State Parks, except on public beaches & in public facilities (bathhouses, visi-

tor centers, park offices, restaurants, etc.). Confined or kept on a 6-ft. leash. **Fires:** Permitted. **Alcoholic Beverages:** Not allowed in public. **Vehicle Maximum Length:** 30 ft.

TO GET THERE
Twin Lakes State Park is near Farmville, about 1 hour southwest of Richmond. To get there, take US 360 west of Burkeville to Hwy. 613. Then go east on Hwy. 629.

GREEN BAY MAP, C-2
Twin Lakes State Park

reserve america™

788 Twin Lakes Rd., P.O. Box 70, 23942. T: (434) 392-3435 or (800) 933-PARK; www.reserveamerica.com.

🚐 ★★★   ⛺ ★★★

Beauty: ★★★   Site Privacy: ★★
Spaciousness: ★★   Quiet: ★★★
Security: ★★★   Cleanliness: ★★★
Insect Control: ★★★   Facilities: ★★★

Green Bay is the home of Twin Lakes State Park, which operated as two parks until 1976. The land for Twin Lakes State Park was initially bought from struggling farmers by the federal government during the Great Depression. Goodwin Lake Park and Prince Edward Lake Park were created in 1939. Until the early 1960s, they were managed as two racially segregated parks. As a result, Twin Lakes State Park has two complete sets of facilities. The campground has 30 sites, all with electric and water hookups. Most of the sites are shaded. Goodwin Lake's day-use area features a 1.5-mile nature trail, a sandy beach, and a playground. A 14-mile multiuse trail winds around the adjacent 6,496-acre Prince Edward-Gallion State Forest. Nearby is Sailor's Creek Historical State Park, where Gen. Robert E. Lee's Confederate troops were soundly defeated by Union troops, leading to General Lee's surrender at Appomattox Court House three days later.

BASICS
Operated By: State of Virginia. **Open:** Mar.–Dec. **Site Assignment:** Reservations and walk-ins accepted. **Registration:** At registration point. **Fee:** $21; V, MC. **Parking:** At site.

FACILITIES
Number of RV-only Sites: 20. **Number of Tent-only Sites:** 10. **Hookups:** Electric (20, 30 amps), water. **Each Site:** Fire ring, picnic table. **Dump Station:** Yes. **Laundry:** No. **Pay Phone:** Yes. **Restrooms and Showers:** Yes. **Fuel:** No. **Propane:** No. **Internal Roads:** Paved, in good condition. **RV Service:** No. **Market:** W/in 10 mi. **Restaurant:** W/in 10 mi. **General Store:** No. **Vending:** Yes. **Swimming:** Yes. **Playground:** Yes. **Other:** Cedar Crest Conference Center, Mistletoe Lodge. **Activities:** Lake swimming, boating, and fishing; hiking trails. **Nearby Attractions:** Sailor's Creek Battlefield State Park, Sandy River Reservoir, Briery Creek Wildlife Management Area, Prince Edward-Gallion State Forest, Lee's Retreat Driving

Tour, Longwood College Visual Arts Center, Jim's Cowboy Museum. **Additional Information:** Virginia Tourism Corp., (800) 371-8164, www.virginia.org.

RESTRICTIONS

Pets: On leash only, $3 per night. **Fires:** At site. **Alcoholic Beverages:** No alcohol permitted. **Vehicle Maximum Length:** 25 ft. **Other:** Max. 14-day stay in 30-day period.

TO GET THERE

From Burkeville, take US 360 west to Hwy. 613, then go east on Hwy. 629. Entrance is on the left.

HILLSVILLE   MAP, C-1
Lake Ridge RV Resort

reserve america

8736 Double Cabin Rd., 24343. T: (276) 766-3703; www.lakeridgerv.com.

🚐 ★★★★   ⛺ ★★★★

Beauty: ★★★★   Site Privacy: ★★★
Spaciousness: ★★   Quiet: ★★
Security: ★★★   Cleanliness: ★★★
Insect Control: ★★★   Facilities: ★★★★

Whether you are an RV park enthusiast, enjoy the comfort of a cabin in the woods, or just like to tent camp and sleep in the great outdoors, Jellystone Park's accommodations, amenities, and activities are top-notch. Amenities and activities include swimming, mini-golf, hay rides, tennis, volleyball, fishing, hiking, and appearances from Yogi Bear and friends.

BASICS

Operated By: Legacy RV. **Parking:** 2 cars.

FACILITIES

Number of RV-only Sites: 106. **Number of Tent-only Sites:** 4. **Hookups:** Yes. **Each Site:** Picnic table. **Dump Station:** Yes. **Laundry:** Yes. **Pay Phone:** Yes. **Restrooms and Showers:** Yes. **Fuel:** No. **Propane:** Yes. **Internal Roads:** Paved. **RV Service:** 68 mi. **Market:** 6 mi. **Restaurant:** On site. **General Store:** Camp store. **Vending:** Yes. **Swimming:** 2 pools. **Playground:** Yes. **Activities:** Water activities, fish pond. **Nearby Attractions:** New River.

RESTRICTIONS

Pets: On leash. **Fires:** Allowed. **Alcoholic Beverages:** At site only. **Vehicle Maximum Length:** 45 ft.

TO GET THERE

From I-77 heading north take Exit 14 for Hillsville. Turn right on Hwy. 221 traveling approx. 1 mi. to town. Continue on Hwy. 221 about 1.5 mi. Turn left on Hwy. 100N and travel about 4 mi. until you see the big Lake Ridge RV Resort sign on the right. Turn right at VA 783 (Deer Ridge Rd.) and travel approx 0.7 mi. Turn right at VA 753 (Double Cabin Rd.) and travel approx 0.5 mi. Lake Ridge RV Resort is on the left.

HUDDLESTON   MAP, C-2
Smith Mountain Lake State Park

reserve america

1235 State Park Rd., 24104-9547. T: (540) 297-6066; www.reserveamerica.com.

🚐 ★★★   ⛺ ★★★★

Beauty: ★★★   Site Privacy: ★★★
Spaciousness: ★★★   Quiet: ★★★
Security: ★★★★   Cleanliness: ★★★
Insect Control: ★★★   Facilities: ★★★

Spread out over 1,246 acres densely wooded with Virginia pine, American beech, and juniper, Smith Mountain Lake State Park is home to and named for Virginia's second largest freshwater lake. The park is located in the foothills of the Blue Ridge Mountains. There are no lake views from the 50-site campground, but the sites are situated in the woods. The park has a 500-foot sandy beach (the park's lone swimming area). There are guided night hikes, hayrides, canoe trips, and other activities. Hike to the water from the Lake View Trail and Chestnut Ridge Trail. The park's visitor center features exhibits on the history and folklore of the area and the lake's aquatic environment. A small gift shop is operated by the Friends of Smith Mountain Lake State Park. Many interpretive programs take place here or at the newly refurbished amphitheater nearby.

BASICS

Operated By: State of Virginia. **Open:** Mar.–Dec. **Site Assignment:** First come, first served; no reservations. **Registration:** At campground office. **Fee:** $19–$24; V, MC. **Parking:** At site.

FACILITIES

Number of RV-only Sites: 24. **Number of Tent-only Sites:** 26. **Hookups:** Electric (20, 30 amps). **Each Site:** Grill, picnic table. **Dump Station:** Yes. **Laundry:** No. **Pay Phone:** Yes. **Restrooms and Showers:** Yes. **Fuel:** No. **Propane:** No. **Internal Roads:** Paved, in good condition. **RV Service:** No. **Market:** W/in 10 mi. **Restaurant:** W/in 12 mi. **General Store:** No. **Vending:** Yes. **Swimming:** Yes. **Playground:** Yes. **Other:** Cabin rentals, interpretive center. **Activities:** Lake swimming and fishing, boating, canoeing, boat rentals, hiking trails. **Nearby Attractions:** Booker T. Washington National Monument, Peaks of Otter, Blue Ridge Parkway. **Additional Information:** Roanoke Valley CVB, (800) 635-5535, www.visitroanoke.com.

RESTRICTIONS

Pets: On leash, $3 per night. **Fires:** In grills and pits. **Alcoholic Beverages:** No alcohol permitted. **Vehicle Maximum Length:** 50 ft. **Other:** Max. 14-day stay in 30-day period.

TO GET THERE

From Hwy. 43, go 14 mi. southwest on Hwy. 626. Follow signs to park.

LANCASTER   MAP, B-4
Belle Isle State Park

reserve america

Rte. 3, Box 550, 22503-9425. T: (804) 462-5030; www.reserveamerica.com.

🚐 ★★★★   ⛺ ★★★★

Beauty: ★★★   Site Privacy: ★★★
Spaciousness: ★★★   Quiet: ★★★★
Security: ★★★★   Cleanliness: ★★★★
Insect Control: ★★★   Facilities: ★★

Located in the rural Northern Neck of Virginia, Belle Isle was the first state park to be purchased with funds from the $95 million 1992 Parks and Recreational Facilities Bond Referendum. The 733-acre site is a window to the beautiful lower Rappahannock River in Lancaster County. Waterfront in the area has been developed extensively by private landowners with little public recreational access. This fact made the lower Rappahannock a priority for purchasing land for a new state park. The park has 7 miles of frontage on the north shore of the Rappahannock, and it borders Deep and Mulberry creeks. It features diverse tidal and nontidal wetlands, lowland marshes, tidal coves, and upland forests. The diverse habitats found in the park provide homes to many predator birds, such as blue herons, osprey, hawks, and bald eagles, as well as wildlife such as white-tailed deer, turkeys, groundhogs, rabbits, squirrels, moles, reptiles, and amphibians. There are eight distinct types of wetlands within the park. These diverse ecosystems make Belle Isle an excellent outdoor laboratory for environmental education.

BASICS

Operated By: Virginia State Parks. **Open:** All year. **Site Assignment:** Reservations can be made 11 months in advance. **Registration:** At office. **Fee:** Picnic shelter, $30–$45; single house, $78–$103; single mansion, $191–$257. **Parking:** At site.

FACILITIES

Number of Multipurpose Sites: 31. **Hookups:** None. **Each Site:** Fire ring. **Dump Station:** No. **Laundry:** No. **Pay Phone:** No. **Restrooms and Showers:** Yes. **Fuel:** No. **Propane:** No. **Internal Roads:** Paved. **RV Service:** No. **Market:** No. **Restaurant:** No. **General Store:** No. **Vending:** No. **Swimming:** No. **Playground:** Yes. **Other:** Overnight Facilities: Bel Air Overnight Area. Primitive group camping available by permit arranged through the park. **Activities:** Biking, boating, fishing, hiking, picnicking.

RESTRICTIONS

Fires: Fire ban in effect during certain times of the year.

TO GET THERE

Belle Isle State Park is located in Lancaster County on the Rappahannock River. From Warsaw, take VA 3 east to SR 354. Turn right and follow 3 mi. Turn right onto SR 683 near Litwalton to the park entrance. From Kilmarnock, take VA 3 west to Lively, then left on SR 201 3 mi., then right on SR 354 3 mi. and left onto SR 683 to the park entrance.

LANEXA — MAP, C-3
Ed Allen's Campgrounds and Cottages

Chickahominy Recreational Park, 13501 Campground Rd., 23089. T: (804) 966-2582; www.edallens.com.

🚐 ★★★★ ▲ ★★★★

Beauty: ★★★★ | Site Privacy: ★★★★
Spaciousness: ★★★★ | Quiet: ★★★★
Security: ★★★★ | Cleanliness: ★★★★
Insect Control: ★★★★ | Facilities: ★★★★

Located along the shores of Chickahominy Lake, which is renowned for its bass fishing, perhaps it's appropriate that Ed Allen's Campgrounds and Cottages features what it calls the world's largest bass-shaped swimming pool. Consisting of 1,100 acres, Chickahominy Lake is a stunning sight, especially with the setting sun reflecting in the glassy water. Ed Allen's is a fisherman's haven. Boat rentals are available at the lake, and there is a lakeside restaurant where prime rib, steaks, fresh seafood, and pasta grace the menu. Many of the campsites are shaded by cypress trees; there are 50 pull-throughs. Cottages and motel rooms are also available, as are lakeside tent sites. For children, Ed Allen's has a kiddie pool, a stocked fishing pond, hayrides, and a game room. Of course, most children flock to the bass-shaped swimming pool. The campground is a short drive to Colonial Williamsburg and Richmond.

BASICS
Operated By: Ed Allen Jr. **Open:** Apr. 1–Nov. 1. **Site Assignment:** Reservations accepted online, walk-ins accepted. **Registration:** At campground headquarters. **Fee:** $16–$23; V, MC. **Parking:** At designated spot.

FACILITIES
Number of RV-only Sites: 300. **Number of Tent-only Sites:** 75. **Hookups:** Electric (20, 30 amps), water, phone. **Each Site:** Fire ring, picnic table. **Dump Station:** Yes. **Laundry:** Yes. **Pay Phone:** Yes. **Restrooms and Showers:** Yes. **Fuel:** Yes. **Propane:** Yes. **Internal Roads:** Gravel & paved, in good condition. **RV Service:** No. **Market:** W/in 5 mi. **Restaurant:** On premises. **General Store:** Yes. **Vending:** Yes. **Swimming:** Yes. **Playground:** Yes. **Other:** Bass-shaped swimming pool. **Activities:** Swimming, wading pool, game room, rec hall, boating, canoeing, kayaking, boat rentals, lake and pond fishing, basketball, planned activities on weekends, horseback riding, sports field, horseshoes, hiking trails, volleyball. **Nearby Attractions:** Colonial Williamsburg, Busch Gardens, Historic Jamestown Settlement, Richmond, Yorktown, James River. **Additional Information:** Virginia Tourism Corp., (800) 371-8164, www.virginia.org.

RESTRICTIONS
Pets: On leash only. **Fires:** At site. **Alcoholic Beverages:** At site. **Vehicle Maximum Length:** No limit.

TO GET THERE
From Hwy. 155, go 5.5 mi. east on US 60 and 0.5 mi. south on Hwy. 649. Entrance is on the right.

LORTON — MAP, B-3
Pohick Bay Regional Park

6501 Pohick Bay Dr., 22709. T: (703) 339-6104; www.nvrpa.org.

🚐 ★★★★ ▲ ★★★★

Beauty: ★★★★ | Site Privacy: ★★★
Spaciousness: ★★★ | Quiet: ★★★
Security: ★★★★ | Cleanliness: ★★★★
Insect Control: ★★★★ | Facilities: ★★★★

Located 25 miles south of Washington, D.C., the Pohick Bay Regional Park is situated on a bay on the historic Mason Neck peninsula in Fairfax County. The park has a marina, boat launch, and a fleet of pedal boats, sailboats, and job boats available for rent. The campsites are nestled under pine, beech, and holly trees, providing ample shade on sweltering days. Local golf magazines have repeatedly name Pohick Bay as one of the area's most challenging courses. If you would rather explore nature without a bag of golf clubs, make a short drive to Mason Neck State Park, where more than 200 species of birds reside. Chances are you'll see great blue heron and even bald eagles. If you prefer to mix nature with visiting historic landmarks, remember that Washington, D.C. is a short drive away, and when you return to Pohick Bay, you'll appreciate nature's splendor—and serenity—even more.

BASICS
Operated By: Northern Virginia Regional Park Authority. **Open:** All year. **Site Assignment:** First come, first served; no reservations. **Registration:** At campground office. **Fee:** $7; V, MC. **Parking:** At site.

FACILITIES
Number of RV-only Sites: 100. **Number of Tent-only Sites:** 50. **Hookups:** Electric (30 amps). **Each Site:** Grill, picnic table. **Dump Station:** Yes. **Laundry:** Yes. **Pay Phone:** Yes. **Restrooms and Showers:** Yes. **Fuel:** No. **Propane:** No. **Internal Roads:** Paved, in good condition. **RV Service:** No. **Market:** W/in 4 mi. **Restaurant:** On premises. **General Store:** Yes. **Vending:** Yes. **Swimming:** Yes. **Playground:** Yes. **Other:** 18-hole golf course. **Activities:** Golf, mini-golf, Frisbee golf, horseback riding, hiking trails, boating, canoeing, boat rentals, river fishing, driving range, putting green. **Nearby Attractions:** Washington, D.C. **Additional Information:** Washington, D.C., CVB, (202) 789-7000, www.washington.org.

RESTRICTIONS
Pets: On leash only. **Fires:** Camp stove or fire ring. **Alcoholic Beverages:** Not allowed. **Vehicle Maximum Length:** 33 ft. **Other:** 7-day stay limit.

TO GET THERE
From US 1, go 4 mi. east on Hwy. 242. Entrance is on the left.

LURAY — MAP, B-2
Big Meadows Campground

3655 US 211 East, 22835-9036. T: (540) 999-3500; www.nps.gov/shen.

🚐 ★★★★ ▲ ★★★★

Beauty: ★★★★ | Site Privacy: ★★★★
Spaciousness: ★★★★ | Quiet: ★★★★
Security: ★★★★ | Cleanliness: ★★★★★
Insect Control: ★★★★ | Facilities: ★★★★

On July 3, 1936, President Franklin D. Roosevelt helped formally open Shenandoah National Park during a ceremony at Big Meadows near Luray. Big Meadows is the park's most expansive treeless area at 640 acres. In a region dominated by mature forests, a tree-barren plateau like Big Meadows is indeed unique. Historians believe that Native Americans may have cleared the area to promote better grazing conditions. Big Meadows Campground has some grassy and open sites; others are wooded. Big Meadows Campground is the only one at the park that accepts reservations. Overall, Shenandoah National Park consists of more than 500 miles of trails, including 101 miles of the Appalachian Trail. Trails may follow a ridge crest, lead to high places with panoramic views, or wander to waterfalls in deep canyons. Many animals, including deer, black bears, and wild turkeys flourish among the rich growth of an oak-hickory forest.

BASICS
Operated By: National Park Service. **Open:** May–Oct. **Site Assignment:** Reservations recommended, walk-ins accepted. **Registration:** At campground office. **Fee:** $16–$19; plus park entrance fee, $10; V, MC. **Parking:** At site.

FACILITIES
Number of RV-only Sites: 39. **Number of Tent-only Sites:** 178. **Hookups:** None. **Each Site:** Grill, picnic table. **Dump Station:** Yes. **Laundry:** Yes. **Pay Phone:** Yes. **Restrooms and Showers:** Yes. **Fuel:** No. **Propane:** No. **Internal Roads:** Paved, in good condition. **RV Service:** No. **Market:** W/in 16 mi. **Restaurant:** On premises. **General Store:** Yes. **Vending:** Yes. **Swimming:** No. **Playground:** No. **Other:** Lodge & restaurant. **Activities:** Stream fishing, hiking trails. **Nearby Attractions:** Shenandoah National Park, Appalachian Trail, Skyline Drive. **Additional Information:** Shenandoah Valley Travel Assoc., (540) 740-3132, www.svta.org.

RESTRICTIONS
Pets: On leash only. **Fires:** In camp stoves and fireplaces. **Alcoholic Beverages:** At site. **Vehicle Maximum Length:** No limit. **Other:** Max. 6 people per site.

TO GET THERE
From US 33, go 16 mi. north on Skyline Dr. to milepost 51. Follow signs to campground.

LURAY   MAP, B-2
Lewis Mountain Campground

3655 US 211 East, 22835-9036. T: (540) 999-3500; www.nps.gov/shen.

🚐 ★★★   ▲ ★★★★

Beauty: ★★★★   Site Privacy: ★★★
Spaciousness: ★★★   Quiet: ★★★★
Security: ★★★★   Cleanliness: ★★★★★
Insect Control: ★★★★   Facilities: ★★★★

The smallest of Shenandoah National Park's five campgrounds (and the only one with no dump station), Lewis Mountain Campground's sites are situated amid massive maple, pine, hemlock, and oak trees. No reservations are accepted at Lewis Mountain. This can pose a problem during the fall, when colors are their most vibrant and campgrounds at the park are full on weekends. The solution: Arrive at Lewis Mountain on a weekday. It's difficult to miss—and important to obey—the sign at the campground that reads, "Bear Country—Protect Your Property and Food, Proper Food Storage is Required." The campground has food storage poles for tenters. If you don't have an RV or tent, Lewis Mountain has several rustic, furnished cabins with private baths. For an interesting hike, drive to milepost 59.5 and walk along the Pocosin Mission Trail. The path leads past an old Episcopal mission from the early 1900s and an overgrown cemetery.

BASICS

Operated By: National Park Service. **Open:** May–Nov. **Site Assignment:** First come, first served; no reservations. **Registration:** At campground office. **Fee:** $17; plus park entrance fee, $10; V, MC. **Parking:** At site.

FACILITIES

Number of RV-only Sites: 16. **Number of Tent-only Sites:** 16. **Hookups:** None. **Each Site:** Picnic table & fire grill. **Dump Station:** No. **Laundry:** Yes. **Pay Phone:** Yes. **Restrooms and Showers:** Yes. **Fuel:** No. **Propane:** No. **Internal Roads:** Paved, in good condition. **RV Service:** No. **Market:** W/in 10 mi. **Restaurant:** W/in 6 mi. **General Store:** Yes. **Vending:** Yes. **Swimming:** No. **Playground:** No. **Other:** Cabin rentals. **Activities:** Stream fishing, hiking trails. **Nearby Attractions:** Shenandoah National Park, Appalachian Trail, Skyline Drive. **Additional Information:** Shenandoah Valley Travel Assoc., (540) 740-3132, www.svta.org.

RESTRICTIONS

Pets: On leash only. **Fires:** In camp stoves and fireplaces. **Alcoholic Beverages:** At site. **Vehicle Maximum Length:** 30 ft. **Other:** Max. 6 people per site.

TO GET THERE

From US 33, go 8 mi. northeast on Skyline Dr. to milepost 57.5 and 1.5 mi. east on park road.

LURAY   MAP, B-2
Loft Mountain Campground

3655 US 211 E., 22835-9036. T: (540) 999-3500; www.nps.gov/shen.

🚐 ★★★   ▲ ★★★★

Beauty: ★★★★   Site Privacy: ★★★
Spaciousness: ★★★   Quiet: ★★★★
Security: ★★★★   Cleanliness: ★★★★
Insect Control: ★★★★   Facilities: ★★★

The largest campground in Shenandoah National Park, Loft Mountain Campground actually sits atop Big Flat Mountain, which affords panoramic views of the neighboring peaks and valley to east and west from 3,400 feet. Loft Mountain is the southernmost campground in the park. This mountaintop area has thick, low-growing shrubs instead of the mature hardwoods that dominate most of Shenandoah National Park's landscape. Many of the campground's 219 sites are private and spacious. Weekends—especially fall weekends—are the most difficult time to find a site. Arriving at Loft Mountain on a weekday is advisable. The 1.3-mile Deadening Nature Trail, which has two rocky observation points, and the 2.7-mile Loft Mountain Loop, which leads to a 3,290-foot lookout, are among the many hiking trails that start at or near the campground. Loft Mountain also has a visitor center with restrooms, an information desk, and first aid items. Many ranger-led programs and hikes begin here.

BASICS

Operated By: National Park Service. **Open:** May–Oct. **Site Assignment:** First come, first served; no reservations. **Registration:** At campground office. **Fee:** $14; plus park entrance fee, $10; V, MC. **Parking:** At site.

FACILITIES

Number of RV-only Sites: 165. **Number of Tent-only Sites:** 54. **Hookups:** None. **Each Site:** Grill, picnic table. **Dump Station:** Yes. **Laundry:** Yes. **Pay Phone:** Yes. **Restrooms and Showers:** Yes. **Fuel:** No. **Propane:** No. **Internal Roads:** Paved, in good condition. **RV Service:** No. **Market:** W/in 12 mi. **Restaurant:** On premises. **General Store:** Yes. **Vending:** Yes. **Playground:** No. **Other:** Restaurant. **Activities:** Stream fishing, hiking trails. **Nearby Attractions:** Shenandoah National Park, Appalachian Trail. **Additional Information:** Shenandoah Valley Travel Assoc., (540) 740-3132, www.svta.org.

RESTRICTIONS

Pets: On leash only. **Fires:** In camp stoves and designated fireplaces. **Alcoholic Beverages:** At site. **Vehicle Maximum Length:** 30 ft. **Other:** Max. 6 people per site.

TO GET THERE

From US 33, go 10 mi. southwest on Skyline Dr. to milepost 79.5 and 1.5 mi. east on park road.

LURAY   MAP, B-2
Mathews Arm Campground

3655 US 211 East, 22835-9036. T: (540) 999-3500; www.nps.gov/shen.

🚐 ★★★   ▲ ★★★★

Beauty: ★★★★   Site Privacy: ★★★
Spaciousness: ★★★   Quiet: ★★★★
Security: ★★★★   Cleanliness: ★★★★★
Insect Control: ★★★★   Facilities: ★★★

The northernmost campground in Shenandoah National Park, Mathews Arm Campground has 179 sites, most of which are level. There are no electric hookups, and no reservations are accepted. At this or any of the Shenandoah National Park campgrounds that don't accept reservations, weekends are the busiest time. The campground is shaded by hickory and oak trees, and there are many desirable sites. However, to have a wider choice of sites, consider arriving at Mathews Arm on a weekday. Several scenic hiking trails sprout near the campground. The 1.7-mile Traces Nature Trail begins near the campground registration station's parking area and connects with the Mathews Arm Trail, which in turn intersects with the Tuscarora–Overall Run Trail. A 2-mile walk down this trail leads to Overall Run Falls, the tallest waterfall in Shenandoah National Park. Two miles from the campground entrance, Elkwallow Wayside has camping supplies and food service.

BASICS

Operated By: National Park Service. **Open:** May–Oct. **Site Assignment:** First come, first served; no reservations. **Registration:** At registration station. **Fee:** $14; plus park entrance fee, $10; V, MC. **Parking:** At site.

FACILITIES

Number of RV-only Sites: 166. **Number of Tent-only Sites:** 13. **Hookups:** None. **Each Site:** Grill, picnic table. **Dump Station:** Yes. **Laundry:** No. **Pay Phone:** Yes. **Restrooms and Showers:** Yes (no showers). **Fuel:** No. **Propane:** No. **Internal Roads:** Paved, in good condition. **RV Service:** No. **Market:** W/in 10 mi. **Restaurant:** W/in 2 mi. **General Store:** No. **Vending:** No. **Swimming:** No. **Playground:** No. **Other:** Amphitheater. **Activities:** Stream fishing, hiking trails. **Nearby Attractions:** Shenandoah National Park, Appalachian Trail. **Additional Information:** Shenandoah Valley Travel Assoc., (540) 740-3132, www.svta.org.

RESTRICTIONS

Pets: On leash only. **Fires:** In camp stoves and fireplaces. **Alcoholic Beverages:** At site. **Vehicle Maximum Length:** No limit. **Other:** Max. 6 people per site.

TO GET THERE

From Thornton Gap entrance to park at milepost 31.5, go north on Skyline Dr. to campground entrance at milepost 22.2.

LURAY   MAP, B-2
Yogi Bear's Jellystone Park Camp-Resort

reserve america

P.O. Box 191, 22835. T: (540) 743-4002 or (800) 420-6679; www.reserveamerica.com.

🚐 ★★★★   ⛺ ★★★★

Beauty: ★★★★	Site Privacy: ★★
Spaciousness: ★★	Quiet: ★★★
Security: ★★★★	Cleanliness: ★★★★
Insect Control: ★★★★	Facilities: ★★★★★

Located at the base of the Blue Ridge Mountains 5 miles from the entrance to Shenandoah National Park and Skyline Drive, Yogi Bear's Jellystone Park Camp Resort in Luray has wooded and open sites that offer panoramic views of the Blue Ridge Mountains. The campground has 63 pull-through sites, a 24-hour Laundromat, and a full-service camp store on the premises. Shenandoah National Park is a sanctuary for 100 varieties of trees, 200 species of birds, and 43 species of mammals. The numerous hiking trails—many accessible off Skyline Drive—lead to stunning views of mountain peaks and valleys. Luray Caverns isn't limited to its network of underground passages; the attraction also includes the Car and Carriage Museum, the Garden Maze, and the Singing Tower. The New Market Battlefield Park and Hall of Valor Museum in nearby New Market offer tours and movies about the battle and Stonewall Jackson.

BASICS
Operated By: Jellystone Park. **Open:** Apr. 1–Nov. 15. **Site Assignment:** Reservations accepted (deposit forfeit for no-shows and less than 7-day cancellation notice), walk-ins accepted. **Registration:** At campground office. **Fee:** $35–$40; V, MC, D. **Parking:** At site.

FACILITIES
Number of RV-only Sites: 132. **Number of Tent-only Sites:** 68. **Hookups:** Electric (20, 30, 50 amps), water. **Each Site:** Fire ring, picnic table. **Dump Station:** Yes. **Laundry:** Yes. **Pay Phone:** Yes. **Restrooms and Showers:** Yes. **Fuel:** No. **Propane:** Yes. **Internal Roads:** Gravel, in good condition. **RV Service:** No. **Market:** W/in 2 mi. **Restaurant:** W/in 2 mi. **General Store:** Yes. **Vending:** Yes. **Swimming:** Yes. **Playground:** Yes. **Other:** Waterslide. **Activities:** Swimming, wading pool, waterslide, pond fishing, boat rentals, rec hall, game room, mini-golf, planned activities, movies, sports field, horseshoes, hiking trails, volleyball. **Nearby Attractions:** Luray Caverns, Shenandoah National Park, Shenandoah River, Natural Bridge of Virginia. **Additional Information:** Shenandoah Valley Travel Assoc., (540) 740-3132, www.svta.org.

RESTRICTIONS
Pets: On leash only. **Fires:** At site. **Alcoholic Beverages:** At site. **Vehicle Maximum Length:** No limit. **Other:** Children must be accompanied by adult at swimming pool.

TO GET THERE
From US 340, go 4 mi. east on US 211. Entrance is on the right.

MADISON   MAP, B-2
Shenandoah Hills Campground

R.R. 1 Box 7, 110 Campground Lane, 22727. T: (540) 948-4186 or (800) 321-4186; www.gocampingamerica.com/shenandoahhills.

🚐 ★★★★   ⛺ ★★★★

Beauty: ★★★★★	Site Privacy: ★★★
Spaciousness: ★★★★	Quiet: ★★★★
Security: ★★★★	Cleanliness: ★★★★
Insect Control: ★★★★	Facilities: ★★★★

Located in the foothills of the Blue Ridge Mountains, Shenandoah Hills Campground has wooded and open sites, including 16 pull-throughs. There are cool and comfortable waterside sites, remote wooded tent sites, and rustic log cabin rentals. The campground is a short distance from Shenandoah National Park, Luray Caverns, and Endless Caverns. Shenandoah Hills is also near Thomas Jefferson's Monticello, a must-see for history and architectural enthusiasts. In Fredericksburg, George Washington's Mount Vernon is another presidential day trip from Shenandoah Hills. More than a dozen outbuildings are meticulously restored, including the slave quarters and greenhouse.

BASICS
Operated By: Private operator. **Open:** Mar.–Dec. **Site Assignment:** Reservations recommended (3-night min. for holiday weekend), walk-ins accepted. **Registration:** At camp store. **Fee:** $24–$35; V, MC. **Parking:** At site.

FACILITIES
Number of RV-only Sites: 65. **Number of Tent-only Sites:** 16. **Hookups:** Electric (20, 30 amps), water, cable TV. **Each Site:** Fire ring, picnic table. **Dump Station:** Yes. **Laundry:** Yes. **Pay Phone:** Yes. **Restrooms and Showers:** Yes. **Fuel:** No. **Propane:** Yes. **Internal Roads:** Gravel & paved, in good condition. **RV Service:** No. **Market:** W/in 2 mi. **Restaurant:** W/in 1 mi. **General Store:** Yes. **Vending:** Yes. **Swimming:** Yes. **Playground:** Yes. **Other:** Hayrides. **Activities:** Game room, rec hall, swimming, basketball, planned activities on weekends, tennis, sports field, horseshoes, hiking trails, volleyball. **Nearby Attractions:** Monticello, Montpelier, Skyline Drive, Luray Caverns, Endless Caverns, Shenandoah National Park, wineries, antique shops. **Additional Information:** Shenandoah Valley Travel Assoc., (540) 740-3132, www.svta.org.

RESTRICTIONS
Pets: On leash only. **Fires:** At site. **Alcoholic Beverages:** At site. **Vehicle Maximum Length:** 45 ft.

TO GET THERE
From Hwy. 230, go 0.1 mi. south on US 29. Entrance is on the right.

MARION   MAP, A-2
Hungry Mother State Park

reserve america

2854 State Park Blvd., 24354. T: (276) 781-7400 or (800) 933-PARK; www.reserveamerica.com.

🚐 ★★★★   ⛺ ★★★★

Beauty: ★★★★	Site Privacy: ★★★★
Spaciousness: ★★★★	Quiet: ★★★★
Security: ★★★★	Cleanliness: ★★★★
Insect Control: ★★★★	Facilities: ★★★★

According to legend, at a time when Native Americans were destroying settlements along the New River, a woman named Molly Marley and her child were captured. They later escaped and wandered through the wilderness eating only wild berries. Molly eventually collapsed, and her child later found help. The child's only words were "hungry, mother" when found. The search party found Molly dead. To honor her, the base at the mountain where she was found was named Molly's Knob, and the creek where her child followed to seek help was called Hungry Mother Creek. The creek was later dammed and renamed Hungry Mother Lake. The 108-acre lake is a popular spot for boating and fishing, and the park's 2,180 acres are ideal for hiking and horseback riding. The 43 camping sites are actually distributed over three campgrounds. The RV sites offer electric hookups, and the park has a dump station and hot showers. One of the original CCC facilities, the Restaurant at Hungry Mother overlooks the lake.

BASICS
Operated By: State of Virginia. **Open:** Mar.–Dec. **Site Assignment:** First come, first served; no reservations. **Registration:** At campground office. **Fee:** $19–$24; V, MC. **Parking:** At site.

FACILITIES
Number of RV-only Sites: 32. **Number of Tent-only Sites:** 11. **Hookups:** Electric (15 amps). **Each Site:** Grill, picnic table. **Dump Station:** Yes. **Laundry:** No. **Pay Phone:** Yes. **Restrooms and Showers:** Yes. **Fuel:** No. **Propane:** No. **Internal Roads:** Paved, in fair condition. **RV Service:** No. **Market:** W/in 3 mi. **Restaurant:** On premises. **General Store:** Yes. **Vending:** Yes. **Swimming:** Yes. **Playground:** Yes. **Other:** Hungry Mother Lake, Hemlock Haven Conference Center, Hungry Mother Lodge. **Activities:** Horseback riding, lake fishing and swimming, boating, boat rentals, planned activities, hiking trails. **Nearby Attractions:** Grayson Highlands State Park, Mt. Rogers National Recreation Area, Historic Saltville, Historic Abingdon, Wytheville, Bristol Motor Speedway. **Additional Information:** Virginia Tourism Corp. (800) 371-8164, www.virginia.org.

RESTRICTIONS
Pets: On leash only. **Fires:** In camp stove or fire ring. **Alcoholic Beverages:** No alcohol permitted. **Vehicle Maximum Length:** 30 ft. **Other:** Swimming only permitted in designated areas.

TO GET THERE

From Marion, go 3 mi. north on Hwy. 16. Follow signs to the park.

MEADOWS OF DAN   MAP, C-1
Meadows of Dan Campground

2182 Jeb Stuart Hwy., 24120. T: (276) 952-2292; www.meadowsofdancampground.

🚐 ★★★★   ▲ ★★★★

Beauty: ★★★★	Site Privacy: ★★★★
Spaciousness: ★★★★	Quiet: ★★★★★
Security: ★★★★★	Cleanliness: ★★★★
Insect Control: ★★★★	Facilities: ★★★★

Located in the Blue Ridge Mountains, less than a mile from the Blue Ridge Parkway, Meadows of Dan Campground is not the place to stay if you have children with visions of swimming pools, waterslides, and mini-golf courses. It is ideal, though, if you are searching for solitude in a clean, scenic environment. There are two pull-through sites. The bathhouse is clean and well kept, and there is a washer and dryer. Two cabin rentals are also available. With its proximity to the Blue Ridge Parkway, Meadows of Dan is convenient to numerous hiking trails. The Pinnacles of Dan and Lover's Leap are two nearby overlooks worth a visit. About 50 miles northeast is Roanoke, where you'll find the Virginia Museum of Transportation and its early automobiles and locomotives. For more modern transportation, a NASCAR speedway in Martinsville is nearby.

BASICS

Operated By: Kevin Johnson. **Open:** All year. **Site Assignment:** Reservations and walk-ins accepted. **Registration:** At campground office. **Fee:** $16–$21; V, MC, AF, D. **Parking:** At designated area.

FACILITIES

Number of RV-only Sites: 20. **Number of Tent-only Sites:** 11. **Hookups:** Electric (30, 50 amps), water. **Each Site:** Fire ring, picnic table. **Dump Station:** Yes. **Laundry:** Yes. **Pay Phone:** Yes. **Restrooms and Showers:** Yes. **Fuel:** No. **Propane:** No. **Internal Roads:** Gravel & paved, in good condition. **RV Service:** No. **Market:** W/in 3 mi. **Restaurant:** W/in 4 mi. **General Store:** No. **Vending:** Yes. **Swimming:** No. **Playground:** Yes. **Other:** Fishing pond. **Activities:** Basketball, pond fishing, badminton, horseshoes, volleyball. **Nearby Attractions:** Blue Ridge Parkway, Mayberry USA, Wytheville, Historic Crab Orchard Museum and Pioneer Park. **Additional Information:** Virginia Tourism Corp., (800) 371-8164, www.virginia.org.

RESTRICTIONS

Pets: On leash only. **Fires:** At site. **Alcoholic Beverages:** At site. **Vehicle Maximum Length:** No limit.

TO GET THERE

From Blue Ridge Pkwy., at milepost 177.7 go 0.1 mi. west on US 58. Entrance is on the left.

MIDDLETOWN   MAP, A-2
Battle of Cedar Creek Campground

8950 Valley Pike, 22645.
T: (540) 869-1888 or (800) 343-1562.

🚐 ★★★   ▲ ★★★★

Beauty: ★★★★	Site Privacy: ★★★★
Spaciousness: ★★★	Quiet: ★★★★
Security: ★★★★	Cleanliness: ★★★★
Insect Control: ★★★★	Facilities: ★★★★

On the banks of Cedar Creek, where Union and Confederate troops clashed during the Civil War, the Battle of Cedar Creek Campground offers 59 sites, including 20 full hookups and two pull-throughs. The tent camping is especially good here, with private sites and quiet surroundings. The campground, which has a swimming pool and a mini-golf course, is not far from the entrance to the 105-mile-long Skyline Drive in Front Royal, and Shenandoah National Park is a short drive away. The main attraction close to the campground is the 158-acre Cedar Creek Battlefield, which includes the Heater House and a 5,000-square-foot visitors center. A mile south of the campground is Belle Grove Plantation, an 18th-century grain and livestock farm. The plantation includes the main house and gardens, original outbuildings, a classic 1918 barn, an overseer's house, the slave cemetery, a heritage apple orchard, fields and meadows, and scenic mountain views.

BASICS

Operated By: Private operator. **Open:** All year. **Site Assignment:** Reservations and walk-ins accepted. **Registration:** At campground office. **Fee:** $17; V, MC. **Parking:** At site.

FACILITIES

Number of RV-only Sites: 46. **Number of Tent-only Sites:** 13. **Hookups:** Electric (20, 30 amps), water, phone. **Each Site:** Fire ring, picnic table. **Dump Station:** Yes. **Laundry:** Yes. **Pay Phone:** Yes. **Restrooms and Showers:** Yes. **Fuel:** No. **Propane:** Yes. **Internal Roads:** Gravel, in good condition. **RV Service:** No. **Market:** W/in 2 mi. **Restaurant:** W/in 2 mi. **General Store:** No. **Vending:** Yes. **Swimming:** Yes. **Playground:** Yes. **Other:** Located on Civil War battlefield. **Activities:** Swimming, rec hall, stream fishing, mini-golf, shuffleboard, horseshoes, volleyball, disc golf, tubing, canoeing. **Nearby Attractions:** Shenandoah National Park, Shenandoah River, Skyline Drive, Battle of Cedar Creek battlefield, Belle Grove Plantation, Museum of American Presidents. **Additional Information:** Shenandoah Valley Travel Assoc., (540) 740-3132, www.svta.org.

RESTRICTIONS

Pets: On leash only. **Fires:** At site. **Alcoholic Beverages:** At site. **Vehicle Maximum Length:** 42 ft.

TO GET THERE

From I-66, go 2 mi. south on I-81 and 1 mi. north on US 11. Entrance is on the left.

MILLBORO   MAP, B-1
Douthat State Park

reserve america

Hwy. 1 , P.O. Box 212, 24460.
T: (540) 862-8100 or (800) 933-PARK;
www.reserveamerica.com.

🚐 ★★★   ▲ ★★★★

Beauty: ★★★★	Site Privacy: ★★★
Spaciousness: ★★★	Quiet: ★★★
Security: ★★★★	Cleanliness: ★★★★
Insect Control: ★★★★	Facilities: ★★★★

Straddling Bath and Allegheny Counties and located in a valley between Beards and Middle Mountains, Douthat State Park has received its share of recognition. Editors of the 1999 *Outside Family Vacation Guide* named it one of the nation's top 10 state park family vacation destinations. In addition to 50-acre Douthat Lake, more than 40 miles of hiking trails and this 77-site campground can be found in the park. Campsites are open with lake and mountain views. Douthat Lake and adjoining Wilson Creek are stocked regularly with trout, water conditions permitting. The renovated Douthat Lakeview Restaurant, one of the original CCC facilities, overlooks the lake and features a glass-enclosed porch. Adjacent to the restaurant is Douthat Camp Store. At 4.5 miles, Stony Run Trail is Douthat's longest. Mountain bikers favor the trails on Middle Mountain, which rises to more than 3,000 feet on Douthat's west end.

BASICS

Operated By: State of Virginia. **Open:** Mar.–Dec. **Site Assignment:** Reservations and walk-ins accepted. **Registration:** At campground office. **Fee:** $23–$24; V, MC. **Parking:** At site.

FACILITIES

Number of RV-only Sites: 77. **Hookups:** Electric (30 amps). **Each Site:** Picnic table, grill, lantern pole. **Dump Station:** Yes. **Laundry:** No. **Pay Phone:** Yes. **Restrooms and Showers:** Yes. **Fuel:** No. **Propane:** No. **Internal Roads:** Paved, in good condition. **RV Service:** No. **Market:** W/in 5 mi. **Restaurant:** W/in 3 mi. **General Store:** Yes. **Vending:** Yes. **Swimming:** Yes. **Playground:** Yes. **Other:** Douthat Lake. **Activities:** Lake fishing and swimming, boating, boat rentals, horseshoes, planned activities, hiking trails. **Nearby Attractions:** The Homestead, Warm Springs Baths, Lexington, Virginia Military Institute, Lee Chapel, Stonewall Jackson House, Roanoke. **Additional Information:** Virginia Tourism Corp., (800) 371-8164, www.virginia.org.

RESTRICTIONS

Pets: On leash only. **Fires:** At site. **Alcoholic Beverages:** No alcohol permitted. **Vehicle Maximum Length:** No limit. **Other:** Max. 14-day stay in 30-day period.

TO GET THERE

From US 60, go 2.5 mi. north on Hwy. 629. Follow signs to park.

MINERAL
Christopher Run Campground
MAP, B-3

7149 Zachary Taylor Hwy., 23117.
T: (540) 894-4744;
www.christopherruncampground.com.

🚐 ★★★★   ⛺ ★★★★

Beauty: ★★★★	Site Privacy: ★★
Spaciousness: ★★	Quiet: ★★★★
Security: ★★★★★	Cleanliness: ★★★★
Insect Control: ★★★★	Facilities: ★★★★

With more than 200 miles of shoreline and 13,600 acres, Lake Anna is a haven for water sports, and Christopher Run Campground is in the middle of the action. The campground hosts a bluegrass festival every second weekend in June. Since Lake Anna is the campground's big draw, Christopher Run offers rowboat, canoe, and pedal-boat rentals. It has a dock and a ramp for campers who own boats, and there's marine gas at the bait and tackle shop. The best spots are the cozy water view sites looking at Lake Anna and a cluster of sites bordering a mature forest near the center of the campground. Lake Anna was formed in 1972 when the North Anna River was damned to form a cooling reservoir for the North Anna Nuclear Power Reactor The lake consists of two sections: a 3,400-acre impoundment that provides the water for the power plant's cooling, and the 9,600-acre main lake impoundment used to distribute the warmer water that results from the reactor cooling process. The smaller impoundment is accessible only to property owners. The larger lake is the area open to the public.

BASICS
Operated By: Childs family. **Open:** Apr. 1–Oct. 31. **Site Assignment:** Reservations accepted (1-night deposit required), walk-ins accepted. **Registration:** At campground office. **Fee:** $23–$26; V, MC, AE, D. **Parking:** At site.

FACILITIES
Number of RV-only Sites: 190. **Number of Tent-only Sites:** 10. **Hookups:** Electric (20, 30 amps), water, phone. **Each Site:** Picnic table. **Dump Station:** Yes. **Laundry:** Yes. **Pay Phone:** Yes. **Restrooms and Showers:** Yes. **Fuel:** Yes. **Propane:** Yes. **Internal Roads:** Paved, in good condition. **RV Service:** No. **Market:** W/in 5 mi. **Restaurant:** W/in 3 mi. **General Store:** Yes. **Vending:** Yes. **Swimming:** Yes. **Playground:** Yes. **Other:** Lake Anna. **Activities:** Lake swimming and fishing, boating, canoeing, kayaking, boat rentals, game room, rec hall, basketball, shuffleboard, planned activities on weekends, horseshoes, volleyball. **Nearby Attractions:** Lake Anna, Fredericksburg and Spotsylvania National Military Park, Historic Fredericksburg, North Anna Nuclear Power Station. **Additional Information:** Virginia Tourism Corp., (800) 371-8164, www.virginia.org.

RESTRICTIONS
Pets: On leash only. **Fires:** In designated areas. **Alcoholic Beverages:** At site. **Vehicle Maximum Length:** No limit. **Other:** Do not cross any fence lines; adjoining property is private.

TO GET THERE
From junction of Hwy. 208 and US 522, go 5 mi. north on Hwy. 208 and 1.5 mi. north on US 522. Entrance is on the right.

MONROE
Wildwood Campground
MAP, C-2

6252 Elon Rd., 24574. T: (434) 299-5228; www.wildwoodcampground.com.

🚐 ★★★★   ⛺ ★★★★

Beauty: ★★★★	Site Privacy: ★★★
Spaciousness: ★★★	Quiet: ★★★★
Security: ★★★★	Cleanliness: ★★★★
Insect Control: ★★★★	Facilities: ★★★★

Surrounded by the Blue Ridge Mountains near Big Island, Wildwood Campground has 75 wooded sites for tents and RVs, including 40 pull-throughs. The area around Wildwood's stocked fishing lake is especially scenic when fall colors are their most vibrant. Wildwood has a network of hiking trails on its grounds. Natural Bridge, though, is what lures many Wildwood campers. Situated between the Blue Ridge and Appalachian Mountains, Natural Bridge is the site of Natural Bridge Cavern and the Natural Bridge of Virginia. The cavern is 34 stories below the earth's surface. Beware—the tour can be strenuous. Spanning 90 feet, the Natural Bridge of Virginia is regarded as one of the seven natural wonders of the world. If you're not weary from exploring the area's natural sites, you can visit the Natural Bridge Wax Museum, where more than 125 life-size replicas depict Native American folklore.

BASICS
Operated By: Brian, Denise, and Nick Hess. **Open:** All year. **Site Assignment:** Reservations accepted (7-day notice required for cancellations), walk-ins accepted. **Registration:** At campground office. **Fee:** $24–$28; V, MC, D, cash. **Parking:** At designated spot.

FACILITIES
Number of RV-only Sites: 67. **Number of Tent-only Sites:** 8. **Hookups:** Electric (20, 30, 50 amps), water, phone. **Each Site:** Fire ring, picnic table. **Dump Station:** Yes. **Laundry:** Yes. **Pay Phone:** Yes. **Restrooms and Showers:** Yes. **Fuel:** No. **Propane:** Yes. **Internal Roads:** Gravel, in good condition. **RV Service:** Available w/in 25 mi. **Market:** W/in 8 mi. **Restaurant:** W/in 8 mi. **General Store:** Yes. **Vending:** Yes. **Swimming:** Pool. **Playground:** Yes. **Other:** Circus train rides. **Activities:** Rec room, game room, swimming, pond fishing, basketball, shuffleboard, badminton, horseshoes, hiking trails, volleyball. **Nearby Attractions:** Blue Ridge Parkway, Peaks of Otter, Natural Bridge of Virginia, Appalachian Trail, James River, Thomas Jefferson's Poplar Forest, Historic Appomattox, Lynchburg, Lexington Caverns. **Additional Information:** Roanoke Valley CVB, (800) 635-5535, www.visitroanokeva.com.

RESTRICTIONS
Pets: On leash only. **Fires:** At site. **Alcoholic Beverages:** At site. **Vehicle Maximum Length:** No limit.

TO GET THERE
From Blue Ridge Pkwy., go 1 mi. east on Hwy. 130. Entrance is on the left.

MONTROSS
Westmoreland State Park
MAP, B-3

reserve america

1650 State Park Rd., 22520-9717.
T: (804) 493-8821; www.reserveamerica.com.

🚐 ★★★★   ⛺ ★★★★

Beauty: ★★★★	Site Privacy: ★★★
Spaciousness: ★★★	Quiet: ★★★★
Security: ★★★★	Cleanliness: ★★★★
Insect Control: ★★★	Facilities: ★★★★

This park lies on 1,299 acres along the Potomac River on Virginia's Northern Neck. The spectacular cliffs are just one of the highlights of this park. This was one of Virginia's first state parks built by the Civilian Conservation Corps and dedicated on June 15, 1936. The park is flanked by the birthplace of George Washington and birthplace and boyhood home of Robert E. Lee. The Horsehead Cliffs provide visitors with a spectacular view. An Olympic-size swimming pool, camping, boating, beautiful nature trails, and a large children's playground make this park memorable. This park offers hiking, camping, cabins, fishing, boating/kayaking, and swimming. The visitor center, open during the summer months, gives an informative historical and ecological perspective to the coastal plain. Three popular day trips just minutes from the park are George Washington's birthplace, a national monument; Stratford Hall, birthplace and boyhood home of Robert E. Lee; and the Ingleside Winery, which offers winery tours and tastings.

BASICS
Operated By: Virginia State Parks. **Open:** All year. **Site Assignment:** Reservations can be made 11 months in advance. **Registration:** At office. **Fee:** Single, $19–$24; picnic shelter, $30; buddy site, $74; cabin, $54–$97. **Parking:** At site.

FACILITIES
Number of Multipurpose Sites: 196. **Hookups:** Electric (30 amps). **Each Site:** Fire ring, grill. **Dump Station:** Yes. **Laundry:** No. **Pay Phone:** No. **Restrooms and Showers:** Yes. **Fuel:** No. **Propane:** No. **Internal Roads:** Paved. **RV Service:** No. **Market:** No. **Restaurant:** Yes. **General Store:** No. **Vending:** No. **Swimming:** Yes. **Playground:** Yes. **Activities:** Boating, fishing, hiking, picnicking.

RESTRICTIONS
Fires: In designated fireplaces. **Vehicle Maximum Length:** 40 ft.

TO GET THERE
Facing the Potomac River, the park is 6 mi. northwest of Montross and just off Hwy. 3. From Fredericksburg (I-95), take Hwy. 3 east, go about 40 mi. to the park's entrance, turning left onto Hwy. 347. From Tappahannock, take US 360 east to Warsaw. Turn left onto Hwy. 3 west at the second stop light.

Stay on this road until about 6 mi. past Montross. Turn right into the park's entrance on Hwy. 347. From Richmond, take US 360 east, then follow Tappahannock directions. From Tidewater, take Hwy. 17 north to Tappahannock. At the second light, past Lowrey's Restaurant, turn right onto US 360 east, then follow Tappahannock directions.

MOUTH OF WILSON   MAP, A-2
Grayson Highlands State Park

829 Grayson Highland Ln., 24363.
T: (276) 579-7092 or (800) 933-PARK;
www.reserveamerica.com.

🚐 ★★★   ⛺ ★★★★

Beauty: ★★★★	Site Privacy: ★★★
Spaciousness: ★★★	Quiet: ★★★
Security: ★★★★	Cleanliness: ★★★★
Insect Control: ★★★★	Facilities: ★★★

Located adjacent to the Mount Rogers National Recreation Area, Grayson Highlands State Park was originally named Mount Rogers State Park. With elevations as high as 5,089 feet, Grayson Highlands is the loftiest state park in Virginia. From the park's highest point, stunning views await of surrounding mountains—including Mt. Rogers at 5,729 feet. Though the campground itself does not offer many activities, the park does. Anglers cast their lines into Cabin and Wilson Creeks. More than 2 miles of bridle paths wander through the park. The park has nine hiking trails averaging a mile in length. These trails lead to panoramic vistas, scenic waterfalls, and a 200-year-old pioneer cabin. The park also offers access to the Appalachian Trail and trails in the surrounding Jefferson National Forest. Mountain bikers love the Virginia Creeper Trail, a 33.4-mile multiuse trail extending from Whitetop to Abingdon.

BASICS
Operated By: State of Virginia. **Open:** Mar.–Dec. **Site Assignment:** First come, first served; no reservations. **Registration:** At campground office. **Fee:** $19–$24; V, MC. **Parking:** At site.

FACILITIES
Number of RV-only Sites: 75. **Hookups:** Electric (30 amps), water. **Each Site:** Fire ring, picnic table. **Dump Station:** Yes. **Laundry:** No. **Pay Phone:** Yes. **Restrooms and Showers:** Yes. **Fuel:** No. **Propane:** No. **Internal Roads:** Gravel, in good condition. **RV Service:** No. **Market:** W/in 5 mi. **Restaurant:** W/in 5 mi. **General Store:** Yes. **Vending:** Yes. **Swimming:** No. **Playground:** No. **Other:** Visitor center. **Activities:** Hiking trails, biking, horseback riding, fishing, boating. **Nearby Attractions:** Blue Ridge Parkway, Barter Theater, Bristol International Raceway, Mt. Rogers Recreation Area, Jefferson National Forest, Virginia Creeper Trail. **Additional Information:** Grayson County Visitors Bureau, (540) 773-3711, www.grayson.va.us.

RESTRICTIONS
Pets: On leash only, at campsite. **Fires:** In grills, stoves, & fire rings. **Alcoholic Beverages:** No alcohol permitted. **Vehicle Maximum Length:** 40 ft. **Other:** 14-day stay in 30-day period.

TO GET THERE
From Hwy. 16, go 5 mi. west on US 58. Follow signs to campground.

NATURAL BRIDGE   MAP, C-1, C-2
STATION
Yogi Bear's Jellystone Park at Natural Bridge

16 Recreation Lane, 24579.
T: (800) 258-9832 or (540) 291-2727;
www.campnbr.com.

🚐 ★★★★   ⛺ ★★★★

Beauty: ★★★★	Site Privacy: ★★
Spaciousness: ★★	Quiet: ★★★★
Security: ★★★★	Cleanliness: ★★★★
Insect Control: ★★★★	Facilities: ★★★★★

In 1774, Thomas Jefferson purchased the 215-foot-high and 90-foot-long limestone arch called the Natural Bridge from King George III. Today, traffic on US 11 passes over the incredible site in the Shenandoah Valley. Located 5 miles from the bridge, Yogi Bear's Jellystone Park at Natural Bridge is situated in the Blue Ridge Mountains on the James River. Some sites are along the waterfront; others are nestled deep in the woods. Several hiking trails sprout from the adjoining Jefferson National Forest. Lexington, home to Lee's Chapel and the Stonewall Jackson House, is a short drive from the campground. You can take a self-guided tour of the Natural Bridge. Other attractions include the Caverns of Natural Bridge, with passages on three levels as far as 300 feet underground; the Natural Bridge Wax Museum, where wax figures depict important people in Shenandoah Valley history; and the Natural Bridge Zoo, which is the largest zoo in Virginia.

BASICS
Operated By: Maurice and Margie Dettman. **Open:** Mar. 15–Dec. 1. **Site Assignment:** Reservations recommended (1-night deposit required), walk-ins accepted. **Registration:** At campground office. **Fee:** $27–$36; cabins, $60–$120; for 2 people; extra adult, $5.50; children (6–15 years old), $2.50; children (5 and younger), N/C; cable, $4; free Wi-Fi; V, MC, D. **Parking:** At site.

FACILITIES
Number of RV-only Sites: 180. **Number of Tent-only Sites:** 22. **Hookups:** Electric (20, 30, 50 amps), water, cable TV, phone, Wi-Fi. **Each Site:** Fire ring, picnic table. **Dump Station:** Yes. **Laundry:** Yes. **Pay Phone:** Yes. **Restrooms and Showers:** Yes. **Fuel:** No. **Propane:** Yes. **Internal Roads:** Gravel, in good condition. **RV Service:** No. **Market:** W/in 18 mi. **Restaurant:** W/in 1.5 mi. **General Store:** Yes. **Vending:** Yes. **Swimming:** Yes. **Playground:** Yes. **Other:** Swimming lake. **Activities:** Lake swimming, river and pond fishing, boating, canoeing, kayaking, mini-golf, basketball, planned activities on weekends,

horseback riding, sports field, hiking trails, horseshoes. **Nearby Attractions:** James River, Natural Bridge of Virginia, Historic Lexington, Shenandoah National Park, Roanoke, Skyline Drive, Blue Ridge Parkway, Endless Caverns, Luray Caverns. **Additional Information:** Shenandoah Valley Travel Assoc., (540) 740-3132, www.svta.org.

RESTRICTIONS
Pets: On leash only. **Fires:** At site. **Alcoholic Beverages:** At site. **Vehicle Maximum Length:** 45–50 ft.

TO GET THERE
From I-81, take Exit 175 and go 2 mi. north on US 11N, 3 mi. east on Hwy. 130, and 2 mi. southeast on Hwy. 759/782. Entrance is on the left.

NEW POINT   MAP, C-4
New Point Campground

P.O. Box 39, 23125. T: (804) 725-5120;
www.newpointcampground.com.

🚐 ★★★★   ⛺ ★★★★

Beauty: ★★★★	Site Privacy: ★★
Spaciousness: ★★★	Quiet: ★★★★
Security: ★★★★	Cleanliness: ★★★★
Insect Control: ★★★★	Facilities: ★★★★

Situated at the Horn Harbor entrance to Chesapeake Bay, New Point Campground is a place where clean, salt air blows in on ocean breezes. From the campground's observation pier, the 1804 New Point comfort light graces the shoreline as a beacon for ships. Some campsites are semi-wooded, others are waterside. All sites are equipped with full hookups. Crabbing and clamming are popular activities at New Point. Of course, saltwater fishing, swimming, and boating also lure campers. New Point has an inviting white-sand beach, as well as a spacious swimming pool. An hour east of Richmond, New Point is a short drive from attractions in Newport News, Virginia Beach, and Norfolk. Worthwhile day trips include the 25-acre Jamestown Settlement, where costumed interpreters depict life in the 17th century, and the Yorktown Victory Center, which highlights the Revolutionary War at the site of the British surrender to Gen. George Washington.

BASICS
Operated By: Private operator. **Open:** Apr. 1–Oct. 31. **Site Assignment:** Reservations recommended, walk-ins accepted. **Registration:** At campground office. **Fee:** $23–$25; V, MC, D. **Parking:** At site.

FACILITIES
Number of RV-only Sites: 300. **Hookups:** Electric (30 amps), phone. **Each Site:** Fire ring, picnic table. **Dump Station:** Yes. **Laundry:** Yes. **Pay Phone:** Yes. **Restrooms and Showers:** Yes. **Fuel:** No. **Propane:** Yes. **Internal Roads:** Gravel & dirt, in good condition. **RV Service:** No. **Market:** W/in 7 mi. **Restaurant:** W/in 7 mi. **General Store:** Yes. **Vending:** Yes. **Swimming:** Yes. **Playground:** Yes. **Other:** White-sand beach on Chesapeake Bay. **Activities:** Crabbing, clamming, ocean fishing, game room, rec hall, wading pool, ocean swimming, mini-golf, planned activities, sports field, horseshoes, hiking trails, volleyball. **Nearby Attractions:** Chesapeake

Bay, Newport News, Colonial Williamsburg, Yorktown, Historic Jamestown Settlement. **Additional Information:** Mathews County Chamber of Commerce, (804) 725-9029, www.mathewsva.org.

RESTRICTIONS

Pets: On leash only. No pets permitted in rental units. **Fires:** At site. **Alcoholic Beverages:** At site. **Vehicle Maximum Length:** No limit.

TO GET THERE

From Hwy. 198 in Mathews, go 7 mi. southeast on Hwy. 14E, 0.75 mi. east on Hwy. 602, and 500 ft. south on Hwy. 601. Entrance is on the left.

NEWPORT NEWS MAP, C-3, C-4
Newport News Park Campground

13564 Jefferson Ave., 23603. T: (800) 203-8322; www.newport-news.va.us/parks.

🚐 ★★★   ▲ ★★★

Beauty: ★★★★	Site Privacy: ★★★
Spaciousness: ★★★	Quiet: ★★★
Security: ★★★★★	Cleanliness: ★★★★
Insect Control: ★★★★	Facilities: ★★★

Adjacent to the Lee Hall Reservoir, Newport News Park Campground offers 188 wooded sites in one of the largest municipal parks east of the Mississippi River. Newport News Park has several special events throughout the year, including the Children's Festival of Friends, the Newport News Fall Festival of Folklife, and Celebration in Lights. In Newport News, visitors flock to the Mariners Museum, where the history of shipbuilding, ocean navigation, and cartography are explored; the Virginia Living Museum, which displays a 60-foot scale model of the James River; and the Virginia War Museum, which contains more than 60,000 artifacts related to US military history from the Revolutionary War to present day.

BASICS

Operated By: City of Newport News. **Open:** All year. **Site Assignment:** Reservations and walk-ins accepted. **Registration:** At campground headquarters. **Fee:** $18.50–$21; V, MC. **Parking:** At designated area.

FACILITIES

Number of RV-only Sites: 164. **Number of Tent-only Sites:** 24. **Hookups:** Electric (20, 30 amps), water. **Each Site:** Fire ring, grill. **Dump Station:** Yes. **Laundry:** Yes. **Pay Phone:** Yes. **Restrooms and Showers:** Yes. **Fuel:** No. **Propane:** Yes. **Internal Roads:** Paved, in good condition. **RV Service:** No. **Market:** W/in 2 mi. **Restaurant:** W/in 2 mi. **General Store:** Yes. **Vending:** Yes. **Playground:** Yes. **Other:** Lee Hall Reservoir. **Activities:** Boating, canoeing, boat rentals, lake fishing, hiking trails, golf, driving range, putting green, disc golf, bike rentals, planned activities, horseback riding, sports field, horseshoes, volleyball. **Nearby Attractions:** Virginia Living Museum, Mariners Museum, Lee Hall Mansion, Norfolk, Virginia Beach, Yorktown, Historic Jamestown Settlement, Colonial Williamsburg. **Additional Information:** Virginia Tourism Corp., (800) 371-8164, www.virginia.org.

RESTRICTIONS

Pets: On leash only. **Fires:** At site. **Alcoholic Beverages:** No alcohol permitted. **Vehicle Maximum Length:** No limit. **Other:** 21-day stay limit.

TO GET THERE

From I-64, take Exit 250B and go 1 mi. northwest on Hwy. 143. Entrance is on the right.

PETERSBURG MAP, C-3
Picture Lake Campground

7818 Boydton Plank Rd., 23803. T: (804) 861-0174.

🚐 ★★★★   ▲ ★★★★

Beauty: ★★★★	Site Privacy: ★★
Spaciousness: ★★★	Quiet: ★★★★
Security: ★★★★	Cleanliness: ★★★★
Insect Control: ★★★★	Facilities: ★★★★

Situated on Picture Lake west of Petersburg, Picture Lake Campground has shaded sites (some located on the water), 120 of them pull-throughs. With its proximity to Petersburg, Picture Lake is near several attractions, many of which relate to the Civil War. The 2,700-acre Petersburg National Battlefield is actually the scene where 10 months of skirmishes took place on several battlefields. The visitor center is the starting point for a 4-mile self-guided walking tour. If you choose to drive the countryside, an audiotape is available for a 37-mile driving tour. Pamplin Historical Park and the National Museum of the Civil War Soldier serves a dual purpose. The park preserves the battlefield of the April 2, 1865 event when Union troops overwhelmed Confederate defense lines. The museum describes the daily life of a Civil War soldier. Picture Lake is also 40 miles south of Richmond and 15 miles west of water activities on the James River.

BASICS

Operated By: Anne Blazek. **Open:** All year. **Site Assignment:** Reservations and walk-ins accepted. **Registration:** At campground office. **Fee:** $23–$25; V, MC, AE, D. **Parking:** At site.

FACILITIES

Number of RV-only Sites: 207. **Hookups:** Electric (20, 30, 50 amps), water, phone. **Each Site:** Fire ring, picnic table. **Dump Station:** Yes. **Laundry:** Yes. **Pay Phone:** Yes. **Restrooms and Showers:** Yes. **Fuel:** No. **Propane:** Yes. **Internal Roads:** Gravel & paved, in good condition. **RV Service:** No. **Market:** W/in 3 mi. **Restaurant:** W/in 3 mi. **General Store:** Yes. **Vending:** Yes. **Swimming:** Yes. **Playground:** Yes. **Other:** Picture Lake. **Activities:** Swimming, boating, canoeing, kayaking, boat rentals, lake fishing, basketball, shuffleboard, badminton, sports field, horseshoes, hiking trails, volleyball. **Nearby Attractions:** Petersburg National Battlefield, Centre Hill Mansion, Ft. Lee, Lee's Retreat Driving Tour, National Museum of the Civil War Solider, Pamplin Park Civil War Site, Siege Museum, Trapezium House. **Additional Information:** Petersburg Visitors Center, (800) 368-3595.

RESTRICTIONS

Pets: On leash only. **Fires:** At site. **Alcoholic Beverages:** At site. **Vehicle Maximum Length:** No limit.

TO GET THERE

From I-95, go 4.5 mi. southwest on I-85 to Exit 63A. Then go 3 mi. south on US 1. Entrance is on the right.

POWHATAN MAP, C-3
Cozy Acres Campground

2177 Ridge Rd., 23139. T: (804) 598-2470; www.cozyacres.com.

🚐 ★★★★   ▲ ★★★★

Beauty: ★★★★	Site Privacy: ★★★★
Spaciousness: ★★★★	Quiet: ★★★★
Security: ★★★★	Cleanliness: ★★★★
Insect Control: ★★★★	Facilities: ★★★★

Bordered on the north by the James River and on the south by the Appomattox River, Powhatan is 20 miles west of Richmond. Cozy Acres Campground is a clean and quiet park with spacious, semi-wooded sites, including 97 pull-throughs. Sites on the north end of the campground are close to two of the three ponds. With its remote location and tranquil setting, Cozy Acres is an ideal place to camp if you want to visit the attractions in Richmond but prefer to stay away from the traffic and crowds of Virginia's capital city. The State Capitol was designed by Thomas Jefferson and is the site where Aaron Burr was tried for treason and Gen. Robert E. Lee accepted command of Virginia's forces. Another interesting spot is the Hollywood Cemetery, where notable figures like James Monroe, James Tyler, and Jefferson Davis are buried, as arc 18,000 Confederate soldiers.

BASICS

Operated By: Private operator. **Open:** Apr. 1–Dec. 1. **Site Assignment:** Reservations and walk-ins accepted. **Registration:** At campground office. **Fee:** $30–$34; V, MC. **Parking:** At designated area.

FACILITIES

Number of RV-only Sites: 105. **Number of Tent-only Sites:** 8. **Hookups:** Electric (20, 30, 50 amps), water, phone. **Each Site:** Fire ring, picnic table. **Dump Station:** Yes. **Laundry:** Yes. **Pay Phone:** Yes. **Restrooms and Showers:** Yes. **Fuel:** No. **Propane:** Yes. **Internal Roads:** Gravel & paved, in good condition. **RV Service:** No. **Market:** W/in 5 mi. **Restaurant:** W/in 4 mi. **General Store:** Yes. **Vending:** Yes. **Swimming:** Yes. **Playground:** Yes. **Other:** Three fishing ponds. **Activities:** Game room, rec hall, swimming, wading pool, sports field, horseshoes, hiking trails, volleyball. **Nearby Attractions:** Richmond, Edgar Allan Poe Museum, Richmond International Speedway, Museum and White House of the Confederacy, Paramount's Kings Dominion, Virginia Museum of Fine Arts. **Additional Information:** Richmond CVB, (800) 370-9004, www.richmondva.org.

RESTRICTIONS

Pets: On leash only. **Fires:** At site. **Alcoholic Beverages:** At site. **Vehicle Maximum Length:** No limit.

TO GET THERE

From US 522, go 4 mi. west on US 60 and 2 mi. south on Hwy. 627. Entrance is on the right.

QUINBY   MAP, C-4
Thousand Trails—Virginia Landing

40226 Upshur Neck Rd., 23423.
T: (800) 723-6226; www.thousandtrails.com.

🚐 ★★★★   ⛺ ★★★★★

Beauty: ★★★★   Site Privacy: ★★★★
Spaciousness: ★★★★   Quiet: ★★★★
Security: ★★★★★   Cleanliness: ★★★★
Insect Control: ★★★★   Facilities: ★★★★

Situated on the Virginia Peninsula along Hog Island Bay on the Atlantic Ocean, Thousand Trails—Virginia Landing is a beautiful 800-acre preserve with open and shaded sites. With its perch on the shorefront, this Thousand Trails facility offers ample boating and fishing opportunities. Located 35 miles from the Maryland line and an hour's drive from Virginia Beach, the campground has a 9-hole pitch-and-putt golf course, mini-golf course, adult lodge, and a well-stocked country store among other features. Assateague Island, which includes Chincoteague National Wildlife Refuge and Assateague Island National Seashore, is a short drive away. The 37-mile barrier island combines stretches of ocean, sand dunes, forests, and marshes teeming with wildlife, including Sitka deer and the famous Chincoteague wild ponies. Thousand Trails is about an hour's drive to the NASA Visitor Center on Wallops Island.

BASICS
Operated By: Thousand Trails. **Open:** Apr. 1–Oct. 31. **Site Assignment:** Reservations and walk-ins accepted. **Registration:** At campground office. **Fee:** $25; V, MC, AE, D. **Parking:** At site.

FACILITIES
Number of RV-only Sites: 215. **Hookups:** Electric (20, 30 amps), water, phone. **Each Site:** Grill, picnic table. **Dump Station:** Yes. **Laundry:** Yes. **Pay Phone:** Yes. **Restrooms and Showers:** Yes. **Fuel:** No. **Propane:** Yes. **Internal Roads:** Gravel & paved, in good condition. **RV Service:** No. **Market:** W/in 5 mi. **Restaurant:** W/in 5 mi. **General Store:** Yes. **Vending:** Yes. **Swimming:** Yes. **Playground:** Yes. **Other:** Adult & family lodges. **Activities:** River swimming, game room, rec hall, boating, canoeing, kayaking, boat rentals, ocean and pond fishing, mini-golf, bike rentals, shuffleboard, sports field, horseshoes, hiking trails, volleyball. **Nearby Attractions:** Assateague Island National Seashore, Chincoteague National Wildlife Refuge. **Additional Information:** Eastern Shore of Virginia Tourism Commission, (757) 787-2460, www.esva.net/~esvatourism.

RESTRICTIONS
Pets: On leash only. **Fires:** At site. **Alcoholic Beverages:** At site. **Vehicle Maximum Length:** No limit.

TO GET THERE
From SR 182, go 6.75 mi. south on SR 605. Entrance is at the end.

REEDVILLE   MAP, B-4
Chesapeake Bay/
Smith Island KOA

382 Campground Rd., 22539.
T: (804) 453-3430 or (804) 453-4051;
www.eaglesnest.net/smithislandcruise.

🚐 ★★★★   ⛺ ★★★★

Beauty: ★★★★   Site Privacy: ★★★
Spaciousness: ★★★   Quiet: ★★★★
Security: ★★★★   Cleanliness: ★★★★
Insect Control: ★★★★   Facilities: ★★★★

Located on Slough Creek near Reedville, Chesapeake Bay/Smith Island KOA has one of the most interesting spots in Virginia. There are shaded waterfront sites, including 55 pull-throughs. Cabins are also available for rent. The campground is home to the Smith Island Cruise, which departs from the premises. Aboard the Capt. Evans, passengers see historic Smith Point, where the Potomac River meets the Chesapeake Bay, as well as the Smith Point Lighthouse 2 miles offshore. Known as the Soft-Shelled Crab Capital of the World, Smith Island has three picturesque fishing villages: Ewell, Rhodes Point, and Tylerton, each on its own island in this archipelago of the Chesapeake, with interlacing creeks, canals, marsh, and meadows. Smith Island's roots date back to 1608, when Capt. John Smith sailed up Chesapeake Bay and came ashore on the island that now bears his name. The campground is also near Hughlett Point Nature Preserve on Chesapeake Bay, where hiking and bird-watching are popular activities.

BASICS
Operated By: KOA. **Open:** Apr. 1–Nov. 1. **Site Assignment:** Reservations and walk-ins accepted. **Registration:** At campground office. **Fee:** $30–$50; V, MC. **Parking:** At designated area.

FACILITIES
Number of RV-only Sites: 86. **Hookups:** Electric (20, 30, 50 amps), water. **Each Site:** Picnic table. **Dump Station:** Yes. **Laundry:** Yes. **Pay Phone:** Yes. **Restrooms and Showers:** Yes. **Fuel:** No. **Propane:** No. **Internal Roads:** Dirt & gravel, in good condition. **RV Service:** No. **Market:** W/in 3 mi. **Restaurant:** W/in 4 mi. **General Store:** Yes. **Vending:** Yes. **Swimming:** Yes. **Playground:** Yes. **Other:** Smith Island Cruises. **Activities:** Swimming, boating, canoeing, boat rentals, river fishing, mini-golf, planned activities on weekends. **Nearby Attractions:** Smith Point, Smith Island, Chesapeake Bay, Colonial Williamsburg, Stratford Hall Plantation, George Washington's Birthplace and National Monument, Ingleside Winery. **Additional Information:** Virginia Tourism Corp., (800) 371-8164, www.virginia.org.

RESTRICTIONS
Pets: On leash only. **Fires:** At site. **Alcoholic Beverages:** At site. **Vehicle Maximum Length:** No limit.

TO GET THERE
From US 360, go 2.5 mi. east on CR 652/CR 650 and 0.5 mi. northeast on Campground Rd. Entrance is on the right.

RESTON   MAP, A-3
Lake Fairfax Park

1400 Lake Fairfax Dr., 22090.
T: (703) 471-5415 or (703) 757-9242;
www.co.fairfax.va.us.

🚐 ★★★★   ⛺ ★★★★

Beauty: ★★★★   Site Privacy: ★★
Spaciousness: ★★   Quiet: ★★★
Security: ★★★★   Cleanliness: ★★★★
Insect Control: ★★★★   Facilities: ★★★★

With a carousel, playgrounds, and one of the nicest municipal water parks you will find anywhere, Lake Fairfax Park in Reston was definitely designed with children in mind. The 20-acre Lake Fairfax provides a tranquil setting for fishing and pedal boating. The park's star attraction is the Water Mine Family Swimmin' Hole, a western-themed activity pool with an acre of interactive play features, including Box Canyon Crossing, slides, and flumes. The water park is circled by Rattlesnake River, which has a 2.5-mile-per-hour current that gently nudges the tubes along. Kids careen off covered wagons, float on rattlesnakes, and dash through showers tipped from water-filled ore carts. Of the campground's 136 sites, 70 have electric hookups. These sites offer little privacy. With the Metro Rail, Washington, D.C., is a short ride away. From Lake Fairfax Park, the Metro Rail's closest stop is the Nutley St. or Dunn Loring station, about 10 miles away.

BASICS
Operated By: Fairfax County Park Authority. **Open:** Mar. 1–Dec. 1. **Site Assignment:** Reservations and walk-ins accepted. **Registration:** At campground office. **Fee:** $20–$25; V, MC. **Parking:** At designated spot.

FACILITIES
Number of RV-only Sites: 136. **Hookups:** Electric (30 amps). **Each Site:** Grill, picnic table. **Dump Station:** Yes. **Laundry:** Yes. **Pay Phone:** Yes. **Restrooms and Showers:** Yes. **Fuel:** No. **Propane:** No. **Internal Roads:** Gravel, in good condition. **RV Service:** No. **Market:** W/in 4 mi. **Restaurant:** W/in 2 mi. **General Store:** Yes. **Vending:** Yes. **Swimming:** Pool. **Playground:** Yes. **Other:** Lake Fairfax, water park. **Activities:** Swimming, waterslide, wading pool, paddle-boat rentals, lake fishing, sports field, hiking trails. **Nearby Attractions:** Washington, D.C. **Additional Information:** Washington, D.C., CVB, (202) 789-7000, www.washington.org.

RESTRICTIONS
Pets: On leash only. **Fires:** At site. **Alcoholic Beverages:** At site. **Vehicle Maximum Length:** 35 ft. **Other:** No swimming permitted in lake.

TO GET THERE
From I-495, take Exit 10 and go 6.5 mi. northwest on Hwy. 7 and south on Hwy. 606 to Lake Fairfax Dr. Entrance is on the left.

ROANOKE MAP, C-1
Morris Hill Spur—George Washington and Jefferson National Forest

reserve america

5162 Valley Pointe Parkway, 24091.
T: (540) 962-2214; www.reserveamerica.com.

🚐 ★★★★ ⛺ ★★★★

Beauty: ★★★★	Site Privacy: ★★★★
Spaciousness: ★★★	Quiet: ★★★
Security: ★★★★	Cleanliness: ★★★★
Insect Control: ★★★★	Facilities: ★★★★

This national forest outside of Covington, Virginia, just a few miles away from West Virginia, has an altitude of 9,000 feet and offers 54 sites in the woods. Each site has a tent pad, lantern post, and a fire pit with grill. The sites are far enough apart that you will not disturb your fellow campers, and bathrooms with hot and cold water are close by. You have Lake Moomaw and the Gaithright Dam within a 5-mile radius, which makes for excellent fishing and water sports. The lake has a small sandy beach and beautiful views. If you like being in tune with nature, this is the perfect place to be. Morris Hill Spur is located within the George Washington National Forest was established in 1917, and Jefferson National Forest was established in 1936. The two forests were administratively combined in 1995. North of the James River the forest is called George Washington National Forest. South of the James River it is called Jefferson National Forest. The forest covers 1.8 million acres (7,300 km) of land in the Appalachian Mountains of Virginia, West Virginia, and Kentucky. The forest extends the along the entire length of the Blue Ridge Mountains and the Alleghany Mountains to the North Carolina border. Just over one third of the forest is actively used for timber harvesting, with the bulk of that used for furniture manufacturing and pulp for paper products. Approximately one million acres (4,000 km) of the forest are remote and undeveloped and 89,862 acres have been designated as wilderness areas, which eliminates future development.

BASICS

Operated By: U.S. Forest Service. **Open:** Apr. 27–Oct. 28. **Site Assignment:** Reservations must be made at least 10 days in advance. **Registration:** At office. **Fee:** Single, $10. **Parking:** At park.

FACILITIES

Number of Multipurpose Sites: 64. **Hookups:** None. **Each Site:** Call ahead. **Dump Station:** No. **Laundry:** No. **Pay Phone:** Yes. **Restrooms and Showers:** Yes. **Fuel:** No. **Propane:** No. **Internal Roads:** Paved. **RV Service:** No. **Market:** No. **Restaurant:** No. **General Store:** No. **Vending:** No. **Swimming:** Yes. **Playground:** Yes. **Other:** Tents are allowed on tent pads only. **Activities:** Boating, hiking.

RESTRICTIONS

Pets: Restrained or on a leash at all times while in developed recreation areas. **Fires:** In fire rings, stoves, grills, or fireplaces provided for that purpose. **Alcoholic Beverages:** Not allowed. **Vehicle Maximum Length:** Call ahead.

TO GET THERE

From Covington take US 220 north to SR 687, left on SR 687 to intersection of SR 641, left on SR 641 (becomes SR 666). Continue with SR 666 to SR 605 and bear right. SR 605 is marked with USFS direction signs to campground.

SCOTTSBURG MAP, C-2
Staunton River State Park

reserve america

1170 Staunton Trail, 24589.
T: (434) 572-4623 or (800) 933-PARK;
www.reserveamerica.com.

🚐 ★★★★ ⛺ ★★★★

Beauty: ★★★	Site Privacy: ★★★
Spaciousness: ★★★	Quiet: ★★★
Security: ★★★★	Cleanliness: ★★★★
Insect Control: ★★★★	Facilities: ★★★

Staunton River State Park is made up of 1,597 acres along the shoreline of the John H. Kerr Reservoir (also known as Buggs Island Lake), as well as the Dan and Staunton Rivers. Set under a forest of oak and pine trees, the campsites are spread in a figure-eight, with the bathhouse and hot showers in the center. Staunton River State Park is actually located on a peninsula at the narrow end of Buggs Island Lake. Hikers, equestrians, and bikers take advantage of the 7.5-mile River Bank Multiuse Trail, which follows the peninsula. Swimming is not allowed from the park's shoreline, so campers must cool themselves in the park's swimming pool. A short drive away is the Staunton River Battlefield Park, where Confederate soldiers stymied Union troops at a bridge that crossed the river. The 300-acre battlefield has a visitor center and a self-guided walking trail.

BASICS

Operated By: State of Virginia. **Open:** Mar.–Dec. **Site Assignment:** First come, first served; no reservations. **Registration:** At campground office. **Fee:** $19–$24; V, MC. **Parking:** At site.

FACILITIES

Number of RV-only Sites: 34. **Number of Tent-only Sites:** 14. **Hookups:** Electric (30 amps). **Each Site:** Fire ring, picnic table. **Dump Station:** Yes. **Laundry:** No. **Pay Phone:** Yes. **Restrooms and Showers:** Yes. **Fuel:** No. **Propane:** No. **Internal Roads:** Paved, in good condition. **RV Service:** No. **Market:** W/in 9 mi. **Restaurant:** W/in 9 mi. **General Store:** No. **Vending:** Yes. **Swimming:** Yes. **Playground:** Yes. **Other:** John H Kerr Reservoir (Buggs Island Lake). **Activities:** Swimming, boating, canoeing, boat rentals, lake fishing, planned activities, tennis court, hiking trails. **Nearby Attractions:** John H. Kerr Reservoir, Lake Gaston. **Additional Information:** Virginia Tourism Corp., (800) 371-8164, www.virginia.org.

RESTRICTIONS

Pets: On leash only; $3 per night. **Fires:** In camp stove or fire ring. **Alcoholic Beverages:** No alcohol permitted. **Vehicle Maximum Length:** 30 ft. **Other:** 14-day stay limit in 30-day period.

TO GET THERE

From Scottsburg, go 9 mi. southeast on Hwy. 344. Follow signs to park.

SPOTSYLVANIA MAP, B-3
Lake Anna State Park

reserve america

6800 Lawyers Rd., 22553-9645. T: (540) 854-5503;
www.reserveamerica.com.

🚐 ★★★★ ⛺ ★★★★

Beauty: ★★★★	Site Privacy: ★★★
Spaciousness: ★★★	Quiet: ★★★★
Security: ★★★★	Cleanliness: ★★★★
Insect Control: ★★★	Facilities: ★★★★

The land in Lake Anna State Park used to be known as Gold Hill and contained the Goodwin Gold Mine. Gold was first discovered in 1829, with mining reaching its peak in the 1880s. The last gold to be found was in a zinc mine during the 1940s. In 1971 Lake Anna was created to serve as a water coolant for Virginia Power's nuclear plant. In 1972 work began on the acquisition and development of a water-oriented state park. Lake Anna State Park opened in 1983. While boating and fishing on this beautiful lake are major attractions, these are only some of the park's offerings. Lakefront picnic areas and wooded hiking trails are also popular. During the summer, interpretive programs on the nature and history of the area complement exhibits and displays in the visitor center. Lake Anna State Park has 13 miles of hiking trails, lakeshore picnicking, a guarded swimming beach, a children's play area, a boat ramp, a food concession stand, a bathhouse, and a children's and wheelchair-accessible fishing pond.

BASICS

Operated By: Virginia State Parks. **Open:** All year. **Site Assignment:** Reservations can be made 11 months in advance. **Registration:** At office. **Fee:** Single, $23–$29; single cabin, $83–$124. **Parking:** At site.

FACILITIES

Number of Multipurpose Sites: 82. **Hookups:** None. **Dump Station:** No. **Laundry:** No. **Pay Phone:** No. **Restrooms and Showers:** Yes. **Fuel:** No. **Propane:** No. **Internal Roads:** Paved. **RV Service:** No. **Market:** No. **Restaurant:** No. **General Store:** Yes. **Vending:** Yes. **Swimming:** Yes. **Playground:** Yes. **Other:** Primitive group camping available by permit only. **Activities:** Beach, biking, boating, fishing, hiking, picnicking.

RESTRICTIONS

Fires: In designated fireplaces.

TO GET THERE

The park lies adjacent to Hwy. 601 off Hwy. 208, 25 mi. southwest of Fredericksburg and 60 mi. northwest of Richmond.

STAFFORD   MAP, B-3
Aquia Pines Camp Resort

3071 Jefferson Davis Hwy., 22554.
T: (800) 726-1710 or (540) 659-3447;
www.gocampingamerica.com/aquiapines.

🚐 ★★★★   ⛺ ★★★★

Beauty: ★★★	Site Privacy: ★★
Spaciousness: ★★	Quiet: ★★★★
Security: ★★★★	Cleanliness: ★★★★
Insect Control: ★★★★	Facilities: ★★★★

Located southwest of Washington, D.C. and northeast of Fredericksburg, Aquia Pines Camp Resort is definitely a recommended base for exploring the nation's capital and the surrounding historical sites. The sites are open and wooded. They are clean and well maintained, but offer little privacy. This is a campground with very clean bathroom and shower facilities. Aquia Pines offers daylong guided tours aboard the campground's comfortable bus. Stops include the White House, Capitol Hill, and Arlington National Cemetery among other monuments. Aquia Pines also offers shuttle bus service to the Smithsonian Museum. Recreation at the campground includes a large swimming pool and a mini-golf course. Aquia Pines is 10 minutes from a free private beach on the Potomac River. The Fredericksburg and Spotsylvania National Military Park and George Washington's Mt. Vernon are a short drive from the campground, as is Washington's birthplace, Wakefield, and his childhood home, Ferry Farm.

BASICS
Operated By: Private operator. **Open:** All year. **Site Assignment:** Reservations and walk-ins accepted. **Registration:** At campground headquarters. **Fee:** $39–$50, V, MC. **Parking:** At designated area.

FACILITIES
Number of RV-only Sites: 102. **Number of Tent-only Sites:** 18. **Hookups:** Electric (20, 30, 50 amps), water, cable TV, phone. **Each Site:** Picnic table. **Dump Station:** Yes. **Laundry:** Yes. **Pay Phone:** Yes. **Restrooms and Showers:** Yes. **Fuel:** No. **Propane:** Yes. **Internal Roads:** Gravel & paved, in good condition. **RV Service:** No. **Market:** W/in 2 mi. **Restaurant:** W/in 2 mi. **General Store:** Yes. **Vending:** Yes. **Swimming:** Yes. **Playground:** Yes. **Other:** Washington, D.C. tours aboard Aquia Pines tour bus. **Activities:** Rec hall, game room, swimming, mini-golf, basketball, planned activities on weekends, horseshoes, volleyball. **Nearby Attractions:** Washington, D.C., Fredericksburg and Spotsylvania National Military Park, Manassas National Battlefield Park, Mt. Vernon. **Additional Information:** Virginia Tourism Corp., (800) 371-8164, www.virginia.org.

RESTRICTIONS
Pets: On leash only. **Fires:** At site. **Alcoholic Beverages:** At site. **Vehicle Maximum Length:** No limit.

TO GET THERE
From I-95, take Exit 143A, go north at light onto US 1, then 0.5 mi. north on US 1. Entrance is on the left.

STAUNTON   MAP, B-2
Shenandoah Valley KOA

P.O. Box 98, 296 Riner Lane, 24482.
T: (540) 248-2746 or (800) 562-9949;
www.koa.com.

🚐 ★★★★   ⛺ ★★★★

Beauty: ★★★★	Site Privacy: ★★★
Spaciousness: ★★★	Quiet: ★★★
Security: ★★★★	Cleanliness: ★★★★
Insect Control: ★★★★	Facilities: ★★★★

Located in the Shenandoah Valley, where the Skyline Drive and Blue Ridge Parkway wind past stunning mountain vistas, Shenandoah Valley KOA is bordered by 1.5 miles of the Middle River, where a waterfall cascades and outdoor enthusiasts enjoy tubing, boating, and fishing. The campground has its own stocked fishing lake, a swimming pool, and four indoor whirlpools. There's also a spacious game room. On weekends Memorial Day–Labor Day, a country band performs on Saturday nights, and several special events are held. The mostly wooded sites include 104 pull-throughs. With its proximity to Shenandoah National Park, the campground is near numerous hiking trails and scenic overlooks. In nearby Staunton, the Museum of American Frontier Culture consists of working farms from the 17th, 18th, and 19th centuries, representing English, German, Irish, and American farmers. Presidential history enthusiasts will want to visit the Woodrow Wilson Birthplace and National Museum, also in Staunton.

BASICS
Operated By: KOA. **Open:** Mar. 15–Nov. 1. **Site Assignment:** Reservations and walk-ins accepted. **Registration:** At campground office. **Fee:** $34–$53; V, MC, D. **Parking:** At site.

FACILITIES
Number of RV-only Sites: 100. **Number of Tent-only Sites:** 50. **Hookups:** Electric (20, 30, 50 amps), water, cable TV, phone. **Each Site:** Fire ring, picnic table. **Dump Station:** Yes. **Laundry:** Yes. **Pay Phone:** Yes. **Restrooms and Showers:** Yes. **Fuel:** No. **Propane:** Yes. **Internal Roads:** Gravel & paved, in good condition. **RV Service:** No. **Market:** W/in 2 mi. **Restaurant:** W/in 2 mi. **General Store:** Yes. **Vending:** Yes. **Swimming:** Yes. **Playground:** Yes. **Other:** Middle River. **Activities:** Lake and river fishing, rec hall, game room, swimming, whirlpool, basketball, planned activities, sports field, horseshoes, hiking trails, volleyball. **Nearby Attractions:** Shenandoah National Park, Statler Brothers Museum, Blue Ridge Parkway, Skyline Drive, Frontier Culture Museum, Woodrow Wilson Birthplace and Museum. **Additional Information:** Shenandoah Valley Travel Assoc., (540) 740-3132, www.svta.org.

RESTRICTIONS
Pets: On leash only. **Fires:** At site. **Alcoholic Beverages:** At site. **Vehicle Maximum Length:** No limit.

TO GET THERE
From I-81, take Exit 227 and go 1 mi. west on Hwy. 612, 0.5 mi. north on US 11, and 1 mi. west on CR 781. Entrance is on the left.

STAUNTON   MAP, B-2
Walnut Hills Campground

484 Walnut Hills Rd., 24401.
T: (540) 337-3920 or (800) 699-2568;
www.walnuthillscampground.com.

🚐 ★★★★   ⛺ ★★★★

Beauty: ★★★★	Site Privacy: ★★★
Spaciousness: ★★★	Quiet: ★★★★
Security: ★★★★	Cleanliness: ★★★★
Insect Control: ★★★★	Facilities: ★★★★

Located in Staunton, the Queen City of the Shenandoah Valley, Walnut Hills Campground is a quiet and comfortable base for exploring Shenandoah National Park, Skyline Drive, and the Blue Ridge Parkway. The open and semi-wooded sites are large and level, including 20 pull-throughs. Some of the sites are situated on the waterfront, and the campground has a separate area for tenters. We like the sites located on Kerplonken Lake; the sites on the west end are also inviting. The lake is stocked with bass, perch, blue gill, and channel catfish. Cabins and cottages are available for rent. The south tip of Shenandoah National Park is a short drive from Walnut Hills. Along Skyline Drive in Shenandoah National Park, there are an estimated 70 overlooks where you can stretch your legs and gaze at the mountains and valleys; hiking trails also sprout from numerous points in the park.

BASICS
Operated By: Albrecht family. **Open:** Mar. 1–Nov. 15. **Site Assignment:** Reservations recommended (holidays require 3-night min. and $30 deposit), walk-ins accepted. **Registration:** At campground office. **Fee:** $19–$27; V, MC. **Parking:** At site.

FACILITIES
Number of RV-only Sites: 108. **Number of Tent-only Sites:** 25. **Hookups:** Electric (20, 30, 50 amps), water, cable TV, phone. **Each Site:** Fire ring, picnic table. **Dump Station:** Yes. **Laundry:** Yes. **Pay Phone:** Yes. **Restrooms and Showers:** Yes. **Fuel:** No. **Propane:** Yes. **Internal Roads:** Gravel & paved, in good condition. **RV Service:** No. **Market:** W/in 4 mi. **Restaurant:** W/in 4 mi. **General Store:** Yes. **Vending:** Yes. **Swimming:** Yes. **Playground:** Yes. **Other:** Fishing lake. **Activities:** Swimming, game room, rec hall, lake fishing, wading pool, horseshoes, volleyball. **Nearby Attractions:** Historic Lexington, Shenandoah National Park, Statler Brothers Museum, Blue Ridge Parkway, Skyline Drive, Frontier Culture Museum, Woodrow Wilson Birthplace and Museum. **Additional Information:** Shenandoah Valley Travel Assoc., (540) 740-3132, www.svta.org.

RESTRICTIONS
Pets: On leash only. **Fires:** At site. **Alcoholic Beverages:** At site. **Vehicle Maximum Length:** 50 ft.

TO GET THERE
From I-81, take Exit 217 and go 0.5 mi. west on Hwy. 654, 1.5 mi. south on US 11, and 1 mi. east on Hwy. 655. Entrance is on the left.

STUART   MAP, C-1
Fairy Stone State Park

reserve america

967 Fairy Stone Lake Dr., 24171-9588.
T: (276) 930-2424 or (800) 933-PARK;
www.reserveamerica.com.

🚐 ★★★   ▲ ★★★

Beauty: ★★★	Site Privacy: ★★★
Spaciousness: ★★★	Quiet: ★★★
Security: ★★★★★	Cleanliness: ★★★★
Insect Control: ★★★	Facilities: ★★★

Fairy stones are brown staurolite, a combination of silica, iron, and aluminum. Together, these minerals crystallize in twin form, accounting for the cross like structure. These stones are also found in the mountains of North Carolina and in Switzerland, but nowhere else in the world are they found in such abundance and shaped so nearly like crosses as in the vicinity of Fairy Stone State Park. Fairy Stone's campground has 51 sites. Each site is shaded by a pine grove and scattered oaks. The best place to search for the fairy stones is within a 2.5-mile drive from the park. At Haynes Store, an old gas station on US 57, a sign leads visitors to a streambed where the crosses can be collected. Campers at Fairy Stone aren't limited to searching for rocks. The park consists of 4,868 acres, including 168-acre Fairy Stone Lake, where fishing, swimming, and boating are options.

BASICS

Operated By: State of Virginia. **Open:** Mar.–Dec. 1. **Site Assignment:** Reservations and walk-ins accepted. **Registration:** At campground office. **Fee:** $24; plus tax; V, MC, check, cash. **Parking:** At site.

FACILITIES

Number of RV-only Sites: 50. **Hookups:** Electric (15 amps), water. **Each Site:** Fire ring, picnic table. **Dump Station:** Yes. **Laundry:** No. **Pay Phone:** Yes. **Restrooms and Showers:** Yes. **Fuel:** No. **Propane:** No. **Internal Roads:** Gravel, in good condition. **RV Service:** Yes. **Market:** W/in 5 mi. **Restaurant:** W/in 5 mi. **General Store:** No. **Vending:** Yes. **Swimming:** Lake. **Playground:** Yes. **Other:** Lodge & cabins. **Activities:** Lake swimming, boating, lake fishing, canoeing, boat rentals, hiking trails. **Nearby Attractions:** Blue Ridge Parkway, Philpott Lake, Virginia Museum of Natural History, J.E.B. Stuart Birthplace, covered bridges. **Additional Information:** Roanoke Valley CVB, (800) 635-5535, www.visitroanokeva.com.

RESTRICTIONS

Pets: On leash only. **Fires:** At site. **Alcoholic Beverages:** No alcohol permitted. **Vehicle Maximum Length:** 30 ft. **Other:** 14-day stay limit in 30-day period.

TO GET THERE

From I-81, take I-581 to US 220, turn right onto US 57 and right onto SR 346.

SURRY   MAP, C-3
Chippokes Plantation State Park

reserve america

695 Chippokes Park Rd., 23883-9728.
T: (757) 294-3728; www.reserveamerica.com.

🚐 ★★★   ▲ ★★★

Beauty: ★★★	Site Privacy: ★★
Spaciousness: ★★	Quiet: ★★★★
Security: ★★★★	Cleanliness: ★★★★
Insect Control: ★★★	Facilities: ★★★★

Chippokes Plantation State Park is one of the oldest working farms in the United States. Chippokes is a living historical exhibit located in a rural agricultural area along the James River in Surry County. In addition, the park has a wide variety of traditional park offerings, including a swimming complex, visitor center, picnic facilities, and hiking and biking trails. The plantation has kept its original boundaries since the 1600s and has a variety of cultivated gardens and native woodland. The formal gardens surrounding the Chippokes Mansion are accented by azaleas, crepe myrtle, boxwood and seasonal flowers. The plantation grounds are also home to the Chippokes Farm and Forestry Museum. Chippokes Plantation State Park is operated by the Department of Conservation and Recreation in cooperation with the Chippokes Plantation Farm Foundation. The Virginia General Assembly created the foundation in 1977 to establish, administer and maintain the model farm. Funding for the foundation comes from farmland rent payments, donations, admissions and gift shop sales.

BASICS

Operated By: Virginia State Parks. **Open:** All year. **Site Assignment:** Reservations can be made 11 months in advance. **Registration:** At office. **Fee:** Single, $23; picnic shelter, $30–$45; cabin, $59–$142. **Parking:** At site.

FACILITIES

Number of Multipurpose Sites: 119. **Hookups:** Electric (30 amps). **Each Site:** Fire ring. **Dump Station:** Yes. **Laundry:** No. **Pay Phone:** No. **Restrooms and Showers:** Yes. **Fuel:** No. **Propane:** No. **Internal Roads:** Paved. **RV Service:** No. **Market:** No. **Restaurant:** No. **General Store:** Yes. **Vending:** No. **Swimming:** Yes. **Playground:** Yes. **Other:** Camping equipment & vehicles must fit w/in designated site borders. Additional vehicles should use the parking lot at the pool complex. We protect the natural terrain of our camping areas, some sites are more level than others. **Activities:** Beach, biking, fishing, hiking, picnicking.

RESTRICTIONS

Fires: In designated fireplaces.

TO GET THERE

Chippokes Plantation State Park is located in Surry County. From I-95 and I-295, take Hwy. 10 toward Hopewell. Follow Hwy. 10 east approx. 40 mi. to Surry. Turn left at the intersection of Hwys. 10 and 31 (this continues on Hwy. 10). Turn right at the blinking light. Turn left at Hwy. 634 (Alliance Rd.), and the park entrance is 4 mi. on the left.

TRIANGLE   MAP, B-3
Prince William Forest Park

P.O. Box 209, 18100 Park Headquarters Rd., 22172-0209. T: (703) 221-7181; www.nps.gov/prwi.

🚐 ★★★★   ▲ ★★★★

Beauty: ★★★★	Site Privacy: ★★★
Spaciousness: ★★★	Quiet: ★★★★
Security: ★★★★	Cleanliness: ★★★
Insect Control: ★★★★	Facilities: ★★★★

Located 32 miles from Washington, D.C., 17,000-acre Prince William Forest Park certainly has an interesting menu of camping options. This national park has Oak Ridge Campground, which is operated by the National Park Service, but it also has the privately operated Prince William Travel Trailer Village. The trailer village is located on the north side of the park and provides full hookups, hot showers, a dump station, a swimming pool, laundry facilities, and a playground. Oak Ridge is situated 5.5 miles from the park visitor center; there are 80 sites, none with electric hookups, and there are no shower facilities. Sites are spacious and private, shaded by oaks and pines. If you like hiking and biking, Prince William has 37 miles of hiking trails and fire roads for mountain biking along ridges, into valleys, and alongside the two main creeks in the park. Prince William also consists of the Chopawamsic Backcountry Area, which offers 400 acres of undeveloped terrain for hiking and camping. Permits are required and can be obtained for free at the visitor center.

BASICS

Operated By: National Park Service. **Open:** All year. **Site Assignment:** First come, first served; no reservations. **Registration:** Self-register on site. **Fee:** $10; plus entry fee, $4; V, MC. **Parking:** At site.

FACILITIES

Number of RV-only Sites: 100. **Number of Tent-only Sites:** 80. **Hookups:** None. **Each Site:** Picnic table, grill, lantern pole. **Dump Station:** Yes. **Laundry:** Yes. **Pay Phone:** Yes. **Restrooms and Showers:** Yes. **Fuel:** No. **Propane:** Yes. **Internal Roads:** Gravel & paved, in good condition. **RV Service:** No. **Market:** W/in 2 mi. **Restaurant:** W/in 2 mi. **General Store:** Yes. **Vending:** Yes. **Swimming:** Yes. **Playground:** Yes. **Other:** Separate national park campground & private RV park on park grounds. **Activities:** Lake and stream fishing, swimming pool, planned activities on weekends, hiking trails. **Nearby Attractions:** Quantico Marine Base, Washington, D.C., Fredericksburg and Spotsylvania National Military Park, Manassas National Battlefield Park, Mt. Vernon. **Additional Information:** Prince William County/Manassas CVB, (800) 432-1792, www.visitpwc.com.

RESTRICTIONS

Pets: On leash only. **Fires:** Grill only. **Alcoholic Beverages:** At site. **Vehicle Maximum Length:** 30 ft. **Other:** 14-day stay limit.

TO GET THERE
From I-95, go 0.25 mi. west on Hwy. 619 to park entrance and follow signs 7 mi.

TROUTDALE — MAP, A-2
Grindstone—George Washington/Jefferson National Forest

reserve america

1946 Laurel Valley Rd., 24378. T: (276) 388-3983; www.reserveamerica.com.

🚐 ★★★★   ⛺ ★★★★

Beauty: ★★★   Site Privacy: ★★★
Spaciousness: ★★★★   Quiet: ★★★
Security: ★★★★   Cleanliness: ★★★★
Insect Control: ★★★★   Facilities: ★★

Located in the Mount Rogers National Recreation Area. Grindstone is in Fairwood Valley, with pastures and wooded hillsides. The valley is known for outstanding trout fishing in Fox Creek. Facilities provided include restrooms, picnic tables, and two impact areas. Popular activities include fishing, hiking the nature trails, horseback riding, and interpretive programs. Firewood is sold at the campground. There is a local store within 10 miles of the site. Water play area and playground equipment available. Grindstone Campground is located within the George Washington National Forestand the Jefferson National Forest. North of the James River the forest is called George Washington National Forest. South of the James River it is called Jefferson National Forest. The forest covers 1.8 million acres of land in the Appalachian Mountains of Virginia, West Virginia, and Kentucky.

BASICS
Operated By: U.S. Forest Service. **Open:** Apr. 8–Dec. 1. **Site Assignment:** Reservations must be made at least 4 days in advance. **Registration:** At office. **Fee:** Single, $17–$20; double, $36. **Parking:** At park.

FACILITIES
Number of Multipurpose Sites: 184. **Hookups:** Yes. **Each Site:** Call ahead. **Dump Station:** No. **Laundry:** No. **Pay Phone:** No. **Restrooms and Showers:** Yes. **Fuel:** No. **Propane:** No. **Internal Roads:** Paved. **RV Service:** No. **Market:** No. **Restaurant:** No. **General Store:** No. **Vending:** No. **Swimming:** No. **Playground:** No. **Activities:** Fishing, hiking, interpretive trails, horseback riding.

RESTRICTIONS
Pets: Restrained or on a leash at all times while in developed recreation areas. **Fires:** In fire rings, stoves, grills, or fireplaces provided for that purpose. **Alcoholic Beverages:** Not allowed. **Vehicle Maximum Length:** Call ahead.

TO GET THERE
Grindstone Campground is located in Smyth County, 22 mi. south of Marion, between Konnarock and Troutdale. From I-81N, take Exit 35. Turn right off the exit approx. 10 mi., and take a left onto Hwy. 603. Look for the Grindstone entrance.

URBANNA — MAP, B-4
Bethpage Camp-Resort

reserve america

P.O. Box 178, 23175. T: (804) 758-4349; www.reserveamerica.com.

🚐 ★★★★★   ⛺ n/a

Beauty: ★★★★   Site Privacy: ★★
Spaciousness: ★★★   Quiet: ★★★★
Security: ★★★★   Cleanliness: ★★★★
Insect Control: ★★★★   Facilities: ★★★★★

Set on the southern reach of the Rappahannock River near Chesapeake Bay, Bethpage Camp-Resort is not only the best all-around campground in Virginia, it is one of the top five in the mid-Atlantic region. Bethpage has 1000 wooded sites on 150 acres, including 300 pull-throughs and 300 double slideouts. Many of the larger sites are located along the banks of the Rappahannock River. There are two swimming pools, a swimming lake with a soft-sanded beach, a lake pier with a band gazebo, and two recreation centers. For boaters and anglers, the campground has a marina, fish-cleaning stations, a boat ramp, and a high-pressure boat and RV wash. Bethpage can charter fishing boat excursions too. There are numerous special events during the year. Our favorite is the Steamed Crab Feast Weekend, which features all-you-can-eat Chesapeake Bay blue crabs. Colonial Williamsburg and Jamestown are nearby. Urbanna is the site of the annual Urbanna Oyster Festival, another treat for seafood lovers.

BASICS
Operated By: Private operator. **Open:** Apr. 1–Nov. 15. **Site Assignment:** Reservations accepted (3-night min. on holiday weekends, 2-night min. Oyster Festival Weekend, $20 deposit), walk-ins accepted. **Registration:** At campground office. **Fee:** $29.95–$44.95; V, MC. **Parking:** At designated area.

FACILITIES
Number of RV-only Sites: 1000. **Hookups:** Electric (30, 50 amps), water, sewer, phone. **Each Site:** Fire ring, picnic table. **Dump Station:** Yes. **Laundry:** Yes. **Pay Phone:** Yes. **Restrooms and Showers:** Yes. **Fuel:** Yes. **Propane:** Yes. **Internal Roads:** Paved, in good condition. **RV Service:** No. **Market:** On site. **Restaurant:** W/in 5 mi. **General Store:** Yes. **Vending:** Yes. **Swimming:** Yes. **Playground:** Yes. **Other:** Marina & boat ramp. **Activities:** 2 swimming pools, wading pool, game room, rec hall, pond swimming, boating, boat rentals, pond and saltwater fishing, basketball, bike rentals, planned activities, tennis, shuffleboard, volleyball, sports field, horseshoes. **Nearby Attractions:** Chesapeake Bay, Colonial Williamsburg, Urbanna Oyster Festival, Busch Gardens, Historic Jamestown Settlement, Yorktown. **Additional Information:** Virginia Tourism Corp. (800) 371-8164, www.virginia.org.

RESTRICTIONS
Pets: On leash only. **Fires:** At site. **Alcoholic Beverages:** At site. **Vehicle Maximum Length:** 45 ft.

TO GET THERE
From US 17, go 4 mi. east on SR 602 and 0.5 mi. east on SR 684. Entrance is on the left.

VIRGINIA BEACH — MAP, C-4
False Cape State Park

reserve america

4001 Sandpiper Rd., 23456-4347. T: (757) 426-7128; www.reserveamerica.com.

🚐   ⛺ ★★★

Beauty: ★★★   Site Privacy: ★★★★★
Spaciousness: ★★★★★   Quiet: ★★★★
Security: ★★★★   Cleanliness: ★★★★
Insect Control: ★★★   Facilities: ★★

Located in southern Virginia Beach, False Cape State Park is a mile-wide barrier spit between Back Bay and the Atlantic Ocean. Access is through the Back Bay National Wildlife Refuge and is limited to hiking, bicycling, or boating. The park features primitive camping and an extensive environmental education program in one of the last undisturbed coastal environments on the East Coast. In the 1800s, False Cape gained a reputation as a ship's graveyard. The area got its name because its land mass resembled Cape Henry, luring boats into shallow waters. One of the area's first communities, Wash Woods, was developed by survivors of such a shipwreck. The village's church and other structures were built using cypress wood that washed ashore from a wreck. False Cape State Park is situated on 4,321 acres. Beach Size: 5.9 miles of beachfront, extending to North Carolina line. To get a taste of the park, the Back Bay Restoration Foundation operates a tram that leaves from Little Island City Park, drives through the wildlife refuge, and lets visitors explore the park for an hour in the Barbour Hill contact station area. The tram provides a round-trip ride and is not available for overnight guests. Overnight guests must either hike or bike through the refuge, or canoe or boat in. Both day-use and overnight visitors are advised to read all warnings regarding visiting the park to learn what is expected and about preparation. All visitors must follow refuge regulations while on refuge property.

BASICS
Operated By: Virginia State Parks. **Open:** All year. **Site Assignment:** Reservations can be made 11 months in advance. **Registration:** At office. **Fee:** Single, $9. **Parking:** At site.

FACILITIES
Number of Multipurpose Sites: 48. **Hookups:** None. **Dump Station:** No. **Laundry:** No. **Pay Phone:** No. **Restrooms and Showers:** Yes. **Fuel:** No. **Propane:** No. **RV Service:** No. **Market:** No. **Restaurant:** No. **General Store:** No. **Vending:** No. **Swimming:** No. **Playground:** No. **Other:** No vehicular access to this park. Must follow refuge regulations. Groups of 10 or more are required to obtain a special-use permit from Back Bay Wildlife Refuge 2 weeks in advance of trip. **Activities:** Beach, biking, boating, fishing, hiking.

RESTRICTIONS

Fires: Fire ban in effect during certain times of the year.

TO GET THERE

From I-64, exit onto Indian River Rd. East. Go 13 mi., then turn left onto Newbridge Rd., then right onto Sandbridge Rd. Next, turn right onto Sandpiper Rd. to Little Island City Park. Parking fees required Memorial Day–Labor Day. Day-use parking is also available at Back Bay Wildlife Refuge. From First Landing State Park and oceanfront, turn east onto Shore Dr. (Hwy. 60); follow Pacific Ave. to General Booth Blvd., then left on Princess Anne Rd. and left onto Sandbridge Rd. Turn right onto Sandpiper Rd. to Little Island City Park.

VIRGINIA BEACH MAP, C-4
First Landing State Park

reserve america

2500 Shore Dr., 23451.
T: (757) 412-2300 or (800) 933-PARK;
www.reserveamerica.com.

🚐 ★★★   ⛺ ★★★★

Beauty: ★★★	Site Privacy: ★★★
Spaciousness: ★★★	Quiet: ★★★
Security: ★★★	Cleanliness: ★★★
Insect Control: ★★★★	Facilities: ★★★

Virginia Beach is regarded as the world's largest resort city. Long before Virginia Beach was settled, the Virginia Company landed at a site on Chesapeake Bay on April 26, 1607—more than two weeks before arriving at Jamestown. Today, that site is First Landing State Park, visited by 1.2 million people a year. Though Virginia Beach and the state park are both crowded with tourists in warmer months, First Landing's beachfront swimming area is limited to campers, which minimizes the chance you will have to step over countless sunbathers to find a patch of sand. The campground's sites are separated by small sand dunes and trees. Though there are no hookups, the campground has hot showers, a Laundromat with large capacity dryers and a well-stocked camp store. There are many hiking trails; the most popular path is the 1.5-mile Bald Cypress Loop Trail, which sprouts from the visitor center and takes you along boardwalks and through cypress swamps.

BASICS

Operated By: State of Virginia. **Open:** Mar.–Dec. **Site Assignment:** Reservations strongly recommended, walk-ins accepted. **Registration:** At campground office. **Fee:** $23–$29; V, MC. **Parking:** At site.

FACILITIES

Number of RV-only Sites: 233. **Hookups:** Water/electric. **Each Site:** Grill, picnic table. **Dump Station:** No. **Laundry:** Yes. **Pay Phone:** Yes. **Restrooms and Showers:** Yes. **Fuel:** No. **Propane:** No. **Internal Roads:** Paved, in good condition. **RV Service:** No. **Market:** W/in 5 mi. **Restaurant:** W/in 5 mi. **General Store:** Yes. **Vending:** Yes. **Swimming:** Yes. **Playground:** No. **Other:** Bay Store. **Activities:** Boating, kayaking, saltwater

fishing, hiking trails, crabbing, biking, bike rentals, Chesapeake Bay swimming (at own risk). **Nearby Attractions:** Chesapeake Bay, Virginia Beach, Ocean Breeze Water Park, Old Cape Henry Lighthouse and Memorial Park, Old Coast Guard Station, Virginia Marine Science Museum, Motor World Family Thrill Park. **Additional Information:** Virginia Beach Dept. of Convention Visitor Development, (800) 700-7702, www.vabeach.com.

RESTRICTIONS

Pets: On leash only. **Fires:** In fire rings, stoves, & grills. **Alcoholic Beverages:** No alcohol permitted. **Vehicle Maximum Length:** 34 ft. **Other:** 14-day stay limit in 30-day period.

TO GET THERE

From I-64, take Exit 282 and go northeast on US 13 and 5 mi. east on Shore Dr. Follow signs to campground.

VIRGINIA BEACH MAP, C-4
Holiday Trav-L-Park

reserve america

1075 General Booth Blvd., 23451.
T: (800) 548-0223 or (757) 425-0249;
www.htpvabeach.com.

🚐 ★★★★   ⛺ ★★★★

Beauty: ★★★★	Site Privacy: ★
Spaciousness: ★	Quiet: ★★★
Security: ★★★★★	Cleanliness: ★★★★
Insect Control: ★★★★	Facilities: ★★★★★

Amid forests and meadows, Holiday Trav-L-Park in Virginia Beach is like a small town in itself, with 1,000 sites, three grocery stores, Laundromats, a full-service restaurant, six playgrounds, an 18-hole mini-golf course, and more. There are 550 pull-through sites. Campers have their choice of shaded, open, and wooded sites. In the busy season, the campground is stirring with live entertainment, bingo games, and hayrides. There is a bike path that leads to the beach; campers also have access to free parking one block from the beach. The Ocean Breeze Festival Park and the Motor World Family Thrill Park are close by as well. So is the Virginia Marine Science Museum, where visitors can see sharks, sea turtles, seals, and other ocean life, in addition to enjoying a 300-seat IMAX theater.

BASICS

Operated By: Holiday Trav-L-Park. **Open:** All year. **Site Assignment:** Reservations accepted (recommended Memorial Day–Labor Day), walk-ins accepted. **Registration:** At campground office. **Fee:** $20–$35; V, MC, D. **Parking:** At site.

FACILITIES

Number of RV-only Sites: 700. **Number of Tent-only Sites:** 300. **Hookups:** Electric (20, 30, 50 amps), water, phone. **Each Site:** Picnic table. **Dump Station:** Yes. **Laundry:** Yes. **Pay Phone:** Yes. **Restrooms and Showers:** Yes. **Fuel:** Yes. **Propane:** Yes. **Internal Roads:** Gravel & paved, in good condition. **RV Service:** No. **Market:** On site. **Restaurant:** On site. **General Store:** Yes. **Vend-**

ing: Yes. **Swimming:** Yes. **Playground:** Yes. **Other:** Four large pools & 18-hole mini-golf course. **Activities:** Swimming, game room, rec hall, wading pool, whirlpool, mini-golf, basketball, bike rentals, shuffleboard, planned activities, movies, badminton, sports field, horseshoes, volleyball. **Nearby Attractions:** Virginia Beach, Virginia Marine Science Museum, Back Bay Wildlife Refuge, First Landing State Park, Jamestown, Yorktown, Colonial Williamsburg. **Additional Information:** Virginia Beach Dept. of Convention Visitor Development, (800) 700-7702, www.vabeach.com.

RESTRICTIONS

Pets: On leash only. **Fires:** At site. **Alcoholic Beverages:** At site. **Vehicle Maximum Length:** No limit. **Other:** Max. 6 people per campsite.

TO GET THERE

From I-264, take Exit 22 and go 3 mi. southeast on Birdneck Rd. and 0.25 mi. south on General Booth Blvd. Entrance is on the right.

VIRGINIA BEACH MAP, C-4
Outdoor Resorts—Virginia Beach

3665 Sandpiper Rd., 23456. T: (800) 333-7515 or (757) 721-2020; www.outdoor-resorts.com.

🚐 ★★★★   ⛺ n/a

Beauty: ★★★★	Site Privacy: ★★
Spaciousness: ★★	Quiet: ★★★
Security: ★★★★★	Cleanliness: ★★★★
Insect Control: ★★★★	Facilities: ★★★★

Located along the outer banks near Virginia Beach, Outdoor Resorts—Virginia Beach has 250 sites on Back Bay. The nicely landscaped grounds include two lighted tennis courts, a large swimming pool with a whirlpool and a nearby sauna, bicycle trails, and a boating ramp and dock. There are no tent sites here, and vans, pop-ups, and truck campers are not permitted. The fishing is good at this campground, with choices of casting your line into the bay, the lake, or the ocean. The campground is a short walk to Back Bay National Wildlife Refuge. The 7,000-acre preserve is bordered by the Atlantic Ocean on one side and Back Bay on the other. A network of trails and boardwalks meanders through the park. If you are longing for a unique drive, head for the Chesapeake Bay Bridge-Tunnel. Stretching 17.6 miles, the incredible engineering feat carries traffic on US 13 from Virginia Beach to Virginia's eastern shore.

BASICS

Operated By: Outdoor Resorts. **Open:** All year. **Site Assignment:** Reservations recommended, walk-ins accepted. **Registration:** At campground headquarters. **Fee:** $50–$70; V, MC. **Parking:** At designated spot.

FACILITIES

Number of RV-only Sites: 250. **Hookups:** Electric (20, 30, 50 amps), water, sewer, cable TV, phone. **Each Site:** Picnic table, patio. **Dump Station:** Yes. **Laundry:** Yes. **Pay Phone:** Yes. **Restrooms and Showers:** Yes. **Fuel:** No. **Propane:** No. **Internal Roads:** Paved, in good condition. **RV Service:** No. **Market:** W/in 6 mi. **Restaurant:** W/in 5 mi.

General Store: No. **Vending:** Yes. **Swimming:** Yes. **Playground:** Yes. **Other:** Boating ramp & dock. **Activities:** Swimming, sauna, whirlpool, boating, ocean fishing, bike rentals, tennis. **Nearby Attractions:** Virginia Beach, Virginia Marine Science Museum, Back Bay Wildlife Refuge, First Landing State Park, Jamestown, Yorktown, Colonial Williamsburg. **Additional Information:** Virginia Beach Dept. of Convention Visitor Development, (800) 700-7702, www.vabeach.com.

RESTRICTIONS

Pets: On leash only. **Fires:** At site. **Alcoholic Beverages:** At site. **Vehicle Maximum Length:** 18 ft. **Other:** No vans, pop-ups, or truck campers.

TO GET THERE

From I-64, take Exit 22 and go 3.5 mi. southeast on Birdneck Rd, 7 mi. south on General Booth Blvd., 1 mi. east on Princess Anne Rd., 7 mi. east on Sandbridge Rd., and 3.5 mi. south on Sandpiper Rd. Entrance is on the right.

VIRGINIA BEACH   MAP, C-4
Virginia Beach KOA

1240 General Booth Blvd., 23451.
T: (800) 562-4150 or (757) 428-1444;
www.koa.com.

🚐 ★★★★   ▲ ★★★★

Beauty: ★★★★   Site Privacy: ★★
Spaciousness: ★★   Quiet: ★★★
Security: ★★★★   Cleanliness: ★★★★
Insect Control: ★★★★   Facilities: ★★★★

Located close to the lively resort strip on Virginia Beach, Virginia Beach KOA has 100 acres (just like Holiday Trav-L-Park), but the campground has 600 fewer sites. Campers who want proximity to the ocean but desire a less crowded environment will likely prefer this campground. KOA does not have the wealth of amenities that Holiday boasts, but it does have two swimming pools, a Laundromat, and a well-stocked store. A trolley provides free rides to the beach for campers, departing every half-hour 8 a.m.–midnight. There are 400 open and partially wooded sites, including 350 pull-throughs. Ocean Breeze Festival Park and the Virginia Marine Science Museum are nearby. Lighthouse enthusiasts will enjoy the Old Cape Henry Lighthouse, located on the grounds of the Ft. Story Military Reservation.

BASICS

Operated By: KOA. **Open:** All year. **Site Assignment:** Reservations and walk-ins accepted. **Registration:** At campground office. **Fee:** $18–$46; V, MC, D. **Parking:** At designated area.

FACILITIES

Number of RV-only Sites: 330. **Number of Tent-only Sites:** 70. **Hookups:** Electric (20, 30, 50 amps), water. **Each Site:** Fire ring, picnic table. **Dump Station:** Yes. **Laundry:** Yes. **Pay Phone:** Yes. **Restrooms and Showers:** Yes. **Fuel:** No. **Propane:** Yes. **Internal Roads:** Gravel & paved, in good condition. **RV Service:** No. **Market:** W/in 1 mi. **Restaurant:** W/in 1 mi. **General Store:** Yes. **Vending:** Yes. **Swimming:** Yes. **Playground:** Yes. **Other:** Trolley to beach. **Activities:** Swimming,

mini-golf, game room, rec hall, planned activities, sports field, badminton, horseshoes, volleyball, tennis. **Nearby Attractions:** Virginia Beach, Virginia Marine Science Museum, Back Bay Wildlife Refuge, First Landing State Park, Jamestown, Yorktown, Colonial Williamsburg. **Additional Information:** Virginia Beach Dept. of Convention Visitor Development, (800) 700-7702, www.vabeach.com.

RESTRICTIONS

Pets: On leash only. **Fires:** At site. **Alcoholic Beverages:** At site. **Vehicle Maximum Length:** No limit.

TO GET THERE

From Hwy. 44E, go 1 mi. south on Pacific Ave. and 3 mi. south on General Booth Blvd. Entrance is on the left.

WILLIAMSBURG   MAP, C-3
Colonial Central KOA

4000 Newman Rd., 23188.
T: (800) 562-7609 or (757) 565-2734;
www.williamsburgkoa.com.

🚐 ★★★★   ▲ ★★★★

Beauty: ★★★★★   Site Privacy: ★★
Spaciousness: ★★   Quiet: ★★★
Security: ★★★★   Cleanliness: ★★★★
Insect Control: ★★★★   Facilities: ★★★★

Featuring 200 grassy and partially wooded sites, Colonial Central KOA is connected to its sister property (Williamsburg KOA) by a winding nature trail. Guests at one property can use facilities at the other. Colonial Central is 7 miles from Colonial Williamsburg, and a short drive from an abundance of restaurants on Hwy. 60. There are so many eateries on this portion of Hwy. 60 that locals call it Restaurant Row. The campground has 180 pull-through sites. Full-hookup sites with 50-amp service are located on the east end, while the remaining full hookups are situated on the west side. A free shuttle service transports campers to attractions like Colonial Williamsburg and Busch Gardens. Yorktown Battlefield, which is part of the Colonial National Historical Park which includes Williamsburg and Jamestown, is located 20 miles from the campground. Colonial Central KOA is near several golf courses, including the much-heralded Colonial Golf Course set amid forests and tidal wetlands.

BASICS

Operated By: KOA. **Open:** Mar. 1–Nov. 15. **Site Assignment:** Reservations accepted ($25 deposit), walk-ins accepted. **Registration:** At campground office. **Fee:** $19.95–$54.95; V, MC. **Parking:** At site.

FACILITIES

Number of RV-only Sites: 175. **Number of Tent-only Sites:** 25. **Hookups:** Electric (20, 30, 50 amps), water, cable TV, phone. **Each Site:** Fire ring, picnic table. **Dump Station:** Yes. **Laundry:** Yes. **Pay Phone:** Yes. **Restrooms and Showers:** Yes. **Fuel:** No. **Propane:** Yes. **Internal Roads:** Gravel & paved, in good condition. **RV Service:** No. **Market:** W/in 2 mi. **Restaurant:** W/in 2 mi. **General Store:** Yes. **Vending:** Yes. **Swimming:** Yes. **Playground:** Yes. **Other:** Shuttle service to Williamsburg attractions.

Activities: Game room, rec hall, swimming, wading pool, basketball, sports field, horseshoes. **Nearby Attractions:** Colonial Williamsburg, College of William and Mary, Busch Gardens, Historic Jamestown Settlement, Yorktown. **Additional Information:** Williamsburg Area CVB, (757) 253-0192, www.visitwilliamsburg.com.

RESTRICTIONS

Pets: On leash only. Dogs, cats, & ferrets are the only pets permitted. **Fires:** At site. **Alcoholic Beverages:** At site. **Vehicle Maximum Length:** No limit.

TO GET THERE

From I-64, take Exit 234 and go 1 mi. northeast on Hwy. 199, which turns into Hwy. 646. Entrance is on the right.

WILLIAMSBURG   MAP, C-3
Jamestown Beach Campsites

P.O. Box CB, 23187.
T: (757) 229-7609 or (800) 446-9228.

🚐 ★★★★   ▲ ★★★★

Beauty: ★★★★   Site Privacy: ★★
Spaciousness: ★★   Quiet: ★★★★
Security: ★★★★   Cleanliness: ★★★★
Insect Control: ★★★★   Facilities: ★★★★

Situated along the James River, Jamestown Beach Campsites' location is perfect for travelers interested in visiting the area's rich historical attractions. The campground is adjacent to the Jamestown Settlement and near the Colonial Parkway that links Jamestown, Williamsburg, and Yorktown. If you like the water, Jamestown Beach Campsites has a sandy beach where you can soak in the sun and swim in the James River. There is a dock and ramp for boats, and a place to get bait and fishing supplies. Most sites are nestled in the woods and near the water. During warmer months, the campground has dances on the beach and live entertainment in the recreation hall. The nearby Jamestown Colonial National Historical Park is a fascinating place where the first permanent English settlement in the New World was founded on May 13, 1607. Here, you can visit a living history museum which recreates the Jamestown of the 1600s.

BASICS

Operated By: Robert Vermillion. **Open:** All year. **Site Assignment:** Reservations required. **Registration:** At campground office. **Fee:** $18–$25; V, MC. **Parking:** At site.

FACILITIES

Number of RV-only Sites: 300. **Number of Tent-only Sites:** 300. **Hookups:** Electric (20, 30, 50 amps), water, phone. **Each Site:** Fire ring, picnic table. **Dump Station:** Yes. **Laundry:** Yes. **Pay Phone:** Yes. **Restrooms and Showers:** Yes. **Fuel:** No. **Propane:** Yes. **Internal Roads:** Gravel & paved, in good condition. **RV Service:** No. **Market:** W/in 3 mi. **Restaurant:** On site. **General Store:** Yes. **Vending:** Yes. **Swimming:** Yes. **Playground:** Yes. **Other:** James River. **Activities:** Swimming, wading pool, boating, canoeing, kayaking, river fishing, mini-golf, game room, rec hall, shuffleboard, horseshoes, volleyball, sports field. **Nearby Attractions:** Colonial Williamsburg,

College of William and Mary, Busch Gardens, Historic Jamestown Settlement, Yorktown. **Additional Information:** Williamsburg Area CVB, (757) 253-0192, www.visitwilliamsburg.com.

RESTRICTIONS

Pets: On leash only. **Fires:** At site. **Alcoholic Beverages:** At site. **Vehicle Maximum Length:** No limit.

TO GET THERE

From I-64, take Exit 242A and go 4 mi. west on Hwy. 199 and 4 mi. south on Hwy. 31. Entrance is on the right.

WILLIAMSBURG — MAP, C-3
Outdoor World—
Williamsburg Campground

4301 Rochambeau Dr., 23188.
T: (800) 222-5557 or (757) 566-3021;
www.campoutdoorworld.com.

🚐 ★★★★   ⛺ ★★★★

Beauty: ★★★★★   Site Privacy: ★★★
Spaciousness: ★★★   Quiet: ★★★★
Security: ★★★★   Cleanliness: ★★★★
Insect Control: ★★★★   Facilities: ★★★★★

Outdoor World—Williamsburg Campground sites are spacious, and there are 30 pull-throughs. What we especially like here is the menu of special events. There's a Roaring 1920s Weekend, when male campers dress in gangster-like pinstripe suits and females don flapper dresses with strands of long pearls; and Disco Fever Weekend, when polyester suits and platform shoes take over and campers dance to music from the Bee Gees and the Village People. Good Old Days Weekend and Island Escape Weekend are other noteworthy special events. We were here during Star Search Weekend, but since we can't dance like Fred Astaire or sing like Frank Sinatra or Celine Dion, we chose to watch rather than participate. Of course, we could have sang a tune and entered it into the stand-up comedian category.

BASICS

Operated By: Outdoor World. **Open:** All year. **Site Assignment:** Reservations recommended (3-night min. on holiday weekends, otherwise 2-night min.), walk-ins accepted. **Registration:** At campground office. **Fee:** $37; V, MC, AE. **Parking:** At site.

FACILITIES

Number of RV-only Sites: 125. **Number of Tent-only Sites:** 30. **Hookups:** Electric (20, 30, 50 amps), water, phone. **Each Site:** Fire ring, picnic table. **Dump Station:** Yes. **Laundry:** Yes. **Pay Phone:** Yes. **Restrooms and Showers:** Yes. **Fuel:** No. **Propane:** No. **Internal Roads:** Gravel & paved, in fair condition. **RV Service:** No. **Market:** W/in 4 mi. **Restaurant:** W/in 2 mi. **General Store:** Yes. **Vending:** Yes. **Swimming:** Yes. **Playground:** Yes. **Other:** Mini-golf course. **Activities:** Swimming, wading pool, game room, rec hall, mini-golf, whirlpool, basketball, shuffleboard, planned activities, movies, sports field, horseshoes, volleyball. **Nearby Attractions:** Colonial Williamsburg, College of William and Mary, Busch

Gardens, Historic Jamestown Settlement, Yorktown. **Additional Information:** Williamsburg Area CVB, (757) 253-0192, www.visitwilliamsburg.com.

RESTRICTIONS

Pets: On leash only. **Fires:** At site. **Alcoholic Beverages:** At site. **Vehicle Maximum Length:** No limit.

TO GET THERE

From I-64, take Exit 231A and go 0.2 mi. south on Hwy. 607 and 0.25 mi. north on Rochambeau Rd./Hwy. 30. Entrance is on the left.

WILLIAMSBURG — MAP, C-3
Williamsburg KOA

5210 Newman Rd., 23188.
T: (757) 565-2907 or (800) 562-1733;
www.williamsburgkoa.com.

🚐 ★★★★   ⛺ ★★★★

Beauty: ★★★★   Site Privacy: ★★
Spaciousness: ★★★   Quiet: ★★★
Security: ★★★★   Cleanliness: ★★★★
Insect Control: ★★★★   Facilities: ★★★★

Williamsburg KOA and Colonial Central KOA are separate campgrounds connected by a nature trail. Campers have access to activities at either location. Williamsburg KOA offers more activities than its sister property, however. At this campground, you can watch movies, fish in a creek, and enjoy cable TV at every site. There are 12 pull-through sites at Williamsburg KOA compared to 180 at Colonial Central. Both campgrounds are elegantly landscaped, offer clean restrooms and showers, and have nice swimming pools. Full hookup sites along the creek and near the restrooms and showers are favorite spots at Williamsburg KOA. The campground offers a free shuttle service to area attractions, which include Colonial Williamsburg and Busch Gardens. There are also several summer programs for children. The campground also sells tickets to area attractions.

BASICS

Operated By: KOA. **Open:** Mar. 1–Oct. 31. **Site Assignment:** Reservations recommended, walk-ins accepted. **Registration:** At campground office. **Fee:** $19.95–$89.95; V, MC. **Parking:** At site.

FACILITIES

Number of RV-only Sites: 140. **Number of Tent-only Sites:** 17. **Hookups:** Electric (20, 30, 50 amps), water, cable TV, phone. **Each Site:** Picnic table. **Dump Station:** Yes. **Laundry:** Yes. **Pay Phone:** Yes. **Restrooms and Showers:** Yes. **Fuel:** No. **Propane:** No. **Internal Roads:** Gravel, in good condition. **RV Service:** No. **Market:** W/in 3 mi. **Restaurant:** W/in 3 mi. **General Store:** Yes. **Vending:** Yes. **Swimming:** Yes. **Playground:** Yes. **Other:** Shuttle service to Williamsburg attractions. **Activities:** Game room, rec hall, swimming, basketball, planned activities, movies, horseshoes, volleyball. **Nearby Attractions:** Colonial Williamsburg, College of William and Mary, Busch Gardens, Historic Jamestown Settlement, Yorktown. **Additional Information:** Williamsburg Area CVB, (757) 253-0192, www.visitwilliamsburg.com.

RESTRICTIONS

Pets: On leash only. Dogs, cats, & ferrets are the only pets permitted. **Fires:** At site. **Alcoholic Beverages:** At site. **Vehicle Maximum Length:** No limit.

TO GET THERE

From I-64, take Exit 234 and go 1.5 mi. east on Hwy. 199, which turns into Hwy. 646. Entrance is on the right.

WINCHESTER — MAP, A-2
Candy Hill Campground

165 Ward Ave., 22602.
T: (540) 662-8010 or (800) 462-0545;
www.candyhill.com.

🚐 ★★★★   ⛺ ★★★★

Beauty: ★★★★★   Site Privacy: ★★★
Spaciousness: ★★★   Quiet: ★★★★
Security: ★★★★   Cleanliness: ★★★★
Insect Control: ★★★★   Facilities: ★★★★

Situated atop Shenandoah Valley in northern Virginia, Candy Hill Campground has 103 level sites, some open and some shaded. The facilities at Candy Hill are well maintained and clean. Groups of 12 or more can use the Candy Hill Trolley at no cost to travel to area attractions. If you are interested in a unique lodging experience, stay in an authentic B&O Railroad caboose. Candy Hill is a short drive from the northern entrance of Skyline Drive in Front Royal. Endless Caverns and Luray Caverns are also nearby. The town of Winchester is an interesting place; it changed hands 72 times during the Civil War, including 13 times in one day. Stonewall Jackson's Headquarters is now a museum where you can peruse Confederate artifacts. Today, about 3.5 million bushels of apples are harvested in the area. The Shenandoah Apple Blossom Festival is held annually in late April and early May.

BASICS

Operated By: Art and Wendy Littman. **Open:** All year. **Site Assignment:** Reservations recommended (1-night deposit), walk-ins accepted. **Registration:** At campground office. **Fee:** $30–$35; V, MC, D. **Parking:** At site.

FACILITIES

Number of RV-only Sites: 103. **Hookups:** Electric (20, 30, 50 amps), water, phone. **Each Site:** Fire ring, picnic table. **Dump Station:** Yes. **Laundry:** Yes. **Pay Phone:** Yes. **Restrooms and Showers:** Yes. **Fuel:** No. **Propane:** Yes. **Internal Roads:** Paved, in good condition. **RV Service:** No. **Market:** W/in 2 mi. **Restaurant:** W/in 1 mi. **General Store:** Yes. **Vending:** Yes. **Swimming:** Yes. **Playground:** Yes. **Other:** Cabin & caboose rentals. **Activities:** Swimming, basketball, game room, rec hall, badminton, sports field, horseshoes, volleyball. **Nearby Attractions:** Winchester Speedway, Skyline Drive, Harper's Ferry, Stonewall Jackson's Headquarters, Luray Caverns, Endless Caverns, Belle Grove Plantation. **Additional Information:** Virginia Tourism Corp., (800) 371-8164, www.virginia.org.

RESTRICTIONS

Pets: On leash only. **Fires:** At site. **Alcoholic Beverages:** At site. **Vehicle Maximum Length:** 45 ft.

TO GET THERE

From I-81, take Exit 310 and go 5.5 mi. north on Hwy. 37, 300 yards west on US 50, and 0.25 mi. south on Ward Ave. Entrance is on the left.

| WYTHEVILLE | MAP, A-2 |
| Wytheville KOA | |

231 KOA Rd., P.O. Box 122, 24382.
T: (276) 228-2601 or (800) KOA-3380;
www.wythevillekoa.com.

🚐 ★★★★   ▲ ★★★★

Beauty: ★★★★	Site Privacy: ★★
Spaciousness: ★★	Quiet: ★★★
Security: ★★★★	Cleanliness: ★★★★
Insect Control: ★★★★	Facilities: ★★★★

Nestled between the Blue Ridge and Allegheny mountains in western Virginia, Wytheville KOA is one of the cleanest KOA campgrounds you will find in Virginia and the mid-Atlantic. There are 110 RV sites, including 65 pull-throughs. While using the restroom or taking a shower, you can listen to classical music played through the speakers. A 12,500-square-foot recreation center houses batting cages, a mini-golf course, a rock climbing wall, and the Family Fun Center with video games, dart boards, pool tables, and skeeball. Children flock to the campground's petting zoo to see rabbits, cats, goats, lambs, and horses. Beyond the campground, scenic drives and outdoor activities beckon. Rural Retreat Lake is nearby, as is the George Washington and Jefferson National Forest. Rafting trips in Virginia's Outback on the New River are popular. Shot Tower Historical Park in Wytheville is perched on a bluff overlooking the New River.

BASICS

Operated By: Gene and Donna Metzger. **Open:** All year. **Site Assignment:** Reservations and walk-ins accepted. **Registration:** At campground office. **Fee:** $20–$50; V, MC, AE, D. **Parking:** At site.

FACILITIES

Number of RV-only Sites: 110. **Number of Tent-only Sites:** 15. **Hookups:** Electric (20, 30, 50 amps), water, cable TV, phone. **Each Site:** Fire ring, picnic table. **Dump Station:** Yes. **Laundry:** Yes. **Pay Phone:** Yes. **Restrooms and Showers:** Yes. **Fuel:** No. **Propane:** Yes. **Internal Roads:** Gravel & paved, in good condition. **RV Service:** No. **Market:** W/in 2 mi. **Restaurant:** W/in 2 mi. **General Store:** Yes. **Vending:** Yes. **Swimming:** Yes. **Playground:** Yes. **Other:** Shuttle service to area attractions. **Activities:** Float trips, mini-golf, game room, rec hall, basketball, shuffleboard, planned activities, movies, badminton, horseshoes, hiking trails, volleyball. **Nearby Attractions:** Museum of the Middle Appalachians, Appalachian Trail, Wytheville State Fish Hatchery, New River Trail, Shot Tower Historical Park, Big Walker Lookout, Rural Retreat Lake. **Additional Information:** Wytheville-Wythe-Bland Chamber of Commerce, (540) 223-3365, www.wytheville.org/chamber.

RESTRICTIONS

Pets: On leash only. **Fires:** At site. **Alcoholic Beverages:** At site. **Vehicle Maximum Length:** 45 ft.

TO GET THERE

From I-77, take Exit 77 and go 0.5 mi. south on Hwy. 758. Entrance is at the end.

Washington

A beautiful place to tour all year, Washington State boasts a variety of natural and urban environments to explore. Although the region most popular for tourism lies along the Interstate 5 corridor, astounding natural beauty, cultural events, and man-made curiosities await across the 42nd state.

The I-5 corridor, the most widely traveled and promoted section of the state, includes the major destinations of **Seattle, Tacoma, Olympia, Bellingham,** the **Canadian border,** volcanoes, the **North Cascades,** the **Olympic Peninsula,** and **Vancouver.** Although Washington experiences above-average rainfall, this region has mild, temperate weather all year.

The **San Juan Islands, Victoria (Canada),** and **Bellingham** are truly the gems of the Northwestern region; the geography included in this region blends mountains to the east, myriad inlets and bays to the west, and more mountains rising from the islands beyond. Bellingham houses **Western Washington University** and is a small and particularly interesting college town. The absolute best views in the region are from overlooks on **Chuckanut Drive.** If you're in a small enough vehicle, continue on south through the beautiful **Skagit County** farmland as the road makes its way back to the interstate.

A major geographic region of the state, the **Olympic Peninsula** offers tremendous natural beauty, vibrancy, and diversity. For a push-off point, **Port Angeles** has the most services of any city on the northern peninsula, provides the best access to the **Olympic Mountains,** and, along with the surrounding area, handles the bulk of the tourist traffic. If you can only visit one area in the state, a trip to the peninsula will not leave you disappointed.

Traveling east across the Evergreen State, the climate and environment change dramatically. The **North Cascades** have snow on the ground all year in some places as the mountainous belt drops a couple of thousand feet into high-altitude deserts. The red earth of north-central Washington is home to a mix of desert, valleys, canyons, farms, rivers, lakes, and the occasional ponderosa pine forest. For fringe culture and thrill seekers traveling through **Okanogan County** in January, seek out the city of **Conconully** for its annual **Outhouse Races.** The **Coulee region** has scenery different from any other area, with many pullouts and vistas along **Banks Lake Road.** South-central Washington has a flat, desolate, arid terrain with numerous farms and wineries. The **Yakima** region of the state produces copious amounts of wine, which makes it a popular tourist destination. In both central and eastern Washington, lake fishing is the sport of choice and attracts a lot of travelers.

Moving east from south-central Washington, the landscape changes to rolling hills around the Idaho border and the **Snake River** area. To the north in **Spokane,** the landscape changes yet again to smoothly rolling farms and dry ponderosa pine forests. If you plan to travel around this area for a while, www.spokanegasprices.com is a valuable resource for RVers seeking the best rates on fuel. Although it is a popular escape for locals, the eastern side of the state receives very little state-sponsored tourism publicity, a fact not lost on residents. However, if you happen to be passing through **Adams County** the second week in June, head to **Lind** for the annual **Combine Demolition Derby** for a smash-up good time. Goods and services on the eastern side of the state don't cost quite as much as those in the **Puget Sound** region, particularly hotels and restaurants, because the tourism infrastructure is not as marketed as it is around **Seattle.**

Campground Profiles

ANATONE   MAP, C-4
Fields Spring State Park

P.O. Box 37, 99401. T: (509) 256-3332;
www.parks.wa.gov.

🚐 ★★★   ⛺ ★★★★

Beauty: ★★★★★   Site Privacy: ★★★
Spaciousness: ★★★★★   Quiet: ★★★★
Security: ★★★★   Cleanliness: ★★★★★
Insect Control: ★★   Facilities: ★★★

Anatone is quite small. It is the last stop for any kind of services before continuing on to Fields Spring State Park. Beyond Fields Spring to the south lies wilderness, national forest, and wild river canyons. Sitting on a basalt foundation at 4,000 feet on the eastern edge of Washington's Blue Mountains, Fields Spring State Park is a place of unusual beauty in an otherwise harsh and rugged terrain. Escaping the heat of the summer is one of the biggest draws to Fields Spring. Although the park sits on what is essentially an arid, desert-like plateau, with prickly pear cactus growing down along the Grande Ronde's banks, the difference in elevation makes all the difference in temperature. While Clarkston and Lewiston swelter in 100-degree agony in midsummer, Fields Spring rarely gets above a tolerable 85. Fields Spring is a true oasis in a region otherwise parched for camping options.

BASICS

Operated By: Washington State Parks & Recreation Commission. **Open:** All year; weather permitting. **Site Assignment:** First come, first served. **Registration:** Self-registration. **Fee:** $15–$21. **Parking:** At site.

FACILITIES

Number of Multipurpose Sites: 20. **Hookups:** None. **Dump Station:** Yes. **Laundry:** No. **Pay Phone:** Yes. **Restrooms and Showers:** Yes. **Fuel:** 31 mi. in Clarkston. **Propane:** 31 mi. in Clarkston. **Internal Roads:** Paved. **RV Service:** No. **Market:** 31 mi. in Clarkston. **Restaurant:** No. **General Store:** 31 mi. in Clarkston. **Vending:** No. **Swimming:** No. **Playground:** Yes. **Other:** 2 lodges, 2 kitchen shelters w/ electricity, 2 sheltered fire circles, teepee camp (6 can be reserved for $20 per night). **Activities:** Environmental Learning Center, hiking, biking, horseshoe pits, softball field, volleyball fields, hang gliding, paragliding. **Nearby Attractions:** Puffer Butte, Snake River. **Additional Information:** www.parks.wa.gov.

RESTRICTIONS

Pets: On leash. **Fires:** Fire pit only. **Alcoholic Beverages:** Allowed. **Vehicle Maximum Length:** Call ahead for details.

TO GET THERE

From Clarkston (roughly 110 mi. south of Spokane), follow SR 129 south through Asotin and Anatone for about 25 mi. to the park entrance.

ASHFORD   MAP, B-2
Mounthaven Resort

38210 SR 706 East, 98304.
T: (360) 569-2594 or (800) 456-9380;
www.mounthaven.com.

🚐 ★★★★   ⛺ ★

Beauty: ★★★★   Site Privacy: ★
Spaciousness: ★★★   Quiet: ★★★
Security: ★   Cleanliness: ★★★★
Insect Control: ★★   Facilities: ★★

Mounthaven Resort, half a mile west of the entrance to Mount Rainier National Park, offers a beautiful woodland setting. The quaint park lacks on-site indoor recreation, but people don't often come to the area to "stay at home." Sixteen shady RV sites are arranged in two rows. The intimate campground sits among cedars and firs, and is visited by friendly deer. Adjacent sites have dirt surfaces and come in a variety of sizes. Sites 6–13 make up the nicest sites in the park, due to size and quiet; sites 1–5 sit near the sometimes busy Hwy. 706. The campground also has an array of cabins for travelers looking for indoor accommodations. Visit during the early or late summer shoulder seasons for optimal conditions.

BASICS

Operated By: Mt. Haven Resort. **Open:** All year. **Site Assignment:** On arrival or by reservation (deposit required for holidays, 15-day cancellation notice for refund). **Registration:** At office, late arrivals pay in morning. **Fee:** Full $25; extra campers (more than 4) & dogs, $2; V, MC, cash. **Parking:** At site.

FACILITIES

Number of RV-only Sites: 16. **Hookups:** Electric (20, 30 amps), water, sewer. **Each Site:** Picnic table, fire ring. **Dump Station:** Yes. **Laundry:** Yes. **Pay Phone:** Yes. **Restrooms and Showers:** Yes. **Fuel:** No. **Propane:** No. **Internal Roads:** Gravel, dirt. **RV Service:** No. **Market:** Convenience stores, 1–5 mi.; larger store 30 mi. west. **Restaurant:** 1–5 mi. **General Store:** No. **Vending:** Yes. **Swimming:** No. **Playground:** Yes. **Other:** Cabins, firewood, horseshoes, volleyball, basketball, badminton, board games, hot tub (by reservation only, $10 per hour for 2 people). **Activities:** Mt. Rainier. **Nearby Attractions:** Mt. Rainier. **Additional Information:** Mount Ranier NPS Office, (360) 569-2212.

RESTRICTIONS

Pets: On leash only, 2 per site max. **Fires:** Fire pit only. **Alcoholic Beverages:** At site only. **Vehicle Maximum Length:** No limit.

TO GET THERE

Located on SR 706, 0.5 mi. west of the southwestern park gate (Nisqually entrance).

BAKER LAKE   MAP, A-2
Panorama Point Campground

reserve america

2105 WA 20, 98284. T: (360) 856-5700;
www.reserveamerica.com.

🚐 ★★★   ⛺ ★★★★

Beauty: ★★★★★   Site Privacy: ★★★★
Spaciousness: ★★★★   Quiet: ★★★
Security: ★★★★   Cleanliness: ★★★★★
Insect Control: ★★★   Facilities: ★★★

Many purist northwest wilderness goers purposefully overlook camping options at places like Baker Lake simply because they don't feel that they're truly getting a pristine experience if they're within earshot of mechanized sounds. In the case of Panorama Point Campground, midway up the western shore, that sound will most likely be the gentle buzz of small outboard motors as anglers putt-putt around in search of the best spots to hook their daily catch. They have their choice of such delights as rainbow, cutthroat, or Dolly Varden trout; kokanee salmon; and whitefish. This is, indeed, an angler's lake. But one can hardly complain that there's no getting away from civilization here thanks to miles and miles of Forest Service roads and trails that can lead you to soothing hot springs and deep into two designated wildernesses, a national recreation area, and a national park. Just make sure you have a good map and trail guides of the area before you find yourself at the mercy of the purists.

BASICS

Operated By: Mount Baker–Snoqualmie National Forest; Conservation Resources, Inc. **Open:** May–mid-Sept. **Site Assignment:** Reservations required, call (877) 444-6777. **Registration:** Self-registration on-site. **Fee:** $16. **Parking:** At site.

FACILITIES

Number of Multipurpose Sites: 16. **Hookups:** Water. **Dump Station:** No. **Laundry:** No. **Pay Phone:** No. **Restrooms and Showers:** Vault toilets. **Fuel:** 6 mi. in Concrete. **Propane:** 6 mi. in Concrete. **Internal Roads:** Paved. **RV Service:** No. **Market:** 6 mi. in Concrete. **Restaurant:** 6 mi. in Concrete. **General Store:** 6 mi. in Concrete. **Vending:** No. **Swimming:** No. **Playground:** No. **Activities:** Fishing, hiking, backpacking, skiing, climbing. **Nearby Attractions:** Hot springs, Mt. Baker, designated wildernesses, Mt. Shuksan. **Additional Information:** www.fs.fed.us/r6/mbs or www.reserveusa.com.

RESTRICTIONS

Pets: On leash only. **Fires:** Fire pit only. **Alcoholic Beverages:** Allowed. **Vehicle Maximum Length:** 21 ft. **Other:** Permit required for overnight backpacking or to park at trailhead; 2-day min. weekend stay, 3-day min. on holidays.

TO GET THERE

Drive north on Baker Lake Rd. from its junction with SR 20, about 6 mi. west of Concrete (named for the primary industry that converts local limestone into cement).

BELLINGHAM — MAP, A-2
Larrabee State Park

245 Chuckanut Dr., 98226. T: (360) 676-2093; www.parks.wa.gov.

🚐 ★★★ ▲ ★★★★

Beauty: ★★★★★ — Site Privacy: ★★★★
Spaciousness: ★★★★ — Quiet: ★★★
Security: ★★★ — Cleanliness: ★★★★★
Insect Control: ★★★ — Facilities: ★★★

Located on 1,885 acres along the saltwater shores of Samish Bay south of Bellingham, Larrabee is the oldest state park in Washington. Its designation in 1915 has protected throughout the years such a lush growth of northwest foliage that it is difficult not to feel you have ventured miles into a remote and primeval place. There are plenty of hiking trails, pebbled beaches, and rocky tide pools to explore, and sea kayaking is also an option, with numerous coves, bays, points, rocks, and islets within easy paddling range. For freshwater anglers, both Fragrance Lake and Lost Lake are stocked, but you have to take a 2-mile trail to reach them. If you simply want fresh air and a look at the lay of the land, take a drive up Cleator Road to 1,900-foot Cyrus Gates Overlook for the best possible view of the San Juans. For views of Mount Baker and the North Cascades, take the short trail to the East Overlook.

BASICS
Operated By: Washington State Parks & Recreation Commission. **Open:** All year. **Site Assignment:** First come, first served; reservations accepted mid-May–mid-Sept. **Registration:** Self-registration. **Fee:** $10–$21. **Parking:** At site.

FACILITIES
Number of RV-only Sites: 26. **Number of Tent-only Sites:** 59. **Hookups:** Electric, water, sewer. **Each Site:** Picnic table, fire pit w/ grill, shade trees. **Dump Station:** Yes. **Laundry:** No. **Pay Phone:** Yes. **Restrooms and Showers:** Yes. **Fuel:** 6 mi. north in Bellingham. **Propane:** 6 mi. north in Bellingham. **Internal Roads:** Paved. **RV Service:** No. **Market:** 6 mi. north in Bellingham. **Restaurant:** 6 mi. north in Bellingham. **General Store:** 6 mi. north in Bellingham. **Vending:** Yes. **Swimming:** Yes. **Playground:** Yes. **Other:** Boat launch, security, amphitheater, working train track that runs through the park. **Activities:** Boating, hiking, fishing, diving, clamming & crabbing. **Nearby Attractions:** Fragrance Lake, Lost Lake. **Additional Information:** www.parks.wa.gov.

RESTRICTIONS
Pets: On leash only. **Fires:** Fire pit only. **Alcoholic Beverages:** In designated areas. **Vehicle Maximum Length:** No limit.

TO GET THERE
Drive north on I-5 to the turnoff for Chuckanut Dr. and Fairhaven. Follow the signs to SR 11, and head south. The entrance to the park is about 7 mi. on the right.

CENTRALIA — MAP, B-1
Midway RV Park

3200 Galvin Rd., 98531. T: (360) 736-3200; www.midwayrv.com.

🚐 ★★★★ ▲ n/a

Beauty: ★★★ — Site Privacy: ★
Spaciousness: ★★★★ — Quiet: ★★
Security: ★★★ — Cleanliness: ★★★★
Insect Control: ★★ — Facilities: ★★

Midway RV in Centralia has the nicest accommodations among RV parks located roughly halfway between Portland and Puget Sound. The grounds have friendly, yet not overdone, landscaping with small, manicured conifers, red Japanese Maples, and maintained grass. Sites lack substantial privacy and shade, and the city location has some noise. Still, the pleasant grounds and the limited facilities have a well-maintained, newer look, and sites have lots of space. Back-ins on the back perimeter row, numbers 12–24, have the longest diagonal measurements. The rows of sites also have wide access roads. The best time to tour in the region is late summer when weather is the most amicable.

BASICS
Operated By: Midway RV. **Open:** All year. **Site Assignment:** On arrival, reservations (deposit of 1-night stay; refund w/ 72-hour cancellation notice). **Registration:** At office; late arrivals see sign outside office. **Fee:** $23; extra campers (more than 2), $2; family rate, $28 (2 adults & up to 3 children); V, MC, cash, personal check. **Parking:** At site.

FACILITIES
Number of RV-only Sites: 60. **Hookups:** Electric (30, 50 amps), water, sewer, cable TV. **Dump Station:** No. **Laundry:** Yes. **Pay Phone:** Yes. **Restrooms and Showers:** Yes. **Fuel:** No. **Propane:** Yes. **Internal Roads:** Paved. **RV Service:** No. **Market:** Down the street. **Restaurant:** Down the street. **General Store:** Yes. **Vending:** Yes. **Swimming:** No. **Playground:** No. **Other:** Horseshoes, movies for loan, rec room, meeting room (reservable). **Activities:** Monthly potluck. **Nearby Attractions:** The Vintage Antique Motorcycle Museum, skiing, wineries, casino gambling, Puget Sound & big cities, Washington's Pacific coast. **Additional Information:** Centralia, Chehalis, & Greater Lewis County Chamber of Commerce, (360) 748-8885.

RESTRICTIONS
Pets: On leash only. **Fires:** No open fires. **Alcoholic Beverages:** At site only. **Vehicle Maximum Length:** No limit. **Other:** Do not park in grassy areas or vacant spaces.

TO GET THERE
From I-5 Exit 82, drive west on Harrison Ave. to Galvin Rd. Turn left and continue driving for about 0.3 mi. Midway RV Park is on the left side of the road.

CHENEY — MAP, B-4
Yogi Bear's Camp-Resort

reserve america

7520 South Thomas Mallen Rd., 99004. T: (509) 747-9415 or (800) 494-PARK; www.jellystonewa.com.

🚐 ★★★★ ▲ ★★

Beauty: ★★ — Site Privacy: ★
Spaciousness: ★★ — Quiet: ★★★
Security: ★★★★★ — Cleanliness: ★★★
Insect Control: ★★ — Facilities: ★★★★★

Yogi Bear's Camp-Resort, 10 miles east of Spokane, offers a wide array of in-house resort-like activities. The quality of the recreational facilities here far surpasses that of competitors, with tons of planned activities during the on-season and good facilities. These facilities include a well-kept mini-golf course with lots of flowing water under the shade of ponderosa pines. Within the shady grounds, sites vary in quality, and accommodations consist of both back-in and pull-through sites. Flat, gravel pull-through rows R, G, and B make up the best sites in the campground; avoid row Y. Back-in sites exist throughout the grounds, but unfortunately many are not totally flat. The tent sites at Yogi Bear's lack a Jellystone forest feel; all have gravel floors. Additionally, the camp resort offers several varieties of permanent fixture lodging, including bungalows and cabins. The busiest time to visit is June 16 through Labor Day; visit in the late spring or early fall to avoid the crowds.

BASICS
Operated By: Private operator. **Open:** All year. **Site Assignment:** First come, first served; reservations require 2-night min. (deposit 50% of total stay; refund on cancellation before 2 weeks, after 2 weeks no refund or rain check). **Registration:** At office; after hours must wait until morning to enter park. **Fee:** Pull-through, $33; back-in, $30; tent, $19. Fri./Sat.: add $5-base; extra adult, $8; extra child, $3; extra tent (1 per site), $11, $13 on weekends; extra car (2-car max), $2; V, MC, cash. **Parking:** At site.

FACILITIES
Number of RV-only Sites: 64. **Number of Tent-only Sites:** 21. **Hookups:** Electric (20, 30, 50 amps), water, sewer, cable TV, phone. **Each Site:** Picnic table. **Dump Station:** Yes. **Laundry:** Yes. **Pay Phone:** Yes. **Restrooms and Showers:** Yes. **Fuel:** No. **Propane:** Yes. **Internal Roads:** Gravel. **RV Service:** No. **Market:** 5 mi. east on I-90. **Restaurant:** 5 mi. east on I-90. **General Store:** Yes. **Vending:** Yes. **Swimming:** Yes. **Playground:** Yes. **Other:** Volleyball, pickleball, & basketball courts; 18-hole mini-golf, horseshoes, water balloon slingshot range, kiddie lagoon, hot tub, arcade w/ pool table, birthday party room, exercise room (small, equipped w/ weight, aerobic machines). **Activities:** Planned activities every weekend; more frequent June 16–end of Aug. **Nearby Attractions:** Cheney Cowles Museum, Manito Park & Japanese Gardens, Riverfront Park, golf, Centennial Trail, regional special events. **Additional Information:** Spokane Chamber of Commerce, (509) 624-1393.

RESTRICTIONS

Pets: On leash only. Some breeds not allowed. **Fires:** No open fires. **Alcoholic Beverages:** At site only. **Vehicle Maximum Length:** No limit. **Other:** All holiday weekends 3-night min. stay.

TO GET THERE

From I-90 Exit 172 (eastbound turn right; westbound turn left), take next left at stop sign onto Westbow; road becomes Hallet St. Follow Hallet for 1.1 mi., and then turn right on Thomas Mallen Rd. Follow Thomas Mallen Rd. for 1.1 mi.; entrance is on right.

COUGAR   MAP, C-2
Merrill Lake Campground

601 Bond Rd., P. O. Box 280, 98611.
T: (360) 577-2025.

🚐 n/a   ⛺ ★★★★

Beauty: ★★★★   Site Privacy: ★★★★
Spaciousness: ★★★★★   Quiet: ★★★★★
Security: ★★   Cleanliness: ★★★★
Insect Control: ★★★   Facilities: ★★

Campers who were enjoying the serene quiet of Merrill Lake on the fateful May morning when Mount St. Helens erupted must have been doing so with one eye nervously fixed in the direction of the mountain (which is roughly 6 air miles to the northeast). When the mountain blew, those lucky enough to have chosen a weekend outing on the south side probably thought that the plume of ash rising to an eventual height of 63,000 feet was the extent of the show. It wouldn't be until they returned home later that evening that television news reports showed them the full extent of the horror. Today, more than a decade later, Merrill Lake Campground sits in wooded isolation just outside the boundaries of Gifford Pinchot National Forest and Mount St. Helens National Volcanic Monument. In summer, most of the tourist throngs inundate Mount St. Helens from the north, leaving you free to explore lands around the geologic wonder in relative solitude.

BASICS

Operated By: Dept. of Natural Resources. **Open:** Memorial Day–Nov. 30. **Site Assignment:** First come, first served. **Registration:** Not necessary. **Fee:** None. **Parking:** At site.

FACILITIES

Number of RV-only Sites: 0. **Number of Tent-only Sites:** 7. **Hookups:** None. **Each Site:** Picnic table, fire grill, tent pad. **Dump Station:** No. **Laundry:** No. **Pay Phone:** No. **Restrooms and Showers:** Vault toilets. **Fuel:** No. **Propane:** No. **Internal Roads:** None. **RV Service:** No. **Market:** No. **Restaurant:** No. **General Store:** No. **Vending:** No. **Swimming:** Yes. **Playground:** No. **Other:** Boat launch, disabled access. **Activities:** Boating, fishing, hiking, biking, caving, bird-watching. **Nearby Attractions:** Mount St. Helens, Ape Cave, Cedar Flats Northern Research Natural Area.

RESTRICTIONS

Pets: On leash. **Fires:** Fire pit only. **Alcoholic Beverages:** Allowed. **Vehicle Maximum Length:** Call ahead for details. **Other:** RVs prohibited.

TO GET THERE

Take Lewis River Rd. east from Woodland off I-5 to the small settlement of Cougar. Turn north, away from Yale Lake, onto FS 81, and travel 4.5 mi. to the access road that leads to the campground.

COULEE DAM   MAP, B-3
Keller Ferry Campground

reserve america

1008 Crest Dr., 99116. T: (828) 963-5911; www.reserveamerica.com.

🚐 ★★★   ⛺ ★★★★

Beauty: ★★★★   Site Privacy: ★★★
Spaciousness: ★★★★   Quiet: ★★★
Security: ★★★★★   Cleanliness: ★★★★
Insect Control: ★★★   Facilities: ★★★★

Keller Ferry Campground is located in the Lake Roosevelt National Recreation Area, which is renowned for towering trees, soaring mountains, deep gorges, and expansive wilderness. Lake Roosevelt National Recreation Area can rightfully claim a place among the Pacific Northwest's outstanding resources. The largest lake in the area, Lake Roosevelt is ideal for motor boating, water-skiing, sailing, and fishing. In the surrounding sagebrush hills and forested mountains, you can camp, picnic, hike, hunt, and sight-see. The creation of this sprawling recreation area began with 24 million tons of concrete and steel: Grand Coulee Dam. A Goliath of a dam, it was built to turn the power of the Columbia River into electricity and turn vast deserts into productive farmlands. Today the recreation area preserves in their natural setting reminders of the days when Native Americans fished the free-flowing Columbia River, and fur trappers, farmers, missionaries, and soldiers first worked and settled this region. Here, the new and old coexist side by side.

BASICS

Operated By: National Park Service. **Open:** May 11–Oct. 27. **Site Assignment:** Reservations must be made 7 days in advance. **Registration:** At registration office. **Fee:** Single, $5–$10. **Parking:** At site.

FACILITIES

Number of Multipurpose Sites: 160. **Hookups:** None. **Each Site:** Call ahead. **Dump Station:** Yes. **Laundry:** No. **Pay Phone:** Yes. **Restrooms and Showers:** Yes. **Fuel:** No. **Propane:** No. **Internal Roads:** Paved. **RV Service:** No. **Market:** No. **Restaurant:** No. **General Store:** Yes. **Vending:** No. **Swimming:** Yes. **Playground:** Yes. **Other:** No metal detectors allowed, or collecting of artifacts. No livestock. No ATVs or ORVs allowed. **Activities:** Amphitheater, biking, bird-watching, boating, campfire programs, canoeing, fishing, hiking, photography, sightseeing, skiing, snowshoeing.

RESTRICTIONS

Pets: Pets must be on a leash at all times. **Fires:** Allowed; Campfire Program. **Alcoholic Beverages:** Not allowed. **Vehicle Maximum Length:** Varies; call ahead.

TO GET THERE

Take Hwy. 2 west of Spokane for 54 mi. to the town of Wilbur. Turn north on Hwy. 21 (follow road signs) and travel 14 mi. to the Keller Ferry Campground.

DAVENPORT   MAP, B-4
Fort Spokane

reserve america

44150 District Office Lane, 99122. T: (509) 633-3830; www.reserveamerica.com.

🚐 ★★★★   ⛺ ★★★★

Beauty: ★★★★   Site Privacy: ★★★
Spaciousness: ★★★★   Quiet: ★★★★
Security: ★★★★★   Cleanliness: ★★★★
Insect Control: ★★★   Facilities: ★★★★

Fort Spokane is one of the cultural jewels of Lake Roosevelt National Recreation Area. For thousands of years, the area was a gathering place for native tribes fishing the rapids of the Spokane River. In 1880, the U.S. Army established a fort above the confluence of the Spokane and Columbia rivers. In 1898, the fort was closed and used as an Indian boarding school and tuberculosis hospital. In many ways, the Indian experience at Fort Spokane is a microcosm of the Indian experience across the United States. The National Park Service recognizes the significance of the site as a tool for teachers and students to explore this nation's past and developed a curriculum-based education program to explore both the European and Indian experiences on the site. In addition to classroom lessons, the program will include a cyber-tour of the fort in the 1800s.

BASICS

Operated By: National Park Service. **Open:** All year. **Site Assignment:** Reservations must be made 7 days in advance. **Registration:** At registration office. **Fee:** Single, $5–$10. **Parking:** At park.

FACILITIES

Number of Multipurpose Sites: 140. **Hookups:** None. **Each Site:** Call ahead. **Dump Station:** Yes. **Laundry:** No. **Pay Phone:** No. **Restrooms and Showers:** Yes. **Fuel:** No. **Propane:** No. **Internal Roads:** Paved. **RV Service:** No. **Market:** Less than 1 mi. **Restaurant:** Less than 1 mi. **General Store:** No. **Vending:** No. **Swimming:** Yes. **Playground:** Yes. **Activities:** Biking, bird-watching, boating, campfire programs, canoeing, fishing, hiking, hunting, photography, scuba diving, sightseeing, skiing, snowshoeing, waterskiing, wildlife viewing, windsurfing.

RESTRICTIONS

Pets: Pets must be on a leash at all times. **Fires:** Allowed; Campfire Program. **Alcoholic Beverages:** Not allowed. **Vehicle Maximum Length:** Varies; call ahead. **Other:** No ATVs or ORVs, no metal detectors or collecting artifacts. No livestock.

TO GET THERE

Take Hwy. 2 west of Spokane 32 mi. Turn north on WA 25 at the town of Davenport, travel 24 mi. (follow the signs).

DAVENPORT
Two Rivers RV Park

MAP, B-4

68 B. Hwy. 25S, 99122. T: (509) 722-4029;
www.tworiverscasinoandresort.com.

🚐 ★★★★   ⛺ ★★

Beauty: ★★★   Site Privacy: ★
Spaciousness: ★★★   Quiet: ★★★★
Security: ★★   Cleanliness: ★★★★
Insect Control: ★★   Facilities: ★★★★

Two Rivers RV Resort, a half hour north of Davenport on Hwy. 25, provides a convenient location for visiting the adjacent casino and Fort Spokane. The campground sits on high bluffs overlooking the giant, gray-blue Spokane River, with an organizational scheme of several loops plus two rows of campsites surrounded by lots of grass and some small flowering shrubs. The sites lack privacy or shade, but most have views of the surrounding semi-arid rolling highlands that fall toward the river; sites with views of the river exist on G and F loops. Half the sites in section E back into a hill, diminishing their scenic views. The park has a few large pull-throughs, but it consists mostly of paved, spacious back-ins. The tent section of the campground has a cramped arrangement of picnic areas with some grassy patches for tents; sites 15–18 and 23–26 sit on the edge of bluffs overlooking the river. The park boasts two unusually large playground areas, but there's not much more in the way of on-site family recreation. Winters here are snowy and cold; visit during the late spring or summer for warm temperatures.

BASICS

Operated By: Spokane Tribe of Indians. **Open:** All year. **Site Assignment:** Reservations (deposit 1-night stay; refund). **Registration:** At office; after hours pay in morning. **Fee:** Full pull-through, $23; full back-in, $19; tent, $14; for 6 people; extra person, $2; maximum people per site, 10; RV overflow parking, $10; V, MC, check, cash. **Parking:** At site, some off site.

FACILITIES

Number of RV-only Sites: 100. **Number of Tent-only Sites:** 32. **Hookups:** Electric (20, 30, 50 amps), water, sewer. **Each Site:** Picnic table, grill. **Dump Station:** Yes. **Laundry:** Yes. **Pay Phone:** Yes. **Restrooms and Showers:** Yes. **Fuel:** Yes. **Propane:** Yes. **Internal Roads:** Paved & gravel. **RV Service:** No. **Market:** 25 mi. south in Davenport. **Restaurant:** 25 mi. south in Davenport. **General Store:** No. **Vending:** Yes. **Swimming:** No. **Playground:** Yes. **Other:** Horseshoe pit, marina w/ houseboat rentals, casino. **Activities:** Fishing, 4th of July fireworks show, hiking, swimming, gambling, boating. **Nearby Attractions:** Fort Spokane, Two River's Casino, hiking, fishing. **Additional Information:** Davenport Chamber of Commerce, (509) 725-6711.

RESTRICTIONS

Pets: On leash only, pick up after pets. **Fires:** Fire pit only. **Alcoholic Beverages:** At site only. **Vehicle Maximum Length:** 40 ft. **Other:** No refund once checked in; 3-day min. stay on holidays.

TO GET THERE

From the junction of Hwys. 2 and 25 on east side of Davenport: Drive 23.5 mi. north on Hwy. 25, then turn left on Confluence Drive just after Fort Spokane and Spokane River Bridge; entrance to campground is on left.

ELECTRIC CITY
Sunbanks Resort

MAP, B-3

reserve america

57662 Hwy. 155 N, 99123. T: (888) 822-7195;
www.reserveamerica.com.

🚐 ★★★★   ⛺ ★★★

Beauty: ★★★★   Site Privacy: ★★
Spaciousness: ★★   Quiet: ★★★★
Security: ★★★   Cleanliness: ★★★★
Insect Control: ★★★   Facilities: ★★★★★

Sunbanks Resort, on the edge of deep, blue Banks Lake just south of Electric City, comes stocked with beautiful views of surrounding scenery and nicely furnished facilities. A mix of arid and irrigated areas creates an intriguing landscape inside the grounds. Sites consist of grass or gravel in a seemingly random organization running downhill to the lake's edge. The shady, gravel, back-in, full hookups sit in cramped, adjacent rows near the office. Most RV sites on the property have water and electric hookups; of these, sites 85–95, 60–63, and 68–74 make up the least-crowded areas. Sites A and B sit on a flat hill with a crow's-nest view of shear, jagged coulee walls and the lake, but they have no hookups and access limited by vehicle size. The best tent options, sites 1–39, sit on the shores of Banks Lake in a semishaded, grassy area. Inter-site privacy does not exist here, and the grounds become extremely cramped when full. Just before or after the summer season make the best times to visit and avoid crowds.

BASICS

Operated By: Precision Management. **Open:** All year; fully operational Apr. 1–Oct. **Site Assignment:** First come, first served; reservations (nonrefundable deposit of 1-night stay). **Registration:** At gate or lodge; after hours pay in morning. **Fee:** Full, $34; waterfront tent, $34; water/electric, $30; non-waterfront tent, $30; view site, $26; for 6 people. **Parking:** At site.

FACILITIES

Number of RV-only Sites: 125. **Number of Tent-only Sites:** 82. **Hookups:** Electric (20, 30, 50 amps), water, sewer. **Each Site:** Picnic table, grated fire pits. **Dump Station:** Yes. **Laundry:** Yes. **Pay Phone:** Yes. **Restrooms and Showers:** Yes. **Fuel:** No. **Propane:** No. **Internal Roads:** Well-maintained gravel. **RV Service:** No. **Market:** 5 mi. north in Electric City. **Restaurant:** Yes. **General Store:** Yes. **Vending:** Yes. **Swimming:** Yes. **Playground:** No. **Other:** Cafe, boat launch & moorage, outdoor stage, game room (2 pool tables), paddleboat rentals, horseshoes, play field. **Activities:** Swimming, fishing, boating, waterskiing & other water sports (BYOB-Bring Your Own Boat). **Nearby Attractions:** Grand Coulee Dam, tons of lakes for fishing, 2 golf courses, Steamboat Rock State Park, hiking trails, rock climbing, various local events, Coulee Dam Casino, Coville

Tribes Museum. **Additional Information:** Grand Coulee Dam Area Chamber of Commerce, (800) 268-5332.

RESTRICTIONS

Pets: On leash only; watch for no-pet areas. **Fires:** Fire pit only. **Alcoholic Beverages:** At site only. **Vehicle Maximum Length:** No limit. **Other:** 2-night min. stay on all reservations; site requests not guaranteed; tents must be moved every 3 days.

TO GET THERE

From the junction of Hwys. 174 and 155, go 3 mi. south on 155; entrance on right just before bridge.

ENUMCLAW
Corral Pass Campground

MAP, B-2

White River Ranger District, 98022.
T: (360) 825-6585; www.fs.fed.us/r6/mbs.

🚐 n/a   ⛺ ★★★★

Beauty: ★★★★   Site Privacy: ★★★★★
Spaciousness: ★★★★★   Quiet: ★★★★★
Security: ★★   Cleanliness: ★★★
Insect Control: ★★★   Facilities: ★★

For your own personal, unsurpassed view of the north face of Mount Rainier and for a different perspective of Crystal Mountain Ski Area, take a hard left off WA 410 about 30 miles out of Enumclaw, onto FS 7174, to Corral Pass Campground. But bring plenty of water because there is no piped water here. Hopefully, you've come to Corral Pass for the backcountry hiking options, which are plentiful. Among a number of choices, there's Norse Peak Wilderness brushing the ridge top just east of the campground, covering more than 50,000 acres of diverse terrain dissected by 52 miles of hiking trails. There is a surprising variety of wildlife and vegetation to enjoy as well—mountain goats, elk, and deer, to name a few. The wildflowers in the meadows around Noble Knob are known to rival those at Paradise on Mount Rainier's southern slope when in full bloom (late June to early August, depending on the elevation), and berry-picking is prime in late August and early September.

BASICS

Operated By: Mount Baker-Snoqualmie National Forest. **Open:** July–late Sept. **Site Assignment:** First come, first served. **Registration:** Not necessary. **Fee:** None. **Parking:** At site.

FACILITIES

Number of RV-only Sites: 0. **Number of Tent-only Sites:** 20. **Hookups:** None. **Each Site:** Picnic table, fire grill. **Dump Station:** No. **Laundry:** No. **Pay Phone:** No. **Restrooms and Showers:** Vault toilets. **Fuel:** No. **Propane:** No. **Internal Roads:** Call ahead for details. **RV Service:** No. **Market:** No. **Restaurant:** No. **General Store:** No. **Vending:** No. **Swimming:** No. **Playground:** No. **Other:** Firewood. **Activities:** Hiking, fishing, horseback riding. **Nearby Attractions:** Norse Peak Wilderness, Noble Knob, Echo Lake/Greenwater River Trail, Naches Trail. **Additional Information:** www.fs.fed.us/r6/mbs.

RESTRICTIONS

Pets: On leash only. **Fires:** Fire pit only. **Alcoholic Beverages:** Allowed. **Vehicle Maximum Length:** RVs & trailers not recommended. **Other:** No piped water.

TO GET THERE

From Enumclaw (roughly 40 mi. southeast of Seattle), take SR 410 southeast for about 30 mi. Turn left onto FS 7174 and follow to its end (6 mi.). The highway marker for FS 7174 can be obscured by overhanging foliage, so keep a sharp lookout for it on the right side of the road. If you find yourself at the turnoff to Crystal Mountain Ski Area and the entrance to Mount Rainier National Park, you've gone about 1 mi. too far.

GIG HARBOR   MAP, B-2
Gig Harbor RV Resort

reserve america

9515 Burnham Dr. NW, 98332.
T: (253) 858-8138 or (800) 526-8311;
www.reserveamerica.com.

🚐 ★★★   ⛺ ★★

Beauty: ★★★	Site Privacy: ★★
Spaciousness: ★★★	Quiet: ★★★
Security: ★	Cleanliness: ★★★★
Insect Control: ★★	Facilities: ★★★

Gig Harbor RV Resort, located off Hwy. 16 and 45 minutes southwest of Seattle, provides lodging near a beautiful harbor area. Large terraced, gravel sites crown this park's accommodations. The park also has some adjacent sites at the top of the terraced hill. In the upper section, foliage provides a small amount of privacy; the actual terraces in the terraced section give a feeling of semiprivacy and open space. The upper section has some shade from trees; although ringed by forests of fir, the lower section has less shade and foliage among sites. Tenting within the park is limited, as the tenting area has small sites with no privacy and a little gravel, but lots of shade. Gig Harbor is a beautiful coastal area on Puget Sound. Visit during summer for the best weather.

BASICS

Operated By: PCF Management. **Open:** All year. **Site Assignment:** By reservation; first come, first served. **Registration:** At office; after hours check welcome board out front. **Fee:** Full, $37.81; water/electric, $32.24; tent, $20; cabins, $30.85; V, MC, D, personal check, cash. **Parking:** At site, limited off site.

FACILITIES

Number of RV-only Sites: 93. **Number of Tent-only Sites:** 12. **Hookups:** Electric (20, 30, 50 amps), water, sewer. **Each Site:** Picnic table. **Dump Station:** Yes. **Laundry:** Yes. **Pay Phone:** Yes. **Restrooms and Showers:** Yes. **Fuel:** No. **Propane:** Yes. **Internal Roads:** Paved. **RV Service:** No. **Market:** 3 mi. west in Gig Harbor. **Restaurant:** 3 mi. west in Gig Harbor. **General Store:** Yes. **Vending:** Yes. **Swimming:** Yes. **Playground:** Yes. **Other:** Basketball, volleyball, badminton, club room, horse-

shoes. **Activities:** Inquire at campground. **Nearby Attractions:** Scuba diving, sailing, kayaks, power boats, jet skis, wind surfing, waterskiing, fishing, Seattle-Tacoma area, Puget Sound. **Additional Information:** Gig Harbor Chamber of Commerce, (253) 851-6865; Seattle Visitor Info Center, (206) 461-5840, www.seeseattle.org.

RESTRICTIONS

Pets: On leash only, no fencing or kenneling. **Fires:** No open fires, charcoal is okay. **Alcoholic Beverages:** At site only. **Vehicle Maximum Length:** No limit.

TO GET THERE

From I-5, take Exit 132 and follow Hwy. 16 west, cross the Tacoma Narrows Bridge. Turn right at Burnham Dr.–North Rosedale Exit. Drive 1.2 mi. on Burnham; entrance is on the left.

GOLDENDALE   MAP, C-3
Brooks Memorial State Park

2465 US 97, 98620. T: (509) 773-4611;
www.parks.wa.gov.

🚐 ★★★   ⛺ ★★★★

Beauty: ★★★★★	Site Privacy: ★★★
Spaciousness: ★★★	Quiet: ★★★★★
Security: ★★★★	Cleanliness: ★★★★★
Insect Control: ★★★	Facilities: ★★★

From its 3,000-foot location in the Simcoe Mountains, Brooks Memorial State Park is not only a good base for exploring the Klickitat Valley, but also for sights farther south to the Columbia River, west into the untamed Klickitat River region and Mount Adams, and north into the Yakima Indian Reservation and the viticultural lands of the Yakima Valley. Points of interest abound in all directions. Central to the area is Goldendale, a quiet community that is home to the Goldendale Observatory State Park Interpretive Center and has one of the largest telescopes available for public use in the country. Wildflowers bloom in the park from March until July, and there is quite a variety of park wildlife—turkeys, deer, raccoons, porcupines, beavers, bobcats, coyotes, red-tailed hawks, and owls. The Little Klickitat River follows US 97 from Brooks Memorial down into Goldendale, and it is not uncommon to observe beavers going about their business of damming the river.

BASICS

Operated By: Washington State Parks & Recreation Commission. **Open:** All year. **Site Assignment:** First come, first served. **Registration:** Self-registration at self-pay station across from the restrooms. **Fee:** $11–$16. **Parking:** At site.

FACILITIES

Number of RV-only Sites: 23. **Number of Tent-only Sites:** 22. **Hookups:** Electric (20 amps), water. **Dump Station:** Yes. **Laundry:** No. **Pay Phone:** Yes. **Restrooms and Showers:** Yes. **Fuel:** 13 mi. in Goldendale. **Propane:** 13 mi. **Internal Roads:** Paved. **RV Service:** No. **Market:** 13 mi. in Goldendale. **Restaurant:** 13 mi. **General Store:** 13 mi. **Vending:** No. **Swimming:** No. **Playground:** Yes. **Other:** Kitchen shelters w/ water & electricity,

group accommodations. **Activities:** Hiking, fishing, nature talks in Environmental Learning Center upon request, horseshoe pit, softball field. **Nearby Attractions:** Goldendale Observatory, Maryhill Museum, historic Columbia Highway. **Additional Information:** www.parks.wa.gov.

RESTRICTIONS

Pets: On leash only. **Fires:** Fire pit only. **Alcoholic Beverages:** At site, picnic area. **Vehicle Maximum Length:** 40 ft. **Other:** No firewood gathering.

TO GET THERE

From Yakima, follow US 97 south for 55 mi., crossing Satus Pass (elevation 3,107 ft.) to the park entrance.

GRAND COULEE   MAP, B-3
Spring Canyon

reserve america

46000 Campground Dr., 99133 T: (509) 633-9188;
www.reserveamerica.com.

🚐 ★★★★   ⛺ ★★★★

Beauty: ★★★★	Site Privacy: ★★★★
Spaciousness: ★★★★	Quiet: ★★★
Security: ★★★★★	Cleanliness: ★★★★
Insect Control: ★★★	Facilities: ★★★★

Pack a Frisbee and beach toys for the kds for one of Grand Coulee's main summer hangouts. The Park at Spring Canyon at the shores of Lake Roosevelt. Hundreds of feet of sandy beach and tens of acres of grassy park, complete with barbecue pits, picnic tables, and shade trees makes for old-fashioned family summertime fun. There is a designated swimming area, which hosts a 20-foot square dock in the center surrounded by a huge log boom. You will also find monkey bars, slides, merry-go-rounds, and other permanent playground toys for the kids, plus a regulation-size sand volleyball court for the adults. The view at Spring Canyon is spectacular. Lake Roosevelt stretches out forever to the East, giving way to the granite and basalt cliffs that form the Coulee Walls. In the distance, only a couple miles away, is the Grand Coulee Dam, holding back the mighty Columbia River, converted to the 152-mile-long Lake Roosevelt. Spring Canyon boat ramp is one of the few entry points into the Grand Coulee end of Lake Roosevelt for the fisherman and camping enthusiast alike. Grand Coulee Dam is a large hydroelectric dam located on the Columbia River in Central Washington. Made from 12 million cubic yards of concrete, Grand Coulee Dam is the largest concrete structure in the United States and the third largest hydroelectric facility in the world. Sharing the river with ten other U.S. dams, Grand Coulee is the first dam encountered on the Columbia after the river enters the United States from Canada. Lake Roosevelt, the reservoir created by the dam, contains 9 million acre-feet of water and stretches over 150 miles back to the border.

BASICS

Operated By: National Park Service. **Open:** All year. **Site Assignment:** Reservations must be made at least 7 days in advance. **Registration:** At registration office. **Fee:** Single, $5–$10. **Parking:** At park.

FACILITIES

Number of Multipurpose Sites: 152. **Hookups:** None. **Each Site:** Call ahead. **Dump Station:** No. **Laundry:** No. **Pay Phone:** Yes. **Restrooms and Showers:** Yes. **Fuel:** No. **Propane:** No. **Internal Roads:** Paved. **RV Service:** No. **Market:** No. **Restaurant:** 4 mi. north. **General Store:** No. **Vending:** No. **Swimming:** Yes. **Playground:** Yes. **Activities:** Amphitheater, biking, bird-watching, boating, campfire programs, canoeing, fishing, hiking, hunting, photography, scuba diving, sightseeing, skiing, snowshoeing, waterskiing, wildlife viewing.

RESTRICTIONS

Pets: Pets must be on a leash at all times. **Fires:** Allowed; Campfire Program. **Alcoholic Beverages:** Not allowed. **Vehicle Maximum Length:** Varies; call ahead. **Other:** No metal detectors allowed, or collecting of artifacts. No livestock. No ATVs or ORVs allowed. No beach fires Nov. 1–May 1.

TO GET THERE

Spring Canyon is located just above Grand Coulee Dam.

KETTLE FALLS MAP, A-4
Haag Cove Campground

1368 South Kettle Park Rd., 99141.
T: (509) 738-6366; www.nps.gov/laro.

🚐 ★★★★ ⛺ ★★★★

Beauty: ★★★★★	Site Privacy: ★★★★
Spaciousness: ★★★★★	Quiet: ★★★★★
Security: ★★★	Cleanliness: ★★★★
Insect Control: ★★★	Facilities: ★★★

Set on the shore of Lake Roosevelt, against the sprawling backdrop of Colville National Forest—a 1,095,368-acre parcel in central northeastern Washington—Haag Cove is one of 32 campgrounds within the magnificent Coulee Dam National Recreation Area managed by the National Park Service. Deep canyons, sagebrush hills, and forested mountains are home to many kinds of animal and bird populations. One of the best spots for observing and shooting (with a camera) is just north of Haag Cove in Sherman Creek Habitat Management Area. The confluence of Sherman Creek and Lake Roosevelt produces a quality fly-fishing spot. The only other campground in the vicinity is Sherman Creek. However, it is boat-in only—one of the few campgrounds in eastern Washington accessible only via watercraft. Hiking options are plentiful and relatively uncrowded in Colville National Forest. A gentler terrain, drier climate, and longer season compared to the Cascade area make for ideal conditions for treks into the backcountry here.

BASICS

Operated By: National Park Service. **Open:** All year. **Site Assignment:** First come, first served. **Registration:** Not necessary. **Fee:** $10; winter, $5. **Parking:** At site.

FACILITIES

Number of Multipurpose Sites: 16. **Hookups:** None. **Dump Station:** No. **Laundry:** No. **Pay**

Phone: No. **Restrooms and Showers:** Vault toilets. **Fuel:** 3 mi. in Kettle Falls. **Propane:** 3 mi. **Internal Roads:** Paved. **RV Service:** No. **Market:** 3 mi. in Kettle Falls. **Restaurant:** 3 mi. **General Store:** 3 mi. **Vending:** No. **Swimming:** No. **Playground:** No. **Other:** Boat launch (in Kettle Falls). **Activities:** Fishing, boating, hiking, biking, badminton, bird-watching. **Nearby Attractions:** Lake Roosevelt, Colville National Forest. **Additional Information:** www.nps.gov/laro.

RESTRICTIONS

Pets: On leash only. **Fires:** Fire pit only. **Alcoholic Beverages:** At site only. **Vehicle Maximum Length:** 26 ft. **Other:** Fishing license & boat launch permit required. Extended stay of 2 or more weeks not recommended due to lead smelting plant (closed, but still contaminated).

TO GET THERE

From Kettle Falls (81 mi. northwest of Spokane), drive west on SR 20 across this upper portion of the Columbia River, and stay on SR 20 as it turns south along the river to the turnoff for Inchelium–Kettle Falls Rd. at about 7 mi. Take Inchelium–Kettle Falls Rd. south for 5 mi. to the campground.

KETTLE FALLS MAP, A-4
Kettle Falls Campground

1368 Kettle Park Rd., 99141. T: (509) 738-6266; www.reserveamerica.com.

🚐 ★★★★ ⛺ ★★★★

Beauty: ★★★★	Site Privacy: ★★★
Spaciousness: ★★★★	Quiet: ★★★★
Security: ★★★★★	Cleanliness: ★★★★
Insect Control: ★★★	Facilities: ★★★★

Kettle Falls are actually dormant under 80 feet of water formed by the backwaters of Grand Coulee Dam. There are approximately 50 first-come, first-served sites designated in this campground. St. Paul's Mission is located about 2 miles from the campground. Also in the area are Fort Colville and the Hudson Bay Company Post on the Upper Columbia. Extensive Native American history dates back 9,000 years in area. Kettle Falls is located within Lake Roosevelt National Recreation Area, a region renowned for towering trees, soaring mountains, deep gorges, and expansive wilderness. Lake Roosevelt National Recreation Area can rightfully claim a place among the Pacific Northwest's outstanding resources. The largest lake in the area, Lake Roosevelt is ideal for motor boating, water-skiing, sailing, and fishing. In the surrounding sagebrush hills and forested mountains, you can camp, picnic, hike, hunt, and sightsee. The creation of this sprawling recreation area began with 24 million tons of concrete and steel: Grand Coulee Dam. A Goliath of a dam, it was built to turn the power of the Columbia River into electricity and turn vast deserts into productive farmlands. Today the recreation area preserves in their natural setting reminders of the days when Native Americans fished the free-flowing

---

Columbia River, and fur trappers, farmers, missionaries, and soldiers first worked and settled this region. Here, the new and old coexist side by side.

BASICS

Operated By: National Park Service. **Open:** All year. **Site Assignment:** Reservations must be made at least 7 days in advance w/ a nonrefundable reservation fee. **Registration:** At registration office. **Fee:** Single, $5–$10. **Parking:** At park.

FACILITIES

Number of Multipurpose Sites: 184. **Hookups:** None. **Each Site:** Picnic table, fire ring. **Dump Station:** Yes. **Laundry:** No. **Pay Phone:** No. **Restrooms and Showers:** Yes. **Fuel:** No. **Propane:** No. **Internal Roads:** Paved. **RV Service:** No. **Market:** No. **Restaurant:** W/in 20 mi. **General Store:** Yes. **Vending:** No. **Swimming:** Yes. **Playground:** Yes. **Activities:** Biking, bird-watching, boating, campfire programs, canoeing, fishing, hiking, hunting, photography, scuba diving, skiing, showshoeing, softball, water-skiing, wildlife viewing.

RESTRICTIONS

Pets: Under physical control at all times, must not be left alone. **Fires:** Allowed; campfire program. **Alcoholic Beverages:** Not allowed. **Vehicle Maximum Length:** Varies; call ahead. **Other:** No ATVs or ORVs allowed. There are no electricity/water/sewer site hookups at this campground. No metal detectors or collecting of artifacts allowed.

TO GET THERE

Located 87 mi. north of Spokane. Take US 395 north to the town of Kettle Falls. Turn south on Boise Rd. at Barney's Bridge and travel 3 mi. to the campground.

LA PUSH MAP, B-1
Mora Campground

3283 Mora Rd., 98331. T: (360) 374-5460 or (360) 565-3130; www.northolympic.com.

🚐 ★★★★ ⛺ ★★★★

Beauty: ★★★★★	Site Privacy: ★★★★
Spaciousness: ★★★★	Quiet: ★★★★★
Security: ★★★	Cleanliness: ★★★★
Insect Control: ★★★★★	Facilities: ★★★

Mora Campground, part of the network of well-attended Olympic National Park facilities, is among the elite when it comes to its location (only a mile or so from the Pacific Ocean). For a total of 57 unspoiled and challenging miles, the saltwater frontage of the Pacific Ocean is a panoply of protruding headlands, swirling tidepools, crashing surf, and stalwart "sea-stacks." Situated at sea level, Mora is open all year and is an ideal choice for off-season travel. Actually, winter months and early spring can be some of the best times weather-wise at the Washington coast. You'll have an opportunity to watch the migratory gray whales pass on their way to southern California and Mexico. A word of warning: Coastal hiking requires a tide table at all times of the year. The "Strip of Wilderness" brochure available at the Mora Ranger Station is full of information about the pleasures and precautions of coastal hiking. Check at either the Mora station or information stations along US 101 for other options in this part of Olympic National Park and the surrounding national forest. One last word: The Native American reservations that border the Park along the coast are private property.

BASICS

Operated By: Olympic National Park, National Park Service, U.S. Dept. of Interior. **Open:** All year. **Site Assignment:** First come, first served. **Registration:** Self-registration. **Fee:** $10. **Parking:** At site.

FACILITIES

Number of RV-only Sites: 6. **Number of Tent-only Sites:** 94. **Hookups:** None. **Dump Station:** Yes. **Laundry:** No. **Pay Phone:** No. **Restrooms and Showers:** Yes (no showers). **Fuel:** 12 mi. in Forks. **Propane:** 12 mi. **Internal Roads:** Paved. **RV Service:** No. **Market:** 12 mi. in Forks. **Restaurant:** 12 mi. **General Store:** 1 mi. **Vending:** No. **Swimming:** No (1 mi. to coast). **Playground:** No. **Other:** Amphitheater. **Activities:** Hiking, campfire programs, tide pool walks. **Nearby Attractions:** Olympic Wilderness Area. **Additional Information:** www.northolympic.com.

RESTRICTIONS

Pets: On leash only. **Fires:** Fire pit only. **Alcoholic Beverages:** Allowed. **Vehicle Maximum Length:** 21 ft. **Other:** No vehicles allowed off park roads, permits required for extended hikes.

TO GET THERE

From either north or south, take US 101 around the Olympic Peninsula to the town of Forks (between 125 and 200 mi. from Seattle, depending on which route you take). About 1 mi. north of Forks, turn west onto La Push Rd. and drive for about 10 mi. to Mora Rd. Turn right onto Mora Rd. and follow the signs to the campground.

LEAVENWORTH   MAP, B-3
Icicle River RV Resort

7305 Icicle Rd., 98826. T: (509) 548-5420; www.icicleriverrv.com.

🚐 ★★★★★	🏕 n/a
Beauty: ★★★★★	Site Privacy: ★
Spaciousness: ★★★	Quiet: ★★★★★
Security: ★★★	Cleanliness: ★★★★
Insect Control: ★★	Facilities: ★

Icicle River RV Resort, a few minutes from the western edge of Leavenworth, has to have the most spectacular localized scenery of any RV park in Washington State. The grounds, partially shaded by birch and pines, sit very near Wenatchee National Forest boundaries and on a small alpine river, across which beautifully gray, rocky hills rise steeply toward the sky. No truly undesirable sites exist in this park; the best full-hookup options sit on the river (sites 15–28 and 59–62). Full-hookup sites 42–56 also have spectacular views. The park has a few water and electric sites, and some sites have gravel while others have concrete surfaces. Most sites have grass perimeters and some shade. The resort provides a very quiet, mellow place to relax away from the tourist hustle of Leavenworth, feeling worlds apart from the

Bavarian tourist trap; the park seldom feels crowded, even when full. Mild mountain summers are the best time to travel here; winters bring snow and cold weather.

BASICS

Operated By: Icicle River RV. **Open:** Apr. 1–Nov. 30. **Site Assignment:** First come, first served; by reservation ($25 deposit; refund w/ 48-hour cancellation notice). **Registration:** At office; after hours ring management from facility outside office. **Fee:** Full (50 amps), $30; full, $27; water/electric, $25; for 2 people; extra adult, $4; extra child (6–16), $3; extra vehicle, $4; V, MC, cash. **Parking:** At site, some off site.

FACILITIES

Number of RV-only Sites: 106. **Hookups:** Electric (20, 30, 50 amps), water, sewer, cable TV, central data port. **Each Site:** Picnic table. **Dump Station:** No. **Laundry:** Yes. **Pay Phone:** Yes. **Restrooms and Showers:** Yes. **Fuel:** No. **Propane:** Yes. **Internal Roads:** Paved, gravel. **RV Service:** No. **Market:** East 5 min. in Leavenworth. **Restaurant:** East 5 min. in Leavenworth. **General Store:** Yes. **Vending:** No. **Swimming:** Yes. **Playground:** No. **Other:** Small creek-side beach, hot tub, 2 reservable & fully enclosed pavilions, croquet, putting green. **Activities:** Putting, river fishing, hiking, biking, river swimming. **Nearby Attractions:** Wenatchee Nat'l Forest, Leavenworth Bavarian Village, Ohme Gardens, Icicle Junction Family Fun Center, Rocky Reach Dam. **Additional Information:** Leavenworth Chamber of Commerce, (509) 548-5807.

RESTRICTIONS

Pets: On leash only. **Fires:** Fire pit only. **Alcoholic Beverages:** At site only. **Vehicle Maximum Length:** No limit. **Other:** No tents.

TO GET THERE

From the center of Leavenworth, go 1 mi. west on Hwy. 2, then turn left on Icicle Rd. Icicle River RV Resort's entrance is on the left.

LEAVENWORTH   MAP, B-3
Lake Wenatchee State Park

21588A Hwy. 207, 98826. T: (509) 763-3101; www.parks.wa.gov.

🚐 ★★★	🏕 ★★★★
Beauty: ★★★★★	Site Privacy: ★★★
Spaciousness: ★★★	Quiet: ★★★
Security: ★★★★	Cleanliness: ★★★★
Insect Control: ★★	Facilities: ★★★

Although it is quite large, Lake Wenatchee State Park is a pretty nice spot with spacious, secluded campsites and oodles of choices for enjoying the outdoor recreation of one of Washington State's most scenic and untainted areas. It is a sprawling 489-acre complex divided into north and south campgrounds. The sites are available on a first-come, first-serve basis, and if you can manage it, go for the sites in the northern section. They're closer to the river and more spacious. On this eastern slope of the Cascades, summers are hot and dry. Thunderstorms materialize out of nowhere, and lightning

strikes can quickly ignite the forests in late summer and early fall. Be aware of the fire danger at all times. Also be aware that this is bear country. Food should be stored in bear-proof containers (or at least the car) when not being consumed; a tent is not much of a deterrent to a hungry bear.

BASICS

Operated By: Washington State Parks & Recreation Commission. **Open:** All year. **Site Assignment:** First come, first served; reservations May 15–Sept. 15; call (800) 452-5687; $6 fee. **Registration:** Self-registration. **Fee:** $12. **Parking:** At site.

FACILITIES

Number of RV-only Sites: 42. **Number of Tent-only Sites:** 155. **Hookups:** None. **Dump Station:** Yes. **Laundry:** No. **Pay Phone:** Yes. **Restrooms and Showers:** Yes. **Fuel:** 21 mi. in Leavenworh. **Propane:** Yes. **Internal Roads:** Paved. **RV Service:** No. **Market:** 21 mi. in Leavenworth. **Restaurant:** No. **General Store:** Yes. **Vending:** No. **Swimming:** Yes. **Playground:** No. **Other:** Amphitheater, boat launch, boat rentals, group camp, firewood, kitchen shelters (w/o electricity). **Activities:** Boating, horseback riding, campfire programs, nature walks, golf, junior ranger programs, rock climbing, volleyball field. **Nearby Attractions:** Alpine Lakes Wilderness. **Additional Information:** www.parks.wa.gov.

RESTRICTIONS

Pets: On leash only. **Fires:** Fire pit only. **Alcoholic Beverages:** At site or picnic area. **Vehicle Maximum Length:** No limit. **Other:** No firewood gathering.

TO GET THERE

From Leavenworth (23 mi. west of Wenatchee), take US 2 west for 16 mi. to SR 207. The state park and campground are 5 mi. up SR 207.

LEAVENWORTH   MAP, B-3
Pine Village KOA

11401 River Bend Dr., 98826. T: (509) 548-7709 or (800) 562 5709; www.koa.com.

🚐 ★★★★	🏕 ★★★
Beauty: ★★★★	Site Privacy: ★
Spaciousness: ★★★	Quiet: ★★★
Security: ★★	Cleanliness: ★★★
Insect Control: ★★	Facilities: ★★★★

Pine Village KOA, located minutes east of the tourist mecca of Leavenworth, has to be one of the busiest campgrounds in Washington State, mostly due to its scenic location. The nearby Wenatchee National Forest houses some of the most beautiful alpine scenery around. Since it has an array of in-house recreation opportunities, the KOA stays buzzing with families, but the grounds do have some quieter areas amid all of the chaos. Sites have a seemingly arbitrary arrangement over a pine-shaded, hilly area near the Wenatchee River. Full-hookup RV sites 1–17 and 19–38 have a crowded feel, as do tent sites T4–T9 and T11–T24 located in and around a large field of grass. The least traffic-prone areas provide a less-crowded feel; gravel full-hookup sites H1–H8 and R1–R4 and dirt tent sites R5–R21 make up the best of these. Be prepared for plenty of people regardless, as the common areas stay packed during the summer. Even so, summer provides the best season to visit this alpine area.

BASICS

Operated By: Pine Village KOA. **Open:** Mar. 20–Nov. 1. **Site Assignment:** First come, first served; reservations require 1-night deposit; refund w/ 5-day cancellation notice). **Registration:** At office; after hours at drop by office. **Fee:** Full, $36; water/electric, $34; tent, $29; for 2 people; extra adult, $4.50; extra child (age 5–17), $4; extra vehicles, $5; children (age 5 & under), free; V, MC, cash. **Parking:** At site, some off site.

FACILITIES

Number of RV-only Sites: 135. **Number of Tent-only Sites:** 45. **Hookups:** Electric (20, 30, 50 amps), water, sewer, cable TV. **Each Site:** Picnic table, grill. **Dump Station:** Yes. **Laundry:** Yes. **Pay Phone:** Yes. **Restrooms and Showers:** Yes. **Fuel:** No. **Propane:** No. **Internal Roads:** Paved. **RV Service:** No. **Market:** 3 mi. west in Leavenworth. **Restaurant:** 3 mi. west in Leavenworth. **General Store:** Yes. **Vending:** Yes. **Swimming:** Yes. **Playground:** Yes. **Other:** Spa, game room, horseshoes, large covered pavilion, basketball, group areas, volleyball, horseshoes. **Activities:** Sat. night hay rides, train rides (small motorized cart pulling small cars), hiking, swimming, shuttle to Leavenworth, free coffee. **Nearby Attractions:** Ohme Gardens, Rocky Reach Dam, Icicle Junction Family Fun Center, Nutcracker Museum, North Central Washington Museum, Lake Wenatchee, Wenatchee National Forest. **Additional Information:** Leavenworth Chamber of Commerce, (509) 548-5807.

RESTRICTIONS

Pets: On leash only, not allowed in recreation areas. **Fires:** Fire pits, grills only. **Alcoholic Beverages:** At site only. **Vehicle Maximum Length:** No limit. **Other:** Don't tie clotheslines to trees or damage trees.

TO GET THERE

From Hwy. 2 east of town heading west, turn right onto River Bend Dr., located by a Safeway. Follow signs for 0.5 mi.; entrance is on the right.

LOPEZ   MAP, A-1
Spencer Spit State Park

Hwy. 2, P.O. Box 3600, 98261. T: (360) 468-2251; www.parks.wa.gov.

🚐 ★★★★	🛖 ★★★★
Beauty: ★★★★★	Site Privacy: ★★★★
Spaciousness: ★★★★	Quiet: ★★★★★
Security: ★★★	Cleanliness: ★★★★
Insect Control: ★★★★	Facilities: ★★★

Spencer Spit is an excellent base camp for enjoying Lopez and its sister islands by car, foot, or bicycle. The only drawback to lovely little Spencer Spit is the Washington State ferry system. Plan on becoming a veritable scholar of the ferry schedule. One of the most appealing aspects of Spencer Spit State Park is

that you can camp right on the beach—in designated areas, of course. You will have to pack your gear down from the parking lot above. Lopez Island is, in our opinion, the premier bicycling island of the San Juans and can easily be covered in a day of riding if you're accustomed to 40 miles or so. A terrific excursion on Lopez is to ride out to Shark Reef Park to watch the sea lions that sprawl en masse on the offshore rocks. You can also look far across the San Juan Channel to windswept Cattle Point on San Juan Island, where the only sand dunes in the entire island group exist.

BASICS

Operated By: Washington State Parks & Recreation Commission. **Open:** Mar.–Oct. **Site Assignment:** Reservations required; call (800) 452-5687; $6. **Registration:** Self-registration. **Fee:** $6–$12. **Parking:** In campground & at some sites; parking for beach sites near trailhead.

FACILITIES

Number of Multipurpose Sites: 41. **Hookups:** Sewer (dump station). **Dump Station:** Yes. **Laundry:** No. **Pay Phone:** No. **Restrooms and Showers:** Yes. **Fuel:** On island. **Propane:** On island. **Internal Roads:** Paved. **RV Service:** No. **Market:** On island. **Restaurant:** On island. **General Store:** On island. **Vending:** No. **Swimming:** No. **Playground:** No. **Other:** 2 kitchen shelters w/o electricity. **Activities:** Boating, diving, fishing, clamming, crabbing, wildlife viewing, biking, water craft launch site, nightly moorage available for fee. **Nearby Attractions:** San Juan Islands National Wildlife Refuge, Shark Reef Park, Cattle Point, Village of Lopez, Richardson & Mackay. **Additional Information:** www.parks.wa.gov.

RESTRICTIONS

Pets: On leash only. **Fires:** Fire pit only. **Alcoholic Beverages:** At site only. **Vehicle Maximum Length:** 28 ft.

TO GET THERE

From the ferry terminal at the north end of Lopez Island, take Ferry Rd. south, and follow the signs to the park. The total distance from the ferry terminal is barely 5 mi.

NORTH BEND   MAP, B-2
Denny Creek Campground

reserve america

42404 SE North Bend Way, 98045. T: (425) 888-1421; www.reserveamerica.com.

🚐 ★★★★	🛖 ★★★
Beauty: ★★★★★	Site Privacy: ★★
Spaciousness: ★★★	Quiet: ★★★★
Security: ★★	Cleanliness: ★★
Insect Control: ★★	Facilities: ★★

Denny Creek Campground, a National Forest Campground around an hour east of Seattle and in the vicinity of Snoqualmie Pass, provides a beautiful alpine forest landscape. The limited facilities include flush toilets only, and a few electric hookups; the park's facilities almost fit a description of rustic. Of the electric sites, paved pull-throughs 30–33 have

the best location. Back-in sites 16–22 sit in an area with semiprivacy for each site and near a south fork of the Snoqualmie River. All back-in sites have paved parking, with a large adjacent area used for tenting. Shaded by firs and birch, the whole park provides a peaceful, quiet retreat. Summers bring the best time to visit the area, but nights can still be cool at this altitude.

BASICS

Operated By: Recreational Resource Mgmt. for National Forest Service. **Open:** Mid-May–mid-Oct.; weather permitting. **Site Assignment:** On arrival, reservations (877) 444-6777. **Registration:** At self-pay station. **Fee:** Electric, $20; extra vehicle, $7; no hookup, $16; second vehicle, $6; cash upon arrival. **Parking:** At site.

FACILITIES

Number of Multipurpose Sites: 33. **Hookups:** Electric (20 amps). **Each Site:** Picnic table, fire ring. **Dump Station:** No. **Laundry:** No. **Pay Phone:** No. **Restrooms and Showers:** Flush toilets only. **Fuel:** No. **Propane:** No. **Internal Roads:** Paved. **RV Service:** No. **Market:** Up the Interstate a few mi. **Restaurant:** Up the Interstate a few mi. **General Store:** No. **Vending:** No. **Swimming:** No. **Playground:** No. **Activities:** Inquire at campground. **Nearby Attractions:** Hiking trails, Mt. Baker-Snoqualmie National Forest, skiing, fishing, golf, Seattle. **Additional Information:** Washington State Tourism Office, (360) 725-5052.

RESTRICTIONS

Pets: On 6-ft. leash only. **Fires:** Fire pit only. **Alcoholic Beverages:** At site only. **Vehicle Maximum Length:** 35 ft. (a few 40s). **Other:** Ask about collecting dead & down wood for campfires.

TO GET THERE

Take Exit 47 off I-90. Go north, then turn right at the T intersection. Travel 0.25 mi. and turn left on Denny Creek Rd. 58. Continue for 2 mi. to the campground entrance on the left.

OCEAN PARK   MAP, C-1
Evergreen Court Campground

222nd Ave. and WA 103, 98640. T: (360) 665-6351.

🚐 n/a	🛖 ★★★
Beauty: ★★★	Site Privacy: ★★★
Spaciousness: ★★★	Quiet: ★★★★
Security: ★★★★★	Cleanliness: ★★★★★
Insect Control: ★★★★	Facilities: ★★

Long Beach Peninsula, so named by its claim to be the world's longest beach, struggles to find a workable balance between tourism promoters, real estate developers, oyster farmers, and cranberry harvesters. In the midst of this multiple-use stretch of surf and sand is Evergreen Court Campground, a five-acre haven for those willing to make the circuitous journey to this place of subtle beauty. Its proximity to Leadbetter Point State Park and the 11,000-acre Willapa National Wildlife Refuge makes Evergreen Court the perfect choice for those interested in all that these state and federal managed areas offer. For ocean access, Klipsan Beach Trail can be found about a half mile north of the campground, and a place to clean fish is provided for those who have a bit of luck at freshwater Loomis Lake, which is connected to the campground.

BASICS

Operated By: John & Deanna Klattenhoff. **Open:** All year. **Site Assignment:** Reservations or first come, first served. **Registration:** At camp office or by mail w/ deposit. **Fee:** $12; for 2 people; each additional person, $1. **Parking:** At site or in main lot.

FACILITIES

Number of RV-only Sites: 0. **Number of Tent-only Sites:** 8. **Hookups:** None. **Each Site:** Picnic table, fire pit w/ grill. **Dump Station:** No. **Laundry:** No. **Pay Phone:** Yes. **Restrooms and Showers:** Yes. **Fuel:** No. **Propane:** No. **Internal Roads:** Gravel. **RV Service:** No. **Market:** 2 mi. in Ocean Park. **Restaurant:** 2 mi. **General Store:** 2 mi. **Vending:** No. **Swimming:** No. **Playground:** Yes. **Activities:** Year-round renters participate in community activities. **Nearby Attractions:** Willapa National Wildlife Refuge.

RESTRICTIONS

Pets: On leash only. **Fires:** Fire pit only. **Alcoholic Beverages:** Allowed. **Vehicle Maximum Length:** Call ahead for details.

TO GET THERE

From Seattle, take I-5 to Kelso/Longview (133 mi.). Go west on SR 4 for 62 mi. to Johnson's Landing. Turn south onto US 101 across the Naselle River and around the southern end of Willapa Bay to the turnoff for SR 103 and Long Beach Peninsula. Take SR 103 north. Evergreen Court Campground is 7 mi. north of Long Beach at the intersection of SR 103 and 222nd Ave. From Portland, take US 30 northwest along the Columbia River for 95 mi. to Astoria. Cross the bridge into Washington on US 101, turning left (west) onto SR 103 after 10 mi. From there, the directions are the same as from Seattle.

OLYMPIA   MAP, B-1
American Heritage Campground

9610 Kimmie St. SW, 98512. T: (360) 943-8778; www.americanheritagecampground.com.

🚐 ★★★★   ⛺ ★★★

Beauty: ★★★★	Site Privacy: ★★★★
Spaciousness: ★★★	Quiet: ★★
Security: ★	Cleanliness: ★★★
Insect Control: ★★	Facilities: ★★★★

American Heritage, the family-oriented sister campground of Olympia Campground, puts in a bid as a destination park. The older park has sites set within a well-manicured forest; the RV section has wide, paved sites, and the tenting section has a manicured yet unimproved feeling. Most sites create semiprivate environments and receive lots of shade from tall conifers overhead. The best sites for both types of camping sit on the perimeters of their respective sections; sites on the medians of sections often lack any seclusion. As far as recreation goes, the destination section of the park kind of feels like a Florida reptile

farm, but kids won't notice. The park offers easy access to the interstate and a good amount of quiet; though it's open only in summer, you will still need a jacket for the cool western Washington nights.

BASICS

Operated By: Olympia Campgrounds. **Open:** Memorial Day–Labor Day. **Site Assignment:** First come, first served & by reservation. **Registration:** At office; after hours see instructions outside office. **Fee:** Full, $28; water/electric, $27; tent, $20; for 2 adults & 2 children; extra person, $4. **Parking:** At site.

FACILITIES

Number of RV-only Sites: 74. **Number of Tent-only Sites:** 25. **Hookups:** Electric (20, 30 amps), water, sewer. **Each Site:** Picnic table, fire ring. **Dump Station:** Yes. **Laundry:** Yes. **Pay Phone:** Yes. **Restrooms and Showers:** Yes. **Fuel:** No. **Propane:** Yes. **Internal Roads:** Paved. **RV Service:** No. **Market:** 5 mi. north in Olympia. **Restaurant:** 4 mi. north in Olympia. **General Store:** Yes. **Vending:** No. **Swimming:** Yes. **Playground:** Yes. **Other:** Movie room, kiddie farm, bike rentals, horseshoes, volleyball, badminton, rec hall, pavilion, bike track. **Activities:** Movies nightly, hay rides, various planned activities. **Nearby Attractions:** Olympia Farmers Market, Tumwater Falls Park, Monarch Sculpture Park, Yashiro Japanese Garden, Puget Sound, Seattle. **Additional Information:** Olympia Thurston County Visitor & Convention Bureau, (360) 704-7544 or (877) 704-7500.

RESTRICTIONS

Pets: On leash only, quiet. **Fires:** Fire pit only. **Alcoholic Beverages:** At site only. **Vehicle Maximum Length:** 40 ft. **Other:** Check in at 1 p.m.

TO GET THERE

Take Exit 99 off I-5, go 0.3 mi. east on 93rd Ave., then left on Kimmie St. SW for 0.3 mi.; the road dead-ends into campground.

PACKWOOD   MAP, C-2
Ohanapecosh Campground

Mount Rainier National Park, Tahoma Woods, Star Rte., 98304-9751. T: (360) 569-2211.

🚐 ★★★★   ⛺ ★★★★

Beauty: ★★★★★	Site Privacy: ★★
Spaciousness: ★★★	Quiet: ★★★★
Security: ★★	Cleanliness: ★★★
Insect Control: ★★	Facilities: ★★★

Ohanapecosh Campground, on the east side of Mt. Rainier National Park, offers a more open feeling than Cougar Creek. Located in an old-growth forest near a rocky, cascading alpine river, the campground draws lots of campers year-round. Sites have less low-growing foliage than those at Cougar Creek, sacrificing privacy but creating a more spacious feeling below a canopy of tall evergreens. The campground has an organization of several shady loops; loop C has sites on the river, with several walk-in tent sites right on the banks. Other loops lack riverfront property but still provide a beautiful camping environment. The only loop to really avoid, B loop, has higher traffic

and a location among campground facilities. Visit during the summer for the best temperatures, although you might still need a jacket at night.

BASICS

Operated By: National Park Service. **Open:** Late May–mid-Oct.; weather permitting. **Site Assignment:** On arrival; reservations highly recommended & available July 1–Labor Day; call (800) 365-CAMP; 1-night deposit; refund w/ 24-hour cancellation notice less $13.25 fee. **Registration:** At self-pay station. **Fee:** Reserved, $15; self-pay, $12; V, MC, D, cash. **Parking:** At site.

FACILITIES

Number of Multipurpose Sites: 188. **Hookups:** Sewer (dump station). **Each Site:** Picnic table, fire ring. **Dump Station:** Yes. **Laundry:** No. **Pay Phone:** Yes. **Restrooms and Showers:** No showers, but flush toilets. **Fuel:** No. **Propane:** No. **Internal Roads:** Paved, gravel. **RV Service:** No. **Market:** 11 mi. in Packwood. **Restaurant:** 11 mi. in Packwood. **General Store:** No. **Vending:** No. **Swimming:** No. **Playground:** No. **Other:** Amphitheater, hiking trails, visitor center. **Activities:** Interpretive programs, hiking. **Nearby Attractions:** Mount Rainier, hiking, fishing, backcountry camping. **Additional Information:** Ohanapecosh Visitor Center, (360) 569-2211, ext. 2352.

RESTRICTIONS

Pets: On leash only (6 ft. max length, pets not allowed on National Park trails). **Fires:** Fire pit only. Fires must be small & controlled. **Alcoholic Beverages:** At site only. **Vehicle Maximum Length:** 32 ft. **Other:** Max. of 6 people (or immediate family), 2 tents & 2 vehicles per site.

TO GET THERE

The campground is located off Hwy. 123 in the southeast corner of the park, between mile markers 4 and 3. The road in the immediate area briefly changes to 4 lanes to accommodate park traffic; if headed southbound, campground entrance is on the right.

PASCO   MAP, C-3
Sandy Heights RV Park

8801 St. Thomas Dr., 99301. T: (509) 547-3521 or (877) 894-1357; www.nwfamilyrvresorts.com.

🚐 ★★★★   ⛺ ★★★

Beauty: ★★★	Site Privacy: ★
Spaciousness: ★★★	Quiet: ★★★
Security: ★★★★	Cleanliness: ★★★★★
Insect Control: ★★	Facilities: ★★★

Sandy Heights RV Park, off I-182 in Pasco, provides a good base for exploring the tri-cities area. The grounds have a suburban park-like feel, lots of grass, the occasional red or green seedling, and well-kept facilities. Recreational facilities include a basketball court with opposing goals and a large hot tub. The grass-perimetered, flat, paved, full-hookup sites come in both the pull-through and back-in variety. The park has no official tent sites, but tents are allowed. The best back-in sites, 114–185, sit on the perimeter of the park with no neighbors to the rear;

the pull-through sites lack any distinguishable differences. Security fences around the perimeter help to keep outsiders out, but also obscure views of the surrounding barren hills. Summers here stay hot, and winters stay cold; avoid visits during the hottest of summer months.

BASICS

Operated By: Sandy Heights RV. **Open:** All year. **Site Assignment:** On arrival; reservation requires 1-night deposit; refund w/ 24-hour cancellation notice. **Registration:** At office; after hours pay in morning. **Fee:** RV, $22.50; tent, $18; for 2 people; extra adult, $2.50; phone, $3; no charge for kids; V, MC, cash. **Parking:** At site, some off site.

FACILITIES

Number of RV-only Sites: 185. **Hookups:** Electric (20, 30, 50 amps), water, sewer, cable TV, phone. **Each Site:** Picnic table. **Dump Station:** Yes. **Laundry:** Yes. **Pay Phone:** Yes. **Restrooms and Showers:** Yes. **Fuel:** No. **Propane:** Yes. **Internal Roads:** Paved. **RV Service:** No. **Market:** 5 mi. west on I-182. **Restaurant:** 5 mi. west on I-182. **General Store:** Yes. **Vending:** No. **Swimming:** Yes. **Playground:** Yes. **Other:** Hot tub, basketball court, horseshoes, volleyball, barbecue area, reservable meeting hall. **Activities:** Occasional potluck, ice-cream socials on Sun. (seasonal). **Nearby Attractions:** Wineries, golf, rodeos, boating, waterskiing, fishing, Oasis Waterworks (water park), Lewis & Clark Trail historical sites. **Additional Information:** Pasco Chamber of Commerce, (509) 547-9755.

RESTRICTIONS

Pets: On leash only. **Fires:** No open fires. **Alcoholic Beverages:** At site only. **Vehicle Maximum Length:** No limit. **Other:** 3-day stay limit for tents.

TO GET THERE

From I-182 Exit 7 (westbound, turn left) onto Broadmoor, drive 0.1 mi. south and turn at the first left onto St. Thomas Dr. Drive 1 mi. on St. Thomas, and the park is at the end of the road. on the left.

PORT ANGELES   MAP, B-1
Heart o' the Hills Campground

Olympic National Park, Olympic Hot Springs Rd., 98362-6798. T: (360) 565-3130; www.nps.gov.

🚐 ★★★★	⛺ ★★★★★
Beauty: ★★★★★	Site Privacy: ★★★
Spaciousness: ★★	Quiet: ★★★★
Security: ★★	Cleanliness: ★★★★
Insect Control: ★★	Facilities: ★

Heart o' the Hills Campground, the closest Olympic National Park campground in relation to Port Angeles (the largest city in the national park area), has the best variety in nearby recreation of any of the park campgrounds. Laid out over rolling hills, campsites sit under the canopy of an old-growth forest. Every site has a dirt area where a tent can be erected; parking areas have pavement. The surrounding forest has a vibrancy hard to find anywhere else, with lots of symbiotic plant and fungal relationships, wildlife, and atmosphere. Of the five single-loop sections, E loop has the least-open feel. All sites have at least a

little privacy and lots of shade. Summers on the Olympic Peninsula bring lots of tourists, as the region has a look and feel like no other; if it's the on-season, be prepared for some crowds. Local weather is temperate, and summers can be cool, so bring rain gear and cold-weather clothes.

BASICS

Operated By: National Park Service. **Open:** All year. **Site Assignment:** First come, first served. **Registration:** At self-pay station. **Fee:** $10. **Parking:** At site.

FACILITIES

Number of Multipurpose Sites: 105. **Hookups:** None. **Each Site:** Picnic table, fire ring. **Dump Station:** No. **Laundry:** No. **Pay Phone:** At park entrance. **Restrooms and Showers:** No showers. **Fuel:** No. **Propane:** No. **Internal Roads:** Paved. **RV Service:** No. **Market:** In Port Angeles. **Restaurant:** In Port Angeles. **General Store:** No. **Vending:** No. **Swimming:** No. **Playground:** No. **Other:** Amphitheater. **Activities:** Hiking, salt-water fishing, boating, interpretive programs. **Nearby Attractions:** Olympic National Park, Hurricane Ridge. **Additional Information:** ONP Info, (360) 452-0330; Port Angeles Chamber of Commerce, (360) 452-2363.

RESTRICTIONS

Pets: On leash only (6 ft. max length, not allowed on any park trails). **Fires:** Fire pit only. **Alcoholic Beverages:** At site only. **Vehicle Maximum Length:** 21 ft. (limited availability up to 32 ft.). **Other:** Store all food in a bear-proof location, wash all dishes promptly & don't drop food scraps. In campgrounds where wood is not available, dead & down wood along public roads may be collected. Max. occupancy 8 people per site. 14-day stay limit.

TO GET THERE

From Hwy. 101 southbound in Port Angeles, turn left on Race St. (at traffic light). Drive 1 mi., and after NPS Visitor's Center road forks, follow the right side of the fork. Drive 5.5 mi., through the entrance gate, and the campground is on the left.

PORT ANGELES   MAP, B-1
Hoh Rain Forest Campground

Olympic National Park, Olympic Hot Springs Rd., 98362-6798. T: (360) 452-4501; www.nps.gov.

🚐 ★★★★★	⛺ ★★★★★
Beauty: ★★★★★	Site Privacy: ★★★
Spaciousness: ★★	Quiet: ★★★★★
Security: ★★	Cleanliness: ★★★
Insect Control: ★★	Facilities: ★

Well off Highway 101, on the western edge of Olympic National Park sits the Hoh Rain Forest visitor center, and close by, the Hoh Rain Forest Campground. Although a popular spot for tourists, the area has a quiet, private feel during the off-season and the surrounding natural environment breathes beauty year-round. The campground has three loops; B and C loops have a similar layout with dense foliage, paved parking, and gravel-and-grass mixed areas for tents on many sites. A loop has more grass than the others, but it also has more open sites. The

benefits of such obscured views of the mountains are best reaped in sites A1–A15. Plant life throughout the area has a unique look and wide diversity; rivers and streams abound; and many hiking trails start at the visitor center and are usually open even if the center is not. Summer provides the mildest time to visit (it still can be rainy), but be warned: the park has lots of visitors June 17 through Labor Day.

BASICS

Operated By: National Park Service. **Open:** All year; some sections seasonal. **Site Assignment:** First come, first served. **Registration:** At self-pay station. **Fee:** $10; cash. **Parking:** At site, additional parking at visitor center.

FACILITIES

Number of Multipurpose Sites: 82. **Hookups:** None. **Each Site:** Picnic table, fire ring. **Dump Station:** Yes. **Laundry:** No. **Pay Phone:** No. **Restrooms and Showers:** Flush & nonflush only (no shower). **Fuel:** No. **Propane:** No. **Internal Roads:** Paved. **RV Service:** No. **Market:** A long way. **Restaurant:** A long way. **General Store:** No. **Vending:** No. **Swimming:** No. **Playground:** No. **Other:** Visitor center. **Activities:** Interpretive programs, hiking. **Nearby Attractions:** Hoh Rain Forest, Hoh River, Olympic National Park, hiking, fishing. **Additional Information:** ONP Info, (360) 452-0330.

RESTRICTIONS

Pets: On leash only (6 ft. max length, not allowed on any park trails). **Fires:** Fire pit only. **Alcoholic Beverages:** At site only. **Vehicle Maximum Length:** 28 ft. **Other:** Store all food in a bear-proof location, wash all dishes promptly & don't drop food scraps. In campgrounds where wood is not available, dead & down wood along public roads may be collected. Max. occupancy 8 people per site. 14-day stay limit.

TO GET THERE

From Hwy. 101 southbound, turn left between mile markers 179 and 178; you're looking for an unnamed (and practically unmarked) access road. Drive 12.3 mi. to the park gate; proceed through gate and drive 5.4 mi. Campground entrance is on the right.

PORT ANGELES   MAP, B-1
Log Cabin Resort

3183 East Beach Rd., 98363. T: (360) 928-3325; www.logcabinresort.net.

🚐 ★★★★	⛺ n/a
Beauty: ★★★★★	Site Privacy: ★
Spaciousness: ★★	Quiet: ★★★★
Security: ★	Cleanliness: ★★★★
Insect Control: ★★	Facilities: ★

Log Cabin Resort, west of Port Angeles and off Hwy. 101, has a small, no-frills RV area in a beautiful fishing lodge environment. The resort also has convenient access to much of Olympic National Park. Located on big, blue Lake Crescent, the shady, rust red-painted wood lodge has nonpowered boat and fishing gear rentals, a restaurant (open at volume), and a Laundromat. When occupancy in the RV section is low, individual sites have an outstanding view; when full, such is only a short walk away. Across the cold-blue lake, the Olympic mountains rise into the sky. And the whole joint's pretty quiet too. The area has sunny, mild weather most of the time, summers being most pleasant.

BASICS

Operated By: Log Cabin Resort for National Park Service. **Open:** Apr. 1–Oct. 31. **Site Assignment:** On arrival; reservations require 1-night deposit; refund less $12 fee w/ 48-hour cancellation notice. **Registration:** At office; after hours see office door; online or by mail. **Fee:** Full, $35; extra vehicle, $5; fee per pet, $12; pay showers; V, MC, cash. **Parking:** At site.

FACILITIES

Number of RV-only Sites: 38. **Hookups:** Electric (30 amps), water, sewer. **Each Site:** Picnic table, fire ring. **Dump Station:** Yes. **Laundry:** Yes. **Pay Phone:** Yes. **Restrooms and Showers:** Yes. **Fuel:** No. **Propane:** No. **Internal Roads:** Gravel. **RV Service:** No. **Market:** East in Port Angeles. **Restaurant:** On site (May to Oct.). **General Store:** Yes. **Vending:** No. **Swimming:** No. **Playground:** No. **Other:** Nonpowered-boat rentals, fishing gear rentals, lake access. **Activities:** Fishing, boating. **Nearby Attractions:** Olympic National Park. **Additional Information:** ONP Info, (360) 452-0330; Port Angeles Chamber of Commerce, (360) 452-2363.

RESTRICTIONS

Pets: In cabins & RVs only. **Fires:** Fire pit only. **Alcoholic Beverages:** At site only. **Vehicle Maximum Length:** 40 ft. (limited capacity at that length). **Other:** No tents.

TO GET THERE

From Hwy. 101 west of Port Angeles, and if driving west, turn left just after mile marker 232 onto East Beach Rd. Drive 3.2 mi., and the entrance is

PORT TOWNSEND   MAP, B-2
Fort Flagler State Park

10542 Flagler Rd., 98348. T: (360) 385-1259; www.parks.wa.gov.

🚐 ★★★★	⛺ ★★★★★
Beauty: ★★★★★	Site Privacy: ★★★
Spaciousness: ★★★	Quiet: ★★★
Security: ★	Cleanliness: ★★★
Insect Control: ★★	Facilities: ★★

Fort Flagler, situated between Port Townsend Bay and Kilisut Harbor, has 19,100 feet of saltwater shoreline. The park has two campgrounds, and both have good views. Better suited for RVs, the grassy lower campground also has better localized views than the upper. Gravel sites 97–116 have almost totally unobstructed 270-degree views of water, horizon, and mountains (and smokestacks) rising from the Washington mainland. These sites don't have any shade; sites 52–76 have shade from short coastal pines but no view. All utility sites reside in the lower campground; the upper campground lacks utilities, is only open seasonally, and has a totally different vibe. Sitting on the edge of a lush, green, heavily forested cliff, the upper campground has limited

views of the harbor below. With dirt site surfaces, narrow roads, semiprivacy, and shade, upper campground sites hold the most appeal for tent campers. Summers make the best time to visit here.

BASICS

Operated By: Washington State Parks & Recreation Commission. **Open:** Oct. 28–Mar. 1; open for day use only. **Site Assignment:** First come, first served & by reservation. **Registration:** At self-pay station or entrance gate. **Fee:** Utility, $21; standard, $15; primitive, $10; for 4 adults; extra adult, $2; extra vehicle, $6; V, MC, cash. **Parking:** At site, off site.

FACILITIES

Number of RV-only Sites: 14. **Number of Tent-only Sites:** 101. **Hookups:** None. **Each Site:** Picnic table. **Dump Station:** Yes. **Laundry:** No. **Pay Phone:** No. **Restrooms and Showers:** Yes. **Fuel:** No. **Propane:** No. **Internal Roads:** Paved. **RV Service:** No. **Market:** In Port Townsend. **Restaurant:** In Port Townsend. **General Store:** Yes. **Vending:** No. **Swimming:** No. **Playground:** No. **Other:** Fort Flagler Environmental Learning Center (call for info), boat ramp, moorage. **Activities:** Boating, fishing, swimming, crabbing, clamming. **Nearby Attractions:** The ocean, Fort Worden Military Park (historical), Olympic National Park & Forest, ferries, golf, hiking, biking. **Additional Information:** Port Townsend Chamber of Commerce, (360) 385-2722.

RESTRICTIONS

Pets: On leash only (6 ft. max length). **Fires:** Fire pit only. **Alcoholic Beverages:** At site only. **Vehicle Maximum Length:** 40 ft. **Other:** Don't play in drift wood.

TO GET THERE

From the junction of Hwy. 20 and Hwy. 19 near Port Townsend, drive 5.4 mi. on Hwy. 19 south. Turn left onto SR 116 (Oak Bay Rd.). Go through Port Hadlock 2 mi. and take a sharp left, staying on SR 116. Follow to park entrance at end of highway. Park is about 10 mi. from Oak Bay Rd. turnoff.

PORT TOWNSEND   MAP, B-2
Fort Worden State Park

200 Battery Way, 98368. T: (360) 344-4400; www.fortworden.org.

🚐 ★★★★★	⛺ ★★★
Beauty: ★★★★★	Site Privacy: ★
Spaciousness: ★★★	Quiet: ★★★★
Security: ★★	Cleanliness: ★★
Insect Control: ★★	Facilities: ★★★★

Fort Worden State Park, a military history park in Port Townsend, has two campground sections. One has spectacular views—absolutely amazing views of the water and nonpeninsular Washington beyond. Within the aptly titled "Beach Campground" sites, 1–17 have the most unobstructed views; sites 24–50 sit on a loop surrounded by dunes. The whole section hears the waves crashing on the flat beach, providing a peaceful aural backdrop. Waterfront areas have no shade or privacy to speak of; the upper area has some shade. Beach sites have flat, paved parking, while the upper campground sites have gravel park-

ing, a few primitive sites, and no views. Weather here has a knack for changing, so bring cold-weather rain gear just in case.

BASICS

Operated By: Washington State Parks & Recreation Commission. **Open:** All year. **Site Assignment:** First come, first served & by reservation. **Registration:** At park office or self-pay station in campground. **Fee:** Apr.1–Sept.30, $22 or $27; Oct.1–Mar.30, $22; extra vehicle, $10; V, MC, D, cash, check. **Parking:** At site.

FACILITIES

Number of RV-only Sites: 85. **Number of Tent-only Sites:** 5. **Number of Multipurpose Sites:** 35. **Hookups:** Electric (20, 30 amps), water, sewer. **Each Site:** Picnic table, fire ring. **Dump Station:** Yes. **Laundry:** No. **Pay Phone:** Yes. **Restrooms and Showers:** Yes. **Fuel:** No. **Propane:** No. **Internal Roads:** Paved. **RV Service:** No. **Market:** 5 mi. south in Port Townsend. **Restaurant:** 5 mi. south in Port Townsend. **General Store:** No. **Vending:** No. **Swimming:** Yes. **Playground:** No. **Other:** Boat launch, beach, convention center, military museums, hiking trails. **Activities:** Hiking, boating, fishing (check on regulations & seasons). **Nearby Attractions:** Whale-watching, fishing, boating, Olympic National Park, Olympic National Forest, shell fishing. **Additional Information:** Port Townsend Chamber of Commerce, (360) 385-2722.

RESTRICTIONS

Pets: On leash only (6 ft. max. length). **Fires:** Fire pit only. **Alcoholic Beverages:** At site only. **Vehicle Maximum Length:** 40 ft. **Other:** Do not collect driftwood for fires, do not play in driftwood (very dangerous).

TO GET THERE

From I-20 east, follow hwy. into Port Towsend, turn left on Kearney St., drive 0.4 mi., then turn right on Blaine St. Drive 1 block and turn left on Walker, which changes names several times and even forks once (take the left side). When the road dead-ends, turn right and drive 1 block; campground entrance is on the left.

RANDLE   MAP, C-2
Takhlakh Lake Campground

Cowlitz Valley Ranger District, P.O. Box 59, 98377. T: (360) 497-1100; www.reserveamerica.com.

🚐 n/a	⛺ ★★★★
Beauty: ★★★★★	Site Privacy: ★★
Spaciousness: ★★★	Quiet: ★★★★★
Security: ★★★★	Cleanliness: ★★★★
Insect Control: ★★★	Facilities: ★★★

Just imagine: you're sitting at your site at Takhlakh Lake gazing out at a picture-perfect view of Mount Adams. Most of the 54 tent sites offer views of the lake and the mountain through stands of Douglas fir, Engelmann spruce, pine, and sub alpine fir. There is a campground host in attendance at Takhlakh, so anything you can't find, feel free to inquire. There is no easy way to get to Takhlakh, which is part of its appeal. The confusing network of Forest Service roads can be downright irritating, too, if you don't have a good map of the area. If you've come in search of lazy fishing opportunities, Takhlakh is a treat. Only nonmotorized boats are allowed on the glassy waters. With an Ansel Adams–like scene at your back, cast your line, and wait for the trout lurking in the frigid glacial depths to find you.

BASICS

Operated By: Northwest Land Management. **Open:** Mid-June–Oct. **Site Assignment:** 70% of sites are reservable; call (877) 444-6777; $8.25 fee. **Registration:** Not necessary. **Fee:** $11. **Parking:** At site.

FACILITIES

Number of Multipurpose Sites: 54. **Hookups:** Water. **Dump Station:** No. **Laundry:** No. **Pay Phone:** No. **Restrooms and Showers:** Pit toilets. **Fuel:** Inquire at campground. **Propane:** 3 mi. in Randle. **Internal Roads:** Paved. **RV Service:** No. **Market:** 3 mi. in Randle. **Restaurant:** 3 mi. **General Store:** Yes. **Vending:** No. **Swimming:** No. **Playground:** No. **Other:** Campground host. **Activities:** Fishing, hiking, mountain biking. **Nearby Attractions:** Gifford Pinchot National Forest, Mount Adams Wilderness, Trout Lake, Lava Fields, New Takhtakh Meadow. **Additional Information:** www.fs.fed.us/gpnf.

RESTRICTIONS

Pets: On leash only. **Fires:** Fire pit only. **Alcoholic Beverages:** Allowed. **Vehicle Maximum Length:** 22 ft. **Other:** Nonmotorized boats only.

TO GET THERE

From Randle, take CR 3 off WA 12 at Randle. Go south for 2 mi. to FS 23. In another 29 mi., turn north onto FS 2329. The campground is a little over 1 mi. in. From Trout Lake, take FS 80 north to its intersection with FS 23. The campground is nearly the same distance from Trout Lake as from Randle, but the road twists and turns with vaguely marked intersections. The turnoff onto FS 2329 will be to the right coming from Trout Lake.

REPUBLIC — MAP, A-4
Swan Lake Campground

Republic Ranger Station, P.O. Box 468, 99166.
T: (509) 775-3305; www.fs.fed.us/r6/colville.

🚐 ★★★	🏕 ★★★
Beauty: ★★★	Site Privacy: ★★★
Spaciousness: ★★★	Quiet: ★★★★
Security: ★★★★	Cleanliness: ★★★★
Insect Control: ★★	Facilities: ★★★

Swan Lake Campground has no headliner attractions. That's why people who have checked out the area come back year after year. It has a little bit of everything, but not enough of anything to attract crowds. Once a ranger station, Swan Lake retains much of the Civilian Conservation Corps' handiwork. The kitchen shelter built by the CCC in 1933 is the only structure of its kind in the Colville forest. The structure is the epicenter of all campground activity; it is a sanctuary in storms and the gathering

place for everything from mountain biking groups to wedding parties. The nifty 2.2-mile trail circumnavigating the lake is particularly attractive to seniors and parents with kids. Although it's fun for mountain biking, most fat-tire enthusiasts head out to roughly 50 miles of single- and double-track trails that are blossoming on logging routes closed to motor vehicles. Popular routes go past beaver ponds, where the occasional moose can be found, and along Sheep Mountain, with views of the Kettle River Range.

BASICS

Operated By: Colville National Forest. **Open:** All year. **Site Assignment:** First come, first served. **Registration:** Not necessary. **Fee:** $8. **Parking:** At site & at boat launch & trailhead.

FACILITIES

Number of Tent-only Sites: 4. **Number of Multipurpose Sites:** 21. **Hookups:** Water. **Each Site:** Fire pit. **Dump Station:** No. **Laundry:** No. **Pay Phone:** Yes. **Restrooms and Showers:** Vault toilets. **Fuel:** No. **Propane:** No. **Internal Roads:** Paved. **RV Service:** No. **Market:** No. **Restaurant:** No. **General Store:** No. **Vending:** No. **Swimming:** Yes. **Playground:** No. **Other:** Group site, common cooking shelter, 12 water spigots, boat launch. **Activities:** Fishing, boating, biking, hiking. **Nearby Attractions:** Long Lake (dedicated to fly-fishing only), Stonerose Interpretive Center (in Republic). **Additional Information:** www.fs.fed.us/r6/colville.

RESTRICTIONS

Pets: On leash only. **Fires:** Fire pit only. **Alcoholic Beverages:** At site only. **Vehicle Maximum Length:** 24 ft. (several pull-throughs available for big rigs). **Other:** Fishing license required, gas motors prohibited.

TO GET THERE

From Republic on SR 20, drive south on SR 21 for 8.5 mi. and turn west on Scatter Creek Rd. (No. 53). Follow this paved road about 12 mi., turning right just before Long Lake to reach the Swan Lake Campground.

SEATTLE — MAP, B-2
Lake Pleasant RV Park

24025 Bothell Everett Hwy. SE, 98021.
T: (800) 742-0386 or (425) 487-1785;

🚐 ★★★	🏕 n/a
Beauty: ★★★	Site Privacy: ★★★
Spaciousness: ★★	Quiet: ★★
Security: ★★★	Cleanliness: ★★★★
Insect Control: ★★	Facilities: ★★★

Lake Pleasant RV Park, off I-405 in the northeast suburbs of Seattle, has to be the nicest RV park in the metro area. The garden-like grounds, surrounded by oak, pine, and blackberry bramble–covered hills, sit on the edge of small, man-made Lake Pleasant. The willows on the lake's edge, the occasional red Japanese maple, and the ducks only add to the charm of this very green park with paved, grass-encircled sites. The best back-ins (sites 1–14) and the best pull-throughs (sites 15–33) have privacy created by hedges of small pines and cedars, and they sit on the lake's edge. Most other sites also have some form of

privacy hedging. The least-desirable sites (back-in sites 201–228) are cramped with no privacy. The quiet grounds' location in relation to downtown Seattle is less than 20 miles, but unless the day is Sunday at six in the morning, expect lots of traffic. Chilly temperatures and rain abound in all seasons except summer, making summers the best time to visit the Puget Sound area.

BASICS

Operated By: Lake Pleasant RV Park. **Open:** All year. **Site Assignment:** First come, first served & by reservation. **Registration:** At office; after hours at drop box in front of office. **Fee:** $28; cash, check, V, MC. **Parking:** At site.

FACILITIES

Number of RV-only Sites: 186. **Hookups:** Electric (30 amps), water, sewer. **Each Site:** Picnic table. **Dump Station:** Yes. **Laundry:** Yes. **Pay Phone:** Yes. **Restrooms and Showers:** Yes. **Fuel:** No. **Propane:** Yes. **Internal Roads:** None. **RV Service:** No. **Market:** 2 mi. south in Bothell. **Restaurant:** 2 mi. south in Bothell. **General Store:** No. **Vending:** Yes. **Swimming:** No. **Playground:** Yes. **Other:** Footpaths, volleyball net, horseshoe pit. **Activities:** Pancake breakfasts (monthly in summer), license-less fishing, blueberry picking, hiking. **Nearby Attractions:** Puget Sound, Seattle Center, Pike Place Market, fishing, nightlife, hiking, whale-watching charter. **Additional Information:** Greater Seattle Chamber of Commerce, (206) 389-7200.

RESTRICTIONS

Pets: On leash only, max length 8 ft.; no fighting breeds. **Fires:** No open fires. **Alcoholic Beverages:** At site only. **Vehicle Maximum Length:** No limit. **Other:** No swimming, boating in lake; no feeding of waterfowl.

TO GET THERE

From I-405 Exit 26, drive south on Hwy. 27 for 1.2 mi.; entrance on right.

SEATTLE — MAP, B-2
Trailer Inns RV Park

15531 SE 37th, 98006. T: (425) 747-9181; www.trailerinnsrv.uswestdex.com/page3.html.

🚐 ★★★★	🏕 ★
Beauty: ★★	Site Privacy: ★
Spaciousness: ★★★	Quiet: ★
Security: ★★	Cleanliness: ★★★★★
Insect Control: ★★	Facilities: ★★★★★

Trailer Inns, in the east Seattle suburb of Bellevue, offers the most amenities of any park near the city. A pool table, indoor pool, and sauna are just a few of the facilities that make this park stand out. Totally paved over, the flat camping area's layout of parallel rows doesn't have any grass, but it does have some trees and landscaping. The small campground makes good use of its allotted space; campsites have a good amount of room for an urban park. Recommended sites include back-ins 2–7 and 21–42. The pull-throughs here provide less room to the sides than back-ins do. Campsites 43–66, which are back-ins with no dividers in the rear, have more of a cramped feeling than other back-ins in the park. Like all urban parks, this one has some ambient urban noise, but it's not intolerable. Also, for pop-up tent trailers or pick-up piggy backs, there are some smaller sites near the office. Visit Seattle during summer for the best weather.

BASICS

Operated By: Trailer Inns RV Park. **Open:** All year. **Site Assignment:** On arrival; reservations require $25 deposit; refund w/ 24-hour cancellation notice. **Registration:** At office; after hours see info at door. **Fee:** Supersite, $40; pull-through, $37; double, $30; single, $25; tent, $20; for 2 adults/2 children/2 pets; extra person, $5; V, MC, cash. **Parking:** At site.

FACILITIES

Number of RV-only Sites: 109. **Hookups:** Electric (30, 50 amps), water, sewer, cable TV. **Dump Station:** No. **Laundry:** Yes. **Pay Phone:** Yes. **Restrooms and Showers:** Yes. **Fuel:** No. **Propane:** Yes. **Internal Roads:** Paved. **RV Service:** No. **Market:** A few blocks west. **Restaurant:** A few blocks west. **General Store:** No. **Vending:** Yes. **Swimming:** Yes. **Playground:** Yes. **Other:** Game room w/ pool table & arcade, indoor hot tub, indoor sauna, indoor barbecue, TV room w/ big screen & fireplace, outdoor gas grill. **Activities:** Inquire at campground. **Nearby Attractions:** Seattle & Puget Sound, Snoqualmie Falls, skiing. **Additional Information:** Seattle Visitor Info Center, (206) 461-5840, www.seeseattle.org.

RESTRICTIONS

Pets: On leash only, 2 pets max. **Fires:** No open fires, no charcoal. **Alcoholic Beverages:** At site only. **Vehicle Maximum Length:** No limit. **Other:** Properly maintained RVs only allowed on property.

TO GET THERE

From I-90 Exit 11, take the third exit ramp to 150 Ave. SE. Drive south and turn left at first light onto Frontage Rd. Drive a few blocks on Frontage; when the road separates with a median, stay on far right. The campground entrance is the third driveway after the median starts.

SEATTLE MAP, B-2
Twin Cedars RV Park

reserve america

17826 Hwy. 99 North, 98037.
T: (425) 742-5540 or (800) 878-9304;
www.reserveamerica.com.

🚐 ★★	🏕 n/a
Beauty: ★	Site Privacy: ★
Spaciousness: ★★	Quiet: ★★
Security: ★★	Cleanliness: ★
Insect Control: ★★	Facilities: ★

Twin Cedars RV Park in Lynnwood has a very convenient location on Hwy. 99 just north of Seattle; location is the only draw here. Sites consist of gravel with a small amount of surrounding grass. The best campsites, sites 10–20, are the farthest from the loud industrial facility next door; conversely, the worst, sites 58–70, sit closest to the industrial area. The

park has no landscaping, a drainage ditch running through it, and patchy grass at best. In Seattle, the best weather happens during the summer, but the city has tourist attractions open year-round.

BASICS

Operated By: PCF Management. **Open:** All year. **Site Assignment:** On arrival; reservations require 1-night deposit; refund w/ 24-hour cancellation notice less $6 fee. **Registration:** At office; after hours check board at office, pay in morning. **Fee:** Full, $31.66; 7th day free; V, MC, cash. **Parking:** At site, limited off site.

FACILITIES

Number of RV-only Sites: 69. **Hookups:** Electric (20, 30, 50 amps), water, sewer, cable TV. **Dump Station:** Yes. **Laundry:** Yes. **Pay Phone:** Yes. **Restrooms and Showers:** Yes. **Fuel:** No. **Propane:** Yes. **Internal Roads:** Paved. **RV Service:** No. **Market:** Across Hwy. 99. **Restaurant:** Across Hwy. 99. **General Store:** No. **Vending:** Yes. **Swimming:** Yes. **Playground:** No. **Other:** Clubhouse w/ TV, VCR, & small aerobic area; horseshoes, common picnic area. **Activities:** Inquire at campground. **Nearby Attractions:** Seattle. **Additional Information:** Seattle Visitor Info Center, (206) 461-5840, www.seeseattle.org.

RESTRICTIONS

Pets: On leash only. **Fires:** No open fires. **Alcoholic Beverages:** At site only. **Vehicle Maximum Length:** 40 ft.

TO GET THERE

From I-5 Exit 183, drive west 1.6 mi. on 164th Southwest. This turns into 44th Ave West. Drive 0.5 mi., turn right on 176th St. SW, and drive 0.3 mi., then turn left on SR 99, go 0.2 mi., and the entrance is on the right behind Avis Rent-A-Car.

SEATTLE (EVERETT) MAP, B-2
Lakeside RV Park

reserve america

12321 Hwy. 99 South, 98204.
T: (425) 347-2970 or (425) 742-7333;
www.reserveamerica.com.

🚐 ★★★	🏕 ★★
Beauty: ★★★	Site Privacy: ★★★
Spaciousness: ★★	Quiet: ★★
Security: ★★★	Cleanliness: ★★★★
Insect Control: ★★	Facilities: ★★

Lakeside RV Park, located in the suburban burg of Everett, has easy access to services (such as groceries and shops) and a quick route to Seattle, some 20 minutes south. The park has laundry, bathroom facilities, and a stocked lake for fishing (runoff feeds the lake, so eat your catch at your own risk). All back-in RV sites come with paved surfaces and are divided by cedar hedges that create a little privacy. The grounds have a cramped feeling but a good location. Back-in sites 127–139 back up to a hedge of deciduous shrubbery and provide the best space and privacy. The even-numbered sites 76–104 are the

best paved pull-throughs (for space). Other than the above, the RV sites have a fairly homogenous layout, and sites 1–15 sit in a high traffic area. The tenting area has fine-grit gravel pads surrounded by grass, no privacy, and cannot accommodate large tents. Seattle has tourism year-round, but summer brings the best weather and avoids the stereotypical rains of winter.

BASICS

Operated By: PCF Management. **Open:** All year. **Site Assignment:** On arrival; reservations require 1-night deposit; refund w/ 24-hour cancellation notice less $6 fee. **Registration:** At office; after hours pay in morning or drop in office door. **Fee:** Full, $38.59; tent, $15.33; V, MC, D, personal check, cash. **Parking:** At site, additional parking available.

FACILITIES

Number of RV-only Sites: 150. **Number of Tent-only Sites:** 9. **Hookups:** Electric (20, 30, 50 amps), water, sewer, cable TV. **Dump Station:** No. **Laundry:** Yes. **Pay Phone:** Yes. **Restrooms and Showers:** Yes. **Fuel:** No. **Propane:** Yes. **Internal Roads:** Paved. **RV Service:** No. **Market:** South or north on Hwy. 99 (close by). **Restaurant:** South or north on Hwy. 99 (close by). **General Store:** No. **Vending:** Yes. **Swimming:** No. **Playground:** Yes. **Other:** RV & boat storage, horseshoes, lake fishing, fishing dock, jogging path around lake, espresso stand (just in front of park, separate enterprise). **Activities:** Fishing (per fish charges & per site limits apply). **Nearby Attractions:** Seattle. **Additional Information:** Seattle Visitor Info Center, (206) 461-5840, www.seeseattle.org.

RESTRICTIONS

Pets: Short leash only. **Fires:** No open fires. **Alcoholic Beverages:** At site only. **Vehicle Maximum Length:** No limit. **Other:** Visitor parking for short-term use (2 hours).

TO GET THERE

From I-5 Exit 186 (128th St. SW), drive west on 128th for 1.3 mi. Turn left on Hwy. 99 at Home Depot.

SEQUIM MAP, B-1
Dungeness Recreation Area

223 East 4th St., 98362. T: (360) 683-5847;
www.clallam.net/countyparks/html/
parks_dungeness.htm.

🚐 ★★★	🏕 ★★★★
Beauty: ★★★★★	Site Privacy: ★★★★★
Spaciousness: ★★★★	Quiet: ★★★★
Security: ★★★★	Cleanliness: ★★★★
Insect Control: ★★★	Facilities: ★★

Dungeness Spit, the main attraction in the Dungeness Recreation Area/National Wildlife Refuge, is the longest natural sand spit in the United States. Arching nearly 7 miles into the Strait of Juan de Fuca from the Olympic Peninsula, this unique landform averages only 100 yards wide for its entire length. The entire expanse of spits, tidelands, wetlands, landmarks, and adjoining surf forms Dungeness National Wildlife Refuge. The Dungeness Recreation Area campsites are well designed around two loops, affording ultimate privacy with dense undergrowth between sites. About a third of the sites are spaced along a high bluff that overlooks the Strait of Juan de Fuca with million-dollar views. Despite the moderate year-round climate, the campground is open only from February 1 to October 1. Summer can be quite busy, so you may want to try the off-season. In addition to the ever-popular beachcombing, other activities in the park include horseback riding (separate equestrian trail and unloading area), game bird hunting in designated areas, and good old-fashioned picnicking.

BASICS

Operated By: Clallam County Parks Dept. **Open:** Feb. 1–Oct. 1. **Site Assignment:** First come, first served. **Registration:** At park information booth daylight–dusk. **Fee:** $14–$16. **Parking:** At site.

FACILITIES

Number of Multipurpose Sites: 67. **Hookups:** None. **Each Site:** Picnic table, fire pit, shade trees. **Dump Station:** Yes. **Laundry:** No. **Pay Phone:** Yes. **Restrooms and Showers:** Yes. **Fuel:** 5 mi. in Sequim. **Propane:** 5 mi. **Internal Roads:** Paved. **RV Service:** No. **Market:** 5 mi. **Restaurant:** 5 mi. **General Store:** 5 mi. **Vending:** No. **Swimming:** Yes. **Playground:** No. **Other:** Firewood. **Activities:** Equestrian trails, hiking, hunting, shell fishing, beachcombing. **Nearby Attractions:** Dungeness Wildlife Refuge, Agriculture Tour, Cungeness Lighthouse. **Additional Information:** www.clallam.net/countyparks/html/parks_dungeness.htm.

RESTRICTIONS

Pets: On leash only. No dogs on beach. **Fires:** Fire pit only. **Alcoholic Beverages:** Not allowed. **Vehicle Maximum Length:** No limit.

TO GET THERE

From Sequim (17 mi. east of Port Angeles), drive 5 mi. west on US 101 to Kitchen-Dick Ln. Turn north and drive 3 mi., watching for signs to the recreation area campground entrance.

SILVER CREEK   MAP, C-2
Harmony Lakeside RV Park

563 Hwy. 122, 98585. T: (360) 983-3804; www.harmonylakesidervpark.com.

🚐 ★★★★		▲ ★★	
Beauty: ★★★★★		Site Privacy: ★★	
Spaciousness: ★★★		Quiet: ★★★★	
Security: ★		Cleanliness: ★★★★	
Insect Control: ★★		Facilities: ★★★	

Harmony Lakeside RV Park on Mayfield Lake is between I-5 and routes to Mt. Rainier and St. Helens. The beautifully manicured grounds run up to the lake's edge; the park also has several small, river-stone-lined ponds with fountains, brightly colored koi, and small bronze statues. The sites and roads are well-maintained gravel. There are no tent sites, but tent campers can set up in a water and electric site if they don't mind the gravel. Sites 1–27 stand on two loops in a grassy field with shade and painstakingly shaped hedges. This section is often reserved well in advance, making it hard to get into. Sites 1–8 have a beautiful view of the water. The sec-

ond set of loops run through a manicured fairy tale–like forest of beautiful moss interspersed with grass, tall cedars, large dead tree trunks with beautiful secondary growth, and views of the lake some 20 feet below. Sites 66–69 in this section have lots of space and sit right on the edge of the cliffs. The bonsai-like artfulness of the groundskeepers makes this already small, quiet campground even more charming. Visit late in spring or early fall for the best weather and slowest-paced days.

BASICS

Operated By: Harmony Lakeside RV. **Open:** All year. **Site Assignment:** First come, first served & by reservation. **Registration:** At office, online or by phone. **Fee:** Full, $27; water/electric, $24; extra daily fee per pet, $2.50; V, MC, cash. **Parking:** At site.

FACILITIES

Number of RV-only Sites: 80. **Number of Tent-only Sites:** 38. **Hookups:** Electric (20, 30, 50 amps), water, sewer, cable TV, Wi-Fi. **Each Site:** Picnic table, fire ring. **Dump Station:** Yes. **Laundry:** No. **Pay Phone:** Yes. **Restrooms and Showers:** Yes. **Fuel:** No. **Propane:** No. **Internal Roads:** Gravel. **RV Service:** No. **Market:** Near Mossyrock. **Restaurant:** Near Mossyrock. **General Store:** Yes. **Vending:** Yes. **Swimming:** No. **Playground:** No. **Other:** Reception hall, both powered & nonpowered boats, volleyball, badminton, horseshoes. **Activities:** Fishing, water sports. **Nearby Attractions:** Mt. Rainier, Mt. St. Helens, fish hatcheries, Seattle, Olympia. **Additional Information:** Washington State Tourism Board, (360) 725-5052.

RESTRICTIONS

Pets: On leash only (fee required). **Fires:** Fire pit only. **Alcoholic Beverages:** At site only. **Vehicle Maximum Length:** No limit. **Other:** No firewood gathering.

TO GET THERE

On I-5, drive to Exit 68 (Hwy. 12 Morton-Yakima). Once on US 12, go east 21 mi. At the Mossyrock blinker, turn left. Drive 2.5 mi. on SR 122, and the entrance is on the left.

SKYKOMISH   MAP, C-3
Beckler River Campground

reserve america

Skykomish Ranger District, P.O. Box 305, 98288. T: (360) 677-2414; www.reserveamerica.com.

🚐 ★★		▲ ★★★★	
Beauty: ★★★★★		Site Privacy: ★★★	
Spaciousness: ★★★		Quiet: ★★★★	
Security: ★★★★★		Cleanliness: ★★★★	
Insect Control: ★★		Facilities: ★★	

Only 60 miles from Seattle, Beckler sits on the banks of the Beckler River 3 miles from the town of Skykomish. A heavy canopy of western Washington foliage drapes the area around the campground as well as the numerous steep-sided river and creek valleys that drain their tributaries into the Beckler River. Trips into the Beckler backcountry should be prefaced by a visit to the Skykomish Ranger Station.

Heavy snow can often keep trails blocked longer than one would imagine. The Henry M. Jackson Wilderness (named for a former Washington State senator) lies to the north. It has 49 miles of hiking trails that were once the cross-Cascade routes used by early Native Americans and later by exploration teams. Follow the Forest Service road past Garland Hot Springs to reach the trailheads. To the south is the fabled Alpine Lakes Wilderness. Trailheads into Alpine Lakes are just west of Skykomish on Miller River Rd., which becomes FS 6412.

BASICS

Operated By: Mount Baker-Snoqualmie National Forest. **Open:** Memorial Day–mid-Sept. **Site Assignment:** First come, first served & by reservation. **Registration:** At camp office. **Fee:** $16. **Parking:** At site.

FACILITIES

Number of Multipurpose Sites: 27. **Hookups:** None. **Each Site:** Picnic table, fire pit w/ grill, shade trees, piped water nearby. **Dump Station:** No. **Laundry:** No. **Pay Phone:** No. **Restrooms and Showers:** Vault toilets. **Fuel:** 1 mi. in Skykomish. **Propane:** 1 mi. **Internal Roads:** Paved. **RV Service:** No. **Market:** No. **Restaurant:** No. **General Store:** 1 mi. **Vending:** No. **Swimming:** No. **Playground:** No. **Activities:** Fishing, hiking. **Nearby Attractions:** Mount Baker, Becker River. **Additional Information:** www.fs.fed.us/r6/mbs or www.reserveusa.com.

RESTRICTIONS

Pets: On leash only. **Fires:** Fire pit only. **Alcoholic Beverages:** Allowed. **Vehicle Maximum Length:** 21 ft.

TO GET THERE

Drive 1 mi. east of Skykomish on US 2, turn left onto FS 65, and go 2 mi. to the campground.

TOPPENISH   MAP, C-3
Yakama Nation Resort RV Park

280 Buster Rd., 98948. T: (509) 865-2000 or (800) 874-3087; www.yakamanation.com.

🚐 ★★★★		▲ ★★★	
Beauty: ★★★		Site Privacy: ★	
Spaciousness: ★★★		Quiet: ★★★	
Security: ★★★		Cleanliness: ★★★★	
Insect Control: ★★		Facilities: ★★★★★	

The Yakama Nation RV Resort, located 20 miles south of Yakima off I-84, provides easy access to Native American cultural events and obscured views of the surrounding arid hill country. The grounds consist of a flat field of grass, with paved avenues creating islands containing paved sites with grass; additional sites ring the park's perimeter. The grassy tent area has some shade from a few tall deciduous trees; the RV section has little protection from the high desert sun. The pull-through section consists of pavement with no surrounding grass. The best RV choices in the park (sites 30–54) sit farthest from nearby Hwy. 97 and on a perimeter with no rear neighbors. The park has nice and wide-ranging recreational facilities, including two very large unisex cedar saunas. The adjacent Yakama Nation Cultural Center adds to nearby recreational opportunities. Winters here stay cold, and summers stay hot with cooler nights; the month of June offers the largest number of Native American cultural events.

BASICS

Operated By: Private operator. **Open:** All year. **Site Assignment:** First come, first served & by reservation (no deposit). **Registration:** At office; after hours pay in morning. **Fee:** Full (2 people), $23; additional person, $2; teepee (5 people), $30; additional person (up to10 people), $5; cot rentals, $2; tent area (4 people), $16; additional person per tent, $5; children (3 & younger), free; V, MC, cash, check. **Parking:** At site.

FACILITIES

Number of RV-only Sites: 125. **Number of Tent-only Sites:** 10. **Hookups:** Electric (20, 30, 50 amps), water, sewer, cable TV. **Each Site:** Picnic table. **Dump Station:** Yes. **Laundry:** Yes. **Pay Phone:** Yes. **Restrooms and Showers:** Yes. **Fuel:** No. **Propane:** Yes. **Internal Roads:** Paved. **RV Service:** No. **Market:** 1 mi. north on 97. **Restaurant:** Next door. **General Store:** No. **Vending:** Yes. **Swimming:** Yes. **Playground:** Yes. **Other:** Hot tub, large saunas (2), exercise room, arcade, volleyball, horseshoes, basketball, running trail, putting green, 2 reservable meeting rooms, Cultural Center adjacent to park. **Activities:** Putting, running. **Nearby Attractions:** Yakama Nation Cultural Center, Old Depot Museum, American Hop Museum, Toppenish Murals (narrated wagon rides available Apr.–Oct), golf. **Additional Information:** Yakima Chamber of Commerce, (509) 248-2021.

RESTRICTIONS

Pets: On leash only. **Fires:** Fire pit only. **Alcoholic Beverages:** Absolutely not allowed. **Vehicle Maximum Length:** No limit. **Other:** Teepees don't come w/ bedding, must supply your own.

TO GET THERE

From I-82 Exit 50, drive 3.1 mi. southeast on Buena Way/East 22. Turn right at stoplight onto West 1st Ave and drive for 0.4 mi. Turn right at stoplight onto 97 North and follow 0.7 mi.; the entrance is on left through Yakama Nation Cultural Center.

WASHINGTON — MAP, B-2
Clear Creek—Wenatchee National Forest

21905 64th Ave., West Mountlake Terrace, 98043-2278; T: (360) 691-1877; www.reserveamerica.com.

🚐 ★★★★	⛺ ★★★★

Beauty: ★★★	Site Privacy: ★★★★
Spaciousness: ★★★★	Quiet: ★★★
Security: ★★★★	Cleanliness: ★★★★
Insect Control: ★★★★	Facilities: ★★★

This nice, secluded spot is set in old-growth fir on the water, but doesn't get heavy use. It's set at the confluence of Clear Creek and the Sauk River, a designated Wild and Scenic River. A trail from camp leads about 1 mile up to Frog Lake. Clear Creek is located within the Wenatchee National Forest, which covers an area approximately 40 miles wide and 140 miles in length, encompassing much of Chelan, Kittitas, and Yakima counties. It stretches from upper Lake Chelan on the north to the Yakama Indian Reservation on the south. The vegetation varies with the elevation, from the sagebrush and pine-covered slopes at 2,000 feet, to higher elevation areas with alpine fir and mountain huckleberry, to the crest of the Cascade Mountain range at 8,000 feet and above where vegetation is sparse. Approximately 40 percent of the Wenatchee Forest is designated as Wilderness in seven Wilderness Areas: Lake Chelan-Sawtooth, Glacier Peak, Henry M. Jackson, Alpine Lakes, William O. Douglas, Norse Peak, and Goat Rocks. Here, foot travel is the only method of transportation allowed, and the land is managed in such a way as to preserve its natural, primitive condition. There are no developments or roads in Wilderness. Wenatchee Forest campgrounds meet a variety of camping needs. Over 100 campgrounds and picnic sites provide room for a total of 13,000 people at any one time. Some campgrounds have sites designed for tent camping, for camper truck use, and for use by those pulling a trailer. Other campgrounds have areas specially designed for campers who bring their horses for trail riding. Still other areas have been developed with the trail bike enthusiasts camping needs in mind. Both single-family and multifamily camping sites may be found.

BASICS

Operated By: U.S. Forest Service. **Open:** May 27–Sept. 11. **Site Assignment:** Reservations must be made at least 4 days in advance. **Registration:** At office. **Fee:** Single, $12. **Parking:** At park.

FACILITIES

Number of Multipurpose Sites: 13. **Hookups:** No. **Each Site:** Call ahead. **Dump Station:** No. **Laundry:** Nearby. **Pay Phone:** Nearby. **Restrooms and Showers:** Yes. **Fuel:** Nearby. **Propane:** Nearby. **Internal Roads:** Paved. **RV Service:** No. **Market:** Nearby. **Restaurant:** Nearby. **General Store:** No. **Vending:** No. **Swimming:** Yes. **Playground:** No. **Activities:** Biking, bird-watching, canoeing, climbing, fishing, hiking, kayaking, photography, rafting, tubing.

RESTRICTIONS

Pets: Pets must be restrained or on a leash at all times while in developed recreation areas. **Fires:** In fire rings, stoves, grills, or fireplaces provided for that purpose. **Alcoholic Beverages:** Not allowed. **Vehicle Maximum Length:** 16 ft. **Other:** There is no water available at this campground.

TO GET THERE

From Seattle go north on I-5 to Arlington exit. East on Hwy. 30 to town of Darrington. South on Mt. Loop Hwy. 3 mi. to Clear Creek Campground.

WOODLAND — MAP, C-2
Columbia Riverfront RV Park

1881 Dike Rd., 98674. T: (360) 225-8051 or (800) 845-9842; www.reserveamerica.com.

🚐 ★★★	⛺ n/a

Beauty: ★★★	Site Privacy: ★
Spaciousness: ★★★	Quiet: ★★★★
Security: ★★	Cleanliness: ★★★
Insect Control: ★★	Facilities: ★★★★

Columbia Riverfront RV Park, a few minutes off I-5 and a half hour north of Vancouver, sits on the south shore of the Columbia in a rural area. Across the expansive Columbia stand rolling green hills and some industrial development. The partially landscaped gravel-covered grounds consist of back-in rows with views of the river. People come to this park to watch big ships navigate up and down the industrial corridor of the river, and the best campsites for this sit near the water (sites 1–10, 50–58, and 76). Other sites in the park have limited or no views of the water, and sites 17–25 and 32–40 have a road behind them. Still, the whole area is quiet and scenic with the local pastoral lands and RV park surrounded by blunt, tree-covered hills. Weather in the area stays mild and rainy during all seasons but the summer.

BASICS

Operated By: Columbia Riverfront RV Park. **Open:** All year. **Site Assignment:** First come, first served; reservations. **Registration:** At office; after hours in front of office. **Fee:** Riverfront full, $26.27; other full, $24.08, for 4 people; extra person, $2; extra vehicle, $10; daily fee per pet, $1; V, MC, cash. **Parking:** At site.

FACILITIES

Number of RV-only Sites: 76. **Hookups:** Electric (20, 30, 50 amps), water, sewer, cable TV. **Each Site:** Picnic table. **Dump Station:** No. **Laundry:** Yes. **Pay Phone:** Yes. **Restrooms and Showers:** Yes. **Fuel:** No. **Propane:** Yes. **Internal Roads:** Wide, well-maintained gravel. **RV Service:** No. **Market:** 2 mi. east in Woodland. **Restaurant:** 2 mi. east in Woodland. **General Store:** Yes. **Vending:** No. **Swimming:** Yes. **Playground:** Yes. **Other:** Riverfront beach, volleyball, horseshoe pits, clubhouse w/ kitchen (only reservable). **Activities:** Fishing, swimming, ship watching, kite flying, hiking. **Nearby Attractions:** Golf, Mt. St. Helens, Hilda Klaegars' Lilac Gardens, The Old Grist Mill, the Columbia River, Ape Caves, Vancouver. **Additional Information:** Woodland Chamber of Commerce, (360) 225-9552.

RESTRICTIONS

Pets: On leash only. **Fires:** Beach only. **Alcoholic Beverages:** At site only. **Vehicle Maximum Length:** 40 ft. **Other:** No vehicle repairs or washing, no clotheslines, be aware of ship wakes & undertows.

TO GET THERE

From I-5 Exit 22: northbound turn left, southbound turn right onto Dike Access Rd., and follow west for

1.7 mi. When the road forks, take the left fork and follow for another 1.1 mi.; entrance is on the right.

YAKIMA   MAP, C-3
Trailer Inns RV Park

1610 North First St., 98901.
T: (509) 452-9561 or (800) 659-4784;
www.trailerinnsrv.com/yakima/index.html.

🚐 ★★★★   ▲ ★★

Beauty: ★★	Site Privacy: ★
Spaciousness: ★★★	Quiet: ★★
Security: ★★★	Cleanliness: ★★★★★
Insect Control: ★★	Facilities: ★★★★★

Trailer Inns RV Park, right on the edge of downtown Yakima, offers convenient access to both the city and the interstate. The older, well-maintained facilities offer a wide array of furnishings. One of the more notable and above-average facilities, an indoor barbecue room, has two gas grills and a fireplace. Further, an indoor pool and two small hot tubs provide year-round swimming and relaxation. Regarding accommodations, the park's level, grassy tent sites lack shade or privacy and sit behind the office/clubhouse. The RV sites, predominately arranged into parallel rows, have some shade, and many also have adjacent grass areas. Avoid RV sites 55–71 because they lack shade and consist solely of blacktop. The best RV options are sites 103–115; they have shade, grass, and a reasonable amount of space. The high desert climate is arid and hot during the summers, and the sun's heat can be intense; visit during the spring, early summer, or early fall for optimal conditions.

BASICS

Operated By: Trailer Inns. **Open:** All year. **Site Assignment:** On arrival; reservations require 1-night deposit; refund w/ 72-hour cancellation notice. **Registration:** At office; after hours pay at drop or in morning. **Fee:** RV, $18–$36; tent, $18; V, MC, cash. **Parking:** At site, limited off site.

FACILITIES

Number of RV-only Sites: 60. **Number of Tent-only Sites:** 22. **Hookups:** Electric (15, 30, 50 amps), water, sewer, cable TV. **Each Site:** Picnic table.

Dump Station: Yes. **Laundry:** Yes. **Pay Phone:** Yes. **Restrooms and Showers:** Yes. **Fuel:** No. **Propane:** Yes. **Internal Roads:** Paved. **RV Service:** No. **Market:** Nearby in Yakima. **Restaurant:** Nearby in Yakima. **General Store:** Yes. **Vending:** Yes. **Swimming:** Yes (indoor). **Playground:** Yes. **Other:** Arcade, TV room, indoor barbecue room, outdoor barbecue area, indoor hot tubs (2, small), outdoor porch, shuffleboard. **Activities:** Occasional potlucks (seasonal). **Nearby Attractions:** Golfing, hunting, fishing, rafting, horseback riding, wineries, Yakima Electric Railway Museum, Yakima Valley Museum. **Additional Information:** Yakima Chamber of Commerce, (509) 248-2021.

RESTRICTIONS

Pets: On leash only, limit of 2 per space. **Fires:** No open fires, no charcoal. **Alcoholic Beverages:** At site only. **Vehicle Maximum Length:** No limit. **Other:** No eye-sore vehicles.

TO GET THERE

From I-82 Exit 31, go 0.1 mi. south on First St. and the entrance is on the right.

West Virginia

John Denver certainly was not bending the truth when he sang that West Virginia was "almost heaven." Of course, there is more to the 35th state than mountain peaks and rapids. The state also boasts the therapeutic waters of **White Sulphur Springs** and **Berkeley Springs;** the subterranean wonders of **Lost World Caverns, Smoke Hole Caverns,** and **Seneca Caverns;** the Victorian historic districts and cultural heritage of **Charleston, Parkersburg,** and **Wheeling;** and the significant pre–Civil War history of **Harpers Ferry.**

The West Virginia nature lovers' vision is best exemplified in the northern section of the state, called the highlands. Rugged and isolated, the area is defined by mountain peaks that stretch to the sky, postcard-perfect waterfalls, jutting cliffs, and unspoiled forests. The highlands has 1.5 million acres of national parks and forests, as well as a dozen state parks. Covering 901,000 acres, **Monongahela National Forest** includes the Mountain State's highest peak, 4,862-foot **Spruce Knob.** Within the park are **Spruce Knob/Seneca Rocks National Recreation Area** near **Petersburg** and **Blue Bend** and **Lake Sherwood** recreation areas near **White Sulphur Springs,** which is also where you will find the 5,100-acre **Greenbrier State Forest** and the famous **Greenbrier** resort. The Greenbrier ghost is more than famous for being the only apparition on record in the history of the courts whose testimony helped solve a murder case. **Marlinton** is home not only to the **Cass Scenic Railroad State Park** but also to the ever increasingly popular annual **Roadkill Cookoff** at the end of September. The 43-mile **Highland National Scenic Highway,** stretching along mountaintops from Richwood to Cass, is an ideal way to experience the natural splendor of the highlands.

Whitewater rafting is an integral part of West Virginia's tourism, and some of the most challenging rapids in the country are found on the **New River** in the **New River Gorge National River** and the **Greenbrier River.** Numerous outfitters operate from small towns along these rivers. **Pipestem Resort State Park** in Pipestem, **Babcock State Park in Clifftop,** and **Twin Falls Resort State Park** in Beckley, the self-proclaimed "Town with a Mine of Its Own," are just a few of the many camping and recreational spots in the region. **Lost World Caverns** north of Lewisburg, **Organ Cave** in Ronceverte, and several covered bridges provide more options for travelers wanting to explore back roads or simply get lost in the grandeur of some of nature's most fascinating geological anomalies.

Harpers Ferry National Historical Park is a major draw in the eastern panhandle of West Virginia. Located at the junction of the Potomac and Shenandoah rivers, where West Virginia meets Maryland and Virginia, Harpers Ferry is preserved to appear much like it did in the 19th century. In 1859, abolitionist John Brown and 16 other men seized the town's armory and rifle factory. Brown was captured by 90 marines under the command of Robert E. Lee and J. E. B. Stuart. Ten of Brown's men were killed, and Brown was later hanged in nearby Charles Town for treason, murder, and inciting slaves to revolt. The uprising at Harpers Ferry is credited with sparking a series of events that led to the Civil War. To learn more, visit the official museum dedicated to John Brown; for a less informative but more kitschy perspective, pay a small fee to witness the spectacle firsthand at the **John Brown Wax Museum.**

Charleston, the state capital, is proud of its **Capitol Building,** which is crowned by a 293-foot-high gold-leaf dome. The Kanawha River cuts through Charleston, and just minutes away from the downtown bustle is the tranquility of 9,300-acre **Kanawha State Forest.** A railroad town along the Ohio River, **Huntington** boasts the state's largest art museum, and fans of broadcast will also be intrigued by the city's **Museum of Radio and Technology.** While around town, see if you can spot the pink elephant. The 500-acre **Blennerhassett Island Historical State Park** in Parkersburg, where Aaron Burr's plan to create his own empire failed, is only accessible by stern-wheeler. Other major towns in West Virginia include **Morgantown,** home of **West Virginia University** and **Cooper's Rock State Forest;** and Wheeling, where the famous **City of Lights** display draws thousands to **Oglebay Resort Park** during the holiday season. Located just outside Wheeling in New Vrindaban is the sprawling tourist attraction **Prabhupada's Palace of Gold and City of Gold,** otherwise known as America's Taj Mahal.

Campground Profiles

BARBOURSVILLE   MAP, C-1
Beech Fork State Park

5601 Long Branch Rd., 25504.
T: (304) 528-5794 or (800) CALLWVA;
www.beechforksp.com.

🚐 ★★★   ⛺ ★★★★

Beauty: ★★★★	Site Privacy: ★★★
Spaciousness: ★★★	Quiet: ★★★★
Security: ★★★	Cleanliness: ★★★★
Insect Control: ★★★★	Facilities: ★★★★

Located 12 miles south of Huntington and Barboursville, Beech Fork State Park has the largest camping area in West Virginia's state park system. The campground features four distinctly different areas. Approximately 80 sites front the lake. Old Orchard, a 49-site campground, is open year-round. Moxley Branch, Four Coves, and Lakeview each are equipped with 20- and 30-amp service. Hiking trails range from the 0.75-mile Nature Trail to the 5-mile Lost Trail; the latter is open to both hikers and mountain bikers. Beech Fork Lake is known for largemouth and hybrid striped bass, catfish, walleye, saugeye (a cross of walleye and sauger), and bluegill. A fishing license is required and is available in the Camper's Corner store located in the Administration Building. The store is open for business March 15 through October 31. Beech Fork also has vacation cottages overlooking Beech Fork Lake.

BASICS
Operated By: State of West Virginia. **Open:** All year. **Site Assignment:** Reservations accepted (2-night min. on weekends), walk-ins accepted. **Registration:** At campground store. **Fee:** $15–$23; V, MC. **Parking:** At site.

FACILITIES
Number of Multipurpose Sites: 324. **Hookups:** Electric (20, 30, 50 amps), water, sewer. **Each Site:** Fire grate, picnic table. **Dump Station:** Yes. **Laundry:** Yes. **Pay Phone:** Yes. **Restrooms and Showers:** Yes. **Fuel:** No. **Propane:** No. **Internal Roads:** Paved, in fair condition. **RV Service:** No. **Market:** W/in 10 mi. **Restaurant:** W/in 10 mi. **General Store:** Yes. **Vending:** Yes. **Swimming:** Yes. **Playground:** Yes. **Activities:** Lake fishing & swimming, boating, rec hall, horseshoes, game room, planned activities, sports field, hiking trails, mountain biking. **Nearby Attractions:** Marshall University, Huntington Museum of Art, Pilgrim Glass & Blenko Glass factory, Ritter Park, River Front Park. **Additional Information:** Cabell Co./Huntington CVB, (800) 635-6329, www.wvvisit.org.

RESTRICTIONS
Pets: On leash only. **Fires:** At site. **Alcoholic Beverages:** Not permitted. **Vehicle Maximum Length:** No limit. **Other:** Quiet hours 10 p.m.–7 a.m.

TO GET THERE
From I-64, take Exit 11 (Hal Greer Blvd.). Take Hwy. 10 south. Continue 4 mi. Turn right onto Hughes Branch Rd. and follow to the end (another 4 mi.). Turn left and the park is about 2 mi. straight ahead (30 minutes).

BOWDEN   MAP, B-3
Revelle's River Retreat

reserve america

P.O. Box 96, 26254.
T: (304) 636-0023 or (877) 988-2267;
www.reserveamerica.com.

🚐 ★★★★   ⛺ ★★★★

Beauty: ★★★★	Site Privacy: ★★
Spaciousness: ★★★	Quiet: ★★★
Security: ★★★	Cleanliness: ★★★★
Insect Control: ★★★★	Facilities: ★★★★

Located in the Potomac highlands on the banks of Shavers Fork off the Cheat River, the spacious Revelle's River Retreat is West Virginia's largest campground with more than 250 fully developed campsites. Open all year, Revelle's is an ideal place for fishing as Shaver's Fork is stocked with rainbow trout. Back-in and pull-through shaded and open campsites are available. Tent sites are available in the rear of the campground. The Bowden Train Depot, which is located on Revelle's grounds and was last operated in the early 1900s, has been restored and is open again. Passengers can board the historic Durban and Greenbrier Railroad here.

BASICS
Operated By: Brenda & Barry Burrows. **Open:** All year. **Site Assignment:** Reservations accepted w/ 1-night deposit, otherwise first come, first served; refund w/ 7-day notice (less $10). **Registration:** At campground office. **Fee:** $19–$29; V, MC, D, AE. **Parking:** At site.

FACILITIES
Number of RV-only Sites: 250. **Number of Tent-only Sites:** 20. **Hookups:** Electric (20, 30, 50 amps), cable TV, phone. **Each Site:** Fire ring, picnic table. **Dump Station:** Yes. **Laundry:** Yes. **Pay Phone:** Yes. **Restrooms and Showers:** Yes. **Fuel:** No. **Propane:** No. **Internal Roads:** Gravel, in good condition. **RV Service:** No. **Market:** 9 mi. west in Elkins. **Restaurant:** On site. **General Store:** Yes. **Vending:** Yes. **Swimming:** Yes (Jellystone Park). **Playground:** Yes. **Other:** Clubhouse; e-mail, fax, copy service. **Activities:** Hiking, fishing, canoeing, basketball, volleyball, swimming. **Nearby Attractions:** Otter Creek Wilderness Area, Smoke Hole Cavern, Bowden Cave, Blackwater Falls State Park, Rich Mountain Battlefield, Cheat Summit Fort, Durbin & Greenbrier Valley Railroad, the Old Mill, Downtown Elkins Historic District, Davis & Elkins College, Halliehurst Mansion. **Additional Information:** West Virginia Visitors Bureau, (800) CALLWVA, www.westvirginia.com.

RESTRICTIONS
Pets: On leash only. **Fires:** At site. **Alcoholic Beverages:** At site. **Vehicle Maximum Length:** 45 ft.

Other: More than 30 sites have no hookups. Cabins & cottages also available.

TO GET THERE
Take US 33 9 mi. east from Elkins. At the end of 4-lane highway (Corridor H US 33), turn left. Drive 0.25 mi. and turn left onto Faulkner Rd.

BOWDEN   MAP, B-3
Yogi Bear's Jellystone Park

reserve america

Faulkner Rd., 26254.
T: (304) 637-8898 or (866) 988-5267;
www.jellystonewestvirginia.com.

🚐 ★★★★   ⛺ ★★★★

Beauty: ★★★★	Site Privacy: ★★★
Spaciousness: ★★	Quiet: ★★
Security: ★★★★	Cleanliness: ★★★
Insect Control: ★★★	Facilities: ★★★★

Whether you are an RV park enthusiast, enjoy the comfort of a cabin in the woods, or just like to tent camp and sleep in the great outdoors, Jellystone Park's accommodations, amenities, and activities are top-notch. Amenities and activities include swimming, mini-golf, hay rides, tennis, volleyball, fishing, hiking, and appearances from Yogi Bear and friends.

BASICS
Operated By: Barrows. **Open:** Apr. 1–Oct. 31. **Site Assignment:** Reservations recommended. **Registration:** At ranger station. **Fee:** $26–$33.

FACILITIES
Number of Multipurpose Sites: 156. **Hookups:** Water, electric (50 amps), sewer, cable. **Dump Station:** Yes. **Laundry:** Yes. **Pay Phone:** Yes. **Restrooms and Showers:** Yes. **Fuel:** No. **Propane:** No. **Internal Roads:** Gravel. **General Store:** Camp store. **Vending:** Yes. **Swimming:** Yes. **Playground:** Yes. **Activities:** Tube rentals, pavilion, trout stream. **Nearby Attractions:** Riding stables.

RESTRICTIONS
Pets: On leash attended only. **Fires:** Allowed.

TO GET THERE
From Elkins, WV, take US 33 east 7 mi. Take Faulkner Rd. exit. Turn right on Faulkner Rd; it's 0.25 mi. to park.

BUCKHANNON   MAP, B-3
Audra State Park

Hwy. 4 , P.O. Box 564, 26201.
T: (800) CALLWVA or (304) 457-1162;
www.audrastatepark.com.

🚐 ★★★   ⛺ ★★★★

Beauty: ★★★★★	Site Privacy: ★★★★
Spaciousness: ★★★	Quiet: ★★★★★
Security: ★★★★	Cleanliness: ★★★★★
Insect Control: ★★★★	Facilities: ★★★★

Want solitude and modern amenities both? Head to Audra State Park, located in the northeastern part of West Virginia, 6 miles east off US 119 and 15 miles east of Buckhannon. The 65-site campground does not have electric hookups, but it certainly has scenery. Situated in a flat with the Middle Fork River cascading in the distance, the campground is nestled amid large boulders and thick hemlock forests. Scenic overlooks beckon along the Alum Cave Trail and the Rock Cliff Trail, the latter of which leaves the campground and climbs the bluffs behind the campsites. There is no swimming pool here, but you can swim in Middle Fork at the campground and tube downstream to a swimming beach. Remember, Audra State Park does not accept reservations. Sites are given on a first-come, first-serve basis.

BASICS

Operated By: State of West Virginia. **Open:** Apr.–Oct. **Site Assignment:** First come, first served. **Registration:** Ranger will greet you. **Fee:** $17. **Parking:** At site.

FACILITIES

Number of RV-only Sites: 50. **Number of Tent-only Sites:** 15. **Hookups:** None. **Each Site:** Fire ring, picnic table. **Dump Station:** Yes. **Laundry:** Yes. **Pay Phone:** Yes. **Restrooms and Showers:** Yes. **Fuel:** No. **Propane:** No. **Internal Roads:** Paved, in good condition. **RV Service:** No. **Market:** W/in 5 mi. **Restaurant:** W/in 12 mi. **General Store:** No. **Vending:** No. **Playground:** Yes. **Activities:** River swimming, hiking trails. **Nearby Attractions:** Carrolton Covered Bridge (Buckhannon River), Philippi Covered Bridge & Museum, Teter Creek Public Hunting & Fishing Area, Alderson-Broaddus College, West Virginia Wesleyan College, Tygart Lake State Park, Valley Falls State Park, Holly River State Park. **Additional Information:** Randolph County CVB, (800) 422-3304, www.randolphcountywv.com.

RESTRICTIONS

Pets: On leash only. **Fires:** At site. **Alcoholic Beverages:** Not permitted. **Vehicle Maximum Length:** 35 ft. **Other:** 14-day stay limit.

TO GET THERE

From I-79, take Exit 99 and follow US 33 east to Talbot Rd. Turn left and follow signs to park.

CALDWELL   MAP, C-2
Greenbrier River State Forest

HC 30, P.O. Box 154, 24925.
T: (800) CALLWVA or (304) 536-1944;
www.greenbriersf.com.

🚐 ★★★   ⛺ ★★★★

Beauty: ★★★★   Site Privacy: ★★★
Spaciousness: ★★★   Quiet: ★★★
Security: ★★★★★   Cleanliness: ★★★★★
Insect Control: ★★★★   Facilities: ★★★

Located in the southeastern corner of the state near the border of Virginia, Greenbrier State Forest provides over 5,100 acres of heavily forested, mountainous terrain perfect for outdoor recreation. The imposing, 3,280-foot-high Kate's Mountain affords magnificent views of the surrounding countryside.

Greenbrier State Forest's campsites are shaded and bordered by thick forests of pine, maple, buckeye, oak, and hemlock. Twelve standard one- and two-bedroom cabins are also available. The Greenbrier River Trail is just a few miles away. Hiking and biking trails are plentiful, and the Greenbrier River is a popular canoeing spot. Worthwhile side trips include Organ Cave, used by the Confederates for saltpeter in the Civil War, and Lewisburg, where the downtown area is a National Registered Historic District. Lewisburg is home to the 1796 Old Stone Church—the oldest continuously used church west of the Alleghenies.

BASICS

Operated By: State of West Virginia. **Open:** Apr. 15–Nov. 30. **Site Assignment:** Reservations accepted w/ full deposit & $5 fee (2-night min.); walk-ins accepted; refund (minus $5 & 1-night charge) w/ 7-day notice. **Registration:** At campground office. **Fee:** $17–$20; V, MC. **Parking:** At site.

FACILITIES

Number of Multipurpose Sites: 16. **Hookups:** Electric (20, 30 amps). **Each Site:** Fire grate, picnic table. **Dump Station:** No. **Laundry:** No. **Pay Phone:** Yes. **Restrooms and Showers:** Yes. **Fuel:** No. **Propane:** No. **Internal Roads:** Paved, in fair condition. **RV Service:** No. **Market:** W/in 7 mi. **Restaurant:** W/in 5 mi. **General Store:** No. **Vending:** Yes. **Swimming:** Yes. **Playground:** Yes. **Activities:** Hiking trails, badminton, horseshoes, volleyball. **Nearby Attractions:** The Greenbrier Resort, Lewisburg, Greenbrier River Trail, Moncove Lake State Park, Organ Cave, Lost World Caverns, Greenbrier River, National Fish Hatchery, Old Stone Church, West Virginia State Fair, Monongahela National Forest. **Additional Information:** Southern West Virginia CVB, (800) VISIT-WV, www.visitwv.org.

RESTRICTIONS

Pets: On leash only. **Fires:** At site. **Alcoholic Beverages:** Not permitted. **Vehicle Maximum Length:** 34 ft. **Other:** Quiet time 10 p.m.–7 a.m.

TO GET THERE

From I-64, take Exit 175. Go 2 mi. south on Hart's Run Rd. Entrance is on the right.

CAMP CREEK   MAP, C-2
Camp Creek State Park and Forest

2390 Camp Creek Rd., P.O. Box 119, 25820.
T: (304) 425-9481 or (800) CALLWVA;
www.campcreekstatepark.com.

🚐 ★★★★   ⛺ ★★★★

Beauty: ★★★   Site Privacy: ★★★
Spaciousness: ★★★   Quiet: ★★★★
Security: ★★★★   Cleanliness: ★★★★
Insect Control: ★★★★ Facilities: ★★★★

Located in the southern part of West Virginia, between Beckley and Princeton, Camp Creek State Park was formed from Camp Creek State Forest in 1987. The park is situated just 2 miles off I-77. Surrounded by the breathtaking mountains of southern West Virginia, Camp Creek actually has two camp-

grounds. Marsh Fork Campground contains 26 RV and tent sites with electrical hookups and a bathhouse with hot showers. Near Campbell Falls, the shady Blue Jay Campground consists of 13 creekside tent sites amid a forest of hemlock and ironwood. Blue Jay campers can use the showers at Marsh Fork, which is a mile away. Campbell Falls is worth the brief walk from Blue Jay. Still adjacent to the park lies Camp Creek State Forest; with about 5,300 acres of land, the state forest has several trails for hiking and mountain biking. Camp Creek is one of West Virginia's best-stocked trout streams.

BASICS

Operated By: State of West Virginia. **Open:** All year. **Site Assignment:** Reservations w/ full deposit & $5 fee; walk-ins accepted; refund w/ 7-day notice. **Registration:** At campground office. **Fee:** $13–$21; V, MC. **Parking:** At site.

FACILITIES

Number of RV-only Sites: 26. **Number of Tent-only Sites:** 13. **Hookups:** Electric (30 amps). **Each Site:** Fire ring, grill, picnic table. **Dump Station:** Yes. **Laundry:** Yes. **Pay Phone:** No. **Restrooms and Showers:** Yes. **Fuel:** No. **Propane:** No. **Internal Roads:** Paved, in good condition. **RV Service:** No. **Market:** W/in 5 mi. **Restaurant:** W/in 5 mi. **General Store:** Yes, limited. **Vending:** Yes. **Playground:** Yes. **Activities:** Stream fishing, shuffleboard, badminton, sports field, horseshoes, hiking trails, volleyball. **Nearby Attractions:** Beckley Exhibition Coal Mine, Bluestone State Park, Bluestone Wildlife Management Area, Bramwell Historic District, Grandview Park & Outdoor Dramas, Pipestem Resort State Park, Pinnacle Rock State Park, Twin Falls Resort State Park, New River Gorge. **Additional Information:** Southern West Virginia CVB, (800) VISIT-WV, www.visitwv.org.

RESTRICTIONS

Pets: On leash only. **Fires:** At site. **Alcoholic Beverages:** Not permitted. **Vehicle Maximum Length:** 45 ft. **Other:** 14-day stay limit.

TO GET THERE

From I-77, take Exit 20 and follow signs to state park.

CHARLESTON   MAP, C-2
Kanawha State Forest

Rte. 2 Box 285, 25314.
T: (304) 558-3500 or (800) CALLWVA;
www.kanawhastateforest.com.

🚐 ★★★★   ⛺ ★★★★

Beauty: ★★★★   Site Privacy: ★★★
Spaciousness: ★★★   Quiet: ★★★★
Security: ★★★★   Cleanliness: ★★★★★
Insect Control: ★★★★ Facilities: ★★★★

It's hard to believe that the sprawling state capital of Charleston is only 7 miles away from the hills and valleys of Kanawha State Forest. With 11,000 acres of terrain, Kanawha is a haven for hikers and mountain bikers who embark along the maze of trails. Davis Creek Campground is served by two bathhouses, coin-operated laundry facilities, a swimming pool, and a well-kept playground. Hemlocks shade part of the intimate campground, which borders Davis Creek. One of the best hiking paths for families is the Spotted Salamander trail—a paved, level walkway with Braille-signed interpretive nature stations designed for both visually impaired and physically challenged guests. Store Hollow and David Creek trails sprout from the campground as well. The capitol complex and 19th-century Old Charleston Village are a short drive away from the campground.

BASICS

Operated By: State of West Virginia. **Open:** Apr. 15–Oct. 31. **Site Assignment:** Reservations recommended, especially holiday weekends; reservations require full deposit; walk-ins accepted; refund (minus $5 & 1-night fee) w/ 7-day notice. **Registration:** At campground office. **Fee:** $17–$20; V, MC. **Parking:** At site.

FACILITIES

Number of RV-only Sites: 25. **Number of Tent-only Sites:** 21. **Hookups:** Electric (20 amps). **Each Site:** Fire ring, grill, picnic table. **Dump Station:** Yes. **Laundry:** Yes. **Pay Phone:** Yes. **Restrooms and Showers:** Yes. **Fuel:** No. **Propane:** No. **Internal Roads:** Paved, in good condition. **RV Service:** No. **Market:** W/in 6 mi. **Restaurant:** W/in 5 mi. **General Store:** No. **Vending:** No. **Swimming:** Yes. **Playground:** Yes. **Activities:** Lake fishing, hiking trails, swimming, mountain biking. **Nearby Attractions:** State Capitol, Governor's Mansion, Cultural Center w/ State Museum, "Mountain Stage" live radio show, Charleston East End Historical District, P.A. Denny Sternwheeler, Sunrise Museum, Charleston Sternwheel Regatta, antique malls in South Charleston & Nitro. **Additional Information:** Charleston CVB, (800) 733-5469, www.charlestonwv.com.

RESTRICTIONS

Pets: On leash only. **Fires:** At site. **Alcoholic Beverages:** Not permitted. **Vehicle Maximum Length:** 26 ft. **Other:** 14-day stay limit.

TO GET THERE

From I-64, take Exit 58A and go south on US 119, east on Oakwood Rd., and follow signs for 6 mi.

CLARKSBURG   MAP, B-2
Wilderness Waterpark and Campground

RR 1 Box 141, 26301. T: (304) 622-7528.

🚐 ★★★	🏕 ★★★
Beauty: ★★★	Site Privacy: ★★★
Spaciousness: ★★★	Quiet: ★★★★
Security: ★★★	Cleanliness: ★★★
Insect Control: ★★★	Facilities: ★★★★

They call West Virginia "Mountaineer Country," and that slogan is especially fitting in the north-central part of the state. This is where you will find Clarksburg and the Wilderness Waterpark and Campground. All 51 sites have full hookups and accommodate pull-throughs. The lake, created from strip mining years ago, is popular for its fishing, paddleboating, canoeing, and waterslide. There are interesting historical attractions nearby. Nearby Fort

New Salem is a collection of relocated log structures representing a West Virginia frontier settlement. Watters Smith Memorial State Park is a 532-acre historical park. Jackson's Mill is the boyhood home of Gen. Thomas J. "Stonewall" Jackson, complete with working grist mill and walking tours. Jackson's Mill is also the site of the Jubilee, an arts and crafts festival held on Labor Day weekend.

BASICS

Operated By: Private operator. **Open:** All year. **Site Assignment:** Reservations w/ 1-night deposit; walk-ins accepted; 50% refund w/ 7-day notice. **Registration:** At campground headquarters. **Fee:** $16–$20; cash, check. **Parking:** At site.

FACILITIES

Number of RV-only Sites: 51. **Hookups:** Electric (15, 30 amps), water, sewer, phone. **Each Site:** Fire ring, picnic table. **Dump Station:** Yes. **Laundry:** No. **Pay Phone:** No. **Restrooms and Showers:** Yes. **Fuel:** No. **Propane:** No. **Internal Roads:** Gravel, in good condition. **RV Service:** No. **Market:** W/in 6 mi. **Restaurant:** W/in 10 mi. **General Store:** Yes. **Vending:** No. **Playground:** Yes. **Other:** Waterslide. **Activities:** Rec hall, game room, lake swimming, boating, lake fishing, basketball, planned activities on weekends, horseback riding, sports field, horseshoes, hiking trails, volleyball. **Nearby Attractions:** Historic Jackson's Mill, Stonewall Jackson Lake State Park, Clarksburg, Fort New Salem, Blennerhasset Island. **Additional Information:** Marion County CVB, (800) 834-7365, www.marioncvb.com.

RESTRICTIONS

Pets: On leash only. **Fires:** At site. **Alcoholic Beverages:** At site. **Vehicle Maximum Length:** No limit.

TO GET THERE

From I-79, go 10 mi. west on US 50, 1 mi. south on Sycamore Rd., and follow signs for 1.5 mi. west on blacktop and then gravel road. Entrance is at the end.

CLIFFTOP   MAP, C-2
Babcock State Park

HC 35 Box 150, 25831.
T: (304) 438-3004 or (800) CALLWVA;
www.babcocksp.com.

🚐 ★★★	🏕 ★★★
Beauty: ★★★★	Site Privacy: ★★★
Spaciousness: ★★	Quiet: ★★★
Security: ★★★★	Cleanliness: ★★★★
Insect Control: ★★★★	Facilities: ★★★★

One of West Virginia's first state parks, the 4,127-acre Babcock State Park borders New River Gorge National River. The park is graced with a fast-flowing trout stream in a boulder-strewn canyon, where mountainous vistas can be viewed from scenic overlooks. The 52-site campground, set amid hemlock, white pine, oak, and hickory, has open and shaded sites. The park itself has more than 20 miles of hiking and mountain biking trails. Also on the park grounds is the Glade Creek Grist Mill, which was completed in 1976 at Babcock. This fully operational replica was built by combining parts from

three vintage mills. A living monument to the hundreds of mills which thrived in West Virginia at the turn of the century, the Glade Creek Grist Mill provides freshly ground cornmeal and buckwheat flour. Of course, many campers at Babcock prefer white-water to grist mills. New River Gorge and numerous river outfitters are a short drive from Babcock.

BASICS

Operated By: State of West Virginia. **Open:** Apr. 15–Oct. 31. **Site Assignment:** Reservations w/ full deposit; walk-ins accepted; refund (minus $5 & 1-night fee) w/ 7-day notice. **Registration:** At campground office. **Fee:** $17–$20; V, MC. **Parking:** At site.

FACILITIES

Number of RV-only Sites: 28. **Number of Tent-only Sites:** 24. **Hookups:** Electric (20 amps). **Each Site:** Fire grate, picnic table. **Dump Station:** Yes. **Laundry:** Yes. **Pay Phone:** Yes. **Restrooms and Showers:** Yes. **Fuel:** No. **Propane:** No. **Internal Roads:** Paved, in good condition. **RV Service:** No. **Market:** W/in 10 mi. **Restaurant:** W/in 12 mi. **General Store:** Yes. **Vending:** Yes. **Swimming:** Yes. **Playground:** Yes. **Activities:** Boating, boat rentals, lake & stream fishing, shuffleboard, tennis, hiking trails, volleyball. **Nearby Attractions:** New River Gorge National River, Beckley, Exhibition Coal Mine & Coal Museum. **Additional Information:** Southern West Virginia CVB, (800) VISIT-WV, www.visitwv.org.

RESTRICTIONS

Pets: On leash only. **Fires:** At site. **Alcoholic Beverages:** Not permitted. **Vehicle Maximum Length:** No limit. **Other:** 14-day stay limit.

TO GET THERE

At the US 60 exit, travel east 10 mi. to Hwy. 41 South. Babcock's Campground is 2 mi. south of Hwy. 60 at Clifftop, while the main park entrance is 2 mi. south of Clifftop.

DAVIS   MAP, B-3
Blackwater Falls State Park

P.O. Box 490, 26260.
T: (304) 259-5216 or (800) CALLWVA;
www.blackwaterfalls.com.

🚐 ★★★	🏕 ★★★
Beauty: ★★★	Site Privacy: ★★★
Spaciousness: ★★★	Quiet: ★★★★
Security: ★★★★	Cleanliness: ★★★★
Insect Control: ★★★★	Facilities: ★★★★

Located in the mountainous Potomac Highlands outside of Davis, Blackwater Falls State Park is named for the falls of the Blackwater River, whose amber-colored waters plunge five stories, then twist and tumble through an 8-mile gorge. The black water is a result of tannic acid from fallen hemlock and red spruce needles. The 65-site campground has 39 pull-through sites. A short walk along the Elakala Trail from the lodge will take hikers over the upper section of Elakala Falls. Pendleton Falls can be viewed at a roadside pull-off about 0.5 miles from the lodge. Like Elakala, these falls are the cascades of Pendleton Run coming from the park's swimming and boating lake. Accommodating non-RVers and tenters, Blackwater Lodge sits on the canyon's south rim, providing a sweeping view of the densely forested gorge. Each one of the 54 air-conditioned guest rooms has a private bath, phone, and color television. The lodge also features a game room, a sitting room with a cozy fireplace, and an indoor pool.

BASICS

Operated By: State of West Virginia. **Open:** May 1–Oct. 31. **Site Assignment:** Reservations w/ full deposit & $5 fee; walk-ins accepted. **Registration:** At campground office. **Fee:** $17–$20; V, MC, AE, DC. **Parking:** At site.

FACILITIES

Number of Tent-only Sites: 35. **Number of Multipurpose Sites:** 30. **Hookups:** Electric (20 amps). **Each Site:** Fire ring, picnic table. **Dump Station:** Yes. **Laundry:** Yes. **Pay Phone:** Yes. **Restrooms and Showers:** Yes. **Fuel:** No. **Propane:** No. **Internal Roads:** Paved, in good condition. **RV Service:** No. **Market:** W/in 5 mi. **Restaurant:** W/in 5 mi. **General Store:** Yes, limited. **Vending:** Yes. **Playground:** Yes. **Other:** State park has lodge w/ indoor pool. **Activities:** Rec hall, lake swimming, boating, boat rentals, river fishing, planned activities, tennis, badminton, sports field, horseshoes, hiking trails, volleyball. **Nearby Attractions:** Harper's Old Country Store, Monongahela National Forest, Seneca Caverns. **Additional Information:** Potomac Highlands Travel Council, (304) 257-9315.

RESTRICTIONS

Pets: On leash only. **Fires:** At site. **Alcoholic Beverages:** Not permitted. **Vehicle Maximum Length:** No limit. **Other:** 14-day stay limit.

TO GET THERE

From Hwy. 32, go 2 mi. southwest on CR 29. Entrance is on the right.

DUNLOW   MAP, C-1
Cabwaylingo State Forest

Rte. 1 Box 85, 25511.
T: (304) 385-4255 or (800) CALLWVA;
www.cabwaylingo.com.

🚐 ★★★	🏕 ★★★★
Beauty: ★★★★	Site Privacy: ★★★
Spaciousness: ★★★	Quiet: ★★★★
Security: ★★★★	Cleanliness: ★★★★
Insect Control: ★★★★	Facilities: ★★★★

Located in Wayne County in southwestern West Virginia, Cabwaylingo State Forest is midway between Huntington and Williamson. Consisting of 8,123 densely wooded acres, the state forest offers two campgrounds to choose from. Spruce Creek is a newer 11-site campground with water and electric hookups and shower facilities. Tick Ridge is a more rustic camping area surrounded by a pine and oak forest. There are about 25 miles of trails to explore at Cabwaylingo, including the Indian Trail that starts at the campground. Located near the McClintic Group Camp, the swimming area features a remodeled pool, bathhouse, and a wading pool for children. Lifeguards are on duty during pool hours. Cabwaylingo State Forest is steeped in the history of the

Civilian Conservation Corps (CCC); the CCC built log cabins with stone fireplaces, the superintendent's residence, picnic areas, hiking trails, and a fire tower.

BASICS

Operated By: State of West Virginia. **Open:** Apr. 1–Oct. 31. **Site Assignment:** First come, first served; no reservations. **Registration:** Ranger will stop at campsite & register campers. **Fee:** $11–$20; V, MC. **Parking:** At site.

FACILITIES

Number of RV-only Sites: 6. **Number of Tent-only Sites:** 15. **Hookups:** Electric (20 amps). **Each Site:** Fire grate, picnic table. **Dump Station:** Yes. **Laundry:** No. **Pay Phone:** Yes. **Restrooms and Showers:** Yes. **Fuel:** No. **Propane:** No. **Internal Roads:** Paved, in good condition. **RV Service:** No. **Market:** W/in 12 mi. **Restaurant:** W/in 12 mi. **General Store:** No. **Vending:** Yes. **Swimming:** Yes. **Playground:** Yes. **Activities:** Fishing, hiking trails, swimming, basketball, volleyball. **Nearby Attractions:** Huntington, Heritage Farm Museum & Village, Mountain State Mystery Train. **Additional Information:** Cabell Co./Huntington CVB, (800) 635-6329, www.wvvisit.org.

RESTRICTIONS

Pets: On leash only. **Fires:** At site. **Alcoholic Beverages:** Not permitted. **Vehicle Maximum Length:** No limit. **Other:** 14-day stay limit.

TO GET THERE

Follow US 152 for about 42 mi. south of Huntington and turn off at Missouri Branch.

ELKINS   MAP, B-3
Alpine Shores Campground

HC. 73 Box 3, 26254. T: (304) 636-4311.

🚐 ★★★	🏕 ★★★
Beauty: ★★★★	Site Privacy: ★★★★
Spaciousness: ★★★★	Quiet: ★★★★
Security: ★★★★	Cleanliness: ★★★
Insect Control: ★★★★	Facilities: ★★★★

Just east of Elkins, Alpine Shores Campground lies on 260 acres of beautiful mountain woodland along a mile of shoreline of the Cheat River's Shaver's Fork. The campground has 166 level, grassy, and open sites. Fishing and swimming are popular activities in Shaver's Fork. Nearby Monongahela National Forest offers a wealth of opportunities for outdoor enthusiasts, including skiing, golfing, canoeing, and whitewater rafting. Alpine Shores is a short drive from the antique shops of Elkins. Another worthwhile side trip is Spruce Knob; at 4,861 ft. above sea level, this is West Virginia's highest peak. From this rugged alpine height, you can view grassy meadows and pastures or look down on forested ridges as far as the eye can see. A stone-and-steel observation tower sits atop Spruce Knob, providing visitors with a panoramic view. The 0.5-mile Whispering Spruce Trail circles Spruce Knob, providing breathtaking views of West Virginia's mountains and valleys.

BASICS

Operated By: Private operator. **Open:** Apr. 15–Nov. 15. **Site Assignment:** Reservations & walk-ins

accepted. **Registration:** At campground headquarters. **Fee:** $18–$20; V, MC. **Parking:** At site.

FACILITIES

Number of RV-only Sites: 141. **Number of Tent-only Sites:** 25. **Hookups:** Electric (15, 20, 30 amps), water. **Each Site:** Fire ring, picnic table. **Dump Station:** Yes. **Laundry:** Yes. **Pay Phone:** Yes. **Restrooms and Showers:** Yes. **Fuel:** No. **Propane:** No. **Internal Roads:** Gravel, in good condition. **RV Service:** No. **Market:** W/in 7 mi. **Restaurant:** On premises. **General Store:** Yes. **Vending:** Yes. **Playground:** Yes. **Other:** Alpine Lodge. **Activities:** River swimming & fishing, basketball, horseshoes, volleyball. **Nearby Attractions:** Blackwater Falls, Seneca Caverns, Spruce Knob, Davis & Elkins historic sites, Augusta Heritage Center. **Additional Information:** Randolph County CVB, (800) 422-3304, www.randolphcountywv.com.

RESTRICTIONS

Pets: On leash only. **Fires:** At site. **Alcoholic Beverages:** At site. **Vehicle Maximum Length:** 40 ft.

TO GET THERE

From Elkins, travel east on US 33 for 7 mi. to find Alpine Shores on the right.

GAP MILLS   MAP, C-2
Moncove Lake State Park

Hwy. 4, P.O. Box 73-A, 24941.
T: (304) 772-3450 or (800) CALLWVA;
www.moncovelakestatepark.com.

🚐 ★★★	🏕 ★★★★
Beauty: ★★★★	Site Privacy: ★★★
Spaciousness: ★★★	Quiet: ★★★
Security: ★★★★	Cleanliness: ★★★★★
Insect Control: ★★★★	Facilities: ★★★

Located in Monroe County's Sweet Spring Valley near Gap Mills, Moncove Lake State Park is home to an abundance of wildlife—foxes, white-tail deer, squirrels, and beavers are among the many animals you are likely to see. The park is located near a major flyway for hawks migrating in the fall and spring. In September, on Peter's Mountain, hundreds of hawks can be seen daily heading south for the winter. All campsites are level; some sites are open, others are shaded by hickory and oak. The 144-acre Moncove Lake provides fishing for largemouth bass, bluegill, trout, and catfish. Rowboats and paddleboats are available for rent. Hikers flock to the Devil's Creek Trail, which departs from the campground and links with other trails such as Diamond Hollow and Roxalia Springs. Underground hiking is the draw at Organ Cave and Lost World Caverns, a short drive from Moncove Lake.

BASICS

Operated By: State of West Virginia. **Open:** Apr. 15–Dec. 31. **Site Assignment:** First come, first served; no reservations. **Registration:** At campground office. **Fee:** $17–$20; cash, check. **Parking:** At site.

FACILITIES

Number of RV-only Sites: 50. **Hookups:** Electric (20, 30 amps). **Each Site:** Fire ring, picnic table.

Dump Station: Yes. **Laundry:** No. **Pay Phone:** Yes. **Restrooms and Showers:** Yes. **Fuel:** No. **Propane:** No. **Internal Roads:** Gravel, in fair condition. **RV Service:** No. **Market:** W/in 6 mi. **Restaurant:** W/in 6 mi. **General Store:** No. **Vending:** Yes. **Swimming:** Yes. **Playground:** Yes. **Activities:** Lake fishing, boating, boat rentals, badminton, sports field, horseshoes, hiking trails, volleyball. **Nearby Attractions:** Greenbrier River, Greenbrier River Rail Trail, Organ Cave, Lost World Caverns, Historic Lewisburg, Harding Rock Hawk Tower on Peter's Mountain. **Additional Information:** Southern West Virginia CVB, (800) VISIT-WV, www.visitwv.org.

RESTRICTIONS

Pets: On leash only. **Fires:** At site. **Alcoholic Beverages:** Not permitted. **Vehicle Maximum Length:** No limit. **Other:** 14-day stay limit.

TO GET THERE

From Gap Mills, go 6 mi. north on CR 8. Follow signs to the park.

GLENVILLE   MAP, B-2
Cedar Creek State Park

Rte. 1 Box 9, 2947 Cedar Creek Rd., 26351.
T: (304) 462-7158 or (800) CALLWVA;
www.cedarcreeksp.com.

🚐 ★★★★   ▲ ★★★★

Beauty: ★★★★   Site Privacy: ★★★
Spaciousness: ★★★   Quiet: ★★★★
Security: ★★★★   Cleanliness: ★★★★★
Insect Control: ★★★★   Facilities: ★★★★

The 2,483-acre Cedar Creek State Park is located 25 miles west of I-79 near Glenville. The 57-site campground is clean, and there are three bathhouses, alleviating long waits at prime shower times. Some of the open and shaded sites are creek side. One of the unique aspects of the campground is the check-in station—a restored log cabin that was formerly a Gilmer County historical landmark. Further adding to the charming ambiance of the park, a reconstructed one-room schoolhouse has been erected as a testimonial to the early years of education. Hikers will enjoy the Stone Trough and Park View trails. The three lakes at Cedar Creek are seasonally stocked for fishing. Trout are stocked in late winter and early spring, and muskie in summer. Bass and catfish may be caught year-round.

BASICS

Operated By: State of West Virginia. **Open:** Apr. 15–Oct. 15. **Site Assignment:** Reservations w/ full deposit & $5 fee; walk-ins accepted. **Registration:** At campground office. **Fee:** $17–$20; credit card. **Parking:** At site.

FACILITIES

Number of RV-only Sites: 57. **Number of Tent-only Sites:** 8. **Hookups:** Electric (20, 30 amps). **Each Site:** Fire grate, picnic table. **Dump Station:** Yes. **Laundry:** Yes. **Pay Phone:** Yes. **Restrooms and Showers:** Yes. **Fuel:** No. **Propane:** No. **Internal Roads:** Paved, in good condition. **RV Service:** No. **Market:** W/in 10 mi. **Restaurant:** W/in 8 mi. **General Store:** Yes. **Vending:** Yes. **Swimming:** Yes. **Playground:** Yes. **Other:** Activity building.

Activities: Boating, boat rentals, stream & pond fishing, mini-golf, planned activities, tennis, sports field, horseshoes, hiking trails, volleyball. **Nearby Attractions:** Blennerhassett Historical State Park, Bulltown Historic District. **Additional Information:** Parkersburg/Wood Co. CVB, (800) 752-4982, www.parkersburgcvb.com.

RESTRICTIONS

Pets: On leash only. **Fires:** At site. **Alcoholic Beverages:** Permitted. **Vehicle Maximum Length:** No limit. **Other:** 14-day stay limit.

TO GET THERE

From I-79, take the Burnsville/Glenville exit and follow Hwy. 5 west to Glenville. The park is located south of Glenville and 4 mi. east of US 33/119.

GRAFTON   MAP, B-3
Tygart Lake State Park

Hwy. 1 , P.O. Box 260, 26354.
T: (304) 265-6144 or (800) CALLWVA;
www.tygartlake.com.

🚐 ★★★★   ▲ ★★★★

Beauty: ★★★★   Site Privacy: ★★★
Spaciousness: ★★★   Quiet: ★★★★
Security: ★★★★   Cleanliness: ★★★★
Insect Control: ★★★★   Facilities: ★★★★

Nestled in the foothills of the Allegheny Mountains in north central West Virginia near Grafton, Tygart Lake State Park is home to the 1,740-acre Tygart Lake. The centrally located bathhouse has hot showers. Though there is no general store, bagged ice and firewood are sold at the check-in station. Perched on a promontory overlooking the lake, Tygart Lake Lodge has 20 wood-paneled guest rooms. The lodge's 100-seat restaurant offers panoramic views of the waterfront. The restaurant can cater banquets and receptions for special groups such as business meetings, family reunions, and weddings. Dinner theaters are also scheduled throughout the year. The park has five hiking trails. Swimming is offered in the roped-off beach area, monitored by a staff of lifeguards. Fishing and pontoon boats can be rented from the marina. You can also hit the links at Tygart Lake Country Club.

BASICS

Operated By: State of West Virginia. **Open:** Apr. 15–Oct. 31. **Site Assignment:** First come, first served; no reservations. **Registration:** At campground office. **Fee:** $17–$20; V, MC. **Parking:** At site.

FACILITIES

Number of RV-only Sites: 14. **Number of Multipurpose Sites:** 26. **Hookups:** Electric (20 amps). **Each Site:** Fire ring, picnic table. **Dump Station:** Yes. **Laundry:** No. **Pay Phone:** Yes. **Restrooms and Showers:** Yes. **Fuel:** No. **Propane:** No. **Internal Roads:** Paved, in good condition. **RV Service:** No. **Market:** W/in 5 mi. **Restaurant:** At park lodge. **General Store:** No. **Vending:** Yes. **Swimming:** Lake. **Playground:** Yes. **Other:** Lodge. **Activities:** Rec hall, equipped pavilion, lake swimming, boating, lake fishing, shuffleboard, planned activities, sports field, hiking trails, volleyball. **Nearby Attractions:**

Tygart Lake Dam Visitor Center, International Mother's Day Shrine, Grafton National Cemetery, Pleasant Creek Wildlife Management Area, Valley Falls State Park, Pricketts Fort Memorial State Park, Phillipi Covered Bridge, Anna Jarvis House, Durbin & Greenbrier Railroads, Weston Glass Factory. **Additional Information:** Marion County CVB, (800) 834-7365, www.marioncvb.com.

RESTRICTIONS

Pets: On leash only. **Fires:** At site. **Alcoholic Beverages:** Permitted. **Vehicle Maximum Length:** 30 ft. **Other:** 14-day stay limit.

TO GET THERE

Take US 119 or Hwy. 50 to Grafton. From Grafton, take Hwy. 50 to South Grafton and follow signs to the park.

HACKER VALLEY   MAP, B-2
Holly River State Park

P.O. Box 70, 26222.
T: (304) 493-6353 or (800) CALLWVA;
www.hollyriver.com.

🚐 ★★★   ▲ ★★★★

Beauty: ★★★   Site Privacy: ★★★
Spaciousness: ★★★   Quiet: ★★★★
Security: ★★★★   Cleanliness: ★★★★
Insect Control: ★★★   Facilities: ★★★★

Located near the center of the state in Webster County, Holly River State Park is far from the hustle and bustle of city life, making it a perfect vacation getaway. Weighing in at 8,101 acres, Holly River is the second-largest park in the West Virginia park system. Nestled in a narrow valley, the park is surrounded by heavily forested mountains, some reaching heights of over 2,800 feet. Most of the campsites are stretched alongside Laurel Fork before that body of water merges with Left Fork Holly River. The campground offers a homey, wood-paneled restaurant with wood-burning fireplace for those who want a delicious break from the picnics, campsite cookouts, and cabin-cooked meals. Tecumseh and Tenskwatawa trails, named for two legendary Native American chiefs of the area, are popular routes to view waterfalls. Another great hike is the trail to Potato Knob, featuring a view at 2,480 feet. At the bottom, you can't miss the Shupe's Chute waterfall.

BASICS

Operated By: State of West Virginia. **Open:** Apr. 15–Nov. 15. **Site Assignment:** Reservations w/ full deposit & $5 fee; 2-day min.; refund (minus $15) w/ 30-day notice; walk-ins accepted. **Registration:** At campground office. **Fee:** $20; credit card. **Parking:** At site.

FACILITIES

Number of RV-only Sites: 88. **Number of Multipurpose Sites:** 88. **Hookups:** Electric (20, 30 amps). **Each Site:** Fire grate, picnic table. **Dump Station:** Yes. **Laundry:** Yes. **Pay Phone:** Yes. **Restrooms and Showers:** Yes. **Fuel:** No. **Propane:** No. **Internal Roads:** Paved, in good condition. **RV Service:** No. **Market:** W/in 12 mi. **Restaurant:** On site. **General Store:** Yes. **Vending:** Yes. **Swimming:** Yes. **Playground:** Yes.

Activities: Lake fishing, hiking trails, swimming, horseshoes, planned activities, sports field, tennis, basketball, croquet. **Nearby Attractions:** Sutton Lake, Burnsville Lake, West Virginia Wildlife Center, Elk River Public Hunting & Fishing Area, Kumbrabow State Forest, Helvetia. **Additional Information:** Randolph County CVB, (800) 422-3304, www.randolphcountywv.com.

RESTRICTIONS

Pets: On leash only. **Fires:** At site. **Alcoholic Beverages:** Permitted. **Vehicle Maximum Length:** No limit. **Other:** 14-day stay limit.

TO GET THERE

From SR 15, go 12 mi. north on SR 20. Follow signs to the park.

HARPERS FERRY   MAP, B-2
Harpers Ferry/Washington, D.C., Northwest KOA

343 Campground Rd., 25425.
T: (304) 535-6895 or (800) KOA-9497;
www.harpersferrykoa.com.

🚐 ★★★★   ⛺ ★★★★

Beauty: ★★★★   Site Privacy: ★★
Spaciousness: ★★★   Quiet: ★★★
Security: ★★★★   Cleanliness: ★★★★
Insect Control: ★★★★   Facilities: ★★★★★

Located at the confluence of the Potomac and Shenandoah Rivers, Harpers Ferry/Washington, D.C. Northwest KOA is packed with Civil War history. With the ferry across the Potomac, the Hall Rifle Works, the Chesapeake and Ohio Canal (which connected Harpers Ferry to Washington, D.C.), and the B&O Railroad, the town had definite strategic value. Usually occupied by Federal troops, Harpers Ferry also became a refugee camp for thousands of runaway slaves making their way north. The campground, one of the top three in West Virginia, is the same place where Civil War troops camped, and it's an ideal base for families exploring the Harpers Ferry area and Washington, D.C. The campground has 104 pull-through sites. A movie theater, spacious swimming pool, and well-stocked camp store are among the amenities. The campground will help arrange local and Washington, D.C. tours.

BASICS

Operated By: KOA. **Open:** All year. **Site Assignment:** Reservations recommended w/ 1-night deposit; refund (minus $5) w/ 48-hour notice. **Registration:** At campground office. **Fee:** $25–$55; V, MC, D. **Parking:** At site.

FACILITIES

Number of RV-only Sites: 209. **Number of Tent-only Sites:** 97. **Hookups:** Electric (20, 30, 50 amps), water, phone, Wi-Fi. **Each Site:** Fire ring, picnic table. **Dump Station:** Yes. **Laundry:** Yes. **Pay Phone:** Yes. **Restrooms and Showers:** Yes. **Fuel:** No. **Propane:** Yes. **Internal Roads:** Gravel & paved, in good condition. **RV Service:** No. **Market:** W/in 3 mi. **Restaurant:** W/in 3 mi. **General Store:** Yes. **Vending:** Yes. **Swimming:** Yes. **Playground:** Yes. **Other:** Located on Civil War battlefield. **Activities:**

Rec hall, game room, swimming, wading pool, kayaking, float trips, planned activities, movies, sports field, horseshoes, hiking trail, volleyball, local tours. **Nearby Attractions:** Harpers Ferry National Historic Park, Harpers Ferry Overlook, Appalachian Trail, Antietam Battlefield, Washington, D.C., George Washington's Headquarters, National Museum of Civil War Medicine, Berkeley Castle. **Additional Information:** Jefferson Co. CVB, (800) 848-TOUR, www.jeffersoncountycvb.com.

RESTRICTIONS

Pets: On leash only. **Fires:** At site. **Alcoholic Beverages:** At site. **Vehicle Maximum Length:** 65 ft.

TO GET THERE

From the junction of US 340 and Harpers Ferry exit, go south 100 ft. to Campground Rd. Follow signs to entrance.

HINTON   MAP, C-2
Bluestone State Park

HC 78 , P.O. Box 3, 25951.
T: (304) 466-2805 or (800) CALLWVA;
www.bluestonesp.com.

🚐 ★★★   ⛺ ★★★

Beauty: ★★★   Site Privacy: ★★★
Spaciousness: ★★★   Quiet: ★★★★
Security: ★★★★   Cleanliness: ★★★★
Insect Control: ★★★★   Facilities: ★★★

Adjacent to 2,000-acre Bluestone Lake, Bluestone State Park consists of 2,100 acres of rugged and mountainous terrain. Located 5 miles south of Hinton, the park has Meador Campground and Old Mill Campground, both with grassy sites along Bluestone Lake. Set on the eastern shore of Bluestone Lake is a primitive 50-site campground accessible by boat only. The campgrounds are located in the flood storage basin of Bluestone Lake and are open early May–late October, depending on the water level. Several points of historical and recreational interest are located in the Bluestone area. Outdoor musical dramas such as "Hatfields and McCoys" are performed at Grandview Park, near Beckley. Just north of the park are Bluestone Dam, historic Hinton, and the New River Gorge National River.

BASICS

Operated By: State of West Virginia. **Open:** Apr. 31–Oct. 31. **Site Assignment:** By reservation; first come, first served. **Registration:** At campground office. **Fee:** $9–$20; V, MC. **Parking:** At site.

FACILITIES

Number of RV-only Sites: 76. **Number of Tent-only Sites:** 8. **Hookups:** Electric (30 amps). **Each Site:** Fire ring, picnic table, lantern pole. **Dump Station:** Yes. **Laundry:** Yes. **Pay Phone:** Yes. **Restrooms and Showers:** Yes. **Fuel:** No. **Propane:** No. **Internal Roads:** Paved, in good condition. **RV Service:** No. **Market:** W/in 5 mi. **Restaurant:** W/in 5 mi. **General Store:** Yes. **Vending:** Yes. **Swimming:** Yes. **Playground:** Yes. **Other:** Cabin rentals. **Activities:** Rec hall, boating, canoeing, boat rentals, lake & stream fishing, planned activities, badminton, horseshoes, hiking trails, volleyball. **Nearby Attractions:** Bluestone Gorge, Hinton his-

toric district, Pipestem Resort State Park, New River Gorge National River, Railroad Museum. **Additional Information:** Summers County CVB, (304) 466-5420, www.summerscvb.com.

RESTRICTIONS

Pets: On leash only. **Fires:** At site. **Alcoholic Beverages:** Not permitted. **Vehicle Maximum Length:** 40 ft. **Other:** 14-day stay limit.

TO GET THERE

From Hinton, go 4 mi. south on Hwy. 20. Follow signs to park entrance.

LOGAN   MAP, C-1
Chief Logan State Park

Chief Logan State Park, 25601.
T: (304) 792-7125 or (800) CALLWVA;
www.wvparks.com/chieflogan.

🚐 ★★★   ⛺ ★★★★

Beauty: ★★★   Site Privacy: ★★★
Spaciousness: ★★★   Quiet: ★★★★
Security: ★★★★   Cleanliness: ★★★★
Insect Control: ★★★★   Facilities: ★★★

Located in West Virginia's southern coalfields near Logan, Chief Logan State Park is situated in wooded hills around Buffalo Creek. The campground has 25 sites, seven of which accommodate pull-throughs. The 3,300-acre park has 18 acres of trails for hiking and mountain biking. There's even a fitness trail dotted with exercise stations along the way. The Coal Mine Trail traces an old mine-tram road, complete with coal silo and mine openings. Chief Logan State Park has several attractions where the area's natural and Mingo Indian history are detailed. "The Aracoma Story," a play about the era when the Mingo tribe first encountered British settlers, is performed at the outdoor theater. An old steam locomotive, typical of those that once pulled coal cars from the surrounding mountains to market, is enshrined as a memorial to a bygone era. Also, a small wildlife exhibit featuring live animals native to the state—such as birds, bears, and snakes—is a much-visited attraction.

BASICS

Operated By: State of West Virginia. **Open:** Mar. 1–Nov. 30. **Site Assignment:** By reservation; first come, first served. **Registration:** Ranger will stop by your campsite & register you. **Fee:** $23; V, MC. **Parking:** At site.

FACILITIES

Number of Multipurpose Sites: 26. **Hookups:** Electric (20, 30 amps), water, sewer. **Each Site:** Fire grate, picnic table. **Dump Station:** Yes. **Laundry:** No. **Pay Phone:** Yes. **Restrooms and Showers:** Yes. **Fuel:** No. **Propane:** No. **Internal Roads:** Paved, in good condition. **RV Service:** No. **Market:** W/in 1 mi. **Restaurant:** On state park grounds (15-minute drive). **General Store:** No. **Vending:** Yes. **Swimming:** Yes. **Playground:** Yes. **Other:** Outdoor theater. **Activities:** Mini-golf, hiking trails, tennis court. **Nearby Attractions:** Hatfield & McCoy Interpretive Driving Tour, Lost World Caverns, Organ Cave, New River Gorge National River. **Additional Information:** Southern West Virginia CVB, (800) VISIT-WV, www.visitwv.org.

RESTRICTIONS

Pets: On leash only. **Fires:** At site. **Alcoholic Beverages:** Not permitted. **Vehicle Maximum Length:** No limit. **Other:** 14-day stay limit.

TO GET THERE

From Logan, go 3 mi. north on Hwy. 10. Entrance is on the left.

LOST RIVER   MAP, B-4
Lost River Campground

HC 83 Box 2, 26810. T: (304) 897-5415.

🚐 ★★★★   ⛺ ★★★★

Beauty: ★★★★   Site Privacy: ★★★
Spaciousness: ★★★   Quiet: ★★★★
Security: ★★★   Cleanliness: ★★★★
Insect Control: ★★★★   Facilities: ★★★★

Located in the eastern panhandle of West Virginia, Lost River Campground is about 10 miles north of the Virginia state line. The campground is a short drive from Lost River State Park, which has several miles of hiking trails, a swimming pool, and naturalist activities. Lost River Campground's main draw is its 63-acre stocked lake, a perfect spot for fishing and boating. The campground has 37 sites, all nice and level, and 11 pull-throughs. As is the case for most campgrounds in West Virginia, eye-catching natural wonders surround Lost River. Seneca Rocks, Spruce Knob, Smoke Hole, and Wolf Gap Recreation Area are nearby. Of course, Lost River State Park has its own share of natural splendor. One trail leads to Cranny Crow Overlook, where there are stunning views of the park from 3,200 feet up. Hikes, stream searches, films, slide shows, cookouts, campfires, and family fun athletic competitions are among the park's organized events.

BASICS

Operated By: Teets Farms. **Open:** All year. **Site Assignment:** By reservation; first come, first served. **Registration:** At campground office. **Fee:** $16–$18; V, MC. **Parking:** At site.

FACILITIES

Number of RV-only Sites: 37. **Hookups:** Electric (20, 30, 50 amps). **Each Site:** Grill, picnic table. **Dump Station:** Yes. **Laundry:** No. **Pay Phone:** Yes. **Restrooms and Showers:** Yes. **Fuel:** No. **Propane:** No. **Internal Roads:** Gravel, in good condition. **RV Service:** No. **Market:** W/in 8 mi. **Restaurant:** W/in 6 mi. **General Store:** Yes. **Vending:** Yes. **Playground:** Yes. **Other:** 63-acre stocked lake. **Activities:** Lake & river fishing, boating, canoeing, kayaking, sports field, horseshoes, hiking trails. **Nearby Attractions:** Lost River State Park, Lost River Museum, the Potomac Eagle Train, Smoke Hole Caverns, Seneca Rocks. **Additional Information:** Potomac Highlands Travel Council, (304) 257-9315, www.potomachighlands.org.

RESTRICTIONS

Pets: On leash only. **Fires:** At site. **Alcoholic Beverages:** At site. **Vehicle Maximum Length:** No limit.

TO GET THERE

From SR 55, go 7 mi. south on SR 259 and 0.5 mi. west on Dove Hollow Rd. Entrance is on the left.

MILTON   MAP, B-1
Fox Fire Resort

Hwy. 2, P.O. Box 655, 25541. T: (304) 743-5622; www.foxfirewv.com.

🚐 ★★★★   ⛺ n/a

Beauty: ★★★★   Site Privacy: ★★★
Spaciousness: ★★★   Quiet: ★★★★
Security: ★★★★★   Cleanliness: ★★★★
Insect Control: ★★★★   Facilities: ★★★★★

A 240-foot waterslide. A whirlpool, sauna, and two swimming pools. Mini-golf. Hot-air balloon rides. Around-the-clock security. Clean, comfortable, open, grassy sites—all with full hookups. Consisting of 72 acres located in Milton between Huntington and Charleston, Fox Fire Resort is hands-down the finest private campground in West Virginia. Sites are spacious, and the campground accommodates 34 pull-throughs. Boating and fishing is available on Fox Fire's five spring-fed lakes, and there are several wooded trails for hikers and bikers to explore. After a long tennis match, soaking in the whirlpool is the perfect form of relaxation. For adventure, I.V. Cunningham will take you for a hot-air balloon ride. Hot-air balloon flights last about one hour or more, and it's a great way to see West Virginia's mountains.

BASICS

Operated By: Marie Cunningham. **Open:** All year. **Site Assignment:** First come, first served; no reservations. **Registration:** At campground office. **Fee:** $25.70–$33.70; V, MC, cash, check. **Parking:** At designated spot.

FACILITIES

Number of RV-only Sites: 110. **Hookups:** Electric (20, 30, 50 amps), water, sewer, phone, Wi-Fi. **Each Site:** Picnic table. **Dump Station:** Yes. **Laundry:** Yes. **Pay Phone:** Yes. **Restrooms and Showers:** Yes. **Fuel:** No. **Propane:** Yes. **Internal Roads:** Paved, in good condition. **RV Service:** No. **Market:** W/in 6 mi. **Restaurant:** W/in 6 mi. **General Store:** Yes. **Vending:** Yes. **Swimming:** Yes. **Playground:** Yes. **Other:** 240-ft. waterslide. **Activities:** Rec hall, game room, 2 swimming pools, lake swimming, sauna, whirlpool, waterslide, boat rentals, mini-golf, basketball, tennis, badminton, sports field, horseshoes, hiking trails, volleyball. **Nearby Attractions:** West Virginia Capitol Complex, West Virginia Cultural Center, Old Charleston Village, Kanawha State Forest. **Additional Information:** Charleston CVB, (800) 733-5469, www.charlestonwv.com.

RESTRICTIONS

Pets: On leash only. **Fires:** At site. **Alcoholic Beverages:** At site. **Vehicle Maximum Length:** No limit. **Other:** No tent camping.

TO GET THERE

From I-64, take Exit 28, go 3 mi. west on US 60, and 0.25 mi. northeast on Fox Fire Rd. Entrance is at the end.

MORGANTOWN   MAP, A-3
Chestnut Ridge Park and Campground

Rte. 1 Box 267/ Bruceton Mills, 26525. T: (304) 594-1773 or (888) 594-3111; www.chestnutridgepark.com.

🚐 ★★★★   ⛺ ★★★★

Beauty: ★★★   Site Privacy: ★★★
Spaciousness: ★★★   Quiet: ★★★★
Security: ★★★★   Cleanliness: ★★★★
Insect Control: ★★★★   Facilities: ★★★★

Rolling woodlands, mountain streams, and shaded trails define the landscape of 150-acre Chestnut Ridge Regional Park, located outside of Morgantown. Like nearby Sand Springs Camping Area, Chestnut Ridge is operated by Monongalia County; it features 18 graveled RV sites and 50 tent sites set on a mountainside forest. Paddleboating and fishing are options at Lake Harris and Feather Lake on the park's grounds. Sites at Area E near the Sand Springs Trail offer the most privacy. Chestnut Ridge hosts several special events, including a fishing rodeo, a 5K run, and a toboggan festival. Though Chestnut Ridge does not have a swimming pool, nearby Sand Springs has a pool and a mini-golf course, available to Chestnut Ridge campers for a fee. Hiking trails meander around Chestnut Ridge, but the best hiking nearby is at Cooper's Rock State Forest, where a lookout atop a massive rock formation looks down at the Cheat River Gorge. During college football season, the campground is swarmed when the West Virginia University Mountaineers are playing at home.

BASICS

Operated By: Monongalia County. **Open:** All year. **Site Assignment:** By reservation; first come, first served; refunds w/30-day notice in writing. **Registration:** At park office. **Fee:** $15–$20; V, MC. **Parking:** At designated spot.

FACILITIES

Number of RV-only Sites: 18. **Number of Tent-only Sites:** 50. **Hookups:** Electric (30 amps), water. **Each Site:** Fire ring, picnic table. **Dump Station:** Yes. **Laundry:** Yes. **Pay Phone:** Yes. **Restrooms and Showers:** Yes. **Fuel:** No. **Propane:** No. **Internal Roads:** Gravel, in good condition. **RV Service:** No. **Market:** W/in 7 mi. **Restaurant:** W/in 5 mi. **General Store:** Yes. **Vending:** Yes. **Playground:** Yes. **Other:** Lodge & cabins, nature center. **Activities:** Pond swimming & boating, boat rentals, pond fishing, basketball, badminton, sports field, horseshoes, volleyball, hiking trails. **Nearby Attractions:** Morgantown, West Virginia University, Cooper's Rock State Forest, Circle H Outfitters, Lakeview Scanticon Resort, Cheat Lake & Cheat River. **Additional Information:** Morgantown CVB, (800) 458-7373, www.mgtn.com.

RESTRICTIONS

Pets: On leash only. **Fires:** At site. **Alcoholic Beverages:** Not permitted. **Vehicle Maximum Length:** 40 ft.

TO GET THERE

From I-68, take Exit 15 and go 0.25 mi. east on Old Hwy. 73, 1.5 mi. on Sand Springs Rd., and left at the fork 1 mi. away. Entrance is on the left.

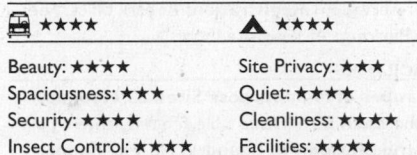

MORGANTOWN   MAP, A-3
Sand Springs Camping Area

Rte. 1 Box 267, Sand Springs Rd., 26525.
T: (304) 594-2415 or (877) 817-9395.

🚐 ★★★★   ⛺ ★★★★

Beauty: ★★★★   Site Privacy: ★★★
Spaciousness: ★★★   Quiet: ★★★★
Security: ★★★★   Cleanliness: ★★★★
Insect Control: ★★★★ Facilities: ★★★★

Located outside of Morgantown, Sand Springs Camping Area is larger than the nearby Chestnut Ridge Regional Park. Sand Springs has 36 RV sites, including 10 pull-throughs. Most of the RV sites are located in the center of the park. Sand Springs also offers 40 tent sites, the best being those at the northeast tip of the campground. Pond fishing and paddleboating are options at nearby Chestnut Ridge; hiking and other outdoor pursuits are available at Cooper's Rock State Forest. The Morgantown area is also home to the Allegheny Trail, which stretches 270 miles through West Virginia. Like Chestnut Ridge, Sand Springs is best visited during the spring and fall, when the colors of the mountains are especially vibrant.

BASICS
Operated By: Robert Christopher. **Open:** May–Dec. 1. **Site Assignment:** By reservation; first come, first served; refunds w/30-day notice in writing. **Registration:** At camp office. **Fee:** $20–$36; V, MC. **Parking:** At designated spot.

FACILITIES
Number of RV-only Sites: 36. **Number of Tent-only Sites:** 40. **Hookups:** Electric (20, 30, 50 amps), water, phone. **Each Site:** Fire ring, picnic table. **Dump Station:** Yes. **Laundry:** Yes. **Pay Phone:** Yes. **Restrooms and Showers:** No. **Fuel:** No. **Propane:** No. **Internal Roads:** Gravel, in good condition. **RV Service:** No. **Market:** W/in 7 mi. **Restaurant:** W/in 7 mi. **General Store:** Yes. **Vending:** Yes. **Swimming:** Yes. **Playground:** No. **Other:** Mini-golf course. **Activities:** Rec room, game room, swimming, mini-golf, hiking trails, horseshoes, karaoke, live music. **Nearby Attractions:** Morgantown, West Virginia University, Cooper's Rock State Forest, Circle H Outfitters, Lakeview Scanticon Resort, Cheat Lake & Cheat River. **Additional Information:** Morgantown CVB, (800) 458-7373, www.mgtn.com.

RESTRICTIONS
Pets: On leash only. **Fires:** At site. **Alcoholic Beverages:** Permitted. **Vehicle Maximum Length:** 45 ft.

TO GET THERE
From I-68, take Exit 15 and go 0.5 mi. northeast on Old Hwy. 73 and 2.25 mi. north on Sand Springs Rd. Entrance is on the right.

MULLENS   MAP, C-2
Twin Falls Resort State Park

Hwy. 97, P.O. Box 667, 25882.
T: (304) 294-4000 or (800) CALLWVA;
www.twinfallsresort.com.

🚐 ★★★★   ⛺ ★★★★

Beauty: ★★★★   Site Privacy: ★★★★
Spaciousness: ★★★   Quiet: ★★★★★
Security: ★★★★★   Cleanliness: ★★★★
Insect Control: ★★★★ Facilities: ★★★★★

Located southwest of Beckley, Twin Falls Resort State Park is named for the falls that majestically grace this rugged mountain wilderness. The campground features wooded and open campsites, including three pull-throughs. The contact center houses a Laundromat, a small store with convenience items, and the camper registration area. Twin Falls has a swimming pool and a tennis court, but its prime recreation draw is the 18-hole, par 71 championship golf course. Nine hiking trails vary from remote wooded paths to scenic walks en route to the Twin Falls. The Pioneer Farm is a restored homeplace on Bowers Ridge; this living history farm provides a glimpse of the 1830s way of life in the Twin Falls area. Twin Falls Lodge is located on a high wooded ridge with a picturesque view of the golf course. The lodge also houses a restaurant that serves breakfast, lunch, and dinner.

BASICS
Operated By: State of West Virginia. **Open:** All year. **Site Assignment:** By reservation; first come, first served. **Registration:** At campground office. **Fee:** $17–$20; V, MC. **Parking:** At designated spot.

FACILITIES
Number of RV-only Sites: 25. **Number of Tent-only Sites:** 25. **Hookups:** Electric (30 amps). **Each Site:** Fire ring, picnic table. **Dump Station:** Yes. **Laundry:** Yes. **Pay Phone:** Yes. **Restrooms and Showers:** Yes. **Fuel:** No. **Propane:** No. **Internal Roads:** Paved, in good condition. **RV Service:** No. **Market:** W/in 5 mi. **Restaurant:** On park grounds. **General Store:** Yes. **Vending:** Yes. **Playground:** Yes. **Other:** Lodge & restaurant. **Activities:** Swimming, tennis, badminton, planned activities, hiking trails, volleyball. **Nearby Attractions:** Beckley, New River Gorge National River, Exhibition Coal Mine & Coal Museum. **Additional Information:** Southern West Virginia CVB, (800) VISIT-WV, www.visitwv.org.

RESTRICTIONS
Pets: On leash only. **Fires:** At site. **Alcoholic Beverages:** Not permitted. **Vehicle Maximum Length:** No limit. **Other:** 14-day stay limit.

TO GET THERE
From Hwy. 54, go 5.5 mi. west on Hwy. 97. Follow signs to park.

NEW MANCHESTER   MAP, A-2
Tomlinson Run State Park

P.O. Box 97, 26056. T: (304) 564-3651;
www.tomlinsonrunsp.com.

🚐 ★★★★   ⛺ ★★★★

Beauty: ★★★★   Site Privacy: ★★★
Spaciousness: ★★★   Quiet: ★★★★
Security: ★★★★   Cleanliness: ★★★★
Insect Control: ★★★★ Facilities: ★★★★

Located at the tip of West Virginia's northern panhandle, Tomlinson Run State Park is 5 miles in either direction of the Ohio and Pennsylvania borders. The spacious sites are situated at the Chief Big Foot and Chief Logan camping areas. Eleven sites accommodate pull-throughs, and there are six rent-a-campsites with cabin-style tents sans electricity. Four ponds at Tomlinson Run are stocked with bass and bluegill. Swimming is even a unique adventure at Tomlinson Run; the Z-shaped pool can accommodate 1,600 people and has a 182-foot figure-8 waterslide. Hiking trails offer spectacular views of the valleys and ridges that surround Tomlinson Run Lake. The Poe Trail, Big Foot Trail, and Laurel Trail are just a few pathways where hikers can immerse themselves in this park's natural splendor.

BASICS
Operated By: State of West Virginia. **Open:** Apr. 1–Oct. 31. **Site Assignment:** Reservations w/ $5 fee & 2-night min.; walk-ins accepted; refund (minus $5 & 1-night fee) w/ 7-day notice. **Registration:** At campground office. **Fee:** $17–$20; V, MC. **Parking:** At site.

FACILITIES
Number of RV-only Sites: 48. **Number of Tent-only Sites:** 6. **Hookups:** Electric (30 amps). **Each Site:** Fire grate, picnic table, lantern pole. **Dump Station:** Yes. **Laundry:** Yes. **Pay Phone:** Yes. **Restrooms and Showers:** Yes. **Fuel:** No. **Propane:** No. **Internal Roads:** Paved, in good condition. **RV Service:** No. **Market:** W/in 8 mi. **Restaurant:** W/in 8 mi. **General Store:** Yes. **Vending:** No. **Playground:** Yes. **Other:** Tomlinson Run Lake. **Activities:** Lake swimming, boating, boat rentals, pond & stream fishing, mini-golf, tennis courts, hiking trails, volleyball. **Nearby Attractions:** Wheeling, Oglebay Park Resort, Point Overlook Museum, Wheeling Suspension Bridge, Independence Hall. **Additional Information:** Wheeling CVB, (800) 828-3097, www.wheelingcvb.com.

RESTRICTIONS
Pets: On leash only. **Fires:** At site. **Alcoholic Beverages:** At site. **Vehicle Maximum Length:** No limit. **Other:** 14-day stay limit.

TO GET THERE
From SR 2, go 3 mi. north on SR 8. Entrance is on the left.

PIPESTEM   MAP, C-2
Pipestem Country Campground

HC 78 Box 37B, 25979.
T: (800) 562-5418 or (304) 466-9121.

🚐 ★★★   ⛺ ★★★★

Beauty: ★★★★   Site Privacy: ★★★★
Spaciousness: ★★★   Quiet: ★★★
Security: ★★★★   Cleanliness: ★★★★
Insect Control: ★★★★ Facilities: ★★★

Located in southeast West Virginia 14 miles north of Princeton, Pipestem KOA is smaller than most KOA campgrounds, and it has few amenities. Yet its proximity to whitewater rafting at the New River Gorge National River and outdoor activities at Pipestem Resort State Park, Bluestone Lake, and the Greenbrier River Trail make it an inviting place to stay nonetheless. Pipestem KOA has open and shaded sites, including 21 pull-throughs. The campground has a full-service store. Nearby, Pipestem

Resort State Park has two golf courses, a restaurant, an outdoor amphitheater, a nature center, and several hiking trails. New River Gorge also offers several miles of hiking trails with incredible cliff views. East of Lewisburg, where the historic district includes the 1796 Old Stone Church, the Greenbrier River Trail offers another 76 miles of trails for hiking and biking.

BASICS

Operated By: Matt & Donna Jeffe. **Open:** All year. **Site Assignment:** Reservations w/ 25% deposit; walk-ins accepted; refund w/ 7-day notice. **Registration:** At campground office. **Fee:** $20–$25; tent, $14; V, MC, D. **Parking:** At designated spot.

FACILITIES

Number of RV-only Sites: 24. **Number of Tent-only Sites:** 6. **Hookups:** Electric (20, 30, 50 amps), Wi-Fi. **Each Site:** Fire ring, picnic table. **Dump Station:** Yes. **Laundry:** Yes. **Pay Phone:** Yes. **Restrooms and Showers:** Yes. **Fuel:** No. **Propane:** Yes. **Internal Roads:** Gravel, in good condition. **RV Service:** No. **Market:** W/in 3 mi. **Restaurant:** W/in 3 mi. **General Store:** Yes. **Vending:** Yes. **Swimming:** Yes, off property. **Playground:** Yes. **Activities:** Hiking trails, golf. **Nearby Attractions:** Bluestone Lake, Historic Lewisburg, Greenbrier River Trail, Exhibition Coal Mine & Coal Museum, Pipestem Resort State Park. **Additional Information:** Southern West Virginia CVB, (800) VISIT-WV, www.visitwv.org.

RESTRICTIONS

Pets: On leash only. **Fires:** At site. **Alcoholic Beverages:** At site. **Vehicle Maximum Length:** No limit.

TO GET THERE

From I-77, take Exit 14 and go 3.5 mi. north on CR 7 and 13.5 northeast on SR 20. Follow signs to park entrance.

PIPESTEM   MAP, C-2
Pipestem Resort State Park

P.O. Box 150, 25979.
T: (304) 466-1800 or (800) CALLWVA;
www.pipestemresort.com.

  🚐 ★★★★   ⛺ ★★★★

Beauty: ★★★★	Site Privacy: ★★★
Spaciousness: ★★★	Quiet: ★★★★
Security: ★★★★	Cleanliness: ★★★★
Insect Control: ★★★★	Facilities: ★★★★★

Pipestem Resort State Park is the crown jewel of West Virginia's state parks. There are several amenities, including two lodges and a full menu of recreational activities (five tennis courts, two golf courses, and mini-golf to name a few). Pipestem's scenic highlight is the aerial tramway that carries passengers on a six-minute ride over Bluestone Gorge and Bluestone River, 3,600 ft. below. The campground has 23 pull-through sites. Pipestem State Park also has two lodges. McKeever Lodge has 112 modern guest rooms and suites, some rooms with gorge views. This lodge has an indoor heated pool, game room, saunas, exercise room, a full-service restaurant, and snack bar. Mountain Creek Lodge is solely accessible by the

aerial tramway; this lodge also has a restaurant. Pipestem features two golf courses—one an 18-hole, par 72 championship course with views of Bluestone Canyon, and the other a nine-hole course.

BASICS

Operated By: State of West Virginia. **Open:** All year. Reservations Memorial Day–Labor Day. **Site Assignment:** Reservations w/ full deposit & $5 fee; walk-ins accepted; refund (minus $5 & 1-night fee) w/ 7-day notice. **Registration:** At campground office. **Fee:** $15–$23; V, MC, AE, D. **Parking:** At designated spot.

FACILITIES

Number of RV-only Sites: 51. **Number of Tent-only Sites:** 31. **Hookups:** Electric (30, 50 amps). **Each Site:** Fire ring, picnic table. **Dump Station:** Yes. **Laundry:** Yes. **Pay Phone:** Yes. **Restrooms and Showers:** Yes. **Fuel:** No. **Propane:** No. **Internal Roads:** Paved, in good condition. **RV Service:** No. **Market:** W/in 5 mi. **Restaurant:** On park grounds. **General Store:** Yes. **Vending:** Yes. **Swimming:** Yes. **Playground:** Yes. **Other:** 2 swimming pools, indoor & outdoor. **Activities:** Swimming, canoeing, boat rentals, lake & river fishing, shuffleboard, mini-golf, tennis courts, planned activities, badminton, horseshoes, hiking trails, volleyball, horseback riding. **Nearby Attractions:** Bluestone Lake, Historic Lewisburg, Greenbrier River Trail, Exhibition Coal Mine & Coal Museum. **Additional Information:** Southern West Virginia CVB, (800) VISIT-WV, www.visitwv.org.

RESTRICTIONS

Pets: On leash only. **Fires:** At site. **Alcoholic Beverages:** At site. **Vehicle Maximum Length:** No limit. **Other:** 14-day stay limit.

TO GET THERE

From I-77, go 3.5 mi. north on CR 7 and 13.5 mi. northeast on SR 20. Follow signs to park and campground.

RICHWOOD   MAP, C-2
Summit Lake Campground

932 North Fork Cherry Rd., 26261.
T: (304) 846-2695; www.fs.fed.us/r9/mnf.

  🚐 ★★★   ⛺ ★★★★

Beauty: ★★★	Site Privacy: ★★★
Spaciousness: ★★★	Quiet: ★★★★
Security: ★★★	Cleanliness: ★★★★
Insect Control: ★★★	Facilities: ★★★

Located about 10 miles east of Richwood in the Monongahela National Forest, Summit Lake Campground is adjacent to 43-acre Summit Lake. Many campsites are level and perched on a mountainside. Summit Lake is stocked with trout by the West Virginia Division of Natural Resources. The lake has an accessible fishing pier and boat launch. Brook trout, rainbow trout, brown trout, largemouth bass, and crappie are among the fish swimming in the lake. Hiking and mountain biking are available on Summit Lake Trail and Pocahontas Trail. Nearby are Bishop Knob Campground and Cranberry Campground. Also close is the Cranberry Backcountry, teeming with hiking and fishing spots. Overall, the

Monongahela National Forest consists of 900,000 acres, including 850 miles of hiking trails.

BASICS

Operated By: U.S. Forest Service. **Open:** Apr. 8–Dec. 8. **Site Assignment:** First come, first served; no reservations. **Registration:** At park office. **Fee:** $8. **Parking:** At designated spot.

FACILITIES

Number of Multipurpose Sites: 33. **Hookups:** None. **Each Site:** Picnic table, fire ring, lantern pole. **Dump Station:** No. **Laundry:** No. **Pay Phone:** No. **Restrooms and Showers:** No. **Fuel:** No. **Propane:** No. **Internal Roads:** Paved, in good condition. **RV Service:** No. **Market:** W/in 5 mi. **Restaurant:** W/in 5 mi. **General Store:** No. **Vending:** No. **Playground:** No. **Other:** Summit Lake. **Activities:** Lake fishing, boating, volleyball, sports field. **Nearby Attractions:** Monongahela National Forest. **Additional Information:** Summersville CVB, (304) 872-3722, www.richwoodwv.com.

RESTRICTIONS

Pets: On leash only. **Fires:** At site. **Alcoholic Beverages:** At site. **Vehicle Maximum Length:** 22 ft. **Other:** 14-day stay limit.

TO GET THERE

From Hwy. 39, go 2 mi. north on Hwy. 77. Follow signs to park.

ROANOKE   MAP, B-2
Stonewall Jackson State Park Campground

940 Resort Dr., 26447.
T: (304) 269-0523 or (800) CALLWVA;
www.stonewalljacksonsp.com.

  🚐 ★★★   ⛺ ★★★

Beauty: ★★★★	Site Privacy: ★★★
Spaciousness: ★★★	Quiet: ★★★★
Security: ★★★★	Cleanliness: ★★★★
Insect Control: ★★★	Facilities: ★★★★

Located in the heart of West Virginia about 13 miles south of Weston and named for the esteemed Civil War general, Stonewall Jackson Lake State Park Campground has 40 sites, all fully equipped. Open April–December, the campground is near the 2,650-acre Stonewall Jackson Lake, where houseboats, pontoons, and motor boats can be rented. The lake also features a fishing pier and a fully equipped marina. Hiking and biking trails are available, as is a pavilion for picnicking and a playground for the children.

BASICS

Operated By: Benchmark Hospitality International. **Open:** Apr. 1–Dec. 15. **Site Assignment:** Reservations recommended w/ full deposit; first come, first served for walk-ins.; refund (minus $15) w/ 7-day notice.; less than 7 days, $15 plus 1-night stay. **Registration:** At campground headquarters. **Fee:** $33. **Parking:** At site only.

FACILITIES

Number of RV-only Sites: 40. **Hookups:** Electric (30, 50 amps), water, sewer. **Each Site:** Grill, picnic table. **Dump Station:** Yes. **Laundry:** Yes. **Pay Phone:** Yes. **Restrooms and Showers:** Yes.

Fuel: No. Propane: No. Internal Roads: Gravel, in fair condition. RV Service: No. Market: 2.5 mi. north in Roanoke. Restaurant: 2.5 mi. north in Roanoke. Playground: Yes. Other: Cottages & houseboats, 200-room lodge, 18-hole championship golf course, 10 cabins. Activities: Boating, swimming, hiking, bicycling. Nearby Attractions: Stonewall Jackson Lake, Jackson's Mill Historic Area, Lambert's Vintage Winery, Masterpiece Crystal, Glass Works Factory Outlet, Weston. Additional Information: Lewis County CVB, (304) 269-7328, www.stonewallcountry.com.

RESTRICTIONS

Pets: On leash only. Fires: At site only. Alcoholic Beverages: At site only. Vehicle Maximum Length: No limit. Other: 14-day stay limit.

TO GET THERE

From I-79, take Exit 91 (Roanoke) and follow US 19 south for 2.5 mi. to the park entrance.

ROANOKE   MAP, B-2
Whisper Mountain Campground and RV Park

4897 Three Lick Rd., 26447. T: (304) 452-9723; www.whispermountaincampground.com.

🚐 ★★★★   ▲ ★★★★

Beauty: ★★★★	Site Privacy: ★★★
Spaciousness: ★★★	Quiet: ★★★★
Security: ★★★★	Cleanliness: ★★★★
Insect Control: ★★★★	Facilities: ★★★★

Located near Stonewall Jackson Lake and State Park, and Weston, Whisper Mountain Campground and RV Park has 69 level and grassy sites with 10 pull-throughs, all situated amid mountain scenery. Hiking and biking trails (as well as boat rentals) can be found at 2,650-acre Stonewall Jackson Lake. The lake also features a fishing pier and a fully equipped marina. A short drive from Whisper Mountain, Jackson's Mill Historic Area, where Confederate Gen. Thomas "Stonewall" Jackson's boyhood home is located, also houses an assortment of 19th-century buildings.

BASICS

Operated By: Chyreck family. Open: All year. Site Assignment: By reservation & first come, first served. Registration: At campground office. Fee: $22–$27; no credit cards. Parking: At designated spot.

FACILITIES

Number of RV-only Sites: 49. Number of Tent-only Sites: 20. Hookups: Electric (20, 30, 50 amps), water. Each Site: Fire ring, picnic table. Dump Station: Yes. Laundry: Yes. Pay Phone: Yes. Restrooms and Showers: Yes. Fuel: No. Propane: No. Internal Roads: Paved, in good condition. RV Service: No. Market: W/in 6 mi. Restaurant: W/in 6 mi. General Store: Yes. Vending: Yes. Swimming: Yes. Playground: Yes. Activities: Swimming, paddleboat rentals, pond fishing, sports field, horseshoes, hiking trails, volleyball, picnic pavilion. Nearby Attractions: Stonewall Jackson Lake & State Park, Jackson's Mill Historic Area, Weston Christmas Town, Glass Works Factory Out-

let. Additional Information: Lewis County CVB, (304) 269-7328, www.stonewallcountry.com.

RESTRICTIONS

Pets: On leash only. Fires: At site. Alcoholic Beverages: At site. Vehicle Maximum Length: No limit.

TO GET THERE

From I-79, take Exit 91. At bottom of exit ramp, stop, turn right (north) onto US 19. Approximately 200 yards on the left is Goosepen Rd. Turn left onto Goosepen Rd. Go 5 mi. on paved road to Three Lick Rd. on left. Turn left. Whisper Mountain Campground entrance is on the right.

RONCEVERTE   MAP, C-2
Greenbrier River Campground

282 Greenbrier Rd., P. O. Box 265, 24970. T: (800) 775-2203; www.greenbrierriver.com.

🚐 ★★★★   ▲ ★★★★

Beauty: ★★★★	Site Privacy: ★★★
Spaciousness: ★★★	Quiet: ★★★★
Security: ★★★	Cleanliness: ★★★★
Insect Control: ★★★	Facilities: ★★★★

Overlooking the Greenbrier River, the 8-acre Greenbrier River Campground offers wooded, open, and riverside grassy campsites. RV campsites average 33 by 68 feet and offer partial shading and scenic views of the river. Greenbrier's grounds are well lit and well maintained. Five sites along the river are reserved for tent camping. Most campsites are equipped with electric, water, cable TV, and sewer service. River swimming is popular at Greenbrier, as are kayaking, canoeing, and tubing.

BASICS

Operated By: Greenbrier River Company. Open: Apr. 15–Oct. 15. Site Assignment: Reservations strongly recommended (50% deposit); walk-ins accepted. Registration: At campground office. Fee: $18.50–$26.50; cash, check. Parking: At site.

FACILITIES

Number of RV-only Sites: 34. Number of Tent-only Sites: 10. Hookups: Electric (20, 30, 50 amps), water, sewer, cable TV. Each Site: Fire ring, picnic table, lantern hook. Dump Station: Yes. Laundry: Yes. Pay Phone: No. Restrooms and Showers: Yes. Fuel: No. Propane: Yes. Internal Roads: Gravel, in good condition. RV Service: No. Market: 4 mi. west in Alderson. Restaurant: 4 mi. west in Alderson. General Store: Yes. Vending: Yes. Swimming: Yes (river). Playground: No. Other: Duckies & boats available for rent. Activities: Canoeing, kayaking, fishing, river swimming, beach volleyball, basketball, badminton, croquet, tubing, mountain biking, soccer, football, softball. Nearby Attractions: Trout fishing streams, Greenbrier Valley Theater, Lewisburg, Lost World & Organ Cave, North House Museum. Additional Information: The Greenbrier River Company, which operates the campground, offers Class I–Class III whitewater rafting adventures on the Greenbrier River.

RESTRICTIONS

Pets: On leash only. Fires: At site. Alcoholic Beverages: At site. Vehicle Maximum Length: No limit.

TO GET THERE

From I-64, take Exit 161 (Alta) and follow Hwy. 12 south for 10 mi. In Alderson, turn left onto Hwy. 63 east. The campground is located 4 mi. east of Alderson on Hwy. 63.

RONCEVERTE   MAP, C-2
Organ Cave Campground

417 Masters Rd., 24970. T: (304) 645-7600; www.organcave.com.

🚐 ★★★★   ▲ ★★★★

Beauty: ★★★★	Site Privacy: ★★★★
Spaciousness: ★★★★	Quiet: ★★★★
Security: ★★★	Cleanliness: ★★★★
Insect Control: ★★★★	Facilities: ★★★

Organ Cave Campground, located in southeastern West Virginia's Greenbrier Valley near Ronceverte, features 37 sites—including four pull-throughs—adjoining Organ Cave, a National Natural Historic Landmark. The campground itself has no restrooms, but its beautiful mountain setting provides lots of serenity and scenery. Tours are given in Organ Cave, one of the longest caves in the United States with more than 40 miles of mapped passageways. Pioneers have known of Organ Cave since 1704, and the cave also played a role during the Civil War. Religious services for 1,100 of Gen. Robert E. Lee's men were given in the shelter of the huge entrance room of the cave. The cave was a significant source of saltpeter, one of the ingredients necessary for making gunpowder. Organ Cave's grounds also feature a rodeo arena, where several rodeos are held throughout the year.

BASICS

Operated By: Organ Cave. Open: Apr.–Sept. Site Assignment: By reservation & first come, first served; credit card. Registration: At campground office. Fee: $16; V, MC, AE, D. Parking: At designated spot.

FACILITIES

Number of RV-only Sites: 37. Hookups: Electric (20, 30, 50 amps), water. Dump Station: No. Laundry: No. Pay Phone: No. Restrooms and Showers: No. Fuel: No. Propane: No. Internal Roads: Paved, in good condition. RV Service: No. Market: W/in 6 mi. Restaurant: W/in 6 mi. General Store: No. Vending: No. Playground: Yes. Other: Rodeo arena, Organ Cave. Activities: Basketball, horseshoes, volleyball, sports field, hiking trails. Nearby Attractions: Organ Cave, Exhibition Coal Mine & Coal Museum, Beckley, Hinton, Lewisburg. Additional Information: Southern West Virginia CVB, (800) VISIT-WV, www.visitwv.org.

RESTRICTIONS

Pets: On leash only. Fires: At site. Alcoholic Beverages: At site. Vehicle Maximum Length: No limit.

To Get There

From I-64, take Exit 169 and go south to Hwy. 63E, and 0.5 mi. east on Hwy. 63E. Entrance is on the right.

SENECA ROCKS	**MAP, B-3**
Yokum's Vacationland	

HC 59 Box 3, 26884.
T: (304) 567-2351 or (800) 772-8342;
www.yokum.com.

🚐 ★★★★   🏕 ★★★★

Beauty: ★★★	Site Privacy: ★★
Spaciousness: ★★★	Quiet: ★★★★
Security: ★★★★	Cleanliness: ★★★
Insect Control: ★★★	Facilities: ★★★★

Located in the center of Pendleton County amid the Spruce Knob–Seneca Rocks National Recreation Area and Monongahela National Forest, Yokum's Vacationland is situated on a 1,000-acre cattle farm. Some sites are open; others are shaded. The campground is located along the north fork of the Potomac River. Princess Snowbird Campground, set on Seneca Creek and facing a majestic view of the Seneca Rocks, has primitive sites with teepees in the Indian Village. Fishing and swimming are popular in the river. The campground also has a heated indoor pool. Adventure seekers have several options in the area, including whitewater rafting. Rock climbers can rent equipment and climb the 960-foot-high Seneca Rocks with qualified instructors. Seneca Caverns offers guided tours through its trails.

BASICS

Operated By: Yokum family. **Open:** All year. **Site Assignment:** First come, first served; no reservations. **Registration:** At campground office. **Fee:** $16–$18; V, MC, AE, D. **Parking:** At designated spot.

FACILITIES

Number of RV-only Sites: 150. **Number of Tent-only Sites:** 50. **Hookups:** Electric (15, 20, 30 amps), water. **Each Site:** Fire ring, picnic table. **Dump Station:** Yes. **Laundry:** Yes. **Pay Phone:** Yes. **Restrooms and Showers:** Yes. **Fuel:** No. **Propane:** No. **Internal Roads:** Gravel, in good condition. **RV Service:** No. **Market:** W/in 5 mi. **Restaurant:** On premises. **General Store:** Yes. **Vending:** Yes. **Swimming:** Yes. **Playground:** Yes. **Activities:** Rec room, swimming, river swimming, canoeing, river fishing, hiking trails, sports field, volleyball. **Nearby Attractions:** Seneca Caverns, Blackwater Falls, Cass Scenic Railroad, Seneca Rocks, Spruce Knob. **Additional Information:** Tucker Co. CVB, (800) 782-2775, www.canaanvalley.org.

RESTRICTIONS

Pets: On leash only. **Fires:** At site. **Alcoholic Beverages:** At site. **Vehicle Maximum Length:** No limit.

To Get There

From US 33, go 0.5 mi. north on Hwy. 28. Entrance is on the right.

SUMMERSVILLE	**MAP, C-2**
Mountain Lake Campground	

reserve america

1868 Summersville Airport Rd., 26651.
T: (304) 872-6222; www.reserveamerica.com.

🚐 ★★★★   🏕 ★★★★

Beauty: ★★★★	Site Privacy: ★★★
Spaciousness: ★★★	Quiet: ★★★★
Security: ★★★★	Cleanliness: ★★★★
Insect Control: ★★★★	Facilities: ★★★★

Located in Summersville in south-central West Virginia, Mountain Lake Campground is situated near Summersville Lake, the largest lake in the state. The campground has shaded and open sites, including 15 pull-throughs. Campers at Mountain Lake can swim and fish in Summersville Lake, called "the little Bahamas of the East" by *Skin Diver Magazine* because of its excellent visibility—scuba diving is popular since the visibility in the lake is 20–45 feet (sometimes as much as 80 feet). The lake was built by the U.S. Army Corps of Engineers, and the dam is on Gauley River near Summersville. The dam is the second largest of its type in the eastern US. In fact, the dam is about as tall as a 40-story building and is 2,280 feet long. The hiking is remarkable, too, especially at the Battle Run Recreation Area.

BASICS

Operated By: Private operator. **Open:** Mar. 1–Nov. 30. **Site Assignment:** Reservations w/ 1-night deposit; walk-ins accepted; voucher refund before morning on day of arrival; no cash refund. **Registration:** At camp headquarters. **Fee:** $14–$20; no checks. **Parking:** At designated spot.

FACILITIES

Number of RV-only Sites: 150. **Number of Tent-only Sites:** 50. **Hookups:** Electric (20, 30 amps), water. **Each Site:** Fire ring, picnic table. **Dump Station:** Yes. **Laundry:** Yes. **Pay Phone:** No. **Restrooms and Showers:** Yes. **Fuel:** No. **Propane:** No. **Internal Roads:** Gravel, in good condition. **RV Service:** No. **Market:** W/in 4 mi. **Restaurant:** On premises. **General Store:** Yes. **Vending:** No. **Swimming:** Yes. **Playground:** Yes. **Activities:** Rec hall, game room, lake swimming & fishing, boating, canoeing, kayaking, mini-golf, basketball, badminton, sports field, horseshoes, hiking, volleyball. **Nearby Attractions:** New River Gorge National River, Gauley River National Recreation Area, Carniex Ferry Battlefield SP, Hawk's Nest State Park. **Additional Information:** Southern West Virginia CVB, (800) VISIT-WV, www.visitwv.org.

RESTRICTIONS

Pets: On leash only. **Fires:** At site. **Alcoholic Beverages:** At site. **Vehicle Maximum Length:** 50 ft.

To Get There

From Summersville, go 1 mi. south on US 19 and 2 mi. west on Airport Rd. Entrance is on the right.

Wisconsin

Along with its famed cheese and cherries, Wisconsin offers up an irresistible vacationer's paradise. From its rugged **Door County** peninsula to the state's biggest city of **Milwaukee** and on to the out-of-this-world wacky **Dells,** America's Dairyland provides a variety of attractions as much as it does a genuine opportunity for escape from the everyday.

The **St. Croix River** shares gorgeous gorges, rock formations, and waterfalls, and the national lakeshore has more lighthouses than any other national park. With 15,000 inland lakes and 25,000 miles of waterways—along with borders on Lakes Michigan and Superior; the St. Croix, Menomonie, and Brule rivers; and the mighty Mississippi—Wisconsin is a water wonderland. Scuba divers explore shipwrecks waiting at death's door, the watery passage between **Door County** and **Washington Island.** Navigable its entire length, the winding **Kickapoo** is called the most crooked river in the world. For heights, head to **Devils Lake State Park** near **Baraboo** for the 500-foot bluffs or to **Granddad Bluff,** which towers 600 feet above **La Crosse.** Stretches of Class V rapids make the **Montreal River** a popular spot for expert kayakers. For exploration, the rugged sea caves dotting the bases of sandstone cliffs are a great choice.

To turn back the clock, visit the living history village in **New Glarus,** often called Little Switzerland. The great architecture of Frank Lloyd Wright is preserved in **Madison** and **Spring Green** at **House on the Rock.** If not arty enough for you, then perhaps check out **Rock in the House** in **Fountain City,** where an errant, 55-ton boulder tumbled from its perch and remains to this day in the exact location it came to rest in the former home of Dwight and Maxine Anderson. A universe of circus memorabilia can be found at the **Circus World Museum** in the former winter home of the Ringling Brothers, Baraboo. For those more inclined to get their kicks from science fiction and within the immediate vicinity, a visit to the world's largest sculpture, the **Forevertron,** is a must. If looking for another feel for steel, climb aboard the **Lumberjack Special** steam-powered train, puffing from the **Laona** historic depot to **Camp Five Museum Complex,** to learn about logging. To see the world's largest replica of cheese commemorating the original from the 1965 World's Fair, make a voyage over to **Neillsville,** which also shares the lot with **Chatty Belle,** the world's largest talking cow.

As Wisconsin's oldest state park, **Interstate State Park** in **St. Croix Falls** is home to an unusual rock outcropping known as the **Old Man of the Dalles.** Climb aboard a boat in the **Wisconsin Dells** for a cruise past rock formations, canyons, islands, and sandstone cliffs. In **Green Bay,** the Packers, founded in 1919, lay claim to being the oldest professional team in the National Football League.

Anglers of all ages will enjoy seeing the **National Fresh Water Fishing Hall of Fame** in **Hayward.** Housed in a building designed to resemble a muskellunge, the facility is complete with an observation deck in the mouth of the giant fish. Horicon offers boat tours of a wetland inhabited by more than 260 species of birds.

More than likely one of the most bizarre, enjoyable, and literally overwhelming destinations in the Badger State, let alone the country, is that of Lake Welton's Wisconsin Dells. Equal parts tourist trap and tourist mecca, the Dells baffles all who pass through, namely with its **Wonder Spot,** in which the laws of gravity and physics do not apply, ostensibly due to the presence of a vortex, according to local lore. If you make it there, however, don't miss **Robot World** or the pool lined with oversized candy. For the gourmand on the go, check out the **Mustard Museum** in **Mount Horeb.**

True to its name, the lovely village of **Land O' Lakes** is surrounded by about 135 lakes. Stroll the tree-shaded streets of Madison, where the impressive 1917 State Capitol offers free tours showcasing state history and artwork. The city's quaint ambiance is further enhanced by its weekly seasonal farmers markets; the jazz, blues, and film festivals; and its decorative festiveness around the holidays.

Campground Profiles

BAGLEY
MAP, D-1
Yogi Bear's Jellystone Park Camp-Resort

11354 CR X, 53801. T: (608) 996-2201 or (800) 999-6557; www.jellystonebagley.com.

🚐 ★★★★   ⛺ ★★★

Beauty: ★★★	Site Privacy: ★★★
Spaciousness: ★★★	Quiet: ★★★
Security: ★★★★	Cleanliness: ★★★★
Insect Control: ★★	Facilities: ★★★★

Campers know what to expect when they go to a Yogi Bear's Jellystone Park Camp-Resort: clean facilities, a quiet, secure campground, and plenty of activities for children. The Bagley campground offers all that, plus a valley site with hills on both sides and the Mississippi River across the road. A railroad track also runs right by the campground. Laid out in a series of loops, the campground has sites that are flat, grassy, and mostly open. Many of the trees were wiped out by a 1998 tornado. Site sizes vary, with some as large as 40 feet wide and 100 feet deep. The campground has seven pull-throughs and 62 seasonal campers. Noncampers are allowed to use the recreational facilities from Sunday through Thursday, holidays excluded. Located 1 mile north of Bagley, the campground enforces quiet time from 10:30 p.m. to 8 a.m., and no mini-bikes, dirt bikes, three- or four-wheelers, or ATVs are allowed in the park at any time. Motorcycles are permitted only to and from the campsite. A five-mph speed limit includes bicycles, too. Security measures include a campground gate that is closed after 10 p.m., as well as "rangers" who patrol the park regularly.

BASICS
Operated By: Mike & Kim Esler. **Open:** May 5–Oct. 15. **Site Assignment:** Reservations w/ deposit of half total fee; 2-day min. on weekends; refunds (minus $7) w/ 14-day notice; less than 14-day notice, 1-night fee. **Registration:** At campground office. **Fee:** $28–$42; cash, check, credit card. **Parking:** At site.

FACILITIES
Number of RV-only Sites: 206. **Number of Tent-only Sites:** 11. **Hookups:** Electric (30, 50 amps), water, sewer. **Each Site:** Picnic table, fire ring. **Dump Station:** Yes. **Laundry:** Yes. **Pay Phone:** Yes. **Restrooms and Showers:** Yes. **Fuel:** No. **Propane:** Yes. **Internal Roads:** Paved/gravel, in good condition. **RV Service:** No. **Market:** 15 mi. north in Prairie du Chien. **Restaurant:** 1 mi. south in Bagley. **General Store:** Yes. **Vending:** Yes. **Swimming:** Yes. **Playground:** Yes. **Other:** Pavilion, mini-golf, Yogi cartoons at outdoor theatre/amphitheatre, ranger station w/ fireplace & lounge, game room, snack bar, shuffleboard, horseshoes, ping-pong, basketball, volleyball, walking trails, rental cabins. **Activities:** Swimming, activity director, scheduled activities. **Nearby Attractions:** House on the Rock, Villa Louis, Mississippi River boat rides, antiques, state parks, golf, caves, mines, locks & dams, fishing, water sports. **Additional Information:** Prairie du Chien Chamber of Commerce, (800) 732-1673.

RESTRICTIONS
Pets: On leash only. **Fires:** Fire ring only. **Alcoholic Beverages:** At sites only. **Vehicle Maximum Length:** No limit.

TO GET THERE
From the junction of CR A and CR X in Bagley, drive 1 mi. north on CR X. Roads are wide and well maintained, with good shoulders.

BANCROFT
MAP, C-2
Vista Royalle Campground

8025 Isherwod Rd., 54921. T: (715) 335-6860; www.vistaroyalle.com.

🚐 ★★★★   ⛺ ★★★★

Beauty: ★★★★	Site Privacy: ★★★★
Spaciousness: ★★★★	Quiet: ★★★★
Security: ★★★★★	Cleanliness: ★★★★★
Insect Control: ★★★	Facilities: ★★★★★

As avid campers, Jim and Judy Kollock decided 26 years ago to open a campground with the amenities they looked for when camping. To be sure they got off on the right foot, the Kollocks worked with a landscape architect to create the initial layout. It shows. Tall pine trees, spacious (40 by 60 feet) sites, and a man-made lake with a sandy bottom and big sandy beach set Vista Royalle Campground apart from others. The lake is aerated and treated to keep it clean. Favorite RV campsites for families are sites 1–10 along the beach. A lodge with a fireplace, video games, movies, and a television welcome children (wholesome, nonraunchy movies and games only). Security is also tops, as the campground has one video-monitored access road and owners who live on site and patrol.

BASICS
Operated By: Jim & Judy Kollock. **Open:** Apr. 15–Oct. 15. **Site Assignment:** Reservations w/ 1-night deposit; full refund (minus $5) w/ 14-day notice. **Registration:** At campground office. **Fee:** $23–$31; cash, check, credit card. **Parking:** At site.

FACILITIES
Number of Multipurpose Sites: 200. **Hookups:** Electric (20, 30, 50 amps), water, sewer. **Each Site:** Picnic table, fire ring. **Dump Station:** Yes. **Laundry:** Yes. **Pay Phone:** Yes. **Restrooms and Showers:** Yes. **Fuel:** No. **Propane:** Yes. **Internal Roads:** Gravel, in good condition. **RV Service:** No. **Market:** 1 mi. south to Bancroft. **Restaurant:** 1 mi. south to Bancroft. **General Store:** Yes. **Vending:** Yes. **Swimming:** No. **Playground:** Yes. **Other:** Swimming pond w/ sandy beach, mini-golf, snack shack, fishing pond, rec hall, shuffleboard, horseshoes, shelter house, video games, basketball. **Activities:** Swimming, fishing, planned activities. **Nearby Attractions:** Chain of lakes, several golf courses, water park, tours of vegetable farming & paper mills. **Additional Information:** Stevens Point Area CVB, (715) 344-2556.

RESTRICTIONS
Pets: On leash only. **Fires:** Fire ring only. **Alcoholic Beverages:** Allowed. **Vehicle Maximum Length:** 50 ft.

TO GET THERE
From Exit 143 at the junction of US 51 and CR W, drive east 0.75 mi. to Isherwood Rd., drive north 1 mi. Roads are wide and well maintained, with broad shoulders.

BARABOO
MAP, D-2
Rocky Arbor State Park

reserve america

E10320 Fern Dell Rd., 53913. T: (608) 253-1173; www.reserveamerica.com.

🚐 ★★★★   ⛺ ★★★★

Beauty: ★★★★	Site Privacy: ★★★
Spaciousness: ★★	Quiet: ★★★★
Security: ★★★★	Cleanliness: ★★★★
Insect Control: ★★★★	Facilities: ★★★

Rocky Arbor State Park opened in 1932. From that time forward the park has served as a respite from the busy day adventures at Wisconsin Dells. Serving as a base camp, folks come to rejuvenate and prepare for the following day's events at the nearby amusement Mecca. The park exhibits a scenic sandstone gorge believed to be 500 million years old. Only 1.5 miles east of the park runs the Wisconsin River, the original creator of the sandstone gorge. Picturesque rock walls, ledges, and formations dominate the pine-shaded park. A variety of woodland shrubs and wildflowers decorate the park floor. Rocky Arbor State Park is a seasonal park open Memorial Day weekend to Labor Day. The 229-acre park offers an 89-site shaded campground with picnic tables, fire rings, wheelchair-accessible site, and electric hookup. Firewood is for sale. Raspberry picking is permitted throughout the campground. The day-use area of the park consists of picnic tables, grills, hand water pump, small playground, and a short nature trail with accompanying brochure available at the check-in station.

BASICS
Operated By: Wisconsin State Parks. **Open:** May 23–Sept. 2. **Site Assignment:** Reservations can be made 11 months in advance or as late as 2 days before arrival. **Registration:** At office. **Fee:** Single, $10–$22; group, $40–$140. **Parking:** At site.

FACILITIES
Number of Multipurpose Sites: 90. **Hookups:** Yes. **Dump Station:** Yes. **Laundry:** No. **Pay Phone:** No. **Restrooms and Showers:** Yes. **Fuel:** No. **Propane:** No. **Internal Roads:** Paved. **RV Service:** No. **Market:** No. **Restaurant:** No. **General Store:** No. **Vending:** No. **Swimming:** No. **Playground:** No. **Other:** Out-of-State campfire wood is prohibited. Vehicle admission stickers are required.

RESTRICTIONS

Pets: On a leash no longer than 8 ft.; under control at all times; not allowed in the general picnic areas. **Fires:** In authorized fireplaces or rings only. Do not leave unattended; extinguish all fires before leaving the campsite. Burning of household refuse is prohibited. **Alcoholic Beverages:** People of legal drinking age may bring alcoholic beverages along for their picnic or campsite meals in Wisconsin state parks & forests.

TO GET THERE

Take I-90/94 to Wisconsin Dells, and take Exit 85. Go south 0.5 mi. on Hwy. 12 to the entrance for Rocky Arbor.

BELOIT — Turtle Creek Campsite   MAP, D-2

3513 East CR S, 53511.

🚐 ★★★   ⛺ ★★★

Beauty: ★★★		Site Privacy: ★★★	
Spaciousness: ★★★		Quiet: ★★★	
Security: ★★★★		Cleanliness: ★★★★	
Insect Control: ★★		Facilities: ★★★	

Located 500 feet off I-90 in Beloit, Turtle Creek Campsite is a good stopping-off point, as well as a destination for campers seeking activities along the creek. With such a convenient highway location, however, the sounds of traffic do float over the campground. The facility has 75 pull-through sites and a typical site width of 30 feet. Spots are level, grassy, and semiwooded. An open field is popular with big rigs and campers with satellite TV. Laid out in a series of loops, the campground offers sites right along Turtle Creek and in a beautiful oak grove. Paddlers can access the creek here for a leisurely canoe trip (no motors allowed). Safety and security measures include quiet time enforced at 10:30 p.m., one entrance/exit road, and owners who live on site and provide regular patrols. Visitors must register and pay $2 per adult and child but are not allowed to use the swimming facilities and must leave at dark.

BASICS

Operated By: The George Denu family. **Open:** May 15–Oct. 1. **Site Assignment:** Reservations w/ 1-night deposit; no refunds. **Registration:** At campground office. **Fee:** $18; cash. **Parking:** At site.

FACILITIES

Number of RV-only Sites: 48. **Number of Tent-only Sites:** 52. **Hookups:** Electric (20, 30 amps), water. **Each Site:** Picnic table, fire ring. **Dump Station:** Yes. **Laundry:** No. **Pay Phone:** Yes. **Restrooms and Showers:** Yes. **Fuel:** No. **Propane:** No. **Internal Roads:** Gravel, in good condition. **RV Service:** No. **Market:** 3 mi. west in Beloit. **Restaurant:** 3 mi. west in Beloit. **General Store:** Yes. **Vending:** No. **Swimming:** Yes. **Playground:** Yes. **Other:** Turtle Creek, air-conditioned rec hall, pavilion, coin games, fishing river, basketball, sports field, horseshoes, hiking trails, volleyball. **Activities:** Swimming, hiking, fishing, boating (no motors). **Nearby Attractions:** Golf, the Angel Museum, Beloit College, historic districts, Logan Museum of Anthropology, Pohlman Field, self-guided

walking tours, antiques, arts & crafts. **Additional Information:** Beloit Convention & Visitor Bureau, (800) 423-5648.

RESTRICTIONS

Pets: On leash only; 1 pet per site. **Fires:** Fire ring only. **Alcoholic Beverages:** Allowed. **Vehicle Maximum Length:** No limit. **Other:** 3-day stay limit for tents.

TO GET THERE

From the junction of I-43 and I-90, take Exit 183 (Shopiere Rd.), drive 2 mi. north on I-90, then 500 feet east on CR S. Roads are wide and well maintained, with broad shoulders.

BLACK RIVER FALLS   MAP, C-1
Black River State Forest

reserve america

901 Hwy. 54 East, 54615-9276. T: (715) 284-4103; www.reserveamerica.com.

🚐 ★★★★   ⛺ ★★★★

Beauty: ★★★		Site Privacy: ★★★	
Spaciousness: ★★★		Quiet: ★★★★	
Security: ★★★★		Cleanliness: ★★★★	
Insect Control: ★★★★		Facilities: ★★★	

Established in 1957, The Black River State Forest encompasses 67,000 acres of which 800 remain natural and the balance managed for timber harvesting and recreation opportunities. The area's geology helps make the Black River State Forest unique among the state forests. The property lies at the edge of the glaciated central plains, east of the driftless area of Wisconsin. Hiking to the top of Castle Mound provides views of the former bed of glacial Lake Wisconsin, as well as the unglaciated buttes, sandstone hills, and castellated bluffs that dot the vast forest landscape. This massive state forest has three family campgrounds, one horse campground, and the opportunity to backpack. Amenities at the campgrounds vary from modern or rustic facilities, to reservable or first-come, first-serve sites. The campgrounds offer swimming beaches, boat landings, mountain bike access, winter camping opportunities, and more. Horse camping is available on a first-come, first-serve basis with sites featuring hitching post, hand pump water, and rustic toilets. For those who enjoy backpacking, group camping, or lodging indoors, the park offers these opportunities as well. Picnicking is enjoyed throughout the Forest with developed sites near several of the campgrounds. Over 20 miles of trail are open to a variety of users including hikers, equestrians, mountain bikers, and cross-country skiers. Slicing through the landscape are the darkened Black River, East Fork River, and Morrison Creek. Fishing from shore or canoe rewards anglers with stringers of walleye and smallmouth bass. Black River State Forest also features two canoe campsites downriver from Black River Falls below Hawk Island. Bird-watchers fancy the forestland during spring and fall migrations, which boast routes along the Mississippi Flyway. Bird-watching has expanded to include observations

of the Karner blue butterfly, an endangered native species to Black River State Forest.

BASICS

Operated By: Wisconsin State Parks. **Open:** May 11–Sept. 30. **Site Assignment:** Reservations can be made 11 months in advance or as late as 2 days before arrival. **Registration:** At office. **Fee:** Single, $9–$19. **Parking:** At site.

FACILITIES

Number of Multipurpose Sites: 35. **Hookups:** Yes. **Each Site:** Fire ring, picnic table. **Dump Station:** Yes. **Laundry:** No. **Pay Phone:** No. **Restrooms and Showers:** Yes. **Fuel:** No. **Propane:** No. **Internal Roads:** Paved. **RV Service:** No. **Market:** No. **Restaurant:** No. **General Store:** No. **Vending:** No. **Swimming:** Less than 1 mi. **Playground:** No. **Other:** Out-of-state campfire wood is prohibited. **Activities:** Hiking, hunting, picnicking.

RESTRICTIONS

Pets: On a leash no longer than 8 ft.; under control at all times; not allowed in the general picnic areas. **Fires:** In authorized fireplaces or rings only. Do not leave unattended; extinguish all fires before leaving the campsite. Burning of household refuse is prohibited. **Alcoholic Beverages:** People of legal drinking age may bring alcoholic beverages along for their picnic or campsite meals in Wisconsin state parks & forests.

TO GET THERE

From I-94, take Black River Falls Exit 116, Hwy. 54. Drive to the first set of traffic lights. Turn left (south) onto Hwy. 12/27. Then turn left (east) onto Hwy. 12. The campground is located 1 mi. east on Hwy. 12.

BLANCHARDVILLE   MAP, D-2
Yellowstone Lake State Park

reserve america

8495 Lake Rd., 53516. T: (608) 523-4427; www.reserveamerica.com.

🚐 ★★★★   ⛺ ★★★★

Beauty: ★★★★		Site Privacy: ★★★	
Spaciousness: ★★		Quiet: ★★★★	
Security: ★★★★		Cleanliness: ★★★★	
Insect Control: ★★★★		Facilities: ★★★	

Yellowstone Lake State Park is comprised of 968 acres with a 455-acre man-made lake. The park's steep hills, deep valleys, and beautiful vistas attract visitors to the Driftless Area of Southwest Wisconsin. In 1949 federal and state financing permitted the purchase of acreage in Lafayette County. The land was excavated, and dams and dikes were built along a 2.5-mile basin. Once the man-made lake filled, bass, walleye, pike, and pan fish were stocked. The development of the fishery has been marginal. Today, anglers consider the fishing good year-round. Hundreds come to ice fish. The artificial lake provides a great setting for park recreation. Campers find two campgrounds containing 128 sites—38 sites offer electric hookup. The east side is open all year and has

36 campsites, while the west side is open from May to October and has 93 campsites. In addition to the family sites, there are six groups sites, four with electricity. A new flush toilet and shower building, completed in 2002, provides campers with excellent accommodations. Fishing Yellowstone Lake State Park entails shoreline fishing along a tree-lined shore or launching your boat from the main two-lane ramp. Day-use areas include nine picnic areas, shelters, beach area, and rifle range. Picnic areas have tables, grills, and restrooms. There is also a large playground near the park office. Swimmers will find a 40-yard-long beach with a smattering of tables, changing facilities, restrooms, and a sunbathing area. The beach is unguarded. At least seven short hiking trails are offered at the park. They range in difficulty from easy to difficult.

BASICS

Operated By: Wisconsin State Parks. **Open:** May 1–Oct. 31. **Site Assignment:** Reservations can be made 11 months in advance or as late as 2 days before arrival. **Registration:** At office. **Fee:** Single, $10–$22; group, $40–$140. **Parking:** At site.

FACILITIES

Number of Multipurpose Sites: 134. **Hookups:** Yes. **Dump Station:** Yes. **Laundry:** No. **Pay Phone:** No. **Restrooms and Showers:** Yes. **Fuel:** No. **Propane:** No. **Internal Roads:** Paved. **RV Service:** No. **Market:** No. **Restaurant:** No. **General Store:** No. **Vending:** No. **Swimming:** No. **Playground:** Yes. **Other:** Out-of-state campfire wood is prohibited. Vehicle admission stickers are required.

RESTRICTIONS

Pets: On a leash no longer than 8 ft.; under control at all times; not allowed in the general picnic areas. **Fires:** In authorized fireplaces or rings only. Do not leave unattended; extinguish all fires before leaving the campsite. Burning of household refuse is prohibited. **Alcoholic Beverages:** People of legal drinking age may bring alcoholic beverages along for their picnic or campsite meals in Wisconsin state parks & forests.

TO GET THERE

Yellowstone Lake State Park is located 50 mi. southwest of Madison off County Hwy. F, between Blanchardville and Darlington.

BOULDER JUNCTION MAP, B-2
Camp Holiday

P.O. Box 67, 54512. T: (715) 385-2264; www.camp-holiday.com.

🚐 ★★★★	⛺ ★★★
Beauty: ★★★	Site Privacy: ★★★
Spaciousness: ★★★	Quiet: ★★★
Security: ★★★★	Cleanliness: ★★★
Insect Control: ★★	Facilities: ★★★★

Set in the heart of the Northern Highland–American Legion State Forest, Camp Holiday has nearly 200 lakes within a 10-mile radius. The campground, 4 miles southwest of Boulder Junction, offers a choice of shaded or open sites alongside Rudolph Lake. Camp Holiday has 100 seasonal campers, 21 pull-through sites, and a typical site width of 40 feet. The lake offers excellent fishing for largemouth bass and panfish, and the area is known as the musky capital of the world. Laid out in a series of loops, the facility's most popular sites are by the lake. Sightings of eagles, nesting loons, and beaver are common in the area. Security and safety measures include a ten-mph speed limit (rather high with all the activities going on), a ban on motors on the lake, quiet time from 10:30 p.m. to 7:30 a.m., and owners who live on site and offer regular patrols of the campground. Since it is open until November 1, Camp Holiday is a good place to enjoy the fall foliage.

BASICS

Operated By: Al & Lila Vehrs. **Open:** May 1–Nov. 1. **Site Assignment:** Reservations held w/ credit card; no fee w/ 7-day cancellation notice. **Registration:** At campground office. **Fee:** $24–$31; cash, check, credit card. **Parking:** At site.

FACILITIES

Number of RV-only Sites: 235. **Number of Tent-only Sites:** 1. **Hookups:** Electric (20, 30, 50 amps), water, sewer, phone. **Each Site:** Picnic table, fire ring. **Dump Station:** Yes. **Laundry:** Yes. **Pay Phone:** No. **Restrooms and Showers:** Yes. **Fuel:** No. **Propane:** Exchange only. **Internal Roads:** Paved/gravel, in good condition. **RV Service:** No. **Market:** 4 mi. northeast in Boulder Junction. **Restaurant:** 4 mi. northeast in Boulder Junction. **General Store:** Yes, limited. **Vending:** No. **Swimming:** No. **Playground:** Yes. **Other:** Rudolph Lake, swimming beach, horseshoes, volleyball, basketball, shuffleboard, rec hall, game room, trails, boat launch, fishing lake. **Activities:** Swimming, fishing, boating (rental rowboats, canoes, kayaks available), scheduled weekend activities, hiking. **Nearby Attractions:** Lakes, forest, antiques, hiking, boating, cross-county skiing, bicycling, arts & crafts, scenic drive. **Additional Information:** Boulder Junction Chamber of Commerce, (800) 466-8579.

RESTRICTIONS

Pets: On leash only. **Fires:** Fire ring only. **Alcoholic Beverages:** Allowed. **Vehicle Maximum Length:** 45 ft.

TO GET THERE

From the junction of US 51 and CR H, drive 3 mi. northeast on CR H, then 500 feet east on Rudolph Lake Ln. Roads are generally wide and well maintained, with narrow shoulders in some areas.

BOULDER JUNCTION MAP, B-2
NH–AL Crystal Lake Area

reserve america

1020 Hwy. North, 54512. T: (715) 385-2704; www.reserveamerica.com.

🚐 ★★★★	⛺ ★★★★
Beauty: ★★★	Site Privacy: ★★★
Spaciousness: ★★★	Quiet: ★★★★
Security: ★★★★	Cleanliness: ★★★★
Insect Control: ★★★★	Facilities: ★★★

Established in 1925 to protect the headwaters of the Wisconsin, Flambeau, and Manitowish rivers, the Northern Highland–American Legion (NH–AL) State Forest occupies more than 225,000 acres in Vilas, Oneida, and Iron counties. The forest offers a diverse array of recreational opportunities, such as camping, canoeing, hiking, bird-watching, snowmobiling, biking, and hunting, as well as the chance to simply sit quietly and enjoy its natural beauty. In addition, the forest provides habitat for a wide range of plant and animal species. There are 18 campgrounds offering 900 campsites. Varying styles of camping are offered: 100 primitive canoe campsites are found along the 247 miles of waterways; two group camps accommodate 100 people; winter camping is permitted at designated grounds; and wilderness sites afford a backcountry experience. Five family campgrounds (Crystal Lake, Muskie Lake, Clear Lake, Firefly Lake, and Indian Mounds), two group campgrounds, and four wilderness campgrounds accept reservations through the Wisconsin State Park's central reservation system. Thirteen campgrounds are first-come, first-served. Canoe campers have over 70 sites for one night only at each site camping.

BASICS

Operated By: Wisconsin State Parks. **Open:** May 24–Sept. 2. **Site Assignment:** Reservations can be made 11 months in advance or as late as 2 days before arrival. **Registration:** At office. **Fee:** Single, $10–$22; group, $40–$140. **Parking:** At site.

FACILITIES

Number of Multipurpose Sites: 303. **Hookups:** Yes. **Each Site:** Fire ring, picnic table. **Dump Station:** Yes. **Laundry:** No. **Pay Phone:** No. **Restrooms and Showers:** Yes. **Fuel:** No. **Propane:** No. **Internal Roads:** Paved. **RV Service:** No. **Market:** No. **Restaurant:** No. **General Store:** No. **Vending:** No. **Swimming:** No. **Playground:** No. **Other:** Out-of-state campfire wood is prohibited. Vehicle admission stickers are required. **Activities:** Boating, picnicking.

RESTRICTIONS

Pets: On a leash no longer than 8 ft.; under control at all times; not allowed in the general picnic areas. **Fires:** In authorized fireplaces or rings only. Do not leave unattended; extinguish all fires before leaving the campsite. Burning of household refuse is prohibited. **Alcoholic Beverages:** People of legal drinking age may bring alcoholic beverages along for their picnic or campsite meals in Wisconsin state parks & forests.

TO GET THERE

To Crystal Lake Contact Station from the intersection of Hwys. 51 and 47, travel north on Hwy. 51, 6.2 mi. to CR M. Turn right on CR M and go 2.7 mi. to CR N. Turn right (north) on CR N and go 2 mi. The Crystal Lake Contact Station is on the left. To Jag Lake Group Campground from the intersection of Hwys. 51 and 47, travel north on Hwy. 51 13 mi. to CR H. Turn right on CR H, go 1.5 mi. to North Creek Rd. Turn right on North Creek Rd., go 1 mi. The group camp is on the left. To North Muskellunge Group Campground from the intersection of Hwys. 51 and 47, travel north on Hwy. 51, 6.2 mi. to CR M. Go right on CR M 3 mi. to Big Muskellunge Lake Rd. Turn right on Big Muskellunge Lake Rd., go 2.5 mi. The group camp is on the right.

BRISTOL MAP, D-3
Happy Acres Kampground

22230 45th St., 53104. T: (262) 857-7373;
www.happyacres.com.

🚐 ★★★ ⛺ ★★★

Beauty: ★★★ Site Privacy: ★★★
Spaciousness: ★★★ Quiet: ★★★★
Security: ★★★★ Cleanliness: ★★★
Insect Control: ★★★ Facilities: ★★★

Established by veteran campers in 1970, Happy Acres Kampground is a popular place with families. Reservations are recommended for all weekends between Memorial Day and Labor Day. Reservations are mandatory and must be finalized at least one week prior to a holiday weekend. Located halfway between Chicago and Milwaukee about 9 miles off I-94, Happy Acres offers convenient access for travelers. Laid out in a series of loops, the campground has 46 seasonal campers and 13 pull-through sites. A rolling, grassy campground, Happy Acres has open and wooded sites. The best sites are 61, 62, and 64 because they are by the lake and offer more green space. A separate tenting area allows privacy from RVs and more trees and greenery. The campground has 25 acres of walking trails. The speed limit is ten mph, and rules note that the facility is not a drivers education training site. Mini-bikes, dirt bikes, mopeds, go-carts, and golf carts are not allowed. Quiet time from 10 p.m. to 9 a.m. is strictly enforced. The owners live on site and provide 24-hour security protection for the campground.

BASICS

Operated By: Greg & Kevin Myers families. **Open:** May 1–Sept. 30. **Site Assignment:** Reservations w/ 1-night deposit; refund (minus $5) w/ 3-day notice; 7 days for holidays. **Registration:** At campground office. **Fee:** $29.95–$41.95; cash, check, credit card. **Parking:** At site.

FACILITIES

Number of RV-only Sites: 150. **Number of Tent-only Sites:** 30. **Number of Multipurpose Sites:** 33. **Hookups:** Electric (20, 30, 50 amps), water. **Each Site:** Picnic table, fire ring. **Dump Station:** Yes. **Laundry:** Yes. **Pay Phone:** Yes. **Restrooms and Showers:** Yes. **Fuel:** No. **Propane:** No. **Internal Roads:** Gravel, in good condition. **RV Service:** No. **Market:** 3 mi. south in Padlock Lake. **Restaurant:** 1 mi. east. **General Store:** Yes. **Vending:** Yes. **Swimming:** Yes. **Playground:** Yes, several. **Other:** Mini zoo, pond, hiking trails, pavilion, swimming beach, mini-golf, horseshoes, volleyball, basketball, lounge, game room, boat dock, rental cabins, rental trailers. **Activities:** Swimming, fishing, hiking, boating (rental rowboats, paddleboats available), scheduled weekend activities. **Nearby Attractions:** Six Flags Great America, Milwaukee Zoo, Dairyland Dog Track, Lake Geneva, Lake Michigan, outlet malls, antiques, arts & crafts, golf, scenic drive. **Additional Information:** Kenosha Area Chamber of Commerce, (800) 654-7309.

RESTRICTIONS

Pets: On leash only; leave nervous watch dogs home. **Fires:** Fire ring only. **Alcoholic Beverages:** Allowed. **Vehicle Maximum Length:** No limit.

TO GET THERE

From the junction of Hwy. 50 and US 45, drive 2 mi. north on US 45, then 1.5 mi. west on CR NN. Roads are wide and well maintained, with sometimes narrow shoulders.

BRUSSELS MAP, C-3
Quietwoods South Camping Resort

9245 Lovers Ln., 54204.
T: (888) 378-2005 or (920) 825-7065;
www.quietwoodsrv.com/qwso.

🚐 ★★★ ⛺ ★★★

Beauty: ★★★ Site Privacy: ★★★
Spaciousness: ★★★ Quiet: ★★★
Security: ★★★★ Cleanliness: ★★★★
Insect Control: ★★★ Facilities: ★★★

Quietwoods South Camping Resort, located 4 miles north of Brussels, is the first campground as you enter Door County. Many of its campers are returnees, along with 65 seasonals. The campground offers secluded, wooded sites in a rural area. The typical site width is 36 feet, with eight pull-throughs. Tents are in a separate area with more green space and privacy. Security measures include one-way roads and an owner who lives on site and provides regular patrols of the campground.

BASICS

Operated By: Michael & Christine Marchant. **Open:** Apr. 28–Oct. 15. **Site Assignment:** Reservations w/ $25 deposit; refund w/ 1-week notice (minus $5). **Registration:** At campground office. **Fee:** $24–$30; cash, check, credit card. **Parking:** At site.

FACILITIES

Number of RV-only Sites: 175. **Number of Tent-only Sites:** 10. **Hookups:** Electric (30, 50 amps), water. **Each Site:** Picnic table, fire ring. **Dump Station:** Yes. **Laundry:** Yes. **Pay Phone:** Yes. **Restrooms and Showers:** Yes. **Fuel:** No. **Propane:** No. **Internal Roads:** Paved/gravel, in good condition. **RV Service:** No. **Market:** 4 mi. south in Brussels. **Restaurant:** 4 mi. south in Brussels. **General Store:** Yes. **Vending:** Yes. **Swimming:** Yes. **Playground:** Yes. **Other:** Game room, pavilion, mini-golf, volleyball, game room, adult lounge, horseshoes, baseball, fishing pond, rental trailers & pop-ups, small bar. **Activities:** Swimming, fishing, scheduled weekend activities. **Nearby Attractions:** Door County, cherry & apple orchards, fishing, golf, hiking, boating, Lake Michigan, Green Bay, historic sites, antiques, arts & crafts shops, summer stock theatre, parks, bike trails. **Additional Information:** Door County Chamber of Commerce, (800) 527-3529.

RESTRICTIONS

Pets: On leash only. **Fires:** Fire ring only. **Alcoholic Beverages:** Allowed. **Vehicle Maximum Length:** No limit.

TO GET THERE

From the junction of Hwy. 57 and CR C, drive 2.5 mi. north on CR C, then 1.5 mi. east on CR K, then 0.5 mi. north on Lovers Ln. The roads are wide and well maintained, with broad shoulders.

CALEDONIA MAP, D-3
Yogi Bear's Jellystone Park Camp-Resort

reserve america

8425 WI 38, 53108. T: (262) 835-2565;
www.jellystone-caledonia.com.

🚐 ★★★★ ⛺ ★★★

Beauty: ★★★ Site Privacy: ★★★
Spaciousness: ★★★ Quiet: ★★★
Security: ★★★★ Cleanliness: ★★★
Insect Control: ★★ Facilities: ★★★★

Located 1 mile south of Oak Creek, Yogi Bear's Jellystone Camp-Resort is a popular destination in itself as well as a camping spot for Milwaukee visitors. Most sites are level and shaded with gravel spots for RVs. The campground has no seasonal campers and offers 22 pull-throughs. Tent campers have a separate area with more green space and privacy. The best sites for RVs are on Jellystone Ave. because they are bigger and located near the pool and other facilities. A five-mph speed limit is enforced, as is quiet time from 11 p.m. to 8 a.m. Ill-mannered conduct is not tolerated, nor is the use of foul language. Security measures include one entrance/exit to the campground, security guards, and a park manager who lives on site.

BASICS

Operated By: Randy, Theresa, & Bridget Isaacson, Ed Van Der Molen. **Open:** Apr. 15–Oct. 10. **Site Assignment:** Reservations w/ 50% deposit; 2-night min.; full deposit for holidays; refund (minus $10) w/ 14-day notice. **Registration:** At campground office. **Fee:** $20–$45; cash, check, credit card. **Parking:** At site.

FACILITIES

Number of RV-only Sites: 222. **Number of Tent-only Sites:** 25. **Hookups:** Electric (20, 30, 50 amps), water, sewer. **Each Site:** Picnic table, fire ring. **Dump Station:** Yes. **Laundry:** Yes. **Pay Phone:** Yes. **Restrooms and Showers:** Yes. **Fuel:** No. **Propane:** Yes. **Internal Roads:** Paved/gravel, in good condition. **RV Service:** No. **Market:** 1 mi. north in Oak Creek. **Restaurant:** 1 mi. north in Oak Creek. **General Store:** Yes. **Vending:** Yes. **Swimming:** Yes. **Playground:** Yes. **Other:** Adult lounge, cafe, mini-golf, volleyball, basketball, game room, fishing pond, rental cabins, kiddie pool, recreation field, cartoon theatre. **Activities:** Swimming, kiddie fishing, scheduled activities. **Nearby Attractions:** Zoo, brewery tours, golf, antiques, arts & crafts, museum, historic homes, nature center, baseball. **Additional Information:** Greater Milwaukee CVB, (800) 554-1448.

RESTRICTIONS

Pets: On leash only. **Fires:** Fire ring only. **Alcoholic Beverages:** At sites only. **Vehicle Maximum Length:** 40 ft.

TO GET THERE

From I-94, take Exit 326 and drive 2 mi. east on Seven Mile Rd., then 0.25 mi. north on Hwy. 38. Roads are wide and well maintained, with broad shoulders.

CAMP DOUGLAS   MAP, C-2
Mill Bluff State Park

reserve america

15819 Funnel Rd., 54618. T: (608) 337-4775; www.reserveamerica.com.

🚐 ★★★★   ⛺ ★★★★

Beauty: ★★★	Site Privacy: ★★★
Spaciousness: ★★★	Quiet: ★★★★
Security: ★★★★	Cleanliness: ★★★★
Insect Control: ★★★★	Facilities: ★★★★

Mill Bluff is a unique 203-foot bluff that is flat-topped in nature and rises abruptly from surrounding flat, sand plain. Large mesas and small buttes characterize the park's region. Slender pinnacles range in height from 80 to over 120 feet. The bluffs have withstood the test of nature's elements due to their dense, hard rock cap. All once stood as islands in Glacial Lake Wisconsin that extended over 70 miles long and 150 feet deep. Plant life is particularly interesting at the park due to the steadfast shade resulting from the tall rock formations. Morel mushrooms and lady's slippers are just two of the shade-loving species found in the park. Other interesting wildflowers observed in the park include false wild indigo, blue lupine, starflower, and prickly pear. Scenic Mill Bluff State Park offers the usual state park amenities. A campground invites tenters, RVers, and those with physical impairments. All sites are first come, first served. Firewood is for sale seasonally. Several hiking opportunities exist, including the 185-step stairway to Mill Bluff. Picnic opportunities and a swimming beach attract warm-weather visitors. The beach is located on a 2.5-acre pond with enhancements that include changing area, picnic tables, grills, and toilets. The beach and easy water entrance is particularly suitable for families with small children.

BASICS

Operated By: Wisconsin State Parks. **Open:** May 25–Sept. 30. **Site Assignment:** Reservations can be made 11 months in advance or as late as 2 days before arrival. **Registration:** At office. **Fee:** Single, $10–$22; group, $40–$140. **Parking:** At site.

FACILITIES

Number of Multipurpose Sites: 25. **Hookups:** Yes. **Dump Station:** No. **Laundry:** No. **Pay Phone:** No. **Restrooms and Showers:** Yes. **Fuel:** No. **Propane:** No. **Internal Roads:** Paved. **RV Service:** No. **Market:** No. **Restaurant:** No. **General Store:** No. **Vending:** No. **Swimming:** Yes. **Playground:** Yes. **Other:** Out-of-state campfire wood is prohibited. Vehicle admission stickers are required. **Activities:** Picnicking.

RESTRICTIONS

Pets: On a leash no longer than 8 ft.; under control at all times; not allowed in the general picnic areas.

Fires: In authorized fireplaces or rings only. Do not leave unattended; extinguish all fires before leaving the campsite. Burning of household refuse is prohibited. **Alcoholic Beverages:** People of legal drinking age may bring alcoholic beverages along for their picnic or campsite meals in Wisconsin state parks & forests.

TO GET THERE

The park can be reached from Hwy. 12/16, which runs parallel to I-90/94. Exit ramps from I-90 to Hwy. 12/16 are located from the west about 5 mi. from the park at Oakdale. Take Exit 48 or Exit 55 3 mi. east of the park at Camp Douglas.

CAMPBELLSPORT   MAP, C-3
Kettle Moraine State Forest
(Northern 2)

reserve america

N1765 Hwy. G, 53010. T: (920) 533-8612; www.reserveamerica.com.

🚐 ★★★★   ⛺ ★★★★

Beauty: ★★★★	Site Privacy: ★★★
Spaciousness: ★★★	Quiet: ★★★★
Security: ★★★★	Cleanliness: ★★★★
Insect Control: ★★★★	Facilities: ★★★★

A visit to the Kettle Moraine State Forest reveals the natural beauty of the region. More than 22,000 acres of glacial hills, kettles, lakes, prairie restoration sites, pine woods, and hardwood forests can be found in the Southern Unit, making this facility a popular area for a wide variety of users. Visitors to the forest can camp in one of three family campgrounds, an equestrian camp, or one of two group camps; hike, mountain bike, ride a horse, snowmobile, or ski on the 160+ miles of trail, swim at one of two beaches, backpack to an overnight shelter on the Ice Age Trail, picnic, fish, hunt, or tour three historic cabin sites. There are also facilities for use by those with disabilities, including a cabin in the campground and an accessible nature trail. Visit the Southern Unit, experience the beauty, and take advantage of the diversity of facilities it has to offer.

BASICS

Operated By: Wisconsin State Parks. **Open:** Apr. 27–Oct. 7. **Site Assignment:** Reservations can be made 11 months in advance or as late as 2 days before arrival. **Registration:** At office. **Fee:** Single, $10–$22; group, $40–$140. **Parking:** At site.

FACILITIES

Number of Multipurpose Sites: 200. **Hookups:** Yes. **Each Site:** Fire ring, picnic table. **Dump Station:** No. **Laundry:** No. **Pay Phone:** Yes. **Restrooms and Showers:** Yes. **Fuel:** No. **Propane:** No. **Internal Roads:** Paved. **RV Service:** No. **Market:** No. **Restaurant:** No. **General Store:** No. **Vending:** No. **Swimming:** Yes. **Playground:** No. **Other:** Out-of-state campfire wood is prohibited. Vehicle admission stickers are required. **Activities:** Boating, fishing, hiking, picnicking.

RESTRICTIONS

Pets: Has a designated pet picnic area w/ tables & grills, a wet dog training area where dogs can be trained in water skills, dry dog training area where dogs can be trained in upland bird skills. **Fires:** In authorized fireplaces or rings only. Do not leave unattended; extinguish all fires before leaving the campsite. Burning of household refuse is prohibited. **Alcoholic Beverages:** No one except registered campers in their family campsites may have open containers of or drink alcoholic beverages between Mar. 31 & the Sat. of Memorial Day weekend.

TO GET THERE

Do not use a computerized mapping program to obtain directions. The Long Lake Recreation Area is easily reached off WI 45, north of Kewaskum. Turn right onto WI 67 North and travel to the Village of Dundee. In Dundee, follow CR F straight east for about 1 mi. At a sweeping curve you will turn left onto Division Rd. Travel north 0.75 mi. to the entrance of the Long Lake Recreation Area.

CASSVILLE   MAP, D-1
Nelson Dewey State Park

reserve america

Box 658, 53806. T: (608) 725-5374; www.reserveamerica.com.

🚐 ★★★★   ⛺ ★★★★

Beauty: ★★★	Site Privacy: ★★★
Spaciousness: ★★★	Quiet: ★★★★
Security: ★★★★	Cleanliness: ★★★★
Insect Control: ★★★★	Facilities: ★★★

Nelson Dewey State Park is located in southwest Wisconsin along the banks of the mighty Mississippi River. The park features several miles of recreation space, 20 acres of prairie designated during the mid-1950s as a State Natural Area, photogenic views from towering bluffs, and adjacent properties with Stonefield State Historic Site and Wisconsin State Agricultural Museum. River views from the state park extend north and south and into sections of the Upper Mississippi River Wildlife and Fish Refuge, a 100,000-acre tract. The refuge encompasses land from Waubasha to Rock Island and protects migratory birds, native wildlife, and fish while providing hunting and fishing opportunities. Nelson Dewey State Park, Stonefield Historic Site, and the Wisconsin State Agricultural Museum offer recreation opportunities where history comes to life and nature soars. The state park boasts spectacular scenery, including wildflower prairies, several hiking trails, bluff-top campsites, a bird-watching area, ancient Native American mounds, and breathtaking sunsets along the mighty Mississippi. Campers find 40 campsites, some with electric hookup. Two walk-in sites are available. Sites are located on high hardwood bluffs overlooking the majestic Mississippi River. Conveniences include dump station, showers, flush toilets, and trail access. Rustic group camping is available for up to 100 persons. Eight picnic areas are available to day users. Visitors to the area may also enjoy hiking at nearby Wyalusing State Park and Effigy Mounds Park.

BASICS

Operated By: Wisconsin State Parks. **Open:** All year. **Site Assignment:** Reservations can be made 11 months in advance or as late as 2 days before arrival. **Registration:** At office. **Fee:** Single, $10–$22; group, $40–$140. **Parking:** At site.

FACILITIES

Number of Multipurpose Sites: 48. **Hookups:** Yes. **Dump Station:** Yes. **Laundry:** No. **Pay Phone:** No. **Restrooms and Showers:** Yes. **Fuel:** No. **Propane:** No. **Internal Roads:** Paved. **RV Service:** No. **Market:** No. **Restaurant:** No. **General Store:** No. **Vending:** No. **Swimming:** No. **Playground:** No. **Other:** Out-of-state campfire wood is prohibited. Vehicle admission stickers are required.

RESTRICTIONS

Pets: On a leash no longer than 8 ft.; under control at all times; not allowed in the general picnic areas. **Fires:** In authorized fireplaces or rings only. Do not leave unattended; extinguish all fires before leaving the campsite. Burning of household refuse is prohibited. **Alcoholic Beverages:** People of legal drinking age may bring alcoholic beverages along for their picnic or campsite meals in Wisconsin state parks & forests.

TO GET THERE

From downtown Cassville take Hwy. 133 North. Turn left onto County Hwy. VV and travel 1 mi. to the park's entrance.

CHETEK MAP, B-1
Chetek River Campground

590 24th St., 54728. T: (715) 924-2440; www.chetekriver.com.

🚐 ★★★★   ⛺ ★★★

Beauty: ★★★	Site Privacy: ★★★★
Spaciousness: ★★★★	Quiet: ★★★★
Security: ★★★★	Cleanliness: ★★★★
Insect Control: ★★	Facilities: ★★★

Chetek River Campground does so many little things right, and that all adds up to a very pleasant campground. Some of the extras: guests may visit campers free of charge (there is a $2 charge to swim), and free doggie bags for cleaning up after pets are available at the office. The campground is chock full of activities for children, including a local high school basketball coach who offers clinics and games every Saturday. Located less than a mile west of Chetek, the campground is situated on the Chetek River, where you can take a tubing trip or rent a canoe. The rural campground has 50 seasonals and is booked up almost every weekend, so reservations are strongly recommended. Laid out in a series of loops, the campground has a typical site width of 36 feet, with back-in, grassy, open sites. A popular spot for family reunions, the campground has a giant grill that can hold 50 pieces of chicken. Quiet hours from 10 p.m. to 8 a.m. are enforced, as is a five-mph speed limit. Owners live on site and provide 24-hour security. With all those children enjoying river activities

and other outdoors play, it sure would be nice to have laundry facilities at such a top-notch family campground.

BASICS

Operated By: Jan Gebhardt & Christine Gay. **Open:** May 1–Sept. 30. **Site Assignment:** Reservations w/ 1-night deposit; refund w/ 7-day notice. **Registration:** At campground office. **Fee:** $24–$26; cash, check. **Parking:** At site.

FACILITIES

Number of Multipurpose Sites: 100. **Hookups:** Electric (20, 30 amps), water. **Each Site:** Picnic table, fire ring. **Dump Station:** Yes. **Laundry:** No. **Pay Phone:** Yes. **Restrooms and Showers:** Yes. **Fuel:** No. **Propane:** No. **Internal Roads:** Paved/gravel, in good condition. **RV Service:** No. **Market:** 1 mi. east in Chetek. **Restaurant:** 1 mi. east in Chetek. **General Store:** No. **Vending:** Yes. **Swimming:** Yes. **Playground:** Yes. **Other:** Red Cedar River, basketball, volleyball, shuffleboard, horseshoes, mini-golf, pool table, ping pong, air hockey, video games, TV room, badminton, recreation field, scheduled weekend activities. **Activities:** Swimming, fishing, tubing trips, boating (rental canoes available), biking, (rental pedal karts available). **Nearby Attractions:** Museums, golf, fishing lakes, antiques. **Additional Information:** Chippewa Valley CVB, (888) 523-3866.

RESTRICTIONS

Pets: On leash only. **Fires:** Fire ring only. **Alcoholic Beverages:** Allowed. **Vehicle Maximum Length:** 40 ft. **Other:** Bury fish guts in a designated area. Shovels are provided.

TO GET THERE

From the junction of US 53 and Hwy. 1, take Exit 126, drive 0.25 mi. south on Hwy. 1 to River Rd., then 0.75 mi. south on River Rd. Roads are wide and well maintained, with good shoulders.

CHIPPEWA FALLS MAP, C-1
Lake Wissota State Park

reserve america

18127 County Hwy., 54729. T: (715) 382-4574; www.reserveamerica.com.

🚐 ★★★★   ⛺ ★★★★

Beauty: ★★★★	Site Privacy: ★★★
Spaciousness: ★★★	Quiet: ★★★★
Security: ★★★★	Cleanliness: ★★★★
Insect Control: ★★★★	Facilities: ★★★★

Lake Wissota State Park lies northeast of Chippewa Falls encompassing 1,062 acres of primarily young, rich forests and open prairie on a 6,300-acre man-made lake. The lake was created in 1918 when the Wisconsin-Minnesota Power and Light Company built a dam on the Chippewa River. The region's early history goes back more than 150 years to 1836, when Frenchman Jean Brunet built the region's first sawmill at the falls of the Chippewa River. Within a year it was ranked as one of the world's largest sawmills. The Chippewa long since has been harnessed to provide electrical power. Pine

forests, mixed hardwood timbers, prairie, and marshes are found in the park. Boating, canoeing, swimming, and waterskiing are popular summer activities on Lake Wissota. There are two boat launches, and motors are allowed. Canoes can be rented at the park. The park has a bathhouse at the 100-yard beach. Lake Wissota State Park has two picnic areas and four shelters. There are two ball diamonds and a volleyball court. Campers find 81 wooded, secluded family campsites; 17 have electricity. Two tents-only group campgrounds accommodate up to 100 people each. Hikers enjoy 17.4 miles of scenic hiking trails within the park. The park also has 6.5 miles of trails available for daytime horseback riding. Bicycling is a popular activity. While most of the park is level, there are 11.3 miles of park trails open to mountain biking. Ice fishing, cross-country skiing, and snowmobiling await winter visitors to Wissota State Park. While the park is open all year, the campground roads are not plowed for snow.

BASICS

Operated By: Wisconsin State Parks. **Open:** May 1–Oct. 1. **Site Assignment:** Reservations can be made 11 months in advance or as late as 2 days before arrival. **Registration:** At office. **Fee:** Single, $10–$22; group, $40–$140. **Parking:** At site.

FACILITIES

Number of Multipurpose Sites: 83. **Hookups:** Yes. **Dump Station:** Yes. **Laundry:** No. **Pay Phone:** Yes. **Restrooms and Showers:** Yes. **Fuel:** No. **Propane:** No. **Internal Roads:** Paved. **RV Service:** No. **Market:** No. **Restaurant:** No. **General Store:** No. **Vending:** No. **Swimming:** Yes. **Playground:** Yes. **Other:** Out-of-state campfire wood is prohibited. Vehicle admission stickers are required. **Activities:** Biking, boating, fishing, hiking.

RESTRICTIONS

Pets: On a leash no longer than 8 ft.; under control at all times; not allowed in the general picnic areas. **Fires:** In authorized fireplaces or rings only. Do not leave unattended; extinguish all fires before leaving the campsite. Burning of household refuse is prohibited. **Alcoholic Beverages:** People of legal drinking age may bring alcoholic beverages along for their picnic or campsite meals in Wisconsin state parks & forests.

TO GET THERE

Lake Wissota State Park is located 7 mi. northeast of Chippewa Falls. From Hwy. 53 North, take Exit 99 (CR S). Travel east on CR S for about 5.5 mi. Cross the bridge over Lake Wissota and turn right on CR O. Drive east 2 mi. on CR O; the park entrance is on the right.

CHIPPEWA FALLS   MAP, C-1
O'Neil Creek Campground and RV Park

14912 105th Ave., 54729. T: (715) 723-6581;
www.discover-net.net/~oneilcreek.

🚐 ★★★★   ⛺ ★★★★

Beauty: ★★★★   Site Privacy: ★★★
Spaciousness: ★★★   Quiet: ★★★★
Security: ★★★★   Cleanliness: ★★★★
Insect Control: ★★   Facilities: ★★★★

Located 4 miles north of Chippewa Falls, O'Neil Creek Campground and RV Park has level, shaded, wooded sites, some along a gently flowing creek. The campground has 200 seasonal campers, 16 pull-through sites, and a typical site width of 28 feet. Be aware that all full hookups are occupied by seasonals. Campers have direct access to Lake Wissota and the Chippewa River system. Motor downstream from the campground on O'Neil Creek to Lake Wissota (15 miles long and 3 miles wide) and the Chippewa River system. Tent sites are in a separate area with privacy from RVs and more green space. Showers and restrooms are tiled and very clean. A nice benefit is no visitor fee. However, all visitors must leave the campground by 11 p.m., or they will be charged as an overnight guest.

BASICS
Operated By: Brian & Anne Mitchell. **Open:** Apr. 15–Oct. 15. **Site Assignment:** Reservations w/ 1-night deposit; refund (minus $5) w/ 7-day notice. **Registration:** At campground office. **Fee:** $17–$30; cash, check, credit card. **Parking:** At site.

FACILITIES
Number of RV-only Sites: 390. **Number of Tent-only Sites:** 35. **Hookups:** Electric (20, 30, 50 amps), water, sewer, phone. **Each Site:** Picnic table, fire ring. **Dump Station:** Yes. **Laundry:** Yes. **Pay Phone:** No. **Restrooms and Showers:** Yes. **Fuel:** No. **Propane:** Yes. **Internal Roads:** Paved/gravel, in good condition. **RV Service:** No. **Market:** 4 mi. south in Chippewa Falls. **Restaurant:** 4 mi. south in Chippewa Falls. **General Store:** Yes. **Vending:** Yes. **Swimming:** No. **Playground:** Yes. **Other:** O'Neil Creek, nature trails, boat ramp, rec room, horseshoes, volleyball, mini-golf, boat dock, rental cabins, pavilion, coin games, basketball, sports field. **Activities:** Swimming, hiking, boating (rental paddleboats, rowboats, & canoes available), fishing, float trips, scheduled activities. **Nearby Attractions:** Golf, Lake Wissota, Chippewa Rose Society Garden, Irvine Park, zoo, swimming pool, tennis, Glen Loch Dam & Overlook, museum, Leinenkugel Brewery, antiques, arts & crafts. **Additional Information:** Chippewa Falls Area Chamber of Commerce, (888) 723-0024.

RESTRICTIONS
Pets: On leash only. **Fires:** Fire ring only. **Alcoholic Beverages:** Allowed. **Vehicle Maximum Length:** No limit.

TO GET THERE
From the junction of Hwy. 124 and US 53, drive 5 mi. north on US 53, then 2 mi. east on County Trunk S, then 2 mi. north on Hwy. 124, then 0.75 mi. east on 105th Ave. Roads are generally wide and well maintained, with broad shoulders, though there is one bad curve down to campground.

COLOMA   MAP, C-2
Coloma Camperland

N 1130 5th Rd., 54930. T: (715) 228-3600.

🚐 ★★★   ⛺ ★★★

Beauty: ★★★   Site Privacy: ★★★
Spaciousness: ★★★   Quiet: ★★★★
Security: ★★★★   Cleanliness: ★★★★
Insect Control: ★★   Facilities: ★★★

It's not a pleasant subject to mention, but if an RV had to break down, this would be the place to do it. Coloma Camperland offers camper sales, RV parts, supplies, and services—along with being a nice place to stay. Located off Hwys. 39 and 21 in Coloma, Camperland has six large (40 by 50 feet), grassy pull-through sites, the most requested ones in the campground. Laid out in a series of loops, the campground offers both wooded and open sites. A family campground and a comfortable spot for overnight travelers, Camperland has good security with only one way into the facility, owners who live on site, and patrols by night personnel. For safety, bike riding is not allowed in the campground after dark.

BASICS
Operated By: Dave & Vicky Peachey. **Open:** All year. **Site Assignment:** Reservations w/ $20 deposit, refund w/ 2-week notice. **Registration:** At campground office. **Fee:** $15–$21. **Parking:** At site.

FACILITIES
Number of RV-only Sites: 85. **Number of Tent-only Sites:** 15. **Hookups:** Electric (30 amps), water, sewer. **Each Site:** Picnic table, fire ring. **Dump Station:** Yes. **Laundry:** Yes. **Pay Phone:** No. **Restrooms and Showers:** Yes. **Fuel:** No. **Propane:** Yes. **Internal Roads:** Gravel, in fair condition. **RV Service:** Yes. **Market:** 0.5 mi. north in Coloma. **Restaurant:** 0.5 mi. north in Coloma. **General Store:** No. **Vending:** Yes. **Swimming:** Yes. **Playground:** Yes. **Other:** Game room, shelter, volleyball, shuffleboard, horseshoes, sports field. **Activities:** Swimming, planned weekend activities. **Nearby Attractions:** Fishing, hunting, snowmobile trail, golf, biking, horseback riding, scenic drive, 35 minutes to casino, Wisconsin Dells. **Additional Information:** Wisconsin Dells Visitor & Convention Bureau, (800) 223-3557.

RESTRICTIONS
Pets: On leash only. **Fires:** Fire pit only. **Alcoholic Beverages:** At sites only. **Vehicle Maximum Length:** No limit.

TO GET THERE
From the junction of Hwys. 51 and 21, drive 0.25 mi. east on Hwy. 21, then 1 mi. south on CR CH. Roads are wide and well maintained, with good shoulders.

CORNELL   MAP, B-1
Brunet Island State Park

reserve america™

23125 255th St., 54732. T: (715) 239-6888;
www.reserveamerica.com.

🚐 ★★★★   ⛺ ★★★★

Beauty: ★★★   Site Privacy: ★★★
Spaciousness: ★★★   Quiet: ★★★★
Security: ★★★★   Cleanliness: ★★★★
Insect Control: ★★★★   Facilities: ★★★★

Brunet Island State Park, on the Chippewa and Fisher rivers, contains more than 1,200 acres of scenic beauty, wildlife, and recreational opportunities. Each summer, thousands of visitors come to camp, fish, boat, canoe, hike, swim, and picnic. During the winter they can ski, snowshoe, and ice fish. Quiet lagoons and channels are excellent for canoeing and wildlife watching. Brunet Island State Park has 69 campsites divided between two campgrounds. The south campground offers modern amenities, including hot showers, while the north campground remains primitive. Both campgrounds have easy access to the water; however, canoeists prefer the north campground due to its location near gentle river channels. Many waterside tent and medium-sized RV campsites are available and do fill quickly during the warm summer months. Firewood is available for sale. Brunet Island State Park provides a boat landing and launching area at the island for a variety of boaters. Local marinas rent watercraft. In addition, the park features a new handicapped fishing pier. The landscape here in Chippewa County is a product of the most recent Ice Age (the Pleistocene Epoch). The rolling terrain carries a wide variety of forest types and is home to a multitude of wildlife.

BASICS
Operated By: Wisconsin State Parks. **Open:** North Campground: Apr. 27–Sept. 3; South Campground: All year. **Site Assignment:** Reservations can be made 11 months in advance or as late as 2 days before arrival. **Registration:** At office. **Fee:** Single, $10–$22; group, $40–$140. **Parking:** At site.

FACILITIES
Number of Multipurpose Sites: 69. **Hookups:** Yes. **Each Site:** Fire ring, picnic table. **Dump Station:** Yes. **Laundry:** No. **Pay Phone:** Yes. **Restrooms and Showers:** Yes. **Fuel:** No. **Propane:** No. **Internal Roads:** Paved. **RV Service:** No. **Market:** No. **Restaurant:** No. **General Store:** No. **Vending:** No. **Swimming:** Yes. **Playground:** Yes. **Other:** Out-of-state campfire wood is prohibited. Vehicle admission stickers are required. **Activities:** Boating, fishing, hiking, nature trail, picnicking.

RESTRICTIONS
Pets: On a leash no longer than 8 ft.; under control at all times; not allowed in the general picnic areas. **Fires:** In authorized fireplaces or rings only. Do not leave unattended; extinguish all fires before leaving the campsite. Burning of household refuse is prohibited. **Alcoholic Beverages:** People of legal drinking

age may bring alcoholic beverages along for their picnic or campsite meals in Wisconsin state parks & forests.

TO GET THERE

Brunet Island is located just north of the city of Cornell in northern Chippewa County. Take WI 64 to Park Rd. Take Park Rd. north about 1 mi. to park entrance.

CRIVITZ   MAP, B-3
Peshtigo River Campground

W7948 Airport Rd., 54114. T: (715) 854-2986; www.peshtigorivercampground.com.

🚐 ★★★   ⛺ ★★★★

Beauty: ★★★	Site Privacy: ★★★
Spaciousness: ★★★★	Quiet: ★★★
Security: ★★★★	Cleanliness: ★★★★
Insect Control: ★★★	Facilities: ★★★

The Peshtigo River Campground calls it stress reduction therapy—floating down the historic Peshtigo River in a big Innertube, stopping along the way for a sandbar picnic, if you want. After the two-to-six-hour trip, all pressure (except that in the tubes) should be gone, they say. The campground offers free shuttles to the put-in. Camping sites are level and shaded, with most backing up into the woods. To ensure future shade, small trees have been planted, and campers are welcome to adopt a tree and water it during their stay. The typical site width is 50 feet, with eight pull-throughs and 40 seasonal campers. A separate area for tent campers provides more green space and privacy. Some open sites for RVs are located near the front of the campground, which is 1 mile south of Crivitz. Quiet time between 11 p.m. and 7 a.m. is enforced. Safety measures include one-way roads and a ten-mph speed limit, rather high for such a child-friendly campground. Security is provided by one entrance and exit, regular patrols, and owners who live on site.

BASICS

Operated By: John & Rosie Wocelka. **Open:** May 1–Oct. 15. **Site Assignment:** Reservations w/ full deposit; refund (minus $20) w/ 2-week notice; less than 14 days, 1-night cancellation fee. **Registration:** At campground office. **Fee:** $20–$26; cash, check, credit card. **Parking:** At site.

FACILITIES

Number of RV-only Sites: 100. **Number of Tent-only Sites:** 10. **Hookups:** Electric (20, 30 amps), water. **Each Site:** Picnic table, fire ring. **Dump Station:** Yes. **Laundry:** Yes. **Pay Phone:** Yes. **Restrooms and Showers:** Yes. **Fuel:** No. **Propane:** No. **Internal Roads:** Gravel, in good condition. **RV Service:** Yes. **Market:** 1 mi. north in Crivitz. **Restaurant:** 1 mi. north in Crivitz. **General Store:** Yes. **Vending:** Yes. **Swimming:** No. **Playground:** Yes. **Other:** Peshtigo River, swimming area, horseshoes, volleyball, nature trails, fish freezer, rental cabins, rec room, pavilion, sports field. **Activities:** Swimming, river tubing (rental tubes available), boating (rental canoes available), fishing, hiking, scheduled activities. **Nearby Attractions:** Golf, tennis, waterski shows, river & lake fishing, whitewater rafting, rid-

ing stables, flea markets, antiques, museums, waterfalls. **Additional Information:** Marinette County Area Chamber of Commerce, (800) 236-6681.

RESTRICTIONS

Pets: On leash only. **Fires:** Fire ring only. **Alcoholic Beverages:** Allowed. **Vehicle Maximum Length:** No limit.

TO GET THERE

From the junction of US 141 and CR W, drive 2 mi. south on US 141, then 500 feet west on Airport Rd. Roads are wide and well maintained, with broad shoulders.

DODGEVILLE   MAP, D-2
Governor Dodge State Park

reserve america

4175 WI 23N, 53533. T: (608) 935-2315; www.reserveamerica.com.

🚐 ★★★★   ⛺ ★★★★

Beauty: ★★★	Site Privacy: ★★★★★
Spaciousness: ★★★★★	Quiet: ★★★★
Security: ★★★★	Cleanliness: ★★★★
Insect Control: ★★★★	Facilities: ★★★★

Governor Dodge, in southwestern Wisconsin, is one of the state's largest state parks, with 5,270 scenic acres of steep hills, bluffs, and deep valleys plus two lakes and a waterfall. Governor Dodge maintains nearly 40 miles of trails. All are open to hiking, and many of them for cross-country skiing, mountain biking, horseback riding, and snowmobiling. The park also is adjacent to the 40-mile Military Ridge State Trail, which goes to Madison. Two designated hiking trails begin at the Enee Point Picnic Shelter—the self-guided Pine Cliff Nature Trail and the 4.5-mile White Oak Trail. Governor Dodge has more than 20 miles of ski trails. All trails can be reached from the Cox Hollow Beach trailhead. Water, picnic tables, and flush toilet facilities are also available at the trailhead. A state trail pass is required of all skiers age 16 and over (in addition to the vehicle admission sticker). Narrow, twisting, gorge-like valleys and soaring rock sculptures mark this beautiful park named after Henry Dodge, the state's territorial governor. The park brochure glosses over Dodge's career by saying he made peace with Native Americans. It doesn't mention that he did it with a gun. Dodge came up from Missouri and began mining illegally on Ho-Chunk (Winnebago) land in the 1820s. Good riding here, though, on more than 10 challenging miles between two loops with long, steep grades on both. The overlook into Lost Canyon is well worth the climb, and there are many more grand views as well. A paved connector runs past the Mill Creek Trail to the Military Ridge State Trail. An excellent aerobic workout on non-technical, well-signed, mostly grassy trails in a beautiful setting—a nice swimming beach makes for a perfect end-of-ride experience. Scenery includes beautiful ridge and valley views of forested slopes punctuated by stone outcrops.

BASICS

Operated By: Wisconsin State Parks. **Open:** All year. **Site Assignment:** Reservations can be made 11 months in advance or as late as 2 days before arrival. **Registration:** At office. **Fee:** Single, $10–$22; group, $40–$140. **Parking:** At site.

FACILITIES

Number of Multipurpose Sites: 301. **Hookups:** Yes. **Each Site:** Fire ring, picnic table. **Dump Station:** Yes. **Laundry:** No. **Pay Phone:** No. **Restrooms and Showers:** Yes. **Fuel:** No. **Propane:** No. **Internal Roads:** Paved. **RV Service:** No. **Market:** No. **Restaurant:** No. **General Store:** No. **Vending:** No. **Swimming:** Yes. **Playground:** Yes. **Other:** Out-of-state campfire wood is prohibited. Vehicle admission stickers are required. **Activities:** Biking, boating, canoeing, fishing, hiking, picnicking.

RESTRICTIONS

Pets: Has a pet swim area adjacent to each swimming beach. There are also designated pet picnic areas close to each beach were pets are also permitted. **Fires:** In authorized fireplaces or rings only. Do not leave unattended; extinguish all fires before leaving the campsite. Burning of household refuse is prohibited. **Alcoholic Beverages:** People of legal drinking age may bring alcoholic beverages along for their picnic or campsite meals in Wisconsin state parks & forests.

TO GET THERE

Governor Dodge State Park is located 3 mi. north of Dodgeville on Hwy. 23 North. The park is 45 mi. west of Madison.

EAGLE   MAP, D-3
Kettle Moraine State Forest—
South Unit 2

reserve america

S91 W39091 Hwy. 59, 53119. T: (262) 594-6200; www.reserveamerica.com.

🚐 ★★★★   ⛺ ★★★★

Beauty: ★★★★	Site Privacy: ★★★
Spaciousness: ★★★	Quiet: ★★★★
Security: ★★★★	Cleanliness: ★★★★
Insect Control: ★★★★	Facilities: ★★★★

A visit to the Kettle Moraine State Forest reveals the natural beauty of the region. More than 22,000 acres of glacial hills, kettles, lakes, prairie restoration sites, pine woods, and hardwood forests can be found in the Southern Unit, making this facility a popular area for a wide variety of users. Visitors to the forest can camp in one of three family campgrounds, an equestrian camp, or one of two group camps; hike, mountain bike, ride a horse, snowmobile or ski on the 160+ miles of trail, swim at one of two beaches, backpack to an overnight shelter on the Ice Age Trail, picnic, fish, hunt, or tour three historic cabin sites. There are also facilities for use by those with disabilities, including a cabin in the campground and an accessible nature trail. Visit the

Southern Unit, experience the beauty, and take advantage of the diversity of facilities it has to offer.

BASICS

Operated By: Wisconsin State Parks. **Open:** Apr. 1–Nov. 30. **Site Assignment:** Reservations can be made 11 months in advance or as late as 2 days before arrival. **Registration:** At office. **Fee:** Single, $10–$22; group, $40–$140. **Parking:** At site.

FACILITIES

Number of Multipurpose Sites: 345. **Hookups:** Yes. **Each Site:** Fire ring, picnic table. **Dump Station:** Yes. **Laundry:** No. **Pay Phone:** Yes. **Restrooms and Showers:** Yes. **Fuel:** No. **Propane:** No. **Internal Roads:** Paved. **RV Service:** No. **Market:** No. **Restaurant:** No. **General Store:** No. **Vending:** No. **Swimming:** No. **Playground:** Yes. **Other:** Out-of-state campfire wood is prohibited. Vehicle admission stickers are required. **Activities:** Boating, fishing, hiking, nature center, picnicking.

RESTRICTIONS

Pets: Has a designated pet picnic area w/ tables & grills, a wet dog training area where dogs can be trained in water skills, & dry dog training area where dogs can be trained in upland bird skills. **Fires:** In authorized fireplaces or rings only. Do not leave unattended; extinguish all fires before leaving the campsite. Burning of household refuse is prohibited. **Alcoholic Beverages:** No one except registered campers in their family campsites may have open containers of or drink alcoholic beverages between Mar. 31 & the Sat. of Memorial Day weekend.

TO GET THERE

The Southern Unit of the Kettle Moraine State Forest is located 61 mi. east of Madison, and 37 mi. southwest of Milwaukee. The forest is 30 mi. in length, extending from the village of Dousman to near the city of Whitewater.

EAGLE RIVER — MAP, B-2
Franklin Lake—Chequamegon-Nicolet National Forest

reserve america

P.O. Box 1809, 54521. T: (715) 479-2827; www.reserveamerica.com.

🚐 ★★★★ ⛺ ★★★★

Beauty: ★★★		Site Privacy: ★★★
Spaciousness: ★★★★		Quiet: ★★★
Security: ★★★★		Cleanliness: ★★★★
Insect Control: ★★★★		Facilities: ★★

Take the time to stroll along the Avenue of the Giants. Enjoy northern hardwood, pine, and hemlock forests with some trees over 400 years old. Franklin Lake is located within the Nicolet National Forest, which is located in northern Wisconsin, where towering pine and hardwood forests are interspersed with hundreds of crystal clear lakes and streams. The Nicolet National Forest offers you a wealth of opportunities to enjoy the outdoors. Within a day's drive of the Chicago, Milwaukee, St. Paul, and Minneapolis metropolitan areas, the Nicolet is a place where you can truly get away from it all in the scenic beauty of the

northwoods. Four seasons of recreation await you, from spring fishing or canoeing to summer camping, hiking, mountain biking, or horseback riding. Come in autumn for hunting or to see our famous fall color. For your driving pleasure there are 3,600 miles of back roads. Please drive slowly. Snow season gears up with cross-country skiing and snowmobiling. Or come anytime to get close to nature in a tranquil and secluded spot. Opportunities for exhilarating views, relaxation, and quiet nature study abound. Experience all the beauty and recreational opportunities of Wisconsin's National Forests. Native American tribes were the first to explore and eventually settle this region, followed by voyageurs, missionaries, loggers, farmers, and miners. Much of this natural beauty and colorful human history can be enjoyed today in the Nicolet. In 1634, Jean Nicolet, a French explorer, discovered what the Native American tribes already knew to be a beautiful resource-rich land. Little did Nicolet know that 300 years later a national forest would be named in his honor. The Nicolet was established in 1933 and now comprises over 661,000 acres in northeastern Wisconsin. Later that same year, the Nicolet evolved into two national forests. The western portion of the Nicolet was proclaimed as a separate forest, the Chequamegon. The name Chequamegon originates from the Ojibway or Chippewa language and is thought to mean "the place of shallow water." The Chequamegon now encompasses 857,000 acres in northern Wisconsin.

BASICS

Operated By: U.S. Forest Service. **Open:** May 19–Sept. 6. **Site Assignment:** Reservations must be made at least 4 days in advance. **Registration:** At office. **Fee:** Single, $10. **Parking:** At park.

FACILITIES

Number of Multipurpose Sites: 52. **Hookups:** None. **Each Site:** Call ahead. **Dump Station:** No. **Laundry:** No. **Pay Phone:** No. **Restrooms and Showers:** Yes. **Fuel:** No. **Propane:** No. **Internal Roads:** Paved. **RV Service:** No. **Market:** No. **Restaurant:** No. **General Store:** No. **Vending:** No. **Swimming:** Yes. **Playground:** No. **Activities:** Fishing, hiking, interpretive programs.

RESTRICTIONS

Pets: Restrained or on a leash at all times while in developed recreation areas. **Fires:** In fire rings, stoves, grills, or fireplaces provided for that purpose. **Alcoholic Beverages:** Not allowed. **Vehicle Maximum Length:** Call ahead. **Other:** Please do not bring firewood from home.

TO GET THERE

Drive 10 mi. east from Eagle River on Hwy. 70. Turn right (south) on Military Rd. (FS 2178). Follow Military Rd. for about 2 mi. to Butternut Lake Rd. (FS 2181). Follow Butternut Lake Rd. to the campground.

EDGERTON — MAP, D-2
Hickory Hills Campground

856 Hillside Rd., 53534. T: (608) 884-6327; www.camphickoryhills.com.

🚐 ★★★★ ⛺ ★★★★

Beauty: ★★★★		Site Privacy: ★★★★★
Spaciousness: ★★★★★		Quiet: ★★★★★
Security: ★★★★★		Cleanliness: ★★★★★
Insect Control: ★★		Facilities: ★★★★

Hickory Hills Campground, located 4 miles north of Edgerton, certainly has personality. It's not all neatly laid out with same-size, same-look sites. Most sites are spacious, ranging from 40 by 60 to 30 by 45 feet. About evenly split between grassy and gravel sites, the wilderness setting offers mostly shady spots sheltered by mature hickory and oak trees. The campground store is not a jumble of odds and ends but an attractive arrangement of light groceries, ice cream, snacks, pop, camping supplies, toiletries, and bait, along with souvenirs and gift items. About half the camping sites are occupied by seasonals. All campers probably wish that Hickory Hills offered laundry facilities.

BASICS

Operated By: Richard & Kelly Poff. **Open:** May 1–Oct. 15. **Site Assignment:** Reservations for 2 nights or more w/ 1-night deposit; refund (minus $10) w/ 14-day notice. **Registration:** At campground office. **Fee:** $35; cash, check. **Parking:** At site.

FACILITIES

Number of Multipurpose Sites: 300. **Hookups:** Electric (20, 30, 50 amps), water, sewer. **Each Site:** Picnic table. **Dump Station:** Yes. **Laundry:** No. **Pay Phone:** Yes. **Restrooms and Showers:** Yes. **Fuel:** No. **Propane:** Yes, exchange. **Internal Roads:** Gravel/paved, in good condition. **RV Service:** No. **Market:** 4 mi. south in Edgerton. **Restaurant:** 4 mi. south in Edgerton. **General Store:** Yes. **Vending:** Yes. **Swimming:** Yes. **Playground:** Yes. **Other:** Mini-golf, shuffleboard, game room, snack bar, spring-fed lake, juke box, lodge, horseshoes. **Activities:** Swimming, biking (rental bikes available), fishing, boating (rental boats available), planned weekend activities. **Nearby Attractions:** Horseback riding, golf, Lake Koshkonong, historic Milton House. **Additional Information:** Milton Area Chamber of Commerce, (608) 868-6222.

RESTRICTIONS

Pets: On leash only. **Fires:** Fire ring only. **Alcoholic Beverages:** Allowed. **Vehicle Maximum Length:** No limit.

TO GET THERE

From the junction of I-90 and Hwy. 73, take Exit 160, drive 0.5 mi. north on Hwy. 73, then 0.75 mi. east on Hwy. 106, then 0.75 mi. north on Hillside Rd. Roads are wide and well maintained, with broad shoulders.

EGG HARBOR — MAP, B-3
Door County Camping Retreat

4906 Court Rd., 54209. T: (866) 830-5145 or (920) 868-3151; www.doorcountycamp.com.

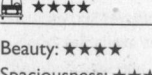
🚐 ★★★★ ⛺ ★★★

Beauty: ★★★★		Site Privacy: ★★★★
Spaciousness: ★★★★		Quiet: ★★★★
Security: ★★★★		Cleanliness: ★★★★
Insect Control: ★★		Facilities: ★★★★

Door County Camping Retreat, located 3 miles south of Egg Harbor, offers wooded campsites and a grassy, open meadow. Average site width is 30 feet, with 12 pull-throughs and 30 seasonal campers. Sites generally have a nice buffer of trees and bushes for privacy. Tent sites are separate from RV area with more green space. Speed limit is five mph, and quiet hours are 10 p.m. to 8 a.m. All radios, TVs, and stereos must be off by 10 p.m., and children must be on sites by 10:30 p.m. Only one warning for noise will be given, and then violators will be evicted without refund. Profanity also is not tolerated, and violators will be evicted without refund. Security measures include one entrance/exit, one-way roads, and regular patrols of the campground.

BASICS

Operated By: John Moravec. **Open:** May 1–Oct. 17. **Site Assignment:** Reservations w/ $25 deposit; no refund except credit on account for next stay w/ 3-day notice. **Registration:** At campground office. **Fee:** $24–$32; cash, check, credit card. **Parking:** At site.

FACILITIES

Number of RV-only Sites: 160. **Number of Tent-only Sites:** 50. **Hookups:** Electric (30, 50 amps), water, sewer, Wi-Fi. **Each Site:** Picnic table, fire ring. **Dump Station:** Yes. **Laundry:** Yes. **Pay Phone:** Yes. **Restrooms and Showers:** Yes. **Fuel:** No. **Propane:** Yes. **Internal Roads:** Gravel, in good condition. **RV Service:** No. **Market:** 3 mi. north in Egg Harbor. **Restaurant:** 3 mi. north in Egg Harbor. **General Store:** Yes. **Vending:** Yes. **Swimming:** Yes. **Playground:** Yes. **Other:** Nature trails, pavilion, game room, arcade games, pool table, pop-up rentals, camping cabins, volleyball, basketball, horseshoes, badminton, sports field. **Activities:** Swimming, hiking, biking (rental bikes available), scheduled weekend activities. **Nearby Attractions:** Door County, cherry & apple orchards, fishing, golf, hiking, boating, Lake Michigan, historic sites, antiques, arts & crafts, parks, bike trails, museums. **Additional Information:** Door County Chamber of Commerce, (800) 527-3529.

RESTRICTIONS

Pets: On leash only. **Fires:** Fire ring only. **Alcoholic Beverages:** Allowed. **Vehicle Maximum Length:** 45 ft. **Other:** No bug lights allowed.

TO GET THERE

From the junction of CR E and Hwy. 42, drive 3.75 mi. south on Hwy. 42, then 0.25 mi. east on Sunny Point Rd., then 0.5 mi. north on Court Rd. Roads are wide and well maintained, with broad shoulders.

EGG HARBOR   MAP, B-3
Frontier Wilderness Campground

4375 Hillside Rd., 54209. T: (920) 868-3349; www.frontierwildernesscampground.com.

🚐 ★★★★★   ⛺ ★★★★

Beauty: ★★★★	Site Privacy: ★★★★
Spaciousness: ★★★★	Quiet: ★★★★
Security: ★★★★	Cleanliness: ★★★★★
Insect Control: ★★★	Facilities: ★★★★★

Nope, it was no hallucination. The voice of Clint Black was actually singing in the women's outhouse at Frontier Wilderness Campground. The campground, located 2.5 miles south of Egg Harbor, has the distinction of providing music in its outhouses. Ask the owners how they do it. That is just one indication that this is no run-of-the-mill camping spot. Other special touches are a big indoor pool, complete with sauna and exercise site; a dumpster station inside a fancy little wooden enclosure; toilet rooms with real slate floors and blue fixtures; and private washrooms with mirrors. Instead of shower stalls with concrete floors and peek-a-boo curtains, Frontier Wilderness offers individual private shower rooms. An adult center has TV, carpet, reading chairs, sofas, tables, and other nice furnishings, instead of just a couple of rickety old chairs and worn-out furniture often found in some facilities. The campground has a typical site width of 36 feet, seven pull-throughs, and 180 seasonal campers. Laid out in a series of loops, the campground offers gravel sites for RVs and sand-bed sites for tents—either a drive-up site or a short walk-in site. A five-mph speed limit is enforced, as are quiet hours from 10 p.m. to 8 a.m. Security measures include surveillance cameras, one entrance/exit, owners who live on site, and regular patrols. Although Frontier Wilderness Campground lacks some amenities, such as sewer hookup, it more than makes up for the deficit with an abundance of other features, including top-notch cleanliness, beautiful landscaping with real flowers, and hanging baskets even at the outhouses.

BASICS

Operated By: Orville & Jeri Rasmussen. **Open:** May 1–Oct. 31. **Site Assignment:** Reservations w/ $25 deposit; refund w/ 14-day notice (minus $5). **Registration:** At campground office. **Fee:** $25.95–$31.95; cash, check, credit card. **Parking:** At site.

FACILITIES

Number of RV-only Sites: 240. **Hookups:** Electric (20, 30, 50 amps), water, Wi-Fi. **Each Site:** Picnic table, fire ring. **Dump Station:** Yes. **Laundry:** Yes. **Pay Phone:** Yes. **Restrooms and Showers:** Yes. **Fuel:** No. **Propane:** Exchange. **Internal Roads:** Paved/gravel, in good condition. **RV Service:** No. **Market:** 2.5 mi. north in Egg Harbor. **Restaurant:** 2.5 mi. north in Egg Harbor. **General Store:** Yes. **Vending:** Yes. **Swimming:** Yes. **Playground:** Yes. **Other:** Cedar-lined sauna, exercise dome, mini-golf, game room, pavilion, activity center, adult lounge, badminton, sports field, volleyball, recreation field. **Activities:** Swimming, live music on holiday weekends. **Nearby Attractions:** Door County, Lake Michigan, cherry & apple orchards, golf, fishing, hiking, boating, historic sites, antiques, arts & crafts, bike trails, Green Bay, parks. **Additional Information:** Door County Chamber of Commerce, (800) 527-3529.

RESTRICTIONS

Pets: On leash only. **Fires:** Fire ring only. **Alcoholic Beverages:** Allowed. **Vehicle Maximum Length:** No limit. **Other:** No smoking in any public buildings.

TO GET THERE

From the junction of CR E and Hwy. 42, drive 2.5 mi. south on Hwy. 42, then 1.5 mi. east on Hillside Rd. Roads are wide and well maintained, with broad shoulders.

ELLISON BAY   MAP, B-3
Wagon Trail Campground

1190 CR ZZ, 54210. T: (920) 854-4818; www.wagontrailcampground.com.

🚐 ★★★★   ⛺ ★★★★

Beauty: ★★★★	Site Privacy: ★★★★
Spaciousness: ★★★★	Quiet: ★★★★
Security: ★★★★	Cleanliness: ★★★★★
Insect Control: ★★	Facilities: ★★★★

Think of the things you want in a campground—Wagon Trail probably has most of them. Secluded and wooded with an average site width of 30 feet, Wagon Trail is the northernmost campground on the Door County peninsula. Most sites are sandy, with some grassy ones for tents. Laid out in a series of loops, Wagon Trail has four pull-throughs and 26 seasonals in a separate area. Located 3.5 miles northwest of Ellison Bay, Wagon Trail is one of the few campgrounds with direct access to the water. With a name like Wagon Trail, it's no surprise the campground features a western motif, including tree branches for curtain rods, branch-trim bed frames, and mirrors in the restrooms. Other nice touches include a heated restroom and rec room. Fresh-brewed coffee is served mornings in the well-stocked camp store, and the restroom features free hot showers with plenty of electric outlets. The best RV sites are on Lady Slipper Lane, which is more secluded. The best tent sites are the three hideaways that have their own driveway for more privacy. Quiet time is from 10 p.m. to 8 a.m., with no radios allowed during those hours. Owners and the manager walk the grounds at night to be sure it is quiet and safe. Campfires must be out by midnight. Dogs are not allowed to sleep outside the camping unit at night.

BASICS

Operated By: Dick Bartlett & Cheri Ault. **Open:** May 12–Oct. 17. **Site Assignment:** Reservations w/ $45 deposit; refund (minus $8) w/ 7-day notice. **Registration:** At campground office. **Fee:** $29–$44; cash, check, credit card. **Parking:** At site.

FACILITIES

Number of RV-only Sites: 88. **Number of Tent-only Sites:** 28. **Hookups:** Electric (30, 50 amps), water, sewer. **Each Site:** Picnic table, fire ring. **Dump Station:** Yes. **Laundry:** Yes. **Pay Phone:** Yes. **Restrooms and Showers:** Yes. **Fuel:** No. **Propane:** Yes. **Internal Roads:** Paved/gravel, in good condition. **RV Service:** No. **Market:** 3.5 mi. northwest in Ellison Bay. **Restaurant:** Walking distance. **General Store:** Yes. **Vending:** Yes. **Swimming:** No. **Playground:** Yes. **Other:** Lake, swimming beach, rec room, hiking trails, volleyball, recreation field, rental cabins, badminton, horseshoes, adult room. **Activities:** Swimming, fishing, hiking. **Nearby Attractions:** Door County, Lake Michigan, cherry & apple orchards, fishing, boating, golf, historic sites, antiques, arts & crafts, parks, bike trails, nature conservancy. **Additional Information:** Door County Chamber of Commerce, (800) 527-3529.

RESTRICTIONS

Pets: On leash only. **Fires:** Fire ring only. **Alcoholic Beverages:** Allowed. **Vehicle Maximum Length:** 45 ft.

TO GET THERE

From the junction of Hwy. 42 and CR ZZ in Sister Bay, drive 6 mi. northeast on CR ZZ. Roads are wide and well maintained, with broad shoulders.

FISH CREEK   MAP, B-3
Path O' Pines Campground

3709 CR F, 54212.
T: (800) 868-7802 or (920) 868-3332;
www.pathofpines.com.

🚐 ★★★   ⛺ ★★★

Beauty: ★★★   Site Privacy: ★★★
Spaciousness: ★★★   Quiet: ★★★
Security: ★★★   Cleanliness: ★★★
Insect Control: ★★   Facilities: ★★★

Located in the heart of Wisconsin vacationland, Path O' Pines Campground offers level, mostly shaded spots near a good access road. About a mile east of Fish Creek, the campground has 20 seasonal campers, 40 pull-through sites, and a typical site width of 30 feet. Laid out in a series of loops, the campground has gravel sites for RVs to park on. Security and safety measures include a five-mph speed limit and owners who live on site. The office staff is very good about sharing information concerning activities in Door County. Although the campground doesn't offer swimming, it is located near three beaches within a 3-mile area. Quiet hours beginning at 10 p.m. are enforced. Violators receive one warning, then are asked to leave if the disturbance continues.

BASICS

Operated By: Tim & Janet Johnson. **Open:** May 15–Oct. 10. **Site Assignment:** Reservations w/ $25 deposit (2-night min.); refund (minus $10) w/ 7-day notice; holiday deposits nonrefundable. **Registration:** At campground office. **Fee:** $18–$38; cash, check, credit card. **Parking:** At site.

FACILITIES

Number of RV-only Sites: 72. **Number of Tent-only Sites:** 23. **Number of Multipurpose Sites:** 20. **Hookups:** Electric (30, 50 amps), water. **Each Site:** Picnic table, fire ring. **Dump Station:** Yes. **Laundry:** Yes. **Pay Phone:** Yes. **Restrooms and Showers:** Yes. **Fuel:** No. **Propane:** Yes. **Internal Roads:** Paved/gravel, in good condition. **RV Service:** No. **Market:** 1 mi. west in Fish Creek. **Restaurant:** 1 mi. west in Fish Creek. **General Store:** Yes. **Vending:** Yes. **Swimming:** No. **Playground:** Yes. **Other:** Fish Creek, rec room, TV & game room, adult room, recreation field. **Nearby Attractions:** Door County, cherry & apple orchards, fishing, swimming, hiking, golf, boating, Lake Michigan, historic sites, antiques, arts & crafts, parks, bike trails. **Additional Information:** Fish Creek Information Center, (800) 577-1880.

RESTRICTIONS

Pets: On leash only. **Fires:** Fire ring only. **Alcoholic Beverages:** Allowed. **Vehicle Maximum Length:** No limit.

TO GET THERE

From the junction of Hwy. 42 and CR F, drive 0.5 mi. east on CR F. Road is wide and well maintained, with broad shoulders.

FISH CREEK   MAP, B-3
Peninsula State Park

reserve america

9462 Shore Rd., 54212-0218. T: (920) 868-3258;
www.reserveamerica.com.

🚐 ★★★★   ⛺ ★★★★

Beauty: ★★★   Site Privacy: ★★★
Spaciousness: ★★★   Quiet: ★★★★
Security: ★★★★   Cleanliness: ★★★★
Insect Control: ★★★★   Facilities: ★★★★

Peninsula State Park, established in 1909, is a 3,776-acre state treasure on Wisconsin's Door County peninsula. Considered Wisconsin's most complete park, Peninsula is also its most popular camping destination. The park has four family campsites with a total of 469 regular sites, of which 102 have electric hookup. Facilities include nearby modern bathhouses. The parks has a sanitary fill/dump station, but no water/sewer hookups. Peninsula State Park is also home to three reservable group camps. Only tent camping is allowed. Electric service is not available at the group sites, and pit toilets and water fountains are located centrally between the campsites. Peninsula State Park is surrounded by water on three sides. The shoreline extends for 7 miles offering landscapes from 180-foot bluffs to cobblestone and natural sand beaches. Visitors enjoy sunbathing, swimming, sailing, boating, and fishing. One of the best avenues for exploring this busy park is on foot or bike. Twenty miles of trails varying in difficulty course through all areas of the park. Bicyclists are offered 5 miles of path along Sunset Bike Trail and an 8-mile section of park road for touring. A visit to the White Cedar Nature Center is a wonderful way to acquaint oneself with the park's natural and cultural history. Six picnic areas are offered, each featuring tables, grills, and toilets: Day-use opportunities at Peninsula State Park extend far beyond the typical park amenities. Visitors will find the 75-foot Eagle Tower rising 250 feet above Green Bay. The park is home to the 1868 Eagle Bluff Lighthouse, whose beacon shines 16 miles along the rugged shoreline. Peninsula offers a single paved tennis court. Two regulation size sand volleyball courts are also available. Rapidly approaching its century-old status is the park's 18-hole, par 71 golf course.

BASICS

Operated By: Wisconsin State Parks. **Open:** May 1–Nov. 30. **Site Assignment:** Reservations can be made 11 months in advance or as late as 2 days before arrival. **Registration:** At office. **Fee:** Single, $10–$22; group, $40–$140. **Parking:** At site.

FACILITIES

Number of Multipurpose Sites: 472. **Hookups:** Yes. **Each Site:** Fire ring, picnic table. **Dump Station:** No. **Laundry:** No. **Pay Phone:** Yes. **Restrooms and Showers:** Yes. **Fuel:** No. **Propane:** No. **Internal Roads:** Paved. **RV Service:** No. **Market:** No. **Restaurant:** No. **General Store:** Yes. **Vending:** No. **Swimming:** Yes. **Playground:** Yes. **Other:** Out-of-state campfire wood is prohibited. Vehicle admission stickers are required. **Activities:** Boating, fishing, picnicking.

RESTRICTIONS

Pets: On a leash no longer than 8 ft.; under control at all times; not allowed in the general picnic areas. **Fires:** In authorized fireplaces or rings only. Do not leave unattended; extinguish all fires before leaving the campsite. Burning of household refuse is prohibited. **Alcoholic Beverages:** People of legal drinking age may bring alcoholic beverages along for their picnic or campsite meals in Wisconsin state parks & forests.

TO GET THERE

From Green Bay take Hwy. 42/57 North. Once north of Sturgeon Bay remain on Hwy. 42 North to Fish Creek. The park is located 1 mi. from the village limits. Turn left at the large entrance sign.

FOND DU LAC   MAP, C-3
Westward Ho Camp Resort

N5456 Division Rd., 53023. T: (920) 526-3407;
www.westwardhocampresort.com.

🚐 ★★★★   ⛺ ★★★★

Beauty: ★★★★   Site Privacy: ★★★★
Spaciousness: ★★★★   Quiet: ★★★★
Security: ★★★★   Cleanliness: ★★★★
Insect Control: ★★   Facilities: ★★★★

The first all-western theme park in Wisconsin and nestled in the North Kettle Moraine, Westward Ho Camp Resort is only minutes away from the historic Wade House—the old stagecoach stop for the early settlers going west or east. The rolling, grassy campground offers a choice of wooded, semiwooded, or open sites, and enough activities to wear out any child or parent. The typical site width is 40 feet, and there are no pull-throughs. Laid out in a series of loops, the campground has a five-mph speed limit and does not permit skateboards. Rollerblades and bikes are not allowed after dark. Quiet time is 10:30 p.m. to 8 a.m., with no radios after 10:30 p.m. The Trading Post offers a pool table and color TV, plus a well-stocked general store and souvenir shop. Security includes one entrance/exit with a gate that is locked from 11 p.m. to 8 a.m., owners who live on site, and a sheriff's patrol of the campgrounds.

BASICS

Operated By: James & Linda Schott. **Open:** Apr. 28–Oct. 6. **Site Assignment:** Reservations w/ full deposit; refunds (minus $15) w/ 14-day notice. **Registration:** At campground office. **Fee:** $28.50–$38.50; cash, check, credit card. **Parking:** At site.

FACILITIES

Number of RV-only Sites: 234. **Number of Tent-only Sites:** 66. **Hookups:** Electric (30, 50 amps), water, sewer. **Each Site:** Picnic table, fire ring. **Dump Station:** Yes. **Laundry:** Yes. **Pay Phone:** No. **Restrooms and Showers:** Yes. **Fuel:** No. **Propane:** No. **Internal Roads:** Paved, in good condition. **RV Service:** No. **Market:** 12 mi. east in Plymouth. **Restaurant:** 5 mi. north in St. Cloud. **General Store:** Yes. **Vending:** Yes. **Swimming:** Yes. **Playground:** Yes. **Other:** Frontier Theater, live petting farm, chuck wagon, music hall, game room, children's fishing, 10-station exercise trail, mini-golf, tetherball, baseball, basketball, volleyball, shuffleboard, horseshoes, hiking trail, wading pool, coin games. **Activities:** Swimming, fishing, hiking, movies, scheduled activities. **Nearby Attractions:** Wildlife refuge, trout & Coho fishing, museums, horseback riding, Lake Michigan, sailing, summer stock theatre, antiques, arts & crafts, historic site. **Additional Information:** Fond du Lac Area CVB, (800) 937-9123.

RESTRICTIONS

Pets: On leash only. **Fires:** Fire rings only; fires not permitted past midnight (township ordinance). **Alcoholic Beverages:** Allowed. **Vehicle Maximum Length:** 40 ft.

TO GET THERE

From the junction of US 41 and Hwy. 23, drive 16 mi. east on Hwy. 23, then 3 mi. south on CR G, then 0.5 mi. east on CR T. Roads are wide and well maintained, with broad shoulders.

FORT ATKINSON   MAP, D-2
Jellystone Park at Fort Atkinson

N551 Wishing Well Dr., 53538.
T: (920) 568-4100 or (877) BEARFUN;
www.bearsatfort.com.

🚐 ★★★★   ⛺ ★★★★

Beauty: ★★★★   Site Privacy: ★★★★
Spaciousness: ★★★★   Quiet: ★★★★
Security: ★★★★   Cleanliness: ★★★★
Insect Control: ★★   Facilities: ★★★★

Check out the facilities and the activities, and you'll see why so many seasonal campers (380) choose to stay at Jellystone Park of Fort Atkinson. With a full-time activities director, the campground has enough going on to keep anyone busy. The grassy hilltop campground is pleasant enough just to sit around and do nothing. The campground has back-in sites and a typical site width of 35 feet. Laid out in a series of loops, the campground has level sites with a choice of shaded or open. Security and safety measures include a ban on motorcycles and scooters, proof of license and insurance for golf cart drivers, and a nightly quiet time. All guests/visitors must wear wristbands, and all vehicles must display a vehicle pass. Rangers patrol the campground.

BASICS

Operated By: Steve Cline. **Open:** May 15–Sept. 15. **Site Assignment:** Reservations w/ 50% deposit; refund (minus $10) w/ 14-day notice; full deposit for holiday weekends. **Registration:** At campground office. **Fee:** $30–$36; cash, check, credit card. **Parking:** At site.

FACILITIES

Number of RV-only Sites: 569. **Number of Tent-only Sites:** 75. **Hookups:** Electric (30, 50 amps), water. **Each Site:** Picnic table, fire ring. **Dump Station:** Yes. **Laundry:** Yes. **Pay Phone:** No. **Restrooms and Showers:** Yes. **Fuel:** No. **Propane:** Yes. **Internal Roads:** Paved/gravel, in good condition. **RV Service:** No. **Market:** 4 mi. north in Fort Atkinson. **Restaurant:** 4 mi. north in Fort Atkinson. **General Store:** Yes. **Vending:** Yes. **Swimming:** Yes. **Playground:** Yes. **Other:** Pond, snack bar, baseball, full-time activities director, mini-

golf, tennis, horseshoes, volleyball, basketball, shuffleboard, lounge, game room, pavilion, trails, kids' fishing pond, rangers kitchen, wading pool, coin games. **Activities:** Swimming, hiking, fishing, movies, scheduled activities. **Nearby Attractions:** Aquatic park, boat launch, horseback riding, Lake Koshkonong, Fireside Dinner Theatre, golf, bicycle trails, roller skating, bowling, hang gliding, archery range, Hoard Historical Museum, National Dairy Shrine & Jones Dairy Farm, Dwight Foster House, Milton House Museum, Hexagon Stagecoach Inn, Replica of Old Fort Koshkonong. **Additional Information:** Fort Atkinson Area Chamber of Commerce, (888) 733-3678.

RESTRICTIONS

Pets: On leash only. **Fires:** Fire ring only. **Alcoholic Beverages:** At sites only. **Vehicle Maximum Length:** No limit.

TO GET THERE

From the junction of US 12 and Hwy. 26, drive 5.25 mi. southwest on Hwy. 26, then 0.75 mi. west on Koshkonong Lake Rd., then 0.25 mi. south on Wishing Well Dr. Roads are wide and well maintained, with broad shoulders.

FOUNTAIN CITY   MAP, C-1
Merrick State Park

reserve america

Box 127, 54629-0127. T: (608) 687-4936;
www.reserveamerica.com.

🚐 ★★★   ⛺ ★★★★

Beauty: ★★★   Site Privacy: ★★★
Spaciousness: ★★★   Quiet: ★★★★
Security: ★★★★   Cleanliness: ★★★★
Insect Control: ★★★★   Facilities: ★★★★

Merrick State Park encompasses 320 acres along the craggy and diverse Mississippi River landscape. The park rests between stately 500-foot sandstone bluffs and America's mighty river. This watery bottomland is characterized by sloughs, backwaters, and slackens. Nature lovers find endless enjoyment paddling, wildlife watching, and hunting. Stealthy visitors may see egrets, herons, muskrats, and otters. As much as one quarter of the majestic park may be covered by water during the wet spring season. The very scenic Merrick State Park boasts a variety of park amenities, including a north and south campground featuring electric hookup, showers, waterfront sites with boat mooring, and walk-in sites. Firewood is for sale during the warmer months. Three miles of hiking trails course through majestic terrain. These ungroomed trails are available in winter for cross-country skiing. Boating is a popular recreation at Merrick State Park. Two ramps give access to anglers, boaters, and canoeists. Canoes may be rented from the park office. The larger of the two launches offers a picnic shelter and mooring dock. Picnic areas of the park may be found at the log shelter, boat ramps, and campground areas. Adjoining the park is Whitman Dam State Wildlife Area, where hunters enjoy waterfowl and deer hunting.

BASICS

Operated By: Wisconsin State Parks. **Open:** May 1–Nov. 30. **Site Assignment:** Reservations can be made 11 months in advance or as late as 2 days before arrival. **Registration:** At office. **Fee:** Single, $10–$22; group, $40–$140. **Parking:** At site.

FACILITIES

Number of Multipurpose Sites: 66. **Hookups:** Yes. **Dump Station:** Yes. **Laundry:** No. **Pay Phone:** Yes. **Restrooms and Showers:** Yes. **Fuel:** No. **Propane:** No. **Internal Roads:** Paved. **RV Service:** No. **Market:** No. **Restaurant:** No. **General Store:** No. **Vending:** No. **Swimming:** No. **Playground:** No. **Other:** Out-of-state campfire wood is prohibited. Vehicle admission stickers are required. **Activities:** Boating.

RESTRICTIONS

Pets: On a leash no longer than 8 ft.; under control at all times; not allowed in the general picnic areas. **Fires:** In authorized fireplaces or rings only. Do not leave unattended; extinguish all fires before leaving the campsite. Burning of household refuse is prohibited. **Alcoholic Beverages:** People of legal drinking age may bring alcoholic beverages along for their picnic or campsite meals in Wisconsin state parks & forests.

TO GET THERE

From Madison, Milwaukee, and Chicago areas: follow I-90 west to Exit 4 (Hwy. 35). Follow Hwy. 35 north through Fountain City. The park is 2 mi. north of Fountain City on the left side of the road. From the Twin Cities: take Hwy. 61 south to Wabasha, MN. Cross the Mississippi River on Hwy. 25. Take Hwy. 35 south through Cochrane, WI. The park is 6 mi. south of Cochrane on the right side of the road.

FREMONT   MAP, C-2
Yogi Bear's Jellystone Park Camp-Resort

reserve america

P.O. Box 497, 54940. T: (800) 258-3315;
www.fremontjellystone.com.

🚐 ★★★★   ⛺ ★★★★

Beauty: ★★★★   Site Privacy: ★★★★
Spaciousness: ★★★★   Quiet: ★★★★
Security: ★★★★   Cleanliness: ★★★★
Insect Control: ★★★★   Facilities: ★★★★

Campers can usually count on a wealth of activities at Yogi Bear campgrounds. The Yogi Bear Jellystone Park Camp-Resort at Fremont has a huge bonus by being located on the shores of Partridge Lake. The 990-acre lake is part of the Wolf River Flowage. From the Yogi Bear boat ramp, there are more than 125 miles of navigable waterways. Not surprisingly, the most popular sites are the ones on the lake with private docks. Laid out in a series of loops, the campground has 50 seasonal campers, 28 pull-through sites, and a typical site width of 50 feet. Sites are level, with a choice of open or shaded. To accompany this water wonderland, the campground has a bait and tackle shop and an array of rental boats with enough good fishing to keep big and little kids happy. Quiet hours, from 11 p.m. to 7 a.m., are enforced. Security is tops, with rangers who keep a close eye on the campground.

BASICS

Operated By: Rick Walker. **Open:** Apr. 15–Oct. 15. **Site Assignment:** Reservations w/ full deposit; refund (minus $25) w/ 14-day notice; reservations w/ 2-night min. on weekends; 3-night min. on holidays. **Registration:** At campground office. **Fee:** $25–$63; cash, check, credit card. **Parking:** At site.

FACILITIES

Number of RV-only Sites: 240. **Number of Tent-only Sites:** 35. **Hookups:** Electric (20, 30, 50 amps), water, sewer. **Each Site:** Picnic table, fire ring. **Dump Station:** Yes. **Laundry:** Yes. **Pay Phone:** Yes. **Restrooms and Showers:** Yes. **Fuel:** No. **Propane:** Yes. **Internal Roads:** Paved/gravel, in good condition. **RV Service:** No. **Market:** 2 mi. east in Fremont. **Restaurant:** 2 mi. east in Fremont. **General Store:** Yes. **Vending:** Yes. **Swimming:** Yes. **Playground:** Yes. **Other:** Partridge Lake, arcade, mini-golf, horseshoes, volleyball, basketball, shuffleboard, rec hall, game room, pavilion, nature trails, boat launch, gift shop, rental cabins, rental cottages, bait & tackle shop, boat ramp, badminton, sports field. **Activities:** Swimming, fishing (fishing guides available), hiking, boating (rental pontoons, rowboats, canoes, kayaks, jon boats available), scheduled activities. **Nearby Attractions:** Golf, horseback riding, waterslide, go-karts, cheese factories, bowling, canoeing, tubing, outlet mall, biking trails, Amish arts & crafts, antiques, harbor boat rides, Green Bay Packer Hall of Fame, zoo. **Additional Information:** Fremont Chamber of Commerce, (920) 446-3838.

RESTRICTIONS

Pets: On leash only. **Fires:** In fire ring only. **Alcoholic Beverages:** Allowed. **Vehicle Maximum Length:** No limit.

TO GET THERE

From the junction of CR H and US 10, drive 1.5 mi. west on US 10. Roads are wide and well maintained, with broad shoulders.

FRIENDSHIP
Roche-A-Cri State Park   MAP, C-2

1767 Hwy. 13, 53934. T: (608) 339-6881; www.reserveamerica.com.

🚐 ★★★★	⛺ ★★★★
Beauty: ★★★★	Site Privacy: ★★★
Spaciousness: ★★★	Quiet: ★★★★
Security: ★★★★	Cleanliness: ★★★★
Insect Control: ★★★★	Facilities: ★★★★

Roche-A-Cri State Park, established in 1948, includes a 605-acre park area. Roche-A-Cri comes from French words meaning "crevice in the rock." The park has a prominent butte rising 300-feet above surrounding flatland. Composed of 480-million-year-old Cambrian sandstone, this outcropping was once an island in ancient glacial Lake Wisconsin. Native Americans used the rock as a median for petroglyphs. Today, visitors are invited to climb the rock using the 303-step staircase to the flat top. Resting benches and interpretive signage accompany the ascent. A variety of attractions draw visitors to Roche-A-Cri State Park. There are more than 5 miles of hiking trails through hardwoods and prairie that teem with wildlife and wildflowers. In fact, there are several areas of prairie restoration. Native trout can be caught in Carter Creek. Roche-A-Cri has 41 rustic campsites beneath a grove of white pines and red oaks. There are no showers or electric hookup, with the exception of one wheelchair-accessible site that offers electric. There are three picnic areas in the park. There is play equipment at the park office picnic area, in the campground, and at the kiosk area. Roche-A-Cri has the only interpreted rock art site in the state. The observation area is west of the office. The accessible ramp and observation deck allow all visitors to view the petroglyphs and pictographs. A marker describing the park's glacial history can be found on the west side of the mound.

BASICS

Operated By: Wisconsin State Parks. **Open:** May 18–Sept. 9. **Site Assignment:** Reservations can be made 11 months in advance or as late as 2 days before arrival. **Registration:** At office. **Fee:** Single, $10–$22; group, $40–$140. **Parking:** At site.

FACILITIES

Number of Multipurpose Sites: 41. **Hookups:** Yes. **Dump Station:** Yes. **Laundry:** No. **Pay Phone:** Yes. **Restrooms and Showers:** Yes. **Fuel:** No. **Propane:** No. **Internal Roads:** Paved. **RV Service:** No. **Market:** No. **Restaurant:** No. **General Store:** No. **Vending:** No. **Swimming:** No. **Playground:** Yes. **Other:** Out-of-state campfire wood is prohibited. Vehicle admission stickers are required. **Activities:** Picnicking.

RESTRICTIONS

Pets: Pets must be on a leash no longer than 8 ft must be in control at all times. Pets are not allowed in the general picnic areas. **Fires:** Fires are allowed in authorized fireplaces or rings only. Do not leave fires unattended; extinguish all fires before leaving the campsite. Burning of household refuse is prohibited. **Alcoholic Beverages:** People of legal drinking age may bring alcoholic beverages along for their picnic or campsite meals in Wisconsin state parks & forests.

TO GET THERE

Roche-A-Cri State Park is situated 28 mi. north of the Wisconsin Dells on Hwy. 13 and midway between the Wisconsin Dells and Wisconsin Rapids on Hwy. 13. From the intersection of Hwy. 21 and I-39: head west 14 mi. to the intersection of Hwy. 21 and Hwy. 13. Take Hwy. 13 south for 1.5 mi. to the park entrance. From the intersection of Hwy. 21 and I-94: head east 33 mi., turn south on Hwy. 13 and travel 1.5 mi. to the park entrance.

FT. ATKINSON
Yogi Bear's Jellystone Park   MAP, D-2, D-3

N551 Wishing Well Dr., 53538.
T: (920) 568-4100 or (877) BEARFUN; www.bearsatfort.com.

🚐 ★★★★	⛺ ★★★★
Beauty: ★★★★	Site Privacy: ★★★
Spaciousness: ★★	Quiet: ★★
Security: ★★★★	Cleanliness: ★★★
Insect Control: ★★★	Facilities: ★★★★

Whether you are an RV park enthusiast, enjoy the comfort of a cabin in the woods, or just like to tent-camp and sleep in the great outdoors, Jellystone Park's first-rate accommodations, amenities, and activities are waiting for you and your family. From swimming, mini-golf, hayrides, tennis, and volleyball to fishing, hiking, and appearances from Yogi Bear and friends, you'll notice that family fun is the main attraction.

BASICS

Operated By: Steve Cline. **Open:** May 13–Sept. 26. **Site Assignment:** Reservations recommended. **Registration:** At ranger station. **Fee:** RV, $20–$36; cabin, $49–$140.

FACILITIES

Number of Multipurpose Sites: 569. **Hookups:** Water, electric. **Dump Station:** Yes. **Laundry:** Yes. **Pay Phone:** Yes. **Restrooms and Showers:** Yes. **Fuel:** No. **Propane:** Yes. **General Store:** Camp store. **Vending:** Yes. **Swimming:** Yes. **Playground:** Yes. **Activities:** Tennis courts, basketball, baseball, volleyball, shuffleboard.

RESTRICTIONS

Pets: On leash and always attended.

TO GET THERE

Located south of Fort Atkinson off Hwy. 26. Take I-90 from Chicago (2 hours) to Hwy. 26N.

HAYWARD
Day Lake—Chequamegon-Nicolet National Forest   MAP, B-1

P.O. Box 896, 54843. T: (715) 634-4821; www.reserveamerica.com.

🚐 ★★★★	⛺ ★★★★
Beauty: ★★★★	Site Privacy: ★★★
Spaciousness: ★★★	Quiet: ★★★
Security: ★★★★	Cleanliness: ★★★★
Insect Control: ★★★★	Facilities: ★★

Campsite beauty is second only to the natural beauty here at Day Lake. The beautiful 640-acre lake that the campground sits on serves as a haven for wildlife. Waterfowl, especially loons, congregate on the lakes' many floating islands. But the first you will notice is the very large campground. Under most circumstances, a campground this large would hold twice the number of campsites here at Day Lake, but those responsible for developing the campground gave each site more than ample room. And a myriad of outdoor activities are quite convenient. Boating, fishing, swimming, and hiking are just feet away, so pack your tent, bring your watercraft and fishing pole, and be prepared to have a good time. Day Lake is located within the Nicolet National Forest in northern Wisconsin, where towering pine and hardwood forests are interspersed with hundreds of crystal clear lakes and streams. The Nicolet National Forest offers you a wealth of opportunities to enjoy the outdoors. Within a day's drive of the Chicago, Milwaukee, St. Paul, and Minneapolis metropolitan areas, the Nicolet is a place where you can truly get away from it all in the scenic beauty of the north woods. Four seasons of recreation await you, from spring fishing or canoeing to summer camping, hiking, mountain biking, or horseback riding. Come in autumn for hunting or to see our famous fall color. For your driving pleasure there are 3,600 miles of back roads. Please drive slowly. Snow season gears up with cross-country skiing and snowmobiling. Or come anytime to get close to nature in a tranquil and secluded spot. Opportunities for exhilarating views, relaxation, and quiet nature study abound. Experience all the beauty and recreational opportunities of Wisconsin's National Forests. Native American tribes were the first to explore and eventually settle this region, followed by voyageurs, missionaries, loggers, farmers, and miners. Much of this natural beauty and colorful human history can be enjoyed today in the Nicolet. In 1634, Jean Nicolet, a French explorer, discovered what the Native American tribes already knew to be a beautiful resource-rich land. Little did Nicolet know that 300 years later a National Forest would be named in his honor. The Nicolet was established in 1933 and now comprises over 661,000 acres in northeastern Wisconsin. Later that same year, the Nicolet evolved into two national forests. The western portion of the Nicolet was proclaimed as a separate forest, the Chequamegon. The name Chequamegon originates from the Ojibway or Chippewa language and is thought to mean "the place of shallow water." The Chequamegon now encompasses 857,000 acres in northern Wisconsin.

BASICS

Operated By: U.S. Forest Service. **Open:** May 1–Oct. 24. **Site Assignment:** Reservations must be made at least 4 days in advance. **Registration:** At office. **Fee:** Single, $12. **Parking:** At park.

FACILITIES

Number of Multipurpose Sites: 124. **Hookups:** None. **Each Site:** Call ahead. **Dump Station:** No. **Laundry:** No. **Pay Phone:** No. **Restrooms and Showers:** Yes. **Fuel:** No. **Propane:** No. **Internal Roads:** Paved. **RV Service:** No. **Market:** No. **Restaurant:** No. **General Store:** No. **Vending:** No. **Swimming:** Yes. **Playground:** No. **Activities:** Fishing.

RESTRICTIONS

Pets: Restrained or on a leash at all times while in developed recreation areas. **Fires:** In fire rings, stoves, grills, or fireplaces provided for that purpose.

Alcoholic Beverages: Not allowed. **Vehicle Maximum Length:** Call ahead. **Other:** Do not bring firewood from home.

TO GET THERE

Travel 1 mi. north of Clam Lake, Wisconsin, on Hwy. GG.

HAYWARD   MAP, B-1
Lake Chippewa Campground

8380 North CTH CC, 54843. T: (715) 462-3672; www.lakechip.com.

🚐 ★★★★   ⛺ ★★★★

Beauty: ★★★★	Site Privacy: ★★★★
Spaciousness: ★★★★	Quiet: ★★★★
Security: ★★★★	Cleanliness: ★★★★
Insect Control: ★★	Facilities: ★★★★

Lake Chippewa Campground is located on an island in the heart of Lake Chippewa. Connected by a bridge and a causeway to the mainland, the campground offers great water activities. The 17,000-acre Chippewa Flowage is Wisconsin's largest wilderness lake, with most of its lakeshore undeveloped, wild, and scenic. The campground offers level, shaded, wooded sites, with 16 seasonal campers, 20 pull-through sites, and a typical site width of 30 feet. Campers can beach their boat or canoe right outside their RV door. Unobstructed views of water and seasonal foliage are also available. Reservations are recommended, especially for weekends and holidays. Since the campground stays open until November 1, campers can enjoy the great fall foliage. Muskie is king here, but other popular fish are walleye, crappie, bluegill, and perch. The best sites, of course, are by the lake.

BASICS

Operated By: Don & Judy Robinson. **Open:** May 1–Nov. 1. **Site Assignment:** Reservations w/ 1-night deposit; refund (minus $5) w/ 10-day notice. **Registration:** At campground office. **Fee:** $23–$34; cash, check. **Parking:** At site.

FACILITIES

Number of RV-only Sites: 170. **Number of Tent-only Sites:** 10. **Hookups:** Electric (20, 30, 50 amps), water, sewer. **Each Site:** Picnic table, fire ring. **Dump Station:** Yes. **Laundry:** Yes. **Pay Phone:** Yes. **Restrooms and Showers:** Yes. **Fuel:** No. **Propane:** Yes. **Internal Roads:** Paved/gravel, in good condition. **RV Service:** No. **Market:** 7 mi. south. **Restaurant:** 2 mi. **General Store:** Yes, limited. **Vending:** Yes. **Swimming:** No. **Playground:** Yes. **Other:** Chippewa Flowage, snack shop, sandy beach, baseball, mini-golf, horseshoes, volleyball, basketball, rec hall, game room, trails, fish-cleaning station, rental RVs, rental cabins, boat landing, boat dock. **Activities:** Swimming, fishing, boating (rental motorboats, canoes, paddleboats available), scheduled activities. **Nearby Attractions:** National Freshwater Fishing Hall of Fame, lumberjack shows, zoo, golf, horseback riding, national forest, fishing, casinos, antiques, arts & crafts, Sawyer County Historical Society & Museum. **Additional Information:** Hayward Area Chamber of Commerce, (715) 634-8662.

RESTRICTIONS

Pets: On leash only. **Fires:** Fire ring only. **Alcoholic Beverages:** Allowed. **Vehicle Maximum Length:** No limit.

TO GET THERE

From the junction of US 63 and Hwy. 27, drive 0.5 mi. south on Hwy. 27, then 13 mi. east on CR B, then 5 mi. south on CR CC. Roads are mostly wide and well maintained, with narrow shoulders in spots.

HIXTON   MAP, C-1
Hixton–Alma Center KOA

N9657 SR 95, 54611.
T: (800) 562-2680 or (715) 964-2508.

🚐 ★★★★   ⛺ ★★★★

Beauty: ★★★★	Site Privacy: ★★★★
Spaciousness: ★★★★	Quiet: ★★★★
Security: ★★★★	Cleanliness: ★★★★★
Insect Control: ★★★	Facilities: ★★★★

This is not a party campground. The Hixton–Alma Center KOA, 12 miles east of Black River Falls, is where families and campers come to enjoy a peaceful country setting with plenty of birds and flowers. The campground owner has an iron fist when it comes to rowdiness, but she also has a green thumb and spends a good number of hours tending her tulips and lilacs. She feeds birds year-round and uses a garlic spray to control mosquitoes without harming wildlife. A small spring-fed pond provides catch-and-release fishing for youngsters. An immaculate bathroom not only has shiny waxed floors, but also features bouquets of fresh flowers. Each large (40 by 50 feet) campsite has a tree, grass, and a gravel pad for RVs; most are pull-throughs. Secluded wilderness sites are available for tent campers.

BASICS

Operated By: Jim & Donna Rankin. **Open:** May 1–Oct. 31. **Site Assignment:** Reservations w/ 1-night deposit; refund w/ 48-hour notice. **Registration:** At campground office. **Fee:** $18–$36; cash, check, credit card. **Parking:** At site.

FACILITIES

Number of RV-only Sites: 60. **Number of Tent-only Sites:** 15. **Hookups:** Electric (30, 50 amps), water, sewer, Wi-Fi, cable TV, telephone. **Each Site:** Picnic table, fire ring. **Dump Station:** Yes. **Laundry:** Yes. **Pay Phone:** No. **Restrooms and Showers:** Yes. **Fuel:** No. **Propane:** No. **Internal Roads:** Gravel, in good condition. **RV Service:** No. **Market:** 3.5 mi. west in Hixton. **Restaurant:** 3.5 mi. west in Hixton. **General Store:** Yes. **Vending:** No. **Swimming:** Yes. **Playground:** Yes. **Other:** Hiking trails, small fishing pond for children, volleyball, horseshoes, pavilion w/ juke box, videos, pool table. **Activities:** Hiking, swimming, fishing, bird-watching, biking (rental bikes available). **Nearby Attractions:** Golf, diving, canoeing, orchard, casino, Thunderbird Museum, antique & craft shops. **Additional Information:** Black River Falls Area Chamber of Commerce, (800) 404-4008.

RESTRICTIONS

Pets: On leash only. **Fires:** Fire ring only. **Alcoholic Beverages:** At sites only. **Vehicle Maximum Length:** No limit.

TO GET THERE

From the junction of I-94 and Hwy. 95, take Exit 105, drive 3.5 mi. east on Hwy. 95. The roads are wide and well maintained, with broad shoulders.

KANSASVILLE MAP, D-3
Richard Bong State Recreation Area

reserve america

26313 Burlington Rd., 53139. T: (262) 878-5600; www.reserveamerica.com.

🚐 ★★★★	⛺ ★★★★
Beauty: ★★★	Site Privacy: ★★★
Spaciousness: ★★★	Quiet: ★★★★
Security: ★★★★	Cleanliness: ★★★★
Insect Control: ★★★★	Facilities: ★★★★

Once designated to be a jet fighter base, Richard Bong State Recreation Area is fittingly named after Major Richard I. Bong, a Poplar, Wisconsin, native who was America's leading air ace during World War II. The project was abandoned three days before concrete was to be poured for a 12,500-foot runway. Local citizens had the foresight to protect this open space for future generations. In 1974 the state bought the land, and it became the state's first recreation area. A recreation area differs from a state park or forest in that it offers additional activities not traditionally found in state parks. Appropriate to its name, Richard Bong SRA offers an area where visitors may fly model airplanes, rockets, hang gliders, and hot-air balloons. Richard Bong also has space to train both hunting and sled dogs, train falcons, ride an ATV trail, ride horseback on trails, and hunt in season. All such activities take place in the special-use zone or managed hunt areas. The recreation area encompasses 4,515 acres of rolling grassland, savanna, wetlands, and scattered woodland. Richard Bong State Recreation Area is open year-round and has 41.1 miles of trails for hiking, mountain biking, cross-country skiing, horseback riding, snowshoeing, and dirt-bike riding.

BASICS

Operated By: Wisconsin State Parks. **Open:** May 4–Oct. 6; some sites reservable year-round. **Site Assignment:** Reservations can be made 11 months in advance or as late as 2 days before arrival. **Registration:** At office. **Fee:** Single, $10–$22; group, $40–$140. **Parking:** At site.

FACILITIES

Number of Multipurpose Sites: 223. **Hookups:** Yes. **Each Site:** Fire ring, picnic table. **Dump Station:** Yes. **Laundry:** No. **Pay Phone:** Yes. **Restrooms and Showers:** Yes. **Fuel:** No. **Propane:** No. **Internal Roads:** Paved. **RV Service:** No. **Market:** No. **Restaurant:** No. **General Store:** No. **Vending:** No. **Swimming:** Yes. **Playground:** Yes. **Other:** Out-of-state campfire wood is

prohibited. Vehicle admission stickers are required. **Activities:** Baseball, boating, fishing, hiking, hunting, picnicking.

RESTRICTIONS

Pets: Has a designated area for teaching dogs to retrieve, point, flush, or track game for the purpose of hunting or dog trial competition. The area is used for training on foot, w/ horses in the water. It is in the special-uses zone in the southwest. **Fires:** In authorized fireplaces or rings only. Do not leave unattended; extinguish all fires before leaving the campsite. Burning of household refuse is prohibited. **Alcoholic Beverages:** People of legal drinking age may bring alcoholic beverages along for their picnic or campsite meals in Wisconsin state parks & forests.

TO GET THERE

Richard Bong State Recreation Area is located in western Kenosha County 35 mi. southwest of Milwaukee and 9 mi. east of Burlington. The entrance is on Hwy. 142, 1 mi. west of Hwy. 75.

KEWAUNEE MAP, C-3
Kewaunee Village RV Park

333 Terraqua Dr., 54216. T: (800) 274-9684 or (920) 388-4851; www.kewauneevillage.com.

🚐 ★★★★	⛺ ★★★
Beauty: ★★★	Site Privacy: ★★
Spaciousness: ★★	Quiet: ★★★
Security: ★★★★	Cleanliness: ★★★★
Insect Control: ★★	Facilities: ★★★★

Location is everything, and Kewaunee Village RV Park certainly has a prime spot. Situated just over 1 mile north of downtown Kewaunee, the campground is right off the main road of Hwy. 42. It is also next to Lake Michigan on a beautiful harbor with a boat launch, charter fishing, and marina facilities. There is even a fish-cleaning house at the harbor and fish-freezing services for campers at the campground. Campsites are level and mostly open, with a typical site width of 40 feet. Kewaunee Village RV Park has 64 pull-through sites, 24 seasonal campers, and city water and sewer. The campground has some shade trees, but it is not a wooded facility. RVs must be parked only on gravel pad areas, not on the grass. A ten-mph speed limit is enforced (a lower one might be better with so many children on site), as is quiet time from 11 p.m. to 7 a.m. Young adults and children must be on their sites by 10 p.m. Security measures include one entrance/exit, a regular patrol, and owners who live on site.

BASICS

Operated By: Nanette & Katie Kulm; Warren & Kathy Clark. **Open:** May 15–Oct. 15. **Site Assignment:** Reservations w/ 1-night deposit; refund (minus $5) w/ 3-day notice. **Registration:** At campground office. **Fee:** $22–$33; cash, check, credit card. **Parking:** At site.

FACILITIES

Number of RV-only Sites: 74. **Number of Tent-only Sites:** 15. **Hookups:** Electric (20, 30, 50 amps), water, sewer. **Each Site:** Picnic table, fire ring. **Dump Station:** Yes. **Laundry:** Yes. **Pay Phone:**

Courtesy. **Restrooms and Showers:** Yes. **Fuel:** No. **Propane:** Yes. **Internal Roads:** Paved/gravel, in good condition. **RV Service:** No. **Market:** 1.5 mi. south in Kewaunee. **Restaurant:** 1.5 mi. south in Kewaunee. **General Store:** Yes. **Vending:** No. **Swimming:** Yes. **Playground:** Yes. **Other:** Pavilion, game & video room, mini-golf, recreation field, horseshoes, fish freezing, shuffleboard. **Activities:** Swimming, scheduled weekend activities. **Nearby Attractions:** Lake Michigan, boating, charter fishing, harbor, boat launch, cheese factories, antiques, arts & crafts shops, Door County, zoo, jail museum, golf, art galleries, nautical museum, nature walk. **Additional Information:** Kewaunee Chamber of Commerce, (800) 666-8214.

RESTRICTIONS

Pets: On leash only, max. of 2 pets per site. **Fires:** Fire ring only; all fires must be extinguished by 11 p.m.; must be put out w/ water until no glowing embers remain. **Alcoholic Beverages:** Allowed. **Vehicle Maximum Length:** No limit.

TO GET THERE

From the junction of Hwy. 29 and Hwy. 42, drive 0.75 mi. north on Hwy. 42. Roads are wide and well maintained, with broad shoulders.

LAKE GENEVA MAP, D-3
Big Foot Beach State Park

reserve america

1452 S. Wells St., 53147. T: (262) 248-2528; www.reserveamerica.com.

🚐 ★★★★	⛺ ★★★★
Beauty: ★★★	Site Privacy: ★★★
Spaciousness: ★★★	Quiet: ★★★★
Security: ★★★★	Cleanliness: ★★★★
Insect Control: ★★★★	Facilities: ★★★

This 271-acre park on the shore of Lake Geneva offers wooded campsites, a sand beach, and picnic areas. Big Foot Beach State Park has 100 campsites. The campground has showers and pit toilets. RV sites have a gravel pad, fire ring, and picnic table. There is a sewage dump station but no electric or water hookups. Tent sites are a short walk from your vehicle (30–100 feet) and have a fire ring and picnic table. Lake Geneva is known for its clear, clean water. A 100-foot swimming area is about a ten-minute walk and across Highway 120 from the campground. The bathroom buildings near the beach have flush toilets and sinks. Share in family fun fishing in Ceylon Lagoon. You can reel them in from the pier, two bridges, or the lagoon bank. Fishing equipment is loaned free of charge at the office. A fishing license is required of anyone age 16 and over who is fishing. Big Foot Beach State Park offers 40 acres of picnic area with about 250 tables and a limited number of charcoal grills. Volleyball and horseshoe courts are available. Horseshoes and volleyballs are loaned free of charge at the office.

BASICS

Operated By: Wisconsin State Parks. **Open:** May 15–Oct. 29. **Site Assignment:** Reservations can be made 11 months in advance or as late as 2 days before arrival. **Registration:** At office. **Fee:** Single, $10–$22; group, $40–$140. **Parking:** At site.

FACILITIES

Number of Multipurpose Sites: 101. **Hookups:** Yes. **Each Site:** Fire ring, picnic table. **Dump Station:** No. **Laundry:** No. **Pay Phone:** No. **Restrooms and Showers:** Yes. **Fuel:** No. **Propane:** No. **Internal Roads:** Paved, gravel. **RV Service:** No. **Market:** No. **Restaurant:** No. **General Store:** No. **Vending:** No. **Swimming:** Yes. **Playground:** No. **Other:** Out-of-state campfire wood is prohibited. **Activities:** Fishing, hiking, picnicking, volleyball.

RESTRICTIONS

Pets: On a leash no longer than 8 ft; under control at all times; not allowed in the general picnic areas. **Fires:** In authorized fireplaces or rings only. Do not leave unattended; extinguish all fires before leaving the campsite. Burning of household refuse is prohibited. **Alcoholic Beverages:** Not allowed.

TO GET THERE

Big Foot Beach State Park entrance is located at 1550 S. Lake Shore Dr., 1 mi. north of WI 120 and Hwy. BB, 1.5 mi. south of Main St. in the city of Lake Geneva.

LAKEWOOD   MAP, B-3
Heaven's Up North Family Campground

18344 Lake John Rd., 54138. T: (715) 276-6556; www.heavensupnorth.com.

🚐 ★★★★   ⛺ ★★★★

Beauty: ★★★★	Site Privacy: ★★★★
Spaciousness: ★★★★	Quiet: ★★★★
Security: ★★★★	Cleanliness: ★★★★★
Insect Control: ★★	Facilities: ★★★★

Located 3 miles west of Lakewood, Heaven's Up North Family Campground is a wooded facility with some steep hills leading to some of the campsites. But that hilly terrain also adds to the beauty. Quiet is maintained at the wilderness campground by having plenty of trees and other green space as buffers between sites and by enforcing 10 p.m. to 7 a.m. quiet times. No loud or amplified music is allowed at any time. Group-camping sites are not available in order to cut down on noise. The typical site width is 50 feet, and the campground has four pull-through sites and 76 seasonal campers. Laid out in a series of loops, the campground has a five-mph speed limit and one-way roads. Security measures include one entrance/exit, owners who live on site, and regular campground patrols. Open year-round, the campground is kept plowed in the winter for campers who want to hunt or go snowmobiling or ice fishing.

BASICS

Operated By: Jeff & Colleen Netcoft. **Open:** All year. **Site Assignment:** Reservations w/ credit card; refunds w/ 2-week notice. **Registration:** At campground office. **Fee:** $19–$26; cash, check, credit card. **Parking:** At site.

FACILITIES

Number of Multipurpose Sites: 116. **Hookups:** Electric (20, 30 amps), water. **Each Site:** Picnic table, fire ring. **Dump Station:** Yes. **Laundry:** Yes. **Pay Phone:** No. **Restrooms and Showers:** Yes. **Fuel:** No. **Propane:** No. **Internal Roads:** Gravel, in good condition. **RV Service:** No. **Market:** 3 mi. east in Lakewood. **Restaurant:** 3 mi. east in Lakewood. **General Store:** Yes, limited. **Vending:** Yes. **Swimming:** Yes. **Playground:** Yes. **Other:** Game room, coin games, mini-golf, horseshoes, recreation field, volleyball. **Activities:** Swimming. **Nearby Attractions:** Casino, bingo, gingerbread houses, fish hatchery, logging camp, golf, fishing & boating lakes, winery, art studio. **Additional Information:** Lakewood Area Chamber of Commerce, (715) 276-6500.

RESTRICTIONS

Pets: On leash only. **Fires:** Fire ring only. **Alcoholic Beverages:** Allowed. **Vehicle Maximum Length:** 36 ft.

TO GET THERE

From the junction of Hwy. 32 and CR F in Lakewood, drive 2 mi. northeast on CR F, then 3 mi. north on Lake John Rd. Roads are wide and well maintained, with broad shoulders.

LAKEWOOD   MAP, B-3
Maple Heights Campground

P.O. Box 130, 16091 East Chain Lake Rd., 54138. T: (715) 276-6441.

🚐 ★★★   ⛺ ★★★

Beauty: ★★★	Site Privacy: ★★★
Spaciousness: ★★★	Quiet: ★★★★
Security: ★★★★	Cleanliness: ★★★★
Insect Control: ★★	Facilities: ★★★

Maple Heights Campground, located 1.5 miles north of Lakewood, has two notable landmarks—a canopy of huge maple, beech, and hemlock trees, and a giant statue of Paul Bunyan's Babe the Blue Ox, a favorite photo op. The campground borders the Nicolet National Forest and offers a wealth of nearby water activities. Over 60 lakes are within 10 miles. The McCaslin Brook trout stream meanders around the campground, and it is located between two popular rafting rivers, the Wolf and Peshtigo. The campground's 50-foot heated pool is also hard to ignore. Laid out in a series of loops, Maple Heights offers a typical site width of 30 feet, 85 pull-throughs, and 50 seasonal campers. Sites in the secluded, wooded campground are level and mostly shady. Seasonal campers are mostly clumped in sections. The best RV site is LB because it is larger, has water and electricity, and is close to the pool and other facilities. The best tent site is B13 because it is large and backs up into the national forest. Speed limit is five mph, and quiet time between 11 p.m. and 7:30 a.m. means music must be turned off and voices kept low. Security includes one entrance/exit road, owners who live on site, and regular patrols of the campground.

BASICS

Operated By: Mike & Carolyn Kubitz. **Open:** Apr. 1–Dec. 1. **Site Assignment:** Reservations w/ $20 deposit; no refunds, camping certificates. **Registra-**

tion: At campground office. **Fee:** $18–$24; cash, check, credit card. **Parking:** At site.

FACILITIES

Number of RV-only Sites: 93. **Number of Tent-only Sites:** 7. **Hookups:** Electric (30, 50 amps), water. **Each Site:** Picnic table, fire ring. **Dump Station:** Yes. **Laundry:** Yes. **Pay Phone:** No. **Restrooms and Showers:** Yes. **Fuel:** No. **Propane:** No. **Internal Roads:** Gravel, in good condition. **RV Service:** No. **Market:** 1.5 mi. south in Lakewood. **Restaurant:** 1.5 mi. south in Lakewood. **General Store:** Yes. **Vending:** Yes. **Swimming:** Yes. **Playground:** Yes. **Other:** McCaslin Brook trout stream, rec room, snack bar, mini-golf, volleyball, horseshoes, ping pong, pavilion, hiking trail, sports field. **Activities:** Swimming, fishing, hiking. **Nearby Attractions:** Casino, bingo, gingerbread houses, fish hatchery, logging camp, golf, fishing & boating lakes, winery, art studio. **Additional Information:** Lakewood Area Chamber of Commerce, (715) 276-6500.

RESTRICTIONS

Pets: On leash only. **Fires:** Fire ring only. **Alcoholic Beverages:** Allowed. **Vehicle Maximum Length:** 45 ft.

TO GET THERE

From the junction of CR F and Hwy. 32, drive 2 mi. north on Hwy. 32. Roads are wide and well maintained, with broad shoulders.

MERRILL   MAP, B-2
Council Grounds State Park

reserve america

N1895 Council Grounds Dr., 54452. T: (715) 536-8773; www.reserveamerica.com.

🚐 ★★★★   ⛺ ★★★★

Beauty: ★★★	Site Privacy: ★★★
Spaciousness: ★★★	Quiet: ★★★★
Security: ★★★★	Cleanliness: ★★★★
Insect Control: ★★★★	Facilities: ★★★★

Before Whiteman's invasion of the region, Council Grounds State Park was home to Native American tribal festivals, thus the park's name. With its dense forests of white pine and its prime access to the Wisconsin River, logging became the region's dominant occupation during the late 19th century and into the 20th century. The state acquired the property in 1978 after a series of public owners. Today, this lovely park still exhibits ancient trees and scenic Wisconsin River and Lake Alexander views punctuated by rock outcroppings and thriving blue heron and white-tailed deer populations. Council Grounds State Park features 55 campsites, electric hookups, a modern bathhouse, and a small nature center. Numerous picnic facilities provide plenty of day-use space, including a 100-yard-long beach framed by beautiful old hardwoods and pines. The beach area is guarded and features a modern bathhouse and concession stand. Boating and canoeing are popular summertime pursuits both along the lazy Wisconsin River and on Lake Alexander. A boat launch, canoe portage, and shoreline fishing access are available.

The ADA fishing pier is also available. Nature lovers will enjoy watching the large herd of white-tailed deer seen throughout the park. Bird-watchers can observe several active bald eagle and osprey nests in addition to the very fascinating blue heron rookery located on the second island behind the dam. Other recreations pursued at Council Grounds State Park include waterskiing, cross-country skiing, hiking, fitness trail, and nature study.

BASICS

Operated By: Wisconsin State Parks. **Open:** All year. **Site Assignment:** Reservations can be made 11 months in advance or as late as 2 days before arrival. **Registration:** At office. **Fee:** Single, $10–$22; group, $40–$140. **Parking:** At site.

FACILITIES

Number of Multipurpose Sites: 55. **Hookups:** Yes. **Each Site:** Fire ring, picnic table. **Dump Station:** Yes. **Laundry:** No. **Pay Phone:** Yes. **Restrooms and Showers:** Yes. **Fuel:** No. **Propane:** No. **Internal Roads:** Paved. **RV Service:** No. **Market:** No. **Restaurant:** No. **General Store:** No. **Vending:** No. **Swimming:** Yes. **Playground:** No. **Other:** Out-of-state campfire wood is prohibited. Vehicle admission stickers are required. **Activities:** Boating, fishing, hiking, picnicking.

RESTRICTIONS

Pets: On a leash no longer than 8 ft.; under control at all times; not allowed in the general picnic areas. **Fires:** In authorized fireplaces or rings only. Do not leave unattended; extinguish all fires before leaving the campsite. Burning of household refuse is prohibited. **Alcoholic Beverages:** People of legal drinking age may bring alcoholic beverages along for their picnic or campsite meals in Wisconsin state parks & forests.

TO GET THERE

Council Grounds State Park is located on the northwest edge of Merrill, on Council Grounds Drive. Exit Hwy. 51 at the Hwy. 64 exit. Take Hwy. 64 west 3 mi. to Hwy. 107 North. Take Hwy. 107 north 1.8 mi. to Council Grounds Drive. Take Council Grounds Drive south 0.5 mi. to the park entrance.

MILTON   MAP, D-2, D-3
Hidden Valley RV Resort and Campground

872 East Hwy. 59, 53563. T: (800) 469-5515; www.hiddenvalleyrvresort.com.

🚐 ★★★★	🔺 ★★★
Beauty: ★★★★	Site Privacy: ★★★★★
Spaciousness: ★★★★★	Quiet: ★★★★★
Security: ★★★★★	Cleanliness: ★★★★★
Insect Control: ★★	Facilities: ★★★★★

Hidden Valley RV Resort and Campground, 2 miles east of Edgerton, makes a wonderful first impression with its stone waterfall at the entrance. And the rural campground lives up to that impression. Grounds are manicured almost like a golf course; sites are spacious (40 feet wide), mostly grassy with gravel pads, and adjoin a grassy park area. The campground opened in 1993, and most of the trees are still rather small to provide much shade. Exceptionally clean, modern facilities and a large, three-level clubhouse add luxury touches. Tent campers are permitted to use RV sites, but the campground may be a bit too organized for many tent enthusiasts. The campground has a manager who lives on site, regular patrols, and one-way roads throughout the facility for security.

BASICS

Operated By: Jim & Marcia Kersten. **Open:** Apr. 21–Oct. 21. **Site Assignment:** Reservations accepted w/ 1-night deposit; refund (minus $10) w/ 7-day notice; 2-night min. on weekends, 3-night min. on holidays. **Registration:** At campground office. **Fee:** $27–$57; cash, check, credit card. **Parking:** At site.

FACILITIES

Number of RV-only Sites: 132. **Hookups:** Electric (20, 30, 50 amps), water, sewer. **Each Site:** Picnic table, fire ring. **Dump Station:** Yes. **Laundry:** Yes. **Pay Phone:** Yes. **Restrooms and Showers:** Yes. **Fuel:** No. **Propane:** Yes. **Internal Roads:** Gravel, in good condition. **RV Service:** No. **Market:** 2 mi. west in Edgerton. **Restaurant:** 0.1 mi. in any direction. **General Store:** Yes. **Vending:** No. **Swimming:** Yes. **Playground:** Yes. **Other:** Hot tub, video game room, lounge areas, meeting room, deck, TV room, 4-acre recreation area including softball, volleyball, horseshoes. **Activities:** Swimming, biking (rental bikes available), planned weekly activities. **Nearby Attractions:** Waterskiing, boating, fishing, swimming on Lake Koshkonong, golf, Milton House Museum. **Additional Information:** Milton Area Chamber of Commerce, (608) 868-6222.

RESTRICTIONS

Pets: On leash only. **Fires:** Fire ring only. **Alcoholic Beverages:** Allowed. **Vehicle Maximum Length:** No limit.

TO GET THERE

From the junction of I-90 and Hwy. 59, take Exit 163 and drive 0.75 mi. east on Hwy. 59. Roads are wide and well maintained, with broad shoulders.

MILTON   MAP, D-2, D-3
Lakeland Camping Resort

2803 E. WI 59, 53563. T: (608) 868-4700; www.lakelandcampingresort.com.

🚐 ★★★	🔺 n/a
Beauty: ★★★	Site Privacy: ★★★
Spaciousness: ★★★	Quiet: ★★★★
Security: ★★★★	Cleanliness: ★★★★
Insect Control: ★★	Facilities: ★★★★

The statistics are impressive: about 575 total campground sites on beautiful Lake Koshkonong (the state's second-largest lake), a well-stocked campground store, and a wealth of recreational activities. But Lakeland Camping Resort is filled mostly with seasonal campers. Only 30 overnight sites are available, so reservations are strongly recommended. The sites are mostly shaded, with nine pull-throughs (30 by 60 feet) and eight with sewer. Laid out in a series of loops, the campground offers a pleasant wilderness with over a mile of lakeshore. The complex, 2.5 miles north of Edgerton, includes Lakeland Custom Coach RV Sales and Service Center.

BASICS

Operated By: Lakeland Leisure Corp. **Open:** May 1–Nov. 1. **Site Assignment:** Reservations w/ 1-night deposit, 3-night deposit for holidays; refund w/ 1-week notice. **Registration:** At campground office. **Fee:** $36.50–$41.75; cash, check, credit card. **Parking:** At site.

FACILITIES

Number of RV-only Sites: 500. **Number of Tent-only Sites:** 10. **Hookups:** Electric (20, 30, 50 amps), water, sewer. **Each Site:** Picnic table, fire ring. **Dump Station:** Yes. **Laundry:** Yes. **Pay Phone:** Yes. **Restrooms and Showers:** Yes. **Fuel:** No. **Propane:** Yes. **Internal Roads:** Paved, in good condition. **RV Service:** Yes. **Market:** 2.5 mi. west in Edgerton. **Restaurant:** 2.5 mi. west in Edgerton. **General Store:** Yes. **Vending:** Yes. **Swimming:** Yes. **Playground:** Yes. **Other:** Lake, sandy beach, tennis courts, rec center, boat launch, game room, nature trails, cross-country & snowmobile trails, bait shop. **Activities:** Swimming, fishing, boating (rental boats available), hiking. **Nearby Attractions:** Golf, Milton House Museum, hunting preserve, horseback riding, antique shops, county fairs & festivals, 35 miles to Madison. **Additional Information:** Greater Madison CVB, (800) 373-6376.

RESTRICTIONS

Pets: On 7-ft. leash only. **Fires:** In fire pit only. **Alcoholic Beverages:** Allowed. **Vehicle Maximum Length:** No limit. **Other:** Limit of 2 trout per day, per person in the pond.

TO GET THERE

From the junction of I-90 and WI 59, drive 2 mi. east on WI 59. Roads are wide and well maintained, with broad shoulders.

MINOCQUA   MAP, B-2
Patricia Lake Campground

8505 Camp Pinemere Rd., 54548. T: (715) 356-3198; www.patricialakecampground.com.

🚐 ★★★	🔺 ★★★
Beauty: ★★★	Site Privacy: ★★★
Spaciousness: ★★★	Quiet: ★★★
Security: ★★★	Cleanliness: ★★★★
Insect Control: ★★★	Facilities: ★★★★

Situated on the Oneida-Vilas County border near Chequamegon National Forest in Minocqua, Patricia Lake Campground features wooded sites on Patricia Lake. A small, deep, spring-fed lake with no wake, Patricia Lake has good fishing for bass, northern pike, and crappies. Nearby is the famous Minocqua Chain of Lakes for more excellent fishing. Sites are level and mostly wooded. A separate tenting area offers tenters more green space and privacy. The campground has four pull-through sites, 69 seasonal campers, and a typical site width of 30 feet. The campground is conveniently located 1 mile from an 18-hole golf course and petting zoo and 3 miles from downtown shops. Most popular sites are closest to the lake. Campground owners provide security and make sure the campground is kept quiet and orderly.

BASICS

Operated By: David & Joy Taber. **Open:** May 1–Oct. 15. **Site Assignment:** Reservations w/ 1-night deposit; refund (minus $5) w/ 2-week notice. **Registration:** At campground office. **Fee:** $20–$30; cash, check, credit card. **Parking:** At site.

FACILITIES

Number of RV-only Sites: 97. **Number of Tent-only Sites:** 3. **Hookups:** Electric (20, 30 amps), water, sewer, Wi-Fi. **Each Site:** Picnic table, fire ring. **Dump Station:** Yes. **Laundry:** Yes. **Pay Phone:** Yes. **Restrooms and Showers:** Yes. **Fuel:** No. **Propane:** No. **Internal Roads:** Gravel, in fair condition. **RV Service:** No. **Market:** 2 mi. south. **Restaurant:** 2 mi. south. **General Store:** Yes. **Vending:** Yes. **Swimming:** No. **Playground:** Yes. **Other:** Patricia Lake, swimming beach, horseshoes, volleyball, basketball, game room, pavilion, boat launch, recreation field, hiking trails. **Activities:** Swimming, fishing, hiking, boating (rental canoes, paddleboats, rowboats available). **Nearby Attractions:** Golf, Peck's Wildwood Wildlife Park & Nature Center, casino, antiques, arts & crafts, cross-country skiing, snowmobiling, professional repertory theater, Circle M Corral amusement park. **Additional Information:** Minocqua-Arbor Vitae-Woodrull Area Chamber of Commerce, (800) 446-6784.

RESTRICTIONS

Pets: On leash only. **Fires:** Fire ring only. **Alcoholic Beverages:** Allowed. **Vehicle Maximum Length:** No limit.

TO GET THERE

From south junction US 51 and Hwy. 70, drive 2.5 mi. west on Hwy. 70, then 0.5 mi. south on Camp Pinemere Rd. Roads are mostly wide and well maintained, with broad shoulders.

MONTELLO   MAP, C-2
Buffalo Lake Camping Resort

555 Lake Ave., 53949.
T: (888) 297-2915 or (608) 297-2915;
www.buffalolakecamping.com.

🚐 ★★★★   ⛺ ★★★

Beauty: ★★★★	Site Privacy: ★★★★
Spaciousness: ★★★★	Quiet: ★★★★
Security: ★★★★★	Cleanliness: ★★★★
Insect Control: ★★	Facilities: ★★★★

Buffalo Lake Camping Resort has the benefits of being located within the town of Montello, without the drawbacks of city noise and traffic. With a barrier of trees and large grassy areas, the campground is secluded and quiet. The campground is situated on 2,200-acre Buffalo Lake, the largest in Marquette County. The lake is well known for its northern pike, bass, crappie, bluegill, and perch. A well-stocked campground store carries groceries, beer, ice, firewood, camping supplies, snacks, clothing, souvenirs, fishing licenses, live bait, tackle, and boat rentals. The laundry room, restrooms, and showers are kept clean, and rules about cleanliness and quiet are

enforced. Recycling is mandatory, with recycling areas located throughout the campground. Quiet hours are 11 p.m. to 7 p.m., and children under 18 years old must remain in their campsite with adult supervision after 10 p.m. Owners live next door, the back gate to the campground is locked at night, and city police patrol the campground for security.

BASICS

Operated By: Linda & Gary Doudna. **Open:** Apr. 12–Oct. 14. **Site Assignment:** Reservations w/ 1-night deposit; refund (minus $5) w/ 14-day notice; 2-night min. **Registration:** At campground office. **Fee:** $23–$35; cash, check, credit card. **Parking:** At site.

FACILITIES

Number of Multipurpose Sites: 110. **Hookups:** Electric (20, 30, 50 amps), water, sewer, Wi-Fi. **Each Site:** Picnic table, fire ring. **Dump Station:** Yes. **Laundry:** Yes. **Pay Phone:** Yes. **Restrooms and Showers:** Yes. **Fuel:** No. **Propane:** Yes. **Internal Roads:** Gravel, in good condition. **RV Service:** No. **Market:** 1 mi. south in Montello. **Restaurant:** Across the road. **General Store:** Yes. **Vending:** Yes. **Swimming:** Yes. **Playground:** Yes. **Other:** Arcade, bait & tackle, horseshoes, covered pavilion, basketball, volleyball, lake boat dock, 4 piers, boat ramp, fish-cleaning house. **Activities:** Swimming, fishing, boating (rental canoes, kayaks, & rowboats available), planned activities. **Nearby Attractions:** Rivers & trout streams, scenic country roads, 30 miles to Wisconsin Dells. **Additional Information:** Wisconsin Dells Visitor & Convention Bureau, (800) 223-3557.

RESTRICTIONS

Pets: On leash only. **Fires:** Fire pit only. **Alcoholic Beverages:** Allowed. **Vehicle Maximum Length:** No limit.

TO GET THERE

From Madison, take I-90/94 to Exit 108B to WI 23 East. Drive 8 mi. to CR C (Lake Ave.), then 0.75 mi. to entrance. Roads are wide and well maintained, with broad shoulders.

MONTELLO   MAP, C-2
Wilderness Campground

N 1499 WI 22, 53949. T: (608) 297-2002;
www.wildernesscampground.com.

🚐 ★★★★   ⛺ ★★★★

Beauty: ★★★★	Site Privacy: ★★★★
Spaciousness: ★★★★	Quiet: ★★★★
Security: ★★★★	Cleanliness: ★★★★
Insect Control: ★★	Facilities: ★★★★

Under the same ownership for more than three decades, Wilderness Campground offers easy access and a quiet facility away from highway noise. Located 7 miles south of Montello, in the heart of Wisconsin's vacation land, the campground is on the shores of beautiful Bonnie and Hidden lakes. The three private lakes provide plenty of water recreation, along with a large heated swimming pool. Laid out in a series of loops, the campground has 100 seasonal campers, 75 pull-through sites, and a typical site width of 45 feet. Sites are grassy, level, and mostly shaded in a rambling oak woodland. A separate tent

area provides privacy from RVs and more green space. The best sites for tents and RVs are along the lakes. Tons of turtles and frogs keep down the mosquito population without insecticides. Security and safety measures include a 10 p.m. curfew for youngsters, a ban on bicycles on the roads after 8 p.m., quiet time starting at 11 p.m., and owners who live on site and provide regular campground patrols.

BASICS

Operated By: Bea Weiss. **Open:** Apr. 15–Oct. 15. **Site Assignment:** Reservations w/ full deposit; 50% deposit for reservations over 3 days; 2-night min.; camping certificates w/ 14-day cancellation notice. **Registration:** At campground office. **Fee:** $32–$39.94; cash, check, credit card. **Parking:** At site.

FACILITIES

Number of RV-only Sites: 300. **Number of Tent-only Sites:** 0. **Hookups:** Electric (15, 20, 30, 50 amps), water, sewer, phone. **Each Site:** Picnic table, fire ring. **Dump Station:** Yes. **Laundry:** Yes. **Pay Phone:** Yes. **Restrooms and Showers:** Yes. **Fuel:** No. **Propane:** Yes. **Internal Roads:** Paved/gravel, in good condition. **RV Service:** No. **Market:** 6 mi. north in Montello. **Restaurant:** 6 mi. north in Montello. **General Store:** Yes. **Vending:** Yes. **Swimming:** Yes. **Playground:** Yes. **Other:** Three private lakes, dance hall, petting zoo, hiking trails, rental cabins, rental RVs, mini-golf, rec hall, mini farm, pavilion, coin games, snack bar, boat ramp, badminton, sports field, volleyball, sandy beach. **Activities:** Hiking, swimming, fishing, boating (no motors allowed, rental rowboats, canoes, & paddleboats available), scheduled activities. **Nearby Attractions:** Wisconsin Dells, golf, horseback riding, wildlife refuge, granite quarries, historic homes, museums, fish hatchery, Circus World museum, Devil's Lake, casino, stock-car racing, antiques, arts & crafts. **Additional Information:** Wisconsin Dells Visitor & Convention Bureau, (800) 223-3557.

RESTRICTIONS

Pets: On leash only. **Fires:** Fire ring only. **Alcoholic Beverages:** Allowed. **Vehicle Maximum Length:** No limit.

TO GET THERE

From the junction of Hwys. 23 and 22 southbound, drive 7 mi. south on Hwy. 22. Roads are wide and well maintained, with mostly broad shoulders.

NECEDAH   MAP, C-2
Buckhorn State Park

W8450 Buckhorn Ave., 54646-7338.
T: (608) 565-2789; www.reserveamerica.com.

🚐 ★★★   ⛺ ★★★★

Beauty: ★★★★	Site Privacy: ★★★
Spaciousness: ★★★	Quiet: ★★★★
Security: ★★★★	Cleanliness: ★★★★
Insect Control: ★★★★	Facilities: ★★★★

Buckhorn State Park features a 2,500-acre day-use park within the Buckhorn Peninsula on the 13,955-acre Castle Rock Flowage. Located on the state's fourth-largest body of water, the park is a rich nature resource attracting anglers, boaters, hunters, and hikers. With its many marshes, bays, and beautiful forestland, the park is one of the most popular fishing destinations in Wisconsin. Originally inhabited by the Winnebago Indians and comprised of primarily white pine, the land was referred to as "unbroken wilderness." By the mid-1800s, the lumber industry moved in and lumbered heavily for nearly two decades. Eventually the Wisconsin and Yellow rivers were dammed, creating the Castle Rock Flowage. Camping is popular at Buckhorn State Park. There are backpack sites, walk-in sites, and group sites. The park also has an accessible cabin for use by people with disabilities. Hikers enjoy 4 miles of earthen path that explore a variety of forest types while providing scenic lake views. Osprey inhabit the park and are oftentimes seen soaring overhead. Sandhill cranes using the Mississippi flyway visit the park each spring and fall. This quiet park features a swimming beach, picnic grove, shelter, changing stalls, grills, volleyball court, horseshoe pits, and playground. A boat launch for small and medium-sized boats is separate from the canoe launch located on the eastern side of the park where canoeists find quieter waters. Castle Rock Flowage is one of the most popular fishing lakes in Wisconsin. A bounty of fish resides in the lake, offering anglers year-round enjoyment. In winter, not only are there an abundance of anglers enjoying ice fishing, but also cross-country skiers and snowmobilers frequent the park.

BASICS

Operated By: Wisconsin State Parks. **Open:** All year; some sites subject to closure. **Site Assignment:** Reservations can be made 11 months in advance or as late as 2 days before arrival. **Registration:** At office. **Fee:** Single, $10–$22; group, $40–$140. **Parking:** At site.

FACILITIES

Number of Multipurpose Sites: 58. **Hookups:** Yes. **Each Site:** Fire ring, picnic table. **Dump Station:** No. **Laundry:** No. **Pay Phone:** Yes. **Restrooms and Showers:** Yes. **Fuel:** No. **Propane:** No. **Internal Roads:** Paved. **RV Service:** No. **Market:** No. **Restaurant:** No. **General Store:** No. **Vending:** Less than 1 mi. **Swimming:** Yes. **Playground:** Yes. **Other:** Out-of-state campfire wood is prohibited. Vehicle admission stickers are required. **Activities:** Boating, fishing, hiking, hunting, nature center, picnicking.

RESTRICTIONS

Pets: Pets must be on a leash no longer than 8 ft must be in control at all times. Pets are not allowed in the general picnic areas. **Fires:** Fires are allowed in authorized fireplaces or rings only. Do not leave fires unattended; extinguish all fires before leaving the campsite. Burning of household refuse is prohibited. **Alcoholic Beverages:** People of legal drinking age may bring alcoholic beverages along for their picnic or campsite meals in Wisconsin state parks & forests.

TO GET THERE

Traveling north on I-90/94 from Madison, take Exit 69 (Mauston) and turn west on Hwy. 82. At the stoplight turn north on Hwy. 58. At CR G (12–15 mi.), turn right and go 4 mi. to the park entrance.

NEW GLARUS   MAP, D-2
New Glarus Woods State Park

reserve america

P.O. Box 805, 53574. T: (608) 527-2335; www.reserveamerica.com.

🚐 ★★★★   ⛺ ★★★★

Beauty: ★★★★	Site Privacy: ★★★
Spaciousness: ★★★	Quiet: ★★★★
Security: ★★★★	Cleanliness: ★★★★
Insect Control: ★★★★	Facilities: ★★★

Located in southeast Wisconsin, New Glarus Woods State Park encompasses 350 acres near the Sugar River State Trail. The park's terrain is comprised of a dense ridgeline and valleys where oak, hickory, elm, and black walnut dominate. The understory is a rich blend of botanicals that include ferns, wildflowers, and berry bushes. The undisturbed habitat of New Glarus Woods attracts marvelous bird life. Commonly seen year-round residents include cardinals, woodpeckers, nuthatches, and chickadees. Summer migrants include stunning visuals such as scarlet tanagers, orioles, vireos, red-headed woodpeckers, and several species of thrush. Campers find drive-in or hike-in campsites of quiet solitude. Camping is divided into three sections: family, group, and primitive, yet none of the camp areas offer electric hookups or hot showers. Firewood is available for sale. Sites accommodate small to large RVs. Fourteen primitive campsites are designed for mountain bikers. A popular picnic grove features tables and grills, children's play area, volleyball court, drinking water, and pit toilets. Hiking trails are easily accessed from the picnic grove.

BASICS

Operated By: Wisconsin State Parks. **Open:** All year. **Site Assignment:** Reservations can be made 11 months in advance or as late as 2 days before arrival. **Registration:** At office. **Fee:** Single, $10–$22; group, $40–$140. **Parking:** At site.

FACILITIES

Number of Multipurpose Sites: 38. **Hookups:** Yes. **Dump Station:** No. **Laundry:** No. **Pay Phone:** No. **Restrooms and Showers:** Yes. **Fuel:** No. **Propane:** No. **Internal Roads:** Paved. **RV Service:** No. **Market:** No. **Restaurant:** No. **General Store:** No. **Vending:** No. **Swimming:** No. **Playground:** No. **Other:** Out-of-state campfire wood is prohibited. Vehicle admission stickers are required. **Activities:** Picnicking.

RESTRICTIONS

Pets: On a leash no longer than 8 ft.; under control at all times; not allowed in the general picnic areas. **Fires:** In authorized fireplaces or rings only. Do not leave unattended; extinguish all fires before leaving the campsite. Burning of household refuse is prohibited. **Alcoholic Beverages:** People of legal drinking age may bring alcoholic beverages along for their picnic or campsite meals in Wisconsin state parks & forests.

TO GET THERE

New Glarus Woods State Park is located 1.5 mi. south of New Glarus on Hwy. 69. Turn onto CR NN, and the ranger station is the first building on the right.

NEW LONDON   MAP, C-3
Wolf River Trips and Campground

E8041 CR X, 54961. T: (920) 982-2458; www.wolfrivertrips.com.

🚐 ★★★   ⛺ ★★★

Beauty: ★★★	Site Privacy: ★★★
Spaciousness: ★★★	Quiet: ★★★
Security: ★★★★	Cleanliness: ★★★★
Insect Control: ★★	Facilities: ★★★

Located 5 miles southwest of New London, Wolf River Trips and Campground offers wooded sites along Little Wolf River and rustic sites on Big Wolf River. Tubing trips start at the campground, where a shuttle bus takes tubers to the put-in point on the Wolf River. From there, the river takes tubers through rocks, rapids, and quiet drifting areas back to the campground. The typical site width is 24 feet, and the campground has ten pull-throughs and 20 seasonal campers. The most desirable sites for both RVs and tents are along the river. All sites are either grassy or sand. An on-site lounge serves fast food and drinks. Security measures include one entrance/exit road, owners who live on site, regular patrols, and a 24-hour staffed security phone.

BASICS

Operated By: Mark & Gary Flease & Janet Koplien. **Open:** May 14–Oct. 17. **Site Assignment:** Reservations w/ 1-night deposit; refund (minus $7) w/ 10-day notice; 2-night min. weekends ($27 deposit); 3-night min. holidays ($54 deposit). **Registration:** At campground office. **Fee:** $17–$27; cash, check. **Parking:** At site.

FACILITIES

Number of RV-only Sites: 105. **Number of Tent-only Sites:** 30. **Hookups:** Electric (30, 50 amps), water, sewer. **Each Site:** Picnic table, fire ring. **Dump Station:** Yes. **Laundry:** Yes. **Pay Phone:** No. **Restrooms and Showers:** Yes. **Fuel:** No. **Propane:** No. **Internal Roads:** Paved/gravel, in good condition. **RV Service:** No. **Market:** 5 mi. northeast in New London. **Restaurant:** 5 mi. northeast in New London. **General Store:** Yes, limited. **Vending:** Yes. **Swimming:** No. **Playground:** Yes. **Other:** Wolf River, tennis, ball diamond, volleyball, rec hall, lounge, horseshoes, shuffleboard, pavilion, hiking trails, boat ramp, boat dock. **Activities:** Swimming, fishing, canoeing (rental canoes available), tubing. **Nearby Attractions:** Chapel in the Woods, covered bridges, snowmobile trails, Red Mill, sternwheeler cruises, golf, museums, historic sites, antiques, Wisconsin Veterans Museum. **Additional Information:** Waupaca Area Chamber of Commerce, (888) 417-4040.

RESTRICTIONS

Pets: On leash only. **Fires:** Fire ring only. **Alcoholic Beverages:** Allowed. **Vehicle Maximum Length:** No limit.

TO GET THERE

From the junction of US 45 and Hwy. 54, drive 4 mi. west on Hwy. 54, then 1 mi. south on Larry Rd., then 2 blocks west on CR X. The roads are wide and well maintained, with broad shoulders.

NORMAN — MAP, C-3
Maple View Campground

N1267 Norman Rd., 54216. T: (920) 776-1588.

🚐 ★★★　　　🏕 ★★★

Beauty: ★★★	Site Privacy: ★★★★
Spaciousness: ★★★★	Quiet: ★★★★
Security: ★★★	Cleanliness: ★★★
Insect Control: ★★	Facilities: ★★★

Perched on a high ridge, Maple View Campground is wooded with maple trees, of course. It may be the only campground that makes its own maple syrup from its own maple trees. The syrup is for sale in the camp store. Located 8 miles south of Kewaunee, Maple View has level sites; most are shaded, but some open ones are available for those who worry about satellite TV reception. Laid out in a series of loops, the campground offers four pull-throughs, 35 seasonals, and a typical site width of 36 feet. Most sites have a green buffer of trees and bushes for privacy and quietness. The best RV site is 22, known as the "honeymoon suite," offering a bigger spot and closeness to facilities. But you don't have to be a newlywed to stay there. The best tent sites are in a separate area down by the lake where they offer privacy away from RVs. Facilities are smoke-free. You don't need a license to fish in the private lake, which is stocked with perch, bluegill, and largemouth bass. Quiet time is 11 p.m. to 8 a.m., the speed limit is five mph, and the owners live on site to ensure safety and quietness.

BASICS

Operated By: Joyce LaCrosse. **Open:** May 1–Oct. 15. **Site Assignment:** Reservations w/ 1-night deposit; refund w/ 7-day notice. **Registration:** At campground office. **Fee:** $18; cash, check. **Parking:** At site.

FACILITIES

Number of RV-only Sites: 65. **Number of Tent-only Sites:** 10. **Hookups:** Electric (20, 30, 50 amps), water. **Each Site:** Picnic table, fire ring. **Dump Station:** Yes. **Laundry:** Yes. **Pay Phone:** Yes. **Restrooms and Showers:** Yes. **Fuel:** No. **Propane:** No. **Internal Roads:** Gravel, in good condition. **RV Service:** No. **Market:** 8 mi. north in Kewaunee. **Restaurant:** 8 mi. north in Kewaunee. **General Store:** Yes, limited. **Vending:** Yes. **Swimming:** No. **Playground:** Yes. **Other:** Lake, swimming beach, pavilion, ball diamond, horseshoes, volleyball, basketball, rental cabins, hiking trails, badminton. **Activities:** Swimming, fishing, hiking, boating (no motors), scheduled weekend activities. **Nearby Attractions:** Lake Michigan, boating, charter fishing, harbor, boat launch, cheese factories, antiques, arts & crafts, Door County, zoo, jail museum, golf, nautical museum, nature walk. **Additional Information:** Kewaunee Chamber of Commerce, (800) 666-8214.

RESTRICTIONS

Pets: On leash only. **Fires:** Fire ring only. **Alcoholic Beverages:** Allowed. **Vehicle Maximum Length:** No limit.

TO GET THERE

From the junction of Hwy. 42 and CR G, drive 3 mi. west on CR G, then 500 feet south on Norman Rd. Roads are wide and well maintained, with broad shoulders.

OAKDALE — MAP, C-2
Oakdale KOA

P.O. Box 150, 200 Jay St., 54649.
T: (800) KOA-1737 or (608) 372-5622.

🚐 ★★★★　　　🏕 ★★

Beauty: ★★★	Site Privacy: ★★★
Spaciousness: ★★★	Quiet: ★★
Security: ★★★★	Cleanliness: ★★★★
Insect Control: ★★	Facilities: ★★★★

It's inevitable: Access this convenient (just one block) to the interstate also means a noisy campground with the rumbling of trucks and cars passing by. This is probably more of a distraction for tent campers than RVs. But convenience is what Oakdale KOA has in abundance. Located in the heart of cranberry country, 6 miles southeast of Tomah, the campground is a popular site during the annual Cranberry Festival in September, as well as for bike riders on the nearby state bike trails. The pluses are mature pine and oak trees (with beautiful fall foliage) and mostly pull-through, level sites with water and electric hookups. Shade is abundant, but some trees have been cut for those RVs with satellite dishes. Tent sites with concrete curbing outlining tent placement areas offer dependability for campers.

BASICS

Operated By: William Rood. **Open:** May 12–Oct. 15. **Site Assignment:** Reservations w/ 1-night deposit; refunds w/ 24-hour notice. **Registration:** At campground office. **Fee:** $22–$28; cash, check, credit card. **Parking:** At site.

FACILITIES

Number of RV-only Sites: 47. **Number of Tent-only Sites:** 6. **Hookups:** Electric (20, 30, 50 amps), water, sewer, cable TV, phone, Wi-Fi. **Each Site:** Picnic table, fire ring. **Dump Station:** Yes. **Laundry:** Yes. **Pay Phone:** Yes. **Restrooms and Showers:** Yes. **Fuel:** No. **Propane:** Yes. **Internal Roads:** Gravel, in good condition. **RV Service:** No. **Market:** 6 mi. northwest in Tomah. **Restaurant:** 6 mi. northwest in Tomah. **General Store:** Yes. **Vending:** No. **Swimming:** Yes. **Playground:** Yes. **Other:** Game room, heated & air-conditioned pavilion, horseshoes, volleyball. **Activities:** Swimming, biking. **Nearby Attractions:** State bike trails, cranberry festival & tours, Tomah tractor pull, golf, roller skating. **Additional Information:** Warrens Area Business Assoc., (608) 378-4878.

RESTRICTIONS

Pets: On leash only. **Fires:** Fire pit only. **Alcoholic Beverages:** At sites only. **Vehicle Maximum Length:** No limit.

TO GET THERE

From the junction of I-90/94 and CR PP, take Exit 48, drive 1 block north on CR PP, then 2 blocks east on Woody Dr., 1 block south on Jay St. Roads are well maintained, with broad shoulders.

ONTARIO — MAP, C-2
Wildcat Mountain State Park

reserve america

Box 99, E 13660 Hwy. 33, 54651.
T: (608) 337-4775; www.reserveamerica.com.

🚐 ★★★　　　🏕 ★★★★

Beauty: ★★★★	Site Privacy: ★★★
Spaciousness: ★★	Quiet: ★★★★
Security: ★★★★	Cleanliness: ★★★★
Insect Control: ★★★★	Facilities: ★★

In 1948 Amos Theodore Saunders donated a mere 40 acres of land to the state of Wisconsin for the enjoyment of all its citizens. Today Wildcat Mountain State Park boasts 3,643 acres located on a ridge rising steeply above the meandering Kickapoo River. This picturesque park is open all year and offers many wheelchair-accessible facilities. Wildcat Mountain State Park features several recreation opportunities for the outdoor enthusiast. A trail system accommodates varied users and includes 26 miles for the hiker, 15 miles for the horseback rider, 7 miles to the cross-country skier, and a 1-mile path along a nature trail. The park offers several overnight choices, including a 30-site family campground featuring showers and drinking water during the warmer season. A 24-site campground suits the equestrian, while three large sites accommodate youths and other organized groups. Canoeists will find their own primitive riverside sites. Winter camping is also permitted at the park. A nature center enlightens visitors about their surroundings through exhibits and seasonal programs. An observation point overlooks the Kickapoo Valley. Both picnic and camp areas are handicapped accessible.

BASICS

Operated By: Wisconsin State Parks. **Open:** May 1–Nov. 15. **Site Assignment:** Reservations can be made 11 months in advance or as late as 2 days before arrival. **Registration:** At office. **Fee:** Single, $10–$22; group, $40–$140. **Parking:** At site.

FACILITIES

Number of Multipurpose Sites: 69. **Hookups:** None. **Dump Station:** Yes. **Laundry:** No. **Pay Phone:** Yes. **Restrooms and Showers:** Yes. **Fuel:** No. **Propane:** No. **Internal Roads:** Paved. **RV Service:** No. **Market:** No. **Restaurant:** No. **General Store:** No. **Vending:** No. **Swimming:** No. **Playground:** No. **Other:** Out-of-state campfire wood is prohibited. Vehicle admission stickers are required. **Activities:** Horseback riding, picnicking.

RESTRICTIONS

Pets: On a leash no longer than 8 ft.; under control at all times; not allowed in the general picnic areas. **Fires:** In authorized fireplaces or rings only. Do not leave unattended; extinguish all fires before leaving the campsite. Burning of household refuse is prohibited. **Alcoholic Beverages:** People of legal drinking age may bring alcoholic beverages along for their picnic or campsite meals in Wisconsin state parks & forests.

TO GET THERE

Family campsites are located 3 mi. east of Ontario, off Hwy. 33. Horse campsites are located 1 mi. east of Ontario. Take Taylor Valley Rd. to horse camp. Horse campers please drive directly to horse campsite. Ranger or camp host will take care of you there. *Do not* drive up the hill to the main park office with a trailer loaded with animals.

OSSEO   MAP, C-1
Osseo Camping Resort

50483 Oak Grove Rd., 54758. T: (715) 597-2102.

🚐 ★★★   ⛺ ★★★

Beauty: ★★★★	Site Privacy: ★★★
Spaciousness: ★★★	Quiet: ★★★★
Security: ★★★★	Cleanliness: ★★★
Insect Control: ★★★	Facilities: ★★★

Osseo Camping Resort is a wonderful campground. With a typical site size of 40 by 60 feet, the campground features mostly shaded, level, grassy sites. With one entrance, owners who live on site, and a night patrol, the campground boasts a good safety record. Remote wooded sites also are available for tent campers. The campground is conveniently located near I-90, 1 mile east of Osseo. It is 90 miles from the Wisconsin Dells, 156 miles from Madison, 88 miles from the Minnesota state line, and 125 miles from the Mall of America.

BASICS

Operated By: Tom & Joy Levake. **Open:** Apr. 1–Nov. 1. **Site Assignment:** Reservations w/ 1-night deposit; refunds w/ 1-week notice. **Registration:** At campground office. **Fee:** $29–$36; cash, check, credit card. **Parking:** At site.

FACILITIES

Number of RV-only Sites: 101. **Number of Tent-only Sites:** 8. **Hookups:** Electric (20, 30, 50 amps), water, sewer. **Each Site:** Picnic table, fire ring. **Dump Station:** Yes. **Laundry:** Yes. **Pay Phone:** Yes. **Restrooms and Showers:** Yes. **Fuel:** No. **Propane:** No. **Internal Roads:** Gravel, in good condition. **RV Service:** No. **Market:** 1 mi. west in Osseo. **Restaurant:** 1 mi. west in Osseo. **General Store:** Yes. **Vending:** No. **Swimming:** Yes. **Playground:** Yes. **Other:** Video & TV game room, basketball, volleyball, horseshoes, outdoor stage, community fire ring, mini-golf, nature trails. **Activities:** Swimming, hiking, Sat. hayrides & dances, theme weekends. **Nearby Attractions:** Lakes, Northland Fishing Museum, golf, buffalo farm, hunting, Amish shops & farm tours, casino, antique & craft shops. **Additional Information:** Chippewa Valley CVB, (999) 523-3866.

RESTRICTIONS

Pets: On leash only. **Fires:** Fire ring only. **Alcoholic Beverages:** Allowed. **Vehicle Maximum Length:** No limit.

TO GET THERE

From the junction of I-94 and US 10, take Exit 88, drive 0.25 mi. east on US 10, then 0.25 mi. south on Oak Grove Rd. Roads are wide and well maintained, with broad shoulders.

OXFORD   MAP, C-2
Coon's Deep Lake Campground

348 Fish Ln., 53952. T: (608) 586-5644; www.coonscampground.com.

🚐 ★★★   ⛺ ★★★

Beauty: ★★★	Site Privacy: ★★★
Spaciousness: ★★★	Quiet: ★★★★
Security: ★★★★	Cleanliness: ★★★★
Insect Control: ★★	Facilities: ★★★

Coon's Deep Lake Campground is popular because of its lake for fishing and swimming. Arranged in three layers of terraces, the campground overlooks the lake, which is down the hillside. Sites are grassy, shaded, and level. The campground is surrounded by farm fields and woods, which gives it a quiet setting. Quiet hours are between 10 p.m. and 7 a.m. The best tent sites are in the woods away from RVs. The best available RV sites are 17–22 because they are larger and offer a nice view. There are no pull-through sites. A family-owned campground 3 miles west of Oxford, Coon's Deep Lake Campground is about 15 minutes from the Wisconsin Dells. But given the scarcity of overnight sites, it is recommended that you call ahead for reservations.

BASICS

Operated By: George & Delores Benish. **Open:** May 1–Sept. 15. **Site Assignment:** Reservations w/ 2-night deposit; refund w/ 7-day notice. **Registration:** At campground office. **Fee:** $24; cash, check. **Parking:** At site.

FACILITIES

Number of RV-only Sites: 54. **Number of Tent-only Sites:** 8. **Hookups:** Electric (30, 50 amps), water. **Each Site:** Picnic table, fire ring. **Dump Station:** Yes. **Laundry:** Yes. **Pay Phone:** No. **Restrooms and Showers:** Yes. **Fuel:** No. **Propane:** No. **Internal Roads:** Gravel, in good condition. **RV Service:** No. **Market:** 3 mi. east in Oxford. **Restaurant:** 3 mi. east in Oxford. **General Store:** No. **Vending:** Yes. **Swimming:** No. **Playground:** Yes. **Other:** Deep Lake, swimming beach, rec room, sports field, horseshoes. **Activities:** Swimming, fishing, boating (rental rowboats, canoe, paddleboats available). **Nearby Attractions:** Wisconsin Dells, scenic drives, golf. **Additional Information:** Wisconsin Dells Visitor & Convention Bureau, (800) 223-3557.

RESTRICTIONS

Pets: On leash only. **Fires:** Fire ring only. **Alcoholic Beverages:** Allowed. **Vehicle Maximum Length:** No limit.

TO GET THERE

From the junction of CR A and Hwy. 82, drive 4 mi. west on Hwy. 82, then 1,000 feet north on paved access road. Roads are wide and well maintained, with adequate shoulders.

PITTSVILLE   MAP, C-2
Dexter Park

8200 WI 54, 54466. T: (715) 421-8422.

🚐 ★★★   ⛺ ★★★★

Beauty: ★★★★	Site Privacy: ★★★★
Spaciousness: ★★★★	Quiet: ★★★★
Security: ★★★★	Cleanliness: ★★★
Insect Control: ★★	Facilities: ★★★

Dexter Park is long on scenic beauty and short on man-made amenities. But that is exactly what some campers are seeking. Others should be forewarned that there is no handy laundry for those wet and dirty clothes, no well-stocked camp store for forgotten or used-up items, and no heated swimming pool for when it is too cold to set foot in the lake. Water and sewer hookups for RVs are nonexistent, the electricity is 20 and 30 amps, and the restroom/shower facilities are adequate and passably clean. The beauty, however, is top-rate. The park is located on 1,235 acres around 298-acre Lake Dexter, 5 miles south of Pittsville, and it offers over 1,000 acres of wild or undeveloped land with abundant wildlife and game fish. Internal roads are paved and in excellent condition, and blacktop camp pads are provided on all campsites, most of which are wooded and secluded.

BASICS

Operated By: Wood County. **Open:** May 1–Nov. 30. **Site Assignment:** Reservations cannot be made at campgrounds, must be made by telephone (715) 421-8422 or in person at county office Mon.–Fri., 9 a.m.–3 p.m.; refund (minus $7) w/ 7-day notice; 2-night min. **Registration:** At park ranger station. **Fee:** $14; cash, Wisconsin check; credit card accepted only for reservation. **Parking:** At site.

FACILITIES

Number of RV-only Sites: 69. **Number of Tent-only Sites:** 28. **Hookups:** Electric (20, 30 amps). **Each Site:** Some picnic table, fire ring. **Dump Station:** Yes. **Laundry:** No. **Pay Phone:** No. **Restrooms and Showers:** Yes. **Fuel:** No. **Propane:** No. **Internal Roads:** Paved, in excellent condition. **RV Service:** No. **Market:** 5 mi. north in Pittsville. **Restaurant:** 4 mi. north in Pittsville. **General Store:** No. **Vending:** Yes. **Swimming:** No. **Playground:** Yes. **Other:** Dexter Lake, beach, enclosed shelter, tennis courts, hiking trail, volleyball court, fish-cleaning house, basketball court, boat launch. **Activities:** Swimming, fishing, hiking, boating. **Nearby Attractions:** Hunting, berry picking, all-terrain vehicle areas, speedway, snowmobiling, golf, zoo. **Additional Information:** Wisconsin Rapids Area CVB, (800) 554-4484.

RESTRICTIONS

Pets: On leash only. **Fires:** Fire pit only. **Alcoholic Beverages:** Allowed. **Vehicle Maximum Length:** No limit. **Other:** 2-night min. for weekends, 3-night for holidays.

TO GET THERE

From the junction of Hwys. 80 and 54, drive 0.5 mi. west on 54. Roads are wide and well maintained, with broad shoulders.

RICE LAKE MAP, B-1
Rice Lake–Haugen KOA

1876 29 3/4 Ave., 54868. T: (715) 234-2360 or (800) 562-3460; www.koa.com.

🚐 ★★★★   ▲ ★★★★

Beauty: ★★★★	Site Privacy: ★★★★
Spaciousness: ★★★★	Quiet: ★★★★
Security: ★★★★	Cleanliness: ★★★★
Insect Control: ★★★★	Facilities: ★★★★

Rice Lake–Haugen KOA, located 10 miles north of Rice Lake, offers relief from highway noise. Situated on Upper Devil's Lake, the campground has a nice beach and a dock where campers can fish. There is no charge to fish—a welcome break from campgrounds that charge that extra fee. The most popular camping spots are as close to the lake as possible. The campground has ten seasonal campers, eight pull-through sites, and a typical site width of 30 feet. The semiwooded campground offers level, open, or shaded sites. Security is good—owners keep an eye on the facility and ensure that it is a quiet, family spot.

BASICS

Operated By: Dave & Mary Jo Nelson. **Open:** Apr. 15–Oct. 15. **Site Assignment:** Reservations w/ 1-night deposit; refund (minus $5) w/ 7-day notice. **Registration:** At campground office. **Fee:** $24–$48; cash, check, credit card. **Parking:** At site.

FACILITIES

Number of RV-only Sites: 99. **Number of Tent-only Sites:** 11. **Hookups:** Electric (20, 30, 50 amps), water, sewer. **Each Site:** Picnic table, fire ring. **Dump Station:** Yes. **Laundry:** Yes. **Pay Phone:** Courtesy. **Restrooms and Showers:** Yes. **Fuel:** No. **Propane:** Yes. **Internal Roads:** Gravel, in good condition. **RV Service:** No. **Market:** 2 mi. south in Haugen. **Restaurant:** 2 mi. south in Haugen. **General Store:** Yes, limited. **Vending:** Yes. **Swimming:** Yes. **Playground:** Yes. **Other:** Upper Devil's Lake, beach, horseshoes, volleyball, basketball, game room, hiking trails, biking trails, boat launch, rental cabins, rental cottages, snack bar, sports field. **Activities:** Swimming, fishing, hiking, boating (rental rowboats, canoes, paddleboats available), scheduled activities. **Nearby Attractions:** Golf, stock-car racing, nature preserve, horseback riding, Museum of Woodcarving, Barron County Historical Society Pioneer Village Museum, amusement center, casinos, antiques, cheese factories. **Additional Information:** Rice Lake Area Chamber of Commerce, (800) 523-6318.

RESTRICTIONS

Pets: On leash only. **Fires:** Fire ring only. **Alcoholic Beverages:** Allowed. **Vehicle Maximum Length:** No limit.

TO GET THERE

From the junction of US 53 and Hwy. 48, drive 10 mi. north on Hwy. 53, then 1 mi. east on the campground driveway. Roads are mostly wide and well maintained, with broad shoulders.

SHELL LAKE MAP, B-1
Red Barn Campground

W6820 CR B, 54871. T: (715) 468-2575 or (877) 468-2575; www.redbarncampground.com.

🚐 ★★★   ▲ ★★★

Beauty: ★★★	Site Privacy: ★★★
Spaciousness: ★★★★	Quiet: ★★★★
Security: ★★★★	Cleanliness: ★★★
Insect Control: ★★★	Facilities: ★★★

Many youngsters don't have a grandma and grandpa to visit on the farm. The Red Barn Campground gives them a taste of that farm life. Located 2 miles east of Shell Lake, the Red Barn has rabbits, goats, chickens, horses, and other animals to pet. A rooster's crow greets the break of dawn, and children can gather their own eggs for breakfast. Campers also can pick strawberries in season (late June through early July) in the U-Pick Patch. The campground has 15 seasonal campers, ten pull-through sites, and a typical site width of 30 feet. A grassy, semiwooded facility, the Red Barn offers a choice of open or shaded sites. A separate tent area allows for more green space and privacy. Lake access is available, as are nature trails through the woods and fields.

BASICS

Operated By: Lee & Dotty Swan. **Open:** May 1–Oct. 7. **Site Assignment:** Reservations w/ 1-night deposit; refund w/ 7-day notice. **Registration:** At campground office. **Fee:** $18–$29; cash, check. **Parking:** At site.

FACILITIES

Number of RV-only Sites: 55. **Number of Tent-only Sites:** 15. **Hookups:** Electric (20, 30, 50 amps), water. **Each Site:** Picnic table, fire ring. **Dump Station:** Yes. **Laundry:** No. **Pay Phone:** Yes. **Restrooms and Showers:** Yes. **Fuel:** No. **Propane:** No. **Internal Roads:** Gravel, in good condition. **RV Service:** No. **Market:** 2 mi. west in Shell Lake. **Restaurant:** 2 mi. west in Shell Lake. **General Store:** No. **Vending:** No. **Swimming:** No. **Playground:** Yes. **Other:** Petting zoo, mini-golf, horseshoes, volleyball, basketball, sports field, hiking trails. **Activities:** Hiking, scheduled activities. **Nearby Attractions:** Shell Lake beach, golf, walking tour, historic sites, Railroad Memories Museum, float trip, Wisconsin Great Northern Railroad, Museum of Woodcarving, Indianhead Art Center, fish hatchery. **Additional Information:** Washburn County Tourism Information Center, (800) 367-3306.

RESTRICTIONS

Pets: On leash only. **Fires:** Fire ring only. **Alcoholic Beverages:** Allowed. **Vehicle Maximum Length:** No limit.

TO GET THERE

From center of town, drive 0.5 mi. north on US 63, then 2 mi. east on CR B. Roads are wide and well maintained, with mostly broad shoulders.

SISTER BAY MAP, B-3
Aqualand Camp Resort

P.O. Box 538, 2445 CR Q, 54234. T: (920) 854-4573; www.aqualandcamping.com.

🚐 ★★★   ▲ ★★

Beauty: ★★★★	Site Privacy: ★★★
Spaciousness: ★★★	Quiet: ★★★★
Security: ★★★★	Cleanliness: ★★★★
Insect Control: ★★	Facilities: ★★★

In the heart of scenic Door County, Aqualand Camp Resort is a semiwooded campground with level gravel sites. The campground is occupied by almost all seasonals. Only ten sites are left for overnighters, so reservations are recommended. The typical site width is 40 feet, and the campground has seven pull-throughs. Seasonal campers take good care of their sites, including landscaping and other knick-knacks, which adds to the beauty of the campground. The speed limit is five mph, and quiet times are enforced between 10 p.m. to 8 a.m., requiring absolute quiet, according to campground rules. Just in time to provide supper, rainbow trout fishing is allowed (no license required) between the hours of 2–4 p.m. The campground furnishes the poles and bait and even cleans the fish. You only pay for what you catch at $4 a fish—but you must keep all the fish you catch. Security includes one entrance/exit road, owners who live on site, and regular patrols of the campground.

BASICS

Operated By: Mike & Karen McAndrews. **Open:** May 25–Oct. 15. **Site Assignment:** Reservations w/ 2-night deposit; refund w/ 1-week notice. **Registration:** At campground office. **Fee:** $26; cash, check. **Parking:** At site.

FACILITIES

Number of RV-only Sites: 150. **Hookups:** Electric (30 amps), water. **Each Site:** Picnic table, fire ring. **Dump Station:** Yes. **Laundry:** No. **Pay Phone:** Yes. **Restrooms and Showers:** Yes. **Fuel:** No. **Propane:** No. **Internal Roads:** Gravel, in good condition. **RV Service:** No. **Market:** 2 mi. north in Sister Bay. **Restaurant:** 2 mi. north in Sister Bay. **General Store:** No. **Vending:** No. **Swimming:** Yes. **Playground:** Yes. **Other:** Fish-cleaning station, fish freezer, trout ponds, shuffleboard, sports field, volleyball. **Activities:** Swimming, fishing. **Nearby Attractions:** Door County, cherry & apple orchards, fishing, golf, hiking, boating, Lake Michigan, historic sites, antiques, arts & crafts, parks, bike trails. **Additional Information:** Door County Chamber of Commerce, (800) 527-3529.

RESTRICTIONS

Pets: On leash only. **Fires:** Fire rings only; fires must be extinguished by midnight. **Alcoholic Beverages:** Allowed. **Vehicle Maximum Length:** No limit.

TO GET THERE

From the junction of Hwys. 42 and 57, drive 2.25 mi. south on Hwy. 57, then 0.25 mi. east on CR Q. Roads are wide and well maintained, with broad shoulders.

SPARTA MAP, C-2
Leon Valley Campground

9050 Jancing Ave., 54656. T: (608) 269-6400; www.campleonvalley.net.

🚐 ★★★   ⛺ ★★★★

Beauty: ★★★★	Site Privacy: ★★★★
Spaciousness: ★★★	Quiet: ★★★★
Security: ★★★★	Cleanliness: ★★★★★
Insect Control: ★★	Facilities: ★★★

Leon Valley is out in the middle of nowhere, a valley surrounded by trees and hills. It's a great location for a peaceful, scenic campground. An attractive entranceway has an old wagon wheel, shrubs, and bushes. Thirty of the 105 RV sites are taken by seasonals. Sites are grassy with gravel pads for RVs, mostly shady, and level. Laid out in a series of loops, the campground offers a wilderness setting with 12 pull-through sites and an average site of 27 by 50 feet. The best RV sites are in the A 40 section near the playground and bathrooms. Tent sites are spread out in the campground, including some secluded areas. The best tent sites are B 1–37 because they are more wooded and away from people. Security measures are good since the owners live on site, have a regular patrol, and lock up the entrance gate at midnight.

BASICS

Operated By: Bernard & JoAnn Waege. **Open:** Apr. 1–Nov. 30. **Site Assignment:** Reservations w/ 1-night deposit; refund w/ 7-day notice, 14-day notice for holidays; 2-night min. weekends, 3-night min. holidays. **Registration:** At campground office. **Fee:** $22–$28; cash, check, credit card. **Parking:** At site.

FACILITIES

Number of RV-only Sites: 105. **Number of Tent-only Sites:** 20. **Hookups:** Electric (20, 30, 50 amps), water. **Each Site:** Picnic table, fire ring. **Dump Station:** Yes. **Laundry:** No. **Pay Phone:** Yes. **Restrooms and Showers:** Yes. **Fuel:** No. **Propane:** No. **Internal Roads:** Gravel, in good condition. **RV Service:** No. **Market:** 4 mi. north in Sparta. **Restaurant:** 4 mi. north in Sparta. **General Store:** Yes. **Vending:** Yes. **Swimming:** Yes. **Playground:** Yes. **Other:** Basketball, volleyball, pavilion, horseshoes, snack bar, game room, hiking trail, sports field. **Activities:** Swimming, hiking. **Nearby Attractions:** Fort McCoy, 32-mile bike trail, fishing, boating, hunting, horseback riding, canoeing, specialty shops, museums, craft mall, tennis, trap shooting, 2 self-guided historical walking tours. **Additional Information:** Sparta Tourism Bureau, (800) 354-BIKE.

RESTRICTIONS

Pets: On leash only. **Fires:** Fire ring only. **Alcoholic Beverages:** Allowed. **Vehicle Maximum Length:** No limit.

TO GET THERE

From the junction of I-90 and Hwy. 27, drive 4 mi. south on Hwy. 27, then 1.25 mi. east on Jancing Ave. Roads are wide and well maintained, with broad shoulders (except for the paved access road, which has little shoulder room). The road also takes a couple of whopping big turns on the way in.

SPOONER MAP, B-1
Scenic View Campground

24560 Scenic View Ln., 54801. T: (715) 468-2510; www.scenicviewcampground.com.

🚐 ★★★   ⛺ ★★★★

Beauty: ★★★★	Site Privacy: ★★★
Spaciousness: ★★★	Quiet: ★★★
Security: ★★★	Cleanliness: ★★★
Insect Control: ★★★	Facilities: ★★★

Activities revolve around Poquette Lake at Scenic View Campground, located 9 miles west of Spooner. Laid out in a series of loops, the campground has 20 seasonal campers and two pull-through sites. The best sites for tent campers are Areas 5 and 6, which offer more privacy and green space. Sites 5 and 6 offer no water or electric hookups, but water is handy nearby. The best RV sites are in Area 1, which features shaded, level spots overlooking the beautiful 100-acre lake. The sites are also near the beach and the main building that houses the bar and bathrooms. RVers who are camping with friends and might want several sites together would probably prefer Area 2, which is west of the main building and has sites with greater depth. Fed with clean, sparkling water, Poquette Lake is ideal for swimming and water sports. It has a sandy beach, swimming raft, and roped-off area for small children. The lake is brimming with bass, walleye, northern pike, and panfish. Check out the 11-pound pike caught in the lake and now hanging on a wall in the bar. Security measures include one way in and out.

BASICS

Operated By: Carol Haseltine. **Open:** May 1–Oct. 10. **Site Assignment:** Reservations w/ 1-night deposit; refund (minus $5) w/ 2-week notice. **Registration:** At campground office. **Fee:** $20–$30; cash. **Parking:** At site.

FACILITIES

Number of RV-only Sites: 40. **Number of Tent-only Sites:** 5. **Hookups:** Electric (30 amps), water. **Each Site:** Picnic table, fire ring. **Dump Station:** Yes. **Laundry:** No. **Pay Phone:** No. **Restrooms and Showers:** Yes. **Fuel:** No. **Propane:** No. **Internal Roads:** Gravel, in good condition. **RV Service:** No. **Market:** 9 mi. east in Spooner. **Restaurant:** 9 mi. east in Spooner. **General Store:** No. **Vending:** No. **Swimming:** Yes. **Playground:** Yes. **Other:** Swimming beach, pavilion, lounge, boat ramp, boat dock, horseshoes, volleyball, basketball, rec hall, game room rental campers, fishing lake, badminton, hiking trails. **Activities:** Swimming, fishing, hiking, boating (rental rowboats, paddleboats, motorboats available). **Nearby Attractions:** Golf, casinos, supper clubs, walking tour, historic sites, Wisconsin Great Northern Railroad, Railroad Memories Museum, fish hatchery, Indianhead Art Center, snowmobile trails, horseback riding. **Additional Information:** Burnett County Tourism Office, (800) 788-3164.

RESTRICTIONS

Pets: On leash only. **Fires:** Fire ring only. **Alcoholic Beverages:** Allowed. **Vehicle Maximum Length:** No limit.

TO GET THERE

From the junction of US 63 and Hwy. 70, drive 9.25 mi. west on Hwy. 70, then 0.5 mi. south on Scenic View Ln. Hwy. 70 is mostly wide and well maintained, with broad shoulders. Scenic View Lane has narrow shoulders in spots.

ST. GERMAIN MAP, B-2
Lynn Ann's Campground

P.O. Box 8, 54558. T: (715) 542-3456; www.lynnannscampground.com.

🚐 ★★★   ⛺ ★★★

Beauty: ★★★	Site Privacy: ★★★
Spaciousness: ★★★	Quiet: ★★★
Security: ★★★	Cleanliness: ★★★★
Insect Control: ★★★	Facilities: ★★★★

Located on Big St. Germain Lake in St. Germain, Lynn Ann's Campground offers open and wooded sites. The facility has ten seasonal campers, one pull-through site, and a typical site width of 36 feet. Laid out in a series of loops, campsites are level and grassy. The campground offers a variety of water activities and rents boats and other water equipment. The lake is a popular fishing spot for muskies, walleye, bass, northerns, and panfish. No glass, bottles, or cans are permitted near the beach or water. To ensure a neat appearance, the campground requires that campsites be cleaned daily. Ceramic-tiled showers are a nice touch, but the showers are coin-operated. Owners keep a close watch on the campground for security measures.

BASICS

Operated By: Mike & Heather Davidson. **Open:** May 5–Oct. 10. **Site Assignment:** Reservations w/ 1-night deposit; refund w/ 15-day notice. **Registration:** At campground office. **Fee:** $24.50–$27.50; cash, check, credit card. **Parking:** At site.

FACILITIES

Number of RV-only Sites: 40. **Number of Tent-only Sites:** 50. **Hookups:** Electric (30 amps), water, sewer, Internet, cable TV. **Each Site:** Picnic table, fire ring. **Dump Station:** Yes. **Laundry:** Yes. **Pay Phone:** Yes. **Restrooms and Showers:** Yes. **Fuel:** Yes. **Propane:** Yes. **Internal Roads:** Gravel, in good condition. **RV Service:** No. **Market:** 3 mi. south. **Restaurant:** 3 mi. south. **General Store:** Yes. **Vending:** Yes. **Swimming:** No. **Playground:** Yes. **Other:** Sandy beach, game room, hiking trails, horseshoes, volleyball, basketball, shuffleboard, boat launch, boat harbor, marina, rental trailers. **Activities:** Swimming, fishing, hiking, boating (rental pontoons, kayaks, wave runners, tubes, motor boats, sailboats, waterskis, canoes available). **Nearby Attractions:** Golf, casino, tennis, historic sites, national forest, museums, snowmobile trails, antiques, arts & crafts. **Additional Information:** St. Germain Chamber of Commerce, (800) 727-7203.

RESTRICTIONS

Pets: On leash only. **Fires:** Fire ring only. **Alcoholic Beverages:** Allowed. **Vehicle Maximum Length:** No limit. **Other:** No oversized tents; trailers must provide drain containers.

TO GET THERE

From the junction of Hwy. 70 and Hwy. 155, drive 2 mi. west on Hwy. 70, then 0.5 mi. north on Normandy Court, then 0.25 mi. east on South Shore Dr. Roads are mostly wide and well maintained, with broad shoulders.

STEVENS POINT   MAP, C-2
Rivers Edge Campground

3368 Campsite Dr., 54481. T: (715) 344-8058.

🚐 ★★★   ⛺ ★★★

Beauty: ★★★★	Site Privacy: ★★★
Spaciousness: ★★★	Quiet: ★★★
Security: ★★★★	Cleanliness: ★★★★
Insect Control: ★★	Facilities: ★★

With 12 miles of frontage on the beautiful Wisconsin River, Rivers Edge Campground has a head start on appealing to campers. The river is known for its good fishing and boating. The campground, located 7 miles north of Stevens Point, offers waterfront or wooded campsites featuring a tree buffer to muffle highway noise. Easy access off I-51 and well-maintained connecting roads also give the campground an edge. Rivers Edge could really use a laundry and general store for the convenience of its campers and seasonal residents. Security gets high marks because the campground has one entrance, the manager lives on site, access to the fenced swimming pool is only through the office, and the grounds are patrolled. In addition, there are two rules that are strictly enforced: a speed limit of five mph (or violators will be asked to leave) and a 10 p.m. quiet time on weekdays (11 p.m. on Fridays and Saturdays).

BASICS

Operated By: Jerry Fahrner. **Open:** May 1–Oct. 7. **Site Assignment:** No reservations; full deposit in advance for holiday weekends. **Registration:** At campground office. **Fee:** $26; cash, check. **Parking:** At site.

FACILITIES

Number of RV-only Sites: 108. **Number of Tent-only Sites:** 6. **Hookups:** Electric (20, 30, 50 amps), water. **Each Site:** Picnic table, fire ring. **Dump Station:** Yes. **Laundry:** No. **Pay Phone:** Yes. **Restrooms and Showers:** Yes. **Fuel:** No. **Propane:** Yes. **Internal Roads:** Gravel, in good condition. **RV Service:** No. **Market:** 7 mi. south in Stevens Point. **Restaurant:** Next door. **General Store:** No. **Vending:** Yes. **Swimming:** Yes. **Playground:** Yes. **Other:** Boat launch, boat docks, rec hall w/ game room, sandy beach, volleyball courts, horseshoes. **Activities:** Swimming, fishing, boating, waterskiing, planned weekend activities. **Nearby Attractions:** 4 public golf courses w/in 25-mi. radius, Cedar Creek Manufacturer's Direct Mall, Rainbow Falls Water Park, Rib Mountain, Grotto Shrine, Mead Wildlife Refuge. **Additional Information:** Stevens Point Area CVB, (800) 236-4626.

RESTRICTIONS

Pets: On leash only. **Fires:** Fire pit only. **Alcoholic Beverages:** Allowed. **Vehicle Maximum Length:** 40 ft. **Other:** 3-day min. on holiday weekends.

TO GET THERE

From Exit 165 on US 51 northbound, drive 0.4 mi. east on CR X, 20.5 mi. north on Sunset Dr., 0.5 mi. west on Maple Dr., 0.25 mi. north on Campsite Dr. Roads are wide and well maintained, with good shoulders.

STOUGHTON   MAP, D-2
Lake Kegonsa State Park

reserve america

2405 Door Creek Rd., 53589. T: (608) 873-9695; www.reserveamerica.com.

🚐 ★★★★   ⛺ ★★★★

Beauty: ★★★★	Site Privacy: ★★★
Spaciousness: ★★★	Quiet: ★★★★
Security: ★★★★	Cleanliness: ★★★★
Insect Control: ★★★★	Facilities: ★★★★

Lake Kegonsa State Park encompasses 342 acres of land accentuated by 3,209 acres of water. Once inhabited by the ancient Effigy Mound Builders, evidence of their efforts is still visible along the White Oak Nature Trail. Wildlife habitats at the park vary from white oak woodlands to prairie restoration to pine plantation, including virgin timber. Much of the Lake Kegonsa State Park activities evolve around the 3,029-acre lake. Good populations of walleye, pike, muskie, and pan fish exist. Two launches give access to anglers, boaters, and water-skiers. Camping at the state park includes 80 rustic sites located under large shade trees. Modern amenities and firewood are for sale during the warmer months. Three tent group sites accommodate groups as large as 20 persons. Amenities at the group sites include water, horseshoe pits, picnic shelter, and vault toilets. A trail connects the campground to the swimmer's beach. Day-use areas are scattered throughout the park. Two reservable picnic shelters, play areas, and easy-to-moderate trails are found at most sites. The beach area features picnic tables and grills, a changing area, outdoor showers, a drink machine, and a pay telephone. Visitors may borrow horseshoes, volleyballs, and children's fishing poles. Four miles of earthen path explore white oak woodlands, prairie restoration tract, and pine forests. One of the most visited trails is the White Oak Nature Trail, which leads to ancient effigies. The interpretive trail informs visitors about the park's habitats. Park roads are great for in-line skating and hiking. Over 5 miles of trail is groomed for winter cross-country skiing.

BASICS

Operated By: Wisconsin State Parks. **Open:** May 1–Oct. 31. **Site Assignment:** Reservations can be made 11 months in advance or as late as 2 days before arrival. **Registration:** At office. **Fee:** Single, $10–$22; group, $40–$140. **Parking:** At site.

FACILITIES

Number of Multipurpose Sites: 83. **Hookups:** Yes. **Each Site:** Fire ring, picnic table. **Dump Station:** Yes. **Laundry:** No. **Pay Phone:** No. **Restrooms and Showers:** Yes. **Fuel:** No. **Propane:** No. **Internal Roads:** Paved. **RV Service:**

No. **Market:** No. **Restaurant:** No. **General Store:** No. **Vending:** No. **Swimming:** Yes. **Playground:** Yes. **Other:** Out-of-state campfire wood is prohibited. Vehicle admission stickers are required. **Activities:** Boating, fishing, hiking, picnicking.

RESTRICTIONS

Pets: Has a pet beach (swim) area. Pets must be on leash unless they are in the water. Normally the beach has a pier to teach pets to jump into the water, but due to high water levels the pier is out. **Fires:** In authorized fireplaces or rings only. Do not leave unattended; extinguish all fires before leaving the campsite. Burning of household refuse is prohibited. **Alcoholic Beverages:** People of legal drinking age may bring alcoholic beverages along for their picnic or campsite meals in Wisconsin state parks & forests.

TO GET THERE

Exit I-90 at Exit 147, Hwy. N. Go south on Hwy. N, then turn west on Koshkonong Rd., turn south on Door Creek Rd. It is 4 mi. from the freeway exit to the park. There are signs to direct you at every intersection.

STURGEON BAY   MAP, C-3
Field Campground

Potawatomi State Park, 3740 CR PD, 54235. T: (920) 746-2890 or (888) 947-2757.

🚐 ★★★★   ⛺ ★★★★

Beauty: ★★★★	Site Privacy: ★★★
Spaciousness: ★★★	Quiet: ★★★★
Security: ★★★★	Cleanliness: ★★★★
Insect Control: ★★	Facilities: ★★★

Natural beauty is the basic asset of Potawatomi State Park. Located only a few miles from Sturgeon Bay on the Wisconsin Door County peninsula, the park consists of 1,200 acres of flat to gently rolling upland terrain bordered by steep slopes and rugged limestone cliffs along Sturgeon Bay. Laid out in a series of loops, campsites are level and mostly shaded, with two pull-through sites. The park also offers two camping options for people with accessibility limitations. Two accessible campsites are located in the south campground adjacent to the toilet/shower building. In addition, the Cabin by the Bay is a fully accessible indoor facility that can be reserved by people who are unable to use the more traditional campsites. The biggest drawback of the park and campground is lack of swimming facilities. Since there is not a sandy beach, swimming is not recommended. However, park staff will direct campers to the nearest public beach. The restroom facilities are cleaner than most state facilities, and the campground has excellent security, including one entrance/exit road past the ranger station, along with regular campground patrols by rangers.

BASICS

Operated By: State of Wisconsin. **Open:** All year. **Site Assignment:** Reservations w/ full deposit (2-night min.); refund (minus $9.50) w/ 2-day notice. **Registration:** At campground office. **Fee:** $10; cash, check, credit card; plus $7 daily park fee or $25 annual fee if Wisconsin resident; $12 daily fee plus

$10 daily park fee or $35 annual fee if not Wisconsin resident. **Parking:** At site.

FACILITIES

Number of RV-only Sites: 25. **Number of Tent-only Sites:** 98. **Hookups:** Electric (20, 30 amps). **Each Site:** Picnic table, fire ring. **Dump Station:** Yes. **Laundry:** No. **Pay Phone:** Yes. **Restrooms and Showers:** Yes. **Fuel:** No. **Propane:** No. **Internal Roads:** Paved, in good condition. **RV Service:** No. **Market:** 3 mi. northeast in Sturgeon Bay. **Restaurant:** 3 mi. northeast in Sturgeon Bay. **General Store:** Yes, limited. **Vending:** No. **Swimming:** No. **Playground:** Yes. **Other:** Sturgeon Bay, fishing lake, hiking trails, boat launch, observation tower, nature center, bike trails, pavilion, boat dock. **Activities:** Fishing, hiking, biking, boating, scheduled activities. **Nearby Attractions:** Lake Michigan, hiking trails, biking trails, fishing, Door County, golf, antiques, arts & crafts, historic sites, swimming. **Additional Information:** Door County Chamber of Commerce, (800) 527-3529.

RESTRICTIONS

Pets: Leash only, some areas are pet free. **Fires:** Fire ring only. **Alcoholic Beverages:** Allowed. **Vehicle Maximum Length:** No limit. **Other:** 21-day stay limit.

TO GET THERE

From Sturgeon Bay, drive 1.5 mi. west on CR C, then 2 mi. north on park road. Roads are wide and well maintained, with mostly broad shoulders.

STURGEON BAY　　MAP, C-3
Monument Point Camping

5718 West Monument Point Rd., 54235.
T: (920) 743-9411.

🚐 ★★★　　　🅰 ★★★★

Beauty: ★★★	Site Privacy: ★★★★
Spaciousness: ★★★★	Quiet: ★★★★
Security: ★★★★	Cleanliness: ★★★★
Insect Control: ★★	Facilities: ★★★

Located 5 miles south of Egg Harbor, Monument Point Camping offers secluded, wooded spots in the Door County area. Sites are level and surrounded by green space for little private nooks. Tall trees, shrubs, and other greenery help buffer noise and add to privacy. Laid out in a series of loops, the campground features gravel RV pads and dirt tent pads. The typical site width is 50 feet, with five pull-throughs and 24 seasonal campers. The biggest drawbacks include no water hookups, pool, or laundry, but the tradeoff might be worth it for the serenity of the camping site. The speed limit is five mph, with quiet hours from 10:30 p.m. to 8 a.m. Security measures include one entrance/exit, one-way roads, owners who live on site, and regular patrols of the campground.

BASICS

Operated By: Doug & Debbie Krauel. **Open:** May 1–Oct. 15. **Site Assignment:** Reservations w/ $10 deposit; refunds (minus $5) w/ 7-day notice. **Registration:** At campground office. **Fee:** $24; cash, check. **Parking:** At site.

FACILITIES

Number of RV-only Sites: 76. **Number of Tent-only Sites:** 9. **Hookups:** Electric (30 amps). **Each Site:** Picnic table, fire ring. **Dump Station:** Yes. **Laundry:** No. **Pay Phone:** No. **Restrooms and Showers:** Yes. **Fuel:** No. **Propane:** No. **Internal Roads:** Gravel, in good condition. **RV Service:** No. **Market:** 5 mi. north in Egg Harbor. **Restaurant:** 5 mi. north in Egg Harbor. **General Store:** Yes, limited. **Vending:** Yes. **Swimming:** No. **Playground:** Yes. **Other:** Game room, volleyball, horseshoes, recreation field, badminton, hiking trails. **Activities:** Hiking. **Nearby Attractions:** Door County, cherry & apple orchards, fishing, golf, hiking, boating, swimming, Lake Michigan, historic sites, antiques, arts & crafts, parks, Green Bay. **Additional Information:** Door County Chamber of Commerce, (800) 527-3529.

RESTRICTIONS

Pets: On leash only. **Fires:** Fire ring only. **Alcoholic Beverages:** Allowed. **Vehicle Maximum Length:** 40 ft.

TO GET THERE

From north junction of Hwys. 42 and 57 near Sturgeon Bay, drive 8 mi. north on Hwy. 42, then 1.25 mi. northwest on Monument Point Rd. Roads are wide and well maintained, with broad shoulders.

STURGEON BAY　　MAP, C-3
Potawatomi State Park

reserve america

3740 CR PD, 54235. T: (920) 746-2890;
www.reserveamerica.com.

🚐 ★★★　　　🅰 ★★★★

Beauty: ★★★★	Site Privacy: ★★★
Spaciousness: ★★★	Quiet: ★★★★
Security: ★★★★	Cleanliness: ★★★★
Insect Control: ★★★★	Facilities: ★★★★

Potawatomi State Park is comprised of 1,127 forested acres that jut out into the sparkling Sturgeon Bay. Sitting atop the Niagara Escarpment, a limestone ledge that forms the spine of Door County, the park is characterized by flat to gently rolling land imprinted with granite boulders and rugged cliffs. A 75-foot lookout tower offers views that on a clear day reach 16 miles across Green Bay to Menomonee, Michigan, and Chambers Island, 20 miles to the northeast. From its forested trails, hikers can enjoy expansive views of the bay and geological features. The land is densely forested in pine and hardwoods, providing habitat for white-tailed deer, porcupine, foxes, raccoon, and 200 bird species of which 50 are nesting birds. This linear park is named for the peaceful Native American tribe, the Potawatomi. Two camping areas offer 125 sites, 25 of which have electric hookup. Flush toilets, hot showers, picnic tables, fire rings, and several wheelchair-accessible sites round out the offerings. Sites are located in both sun and shade. The park does have a wheelchair-accessible cabin. Winter camping is available. This 1,225-acre park offers trails for hiking (9 miles), mountain biking (8 miles),

skiing (8.5 miles, groomed and tracked, some for skate skiing), and snowmobiling (8.3 miles).

BASICS

Operated By: Wisconsin State Parks. **Open:** Apr. 1–Nov. 30. **Site Assignment:** Reservations can be made 11 months in advance or as late as 2 days before arrival. **Registration:** At office. **Fee:** Single, $10–$22; group, $40–$140. **Parking:** At site.

FACILITIES

Number of Multipurpose Sites: 123. **Hookups:** Yes. **Dump Station:** Yes. **Laundry:** No. **Pay Phone:** Yes. **Restrooms and Showers:** Yes. **Fuel:** No. **Propane:** No. **Internal Roads:** Paved. **RV Service:** No. **Market:** No. **Restaurant:** No. **General Store:** No. **Vending:** No. **Swimming:** No. **Playground:** Yes. **Other:** Out-of-state campfire wood is prohibited. Vehicle admission stickers are required. **Activities:** Boating, fishing, picnicking.

RESTRICTIONS

Pets: On a leash no longer than 8 ft.; under control at all times; not allowed in the general picnic areas. **Fires:** In authorized fireplaces or rings only. Do not leave unattended; extinguish all fires before leaving the campsite. Burning of household refuse is prohibited. **Alcoholic Beverages:** People of legal drinking age may bring alcoholic beverages along for their picnic or campsite meals in Wisconsin state parks & forests.

TO GET THERE

From I-43 in Green Bay, take Hwy. 57N to Door County. Turn left on CR PD and follow 2.5 mi. to the park entrance.

STURGEON BAY　　MAP, C-3
Yogi Bear's Jellystone Park Camp-Resort of Door County

reserve america

3677 May Rd., 54235. T: (920) 743-9001;
www.doorcountyjellystone.com.

🚐 ★★★★　　　🅰 ★★★★

Beauty: ★★★★	Site Privacy: ★★★★
Spaciousness: ★★★★	Quiet: ★★★★
Security: ★★★★	Cleanliness: ★★★★
Insect Control: ★★★★	Facilities: ★★★★

Enjoy camping in Door County with numerous amenities and activities tailored for a wonderful family camping experience. Come take advantage of the quiet outdoors and all of the nearby benefits of Door County and the waters of Green Bay and Lake Michigan. Whether you are an RV park enthusiast, enjoy the comfort of a cabin in the woods, or just like to tent camp and sleep in the great outdoors, Jellystone Park offers something for everyone. From swimming, mini-golf, hay rides, tennis, and volleyball to fishing, hiking, and of course appearances from Yogi Bear and friends, you'll notice that family fun is the main attraction.

BASICS

Operated By: Jim & Jill Kavicky. **Open:** May–Sept. **Site Assignment:** First come, first served;

reservations recommended; deposits taken at time of reservation; see Web site for cancellation policy. **Registration:** At ranger station 9 a.m.–9 p.m. in season; register next day for late arrivals. **Fee:** Electric/water (Sun. & weekdays), $29; (Fri. & Sat.), $32; (holidays), $35; for 2 people; extra adult per night, $15; extra child per night, $1; sewer per night, $5. **Parking:** Limit 2 cars per site; extra fee for second car, $2; free overflow parking available.

FACILITIES

Number of Multipurpose Sites: 270. **Hookups:** Electric (30, 50 amps), water, sewer (17 sites), 4 sites w/ 50 amp. **Each Site:** Electric, water, picnic table, fire pit. **Dump Station:** Yes. **Laundry:** Yes. **Pay Phone:** Yes. **Restrooms and Showers:** Yes. **Fuel:** No. **Propane:** No. **Internal Roads:** Mix of paved, gravel. **RV Service:** No. **Market:** 9 mi. east to Sturgeon Bay. **Restaurant:** 9 mi. east to Sturgeon Bay. **General Store:** Yes. **Vending:** Yes. **Swimming:** 3 on-site pools; beach swimming w/in 0.33 mi. **Playground:** Yes (3). **Other:** Yogi Bear™ Theater & Goodie Shoppe. **Activities:** Mini-golf, 3 playgrounds, basketball, horseshoes, soccer, softball, shuffleboard, funnel ball, volleyball, tetherball. **Nearby Attractions:** Golf, shopping, fishing, boat launch, beach swimming. **Additional Information:** Door County Chamber of Commerce, (www.door-county.com).

RESTRICTIONS

Pets: On leash & attended only. **Fires:** Allowed; out by 1 a.m. **Alcoholic Beverages:** Responsible consumption allowed. **Vehicle Maximum Length:** 45 ft.

TO GET THERE

From Hwy. 57 N, take CR MM north to CR C and follow Yogi Bear signs. From Hwy. 42 N, take CR MM north to CR C and follow signs.

TOMAHAWK   MAP, B-2
The Out-Post Campground

9507 CR N, 54487. T: (715) 453-3468.

🚐 ★★★   ⛺ ★★★

Beauty: ★★★	Site Privacy: ★★★
Spaciousness: ★★★	Quiet: ★★★
Security: ★★★	Cleanliness: ★★★
Insect Control: ★★★	Facilities: ★★★

Located on Deer Lake and Lake Nokomis 3 miles west of Tomahawk, The Out-Post Campground features a wide array of water activities. Sites are level and mostly shaded. The campground has 30 seasonal campers, 31 pull-through sites, and a typical site width of 30 feet. A separate area for tents offers more green space and privacy. The wooded campground offers plenty of hot water in its free showers. A rental housekeeping cottage is available year-round for winter enthusiasts. A concrete launching pad offers easy access to the water. Folks say fishing is good in the area, and swimmers like the sandy beach. The most popular sites are closest to the water. Security measures include a traffic-control gate.

BASICS

Operated By: Lou & Kitty Miller. **Open:** Apr. 15–Oct. 15. **Site Assignment:** Reservations w/ 1-night deposit; refund w/ 2-week notice. **Registra-**

tion: At campground office. **Fee:** $33; cash & check. **Parking:** At site.

FACILITIES

Number of RV-only Sites: 230. **Number of Tent-only Sites:** 40. **Hookups:** Electric (20, 30, 50 amps), water, sewer. **Each Site:** Picnic table, fire ring. **Dump Station:** Yes. **Laundry:** Yes. **Pay Phone:** Yes. **Restrooms and Showers:** Yes. **Fuel:** No. **Propane:** Yes. **Internal Roads:** Gravel, in fair condition. **RV Service:** No. **Market:** 3 mi. east in Tomahawk. **Restaurant:** 3 mi. east in Tomahawk. **General Store:** Yes, limited. **Vending:** Yes. **Swimming:** No. **Playground:** Yes. **Other:** Snack bar, swimming beach, Lake Nokomis, Deer Lake, marina, horseshoes, volleyball, basketball, shuffleboard, rec hall, lounge, game room, boat launch, hiking trail, bar. **Activities:** Swimming, fishing, boating (rental paddleboats, canoes, motorboats, rowboats available). **Nearby Attractions:** Golf, local park, Hiawatha Bike Trail, snowmobiling, antiques, arts & crafts, waterski shows, cross-country skiing, ice fishing. **Additional Information:** Tomahawk Regional Chamber of Commerce, (800) 569-2160.

RESTRICTIONS

Pets: On leash only. **Fires:** Fire ring only. **Alcoholic Beverages:** Allowed. **Vehicle Maximum Length:** No limit.

TO GET THERE

From the junction of US 51 and US 8 West, drive 3 mi. west on US 8, then 0.25 mi. north on CR L, then 1 mi. east on CR N. Roads are mostly wide and well maintained, with adequate shoulders.

WARRENS   MAP, C-2
Yogi Bear's Jellystone Park Camp-Resort

CR EW Box 67, 1500 Jellystone Park Dr., 54666. T: (888) FUN-YOGI; www.jellystonewarrens.com.

🚐 ★★★★★   ⛺ ★★★★

Beauty: ★★★★	Site Privacy: ★★★★
Spaciousness: ★★★★	Quiet: ★★★★
Security: ★★★★★	Cleanliness: ★★★★★
Insect Control: ★★	Facilities: ★★★★★

Ask a child to design the perfect campground, and this might be the result. Yogi Bear's Jellystone Park Camp-Resort is a children's wonderland. With a full-time summer activity director, the campground offers a huge smorgasbord of activities, handy snack bars, heated swimming pools, and a lake with a big sandy beach. Fifty pull-through sites (35 by 65 feet) and back-ins (40 by 50 feet) offer easy access and a fair amount of privacy. Arranged in a series of loops, the nicely landscaped campground features mostly shady, grassy sites. One entrance to the campground and a security patrol help keep the campground safe and quiet. For such a popular family facility with a large number of children, the campground is surprisingly peaceful, mainly because most of the play areas are located in a clump away from the campsites.

BASICS

Operated By: Ed Van Der Molen. **Open:** All-year. **Site Assignment:** Reservations w/ full deposit;

refunds (minus $25) w/ 14-day notice; 2-night min., 3-night min. on holidays. **Registration:** At campground office. **Fee:** $40–$60; cash, check, credit card. **Parking:** At site.

FACILITIES

Number of RV-only Sites: 560. **Number of Tent-only Sites:** 30. **Hookups:** Electric (30, 50 amps), water, sewer, Wi-Fi. **Each Site:** Picnic table, fire ring. **Dump Station:** Yes. **Laundry:** Yes. **Pay Phone:** Yes. **Restrooms and Showers:** Yes. **Fuel:** Yes. **Propane:** Yes. **Internal Roads:** Paved, in good condition. **RV Service:** No. **Market:** 8 mi. south in Tomah. **Restaurant:** In campground. **General Store:** Yes. **Vending:** Yes. **Swimming:** Yes. **Playground:** Yes. **Other:** 400-ft. waterslide, adventure golf, mini-golf, game room, Yogi's playroom, sand volleyball court, shuffleboard, horseshoes, pavilions, basketball, tennis, baseball, bandstand. **Activities:** Swimming, paddleboat rental, a full-time activity director w/ over 100 activities offered weekly. **Nearby Attractions:** Cranberry festival, cranberry bog tours, Amish country, antique shops, art galleries, golf, casino. **Additional Information:** Tomah CVB, (800) 04-TOMAH.

RESTRICTIONS

Pets: On leash only. **Fires:** Fire pit only. **Alcoholic Beverages:** Allowed. **Vehicle Maximum Length:** 45 ft.

TO GET THERE

From the junction of I-94 and CR E, take Exit 135 and drive 0.5 mi. east on CR EW.

WASHINGTON ISLAND   MAP, B-3
Rock Island State Park

reserve america

1924 Indian Point Rd., 54246-9728. T: (920) 847-2235; www.reserveamerica.com.

🚐 n/a   ⛺ ★★★★

Beauty: ★★★	Site Privacy: ★★★
Spaciousness: ★★★	Quiet: ★★★★
Security: ★★★★	Cleanliness: ★★★★
Insect Control: ★★★★	Facilities: ★★★★

Wealthy inventor, Chester Thordarson, owned the island between 1910 and 1945. He developed 30 acres, including Viking Hall, a massive stone building that today houses exhibits. This quiet, remote island is known for the primitive camping opportunities, 10 miles of wooded trails, fabulous Green Bay and Lake Michigan views, 120 bird species, three cemeteries, and Wisconsin's oldest lighthouse, Potawatomi Lighthouse. The lighthouse was originally constructed in 1836 and then replaced in 1858. The island's wildlife consists of white-tailed deer, coyote, muskrat, and perhaps bear. Having supported a population up to 200 residents, Rock Island became a state park in 1965. Cars and even bikes are not allowed on 912-acre Rock Island, making for an experience unlike any other Wisconsin state park. You'll find 5,000 feet of beach. Visitors may take their boats to Rock Island, but caution is urged since Lake Michigan and Green Bay can be hazardous due to reefs and storms. Rock Island has 40 primitive campsites. Pit toilets, picnic tables, and fire rings are provided; there is drinking water near the dock and boathouse. Swimming the beach at Rock Island is quite memorable. The half-mile stretch of wilderness beach is reached via a half-mile hike along Thordarson Trail from the stone boathouse. Changing stalls provided. Water temperature in July averages in the mid-40s.

BASICS

Operated By: Wisconsin State Parks. **Open:** May 25–Oct. 8. **Site Assignment:** Reservations can be made 11 months in advance or as late as 2 days before arrival. **Registration:** At office. **Fee:** Single, $10–$22; group, $40–$140. **Parking:** At site.

FACILITIES

Number of Multipurpose Sites: 42. **Hookups:** None. **Dump Station:** No. **Laundry:** No. **Pay Phone:** No. **Restrooms and Showers:** No. **Fuel:** No. **Propane:** No. **Internal Roads:** Paved. **RV Service:** No. **Market:** No. **Restaurant:** No. **General Store:** No. **Vending:** No. **Swimming:** No. **Playground:** No. **Other:** Out-of-state campfire wood is prohibited. Vehicle admission stickers are required.

RESTRICTIONS

Pets: On a leash no longer than 8 ft.; under control at all times; not allowed in the general picnic areas. **Fires:** In authorized fireplaces or rings only. Do not leave unattended; extinguish all fires before leaving the campsite. Burning of household refuse is prohibited. **Alcoholic Beverages:** People of legal drinking age may bring alcoholic beverages along for their picnic or campsite meals in Wisconsin state parks & forests.

TO GET THERE

Located north of Sturgeon Bay, take either Hwy. 57 (less congested) or Hwy. 42 to Northport (2 mi. beyond Gill's Rock). Take a half-hour ride on the Washington Island Ferry to Washington Island. Using the map printed inside of your ferry schedule, drive 9 mi. across Washington Island (20 minutes) to the Rock Island parking lot, located at Jackson Harbor on Washington Island. Take the Rock Island Ferry to Rock Island.

WAUPACA   MAP, C-2
Hartman Creek State Park

reserve america

N2480 Hartman Creek Rd., 54981-9727.
T: (715) 258-2372; www.reserveamerica.com.

🚐 ★★★★	⛺ ★★★★
Beauty: ★★★	Site Privacy: ★★★
Spaciousness: ★★★	Quiet: ★★★★
Security: ★★★★	Cleanliness: ★★★★
Insect Control: ★★★★	Facilities: ★★★★

Canoeists and kayakers looking for quiet lakes, and hikers, off-road bikers, and horseback riders looking for a variety of trails should consider a visit to Hartman Creek State Park, in the center of Wisconsin near Waupaca. The 1,417-acre park provides outdoor recreation experiences in all seasons. Hartman Creek State Park was established on June 22, 1966 and offers a 101-site family campground and five group camping sites. The campsites are in either a red pine forest or an old apple orchard/hardwood mix of trees. The campground has spacious sites and two shower and flush toilet buildings. Some campsites are open all winter on a first-come, first-serve basis. The Allen Lake Picnic Area is a short walk from the campground on an accessible trail. The picnic area includes tables, benches, grills, and swing sets. Volunteer naturalists normally offer some interpretive programs, usually at the amphitheater, throughout the summer.

BASICS

Operated By: Wisconsin State Parks. **Open:** All year; some sites subject to closure. **Site Assignment:** Reservations can be made 11 months in advance or as late as 2 days before arrival. **Registration:** At office. **Fee:** Single, $10–$22; group, $40–$140. **Parking:** At site.

FACILITIES

Number of Multipurpose Sites: 109. **Hookups:** Yes. **Each Site:** Fire ring, picnic table. **Dump Station:** Yes. **Laundry:** No. **Pay Phone:** Yes. **Restrooms and Showers:** Yes. **Fuel:** No. **Propane:** No. **Internal Roads:** Paved. **RV Service:** No. **Market:** No. **Restaurant:** No. **General Store:** No. **Vending:** No. **Swimming:** Yes. **Playground:** Yes. **Other:** Out-of-state campfire wood is prohibited. Vehicle admission stickers are required. **Activities:** Amphitheater, biking, boating, fishing, hiking, nature center, picnicking.

RESTRICTIONS

Pets: On a leash no longer than 8 ft.; under control at all times; not allowed in the general picnic areas. **Fires:** In authorized fireplaces or rings only. Do not leave unattended; extinguish all fires before leaving the campsite. Burning of household refuse is prohibited. **Alcoholic Beverages:** People of legal drinking age may bring alcoholic beverages along for their picnic or campsite meals in Wisconsin state parks & forests.

TO GET THERE

Hartman Creek State Park is located 6 mi. west of Waupaca off Hwy. 54. Exit south on Hartman Creek Rd. and travel 1.5 mi. to the park entrance.

WEST BEND   MAP, D-3
Lake Lenwood Beach and Campground

7053 Lenwood Dr., 53090. T: (262) 334-1335; www.lakelenwood.com.

🚐 ★★★★	⛺ ★★★★
Beauty: ★★★★	Site Privacy: ★★★★
Spaciousness: ★★★★	Quiet: ★★★★
Security: ★★★★	Cleanliness: ★★★★
Insect Control: ★★	Facilities: ★★★★

Want to know if a campground is well maintained? Check out the bathrooms. At Lake Lenwood Beach and Campground, the restrooms are clean and nicely decorated, and so is the rest of the campground. Located 1.5 miles southwest of West Bend, the campground offers shaded and open sites around a beautiful lake. Almost every site has a tree or a shrub, the typical site width is 45 feet, there are gravel pads for RVs, and the campground has ten pull-throughs and 55 seasonal campers. An unusual 25-foot-high enclosed tower with a spiral slide is a thriller for children. The best RV sites are on the lakefront; the best tent sites are on the lakeshore in an isolated area. Quiet time is enforced between 9:30 p.m. and 8 a.m., with no radios allowed. Children must be at their campsites after dark. Owners are serious about no barking dogs allowed. Security includes one entrance/exit road, owners who live on site, and regular patrols of the campground.

BASICS

Operated By: Mike & Mary Dricken. **Open:** Apr. 20–Oct. 14. **Site Assignment:** Reservations w/ 2-day min. & 2-day deposit; refunds (minus 15%) w/ 2-week notice. **Registration:** At campground office. **Fee:** $28–$32; cash, check, credit card. **Parking:** At site.

FACILITIES

Number of RV-only Sites: 125. **Number of Tent-only Sites:** 20. **Hookups:** Electric (30, 50 amps), water, sewer, cable TV, phone. **Each Site:** Picnic table, fire ring. **Dump Station:** Yes. **Laundry:** Yes. **Pay Phone:** Yes. **Restrooms and Showers:** Yes. **Fuel:** No. **Propane:** No. **Internal Roads:** Gravel, in good condition. **RV Service:** No. **Market:** 1.5 mi. northwest in West Bend. **Restaurant:** 1 block. **General Store:** Yes, limited. **Vending:** Yes. **Swimming:** No. **Playground:** Yes. **Other:** Lake Lenwood, beach, pier, basketball, horseshoes, hiking trails, volleyball, pavilion, sports field. **Activities:** Swimming, fishing, hiking, boating (rental fishing boats, canoes, kayaks, paddleboats, hydro-bikes & inner tubes available). **Nearby Attractions:** Parks, Old Courthouse Square Museum, art museum, golf, indoor go karts, historic homes, antiques, arts & crafts, bike trail, hiking trail, outlet shops, nature areas. **Additional Information:** West Bend Chamber of Commerce, (888) 338-8666.

RESTRICTIONS

Pets: Leash only, no barking. **Fires:** Fire ring only. **Alcoholic Beverages:** Allowed. **Vehicle Maximum Length:** No limit.

TO GET THERE

From the junction of US 45 and CR D, drive 1 mi. east on CR D, then 1 mi. north on Hwy. 144, then 1 block east on Wallace Lake Rd. Roads are wide and well maintained, with broad shoulders.

WEST BEND   MAP, D-3
Timber Trail Campground

7590 Good Luck Ln., 53090.
T: (262) 338-8561 or (414) 282-6394; www.timbertrailcampground.com.

🚐 ★★★	⛺ ★★★
Beauty: ★★★	Site Privacy: ★★★★
Spaciousness: ★★★★	Quiet: ★★★★
Security: ★★★★	Cleanliness: ★★★★
Insect Control: ★★	Facilities: ★★★

Timber Trail Campground is like camping under a canopy of maple and beechwood trees, except that

100 seasonal campers are there too. Located adjacent to Kettle Moraine Ice Age Trail 4 miles northwest of West Bend, Timber Trail offers mostly wooded gravel sites. If you're looking for an open spot for that satellite dish, this is not the place for you. But it is a very secluded, woodsy campground. Laid out in a series of loops, the rural campground has two pull-throughs and a typical site width of 45 feet. The best RV site is 216 because it offers full hookups and is close to facilities. The best tent site is 42 because it is very wooded and private, with a sandy spot for the tent. Tent-only sites are available in two separate areas. Security measures include owners who live on site and provide regular patrols of the campground.

BASICS

Operated By: Brent & Judy Lange. **Open:** May 15–Oct. 15. **Site Assignment:** Reservations w/ 1-night deposit; refund w/ 5-day notice. **Registration:** At campground office. **Fee:** $22–$30; cash, check, V, MC. **Parking:** At site.

FACILITIES

Number of RV-only Sites: 130. **Number of Tent-only Sites:** 5. **Hookups:** Electric (30 amps), water, sewer. **Each Site:** Picnic table, fire ring. **Dump Station:** Yes. **Laundry:** Yes. **Pay Phone:** No. **Restrooms and Showers:** Yes. **Fuel:** No. **Propane:** Yes. **Internal Roads:** Paved/gravel, in good condition. **RV Service:** No. **Market:** 5 mi. southeast in West Bend. **Restaurant:** 5 mi. southeast in West Bend. **General Store:** Yes, limited. **Vending:** Yes. **Swimming:** Yes. **Playground:** Yes. **Other:** Whirlpool, recreation building, snack bar, ball field, tennis court, basketball, volleyball, hiking trails, horseshoes, fishing pond. **Activities:** Swimming, hiking, fishing, boating (no motors), scheduled weekend activities. **Nearby Attractions:** Parks, Old Courthouse Square Museum, art museum, golf, indoor go-karts, historic homes, antiques, arts & crafts, bike trail, hiking trail, outlet shops, nature areas, Kettle Moraine Ice Age Trail. **Additional Information:** West Bend Chamber of Commerce, (888) 338-8666.

RESTRICTIONS

Pets: On leash only. **Fires:** Fire ring only. **Alcoholic Beverages:** Allowed. **Vehicle Maximum Length:** No limit.

TO GET THERE

From the junction of US 45 and CR D, drive 1.5 mi. west on CR D, then 0.75 mi. north on Good Luck Ln. Roads are wide and well maintained, with broad shoulders, but they are winding in spots.

WEST SALEM   MAP, C-1, C-2
Neshonoc Lakeside Campground

N5334 Neshonoc Rd., 54669.
T: (888) 783-0035 or (608) 786-1792;
www.neshonoclakeside.com.

🚐 ★★★★★	🏕 ★★★★
Beauty: ★★★★★	Site Privacy: ★★★★★
Spaciousness: ★★★★★	Quiet: ★★★★★
Security: ★★★★★	Cleanliness: ★★★★★
Insect Control: ★★	Facilities: ★★★★★

Neshonoc Lakeside Camp has natural beauty galore, along with some great touches added over the years.

Located on Lake Neshonoc 1 mile east of West Salem, the campground offers beautiful views of the water and bluffs on the other shore. Not surprisingly, the most popular sites are 168–205 up on the hillside, where campers can see spectacular sunsets over the 600-acre lake. Also, not surprisingly, the most desirable lakeside spots have been snapped up by seasonal campers. Tent campers might yearn for a more wilderness that affords some privacy away from RV campers. Exceptionally manicured grounds, mighty clean bathrooms, and color-coordinated reddish-brown paint on campground facilities adds to the visual appeal. Lighted wooden stairs with railings on both sides provide safe passage from the hillside to the heated pool and well-stocked camp store, which features cappuccino every day and sweet rolls from a local bakery every weekend.

BASICS

Operated By: Diversified Investments. **Open:** Apr. 15–Oct. 15. **Site Assignment:** Reservations w/ 1-night deposit, refund (minus $10) w/ 7-day notice. **Registration:** At campground office. **Fee:** $30–$39; cash, check, credit card. **Parking:** At site.

FACILITIES

Number of RV-only Sites: 240. **Hookups:** Electric (20, 30, 50 amps), water, sewer. **Each Site:** Picnic table, fire ring. **Dump Station:** Yes. **Laundry:** Yes. **Pay Phone:** Yes. **Restrooms and Showers:** Yes. **Fuel:** No. **Propane:** Yes. **Internal Roads:** Paved, in good condition. **RV Service:** No. **Market:** 1 mi. west in West Salem. **Restaurant:** 2.5 mi. west in West Salem. **General Store:** Yes. **Vending:** Yes. **Swimming:** Yes. **Playground:** Yes. **Other:** Sandy beach, boat dock, video game room, sand volleyball court, horseshoes, basketball, croquet, softball. **Activities:** Swimming, boating (rental rowboats, paddleboats, kayaks & canoes available), hay wagon rides, scheduled activities. **Nearby Attractions:** Bike trails, shopping center, golf, speedway, zoo, boat tours, historic homes, La Crosse's Riverfest & Oktoberfest. **Additional Information:** Onalaska Center for Commerce & Tourism, (800) 873-1901.

RESTRICTIONS

Pets: On leash only. **Fires:** Fire pit only. **Alcoholic Beverages:** Allowed. **Vehicle Maximum Length:** No limit.

TO GET THERE

From the junction of I-90 and CR 3, take Exit 12, drive 1.5 mi. north on CR C through village, then 1.5 mi. east on Hwy. 16, then 1,000 feet south on paved road. Roads are wide and well maintained, with broad shoulders.

WEST SALEM   MAP, C-1, C-2
Veterans Memorial Campground

N4668 CR VP, 54669. T: (608) 786-4011;
www.co.la-crosse.wi.us.

🚐 ★★★	🏕 ★★★★
Beauty: ★★★★	Site Privacy: ★★★★
Spaciousness: ★★★	Quiet: ★★★★
Security: ★★★★	Cleanliness: ★★★★
Insect Control: ★★★	Facilities: ★★★

At Veterans Memorial Campground, visitors can camp so close to the La Crosse River that they can almost fish from their RV or tent. The La Crosse County park, located in West Salem, lacks many of the amenities campers often want—a laundry, swimming pool, general store, games, and activities—but it has that beautiful river. Wonderful views and unfettered access to the river more than compensate for the shortage of amenities. Located less than 3 miles from I-90, the campground offers easy access for travelers, including 50 pull-through sites. The most popular sites, of course, are on the river, and tenters have private areas of their own. Security is tops, as a manager lives on site and city police patrol every night. As a friendly touch, the campground provides free firewood—and a little wagon to haul it to the campsite.

BASICS

Operated By: La Crosse County. **Open:** Apr. 15–Oct. 15. **Site Assignment:** First come, first served. **Registration:** At campground office. **Fee:** $18–$20; cash, check. **Parking:** At site.

FACILITIES

Number of RV-only Sites: 120. **Number of Tent-only Sites:** 17. **Hookups:** Electric (20, 30, 50 amps). **Each Site:** Picnic table, fire ring. **Dump Station:** Yes. **Laundry:** No. **Pay Phone:** Yes. **Restrooms and Showers:** Yes. **Fuel:** No. **Propane:** No. **Internal Roads:** Paved, in good condition. **RV Service:** No. **Market:** 1.5 mi. east in West Salem. **Restaurant:** 1.5 mi. east in West Salem. **General Store:** Yes. **Vending:** Yes. **Swimming:** No. **Playground:** Yes. **Other:** Shelter house, 4-acre fishing pond, shuffleboard, volleyball, canoe landing, state bike trail. **Activities:** Fishing, biking, scheduled twice-monthly activities. **Nearby Attractions:** Biking, hunting, bird-watching, golf, Onalaska Historical Society Museum, historic homes, aquatic center w/ 200-ft. waterslide, antique shops. **Additional Information:** Onalaska Center for Commerce & Tourism, (800) 873-1901.

RESTRICTIONS

Pets: On leash only. **Fires:** Fire ring only. **Alcoholic Beverages:** At sites only. **Vehicle Maximum Length:** No limit.

TO GET THERE

From the junction of I-90 and CR C, drive 1.5 mi. north and west on CR C, then 2 mi. west on Hwy. 16, Roads are wide and well maintained, with broad shoulders.

WILTON   MAP, C-2
Tunnel Trail Campground

26983 WI 71, 54670.
T: (608) 435-6829 or (920) 294-3742 off season;
www.tunneltrail.com.

🚐 ★★★★	🏕 ★★★★
Beauty: ★★★★	Site Privacy: ★★★
Spaciousness: ★★★	Quiet: ★★★★
Security: ★★★★	Cleanliness: ★★★
Insect Control: ★★	Facilities: ★★★★

A rural campground adjacent to the Elroy-Sparta State Bicycle Trail, Tunnel Trail Campground offers terraced, shaded sites in a valley. Located 4 miles east of Wilton, the campground has nine pull-throughs and a typical site width of 30 feet. Sites are level and grassy in a quiet, park-like setting. Besides the convenient access from the highway, the campground has a major plus in its proximity to the popular bike trail, formerly the old Chicago-Northwestern railroad bed. The trail is 32 level miles in length and passes through three tunnels and the beautiful hills of the Coulee Region. For campers who don't feel like hauling bikes, the campground rents well-maintained mountain bikes, hybrids, bike trailers, third-wheels, tandems, and recumbent bikes. The campground is also blessed by being relatively free of mosquitoes without having to use insecticides. Quiet hours are from 10:30 p.m. to 7 a.m., with all radios required to be off after 10:30 p.m.

BASICS

Operated By: Scott & Julie Grenon. **Open:** May 1–Oct. 15. **Site Assignment:** Reservations w/ $54 deposit, 2-night min. on weekend, 3-night min. on holidays; refund (minus $10) w/ 2-week notice. **Registration:** At campground office. **Fee:** $25–$28; cash, check, credit card. **Parking:** At site.

FACILITIES

Number of RV-only Sites: 63. **Number of Tent-only Sites:** 20. **Hookups:** Electric (20, 30 amps), water. **Each Site:** Picnic table, fire ring. **Dump Station:** Yes. **Laundry:** Yes. **Pay Phone:** Yes. **Restrooms and Showers:** Yes. **Fuel:** No. **Propane:** Yes. **Internal Roads:** Paved/gravel, in good condition. **RV Service:** No. **Market:** 4 mi. west in Wilton. **Restaurant:** 4 mi. west in Wilton. **General Store:** Yes, limited. **Vending:** Yes. **Swimming:** Yes. **Playground:** Yes. **Other:** Mini-golf, horseshoes, volleyball, basketball, game room, trails, rental cabins, pavilion, badminton, sports field, adults room. **Activities:** Swimming, hiking, biking (rental bikes available). **Nearby Attractions:** Kickapoo River, horseback riding, canoeing, fishing, Amish community, scenic drive, antiques, arts & crafts. **Additional Information:** La Crosse Area CVB, (800) 658-9424.

RESTRICTIONS

Pets: On leash only. **Fires:** Fire ring only. **Alcoholic Beverages:** Allowed. **Vehicle Maximum Length:** No limit.

TO GET THERE

From the east junction of Hwys. 131 and 71, drive 1 mi. east on Hwy. 71. Roads are wide and well maintained, with broad shoulders.

WOODRUFF — MAP, B-2
NH–AL Clear Lake Area

reserve america

8282 Woodruff Rd., 54568. T: (715) 385-2704; www.reserveamerica.com.

🚐 ★★★★   ▲ ★★★★

Beauty: ★★★	Site Privacy: ★★★★★
Spaciousness: ★★★★★	Quiet: ★★★★
Security: ★★★★	Cleanliness: ★★★★
Insect Control: ★★★★	Facilities: ★★★

Established in 1925 to protect the headwaters of the Wisconsin, Flambeau, and Manitowish rivers, the Northern Highland–American Legion (NH–AL) State Forest occupies more than 225,000 acres in Vilas, Oneida, and Iron counties. The forest offers a diverse array of recreational opportunities, such as camping, canoeing, hiking, bird-watching, snowmobiling, biking, and hunting, as well as the chance to simply sit quietly and enjoy its natural beauty. In addition, the forest provides habitat for a wide range of plant and animal species. There are 18 campgrounds offering 900 campsites. Varying styles of camping are offered: 100 primitive canoe campsites are found along the 247 miles of waterways; two group camps accommodate 100 people; winter camping is permitted at designated grounds; and wilderness sites afford a backcountry experience. Five family campgrounds (Crystal Lake, Muskie Lake, Clear Lake, Firefly Lake, and Indian Mounds), two group campgrounds, and four wilderness campgrounds accept reservations through the Wisconsin State Park's central reservation system. Thirteen campgrounds are first come, first served. Canoe campers have over 70 sites for one night only at each site camping.

BASICS

Operated By: Wisconsin State Parks. **Open:** May 24–Sept. 2. **Site Assignment:** Reservations can be made 11 months in advance or as late as 2 days before arrival. **Registration:** At office. **Fee:** Single, $10–$22; group, $40–$140. **Parking:** At site.

FACILITIES

Number of Multipurpose Sites: 163. **Hookups:** Yes. **Dump Station:** No. **Laundry:** No. **Pay Phone:** Yes. **Restrooms and Showers:** Yes. **Fuel:** No. **Propane:** No. **Internal Roads:** Paved. **RV Service:** No. **Market:** No. **Restaurant:** No. **General Store:** No. **Vending:** No. **Swimming:** Yes. **Playground:** No. **Activities:** Boating, fishing.

RESTRICTIONS

Pets: On a leash no longer than 8 ft.; under control at all times; not allowed in the general picnic areas. **Fires:** In authorized fireplaces or rings only. Do not leave unattended; extinguish all fires before leaving the campsite. Burning of household refuse is prohibited. **Alcoholic Beverages:** People of legal drinking age may bring alcoholic beverages along for their picnic or campsite meals in Wisconsin state parks & forests. **Other:** Out-of-state campfire wood is prohibited. Vehicle admission stickers are required.

TO GET THERE

To the Clear Lake Contact Station from the intersection of Hwys. 51 and 47, travel south on Hwy. 47 for 3.5 mi. and turn left on Woodruff Rd. Clear Lake Contact Station will be on the right.

WYEVILLE — MAP, C-2
Holiday Lodge Golf Resort

10555 Freedom Rd., 54660. T: (608) 372-2671 or (800) 236-2670; www.holidaylodgegolf.com.

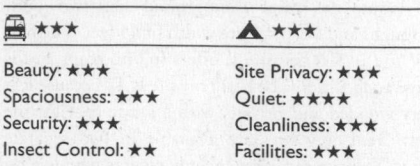

🚐 ★★★   ▲ ★★★

Beauty: ★★★	Site Privacy: ★★★
Spaciousness: ★★★	Quiet: ★★★★
Security: ★★★	Cleanliness: ★★★
Insect Control: ★★	Facilities: ★★★

The name says it all. Holiday Lodge Golf Resort caters to golfers or campers looking for a quiet overnight stay. No other activities are offered. Located 6 miles east of Tomah, the campground is across the street from an 18-hole golf course, a well-stocked pro shop, and a lounge serving sandwiches and drinks. The 71-par course offers gas carts, rental clubs, and watered fairways. Golfing, which includes green fees and a cart, costs $50 per person with a discount for campground guests. The campground's flat, shaded sites are generally spacious (36 feet wide) with 14 full hookups and 14 pull-throughs. The most popular sites are 12–22 because they are larger pull-throughs. The campground offers good security, with one entrance, a manager who lives on site, and a night patrol. For someone who wants to golf and sleep, Holiday Lodge Golf Resort is a popular destination.

BASICS

Operated By: Holiday Lodge Inc. **Open:** May 1–Oct. 15. **Site Assignment:** Reservations accepted w/o deposit. **Registration:** At campground office. **Fee:** $22.16; cash, check, credit card. **Parking:** At site.

FACILITIES

Number of RV-only Sites: 27. **Number of Tent-only Sites:** 4. **Hookups:** Electric (30 amps), water, sewer. **Each Site:** Picnic table, fire ring. **Dump Station:** Yes. **Laundry:** Yes. **Pay Phone:** Yes. **Restrooms and Showers:** Yes. **Fuel:** No. **Propane:** No. **Internal Roads:** Gravel, in good condition. **RV Service:** No. **Market:** 6 mi. west in Tomah. **Restaurant:** 6 mi. west in Tomah. **General Store:** No. **Vending:** Yes. **Swimming:** No. **Playground:** No. **Other:** Golf course, pro shop. **Activities:** Golfing. **Nearby Attractions:** Telecommunications Historical Museum, tractor pull, bicycle trails, cranberry fest. **Additional Information:** Warrens Area Business Assoc., (608) 378-4878.

RESTRICTIONS

Pets: On leash only. **Fires:** Fire pit only. **Alcoholic Beverages:** Allowed. **Vehicle Maximum Length:** No limit.

TO GET THERE

From the junction of I-94 and Hwy. 21, drive 6 mi. east on Hwy. 21, then 0.75 mi. south on Excelsior Ave. Roads are wide and well maintained, with broad shoulders.

Wyoming

Wyoming's clean, geometric borders belie the topographical variety found in its interior. With an amalgam of winding rivers, scenic gorges, vast plains, craggy mountain peaks, pristine lakes, and lonely buttes, Wyoming is a prime destination for campers and outdoor enthusiasts alike. The Equality State is probably most popular for containing the country's first national park, **Yellowstone.** This storied park's **Old Faithful** geyser, though it is not the largest in the park, garnered its reputation and popularity from the regularity of its eruptions. However, if touring the state, don't forget to give yourself plenty of time to visit the other points of interest.

From the eastern border of Yellowstone, in **Shoshone National Forest,** you'll find the **Absakora** and **Wind River Mountain Ranges** as well as the Shoshone River's north and south forks. Camping here provides easy access to hiking, rafting, fishing, and exploration. Southeast of Yellowstone is **Hot Springs State Park,** where you can take in a glimpse of the past from the 2,000-year-old petroglyphs painted onto the sandstone cliffs at **Legend Rock.** If early art is not your flavor, then try out the world's largest mineral hot springs on your road-weary body. Nearby is **Pinedale** where, the second weekend in July, the annual **Green River Rendezvous** festival is held to commemorate the pioneer days of America—the Wild West as it once was. Just south of Yellowstone on Interstate 89 is the **Grand Teton National Park,** where the majestic **Tetons** stand 7,000 feet tall and shadow the famous ski area of **Jackson Hole.** Here, off I-191, are the headwaters of the **Snake River,** making this an ideal spot for campers interested in hiking, river rafting, and fishing. The 25,000-acre **National Elk Preserve** in **Jackson,** which more than 7,500 of the majestic creatures call home from October to May, might give you the opportunity to view a herd of elk or to hear their strange bugle call.

Farther south, the **Fossil Butte National Monument** is an interesting sight for curious observers and budding archaeologists—the 50-million-year-old lake bed is said to contain the highest concentration of pristinely preserved fossils in the world. **Flaming Gorge National Recreation Area** near the **Green River** is a veritable outdoors playground. Both the **Flaming Gorge Lake,** 90 miles long with 375 miles of shoreline, and the Green River provide limitless water recreation. Campers enjoy watching the play of the sun and shadows dance among the rock formations, transforming the area into a circus of lights and color. Nestled in the southeast corner of Wyoming is "the Magic City of the Plains," the state capital, **Cheyenne.** The design of the capitol building here was inspired by a certain capitol located 1,643 miles away in Washington, D.C.

Through the central portion of the 44th state, you can travel the **Oregon Trail** and view the land as Oregon-bound pioneers would have. There are a number of historical sites and opportunities for recreation. **Sink Canyon State Park**, 6 miles south of **Lander** off Highway 131, is where the **Popo Agie River** flows from the **Wind River Mountains** into a limestone cavern in the Sink Canyon. The area offers numerous opportunities for camping, hiking, and fishing. **Casper,** Wyoming's second-largest city, is a nice stop too. In eastern Wyoming, you'll find all 2,883,943 acres of forest and plains at **Medicine Bow** and **Routt National Forests** at **Thunder Basin National Grassland,** where a smattering of private campgrounds are located. If you happen to be in Converse County in mid-June, make your way over to its seat, **Douglas,** for the annual **Jackelope Days** festival. According to local lore, the jackelope has the body of a jackrabbit with the horns of an antelope. When you're there be sure to check out the world's largest jackelope, standing at more than eight feet, located at **Jackelope Square** at the corner of 3rd and Center streets. Traveling north from there, **Devil's Tower,** America's first national monument, and Buffalo Bill country provide ample opportunity for picnics, scenic drives, fishing, and magical views of waterfalls. No matter the direction or destination, Wyoming is rich beyond your wildest imagination with opportunities to experience the beauty of its seemingly never-ending grandeur.

Campground Profiles

BUFFALO
Buffalo KOA
MAP, A-3

P.O. Box 189, 87 US 16 East, 82834.
T: (307) 684-5423 or (800) 562-5403;
www.koa.com.

🚐 ★★★★　　🏕 ★★★★

Beauty: ★★★　　　　Site Privacy: ★★★★
Spaciousness: ★★★★　Quiet: ★★★★
Security: ★★★★　　　Cleanliness: ★★★★
Insect Control: ★★★★　Facilities: ★★★★

Just east of town, set in an attractive and inviting atmosphere, is the Buffalo KOA. This KOA campground has truly earned its gold rating. In a state where grass is a luxury, this KOA is beautifully landscaped and impeccably kept. There are Russian olives and quaking aspen trees giving shade and adding warmth. Campsites are set in a series of rows, with a separate tenting area. All sites have a level parking pad, covered picnic table, and grill. There are both pull-through and back-in sites, most being pull-throughs. In addition, the campground has the only deluxe campsite in the KOA system with a private fence, yard, patio, and hot tub (special rates apply). The campground offers a daily pancake breakfast June–August, and propane service 8 a.m. to dusk. The weather is always windy, and summers are smoldering. The camp staff are friendly and happy to assist.

BASICS
Operated By: Don & Sue Gill. **Open:** All year. **Site Assignment:** By reservation. **Registration:** At camp store. **Fee:** RV, $25–$36; tent, $19–$25; for 2 people; each extra person (over 6 years old), $3. **Parking:** Yes; extra vehicle fee, $5.

FACILITIES
Number of RV-only Sites: 63. **Number of Tent-only Sites:** 28. **Hookups:** Electric (20, 30, 50 amps), water, sewer. **Each Site:** Picnic table, some fire pits. **Dump Station:** Yes. **Laundry:** Yes. **Pay Phone:** Yes. **Restrooms and Showers:** Yes. **Fuel:** No. **Propane:** Yes. **Internal Roads:** Gravel, in good condition. **RV Service:** Local service. **Market:** In town. **Restaurant:** In town. **General Store:** Yes. **Vending:** Yes. **Swimming:** Yes, w/ a hot tub. **Playground:** Yes. **Other:** 5 cabins, a fishing stream, covered picnic areas, camp kitchen, teepees, & a wonderful deluxe site w/ hot tub, Internet data port. **Activities:** Fishing, hiking, game room, playground, horseshoes, mini-golf. **Nearby Attractions:** The White Buffalo, Jim Gatchell Museum, the rodeo. **Additional Information:** Buffalo Chamber of Commerce, (307) 684-5544.

RESTRICTIONS
Pets: On leash. **Fires:** Fire ring only. **Alcoholic Beverages:** Allowed. **Vehicle Maximum Length:** No limit.

TO GET THERE
On Hwy. 16 between I-90 Exit 58 and I-25 Exit 299.

BUFFALO
Lake DeSmet, Lake Stop Resort
MAP, A-3

P.O. Box 578, 9 Lake Stop Rd., 82834.
T: (307) 684-9051.

🚐 ★★★　　🏕 ★★★

Beauty: ★★★★　　　Site Privacy: ★★★★
Spaciousness: ★★★★　Quiet: ★★★★
Security: ★★★★　　　Cleanliness: ★★★
Insect Control: ★★★　Facilities: ★★★

Lake DeSmet, the Lake Stop, is positioned at the base of the Big Horn Mountains on the splendid Lake DeSmet. This small lakeside campground is only a small part of the Lake Stop experience, which offers an 18-site circular campground with full hookups, pool, and clean facilities. The campsites are on a bed of red shale, and each have a table and light post. Although the campsites are not on the lake, there is lake access and a boat launch. There is also a full-service bait/tackle shop, cafe, motel, boat repair shop, professional fishing outfitters, and boat rentals. The Lake Stop has a small decorative pond up by the campground, and the motel is beautifully landscaped with a nice grotto. The owners also have their own private residence across from the campground and are there to assist in any way. Lake DeSmet is 6 miles north of Buffalo, which is a nice community that offers a variety of activities, rodeos, and Native American history.

BASICS
Operated By: Ted & Bambi Schumacher. **Open:** All year. **Site Assignment:** By reservation. **Registration:** At lake shop. **Fee:** RV, $19; tent, $10. **Parking:** At site.

FACILITIES
Number of RV-only Sites: 18. **Number of Tent-only Sites:** Undesignated sites. **Hookups:** Electric (20, 30, 50 amps), water, sewer. **Each Site:** Picnic table, grill, & light post. **Dump Station:** Yes. **Laundry:** Yes. **Pay Phone:** Yes. **Restrooms and Showers:** Yes. **Fuel:** Yes. **Propane:** Yes. **Internal Roads:** Red Shale. **RV Service:** Buffalo. **Market:** In town. **Restaurant:** On site. **General Store:** Yes. **Vending:** Yes. **Swimming:** Yes. **Playground:** Yes. **Other:** Full-service grocery store, tackle shop, boat repair shop, boat ramp, motel, small pond w/ grotto; fishing packages available. **Activities:** Fishing (rainbow, brown, & eagle lake trout), guided fishing tours, boating, jet skiing, basketball, volleyball, lake access. **Nearby Attractions:** 6 miles from Buffalo, stream fishing, golf, scenic drives, rodeo. **Additional Information:** Buffalo Chamber of Commerce, (307) 684-5544.

RESTRICTIONS
Pets: On leash. **Fires:** Grill only. **Alcoholic Beverages:** Allowed. **Vehicle Maximum Length:** 40 ft. (limited room for extra-long RV).

TO GET THERE
Off I-90 (Exit 51), then follow signs 7 mi. north.

CHEYENNE
Cheyenne KOA
MAP, C-4

8800 Archer Frontage Rd., 82007.
T: (307) 638-8840 or (800) 562-1507;
www.cheyennekoa.com.

🚐 ★★★★　　🏕 ★★★

Beauty: ★★★　　　　Site Privacy: ★★★★
Spaciousness: ★★★★　Quiet: ★★★
Security: ★★★★　　　Cleanliness: ★★★★★
Insect Control: ★★★★　Facilities: ★★★★★

Conveniently located off I-80, the Cheyenne KOA presents a comfortable and well-maintained campground with full amenities to meet the entire family's needs. The Cheyenne KOA has reasonably sized gravel camping sites, with some lawn and trees, configured into rows with both back-in and pull-through sites. The campground has several cabins, a snack bar, pool, and mini-golf. The nearby city of Cheyenne is the capital of Wyoming, and it's also the largest city in the state, boasting a variety of activities and events. There are several state and federal parks in the area, as well as museums and galleries. Several tours of the area include downtown and the Wyoming state capitol building and grounds. Cheyenne has a very dry climate with relentless winds. The winters can be very harsh, and the summers very warm. The staff at the Cheyenne KOA are friendly and helpful, and the campground is secure.

BASICS
Operated By: Mike & Donna Lawrance & Don Lonergan. **Open:** All year. **Site Assignment:** By reservation. **Registration:** At camp store. **Fee:** RV, $22.45–$33.45; tent, $22.45; per 2 people; each extra person (5 & over), $3. **Parking:** At site.

FACILITIES
Number of RV-only Sites: 42. **Number of Tent-only Sites:** 11. **Hookups:** Electric (20, 30, 50 amps), water, sewer. **Each Site:** Picnic table & grill in the tent & cabin area. **Dump Station:** Yes. **Laundry:** Yes. **Pay Phone:** Yes. **Restrooms and Showers:** Yes. **Fuel:** 3 mi. east in town. **Propane:** Yes. **Internal Roads:** Gravel, in good condition. **RV Service:** Local service. **Market:** In town. **Restaurant:** In town. **General Store:** Yes. **Vending:** Yes. **Swimming:** Yes. **Playground:** Yes. **Other:** 6 cabins, store, Internet data port, pavilion w/ kitchen. **Activities:** Game room, playground, horseshoes, mini-golf, basketball. **Nearby Attractions:** Golf, State Capitol, trolley tours. **Additional Information:** Cheyenne Chamber of Commerce, (307) 638-3388.

RESTRICTIONS
Pets: On leash. **Fires:** Fire ring only. **Alcoholic Beverages:** Allowed. **Vehicle Maximum Length:** No limit.

TO GET THERE
Right off I-80 Exit 367 on the north side.

CODY
MAP, A-2
Cody KOA

5561 Greybull Hwy., 82414.
T: (307) 587-2369 or (800) 562-8507;
www.koa.com.

🚐 ★★★   ⛺ ★★★

Beauty: ★★★   Site Privacy: ★★★
Spaciousness: ★★★   Quiet: ★★★
Security: ★★★   Cleanliness: ★★★
Insect Control: ★★★   Facilities: ★★★

The Cody KOA is just east of Cody, conveniently located off Hwy 20. This full-service campground comes fully equipped to meet your needs. The campground offers close to 200 sites, 20 cabins, and a cottage. The comfortable sites come in both back-in and pull-through flavors, with quite a bit of grass and shade for the region. Each campsite has a gravel parking area. There is a large pool with a hot tub to escape Wyoming's blistering summer heat, as well as a game room and trail rides for your enjoyment. The community of Cody is warm and friendly, and there are a number of shops and restaurants to enjoy. Cody also conducts a nightly summer rodeo and serves as the east entrance to Yellowstone National Park.

BASICS
Operated By: Jean Mickelson, manager. **Open:** May–Oct. 1. **Site Assignment:** By reservation. **Registration:** At camp store. **Fee:** RV, $28–$36; tent, $23–$29; per 2 people; each extra child/adult, $3. **Parking:** At site.

FACILITIES
Number of RV-only Sites: 120. **Number of Tent-only Sites:** 84. **Hookups:** Electric (20, 30 amps), water, sewer. **Each Site:** Picnic table & fire pit in tent sites. **Dump Station:** Yes. **Laundry:** Yes. **Pay Phone:** Yes. **Restrooms and Showers:** Yes. **Fuel:** No. **Propane:** Yes. **Internal Roads:** Gravel, in good condition. **RV Service:** In Cody. **Market:** In Cody. **Restaurant:** In Cody. **General Store:** Yes. **Vending:** Yes. **Swimming:** Yes, w/ hot tub. **Playground:** Yes. **Other:** 20 cabins, 1 cottage, covered pavilion w/ 2 gas grills, game room w/ TV & cable, hot tub, dish sink, data port. **Activities:** Swimming, playground, games, trail rides, volleyball, horseshoes. **Nearby Attractions:** The east entrance to Yellowstone National Park, nightly summer rodeo, float trips, Buffalo Bills Historical Center. **Additional Information:** Cody Chamber of Commerce, (307) 587-2777.

RESTRICTIONS
Pets: On leash only. **Fires:** Fire pit only. **Alcoholic Beverages:** Allowed. **Vehicle Maximum Length:** 45 ft.

TO GET THERE
On US 20 just east of Cody.

DOUGLAS
MAP, B-4
Jackalope KOA

P.O. Box 1190, 168 Cold Springs Rd., 82633.
T: (307) 358-2164 or (800) 562-2469;
www.koa.com.

🚐 ★★★   ⛺ ★★★

Beauty: ★★★   Site Privacy: ★★★
Spaciousness: ★★★   Quiet: ★★★
Security: ★★★   Cleanliness: ★★★
Insect Control: ★★★   Facilities: ★★★

If you are looking for a quiet place to stay or just passing through, the Jackalope KOA is a delightful, well-maintained, and comfortable place to lodge. The Jackalope KOA offers a more rustic, woodsy setting, with all the amenities you would expect from a full-service campground. The campsites are moderate in size and have gravel parking spurs; there are both pull-through and back-in sites. The community of Douglas is listed as number 72 in Norman Crampton's *The 100 Best Small Towns in America,* and it is home to Fort Fetterman and the Wyoming Pioneer Memorial Museum. This area of Wyoming is rich in Native American history, and the Oregon, Emigrant, Mormon, and Bozeman trails, which cross through the area, are full of untold stories. The Jackalope KOA has a safe and secure atmosphere and a kind and caring staff.

BASICS
Operated By: Bob & Delores Kessner. **Open:** Apr. 1–Nov. 1. **Site Assignment:** By reservation. **Registration:** At camp store. **Fee:** RV, $24–$31; tent, $15–$18.50; per 2 people; each extra person, $3. **Parking:** At site.

FACILITIES
Number of RV-only Sites: 68. **Number of Tent-only Sites:** 16. **Hookups:** Electric (20, 30, 50 amps), water, sewer, cable TV. **Each Site:** Picnic table & grill in the tent & cabin area. **Dump Station:** Yes. **Laundry:** Yes. **Pay Phone:** Yes. **Restrooms and Showers:** Yes. **Fuel:** No. **Propane:** Yes. **Internal Roads:** Gravel, in good condition. **RV Service:** Casper. **Market:** In town. **Restaurant:** In town. **General Store:** Yes. **Vending:** Yes. **Swimming:** Yes. **Playground:** Yes. **Other:** 1 cabin, store, Internet data port, pavilion. **Activities:** Game room, playground, horseshoes, mini-golf, basketball. **Nearby Attractions:** Pioneer Museum, natural bridge, national speedway, Ft. Fetterman. **Additional Information:** Douglas Chamber of Commerce, (307) 358-2950.

RESTRICTIONS
Pets: On leash. **Fires:** No open wood fires. **Alcoholic Beverages:** Allowed. **Vehicle Maximum Length:** No limit.

TO GET THERE
From I-25 take Exit 140, go right on Hwy. 91, and drive for about 1.5 mi.

GLENROCK
MAP, B-3
Deer Creek Village RV Park

P.O. Box 1003, 302 Miller Lane, 82637.
T: (307) 436-8121.

🚐 ★★★   ⛺ ★★

Beauty: ★★★   Site Privacy: ★★★
Spaciousness: ★★★   Quiet: ★★★
Security: ★★★   Cleanliness: ★★★
Insect Control: ★★★   Facilities: ★★

Deer Creek Village RV Park is nestled behind a large community park in Glenrock. Deer Creek has the advantage of activities offered by the Glenrock Community Park while maintaining a separate private area for its visitors. The Deer Creek RV Park has extra-large sites, with lush green grass and large, hearty shade trees. In addition, it offers full hookups and cable TV at a reasonable price. The facilities are adequately maintained, and the owner resides on the property. The Glenrock Community Park has a large playground, baseball diamond, and tennis courts, all in walking distance from any campsite. There is plenty of room for children to ride bikes without the fear of major road traffic. There are a few full-time residents in the RV park as well as a few mobile homes. The weather has a tendency to be cool in the evening, and Wyoming is always windy.

BASICS
Operated By: Cindy Yuker. **Open:** All year. **Site Assignment:** By reservation. **Registration:** At camp store. **Fee:** $40–$52; cable, $1; heat, $3. **Parking:** At site.

FACILITIES
Number of RV-only Sites: 80. **Number of Tent-only Sites:** 10. **Hookups:** Electric (20, 30, 50 amps), water, sewer, cable TV. **Each Site:** None. **Dump Station:** No. **Laundry:** Yes. **Pay Phone:** No. **Restrooms and Showers:** Yes. **Fuel:** No. **Propane:** Yes. **Internal Roads:** Gravel, in good condition. **RV Service:** In Casper. **Market:** In town. **Restaurant:** In town. **General Store:** Yes. **Vending:** Yes. **Swimming:** No. **Playground:** Yes. **Other:** Gift shop. **Activities:** Next door to a nice city park w/ basketball, baseball, tennis, walking trails. **Nearby Attractions:** A Mane Attraction in Casper, Wagon Wheel Roller Skating in Mills. **Additional Information:** Glenrock Chamber of Commerce, (307) 436-5652.

RESTRICTIONS
Pets: On leash. **Fires:** At approved sites only. **Alcoholic Beverages:** Allowed. **Vehicle Maximum Length:** No limit.

TO GET THERE
From I-25, take US 20/26/87 into Glenrock. Campground is behind Glenrock Community Park.

GREEN RIVER   MAP, C-1
Buckboard Crossing—
Ashley National Forest

reserve america

Star Rte. 1, 82935. T: (435) 784-3445;
www.reserveamerica.com.

🚐 ★★★★   ⛺ ★★★★

Beauty: ★★★   Site Privacy: ★★★
Spaciousness: ★★★   Quiet: ★★★
Security: ★★★★   Cleanliness: ★★★★
Insect Control: ★★★★   Facilities: ★★★★

Flaming Gorge Corporation operates this campground under a special-use permit with the U.S. Forest Service. Situated at 6,100 feet, this campground is representative of a high-desert community. The landscape is mainly sagebrush, and temperatures can fluctuate from warm days to cool nights. There are 66 single-family campsites in Loops A and B, 43 of which can be reserved. Most sites have a cabana, picnic table, and a fire ring. The campground area offers a boat ramp, fish-cleaning station, restrooms with electricity, potable water, and a dump station. The campground is located next to Buckboard Marina where campers are able to participate in many water recreational opportunities. The campground is located within the Ashley National Forest in northeastern Utah and Wyoming. It encompasses 1,384,132 national forest acres, (1,287,909 in Utah and 96,223 in Wyoming). Of the total acreage, 276,175 are High Uinta Wilderness (180,530 additional acres of High Uinta Wilderness is located on the Wasatch/Cache National Forest). Elevations on the Ashley National Forest range from 6,000 feet to over 13,500 feet. The Ashley National Forest was established by President Theodore Roosevelt in 1908. Its forest and range lands are protected and managed to ensure timber, grazing, minerals, water, and outdoor recreation for the American people.

BASICS

Operated By: U.S. Forest Service. **Open:** May 19–Sept. 10. **Site Assignment:** Reservations must be made at least 4 days in advance. **Registration:** At office. **Fee:** Single, $14–$17.50. **Parking:** At park.

FACILITIES

Number of Multipurpose Sites: 161. **Hookups:** Yes. **Each Site:** Fire ring, picnic table. **Dump Station:** Yes. **Laundry:** No. **Pay Phone:** No. **Restrooms and Showers:** Yes. **Fuel:** Yes. **Propane:** Yes. **Internal Roads:** Paved. **RV Service:** No. **Market:** No. **Restaurant:** No. **General Store:** Yes. **Vending:** No. **Swimming:** No. **Playground:** No. **Other:** No refunds for bad weather. All vehicles must fit on the designated parking spur. **Activities:** Fishing.

RESTRICTIONS

Pets: Pets must be restrained or on a leash at all times while in developed recreation areas. **Fires:** In fire rings, stoves, grills, or fireplaces provided for that purpose. **Alcoholic Beverages:** Not allowed. **Vehicle Maximum Length:** Call ahead.

TO GET THERE

On Hwy. 530 travel 25 mi. south from Green River, WY. Go 2 mi. east on FS 009 (adjacent to Buckboard Marina).

GREYBULL   MAP, A-2
Greybull KOA

P.O. Box 387, 333 North 2nd St., 82426.
T: (307) 765-2555 or (800) 562-7508;
www.koa.com.

🚐 ★★★   ⛺ ★★★

Beauty: ★★★   Site Privacy: ★★★
Spaciousness: ★★★   Quiet: ★★★
Security: ★★★   Cleanliness: ★★★
Insect Control: ★★★   Facilities: ★★★

Situated just outside of the Big Horn National Forest and the Cloud Peak Wilderness, Greybull KOA is an excellent base camp for the outdoor sports enthusiast. This area of Northeast Wyoming is renowned for its blue-ribbon trout fishing, its miles of hiking trails, and rocks that would challenge even the most experienced rock climbers. It offers excellent mountain biking for the serious biker, and there's also great snow in the winter for those who like to ski. Greybull KOA is a full-service RV park with full amenities, a pool, a snack bar, and cable TV. They offer a comfortable, affordable, well-maintained campground. The staff is friendly, helpful, and always willing to make your visit more pleasurable. The campground offers both pull-through and back-in sites, as well as gravel parking spurs. There is some grass; however, grass is not very common due to dry weather.

BASICS

Operated By: Bob & Marilyn Patterson. **Open:** Apr. 15–Oct. 30. **Site Assignment:** By reservation. **Registration:** At camp store. **Fee:** RV, $30–$45; tent, $20–$25; per 2 people; each extra person (3 & over), $3; no personal checks. **Parking:** At site.

FACILITIES

Number of RV-only Sites: 33. **Number of Tent-only Sites:** 24. **Hookups:** Electric (20, 30 amps), water, sewer, cable TV, phone, Internet. **Each Site:** Picnic table, grill. **Dump Station:** Yes. **Laundry:** Yes. **Pay Phone:** Yes. **Restrooms and Showers:** Yes. **Fuel:** No. **Propane:** Yes. **Internal Roads:** Gravel, in good condition. **RV Service:** In town. **Market:** In town. **Restaurant:** In town. **General Store:** Yes. **Vending:** No. **Swimming:** Yes. **Playground:** Yes. **Other:** 3 cabins, store, cafe, Internet data port. **Activities:** Game room, playground, horseshoes, volleyball, basketball. **Nearby Attractions:** Dinosaur Beds, Shell Falls, horseback riding. **Additional Information:** Greybull Chamber of Commerce, (307) 765-2100.

RESTRICTIONS

Pets: On leash. **Fires:** At approved sites only. **Alcoholic Beverages:** Allowed. **Vehicle Maximum Length:** No limit.

TO GET THERE

Go 4 blocks north of Hwy. 14 off Second St. or 4 blocks east of Hwy. 16/20 off Third Ave. in Greybull.

JACKSON HOLE   MAP, B-1
Snake River Park KOA
Jackson Hole Campground
(Jackson South KOA)

9705 South Hwy. 89, 83001. T: (307) 733-7078;
www.koa.com or www.snakeriverpark.com.

🚐 ★★★★   ⛺ ★★★★

Beauty: ★★★★   Site Privacy: ★★★★
Spaciousness: ★★★★   Quiet: ★★★★
Security: ★★★★   Cleanliness: ★★★★
Insect Control: ★★★★   Facilities: ★★★★

Snake River Park KOA is positioned between the Snake River and Horse Creek only a few short miles south of Jackson Hole. The Snake River runs directly behind the facility and adds to the rustic atmosphere. The Snake River Park KOA is a full-service camping facility that offers grass sites and large shade trees along the water's edge. All sites have a gravel parking area, and both pull-through and back-in sites are available. This particular KOA is also a fully licensed float trip outfitter by the Bridger-Teton National Forest and specializes in packaged float trips both for individuals and for groups. They have Coast Guard–approved equipment and provide both food and transportation. The campground itself has a large convenience store, gift shop, game room, and snacks. This is a very lively KOA that caters to patrons utilizing their float service.

BASICS

Operated By: Snake River Park, Inc. **Open:** Apr.–mid-Oct. **Site Assignment:** By reservation; cabin deposit required; checks taken on deposits only until Apr. 1. **Registration:** At camp store. **Fee:** RV, $48.95–$50.95; tent, $34.95; per 2 people; each extra person (5 & over), $6; max. of 6 people per site. **Parking:** Yes; extra vehicle fee, $10; campers allowed 1 tow.

FACILITIES

Number of RV-only Sites: 47. **Number of Tent-only Sites:** 28. **Hookups:** Electric (30, 50 amps), water, sewer. **Each Site:** Picnic table, fire pit. **Dump Station:** Yes. **Laundry:** Yes. **Pay Phone:** Yes. **Restrooms and Showers:** Yes. **Fuel:** 1 mi. south in town. **Propane:** 1 mi. south in town. **Internal Roads:** Gravel, in good condition. **RV Service:** Mobile service from Jackson. **Market:** In Jackson. **Restaurant:** Cafe on site, restaurant across the street, or in Jackson. **General Store:** Yes. **Vending:** General store. **Swimming:** No. **Playground:** Yes. **Other:** River access, whitewater rafting outfitters, 17 cabins, float packages. **Activities:** Rafting, fishing, tubing. **Nearby Attractions:** Jackson Hole, skiing, the Grand Tetons, Yellowstone National Park. **Additional Information:** Jackson Hole Chamber of Commerce, (307) 733-3316.

RESTRICTIONS

Pets: On leash only. **Fires:** At approved sites only. **Alcoholic Beverages:** Allowed. **Vehicle Maximum Length:** No limit. **Other:** 10-day stay limit; KOA discount.

TO GET THERE

From Jackson, go south on US 26/89 for about 5 mi. Campground is on the right.

JACKSON HOLE MAP, B-1
Virginian Lodge and RV Resort

750 West Broadway, 83001.
T: (307) 733-2792 or (800) 321-6982.

🚐 ★★★ ⛺ n/a

Beauty: ★★★	Site Privacy: ★★★
Spaciousness: ★★	Quiet: ★★★
Security: ★★★	Cleanliness: ★★★
Insect Control: ★★★	Facilities: ★★★

The Virginian Lodge and RV Resort is suitably located in downtown Jackson Hole. The property is convenient to a vast number of novelty shops and excellent restaurants. The campground is open to RVs only and offers a full array of camping amenities. The campsites are gravel with some grass and shade. The facility offers both pull-through and back-in sites and has room to accommodate large RVs. There is a nice-sized swimming pool, hot tub, and full-service lodge. Jackson Hole is but a short drive from the Grand Teton National Park and serves as the south entrance to Yellowstone National Park. The area is a great base camp for those patrons wishing to experience the parks or take a float trip down the Snake River. The resort staff is very friendly and will be more than happy to assist with any needs. The weather can be a bit windy and dry, so it is always best to be prepared.

BASICS

Operated By: Wayne & Lynn Simons. **Open:** May 1–Oct. 15. **Site Assignment:** By reservation. **Registration:** At camp registration office, located at the front gate. **Fee:** $37–$45; no personal checks. **Parking:** At site.

FACILITIES

Number of RV-only Sites: 105. **Hookups:** Electric (20, 30, 50 amps), water, sewer, cable TV. **Each Site:** Picnic table, grill. **Dump Station:** Yes. **Laundry:** Yes. **Pay Phone:** Yes. **Restrooms and Showers:** Yes. **Fuel:** Less than a mi. in any direction. **Propane:** Same as above. **Internal Roads:** Gravel, in good condition. **RV Service:** 65 mi. west in Idaho Falls, Idaho. **Market:** In Jackson. **Restaurant:** On site. Large selection in town. **General Store:** No. **Vending:** Yes. **Swimming:** Yes w/ Jacuzzi at the lodge. **Playground:** Yes. **Other:** Hotel, meeting rooms, central data port in office. **Activities:** There are no activities on site other than the pool & playground. **Nearby Attractions:** Yellowstone National Park, the Grand Tetons, Jackson Hole, Jackson National Fish Hatchery, National Museum of Wildlife Art, Snow King Mountain Ski Area, Jackson Hole Ski Area. **Additional Information:** Jackson Hole Chamber of Commerce, (307) 733-3316.

RESTRICTIONS

Pets: On leash only. **Fires:** No open fires, charcoal grills only. **Alcoholic Beverages:** Allowed. **Vehicle Maximum Length:** 45 ft. **Other:** AAA, Good Sam.

TO GET THERE

Once in Jackson Hole, US 26/89 will be W. Broadway. The campground is behind the lodge on Virginian Lane, heading northeast toward the Tetons.

LYMAN MAP, C-1
Lyman KOA

HC 66 Box 55, 1531 North Hwy. 413, 82937.
T: (307) 786-2188 or (800) 562-2762;
www.koa.com.

🚐 ★★★★ ⛺ ★★★

Beauty: ★★★	Site Privacy: ★★★
Spaciousness: ★★★	Quiet: ★★★★
Security: ★★★★	Cleanliness: ★★★
Insect Control: ★★★	Facilities: ★★★

Located between Evanston and Rock Springs, this delightful medium-sized campground is set in a rural atmosphere. The Lyman KOA is charming and inviting. The campground has a beautiful green lawn, with just enough shade from a few large trees, and a large outdoor swimming pool. The owners are friendly and genuinely pleased to assist their customers. Each campsite has a gravel parking area, and both pull-through and back-in sites are available. There is a large covered pavilion great for family outings, along with a small basketball court and other games. The town of Lyman is small, and this is a great place to read a book and enjoy a nice spring breeze. The historic Ft. Bridger is only a short drive away, and the Mountain Man Rendezvous is celebrated Labor Day weekend.

BASICS

Operated By: Clark Anderson. **Open:** May 15–Oct. 1. **Site Assignment:** By reservation. **Registration:** At camp store. **Fee:** RV, $40–$68; tent, $17; per 2 people; each extra person (over age 4), $1.50. **Parking:** At site.

FACILITIES

Number of RV-only Sites: 36. **Number of Tent-only Sites:** 17. **Hookups:** Electric (20, 30, 50 amps), water, sewer. **Each Site:** Picnic table, some fire pits. **Dump Station:** Yes. **Laundry:** Yes. **Pay Phone:** Yes. **Restrooms and Showers:** Yes. **Fuel:** 7 mi. in Mt. View. **Propane:** 7 mi. in Mt. View. **Internal Roads:** Gravel, in good condition. **RV Service:** Local service. **Market:** Mt. View. **Restaurant:** In town. **General Store:** Yes. **Vending:** Yes. **Swimming:** Yes. **Playground:** Yes. **Other:** 2 cabins, pavilion w/ kitchen, horseshoes, Internet data port. **Activities:** Game room, playground, horseshoes, basketball, volleyball. **Nearby Attractions:** Flaming Gorge, Rock City. **Additional Information:** Bridger Valley Chamber of Commerce, (307) 787-6738.

RESTRICTIONS

Pets: On leash. **Fires:** Fire ring only. **Alcoholic Beverages:** Allowed. **Vehicle Maximum Length:** No limit.

TO GET THERE

Campground is 1 mi. south of I-80 at Exit 44.

MOOSE MAP, B-1
Grand Tetons

P.O. Drawer 170, 83012. T: (307) 739-3300;
www.grand.teton.national-park.com.

🚐 ★★★ ⛺ ★★★★

Beauty: ★★★★★	Site Privacy: ★★★
Spaciousness: ★★	Quiet: ★★★
Security: ★★★★	Cleanliness: ★★★
Insect Control: ★★	Facilities: ★★★

Regal and proud, the Grand Tetons stand tall over the Snake River and peer down from the heavens. This natural marvel represents the most intact temperate ecosystem in North America. Renowned for its world-famous wildlife viewing and unparalleled beauty, the Grand Teton National Park portrays an image of strength and majesty. The park has a total of six large campgrounds with over 1,000 campsites. The sites range from primitive to modern, with Colter Bay Trailer Village offering full hookups. The Grand Teton Lodge Company is the in-park concessionaire and oversees the majority of guest services, including camping reservations in three of the six campgrounds. The campgrounds are configured in loops, with paved parking pads, potable water, and restroom facilities. Showers are available in the Colter Bay Service Area at the laundry. The Grand Tetons, like any national park, is home and refuge to many forms of wildlife—including bear, moose, and elk—therefore it is very important for your safety to please follow all the regulations put forth by the National Park Service.

BASICS

Operated By: National Park Service. **Open:** All year; most camping areas open mid-May–end of Sept. **Site Assignment:** First come, first served w/ exception of Colter Bay Trailer Village; call (307) 739-3399 for visitor information. **Registration:** At registration office. **Fee:** $10–$30; based on which campground is chosen & the amenities they provide. **Parking:** At site.

FACILITIES

Number of RV-only Sites: 112. **Number of Multipurpose Sites:** 905. **Hookups:** Electric (20, 30, 50 amps), water, sewer in Colter Bay Trailer Village Park only; no hookups at the other 5 campgrounds inside the park. **Each Site:** Picnic table, fire pit (except Colter Bay trailer Village). **Dump Station:** Yes, at Gros Ventre, Signal Mountain, & Colter Bay. **Laundry:** Yes, in the service area at Colter Bay. **Pay Phone:** Pay phones are located throughout the park, but not necessarily at each campground, primarily in the service areas. **Restrooms and Showers:** Restrooms in every campground, showers in the service areas near Colter Bay for a fee. **Fuel:** 3 service areas: Colter Bay, Jenny Lake, & Moose Junction. **Propane:** Yes, in several service areas. **Internal Roads:** Paved but in need of repair. **RV Service:** Minor repair service available at Colter Bay. **Market:** Several in the park, or in Jackson Hole, WY. **Restaurant:** Several restaurants in the park, Jenny Lake Lodge, Signal Mountain Lodge, Jackson Lake Lodge, & Flagg Ranch. **General Store:** 3 general stores at Colter Bay, Jenny Lake, Jackson Lake. **Vending:** In the major service areas of the park. **Swimming:** No. **Playground:** No. **Other:** The Grand Teton National Park is its own community w/ lodging, food, transportation, laundry, stores, restaurants, & medical clinic. Each guest will be given a newsletter upon arrival w/ a complete listing of the parks amenities & services. **Activities:** Horseback riding, motor coach tours, photo safaris, hiking, backpacking, ranger-led

programs, evening programs, photo hikes, lectures, boating, tennis, golf, biking tours. **Nearby Attractions:** Yellowstone National Park, Jackson Hole, Jackson National Fish Hatchery, National Museum of Wildlife Art, Snow King Mountain Ski Area, Jackson Hole Ski Area. **Additional Information:** Grand Teton Lodge Company, (307) 543-2811; Jackson Hole Chamber of Commerce, (307) 733-3316; National Park Service U.S. Dept. of the Interior, or there are many Internet links to Yellowstone National Park.

RESTRICTIONS

Pets: On a leash only. However, we strongly discourage bringing them. Pets are not allowed out of the camping areas or off the main roads. Pets are not allowed in the backcountry. **Fires:** Fire pit only (fires may be prohibited due to weather conditions, please ask before starting any open fire). **Alcoholic Beverages:** Allowed. **Vehicle Maximum Length:** 45 ft. (varies by campground).

TO GET THERE

Three main gates into the Grand Tetons—the most popular is through Jackson on Hwy. 191.

MORAN   MAP, A-1
The Flagg Ranch Resort

P.O. Box 187, 83013.
T: (800) 443-2311 or (307) 543-2861;
www.flaggranch.com.

🚐 ★★★   ⛺ ★★★

Beauty: ★★★★★	Site Privacy: ★★★
Spaciousness: ★★★	Quiet: ★★★★
Security: ★★★	Cleanliness: ★★★
Insect Control: ★★★	Facilities: ★★★

The Flagg Ranch Resort Campground is in one of the most ideal locations in Wyoming. It is situated between the Grand Tetons National Park and the south entrance to Yellowstone National Park along Hwy 89. This campground is privately owned in conjunction with a full-service lodge and service station. The campground sits in a forest of large evergreens and offers a real sense of tranquility. A great base for visiting both national parks, this campground offers all the amenities expected of a full-service RV camp. Each campsite has a gravel parking pad, hookups, and fire ring, as well as a natural forest floor and towering pines. Due to the location of this camping facility and the fact that there is only one trailer campground with hookups in either park, reservations must be made far in advance. Also, there is no access to this campground except through one of the national parks; therefore, expect to pay a park entrance fee.

BASICS

Operated By: Bob Walker. **Open:** All year. **Site Assignment:** By reservation. **Registration:** At camp store. **Fee:** RV, $45; tent, $20; per 2 people; extra child/adult, $2. **Parking:** At site.

FACILITIES

Number of RV-only Sites: 97. **Number of Tent-only Sites:** 74. **Hookups:** Electric (20, 30 amps), water, sewer. **Each Site:** Picnic table & fire pit in tent sites. **Dump Station:** No. **Laundry:** Yes. **Pay Phone:** Yes. **Restrooms and Showers:** Yes. **Fuel:** Yes. **Propane:** Yes. **Internal Roads:** Gravel, in good

condition. **RV Service:** At Colter Bay Village. **Market:** At Colter Bay Village. **Restaurant:** On site at the lodge. **General Store:** Yes. **Vending:** Yes. **Swimming:** No. **Playground:** Yes. **Other:** Main lodge w/ dining area, fireplace, gift shop, store, service station, meeting rooms, cabins, hotel, Internet data ports. **Activities:** Fishing, hiking, float tours, biking, horseback riding, coach tours. **Nearby Attractions:** Yellowstone National Park, the Grand Tetons, Jackson Hole, Jackson National Fish Hatchery, National Museum of Wildlife Art, Snow King Mountain Ski Area, Jackson Hole Ski Area, fishing, float trips, covered wagon cookouts. **Additional Information:** Jackson Hole Chamber of Commerce, (307) 733-3316.

RESTRICTIONS

Pets: On leash only. **Fires:** Fire pit only. **Alcoholic Beverages:** Allowed. **Vehicle Maximum Length:** 45 ft. **Other:** Expect to pay a national park entrance fee, unless you have a park pass.

TO GET THERE

The campground is located directly between the south gate of Yellowstone National Park and north gate of the Grand Tetons National Park on Hwy. 89 (you will have to enter through one of the two parks, so expect to pay a park entrance fee).

MORAN   MAP, A-1
Grand Teton Park RV Resort

P.O. Box 92, Hwy. 26/287, 83013.
T: (800) 563-6469 or (307) 733-1980;
www.yellowstonerv.com.

🚐 ★★★   ⛺ ★★★

Beauty: ★★★★★	Site Privacy: ★★★
Spaciousness: ★★★	Quiet: ★★★★
Security: ★★★	Cleanliness: ★★★
Insect Control: ★★★	Facilities: ★★★

The Grand Teton Park RV Resort is just 1 mile east of the Grand Tetons National Park and 32 miles from the south gate of Yellowstone. Few other full-service RV campgrounds are more convenient to the national parks (though there is at least one—see profile for Flagg Ranch Resort). The Grand Teton Park RV Resort offers a spectacular panoramic view of the majestic Grand Tetons, in addition to comfortable and affordable lodging year-round. The campground offers over 200 campsites, large, open tenting areas, and five teepees. They have both pull-through and back-in sites, as well as level parking spaces. The campground has full amenities, including a deli, pizza, and fuel. The property also offers a variety of services such as snowmobile and van rentals. This campground is also in close proximity to the scenic Snake River and many rafting outfitters. The weather in summer is comfortable, and the winter is harsh—but regardless of the season, this campground is always inviting.

BASICS

Operated By: Private operator. **Open:** All year. **Site Assignment:** By reservation. **Registration:** At camp store. **Fee:** RV, $32–$40; tent, $29; per 2 people; extra child, $4; extra adult, $5. **Parking:** At site.

FACILITIES

Number of RV-only Sites: 140. **Number of Tent-only Sites:** 60. **Hookups:** Electric (20, 30, 50 amps), water, sewer. **Each Site:** Picnic table & fire pit in tent sites. **Dump Station:** Yes. **Laundry:** Yes. **Pay Phone:** Yes. **Restrooms and Showers:** Yes. **Fuel:** Yes. **Propane:** Yes. **Internal Roads:** Gravel, in good condition. **RV Service:** Mobile service. **Market:** 36 mi. southwest in Jackson. **Restaurant:** 2 mi. in any direction, including The Buffalo Valley Ranch Café. **General Store:** Yes. **Vending:** No. **Swimming:** Yes, w/ hot tub. **Playground:** Yes. **Other:** 18 cabins, game room, 5 tepees, pizza & deli, central data port in office. **Activities:** Pool, playground. **Nearby Attractions:** Yellowstone National Park, the Grand Tetons, Jackson Hole, Jackson National Fish Hatchery, National Museum of Wildlife Art, Snow King Mountain Ski Area, Jackson Hole Ski Area, fishing, float trips, covered wagon cookouts. **Additional Information:** Jackson Hole Chamber of Commerce, (307) 733-3316.

RESTRICTIONS

Pets: On leash only. **Fires:** Fire pit only. **Alcoholic Beverages:** Allowed. **Vehicle Maximum Length:** 45 ft. **Other:** AAA, Good Sam, KOA discounts.

TO GET THERE

The campground is 6 mi. east of the Moran junction on Hwys. 26 and 287.

RAWLINS   MAP, C-3
Rawlins KOA

205 East Hwy. 71, 82301.
T: (307) 328-2021 or (800) 562-7559;
www.koa.com.

🚐 ★★★   ⛺ ★★

Beauty: ★★★	Site Privacy: ★★★
Spaciousness: ★★★	Quiet: ★★★
Security: ★★★★	Cleanliness: ★★★
Insect Control: ★★★	Facilities: ★★★★

The Rawlins KOA is located directly off I-80 and offers convenient lodging in a clean and well-maintained atmosphere. The Rawlins KOA is nicely landscaped in a desert area where it is hard for anything to grow. The campsites can accommodate newer and longer RVs. Each site has a level, gravel parking area, as well as free cable TV. The tent sites have tent pads and wind shields. The weather is very dry, and there is a considerable amount of sand in this region. In addition, the campground has a nice swimming pool and a camp kitchen. There is fishing in the Seminoe Reservoir or the North Platte River nearby, and hunting for antelope and deer. The community of Rawlins is full of interesting places to see, such as the Frontier Prison and Fort Steele.

BASICS

Operated By: Fran & Jean Farrell. **Open:** Apr.–Oct. 31. **Site Assignment:** By reservation. **Registration:** At camp store. **Fee:** RVs, $22–$32; tent, $18–$22; per 2 people; each extra person (over age 5), $3. **Parking:** At site.

FACILITIES

Number of RV-only Sites: 56. **Number of

Tent-only Sites: 6. **Hookups:** Electric (20, 30, 50 amps), water, sewer. **Each Site:** Picnic table & fire pit in the tent & cabin area. **Dump Station:** Yes. **Laundry:** Yes. **Pay Phone:** Yes. **Restrooms and Showers:** Yes. **Fuel:** No. **Propane:** Yes. **Internal Roads:** Gravel, in good condition. **RV Service:** In Laramie. **Market:** In town. **Restaurant:** In town. **General Store:** Yes. **Vending:** Yes. **Swimming:** Yes. **Playground:** Yes. **Other:** 5 cabins, store, Internet data port. **Activities:** Game room, playground, horseshoes, basketball. **Nearby Attractions:** Carbon County Museum, Frontier Prison, Snowy Ridge Scenic Byway. **Additional Information:** Rawlins Chamber of Commerce, (307) 324-4111 or (800) 935-4821.

RESTRICTIONS

Pets: On leash. **Fires:** Fire ring only. **Alcoholic Beverages:** Allowed. **Vehicle Maximum Length:** No limit.

TO GET THERE

The campground is near Exit 214 off I-80 in central Rawlins.

RIVERTON   MAP, B-2
Owl Creek Kampground

11124 US 26/789, 82501. T: (307) 856-2869; www.campowlcreek.com.

🚐 ★★★★   ▲ ★★★★

Beauty: ★★★★	Site Privacy: ★★★★
Spaciousness: ★★★★	Quiet: ★★★★
Security: ★★★★	Cleanliness: ★★★★
Insect Control: ★★★★	Facilities: ★★★

Owl Creek Kampground in Riverton is a lovely, established campground. Owl Creek was one of the original KOA campgrounds. The original KOA structure and open breezeway still stand. The campground is one of the only campgrounds in Wyoming with thick, lush, green grass and mature, large, deciduous shade trees. The campground is beautifully maintained and has nostalgia for the past. This reminiscence is apparent in the owners' display of antiques and the older facilities. The owners live in a large colonial home on the property, and the house is the focal point of the park. Owl Creek caters to more mature visitors that appreciate the calm atmosphere and picturesque setting. Simply due to the age of this campground, sites needed to accommodate large RVs are very limited.

BASICS

Operated By: Frank & Pat Petek. **Open:** May 15–Sept. 15. **Site Assignment:** By reservation. **Registration:** At camp office. **Fee:** $18.50; per 2 people. **Parking:** At site.

FACILITIES

Number of RV-only Sites: 21. **Number of Tent-only Sites:** 20. **Number of Multipurpose Sites:** 11. **Hookups:** Electric (20, 30, 50 amps), water, sewer, a few phones. **Each Site:** Picnic table, grill. **Dump Station:** Yes. **Laundry:** Yes. **Pay Phone:** Yes. **Restrooms and Showers:** Yes. **Fuel:** No, but in town. **Propane:** No. **Internal Roads:** Paved. **RV Service:** Local service. **Market:** In town. **Restaurant:** In town. **General Store:** Yes. **Vending:** Yes.

Swimming: No. **Playground:** Yes. **Other:** Orchard, utility sink. **Activities:** Playground, tetherball. **Nearby Attractions:** Fishing, hunting, boating, biking, hiking, & scenic byways. **Additional Information:** Riverton Chamber of Commerce, (307) 856-4801.

RESTRICTIONS

Pets: On leash. **Fires:** At approved sites. **Alcoholic Beverages:** Allowed. **Vehicle Maximum Length:** 40 ft. (limited room for extra-long RV).

TO GET THERE

The campground is 5 mi. northeast of Riverton on Hwy. 26.

THERMOPOLIS   MAP, B-2
Country Campin' RV and Tent Park

790 East Sunnyside Lane, 82443. T: (800) 609-2244; www.countrycamp.net.

🚐 ★★★★★   ▲ ★★★★

Beauty: ★★★★	Site Privacy: ★★★★
Spaciousness: ★★★★	Quiet: ★★★★★
Security: ★★★★★	Cleanliness: ★★★★★
Insect Control: ★★★★	Facilities: ★★★★

Located on the owners' private ranch, Country Campin' RV and Tent Park is a charming, small, private campground 5 miles north of Thermopolis. The campground offers full amenities with waterfront access. Campsites are mostly pull-throughs, large, level, and with gravel parking spurs. There is a small store and gift shop, laundry, clean restrooms and showers. The owners have a few farm animals for children to pet and two friendly dogs that watch over the campground. The campground is nicely landscaped, and the sprinklers are on frequently. There is a small boat dock for nonmotorized boats, and there's great fishing along the Big Horn River. The campground has a large open common area, and it's decorated with large, colorful dinosaur statues. Thermopolis is home of Wyoming's Dinosaur Center and earth's largest mineral hot springs, which are open 365 days a year.

BASICS

Operated By: Darvin & Spring Longwell. **Open:** Mar. 15–Nov. 1. **Site Assignment:** By reservation. **Registration:** At camp store. **Fee:** RV, $22.50; tent, $16.50; per 2 people; extra people, $1.50. **Parking:** At site.

FACILITIES

Number of RV-only Sites: 42. **Number of Tent-only Sites:** 25. **Hookups:** Electric (20, 30, 50 amps), water, sewer. **Each Site:** Picnic table. **Dump Station:** Yes. **Laundry:** Yes. **Pay Phone:** Yes. **Restrooms and Showers:** Yes. **Fuel:** No, but local. **Propane:** Yes. **Internal Roads:** Gravel, in good condition. **RV Service:** In town. **Market:** In town. **Restaurant:** In town. **General Store:** Yes. **Vending:** Yes. **Swimming:** No (No swimming in the river). **Playground:** Yes. **Other:** Boat launch, petting zoo, gift shop, teepees, horseback riding & boarding. **Activities:** Playground, hiking, blue ribbon–level trout fishing, boating. **Nearby Attractions:** World's

largest mineral hot spring, Wyoming's Dinosaur Center. **Additional Information:** Thermopolis Chamber of Commerce, (307) 864-3192.

RESTRICTIONS

Pets: On leash. **Fires:** In approved areas & out by 10 p.m. **Alcoholic Beverages:** Allowed. **Vehicle Maximum Length:** No limit.

TO GET THERE

5.4 mi. north of Thermopolis off US 20 on E. Sunnyside Lane. This campground is on a private farm.

THERMOPOLIS   MAP, B-2
Eagle RV Park

204 Hwy. 20 South, 82443. T: (307) 864-5262 or (888) 865-5707; www.eaglervpark.com.

🚐 ★★★   ▲ ★★★

Beauty: ★★★	Site Privacy: ★★★
Spaciousness: ★★★	Quiet: ★★★★
Security: ★★★★	Cleanliness: ★★★
Insect Control: ★★★	Facilities: ★★★

Eagle RV Park is located in the city of Thermopolis on Highway 20. Thermopolis is home of the world's largest mineral pool and hot springs. Eagle RV Park is only a few miles from Hot Springs State Park, where visitors from all over the world come to see and enjoy the pools. The Eagle RV Park is convenient to the Big Horn River and offers float trip packages to its patrons. Internal roads are paved. Restrooms and showers are clean, and the grounds are well kept. Campsites are updated. The owners are very gracious hosts, and they are always there to assist. The weather is dry here, and skin protection is always needed, especially in the mineral pools.

BASICS

Operated By: Harold & Katrina Anton. **Open:** All year. **Site Assignment:** By reservation. **Registration:** At camp office. **Fee:** RV, $25; tent, $19; per 2 people; extra person, $1.50. **Parking:** At site.

FACILITIES

Number of RV-only Sites: 35. **Number of Tent-only Sites:** 9. **Hookups:** Electric (20, 30, 50 amps), water, sewer, cable TV, phone, Wi-Fi. **Each Site:** Picnic tables, grills. **Dump Station:** Yes. **Laundry:** Yes. **Pay Phone:** Yes. **Restrooms and Showers:** Yes. **Fuel:** No, but in town. **Propane:** Yes. **Internal Roads:** Paved asphalt. **RV Service:** Local service. **Market:** In town. **Restaurant:** In town. **General Store:** Yes. **Vending:** Yes. **Swimming:** No. **Playground:** Yes. **Other:** Tube rentals, float trips, 4 cabins, pet walk area, horseshoes, basketball. **Activities:** Playground, rafting, game room. **Nearby Attractions:** Thermopolis hot springs, Wyoming Dinosaur Center, several small museums, blue ribbon–level trout fishing, golf, Hot Springs State Park. **Additional Information:** Thermopolis Chamber of Commerce, (307) 864-3192.

RESTRICTIONS

Pets: On leash. **Fires:** At approved sites. **Alcoholic Beverages:** Allowed. **Vehicle Maximum Length:** 40 ft. (limited room for extra-long RV).

To Get There

The campground is located on Hwy. 20, 2 mi. south of the stop sign in Thermopolis.

YELLOWSTONE NATIONAL PARK
Yellowstone National Park

MAP. A-1

P.O. Box 168, 82190-0168.
T: (307) 344-7381 or (307) 344-2386 (TDD);
www.nps.gov/yell/index.htm.

🚐 ★★★   ⛺ ★★★★

Beauty: ★★★★★   Site Privacy: ★★★
Spaciousness: ★★   Quiet: ★★★
Security: ★★★★   Cleanliness: ★★★
Insect Control: ★★   Facilities: ★★★

Yellowstone National Park encompasses the entire northwestern corner of Wyoming, with over 2.2 million acres of federal land serving as the world's first and oldest national park. The park has five major entrances and a total of 12 campgrounds with over a 2,000 campsites among them. The campsites range from very primitive to full hookups. Most are RV-friendly, with level parking pads, grated fire pits, potable water, and restrooms in a wooded location. Most all of the campgrounds are configured as large multiple loops. Amfac Parks and Resorts are the primary in-park concessionaire and provide the majority of guest services, overseeing the five major campgrounds. Campsites managed by Amfac may be reserved up to a year in advance. Yellowstone Park is open all year; however, there is very limited camping after September. Yellowstone National Park is a wonderful natural attraction, but first and foremost it is a home and refuge to the wildlife that inhabit the land.

Therefore, we are all guests of these majestic animals and must respect the regulations put forth by the National Park Service for our protection as well as that of the wildlife. If you're considering a trip to Yellowstone National Park, please plan far in advance and contact visitor services.

BASICS

Operated By: National Park Service. **Open:** Park, open all year; most camping areas open mid-May–end of Sept. Mommoth open all year. Fishing Lodge, May 18–Sept. 23. **Site Assignment:** First come, first served, except Fishing Bridge RV Park, which is by reservation & concessioned by Amfac Parks & Resorts; call (800) 329-9205 or (307) 344-7311. **Registration:** At registration office. **Fee:** $10–$30. **Parking:** At site.

FACILITIES

Number of RV-only Sites: 340 (Fishing Bridge only). **Number of Tent-only Sites:** 454. **Number of Multipurpose Sites:** 1406. **Hookups:** Electric (20, 30, 50 amps), water, sewer at Fishing Bridge RV Park only; no hookups at the other 11 campgrounds inside the park. **Each Site:** Picnic tables, fire pits (except Fishing Bridge). **Dump Station:** Yes, at Bridge Bay, Canyon, Fishing Bridge, Grant Village, & Madison. **Laundry:** Yes, in the service area near Canyon, Fishing Bridge, & Grant Village. **Pay Phone:** Located throughout the park, but not necessarily at each campground. **Restrooms and Showers:** Restrooms located in every campground; showers in the service areas near Canyon, Fishing Bridge, & Grants Village. **Fuel:** Yes, 8 service areas throughout the park. **Propane:** Yes, in several service areas throughout the park. **Internal Roads:** The majority are paved. **RV Service:** There are several repair stations in the park. **Market:** Several in the park, or West Yellowstone, MT. **Restaurant:** 17 restaurants

in the park, 5 by Old Faithful, 2 in Grants Village, 3 in Canyon Village, 3 in Lake Village, 2 in Tower Roosevelt. **General Store:** 13 general stores throughout the park. **Vending:** In the major service areas of the park. **Swimming:** No. **Playground:** No. **Other:** Yellowstone National Park is a community w/ lodging, food, transportation, laundry, stores, restaurants, & hospital. Each guest will be given a newsletter upon arrival w/ a complete listing of the park's amenities & services. **Activities:** Horseback riding, Stagecoach rides, Bridge Bay Guided Fishing Trips, motor coach tours, Old West Cookouts, photo safaris, hiking, backpacking, ranger-led programs, evening programs, Yellowstone for kids, photo hikes, lectures. **Nearby Attractions:** West Yellowstone, MT, visitors center, Imax, 15 museums, rodeos, the Grand Tetons, Jackson Hole, WY, Cody, WY, shopping. **Additional Information:** West Yellowstone Chamber of Commerce, (406) 646-7701, or there are many Internet links to Yellowstone National Park.

RESTRICTIONS

Pets: Although pets are allowed in Yellowstone National Park on a leash only, we strongly discourage bringing them. Pets are not allowed out of the camping areas or off the main roads. Pets are not allowed in the backcountry or in any public viewing areas. **Fires:** Fire pit only in approved areas. No open fires in Fishing Bridge. Note: fires may be prohibited due to weather conditions. Ask staff before starting any open fire. **Alcoholic Beverages:** Allowed. **Vehicle Maximum Length:** Varies by campground; call reservation line (800) 329-9205 or (307) 344-7311.

To Get There

There are 5 entrances into Yellowstone. Visit www.yellowstone.com.

British Columbia

Southwest British Columbia extends from the southeast end of the **Fraser Valley** in **Hope,** through the start of the **Coast Mountains** just north of **Vancouver,** and ends in **Pemberton.** Within this small section of the large province, travelers can find a diverse array of activities and sights, from cosmopolitan to wilderness.

Squamish and **Whistler** provide the major ecotourism and outdoor sports centers for southwest British Columbia. Squamish prides itself on being cheaper than Whistler, and it's only a short drive away. Squamish has the same outdoor opportunities as Whistler, with one exception—skiing. Whistler is the province's premier Western ski-resort town. Organized recreation north of Whistler exists, but on a smaller scale.

If traveling between Whistler and Pemberton, make sure to have plenty of gas in your tank. Though the distance is short, filling stations come in short supply anywhere north of Whistler. In some of northern British Columbia and the Yukon, it is a good idea to fill up at every gas station along the way.

When going from Vancouver to Alaska or the Yukon, travelers have an alternative to the British Columbia leg of the Alaska Highway. Take the **Cassiar Highway** (Highway 37) running south from Highway 1 near **Upper Liard, Yukon,** to Highway 16 and continuing to **Prince George.** However, be advised: this road is extremely rugged (both in environment and construction), very long, and scarcely populated or traversed along the northernmost 550 miles. Services exist, but just barely.

Camping in northern British Columbia and the Yukon involves little more than stopping at a pull-out (do not camp in a slow vehicle turnout). Empty septic tanks at designated dump stations only, pack all trash to a commercial waste disposal pickup (gas station, etc.), be aware of bears and other animals (consider any wild animal potentially dangerous on approach or confrontation), help people out with car trouble in wilderness areas (otherwise they may be stranded for hours), and carry plenty of water. But if time doesn't permit the lengthy trip through the north country, enjoy the stay in southwest British Columbia.

A note on customs: some products commercially available in the United States will cause trouble at the border. Melatonin is one, alligator meat is another. Anything that seems like drugs or paraphernalia without prescription will cause trouble. Do not take weapons into Canada. If arrested by customs for anything, you will be summarily fined and detained until you pay the fine, and your vehicle will be impounded (to be extricated only by payment of another, usually larger fine). If the offense is deemed large enough, the Royal Canadian Mounted Police will be called, and criminal charges may also be brought.

ABBOTSFORD MAP, C-3
Abbotsford Camp and RV Park

36114 Lower Sumas Mountain Rd., V3G 2J3.
T: (604) 855-3330.

🚐 ★★★★   ⛺ ★★★★

Beauty: ★★★★   Site Privacy: ★★★
Spaciousness: ★★★   Quiet: ★★★
Security: ★★★   Cleanliness: ★★★★
Insect Control: ★★   Facilities: ★★★

Abbotsford Campground, 10 minutes north of the Sumas border crossing and just off Hwy. 1, has attractive landscaping and private tent sites. The hilly grounds have an enormous pool, two smaller hot tubs, a little shade from cedar trees, beautifully maintained grass, and a subtle scheme of potted flowers and shrubs. RV sites come in several flavors: flat grass, gravel, or paved, each with full hookups, and all positioned over gently rolling hills. Most RV sites lack privacy; sites 53–59 lack the flatness most other sites provide. The best paved, grass sites with full hookups, 60–69, sit on the south edge of the park. Extremely thick, tall cedar hedges mark the boundaries for most grass tent sites, creating walls of privacy. On the south edge of the park, there is a hill providing a small viewpoint with a spectacular view of Snowy Mount Baker rising from the horizon (no individual sites have any particularly striking views). Tent sites A1–A10 have the best privacy with cedar hedges on two sides and a hill on the third. Summer provides the best weather for visiting the area, however some grass RV sites may be closed during rainy periods.

BASICS

Operated By: Abbotsford Camp & RV Park. **Open:** All year. **Site Assignment:** Reservations recommended; 1-night deposit; refund w/ 72-hour cancellation notice. **Registration:** At office, gate locked at 11 p.m. **Fee:** Full, $28; water/electric, $26; tent, $23. For 2 people; V, MC, cash, personal check (Canadian). **Parking:** At site, limited off site.

FACILITIES

Number of RV-only Sites: 71. **Number of Tent-only Sites:** 17. **Hookups:** Electric (15, 30 amps), water, sewer, cable TV. **Each Site:** Picnic table. **Dump Station:** Inquire at campground. **Laundry:** Inquire at campground. **Pay Phone:** Inquire at campground. **Restrooms and Showers:** Inquire at campground. **Fuel:** Inquire at campground. **Propane:** Inquire at campground. **Internal Roads:** Paved. **RV Service:** No. **Market:** 4 mi. west. **Restaurant:** 1 mi. south. **General Store:** No. **Vending:** Yes. **Swimming:** Pool (June–Sept.). **Playground:** Yes. **Other:** 2 hot tubs, reservable cabin (meeting hall), view point. **Activities:** Swimming. **Nearby Attractions:** Vancouver (45 minutes east), BC Farm Machinery & Agricultural Museum, Aldergrove Telephone Museum, Cheam Lake Wetlands Regional Park, Minter Gardens, golf, fun castle.

RESTRICTIONS

Pets: On leash only. **Fires:** No open fires. **Alcoholic Beverages:** At site only. **Vehicle Maximum Length:** No limit. **Other:** Gates closed 11 p.m.– 7 a.m.

TO GET THERE

From Hwy. 1 Exit 95 (Whatcom Rd.), go north 3 mi. and take first right onto Lower Sumas Mountain, drive 0.1 mi. and entrance is on the right.

CULTUS LAKE MAP, C-3
Sunnyside Family Campground

3405 Columbia Valley Hwy., 209-192 Sunnyside Rd., K0G 1X0. T: (613) 273-3124; www.sunnysidecampground.on.ca.

🚐 ★★★★   ⛺ ★★★

Beauty: ★★★★★   Site Privacy: ★
Spaciousness: ★★★   Quiet: ★★★
Security: ★★★★   Cleanliness: ★★★
Insect Control: ★★   Facilities: ★★★

Sunnyside Campground, a few minutes south of Hwy. 1 in the Fraser Valley, sits in the very popular vacation area of Cultus Lake. During summer, there exists no chance of entrance without a reservation; the campground teems with people and remains a cluttered sea of trailers and tents. The campground receives shade from a thick canopy of evergreens; individual sites consist of mostly dirt, with some gravel surfaces in the RV areas. In the overnighter area, RV sites sit arranged in parallel rows and tent sites line several avenues winding their way down to the lakefront. The best RV sites, numbered 1–18, back up to the northern perimeter of the park. Tent sites 121–127 sit very near the lake, isolated from the rest of the grounds; all tent sites have close neighbors and no privacy. The lengthy beach and some tent sites have beautiful vistas of the mountains that rise sharply beyond Cultus Lake's southern banks. In addition to the lake, the campground has an arcade, a large general store, and a rec room frequently hosting family-oriented planned activities. The best time for good weather and swimming is during the summer, and the best time to avoid crowds is a weekday during the off-season.

BASICS

Operated By: Cultus Lakes Parks Board. **Open:** Apr. 1–Sept. 30. **Site Assignment:** Reservations highly recommended; 1-night or 10% deposit; refund w/ 7-day cancellation notice; first come, first served. **Registration:** At gate, no after-hours entrance w/o prior notification of office. **Fee:** Full, $35–$37; tent (reg.), $24; tent (view), $27; tent (waterfront), $40; Rates for 2 people. Children under 16 free; extra vehicle, half of site charge; extra RV or tent, full site charge; extra adults, $5; pets, $2; V, MC, cash. **Parking:** At site.

FACILITIES

Number of RV-only Sites: 104. **Number of Tent-only Sites:** 133. **Hookups:** Electric (30 amps), water, sewer. **Each Site:** Picnic table, fire ring. **Dump Station:** Inquire at campground. **Laundry:** Inquire at campground. **Pay Phone:** Inquire at campground. **Restrooms and Showers:** Inquire at campground. **Fuel:** Inquire at campground. **Propane:** Inquire at campground. **Internal Roads:** Call ahead for details. **RV Service:** No. **Market:** 3 mi. north. **Restaurant:** 1.5 mi. north. **General Store:** Yes. **Vending:** Yes. **Swimming:** No. **Playground:** Yes. **Other:** Boat launch, horseshoes, basketball, rec room, group barbecue, arcade, beach, moorage. **Activities:** Swimming, planned activities, daily kids programs. **Nearby Attractions:** Golf, water sports, hiking, Cultus Lake Provincial Park, Bridal Veil Falls, sport fishing, mountain biking, bird-watching, mountain climbing, ATVs. **Additional Information:** Chilliwack Visitor Info Center, (800) 567-9535, www.tourismchilliwack.com.

RESTRICTIONS

Pets: Leash only, not allowed on beach; $3 per night per dog. **Fires:** Fire pit only. **Alcoholic Beverages:** At site. **Vehicle Maximum Length:** 45 ft. **Other:** No fishing from shore; no semis pulling fifth wheels.

TO GET THERE

From Hwy. 1, take Exit 119B (Cultus Lake/Sardis), drive 3.8 mi. south on Vedder Rd. Turn left at light onto Cultus Lake Rd. Drive 2.8 mi. south on Cultus Lake, entrance on right with big wooden sign.

HOPE MAP, C-3
Wild Rose Campground

62030 Flood Hope Rd., V0X 1L2.
T: (604) 869-9842; www.wildrosecamp.com.

🚐 ★★★★   ⛺ ★★★

Beauty: ★★★★   Site Privacy: ★★
Spaciousness: ★★★   Quiet: ★★★
Security: ★★   Cleanliness: ★★★★
Insect Control: ★★   Facilities: ★★

Wild Rose Campground, off Hwy. 1 in Hope, offers a more adult-oriented setting in the beautiful, wild landscape of Hope. Lacking the in-house recreation most families seek, Wild Rose consists primarily of two rows of well-manicured, grassy sites. Much of the grounds receives shade from numerous beautiful fir trees, and most sites have good views of the rugged mountains surrounding the Fraser Valley. The tent section, numbers 61–68, lacks an abundance of shade, but individual sites have some privacy created by cedars and the best, unobstructed mountain views. The largest RV sites, 22–26 and 41–45, have a mixture of shade and views. The pull-through section is extremely shady. The least attractive sites, 51–60, receive such a label due to their smaller size. Even during the summer the weather tends to be cool and rainy, so make sure and keep rain gear handy.

BASICS

Operated By: Wild Rose Campground. **Open:** Apr. 1–Sept. 30. **Site Assignment:** First come, first served & by reservation; 1-night deposit; refund w/ 48-hour cancellation notice. **Registration:** At office. **Fee:** $26–$34; no hookup, $22; rates for 2 people; extra person, $3; V, MC, cash. **Parking:** At site.

FACILITIES

Number of RV-only Sites: 60. **Number of Tent-only Sites:** 8. **Hookups:** Electric (15, 30, 50 amps), water, sewer, cable TV. **Each Site:** Picnic table, fire pits. **Dump Station:** Inquire at campground. **Laundry:** Yes. **Pay Phone:** Yes. **Restrooms and Showers:** Yes. **Fuel:** Yes, service station w/in walking distance. **Propane:** Inquire at campground. **Internal Roads:** Call ahead for details. **RV Service:** No.

Market: 3 mi. east in Hope. **Restaurant:** 0.1 mi. west. **General Store:** Yes. **Vending:** No. **Swimming:** No. **Playground:** Yes. **Other:** Rec room, volleyball, horseshoes. **Activities:** Inquire at campground. **Nearby Attractions:** Dinotown, Hell's Gate AirTram, hiking, Japanese Friendship Gardens, Trans-Canada Waterslide, (*Rambo: First Blood* was filmed in Hope). **Additional Information:** Hope Visitor Info Center, (604) 869-2021, www.fraser valleyguide.com.

RESTRICTIONS

Pets: Short leash only, quiet dogs only. **Fires:** Fire pit only. **Alcoholic Beverages:** At site. **Vehicle Maximum Length:** No limit. **Other:** No outdoor music.

TO GET THERE

From Hwy. 1W, take Exit 165 and turn left off exit ramp. Road dead-ends after 0.1 mi. Turn right onto Flood Hope Rd., drive 0.5 mi. and entrance is on the right. From Hwy. 1E, take Exit 168 and turn right onto Flood Hope Rd., drive 1.3 mi. and entrance on left.

PEMBERTON   MAP, C-3
Nairn Falls Provincial Park

P.O. Box 220, V0N 1H0.
T: (604) 986-9371 or (800) 689-9025;
www.env.gov.bc.ca/bcparks/explore/explore.html.

🚐 ★★★★   ⛺ ★★★★

Beauty: ★★★★★   Site Privacy: ★★★
Spaciousness: ★★★   Quiet: ★★★★
Security: ★★★   Cleanliness: ★★★
Insect Control: ★★   Facilities: ★★

Nairn Falls Provincial Park, just south of Pemberton, offers a quiet, wilderness setting just out of reach of the heavy tourist traffic found to the south in Whistler. Best described as primitive, the campground does not have flush toilets but does have potable water. Nonadjacent sites sit in an arrangement of parallel rows, creating a semiprivate environment. Further, some sites have amazing views of nearby Green River and the mountains. These sites, 48–51, lack the privacy that can be found in the rest of the park and sit on a ridge, subject to a cold breeze at times. Sites with the most privacy sit on the exterior perimeters of the park and have no neighbors to the rear. All sites have gravel surfaces, a fair amount of room, and lots of shade from the overhead forest. The scenery here is incredible. The summers provide the best time to visit; even so, the mountain weather seldom gets very warm, so be prepared for cool temperatures.

BASICS

Operated By: BC Parks. **Open:** May 5–Oct. 1; gates closed, no fees taken & no services during this time. **Site Assignment:** First come, first served & by reservation; reservation & campsite fees must be paid in full by V or MC at time of booking; campers are charged a nonrefundable fee of $6.42 per night to a max. of $19.26; cancel 7 days prior to arrival less $6.42 cancellation fee. **Registration:** Fees collected at sites by attendants; after hours pay in morning w/ host or at drop box located by info station. **Fee:** $14; extra vehicle, $7; for 4 adults, 4 children (under

16 years old); cash only upon arrival. **Parking:** At site, limited off site.

FACILITIES

Number of Multipurpose Sites: 94. **Hookups:** None. **Each Site:** Picnic table, fire ring. **Dump Station:** No. **Laundry:** Inquire at campground. **Pay Phone:** Inquire at campground. **Restrooms and Showers:** Pit toilets, no showers. **Fuel:** Inquire at campground. **Propane:** Inquire at campground. **Internal Roads:** Call ahead for details. **RV Service:** No. **Market:** North in Pemberton; limited. **Restaurant:** North in Pemberton, limited. **General Store:** No. **Vending:** No. **Swimming:** No (2 km. north at One Mile Lake). **Playground:** No. **Other:** Hiking trails, wheelchair-accessible facilities. **Activities:** Fishing (must have license), hiking, wildlife viewing, bird-watching, picnicking. **Nearby Attractions:** River rafting, mountain biking, ecotourism. **Additional Information:** Pemberton District Chamber of Commerce, (604) 894-6175.

RESTRICTIONS

Pets: On leash only. Be aware of areas designated no pets. **Fires:** Fire pit only. **Alcoholic Beverages:** At site. **Vehicle Maximum Length:** 38 ft. **Other:** Do not gather dead or down foliage, habitat sensitive. Use suitable grey water containers. Be aware of bear procedures.

TO GET THERE

Driving north on Hwy. 99, entrance is on right just south of Pemberton and about 30 minutes north of Whistler.

SQUAMISH   MAP, C-3
Dryden Creek Resort
and Campground

P.O. Box 1012, V0N 1T0. T: (604) 898-9726;
www.drydencreek.com.

🚐 ★★★★   ⛺ ★★★

Beauty: ★★★★   Site Privacy: ★★
Spaciousness: ★★★   Quiet: ★★★
Security: ★★   Cleanliness: ★★★★
Insect Control: ★★   Facilities: ★★

Dryden Creek Resort and Campground, located just north of Squamish on Hwy. 99, offers close access to a plethora of outdoor recreation. The small campground has a quaint, enchanted forest feel, and offers a variety of sites. On top of backing up to a beautiful gray, rocky ridge forested with evergreens, the park also has a Salmon spawning creek running through it. RV sites in the west section of the park offer a more forested feel, but sit in a higher traffic area. The best gravel RV sites, E1–E8, sit in the east section of the park, half of which back up to the cliffs at the rear of the park. These sites have an open feel, no privacy, and grass perimeters. Within the tenting section there exist two types of sites, ones positioned in a grassy area with little shade or privacy, and ones that sit in a wooded area with more privacy but also gravel and dirt surfaces. The latter, sites N10–N14, have the most shade from tall cedars characteristic of the area. Surrounding areas provide year-round outdoor recreation. Summers have mild and sometimes

rainy weather; winters bring snow and world-class skiing.

BASICS

Operated By: Dryden Creek Resorts. **Open:** All year. **Site Assignment:** First come, first served & by reservation; deposit is full cost of stay; refund w/ 48-hour cancellation notice less $6. **Registration:** At office; after hours arrival call ahead before close. **Fee:** Full, $28; tent, $22; for 2 people; weekly rates 10% off, extra people older than 18 or traveling w/out parents $2.80, extra people 18 & younger $1.50; V, MC, cash. **Parking:** At site.

FACILITIES

Number of RV-only Sites: 29. **Number of Tent-only Sites:** 20. **Hookups:** Electric (30 amps), water, sewer, cable TV, phone. **Each Site:** Picnic table, fire ring. **Dump Station:** Each site has sewer. **Laundry:** Yes. **Pay Phone:** Yes. **Restrooms and Showers:** Yes. **Fuel:** No. **Propane:** No. **Internal Roads:** Gravel. **RV Service:** No. **Market:** South in Squamish. **Restaurant:** South in Squamish. **General Store:** Yes. **Vending:** No. **Swimming:** No. **Playground:** No. **Other:** Motel, group camping, one canoe for rental, German & Spanish speaking staff. **Activities:** Occasional church on Sun., stream fishing. **Nearby Attractions:** Mountain biking, wind surfing, rock climbing, salmon spawning trails, ecotourism, eagle viewing. **Additional Information:** Squamish Chamber of Commerce, (604) 892-9244, www.squamishchamber.bc.ca.

RESTRICTIONS

Pets: On leash only. **Fires:** Fire pit only. **Alcoholic Beverages:** At site. **Vehicle Maximum Length:** 40 ft. **Other:** Check in 3 p.m. Stream regulated for fishing, check w/ office before fishing.

TO GET THERE

On Hwy. 99, drive 1.7 mi. north of Burger King on north edge of Squamish/Brackendale. Turn right onto Depot Rd., take an almost immediate left and drive up entry drive into campground.

VANCOUVER   MAP. C-3
(SURREY)
Peace Arch RV Park

14601 40th Ave., V4P 2J9. T: (604) 594-7009.

🚐 ★★★★   ⛺ ★★

Beauty: ★★★   Site Privacy: ★★★★
Spaciousness: ★★★   Quiet: ★★★
Security: ★★★   Cleanliness: ★★★★
Insect Control: ★★   Facilities: ★★★★

Peace Arch RV Park, located about ten minutes north of the Blaine, WA, border crossing, houses beautiful, flowering shrubs and many private pull-throughs. Colored by densely packed flowers, the common areas stay in bloom throughout the summer. Facilities have a well-kept, clean appearance. The sites are arranged in many rows of gravel pull-throughs and back-ins parallel to each other. Back-in sites lack much shade or privacy, but all pull-through sites, rows B–D, have huge fir tree buffers on either side, creating a private, almost forest feeling and shade; they also have some grass within each site. The firs have an overgrown look, but do not encroach upon the spaciousness of the sites. Tent sites in the park sit in a small field without much shade or privacy; this field does, however, have many seedling hardwoods. Also, the tenting section has a small covered area with a sink for dishes. Summers bring flowers and the best time to visit the Vancouver area, but nights can be especially chilly even in August.

BASICS

Operated By: Peace Arch RV Park. **Open:** All year. **Site Assignment:** First come, first served & by reservation; 1-night deposit; refund w/24-hour cancellation notice. **Registration:** At office; after hours at drop box. **Fee:** Full, $36; tent, $18.50; for 2 people; extra people over 7 years old, $2; under 7 years old, free; V, MC, US & Canadian cash, traveler's checks. **Parking:** At site, off site.

FACILITIES

Number of RV-only Sites: 202. **Number of Tent-only Sites:** 70. **Hookups:** Electric (30 amps), water, sewer, phone (pull-throughs only), cable TV. **Each Site:** Picnic table. **Dump Station:** Yes, requires a fee. **Laundry:** Yes. **Pay Phone:** Yes. **Restrooms and Showers:** Yes. **Fuel:** No. **Propane:** Yes. **Internal Roads:** Paved. **RV Service:** Yes. **Market:** 5 min. north in Cloverdale. **Restaurant:** No. **General Store:** No. **Vending:** Yes. **Swimming:** Yes. **Playground:** Yes. **Other:** Mini-golf, horseshoes, basketball, rec room w/ pool table & 2 arcade games, RV storage; meeting/banquet facilities. **Activities:** Winter social clubs, occasional barbecues in summer. **Nearby Attractions:** Stanley Park & Zoo, Vancouver Aquarium, Transportation Museum, Capilano Suspension Bridge, Gastown, White Rock Beach. **Additional Information:** City of Surrey, (604) 591-4811, www.city.surrey.bc.ca; Vancouver Tourist Info Center, (604) 683-2000, www.tourism-vancouver.org.

RESTRICTIONS

Pets: On leash only. **Fires:** Not allowed. **Alcoholic Beverages:** At site. **Vehicle Maximum Length:** 45 ft. **Other:** No parking on grass, do not tie lines to trees.

TO GET THERE

From Hwy. 99, take Exit 10, turn onto 99A northbound. After less than one block, turn right onto 40th Ave., drive 0.5 mi., entrance on the left.

WHISTLER	MAP, C-3
Riverside RV Resort and Campground	

8018 Mons Rd., V0N 1B8.
T: (604) 905-5533 or (877) 905-5533;
www.whistlercamping.com.

🚐 ★★★★   ⛺ ★★★★

Beauty: ★★★★	Site Privacy: ★★★
Spaciousness: ★★	Quiet: ★★★
Security: ★★★	Cleanliness: ★★★★★
Insect Control: ★★	Facilities: ★★★★★

Riverside RV Resort and Campground, located in the expensive resort town of Whistler, provides convenient access to world-class, year-round outdoor recreation, restaurants, and clubs. This campground has top-of-the-line, well-equipped facilities and a variety of in-house recreation—notably a high-quality all-grass, 18-hole putting course. Landscaping within the grounds is garden-like, well maintained, and classy. The RV section has obscured views of the surrounding mountains. In the RV section, consisting of several parallel rows of flat, paved back-in sites, the best sites, D1–D9 and E1–E8, sit toward the back of the grounds with some shade trees overhead and a little privacy. The tenting area, heavily shaded by pine and birch, consists of walk-in, semiprivate dirt and gravel sites; the only sites to avoid, T1, T25, and T26, lack the privacy found in other sites. Any time makes a good time to visit Whistler; the town draws crowds for both summer and winter recreation.

BASICS

Operated By: Riverside RV Resort. **Open:** All year. **Site Assignment:** First come, first served & by reservation; 1-night deposit; refund w/ 2-week cancellation notice; for notice less than 2 weeks, 50% refund; w/in 48 hours of arrival, no refund. **Registration:** At office; after-hours info in front of office. **Fee:** Full, $40 (for 2 people); overflow RV, $25; extra RV adults, $5; tent, $25; extra tent adults, $5 (16 years & older, flexible for families). Summer Rate: full, $45; tent, $30. **Parking:** At site; tent sites walk-in w/ separate parking lot.

FACILITIES

Number of RV-only Sites: 67. **Number of Tent-only Sites:** 31. **Hookups:** Electric (15, 30, 50 amps), water, sewer, cable TV ($2/day). **Each Site:** Picnic table, fire ring. **Dump Station:** Yes. **Laundry:** Yes. **Pay Phone:** Yes. **Restrooms and Showers:** Yes. **Fuel:** No. **Propane:** Yes. **Internal Roads:** Paved. **RV Service:** No. **Market:** Across street. **Restaurant:** On grounds. **General Store:** Yes. **Vending:** Yes. **Swimming:** Creek. **Playground:** Yes. **Other:** PGA regulation 18-hole grass putting green, arcade w/ pool table, ping pong, Internet terminal, cafe, rentals (Rollerblades, foot scooters, mountain bikes, movies, TVs, VCRs). **Activities:** Putting, volleyball, horseshoes, free shuttles to & from Whistler Village twice in morning & twice in afternoon. **Nearby Attractions:** Mountain biking, golf, hiking, fishing, tons of winter recreation (in winter), ecotourism; restaurants, shopping, & nightlife at Whistler resort complex. **Additional Information:** Tourism Whistler, (800)-WHISTLER, www.tourism.whistler.com; Squamish Chamber of Commerce, (604) 892-9244, www.squamishchamber.bc.ca.

RESTRICTIONS

Pets: On leash only; not allowed in beach (stream), playground area. **Fires:** At site, in pits. **Alcoholic Beverages:** At site. **Vehicle Maximum Length:** No limit. **Other:** Be aware of bear regulations. No refunds for early departures.

TO GET THERE

On Hwy. 99 heading north, drive 1.1 mi. north of Whistler Village (main entrance to the north edge of town) and turn right onto Spruce Grove Park/Blackcomb Way. Take an almost immediate left onto the access road and follow for 0.3 mi. to entrance.

Supplemental Directory of Campgrounds

ALABAMA

Alberta

Chilatchee Creek Park, Chilatchee Cr. Rd., 36720. T: (334) 573-2562. www.reserveusa.com. RV/tent: 53. $$. Hookups: electric (30, 50 amp), water.

Alpine

Logan Landing RV Resort & Campground, 1036 Bear Bryant Rd., 35014. T: (256) 268-0045 or (888) 564-2671. www.loganlanding.com. RV/tent: 140. $$. Hookups: electric (30, 50 amp), sewer, water.

Andalusia

Conecuh National Forest (Open Pond Campground), Rte. 5 Box 157, 36420. T: (334) 222-2555. gorp.away.com/dow/southern/ conecmp.htm. RV/tent: 55. $. Hookups: electric (30 amp), water.

Ariton

Camp Bama RV Resort & Campgrounds, Hwy. 231 North, 36311. T: (800) 435-8259. RV/tent: 16. $. Hookups: electric (20, 30 amp), water, sewer.

Athens

Lucy's Branch Resort & Marina, 5381 Bay Village Dr., 35611. T: (256) 729-6443. RV/tent: 204. $$. Hookups: electric (20, 30, 50 amp), water, sewer.

Atmore

Claude D. Kelley State Park, 580 H. Kyle, 36502. T: (251) 862-2511. www.alapark.com. RV/tent: 25. $. Hookups: electric, water, sewer.

Auburn

Chewacla State Park, 124 Shell Toomer Pkwy., 36830. T: (334) 887-5621. www.alapark.com. RV/tent: 36. $. Hookups: electric (30 amp), water, sewer.

Leisure Time Campgrounds, 2670 South College St., 36830. T: (334) 821-2267. RV/tent: 60. $$. Hookups: electric (20, 30, 50 amp), water, sewer, phone.

Birmingham

M & J RV Park, 556 Bessemer Super Hwy., 35228. T: (205) 788-2605. RV/tent: 72. $. Hookups: electric (50 amp), water, sewer.

Boaz

Barclay RV Parking, Billy Dyer Blvd., 35957. T: (256) 593-8769. RV/tent: 22. $. Hookups: electric (30, 50 amp), water, sewer, cable.

Castleberry

Country Sunshine RV Park, Rte. 2 Box 290, 36432. T: (251) 966-5540. RV/tent: 11. $$. Hookups: electric (30, 50 amp), water, sewer.

Centre

John's Campground & Grocery, 6480 CR 22, 35960. T: (256) 475-3234. RV/tent: 58. $$. Hookups: electric (30, 50 amp), water, sewer, cable.

Centreville

Payne Lake West Side, Talladega National Forest, U.S. 82/AL 5 North, 35042. T: (205) 926-9765. RV/tent: 77. $. Hookups: none.

Citronelle

Lakeview RV Park, 17850 Municipal Park Dr., 36522. T: (251) 866-9647. RV/tent: 32. $$. Hookups: electric (30, 50 amp), water, sewer.

Clio

Blue Springs State Park, 2595 Hwy. 10, 36017. T: (334) 397-4875. www.alapark.com. RV/tent: 50. $. Hookups: electric (30 amp), water, sewer.

Coaling

Candy Mountain RV Park, 11742 Hagler Coaling Rd., 35449. T: (205) 553-5428. www.goldorb.com/candy2.htm. RV/tent: 40. $$. Hookups: electric (30, 50 amp), water, sewer.

Cottondale

Sunset II Travel Park, 5001 JVC Rd., 35453. T: (205) 553-9233. RV/tent: 36. $$. Hookups: electric (20, 30, 50 amp), water, sewer.

Creola

I-65 RV Campground, 730 Jackson Rd., 36525. T: (800) 287-3208. www.i65rvcampground.com. RV/tent: 76. $$. Hookups: electric (30, 50 amp), sewer, phone.

KOA Mobile North/River Delta, 2350 Dead Lake Marina Rd., 36525. T: (800) KOA-0362 or (251) 675-0320. www.koa.com. RV/tent: 42. $$. Hookups: electric (20, 30, 50 amp), water, sewer.

Cullman

Cullman Campground, 215 CR 1185, 35056. T: (256) 734-9794. RV/tent: 75. $$. Hookups: electric (20, 30, 50 amp), water, sewer.

Good Hope Campground, 330 Super Saver Rd., 35055. T: (256) 739-1319. RV/tent: 50. $$. Hookups: electric (15, 30 amp), water, sewer.

Dauphin Island

Dauphin Island Campground, 109 Bienville Blvd., 36528. T: (251) 861-2742. www.dauphinisland.org. RV/tent: 150. $$. Hookups: electric (30, 50 amp), water, sewer.

Decatur

Point Mallard Campground, 1800 Point Mallard Dr., 35601. T: (256) 351-7772. www.pointmallard park.com/campground. RV/tent: 210. $. Hookups: electric (20, 30, 50 amp), water, sewer.

Demopolis

Forkland Park, 384 Resource Dr., 12 miles north of Demopolis, 36732. T: (334) 289-5530. www.reserveusa.com. RV/tent: 42. $$. Hookups: electric (30 amp), water.

Foscue Creek Park, 1800 Lockin Dam Rd., 36732. T: (334) 289-5535. www.reserveusa.com. RV/tent: 45. $$. Hookups: electric (20, 30, 50 amp), water, sewer.

Dothan

Clean Park RV Park, 4100 South Oates St., 36301. T: (334) 792-2000. RV/tent: 150. $$. Hookups: electric (30, 50 amp), water, sewer, cable.

Elberta

Lazy Acres RV Park & Campground, 12160 Wortel Rd., 36530. T: (877) 986-5266. www .lazyacrescampground.com. RV/tent: 78. $$. Hookups: electric (15, 30, 50 amp), water, sewer, phone.

Elkmont

Mill Creek RV Park, 28861 Veto Rd., 35620. T: (256) 732-3686. www.millcreekrv.com. RV/tent: 125. $. Hookups: electric (30, 50 amp), sewer, water.

ALABAMA (continued)

Equality

Lakeway Pub & Grill and RV Park, P.O. Box 176, 36026. T: (334) 541-2010. www.lakeywaypubrv .com. RV/tent: 17. $$. Hookups: electric (30, 50 amp), water, sewer.

Eufaula

Lake Eufaula Campground, 151 West Chewalla Creek Dr., 36027. T: (334) 687-4425. RV/tent: 100. $$. Hookups: electric (30 amp), water, sewer.

Fairhope

Driftwood RV Park, 9318 Hwy. 98, 36532. T: (251) 928-8233. RV/tent: 24. $$. Hookups: electric (30, 50 amp), water, sewer.

East Park Plaza, 7625 Parker Rd., 36532. T: (251) 928-7619. RV/tent: 15. $$. Hookups: electric (30, 50 amp), water, sewer.

Safe Harbor RV Resort & Marina, 11401 US 98, 36532. T: (800) 928-4544. RV/tent: 105. $$. Hookups: electric (30, 50 amp), water, sewer.

Florala

Florala State Park, P.O. Box 322, 36442-0322. T: (334) 858-6425. RV/tent: 23. $$. Hookups: electric (30 amp), water.

Florence

McFarland Park, South Seminary St., 35630. T: (256) 760-6416. RV/tent: 50. $$. Hookups: electric (30, 50 amp), water.

Veterans Memorial Park, Wilson Dam Rd., 35630. T: (256) 760-6416. RV/tent: 22. $. Hookups: electric (20, 30 amp), water.

Foley

Helen's RV Park, 10340 South Juniper St., 36535. T: (251) 943-1227. RV/tent: 18. $. Hookups: electric (30, 50 amp), sewer, water, phone, cable.

Palm Lake RV Court, 15810 Hwy. 59, 36535. T: (251) 970-3773. RV/tent: 62. $$. Hookups: electric (20, 30, 50 amp), water, sewer, phone.

Franklin

Isaac Creek Park, Rte. 1 Box 51B, 36444. T: (251) 282-4254. www.sam.usace.army.mil/op/rec/al_ lakes/camp.htm. RV/tent: 50. $$. Hookups: electric (30, 50 amp), water.

Gadsden

River Country Campground, 1 River Rd., 35901. T: (256) 543-7111. www.rivercountrycamp ground.com. RV/tent: 185. $$. Hookups: electric (30, 50 amp), sewer, water, phone, cable, internet.

Gallion

Chickasaw State Park, 26955 US 43, 36742. T: (334) 295-8230. www.alapark.com. RV/tent: 15. $. Hookups: electric (30 amp), water.

Gardendale

Gardendale Kampground, 2128 Moncrief Rd., 35071. T: (205) 631-7364. RV/tent: 30. $. Hookups: electric (30 amp), water, sewer.

Gulf Shores

Luxury RV Resort, 590 Gulf Shores Pkwy., 36542. T: (800) 982-3510. RV/tent: 89. $$. Hookups: electric (30, 50 amp), sewer, water, cable.

Southport Campgrounds, 108 West 28th Ave., 36542. T: (251) 968-6220. RV/tent: 116. $$. Hookups: electric (20, 30 amp), water, sewer, phone.

Sun Runners RV Park, 19436 C.R. 8, 36542. T: (251) 955-5257. RV/tent: 60. $$. Hookups: electric (20, 30 amp), water, sewer.

Guntersville

Seibold Campground, 54 Seibold Creek Rd., 35976. T: (256) 582-0040. RV/tent: 134. $$. Hookups: electric (20, 30, 50 amp), water.

Hamilton

U.S. 78 Campgrounds, 3194 C.R. 55, 35570. T: (205) 886-9505. RV/tent: 14. $. Hookups: electric (20, 30, 50 amp), water, sewer.

Hanceville

Country RV Park, 15959 Hwy. 91, 35077. T: (256) 352-4678. RV/tent: 32. $$. Hookups: electric (30, 50 amp), sewer, water, phone, cable.

Hames Marina & RV Park, 850 C.R. 248, 35077. T: (256) 287-9785. RV/tent: 48. $. Hookups: electric (30, 50 amp), water, sewer.

Heflin

Coleman Lake, Talladega National Forest, 2309 Hwy. 46, 36264. T: (256) 463-2272. RV/tent: 39. $. Hookups: electric (30, 50 amp), water.

Pine Glen, Talladega National Forest, 2309 Hwy. 46, 36264. T: (256) 463-2272. RV/tent: 31. $. Hookups: none.

Helena

Cherokee Beach Kamper Village, 2800 Hwy. 93, 35080. T: (205) 428-8339. RV/tent: 90. $$. Hookups: electric (30 amp), water, sewer.

Hope Hull

KOA Montgomery, 250 Fischer Rd., 36043. T: (800) KOA-5032. www.koa.com. RV/tent: 125. $$. Hookups: electric (20, 30, 50 amp), water, sewer, phone.

Huntsville

Ditto Landing Marina Campground, 293 Ditto Landing Rd., 35815. T: (256) 883-9420. www.nservice.com/ditto_landing. RV/tent: 26. $$. Hookups: electric (30 amp), water.

Ider

Thunder Canyon Campground, 583 Thunder Canyon Rd., 35981. T: (256) 632-2103. RV/tent: 31. $. Hookups: electric (20, 30, 50 amp), water, sewer.

Jemison

Peach Queen Campground, 12986 C.R. 42, 35085. T: (205) 688-2573 or (866) 724-2267. www.peachqueencampground.com. RV/tent: 72. $$. Hookups: electric (30, 50 amp), water, sewer, phone.

Langston

South Sauty Creek Resort, 6845 South Sauty Rd., 35755. T: (256) 582-3367. RV/tent: 85. $$. Hookups: electric (20, 30, 50 amp), water.

Leeds

Holiday Trav-L-Park, 900 Old Ashville Rd., 35094. T: (205) 640-5300. RV/tent: 137. $$. Hookups: electric (20, 30 amp), water, sewer.

Leroy

Double R Campground, H.C. 63 Box 247, 36548. T: (251) 246-9175. RV/tent: 40. $$. Hookups: electric (20, 30, 50 amp), water, sewer.

Magnolia Springs

Southwind RV Park, 12821 CR 9 North, 36555. T: (251) 988-1216. RV/tent: 120. $$. Hookups: electric (20, 30, 50 amp), water, sewer.

McCalla

KOA McCalla/Tannehill, 22191 Hwy. 216, 35111. T: (800) KOA-9505. www.koa.com. RV/tent: 62. $$. Hookups: electric (30, 50 amp), sewer, water, phone.

Millbrook

K & K RV Park, 1810 I-65 Service Rd. East, 36054. T: (334) 285-5251. RV/tent: 46. $$. Hookups: electric (30, 50 amp), water, sewer, phone.

Mobile

Brown's RV Park, 1619 Jasper Rd., 36618. T: (251) 342-3383. www.brownsrvpark.com. RV/tent: 34. $$. Hookups: electric (30, 50 amp), sewer, water, phone, cable.

Pala Verde RV Park, 3525 Demetropolis Rd., 36693. T: (251) 660-7148. RV/tent: 19. $$. Hookups: electric (30, 50 amp), water, sewer.

Moundville

Moundville Archaeological Park, 13075 Moundville Arch Park, 35474. T: (205) 371-2572. www.ua.edu/mndville.htm. RV/tent: 34. $. Hookups: electric (20, 30 amp), water, sewer.

Muscle Shoals

Mallard Creek, P.O. Box 1010 SB1H, 35662. T: (256) 386-2221. RV/tent: 56. $. Hookups: electric (30 amp), water.

Ohatchee

Coosa Willow Point Campground & Marina, 138 Willow Point Dr./ Hwy. 77 North, 36271. T: (800) 566-9906. RV/tent: 74. $$. Hookups: electric (20, 30, 50 amp), water, sewer.

Opelika

Lakeside RV Park, 5664 US 280 East, 36801. T: (334) 745-5414. RV/tent: 27. $$. Hookups: electric (30, 50 amp), water, sewer, cable.

Opp

Frank Jackson State Park, Rte. 3 Box 73-C, 36467. T: (334) 493-6988. www.dcnr.state. al.us/parks/frank_jackson_la.html. RV/tent: 26. $$. Hookups: electric (30 amp), water.

ALABAMA (continued)

Orange Beach
Beech Camping, 4224 Orange Beach Blvd., 36561. T: (251) 981-4136. RV/tent: 90. $$. Hookups: electric (20, 30, 50 amp), water, sewer, cable.

Ozark
Ozark Trav-L-Park, 4000 U.S. 231 North, 36360. T: (800) 359-3218. www.ozarktravelpark.com. RV/tent: 50. $$. Hookups: electric (30, 50 amp), sewer, water, phone, cable.

Pelham
KOA Birmingham South, 222 Hwy. 33, 35124. T: (205) 664-8832. www.koa.com. RV/tent: 113. $$. Hookups: electric (20, 30, 50 amp), water, sewer, phone.

Pittsview Bluff Creek Park, 144 Bluff Creek Rd., 36871. T: (334) 855-2746. RV/tent: 88. $$. Hookups: electric (20, 30 amp), water.

Robertsdale
Hilltop RV Park, 23420 CR 64, 36567. T: (251) 960-1129. RV/tent: 62. $$. Hookups: electric (20, 30, 50 amp), water, sewer.

Russellville
Bear Creek Development Authority, 111 CR 88, 35653. T: (256) 332-4392. www.bearcreeklakes.com. RV/tent: 160. $. Hookups: electric (30 amp), water, sewer.

Scottsboro
Crawford RV Park, 4320 South Broad St., 35769. T: (256) 574-5366. www.crawfordrv.com. RV/tent: 14. $$. Hookups: electric (30, 50 amp), water, sewer, cable.

Goose Pond Colony, 417 Ed Hembree Dr., 35769. T: (256) 259-1808 or (800) 268-2884. www.goosepond.org. RV/tent: 117. $$. Hookups: electric (20, 30 amp), water, sewer, cable.

Selma
Lake Lanier Travel Park, 655 Lake Lanier Rd., 36701. T: (334) 875-1618. RV/tent: 55. $$. Hookups: electric (20, 30, 50 amp), water, sewer.

Paul M. Grist State Park, 1546 Grist Rd., 36701. T: (334) 872-5846. www.dcnr.state.al.us/parks/paul_m_grist_la.html. RV/tent: 6. $. Hookups: electric (30, 50 amp), water, sewer.

Shorter
Wind Drift Campground, I-85 and U.S. 80, 36075. T: (334) 724-9428. RV/tent: 33. $$. Hookups: electric (20, 30, 50 amp), water, sewer, phone.

Silas
Service Park Campground, 451 Service Park Rd., 36919. T: (251) 754-9338. RV/tent: 32. $$. Hookups: electric (20, 30 amp), water.

Theodore
I-10 Kampground, 6430 Theodore Dawes Rd., 36582. T: (800) 272-1263. RV/tent: 193. $$. Hookups: electric (30, 50 amp), sewer, water, cable.

Town Creek
Doublehead Resort, 145 CR 314, 35672. T: (800) 685-9267. www.doublehead.com. RV/tent: 30. $$. Hookups: electric (30, 50 amp), water.

Troy
Deer Run RV Park, 3736 Hwy. 231 North, 36081. T: (800) 552-3036. www.deerrunrvpark.com. RV/tent: 70. $$. Hookups: electric, water, sewer, cable.

ALASKA

Anchor Point
Kyllonen's RV Park, 74160 Anchor Point Beach Rd., 99556. T: (907) 235-7762 or (907) 235-7451. www.kyllonenrvpark.com. RV/tent: 23. $$. Hookups: electric (30 amp), water, sewer.

Anchorage
Centennial Campground, 8300 Glenn Hwy., 99519. T: (907) 343-4474. RV/tent: 129. $$. Hookups: none.

Electronic Solutions Midtown RV Park, 545 East Northern Lights Blvd., 99503. T: (907) 277-2407. RV/tent: 42. $$. Hookups: electric (20, 30 amp), water, sewer.

Golden Nugget Camper Park, 4100 Debarr, 99508. T: (907) 333-2012 or (800) 449-2012. www.alaskan.com/camperpark. RV/tent: 215. $$. Hookups: electric (20, 30, 50 amp), water, sewer.

Hillside on Gambell Motel & RV Park, 2150 Gambell St., 99503. T: (907) 258-6006 or (800) 478-6005. www.hillside-alaska.com. RV/tent: 68. $$. Hookups: electric (20, 30, 50 amp), water, sewer.

Auke Bay
Auke Bay RV Park, 11930 Glacier Hwy., 99821. T: (907) 789-9467. RV/tent: 41. $$. Hookups: electric (20, 30 amp), water, sewer.

Cantwell
Cantwell RV Park, Mile 209.9 George Parks Hwy., 99729. T: (907) 768-2210 (summer) or (800) 940-2210. www.alaskaone.com/cantwellrv. RV/tent: 82. $$. Hookups: electric (20, 30 amp), water.

Cooper Landing
Cooper Creek Campground, Sterling Hwy. Mile 51, 99572. T: (877) 444-6777. www.reserveusa.com. RV/tent: 30. $$. Hookups: none.

Russian River Campground, Mile 53 Sterling Hwy., 99572. T: (800) 280-CAMP or (877) 444-6777. www.reserveusa.com. RV/tent: 84. $$. Hookups: none.

Sunrise Inn RV Park, Mile 35 Sterling Hwy., 99572. T: (907) 595-1222. www.alaskasunriseinn.com. RV/tent: 19. $$. Hookups: electric (20, 30, 50 amp).

Copper Center
Kenny Lake Mercantile/RV Park, Mile 7.2 Edgerton Hwy., 99573. T: (907) 822-3313. www.alaskaoutdoors.com/KennyLake.knny. RV/tent: 19. $. Hookups: electric (20 amp).

Delta Junction
Smith's Green Acres, 2428 Richardson Hwy. Mile 268, 99737. T: (907) 895-4369 or (800) 895-4369. www.greenacresrvpark.com. RV/tent: 97. $. Hookups: electric (30 amp), water, sewer.

Fairbanks
Chena Hotsprings Resort, P.O. Box 58740, 99711. T: (907) 452-7867 or (800) 478-4681. www.chenahotsprings.com. RV/tent: 80. $$. Hookups: none.

Chena Marina RV Park, 1145 Shypoke Dr., 99709. T: (907) 479-4653. www.chenarvpark.com. RV/tent: 67. $$. Hookups: electric (30 amp), water, sewer, cable, phone.

Tanana Valley Campground, 1800 College Rd., 99709. T: (907) 456-7956 (summer) or (907) 452-3750 (winter). www.tananavalleyfair.org/campground. RV/tent: 50. $. Hookups: electric (30 amp).

Glennallen
Tazlina River RV Park, Mile 110.2 Richardson Hwy., 99588. T: (907) 822-3546. RV/tent: 12. $. Hookups: electric (20 amp), water.

Haines
Haines Hitch-up RV Park, 851 Main St., 99827. T: (907) 766-2882. www.hitchuprv.com. RV/tent: 92. $$. Hookups: electric (30, 50 amp), water, sewer, cable, phone.

Port Chilkoot Camper Park, P.O. Box 1589, 99827. T: (907) 766-2755 or (800) 542-6363. www.haines.ak.us/halsingland. RV/tent: 25. $$. Hookups: electric (20, 30, 50 amp), water, sewer.

Salmon Run Campground & Cabins, Mile 6.5 Lutak Rd., 99827. T: (907) 766-3240. RV/tent: 30. $$. Hookups: none.

Healy
Carlo Creek Lodge and Campground, Mile 223.9 Parks Hwy., 99743. T: (907) 683-2576 (summer) or (907) 683-2573 (winter). www.alaskaone.com/carlocreek. RV/tent: 25. $$. Hookups: electric (20 amp).

McKinley RV and Campground, Mile 248.3 Parks Hwy., 99743. T: (907) 683-2379 or (800) 478-2562. RV/tent: 100. $$. Hookups: electric (20, 30 amp), water, sewer.

Homer
Driftwood Inn RV Park, 135 West Bunnell Ave., 99603. T: (907) 235-8019 or (800) 478-8019. www.thedriftwoodinn.com. RV/tent: 27. $$$. Hookups: electric (20, 30, 50 amp), water, sewer, cable.

Hope
Henry's One Stop, Mile 15.5 Hope Hwy., 99605. T: (907) 782-3222. RV/tent: 12. $$. Hookups: electric (20 amp), water, sewer.

ALASKA (continued)

Hyder

Camp Run-A-Muck, 1001 Premier Ave., 99923. T: (250) 636-9006 or (888) 393-1199. www.sealaskainn.com. RV/tent: 65. $. Hookups: electric (30 amp), water, sewer.

Juneau

Spruce Meadow RV Park, 10200 Mendenhall Loop Rd., 99801. T: (907) 789-1990. www.juneaurv.com. RV/tent: 69. $$. Hookups: electric (30 amp), water, sewer, cable.

Kasilof

Crooked Creek RV Park, 111 Sterling Hwy., 99610. T: (907) 262-1299. RV/tent: 45. $$. Hookups: electric (20, 30, 50 amp), water, sewer.

Ketchikan

Clover Pass Resort, P.O. Box 7322, 99901. T: (907) 247-2234 or (800) 410-2234. www.cloverpass resort.com. RV/tent: 32. $$$. Hookups: electric (30 amp), water, sewer, cable.

Moose Pass

Moose Pass RV Park, Mile 29 Seward Hwy., 99631. T: (907) 288-5624. www.moosepassrvpark.com. RV/tent: 31. $. Hookups: electric (30 amp).

Ptarmigan Creek, Mile 23 Seward Hwy., 99631. T: (800) 280-CAMP. www.reserveusa.com. RV/tent: 16. $. Hookups: none.

Trail River Campground, Mile 24 Seward Hwy., 99631. T: (800) 280-CAMP. www.reserveusa.com. RV/tent: 65. $. Hookups: none.

Ninilchik

Alaskan Angler RV Resort, P.O. Box 39388, 99639. T: (907) 567-3393 or (800) 347-4114. www.afishunt.com. RV/tent: 70. $. Hookups: electric (20, 30, 50 amp), water, sewer, cable, phone.

North Pole

Riverview RV Park, 1316 Badger Rd., 99707. T: (907) 488-6281 or (888) 488-6392. www.alaskaone.com/riverview. RV/tent: 180. $$. Hookups: electric (20, 30, 50 amp), water, sewer, cable.

Road's End RV Park, 1463 Westcott Ln., 99705. T: (907) 488-0295. www.roadsendrvpark.com. RV/tent: 73. $. Hookups: electric (20, 30, 50 amp), water, sewer.

Santaland RV Park, 125 St. Nicholas Dr., 99705. T: (907) 488-9123 or (888) 488-9123. www.san talandrv.com. RV/tent: 94. $$. Hookups: electric (20, 30, 50 amp), water, sewer, cable.

Palmer

Grandview Lodge & RV Park, Mile 109.75 Glenn Hwy., 99645. T: (907) 746-4480. www.grand viewrv.com. RV/tent: 19. $$. Hookups: electric (30, 50 amp), water, sewer.

The Homestead RV Park, P.O. Box 354, 99645. T: (907) 745-6005. RV/tent: 64. $$. Hookups: electric (30 amp), water.

Petersburg

Twin Creek RV Park, Mile 7 Mitkof Hwy., 99833. T: (907) 772-3244. RV/tent: 22. $$. Hookups: electric (30 amp), water, sewer, cable.

Prince Wales Island

Log Cabin Resort, P.O. Box 54, 99925. T: (907) 755-2205 or (800) 544-2205. www.logcabinresor tandrv.com. RV/tent: 14. $. Hookups: electric (30 amp), water, sewer.

Seward

Miller's Landing Campground, P.O. Box 81, 99664. T: (907) 224-5739. www.millerslandingak.com. RV/tent: 53. $$. Hookups: electric (30 amp).

Sitka

Sitka Sportsman's Association RV Park, P.O. Box 3030, 99835. T: (907) 747-6033. RV/tent: 16. $$. Hookups: electric (30 amp), water.

Skagway

Garden City RV Park, P.O. Box 228, 99840. T: (907) 983-2378. www.gardencityrv.com. RV/tent: 100. $$. Hookups: electric (30 amp), water, sewer, cable.

Skagway Mountainview RV Park, 12th and Broadway, 99840. T: (907) 983-3333 or (888) 778-7700. www.alaskarv.com. RV/tent: 147. $$. Hookups: electric (20, 30, 50 amp), water.

Soldotna

Diamond M Ranch, B&B, Cabins, and RV Park, Mile 16.5 Kalifornsky Beach Rd., 99669. T: (907) 283-9424. www.diamondmranch.com. RV/tent: 30. $$. Hookups: electric (30, 50 amp), water, sewer, modem.

Kasilof RV Park, P.O. Box 1333, 99669. T: (907) 262-0418 or (800) 264-0418. www.kasilofrvpark.com. RV/tent: 39. $$. Hookups: electric (30 amp), water, sewer.

River Terrace RV Park, 44761 Sterling Hwy. (Kenai River Bridge), 99669. T: (907) 262-5593. RV/tent: 70. $$. Hookups: electric (20, 30, 50 amp), water, sewer.

Talkeetna

Talkeetna River Adventures Campground, P.O. Box 473, 99676. T: (907) 733-2604. www.karo-ent.com/riveradv.htm. RV/tent: 45. $$. Hookups: none.

Tok

Bull Shooter RV Park, Mile 1313.3 Alaska Hwy., 99780. T: (907) 883-5625. www.tokalaska.com. RV/tent: 24. $$. Hookups: electric (30 amp), water, sewer.

Sourdough Campground, Mile 122.8 Tok Cutoff Rd., 99780. T: (907) 883-5543 or (800) 789-5543. www.tokalaska.com. RV/tent: 75. $$. Hookups: electric (20, 30 amp), water, sewer.

Tok RV Village, Mile 1313.3 Alaska Hwy., 99780. T: (907) 883-5877. RV/tent: 115. $$. Hookups: electric (30, 50 amp), water, sewer.

Tundra RV Park, Mile 1315 Alaska Hwy., 99780. T: (907) 883-7875 (summer) or (907) 883-5885 (winter). www.tokalaska.com. RV/tent: 78. $$. Hookups: electric (20, 30, 50 amp), water, sewer.

Two Rivers

Pleasant Valley RV Park, 7435 Chena Hot Springs Rd., 99716. T: (907) 488-8198. RV/tent: 16. $$. Hookups: electric (30 amp), water.

Valdez

Bear Paw Camper Park, 101 North Harbor Dr., 99686. T: (907) 835-2530. www.bearpawrv park.com. RV/tent: 100. $$. Hookups: electric (30 amp), water, sewer, cable, modem.

Eagle's Rest RV Park, 139 East Pioneer Dr., 99686. T: (800) 553-7275 or (907) 835-2373. www.eaglesrestrv.com. RV/tent: 300. $$. Hookups: electric (20, 30, 50 amp), water, sewer, cable, phone.

Wasilla

Bestview RV Park, 7701 Parks Hwy., 99687. T: (907) 745-7400 or (800) 478-6600. RV/tent: 61. $$. Hookups: electric (30 amp), water, sewer.

Iceworm RV Park & Country Store, Mile 50.2 Parks Hwy., 99687. T: (907) 892-8200 or (888) 484-9088. www.icewormrvp.com. RV/tent: 22. $. Hookups: electric (20, 30, 50 amp), water, sewer, phone, modem.

Willow

Pioneer Lodge Inc., Mile 71.4 Parks Hwy., 99688. T: (907) 495-1000. RV/tent: 25. $$. Hookups: electric (30 amp), water, sewer.

Susitna Landing, Mile 82.5 Parks Hwy., 99688. T: (907) 495-7700. www.ronsriverboat.com. RV/tent: 35. $. Hookups: electric (30 amp).

Wrangell

Wrangell RV Park, P.O. Box 531, 99929. T: (907) 874-2444. RV/tent: 26. $. Hookups: electric (30 amp).

ARIZONA

Aguila

Fairhaven RV Park, 52227 West Hwy. U.S. 60, 85320. T: (928) 685-2412. RV/tent: 55. $. Hookups: electric (30 amp), water, sewer.

Ajo

Ajo Heights RV Park, 2000 North Hwy. 85, 85321. T: (520) 387-6796. www.arizonawebsites.net. RV/tent: 40. $$. Hookups: electric (30, 50 amp), water, sewer, cable , phone.

Belly Acres RV Park, 2050 North Hwy. 85, 85321. T: (520) 387-5767. www.campsites411.com. RV/tent: 43. $$. Hookups: electric (30 amp), water, sewer, cable.

La Siesta Motel & RV Resort, 2561 North Ajo-Gila Bend Hwy., 85321. T: (520) 387-6569. RV/tent: 20. $$. Hookups: electric (30 amp), water, sewer, cable.

Shadow Ridge RV Resort, 431 North 2nd Ave., 85321. T: (520) 387-5055. www.shadow ridgervresort.com. RV/tent: 125. $. Hookups: electric (30, 50 amp), water, sewer, cable.

Apache Junction

Apache Skies Mobile Home Park, 102 South Ironwood, 85220. T: (480) 982-6916 or (480) 296-1878. RV/tent: 38. $$. Hookups: electric (20, 30, 50 amp), water, sewer, phone (modem).

Arizonian Travel Trailer Resort, 15976 East Hwy. 60, 85219. T: (480) 474-2700. www.camp sites411.com. RV/tent: 300. $$. Hookups: electric (30, 50 amp), water, sewer.

Budget RV Park, 2024 South Cortez, 85219. T: (480) 982-5856. RV/tent: 176. $$. Hookups: electric (30, 50 amp), water, sewer.

Countryside Travel Trailer Resort, 2701 South Idaho Rd., 85219. T: (480) 982-1537. www.gocampingamerica.com. RV/tent: 560. $$$. Hookups: electric (30, 50 amp), water, sewer, phone.

Dana's Trailer Ranch, 10712 East Apache Trail, 85220. T: (480) 986-1471. RV/tent: 60. $$. Hookups: electric (20, 30 amp), water, sewer, phone.

Gold Canyon RV Resort, 7151 East Hwy. 60, 85218. T: (480) 982-5800 or (877) 465-3266. www.goldcanyonrvresort.com. RV/tent: 754. $$$. Hookups: electric (30, 50 amp), water, sewer.

Golden Sun RV Resort, 999 West Broadway, 85220. T: (480) 983-3760 or (888) 593-9632. www.gocampingamerica.com. RV/tent: 329. $$$. Hookups: electric (30, 50 amp), water, sewer, phone.

La Hacienda RV Resort, 1797 West 28th Ave., 85220. T: (480) 982-2808. www.haciendaRV.com. RV/tent: 280. $$$. Hookups: electric (30, 50 amp), water, sewer, cable, phone (modem).

Rock Shadows RV Resort, 600 South Idaho Rd., 85219. T: (480) 982-0450 or (800) 521-7096. www.rockshadows.com. RV/tent: 683. $$. Hookups: electric (30, 50 amp), water, sewer, phone.

Sunrise RV Resort, 1403 West Broadway Ave., 85220. T: (480) 983-2500 or (877) 633-3133. www.sunriservresort.com. RV/tent: 484. $$$. Hookups: electric (30, 50 amp), water, sewer.

Superstition Lookout RV Resort, 1371 East 4th Ave., 85219. T: (480) 982-2008. www.gocamping america.com. RV/tent: 192. $$$. Hookups: electric (30, 50 amp), water, sewer, phone.

Superstition Sunrise RV Resort, 702 South Meridian Dr., 85220. T: (480) 986-4524 or (800) 624-7027. www.azrvresort.com. RV/tent: 1,119. $$$. Hookups: electric (30, 50 amp), water, sewer, cable.

VIP RV Resort, 401 South Ironwood Dr., 85220. T: (480) 983-0847. RV/tent: 128. $$. Hookups: electric (20, 30, 50 amp), water, sewer.

Weaver's Needle Travel Trailer Resort, 250 South Tomahawk Rd., 85219. T: (480) 982-3683. www.weaversneedle.com. RV/tent: 400. $$$. Hookups: electric (20, 30, 50 amp), water, sewer.

Arizona City

Quail Run RV Resort, 14010 South Amado Blvd., 85223. T: (520) 466-6000 or (800) 301-8114. www.rvnetlinx.com. RV/tent: 324. $$. Hookups: electric (20, 30, 50 amp), water, sewer, cable.

Benson

Benson I-10 RV Park, 840 North Ocotillo, 85602. T: (520) 586-4262 or (800) 599-0081. www.bensonaz.com. RV/tent: 88. $$. Hookups: electric (30, 50 amp), water, sewer, cable.

Benson KOA, 180 Four Feathers Ln., 85602. T: (520) 586-9815 or (800) 562-6823. www.koakampgrounds.com. RV/tent: 107. $$. Hookups: electric (20, 30, 50 amp), water, sewer, cable, phone (modem).

Butterfield RV Resort, 251 South Ocotillo Ave., 85602. T: (520) 586-4400 or (800) 863-8160. www.rvnetlinx.com. RV/tent: 173. $$. Hookups: electric (30, 50 amp), water, sewer, cable, phone (modem).

Pato Blanco Lakes RV Park, 635 East Pearl St., 85602. T: (520) 586-8966. www.rvnetlinx.com. RV/tent: 104. $$$. Hookups: electric (20, 30, 50 amp), water, sewer, cable.

Quarter Horse RV Park, 800 West 4th St., 85602. T: (800) 527-5025. RV/tent: 50. $$. Hookups: electric (20, 30, 50 amp), water, sewer, cable, phone (modem).

Red Barn Campground, North Ocotillo Rd. at I-10, 85602. T: (520) 586-2035. RV/tent: 46. $$. Hookups: electric (30 amp), water, sewer.

San Pedro Territory 55+ Mobile Home & RV Resort, 1110 South Hwy. 80 Box 1, 85602. T: (520) 586-9546 or (877) 235-9100. www.sanpedrorv.com. RV/tent: 169. $$. Hookups: electric (20, 30, 50 amp), water, sewer.

Bisbee

San Jose Lodge & RV Park, 1002 Naco Hwy., 85603. T: (520) 432-5761. www.sanjoselodge.com. RV/tent: 50. $$. Hookups: electric, water, sewer, cable.

Brenda

Desert Gold RV Park, 46628 East Hwy. 60, 85348. T: (520) 927-7800 or (800) 927-2101. www.rvnetlinx.com. RV/tent: 551. $$. Hookups: electric (30, 50 amp), water, sewer, modem, cable.

Buckeye

Blackstone RV Park, 3299 Boundary Cone Rd., 86440. T: (928) 768-3303. www.bullheadcity az.com. RV/tent: 136. $$. Hookups: electric (20, 30, 50 amp), water, sewer, phone (modem).

Leaf Verde RV Park, 1500 South Apache Rd., 85326. T: (623) 386-3132. RV/tent: 400. $$$. Hookups: electric (30, 50 amp), water, sewer, cable, phone (modem).

Bullhead City

Ridgeview RV Resort, 775 Bullhead Pkwy, 86429. T: (928) 754-2595 or (800) 392-8560. www.sun riseresorts.com. RV/tent: 302. $$. Hookups: electric (30, 50 amp), water, sewer, phone (modem), cable.

River City RV Park, 2225 Merrill Ave., 86442. T: (928) 754-2121. www.rivercityrvpark.com. RV/tent: 134. $$. Hookups: electric (30, 50 amp), water, sewer.

Silver Creek RV Park, 1515 Gold Rush Rd., 86442. T: (928) 763-2444. RV/tent: 140. $$. Hookups: electric, water, sewer, cable.

Snowbird RV Resort, 1600 Joy Ln., 86426. T: (928) 768-7141. RV/tent: 124. $$. Hookups: electric (30, 50 amp), water, sewer, phone (modem).

Casa Grande

Campground Buena Tierra, 1995 South Cox Rd., 85222. T: (520) 836-3500 or (888) 520-8360. www.campgroundbuenatierra.com. RV/tent: 266. $$. Hookups: electric (20, 30, 50 amp), water, sewer.

Fiesta Grande RV Resort, 1511 East Florence Blvd., 85222. T: (520) 836-7222 or (888) 934-3782. www.rvinthesun.com/FiestaGrandeRV/Fiesta GrandeHome.htm. RV/tent: 767. $$$. Hookups: electric (30, 50 amp), water, sewer, phone (modem).

Foothills West RV Resort, 19501 West Hopi Dr., 85222. T: (520) 836-2531. www.rvinthesun.com/ FoothillsRV/Foot-hillsHome.htm. RV/tent: 180. $$. Hookups: electric (30, 50 amp), water, sewer, phone (modem).

Leisure Valley RV Resort, 9985 North Pinal Ave., 85222. T: (520) 836-9449 or (800) 993-9449. www.gocampingamerica.com/leisurevalleyaz. RV/tent: 126. $$. Hookups: electric (20, 30, 50 amp), water, sewer.

Palm Creek Golf and RV Resort, 1110 North Henness Rd., 85222. T: (800) 421-7004 or (520) 421-7000. www.palmcreekgolf.com. RV/tent: 1,089. $$$. Hookups: electric (30, 50 amp), water, sewer, cable, phone (modem).

Sundance 1 RV Resort, 1920 North Thornton Rd., 85222. T: (520) 426-9662 or (888) 332-5335. www.sundance1rv.com. RV/tent: 711. $$$. Hookups: electric (30, 50 amp), water, sewer.

Val Vista Winter Village RV Resort, 16680 West Val Vista Rd., 85222. T: (520) 836-7800 or (877) 836-7801. www.valvistawintervillage.com. RV/tent: 344. $$. Hookups: electric (20, 30, 50 amp), water, sewer, phone (modem).

ARIZONA (continued)

Chloride

Chloride Western RV Park, 5123 Tennessee Ave., 86431. T: (928) 565-4492 or (800) 575-4492. RV/tent: 93. $. Hookups: electric (30, 50 amp), water, sewer.

Shep's RV Park, 9827 2nd Ave., 86431. T: (928) 565-4251. RV/tent: 7. $. Hookups: electric, water, sewer.

Dateland

The Oasis at Aztec Hills, P.O. Box 324, 85333. T: (928) 454-2229. RV/tent: 37. $$. Hookups: electric (30, 50 amp), water, sewer, phone (modem).

Dewey

Orchard RV Ranch, 11250 East Hwy. 69, 86327. T: (928) 772-8266 or (800) 352-6305. RV/tent: 315. $$. Hookups: electric (20, 30, 50 amp), water, sewer, phone (modem), cable.

Ehrenberg

Ehrenberg/Colorado River KOA, 50238 Ehrenberg-Parker Hwy., 85334. T: (928) 923-7863 or (800) 378-3709. RV/tent: 169. $$. Hookups: electric (20, 30, 50 amp), water, sewer.

Flagstaff

Flagstaff KOA, 5803 North Hwy. 89, 86004. T: (928) 526-9926 or (800) KOA-FLAG. RV/tent: 150. $$. Hookups: electric (20, 30 amp), water, sewer, phone (modem).

J&H RV Park, 7901 North Hwy. 89, 86004. T: (520) 526-1829 or (623) 879-3215 (winter). www.jandhrvpark.com. RV/tent: 65. $$$. Hookups: electric (20, 30, 50 amp), water, sewer, phone (modem).

Woody Mountain Campground & RV Park, 2727 West Rte. 66, 86001. T: (928) 774-7727 or (800) 732-7986. www.woodymoutain-camp ground.com. RV/tent: 146. $$. Hookups: electric (20, 30 amp), water, sewer, phone (modem).

Florence

Desert Gardens RV Park, P.O. Box 1186, 85232. T: (520) 868-3800 or (800) 868-4888. www.desertgardensrvpark.com. RV/tent: 84. $$. Hookups: electric (20, 30, 50 amp), water, sewer, phone (modem).

Globe

Gila County RV Park & Batting Range, 300 South Pine St., 85501. T: (800) 436-8083. RV/tent: 24. $$. Hookups: electric (30, 50 amp), water, sewer, modem, cable.

Gold Canyon

Canyon Vistas RV Resort, 6601 East Hwy. 60, 85219. T: (480) 288-8844. www.cal-am.com. RV/tent: 637. $$$. Hookups: electric (30, 50 amp), water, sewer, cable, phone (modem).

Golden Valley

Adobe RV Park, 4950 Apache Way, 86413. T: (520) 565-3010. RV/tent: 75. $$. Hookups: electric (20, 30, 50 amp), water, sewer.

Goodyear

Destiny Phoenix RV Resort, 416 North Citrus Rd., 85338. T: (888) 667-2454. www.destinyrv.com. RV/tent: 285. $$$. Hookups: electric (20, 30, 50 amp), water, sewer, phone (modem).

Grand Canyon

Desert View, P.O. Box 129, 86023. T: (928) 638-7888. RV/tent: 50. $. Hookups: none.

Grand Canyon Camper Village, Box 490, 86023. T: (520) 638-2887. RV/tent: 300. $$. Hookups: electric (20, 30 amp), water, sewer, phone (modem).

Ten-X, FR 7302C, 86023. T: (928) 638-2443. RV/tent: 70. $. Hookups: none.

Happy Jack

Happy Jack Lodge & RV Resort, P.O. Box 19569, 86024. T: (928) 477-2805 or (800) 430-0385. RV/tent: 73. $. Hookups: electric (20, 30, 50 amp), water, sewer.

Hereford

Lakeview Campground, 5990 South Hwy. 92, 85615. T: (520) 378-0311. www.fs.fed.us/r3/coronado. RV/tent: 65. $. Hookups: none.

Huachuca City

Mountain View RV Park, 99 West Vista Ln., 85616. T: (520) 456-2860 or (800) 772-4103. www.mountainviewrvpark.com. RV/tent: 100. $$. Hookups: electric (30, 50 amp), water, sewer, cable, phone (modem).

Tombstone Territories RV Park, 2111 East Hwy. 82, 85616. T: (520) 457-2584 or (877) 316-6714. www.tombstoneterritories.com. RV/tent: 102. $$$. Hookups: electric (20, 30, 50 amp), water, sewer, phone (modem).

Kingman

A Quality Star RV Park, 3131 McDonald Ave., 86401. T: (928) 753-2277. RV/tent: 49. $$. Hookups: electric (20, 30 amp), water, sewer, phone (modem), cable.

Blake RV Ranch, 9315 East Blake Ranch Rd., 86401. T: (928) 757-3336 or (800) 270-1332. RV/tent: 58. $$. Hookups: electric (20, 30, 50 amp), water, sewer.

Hualapai Mountain Park, P.O. Box 7000, 86402. T: (928) 757-3859. RV/tent: 75. $. Hookups: electric (30 amp), water, sewer.

Zuni Village RV, 2840 Airway Ave., 86401. T: (928) 692-6202. RV/tent: 84. $$. Hookups: electric (20, 30, 50 amp), water, sewer.

Lake Havasu City

Beachcomber RV Resort, 601 Beachcomber Blvd., 86403. T: (928) 855-2322. www.rentor.com/lake havasu/rvcamp/beachcomber.htm. RV/tent: 50. $$$. Hookups: electric (30 amp), water, sewer, phone (modem), cable.

Cattail Cove State Park, P.O. Box 1990, 86405. T: (928) 855-1223. www.pr.state.az.us/parks/ parkhtml/cattail.html. RV/tent: 61. $. Hookups: electric (30 amp), water.

Crazy Horse Campgrounds, 1534 Beachcomber Blvd., 86403. T: (928) 855-4033. www.crazy horsecampgrounds.com. RV/tent: 777. $$.

Hookups: electric (30, 50 amp), water, sewer, cable, phone.

London Bridge RV Park, 3405 London Bridge Rd., 86405. T: (928) 764-3700. RV/tent: 58. $$. Hookups: electric (20, 30 amp), water, sewer.

Marana

A Bar A RV Park, 9015 West Tangerine Rd., 85653. T: (520) 682-4333. RV/tent: 85. $$. Hookups: electric (20, 30, 50 amp), water, sewer, phone (modem).

Valley of the Sun RV Mobile Home Park, 13377 North Sandario Rd., 85653. T: (520) 682-3434. RV/tent: 65. $$$. Hookups: electric (30, 50 amp), water, sewer, phone (modem).

McNeal

Double Adobe Campground, 5057 West Double Adobe Rd., 85617. T: (520) 364-4000 or (800) 694-4242. www.doubleadobe.com. RV/tent: 70. $. Hookups: electric (30 amp), water, sewer, cable.

Mesa

Apache Wells RV Resort, 2656 North 56th St., 85215. T: (480) 832-4324. www.cal-am.com/ apache.html. RV/tent: 320. $$$. Hookups: electric (30, 50 amp), water, sewer, phone (modem).

Canyon Lake Marina, 26 North MacDonald, 85211. T: (830) 935-4333. www.clmarina.com. RV/tent: 5. $$. Hookups: none.

Fiesta RV Resort, 3811 East University Dr., 85205. T: (480) 832-6490 or (877) 506-0071. www.fies tarv.net. RV/tent: 336. $$$. Hookups: electric (20, 50 amp), water, sewer, phone (modem).

Good Life RV Resort, 3403 East Main St., 85213. T: (480) 832-4990 or (800) 999-4990. www.gocampingamerica.com/goodlife. RV/tent: 1,170. $$$. Hookups: electric (30, 50 amp), water, sewer, phone (modem).

Greenfield Village RV Resort, 111 South Greenfield Rd., 85206. T: (480) 832-6400. www.greenfield village.com. RV/tent: 1,184. $$$. Hookups: electric (30, 50 amp), water, sewer.

Las Palmas Grand, 2550 South Ellsworth Rd., 85212. T: (480) 380-3000 or (800) 982-2250. RV/tent: 63. $$$. Hookups: electric (20, 30, 50 amp), water.

Mesa Regal RV Resort, 4700 East Main St., 85205. T: (480) 830-2821 or (800) 845-4752. www.cal-am.com/mesa.html. RV/tent: 2,005. $$$. Hookups: electric (30, 50 amp), water, sewer, phone (modem).

Mesa Spirit RV and Mobile Home Park, 3020 East Main St., 85213. T: (480) 832-1770 or (877) 924-6709. www.mesaspirit.com. RV/tent: 1,800. $$$. Hookups: electric (20, 30, 50 amp), water, sewer, phone (modem).

Orangewood Shadows RV Resort, 3165 East University, 85213. T: (480) 832-9080 or (800) 826-0909. www.orangewoodshadows.com. RV/tent: 474. $$$. Hookups: electric (30, 50 amp), water, sewer.

Palm Gardens Mobile Home/RV Community, 2929 East Main St., 85213. T: (480) 832-0290. www.palmgardens.net. RV/tent: 115. $$$. Hookups: electric (30, 50 amp), water, sewer, phone (modem).

ARIZONA (continued)

Paradise Palms Resort, 1608 East Main St., 85203. T: (480) 964-3552. RV/tent: 25. $$. Hookups: electric (30 amp), water, sewer, phone (modem).

Park Place Travel RV Resort, 306 South Recker Rd., 85206. T: (480) 830-1080. www.gocampingamer ica.com. RV/tent: 288. $$. Hookups: electric (30, 50 amp), water, sewer.

Silveridge RV Resort, 8265 East Southern, 85208. T: (480) 373-7000 or (800) 354-0054. www.silver idge.com. RV/tent: 687. $$$. Hookups: electric (30, 50 amp), water, sewer, cable, phone (modem).

Sun Life RV Resort, 5055 East University, 85205. T: (480) 981-9500. www.cal-am.com/sunlife.html. RV/tent: 761. $$. Hookups: electric (30, 50 amp), water, sewer, phone (modem).

The Resort, 1101 South Ellsworth Rd., 85208. T: (480) 986-8404 or (866) 386-1101. www.theresortrvpark.com. RV/tent: 792. $$$. Hookups: electric (30, 50 amp), water, sewer, cable, phone (modem).

Tortilla, 26 North MacDonald, 85211. T: (602) 467-2511 or (602) 379-6446. RV/tent: 77. $. Hookups: water.

Towerpoint RV Resort, 4860 East Main, 85205. T: (480) 832-4996 or (800) 444-4996. www.towerpointresort.com. RV/tent: 1115. $$$. Hookups: electric (20, 30, 50 amp), water, sewer, phone (modem).

Trailing Ranch, 8730 East Apache Trail, 85208. T: (480) 984-0592 or (800) 625-7266. RV/tent: 55. $$. Hookups: electric (30, 50 amp), water, sewer, phone (modem).

Val Vista Village RV Resort, 233 North Val Vista Dr., 85213. T: (480) 832-2547. www.cal-am.com/ valvista.html. RV/tent: 1016. $$$. Hookups: electric (30, 50 amp), water, sewer, phone (modem).

Valle de Oro RV Resort, 1452 South Ellsworth Rd., 85208. T: (480) 984-1146 or (800) 626-6686. www.valledeoro.com. RV/tent: 1802. $$$. Hookups: electric (30, 50 amp), water, sewer, phone (modem).

Venture Out RV Resort, 5001 East Main St., 85205. T: (480) 832-0200. www.ventureoutrvresort .com. RV/tent: 1749. $$. Hookups: electric (30, 50 amp), water, sewer.

View Point RV & Golf Resort, 8700 East University, 85207. T: (480) 373-8700 or (800) 822-4404. www.viewpointrv.com. RV/tent: 1784. $$$. Hookups: electric (30, 50 amp), water, sewer, cable, phone (modem).

Mormon Lake

Mormon Lake Lodge RV Park and Campground, Main St., 86038. T: (928) 354-2227. www.mor monlakelodge.com. RV/tent: 74. $. Hookups: electric (20, 30, 50 amp), water, sewer, phone (modem).

Naco

Turquoise Valley Golf Course & RV Park, 1794 West Newell St., 85620. T: (520) 432-3091. www.turquoisevalley.com. RV/tent: 100. $$. Hookups: electric (30, 50 amp), water, sewer, cable, phone (modem).

Overgaard

Elk Pines RV Resort, 2256 East Hwy. 260, 85933. T: (928) 535-3833. www.gocampingamerica .com/elkpinesrv. RV/tent: 68. $$. Hookups: electric (20, 30, 50 amp), water, sewer, phone (modem).

Page

Page-Lake Powell Campground, 849 South Coppermine Rd., 86040. T: (928) 645-3374. www.camp ground.page-lakepowell.com. RV/tent: 133. $$. Hookups: electric (20, 30, 50 amp), water, sewer, modem, cable.

Parker

Fox's Pierpoint Landing RV Resort and Restaurant, 6350 Riverside Dr., 85344. T: (928) 667-3444 or (800) 335-FOXS. www.foxsresort.com. RV/tent: 70. $$. Hookups: electric (50 amp), water, sewer, cable.

Road Runner RV Park, 7000 Riverside Dr., 85344. T: (928) 667-4252. RV/tent: 35. $$$. Hookups: electric (20, 30) amp), water, sewer, phone (modem), cable.

Peoria

Grand Inn Hotel and RV Park, 8955 NW Grand Ave., 85382. T: (800) 572-9295 or (623) 979-7200. www.theworldlinks.com/GRANDIN.html. RV/tent: 72. $$$. Hookups: electric (20, 30 amp), water, sewer.

Pleasant Harbor RV Resort, 8708 West Harbor Blvd., 85382. T: (800) 475-3272 or (928) 501-LAKE. www.pleasantharbor.com. RV/tent: 200. $$$. Hookups: electric (20, 30, 50 amp), water, sewer, phone (modem).

Sundial Mobil & RV Park, 9250 North 75th Ave., 85345. T: (623) 979-1921. RV/tent: 102. $$. Hookups: electric (30, 50 amp), water, sewer.

Phoenix

Desert Shadows Travel Trailer Resort, 19203 North 29th Ave., 85027. T: (623) 869-8178 or (800) 595-7290. www.arizonarvresorts.com/ ds_index.htm. RV/tent: 638. $$. Hookups: electric (30, 50 amp), water, sewer.

Desert's Edge RV Village, 22623 North Black Canyon Hwy., 85027. T: (623) 587-0940 or (888) 633-7677. www.desertsedgerv.com. RV/tent: 250. $$. Hookups: electric (30, 50 amp), water, sewer, phone (modem).

Prescott

Point of Rocks Campground, 3025 North Hwy. 89, 86301. T: (928) 445-9018. www.rvparksusa.com/ az/point.htm. RV/tent: 96. $$. Hookups: electric (20, 30 amp), water, sewer.

Willow Lake RV & Camping Park, 1617 Heritage Park Rd., 86301. T: (928) 445-6311 or (800) 940-2845. www.gocampingamerica.com/willowlakeaz. RV/tent: 200. $$. Hookups: electric (20, 30, 50 amp), water, sewer, phone (modem), cable.

Quartzsite

88 Shades RV Park, 575 West Main St., 85346. T: (928) 927-6336 or (800) 457-4392. www.G7inc.org/88shades. RV/tent: 255. $$. Hookups: electric (30 amp), water, sewer, cable.

B-10 Campground, 615 West Main St., 85346. T: (928) 927-4393. RV/tent: 200. $$. Hookups: electric (30, 50 amp), water, sewer.

Desert Gardens, 1240 Acacia, 85346. T: (928) 927-6361. RV/tent: 270. $$. Hookups: electric (20, 30, 50 amp), water, sewer, phone (modem).

Holiday Palms RV Park, P.O. Box 4800, 85346. T: (928) 927-5666. RV/tent: 245. $$. Hookups: electric (20, 30) amp), water, sewer.

Queen Valley

Encore RV Park, 50 West Oro Viejo Dr., 85218. T: (480) 982-2300. www.gocampingamerica.com. RV/tent: 210. $$. Hookups: electric (30, 50 amp), water, sewer.

Roosevelt

Apache Lake Resort, Hwy. 88, HCO 2 Box 4800, 85545. T: (928) 467-2511. www.apachelake.com. RV/tent: 12. $$. Hookups: yes (unspecified).

Safford

Roper Lake State Park, 101 East Roper Lake Rd., 85546. T: (520) 428-6760. www.roperlake.com. RV/tent: 71. $. Hookups: electric, water.

Sahuarita

Rancho Resort RV Park, 1300 West Sahuarita Rd., 85629. T: (888) 363-8616 or (520) 399-3900. www.ranchoresort.com. RV/tent: 100. $$. Hookups: electric, water, sewer, cable, phone.

Salome

Desert Palms Golf & RV Resort, 39258 Harquahala Rd., 85348. T: (866) 725-6778. www.desertpalms rv.com. RV/tent: 195. $$. Hookups: electric (30, 50 amp), water, sewer.

Tomahawk RV Park, 48710 Vicksburg Rd., 85348. T: (520) 859-3843 or (800) 925-2407. www.gocampingamerica.com. RV/tent: 95. $. Hookups: electric (20, 30, 50 amp), water, sewer.

Sedona

Rancho Sedona RV Park, 135 Bear Wallow Ln., 86336. T: (888) 641-4261. www.ranchosedona.com. RV/tent: 84. $$$. Hookups: electric (30, 50 amp), water, sewer, modem, cable.

Show Low

K-Bar RV Park, 300 North 15th Ave., 85901. T: (928) 537-2886. RV/tent: 92. $$. Hookups: electric (20, 30, 50 amp), water, sewer, cable.

Waltner's RV Park, 4800 South 28th St., 85901. T: (928) 537-4611. RV/tent: 146. $$. Hookups: electric (30 amp), water, sewer, cable.

Sierra Vista

Pueblo del Sol RV Resort, 3400 Resort Dr., 85650. T: (888) 551-1432. www.pdsrvresort.com. RV/tent: 135. $$. Hookups: electric (30, 50 amp), water, sewer, cable.

St. David

Holy Trinity Monastery/Monte Cassino RV Park, 401 Hwy. 80, 85630. T: (520) 720-4016. www.holytrinitymonastery.org. RV/tent: 26. $$. Hookups: electric (20, 30 amp), water, sewer.

Sun City

Paradise RV Resort, 10950 West Union Hills Dr., 85373. T: (800) 847-2280. RV/tent: 100. $$$$. Hookups: electric (30, 50 amp), water, sewer, cable.

Surprise

Donorma RV Park, 15637 Norma Ln., 85374. T: (623) 583-8195. RV/tent: 66. $$$. Hookups: electric (20, 30, 50 amp), water, sewer.

Sunflower Resort, 16501 North El Mirage Rd., 85374. T: (800) 627-8637. www.cal-am.com. RV/tent: 160. $$$$. Hookups: electric (30, 50 amp), water, sewer, cable.

Tempe

Apache Palms RV Park, 1836 East Apache Blvd., 85281. T: (480) 966-7399. www.apachepalmsrv park.com. RV/tent: 80. $$. Hookups: electric (20, 30, 50 amp), water, sewer, cable, phone (modem).

Tombstone

Stampede RV Park, 201 West Allen, 85638. T: (520) 457-3738. www.tombstone-stampede.com. RV/tent: 50. $$. Hookups: electric (20, 30, 50 amp), water, sewer.

Tombstone Hills RV Park & Campground, Rte. 80, 85638. T: (800) 348-3829. www.desert-gold.com/tombstonehills. RV/tent: 86. $$. Hookups: electric (50 amp), water, sewer.

Tonopah

Saddle Mountain RV Park, 3607 North 411th St., 85354. T: (623) 386-3892. www.holidayguide.com. RV/tent: 116. $$. Hookups: electric (30, 50 amp), water, sewer.

Stage Stop RV Park, 2614 South Wintersberg Rd., 85354. T: (623) 386-1601. RV/tent: 146. $$. Hookups: electric (20, 30, 50 amp), water, sewer.

Tucson

Beaudry RV Resort, 5151 South Country Club Rd., 85706. T: (888) 318-9119. www. beaudryrv resort.com. RV/tent: 400. $$. Hookups: electric (50 amp), water, sewer, cable.

Cactus Country RV Resort, 10195 South Houghton Rd., 85747. T: (800) 777-8799. www.cactuscountryrvresort.com. RV/tent: 263. $$. Hookups: electric (20, 30, 50 amp), water, sewer, cable, phone (modem).

Desert Trails RV Park & Water World, 3551 South San Joaquin Rd., 85735. T: (888) 883-8340. RV/tent: 220. $$. Hookups: electric (30, 50 amp), water, sewer, phone (modem).

Far Horizons Trailer Village, 555 North Pantano Rd., 85710. T: (520) 296-1234. www.tucsonvil lage.com. RV/tent: 514. $$$. Hookups: electric (30, 50 amp), water, sewer, phone (modem).

Miracle RV Park, 333 West Glenn St., 85705. T: (520) 624-0142 or (888) 624-0142. RV/tent: 86. $$. Hookups: electric (20, 30 amp), water, sewer, phone (modem).

Mission View RV Resort, 31 West Los Reales Rd., 85735. T: (800) 444-8439 or (520) 741-1945. RV/tent: 152. $$$. Hookups: electric (30, 50 amp), water, sewer.

Prince of Tucson, 3501 North Freeway, 85705. T: (520) 887-3501 or (800) 955-3501. RV/tent: 212. $$$. Hookups: electric (20, 30, 50 amp), water, sewer.

Rincon Country East RV Resort, 8989 East Escalante, 85730. T: (520) 886-8431. www.gocampingamerica.com/rinconeast. RV/tent: 460. $$$. Hookups: electric (30, 50 amp), water, sewer.

Rincon Country West RV Resort, 4555 South Mission Rd., 85746. T: (520) 294-5608 or (800) 782-7275. www.gocampingamerica.com/rinconwest. RV/tent: 1,101. $$$. Hookups: electric (30, 50 amp), water, sewer, cable, phone (modem).

Rose Canyon, Catalina Hwy., Mile Marker 17, 85750. T: (520) 749-8700. RV/tent: 74. $$. Hookups: none.

South Forty RV Ranch, 3600 West Orange Grove Rd., 85741. T: (520) 297-2503. RV/tent: 229. $$$. Hookups: electric (20, 30 amp), water, sewer, phone (modem).

Spencer Canyon, Catalina Hwy., Mile Marker 22, 85750. T: (520) 749-8700. www.azstarnet. com.public/nonprofit/coronado/d5home.html. RV/tent: 77. $$. Hookups: none.

Western Way RV Resort, 3100 South Kinney Rd., 85713. T: (520) 578-1715 or (800) 292-8616. RV/tent: 300. $$$. Hookups: electric (20, 30 amp), water, sewer.

Whispering Palms RV Trailer Park, 3445 North Romero Rd., 85705. T: (520) 888-2500 or (800) 266-8577. RV/tent: 103. $$. Hookups: electric (30 amp), water, sewer.

Wellton

M&M RV Village, 28541 West AZ Ave., 85356. T: (928) 785-4273. RV/tent: 90. $$. Hookups: electric (30 amp), water, sewer, phone (modem).

West Sedona

Lo Lo Mai Springs Outdoor Resort, 11505 Lo Lo Mai Rd., 86340. T: (928) 634-4700. www.lolo mai.com. RV/tent: 90. $$$. Hookups: electric (30 amp), water, sewer.

Why

Coyote Howls Campground, P.O. Box 1134, 85321. T: (520) 387-5209. RV/tent: 600. $. Hookups: none.

Hickiwan Trails RV Park, South US 86, 85321. T: (520) 362-3267. RV/tent: 95. $$. Hookups: electric (20, 30 amp), water, sewer.

Las Palmas RV Park, Hwy. 85, 85321. T: (520) 387-3300. RV/tent: 47. $$. Hookups: electric (20, 30 amp), water, sewer.

Robert Ranch Resort, 1600 North Ajo Way, 85321. T: (800) 699-7983 or (520) 387-7275. RV/tent: 85. $. Hookups: electric (20, 30, 50 amp), water, sewer.

Wickenburg

Desert Cypress Trailer Ranch, 610 Jack Burden Rd., Space No. 1, 85390. T: (928) 684-2153. RV/tent: 32. $$. Hookups: electric (20, 30, 50 amp), water, sewer, cable.

Willcox

Fort Willcox RV Park, RR 2 Box 512, 85643. T: (520) 384-4986. RV/tent: 35. $$. Hookups: electric (20, 30, 50 amp), water, sewer.

Grande Vista RV Park, 711 Prescott Ave. North, 85643. T: (520) 384-4002. RV/tent: 40. $$. Hookups: electric (30, 50 amp), water, sewer, cable, phone (modem).

Lifestyle RV Resort, 622 North Haskell Ave., 85643. T: (520) 384-3303. RV/tent: 60. $$. Hookups: electric (20, 30, 50 amp), water, sewer, cable, modem.

Magic Circle RV Park, 700 North Virginia Ave., 85643. T: (520) 384-3212 or (800) 333-4720. www.gocampingamerica.com/magiccircle. RV/tent: 56. $$. Hookups: electric (20, 30, 50 amp), water, sewer, cable, phone (modem).

Williams

Canyon Gateway RV Park, 1060 North Grand Canyon Blvd., 86046. T: (888) 635-0329 or (928) 635-2718. www.grandcanyonrvparks.com. RV/tent: 101. $$. Hookups: electric (30, 50 amp), water, sewer.

Circle Pines KOA, 1000 Circle Pines Rd., 86046. T: (928) 635-2626 or (800) 562-9379. www.koakampgrounds.com. RV/tent: 149. $$. Hookups: electric (20, 30 amp), water, sewer, phone (modem).

Flintstone's Bedrock City Camping, H CR-34 Box A, 86046. T: (928) 635-2600. www.flintstones bedrockcity.com. RV/tent: 60. $$. Hookups: electric (30 amp).

Railside RV Ranch, 877 Rodeo Rd., 86046. T: (928) 635-4077 or (888) 635-4077. www.thegrand canyon.com/railside. RV/tent: 96. $$. Hookups: electric (20, 30, 50 amp), water, sewer, modem, cable.

Yuma

Araby Acres Travel Trailer Park, 6649 East Hwy. 80, 85365. T: (928) 344-8666. RV/tent: 338. $$$. Hookups: electric (30, 50 amp), water, sewer, phone (modem).

Arizona Sands RV Park, 5510 East US 80, 85365. T: (928) 726-0286. RV/tent: 200. $$. Hookups: electric (30, 50 amp), water, sewer.

Blue Sky RV Park, 10247 South Frontage Rd., 85365. T: (877) 367-5220 or (928) 342-1444. www.blueskyyuma.com. RV/tent: 276. $$. Hookups: electric (30, 50 amp), water, sewer.

Bonita Mesa RV Resort, 9400 East North Frontage Rd., 85365. T: (928) 342-2999. www.gocamping america.com/bonitamesa/index.html. RV/tent: 470. $$. Hookups: electric (30, 50 amp), water, sewer, phone (modem), cable.

Caravan Oasis RV Park, 10500 North East Frontage Rd., 85365. T: (928) 342-1480. RV/tent: 742. $$. Hookups: electric (30, 50 amp), water, sewer, phone (modem), cable.

Cocopah RV & Golf Resort, 6800 Strand Ave. South, 85366. T: (928) 343-9300 or (800) 537-7901. www.cocopahrv.com. RV/tent: 806. $$. Hookups: electric (30, 50 amp), water, sewer, phone (modem), cable.

Desert Paradise RV Resort, 10537 South Ave. 9E, 85365-8117. T: (928) 342-9313. www.the-camp ground-network.com/DESERTPARADISERVRE SORT.com. RV/tent: 260. $$. Hookups: electric (30, 50 amp), water, sewer, phone (modem), cable.

ARIZONA (continued)

El Prado Estates RV Park, 6200 East Hwy. 95, 85365. T: (520) 726-4006. RV/tent: 120. $$. Hookups: electric (30 amp), water, sewer.

Fortuna de Oro RV Resort, 13650 North Frontage Rd., 85367. T: (928) 342-5051 or (800) 839-0126. www.fortunadeoro.com. RV/tent: 1,294. $$. Hookups: electric (20, 30, 50 amp), water, sewer.

Friendly Acres Trailer Park, 2779 West 8th St., 85364. T: (928) 783-8414. www.friendly-acres.com. RV/tent: 280. $$. Hookups: electric (30 amp), water, sewer, phone (modem), cable.

Hidden Shores RV Village, SR 4 Box 40, 85365. T: (928) 539-6700. www.hiddenshores.com. RV/tent: 354. $. Hookups: electric (20, 30, 50 amp), water, sewer, phone (modem).

Las Quintas Oasis RV Park, 1442 North Frontage Rd., 85365. T: (928) 305-9005 or (877) 975-9005. www.caravanoasisresort.com. RV/tent: 460. $$$. Hookups: electric (30, 50 amp), water, sewer, phone (modem), cable.

Shangri-La RV Park, 10498 North Frontage Rd., 85365. T: (928) 342-9123 or (877) 742-6474. www.shangrilarv.com. RV/tent: 302. $$. Hookups: electric (30, 50 amp), water, sewer.

Sun Vista RV Resort, 7201 East Hwy. 80, 85365. T: (928) 726-8920 or (800) 423-8382. www.sunvistarvresort.com. RV/tent: 1,230. $$$. Hookups: electric (30, 50 amp), water, sewer, phone (modem), cable.

Villa Alameda RV Resort, 11451 South Ave. 5E, 85365. T: (520) 344-8081. RV/tent: 302. $$.

Hookups: electric (30, 50 amp), water, sewer, phone (modem), cable.

Westwind RV & Golf Resort, 9797 East 32nd St., 85365. T: (928) 342-2992 or (866) 440-2992. www.westwindrvgolfresort.com. RV/tent: 1,075. $$$. Hookups: electric (20, 30, 50 amp), water, sewer, phone (modem), cable.

Windhaven RV Park, 6580 East Hwy. 80, 85365. T: (928) 726-0284. RV/tent: 135. $$$. Hookups: electric (20, 30, 50 amp), water, sewer.

Yuma Mesa RV Park, 5990 East Hwy. 80, 85365. T: (928) 344-3369. www.gocampingamerica.com/yumamesa. RV/tent: 183. $$. Hookups: electric (30 amp), water, sewer.

ARKANSAS

Alma

Alma RV Park, 405 Heather Ln., 72921. T: (479) 632-0909. RV/tent: 50. $. Hookups: electric (30, 50 amp), water, sewer.

Ft. Smith/Alma KOA, 3539 North Hwy. 71, 72921. T: (800) 562-2703 or (479) 632-2704. www.koa.com. RV/tent: 78. $$. Hookups: electric (30, 50 amp), water, sewer.

Arkadelphia

Alpine Ridge Campground, 729 Channel Rd., 71923. T: (870) 246-5501. www.reserveusa.com. RV/tent: 49. $. Hookups: electric (20, 30 amp).

Edgewood Campground, 729 Channel Rd., 71923. T: (870) 246-5501. www.reserveusa.com. RV/tent: 51. $. Hookups: electric (20, 30 amp).

Ashdown

Beards Bluff Campground, 1528 Hwy. 32 East, 71822. T: (870) 388-9556. www.reserveusa.com. RV/tent: 30. $$. Hookups: electric (20, 30 amp).

Cottonshed, 1528 Hwy. 32 East, 71822. T: (870) 287-7118. www.reserveusa.com. RV/tent: 46. $$. Hookups: electric (20, 30 amp), water.

Millwood State Park, 1564 Hwy. 32 East, 71822. T: (870) 898-2800. www.ArkansasState Parks.com. RV/tent: 117. $. Hookups: electric (30 amp), water.

Benton

JB's RV Park & Campground, 8601 J. B. Baxely Rd., 72015. T: (501) 778-6050. RV/tent: 44. $$. Hookups: electric (30, 50 amp), water, sewer.

Bismarck

DeGray State Park, 2027 State Park Entrance Rd., 71929. T: (501) 865-2801. www.ArkansasState Parks.com. RV/tent: 113. $$. Hookups: electric (30 amp), water.

Bluff City

White Oak Lake State Park, Rte. 2 Box 28, 71722. T: (870) 685-2748 or (870) 685-2132. www.ArkansasStateParks.com. RV/tent: 42. $$. Hookups: electric (30 amp), water.

Blytheville

Knights of the Road RV Park, 3801 South Division, 72315. T: (501) 763-7161. RV/tent: 12. $$. Hookups: electric (20, 30, 50 amp), water, sewer.

Brinkley

Super 8 RV Park, 2005-A North Main, 72021. T: (870) 734-4680. RV/tent: 34. $$. Hookups: electric (30 amp), water, sewer.

Cotter

White River Campground, Hwy. 62 B, 72626. T: (870) 453-2299. www.southshore.com. RV/tent: 80. $$. Hookups: electric (30, 50 amp), water, sewer, cable.

Dardanelle

Mount Nebo State Park, No. 1 State Park Dr., 72834. T: (479) 229-3655. www.ArkansasState Parks.com. RV/tent: 34. $. Hookups: electric (30 amp), water.

DeQueen

Bellah Mine Campground, 706 DeQueen Lake Rd., 71832. T: (870) 584-4161. www.reserveusa.com. RV/tent: 20. $. Hookups: electric (20, 30 amp), water.

Big Coon Creek Campground, 706 DeQueen Lake Rd., 71832. T: (870) 584-4161. www.reserve usa.com. RV/tent: 30. $$. Hookups: electric (20, 30 amp), water.

Cossatot Reefs Campground, 706 DeQueen Lake Rd., 71832. T: (870) 584-4161. www.reserve usa.com. RV/tent: 26. $. Hookups: electric (20, 30 amp), water.

Dierks

Blue Ridge Campground, 952 Lake Rd. P.O. Box 8, 71833. T: (870) 286-2346. www.reserveusa.com. RV/tent: 17. $. Hookups: electric (20, 30 amp), water.

Eureka Springs

Green Tree Lodge & RV Park, 560 West Van Buren, 72632. T: (479) 253-8807. RV/tent: 24. $$. Hookups: electric (20, 30, 50 amp), water, sewer.

Hidden Cove, 700 CR 1089, 72632. T: (501) 253-2939. www.eurekaweb.com/hiddencove. RV/tent: 80. $. Hookups: electric (20, 30, 50 amp), water, sewer.

Kettle Campground, Hwy. 62 East, 72632. T: (800) 899-CAMP or (479) 253-9100. www.kettlecamp ground.com. RV/tent: 80. $$. Hookups: electric (20, 30, 50 amp), water, sewer.

Starkey Campground, 3994 Mundell Rd., 72631. T: (479) 253-5866. www.reserveusa.com. RV/tent: 23. $$. Hookups: electric (20, 30 amp).

Wanderlust RV Park, 468 Passion Play Rd., 72632. T: (800) 253-7385. RV/tent: 90. $$. Hookups: electric (20, 30, 50 amp), water, sewer.

Flippin

Cedar Hollow RV Park, 76 MC 8119, 72634. T: (877) 747-3633 or (870) 453-8643. www.billy hill.com. RV/tent: 26. $$. Hookups: electric (20, 30, 50 amp), water, sewer.

Garfield

Indian Creek Campground, 13324 Indian Creek Rd., 72732. T: (479) 656-3145. www.reserveusa.com. RV/tent: 20. $$. Hookups: electric (30 amp).

Lost Bridge South Campground, 12001 Buckhorn Cir., 72732. T: (501) 359-3312. www.reserve usa.com. RV/tent: 36. $$. Hookups: electric (20, 30 amp).

Greenbrier

Woolly Hollow State Park, 82 Woolly Hollow Rd., 72058. T: (501) 679-2098. www.ArkansasState Parks.com. RV/tent: 32. $. Hookups: electric (30 amp), water.

Hampton

Silver Eagle RV Campground, Hwy. 167 North, 71744. T: (870) 798-3798. www.silvereagle rv.com. RV/tent: 35. $$. Hookups: electric (20, 30, 50 amp), water, sewer.

Harrisburg

Lake Poinsett State Park, 5752 State Park Ln., 72432. T: (870) 578-2064. www.ArkansasState Parks.com. RV/tent: 30. $. Hookups: electric (30 amp), water.

ARKANSAS (continued)

Harrison

Harrison Village Campground, 2364 Hwy. 65 South, 72601. T: (870) 743-3388. www.woodalls.com/ a/00105_HarrisonVillage.html. RV/tent: 79. $$. Hookups: electric (20, 30, 50 amp), water, sewer.

Shady Oaks Campground and RV Park, 960 Hwy. 206 East, 72601. T: (870) 743-2343. www.camp theoaks.com. RV/tent: 50. $. Hookups: electric (20, 30, 50 amp), water, sewer.

Heber Springs

Hill Creek Campground, 700 Heber Springs Rd. North, 72543. T: (501) 362-2416. www.reserve usa.com. RV/tent: 41. $. Hookups: electric (30, 50 amp), water, sewer.

John F. Kennedy Campground, 700 Heber Springs Rd. North, 72543. T: (501) 362-2416. www.reserveusa.com. RV/tent: 74. $$. Hookups: electric (20, 30 amp), water.

Hot Springs

Camp Lake Hamilton, 6191 Central Ave., 71913. T: (501) 525-8204. RV/tent: 80. $$. Hookups: electric (30, 50 amp), water, sewer.

Hot Springs KOA, 838 McClendon Rd., 71901. T: (800) 562-5903 or (501) 624-5912. www.koa.com/where/AR/04106.htm. RV/tent: 86. $$. Hookups: electric (20, 30, 50 amp), water, sewer, phone(modem).

Lake Catherine State Park, 1200 Catherine Park Rd., 71913. T: (501) 844-4176. www.ArkansasStateParks.com. RV/tent: 70. $$. Hookups: electric (30 amp), water.

Lakeside Trailer Park & Cottages Inc., 451 Lakeland Dr., 71901. T: (501) 525-8878. RV/tent: 20. $$. Hookups: electric (30 amp), water, sewer.

Mill Pond Mobile Home & RV Village, 7 South-1 Peakness Dr., 71913. T: (501) 525-3959. www.hsnp.com. RV/tent: 21. $. Hookups: electric (30, 50 amp), water, sewer.

Pit Stop RV Park & Restaurant, 3040 Albert Pike, 71901. T: (501) 767-6830. RV/tent: 15. $$. Hookups: electric (30, 50 amp), water.

River View Paradise RV Park & Condos, 173 Barbary Rd., 71913. T: (501) 767-9821. RV/tent: 65. $$. Hookups: electric (30 amp), water, sewer.

Timbercrest RV & Mobile Home Park, 3921 Central Ave., 71913. T: (501) 525-8361. RV/tent: 53. $$. Hookups: electric (50 amp), water, sewer.

Wagon Wheel RV Park, 205 Treasure Isle Rd. No. 99, 71913. T: (501) 767-6852. RV/tent: 62. $$. Hookups: electric (30 amp), water, sewer.

Huntsville

Withrow Springs State Park, Rte. 3 Box 29, 72750. T: (501) 559-2593. www.ArkansasState Parks.com. RV/tent: 26. $. Hookups: electric (30 amp), water.

Jonesboro

Lake Frierson State Park, 7904 Hwy. 141, 72401. T: (870) 932-2615. www.ArkansasState Parks.com. RV/tent: 12. $. Hookups: electric (30 amp), water.

Perkins RV Park, 1821 Parker Rd., 72404. T: (870) 935-4152. RV/tent: 44. $. Hookups: electric (30, 50 amp), water, sewer.

Kirby

Daisy State Park, 103 East Park, 71950. T: (870) 398-4487. www.ArkansasStateParks.com. RV/tent: 117. $. Hookups: electric (30 amp), water.

Lake Village

Lake Chicot State Park, 2542 Hwy. 257, 71653. T: (870) 265-5480. www.ArkansasStateParks. com. RV/tent: 127. $. Hookups: electric (30 amp), water, sewer.

Lakeview

Bull Shoals-White River State Park, 129 Bull Shoals Park, 72642. T: (870) 431-5521. www.Arkansas StateParks.com. RV/tent: 105. $. Hookups: electric (30 amp), water, sewer.

Riverside Mobile/RV Park, 449 River Rd., 72642. T: (870) 431-8260. www.riversidervpark.com. RV/tent: 21. $$. Hookups: electric (20, 30, 50 amp), water, sewer.

Lamar

Dad's Dream RV Park, Rte. 2 Box 19, 72846. T: (501) 865-2322. RV/tent: 40. $. Hookups: electric (30, 50 amp), water, sewer.

Lowell

Green Country RV Park, 110 Pleasant Grove Rd., 72745. T: (888) 980-8850. www.greencountry-rvpark.com. RV/tent: 71. $$. Hookups: electric (30, 50 amp), water, sewer.

Hickory Creek Park, 12618 Hickory Creek Rd., 72745. T: (479) 750-2943. www.reserveusa.com. RV/tent: 61. $$. Hookups: electric (20, 30 amp).

Magnolia

Best Western Coachman's Inn, 420 East Main St., 71753. T: (870) 234-6122. www.bestwestern. worldexecutive.com. RV/tent: 10. $$. Hookups: electric (30, 50 amp), water, sewer.

Mena

Queen Wilhelmina State Park, 3877 Hwy. 88 West, 71953. T: (479) 394-2863. www.ArkansasState Parks.com. RV/tent: 41. $. Hookups: electric (30 amp), water.

Morrilton

Cherokee Campground, 1 Quincy Rd., 72110. T: (501) 329-2986. www.reserveusa.com. RV/tent: 33. $$. Hookups: electric (20, 30 amp), water.

Lewisburg Bay RV Park, 1020 South Bridge St., 72110. T: (501) 354-5601. RV/tent: 20. $. Hookups: electric (30 amp), water, sewer.

Mount Ida

Marilyn's RV Park, 3551 Hwy. 270 West, 71957. T: (870) 867-0168. RV/tent: 15. $$. Hookups: electric (20, 30, 50 amp), water.

Mountain Home

Bidwell Point Campground, 324 West 7th St., 72653. T: (870) 467-5375. www.reserveusa .com/nrrs/ar/bidw. RV/tent: 48. $$. Hookups: electric (20, 30 amp).

Buck Creek Campground, 324 West 7th St., 72653. T: (417) 785-4313. www.reserveamerica.com. RV/tent: 39. $$. Hookups: electric (20, 30 amp).

Cranfield Park Campground, P.O. Box 2070, 72654. T: (870) 492-4191. www.reserveusa.com/nrrs/ ar/cran. RV/tent: 69. $$. Hookups: electric (20, 30 amp).

Gamaliel Campground, 324 West 7th St., 72654. T: (870) 425-2700. www.reserveusa.com/nrrs/ ar/gama. RV/tent: 64. $$. Hookups: electric (20, 30 amp).

Jordan Park Campground, 324 West 7th St., 72653. T: (870) 499-7223. www.reserveusa.com/nrrs/ ar/jord. RV/tent: 33. $. Hookups: electric (20, 30 amp).

Panther Bay Campground, P.O. Box 2070, 72654. T: (870) 425-2700. www.reserveamerica.com. RV/tent: 22. $. Hookups: electric (20, 30 amp).

Robinson Point Campground, 324 West 7th St., 72654. T: (870) 492-6853. www.reserveusa.com/ nrrs/ar/robp. RV/tent: 102. $$. Hookups: electric (20, 30, 50 amp).

White Buffalo Resort and Campground, 418 White Buffalo Tr., 72653. T: (870) 425-8555. www.whiteriver.net. RV/tent: 52. $$. Hookups: electric (20, 30, 50 amp), water, sewer.

Mountain Pine

Lake Ouachita State Park, 5451 Mountain Pine Rd., 71956. T: (501) 767-9366. www.ArkansasState Parks.com. RV/tent: 118. $. Hookups: electric (30 amp), water, sewer.

Mountain View Blue Sky RV Park, HC 72 Box 136, 72560. T: (870) 269-8132 or (800) 330-6655. www.blueskyrvpark.com. RV/tent: 100. $$. Hookups: electric (20, 30 amp), water, sewer.

Mountain View

Ozark RV Park, 1022 Park Ave., 72560. T: (501) 269-2542. RV/tent: 73. $$. Hookups: electric (20, 30 amp), water, sewer, cable.

Mountainburg

Lake Fort State Park, P.O. Box 4, 72946. T: (501) 369-2469. www.ArkansasStateParks.com. RV/tent: 12. $$. Hookups: electric (30 amp), water.

Murfreesboro

Cowhide Cove Campground, 155 Dynamite Hill, 71958. T: (870) 285-2151. www.reserveusa .com/nrrs/ar/cown. RV/tent: 50. $. Hookups: electric (20, 30 amp).

Crater of Diamonds State Park, 209 State Park Rd., 71958. T: (870) 285-3113. www.craterof diamondsstatepark.com. RV/tent: 60. $$$$. Hookups: electric (30 amp), water.

Omaha

Cricket Creek Campground, 20110 Boat Dock Rd., 72662. T: (870) 426-3331. www.reserve usa.com/nrrs/ar/cric. RV/tent: 35. $. Hookups: electric (20, 30 amp).

Ozark Vue RV Park, Rte. 1 Box 126D, 72662. T: (501) 426-5166. RV/tent: 31. $$. Hookups: electric (20, 30, 50 amp), water, sewer.

ARKANSAS (continued)

Ozark

Aux Arc Campground, 1314 Aux Arc Park Rd., 72949. T: (501) 667-2129. www.reserveusa.com/ nrrs/ar/auxa. RV/tent: 61. $$. Hookups: electric (20, 30, 50 amp), water, sewer.

Perryville

Coffee Creek Landing & Resort, Hwy. 300 Harris Brake Lake, 72126. T: (501) 889-2745. www. coffeecreekresort.com. RV/tent: 42. $$. Hookups: electric (20, 30, 50 amp), water, sewer.

Plainview Quarry Cove Campground, Nimrod Lake Quarry Cove Park, 3 Hwy. 7 South, 72857. T: (501) 272-4233. www.reserveusa.com/ nrrs/ar/quar. RV/tent: 31. $$. Hookups: electric (20, 30 amp), water.

Sunlight Bay Campground, Sunlight Bay 3, Hwy. 7 South, 72857. T: (501) 272-4234. www.reserve usa.com/nrrs/ar/sunl. RV/tent: 28. $$. Hookups: electric (20, 30 amp), water.

Plainview

Carter Cove Campground, 3 Hwy. 7, 72857. T: (501) 272-4983. www.reserveusa.com/nrrs/ ar/cart. RV/tent: 34. $$. Hookups: electric (20, 30 amp), water.

Powhatan

Lake Charles State Park, 3705 Hwy. 25, 72458. T: (870) 878-6595. www.ArkansasState Parks.com. RV/tent: 61. $$. Hookups: electric (30 amp), water.

Rogers

Lost Bridge North Campground, 2260 North 2nd, 72756. T: (501) 359-3312. www.reserveusa.com/ nrrs/ar/lost. RV/tent: 48. $$. Hookups: electric (20, 30 amp).

Royal

Brady Mountain Campground, 1201 Blakely Dam Rd., 71968. T: (501) 767-2108. www.reserveusa. com/nrrs/ar/bran. RV/tent: 74. $. Hookups: electric (20, 30 amp).

Denby Point Campground, 1201 Blakely Dam Rd., 71968. T: (501) 767-2108. www.reserveusa.com/ nrrs/ar/denb. RV/tent: 67. $. Hookups: electric (20, 30 amp).

Russellville

Lake Dardanelle State Park, 2428 Marina Rd., 72802. T: (479) 967-5516. www.ArkansasState Parks.com. RV/tent: 83. $$. Hookups: electric (30 amp), water, sewer.

Piney Bay Campground, 1598 Lock And Dam Rd., 72802. T: (501) 885-3029. www.reserve usa.com/nrrs/ar/pinb. RV/tent: 91. $. Hookups: electric (20, 30 amp), water.

Shirley

Golden Pond RV Park, Hwy. 330 South, 72153. T: (501) 723-8212. www.goldenpond.com. RV/tent: 50. $$. Hookups: electric (30, 50 amp), water, sewer, cable.

Siloam Springs

County Line, 3 Hwy. 7, 72857. T: (501) 272-4945. www.reserveusa.com/nrrs/ar/coul. RV/tent: 20. $$. Hookups: electric (20, 30 amp), water.

Greentree RV Park, 1800 West Hwy. 412, 72761. T: (479) 524-8898. RV/tent: 37. $$. Hookups: electric (30, 50 amp), water, sewer.

Springdale

Springdale Whistler RV Park, 1101 South Old Missouri Rd., 72764. T: (479) 751-9081. RV/tent: 64. $$. Hookups: electric (30, 50 amp), water, sewer.

Star City

Cane Creek State Park, P.O. Box 96, 71667. T: (870) 628-4714. www.ArkansasStateParks.com. RV/tent: 30. $$. Hookups: electric (30 amp), water.

Van Buren

Park Ridge RV Campground, 1616 Rena Rd., 72956. T: (501) 410-GORV. RV/tent: 50. $$. Hookups: electric (30, 50 amp), water, sewer.

West Fork

Devil's Den State Park, 11333 West Hwy. 74, 72774. T: (479) 761-3325. www.ArkansasState Parks.com. RV/tent: 140. $. Hookups: electric (30 amp), water.

West Memphis

Tom Sawyer's Mississippi River RV Park, 1286 South 8th, 72301. T: (870) 735-9770. RV/tent: 90. $$. Hookups: electric (30, 50 amp), water, sewer.

CALIFORNIA

Acton

The Californian RV Resort, 1535 West Sierra Hwy., 93510. T: (888) 787-8386 or (661) 269-0919. www.calrv.com. RV/tent: 73. $$$. Hookups: electric (20, 30, 50 amp), water, sewer, cable, phone.

Adin

Lower Rush Creek Campground, Modoc National Forest, CR 198A, 96006. T: (530) 233-5811. www.r5.fs.fed.us/modoc/recreation/camping/ lower-rush-creek.html. RV/tent: 10. $. Hookups: none.

Allensworth

Colonel Allensworth State Historic Park, Palmer Ave., 93219. T: (800) 444-7275 or (661) 634-3795. www.reserveamerica.com. RV/tent: 15. $. Hookups: none.

Anaheim

Anaheim Harbor RV Park, 1009 South Harbor Blvd., 92805. T: (714) 535-6495. www.anaheim harborrvpark.com. RV/tent: 198. $$$. Hookups: electric (30, 50 amp), water, sewer, cable, phone.

Anaheim Resort RV Park, 200 West Midway Dr., 92805. T: (714) 774-3860. www.anaheimresort rvpark.com. RV/tent: 150. $$$. Hookups: electric (20, 30, 50 amp), water, sewer, cable, phone.

Angels Camp

Angels Camp RV & Camping Resort, 3069 South Hwy. 49, 95222. T: (888) 398-0404 or (209) 736-0404. www.gocampingamerica.com/angelscamp. RV/tent: 44. $$$. Hookups: electric (20, 30, 50 amp), water, sewer.

Angelus Oaks

Barton Flats, Hwy. 38, 92305. T: (877) 444-6777 or (909) 389-4517. www.reserveusa.com. RV/tent: 52. $$. Hookups: none.

Heart Bar Family Camp, FR 1N02, 92305. T: (877) 444-6777 or (909) 794-1123. www.reserveusa. com. RV/tent: 94. $. Hookups: none.

San Gorgonio, Hwy. 42700 Hwy. 38, 92305. T: (877) 444-6777 or (909) 794-1123. www.reserve usa.com. RV/tent: 54. $$. Hookups: none.

South Fork, Hwy. 38, 92305. T: (877) 444-6777 or (909) 794-1123. RV/tent: 24. $$. Hookups: none.

Anza

Kamp-Anza RV Resort, 41560 Terwilliger Rd., 92539. T: (909) 763-4819. RV/tent: 115. $$. Hookups: electric (30 amp), water.

Arcadia

Santa Anita Village & RV Park, 4241 East Live Oak Ave., 91006. T: (626) 447-3878. RV/tent: 100. $$$. Hookups: electric (30 amp), water, sewer, phone.

Arcata

Mad River Rapids RV Park, 3501 Janes Rd., 95521. T: (800) 822-7776 or (707) 822-7275. www.madriverrv.com. RV/tent: 92. $$$. Hookups: electric (30, 50 amp), water, sewer, cable, phone.

Auburn

Auburn KOA, 3550 KOA Way, 95602. T: (800) 562-6671 or (530) 885-0990. www.koa.com. RV/tent: 80. $$$. Hookups: electric (30, 50 amp), water, sewer.

Bakersfield

Bakersfield Palms RV Park, 250 Fairfax Rd., 93307. T: (888) 725-6778 or (661) 366-6700. www.palmsrv.com. RV/tent: 116. $$. Hookups: electric (30, 50 amp), water, sewer, cable, phone.

Bakersfield Trav-L-Park, 8633 East Brundage Ln., 93307. T: (800) 962-4546 or (661) 366-3550. www.bakersfieldtravelpark.com. RV/tent: 126. $$. Hookups: electric (30, 50 amp), water, sewer, cable, phone.

Orange Grove RV Park, 1452 South Edison Rd., 93307. T: (800) 553-7126 or (661) 366-4662. www.orangegrovervpark.com. RV/tent: 146. $$$. Hookups: electric (30, 50 amp), water, sewer, cable, phone.

CALIFORNIA (continued)

Bakersfield (continued)

Southland RV Park, 9901 Southland Ct., 93307. T: (877) 834-4868. www.gocampingamerica.com/southlandrvpk. RV/tent: 91. $$. Hookups: electric (30, 50 amp), water, sewer, phone.

Banning

Stagecoach RV Park, 1455 South San Gorgonio Ave., 92220. T: (909) 849-7513. RV/tent: 97. $$. Hookups: electric (30, 50 amp), water, sewer, cable, phone.

Bard

Senator Wash Recreation Area, Senator Wash Rd., 92222. T: (520) 317-3200. www.ca.blm.gov/caso/information.html. RV/tent: Undesignated. $. Hookups: none.

Squaw Lake, Senator Wash Rd., 92222. T: (520) 317-3200. www.ca.blm.gov/caso/information.html. RV/tent: 80. $. Hookups: none.

Barstow

Shady Lane RV Camp, 36445 Soap Mine Rd., 92311. T: (760) 256-5332. RV/tent: 33. $$. Hookups: electric (20, 30 amp), water, sewer, phone.

Bass Lake

Chilkoot, Beasore Rd., 93604. T: (559) 877-2218. www.r5.fs.fed.us/sierra. RV/tent: 14. $$. Hookups: none.

Spring Cove, CR 222, 93604. T: (559) 877-2218. www.r5.fs.fed.us/sierra. RV/tent: 65. $$. Hookups: none.

Wishon Point, CR 222, 93604. T: (559) 877-2218. www.r5.fs.fed.us/sierra. RV/tent: 47. $$. Hookups: none.

Beckwourth

Lightning Tree, Lake Davis Rd., 96129. T: (530) 836-2575. www.r5.fs.fed.us/plumas. RV/tent: 38. $$. Hookups: none.

Bethel Island

Lundborg Landing, 6777 Riverview Rd., 94511. T: (925) 684-9351. www.lundborglanding.com. RV/tent: 96. $$. Hookups: electric (30 amp), water, sewer.

Big Bear Lake

Holloway's Marina & RV Park, 398 Edgemoor Rd., 92325. T: (800) 448-5335 or (909) 866-5706. www.bigbearboating.com. RV/tent: 99. $$. Hookups: electric (20, 30, 50 amp), water, sewer, cable.

Big Pine

Sage Flat, Glacier Lodge Rd., 93513. T: (760) 873-2500. www.r5.fs.fed.us/inyo. RV/tent: 28. $. Hookups: none.

Upper Sage Flat, Glacier Lodge Rd., 93513. T: (760) 873-2500. www.r5.fs.fed.us/inyo. RV/tent: 21. $. Hookups: none.

Big Sur

Big Sur Campgrounds & Cabins, Hwy. 1, 93920. T: (831) 667-2322. www.bigsurcalifornia.org/camping.html. RV/tent: 81. $$$. Hookups: electric (20, 30 amp), water.

Bishop

Big Trees, Hwy. 168, 93514. T: (760) 873-2500. www.r5.fs.fed.us/inyo. RV/tent: 9. $$. Hookups: none.

Bishop Park, Hwy. 168, 93514. T: (760) 873-2500. www.r5.fs.fed.us/inyo. RV/tent: 21. $$. Hookups: none.

Brown's Millpond Campground, 219 Wye Rd., 93514. T: (760) 872-6911. www.thesierraweb.com/recreation/browns/millpond.html. RV/tent: 60. $$. Hookups: electric (30 amp), water.

Brown's Owens River Campground, 219 Wye Rd., 93514. T: (760) 920-0975 or (760) 872-6911. www.thesierraweb.com/recreation/browns/owens.html. RV/tent: 75. $$. Hookups: electric (30 amp), water.

Brown's Town Campground, Schober Ln./Rte. 1, 93514. T: (760) 873-8522. www.thesierraweb.com/recreation/browns.html. RV/tent: 150. $$. Hookups: electric (30 amp), water.

Creekside RV Park, South Lake Rd., 93514. T: (760) 873-4483. www.thesierraweb.com/lodging/creekside. RV/tent: 49. $$. Hookups: electric (15, 30 amp), water, sewer.

Four Jeffrey, South Lake Rd., 93514. T: (760) 873-2500. www.r5.fs.fed.us/inyo. RV/tent: 106. $$. Hookups: none.

Highlands RV Park, 2275 North Sierra Hwy., 93514. T: (760) 873-7616. RV/tent: 103. $$. Hookups: electric (15, 30, 50 amp), water, sewer, cable.

Intake, Hwy. 168, 93514. T: (760) 873-2500. www.r5.fs.fed.us/inyo. RV/tent: 15. $$. Hookups: none.

North Lake, FR 8S02, 93514. T: (760) 873-2500. www.r5.fs.fed.us/inyo. RV/tent: 11. $$. Hookups: none.

Sabrina, Hwy. 168, 93514. T: (760) 873-2500. www.r5.fs.fed.us/inyo. RV/tent: 18. $$. Hookups: none.

Blythe

Blythe Destiny's Riviera RV Resort & Marina, 14100 Riviera Dr., 92225. T: (760) 922-5350. www.destinyrv.com/River2.htm. RV/tent: 268. $$$. Hookups: electric (30, 50 amp), water, sewer, cable, phone.

Coon Hollow Campground, Wiley's Well Rd., 92225. T: (760) 251-4800. www.ca.blm.gov/palmsprings/bradshaw.html. RV/tent: 27. $$. Hookups: none.

Destiny's McIntyre RV Resort, 8750 East 26th Ave., 92225. T: (760) 922-8205. www.destinyrv.com/River2.htm. RV/tent: 161. $$$. Hookups: electric (30 amp), water, sewer.

Wiley's Well, Wiley's Well Rd., 92225. T: (760) 251-4800. RV/tent: 13. $$. Hookups: none.

Boca

Boca Rest Campground, CR 270, 96161. T: (877) 444-6777 or (530) 587-3558. www.r5.fs.fed.us/tahoe. RV/tent: 31. $. Hookups: none.

Boca Spring Campground, FR 72, 96161. T: (877) 444-6777 or (530) 587-3558. www.r5.fs.fed.us/tahoe. RV/tent: 22. $. Hookups: none.

Boyington Mill, CR 270, 96161. T: (877) 444-6777 or (530) 587-3558. www.r5.fs.fed.us/tahoe. RV/tent: 10. $. Hookups: none.

Cold Creek, Hwy. 89, 96161. T: (877) 444-6777 or (530) 587-3558. www.r5.fs.fed.us/tahoe. RV/tent: 13. $$. Hookups: none.

Lower Little Truckee, Hwy. 89, 96161. T: (877) 444-6777 or (530) 587-3558. www.r5.fs.fed.us/tahoe. RV/tent: 14. $$. Hookups: none.

Upper Little Truckee, Hwy. 89, 96161. T: (877) 444-6777 or (530) 587-3558. www.r5.fs.fed.us/tahoe. RV/tent: 26. $$. Hookups: none.

Bodega Bay

Bodega Bay RV Park, 2001 Hwy. 1, 94923. T: (800) 201-6864 or (707) 875-3701. www.bodegabayrvpark.com. RV/tent: 72. $$. Hookups: electric (30, 50 amp), water, sewer,.

Doran Regional Park, Hwy. 1, 94923. T: (707) 875-3540. www.sonoma-county.org. RV/tent: 114. $$. Hookups: none.

Sonoma Coast State Beach, Wrights Beach, Hwy. 1, 94923. T: (707) 875-3483 or (800) 444-7275. www.cal-parks.ca.gov. RV/tent: 30. $. Hookups: none.

Westside Regional Park, 2400 Westshore Rd., 94923. T: (707) 875-3540. www.sonomacounty.org. RV/tent: 47. $$. Hookups: none.

Bonita

Sweetwater Regional Park-Summit Site (San Diego County Park), 3218 Summit Meadow Rd., 91902. T: (877) 565-3600 or (858) 694-3049. www.co.san-diego.ca.us/parks/camping/sweetwater.html. RV/tent: 60. $. Hookups: electric (30 amp), water.

Borrego Springs

Anza-Borrego Desert State Park, Arroyo Salado Primitive Camp, CR S22, 92004. T: (760) 767-5311. www.cal-parks.ca.gov. RV/tent: Dispersed. $. Hookups: none.

Anza-Borrego Desert State Park, Tamarisk Grove, Hwy. 78 and Yaqui Pass Rd., 92004. T: (760) 767-5311. www.cal-parks.ca.gov. RV/tent: 27. $. Hookups: none.

Anza-Borrego Desert State Park, Yaqui Pass Primitive Camp, 200 Palm Canyon Dr., 92004. T: (760) 767-5311. www.calparks.ca.gov. RV/tent: Dispersed. $. Hookups: none.

Palm Canyon Resort RV Park, 221 Palm Canyon Dr., 92004. T: (800) 242-0044 or (760) 767-5341. www.pcresort.com. RV/tent: 132. $$$. Hookups: electric (30 amp), water, sewer, cable.

Bradley

Lake Nacimiento Resort, 10625 Nacimiento Lake Dr., 93446. T: (800) 323-3839 or (805) 238-3256. www.nacimientoresort.com. RV/tent: 340. $$. Hookups: electric (30 amp), water, sewer.

Bridgeport

Lower Twin Lakes, Twin Lakes Rd., 93517. T: (760) 932-7070. www.reserveamerica.com. RV/tent: 15. $$. Hookups: none.

Paha Campground, Twin Lakes Rd., 93517. T: (760) 932-7070. www.reserveamerica.com. RV/tent: 22. $$. Hookups: none.

CALIFORNIA (continued)

Bucks Lake

Grizzly Creek, Oroville-Quincy Rd./FR 33, 95971. T: (530) 283-0555 or (530) 836-2575. www.reserveamerica.com. RV/tent: 55. $$. Hookups: none.

Haskins Valley, Bucks Lake Rd., 95971. T: (530) 283-0555. www.fs.fed.us/r5/plumas. RV/tent: 65. $$. Hookups: none.

Lower Bucks, Bucks Lake Dam Rd./FR 33, 95971. T: (530) 283-0555. www.fs.fed.us/r5/plumas. RV/tent: 6. $. Hookups: none.

Mill Creek, Bucks Lake Dam Rd./FR 33, 95971. T: (530) 283-0555. www.fs.fed.us/r5/plumas. RV/tent: 8. $$. Hookups: water.

Sundew, Bucks Lake Dam Rd./FR 33, 95971. T: (530) 283-0555. www.fs.fed.us/r5/plumas. RV/tent: 19. $$. Hookups: water.

Whitehorse, Bucks Lake Rd., 95971. T: (530) 283-0555. www.fs.fed.us/r5/plumas. RV/tent: 20. $$. Hookups: water.

Buellton

Flying Flags RV Park & Campground, 180 Avenue of the Flags, 93427. T: (805) 688-3716. www.flying flags.com. RV/tent: 320. $$. Hookups: electric (20, 30, 50 amp), water, sewer, , phone.

Camp Nelson

Belknap, Nelson Dr., 93208. T: (559) 539-2607. www.fs.fed.us/sequoia. RV/tent: 15. $$. Hookups: none.

Coy Flat, Coy Flat Rd., 93208. T: (559) 539-2607. www.fs.fed.us/r5/sequoia/recreation/camp grounds.html. RV/tent: 20. $$. Hookups: none.

Lower Peppermint, Lloyd Meadow Rd., 93208. T: (559) 539-2607. www.fs.fed.us/r5/sequoia/ recreation/campgrounds.html. RV/tent: 17. $$. Hookups: none.

Camptonville

Cal-Ida, Cal-Ida Rd., 95922. T: (530) 288-3231. www.fs.fed.us/r5/tahoe. RV/tent: 20. $$. Hookups: none.

Carlton Flat, Hwy. 49, 95922. T: (530) 288-3231. www.fs.fed.us/r5/tahoe. RV/tent: 21. $$. Hookups: none.

Dark Day, Dark Day Rd., 95922. T: (530) 692-3200 or (530) 288-3231. www.fs.fed.us/r5/tahoe. RV/tent: 16. $$. Hookups: none.

Fiddle Creek, Hwy. 49, 95922. T: (530) 288-3231. www.fs.fed.us/r5/tahoe. RV/tent: 15. $$. Hookups: none.

Indian Valley, Hwy. 49, 95922. T: (530) 288-3231. www.fs.fed.us/r5/tahoe. RV/tent: 17. $$. Hookups: none.

Ramshorn, Hwy. 49, 95922. T: (530) 288-3231. www.fs.fed.us/r5/tahoe. RV/tent: 16. $$. Hookups: none.

Rocky Nest, Hwy. 49, 95922. T: (530) 288-3231. www.fs.fed.us/r5/tahoe. RV/tent: 10. $$. Hookups: none.

Carmel

Carmel by the River RV Park, 27680 Schulte Rd., 93923. T: (831) 624-9329. www.carmelrv.com. RV/tent: 35. $$$$. Hookups: electric (20, 30 amp), water, sewer, cable, phone.

Carrville

Trinity River, Hwy. 3, 96091. T: (530) 623-2121. www.fs.fed.us/r5/shastatrinity. RV/tent: 7. $. Hookups: none.

Castaic

Castaic Lake RV Park, 31540 Ridge Rte. Rd., 91384. T: (661) 257-3340 or (877) 450-3340. www.gocampingamerica.com/castaiclake. RV/tent: 103. $$. Hookups: electric (30, 50 amp), water, sewer, cable, phone.

Cathedral City

Palm Springs Oasis RV Resort, 36100 Date Palm Dr., 92234. T: (800) 680-0144 or (760) 328-4813. www.mhchomes.com. RV/tent: 140. $$$. Hookups: electric (20, 30, 50 amp), water, sewer, cable.

Chester

Benner Creek, Juniper Lake Rd., 96020. T: (530) 258-2141. www.fs.fed.us/r5/lassen. RV/tent: 9. $$. Hookups: none.

Domingo Springs, CR 311, 96020. T: (530) 258-2141. www.fs.fed.us/r5/lassen. RV/tent: 18. $. Hookups: none.

High Bridge, CR 312, 96020. T: (530) 258-2141. www.fs.fed.us/r5/lassen. RV/tent: 12. $. Hookups: none.

North Shore Campground, Hwy. 36, 96020. T: (530) 258-3376. www.northshorecampground.com/ index.html. RV/tent: 128. $$. Hookups: electric (20, 30 amp), water, phone.

Warner Creek, CR 311, 96020. T: (530) 258-2141. www.fs.fed.us/r5/lassen. RV/tent: 13. $. Hookups: none.

Chico

Almond Tree RV Park, 3124 Esplanade, 95973. T: (530) 899-1271. www.now2000.com/rvpark. RV/tent: 42. $$$. Hookups: electric (30, 50 amp), water, sewer, cable, phone.

Chula Vista

Chula Vista RV Resort & Marina, 460 Sandpiper Way, 91910. T: (619) 422-0111 or (800) 770-2878. www.chulavistarv.com. RV/tent: 237. $$$$. Hookups: electric (30, 50 amp), water, sewer, , phone.

KOA San Diego Metropolitan, 111 North 2nd St., 91910. T: (800) KOA-9877 or (619) 427-3601. www.sandiegokoa.com. RV/tent: 270. $$$. Hookups: electric (30, 50 amp), water, sewer, cable, phone.

Cloverdale

KOA Cloverdale Camping Resort, 26460 River Rd., 95425. T: (707) 894-3337. www.koa.com. RV/tent: 90. $$$. Hookups: electric (30, 50 amp), water, sewer.

Coleville

Bootleg, Bridgeport Ranger District, U.S. 395, 96107. T: (760) 932-7070. RV/tent: 63. $$. Hookups: none.

Chris Flat, Bridgeport Ranger District, U.S. 395, 96107. T: (760) 932-7070. RV/tent: 15. $$. Hookups: none.

Obsidian, Bridgeport Ranger District, U.S. 395, 96107. T: (760) 932-7070. RV/tent: 14. $. Hookups: none.

Coloma

Coloma Resort & RV Park, 6921 Mt. Murphy Rd., 95613. T: (530) 621-2267 or (800) 238-2298. www.colomaresort.com. RV/tent: 165. $$$. Hookups: electric (30 amp), water, sewer.

Columbia

49er RV Ranch, 23223 Italian Bar Rd., 95310. T: (209) 532-4978. www.49rv.com. RV/tent: 45. $$$. Hookups: electric (30 amp), water, sewer, cable.

Marble Quarry RV Park, 11551 Yankee Hill Rd., 95310. T: (209) 532-9539 or (866) 677-8464. www.marblequarry.com. RV/tent: 87. $$. Hookups: electric (30, 50 amp), water, sewer, satellite.

Colusa

Colusa-Sacramento River State Recreation Area, 10th St., 95932. T: (800) 444-7275 or (530) 458-4927. www.reserveamerica.com. RV/tent: 14. $. Hookups: none.

Crescent City

Bayside RV Park, 750 US 101 S, 95531. T: (707) 464-9482 or (800) 446-9482. RV/tent: 110. $$. Hookups: electric (30 amp), water, sewer, phone.

Hiouchi Hamlet RV Resort, 2000 Hwy. 199, 95531. T: (707) 458-3321 or (800) 7229468. www.hiouchihamletrvresort.com. RV/tent: 120. $$. Hookups: electric (20, 30, 50 amp), water, sewer, cable, phone.

KOA Crescent City Redwoods, 4241 Hwy. 101 North, 95531. T: (800) 562-5754 or (707) 464-5744. www.koa.com. RV/tent: 94. $$. Hookups: electric (15, 20, 30 amp), water, sewer, cable.

Sunset Harbor RV Park, 205 King St., 95531. T: (707) 464-3423. RV/tent: 69. $$. Hookups: electric (30, 50 amp), water, sewer, cable, phone.

Village Camper Inn, 1543 Parkway Dr., 95531. T: (707) 464-3544. RV/tent: 143. $. Hookups: electric (20, 30, 50 amp), water, sewer, cable, phone.

Dardanelle

Baker, Hwy. 108, 95314. T: (209) 965-3434. www.r5.fs.fed.us/stanislaus. RV/tent: 44. $$. Hookups: none.

Brightman Flat, Hwy. 108, 95314. T: (209) 965-3434. www.r5.fs.fed.us/stanislaus. RV/tent: 33. $$. Hookups: none.

Cascade Peak, Hwy. 108, 95314. T: (209) 965-3434. www.r5.fs.fed.us/stanislaus. RV/tent: 14. $. Hookups: none.

Dardanelle, Hwy. 108, 95314. T: (209) 965-3434. www.r5.fs.fed.us/stanislaus. RV/tent: 28. $$. Hookups: none.

Deadman Campground, Kennedy Meadow Rd., 95314. T: (209) 965-3434. www.fs.fed.us/r5/ summit/camping/deadman.shtml. RV/tent: 17. $$. Hookups: none.

Eureka Valley, Hwy. 108, 95314. T: (209) 965-3434. www.fs.fed.us.r5.stanislaus/summit/camping/ eureka.shtml. RV/tent: 28. $$. Hookups: none.

CALIFORNIA (continued)

Dardanelle (continued)

Fence Creek Campground, FR 6N06, 95314. T: (209) 965-3434. www.fs.fed.us/r5/stanislaus/ summit/camping/fence.shtml. RV/tent: 38. $. Hookups: none.

Pigeon Flat Campground, Hwy. 108, 95314. T: (209) 965-3434. www.fs.fed.us/r5/stanislaus/ summit/camping/pigeon.shtml. RV/tent: 7. $. Hookups: none.

Sand Flat Campground, Stanislaus National Forest, Clark Fork Rd., 95314. T: (209) 965-3434. www.r5.fs.fed.us/r5/stanislaus/summit/camping/ sandflat.shtml. RV/tent: 68. $. Hookups: none.

Death Valley

Stovepipe Wells, Hwy. 190, 92328. T: (800) 365-2267 or (760) 786-2331. www.nps.gov/dev. RV/tent: 190. $. Hookups: none.

Sunset, Hwy. 190, 92328. T: (800) 365-2267 or (760) 786-2331. www.nps.gov/deva. RV/tent: 1,000. $. Hookups: none.

Texas Spring, Hwy. 190, 92328. T: (800) 365-2267 or (760) 786-2331. www.nps.gov/deva. RV/tent: 92. $. Hookups: none.

Dunnigan

Campers Inn RV & Golf Resort, 2501 CR 88, 95937. T: (800) 79-GOLF-3 or (530) 724-3350. www.campersinnrv.com. RV/tent: 85. $$. Hookups: electric (30, 50 amp), water, sewer.

Dunsmuir

Railroad Park Resort, 100 Railroad Park Rd., 96025. T: (530) 235-0420. www.rrpark.com. RV/tent: 60. $$. Hookups: electric (20, 30 amp), water, sewer, cable.

El Cajon

Circle RV Ranch, 1835 East Main St., 92021. T: (800) 422-1835 or (619) 440-0040. www.gocampingamerica.com/circlervranch/ index.html. RV/tent: 179. $$$. Hookups: electric (30, 50 amp), water, sewer, phone.

Oak Creek RV Resort, 15379 Oak Creek Rd., 92021. T: (619) 390-7132 or (800) 365-1274. www.oakcreekrv.com. RV/tent: 120. $$$. Hookups: electric (30, 50 amp), water, sewer, cable, phone.

El Centro

Desert Trails RV Park & Golf Course, 225 Wake Ave., 92243. T: (760) 352-7275. RV/tent: 388. $$. Hookups: electric (30, 50 amp), water, sewer, phone.

Encinitas

San Elijo State Beach, US 101, 92023. T: (800) 444-7275 or (760) 753-5091. www.reserveamerica .com. RV/tent: 150. $$. Hookups: electric (30 amp), water.

Escondido

Escondido RV Resort, 1740 Seven Oaks Rd., 92026. T: (760) 740-5000 or (800) 331-3556. www.escondidorv.com. RV/tent: 67. $$$. Hookups: electric (20, 30, 50 amp), water, sewer, cable, phone (long term).

Essex

Providence Mountains State Recreation Area, Essex Rd., 92332. T: (760) 928-2586. www.parks.ca.gov. RV/tent: 6. $. Hookups: none.

Etna

Mountain Village RV Park, 30 Commercial Way, 96027. T: (877) 386-2787. www.etnarvp.com. RV/tent: 44. $$. Hookups: electric (20, 30, 50 amp), water, sewer, cable, phone.

Eureka

KOA Eureka, 4050 North Hwy. 101, 95503. T: (800) 562-3136 or (707) 822-4243. www.koa kampgrounds.com. RV/tent: 156. $$. Hookups: electric (20, 30, 50 amp), water, sewer, cable, phone.

Redwood Acres Fairground, 3750 Harris St., 95503. T: (707) 445-3037. www.redwood acres.com. RV/tent: 52. $$. Hookups: electric (30, 50 amp), water, sewer.

Felton

Cotillion Gardens Recreational Vehicle Park, 300 Old Big Trees Rd., 95018. T: (831) 335-7669. RV/tent: 80. $$$. Hookups: electric (20, 30 amp), water, sewer, cable, phone.

Fort Bragg

Pomo RV Park & Campground, 17999 Tregoning Ln., 95437. T: (707) 964-3373. www.infortbragg .com/pomorvpark. RV/tent: 125. $$. Hookups: electric (20, 30, 50 amp), water, sewer, cable, phone.

Woodside RV Park Campground, 17900 North Hwy. Ave., 95437. T: (707) 964-3684. www.go campingamerica.com/woodsiderv/index.html. RV/tent: 104. $$. Hookups: electric (15, 30 amp), water, sewer.

Fouts Springs

Letts Lake Complex, Mendocino National Forest, FR 17N02, 95979. T: (530) 963-3128. www.r5.fs .fed.us/mendocino/recreation/campgrounds/se.h tml. RV/tent: 44. $. Hookups: none.

Mill Valley, Mendocino National Forest, FR 17N02, 95979. T: (530) 963-3128. www.r5.fs.fed.us/ mendocino/recreation/campgrounds/se.html. RV/tent: 15. $. Hookups: none.

Frazier Park

McGill Campground, Mount Piños Hwy., 93222. T: (661) 245-3731. www.rockymountainrec .com/camp/padres-mcgill.html. RV/tent: 73. $. Hookups: none.

Mount Piños Campground, Mount Piños Hwy., 93222. T: (661) 245-3731. www.rockymountain rec.com/camp/padres-mtpinos.html. RV/tent: 19. $. Hookups: none.

Fresno

West Olive Mobile/RV Park, 3147 West Olive Ave., 93722. T: (559) 275-0154. RV/tent: 55. $$. Hookups: electric (20, 30, 50 amp), water, sewer, phone.

Garbervile

Benbow Valley RV Resort & Golf Course, 7000 Benbow Dr., 95542. T: (866) BEN-BOWRV or (707)

923-2777. www.benbowrv.com. RV/tent: 100. $$$. Hookups: electric (20, 30, 50 amp), water, sewer, cable, phone.

Gasquet

Big Flat, Smith River National Recreation Area, FR 15N59, 95543. T: (707) 457-3131. www.fs.fed.us/ r5/sixrivers/recreation/smith-river/campgrounds. RV/tent: 28. $. Hookups: none.

Grassy Flat, Smith River National Recreation Area, US 199, 95543. T: (877) 444-6777 or (707) 457-3131. www.r5.fs.fed.us/sixrivers. RV/tent: 19. $. Hookups: none.

Patrick Creek, Smith River National Recreation Area, US 199, 95543. T: (877) 444-6777 or (707) 457-3131. www.fs.fed.us/r5/sixrivers/recreation/ smith-river/campgrounds. RV/tent: 13. $. Hookups: none.

Gorman

Los Alamos Campground, Pyramid Lake, Smokey Bear Rd., 93243. T: (661) 245-3731. RV/tent: 93. $. Hookups: none.

Groveland

Diamond "O" Campground, Evergreen Rd., 95321. T: (209) 962-7825. www.fs.fed.us/r5/stanislaus/ groveland/camping/diamond.shtml. RV/tent: 38. $$. Hookups: none.

Lost Claim Campground, Hwy. 120, 95321. T: (209) 962-7825. www.fs.fed.us/r5/stanislaus/groveland/ camping/lostclaim.shtml. RV/tent: 10. $. Hookups: none.

Sweetwater Campground, Hwy. 120, 95321. T: (209) 962-7825. www.fs.fed.us/r5/stanislaus/ groveland/camping/sweetwater.shtml. RV/tent: 13. $. Hookups: none.

Thousand Trails Yosemite Lakes, Hwy. 120, 95321. T: (800) 533-1001. www.1000trails.com. RV/tent: 445. $$. Hookups: electric (20, 30, 50 amp), water, sewer, phone.

Yosemite Pines RV Resort & Family Lodging, 20450 Old Hwy. 120, 95321. T: (209) 962-7690 or (877) 962-7690. www.yosemitepines.com. RV/tent: 214. $$. Hookups: electric (20, 30, 50 amp), water, sewer, cable, phone.

Grover Beach

Le Sage Riviera RV Park, 319 Hwy. 1, 93433. T: (805) 489-5506. RV/tent: 82. $$. Hookups: electric (20, 30 amp), water, sewer, phone.

Gustine

San Luis Reservoir State Recreation Area, Basalt Campground, Hwy. 152, 95322-9737. T: (800) 444-7275 or (209) 826-1196. www.cal-parks. ca.gov. RV/tent: 79. $. Hookups: none.

Half Moon Bay

Half Moon Bay State Beach, Kelly Ave., 94019. T: (650) 726-8820. www.parks.ca.gov. RV/tent: 55. $. Hookups: none.

Hamburg

O'Neil Creek Campground, Hwy. 96, 96086. T: (877) 444-6777 or (530) 493-2243. www.fs.fed.us.r5/klamath/recreation/camping/ oneil.shtml. RV/tent: 18. $. Hookups: none.

CALIFORNIA (continued)

Happy Camp

Curly Jack Campground, Curly Jack Rd., 96039. T: (530) 493-2243. www.fs.fed.us/klamath/ recreation/camping/curlyjack.shtml. RV/tent: 17. $. Hookups: none.

West Branch, Indian Creek Rd., 96039. T: (530) 493-2243. www.r5.fs.fed.us/klamath. RV/tent: 15. $. Hookups: none.

Hat Creek

Rancheria RV Park, 15565 Black Angus Ln., 96040. T: (800) 346-3430 or (530) 335-7418. www.rancheriarv.com. RV/tent: 75. $$. Hookups: electric (30, 50 amp), water, sewer, satellite.

Hemet

Casa del Sol RV Resort, 2750 West Acacia, 92545. T: (909) 925-2515 or (888) 925-2516. www.casadelsolrvpark.com. RV/tent: 358. $$. Hookups: electric (30, 50 amp), water, sewer, cable, phone.

Golden Village Palms RV Resort, 3600 West Florida Ave., 92545. T: (800) 323-9610 or (909) 925-2518. www.goldenvillagepalms.com. RV/tent: 65. $$$. Hookups: electric (20, 30, 50 amp), water, sewer, cable.

Mountain Valley RV Park, 235 South Lyon Ave., 92543. T: (800) 926-5593 or (909)-925-5812. www.mountainvalleyrvp.com. RV/tent: 170. $$$. Hookups: electric (20, 30, 50 amp), water, sewer, cable, phone.

Hesperia

Hesperia Lake Park & Campground, Arrowhead Lake Rd., 92345. T: (800) 521-6332 or (760) 244-5951. www.hesperiaparks.com/pages/facilities/camping.html. RV/tent: 86. $. Hookups: electric (30 amp), water.

Hollister

Casa De Fruta RV Orchard Resort, 10031 Pacheco Pass Hwy., 95023. T: (800) 548-3813 or (408) 842-9316. www.casadefruta.com. RV/tent: 301. $$$. Hookups: electric (20, 30 amp), water, sewer, satellite.

Huntington Beach

Huntington By The Sea RV Park, 21871 Newland St., 92646. T: (714) 536-8316 or (800) 439-3486. www.gocampingamerica.com/huntingtonbythe sea. RV/tent: 140. $$. Hookups: electric (30 amp), water, sewer, cable, phone.

Idyllwild

Boulder Basin Campground, San Bernardino National Forest, FR 4S01, 92549. T: (909) 659-2117. www.reserveusa.com. RV/tent: 34. $. Hookups: none.

Dark Canyon Campground, San Bernardino National Forest, FR 4S02, 92549. T: (909) 659-2117. www.reserveusa.com. RV/tent: 20. $. Hookups: none.

Fern Basin Campground, San Bernardino National Forest, FR 4S02, 92549. T: (909) 659-2117. www.reserveusa.com. RV/tent: 22. $. Hookups: none.

Marion Mountain Campground, San Bernardino National Forest, FR 4S02, 92549. T: (909) 659-

2117. www.reserveusa.com. RV/tent: 24. $. Hookups: none.

Pinyon Flat Campground, Hwy. 74, 92549. T: (909) 659-2117. www.bigbeardiscoverycenter.com/pages/camping.html. RV/tent: 18. $. Hookups: none.

Indio

Fiesta RV Park, 46-421 Madison St., 92201. T: (760) 342-2345. www.fiestarvpark.com. RV/tent: 200. $$$. Hookups: electric (30, 50 amp), water, sewer, cable, phone.

Jamestown

Lake Tulloch RV Campground and Marina, 14448 Tulloch Rd., 95327. T: (800) 894-2267 or (209) 881-0107. www.laketullochcampground.com. RV/tent: 130. $$. Hookups: electric (50 amp), water, sewer.

Julian

Pinezanita Trailer Ranch & Campgrounds, 4446 Hwy. 79, 92036. T: (760) 765-0429. www.pinezanita.com. RV/tent: 230. $$. Hookups: electric (20, 30 amp), water, sewer.

June Lake

Gull Lake Campground, Hwy. 158, 93529. T: (760) 647-2408. www.fs.fed.us/r5/inyo/recreation/campgrounds.html. RV/tent: 11. $$. Hookups: none.

June Lake Campground, Hwy. 158, 93529. T: (760) 647-2408. www.fs.fed.us/inyo/recreation/camp grounds.html. RV/tent: 28. $$. Hookups: none.

Oh! Ridge Campground, Oh! Ridge Rd., 93529. T: (760) 647-2408. www.fs.fed.us/r5/inyo/recreation/campgrounds.html. RV/tent: 148. $$. Hookups: none.

Reversed Creek Campground, Hwy. 158, 93529. T: (760) 647-2408. www.fs.fed.us/r5/inyo/recreation/campgrounds.html. RV/tent: 17. $$. Hookups: none.

Silver Lake Campground, Hwy. 158, 93529. T: (760) 647-2408. www.fs.fed.us/r5/inyo/recreation/campgrounds.html. RV/tent: 63. $. Hookups: none.

Kelseyville

Edgewater Resort & RV Park, 6420 Soda Bay Rd., 95451. T: (800) 396-6224 or (707) 279-0208. www.edgewaterresort.net. RV/tent: 61. $$. Hookups: electric (20, 30 amp), water, sewer, cable, phone.

Kernville

Camp 3 Campground, Sequoia National Forest, Sierra Way Rd., 93238. T: (760) 376-3781. www.fs.fed.us/r5/sequoia/recreation/camp-grounds.html. RV/tent: 52. $. Hookups: none.

Headquarters Campground, Sequoia National Forest, Sierra Way Rd., 93238. T: (760) 376-3781. www.fs.fed.us/r5/sequoia/recreation/camp grounds.html. RV/tent: 44. $. Hookups: none.

Hospital Flat Campground, Sequoia National Forest, Sierra Way Rd., 93238. T: (760) 376-3781. www.fs.fed.us/r5/sequoia/recreation/camp grounds.html. RV/tent: 40. $. Hookups: none.

Rivernook Campground, 14001 Sierra Way, 93238. T: (760) 376-2705. RV/tent: 269. $$. Hookups: electric (20, 30, 50 amp), water, sewer, cable.

King City

Ciudad Del Rey, 50557 Wild Horse Rd., 93930. T: (831) 385-4828. RV/tent: 38. $$. Hookups: electric (20, 30, 50 amp), water, sewer, phone.

Kings Canyon National Park

Crystal Springs Campground, Hwy. 180, 93633. T: (559) 565-3341. www.nps.gov/seki. RV/tent: 63. $$. Hookups: none.

Moraine Campground, Hwy. 180, Cedar Grove Village, 93633. T: (559) 565-3341. www.nps .gov/seki. RV/tent: 120. $$. Hookups: none.

Sentinel Campground, Hwy. 180, Cedar Grove Village, 93633. T: (559) 565-3341. www.nps .gov/seki. RV/tent: 83. $$. Hookups: none.

Sheep Creek Campground, Hwy. 180, Cedar Grove Village, 93633. T: (559) 565-3341. www.nps .gov/seki. RV/tent: 111. $$. Hookups: none.

Sunset, Hwy. 180, 93633. T: (559) 565-3341. www.nps.gov/seki. RV/tent: 200. $$. Hookups: none.

Kingsburg

Riverland Resorts, 38743 West Frontage Rd., 38743 Hwy. 99, 93631. T: (559) 897-5166. www.riverlandresorts.com. RV/tent: 200. $$. Hookups: electric (15, 30 amp), water, sewer.

Kit Carson

Caples Lake Campground, El Dorado National Forest, Hwy. 88, 95644. T: (209) 295-4251. RV/tent: 35. $. Hookups: none.

Kirkwood Lake Campground, El Dorado National Forest, Hwy. 88, 95644. T: (209) 295-4251. RV/tent: 12. $. Hookups: none.

Silver Lake East, El Dorado National Forest, Hwy. 88, 95644. T: (877) 444-6777 or (209) 295-4251. www.reserveusa.com/nrrs/ca/sile. RV/tent: 62. $$. Hookups: none.

Woods Lake, Woods Lake Turnoff, 95644. T: (209) 295-4251. RV/tent: 25. $. Hookups: none.

Klamath

Camp Marigold Garden Cottages & RV Park, 16101 Hwy. 101 S, 95548. T: (800) 621-8513 or (707) 482-3585. RV/tent: 45. $$. Hookups: electric (30 amp), water, sewer, cable.

Chinook RV Resort, 17465 Hwy. 101, 95548. T: (707) 482-3511. www.rvdestinations.com/chinook. RV/tent: 70. $$. Hookups: electric (30 amp), water, sewer, cable, phone.

Klamath's Camper Corral, Hwy. 101 at 169 Interchange, 95548. T: (707) 482-5741 or (800) 701-PARK. www.rvdestinations.com/campercorral. RV/tent: 120. $$. Hookups: electric (30 amp), water, sewer, cable.

Mystic Forest RV Park, 15875 US 101, 95548. T: (707) 482-4901. www.rvdestinations.com/mysticforest. RV/tent: 30. $$. Hookups: electric (20, 30 amp), water, sewer, cable, phone.

CALIFORNIA (continued)

La Porte

Black Rock Tent Campground, Feather River Ranger District, CR 514/Little Grass Valley Rd., 95981. T: (530) 534-6500. www.r5.fs.fed.us/plumas. RV/tent: 20. $. Hookups: water.

Little Beaver Campground, Feather River Ranger District, CR 514/Little Grass Valley Rd., 95981. T: (530) 534-6500. www.r5.fs.fed.us/plumas. RV/tent: 120. $$. Hookups: water.

Peninsula Tent Campground, Feather River Ranger District, CR 514/Little Grass Valley Rd., 95981. T: (530) 534-6500. www.r5.fs.fed.us/plumas. RV/tent: 25. $. Hookups: water.

Red Feather Campground, Feather River Ranger District, CR 514/Little Grass Valley Rd., 95981. T: (530) 534-6500. www.r5.fs.fed.us/plumas. RV/tent: 60. $$. Hookups: water.

Running Deer Campground, FR 22N57, 95981. T: (877) 444-6777 or (530) 283-5559. www.r5.fs.fed.us/plumas. RV/tent: 40. $$. Hookups: none.

Wyandotte Campground, Feather River Ranger District, CR 514/Little Grass Valley Rd., 95981. T: (530) 534-6500. www.r5.fs.fed.us/plumas. RV/tent: 28. $$. Hookups: water.

Lake Elsinore

Lake Elsinore West Marina & RV, 32700 Riverside Dr., 92530. T: (800) 328-6844 or (909) 678-1300. www.gocampingamerica.com/elsinorewest/index.html. RV/tent: 200. $$$. Hookups: electric (30, 50 amp), water, sewer, cable, phone.

Lake Isabella

Lake Isabella RV Resort, 11936 Hwy. 178, 93240. T: (800) 787-9920. www.lakeisabellarv.com. RV/tent: 91. $$$. Hookups: electric (30, 50 amp), water, sewer, cable, phone.

Lakehead

Lakeshore Villa RV Park, 20672 Lakeshore Dr., 96051. T: (800) 238-8688. www.gocamping america.com/lakeshorevilla. RV/tent: 92. $$. Hookups: electric (30, 50 amp), water, sewer, cable, phone.

Shasta Lake RV Resort & Campground, 20433 Lakeshore Dr., 96051. T: (800) 374-2782 or (530) 238-8500. www.shastarv.com. RV/tent: 70. $$. Hookups: electric (30 amp), water, sewer.

Lakeside

Rancho Los Coches RV Park, 13468 Hwy. 8 Business, 92040. T: (800) 630-0448 or (619) 443-2025. www.rancholoscochesrv.com. RV/tent: 147. $$. Hookups: electric (30, 50 amp), water, sewer, cable, phone.

Lancaster

Saddleback Butte State Park, 17 miles east of Lancaster on Ave. J East, 93535. T: (661) 942-0662. www.calparksmojave.com/saddleback. RV/tent: 50. $. Hookups: none.

Lee Vining

Big Bend Campground, Inyo National Forest, Hwy. 120, 93541. T: (760) 932-5451. www.fs.fed.us/r5/inyo/recreation/campgrounds.html. RV/tent: 17. $$. Hookups: none.

Boulder Campground, Hwy. 120, 93541. T: (760) 932-5451. www.fs.fed.us/r5/inyo/recreation/campgrounds.html. RV/tent: 32. $. Hookups: none.

Cattle Guard Campground, Hwy. 120, 93541. T: (760) 932-5451. www.fs.fed.us/r5/inyo/recreation/campgrounds.html. RV/tent: 17. $. Hookups: none.

Junction Campground, Saddlebag Lake Rd., 93541. T: (760) 873-2400 or (760) 647-3044. www.fs.fed.us/r5/inyo/recreation/campgrounds. html. RV/tent: 13. $. Hookups: none.

Lower Lee Vining Campground, Hwy. 120, 93541. T: (760) 932-5451. www.fs.fed.us/r5/inyo/recreation/campgrounds.html. RV/tent: 74. $. Hookups: none.

Mono Vista RV Park, US 395, 93541. T: (760) 647-6401. www.thesierraweb.com/recreation/monovista. RV/tent: 63. $$. Hookups: electric (20, 30, 50 amp), water, sewer, cable.

Morraine Campground, Hwy. 120, 93541. T: (760) 932-5451. www.fs.fed.us/r5/inyo/recreation/campgrounds.html. RV/tent: 20. $. Hookups: none.

Saddlebag Lake Campground, Saddlebag Lake Rd., 93541. T: (760) 873-2400 or (760) 647-3044. www.fs.fed.us/r5/inyo/recreation/campgrounds. html. RV/tent: 20. $$. Hookups: none.

Tioga Lake Campground, Hwy. 120, 93541. T: (760) 873-2400 or (760) 647-3044. www.fs.fed.us/r5/inyo/recreation/campgrounds.html. RV/tent: 13. $$. Hookups: none.

Leggett

Redwoods River Resort & Campground, 75000 Hwy. 101, 95585. T: (707) 925-6249. www.red woodriverresort.com. RV/tent: 50. $$. Hookups: electric (30, 50 amp), water, sewer.

Lewiston

Ackerman, Trinity Dam Blvd., 96052. T: (530) 623-2121. www.r5.fs.fed.us/shastatrinity. RV/tent: 66. $. Hookups: none.

Mary Smith, Trinity Dam Blvd., 96052. T: (530) 623-2121. www.r5.fs.fed.us/shastatrinity. RV/tent: 18. $. Hookups: none.

Tunnel Rock, Trinity Dam Blvd., 96052. T: (530) 623-2121. www.r5.fs.fed.us/shastatrinity. RV/tent: 6. $. Hookups: none.

Lodi

Tower Park Resort, 14900 West Hwy. 12, 95242. T: (209) 369-1041 or (800) 77-TOWER. www.westrec.com/towerpark.html. RV/tent: 442. $$. Hookups: electric (30, 50 amp), water, sewer.

Loma Linda

Mission RV Park, Redlands Blvd., 92354. T: (909) 796-7570. www.woodalls.com. RV/tent: 100. $$$. Hookups: electric (20, 30, 50 amp), water, sewer, cable.

Lone Pine

Boulder Creek RV Resort, 2550 South Hwy. 395, 93545. T: (800) 648-8965 or (760) 876-4243. www.bouldercreekrvresort.com. RV/tent: 65. $$. Hookups: electric (30, 50 amp), water, sewer, cable, phone.

Lone Pine Creek

Whitney Portal Campground, Whitney Portal Rd., 93545. T: (760) 876-6200. www.r5.fs.fed.us/inyo. RV/tent: 43. $$. Hookups: none.

Loomis

KOA Loomis, 3945 Taylor Rd., 95650. T: (916) 652-6737. www.koa.com. RV/tent: 81. $$$. Hookups: electric (20, 30 amp), water, sewer.

Lucia

Limekiln State Park, Hwy. 1, 93921. T: (877) 444-6777 or (831) 667-2403. www.reserveusa.com. RV/tent: 28. $$. Hookups: none.

Nacimiento, Nacimiento Fergusson Rd., 93921. T: (831) 385-5434. www.r5.fs.fed.us/lospadres. RV/tent: 8. $. Hookups: none.

Plaskett Creek, Hwy. 1, 93921. T: (831) 385-5434. www.r5.fs.fed.us/lospadres. RV/tent: 45. $$. Hookups: none.

Mammoth Lakes

Pine City, Mammoth Ranger District, Lake Mary Rd., 93546. T: (760) 924-5500. www.r5.fs.fed.us/inyo. RV/tent: 10. $$. Hookups: none.

Mammoth Lakes Basin

Coldwater, Mammoth Ranger District, Lake Mary Rd., 93546. T: (760) 924-5500. www.r5.fs.fed.us/inyo. RV/tent: 77. $$. Hookups: none.

Lake George, Mammoth Ranger District, Lake Mary Rd., 93546. T: (760) 924-5500. www.r5.fs.fed.us/inyo. RV/tent: 16. $$. Hookups: none.

Lake Mary, Mammoth Ranger District, Lake Mary Rd., 93546. T: (760) 924-5500. www.r5.fs.fed.us/inyo. RV/tent: 48. $$. Hookups: none.

Mammoth Mountain RV Park, Hwy. 203, 93546. T: (760) 934-3822. www.mammothweb.com/lodging/mammothrv/mammothrv.html. RV/tent: 164. $$$. Hookups: electric (30, 50 amp), water, cable.

Mammoth Village

New Shady Rest, Mammoth Ranger District, Sawmill Cutoff, 93546. T: (760) 924-5500. www.r5.fs.fed.us/inyo. RV/tent: 94. $$. Hookups: none.

Pine Glen, Mammoth Ranger District, Sawmill Cutoff, 93546. T: (760) 924-5500. www.r5.fs.fed.us/inyo. RV/tent: 11. $$. Hookups: none.

Old Shady Rest, Mammoth Ranger District, Sawmill Cutoff, 93546. T: (760) 924-5500. www.r5.fs.fed.us/inyo. RV/tent: 51. $$. Hookups: none.

Manchester

KOA Manchester Beach, 44300 Kinney Rd., 95459. T: (800) KOA-4188 or (707) 882-2375. www.koa.com. RV/tent: 125. $$$. Hookups: electric (20, 30 amp), water, sewer, cable.

Manchester State Park, Kinney Ln., 95468. T: (707) 882-2463 or (800) 444-7275. www.parks.ca.gov. RV/tent: 46. $. Hookups: none.

Manteca

Oakwood Lake RV Campground, 874 East Woodward Ave., 95337. T: (800) 626-5253 or (209) 249-2500. www.oakwoodlake.com. RV/tent: 357. $$$. Hookups: electric (20, 30 amp), water, sewer.

CALIFORNIA (continued)

Marina

Marina Dunes RV Park, 3330 Dunes Dr., 93933. T: (831) 384-6914. www.marinadunesrv.com. RV/tent: 65. $$$. Hookups: electric (20, 30 amp), water, sewer, cable.

Mariposa

Mariposa Fairgrounds, 5007 Fairgrounds Rd., 95338. T: (209) 966-2432. www.mariposafair.com/camping.htm. RV/tent: 150. $$. Hookups: electric (20, 30, 50 amp), water.

Markleeville

Markleeville, Hwy. 89, 96120. T: (775) 882-2766. RV/tent: 10. $. Hookups: none.

McCloud

Ah-Di-Na, Lake McCloud Rd., 96057. T: (530) 964-2184. www.r5.fs.fed.us/shastatrinity. RV/tent: 16. $. Hookups: none.

Cattle Camp, Hwy. 89, 96057. T: (530) 964-2184. www.r5.fs.fed.us/shastatrinity. RV/tent: 27. $. Hookups: none.

Meeks Bay

Kaspian, West Shore Lake Tahoe, Hwy. 89, 96142. T: (877) 444-6777 or (530) 573-2674. www.r5.fs.fed.us/ltbmu. RV/tent: 9. $$. Hookups: none.

Mendocino

Caspar Beach RV Park, 14441 Point Cabrillo Dr., 95460. T: (707) 964-3306. www.casparbeachrvpark.com. RV/tent: 118. $$$. Hookups: electric (30 amp), water, sewer, cable.

Mineral

Crags, Lassen Volcanic National Park, Lassen Park Rd., 96063. T: (530) 595-4444. www.nps.gov/lavo. RV/tent: 45. $. Hookups: none.

Juniper Lake, Juniper Lake Rd., 96063. T: (530) 595-4444. www.nps.gov/lavo. RV/tent: 18. $. Hookups: none.

Mojave National Preserve Mid Hills, Black Canyon Rd., 92311. T: (760) 255-8801. www.nps.gov/moja. RV/tent: 26. $. Hookups: none.

Southwest, Lassen Park Rd., 96063. T: (530) 595-4444. www.nps.gov/lavo. RV/tent: 21. $. Hookups: none.

Summit Lake North, Lassen Park Rd., 96063. T: (530) 595-4444. www.nps.gov/lavo. RV/tent: 46. $$. Hookups: none.

Summit Lake South, Lassen Park Rd., 96063. T: (530) 595-4444. www.nps.gov/lavo. RV/tent: 48. $$. Hookups: none.

Volcano Country Campground, Hwy. 36 East, 96063. T: (530) 595-3347. www.lassenminerva.com/campground.htm. RV/tent: 30. $$. Hookups: electric (20, 30 amp), water, sewer.

Warner Valley, Warner Valley Rd., 96063. T: (530) 595-4444. www.nps.gov/lavo. RV/tent: 18. $. Hookups: none.

Monterey

Cypress Tree Inn of Monterey, 2227 North Fremont St., 93940. T: (800) 446-8303 or (831) 372-7586. www.cypresstreeinn.com/rv.html. RV/tent: 25. $$. Hookups: electric (20, 30 amp), water.

Morro Bay

Bay Pines Travel Trailer Park, 1502 Quintana Rd., 93442. T: (805) 772-3223. www.baypinesrv.com. RV/tent: 112. $$$. Hookups: electric (30 amp), water, sewer, satellite , phone.

Morro Bay State Park, State Park Rd., 93443. T: (805) 772-7434 or (800) 444-7275. www.reserveamerica.com. RV/tent: 135. $$. Hookups: electric (30 amp), water.

Morro Dunes RV Park, 1700 Embarcadero, 93442. T: (805) 772-2722. www.rvdestinations.com/morrodunes. RV/tent: 175. $$. Hookups: electric (15, 30 amp), water, sewer, cable.

Mount Laguna

Agua Dulce, Sunrise Hwy./Laguna Mountain Rd., 91948. T: (877) 444-6777 or (619) 445-6235. www.r5.fs.fed.us/cleveland. RV/tent: 5. $$. Hookups: none.

Burnt Rancheria, Sunrise Hwy./Laguna Mountain Rd., 91948. T: (877) 444-6777 or (619) 445-6235. www.r5.fs.fed.us/cleveland. RV/tent: 109. $$. Hookups: none.

Cibbets Flat, Kitchen Creek Rd., 91948. T: (619) 445-6235. www.r5.fs.fed.us/cleveland. RV/tent: 25. $. Hookups: none.

Laguna, Sunrise Hwy./Laguna Mountain Rd., 91948. T: (877) 444-6777 or (619) 445-6235. www.r5.fs.fed.us/cleveland. RV/tent: 104. $$. Hookups: none.

Napa

Spanish Flat Resort, 4290 Knoxville Rd., 94558. T: (707) 966-7700. www.spanishflatresort.com. RV/tent: 120. $$. Hookups: electric (50 amp), water.

Needles

KOA Needles, 5400 National Old Trails Hwy., 92363. T: (800) 562-3407 or (760) 326-4207. www.koa.com/where/ca/05366. RV/tent: 101. $$. Hookups: electric (30, 50 amp), water, sewer, phone.

Rainbo Beach Resort, Rte. 4 Box 139, River Rd., 92363. T: (760) 326-3101. www.coloradoriverinfo.com/needles/rainbobeach. RV/tent: 141. $$. Hookups: electric (20, 30, 50 amp), water, sewer, phone.

Niland

Fountain of Youth Spa, 10249 Coachella Canal Rd., 92257. T: (888) 800-0772. www.foyspa.com. RV/tent: 1000. $$. Hookups: electric (50 amp), water, sewer, cable.

North Shore

Salton Sea State Recreation Area, 100-225 State Park Rd., Hwy. 111, 92254. T: (760) 393-3052. www.saltonsea.statepark.org. RV/tent: 110. $. Hookups: electric (30 amp), water.

Northridge

Walnut RV Park, 19130 Nordhoff St., 91324. T: (800)-868-2749. www.walnutrvpark.com. RV/tent: 114. $$$$. Hookups: electric (50 amp), water, sewer, cable, phone (long term).

Novato

Novato RV Park, 1530 Armstrong Ave., 94945. T: (800) 733-6787 or (415) 897-1271. www.novatorvpark.com. RV/tent: 69. $$$$. Hookups: electric (20, 30, 50 amp), water, sewer, phone.

O'Brien

Antlers, Antlers Rd., 96070. T: (877) 444-6777 or (530) 275-1587. www.r5.fs.fed.us/shastatrinity. RV/tent: 59. $$. Hookups: none.

Gregory Creek, Gregory Creek Rd., 96070. T: (877) 444-6777 or (530) 275-1587. www.r5.fs.fed.us/shastatrinity. RV/tent: 18. $$. Hookups: none.

Lakeshore East, Lakeshore Dr., 96070. T: (877) 444-6777 or (530) 275-1587. www.r5.fs.fed.us/shastatrinity. RV/tent: 26. $$. Hookups: none.

Moore Creek, Gilman Rd., 96070. T: (877) 444-6777 or (530) 275-1587. www.r5.fs.fed.us/shastatrinity. RV/tent: 12. $$. Hookups: none.

Old Station

Big Pine Camp, Hwy. 89, 96071. T: (530) 336-5521. www.r5.fs.fed.us/lassen. RV/tent: 19. $. Hookups: none.

Bridge Camp, Hwy. 89, 96071. T: (530) 336-5521. www.r5.fs.fed.us/lassen. RV/tent: 25. $. Hookups: none.

Cave Camp, Hwy. 89, 96071. T: (530) 336-5521. www.r5.fs.fed.us/lassen. RV/tent: 46. $$. Hookups: none.

Crater Lake, FR 32N08, 96071. T: (530) 257-4188. www.r5.fs.fed.us/lassen. RV/tent: 32. $. Hookups: none.

Hat Creek, Hwy. 89, 96071. T: (877) 444-6777 or (530) 336-5521. www.r5.fs.fed.us/lassen. RV/tent: 75. $$. Hookups: none.

Honn Campground, Hwy. 89, 96071. T: (530) 336-5521. www.r5.fs.fed.us/lassen. RV/tent: 6. $. Hookups: none.

Orland

Old Orchard RV Park, 4490 CR HH, 95963. T: (530) 865-5335. RV/tent: 72. $$. Hookups: electric (30, 50 amp), water, sewer.

Orland Buttes, Newville Rd./Rd. 200, 95963-8901. T: (530) 865-4781. www.spk.usace.army.mil/cespkco/lakes/blackbutte.html. RV/tent: 40. $. Hookups: none.

Orleans

Aikens Creek West, Hwy. 96, 95556. T: (530) 626-3291. www.r5.fs.fed.us/sixrivers. RV/tent: Varies. $. Hookups: none.

Dillon Creek, Hwy. 96, 95556. T: (530) 626-3291. www.r5.fs.fed.us/sixrivers. RV/tent: 21. $. Hookups: none.

E-Ne-Luck, Hwy. 96, 95556. T: (530) 626-3291. www.r5.fs.fed.us/sixrivers. RV/tent: 11. $. Hookups: none.

Fish Lake, Fish Lake Rd., 95556. T: (530) 626-3291. www.r5.fs.fed.us/sixrivers. RV/tent: 24. $. Hookups: none.

CALIFORNIA (continued)

Oxnard

Evergreen RV Park, 2135 Oxnard Blvd., 93030. T: (805) 485-1936. www.evergreenrvpark.com. RV/tent: 81. $$$. Hookups: electric (30 amp), water, sewer.

Palmdale

Saddleback Butte State Park, 17 miles east of Lancaster on Ave. J East., 93551. T: (661) 942-0662. www.calparksmojave.com. RV/tent: 50. $. Hookups: none.

Paso Robles

Wine Country RV Resort, Airport Rd., 93446. T: (805) 238-4560 or (866) 927-8669. www .winecountryrvresort.com. RV/tent: 82. $$$. Hookups: electric (30, 50 amp), water, sewer.

Petaluma

KOA San Francisco North-Petaluma, 20 Rainsville Rd., 94952. T: (800) 992-2267 or (707) 763-1492. www.sanfranciscokoa.com. RV/tent: 312. $$$. Hookups: electric (20, 30, 50 amp), water, sewer, cable, phone.

Pine Valley

Boulder Oaks, Old Hwy. 80, 91962. T: (877) 444-6777 or (619) 445-6235. www.r5.fs.fed.us/cleveland. RV/tent: 30. $. Hookups: none.

Pismo Beach

Oceano Campground, Pismo State Beach, Pier Ave., 93445. T: (800) 444-7275 or (805) 489-2684. www.cal-parks.ca.gov. RV/tent: 82. $$. Hookups: electric (30 amp), water.

Pollock Pines

Jones Fork, Ice House Rd., 95726. T: (530) 644-2349. www.r5.fs.fed.us/eldorado. RV/tent: 10. $. Hookups: none.

Northwind, Ice House Rd., 95726. T: (530) 644-2349. www.r5.fs.fed.us/eldorado. RV/tent: 9. $. Hookups: none.

Silver Creek, Ice House Rd., 95726. T: (530) 644-2349. www.r5.fs.fed.us/eldorado. RV/tent: 12. $. Hookups: electric (20, 30, 50 amp), water, phone, cable.

Strawberry Point, Ice House Rd., 95726. T: (530) 644-2349. www.r5.fs.fed.us/eldorado. RV/tent: 10. $. Hookups: none.

Wench Creek, Ice House Rd., 95726. T: (530) 644-6777 or (530) 644-2349. www.r5.fs.fed.us/eldorado. RV/tent: 100. $$. Hookups: none.

Wolf Creek, Union Valley Rd., 95726. T: (877) 444-6777 or (530) 644-2349. www.r5.fs.fed.us/eldorado. RV/tent: 41. $$. Hookups: none.

Yellowjacket, Union Valley Rd., 95726. T: (877) 444-6777 or (530) 644-2349. www.r5.fs.fed.us/eldorado. RV/tent: 40. $$. Hookups: none.

Pomona

KOA Pomona-Fairplex, 2200 North White Ave., 91768. T: (909) 593-8915 or (888) 562-4230. www.koa.com/where/ca/05438.htm. RV/tent: 185. $$. Hookups: electric (30, 50 amp), water, sewer, phone.

Port Hueneme

Point Mugu State Park, Sycamore Canyon Campground, Hwy. 1, 93043. T: (800) 444-7275 or (818) 880-0350. www.reserveamerica.com. RV/tent: 58. $. Hookups: none.

Point Mugu State Park, Thornhill Broome Campground, Hwy. 1, 93043. T: (800) 444-7275 or (818) 880-0350. www.reserveamerica.com. RV/tent: 68. $. Hookups: none.

Porterville

Deer Creek RV Park, 10679 Main St., 93257. T: (559) 781-3337. RV/tent: 78. $$. Hookups: electric (20, 30, 50 amp), water, sewer, phone.

Portola

Sierra Springs Trailer Resort, 70099 Hwy. 70 Box 595, 96122. T: (530) 836-2747. www.psln.com/sstr. RV/tent: 30. $$. Hookups: electric (20, 30 amp), water, sewer, cable.

Praille

Cool Springs, Butt Valley Rd., 95923. T: (916) 386-5164. www.r5.fs.fed.us/lassen. RV/tent: 30. $$. Hookups: none.

Last Chance Creek, Lake Almanor Causeway, 95923. T: (916) 386-5164. www.r5.fs.fed.us/lassen. RV/tent: 12. $$. Hookups: none.

Ponderosa Flat, Butt Valley Rd., 95923. T: (916) 386-5164. www.r5.fs.fed.us/lassen. RV/tent: 63. $$. Hookups: none.

Yellow Creek, CR 307, 95923. T: (916) 386-5164. www.r5.fs.fed.us/lassen. RV/tent: 10. $$. Hookups: none.

Redding

JGW RV Park, 6612 Riverland Dr., 96002. T: (800) 469-5910 or (530) 365-7965. www.jgwrvpark.com. RV/tent: 75. $$$. Hookups: electric (20, 30, 50 amp), water, sewer, cable, phone, wireless internet.

Mountain Gate RV Park, 14161 Holiday Rd., 96003. T: (800) 404-6040 or (530) 275 4600. www.mt-gatervpark.com. RV/tent: 122. $$$. Hookups: electric (30, 50 amp), water, sewer, satellite, phone.

Redding RV Park, 11075 Campers Ct., 96003. T: (800) 428-2089 or (530) 241-0707. www.gocampingamerica.com/redding. RV/tent: 110. $$. Hookups: electric (30, 50 amp), water, sewer, cable, phone.

Red's Meadow

Agnew Meadows, Inyo National Forest, Mammoth Ranger District, Minaret Summit Rd., 93546. T: (760) 924-5500. www.r5.fs.fed.us/inyo. RV/tent: 21. $$. Hookups: none.

Minaret Falls, Inyo National Forest, Mammoth Ranger District, Minaret Summit Rd., 93546. T: (760) 924-5500. www.r5.fs.fed.us/inyo. RV/tent: 27. $$. Hookups: none.

Pumice Flat, Inyo National Forest, Mammoth Ranger District, Minaret Summit Rd., 93546. T: (760) 924-5500. www.r5.fs.fed.us/inyo. RV/tent: 17. $$. Hookups: none.

Red's Meadow, Inyo National Forest, Mammoth Ranger District, Minaret Summit Rd., 93546.

T: (760) 924-5500. www.r5.fs.fed.us/inyo. RV/tent: 56. $$. Hookups: none.

Upper Soda Springs, Inyo National Forest, Mammoth Ranger District, Minaret Summit Rd., 93546. T: (760) 924-5500. www.r5.fs.fed.us/inyo. RV/tent: 29. $$. Hookups: none.

Redwood City

Trailer Villa, 3401 East Bayshore Rd., 94063. T: (650) 366-7880. www.gocampingamerica.com/trailer villarv. RV/tent: 114. $$$. Hookups: electric (20, 30 amp), water, sewer.

Rock Creek

Holiday, White Mountain Ranger District, Rock Creek Rd., 93514. T: (760) 873-2500. www.r5.fs. fed.us/inyo. RV/tent: 35. $$. Hookups: none.

Iris Meadows, White Mountain Ranger District, Rock Creek Rd., 93514. T: (760) 873-2500. www.r5.fs.fed.us/inyo. RV/tent: 14. $$. Hookups: none.

Pine Grove, White Mountain Ranger District, Rock Creek Rd., 93514. T: (760) 873-2500. www.r5.fs. fed.us/inyo. RV/tent: 11. $$. Hookups: none.

Rock Creek Lake, White Mountain Ranger District, Rock Creek Rd., 93514. T: (760) 873-2500. www.r5.fs.fed.us/inyo. RV/tent: 28. $$. Hookups: none.

Tuff, White Mountain Ranger District, US 395, 93514. T: (760) 873-2500. www.r5.fs.fed.us/inyo. RV/tent: 34. $$. Hookups: none.

Upper Pine Grove, White Mountain Ranger District, Rock Creek Rd., 93514. T: (760) 873-2500. www.r5.fs.fed.us/inyo. RV/tent: 8. $$. Hookups: none.

Sacramento

Oak Haven RV Park, 2145 Auburn Blvd., 95821. T: (916) 922-0814. www.gocampingamerica. com/oakhavenrv. RV/tent: 90. $$. Hookups: electric (30, 50 amp), water, sewer, phone.

Stillman Adult RV Park, 3880 Stillman Park Cir., 95824. T: (916) 392-2820 or (800) 570-6562. www.gocampingamerica.com/stillman. RV/tent: 65. $$$. Hookups: electric (20, 30, 50 amp), water, sewer, cable.

Salinas

Laguna Seca Recreation Area, Hwy. 68, 93901. T: (831) 755-4895. www.carmelfun.com/parks. html. RV/tent: 102. $$. Hookups: electric (20, 30 amp), water.

San Bernardino

KOA San Bernardino, 1707 Cable Canyon Rd., 92407. T: (800) KOA-4155 or (909) 887-4098. www.sanbernardinokoa.com. RV/tent: 153. $$. Hookups: electric (20, 30, 50 amp), water, sewer, phone.

San Diego

Campland on the Bay, 2211 Pacific Beach Dr., 92109. T: (800) 4-BAY-FUN. www.campland.com. RV/tent: 750. $$$$. Hookups: electric (50 amp), water, sewer, cable, phone.

La Pacifica RV Park, 1010 West San Ysidro Blvd., 92109. T: (888) 786-6997. www.lapacificarvre sort.com. RV/tent: 177. $$$$. Hookups: electric (30, 50 amp), water, sewer, phone, satellite.

CALIFORNIA (continued)

San Fernando

Buckhorn, Hwy. 2, 91342. T: (818) 899-1900. www.r5.fs.fed.us/angeles. RV/tent: 38. $. Hookups: none.

Chilao, Hwy. 2, 91342. T: (818) 899-1900. www.r5.fs.fed.us/angeles. RV/tent: 111. $. Hookups: none.

Horse Flats, Santa Clara Divide Rd., 91342. T: (818) 899-1900. www.r5.fs.fed.us/angeles. RV/tent: 25. $. Hookups: none.

Messenger Flats, Santa Clara Divide Rd., 91342. T: (818) 899-1900. www.r5.fs.fed.us/angeles. RV/tent: 10. $. Hookups: none.

San Juan Bautista

Betabel RV Resort, 9664 Betabel Rd., 95045. T: (800) 278-7275. www.betabel.com. RV/tent: 172. $$$. Hookups: electric (30, 50 amp), water, sewer, satellite , phone.

Fremont Peak State Park, San Juan Canyon Rd., 95045. T: (831) 623-4255 or (800) 444-PARK. RV/tent: 25. $. Hookups: none.

Mission Farm RV Park, 400 San Juan-Hollister Rd., 95045. T: (831) 623-4456. www.missionfarm.com. RV/tent: 165. $$$. Hookups: electric (20, 30 amp), water, sewer, cable, phone.

San Luis Obispo

Avila Valley Hot Springs Spa & RV Resort, 250 Avila Beach Dr., 93405. T: (805) 595-2359 or (800) 332-2359. www.rvdestinations.com/avila. RV/tent: 100. $$. Hookups: electric (20, 30 amp), water, sewer, cable.

San Rafael

China Camp State Park, North San Pedro Rd., 94903. T: (800) 444-7275 or (415) 456-0766. www.reserveamerica.com. RV/tent: 30. $. Hookups: none.

San Simeon

San Simeon State Park, Washburn Campground, San Simeon Creek Rd., 93452. T: (800) 444-7275 or (805) 927-2035. www.cal-parks.ca.gov. RV/tent: 115. $. Hookups: none.

Santa Barbara

Santa Barbara Sunrise RV Park, 516 South Salinas, 93103. T: (800) 345-5018 or (805) 966-9954. www.gocampingamerica.com/santabarbara. RV/tent: 33. $$$. Hookups: electric (20, 30 amp), water, sewer, cable, phone.

Scott Bar

Indian Scotty, Scott River Rd., 96085. T: (530) 468-5351. www.r5.fs.fed.us/klamath. RV/tent: 28. $. Hookups: none.

Scotts Valley

Carbonero Creek RV Park, 917 Disc Dr., 95066. T: (408) 438-1288 or (800) 546-1288. www.gocampingamerica.com/carbonero. RV/tent: 104. $$$. Hookups: electric (20, 30 amp), water, sewer, cable, phone.

Sequoia National Park

Atwell Mill, Mineral King Rd., 93262. T: (559) 565-3341. www.nps.gov/seki. RV/tent: 23. $. Hookups: none.

Buckeye Flat, Hwy. 198, 93262. T: (559) 565-3341. www.nps.gov/seki. RV/tent: 28. $$. Hookups: none.

Cold Springs, Mineral King Rd., 93262. T: (559) 565-3341. www.nps.gov/seki. RV/tent: 40. $. Hookups: none.

Dorst, Generals Hwy., 93262. T: (559) 565-3341. www.nps.gov/seki. RV/tent: 204. $$. Hookups: none.

Lodgepole, Generals Hwy., 93262. T: (559) 565-3341. www.nps.gov/seki. RV/tent: 214. $$. Hookups: none.

South Fork, South Fork Rd., 93262. T: (559) 565-3341. www.nps.gov/seki. RV/tent: 13. $. Hookups: none.

Shelter Cove

Horse Mountain, Kings Peak Rd., 95589. T: (707) 986-7731 or (707) 825-2300. www.ca.blm.gov/arcata/campground.html. RV/tent: 9. $. Hookups: none.

Nadelos, Chemise Mountain Rd., 95589. T: (707) 986-7731 or (707) 825-2300. www.ca.blm.gov/arcata/campground.html. RV/tent: 8. $. Hookups: none.

Wailaki, Chemise Mountain Rd., 95589. T: (707) 986-7731 or (707) 825-2300. www.ca.blm.gov/arcata/campground.html. RV/tent: 13. $. Hookups: none.

Sierra City

Loganville, Downieville Ranger District, Hwy. 49, 96125. T: (530) 288-3231 or (530) 993-1410. www.r5.fs.fed.us/tahoe. RV/tent: 19. $$. Hookups: none.

Stockton

Tiki Lagun Resort & Marina, 12988 West McDonald Rd., 95206. T: (877) 444-TIKI or (209) 464-2980. www.tikimarina.com. RV/tent: 103. $$. Hookups: electric (30, 50 amp), water, sewer, cable.

Susanville

Christie, CR 231, 96130. T: (877) 444-6777 or (530) 257-4188. www.r5.fs.fed.us/lassen. RV/tent: 69. $$. Hookups: none.

Mariners Resort, 509-725 Stones Rd., 96130. T: (800) 700-5253. www.marinersresort.com. RV/tent: 67. $$. Hookups: electric (30, 50 amp), water, sewer, satellite , phone.

Mountain View RV Park, 3075 Johnstonville Rd., 96130. T: (877) 686-7878. RV/tent: 77. $$. Hookups: electric (30, 50 amp), water, sewer, cable, phone.

Tahoe City

Tahoe State Recreation Area, Hwy. 28, 96145. T: (530) 583-3074. www.reserveamerica.com. RV/tent: 27. $$. Hookups: none.

William Kent, West Shore Lake Tahoe, Hwy. 89, 96145. T: (877) 444-6777 or (530) 573-2674. www.r5.fs.fed.us/ltbmu. RV/tent: 95. $$. Hookups: none.

Tahoma

Emerald Bay State Park, West Shore Lake Tahoe, Hwy. 89, 96142. T: (800) 444-7275 or (530) 525-7277. www.cal-parks.ca.gov. RV/tent: 100. $. Hookups: none.

Temecula

Indian Oaks Trailer Ranch Campground, 38120 East Benton Rd., 92593. T: (909) 302-5399. www.gocampingamerica.com/indianoaks. RV/tent: 62. $$. Hookups: electric (20, 30 amp), water, sewer, phone.

Pechanga RV Resort, 45000 Pala Rd., 92592. T: (909) 587-0484 or (877) 997-8386. www.pechangarvresort.com. RV/tent: 170. $$$. Hookups: electric (20, 30, 50 amp), water, sewer, cable, phone.

Three Rivers

Three Rivers Hideaway, 43365 Sierra Dr., 93271. T: (559) 561-4413. RV/tent: 26. $$. Hookups: electric (15, 30 amp), water, sewer, phone.

Toms Place

Big Meadow, White Mountain Ranger District, Rock Creek Rd., 93514. T: (760) 873-2500. www.r5.fs.fed.us/inyo. RV/tent: 11. $$. Hookups: none.

French Camp, White Mountain Ranger District, Rock Creek Rd., 93514. T: (760) 873-2500. www.r5.fs.fed.us/inyo. RV/tent: 86. $$. Hookups: none.

Trinidad

Azalea Glen RV Park & Campground, 3883 Patricks Point Dr., 95570. T: (707) 677-3068. www.azaleaglen.com. RV/tent: 42. $$. Hookups: electric (30, 50 amp), water, sewer, cable, phone.

Truckee

Goose Meadows, Hwy. 89, 96161. T: (877) 444-6777 or (530) 587-3558. www.r5.fs.fed.us/tahoe. RV/tent: 24. $. Hookups: none.

Granite Flat, Hwy. 89, 96161. T: (877) 444-6777 or (530) 587-3558. www.r5.fs.fed.us/tahoe. RV/tent: 75. $$. Hookups: none.

Silver Creek, Hwy. 89, 96161. T: (877) 444-6777 or (530) 587-3558. www.r5.fs.fed.us/tahoe. RV/tent: 28. $. Hookups: none.

Tulare

Sun & Fun RV Park, 1000 East Rankin Ave., 93274. T: (559) 686-5779. www.tldirectory.com/campgrounds/sunandfun. RV/tent: 89. $$. Hookups: electric (30, 50 amp), water, sewer, cable, phone.

Tulelake

A.H. Hogue, FR 49/Medicine Lake Rd., 96134. T: (530) 667-2246. www.r5.fs.fed.us/modoc. RV/tent: 24. $. Hookups: none.

Headquarters, FR 49/Medicine Lake Rd., 96134. T: (530) 667-2246. www.r5.fs.fed.us/modoc. RV/tent: 9. $. Hookups: none.

Hemlock, FR 49/Medicine Lake Rd., 96134. T: (530) 667-2246. www.r5.fs.fed.us/modoc. RV/tent: 19. $. Hookups: none.

Tulelake

Medicine, FR 49/Medicine Lake Rd., 96134. T: (530) 667-2246. www.r5.fs.fed.us/modoc. RV/tent: 22. $. Hookups: none.

CALIFORNIA (continued)

Tuttletown

Big Oak Campground, Tuttletown Recreation Area, Glory Hole Rd., 95222. T: (209) 536-9094. www.recreation.gov. RV/tent: 176. $. Hookups: none.

Glory Hole Campground, Tuttletown Recreation Area, Glory Hole Rd., 95222. T: (209) 536-9094. www.recreation.gov. RV/tent: 144. $. Hookups: none.

Ironhorse Campground, Tuttletown Recreation Area, Glory Hole Rd., 95222. T: (209) 536-9094. www.recreation.gov. RV/tent: 144. $. Hookups: none.

Twentynine Palms

29 Palms RV and Golf Resort, 4949 Desert Knoll Ave., 92277. T: (800) 874-4548 or (760) 367-3320. www.29palmsgolf.com. RV/tent: 197. $$$. Hookups: electric (30, 50 amp), water, sewer, phone.

Black Rock Canyon, Joshua Tree National Park, Black Rock Canyon Rd., 92277-3597. T: (760) 367-5525. www.nps.gov/jotr. RV/tent: 100. $. Hookups: none.

Indian Cove, Joshua Tree National Park, Indian Cove Rd., 92277-3598. T: (760) 367-5525. www.nps.gov/jotr. RV/tent: 101. $. Hookups: none.

Ukiah

Bu-Shay, Inlet Rd., 95482-9404. T: (877) 444-6777 or (707) 462-7581. www.spn.usace.army.mil/mendocino.html. RV/tent: 264. $$. Hookups: none.

Che-Ka-Ka, Lake Mendocino Dr., 95482-9404. T: (877) 444-6777 or (707) 462-7581. www.spn.usace.army.mil/mendocino.html. RV/tent: 23. $. Hookups: none.

Valencia

Valencia Travel Village, 27946 Henry Mayo Dr., 91384. T: (661) 257-3333. www.gocamping america.com/valencia. RV/tent: 460. $$$$. Hookups: electric (20, 30, 50 amp), water, sewer, cable, phone.

Vallejo

Tradewinds RV Park of Vallejo, 239 Lincoln Rd. West, 94590. T: (707) 643-4000. www.gocampingamerica.com/tradewinds. RV/tent: 78. $$$. Hookups: electric (30, 50 amp), water, sewer, phone.

Ventura

Ventura Beach RV Resort, 800 West Main St., 93001. T: (805) 643-9137. www.caohwy.com/v/venbearv.htm. RV/tent: 168. $$$. Hookups: electric (50 amp), water, sewer.

Visalia

KOA Visalia-Fresno South, 7480 Ave 308, 93291. T: (800) 562-0540 or (559) 651-0544. www.koa.com. RV/tent: 137. $$. Hookups: electric (20, 30 amp), water, sewer, cable.

Watsonville

KOA Santa Cruz-Monterey Bay, 1186 San Andreas Rd., 95076. T: (800) 562-7701 or (831) 722-0551. www.koa.com. RV/tent: 230. $$$. Hookups: electric (30, 50 amp), water, sewer.

Weaverville

Alpine View, Gun Covington Dr., 96093. T: (877) 444-6777 or (530) 623-2121. www.r5.fs.fed.us/shastatrinity. RV/tent: 66. $$. Hookups: none.

Eagle Creek Shasta Trinity National Forest, Hwy. 3, 96093. T: (530) 623-2121. www.fs.fed.us/r5/shastatrinity. RV/tent: 17. $. Hookups: none.

Hayward Flat, FR 35N26Y, 96093. T: (877) 444-6777 or (530) 623-2121. www.r5.fs.fed.us/shastatrinity. RV/tent: 98. $$. Hookups: none.

Preacher Meadow, Hwy. 3, 96093. T: (877) 444-6777 or (530) 623-2121. www.r5.fs.fed.us/shastatrinity. RV/tent: 45. $. Hookups: none.

Sidney Gulch RV Park, Hwy. 299 West & Tinnen St., 96093. T: (530) 623-6621. RV/tent: 40. $$. Hookups: electric (20, 30 amp), water, sewer, cable, phone.

Stoney Point, Hwy. 3, 96093. T: (530) 623-2121. www.r5.fs.fed.us/shastatrinity. RV/tent: 22. $. Hookups: none.

West Sacramento

KOA Sacramento-Metropolitan, 3951 Lake Rd., 95691. T: (800) KOA-2747 or (916) 371-6771. www.koakampgrounds.com; www.sacramento koa.com. RV/tent: 122. $$. Hookups: electric (20, 30 amp), water, sewer, cable, phone.

Sherwood Harbor Marina & RV Park, 35050 South River Rd., 95691. T: (916) 371-3471. RV/tent: 40. $$$. Hookups: electric (20 amp), water, sewer.

Westport

Westport-Union Landing State Beach, Hwy. 1, 95488. T: (707) 937-5804. RV/tent: 100. $. Hookups: none.

Winterhaven

Picacho State Recreation Area, Picacho Rd., 92283. T: (760) 393-3059. www.cal-parks.ca.gov. RV/tent: 135. $$. Hookups: electric, water, sewer.

Wofford Heights

Boulder Gulch, Hwy. 155, 93285. T: (760) 379-5646. www.r5.fs.fed.us/sequoia. RV/tent: 78. $$. Hookups: none.

Camp 9, Sierra Way, 93285. T: (877) 444-6777 or (760) 379-5646. www.r5.fs.fed.us/sequoia. RV/tent: 109. $. Hookups: none.

Hungry Gulch, Hwy. 155, 93285. T: (760) 379-5646. www.r5.fs.fed.us/sequoia. RV/tent: 79. $$. Hookups: none.

Pioneer Point, Hwy. 155, 93285. T: (760) 379-5646. www.r5.fs.fed.us/sequoia. RV/tent: 77. $$. Hookups: none.

Woodfords

Crystal Springs, Hwy. 88, 96120. T: (775) 882-2766. www.r5.fed.fs.us. RV/tent: 20. $. Hookups: none.

Kit Carson, Hwy. 88, 96120. T: (775) 882-2766. www.r5.fed.fs.us. RV/tent: 12. $. Hookups: none.

Yermo

KOA Barstow-Calico, 35250 Outer Hwy. 15, 92398. T: (800) 562-0059 or (760) 254-2311. www.koa.com. RV/tent: 78. $$. Hookups: electric (20, 30, 50 amp), water, sewer, phone.

Yosemite National Park

Bridalveil Creek, Mineral King Rd., 95389. T: (800) 436-7275 or (209) 372-0265. www.nps.gov/yose. RV/tent: 110. $. Hookups: none.

Crane Flat, Hwy. 120, 95389. T: (800) 436-7275 or (209) 372-0265. www.nps.gov/yose. RV/tent: 166. $$. Hookups: none.

Hodgdon Meadow, Hwy. 120, 95389. T: (800) 436-7275 or (209) 372-0265. www.nps.gov/yose. RV/tent: 105. $$. Hookups: none.

Lower Pines, Yosemite Valley, Southside Dr., 95389. T: (800) 436-7275 or (209) 372-0265. www.nps.gov/yose. RV/tent: 60. $$. Hookups: none.

Porcupine Flat, Tioga Rd./Hwy. 120, 95389. T: (800) 436-7275 or (209) 372-0265. www.nps.gov/yose. RV/tent: 52. $. Hookups: none.

Upper Pines, Yosemite Valley, Southside Dr., 95389. T: (800) 436-7275 or (209) 372-0265. www.nps.gov/yose. RV/tent: 238. $$. Hookups: none.

White Wolf, White Wolf Rd., 95389. T: (800) 436-7275 or (209) 372-0265. www.nps.gov/yose. RV/tent: 74. $. Hookups: none.

Yosemite Creek, Yosemite Creek Campground Rd., 95389. T: (800) 436-7275 or (209) 372-0265. www.nps.gov/yose. RV/tent: 75. $. Hookups: none.

COLORADO

Alamosa

Alamosa Economy Campground, 12532 Hwy. 160 East, 81101. T: (719) 589-5574. www.colorado directory.com. RV/tent: 30. $. Hookups: electric (20, 30, 50 amp), water.

Almont

Three Rivers Resort & Outfitting, 130 CR 742, 81210. T: (888) 761-3474 or (970) 641-1303. www.3riversresort.com. RV/tent: 62. $$. Hookups: electric (20, 30 amp), water, sewer.

Amargosa Valley

Fort Amargosa, East Hwy. 95 & South Hwy. 373, 89020. T: (775) 372-1178. RV/tent: 98. $. Hookups: electric (30, 50 amp), water, sewer.

Antonio

Camp Twin Rivers Cabins & RV Park, 34044 Hwy. 17, 81120. T: (888) 689-6787 or (719) 376-5710. www.coloradodirectory.com. RV/tent: 46. $$. Hookups: electric (20, 30, 50 amp), water, sewer.

Conejos River Campground, 26714 Hwy. 17, 81120. T: (719) 376-5943. www.conejosriver campground.com. RV/tent: 56. $$. Hookups: electric (30, 50 amp), water, sewer.

Narrow Gauge RR Inn & RV Park, 5200 CO 285, 81120. T: (800) 323-9469 or (719) 376-5441. www.coloradodirectory.com. RV/tent: 10. $. Hookups: electric (20, 30 amp), water, sewer.

Ponderosa Campground & Cabins, 18234 West Hwy. 17, 81120. T: (719) 376-5857. www.colorado directory.com. RV/tent: 34. $$. Hookups: electric (20, 30 amp), water.

Arboles

Arboles Campground, Navajo State Park, 1526 CR 982, 81121. T: (970) 883-2208. www.parks.state. co.us. RV/tent: 52. $. Hookups: electric (30 amp).

Pinon Park Campground & RV Resort, 19 Lazy Ln., 81121. T: (888) 926-1749 or (970) 883-3636. www.frontier.net/~pinonparkcamp. RV/tent: 55. $$. Hookups: electric (20, 30, 50 amp), water, sewer.

Aurora

Cherry Creek Campground, Cherry Creek State Park, 4201 South Parker Rd., 80014. T: (303) 699-3860. www.parks.state.co.us. RV/tent: 108. $. Hookups: electric (30 amp).

Denver Meadows RV Park, 2075 Potomac St., 80011. T: (800) 364-9487 or (303) 364-9483. www.denvermeadows.com. RV/tent: 289. $$$. Hookups: electric (20, 30, 50 amp), water, sewer.

Bayfield

Five Branches Camper Park & Cabins, 4677 CR 501-A, 81122. T: (970) 884-2582. www.5branches.com. RV/tent: 108. $$. Hookups: electric (20, 30 amp), water, sewer.

Riverside RV Park, 41743 Hwy. 160, 81122. T: (800) 258-9458. RV/tent: 84. $$. Hookups: electric (20, 30 amp), water, sewer, cable.

Vallecito Resort & Grill, 13030 CR 501, 81122. T: (800) 258-9458. RV/tent: 170. $$$. Hookups: electric (20, 30, 50 amp), water, sewer.

Bellevue

Archer's Poudre River Resort, 33021 Poudre Canyon Hwy., 80512. T: (888) 822-0588 or (970) 881-2139. www.poudreriverresort.com. RV/tent: 10. $$. Hookups: electric (20, 30, 50 amp), water, sewer.

Home Moraine Trailer Park, 37797 Poudre Canyon Hwy., 80512. T: (970) 881-2356. RV/tent: 32. $$. Hookups: electric (20, 30, 50 amp), water, sewer.

Mountain Park, Hwy. 14, 80512. T: (970) 881-2157. www.reserveusa.com. RV/tent: 55. $$. Hookups: electric (20, 30 amp).

Rustic Resort Restaurant Lounge & Store, 31443 Poudre Canyon Hwy., 80512. T: (970) 881-2179. RV/tent: 18. $$. Hookups: electric (20, 30 amp), water, sewer.

Sportsman's Lodge & Store, 44174 Poudre Canyon, 80512. T: (800) 270-2272 or (970) 881-2272. www.coloradomountainvacation.com/sports manslodge.html. RV/tent: 14. $$. Hookups: electric (20, 30 amp), water, sewer.

Black Hawk

Reverends Ridge Campground, Golden Gate Canyon State Park, 3873 Hwy. 46, 80403. T: (303) 582-3707. www.parks.state.co.us. RV/tent: 97. $. Hookups: electric (20, 30, 50 amp).

Blanca

Blanca RV Park, 521 Main St., 81123. T: (719) 379-3201. RV/tent: 31. $$. Hookups: electric (20, 30, 50 amp), water, sewer.

Brighton

Barr Lake Campground, 17180 East 136th Ave., 80601. T: (800) 654-7988 or (303) 659-6180. RV/tent: 108. $$. Hookups: electric (20, 30, 50 amp), water, sewer.

Buena Vista

Buena Vista KOA, 27700 CR 303, 81211. T: (800) 562-2672 or (719) 395-8318. www.buenavista koa.com. RV/tent: 77. $$. Hookups: electric (50 amp), water, sewer.

Crazy Horse Camping Resort, 33975 Hwy. 24 North, 81211. T: (800) 888-7320. www.crazy horseresort.com. RV/tent: 85. $$. Hookups: electric (20, 30 amp), water, sewer.

Mt. Princeton RV Park, 30380 CR 383, 81211. T: (719) 395-6206. www.mtprincetonrvpark.com. RV/tent: 62. $$. Hookups: electric (30, 50 amp), water, sewer.

Snowy Peaks RV & Mobile Park, 30430 North Hwy. 24, 81211. T: (719) 395-8481 or (800) 954-8481. www.snowypeaksrvpark.com. RV/tent: 65. $$. Hookups: electric (20, 30, 50 amp), water, sewer.

Canon City

Buffalo Bill's Royal Gorge Campground, 30 CR 3-A, 81212. T: (800) 787-0880 or (719) 269-3211. www.camproyalgorge.com. RV/tent: 46. $$. Hookups: electric (20, 30, 50 amp), water, sewer.

Fort Gorge Campground & RV Park, 45044 Hwy. 50, 81212. T: (719) 275-5111. www.fortgorge. com. RV/tent: 90. $$. Hookups: electric (20, 30, 50 amp), water, sewer.

Indian Springs Ranch, P.O. Box 405, 81215. T: (719) 372-3907. www.coloradodirectory.com/indian springsranch. RV/tent: 80. $$. Hookups: electric (20, 30 amp), water, sewer.

Royal Gorge/Canon City KOA, P.O. Box 528, 81215. T: (800) 562-5689. www.koa.com. RV/tent: 153. $$. Hookups: electric (20, 30, 50 amp), water, sewer.

Royal View Camp Resort, 43590 Hwy. 50 West, 81212. T: (866) 290-2461 or (719) 275-1900. www.royalviewcampground.com. RV/tent: 53. $$. Hookups: electric (20, 30, 50 amp), water, sewer.

Cascade

Lone Duck Campground & Fishing Pond, P.O. Box 25, 80809. T: (800) 776-5925 or (719) 684-9907. RV/tent: 62. $$. Hookups: electric (20, 30, 50 amp), water, sewer.

Cedaredge

Alexander Lake Lodge, P.O. Box 900, 81413. T: (970) 856-2539 or (866) 525-ALEX. RV/tent: 10. $$. Hookups: electric (20, 30, 50 amp), water, sewer.

Shady Creek, 205 North Grand Mesa Dr. (Hwy. 65), 81413. T: (970) 856-7522. RV/tent: 17 RV. $$. Hookups: electric (30, 50 amp), water, sewer.

Central City

Central City/Blackhawk KOA, 661 Hwy. 46, 80403. T: (800) 562-1620 or (303) 582-9979. www.koa.com. RV/tent: 37. $$. Hookups: electric (15, 20, 50 amp), water, sewer.

Cimarron

Black Canyon RV Park & Campground, P.O. Box 128, 81220. T: (970) 249-1147. RV/tent: 28. $$. Hookups: electric (20, 30, 50 amp), water, sewer.

Clark

Pearl Lake State Park Lower Loop, P.O. Box 750, 80428. T: (970) 879-3922 or (800) 678-2267. parks.state.co.us/pearl. RV/tent: 21. $. Hookups: electric.

Clifton

Island Acres Campground, Colorado River State Park, Exit 47 off I-70, 5 miles east of Palisade, 81520. T: (970) 434-3388. parks.state.co.us. RV/tent: 80. $. Hookups: electric (30 amp), water, sewer.

Collbran

Aspen Grove Campground, Vega State Park, SR 330 East, 81624. T: (970) 487-3407. www.parks.state .co.us. RV/tent: 27. $. Hookups: electric, water.

Early Settlers Campground, Vega State Park, SR 330 East, 81624. T: (970) 487-3407. www.parks.state .co.us. RV/tent: 33. $$. Hookups: electric (30 amp), water.

Oak Point Campground, Vega State Park, SR 330 East, 81624. T: (970) 487-3407. parks.state.co.us. RV/tent: 39. $. Hookups: electric.

Wallace Guides & Outfitters, 29781 Kimball Creek Rd, 81624. T: (970) 487-3235. RV/tent: 8. $. Hookups: electric (20, 30 amp), water.

COLORADO (continued)

Colorado Springs

Conifer Ridge Campground, Mueller State Park, South Hwy. 67, 80814. T: (719) 687-2366 or (800) 678-2267.www. parks.state.co.us/mueller. RV/tent: 28. $. Hookups: electric (30, 50 amp).

Cross Creek Campground, Eleven Mile State Park, 4229 CR 92, 80827. T: (719) 748-3401. www.parks.state.co.us/eleven_mile. RV/tent: 13. $$. Hookups: electric.

Fountain Creek RV Park, 3023 1/2 West Colorado Ave., 80904. T: (719) 633-2192. RV/tent: 114. $$$. Hookups: electric (20, 30, 50 amp), water, sewer.

Grouse Mountain Campground, Mueller State Park, South Hwy. 67, 80814. T: (719) 687-2366 or (800) 678-2267.www.parks.state.co.us/ mueller. RV/tent: 32. $$. Hookups: electric (30, 50 amp).

Howbert Point Campground, Eleven Mile State Park, 4229 CR 92, 80827. T: (719) 748-3401. www.parks.state.co.us. RV/tent: 10. $. Hookups: electric (30 amp).

Lazy Boy Campground, Eleven Mile State Park, 4229 CR 92, 80827. T: (719) 748-3401. RV/tent: 14. $. Hookups: electric.

Mountaindale Campground & Cabins, 2000 Barrett Rd., 80926. T: (719) 576-0619. RV/tent: 98. $$. Hookups: electric (20, 30, 50 amp), water, sewer.

North Shore Campground, Eleven Mile State Park, 4229 CR 92, 80827. T: (719) 748-3401. RV/tent: 89. $. Hookups: electric.

Northwoods Village RV Park, 3100 Wood Ave., 80907. T: (719) 633-7564. RV/tent: 143. $$. Hookups: electric (50 amp), water, sewer.

Peak View Campground, Mueller State Park, South Hwy. 67, 80814. T: (719) 687-2366. www.parks.state.co.us. RV/tent: 5. $$. Hookups: electric (30 amp).

Peak View Inn & RV Park, 4950 North Nevada Ave., 80918. T: (800) 551-CAMP or (719) 598-1434. RV/tent: 120. $$. Hookups: electric (20, 30 amp), water, sewer.

Revenuers Ridge Campground, Mueller State Park, South Hwy. 67, 80814. T: (719) 687-2366 or (800) 678-2267. www.parks.state.co.us/mueller. RV/tent: 34. $. Hookups: electric (30 amp).

Rocking Chair Campground, Eleven Mile State Park, 4229 CR 92, 80827. T: (719) 748-3401. www.parks.state.co.us. RV/tent: 13. $. Hookups: electric.

Rocky Ridge Campground, Eleven Mile State Park, 4229 CR 92, 80827. T: (719) 748-3401. www.parks.state.co.us. RV/tent: 140. $. Hookups: electric (30 amp).

Witcher Cove Campground, Eleven Mile State Park, 4229 CR 92, 80827. T: (719) 748-3401. www.parks.state.co.us. RV/tent: 22. $. Hookups: electric.

Wrangler RV Ranch & Motel, 6225 East Platte Ave. (Hwy. 24), 80915. T: (719) 591-1402. RV/tent: 110. $$$. Hookups: electric (20, 30, 50 amp), water, sewer.

Cortez

La Mesa Campground, 2430 East Main St., 81321. T: (970) 565-3610. RV/tent: 45. $$. Hookups: electric (20, 30 amp), water, sewer.

Lazy G Campground, P.O. Box 1048, 81321. T: (800) 628-2183 or (970) 565-8577. RV/tent: 79. $$. Hookups: electric (20, 30, 50 amp), water, sewer.

Sundance RV Park, 815 East Main, 81321. T: (800) 880-9413 or (970) 565-0997. RV/tent: 68. $$. Hookups: electric (30, 50 amp), water, sewer.

Creede

Antlers Rio Grande Resort, 26222 Hwy. 149, 81130. T: (719) 658-2423. RV/tent: 24. $$. Hookups: electric (30, 50 amp), water, sewer.

Cripple Creek

Cripple Creek Gold Campground & Horse Company, P.O. Box 601, 80813. T: (719) 689-2342 or (719) 689-0131. RV/tent: 25. $. Hookups: electric (20, 30 amp).

Cripple Creek Hospitality House & Travel Park, P.O. Box 957, 80813. T: (800) 500-2513 or (719) 689-2513. RV/tent: 90. $$. Hookups: electric (20, 30, 50 amp), water, sewer.

Cripple Creek KOA, P.O. Box 699, 80813. T: (800) 562-9125 or (719) 689-3376. www.koa.com. RV/tent: 82. $$. Hookups: electric (20, 30, 50 amp), water, sewer.

Prospectors RV Park, 202 East May Ave., 80813. T: (719) 689-2006. RV/tent: 27. $$$. Hookups: electric (20, 30 amp), water, sewer.

Del Norte

Woods & River Campground, P.O. Box 64, 81132. T: (877) 354-6922 or (719) 657-4530. RV/tent: 54. $. Hookups: electric (20, 30 amp), water, sewer, cable.

Delta

Four Seasons River Inn & RV Park, 676 Hwy. 50 North, 81416. T: (888) 340-4689 or (970) 874-9659. RV/tent: 38. $$. Hookups: electric (30, 50 amp), water, sewer, cable.

Over-the-Hill RV Ranch, 1675 Hwy. 92, 81416. T: (970) 874-0200. RV/tent: 51. $$. Hookups: electric (20, 30, 50 amp), water, sewer.

Riverwood Inn and RV Park, 677 Hwy. 50 North, 81416. T: (888) 213-2124 or (970) 874-5787. www.riverwoodn.com/rvpark.htm. RV/tent: 39. $. Hookups: electric (30, 50 amp), water, sewer, cable, phone.

Divide

Alpine Lakes Resort, 4145 Omer Rd., 80814. T: (719) 687-7337. RV/tent: 85. $$. Hookups: electric (20, 30, 50 amp), water.

Dolores

Dolores River RV Park & Cabins, 18680 Hwy. 145, 81323. T: (800) 200-2399 or (970) 882-7761. RV/tent: 81. $$. Hookups: electric (20, 30, 50 amp), water, sewer.

Groundhog Lake Fishing Camp & Outfitters, P.O. Box 27, 81323. T: (970) 882-4379. RV/tent: 10. $. Hookups: electric (20, 30 amp).

Outpost Motel Cabins & RV Park, 1800 Central Ave., 81323. T: (800) 382-4892 or (970) 882-7271. www.doloreslodging.com. RV/tent: 15. $$. Hookups: electric (30, 50 amp), water, sewer, cable.

Priest Gulch Campground & RV Park, 276 Hwy. 145, 81323. T: (970) 562-3810. www.priest gulch.com. RV/tent: 99. $$. Hookups: electric (20, 30, 50 amp), water, sewer.

Stoner Creek Cafe, Store, Cabins, & RV Park, 25113 Hwy. 145, 81323. T: (970) 882-2204. RV/tent: 28. $$. Hookups: electric (20, 30, 50 amp), water, sewer.

Durango

Alpen Rose RV Park, 27847 Hwy. 550 North, 81301. T: (877) 259-5791 or (970) 247-5540. www.alpenroservpark.com. RV/tent: 100. $$$. Hookups: electric (30, 50 amp), water, sewer.

Bueno Tiempo Ranch, 27846 Hwy. 550, 81301. T: (877) 247-9796 or (970) 247-9796. www.sun face.com/bueno. RV/tent: 118. $$. Hookups: electric (20, 30 amp), water.

Cottonwood Camper Park, 21636 US 160, 81303. T: (970) 247-1977. RV/tent: 75. $$. Hookups: electric (20, 30, 50 amp), water, sewer.

Durango North KOA, 13391 CR 250, 81301. T: (800) 562-2792 or (970) 247-4499. www.koa.com. RV/tent: 146. $$. Hookups: electric (30, 50 amp), water, sewer, cable.

Golden Terrace South, 17801 West Colfax, 80401. T: (303) 279-6279. RV/tent: 167. $$$. Hookups: electric (30, 50 amp), water, sewer.

Lightner Creek Campground, 1567 CR 207, 81301. T: (970) 247-5406. www.camplightnercreek.com. RV/tent: 97. $$. Hookups: electric (30 amp), water, sewer.

United Campground of Durango, 1322 Animas View Dr., 81301. T: (970) 247-3853. www.united campground.com. RV/tent: 193. $$. Hookups: electric (20, 30, 50 amp), water, sewer, cable.

Eagle

Elk Run Campground, 15000 Brush Creek Rd, 81631. T: (970) 328-2021. www.parks.state.co. us/default.asp?parkID=72&action=park. RV/tent: 34. $. Hookups: none.

Fishermans Paradise Campground, 15000 Brush Creek Rd., 81631. T: (970) 328-2021. www.parks.state.co.us/default.asp?parkID=72&a ction=park. RV/tent: 12. $$. Hookups: none.

Empire

Clear Creek Cabins & RV Park, 7364 US 40, 80438. T: (888) 428-9604 or (303) 569-3066. RV/tent: 9. $$. Hookups: electric (20, 30, 50 amp), water, sewer.

Mountain Meadow Campground, 11961 US 40, 80438. T: (877) 931-2500 or (303) 569-2424. RV/tent: 45. $$. Hookups: electric (20, 30 amp), water, sewer.

Englewood

Flying Saucer RV Park, 2500 West Hampden, 80110. T: (303) 789-1707. RV/tent: 150. $$$. Hookups: electric (20, 30, 50 amp), water, sewer.

Estes Park

Elk Meadow Lodge & RV Park, 1665 Colorado Hwy. 66, 80517. T: (800) 582-5342 or (970) 586-5342. www.elkmeadowrv.com. RV/tent: 170. $$. Hookups: electric (30, 50 amp), water, sewer, cable.

COLORADO (continued)

Estes Park Campground, 3420 Tunnel Rd., 80517. T: (888) 815-2029 or (970) 586-4188. www.estesparkcampground.com. RV/tent: 68. $$. Hookups: electric (20, 30 amp), water.

Manor RV Park & Motel, 815 East Riverside Dr., 80517. T: (800) 344-3256 or (970) 586-3251. www.campestespark.com. RV/tent: 110. $$$. Hookups: electric (20, 30 amp), water, sewer, cable.

Mary's Lake Campground & RV Park, 2120 Mary's Lake Rd., 80517. T: (800) 445-6279 or (970) 586-4411. www.maryslakecampground.com. RV/tent: 150. $$. Hookups: electric (20, 30, 50 amp), water, sewer, cable.

National Park Retreats Campground & Cabins, 3501 Fall River Rd., 80517. T: (970) 586-4563. www.natlparkresort.com. RV/tent: 100. $. Hookups: electric (20, 30 amp), water, sewer, cable.

Spruce Lake RV Park, 1050 Mary's Lake Rd., 80517. T: (970) 586-2889 or (800) 536-1050. www.sprucelakerv.com. RV/tent: 110. $$$. Hookups: electric (30 amp), water, sewer, cable.

Falcon

Falcon Meadow Campground, 11150 Hwy. 24, 80831. T: (719) 495-2694. www.falconmeadow rvcampground.com. RV/tent: 30. $. Hookups: electric (20, 30, 50 amp), water, sewer.

Fort Collins

Blue Spruce Mobile Home & RV Park, 2730 North Shields, 80524. T: (970) 221-3723. RV/tent: 14. $$. Hookups: electric (20, 30, 50 amp), water, sewer.

Heron Lake RV Park, 1910 North Taft Hill Rd., 80524. T: (970) 484-9880 or (877) 254-4063. www.heronlakerv.com. RV/tent: 190. $$. Hookups: electric (20, 30, 50 amp), water, sewer, phone, satellite.

Fort Garland

Ft. Collins KOA, 6670 North Hwy. 287, 80535. T: (970) 568-7486 or (800) 562-8142. www.koa.com. RV/tent: 59. $$. Hookups: electric (20, 30, 50 amp), water, sewer, cable, phone.

Ute Creek Campground, P.O. Box 188, 81133. T: (719) 379-3238. RV/tent: 44. $. Hookups: electric (20, 30 amp), water, sewer.

Glenwood Springs

Rock Gardens Campground, Rafting, & Jeep Tours, 1308 CR 129, 81601. T: (800) 958-6737 or (970) 945-6737. www.rockgardens.com. RV/tent: 77. $$. Hookups: electric (20, 30, 50 amp), water, sewer.

Golden

Dakota Ridge RV Park, 17800 West Colfax Ave., 80401. T: (800) 398-1625 or (303) 279-1625. www.dakotaridgerv.com. RV/tent: 141. $$$. Hookups: electric (20, 30, 50 amp), water, sewer.

Grand Junction

Big J RV Park, 2819 Hwy. 50, 81503. T: (970) 242-2527 or (877) 240-2527. RV/tent: 104. $$. Hookups: electric (30, 50 amp), water, sewer.

Junction West RV Park, 793-22 Rd., 81505. T: (970) 245-8531. RV/tent: 55. $$. Hookups: electric (30, 50 amp), water, sewer.

Mobile City RV Home Park, 2322 Hwys. 6 and 50, 81505. T: (970) 242-9291. RV/tent: 90. $$. Hookups: electric (30, 50 amp), water, sewer.

Grand Lake

Winding River Resort Village & Snowmobiling, 1447 CR 491, 80447. T: (800) 282-5121 or (970) 627-3215. www.windingriverresort.com. RV/tent: 150. $$. Hookups: electric (30 amp), water, sewer.

Green Mountain Falls

Rocky Top Motel and Campground, 10090 West Hwy. 24, 80819. T: (719) 684-9044 or (866) 900-9044. RV/tent: 75. $$. Hookups: electric (20, 30, 50 amp), water, sewer.

Gunnison

Gunnison Lakeside Resort, 28357 Hwy. 50 West, 81230. T: (877) 641-0488 or (970) 641-0477. www.gunnisonlakeside.com. RV/tent: 43. $$. Hookups: electric (20, 30, 50 amp), water, sewer, phone.

Mesa Campground, 36128 West Hwy. 50, 81230. T: (970) 641-3186 or (800) 482-8384. www.gunnison-co.com/main/lodging/mesa.htm. RV/tent: 116. $$. Hookups: electric (30, 50 amp), water, sewer.

Rockey River Resort, 4359 CR 10, 81230. T: (970) 641-0174. RV/tent: 26. $$. Hookups: electric (20, 30 amp), water, sewer.

Shady Island Resort Cabins & RV Park, 2776 Hwy. 135 North, 81230. T: (970) 641-0416. RV/tent: 40. $$. Hookups: electric (20, 30 amp), water, sewer.

Tall Texan Campground, 194 CR 11, 81230. T: (970) 641-2927. RV/tent: 116. $$. Hookups: electric (20, 30 amp), water, sewer.

Hayden

Juniper Springs Campground, Yampa River State Park, I-40 and SR 13, 81639. T: (970) 276-2061. www.parks.state.co.us/Yampa. RV/tent: 6. $. Hookups: none.

Maybell Bridge Campground, US 40, 81639. T: (970) 276-2061. www.parks.state.co.us. RV/tent: 5. $$. Hookups: none.

The Elks Campground, Yampa River State Park, I-40 and SR 13, 81639. T: (970) 276-2061. www.parks.state.co.us. RV/tent: 15. $$. Hookups: none.

Yampa River State Park Headquarters, P.O. Box 759, 81639. T: (970) 276-2061. www.parks.state.co.us. RV/tent: 35. $$. Hookups: electric (30 amp).

Hooper

UFO Watchtower & Campground, P.O. Box 583, 81136. T: (719) 378-2271. www.ufowatchtower.com. RV/tent: 24. $. Hookups: electric (20, 30 amp), water, sewer.

Hotchkiss

Clear Fork Campground, Crawford State Park, Hwy. 92, 1 mile south of Crawford, 81415.

T: (970) 921-5721. www.parks.state.co.us/crawford. RV/tent: 16. $. Hookups: none.

Iron Creek Campground, Crawford State Park, Hwy. 92, 1 mile south of Crawford, 81415. T: (970) 921-5721. www.parks.state.co.us. RV/tent: 16. $. Hookups: electric (30 amp).

Howard

Pleasant Valley RV Park of Howard, 0018 CR 47, 81233. T: (719) 942-3484. RV/tent: 61. $$. Hookups: electric (20, 30, 50 amp), water, sewer.

Idaho Springs

Cottonwood RV Park, 1485 Hwy. 103, 80452. T: (303) 567-2617. RV/tent: 20. $$. Hookups: electric (20, 30, 50 amp), water, sewer.

Indian Springs Resort & Campground, P.O. Box 1990, 80452. T: (303) 989-6666. www.indian springsresort.com. RV/tent: 32. $$. Hookups: electric (20, 30 amp), water.

La Jara

Aspen Glade, Conejos Peak Rd., 81140. T: (719) 852-5941. www.reserveusa.com/nrrs/co/asgl. RV/tent: 34. $$. Hookups: none.

La Veta

Bearadise Cabins & RV Park, 404 South Oak, 81055. T: (719) 742-6221. www.bearadisecabins .com. RV/tent: 12. $$. Hookups: electric (20, 30 amp), water, sewer.

Elk Valley RV Park & Fly Shop, 5535 Hwy. 12, 81055. T: (866) 733-5533. www.colorado directory.com/elkvalley. RV/tent: 24. $$. Hookups: electric (50 amp), water, sewer.

Lake City

Castle Lakes Campground Resort & Cabins, CR 30, 81235. T: (800) 862-6166 or (970) 944-2622. www.coloradodirectory.com/castlelakeresort. RV/tent: 51. $$. Hookups: electric (30 amp), water, sewer.

Highlander RV Campground, Complete Jeep Rentals & Gifts, 3445 CR 30, 81235. T: (888) 580-4636 or (970) 944-2878. www.ithat.com/ highlandercampground.htm. RV/tent: 28. $$. Hookups: electric (20, 30, 50 amp), water, sewer.

Woodlake Park Campground & Cabins, P.O. Box 400, 81235. T: (800) 201-2694 or (970) 944-2283 (June–Sept) or (817) 536-4079 (Oct–May). www.coloradodirectory.com/woodlakeparkcamp. RV/tent: 25. $$. Hookups: electric (30, 50 amp), water, sewer.

Lake George

Lake George Cabins & RV Park, 8966 CR 90, 80827. T: (719) 748-3822. www.coloradodirectory .com/lakegcabinsrv. RV/tent: 13. $$. Hookups: electric (20, 30 amp), water, sewer.

Lamar

Lamar Country Acres, 29151 US 28, 81052. T: (719) 336-1031. www.lamarcountryacres.com. RV/tent: 8. $$. Hookups: electric (20, 30, 50 amp), water, sewer, cable.

Leadville

Baby Doe, Turquoise Lake, 80461. T: (877) 444-6777. www.reserveamerica.com. RV/tent: 50. $$. Hookups: none.

COLORADO (continued)

Leadville (continued)

Sugar Loafin' RV Park and Campground, 303 Hwy. 300, 80461. T: (719) 486-1013. www.leadville.com/sugarloafin. RV/tent: 98. $$. Hookups: electric (20, 30, 50 amp), water, sewer.

Loma

Bookcliff Campground, Highline Lake State Park, Off of Q Rd. on 11.8 Rd., 81524. T: (970) 858-7208. www.parks.state.co.us. RV/tent: 30. $. Hookups: none.

Longmont

Westwood Inn Motel & Campground, 1550 North Main, 80501. T: (303) 776-2185. RV/tent: 20. $$. Hookups: electric (20, 30, 50 amp), water, sewer.

Loveland

Fireside RV Park & Cabins, 6850 West Hwy. 34, 80537. T: (970) 667-2903. www.colorado directory.com/firesidervpark. RV/tent: 36. $$. Hookups: electric (30, 50 amp), water, sewer.

Loveland RV Village, 4421 East Hwy. 34, 80537. T: (970) 667-1204 or (888) 571-3350. www.lovelandrvcampground.com. RV/tent: 210. $$. Hookups: electric (30, 50 amp), water, sewer, cable.

Riverview RV Park & Campground, 7806 West Hwy. 34, 80537. T: (800) 447-9910 or (970) 667-9910. www.coloradodirectory.com/riverview camp. RV/tent: 160. $$. Hookups: electric (20, 30, 50 amp), water, sewer.

Lyons

Stone Mountain Lodge & Cabins, 18055 North St. Vrain Dr., 80540. T: (800) 282-5612 or (303) 823-6091. www.stonemountainlodge.com. RV/tent: 16. $$. Hookups: electric (20, 30 amp).

Mancos

A & A Mesa Verde RV Park, 34979 Hwy. 160, 81328. T: (800) 972-6620. www.mesaverdecamp ing.com. RV/tent: 75. $$. Hookups: electric (30, 50 amp), water, sewer.

Echo Basin Guest Ranch Resort & RV Park, 43747 Rd. M, 81328. T: (800) 426-1890 or (970) 533-7000. www.coloradodirectory.com/echobasin ranch. RV/tent: 75. $$. Hookups: electric (20, 30, 50 amp), water, sewer.

Mancos State Park, 42545 CRN 81328. T: (970) 883-2213 or (970) 533-7065. www.parks.state. co.us. RV/tent: 33. $. Hookups: none.

Morefield Campground in Mesa Verde, P.O. Box 277, 81328. T: (800) 449-2288. www.visitmesa verde.com. RV/tent: 440. $$. Hookups: electric (20, 30 amp), water, sewer.

Marble

Meri Daes RV Park, 220 West Park, 81623. T: (970) 963-1831 (June–Sept) or (303) 756-0566 (Oct–May). www.coloradodirectory.com/ meridaesrvpark. RV/tent: 15. $$. Hookups: electric (20, 30 amp), water.

Meeker

Buford Hunting & Fishing Lodge Store Horse Boarding & Chuckwagon, 20474 CR 8, 81641. T: (970) 878-4745. www.coloradodirectory.com/ bufordlodge. RV/tent: 4. $$. Hookups: electric (20, 30 amp), water.

North Fork Campground and Group Site, CR 8, 81641. T: (970) 878-4039. www.reserveusa.com/ nrrs/co/nor2. RV/tent: 40. $$. Hookups: none.

Ute Lodge, 393 RBC 75, 81641. T: (888) 414-2022 or (970) 878-4669. www.utelodge.com. RV/tent: 12. $$. Hookups: electric (20, 30, 50 amp), water, sewer.

Mesa

Sundance RV Camp & Cabins, 11674 Hwy. 65, 81643. T: (970) 268-5651. www.colorado directory.com/sundancervcamp. RV/tent: 37. $$. Hookups: electric (20, 30, 50 amp), water, sewer.

Montrose

Cedar Creek RV Park & Mini Golf, 126 Rose Ln., 81401. T: (877) 425-3884 or (970) 249-3884. www.cedarcreekrv.com. RV/tent: 47. $$. Hookups: electric (20, 30, 50 amp), water, sewer.

Hangin Tree RV Park Campground Convenience Store & Gas, 17250 Hwy. 550 South, 81401. T: (888) 657-4131. www.coloradodirectory.com/ hangintree. RV/tent: 31. $$. Hookups: electric (20, 30, 50 amp), water, sewer.

King's River Bend RV Park, 65100 Old Chipeta Tr., 81401. T: (970) 249-8235. www.colorado directory.com/riverbendrv. RV/tent: 70. $$. Hookups: electric (20, 30, 50 amp), water, sewer.

Monument

Lake of the Rockies Retreat Camping & Cabin Resort, 99 Mitchell Ave., 80132. T: (800) 429-4228 or (719) 481-4227. www.lakeoftherockies.com. RV/tent: 235. $$. Hookups: electric (20, 30, 50 amp), water, sewer.

Mosca

Great Sand Dunes Oasis, 5400 Hwy. 150 North, 81146. T: (719) 378-2222. www.colorado directory.com/greatsanddunesoasis. RV/tent: 90. $. Hookups: electric (20, 30, 50 amp), water, sewer.

Nathrop

Chalk Creek Campground, 11430 CR 197, 81236. T: (800) 643-9727 or (719) 395-8301. www.coloradodirectory.com/chalkcreekcamp. RV/tent: 77. $$. Hookups: electric (20, 30, 50 amp), water, sewer.

New Castle

New Castle/Glenwood Springs KOA, 0581 CR 241, 81647. T: (800) 562-3240 or (970) 984-2240. www.koa.com/where/co/06122.htm. RV/tent: 57. $$. Hookups: electric (20, 30, 50 amp), water, sewer.

Oak Creek

Harding Spur Campground, Stagecoach State Park, 25500 R CR 14, 80467. T: (970) 736-2436. www .parks.state.co.us. RV/tent: 18. $. Hookups: none.

Junction City Campground, Stagecoach State Park, 25500 R CR 14, 80467. T: (970) 736-2436. www.parks.state.co.us. RV/tent: 26. $$. Hookups: electric (30 amp).

Pinnacle Campground, Stagecoach State Park, 25500 R CR 14, 80467. T: (970) 736-2436. www.parks.state.co.us. RV/tent: 36. $$. Hookups: electric (30 amp).

Ohio City

Rowe's RV Park Gun Shop & 1886 Gen'l Store, P.O. Box 61, 81237. T: (970) 641-4272. RV/tent: 8. $. Hookups: electric (20, 30, 50 amp), water, sewer.

Orchard

Dunes Campground, Jackson Lake State Park, 26363 CR 3, 80649. T: (970) 645-2551. www.parks.state.co.us/default.asp?parkID=65& action=park. RV/tent: 18. $$. Hookups: electric.

Foxhills Campground, Jackson Lake State Park, 26363 CR 3, 80649. T: (970) 645-2551. www.parks.state.co.us/default.asp?park ID=65&action=park. RV/tent: 89. $$. Hookups: electric.

Lakeside Campground, Jackson Lake State Park, 26363 CR 3, 80649. T: (970) 645-2551. www.parks.state.co.us/default.asp?parkID=65&a ction=park. RV/tent: 58. $$. Hookups: electric.

Northview Campground, Jackson Lake State Park, 26363 CR 3, 80649. T: (970) 645-2551. www.parks.state.co.us/default.asp?parkID=65& action=park. RV/tent: 10. $$. Hookups: electric (30 amp).

Pelican Campground, Jackson Lake State Park, 26363 CR 3, 80649. T: (970) 645-2551. www.parks.state.co.us/default.asp?park ID=65&action=park. RV/tent: 37. $$. Hookups: electric.

Sandpiper Campground, Jackson Lake State Park, 26363 CR 3, 80649. T: (970) 645-2551. www.parks.state.co.us/default.asp?park ID=65&action=park. RV/tent: 28. $. Hookups: electric (30 amp).

Ouray

Ouray KOA, P.O. Box J, 81427. T: (800) 562-8026 or (970) 325-4736. www.koa.com/where/ co/06158.htm. RV/tent: 123. $$. Hookups: electric (20, 30, 50 amp), water, sewer.

Pagosa Springs

160 West Adult RV Park, P.O. Box 28, 81147. T: (970) 264-5873. www.coloradodirectory.com/ 160west. RV/tent: 28. $$. Hookups: electric (20, 30, 50 amp), water, sewer.

Acres Green RV Park, 10 Leisure Ct., 81147. T: (888) 724-6727 or (970) 264-9264. www.acresgreenrvpark.com. RV/tent: 20. $$. Hookups: electric (30, 50 amp), water, sewer.

Blanco River RV Park, 97 Leisure Ct., 81147. T: (800) 280-9429 or (970) 264-5547. www.coloradodirectory.com/blancoriverrvpark. RV/tent: 64. $$. Hookups: electric (20, 30, 50 amp), water, sewer.

Elk Meadows Campground, P.O. Box 238, 81147. T: (970) 264-5482 or (866) 264-5482. www.elk meadowresort.com. RV/tent: 35. $$. Hookups: electric (20, 30, 50 amp), water, sewer.

Happy Camper RV Park & Cabin, 9260 West Hwy. 160, 81147. T: (970) 731-5822. www.coloradodi rectory.com/happycamper.com. RV/tent: 60. $$. Hookups: electric (20, 30, 50 amp), water, sewer.

Hide-A-Way RV Park & Campground, 8880 West Hwy. 160, 81147. T: (970) 731-5112. RV/tent: 40. $. Hookups: electric (20, 30, 50 amp), water, sewer.

COLORADO (continued)

Pagosa Riverside Campground & Camper Cabins, P.O. Box 268, 81147. T: (888) 785-3234 or (970) 264-5874. www.coloradodirectory.com/pagosa riversidecamp. RV/tent: 87. $$. Hookups: electric (20, 30 amp), water, sewer.

Sportsman's Supply Campground & Cabins, 2095 Taylor Ln., 81147. T: (970) 731-2300. www.coloradodirectory.com/sportsmanssupply camp. RV/tent: 40. $$. Hookups: electric (20, 30 amp), water, sewer.

The Spa at Pagosa Springs, Destination Spa, & RV Resort, 317 Hot Springs Blvd., 81147. T: (800) 832-5523 or (970) 264-5910. www.thespaat pagosasprings.com. RV/tent: 8. $$$. Hookups: electric (20, 30, 50 amp), water, sewer.

Paonia

Redwood Arms Motel & RV Park, 1478 Hwy. 133, 81428. T: (970) 527-4148. www.colorado directory.com/redwoodarms. RV/tent: 20. $$. Hookups: electric (20, 30, 50 amp), water, sewer.

Parlin

7-11 Ranch, 5291 CR 76, 81239. T: (970) 641-0666. www.coloradodirectory.com/711ranch. RV/tent: 11. $. Hookups: electric (20, 30, 50 amp), water, sewer.

Penrose

Floyd's RV Park, 1438 Hwy. 50, 81240. T: (719) 372-3385. www.coloradodirectory.com/floydsrvpark. RV/tent: 47. $. Hookups: electric (20, 30 amp), water, sewer.

Piru

Green Ridge, P.O. Box 249, 93040. T: (970) 887-4100. www.reserveusa.com/nrrs/co/grer. RV/tent: 78. $$. Hookups: none.

Pueblo

Arkansas Point Campground, Lake Pueblo State Park, 640 Pueblo Reservoir Rd., 81005. T: (719) 561-9320. www.parks.state.co.us/default .asp?parkID=85&action=park. RV/tent: 95. $. Hookups: electric (30 amp).

Fort's RV Park, 3015 Lake Ave., 81004. T: (719) 564-2327. www.coloradodirectory.com/fortsrvpark. RV/tent: 55. $$$. Hookups: electric (20, 30, 50 amp), water, sewer.

Fowler RV Park, P.O. Box 306, 81039. T: (719) 263-4287. www.coloradodirectory.com/fowlerrv park. RV/tent: 41. $. Hookups: electric (20, 30 amp), water, sewer.

Haggard's RV Campground, 7910 West Hwy. 50, 81007. T: (719) 547-2101. www.colorado directory.com/haggardsrvcamp. RV/tent: 180. $$. Hookups: electric (20, 30 amp), water, sewer.

Juniper Breaks Campground, Lake Pueblo State Park, 640 Pueblo Reservoir Rd., 81005. T: (719) 561-9320. www.parks.state.co.us/default. asp?parkID=85&action=park. RV/tent: 84. $. Hookups: electric.

Kettle Creek Campground, Lake Pueblo State Park, 640 Pueblo Reservoir Rd., 81005. T: (719) 561-9320. www.parks.state.co.us/default.asp parkID=85&action=park. RV/tent: 34. $. Hookups: none.

Prairie Ridge Campground, Lake Pueblo State Park, 640 Pueblo Reservoir Rd., 81005. T: (719) 561-9320. www.parks.state.co.us/default.asp ?parkID=85&action=park. RV/tent: 83. $. Hookups: electric (30 amp).

Pueblo South/Colorado City KOA, 9040 I-25 South, 81004. T: (800) 562-8646 or (719) 676-3376. www.koa.com/where/co/06105.htm. RV/tent: 82. $$. Hookups: electric (30, 50 amp), water, sewer.

Pueblo West Campground, Cabins, & Arena, 480 East McCulloch Blvd., 81007. T: (877) 547-7070 or (719) 547-9887. www.coloradodirectory. com/pueblowest. RV/tent: 63. $$. Hookups: electric (20, 30, 50 amp), water, sewer.

Yucca Flats Campground, Lake Pueblo State Park, 640 Pueblo Reservoir Rd., 81005. T: (719) 561-9320. www.parks.state.co.us/default.asp parkID=85&action=park. RV/tent: 86. $. Hookups: electric (30 amp).

Red Feather Lakes

Alpine Lodge, 157 Prairie Divide Rd., 80545. T: (970) 881-2933. RV/tent: 10. $. Hookups: electric (20, 30 amp), water, sewer.

Rye

Lodge at San Isabel RV Park & General Store, 59 CR 371, 81069. T: (719) 489-2280 (lodge) or (719) 489-2601 (store). www.colorado directory.com/lodgesanisabel. RV/tent: 13. $$. Hookups: electric (20, 30 amp), water, sewer.

Salida

Five Points Campground, Arkansas Headwaters Recreation Area, US 50, Mile Marker 260, 81201. T: (719) 539-7289. www.parks.state.co .us/default.asppparkID=96&action=park. RV/tent: 20. $. Hookups: none.

Heart of the Rockies RV & Tent Campground, 16105 Hwy. 50, 81201. T: (800) 496-2245 or (719) 539-4051. RV/tent: 65. $$. Hookups: electric (20, 30 amp), water, sewer.

Hecla Junction Campground, Arkansas Headwaters Recreation Area, CR 194, 81201. T: (719) 539-7289. www.parks.state.co.us/default.asp parkID=96&action=park. RV/tent: 22. $. Hookups: none.

Monarch Spur RV Park and Campground, 18989 West Hwy. 50, 81201. T: (719) 530-0341 or (888) 814-3001. www.monarchspurrvpark.com. RV/tent: 49. $$. Hookups: electric (20, 30, 50 amp), water, sewer.

Railroad Bridge Campground, Arkansas Headwaters Recreation Area, CR 371, 81201. T: (719) 539-7289. www.parks.state.co.us/default .asppparkID=96&action=park. RV/tent: 14. $. Hookups: none.

Rincon Campground, Arkansas Headwaters Recreation Area, US 50, Mile Marker 231, 81201. T: (719) 539-7289. www.parks.state.co.us/ default.asp?parkID=96&action=park. RV/tent: 5. $. Hookups: none.

Ruby Mountain Campground, Arkansas Headwaters Recreation Area, CR 300, 81201. T: (719) 539-7289. www.parks.state.co.us/default.asp parkID=96&action=park. RV/tent: 22. $. Hookups: none.

Silt

Viking RV Park & Campground, 32958 River Frontage Rd., 81652. T: (970) 876-2443. www.coloradodirectory.com/vikingrvpark. RV/tent: 77. $$. Hookups: electric (20, 30, 50 amp), water, sewer.

Silverton

Molas Lake Camping Stables & Snowmobile Tours, P.O. Box 776, 81433. T: (970) 759-5557 or (800) 752-4494. www.coloradodirectory.com/ molaslakecamp. RV/tent: 60. $$. Hookups: electric (20, 30 amp), water, sewer.

Red Mountain Motel, RV Park, Cabin, & Jeep Rental, 664 Greene St., 81433. T: (888) 970-5512 or (970) 387-5512. www.redmtmotelrvpark.com. RV/tent: 25. $$. Hookups: electric (20, 30, 50 amp), water, sewer.

Silverton Lakes Campground, P.O. Box 126, 81433. T: (970) 387-5721. www.gimi.com/silverton-lakes. RV/tent: 75. $$. Hookups: electric (20, 30, 50 amp), water, sewer.

Somerset

Crystal Meadows Resort, 30682. CR 12, 81434. T: (970) 929-5656 or (877) 886-9678. www.crystalmeadowsresort.com. RV/tent: 23. $. Hookups: electric (30, 50 amp), water, sewer.

South Fork

Aspen Ridge Cabins & RV Park, 0710 West Hwy. 149, 81154. T: (719) 873-5921. www.aspenridge colorado.com. RV/tent: 40. $$. Hookups: electric (30 amp), water, sewer.

Blue Creek Lodge, Cabins, RV Park, & Campground, 11682 Hwy. 149, 81154. T: (800) 326-6408 or (719) 658-2479. www.coloradodirectory.com/ bluecreeklodge. RV/tent: 31. $$. Hookups: electric (30, 50 amp), water, sewer.

Budget Hostó Ute Bluff Lodge, Cabins, Motel, & RV Park, 27680 West Hwy. 160, 81154. T: (719) 873-5595 or (800) 473-0595. www.utebflodge.com. RV/tent: 38. $$. Hookups: electric (30, 50 amp), water, sewer.

Chinook Lodge, Cabins, Smokehouse, RV Park, & Trail Rides, 29666 West US 160, 81154. T: (888) 890-9110 or (719) 873-1707. www.colorado directory.com/chinooklodge. RV/tent: 20. $$. Hookups: electric (20, 30, 50 amp), water.

Cottonwood Cove, 13046 Hwy. 149, 81154. T: (719) 658-2242. www.cottonwoodcove.com. RV/tent: 41. $$. Hookups: electric (20, 30, 50 amp), water, sewer.

Goodnight's Lonesome Dove Cabins & RVs, Hwy. 160, 81154. T: (800) 551-3683 or (719) 873-1072. www.coloradodirectory.com/goodnight cabins. RV/tent: 44. $$. Hookups: electric (20, 30 amp), water, sewer.

Moon Valley Ranch Resort Campground & Guided Fishing & Hunting, Hwy. 160 West, 81154. T: (719) 873-5216. www2.amigo.net/ wilderness-adv. RV/tent: 61. $$. Hookups: electric (20, 30 amp), water, sewer.

Rainbow Lodge Cabins & RV Park, 30359 West Hwy. 160, 81154. T: (888) 873-5174 or (719) 873-5571. www.rainbowsouthfork.biz. RV/tent: 24. $$. Hookups: electric (20, 30 amp), water, sewer.

COLORADO (continued)

South Fork (continued)

Riverbend Resort Cabins & RV Park, P.O. Box 1270, 81154. T: (800) 621-6512 or (719) 873-5344. www.riverbend-resort.com. RV/tent: 57. $$. Hookups: electric (20, 30 amp), water, sewer.

Steamboat Springs

Hahns Peak Lake, USFS 486, 80487. T: (970) 870-2161. www.reserveamerica.com. RV/tent: 26. $. Hookups: none.

Sterling

Chimney Grove Campground, North Sterling State Park, 24005 CR 330, 80751. T: (970) 522-3657. www.parks.state.co.us. RV/tent: 44. $. Hookups: none.

Elks Campground, North Sterling State Park, 24005 CR 330, 80751. T: (970) 522-3657. www.parks.state.co.us. RV/tent: 50. $$. Hookups: electric (30 amp).

Inlet Grove Campground, North Sterling State Park, 24005 CR 330, 80751. T: (970) 522-3657. www.parks.state.co.us. RV/tent: 47. $$. Hookups: electric (30 amp).

Strasburg

Denver East/Strasburg KOA, Exit 310/Frontage Rd., 80136. T: (800) 562-6538 or (303) 622-9274. www.koa.com. RV/tent: 75. $$. Hookups: electric (20, 30, 50 amp), water, sewer.

Stratton

Marshall Ash Village RV Park, 818 Colorado Ave., 80836. T: (800) 577-5795 or (719) 348-5141. RV/tent: 33. $$. Hookups: electric (30, 50 amp), water, sewer.

Texas Creek

Whispering Pines Resort, 24871 Hwy. 50 West, 81223. T: (888) 275-3827 or (719) 275-3827.

www.coloradodirectory.com/whisperingpines resort. RV/tent: 118. $. Hookups: electric (20, 30 amp), water, sewer.

Trinidad

Budget Hostó Derrick RV Park & Motel, 10301 Santa Fe Trail Dr., 81082. T: (719) 846-3307. www.coloradodirectory.com/budgethostrvpark. RV/tent: 18. $$. Hookups: electric (20, 30, 50 amp), water, sewer.

Carpios Ridge Campground, Trinidad Lake State Park, 32610 Hwy. 12, 81082. T: (719) 846-6951. www.parks.state.co.us. RV/tent: 62. $. Hookups: electric (30 amp).

Walden

Bockman Campground, 56750 Hwy. 14, 80480. T: (970) 723-8366. www.parks.state.co.us. RV/tent: 52. $. Hookups: none.

CONNECTICUT

Bantam

Looking Glass Hill Campgrounds, 14 Cozy Hill, 06750. T: (860) 567-2050. RV/tent: 50. $$. Hookups: electric, water.

Bozrah

Odetah, 38 Bozrah St., 06334. T: (860) 889-4144. RV/tent: 250. $$. Hookups: electric, water, sewer

Chaplin

Nickerson Park Family Campground, 1036 Phoenixville Rd., 06235. T: (860) 455-0007. www.nickersonpark.com. RV/tent: 150. $$. Hookups: electric, water, sewer, cable, phone.

Clinton

River Road Campsites, 13 River Rd., 06413. T: (860) 669-2956. RV/tent: 50. $$. Hookups: electric, water.

Riverdale Farm Campsites, 111 River Rd., 06413. T: (860) 669-5388. RV/tent: 250. $$$. Hookups: electric, water, sewer.

Cornwall Bridge

Housatonic Meadows State Park, Rte. 7, 06754. T: (860) 676-6772. RV/tent: 95. $$. Hookups: none.

Deep River

Dale River Campsites, River Rd., 06417. T: (860) 669-5388. RV/tent: 96. $$$. Hookups: electric (30, 50 amp), water, sewer, cable.

East Hampton

Nelson's Family Campground, 71 Mott Hill Rd., 06424. T: (860) 267-5300. www.nelsonscamp ground.com. RV/tent: 270. $$$. Hookups: electric (30, 50 amp), water, sewer, cable, phone.

East Killingly

Stateline Camp Resort, Rte. 101, 06243. T: (860) 774-3016. www.resortcamplands.com. RV/tent: 226. $$. Hookups: electric, water, sewer, phone.

Eastford

Silvermine Horse Camp, Pilfershire Rd., 06242. T: (860) 974-1562. RV/tent: 15. $. Hookups: none.

Goshen

Mohawk Campground, 708 Sharon Turnpike, 06756. T: (860) 491-2231. RV/tent: 80. $$. Hookups: electric, water.

Valley in the Pines Campground, Lucas Rd., 06756. T: (860) 491-2032. RV/tent: 35. $$. Hookups: electric, water, sewer.

Higganum

Little City Campground, 741 Little City Rd., 06438. T: (860) 345-8469. RV/tent: 50. $$$. Hookups: electric (15, 30 amp), water, sewer.

Jewett City

Ross Hill Park, 170 Ross Hill Rd., 06351. T: (860) 376-9606. RV/tent: 250. $$$. Hookups: electric, water, sewer, cable.

Kent

Treetops Camp Resort, Spectacle Lake, 06757. T: (860) 927-3555. RV/tent: 262. $$. Hookups: electric, water, sewer.

Lebanon

Water's Edge Family Campground, 271 Leonard Bridge Rd., 06249. T: (860) 642-7470. RV/tent: 200. $$. Hookups: electric, water, cable.

Litchfield

White Memorial Campground, P.O. Box 368, 06759. T: (860) 567-0069. RV/tent: 65. $. Hookups: none.

North Grosvenor

West Thompson Lake Campground, 449 Reardon Rd., 06255. T: (203) 923-2982. www.nae.usace .army.mil/recreati/wtl/wtlcamp.htm. RV/tent: 22. $. Hookups: electric, water.

Oakdale

Laurel-Lock Campgrounds, 15 Cottage Rd., 06370. T: (860) 859-1424. RV/tent: 130. $$. Hookups: electric, water, sewer, cable.

Pequot Ledge Campgrounds, 157 Doyle Rd., 06370. T: (860) 859-0682. RV/tent: 92. $$$. Hookups: electric, water, sewer.

Oneco

River Bend Campground, Rte. 14A, 06373. T: (860) 564-3440. www.riverbendcamp.com. RV/tent: 160. $$$. Hookups: electric, water, sewer.

Preston

Strawberry Park Resort Campground, 42 Pierce Rd., 06365. T: (860) 886-1944. RV/tent: 440. $$$$. Hookups: electric, water, sewer.

Salem

Salem Farms Campground Inc., 39 Alexander Rd., 06420. T: (860) 859-2320 or (800) 479-9238. www.salemfarmscampground.com. RV/tent: 191. $$$. Hookups: electric (30 amp), water, sewer.

Witch Meadow Lake Campsites, 139 Witch Meadow Rd., 06420. T: (860) 859-1542. RV/tent: 280. $$. Hookups: electric, water, sewer.

Stafford Springs

Mineral Springs Family Campground, 135 Leonard Rd., 06076. T: (860) 684-2993. RV/tent: 150. $$. Hookups: electric, water.

Sterling

Sterling Park Campground, 177 Gibson Hill Rd., 06377. T: (860) 564-8777. RV/tent: 100. $$. Hookups: electric, water, sewer, cable.

Thomaston

Black Rock State Park, Rte. 6, 06787. T: (860) 283-8088. RV/tent: 96. $. Hookups: none.

CONNECTICUT (continued)

Voluntown

Frog Hollow Horse Camp, RFD 1, 06384. T: (860) 376-4075. RV/tent: 18. $. Hookups: electric, water, sewer.

Green Falls Campground, Pachaug State Forest, 06384. T: (860) 376-4075. RV/tent: 18. $$. Hookups: electric, water, sewer.

Mt. Misery Campground, Pachaug State Forest, 06384. T: (860) 376-4075. RV/tent: 22. $. Hookups: electric, water, sewer.

Nature's Campsite, Rte. 49, 06384. T: (860) 376-4203. RV/tent: 185. $$. Hookups: electric, water, sewer.

Wethersfield

Roaring Brook, 308 Silas Deane Hwy., 06109. T: (860) 563-2199. RV/tent: 400. $. Hookups: electric, water, sewer.

Willington

Moosemeadow Camping Resort, 28 Kechkes Rd., 06279. T: (860) 429-7451. RV/tent: 100. $$$.

Hookups: electric (20, 30 amp), water, sewer, cable.

Rainbow Acres Family Campground, 166 Village Hill Rd., 06279. T: (860) 684-5704. RV/tent: 135. $$. Hookups: electric, water.

Woodstock

Solair Family Nudist Campground, 65 Ide Perrin Rd., 06281. T: (860) 928-9174. www.solairrl.com. RV/tent: 140. $$. Hookups: electric, water.

DELAWARE

Fenwick Island

Lost Lands RV Park, Bearhole Rd., 19975. T: (302) 436-9450 or (302) 242-8912. www.lostlandsrvpark.com. RV/tent: 66. $$$. Hookups: electric, water, sewer.

Houston

G & R Campground, 4075 Gun and Rod Club Rd., 19954. T: (302) 398-8108. www.gnrcampground.com. RV/tent: 190. $$. Hookups: electric (30, 50 amp), water, sewer.

Lincoln

Pine Haven Campground, Pine Haven Trailer Park, 19963. T: (302) 422-7117. RV/tent: 140. $$. Hookups: electric (20, 30 amp), water.

Long Neck

Leisure Point Resort, Box A-1 Leisure Point, 19966. T: (302) 945-2000. www.leisurepoint.com. RV/tent: 319. $$$$. Hookups: electric, water, sewer.

Millsboro

Shawn's Hideaway Trailer, RR 24, 19966. T: (302) 945-3133. RV/tent: 120. $$$. Hookups: electric (20, 30 amp), water.

Milton

Eagles Nest Family Campground, Rtes. 1 & 16, 19968. T: (302) 684-4031. RV/tent: 67. $$. Hookups: electric (20, 30 amp), water.

Pine Tree Campsites, RR 1 Box 331, 19970. T: (302) 539-7006. RV/tent: 115. $$. Hookups: electric (20, 30 amp), water, sewer.

Ocean View

Ocean View Bayshore RV Campground, RR 1 Box 252, 19970. T: (302) 539-7200. www.bayshorecampground.com. RV/tent: 324. $$$. Hookups: electric (30 amp), water, sewer.

FLORIDA

Alligator Point

KOA Alligator Point Kampground Resort, 1320 Alligator Dr., 32346. T: (850) 349-2525 or (800) 562-0848. www.alligatorpointkoa.com. RV/tent: 148. $$$. Hookups: electric (30, 50 amp), water, sewer.

Arcadia

Lettuce Lake Travel Resort, 8644 SW Reese St., 34269. T: (863)-494-6057. www.lettucelake.com. RV/tent: 250. $$. Hookups: electric (30, 50 amp), water, sewer, phone.

Riverside RV Resort and Campground, 9770 SW CR 769 (Kings Hwy.), 34269. T: (863) 993-2111 or (800) 795-9733. www.riversidervresort.com. RV/tent: 250. $$. Hookups: electric (30, 50 amp), water, sewer, phone.

Astor

St. Johns River Campground, 1520 SR 40, 32102. T: (386) 749-3995. www.stjohnsrivercampground.com. RV/tent: 85. $$. Hookups: electric (20, 30, 50 amp), water, sewer.

Big Pine Key

Bahia Honda State Park, 36850 Overseas Hwy., 33043. T: (305) 872-2353 or (800) 326-3521. www.bahiahondapark.com. RV/tent: 80. $$. Hookups: electric, water, dump station.

Big Pine Key Fishing Lodge, 33000 Overseas Hwy., 33043. T: (305) 872-2351. RV/tent: 155. $$$$. Hookups: electric (30 amp), water, sewer, solar, cable.

Bokeelia

Tropic Isle RV Park, 15175 Stringfellow Rd. NW (CR 767), 33922. T: (239) 283-4456. RV/tent: 55. $$$$. Hookups: electric (20, 30 amp), water, sewer.

Bradenton

Encore RV Resort–Sarasota North, 800 Kay Rd. NE, 34202. T: (941) 745-2600 or (800) 678-2131. www.rvonthego.com. RV/tent: 415. $$$. Hookups: electric (30, 50 amp), water, sewer, cable, phone.

Pleasant Lake RV Resort, 6653 53rd Ave. East, 34203. T: (941) 756-5076 or (800) 283-5076. www.pleasantlakervresort.com. RV/tent: 343. $$$. Hookups: electric (30, 50 amp), water, sewer, cable, phone.

Cape Canaveral

Mango Manor, 190 Oak Manor Dr., 32920. T: (321) 799-0741. RV/tent: 51. $$. Hookups: electric (20, 30, 50 amp), water, sewer, cable, phone.

Carrabelle

Ho-Hum RV Park, 2132 Hwy. 98E, 32322. T: (850) 697-3926 or (888) 884-6486. www.hohorvpark.com. RV/tent: 50. $$. Hookups: electric, water, sewer.

Chattahoochee

KOA Chattahoochee, 2309 Flat Creek Rd., 32324. T: (850) 442-6657 or (800) 562-2153. www.koa.com/where/fl/09323.htm. RV/tent: 46. $$. Hookups: electric (30, 50 amp), water, sewer.

Clearwater

Travel World RV Park, 12400 US 19 North, 33764. T: (727) 536-1765. RV/tent: 200. $$. Hookups: electric (50 amp), water, sewer, cable, phone.

Clewiston

Clewiston/Lake Okeechobee Holiday Trav-L Park, Rte. 2, Box 242, 33440. T: (863) 983-7078 or (877) 983-7078. RV/tent: 124. $$. Hookups: electric (30 amp), water, sewer, phone.

Crooked Hook RV Resort, 51700 US 27, 33440. T: (863) 983-7112. RV/tent: 20. $$$. Hookups: electric (30 amp), water, sewer.

Cocoa Beach

Oceanus Mobile Village Campground, 152 Crescent Beach Dr. (23rd), 32931. T: (321) 783-3871. RV/tent: 38. $$$. Hookups: electric (30, 50 amp), water, sewer.

Dade City

Traveler's Rest Resort, 29129 Johnston Rd., 33525. T: (352) 588-2013 or (800) 565-8114. www.travelersrestresort.com. RV/tent: 654. $$. Hookups: electric (15, 30, 50 amp), water, sewer, cable.

FLORIDA (continued)

Daytona Beach

Daytona Beach Campground, 4601 Clyde Morris Blvd., 32129. T: (386) 761-2663. www.rvdayton. com. RV/tent: 224. $$$. Hookups: electric (30, 50 amp), water, sewer, cable.

International RV Park and Campground, 3175 West International Speedway Blvd., 32124. T: (386) 239-0249 or (866) 261-3698. www.international rvdaytona.com. RV/tent: 137. $$. Hookups: electric (30, 50 amp), water, sewer.

Nova Family Campground, 1190 Herbert St., 32129. T: (386) 767-0095. www.novacamp.com. RV/tent: 200. $$. Hookups: electric (20, 30, 50 amp), water, sewer, cable.

DeBary

High Banks Marina & RV, 488 West High Banks Rd., 32713. T: (386) 668-4491. RV/tent: 227. $$$. Hookups: electric (30, 50 amp), water, sewer.

Delray Beach

Del-Raton Travel Trailer Park, 2998 South Federal Hwy., 33483-3246. T: (561) 278-4633. RV/tent: 60. $$$. Hookups: electric (20, 30, 50 amp), water, sewer, phone.

Destin

Camping on the Gulf Holiday Travel Park, 10005 West Emerald Coast Pkwy., 32550. T: (850) 837-6334 or (877) 226-7485. www.campgulf.com. RV/tent: 192. $$$. Hookups: electric (20, 30, 50 amp), water, sewer.

Dover

Citrus Hills RV Park, 5311 St. 60 East, 33527-9763. T: (813) 737-4770. RV/tent: 225. $$. Hookups: electric (30, 50 amp), water, sewer.

Dunedin

Dunedin Beach Campground, 2920 Alternate 19 North, 34698. T: (727) 784-3719 or (800) 345-7504. www.gocampingamerica.com/dunedin beach. RV/tent: 233. $$$. Hookups: electric (50 amp), water, sewer, cable, phone.

Flagler Beach

Bulow Resort, 345 Old Kings Rd. South, 32136. T: (386) 439-9200 or (800) 782-8569. www.bulow.com. RV/tent: 350. $$$. Hookups: electric, water, sewer, cable.

Picnickers Campground/Shelltown, 2455 North Oceanshore Blvd., 32136. T: (386) 439-5337 or (800) 553-2381. RV/tent: 56. $$$. Hookups: electric, water, sewer, cable.

Fort Lauderdale

Yacht Haven Park & Marina, 2323 State Rd. 84, 33312-4889. T: (954) 583-2322 or (800) 581-2322. www.yachthavenpark.com. RV/tent: 250. $$$. Hookups: electric (20, 30, 50 amp), water, sewer.

Fort Myers

Shady Acres RV Travel Park, 19370 South Tamiami Trail, 33908. T: (239) 267-8448. www.shadyacres fl.com. RV/tent: 316. $$$. Hookups: electric (20, 30, 50 amp), water, sewer, cable, phone.

The Groves RV Resort, 16175 John Morris Rd., 33908. T: (239) 466-4300 or (800) 828-6992. www.suncommunities.com. RV/tent: 306. $$$. Hookups: electric (30, 50 amp), water, sewer, cable, phone.

Fort Myers Beach

Red Coconut RV Resort on the Beach, 3001 Estero Blvd., 33931. T: (239) 463-7200 or (888) 262-6226. www.redcoconut.com. RV/tent: 247. $$$. Hookups: electric (50 amp), water, sewer, cable, phone.

Fort Pierce

Road Runner Travel Resort, 5500 St. Lucie Blvd., 34946. T: (772) 464-0969 or (800) 833-7108. www.roadrunnertravelresort.com. RV/tent: 450. $$$. Hookups: electric (50 amp), water, sewer, cable, phone.

Fort Walton Beach

Playground RV Park, 777 Beal Pkwy., 32547. T: (850) 862-3513. RV/tent: 54. $$$. Hookups: electric (20, 30, 50 amp), water, sewer, cable.

Fountain

Pine Lake RV Park, 21036 US 231, 32428. T: (850) 722-1401. RV/tent: 75. $$. Hookups: electric (30, 50 amp), water, sewer, cable.

Freeport

Lazy Days RV Park, 18655 US 331 South, 32439. T: (850) 835-4606. www.lazydaysrv.net. RV/tent: 27. $$. Hookups: electric (20, 30, 50 amp), water, sewer, cable, phone.

Georgetown

Riverwood RV Village, 1389 CR 309, 32139. T: (386) 467-7144. RV/tent: 25. $$. Hookups: electric (30, 50 amp), water, sewer.

Gulf Islands National Seashore

Fort Pickens Area Campground, 1400 Fort Pickens Rd., 32561. T: (850) 934-2622 or (800) 365-2267. www.nps.gov/guis/pphtml/camping.html. RV/tent: 200. $$. Hookups: electric, water.

Haines City

Paradise Island RV Park, 2900 South Hwy. 27, 33844. T: (863) 439-1350. RV/tent: 181. $$. Hookups: electric (15, 30, 50 amp), water, sewer, cable, phone.

High Springs

Ginnie Springs Resort, 7300 NE Ginnie Springs Rd., 32643. T: (386) 454-7188. www.ginnie springsoutdoors.com. RV/tent: 252. $$. Hookups: electric (20, 30, 50 amp), water.

Holiday

Holiday Travel Park, 1622 Aires Dr., 34690. T: (727) 934-6782. www.campgulf.com. RV/tent: 703. $$. Hookups: electric (50 amp), water, sewer, cable, phone.

Holt

River's Edge RV Campground, 4001 Log Lake Rd., 32564. T: (850) 537-2267. riversedgerv.com.

RV/tent: 114. $$. Hookups: electric, water, sewer, phone.

Homosassa

Camp N' Water Outdoor Resort, 11465 West Priest Ln., 34448. T: (352) 628-2000. RV/tent: 91. $$. Hookups: electric (30, 50 amp), water, sewer, cable, phone.

Chassahowitzka River Campground, 8600 Miss Maggie Dr., 32623. T: (352) 382-2200. RV/tent: 85. $$. Hookups: electric, water, sewer.

Indian Rocks Beach

Indian Rocks Beach RV Resort, 601 Gulf Blvd., 33785. T: (727) 596-7743 or (800) 354-7559. RV/tent: 55. $$$. Hookups: electric (30, 50 amp), water, sewer, cable, phone.

Jacksonville

Flamingo Lake RV Resort Park, 3640 Newcomb Rd., 32218. T: (904) 766-0672 or (800) 326-3521. www.flamingolake.com. RV/tent: 152. $$$. Hookups: electric (20, 30, 50 amp), water, sewer, cable, phone.

Huguenot Memorial Park, 10980 Heckscher Dr., 32226. T: (904) 251-3335. RV/tent: 71. $. Hookups: none.

Little Talbot Island State Park, 12157 Heckscher Dr., 32226. T: (904) 251-2320. www.florida stateparks.org/littletalbotisland/default.asp. RV/tent: 40. $. Hookups: electric, water.

Jennings

Jennings Outdoor Resort, 2039 Hamilton Ave., 32053. T: (386) 938-3321. RV/tent: 102. $$. Hookups: electric (20, 30, 50 amp), water, sewer, cable, phone.

Juno Beach

Juno Beach RV Park, 900 Juno Ocean Walk, 33408. T: (561) 622-7500. RV/tent: 246. $$$. Hookups: electric (30, 50 amp), water, sewer.

Jupiter

West Jupiter Camping Resort, 17801 130th Trail North, 33478. T: (561) 746-6073 or (888) 746-6073. www.westjupitercampingresort.com. RV/tent: 103. $$. Hookups: electric (20, 30, 50 amp), water, sewer, cable, phone.

Key West

Boyd's Key West Campground, 6401 Maloney Ave., 33040. T: (305) 294-1465. www.boydscamp ground.com. RV/tent: 203. $$$. Hookups: electric (30, 50 amp), water, sewer, cable, phone.

Jabours Trailer Court, 223 Elizabeth St., 33040. T: (305) 294-5723. www.kwcamp.com. RV/tent: 74. $$$$. Hookups: electric (30 amp), water, sewer.

Kissimmee

Cypress Cove Nudist Resort, 4425 Pleasant Hill Rd., 34746. T: (407) 933-5870 or (888) 683-3140. www.cypresscoveresort.com. RV/tent: 100. $$. Hookups: electric, water, sewer.

Mill Creek RV Resort, 2775 Michigan Ave., 34744. T: (407) 847-6288. RV/tent: 183. $$. Hookups: electric (30 amp), water, sewer, phone.

FLORIDA (continued)

Southport Park Campground and Marina, 2001 West Southport Rd., 34746. T: (407) 933-5822. www.southportpark.com. RV/tent: 61. $. Hookups: electric (30, 50 amp), water, sewer.

Tropical Palms Resort, 2650 Holiday Trail, 34746. T: (407) 396-4595. RV/tent: 500. $$$. Hookups: electric (50 amp), water, sewer, cable, phone.

LaBelle

Whisper Creek RV Resort, 1980 Hickory Dr., 33935. T: (863) 675-6888. www.whispercreek .com. RV/tent: 396. $$. Hookups: electric (30, 50 amp), water, sewer, cable, phone.

Lake Buena Vista

Fort Summit Camping Resort, 4200 US 27 North, 32830. T: (863) 424-1880 or (800) 424-1880. www.fortsummit.com. RV/tent: 300. $$$. Hookups: electric (50 amp), water, cable, phone.

Lake City

Waynes RV Resort Inc., Rte. 21 Box 501, 32024. T: (386) 752-5721. www.waynesrvresort.net. RV/tent: 102. $$. Hookups: electric (30 amp), water, sewer.

Lake Placid

Camp Florida Resort/Lake Placid, 100 Shoreline Dr., 33852. T: (863) 699-1991 or (800) 266-5188. www.campfla.com. RV/tent: 396. $$$. Hookups: electric (30, 50 amp), water sewer.

Lake Worth

Camping Resort of the Palm Beaches, 5332 Lake Worth Rd., 33463. T: (561) 965-1653. RV/tent: 150. $$$. Hookups: electric (30 amp), water, sewer, cable, phone.

Lakeland

Sanlan Ranch Campground, 3929 US 98 South, 33813. T: (863) 665-1726 or (800) 524-5044. www.sanlan.com. RV/tent: 500. $$. Hookups: electric (30, 50 amp), water, sewer, phone.

Lakeport

Aruba RV Resort, 1825 Old Lakeport Rd., 33471. T: (863) 946-1324. www.okeedirect.com/aruba rv.htm. RV/tent: 156. $$. Hookups: electric (30, 50 amp), water, sewer, cable, phone.

Lamont

A Camper's World Campground, Rte. 1 Box 164B, 32336. T: (850) 997-3300. RV/tent: 63. $$. Hookups: electric (20, 30, 50 amp), water, sewer, phone.

Largo

Indian Rocks Travel Park, 12121 Vonn Rd., 33774. T: (727) 595-2228. RV/tent: 30. $$. Hookups: electric (30 amp), water, sewer, cable, phone.

Yankee Traveler RV Park, 8500 Ulmerton Rd. (Hwy. 688), 33771. T: (727) 531-7998 or (866) 202-9232. www.yankeetraveler.net. RV/tent: 210. $$. Hookups: electric (30, 50 amp), water, sewer.

Leesburg

Holiday Travel Resort, 28229 CR 33, 34748. T: (352) 787-5151 or (800) 428-5334. www .holidaytravelresort.com. RV/tent: 935. $$$.

Hookups: electric (30 amp), water, sewer, cable, phone.

Long Key

KOA Fiesta Key Kampground, US 1, Mile Marker 70, 33001. T: (305) 664-4922 or (800) 562-7730. www.koa.com/where/fl/09250.html. RV/tent: 341. $$$$. Hookups: electric, water, sewer, cable, phone.

Marathon

Jolly Roger Travel Park, 59275 Overseas Hwy., 33050-9756. T: (305) 289-0404 or (800) 995-1525. www.jrtp.com. RV/tent: 170. $$$. Hookups: electric (20, 30, 50 amp), water, sewer.

Mexico Beach

Islander RV Park, 2600 US 98, 32410. T: (850) 648-4006. RV/tent: 40. $$. Hookups: electric (30 amp), water, sewer, phone, cable.

Miami

Larry and Penny Thompson Park and Campground, 12451 SW 184th St., 33177. T: (305) 232-1049. www.co.miami-dade.fl.us/parks/mparks2.htm. RV/tent: 300. $$. Hookups: electric (20, 30, 50 amp), water, sewer.

Milton

Adventures Unlimited, 8974 Tomahawk Landing Rd., 32570. T: (850) 623-6197 or (800) 239-6864. www.adventuresunlimited.com. RV/tent: 30. $$. Hookups: electric (30 amp), water.

Mims

KOA Cape Kennedy, 4513 West Main St., 32754. T: (352) 269-7361. www.koa.com. RV/tent: 100. $$$. Hookups: electric (30, 50 amp), water, sewer, cable, phone.

Naples

Club Naples RV Resort, 3180 Beck Blvd., 34114. T: (239) 455-7275 or (888) 795-2780. www. clubnaplesrv.com. RV/tent: 309. $$. Hookups: electric (30, 50 amp), water, cable, phone.

Greystone Park, 13300 East Tamiami Trail, 34104. T: (239) 774-4044 or (877) 447-3978. RV/tent: 40. $$$. Hookups: electric (30, 50 amp), water, sewer.

KOA Naples/Marco Island, 1700 Barefoot Wiliams Rd., 34113. T: (239) 774-5455 or (800) 562-7734. www.koa.com/where/fl/09109.htm. RV/tent: 186. $$$. Hookups: electric (20, 30 amp), water, sewer.

Kountree Kampinn RV Resort, 8230 Collier Blvd., 34114. T: (239) 775-4340. www.kountree kampinn.com. RV/tent: 161. $$$. Hookups: electric (30, 50 amp), water, sewer.

Port of the Islands RV Resort, 12425 Union Rd., 34114. T: (239) 642-5343 or (800) 319-4447. www.portoftheislands.com. RV/tent: 99. $$. Hookups: electric (30 amp), water, sewer, phone.

Nokomis

Caribbean Bay Club, 899 Knights Trail, 34275. T: (941) 485-1800. RV/tent: 398. $$$. Hookups: electric (50 amp), water, cable, phone.

Encore SuperPark–Sarasota South, 1070 Laurel Rd., 34275. T: (800) 548-8678. www.rvonthego.com.

RV/tent: 558. $$$. Hookups: electric (30, 50 amp), water, cable, phone.

O'Brien

Ichetucknee Family Campground, RR 1 Box 1576, 32071. T: (386) 497-2150 or (866) 224-2064. www.ichetuckneecanoeandcabins.com. RV/tent: 50. $. Hookups: electric (30, 50 amp), water, sewer.

Ocala

KOA Silver Springs, 3200 SW 38th Ave., 34474. T: (352) 237-2138 or (800) 562-7798. www .koa.com/where/fl/09258.htm. RV/tent: 205. $$$. Hookups: electric (20, 30, 50 amp), water, sewer.

Okeechobee

Bob's Big Bass RV Park, 12766 SE Hwy. 441, 34974. T: (863) 763-2638. RV/tent: 43. $$. Hookups: electric (20, 30, 50 amp), water, sewer.

Buckhead Ridge Marina, 670 Hwy. 78B, 34974. T: (863) 763-2826. RV/tent: 112. $$. Hookups: electric (20, 30 amp), water, sewer.

KOA Okeechobee Kampground and Golf Course, 4276 Hwy. 441 South, 34974. T: (863) 763-0231. www.koa.com/where/fl/09325.htm. RV/tent: 465. $$$. Hookups: electric (30, 50 amp), water sewer, cable, phone.

Ormond Beach

Encore Superpark Daytona Beach North, 1701 North US 1, 32174. T: (386) 672-3045. RV/tent: 336. $$$. Hookups: electric, water, sewer, cable, phone.

Ocean Village Camper Resort, 2162 Ocean Shore Blvd., 32176. T: (386) 441-1808. RV/tent: 60. $$. Hookups: electric (30 amp), water, sewer, cable.

Palm Harbor

Caladesi RV Park, 205 Dempsey Rd., 34683. T: (727) 784-3622. RV/tent: 86. $$$. Hookups: electric (20, 30 amp), water, sewer.

Palmetto

Frog Creek Campground, 8515 Bayshore Rd., 34221. T: (941) 722-6154 or (800) 771-3764. www.frogcreekrv.com. RV/tent: 174. $$$. Hookups: electric (30 amp), water, sewer, phone.

Panacea

Holiday Campground, 14 Coastal Hwy., 32346. T: (850) 984-5757. www.holidaycampground.com. RV/tent: 75. $$. Hookups: electric (30, 50 amp), water, sewer.

Pensacola

Playa del Rio Park and Yacht Club, 16990 Perdido Key Dr., 32507. T: (850) 492-0904 or (888) 200-0904. www.playadelrio.com. RV/tent: 30. $$. Hookups: electric (20, 30 50 amp), water, sewer, cable, phone.

Perdido Key

Playa Del Rio RV Resort, 13621 Perdido Key Dr., 32507. T: (850) 492-0041 or (800) 245-3602. www.playadelrio.com. RV/tent: 30. $$$$. Hookups: electric (20, 30, 50 amp), water, sewer, cable, phone.

FLORIDA (continued)

Perry

Southern Oaks RV Campground and Resort, 3641 Hwy. 19 South, 32347. T: (850) 584-3221 or (800) 339-5421. www.gocampingamerica.com/southernoaks. RV/tent: 100. $$. Hookups: electric (15, 30, 50 amp), water, sewer, cable, phone.

Port Richey

Suncoast RV Resort, 9029 US 19, 34668. T: (727) 842-9324 or (888) 922-5603. www.suncoastrvresort.com. RV/tent: 145. $$$. Hookups: electric (20, 30, 50 amp), water, sewer, cable, phone.

Port St. Joe

Presnell's Bayside Marina and RV Resort, 2115 Hwy. C30, 32456. T: (850) 229-2710. RV/tent: 27. $$. Hookups: electric (50 amp), water.

Punta Gorda

Hidden River Travel Resort, 12500 McMullen Loop, 33569. T: (813) 677-1515. RV/tent: 340. $$. Hookups: electric (20, 30, 50 amp), water, sewer.

Riverview Alafia River RV Resort, 9812 Gibsonton Dr., 33569-5399. T: (813) 677-1997 or (800) 555-4384. www.alafiariverresort.com. RV/tent: 203. $$. Hookups: electric (20, 30 amp), water, sewer.

Water's Edge RV Resort, 6800 Golf Course Blvd., 33982. T: (941) 637-4677 or (800) 637-9224. www.watersedgervresort.com. RV/tent: 176. $$$. Hookups: electric (20, 30, 50 amp), water, sewer.

Rockledge

Space Coast RV Resort, 820 Barnes Blvd., 32955. T: (321) 636-2873 or (800) 482-4233. www.spacecoastrv.net. RV/tent: 240. $$. Hookups: electric (30, 50, 100 amp), water, sewer.

Ruskin

Hide-A-Way RV Resort, 2206 Chaney Dr., 33570. T: (813) 645-6037 or (800) 607-2532. www.gocampingamerica.com/hideawayfl. RV/tent: 292. $$. Hookups: electric (30, 50 amp), water, sewer, cable, phone.

River Oaks RV Resort, 201 Stephens Rd., 33570. T: (813) 645-2439 or (800) 645-6311. www.riveroaksrv.com. RV/tent: 97. $$. Hookups: electric (20, 30, 50 amp), water, sewer.

Salt Springs

Elite Resorts at Salt Springs, 25250 East Hwy. 316, 32134. T: (352) 685-1900 or (800) 356-2460. www.eliteresorts.com/saltsprings.htm. RV/tent: 465. $$$. Hookups: electric (20, 30 amp), water, sewer.

Sanford

Twelve Oaks RV Resort, 6300 State Rte. 46 West, 32771-9290. T: (407) 323-0880 or (800) 633-9529. RV/tent: 247. $$$. Hookups: electric (30, 50 amp), water, sewer.

Sarasota/Siesta Key

Gulf Beach Campground, 8862 Midnight Pass Rd., 34242. T: (941) 349-3839. www.gulfbeachcampground.com. RV/tent: 48. $$$. Hookups: electric (20, 30, 50 amp), water, sewer, cable, phone.

Sopchoppy

Ochlockonee River State Park, P.O. Box 5, 32358. T: (850) 962-2771 or (800) 326-3521. www.floridastateparks.org/ochlockoneeriver/default.asp. RV/tent: 30. $. Hookups: electric, water.

South Bay

South Bay RV Campground, 100 Levee Rd., 33493. T: (561) 992-9045. RV/tent: 96. $$. Hookups: electric (30, 50 amp), water, cable.

St. Augustine

North Beach Camp Resort, 4125 Coastal Hwy. (A1A), 32084. T: (904) 824-1806 or (800) 542-8316. www.northbeachcamp.com. RV/tent: 125. $$$. Hookups: electric (30, 50 amp), water, sewer, cable, phone.

St. Augustine Beach

Bryn Mawr Ocean Resort, 4850 A1A South, 32800. T: (904) 471-3353. www.brynmawroceanresort.com. RV/tent: 130. $$$$. Hookups: electric (20, 30, 50 amp), water, sewer, cable, phone.

Cooksey's Camping Resort, 2795 A1A South, 32085. T: (904) 824-4016. www.koa.com/where/fl/09205. RV/tent: 250. $$$. Hookups: electric (15, 30, 50 amp), water, sewer, phone.

KOA St. Augustine Beach Kampground Resort, 525 West Pope Rd., 32080. T: (904) 471-3113 or (800) 562-4022. www.koa.com/where/fl/09205. RV/tent: 71. $$$. Hookups: electric (30, 50 amp), water, sewer, cable.

Ocean Grove Camp Resort, 4225 Hwy. A1A South, 32084. T: (904) 471-3414 or (800) 342-4007. www.oceangroveresort.com. RV/tent: 198. $$$. Hookups: electric (20, 30, 50 amp), water, sewer, cable, phone.

St. Petersburg

KOA St. Petersburg/Madeira Beach Kampground, 5400 95th St. North, 33708. T: (727) 392-2233 or (800) 562-7714. www.koakampgrounds.com/where/fl/09144.htm. RV/tent: 390. $$$. Hookups: electric (20, 30, 50 amp), water, phone.

Robert's Mobile Home and RV Resort

Robert's Mobile Home and RV Resort, 3390 Gandy Blvd., 33702. T: (727) 577-6820 or (727) 577-6320. www.robertsrv.com. RV/tent: 430. $$. Hookups: electric (30, 50 amp), water, sewer, cable, phone.

Thonotassa

Happy Traveler RV Park, 9401 Fowler Ave., 33592. T: (813) 986-3094. RV/tent: 224. $$. Hookups: electric (20, 30, 50 amp), water, sewer, phone.

Titusville

The Great Outdoors RV and Golf Resort, 135 Plantation Dr., 32780. T: (800) 621-2267 or (321) 269-5004. www.tgoresort.com. RV/tent: 200. $$$. Hookups: electric (30, 50 amp), water, sewer, cable.

Venice

Venice Campground and RV Park, 4085 East Venice Ave., 34292. T: (941) 488-0850. www.campvenice.com. RV/tent: 133. $$$$. Hookups: electric (30 amp), water, sewer.

Wabasso

Vero Beach Kamp RV Resort, 8850 North US 1, 32970. T: (772) 589-5665. RV/tent: 120. $$$. Hookups: electric (30, 50 amp), water, cable.

West Palm Beach

Pine Lake Camp Resort, 7000 Okeechobee Blvd., 33411. T: (561) 686-0714. RV/tent: 194. $$. Hookups: electric (20, 30 amp), water, sewer, phone.

White Springs

Kelly's RV Park, Rte. 41 South, 32096. T: (386) 397-2616. RV/tent: 76. $$. Hookups: electric (30, 50 amp), water, sewer, phone.

Yulee

Hance's First in Florida RV Park, 3111 Hance Pkwy. (US 17), 32097. T: (904) 225-2080 or (800) 628-9953. www.floridarvparks.com. RV/tent: 73. $$. Hookups: electric (30, 50 amp), water, sewer, cable, phone.

Zephyrhills

Jim's RV Park, 35120 Hwy. 54 West, 33541-1400. T: (813) 782-5610. RV/tent: 50. $$. Hookups: electric (20, 30, 50 amp), water, sewer.

GEORGIA

Acworth

Holiday Marina Harbor & Campground, 5989 Groover's Landing, 30102. T: (770) 974-2575. RV/tent: 15. $$. Hookups: electric (20, 30 amp), water.

Lakemont Campground, 5134 North Shores Rd., 30101. T: (770) 966-0302. RV/tent: 100. $$. Hookups: electric (20, 30, 50 amp), water, sewer, phone (modem).

Adel

Reed Bingham State Park, Rte. 2, 31620. T: (229) 896-3552. www.reedbinghamstatepark.org. RV/tent: 46. $$. Hookups: electric (20, 30 amp), water, sewer, cable, phone.

GEORGIA (continued)

Albany

Albany RV Resort, 1218 Liberty Expy SE, 31705. T: (229) 878-6595 or (866) 778-7735. www.travelingusa.com/albanyrv/. RV/tent: 78. $$. Hookups: electric (20, 30, 50 amp), water, sewer, cable, phone (modem).

Creekside Plantation RV Campground, 2700 Liberty Expy SE, 31705. T: (229) 883-7996. RV/tent: 60. $$. Hookups: electric (30, 50 amp), water, sewer, cable, phone (modem).

Devencrest Travel Park, 1833 Liberty Expy SE, 31705. T: (229) 432-2641. www.devencresttravel park.com. RV/tent: 100. $$. Hookups: electric (15, 20, 30 amp), water, sewer, laundry.

Americus

Brickyard Plantation RV & Tent Campground, 1619 US 280 East, 31709. T: (229) 874-1234. www.brickyardgolfclub.com. RV/tent: 12. $$. Hookups: electric (20, 30 amp), water, sewer.

Andersonville

City Campground, Rte. 1 Box 800, 31711. T: (229) 924-2558. www.andersonvillega.freeservers.com. RV/tent: 40. $. Hookups: electric (15, 20 amp), water, sewer.

Arabi

Southern Gates RV Park & Campground, 138 Campsite Rd., 31712. T: (229) 273-6464. www.southerngates.com. RV/tent: 55. $. Hookups: electric (20, 30, 50 amp), water, sewer, phone (modem).

Ashburn

Knights Inn & RV Park, 1971 North St., 31714. T: (229) 567-3334. RV/tent: 77. $. Hookups: electric (20, 30 amp), water, sewer.

Augusta

Flynn's Inn Camping Village, 3746 Peach Orchard Rd., 30906. T: (706) 798-6912. RV/tent: 61. $$. Hookups: electric (30, 50 amp), water, sewer, phone (modem).

Austell

Arrowhead Campground, 7400 Six Flags Dr. SW, 30001. T: (770) 732-1130 or (800) 631-8956. RV/tent: 200. $$$. Hookups: electric (20, 30, 50 amp), water, sewer, phone (modem).

Barnesville

High Falls Campground, 1046 High Falls Park Rd., 30204. T: (770) 358-2205 or (800) 428-0132. gastateparks.org/info/highfalls. RV/tent: 112. $$. Hookups: electric (20, 30, 50 amp), water, sewer, phone, laundry.

Blairsville

Goose Creek Cabins & Campground, 7061 Goose Creek, 30512. T: (706) 745-5111. www.goose creekcabins.com. RV/tent: 24. $$. Hookups: electric (20 amp), water, sewer.

Lake Nottely RV Park, 350 Haley Cir., 30512. T: (706) 745-4523. www.the-campground-network.com/lakenottellyrvparkinc.html. RV/tent: 80. $$. Hookups: electric (20, 30, 50 amp), water, sewer, phone (modem).

Mountain Oak Cabins & Campgrouds, 2388 Mulky Gap Rd., 30512. T: (706) 781-6867 or (888) 781-6867. www.mountainoak.com. RV/tent: 35. $$. Hookups: electric (20, 30, 50 amp), water, sewer, phone (modem).

Trackrock Campgrounds & Cabins, 4887 Trackrock Campground Rd., 30512. T: (706) 745-2420. www.trackrock.com. RV/tent: 90. $$. Hookups: electric (20, 30 amp), water, sewer, phone (modem), laundry.

Blakely

Kolomoki Mounds State Park, 205 Indian Mounds Rd., 39823. T: (229) 724-2150. RV/tent: 43. $$. Hookups: electric (30 amp), water.

Blue Ridge

Cooper Creek Campground, Chattahoochee National Forest, USFS 4, off of Hwy. 60 South, 30513. T: (706) 632-3031. www.fs.fed.us/conf/coopercp.htm. RV/tent: 17. $. Hookups: water, picnic table, restrooms, showers, tent pads.

Deep Hole Campground, Chattahoochee National Forest, Hwy. 60 South, 30513. T: (706) 632-3031. www.fs.fed.us/conf/dpholecp.shtml. RV/tent: 8. $. Hookups: water, picnic table, restrooms, showers, tent pads.

Frank Gross Campground, Chattahoochee National Forest, USFS 69, off of Hwy. 60 South, 30513. T: (706) 632-3031. www.fs.fed.us/conf/frankcmp.shtml. RV/tent: 9. $. Hookups: water, picnic table, restrooms, showers, tent pads.

Lake Blue Ridge Campground, 1755 Green Creek Rd., 30513. T: (706) 632-8331. www.fs.fed.us/conf/lkblurcp.htm. RV/tent: 58. $. Hookups: water, restrooms, showers, tent pads.

Morganton Point, Chattahoochee National Forest, CR 616, 30513. T: (706) 632-3031. www.fs.fed.us/conf/mgntncmp.htm. RV/tent: 37. $. Hookups: water, picnic table, restrooms, showers, tent pads.

Mulky Campground, Chattahoochee National Forest, USF.S. 4, off of Hwy. 60 South, 30513. T: (706) 632-3031. www.fs.fed.us/conf/mlky camp.htm. RV/tent: 11. $. Hookups: water, picnic table, restrooms, showers, tent pads.

Brunswick

Golden Isles Vacation Park, 7445 Blythe Hwy., 31523. T: (912) 261-1025. RV/tent: 110. $$. Hookups: electric (20, 30, 50 amp), water, sewer, cable.

Ocean Breeze Campround, Dover Bluff Rd., 31523. T: (912) 264-6692. RV/tent: 37. $$. Hookups: electric (20, 30 amp), water, sewer, phone.

Buena Vista

Country Vista Campground, South Hwy. 41, 31803. T: (229) 649-2267. RV/tent: 44. $$. Hookups: electric (20, 30, 50 amp), water, sewer, phone (modem), cable.

Byron

Interstate Camping, 305 Chapman Rd., 31008. T: (229) 956-5511 or (888) 817-0906. www.interstatervcenter.com. RV/tent: 104. $$. Hookups: electric (30, 50 amp), water, sewer, phone (modem).

Calhoun

KOA Calhoun, 2523 Redbud Rd. NE, 30701. T: (800) 562-7512. RV/tent: 87. $$. Hookups: electric (15, 20, 30 amp), water, sewer, laundry.

Carrollton

John Tanner State Park, 354 Tanner Beach Rd., 30117. T: (770) 830-2222. RV/tent: 32. $$. Hookups: electric (30, 50 amp), water, cable.

Cartersville

Clark Creek South, P.O. Box 487, 30120-0487. T: (770) 382-4700. RV/tent: 40. $$. Hookups: electric (30 amp), water.

KOA Cartersville, 800 Cassville-White Rd., 30121. T: (770) 382-7330 or (800) 562-2841. RV/tent: 117. $$. Hookups: electric (20, 30, 50 amp), water, sewer, cable, phone, laundry.

McKinney Campground, P.O. Box 487, 30120. T: (770) 382-4700. www.reserveusa.com. RV/tent: 150. $$. Hookups: electric (30, 50 amp), water, sewer.

Payne Campground, P.O. Box 487, 30120. T: (770) 382-4700 or (678) 721-6700. RV/tent: 60. $$. Hookups: electric (30 amp), water, sewer.

Cave Spring

Cedar Creek Park, 6770 Cave Springs Rd., 30124. T: (706) 777-3030. RV/tent: 60. $$. Hookups: electric (30, 50 amp), water, sewer.

Cecil

Cecil Bay RV Park, Old Coffee Rd., 31627. T: (229) 794-1484. RV/tent: 100. $$. Hookups: electric (20, 30, 50 amp), water, sewer.

Chatsworth

Fort Mountain State Park, 181 Ft. Mountain Park Rd., 30705. T: (706) 695-2621 or (800) 864-7275. RV/tent: 70. $. Hookups: electric (30 amp), water, sewer, cable.

Chauncey

Jay Bird Springs Resort, Inc., 1221 Jay Bird Springs Rd., 31011. T: (229) 868-2728. RV/tent: 22. $$. Hookups: electric (15, 30 amp), water, sewer, phone.

Cleveland

Gold 'n' Gem Grubbin, 75 Gold Nugget Ln., 30528. T: (706) 865-5454. www.goldngem.com. RV/tent: 50. $. Hookups: electric (20, 30, 50 amp), water, sewer, bathhouse.

Colquitt

Emerald Lake RV Park & Music Showcase, 698 Enterprise Rd., 31737. T: (229) 758-2929. RV/tent: 20. $$. Hookups: electric (30, 50 amp), water, sewer, laundry.

Comer

Watson Mill Bridge State Park, 650 Watson Mill Rd., 30629. T: (706) 783-5349. www.negia.net/~wat son. RV/tent: 21. $. Hookups: electric (30 amp), water, sewer, laundry.

Commerce

Country Boys RV Park, CR 466, 30529. T: (706) 335-5535. RV/tent: 71. $$. Hookups: electric (20, 30, 50 amp), water, sewer, phone (modem).

Cordele

KOA Cordele, 373 Rockhouse Rd., 31015. T: (229) 273-5454 or (800) 562-0275. www.koakamp grounds.com. RV/tent: 73. $$. Hookups: electric (20, 30 amp), water, sewer.

Cornelia

Lake Russell Campground, 1756 Cleveland Hwy., 30501. T: (706) 754-6221. www.fs.fed.us/conf/ lkrslcmp.htm. RV/tent: 42. $. Hookups: water, sewer, table, grill.

Covington

Riverside Estates RV & Camping, 1891-2 Access Rd., 30014. T: (770) 787-3707. RV/tent: 172. $$. Hookups: electric (30, 50 amp), water, sewer, phone (modem), cable.

Crawfordsville

Alexander H. Stephens State Historic Park, Hwy. 22 & US 278, 30631. T: (706) 456-2602. www. travelthepast.com. RV/tent: 25. $$. Hookups: electric (20, 30 amp), water, sewer, laundry.

Cumming

Sawnee Campground, 3200 Bufford Dam Rd., 30041. T: (770) 887-0592. RV/tent: 56. $$. Hookups: electric (20 amp), water, sewer, laundry.

Shady Grove Campground, 7800 Shadburn Ferry Rd.; 5620 Shady Grove Rd., 30041. T: (770) 887-2067. RV/tent: 115. $$. Hookups: electric (20 amp), water, sewer, laundry.

Twin Lakes RV Park, 3300 Shore Dr., 30040. T: (770) 887-4400. www.geocities.com/ tl_rv_park/homex.html. RV/tent: 95. $$. Hookups: electric (30, 50 amp), water, sewer.

Darien

Tall Pines Campground, Hwy. 251, 31305. T: (912) 437-3966. RV/tent: 45. $$. Hookups: electric (30, 50 amp), water, sewer, laundry.

Dawsonville

Amicalola Falls State Park & Lodge, 418 Amicalola Falls Lodge Rd., 30534. T: (706) 265-8888. www.visitamicalolafalls.com. RV/tent: 20. $$. Hookups: electric (20, 30 amp), water, sewer, laundry.

Dillard

River Vista Mountain Village, 960 Hwy. 246, 30537. T: (888) 850-7275. www.rvmountainvillage.com. RV/tent: 127. $$$. Hookups: electric (30, 50 amp), water, sewer, cable, laundry.

Donalsonville

Seminole Sportsman Lodge & Marina, Marina & Campground, 7966 Marina Rd., 39845. T: (229) 861-3862 or (877) 258-1080. www.seminole sportsmanlodgeandmarina.com. RV/tent: 24. $. Hookups: electric (20, 30 amp), water, gas, sewer.

Seminole State Park, 7870 State Park Dr., Rte. 2 & Hwy. 39, 39845. T: (229) 861-3137 or (800) 864-7275. gastateparks.org/info/seminole. RV/tent:

50. $$. Hookups: electric (30 amp), water, sewer, firewood, grill, laundry.

Eatonton

Lawrence Shoals Park, US 129 & Hwy. 16, 31024. T: (706) 485-5494. www.georgiapower.com/ gpclake. RV/tent: 49. $$. Hookups: electric (20, 30 amp), water, firewood, grill, laundry.

Oconee Springs Park at Lake Sinclair, US 129 & Hwy. 16, 31024. T: (706) 485-8423. www.lakesin clair.org. RV/tent: 52. $. Hookups: electric (20, 30 amp), water, sewer, firewood, grill, laundry (no pets).

Old Federal Rd. Park, Hwy. 369 & Hwy. 53, 31024. T: (770) 967-6757. www.reserveusa.com. RV/tent: 84. $$. Hookups: electric (30, 50 amp), water, laundry.

Ellijay

Camp Cherry Log, Little Rock Creek Rd., 30540. T: (706) 635-5006. www.batesrv.com/cherry.htm. RV/tent: 43. $$. Hookups: electric (30, 50 amp), water, sewer.

Plum Nelly Campground, 15828 South Hwy. 515, 30540. T: (404) 317-2458. www.geocities.com/ plumnellycampground. RV/tent: 32. $$. Hookups: electric (30, 50 amp), water, sewer.

Fitzgerald

Colony City Campground, Perry House Rd., 31750. T: (229) 423-5050. RV/tent: 36. $. Hookups: electric (30 amp), water, sewer, firewood, grill, laundry (no showers).

Florence

Florence Marina State Park, 39 C & Hwy. 39, 31821. T: (229) 838-4244 or (800) 864-7275. gastateparks.org/info/flormarin. RV/tent: 43. $$. Hookups: electric (30, 50 amp), water, sewer.

Folkston

Okefenokee Pastimes, Rte. 2 Box 3090, 31537. T: (912) 496-4472. www.okefenokee.com. RV/tent: 22. $$. Hookups: electric (30 amp), water, sewer, firewood, grill, laundry.

Forsyth

L & D RV Park & Campgrounds, 1655 Dames Ferry Rd., Rte. 3 Box 62A, 31029. T: (478) 994-8977. RV/tent: 29. $$. Hookups: electric (20, 30, 50 amp), water, sewer, laundry.

Fort Benning

Uchee Creek Campground/Fort Benning Manor, Miller Hall Bldg. 241, 31905. T: (706) 545-4053 or (706) 545-7238. ww.gocampingamerica. com/ucheecreek/index.html. RV/tent: 85. $$. Hookups: electric (20, 30, 50 amp), water, sewer, cable, phone (modem).

Gainesville

Bolding Mill Campground, 4055 Chestatee Rd., 30506. T: (770) 532-3650. RV/tent: 97. $$. Hookups: electric (20 amp), water, sewer, laundry.

Duckett Mill Campground, 3720 Duckett Mill Rd., Hwy. 400 & Duckett Mill Rd., 30506. T: (770) 532-9802. RV/tent: 54. $$. Hookups: electric, water, sewer, table, tent pad, grill.

Hephzibah

Fox Hollow Campgrounds, 4032 Peach Orchard Rd., 30815. T: (706) 592-4563. www.gocamping america.com/foxhollowcpgrdga/index.html. RV/tent: 21. $$. Hookups: electric (30 amp), water, phone (modem).

Hiawassee

Enota Campground & Resort, 1000 Hwy. 180, 30546. T: (706) 896-9966 or (800) 990-8869. www.enota.com. RV/tent: 92. $$. Hookups: electric (30, 50 amp), water, laundry, sewer, phone.

Georgia Mountain Campground, US 76 West, 30546. T: (706) 896-4191. www.georgia-mountain-fair.com/campground.html. RV/tent: 189. $$. Hookups: electric (30, 50 amp), water, sewer, cable, phone (modem).

Jenny

Jenny's Creek Family Campground, 4542 Hwy. 129 North, 30528. T: (706) 865-6955. www.jennys creek.com. RV/tent: 70. $$. Hookups: electric (15, 20, 30 amp), water, sewer, laundry.

Leisure Acres Campground, 3840 Westmoreland Rd., 30528. T: (706) 865-4114 or (888) 748-6344. www.leisureacrescampground.com. RV/tent: 92. $$. Hookups: electric (30, 50 amp), water, sewer, phone (modem).

Mountain Creek Grove, 258 Grove Ln., 30528. T: (706) 865-6930 or (800) 863-nude. www.mountaincreekgrove.com. RV/tent: 17. $$. Hookups: electric (20, 30, 50 amp), water, sewer.

Mountain Creek Grove Campgrounds, 338 Mountain Creek Cir., 30528. T: (706) 865-6930 or (800) 863-nude. www.mountaincreekgrove.com. RV/tent: 110. $. Hookups: electric (30 amp), water, sewer, shower, bathhouse.

Serendipity Nudist Resort, 95 Cedar Hollow Dr., 30528. T: (706) 219-3993 or (888) NUDE-ONE. www.serendipity-park.com. RV/tent: 42. $. Hookups: electric (50 amp), water, sewer, phone (modem).

Turner Campsite, 142 Turner Campsite Rd., 30528. T: (706) 865-4757. www.turnercampsites.com. RV/tent: 126. $$. Hookups: electric (30 amp), water, sewer, laundry.

La Grange

Three Creeks Campground, 305 Old Roanoke Rd., 30240. T: (706) 884-0899. www.troop county.com. RV/tent: 38. $$. Hookups: electric (30, 50 amp), water, sewer, phone, laundry.

Metter

Beaver Run RV Park & Campground, Rte. 3 Box 168, 30439. T: (912) 685-2594. www.turnstone cabins.com/beaverrun.html. RV/tent: 71. $$. Hookups: electric (30, 50 amp), water, sewer, phone (modem).

Midland

Lake Pines RV Park & Campground, 6404 Garrett Rd., 31820. T: (706) 561-9675. www.lakepines.net. RV/tent: 68. $$. Hookups: electric (20, 30, 50 amp), water, sewer, phone (modem).

Morganton

Whispering Pines Campground, 290 Whipering Pines Rd., 30560. T: (706) 374-6494. RV/tent: 30. $$. Hookups: electric (15, 20 amp), water, sewer.

GEORGIA (continued)

Mountain City
Black Rock Mountain State Park, 3085 Black Rock Mountain Pkwy., 30562. T: (706) 746-2141. RV/tent: 48. $$. Hookups: electric (30 amp), water.

Perry
Boland's Perry Overnight Park, 800 Perimeter Rd., 31069. T: (478) 987-1000. RV/tent: 65. $$. Hookups: electric (20, 30 amp), water, laundry, sewer, cable, phone (modem).

Crossroads Travel Park, 1513 Sam Nunn Blvd., 31069. T: (478) 987-3141. RV/tent: 56. $$. Hookups: electric (20, 30 amp), water, sewer, phone (modem).

Rincon
Green Peace RV Park, 155 Caroni Dr., 31326. T: (912) 826-5540. RV/tent: 50. $. Hookups: electric (30 amp), water, sewer, phone (modem).

Whispering Pines RV Park, 1755 Hodgeville Rd., 31326. T: (912) 728-7562. www.gocampingamerica.com/whisperingpinesga/index.html. RV/tent: 53. $$. Hookups: electric (20, 30, 50 amp), water, sewer, phone (modem).

Rome
Coosa River Campground, 181 Lock & Dam Rd., 30161. T: (706) 234-5001. rfpra.com/lock_dam_park.html. RV/tent: 31. $$. Hookups: electric (30, 50 amp), water, sewer, phone (modem), laundry.

Sautee
Cherokee Campground of White County, 45 Bethel Rd., 30571. T: (706) 878-2267 or (888) 878-2268. www.mindlessdrivel.org. RV/tent: 48. $$. Hookups: electric (20, 30 amp), water, sewer, cable, phone (modem).

Creekwood Cabins & Campground, 5730 Hwy. 356, 30571. T: (706) 878-2164. www.creekwoodresort.info. RV/tent: 168. $. Hookups: electric (30, 50 amp), water, sewer, cable, bathhouse.

Sleepy Hollow Campground, 307 Sleepy Hollow Rd., 30571. T: (706) 878-2618. www.helenga.com/sleepyhollow/default.htm. RV/tent: 73. $$. Hookups: electric (20, 30 amp), water, sewer, hot showers, playground.

St. George
Hidden River Resort, 885 Reynolds Bridge Road St., 9988 CR 120, 31646. T: (912) 843-2603. www.hiddenriverresort.com. RV/tent: 30. $. Hookups: electric (30, 50 amp), water, sewer, phone (modem), laundry.

Statesboro
Parkwood Motel & RV Park, 12188 Hwy. 301 South, 30458. T: (912) 681-3105. www.parkwoodrv.com. RV/tent: 37. $$. Hookups: electric (30, 50 amp), water, sewer, cable, phone.

Tifton
Amy's South Georgia RV Park, 4632 Union Rd., 31794. T: (912) 386-8441 or (800) 813-3274. RV/tent: 88. $$. Hookups: electric (20, 30, 50 amp), water, sewer, phone.

Townsend
Lake Harmony RV Park, Rte. 3 Box 3128, 31331. T: (912) 832-4338 or (888) 767-7864. www.lakeharmonypark.com. RV/tent: 50. $$. Hookups: electric (30 amp), water, sewer, cable, phone (modem).

Tybee Island
River's End Campground & RV Park, 915 Polk St., 31328-0988. T: (912) 786-5518 or (800) 786-1016. www.gocampingamerica.com/riversendga/index.html. RV/tent: 127. $$. Hookups: electric (20, 30, 50 amp), water, sewer, phone (modem).

Unadilla
South Prong Creek Campground, 627 Hwy. 230, 31091. T: (912) 783-2551. RV/tent: 150. $. Hookups: electric (20, 30 amp), water, sewer, laundry.

Yatesville
Heart of Georgia RV Park, 6722 Hwy. 74, 31097. T: (706) 472-3437. RV/tent: 33. $$. Hookups: electric (30, 50 amp), water, sewer, laundry.

IDAHO

American Falls
Indian Springs RV Campground, 3249 Indian Springs Rd., 83211. T: (208) 226-2174. RV/tent: 125. $$. Hookups: electric (15, 20, 30 amp), water, sewer.

Massacre Rocks State Park, 3592 North Park Ln., 83211. T: (208) 548-2672. www.idahoparks.org. RV/tent: 48. $. Hookups: electric (30, 50 amp), water, sewer.

Willow Bay Recreation Area, 2830 Marina Rd., 83211. T: (208) 226-2688. www.visitid.com. RV/tent: 26. $. Hookups: electric (30 amp), water, sewer.

Arco
Landing Zone RV Park, 2424 No. 3000 West, 83213. T: (877) 563-0663. www.geocities.com/landingzone_2000. RV/tent: 37. $$. Hookups: electric (30 amp), water, sewer, modem.

Mountain View RV Park, 705 West Grand Ave., 83213. T: (800) 845-1460 or (208) 527-3707. RV/tent: 40. $$. Hookups: electric (20, 30 amp), water, sewer, modem.

Ashton
Jessen's RV Park, 1146 North 3400 East Hwy. 20, 83420. T: (800) 747-3356 or (208) 652-3356. RV/tent: 55. $$. Hookups: electric (30 amp), water, sewer, modem.

Boise
Americana RV Park, 3600 Americana Ter., 83706. T: (208) 344-5733. RV/tent: 107. $$. Hookups: electric (30, 50 amp), water, sewer, modem.

Fiesta RV Park, 11101 Fairview Ave., 83713. T: (888) 784-3246 or (208) 375-8207. www.fiestarv.com. RV/tent: 142. $$. Hookups: electric (20, 30 amp), water, sewer, modem.

Hi Valley RV Park, 10555 Horshoe Bend Rd., 83714. T: (888) 457-5959 or (208) 939-8080. www.g7inc.org/hivalley.htm. RV/tent: 194. $$. Hookups: electric (30, 50 amp), water, sewer, cable, phone.

On the River RV Park, 6000 North Glenwood, 83714. T: (800) 375-7432. www.camplan.com/ontheriver. RV/tent: 238. $$. Hookups: electric (20, 30, 50 amp), water, sewer, cable, modem.

Bonners Ferry
Blue Lake RV Park, H CR 61 Box 501, 83805. T: (208) 267-2029 or (888) 441-1031. RV/tent: 55. $$. Hookups: electric (20, 30 amp), water, sewer.

Deep Creek Resort, Rte. 4 Box 628, 83805. T: (800) 689-2729 or (208) 267-2729. RV/tent: 52. $. Hookups: electric, water, sewer.

Idyl Acres RV Park, H CR 61 Box 170, 83805. T: (208) 267-3629. RV/tent: 10. $$. Hookups: electric (20, 30 amp), water, sewer.

Caldwell
Caldwell Campground, 218 Town Cir. #34, 83607. T: (888) 675-0279 or (208) 454-0279. RV/tent: 125. $$. Hookups: electric (30, 50 amp), water, sewer, cable, modem.

Country Corners Campground, 17671 Oasis Rd., 83607. T: (208) 453-8791. www.rverschoice.com/countrycornersrvpark. RV/tent: 69. $$. Hookups: electric (30, 50 amp), water, sewer, cable, modem.

Challis
Challis All Valley RV Park, Hwy. 93 South, 83226. T: (208) 879-2393. RV/tent: 48. $$. Hookups: electric (30, 50 amp), water, sewer, cable.

Challis Hot Springs Campground, HC 63 Box 1779, Hot Springs Rd., 83226. T: (208) 879-4442. RV/tent: 36. $$. Hookups: electric (30 amp), water, modem.

Clark Fork
River Delta Resort, 60190 Hwy. 200 East, 83811. T: (208) 266-1335. RV/tent: 57. $$. Hookups: electric (30, 50 amp), water, sewer.

River Lake RV Park, 145 North River Lake Dr., 83811. T: (208) 266-1115. RV/tent: 31. $$. Hookups: electric (30 amp), water, sewer.

Clayton
Torrey's Burnt Creek Inn, HC 67 Box 725, 83227. T: (208) 838-2313. RV/tent: 27. $$. Hookups: electric (30, 50 amp), water, sewer.

IDAHO (continued)

Cocolalla

Sandy Beach Resort, 4405 Loop Rd., 83813. T: (208) 263-4328 or (888) 276-5755. www.sandy-beach-campground.com. RV/tent: 90. $$. Hookups: electric, water, sewer.

Coeur d'Alene

Bambi RV Park, 3113 North Government Way, 83815. T: (877) 381-5534 or (208) 664-6527. RV/tent: 21. $$. Hookups: electric, water, sewer.

Blackwell Island RV Park, 800 South Marina Dr., 83814. T: (888) 571-2900 or (208) 665-1300. www.idahorvpark.com. RV/tent: 122. $$. Hookups: electric (20, 30, 50 amp), water, sewer, cable, modem.

River Walk RV Park, 1214 Mill Ave., 83814. T: (888) 567-8700 or (208) 765-5943. RV/tent: 42. $$. Hookups: electric (30, 50 amp), water, sewer, cable, modem.

Robin Hood Campground & RV Park, 703 Lincoln Way South, 83814. T: (208) 664-2306. RV/tent: 80. $$. Hookups: electric (20, 30, 50 amp).

Shady Acres RV Park, 3630 North Government Way, 83814. T: (877) 212-0523 or (206) 664-3087. www.angelfire.com/id2/shadyacresrv. RV/tent: 30. $$. Hookups: electric (20, 30 amp), water, sewer.

Squaw Bay Camping Resort, 17505 South Hwy. 97, 83816. T: (208) 664-6782. www.squawbayresort .com. RV/tent: 50. $$. Hookups: electric, water, sewer, cable, modem.

Wolf Lodge Campground, 12329 East Frontage Rd., 83814. T: (208) 664-2812. RV/tent: 100. $$. Hookups: electric, water, sewer, cable, modem.

Declo

Travel Stop 216 RV Park, Exit 216 Interstate 84, 83323. T: (208) 654-2133. www.travelstop216. com. RV/tent: 120. $$. Hookups: electric (30, 50 amp), water, sewer, cable.

Donnelly

Chalet RV Resort, P.O. Box 100, 83615. T: (888) 457-5959 or (208) 325-8223. www.g7inc.org/chalet.htm. RV/tent: 76. $$. Hookups: electric (30 amp), water, sewer.

Mountain View RV Park, 1140 West Roseberry Rd., 83615. T: (208) 325-8055. RV/tent: 40. $$. Hookups: electric, water, sewer.

Southwestern Idaho Senior Citizens Recreation Association, P.O. Box 625, 83615. T: (208) 325-8130. RV/tent: 175. $. Hookups: electric, water, sewer.

Downey

Downata Hot Springs, 25900 Downata Rd., 83234. T: (208) 897-5736. www.downatahot springs.com. RV/tent: 90. $. Hookups: electric (20, 30 amp), water, modem.

Eden

Anderson Best Holiday Trav-L-Park, 1188 East 990 South, 83325. T: (888) 480-9400 or (208) 825-9800. www.bestholiday.org. RV/tent: 125. $$. Hookups: electric (30, 50 amp), water, sewer, modem.

Fruitland

Neat Retreat RV Park, 2700 Hwy. 95, 2701 Alder Space, 83619. T: (208) 452-4324. www.neat retreat.com. RV/tent: 80. $$. Hookups: electric (30, 50 amp), water, sewer, cable, modem.

Glenns Ferry

Trails West RV Park, 510 North Bannock Ave., 83623. T: (208) 366-7745. RV/tent: 52. $$. Hookups: electric, water, sewer, cable.

Grangeville

Mountain View RV Park, 127 Cunningham St. No. 4, 83530. T: (208) 983-2328. www.mountain viewmhrvpark.com. RV/tent: 75. $$. Hookups: electric (15, 30, 50 amp), water, sewer.

Hagerman

Hagerman RV Village, 18049 Hwy. 30 North, 83332. T: (208) 837-4906. RV/tent: 54. $$. Hookups: electric (30, 50 amp), water, sewer, modem.

Harvard

Pines RV Park & Campground, 4510 Hwy. 6, 83834. T: (208) 875-0831. www.pinesrv.freeyellow.com. RV/tent: 17. $. Hookups: electric (15, 30 amp).

Hayden Lake

Coeur D'Alene North/Hayden Lake KOA, 4850 East Garwood Rd., 83825. T: (800) KOA-0250 or (208) 664-4471. www.koa.com. RV/tent: 66. $$. Hookups: electric (30 amp), water, sewer.

Heise

Heise Hot Springs, 5116 Heise Rd. East, 83443. T: (208) 538-7312 or (208) 538-7944. www.srv.net/~heise/heise.html. RV/tent: 50. $$. Hookups: electric, water, sewer.

Homedale

Snake River RV Resort, 1 East Pioneer Rd., Rte. 1 Box 1062, 83628. T: (208) 337-3744. RV/tent: 50. $$. Hookups: electric (30, 50 amp), water, sewer, modem.

Hope

Beyond Hope Resort, 248 Beyond Hope, 1267 Peninsula Rd., 83836. T: (877) 270-HOPE or (208) 264-5251. RV/tent: 91. $$. Hookups: electric (30, 50 amp), water, sewer, cable, modem.

Idaho Country Resort, 141 Idaho Country Rd., 83836. T: (800) 307-3050 or (208) 264-5505. www.keokee.com/idahoresorts. RV/tent: 90. $$. Hookups: electric (30 amp), water, sewer, cable.

Sam Owen Campground, Idaho Panhandle National Forest, Rd. 136/Hope Peninsula Rd., 83836. T: (877) 444-6777 or (208) 263-5111. www.reserveusa.com. RV/tent: 80. $$. Hookups: none.

Idaho Falls

Sunnyside Acres Park, 905 West Sunnyside Rd., 83401. T: (208) 523-8403. RV/tent: 25. $$. Hookups: electric (30, 50 amp), water, sewer.

Island Park

Aspen Lodge, HC 66 Box 269, 83429. T: (208) 558-7407. RV/tent: 8. $$$$. Hookups: electric, water, sewer.

Big Springs (Caribou National Forest), Big Springs Loop Rd., 83429. T: (208) 558-7301. www.reserve usa.com. RV/tent: 29. $. Hookups: none.

Red Rock RV & Camping Park, Red Rock Rd., Hwy. 20, HC 66 Box 256, 83429. T: (800) 473-3762. www.8004redrock.com. RV/tent: 52. $$. Hookups: electric (20, 30 amp), water, sewer, modem.

Snowy River Campground, 3502 North Hwy. 20, 83429. T: (208) 558-7112 or (888) 897-3434. RV/tent: 57. $$. Hookups: electric (20, 30 amp), water, sewer, modem.

Valley View General Store & RV Park, 5152 North Hwy. 20, HC 66 Box 26, 83429. T: (208) 558-7443 or (888) 558-7443. www.valleyviewrv.com. RV/tent: 53. $. Hookups: electric (30, 50 amp), water, sewer.

Jerome

KOA Twin Falls/Jerome, 5431 US 93, 83338. T: (800) 562-4169 or (208) 324-4169. www.koa.com. RV/tent: 91. $$. Hookups: electric (30, 50 amp), water, sewer, satelite, modem.

Kamiah

Lewis-Clark Resort, Rte. 1 Box 17X, Hwy. 12, 83536. T: (208) 935-2556. www.lewisclarkresort .com. RV/tent: 200. $$. Hookups: electric (30 amp), water, sewer, modem.

Ketchum

The Meadows RV Park, Hwy. 75, 83353. T: (208) 726-5445. RV/tent: 45. $$. Hookups: electric (30 amp), water, sewer, cable.

Kooskia

Harpster Riverside RV Park, HC 66 Box 337, 83539. T: (208) 983-2312 or (800) 983-1918. www.harpsterriversidervpark.com. RV/tent: 29. $. Hookups: electric (30, 50 amp), water, sewer, satellite, modem.

River Junction RV Park, Hwy. 12, 83539. T: (208) 926-7865. RV/tent: 35. $. Hookups: electric, water, sewer.

Lava Hot Springs

Cottonwood Family Campground, 100 Bristol Park Ln., 83246. T: (208) 776-5295. www.lavasprings. org/cottonwoodfcg. RV/tent: 110. $$. Hookups: electric (20, 30 amp), water, sewer.

Lucille

Prospector's Gold RV & Campground, P.O. Box 313, 83542. T: (208) 628-3773. RV/tent: 50. $. Hookups: electric (30, 50 amp), water, modem.

McCall

Lakeview Village RV Park, 8 Pearl St., 83638. T: (208) 634-5280. RV/tent: 84. $. Hookups: electric (30 amp), water, sewer.

McCall Campground, 190 Krahn Ln., 83638. T: (208) 634-5165. RV/tent: 29. $$. Hookups: electric, water, sewer.

Melba

Given's Hot Springs, HC 79 Box 103, 83641. T: (208) 495-2000. www.givenshotsprings.com. RV/tent: 18. $$. Hookups: electric, water, sewer.

IDAHO (continued)

Meridian

The Playground RV Park, 1780 East Overland Rd., 83642. T: (800) 668-PLAY or (208) 887-1022. www.geocites.com/playgroundrv. RV/tent: 72. $$. Hookups: electric (30 amp), water, sewer, satellite, modem.

Montpelier

Emigration, Caribou National Forest, SR 36, 83254. T: (877) 444-6777. www.reserveusa.com. RV/tent: 23. $. Hookups: none.

Montpelier Canyon, Caribou National Forest, US Rte. 89, 83254. T: (877) 444-6777 or (208) 847-0375. www.reserveusa.com. RV/tent: 14. $. Hookups: none.

Moyie Springs

Herman Lake Campground, 158 Rd. 72, 83845. T: (208) 267-5120. RV/tent: 10. $. Hookups: electric, water, sewer.

Twin Rivers Canyon Resort, HCR 62 Box 25, 83845. T: (208) 267-5932 or (888) 258-5952. www.twinriversresort.com. RV/tent: 66. $$. Hookups: electric, water, sewer.

Nampa

Garrity RV Park, 3515 Garrity Blvd., 83687. T: (877) 442-9090 or (208) 442-9000. www.passport-america.com. RV/tent: 88. $. Hookups: electric (30, 50 amp), water, sewer, cable.

Mason Creek RV Park, 807 Franklin Blvd., 83687. T: (208) 465-7199. RV/tent: 88. $$. Hookups: electric (30, 50 amp), water, sewer, cable.

New Meadows

Meadows RV Park, 3278 Hwy. 55, 83654. T: (208) 347-2325 or (800) 603-2325. RV/tent: 37. $$$. Hookups: electric (30 amp), water, sewer.

Zim's Hot Springs, P.O. Box 314, 83654. T: (208) 347-2686. RV/tent: 35. $. Hookups: electric (30 amp), water.

Nordman

Kaniksu Resort, 485 Jim Low Rd., HCO 1 Box 152, 83848. T: (208) 443-2609. www.kaniksu-rv-park.com. RV/tent: 80. $$. Hookups: electric (30, 50 amp), water, sewer.

North Fork

Wagonhammer Springs Campground, Hwy. 93, 83466. T: (208) 865-2477. www.wagonhammer.com. RV/tent: 28. $$. Hookups: electric (20, 30 amp), water, sewer.

Osburn

Blue Anchor Trailer & RV Park, 300 West Mullin Ave., 83849. T: (208) 752-3443. RV/tent: 38. $$. Hookups: electric (30, 50 amp), water, sewer, cable.

Paris

Bear Lake State Park, P.O. Box 297, 83261. T: (208) 847-1045. www.reserveamerica.com. RV/tent: 100. $. Hookups: none.

Pinehurst

KOA Kellogg/Silver Valley Kampground, P.O. Box 949, 83850. T: (208) 682-3612 or (800) 562-0799. www.koakampgrounds.com. RV/tent: 66. $$. Hookups: electric (20, 30, 50 amp), water, sewer, cable, modem.

Pocatello

Cowboy RV Park, 845 Barton Rd., 83204. T: (208) 232-4587. RV/tent: 41. $$. Hookups: electric (30, 50 amp), water, sewer, cable, modem.

Scout Mountain (Caribou National Forest), 322 North 4th, 83254. T: (877) 444-6777 or (208) 236-7500. www.reserveusa.com. RV/tent: 25. $. Hookups: none.

Post Falls

Suntree RV Park, 350 North Idahine Rd., 83854. T: (208) 773-9982. RV/tent: 111. $$. Hookups: electric (30 amp), water, sewer, modem.

Preston

Willow Flat, Caribou National Forest, Cub River Canyon Rd., 83254. T: (877) 444-6777 or (208) 847-0375. www.reserveusa.com. RV/tent: 47. $. Hookups: none.

Priest Lake

Priest Lake RV Resort & Marina, HCR 5 Box 172, 83856. T: (208) 443-2405. www.priestlake.org. RV/tent: 16. $$. Hookups: electric, water, sewer.

Priest River

Luby Bay (Idaho Panhandle National Forest), 5538 West Lakeshore Rd., 83856. T: (800) 280-2267 or (208) 443-1801. www.reserveusa.com. RV/tent: 54. $$. Hookups: none.

Rexburg

Rainbow Lake & Campground, 2245 South 2000 West, 83440. T: (208) 356-3681. RV/tent: 60. $$. Hookups: electric (30 amp), water, sewer, modem.

Sheffield RV Park, 5362 South Hwy. 191, 83440. T: (208) 356-4182. RV/tent: 25. $$. Hookups: electric (30, 50 amp), water, sewer.

Ririe

7N Ranch, 5156 East Heise Rd., 83443. T: (208) 538-5097. RV/tent: 28. $. Hookups: electric (20, 30, 50 amp), water.

Mountain River Ranch RV Park, 98 North 5050 East, 83443. T: (208) 538-7337. RV/tent: 28. $. Hookups: electric (30 amp), water.

Rogerson

Desert Hot Springs, Hwy. 93, 83302. T: (208) 857-2233. RV/tent: 12. $. Hookups: electric, water, sewer.

Sagle

Alpine Park, Sagle Rd. & Hwy. 95, 83860. T: (208) 265-0179. RV/tent: 23. $$. Hookups: electric, water, sewer.

Travel America Plaza, Hwy. 95, 83860. T: (208) 263-6522. RV/tent: 80. $. Hookups: electric (20, 30, 50 amp), water, sewer.

Salmon

Century II Campground, 603 Hwy. 93 North, 83467. T: (208) 756-3063. RV/tent: 25. $. Hookups: electric (30, 50 amp), water, sewer.

Heald's Haven, 22 Heald Haven Dr., 83467. T: (208) 756-3929. RV/tent: 20. $. Hookups: electric (20, 30 amp), water.

Salmon Meadows

Salmon Meadows Campground, 400 North Saint Charles, Rte. 1 Box 25AB, 83467. T: (888) 723-2640 or (208) 756-2640. RV/tent: 70. $$. Hookups: electric (30, 50 amp), water, sewer.

Spirit Lake

Silver Beach Resort, 9484 West Spirit Lake, 83869. T: (208) 623-4842. www.silverbeachresort.com. RV/tent: 40. $$. Hookups: electric, water, sewer.

St. Anthony

Riverside Campground (Targhee National Forest), Hwy. 20, 83445. T: (208) 652-7442. RV/tent: 63. $. Hookups: none.

St. Charles

Bear Lake North RV Park & Campgrounds, 220 North Main St., 83201. T: (208) 945-2941. RV/tent: 66. $$. Hookups: electric (20, 30 amp), water.

Twin Falls

Nat-Soo-Pah Hot Springs, 2738 East 2400 North, 83301. T: (208) 655-4337. RV/tent: 75. $. Hookups: electric (30 amp), water, sewer.

Oregon Trail Campground & Family Fun Center, 2733 Kimberly Rd., 83301. T: (800) 733-0853 or (208) 733-0853. RV/tent: 41. $$. Hookups: electric, water, sewer.

Victor

Teton Valley Campground, 128 Hwy. 31 or P.O. Box 49, 83455. T: (877) 787-3036 or (208) 787-2647. www.tetonvalleycampground.com. RV/tent: 65. $$. Hookups: electric (20, 30, 50 amp), water, sewer, modem.

Wallace

Down by the Depot RV Park, 108 Nine Mile Rd., 83873. T: (208) 753-7121. RV/tent: 45. $$. Hookups: electric (30 amp), water, sewer.

Weiser

Gateway RV Park, 229 East 7th St., 83672. T: (208) 549-2539. RV/tent: 20. $$. Hookups: electric (20, 30 amp), water, sewer, cable.

Monroe Creek Campground & RV Park, 822 US 95, 83672. T: (208) 549-2026. RV/tent: 46. $. Hookups: electric (30 amp), water, modem.

Wendell

Intermountain RV Park, 1894 North Frontage Rd., 83355. T: (208) 536-2301. RV/tent: 25. $. Hookups: electric (20, 30 amp), water, modem.

Wilder

Rivers Edge RV Park, 28522 Lower Pleasant Rd., 83676. T: (208) 482-6560. RV/tent: 14. $$. Hookups: electric (30, 50 amp), water, sewer.

ILLINOIS

Algonquin

Buffalo Park, 4 Alan Dr., 60102. T: (847) 658-1188. RV/tent: 54. $$. Hookups: electric (30, 50 amp), water.

Amboy

Mendota Hills Resort, 642 US 52, 61310. T: (815) 849-5930 or (888) 436-3682. RV/tent: 250. $$$. Hookups: electric (30, 50 amp), water sewer, phone.

Arcola

Arcola Camper Stop, 472 Davis St., 61910. T: (217) 268-4616. RV/tent: 30. $$. Hookups: electric (30 amp), water, cable.

Campalot, 55 Industrial Dr., 61910. T: (217) 268-3563. RV/tent: 10. $$. Hookups: electric (20, 30, 50 amp), water, sewer.

Atlanta

Hickory Lane Camping, RR 2, 61723. T: (217) 648-2778. RV/tent: 178. $$. Hookups: electric (20, 30, 50 amp), water, sewer.

Barstow

Lundeen's Landing (East Moline), 21119 Barstow Rd., 61236. T: (309) 496-9956. www.lundeens landing.com. RV/tent: 65. $$. Hookups: electric (30 amp), water.

Belvidere

Outdoor World-Pine Country Campground, 5710 Shattuck Rd., 61008. T: (815) 547-5517 or (800) 222-5557. RV/tent: 107. $$. Hookups: electric (30 amp), water, sewer.

Benton

Gun Creek Campground, 12220 Rend City Rd., 62812. T: (618) 724-2493. RV/tent: 100. $. Hookups: electric (30 amp).

North Sandusky Creek Recreation Area, SR 154, 62812. T: (618) 625-6115. RV/tent: 141. $$. Hookups: electric (30 amp), water, sewer.

South Marcum Recreation Area, 11623 Trail Head Ln., 62812. T: (618) 435-3549. RV/tent: 143. $$. Hookups: electric (50 amp).

South Sandusky Creek Recreation Area, Red Oak Ln., 62812. T: (618) 625-3011. RV/tent: 121. $$. Hookups: electric (50 amp), water, sewer.

Biggsville

Hend-CoHills, Rte. 34, 61418. T: (309) 627-2779. RV/tent: 34. $$. Hookups: electric (20, 30 amp), water, sewer.

Bourbonnais

Kankakee River State Park, 5314 West Rte. 102, 60914. T: (815) 933-1383. dnr.state.il.us. RV/tent: 250. $$. Hookups: electric (30 amp).

Bushnell

Timberview Lakes Campground, 23200 North 2000 Rd., 61422. T: (309) 772-3609. RV/tent: 108. $$. Hookups: electric (20, 30, 50 amp), water, sewer, phone.

Byron

Lake Louise, 8840 Rte. 2, 61010. T: (815) 234-8483. www.lakelouisellc.com. RV/tent: 317. $$$. Hookups: electric (20, 30, 50 amp), water, sewer.

Cahokia

Cahokia RV Parque, 4060 Mississippi Ave., 62206. T: (618) 332-7700. www.cahokiarv.com. RV/tent: 116. $$$. Hookups: electric (30, 50 amp), water, sewer.

Cambridge

Gibson's RV Park and Campground, 10768 East 1600 St., 61238. T: (309) 937-2314. www.home town.aol.com/gibsoncmp. RV/tent: 125. $. Hookups: electric (20, 30, 50 amp), water.

Carbondale

Crab Orchard Lake Campground, 10067 Campground Dr., 62901. T: (618) 985-4983. RV/tent: 250. $. Hookups: electric (20, 30 amp), water.

Little Grassy Campground and Boatdock, 788 Hidden Bay, 62958. T: (618) 457-6655. RV/tent: 152. $$. Hookups: electric (30 amp), water, sewer.

Carlyle

Cole's Creek Recreation Area (Boulder), 16225 Cole's Creek Rd., 62231. T: (618) 226-3211. RV/tent: 148. $. Hookups: electric (30, 50 amp), water, sewer.

Dam West Recreation Area, 801 Lake Rd., 62231. T: (618) 594-4410 or (618) 594-2484. www.reserveusa.com. RV/tent: 113. $$. Hookups: electric (30 amp).

Eldon Hazlet State Park, 20100 Hazlet Park Rd., 62231. T: (618) 594-3015. dnr.state.il.us. RV/tent: 363. $. Hookups: electric (30, 50 amp).

McNair Campground, 801 Lake Rd., 62231. T: (618) 594-2484 or (618) 594-5253. www.reserve america.com. RV/tent: 25. $. Hookups: electric (30 amp), water.

Carmi

Burrell Park Campground, 6th & Stewart Sts., 62821. T: (618) 382-2693. RV/tent: 20. $$. Hookups: electric (30, 50 amp), water, sewer.

Champaign

D & W Camping and Fishing Lake, 411 West Hensley Rd., 61821. T: (217) 356-3732. RV/tent: 60. $$. Hookups: electric (20, 30, 50 amp), water, sewer.

Clayton

Siloam State Park, 938 East 300 3rd Ln., RR 1 Box 204, 62324. T: (217) 894-6205. www.dnr.state. il.us. RV/tent: 186. $. Hookups: electric (30 amp).

Clinton

Weldon Springs State Park, 1159 500 North, RR 2 Box 87, 61727. T: (217) 935-2644. dnr.state.il.us. RV/tent: 77. $. Hookups: electric (30 amp).

Crete

Emerald Trails Campground, 3132 East Goodnow Rd., 60417. T: (800) 870-8357. RV/tent: 94. $$. Hookups: electric (30 amp), water, sewer.

De Witt

Clinton Lake-Mascoutin State Recreation Complex, RR 1 Box 4, 61735. T: (217) 935-8722. dnr.state.il.us. RV/tent: 308. $. Hookups: electric (20, 30, 50 amp).

Durand

Sugar Shores Camping Resort, 9938 West Winslow Rd., 61024. T: (815) 629-2568. www.sugar shoresresort.com. RV/tent: 90. $$. Hookups: electric (20, 30, 50 amp), water, phone.

East St. Louis

Casino Queen RV Park, River Park Drive, 62201. T: (618) 874-5000 or (800) 777-0777. www .casinoqueen.com. RV/tent: 132. $$. Hookups: electric (50 amp), water, cable, Internet.

Edwardsville

Red Barn Rendezvous, 3955 Blackburn Rd., 62025. T: (618) 692-9015. RV/tent: 22. $$. Hookups: electric (20, 30, 50 amp), water, sewer.

Effingham

Lake Sara Campground and Beach, 70 Wildwood Dr., 62401. T: (217) 868-2964. RV/tent: 315. $$. Hookups: electric (20, 30 amp), water, sewer.

Fithian

Five Bridges Campground, IL 49 North, 61844. T: (217) 583-3200. RV/tent: 37. $$. Hookups: electric (30 amp), water.

Gages Lake

Gages Lake Camping, 18887 West Gages Lake Rd., 60030. T: (847) 223-5541. RV/tent: 100. $$$. Hookups: electric (30 amp), water.

Garden Prairie

Holiday Acres, 7050 Epworth Rd., 61038. T: (815) 547-7846. RV/tent: 520. $$. Hookups: electric (20, 30 amp), water.

Paradise Park, 11122 Station St., 61038. T: (815) 597-1671. www.paradiservpark.com. RV/tent: 170. $$$. Hookups: electric (15, 20, 30, 50 amp), water.

Geneseo

Spirit in the Oaks, 27340 East 1350 St., 61254. T: (309) 944-3889 or (309) 944-3891. www .fulltiming-america.com/spirits/. RV/tent: 90. $$. Hookups: electric (20, 30, 50 amp), water, sewer.

Glenarm

Holiday RV Center & Trav-L-Park, 9683 Palm Rd., 62629. T: (260) 483-9998. RV/tent: 110. $$. Hookups: electric (50 amp), water, sewer.

Golconda

Dixon Springs State Park (Dixon), Rte. 146, 62938. T: (618) 949-3394. dnr.state.il.us. RV/tent: 50. $. Hookups: electric (30 amp).

Goreville

Ferne Clyffe State Park, Rte. 37, 62939. T: (618) 995-2411. dnr.state.il.us. RV/tent: 65. $. Hookups: electric (30 amp).

ILLINOIS (continued)

Hilltop Campgrounds, 255 Baker Ln., 62939. T: (618) 995-2189. RV/tent: 52. $$. Hookups: electric (30, 50 amp), water, sewer.

Grafton

Pere Marquette State Park, Rte. 100, 62037. T: (618) 786-3323. www.greatriverroad.com. RV/tent: 117. $. Hookups: electric (30 amp).

Havana

Havana Park District Riverfront Park Campground, 200 South McKinley, 62644. T: (309) 543-6240. www.havana.lib.il.us. RV/tent: 12. $$. Hookups: electric (30 amp), water.

Joliet

Martin Campground, 725 Cherry Hill Rd., 60433. T: (815) 726-3173. RV/tent: 110. $$. Hookups: electric (20, 30 amp), water, sewer.

Le Roy

Moraine View State Park, 27374 Moraine View Park Rd., 61752. T: (309) 724-8032. dnr.state.il.us. RV/tent: 199. $$. Hookups: electric (30 amp).

Leland

Hi-Tide Recreation, 4611 East 22nd Rd., 60531. T: (815) 495-9032. www.gocampingamerica .com/hitide. RV/tent: 33. $$. Hookups: electric (20, 30, 50 amp), water, sewer, propane.

Lincoln

Camp-A-While, 1779 1250 Ave., 62656. T: (888) 593-5102. RV/tent: 27. $$. Hookups: electric (20, 30, 50 amp), water, sewer.

Litchfield

Kamper Kompanion Campground, 18388 East Frontage Rd., 62056. T: (217) 324-4747. RV/tent: 24. $$. Hookups: electric (20, 30 amp), water, sewer.

Mackinaw

Kentuckiana Campground, 27585 Kentuckiana Rd., 61755. T: (309) 449-3274. www.gocamping america.com/kentuckiana. RV/tent: 340. $$. Hookups: electric (20, 30, 50 amp), water, sewer.

Makanda

Giant City State Park, 235 Grant City Rd., 62958. T: (618) 457-4836. www.dnr.state.il.us. RV/tent: 99. $. Hookups: electric (20, 30, 50 amp).

Marengo

Best Holiday Lehman's Lakeside RV Resort, 19609 Harmony Rd., 60152. T: (877) 242-8533 or (815) 923-4533. www.bestholiday.org/il.html. RV/tent: 290. $$$. Hookups: electric (20, 30, 50 amp), water, sewer, cable, phone.

Marion

Motel Marion Campground, 2100 West Main St., 62959. T: (618) 993-2101. www.motelmarion .com. RV/tent: 25. $$. Hookups: electric (30, 50 amp), water, sewer.

Marseilles

Illini State Park, 2660 East 2350th Rd., 61341. T: (815) 795-2448. www.dnr.state.il.us. RV/tent: 102. $. Hookups: electric (30 amp).

Whispering Pines Campground, 2776 East 2625 Rd., 61341. T: (815) 795-5720. RV/tent: 400. $$. Hookups: electric (15, 20, 30, 50 amp), water, sewer.

Marshall

Mill Creek Park Campground, 20482 North Park Entrance Rd., 62441. T: (217) 889-3601 or (217) 889-3901. www.clarkcountyparkdistrict.com/ millcreek. RV/tent: 139. $. Hookups: electric (20, 30 amp).

Mendon

Whispering Oaks Campground, 2124 East 1300th Place, 62351. T: (217) 936-2500. RV/tent: 235. $$. Hookups: electric (30 amp), water, sewer.

Mount Vernon

Quality Times, 9746 East IL Hwy. 15, 62864. T: (618) 244-0399. www.gocampingamerica .com/qualitytimes/index.html. RV/tent: 42. $$. Hookups: electric (20, 30 amp), water, sewer, propane.

Murphysboro

Lake Murphysboro State Park, 52 Cinder Hill Dr., 62966. T: (618) 684-2867. www.murphysboro .com/lakemurphysboro/index.html. RV/tent: 74. $. Hookups: electric (50 amp).

Nauvoo

Nauvoo Campground, 2205 Mulholland St., 62354. T: (217) 453-2253. www.campingconnection .com/u/u145.shtml. RV/tent: 30. $. Hookups: electric (20, 30, 50 amp), water, sewer.

New Windsor

Shady Lakes Camping & Recreation, 3355 75th Ave., 61465. T: (309) 667-2709. web.winco .net/~shadylak/. RV/tent: 243. $$. Hookups: electric (20, 30, 50 amp), water.

Oakland

Hebron Hills Camping, 14349 North City Rd. 2350 East, 61943. T: (217) 346-3385. www.Hebron Hills.com. RV/tent: 45. $$. Hookups: electric (20, 30, 50 amp), water, sewer, phone.

Oakwood

Kickapoo State Park, 10906 Kickapoo Park Rd., 61858. T: (217) 442-4915. dnr.state.il.us. RV/tent: 217. $. Hookups: electric (30 amp).

Onarga

Lake Arrowhead, 1478 North 500 East Rd., 60955. T: (815) 268-4849. RV/tent: 50. $$. Hookups: electric (30 amp), water.

Oquawka

Delabar State Park, RR 2 Box 27, 61469. T: (309) 374-2496. www.dnr.state.il.us/lands/landmgt /parks/r1/delabar.htm. RV/tent: 124. $. Hookups: electric (30 amp), water, sewer.

Oregon

Hansen's Hide Away Ranch & Family Campground, 2936 South Harmony Rd., 61061. T: (815) 732-6489. www.hansenscampground.com. RV/tent: 102. $$. Hookups: electric (20, 30 amp), water, sewer.

Pearl City

Emerald Acres Campground, 3351 South Mill Grove Rd., 61062. T: (815) 443-2550 or (815) 633-3279. www.emeraldacrescampground.com. RV/tent: 140. $$. Hookups: electric (20, 30 amp), water, sewer.

Peoria

Mt. Hawley RV Park, 8327 North Knoxville Ave., 61615. T: (309) 692-2223 or (888) 862-5494. www.gocampingamerica.com/mt.hawleyrvpk. RV/tent: 90. $$. Hookups: electric (20, 30, 50 amp), water, sewer, phone.

Plainview Beaver Dam State Park, 14548 Beaver Dam Ln., 62676. T: (217) 854-8020. www.dnr.state.il.us. RV/tent: 84. $. Hookups: electric (30 amp), water, sewer.

Rochester

KOA Springfield, 4320 KOA Rd., 62563. T: (417) 831-3645 or (800) 562-1228. www.koa.com/ where/mo/25137.htm. RV/tent: 96. $$. Hookups: electric (20, 30 amp), water, sewer, phone.

Rock

Cave-In-Rock State Park, 1 New State Park Rd. Box 338, 62919. T: (618) 289-4325. www.dnr.state.il.us. RV/tent: 59. $. Hookups: electric (30 amp), water, sewer.

Rock Falls

Leisure Lake Campground, 2304 French St., 61071. T: (815) 626-0005. RV/tent: 68. $$. Hookups: electric (20, 30 amp), water, sewer, phone.

Rock Island

Camelot Campground & Recreation, 2311 78 Ave. West, 61201. T: (309) 787-0665. RV/tent: 158. $$. Hookups: electric (30, 50 amp), water, sewer.

Rockford

Blackhawk Valley Campground, 6540 Valley Trail Rd., 61109. T: (815) 874-9767. RV/tent: 130. $$. Hookups: electric (30 amp), water, sewer.

Salem

Stephen A. Forbes State Park, 4577 Rte. 84N, 61074. T: (618) 547-33381. RV/tent: 115. $. Hookups: electric (30 amp).

Shelbyville

Bo Wood Recreation Area, RR 4, 62565. T: (217) 774-2014. RV/tent: 82. $$. Hookups: electric (30 amp).

Sheridan

Mallard Bend Campground & RV Park, 2838 North 4351st St., 60551. T: (815) 496-2496. www .mallardbend.com. RV/tent: 168. $$. Hookups: electric (20, 30, 50 amp), water, sewer.

Rolling Oaks Campground, 2743 North 1st Rd., 60551. T: (815) 496-2334. RV/tent: 670. $$. Hookups: electric (20, 30 amp), water, sewer.

Spring Grove

Chain O'Lakes State Park, Oak Point (Fox Lake), 8916 Wilmot Rd., 60081. T: (847) 587-5512. RV/tent: 238. $. Hookups: electric (30 amp).

ILLINOIS (continued)

St. Elmo

Bell's Timberline Lake Campground, P. O. Box 15, 62458. T: (618) 829-3383. RV/tent: 100. $. Hookups: electric (30 amp), water, sewer.

Sumner

Red Hills Lake State Park (Lawrencville), RR 2, 62466. T: (618) 936-2469. RV/tent: 104. $. Hookups: electric (20, 30 amp).

Tinley Park

Windy City Campground & Beach, 18701 South 80th Ave., 60477. T: (708) 720-0030. RV/tent: 100. $$$. Hookups: electric (20, 30, 50 amp), water, sewer, phone.

Tokeka

Evening Star Camping Resort, 23049 US 136, 61567. T: (309) 562-7590. www.passport-america.com. RV/tent: 325. $$. Hookups: electric (20, 30, 50 amp), water, sewer.

Union

KOA Chicago Northwest (Marengo), 8404 South Union Rd., 60180. T: (800) KOA-2827. RV/tent: 138. $$. Hookups: electric (15, 20, 30, 50 amp), water.

Wilmington

Fossil Rock Campground, 24615 West Strip Mine Rd., 60481. T: (815) 476-6784. RV/tent: 215. $$$.

Hookups: electric (20, 30, 50 amp), water, sewer, phone.

Windsor

Wolf Creek State Park, RR 1 Box 99, 61957. T: (217) 459-2831. www.dnr.state.il.us. RV/tent: 406. $. Hookups: electric (30 amp).

Yorkville

Hide-A-Way Lakes, 8045 Van Emmon Rd., 60560. T: (630) 553-6323. www.hideawaylakes.com. RV/tent: 800. $$. Hookups: electric (30, 50 amp), water, sewer, phone.

INDIANA

Albion

Chain O'Lakes State Park, 2355 East 75S, 46701. T: (260) 636-2654. RV/tent: 413. $. Hookups: electric (30 amp), water, sewer.

Anderson

Mounds State Park, 4306 Mounds Rd., 46017. T: (765) 642-6627. RV/tent: 75. $$. Hookups: electric (30 amp), water.

Andrews

Lost Bridge West SRA. Salamonie Lake, 9214 West Lost Bridge West, 46702. T: (260) 468-2125. RV/tent: 290. $. Hookups: electric (30 amp).

Angola

Camp Sack-In, 8740 East 40S, 46703. T: (260) 665-5166. www.campsackin.com. RV/tent: 150. $$. Hookups: electric (30 amp), water.

Circle B Park, 340 Ln. 100, 46703. T: (260) 665-5353. www.circlebpark.com. RV/tent: 50. $$$. Hookups: electric (50 amp), water, sewer.

Cook's Happy Acres RV Park, 1940 South 300W, 46703. T: (888) 318-8797. RV/tent: 100. $$. Hookups: electric (20, 30, 50 amp), water, sewer.

Pokagon State Park, 450 Ln. 100 Lake James, 46703. T: (219) 833-2012. www.in.govdnr. RV/tent: 273. $. Hookups: electric (30 amp).

Attica

Summers Campground, 5509 North 200E, 47918. T: (765) 762-2832. RV/tent: 100. $$. Hookups: electric (30 amp), water.

Birdseye

Newton-Stewart SRA. Patoka Lake, 3084 North Dillano Rd., 47513. T: (812) 685-2464. www.in.gov/dnr. RV/tent: 563. $$. Hookups: electric (30 amp).

Bloomington

Paynetown State Recreation Area, 4850 South SR 446, 47401. T: (812) 837-9546. www.dnr.in.gov. RV/tent: 320. $. Hookups: electric (30 amp), water.

Bluffton

Quabache State Park, 4930 East SR 201, 46714. T: (866) 622-6746. www.campin.gov. RV/tent: 124. $$. Hookups: electric (30 amp).

Boonville

Scales Lake Park, 800 West Tennyson Rd., 47601. T: (812) 897-6200. www.scaleslakepark.com. RV/tent: 141. $. Hookups: electric (30 amp), sewer.

Borden

Deam Lake State Recreation Area, 1217 Deam Lake Rd., 47106. T: (574) 546-2657. www.ru destinations.com. RV/tent: 100. $. Hookups: electric (30 amp).

Bremen

Rupert's Resort Campground, 3408 West Shore Dr., 46506. T: (219) 546-2657. RV/tent: 120. $$. Hookups: electric (30 amp), water.

Brookville

Mounds State Recreation Area, SR 101, 47012. T: (765) 647-2657. www.state.in.us/dnr. RV/tent: 379. $$. Hookups: electric (30 amp), water, sewer.

Cedar Lake

Cedar Lake Bible Conference, 13701 Lauerman, 46303. T: (219) 374-5941. www.cedarlake ministries.org. RV/tent: 40. $$. Hookups: electric (30 amp), water, sewer.

Charlestown

Charlestown State Park, 12500 St. Rd. 62, 47111. T: (866) 622-6746. www.camp.in.gov. RV/tent: 192. $$. Hookups: electric (30 amp), water, sewer.

Chesteron

Indiana Dune State Park, 1600 North 25E, 46304. T: (219) 926-1952. www.state.in.us/dn. RV/tent: 201. $. Hookups: electric (30 amp).

Sand Creek Campground, 1000 North 350 East, 46304. T: (219) 926-7482. www.duneland.com. RV/tent: 146. $$. Hookups: electric (50 amp), water, sewer.

Cicero

White River Campground, 11299 East 234th St., 46034. T: (317) 984-2705. www.co.hamilton.in.us. RV/tent: 106. $$. Hookups: electric (30 amp), water, sewer.

Clarksville

Louisville Metro KOA Kampground, 900 Marriott Dr., 47129. T: (812) 282-4474 or (800) 562-4771. www.koakampgrounds.com. RV/tent: 92. $$. Hookups: electric (50 amp), water, sewer, cable, phone.

Cloverdale

Blackhawk Campground, 2046 West CR 1050S, 46120. T: (765) 795-4795. www.campindiana. com. RV/tent: 141. $$. Hookups: electric (30 amp), water, sewer.

Colfax

Broadview Lake, 4850 South Broadview Rd., 46035. T: (317) 324-2622. RV/tent: 170. $$. Hookups: electric (30 amp), water, sewer.

Dillsboro

Brownings Camp, 3622 East CR 200S, 47018. T: (812) 689-6464. RV/tent: 257. $. Hookups: electric (50 amp), water, sewer.

Edinburgh

Driftwood Camp-RV Park, 12180 US 31N, 46124. T: (812) 526-6422. RV/tent: 62. $$. Hookups: electric (30, 50 amp), water, sewer.

Elkhart

Elkhart Campground, 25608 CR 4E, 46514. T: (574) 264-2914. RV/tent: 450. $$. Hookups: electric (50 amp), water, sewer.

Fort Wayne

Gordon's Camping, 1010 Ansely Dr., 46804. T: (260) 351-3383 or (260) 436-6823. www .gordonscamping.com. RV/tent: 321. $$. Hookups: electric (50 amp), water.

INDIANA (continued)

Geneva
Amishville USA, 844 East 900S, 46740. T: (219) 589-3536. www.amishville.com. RV/tent: 284. $. Hookups: electric (30 amp), water.

Granger
South Bend East KOA, 50707 Princess Way, 46530. T: (574) 277-1335. www.koa.com/where/in/14153.htm. RV/tent: 80. $$. Hookups: electric (30, 50 amp), water.

Greenfield
Heartland Resort, 1613 West 300N, 46140. T: (317) 326-3181. RV/tent: 309. $$. Hookups: electric (50 amp), water, sewer.

Mohawk Campground & RV Park, 756 West 375 N, 46140. T: (317) 326-3393. RV/tent: 104. $$. Hookups: electric (30 amp), water, sewer.

Hartford City
Wildwood Acres Campground, 520 West 300N, 47348. T: (765) 348-2100. RV/tent: 120. $$. Hookups: electric (30 amp), water.

Indianapolis
Indiana State Fairgrounds Campground, 1202 East 38th St., 46205. T: (317) 927-7510. RV/tent: 170. $$. Hookups: electric (20 amp), water, sewer.

Jasonville
Shakamak State Park, 6265 West SR 48, 47438. T: (812) 665-2158. www.in.gov/dnr/parklake/parks/shakamak.html. RV/tent: 196. $. Hookups: electric (30 amp).

Knox
Bass Lake State Park, 5838 South SR 10, 46534. T: (219) 772-3382. RV/tent: 60. $. Hookups: electric (30 amp).

Kokomo
Springhill Campground, 623 South 750 W, 46901. T: (765) 883-7433. RV/tent: 122. $$. Hookups: electric (30 amp), water.

Kouts
Donna-Jo Camping Area, 1255 South CR 350E, 46347. T: (219) 766-2186. RV/tent: 75. $$. Hookups: electric (30, 50 amp), water.

Liberty
Whitewater Memorial State Park, 1418 South SR 101, 47353. T: (765) 458-5565. www.in.gov/dnr/parklake/parks/whitewater.html. RV/tent: 281. $. Hookups: electric (30 amp).

Lincoln City
Lincoln State Park, P.O. Box 216, 47552. T: (812) 937-4710. www.in.gov/dnr/parklake/parks/lincoln.html. RV/tent: 270. $. Hookups: electric (30 amp), water.

Logansport
France Park, 4505 US 24W, 46947-9083. T: (574) 753-2928. www.francepark.com. RV/tent: 300. $. Hookups: electric (30 amp), water.

Tall Sycamore Campground, 355 South CR 600E, 46947. T: (574) 753-4898. RV/tent: 125. $. Hookups: full.

Loogootee
West Boggs Park, P.O. Box 245, 47553. T: (812) 295-3421. RV/tent: 220. $$. Hookups: electric (30 amp), water, sewer.

Lynnville
Lynnville Park, P.O. Box 309, 47619. T: (812) 922-5144. RV/tent: 47. $$. Hookups: electric (30 amp), water, sewer.

Marshall
Turkey Run State Park, P.O. Box 37, 47859. T: (765) 597-2635. www.in.gov/dnr/parklake/parks/turkeyrun.html. RV/tent: 213. $. Hookups: electric (30 amp).

Michigan City
Michigan City Campground, 1601 US 421N, 46360. T: (219) 872-7600 or (800) 813-2267. RV/tent: 150. $$. Hookups: electric (30 amp), water, sewer.

Middlebury
Elkhart Co./Middlebury Exit KOA, 52867 SR 13, 46540. T: (574) 825-5932 or (800) 562-5892. www.koa.com. RV/tent: 120. $$. Hookups: electric (50 amp), water, sewer.

Mitchell
Spring Mill State Park, P.O. Box 376, 47446. T: (812) 849-4129. www.in.gov/dnr/parklake/parks/springmill.htm. RV/tent: 223. $. Hookups: electric (30 amp).

Modoc
Kamp Modoc, 8773 South 800W, 47358. T: (765) 853-5290. www.kampmodoc.com. RV/tent: 260. $$. Hookups: electric (30 amp), water.

Montgomery
Glendale State Fish & Wildlife Area, P.O. Box 300, 47558. T: (812) 644-7711. RV/tent: 121. $. Hookups: electric (30 amp).

Monticello
Arrowhead Campground, CR 400 East, 47960. T: (574) 583-5198. RV/tent: 194. $$$. Hookups: electric (30 amp), water, sewer.

Holiday Resort, 101 Penson Dr., 47960. T: (574) 583-7396. RV/tent: 36. $$. Hookups: electric (30 amp), water.

Indiana Beach Camp Resort, 5224 East Indiana Beach Rd., 47960. T: (800) 583-5306. www.indiabeach.com/IBCampResort.html. RV/tent: 301. $$. Hookups: electric (50 amp), water, sewer.

Nashville
Brown County State Park, SR 46, 47448. T: (812) 988-6406. www.browncountystatepark.com. RV/tent: 412. $$. Hookups: electric (30 amp).

Westward Ho Campground, 4557 East SR 46, 47448. T: (812) 988-0008. RV/tent: 91. $$. Hookups: electric (30, 50 amp), water, sewer.

New Carlisle
Mini Mountain Camp Resort, 32351 State Rd. 2, 46552. T: (574) 654-3307. www.minimountaincampground.com. RV/tent: 199. $$. Hookups: electric (50 amp), water, sewer.

New Castle
Summit Lake State Park, 5993 North Messick Rd., 47362. T: (765) 766-5873. www.in.gov/dnr/parklake/parks/summitlake.html. RV/tent: 125. $. Hookups: electric (30 amp).

Walnut Ridge Resort Campground, 408 North CR 300W, 47362. T: (765) 533-6611 or (877) 61-WALLY. www.walnutridgerv.com/campground. RV/tent: 150. $$. Hookups: electric (30 amp), water.

New Harmony
Harmonie State Park, 3451 Harmonie State Park Rd., 47631. T: (812) 682-4821. www.in.gov/dnr/parklake/parks/harmonie.html. RV/tent: 200. $. Hookups: electric (30 amp).

North Liberty
Potato Creek State Park, 25601 SR 4, 46554. T: (574) 656-8186. www.in.gov/dnr/parklake/parks/potatocreek.html. RV/tent: 287. $. Hookups: electric (30 amp).

Pendleton
Glowood Campground, 9384 West 700S, 46064. T: (317) 485-5239. RV/tent: 100. $$. Hookups: electric (30, 50 amp), water.

Peru
Mississinewa Lake-Miami Recreation Area, Box 194, 46970. T: (765) 473-6528 or (765) 395-7038. www.state.in.us/dnr/parklake/reservoirs/mississinewa. RV/tent: 620. $. Hookups: electric (50 amp), water, sewer.

Pierceton
Yogi Bear's Jellystone Park Camp-Resort Pierceton, 1916 North 850E, 46562. T: (574) 594-2124. RV/tent: 150. $$$. Hookups: electric (30 amp), water, sewer.

Portland
Hickory Grove Lakes Campground, 7424 South 300E, 47371. T: (260) 637-3524. RV/tent: 78. $$. Hookups: electric (30 amp), water, sewer.

Richmond
Deer Ridge Camping Resort, 3696 Smyrna Rd., 47374. T: (765) 939-0888 or (800) 578-5267. www.deerridgecampingresort.com. RV/tent: 70. $$. Hookups: electric (30 amp), water, sewer.

Grandpa's Farm, 4244 SR 227 North, 47374. T: (765) 962-7907 or (888) 756-4490. www.grandpasfarmcamp.com. RV/tent: 85. $$. Hookups: electric (30, 50 amp), water, sewer.

Richmond KOA, 3101 Cart Rd., 47374. T: (765) 962-1219 or (800) 562-0611. www.koa.com. RV/tent: 75. $$. Hookups: electric (30 amp), water, sewer.

Rockville
Covered Bridge Campground, 211 South Erie St., 47874. T: (765) 569-3911. RV/tent: 100. $$. Hookups: electric (30 amp), water, sewer.

Raccoon State Recreation Area, 160 South Raccoon Pkwy, 47872. T: (765) 344-1412. www.in.gov/dnr/parklake/reservoirs/cecil.html. RV/tent: 306. $. Hookups: electric (30 amp).

INDIANA (continued)

Scottsburg

Hardy Lake State Recreation Area, 4171 East Harrod Rd., 47170. T: (812) 794-3800. www.in .gov/dnr/parklake/reservoirs/hardy.html. RV/tent: 168. $. Hookups: electric (30 amp).

Shelbyville

Fairland Recreation Park, 3779 North Frontage Rd., 46176. T: (317) 392-0525. RV/tent: 44. $$. Hookups: full.

Shipshewana

Riverside Campground, 5910 North CR 450W, 46565. T: (260) 562-3742. RV/tent: 30. $$. Hookups: electric (30 amp), water.

Shipshewana Campground & Amish Log Cabin Lodging, 5970 North SR 5, 46565-0172. T: (260) 768-7770. www.amish.org. RV/tent: 45. $$. Hookups: electric (30 amp), water, sewer.

Shipshewana Campground South, 1105 South Van-Buren St., 46565. T: (260) 768-4669. RV/tent: 70. $$$. Hookups: electric (30 amp), water.

Spencer

McCormick's Creek State Park, RR 5 Box 282, 47460. T: (812) 829-2235. www.in.gov/dnr/park lake/parks/mccormickscreek.html. RV/tent: 289. $. Hookups: electric (30 amp).

St. Paul

Hidden Paradise Campground, 802 East Jefferson St., 47272. T: (765) 525-6582. RV/tent: 168. $$. Hookups: electric (50 amp), water, sewer.

Terre Haute

KOA Terre Haute, 5995 East Sony Dr., 47802. T: (812) 232-2457 or (800) 562-4179. www.koa .com. RV/tent: 77. $$. Hookups: electric (30, 50 amp), water, sewer.

Vallonia

Starve Hollow State Recreation Area, 4345 South CR 275W, 47281. T: (812) 358-3464 or (888) 524-0000. RV/tent: 191. $$. Hookups: electric (30 amp).

Valparaiso

Candy Stripe Campsite, 446 West Division Dr., 46383. T: (219) 462-0784. RV/tent: 100. $$. Hookups: electric (50 amp), water, sewer.

Warsaw

Hoffman Lake Camp, 7638 West 300N, 46582. T: (800) 289-8256 or (574) 858-9628. camp indiana.com/hoffmanlake. RV/tent: 193. $$. Hookups: electric (20, 30, 50 amp), water, sewer.

Pic-A-Spot Campground, 6402 East McKenna Rd., 46580. T: (574) 594-2635. www.mytownlink.com/picaspot. RV/tent: 168. $$. Hookups: electric (30 amp), water.

Pike Lake Campground, 117 East Canal St., 46580. T: (219) 269-1439. RV/tent: 110. $$. Hookups: electric (30 amp), water.

Winamac

Tippecanoe River State Park, 4200 North US 35, 46996. T: (574) 946-3213. www.in.gov/dnr/park lake/parks/tippecanoeriver.html. RV/tent: 178. $. Hookups: electric (30 amp).

Williams Broken Arrow Campground, RR 1 Box 391, 46996. T: (574) 946-4566. RV/tent: 990. $$. Hookups: electric (30, 50 amp), water, sewer.

IOWA

Amana

Amana Colonies RV Park, P.O. Box 345, 52203. T: (319) 622-7616 or (800) 471-7616. www .amanarvpark.com. RV/tent: 420. $. Hookups: full.

Anita

Lake Anita State Park, 55111 750th St., 50020. T: (712) 762-3564. www.state.ia.us/dnr/organiza/ ppd.anita.htm. RV/tent: 144. $. Hookups: full.

Arnolds Park

Arnolds Park City Park, P.O. Box 437, City Hall, Broadway, 51331. T: (712) 332-2341. RV/tent: 25. $. Hookups: electric (20 amp).

Auburn

Grants Park, 3531 365th St., 51433. T: (712) 662-4530. RV/tent: 30. $. Hookups: electric, water.

Augusta

Lower Skunk River Access (Des Moines County Park), 512 North Main St., 52601. T: (319) 753-8260. RV/tent: 47. $. Hookups: electric.

Avoca

Parkway Cafe & Campground, 857 South Chestnut St., 51521. T: (712) 343-6652. www.geocities .com/parkwaycafe. RV/tent: 80. $. Hookups: full.

Bedford

Lake of Three Fires State Park, 2303 IA 49, 50833. T: (712) 523-2700. www.state.ia.us/dnr/organiza /ppd/lakefire.htm. RV/tent: 140. $. Hookups: full.

Bellevue

Bellevue State Park, 21466 429th Ave., 52031. T: (563) 872-4019. www.state.ia.us/dnr/orga niza/ppd/camping.htm. RV/tent: 48. $. Hookups: electric, water.

Hannen Park (Benton County Park), 1949 Benton Iowa Rd., 52209. T: (319) 454-6382. RV/tent: 55. $$. Hookups: electric.

Spruce Creek Park (Jackson County Park), Jackson County Courthouse, 52060. T: (563) 872-3621. www.jacksoncountyiowa.com/tourismpark index.cfm. RV/tent: 85. $. Hookups: electric (30 amp).

Bloomfield

Lakeside Village Campground, Rte. 3 Box 39, 52537. T: (647) 664-3364. RV/tent: 180. $. Hookups: full.

Brighton

Lake Darling State Park, 111 Lake Darling Rd., 52540. T: (319) 694-2323. www.state.ia.us/dnr/ organiza/ppd/darling.htm. RV/tent: 118. $. Hookups: electric.

Clermont

Skip-A-Way RV Park and Campground, 3825 Harding Rd., 52135. T: (800) 728-1167 or (563) 423-7338. RV/tent: 77. $$. Hookups: electric (20, 30, 50 amp), water, phone (modem),.

Colo

Twin Anchors RV Park, 68132 US 30, 50056. T: (641) 377-2243. RV/tent: 210. $$. Hookups: electric (30, 50 amp), water.

Council Bluffs

Bluffs Run Casino RV Park, 2701 23rd Ave., 51502-0420. T: (800) 238-2946 or (712) 323-2500. RV/tent: 123. $$. Hookups: electric (30, 50 amp), water.

Tomes Country Club Acres, 706 SW Omaha Bridge Rd., 51501. T: (712) 366-0363. RV/tent: 25. $$. Hookups: electric (15, 20, 30 amp).

Creco

Chimney Rock Canoe Rental and Campground, 3312 Chimney Rock Rd., 52136. T: (563) 735-5786 or (877) 787-2267. www.chimneyrocks .com. RV/tent: 28. $. Hookups: electric (20 amp).

Dubuque

Dubuque Yacht Basin and RV Park, 1630 East 16th St., 52001. T: (563) 588-9564. www.dubuque yachtbasin.com. RV/tent: 60. $$. Hookups: full.

Forest City

Three Fingers Campground, 14300 355th St., 50436. T: (641) 581-5856. RV/tent: 75. $$. Hookups: electric, water.

Garnavillo

J-Wood Campground, 31848 Clayton Rd., 52049. T: (563) 964-2236. www.mcgreg-marq.org/ jwood.htm. RV/tent: 97. $. Hookups: electric, water.

Paradise Valley Campground, 19745 Keystone Rd., Unit 4, 52049. T: (563) 873-9632. RV/tent: 210. $. Hookups: electric (30 amp), water.

Kalona

Windmill Ridge Campground, 2114 140th St., 52247. T: (319) 656-4488. RV/tent: 70. $. Hookups: electric (15, 30, 50 amp).

Kellogg

Lake Pla-Mor, 12725 Killdeer Ave., 50135. T: (641) 526-3169. RV/tent: 84. $. Hookups: electric (20, 30 amp), water.

IOWA (continued)

Keokuk

Hickory Haven Campground, 2413 353rd St., 52632. T: (800) 890-8459 or (319) 524-8459. www.inter1.net/~ginsberg/index.htm. RV/tent: 40. $$. Hookups: electric (20, 30, 50 amp), water.

Lansing

Red Barn Resort & Campground, 2609 Main St., Hwy. 9, 52151. T: (563) 538-4956 or (888) 538-4956. www.lansingiowa.com/redbarncamp ground.htm. RV/tent: 117. $. Hookups: electric (20, 30, 50 amp), water.

Madrid

Ledges State Park, 1519 250th St., 50156. T: (515) 432-1852. www.state.ia.us/dnr/organiza/ppd/ledges.htm. RV/tent: 94. $. Hookups: electric.

Marshalltown

Shady Oaks Campground, 2370 Shady Oaks Rd., 50138. T: (641) 752-2946. www.bigtreehouse .net/shadyoaks.html. RV/tent: 22. $$. Hookups: electric (20, 30, 50 amp).

McCregor

Spook Cave and Campground, 13899 Spook Cave Rd., 52157. T: (563) 873-2114. www.spookcave.com. RV/tent: 73. $$. Hookups: electric (15, 20, 30, 50 amp), water.

Monticello

Walnut Acres Campground, Hwy. 38 North, 52310. T: (319) 465-4665. www.gocampingamerica .com/walnutacres/index.html. RV/tent: 189. $$. Hookups: electric (20, 30, 50 amp), water, phone (modem), propane.

Mount Pleasant

J & J Camping, 105 North J & J Ln., 52641. T: (319) 986-6398. RV/tent: 100. $$. Hookups: electric, water, sewer.

Nashua

River Ranch Camping, 2575 Cheyenne Ave., 50658-9615. T: (641) 435-2108. www.gocamping america.com/riverranchia. RV/tent: 111. $. Hookups: electric, water.

Newton

Rolling Acres RV Park and Campground, 1601 East 36th St. South, 50208. T: (641) 792-2428 or (877) 792-2428. www.midiowa.com/rollacrs. RV/tent: 82. $$. Hookups: electric (20, 30, 50 amp), water.

North Liberty

Colony County Campground, 1275 West Forever-green Rd., 52240. T: (319) 626-2221. RV/tent: 45. $$. Hookups: electric (20, 30 amp), water.

Jolly Roger Campground and Harper's Marina, 1858 Scales Bend Rd., 52317. T: (319) 626-2171.

www.jollyrogercampground.com. RV/tent: 190. $. Hookups: electric (15, 20, 30, 50 amp), water.

Onawa

Interchange RV Park, Box 324, 51040. T: (712) 423-1387. RV/tent: 28. $$. Hookups: electric (20, 30, 50 amp), water.

Oxford

Sleepy Hollow RV Park and Campground, 3340 Black Hawk Ave. NW, 52322. T: (319) 828-4900. RV/tent: 105. $$. Hookups: electric (30, 50 amp), water, phone (modem).

Palo

Pleasant Creek State Recreation Area, 4530 McClintock Rd., 52324. T: (319) 436-7716. www.state.ia.us/dnr/organiza/ppd/pleascrk.htm. RV/tent: 69. $. Hookups: none.

Waukee

Timberline Campground, 3165 Ashworth Rd., 50263. T: (515) 987-1714. www.timberlineiowa.com. RV/tent: 100. $$. Hookups: full.

Westphalia

Nielson RV Park, 1244 1600th, 51578. T: (712) 627-4640. RV/tent: 17. $$. Hookups: electric (20, 30 amp), water, sewer.

KANSAS

Arkansas City

LouAnn's Campground, 9423 292nd Rd., 67005. T: (620) 442-4458. RV/tent: 20. $$. Hookups: electric (30 amp), water, sewer.

Assaria

Shepherd's Gate RV & Recreational Park, 1288 East Lapsley Rd., 67416. T: (785) 667-5795 or (785) 822-8463. RV/tent: 35. $$. Hookups: electric (30 amp), water, sewer.

Bonner Springs

Cottonwood Camping RV Park & Campground, 115 South 130th St., 66012. T: (913) 422-8038. www.cottonwoodcamping.com. RV/tent: 100. $$. Hookups: electric (20, 30, 50 amp), water, sewer.

Burlington

Damsite Campground, 1565 Embankment Rd. Sw, 66839. T: (316) 364-8613. www.reserveusa.com/nrrs/ks/dams/index.html. RV/tent: 26. $. Hookups: electric (30 amp), water.

Riverside East Campground, 1565 Embankment Rd. Sw, 66839. T: (620) 364-8613. www.reserveusa.com. RV/tent: 53. $. Hookups: electric (30 amp), water.

Riverside West Campground, 1565 Embankment Rd. Sw, 66839. T: (620) 364-8613. www.reserve usa.com. RV/tent: 43. $. Hookups: electric (30, 50 amp).

Coffeyville

Walter Johnson Park Campground, Hwy. 166 and 169, 508 Park, 67337. T: (800) 626-3357. www.coffeyville.com. RV/tent: 72. $. Hookups: electric (20, 30, 50 amp), water.

Columbus

T&S RV Park, 1308 East Hwy. 160, 66725. T: (620) 674-3304. RV/tent: 23. $$. Hookups: electric (30, 50 amp), water, sewer.

Council Grove

Canning Creek, 945 Lake Rd., 66846. T: (620) 767-5195. www.reserveusa.com. RV/tent: 42. $. Hookups: electric (30, 50 amp), water.

Richey Cove, 945 Lake Rd., 66846. T: (620) 767-5195. www.reserveusa.com. RV/tent: 49. $. Hookups: electric (30 amp), water.

Santa Fe Trail Campground, 945 Lake Rd., 66846. T: (620) 767-5195. www.reserveusa.com. RV/tent: 39. $. Hookups: electric (20, 30, 50 amp), water, sewer.

Dodge City

Gunsmoke Trav-L Park, 11070 108 Rd., 67801. T: (800) 789-8247 or (620) 227-8247. RV/tent: 114. $$. Hookups: electric (30, 50 amp), water, sewer, cable.

El Dorado

Bluestem Point Campground, Rte. 3, 67042. T: (316)

321-7180. RV/tent: 286. $$. Hookups: electric (30 amp), water, sewer.

Walnut River Campground, Rte. 3, 67042. T: (316) 321-7180. RV/tent: 177. $$. Hookups: electric (30 amp), water, sewer.

Ellis

Cedar Bluff State Park, Rte. 2 Box 76A, 67637. T: (785) 726-3212. www.kdwp.state.ks.us/pm forum/cedarbluff.htm. RV/tent: 121. $. Hookups: electric (20, 30, 50 amp), water, sewer.

Ellis Lakeside Campground, Jefferson St., 67637. T: (785) 726-4812. www.ellis.ks.us/camp.htm. RV/tent: 28. $. Hookups: electric (20 amp).

Fall River

Damsite, P.O. Box 37, 67047. T: (620) 658-4445. www.reserveusa.com. RV/tent: 33. $. Hookups: electric (20, 30, 50 amp), water, sewer.

Whitehall Bay, P.O. Box 37, 67047. T: (620) 658-4445. www.reserveusa.com. RV/tent: 29. $. Hookups: electric (20, 30, 50 amp), water, sewer.

Fredonia

Cottonwood Court, 703 North 7th St., 66736. T: (620) 378-3468. RV/tent: 13. $. Hookups: electric (20, 30, 50 amp), water, sewer, cable.

Garden City

Fosters RV Park, 4100 East Hwy. 50, 67846. T: (620) 276-8741. RV/tent: 96. $$. Hookups: electric (50 amp), water, sewer.

KANSAS (continued)

Goodland

Mid-America Camp Inn, 2802 Commerce Rd., 67735. T: (785) 899-5431. RV/tent: 109. $$. Hookups: electric (30, 50 amp), water, sewer.

Halstead

Spring Lake RV Resort, 1308 South Spring Lake Rd., 67056. T: (316) 835-3443. www.spring lakervresort.com. RV/tent: 180. $$. Hookups: electric (30, 50 amp), water, sewer.

Hays

El Charro RV Park, 2020 East 8th St., 67601. T: (785) 625-3423. RV/tent: 25. $$. Hookups: electric (30, 50 amp), water, sewer.

Sunflower Creek Campground & RV Park, 501 Vine St., 67601. T: (785) 625-2313. RV/tent: 24. $$. Hookups: electric (30, 50 amp), water, sewer.

Hesston

Cottonwood Grove Campground, 1001 East Lincoln Blvd., 67062. T: (620) 327-4173. www.cotton woodgrove.com. RV/tent: 22. $$. Hookups: electric (30 amp), water, sewer, phone.

Junction City

Curtis Creek Park, 4020 West Hwy. K-57, 66441. T: (785) 238-4636. www.reserveusa.com. RV/tent: 131. $. Hookups: electric (20, 30 amp), water.

Dam Site, 2105 North Pawnee Rd., 66839. T: (316) 364-8613. RV/tent: 32. $. Hookups: electric (20, 30 amp), water.

Rolling Hills Park West, 4020 West Hwy. K-57, 66441. T: (785) 238-5714. www.reserveusa.com. RV/tent: 72. $. Hookups: electric (30, 50 amp), water.

Thunderbird Marina, West Rolling Hills Rd., 66441. T: (785) 238-5864. RV/tent: 163. $$. Hookups: electric (15, 20, 30, 50 amp), water.

La Crosse

Double D RV Park, P.O. Box 699, 67548. T: (785) 222-2457. RV/tent: 14. $$. Hookups: electric (20, 30 amp), water, sewer.

Lawrence

Cedar Ridge, 872 North 1402 Rd., 66049. T: (785) 843-7665. www.reserveusa.com. RV/tent: 101. $$. Hookups: electric (30, 50 amp), water.

Hickory Campground, 872 North 1402 Rd., 66049. T: (785) 843-7665. www.reserveusa.com. RV/tent: 196. $. Hookups: electric (30 amp).

Walnut, 872 North 1402 Rd., 66049. T: (785) 843-7665. www.reserveusa.com. RV/tent: 145. $. Hookups: electric (30 amp).

Leavenworth

Leavenworth RV Park, 24836 Tonganoxie Rd., 66048. T: (913) 351-0505. RV/tent: 5. $$. Hookups: electric (30, 50 amp), water.

Lebo

Sundance Campground, 31051 Melvern Lake Pkwy., 66510. T: (785) 549-3318. RV/tent: 30. $. Hookups: none.

Lindsborg

Coronado Motel/RV Park, 305 Harrison, 67456. T: (800) 747-2793 or (785) 227-3943. www.coronadomotel.com. RV/tent: 18. $$. Hookups: electric (20, 30, 50 amp), water, sewer.

Louisburg

Middle Creek RV Park, 33565 South Metcalf, 66053. T: (866) 888-6779. www.rutladeroutpost. com. RV/tent: 48. $$. Hookups: electric (30, 50 amp), water, sewer.

Lucas

Lucas RV Park & Laundry, 119 North Wolf, 67648. T: (785) 525-6236. RV/tent: 5. $. Hookups: electric (20, 50 amp), water, sewer.

Lyndon

Crossroads RV Park & Campground Inc., P.O. Box 721, 66451. T: (785) 221-5482. RV/tent: 47. $. Hookups: electric (20, 30, 50 amp), water, sewer.

Marion

Cottonwood Point, 2105 North Pawnee, 66861. T: (620) 382-2101. www.reserveamerica.com. RV/tent: 94. $$. Hookups: electric (20, 30, 50 amp).

Hillsboro Cove, 2105 North Pawnee, 66861. T: (620) 382-2101. www.reserveusa.com/nrrs/ ks/hilc. RV/tent: 52. $$. Hookups: electric (30, 50 amp), water.

Marquette

Horse Thief Campground, 200 Horse Thief Rd., 67464. T: (785) 546-2565. RV/tent: 40. $. Hookups: electric (30 amp), water, sewer.

Riverside, 105 Riverside Dr., 67464. T: (785) 546-2294. www.reserveusa.com/nrrs/ks/rive. RV/tent: 40. $. Hookups: electric (20, 30 amp).

Mayetta

Prairie Schooner RV Park & Campground, 15680 Pacific St., 66509. T: (785) 966-2952. RV/tent: 39. $$. Hookups: electric (20, 30, 50 amp), water, sewer.

McPherson

Mustang Mobile Park, 1909 Millers Ln., 67460. T: (620) 241-0237. www.allstays.com/camp grounds/kansas-campgrounds.htm-46k. RV/tent: 28. $. Hookups: electric (20, 50 amp), water, sewer.

Melvern

Arrow Rock Campground, 31051 Melvern Lake Pkwy., 66510-9179. T: (785) 549-3318. www.nwk.usa.ce.army.mil/melvern/melvern_ home.htm. RV/tent: 33. $. Hookups: electric (30 amp), water.

Coeur d'Alene Campground, 31051 Melvern Lake Pkwy., 66510-9179. T: (785) 549-3318. www.nwk .usa.ce.army.mil/melvern/melvern_home.htm. RV/tent: 60. $. Hookups: electric (30 amp).

Eisenhower Campground, 31051 Melvern Lake Pkwy., 66510-9179. T: (785) 528-4102. www.nwk.usa.ce.army.mil/melvern/melvern_ home.htm. RV/tent: 190. $. Hookups: electric (30, 50 amp), water, sewer.

Outlet Campground, 31051 Melvern Lake Pkwy., 66510-9179. T: (785) 549-3318. www.nwk.usa .ce.army.mil/melvern/melvern_home.htm. RV/tent: 150. $$. Hookups: electric (20, 30, 50 amp), water, sewer.

Turkey Point Campground, 31051 Melvern Lake Pkwy., 66510-9179. T: (785) 549-3318. www.nwk .usa.ce.army.mil/melvern/melvern_home.htm. RV/tent: 50. $. Hookups: electric (20, 30, 50 amp), water.

Merriam

Walnut Grove RV Park, 10218 Johnson Dr., 66203. T: (913) 262-3023. www.walnutgroverv.com. RV/tent: 55. $$. Hookups: electric (30, 50 amp), water, sewer.

Milford

Flagstop Resort & RV Park, 105 8th & Whiting, 66514. T: (800) 293-1465 or (785) 463-5537. www.lasr.net/leisure/kansas/geary/flagstop.html. RV/tent: 190. $$. Hookups: electric (50 amp), water, sewer.

Langley Point, 4020 West Hwy. K57, 66441. T: (785) 546-2565. www.kdwp.state.ks.us/pmforum/ kanopolis.html. RV/tent: 57. $. Hookups: electric (20, 30, 50 amp), water, sewer.

Timber Creek Park, 4020 West Hwy. K57, 66441. T: (785) 238-5714. www.nwk.usa.ce.army.mil/ milford/milford_home.htm. RV/tent: 35. $. Hookups: water, sewer.

Morrill

Mulberry Creek Family Retreat, 551 270th St., 66515. T: (785) 459-2279. RV/tent: 70. $$. Hookups: electric (30, 50 amp), water, sewer.

Mound Valley

Big Hill Lake, 19065 Cherryvale Pkwy., 67335. T: (620) 336-2741. www.naturalkansas.org/bighill .htm. RV/tent: 72. $. Hookups: electric (20, 30, 50 amp), water, sewer.

Nickerson

Hedrick's Capybara Lake, 7910 North Roy L. Smith Rd., 67561. T: (888) 489-8039. www.hedricks .com/lake.htm. RV/tent: 16. $$. Hookups: electric (20, 30, 50 amp), water, sewer.

Oakley

Kansas Kountry Inn, 3538 Hwy. 40, 67748. T: (800) 211-6917 or (785) 672-3131. RV/tent: 16. $. Hookups: electric (20, 30, 50 amp), water, sewer.

Paola

Hillsdale State Park, 26001 West 255th St., 66071. T: (913) 783-4507. www.kdwparks.state.ks.us/pm forum/hillsdale.html. RV/tent: 80. $. Hookups: electric (20, 30, 50 amp), water.

Paxico

Mill Creek Campground, 22450 Campground Rd., 66526. T: (785) 636-5321 or (888) 645-6647. www.millcreekcampground.com. RV/tent: 46. $$. Hookups: electric (20, 30, 50 amp), water, sewer.

KANSAS (continued)

Perry

Locust Campground, 10419 Perry Park Dr., 66073. T: (785) 597-5144. www.nwk.usace.army.mil. RV/tent: 14. $$. Hookups: electric (20, 30 amp), water.

Longview, 10419 Perry Park Dr., 66073. T: (785) 597-5144. www.reserveusa.com/nrrs/ks/lonv. RV/tent: 52. $. Hookups: electric (20, 30 amp).

Perry Southpoint Campground, 10419 Perry Park Dr., 66073. T: (785) 597-5144. www.reserveusa.com/nrrs/ks/peRR RV/tent: 24. $$. Hookups: electric (20, 30 amp), water.

Rock Creek Peninsula Campground, 10419 Perry Park Dr., 66073. T: (785) 597-5144. www.reserveusa.com/nrrs/ks/rocr. RV/tent: 77. $. Hookups: electric (20, 30 amp), water.

Slough Creek Campground, 10419 Perry Park Dr., 66073. T: (785) 597-5144. www.reserveusa.com/nrrs/ks/slou. RV/tent: 273. $. Hookups: electric (20, 30 amp), water.

Worthington Campground, 10419 Perry Park Dr., 66073. T: (785) 597-5144. www.reserveusa.com/nrrs/ks/slou. RV/tent: 62. $. Hookups: electric (20, 30 amp).

Quinter

Sunflower Campground, 1130 Castle Rock Rd., 67752-9400. T: (913) 754-3451. RV/tent: 40. $$. Hookups: electric (30 amp), water, sewer.

Rexford

Shepherd's Staff RV Park, 315 Main St., 67753. T: (888) 687-2565 or (785) 687-2565. www.gospelcom.net/shepherdstaff. RV/tent: 12. $$. Hookups: electric (20, 30, 50 amp), water, sewer.

Richmond

V & P RV Park, 532 East South St., 66080. T: (785) 835-6369. RV/tent: 25. $$. Hookups: electric (30, 50 amp), water, sewer.

Russel

Dumler Estates RV Park, P.O. Box 180, 67665. T: (785) 483-2603. RV/tent: 30. $$. Hookups: electric (20, 30, 50 amp), water, sewer.

Salina

Salina KOA, 1109 West Diamond Dr., 67401. T: (800) 562-3126 or (785) 827-3182. www.koa.com. RV/tent: 82. $$. Hookups: electric (20, 30, 50 amp), water, sewer.

Sundowner West Park, 2745 North Hedville Rd., 67402. T: (785) 823-8335. www.sundownerwest.com. RV/tent: 79. $$. Hookups: electric (30, 50 amp), water, sewer.

Scott City

Pine Tree RV Park, 402 North Main St., 67871. T: (620) 872-3076. RV/tent: 25. $. Hookups: electric (20, 30, 50 amp), water, sewer.

Smith Center

Sunset Park Campground, West Hwy. 36, 705 White Rock, 66967. T: (785) 282-6037. RV/tent: 16. $$. Hookups: electric (20, 30 amp), water, sewer.

South Haven

Oasis RV Park, Hwy. 166, east of I-35, 67140. T: (620) 892-5115. RV/tent: 25. $$. Hookups: electric (20, 30, 50 amp), water, sewer.

St. Francis

Homesteader Motel & RV Park, 414 West Hwy. 36, 67756. T: (800) 750-2169 or (785) 332-2168. RV/tent: 9. $$. Hookups: electric (30, 50 amp), water, sewer.

St. John

Pine Haven Retreat, 217 East US 50, 67576. T: (888) 549-CAMP or (620) 549-3444. RV/tent: 40. $$. Hookups: electric (20, 30, 50 amp), water, sewer.

Sylvan Grove

Minooka Park, 4860 Outlet Blvd., 67481. T: (785) 658-2551. www.reserveamerica.com. RV/tent: 160. $. Hookups: electric (20, 30 amp), water.

Topeka

Capital City RV Park, 1949 Sw 49th St., 66609. T: (785) 862-KAMP. www.capitalcityrvpark.com. RV/tent: 51. $. Hookups: electric (20, 30, 50 amp), water, sewer.

Lake Shawnee Camping Area, 3435 SE Edge Rd., 66609. T: (785) 267-PLAY. RV/tent: 154. $$. Hookups: electric (30 amp), water.

Toronto

Holiday Hill Campground, 144 Hwy. 105, 66777. T: (316) 637-2213. RV/tent: 30. $. Hookups: electric (30 amp).

Toronto Point Campground, 144 Hwy. 105, 66777. T: (316) 637-2213. RV/tent: 200. $. Hookups: electric (20, 30 amp), water.

Vassar

Carbolyn Park, 5260 Pomona Dam Rd., 66543. T: (785) 453-2201. www.reserveamerica.com. RV/tent: 29. $. Hookups: electric (20, 30 amp), water.

Michigan Valley, 5260 Pomona Dam Rd., 66543. T: (785) 453-2201. www.reserveamerica.com. RV/tent: 91. $. Hookups: electric (20, 30 amp), water.

Pomona Lake Outlet Campground, 5260 Pomona Dam Rd., 66543. T: (785) 453-2201. www.reserveamerica.com. RV/tent: 36. $. Hookups: electric (20, 30 amp), water.

Wolf Creek, 5260 Pomona Dam Rd., 66543. T: (785) 453-2201. www.reserveamerica.com. RV/tent: 87. $. Hookups: electric (20, 30 amp).

Washington

Rose Garden RV Camp, 127 East 9th St., 66968. T: (785) 325-2411. RV/tent: 9. $. Hookups: electric (20, 30, 50 amp), water, sewer.

Wellington

Wheatlands of Wellington RV Park, Rte. 1 Box 227, 67152. T: (877) 914-6114 or (316) 326-6114. RV/tent: 72. $$. Hookups: electric (30, 50 amp), water, sewer.

Wichita

All Seasons RV Park, 15520 Maple Ave., 67052. T: (316) 722-1154. RV/tent: 76. $$. Hookups: electric (20, 30, 50 amp), water, sewer.

Blasi Campgrounds, 11209 West Hwy. 54, 67209. T: (316) 722-2681. RV/tent: 110. $$. Hookups: electric (20, 30, 50 amp), water, sewer.

K & R Tratel RV Park, 3200 SE Blvd., 67216. T: (316) 684-1531. RV/tent: 90. $$. Hookups: electric (30, 50 amp), water, sewer.

Waco Wego Campground, 9747 South Broadway, 67120. T: (316) 522-1400. RV/tent: 9. $$. Hookups: electric (20, 30, 50 amp), water, sewer.

Wilson

Hell Creek Campground, Rte. 1 Box 181, 67841. T: (785) 658-2465. RV/tent: 400. $. Hookups: electric (20, 30 amp), water.

Otoe Campground, Rte. 1 Box 181, 67841. T: (785) 658-2465. RV/tent: 235. $. Hookups: electric (20, 30 amp), water.

KENTUCKY

Aurora

Aurora Oaks Campground, 55 KOA Ln., 42048. T: (888) 886-8704 or (270) 474-2778. RV/tent: 60. $$. Hookups: full.

Lakeside Campground & Marina, 12363 US 68 East, 42025. T: (270) 354-8157. www.lakesidecampground.net. RV/tent: 140. $$. Hookups: full.

Bardstown

Holt's Campground, 2351 Templin Ave., 40004. T: (502) 348-6717. RV/tent: 60. $$. Hookups: full.

White Acres Campground & Gifts, 3022 Boston Rd., 40004. T: (502) 348-9677. RV/tent: 100. $. Hookups: electric, water.

Bee Spring

Dog Creek, 2150 Nolin Dam Rd., 42207. T: (270) 524-5454. RV/tent: 70. $. Hookups: electric, water.

Wax, Nolin River Lake, 2150 Nolin Dam Rd., 42207-0339. T: (270) 242-7578. RV/tent: 110. $$. Hookups: electric, water.

Benton

Big Bear Resort, 30 Big Bear Resort Rd., 42025. T: (800) 922-BEAR or (270) 354-6414. www.bigbearkentuckylake.com. RV/tent: 75. $$. Hookups: electric, water.

KENTUCKY (continued)

Berea

Oh Kentucky Campground, 1142 Hwy. 21 West, 40403-9502. T: (859) 986-1150. www.okcg2.homestead.com/okcg2.html. RV/tent: 112. $. Hookups: full.

Walnut Meadow Campground, 1201 Paint Lick Rd., 40403. T: (859) 986-6180. www.walnutmeadow rv.com. RV/tent: 123. $. Hookups: electric, water.

Bowling Green

Beech Bend Family Campground, 798 Beech Bend Rd., 42101. T: (270) 781-7634. www.beech bend.com. RV/tent: 500+. $$. Hookups: electric, water.

Bronston

Lake Cumberland RV Park, 499 Gibson Ln., 42518. T: (606) 561-8222 or (877) 461-2404. www.lakecumberlandrvpark.com. RV/tent: 40. $$. Hookups: electric (20, 30, 50 amp), water.

Buckhorn

Buckhorn Dam Recreation Area (Corps of Engineers—Buckhorn Lake), 104 Tailwater Camp Rd., 41721. T: (606) 398-7251. RV/tent: 35. $. Hookups: electric, water.

Burkesville

Sulphur Creek Resort, 3498 Sulphur Creek Rd., 42717. T: (270) 433-7272. www.sulphur creek.com. RV/tent: 22. $$. Hookups: electric, water.

Cadiz

Devil's Elbow Campground (Corps of Engineers—Trigg), 100 Devil's Elbow Rd., 42211. T: (270) 362-4632. RV/tent: 22. $. Hookups: electric, water.

Prizer Point Marina & Resort, 1777 Prizer Point Rd., 42211. T: (270) 522-3762 or (800) 548-2048. www.prizerpoint.com. RV/tent: 102. $$. Hookups: electric, water.

Rockcastle RV Park & Campground, 1049 Goose Hollow Rd., 42211. T: (270) 522-1955. RV/tent: 57. $. Hookups: electric, water.

Calvert City

Cypress Lakes RV Park, 54 Stillion Dr., 42029. T: (270) 395-4267. RV/tent: 130. $$. Hookups: full.

KOA Paducah, 4793 US 62, 42029. T: (270) 395-5841or (800) 562-8540. www.koa.com. RV/tent: 85. $$. Hookups: electric, water.

Campbellsville

Smith Ridge, 2882 Smith Ridge Rd., 42718. T: (270) 789-2743. RV/tent: 80. $$. Hookups: electric, water.

Corbin

Grove Campground-Daniel Boone National Forest, 3035 Grove Rd., 40391. T: (800) 280-CAMP (606) 528-6156. RV/tent: 56. $$. Hookups: electric, water.

Danville

Pioneer Playhouse Trailer Park, 840 Stanford Rd./US 150, 40422. T: (859) 236-2747. RV/tent: 70. $. Hookups: electric, water.

Dry Ridge

I-75 Camper Village, 940 Currey Ln., 41035. T: (859) 824-5836. RV/tent: 70. $$. Hookups: full.

Dunmor

Dogwood Lake Camping Resort & Funpark, 7777 State Rte. 973, 42339-0165. T: (270) 657-8380. www.dogwoodlakes.com. RV/tent: 95. $$. Hookups: full.

Eddyville

Holiday Hills Resort, 5631 KY 93 South, 42038. T: (800) 337-8550 or (270) 388-7236. www.lakebarkleyholiday.com. RV/tent: 150. $$. Hookups: full.

Lake Barkley RV Resort, 4481 KY 93 South, 42038. T: (800) 910-PARK. RV/tent: 102. $$. Hookups: full.

Elizabethtown

Glendale Campground, 4566 Sportsman Lake Rd., 42701. T: (270) 369-7755. RV/tent: 60. $$. Hookups: full.

KOA Elizabethtown, 209 Tunnel Hill Rd., 42701. T: (270) 737-7600 or (800) 562-7605. www.koa.com. RV/tent: 68. $$. Hookups: full.

Frankfort

Elkhorn Campground, 165 Scruggs Ln., 40601. T: (502) 695-9154. RV/tent: 125. $$. Hookups: electric, water.

Franklin

KOA Franklin, P.O. Box 346, 42135. T: (800) 562-5631 or (270) 586-5622. www.koa.com. RV/tent: 104. $$. Hookups: electric, water.

Glasgow

Bailey's Point Campground (Corps of Engineers—Barren River Lake), 11088 Finney Rd., 42141-9683. T: (270) 646-2055. RV/tent: 215. $$. Hookups: electric, water.

Golden Pond

Energy Lake (LBL) National Recreation Area, 100 Van Morgan Dr., 42211. T: (270) 924-2270. RV/tent: 48. $. Hookups: electric, water.

Fenton (LBL) National Recreation Area, 100 Van Morgan Dr., 42211. T: (270) 924-2000. RV/tent: 29. $. Hookups: electric.

Rushing Creek (LBL) National Recreation Area, 100 Van Morgan Dr., 42211. T: (270) 924-2000. gorp.away.com/dow/southern/blbcmp.htm# rushing%20creek. RV/tent: 38. $. Hookups: electric, water.

Wrangler (LBL) National Recreation Area, 100 Van Morgan Dr., 42211. T: (270) 924-2000. RV/tent: 400. $. Hookups: electric, water, sewer.

Grand Rivers

Birmingham Ferry (LBL) National Recreation Area, 100 Van Morgan Dr., 42211. T: (270) 924-2000. RV/tent: 400. $$. Hookups: electric, water, sewer.

Boyd's Landing Campground (Corps of Engineers), P.O. Box 218, 42045-0218. T: (270) 362-4236. RV/tent: 14. $. Hookups: electric, water.

Cravens Bay (LBL) National Recreation Area, 100 Van Morgan Dr., 42211. T: (270) 924-2000. gorp.away.com/dow/southern/blbcmp.htm#crav ens%bay. RV/tent: 30. $. Hookups: electric, water.

Hillman Ferry (LBL) National Recreation Area, 820 Hillman Ferry Rd., 47045. T: (270) 362-8230. RV/tent: 379. $. Hookups: electric, water, sewer.

Hurricane Creek Recreational Area (Corps of Engineers—Lake Barkle), Box 218, 42045-0218. T: (270) 362-4236. RV/tent: 51. $. Hookups: electric, water.

Harrodsburg

Chimney Rock Campground, 160 Chimney Rock Rd., 40330. T: (606) 748-5252 or (859) 748-5252. www.chimneyrockrvpark.com. RV/tent: 65. $$. Hookups: electric, water, sewer.

Hartford

Ohio County Park, 1802 Country Club Ln., 42347. T: (270) 298-4466. RV/tent: 50. $. Hookups: electric, water, sewer.

Horse Cave

KOA Horse Cave, Box 87, 42749. T: (270) 786-2819 or (800) 562-2809. www.koa.com. RV/tent: 100. $$. Hookups: full.

Hyden

Trace Branch (Corps of Engineers—Buckhorn Lake), 1325 Buckham Dam Rd., 41721. T: (606) 398-7251. RV/tent: 15. $. Hookups: none.

Jamestown

Kendall Recreation Area, 80 Kendall Rd., 42501-0450. T: (606) 343-4660. RV/tent: 83. $$. Hookups: electric, water.

London

Holly Bay Campground, London Ranger District, Daniel Boone Nat'l Forest, 40744. T: (877) 444-6777 or (606) 864-4163. www.r8web.com. RV/tent: 94. $. Hookups: electric, water.

Westgate RV Camping, 254 West Daniel Boone Pkwy, 40741. T: (606) 878-7330. RV/tent: 14. $$. Hookups: full.

White Oak Boat-In Campground, Daniel Boone National Forest, 2-mile walk from FR 774, 42653. T: (606) 864-4163 or (877) 444-6777. www.r8web.com. RV/tent: 51. $. Hookups: none.

Louisa

The Falls Campground, SR 3, 41230. T: (606) 686-3398. RV/tent: 111. $$. Hookups: electric, water, cable.

McDaniels

Axtel Campground (Corps of Engineers—Rough River Lake), 14500 Falls of Rough R, 40119-6316. T: (270) 257-2584. RV/tent: 158. $$. Hookups: electric, water.

Laurel Branch Campground (Corps of Engineers—Rough River Lake), 14500 Falls of Rough R, 40152. T: (270) 257-8839. RV/tent: 77. $. Hookups: electric, water.

Monticello

Conley Bottom Resort, Rte. 5 Box 5360, 42633. T: (606) 348-6351. www.conleybottom.com. RV/tent: 170. $. Hookups: full.

KENTUCKY (continued)

Mortons Gap

Pennyrile Campground, P.O. Box 612, 42440. T: (270) 258-5201. RV/tent: 15. $$. Hookups: electric, water.

Mount Vernon

Nicely's Campground, Rte. 2 Box 38, 40456. T: (606) 256-5637. RV/tent: 99. $$. Hookups: electric, water.

Muldraugh

Military Park (Camp Carlson Army Travel Camp), 9186 US 60, 40155. T: (502) 624-4836. RV/tent: 25. $. Hookups: electric, water, sewer.

Murray

Wildcat Creek Recreation Area, 28 Wildcat Beach Rd., 42071. T: (270) 436-5628. www.wildcat-creek.com. RV/tent: 50. $$. Hookups: electric (20, 30, 50 amp), water.

Nancy

Cumberland Point Public Use Area, 10000 Hwy. 761, 42544. T: (606) 871-7886. RV/tent: 30. $$. Hookups: electric, water.

Owensboro

Diamond Lake Resort Campground, 7301 Hobbs Rd., 42301. T: (270) 229-4961. RV/tent: 440. $$. Hookups: full.

Windy Hollow Campground & Recreation Area, 5141 Windy Hollow Rd., 42301. T: (270) 785-4150. www.windyhollowcampground.com. RV/tent: 175. $$. Hookups: full.

Paducah

Fern Lake Campground, 5535 Cairo Rd., 42001. T: (270) 444-7939. RV/tent: 70. $. Hookups: electric, water.

Park City

Cedar Hill Campground, P.O. Box 305, 42160. T: (270) 749-3114. RV/tent: 117. $$. Hookups: electric, water, sewer.

Renfro Valley

Renfro Valley RV Park, US 25, 40473. T: (800) 765-7464 or (606) 256-2638. www.renfrovalley.com. RV/tent: 199. $$. Hookups: full.

Salt Lick

Outpost RV Park & Campground, 340 Cave Run Lake Rd., 40371. T: (606) 683-2311. RV/tent: 89. $$. Hookups: full.

Salvisa

Cummins Ferry Campground & Marina, 2558 Cummins Ferry Rd., 40372. T: (859) 856-2003. www.geocities.com/cfcpgd/index.html. RV/tent: 120. $$. Hookups: full.

Sanders

Eagle Valley Camping Resort, 1100 Eagle Valley Rd., 41083. T: (502) 347-9361. www.eaglevalley resort.com. RV/tent: 225. $$. Hookups: electric, water.

Shelbyville

Guist Creek Marina & Campground, 11990 Boat Dock Rd., 40065. T: (502) 633-1934. RV/tent: 50. $$. Hookups: electric, water.

Slade

Koomer Ridge Campground, Daniel Boone National Forest, Bert T. Combs Mountain Pkwy., 40380. T: (606) 663-2852. www.r8web.com. RV/tent: 54. $. Hookups: none.

Somerset

Fishing Creek Campground (Corps of Engineers–Lake Cumberland), 1611 Hwy. 1248, 42501-0450. T: (606) 679-5174. RV/tent: 47. $$. Hookups: electric, water.

Waitsboro Recreation Area, Lake Cumberland, 500 Waitsboro Rd., 42501. T: (606) 561-5513. RV/tent: 25. $$. Hookups: electric, water.

Stearns

Big South Forks Nat'l. River & Rec. Area (Blue Heron), Park Headquarters, 4564 Leatherwood Rd., 37841. T: (423) 569-9778. RV/tent: 146. $$. Hookups: electric, water.

Walton

Oak Creek Campground, P.O. Box 161, 41094. T: (859) 485-9131. www.oakcreekcampground. com. RV/tent: 105. $$. Hookups: electric, water, cable.

Williamsburg

Williamsburg Travel Trailer Park, 50 Balltown Rd., 40769. T: (800) 426-3267. RV/tent: 56. $. Hookups: electric, water.

LOUISIANA

Ajax

Country Livin' RV Park, 1115 Hwy. 174, 71450. T: (318) 796-2543. www.passport-america.com. RV/tent: 21. $$. Hookups: electric (30, 50 amp), water, sewer, laundry.

Alexandria

Fish'n Heav'n RV Park, 402 Monroe St., 71303. T: (318) 448-9269. RV/tent: 31. $$. Hookups: electric (30, 50 amp), water, sewer, laundry, row boat rentals.

Angie

Great Southern RC & Bluegrass Park, Hwy. 21 & Main St., 70426. T: (985) 986-8411. RV/tent: 100. $$. Hookups: electric (30, 50 amp), water, sewer, phone (modem).

Arcadia

Bonnie & Clyde Trade Days & Campground, South Hwy. 9, 71001. T: (318) 263-2437. RV/tent: 109. $$. Hookups: electric (30, 50 amp), water, sewer, phone (modem).

Avoyselles

Grand Avoyelles RV Resort, Hwy. 1, 70648. T: (800) 578-7275. RV/tent: 186. $$. Hookups: electric (20, 30, 50 amp), water, sewer, cable, phone (modem), playground.

Baker

Azalea Gardens Mobile Home and RV Park, 3300 Baker Blvd., 70714. T: (225) 775-1123. RV/tent: 52. $$. Hookups: electric (20, 30 amp), water, sewer, laundry.

Baton Rouge

Farr Park Campground, 6400 River Rd., 70820. T: (225) 769-7805. www.brec.org/nature/6.html. RV/tent: 180. $. Hookups: electric (30 amp), water, sewer, phone (modem), laundry, playground.

Greenwood Park, 13350 Louisiana Hwy. 19, 70821. T: (225) 775-3877. www.brec.org/nature/6.html. RV/tent: 75. $. Hookups: electric (30, 50 amp), water, sewer, phone (modem), laundry.

Night's RV Park, 14740 Florida Blvd., 70819. T: (225) 275-0679. RV/tent: 78. $. Hookups: electric (20, 30, 50 amp), water, sewer.

Benton

Cypress–Black Bayou Recreation, 135 Cypress Park Dr., 71006. T: (318) 965-0007. www.cypressblackbayou.com. RV/tent: 73. $. Hookups: electric (20, 30, 50 amp), water, sewer.

Bossier

Maplewood RV Park, 452 Maplewood Dr., 71111. T: (800) 569-2264. RV/tent: 42. $$. Hookups: electric (30, 50 amp), water, sewer, phone.

Bourg

Grand Bois Campsite, 470 Bourg-larose Hwy. 24, 70343. T: (985) 594-7410. RV/tent: 41. $. Hookups: electric (30, 50 amp), water.

Boyce

KOA Alexandria West, 64 Kisatchie Ln., 71409. T: (800) 562-5640 or (318) 445-5227. RV/tent: 52. $. Hookups: electric (50 amp), water, sewer.

KOA Kincaid Lake Campground, South Kisatchie Ln., 71409. T: (318) 445-5227 or (800) 562-5640. RV/tent: 57. $. Hookups: electric (20, 30, 50 amp), water, sewer.

Broussard

Maxie's Campground, 4350 US 90, 70518. T: (337) 837-6200. www.maxiescampground.com. RV/tent: 70. $$. Hookups: electric (20, 30, 50 amp), water, sewer, phone (modem), laundry.

LOUISIANA (continued)

Florien

Hodges Wilderness Campground, 3894 Hodges Loop, 71429. T: (318) 586-3523 or (800) 354-3523. www.hodgespark.com. RV/tent: 19. $. Hookups: electric (30, 50 amp), water, sewer.

Greenwood

Kelly's RV Park, 8560 Greenwood Rd., 71033. T: (318) 938-6360. RV/tent: 45. $$. Hookups: electric, water, sewer.

Hammond

Punkin Park Campground, 43037 North Billville Rd., 70404. T: (225) 567-3418. RV/tent: 52. $$. Hookups: electric (30, 50 amp), water, sewer.

Haughton

Pine Hill Mobile Home and RV, 2 Pine Hill Cir., 71037. T: (318) 949-3916. RV/tent: 28. $$. Hookups: electric (30, 50 amp), water, sewer, bathhouse, showers.

Kinder

Grand Casino Coushatta Luxury RV Resort, 1240 711 Pow Wow Pkwy., 70648. T: (888) 867-8727. RV/tent: 156. $$. Hookups: electric, water, sewer.

Quiet Oaks RV Park, 18159 Tower Rd., 70648. T: (888) 755-2230. www.quietoaks.com. RV/tent: 40. $$. Hookups: electric (30, 50 amp), water, sewer, boat rentals.

Leesville

Shady Lake RV Park, 168 Sapphire Ln., 71446. T: (337) 239-4674. www.shadylakervpark.com. RV/tent: 25. $$. Hookups: electric (30, 50 amp), water, sewer, phone (modem).

Longville

Longville Lake Park, Hwy. 110, 70652. T: (337) 725-3395. RV/tent: 175. $$. Hookups: electric (30, 50 amp), water.

Many

Cypress Bend Park (Toledo Bend Lake), 3462 Cypress Bend Dr., 71449. T: (318) 256-4118. www.toledo-bend.com. RV/tent: 63. $. Hookups: electric (20, 30 amp), water, sewer.

Monroe

Monroe Shilo RV and Travel, 7300 Frontage Rd., 71202. T: (318) 343-6098. www.shresorts.com. RV/tent: 81. $$. Hookups: electric (30 amp), water, sewer.

Morgan City

Morgan City RV Park, 7100 Hwy. 182 East, 70380. T: (985) 385-4813. RV/tent: 99. $$. Hookups: electric (30, 50 amp), water, sewer.

Natchitoches

Nakatosh RV Park, 5428 Hwy. 6, 71457. T: (318) 352-0911. RV/tent: 41. $. Hookups: electric, water, sewer.

Pine Prairie

Crooked Creek Campground, 1300 Sandy Beach Rd., 70586. T: (337) 599-2661. RV/tent: 100. $$. Hookups: electric (30 amp), water, sewer, laundry.

Port Allen

Cajun Country Campground, 4667 Rebelle Ln., 70767. T: (800) 264-8554. RV/tent: 77. $$. Hookups: electric (30, 50 amp), water, sewer, phone (modem), laundry.

Rosepine

Sadler RV Park and Mobile Home, 7196 Main St., 70659. T: (337) 463-5561. RV/tent: 72. $. Hookups: electric (30, 50 amp), water, sewer, laundry.

Ruston

Lincoln Parish Park, 198 Parish Park Rd., 71270. T: (318) 251-5156. RV/tent: 33. $$. Hookups: electric, water, sewer.

Shreveport

Campers RV Center, 7700 West 70th St., 71129. T: (318) 687-4567 or (800) 426-1352. www.campersrvcenter.com. RV/tent: 56. $$. Hookups: electric, water, sewer.

Tallulah

Roudaway RV Park, Hwy. 602, 71282. T: (318) 574-9026. RV/tent: 48. $. Hookups: electric (20 amp), water, sewer.

West Monroe

Cheniere Lake Park–Area 1, 337 Well Rd., 71292. T: (318) 387-2383. RV/tent: 10. $. Hookups: electric, water.

Pavilion RV Park, 309 Well Rd., 71292. T: (318) 322-4216. RV/tent: 62. $$. Hookups: electric (30, 50 amp), water, sewer.

MAINE

Acton

Apple Valley Campground, P.O. Box 92, Rte. 109, 04001. T: (207) 636-2285. RV/tent: 145. $$. Hookups: electric (30 amp), water, sewer, cable.

Addison

Pleasant River RV Park, 8 West Side Rd., 04606. T: (207) 483-4083. www.camp.com/pleas antriver. RV/tent: 6. $$. Hookups: electric (20, 30, 50 amp), water, sewer, phone.

Alfred

Bunganut Lake Camping Area, P.O. Box 141, 04002. T: (207) 247-3875. www.americatravelguide.com. RV/tent: 110. $$. Hookups: electric (20, 30 amp), water.

Scott's Cove Camping Area, Box 761, Rte. 202, 04002. T: (207) 324-6594. www.scottscovecamp ing.com. RV/tent: 50. $$$. Hookups: electric (20, 30 amp), water, sewer.

Walnut Grove Campground, 599 Gore Rd., 04002. T: (207) 324-1207. www.gocampingamerica.com/ walnutgroveme. RV/tent: 93. $$. Hookups: electric (20, 30 amp), water.

Baileyville

Sunset Acres Campground, 162 Airline Rd., 04694. T: (207) 454-1440. www.camp.com/sunsetacres. RV/tent: 15. $. Hookups: electric (30, 50 amp), water, sewer.

Bangor

Shady Acres RV & Campground, RR 2 Box 7890, 04419. T: (207) 848-5515. RV/tent: 50. $$. Hookups: electric (30 amp), water, sewer.

Wheeler Stream Camping Area, RR 2 Box 2800, 04401. T: (207) 848-3713. RV/tent: 18. $$. Hookups: electric (20, 30 amp), water.

Berwick

Beaver Dam Campground, 551 Rte. 9, 03901. T: (207) 698-2267. www.beaverdamcamp ground.com. RV/tent: 61. $$. Hookups: electric (20, 30, 50 amp), water, sewer.

Bethel

Bethel Outdoor Adventures & Campground, 121 Mayville Rd., 04217. T: (207) 824-4224. www.betheloutdooradventure.com. RV/tent: 25. $$. Hookups: electric (50 amp), water, sewer.

Biddeford

Shamrock RV Park, 391 West St., 04005. T: (207) 284-4282. www.lamere.net/shamrock. RV/tent: 60. $$$. Hookups: electric (20, 30 amp), water, sewer.

Boothbay

Camper's Cove Campground, P.O. Box 136, 04537. T: (207) 633-5013 or (207) 633-0050. RV/tent: 56. $$. Hookups: electric (30 amp), water, sewer.

Bridgton

Vicki-Lin Camping Area, RR 2, 04009. T: (207) 647-2630. RV/tent: 87. $$. Hookups: electric (30 amp), water, sewer.

Brownfield

Shannon's Saco River Sanctuary, Rte. 160 North, 04010. T: (207) 452-2274. www.angelfire.com/ me3/shannonsanctuary. RV/tent: 55. $$. Hookups: electric (30 amp), water.

Bucksport

Masthead Campground, 444 Masthill Rd., 04416. T: (207) 469-3482. RV/tent: 38. $$. Hookups: electric (15, 20 amp), water.

MAINE (continued)

Danforth

Greenland Cove Campground, East Grand Lake, 04424. T: (207) 448-2863. www.mainerec.com/gov/index.shtml. RV/tent: 85. $$. Hookups: electric (20, 30 amp), water.

Deer Isle

Sunshine Campground, RR 2 Box 521E, 04627. T: (207) 348-2663. www.sunshinecampground.com. RV/tent: 22. $$. Hookups: electric (15, 20, 50 amp), water.

Denmark

Granger Pond Camping Area, P.O. Box 47, 04022. T: (207) 452-2342. RV/tent: 45. $$. Hookups: electric (15 amp), water, sewer.

Pleasant Mountain Camping Area, RR 1, 04022. T: (207) 452-2170. RV/tent: 40. $$. Hookups: electric (30 amp), water, sewer.

Dixfield

Mountain View Campground, 208 Weld St., 04224. T: (207) 562-8285. www.exploremaine.com/~jenndon/mountainview. RV/tent: 32. $$. Hookups: electric (50 amp), water, sewer.

East Hebron

Hebron Pines Campground, RR 1, 04238. T: (207) 966-2179. RV/tent: 24. $$. Hookups: electric (30 amp), water.

East Machias

River's Edge Campground, HCR 74, Box 265, 04630. T: (207) 255-5987. RV/tent: 30. $$. Hookups: electric (20, 30, 50 amp), water, sewer.

Eastbrook

Eastbrook Campground, RR 1 Box 465M, 04634. T: (888) 565-2319. www.eastbrookcamp.com. RV/tent: 25. $. Hookups: electric (20, 30, 50 amp), water, sewer.

Eastport

Seaview Campground, 16 Norwood Rd., 04631. T: (207) 853-4471. www.Eastportmaine.com/index. RV/tent: 74. $$. Hookups: electric (20, 30 amp), water, sewer, cable.

Ellsworth

Hospitality Woods RV Park, 2 Our Way, 04605. T: (207) 667-2668 or (800) 773-2668. www.hospitalitywoodsrvpark.com/pages/750352. RV/tent: 47. $$$. Hookups: electric (20, 30, 50 amp), water, sewer, cable, phone.

Farmingdale

Foggy Bottom RV Campground, 331 Maine Ave., 04344. T: (207) 582-0075. www.foggybottommarine.com. RV/tent: 9. $$. Hookups: electric (50 amp), water, sewer.

Troll Valley Campground, 203 Schoolhouse Rd., 04938. T: (207) 778-3656. RV/tent: 25. $$. Hookups: electric (50 amp), water.

Freeport

Blueberry Pond Campground, 218 Poland Range Rd., 04069. T: (207) 688-4421 or (877) 290-1381. www.blueberrycampground.com. RV/tent: 40. $$. Hookups: electric (20, 30 amp), water, sewer.

KOA Freeport, 1430 Hallowell, 04222. T: (207) 688-4288. www.koakampgrounds.com. RV/tent: 212. $$. Hookups: electric (30 amp), water, sewer.

Recompence Shore Campsites, 134 Burnett Rd., 04032. T: (207) 865-9307. www.freeportcamping.com. RV/tent: 104. $$. Hookups: electric (15 amp), water.

Fryeburg

Canal Bridge Campground, Rte. 5, 04037. T: (207) 935-2286. RV/tent: 50. $$. Hookups: electric (20 amp), water.

Georgetown

Sagahadoc Bay Campground, Sagahadoc Bay Rd., 04548. T: (207) 371-2014. www.sagbaycamping.com. RV/tent: 45. $$. Hookups: electric (50 amp), water, sewer.

Greene

Lewiston-Auburn North Allen Pond Campground, 102 North Mountain Rd., 04236. T: (207) 946-7439. RV/tent: 65. $$. Hookups: electric (30 amp), water.

Greenville

Allagash Gateway Campsite, P.O. Box 675, 04441. T: (207) 723-9215. www.allagashgateway.com. RV/tent: 30. $$. Hookups: none.

Frost Pond Campground, P.O. Box 620, HCR 76, 04441. T: (207) 695-2821. www.frostpondcamps.com. RV/tent: 10. $$. Hookups: none.

Moosehead Family Campground, 312 Moosehead Lake Rd., 04441-0307. T: (207) 695-2210. www.mooseheadcampground.com. RV/tent: 35. $$. Hookups: electric (20, 30, 50 amp), water.

Greenwood

Littlefield Beaches Campground, 13 Littlefield Ln., 04255. T: (207) 875-3290. www.littlefieldbeaches.com. RV/tent: 130. $$. Hookups: electric (30 amp), water, sewer.

Hanover

Stony Brook Recreation, 42 Powell Pl., 04237. T: (207) 824-2836 or (888) 439-5625 ext 0604. www.stonybrookrec.com. RV/tent: 140. $$. Hookups: electric (30 amp), water, sewer, cable.

Harrison

Bear Mountain Village Cabins and Sites, RR 2, 04040. T: (207) 583-2541. RV/tent: 65. $$. Hookups: electric (30 amp), water.

Vacationland Campground, 233 Vacationland Rd. RFD #2, 04040. T: (207) 583-4953. www.vacationlandcampground.com. RV/tent: 90. $$. Hookups: electric (30 amp), water, sewer, phone, modem.

Hermon

Pumpkin Patch RV Resort, 149 Billings Rd., 04401. T: (207) 848-2231. www.pumpkinpatchrv.com. RV/tent: 35. $$. Hookups: electric (30, 50 amp), water, sewer, cable.

Holden

Red Barn RV Park, 602 Main Rd., 04429. T: (207) 843-6011. RV/tent: 125. $$. Hookups: electric (20, 30, 50 amp), water, sewer, cable, phone.

Jackman

Jackman Landing, Main St., 04945. T: (207) 668-3301 or (207) 668-4436. RV/tent: 24. $$. Hookups: electric (30 amp), water.

John's Four Season Accomodations, 37 John St., 04945. T: (207) 668-7683 or (888) 668-0098. www.johnsfourseasons.com. RV/tent: 14. $. Hookups: electric (30 amp), water, sewer, cable.

Loon Echo Family Campground, Rte. 201, 04945. T: (207) 668-4829. www.campmaine.com/loon echo. RV/tent: 15. $$. Hookups: none.

Moose Alley Campground, Rte. 201, Box 298, 04945. T: (207) 668-2781. www.moosealley.com. RV/tent: 21. $. Hookups: electric (30 amp), water, cable.

Jefferson

Town Line Campsites, 483 East Pond Rd., 04348. T: (207) 832-7055. RV/tent: 55. $. Hookups: electric (15 amp), water.

Kennebunk

Hemlock Grove Campground, 1299 Portland Rd., 04046. T: (207) 985-0398. RV/tent: 100. $$. Hookups: electric (30, 50 amp), water, sewer.

Red Apple Campground, 111 Sinnott Rd., 04046. T: (207) 967-4927. www.redapplecampground.com. RV/tent: 140. $$. Hookups: electric (20, 30 amp), water, sewer, cable, phone.

Salty Acres, 272 Mills Rd., Rte. 9, 04046. T: (207) 967-2483. www.beachwoodmotel.com/salty acres.html. RV/tent: 225. $$. Hookups: electric (20, 30 amp), water, sewer.

Kezar Falls

Windsong Campground, P.O. Box 547, 04047. T: (207) 625-4389. RV/tent: 60. $$. Hookups: electric (20, 30 amp), water.

Kingfield

Deer Farm Campground, Tufts Pond Rd., 04947. T: (207) 265-4599 or (207) 265-2241. www.deerfarmcamps.com. RV/tent: 47. $$. Hookups: electric (30 amp), water.

Lebanon

Heavenlee Acres Campground, 75 Cemetery Rd., 04027. T: (207) 457-1260. www.heavenleeacres.com. RV/tent: 70. $$. Hookups: electric (20, 30, 50 amp), water, sewer.

King & Queens Court Resort, 21 Flat Rock Bridge Rd., 04027. T: (207) 339-9465. www.kingandqueenscamping.com. RV/tent: 400. $$$. Hookups: electric (20 amp), water, sewer.

Potter's Place Adult Camping Area, 89 Baker's Grant Rd., 04027. T: (207) 457-1341. pottersplacecampground.com. RV/tent: 100. $$. Hookups: electric (20, 30 amp), water.

Lee

Sleeping Bear Camping, P.O. Box 37, 04455. T: (207) 738-3148. www.sleepingbearcamping.com. RV/tent: 9. $$. Hookups: electric (30 amp), water.

Lincoln

Lakeside Camping and Cabins, P.O. Box 38, 04457. T: (207) 732-4241. RV/tent: 40. $$. Hookups: electric (15 amp), water, sewer.

Litchfield

Birches Family Campground, Cobbossee Rd, Box 302, 04350. T: (207) 268-4330. www.the birches.com. RV/tent: 106. $$. Hookups: electric (30 amp), water, modem.

Livermore

Rol-Lin Hills, RR 2, 04254. T: (207) 897-6394. RV/tent: 30. $$. Hookups: electric (30 amp), water, sewer.

Lubec

South Bay Campground, RR 1 Box 6565, 04652. T: (207) 733-1037. RV/tent: 42. $$. Hookups: electric (30 amp), water, sewer.

Sunset Point Trailer Park, P.O. Box 180, 04652. T: (207) 733-2272. RV/tent: 45. $$. Hookups: electric (20, 50 amp), water.

Madison

Abnaki Family Camping Center, Abnaki Rd., 04950. T: (207) 474-2070. RV/tent: 95. $$. Hookups: electric (20 amp), water.

Yonder Hill Campground, 221 Lakewood Rd., Rte. 201, 04950. T: (207) 474-7353 or (207) 474-6688. www.yonderhill.com. RV/tent: 100. $$. Hookups: electric (30 amp), water, sewer.

Medway

Pine Grove Campground and Cottages, P.O. Box 604, 04460. T: (207) 746-5172. www.mainerec.com/pinegrov.shtml. RV/tent: 45. $$. Hookups: electric (30 amp), water, sewer, modem.

Millinocket

Abol Bridge Campground, Bowater Great Northern Paper Co. Rd., 04462. T: No phone. www.campstorent.com. RV/tent: 36. $$. Hookups: none.

Chewonki's Big Eddy Campground, P.O. Box 238, 04462. T: (207) 350-1599. www.bigeddy.org. RV/tent: 80. $. Hookups: electric (15 amp), water.

Hidden Springs Campground, 224 Central St., 04462. T: (207) 723-6337 or (888) 685-4488. www.hiddenspring.com. RV/tent: 103. $$. Hookups: electric (50 amp), water.

Jo-Mary Lake Campground, P.O. Box 329, 04462. T: (207) 746-5512. www.campmaine.com/jo-mary. RV/tent: 60. $$. Hookups: none.

Nesowadnehunk Lake Wilderness Campground, P.O. Box 345, 04462. T: (207) 458-1551 (summer) or (207) 723-9595 (winter). www.mainerec.com/nesowadnehunk. RV/tent: 46. $. Hookups: electric (15 amp), water.

Moody

Outdoor World-Moody Beach Campground, US 1, 04054. T: (207) 646-4586. www.campoutdoor world.com. RV/tent: 145. $$$$. Hookups: electric (30, 50 amp), water, sewer.

Mount Vernon

Five Seasons Family Resort, 156 Five Seasons Rd., 04352. T: (207) 685-9141. www.5seasonsfamily resort.com. RV/tent: 50. $$. Hookups: electric (30 amp), water.

Naples

Brandy Pond Park, P.O. Box 1617, 04055. T: (207) 693-3129. RV/tent: 75. $. Hookups: electric (20 amp), water, sewer.

Colonial Mast Campground, Kansas Rd., 04055. T: (207) 693-6652. www.colonialmast.com. RV/tent: 79. $$$. Hookups: electric (30 amp), water, sewer.

Loon's Haven Family Campground, Rte. 114, Box 557, 04055. T: (207) 693-6881. www.loons haven.com/index.html. RV/tent: 135. $$. Hookups: electric (20 amp), water.

New Harbor

Pemaquid Point Campground, 9 Pemaquid Point Campground Rd., 04554. T: (207) 677-CAMP. www.midcoast.com/med. RV/tent: 50. $$. Hookups: electric (50 amp), water.

Newport

Christie's Lakeside Campground, Rte. 2 Box 565, 04953. T: (207) 368-4645 or (800) 688-4645. www.americantravelguide.com/northeast/maine/ads/christies/index.htm. RV/tent: 50. $$. Hookups: electric (20, 30 amp), water, sewer.

Tent Village Travel Trailer Park, RR 2 Box 580, 04953. T: (207) 368-5047 or (800) 319-9333. www.americantravelguide.com/northeast/maine/ads/tenill/index.html. RV/tent: 50. $$. Hookups: electric (20, 30 amp), water, sewer.

Nobleboro

Duck Puddle Campground, P.O. Box 176, 04555. T: (207) 563-5608. www.duckpuddlecamp ground.com. RV/tent: 120. $$. Hookups: electric (30 amp), water, sewer.

North Bridgton

Lakeside Pines Campground, P.O. Box 182, 04057. T: (207) 647-3935. www.lakesidepinescamping.com. RV/tent: 185. $$. Hookups: electric (30 amp), water, sewer.

Old Orchard Beach

Acorn Village, 42 Walnut St., 04064. T: (207) 934-4154. www.campmaine.com/acornvillage. RV/tent: 75. $$. Hookups: electric (20 amp), water, sewer.

Ne're Beach Family Campground, 38 Saco Ave. (Rte. 5), 04064. T: (207) 934-7614. www.old orchardbeachonline.com/nere/beach/family/camp ground.htm. RV/tent: 60. $$$. Hookups: electric (20, 30 amp), water, sewer.

Virginia Tent & Trailer Park, Box 242, 04064. T: (207) 934-4791. www.virginiaparkcamp ground.com. RV/tent: 130. $$$. Hookups: electric (20, 30, 50 amp), water, sewer.

Wagon Wheel Campground & Cabins, 27 Ocean Park Rd., 04064. T: (207) 934-4477. www.gocamping.com. RV/tent: 400. $$$. Hookups: electric (20, 30 amp), water, sewer.

Oxford

Mirror Pond Campground, 210 Tiger Hill Rd., 04270. T: (207) 539-4888. RV/tent: 40. $$. Hookups: electric (30 amp), water.

Parsonfield

Locklin Camping Area, Tripp Town Rd., 04047. T: (207) 625-8622. RV/tent: 50. $$. Hookups: electric (50 amp), water.

Patten

Shin Pond Village Campground & Cottages, Shin Pond Rd., 04765. T: (207) 528-2900. www.shin pond.com. RV/tent: 30. $$. Hookups: electric (30 amp), water.

Phippsburg

Ocean View Park Campground & Cottages, Rte. 209, Popham Beach, 04562. T: (207) 389-2564 (summer) or (207) 443-1000 (winter). RV/tent: 48. $$. Hookups: electric (20 amp), water, sewer.

Poland

Range Pond Campground, 94 Plains Rd., 04274. T: (207) 998-2624. www.rangepondcamp.com. RV/tent: 80. $$. Hookups: electric (30 amp), water, sewer.

Robinston

Hilltop Campground, 317 Ridge Rd., 04671. T: (207) 454-3985. www.hilltopcamping.com. RV/tent: 81. $$. Hookups: electric (20, 30, 50 amp), water, sewer.

Rockwood

Old Mill Campground, Cabins, & Marina, Rte. 15, 04478. T: (207) 534-7333. www.maineguide. com/moosehead/oldmill/oldmill1.html. RV/tent: 50. $$. Hookups: electric (20 amp), water, sewer.

Seboomook Wilderness Campground, P.O. Box 560, HC 85, 04478. T: (207) 534-8824. www.seboomookwildernesscampground.com. RV/tent: 39. $$. Hookups: electric (15 amp), water, sewer.

Roxbury

Silver Lake Campground, P.O. Box 32, 04275. T: (207) 545-0416. www.campme.com. RV/tent: 25. $$. Hookups: electric (30 amp), water.

Rumford

Madison Resort Inn & Campground, Rte. 2, Box 398, 04276. T: (207) 364-7973 or (800) 258-MADISON. www.madisoninn.com. RV/tent: 61. $$. Hookups: electric (30, 50 amp), water.

Saco

Homestead by the River, Rte. 5, Box 107, 04072. T: (207) 282-6445. www.homesteadbytheriver. com. RV/tent: 110. $$. Hookups: electric (30, 50 amp), water, sewer.

Sanford

Apache Campground, 165 Bernier Rd., 04073. T: (207) 324-5652. www.camp.com/apachecamp ground. RV/tent: 150. $$. Hookups: electric (20, 30 amp), water, sewer.

Jellystone Park Camp Resort, 1175 Main St., 04073. T: (207) 324-7782. www.jellystoneme.com. RV/tent: 102. $$$. Hookups: electric (30, 50 amp), water, sewer.

Sand Pond Campground, 149 Sandpond Rd., 04073. T: (207) 324-1752. www.sandpond.com. RV/tent: 48. $$. Hookups: electric (30, 50 amp), water, sewer.

MAINE (continued)

Scarborough

Twin Brooks Camping Area, 5 Ward St., 04039-0194. T: (207) 428-3832 or (207) 883-9959. www.campmaine.com/twinbrooks. RV/tent: 24. $$. Hookups: electric (20 amp), water, sewer.

Wild Duck Campground, 39 Dunstan Landing Rd., 04074. T: (207) 883-4432. www.wildduckcampground.com. RV/tent: 70. $$. Hookups: electric (30, 50 amp), water, sewer.

Sebago

Nason's Beach & Campground, 771 Sebago Rd., 04029. T: (207) 787-2345. RV/tent: 50. $$. Hookups: electric (20, 30 amp), water.

Skowhegan

Eaton Mountain Ski Area and Campground, 89 Lambert Rd., 04976. T: (207) 474-2666. www.eatonmountain.com. RV/tent: 32. $. Hookups: electric (20, 30 amp), water, sewer.

Two Rivers Campground, HCR 71, 04976. T: (207) 474-6482. www.twors.com. RV/tent: 65. $$. Hookups: electric (30 amp), water, cable, phone.

Solon

The Evergreens Campground, Ferry St., 04979. T: (207) 643-2324. www.evergreenscampground.com. RV/tent: 40. $$. Hookups: electric (20, 30 amp), water.

South Thomaston

Lobster Buoy Campsites, 280 Waterman Beach Rd., 04858. T: (207) 594-7546. RV/tent: 40. $$. Hookups: electric (30 amp), water.

Stetson

Stetson Shores, P.O. Box 86M, Rte. 143, 04488. T: (207) 296-2041. www.campmaine.com/stetson. RV/tent: 47. $$. Hookups: electric (20, 30 amp), water, sewer.

Steuben

Mainayr Campground, 321 Village Rd., 04680. T: (207) 546-2690. www.mainayr.com. RV/tent: 35. $$. Hookups: electric (20, 30 amp), water, sewer.

Stonington

Greenlaw's RV Tent & Rental, P.O. Box 72, 04681. T: (207) 367-5049. RV/tent: 27. $$. Hookups: electric (15, 20, 30 amp), water, sewer.

The Forks

Indian Pond Campground, H.CR 63, 04985. T: (800) 371-7774. RV/tent: 27. $$. Hookups: none.

Northern Outdoors Adventure Resort, Rte. 201, Box 100, 04985. T: (800) 765-7238. www.northernoutdoors.com. RV/tent: 10. $. Hookups: none.

Tremont

Quietside Campground & Cabins, P.O. Box 10, Rte. 102, 04653. T: (207) 244-5992. www.quietsidecampground.com. RV/tent: 35. $$. Hookups: electric (20, 30 amp), water.

Vassalboro

Green Valley Campground, 1248 Cross Hill Rd., 04989. T: (207) 923-3000. www.greenvalleycampground.us. RV/tent: 80. $$. Hookups: electric (15, 30 amp), water, sewer.

Warren

Sandy Shores RV Resort, 459 Sandy Shores Rd., 04864. T: (207) 273-2073. RV/tent: 10. $$. Hookups: electric (50 amp), water, sewer, cable.

Waterville

Countryside Campground, West River Rd., 04903. T: (207) 873-4603. RV/tent: 25. $$. Hookups: electric (30 amp), water, sewer, phone, cable.

Weld

Dummer's Beach Campground, P.O. Box 82, 04285. T: (207) 585-2200. RV/tent: 200. $$. Hookups: electric (30 amp), water.

Wells

Beach Acres Campground, 563M Post Rd., Rte. 1, 04090. T: (207) 646-5612. www.beachacres.com. RV/tent: 71. $$. Hookups: electric (20, 30, 50 amp), water, sewer.

Gregoire's Campground, 697 Sanford Rd., 04090. T: (207) 646-3711. RV/tent: 130. $$. Hookups: electric (20, 30 amp), water, sewer.

Pinederosa Camping Area, 128 North Village Rd., 04090. T: (207) 646-2492. www.pinederosa.com. RV/tent: 122. $$. Hookups: electric (20, 30 amp), water, sewer.

Riverside Campground, 2295 Post Rd., 04090. T: (207) 646-3145 (summer) or (207) 725-6418 (winter). www.riversidecampgroundwells.com. RV/tent: 130. $$. Hookups: electric (20, 30, 50 amp), water, sewer, cable, phone.

Stadig Mobile Park & Campground, 146 Bypass Rd., 04090. T: (207) 646-2298. www.stadig.com. RV/tent: 150. $$. Hookups: electric (20, 30 amp), water, sewer.

West Bethel

Pleasant River Campground, 800 West Bethel Rd./Rte. 2, 04286. T: (207) 836-2000. RV/tent: 75. $$. Hookups: electric (50 amp), water, sewer.

West Poland

Hemlocks Camping Area, P.O. Box 58, 04291. T: (888) 578-9251. www.hemlockscampground.com. RV/tent: 75. $$. Hookups: electric (30 amp), water, sewer.

Mac's Campground, Tripp Lake Rd., 04291. T: (207) 998-4238. RV/tent: 30. $$. Hookups: electric (20 amp), water, sewer.

Wilsons Mills

Aziscoos Valley Camping Area, H.CR 10, 03579. T: (207) 486-3271. RV/tent: 34. $$. Hookups: electric (30 amp), water.

Windham

Highland Lake Park, 19 Roosevelt Trail, Rte. 302, 04062. T: (207) 892-8911. RV/tent: 40. $$. Hookups: electric (20, 30 amp), water, sewer, cable.

Winslow

Giordano's Camping and Recreation, RR 2, 04901. T: (207) 873-2408. RV/tent: 45. $$. Hookups: electric (15 amp), water.

Winthrop

Augusta West Kampground, East Monmouth Rd., 04364. T: (207) 377-9993. RV/tent: 81. $$. Hookups: electric (30 amp), water, sewer, phone, modem.

York Beach

York Beach Camper Park, 11 Cappy's Ln., 03910. T: (207) 363-1343. RV/tent: 46. $$$. Hookups: electric (30, 50 amp), water, sewer.

York Harbor

Camp Eaton, Rte. 1A, 03911. T: (207) 363-3424. www.campeaton.com. RV/tent: 307. $$$. Hookups: electric (20, 30, 50 amp), water, sewer, cable.

MARYLAND

Callaway

Take-It-Easy Campground, 45285 Take It Easy Ranch Rd., 20620. T: (301) 994-0494. www.takeiteasycampground.com. RV/tent: 250. $$$. Hookups: electric, water, sewer, cable.

Delmar

Woodlawn Campground, 1209 Walnut St., 21875. T: (410) 896-2979. RV/tent: 35. $$. Hookups: electric (30 amp), water.

Elkton

Woodlands Camping Resort, 265 Starkey Ln., 21921. T: (410) 398-4414 or (800)-972-2674. RV/tent: 155. $$. Hookups: electric (30, 50 amp), water, sewer.

Frostburg

Mason Dixon Campground, 4121 Greenville Rd., 21532. T: (888) MAPLECAMP. RV/tent: 70. $$. Hookups: electric (20, 30 amp), water, sewer.

Grantsville

New Germany State Park, 349 Headquarters Ln., 21536. T: (301) 895-5453 or (888) 432-2267. www.dnr.state.md.us. RV/tent: 37. $$. Hookups: none.

Hancock

Happy Hills Campground, 12617 Seavolt Rd., 21750. T: (301) 678-7760. www.happyhillscampground-md.com. RV/tent: 280. $$. Hookups: electric (20, 30 amp), water, sewer.

MARYLAND (continued)

Indian Springs

Indian Springs Campground, 10809 Big Pool Rd., 21711. T: (301) 842-3336. RV/tent: 95. $$. Hookups: electric (20, 30 amp), water, sewer.

Leonardtown

LaGrande Estate Camping Resort, 23285 Pt. Lookout Rd., 20650. T: (301) 475-8550. www.lagranderesort.com. RV/tent: 109. $$. Hookups: electric (30 amp), water, sewer.

Newburg

Aqua-Land Campground, US 301 South, 20664. T: (301) 259-2575. RV/tent: 136. $$. Hookups: electric (20, 30, 50 amp), water, sewer.

North East

Elk Neck State Park, 4395 Turkey Point Rd., 21901. T: (410) 287-5333. www.dnr.state.md.us.com.

RV/tent: 279. $$. Hookups: electric (20), water, sewer.

Perryville

Riverview Campground, 1200 Frenchtown Rd., 21903. T: (410) 642-6200. RV/tent: 64. $$. Hookups: electric (30, 50 amp), water, sewer.

Queen Anne

Tuckahoe State Park, 13070 Crouse Mill Rd., 21657. T: (410) 820-1668 or (888) 432-CAMP. www.dnr.state.md.us. RV/tent: 35. $$. Hookups: none.

Snow Hill

Pocomoke River State Park, 3461 Worecester Hwy., 21863. T: (410) 632-2566. www.dnr.state.md.us. RV/tent: 200. $$. Hookups: electric (20, 30).

Thurmont

Catoctin Mountain National Park, 6602 Foxville Rd., 21788. T: (301) 663-9388. www.nps.gov/cato. RV/tent: 51. $$. Hookups: none.

Crow's Nest Campground, Rte. 77 West, 21788. T: (301) 271-7632 or (800) 866-1959. RV/tent: 110. $$. Hookups: electric (15, 20, 30), water, sewer.

Westover

Lake Somerset Campground, 8658 Lake Somerset Ln., 21871. T: (410) 957-9897. www.lakesomerset.com. RV/tent: 140. $$$. Hookups: electric (30 amp), water.

MASSACHUSETTS

Amesbury

Powow Cove Campground, 2 Powow Cove Ln., 01913. T: (978) 388-4022. RV/tent: 73. $$$. Hookups: electric (30 amp), water.

Ashburnham

Howe's Camping, 133 Sherbert Rd., 01430. T: (978) 827-4558 or (800) 766-4807. www.howes camping.com. RV/tent: 30. $$. Hookups: electric (20 amp), water.

Ashby

The Pines, 39 Davis Rd., 01431. T: (978) 386-7702. RV/tent: 60. $$. Hookups: electric (50 amp), water.

Assonet

Forge Pond Campground, 62 Forge Rd., 02702. T: (508) 644-5701. RV/tent: 65. $$. Hookups: electric (15 amp), water.

Barre

Coldbrook Campground, 864 Old Coldbrook Rd., 01005. T: (978) 355-2090. www.coldbrook country.com. RV/tent: 195. $$. Hookups: electric (30 amp), water.

Becket

Bonny Rigg Campground, P.O. Box 14, 01011. T: (413) 623-5366. www.bonnyriggcampground. com. RV/tent: 215. $$. Hookups: electric (30 amp), water.

Bedford

Military Park (Hanscom AFB Family Camp), P.O. Box 479, 02047. T: (781) 377-4670. www.army mwr.com/portal/travel/paths/ma.asp. RV/tent: 66. $. Hookups: electric (20, 30, 50 amp), water.

Bernardston

Purple Meadow Campground, P.O. Box 192, 01337. T: (413) 648-9289. RV/tent: 40. $$. Hookups: electric (50 amp), water.

Travelers Woods of New England, 152 River St., 01337. T: (413) 648-9105. www.travelerswoods .com. RV/tent: 94. $$. Hookups: electric (30 amp), water, sewer.

Bolton

Crystal Springs Campground, Hwy. 117, 01740. T: (978) 779-2711. RV/tent: 200. $$$. Hookups: electric (30 amp), water, sewer.

Brimfield

Village Green Family Campground, 228 Sturbridge Rd. Rte. 20, 01010. T: (413) 245-3504. www .villagegreencampground.com. RV/tent: 131. $$. Hookups: electric (30 amp), water.

Charlemont

Mohawk Park, P.O. Box 668, 01339. T: (413) 339-4470. RV/tent: 80. $$$. Hookups: electric (20 amp), water, sewer.

Dennisport

Grindell's Ocean View Park, 61 Old Wharf Rd., 02639. T: (508) 398-2671. RV/tent: 160. $$$. Hookups: electric (20 amp), water, sewer, cable.

East Douglas

Lake Manchaug Camping, 76 Oak St., 01516. T: (508) 476-2471. RV/tent: 192. $$$. Hookups: electric (50 amp), water, sewer.

East Otis

Laurel Ridge Camping Area, 40 Old Blandford Rd., 01029. T: (413) 269-4804 or (800) 538-CAMP. RV/tent: 180. $$. Hookups: electric (30 amp), water.

East Wareham

Maple Park Family Campground, 290 Glen Charlie Rd., 02538. T: (508) 295-4945 or (508) 291-CAMP. www.mapleparkfamilycampground.com. RV/tent: 400. $$. Hookups: electric (20 amp), water, sewer.

Hancock

Berkshire Vista Nudist Resort, P.O. Box 1177, 01237. T: (413) 738-5154. www.berkshire vista.com. RV/tent: 180. $$. Hookups: electric (50 amp), water, sewer.

Hinsdale

Fernwood Forest, P.O. Box 896, 01235. T: (413) 655-2292. www.topcities.com/Business/fernwood/ index.htm. RV/tent: 36. $$. Hookups: electric (30 amp), water.

Mashpee

Johns Pond Campground/Otis Trailer Village, P.O. Box 586, 02541. T: (508) 477-0444. www.johns pondcampground.com. RV/tent: 90. $$. Hookups: electric (30 amp), water, sewer.

Monson

Partridge Hollow, 72 Sutcliffe Rd. South, 01057. T: (413) 267-5122. RV/tent: 240. $$. Hookups: electric (50 amp), water.

North Egremont

Prospect Lake Park, 50 Prospect Lake Rd., 02152. T: (413) 528-4158 or (877) 860-4757. www.prospectlakepark.com. RV/tent: 140. $$. Hookups: electric (30 amp), water, sewer.

North Rutland

Pout & Trout Family Campground, 94 River Rd., 01543. T: (508) 886-6677. RV/tent: 156. $$. Hookups: electric (30 amp), water, sewer.

North Truro

North of Highland, 52 Head of the Meadow Rd., 02652. T: (508) 487-1191. www.capecodcamp ing.com. RV/tent: 237. $$. Hookups: none.

Northfield

Barton Cove Campground and Canoe Shuttle Service, 90 Millers Falls Rd., 01360. T: (413) 863-9300. www.nv.com/northfield/camping.asp. RV/tent: 31. $$. Hookups: none.

MASSACHUSETTS (continued)

Otis

Camp Overflow, P.O. Box 645, 01253. T: (413) 269-4036. www.campoverflow.com. RV/tent: 175. $$. Hookups: electric (20, 30 amp), water, dump station.

Mountain View Campground, P.O. Box 162, 01253. T: (413) 269-8928. RV/tent: 50. $$. Hookups: electric (50 amp), water, sewer.

Phillipston

Lamb City Campground, 85 Royalston Rd., 01331. T: (978) 249-2049 or (800) 292-5262. www.lambcity.com. RV/tent: 228. $$. Hookups: electric (30 amp), water, sewer, cable.

Pittsfield

Bonnie Brae Cabins & Campsites, 108 Broadway St., 01201. T: (413) 442-3754 or (413) 445-9358. www.bonniebraecampground.tripod.com. RV/tent: 42. $$$. Hookups: electric (30 amp), water, sewer.

Plymouth

Indianhead Resort, 1929 State Rd., Rte. 3A, 02360. T: (508) 888-3688. www.indianhead-resort.com/home. RV/tent: 200. $$. Hookups: electric (50 amp), water.

Sandy Pond Campground, 834 Bourne Rd., 02360. T: (508) 759-9336. www.sandypond.com. RV/tent: 200. $$$. Hookups: electric (50 amp), water, sewer.

Rochester

Knight and Look Campground, 241 Marion Rd., 02770. T: (508) 763-2454 or (866) 463-2454. geocities.com/knlcamp. RV/tent: 120. $$. Hookups: electric (20 amp), water, sewer.

Sandwich

Dunroamin' Trailer Park, 5 John Ewer Rd., RR 3, 02563. T: (508) 477-0541 or (508) 477-0859 (winter). www.hometown.aol.com/dunroamin trailer. RV/tent: 64. $$$. Hookups: electric (30 amp), water, sewer.

South Dennis

Old Chatham Road RV Resort, 310 Old Chatham Rd., 02660. T: (508) 385-3616. RV/tent: 10. $$$. Hookups: electric (15, 30 amp), water.

South Wellfleet

Paine's Campground, 180 Old County Rd., 02663. T: (508) 349-3007. www.campingcapecod.com. RV/tent: 50. $$. Hookups: electric (30 amp), water.

Southwick

Southwick Acres, 256 College Hwy., Rte. 10 & 202, 01077. T: (413) 569-6339. www.southwickacres.com. RV/tent: 40. $$. Hookups: electric (30 amp), water.

Vineyard Haven

Martha's Vineyard Family Campground, 569 Edgartown Rd., 02568. T: (508) 693-3772. www.campmvfc.com. RV/tent: 40. $$$. Hookups: electric (30 amp), water, sewer, cable.

Warwick

Wagon Wheel Camping Area, 909 Wendell Rd., 01378. T: (978) 544-3425. RV/tent: 102. $$. Hookups: electric (30 amp), water, sewer.

Washington

Summit Hill Campground, Summit Hill Rd., 01223. T: (413) 623-5761. RV/tent: 106. $$$. Hookups: electric (15 amp), water.

West Brookfield

Highview Campground, 58 John Gilbert Rd., 01585. T: (508) 867-7800. RV/tent: 212. $$$. Hookups: electric (30 amp), water.

The Old Sawmill Campground, Long Hill Rd., Box 377, 01585. T: (508) 867-2427. RV/tent: 125. $$. Hookups: electric (20, 30 amp), water.

West Sutton

Sutton Falls Camping Area, 90 Manchaug Rd., 01590. T: (508) 865-3898. www.suttonfalls.com. RV/tent: 119. $$. Hookups: electric (30 amp), water.

Westhampton

Windy Acres Campground, 139 South St., 01027. T: (413) 527-9862. www.windyacres.com. RV/tent: 135. $$. Hookups: electric (30 amp), water.

Whately

White Birch Campground, 214 North St., 01093. T: (413) 665-4941 or (800) 244-4941. RV/tent: 60. $$. Hookups: electric (30 amp), water.

Worthington

Berkshire Park Camping Area, 350 Harvey Rd., 01237. T: (413) 238-5918. www.erols.com/bpca. RV/tent: 134. $$. Hookups: electric (30 amp), water.

MICHIGAN

Acme

Traverse Bay RV Park, 555 M-72 East, 49610. T: (231) 938-5800. www.traversebayrv.com. RV/tent: 133. $$$. Hookups: electric (20, 30, 50 amp), water, sewer, cable.

Alanson

Crooked River RV Park, 7384 Cheboygan St., 49706. T: (231) 548-5534 or (888) 564-5534. www.michcampgrounds.com/crookedriver. RV/tent: 15. $$. Hookups: electric (30 amp), water, sewer, cable.

Alger

Greenwood Campground, 636 West Greenwood Rd., 48610. T: (989) 345-2778. www.michcampgrounds.com/greenwood. RV/tent: 45. $$. Hookups: electric (50 amp), water, sewer.

Algonac

Algonac State Park, 8732 River Rd., 48039. T: (810) 765-5605. RV/tent: 300. $$. Hookups: electric (30 amp).

Alpena

Thunder Bay RV Park & Campground, 4250 US 23 South, 49707. T: (989) 354-2528. RV/tent: 45. $. Hookups: electric (30 amp), water.

Alto

Tyler Creek Golf Club & Campground, 13495 92nd St., 49302. T: (616) 868-6751. RV/tent: 206. $$. Hookups: electric (30 amp), water.

Atlanta

Clear Lake State Park, 20500 M-33, 49709. T: (989) 785-4388. RV/tent: 200. $$. Hookups: electric (30 amp).

Au Gres

Pt. Au Gres Marina & Fish Camp, 2325 Green Dr., 48703. T: (989) 876-7314. RV/tent: 44. $$. Hookups: electric (30 amp), water.

Augusta

Fort Custer Recreation Area, 5163 West Fort Custer Dr., 49012. T: (269) 731-4200. RV/tent: 217. $$. Hookups: electric (30 amp).

Shady Bend Campground, 15320 Augusta Dr., 49012. T: (269) 731-4503. RV/tent: 62. $$. Hookups: electric (30 amp), water.

Baraga

Baraga State Park, 1300 US 41S, 49908. T: (906) 353-6558. RV/tent: 188. $. Hookups: electric (30 amp).

Bark River

Bayside Resort & Campground, 376 Hwy. M-35, 49807. T: (906) 786-7831. RV/tent: 30. $$. Hookups: electric (30 amp), water, sewer.

Bay City

Bay City State Park, 3582 State Park Dr., 48706. T: (989) 684-3020. RV/tent: 193. $. Hookups: electric (30 amp).

Bay View Petoskey KOA, 1800 North US 31, 49770. T: (231) 347-0005. RV/tent: 206. $$. Hookups: electric (30, 50 amp), water, sewer, phone, cable.

MICHIGAN (continued)

Beaverton

Lost Haven Campground, 5300 Townhall Rd., 48612. T: (989) 435-7623. RV/tent: 100. $$. Hookups: electric (30 amp), water.

Bellaire

Chain-O-Lakes Campground, 7231 South M-88, 49615. T: (231) 533-8432. RV/tent: 78. $$. Hookups: electric (50 amp), water, sewer.

Belmont

Grand Rogue Campground, Canoe, & Tube Livery, 6400 West River Dr., 49306. T: (616) 361-1053. RV/tent: 82. $$. Hookups: electric (30 amp), water.

Benzonia

Timberline Campground, 2788 Benzie Hwy, 49616. T: (231) 882-9548. RV/tent: 189. $$. Hookups: electric, water, sewer.

Beulah

Turtle Lake Campground, 854 Miller Rd., 49617. T: (231) 275-7353. RV/tent: 59. $$. Hookups: electric (30 amp).

Birch Run

Pine Ridge RV Campground, 11700 Gera Rd., 48415. T: (989) 624-9029. RV/tent: 157. $$$. Hookups: electric (50 amp), water, sewer.

Bitely

Pettibone Lake, Pettibone Lake Rd., 51408. T: (231) 689-2021. RV/tent: 16. $. Hookups: electric (30 amp).

Pickerel Lake Lakeside Campground & Cottages, 12666 North Woodbridge, 49309. T: (231) 745-7268. www.travel.michigan.org/lodging. RV/tent: 42. $$. Hookups: electric (20, 30, 50 amp).

Boyne City

Young State Park, 2280 Boyne City Rd., 49712. T: (231) 582-7523. RV/tent: 240. $$. Hookups: electric (20, 30, 50 amp).

Breckenridge

River Ridge Campground, 1989 West Pine River Rd., 48615. T: (989) 842-5184. RV/tent: 82. $$. Hookups: electric (50 amp), water, sewer.

Brimley

Brimley State Park, 9200 West 6 Mile Rd., 49715. T: (906) 248-3422. RV/tent: 269. $$. Hookups: electric (30 amp).

Byron Center

Dome World Recreation, 400 84th St. Sw, 49315. T: (616) 878-1518. www.domeworld.com/pages/_newpages/campground.asp. RV/tent: 50. $$. Hookups: electric (30 amp), water, sewer, phone, cable.

Woodchip Campground, 7501 Burlingame Ave. SW, 49315. T: (616) 878-9050. www.michcamp grounds.com/woodchip. RV/tent: 122. $$. Hookups: electric (30, 50 amp), water, sewer.

Cadillac

Birchwood Resort and Campground, 6545 East M-115, 49601. T: (231) 775-9101. RV/tent: 28. $$$. Hookups: electric (20, 30, 50 amp), water, sewer.

Mitchell State Park, 6093 E-M115, 49601. T: (231) 775-7911. RV/tent: 200. $$. Hookups: electric (30 amp).

Calumet

McLain State Park, M-203, 49930. T: (906) 482-0278. RV/tent: 103. $$. Hookups: electric (30 amp).

Carp Lake

Wilderness State Park, 898 Wilderness Park Dr., 49718. T: (231) 436-5381. RV/tent: 250. $$. Hookups: electric (30 amp).

Caseville

Sleeper State Park, 6573 State Park Rd., 48725. T: (989) 856-4411. RV/tent: 223. $$. Hookups: electric (30 amp).

Cedar River

J. W. Wells State Park, North 7670 Hwy. M-35, 49813. T: (906) 863-9747. RV/tent: 178. $$. Hookups: electric (30 amp).

Cedar Springs

Duke Creek Campground, 15190 White Creek Ave., 49319. T: (616) 696-2115. RV/tent: 114. $$. Hookups: electric (30 amp), water, sewer.

Cedarville

Cedarville RV Park & Campground, Box 328, 49719. T: (800) 906-3351. RV/tent: 57. $$. Hookups: electric (50 amp), water, sewer.

Lazy Days Campground, 266 Mary, 49719. T: (888) 813-2564. RV/tent: 22. $$. Hookups: electric (30 amp), water.

Champion

Van Riper State Park, P.O. Box 88/US 41 West, 49814. T: (906) 339-4461 or (800) 447-2757. www.michigandnr.com/parksandtrails/parklist .asp. RV/tent: 106. $$. Hookups: electric (30 amp).

Cheboygan

Aloha State Park, 4347 3rd St., 49721. T: (231) 625-2522. www.michigan.state-park.org. RV/tent: 285. $$. Hookups: electric (30 amp).

Cheboygan State Park, 4490 Beach Rd., 49721. T: (231) 627-2811. RV/tent: 78. $. Hookups: electric (30 amp).

Chelsea

Portage Campground, Waterloo Recreation Area, 16345 McClure Rd., 48118. T: (734) 475-8307 or (800) 447-2757. www.michigandnr.com/parks andtrails.parklist.asp. RV/tent: 136. $$. Hookups: electric (30 amp).

Sugarloaf Campground, Waterloo Recreation Area, 16345 McClure Rd., 48118. T: (734) 475-8307 or (800) 447-2757. www.lmichigandnr.com/parks andtrials/parklist.asp. RV/tent: 164. $$. Hookups: electric (30 amp).

Clare

Herrick Recreation Area, 6320 East Herrick Rd., 48617. T: (989) 772-0911. RV/tent: 73. $$. Hookups: electric (30 amp).

Clarkston

Holly State Recreation Area, 8100 Grange Hall Rd., 48442. T: (248) 634-8811. RV/tent: 161. $$. Hookups: electric (30 amp).

Clinton

W. J. Hayes State Park, 1220 Wampler's Lake Rd., 49265. T: (517) 467-7401. RV/tent: 185. $$. Hookups: electric (30 amp).

Clyde

Fort Trodd Family Campground Resort, 6350 Lapeer Rd., 48049. T: (810) 987-4889. RV/tent: 120. $$. Hookups: electric (50 amp), water, sewer.

Commerce

Proud Lake State Recreation Area, 3500 Wixom Rd., 48382. T: (248) 685-2433 or (800) 447-2757. www.michigan.gov/dnr. RV/tent: 130. $$. Hookups: electric (30 amp).

Concord

Swains Lake County Park & Campground, 117 Swains Lake Dr., 49237. T: (517) 524-7666 or (517) 788-4320. www.co.jackson.mi.us/parks/ swainslakepark.asp. RV/tent: 56. $$. Hookups: electric (30 amp), water.

Cooks

Fish Dam Campground, Box 24, 49817. T: (906) 644-7660. RV/tent: 19. $$. Hookups: electric (30 amp).

Coopersville

Conestoga Grand River Campground, 9720 Oriole Dr., 49404. T: (616) 837-6323. www.michcamp grounds.com/conestoga. RV/tent: 81. $$. Hookups: electric (50 amp), water, sewer.

Copper Harbor

Fort Wilkins State Park, P.O. Box 71, 49918. T: (906) 289-4215. RV/tent: 165. $$. Hookups: electric (30 amp).

Lake Fanny Hooe Resort & Campground, 505 Second St., 49918. T: (800) 426-4451. www.fanny hooe.com. RV/tent: 64. $$. Hookups: electric (30, 50 amp), water, sewer, cable.

Crystal Falls

Bewabic State Park, 1933 US 2 W, 49920. T: (906) 875-3324. RV/tent: 144. $$. Hookups: electric (30 amp).

Pentoga Park, 1630 CR 424, 49920. T: (906) 265-3979. www.pentogapark.com. RV/tent: 100. $$. Hookups: electric (30 amp), water.

Dafter

Clear Lake Campground, 13301 South Mackinaw Trail, 49724. T: (906) 635-0201. RV/tent: 60. $$. Hookups: electric (30 amp), water.

MICHIGAN (continued)

Davison

Davison Wolverine Campground, G-7698 North Baxter Rd., 48506. T: (810) 736-7100 or (810) 793-6613. www.geneseecountyparks.org/wolverine.htm. RV/tent: 195. $$. Hookups: electric (30 amp).

Timber Wolf Campground, 7004 North Irish Rd., 48463. T: (810) 736-7100 or (810) 640-1600. www.geneseecountyparks.org/timberwolf.htm. RV/tent: 196. $$. Hookups: electric (30 amp), water, sewer.

Dundee

Wilderness Retreat Campground, 1350 Meanwell Rd., 48131. T: (734) 529-5122. RV/tent: 44. $$. Hookups: electric (30 amp), water.

East Tawas

East Tawas City Park, 407 West Bay, 48730. T: (989) 362-5562. www.myvoyager.net/~easttawas/park.htm. RV/tent: 170. $$. Hookups: electric (30 amp), water, sewer, cable.

Tawas Point State Park, 686 Tawas Beach Rd., 48730. T: (989) 362-5041. www.dnr.state.mi.us. RV/tent: 194. $$. Hookups: electric (30 amp).

Elk Rapids

Vacation Village Campground, 509 Lake St., 49629. T: (231) 264-8636. RV/tent: 31. $$. Hookups: electric (30 amp), water, sewer.

Emmett

Emmett KOA, 3864 Breen Rd., 48022. T: (810) 395-7042 or (888) 562-5612. www.koa.com. RV/tent: 100. $$$. Hookups: electric (30 amp), water.

Escanaba

Park Place of the North, E4575 Hwy. M-35, 49829. T: (906) 786-8453. RV/tent: 25. $$. Hookups: electric (30 amp), water.

Evart

Muskegon River Camp & Canoe, 6281 River Rd., 49631. T: (231) 734-3808. www.campand canoe.com. RV/tent: 116. $$. Hookups: electric (30 amp), water, sewer.

Fenton

Seven Lakes, 2220 Tinsman, 48430. T: (810) 634-7271. RV/tent: 71. $. Hookups: electric (50 amp).

Forester

Forester Park, 2820 North Lakeshore Dr., 48419. T: (810) 622-8715. RV/tent: 120. $$. Hookups: electric (30 amp), water.

Fountain

Timber Surf Campground, 6575 Dewey Rd., 48410. T: (231) 462-3468. RV/tent: 75. $$. Hookups: electric (30 amp), water, sewer.

Frankfort

Betsie River Campsite, 1923 River Rd., 49635. T: (231) 352-9535. www.michcampgrounds.com/betsieriver. RV/tent: 100. $$. Hookups: electric (20 amp), water.

Garden

Fayette State Park, 13700 13.25 Ln., 49835. T: (906) 644-2603. www.dnr.state.mi.us. RV/tent: 61. $. Hookups: electric (30 amp).

Gaylord

Gaylord KOA, 5101 Campfires Pkwy, 49735. T: (989) 939-8723 or (800) 562-4146. ww.koa.com. RV/tent: 130. $$. Hookups: electric (30 amp), water, sewer.

Otsego Lake State Park, 7136 Old 27 South, 49735. T: (989) 732-5485. www.dnr.state.mi.us. RV/tent: 156. $$. Hookups: electric (30 amp).

Germfask

Big Cedar Campground & Canoe Livery, Hwy. M-77, 49836. T: (906) 586-6684. www.bigcedar campground.com. RV/tent: 52. $$. Hookups: electric (30 amp), water.

Northland Outfitters Camping Resort, Hwy. M-77, 49836. T: (800) 808-3FUN or (906) 586-9801. www.exploringthenorth.com/northland/outfitters.html. RV/tent: 15. $$. Hookups: electric (30 amp), water.

Gladwin

River Valley RV Park, 2165 South Bailey Lake Ave., 48624. T: (989) 386-7844. www.rivervalleyrv.com. RV/tent: 68. $$. Hookups: electric (30 amp), water, sewer.

Glennie

Alcona Park-Full Service Area, 2550 Au Sable Rd., 48737. T: (989) 735-3881. www.alconapark.com. RV/tent: 48. $$. Hookups: electric (50 amp), water, sewer.

Alcona Park-Modern Area, 2550 Au Sable Rd., 48737. T: (989) 735-3881. www.alconapark.com. RV/tent: 104. $$. Hookups: electric (30 amp).

Gould City

Michihistrigan Campground, HCR Box 20, 49838. T: (906) 477-6983 or (800) 924-8873. www.michihistrigan.com. RV/tent: 47. $$. Hookups: electric (30 amp), water, sewer.

Gowen

Camp Concordia, 13400 Pinewood NE, 49326. T: (616) 754-3785. RV/tent: 38. $$. Hookups: electric (50 amp).

Grand Haven

Grand Haven State Park, 1001 Harbor Ave., 49417. T: (616) 798-3711 or (800) 44-PARKS. www.grandhavenlive.com. RV/tent: 174. $$. Hookups: electric (30 amp).

Grant

Chinook Camping, 5471 West 112th St., 49327. T: (231) 834-7505. RV/tent: 56. $$. Hookups: electric (30 amp), water.

Salmon Run Campground & Vic's Canoes, 8845 Felch Ave., 49327. T: (231) 834-5494. RV/tent: 80. $$. Hookups: electric (20, 30 amp), water.

Grass Lake

Applecreek Resort & RV Park, 11185 Orban Rd., 49240. T: (517) 522-3467. RV/tent: 95. $$. Hookups: electric (20, 30 amp), water.

Hideaway RV Park, 3500 Updyke Rd., 49240. T: (517) 522-5858. RV/tent: 55. $$. Hookups: electric (50 amp), water, sewer.

Grayling

Hartwick Pines State Park, 4216 Ranger Rd., 49738. T: (989) 348-7068. RV/tent: 100. $$. Hookups: electric (30 amp).

Greenville

Three Seasons RV Park, 6956 Fuller Rd., 48838. T: (616) 754-5717. www.threeseasonsrvpark.com. RV/tent: 25. $$. Hookups: electric (30 amp), water.

Gwinn

Horseshoe Lake Campground, 840 North Horseshoe Lake Rd., 49841. T: (906) 346-9937. RV/tent: 125. $$. Hookups: electric (30 amp), water, sewer.

Hanover

Twin Pines Campground & Canoe Livery, 9800 Wheeler Rd., 49241. T: (517) 524-6298. RV/tent: 81. $$. Hookups: electric (30 amp), water.

Harbor Beach

North Park Campground, 836 North Huron Ave., 48441. T: (989) 479-9554 or (989) 479-3363. RV/tent: 184. $$. Hookups: electric (30, 50 amp), water, sewer, cable.

Harrisville

Harrisville State Park, P.O. Box 326, 48740. T: (989) 724-5126. RV/tent: 200. $$. Hookups: electric (30 amp).

Hastings

Camp Michawana, 5800 Head Lake Rd., 49058. T: (269) 623-5168. RV/tent: 54. $$. Hookups: electric (30 amp), water.

Hesperia

Leisure Haven Campground, 3056 East M-20, 49421. T: (231) 861-7262. RV/tent: 47. $$. Hookups: electric (30 amp).

Hillman

Heine's Landing, 24650 Landing Rd., 49746. T: (517) 742-4029. RV/tent: 62. $$. Hookups: electric (30 amp).

Sorensen's Grass Lake Resort, 18680 Sorensen Rd., 49746. T: (989) 742-3412. RV/tent: 20. $$. Hookups: electric (30 amp), water.

Holland

Drew's Country Camping, 12850 Ransom Rd., 49424. T: (616) 399-1886. RV/tent: 75. $$. Hookups: electric (20, 30 amp), water.

Holland State Park, 2215 Ottawa Beach Rd., 49424. T: (616) 399-9390 or (800) 44-PARKS. www.michigan.gov/dnr. RV/tent: 309. $$. Hookups: electric (20, 30, 50 amp), water, sewer.

Holly

Groveland Oaks County Park, 14555 Dixie Hwy., 48442. T: (248) 634-9811 or (888) 677-2757. RV/tent: 269. $$$. Hookups: electric (50 amp), water.

MICHIGAN (continued)

Hopkins

Miller Lake Campground, 2130 Miller Lake Rd., 49328. T: (269) 672-7139. RV/tent: 42. $$. Hookups: electric (50 amp), water, sewer.

Howell

Brighton State Recreation Area, 6360 Chilson Rd., 48843. T: (810) 229-6566. www.mich.info/ michigan/recreation/stateparks.htm. RV/tent: 215. $$. Hookups: electric (30 amp).

Indian River

Burt Lake State Park, 6635 State Park Dr., 49749. T: (231) 238-9392 or (800) 44-PARKS. www.michigan.gov/dnr. RV/tent: 333. $$. Hookups: electric (30 amp).

Ionia

Ionia Recreation, 2880 David Hwy., 48846. T: (616) 527-3750 or (800) 447-2757. www.michigan.gov/dnr. RV/tent: 100. $$. Hookups: electric (30 amp).

Iron Mountain

Lake Antoine Park, North 3393 Lake Antoine Rd., 49801. T: (906) 774-8875. RV/tent: 90. $. Hookups: electric (30 amp), water.

Summer Breeze, West 8576 Twin Falls Rd., 49801. T: (906) 774-7701. www.summerbreezecamp ground.com. RV/tent: 65. $$. Hookups: electric (30 amp), water, sewer.

Irons

Leisure Time Campground, 9214 West 5 Mile Rd., 49644. T: (800) 266-8214 or (269) 266-8214. RV/tent: 100. $$. Hookups: electric (50 amp), water, sewer.

Ironwood

Curry Park, Cloverland Dr., 49938. T: (906) 932-5050. RV/tent: 56. $$. Hookups: electric (30 amp), water, sewer.

Jackson

Greenwood Acres, 2401 Hilton Rd., 49201. T: (517) 522-8600. RV/tent: 1160. $$. Hookups: electric (50 amp), water, sewer.

Pleasant Lake County Park & Campground, 1000 Styles Rd., Pleasant Lake, 49201. T: (517) 769-6401. RV/tent: 69. $$. Hookups: electric (30 amp), water.

Jones

Camelot Campground LLC, 14630 M-60, 49061. T: (269) 476-2473. RV/tent: 76. $$. Hookups: electric (30, 50 amp), water, sewer, cable.

Kinross

Kinross RV Park East, Riley Rd., 49783. T: (906) 495-3023. RV/tent: 64. $. Hookups: electric (30 amp), water, sewer.

Laingsburg

Sleepy Hollow State Park, 7835 East Price Rd., 48848. T: (517) 651-6217. RV/tent: 181. $$. Hookups: electric (30 amp).

Lake City

Maple Grove Campground, East Union St., 49651. T: (231) 839-4429. www.lakecitymich.com/ parks.shtml. RV/tent: 23. $. Hookups: electric (30 amp), water.

Lansing

Lansing Cottonwood Campground, 5339 South Aurelius Rd., 48911. T: (517) 393-3200. RV/tent: 110. $$. Hookups: electric (20, 30, 50 amp), water, sewer.

Lapeer

Hilltop Campground, 1260 Piper Dr., 48446. T: (810) 664-2782. RV/tent: 60. $$. Hookups: electric (30 amp), water.

Leonard

Addison Days, 1480 West Romeo Rd., 48367. T: (248) 693-2432. RV/tent: 133. $$$. Hookups: electric (30, 50 amp), water.

Family Park Campground, 120 Yule Rd., 48367. T: (248) 628-4204. RV/tent: 30. $$. Hookups: electric (20 amp), water.

Lewiston

Lewiston Shady Acres Campground & Cottages, CR 489 South, 49756. T: (800) 357-2494 or (989) 786-3000. www.lewistonshadyacres.com. RV/tent: 40. $$. Hookups: electric (30, 50 amp), water, sewer, cable.

Lexington

Lexington RV Resort, 7181 Lexington Blvd., 48450. T: (810) 359-2054. www.greatlakes.net/~rv resort. RV/tent: 210. $$$. Hookups: electric (30, 50 amp), water, sewer, cable.

Linwood

Hoyle's Marina & Campground, 135 South Linwood Beach Rd., 48634. T: (989) 697-4415. www.hoylesmarina.com. RV/tent: 80. $$. Hookups: electric (50 amp), water, sewer.

Ludington

Kibby Creek Travel Park, 4900 Deren Rd., 49431. T: (231) 843-3995 or (800) 574-3995. www.michcampground.com/kibbycreek. RV/tent: 113. $$. Hookups: electric (30 amp), water, sewer.

Lakeview Campsite, 6181 Peterson Rd., 49431. T: (231) 843-3702. www.hamilinlake.com/lake view. RV/tent: 88. $$. Hookups: electric (30 amp), water.

Ludington State Park, SR 116, 49431. T: (231) 843-8671 or (800) 44-PARKS. RV/tent: 341. $$. Hookups: electric (30 amp).

Mason County Campground, 5906 West Chauvez Rd., 49431. T: (231) 845-7609. RV/tent: 50. $$. Hookups: electric (30 amp).

Tamarac Village Mobile Homes & RV Park, 2875 North Lakeshore Dr., 49431. T: (231) 843-4990. RV/tent: 20. $$. Hookups: electric (30 amp), water, sewer.

Mackinaw City

Mackinaw City KOA, 566 Trailsend Rd., 49701. T: (231) 436-5643 or (800) 562-1738. RV/tent: 110. $$. Hookups: electric (50 amp), water, sewer.

Mancelona

Rapid River Campground/Cabins, 7182 US 131, 49659. T: (231) 258-2042. www.michcamp grounds.com/rapidriver. RV/tent: 63. $$. Hookups: electric (30 amp), water.

Manistee

Orchard Beach State Park, 2064 Lakeshore Dr., 49660. T: (231) 723-7422 or (800) 447-2757. www.michigan.gov/dnr. RV/tent: 168. $$. Hookups: electric (30 amp).

Manistique

Kewadin Inn Campground, Lakeshore Dr., US-2, 49854. T: (906) 341-6911 or (800) 770-9736. RV/tent: 40. $$. Hookups: electric (30 amp), water, sewer.

Matson's Big Manistee River Campground, 2680 Bialik Rd., 49660. T: (888) 556-2424 or (231) 723-5705. RV/tent: 65. $$. Hookups: electric (50 amp), water, sewer.

Woodstar Beach Campground, Little Harbor Rd., 49854. T: (906) 341-6514. www.manistique.com/ camp/woodstar/home.htm. RV/tent: 44. $$. Hookups: electric (20, 30 amp), water.

Marenisco

Lake Gogebic State Park, HC 1 Box 139, 49947. T: (906) 842-3341 or (800) 447-2757. www.michigan.gov/dnr. RV/tent: 127. $$. Hookups: electric (30 amp).

Marquette

Gitche Gumee RV Park & Campground, 2048 SR 28E, 49855. T: (906) 249-9102. www.gitche gumeervpark.com. RV/tent: 102. $$$. Hookups: electric (30, 50 amp), water, sewer, cable.

Marquette Tourist Park & Campground, CR 550, 49855. T: (906) 228-0465. RV/tent: 110. $. Hookups: electric (30 amp), water, sewer.

Martin

Schnable Lake Family Campground, 1476 115th Ave., 49070. T: (269) 672-7367. RV/tent: 62. $$. Hookups: electric (50 amp), water, sewer.

Mears

Hide-A-Way Campground/Waterslide, 9671 West Silver Lake Rd., 49436. T: (231) 873-4428. www.hideawaycampground.com. RV/tent: 220. $$. Hookups: electric (30 amp), water.

Silver City II Campground, 1786 North 34th Ave., 49436. T: (800) 359-1909 or (231) 873-7199. RV/tent: 270. $$. Hookups: electric (30 amp), water.

Silver Hills Camp/Resort, 7594 West Hazel Rd., 49436. T: (800) 637-3976 or (231) 873-3976. www.silverhillscampresort.com. RV/tent: 105. $$$. Hookups: electric (50 amp), water.

Silver Lake State Park, 9679 West State Park Rd., 49436. T: (231) 873-3083 or (800) 447-2757. www.michigan.gov/dnr. RV/tent: 196. $$. Hookups: electric (30 amp).

MICHIGAN (continued)

Mecosta

Blue Gill Lake Campground, 15854 Pretty Lake Dr., 49332. T: (231) 972-7410. RV/tent: 60. $$. Hookups: electric (20, 30, 50 amp), water.

School Section Lake Park, 9003 90th Ave., 49332. T: (231) 972-7450. www.mecostacountyparks .com/school-section.htm. RV/tent: 166. $$. Hookups: electric (30 amp), water.

Mesick

Northern Exposure Campground, 285 Manistee River Dr., 49668. T: (231) 885-1199. www. northernexposureinc.com. RV/tent: 260. $. Hookups: electric (30, 50 amp), water.

Metamora

Metamora-Hadley Recreation Area, 3871 Herd Rd., 48455. T: (810) 797-4439 or (800) 447-2757. www.michigan.gov/dnr. RV/tent: 214. $$. Hookups: electric (30 amp).

Middleville

Gun Lake Parkside Park, 2430 Briggs Rd., 49333. T: (269) 795-3140. RV/tent: 80. $$. Hookups: electric (30 amp), water, sewer.

Yankee Springs State Recreational Area, 2104 South Briggs Rd., 49333. T: (616) 795-9081 or (800) 447-2757. www.michigan.gov/dnr. RV/tent: 345. $$. Hookups: electric (30 amp).

Mio

Mio Pines Acres, 1215 West 8th St., 48647. T: (800) 289-2845 or (989) 826-5590. www.michcamp grounds.com/miopines. RV/tent: 90. $$. Hookups: electric (30 amp), water.

Monroe

Sterling State Park, 2800 State Park Rd., 48162. T: (734) 289-2715. www.michigan.gov/dnr. RV/tent: 256. $$. Hookups: electric (50 amp), water, sewer.

Montague

White River Campground, 735 Fruiale Rd., 49437. T: (231) 894-4708. www.whiterivercamp ground.com. RV/tent: 182. $$. Hookups: electric (30 amp), sewer, water.

Morley

Mecosta Pines RV Park, 550 South Talcott, 49336. T: (231) 856-4556. RV/tent: 30. $$. Hookups: electric (30, 50 amp), water.

Mount Pleasant

Coldwater Lake Family Park, 1703 North Little-field, 48893. T: (989) 772-0911. RV/tent: 95. $$. Hookups: electric (20, 30 amp), water.

Munising

Buckhorn/Otter Lake Campground, HC 50, 49862. T: (906) 387-3559. RV/tent: 72. $$. Hookups: electric (30 amp).

Munith

The Oaks Resort, 7800 Cutler Rd., 49259. T: (517) 596-2747. RV/tent: 75. $$. Hookups: electric (30 amp), water.

Muskegon

Hoffmaster State Park, 6585 Lake Harbor Rd., 49441. T: (231) 798-3711. RV/tent: 293. $$. Hookups: electric (30 amp).

Muskegon KOA, 3500 North Strand, 49445. T: (231) 766-3900. RV/tent: 82. $$. Hookups: electric (30 amp), water, sewer.

Nashville

Camp Thornapple Inc., 5625 Thornapple Lake Rd., 49073. T: (517) 852-9645. RV/tent: 143. $$. Hookups: electric (50 amp), water, sewer.

New Era

Stony Haven Campground, 8079 West Stony Lake Rd., 49446. T: (800) 962-1117. RV/tent: 45. $$. Hookups: electric (30 amp), water.

New Hudson

Green Valley Park, P.O. Box 298, 48165. T: (248) 437-4136. RV/tent: 112. $$. Hookups: electric (30 amp), water, sewer.

Haas Lake Park, 25800 Haas Rd., 48165. T: (248) 437-0900. RV/tent: 110. $$. Hookups: electric (50 amp), water, sewer.

Newaygo

Ed H. Henning Park, 500 East Croton Rd., 49337. T: (231) 689-7383. RV/tent: 60. $$. Hookups: electric (30 amp).

Little Switzerland Resort and Campground, 254 Pickeral Lake Dr., 49337. T: (231) 652-7939. RV/tent: 80. $$. Hookups: electric (30 amp), water.

Newaygo

Muskallonge Lake State Park, P.O. Box 245, 49868. T: (906) 658-3338. RV/tent: 175. $$. Hookups: electric (30 amp).

Mystery Creek Campground, 9419 Wisner, 49337. T: (231) 652-6915. RV/tent: 65. $$. Hookups: electric (30 amp), water.

Northcountry Campground & Cabins, RR 1 Box 94, 49868. T: (906) 293-8562. RV/tent: 50. $$. Hookups: electric (30 amp), water, sewer.

Newberry

Newberry KOA, Box 783 M-28, 49868. T: (800) 562-5853. RV/tent: 130. $$$. Hookups: electric (50 amp), water.

North Branch

Sutter's Recreation Area, 1601 Tozer Rd., 48461. T: (810) 688-3761. RV/tent: 40. $$. Hookups: electric (30 amp), water, sewer.

North Muskegon

Muskegon State Park, 3560 Memorial Dr., 49445. T: (231) 744-3483. RV/tent: 284. $$. Hookups: electric (30 amp).

Omer

Big Bend Campground, 513 Conrad Rd., 48658. T: (989) 653-2267. www.bigbendcamp.com. RV/tent: 100. $$. Hookups: electric (20 amp), water.

Riverbend Campground & Canoe Rental, P.O. Box 6, 48749. T: (989) 653-2576. RV/tent: 80. $$. Hookups: electric (30 amp), water, sewer.

Russell's Canoe & Campground, 146 Carrington, 48749. T: (517) 653-2644. RV/tent: 30. $$. Hookups: electric (30 amp).

Onaway

Onaway State Park, Rte. 1 Box 112, 49765. T: (989) 733-8279. RV/tent: 98. $. Hookups: electric (30 amp).

Onsted

Lake Hudson Recreation Area, 1220 Wampler, 49265. T: (517) 445-2265. RV/tent: 50. $. Hookups: electric (30 amp).

Ossineke

Paul Bunyan Campgrounds, 6969 North Huron, 48762. T: (989) 471-2921. RV/tent: 80. $$. Hookups: electric (30 amp), water, sewer.

Otter Lake

Genesee Otterlake Campground, 12260 Farrand Rd., 48464. T: (810) 793-2725. RV/tent: 129. $$. Hookups: electric (30 amp), water.

Paradise

Tahquamenon Falls State Park, Lower Falls, 49768. T: (906) 492-3415. RV/tent: 171. $. Hookups: electric (30 amp).

Tahquamenon Falls State Park, River Mouth Unit, 49768. T: (906) 492-3415. RV/tent: 130. $. Hookups: electric (30 amp).

Paris

Paris Park Campground, US 131, 49512. T: (231) 796-3420. RV/tent: 68. $$. Hookups: electric (30 amp), water, sewer.

Pentwater

Hill & Hollow Campground, 8915 North Business 31, 49449. T: (231) 869-5811. RV/tent: 150. $$$. Hookups: electric (30 amp), water, sewer.

Mears State Park, P.O. Box 370, 49449. T: (231) 869-2051. RV/tent: 179. $$. Hookups: electric (30 amp).

Perry

Hickory Lake Camping, 11433 South Beardslee Rd., 48872. T: (517) 625-3113. RV/tent: 62. $$. Hookups: electric (30 amp), water, sewer.

Petoskey

Petoskey State Park, Rte. 4 Box 121 A, 49770. T: (231) 347-2311. RV/tent: 170. $$. Hookups: electric (30 amp).

Pinckney

Pinckney Recreation Area, 8555 Silver Hill, 48169. T: (734) 426-4913. RV/tent: 225. $$. Hookups: electric (30 amp).

Port Austin

Port Crescent State Park, 1775 Port Austin Rd., 48467. T: (989) 738-8663. RV/tent: 135. $$. Hookups: electric (30 amp).

Port Huron

Lakeport State Park, 7605 Lakeshore Rd., 48060. T: (810) 327-6224. RV/tent: 284. $$. Hookups: electric (30 amp).

MICHIGAN (continued)

Rapid River

Camper's Paradise Resort, 8733 EE 25 Rd., 49878. T: (906) 474-6106. RV/tent: 19. $$. Hookups: electric (30 amp), water.

Vagabond Resort & Campground, 8935 CR 513T, 49878. T: (906) 474-6122. RV/tent: 50. $$. Hookups: electric (50 amp), water, sewer.

Whispering Valley Campground & RV Park, 8410 US 2, 49878. T: (906) 474-7044. RV/tent: 26. $$. Hookups: electric (50 amp), water, sewer.

Riverdale

Half Moon Lake Campground & RV Park, 11394 Lumberjack Rd., 48877. T: (989) 833-7852. RV/tent: 42. $$. Hookups: electric (30 amp), water.

Riverside

Benton Harbor KOA, 3527 Coloma Rd., 49084. T: (269) 849-3333. RV/tent: 113. $$$. Hookups: electric (30 amp), water, sewer.

Rogers City

Hoeft State Park, US 23 North, 49779. T: (989) 734-2543. RV/tent: 144. $$. Hookups: electric (30 amp).

Roscommon

Great Circle Campground, 5370 Marl Lake Rd., 48653. T: (989) 821-9486. RV/tent: 45. $$. Hookups: electric (30 amp), water.

Higgins Lake Family Campground & Mobile Resort, 2380 West Burdell Rd., 48653. T: (989) 821-6891. RV/tent: 35. $$. Hookups: electric (20 amp), water.

North Higgins Lake State Park, RR 1 Box 436, 48653. T: (989) 821-6125. RV/tent: 195. $$. Hookups: electric (30 amp).

Paddle Brave Campground & Canoe Livery, 10610 Steckert Bridge Rd., 48653. T: (989) 275-5273. RV/tent: 45. $$. Hookups: electric (30 amp).

South Higgins Lake State Park, RR 2 Box 360, 48653. T: (517) 821-6374. RV/tent: 395. $$. Hookups: electric (30 amp).

Rose City

Rifle River State Recreation Area, P.O. Box 98, 48635. T: (517) 473-2258. RV/tent: 181. $. Hookups: electric (30 amp).

Saugatuck

Saugatuck RV Resort, P.O. Box 683, 49453. T: (269) 857-3315. RV/tent: 195. $$$. Hookups: electric (50 amp), water, sewer.

Sault Ste. Marie

Chippewa Campground, P.O. Box 786, 49783. T: (906) 632-8581. RV/tent: 100. $$. Hookups: electric (50 amp), water, sewer.

Sawyer

New Life Campground, 12033 Red Arrow Hwy., 49125. T: (269) 426-4971. RV/tent: 110. $$. Hookups: electric (30 amp), water, sewer.

Warren Dunes State Park, 12032 Red Arrow Hwy.,
49125. T: (269) 426-4013. RV/tent: 280. $$. Hookups: electric (30 amp).

Scotille

Crystal Lake Campground, 1884 West Hansen Rd., 49454. T: (231) 757-4510. RV/tent: 130. $$$. Hookups: electric (30 amp), water, sewer.

Scotille Riverside Park, 105 North Main St., 49454. T: (231) 757-4729. RV/tent: 52. $$. Hookups: electric (30 amp), water.

Sears

Merrill Lake Park, SR 66, 49679. T: (517) 382-7158. RV/tent: 74. $$. Hookups: electric (30 amp), water.

Shepherd

Salt River Acres Inc., 926 Greendale Rd., 48883. T: (989) 631-7659. RV/tent: 88. $$. Hookups: electric (30 amp), water.

Silver City

Porcupine Mountains Wilderness State Park, 412 South Boundry Rd., 49953. T: (906) 885-5275. RV/tent: 188. $$. Hookups: electric (30 amp).

South Boardman

Ranch Rudolf Campground, 6841 Brownbridge Rd., 49686. T: (231) 947-9529. RV/tent: 25. $$. Hookups: electric (30 amp), water.

South Haven

Van Buren State Park, 23960 Ruggles Rd., 49090. T: (269) 637-2788 or (800) 447-2757. www.michigandnr.com/parksandtrail./parklist.asp. RV/tent: 220. $$. Hookups: electric (30 amp).

St. Ignace

Lakeshore Park, 416 Pte LaBarbe Rd., 49781. T: (800) 643-9522. RV/tent: 100. $$. Hookups: electric (50 amp), water, sewer.

Straits State Park, 720 Church St., 49781. T: (906) 643-8620. RV/tent: 275. $$. Hookups: electric (30 amp).

Tiki Travel Park, 200 South Airport Rd., 49781. T: (906) 643-7808. RV/tent: 100. $$. Hookups: electric (30 amp), water, sewer.

Stanwood

Brower County Park, 8 Mile and Old State Rd., 49346. T: (231) 823-2561. RV/tent: 230. $$. Hookups: electric (50 amp), water.

Sterling

Rifle River AAA Canoe Rental, 2148 South School Rd., 48659. T: (989) 654-2333. RV/tent: 65. $$. Hookups: electric (30 amp), water.

River View Campground and Canoe Livery, 5755 Townline Rd., 48659. T: (989) 654-2447. www.riverviewcampground.com. RV/tent: 250. $$. Hookups: electric (30 amp), water, sewer.

Sturgis

Green Valley Campgrounds, 25499 West Fawn River Rd., 49091. T: (616) 651-8760. RV/tent: 220. $$. Hookups: electric (20 amp), water.

Tawas City

Brown's Landing RV Park, 1129 Dyer Rd., 48763. T: (989) 362-3737. RV/tent: 74. $$. Hookups: electric (50 amp), water, sewer.

Tawas RV Park, 1453 Townline Rd., 48673. T: (989) 362-0005. RV/tent: 39. $$. Hookups: electric (30 amp), water, sewer.

Tecumseh

Indian Creek Camp & Conference Center, 9415 Tangent Hwy., 49286. T: (517) 423-5659. RV/tent: 47. $$. Hookups: electric (30 amp), water, sewer.

Thompson

Indian Lake State Park, South Campground, Rte. 2 Box 2500, 49854. T: (906) 341-2355. RV/tent: 302. $$. Hookups: electric (30 amp).

Traverse City

Traverse City State Park, 1132 US 31 North, 49686. T: (231) 922-5270. RV/tent: 342. $$. Hookups: electric (30 amp).

Tustin

Cadillac KOA, 13163 M-115, 49688. T: (231) 825-2012. RV/tent: 35. $$. Hookups: electric (30 amp), water.

Union

Hollywood Shores Resort, 70901 Wayne St., 49130. T: (269) 641-7307. RV/tent: 28. $$. Hookups: electric (20 amp), water.

Union City

Rustic Potawatomie Recreation Area, 1126 Bell Rd., 49094. T: (517) 278-4289. RV/tent: 70. $$. Hookups: electric (50 amp), water, sewer.

Vassar

Ber-Wa-Ga-Na Campground, 3526 Sanilac Rd., 48768. T: (517) 673-7125. RV/tent: 74. $$. Hookups: electric (30 amp), water, sewer.

Walkerville

Pine Haven Campground, 7792 North 186th Ave., 49459. T: (231) 898-2722. RV/tent: 25. $$. Hookups: electric (30 amp), water, sewer.

Waterford

Pontiac Lake State Recreation Area, 7800 Gale Rd., 48054. T: (248) 666-1020. RV/tent: 176. $. Hookups: electric (30 amp).

Wellston

Sportsman's Port Canoes & Campground, 10487 West M-55 Hwy, 49689. T: (888) 226-6301. RV/tent: 51. $. Hookups: electric (30 amp).

Twin Oaks Campground, 233 Moss Rd., 49689. T: (877) 442-3102. www.twinoakscamping.com. RV/tent: 60. $$. Hookups: electric (30 amp).

MINNESOTA

Annandale
Schroeder County Park, 9201 Ireland Ave. NW, 55302. T: (320) 274-8870. RV/tent: 50. $$. Hookups: electric (30 amp).

Apple Valley
Lebanon Hills Regional Park, 12100 Johnny Cake Ridge Rd., 55124. T: (952) 454-9211 or (651) 488-4737. www.co.dakota.mn.us/parks/hills camp.htm. RV/tent: 93. $$. Hookups: electric (30, 50 amp), water, sewer.

Argyle
Old Mill State Park, Rte. 1 Box 43, 56713. T: (218) 437-8174. www.dnr.state.mn.us/state_parks/old_mill/index.html. RV/tent: 26. $. Hookups: electric (30 amp), water.

Ashby
Sundown RV Park & Campground, 29188 Hwy. 78, 56309. T: (218) 747-2931. RV/tent: 30. $$. Hookups: electric (30 amp), water, sewer.

Backus
Eagle Wing Campground, 1588 36th Ave. Sw, 56435. T: (218) 587-2090. RV/tent: 45. $$. Hookups: electric (30 amp), water.

Lindsey Lake Campground, 3781 State 87 NW, 56435. T: (218) 947-4728. www.lindseylake.com. RV/tent: 40. $$. Hookups: electric (30 amp), water.

Barnum
Bent Trout Lake Campground, 2928 Bent Trout Lake Rd., 55707. T: (218) 389-6322. RV/tent: 100. $$. Hookups: electric (30 amp), water.

Barrett
Barrett Lake Resort & Campground, 427 CR 2, 56311. T: (320) 528-2598. RV/tent: 34. $$. Hookups: electric (50 amp), water, sewer.

Battle Lake
Battle Lake Sunset Beach Resort & Campground, 42502 240th St., 56515. T: (888) 583-2750. RV/tent: 49. $$. Hookups: electric (30 amp), water, sewer.

Bemidji
Hamilton's Fox Lake Campground, 2555 Island View Dr. NE, 56601. T: (218) 586-2231 or (800) 752-3309. www.hamfoxlakecampgrd.com. RV/tent: 70. $$. Hookups: electric (20, 30, 50 amp), water, sewer, cable.

Lake Bemidji State Park, 3401 State Park Rd. NE, 56601. T: (218) 755-3843. www.dnr.state.mn.us/state_parks/lake_bemidji/index.html. RV/tent: 98. $$. Hookups: electric (30 amp), water.

Bena
New Leech Lake Campground, 12962 Sunset Beach Rd., 56626. T: (800) 272-3785. RV/tent: 73. $$. Hookups: electric (30 amp), water.

Bigfork
Scenic State Park, 56956 Scenic Hwy. 7, HCR 2 Box 17, 56628. T: (218) 743-3362. RV/tent: 117. $$. Hookups: electric (30 amp).

Blackduck
Lost Acres Resort & Campground, 26772 Birchmont Beach Rd. NE, 56630. T: (800) 835-6414. www.lostacresresort.com. RV/tent: 8. $$. Hookups: electric (30 amp), water, sewer.

Blooming Prairie
Brookside Campground, 52482 320th St., 55917. T: (507) 583-2979. RV/tent: 60. $$. Hookups: electric (30 amp), water.

Brainerd
Crow Wing State Park, 7100 State Park Rd. Sw, 56401. T: (218) 829-8022. RV/tent: 61. $$. Hookups: electric (30 amp).

Hidden Paradise Resort & Campground, 20621 Hidden Paradise Rd., 56401. T: (218) 963-3180 or (888) 963-3180. www.brainerd.com/hidden. RV/tent: 10. $$$. Hookups: electric (50 amp), water, sewer.

Lum Park Campground, 1619 NE Washington St., 56401. T: (218) 828-2320. www.brainerdparks.com/parks/lumpark.htm. RV/tent: 18. $$. Hookups: electric (30 amp), water, cable.

Breezy Point
Highview Campground & RV Park, 11090 Old CR 39, 56472. T: (877) 543-4526. RV/tent: 132. $$. Hookups: electric (30 amp), water, sewer.

Burtrum
Big Swan Lake Resort, RR 1 Box 256, 56318. T: (320) 732-6065. RV/tent: 21. $$. Hookups: electric (30 amp), water, sewer.

Caledonia
Beaver Creek Valley State Park, 159 CR 1, 55921. T: (507) 724-2107. RV/tent: 48. $. Hookups: electric (30 amp).

Dunromin' Park, 12757 Dunromin' Drive, 55921. T: (507) 724-2514. www.dunrominpark.com. RV/tent: 92. $$. Hookups: electric (30 amp), water.

Canby
Stonehill Regional Park, P.O. Box 2, 56220. T: (507) 223-7586. RV/tent: 40. $$. Hookups: electric (30 amp), water.

Cannon Falls
Cannon Falls Campground, 30365 Oak Ln., 55009. T: (507) 263-3145. RV/tent: 100. $$. Hookups: electric (50 amp), water.

Lake Byllesby Regional Park Campground, 7650 Echo Point Rd., 55009. T: (507) 263-4447. www.co.dakota.mn.us/parks/activities/camping.htm. RV/tent: 58. $. Hookups: electric (30 amp), water.

Carlos
Lake Carlos State Park, 2601 CO 38 NE, 56319. T: (320) 852-7200. RV/tent: 126. $$. Hookups: electric (30 amp).

Cass Lake
Cass Lake Lodge, Resort, & RV Park, 16293 60th Ave. NW, 56633. T: (218) 335-6658. www.casslakelodge.com. RV/tent: 50. $$. Hookups: electric (30 amp), water, sewer.

Marclay Point
Marclay Point Campground, Rte. 2 Box 80, 56633. T: (218) 335-6589. www.marclaypoint.com. RV/tent: 94. $$. Hookups: electric (30 amp), water, sewer.

Center City
Wild River State Park, 39755 Park Trace, 55012. T: (651) 583-2125. www.dnr.state.mn.us/state_parks/wild_river/camping.html. RV/tent: 96. $$. Hookups: electric (30 amp).

Clearwater
KOA St. Cloud-Clearwater, 2454 CR 143, 55320. T: (320) 558-2876 or (800) 562-5025. www.koa.com/where/23131.htm. RV/tent: 93. $$. Hookups: electric (50 amp), water, sewer.

Cokato
Collinwood Regional Park, 17251 70th St. SW, 55321. T: (320) 286-2801. RV/tent: 49. $$. Hookups: electric (30 amp).

Coon Rapids
Bunker Hills Campground, 550 Bunker Lake Blvd., Hwy. 242 & Foley Blvd., 55304. T: (763) 757-3920. www.anokacountyparks.com/qlink/parks/bunkerhills/bunker.htm. RV/tent: 50. $$. Hookups: electric (30 amp), water.

Crane Lake
Beddow's Campground, 7516 Bayside Dr., 55725. T: (218) 993-2389. www.visitcranelake.com/resorts/crnlkb02.html. RV/tent: 22. $$. Hookups: electric (30 amp), water, sewer.

Cromwell
Island Lake Campground, 1391 Middle Rd., 55726. T: (218) 644-3543. RV/tent: 15. $$. Hookups: electric (50 amp), water.

Currie
Lake Shetek State Park, 163 State Park Rd., 56123. T: (507) 763-3256. www.dnr.state.mn.us/state_parks/lake_shetek/index.html. RV/tent: 108. $. Hookups: electric (30 amp).

Schreier's on Shetek, 35 Resort Rd., 56123. T: (507) 763-3817. RV/tent: 110. $$. Hookups: electric (50 amp), water, sewer.

Cushing
Fish Trap Lake Campground, 30894 Fish Trap Lake Dr., 56443. T: (218) 575-2603. RV/tent: 47. $$. Hookups: electric (30 amp), water, sewer.

Fish Trap Resort, 30894 Fish Trap Lake Drive, 56443. T: (218) 575-2603. www.scenic lodging.com/fish_trap/fish_trap.htm. RV/tent: 130. $$$. Hookups: electric (50 amp), water, sewer.

Dassel
Lake Dale Campground, 650 Parker Ave. West, 55325. T: (320) 275-3387. RV/tent: 45. $$. Hookups: electric (30 amp).

Deer River
Jessie View Resort & Campground, 45756 CO 35, 56636. T: (218) 832-3678 or (877) 537-7438. RV/tent: 37. $$. Hookups: electric (30, 50 amp), water, sewer.

MINNESOTA (continued)

Deer River (continued)

Lake Winnibigoshish Recreation Area, 34385 US 2, 56636. T: (218) 326-6128. RV/tent: 44. $$. Hookups: electric (30 amp).

Deerwood

Camp Holiday Resort & Campground, 17467 Round Lake Rd., 56444. T: (218) 678-2495 or (800) 450-2495. www.campholiday.com. RV/tent: 40. $$. Hookups: electric (30 amp), water, sewer.

Sisselbagamah RV Resort on Bay Lake, 685 Katrine Dr. NE, 56444. T: (218) 678-3393. RV/tent: 35. $$. Hookups: electric (30 amp), water, sewer.

Detroit Lakes

American Legion Campground, 810 West Lake Dr., 56501. T: (218) 847-3759. www.angelfire.com/mn/legioncampground. RV/tent: 97. $$. Hookups: electric (30 amp), water, sewer, cable.

Duluth

Duluth Tent & Trailer Camp, 7408 Grand Ave., 55804. T: (218) 525-1350. RV/tent: 54. $$. Hookups: electric (30 amp), water.

Indian Point Campground, 902 South 69th Ave., 55807. T: (218) 624-5637 or (800) 982-2453. www.indianpointcampground.com. RV/tent: 70. $$. Hookups: electric (30 amp), water, sewer.

Elbow Lake

Tipsinah Mounds Campground & Park, 26527 Tipsinah Mounds Rd., 56531. T: (218) 685-5114. www.tipsinahmoundscampground.com. RV/tent: 79. $$. Hookups: electric (30 amp), water, sewer.

Elk River

Wapiti Park Campground, 18746 Troy St., 55330. T: (763) 441-1396. RV/tent: 142. $$. Hookups: electric (30 amp), water, sewer.

Ely

Canoe Country Campground & Cabins, 629 East Sheridan St., 55731. T: (218) 365-4046. www.canoecountryoutfitters.com/cabins&campground.html. RV/tent: 15. $$. Hookups: electric (30 amp), water, sewer.

Timber Wolf Lodge, 9130 Escape Rd., 55731. T: (218) 827-3512. www.timberwolflodge.com. RV/tent: 23. $$. Hookups: electric (30 amp), water.

Erskine

Lake Cameron RV Park & Campground, RR 3 Box 24, 56535. T: (218) 687-4678. RV/tent: 15. $$. Hookups: electric (50 amp), water, sewer, cable.

Fairmont

Dawson's Lakeside Campground, 248 Cottonwood Rd., 56031. T: (507) 235-5753. RV/tent: 140. $$. Hookups: electric (50 amp), water, sewer.

Flying Goose Campground, 2521 115th St., 56031. T: (507) 235-3458. www.flyinggoosecampground.com. RV/tent: 115. $$. Hookups: electric (50 amp), water, sewer.

Faribault

Camp Maiden Rock, 9870 Morristown Blvd., 55052. T: (507) 685-2240. www.campmaidenrock.com. RV/tent: 100. $$. Hookups: electric (30 amp), water.

Roberds Lake Resort & Campground, 18192 Roberds Lake Blvd., 55021. T: (800) 879-5091. RV/tent: 40. $$. Hookups: electric (50 amp), water, sewer.

Fergus Falls

Elks Point, Rte. 1, 56537. T: (218) 736-4292. RV/tent: 40. $$. Hookups: electric (30 amp), water.

Fifty Lakes

Fifty Lakes Campground, P.O. Box 158, 56448. T: (218) 763-2616. RV/tent: 82. $$. Hookups: electric (50 amp), water, sewer.

Forest Lake

Timm's Marina & Campground, 9080 North Jewel Ln., 55025. T: (612) 464-9965. RV/tent: 30. $$. Hookups: electric (30 amp), water, sewer.

Frazee

Birchmere Family Resort & Campground, 18346 Birchmere Rd., 56544. T: (800) 642-9554. RV/tent: 30. $$. Hookups: electric (30 amp), water, sewer.

Garden City

Shady Oaks Campground, P.O. Box 284, 56034. T: (507) 546-3986. RV/tent: 55. $. Hookups: electric (30 amp), water.

Garfield

Oak Park Campground, 9561 CO 8 NW, 56332. T: (320) 834-2345. RV/tent: 55. $$. Hookups: electric (30 amp), water, sewer.

Garrison

Wilderness of Minnesota, Box 387, 56450. T: (320) 692-4347. RV/tent: 132. $$. Hookups: electric (50 amp), water, sewer.

Glenwood

Chalet Campground, Hwy. 104, 56334. T: (651) 634-5433. RV/tent: 36. $$. Hookups: electric (30 amp), water, sewer.

Grand Marais

Grand Marais RV Park & Campground, P.O. Box 820, 55604. T: (218) 387-1712. RV/tent: 200. $$. Hookups: electric (50 amp), water, sewer.

Gunflint Pines Resort & Campground, 217 South Gunflint Lake Rd., 55604. T: (218) 388-4454. RV/tent: 20. $$. Hookups: electric (20, 30, 50 amp), water.

Grand Rapids

Birch Cove Resort & Campground, 32382 Southwood Rd., 55744. T: (218) 326-8754. RV/tent: 14. $$. Hookups: electric (20 amp), water, sewer.

Pokegama Recreation Area, 34385 US 2, 55744. T: (218) 326-6128. RV/tent: 40. $$. Hookups: electric (30 amp).

Sal's Campground, P.O. Box 363, 55744. T: (218) 492-4297. RV/tent: 44. $$. Hookups: electric (30 amp), water, sewer.

Hackensack

Quietwoods Campground, 4755 Alder Ln. NW, 56452. T: (218) 675-6240. RV/tent: 20. $$. Hookups: electric (20 amp), water.

Ham Lake

Ham Lake Campground, 2400 Constance Blvd., 55304. T: (763) 434-5337. RV/tent: 130. $$. Hookups: electric (50 amp), water.

Hastings

St. Croix Bluffs Regional Park Campground, 10191 St. Croix Trail, 55033. T: (651) 430-8240. RV/tent: 73. $$. Hookups: electric (50 amp), water.

Hawick

Old Wagon Campground, 21611 132nd St. NE, 56246. T: (320) 354-2165. RV/tent: 25. $$. Hookups: electric (30 amp), water.

International Falls

Arnold's Campground & RV Park, Hwy. 53 and 21st St., 56649. T: (218) 285-9100. RV/tent: 24. $. Hookups: electric (30 amp), water, sewer.

Isanti

Country Camping RV Tent & RV Park on the Rum River, 750 273rd Ave., 55040. T: (763) 444-9626. www.country-camping.com. RV/tent: 58. $$. Hookups: electric (30 amp), water.

Isle

Father Hennepin State Park, P.O. Box 397, 56342. T: (320) 676-8763. RV/tent: 103. $$. Hookups: electric (30 amp).

Jackson

Jackson KOA Campground, 2035 Hwy. 71, 56143. T: (507) 847-3825. RV/tent: 60. $$. Hookups: electric (30 amp), water, sewer.

Loon Lake Campground, 405 4th St., 56143. T: (507) 847-2240. RV/tent: 80. $. Hookups: electric (30 amp), water.

Jasper

Split Rock Creek State Park, 336 50th Ave., 56144. T: (507) 348-7908. RV/tent: 28. $$. Hookups: electric (30 amp), water.

Jordan

Minneapolis SW KOA, 3315 West 166th St., 55352. T: (952) 492-6440. RV/tent: 111. $$. Hookups: electric (50 amp), water.

Kabetogama Lake

Cedar Cove Campsites & Resort, 9940 Gappa Rd., 56669. T: (218) 875-3851. RV/tent: 30. $$. Hookups: electric (30 amp), water, sewer.

Kandiyohi

Kandiyohi County Park No. 3, 6920 CO 4, 56251. T: (612) 974-8520. RV/tent: 65. $$. Hookups: electric (30 amp).

Kelliher

Rogers' On Red Lake Campground & RV Park, HC 78 Box 20, 56650. T: (218) 647-8262. RV/tent: 51. $$. Hookups: electric (30 amp), water, sewer.

Kerrick

Hoffman's Oak Lake Campground, HC1 Box 80, 55756. T: (218) 496-5678. RV/tent: 14. $$$. Hookups: electric (30 amp), water, sewer.

MINNESOTA (continued)

Knife River

Depot Campground, P.O. Box 115, 56149. T: (218) 834-5044. RV/tent: 32. $$. Hookups: electric (30 amp), water.

Lake Benton

Hole-in-the-Mountain County Park, Hwy. 14 West, 56149. T: (507) 368-9350. RV/tent: 70. $. Hookups: electric (30 amp), water.

Lake Bronson

Lake Bronson State Park, Box 9, 56734. T: (218) 754-2200. RV/tent: 194. $$. Hookups: electric (30 amp).

Lakefield

Kilen Woods State Park, Rte. 1 Box 122, 56150. T: (507) 662-6258. RV/tent: 33. $$. Hookups: electric (30 amp).

Lanesboro

Sylvan Park, P.O. Box 333, 55949. T: (507) 467-3722. RV/tent: 42. $. Hookups: electric (30 amp).

Le Roy

Lake Louise State Park, 12385 766th Ave., 55951. T: (507) 324-5249. RV/tent: 22. $$. Hookups: electric (30 amp).

Le Sueur

Peaceful Valley Campsite, 213 Peaceful Valley Rd., 56058. T: (507) 665-2297. RV/tent: 38. $$. Hookups: electric (50 amp), water, sewer.

Lindstrom

Hillscrest RV Park, 32741 North Lakes Trail, 55045. T: (651) 257-5352. RV/tent: 70. $$. Hookups: electric (30 amp), water, sewer.

Lino Lakes

Rice Creek Campground, 7401 Main St., 55038. T: (612) 757-3928. RV/tent: 78. $$. Hookups: electric (30 amp), water.

Mahnomen

Shooting Star Casino, Hotel, & RV Park, 777 Casino Dr., 56557. T: (800) 453-STAR. RV/tent: 47. $$. Hookups: electric (30 amp), water, sewer.

Mankato

Minneopa State Park, RR 9 Box 143, 56001. T: (507) 389-5464. RV/tent: 62. $$. Hookups: electric (30 amp).

Maple Grove

Minneapolis Northwest/Maple Grove KOA, 10410 Brockton Ln., 55311. T: (763) 420-2255 or (888) KOA-0261. RV/tent: 160. $$$. Hookups: electric (50 amp), water, sewer, phone.

Maple Plain

Baker Park Reserve, 2931 CO 19, 55359. T: (612) 479-2258. RV/tent: 213. $$. Hookups: electric (30 amp).

Marine on St. Croix

William O'Brien State Park, 16821 O'Brien Trail North, 55047. T: (651) 433-0500. RV/tent: 125. $. Hookups: electric (30 amp).

Mazeppa

Ponderosa Campground, RR 1 Box 209, 55956. T: (800) 895-0328. RV/tent: 80. $$. Hookups: electric (50 amp), water.

McGregor

Sandy Lake Recreation Area, HCR 4 Box 362, 55760. T: (218) 426-3482. RV/tent: 110. $$. Hookups: electric (30 amp).

Savanna Portage State Park, HCR 3 Box 591, 55760. T: (218) 426-3271. RV/tent: 72. $$. Hookups: electric (30 amp).

Merrifield

Shing Wako Resort & Campground, HC 87 Box 9580, 51465. T: (218) 765-3226. RV/tent: 33. $$. Hookups: electric (30 amp), water, sewer.

Sunset Bay Resort & Campground, HC 86 Box 1000, 56465. T: (800) 715-2267. RV/tent: 75. $$. Hookups: electric (30 amp), water, sewer.

Montevideo

Lac Qui Parle State Park, Rte. 5 Box 74A, 56265. T: (612) 752-4736. RV/tent: 66. $$. Hookups: electric (30 amp).

Moorhead

Buffalo River State Park, P.O. Box 352, 56547. T: (218) 498-2124. RV/tent: 44. $$. Hookups: electric (30 amp).

Fargo-Moorhead KOA, 4396 28th Ave. S, 56560. T: (218) 233-0671 or (800) 562-0271. RV/tent: 95. $$. Hookups: electric (50 amp), water, sewer, cable.

Mora

Camperville, 2351 310th Ave., 55051. T: (320) 679-2326. RV/tent: 49. $$. Hookups: electric (50 amp), water.

Captain Dan's Crow's Nest Resort, 2743 Hwy. 65, 55051. T: (320) 679-1977. RV/tent: 51. $$. Hookups: electric (30 amp), water, sewer.

Morton

Jackpot Junction Casino Hotel Campground, 39375 CO 24, 56270. T: (507) 644-3000 or (800) 946-0077. www.jackpotjunction.com/lodging/campground.htm. RV/tent: 42. $$. Hookups: electric (30 amp), water, sewer.

Nerstrand

Nerstrand Big Woods State Park, 9700 170th St. East, 55053. T: (507) 333-4840. www.dnr.state.mn.us. RV/tent: 68. $$. Hookups: electric (30 amp), water.

Nevis

Whispering Pines Resort & Campgrounds, 25401 CR 86, 56467. T: (218) 652-4362. www.whispering-pines-resort.com. RV/tent: 10. $$. Hookups: electric (20, 30 amp), water, sewer.

New London

Hide-Away Campground, 199th Ave. NE, 56273. T: (320) 354-2148. RV/tent: 11. $$. Hookups: electric (30 amp), water.

Sibley State Park, 800 Sibley Park Rd., 56273. T: (320) 354-2055. www.dnr.state.mn.us. RV/tent: 138. $$. Hookups: electric (30 amp).

New Ulm

Flandrau State Park, 1300 Summit Ave., 56073. T: (507) 233-9800. www.dnr.state.mn.us/parks. RV/tent: 90. $$. Hookups: electric (30 amp).

Ogema

Woodland Trails Resort & Campground, 33616 Loon Dr., 56569. T: (218) 983-3230 or (800) 879-7829. www.woodlandtrailsresort.com. RV/tent: 35. $$. Hookups: electric (30 amp), water, sewer.

Orr

Cabin O'Pines Resort & Campground, 4378 Pelican Rd., 55771. T: (218) 757-3122 or (800) 757-3122. www.cabinopines.com. RV/tent: 30. $$. Hookups: electric (30 amp), water.

Pine Acres Resort & Campground, 4498 Pine Acres Rd., 55771. T: (218) 757-3144 or (800) 777-7231. www.pineacres.com. RV/tent: 80. $$. Hookups: electric (30 amp), water, sewer.

Ortonville

Big Stone Lake State Park, RR 1 Box 153, 56278. T: (320) 839-3663. www.dnr.state.mn.us. RV/tent: 40. $$. Hookups: electric (30 amp).

Osage

R&D Resort & Campground, 54097 Grant St., 56570. T: (218) 573-3182 or (800) 895-5050. www.randdresort.com. RV/tent: 26. $$. Hookups: electric (30 amp), water.

Osakis

Black's Cresent Beach, P.O. Box 416, 56360. T: (320) 859-2127. RV/tent: 10. $$. Hookups: electric (30 amp), water, sewer.

Midway Beach Resort & Campground, 1821 Lake St. East, 56360. T: (320) 859-4410 or (800) 367-2547. www.midwaybeach.com. RV/tent: 9. $$$. Hookups: electric (30 amp), water, sewer.

Owatonna

Riverview Campground, 2554 SW 28th St., 55060. T: (507) 451-8050. RV/tent: 142. $$. Hookups: electric (50 amp), water, sewer.

Park Rapids

Breeze Camping & RV Resort on Eagle Lake, 25824 CR 89, HCO 5 Box 321, 56470. T: (218) 732-5888. www.sceniclodging.com/information/information.htm. RV/tent: 69. $$. Hookups: electric (20, 30 amp), water, sewer.

Pelican Rapids

Pelican Hills Park, 20098 South Pelican Drive, RR 4 Box 218B, 56572. T: (800) 430-2267. www.pelicanhillspark.com. RV/tent: 83. $$. Hookups: electric (30 amp), water, sewer.

Pengilly

Swan Lake Campground & Resort, 29995 East Shore Dr., 55775. T: (218) 885-3385. RV/tent: 24. $$. Hookups: electric (30 amp), water.

Perham

Golden Eagle Vacationland, Golden Eagle Rd., 56573. T: (218) 346-4386. RV/tent: 131. $$. Hookups: electric (30 amp), water, sewer.

MINNESOTA (continued)

Preston

Foresille Mystery Cave State Park, Rte. 2 Box 128, 55965. T: (507) 352-5111. www.dnr.state.mn.us. RV/tent: 73. $$. Hookups: electric (30 amp).

Prior Lake

Dakotah Meadows Campground, 2341 Park Place, 55372. T: (800) 653-CAMP. www.ccsmdc.org/dak mead. RV/tent: 122. $$. Hookups: electric (50 amp), water, sewer.

Red Wing

Haycreek Valley Campground, 31673 Hwy. 58 Blvd., 55066. T: (651) 388-3998 or (888) 388-3998. RV/tent: 122. $$. Hookups: electric (30, 50 amp), water.

Richmond

Cozy Corners, 19897 Hwy. 22, 56368. T: (320) 597-3587. RV/tent: 17. $$. Hookups: electric (30 amp), water.

Your Haven Campground, 18337 SR 22, 56368. T: (320) 597-2450. RV/tent: 18. $$. Hookups: electric (30 amp), water, sewer.

Rochester

Brookside RV Park, 516 17th Ave., 55901. T: (507) 288-1413. RV/tent: 25. $$. Hookups: electric (50 amp), water, sewer, cable, telephone.

Roseau

Roseau City Park, 900 11th St. SE, 56751. T: (218) 463-1791 or (218) 463-1542. city.roseau.mn.us/tourism/citypark.htm. RV/tent: 20. $$. Hookups: electric (30 amp), water.

Sandstone

Banning State Park, P.O. Box 643, 55072. T: (320) 245-2668. www.dnr.state.mn.us. RV/tent: 39. $$. Hookups: electric (30 amp).

Savage

Town and Country Campground, 12630 Boone Ave., 55378. T: (952) 445-1756. www.townand countrycampground.com. RV/tent: 46. $$$. Hookups: electric (30 amp), water, sewer.

Sebeka

Sebeka Municipal Park, P.O. Box 305, 56477. T: (218) 837-5773. RV/tent: 10. $. Hookups: electric (30 amp).

Silver Bay

Northern Exposure Campground, 5346 Hwy. 61, 55614. T: (218) 226-3324. RV/tent: 55. $$. Hookups: electric (30 amp), water, sewer.

South Haven

Timberwoods Resort & Campground, 10255 Nevens Ave. NW, 55382. T: (320) 274-5140. www.timberwoodsresort.com. RV/tent: 65. $$. Hookups: electric (30 amp), water, sewer.

South Isle

South Isle Family Campground, 39002 SR 47, 56342. T: (320) 676-8538. RV/tent: 47. $$. Hookups: electric (30 amp), water.

Starbuck

Glacial Lakes State Park, 25022 CO 41, 56381. T: (320) 239-2860 or (866) 857-2757. www.stayatmnparks.com. RV/tent: 46. $$. Hookups: electric (30 amp).

Tenstrike

Gull Lake Campground, Rte. 1 Box 28, 56683. T: (218) 586-2842. RV/tent: 92. $$. Hookups: electric (30 amp), water, sewer.

Moen's Birch Haven Campground & Resort, Rte. 1 Box 138, 56683. T: (218) 586-2863. RV/tent: 42. $$. Hookups: electric (30 amp), water.

Thief River Falls

Thief River Falls Tourist Park, Oakland Park Rd., 56701. T: (218) 681-2519. RV/tent: 64. $. Hookups: electric (30 amp), water, sewer.

Thomson

Knife Island Campgrounds, 234 Hwy. 61 Box 361, 55720. T: (218) 879-6063. RV/tent: 20. $$. Hookups: electric (30 amp), water.

Two Harbors

Burlington Bay Campsite, 522 1st Ave., 55616. T: (218) 834-2021. RV/tent: 111. $$. Hookups: electric (30 amp), water, sewer.

Penmarallter Campsite, 725 Scenic Dr., 55616. T: (218) 834-4603. RV/tent: 19. $$. Hookups: electric (30 amp), water.

Walker

Waters Edge RV Park, 10634 SR 371 NW, 56484. T: (218) 547-3552. RV/tent: 26. $$. Hookups: electric (30 amp), water, sewer.

Warroad

Warroad Campground, P.O. Box 50, 56763. T: (218) 386-1004. RV/tent: 180. $$. Hookups: electric (30 amp), water, sewer, cable.

Waterville

Sakatah Lake State Park, RR 2 Box 19, 56096. T: (507) 362-4438 or (866) 857-2757. RV/tent: 68. $. Hookups: electric (30 amp).

Waubun

Elk Horn Resort & Campground, Rte. 2 Box 323, 56589. T: (218) 935-5437. RV/tent: 24. $$. Hookups: electric (30 amp), water, sewer.

Williams

Zippel Bay Resort, 6080 39th St. NW, 56686. T: (800) 222-2537. www.zippelbay.com. RV/tent: 57. $$. Hookups: electric (30 amp), water.

Woodbury

KOA St. Paul East, 568 Cottage Grove Dr., 55129. T: (651) 436-6436. RV/tent: 76. $$$. Hookups: electric (50 amp), water, sewer, telephone.

Zimmerman

Camp in the Woods, 14791 289th Ave., 55398. T: (763) 427-5050. RV/tent: 78. $$. Hookups: electric (30 amp), water, sewer.

Zumbrota

Shades of Sherwood Camping Park, 14334 Sherwood Trail, 55992. T: (507) 732-5100. RV/tent: 140. $$. Hookups: electric (30 amp), water.

MISSISSIPPI

Ackerman

Tombigbee National Forest Choctaw Lake Rec. Area, Hwy. 15 South, 39735. T: (662) 285-3264 or (800) 280-2267. www.reserveusa.com. RV/tent: 21. $$. Hookups: electric (30, 50 amp), water.

Bay St. Louis

Bay Marina, RV Park, & Lodging, 100 Bay Marina Dr., 39520. T: (228) 466-4970. www.baymarina.com. RV/tent: 33. $$. Hookups: electric (20, 30, 50 amp).

KOA Bay St. Louis/Gulfport, 814 Hwy. 90, 39520. T: (800) 562-2790 or (228) 467-2080. www.koa.com. RV/tent: 78. $$. Hookups: electric (20, 30, 50 amp).

Belden

Trace State Park, 2139 Faulkner Rd., Rte. 1 Box 254, 38826. T: (662) 489-2958. www.mdwfp.com. RV/tent: 62. $. Hookups: electric (20, 30 amp), water.

Biloxi

Biloxi Southern Comfort Camping Resort, 1766 Beach Blvd., 39531. T: (877) 302-1700. RV/tent: 123. $$. Hookups: electric (20, 30, 50 amp), water, sewer, cable.

Cajun RV Park, 1860 Beach Blvd., 39531. T: (228) 388-5590. RV/tent: 126. $$. Hookups: electric (20, 30, 50 amp), water, sewer, cable.

Fox's RV Park & Complex, 190 Beauvoir Rd., 39531. T: (800) 736-7275. RV/tent: 144. $$. Hookups: electric (30, 50 amp).

Brandon

Goshen Springs Campground (Pearl River Valley Water Supply District), 1684 Hwy. 43 North, 39042. T: (601) 829-2751 or (877) 388-2267. RV/tent: 68. $. Hookups: electric (30 amp), water, sewer.

Clinton

Springridge RV Park, 499 Springridge Rd., 39056. T: (601) 924-0947. RV/tent: 42. $$. Hookups: electric (20, 30, 50 amp).

MISSISSIPPI (continued)

Coldwater

Dub Patton Campground, 3905 Arkabutla Dam Rd., 38618. T: (662) 562-6261. www.reserve america.com. RV/tent: 66. $. Hookups: electric, water.

Hernando Point, 3905 Arkabutla Dam Rd., 38618. T: (662) 562-6261. RV/tent: 83. $. Hookups: electric, water.

Memphis South Campground & RV Park, 256 Campground Dr., 38618. T: (662) 622-0056. RV/tent: 82. $$. Hookups: electric (20, 30, 50 amp), water, sewer.

Columbia

Whispering Pines RV Park, 7836 Hwy. 49 South, 39402-9169. T: (601) 943-6290. RV/tent: 10. $$. Hookups: electric (20, 50 amp), water.

Columbus

Brown's RV Trailer Park, 2002 Bluecutt Rd., 39705. T: (662) 328-1976. RV/tent: 24. $$. Hookups: electric (20, 30 amp).

Decatur

Turkey Creek Water Park, 142 Parkway Dr., 39327. T: (601) 635-3314. www.phwd.net. RV/tent: 22. $$. Hookups: electric (20 amp).

Durant

Holmes County State Park, 5369 State Park Rd., 39063. T: (662) 653-3351. RV/tent: 28. $. Hookups: electric, water (50 amp).

Edwards

Askew's Landing Campground, 3412 Askew Ferry Rd., 39066. T: (601) 852-2331 or (877) 601-2331. www.askewslanding.com. RV/tent: 89. $$. Hookups: electric (20, 30, 50 amp) water, sewer.

Enid

Persimmon Hill–South Abutment, 931 CR 36, 38927. T: (662) 563-4571. www.reserveamerica. com. RV/tent: 72. $. Hookups: electric (30 amp), water.

Water Valley Landing Campground, 931 CR 36, 38927. T: (662) 563-4571. www.reserveamerica. com. RV/tent: 29. $. Hookups: electric (30 amp), water.

Enterprise

Dunn's Falls Water Park (Pat Harrison Waterway District), 6890 Dunn's Falls Rd., 39330. T: (601) 655-8550. RV/tent: 15. $. Hookups: none.

Escatawpa

Riverbend RV Resort, 10707 Hwy. 613, 39552. T: (228) 475-2429. www.riverbendinc.com. RV/tent: 77. $$. Hookups: electric (20, 30, 50 amp).

Flora

Mississippi Petrified Forest Campground, 124 Forest Park Rd., 39071. T: (601) 879-8189. www.mspetrifiedforest.com. RV/tent: 37. $$. Hookups: electric (20, 30 amp), water.

Forest

Bienville National Forest, 3437 Hwy. 35 South, 39074. T: (601) 469-3811. RV/tent: 32. $. Hookups: electric (20, 30 amp), water.

Greenville

Delta Village Park, 3836 Hwy. 82 East, 38701. T: (662) 378-3655. RV/tent: 16. $. Hookups: electric (20, 30, 50 amp).

Grenada

Frog Hollow Campground & RV, 601 Hwy. 7 North, 38901-8656. T: (662) 226-9042. www.frog-hollow.com. RV/tent: 49. $$. Hookups: electric (20, 30, 50 amp), water, sewer.

Hugh White State Park, 3170 Hugh White State Park Rd., 38901. T: (662) 226-4934. RV/tent: 185. $$. Hookups: electric (30 amp), water.

Gulfport

Campground of the South, 10406 Three Rivers Rd., 39503. T: (228) 539-2922. www.campgrounds ofthesouth.com. RV/tent: 90. $$. Hookups: electric (20, 30, 50 amp), water, sewer.

Hattiesburg

Quilla's RV Park, 558 South Gate Rd., 39401-9410. T: (601) 544-6837. RV/tent: 28. $$. Hookups: electric (20, 30, 50 amp), water.

Shady Cove RV Park, 7836 Hwy. 49 North, 39402. T: (877) 251-8169. www.shadycovervpark.com. RV/tent: 53. $$. Hookups: electric (20, 30, 50 amp), water.

Hollandale

Leroy Percy State Park, Hwy. 12 West, 38748. T: (662) 827-5436. RV/tent: 16. $. Hookups: electric (30, 50 amp), water.

Holly Springs

Wall Doxey State Park, 3946 Hwy. 7 South, 38635. T: (662) 252-4231. RV/tent: 64. $. Hookups: electric (20, 30 amp), water.

Iuka

J. P. Coleman State Park, 613 CR 321, 38852. T: (662) 423-6515. www.jpcolemanstatepark .com. RV/tent: 87. $. Hookups: electric, water, sewer, cable.

Jackson

Swinging Bridge RV Park, 5750 I-55 South Frontage Rd., 39272. T: (601) 502-1101 or (800) 297-9127. www.rvresort.net. RV/tent: 95. $$$. Hookups: electric (20, 30, 50 amp), water, sewer.

Laurel

KOA Laurel, 2920 Hwy. 11 North, 39443. T: (601) 426-6444 or (800) 562-0378. RV/tent: 88. $$. Hookups: electric (50 amp), water, sewer, cable, phone.

Long Beach

Plantation Pines Campground and RV Park, 19391 28 St., 39560. T: (228) 863-6550. RV/tent: 70. $$. Hookups: full.

Louisville

Legion State Park, 635 Legion St. Park Rd., 39339. T: (662) 773-8323. www.mdwfp.com. RV/tent: 15. $. Hookups: electric, water, sewer.

Ludlow

Coal Bluff Park (Pearl River Valley Water Supply District), 1319 Coal Bluff Rd., 39200. T: (601) 654-7726 or (877) 388-CAMP. RV/tent: 68. $. Hookups: electric (20, 30 amp), water, sewer.

Lumberton

Little Black Creek Water Park (Pat Harrison Waterway District), 2159 Little Black Creek Rd., 39455. T: (601) 794-2957. www.phwd.net. RV/tent: 106. $$. Hookups: electric (30, 50 amp), water, sewer, cable.

Mendenhall

D'Lo Water Park, P.O. Box 278, 39114. T: (601) 847-4310. RV/tent: 12. $. Hookups: electric, water.

Meridian

Campground RV and Trailer Park, Hwy. 45 North, 39301. T: (601) 485-4549. RV/tent: 58. $$. Hookups: full.

Mount Olive

Dry Creek Water Park (Pat Harrison Waterway District), Hwy. 35, 39119. T: (601) 797-4619. www.phwd.net. RV/tent: 28. $. Hookups: electric (20 amp), water.

Natchez

Natchez State Park, 40 Wickcliff Rd., 39120. T: (601) 442-2658. www.mdwfp.com. RV/tent: 58. $. Hookups: electric (20, 30 amp), water, sewer.

Traceway Campground, 1113 Hwy. 61 North, 39120. T: (601) 445-8278. RV/tent: 40. $$. Hookups: electric (15, 20, 30, 50 amp), water, sewer.

Ocean Springs

RV-Tel, 2302 Beinville Blvd., 39564. T: (228) 826-3958. RV/tent: 20. $$. Hookups: electric (20, 30, 50 amp).

Philadelphia

Frog Level RV Park, 1532 Hwy. 16 West, 39350. T: (601) 650-0044. RV/tent: 52. $$. Hookups: electric, water, sewer, cable.

Port Gibson

Grand Gulf Military Park Campground (State), 12006 Grand Gulf Rd., 39150. T: (601) 437-5911. www.grandgulfpark.state.ms.us. RV/tent: 42. $. Hookups: electric (20, 30, 50 amp), water, sewer.

Quitman

Clarkco State Park, 386 Clarkco Rd., 39355. T: (601) 776-6651. www.mdwfp.com. RV/tent: 58. $$. Hookups: electric (20, 30 amp), water, sewer.

Rosedale

Great River Road State Park, Hwy. 1 South, 38769. T: (662) 759-6762. www.mdwfp.com. RV/tent: 61. $. Hookups: electric (30 amp), water.

MISSISSIPPI (continued)

Russell

Nanabe Creek Campground, 1933 Russell–Mt. Gilead Rd., 39301. T: (601) 485-4711. RV/tent: 95. $$. Hookups: electric (20, 30, 50 amp), water.

Saucier

Country Side RV Park & Tradin' Post, 20278 Hwy. 49, 39574. T: (228) 539-0807. www.country sidervpark.com. RV/tent: 32. $$. Hookups: electric (20, 30, 50 amp), water, sewer, cable, phone.

Shannon

Natchez Trace RV Park, 189 Co. Rd. 506, 38868. T: (662) 767-8609. RV/tent: 72. $$. Hookups: electric (20, 30, 50 amp), water.

Tishomingo

Tishomingo State Park, 105 CR 90, 38873. T: (662) 438-6914. www.mdwfp.com. RV/tent: 62. $. Hookups: electric (20, 30, 50 amp), water.

Tunica

Hollywood Casino RV Resort, 1150 Casino Strip Resort, 38676. T: (662) 357-7700 or (800) 871-0711. RV/tent: 123. $. Hookups: electric, water, sewer, cable, phone.

Sam's Town RV Park, 1477 Casino Strip Resorts Blvd., 38664. T: (800) 456-0711. RV/tent: 100. $$. Hookups: electric, water, sewer, cable, phone.

Tupelo

RV Campground at Barnes Crossing, 125 Rd. 1698, 38801. T: (662) 844-6063 or (662) 767-8609. RV/tent: 40. $$. Hookups: electric, water, sewer, cable.

Vaiden

Vaiden Campground, Hwy. I-55, 39176. T: (662) 464-9336. RV/tent: 90. $$. Hookups: electric (20, 30, 50 amp), water, sewer.

Vicksburg

Vicksburg Battlefield Campground, 4407 I-20 Frontage Rd., 39183. T: (601) 636-2025. RV/tent: 81. $$. Hookups: electric (20, 30 amp), water, sewer, cable.

Wesson

Lake Lincoln State Park, 2573 Sunset Rd. NE, 39191. T: (601) 643-9044 or (601) 735-4365. www.mdwfp.com. RV/tent: 75. $. Hookups: electric (30 amp), water, sewer.

Wiggins

Flint Creek Water Park (Pat Harrison Waterway District), 1216 Parkway Dr., 39577. T: (601) 928-3051. www.waterparkin.com. RV/tent: 174. $$. Hookups: electric (30, 50 amp), water, sewer, cable.

MISSOURI

Anderson

Indian Creek RV Park & Campground, Hwy. 71, 64831. T: (417) 845-6400. RV/tent: 120. $. Hookups: electric (20, 30, 50 amp), water, sewer.

Arrow Rock

Arrow Rock State Historic Site State Park, P.O. Box 1, 65320. T: (660) 837-3330 or (800) 334-6946. www.mostateparks.com. RV/tent: 45. $. Hookups: electric (20, 30 amp), water.

Bigelow

Big Lake State Park, 204 Lake Shore Dr., 64437. T: (660) 442-3770. www.mostateparks.com. RV/tent: 76. $. Hookups: electric (20, 30 amp).

Blue Eye

Old Hwy. 86, 1791 MO UU, 65615. T: (417) 779-5376. www.reserveusa.com. RV/tent: 71. $. Hookups: electric (20, 30 amp).

Bonne Terre

St. Francois State Park, 8920 US 67 North, 63628. T: (573) 358-2173 or (800) 334-6946. www.mostateparks.com. RV/tent: 110. $. Hookups: electric (20, 30 amp), water.

Branson

Acorn Acres, 159 Acorn Acres Ln., 65737. T: (417) 338-2500 or (800) 338-2504. www.bestbranson rvpark.com. RV/tent: 75. $$. Hookups: electric (30, 50 amp), water, sewer.

America's Best Campground, 499 Buena Vista Rd., 65616. T: (417) 336-4399 or (800) 671-4399. www.abc-branson.com. RV/tent: 138. $$. Hookups: electric (30, 50 amp), water, sewer.

Andrew's Landing Resort & RV Park, 5329 Hwy. 165, 65616. T: (800) 678-9780 or (417) 334-5071. www.andrewslanding.com. RV/tent: 25. $. Hookups: electric (20, 30, 50 amp), water, sewer.

Bar M Resort & Campground, 207 Bar M Ln., 65737. T: (417) 338-2593.

www.Barmresort.com. RV/tent: 12. $$. Hookups: electric (30 amp), water, sewer.

Branson City Campground, 300 Boxcar Willie Dr., 65616. T: (417) 334-2915. www.cityofbranson .org. RV/tent: 350. $$. Hookups: electric (30, 50 amp), water, sewer.

Branson KOA, 1025 Headwaters Rd., 65616. T: (800) 562-4177 or (417) 334-7450. www.koa.com. RV/tent: 180. $$. Hookups: electric (30, 50 amp), water, sewer.

Branson Shenanigans RV Park, 3675 Keeter St., 65616. T: (800) 338-7275 or (417) 334-1920. www.bransonrvparks.com. RV/tent: 40. $$. Hookups: electric (30, 50 amp), water, sewer, cable.

Branson Stagecoach RV Park, 5751 Hwy. 165, 65616. T: (800) 446-7110 or (417) 335-8185. www.gocampingamerica.com. RV/tent: 51. $$. Hookups: electric (20, 30, 50 amp), water, sewer.

Branson View Campground, 2362 Hwy. 265, 65616. T: (800) 992-9055 or (417) 338-8716. www.rvnetlinx.com. RV/tent: 38. $$. Hookups: electric (20, 30, 50 amp), water, sewer, cable.

Branson's Ozark Country Campground, 679 Quebec Dr., 65616. T: (800) 968-1300 or (417) 334-4681. www.bransoncampground.com. RV/tent: 67. $$. Hookups: electric (20, 30, 50 amp), water, sewer.

Compton Ridge Campground, 5040 Hwy. 265, 65616. T: (800) 233-8648 or (417) 338-2911. www.comptonridge.com. RV/tent: 180. $$. Hookups: electric (20, 30, 50 amp), water, sewer, cable.

Cooper Creek Resort & Campground, 471 Cooper Creek Rd., 65616. T: (800) 261-8398 or (417) 334 5250. www.coopercreekcampground. com. RV/tent: 85. $$. Hookups: electric (20, 30, 50 amp), water, sewer, cable.

Gerth Camper Park, 139 Irish Ln., 65616. T: (417) 334-5849. www.gerthcamperpark.com. RV/tent: 200. $$. Hookups: electric (30, 50 amp), water, sewer.

Indian Point, 3125 Indian Point Rd., 65616. T: (417) 338-2121. www.reserveusa.com. RV/tent: 76. $$. Hookups: electric (20, 30 amp).

Lakeview Campground, 2820 Indian Point Rd., 65616. T: (800) 396-2232 or (417) 338-5211. www.lakeviewcampground.com. RV/tent: 45. $$. Hookups: electric (30, 50 amp), water, sewer.

Musicland Kampground, 116 North Gretna Rd., 65616. T: (417) 334-0848 or (888) 248-9080. www.musiclandkampground.com. RV/tent: 112. $$$. Hookups: electric (30, 50 amp), water, sewer.

Stormy Point Camp & Resort, 1318 Stormy Point Rd., 65616. T: (417) 338-2255 or (800) 933-5175. www.stormypoint.us. RV/tent: 55. $$. Hookups: electric (20, 30, 50 amp), water, sewer.

Table Rock State Park, 5272 Hwy. 165, 65616. T: (417) 334-4704 or (877) 422-6766. www.mostateparks.com/tablerock.htm. RV/tent: 152. $. Hookups: electric (20, 30, 50 amp), water, sewer.

Tall Pines Campground, 5558 Hwy. 265, 65616. T: (417) 338-2445 or (800) 425-2300. www.tallpinescampground.com. RV/tent: 83. $$. Hookups: electric (30, 50 amp), water, sewer.

Camdenton

Bull Run Bluff RV Park & Campground, 54–82 Lake Rd., H.CR 80 Box 775, 65020. T: (573) 346-7815. www.funlake.com/accommodations/bullrunbluff. RV/tent: 72. $$. Hookups: electric (30, 50 amp), water, sewer.

Cameron

Wallace State Park, 10621 NE Hwy. 121, 64429. T: (816) 632-3745. www.mostateparks.com. RV/tent: 87. $. Hookups: electric (20, 30 amp), water.

Cape Fair

Cape Fair, 1092 Shadrack Rd., 65624. T: (417) 538-9999. www.reserveusa.com. RV/tent: 82. $. Hookups: electric (20, 30 amp), water.

MISSOURI (continued)

Carthage
Big Red Barn RV Park, 5089 CL 138, 64836. T: (888) 244-2276 or (417) 358-2432. www.bigredbarnrvpark.com. RV/tent: 65. $$. Hookups: electric (30, 50 amp), water, sewer, cable, phone.

Cassville
Big M, HCR 81 Box 9251, 65625. T: (417) 271-3190. www.reserveusa.com. RV/tent: 92. $. Hookups: electric (20, 30 amp), water, sewer.

Roaring River State Park, Rte. 4 Box 4100, 65625. T: (417) 847-2539. www.mostateparks.com. RV/tent: 185. $. Hookups: electric (20, 30 amp), water.

Columbia
Finger Lakes State Park, 1505 East Peabody Rd., 65202. T: (573) 443-5315. www.mostateparks. com. RV/tent: 35. $. Hookups: electric (20, 30 amp), water.

Cuba
Blue Moon RV & Horse Park, 355 Hwy. F, 65453. T: (877) 440-CAMP or (573) 885-3662. www.fidnet.com/~blmoonrv. RV/tent: 55. $$. Hookups: electric (30, 50 amp), water, sewer.

Dadeville
Stockton State Park, Rte. 1 Box 1715, 65635. T: (417) 276-4259. www.mostateparks.com. RV/tent: 75. $. Hookups: electric (20, 30 amp), water.

DeSoto
Washington State Park, Rte. 2 Box 450, 63020. T: (636) 586-2995. www.mostateparks.com. RV/tent: 51. $. Hookups: electric (20, 30 amp), water.

Eagle Rock
Eagle Rock, HC 1 Box 1037, 65641. T: (417) 271-3215. www.reserveusa.com. RV/tent: 63. $. Hookups: electric (20, 30 amp), water, sewer.

Paradise Cove Camping Resort, HCR 1 Box 1067, 65641. T: (417) 271-4888. RV/tent: 21. $. Hookups: electric (20, 30 amp), water, sewer.

Forsyth
Forsyth KOA, 11020 MO 76, 65653. T: (800) 562-7560 or (417) 546-5364. www.koa.com. RV/tent: 67. $$. Hookups: electric (20, 30, 50 amp), water, sewer.

Genevieve
Hawn State Park, 12096 Park Dr., 63670. T: (573) 883-3603. www.mostateparks.com. RV/tent: 50. $. Hookups: electric (20, 30 amp), water.

Golden
Viney Creek, Rte. 1 Box 1023, 65658. T: (417) 271-3860. www.reserveusa.com. RV/tent: 46. $. Hookups: electric (20, 30 amp), water.

Hermitage
Lightfoot Landing, Rte. 2 Box 2160, 65668. T: (417) 282-6890. www.reserveusa.com. RV/tent: 40. $. Hookups: electric (20, 30, 50 amp), water.

Nemo Landing, Rte. 2 Box 2160, 65668. T: (417) 993-5529. www.reserveusa.com. RV/tent: 128. $. Hookups: electric (20, 30, 50 amp), water, sewer.

Outlet Park, Rte. 2 Box 2160, 65668. T: (417) 745-2290. www.reserveusa.com. RV/tent: 28. $. Hookups: electric (20, 30 amp).

Jamesport
Countryside RV Park, 106 East 2nd, 64648. T: (660) 684-6392. RV/tent: 16. $$. Hookups: electric (20, 30 amp), water, sewer.

Jonesburg
Jonesburg/Warrenton KOA, P.O. Box H, 63351. T: (800) 562-5634 or (636) 488-5630. www.koa.com. RV/tent: 52. $$. Hookups: electric (20, 30, 50 amp), water, sewer.

Joplin
Joplin KOA, 4359 Hwy. 43, 64804. T: (800) 562-5675 or (417) 623-2246. www.koa.com. RV/tent: 74. $$. Hookups: electric (20, 30, 50 amp), water, sewer.

Kimberling City
Kimberling City KOA, HCR 5 Box 465, 65686. T: (800) 562-5685 or (417) 739-4627. www.koa.com/where/MO/25107. RV/tent: 94. $$. Hookups: electric (30, 50 amp), water, sewer, cable.

Knob Noster
Knob Noster State Park, 801 SE Hwy. 10, 65336. T: (660) 563-2463. www.mostateparks.com. RV/tent: 72. $. Hookups: electric (20, 30 amp), water.

Laclede
Pershing State Park, 29277 Hwy. 130, 64651. T: (660) 963-2299. www.mostateparks.com. RV/tent: 39. $. Hookups: electric (20, 30 amp), water.

LaGrange
Wakonda State Park, Rte. 1 Box 242, 63448. T: (573) 655-2280. www.mostateparks.com. RV/tent: 79. $. Hookups: electric (20, 30 amp), water.

Lake Ozark
Cross Creek RV Park, P.O. Box 936, 65049. T: (888) 250-3885. RV/tent: 76. $. Hookups: electric (30, 50 amp), water, sewer.

Lake of the Ozarks State Park, 403 Hwy. 134, 65049. T: (573) 348-2694. www.mostateparks .com. RV/tent: 182. $. Hookups: electric (20, 30 amp), water.

Majestic Oaks Park, P.O. Box 525, 65049. T: (573) 365-1890. www.majesticoakspark.com. RV/tent: 85. $$. Hookups: electric (30, 50 amp), water, sewer, cable.

Lampe
Baxter Campground, 4631 MO H, 65681. T: (417) 779-5370. www.reserveusa.com. RV/tent: 54. $. Hookups: electric (20, 30 amp).

Mill Creek, 1236 Long Creek Rd, 65681. T: (417) 779-5378. www.reserveusa.com. RV/tent: 68. $. Hookups: electric (20, 30 amp), water.

Lawson
Watkins Woolen Mill State Park, 26600 Park Rd. North, 64602. T: (816) 296-3357. www.mostateparks.com. RV/tent: 98. $. Hookups: electric (20, 30 amp), water.

Leasburg
Onondaga Cave State Park, 7556 Hwy. H, 65535. T: (573) 245-6576. www.mostateparks.com. RV/tent: 71. $. Hookups: electric (20, 30 amp), water.

Ozark Outdoors, 205 Ozark Outdoor Ln., 65535. T: (800) 888-0023 or (573) 245-6839. www.ozarkoutdoors.net. RV/tent: 260. $. Hookups: electric (20, 30, 50 amp), water, sewer.

Lebanon
Bennett Spring State Park, 26250 Hwy. 64A, 65536. T: (417) 532-4338. www.mostateparks.com. RV/tent: 140. $. Hookups: electric (20, 30 amp), water, sewer.

Mansfield
Mansfield House B&B/RV Park, 2991 Hwy. A, 65704. T: (417) 924-2222. www.themansfield house.com. RV/tent: 52. $. Hookups: electric (20, 30, 50 amp), water, sewer.

Miami
Van Meter State Park, Rte. 1, 65344. T: (660) 886-7537. www.mostateparks.com/vanmeter.htm. RV/tent: 21. $. Hookups: electric (20, 30 amp), water.

Monroe City
Frank Russell, 20642 Hwy. J, 63456. T: (573) 735-4097. www.reserveusa.com. RV/tent: 65. $$. Hookups: electric (20, 30 amp).

Indian Creek, 20642 Hwy. J, 63456. T: (573) 735-4097. www.reserveusa.com. RV/tent: 190. $. Hookups: electric (20, 30 amp), sewer, water.

Ray Behrens, 20642 Hwy. J, 63456. T: (573) 735-4097. www.reserveusa.com/nrrs/mo/rabe. RV/tent: 168. $$. Hookups: electric (20, 30 amp), water, sewer.

Montgomery City
Graham Cave State Park, 217 Hwy. TT, 63361. T: (573) 564-3476. www.mostateparks.com. RV/tent: 52. $. Hookups: electric (20, 30 amp), water.

Mountain Home
Beaver Creek Resort, P.O. Box 2070, 72654. T: (870) 546-3708. www.reserveusa.com/nrrs/ mo/bec3. RV/tent: 37. $$. Hookups: electric (20, 30 amp).

Mountain Springs RV Park, 5400 CR 3200 No. J 9, 65548. T: (417) 469-3351. RV/tent: 25. $$. Hookups: electric (20, 30, 50 amp), water, sewer. Pontiac Park, P.O. Box 2070, 72654. T: (870) 425-2700. www.reserveusa.com/nrrs/mo/pont. RV/tent: 38. $$. Hookups: electric (20, 30 amp).

River Run, P.O. Box 2070, 72654. T: (870) 546-3646. www.reserveusa.com/nrrs/mo/rivn. RV/tent: 32. $$. Hookups: electric (20, 30 amp).

MISSOURI (continued)

Newburg

Arlington RV Campground, 13003 Arlington Outer Rd., 65550. T: (573) 762-2714. www.arlingtonrv campground.com. RV/tent: 60. $$. Hookups: electric (30, 50 amp), water, sewer.

Park Hills

St. Joe State Park, 2800 Pimville Rd., 63601. T: (573) 431-1069 or (877) 422-6766. RV/tent: 80. $. Hookups: electric (20, 30 amp).

Patterson

Sam A. Baker State Park, Hwy. 143, RFD 1 Box 114, 63956. T: (573) 856-4411. www.mostateparks .com/baker. RV/tent: 192. $. Hookups: electric (20, 30 amp).

Piedmont

Bluff View (Clearwater Lake), Rte. 3 Box 3559-D, 63957. T: (573) 223-7777. www.reserveusa.com/ nrrs/mo/blu2. RV/tent: 69. $. Hookups: electric (20, 30, 50 amp), water.

Highway K, Rte. 3 Box 3559-D, 63957. T: (573) 223-7777. www.reserveusa.com/nrrs/mo/higw. RV/tent: 61. $. Hookups: electric (20, 30 amp).

River Road L. Bank, Rte. 3 Box 3559-D, 63957. T: (573) 223-7777. www.reserveusa.com/nrrs/mo/rilb. RV/tent: 120. $$. Hookups: electric (20, 30, 50 amp).

Webb Creek, Rte. 3 Box 3559-D, 63957. T: (573) 223-7777. www.reserveusa.com/nrrs/mo/webb. RV/tent: 39. $. Hookups: electric (20, 30, 50 amp), water.

Pittsburg

Pomme de Terre State Park, HC 77 Box 890, 65724. T: (417) 852-4291. RV/tent: 257. $. Hookups: electric (20, 30, 50 amp), water.

Poplar Bluff

Camelot RV Campground, 4728 Hwy. 67 North, 63901. T: (573) 785-1016. RV/tent: 76. $$. Hook-ups: electric (30, 50 amp), water, sewer, cable.

Reeds Spring

Aunts Creek, Rte. 5 Box 585, 65737. T: (417) 739-2792. www.reserveusa.com. RV/tent: 56. $. Hookups: electric (20, 30 amp).

Ridgedale

Long Creek, 1036 Long Creek Rd., 65639. T: (417) 334-8427. www.reserveusa.com. RV/tent: 47. $. Hookups: electric (20, 30, 50 amp), water.

Robertsville

Robertsville State Park, 902 St. Park Dr., 63072. T: (636) 257-3788 or (800) 334-6946. www.mostateparks.com. RV/tent: 27. $. Hookups: electric (20, 30 amp), water.

Rock Port

Rock Port KOA, 1409 Hwy. 136 West, 64482. T: (800) 562-5415 or (660) 744-5485. www.koa.com/where/MO/25148. RV/tent: 56. $$. Hookups: electric (20, 30, 50 amp), water, sewer, phone.

Rushville

Lewis and Clark State Park, 801 Lake Crest Blvd., 64484. T: (816) 579-5564. RV/tent: 70. $. Hookups: electric (30 amp), water.

Salem

Jason Place Campground, HCR 81 Box 90, 65560. T: (800) 333-5628 or (573) 858-3224. RV/tent: 175. $. Hookups: electric (20, 30, 50 amp), water.

Montauk State Park, Rte. 5 Box 279, 65560-9025. T: (573) 548-2201. www.mostateparks.com/ montauk/camp. RV/tent: 154. $. Hookups: electric (20, 30 amp).

Sarcoxie

WAC RV Park, 2041 Cimarron Rd., 64862. T: (417) 548-2258. RV/tent: 144. $$. Hookups: electric (30, 50 amp), water, sewer.

Sedalia

Chaplin's RVs, 22415 Main St., 65301. T: (660) 826-8549 or (888) 816-4663. RV/tent: 15. $. Hookups: electric (30, 50 amp), water, sewer.

Shell Knob

Campbell Point, 792 Campbell Point Rd., 65747. T: (417) 858-3903. www.reserveusa.com. RV/tent: 76. $. Hookups: electric (20, 30 amp).

Viola Park, Rte. 5 Box 5210, 65747. T: (417) 858-3904. www.reserveusa.com. RV/tent: 57. $. Hookups: electric (20, 30 amp), water.

Sikeston

Town & Country Camping & RV Park, Hwy. 62 East, 63801. T: (800) 771-1339 or (573) 472-1339. RV/tent: 60. $$. Hookups: electric (30, 50 amp), water, sewer.

Silver Dollar City

Trail's End Resort & RV Park, 71 Dogwood Park Tr., 65616. T: (800) 888-1891 or (417) 338-2633. www.indianpoint.com/lodging/trailsendresort. RV/tent: 12. $. Hookups: electric (30, 50 amp), water, sewer.

Springfield

Springfield Missouri KOA, 5775 West Farm Rd., 65802. T: (800) 562-1228 or (417) 831-3645. www.koa.com. RV/tent: 99. $$. Hookups: electric (20, 30, 50 amp), water, sewer.

St. Charles

Sundermeier RV Park & Conference Center, 111 Transit St., 63301. T: (800) 929-0832 or (314) 940-0111. RV/tent: 106. $$$. Hookups: electric (30, 50 amp), water, sewer.

St. Louis

KOA St. Louis South, 8000 Metropolitan Blvd., 63012. T: (800) 562-3049 or (636) 479-4449. www.koa.com. RV/tent: 113. $$. Hookups: electric (20, 30, 50 amp), water, sewer.

KOA St. Louis West at Six Flags, Box 128, 63025. T: (800) 562-6249 or (636) 257-3018. www.koa.com. RV/tent: 159. $$$. Hookups: electric (20, 30, 50 amp), water, sewer.

Stanton

KOA Stanton/Meramec, Box 177, 63079. T: (800) 562-4498 or (573) 927-5215. www.koa.com. RV/tent: 51. $$. Hookups: electric (20, 30, 50 amp), water, sewer.

Stockton

Cedar Ridge, 16435 East Stockton Lake Dr., 65785. T: (660) 995-2045 disconnected during off-season. www.reserveusa.com. RV/tent: 54. $$. Hookups: electric (20, 30 amp).

Crabtree Cove, 16435 East Stockton Lake Dr., 65785. T: (660) 276-6799 disconnected during off-season. www.reserveusa.com. RV/tent: 58. $. Hookups: electric (20, 30 amp), water.

Hawker Point, 16435 East Stockton Lake Dr., 65785. T: (660) 276-7266 disconnected during off-season. www.reserveusa.com. RV/tent: 62. $. Hookups: electric (20, 30 amp).

Ruark Bluff East, 16435 East Stockton Lake Dr., 65785. T: (660) 637-5303 disconnected during off-season. www.reserveusa.com. RV/tent: 91. $. Hookups: electric (20, 30 amp).

Ruark Bluff West, 16435 East Stockton Lake Dr., 65785. T: (660) 637-5279 disconnected during off-season. www.reserveusa.com. RV/tent: 74. $. Hookups: electric (20, 30 amp).

Stoutsville

Mark Twain State Park, 20057 State Park Office Rd., 65283. T: (573) 565-3440. RV/tent: 101. $. Hookups: electric (30, 50 amp), water, dump station.

Sullivan

Meramec State Park, 2800 South Hwy. 185, 63080. T: (573) 468-6072. RV/tent: 190. $$. Hookups: electric (20, 30, 50 amp), water, sewer.

Trenton

Crowder State Park, 76 Hwy. 128, 64683. T: (660) 359-6473. RV/tent: 42. $. Hookups: electric (30 amp).

Troy

Cuivre River State Park, 678 SR 147, 63379. T: (636) 528-7247. RV/tent: 80. $. Hookups: electric (30, 50 amp), water, sewer.

Wappapello

Peoples Creek Campground, 10992 Hwy. T, 63966. T: (573) 222-8234. www.reserveusa.com. RV/tent: 37. $$. Hookups: electric (20, 30 amp).

Peoples Creek Upper Campground, HC 2 Box 2349, 63966. T: (573) 222-8234. www.Reserve USA.com/nrrs/mo/pecr/pecr1. RV/tent: 20. $$. Hookups: electric (20, 30 amp).

Redman Creek East, 10992 Hwy. T, 63966. T: (573) 222-8233. www.reserveusa.com. RV/tent: 68. $. Hookups: electric (20, 30 amp).

Redman Creek West, 10992 Hwy. T, 63966. T: (573) 222-8233. www.reserveusa.com. RV/tent: 38. $$. Hookups: electric (20, 30 amp), water, sewer.

MISSOURI (continued)

Warsaw

Harry S Truman State Park, H.CR 66 Box 14, 65355. T: (660) 438-7711. www.mostateparks.com/trumanpark. RV/tent: 201. $. Hookups: electric (20, 30 amp), water.

Long Shoal, Rte. 2 Box 29A, 65355. T: (660) 438-7317. www.reserveusa.com. RV/tent: 123. $. Hookups: electric (20, 30, 50 amp), water.

Osage Bluff, Rte. 2 Box 29A, 65355. T: (660) 438-7317. www.reserveusa.com. RV/tent: 68. $. Hookups: electric (20, 30 amp).

Weston

Weston Bend State Park, 16600 St. Rte. 45 North, 64098. T: (816) 640-5443. www.mostateparks.com/westonbend. RV/tent: 36. $. Hookups: electric (20, 30 amp), water.

Wildwood

Dr. Edmund A. Babler Memorial State Park, 800 Guy Park Dr., 63005. T: (636) 458-3813. RV/tent: 77. $. Hookups: electric (30, 50 amp), water.

MONTANA

Arlee

Jocko Hollow, 19001 US 93 North, 59821. T: (406) 726-3336. RV/tent: 16. $$. Hookups: electric (30 amp).

Augusta

Lewis & Clark National Forest (Benchmark Campground), P.O. Box 869, 59403. T: (406) 466-5341. RV/tent: 25. $. Hookups: none.

Basin

Merry Widow Health Mine Campground & Motel, Box 129, 59631. T: (406) 225-3220 or (877) 225-3220. www.merrywidowmine.com. RV/tent: 55. $. Hookups: electric (20, 30, 50 amp), water, sewer.

Big Sky

Gallatin/Red Cliff, US 191, 59718. T: (406) 522-2520 or (877) 444-6777. RV/tent: 63. $. Hookups: electric, water.

Greek Creek/Deerlodge National Forest, US 191 North, 59718. T: (406) 444-6777 or (877) 444-6777. RV/tent: 14. $. Hookups: none.

Big Timber

Spring Creek Campground and Trout Ranch, P.O. Box 1435, 59011. T: (406) 932-4387. www.springcreekcampground.com. RV/tent: 65. $$. Hookups: full.

Bigfork

Outback Montana, 27202 East Lakeshore, 59911. T: (888) 900-6973 or (406) 837-6973. www.outbackmontana.com. RV/tent: 50. $. Hookups: electric (20, 30 amp), water, sewer.

Timbers RV Park & Campground, 8550 Hwy. 35 South, 59911. T: (800) 821-4546 or (406) 837-6200. RV/tent: 30. $$. Hookups: electric (20, 30, 50 amp), water, sewer.

Billings

Big Sky Campground, 5516 Laurel Rd., 59101. T: (406) 259-4110. www.visitmt.com. RV/tent: 54. $$. Hookups: electric (30, 50 amp), water, sewer.

Bozeman

Bear Canyon Campground, 4000 Bozeman Trail Rd., 59715. T: (800) 438-1575 or (406) 587-1575. www.bearcanyoncampground.com. RV/tent: 130. $$. Hookups: electric (30, 50 amp), water, sewer.

Sunrise Campground, 31842 Frontage Rd., 59715. T: (877) 437-2095 or (406) 587-4797. RV/tent: 70. $$. Hookups: electric (30, 50 amp), water, sewer.

Broadus

Wayside Park, Box 568, 59317. T: (406) 436-2510. RV/tent: 21. $. Hookups: electric (20, 30, 50 amp), water, sewer.

White Buffalo Campground, P.O. Box 387, 59317. T: (406) 436-2595. RV/tent: 17. $. Hookups: electric, water, sewer.

Browning

Chewing Black Bones Resort & Campground, P.O. Box 2809, 59417. T: (406) 732-9263. RV/tent: 127. $. Hookups: electric, water, sewer, cable, phone.

Sleeping Wolf Campground, Box 607, 59417. T: (406) 338-3251. RV/tent: 21. $$. Hookups: electric (20, 30, 50 amp), water.

Butte

2 Bar Lazy H RV Park, 122015 West Browns Gulch Rd., 59701. T: (406) 782-5464. RV/tent: 24. $$. Hookups: electric (30, 50 amp), phone.

Clancy

Alhambra RV Park, Hwy. 282 South No. 515, 59634. T: (406) 933-8020-. RV/tent: 38. $. Hookups: electric (20, 30 amp), water.

Clinton

Beavertail Hill State Park, 3201 Spurgin Rd., 59804. T: (406) 542-5500. www.fwp.state.mt.us. RV/tent: 28. $$. Hookups: none.

Elkhorn RV Ranch, 408 Rock Creek Rd., 59825. T: (406) 825-3220. www.montana.com/elkhorn. RV/tent: 120. $$. Hookups: electric (20, 30 amp), water, sewer, modem.

Columbia Falls

Glacier Mountain Shadows Resort, 7285 Hwy. 2 East, 59912. T: (406) 892-7686. www.glacieradventure.com. RV/tent: 28. $$. Hookups: electric (20, 30 amp), water, sewer, cable.

Glacier Peaks Campground, P.O. Box 492, 59912. T: (800) 268-4849. www.digisys.net/rvs/. RV/tent: 76. $$. Hookups: electric (30, 50 amp), water, cable, phone.

Conner

Moosehead Campground, 6457 Hwy. 93 South, 59827. T: (406) 821-3327. RV/tent: 91. $$. Hookups: electric (20 amp), water, sewer.

Dillon

Red Mountain Campgrounds, 1005 Selway Dr., 59725. T: (406) 683-2337. www.blm/for/state. RV/tent: 14. $. Hookups: electric, water.

Skyline RV Park Campground, 3525 North US 91, 59725. T: (406) 683-4692. RV/tent: 34. $$. Hookups: electric (30 amp), water, sewer, cable.

Drummond

Good Time Camping & RV Park, 239 Frontage Rd. West, 59832. T: (406) 288-3608. www.experiencegoldwest.com. RV/tent: 16. $$. Hookups: electric (20, 30, 50 amp), water.

East Glacier Park

Firebrand Campground, P.O. Box 146, 59434. T: (406) 226-5573. RV/tent: 30. $$. Hookups: electric (20, 30 amp).

Glacier/Two Medicine, P.O. Box 128, 59936. T: (406) 888-7800 or (800) 365-CAMP. RV/tent: 99. $$. Hookups: none.

Three Forks Campground, P.O. Box 124, 59434. T: (406) 226-4479. RV/tent: 42. $$. Hookups: electric (20, 30 amp), water, sewer, modem.

Y Lazy R Camper Trailer Park, P.O. Box 146, 59434. T: (406) 226-5573. RV/tent: 41. $$. Hookups: electric (20, 30 amp), water.

Gardiner

Rocky Mountain Campground, 14 Gardine Rd., 59030. T: (406) 848-7251 or (877) 534-6931. www.rockymountaincampground.com. RV/tent: 87. $$. Hookups: electric (20, 30 amp), water, sewer, modem.

Georgetown

Georgetown Lake Lodge, 2015 Georgetown Lake Rd., 59711. T: (406) 563-7020. RV/tent: 63. $$. Hookups: electric (30, 50 amp), water, sewer, modem.

Glasgow

Trails West Campground, Rte. 1-4404, 59230. T: (406) 228-2778. RV/tent: 66. $$. Hookups: electric (30, 50 amp), water, sewer, modem.

Glendive

Green Valley Campground, 124 Green Valley Ln., 59330. T: (406) 377-1944. www.greenvalley-campground.com. RV/tent: 87. $$. Hookups: electric (20, 30, 50 amp), water.

MONTANA (continued)

Great Falls

Dick's RV Park, 1403 11th St. South, 59404. T: (406) 452-0333. www.dicksrvpark.com. RV/tent: 137. $$$. Hookups: electric (30, 50 amp), water, sewer, modem.

Hamilton

Angler's Roost Campground, 815 US 93 South, 59840. T: (406) 363-1268. www.anglersroost-montana.com. RV/tent: 70. $$. Hookups: full.

Bitterroot Family Campground, 1744 Hwy. 93 South, 59840. T: (800) 453-2430. RV/tent: 52. $. Hookups: electric (15, 20, 30 amp), water.

Lick Creek Campground, 2251 US 93 South, 59840. T: (406) 363-3744. RV/tent: 34. $$$. Hookups: electric (30, 50 amp), water, sewer, cable.

Hardin

Grandview Campground, 1002 North Mitchell Ave., 59034. T: (800) 622-9890 or (406) 665-2489. www.grandviewcamp.com. RV/tent: 50. $$. Hookups: electric (20, 30, 50 amp), water, sewer, cable, modem.

Harlowton

Chief Joseph Park, Box 292, 59036. T: (406) 632-5523. RV/tent: 23. $. Hookups: electric (20, 30 amp).

Havre

Havre Family Campground, HC Box 200, 59501. T: (406) 265-9722. www.chinookmontana.com/familycampground.html. RV/tent: 108. $$. Hookups: electric (30 amp), water, sewer.

Helena

Hauser Lake SRA/Black Sandy, 930 Custer Ave., 59601. T: (406) 495-3260. www.fwp.state.mt.us. RV/tent: 33. $. Hookups: electric, water.

Hungry Horse

Flathead/Lid Creek, Ranger District, Box 190340, 59919. T: (406) 387-3800. www.gorp.away.com/dow/northern/flat.htm. RV/tent: 22. $. Hookups: electric, water.

Sundance RV Park & Campground, 10545 Hwy. 2 East, 59919. T: (406) 387-5016. RV/tent: 64. $$. Hookups: electric (20, 30 amp), water.

Joliet

Cooney Reservoir State Park, P.O. Box 253, 59041. T: (406) 247-2940 or (406) 445-2326. www.fwp .state.mt.us. RV/tent: 75. $. Hookups: none.

Kalispell

Glacier Pines RV Park, 1850 Hwy. 35 East, 59901. T: (800) 533-4029 or (406) 752-2760. www.glacierpines.com. RV/tent: 160. $$. Hookups: electric (20, 30, 50 amp), modem.

Greenwood Village Campgrounds, 1100 East Oregon St., 59901. T: (406) 257-7719. RV/tent: 38. $. Hookups: electric (20, 30, 50 amp), phone.

Rocky Mountain HI Campground, 825 Helena Flats Rd., 59901. T: (800) 968-5637 or (406) 755-9573. www.glaciercamping.com. RV/tent: 102. $$. Hookups: electric (20, 30 amp), water, phone.

Spruce Park Campground, 1985 Hwy. 35, 59901. T: (888) 752-6321 or (406) 752-6321. www.spruceparkrv.com. RV/tent: 160. $$. Hookups: electric (15, 20, 30, 50 amp), water, sewer, cable, phone.

Laurel

Clark's Riverfront Campground & Resort, 3001 Thiel Rd., 59044. T: (406) 628-2984. RV/tent: 33. $$. Hookups: electric.

Pelican's RV Campground, 3444 South Frontage Rd., 59044. T: (406) 628-4324. RV/tent: 54. $$. Hookups: electric (30, 50 amp), water, sewer.

Lewiston

Mountain Acres Mobile Home Park, 103 Rocklyn Ave., 59457. T: (406) 538-7591. RV/tent: 36. $$. Hookups: electric (20, 30 amp), water, sewer.

Libby

Sportsman's RV Park, 11741 Hwy. 37, 59923. T: (406) 293-2267. RV/tent: 22. $$. Hookups: full.

Two Bit Outfit RV Park, 716 Hwy. 2 West, 59923. T: (406) 293-8323. RV/tent: 40. $. Hookups: electric (30, 50 amp), water, sewer.

Livingston

Livingston Campground, 9 Rogers Ln., 59047. T: (406) 222-1122. RV/tent: 42. $$$. Hookups: electric (20, 50 amp), water, sewer, cable.

Osen's Campground, 20 Merrill Ln., 59047. T: (406) 222-0591. www.montanarvpark.com. RV/tent: 57. $$. Hookups: electric (20, 30, 50 amp), water, sewer, cable.

Rock Canyon RV Park, 5070 US 89 South, 59047. T: (406) 222-1096. RV/tent: 36. $. Hookups: electric (30 amp), water, sewer.

Lolo

Lolo Hot Springs RV Park & Campground, 38500 Hwy. 12 West, 59847. T: (406) 273-2290 or (800) 273-2290 or (877) 541-5117. www.lolo hotsprings.com. RV/tent: 116. $$. Hookups: electric (20, 30 amp), water, sewer.

Square Dance Center & Campground, 9955 Hwy. 12 West, 59847. T: (406) 273-0141. www.missoula .bigsky.net/sqrdance. RV/tent: 71. $. Hookups: electric (20, 30 amp), water, sewer, cable, modem.

Marion

Moose Crossing, 8405 Hwy. 2 West, 59925. T: (406) 854-2070. RV/tent: 24. $$. Hookups: electric (15 amp), water, phone.

Miles City

Big Sky Camp & RV Park, RR 1 Hwy. 12, 59301. T: (406) 232-1511. RV/tent: 74. $$. Hookups: electric (30 amp), water.

Missoula

Jim & Mary's RV Park, 9800 US 93 North, 59802. T: (406) 549-4416. RV/tent: 45. $$. Hookups: electric (30, 50 amp), water, sewer.

Outpost Campground, 11600 US 93 North, 59808. T: (406) 549-2016. RV/tent: 45. $$. Hookups: electric (20, 30 amp), water, sewer.

Yogi Bear's Jellystone Park Missoula, 9900 Jellystone Drive, 59802. T: (406) 543- 9400 or (800)

318-9644. www.campjellystonemt.com. RV/tent: 110. $$. Hookups: electric (20, 30, 50 amp), water, sewer, phone.

Noxon

Cabinet Gorge RV Park & Campground, 30 Blue Jay Ln., 59853. T: (406) 847-2291 or (800) 639-9692. RV/tent: 35. $$. Hookups: electric (30, 50 amp), water, sewer.

Phillipsburg

Deerlodge/Piney Campground, Phillipsburg Ranger District H, 59851. T: (406) 859-3211. RV/tent: 47. $. Hookups: none.

Polson

Flathead River Resort, 9 Regatta Rd., 59860. T: (406) 883-6400. www.flatheadrv.com. RV/tent: 36. $$. Hookups: electric (20, 30, 50 amp), phone.

Montana Pines RV Resort, 6913 East Shore Rte., 59860. T: (406) 887-2537. RV/tent: 87. $. Hookups: electric (20, 30 amp), water, modem.

Red Lodge

Perry's RV Park & Campground, HC 49 Box 3586, 59068. T: (406) 446-2722. RV/tent: 40. $$. Hookups: electric (20 amp), water.

Rexford

Mariners Haven Campground, 101 Mariners Dr., 59930. T: (406) 296-3252. RV/tent: 54. $$. Hookups: electric (20, 30 amp), water, sewer.

Ronan

Mission Meadows, 298 Mission Meadows Dr., 59364. T: (406) 676-5182. RV/tent: 42. $$. Hookups: electric (20, 30, 50 amp), water, sewer.

Shelby

Lake Shel-oole Campground, I-15, 59474. T: (406) 434-5222. RV/tent: 42. $$. Hookups: electric (30 amp), water.

St. Ignatius

St. Ignatius Campground & Hostel, 33076 Hwy. 93, 59865. T: (406) 745-3959. www.camp-hostel.com. RV/tent: 14. $. Hookups: electric (30 amp), water, sewer.

Sula

Lost Trail Hot Springs Resort, 8321 Hwy. 93 South, 59871. T: (406) 821-3574 or (800) 825-3574. www.losttrailhotsprings.com. RV/tent: 16. $. Hookups: full.

Terry

Terry's RV Oasis, 510 Jane St., 59349. T: (406) 637-5520. RV/tent: 18. $. Hookups: electric (30, 50 amp), water, sewer, cable.

Thompson Falls

The Riverfront, 4907 Hwy. 200, 59873. T: (406) 827-3460. www.riverfrontmotel.com. RV/tent: 8. $$. Hookups: electric (20, 30, 50 amp), water, sewer, phone.

MONTANA (continued)

Three Forks

Fort Three Forks RV Park & Motel, 10776 Hwy. 287, 59752. T: (800) 477-5690 or (406) 285-3233. www.fortthreeforks.com. RV/tent: 12. $$. Hookups: electric (30, 50 amp) water, sewer.

Townsend

Roadrunner RV Park, 704 North Front Rd., 192 Hwy. 12 East, 59644. T: (406) 266-3278. RV/tent: 25. $$. Hookups: electric (30, 50 amp), water, sewer.

Silos RV Park & Fishing Camp, 81 Silos Rd., 59644. T: (406) 266-3100. RV/tent: 57. $$. Hookups: electric (30, 50 amp), water, sewer.

Troy

Kootenai River Campground, 2898 Hwy. 2 North, 59935. T: (406) 295-4090. RV/tent: 48. $$. Hookups: electric (20, 30 amp), water.

Twin Bridges

Jefferson River Camp, 5162 MT 41, 59754. T: (406) 684-5225. RV/tent: 14. $. Hookups: electric (20, 30 amp), water.

Valier

Lake Francis City Park Campground, P.O. Box 512, 59486. T: (406) 279-3361. RV/tent: 32. $. Hookups: electric.

Virginia City

Virginia City Campground & RV Park, P.O. Box 352, 59755. T: (406) 843-5493 or (888) 833-5493. www.virginiacitycampground.com. RV/tent: 17. $$. Hookups: electric (30 amp), water, sewer.

West Glacier

San-Suz-Ed Trailer Park & Campground, 11505 Hwy. 2 East, 59936. T: (406) 387-5280 or (800) 305-4616. www.san-suz-edrvpark.com. RV/tent: 68. $$. Hookups: electric (30, 50 amp), water, sewer, phone.

West Yellowstone

Gallatin/Beaver Creek, P.O. Box 520, 59758. T: (406) 823-6961. RV/tent: 64. $. Hookups: none.

Hideaway RV Park, 310 Electric, 59758. T: (406) 646-9049. www.hideawayrv.com. RV/tent: 14. $$.

Hookups: electric (30, 50 amp), water, sewer, cable.

Rustic Wagon RV Campground & Cabins, 634 Hwy. 20 & Gibbon Ave., 59758. T: (406) 646-7387. www.rusticwagonrv.com. RV/tent: 52. $$$. Hookups: electric (20, 30, 50 amp), water.

Wagon Wheel RV Campground & Cabins, 408 Gibbon Ave., 59758. T: (406) 646-7872. www.wyellowstone.com. RV/tent: 51. $$. Hookups: electric (20, 30 amp), water, sewer, cable, modem.

Yellowstone Holiday RV Campground & Marina, 16990 Hebgen Lake Rd., 59758. T: (877) 646-4242 or (406) 646-4242. www.yellowstone holiday.com. RV/tent: 27. $$. Hookups: electric (20, 30, 50 amp), water, sewer, modem.

Wolf Point

Rancho Campground, Hwy. 2 West, 59201. T: (406) 653-1940. RV/tent: 25. $. Hookups: electric (30 amp), water, sewer.

NEBRASKA

Alliance

J & C RV Park, 2491 South US 385, 69301. T: (308) 762-3860. RV/tent: 13. $$. Hookups: electric, water, sewer.

Anselmo

Victoria Springs State Recreation Area, HC 69 P.O. Box 117, 68813. T: (308) 749-2235. www.npgc .state.ne.us. RV/tent: 75. $. Hookups: electric.

Bellevue

Haworth Park, 2502 Payne Drive, 68005. T: (402) 293-3098. www.bellevue.net. RV/tent: 129. $. Hookups: electric, water.

Big Springs

McGreer Camper Park, Rte. 2 Box 96, 69122. T: (308) 889-3489. RV/tent: 40. $. Hookups: electric, water.

Bridgeport

Golden Acres Motel and RV Park, NW Hwy. 385, 69336. T: (308) 262-0410. RV/tent: 18. $$. Hookups: electric, water, sewer.

Broken Bow

Wagon Wheel Motel and Campground, 1545 South "E" St., 68822. T: (308) 872-2433. RV/tent: 10. $$. Hookups: electric, water, sewer, phone, cable.

Brule

Riverside Park, 1000 South State St., 69127. T: (308) 287-2474. RV/tent: 38. $$. Hookups: electric, water, sewer.

Burwell

Calamus Reservoir State Recreation Area, HC 79 P.O. Box 20-L, 68823. T: (308) 346-5666.

www.ngpc.state.ne.us. RV/tent: 172. $. Hookups: electric.

Chadron

J & L RV Park, J & L No. 13, 69337. T: (308) 432-4349. RV/tent: 58. $. Hookups: electric, water, sewer.

Chappell

Creekside RV Park and Campground, P.O. Box 912, 69129. T: (308) 874-CAMP. RV/tent: 55. $$. Hookups: electric, water, sewer.

Elm Creek

Sunny Meadows Campground, 234 East Front St., 68836. T: (308) 856-4792. RV/tent: 30. $. Hookups: electric, water, sewer.

Gibbon

Windmill State Recreation Area, 2625 Lowell Rd., 68840. T: (308) 468-5700. www.ngpc.state.ne.us. RV/tent: 89. $. Hookups: electric (20, 30, 50 amp).

Grand Island

Grand Island KOA, 904 South B Rd., 68832. T: (402) 886-2249. RV/tent: 71. $$. Hookups: electric.

Gretna

KOA West Omaha, 14601 Hwy. 6, 68028. T: (402) 332-3010. RV/tent: 86. $$. Hookups: electric, water.

Harrison

Corral Campground, 410 East Hwy. 20, 69346. T: (308) 668-2441. RV/tent: 12. $$. Hookups: electric, water, sewer.

Hemingford

Box Butte Reservoir State Recreation Area, P.O.

Box 392, 69339. T: (308) 665-2900. RV/tent: 50. $. Hookups: electric, water, sewer.

Kearney

Claude and Vi's Campground, 300 3rd Ave., 68847. T: (308) 234-1532. RV/tent: 110. $$. Hookups: electric, water.

Kimball

KOA Kimball, 4334 Link 53 East, 69145. T: (308) 235-4404. RV/tent: 45. $$. Hookups: electric, water, sewer.

Maxwell

Fort McPherson Campground, 12568 Valley View Rd., 69151. T: (308) 582-4320. RV/tent: 75. $$. Hookups: electric, water, sewer.

Minden

Pioneer Village Motel and Campground, Harold Wrap Memorial Dr., 68959. T: (800) 445-4447. RV/tent: 165. $$. Hookups: electric, water, sewer.

Nebraska City

Victorian Acres RV Park and Campground, 6591 Hwy. 2, 68410. T: (402) 873-6866. RV/tent: 66. $$. Hookups: electric, water.

North Plate

A-1 Sunset RV Park, 3120 Rodeo Rd., 69101. T: (308) 532-9182. RV/tent: 24. $$. Hookups: electric (20, 30, 50 amp), water, sewer, cable.

Holiday Park, 601 Hullingan Dr., 69101. T: (308) 534-2265 or (800) 424-4531. RV/tent: 100. $$. Hookups: electric (50 amp), water, sewer.

The Rockin' DH Campground, 3800 Hadley Dr., 69101. T: (308) 534-5300 or (877) 994-2267. RV/tent: 67. $$. Hookups: electric (30, 50 amp), water, sewer, cable.

NEBRASKA (continued)

Ogallala

Area's Finest Meyer Camper Court, 120 Rd. East 80, 69153. T: (308) 284-2415. RV/tent: 112. $. Hookups: electric, water, sewer.

Corral Campground and RV Park, 221 Rd. East 85, 69153. T: (308) 284-4327. RV/tent: 68. $$. Hookups: electric, water, sewer.

Van's Lakeview Fishing Camp, No. 1 Lakeview, 69127. T: (308) 284-4965. RV/tent: 122. $. Hookups: electric, water, sewer.

Paxton

Ole's Lodge and RV Park, 851 Paxton-Elsie Rd., 69155. T: (308) 239-4510. RV/tent: 12. $. Hookups: full.

Schuyler

Schuyler Campground, 1103 B St., 68661. T: (402) 352-2057. RV/tent: 30. $. Hookups: electric, water.

Shubert

Indian Cave State Park, RR 1 Box 30, 68437. T: (402) 883-2575. RV/tent: 234. $. Hookups: electric.

Sidney

Bear Family RV Park, 921 Greenwood Rd., 69162. T: (308) 254-6000. RV/tent: 44. $$. Hookups: electric, water, sewer, cable.

Cabela's RV Park, 1 Anglers Ln., 69162. T: (308) 254-7177. RV/tent: 37. $$. Hookups: full.

South Sioux

Scenic Park, 1615 1st Ave., 68776. T: (402) 494-7531. RV/tent: 53. $$. Hookups: full.

Sutherland

Oregon Trail Trading Post and Campground, Rte. 1 Box 606, 69165. T: (308) 386-4653. RV/tent: 30. $. Hookups: electric, water.

Valentine

River of Life Camp, East Hwy. 20, 96201. T: (402) 376-2958. RV/tent: 37. $$. Hookups: electric, water.

Valentine Motel and RV Park, P.O. Box A, 69201. T: (800) 376-2450. RV/tent: 36. $$. Hookups: electric, water, sewer, cable.

Wacky West Travel Park, 224 North Wood St., 69201. T: (402) 376-1771. RV/tent: 22. $$. Hookups: electric, water.

York

Double Nickel Campground and County Store, 907 Rd. South, 68460. T: (402) 728-5558. RV/tent: 110. $$. Hookups: electric, water, sewer.

NEVADA

Amargosa Valley

Fort Amargosa, P.O. Box 245, 89020. T: (775) 372-1178. RV/tent: 98. $. Hookups: electric (20, 30, 50 amp), water, sewer.

Austin

Austin RV Park, US 50, 89310. T: (775) 964-1011. RV/tent: 21. $$. Hookups: electric (20, 30 amp), water, sewer.

Big Creek Campground, P.O. Box 130, 89310. T: (775) 964-2671. RV/tent: 9. $. Hookups: none.

Bob Scott Campground, P.O. Box 130, 89310. T: (702) 964-2671. RV/tent: 10. $. Hookups: none.

Baker

Baker Creek Campground, 100 Great Basin National Park, 89311. T: (775) 234-7331. www.nps.gov/grba. RV/tent: 30. $. Hookups: none.

Wheeler Creek Campground, 100 Great Basin National Park, 89311. T: (775) 234-7331. www.nps.gov/grba. RV/tent: 37. $. Hookups: none.

Whispering Elms RV Park, P.O. Box 105, 89311. T: (775) 234-7343. www.greatbasinpark.com/whisperingelms. RV/tent: 20. $. Hookups: electric (20, 30 amp), water, sewer.

Battle Mountain

Broadway Flying J Service Center, 650 West Front, 89820. T: (775) 635-5424. RV/tent: 96. $$. Hookups: electric (20, 30, 50 amp), water, sewer.

Beatty

Burro Inn, 851 Hwy. 95 South, 89003. T: (775) 553-2225 or (800) 843-2078. www.burroinn.com. RV/tent: 43. $$. Hookups: electric (20, 30, 50 amp), water, sewer.

Kay's Korral RV Park, US 95, 89003. T: (775) 553-2732. RV/tent: 25. $. Hookups: electric, water, sewer.

Rio Rancho RV Park, US 95 North, 89003. T: (775) 553-2238 or (800) 448-4423. RV/tent: 35. $$. Hookups: electric (30, 50 amp), water, sewer.

Space Station RV Park & Market, 400 East Hwy. 95 North, 89003. T: (775) 553-9039. RV/tent: 24. $. Hookups: electric (30 amp), water, sewer.

Boulder City

Boulder Oaks RV Resort, 1010 Industrial Rd., 89005. T: (702) 294-4425 or (800) 478-5687. www.aardvarkrv/boulderoaks. RV/tent: 275. $$$. Hookups: electric (30, 50 amp), water, sewer, cable, phone (modem).

Canyon Trail RV Park, 1200 Industrial Rd., 89005. T: (702) 293-1200. RV/tent: 156. $$. Hookups: electric (30, 50 amp), water, sewer.

Lakeshore Trailer Village, 268 Lakeshore Rd., 89005. T: (702) 293-2540. RV/tent: 80. $$. Hookups: electric (30 amp), water, sewer, cable.

Cal Nev Ari

Cal Nev Ari, 2 Spirit Mountain, 89039. T: (702) 297-1115. RV/tent: 58. $$. Hookups: electric (20, 30, 50 amp), water, sewer.

Caliente

Agua Caliente Trailer Park, US 93 North, 89008. T: (775) 726-3399. RV/tent: 5. $. Hookups: electric (20 amp), water, sewer.

Beaver Dam State Park, H.CR 64 Box 3, 89042. T: (775) 726-3564. www.state.nv.us/stparks. RV/tent: 42. $. Hookups: none.

Carson City

Camp-N-Town, 2438 North Carson St., 89706. T: (775) 883-1132 or (800) 872-1132. RV/tent: 130. $$. Hookups: electric (30, 50 amp), water, sewer, cable, phone (modem).

Comstock Country RV Resort, 5400 South Carson St., 89701. T: (775) 882-2445 or (800) NEVADA-1. www.comstocknv.com. RV/tent: 156. $$. Hookups: electric (20, 30, 50 amp), water, sewer, cable.

Crystal Springs Campground, 1536 South Carson St., 89701. T: (775) 882-2766. RV/tent: 22. $. Hookups: none.

Indian Creek Campground, 5665 Morgan Hill Rd., 89701. T: (775) 885-6000. www.nv.blm.gov/carson. RV/tent: 29. $. Hookups: none.

Kit Carson Campground, 1536 South Carson St., 89701. T: (775) 882-2766. RV/tent: 12. $. Hookups: none.

Mount Rose Campground, 431 Mt. Rose Hwy., 89701. T: (775) 882-2766. RV/tent: 24. $. Hookups: none.

Oasis RV Park, 4550 South Carson St., 89701. T: (775) 882-1375. RV/tent: 28. $$. Hookups: electric (20, 30 amp), water, sewer, cable.

Piñon Plaza Casino Resort & RV Park, 2171 US 50 East, 89701. T: (775) 885-9000 or (877) 519-5567. www.pinonplaza.com. RV/tent: 47. $$. Hookups: electric (30, 50 amp), water, sewer, cable, phone (modem).

Cottonwood Cove

Cottonwood Cove Marina & Resort, 1000 Cottonwood Cove Rd., 89046. T: (702) 297-1464. www.foreverresorts.com. RV/tent: 73. $. Hookups: electric (30, 50 amp), water, sewer, cable.

Dayton

Dayton State Park, P.O. Box 412, 89403. T: (775) 687-4379. RV/tent: 10. $. Hookups: none.

Denio

Royal Peacock RV Park, Virgin Valley Rd., 89404. T: (775) 941-0374 or (775) 272-3201. RV/tent: 15. $$. Hookups: electric (20, 30 amp), water, sewer.

Elko

Best Western Gold Country RV Park, 2050 Idaho St., 89801. T: (775) 738-8421 or (800) 621-1332. www.bestwesternnevada.com. RV/tent: 26. $$. Hookups: electric (20, 30, 50 amp), water, sewer.

NEVADA (continued)

Double Dice RV Park, 3730 East Idaho St., 89801. T: (775) 738-5642 or (888) 738-3423. www.gocampingamerica.com/doubledice. RV/tent: 140. $$. Hookups: electric (30, 50 amp), water, sewer, cable, phone (modem).

Dunn's Wildhorse Resort, HC 31 Box 213 (62 mi. north of Elko), 89801. T: (775) 758-6472. www.nevadaadventures.com/client/wildhorse/ wildhorseevents.html. RV/tent: 34. $$. Hookups: electric (20, 30 amp), water, sewer.

Hidden Valley Guest & RV Resort, P.O. Box 1454, 89803. T: (775) 738-2347. RV/tent: 27. $. Hookups: electric (30 amp), water, sewer.

North Wildhorse Campground, 3900 East Idaho St., 89801. T: (775) 753-0200. RV/tent: 18. $. Hookups: none.

Ryndon RV Park, 303-11 Ryndon, 89801. T: (775) 738-3448. RV/tent: 54. $$. Hookups: electric (30, 50 amp), water, sewer, phone (modem).

Wildhorse State Recreation Area, HC 31 Box 265 (67 mi. north of Elko), 89801. T: (775) 758-6493. www.parks.nv.gov/wh.html. RV/tent: 33. $. Hookups: none.

Wilson Reservoir Campground, 3900 East Idaho St., 89801. T: (775) 753-0200. RV/tent: 15. $. Hookups: none.

Ely

Harry's Wilderness RV, No. 58 McGill Hwy., 89301. T: (775) 289-4900. RV/tent: 10. $. Hookups: electric (30 amp), water, sewer.

KOA of Ely, US 93S, 89301. T: (775) 289-3413 or (800) 526-3413. www.elykoa.com. RV/tent: 107. $$. Hookups: electric (20, 30, 50 amp), water, sewer, cable, phone (modem).

Lanes Ranch Motel, HC 34 (Preston) Box 34145, 89301. T: (775) 238-5246. RV/tent: 7. $. Hookups: electric (30 amp), water, sewer.

Major's Station RV Park, US 93 & US 50 Junction, 89301. T: (775) 591-0430. RV/tent: 7. $$. Hookups: electric (30 amp), water, sewer, phone.

Prospector Casino RV Park (Holiday Inn), US 93, 1501 East Aultman St., 89301-0958. T: (775) 289-8900. RV/tent: 22. $. Hookups: electric (20, 30, 50 amp), water, sewer.

Stage Stop, HCR 33 Box 33900, 89301. T: (775) 591-0397. RV/tent: 4. $. Hookups: electric (30 amp), water.

Timber Creek, 350 8th St., 89301. T: (775) 289-3031. RV/tent: 10. $. Hookups: none.

Valley View RV Park, No. 65 McGill Hwy., 89301. T: (775) 289-3303. RV/tent: 46. $$. Hookups: electric (20, 30, 50 amp), water, sewer, cable, phone (modem).

West End RV Park, No. 50 Aultman St., 89301. T: (775) 289-8900. RV/tent: 11. $. Hookups: electric (30 amp), water, sewer.

Eureka

Eureka RV Park, P.O. Box 734, 89316. T: (775) 237-7203. RV/tent: 25. $. Hookups: electric (30 amp), water, sewer, cable.

Pita RV, P.O. Box 27, 89316. T: (775) 237-5281. RV/tent: 11. $. Hookups: electric (30 amp), water, sewer, cable.

Silver Sky RV Park, Hwy. 50 No. 1 South Main, 89316. T: (775) 237-7146. www.eurekacounty. com/directory/silversky.htm. RV/tent: 15. $. Hookups: electric (30 amp), water, sewer.

T/C Trailer Park, P.O. Box 176, 89316. T: (775) 237-5331. RV/tent: 14. $. Hookups: electric (30 amp), water, sewer, cable.

Fallon

Bonanza RV Park, 855 West Williams, 89407. T: (775) 423-6031. www.travelnevada.com/rv parks2.asp. RV/tent: 20. $. Hookups: electric (30 amp), water, sewer.

Fallon RV Park, 5787 Reno Hwy., 89406. T: (775) 867-2332. www.travelnevada.com/rvparks2.asp. RV/tent: 64. $$. Hookups: electric (30, 50 amp), water, sewer.

The Hub Hotel RV Park, 4800 Reno Hwy. (US 50), 89406. T: (775) 867-3636. www.travelnevada.com /rvparks2.asp. RV/tent: 44. $$. Hookups: electric (20, 30 amp), water, sewer, cable, phone (modem).

Fernley

Desert Rose RV Park, 3285 Hwy. 50 East, 89408. T: (775) 575-9399 or (877) 767-3478. www.desertroserv.com. RV/tent: 112. $$. Hookups: electric (30, 50 amp), water, sewer, cable, phone (modem).

Fernley RV Park, 550 West Main St., 89408. T: (775) 575-5222. RV/tent: 40. $$. Hookups: electric (30, 50 amp), water, sewer, cable, phone (modem).

Gardnerville

Topaz Lodge & Casino RV Park, 1995 US 395 South, 89410. T: (775) 266-3338 or (800) 962-0732. www.enterit.com. RV/tent: 59. $. Hookups: electric, water, sewer, cable.

Goldfield

Goldfield RV Park, 410 South 4th St., 89013. T: (775) 485-3280. RV/tent: 10. $. Hookups: electric (30, 50 amp), water, sewer.

Hawthorne

Desert Lake Campground, 850 US 95 Walker Lake, 89415. T: (775) 945-3373. RV/tent: 25. $. Hookups: electric (30 amp), water, sewer.

Frontier RV Park, 1121 5th & L St., 89415. T: (775) 945-2733. RV/tent: 27. $. Hookups: electric (30, 50 amp), water, sewer.

Scotty's RV Park, 1005 5th St., 89415. T: (775) 945-2079. RV/tent: 16. $$. Hookups: electric (20, 30, 50 amp), water, sewer, cable.

Henderson

Desert Sands RV Park, 1940 North Boulder Hwy., 89015. T: (702) 565-1945. RV/tent: 300. $$. Hookups: electric (20, 30, 50 amp), water, sewer.

Jackpot

Cactus Pete's Saquaro RV Park, 1385 Hwy. 93, 89825. T: (775) 755-2321 or (800) 821-1103. www.ameristarcasinos.com/cactus_petes.asp. RV/tent: 91. $. Hookups: electric (20, 30 amp), water, sewer, cable, phone (modem).

Spanish Gardens RV Park, US 93 & Gurley Drive, 89825. T: (775) 755-2396 or (800) 422-8233. RV/tent: 38. $$. Hookups: electric (30, 50 amp), water, sewer, cable.

Las Vegas

Arizona Charlie's East Hotel Casino & RV Park, 4445 Boulder Hwy, 89121. T: (702) 951-5911 or (800) 970-7280. RV/tent: 200. $$. Hookups: electric (20, 30, 50 amp), water, sewer, phone (modem).

Arizona Charlie's RV Park, 4445 Boulder Hwy., 89121. T: (702) 458-7275 or (800) 970-7280. www.arizonacharliesboulder.com. RV/tent: 239. $$. Hookups: electric (30, 50 amp), water, sewer, phone (modem).

Boulder Lakes RV Resort, 6201 Boulder Hwy., 89122. T: (702) 435-1157. RV/tent: 417. $$. Hookups: electric (20, 30, 50 amp), water, sewer, cable, phone (modem).

Castaways RV Park, 2800 East Fremont St., 89104. T: (702) 383-9333 or (800) 826-2800. www.showboat-lv.com. RV/tent: 84. $$. Hookups: electric (20, 30, 50 amp), water, sewer, cable, phone (modem).

Circusland RV Park, 500 Circus Circus Dr., 89109. T: (702) 794-3757 or (877) 224-7287. www.circuscircus.com. RV/tent: 399. $$. Hookups: electric (30, 50 amp), water, sewer, phone (modem).

Destiny's Oasis Las Vegas RV Resort, 2711 Windmill Rd., 89123. T: (702) 260-2020 or (800) 566-4707. www.destinyrv.com. RV/tent: 701. $$. Hookups: electric (30, 50 amp), water, sewer, cable, phone (modem).

Hitchin' Post RV Park, 3640 Las Vegas Blvd. North, 89115. T: (702) 644-1043 or (888) 433-8402. RV/tent: 184. $$. Hookups: electric (20, 30, 50 amp), water, sewer, cable, phone (modem).

Holiday Travel Park, 3890 South Nellis Blvd., 89121. T: (702) 451-8005. RV/tent: 403. $$. Hookups: electric (30, 50 amp), water, sewer, phone (modem).

KOA Las Vegas, 3333 Blue Diamond Rd., 89139. T: (702) 451-5527 or (800) 562-7782. RV/tent: 323. $$$. Hookups: electric (20, 30, 50 amp), water, sewer, phone (modem).

Nevada Palace VIP Travel Trailer Park, 5325 Boulder Hwy., 89122. T: (702) 451-0232 or (800) 634-6283. www.nvpalace.com. RV/tent: 168. $$. Hookups: electric (30 amp), water, sewer.

Riviera RV Park, 2200 Palm, 89104. T: (702) 457-8700. RV/tent: 135. $$. Hookups: electric (20, 30, 50 amp), water, sewer, phone (modem).

Road Runner RV Park, 4711 Boulder Hwy., 89121. T: (702) 456-4711. RV/tent: 200. $$. Hookups: electric (30, 50 amp), water, sewer.

Sam's Town Boulder RV Park, 5225 Boulder Hwy., 89122. T: (702) 454-7777 or (800) 897-8696. RV/tent: 291. $$. Hookups: electric (20, 30, 50 amp), water, sewer, cable.

Sam's Town Nellis RV Park, 4040 South Nellis Blvd., 89121. T: (702) 456-7777 or (800) 897-8696. www.samstownlv.com/rvpark/index.cfm. RV/tent: 207. $$. Hookups: electric (20, 30, 50 amp), water, sewer, cable, phone.

Western RV Park, 1023 East Fremont, 89101. T: (702) 384-1033. RV/tent: 69. $. Hookups: electric (20, 30, 50 amp), water, sewer.

Laughlin

Avi RV Park, 10000 Aha Macave Pkwy., 89028. T: (702) 535-5555. RV/tent: 260. $$. Hookups: electric (50 amp), water, sewer, cable, phone (modem).

Lovelock

Rye Patch Reservoir State Recreation Area, 2505 Rye Patch Reservoir Rd., 89419. T: (775) 538-7321. www.parks.nv.gov/rp.htm#camp. RV/tent: 44. $. Hookups: none.

Mesquite

Casablanca RV Park, 950 West Mesquite Blvd., 89024. T: (702) 346-7529 or (800) 459-7529. www.casablancaresort.com. RV/tent: 45. $$. Hookups: electric (20, 30, 50 amp), water, sewer, cable.

Desert Skies RV Resort, 99 Peppermill Palms Dr., 89024. T: (520) 347-6000 or (800) 818-2773. RV/tent: 189. $$. Hookups: electric (20, 30, 50 amp), water, sewer, cable.

Si Redd's Oasis Resort RV Park, 897 West Mesquite Blvd, 89027. T: (702) 346-5232 or (800) 21-oasis. www.oasisresort.com. RV/tent: 91. $$. Hookups: electric (20, 30, 50 amp), water, sewer, cable.

Virgin River RV Park, I-15, Exit 122, 89027. T: (702) 346-7777 or (800) 346-7721. www.virginriver.com. RV/tent: 55. $$. Hookups: electric (20, 30 amp), water, sewer, cable.

Mina

Sunrise Valley RV Park LLC, US 95, 89422. T: (775) 573-2214. www.sunrisevalley.com. RV/tent: 26. $$. Hookups: electric (30, 50 amp), water, sewer, cable, phone.

Minden

Carson Valley Inn Hotel Casino RV Resort, 1627 US 395 North, 89423. T: (775) 782-9711 or (800) 321-6983. www.cvinn.com. RV/tent: 59. $$. Hookups: electric (20, 30, 50 amp), water, sewer, cable, phone (modem).

Silver City RV Resort, 3165 Hwy. 395, 89423. T: (775) 267-3359 or (800) 997-6393. www.silvercityrvresort.com. RV/tent: 206. $$. Hookups: electric (30, 50 amp), water, sewer, cable, phone (modem).

Overton

Robbin's Nest Mobile Village, 479 South Moapa Dr., 89040. T: (702) 397-2364. www.robbinsnest mv.com. RV/tent: 50. $$. Hookups: electric (30, 50 amp), water, sewer, phone (modem).

Pahrump

Pahrump Station RV Park, 1101 South Hwy. 160, 89048. T: (775) 727-5100. RV/tent: 90. $$. Hookups: electric (20, 30, 50 amp), water, sewer, cable, phone (modem).

Saddle West Hotel, Casino, & RV Resort, 1220 South Hwy. 160, 89048. T: (775) 727-1111 or (800) 433-3987. www.saddlewest.com. RV/tent: 80. $$. Hookups: electric (20, 30, 50 amp), water, sewer, cable.

Seven Palms RV Park, 101 South Linda St., 89048. T: (775) 727-6091. RV/tent: 59. $$. Hookups: electric (20, 30, 50 amp), water, sewer.

Terrible's Lakeside Casino & RV Resort, 5870 South Homestead Rd., 89048. T: (775) 751-7770 or (888) 558-LAKE. www.terribleherbst.com. RV/tent: 159. $$. Hookups: electric (50 amp), water, sewer, cable, phone (modem).

Primm

Primadonna RV Village, 31900 South Las Vegas Blvd., 89019. T: (702) 382-1212 or (800) 386-7867. www.primadonna.com. RV/tent: 197. $. Hookups: electric (30, 50 amp), water, sewer, cable.

Reno

Bordertown Casino RV Resort, 19575 US 395 North, 89506. T: (775) 677-0169 or (800) 218-9339. RV/tent: 50. $$. Hookups: electric (20, 30, 50 amp), water, cable, phone (modem).

Chism Trailer Park, 1300 West 2nd St., 89503. T: (775) 322-2281 or (800) 638-2281. www.chismtrailerpark.com. RV/tent: 152. $$. Hookups: electric (20, 30, 50 amp), water, sewer, cable.

Keystone RV Park, 1455 West 4th St., 89503. T: (775) 324-5000 or (800) 686-8559. RV/tent: 102. $$. Hookups: electric (20, 30, 50 amp), water, sewer, cable, phone (modem).

KOA at the Reno Hilton, 2500 East 2nd St., 89595. T: (775) 789-2147 or (888) 562-5698. RV/tent: 230. $$. Hookups: electric (30, 50 amp), water, sewer, phone (modem).

Reno RV Park, 735 Mill St., 89502. T: (775) 323-3381 or (800) 445-3381. RV/tent: 46. $$. Hookups: electric (30 amp), water, sewer, cable, phone (modem).

Shamrock RV Park, 260 Parr Blvd., 89512. T: (775) 329-5222 or (800) 322-8248. RV/tent: 121. $$. Hookups: electric (20, 30, 50 amp), water, sewer, cable, phone (modem).

Silver Sage RV Park, 2760 South Virginia St., 89502. T: (775) 829-1919 or (888) 823-2002. www.cris.com/~rvparks. RV/tent: 43. $$. Hookups: electric (30, 50 amp), water, sewer, cable, phone (modem).

Searchlight

Cree's, US 164 West 701, 89046. T: (702) 297-1532. RV/tent: 10. $. Hookups: electric (20, 30 amp), water, sewer, cable.

Smith

Walker River Resort, 1 Hudson Way, 89430. T: (775) 465-2573. RV/tent: 130. $$. Hookups: electric (30, 50 amp), water, sewer, phone (modem).

Sparks

Rivers Edge RV Park, 1405 South Rock Blvd., 89431. T: (775) 358-8533 or (800) 621-4792. RV/tent: 164. $$. Hookups: electric (30, 50 amp), water, sewer.

Victorian RV Park, 205 Nichols Blvd., 89431. T: (775) 356-6400 or (800) 955-6405. RV/tent: 92. $$. Hookups: electric (20, 30, 50 amp), water, sewer.

Spring Creek

South Fork State Recreation Area, 353 Lower South Fork #8, 89815. T: (775) 744-4346. RV/tent: 25. $. Hookups: none.

Tonopah

Twister Inn RV Park, Ketten Rd. & US 6, 89049. T: (775) 482-9444. RV/tent: 13. $. Hookups: electric (30 amp), water, sewer, cable.

Verdi

Boomtown RV Park, I-80. Exit 4, 89439. T: (775) 345-8650 or (877) 626-6686. www.boomtown casinos.com. RV/tent: 203. $$$. Hookups: electric (30, 50 amp), water, sewer, cable, phone (modem).

Gold Ranch Casino RV Park, I-80, Exit 2, 89439. T: (775) 345-6789 or (877) 914-6789. RV/tent: 105. $$. Hookups: electric (20, 30, 50 amp), water, sewer, cable, phone (modem).

Virginia City

Virginia City RV Park, 355 North F St., 89440. T: (775) 847-0999 or (800) 889-1240. www.vcrvpark.com. RV/tent: 50. $$. Hookups: electric (30, 50 amp), water, sewer, phone (modem).

Wells

Angel Creek Campground, P.O. Box 246, 89825. T: (775) 752-3357. RV/tent: 18. $. Hookups: none.

Angel Lake Campground, 140 Pacific Ave., 89825. T: (775) 752-3357 or (775) 738-5171. www.nevadaadventures.com. RV/tent: 26. $. Hookups: none.

Beverly Hills RV Ranch, I-80, Exit 348, 89835. T: (775) 752-3800. RV/tent: 44. $$$. Hookups: electric (20, 30 amp), water, sewer, phone (modem).

Crossroads RV Park, SR 40 & Shoshone, 89835. T: (775) 752-3012. RV/tent: 24. $$. Hookups: electric (30 amp), water, sewer, cable, phone.

Thomas Canyon Campground, P.O. Box 246, 89825. T: (775) 752-3357. RV/tent: 42. $$. Hookups: none.

Wendover

KOA Wendover, 651 North Camper Dr., 89883. T: (775) 664-3221 or (800) 562-8552. RV/tent: 122. $$. Hookups: electric (20, 30, 50 amp), water, sewer, cable.

Stateline RV Park, P.O. Box 789, 89883. T: (775) 664-2221 or (800) 848-7300. RV/tent: 56. $$. Hookups: electric (30, 50 amp), water, sewer.

Winnemucca

Model T Hotel/Casino/RV Park, 1130 West Winnemucca Blvd., 89445. T: (775) 623-2588. www.ModelT.com. RV/tent: 58. $$. Hookups: electric (30, 50 amp), water, sewer, phone (modem).

Westerner Trailer Lodge, 800 East 4th St., 89445. T: (775) 623-2907. RV/tent: 20. $$. Hookups: electric (30 amp), water, sewer.

Winnemucca RV Park, 5255 East Winnemucca Blvd., 89445. T: (775) 623-4458 or (877) 787-2750. RV/tent: 121. $$. Hookups: electric (30, 50 amp), water, sewer, cable, phone (modem).

Zephyr Cove

Nevada Beach Campground, Lake Tahoe Basin, 94301. T: (775) 588-5562 or (877) 444-6777. RV/tent: 54. $$. Hookups: none.

NEW HAMPSHIRE

Alton Bay
Viewland Campground, Bay Hill Rd., 03810. T: (603) 875-7100. RV/tent: 56. $$. Hookups: electric, water, sewer.

Ashland
Squam Lakes Camp Resort, RFD 1 Box 42 Rte. 3, 03217. T: (603) 968-7227. www.squamlakes resort.com. RV/tent: 119. $$. Hookups: electric (20, 30, 50 amp), water, sewer, cable.

Bath
Twin River Campground & Cottages, P.O. Box 212, 03740. T: (603) 747-3640 or (800) 811-1040. www.ucampnh.com/twinriver. RV/tent: 116. $$. Hookups: electric (20, 30, 50 amp), water, sewer, modem.

Bethlehem
Apple Hill Campground, P.O. Box 388, Rte. 142 North, 03574. T: (603) 869-2238 or (800) 284-2238. www.musar.com/applehill. RV/tent: 66. $$. Hookups: electric (20, 30 amp), water, sewer.

Snowy Mountain Campground & Motel, 1225 Main St., Rte. 302, 03574. T: (603) 444-7789. RV/tent: 40. $$. Hookups: electric (15 amp), water.

Bristol
Davidson's Countryside Campground, 100 Schofield Rd., 03222. T: (603) 744-2403. www.worldpath.net/~davcamp. RV/tent: 273. $$$. Hookups: electric (20, 30 amp), water, sewer.

Brookline
Field & Stream Park, 5 Dupaw Gould Rd., 03033. T: (603) 673-4677. www.fsttp.com. RV/tent: 40. $$. Hookups: electric (20, 30 amp), water, sewer, cable, modem.

Campton
Branch Brook Four Season Campground, P.O. Box 390, Rte. 49, 03223. T: (603) 726-7001. www.campnh.com. RV/tent: 168. $$. Hookups: electric (20, 30, 50 amp), water, sewer.

Canaan
Crescent Campsites, P.O. Box 238, 03741. T: (603) 523-9910 or (800) 494-5118. www.ucampnh .com/crescent/area.asp. RV/tent: 80. $$. Hookups: electric (20, 30 amp), water, sewer.

Center Ossipee
Deer Cap Campground, P.O. Box 332, 03814. T: (603) 539-6030. www.geocities.com/deercap/home.htm. RV/tent: 75. $$. Hookups: electric (30 amp), water, sewer.

Terrace Pines Campground, P.O. Box 98 Z, 03814. T: (603) 539-6210. www.terracepines.com. RV/tent: 65. $$$. Hookups: electric (20, 30 amp), water, sewer, cable.

Chester
Silver Sands Campground, 603 Raymond Rd., 03036. T: (603) 887-3638. RV/tent: 206. $$. Hookups: electric (30 amp), water, sewer.

Colebrook
Notch View Country Inn & RV Resort, Box 114, 03576. T: (603) 237-4237. www.notch-view.com. RV/tent: 400. $$. Hookups: electric (30 amp), water, sewer.

Conway Lake
Cove Camping Area, P.O. Box 778A, 03818. T: (603) 447-6734. www.covecamping.com. RV/tent: 155. $$. Hookups: electric (20, 30 amp), water.

Derry
Hidden Valley Campground, 81 Damren Rd., 03038. T: (603) 887-3767 or (800) 336-3107. www.hiddenvalleyrv.com. RV/tent: 72. $$. Hookups: electric (20, 30 amp), water, sewer.

Dover
Old Stage Campground, 46 Old Stage Rd., 03820. T: (603) 742-4050. RV/tent: 157. $$$. Hookups: electric (20, 30 amp), water, sewer.

Durham/Lee
Forest Glen Campground, P.O. Box 676, 03824. T: (603) 659-3416. RV/tent: 130. $$. Hookups: electric (30 amp), water, sewer, cable.

East Lempster
Tamarack Trails Campground, Dodge Hollow Rd., 03605. T: (603) 863-6443. RV/tent: 28. $$. Hookups: electric (30 amp), water, sewer.

East Wakefield
Beachwood Shores Campground, HC 66 Box 228, Bonnyman Rd., 03830. T: (603) 539-4272 or (800) 371-4282. www.ucampnh.com/beachwood shores. RV/tent: 90. $$$. Hookups: electric (20, 30 amp), water, sewer.

Lake Forest Resort, P.O. Box 713, Wolfeboro Falls, 03839. T: (603) 522-3306 or (603) 569-6186. www.lakeforestrvresort.com. RV/tent: 130. $$$. Hookups: electric (20, 30 amp), water, sewer.

Epsom
Blake's Brook Campground, 76 Mountain Rd., 03234. T: (603) 736-4793. www.blakesbrook.com. RV/tent: 68. $$. Hookups: electric (20, 30 amp), water, sewer.

Errol
Log Haven Campground, Rte. 26, Millsfield, 03579. T: (603) 482-3294. www.loghaven.com. RV/tent: 90. $$. Hookups: electric (20, 30 amp), water, sewer.

Exeter
Green Gate Camping Area, Rte. 108, 03833. T: (603) 772-2100. www.ucampnh.com/green gate. RV/tent: 109. $$. Hookups: electric (20, 30, 50 amp), water, sewer.

Fitzwilliam
Laurel Lake Campground, Laurel Lake Rd., 03447. T: (603) 585-3304. RV/tent: 65. $$. Hookups: electric (20, 30 amp), water, sewer.

Franconia
Fransted Campground, Rte. 18, 03580. T: (603) 823-5675. www.franstedcampground.com. RV/tent: 95. $$. Hookups: electric (20, 30 amp), water, sewer.

Franklin
Thousand Acres Campground, Rte. 3, Franklin, 03235. T: (603) 934-4440. www.thousandacres camp.com. RV/tent: 150. $$. Hookups: electric (20, 30 amp), water, sewer.

Glen
Green Meadow Camping Area, Rte. 16, 03838. T: (603) 383-6801. www.ucampnh.com/green meadow. RV/tent: 93. $$. Hookups: electric (15 amp), water, sewer, cable.

Hampstead
Sanborn Shore Acres Campground, Rte. 121, Box 626,, 03841. T: (603) 329-5247. RV/tent: 140. $$. Hookups: electric, water, sewer.

Sunset Park Campground, 104 Emerson Rd., 03841. T: (603) 329-6941. RV/tent: 151. $$. Hookups: electric (30 amp), water, sewer.

Hampton
Shel-Al Camping Area, Rte. 1 Box 700, 03862. T: (603) 964-5730. www.shel-al.com. RV/tent: 208. $$$. Hookups: electric (20, 30 amp), water, sewer.

Holderness
Bethel Woods Campground, Rte. 3 Box 201, 03245. T: (603) 279-6266. www.bethelwoods.com. RV/tent: 380. $$. Hookups: electric (20, 30 amp), water, sewer.

Jaffrey
Emerald Acres, 39 Ridgecrest Rd., 03452. T: (603) 532-8838. RV/tent: 52. $$. Hookups: electric (20, 30 amp), water, sewer.

Jefferson
Israel River Campground, 111 Israels River Rd., 03583. T: (603) 586-7977. RV/tent: 119. $$. Hookups: electric (30 amp), water, sewer.

Jefferson Campground, 1468 Presidential Hwy., 03583. T: (603) 586-4510. www.jeffersoncamp ground.com. RV/tent: 100. $$. Hookups: electric (20, 30 amp), water, sewer.

Kingston
Country Shore Camping Area, Rte. 125, 03865. T: (603) 642-5072. www.ucampnh.com/country shore. RV/tent: 100. $$$. Hookups: electric (20, 30, 50 amp), water, sewer.

Laconia
Hack-Ma-Tack Campground, 713 Endicott St. North, 03246. T: (603) 366-5977. www.hackmat ackcampground.com. RV/tent: 80. $$. Hookups: electric (30 amp), water, sewer.

Paugus Bay Campground, 96 Hilliard Rd., 03246. T: (603) 366-4757. www.geocities.com/weirs_ pbc. RV/tent: 173. $$$. Hookups: electric (20, 30 amp), water, sewer.

NEW HAMPSHIRE (continued)

Lancaster
Beaver Trails Campground, RR 2 Bridge St., 03584. T: (603) 788-3815 or (888) 788-3815. www.beavertrailsnh.com. RV/tent: 92. $$. Hookups: electric (20, 30, 50 amp), water, sewer, modem.

Lee
Wadleigh Falls Campground, 16 Campground Rd., 03824. T: (603) 659-1751. www.wadleighfalls.com. RV/tent: 50. $$. Hookups: electric (20, 30, 50 amp), water, sewer.

Lincoln
Country Bumpkins Campground & Cabins, Rte. 3 Box 83, 03251. T: (603) 745-8837. www.country bumpkins.com. RV/tent: 45. $$. Hookups: electric (20, 30 amp), water, sewer.

Lochmere
Silver Lake Park Campground, 389 Jamestown Rd., 03220. T: (603) 524-6289. www.onlinevacation .com/silverlake. RV/tent: 77. $$. Hookups: electric (20, 30 amp), water, sewer.

Moultonboro
Pine Woods Campground, P.O. Box 776, 03254. T: (603) 253-6251. www.pinewoods.com. RV/tent: 97. $$. Hookups: electric (20, 30, 50 amp), water, sewer.

Newport
Northstar Campground, 43 Coon Brook Rd., 03773. T: (603) 863-4001. www.northstarcamp ground.com. RV/tent: 69. $$. Hookups: electric (20, 30 amp), water, sewer.

Orford
Jacobs Brook Campground, High Bridge Rd., 03777. T: (603) 353-9210. jacobsbrook .homestead.com/home.html. RV/tent: 65. $$. Hookups: electric (20, 30 amp), water, sewer.

Pittsburg
Mountain View Cabins & Campground, RR 1 Box 30, 03592. T: (603) 538-6305. www.mountain viewcabinsandcampground.com. RV/tent: 53. $$. Hookups: electric (20 amp), water, sewer.

Plymouth
Plymouth Sands Campground, 3 Quincy Rd., 03264. T: (603) 536-2605. RV/tent: 84. $$. Hookups: electric (20 amp), water, sewer.

Rochester
Crown Point Campground, 44 First Crown Point Rd., 03867. T: (603) 332-0405. RV/tent: 135. $$$. Hookups: electric (20, 30 amp), water, sewer.

Grand View Camping Area, 51 Four Rod Rd., 03867. T: (603) 332-1263. www.grandview camping.com. RV/tent: 70. $$. Hookups: electric (20, 30 amp), water, sewer.

Rumney
Baker River Campground, 56 Campground Rd., 03266. T: (603) 786-9707. RV/tent: 40. $$. Hookups: electric (20, 30 amp), water, sewer.

Sandown
Angle Pond Grove Camping Area, P.O. Box 173, 03826. T: (603) 887-4434 or (888) 226-7436. www.anglepondgrove.com. RV/tent: 15. $$. Hookups: electric (30, 50 amp), water, sewer.

Shelburne
White Birches Camping Park, 218 State St., 03581. T: (603) 466-2022. www.gocampingamerica/ whitebirches. RV/tent: 91. $$. Hookups: electric (30 amp), water, sewer.

Tamworth
Foothills Campground, 506 Maple Rd., 03886. T: (603) 323-8322. www.thefoothills.com. RV/tent: 40. $$. Hookups: electric (20, 30 amp), water, sewer.

Thornton
Pemi River Campground, 2458 US Rte. 3, 03223. T: (603) 726-7015 or (603) 625-2879. www.pemirivercampground.com. RV/tent: 71. $$$. Hookups: electric (15, 30, 50 amp), water.

Twin Mountain
Ammonoosuc Campground, US 3, 03595. T: (603) 846-5527. www.ucampnh.com/ammonoosuc. RV/tent: 112. $$. Hookups: electric (20, 30 amp), water, sewer.

Warren
Scenic View Campground, 193AA South Main St., 03279. T: (603) 764-9380. www.scenicview nh.com. RV/tent: 98. $$. Hookups: electric (20, 30 amp), water, cable, phone, modem.

Washington
Happy Days Campground, 928 Valley Rd., 03280. T: (603) 495-0150 or (888) 293-4556. www.campingnh.com. RV/tent: 18544. $$. Hookups: electric (20, 30 amp), water, sewer.

Weare
Autumn Hills Campground, 285 South Stark Hwy., Rte. 114, 03281. T: (603) 529-2425. www.autumnhillscampground.com. RV/tent: 159. $$. Hookups: electric (20, 30 amp), water, sewer.

Webster
Cold Brook Campground, 541 Battle St. Rte. 127, 03303. T: (603) 746-3390. www.coldbrookcamp ground.com. RV/tent: 50. $$. Hookups: electric (15, 20 amp), water, sewer.

Weirs Beach
Weirs Beach Tent and Trailer Park, 198 Endicott St. North, 03246. T: (603) 366-4747. www.ucampnh.com/weirsbeach. RV/tent: 180. $$. Hookups: electric (30 amp), water, sewer.

West Milan
Nay Pond Campground, 7 Nay Pond Rd., 03588. T: (603) 449-2122. www.naypond.com. RV/tent: 33. $$. Hookups: electric (30 amp), water, sewer.

West Ossipee
Bearcamp River Campground, 330 Newman Drew Rd., 03890. T: (603) 539-4898. www.bearcamp. com. RV/tent: 112. $$. Hookups: electric (20, 30 amp), water, sewer.

Winchester
Forest Lake Campground, 331 Keene Rd., 03470. T: (603) 239-4267. www.ucampnh.com/forest lake. RV/tent: 150. $$. Hookups: electric (20, 30 amp), water, sewer.

Wolfeboro
Robie's RV Park, 139 Governor Wentworth Hwy., 03894. T: (603) 569-2732. RV/tent: 50. $$. Hookups: electric (30, 50 amp), water, sewer.

Willey Brook Campground, 883 Center St., 03894. T: (603) 569-9493. www.WilleyBrookCamp ground.com. RV/tent: 33. $$. Hookups: electric (30 amp), water, sewer.

NEW JERSEY

Andover
Columbia Valley Campground, 3 Ghost Pony Rd., 07821. T: (973) 691-0596. RV/tent: 150. $$. Hookups: electric, water, sewer.

Barnegat
Brookville Campground, 224 Jones Rd., 08005. T: (609) 698-3134. RV/tent: 100. $$. Hookups: electric (20, 30 amp), water, sewer.

Beach Haven
Long Beach Island Trailer Park, 19 Harding Ave., 08008. T: (609) 492-9151. www.lbinet.com/lbitp. RV/tent: 140. $$$$. Hookups: electric (30 amp), water, sewer.

Cape May
Cape May Mobile Homes, 755 Rte. 9, 08204. T: (609) 884-3203. www.cmmobileestates. com/trailer.htm. RV/tent: 86. $$$. Hookups: electric (20, 30 amp), water, sewer.

Lake Laurie Campground, 669 Rte. 9, 08204. T: (609) 884-3567. www.lakelaurie.com. RV/tent: 700. $$$. Hookups: electric (30, 50 amp), water, sewer.

Cape May Court House
Ponderosa Campground, 18 West Beaver Dam Rd., 08210. T: (609) 465-7794 or (866) 465-7794. www.ponderosacampground.com. RV/tent: 100. $$. Hookups: electric, water, sewer.

Shellbay Campground, Shellbay Ave., 08210. T: (609) 465-4770. RV/tent: 300. $$$. Hookups: electric (20, 30, 50 amp), water sewer.

NEW JERSEY (continued)

Clermont

Avalon Campground, 1917 North Rte. 9, 08210. T: (609) 624-0075 or (800) 814-CAMP. www.avaloncampground.com. RV/tent: 360. $$$. Hookups: electric (30 amp), water, sewer, cable.

Clinton

Spruce Run State Recreation Area, 1 Van Syckels Rd., 08809. T: (908) 638-8572. www.state.nj .us/dep/parksandforests/parks/spruce.html. RV/tent: 70. $$. Hookups: none.

Columbia

Worthington State Forest, HC 62, 07832. T: (908) 841-9575. www.state.nj.us/dep/parksandforests/ parks/worthington.html. RV/tent: 69. $$. Hookups: none.

Delaware

Delaware River Family Campground, 100 Rte. 46, 07833. T: (908) 475-4517 or (888) 543-0271. www.drfcnj.com. RV/tent: 171. $$. Hookups: electric, water, cable.

Flanders

Fla-Net-Park Campground, 23 Flanders Netcong Rd., 07836. T: (973) 347-4467. RV/tent: 100. $$. Hookups: electric (20, 30 amp), water, sewer.

Freehold

Pine Cone Campground, 340 Georgia Rd., 07728. T: (732) 462-2230. www.beachcomber.com/nj/ camping/shore/pinecone.html. RV/tent: 125. $$$. Hookups: electric (20, 30 amp), water, sewer.

Turkey Swamp/Monmouth County Park, 66 Nomoco Rd., 07728. T: (732) 462-7286. www.monmouthcountyparks.com/campsites/ family.asp. RV/tent. 64. $$. Hookups: electric (20, 30 amp), water.

Hackettstown

Stephens State Park, 800 Willow Grove St., 07840. T: (908) 852-3790. www.state.nj.us/dep/parks andforests/parks/stephens.html. RV/tent: 40. $$. Hookups: none.

High Bridge

Voorhees State Park, 251 Circle-513, 08829. T: (908) 638-6969. www.state.nj.us/dep/parks andforests/parks/voorhees.html. RV/tent: 50. $$. Hookups: none.

Highpoint

High Point State Park, Rte. 23, 07461. T: (973) 875-4800. www.state.nj.us/dep/parksandforests/ parks/highpoint.html. RV/tent: 50. $$. Hookups: none.

Hope

Jenny Jump State Forest, 330 State Park Rd., 07844. T: (908) 459-4366. www.state.nj.us/dep/parks andforests/parks/jennyjump.html. RV/tent: 22. $$. Hookups: none.

Jackson

Maple Lake Campground, 980 East Veterans Hwy., 08527. T: (732) 367-0177 or (800) 428-1202. RV/tent: 150. $$$. Hookups: electric (20, 30 amp), water, sewer.

Lebanon

Round Valley State Recreational Area, 1220 Lebanon-Stanton Rd., 08833-3115. T: (908) 236-6355. www.state.nj.us/dep/parksandforests/ parks/round.html. RV/tent: 85. $. Hookups: none.

Leektown

Union Hill Campground, 163 Chatsworth Leektown Rd., 08215. T: (609) 296-8599. www.kiz.com/camp net/html/zp/nj/0735/0735.htm. RV/tent: 25. $$. Hookups: electric, water, sewer.

Monroeville

Old Cedar Campground, 274 Richwood Rd., 08343. T: (856) 358-2406. RV/tent: 200. $$. Hookups: electric (30 amp), water, sewer.

Montague

Cedar Ridge Campground, 205 River Rd., 07827. T: (973) 293-3512 or (800) 813-8639. www.cedarridgecampground.com. RV/tent: 220. $$. Hookups: electric (20, 30 amp), water, sewer.

New Gretna

Chips Folly Family Campgrounds, P.O. Box 56, 08224. T: (609) 296-4434. www.chipsfolly.com. RV/tent: 300. $$. Hookups: electric (20, 30, 50 amp), water, sewer.

Pilgrims Lake Campground, Stage & Allen Rd., 08224. T: (609) 296-4725. RV/tent: 116. $$. Hookups: electric (30 amp), water, sewer.

New Llisbon

Brendon T. Byrne State Forest, Rte. 72, 08064. T: (609) 726-1191. www.state.nj.us/dep/parks andforests/parks/byrne.html. RV/tent: 82. $$. Hookups: none.

Newton

Swartswood State Park, P.O. Box 123, 07860. T: (973) 383-5230. www.state.nj.us/dep/parks andforests/parks/parkindex.html. RV/tent: 70. $$. Hookups: none.

Ocean View

Ocean View Tamerlane Campground, 2241 Rte. 9, 08230. T: (609) 604-0767. RV/tent: 300. $$$.

Hookups: electric (20, 30 amp), water, sewer, cable.

Parkertown

Baker's Acres Campground, 230 Willets Ave., 08087. T: (609) 296-2664 or (800) 648-2227. www.bakersacres.com. RV/tent: 300. $$. Hookups: electric, water, sewer, cable.

Pilesgrove

Four Seasons Campground, 158 Woodstown-Daretown Rd., 08098. T: (856) 769-3635 or (888) FSC-CAMP. www.fourseasonscamping.com. RV/tent: 480. $$. Hookups: electric (30, 50 amp), water, sewer.

Pomona

Evergreen Woods Lakefront Resort, P.O. Box 197, 08240. T: (609) 652-1577. RV/tent: 175. $$$. Hookups: electric (30 amp), water, sewer.

Pomona Campground, Oak Drive, 08240. T: (609) 965-2123. RV/tent: 125. $$$. Hookups: electric (30 amp), water, sewer.

Port Republic

Atlantic City Blueberry Hill Campground, 283 Clarks Landing Rd., 08241. T: (609) 652-1644 or (800) 732-2036. www.blueberryhillrvpark.com. RV/tent: 171. $$$. Hookups: electric (20, 30, 50 amp), water, sewer.

Sewell

Lake Kandle Campground, 250 Chapel Heights Rd., 08080. T: (800) 905-2653 or (856) 589-2158. RV/tent: 150. $$$. Hookups: electric, water, sewer.

Stockton

Delaware & Raritan Canal State Park, Canal Rd., 08873. T: (732) 873-3050 or (609) 397-2949. www.state.nj.us/dep/parksandforests/parks/drca nal.html. RV/tent: 75. $$. Hookups: none.

Toms River

Albocondo Campground, 1480 Whitesville Rd., 08755. T: (732) 349-4079. RV/tent: 186. $$. Hookups: electric (20, 30 amp), water, sewer.

Wall

Allaire State Park, Allaire Station Rd., 07731. T: (732) 938 2371. www.state.nj.us/dep/parks andforests/parks/allaire.html. RV/tent: 45. $$. Hookups: none.

NEW MEXICO

Alamogordo

Evergreen Park, 2200 North Florida Ave. No. 50, 88310. T: (505) 437-3721. www.gocampingamer ica.com. RV/tent: 49. $$. Hookups: electric (20, 30, 50 amp), water, sewer.

Oliver Lee Memorial State Park, 409 Dog Canyon, 88310. T: (505) 437-8284. www.nmparks.com. RV/tent: 48. $. Hookups: electric (20, 30 amp).

White Sands Community, 602 South White Sands Blvd., 88310. T: (505) 437-8388. RV/tent: 175. $$. Hookups: electric (30 amp), water, sewer.

Albuquerque

Albuquerque North/Bernalillo KOA, P.O. Box 758, 87004. T: (800) 562-3616 or (505) 867-5227. www.koa.com. RV/tent: 89. $$$. Hookups: electric (20, 30, 50 amp), water, sewer.

NEW MEXICO (continued)

Albuquerque (continued)

American RV Park of Albuquerque, 13500 Coronado Freeway SW, 87121. T: (800) 282-8885 or (505) 831-3545. www.americanrvpark.com. RV/tent: 186. $$$. Hookups: electric (30, 50 amp), water, sewer.

Balloon View RV Park, 500 Tyler Rd. NE, 87113. T: (800) 932-9523 or (505) 345-3716. RV/tent: 73. $$. Hookups: electric (30, 50 amp), water, sewer.

Best Western American Motor Inn & RV Park, 12999 Central Ave. NE, 87123. T: (505) 298-7426. RV/tent: 13. $$. Hookups: electric (30, 50 amp), water, sewer, cable.

Enchanted Trails Camping Resort, 14305 Central NW, 87121. T: (800) 326-6317. www.enchanted trails.com. RV/tent: 135. $$. Hookups: electric (30, 50 amp), water, sewer.

Palisades RV Park, 9201 Central NW, 87121. T: (888) 922-9595 or (505) 831-5000. www .palisadesrvpark.com. RV/tent: 112. $$$. Hookups: electric (30, 50 amp), water, sewer.

Alto

Elk Run Cabins & RV Park, Hwy. 48 North at Airport Rd., 88312. T: (800) 687-0620 or (505) 336-4240. www.ruidoso.net/elkrun. RV/tent: 20. $$. Hookups: electric (30, 50 amp), water, sewer, cable.

Angel Fire

Monte Verde RV Park, 3521 Hwy. 434, 87710. T: (505) 377-3404. www.aardvarkrvcom/monte verderv. RV/tent: 34. $$. Hookups: electric (30, 50 amp), water, sewer.

Anthony

El Paso West RV Park, 1415 Anthony Dr., 88021. T: (505) 882-7172 or (800) 754-1543. www1.second.com/elpasowestrvpark.htm. RV/tent: 100. $$. Hookups: electric (20, 30, 50 amp), water, sewer, cable, phone.

Arrey

Arrey RV Park, Hwy. 87, Mile Marker 19, 87930. T: (866) 267-1049 or (505) 267-1049. www.zianet.com/mmoyle. RV/tent: 10. $. Hookups: electric (20, 30, 50 amp), water, sewer.

Aztec

Ruins Road RV Park, 312 Ruins Rd., 87410. T: (505) 334-3160. RV/tent: 45. $$. Hookups: electric (30, 50 amp), water, sewer.

Bloomfield

Bloomfield KOA, 1900 East Blanco Blvd., 87413. T: (800) 562-8513 or (505) 632-8339. www.koa.com/where/NM/31156. RV/tent: 84. $$. Hookups: electric (20, 30, 50 amp), water, sewer, cable, phone.

Caballo

Caballo Lake State Park, P.O. Box 32, 87931. T: (505) 743-3942. www.emnrd.state.nm.us/ nmparks/pages/parks/caballo/caballo.htm. RV/tent: 200. $. Hookups: electric (20, 30 amp), water, sewer.

Percha Dam State Park, P.O. Box 32, 87931. T: (505) 743-3942. www.emnrd.state.nm.us/nmparks/ pages/parks/percha/percha.htm. RV/tent: 29. $. Hookups: electric (20, 30 amp).

Capitan

Mountain High RV Park, HC 71 Box 1220, 88316. T: (505) 336-4236. mthighrv.tripod.com. RV/tent: 39. $$. Hookups: electric (30, 50 amp), water, sewer, cable.

Carlsbad

Brantley Lake State Park, P.O. Box 2288, 88221. T: (505) 457-2384. www.emnrd.state.nm.us/nm parks/pages/parks/brantley/Brantley.htm. RV/tent: 51. $. Hookups: electric (20, 30 amp).

Carlsbad KOA, 2 Manthei Rd., 88220. T: (877) 457-2002 or (505) 457-2000. www.carlsbadkoa.com. RV/tent: 104. $$. Hookups: electric (30, 50 amp), water, sewer.

Cavern Estates Mobile Home & RV Park, 3022 National Parks Hwy., 88220. T: (505) 887-3274. RV/tent: 50. $$. Hookups: electric (30, 50 amp), water, sewer.

Edeal's Pecos River RV Park & Minimart, 320 East Greene St., 88220. T: (505) 885-5201. RV/tent: 16. $$. Hookups: electric (20, 30, 50 amp), water, sewer.

Windmill RV Park, 3624 National Parks Hwy., 88220. T: (888) 349-7275 or (505) 887-1387. RV/tent: 61. $$. Hookups: electric (30, 50 amp), water, sewer.

Carrizozo

Valley of Fires Recreation Area, 101 Valley of Fires Ln., 88301. T: (505) 648-2241. RV/tent: 25. $. Hookups: electric (30, 50 amp), water, sewer.

Cedar Crest

Turquoise Trail Campground & RV Park, 22 Calvary Rd., 87008. T: (505) 281-2005. RV/tent: 87. $$. Hookups: electric (20, 30, 50 amp), water, sewer.

Chama

Little Creel Resort, P.O. Box 781, 87520. T: (505) 756-2382. www.gocampingamerica.com/little creelnm/index.html. RV/tent: 64. $$. Hookups: electric (20, 30, 50 amp), water, sewer.

Twin Rivers RV Park & Campground, P.O. Box 26, 87520. T: (505) 756-2218. www.twinriverson line.net. RV/tent: 85. $$. Hookups: electric (30, 50 amp), water, sewer.

Church Rock

Red Rock State Park, Box 10, 87311. T: (505) 722-3839. www.ci.gallup.nm.us. RV/tent: 135. $. Hookups: electric (30, 50 amp), water.

Cimarron

Cimarron Inn & RV Park, 212 10th St., 87714. T: (505) 376-2268 or (800) 546-2244. www.placestostay.com. RV/tent: 12. $$. Hookups: electric (20, 30 amp), water, sewer, cable.

Cloudcroft

Apache Campground, Lincoln National Forest, SR 244, 88317. T: (505) 682-2551. www.gorp.away .com. RV/tent: 25. $. Hookups: none.

Deerhead Campground, Lincoln National Forest, SR 244, 88317. T: (505) 682-2551. www.reserveamerica.com. RV/tent: 35. $. Hookups: none.

Pine Campground, Lincoln National Forest, SR 244, 88317. T: (505) 682-2551. www.fs.red.us. RV/tent: 12. $. Hookups: none.

Silver Campground, Lincoln National Forest, SR 244, 88310-6995. T: (505) 682-2551. RV/tent: 32. $. Hookups: none.

Sleepy Grass Campground, Lincoln National Forest, FR 24B, 88310-6996. T: (505) 682-2551. RV/tent: 45. $. Hookups: none.

Clovis

Westpark Inn RV Park, 1500 West 7th St., 88101. T: (505) 763-7218. RV/tent: 18. $$. Hookups: electric (20, 30 amp), water, sewer, cable.

Conchas Dam

Conchas Lake State Park, P.O. Box 976, 88416. T: (505) 868-2270 or (877) NM-4-RSVP. www.emnrd.state.nm.us. RV/tent: 215. $. Hookups: electric (20, 30 amp), sewer.

Deming

81 Palms RV Resort, 2800 West Pine St., 88030. T: (505) 546-7434. RV/tent: 106. $$. Hookups: electric (20, 30, 50 amp), water, sewer.

A Deming Roadrunner RV Park, 2849 East Motel Dr., 88030. T: (505) 546-6960 or (800) 226-9937. www.zianet.com/roadrunnerrv. RV/tent: 109. $$. Hookups: electric (20, 30, 50 amp), water, sewer, cable.

A Little Vineyard RV Park & Resort, 2901 Motel Dr. East, 88030. T: (505) 546-3560 or (800) 413-0312. www.littlevinyardrv.com. RV/tent: 158. $$. Hookups: electric (30, 50 amp), water, sewer.

Dream Catcher Escapees RV Park, 4400 East Motel Dr., 88030. T: (505) 544-4004. www.escapees.com. RV/tent: 93. $. Hookups: electric (20, 30, 50 amp), water, sewer, cable.

Hitchin' Post RV Park, 611 West Pine St., 88030. T: (505) 546-9145. RV/tent: 40. $. Hookups: electric (30 amp), water, sewer, cable.

Rockhound State Park, P.O. Box 1064, 88030. T: (505) 546-6182 or (877) NM-4-RSVP. www.emnrd.state.nm.us. RV/tent: 36. $. Hookups: electric (20, 30 amp).

Starlight Village Resort, 2020 Hatch Hwy. NE, 88031. T: (505) 546-9550 or (888) 515-4324. www.starlightresort.com. RV/tent: 46. $$. Hookups: electric (30, 50 amp), water, sewer.

Vista Floridas RV Park, 545 O'Kelley Rd. SE, 88030. T: (505) 544-8366. RV/tent: 21. $$. Hookups: electric (20, 30, 50 amp), water, sewer.

Eagle Nest

Eagle Gem RV Park, 28418 Hwy. 64, 87718. T: (505) 377-2214 or (505) 377-0533. RV/tent: 60. $$. Hookups: electric (20, 30, 50 amp), water, sewer.

Golden Eagle RV Park, Box 458, 87718. T: (800) 388-6188 or (505) 377-6188. RV/tent: 53. $$. Hookups: electric (30, 50 amp), water, sewer.

Lost Eagle RV Park, 155 East Therma Dr., 87718. T: (800) 581-2374 or (505) 377-2374. RV/tent: 41. $$. Hookups: electric (30, 50 amp), water, sewer.

NEW MEXICO (continued)

Elephant Butte

Cozy Cove, Hwy. 195, 87935. T: (505) 476-3355 or (888) NM PARKS. RV/tent: 29. $$. Hookups: electric (20, 30, 50 amp), water, sewer.

Elephant Butte Lake State Park, P.O. Box 13, 87935. T: (505) 476-3355 or (888) NM PARKS. www.emnrd.state.nm.us. RV/tent: 250. $. Hookups: electric (20, 30 amp), sewer.

Enchanted Views RV Park, 104 Roadrunner Circle, 87935. T: (866) 672-8303. www.enchantedview rv.com. RV/tent: 37. $$. Hookups: electric (30, 50 amp), water, sewer.

Espanola

Ohkay RV Park, 2016 North Riverside Dr., 87532. T: (505) 753-5067. RV/tent: 84. $$. Hookups: electric (30, 50 amp), water, sewer.

Farmington

Dad & Ann's RV Park, 202 East Pinon, 87401. T: (505) 564-2222 or (888) 326-3237. RV/tent: 10. $$. Hookups: electric (30 amp), water, sewer, cable.

Downs Hair Salon & RV Park, 5701 Hwy. 64, 87401. T: (505) 325-7094. RV/tent: 35. $$. Hookups: electric (30, 50 amp), water, sewer, cable.

Mom & Pop RV Park, 901 Illinois Ave., 87401. T: (505) 327-3200 or (800) 748-2807. RV/tent: 36. $$. Hookups: electric (30 amp), water, sewer.

Faywood

City of Rocks State Park, P.O. Box 50, 88034. T: (505) 536-2800 or (877) NM-4-RSVP. www.emnrd.state.nm.us. RV/tent: 62. $. Hookups: electric (20, 30 amp).

Fort Sumner

Sumner Lake State Park, HC 64 Box 125, 88119. T: (505) 355-2541 or (877) NM-4-RSVP. www.emnrd.state.nm.us. RV/tent: 68. $. Hookups: electric (20, 30 amp).

Gila Hot Springs

Gila Hot Springs RV Park & Vacation Center, HC 68 Box 80 Hwy. 15, 88061. T: (505) 536-9551. RV/tent: 16. $$. Hookups: electric (30, 50 amp), water, sewer.

Grants

Blue Spruce RV Park, 1708 Zuni Canyon Rd., 87020. T: (505) 287-2560. RV/tent: 26. $$. Hookups: electric (20, 30, 50 amp), water, sewer.

Grants Cibola Sands KOA, 26 Cibola Loop, 87020. T: (505) 287-4376 or (888) 264-5229. www.koa.com. RV/tent: 44. $$. Hookups: electric (20, 30, 50 amp), water, sewer.

Valencia Village Mobile & RV Park, 1400 East Roosevelt Ave., 87020. T: (505) 287-2744. www.rvpark.com. RV/tent: 60. $$. Hookups: electric (30, 50 amp), water, sewer.

Guadalupita

Coyote Creek State Park, P.O. Box 477, 87722. T: (505) 387-2328 or (877) NM-4-RSVP. www.emnrd.state.nm.us. RV/tent: 63. $. Hookups: electric (20, 30 amp).

Morphy Lake State Park, P.O. Box 477, 87722. T: (505) 387-2328 or (877) NM-4-RSVP. www.nm parks.com. RV/tent: 60. $. Hookups: none.

Hobbs

Burnell's RV Park, 100 South Marland, 88240. T: (505) 393-3226. RV/tent: 27. $$. Hookups: electric (30, 50 amp), water, sewer.

Jim's RV Park, 615 North Marland Blvd., 88240. T: (505) 397-2551. RV/tent: 21. $$. Hookups: electric (20, 30, 50 amp), water, sewer.

Jemez Springs

Fenton Lake State Park, 455 Fenton Lake Rd., 87025. T: (505) 829-3630. www.emnrd.state .nm.us. RV/tent: 37. $. Hookups: electric (20, 30 amp).

Las Cruces

Coachlight Motel & RV Park, 301 South Motel Blvd., 88005. T: (505) 526-3301. www.zianet.com/ coachlight. RV/tent: 33. $$. Hookups: electric (30, 50 amp), water, sewer.

Dalmonts RV Trailer Corral, 2224 South Valley Drive, 88005. T: (505) 523-2992. RV/tent: 26. $$. Hookups: electric (15, 20, 30 amp), water, sewer, cable.

RV Doc's Park & Service Center, 1475 Ave. de Mesilla, 88005. T: (505) 526-8401. RV/tent: 64. $. Hookups: electric (30, 50 amp), water, sewer.

Siesta RV Park, 1551 Ave. de Mesilla, 88005. T: (800) 414-6816 or (505) 523-6816. www.siestarv park.com. RV/tent: 54. $$. Hookups: electric (30 amp), water, sewer.

Sunny Acres Mobile Village, 595 North Valley Dr., 88005. T: (877) 800-1716 or (505) 534-1716. www.zianet.com/sunnyacres. RV/tent: 24. $$$. Hookups: electric (30, 50 amp), water, sewer.

Las Vegas

Las Vegas KOA, HC 31 Box 16, 87701. T: (800) 562-3423 or (505) 454-0180. www.koa.com. RV/tent: 60. $$. Hookups: electric (20, 30 amp), water, sewer.

Storrie Lake State Park, HC 33 Box 109 No. 2, 87701. T: (505) 425-7278. www.emnrd.state. nm.us. RV/tent: 112. $. Hookups: electric (20, 30 amp).

Vegas RV Park, 504 Harris Rd., 87701. T: (505) 425-5640. RV/tent: 33. $$. Hookups: electric (30 amp), water, sewer.

Westward Ho RV Park, 857 Airport Rd., 87701. T: (505) 425-6978. www.members.tripod .com/~dukesrv. RV/tent: 20. $$. Hookups: electric (30, 50 amp), water, sewer.

Los Alamos

Bandelier National Monument, H.CR 1 Box 1, 87544. T: (505) 672-3861. www.nps.gov/band. RV/tent: 93. $$. Hookups: none.

Los Ojos

Heron Lake State Park, P.O. Box 159, 87511. T: (505) 588-7470. www.emnrd.state.nm.us. RV/tent: 400. $. Hookups: electric (20, 30 amp).

Magdalena

Western Motel & RV Park, 404 1st St., 87825. T: (505) 854-2417. RV/tent: 12. $$. Hookups: electric (20, 30, 50 amp), water, sewer.

Mesilla

Hacienda RV Resort, 740 Stern Drive, 88046. T: (888) 686-9090 or (505) 528-5800. www. haciendarv.com. RV/tent: 113. $$$. Hookups: electric (30, 50 amp), water, sewer, cable.

Milan

Bar S RV Park, 1860 Pinon Drive, 87021. T: (505) 876-6002. RV/tent: 60. $$. Hookups: electric (20, 30, 50 amp), water, sewer.

Moriarty

Zia RV Park & Campground, 740 East Abraham, 87035. T: (505) 832-9796. RV/tent: 58. $$. Hookups: electric (30, 50 amp), water, sewer.

Navajo Dam

Navajo Lake State Park, 1448 NM 511 No. 1, 87419. T: (505) 632-2278. www.emnrd.state.nm.us/ nmparks/pages/parks/navajo/navajo.htm. RV/tent: 451. $. Hookups: electric (20, 30 amp).

Pena Blanca

Cochiti Lake, 82 Dam Crest Rd., 87041. T: (505) 465-0307. RV/tent: 60. $. Hookups: electric (20, 30 amp).

Tetilla Peak, 82 Dam Crest Rd., 87041. T: (505) 465-0307. RV/tent: 52. $. Hookups: electric (20, 30 amp).

Penasco

Santa Barbara Campground, Carson National Forest, Hwy. 73, 87571. T: (505) 758-6200. www.fs.fed.us/r3/carson/html_main/list_ camping2.html. RV/tent: 22. $. Hookups: none.

Portales

Oasis State Park, 1891 Oasis Rd., 88130. T: (505) 356-5331. RV/tent: 23. $. Hookups: electric (20, 30 amp).

Radium Springs

Leasburg Dam State Park, P.O. Box 6, 88054. T: (505) 524-4068. www.emnrd.state.nm.us/ nmparks/pages/parks/leasburg/leasburg.htm. RV/tent: 54. $. Hookups: electric (20, 30 amp).

Ranchos de Taos

Taos RV Park, 1798 Pasea Del Pueblo Sur, Hwy. 68, 87557. T: (800) 323-6009 or (505) 758-1667. RV/tent: 33. $$. Hookups: electric (20, 30 amp), water, sewer.

Raton

Kickback RV Park, 1025 Frontage Rd., 87740. T: (505) 445-1200. RV/tent: 35. $$. Hookups: electric (30, 50 amp), water, sewer, cable.

KOA Raton, 1330 South 2nd St., 87740. T: (800) 562-9033 or (505) 445-3488. www.koakamp grounds.com/where/nm/. RV/tent: 54. $$. Hookups: electric (20, 30, 50 amp), water, sewer.

NEW MEXICO (continued)

Raton (continued)

Sugarite Canyon State Park, H.CR 63 Box 386, 87740. T: (505) 445-5607. www.emnrd.state.nm.us. RV/tent: 40. $. Hookups: electric (20, 30 amp), water.

Red River

River Ranch, Box 69, 87558. T: (505) 754-2293. www.redrivernm.com. RV/tent: 31. $$. Hookups: electric (30, 50 amp), water, sewer.

Red River Canyon

Columbine Campground, Carson National Forest, Hwy. 38, 87571. T: (505) 758-6200. www.fs.fed.us/r3/carson/html_main/list_camping2.html. RV/tent: 27. $. Hookups: none.

Fawn Lakes Campground, Carson National Forest, Hwy. 38, 87571. T: (505) 758-6200. www.fs.fed.us/r3/carson/html_main/list_camping2.html. RV/tent: 18. $. Hookups: none.

Junebug Campground, Carson National Forest, Hwy. 38, 87571. T: (505) 758-6200. www.fs.fed.us/r3/carson/html_main/list_camping2.html. RV/tent: 22. $. Hookups: none.

Rio Grande Gorge

BLM Orilla Verde, Carson National Forest, SR 570, 87571. T: (505) 758-6200. www.fs.fed.us/r3/carson/html_main/list_camping2.html. RV/tent: 23. $. Hookups: none.

Rio Pueblo

Comales Campground, Carson National Forest, US 64, 87571. T: (505) 758-6200. www.fs.fed.us/r3/carson/html_main/list_camping2.html. RV/tent: 13. $. Hookups: none.

Duran Canyon Campground, Carson National Forest, USFS.76, 87571. T: (505) 758-6200. www.fs.fed.us/r3/carson/html_main/list_camping2.html. RV/tent: 12. $. Hookups: none.

La Junta Campground, Carson National Forest, USFS 76, 87571. T: (505) 758-6200. www.fs.fed.us/r3/carson/html_main/list_camping2.html. RV/tent: 30. $. Hookups: none.

Rio Rancho

Stagecoach Stop RV Resort, 3650 Hwy. 528, 87124. T: (888) 272-PARK. RV/tent: 85. $$. Hookups: electric (30, 50 amp), water, sewer, cable.

Rociada

Pendaries RV Park, P.O. Box 697, 87742. T: (800) 820-8304 or (505) 454-8304. www.pendariesrv park.com. RV/tent: 30. $$. Hookups: electric (20, 30, 50 amp), water, sewer.

Rodeo

Mountain Valley Lodge, Hwy. 80, 88056. T: (505) 557-2267. RV/tent: 6. $. Hookups: electric (30, 50 amp), water, sewer.

Roswell

Bottomless Lakes State Park, HC 12 Box 1200, 88201. T: (505) 624-6058. www.emnrd.State.nm .us/nmparks. RV/tent: 62. $. Hookups: electric (20, 30 amp).

Town & Country RV Park, 331 West Brasher Rd., 88203. T: (800) 499-4364 or (505) 624-1833.

www.roswell-usa.com/tandcrv. RV/tent: 75. $$. Hookups: electric (30, 50 amp), water, sewer, cable.

Ruidoso

Alto Hombre Gordito, Hwy. 37, 88341. T: (877) 466-2734 or (505) 336 7877. www.hombre gordito.com. RV/tent: 20. $$. Hookups: electric (20, 30, 50 amp), water, sewer.

Blue Spruce RV Park, 302 Mechem Drive, 88345. T: (505) 257-7993. RV/tent: 23. $$. Hookups: electric (30 amp), water, sewer.

Bonito Hollow RV Park, Hwy. 37, Alto, 88312. T: (505) 336-4325. www.bonitohollow.com. RV/tent: 71. $$. Hookups: electric (20, 30, 50 amp), water, sewer.

Pine Ridge RV Campground, 124 Glade Dr., 88345. T: (505) 378-4164. www.ruidoso.net/pineridge. RV/tent: 75. $$. Hookups: electric (30, 50 amp), water, sewer.

Twin Spruce RV Park, 621 Hwy. 70 West, 88345. T: (505) 257-4310. RV/tent: 111. $$. Hookups: electric (20, 30, 50 amp), water, sewer, cable.

Ruidoso Downs

Circle B RV Park, Box 1800, 88346. T: (505) 378-4990. RV/tent: 202. $$. Hookups: electric (20, 30, 50 amp), water, sewer.

Seeping Springs Trout Lakes & Campground, P.O. Box 997, 88346. T: (505) 378-4216. RV/tent: 50. $$. Hookups: electric (30 amp), water, sewer, cable.

Santa Fe

Hyde Memorial State Park, 740 Hyde Park Rd., 87501. T: (505) 983-7175. www.emnrd.state.nm .us/nmparks/pages/parks/hyde/hyde.htm. RV/tent: 50. $. Hookups: electric (20, 30 amp).

KOA Santa Fe, 934 Old Las Vegas Hwy., 87505. T: (800) 562-1514 or (505) 466-1419. www.koakampgrounds.com. RV/tent: 51. $$. Hookups: electric (30, 50 amp), water, sewer.

Los Campos de Santa Fe RV Park, 3574 Cerrillos Rd., 87505. T: (800) 852-8160 or (505) 473-1949. RV/tent: 95. $$. Hookups: electric (30, 50 amp), water, sewer.

Rancheros de Santa Fe Campground, 736 Old Las Vegas Hwy., 87505. T: (800) 426-9259 or (505) 466-3482. www.rancheros.com. RV/tent: 121. $$$. Hookups: electric (15, 20, 30, 50 amp), water, sewer.

Trailer Ranch RV Park, 3471 Cerrillos Rd., 87505. T: (505) 471-9970. www.trailerranch.com. RV/tent: 42. $$. Hookups: electric (30, 50 amp), water, sewer.

Santa Rosa

KOA Santa Rosa, Box 423, 88435. T: (800) 562-0836 or (505) 472-3126. www.koa.com/where/NM/31143. RV/tent: 100. $$. Hookups: electric (20, 30, 50 amp), water, sewer.

Santa Rosa Lake State Park, P.O. Box 384, 88433. T: (505) 472-3110. www.emnrd.state.nm.us/nm parks/pages/parks/santa/Santa.htm. RV/tent: 90. $. Hookups: electric (20, 30 amp).

Seneca

Clayton Lake State Park, 141 Clayton Lake Rd., 88437. T: (505) 374-8808. www.nmparks.com. RV/tent: 33. $. Hookups: electric (20, 30 amp).

Silver City

Cedar Ridge RV Park & Campground, 2789 South Hwy. 90, 88061. T: (505) 388-4013. RV/tent: 15. $. Hookups: electric (20, 30 amp), water, sewer.

Silver City KOA, 11824 Hwy. 180 East, 88061. T: (800) 562-7623 or (505) 388-3351. www.koa.com. RV/tent: 77. $$. Hookups: electric (20, 30, 50 amp), water, sewer.

Socorro

Casey's Socorro RV Park, 1101 State Rd. SW, 87801. T: (800) 687-2696 or (505) 835-2234. RV/tent: 103. $$. Hookups: electric (30 amp), water, sewer, cable.

Taos

Enchanted Moon RV Park, 7 Valle Escondido Rd., 87571. T: (505) 758-3338. www.emooncamp ground.com. RV/tent: 69. $$. Hookups: electric (20, 30, 50 amp), water, sewer.

Taos Valley RV Park & Campground, 120 Estes Rd., 87571. T: (800) 999-7571 or (505) 758-4469. www.camptaos.com/rv. RV/tent: 92. $$. Hookups: electric (20, 30, 50 amp), water, sewer.

Taos Canyon

Capulin Campground, Carson National Forest, US 64, 87571. T: (505) 758-6200. www.fs.fed.us/r3/carson/html_main/list_camping2.html. RV/tent: 11. $. Hookups: none.

La Sombra Campground, Carson National Forest, US 64, 87571. T: (505) 758-6200. www.fs.fed.us/r3/carson/html_main/list_camping2.html. RV/tent: 13. $. Hookups: none.

Las Petacas Campground, Carson National Forest, US 64, 87571. T: (505) 758-6200. www.fs.fed.us/r3/carson/html_main/list_camping2.html. RV/tent: 9. $. Hookups: none.

Tierra Amarilla

El Vado Lake State Park, P.O. Box 367, 87575. T: (505) 588-7247. www.emnrd.state.nm.us/nmparks/pages/parks/elvado/elvado.htm. RV/tent: 80. $. Hookups: electric (20, 30 amp).

Tijeras

Hidden Valley Resort, 844B Hwy. 66 East, 87059. T: (800) 326-2024 or (505) 281-3363. RV/tent: 102. $$. Hookups: electric (30, 50 amp), water, sewer.

Mountain View Campground & RV Park, 768 Hwy. 66 East, 87059. T: (888) 284-2343 or (505) 281-2343. RV/tent: 24. $$. Hookups: electric (30 amp), water, sewer.

Truth or Consequences

Cielo Vista RV Park, 501 South Broadway, 97901. T: (888) 414-8478 or (505) 894-3738. RV/tent: 72. $$. Hookups: electric (30, 50 amp), water, sewer, cable.

RJ RV Park, 2103 South Broadway, 87901. T: (505) 894-9777. RV/tent: 47. $$. Hookups: electric (30, 50 amp), water, sewer.

NEW MEXICO (continued)

Tucumcari

Tucumcari KOA, 6299 Quay Rd., 88401. T: (800) 562-1871 or (505) 461-1841. www.koa.com. RV/tent: 111. $$. Hookups: electric (20, 30, 50 amp), water, sewer, cable.

Tularosa

Mountain Meadow RV Park, 240 Mountain Meadow, 88352. T: (505) 585-4979. RV/tent: 20. $$. Hookups: electric (30 amp), water, sewer.

Valle Vidal

Cimmarron Campground, Carson National Forest, Hwy. 522, 87571. T: (505) 758-6200. www.fs.fed.us/r3/carson/html_main/list_camping2.html. RV/tent: 36. $. Hookups: none.

McCrystal Campground, Carson National Forest, Hwy. 64, 87571. T: (505) 758-6200. www.fs.fed.us/r3/carson/html_main/list_camping2.html. RV/tent: 60. $. Hookups: none.

Villanueva

Villanueva State Park, P.O. Box 40, 87504. T: (505) 421-2957. www.emnrd.state.nm.us/nmparks/pages/parks/villanue/villanue.htm. RV/tent: 60. $. Hookups: electric (20, 30 amp).

Williamsburg

Shady Corner RV Park, Broadway & Rio Grande, 87942. T: (505) 894-7698. RV/tent: 6. $. Hookups: electric (30, 50 amp), water, sewer.

NEW YORK

Accord

So-Hi Campground, 425 Woodland Rd., 12404. T: (845) 687-7377. www.reserveamerica.com. RV/tent: 130. $$. Hookups: electric (20, 30 amp), water, sewer.

Acra

Whip-O-Will Campsite, CR 31, 12473-0327. T: (518) 622-3277 or (800) WOW-CAMP. RV/tent: 304. $$. Hookups: electric (20, 30, 50 amp), water, sewer.

Addison

Sunflower Acres Family Campground, 8355 Tinkertown Rd., 14801. T: (607) 523-7756. RV/tent: 91. $$. Hookups: electric (20, 30, 50 amp), water, sewer.

Akron

Sleepy Hollow Lake Campground, 13800 Siehl Rd., 14001. T: (716) 542-4336 or (866) 542-4336. www.sleepyhollowlakecabins.com. RV/tent: 200. $$. Hookups: electric (20, 30, 50 amp), water.

Altamont

Thompson's Lake State Park, 68 Thompson's Lake Rd., 12059. T: (518) 872-1674. www.reserveamerica.com. RV/tent: 140. $$. Hookups: none.

Angelica

Evergreen Trails Campground, Allegany CR 15, 14709. T: (585) 466-7993. www.evergreentrails.com. RV/tent: 25. $$. Hookups: electric (20, 30 amp), water.

Ausable

Holiday Travel Park, 428 Rte. 373, 12944. T: (518) 834-9216. www.adirondackcampgrounds.com. RV/tent: 48. $$. Hookups: electric (20, 30 amp), water, sewer.

Bainbridge

Oquaga Creek State Park, 5995 County Hwy. 20, 13733. T: (607) 467-4160. www.nysparks.state.ny.us. RV/tent: 95. $$. Hookups: none.

Riverside RV Camping, 1303 CR 39, 13733. T: (607) 967-2102. RV/tent: 14. $$. Hookups: electric (20, 30 amp), water, sewer.

Bath

Babcock Hollow Campground, 5932 Babcock Hollow Rd., 14910. T: (607) 776-7185. www.campingnavigator.com. RV/tent: 93. $$. Hookups: electric (20, 30 amp), water, sewer.

Campers Haven

Campers Haven, 6832 Cr-15 Knight Settlement Rd., 14910. T: (607) 776-0328. www.campershavenllc.com. RV/tent: 136. $$. Hookups: electric (15, 20), water, sewer.

Bear Mountain

Harriman State Park, Palisades Interstate, 10911. T: (845) 786-2701 or (800) 456-2267. www.nysparks.com. RV/tent: 200. $$. Hookups: none.

Bemus Point

Wildwood Acres, 506 Brown Rd., 14712. T: (716) 386-7037. RV/tent: 88. $$. Hookups: electric (20, 30, 50 amp), water, sewer.

Blossvale

Ta-Ga-Soke Campgrounds, 7820 Higginsville Rd., 13308. T: (800) 831-1744. www.ta-ga-soke.com. RV/tent: 150. $$. Hookups: electric (15, 20, 50 amp), water.

Bluff Point

Wigwam Keuka Lake Campground, 3324 Esperanza Rd., 14478. T: (315) 536-6352. www.wigwamkeukalakecampground.com. RV/tent: 63. $$. Hookups: electric (30 amp), water.

Bolton Landing

Scenic View Campground, Rte. 9 North, 12814. T: (518) 644-2115. RV/tent: 100. $$. Hookups: electric (20, 30 amp), water.

Boonville

Pixley Falls State Park, 11430 NY 46, 13309. T: (315) 942-4713 or (800) 456-CAMP. www.nysparks.state.ny.us. RV/tent: 22. $$. Hookups: none.

Cambridge

Battenkill Sports Quarters/Campground, 937 State Rte. 313, 12816. T: (518) 677-8868 or (800) 676-8768. RV/tent: 60. $. Hookups: electric (15 amp), water.

Canandaigua

Bristol Woodlands Campground, 4835 South Hill Rd., 14424. T: (585) 229-2290. www.bristolwoodlands.com. RV/tent: 86. $$. Hookups: electric (30 amp), water, sewer.

Creek Side Campground, 2528 Wheeler Station Rd., 14469-9326. T: (585) 657-7746. RV/tent: 40. $$. Hookups: electric (20, 30 amp), water, sewer.

Candor

Buckridge Nudist Park, 215 Turtle Hill Rd., 13743. T: (607) 659-3868 or (888) 231-3268. www.buckridge-park.com. RV/tent: 40. $$$. Hookups: electric (20 amp), water.

Cape Vincent

Burnham Point State Park, 34075 State Rte. 12e, 13618. T: (315) 654-2522. www.nysparks.com. RV/tent: 49. $$. Hookups: electric.

Caroga Lake

Caroga Lake Campgrounds, Rte. 29A, 12032. T: (518) 835-4241 or (800) 456-CAMP. www.reserveamerica.com. RV/tent: 161. $$. Hookups: none.

Cazenovia

Chittenango Falls State Park, 2300 Rathbun Rd., 13035. T: (315) 655-9620. www.nysparks.com. RV/tent: 23. $$. Hookups: none.

Central Bridge

Hide-A-Way Campsites, 107 Janice Ln., 12035. T: (518) 868-0075. RV/tent: 50. $$. Hookups: electric (20, 30, 50 amp), water.

Locust Park Campground, Box 225, 12035. T: (518) 668-9927. RV/tent: 32. $$. Hookups: electric (20, 30 amp), water, sewer.

Chateaugay

High Falls Park Campground, 34 Cemetery Rd., 12920. T: (518) 497-3156 or (518) 483-7299. www.highfallspark.com. RV/tent: 240. $$. Hookups: electric (20, 30, 50 amp), water, sewer.

Chestertown

Rancho Pines, 2794 Schroon River Rd., 12817. T: (518) 494-3645. www.ranchopines.com. RV/tent: 54. $$. Hookups: electric (20, 30 amp), water, sewer, cable.

Riverside Pines Campsites, 1 Carl Turner Rd., 12817. T: (518) 494-2280. RV/tent: 72. $$. Hookups: electric (20, 30 amp), water, sewer.

Clayton

Cedar Point State Park, 36661 Cedar Point Dr, 13624. T: (315) 654-2522. www.nysparks.com. RV/tent: 175. $$. Hookups: electric, water, sewer.

Riverside Acres Campground & Motel, 38447 NY 12E, 13624. T: (315) 686-4001. RV/tent: 72. $$. Hookups: electric (20, 30 amp), water, sewer.

NEW YORK (continued)

Cohocton

Tumble Hill Campground, 10551 Atlanta Back Rd., 14826. T: (585) 384-5248. www.tumblehill.com. RV/tent: 40. $$. Hookups: electric (15, 20, 30 amp), water, sewer.

Conesus

Conesus Lake Campground, 5609 East Lake Rd., 14435. T: (585) 346-5472. www.gocamping america.com/conesuslake. RV/tent: 100. $$. Hookups: electric (15, 20 amp), water.

Cooperstown

Cooperstown Famous Family Tent & Trailer Campground, 230 Petkewec Rd., 13326. T: (607) 293-7766 or (800) 959-2267. RV/tent: 100. $$. Hookups: electric (30, 50 amp), water, sewer.

Cooperstown Ringwood Farms Campground, 7489 NY 80, 13326. T: (607) 547-2896 or (800) 231-9114. www.ringwood.com. RV/tent: 95. $$. Hookups: electric (20, 30 amp), water, sewer.

Glimmerglass State Park, 1527 County Hwy. 31, 13326. T: (607) 547-8662 or (800) 456-CAMP. www.nysparks.state.ny.us/parks. RV/tent: 36. $$. Hookups: none.

Copake Falls

Copake Falls Area (Taconic State Park), 253 Rte. 344, 12517. T: (518) 329-3993. www.reserve america.com. RV/tent: 112. $$. Hookups: none.

Corinth

River Road Campground, 5254 Rte. 9 North, 12822. T: (518) 654-6630 or (518) 654-9995. www.theriverroad.com. RV/tent: 80. $$$. Hookups: electric (20, 30 amp), water, sewer.

Rustic Barn Campsites, 4748 NY Rte. 9 North, 12822. T: (518) 654-6588. www.rusticbarn camping.com. RV/tent: 55. $$. Hookups: electric (20, 30 amp), water.

Cortland

Yellow Lantern Kampground, 1770 NY 13 North, 13045. T: (607) 756-2959. www.usagetaways .com/newyork/yellowlantern. RV/tent: 250. $$. Hookups: electric (20, 30 amp), water, sewer.

Cuba

Uncle Bo's RV Park, 5239 Maple Ln., 14727. T: (585) 968-1677. RV/tent: 34. $$. Hookups: electric (30, 50 amp), water, cable.

Cuddebackville

Oakland Valley Campground, 399 Oakland Valley Rd., 12729. T: (845) 754-8732 or (800) 832-2254. www.oaklandvalleycampground.com. RV/tent: 110. $$. Hookups: electric (15, 30 amp), water, cable.

Cutchogue

Cliff & Ed's Trailer Park, 395 Schoolhouse Rd., 11935. T: (631) 298-4091. RV/tent: 23. $$. Hookups: electric (30, 50 amp), water, sewer.

Dansville

Skybrook Campground, 10861 McCurdy Rd., 14437. T: (585) 335-6880. www.skybrookcamp ground.com. RV/tent: 500. $$. Hookups: electric (15, 20, 30 amp), water, sewer.

Stony Brook State Park, 10820 Rte. 36 South, 14437. T: (585) 335-8111. www.reserveamerica .com. RV/tent: 125. $$. Hookups: electric (15, 20 amp), water, sewer.

Delevan

Arrowhead Camping Area, 10487 Rte. 16, 14042. T: (716) 492-3715. www.arrowheadcamping.com. RV/tent: 200. $$. Hookups: electric (20, 30 amp), water.

Downsville

Catskill Mountain Kampground, Rte. 30, 13755. T: (607) 363-2599. RV/tent: 100. $$. Hookups: electric (15, 20, 30 amp), water, sewer.

Delaware Valley Campsite, Rte. 30, 13755. T: (607) 363-2306. RV/tent: 88. $$. Hookups: electric (15, 20 amp), water, sewer.

East Islap

Heckscher State Park, Heckscher Pkwy. Parkng Field No. 1, 11730. T: (631) 581-2100. www.nys parks.state.ny.us. RV/tent: 69. $. Hookups: none.

Elizaville

Brook–Wood Family Campground, CR 8, 12523. T: (518) 537-6896 or (888) 588-8622. www.brooknwood.com. RV/tent: 150. $$. Hookups: electric (15, 30, 50 amp), water, sewer.

Findley Lake

Paradise Bay Park, 2360 Shady Side Rd., 14736. T: (716) 769-7582. RV/tent: 100. $$. Hookups: electric (15, 20, 30, 50 amp), water.

Forestport

Kayuta Lake Campground, 10892 Campground Rd., 13338. T: (315) 831-5077. RV/tent: 148. $$. Hookups: electric (20, 30, 50 amp), water, sewer.

Fort Ann

Fort Ann Campground, Clay Hill Rd., 12827. T: (518) 639-8840. RV/tent: 50. $$. Hookups: electric (15, 20, 30 amp), water, sewer.

Frankfort

Elmtree Estates, 2842 St. Rte. 5, 13340. T: (315) 724-6678. www.gocampingamerica.com. RV/tent: 36. $$. Hookups: electric (20, 30, 50 amp), water, sewer, cable.

Franklinville

Memory Lake Campground, 3900 Jarecki Rd., 14737. T: (716) 676-2776. RV/tent: 150. $$. Hookups: electric (30, 50 amp), water, sewer.

Gainesville

Woodstream Campsites, 5440 School Rd., 14066. T: (585) 493-5643 or (877) CAMPNOW. RV/tent: 200. $$. Hookups: electric (15, 20, 30, 50 amp), water.

Galway

McConchies Heritage Acres, 2501 Northline Rd., 12074. T: (518) 882-6605. www.gocamping america.com/mcconchies. RV/tent: 190. $$. Hookups: electric (15, 20, 30 amp), water.

Pop's Lake Campground, 518 Centerline Rd., 12074. T: (518) 883-8678.

www.saratoga.org/membersites/popslake. RV/tent: 80. $$. Hookups: electric (15, 20 amp), water, sewer.

Gilboa

Nickerson Park Campground, 378 Stryker Rd., 12076. T: (607) 588-7327 or (860) 455-0007. www.nickersonpark.com. RV/tent: 100. $$. Hookups: electric (15, 20, 30 amp), water, sewer.

Glenville

Arrowhead Marina & RV Park, 2 Van Buren Ln., 12302. T: (518) 382-8966. RV/tent: 64. $$. Hookups: electric (20, 30 amp), water, sewer.

Godeffroy

American Family Campground, 110 Guymard Turnpike, 12739. T: (845) 754-8388 or (800) CAMP-AFC. www.americanfamilycampground.com. RV/tent: 147. $$$. Hookups: electric (20, 30 amp), water, sewer.

Haines Falls

North/South Lake Campground, North Lake Rd., 12436. T: (518) 589-5058. www.reserveamerica .com. RV/tent: 219. $$. Hookups: none.

Hammond

McLear Cottage Colony & Campground, 2477 CR 6, 13646. T: (315) 375-6508. www.mclears.com. RV/tent: 40. $$. Hookups: electric (15, 20, 30 amp), water, sewer.

Harpursville

Belden Hill Campground, 1843 Rte. 7, 13787. T: (607) 693-1645. www.beldenrvpark.com. RV/tent: 142. $$. Hookups: electric (20, 30 amp), water, sewer.

Henderson Harbor

Association Island RV Resort & Marina, 15530 Snowshoe Rd., 13651. T: (315) 938-5887. www.associationislandresort.com. RV/tent: 307. $$$. Hookups: electric (20, 30, 50 amp), water, sewer, cable.

Himrod

Back-Achers Campsite, 3112 Rte. 14, 14842. T: (607) 243-7926. www.linkny.com. RV/tent: 40. $$. Hookups: electric (30 amp), water.

Hubbardsville

Canaan Campground, 8108 Green Rd., 13355. T: (315) 691-2005. RV/tent: 41. $$. Hookups: electric (30 amp), water, sewer.

Hudson

Lake Taghkanic State Park, 1528 State Rte. 82, 12502-5103. T: (518) 851-3631. www.nysparks.com. RV/tent: 30. $$. Hookups: none.

Indian Lake

Lewey Public Campground, Rte. 30, 12864. T: (518) 648-5266 or (800) 456-CAMP. www.reserveamerica.com. RV/tent: 209. $$. Hookups: none.

NEW YORK (continued)

Inlet

Limekiln Lake, Rte. 28, 13360. T: (315) 357-4401.
RV/tent: 271. $$. Hookups: none.

Jamestown

Hidden Valley Camping Area, 299 Kiantone Rd.,
14701. T: (716) 569-5433. www.hiddenvalley
campingarea.com. RV/tent: 215. $$. Hookups:
electric (20, 30 amp), water.

Johnstown

Royal Mountain Campsite, 4948 Hwy. 29, 12095.
T: (518) 762-1946. www.rvparksusa.com.
RV/tent: 65. $. Hookups: electric (15, 20 amp),
water.

Kennedy

Forest Haven Campground, 2329 Page Rd., 14747.
T: (716) 267-5902. RV/tent: 102. $. Hookups:
electric (20, 30 amp), water, sewer.

Keuka

Keuka Lake State Park, 3370 Pepper Rd., 14478.
T: (315) 536-3666. RV/tent: 150. $$. Hookups:
electric, water.

Lake George

King Phillips Family Campsite, Bloody Pond Rd.,
12845. T: (518) 668-5763. RV/tent: 16. $$$.
Hookups: electric (20, 30 amp), water, sewer.

Lake George Battleground Campground, Box 220,
12885. T: (518) 668-3348 or (518) 623-1200.
www.dec.state.ny.us. RV/tent: 68. $$. Hookups:
none.

Mt. Kenyon Family Campground, 1571 Lake Ave.,
12845. T: (518) 696-2905. www.mtkenyon.com.
RV/tent: 110. $$. Hookups: electric (15, 20 amp),
water, sewer.

Rainbow View Family Campground, 3652 State Rte.
9, 12845. T: (863) 424-8362. www.rvdestinations.
com. RV/tent: 200. $$$. Hookups: electric (30
amp), water, sewer.

Whippoorwill Campground, Rte. 9, 12845. T: (518)
668-5565. www.campwhippoorwill.com.
RV/tent: 45. $$. Hookups: electric (20, 30 amp),
water, sewer.

Lake Luzerne

Lake Luzerne State Park, Rte. 9N Lake Ave., 12846.
T: (518) 696-2031. RV/tent: 174. $$. Hookups:
none.

Lake Placid

Whispering Pines Campground, Cascade Rd., Rte.
73, 12946. T: (518) 523-9322 or (800) 437-9322.
RV/tent: 80. $$. Hookups: electric (15, 20 amp),
water, sewer.

Laurens

Gilbert Lake State Park, 18 Ccc Rd., 13796. T: (607)
432-2114. RV/tent: 221. $$. Hookups: electric.

Lewis

Magic Pines Family Campground, HCR 1, Box 411,
12950. T: (518) 873-2288. RV/tent: 37. $$.
Hookups: electric (20, 30 amp), water, sewer.

Lockport

Niagara County Camping Resort, 7369 Wheeler
Rd., 14094. T: (716) 434-3991. www.nycamp
grounds.com. RV/tent: 210. $$. Hookups:
electric (30, 50 amp), water, sewer.

Long Lake

Lake Eaton Campground, Rte. 30, 12847. T: (518)
624-2641. RV/tent: 135. $. Hookups: none.

Lowville

Whetstone Gulf State Park, RD 2, Box 69, 13367.
T: (315) 376-6630. www.nysparks.com. RV/tent:
56. $$. Hookups: none.

Marathon

Country Hills Campground, 1165 Muckey Rd.,
13803. T: (607) 849-3300. www.country
hillscampground.com. RV/tent: 68. $$. Hookups:
electric (20, 30, 50 amp), water, sewer.

Memphis

Sunset Park Campground, 455 Sprague Rd., 13112.
T: (315) 635-6450. RV/tent: 233. $$. Hookups:
electric (20 amp), water.

Mexico

KOA Mexico Campground, 291 Tubbs Rd., 13114.
T: (315) 963-3509. RV/tent: 75. $$. Hookups:
electric (20, 30, 50 amp), water, sewer.

Middlesex

Flint Creek Campgrounds, 1455 Phelps Rd., 14507.
T: (585) 554-3567 or (800) 914-3550. www.flint
creekcampground.com. RV/tent: 109. $$.
Hookups: electric (20, 30 amp), water, sewer.

Montauk

Hither Hill State Park, 50 South Fairview Ave.,
11754. T: (613) 668-2554. RV/tent: 165. $$.
Hookups: none.

Montezuma

Hejamada Campground & RV Park, 748 McDonald
Rd., 13117. T: (315) 776-5887. www.hejamada
campground.com. RV/tent: 200. $$. Hookups:
electric (20, 30, 50 amp), water, sewer.

Montgomery

Winding Hills Park, Rte. 17K, 12549. T: (845) 457-
4918. RV/tent: 51. $. Hookups: electric (15 amp),
water.

Moravia

Fillmore Glen State Park, 1686 St. Rte. 38, 13118.
T: (315) 497-0130. RV/tent: 60. $$. Hookups:
none.

Morristown

Jacques Cartier State Park, River Rd., 13664.
T: (315) 375-6371. www.nysparks.com. RV/tent:
122. $$. Hookups: electric.

Morrisville

Cedar Valley Campsites, South Butler Rd., 13408.
T: (315) 684-3033. RV/tent: 55. $$. Hookups:
electric (30 amp), water, sewer.

Nassau

Dingmans Family Campground, R.D. 2 Box 459,
12123. T: (518) 766-2310. RV/tent: 60. $$.
Hookups: electric (20, 30 amp), water.

Niagara Falls

Cinderella Campsite & Motel, 2797 Grand Island
Blvd., 14072. T: (716) 773-4095. RV/tent: 75. $$$.
Hookups: electric (15, 30, 50 amp), water, sewer.

Niagara Falls Campground & Motel, 2405 Niagara
Falls Blvd., 14304. T: (716) 731-3434.
www.nfcamping.com. RV/tent: 65. $$. Hookups:
electric (15, 20, 30 amp), water, sewer.

Nineveh

Kellystone Park Campsite, 51 Hawkins Rd., 13813.
T: (607) 639-1090. www.keystonepark.com.
RV/tent: 95. $$. Hookups: electric (15, 20, 30
amp), water, sewer.

North Hudson

Sharp Bridge Campground, 4390 US Rte. 9, 12855.
T: (518) 532-7538. www.dec.state.ny.us. RV/tent:
40. $. Hookups: none.

North Java

Rolling Pines Campground & Resort, 5204
Youngers Rd., 14113. T: (716) 457-9644 or
(800) 232-4039. RV/tent: 200. $$. Hookups:
electric (15, 20, 30 amp), water, sewer.

Odessa

Cool-Lea Camps, SR 228, 14869. T: (607) 594-
3500. www.coolleacamp.com. RV/tent: 35. $$.
Hookups: electric, water.

Ogdensburg

Eel Weir State Park, Rd. # 3, 13669. T: (315) 393-
1138. RV/tent: 35. $$. Hookups: none.

KOA Thousand Islands, 4707 Hwy. 37, 13669.
T: (315) 393-3951. RV/tent: 100. $$. Hookups:
electric (15, 20, 30 amp), water, sewer.

Old Forge

Singing Waters Campground, Box 411, 13420.
T: (315) 369-6618. www.singingwaterscamp
.com. RV/tent: 132. $$. Hookups: electric (15, 20
amp), water, sewer.

Onchiota

Buck Pond, HCR 1, Box 9A, 12968. T: (518) 891-
3449. RV/tent: 116. $$. Hookups: none.

Oneonta

Susquehanna Trail Campsites, 4292 St. Hwy. 7,
13820. T: (607) 432-1122. www.gocamping
america.com. RV/tent: 40. $$. Hookups: electric
(15, 30 amp), water, sewer.

Oswego

Sunset RV Park, 45 CR 89, 13126. T: (315) 343-
2166. RV/tent: 38. $$. Hookups: electric (15, 30
amp), water, sewer.

Ovid

Ridgewood Campground, 6590 South Cayuga Lake
Rd., 14521. T: (607) 869-9787. www.ridgewoods
campgrounds.com. RV/tent: 84. $$. Hookups:
electric (20, 30 amp), water, sewer.

NEW YORK (continued)

Palenville
Pine Hollow Campground, 28 Madison Ave., 12463. T: (518) 678-2245 or (518) 678-5507. www.the catskills.com/pinehollow.htm. RV/tent: 31. $$. Hookups: electric (20, 30, 50 amp), water.

Paradox
Paradox Lake Campground, 897 Rte. 74, 12858. T: (518) 532-7451. www.reserveamerica.com. RV/tent: 58. $. Hookups: none.

Peru
Ausable Pines Campground, 3281 Lakeshore Rd., 12972. T: (518) 561-1188. www.ausablepines campground.com. RV/tent: 130. $$. Hookups: electric (30 amp), water, sewer, cable.

Ausable Point Campground, 3346 Lakeshore Rd., 12972. T: (518) 561-7080. RV/tent: 80. $$. Hookups: electric.

Iroquois RV & Campground, 270 Bear Swamp Rd., 12972. T: (578) 643-9057. RV/tent: 170. $$. Hookups: electric (20, 30 amp), water, sewer.

Petersburgh
Acqua Vista Valley Campground, 82 Armsby Rd., 12138. T: (518) 658-3559 or (877) 646-0653. www.fortunecity.com/business/wrigley/256. RV/tent: 156. $$. Hookups: electric (50 amp), water.

Broken Wheel Campground, 61 Broken Wheel Rd., 12138. T: (518) 658-2925. www.brokenwheel campground.com. RV/tent: 75. $$. Hookups: electric (15, 20 amp), water.

Phelps
Junius Ponds Cabins & Campground, 1475 West Townline Rd., 14532. T: (315) 781-5120. RV/tent: 119. $$. Hookups: electric (20, 30, 50 amp), water, sewer.

Pike
Rolling Acres Golf & Campground, 7795 Dewitt Rd., 14130. T: (585) 567-5240. RV/tent: 85. $$. Hookups: electric (20, 30 amp), water.

Plattsburgh
Plattsburgh RV Park, 7182 Rte. 9, 12901. T: (518) 563-3915. www.plattsburghrvpark.com. RV/tent: 170. $$. Hookups: electric (20, 30 amp), water, sewer.

Shady Oaks RV Park, 70 Moffit Rd., 12901. T: (518) 566-9265 or (888) 329-0899. www.shadyacres park.com. RV/tent: 94. $$. Hookups: electric (20, 30 amp), water.

Port Kent
Port Kent Campsite, 93 Port Kent Rd., 12975. T: (518) 834-9011. www.port-kent-campsite.com. RV/tent: 127. $$. Hookups: electric (20, 30 amp), water, sewer.

Pottersville
Ideal Campground, 115 Valley Farm Rd., 12860. T: (518) 494-2096. RV/tent: 68. $$. Hookups: electric (20, 30 amp), water, sewer.

Wakonda Family Campground, 3901 East Schroon River Rd., 12860. T: (518) 494-2610. www .wakondacampground.com. RV/tent: 134. $$$. Hookups: electric (20, 30 amp), water, sewer.

Prattsburgh
Wagon Wheel Campground, 10378 Presler Rd., 14873. T: (607) 522-3270. www.wagonwheel camp.com. RV/tent: 95. $$. Hookups: electric (30, 50 amp), water.

Pulaski
Bear's Sleepy Hollow RV Park, 7065 SR-3, 13142. T: (315) 298-5560. www.sleepyhollowfamily campground.com. RV/tent: 65. $$. Hookups: electric (20, 30 amp), water, sewer.

Rainbow Shores Campsite, 348 Rainbow Shores Rd., 13142. T: (315) 298-4407. www.pulaskiny. com. RV/tent: 200. $$. Hookups: electric (20, 30, 50 amp), water, sewer.

Randolph
JJ's Pope Haven, 11948 Pope Rd., 14772. T: (716) 358-4900. www.whresorts.com. RV/tent: 100. $$. Hookups: electric (30, 50 amp), water.

Raquette Lake
Brown Tract Pond Campground, Raquette Lake, 13436. T: (315) 354-4412. RV/tent: 90. $. Hookups: none.

Golden Beach, Raquette Lake, 13436. T: (315) 354-4230. RV/tent: 205. $$. Hookups: none.

Ray Brook
Meadowbrook Campground, Rte. 86, 12977. T: (518) 891-4351. RV/tent: 62. $. Hookups: none.

Rhinebeck
Interlake RV Park, 428 Lake Dr., 12572. T: (845) 266-5387. www.interlakervpark.com. RV/tent: 159. $$. Hookups: electric (20, 30 amp), water, sewer, cable.

Ripley
Lakeside Campground, 10768 West Lake Rd., 14775. T: (716) 736-3362 or (800) 669-5404. RV/tent: 90. $$. Hookups: electric (30, 50 amp), sewer.

Rome
Delta Lake State Park, 8797 State Rte. 46, 13440. T: (315) 337-4670. RV/tent: 101. $$. Hookups: none.

Romulus
Sampson State Park, 6096 Rte. 96A, 14541. T: (315) 585-6392 or (800) 456-CAMP. www.nysparks .com. RV/tent: 309. $$. Hookups: electric.

Roscoe
Beaverkill Campground, RR 3 Box 243, 12776. T: (845) 439-4281. RV/tent: 108. $$. Hookups: none.

Sackets Harbor
Allen's Boat Livery & Campground, 16750 Allen Dr, 13685. T: (315) 646-2486. RV/tent: 155. $$. Hookups: electric (15, 20, 30 amp), water, sewer.

Wescott Beach State Park, Sackets Harbor, 13685. T: (315) 646-2239. www.nysparks.com. RV/tent: 69. $$. Hookups: electric.

Salamanca
Allegany State Park (Quaker Area), 2373 Rte. 1, 14779. T: (716) 354-2182. RV/tent: 189. $$. Hookups: electric (20 amp).

Allegany State Park (Redhouse Cabins), 2373 Asp Rte. 1, 14779. T: (716) 354-9121. RV/tent: 300. $$$. Hookups: electric.

Saranac
Baker's Acres Campground, Rte. 3, P.O. Box 115, 12981. T: (518) 293-6471. RV/tent: 50. $$. Hookups: electric (15 amp), water, sewer.

Saranac Lake
Rollins Pond Campground, SR Box 75, 12983. T: (518) 891-3239. www.dec.state.ny.us. RV/tent: 287. $$. Hookups: none.

Savannah
Oak Orchard Marina & Campground, Rte. 89 at Mays Point, 13148. T: (315) 365-3000. www.oakorchard.com. RV/tent: 34. $$. Hookups: electric (15, 20, 30 amp), water, sewer.

Schuyler Falls
Macomb Reservation State Park, 201 Campsite Rd., 12985. T: (518) 643-9952. www.reserve america.com. RV/tent: 173. $$. Hookups: none.

Schuylerville
Schuyler Yacht & Campground, 1 Ferry St., 12871. T: (518) 695-3193. www.saratoga.com. RV/tent: 25. $$. Hookups: electric (15, 20 amp), water, sewer.

Seneca Falls
Cayuga Lake Campground, 2546 State Rte. 89, 13148. T: (315) 568-0919. RV/tent: 72. $$. Hookups: electric (15, 20 amp), water, sewer.

Cayuga Lake State Park, 2678 Lower Lake Rd., 13148. T: (315) 568-5163. www.reserve america.com. RV/tent: 36. $$. Hookups: electric.

Smithtown
Blydenburgh, Suffolk County Parks Box 144, 11796. T: (631) 853-4966 or (631) 854-4945. RV/tent: 50. $$. Hookups: none.

Sodus Point
South Shore RV Park, 7867 Lake Rd., 14555. T: (315) 483-8649. www.southshorervpark.com. RV/tent: 50. $$. Hookups: electric (20, 30 amp), water, sewer.

South Colton
Higley Flow State Park, 442 Cold Brook Drive, 13625. T: (315) 262-2880. www.reserve america.com. RV/tent: 135. $$. Hookups: electric.

Springwater
Holiday Hill Campground, 7818 Marvin Hill Rd., 14560. T: (585) 669-2600 or (800) 719-2267. www.holidayhillcampground.com. RV/tent: 170. $$. Hookups: electric (20, 30 amp), water.

NEW YORK (continued)

Swan Lake

Swan Lake Campground, Fulton Rd., 12783. T: (800) 733-0604 or (845) 292-4781. RV/tent: 170. $$$. Hookups: electric (30 amp), water, sewer, cable.

Sylvan Beach

The Landing Campground, 2796 Kellogg Rd., 13157. T: (315) 245-9951 or (800) 318-1318. RV/tent: 94. $$. Hookups: electric (15, 20, 30 amp), water, sewer, phone, cable.

Syracuse

Foland Trailer Park, 407 North Midler Ave., 13206. T: (315) 463-1892. RV/tent: 10. $$. Hookups: electric (15, 20, 30 amp), water, sewer.

Ticonderoga

Putnam Pond Campsite, 763 Patts Pond Rd., 12883. T: (518) 585-7280. www.reserve america.com. RV/tent: 63. $. Hookups: none.

Unadilla

KOA Unadilla/I-88 Campground, R.D. 1 Box 186, 13775. T: (607) 369-9030 or (800) KOA-9032. www.koakampgrounds.com. RV/tent: 72. $$$. Hookups: electric (20, 30, 50 amp), water.

Verona

Peaceful Pines Campground & RV Park, 6591 Blackman's Corner Rd., 13478. T: (315) 336-7318 or (800) 562-7218. www.turning stone.com. RV/tent: 38. $$$. Hookups: electric (15, 20, 30, 50 amp), water, sewer.

Wadding River

Wildwood State Park, Hulse Landing Rd., 11792. T: (631) 929-4314. www.reserveamerica.com. RV/tent: 320. $$. Hookups: electric (15 amp), water, sewer.

Warrensburg

Daggett Lake Campsites, 660 Glen Athol Rd., 12885. T: (518) 623-2198. www.daggettlake.com. RV/tent: 60. $$. Hookups: electric (20 amp), water, sewer.

Glen Hudson Campsite, 172 River Rd., 12885. T: (518) 623-9871. RV/tent: 100. $$. Hookups: electric (15, 20, 30, 50 amp), water, sewer.

Warrensburg Travel Park, P.O. Box 277, 12885. T: (518) 623-9833. www.warrensburgtravel park.com. RV/tent: 130. $$. Hookups: electric (15, 20 amp), water, sewer, cable.

Warsaw

Dream Lake Campground, 4391 Old Buffalo Rd., 14569. T: (585) 786-5172. www.wanttogo.com. RV/tent: 100. $$. Hookups: electric (15, 20, 30 amp), water, sewer.

Waterloo

Welcome Traveler Campground, 672 Packwood Rd., 13165. T: (315) 789-2102. RV/tent: 20. $$. Hookups: electric (20, 30 amp), water.

Watertown

Kelly RV Park, 24949 Eastern Blvd., 13601. T: (315) 782-1451. RV/tent: 17. $$. Hookups: electric (30 amp), water, sewer.

Weedsport

Riverforest Park Campground, 2526 Riverforest Rd., 13166. T: (315) 834-9458. www.gocamping america.com. RV/tent: 250. $$. Hookups: electric (20, 30 amp), water, phone.

Wellsville

Breezy Point Campsite, 2749 Wolf Spring Rd., 14880. T: (716) 593-3085. ww.wnybiz.com. RV/tent: 192. $$. Hookups: electric (20, 30 amp), water, sewer.

Westfield

Brookside Beach Campground, P.O. Box 130, 14787. T: (716) 326-3096. RV/tent: 70. $$. Hookups: electric (30, 50 amp), water.

Westport

Barber Homestead Campground, 68 Barber Ln., 12993. T: (518) 962-8989. www.barberhome steadpark.com. RV/tent: 40. $$. Hookups: electric (20, 30, 50 amp), water, sewer.

Windham

White Birches Campsites, Princess Nauvoo Rd., 12496. T: (518) 734-3266 or (239) 567-0195. RV/tent: 130. $$. Hookups: electric (15, 20 amp), water.

Windsor

Pine Crest Campground, 280 NY 79, 13865. T: (607) 655-1515. www.gocamping america.com. RV/tent: 104. $$. Hookups: electric (15 amp), water, sewer.

Wolcott

Cherry Grove Campground, 12669 Ridge Rd. East, 14590. T: (315) 594-8320. www.lakeontario.net. RV/tent: 90. $$. Hookups: electric (20, 30 amp), water, sewer.

Lake Bluff Campground, 7150 Garner Rd., 14590. T: (315) 587-4517 or (888) 588-4517. www.gocampingamerica.com. RV/tent: 127. $$. Hookups: electric (20, 30 amp), water, sewer.

Woodridge

Lazy "G" Campground, P.O. Box 563, 12789. T: (845) 434-3390. www.lazyg.com. RV/tent: 70. $$. Hookups: electric (20, 30 amp), water, sewer.

Woodville

Southwick State Park, 8119 Southwick Pl., 13650. T: (315) 938-5083. www.reserveamerica.com. RV/tent: 112. $$. Hookups: electric.

Youngstown

Niagara Frontier State Park, 1 Maintenance Ave., 14174. T: (716) 745-7273. RV/tent: 266. $$. Hookups: electric (15 amp).

NORTH CAROLINA

Almond

Turkey Creek Campground, 135 Turkey Creek Rd., 28702. T: (828) 488-8966. www.turkey-creek .com. RV/tent: 70. $$. Hookups: electric (20 amp), water.

Apex

Jordan Lake State Recreation Area (Parkers Creek), 280 State Park Rd., 27523. T: (919) 362-0586. www.ils.unc.edu/parkproject/ncparks. RV/tent: 250. $. Hookups: electric (20, 30 amp), water.

Jordan Lake State Recreation Area (Vista Point), 280 State Park Rd., 27523. T: (919) 362-0586. www.ils.unc.edu/parkproject/ncparks. RV/tent: 50. $. Hookups: electric (20, 30 amp), water.

Ararat

Homeplace Recreational Park, 119 Waterloo Ln., 27007. T: (336) 374-5173. www.wanttogo.com. RV/tent: 160. $$. Hookups: electric (30, 50 amp), water.

Asheboro

Deep River Campground & RV Park, 814 McDowell Country Trail, 27203. T: (336) 629-4069. www.kiz.com/deepriver. RV/tent: 62. $$. Hookups: electric (20, 30, 50 amp), water.

Holly Bluff Family Campground, 4846 NC Hwy. 49 South, 27203. T: (336) 857-2761. RV/tent: 85. $$. Hookups: electric (15, 20, 30, 50 amp), water.

Zooland Family Campground, 3671 Pisgah–Covered Bridge Rd., 27205. T: (336) 381-3422. RV/tent: 100. $$. Hookups: electric (20, 30 amp), water.

Asheville

Asheville–Bear Creek RV Park, 81 South Bear Creek Rd., 28806. T: (828) 253-0798 or (800) 833-0798. www.ashevillebearcreek.com. RV/tent: 100. $$. Hookups: electric (15, 20, 30, 50 amp), water.

Campfire Lodgings, 7 Appalachian Village Rd., 28804. T: (828) 658-8012 or (800) 933-8012. www.campfirelodgings.com. RV/tent: 21. $$. Hookups: electric (20, 30, 50 amp), water.

Taps RV Park, 1327 Tunnel Rd., 28805. T: (828) 299-8277. RV/tent: 52. $$. Hookups: electric (15, 20, 30, 50 amp), water.

The French Broad River Campground, 1030 Old Marshall Hwy., 28804. T: (828) 658-0772. RV/tent: 53. $$. Hookups: electric, water.

NORTH CAROLINA (continued)

Atlantic Beach

Arrowhead Campground, 1550 Salter Path Rd., 28512. T: (252) 247-3838. www.nccoast.com/ virtual/arrowhead/arrowhead.htm. RV/tent: 180. $$. Hookups: electric (20, 30 amp), water, sewer, cable.

Salter Path Family Campground, 1620 Salter Path Rd., 28512-2323. T: (252) 247-3525. www.salter pathcamping.com. RV/tent: 205. $$. Hookups: electric (20, 30 amp), water.

Avon

Sands of Time Campground, 125 North End Rd., 27915. T: (252) 995-5596. www.sandsoftime campground.com. RV/tent: 57. $$. Hookups: electric (20, 30, 50 amp), water, sewer.

Bat Cave

Creekside Mountain Camping, P.O. Box 251, 28710. T: (828) 625-4257. www.creekside camping.com. RV/tent: 121. $$. Hookups: electric (15, 20, 30 amp), water, sewer.

Boone

Appalachian Campground, 339 Ray Brown Rd., 28607. T: (828) 264-4505. RV/tent: 75. $$. Hookups: electric (20, 30 amp), water.

Flintlock Family Campground, 171 Flintlock Campground Dr., 28607. T: (828) 963-5325 or (888) 850-9997. www.rvnetlinx.com. RV/tent: 95. $$. Hookups: electric (15, 20, 30, 50 amp), water.

Grandfather Mountain Campground, 125 Riverside Drive, 28604. T: (828) 963-7275 or (800) 788-2582. www.grandfatherrv.com. RV/tent: 149. $$. Hookups: electric (20, 30, 50 amp), water, cable.

KOA Boone, 123 Harmony Mtn Ln., 28607. T: (828) 264-7250 or (800) 562-2806. RV/tent: 108. $$. Hookups: electric (15, 20, 30, 50 amp), water.

Waterwheel RV Park, 1655 Jefferson Rd., 28607. T: (828) 264-5165. RV/tent: 25. $$. Hookups: electric (15, 30 amp), water.

Boonville

Holly Ridge Family Campground, 5140 River Rd., 27011. T: (336) 367-7756. RV/tent: 62. $$. Hookups: electric (20, 30, 50 amp), water.

Bryson City

Deep Creek Tube Center & Campground, 1090 West Deep Creek Rd., 28713. T: (828) 488-6055. RV/tent: 38. $$. Hookups: electric (20, 30 amp), water.

Smoky Mountain Meadows Family Campground, 755 East Alarka Rd., 28713. T: (828) 488-3672. RV/tent: 53. $. Hookups: electric (15, 30 amp), water, sewer.

Burnsville

Black Mountain Campground, Pisgah National Forest, USFS 472, 28714. T: (877) 444-6777. www.cs.unca.edu/nfsnc. RV/tent: 48. $$. Hookups: none.

Candler

KOA Asheville West, 309 Wiggins Rd., 28715. T: (828) 665-7015. www.koa.com. RV/tent: 78. $$. Hookups: electric (20, 30, 50 amp), water.

Canton

Riverside Campground, 6 Happy Camper Drive, 28716. T: (828) 235-9128. RV/tent: 86. $$. Hookups: electric (15, 30 amp), water, sewer.

Cedar Island

Driftwood Campground, 3575 Cedar Island Rd., 28520. T: (252) 225-4861. www.clis.com/deg. RV/tent: 65. $$. Hookups: electric (15, 20, 30 amp), water, sewer.

Cedar Mountain

Black Forest Family Camping Resort, Summer Rd., Rte. 276, 28718. T: (828) 884-2267. www.black forestcampground.com. RV/tent: 90. $$. Hookups: electric (30, 50 amp), water.

Charlotte

Elmore Mobile Home Park, 4826 North Tryon St., 28213. T: (704) 597-1323. RV/tent: 25. $$. Hookups: electric (15, 20, 30, 50 amp), water, sewer.

Cherokee

Adventure Trail Campground, P.O. Box 1673, 28719. T: (828) 497-3651. RV/tent: 90. $$. Hookups: electric (15, 20, 30 amp), water, sewer.

Bradley's Campground, P.O. Box 88, 28719. T: (828) 497-6051. RV/tent: 42. $$. Hookups: electric (15, 20, 30 amp), water, sewer.

Cherokee Campground, P.O. Box 516, 28719. T: (828) 497-9838. www.cherokeekoa.com. RV/tent: 70. $$. Hookups: electric (15, 20, 30 amp), water, sewer.

Flaming Arrow Campground, US 441 South, 28719. T: (877) 497-6161. www.flamingarrowcamp ground.com. RV/tent: 85. $$. Hookups: electric (20, 30, 50 amp), water, sewer.

Fort Wilderness Campground and RV Resort, P.O. Box 1657, 28719. T: (828) 497-9331. www.fortwilderness.net. RV/tent: 120. $$. Hookups: electric (15, 30, 50 amp), water, sewer.

Great Smoky Mountain RV Camping Resort, 17 Old Soco Rd., 28789. T: (828) 497-2470. RV/tent: 251. $$. Hookups: electric (20, 30 amp), water, sewer.

Indian Creek Campground, 1367 Bunches Creek Rd., 28719. T: (828) 497-4361. www.indiancreek campground.com. RV/tent: 70. $$. Hookups: electric (15 amp), water, sewer.

River Valley Campground, P.O. Box 471, 28719. T: (828) 497-3540. www.mountainshops .com/rvc.html. RV/tent: 200. $$. Hookups: electric (20, 30, 50 amp), water, sewer.

Chimney Rock

Lake Lure RV Park & Campground, 176 Boys Camp Rd., 28746. T: (828) 625-9160. www.lakelurervpark.net. RV/tent: 70. $$$. Hookups: electric (15, 30 amp), water, sewer.

Chocowinity

Twin Lakes Camping Resort & Yacht Basin, 1618 Memory Ln., 27817. T: (252) 946-5700. www.twinlakesnc.com. RV/tent: 379. $$. Hookups: electric (20, 30, 50 amp), water.

Whichard's Beach Campground, 3670 Whichard's Beach Rd., 27817. T: (252) 946-0011. www.whichardsbeach.com. RV/tent: 118. $$. Hookups: electric (20, 30, 50 amp), water.

Coinjock

Hampton Lodge Camping Resort, 1631 Waterlily Rd., 27923. T: (252) 453-2732. RV/tent: 268. $$. Hookups: electric (20, 30 amp), water, sewer.

Columbus

Silver Creek Campground, 410 Silver Creek Rd., 28756. T: (800) 510-1603. www.camptheusa.com/ nc/silvercreek. RV/tent: 62. $$. Hookups: electric (20, 30 amp), water, sewer.

Concord

Fleetwood RV Racing Camping Resort, 6550 Speedway Blvd., 28027. T: (704) 455-4445. www.gospeedway.com. RV/tent: 254. $$. Hookups: electric, water, sewer.

Elizabethtown

Jones Lake State Park, 113 Jones Lake Dr., 28337. T: (910) 588-4550. www.ils.unc.edu/parkproject/ ncparks.html. RV/tent: 20. $. Hookups: none.

Emerald Isle

Miles Motors RV Center & Campground, 15 Patton Cove Rd., 28778. T: (828) 686-3414. RV/tent: 61. $$. Hookups: electric (20, 30, 50 amp), water, cable.

Waterway RV Park, P.O. Box 4847, 28594. T: (252) 393-8715. www.members.aol.com/jsh63/lavon/ index.htm. RV/tent: 245. $$. Hookups: electric (30, 50 amp), water.

Enfield

KOA Enfield/Rocky Mtn., 101 Bell Acres, 27823. T: (252) 445-5925. RV/tent: 78. $$. Hookups: electric (15, 20, 30 amp), water, sewer.

Fayetteville

Fayetteville Spring Valley Park, 4504 US 301 South, 28348. T: (910) 425-1505. www.visitfayette villenc.com. RV/tent: 36. $$. Hookups: electric (20, 30 amp), water.

Fletcher

Rutledge Lake Travel Park, 170 Rutledge Rd., 28732. T: (828) 654-7873. www.campingnorth carolina.com. RV/tent: 75. $$. Hookups: electric (20, 30, 50 amp), water, sewer.

Fontana Village

Cable Cove Campground, Nantahala National Forest, FR 520, 28721. T: (828) 479-6431. www.main.nc.us/graham/hiking/cablecov.html. RV/tent: 26. $. Hookups: none.

Fort Mill

KOA Charlotte/Fort Mill, 940 Gold Hill Rd., 29708. T: (803) 548-1148 or (888) 562-4430. www.koakampgrounds.com. RV/tent: 209. $$$. Hookups: electric (20, 30, 50 amp), water.

NORTH CAROLINA (continued)

Franklin

Carolina Village RV Resort, 20 Carolina Village Cir., 28734. T: (828) 369-5858 or (888) 818-5228. RV/tent: 16. $$. Hookups: electric (20, 30, 50 amp), water.

Cartoogechaye Creek Campground, 91 No Name Rd., 28734. T: (828) 524-8553 or (800) 880-2267. www.franklin-chamber.com/cartoogechaye/index.html. RV/tent: 103. $$. Hookups: electric (30 amp), water.

Franklin RV Park, 145 Addington Bridge Rd., 28734. T: (828) 369-5841 or (877) 370-8787. www.franklinrvpark.com. RV/tent: 25. $$. Hookups: electric (20, 30 amp), water.

Mi Mountain Campground, 151 Mi Mountain Rd., 28734. T: (828) 524-6155 or (800) 441-6155. www.members.aol.com/mimtn1. RV/tent: 48. $$. Hookups: electric (15, 30 amp), water.

Old Corundum Mill Campground, 80–33 Nickajack Rd., 28734. T: (828) 524-4663. www.travel.to/oldcorundum. RV/tent: 86. $$. Hookups: electric (20, 30 amp), water.

Rainbow Springs Campground, 7984 West Old Murphy Rd., 28734. T: (828) 524-6376. www.dnet.net/rainbowsprings. RV/tent: 51. $$. Hookups: electric (15, 30 amp), water.

Frisco

Frisco Woods Campground, Cape Hatteras National Seashore, Hwy. 12, 27936. T: (252) 995-5208 or (800) 948-3942. www.outer-banks.com/friscowoods. RV/tent: 225. $$. Hookups: electric (15, 20, 30 amp), water, sewer, cable.

Gatesville

Merchants Millpond State Park, 71 US 158 East, 27938. T: (252) 357-1191. www.ils.unc.edu/parkproject/vlslt/memi/home.html. RV/tent: 20. $. Hookups: none.

Gatlinburg

Balsam Mountain (Cherokee, NC), Blue Ridge Parkway between Mile Markers 458 and 459 on Balsam Mountain Rd., 37738. T: (423) 436-1200. www.nps.gov/grsm/pphtml/camping.html. RV/tent: 46. $$. Hookups: none.

Glendale Springs

Raccoon Holler Campground, 493 Raccoon Holler Rd., 28629. T: (336) 982-2706. www.raccoonholler.com. RV/tent: 179. $$. Hookups: electric (20, 30 amp), water.

Grandy

Yogi Bear's Jellystone/Currituck Resort Shores, 6671 Caratoke Hwy., 27939. T: (252) 453-226. RV/tent: 138. $$$. Hookups: electric (20, 30, 50 amp), water.

Greensboro

Fields RV Campground, 2317 Campground Rd., 27406. T: (336) 292-1381. RV/tent: 29. $$. Hookups: electric (20, 30 amp), water.

Greensboro Campground, 1896 Trox St., 27406. T: (336) 274-4143 or (877) 274-4143. www.greensborocampground.com. RV/tent: 117. $$. Hookups: electric (20, 30, 50 amp), water.

Hatteras

Hatteras Sands Camping Resort, P.O. Box 295, 27943. T: (252) 986-2422 or (888) 987-2225. www.hatterassands.com. RV/tent: 124. $$$. Hookups: electric (15, 20, 30, 50 amp), water.

Hayesville

Ho Hum Campground, 47 Ho Hum Loop, 28904. T: (828) 389-6740. RV/tent: 87. $$. Hookups: electric (15, 20, 30 amp), water.

Tusquittee Campground & Cabins, 9594 Tusquittee Rd., 28904. T: (828) 389-8520. www.geocities.com/tusquitteecampground. RV/tent: 18. $$. Hookups: electric (15, 20, 30 amp), water.

Henderson

Bullocksville, Kerr Lake State Recreation Area, 6254 Satterwhite Point Rd., 27536. T: (252) 438-7791. www.ils.unc.edu/parkproject/visit/kela/home.html. RV/tent: 69. $. Hookups: electric (30 amp), water.

Henderson Point, Kerr Lake State Recreation Area, 6254 Satterwhite Point Rd., 27536. T: (252) 438-7791. www.ils.unc.edu/parkproject/visit/kela/home.html. RV/tent: 79. $. Hookups: electric (30 amp), water.

Nutbush Bridge, Kerr Lake State Recreation Area, 6254 Satterwhite Point Rd., 27536. T: (252) 438-7791. www.ils.unc.edu/parkproject/visit/kela/home.html. RV/tent: 103. $. Hookups: electric (30 amp), water.

Park Place RV Park, 501 South Allen Rd., 28731. T: (828) 693-3831. www.parkplacervpark.com. RV/tent: 48. $$. Hookups: electric (20, 30, 50 amp), water.

Phil & Ann's RV, 818 Tracy Grove Rd., 28731-9618. T: (828) 696-9089 or (800) 753-8373. www.mdt-bof.org/members/botnick_phil-ann/botnick_phil-ann.htm. RV/tent: 31. $. Hookups: electric (15, 30 amp), water.

Satterwhite Point, Kerr Lake State Recreation Area, 269 Glasshouse Rd., 27536. T: (252) 438-7791. www.ils.unc.edu/parkproject/visit/kela/home.html. RV/tent: 118. $. Hookups: electric (30 amp), water.

Town Mountain Travel Park, 2030 Old Spartanburg Rd., 28792. T: (828) 697-6692. www.townmountaintravelpark.com. RV/tent: 26. $$. Hookups: electric (20, 30, 50 amp), water.

Hendersonville

Apple Valley Travel Park, 1 Apple Orchard Rd., 28792. T: (828) 685-8000. RV/tent: 94. $$. Hookups: electric (30 amp), water.

Lazy Boy Travel Park, 110 Old Sunset Hill Rd., 28792. T: (828) 697-7165. RV/tent: 83. $$. Hookups: electric (20, 30, 50 amp), water.

Red Gates RV Park, 314 Sugarloaf Rd., 28792. T: (828) 685-8787. www.cojoweb.com/red-gates-rv-park.html. RV/tent: 18. $$. Hookups: electric (30, 50 amp), water.

Highlands

Highlands RV Park, 651 Chestnut St., 28741. T: (828) 526-5985. RV/tent: 6. $$$$. Hookups: electric (20, 30, 50 amp), water.

Hot Springs

Hot Springs RV Park & Campground, P.O. Box 428, 28743. T: (828) 622-7676. RV/tent: 110. $$. Hookups: electric (15, 20, 30 amp), water.

Rocky Bluff Campground, Pisgah National Forest, Hwy. 209, 28743. T: (828) 622-3202. www.cs.unca.edu/nfsnc/recreation/RockyBluff.pdf. RV/tent: 30. $. Hookups: none.

Jacksonville

Cabin Creek Campground & Mobile Home Park, 3200 Wilmington Hwy., 28540. T: (910) 346-4808 or (800) 699-5305. www.gocampingamerica.com/cabincreek. RV/tent: 81. $$. Hookups: electric (15, 30, 50 amp), water.

Kitty Hawk

Adventure Bound Campground, 1004 West Kitty Hawk Rd., 27949. T: (252) 255-1130 or (877) 453-2545. www.outerbanks.org/accomodations/north_beach/adventure_bound_campground.asp. RV/tent: 20. $. Hookups: none.

Colington Park Campground, 1608 Colington Rd., 27948. T: (252) 441-6128. RV/tent: 90. $$. Hookups: electric (15, 20, 30 amp), water.

Lake Toxaway

Outdoor Resorts–Blue Ridge, 1 Resorts Blvd., 28747. T: (828) 966-9350. www.outdoor-resorts.com/blueridge. RV/tent: 82. $$$$. Hookups: electric (20, 30, 50 amp), water.

Laurel Springs

Doughton Park Camp, Blue Ridge National Pkwy., Milepost 239.2, 28644. T: (336) 372-8568. www.nps.gov/blri/pphtml/camping.html. RV/tent: 135. $. Hookups: none.

Linville Falls

Linville Falls Camp, Blue Ridge National Pkwy, Milepost 316.4, 28647. T: (828) 298-0398. www.nps.gov/blri/linville.htm. RV/tent: 70. $. Hookups: none.

Linville Falls Trailer Lodge & Campground, P.O. Box 205, 28647. T: (828) 765-2681. www.linvillefalls.com. RV/tent: 46. $$. Hookups: electric (15, 20, 30 amp), water.

Little Switzerland

Crabtree Meadows Camp, Blue Ridge National Pkwy, Milepost 339.5, 28749. T: (828) 298-0398. www.nps.gov/blri/pphtml/camping.html. RV/tent: 93. $. Hookups: none.

Littleton

Outdoor World–Lake Gaston Campground, Rte. 6 Box 236, 27850. T: (252) 586-4121. www.resortusa.com/ow_lg.php. RV/tent: 191. $$. Hookups: electric (30, 50 amp), water, modem.

Lumberton

Sleepy Bear's RV Park, 465 Kenric Rd., 28360. T: (910) 739-4372. www.sleepybearsrvpark.com. RV/tent: 80. $$. Hookups: electric (20, 30, 50 amp), water.

NORTH CAROLINA (continued)

Maggie Valley
Meadowbrook Resort, 102 Meadowbrook Loop, 28751. T: (828) 926-1821. RV/tent: 28. $$. Hookups: electric (15, 20, 30 amp), water.

Stonebridge Campground & RV Park, 1786 Soco Rd. US 19, 28751. T: (828) 926-1904. www.stonebridgervpark.com. RV/tent: 308. $$. Hookups: electric (30, 50 amp), water.

Manteo
Cypress Cove Campground, 818 South Main Hwy. 64, 27954. T: (252) 473-5231. www.outer bankscamping.com. RV/tent: 58. $$. Hookups: electric (15, 20, 30 amp), water.

Marion
Buck Creek Campground, 2576 Tom's Creek Rd., 28752. T: (828) 724-4888. www.buckcreekcamp ground.com. RV/tent: 64. $$. Hookups: electric (15, 20, 30, 50 amp), water.

Murphy
Creekside RV Park, 68 Old Peachtree Rd., 28905. T: (828) 837-4123. RV/tent: 23. $$. Hookups: electric (15, 20, 30, 50 amp), water.

Hanging Dog Campground, Nantahala National Forest, SR 1326 West, 28906. T: (828) 837-5152. www.gorp.away.com/gorp/resource/us_ national_forest/nc/cam_nant.htm. RV/tent: 67. $. Hookups: none.

Jackrabbit Mountain Camp, Nantahala National Forest, SR 1155, 28906. T: (828) 837-5152. www.gorp.away.com/gorp/resource/us_national _forest/nc/cam_nant.htm. RV/tent: 100. $. Hookups: none.

Peace Valley Campground, P.O. Box 606, 28906. T: (828) 837-6223. www.ncvillage.com/peace valley. RV/tent: 87. $$. Hookups: electric (15, 30 amp), water.

Nebo
Lake James State Park, Rte. 2 Lake James Rd., 28761. T: (828) 652-5047. www.ils.unc.edu/ parkproject/visit/laja/home.html. RV/tent: 20. $. Hookups: none.

New Bern
Neuse River Campground, 1565 B St., 28560. T: (252) 638-2556. RV/tent: 83. $. Hookups: electric (20, 30 amp), water, sewer.

Newland
Secluded Valley Campground, 8551 19E South, 28657. T: (828) 765-4810. www.secludedvalletrv campground.com. RV/tent: 58. $$. Hookups: electric (30 amp), water, sewer.

Newport
Waters Edge RV Park, 1463 Hwy. 24, 28570. T: (252) 247-0494 or (252) 247-0709. www.watersedge-rvpark.com. RV/tent: 86. $$. Hookups: electric (30, 50 amp), water.

Whispering Pines Family Campground, 25 Whispering Pines, 28570. T: (252) 726-4902. www.ncpines.com. RV/tent: 135. $$. Hookups: electric (30, 50 amp), water.

Norlina
County Line Park, Kerr Lake State Recreation Area, 6254 Satterwhite Point Rd., 27536. T: (252) 438-7791. www.ils.unc.edu/park project/visit/kela/home.html. RV/tent: 82. $$. Hookups: electric (30 amp), water.

Kimball Point Park, Kerr Lake State Recreation Area, 6254 Satterwhite Point Rd., 27536. T: (252) 438-7791. www.ils.unc.edu/ parkproject/visit/kela/home.html. RV/tent: 91. $. Hookups: electric (30 amp), water.

Oak Island
Long Beach Campground, 5011 East Oak Island Dr., 28465. T: (910) 278-5737. RV/tent: 184. $. Hookups: electric (15, 20, 30 amp), water.

Ocracoke
Beachcomber Campground, 990 Irvin Garrish Hwy., 27960. T: (252) 928-4031. RV/tent: 29. $$. Hookups: electric (30 amp), water.

Old Fort
Catawaba Falls Campground, Rte. 3 Box 230, 28762. T: (828) 668-4831. home.wnclink.com/ camp/index.htm. RV/tent: 44. $$. Hookups: electric (20, 30 amp), water.

Pikeville
Eastern Carolina Athletic Park, 871 Buckswamp Rd., 27863. T: (919) 580-1100. www.ecapark.com. RV/tent: 22. $$. Hookups: electric (20, 30, 50 amp), water.

Pinehurst
Pinehurst RV Park, P.O. Box 5170, 28374. T: (910) 295-5452 or (800) 600-0705. www.pinehurstrv park.com. RV/tent: 55. $$. Hookups: electric (30, 50 amp), water.

Piney Creek
River Camp USA RV Park & Campground, P.O. Box 9, 28663-0009. T: (336) 359-2267 or (800) 748-3722. www.rivercampusa.com. RV/tent: 74. $$. Hookups: electric (20, 30 amp), water.

Pink Hill
Maxwell's Mill Campground, 142 Maxwell's Mill Campground Rd., 28572. T: (252) 568-2022. www.sbhelper.hypermart.net/maxwell. RV/tent: 56. $$. Hookups: electric (30, 50 amp), water.

Pinnacle
Pilot Mountain State Park, 1792 Pilot Knob Park Rd., 27043. T: (336) 325-2355. www.ils.unc.edu/ parkproject/visit/pimo/home.html. RV/tent: 49. $. Hookups: none.

Plumtree
Buck Hill Campground, 6401 South US 19 East Hwy., 28664. T: (828) 765-7387 or (800) 387-5224. www.buckhillcampground.com. RV/tent: 60. $$. Hookups: electric (20, 30 amp), water, sewer.

Raleigh
William B. Umstead State Park, 8801 Glenwood Ave., 27612. T: (919) 571-4170.

www.ils.unc.edu/parkproject/visit/wium/home .html. RV/tent: 28. $. Hookups: none.

Robbinsville
Cheoah Point Recreation Area, Nantahala National Forest, Santeetlah Lake, off US 129 North, 28721. T: (828) 479-6431. www.main.nc.us/ graham/hiking/rangerhq.html. RV/tent: 26. $. Hookups: none.

Hidden Waters RV Park & Campground, 129 South Hwy., 28771. T: (828) 479-3509. RV/tent: 12. $$. Hookups: electric (20, 30, 50 amp), water.

Tsali Recreational Area, Nantahala National Forest, Fontana Lake, on FR 521, 28721. T: (828) 479-6431. www.cs.unca.edu/nfsnc. RV/tent: 40. $$. Hookups: none.

Rodanthe
Camp Hatteras, P.O. Box 10, 27968. T: (252) 987-2777. www.camphatteras.com. RV/tent: 336. $$. Hookups: electric (30, 50 amp), water, sewer.

Rodanthe Watersports & Campground, Hwy. 12, 27968. T: (252) 987-1431. www.watersportsand campground.com. RV/tent: 10. $$. Hookups: electric (30 amp), water.

Salisbury
Dan Nicholas Park (Rowan County Park), 6800 Bringle Ferry Rd., 28146. T: (704) 636-2089 or (866) 767-2757. www.co.rowan.nc.us/parks. RV/tent: 80. $$. Hookups: electric (20, 30 amp), water.

Sea Level
Cedar Creek Campground & Marina, 111 Canal Dr., 28577. T: (252) 225-9571. RV/tent: 70. $$. Hookups: electric (20, 30, 50 amp), water.

Selma
KOA Selma/Smithfield, 428 Campground Rd., 27576. T: (919) 965-5923 or (800) 562-5897. www.koa.com. RV/tent: 93. $$. Hookups: electric (20, 30, 50 amp), water.

Seven Springs
Cliffs of the Neuse State Park, 345-A Park Entrance Rd., 28578. T: (919) 778-6234. www.ils.unc.edu/parkproject/visit/clne/home .html. RV/tent: 35. $. Hookups: none.

Shallotte
S & W RV Park, 532 Holden Beach Rd., 28470-1713. T: (910) 754-8576. RV/tent: 22. $$. Hookups: electric (30 amp), water.

Sea Mist Camping Resort, 4616 Devane Rd. SW, 28459. T: (910) 754-8916. RV/tent: 250. $$$. Hookups: electric (30 amp), water.

Sherrills Ford
Wildlife Woods Campground, 4582 Beaver Blvd., 28673. T: (704) 483-5611. www.woodalls.com/ a/01630_wildlifewoods.html. RV/tent: 305. $$. Hookups: electric (15, 20, 30, 50 amp), water, sewer.

NORTH CAROLINA (continued)

Smithfield

Holiday Trav-L-Park Smithfield, 497 US 701, Four Oaks, 27524. T: (919) 934-3181. www.gocamping america.com/holiday4oaks. RV/tent: 104. $$. Hookups: electric (20, 30 amp), water, sewer.

Statesville

KOA Statesville, 162 KOA Ln., 28677. T: (704) 873-5560 or (800) KOA-5705. www.koakamp grounds.com. RV/tent: 88. $$. Hookups: electric (20, 30, 50 amp), water.

Midway Campground & RV Resort, 114 Midway Dr., 28677. T: (704) 546-7615 or (888) 754-4809. www.kiz.com/campnet/html/zp/nc/0042/ 0042.htm. RV/tent: 83. $$. Hookups: electric (20, 30, 50 amp), water.

Stoneville

Dan River Campground, 724 Webster Rd., 27048. T: (336) 427-8530. RV/tent: 40. $$. Hookups: electric (20, 30, 50 amp), water.

Sunset Beach

Wishing Well Campground, 520 Seaside Rd. SW, 28468. T: (910) 579-7982. RV/tent: 39. $$. Hookups: electric (20, 30 amp), water.

Swannanoa

Mama Gertie's Hideaway Campground, 15 Uphill Rd., 28778. T: (828) 686-4258 or (877) 686-4258. www.mamagerties.com. RV/tent: 28. $$. Hookups: electric (20, 30, 50 amp), water.

Topton

Brookside Campground & Rafting, P.O. Box 93, 28781. T: (828) 321-5209 or (800) 848-RAFT.

www.brooksidecampground.com. RV/tent: 46. $$. Hookups: electric (15, 20 amp), water.

Union Grove

Fiddlers Grove Campground, 1819 West Memorial Hwy., 28689. T: (704) 539-4417. www.fiddlers grove.com. RV/tent: 38. $$. Hookups: electric (20, 30, 50 amp), water.

Van Hoy Farms Family Campground, 742 Jericho Rd., 28634. T: (704) 539-5493. www.vanhoy farms.com. RV/tent: 147. $$. Hookups: electric (15, 30, 50 amp), water.

Vilas

Vanderpool Campground, 1173 Charlie Thompson Rd., 28692. T: (828) 297-3486. RV/tent: 44. $$. Hookups: electric (30 amp), water.

Wade

KOA Fayetteville, P.O. Box 67, 28395. T: (910) 484-5500 or (800) KOA-5350. www.koakamp grounds.com/where/nc/33123.htm. RV/tent: 66. $$. Hookups: electric (20, 30, 50 amp), water.

Waves

Ocean Waves Campground, 25313 Hwy. 12, 27982. T: (252) 987-2556. RV/tent: 68. $$. Hookups: electric (20, 30, 50 amp), water, sewer, cable.

Waxhaw

Cane Creek Park (Union County Park), 5213 Harkey Rd., 28173. T: (704) 843-3919. www.co.union.nc.us/gov_offices/parks/parks .htm. RV/tent: 120. $. Hookups: electric (20, 30 amp), water, sewer.

Waynesville

Winngray Family Campground, 26 Winngray Ln., 28785. T: (828) 926-3170. RV/tent: 150. $$. Hookups: electric (15, 20, 30, 50 amp), water.

White Lake

Camp Clearwater Family Campground, 2038 White Lake Dr., 28337. T: (910) 862-3365. www.campclearwater.com. RV/tent: 1081. $$. Hookups: electric (20, 30, 50 amp), water, sewer.

Whittier

Holly Cove Campground & RV Resort, 341 Holly Cove Rd., 28789. T: (828) 631-0692. www.holly covervresort.com. RV/tent: 60. $$. Hookups: electric (30, 50 amp), water, satellite.

Timberlake Campground, 3270 Conleys Creek Rd., 28789. T: (828) 497-7320. www.campingnc.com/ timberlake. RV/tent: 54. $$. Hookups: electric (15, 20, 30 amp), water.

Wilkesboro

Warrior Creek Park (Corps of Engineers—West Kerr Scott Reservoir), 499 Reservoir Rd., 28697. T: (336) 921-2177. www.reserveusa.com. RV/tent: 88. $$. Hookups: electric (30 amp), water.

Wilmington

Camelot RV Park, 7415 Market St., 28411. T: (910) 686-7705 or (800) 454-7705. RV/tent: 107. $$. Hookups: electric (15, 20, 30 amp), water.

NORTH DAKOTA

Beulah

Dakota Waters Resort, P.O. Box 576, 58523. T: (701) 873-5800 or (800) 473-5803. www.dakotawaters.com. RV/tent: 43. $. Hookups: electric (30 amp).

Bismarck

Bismarck KOA, 3720 Centennial Rd., 58503. T: (701) 222-2662. www.koa.com/where/ nd/34104.htm. RV/tent: 128. $$. Hookups: electric (30, 50 amp), water, sewer, modem.

Colonial Motel & Campground, 4631 Memorial Hwy., 58554. T: (701) 663-9824 or (800) 377-9824. RV/tent: 42. $$. Hookups: electric (30 amp), sewer.

General Sibley RV Park, 5001 South Washington St., 58504. T: (701) 222-1844. RV/tent: 19. $$. Hookups: electric (20, 30 amp), water, sewer.

Hill Crest Acres Campground, 5700 East Main Ave., 58501. T: (701) 255-4334. RV/tent: 74. $$. Hookups: electric (30, 50 amp), water, sewer.

Bowman

Twin Butte Campground & Antiques, Box 983, 58623. T: (701) 523-5569. RV/tent: 26. $$. Hookups: electric (30 amp).

Church's Ferry

Wild Goose RV Park, HCR 1 Box 10, 58325. T: (701) 466-2324. RV/tent: 15. $. Hookups: electric (20, 30 amp).

Devils Lake

Graham's Island State Recreation Area, 152 South Duncan Dr., 58301. T: (800) 807-4723 or (701) 766-4015. www.state.nd.us/ndparks/Parks/ DLSP.htm. RV/tent: 44. $. Hookups: electric (30, 50 amp), water.

Dickinson

Camp on the Heart, 387 South State Ave., 58601. T: (701) 225-9600. www.campontheheart.com. RV/tent: 70. $$. Hookups: electric (20, 30, 50 amp), water, sewer.

Dunseith

International Peace Garden Campground, Rte. 1 Box 116, 58367. T: (701) 263-4390 or (888) 432-6733. www.peacegarden.com. RV/tent: 20, unlimited tent sites. $. Hookups: electric (20 amp), water.

Eckelson

Prairie Haven Family Campground, 10125 36th St. East, 58481. T: (701) 646-2267. www.prairie-haven .com. RV/tent: 31. $$. Hookups: electric (20, 30, 50 amp), water, sewer, modem.

Grafton

Leistikow Park Campground, P.O. Box 122, 58237. T: (701) 352-1842. RV/tent: 38. $. Hookups: electric (30, 50 amp), water, sewer.

Grand Forks

Grand Forks Campground & RV Park, 47965 42nd St., Rte. 1 Box 227, 58201. T: (701) 772-6108. www.gorving.com. RV/tent: 149. $$. Hookups: electric (20, 30, 50 amp), water, sewer, modem.

Hillsboro

Hillsboro Campground & RV Park, 203 6th St. SW, 58045. T: (888) 430-5205 or (701) 436-5205. www.hillsborocampground.com. RV/tent: 34. $$. Hookups: electric (20, 30 amp), water, sewer, modem.

Jamestown

Jamestown Dam/Lakeside Marina, 3225 East Lakeside Rd., 58401. T: (701) 252-9200. RV/tent: 49. $$. Hookups: electric (20, 30 amp), water.

NORTH DAKOTA (continued)

Lamoure

Lamoure County Memorial Park, P.O. Box 128, 58458. T: (701) 683-5856. RV/tent: 90. $. Hookups: electric (15, 20 amp).

Linton

Sunrise Mobile Home Park & RV Camp, 146 Sunrise Ln., 58552. T: (701) 254-4439. RV/tent: 13. $. Hookups: electric (30 amp).

Mandan

Fort Abraham Lincoln State Park, 4480 Fort Lincoln Rd., 58554. T: (800) 807-4723 or (701) 663-9571. www.ndparks.com/parks/flsp.htm. RV/tent: 95. $. Hookups: electric (20, 30, 50 amp).

Medora

Medora Campground, P.O. Box 198, 58645. T: (800) 633-6721 or (701) 623-4444. RV/tent: 210. $$. Hookups: electric (20, 30, 50 amp), water, sewer, modem.

Red Trail Campground, Box 367 G, 58645. T: (800) 621-4317 or (701) 623-4317. RV/tent: 100. $$. Hookups: electric (20, 30, 50 amp), water, sewer, cable, modem.

Theodore Roosevelt/Cottonwood Campground, North of I-94, 58854. T: (701) 842-2333 or (701) 623-4466. www.nps.gov/thro/tr_camps .html. RV/tent: 76. $. Hookups: none.

Menoken

A Prairie Breeze RV Park, 2810 158th St. NE, 58558. T: (701) 224-8215. RV/tent: 41. $$. Hookups: electric (30, 50 amp), water, sewer.

Minot

Casa Motel & Campground, 1900 Hwy. 2 & 52 West, 58701. T: (701) 852-2352. RV/tent: 15. $$. Hookups: electric (30 amp), water, sewer.

KOA Minot, 5261 Hwy. 52 South, 58701. T: (701) 839-7400 or (800) 562-7421. www.koa.com/ where/nd/34102.htm. RV/tent: 74. $$. Hookups: electric (30 amp), water, sewer, modem.

Pat's Motel & Campground, 2025 27th St. SE, 58701. T: (701) 838-5800. RV/tent: 30. $. Hookups: electric (30 amp), water, sewer.

Roughrider Campground, 500 54th St. West, 58703. T: (701) 852-8442. www.minot.com/~roughrid. RV/tent: 94. $$. Hookups: electric (30 amp), water, sewer, modem.

Ray

Red Mike's RV Park, Hwy. 1840, 58849. T: (701) 568-2600. www.thelinksofnorthdakota.com. RV/tent: 17. $$. Hookups: electric (30, 50 amp), water, sewer.

Ross

Dakota West RV Park & General Store, P.O. Box 36, 58776. T: (701) 755-3407. RV/tent: 21. $. Hookups: electric (20, 30, 50 amp).

Steele

OK Motel & Campground, 301 3rd Ave. NE, 58482. T: (701) 475-2440. RV/tent: 17. $. Hookups: electric (30, 50 amp).

Warwick

East Bay Campground, 3892 East Bay Rd., 58381. T: (701) 398-5184 or (701) 740-8368. www.eastbaycampground.com. RV/tent: 16. $. Hookups: electric (20, 30 amp), water, sewer.

Williston

Buffalo Trails Campground, 6700 2nd Ave. West, 58801. T: (701) 572-3206. RV/tent: 110. $$. Hookups: electric (20, 30, 50 amp), water, sewer, modem.

OHIO

Adrian

Adrian Campground and Recreation Park, 190 Hwy. 91, 56110. T: (507) 483-2820. RV/tent: 120. $$. Hookups: electric (20, 30, 50 amp), sewer.

Aitkin

Big "K" Campground, 29510 US 169, 56431. T: (218) 927-6001. RV/tent: 55. $$. Hookups: electric (30 amp), water, sewer.

Farm Island Lake Resort & Campground, 29551 Pioneer Ave., 56431. T: (218) 927-3841. RV/tent: 40. $$. Hookups: electric (30 amp), water, sewer.

Albert Lea

Myre Big Island, 19499 780th Ave, 56007. T: (507) 379-3403. RV/tent: 104. $$. Hookups: electric (30 amp).

Alexandria

Hillcrest RV Park, 715 Birch Ave., 56038. T: (320) 763-6330. RV/tent: 55. $$. Hookups: electric (30 amp), water, sewer.

Andover

Bay Shore, 7124 Pymatuning Lake Rd., 44003. T: (440) 293-7202. RV/tent: 375. $$$. Hookups: electric (30 amp), water, sewer.

Pymatuning State Park, 6260 Pymatuning Lake Rd., 44003-1000. T: (440) 293-6329. www.dnr.state .oh.us/parks/parks/pymatuning.htm. RV/tent: 370. $$. Hookups: electric (20 amp).

Wildwood Acres, 6091 Marvin Rd., 44003. T: (440) 293-6838. RV/tent: 102. $$. Hookups: electric (30 amp), water.

Ashtabula

Hide-A-Way Lakes Campground, 2034 South Ridge W, 44004. T: (440) 992-4431. RV/tent: 200. $$. Hookups: electric (30 amp), water.

Aurora

Six Flags Silverhorn Camping Resort, 250 Treat Rd., 44202. T: (330) 562-9151. RV/tent: 300. $$$. Hookups: electric (30 amp), water.

Woodside Lake Park, 2256 Frost Rd., 44241. T: (330) 626-4251. www.woodsidelake.com. RV/tent: 125. $$$. Hookups: electric (30, 50 amp), water.

Bainbridge

Paint Creek State Park, 14265 US Rte. 50, 45612. T: (937) 365-1401 or (937) 981-706. www.dnr.state.oh.us/parks/paintcrk.htm. RV/tent: 197. $$. Hookups: electric (20 amp).

Pike Lake State Park, 1847 Pike Lake Rd., 45612. T: (740) 493-2212. www.dnr.state.oh.us/parks/ parks/pikelake.htm. RV/tent: 78. $$. Hookups: electric (20 amp).

Baltimore

Rippling Stream Campground, 3640 Reynoldsburg-Baltimore Rd., 43105-9323. T: (740) 862-6065. RV/tent: 120. $$. Hookups: electric (20 amp), water.

Bellefontaine

Eagles Club of Ohio-Alken Lakes, 5118 US 68 North, 43311. T: (937) 593-1565. RV/tent: 263. $$. Hookups: electric (30 amp), water.

Bellville

Yogi Bear's Jellystone Park Camp-Resort Bellville, 6500 Black Rd., 44813. T: (419) 886-2267. RV/tent: 175. $$. Hookups: electric (50 amp), water, sewer.

Belmont

Barkcamp State Park, 65330 Barkcamp Park Rd., 43718. T: (740) 484-4064. RV/tent: 125. $$. Hookups: electric (50 amp).

Blue Rock

Muskingum River Campgrounds, 11206 South River Rd., 43720. T: (740) 674-6918. RV/tent: 24. $. Hookups: electric (30 amp), water, sewer.

Bowerston

Clow's Marina & Campground, 4131 Deer Rd. SW, 44695. T: (740) 269-5371. RV/tent: 88. $$. Hookups: electric (20 amp).

Camden

Cross's Campground Inc., 7777 US Rte.127, 45311. T: (937) 452-1535. RV/tent: 55. $$. Hookups: electric (30 amp), water.

Canfield

Dreamiee Acres, 9727 Columbiana-Canfield Rd., 44406. T: (330) 533-9366. RV/tent: 24. $$. Hookups: electric (20 amp), water.

Carrollton

Camper's Paradise Campground, 4105 Fresno Rd. NW, 44615. T: (330) 735-3220. RV/tent: 55. $$. Hookups: electric (30 amp), water.

OHIO (continued)

Cozy Ridge Campground, 4145 Fresno Rd. NW, 44615. T: (330) 735-2553. RV/tent: 150. $$. Hookups: electric (30 amp), water, sewer.

Petersburg Boat Landing, 2126 Azalea Rd. SW, 44615. T: (330) 627-4270. RV/tent: 78. $$. Hookups: electric (30 amp).

Twin Valley Campground, 2330 Apollo Rd. SE, 44615. T: (330) 739-2811. RV/tent: 100. $$. Hookups: electric (50 amp), water, sewer.

Chillicothe

Scioto Trail State Park, 144 Lake Rd., 45601. T: (740) 663-2125. www.dnr.state.oh.us/parks/parks.sciototr.htm. RV/tent: 73. $. Hookups: electric (30 amp).

Circleville

A.W. Marion State Park, 7317 Warner-Huffer Rd., 43113. T: (740) 474-3386. www.dnr.state.oh.us/parks/parks/awmarion.htm. RV/tent: 58. $$. Hookups: electric (20 amp).

Clyde

Camp Sandusky, 3518 Tiffin Ave., 43410. T: (419) 626-1133. www.sandusky.com. RV/tent: 300. $. Hookups: electric (50 amp), water, sewer.

College Corner

Hueston Woods State Park, 6301 Park Office Rd, 45003. T: (513) 523-1060 or (513) 523-6347. RV/tent: 488. $$. Hookups: electric (30 amp).

Conneaut

Evergreen Lake Park, 703 Center Rd., 44030. T: (440) 599-8802. www.evergreenlake.com. RV/tent: 250. $$. Hookups: electric (50 amp), water.

Deersville

Tappan Lake Park Campground, US 250, 44693. T: (740) 922-3649. RV/tent: 550. $$. Hookups: electric (30 amp).

Delaware

Delaware State Park, 5202 US 23N, 43015. T: (740) 363-4561 or (740) 369-2761. www.dnr.state.oh.us/parks/parks/delaware.htm. RV/tent: 211. $$. Hookups: electric (20 amp).

East Rochester

Bob Boord's Park, 25067 Buffalo Rd., 44625. T: (330) 894-2360. RV/tent: 250. $$. Hookups: electric (30 amp), water, sewer.

Paradise Lake Park, 6940 Rochester Rd., 44625. T: (330) 525-7726. www.gocampingamerica.com/paradiselakeoh. RV/tent: 500. $$. Hookups: electric (20, 30 amp), water.

East Sparta

Bear Creek Ranch KOA, 3232 Downing St. SW, 44626-9741. T: (330) 484-3901 or (800) 562-3903 (reservations). www.bearcreek.us. RV/tent: 103. $$. Hookups: electric (50 amp), water, sewer.

Fayette

Harrison Lake State Park, 26246 Harrison Lake Rd., 43521. T: (419) 237-2593. www.dnr.state.oh.us/parks/parks/harrison.htm. RV/tent: 196. $$. Hookups: electric (20 amp).

Fort Loramie

Hickory Hill Lakes, SR 66, 45845. T: (937) 295-3820. RV/tent: 127. $$. Hookups: electric (30 amp), water.

Frankfort

Lake Hill Campground, 2466 Musselman Station Rd., 45628. T: (740) 998-5648. RV/tent: 95. $$. Hookups: electric (50 amp), water, sewer.

Freeport

Clendening Lake Marina Campground, 79100 Bose Rd., 43973. T: (740) 658-3691. www.clendeninglake.com. RV/tent: 100. $$. Hookups: electric (30 amp).

Piedmont Lake Marina & Campground, SR 8, 43973. T: (740) 658-3735. RV/tent: 67. $$. Hookups: electric (30 amp).

Twin Hills Park, 77720 Cummins Rd., 43973. T: (740) 658-3275. RV/tent: 100. $$. Hookups: electric (30 amp), water.

Fresno

Forest Hill Lake & Campground, 52176 CR 425, 43824. T: (740) 545-9642. RV/tent: 75. $$. Hookups: electric (20 amp), water.

Geneva

Audubon Lakes Campground, 3935 North Broadway, 44041. T: (440) 466-0150. RV/tent: 145. $$. Hookups: electric (30 amp), water.

Geneva State Park, 4499 Padanarum Rd., 44041. T: (440) 466-8400 or (440) 466-7565 (Marina). www.dnr.sate.oh.us/parks/parks/geneva.htm. RV/tent: 88. $$. Hookups: electric (20 amp).

Kenisee's Grand River Camp & Canoe, 4680 Rte. 307E, 44041. T: (440) 466-2320. www.keniseegrc.com. RV/tent: 120. $$. Hookups: electric (50 amp), water.

R & R Camping, 4455 Rte. 307, 44041. T: (440) 466-2550. RV/tent: 120. $$$. Hookups: electric (30 amp), water, sewer.

Geneva-on-the-Lake

Indian Creek Camping & Resort, 4710 Lake Rd. East, 44041. T: (440) 466-8191. www.indiancreekresort.com. RV/tent: 573. $$$. Hookups: electric (50 amp), water, sewer.

Granville

Lazy R Campground, 2340 Dry Creek Rd. NE, 43023. T: (740) 366-4385. RV/tent: 195. $$. Hookups: electric (20, 30, 50 amp), water, sewer.

Greenville

Wildcat Woods Campground, 1355 Wildcat Rd., 45331. T: (937) 548-7921. www.angelfire.com/folk/wildcatwoods. RV/tent: 78. $$. Hookups: electric (30 amp), water, sewer.

Homerville

Wild Wood Lake Campground, 11450 Crawford Rd., Box 26, 44235. T: (330) 625-2817. www.wildwoodlakes.com. RV/tent: 245. $$. Hookups: electric (50 amp), water.

Howard

Kokosing Valley Camp & Canoe, 25860 Coshocton Rd., 43028. T: (740) 599-7056. RV/tent: 170. $$. Hookups: electric (20 amp), water.

Hubbard

Homestead Campground, 1436 Brookfield Rd., 44425. T: (330) 448-2938. www.homesteadrv.com. RV/tent: 77. $$. Hookups: electric (30 amp), water, sewer.

Jefferson

Buccaneer Campsites, 1408 State Rte. 307 West, 44047. T: (440) 576-2881. www.buccaneercampsites.com. RV/tent: 170. $$. Hookups: electric (30 amp), water, sewer.

Kings Mill

Paramount's Kings Island Campground, 6300 Kings Island Dr., 45034. T: (513) 754-5901. www.pki.com. RV/tent: 349. $$$$. Hookups: electric (30 amp), water, sewer.

Lakeside

Indian Lake State Park, 12744 SR 235 North, 43331. T: (937) 843-3553 or (937) 843-2717. www.dnr.state.oh.us/parks/parks/indianlk.htm. RV/tent: 459. $$. Hookups: electric (30 amp).

Lakeside-Marblehead

East Harbor State Park, 1169 North Buck Rd., 43440-9610. T: (419) 734-5857 or (419) 734-4424. RV/tent: 570. $$. Hookups: electric (330 amp).

Lancaster

Lakeview RV Park and Campground, 2715 Old Sugar Grove Rd., 43130. T: (740) 653-4519. RV/tent: 70. $$. Hookups: electric (50 amp), water, sewer.

Lancaster Campground, 2151 West Fair Ave., 43130. T: (740) 653-2119 or (740) 654-7492. RV/tent: 24. $$. Hookups: electric (50 amp), water.

Latham

Cave Lake Park, 1132 Bell Hollow Rd., 45133. T: (937) 588-3252. RV/tent: 300. $$. Hookups: electric (30 amp), water.

Long's Retreat Family Resort, 50 Bell Hollow Rd., 45133. T: (937) 588-3725. www.longsretreat.com. RV/tent: 450. $$. Hookups: electric (20 amp), water, sewer.

Laurelville

Tar Hollow State Park, 16396 Tar Hollow Rd., 43135. T: (740) 887-4818. www.dnr.state.oh.us/parks/parks/tarhollow.htm. RV/tent: 113. $$. Hookups: electric (50 amp).

OHIO (continued)

Lebanon

Cedarbrook Campground, 760 Franklin Rd., 45036. T: (513) 932-7717. www.cedarbrookcamp ground.com. RV/tent: 150. $$. Hookups: electric (50 amp), water, sewer.

Lisbon

Lock 30 Woodlands RV Campground Resort, 45529 Middle Beaver Rd., 44432. T: (330) 424-9197 or (877) 856-2530. www.ohiorvcamp.com. RV/tent: 65. $$$. Hookups: electric (50 amp), water, sewer.

Logan

Hocking Hills State Park, 20160 SR 664 South, 43138. T: (740) 385-6165 or (740) 385-6841. www.hockinghillspark.com. RV/tent: 172. $$. Hookups: electric (30 amp).

Scenic View Campground, 29150 Pattor Rd., 43138. T: (740) 385-4295. www.scenicviewcamp ground.net. RV/tent: 92. $$$. Hookups: electric (30 amp), water, sewer.

Lore City

Salt Fork State Park, 14755 Cadiz Rd., 43725. T: (740) 432-1508 or (740) 439-3521. www.dnr.state.oh.us/parks/parks/saltfork. RV/tent: 212. $$. Hookups: electric (50 amp).

Loudonville

Camp Toodik Family Campground & Canoe Livery, 7700 TR 462, 44842. T: (419) 994-3835 or (800) 322-2663. www.camptoodik.com. RV/tent: 153. $$$. Hookups: electric (50 amp), water, sewer.

Lake Wapusun, 10787 Molter Rd., 44676. T: (330) 496-2355. RV/tent: 150. $$. Hookups: electric (30 amp), water.

Long Lake Park & Campground, 8974 Long Lake Dr., 44638. T: (419) 827-2278. www.longlake campground.com. RV/tent: 215. $. Hookups: electric (30 amp), water.

Mohican Campground & Cabins, 3058 SR 3, 44842. T: (419) 994-2267 or (888) 909-7400. www.mohicancamp.com. RV/tent: 146. $$. Hookups: electric (30 amp), water, sewer.

Mohican State Park, 3116 SR 3, 44842. T: (419) 994-4290 or (419) 994-5125. www.dnr.state .oh.us/parks/parks/mohican.htm. RV/tent: 198. $$. Hookups: electric (50 amp).

River Run Family Campground, 3070 CR 3175, 44842. T: (419) 994-5257. www.riverrunfamily campground.com. RV/tent: 98. $$$. Hookups: electric (50 amp), water.

Mansfield

Charles Mill Lake Park Camp Area, 1271 SR 430, 44903. T: (419) 368-6885. www.mwcdlakes.com. RV/tent: 511. $$. Hookups: electric (30 amp).

Marietta

Camp Civitan, 922 Front St., 45750. T: (740) 373-1347. www.northcountrytrail.org/explore/ guide/f08.htm. RV/tent: 42. $$. Hookups: electric (30 amp), water.

Marion

Hickory Grove Lake Family Campground, 805 Hoch Rd., 43302-9572. T: (740) 382-8584.

RV/tent: 200. $$. Hookups: electric (50 amp), water, sewer.

McArthur

Lake Hope State Park, 22331 SR 278, 45651. T: (740) 596-5253. www.dnr.state.oh.us/parks/ parks/lakehope.htm. RV/tent: 219. $$. Hookups: electric (30 amp).

Medina

Pier-Ion Park, 5960 Vandemark Rd., 44256. T: (330) 667-2311. www.pier-ionpark.com. RV/tent: 150. $$. Hookups: electric (50 amp), water, sewer.

Milan

Milan Trav-L-Park, 11404 SR 250N, 44846. T: (419) 499-4627. RV/tent: 142. $$$. Hookups: electric (50 amp), water, sewer.

Mineral City

Atwood Lake Park, 4956 Shop Rd., 44656. T: (330) 343-6780. RV/tent: 569. $$. Hookups: electric (30 amp).

Minster

Lake Loramie State Park, 4401 Ft. Loramie Swanders Rd., 45865-9311. T: (937) 295-2011. www.dnr.state.oh.us/parks/parks/lkloramie.htm. RV/tent: 162. $$. Hookups: electric (30 amp), water.

Montville

Tri-County Kamp Inn, 17147 Gar Hwy., 44064. T: (440) 968-3400. RV/tent: 125. $$. Hookups: electric (30 amp), water.

Mount Gilead

Dogwood Valley, 4185 Twp Rd. 99, 43338. T: (419) 946-5230. www.dogwoodvalleycampground .com. RV/tent: 200. $$. Hookups: electric (30 amp), water, sewer.

Mount Gilead State Park, 4119 SR 95, 43338. T: (419) 946-1961. www.mtgilead.com/mgsp2 .htm. RV/tent: 60. $. Hookups: electric (50 amp).

Mount Sterling

Deer Creek State Park, 20635 Waterloo Rd., 43143. T: (746) 869-3508 or (740) 869-3124. www.dnr.state.oh.us/parks/parks/deercrk.htm. RV/tent: 227. $$. Hookups: electric (30 amp).

Mount Vernon

Rustic Knolls Campsites, 8664 Keys Rd., 43050. T: (740) 397-9318. RV/tent: 150. $$. Hookups: electric (30, 50 amp), water, sewer.

Nashport

Dillon State Park, 5265 Dillon Hills Dr., 43830. T: (740) 452-1083 or (740) 453-4377. www.dnr.state.oh.us/parks/parks/dillon.htm. RV/tent: 195. $$. Hookups: electric (20 amp).

Wild Bill's Resort, 6819 Newark Rd., 43830. T: (740) 452-0113. RV/tent: 150. $$. Hookups: electric (30 amp), water, sewer.

Navarre

Baylor Beach Park, 8725 Manchester Ave. SW, 44662. T: (330) 767-3031 or (330) 922-9567.

www.baylorbeachpark.com. RV/tent: 60. $$. Hookups: electric (30, 50 amp), water.

Nelsonville

Happy Hills Family Campground, 22245 SR 278, 45764. T: (740) 385-6720. www.hockinghills.com/ happyhills. RV/tent: 63. $$. Hookups: electric (30 amp), water.

Nevada

Foxfire Family Fun Park, 3699 Crawford-Wyandot Rd., 44849. T: (740) 482-2190. RV/tent: 150. $$. Hookups: electric (30, 50 amp), water, sewer.

New London

Indian Trail Campground, 1400 US 250S, 44851. T: (419) 929-1135. www.indiantrailcamp ground.com. RV/tent: 176. $$. Hookups: electric (30 amp), water, sewer.

New Paris

Arrowhead Campground, 1361 Thomas Rd., 45347. T: (937) 996-6203. www.arrowhead-campground .com. RV/tent: 33. $$. Hookups: electric (30 amp), water, sewer.

New Washington

Auburn Lake Park, 555 Michael Ave., 44854. T: (419) 492-2110. RV/tent: 111. $$. Hookups: electric (30 amp), water.

Newbury

Punderson State Park, 11755 Kinsman Rd., 44065-9684. T: (440) 564-2279. www.dnr.state.oh.us/ parks/parks/punderson.htm. RV/tent: 201. $$. Hookups: electric (20 amp).

Newton Falls

Ridge Ranch Campground, 5219 SR 303 NW, 44444-9522. T: (330) 898-8080. RV/tent: 176. $$. Hookups: electric (30, 50 amp), water, sewer.

North Canton

Pine Valley Lake Park, 4936 South Arlington Rd., 44720. T: (330) 896-1381. RV/tent: 90. $$. Hookups: electric (30 amp), water, sewer.

Oak Harbor

Paradise Acres, 4225 North Rider Rd., 43449. T: (419) 898-6411 or (888) 311-0143. www.cros.net/paradise. RV/tent: 300. $$. Hookups: electric (30 amp), water, sewer.

Oberlin

Schaun Acres Campground, 51468 SR 303, 44074. T: (440) 775-7122. RV/tent: 90. $$. Hookups: electric (30 amp), water, sewer.

Oregon

Maumee Bay State Park, 1750 State Park Rd., 43618-9713. T: (419) 836-8828 or (419) 836-7758. www.dnr.state.oh.us/parks/parks/ maumeebay.htm. RV/tent: 252. $$. Hookups: electric (20 amp).

OHIO (continued)

Oregonia
Olive Branch Campground, 6985 Wilmington Rd., 45054. T: (513) 932-2267. RV/tent: 138. $$$. Hookups: electric (50 amp), water, sewer.

Orwell
Pine Lakes Campground, 3001 Hague Rd., 44076. T: (440) 437-6218. RV/tent: 240. $$. Hookups: electric (30 amp), water.

Oxford
Camp America, 8501 Camden College Corner Rd, 45003. T: (800) 818-2267 or (513) 798-2794. www.campamerica.us. RV/tent: 24. $$. Hookups: electric (30 amp), water.

Parkman
Kool Lakes Family Camping & Recreation Resort, 12990 SR 282, 44080. T: (440) 548-8436. www.koollakes.com. RV/tent: 200. $$. Hookups: electric (50 amp), water, sewer.

Paulding
Woodbridge Campground, 8656 Rd. 137, 45879. T: (419) 399-2267. RV/tent: 124. $$. Hookups: electric (30 amp), water.

Perrysburg
Stony Ridge KOA Campgrounds, 24787 Luckey Rd., 43551. T: (419) 837-6848 or (800) 562-6831. RV/tent: 42. $$. Hookups: electric (30, 50 amp), water, sewer.

Perrysville
Pleasant Hill Lake, 3431 SR 95, 44864. T: (419) 938-7884. www.mwcdlakes.com/pleasant.htm. RV/tent: 380. $$. Hookups: electric (30 amp).

Pioneer
Funny Farm Campground, 19452 CR 12, 43554. T: (419) 737-2467. www.loveberrysfunnyfarm.com. RV/tent: 300. $$. Hookups: electric (30 amp), water, sewer.

Lazy River Campground, 12808 US 20, 43554. T: (419) 485-4411. RV/tent: 350. $$. Hookups: electric (30 amp), water, sewer.

Port Clinton
Cedarlane Campground, 2926 NE Catawba Rd., 43452. T: (419) 797-9907. www.gocamping america.com/cederlane. RV/tent: 300. $$. Hookups: electric (50 amp), water.

Tall Timbers Campground, 340 Christy Chapel Rd., 43452. T: (419) 732-3938. www.camplakeerie.com/talltimbers. RV/tent: 409. $$. Hookups: electric (30 amp), water.

Portsmouth
Shawnee Village RV Park & Campground, 13610 US 52, 45663. T: (740) 858-5542. RV/tent: 100. $$. Hookups: electric (30, 50 amp), water.

Randolph
Friendship Acres Campground, 2210 SR 44, 44201. T: (330) 325-9527. www.welcome.to/friendshipacres. RV/tent: 175. $$. Hookups: electric (30 amp), water.

Ravenna
Country Acres Campground, 9850 Minyoung Rd., 44266. T: (330) 358-2774. www.gocamping america.com/countryacres. RV/tent: 200. $$. Hookups: electric (50 amp), water, sewer.

Republic
Clinton Lake Camping, 4990 East Twp Rd. 122, 44867. T: (419) 585-3331. RV/tent: 100. $$. Hookups: electric (30 amp), water.

Rogers
Camp Frederick, 6996 Millrock Rd., 44455. T: (330) 227-3633. RV/tent: 11. $$. Hookups: electric (30 amp), water.

Rushsylvania
Back Forty Ltd., 959 CR 111E, 43347. T: (937) 468-7492. RV/tent: 52. $$. Hookups: electric (30 amp), water.

Salem
Chaparral Family Campground, 10136 Middletown Rd., 44460. T: (330) 337-9381. www.gocamping america.com/chaparralfamily. RV/tent: 225. $$. Hookups: electric (30 amp), water, sewer.

Timashamie Family Campground, 28251 Georgetown Rd., 44460. T: (330) 525-7054. RV/tent: 175. $$. Hookups: electric (50 amp), water, sewer.

Sandusky
Bayshore Estates Campground, 2311 Cleveland Rd., 44870. T: (419) 625-7906. www.mhdcorp.com/campgrounds/bayshore/default.htm. RV/tent: 650. $. Hookups: electric (50 amp), water, sewer.

Crystal Campground, 710 Crystal Rock Ave., 44870. T: (419) 684-7177 or (800) 321-7177. www.mhd corp.com/campgrounds/crystal/default.htm. RV/tent: 124. $. Hookups: electric (30 amp), water, sewer.

Senecaville
Seneca Lake Marina Point, 22172 Park Rd, 43780. T: (740) 685-6013. RV/tent: 500. $$. Hookups: electric (30 amp).

Shelby
Wagon Wheel Campground, 6787 Baker, 44875. T: (419) 347-1392 or (888) 562-5607 for reservations. www.wagonwheelcampground.com. RV/tent: 196. $$$. Hookups: electric (50 amp), water, sewer.

South Bloomingville
Top O' the Caves Family Campground/Resort, 26780 Chapel Ridge Rd., 43152. T: (740) 385-6566 or (800) 967-2434. www.topothe caves.com. RV/tent: 75. $$. Hookups: electric (30 amp), water, sewer.

Southington
Valley Lake Park, 3959 SR 305, 44470. T: (330) 898-1819. RV/tent: 40. $$. Hookups: electric (30 amp), water, sewer.

Spencer
Sunset Lake Campground, 5566 Root Rd., 44275. T: (330) 667-2686. RV/tent: 145. $$. Hookups: electric (30 amp) water.

Springfield
Buck Creek State Park, 1901 Buck Creek Ln., 45502. T: (937) 322-5284 or (937) 325-4211. www.dnr.state.oh.us/parks/parks/buckck. RV/tent: 111. $$. Hookups: electric (30 amp).

St. Mary's
Grand Lake–St. Mary's State Park, P.O. Box 308, 45885. T: (419) 394-2774 or (419) 394-3611. www.dnr.state.oh.us/parks/parks/grndlake.htm. RV/tent: 210. $$. Hookups: electric (50 amp).

Streetsboro
Mar-Lynn Lake Park, 187 SR 303, 44241. T: (330) 650-2522 or (888) 627-5966. www.mar-lynn.com. RV/tent: 250. $$$. Hookups: electric (50 amp), sewer, water.

Sullivan
Rustic Lakes Campground, 44901 New London Eastern Rd., 44880. T: (440) 647-3804. RV/tent: 275. $$. Hookups: electric (30 amp), water.

Thompson
Heritage Hills Campground, 6445 Ledge Rd., 44086. T: (440) 298-1311. RV/tent: 120. $$. Hookups: electric (50 amp), water, sewer.

Tiffin
Walnut Grove Campground, 7325 South Twp Rd. 131, 44883. T: (419) 448-0914. RV/tent: 209. $$. Hookups: electric (30 amp), water, sewer.

Toronto
Austin Lake Park & Campground, 1002 Twp Rd. 285A, 43964. T: (740) 544-5253 or (888) 249-5685. RV/tent: 55. $$. Hookups: electric (50 amp), water.

Urbana
Meadow Lake Resort, 4739 Woodville Pike, 43078. T: (937) 652-3400. RV/tent: 225. $$. Hookups: electric (50 amp), water, sewer.

Van Wert
Pleasant Grove Campground, 10856A Liberty-Union Rd., 45891. T: (419) 238-1124. www.angelfire.com/biz6/pgc. RV/tent: 135. $$. Hookups: electric (30 amp), water, sewer.

Versailles
Cottonwood Lakes, 8549 Althoff Rd., 45380. T: (419) 582-2610. RV/tent: 40. $$. Hookups: electric (30 amp), water.

Williamstown
Sulphur Lake Camp, P.O. Box 19, 45897. T: (419) 365-5374. RV/tent: 100. $$. Hookups: electric (50 amp), water, sewer.

OHIO (continued)

Wilmington
Beechwood Acres, 855 Yankee Rd, 45177. T: (937) 289-2202. www.beechwoodacres.com. RV/tent: 95. $$. Hookups: electric (50 amp), water.

Winesburg
Amish Country Campsite, 1930 SR 62 East, 44690. T: (330) 359-5226. RV/tent: 60. $$. Hookups: electric (30 amp), water.

Zanesville
Campers Grove, Hopewell National Rd. Rte. 40, 43701. T: (740) 453-3973. RV/tent: 45. $$. Hookups: water.

Wolfies Family Kamping, 101 Buckeye Dr., 43701. T: (740) 454-0925. RV/tent: 39. $$. Hookups: electric (30 amp), sewer, water.

OKLAHOMA

Afton
Grand Country Mobile & RV Park, 55015 East 270th Rd., 74331. T: (918) 257-5164. RV/tent: 27. $$. Hookups: electric (20, 30, 50 amp), water, sewer.

Canton
Big Bend, HC 65 Box 120, 73724. T: (580) 886-3576. www.reserveusa.com/nrrs/ok/biok. RV/tent: 115. $. Hookups: electric (20, 30 amp), water.

Canadian, HC 65 Box 120, 73724. T: (580) 886-2989. www.reserveusa.com/nrrs/ok/caok. RV/tent: 77. $. Hookups: electric (20, 30 amp), water.

Sandy Cove, HC 65 Box 120, 73724. T: (580) 274-3576. www.reserveusa.com/nrrs/ok/saco. RV/tent: 37. $$. Hookups: electric (20, 30 amp).

Checotah/Henryetta
Checotah/Henryetta KOA, HC 68 Box 750, 74426. T: (800) 562-7510 or (918) 473-6511. www.koa.com. RV/tent: 83. $$. Hookups: electric (20, 30, 50 amp), water, sewer.

Choctaw
Oklahoma City East KOA, 6200 South Choctaw Rd., 73020. T: (800) 562-5076 or (405) 391-5000. www.koa.com. RV/tent: 85. $$. Hookups: electric (20, 30, 50 amp), water, sewer.

Claremore
Claremore Expo Center, 400 Veterans Pkwy., 74017. T: (918) 342-5357. www.claremore expo.com. RV/tent: 44. $$. Hookups: electric (20, 30, 50 amp), water, sewer.

Clayton
Potato Hills Central, HC 60 Box 175, 74536. T: (918) 569-4131. www.reserveusa.com. RV/tent: 94. $$. Hookups: electric (20, 30 amp), water.

Copan
Post Oak Park, Rte. 1 Box 260, 74022. T: (918) 532-4334. www.reserveusa.com/nrrs/ok/post. RV/tent: 20. $$. Hookups: electric (20, 30 amp).

Washington Cove, Rte. 1 Box 260, 74022. T: (918) 532-4129. www.reserveusa.com/nrrs/ok/wash. RV/tent: 101. $$. Hookups: electric (20, 30, 50 amp), water.

Davis
Turner Falls Park, I-35, Exit 47 or 51, 73030. T: (580) 369-2917 or (580) 369-2988. www.turnerfallspark.com. RV/tent: 344. $. Hookups: electric (30 amp), water.

El Reno
Cherokee KOA, Exit 108/Spur 281, 73036. T: (800) 562-5736 or (405) 884-2595. www.koa.com. RV/tent: 79. $$. Hookups: electric (20, 30, 50 amp), water, sewer.

Hensley's RV Park, Country Club Rd., 73036. T: (405) 262-6490. RV/tent: 26. $$. Hookups: electric (30, 50 amp), water, sewer.

Elk City
Elk City/Clinton KOA, Rte. 66, 73626. T: (800) 562-4149 or (580) 592-4409. www.koa.com. RV/tent: 90. $$. Hookups: electric (20, 30, 50 amp), water, sewer.

Elk Creek RV Park, 20th & South Main, 73644. T: (888) 478-6552 or (580) 225-7865. www.elkcreekrvpark.com. RV/tent: 74. $$. Hookups: electric (30, 50 amp), water, sewer, cable.

Eufala
Terra Starr Park, Rte. 2 Box 2130, 74432. T: (918) 689-2164 or (918) 689-7094. RV/tent: 300. $$. Hookups: electric (30 amp), water, sewer.

Fort Gibson
Blue Bill Point, 8568 OK 251 A, 74434. T: (918) 476-6638. www.reserveusa.com/nrrs/ok/blpo. RV/tent: 43. $. Hookups: electric (20, 30 amp), water.

Dam Site (Fort Gibson Lake), 8568 OK 251 A, 74434. T: (918) 683-6618. www.reserveusa. com/nrrs/ok/dami. RV/tent: 47. $$. Hookups: electric (20, 30 amp), water, phone.

Flat Rock Creek, 8568 OK 251 A, 74434. T: (918) 476-6766. www.reserveusa.com/nrrs/ok/flat. RV/tent: 38. $$. Hookups: electric (20, 30 amp), water.

Rocky Point, 8568 OK 251 A, 74434. T: (918) 682-4314. www.reserveusa.com/nrrs/ok/rocy. RV/tent: 63. $. Hookups: electric (20, 30 amp), water.

Taylor Ferry, 8568 OK 251 A, 74434. T: (918) 485-4792. www.reserveusa.com/nrrs/ok/tafe. RV/tent: 102. $. Hookups: electric (20, 30, 50 amp), water.

Wildwood, 8568 OK 251 A, 74434. T: (918) 682-4314. www.reserveusa.com/nrrs/ok/wilw. RV/tent: 30. $$. Hookups: electric (20, 30, 50 amp), water.

Fort Supply
Supply Park, P.O. Box 248, 73841. T: (580) 766-2001. www.reserveamerica.com/nrrs/ok/supp. RV/tent: 110. $. Hookups: electric (20, 30 amp), water, phone.

Gore
Afton Landing, Rte. 2 Box 21, 74435. T: (918) 489-5541. www.reserveamerica.com/nrrs/ok/afto. RV/tent: 22. $$. Hookups: electric (20, 30 amp), water.

Bluff Landing, Rte. 2 Box 21, 74435. T: (918) 489-5541. www.reserveamerica.com/nrrs/ok/blla. RV/tent: 21. $$. Hookups: electric (20, 30 amp).

Brewers Bend, Rte. 2 Box 21, 74435. T: (918) 489-5541. www.reserveamerica.com/nrrs/ok/brew. RV/tent: 42. $. Hookups: electric (20, 30 amp), water.

Chicken Creek, Rte. 1 Box 259, 74435. T: (918) 487-5252. www.reserveusa.com/nrrs/ok/chok. RV/tent: 102. $$. Hookups: electric (20, 30, 50 amp), water.

Elk Creek Landing, Rte. 1 Box 259, 74435. T: (918) 487-5252. www.reserveusa.com/nrrs/ok/elcl. RV/tent: 42. $. Hookups: electric (20, 30 amp).

Snake Creek, Rte. 1 Box 259, 74435. T: (918) 487-5252. www.reserveusa.com/nrrs/ok/sank. RV/tent: 112. $. Hookups: electric (20, 30, 50 amp), water, sewer.

Spaniard Creek, Rte. 2 Box 21, 74435. T: (918) 489-5541. www.reserveusa.com/nrrs/ok/span. RV/tent: 35. $$. Hookups: electric (20, 30 amp), water.

Strayhorn Landing, Rte. 1 Box 259, 74435. T: (918) 487-5252. www.reserveusa.com/nrrs/ok/strl. RV/tent: 40. $$. Hookups: electric (20, 30 amp), water, sewer.

Grove
Lee's Grand Lake Resort, 24800 South 630 Rd., 74344. T: (918) 786-4289. RV/tent: 48. $$. Hookups: electric (30, 50 amp), water, sewer, cable.

Hodger
Cedar Lake (Oklahoma), Choctaw Ranger District, 52175 US 59, 74939. T: (918) 653-2991 or (877) 444-6777. www.reserveusa.com/nrrs/ok/ced3. RV/tent: 24. $. Hookups: electric (20, 30, 50 amp), water, sewer.

Kansas
Spencer Ridge Resort, Rte. 1 Box 222, 74347. T: (800) 964-6670 or (918) 597-2269. RV/tent: 32. $$. Hookups: electric (20, 30, 50 amp), water, sewer.

Kellyville
Heyburn Park, 27349 West Heyburn Lake Rd., Rte. 2 Box 140, 74039. T: (918) 247-6601. www.reserveusa.com/nrrs/ok/heyb. RV/tent: 46. $$. Hookups: electric (20, 30, 50 amp), water.

OKLAHOMA (continued)

Sheppard Point, 27349 Heyburn Lake Rd., 74039. T: (918) 247-4551. www.reserveusa.com. RV/tent: 38. $. Hookups: electric (20, 30 amp), water.

Kingston

Buncombe Creek, 351 Corps Rd., 75020. T: (903) 465-4990. www.reserveusa.com. RV/tent: 51. $. Hookups: electric (20, 30 amp), water.

Burns Run East, 351 Corps Rd., 75020. T: (903) 465-4990. www.reserveusa.com. RV/tent: 54. $. Hookups: electric (20, 30 amp), water.

Burns Run West, 351 Corps Rd., 75020. T: (903) 465-4990. www.reserveusa.com. RV/tent: 127. $. Hookups: electric (20, 30 amp), water.

Caney Creek, 351 Corps Rd., 75020. T: (903) 465-4990. www.reserveusa.com. RV/tent: 52. $. Hookups: electric (20, 30 amp), water.

Johnson Creek, 351 Corps Rd., 75020. T: (903) 465-4990. www.reserveusa.com. RV/tent: 55. $$. Hookups: electric (20, 30 amp), water.

Lakeside, 351 Corps Rd., 75020. T: (903) 465-4990. www.reserveusa.com. RV/tent: 127. $. Hookups: electric (20, 30 amp), water.

Platter Flats, 351 Corps Rd., 75020. T: (903) 465-4990. www.reserveusa.com/nrrs/ok/plat. RV/tent: 83. $. Hookups: electric (20, 30, 50 amp), water.

McAlester

Super 8 Motel & RV Park, US 69 Business South, 74501. T: (918) 426-5400. RV/tent: 175. $$. Hookups: electric (20, 30 amp), water, sewer, cable.

Miami

Miami Mobile Home & RV Park, 2001 East Steve Owens, 74354. T: (800) 515-2287 or (918) 542-2287. RV/tent: 48. $$. Hookups: electric (30, 50 amp), water, sewer.

Muskogee

Meadowbrook RV Park, 1313 South 30th, 74401. T: (918) 681-4574. RV/tent: 96. $$. Hookups: electric (30, 50 amp), water, sewer.

Oklahoma City

A-OK RV Park, 721 South Rockwell Ave., 73128. T: (405) 787-7356. RV/tent: 33. $$. Hookups: electric (30, 50 amp), water, sewer.

Briscoe's RV Park, 6002 I-35 South, 73149. T: (800) 622-6073. RV/tent: 60. $$. Hookups: electric (20, 30, 50 amp), water, sewer.

Council Road RV Park, 8108 SW 8th St., 73128. T: (405) 789-2103. RV/tent: 102. $$. Hookups: electric (20, 30, 50 amp), water, sewer.

Eastland Hills RV Park, 3100 South Douglas Blvd., 73150. T: (405) 736-1013. RV/tent: 54. $$. Hookups: electric (20, 30, 50 amp), water, sewer, garbage.

Okie RV Park & Campground, 9824 SE 29th St., 73130. T: (405) 732-3093. RV/tent: 150. $. Hookups: electric (30, 50 amp), water, sewer.

Roadrunner RV Park, 4800 South I-35, 73129. T: (405) 677-2373. RV/tent: 80. $$. Hookups: electric (30, 50 amp), water, sewer.

Rockwell RV Park, 720 South Rockwell, 73128. T: (888) 684-3251 or (405) 787-5992.

www.campusa.com/ok/rockwell. RV/tent: 123. $$. Hookups: electric (30, 50 amp), water, sewer.

Oologah

Blue Creek, P.O. Box 700, 74053. T: (918) 341-4244. www.reserveusa.com/nrrs/ok/blcr. RV/tent: 61. $. Hookups: electric (20, 30 amp), phone.

Hawthorn Bluff, P.O. Box 700, 74053. T: (918) 443-2319. www.reserveusa.com/nrrs/ok/hawt. RV/tent: 93. $$. Hookups: electric (20, 30 amp).

Ponca City

Bear Creek Cove, 9400 Lake Rd., 74604. T: (580) 762-5611. www.reserveusa.com/nrrs/ok/brcc. RV/tent: 22. $$. Hookups: electric (20, 30 amp), water.

Coon Creek, 9400 Lake Rd., 74604. T: (580) 762-5611. www.reserveusa.com/nrrs/ok/cooe. RV/tent: 54. $$. Hookups: electric (20, 30 amp), water.

Osage Cove, 9400 Lake Rd., 74604. T: (580) 762-5611. www.reserveusa.com/nrrs/ok/osac. RV/tent: 94. $$. Hookups: electric (20, 30 amp).

Sarge Creek, 9400 Lake Rd., 74604. T: (580) 762-5611. www.reserveusa.com/nrrs/ok/sarg. RV/tent: 51. $$. Hookups: electric (20, 30 amp), water.

Washunga Bay, 9400 Lake Rd., 74604. T: (580) 762-5611. www.reserveusa.com/nrrs/ok/waba. RV/tent: 62. $. Hookups: electric (20, 30, 50 amp), water.

Sallisaw

Applegate Cove, HC 61 Box 238, 74955. T: (918) 775-4475. www.reserveusa.com/nrrs/ok/appg. RV/tent: 27. $$. Hookups: electric (20, 30 amp), water.

Sallisaw KOA, P.O. Box 88, 74955. T: (800) 562-2797 or (918) 775-2792. www.koa.com. RV/tent: 82. $$. Hookups: electric (20, 30, 50 amp), water, sewer.

Short Mountain Cove, Rte. 2 Box 21, 74955. T: (918) 489-5541 or (918) 775-4475. www.reserveamerica.com/nrrs/ok/shmc. RV/tent: 32. $$. Hookups: electric (20, 30 amp).

Sand Springs

New Mannford Ramp, 23115 West Wekiwa Rd., 74063. T: (918) 865-2621. www.reserveusa.com/nrrs/ok/newm. RV/tent: 39. $$. Hookups: electric (20, 30 amp), water.

Salt Creek North, 23115 West Wekiwa Rd., 74063. T: (918) 865-2845. www.reserveusa.com/nrrs/ok/salc. RV/tent: 126. $. Hookups: electric (20, 30 amp), water.

Washington Irving S. Campground, 23115 West Wekiwa Rd., 74063. T: (918) 865-2621. www.reserveusa.com. RV/tent: 41. $. Hookups: electric (20, 30 amp).

Sawyer

Kiamichi Park, P.O. Box 99, 74756. T: (580) 326-3345. www.reserveusa.com/nrrs/ok/kiam. RV/tent: 91. $. Hookups: electric (20, 30 amp), water.

Skiatook

Birch Cove, HC 67 Box 135, 74070. T: (918) 396-3170. www.reserveusa.com/nrrs/ok/birc. RV/tent: 84. $$. Hookups: electric (20, 30 amp).

Tall Chief Cove, HC 67 Box 135, 74070. T: (918) 288-6820. www.reserveusa.com/nrrs/ok/tall. RV/tent: 57. $$. Hookups: electric (20, 30 amp), water.

Twin Points, HC 67 Box 135, 74070. T: (918) 396-3170. www.reserveusa.com/nrrs/ok/twpo. RV/tent: 54. $$. Hookups: electric (20, 30 amp).

Stigler

Belle Starr, Rte. 4 Box 5500, 74462. T: (918) 799-5843. www.reserveusa.com/nrrs/ok/bels. RV/tent: 68. $$. Hookups: electric (20, 30, 50 amp), water.

Brooken Cove, Rte. 4 Box 5500, 74462. T: (918) 799-5843. www.reserveusa.com/nrrs/ok/brco. RV/tent: 71. $$. Hookups: electric (20, 30 amp), water.

Dam Site South (Eufaula Lake), Rte. 4 Box 5500, 74462. T: (918) 799-5843. www.reserveusa.com/nrrs/ok/dam9. RV/tent: 57. $. Hookups: electric (20, 30 amp), water.

Gentry Creek, Rte. 4 Box 5500, 74462. T: (918) 799-5843. www.reserveusa.com/nrrs/ok/gent. RV/tent: 40. $. Hookups: electric (20, 30 amp), water.

Highway 9 Landing, Rte. 4 Box 5500, 74462. T: (918) 799-5843. www.reserveusa.com. RV/tent: 81. $. Hookups: electric (20, 30 amp), water.

Porum Landing, Rte. 4 Box 5500, 74462. T: (918) 799-5843. www.reserveusa.com. RV/tent: 53. $. Hookups: electric (20, 30 amp), water.

Tahlequah

Arrowhead Camp, 7704 Hwy. 10, 74464. T: (800) 749-1140 or (918) 456-1140. www.arrowhead-thunderbird.com. RV/tent: 281. $. Hookups: electric (15, 20, 30 amp), water, sewer.

Diamondhead Resort, 10281 Hwy. 10, 74464. T: (800) 722-2411 or (918) 456-4545. www.diamondresort.us. RV/tent: 118. $. Hookups: electric (30 amp).

Eagle Bluff Resort, 9800 Hwy. 10, 74464. T: (800) OK-RIVER. www.eaglebluffresort.com. RV/tent: 155. $. Hookups: electric (30, 50 amp), water, sewer.

Hanging Rock Camp, 7453 Hwy. 10, 74464. T: (800) 375-3088 or (918) 456-3088. RV/tent: 506. $. Hookups: electric (30 amp), water, sewer.

Peyton's Place, 10298 Hwy. 10, 74464. T: (800) 359-0866 or (918) 456-3847. RV/tent: 85. $. Hookups: electric (20, 30, 40 amp), water, sewer.

Riverside Camp, 5116 Hwy. 10, 74464. T: (918) 456-4787 or (800) 749-CAMP. RV/tent: 48. $. Hookups: electric (30 amp).

Sparrowhawk Camp, 21985 North Ben George Rd., 74464. T: (800) 722-9635 or (918) 456-8371. www.sparrowhawkcamp.com. RV/tent: 100. $. Hookups: electric (30 amp).

Tahlequah Floats, 1 Plaza South, 74464. T: (800) 375-6949. RV/tent: 158. $. Hookups: electric (30 amp).

War Eagle Resort, 13020 Hwy. 10, 74464. T: (800) 722-3834 or (918) 456-6272. www.shop oklahoma.com/wareagle.htm. RV/tent: 532. $. Hookups: electric (30 amp), water.

OKLAHOMA (continued)

Tulsa

Estes Park, 1710 South 79th East Ave., 74112. T: (918) 627-3150. RV/tent: 21. $$. Hookups: electric (30, 50 amp), water, sewer.

Mingo RV Park, 801 North Mingo Rd., 74116. T: (800) 932-8824 or (918) 832-8824. RV/tent: 100. $$. Hookups: electric (30, 50 amp), water, sewer, cable.

Valliant

Lost Rapids, Rte. 1 Box 400, 74764. T: (580) 876-3720. www.reserveusa.com/nrrs/ok/losr. RV/tent: 30. $. Hookups: electric (20, 30 amp), water.

Pine Creek Cove, Rte. 1 Box 400, 74764. T: (580) 933-4215. www.reserveusa.com/nrrs/ok/picr. RV/tent: 41. $. Hookups: electric (20, 30 amp), water.

Turkey Creek, Rte. 1 Box 400, 74764. T: (580) 876-3720. www.reserveusa.com/nrrs/ok/turk. RV/tent: 34. $. Hookups: electric (20, 30 amp).

Watonga

Roman Nose Resort Park, Rte. 1, 73772. T: (800) 892-8690 or (580) 623-4215. www.tourokla-home.com/pages/resort5.html. RV/tent: 175. $. Hookups: electric (20, 30, 50 amp), water, sewer.

Waurika

Chisholm Trail Ridge, P.O. Box 29, 73573. T: (580) 439-8040. www.reserveusa.com. RV/tent: 95. $$. Hookups: electric (20, 30 amp), water.

Kiowa Park I, P.O. Box 29, 73573. T: (580) 963-9031. www.reserveusa.com. RV/tent: 180. $$. Hookups: electric (20, 30 amp), water.

Woodward

Cottonwood RV Park, South Hwy. 270, 73801. T: (580) 256-1068. RV/tent: 22. $. Hookups: electric (30, 50 amp), water, sewer.

OREGON

Agness

Agness RV Park, 04125 Agness Rd., 97406. T: (541) 247-2813. www.agnessrv.com. RV/tent: 90. $$. Hookups: electric (30 amp), water.

Albany

Blue Ox RV Park, 4000 Blue Ox Dr. SE, 97321. T: (541) 926-2886 or (800) 336-2881. RV/tent: 147. $$$. Hookups: electric, water, sewer, cable.

Ashland

Ashland Regency Inn and RV Park, 50 Lowe Rd., 97520. T: (800) 482-4701. RV/tent: 12. $$. Hookups: electric (20, 30 amp), water.

Howard Prairie Lake Resort, 3249 Hyatt Prairie Rd., 97501. T: (541) 482-1979. www.howard prairieresort.com. RV/tent: 268. $$. Hookups: electric (20 amp), water, dump station.

Hyatt Lake Resort, 7979 Hyatt Prarie Rd., 97520. T: (541) 482-3331. RV/tent: 35. $$. Hookups: electric (20, 30, 50 amp), water, dump station.

Baker City

Mountain View Holiday Trav-L-Park, 2845 Hughes Ln., 97814. T: (541) 523-4824. www.miewrv.com. RV/tent: 91. $$. Hookups: electric (20, 30, 50 amp).

Oregon Trails West RV Park, 42534 North Cedar Rd., 97814. T: (541) 523-3236 or (888) 523-3236. www.easy-finder.com. RV/tent: 50. $$. Hookups: electric (30, 50 amp), water, sewer.

Union Creek Campground, Wallowa-Whitman National Forest, Hwy. 7, 97814. T: (541) 523-4476. www.fs.fed.us/r6/w-w/rog/recrep. RV/tent: 58. $$. Hookups: electric (20, 30 amp).

Beaver

Camper Cove RV Park & Campground, 19620 Hwy. 101 South, 97108. T: (503) 398-5334. RV/tent: 20. $$. Hookups: electric (20, 30, 50 amp), water.

Bend

Crane Prairie Resort, Crane Prairie Lake Rd., 97701. T: (541) 383-3939. RV/tent: 20. $$. Hookups: full.

Crown Villa RV Park, 60801 Brosterhaus Rd., 97702. T: (541) 388-1131. RV/tent: 24. $$. Hookups: full.

Gull Point Campground (Deschutes National Forest), USFS 4260, 97701. T: (541) 383-5300. www.fs.fed.us. RV/tent: 79. $$. Hookups: none.

Lava Lake Campground (Deschutes National Forest), USFS. 4600, 97701. T: (541) 383-5300. www.fs.fed.us. RV/tent: 43. $. Hookups: none.

Quinn River Campground (Deschutes National Forest), Hwy. 46, 97701. T: (541) 383-5300. www.fs.fed.us. RV/tent: 41. $. Hookups: none.

Rock Creek Campground (Deschutes National Forest), Hwy. 46, 97701. T: (541) 383-5300. www.fs.fed.us. RV/tent: 31. $. Hookups: none.

Scandia RV and Mobile Park, 61415 South Hwy. 97, 97702. T: (541) 382-6206. RV/tent: 60. $. Hookups: full.

South Twin Lake Recreation Complex, Deschutes National Forest, USFS 4260, 97701. T: (541) 383-5300. www.fs.fed.us. RV/tent: 24. $$. Hookups: none.

Boardman

Driftwood RV Park, 800 West Kunze, 97818. T: (800) 684-5583. www.driftwood-rv.com. RV/tent: 103. $$. Hookups: electric (20, 30, 50 amp), water, sewer, cable.

Bonanza

Gerber Reservoir Campground, Gerber Rd., 97603. T: (541) 883-6916. www.or.blm.gov. RV/tent: 50. $. Hookups: water.

Brookings

At Rivers Edge RV Resort, 98203 South Bank Chetco, 97415. T: (541) 469-3356 or (888) 295-1441. www.atriversedge.com. RV/tent: 121. $$. Hookups: electric (20, 30, 50 amp).

Port of Brookings Harbor Beachfront RV Park, 16035 Boat Basin Rd., 97415. T: (541) 469-5867. www.port-brookings-harbor.org. RV/tent: 150. $$. Hookups: electric (30 amp), water.

Portside RV Park, 16219 Lower Harbor Rd., 97415. T: (541) 469-6616. www.portsidervpark.com. RV/tent: 104. $$. Hookups: full.

Whaleshead Beach Resort, 19921 Whaleshead Rd., 97415. T: (541) 469-7446 or (800) 943-4325. www.whalesheadresort.com. RV/tent: 110. $$. Hookups: electric (30, 50 amp), cable.

Canby

Riverside RV Park, 24310 Hwy. 99 East, 97013. T: (503) 263-3000 or (800) 425-2250. www .woodalls.com. RV/tent: 118. $$. Hookups: full.

Canyonville

Seven Feathers Casino Resort, 146 Chief Miwaleta Ln., 97417. T: (541) 839-1111 or (800) 548-8461. www.sevenfeathers.com. RV/tent: 32. $$. Hookups: electric (20, 30 amp), water, sewer.

Stanton Park (Douglas County Park), 1540 Stanton Park Rd., 97417. T: (541) 839-4483. RV/tent: 40. $. Hookups: electric (30 amp), water, sewer.

Cascade Summit

Shelter Cove Resort, West Odell Lake Rd., 97425. T: (541) 433-2548 or (800) 647-2729. www.sheltercoveresort.com. RV/tent: 69. $. Hookups: electric (20, 30 amp).

Cave Junction

Country Hills, 7901 Caves Hwy., 97523. T: (541) 592-3406. www.cavejunction.com. RV/tent: 28. $$. Hookups: electric (20, 30 amp), water.

Grayback US Forest and Campground, 11575 Caves Hwy. 46, 97523. T: (541) 592-3311. RV/tent: 18. $. Hookups: none.

Shady Acres RV Park, 27550 Redwood Hwy., 97523. T: (541) 592-3702. www.cavejunction .com. RV/tent: 35. $. Hookups: electric (20, 30 amp).

Chiloquin

Agency Lake Resort, 37000 Modoc Point Rd., 97642. T: (541) 783-2489. RV/tent: 30. $$. Hookups: electric (30 amp), water, sewer.

Melita's Highway 97 RV Park, 39500 Hwy. 97, 97624. T: (541) 783-2401. RV/tent: 27. $$. Hookups: electric (30 amp), water, sewer.

Walt's Cozy Camp, P.O. Box 243, 97624. T: (541) 783-2537. RV/tent: 54. $$. Hookups: electric (20 amp), water, sewer.

Water Wheel Campground, 200 Williamson River Dr., 97624. T: (541) 783-2738. RV/tent: 40. $$. Hookups: electric (30, 50 amp), water.

OREGON (continued)

Coos Bay

Alder Acres, 1800 28th Ct., 97420. T: (541) 269-0999 or (888) 400-7275. www.alderacresrv .homestead.com. RV/tent: 70. $$. Hookups: electric (30, 50 amp), cable.

Oregon Dunes KOA, 4135 Coast US 101, 97459. T: (541) 756-4851 or (800) KOA-4236. www .oregonduneskoa.com. RV/tent: 66. $$. Hookups: electric (30, 50 amp), water, sewer.

Cottage Grove

Village Green RV Park, 725 Row River Rd., 97424. T: (541) 942-2491. www.moonstonehotels.com. RV/tent: 42. $$. Hookups: electric (20, 30, 50 amp), water, sewer.

Crater Lake

Mazama Campground, 1211 Ave. C, 97503. T: (541) 594-2511. RV/tent: 200. $$. Hookups: none.

Crescent

Big Pines RV Park, 135151 Hwy. 97 North, 97733. T: (541) 433-2785 or (800) 351-2785. www.rverschoice.com/bigpinesrvpark. RV/tent: 21. $. Hookups: full.

Willamette Pass Inn and RV, Milepost 69, Hwy. 58, 97425. T: (541) 443-2211. www.willamette passinn.com. RV/tent: 19. $. Hookups: electric (20, 30, 50 amp), water.

Dale

Meadowbrook Lodge Inc., P.O. Box 37, 97880. T: (541) 421-3104. RV/tent: 31. $. Hookups: electric (30 amp).

Depoe Bay

Fogarty Creek RV Park, 3340 North Hwy. 101, 97341. T: (541) 764-2228 or (888) 675-7034. www.fogartycreekrv.com. RV/tent: 53. $$. Hookups: electric (20, 30 amp), water, sewer.

Sea and Sand RV Park, 4985 US 101, 97388. T: (541) 764-2313. RV/tent: 109. $$$. Hookups: electric (30, 50 amp), water, sewer.

Detroit

Detroit RV Park, 100 Breinbenbush Rd., 97342. T: (503) 854-3200 or (503) 931-2100. www. hometown.aol.com/detroitrvpark/myhome page/business.html. RV/tent: 14. $$. Hookups: full.

Dexter

Dexter Shores Mobile and RV Park, 39140 Dexter Rd., 97431. T: (541) 937-3711 or (866) 558-9777. www.dextershoresrvpark.com. RV/tent: 56. $$. Hookups: electric (30, 50 amp), water, sewer.

Dodson

Ainsworth State Park, P.O. Box 100, 97019. T: (503) 695-2301. www.oregonstateparks.org/park_ 146.php. RV/tent: 50. $$. Hookups: full.

Dufur

Dufur RV Park, P.O. Box 192, 97021. T: (541) 467-2449. RV/tent: 26. $$. Hookups: electric (20, 30 amp), water, sewer, cable.

Eagle Point

Medford Oaks RV Park, 7049 OR 140, 97524. T: (541) 826-5103. www.medfordoaks.com. RV/tent: 55. $$. Hookups: electric (20, 30, 50 amp), water, phone, modem.

Elkton

Elkton RV Park, 450 River Rd., 97436. T: (541) 584-2832. www.rverschoice.com/elktonrvpark. RV/tent: 53. $$. Hookups: electric (20, 30, 50 amp).

Sawyers Rapids RV Resort, 24828 OR 38, 97436. T: (541) 584-2226 or (888) 478-4426. www.sawyersrapids.com. RV/tent: 32. $$. Hookups: electric (30, 50 amp), water, sewer.

Enterprise

Outpost RV, 66258 Lewiston Hwy., 97828. T: (541) 426-4027. RV/tent: 45. $$. Hookups: full.

Estacada

Promontory Park, 40600 East Hwy. 224, 97023. T: (503) 630-7229 or (503) 630-5153. RV/tent: 48. $$. Hookups: none.

Silver Fox RV Park, 40505 SE Hwy. 224, 97023. T: (503) 630-7000. RV/tent: 70. $$. Hookups: electric (15, 30, 50 amp), water, sewer.

Eugene

Deerwood RV Park, 35059 Seavey Loop Rd., 97405. T: (541) 988-1139 or (877) 988-1139. www.deerwoodrvpark.com. RV/tent: 50. $$$. Hookups: electric (30, 50 amp), water, sewer.

Premier RV Resorts, 33022 Van Duyn Rd., 97408. T: (541) 686-3152. www.premierrvresorts.com. RV/tent: 111. $$$. Hookups: electric (30, 50 amp), water, sewer.

Shamrock Village, 4531 Franklin Blvd., 97403. T: (541) 747-7473. RV/tent: 115. $$. Hookups: electric (20, 30, 50 amp), water, sewer.

Fairview

Portland Fairview RV Park, 21401 NE Sandy Blvd., 97024. T: (503) 661-1047 or (877) 777-1047. www.portlandfairviewrv.com. RV/tent: 407. $$. Hookups: electric (20, 30, 50 amp), cable.

Florence

Darlings Resort, RV Park & Marina, 4879 Darlings Loop, 97439. T: (541) 997-2841. www.darlings resort.com. RV/tent: 41. $$. Hookups: electric (20, 30 amp), water, sewer.

Happy Place RV Park, 4044 Hwy. 101, 97439. T: (541) 997-1434. www.touroregon.com/happy placervpark. RV/tent: 52. $$. Hookups: electric (30, 50 amp), water, sewer.

Lakeshore RV Park, 83763 US 101, 97439. T: (541) 997-2741. www.pacific101.com/lakeshore. RV/tent: 20. $$. Hookups: electric (30 amp), water, sewer, cable.

Thousand Trails South Jetty, 05010 South Jetty Rd., 97439. T: (541) 997-8333 or (877) 902-2024. RV/tent: 192. $$. Hookups: electric (20, 30 amp), water.

Woahink Lake RV Resort, 83570 Hwy. 101 South, 97439. T: (541) 997-6454 or (800) 659-6454. www.ohwy.com/or/w/woahlkrv.htm. RV/tent: 78. $$. Hookups: electric (30, 50 amp), water, sewer.

Fort Klamath

Crater Lake Resort at Fort Creek Campground, 50711 OR 62, 97626. T: (541) 381-2349. www.craterlakeresort.com. RV/tent: 43. $$. Hookups: electric (20, 30, 50 amp), water, sewer.

Fort Klamath Lodge and RV Park, P.O. Box 428, 97601. T: (541) 381-2234. RV/tent: 16. $$. Hookups: electric (20, 30 amp), water, sewer.

Glendale

Meadow Wood RV and Campground, P.O. Box 885, 97442. T: (541) 832-3114 or (800) 606-1274. www.meadow-woodrvpark.com. RV/tent: 64. $$. Hookups: electric (20, 30, 50 amp), water.

Glide

Susan Creek (BLM), 777 NW Garden Valley Blvd., 97470. T: (541) 440-4930. RV/tent: 31. $. Hookups: none.

Gold Beach

Four Seasons RV Resort, 96526 North Bank Rogue, 97444. T: (800) 247-4503. www.four seasonsrv.com. RV/tent: 51. $$. Hookups: full.

Indian Creek Recreation Park, 94680 Jerry's Flat Rd., 97444. T: (541) 247-7704 or (877) 537-7704. www.indiancreekrv.com. RV/tent: 172. $$. Hookups: electric (20, 30 amp), water, sewer.

Irelands Oceanview RV Park, 29272 Ellensburg Ave., 97444. T: (541) 247-0148. www.irelandsrv park.com. RV/tent: 32. $$. Hookups: electric (20, 30, 50 amp), water, sewer.

Kimball Creek Bend RV Resort, 97136 North Bank Rogue River Rd., 97444. T: (541) 247-7580 or (888) 814-0633. www.kimballcreek.com. RV/tent: 69. $$. Hookups: electric (30 amp), water, sewer.

Lucky Lodge RV Park, 32040 Watson Ln., 97444. T: (541) 247-7618. RV/tent: 36. $$. Hookups: full.

Turtle Rock RV Resort, 28788 Hunter Creek Loop Rd., 97444. T: (541) 247-9203 or (800) 353-9754. www.turtlerockresorts.com. RV/tent: 50. $$$. Hookups: electric (20, 30, 50), water, sewer.

Gold Hill

Cypress Grove RV Park, 1679 Rogue River Hwy., 97525. T: (541) 855-9000 or (800) 758-0719. www.cypressgrovervpark.com. RV/tent: 45. $$. Hookups: electric (30, 50 amp), cable.

KOA Medford/Gold Hill, P.O. Box 320, 97525. T: (541) 855-7710 or (800) KOA-7608. www.koa.com/where/or/37109.htm. RV/tent: 69. $$. Hookups: electric (20, 30, 50 amp), water, sewer.

Lazy Acres RV Park and Motel, 1550 2nd Ave., 97525. T: (541) 855-7000. www.lazyacresrv park.com. RV/tent: 68. $$. Hookups: electric (30, 50 amp), phone, modem, dump station.

Grants Pass

Moon Mountain RV Resort, 3290 Pearce Park Rd., 97526. T: (541) 479-1145 or (877) 479-1145. www.moonmountainrv.com. RV/tent: 50. $$. Hookups: electric (20, 30, 50 amp), water, dump station.

Rogue Valley Overnighters, 1806 NW 6th St., 97526. T: (541) 479-2208. RV/tent: 110. $$. Hookups: electric (30, 50 amp), water, sewer, cable.

OREGON (continued)

Hermiston

Hat Rock Campground, Hat Rock Rd., RR 3 Box 3780, 97838. T: (541) 567-4188. RV/tent: 80. $$. Hookups: full.

Idleyld Park

Elk Have RV Resort, 22020 North Umpqua Hwy., 97477. T: (541) 496-3090. www.elkhavenrv.com. RV/tent: 42. $$. Hookups: electric (20, 30, 50 amp), water, sewer.

Klamath Falls

Oregon Motel 8 RV Park, 5225 Hwy. 97 North, 97601. T: (541) 882-0482. RV/tent: 32. $$. Hookups: electric (20, 30 amp), water.

La Pine

Cascade Meadows RV Resort, 53750 Hwy. 97, 97739. T: (541) 536-2244. RV/tent: 100. $$. Hookups: electric (20, 30, 50 amp), water, sewer.

Lakeside

Eel Creek RV Park, 67760 Spin Reel Rd., 97449. T: (541) 759-4462. RV/tent: 41. $$. Hookups: electric (50 amp), water, sewer.

Goose Lake State Recreation Area, US 395, 97630. T: (541) 937-3111. www.oregonstateparks.org/park_1.php. RV/tent: 47. $. Hookups: electric, water.

Hunter's RV Park, US 395, 97630. T: (541) 947-4968. RV/tent: 133. $$. Hookups: full.

Osprey Point RV Resort, 1505 North Lake Rd., 97449. T: (541) 759-2801. www.ospreypoint.net. RV/tent: 164. $$. Hookups: full.

Langlois

Bandon-Port Orford-KOA, 46612 Hwy. 101, 97450. T: (541) 348-2358 or (800) 562-3298. www.koa.com. RV/tent: 72. $$. Hookups: electric (20, 30 amp), water.

Lincoln City

KOA Lincoln City, 5298 NE Parklane, 97368. T: (541) 944-2961 or (800) 562-2791. www.koa.com/where/or/37108.htm. RV/tent: 76. $$. Hookups: full.

McKenzie Bridge

Belknap Lodge and Hot Springs, 59296 Belknap Springs Rd., 97413. T: (541) 822-3512. RV/tent: 40. $$. Hookups: electric (30 amp), water.

McMinnville

Mulkey RV Park, 14325 SW Hwy. 18, 97128. T: (887) 472-2475. RV/tent: 70. $$. Hookups: full.

Olde Stone Village RV Park, 4155 Three Mile Ln., 97128. T: (503) 472-4315 or (877) 472-4315. www.woodalls.com/a/02465_oldestonevlg.html. RV/tent: 71. $$. Hookups: full.

Medford

Fish Lake Resort, P.O. Box 40, 97501. T: (541) 949-8500. RV/tent: 59. $$. Hookups: electric (20, 30 amp), water, sewer.

Pear Tree Motel and RV Park, 3730 Fern Valley, 97504. T: (541) 535-4445. RV/tent: 31. $$. Hookups: electric (20, 30 50 amp).

Myrtle Creek

Rivers West RV Park, 333 Ruckles Dr., 97457. T: (888) 863-7602. RV/tent: 120. $$. Hookups: electric (30, 50 amp), water.

Newport

Harbor Village RV Park, 923 SE Bay Blvd., 97365. T: (541) 265-5088. www.harborvillagervpark.com. RV/tent: 140. $$. Hookups: full.

O'Brien

Neelson Almost Heaven, 38548 Redwood Hwy., 97534-9703. T: (541) 516-2952. RV/tent: 110. $$. Hookups: electric (30 amp), water, sewer.

Ophir

Honey Bear Campground, 34161 Ophir Rd., 97464. T: (541) 247-2765 or (800) 822-4444. www.honeybearrv.com. RV/tent: 120. $$. Hookups: electric (20, 30 amp), water, sewer.

Pendleton

Mountain View RV Park, 1375 SE 3rd St., 97801. T: (541) 276-1041. RV/tent: 70. $$. Hookups: full.

Phoenix

Holiday RV Park, 201 Fern Valley Rd., 97535. T: (541) 535-2183 or (800) 452-7970. RV/tent: 110. $$. Hookups: electric (20, 50 amp), water, sewer.

Prineville

Crook County RV Park, 1040 South Main, 97754. T: (541) 447-2599 or (800) 609-2599. RV/tent: 32. $$. Hookups: full.

Prospect

Rogue River National Forest (Farewell Bend Campground), 333 West 8th St., 97501. T: (541) 770-5146. RV/tent: 61. $. Hookups: none.

Rogue River

Circle W RV Park, 8110 Rogue River Hwy., 97527. T: (541) 582-1686. RV/tent: 25. $$. Hookups: electric (20, 30, 50 amp), water, dump station.

Roseburg

Mt. Nebo Trailer Park, 2071 NE Stephens, 97470. T: (541) 673-4108. RV/tent: 26. $$. Hookups: electric (30 amp).

Rising River RV Park, 5579 SW Grange Rd., 97470. T: (541) 6798-7256 or (800) 854-4279. www.risingriverrv.com. RV/tent: 68. $$. Hookups: full.

Twin Rivers Vacation Park, 433 River Forks Park Rd., 97470. T: (541) 673-3811. RV/tent: 80. $$. Hookups: full.

Western Star Mobile Estates, 101 Ladd Ln., 97470. T: (541) 679-6159. RV/tent: 15. $$. Hookups: electric (20, 30, 50 amp).

Salem

Eola Bend RV Resort, 4700 Salem, Dallas Hwy. 22, 97304. T: (503) 364-7714 or (877) 364-9990. RV/tent: 180. $$. Hookups: full.

Shady Cove

Fly Casters RV Park, 21655 Crater Lake Hwy. 62, 97539. T: (541) 878-2749 or (800) 806-4705.

RV/tent: 47. $$. Hookups: electric (30, 50 amp), cable.

Rogue River RV Park and Resort, 21800 Crater Lake Hwy. 62, 97539. T: (541) 878-2404. RV/tent: 70. $$. Hookups: electric (30, 50 amp).

Shady Trails RV Park and Campground, 1 Meadow Ln., 97539. T: (541) 878-2206 or (800) 606-2206. RV/tent: 50. $$. Hookups: electric (20, 30 amp), water, dump station.

Sunny Valley

Grants Pass/Sunny Valley KOA, 140 Old Stage Rd., 97497. T: (541) 476-6508 or (800) 562-7566. www.koa.com/where/or/37106.htm. RV/tent: 70. $$. Hookups: electric (20, 40 amp), water, dump station.

Trail

Bear Mountain RV Park, 27301 Hwy. 62, 97541. T: (541) 878-2400 or (800) 586-2327. RV/tent: 43. $. Hookups: electric (20, 30, 50 amp), water.

Troutdale

Rolling Hills Mobile Terrace and RV Park, 20145 NE Sandy Blvd., 97024. T: (503) 666-7282. RV/tent: 101. $$. Hookups: electric (30, 50 amp), water, sewer, cable.

Tualatin

Roamer's Rest RV Park, 17585 Sw Pacific Hwy., 97062. T: (503) 692-6350 or (877) 4RV-PARK. RV/tent: 93. $$. Hookups: full.

Waldport

KOA Waldport/Newport, Hwy. 101, 97394. T: (541) 563-2250 or (800) 562-3443. www.oregoncoastkoa.com. RV/tent: 78. $$. Hookups: electric (50 amp), water, sewer.

White City

Lakewood RV Park, 2564 Merry Ln., 97503. T: (541) 830-1957. www.lakewoodrvpark.com. RV/tent: 45. $$. Hookups: electric (20, 30, 50 amp), water, sewer.

Wilderville

Grants Pass/Redwood Hwy. KOA, 13370 Redwood Hwy., 97543. T: (541) 476-6508 or (800) 562-7566. www.koa.com/where/or/37106.htm. RV/tent: 40. $$. Hookups: electric (30, 50 amp), water, dump station.

Wilsonville

Pheasant Ridge RV Park, 8275 Sw Elligsen Rd., 97070. T: (503) 682-7829 or (800) 532-7829. www.pheasantridge.com. RV/tent: 130. $$$. Hookups: electric (20, 30, 50 amp), water, sewer.

Winston

On the River RV Park, P.O. Box 1614, 97470. T: (541) 679-6634 or (800) 521-5556. RV/tent: 30. $$. Hookups: electric (20, 30 amp), water, dump station.

River Bend RV Park, 31 SE Thompson Ave., 97496. T: (541) 679-4000. RV/tent: 63. $$. Hookups: electric (20, 30, 50 amp), dump station.

OREGON (continued)

Umpqua Safari RV Park, 511 NE Main St., 97496. T: (541) 679-6328 or (800) 818-8580. www.umoquasafari.com. RV/tent: 30. $$. Hookups: electric (20, 30, 50 amp).

Wildlife Safari RV Area, P.O. Box 1600, 97496. T: (541) 679-6761 or (800) 350-4848. RV/tent: 20. $. Hookups: electric (20, 30 amp).

Wolf Creek

Creekside RV Resort, 999 Old Hwy. 99, 97497. T: (541) 866-2655. RV/tent: 42. $$. Hookups: electric (20, 30, 50 amp).

Woodburn

Woodburn I-5 RV Park, 115 North Arney Rd., 97071. T: (503) 981-0002 or (888) 988-0002. www.woodburnrv.com. RV/tent: 150. $$$. Hookups: electric (50 amp), water, sewer.

Yachats

Sea Perch Campground/RV Park, 95480 US 101 South, Milepost 171, 97498. T: (541) 547-3505. www.seaperchrvpark.com. RV/tent: 36. $$$. Hookups: full.

Yamhill

Flying M Ranch, 23029 NW Flying M Rd., 97148. T: (503) 662-3222. www.flying-m-ranch.com. RV/tent: 100. $. Hookups: none.

PENNSYLVANIA

Airville

Otter Creek Campground, 1101 Furnace Rd., 17302. T: (717) 862-3628. RV/tent: 85. $$. Hookups: electric (20, 30 amp), water.

Allentown

KOA Allentown, Rte. 100, 18066. T: (610) 298-2160. RV/tent: 103. $$. Hookups: electric (20, 30, 50 amp), water, sewer, phone.

Altoona

Sanderbeck's Campground, Spencer Creek Dr., 16635. T: (814) 695-0501. RV/tent: 20. $$. Hookups: electric (20, 30 amp), water, sewer, phone.

Wright's Orchard Station Campground, US 220, 16635. T: (814) 695-2628. www.gocamping america.com/wrightsorchard. RV/tent: 42. $$. Hookups: electric (20, 30, 50 amp), water, sewer.

Bangor

Camp Charles Campground, 1020 Blue Mountain Rd., 18013. T: (610) 588-0553. RV/tent: 155. $$. Hookups: electric, water.

Bath

Evergreen Lake Camping, 2375 Benders Dr., 18014. T: (610) 837-6401. RV/tent: 375. $$. Hookups: electric (20, 30 amp), water, sewer, phone.

Beavertown

Gray Squirrel Campsites, RR 1 Box 1699, 17813. T: (570) 837-0333. RV/tent: 240. $$. Hookups: electric, water, sewer.

Bedford

Choice Camping Court, 209 Choice Campground Rd., 15550. T: (814) 623-9272. RV/tent: 197. $$. Hookups: electric (20, 30 amp), water, sewer, phone.

Bellefonte

Fort Bellefonte Campground, 2023 Jacksonville Rd., 16823. T: (814) 355-9820. RV/tent: 100. $$. Hookups: electric, water, sewer, phone.

Bentleyville

Campground 70, 824 Bentleyville Rd., 15022. T: (800) 327-6053. RV/tent: 47. $$. Hookups: electric, water, sewer.

Benton

Whispering Pines Camping Estates, 1969 Henderson Ave., 15301. T: (570) 925-6810. RV/tent: 56. $$. Hookups: electric, water, sewer, phone.

Blakeslee

Fern Ridge Campground, P.O. Box 707, 18610. T: (570) 646-2267. RV/tent: 225. $$. Hookups: electric, water.

WT Family Camping, Rte. 115, 18610. T: (570) 646-9255. RV/tent: 110. $$. Hookups: electric, water, sewer.

Bloomsburg

Deihl's Camping Resort, R.D. 4, 17815. T: (717) 683-5212. RV/tent: 101. $$. Hookups: electric (30 amp), water, sewer, phone.

Indian Head Recreational Campground, 340 Reading St., 17815. T: (570) 784-6150. RV/tent: 229. $$. Hookups: electric, water, sewer.

Shady Rest Campground, 119 Eyers Grove Rd., 17846. T: (570) 458-6327. RV/tent: 100. $. Hookups: electric, water.

Turner High View Camping Area, RR 4, 17815. T: (570) 784-6940. RV/tent: 92. $$. Hookups: electric, water.

Boyertown

Schlegel's Grove & Campsites, 102 Township Line Rd., 19505. T: (610) 367-8576. RV/tent: 175. $$. Hookups: electric, water, sewer.

Bradford

KOA Kinzua East, Kinuza Hts. Rte. 59, 16701. T: (814) 368-3662. RV/tent: 120. $$$. Hookups: electric, water, sewer, phone.

Breezewood

Way Bridge Campground, P.O. Box 102, 15522. T: (814) 735-2768. RV/tent: 50. $$. Hookups: none.

Brodheadsville

Chestnut Lake Campground, Frantz Rd., 18322. T: (570) 992-6179. RV/tent: 200. $$. Hookups: electric, water, sewer.

Silver Valley Campsites, 4214 Silver Valley Dr., 18353. T: (570) 992-4824. RV/tent: 125. $$. Hookups: electric, water, sewer, phone.

Bushkill

Outdoor World Timothy Lake South Campground, RD 6 Box 6627, 18301. T: (570) 699-1617. RV/tent: 216. $$. Hookups: electric, water, sewer.

Carlisle

Bienvenu Canadian, 200 Greenview Dr., 17013. T: (717) 243-1179. RV/tent: 256. $$. Hookups: electric (20, 30 amp) water, sewer, phone.

Carlisle Campground, 1075 Harrisburg Pike, 17013. T: (717) 249-4563. RV/tent: 115. $$. Hookups: electric, water, sewer, phone.

Catawissa

J & D Campground, RD 2 Box 358, 17820. T: (717) 356-7700. RV/tent: 225. $$. Hookups: electric, water, phone.

Chambersburg

Twin Bridge Meadow Family Campground, 1345 Twin Bridge Rd., 17201. T: (717) 369-2216. RV/tent: 132. $$. Hookups: electric, water, sewer.

Clarks Mills

Camp Wilhelm, 1401 Creek Rd., 16114. T: (724) 253-2886. RV/tent: 147. $$. Hookups: electric, water, sewer.

Claysville

Four Seasons Camping Resort, 3 Camp Resort Rd., 15377. T: (877) 660-4407. RV/tent: 200. $$. Hookups: electric, water, sewer.

Coatesville

Birchview Farm Campground, RD 9 Box 266, 19320. T: (610) 384-0500. RV/tent: 185. $$. Hookups: electric, water, sewer, phone.

Hidden Acres Camping Grounds, RD 2, 19320. T: (610) 857-3990. RV/tent: 255. $$. Hookups: electric, water, sewer.

Cocalico

Cocalico Creek Campground, 560 Cocalico Rd., 17517. T: (717) 336-2014. RV/tent: 130. $$. Hookups: electric, water, sewer.

Columbia

Prospect Valley Farm Campground, 1334 Prospect Rd., 17512. T: (717) 684-8893. RV/tent: 148. $$. Hookups: electric (20, 30 amp), water, sewer, phone.

Connellsville

River's Edge Family Campground, 1101 River's Edge Rd., 15425. T: (412) 628-4880. RV/tent: 157. $$. Hookups: electric (30 amp), water, sewer.

White's Haven Campground & Cabins, HC 1 Box 81D, 15828. T: (814) 752-2205. RV/tent: 120. $$. Hookups: electric, water, sewer.

Corry

Hare Creek Campground, 375 Sciota St., 16407. T: (814) 664-9684. RV/tent: 160. $$. Hookups: electric, water, sewer, phone, cable.

Covington

Tanglewood Camping, Tanglewood Rd., 16917. T: (570) 549-8299. RV/tent: 100. $$. Hookups: electric, water.

Cranberry Township

Pittsburgh North Campground, 6610 Mars Rd., 16066. T: (724) 776-1150. RV/tent: 126. $$. Hookups: electric (30 amp), water, sewer.

Darlington

Crawford's Camping Park, 273 Hodgson Rd., 16115. T: (724) 846-5964. RV/tent: 125. $$. Hookups: electric, water, sewer.

Denver

Lancaster/Reading KOA, 3 Denver Rd., 17517. T: (800) 562-1621. RV/tent: 144. $$. Hookups: electric (30 amp), water, sewer.

Dingmans Ferry

Dingmans Campground, Rte. 209, 18328. T: (570) 828-2266. RV/tent: 45. $$. Hookups: electric, water, sewer.

Donegal

Donegal Campground, Rte. 31, HC 63 Box 104, 15628. T: (412) 593-7717. RV/tent: 45. $$. Hookups: electric (20, 50 amp), water, sewer.

Laurel Highlands Campground, Rte. 31 East, 15628. T: (724) 593-6325. RV/tent: 300. $$. Hookups: electric, water, sewer.

Downingtown

Shady Acres Campground, Rte. 282, 19335. T: (610) 269-1800. RV/tent: 50. $$$. Hookups: electric, water, sewer.

Drums

Hazelton/Wilkes-Barre Campground, 718 North Old Turnpike Rd., 18222. T: (570) 788-3382. RV/tent: 87. $$. Hookups: electric, water, sewer, phone.

Hazleton KOA, RR 1 Box 1405, 18222. T: (800) 562-9751. RV/tent: 148. $$. Hookups: electric (20, 30 amp), water, sewer.

Du Bois

Clearview Campground, RD 2 Box 355, 15801. T: (814) 371-9947. RV/tent: 70. $. Hookups: electric, water, sewer.

East Berlin

Conewago Isle Campground, Bigmount Rd., 17315. T: (717) 292-1461. RV/tent: 95. $$. Hookups: electric, water, sewer.

Outdoor World Gettysburg Farm Campground, 6200 Big Mount Rd., 17315. T: (717) 292-7191. RV/tent: 275. $$. Hookups: electric, water, sewer.

East Lancaster

Old Mill Stream Camping Manor, 2249 Rte. 30, 17602. T: (717) 299-2314. www.oldmillstream camping.com. RV/tent: 65. $$. Hookups: electric (30, 50 amp), water, sewer, cable.

East Springfield

Pine Lane Campground, 11709 West Lake Rd., 16411. T: (814) 774-4808. www.pinelane campground.com. RV/tent: 45. $$. Hookups: electric (20 amp), water.

Ebensburg

Woodland Park, 220 Campground Rd., 15931. T: (814) 472-9857. www.rvnetlinx.com. RV/tent: 230. $. Hookups: electric (20, 30 amp), water, sewer.

Elizabethtown

Ridge Run Family Campground, 867 Schwanger Rd., 17022. T: (717) 367-3454. RV/tent: 138. $$. Hookups: electric, water, sewer, phone.

Elysburg

Knoebels Grove Campground, Hwy. 487, 17824. T: (570) 672-9555. RV/tent: 500. $$. Hookups: electric.

Emlenton

Gas Light Campground, RD 2 Box 10, 16373. T: (724) 867-6981. RV/tent: 158. $$. Hookups: electric (30 amp), water, sewer.

Entriken

Hemlock Hideaway Camp, Box 189 B1, 16657. T: (814) 658-3663. RV/tent: 63. $$. Hookups: electric, water.

Ephrata

Starlite Camping Resort, 1500 Furnace Hill Rd., 17578. T: (800) 521-3599. RV/tent: 220. $$$. Hookups: electric, water, sewer.

Erie

Hill's Family Campground, 6300 Sterrittania Rd., 16415. T: (814) 833-3272. RV/tent: 136. $$. Hookups: electric, water, sewer.

Etters

Park Away Park Family Campground, 1300 Old Trail Rd., 17319. T: (717) 938-1686. RV/tent: 203. $$. Hookups: electric (20, 30 amp), water, sewer.

Everett

Triangle Acres Family Campground, Bridge St., 15537. T: (814) 784-3363. RV/tent: 25. $$. Hookups: electric, water.

Farmington

Benner's Meadow Run Camping & Cabins, 315 Nelson Rd., 15437. T: (724) 329-4097. RV/tent: 200. $$. Hookups: electric, water, sewer.

Florence

Bennett Acres Campground, Rte. 18 North, 15021. T: (412) 947-5120. RV/tent: 515. $$. Hookups: electric (30 amp), water.

Forksville

Almost Heaven Campground, P.O. Box 63, 18616. T: (717) 924-3458. RV/tent: 200. $$. Hookups: electric (20, 30 amp), water.

Fort Littleton

Ye Olde Mill Campground, 599 Gristmill Rd., 17215. T: (717) 987-3244. RV/tent: 30. $$. Hookups: electric, water.

Gaines

Pine Creek Vista Campgrounds, Elk Run Rd., 16921. T: (814) 435-6398. RV/tent: 88. $. Hookups: electric, water.

Gettysburg

Gettysburg Battlefield Resort, 1960 Emmitsburg Rd., 17325. T: (717) 337-3363. RV/tent: 300. $$. Hookups: electric, water, sewer.

Gettysburg KOA, 20 Knox Rd., 17325. T: (800) 562-1869. RV/tent: 93. $$. Hookups: electric (30 amp), water, sewer, cable.

Glen Iron

Penn's Creek Campground, RD 1 Box 363, 17845. T: (570) 922-1371. RV/tent: 87. $$. Hookups: electric, water, sewer.

Gordonville

Country Aces Family Campground, 20 Leven Rd., 17529. T: (717) 687-8014. RV/tent: 60. $$. Hookups: electric (30 amp), water, sewer.

Greencastle

Keystone RV Campground, 15799 Young Rd., 17225. T: (800) 232-3279. RV/tent: 25. $$. Hookups: electric, water.

Greentown

Ironwood Point Recreation Area (PP&L), RR 3 Box 344, 18426. T: (570) 857-0880. RV/tent: 60. $$. Hookups: electric.

Ledgedale Recreation Area, RR 3 Box 379 C, 18426. T: (570) 689-2181. RV/tent: 70. $$. Hookups: electric.

Harmony

Indian Brave Campground, Mercer St., 16037. T: (724) 452-9204. RV/tent: 250. $$. Hookups: electric, water, sewer.

Harrisburg

Harrisburg East Campground, 1134 Highspire Rd., 17111. T: (717) 939-4331. RV/tent: 74. $$. Hookups: electric, water, sewer.

Harrisville

Kozy Rest Kampground, 449 Campground Rd., 16038. T: (724) 735-2417. RV/tent: 203. $$. Hookups: electric, water, sewer.

PENNSYLVANIA (continued)

Hatfield

Village Scene Park, 2151 Koffel Rd., 19440. T: (215) 362-6030. RV/tent: 10. $$. Hookups: electric, water, sewer.

Hawley

Wilsonville Recreation Area, HC 6 Box 6114, 18428. T: (570) 226-4382. RV/tent: 168. $$. Hookups: electric.

Hegins

Camp-A-While, RD 3 Box 334, 17938. T: (570) 682-8696. RV/tent: 106. $$. Hookups: electric, water, sewer.

Hershey

KOA Hershey/Conewago, Hwy. 743, 17033. T: (717) 367-1179. RV/tent: 151. $$. Hookups: electric, water, sewer.

Hesston

Pleasant Hills Resort, P.O. Box 86, 16647. T: (814) 658-3986. RV/tent: 110. $$. Hookups: electric, water, sewer.

Holtwood

Muddy Run Recreation Park, 172 Bethesda Church Rd. West, 17532. T: (717) 284-4325. RV/tent: 163. $$. Hookups: electric, water, sewer.

Tucquan Park Family Campground, 917 River Rd., 17532. T: (717) 284-2156. RV/tent: 198. $$. Hookups: electric, water, sewer, phone.

Honesdale

Countryside Family Campground, RR 1, 18431. T: (570) 253-0424. RV/tent: 70. $$. Hookups: electric, water.

Ponderosa Pines Campground, Alden Lake Rd., 18431. T: (570) 253-2080. RV/tent: 88. $$. Hookups: electric, water.

Honey Brook

The Berry Patch Campground, Ross Rd., 19344. T: (610) 273-3720. RV/tent: 125. $$. Hookups: electric, water, sewer.

Two Log Campground, 960 Beaver Dam Rd., 19344. T: (610) 273-3068. RV/tent: 75. $$. Hookups: electric, water.

Hop Bottom

Shore Forest Campground, P.O. Box 366, 18824. T: (717) 289-4666. RV/tent: 160. $$. Hookups: electric, water, sewer, phone.

Indiana

L & M Campgrounds, 2743 Campground Rd., 15765. T: (724) 479-3264. RV/tent: 239. $. Hookups: electric (20, 30 amp), water, sewer.

Intercourse

Beacon Camping, West Newport Rd./Rte. 772, 17534. T: (717) 768-8775. www.800padutch.com/beacon.html. RV/tent: 44. $$. Hookups: electric (30, 50 amp), water, sewer.

Irwin

Dusty Rhodes Mobile Home Village, 14940 US 30, 15647. T: (412) 824-7078. RV/tent: 18. $$. Hookups: electric, water, sewer.

Rustic Acres Campground, P.O. Box 253, 15642. T: (814) 226-9850. RV/tent: 132. $. Hookups: electric (30 amp), water, sewer.

Jamestown

Shangri-La by the Lake Campground, 1824 Williamsfield Rd., 16134. T: (724) 932-5044. RV/tent: 280. $$. Hookups: electric, water, sewer.

Jonestown

Jonestown KOA, 500 Old Rte. 22 East, 17038. T: (717) 865-2526. RV/tent: 129. $$. Hookups: electric, water, sewer, phone.

Kinzers

Roamers Retreat Campground, 5005 Lincoln Hwy., 17535. T: (717) 442-4287. www.rvcamping.com/pa/roamers.html. RV/tent: 170. $. Hookups: electric (30, 50 amp), water, sewer.

Kutztown

Pine Hill Campground, 268 Old Rte. 22, 19530. T: (610) 285-6776. RV/tent: 125. $$$. Hookups: electric, water, sewer, phone.

Sacony Park Campsites, RD 3 Box 306, 19530. T: (610) 683-3939. RV/tent: 113. $$. Hookups: electric (20, 30 amp), water.

Lake City

Camp Eriez, 9356 West Lake Rd./Rte. 5, 16423. T: (814) 774-8381. RV/tent: 190. $$. Hookups: electric, water.

Laporte

Pioneer Campground, Rte. 220, 18626. T: (717) 946-9971. RV/tent: 95. $$. Hookups: electric, water, sewer, phone.

Lenhartsville

Blue Rocks Family Campground, 341 Sousley Rd., 19534. T: (610) 756-6366. RV/tent: 200. $$. Hookups: electric, water, sewer.

Loganton

Holiday Pines Campground, RR 1, 17747. T: (570) 725-CAMP. RV/tent: 74. $$. Hookups: electric, water, sewer, phone.

Manheim

Tall Oaks Campground, 2649 Camp Rd., 17545. T: (717) 665-7120. RV/tent: 40. $. Hookups: electric, water, sewer.

Matamoras

Tri-State RV Park, 400 Shay Ln., 18336. T: (800) 562-2663. RV/tent: 130. $$. Hookups: electric, water, sewer, phone.

Mercer

Junction 19-80 Campground, 1266 Old Mercer Rd., 16137. T: (412) 748-4174. RV/tent: 161. $$. Hookups: electric, water, sewer, phone.

Mercer/Grove City KOA, 1337 Butler Pike, 16137. T: (724) 748-3160. RV/tent: 173. $$$. Hookups: electric, water, sewer.

Rocky Springs Campground, 84 Rocky Springs Rd./Rte. 318, 16137. T: (412) 662-4415. www.rockyspringscampground.com.

RV/tent: 115. $$. Hookups: electric (30 amp), water, sewer.

Meshoppen

Slumber Valley Campground, RR 2, 18630. T: (570) 833-5208. RV/tent: 70. $$. Hookups: electric, water, phone.

Milford

River Beach Campsites, Rte. 209 Box 382, 18337. T: (717) 296-7421. RV/tent: 165. $$. Hookups: electric, water, phone.

Montgomery

Riverside Campground, 125 South Main St., 17752. T: (717) 547-6289. www.riversidecampground.com. RV/tent: 172. $$. Hookups: electric (30 amp), water, sewer, cable.

New Castle

Willow Lake Campground, RD 1 Box 551, 17856. T: (717) 538-2790. RV/tent: 100. $$. Hookups: electric (20, 30 amp), water, sewer.

New Holland

Country Haven Campsite, 354 Springville Rd., 17557. T: (717) 354-7926. RV/tent: 55. $$. Hookups: electric, water, sewer, phone.

New Stanton

Fox Den Acres RV Resort, RD 1, 15672. T: (412) 925-7054. RV/tent: 350. $$. Hookups: electric, water, sewer, phone.

North East

Creekside Campgrounds, 10834 Rte. 89, 16428. T: (814) 725-5523. RV/tent: 100. $$. Hookups: electric, water.

Ottsville

Beaver Valley Family Campground, 80 Clay Ridge Rd., 18942. T: (610) 847-5643. RV/tent: 85. $$. Hookups: electric, water.

Palmerton

Don Laine Family Campground, 790 57 Dr., 18071. T: (610) 318-3381 or (800) 635-0152. www.donlaine.com. RV/tent: 92. $$. Hookups: electric (30 amp), water, sewer.

Pequea

Pequea Creek Campground, 86 Fox Hollow Rd., 17565. T: (717) 284-4587. RV/tent: 99. $$. Hookups: electric, water.

Portland

Shady Acres Campground, 1078 Turkey Ridge Rd., 18351. T: (570) 897-6230. RV/tent: 110. $$. Hookups: electric, water, phone.

Quakertown

Melody Lakes Country Estates, 1045 North West End Blvd./US 309, 18951. T: (215) 536-6640. RV/tent: 16. $$. Hookups: electric (30 amp), water, sewer.

Tohickon Family Campground, 8308 Covered Bridge Rd., 18951. T: (215) 536-7951. RV/tent: 200. $$. Hookups: electric, water, sewer, phone.

PENNSYLVANIA (continued)

Ruffsdale
Madison/Pittsburgh SE KOA, RR 2 Box 560, 15679. T: (800) 562-4034. RV/tent: 106. $$. Hookups: electric, water, sewer, phone.

Russell
Red Oak Campground, RD 1 Box 1724, 16345. T: (814) 757-8507. RV/tent: 109. $$. Hookups: electric (20, 30 amp), water, sewer.

Sandy Lake
Goddard Park Vacationland Campground, 867 Georgetown Rd., 16145. T: (724) 253-4645. RV/tent: 534. $$. Hookups: electric, water, sewer.

Schellsburg
Shawnee Sleepy Hollow Campground, RD 1 Box 121, 15559. T: (814) 733-4380. www.dcnr .state.pa.us/stateparks/parks/index.htm. RV/tent: 314. $$. Hookups: electric (30 amp).

Scotrun
Four Seasons Campground, Babbling Brook Rd., 18355. T: (570) 629-2504. RV/tent: 125. $$. Hookups: electric, water, sewer.

Shelocta
Wheel-In Campground, RD 2 Box 147, 15774. T: (412) 354-3693. RV/tent: 100. $$. Hookups: electric, water, sewer, phone.

Sigel
Camper's Paradise Campground & Cabins, RD 1 Rte. 949, 15860. T: (814) 752-2393. RV/tent: 136. $$. Hookups: electric (30 amp), water, sewer.

Strasburg
White Oak Campground, P.O. Box 90, 17579. T: (717) 687-6207. RV/tent: 180. $$. Hookups: electric, water, sewer, phone.

Stroudsburg
Arrowhead Campground, Beaver Valley Rd., 18360. T: (570) 992-7949. RV/tent: 47. $$. Hookups: electric, water, sewer, phone.

Sunbury
Fantasy Island Campground, 401 Park Dr., 17801. T: (570) 286-1307. RV/tent: 35. $$. Hookups: electric (20, 30 amp), water.

Tamaqua
Rosemount Camping Resort, Valley Rd., 18252. T: (570) 668-2580. RV/tent: 200. $$. Hookups: electric, water, sewer, phone.

Tioga
TNT Scenic View Campground, Scenic View Dr., 16946. T: (570) 835-5863. RV/tent: 220. $$. Hookups: electric, water, sewer, phone.

Titusville
Oil Creek Camp Resort, RD 3, 16354. T: (814) 827-1023. RV/tent: 100. $$. Hookups: electric, water, sewer.

Tobyhanna
Hemlock Campground & Cottages, 362 Hemlock Dr., 18466. T: (570) 894-4388. RV/tent: 81. $$. Hookups: electric, water, sewer.

Towanda
Riverside Acres Campground, RR 2 Box 211, 18848. T: (570) 265-3235. www.riverside acres.com. RV/tent: 41. $$. Hookups: electric (30 amp), water, sewer.

Tunkhannock
Tunkhannock, Box 768, 18657. T: (570) 836-4122. RV/tent: 181. $$. Hookups: electric, water, sewer, phone.

Unionville
Philadelphia/West Chester KOA, P.O. Box 920D, 19375. T: (800) 562-1726. RV/tent: 126. $$. Hookups: electric (20, 30 amp), water, sewer.

Upper Black Eddy
Ringing Rocks Family Campground, 75 Woodland Dr., 18972. T: (610) 982-5552. www.ringing rockscampground.com. RV/tent: 100. $$. Hookups: electric, water.

Washington
Washington KOA, 7 Koa Rd., 15301. T: (800) 562-0254 or (724) 225-7590. www.koakamp grounds.com. RV/tent: 167. $$. Hookups: electric (20, 30 amp), water, sewer.

Wellsboro
Canyon Country Campground, RD 6 Box 186, 16901. T: (570) 724-3818. www.campingpa.com. RV/tent: 72. $$. Hookups: electric (20, 30 amp), water, sewer.

West Sunbury
Peaceful Valley Family Campground, 236 Peaceful Valley Rd., 16061. T: (724) 894-2421. RV/tent: 85. $$. Hookups: electric (30 amp), water, sewer.

White Haven
Lehigh Gorge Campground, Rte. 940, 18661. T: (570) 443-9191. www.lehighgorgerv.com. RV/tent: 150. $$. Hookups: electric, water, sewer, phone.

Woodland
Woodland Campground, 314 Egypt Rd., RR 1 Box 474, 16881. T: (814) 857-5388 or (800) 589-1674. www.woodlandpa.com. RV/tent: 90. $$. Hookups: electric, water, phone.

York
Indian Rock Campground, 436 Indian Rock Dam Rd., 17403. T: (717) 741-1764. www.indianrock campground.com. RV/tent: 40. $$$. Hookups: electric, water, sewer.

York Springs
Hershey's Fur Center, 8164 Carlisle Pike, 17372. T: (717) 528-4412. RV/tent: 50. $$. Hookups: electric, water, sewer.

RHODE ISLAND

Charlestown
Charlestown Breachway, Burlingame State Park, 1 Burlingame State Park, off Rte. 1 South, 02908. T: (401) 364-7000. www.riparks.com/charles-breach.htm. RV/tent: 75. $$. Hookups: none.

Ninigret Conservation Area, East Beach Rd., 02813. T: (401) 322-0450 or (401) 322-8910. RV/tent: 20. $$. Hookups: electric, water.

Chepachet
Camp Ponagansett, Bungy Rd., 02814. T: (401) 647-7377. RV/tent: 40. $$. Hookups: electric (20, 30, 50 amp), water.

Foster
Dyer Woods Nudist Campground, 114 Johnson Rd., 02825. T: (401) 397-3007.

www.sunclad.com/dyerwoods. RV/tent: 16. $$. Hookups: electric, water.

Middletown
Meadowlark Park, 132 Prospect Ave., 02842. T: (401) 846-9455. RV/tent: 40. $$$. Hookups: electric (30 amp), water, sewer.

Paradise Motel and Campground, 459 Aquidneck Ave., 02842. T: (401) 847-1500. RV/tent: 16. $$. Hookups: electric, water, sewer.

Second Beach Family Campground, Sachuest Pt. Rd., 02842. T: (401) 846-6273. RV/tent: 44. $. Hookups: electric, water, sewer.

Narragansett
Long Cove Campsite and Marina, 325 Point Judith Rd., 02882. T: (401) 783-4902. RV/tent: 150. $$. Hookups: electric, water, sewer.

Pascoag
Echo Lake Campground, 180 Moroney Rd., 02859. T: (401) 568-7109. RV/tent: 150. $$. Hookups: electric, water, sewer.

Portsmouth
Melville Campground Recreation, 181 Bradford Ave., 02871. T: (401) 682-2424. RV/tent: 133. $$$. Hookups: electric (30 amp), water, sewer.

Wakefield
Worden Pond Family Campground, 1173 Worden Pond Rd., 02879. T: (401) 789-9113. www.wordenpondcampground.com. RV/tent: 250. $$$. Hookups: electric (30 amp), water.

SOUTH CAROLINA

Aiken

Crossroads RV Park & Mobile Home Community, 569 Crossreads Park Dr., 29803. T: (803) 642-5702. RV/tent: 22. $$. Hookups: electric (20, 30, 50 amp), water.

Pine Acres Campground, 205 Duke Dr., 29801. T: (803) 648-5715. RV/tent: 30. $$. Hookups: electric (20, 30, 50 amp), water, sewer.

Anderson

KOA Anderson/Lake Hartwell, 200 Wham Rd., 29625. T: (864) 287-3161. www.koa.com. RV/tent: 70. $$. Hookups: electric (30, 50 amp), water, sewer.

Sadlers Creek State Recreation Park, 940 Sadlers Creek Park Rd., 29626. T: (864) 226-8950. RV/tent: 37. $$. Hookups: electric (20, 30 amp), water.

Thousand Trails Carolina Landing, 120 Carolina Landing Dr., 29643-2703. T: (864) 972-3717 or (864) 972-9892. www.inspire21.com/landing.html. RV/tent: 250. $$. Hookups: electric (30 amp), water.

Bluffton

Stoney Crest Plantation Campground, 419 May River Rd., 29910. T: (843) 757-3249. RV/tent: 30. $$. Hookups: electric (20, 30 amp), water, sewer.

Canadys

Shuman's RV Trailer Park, Hwy. 15 North, 29433. T: (843) 538-8731. RV/tent: 15. $. Hookups: electric (20, 30, 50 amp), water.

Charleston

Fain's RV Park, 6309 Fain Blvd., 29418. T: (843) 744-1005. RV/tent: 34. $$. Hookups: electric (30, 50 amp), water.

Oak Plantation Campground, 3540 Savannah Hwy., 29455. T: (843) 766-5936 or (866) 658-2500. www.oakplantationcampground.com. RV/tent: 250. $$. Hookups: electric (30, 50 amp), water.

Conway

Big Cypress Lake RV Park & Fishing Retreat, 6531 Brownsway Shortcut Rd., Cates Bay Hwy., 29527. T: (843) 397-1800. www.bigcypressfishing.com. RV/tent: 25. $$. Hookups: electric (20, 30, 50 amp), water, sewer, cable, phone.

Dillon

Bass Lake RV Campground, 1149 Bass Lake Pl., 29536. T: (843) 774-2690. RV/tent: 68. $$. Hookups: electric (20, 30 amp), water.

Ehrhardt

Rivers Bridge State Historic Site, 325 St. Park Rd., 29801. T: (803) 267-3675. www.southcarolinaparks.com. RV/tent: 25. $. Hookups: electric (20, 30 amp), water.

Fair Play

Lakeshore Campground, 231 Lakeshore Dr., 29563. T: (864) 972-3330. www.pendleton-district.org/campgrounds. RV/tent: 55. $$. Hookups: electric (20, 30 amp), water.

Florence

KOA Florence, 1115 East Campground Rd., 29506. T: (843) 665-7007 or (800) 562-7807. www.koa.com. RV/tent: 135. $$. Hookups: electric (20, 30, 50 amp), water, cable, phone.

Swamp Fox Camping, 1600 Gateway Rd., 29502. T: (877) 251-2251 or (843) 665-7007. www.swamp-fox-campground.com. RV/tent: 61. $$. Hookups: electric (20, 30, 50 amp), water.

Fort Mill

KOA Charlotte/Fort Mill, 940 Gold Hill Rd., 29708. T: (803) 548-1148 or (888) 562-4430. www.koa.com. RV/tent: 209. $$. Hookups: electric (20, 30, 50 amp), water, sewer.

SPM Defender Lakeside Lodges & Campground, 9600 Regent Pkwy., 29715. T: (803) 547-3500. RV/tent: 127. $$. Hookups: electric (30 amp), water.

Gaffney

Pine Cone Campground, 160 Sarrett School Rd., 29341. T: (864) 489-2022. RV/tent: 110. $$. Hookups: electric (20, 30, 50 amp), water, sewer.

Green Pond

Wood Brothers Campground, 8446 Ace Basin Pkwy., 29446. T: (843) 844-2208. RV/tent: 42. $$. Hookups: electric (20, 30 amp), water.

Greenville

Flowermill RV Park, 31 Stallings Rd., 29687. T: (864) 877-5079. RV/tent: 30. $$. Hookups: electric (20, 30 amp), water.

Paris Mountain State Park, 2401 State Park Rd., 29609. T: (864) 244-5565. www.discoversouthcarolina.com. RV/tent: 40. $$. Hookups: electric (20, 30 amp), water.

Springwood RV Park, 800 Donaldson Rd., 29605. T: (864) 277-9789. RV/tent: 55. $$. Hookups: electric (30, 50 amp), water.

Hartwell

Coneross Campground, P.O. Box 278, 30643. T: (888) 893-0678 or (706) 856-0300. www.reserveamerica.com. RV/tent: 106. $. Hookups: electric (20, 30 amp), water.

Twin Lakes Campground, US 187, Fants Grove Rd.; 5 miles west of Pendleton, 29670. T: (888) 893-0678 or (706) 856-0300. RV/tent: 102. $$. Hookups: electric (20, 30 amp), water.

Hilton Head Island

Outdoor Resorts Motor Coach Resort, 19 Arrow Rd., 29928-3245. T: (800) 722-2365 or (843) 785-7699. www.outdoor-resorts.com/hilton_head. RV/tent: 401. $$$. Hookups: electric (20, 30, 50 amp), water.

Outdoor RV Resort & Yacht Club, 43 Jenkins Rd., 29925. T: (843) 681-3256 or (800) 845-9560. www.outdoor-rv.com. RV/tent: 200. $$$. Hookups: electric (30, 50 amp), water, sewer, cable, phone.

Hollywood

Lake Aire RV Park and Campground, 4375 Hwy. 162, 29449. T: (843) 571-1271. www.lakeairerv.com. RV/tent: 113. $. Hookups: electric (30, 50 amp), water, sewer.

Irmo

Wood Smoke Family Campground, 11302 Broad River Rd., 29063. T: (803) 781-3451. RV/tent: 37. $$. Hookups: electric (30, 50 amp), water, sewer.

James Island

Campground at James Island County Park, 871 Riverland Dr., 29412. T: (843) 795-7275. www.charlestoncampgrounds.com. RV/tent: 125. $$. Hookups: electric (30, 50 amp), water, sewer.

Leesville

Cedar Pond Campground, 4721 Fairview Rd., 29070. T: (803) 657-5993. RV/tent: 25. $$. Hookups: electric (30, 50 amp), water, sewer.

Lexington

Barnyard RV Park, 201 Oak Dr., 4414 Augusta Rd., 29073-7345. T: (803) 957-1238 or (800) 633-6351. www.barnyardrvpark.com. RV/tent: 97. $$. Hookups: electric (30, 50 amp), water, sewer.

Edmund RV Park & Campground, 5920 Edmund Hwy., 29073. T: (800) 955-7957. www.edmundrvpark.com. RV/tent: 265. $$. Hookups: electric (20, 30, 50 amp), water, sewer, laundry.

Liberty Hill

Wateree Lake Campground, 2367 Dolan Rd., 29074. T: (803) 273-3013. RV/tent: 74. $$. Hookups: electric (30 amp), water, sewer.

Lugoff

Columbia/Camden RV Park, 1354 Fort Jackson Rd, 29078. T: (803) 438-8774. www.columbia-camden-rv-park.com. RV/tent: 34. $$. Hookups: electric (30, 50 amp), water, sewer.

Manning

Campers Paradise, 2449 Raccoon Rd., Rte. 6 Box 870, 29102. T: (803) 473-3550. RV/tent: 60. $$. Hookups: electric (30 amp), water, sewer.

McCormick

Hickory Knob State Resort Park, Rte. 4 Box 199B, 29835. T: (800) 491-1764 or (864) 391-2450. www.discoversouthcarolina.com. RV/tent: 44. $$. Hookups: electric (20, 30 amp), water.

Myrtle Beach

Apache Family Campground, 9700 Kings Rd., 29572. T: (800) 553-1749 or (843) 449-7323. www.apachefamilycampground.net. RV/tent: 730. $$. Hookups: electric (20, 30 amp), water, sewer, cable.

Ridgeway

Ridgeway Campground, 7210 St. Hwy. 34 East, 29130. T: (803) 337-4085. RV/tent: 24. $$. Hookups: electric (20, 30 amp), water.

Roebuck

Pine Ridge Family Campground, 199 Pine Ridge Campground Rd., 29376. T: (864) 576-0302. www.pineridgecampground.homestead.com. RV/tent: 47. $$. Hookups: electric (30, 50 amp), water.

SOUTH CAROLINA (continued)

Saint Helena

Tuck in the Wood Campground, 22 Tuc in de Wood Ln., 29920. T: (843) 838-2267. RV/tent: 75. $$. Hookups: electric (30, 50 amp), water, sewer.

Salem

Devils Fork State Park, 161 Holcombe Cir., 29676. T: (864) 944-2639. www.discoversouthcarolina .com. RV/tent: 59. $$. Hookups: electric (30 amp), water.

Santee

Lake Marion Resort & Marina, 510 Rag Time Trail, 29142. T: (803) 854-2136. www.spmresorts.com. RV/tent: 55. $$. Hookups: electric (20, 30, 50 amp), water.

Simpsonville

Scuffletown USA, 603 Scuffletown Rd., 29681. T: (864) 967-2276. www.scuffletownusa.com. RV/tent: 55. $$. Hookups: electric (30, 50 amp), water.

South of the Border

Camp Pedro, 301 Hwy. 501, 29547. T: (843) 774-2411 or (800) 845-6011. RV/tent: 100. $$. Hookups: electric (20, 30, 50 amp), water.

St. Matthews

Sweetwater Lake Campground, 58 Campground Trail, 29135. T: (803) 874-3547 or (800) 553-1749. RV/tent: 50. $$. Hookups: electric (15, 20, 50 amp), water.

Summerton

Taw Caw Campground & Marina, 1328 Joyner Dr., Rte. 4 Box 1740, 29148. T: (803) 478-2171. www.tawtawcampground.com. RV/tent: 80. $$. Hookups: electric (20, 30 amp), water.

Sumter

Military Park, 314 Lance Ave., 29152. T: (803) 432-7976. RV/tent: 13. $. Hookups: electric (20, 30 amp), water.

Swansea

River Bottom Farms RV Park & Campground, 357 Cedar Creek Rd., 29160. T: (803) 568-4182. RV/tent: 60. $$. Hookups: electric (20, 30, 50 amp), water.

Taylors

Rainbow RV Park, 3553 Rutherford Rd., 29687. T: (864) 244-1271. RV/tent: 50. $$. Hookups: electric (30, 50 amp), water.

Timmonsville

Lake Honey Dew Campground, 2028 Cale Yarborough Hwy., 29161. T: (843) 346-0700. RV/tent: 16. $$. Hookups: electric (20, 30, 50 amp), water.

Townville

Hartwell Four Seasons Campground, 400 Ponderosa Point Rd., 29689. T: (864) 287-3223. RV/tent: 110. $$. Hookups: electric (30 amp), water, sewer.

Travelers Rest

Holly Hill RV Park, 219 Stamey Valley Rd., 29690. T: (864) 834-0776. RV/tent: 18. $$. Hookups: electric (20, 30, 50 amp), water.

Walterboro

Green Acres Family Campground, 330 Campground Rd., 29488. T: (800) 474-3450 or (843) 538-3450. www.newgreenacres.com. RV/tent: 125. $$. Hookups: electric (15, 30, 50 amp), water, cable.

West Union

Crooked Creek RV Park, 777 Arve Ln., 29696. T: (864) 882-5040. www.crookedcreek rvpark.com. RV/tent: 97. $$$. Hookups: electric (20, 30, 50 amp), water, cable.

Whitmire

Brickhouse Campground, Hwy. 66, 29178. T: (864) 427-9858. www.fs.fed.us/R8/FMS. RV/tent: 24. $. Hookups: none.

Yemassee

KOA Point South, P.O. Box 1760, 29945. T: (843) 726-5733 or (800) KOA-2948. www.koa.com. RV/tent: 54. $$$. Hookups: electric (30, 50 amp), water, sewer, cable.

The Oaks at Point South RV Resort, Rte. 1, 29945. T: (843) 726-5728. RV/tent: 83. $$. Hookups: electric (30, 50 amp), water, sewer.

SOUTH DAKOTA

Aberdeen

Wylie Park, 616 SE 10th Ave., 57401. T: (888) 326-9693. www.aberdeen.sd.us/parks/wylie.html. RV/tent: 92. $. Hookups: electric (30, 50 amp), water, sewer.

Akaska

D & S Campground, 103 Swan Creek Rd., 57420. T: (605) 229-1739. RV/tent: 16. $$. Hookups: electric (30, 50 amp).

Belle Fourche

Riverside Campground & RV Park, 418 9th St., 57717. T: (605) 892-6446. www.ohwy.com/sd/r/ rivecamp.htm. RV/tent: 50. $. Hookups: electric (15, 20, 30, 50 amp).

Beresford

Windmill Campground, 505 SwW13th St., 57004. T: (605) 763-2029. RV/tent: 60. $. Hookups: electric (20, 30, 50 amp), water.

Chamberlain

Happy Campers Campground, 110 West Clemmer Ave., 57325. T: (888) 734-6655 or (605) 734-4050. RV/tent: 80. $. Hookups: electric (20, 30, 50 amp), water.

Custer

Beaver Lake Campground, 12005 West US 16, 57730. T: (800) 346-4383. www.beaverlakecamp ground.net. RV/tent: 83. $$. Hookups: electric (15, 20, 30 amp).

Big Pine Campground, Rte. 1 Box 52, 57730. T: (800) 235-3981 or (605) 673-4054. RV/tent: 90. $$. Hookups: electric (20, 30 amp).

Custer-Crazy Horse Campground, Rte. 2 Box 3030, 57730. T: (866) 526-7377 or (605) 673-2565. www.rushmorecabins.com. RV/tent: 150. $$. Hookups: electric (20, 30, 50 amp), water, sewer.

Fort WeLiklt Family Campground, 24992 Sylvan Lake Rd., 57730. T: (888) 946-2267 or (605) 673-3600. www.fortwelikit.blackhills.com. RV/tent: 100. $$. Hookups: electric (20, 30, 50 amp), water, cable, sewer.

Deadwood

Fish'n Fry Campground, HC 73 Box 801, 57732. T: (605) 578-2150. www.deadwood.net/fishnfry. RV/tent: 65. $. Hookups: electric, water, sewer.

Hermosa

Heartland Campground and RV Park, 24743 Hwy. 79, 57744. T: (605) 255-5460 or (866) 445-5778. RV/tent: 150. $$. Hookups: electric (20, 30, 50 amp), water, sewer, cable, phone.

Hot Springs

Angostura Reservoir, HC 52 Box 131-A, 57747. T: (605) 745-6996 or (800) 710-CAMP. RV/tent: 159. $. Hookups: electric.

Larive Lake Resort and Campground, 1802 Evans St., 57747. T: (605) 745-3993. www.larivelake.com. RV/tent: 40. $$. Hookups: electric (20, 30 amp).

Keystone

Spokane Creek Resort, 24631 Iron Mountain Rd., 57751. T: (605) 666-4609 or (800) 261-9331. www.spokanecreekresort.com. RV/tent: 15. $$. Hookups: electric (15 amp).

Kimball

Parkway Campground, Hwy. 190 & Hwy. 45, 57751. T: (605) 778-6312. RV/tent: 26. $. Hookups: electric (20, 30, 50 amp).

Mitchell

R & R Campground, 1700 South Burr St., 57301. T: (605) 996-8895. RV/tent: 53. $$. Hookups: electric (20, 30, 50 amp), cable, water, sewer.

Mobridge

Kountry Kamping and Kabins, 2712 West Hwy. 12, 57601. T: (605) 845-2900 or (800) 648-2267. RV/tent: 27. $$. Hookups: electric, water.

Murdo

Camp McKen-Z, 810 5th St., 57559. T: (605) 669-2573. RV/tent: 100. $$. Hookups: electric (30, 50 amp), phone.

Oacoma

Al's Oasis Campground, 1000 East Hwy. 16, 57365. T: (800) 675-6959. www.alsoasis.com. RV/tent: 100. $$. Hookups: electric (30 amp), water, sewer, cable.

SOUTH DAKOTA (continued)

Oasis Campground, P.O. Box 97, 57365. T: (800) 675-6959. RV/tent: 97. $. Hookups: electric (20, 30, 50 amp), water, cable.

Pierre

Lighthouse Pointe, 19602 Lake Place, 57501. T: (888) 420-9340. www.lighthousepoint.com. RV/tent: 60. $. Hookups: electric (50 amp), water.

Rapid City

Lake Park Campground, 2850 Chapel Ln., 57702. T: (605) 341-5320 or (800) 644-2267. www.lakeparkcampground.com. RV/tent: 48. $$.

Hookups: electric (20, 30, 50 amp), water, sewer, cable, phone.

Salem

Camp America Campground, 25495 US 81, 57058. T: (605) 425-9085. RV/tent: 62. $. Hookups: electric (30, 50 amp), water, phone, cable, modem.

Sisseton

Camp Dakotah, Rte. 1 Box 184, 57262. T: (605) 698-7388 or (877) 698-3507. www.sdglacial lakes.com. RV/tent: 33. $. Hookups: electric (30, 50 amp), water, sewer.

Sturgis

Hog Heaven Resort, P.O. Box 477, 57785. T: (800) 551-1283. www.hogheaven-campground.com. RV/tent: 100. $$$$. Hookups: electric (30, 50 amp), water, sewer.

Wall

Sleepy Hollow Campground, 118 4th Ave. West, 57790. T: (605) 279-2100. www.blackhills badlands.com/sleepyhollow. RV/tent: 93. $$. Hookups: electric (20, 30 amp), water, cable, phone.

TENNESSEE

Allons

Lillydale Campground, 5199 Lillydale Rd., 38541. T: (931) 823-4155. www.reserveusa.com. RV/tent: 114. $$. Hookups: electric (20, 30 amp), water.

Willow Grove, 9997 Willow Grove Rd., 38541. T: (931) 823-4285. www.reserveusa.com. RV/tent: 88. $. Hookups: electric (30, 50 amp), water.

Athens

Athens I-75 Campground, 2509 Decatur Pike, Hwy. 30, 37303. T: (423) 745-9199. RV/tent: 63. $$. Hookups: electric (20, 30 amp), water, sewer.

Over-Niter RV Park, 316 Mt Verd Rd., Hwy. 305, 37303. T: (423) 507-0069. RV/tent: 16. $$. Hookups: electric (20, 30, 50 amp), water, sewer.

Baileyton

Baileyton Camp Inn, 7485 Horton Hwy., 37745. T: (423) 234-4992. RV/tent. 44. $$. Hookups: electric (20, 30, 50 amp), water, sewer, modem.

Blounille

KOA Bristol/Kingsport, 425 Rocky Branch Rd., 37617. T: (423) 323-7790 or (800) 562-7640. www.koa.com. RV/tent: 73. $$. Hookups: electric (20, 30, 50 amp), water, sewer, cable, phone, modem.

Rocky Top Campground, 649 Pearl Ln., 37617. T: (423) 323-2535 or (800) 452-6456. www.rockytopcampground.com. RV/tent: 42. $$. Hookups: electric (20, 30, 50 amp), water, sewer.

Buchanan

Paris Landing State Park, 16055 Hwy. 79 North, 38222. T: (731) 641-4465 or (800) 250-8614. www.tnstateparks.com. RV/tent: 44. $$. Hookups: electric (30 amp), water.

Carthage

Defeated Creek Park, SR 85, 37030. T: (615) 774-3141. www.reserveusa.com. RV/tent: 155. $$. Hookups: electric (20, 30 amp), water, sewer.

Indian Creek Park, 71 Corps Ln., North of Chestnut Mound, 37030. T: (615) 889-2233. www.reserveusa.com. RV/tent: 53. $. Hookups: electric (30 amp), water.

Castalian Springs

Shady Cove Resort & Marina, 1115 Shady Cove Rd., 37031. T: (615) 452-8010. RV/tent: 95. $.

Hookups: electric (30, 50 amp), water, sewer, modem.

Celina

Dale Hollow Dam Campground, 5050 Dale Hollow Dam Rd., 38551. T: (931) 243-3554. www.reserveusa.com. RV/tent: 79. $$. Hookups: electric, water.

Chattanooga

Lookout Valley RV Park, 3714 Cummings Hwy., 37419. T: (423) 821-3100. RV/tent: 126. $$. Hookups: electric (30, 50 amp), water, sewer, modem.

Raccoon Mountain Campground & RV Park, 319 West Hills Dr., 37419. T: (423) 821-9403 or (800) 823-2267. www.raccoonmountain.com. RV/tent: 124. $$. Hookups: electric (20, 30, 50 amp), water, sewer.

Shipp's RV Center & Campground, 3728 Ringgold Rd., 37412. T: (800) 222-4551 or (423) 892-8275. www.shippsrv.com. RV/tent: 120. $$. Hookups: electric (20, 30, 50 amp), water, sewer, cable.

Clarksville

Clarksville RV Park & Campground, 1270 Tylertown Rd., 37040. T: (931) 648-8638 or (888) 287-8638. www.clarksvillervpark.com. RV/tent: 59. $$. Hookups: electric (20, 30, 50 amp), water, sewer, modem.

Clinton

Fox Inn Campground, 2423 Andersonville Hwy., 37716. T: (865) 494-9386 or (888) 803-9883. www.foxinncampground.com. RV/tent: 93. $$. Hookups: electric (30, 50 amp), water, sewer.

Cornersville

Texas T Campground, 2499 Lynnville Hwy., 37047. T: (931) 293-2500. www.texastcampground.com. RV/tent: 40. $$$. Hookups: electric (30, 50 amp), water, sewer.

Cosby

Fox Den Campground, 311 South Hwy. 32, 37722. T: (888) 369-3661. RV/tent: 64. $$. Hookups: electric (15, 30, 50 amp), water, sewer.

Crossville

Ballyhoo Family Campground, 256 Werthwyle, 38555. T: (931) 484-0860 or (888) 336-3703.

www.ballyhoocampground.tripod.com. RV/tent: 74. $$. Hookups: electric (20, 30, 50 amp), water, sewer.

Roam & Roost RV Campground, 255 Fairview Dr., 38558. T: (951) 707-1414 or (877) 707-1414. RV/tent: 24. $$. Hookups: electric (20, 30, 50 amp), water, sewer.

Delano

Gee Creek Campground, Spring Creek Rd., 37325. T: (423) 263-0050. www.tnstateparks.com. RV/tent: 43. $. Hookups: none.

Dickson

Dickson RV Park, 150 West Christi Rd., 37055. T: (615) 446-9925. RV/tent: 60. $$. Hookups: electric (20, 30 amp), water, sewer, modem.

Tanbark Campground, 125 South Spradlin Rd., 37055. T: (615) 441-1613. RV/tent: 30. $. Hookups: electric (20, 30, 50 amp), water, sewer.

Dover

Bumpus Mills Recreational Area, 764 Forest Trace, 37058. T: (931) 232-8831. www.reserveusa.com. RV/tent: 33. $. Hookups: electric (30 amp), water.

Gainesboro

Salt Lick Creek Campground, Smith Bend Rd., 38562. T: (931) 678-4718. www.reserveusa.com. RV/tent: 150. $$. Hookups: electric (30 amp), water, sewer.

Gatlinburg

Arrow Creek Campground, 4721 East Pkwy., 37738. T: (865) 430-7433. www.arrowcreek camp.com. RV/tent: 63. $$. Hookups: electric (20, 30 amp), water, cable, sewer.

Crazy Horse Campground & RV Resort, 4609 East Pkwy., 37738. T: (800) 528-9003. www.crazy horsecampground.com. RV/tent: 229. $$. Hookups: electric (20, 30, 50 amp), water, sewer, cable.

Greenbrier Island Campground, 2353 East Pkwy., 37738. T: (865) 436-4243. RV/tent: 116. $$. Hookups: electric (20, 30 amp), water, sewer.

Le Conte Vista Campground Resort, 1739 East Pkwy., 37738. T: (865) 436-5437. RV/tent: 75. $$$. Hookups: electric (15, 30 amp), water, sewer, cable.

TENNESSEE (continued)

Greenback

Lotterdale Cove, 17177 East Coast Tellico Pkwy., 37742. T: (865) 856-3832. RV/tent: 90. $$. Hookups: electric (20, 30, 50 amp).

Heiskell

Jellystone Camping Resort, 9514 Diggs Gap Rd., 37754. T: (865) 938-6600. RV/tent: 100. $$. Hookups: electric (30, 50 amp), water, sewer, cable.

Hendersonville

Cages Bend Campground, 1125 Benders Ferry Rd., 37075. T: (615) 824-4989. www.reserveusa.com. RV/tent: 43. $$. Hookups: electric, water.

Henning

Fort Pillow State Park, 3122 Park Rd., 38041. T: (731) 738-5581. www.tnstateparks.com. RV/tent: 38. $. Hookups: none.

Hermitage

Seven Points Campground, Stewarts Ferry Pike, 37076. T: (615) 889-5198. www.reserveusa.com. RV/tent: 60. $$. Hookups: electric (30, 50 amp), water.

Hixson

Chester Frost County Park, 2318 Gold Point Cir. North, 37343. T: (423) 842-3306. RV/tent: 224. $$. Hookups: electric (30, 50 amp), water.

Hohenwald

Thousand Trails Natchez Trace, 1363 Napier Rd., 38462. T: (931) 796-3211. www.thousandtrails. com. RV/tent: 653. $$. Hookups: electric (30 amp), water, sewer.

Hurricane Mills

KOA Buffalo, 473 Barren Hollow Rd., 37078. T: (931) 296-1306 or (800) 562-0832. www.koa.com. RV/tent: 62. $$. Hookups: electric (20, 30, 50 amp), water, sewer, modem.

Jackson

Jackson Mobile Village & RV Park, 2223 Hollywood Dr., 38305. T: (731) 668-1147. RV/tent: 14. $$. Hookups: electric (15, 30 amp), water, sewer.

Whispering Pines RV Park, 129 McKenzie Rd., 38301. T: (731) 422-3682. RV/tent: 30. $$. Hookups: electric (30, 50 amp), water, sewer.

Jamestown

Maple Hill RV Park, 1386 North York Hwy., 38556. T: (931) 879-3025. www.jamestowntn.us/maple hill.htm. RV/tent: 22. $. Hookups: electric (20, 30, 50 amp), water, sewer, cable, phone.

Kingston

Four Seasons Campground, 120 Farmer Rd., 37763. T: (423) 376-4568 or (800) 990-CAMP. RV/tent: 50. $$. Hookups: electric (20, 30 amp), water, sewer.

Knoxville

Southlake RV Park, 3730 Maryville Pike, 37920. T: (865) 573-1837. RV/tent: 125. $$. Hookups: electric (30, 50 amp), water, sewer, modem.

Kodak

KOA Knoxville East, 241 KOA Dr., 37764. T: (865) 933-6393 or (800) 562-8693. www.koa.com. RV/tent: 153. $$. Hookups: electric (20, 30, 50 amp), water, sewer, cable, modem.

Smoky Mountain Campground, 194 Foretravel Dr., 37764. T: (423) 933-8312 or (800) 864-2267. RV/tent: 280. $. Hookups: electric (30 amp), water, sewer.

Lancaster

Long Branch Campground, 478 Lancaster Rd., 38569. T: (615) 548-8002. www.reserveusa.com. RV/tent: 60. $$. Hookups: electric (20, 30, 50 amp), water, sewer.

Lebanon

Countryside Resort, 2100 Safari Camp Rd., 37087. T: (615) 449-5527. www.gocampingamerica .com/countrysidetn. RV/tent: 120. $$. Hookups: electric (20, 30, 50 amp), water, sewer.

Lenoir City

The Crosseyed Cricket, 751 Country Ln., 37771. T: (865) 986-5435. www.crosseyedcricket.com. RV/tent: 47. $$. Hookups: electric (30, 50 amp), water, sewer.

Limestone

Davy Crockett Birthplace State Park, 1245 Davy Crockett Park Rd., 37681. T: (423) 257-2167 or (423) 257-4500. www.tnstateparks.com. RV/tent: 73. $$. Hookups: electric (30 amp), water, sewer.

Linden

Mousetail Landing State Park, Rte. 3 Box 280B, 37096. T: (731) 847-0841. www.tnstateparks.com. RV/tent: 45. $. Hookups: electric (30, 50 amp), water.

Manchester

KOA Manchester, 586 Kampground Rd., 37355. T: (931) 728-9777 or (800) 562-7785. www.koa .com. RV/tent: 43. $$. Hookups: electric (20, 30, 50 amp), water, sewer, cable, phone, modem.

Whispering Oaks Campground, 812 16th Model Rd., 37355. T: (931) 728-0225. RV/tent: 49. $$. Hookups: electric (20, 30 amp), water, sewer, modem.

Memphis

Camp Memphis/Agricenter International, 7777 Walnut Grove Rd., 38120. T: (901) 757-7777. RV/tent: 600. $$. Hookups: electric (30 amp), water.

Middleton

Thousand Trails Cherokee Landing, Cherokee Landing Rd., 38052. T: (731) 376-0935. www.thousandtrails.com. RV/tent: 296. $$. Hookups: electric (30 amp), water, sewer.

Monroe

Obey River Campground, 100 Park Rd., 38573. T: (931) 864-6388. www.reserveusa.com. RV/tent: 132. $. Hookups: electric (20, 30 amp), water.

Mt. Juliet

Cedar Creek Campground, 9264 Saundersville Rd., 37122. T: (615) 754-4947. RV/tent: 60. $$. Hookups: electric (30 amp), water.

Nashville

Anderson Road Campground, 3737 Bell Rd., 37214. T: (615) 361-1980. www.reserveusa.com. RV/tent: 37. $. Hookups: none.

Holiday Nashville Travel Park, 2572 Music Valley Dr., 37214. T: (615) 889-4225 or (800) 547-4480. www.holidaypark.citysearch.com. RV/tent: 338. $$. Hookups: electric (20, 30, 50 amp), water, sewer, cable, modem.

Nashville Shores, 4001 Bell Rd., Hermitage, 37076. T: (615) 889-7050 or (615) 871-2060. www.nashvilleshores.com. RV/tent: 100. $$. Hookups: electric (20, 30, 50 amp), water, sewer.

Two Rivers Campground, 2616 Music Valley Dr., 37214. T: (615) 883-8559. www.yp.bellsouth.com/ sites/tworiverscampground. RV/tent: 105. $$. Hookups: electric (30, 50 amp), water, sewer.

Newport

KOA Newport I–40/Smoky Mtns, 240 KOA Ln., 37821. T: (423) 623-9004 or (800) 562-9016. www.koa.com. RV/tent: 99. $$. Hookups: electric (20, 30, 50 amp), water, sewer, modem.

Triple Creek Campground, 141 Lower Bogard Rd., 37821. T: (423) 623-2020. RV/tent: 79. $. Hookups: electric (20, 30 amp), water, sewer.

Old Hickory

Shutes Branch Campground, No. 5 Power Plant Rd., Hendersonville, 37075. T: (615) 754-4847. www.reserveusa.com. RV/tent: 35. $$. Hookups: electric (30, 50 amp), water, sewer.

Pickwick Dam

Pickwick Landing State Park, Park Rd./State Rte. 57, 38365. T: (731) 689-3129. www.tnstate parks.com. RV/tent: 48. $$. Hookups: electric (20, 30, 50 amp), water.

Pigeon Forge

Alpine Hideaway Campground, 251 Spring Valley Rd., 37863. T: (865) 428-3285. RV/tent: 80. $$. Hookups: electric (30, 50 amp), water, sewer.

Clabough's Campground & Market, 405 Wears Valley Rd., 37863. T: (800) 965-8524. www.claboughcampground.com. RV/tent: 310. $$. Hookups: electric (30, 50 amp), water, sewer.

Creekside Campground, 2475 Henderson Springs Rd., 37863. T: (865) 498-4801 or (800) 498-4801. www.creeksidervpark.com. RV/tent: 76. $$. Hookups: electric (30, 50 amp), water, sewer, cable.

Eagle's Nest Campground, 1111 Wears Valley Rd., 37863. T: (865) 428-5841 or (800) 892-2714. www.eaglesnestcampground.com. RV/tent: 200. $$. Hookups: electric (20, 30 amp), water, sewer.

Foothills RV Park & Campground, 4235 Huskey St., 37863. T: (888) 428-3818. www.foothillsrvpark .com. RV/tent: 39. $$. Hookups: electric (20, 30 amp), water, sewer, cable.

TENNESSEE (continued)

King's Holly Haven RV Park, 647 Wears Valley Rd., 37863. T: (865) 453-5352 or (888) 204-0247. www.hollyhavenrvpark.com. RV/tent: 170. $$. Hookups: electric (30, 50 amp), water, sewer, cable.

Riverbend Campground, 2479 Riverbend Loop 1, 37863. T: (865) 453-1224. www.river bendcampground.com. RV/tent: 120. $$. Hookups: electric (30, 50 amp), water, sewer.

Z Buda's Smokies Campground, 4020 Pkwy., 37863. T: (865) 453-4129. RV/tent: 300. $$. Hookups: electric (30 amp), water, sewer.

Pocahontas

Big Hill Pond State Park, 984 John Howell Rd., 38061. T: (731) 645-7967. www.tnstate parks.com. RV/tent: 30. $$. Hookups: none.

Roan Mountain

Roan Mountain State Resort Park, 1015 Hwy. 143, 37687. T: (423) 772-0190 or (800) 250-8620. www.tnstateparks.com. RV/tent: 107. $$. Hookups: electric (30 amp), water.

Sevierville

Ripplin' Waters Campground, 1930 Winfield Dunn Pkwy., 37876. T: (865) 453-4169 or (888) 747-7546. RV/tent: 156. $$. Hookups: electric (20, 30, 50 amp), water, sewer.

Riverside RV Park & Resort, 4280 Boyds Creek Hwy., 37876. T: (865) 453-7299 or (800) 341-7534. www.riversidecamp.com. RV/tent: 265. $$. Hookups: electric (30, 50 amp), water, sewer, modem.

Silver Point

Floating Mill Park Campground, 430 Floating Mill Ln., 38582. T: (931) 858-4845. www.reserveusa.com. RV/tent: 118. $$. Hookups: electric (30, 50 amp), water.

Smithville

Holmes Creek, 2620 Casey Cove Rd., 37166. T: (615) 597-7191. www.reserveusa.com. RV/tent: 96. $$. Hookups: electric (30, 50 amp), water.

Smyrna

Nashville I-24 Campground, 1130 Rocky Fork Rd., 37167. T: (615) 459-5818. RV/tent: 150. $$. Hookups: electric (30 amp), water, sewer, modem.

Springville

Buchanan Resort, 785 Buchanan Resort Rd., 38256. T: (731) 642-2828. www.buchanan resort.com. RV/tent: 38. $$. Hookups: electric (20, 30, 50 amp), water, sewer.

Ten Mile

Fooshee Pass (A), Sandy Bottoms Ln., 37880. T: (423) 334-4842. RV/tent: 55. $$. Hookups: electric (30 amp), water, dump station.

Hornsby Hollow (A-Watts Bar Lake), Rte. 1 Box 61, 37880. T: (423) 334-1709. RV/tent: 99. $$. Hookups: electric (30, 50 amp), water.

Townsend

Big Meadow Family Campground, 8215 Cedar Creek Rd., 37882. T: (865) 448-0625 or (888) 497-0625. www.bigmeadowcampground.com. RV/tent: 86. $$. Hookups: electric (30, 50 amp), water, sewer, cable.

Mountaineer Campground, 8451 Hwy. 73, 37882. T: (865) 448-6421. www.gocampingamerica.com/ mountaineer. RV/tent: 49. $$. Hookups: electric (30 amp), water, sewer.

Tuckaleechee Campground, 7301 Punkin Ln., 37882. T: (865) 448-9608. RV/tent: 150. $$. Hookups: electric (30, 50 amp), water, sewer, cable.

Vonore

Notchy Creek Campground, 1235 Corntassle, 37885. T: (423) 884-6280. RV/tent: 51. $$. Hookups: electric (30, 50 amp).

Toqua Beach Campground, 1360 Hwy. 360, 37885. T: (423) 884-2344. RV/tent: 24. $$. Hookups: electric (30, 50 amp), water.

Wildersville

Natchez Trace State Park, 24845 Natchez Trace Rd., 38388. T: (731) 968-3742 or (800) 250-8616. www.tnstateparks.com. RV/tent: 210. $$. Hookups: electric (20, 30, 50 amp), water, sewer.

Yuma

Parkers Crossroads Campground, 22580 Hwy. 22 North, 38390. T: (731) 968-9939. home.aeneas .net/~wksmith/pcamp.htm. RV/tent: 66. $$. Hookups: electric (20, 30, 50 amp), water, sewer.

TEXAS

Abilene

Abilene RV Park, 6195 East Int. Hwy. 20, 79601. T: (325) 672-0657. RV/tent: 60. $$. Hookups: electric (20, 30, 50 amp), phone (modem).

Abilene State Park, 150 Park Rd. 32, 79562. T: (915) 572-3204. RV/tent: 94. $. Hookups: electric, water, sewer.

KOA Abilene, 4851 West Stamford St., 79603. T: (915) 672-3681. RV/tent: 81. $$. Hookups: electric (20, 30, 50 amp), water, cable, central phone (modem), phone (modem).

Alamo

Alamo Rec-Veh Park, 1320 West Frontage Rd., 78516. T: (956) 787-8221. RV/tent: 440. $$. Hookups: electric (20, 30 amp), phone (modem).

Casa Del Valle, 1048 North Alamo Rd., 78516. T: (956) 783-5008. RV/tent: 175. $$$. Hookups: electric (30, 50 amp).

Morningside Mobile & RV Park, 105 North Cesar Chavez, 78589. T: (956) 787-5784. RV/tent: 504. $$. Hookups: electric (30, 50 amp).

Alpine

KOA Amarillo, 1100 Folsom Rd., 79108. T: (800) 562-3431. RV/tent: 142. $$. Hookups: electric (20, 30, 50 amp), water.

Lost Alaskan RV Resort, 2401 North Hwy. 118, 79830. T: (800) 837-3604. RV/tent: 93. $$. Hookups: electric (30, 50 amp), cable, central phone (modem), phone (modem).

Overnite RV Park, 900 South Lakeside Dr., 79118. T: (806) 373-1431. www.overnitervpark.com. RV/tent: 77. $$. Hookups: electric (20, 30, 50 amp), water, cable, central phone (modem), modem.

Amarillo

The Village East RV Park, 1414 Sunrise Dr., 79104. T: (806) 373-4962. RV/tent: 90. $$$. Hookups: electric (20, 30, 50 amp), cable, central phone (modem).

Wesiew RV Park, P.O. Box 2891, 79105. T: (806) 352-8567. RV/tent: 54. $$. Hookups: electric (30, 50 amp), water, sewer.

Aransas Pass

ICW RV Park, 427 East Ransom Rd., 78336. T: (361) 758-1044. RV/tent: 134. $$. Hookups: electric (20, 30, 50 amp), water, sewer.

Portobelo Village RV & Mobile Home Park, 2009 West Wheeler (Hwy. 35 West), 78336. T: (361) 758-3378. RV/tent: 125. $$. Hookups: electric (100 amp), water, sewer.

Argyle

Paradise RV Park, 1217 FM 407W, 76226. T: (940) 648-3573. RV/tent: 91. $$. Hookups: electric (20, 30, 50 amp), water, sewer.

Arroyo City

Seaway RV Village, 35375 FM 2925 Rio Hondo, 78583-3474. T: (956) 748-2276. www.camp southtexas.com/seaway. RV/tent: 70. $$. Hookups: electric (20, 30, 50 amp), central phone (modem), phone (modem).

Austin

McKinney Falls State Park, 5808 McKinney Falls Pkwy, 78744. T: (512) 243-1643. RV/tent: 84. $. Hookups: electric, water.

Oak Forest RV Park, 8207 Canoga Ave., 78724. T: (512) 926-8984. RV/tent: 88. $$$. Hookups: electric (30, 50 amp), cable, phone (modem).

Pecan Grove RV Park, 1518 Barton Springs Rd., 78704. T: (512) 472-1067. www.pecangroverv park.com. RV/tent: 41. $$. Hookups: electric (30 amp), cable, central phone (modem), phone (modem).

TEXAS (continued)

Bacliff

Bayside RV Park, 5437 East FM 646, 77518. T: (281) 339-2131. RV/tent: 110. $$. Hookups: electric (30, 50 amp), water, sewer, central phone (modem).

Bandera

Pomarosa RV Park, 3845 TX 16 South, 78003. T: (830) 796-4339. www.pomarosa.com. RV/tent: 50. $$. Hookups: electric (30, 50 amp), phone (modem).

Skyline Ranch RV Park, 2231 North Hwy. 16, 78003. T: (830) 796-4958. www.gocamping america.com/skylineranchtx. RV/tent: 124. $$. Hookups: electric (20, 30, 50 amp), cable, central phone (modem), phone (modem).

Yogi Bear's Jellystone Camp-Resort Bandera, P.O. Box 1687, 78003. T: (830) 796-3751. RV/tent: 210. $$. Hookups: electric (20, 30, amp), water, sewer.

Baytown

Willow Creek RV Park, 2305 Hwy. 146 North, 77520. T: (281) 422-5423. RV/tent: 62. $$. Hookups: electric (30, 50 amp).

Beaumont

East Lucas RV Park, 2590 East Lucas Dr., 77703-1126. T: (409) 899-9209. RV/tent: 65. $$. Hookups: electric (20, 30, 50 amp), cable, central phone (modem), phone (modem).

Belton

KOA Belton/Temple/Killeen, P.O. Box 118, 76513. T: (254) 939-1961. RV/tent: 99. $$. Hookups: electric (20, 30, 50 amp), water, cable, central phone (modem), phone (modem).

Benbrook

Holiday Park, South Lakeview, 76126-0619. T: (817) 292-2400. RV/tent: 105. $. Hookups: electric, water.

Big Spring

Texas RV Park of Big Spring, 4100 South US 87, 79720. T: (800) 749-4898. www.txrvpark.com. RV/tent: 75. $$. Hookups: electric (20, 30, 50 amp), cable, central phone (modem), phone (modem).

Bracketille

Fort Clark Springs, Hwy. 90 West, 78832. T: (830) 563-9340 or (800) 937-1590. RV/tent: 84. $. Hookups: electric (20, 30, 50 amp), cable, phone (modem).

Breckenridge

Bridgeview RV Park, 5300 Hwy. 180 W, 76424. T: (254) 559-8582. RV/tent: 43. $$. Hookups: electric (30, 50 amp), water.

Brenham

Artesian Park RV Campground, 8601 Hwy. 290 West, 77833. T: (979) 836-0680. www.artesian rvpark.com. RV/tent: 49. $$$. Hookups: electric (20, 30, 50 amp), water, central phone (modem), phone (modem).

Brookshire

KOA Houston West Campground, 35303 Cooper Rd., 77423. T: (281) 375-5678. RV/tent: 84. $$. Hookups: electric (20, 30, 50 amp), water, central phone (modem), phone (modem).

Brownsville

4 Seasons Mobile Home Park & RV Resort, 6900 Coffee Port Rd., 78521. T: (956) 831-4918. RV/tent: 125. $$$. Hookups: electric (30 amp), water, cable, phone (modem).

Breeze Lake Campground, 1710 North Vermillion, 78521. T: (877) 296-3329. RV/tent: 103. $$. Hookups: electric (20, 30, 50 amp), cable, central phone (modem), phone (modem).

Crooked Tree Campland, 605 FM 802, 78520. T: (956) 546-9617. RV/tent: 200. $$. Hookups: electric (20, 30, 50 amp), central phone (modem), phone (modem).

Paul's RV Park, 1129 North Minnesota Ave., 78521. T: (956) 831-4852. www.paulsrvpark.com. RV/tent: 135. $$$. Hookups: electric (20, 30, 50 amp), cable, central phone (modem), phone (modem).

Rio RV Park, 8801 East Boca Chica, 78521. T: (956) 831-4653. www.riorvpark.com. RV/tent: 112. $$$. Hookups: electric (20, 30, 50 amp), water, sewer, cable, phone (modem).

Bryan

Primrose Lane RV & MH Park, 2929 Stevens Dr., 77803. T: (888) 782-2671. RV/tent: 117. $$. Hookups: electric (20, 30, 50 amp).

Buchanan Dam

Shady Oaks RV Park, P.O. Box 725, 78609. T: (512) 793-2718. RV/tent: 64. $$. Hookups: electric (20, 30, 50 amp), cable, phone (modem).

Bulverde

Texas 281 RV Park, 33300 Hwy. 281 North, 78163. T: (830) 980-2282 or (800) 456-2126. RV/tent: 155. $$. Hookups: electric (30, 50 amp), water, sewer, cable.

Burleson

Mockingbird Hill Mobile Home & RV Park, 1990 South Burleson Blvd No. 20, 76028. T: (817) 295-3011 or (877) 736-7699. RV/tent: 60. $$. Hookups: electric (20, 30, 50 amp), water, sewer, phone (modem).

Caddo Mills

Dallas Northeast/Caddo Mills KOA, 4268 FM 36 South, 75135-6782. T: (903) 527-3615 or (866) DALLAS1. RV/tent: 85. $$$. Hookups: electric (20, 30, 50 amp), water, sewer, phone (modem).

Canton

Canton Campground, 30488 TX 64 Wills Point, 75169. T: (903) 865-1511. RV/tent: 74. $$. Hookups: electric (20, 30, 50 amp), water, sewer, central phone (modem).

Canyon Lake

Maricopa Ranch Resort, 12915 FM 306, 78130. T: (877) 964-3731. www.maricoparesort.com. RV/tent: 142. $$. Hookups: electric (30, 50 amp).

Carrollton

Sandy Lake RV Park, 1915 Sandy Lake Rd., 75006. T: (972) 242-6808. RV/tent: 276. $$. Hookups: electric (20, 30, 50 amp), water, sewer.

Cleburne

Cleburne State Park, 5800 Park Rd. 21, 76031. T: (817) 645-4215. RV/tent: 58. $. Hookups: electric, water.

Clint

Cotton Valley RV Park, P.O. Box 1189, 79836. T: (915) 851-2137. RV/tent: 75. $$. Hookups: electric (20, 30, 50 amp), water, sewer.

College Station

University RV Park, 19191 Hwy. 6 South, 77845. T: (979) 690-6056. RV/tent: 42. $$. Hookups: electric (20, 30 amp), water.

Columbus

Columbus RV Park & Campground, 2800 Hwy. 71S, 78934. T: (979) 732-6455 or (800) 657-6108. RV/tent: 49. $$. Hookups: electric (30, 50 amp).

Comanche

Copperas Creek Park, 2180 FM 2861, 76442-9210. T: (817) 893-7545. RV/tent: 66. $$. Hookups: electric (30 amp), water.

Comfort

RV Park USA, 108 Blue Ridge, 78013. T: (830) 995-2900. RV/tent: 52. $$. Hookups: electric (20, 30, 50 amp).

Conroe

Convenience RV Park & Repair Center at the Fish Ponds, 17091 TX 75 North Willis, 77378. T: (936) 344-2027. RV/tent: 52. $$. Hookups: electric (20, 30, 50 amp), water, sewer, phone (modem).

Park on the Lake, 12351 FM 830 Willis, 77378. T: (409) 890-2375. www.parkonthelake.com. RV/tent: 88. $$. Hookups: electric (30, 50 amp), central phone (modem), phone (modem).

Corpus Christi

Greyhound RV Park, 5402 Leopard St., 78408. T: (361) 289-2076 or (866) 704-2483. www.gocampingamerica.com. RV/tent: 90. $$. Hookups: electric (20, 30, 50 amp), water, sewer.

Hatch RV Park, 3101 Up River Rd., 78409. T: (361) 883-9781 or (800) 332-4509. www.hatchrv park.com. RV/tent: 130. $$$. Hookups: electric (20, 30, 50 amp), water, sewer.

Puerto Del Sol RV Park, 5100 Timon Blvd, 78402. T: (361) 882-5373 or (888) 353-5373. RV/tent: 59. $$. Hookups: electric (20, 30, 50 amp), water, central phone (modem), phone (modem).

Corsicana

American RV Park, 4345 West Hwy. 31, 75110. T: (888) 872-0233. RV/tent: 150. $$. Hookups: electric (20, 30, 50 amp), water, sewer, laundry.

TEXAS (continued)

Dallas

Dallas Hi Ho RV Park, 200 West Bear Creek Rd., 75115. T: (972) 223-4834 or (877) 619-3900. www.hihorvpark.com. RV/tent: 127. $$. Hookups: electric (20, 30, 50 amp), water, sewer.

Del Rio

American Campground, HCR 3 Box 44, 78840. T: (830) 775-6484 or (800) 525-3386. www .delrio.com. RV/tent: 87. $$$. Hookups: electric (20, 30, 50 amp), water, sewer, cable.

Holiday Trav-L-Park, HCR 3 Box 40, US 90 West, 78840. T: (830) 775-7275 or (800) 545-2364. www.frommers.com. RV/tent: 176. $$. Hookups: electric (30, 50 amp), water, cable.

Denton

Dallas Destiny RV Park, 7100 I-35 East, 76205. T: (940) 497-3353 or (888) 238-1532. www.destinyrv.com. RV/tent: 178. $$$. Hookups: electric (20, 30, 50 amp).

Dickinson

Green Caye RV Park, 2401 Owens Drive, 77539. T: (281) 337-0289 or (800) 360-6966. www.green cayervpark.com. RV/tent: 75. $$. Hookups: electric (30, 50 amp), water, sewer, central phone.

Donna

Bit-O-Heaven RV & Mobile Home Park, 1051 West US 83, 78537. T: (956) 464-5191. www.bit-o-heaven.com. RV/tent: 824. $$. Hookups: electric (20, 30, 50 amp), water, sewer.

Palm Shadows RV Park, Rte. 6 Box 4452, 78537. T: (956) 464-3324. www.palmshadowspark.com. RV/tent: 469. $$. Hookups: electric (30, 50 amp), water, sewer, phone.

Dumas

Yerby's Mobile Home & RV Park, 1520 Meredith, 79029. T: (806) 935-4940. RV/tent: 49. $$. Hookups: electric (30, 50 amp), water, sewer, phone.

Edinburg

Orange Grove RV Park, 4901 East TX 107, 78539. T: (956) 383-7931. RV/tent: 478. $$. Hookups: electric (20, 30 amp), water, sewer.

Edna

Lake Texana State Park, P.O. Box 760, 77957-0760. T: (361) 782-5718. www.reserveamerica.com. RV/tent: 141. $. Hookups: electric, water.

El Paso

El Paso Roadrunner RV Park, 1212 Lafayette Dr., 79907. T: (915) 598-4469. www.elpasoroad runnerrv.com. RV/tent: 136. $$. Hookups: electric (20, 30 amp), water, sewer.

Ennis

Waxahachie Creek Park, 4000 Observation Dr., 75119. T: (972) 875-5711. www.reserveusa.com. RV/tent: 72. $$. Hookups: electric (20, 30 amp), water.

Eustace

Purtis Creek State Park, 14225 FM 316, 75124. T: (903) 425-2332. RV/tent: 64. $. Hookups: electric, water.

Fannin

Coleto Creek Reservoir and Park, 365 Coleto Park Rd., 77960. T: (361) 575-6366. www.gbra.org. RV/tent: 58. $$. Hookups: electric, water (15, 30, 50 amp).

Fentress

Leisure Camp and RV Park, P.O. Box 277, 79734. T: (512) 488-2563 or (800) 248-4103. www.leisurecamp.net. RV/tent: 109. $$. Hookups: electric (20, 30, 50 amp), water, sewer.

Fort Davis

Davis Mountains State Park, Hwy. 118, 79734. T: (432) 426-3337. www.tpwd.state.tx.us. RV/tent: 100. $. Hookups: electric, water, sewer, cable.

Fort Stockton

Comanche Land RV Park, 1800 West IH 10, 79735. T: (432) 336-6403. RV/tent: 58. $. Hookups: electric (30 amp).

KOA Fort Stockton, I-10 at Warnock Rd., 79735. T: (432) 395-2494 or (800) 562-8607. www.koakampgrounds.com. RV/tent: 79. $$. Hookups: electric (20, 30, 50 amp), water, sewer.

Fort Worth

Sunset RV Park, 4921 White Settlement Rd., 76114. T: (817) 738-0567 or (800) 738-0567. RV/tent: 69. $$. Hookups: electric (20, 30, 50 amp), water, sewer, cable.

Fredericksburg

Fredericksburg-KOA, 5681 East US 290, 78624. T: (830) 997-4796 or (800) 562-0796. www.koakampgrounds.com. RV/tent: 90. $$. Hookups: electric (20, 30, 50 amp), water, sewer, cable.

Oakwood RV Resort, 78 FM 2093, 78624. T: (830) 997-9817 or (800) 366-9396. www.gocamping america.com. RV/tent: 132. $$. Hookups: electric (20, 30, 50 amp), water, sewer, cable, central phone (modem).

Fulton

Woody Acres Mobile Home & RV Resort, 1202 Mesquite St., 78358. T: (361) 729-5636 or (800) 526-9264. woodyacres.us. RV/tent: 225. $$. Hookups: electric (20, 30, 50 amp), water, sewer, cable, central phone (modem), phone (modem).

Galveston

Bayou Shores RV Resort, 6310 Heards Ln., 77551. T: (888) 744-2837. www.bayoushoresrvresort .com. RV/tent: 84. $$. Hookups: electric (20, 30, 50 amp), water, sewer, cable, phone (modem).

Glen Rose

Oakdale Park, P.O. Box 548, 76043. T: (254) 897-2321. www.oakdalepark.com. RV/tent: 300. $$. Hookups: electric (20, 30 amp), water, sewer.

Grapeland

Salmon Lake Park, P.O. Box 483, 75844. T: (936) 687-2594. www.salmonlakervpark.com. RV/tent: 250. $$. Hookups: electric (20, 30 amp), water, sewer.

Grapevine

Silver Lake Park, 1501 North Dooley, 76051. T: (817) 329-8993. RV/tent: 59. $$. Hookups: electric (30 amp), water.

Harlingen

Encore RV Park Harlingen, 1900 Grace Ave., 78550. T: (956) 428-4137. RV/tent: 1066. $$. Hookups: electric (30 amp), water, sewer, cable.

Paradise Park Harlingen, 1201 North Expy. 77, 78552. T: (956) 425-6881 or (800) 425-1201. RV/tent: 309. $$. Hookups: electric (30 amp), water, sewer, cable.

Sunburst RV Park, 4525 Graham Rd,, 78550. T: (956) 423-1170. RV/tent: 300. $$. Hookups: electric (30 amp), water, sewer.

Tropic Winds Mobile Home & RV Park, 1501 North Loop 499, 78550. T: (956) 423-4020 or (800) 458-6086. www.mhcrv.com. RV/tent: 447. $$. Hookups: electric (20, 30, 50 amp), cable, phone (modem).

Hempstead

Yogi Bear's Jellystone Park Hempstead, 34843 Betka Rd. #1, 77445. T: (979) 826-4111. www.campjellystone.com. RV/tent: 135. $$. Hookups: electric (20, 30, 50 amp), water, sewer.

Houston

All Star RV Resort, 10515 Sw Freeway, 77074. T: (713) 981-6814 or (800) 385-9074. www.allstar-rv.com. RV/tent: 120. $$$. Hookups: electric (15, 30, 50 amp), water, sewer, cable, phone (modem).

KOA Houston Central, 1620 Peachleaf, 77039. T: (281) 442-3700 or (800) 562-2132. RV/tent: 75. $$. Hookups: electric (20, 30, 50 amp), water, phone (modem).

South Main RV Park, 10100 South Main, 77025. T: (713) 667-0120. www.smrvpark.com. RV/tent: 108. $$$. Hookups: electric (20, 30, 50 amp), water, sewer, phone (modem).

Traders Village, 7979 Eldridge Rd., 77041. T: (281) 890-8846. www.tradersvillage.com/hnrv.html. RV/tent: 307. $$$. Hookups: electric (20, 30, 50 amp), water, sewer, phone (modem).

Ingram

By the River RV Campground, Riverview Rd., 78025. T: (830) 367-5566. RV/tent: 75. $$. Hookups: electric (30 amp), cable, central phone (modem).

Jefferson

Brushy Creek Park, 2669 FM 726, 75657. T: (903) 777-3491. RV/tent: 103. $$. Hookups: electric, water.

Tres Rios RV River Resort

Tres Rios RV River Resort, 2322 CR 312, 76043. T: (254) 897-4253. www.tresrioscamping.com. RV/tent: 537. $$. Hookups: electric (30, 50 amp), water, sewer, central phone.

Jefferson (continued)

Buckhorn Creek, Farm 726, 75657. T: (903) 665-8261. RV/tent: 96. $$. Hookups: electric (30, 50 amp), water.

Johnson City

Roadrunner RV Park, 503 South US 281, 78636. T: (830) 868-7449. RV/tent: 52. $$. Hookups: electric (20, 30, 50 amp), water, sewer, cable, phone (modem).

Junction

KOA Junction, 2145 North Main St., 76849. T: (325) 446-3138 or (800) 562-7506. www.junction koa.com. RV/tent: 61. $$. Hookups: electric (20, 30, 50 amp), water, sewer, cable, phone.

South Llano River State Park, 1927 Park Rd. 73, 76849. T: (325) 446-3994. www.tpwd.state.tx.us/ park/slano/slano.htm. RV/tent: 64. $. Hookups: electric, water.

Kerrville

Buckhorn Lake Resort, 4071 Goat Creek Rd., I-10, Exit 501, 78028. T: (800) 568-6458. www.buckhornlake.com. RV/tent: 225. $$$. Hookups: electric (30, 50 amp), water, sewer, cable, phone (modem).

Take-It-Easy Resort, 703 Junction Hwy., 78028. T: (830) 257-6636 or (800) 828-6984. RV/tent: 81. $$. Hookups: electric (30, 50 amp), water, sewer, cable, phone (modem).

Kingsville

Oasis RV & Mobile Home Park, Hwy. 77 East Bypass, 78363. T: (361) 592-0764. RV/tent: 147. $$. Hookups: electric (20, 30, 50 amp), phone (modem).

La Feria

Kenwood RV & Mobile Home Plaza Llc, 1221 North Main No. 100, 78559. T: (956) 797-1851. RV/tent: 293. $$$. Hookups: electric (30, 50 amp), cable, phone (modem).

La Feria RV Park, 450 East Frontage Rd., 78559. T: (956) 797-1043. RV/tent: 153. $$. Hookups: electric (30, 50 amp), water, sewer.

VIP Park, 600 East Frontage Rd., 78559. T: (956) 797-1401 or (866) 714-8471. RV/tent: 300. $$. Hookups: electric (20, 30, 50 amp), water, sewer, cable, phone.

La Marque

Lil Thicket Travel Park, 408 Volney, 77568. T: (409) 935-5375. RV/tent: 59. $$. Hookups: electric (20, 30, 50 amp).

Lajitas

Lajitas On The Rio Grande RV Park, HC 70 Box 435, 79852. T: (432) 424-3471. RV/tent: 78. $$$. Hookups: electric (20, 30, 50 amp), cable, phone (modem).

Laredo

Lake Casa Blanca International State Park, 5102 Bob Bullock Loop, 78044. T: (956) 725-3826. www.tpwd.state.tx.us/park/lakecasa. RV/tent: 66. $. Hookups: electric (30 amp), water.

Lavon

Lavonia Park, 3375 Skyview Dr., 75098-7575. T: (972) 442-3141. www.swf-wc.usace.army .mil/lavon/index.htm. RV/tent: 53. $. Hookups: electric, water.

League City

Space Center RV Resort, 301 Gulf Freeway, 77573. T: (281) 554-8800 or (888) 846-3478. www.spacecenterrv.com. RV/tent: 125. $$$. Hookups: electric (20, 30, 50 amp), cable, phone and modem.

Los Fresnos

Palmdale RV Resort, P.O. Box 308, 78566. T: (956) 399-8694 or (800) 456-7683. www.palmdale resort.com. RV/tent: 200. $$. Hookups: electric (30, 50 amp), central phone (modem), phone (modem).

Lubbock

KOA Lubbock, 5502 CR 6300, 79416. T: (806) 762-8653 or (800) 862-8643. www.koa.com/where/ tx/43160.htm. RV/tent: 87. $$. Hookups: electric (20, 30, 50 amp), water.

Loop 289 RV Park, 3436 West Loop 289, 79407. T: (806) 792-4348. RV/tent: 85. $$. Hookups: electric (20, 30, 50 amp), water, sewer.

Luling

Riverbend RV Park, 1881 South TX 80, 78648. T: (830) 875-9548. www.riverbendrvpark.com. RV/tent: 80. $$. Hookups: electric (30, 50 amp), water.

Manvel

Almost Heaven Resort, 4202 Del Bello Rd., 77578. T: (281) 489-8561 or (800) 895-CAMP. www.gocampingamerica.com/almostheaven. RV/tent: 104. $$. Hookups: electric (20, 30, 50 amp), water, central phone (modem).

Marathon

Stillwell Ranch Campground, HC 65 Box 430, 79830. T: (432) 376-2244. RV/tent: 66. $$. Hookups: electric (30 amp), water, sewer.

Marshall

Country Pines RV Park, 5935 US 59 North, 75670. T: (903) 935-4278 or (800) 848-7087. RV/tent: 100. $$. Hookups: electric (20, 30, 50 amp), water, central phone (modem).

Mathis

KOA Lake Corpus Christi, 101 CR 371, 78368. T: (361) 547-5201 or (800) 562-8601. www.koa.com/where/tx/43209. RV/tent: 108. $$. Hookups: electric (20, 30, 50 amp), water.

Wilderness Lakes RV Resort, P.O. Box 518, 78368. T: (361) 547-9995. RV/tent: 133. $$. Hookups: electric (20, 30, 50 amp), water, sewer.

McAllen

Citrus Valley RV Park, 2901 TX 107, 78504. T: (956) 383-8189. RV/tent: 233. $$. Hookups: electric (20, 30 amp), water, sewer.

McAllen Mobile Park, 4900 North McColl Rd., 78504. T: (956) 682-3304 or (800) 845-6077.

www.mcallenmobilepark.com. RV/tent: 318. $$. Hookups: electric (20, 30, 50 amp), phone (modem).

Melissa

Lighthouse RV Resort, Box 350, 75454. T: (972) 838-4600 or (800) 844-2196. RV/tent: 97. $$$. Hookups: electric (20, 30, 50 amp), water, phone (modem).

Mercedes

Encore RV Park-Mercedes, 8000 Paradise South, 78570. T: (956) 565-2044 or (877) 247-2757. www.rvonthego.com/encore-rv-resort-mercedes-8.htm. RV/tent: 490. $. Hookups: electric (30, 50 amp), water, sewer, phone (modem).

Llano Grande Lake Park, 489 Yolanda, 78570. T: (956) 565-2638 or (800) 656-2638. RV/tent: 870. $$. Hookups: electric (30, 50 amp).

Midland

Midessa Oil Patch RV Park, 4220 South CR 1290, Odessa, 79765. T: (432) 5632368 or (800) 864-3204. RV/tent: 160. $$$. Hookups: electric (20, 30, 50 amp), water, sewer, central phone (modem), phone (modem).

Mims

Johnson Creek Camping Area, 2669 FM, 75668. T: (903) 755-2435. RV/tent: 85. $. Hookups: electric (30, 50 amp), water.

Mission

Bentsen Grove Trailer Park, 810 North Bentsen Palm Dr., 78572. T: (956) 585-7011. www .bentsengroveresort.com. RV/tent: 850. $$. Hookups: electric (30, 50 amp), water, sewer, cable, central phone (modem), phone (modem).

Circle T RV Park, 1820 Clay Tolle St., 78572. T: (956) 585-5381. RV/tent: 270. $$. Hookups: electric (20, 30, 50 amp), phone (modem).

Eldorado Acres RV Park, 2404 North Goodwin Rd. (FM 492), 78572. T: (956) 581-6718. RV/tent: 122. $$. Hookups: electric (30 amp), water, sewer.

Seven Oaks Resort & Country Club, 1300 Circle Dr., 78572. T: (956) 581-0068. RV/tent: 232. $$. Hookups: electric (30 amp), water, sewer.

Montgomery

Havens Landing RV Resort, 19785 Hwy. 105 West, 77316. T: (936) 582-1200 or (800) 535-8351. www.havenslandingresort.com. RV/tent: 239. $$$. Hookups: electric (20, 30, 50 amp), water, sewer.

New Braunfels

Hill Country RV Resort, 131 South Ruekle Rd., 78130. T: (830) 625-1919. RV/tent: 300. $$. Hookups: electric (20, 30, 50 amp), water, sewer, cable.

New Caney

Lone Star Lakes RV Park, 20842 US 59, 77357. T: (281) 399-8977 or (800) 290-9301. RV/tent: 82. $$. Hookups: electric (20, 30, 50 amp), water, sewer, cable, phone (modem).

TEXAS (continued)

Orange

Oak Leaf Park Campground, 6900 Oak Leaf Dr., 77632. T: (409) 886-4082. RV/tent: 100. $$. Hookups: electric (20, 30, 50 amp), water, sewer, phone (modem).

Ozona

Circle Bar RV Park, P.O. Box 1498, 76943. T: (325) 392-2611. RV/tent: 128. $$. Hookups: electric (20, 30, 50 amp), water, sewer.

Palacios

Serendipity Resort RV Park & Marina, 1001 Main St., 77465. T: (361) 972-5454 or (800) 556-0534. www.serendipityresort.com. RV/tent: 162. $$. Hookups: electric (30, 50 amp), water, sewer.

Pecos

Trapark RV Park, 3100 Moore St., 79772. T: (432) 447-2137. RV/tent: 61. $. Hookups: electric (20, 30, 50 amp), water, sewer, cable, central phone (modem).

Perrin

Mitchell RV Park, 2730 FM 2210 East, 76486. T: (940) 798-4615. www.mitchellrvpark.com. RV/tent: 245. $$. Hookups: electric (20, 30, 50 amp), water, sewer, central phone (modem), phone (modem).

Pineland

San Augustine Park, FM 1751, 75951-9598. T: (409) 384-5716. RV/tent: 100. $. Hookups: electric (30 amp), water.

Port Aransas

Island RV Resort, 700 6th St., 78373. T: (361) 749-5600. www.islandrvresort.com. RV/tent: 199. $$. Hookups: electric (20, 30, 50 amp), water, sewer, cable, phone (modem).

Surfside RV Resort, 1820 11th St., 78373. T: (361) 749-2208 or (888) 565-5929. RV/tent: 45. $$. Hookups: electric (50 amp), water, sewer, cable, phone (modem).

Port Isabel

Port Isabel Park Center, 702 Champion, 78578. T: (956) 943-7340. www.campsouthtexas.com/portisabel. RV/tent: 225. $$. Hookups: electric (30, 50 amp), cable, central phone (modem), phone (modem).

Portland

Sea Breeze RV Park, 1026 Seabreeze Ln., 78374. T: (361) 643-0744 or (888) 212-7541. www.seabreezerv.com. RV/tent: 177. $$. Hookups: electric (30, 50 amp), water, sewer, cable, central phone (modem), phone (modem).

Proctor

Sowell Creek Park, FM 1476, 76442-9210. T: (817) 879-2322. RV/tent: 60. $. Hookups: electric (30 amp), water, sewer.

Purdon

Wolf Creek Park, 1175 FM 667, 76679. T: (254) 578-1431. www.reserveusa.com. RV/tent: 72. $. Hookups: electric (20, 30 amp), water.

Rio Hondo

River Ranch RV Resort, 20054 Reynolds, 78583-3106. T: (956) 748-2286. RV/tent: 125. $$. Hookups: electric (30, 50 amp), water, sewer.

Rockport

Goose Island State Park, 202 South Palmetto St., 78382. T: (361) 729-2858. www.tpwd.state.tx.us. RV/tent: 97. $$. Hookups: electric, water.

Lagoons RV Resort, 600 Enterprise Blvd., 78382. T: (361) 729-7834. www.lagoonsrv.com. RV/tent: 247. $$$. Hookups: electric (30, 50 amp), cable, central phone (modem), phone (modem).

San Angelo

Spring Creek Marina & RV Park, 45 Fishermans Rd., 76904. T: (915) 944-3850 or (800) 500-7801. RV/tent: 83. $$. Hookups: electric (20, 30, 50 amp), water, cable, central phone (modem), phone (modem).

San Antonio

Blazing Star Luxury RV Resort, 1120 West Loop 1604 North, 78251. T: (210) 680-7827 or (877) 387-5777. www.blazingstarrv.com. RV/tent: 260. $$. Hookups: electric (30, 50 amp), water, sewer, cable, central phone (modem), phone (modem).

Traveler's World RV Resort, 2617 Roosevelt Ave., 78214. T: (210) 532-8310. www.travelersworld.com. RV/tent: 170. $$. Hookups: electric (20, 30, 50 amp), water, sewer, central phone (modem), phone (modem).

Sanger

Ray Roberts Lake State Park, 100 PW 4137 Pilot Point, 76258-8944. T: (940) 686-2148. RV/tent: 151. $$. Hookups: electric (20, 30 amp), water.

Schertz

Stone Creek RV Park, 18905 IH-35 North, 78154. T: (830) 609-7759. www.gocampingamerica.com/stonecreek. RV/tent: 250. $$. Hookups: electric (30, 50 amp), water, sewer, central phone (modem), phone (modem).

Seguin

River Shade RV Park, 3995 TX 123 Bypass, 78155. T: (830) 379-8826 or (800) 364-7275. RV/tent: 87. $$. Hookups: electric (30, 50 amp), water, sewer, cable, central phone (modem), phone (modem).

South Padre Island

Destination South Padre Island, 1 Padre Blvd., 78597. T: (956) 761-5665 or (800) 867-2373. www.destinationsouthpadre.com. RV/tent: 190. $$$. Hookups: electric (20, 30, 50 amp), water, sewer.

Spring

Spring Oaks RV & Mobile Home Community, 22014 Spring Oaks Dr., 77389. T: (281) 350-2606. RV/tent: 65. $$. Hookups: electric (30, 50 amp), central phone (modem), phone (modem).

Sugar Land

USA RV Park, 20825 Sw Freeway, 77479. T: (281) 343-0626. RV/tent: 114. $$. Hookups: electric (30, 50 amp), water, sewer.

Surfside Beach

San Luis Pass County Park, 14001 CR 257 Freeport, 77541. T: (979) 233-6026 or (800) 372-7578. RV/tent: 79. $$. Hookups: electric (20, 30, 50 amp).

Terlingua

Big Bend Motor Inn & RV Campground, Hwy. 118 at 170, 79852. T: (432) 371-2218 or (800) 848-2363. www.texasbesthotels.com/bigbend_motorinn.htm. RV/tent: 126. $$. Hookups: electric (20, 30, 50 amp), water, cable, central phone (modem), phone (modem).

Texarkana

Clear Springs Recreational Area, P.O. Box 1817, 75504-1817. T: (903) 838-8636. RV/tent: 113. $. Hookups: electric (20, 30 amp), water.

The Colony

Hidden Cove Park, 20400 Hackberry Creek Park Rd., Rte. 2 Box 353H, 75034. T: (972) 294-1155 or (972) 294-1443. www.hiddencovepark.com. RV/tent: 50. $. Hookups: electric (20, 30 amp), water, sewer.

Tyler

Tyler State Park, 789 Park Rd. 16, 75706-9141. T: (903) 597-5338. www.tpwd.state.tx.us/park/tyler/tyler.htm. RV/tent: 174. $. Hookups: electric (20, 30 amp), water.

Whispering Pines Campground & Resort, 5583 FM 16 East, 75706. T: (903) 858-2405 or (800) 559-3817. www.gocampingamerica.com/whisperingpinestx. RV/tent: 140. $$. Hookups: electric (20, 30, 50 amp), water, central phone (modem), phone (modem).

Uvalde

Park Chalk Bluff, H.CR 33 Box 566, 78801. T: (830) 278-5515. RV/tent: 87. $$. Hookups: electric (30, 50 amp), water.

Van Horn

KOA Van Horn, P.O. Box 265, 79855. T: (800) 562-0798 or (915) 283-2728. www.koa.com/where/tx/43196. RV/tent: 70. $$. Hookups: electric (20, 30, 50 amp), water.

Vernon

Rocking A RV Park, 3725 Harrison, 76384. T: (940) 552-2821. RV/tent: 83. $$. Hookups: electric (20, 30, 50 amp), water, sewer, central phone (modem), phone (modem).

Victoria

Dad's RV Park, 203 Hopkins, 77901. T: (361) 573-1231. RV/tent: 50. $. Hookups: electric (20, 30, 50 amp), water, cable, central phone (modem), phone (modem).

Waco

KOA Waco North, P.O. Box 157, 76691. T: (254) 826-3869 or (800) 562-4199. www.koa.com/where/tx/43130.htm. RV/tent: 76. $$. Hookups: electric (20, 30, 50 amp), water, central phone (modem), phone (modem).

TEXAS (continued)

Waco (continued)

Speegleville I Park, P.O. Box 8221, 76714. T: (817) 756-5359. RV/tent: 100. $$. Hookups: electric (30 amp), water.

Wallisville

Turtle Bayou RV Park, P.O. Box 185, 77597. T: (409) 389-2468. RV/tent: 63. $$$. Hookups: electric (20, 30, 50 amp), water.

Weslaco

Magic Valley Park, 2300 East TX 83, 78596. T: (956) 968-8242 or (800) 556-5151. RV/tent: 387. $$.

Hookups: electric (20, 30 amp), phone (modem).

Snow to Sun RV & Mobile Home Community, 1701 North International Blvd., 78596. T: (956) 968-0322 or (800) 968-0322. RV/tent: 493. $$. Hookups: electric (30, 50 amp), phone (modem), central phone (modem).

Wichita Falls

Wichita Falls RV Park, 2944 Seymour Hwy. 5th St., 76301. T: (940) 723-1532 or (800) 252-1532. RV/tent: 135. $$. Hookups: electric (20, 30, 50 amp), cable.

Wylie

East Fork Park, 3375 Skyview Dr., 75098. T: (972) 442-3014. RV/tent: 62. $. Hookups: electric (50 amp), water.

Zapata

4 Seasons RV Park, P.O. Box 1007, 78076. T: (956) 765-4241. www.fourseasons-rvpark.com. RV/tent: 175. $$. Hookups: electric (20, 30, 50 amp), water, cable, phone (modem).

UTAH

American Fork

American Campground, 418 East 620 South, 84003. T: (801) 756-5502. RV/tent: 52. $$. Hookups: electric (20, 30 amp), water, sewer.

Antimony

Antimony Mercantile Campground, 70 North Hwy. 22, 84712. T: (435) 624-3253. RV/tent: 20. $$. Hookups: electric (30 amp), water, sewer.

Otter Creek RV & Marina, P.O. Box 43, 84712. T: (435) 624-3268. www.ottercreekrv.com. RV/tent: 35. $$. Hookups: electric (15, 30 amp), water, sewer.

Beaver

Anderson Meadow, 575 South Main, 84713. T: (435) 438-2436. RV/tent: 10. $. Hookups: none.

Beaver Canyon Campground, 1419 East Canyon Rd., 84713. T: (435) 438-5654. RV/tent: 105. $. Hookups: electric (20, 30 amp), water, sewer.

Kents Lake, 575 South Main, 84713. T: (435) 438-2436. RV/tent: 40. $. Hookups: none.

KOA Beaver, 1428 Manderfield Rd., 84713. T: (435) 438-2924. RV/tent: 76. $$. Hookups: electric (20, 30 amp), water, sewer.

Blanding

Kampark, 861 South Main St., 84511. T: (435) 678-2770. RV/tent: 55. $$. Hookups: electric (20, 30, 50 amp), water, sewer, phone (modem).

Bluff

Cottonwood RV Park, 4th Ave., 84512. T: (435) 672-2287. RV/tent: 32. $$. Hookups: electric (20, 30, 50 amp), water, sewer.

Boulder

Boulder Exchange, 425 North Hwy. 12, Box 1418, 84716. T: (435) 335-7304. RV/tent: 4. $$. Hookups: electric (20 amp), water, sewer.

Brigham City

Brigham City/Perry South KOA, 1040 West 3600 South, 84302. T: (435) 723-5503 or (800) 562-0903. www.koa.com. RV/tent: 102. $$. Hookups: electric (20, 30 amp), water, sewer.

Golden Spike RV Park, 1075 South 905 West, 84302. T: (435) 723-8858. RV/tent: 60. $$.

Hookups: electric (20, 30, 50 amp), water, sewer, cable, phone (modem).

Caineville

Sleepy Hollow Campground, HC 70, Box 40, 84775. T: (435) 456-9130. RV/tent: 39. $$. Hookups: electric (30 amp).

Cedar City

Best Western Town & Country RV Park, 189 North Main St., 84720. T: (435) 586-9900. RV/tent: 10. $$. Hookups: electric (20, 30, 50 amp), water, sewer, cable, phone (modem).

KOA Cedar City, 1232 North Main, 84720. T: (435) 586-9872 or (800) 562-9873. RV/tent: 129. $$. Hookups: electric (20, 30 amp), water, sewer, phone.

Navajo Lake, Hwy. 614, 84720. T: (435) 865-3200 or (877) 444-6777. www.fs.fed.us/dxnf/recreation/campgrounds/navajolake.html. RV/tent: 21. $. Hookups: none.

Delta

Antelope Valley RV Park, 776 West Main, 84624. T: (435) 864-1813. www.antelopevalleyrvpark.com. RV/tent: 96. $$. Hookups: electric (20, 30, 50 amp), water, sewer.

Dixie

Te-Ah, Navajo Lake Rd., 84720. T: (435) 865-3200. www.fs.fed.us/dxnf/recreation/campgrounds/teah.html. RV/tent: 42. $. Hookups: none.

Duchesne

Aspen Grove Campground, 85 West Main, Forest Rd. 144, 84021. T: (435) 738-2482. RV/tent: 32. $. Hookups: none.

Hades Campground, 85 West Main, Forest Rd. 144, 84021. T: (435) 738-2482. RV/tent: 14. $. Hookups: none.

Iron Mine Campground, 85 West Main, Forest Rd. 144, 84021. T: (435) 738-2482. RV/tent: 28. $. Hookups: none.

Moon Lake Campground, 85 West Main, Forest Rd. 131. T: (435) 738-2482. RV/tent: 58. $. Hookups: none.

South Fork Campground, 85 West Main, 84021. T: (435) 738-2482. RV/tent: 5. $. Hookups: none.

Yellowpine Campground, Upper Stillwater Dam, 85 West Main, 84021. T: (435) 738-2482. RV/tent: 29. $. Hookups: none.

Dutch John

Skull Creek Campground, Hwy. 44, 84023. T: (801) 784-3448. RV/tent: 17. $$. Hookups: none.

Escalante

Blue Spruce Campground, P.O. Box 246, 84726. T: (435) 826-5400 or (877) 444-6777. RV/tent: 6. $. Hookups: none.

Moqui Motel & RV Park, 480 West Main St., Box 534, 84726. T: (435) 826-4210. RV/tent: 10. $$. Hookups: electric (20, 30 amp), water, sewer.

Pine Lake Campground, P.O. Box 246, 84726. T: (435) 826-5600 or (877) 444-6777. RV/tent: 33. $. Hookups: none.

Posey Lake Campground, P.O. Box 246, 84726. T: (435) 826-5400. RV/tent: 19. $. Hookups: none.

Farmington

Lagoon RV Park & Campground, 375 North Lagoon Dr., 84025. T: (801) 451-8100 or (800) 748-5246. www.lagoonpark.com. RV/tent: 208. $$. Hookups: electric (20, 30, 50 amp), water, sewer.

Fillmore

Wagons West RV Park and Campground, 545 North Main, 84631. T: (435) 743-6188. RV/tent: 50. $$. Hookups: electric (20, 30, 50 amp), water, sewer, cable.

Garden City

Bear Lake KOA, 485 North Bear Lake Blvd., 84028. T: (435) 946-3454 or (800) 562-3442. RV/tent: 160. $$. Hookups: electric (30, 50 amp), water, sewer.

Sweetwater RV Park & Marina, 2415 South Bear Lake Rd., 84028. T: (435) 946-8735. RV/tent: 19. $$. Hookups: electric (30 amp), water, sewer.

Hanksville

Starr Spring Campground, 100 West 400 South, 84734. T: (435) 542-3461. www.utso.ut.blm.gov. RV/tent: 12. $. Hookups: none.

Hatch

Bryce-Zion Midway Resort, US 89, 84735. T: (888) 299-3531 or (435) 735-4199. www.netutah.com/bzrhatch. bzmrhatch@juno.com. RV/tent: 20. $$. Hookups: electric (30 amp), water, sewer.

UTAH (continued)

Heber City

Currant Creek Campground, 2460 South Hwy. 40, 84032. T: (435) 654-0470. RV/tent: 99. $. Hookups: none.

Heber Valley RV Park Resort, 7000 North Hwy. 40, 84032. T: (435) 654-4049. RV/tent: 120. $$. Hookups: electric (20, 30, 50 amp), water, sewer.

High Country Inn & RV Park, 1000 South Main, 84032. T: (435) 654-0201 or (800) 345-9198. RV/tent: 38. $$. Hookups: electric (20, 30, 50 amp), water, sewer.

Jordenelle State Park–Hailstone Campground, SR 319, 84032. T: (435) 649-9540. RV/tent: 186. $$. Hookups: electric (20, 30, 50 amp), water.

Lodgepole Campground, 2460 South Hwy. 40, 84032. T: (435) 654-0470. RV/tent: 50. $. Hookups: none.

Mill Hollow, 2460 South Hwy. 40, 84032. T: (435) 654-0470. RV/tent: 26. $. Hookups: none.

Honeyville

Crystal Hot Springs, 8215 North Hwy. 38, 84314. T: (435) 279-8104. RV/tent: 120. $$. Hookups: electric (20, 30 amp), water, sewer.

Huntington

Huntington State Park, P.O. Box 1343, 84528. T: (435) 687-2491. RV/tent: 22. $$. Hookups: none.

Millsite State Park, P.O. Box 1343, 84528. T: (435) 687-2491. RV/tent: 20. $$. Hookups: none.

Hurricane

The Canyons RV Resort, 36 North 2770 West, 84737. T: (801) 635-0200. www.resortparks.com. RV/tent: 20. $$. Hookups: electric (30, 50 amp), water, sewer.

Jensen

Bedrock Campground & RV Park, 9650 East 6000 South Hwy. 40, 84035. T: (435) 781-6000 or (800) 852-7336. RV/tent: 131. $. Hookups: electric (20, 30, 50 amp), water, sewer.

Kamas

Beaver View Campground, 50 East Center, 84036. T: (435) 783-4338. RV/tent: 8. $. Hookups: none.

Butterfly Lake Campground, 50 East Center, 84036. T: (435) 783-4338. RV/tent: 20. $. Hookups: none.

Christmas Meadows Campground, 50 East Center, 84036. T: (435) 783-4338. RV/tent: 21. $. Hookups: none.

Cobble Rest Campground, 50 East Center, 84036. T: (435) 783-4338. RV/tent: 18. $. Hookups: none.

Hayden Fork Campground, 50 East Center, 84036. T: (435) 783-4338. RV/tent: 9. $. Hookups: none.

Ledgefork Campground, 50 East Center, 84036. T: (435) 783-4338. RV/tent: 73. $. Hookups: none.

Lost Lake Campground, 50 East Center, 84036. T: (435) 783-4338. RV/tent: 35. $. Hookups: none.

Mirror Lake Campground, 50 East Center, 84036. T: (435) 783-4338. RV/tent: 79. $. Hookups: none.

Moose Horn Lake Campground, 50 East Center, 84036. T: (435) 783-4338. RV/tent: 33. $. Hookups: none.

Shady Dell Campground, 50 East Center, 84036. T: (435) 783-4338. RV/tent: 20. $. Hookups: none.

Shingle Creek Campground, 50 East Center, 84036. T: (435) 783-4338. RV/tent: 20. $. Hookups: none.

Smith and Moorehouse Campground, 50 East Center, 84036. T: (435) 783-4338. RV/tent: 34. $. Hookups: none.

Soapstone Basin Campground, 50 East Center, 84036. T: (435) 783-4338. RV/tent: 34. $. Hookups: none.

Stillwater Campground, 50 East Center, 84036. T: (435) 783-4338. RV/tent: 21. $. Hookups: none.

Sulphur Campground, 50 East Center, 84036. T: (801) 783-4338. RV/tent: 21. $. Hookups: none.

Trial Lake Soapstone Campground, 50 East Center, 84036. T: (801) 783-4338. RV/tent: 60. $. Hookups: none.

Kanab

Hitchin' Post RV Park, 196 East 300 South, 84741. T: (435) 644-2142. RV/tent: 50. $$. Hookups: electric (20, 30, 50 amp), water, sewer.

Kanab RV Corral, 483 South 100 East, 84741. T: (435) 644-5330 or (888) 818-5330. RV/tent: 40. $$. Hookups: electric (20, 30, 50 amp), water, sewer, phone (modem).

Kanarraville

Red Ledge RV Park & Campground, 15 North Main, 84742. T: (435) 586-9150. RV/tent: 22. $. Hookups: electric (30, 50 amp), water, sewer.

Leeds

Leeds RV Park & Motel, 97 South Valley Rd., 84746. T: (435) 673-2970. RV/tent: 59. $$. Hookups: electric (20, 30, 50 amp), water, sewer, phone (modem).

Loa

Bowery Campground, 138 South Main St., 84747. T: (435) 638-1033. RV/tent: 43. $. Hookups: none.

Doctor Creek Campground, 138 South Main St., 84747. T: (435) 638-1033. RV/tent: 30. $. Hookups: none.

Mackinaw Campground, 138 South Main St., 84747. T: (435) 836-2811 or (877) 444-6777. RV/tent: 67. $. Hookups: none.

Piute Campground, 138 South Main St., 84747. T: (435) 836-2811 or (877) 444-6777. RV/tent: 47. $. Hookups: none.

Logan

Box Elder Campground, 1500 East Hwy. 89, 84327. T: (435) 755-3620. RV/tent: 26. $. Hookups: none.

Bridger Campground, 1500 East Hwy. 89, 84327. T: (435) 755-3620. RV/tent: 10. $. Hookups: none.

Guinavah-Malibu Campground, 1500 East Hwy. 89, 84327. T: (435) 755-3620. RV/tent: 40. $. Hookups: none.

Lewis M. Turner Campground, 1500 East Hwy. 89, 84327. T: (435) 755-3620. RV/tent: 10. $. Hookups: none.

Lodge Campground, 1500 East Hwy. 89, 84327. T: (435) 755-3620. RV/tent: 10. $. Hookups: none.

LW's Phillips 66, 1936 North Main (US 91), 84327. T: (435) 753-1025. RV/tent: 13. $$. Hookups: electric (20, 50 amp), water, sewer.

Pioneer Campground, 1500 East Hwy. 89, 84327. T: (435) 755-3620. RV/tent: 15. $. Hookups: none.

Red Banks Campground, 1500 East Hwy. 89, 84327. T: (435) 755-3620. RV/tent: 12. $. Hookups: none.

Riverside RV Park & Campground, 447 West 1700 South, 84327. T: (435) 245-4469. RV/tent: 14. $$. Hookups: electric (20, 30 amp), water, sewer.

Spring Hollow Campground, 1500 East Hwy. 89, 84327. T: (435) 755-3620. RV/tent: 12. $. Hookups: none.

Sunrise Campground, 1500 East Hwy. 89, 84327. T: (435) 755-3620 or (877) 444-6777. RV/tent: 27. $. Hookups: none.

Tony Grove Lake, 1500 East Hwy. 89, 84327. T: (435) 755-3620. RV/tent: 36. $. Hookups: none.

Traveland RV Park, 2020 South Hwy. 89-91, 84321. T: (435) 787-2060. RV/tent: 52. $$. Hookups: electric (20, 30, 50 amp), water, sewer.

Western Park Campground, 350 West 800 South, 84321. T: (435) 752-6424. RV/tent: 13. $$. Hookups: electric (20, 30 amp), water, sewer.

Manila

Antelope Flat Campground, P.O. Box 279, 84046. T: (801) 784-3448. RV/tent: 126. $. Hookups: none.

Canyon Rim Campground, US 191, 84046. T: (435) 784-3445 or (877) 444-6777. RV/tent: 18. $$. Hookups: none.

Deep Creek, P.O. Box 279, 84046. T: (435) 784-3445 or (877) 444-6777. RV/tent: 17. $. Hookups: none.

Dripping Springs Campground, Ashley National Forest, FR 075, 84046. T: (435) 784-3445 or (877) 444-6777. RV/tent: 21. $$. Hookups: none.

Firefighters Memorial Campground, Ashley National Forest, 355 North Vernal Ave., 84046. T: (435) 784-3445 or (877) 444-6777. RV/tent: 94. $$. Hookups: none.

Flaming Gorge KOA, P.O. Box 157, 84046. T: (435) 784-3184 or (800) 562-3254. RV/tent: 50. $$. Hookups: electric (20, 30, 50 amp), water, sewer.

Greens Lake Campground, P.O. Box 279, 84046. T: (435) 784-3445 or (877) 444-6777. RV/tent: 20. $$. Hookups: none.

Lucerne Valley Campground, SR 43/Forest Rd. 146, 84046. T: (435) 784-3445 or (877) 444-6777. RV/tent: 147. $$. Hookups: electric (50 amp).

Mustang Ridge Campground, US 191/FR 184, 84046. T: (435) 784-3445 or (877) 444-6777. RV/tent: 73. $$. Hookups: none.

Spirit Lake Campground, P.O. Box 279, 84046. T: (435) 784-3445. RV/tent: 24. $. Hookups: none.

Manti

Manti Campground & RV Park, 490 North 250 East, 84642. T: (435) 835-2267. RV/tent: 79. $. Hookups: electric (20, 30 amp), water, sewer.

UTAH (continued)

Mantua

Mountain Haven RV Park & Country Store, 130 North Main, 84324. T: (435) 723-1292. RV/tent: 57. $$. Hookups: electric (15 amp), water, sewer.

Midway

Deer Creek State Park, P.O. Box 257, 84049. T: (435) 654-0171. RV/tent: 35. $. Hookups: none.

Moab

Devil's Canyon Campground, 2290 South West Resource Blvd., 84532. T: (877) 444-6777. RV/tent: 33. $. Hookups: none.

Moab Valley RV & Campark, 1773 North Hwy. 191, 84532. T: (435) 259-4469. www.moabvalley rv.com. RV/tent: 128. $$. Hookups: electric (20, 30, 50 amp), water, sewer.

O.K. RV Park & Canyonlands Stables, 3310 Spanish Valley Dr., 84532. T: (435) 259-1400. RV/tent: 45. $$. Hookups: electric (20, 30, 50 amp), water, sewer, cable.

Park Creek Campground & RV Park, 1520 Murphy Ln., No. 6, 84532. T: (435) 259-2982. RV/tent: 48. $$. Hookups: electric (20, 30 amp), water, sewer.

Price Canyon, 82 East Dogwood Rd., 84501. T: (435) 637-4584. RV/tent: 18. $. Hookups: none.

Riverside Oasis RV Park, P.O. Box 412, 84532. T: (435) 259-3424. www.riversideoasis.com. Rsoasis@lasal.net. RV/tent: 60. $$. Hookups: electric (20, 30, 50 amp), water, sewer, cable, phone (modem).

Slickrock Campground, 1301 1/2 North Hwy. 191, 84532. T: (435) 259-7660 or (800) 448-8873. www.slickrockcampground. RV/tent: 173. $$. Hookups: electric (20, 30 amp), water, sewer, cable, phone (modem).

Spanish Trail RV Park & Campground, 2980 South Hwy. 191, 84532. T: (800) 787-2751. RV/tent: 73. $$. Hookups: electric (20, 30, 50 amp), water, sewer, cable, phone (modem).

Mount Carmel

East Zion RV Park, US 69 & Hwy. 9, 84755. T: (435) 648-2326. RV/tent: 20. $$. Hookups: electric (30 amp), water, sewer.

Ogden

Anderson Cove, SR 39, 84401. T: (801) 625-5112. RV/tent: 74. $. Hookups: none.

Century RV Park & Campground, 1399 West 2100 South, 84401. T: (801) 731-3800. RV/tent: 168. $$. Hookups: electric (20, 30, 50 amp), water, sewer, cable, phone (modem).

Maple Grove, 2501 Wall Ave., 84401. T: (435) 743-5721. RV/tent: 18. $. Hookups: none.

Meadows Campground, SR 39, 84401. T: (801) 625-5110. RV/tent: 26. $. Hookups: none.

Monte Cristo Campground, SR 39, 84401. T: (801) 625-5110. RV/tent: 47. $. Hookups: none.

Oak Creek, 2501 Wall Ave., 84401. T: (435) 743-5721. RV/tent: 23. $$$$. Hookups: none.

Perception Park Campground, SR 39, 84401. T: (801) 625-5110. RV/tent: 60. $. Hookups: none.

Panguitch

Hitch-N-Post Campground, 420 North Main St., 84759. T: (435) 676-2436. RV/tent: 48. $$. Hookups: electric (20, 30, 50 amp), water, sewer.

Kings Creek Campground, P.O. Box 80, 84759. T: (435) 676-8815. RV/tent: 38. $. Hookups: none.

Panguitch Lake General Store, Gift Shop, & RV Park, 53 West Hwy. 143, 84759. T: (435) 676-2464. www.panguitchlake.net. RV/tent: 14. $$. Hookups: electric (20, 30 amp), water, sewer.

Paradise RV Park & Campground, 2153 North Hwy. 89, 84759. T: (435) 676-8348. www.bryce canyonparadiserv.com. RV/tent: 67. $$. Hookups: electric (20, 30, 50 amp), water, sewer.

Panguitch Lake

Panguitch Lake Resort, 905 South Hwy. 143, 84759. T: (435) 676-2650 or (888) LKE-VIEW. www.panguitchlake.net. RV/tent: 62. $$. Hookups: electric (20, 30 amp), water, sewer.

Park City

Hidden Haven Campground, 2200 Rasmussen Rd., 84098. T: (435) 649-8935 or (800) 553-8269. RV/tent: 88. $$. Hookups: electric (20, 30, 50 amp), water, sewer, cable, phone (modem).

Parowan

Sportsman's Country RV Park & Restaurant, 492 North Main, 84761. T: (435) 477-3714. RV/tent: 28. $. Hookups: electric (20, 30 amp), water, sewer, cable, phone (modem).

Peoa

Rockport State Park, 9040 North Hwy. 302, 84061. T: (435) 336-2241. RV/tent: 102. $. Hookups: electric (20, 30 amp), water, sewer.

Price

Budget Host Inn & RV Park, 145 North Carbon-ville Rd., 84501. T: (435) 637-2424. RV/tent: 40. $$. Hookups: electric (20, 30, 50 amp), water, sewer.

Flat Canyon Campground, 599 West Price River Dr., 84501. T: (801) 756-8616. RV/tent: 12. $. Hookups: none.

Price Old Folks Flat Campground, 599 West Price River Dr., 84501. T: (435) 637-2817. RV/tent: 5. $. Hookups: none.

Scofield State Park, P.O. Box 166, 84501. T: (801) 322-3770. RV/tent: 70. $$. Hookups: none.

Provo

Granite Flat Campground, 88 West 100 North, 84601. T: (801) 342-5100. RV/tent: 90. $. Hookups: none.

Hope Campground, 88 West 100 North, 84601. T: (801) 342-5100. RV/tent: 48. $. Hookups: none.

KOA Provo, 320 North 2050 West, 84601. T: (801) 375-2994 or (800) 562-1894. www.koa.com/where/ut/44108.htm. RV/tent: 95. $$. Hookups: electric (20, 30 amp), water, sewer.

Lakeside RV Campground, 4000 West Center, 84601. T: (801) 373-5267 or (800) 906-5267. www.lakesidervcampground.com. RV/tent: 145. $$. Hookups: electric (20, 30 amp), water, sewer, phone (modem).

Little Mill

Little Mill Campground, 88 West 100 North, 84601. T: (801) 342-5100. RV/tent: 79. $. Hookups: none.

Mt. Timpanogos Campground, 88 West 100 North, 84601. T: (801) 342-5100. RV/tent: 27. $. Hookups: none.

Payson Lakes Campground, 44 West 400 North, Spanish Forks, 84660. T: (435) 548-2554. RV/tent: 92. $. Hookups: none.

Timpooneke Campground, 88 West 100 North, 84601. T: (801) 342-5100. RV/tent: 32. $. Hookups: none.

Richfield

J. R. Munchies Convenience Store, US 89, 84701. T: (435) 896-9340. RV/tent: 21. $$. Hookups: electric (30, 50 amp), water, sewer.

KOA Richfield, 600 West 600 South, 84701. T: (435) 896-6674. www.koa.com. RV/tent: 141. $$. Hookups: electric (20, 30, 50 amp), water, sewer.

Roosevelt

Swift Creek Campground, 244 West Hwy. 40, 84066. T: (801) 722-5018. RV/tent: 13. $. Hookups: none.

Yellowstone Campground, 244 West Hwy. 40, 84066. T: (801) 722-5018. RV/tent: 14. $. Hookups: none.

Salina

Albion Basin Campground, 6944 South 300 East, 84121. T: (801) 943-1794. www.reserveusa.com/nrrs/ut/albi. RV/tent: 26. $. Hookups: none.

Big Bend Group Campsites, 324 South State St., 84145. T: (435) 259-6111 or (435) 259-2100. www.blm.gov/utah/moab/bbg.html. RV/tent: 23. $. Hookups: none.

Bountiful Peak Campground, 6944 South 300 East, 84121. T: (801) 943-1794. www.reserveamerica.com/nrrs/ut/bout. RV/tent: 26. $. Hookups: none.

Bridge Hollow Campground, 170 South 500 East, 84145. T: (435) 885-3307. RV/tent: 12. $. Hookups: none.

Deer Creek Campground, 324 South State St., 84145. T: (435) 826-5499. RV/tent: 5. $. Hookups: none.

Oasis Campground (Little Sahara Recreation Area), 324 South State St., 84145. T: (435) 743-3100. RV/tent: 114. $. Hookups: none.

Redman Campground, 6944 South 300 East, 84121. T: (801) 943-1794 or (877) 444-6777. RV/tent: 37. $. Hookups: none.

Salina Creek RV Camp, 1385 South State St., 84654. T: (435) 529-3711 or (888) 529-3711. RV/tent: 27. $$. Hookups: electric (20, 30, 50 amp), water, sewer.

Spruces Campground, 6944 South 300 East, 84121. T: (801) 524-3900. RV/tent: 97. $$. Hookups: none.

Sunset Campground, 6944 South 300 East, 84121. T: (801) 943-1794. RV/tent: 32. $. Hookups: none.

Tanner's Flat Campground, 6944 South 300 East, 84121. T: (801) 943-1794. RV/tent: 42. $. Hookups: none.

UTAH (continued)

White Sands Campground, Little Sahara Recreation Area, 324 South State St., 84145. T: (435) 896-1551. RV/tent: 99. $. Hookups: none.

Salt Lake City

KOA Salt Lake City, 1400 West North Temple St., 84116. T: (801) 328-0224 or (800) 226-7752. www.campvip.net. RV/tent: 226. $$$. Hookups: electric (30, 50 amp), water, sewer, cable, phone (modem).

Sandy

Ardell Brown's Quail Run RV Park, 9230 South State St., 84070. T: (801) 255-9300. www.quail runrvpark.com. RV/tent: 69. $$. Hookups: electric (20, 30, 50 amp), water, sewer, cable, phone (modem).

Santa Clara

Gunlock State Park, P.O. Box 637, 84525. T: (435) 564-3633 or (435) 628-2255. RV/tent: 30. $$. Hookups: none.

Sevier

Fremont Indian State Park & Museum, 11550 West Clear Creek Canyon Rd., 84766. T: (435) 527-4631. RV/tent: 31. $. Hookups: none.

Snowville

Lottie-Dell Campground, 490 West Main St., Box 601, 84336. T: (435) 872-8273. RV/tent: 51. $$. Hookups: electric (15, 20, 30 amp), water, sewer, phone (modem).

Springville

East Bay RV Park, 1750 West 1600 North, 84663. T: (801) 491-0700. www.eastbayrvpark.com. RV/tent: 155. $$$. Hookups: electric (20, 30, 50 amp), water, sewer, cable, phone (modem).

St. George

Baker Dam, 225 North Bluff, 84770. T: (435) 673-4654. RV/tent: 19. $. Hookups: none.

McArthur's Temple View RV Resort, 975 South Main, 84770. T: (435) 673-6400 or (800) 776-6410. RV/tent: 266. $$. Hookups: electric (20, 30, 50 amp), water, sewer, cable, phone (modem).

Redlands RV Park, 650 West Telegraph, 84770. T: (435) 673-9700 or (800) 553-8269. RV/tent: 200. $$. Hookups: electric (20, 30, 50 amp), water, sewer, cable, phone (modem).

Settler's RV Park, 1333 East 100 South, 84790. T: (435) 628-1624 or (800) 628-2255. www.settlersrv.com. RV/tent: 155. $$. Hookups: electric (20, 30, 50 amp), water, sewer.

St. George RV Park & Campground, 2100 East Middleton Dr., 84770. T: (435) 673-2970. RV/tent: 100. $$. Hookups: electric (20, 30 amp), water, sewer, cable, phone (modem).

Teasdale

Oak Creek Campground, 138 East Main, 84773. T: (435) 425-3702. RV/tent: 9. $. Hookups: none.

Pleasant Creek Campground, 138 East Main, 84773. T: (435) 425-3702. RV/tent: 19. $. Hookups: none.

Single Tree Campground, 138 East Main, 84773. T: (435) 425-3702 or (877) 444-6777. RV/tent: 33. $. Hookups: none.

Ticaboo

Ticaboo Resort, Restaurant, & Campground, Hwy. 276, Box 2110-T, 84533. T: (877) 842-2267. RV/tent: 22. $$. Hookups: electric (30 amp), water, sewer.

Torrey

Sand Creek RV Park, Campground, & Hostel, 540 Hwy. 24, 84775. T: (435) 425-3577 or (877) 425-3578. RV/tent: 24. $. Hookups: electric (30, 50 amp), water, sewer.

Vernal

Dinosaurland KOA, 930 North Vernal Ave., 84078. T: (435) 789-2148 or (800) 562-7524. RV/tent: 110. $$. Hookups: electric (20, 30, 50 amp), water, sewer, cable.

East Park, 353 North Vernal Ave., 84078. T: (435) 648-3011. RV/tent: 21. $. Hookups: none.

Fossil Valley RV Park, 999 West Hwy. 40, 84078. T: (435) 789-6450 or (888) 789-6450. www.fossilvalleyrvpark.com. RV/tent: 50. $$. Hookups: electric (30, 50 amp), water, sewer.

Lodgepole Springs Campground, 353 North Vernal Ave., 84078. T: (435) 789-1181. RV/tent: 35. $$. Hookups: none.

Oaks Park, 353 North Vernal Ave., 84078. T: (435) 789-1181. RV/tent: 11. $. Hookups: none.

Wellington

Mountain View RV Park, 50 South 700 East, 84542. T: (435) 637-7980. RV/tent: 24. $$. Hookups: electric (20, 30 amp), water, sewer.

VERMONT

Addison

Ten Acres Campground, 9 Ten Acre Drive, RR 1 Box 356, 05491. T: (802) 759-2662. www.10acrescampground.com. RV/tent: 87. $$. Hookups: electric, water, sewer.

Andover

Horseshoe Acres Campgrounds, 1978 Weston Andover Rd., 05143. T: (802) 875-2960. RV/tent: 120. $$. Hookups: electric, water, sewer.

Arlington

Camping on the Battenkill, Rte. 7A, 05250. T: (802) 375-6663 or (800) 830-6663. RV/tent: 96. $$. Hookups: electric, water, sewer.

Howell's Camping Area, No Name Rd., 05250. T: (802) 375-6469. RV/tent: 77. $$. Hookups: electric, water, sewer.

Ascutney

Running Bear Camping Area, 6248 Rte. 5, 05030. T: (802) 674-6417. www.runningbearvermont. com. RV/tent: 90. $$. Hookups: electric, water, sewer.

Wilgus State Park Campground, P.O. Box 196, 05030. T: (802) 674-5422. www.campvermont. com. RV/tent: 29. $$. Hookups: none.

Barnard

Silver Lake State Park Campground, Town Rd., 05031. T: (802) 234-9451. RV/tent: 47. $$. Hookups: none.

Barton

Sugar Mill Farm, Box 26, 05822. T: (800) 688-7978. www.sugarmillfarm.com. RV/tent: 18. $$. Hookups: electric, water.

Bennington

Greenwood Lodge and Campsites, Rte. 9, 05201. T: (802) 442-2547. www.campvermont.com/ greenwood. RV/tent: 20. $$. Hookups: electric (20, 30, 50 amp), water, sewer.

Bomoseen

Lake Bomoseen Campground, 18 Campground Drive, Rte. 30, 05732. T: (802) 273-2061. www.lakebomoseen.com. RV/tent: 99. $$. Hookups: electric, water, sewer, phone.

Brandon

Branbury State Park, 3570 Lake Dunmore Rd, Rte. 53, 05733. T: (802) 247-5925 or (800) 658-1622. www.vtstateparks.com. RV/tent: 39. $$. Hookups: none.

Smoke Rise Farm Campground, Rte. 7 North, 05733. T: (802) 247-6472. RV/tent: 60. $$. Hookups: electric, water, sewer.

Bristol

Green Mountain Family Campground, RD 3 Box 850, 05443. T: (802) 453-3123. www.familycamp ground.com. RV/tent: 50. $$. Hookups: electric, water, sewer.

Maple Hill Campground, 690 Quaker St., 05443. T: (802) 453-3687. www.sover.net/-maplehil. RV/tent: 13. $$. Hookups: electric.

Burlington

North Beach Campground, 60 Institute Rd., 05401. T: (800) 571-1198 or (802) 862-0942. www.bpr.ci.burlington.vt.us. RV/tent: 137. $$. Hookups: electric (30, 50 amp), water, sewer.

Cavendish

Caton Place Campground, East Rd., 05142. T: (802) 226-7767. www.vtliving.com/camping/rutl.shtml. RV/tent: 85. $$. Hookups: electric (15, 20, 30 amp), water, sewer.

VERMONT (continued)

Charlotte

Mt. Philo State Park, 5425 Mt. Philo Rd., 05445. T: (802) 425-2390 or (888) 409-7579. www.state.vt.us/anr/fpr/parks/htm/philo.html. RV/tent: 7. $$. Hookups: none.

Chester

Hidden Valley Campgrounds, 1924 Mattson Rd., 05143. T: (802) 886-2497. RV/tent: 32. $$. Hookups: electric, water.

Danby

Otter Creek Campground, Rte. 7, 05739. T: (802) 293-5041. RV/tent: 50. $$. Hookups: electric, water.

Dorset

Dorset RV Park, 1567 Rte. 30, 05251. T: (802) 867-5754. www.campvermont.com. RV/tent: 40. $$. Hookups: electric, water, sewer.

Dummerston

Hidden Acres Campground, 792 US Rte. 5, 05301. T: (802) 254-2098 or (866) 411-CAMP. www.hiddenacresvt.com. RV/tent: 40. $$. Hookups: electric, water, sewer.

East Burke

Burke Mountain Campgrounds, Mountain Rd., 05832. T: (802) 626-1204. RV/tent: 25. $. Hookups: electric, water, sewer.

East Dummerston

KOA, 1238 US 5, 05346. T: (802) 254-5908 or (800) 562-5909. www.koa.com. RV/tent: 42. $$$. Hookups: electric (20, 30, 50 amp), water, sewer.

East Montpelier

Green Valley Campground, RR 2, 05651. T: (802) 223-6217 or (888) 359-1899. www.greenvalley rvpark.com. RV/tent: 36. $$$. Hookups: electric, water, sewer, phone.

East Thetford

Rest 'n' Nest Campground, 300 Latham Rd., 05043. T: (802) 785-2997. www.restnest.com. RV/tent: 90. $$. Hookups: electric (20, 30, 50 amp), water, sewer.

Enosburg Falls

Lake Carmi, 460 Marsh Farm Rd., 05450. T: (802) 933-8383 or (800) 252-2363. www.vtstate parks.com. RV/tent: 140. $$. Hookups: none.

Fair Haven

Bomoseen State Park, 22 Cedar Mountain Rd., 05743. T: (802) 265-4242 or (800) 658-1622. www.vtstateparks.com. RV/tent: 66. $$. Hookups: none.

Gaysville

White River Valley Camping, Rte. 107, P.O. Box 106, 05746. T: (802) 234-9115. www.whiteriver valleycamping.com. RV/tent: 40. $$. Hookups: electric, water, sewer.

Graniteville

Lazy Lions Campground, 281 Middle Rd., 05654-9801. T: (802) 479-2823. www.gocamping america.com/lazy lions. RV/tent: 180. $$. Hookups: electric, water, sewer, phone, cable.

Groton

Ricker Pond State Park, 526 State Forest Rd., 05046. T: (802) 584-3821 or (800) 658-6934. www.state.vt.us. RV/tent: 55. $$. Hookups: none.

Isle La Motte

Lakehurst Campground, 204 Lakehurst Rd., 05463. T: (802) 928-3266. www.campusa.com/frame northbeach.cfm. RV/tent: 160. $$. Hookups: electric, water, sewer.

Summer Place Campground & Cabins, 915 Quarry Rd., 05463. T: (802) 928-3300. RV/tent: 70. $$. Hookups: electric, water.

Jamaica

Jamaica State Park Campground, 285 Salmon Hole Ln., 05343. T: (802) 874-4600 or (800) 299-3071. www.vtstateparks.com. RV/tent: 61. $$. Hookups: none.

Killington

Killington Campground at Alpenhof Lodge, Killington Rd., 05751. T: (802) 422-9787. RV/tent: 10. $$. Hookups: electric, water.

Ludlow

Hideaway Squirrel Hill Camp, 53 Bixby Rd., 05149. T: (802) 228-8800. RV/tent: 24. $$. Hookups: electric, water.

Manchester Center

Greendale Campground, 2539 Depot St., 05255. T: (802) 362-2307. www.fs.fed.us. RV/tent: 11. $. Hookups: water.

Marshfield

Groton Forest Road Campground, Rte. 232, Box 2654, Hwy. 232, 05658. T: (802) 426-4122. www.campvermont.com. RV/tent: 35. $$. Hookups: electric, water.

Meadowcrest Campground, 4239 US Rte. 2, 05658. T: (802) 426-3514. RV/tent: 14. $$. Hookups: electric, water.

Middlebury

Rivers Bend Campground, 1000 Dog Team Rd., 05653. T: (802) 388-9092. www.riversbend campground.com. RV/tent: 65. $$. Hookups: electric (20, 30 amp), water.

Newfane

Kenolie Village Campground, 16 Kenolie Campground Rd., 05345. T: (802) 365-7671. www.campvermont.com. RV/tent: 150. $$. Hookups: electric (20, 30 amp), water.

North Clarendon

Iroquois Land Family, 2334 East Clarendon Rd., 05759. T: (802) 773-2832. RV/tent: 35. $$. Hookups: electric, water, sewer.

North Dorset

Emerald Lake State Park Campground, RD 485, 05251. T: (802) 362-1655. RV/tent: 105. $$. Hookups: none.

North Hero

Carry Bay Campground & Cottages, 5289 Rte. 2, 05474. T: (802) 372-8233. RV/tent: 30. $$. Hookups: electric, water, sewer.

North Hero State Park, 3803 Lakeview Drive, 05474-9698. T: (802) 372-8727 or (800) 252-2363. www.vermont.gov. RV/tent: 99. $. Hookups: none.

Perkinsville

Crown Point Camping Area, 131 Bishops Camp Rd., 05151. T: (802) 263-5555. www.campvermont .com. RV/tent: 36. $$. Hookups: electric, water, sewer.

Winhall Brook Camping Area, RR 1, Box 164B, 05151. T: (802) 874-4881. www.reserveusa.com. RV/tent: 111. $$. Hookups: none.

Peru

Green Mountain/Red Mill Brook, 231 North Main St., 05701-2417. T: (802) 362-2307. RV/tent: 31. $. Hookups: none.

Hapgood Pond Recreation Area, P.O. Box 248, 05152. T: (802) 824-6456. RV/tent: 28. $. Hookups: water.

Plymouth

Coolidge State Park, 855 Coolidge SP Rd., 05056. T: (802) 672-3612 or (800) 299-3071. www.vtstateparks.com. RV/tent: 60. $$. Hookups: none.

Sugarhouse Campground, Rte. 100, 05056. T: (802) 672-5043. RV/tent: 45. $$. Hookups: electric, water.

Randolph

Allis State Park Campground, RD 2, Box 192, 05060. T: (802) 276-3175 or (800) VERMONT. www.vtstateparks.com. RV/tent: 27. $$. Hookups: none.

Randolph Center

Lake Champagne Campground, Furnace Rd., 05061. T: (802) 728-5293. www.lake champagne.com. RV/tent: 68. $$. Hookups: electric, water, sewer.

Rochester

Chittenden Brook Campground, Rte. 100, 05767. T: (802) 767-4261. www.fs.fed.us. RV/tent: 16. $. Hookups: none.

Ryegate

Pleasant Valley Campgrounds, Ticklenaked Rd., 05081. T: (802) 584-3884 or (802) 866-5991. RV/tent: 53. $$. Hookups: electric, water, sewer.

Salisbury

Branbury State Park, 3570 Lake Dunmore Rd., 05769. T: (802) 247-5925 or (888) 409-7579. www.vtstateparks.com. RV/tent: 45. $$. Hookups: none.

VERMONT (continued)

Lake Dunmore Kampersville, SR 53, 05769-9801.
T: (802) 352-4501 or (877) 250-2568. RV/tent:
200. $$. Hookups: electric, water, sewer.

Waterhouse Campground & Marina, 937 West
Shore Rd., 05769. T: (802) 352-4433.
www.waterhouses.com. RV/tent: 60. $$.
Hookups: electric, water, sewer.

Shaftsbury

Lake Shaftsbury State Park, 262 Shaftsbury SP Rd.,
05262. T: (802) 375-9978 or (888) 409-7579.
www.vtstateparks.com. RV/tent: 15. $$.
Hookups: none.

South Hero

Apple Island, Rte. 2, 05486-4008. T: (802) 372-5398.
www.appleislandresort.com. RV/tent: 200. $$$.
Hookups: electric, water, sewer.

South Londonderry

Ball Mountain Lake Project Campground, 98
Reservoir Rd., 05156-2210. T: (802) 824-4570 or
(802) 874-4881. www.reserveamerica.com.
RV/tent: 111. $$. Hookups: electric (20, 30 amp),
water, sewer.

Springfield

Tree Farm Campground, 53 Skitchewaug Trail,
05156. T: (802) 885-2889. RV/tent: 118. $$.
Hookups: electric, water, sewer.

Thetford

Thetford Hill State Park Campground, P.O. Box
132, 05074. T: (802) 785-2266 or (800) 299-
3071. www.vtstateparks.com. RV/tent: 16. $$.
Hookups: none.

Townshend

Bald Mountain Campground, 1760 State Forest
Rd., 05353. T: (802) 365-7510. RV/tent: 200. $$.
Hookups: electric, water, sewer.

Camperama, Depot Rd., 05353. T: (802) 365-4315
or (800) 632-2677. www.gocampingamerica.com/
camperama. RV/tent: 219. $$. Hookups: electric,
water, sewer.

Townshend State Park Campground, 2755 State
Forest Rd., 05353. T: (802) 365-7500 or (800)
299-3071. www.vtstateparks.com. RV/tent: 35.
$$. Hookups: none.

Underhill

South Hill Riverside Campground, RD 2, Box 287,
05489. T: (802) 899-2232. RV/tent: 50. $$.
Hookups: electric, water, sewer.

Vergennes

Button Bay State Park, 5 Button Bay State Park
Rd., 05491. T: (802) 475-2377. RV/tent: 72. $$.
Hookups: none.

D.A.R. State Park, 6750 VT Rte. 17W, 05491.
T: (802) 759-2354. www.vtstateparks.com.
RV/tent: 70. $$. Hookups: none.

Whispering Pines Campground, 1072 Panton Rd.,
05491. T: (802) 475-2264. RV/tent: 40. $$.
Hookups: electric, water.

Waterbury

Duxbury Campground, 2542 VT 100, 05676.
T: (802) 244-7546. RV/tent: 16. $$. Hookups:
electric, water.

Waterbury Center

The Long Trail, 4711 Waterbury-Stowe Rd., 05677.
T: (802) 244-7037. www.greenmountainclub.org.

RV/tent: 70 shelters and lean-tos. $. Hookups:
none.

Westfield

Barrewood Campground, 3201 VT 100, 05874-
9801. T: (802) 744-6340. RV/tent: 46. $$.
Hookups: electric, water, sewer.

White River Junction

Pine Valley RV Resort, 3700 Woodstock Rd., 05001.
T: (802) 296-6711. www.campvermont.com.
RV/tent: 90. $$$. Hookups: electric, water,
sewer.

Quechee Gorge State Park Campground, 760
Dewey Mills Rd., 05001. T: (802) 295-2990 or
(800) 299-3071. www.vtstateparks.com. RV/tent:
54. $$. Hookups: none.

Williamstown

Limehurst Lake, 4104 Rte. 14, 05679. T: (802) 433-
6662 or (800) 242-9876. www.limehurstlake
.com. RV/tent: 76. $$. Hookups: electric, water,
sewer.

Windsor

Ascutney State Park, 1826 Back Mountain Rd.,
5089. T: (802) 674-2060. RV/tent: 39. $$.
Hookups: none.

Woodford

Greenwood Lodge and Campsites, Rte. 9, Box 246,
05201. T: (802) 442-2547. www.campvermont
.com/greenwood. RV/tent: 40. $$. Hookups:
electric (30, 50 amp), water.

Woodford State Park Campground, HCR 65,
05201. T: (802) 447-7169. RV/tent: 103. $$.
Hookups: none.

VIRGINIA

Appomattox

Paradise Lake Family Campground, P.O. Box 478,
24522. T: (434) 993-3332. RV/tent: 117. $$.
Hookups: electric (20, 30, 50 amp), water, sewer.

Bassett

Goose Point/Philpott Lake, 4780 Goose Point Rd.,
24055. T: (276) 629-2703. www.reserveusa.com.
RV/tent: 61. $$. Hookups: electric (30 amp),
water.

Horseshoe Point/Philpott Lake, 3950 Horseshoe
Point Rd., 24102. T: (276) 629-2703 or (276)
365-7385. www.reserveusa.com. RV/tent: 49. $$.
Hookups: electric (30 amp), water.

Bentonville

Low Water Bridge Campground, 192 Panhandle
Rd., 22610. T: (540) 635-7277. www.lowwater
bridge.com. RV/tent: 60. $$. Hookups: none.

Bowling Green

Campground 721, 22089 Sparta Rd., 22427.
T: (804) 633-9516. RV/tent: 43. $. Hookups:
electric, water, sewer.

Boydton

Ivy Hill Park, John H. Kerr Dam & Reservoir, 1930
Mays Chapel Rd., 23917. T: (434) 738-6144.
RV/tent: 25. $. Hookups: none.

Longwood Park / John H Kerr Dam & Resovoir,
1930 Mays Chapel Rd., 23917. T: (434) 738-
6144. RV/tent: 66. $$. Hookups: electric (30
amp), water.

North Bend Park, 1930 Mays Chapel Rd., 23917.
T: (434) 738-6662. RV/tent: 249. $$. Hookups:
electric (20, 30 amp), water.

Bristol

Lee Hwy. Campground, 2671 Lee Hwy., 24203.
T: (276) 669-3616 or (276) 669-1800. RV/tent:
19. $$. Hookups: electric (20, 30 amp), water,
sewer.

Broadway

Harrisonburg/New Market KOA, 12480 Mountain
Valley Rd., 22815. T: (540) 896-8929 or (800)
562-5406. www.koa.com. RV/tent: 48. $$.
Hookups: electric (30, 50 amp), water, sewer.

Buena Vista

Glen Maury Park, 2039 10th St., 24416. T: (540)
261-7321 or (800) 555-8845. www.glenmaury
park.com. RV/tent: 52. $$. Hookups: electric (20,
30 amp), water, sewer.

Chesapeake

Chesapeake Campground, 693 South George
Washington Pkwy., 23323. T: (757) 485-0149 or
(888) 584-2267. RV/tent: 133. $$. Hookups:
electric (20, 30 amp), water.

Chincoteague

Pine Grove Campround & Waterfowl Park, 5283
Deep Hole Rd., 23336. T: (757) 336-5200.
www.pinegrovecampground.com. RV/tent: 150.
$$. Hookups: electric (15, 20, 30 amp), water,
sewer.

Christiansburg

Interstate Overnight Park, 2705 Roakoke St.,
24073. T: (540) 382-1554. RV/tent: 32. $$.
Hookups: electric (20, 30, 50 amp), water, sewer.

VIRGINIA (continued)

Colonial Beach

Monroe Bay Campground, 551 Lafayette St., 22443. T: (804) 224-7544. RV/tent: 325. $$. Hookups: electric (30 amp), water, sewer.

Outdoor World Harbor View Campground, 15 Harbor View Cir., 22443. T: (800) 222-5557 or (804) 224-8164. www.campoutdoorworld.com. RV/tent: 140. $$. Hookups: electric (30, 50 amp), water, sewer.

Cross Junction

Log Cabin Campgrounds, 2058 Morgan Frederick Grade, 22625. T: (540) 888-3461. RV/tent: 60. $$. Hookups: electric (15, 20 amp), water.

Damascus

Ironhorse Family Campground, 30460 Blossom Rd., 24236. T: (276) 475-6008. RV/tent: 18. $$. Hookups: electric (30 amp), water, sewer.

Dumfries

Prince William Travel Trailer Village & RV Park, 16058 Dumfries Rd., 22026. T: (703) 221-2474 or (888) 737-5730. RV/tent: 74. $$. Hookups: electric (20, 30 amp), water, sewer.

Gainesville

Hillwood Camping Park, 14222 Lee Hwy., 20155. T: (703) 753-1221 or (800) 754-4202. www. hillwoodcamping.com. RV/tent: 140. $$$. Hookups: electric (30, 50) water, sewer.

Hayes

Gloucester Point Campground, 3149 Campground Rd., 23072. T: (800) 332-4316. RV/tent: 230 RV. $$. Hookups: electric (30, 50 amp), water, sewer.

Haymarket

Greenville Farm Family Campground, 14004 Shelter Ln., 20169. T: (703) 754-7944. RV/tent: 165 RV. $$. Hookups: electric (20, 30, 50 amp), water, sewer.

Henry

Salthouse Branch Park/Philpott Lake, 620 Salthouse Branch Rd., 24102. T: (540) 629-2703. www.reserveusa.com. RV/tent: 93. $$. Hookups: electric (30 amp), water.

Hillsville

Carrollwood Campground, P.O. Box 175, 24343. T: (276) 728-9312. RV/tent: 100. $$. Hookups: electric (20, 30, 50 amp), water, sewer.

Hot Springs

Bolar Mountain Campground/George Washington National Forest, Warm Springs Ranger District, Hwy. 220 South, 24445. T: (540) 839-2521. RV/tent: 91. $$. Hookups: electric (30 amp).

Hidden Valley Campgrounds/George Washington National Forest, Warm Springs Ranger District, Hwy. 220 South, 24445. T: (540) 839-2521. RV/tent: 30. $. Hookups: none.

Jamaica

Dublfun Campground, HCR 67, Box 2206, 23079. T: (804) 758-5432. www.dublfuncampground .com. RV/tent: 150. $$. Hookups: electric (20, 30 amp), water, sewer.

Lexington

Lake A. Willis Robertson Recreation Area/ Rockbridge County Park, 106 Lake Robertson Drive, 24450. T: (540) 463-4164. www.co.rock bridge.va.us. RV/tent: 53. $$. Hookups: electric (20, 30 amp), water, sewer.

Louisa

Small Country Camping, 4400 Byrd Mill Rd., P.O. Box 343, 23093. T: (540) 967-2431. www.small country.com. RV/tent: 236. $$. Hookups: electric (20, 30 amp), water, sewer.

Luray

The Country Waye RV Resort, 3402 Kimball Rd., 22835. T: (888) 765-7222. www.countrywaye .com. RV/tent: 97. $$. Hookups: electric (30, 50 amp), water, sewer.

Marion

Beartree Campground/Mount Rogers National Recreation Area, 3714 Hwy. 16, Rte. 1, Box 303, 24354. T: (540) 783-5196. RV/tent: 113. $. Hookups: none.

Grindstone Campground/Mount Rogers National Recreation Area, Rte. 1, Box 303, 24354. T: (540) 783-5196 or (800) 628-7202. RV/tent: 100. $$. Hookups: none.

Martinsville

David & Julia's RV Park, Beckham Church Rd., 24115. T: (276) 632-8718. www.kimbanet.com/ ~rvpark. RV/tent: 10. $$. Hookups: electric (20, 30, 50 amp), water, sewer.

Max Meadows

Fort Chiswell RV Campground, 312 Ft. Chiswell Rd., 24360. T: (276) 637-6868. RV/tent: 92. $$$. Hookups: electric (30, 50 amp), water, sewer, cable.

Moneta

Campers Paradise, 1336 Campers Paradise Tr., 24121. T: (540) 297-6109. www.campers paradise. com. RV/tent: 35. $$. Hookups: electric (15, 20, 30, 50 amp), water, sewer.

Montebello

Montebello Camping Resort, 15072 Crabtree Falls Hwy., Rte. 56, 24464. T: (540) 377-2650. www.montebellova.com. RV/tent: 60. $$. Hookups: electric (30 amp), water, sewer.

Natural Bridge

KOA Natural Bridge Campground, US 11, 24578. T: (540) 291-2770 or (800) 562-8514. www.koa.com. RV/tent: 97. $$. Hookups: electric (20, 30, 50 amp), water, sewer.

New Market

Rancho Campground, 15554 North Valley Pike, 22844. T: (540) 740-8313. RV/tent: 65. $$. Hookups: electric (20, 30, 50 amp), water, sewer.

Petersburg

Spring Gardens Mobile Home Park, 2178 Country Dr., 23803. T: (804) 732-8908. RV/tent: 44. $$. Hookups: electric (20, 30, 50 amp), water, sewer.

Sanford

Tall Pines Harbor Waterfront Campground, Box 375, 23426. T: (757) 824-0777. www.tallpines harbor.com. RV/tent: 90. $$. Hookups: electric (30 amp), water, sewer.

Shernando

Shernando Campgrounds, George Washington National Forest, Pedlar Ranger District, USFS. 91, 24579. T: (540) 291-2189. RV/tent: 65. $$. Hookups: electric (30 amp).

Skippers

Cattail RV Park and Campground, 3901 Moore's Ferry Rd., 23879. T: (434) 634-9935 or (877) 888-0324. www.cattailcreek.hypermart.net. RV/tent: 60 RV. $$. Hookups: electric (30, 50 amp), water, sewer.

Stanardsville

Heavenly Acres Campground, 2010 Madison Rd., 22973. T: (804) 985-6601. www.heavenlyacres.net. RV/tent: 35. $$. Hookups: electric (20, 30 amp), water, sewer.

Sugar Grove

Raccoon Branch/Mount Rogers National Recreation Area, 3714 Hwy. 16, 24354. T: (540) 783-5196. RV/tent: 20. $. Hookups: electric, water.

Vesuvius

Tye River Gap Campground, SR 56, 24483. T: (540) 377-6168. www.tyerivergap.com. RV/tent: 50 RV. $$. Hookups: electric, water, sewer.

Vinton

Roanoke Mountain Campground, 2551 Mountain View Rd., 24179. T: (540) 982-9242. RV/tent: 104. $. Hookups: none.

Virginia Beach

Shore Campground, 3257 Colechester Rd., 23456. T: (757) 426-7911. RV/tent: 140 RV. $$. Hookups: electric (20, 30 amp), water, sewer.

Warsaw

Naylors Beach Campground, 4011 Naylors Beach Rd., 22572. T: (804) 333-3951. RV/tent: 100. $$. Hookups: electric (15, 20, 30 amp), water.

Waynesboro

Waynesboro North 340 Campground, Rte. 340 North, 22980. T: (540) 943-9573. RV/tent: 175. $$. Hookups: electric (15, 20, 50 amp), water, sewer.

Williamsburg

American Heritage RV Park, 146 Maxton Ln., 23188. T: (888) 530-2267 or (757) 526-2133. www.americanheritagervpark.com. RV/tent: 95. $$. Hookups: electric (20, 30, 50 amp), water, sewer.

Four Winds Trading Post & Campground, 8758 Pocahontas Tr., Rte. 60, 23185. T: (757) 220-0386 or (888) 999-6236. RV/tent: 50 RV. $$$. Hookups: electric (20, 30, 50 amp), water, sewer.

VIRGINIA (continued)

Willis

Daddy Rabbit's Campground, 2015 Union School Rd. SW, 24380. T: (540) 789-4150. RV/tent: 57. $$. Hookups: electric (20, 30 amp), water, sewer.

Wise

Cane Patch Campground/Jefferson National Forest, Clinch Ranger District, 9416 Darden Dr., 24293. T: (540) 328-2931. RV/tent: 25. $. Hookups: none.

Cave Springs Campground, Jefferson National Forest, Clinch Ranger District, 9416 Darden Dr., 24293. T: (540) 328-2931. RV/tent: 40. $. Hookups: none.

Woolwine

Deer Run Campgrounds, P.O. Box 6, 24185. T: (276) 930-1235. www.virginiacampground.org. RV/tent: 72. $$. Hookups: electric (20, 30, 50 amp), water, sewer.

WASHINGTON

Amanda Park

Graves Creek Campground, 1835 Black Lake Blvd. SW, 98512-5623. T: (360) 452-0330. RV/tent: 30. $. Hookups: none.

American River

Bumping Lake Campground, 215 Melody Ln., 98801. T: (509) 653-2205. RV/tent: 45. $$. Hookups: none.

Anacortes

Fidalgo Bay Resort, 4701 Fidalgo Bay Rd., 98221. T: (888) 777-5355. www.fidalgobay.com. RV/tent: 187. $$. Hookups: electric (20, 30, 50 amp), water.

Bay Center

KOA Bay Center/Willapa Bay, 621 NE Gladwin Beach Rd., 98527. T: (800) 562-7810. www.koa.com. RV/tent: 28. $$$. Hookups: electric, water.

Belfair

Snooze Junction RV Park, P.O. Box 880, 98528. T: (360) 275-2381. RV/tent: 36. $$. Hookups: full.

Birch Bay

Thousand Trails Birch Bay, 8418 Harborview Rd., 98230. T: (360) 371-7432. www.1000trails.com. RV/tent: 215. $$$. Hookups: full.

Burlington

KOA Burlington, 6397 North Green Rd., 98233. T: (800) 562-9154 or (360) 724-5511. www.koa.com. RV/tent: 40. $$. Hookups: electric (30 amp), water.

Chehalis

Chehalis-KOA, 118 Hwy. 12, 98532. T: (800) KOA-9120 or (360) 262-9220. www.koa.com. RV/tent: 19. $$. Hookups: electric (50 amp), water.

Cheney

Williams Lake Resort, 18607 Williams Lake Rd., 99004-9762. T: (509) 235-2391 or (800) 274-1540. www.klinksresort.com. RV/tent: 136. $$. Hookups: electric, water.

Chinook

River's End Campground and RV Park, P.O. Box 280, 98614. T: (360) 777-8317. RV/tent: 72. $$. Hookups: electric, water.

Conconully

Conconully Lake Resort, 102 Sinlahekin Rd., P.O. Box 131, 98819. T: (800) 850-0813 or (509) 826-0813. RV/tent: 11. $$. Hookups: electric.

Shady Pines Resort, P.O. Box 44, 98819. T: (800) 552-2287. www.shadypinesresort.com. RV/tent: 23. $$. Hookups: full (30, 50 amp).

Concrete

Baker Lake Resort, 46110 East Main St., 98237. T: (360) 853-8341 or (888) 711-3033. RV/tent: 90. $$. Hookups: electric, water.

Copalis Beach

Rod's Beach Resort, P.O. Box 507, 98535. T: (360) 289-2222. RV/tent: 90. $$. Hookups: electric.

Cosmopolis

Arctic RV Park and Campground, 893 US 101, Cosmopolis, 98537. T: (360) 533-4470. RV/tent: 20. $$. Hookups: full.

Cougar

Lone Fir Resort, 16806 Lewis River Rd., 98616. T: (360) 238-5210. www.lonefirresort.com. RV/tent: 34. $$. Hookups: full.

Coulee

Laurent's Sun Village Resort, 33575 Park Lake Rd. NE, 99115. T: (509) 632-5664. RV/tent: 90. $$. Hookups: full.

Cusick

Blueslide Resort, 400041 Hwy. 20, 99119. T: (509) 445-1327. www.bluesideresort.com. RV/tent: 46. $$. Hookups: full.

Easton

RV Town, P.O. Box 1203, 98925. T: (509) 656-2360. RV/tent: 72. $$. Hookups: electric, water.

Eastsound

Moran State Park, SR Box 22, 98245. T: (360) 376-2326. RV/tent: 151. $$. Hookups: none.

West Beach Resort-Orcas Island, 190 Waterfront Way, 98245. T: (360) 376-2240 or (877) WESTBCH. www.westbeachresort.com. RV/tent: 45. $$$. Hookups: electric, water.

Ellensburg

KOA Ellensburg, 32 Thorp Hwy. South, 98926. T: (800) 562-7616 or (509) 925-9319. www.koa.com. RV/tent: 152. $$. Hookups: full (50 amp).

Elma

Elma RV Park, P.O. Box 1135, 98541. T: (360) 482-4053 or (866) 211-3939. www.elmarvpark.com. RV/tent: 102. $$. Hookups: full (30, 50 amp).

Everett

Lakeside RV Park, 12321 Hwy. 99 South, 98204. T: (800) HOT-PARK or (425) 347-2970. RV/tent: 150. $$$$. Hookups: electric (50 amp).

Forks

Bogachiel State Park, Hwy. 101, 98331. T: (360) 374-6356. RV/tent: 42. $. Hookups: electric, water.

Goldendale

Maryhill State Park, 50 US 97, 98620. T: (509) 773-5007. RV/tent: 70. $. Hookups: electric, water.

Graham

Lakeside Place, 32919 Benbow Dr. East, 98338. T: (360) 879-5426. www.camplakeview.150m.com. RV/tent: 75. $. Hookups: full (30, 50 amp).

Granite Falls

Gold Basin Campground, 33515 Mt. Loop Hwy., 98252. T: (877) 444-6777. RV/tent: 92. $$. Hookups: none.

Grayland

Ocean Gate Resort, P.O. Box 57, 98547. T: (800) 473-1956. RV/tent: 55. $$. Hookups: electric.

Ilwaco

Fort Canby State Park, P.O. Box 488, 98624. T: (360) 642-3078. RV/tent: 227. $. Hookups: full.

KOA Ilwaco, P.O. Box 549, 98624. T: (360) 642-3292 or (800) 562-3250. www.koa.com. RV/tent: 164. $$. Hookups: full (30 amp).

Inchelium

Rainbow Beach Resort, 18 North Twin Lakes Rd., 99138. T: (509) 722-5901 or (888) 862-0978. RV/tent: 19. $$. Hookups: full.

Ione

Colville National Forest, 765 South Main St., 99114. T: (509) 684-4557. www.fs.fed.us. RV/tent: 300. $. Hookups: none.

Issaquah

Blue Sky RV and Resorts, 9002 302nd Ave. SE, 98027. T: (425) 222-7910. RV/tent: 51. $$$. Hookups: full.

WASHINGTON (continued)

Kelso

Brookhollow RV Park, 2506 Allen St., 98626. T: (800) 867-0453. www.brookhollowrvpark. com. RV/tent: 132. $$. Hookups: electric.

Cedars RV Park, 115 Beauvais Rd., 98626. T: (360) 274-5136. RV/tent: 26. $. Hookups: none.

Kent

KOA Seattle/Tacoma, 5801 South 212th, 98032. T: (253) 872-8652. www.koa.com. RV/tent: 160. $$. Hookups: full (50 amp).

La Conner

Blake's RV Park and Marina, 13739 Rawlins Rd., 98273. T: (360) 445-6533. RV/tent: 76. $$. Hookups: full.

La Push

Lonesome Creek RV Park, P.O. Box 130, 98350. T: (360) 374-4338 or (360) 374-4333. RV/tent: 55. $$. Hookups: full (40 amp).

Leavenworth

Blu-Shastin RV Park, 3300 Hwy. 97, 98826. T: (888) 548-4184. www.blueshastin.com. RV/tent: 86. $$. Hookups: full (20, 30 amp).

Thousand Trails Leavenworth, 20752-4 Chiwawa Loop Rd., 98826. T: (509) 7633217 or (800) 353-1700. RV/tent: 308. $$. Hookups: full.

Long Beach

Anderson's on the Ocean, 1400 138th St., 98631. T: (800) 645-6795. RV/tent: 54. $$$. Hookups: full (50 amp).

Driftwood RV Park, P.O. Box 296, 98631. T: (888) 567-1902 or (360) 642-2711. www.driftwoodrv park.com. RV/tent: 57. $$. Hookups: full.

Loomis

Rainbow Resort, 761 Loomis Hwy., 98855. T: (509) 223-3700. RV/tent: 54. $$. Hookups: full.

Loon Lake

Deer Lake Resort, 3908 North Deer Lake Rd., 99148. T: (509) 233-2081. www.deerlakeresort .com. RV/tent: 65. $$. Hookups: full (50 amp).

Shore Acres Resort, 41987 Shore Acres Rd, 99148. T: (800) 900-2474 or (509) 223-2474. www.shoreacresresort.com. RV/tent: 30. $$$. Hookups: electric.

Lynden

Lynden KOA, 8717 Line Rd., 98264. T: (800) 563-4779. www.koa.com. RV/tent: 160. $$. Hookups: full.

Lynn Wood

Twin Cedars RV Park, 17826 Hwy. 99, 98037. T: (800) 878-9304 or (425) 742-5540. RV/tent: 69. $$$. Hookups: full.

Medical Lake

Rainbow Cove Resort, 12514 South Clear Lake Rd., 99022. T: (509) 299-3717. RV/tent: 17. $$. Hookups: electric (30 amp), water.

Montesano

Friends Landing, 300 Katon Rd., 98563. T: (360) 249-5117. RV/tent: 29. $. Hookups: electric, water.

Lake Sylvia State Park, P.O. Box 701, 98563. T: (360) 249-3621. RV/tent: 35. $. Hookups: none.

Moses Lake

Mar Don Resort, 8198 WA 262 SE, 99344. T: (509) 346-2651 or (800) 416-2736. www.mardon resort.com. RV/tent: 275. $$. Hookups: full.

Mossyrock

Harmony Lakeside RV Park, 563 St. Rte. 122, 98585. T: (360) 983-3804. www.harmony lakesidervpark.com. RV/tent: 80. $$. Hookups: electric, water, sewer.

Mount Vernon

Thousand Trails Mount Vernon, 5409 North Darrk Ln., 98232. T: (360) 724-3331 or (800) 495-2101. www.thousandtrails.com/_vti_bin/ minisitegen.cgi?preserve=204. RV/tent: 227. $$$. Hookups: electric (30, 50 amp), water, sewer.

Naches

Squaw Rock Resort, 45070 State Rte. 410, 98937. T: (509) 658-2926. RV/tent: 64. $$. Hookups: electric, water.

Neaah Bay

Snow Creek Campground, P.O. Box 248, 98357. T: (800) 883-1464. www.snowcreekwa.com. RV/tent: 81. $$. Hookups: electric, water, sewer.

Newhalem

North Cascades NP-Ross Lake NRA, 810 St. Rte. 20, 98284. T: (360) 856-5700. www.nps.gov/noca/ index.htm. RV/tent: 168. $. Hookups: none.

Newport

Thousand Trails Little Diamond, 1002 McGowen Rd., 99156. T: (509) 447-4813 or (800) 994-6654. RV/tent: 300. $$$. Hookups: electric, water.

North Bend

Tinkham Campground, 33515 Mountain Loop Hwy., Granite Falls, 98252. T: (877) 444-6777. RV/tent: 48. $. Hookups: none.

Northport

Upper Columbia RV Park, 4706 Northport Waneta Rd., 99157. T: (509) 732-4367. RV/tent: 30. $$. Hookups: electric (20, 30, 50 amp), water, sewer.

Oak Harbor

Military Park, 3515 Princeton St,. Bldg. 2641, 98278-1900. T: (360) 257-2434. RV/tent: 26. $. Hookups: electric, water.

Ocean Park

Ocean Park Resort, 25904 R St., 98640. T: (800) 835-4634. RV/tent: 83. $$. Hookups: electric (30 amp), water, sewer.

Ocean Shores

Yesterday's RV Park, 512 Damon Rd., 98366. T: (360) 289-9227. www.yesterdaysrvpark.com. RV/tent: 48. $$. Hookups: full.

Okanogan

Okanogan National Forest, 1240 South 2nd Ave., 98840. T: (509) 826-3275. www.fs.fed.us. RV/tent: 426. $. Hookups: none.

Omak

Eastside Park, P.O. Box 1456, 98841. T: (509) 826-0804. RV/tent: 68. $. Hookups: full.

Oroville

Orchard RV Park, 25A Thorndike Loop Rd., 98844. T: (509) 476-2669. www.campingnavigator.com. RV/tent: 41. $$. Hookups: full.

Sun Cove Resort and Guest Ranch, 93 East Wannacut Ln., 98844. T: (509) 476-2223. RV/tent: 38. $$. Hookups: electric (30 amp), water, sewer.

Pacific Beach

Pacific Beach State Park, 148 St. Rte. 115, Hoquiam, 98550. T: (360) 276-4297 or (888) CAMPOUT. RV/tent: 64. $. Hookups: electric.

Pasco

Arrowhead RV Park, 3120 Commercial Ave., 99301. T: (509) 545-8206. RV/tent: 64. $$$. Hookups: none.

Pateros

Alta Lake State Park, 191A Alta Lake Rd., 98846. T: (509) 923-2473. RV/tent: 189. $. Hookups: none.

Port Angeles

Crescent Beach and RV Park, 2860 Crescent Beach Rd., 98363-8703. T: (360) 928-3344. www.olypen .com/crescent/index.htm. RV/tent: 64. $$. Hookups: electric (50 amp), water, sewer.

Peabody Creek RV Park, 127 South Lincoln, 98362. T: (360) 457-7092 or (800) 392-2361. www.peabodyrv.com. RV/tent: 44. $$. Hookups: electric (30 amp), water, sewer.

Port Orchard

Manchester State Park, P.O. Box 338, 98353. T: (360) 871-4065. RV/tent: 53. $. Hookups: none.

Poulsbo

Eagle Tree RV Park, 16280 St. Hwy. 305, 98370. T: (360) 598-5988. www.eagletreerv.com. RV/tent: 93. $$. Hookups: electric (30, 50 amp), water, sewer.

Quinault

Lake Quinault's Rain Forest Resort Village, 516 South Shore Rd., Lake Quinault, 98575. T: (360) 288-2535 or (800) 255-6436. www.rfrv.com. RV/tent: 31. $$. Hookups: electric, water.

Quincy

Crescent Bar Resort Campground, 8894 Crescent Bar Rd. NW, 98848. T: (509) 787-1511 or (800) 824-7090. www.crescentbar.com. RV/tent: 60. $$$. Hookups: electric.

Raymond

Timberland RV Park, 850 Crescent St., 98577. T: (360) 942-3325 or (800) 563-3325. RV/tent: 29. $$. Hookups: full.

Republic

Black Beach Resort, 80 Black Beach Rd., 99166. T: (509) 775-3989. www.blackbeachresort.com. RV/tent: 120. $$. Hookups: electric (20, 30 amp), water, sewer.

Tiffany's Resort, 58 Tiffany Rd., 99166. T: (509) 775-3152. www.tiffanysresort.com. RV/tent: 17. $$. Hookups: full.

Riverside

Glenwood RV Park, Hwy. 97, Mile Marker 300, 98849. T: (509) 826-5228. RV/tent: 20. $$. Hookups: full.

Roosevelt

Crow Butte State Park, 1 Crow Butte State Park Rd., 99345. T: (509) 875-2644 or (509) 948-6069. RV/tent: 50. $. Hookups: full.

Salkum

Barrier Dam Campground, 273 Fuller Rd., 98582. T: (360) 985-2495. RV/tent: 27. $$. Hookups: electric, water, sewer.

San Juan Island

Lakedale Resort, 4313 Roche Harbor Rd., 98250. T: (360) 378-0944 or (800) 617-2350. www.lakedale.com. RV/tent: 117. $$$. Hookups: electric, water.

Seabeck

Scenic Beach State Park, P.O. Box 701, 98380. T: (360) 830-5079. RV/tent: 52. $. Hookups: none.

Seaview Thousand Trails-Long Beach Preserve, 2215 Willows Rd., 98644. T: (360) 642-3091. RV/tent: 120. $$. Hookups: full.

Sekiu

Tretteviks RV Park, 6850 Hwy. 112, 98381. T: (360) 963-2070 or (888) 305-2437. RV/tent: 48. $$. Hookups: electric, water, sewer.

Selah

Stagecoach RV Park, P.O. Box 806, 98937. T: (509) 697-9650. RV/tent: 24. $$. Hookups: full.

Shelton

Lake Nahwatzel Resort, West 12900 Shelton Matlock Rd., 98584. T: (360) 426-8323. RV/tent: 15. $$. Hookups: electric, water, sewer.

Potlatch State Park, P.O. Box 1051, 98548-1051. T: (360) 877-5361. RV/tent: 37. $. Hookups: none.

Silver Lake

Seaquest State Park, 3030 Spirit Lake Hwy., 98611. T: (360) 274-8633. RV/tent: 88. $. Hookups: none.

Skamania

Beacon Rock Resort, 62 Moorage Rd., 98648. T: (509) 427-8473. RV/tent: 50. $$. Hookups: electric, water, sewer.

South Prairie

Prairie Creek RV Park, P.O. Box 17, 98358. T: (888) 270-8465. RV/tent: 125. $$. Hookups: electric (30 amp), water, sewer.

Spokane

KOA Spokane, 3025 North Barker Rd., 99027. T: (509) 924-4722 or (800) 562-3309. www.koa.com/where/wa/47107.htm. RV/tent: 196. $$. Hookups: electric (50 amp), water.

Sprague

Four Sesasons Campround & Resort, 2384 North Bob Lee Rd., 99032. T: (509) 257-2332. www.fourseasonscampground.com. RV/tent: 38. $$. Hookups: electric (30, 50 amp), water, sewer.

Stanwood

Cedar Grove Shores RV Park, 16529 West Lake Goodwin Rd., 98292. T: (360) 652-7083. RV/tent: 62. $$. Hookups: electric (30, 50 amp), water.

Starbuck

Lyons Ferry Marina, P.O. Box 189, 99359. T: (509) 399-2001. RV/tent: 58. $. Hookups: electric.

Sultan

Lake Bronson Club Family Nudist Park, P.O. Box 1135, 98294. T: (360) 793-0286. www.lakebronson.com. RV/tent: 60. $. Hookups: electric (50 amp), water, sewer.

Sumas

Sumas RV Park and Campground, 9600 Easterbrook, 98295. T: (360) 988-8875. RV/tent: 65. $$. Hookups: electric, water, sewer.

Tenino

Offut Lake RV Resort, 4005 120th Ave. SE, 98589. T: (360) 264-2438. www.offutlakeresort.com. RV/tent: 66. $$. Hookups: electric, water, sewer.

Tonasket

Spectacle Lake Resort, 10 McCammon Rd., 98855. T: (509) 223-3433. RV/tent: 40. $$. Hookups: electric, water, sewer.

Toppenish

Yakama Nation RV Resort, 280 Buster Rd., 98948. T: (509) 865-2000 or (800) 874-3087. www.yakamanation.com. RV/tent: 119. $$. Hookups: electric.

Trout Lake

Elk Meadows RV Park and Campground, 78 Trout Lake Creek Rd., 98650. T: (509) 395-2400 or (877) 395-2400. RV/tent: 63. $$. Hookups: electric (30 amp), water, sewer.

Twisp

Riverbend RV Park, 19961 Hwy. 20, 98856. T: (509) 997-3500 or (800) 686-4498. www.riverbendrv.com. RV/tent: 104. $$. Hookups: electric (20, 30, 50 amp), water, sewer.

Valley

Silver Beach Resort, 3323 Waitts Lake Rd., 99181. T: (509) 937-2811. RV/tent: 40. $$. Hookups: electric (30 amp), water, sewer.

Winona Beach Resort, 33022 Winona Beach Rd., 99181. T: (509) 937-2231. RV/tent: 54. $$. Hookups: electric (30, 50 amp), water, sewer.

Vantage

Vantage Riverstone Campground, 551 Main St., 98950. T: (509) 856-2800. RV/tent: 100. $$. Hookups: electric, water, sewer.

Wanapum State Park, P.O. Box 1203, 98950. T: (509) 856-2700. RV/tent: 50. $. Hookups: none.

Walla Walla

RV Resort Four Seasons, 1440 Dallas Military Rd., 99362. T: (509) 529-6072. RV/tent: 89. $$. Hookups: electric (30, 50 amp), water, sewer.

Wenatchee

Daroga State Park, 1 South Daroga Park Rd., 98843. T: (509) 664-6380 or (888) 226-7688. RV/tent: 45. $. Hookups: electric, water.

Lincoln Rock State Park, 1253 US 2, 98802. T: (509) 884-8702. RV/tent: 94. $. Hookups: electric, water.

Westport

Coho RV Park, 2501 North Nyhus, 98595. T: (360) 268-0111 or (800) 572-0177. RV/tent: 76. $$. Hookups: electric, water, sewer.

Jolly Rogers Fishing Camp, 709 Neddie Rose Dr., 98595. T: (360) 268-0265. RV/tent: 25. $$. Hookups: electric, water, sewer.

Twin Harbors State Park, 420 St. Rte. 105, 98595. T: (360) 268-9717 or (888) 226-7688. RV/tent: 299. $. Hookups: electric, water.

White Salmon

Bridge RV Park and Campground, 65271 Hwy. 14, 98672. T: (509) 483-1111 or (888) 550-7275. www.business.gorge.net/bridgerv. RV/tent: 50. $$$. Hookups: electric (30, 50 amp), water, sewer.

Wilbur

Bell RV Park, 712 SE Railroad, 99185. T: (509) 647-5888. RV/tent: 20. $$. Hookups: electric (30 amp), water, sewer.

Winthrop

Big Twin Lake Campground, 210 Twin Lakes Rd., 98862. T: (509) 996-2650. www.methownet.com/bigtwin. RV/tent: 89. $$. Hookups: electric, water, sewer.

Jeffrey's Silverline Resort, 677 Bear Creek Rd., 98862. T: (509) 996-2448. www.jeffreyssilverline.com. RV/tent: 122. $$. Hookups: electric, water, sewer.

KOA Methow River, 1114 Hwy. 20, 98862. T: (509) 562-2158 or (800) 562-2158. www.koa.com/where/wa/47145.htm. RV/tent: 90. $$. Hookups: electric (20, 30, 50 amp), water, sewer.

Woodland

Columbia Riverfront RV Park, 1881 Dike Rd., 98674. T: (360) 225-8051 or (800) 845-9842. www.columbiariverfrontrvpark.com. RV/tent: 76. $$$. Hookups: electric, water, sewer.

WASHINGTON (continued)

Woodland (continued)

Paradise Point State Park, 33914 New Paradise Park Rd., 98642. T: (360) 263-2350 or (888) 226-7688. RV/tent: 78. $. Hookups: none.

Yakima

Circle H RV Ranch, 1107 South 18th St., 98901. T: (509) 457-3683. www.circlehrvranch.com. RV/tent: 76. $$. Hookups: electric (50 amp), water, sewer.

KOA Yakima, 1500 Keys Rd., 98901. T: (509) 248-5882 or (800) 562-5773. www.koa.com/where/wa/47108.htm. RV/tent: 148. $$. Hookups: electric (50 amp), water, sewer.

WEST VIRGINIA

Beckley

Beckley Exhibition Coal Mine & Campground, New River Park, off Ewart Ave., 25802. T: (304) 256-1747. www.beckleymine.com. RV/tent: 17. $$. Hookups: electric (20, 30 amp), water, sewer.

Lake Stephens Campground, 1200 Lake Stephens Rd., RR 3 Box 350, 25801. T: (304) 934-5322 or (800) 330-5458. www.lakestephenswv.com. RV/tent: 125. $. Hookups: electric (30 amp), water, sewer.

Belington

Twin Lakes Campground, Audra Rd., RR 1, Box 73-C, 26250. T: (304) 823-2021. www.bc-net.org. RV/tent: 190. $. Hookups: electric (20, 30 amp), water, sewer.

Bruceton Mills

Coopers Rock State Forest, Rte. 1, Box 270, 26525. T: (304) 594-1561 or (800) CALL-WVA. www.coopersrockstate forest.com. RV/tent: 25. $$. Hookups: electric (20 amp).

Glade Farms Campground, P.O. Box 455, 26525. T: (304) 379-9375. RV/tent: 97. $. Hookups: electric (20, 30 amp), water, sewer.

Buckhannon

Stonecoal Campground, Rte. 7, 26201. T: (304) 472-7226. RV/tent: 33. $. Hookups: electric (20, 30, 50 amp), water, sewer.

Cairo

North Bend State Park, Rte. 1 Box 221, 26337. T: (304) 643-2391 or (800) CALL-WVA. www.northbendsp.com. RV/tent: 49. $$. Hookups: electric.

Caldwell

Greenbrier Mountainaire Campground, HC 30, Box 155, 24925. T: (304) 536-1512. RV/tent: 33. $. Hookups: electric (20, 30 amp), water.

Circleville

Milstead's Grocery & Camping, P.O. Box 125, 26804. T: (304) 567-3171. RV/tent: 38. $. Hookups: electric (20 amp), water, sewer.

Spruce Knob Lake Campground, Monongahela National Forest, FR 1, off of FR 112, 26804. T: (304) 257-4488. www.fs.fed.us/r9/mnf. RV/tent: 42. $. Hookups: none.

Davis

Canaan Valley Resort Park, Rte. 1, Box 330, 26260. T: (304) 866-4121. www.canaanresort.com. RV/tent: 34. $$. Hookups: electric (20, 30, 50 amp), water, sewer.

Dunmore

Seneca State Forest, Rte. 1 Box 140, 24934. T: (304) 799-6213. www.senecastateforest.com. RV/tent: 10. $. Hookups: none.

Durbin

East Fork River Campgrounds, Box 177, 26264. T: (304) 456-3101. RV/tent: 20. $. Hookups: electric (20, 30, 50 amp), water.

Fairmont

Prickett's Creek Campground, RR 3, Box 127B, 26554. T: (304) 363-1910. RV/tent: 22. $$. Hookups: electric (20, 30, 50 amp), water.

Falling Waters

Falling Waters Campsite, 7685 Williamsport Pike, 25419. T: (304) 274-2791 or (800) 527-4902. RV/tent: 40. $$$. Hookups: electric (20, 30, 50 amp), water, sewer.

Fayetteville

Mountain Laurel Campground, Rte. 3, Box 68, 25840. T: (304) 574-0188. www.rvnetlinx.com. RV/tent: 23. $$. Hookups: electric (20 amp), water.

Rifrafters Campground, Rte. 2, Box 140a, 25840. T: (304) 574-1065. www.rifrafters.com. RV/tent: 37. $. Hookups: electric (30 amp), water.

Glen Jean

Whitewater Campground, Box 637, 25951. T: (800) 292-0880. www.newriverscenic.com. RV/tent: 56. $. Hookups: electric (20, 30 amp), water.

Hazelton

Pine Hill Campground & Cabins, RD 3, Box 233aa, 26525. T: (304) 379-4612. RV/tent: 150. $$. Hookups: electric (20, 30, 50 amp), water.

Hinton

Bass Lake Park, HC 74, Box 12, 25951. T: (304) 466-4475. RV/tent: 200. $$. Hookups: electric (15, 20, 30 amp), water, sewer.

Huttonsville

Kumbrabow State Forest, P.O. Box 65, 26273. T: (304) 335-2219 or (800) CALL-WVA. www.kumbrabow.com. RV/tent: 13. $. Hookups: none.

Inwood

Lazy A Campground, 317 Kathy's Ln., 25427. T: (304) 229-8185. RV/tent: 64. $$. Hookups: electric (20, 30 amp), water.

Marlinton

Tea Creek Campground, Monongahela National Forest, Hwy. 150, 24954. T: (304) 799-4334.

www.fs.fed.us/r9/mnf. RV/tent: 29. $. Hookups: none.

Watoga State Park, HC 82, Box 252, 24954. T: (304) 799-4087 or (800) CALL-WVA. www.wotaga.com. RV/tent: 86. $$. Hookups: electric (20 amp).

Meadow Bridge

Summer Wind, Rte. 1, Box 1201, 25976. T: (304) 392-2005. RV/tent: 20. $$. Hookups: electric (30, 50 amp), water.

Panther

Panther State Forest, Box 287, 24872. T: (304) 938-2252 or (800) CALL-WVA. www.pantherstate forest.com. RV/tent: 6. $. Hookups: electric (30 amp).

Parkersburg

Trailer Center Campground, I-77, Exit 173, 26101. T: (304) 428-8203. www.keystonetek.com. RV/tent: 33. $$. Hookups: electric (20, 30 amp), water.

Paw Paw

Avalon Campground, P.O. Box 369, 25434. T: (304) 947-5600. www.avalon-nude.com. RV/tent: 40. $$. Hookups: electric (30, 50 amp), water, sewer.

Pax

Plum Orchard Lake State Wildlife Management Area, Rte. 1, Box 186, 25917. T: (304) 469-9905. www.wvstateparks.com. RV/tent: 43. $. Hookups: none.

Point Pleasant

Krodel Park, WV Rte. 2 North, 400 Viand St., 25550. T: (304) 675-1068. www.pointpleasant wv.org. RV/tent: 55. $. Hookups: electric (20, 30, 50 amp), water, sewer.

Oldtown Campground, Rte. 1, Box 662, 25550. T: (304) 675-3095. www.whresirts.com. RV/tent: 70. $. Hookups: electric (20, 30 amp), water, sewer.

Princeton

Green Acres RV Park & Campground, 5127 Eads Mill Rd., 24740. T: (304) 922-2119. www.want togo.com. RV/tent: 56. $. Hookups: electric (20, 30 amp), water, sewer.

Romney

Middle Ridge Campground, HC 65, Box 4960, 26757. T: (304) 822-8020. RV/tent: 21. $$. Hookups: electric (30, 50 amp), water, sewer.

Wapocoma Campgrounds, HC 66, Box 11, 26757. T: (304) 822-5528. RV/tent: 207. $. Hookups: electric (30, 50 amp), water.

WEST VIRGINIA (continued)

Sandyville
Ruby Lake Campground, Rte. 21 North, 25275. T: (304) 273-3427. RV/tent: 29. $. Hookups: electric (30 amp), water, sewer.

Seneca Rocks
Seneca Shadows Campground, Monongahela National Forest, US Rte. 33, 26884. T: (304) 257-4488. www.fs.fed.us/r9/mnf. RV/tent: 81. $. Hookups: electric (20 amp).

Summersville
Battle Run Recreation Area, Rte. 2, Box 470, 26651. T: (304) 872-3459. www.reserveusa.com. RV/tent: 117. $$. Hookups: electric (30 amp).

Summersville Music Park Campground, SR 41 North, 26651. T: (304) 872-3145. RV/tent: 300. $$. Hookups: electric (20, 30 amp), water.

Weston
Briar Point Campground/Stonewall Jackson Lake State Park, 100 State Park Tr., 26447. T: (304) 269-0523. www.stonewallresort.com. RV/tent: 34. $$$. Hookups: electric (20, 30 amp), water, sewer.

Broken Wheel Campground & Country Store, Rte. 3, Box 299, 26452. T: (304) 269-6097. www .brokenwheelcampground.com. RV/tent: 51. $$. Hookups: electric (30 amp), water.

Wheeling
Dallas Pike Campground, RD 1, Box 231, 26059. T: (304) 547-0940 or (800) 233-0940. RV/tent: 148. $$. Hookups: electric (20, 30, 50 amp), water, sewer.

White Sulphur Springs
Twilight Overnight Campground, US 60 East, 24986. T: (304) 536-1731. RV/tent: 15. $$. Hookups: electric (20, 30, 50 amp), water.

WISCONSIN

Algoma
Ahnapee River Trails Camp Resort Inc., 6053 West Wilson Rd., 54201. T: (920) 487-5777. www.ustourism.net/ahnapee. RV/tent: 65. $$. Hookups: electric (30 amp), water.

Alma Center
KOA Hixton/Alma Center, North 9657 WI 95, 54611. T: (715) 964-2508 or (800) 562-2680. www.koa.com. RV/tent: 65. $$. Hookups: electric (30 amp), water, sewer.

Amherst Junction
Lake Emily Park, 3961 Park Dr., 54406. T: (715) 346-1433. www.florencewisconsin.com. RV/tent: 49. $. Hookups: electric (30 amp).

Antigo
Veterans Memorial Park, West 8375 Park Rd., 54409. T: (715) 623-6214. RV/tent: 41. $. Hookups: electric (30 amp).

Arbor Vitae
Arbor Vitae Campground, 10545 Big Arbor Vitae Dr., 54568. T: (715) 356-5146. www.arborvitae campground.com. RV/tent: 42. $$. Hookups: electric (30 amp), water, sewer.

Ashland
Kreher RV Park, 601 Main St. West, 54806. T: (715) 682-7071. RV/tent: 36. $$. Hookups: electric (20 amp).

Prentice Park, 601 Main St. West, 54806. T: (715) 682-7071. RV/tent: 9. $. Hookups: electric (20 amp).

Athelstane
McCaslin Mountain Campground, West 15720 CR F, 54104. T: (715) 757-3734. www.mccaslin mountain.com. RV/tent: 100. $$. Hookups: electric (20 amp), water, sewer.

Augusta
Coon Fork Lake Campground, CTH CF, off of US 12, 54722. T: (715) 839-4738. RV/tent: 88. $. Hookups: electric (30 amp), water.

Sandy Hill Campground, E2100 ND Rd., 54722. T: (715) 286-2495. RV/tent: 32. $$. Hookups: electric (30 amp), water.

Babcock
Country Aire Campground, 1221 Hwy. 173 South, 54413. T: (715) 884-2300. RV/tent: 39. $$. Hookups: electric (30 amp), water.

Bagley
Wyalusing State Park, 13081 State Park Ln., 53801. T: (608) 996-2261. www.reserveamerica.com. RV/tent: 109. $. Hookups: electric (30 amp).

Balsam Lake
DN Campground, 956 165th Ave., 54810. T: (715) 268-8980. RV/tent: 28. $$. Hookups: electric (30 amp), water.

Baraboo
Baraboo Hills Campground, East 10545 Terry-towne Rd., 53913. T: (608) 356-8505 or (800) CAMP-BHC. RV/tent: 157. $$. Hookups: electric (50 amp), water, sewer.

Dell-Boo Campground, E10562 Shady Ln., 539135. T: (608) 356-5898. www.dells.com/dellboo. RV/tent: 138. $$$. Hookups: electric (20, 30, 50 amp), water, sewer.

Devil's Lake State Park, 5975 Park Rd., 53913. T: (608) 356-8301. www.devilslakewisconsin.com. RV/tent: 407. $. Hookups: electric (30 amp).

Fox Hill RV Park, 11371 North Reedsburg Rd., 53913. T: (608) 356-5890. www.foxhillrvpark .com. RV/tent: 50. $$$. Hookups: electric (30 amp), water.

Mirror Lake State Park, 10320 East Fern Dell Rd., 53913. T: (608) 254-2333. www.reserveamerica .com. RV/tent: 140. $. Hookups: electric (30 amp).

Nordic Pines, E11740 County DL, 53913. T: (608) 356-5810. www.nordicpines.com. RV/tent: 140. $$. Hookups: electric (20 amp).

Red Oak Campground, South 2350 US 12, 53913. T: (608) 356-7304. RV/tent: 120. $$. Hookups: electric (50 amp), water, sewer.

Barron
Barron Motel & RV Campground, 1521 East Division Ave., 54812. T: (715) 637-3154. www.wisconsinvacations.com. RV/tent: 17. $$. Hookups: electric (30 amp), water, sewer.

Bayfield
Apostle Islands Area Campground, 85150 Trailer Ct. Rd., 54814. T: (715) 779-5524 or (715) 779-3398. www.travelwisconsin.com. RV/tent: 59. $$. Hookups: electric (20, 30, 50 amp), water, sewer.

Buffalo Bay Campground & Marina, 88385 Pike Rd. Hwy. 13, 54814. T: (715) 779-3743 or (888) 947-2757. www.ncis.net/bflobay. RV/tent: 50. $$. Hookups: electric (30 amp), water.

Belmont
Lake Joy Campground, 24192 Lake Joy Ln., 53510. T: (608) 762-5150. www.lakejoy.com. RV/tent: 88. $$. Hookups: electric (30 amp), water.

Big Flats
Pineland Camping Park, 916 Hwy. 13, 54613. T: (608) 564-7818. RV/tent: 175. $$. Hookups: electric (50 amp), water, sewer.

Birchwood
Doolittle Park, Hinman Dr., 54817. T: (715) 354-3300. RV/tent: 40. $$. Hookups: electric (30 amp).

Black River Falls
Black River State Forest, 910 Hwy. 54 East, 54615. T: (715) 284-4103 or (715) 284-1417. www.dnr.state.wi.us. RV/tent: 35. $. Hookups: electric (30 amp).

Jamboree Campground, Hwy. 12, 54615. T: (715) 284-7138 or (888) 345-2267. RV/tent: 200. $$. Hookups: electric (30 amp), water, sewer.

Blair
Riverside Memorial Park, 122 South Urberg Ave., 54616. T: (608) 989-2517. RV/tent: 24. $. Hookups: electric (30 amp).

Blue Mounds
Blue Mounds State Park, 4350 Mounds Park Rd., 53517. T: (608) 437-5711. www.wiparks.net. RV/tent: 123. $. Hookups: electric (30 amp).

Blue River
Eagle Cave Natural Park, 16320 Cavern Ln., 53518. T: (608) 537-2988. www.eaglecave.net. RV/tent: 50. $. Hookups: electric (15 amp), water.

Briggsville

Lake Mason Campground, 4035 1st Ln., 53920. T: (608) 981-2444. RV/tent: 50. $$. Hookups: electric (30 amp), water, sewer.

Wagon Wheel Campground, 4016 1st Dr., 53920. T: (608) 981-2161. RV/tent: 150. $$. Hookups: electric (30 amp), water, sewer.

Brodhead

Crazy Horse Campground, North 3201 Crazy Horse Ln., 53520. T: (608) 897-2207. www.crazyhorse.wi.com. RV/tent: 210. $$. Hookups: electric (30 amp), water, sewer.

Sweet Minni Ha Ha Campground, North 4697 County East, 53520. T: (608) 862-3769. RV/tent: 117. $$. Hookups: electric (30 amp), water.

Brule

Brule River Motel & Campground, P.O. Box 126, 54820. T: (715) 372-4815. RV/tent: 65. $. Hookups: electric (30 amp), water, sewer.

Burlington

Meadowlark Acres Campground, North 5146 North Rd., 53105. T: (262) 763-7200. RV/tent: 80. $$. Hookups: electric (30 amp), water.

Butternut

Butternut Lake Campground, Rte. 1, Box 129A, 54514. T: (715) 769-3448. RV/tent: 23. $$. Hookups: electric (20 amp), water, sewer.

Cascade

Hilly Haven Campground, North 2827 Dusty Ln., 53011. T: (920) 528-8966. RV/tent: 70. $$. Hookups: electric (20, 30, 50 amp), water, sewer.

Hoeft's Resort & Campground, West 9070 Crooked Lake Dr., 53011. T: (262) 626-2221. www.wisvacations.com/hoeftsresort. RV/tent: 100. $$. Hookups: electric (50 amp), water.

Cassville

K-7 Korral, 10895 Jack Oak Rd., 53806. T: (608) 725-2267. RV/tent: 45. $. Hookups: electric (30 amp), water, sewer.

Chetek

Northern Exposure Resort & Campground, P.O. Box 222, 54728. T: (715) 859-2887. www.chetek.com/northernexposure. RV/tent: 20. $$. Hookups: electric (30 amp), water, cable.

Six Lakes Resort & Campground, 25358 8th Ave., 54728. T: (800) 203-4624. RV/tent: 180. $$. Hookups: electric (30 amp), water, sewer.

Chippewa Falls

Pine Harbor Campground, 7181 185th St., 54729. T: (715) 723-9865. RV/tent: 45. $$. Hookups: electric (30 amp), water.

Conover

Buckatabon Lodge & Lighthouse Inn, 5630 Rush Rd., 54519. T: (715) 479-4660. www.buckatabon .com. RV/tent: 51. $$. Hookups: electric (20, 30 amp), water.

Cumberland

Camp Brigadoon, 2554 4th St., 54829. T: (800) 715-2744. RV/tent: 131. $$. Hookups: electric (30 amp), water.

Dalton

Grand Valley Campground, 5855 CR B, 53926. T: (920) 394-3643. www.grandvalleycamp ground.com. RV/tent: 190. $$. Hookups: electric (30 amp), water.

De Pere

Happy Hollow Camping Resort, 3831 CR U, 54115. T: (920) 532-4386. RV/tent: 125. $$. Hookups: electric (30 amp), water, sewer.

De Soto

Blackhawk Park, RFD 1, 54624. T: (608) 648-3314. www.reserveamerica.com. RV/tent: 150. $$. Hookups: electric (30 amp).

Delavan

Snug Harbor Inn Campground on Turtle Lake, West 7772-2C WI Pkwy., 53115. T: (608) 883-6999. www.snugharborwi.com. RV/tent: 43. $$$. Hookups: electric (20, 30 50 amp), water, sewer.

Dells

American World RV Park & Resort, 400 Wisconsin Dells Pkwy., 53965. T: (608) 253-4451. RV/tent: 52. $$$. Hookups: electric (50 amp), water, sewer.

Arrowhead Resort Campground, Hwy. 530/Arrowhead Rd., 53965. T: (608) 254-7344. www .arrowheadcampresort.com. RV/tent: 285. $$. Hookups: electric (30 amp), water, sewer.

Blue Lake Campground, 3531 Hwy. G, 53965. T: (608) 586-4376. RV/tent: 42. $$. Hookups: electric (30 amp), water, sewer.

Bonanza Campground, 1770 Wisconsin Dells Pkwy., 53965. T: (608) 254-8124 or (800) 438-8139. www.dells.com. RV/tent: 150. $$$. Hookups: electric (50 amp), water, sewer.

Erickson's Tepee Park Campground, 10096 Trout Rd., 53965. T: (608) 253-3122. www.tepeepark.com. RV/tent: 113. $$. Hookups: electric (30 amp), water, sewer.

Holiday Shores Campground & Resort, 3900 River Rd., 53965. T: (608) 254-2717. www.wisvacations .com/holidayshores. RV/tent: 140. $$$. Hookups: electric (30 amp), water.

K & L Campground, 3503 CR G, 53965. T: (608) 586-4720. www.kandlcampground.com. RV/tent: 96. $$. Hookups: electric (30 amp), water, sewer.

River Bay Campground & Marina, Marina and RV Park, 53965. T: (608) 254-7193 or (800) 443-1112. www.dells-camping.com. RV/tent: 158. $$$. Hookups: electric (50 amp), water, sewer.

Sherwood Forest Campground, 352 Hwys 12 & 16, 53965. T: (608) 254-7080 or (877) 474-3796. www.rvnetlinx.com. RV/tent: 201. $$$. Hookups: electric (50 amp), water, sewer.

Stand Rock Campground, 570 Hwy. N, 53965. T: (608) 253-2169. www.standrock.com. RV/tent: 116. $$$. Hookups: electric (30 amp), water, sewer.

Wisconsin Dells KOA, 235 Stand Rock Rd., 53965. T: (608) 254-4177 or (800) 562-4178. www.koacampgrounds.com. RV/tent: 147. $$. Hookups: electric (50 amp), water, sewer.

Denmark

Shady Acres Campsites, 5422 Shady Acre Ln., 54208. T: (920) 863-8143. RV/tent: 25. $$. Hookups: electric (30 amp), water, sewer.

Eagle River

Chain-O-Lakes Resort & Campground, 3165 Campground Rd., 54521. T: (715) 479-6708. www.colcamp.com. RV/tent: 100. $$. Hookups: electric (30 amp), water.

Elkhart Lake

Plymouth Rock Camping Resort, 7271 North Lando St., 53073. T: (920) 893-8452. www. plymouthrockcamping resort.com. RV/tent: 270. $$$. Hookups: electric (50 amp), water, sewer.

Elton

Glacier Wilderness Campground, 3865 North Elton South Rd, 54430. T: (715) 882-4781. RV/tent: 11. $$. Hookups: electric (30 amp), water.

Exeland

Windfall Lake Family Camping, 632 North SR 40, 54835. T: (715) 943-2625. RV/tent: 25. $$. Hookups: electric (15 amp).

Florence

Keyes Lake Campground, HC1 Box 162, 54121. T: (715) 528-4907. www.geocities.com. RV/tent: 35. $$. Hookups: electric (20, 30 amp), water.

Fort Atkinson

Pilgrim's Campground LLC, West 7271 Hwy. C, 53538. T: (920) 563-8122. RV/tent: 103. $$$. Hookups: electric (50 amp), water, sewer.

Fremont

Blue Top Resort & Campground, 1460 Wolf River Dr., 54940. T: (920) 446-3343. www.bluetop resort.com. RV/tent: 50. $$. Hookups: electric (30 amp), water.

Galesville

Pow-Wow Campground, West 16751 Pow-Wow Ln., 54630. T: (608) 582-2995. RV/tent: 128. $$. Hookups: electric (30 amp), water.

Glidden

Northern Lure Resort & Campground, Gordon Lake Rd., 54527. T: (715) 264-3677. www .northernlure.com. RV/tent: 19. $$. Hookups: electric (30 amp), water, sewer.

Gordon

Adventureland, 7440 East CR Y, 54838. T: (715) 376-4528. RV/tent: 50. $$. Hookups: electric (30 amp), water.

WISCONSIN (continued)

Grantsburg

Cedar Point Resort & Campground, 12480 Cedar Point Ln., 54840. T: (715) 488-2224. www.burnettcounty.com/cedarpoint. RV/tent: 30. $$. Hookups: electric (30 amp), water, sewer.

James N. McNally Campground, 316 South Brad St., 54840. T: (715) 463-2405. www.grantsburg wi.com. RV/tent: 38. $$. Hookups: electric (50 amp), water, sewer.

Green Bay

Brown County Fairgrounds, 305 East Walnut St., 54301. T: (920) 448-4466. www.co.brown.wi.us. RV/tent: 40. $$. Hookups: electric (30 amp), water, sewer.

Green Lake

Green Lake Campground, West 2360 Hwy. 23, 54941. T: (920) 294-3543. www.greenlakecamp ground.com. RV/tent: 200. $$$. Hookups: electric (30 amp), water, sewer.

Greenbeulah

Westward Ho Camp Resort, 5456 North Division Rd., 53023. T: (920) 526-3407. www.westward hocampresort.com. RV/tent: 120. $$$. Hookups: electric (20, 30, 50 amp), water, sewer.

Greenwood

Greenwood Park, Hwy. 73, 54456. T: (715) 743-5140. www.co.clark.wi.us. RV/tent: 24. $. Hookups: electric (30 amp).

Hayward

Sisko's Pine Point Resort, 8677 North CR CC, 54843. T: (715) 462-3700. RV/tent: 33. $$. Hookups: electric (30 amp), water, sewer.

Sunrise Bay Campground & RV Park, 16269 West Jolly Fisherman Rd., 54843. T: (715) 634-2213. www.nelsonlake.net. RV/tent: 51. $$. Hookups: electric (30 amp), water, sewer.

The Hayward KOA, 11544 North Hwy. 63, 54843. T: (715) 634-2331. www.koa.com. RV/tent: 142. $$. Hookups: electric (50 amp), water, sewer.

Trail's End Resort & Campground, 8080 North CR K, 54843. T: (715) 634-2423. www.hayward lakes.com. RV/tent: 16. $$. Hookups: electric (30 amp), water, sewer, cable.

Hazelhurst

Cedar Falls Campground, 6051 Cedar Falls Rd., 54531. T: (715) 356-4953. www.innline.com. RV/tent: 42. $$. Hookups: electric (20 amp).

Hilbert

Calumet County Park, 6150 CR EE, 54129. T: (920) 439-1008. RV/tent: 71. $$. Hookups: electric (30 amp).

Hiles

Hiles Pine Lake Campground, 8896 West Pine Lake Rd., 54511. T: (715) 649-3319. www.wisconsin campgrounds.com. RV/tent: 80. $$. Hookups: electric (15, 20, 30 amp), water.

Holmen

Sandman's Campground, 8905 Hwy. 53 & 93, 54636. T: (608) 526-4956. RV/tent: 50. $$. Hookups: electric (30 amp), water.

Horicon

The Playful Goose Campground, 2001 South Main St., 53032. T: (920) 485-4744. www.theplayful goose.com. RV/tent: 192. $$. Hookups: electric (20, 30, 50 amp), water, sewer.

Hudson

Willow River State Park, 1034 CR A, 54016. T: (715) 386-5931 or (715) 386-9340. RV/tent: 72. $. Hookups: electric (30 amp).

Iola

Iola Pines Campground Inc., 100 Fairway Dr., 54945. T: (715) 445-3489. www.iolapines.com. RV/tent: 50. $$. Hookups: electric (30 amp), water, sewer.

Jefferson

Bark River Campground, 2340 West Hansen Rd., 53549. T: (262) 593-2421. www.wisconsincamp grounds.com. RV/tent: 250 (200 seasonal). $$. Hookups: electric (30 amp), water, sewer.

Kewaskum

Kettle Moraine State Forest, Mauthe Lake Recreation Area, CR Hwy. GG, 53010. T: (262) 626-4305. www.wiparks.net. RV/tent: 137. $. Hookups: electric (30 amp).

Kettle Moraine State Forest-North, North 3450 Division Rd., 53010. T: (920) 533-4305. www.wiparks.net. RV/tent: 200. $. Hookups: none.

Kewaunee

Mapleview Campsites, North 1460 Hwy. B, 54216. T: (920) 776-1588. www.wisconsincamp grounds.com. RV/tent: 75. $$. Hookups: electric (30 amp), water.

Kieler

Rustic Barn Campground, 3854 Dry Hollow Rd., 53812. T: (608) 568-7797. www.rusticbarnrv park.com. RV/tent: 58. $$. Hookups: electric (30, 50 amp), water.

La Crosse

Bluebird Springs Recreation Area, North 2833 Smith Valley Rd., 54601. T: (608) 781-2267. RV/tent: 148. $$. Hookups: electric (50 amp), water, sewer.

Goose Island Camp, Hwy. 35 West, 54658. T: (608) 788-7018. RV/tent: 400. $$. Hookups: electric (30 amp).

Pettibone Resort & Campground, 333 Park Plaza Dr., 54601. T: (608) 782-5858 or (800) 738-8426. www.pettiboneresort.com. RV/tent: 170. $$. Hookups: electric (50 amp), water, cable.

Lac Du Flambeau

Lac Du Flambeau Tribal Campground, P.O. Box 67, 54538. T: (715) 588-9611 or (715) 588-3310. RV/tent: 72. $$. Hookups: electric (30 amp), water, sewer.

Ladysmith

Flambeau River Lodge, North 7870 Flambeau Rd., 54848. T: (715) 532-5392. RV/tent: 25. $$. Hookups: electric (30 amp), water, sewer.

Thornapple River Campground, North 6599 Hwy. 27, 54848. T: (715) 532-7034. www.wisconsin campgrounds.com. RV/tent: 25. $. Hookups: electric (30 amp), water.

Westcove Campground, 1011 Edgewood Ave., Hwy. 8, 54848. T: (715) 532-7812. RV/tent: 15. $$. Hookups: electric (30 amp), water, sewer.

Lake Delton

Yogi Bear's Jellystone Park Camp-Resort Lake Delton, 51915 Ishnala Rd., 53940. T: (608) 254-2568 or (800) 462-9644. www.dells.com. RV/tent: 229. $$. Hookups: electric (50 amp), water, sewer.

Lake Geneva

Coachman's Terrace Park, West 3540 SR 50 West, 53147. T: (262) 248-3636. RV/tent: 63. $$$. Hookups: electric (30 amp), water, sewer.

Lancaster

Klondyke Secluded Acres, 6656 Pine Knob Rd., 53813. T: (608) 723-2844. RV/tent: 37. $$. Hookups: electric (30 amp), water.

Land O'Lakes

Borderline RV Park, 6078 US 45, 54540. T: (715) 547-6169. www.innline.com. RV/tent: 25. $$. Hookups: electric (30 amp), water, sewer.

Laong

Ham Lake Campground, 3490 Hwy. 32, 54541. T: (715) 674-2201. RV/tent: 31. $$. Hookups: electric (30 amp), water, sewer.

Lodi

Crystal Lake Campground, North 550 Gannon Rd., 53555. T: (608) 592-5607. www.crystallake campground.com. RV/tent: 65. $$$. Hookups: electric (30 amp), water.

Smokey Hollow Campground, 9935 McGowan West, 53555. T: (608) 635-4806. www.smokey hollowcampground.com. RV/tent: 100. $$. Hookups: electric (30 amp), water.

Lyndon Station

Bass Lake Campground, 1497 Southern Rd. North, 53944. T: (608) 666-2311. www.basslakecamp ground.com. RV/tent: 50. $$. Hookups: electric (30 amp), water, sewer.

Yukon Trails Camping, 2330 Hwy. HH, 53944. T: (608) 666-3261 or (800) 423-9677. RV/tent: 208. $$. Hookups: electric (30 amp), water, sewer.

Lynxville

River Hills Estates Campground, Box 171, 54640. T: (608) 874-4197 or (612) 724-3442. RV/tent: 40. $$. Hookups: electric (30 amp), water, sewer.

Manawa

Bear Lake Campground, North 4715 Hwy. 22-110, 54949. T: (920) 596-3308. www.wisconsin campgrounds.com. RV/tent: 150. $$. Hookups: electric (20, 30 amp), water.

WISCONSIN (continued)

Maribel

Devil's River Campers Park, 16612 CTH R, 54227. T: (920) 863-2812. www.wisconsinvacations.com. RV/tent: 80. $$$. Hookups: electric (30 amp), water.

Marion

Kastle Kampground, North 11301 Kinney Lake Rd., 54950. T: (715) 754-5900. www.kastle kampground.com. RV/tent: 600. $$. Hookups: electric (50 amp), water, sewer.

Markesan

Shady Oaks Campground, North 2770 Park Rd., 53946. T: (920) 398-3138. www.dotnet.com. RV/tent: 150. $$. Hookups: electric (30 amp), water, sewer.

Marquette

Sportsman's Resort LLC, 222 Lyon St., 53947. T: (920) 394-3421. www.thesportsmanresort. com. RV/tent: 30. $$. Hookups: electric (50 amp), water, sewer.

Mauston

Bavarian Campsites, West 4796 Hwy. G, 53948. T: (608) 847-7039 or (608) 847-7787. RV/tent: 70. $$. Hookups: electric (20 amp).

Mellen

Copper Falls State Park, RR 1 Box 17AA, 54546. T: (715) 274-5123. www.reserveamerica.com. RV/tent: 56. $. Hookups: electric (30 amp).

Menomonie

Twin Springs Resort Campground, 3010 Cedarfalls Rd., 54751. T: (715) 235-9321. RV/tent: 82. $$. Hookups: electric (50 amp), water, sewer.

Mercer

Lake of the Falls, Lake of the Falls Rd., 54534. T: (715) 561-2697. RV/tent: 35. $. Hookups: electric (30 amp).

Merrimac

Merry Mac's Camp'N, East 12540 Halwey Rd., 53561. T: (608) 493-2367. www.wisconsin campground.com. RV/tent: 136. $$. Hookups: electric (30 amp), water.

Milton

Blackhawk Campground, 3407 Blackhawk Dr., 53563. T: (608) 868-2586. www.blackhawk campgrounds.com. RV/tent: 50. $$$. Hookups: electric (30 amp), water.

Minong

Totogatic Park, North 1398 Totogatic Park, 54859. T: (715) 466-2822 or (715) 635-4490. RV/tent: 71. $$. Hookups: electric (30 amp).

Montello

Lake Arrowhead Campground, 781 Fox Ct., 53949. T: (920) 295-3000. www.lakearrowheadcamp grounds.com. RV/tent: 225. $$$. Hookups: electric (30, 50 amp), water, sewer.

Lakeside Campground, North 3510 East Tomahawk Trail, 53949. T: (920) 295-3389. www.wisconsin campground.com. RV/tent: 95. $$. Hookups: electric (50 amp), water, sewer.

Wilderness County Park, North 1499 WI 22, 53949. T: (608) 297-2002. www.wilderness campground.com. RV/tent: 300. $$$. Hookups: electric (30 amp).

Mosinee

Lake DuBay Shores Campground, 1713 DuBay Dr., 54455. T: (715) 457-2484. www.wisconsin campgrounds.com. RV/tent: 150. $$. Hookups: electric (20, 30 amp), water, sewer,.

Mountain

Chute Pond Park, 12436 Chute Dam Rd., 54149. T: (715) 276-6261. www.co.oconto.wi.us. RV/tent: 70. $. Hookups: electric (30 amp), water.

Mukwonago

Country View Campground, 26400 Craig Ave., 53149. T: (262) 662-3654. RV/tent: 150. $$. Hookups: electric (30 amp), water, sewer.

Muscoda

Riverside Park, P.O. Box 293, 53573. T: (608) 739-3786. RV/tent: 32. $. Hookups: electric (30 amp), water.

Necedah

Buckhorn Campground Resort Inc., North 8414 City Trk G, 54646. T: (608) 565-2090. RV/tent: 16. $$. Hookups: electric (50 amp), water.

Ken's Marina & Campground, West 4240 Marina Ln., 54646. T: (608) 565-2426. RV/tent: 35. $. Hookups: electric (30 amp), water.

St. Joseph Resort, West 5630 Hwy. 21, 54646. T: (608) 565-7258. www.stjosephresort.com. RV/tent: 40. $$. Hookups: electric (30, 50 amp), water.

Neillsville

Rock Dam Park & Campground, 10666 Camp Globe Rd., 54456. T: (715) 743-5140 or (715) 267-6845. www.co.clark.wi.us. RV/tent: 140. $$. Hookups: electric (30 amp), water, sewer.

Russell Memorial Park & Campground, West 8180 City Hwy. J, 54456. T: (715) 743-5140 or (715) 333-7948. www.co.clark.wi.us. RV/tent: 230. $$. Hookups: electric (30 amp), water, sewer.

Sherwood Park, Hwy. Z, 54456. T: (715) 743-5140. www.co.clark.wi.us. RV/tent: 36. $. Hookups: electric (30 amp).

Snyder Park, 517 Ct. St., 54456. T: (715) 743-5140. www.co.clark.wi.us. RV/tent: 32. $. Hookups: electric (30 amp).

Nekoosa

Deer Trail Park Campground, 13846 CR Z, 54457. T: (715) 886-3871. www.gocampingamerica .com/deertrailpark. RV/tent: 160. $$. Hookups: electric (50 amp), water.

New Lisbon

Lil' Yellow River Campground, 7989 Hwy. 80, 53950. T: (608) 562-5355. www.mwt.net/~wehman. RV/tent: 50. $$. Hookups: electric (30 amp), water.

Oconto

Holtwood Campsite, Holtwood Way, 54153. T: (920) 834-7732. www.cityofoconto.com. RV/tent: 147. $$. Hookups: electric (30 amp), water.

North Bay Shore Recreation Area, 301 Washington St., 54153. T: (920) 834-6825 or (920) 834-6995. www.co.oconto.wi.us. RV/tent: 33. $$. Hookups: electric (30 amp), water.

Oshkosh

Circle R Campground, 1185 Old Knapp Rd., 54902. T: (920) 235-8909. www.circle-r-camp ground.com. RV/tent: 100. $$. Hookups: electric (20, 30 amp), water, sewer,.

Hickory Oaks Fly In and Campground, 555 Glendale Ave., 3485 Vinland Rd., 54901. T: (920) 235-8076. www.hickoryoakscampground.com. RV/tent: 50. $$. Hookups: electric (20, 30, 50 amp) water.

Palmyra

Circle K Campground, West 1316 Island Rd., 53156. T: (262) 495-2896. RV/tent: 80. $$. Hookups: electric (30 amp), water, sewer.

Pardeeville

Duck Creek Campground, 6560 County Hwy. G, 53954. T: (608) 429-2425. www.duckcreekcamp ground.com. RV/tent: 50. $$. Hookups: electric (30 amp), water.

Indian Trails Campground, 6445 Haynes Rd., 53954. T: (608) 429-3244 or (877) 636-8757. www. indiantrailscampground.com. RV/tent: 300. $$. Hookups: electric (30 amp), water.

Pride of America Camping Resort, 7520 West Bush Rd., 53954. T: (608) 742-6395 or (800) 236-6395. www.camppoa.com. RV/tent: 120. $$. Hookups: electric (50 amp), water, sewer.

Pelican Lake

Weaver's Resort & Campground, 1001 Weaver Rd., 54463. T: (715) 487-5217. RV/tent: 9. $$. Hookups: electric (15, 20, 30 amp), water, sewer.

Pembine

Tranquil Vista Campground, Town Corner Lake Rd., 54156. T: (715) 324-6430. RV/tent: 24. $$. Hookups: electric (30 amp), water.

Phillips

Solberg Lake County Park, 104 South Eyder Ave., 54555. T: (715) 339-6371. RV/tent: 60. $$. Hookups: electric (20, 30, 50 amp).

Plover

Ridgewood Campsite, 4800 River Ridge Rd., 54467. T: (715) 344-8750. RV/tent: 70. $$. Hookups: electric (30 amp), water.

Portage

Kamp Dakota, West 10670 Tritz Rd., 53901. T: (608) 742-5599. RV/tent: 125. $$. Hookups: electric (30 amp), water, sewer.

Sky High Camping Resort, 5740 Sky High Dr., 53901. T: (608) 742-2572 or (877) 743-0720. www.skyhighcampingresort.com. RV/tent: 100. $. Hookups: electric (50 amp), water, sewer.

WISCONSIN (continued)

Rapids

Dexter Park, Hwys. 80 and 54, 54494. T: (715) 421-8422. RV/tent: 96. $. Hookups: electric (20, 30 amp).

North Wood County Park, CR A, 54494. T: (715) 421-8422. RV/tent: 91. $. Hookups: electric (20, 30 amp).

South Wood Park-Lake Wazeecha, CR W, 54494. T: (715) 421-8422. RV/tent: 73. $. Hookups: electric (20, 30 amp).

Redgranite

Flanagan's Pearl Lake Campsite, West 4585 South Pearl Lake Rd., 54970. T: (920) 566-2758. RV/tent: 100. $$. Hookups: electric (20, 30, 50 amp), water.

Reedsburg

Lighthouse Rock Campground, 2330 CR V, 53959. T: (608) 524-4203 or (866) 629-7803. RV/tent: 96. $$. Hookups: electric (30, 50 amp), water, sewer.

Reedsville

Rainbow's End Campground, 18227 US 10, 54230. T: (920) 754-4142. RV/tent: 40. $$. Hookups: electric (30 amp), water.

Rhinelander

Lake George Campsites, 4008 Bassett Rd., 54501. T: (715) 362-6152. RV/tent: 37. $$. Hookups: electric (30 amp), water.

West Bay Camping Resort, 4330 South Shore Dr., 54501. T: (715) 362-3481. RV/tent: 79. $$. Hookups: electric (50 amp), water, sewer.

Richland Center

Alana Springs Lodge & Campground, 22628 Covered Bridge Rd., 53581. T: (608) 647-2600. RV/tent: 23. $. Hookups: electric (20 amp), water.

Rio

Little Bluff Campground, North 4003 Traut Rd., 53960. T: (920) 992-5157. RV/tent: 135. $$. Hookups: electric (30 amp), water, sewer.

Silver Springs Campsites, North 5048 Ludwig Rd., 53960. T: (920) 992-3537. www.silverspringscamp.com. RV/tent: 300. $$. Hookups: electric (30 amp), water, sewer.

Willow Mill Campsite, 5830 CR SS, 53960. T: (920) 992-5355 or (800) 582-0393. www.willowmillcampsite.com. RV/tent: 60. $$. Hookups: electric (20, 30 amp), water.

Saxon

Frontier Bar & Campground, HC 1, Box 477, 54559. T: (715) 893-2461. RV/tent: 25. $$. Hookups: electric (30 amp), water, sewer.

Shawano

Brady's Pine Grove Campground, North 5999 Campground Rd., 54166. T: (715) 787-4555. RV/tent: 200. $$. Hookups: electric (30 amp), water.

Shawano County Park Campground, West 5785 Lake Dr., 54166. T: (715) 524-4986 or (715) 524-4988. RV/tent: 90. $. Hookups: electric (30 amp).

Sheboygan

Kohler/Andre State Park, 1520 Old Park Rd., 53081. T: (920) 451-4080. www.reserveamerica.com. RV/tent: 105. $. Hookups: electric (30 amp).

Sherwood

High Cliff State Park, 7650 State Park Rd., 54169. T: (920) 989-1106. RV/tent: 112. $. Hookups: electric (30 amp).

Silver Cliff

Kosir's Rapid Rafts, West 14073 Cty Hwy. C, 54104. T: (715) 757-3431. www.kosirs.com. RV/tent: 40. $$. Hookups: electric (20 amp), water.

Solon Springs

Swanson's Motel & Campground, P.O. Box 296, 54873. T: (715) 378-2215. RV/tent: 21. $$. Hookups: electric (30 amp), water, sewer.

Somerset

River's Edge Camp Resort, 1820 Raleigh Rd., 54025. T: (715) 247-3305. RV/tent: 277. $$. Hookups: electric (30 amp), water.

Spooner

Country House Lodging & RV Park, 717 South River St., 54801. T: (715) 635-8721. www.washburncounty.com. RV/tent: 21. $$. Hookups: electric (30 amp), water.

Highland Park Campground, 8050 Carlton Rd., 54801. T: (715) 635-2462. RV/tent: 47. $$$. Hookups: electric (20, 30, 50 amp), water, sewer.

Spring Green

Valley RV Park, E5016 Hwy. 14 & 23, 53588. T: (608) 588-2717. RV/tent: 18. $$. Hookups: electric (30 amp), water, sewer.

Spring Valley

Highland Ridge Campground, P.O. Box 190, 54767. T: (715) 778-5562. www.reserveusa.com. RV/tent: 45. $. Hookups: electric (30 amp).

Stevens Point

Collins Park, CR 1, 54481. T: (715) 346-1433. RV/tent: 25. $. Hookups: electric (30 amp).

Dubay Park, CR E, 54481. T: (715) 346-1433. RV/tent: 31. $. Hookups: electric (30 amp).

Jordan Park, SR 66, 54481. T: (715) 346-1433. RV/tent: 25. $$. Hookups: electric (30 amp).

Stoughton

Kamp Kegonsa, 2671 Circle Dr., 53589. T: (608) 873-5800. RV/tent: 100. $$. Hookups: electric (20, 30 amp), water.

Viking Village Campground & Resort Inc., 1648 County Trunk N, 53589. T: (608) 873-6601. www.instoughton.com/vikingvillage.htm. RV/tent: 77. $$$. Hookups: electric (50 amp), water, sewer.

Sturgeon Bay

Door County Yogi Bear's Jellystone Park, 3677 May Rd., 54235. T: (920) 743-9001. www.campdoorcounty.com/yogibear. RV/tent: 175. $$$. Hookups: electric (30, 50 amp), water, sewer.

Sturtevant

Cliffside Park, 14200 Washington Ave., 53177. T: (262) 886-8440. RV/tent: 92. $$. Hookups: electric (30 amp), water.

Travelers' Inn Motel and Campground, 14017 Durand Ave., 53177. T: (262) 878-1415. RV/tent: 25. $$. Hookups: electric (30 amp), water.

Superior

Pattison State Park, 6294 South SR 35, 54880. T: (715) 399-3111. www.reserveamerica.com. RV/tent: 59. $. Hookups: electric (20 amp).

Tilleda

Tilleda Falls Campground, P.O. Box 76, 54978. T: (715) 787-4143. RV/tent: 40. $$. Hookups: electric (30 amp), water.

Tomah

Holiday Lodge Golf Resort & RV Park, 10558 Freedom Rd., 54660. T: (608) 372-9314 or (800) 236-2670. www.holidaylodgegolf.com. RV/tent: 28. $$. Hookups: electric (30 amp), water, sewer.

Tomahawk

Birkensee Resort & Camping, 9350 CR H, 54487. T: (715) 453-5103. RV/tent: 45. $$. Hookups: electric (30 amp), water, sewer.

Terrace View Campsites, West 5220 Terrace View Rd., 54487. T: (715) 453-8352. RV/tent: 50. $$. Hookups: electric (30 amp), water.

Trego

Bay Park Resort & Campground, 8347 Bay Park Rd., 54888. T: (715) 635-2840. www.bayparkresort.com. RV/tent: 64. $$. Hookups: electric (30 amp), water, sewer.

Eagle Lodge Resort & Campground, 8234 Bald Eagle Dr., 54888. T: (715) 466-2728. RV/tent: 17. $$. Hookups: electric (30 amp), water, sewer.

Trego Town Park & Campground, 5665 Trego Park Rd., 54888. T: (715) 635-6075. RV/tent: 50. $$. Hookups: electric (30 amp), water.

Trempealeau

Perrot State Park, West 26247 Sullivan Rd, 54661. T: (608) 534-6409. www.reserveamerica.com. RV/tent: 97. $. Hookups: electric (30 amp).

Tripoli

Buck Snort Resort & Campground, 5129 Boyle Rd., 54564. T: (715) 564-2262. www.bucksnortresort.com. RV/tent: 33. $$. Hookups: electric (30 amp), water, sewer.

Two Rivers

Point Beach State Forest, 9400 County Trunk O, 54241. T: (920) 794-7480. www.reserveamerica.com. RV/tent: 127. $$. Hookups: electric (30 amp), water, sewer.

Viola

Banker Park, P.O. Box 38, 54664. T: (608) 627-1831. RV/tent: 45. $. Hookups: electric (30 amp).

WISCONSIN (continued)

Washington Island

Washington Island Campground, RR 1, Box 144, 54246. T: (920) 847-2622 or (920) 847-2622. www.washingtonisland.com. RV/tent: 100. $$. Hookups: electric (30 amp), water.

Waupaca

Deerhaven Campground, North 3185 Butts Dr., 54981. T: (715) 256-1412. www.deerhavencamp ground.com. RV/tent: 40. $$. Hookups: electric (30 amp), water, sewer.

Royal Oaks Golf Resort Inc., North 4440 Oakland Dr., 54981. T: (715) 258-5103. RV/tent: 25. $$. Hookups: electric (30 amp), water, sewer.

Rustic Woods, East 2585 Southwood Dr., 54981. T: (715) 258-2442. RV/tent: 164. $$$. Hookups: electric (30 amp), water, sewer.

Waupaca Camping Park, 2411 Holmes Rd., 54981. T: (715) 258-8010. www.waupacacamping park.com. RV/tent: 133. $$. Hookups: electric (30 amp), water, sewer.

Wausau

Dells of the Eau Claire Park, CR Y, 54401. T: (715) 261-1566. RV/tent: 27. $. Hookups: electric (30 amp).

Marathon Park, SR 29 West, 54401. T: (715) 261-1570. RV/tent: 35. $. Hookups: electric (30 amp).

Rib Mountain State Park, 4200 Park Rd., 54401. T: (715) 842-2522. RV/tent: 40. $. Hookups: electric (20 amp).

Wautoma

Lake of the Woods Campground, 9070 14th Ave., 54982. T: (920) 787-3601 or (888) 919-9109. www.lakeofthewoodswi.com. RV/tent: 150. $$. Hookups: electric, water, sewer.

Webster

Wagner's Port Sand, 4904 Hwy. 70, 54893. T: (715) 349-2395. RV/tent: 85. $$. Hookups: electric (30 amp), water, sewer.

White Lake

River Forest Rafts & Campground, West 510 CR West, 54491. T: (715) 882-3351. www.wolfriver rafting.com. RV/tent: 45. $. Hookups: electric (15 amp).

Whitewater

Scenic Ridge Campground, West 7991 R & W Townline Rd., 53190. T: (608) 883-2920. RV/tent: 200. $. Hookups: electric (30 amp), water.

Wild Rose

Evergreen Campsites, West 5449 Archer Ln., 54984. T: (920) 622-3498. www.evergreen campsites.com. RV/tent: 400. $$. Hookups: electric (20, 30 amp), water.

Willard

Mead Lake Park, CR G, 54456. T: (715) 743-5140. www.co.clark.wi.us. RV/tent: 75. $. Hookups: electric (30 amp).

Wonewoc

Chapparal Campground & Resort, S320 Hwy. 33, 53968. T: (888) 283-0755 or (608) 464-3200. www.chapparal.com. RV/tent: 72. $$. Hookups: electric (50 amp), water, sewer.

Woodruff

Hiawatha Trailer Resort, 1070 Old 51 South, 54568. T: (715) 356-6111. RV/tent: 60. $$$. Hookups: electric (30, 50 amp), water, sewer.

Indian Shores Resort & RV Sales, P.O. Box 12, 54568. T: (715) 356-5552. RV/tent: 268. $$$. Hookups: electric (30 amp), water, sewer.

WYOMING

Arlington

Arlington Outpost, Hwy. 13, 82083. T: (307) 378-2350. RV/tent: 76. $. Hookups: electric (30 amp), water, sewer.

Beulah

Camp Fish, Main St., 82712. T: (888) 643-2277. www.beulah.com/camping.htm. RV/tent: 16. $$. Hookups: electric (20, 30 amp), water.

Buffalo

Big Horn Mountains Campground, 8935 US 16 West, 82834. T: (307) 684-2307. www.buffalo camping.com. RV/tent: 83. $$. Hookups: full.

Buffalo KOA Campground, 87 Hwy. 16 East, 82834. T: (800) 562-5403 or (307) 684-5423. www .buffalokoa.com. RV/tent: 91. $$. Hookups: full.

Deer Park, US 16, 82834. T: (800) 222-9960. www.deerparkrv.com. RV/tent: 97. $$. Hookups: full.

Indian Campground, US 16, 660 East Hart St., 82834. T: (307) 684-9601 or (866) 808-9601. www.indiancampground.com. RV/tent: 122. $$. Hookups: full.

Mountain View, US 16, 585 Fort St., 82834. T: (307) 684-2881. www.buffalowyoming.com/mtnview. RV/tent: 18. $$. Hookups: full.

Burns

WYO Campground, 4066 Road 211, 82053. T: (307) 547-2244. RV/tent: 143. $$. Hookups: electric (20, 30, 50 amp).

Caspar

Caspar KOA, 2800 East Yellowstone, 82609. T: (800) KOA-3259. www.koa.com. RV/tent: 110. $$. Hookups: full.

Fort Caspar Campground, 4205 Fort Caspar Rd., 82604. T: (888) 243-7709 or (307) 234-3260. RV/tent: 165. $$. Hookups: full.

Cheyenne

Greenway Trailer Park, 3829 Greenway, 82207. T: (307) 635-0220. RV/tent: 42. $$. Hookups: full.

Jolley Rogers RV Campground, US 30, 6102 East Hwy. 30, 82001. T: (307) 634-8457 or (800) 458-7779. www.jolleyrogers.com. RV/tent: 69. $$. Hookups: full.

KOA Cheyenne, 8800 Archer Frontage Rd, 82207. T: (307) 638-8840. www.cheyennekoa.com. RV/tent: 53. $$. Hookups: electric (20, 30, 50 amp), water.

Restway Travel Park, Whitney Rd., 82207. T: (800) 443-2751 or (307) 634-3811. www.traveling usa.com/restway. RV/tent: 102. $$. Hookups: electric (30, 50 amp), water, sewer.

T-Joe's RV Park, 12700 Service Rd. (I-80), 82001. T: (307) 635-8750. RV/tent: 48. $. Hookups: electric (20, 30, 50 amp), water, sewer.

Chugwater

Diamond Guest Ranch, Box 236, 82210. T: (800) YEA-HAAA or (307) 422-3564. www.diamondgr .com. RV/tent: 106. $$. Hookups: electric (20, 30, 50 amp), water.

Cody

7 K's RV Park, 232 West Yellowstone Ave., 82414. T: (307) 587-5890. RV/tent: 37. $$. Hookups: electric (20, 30 amp).

Absaroka Bay RV Park, P.O. Box 953, 82414. T: (800) 557-7440. www.cody-wy.com. RV/tent: 99. $$. Hookups: electric (20, 30, 50 amp).

Camp Cody Campground, 415 Yellowstone Ave., 82414. T: (888) 231- CAMP or (307) 587-9730. RV/tent: 63. $$. Hookups: electric (20, 30, 50 amp), water.

Gateway Motel and Campground, 203 Yellowstone Ave., 82414. T: (307) 587-2561. www.imf.net/ nrodeo/gatewayhtml. RV/tent: 87. $. Hookups: electric (20, 30 amp).

KOA Cody, 5561 Greybull Hwy., 82414. T: (800) KOA-8507 or (307) 507-2364. www.koa.com. RV/tent: 228. $$$. Hookups: electric (20, 30, 50 amp), water.

Parkway Trailer and RV Park, 132 Yellowstone Ave., 82414. T: (307) 527-5927. RV/tent: 25. $. Hookups: electric (20, 30, 50 amp), water.

Dayton

Foothills Motel and Campground, Box 174, 82836. T: (307) 655-2547. www.fiberpipe.net/~foothill/ Home.htm. RV/tent: 45. $. Hookups: electric (20, 30, 50 amp), water.

Devils Tower

Fort Devils Tower Campground, 601 Hwy. 24, 82714. T: (307) 467-5655. RV/tent: 32. $$. Hookups: electric (50 amp), water, sewer.

WYOMING (continued)

KOA Devils Tower, P.O. Box 100, 82714. T: (800) 562-5785. RV/tent: 150. $$. Hookups: electric (20, 30, 50 amp), water, sewer.

Douglas

Douglas Jackalope KOA Kampground, P.O. Box 1150, 82633. T: (800) 562-2469. RV/tent: 101. $$. Hookups: electric (20, 30, 50 amp), water, sewer.

Dubois

Circle Up Camper Court, 225 West Welty, 82513. T: (307) 455-2238. RV/tent: 117. $$. Hookups: electric (20, 30, 50 amp), water, sewer.

Pinnicale Buttes Lodge and Campground, 3577 US 26, 82513. T: (800) 934-3569. RV/tent: 21. $. Hookups: electric (15, 20, 30, 50), water, sewer.

Evanston

Phillips RV Park, 225 Bear River Dr., 82930. T: (307) 789-3805. RV/tent: 58. $$. Hookups: electric (20, 30, 50 amp).

Fort Bridger

Fort Bridger RV Camp, P.O. Box 244, 82933. T: (800) 578-6535. RV/tent: 23. $$. Hookups: electric (20, 30, 50 amp), water, sewer.

Fort Laramie

Chuckwagon RV Park, 306 Pioneer Ct., 82212. T: (307) 837-2828. www.prairieweb.com. RV/tent: 10. $. Hookups: electric (20, 30, 50 amp), water.

Gillette

Green Tree's Crazy Woman Campground, 1001 West 2nd St., 82716. T: (307) 682-3665. RV/tent: 124. $$. Hookups: electric (20, 30, 50 amp), water, sewer.

Green River

Buckbord Marina, H.CR 65, Box 100, 82935. T: (307) 865-6927. RV/tent: 40. $$. Hookups: electric (30, 50 amp).

Tex's Travel Camp, SR 2, Box 101, 82935. T: (307) 875-2630. RV/tent: 89. $$. Hookups: electric (20, 30, 50 amp), water, sewer, cable.

Greybull

Green Oasis Campground, 540 12th Ave. North, 82426. T: (888) 765-2856. www.greenoasis campground.com. RV/tent: 32. $$. Hookups: electric (20, 30, 50 amp), water, sewer, cable.

KOA Greybull, Box 387, 82426. T: (800) 562-7508 or (307) 765-2555. www.koa.com. RV/tent: 57. $$. Hookups: electric (30 amp), water.

Jackson

Lone Eagle Resort, 13055 South US 191, 83001. T: (800) 321-3800 or (307) 733-1090. RV/tent: 154. $$$$. Hookups: electric (20, 30 amp).

Jackson Hole

KOA Snake River Park, 9705 South US 89, 83001. T: (800) 562-1878 or (307) 733-7078. www.srp koa.com. RV/tent: 96. $$$. Hookups: electric (20, 30, 50 amp), water.

Lander

Hart Ranch Hideout RV Park and Campground, 7192 Hwy. 789/287, 82520. T: (800) 914-9226 or (307) 332-3836. RV/tent: 85. $$. Hookups: electric (20, 30, 50 amp), water.

Maverick Mobile Home and RV Park, 1104 North 2nd St., 82520. T: (307) 332-3142. RV/tent: 60. $$. Hookups: electric (15, 20, 30 amp), water.

Sleeping Bear RV Park and Campground, 715 East Main, 82520. T: (888) 737-2327 or (307) 332-5759. www.sleeping-rv-park.com. RV/tent: 54. $$$. Hookups: electric (20, 30, 50 amp), water.

Laramie

KOA Laramie, P.O. Box 1134, 82073. T: (800) KOA-4153 or (307) 742-6553. www.koa.com. RV/tent: 146. $. Hookups: electric (20, 30, 50 amp).

Lingle

Pony Soldier RV Park, 2302 A Hwy. 26, 82223. T: (307) 837-3078. RV/tent: 65. $$. Hookups: electric (20, 30, 50 amp), water, sewer.

Lusk

Prairie View Campground, 3925 US 20, 82225. T: (307) 334-3174. RV/tent: 29. $$. Hookups: electric (15, 20, 30 amp), water.

Lyman

KOA Lyman, HC 66, Box 55, 82937. T: (307) 786-2188 or (800) 562-2762. www.koa.com. RV/tent: 51. $$. Hookups: electric (20, 30, 50 amp), water.

Madison Junction

Madison Junction Campground, P.O. Box 165, Yellowstone National Park, 82190. T: (307) 344-7311. www.travelyellowstone.com. RV/tent: 280. $$. Hookups: none.

Moran Junction

Colter Bay RV Park, P.O. Box 250, 83013. T: (800) 628-9988. RV/tent: 112. $$$$. Hookups: electric (20, 30, 50 amp).

Moran Junction Grand Teton Park RV Resort, Hwy. 26/282, 83013. T: (800) 563-6469 or (307) 733-1980. www.yellowstonerv.com. RV/tent: 204. $$$. Hookups: electric (20, 30, 50 amp), water.

Newcastle

Crystal Park Campground, 2 Fountain Plaza, 82701. T: (307) 746-3339. RV/tent: 70. $$. Hookups: electric (20, 30 amp), water.

Rimrock RV, 2206 West Main, 82701. T: (307) 746-2007. RV/tent: 58. $$. Hookups: electric (20, 30 amp), water.

Pine Bluffs

Pine Bluffs RV Park, 10 Paintbrush, P.O. Box 806, 82082. T: (800) 294-4968 or (307) 245-3665. RV/tent: 108. $$. Hookups: electric (20, 30, 50 amp).

Pinedale

Pinedale RV, 204 South Jackson Ave., P.O. Box 248, 82941. T: (307) 367-4555 or (307) 367-4563. RV/tent: 64. $$. Hookups: electric (20, 30, 50 amp), water.

Ranchester

Lazy R Campground, 348 Dayton, P.O. Box 286, 82839. T: (888) 655-9284. www.lazyrcamp ground.com. RV/tent: 22. $$. Hookups: electric (30, 50 amp).

Rawlins

American Presidents Camp, 2346 West Spruce St., 82301. T: (307) 324-3218 or (800) 294-3218. RV/tent: 67. $. Hookups: electric (20, 30, 50 amp), water, sewer.

KOA Rawlins, 205 East Hwy. 71, 82301. T: (800) 562-7559 or (307) 328-2021. www.koa.com. RV/tent: 57. $$. Hookups: electric (20, 30, 50 amp), water.

RV World Campground, 3101 Wagon Circle Rd., 82301. T: (307) 328-1091 or (800) 478-9752. RV/tent: 135. $$. Hookups: electric (20, 30, 50 amp), water.

Western Hills Campground, 2500 Wagon Circle Rd., 82301. T: (888) 568-3040 or (307) 324-2592. members.tripod.com/~wyo_camping/ index.htm. RV/tent: 179. $$. Hookups: electric (20, 30, 50 amp).

Riverside

Lazy Acres Campground, P.O. Box 641, 82325. T: (307) 327-5968. www.wyomingcarbon county.com. RV/tent: 34. $$. Hookups: electric (15, 20, 30, 50 amp), water, sewer.

Riverton

Owl Creek Kampground, 11124 US 26/789, 82501. T: (307) 856-2869. www.campowlcreek.com. RV/tent: 40. $$. Hookups: electric (20, 30 amp), water.

Wind River RV Park, 1618 East Park, 82501. T: (800) 528-3913. RV/tent: 60. $$. Hookups: electric (20, 30, 50 amp).

Thermopolis

Country Campin' RV and Tent Park, 710 East Sunnyside Ln., 82443. T: (800) 609-2244. RV/tent: 62. $$. Hookups: electric (20, 30, 50 amp), water.

Fountain of Youth RV Park, 250 US 20 North, 82443. T: (307) 864-3265. www.fountainofyouth rvpark.com. RV/tent: 68. $$. Hookups: full.

The Wyoming Waltz RV Park, 720 Shoshoni Hwy. 20 South, 82443. T: (307) 864-2778. RV/tent: 13. $$. Hookups: full.

BRITISH COLUMBIA

Balfour

Birch Grove Campground, 7048 Lee Rd.,V1L 5P6. T: (250) 229-4275. RV/tent: 50. $$. Hookups: full.

Barkerville

Becker's Lodge, P.O. Box 129,V0K 2R0.T: (800) 808-4761. www.beckerslodge.ca. RV/tent: 17. $$. Hookups: none.

Barriere

Dee Jay Camp and Trailer Park, 626 Yellowhead Hwy. 5, Box 198,V0E 1E0.T: (250) 672-5685 or (866) 872-5685. RV/tent: 75. $$. Hookups: electric (30 amp), water.

Bell II

Bell II Lodge, Hwy. 37, Box 49,V0J 3S0. T: (877) 617-2288. www.bell2lodge.com. RV/tent: 10. $. Hookups: full.

Blue River

Eleanor Lake Campsite, 1 Herb Bilton Way,V0E 1J0.T: (250) 673-8316 or (800) 661-9170. www.wiegele.com/summer/eleanorlake.htm. RV/tent: 50. $. Hookups: electric (30 amp).

Boston Bar

Blue Lake Resort, 63452 Blue Lake,V0K 1C0. T: (877) 867-9246. RV/tent: 75. $$. Hookups: electric (15 amp), water.

Canyon Alpine RV Park & Campground, Box 39850490 Trans-Canada Hwy.V0K 1C0.T: (604) 867-9734. RV/tent: 31. $$. Hookups: full.

Boswell

Mountain Shores Resort and Marina, 13485 Hwy. 3A,V0B 1A0.T: (250) 223-8258. www.mtnshores.com. RV/tent: 87. $$. Hookups: full.

Burnaby

Burnaby Cariboo RV Park, 8765 Cariboo Place, V3N 4T2.T: (604) 420-1722 or (800) 667-9901. www.bcrvpark.com. RV/tent: 217. $$. Hookups: full.

Burns Lake

Beaver Point Resort, P.O. Box 587,V0J 1E0.T: (250) 695-6519. www.bcnorth.ca/beaverpoint. RV/tent: 40. $$. Hookups: electric, water, sewer.

Burns Lake KOA, P.O. Box 491,V0J 1E0.T: (800) 562-0905 or (250) 692-3105. www.koa.com. RV/tent: 36. $$. Hookups: full.

Cache Creek

Brookside Campsite, P.O. Box 737,V0H 1H0.T: (250) 457-6633. www.brooksidecampsite.com. RV/tent: 95. $$. Hookups: full.

Campbell River

Shelter Bay Resort, 3860 South Island Hwy.,V9H 1M2.T: (250) 923-5338. www.shelter-bay-rv-resort .com. RV/tent: 50. $$. Hookups: full.

Canim Lake

Canim Lake Resort, P.O. Box 248,V0K 1J0.T: (250) 397-2355. www.canim.com. RV/tent: 25. $$. Hookups: full.

Reynolds Resort, Box 15,V0K 1M0.T: (250) 397-2244 or (888) 659-9977. RV/tent: 29. $$. Hookups: full.

Castlegar

Pine Grove Resort, 1142 Pine Grove Rd., Scotch Creek,V0E 3L0.T: (250) 955-2306. www.pinegroveresorts.com. RV/tent: 15. $$$. Hookups: full.

Chilanko Forks

Poplar Grove Resort, P.O. Box 70,V0L 1H0. T: (250) 481-1186 or (800) 578-6804. www.poplargroveresort.com. RV/tent: 18. $$. Hookups: electric, water.

Chilliwack

Cottonwood Meadows RV Country Club, 44280 Luckakuck Way,V2R 4A7.T: (604) 824-7275. www.cottonwoodrvpark.com. RV/tent: 107. $$. Hookups: full.

Christina Lake

Skands Court, 64 Johnson Rd.,V0H 1E2.T: (250) 447-9295 or (866) 875-2637. www.christina lake.com/skands. RV/tent: 84. $$. Hookups: electric, water.

Clearwater

Birch Island Campground, 88 Walker Rd.,V0E 1N0.T: (250) 674-3991. RV/tent: 42. $$. Hookups: full.

Clinton

Cache Creek, Cariboo Hwy.,V0K 1H0.T: (250) 752-6707. RV/tent: 22. $$. Hookups: full.

Courtenay

Hideaway Resort, 9413 Bracken Rd., Black Creek, V9J 1E3.T: (250) 337-5360. RV/tent: 67. $$. Hookups: none.

Fairmont Hot Springs

Hoodoos Mountain Resort, P.O. Box 67,V0B 1L0. T: (250) 345-6631. www.realtystar.com/hoodoos. RV/tent: 75. $$. Hookups: electric, water, sewer.

Spruce Grove Resort, P.O. Box 993,V0B 1L0. T: (250) 345-6561. www.sprucegrove resort.com. RV/tent: 188. $$$. Hookups: electric, water.

Fanny Bay

Pepper Land Outdoor Resort, 8256 South Island Hwy.,V0R 1W0.T: (250) 336-1521. RV/tent: 24. $$. Hookups: full.

Fort Fraser

Pipers Glen RV Resort, Box 35,V0J 1N0.T: (250) 690-7565. www.pipersglenresort.com. RV/tent: 32. $$. Hookups: electric (15, 30 amp), water.

Fort Langley

Fort Camping Resort, 9451 Glover Rd.,V1M 2R9. T: (604) 888-3678. www.fortcamping.com. RV/tent: 220. $$. Hookups: full.

Fort Nelson

Westend Campground, Mile 300.5 Alaska Hwy., V0C 1R0.T: (250) 774-2340. RV/tent: 160. $$. Hookups: full.

Fort St. James

Pitka Bay Resort, Pitka Bay Rd.,V0J 1P0.T: (250) 996-8585. RV/tent: 17. $$. Hookups: full.

Stuart River Campground, Roberts Rd.,V0J 1P0. T:(250) 996-8690. RV/tent: 34. $$. Hookups: full.

Fort St. John

Sourdough Pete's RV Park, Box 6911,V1J 4J3. T: (800) 227-8388. RV/tent: 88. $$. Hookups: full.

Fort Steele

Fort Steele Campground and RV Park, 335 Kelly Rd.,V0B 1N0.T: (250) 426-5117. www.fort steelecampground.com. RV/tent: 60. $$. Hookups: full.

Fraser Lake

Birch Bay Resort, Birch Bay Rd.,V0J 1S0.T: (250) 699-8484. RV/tent: 31. $$. Hookups: electric (15, 30 amp), water.

Francois Lake Resort, Francois Lake Rd.,V0J 1S0. T: (250) 699-6551. RV/tent: 30. $$. Hookups: full.

Nithi on the Lake, Francois Lake Rd.,V0J 1S0. T: (250) 699-6675. RV/tent: 30. $$. Hookups: full.

Golden

Whispering Spruce Campground and RV Park, 1430 Golden View Rd.,V0A 1H1.T: (250) 344-6680. RV/tent: 135. $$. Hookups: full.

Grand Forks

Riviera RV Park, 6331 Hwy. 3,V0H 1H0.T: (250) 442-2158. RV/tent: 46. $$. Hookups: full.

Harrison Hot Springs

Bigfoot Campground, 670 Hot Springs,V0M 1K0. T: (604) 796-9767. RV/tent: 200. $$. Hookups: full.

Hixon

Canyon Creek Campgound, 39035 Hwy. 97 South, V0K 1S0.T: (250) 998-4384. www.canyoncreek campground.com. RV/tent: 55. $. Hookups: full.

Hope

Coquihalla Campsite, 800 Kawkawa Lake Rd.,V0X 1L0.T: (604) 869-7119. RV/tent: 122. $$. Hookups: electric (15, 30 amp), water.

Kawkawa Lake Resort, P.O. Box 788,V0X 1L0. T: (604) 869-9930. RV/tent: 89. $$. Hookups: electric, water, sewer.

Hornby Island

Bradsdadsland, 1980 Shingle Spit Rd.,V0R 1Z0. T: (250) 335-0757. RV/tent: 50. $$. Hookups: electric (15 amp), water.

Kaslo

Mirror Lake Campground, 5777 Arcola,V0G 1M0. T: (250) 353-7102. RV/tent: 100. $$. Hookups: electric (15 amp), water.

BRITISH COLUMBIA (continued)

Madeira Park

Sunshine Coast Resort, 12695 Hwy. 101, V0N 2H0.
T: (604) 883-9177. RV/tent: 10. $$. Hookups: full.

Monte Lake

Heritage Campsite and RV Park, P.O. Box 42, V0E
2N0. T: (877) 881-5150. RV/tent: 34. $$.
Hookups: full.

Nakusp

Coachman Campsite, 1701 Hwy. 23, V0G 1R0.
T: (250) 265-4212. RV/tent: 44. $$. Hookups: full.

Osoyoos

Wild Rapids Campground, RR. 1 Lakeshore Dr.,
V0H 1R0. T: (250) 495-7696. RV/tent: 150. $$.
Hookups: full.

Parksville

Park Sands Beach Resort, P.O. Box 179, V9P 2G4.
T: (250) 248-3171. www.parksands.com.
RV/tent: 99. $$. Hookups: full.

Port Alberni

Arrowvak Riverside Campground, 5955 Hector
Rd., RR 3, V9Y 7L7. T: (250) 723-7948. RV/tent:
44. $$. Hookups: electric, water.

Prince George

Sintich Trailer Park, P.O. Box 1022, V2L 4V1.
T: (250) 963-9862 or (877) 963-9862.
www.sintichpark.bc.ca. RV/tent: 51. $$.
Hookups: full.

Quesnel

Cariboo Place Campsite, 6905 Hwy. 97 South, V2J
6M2. T: (250) 747-8555. RV/tent: 50. $$.
Hookups: electric, water.

Revelstoke

Williamson's Lake Campground, P.O. Box 1791, V0E
2S0. T: (250) 837-5512. RV/tent: 41. $$.
Hookups: full.

Salmon Arm

Salmon Arm KOA, 381 Hwy. 97 B, V1E 4M4.
T: (250) 832-6489. RV/tent: 78. $$$.
Hookups: full.

Sicamous

Cedars Campground, 3499 Luoma Rd., V0E 2V0.
T: (250) 836-2265. www.campingcompanion.com.
RV/tent: 102. $$. Hookups: electric, water.

Dogwood Campground and RV Park, 15151 112th
Ave., V3R 6G8. T: (604) 583-5585. RV/tent: 300.
$$. Hookups: full.

Peace Arch RV Park, 14601 40th Ave., V4P 2J9.
T: (604) 594-7009. RV/tent: 350. $$. Hookups:
full, cable .

Victoria

Weir's Beach RV Resort, 5191 William Head Rd.,
V9C 4H5. T: (250) 478-3323. RV/tent: 60. $$.
Hookups: full.

Westbay Marine Village RV Park, 453 Head St., V9A
5S1. T: (250) 385-1831. www.westbay.bc.ca.
RV/tent: 61. $$. Hookups: full.

Index

North Dakota